EVERYTHING IRISH

EVERYTHING IRISH

The History, Literature, Art, Music, People, and Places of Ireland from A to Z

EDITED BY
Lelia Ruckenstein AND James A. O'Malley

Ballantine Books · New York

2005 Ballantine Books Trade Paperback Edition

Published in the United States by Ballantine Books, an imprint of Random House Publishing Group, a division of Random House, Inc., New York.

Originally published in hardcover in the United States by Ballantine Books, an imprint of The Random House Publishing Group, a division of Random House, Inc., in 2003.

Library of Congress Cataloging-in-Publication Data

Everything Irish : the history, literature, art, music, people, and places of Ireland, from A to Z / edited by Lelia Ruckenstein and James A. O'Malley.
p. cm.
ISBN 0-345-44129-X
1. Ireland—Encyclopedias. 2. Northern Ireland—Encyclopedias. I. Ruckenstein, Lelia. II. O'Malley, James A.

DA906.E94 2003
941.5'003—dc21 2003043672

Printed in the United States of America

www.ballantinebooks.com

9 8 7 6 5 4 3 2 1

Text design by Joseph Rutt

General Editorial Advisor

Lawrence J. McCaffrey

Editorial Consultant for Literature

José Lanters

Contributors

John Allen (J.A.)
Deputy Music Critic for the *Irish Times*; lecturer, broadcaster, and writer on opera

Linda D. Almeida (L.D.A.)
Adjunct Professor, New York University

Bernadette Andreosso (B.A.)
Head of the Economics Department, University of Limerick

Stephen Andrew Ball (S.A.B.)
Archivist at the National Library of Ireland, Manuscripts Department

Frank Biletz (F.B.)
Lecturer in History, Loyola University of Chicago

Sighle Breathnach-Lynch (S.B-L.)
Curator of Irish paintings, National Gallery of Ireland, Dublin

Terence Brown, (T.B.)
Professor of Literature, Trinity College, Dublin

Robert Burns (R.B.)
Professor of History, Emeritus, University of Notre Dame

Michael P. Cahill (M.P.C.)
Ph.D., University of Chicago; Adjunct Professor, University of St. Mary of the Lake, Illinois

Tony Canavan (T.C.)
Cofounder of *History Ireland*; Parliamentary Reporter at Oireachtas Éireann (the Irish Parliament)

Caitriona Clear (C.C.)
Lecturer in History, National University of Ireland, Galway

Tony Clayton-Lea (T.C.-L.)
Writer on Popular Music

Eileen Connolly (E.C.)
Lecturer in Politics, Dublin City University

Mary Cosgrove (M.C.)
Lecturer in Art History, Queens University, Belfast

Thomas Oliver Coughlan (T.O.C.)
Solicitor and Lecturer at National University of Ireland, Cork

John Cronin (J.C.)
Researcher in History and Civilization, European University Institute in Florence

Troy D. Davis (T.D.)
Assistant Professor of History, Stephen F. Austin State University, Texas

Ciaran Deane (C.D.)
Editor and Author of *The Guinness Book of Irish Facts & Feats*

Breandán Delap (B.D.)
Editor of the Irish Language Magazine, *Foinse*

Michael Dervan (M.D.)
Classical Music Critic for the *Irish Times*

Paul Dillon (P.D.)
Ph.D. History, National University of Ireland, Dublin

Donal A. Dineen (D.A.D.)
Dean, Kemmy Business School, University of Limerick

John Doyle (J.D.)
Director of the Centre for International Studies, Dublin City University

Ryan Dye (R.D.)
Assistant Professor of History, St. Ambrose University, Davenport, Iowa

Patrick J. Egan (P.E.)
Head of the History Department, Riversdale Community College, Dublin

Co-Contributors

Patricia M. Deane (P.M.D.), Science Department, Riversdale Community College
Marie T. Denny (M.T.D.), History Department, Riversdale Community College
Patrick Nulty (P.N.), History Department, Riversdale Community College
Toyah O'Connell (T.OCon.), History Department, Riversdale Community College

Michael Ellison (M.E.)
Journalist for the *Guardian*

Tyler Farrell (T.F.)
Lecturer in English, University of Wisconsin, Milwaukee

Thomas Gilbert (T.G.)
Writer

Dermot Gilleece (D.G.)
Sports Writer for the *Irish Times*

Brian Griffin (B.G.)
Professor of History, Bath Spa University College, UK

Thomas E. Hachey (T.E.H.)
Executive Director of the Center for Irish Studies, Boston College

Peter Harbison (P.H.)
Archeologist, writer; former Editor of *Ireland of the Welcomes*

Cheryl Herr (C.H.)
Professor of English, University of Iowa

Patrick Hicks (P.J.H.)
Assistant Professor of English, Augustana College, Sioux Falls, South Dakota

John Horgan (J.H.)
Professor of Journalism, Dublin City University

Nainsí Houston (N.H.)
Assistant Professor of English, Irish Studies Program, Creighton University, Omaha, Nebraska

Elmer Kennedy-Andrews (E.K-A.)
Head of the English Department, University of Ulster at Coleraine

Andrew Kincaid (A.K.)
Assistant Professor of English, University of Wisconsin, Milwaukee

José Lanters (J.C.E.L.)
Professor of English, Co-Director, Center for Celtic Studies, University of Wisconsin, Milwaukee

Padraig Lenihan (P.L.)
Lecturer in History, University of Limerick

Colm Lennon (C.L.)
Senior Lecturer in History, St. Patrick's College, Maynooth

James Liddy (J.L.)
Poet and Professor of English, University of Wisconsin, Milwaukee

Hugh Linehan (H.L.)
Entertainment Editor, the *Irish Times*

Michael Liston (M.L.)
Chairman of the Department of Logic, University of Wisconsin, Milwaukee

P. J. Mathews (P.J.M.)
Lecturer in English, St. Patrick's College, (DCU), Dublin

Alan Matthews (A.M.)
Head of the Economics Department, Trinity College, Dublin

Lawrence W. McBride (L.MB.)
Professor of History, Illinois State University

John P. McCarthy (J.P.MC.)
Professor of History and Director, Institute of Irish Studies at Fordham University, New York

Lawrence McCaffrey (L.J.MC.)
Professor of History, Emeritus, Loyola University of Chicago

Jim McDonnell (J.McD.)
Professor of English, Carleton College, Northfield, Minnesota

Joe McDowell (J.MD.)
Assistant Professor of English, Augustana College, Rock Island, Illinois

Kathleen McInerney (K.MI.)
Assistant Professor of English, Chicago State University

Eileen McMahon (E.McM.)
Assistant Professor of History, Lewis University, Romeoville, Illinois

Ailfrid MacLochlainn (A.ML.)
Former Director of the National Library in Dublin and the National University of Ireland, Galway Libraries

Elizabeth S. Meloy (E.S.M.)
Ph.D. Candidate in History Department, Brown University

Sean Moran (S.M.)
Sports Writer for the *Irish Times*

Eileen Morgan (E.M.)
Assistant Professor of English, State University of New York—Oneonta

Marc E. Mullholland (M.M.)
Lecturer in History, St. Catherine's College, Oxford University

John A. Murphy (J.A.M.)
Professor of History, Emeritus, National University of Ireland, Cork

Shakir M. Mustafa (S.M.M.)
Assistant Professor of English, Boston University

George O'Brien (G.OB.)
Professor of English, Georgetown University

Brian O'Connor (B.OC.)
Sports Writer for the *Irish Times*

Thomas H. O'Connor (T.H.OC.)
University Historian, Boston College

Ruan O'Donnell (R.OD.)
Lecturer in History, University of Limerick

Nollaig Ó Gadhra (N.ÓG.)
Journalist, Historian, and Writer

Daithi O hOgain (D.Oh.)
Head of the Department of Irish Folklore, National University of Ireland, Dublin

James A. O'Malley (J.OM.)
Writer, Editor

Fionan O'Muircheartaigh (F.OM.)
Chief Economic Advisor of Enterprise Ireland

Gearoid O Tuathaigh (G.OT.)
Professor of History, National University of Ireland, Galway

Jim Patterson (J.P.)
Assistant Professor of History, Centenary College, New Jersey

Jody AllenRandolph, (J.AR.)
Poetry Critic

Lelia Ruckenstein (L.R.)
Writer, Editor

Michael Seaver (M.S.)
Director of Kinetic Reflex dance publishing house; Dance Critic for the *Irish Times*

Andrew Shields (A.S.)
Tutor in History, University of New South Wales, Australia

Frank Shouldice (F.S.)
Writer; Journalist for the *Irish Voice* and RTÉ

David Sprouls (D.S.)
Director of Admissions, New York School of Interior Design

Mary S. Thompson (M.S.T.)
Lecturer in English, St. Patrick's College, (DCU) Dublin

Alan Titley (A.T.)
Head of the Irish Department, St. Patrick's College, (DCU) Dublin

Paul A. Townend (P.A.T.)
Assistant Professor of British and Irish History, University of North Carolina at Wilmington

Gearóidín Uí Laighléis (G.U.L.)
Lecturer in Irish, St. Patrick's College, (DCU), Dublin

Fintan Vallely (F.V.)
Lecturer in Traditional Irish Music, Dundalk Institute of Technology, County Louth; editor of *The Companion to Irish Traditional Music*

Gordon M. Weiner (G.M.W.)
Professor of History and Jewish Studies, Emeritus, Arizona State University

Kevin Whelan (K.W.)
Director of Notre Dame Center of Irish Studies, Dublin

Timothy White (T.W.)
Professor of Political Science, Xavier University, Cincinnati

Sabine Wichert (S.W.)
Senior Lecturer in History, Queens University, Belfast

Ireland

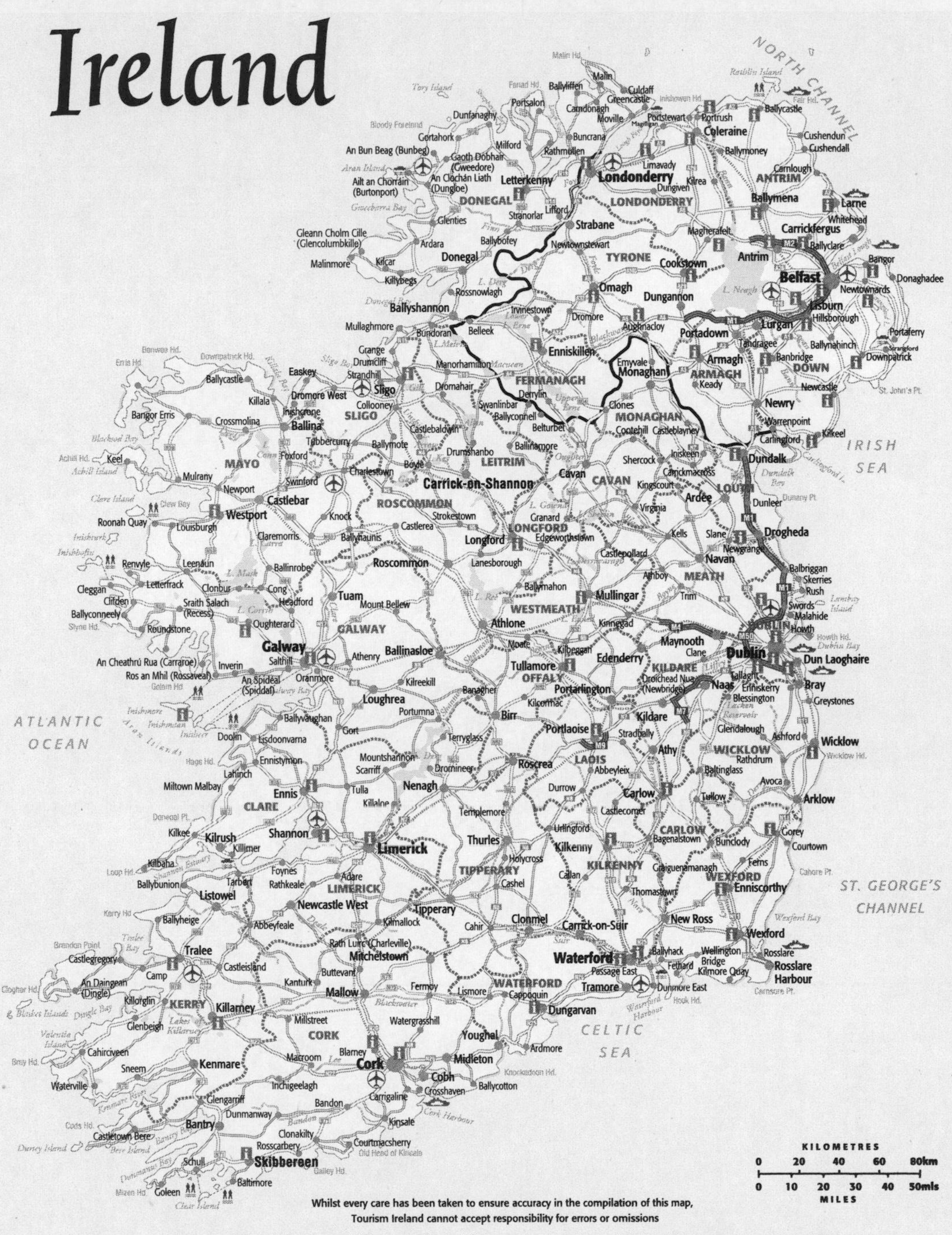

NORTH CHANNEL
Malin Hd.
Malin
Ballyliffen
Culdaff
Greencastle
Carndonagh
Moville
Fanad Hd.
Portsalon
Tory Island
Dunfanaghy
Bloody Foreland
Gortahork
An Bun Beag (Bunbeg)
Gaoth Dobhair (Gweedore)
Aran Island
Ailt an Chorráin (Burtonport)
An Clochán Liath (Dungloe)
Milford
Rathmullen
Buncrana
Portstewart
Portrush
Coleraine
Ballycastle
Rathlin Island
Fair Hd.
Cushendun
Cushendall
Ballymoney
Limavady
Londonderry
Dungiven
Kilrea
Carnlough
ANTRIM
Letterkenny
DONEGAL
Lifford
LONDONDERRY
Ballymena
Larne
Whitehead
Carrickfergus
Glenties
Stranorlar
Strabane
Magherafelt
Gleann Cholm Cille (Glencolumbkille)
Ardara
Ballybofey
Newtownstewart
Ballyclare
Malinmore
Kilcar
Donegal
TYRONE
Cookstown
Antrim
Bangor
Killybegs
Omagh
Belfast
Donaghadee
Newtownards
Rossnowlagh
Dungannon
L. Neagh
Lisburn
Ballyshannon
Irvinestown
Hillsborough
Mullaghmore
Bundoran
Belleek
Dromore
Aughnacloy
Lurgan
Portadown
Portaferry
Tandragee
Ballynahinch
Grange
Drumcliff
Enniskillen
Banbridge
Downpatrick
Manorhamilton
Emyvale
Armagh
DOWN
Easkey
Strandhill
Sligo
Dromahair
FERMANAGH
Monaghan
ARMAGH
Keady
Newcastle
Erris Hd.
Ballycastle
Killala
Dromore West
Inishcrone
Collooney
Derrylin
Clones
Newry
St. John's Pt.
Bangor Erris
Crossmolina
Ballina
SLIGO
Swanlinbar
Ballyconnell
MONAGHAN
Warrenpoint
Castlebaldwin
Belturbet
Cootehill
Castleblayney
Kilkeel
Tubbercurry
Ballymote
Ballinamore
Carlingford
Achill Hd.
Keel
Achill Island
Foxford
Drumshanbo
Iniskeen
IRISH SEA
MAYO
Boyle
LEITRIM
Cavan
Shercock
Dundalk
Mulranny
Newport
Charlestown
Carrickmacross
Swinford
Carrick-on-Shannon
CAVAN
Kingscourt
LOUTH
Clare Island
Clew Bay
Castlebar
ROSCOMMON
Ardee
Dunleer
Westport
Knock
Strokestown
Virginia
Roonah Quay
Louisburgh
Castlerea
Granard
LONGFORD
Claremorris
Ballyhaunis
Longford
Edgeworthstown
Kells
Slane
Drogheda
Inishturk
Newgrange
Renvyle
Leenaun
Ballinrobe
Roscommon
Lanesborough
Castlepollard
Navan
Cleggan
Letterfrack
Clonbur
Cong
Ballymahon
Athboy
MEATH
Balbriggan
Skerries
Clifden
Headford
Tuam
Mount Bellew
Mullingar
Rush
Ballyconneely
Slyne Hd.
Sraith Salach (Recess)
WESTMEATH
Trim
Swords
Malahide
Roundstone
Oughterard
GALWAY
Athlone
Kinnegad
Howth
Galway
Ballinasloe
Moate
Maynooth
Dublin
Dun Laoghaire
An Cheathrú Rua (Carraroe)
Inverin
Salthill
Athenry
Kilbeggan
Clane
Ros an Mhíl (Rossaveal)
An Spidéal (Spiddal)
Oranmore
Tullamore
OFFALY
Edenderry
KILDARE
Naas
Bray
Kilreekill
Portarlington
Droichead Nua (Newbridge)
Tallaght
Enniskerry
Blessington
Greystones
Loughrea
Banagher
Kilcormac
Portumna
Birr
ATLANTIC OCEAN
Aran Islands
Ballyvaughan
Kildare
Doolin
Gort
Portlaoise
Stradbally
Glendalough
Ashford
Wicklow
Lisdoonvarna
Terryglass
Athy
WICKLOW
Rathdrum
Ennistymon
Mountshannon
Scarriff
Dromineer
Roscrea
LAOIS
Abbeyleix
Baltinglass
Lahinch
Avoca
Miltown Malbay
Ennis
Tulla
Nenagh
Durrow
Carlow
Tullow
CLARE
Killaloe
Templemore
Castlecomer
Arklow
Kilkee
Kilrush
Shannon
Urlingford
CARLOW
Gorey
Killimer
Limerick
Thurles
Kilkenny
Bagenalstown
Bunclody
Courtown
Holycross
KILKENNY
Kilbaha
Foynes
Adare
TIPPERARY
Graiguenamanagh
Ferns
Loop Hd.
Ballybunion
Tarbert
Rathkeale
Callan
WEXFORD
Listowel
LIMERICK
Cashel
Enniscorthy
ST. GEORGE'S CHANNEL
Newcastle West
Tipperary
Thomastown
Kerry Hd.
Ballyheige
Abbeyfeale
Kilmallock
Cahir
Clonmel
Carrick-on-Suir
New Ross
Wexford
Rath Luirc (Charleville)
Tralee
Mitchelstown
Waterford
Ballyhack
Wellington Bridge
Rosslare
Rosslare Harbour
Castlegregory
Castleisland
Buttevant
Passage East
Fethard
Kilmore Quay
Camp
Kanturk
Fermoy
WATERFORD
Tramore
Dunmore East
An Daingean (Dingle)
Mallow
Lismore
Cappoquin
Killorglin
KERRY
Killarney
Dungarvan
Glenbeigh
Millstreet
Watergrasshill
CELTIC SEA
CORK
Youghal
Ardmore
Cahirciveen
Blarney
Kenmare
Macroom
Cork
Midleton
Sneem
Cobh
Ballycotton
Waterville
Inchigeelagh
Crosshaven
Carrigaline
Glengarriff
Bandon
Dunmanway
Kinsale
Bantry
Clonakilty
Castletown Bere
Rosscarbery
Courtmacsherry
Schull
Skibbereen
Baltimore
Goleen
Mizen Hd.
KILOMETRES
0 20 40 60 80km
0 10 20 30 40 50mls
MILES
Whilst every care has been taken to ensure accuracy in the compilation of this map,
Tourism Ireland cannot accept responsibility for errors or omissions
Because of the small scale of this map, not all holiday centres can be shown. The information on this map is correct at the time of going to press. © July 2002 Tourism Ireland

Abbey Theatre, the. Ireland's national theater. Considered one of the most prestigious theater companies in the world, the Abbey is one of the important institutions to emerge from the *Irish Revival of the late nineteenth century. In 1899, Lady *Gregory, W. B. *Yeats, and others created the Irish Literary Theatre, which became known as the Abbey Theatre in 1904. As a writers' theater, its main objective was to encourage the staging of Irish plays for Irish audiences at a time when *theater in Ireland was dominated by the offerings of British touring companies. The Abbey also aimed to uphold the highest artistic principles and to provide an alternative to the melodrama and vaudeville of the commercial theaters. Early on, the movement produced a crop of talented playwrights, including Yeats, Lady Gregory, J. M. *Synge, and Seán *O'Casey, whose contribution to world drama has been widely acknowledged. The Abbey's initial success was considerably enhanced by the acting talents of Frank and Willie *Fay. Some of the early productions became embroiled in the politics of the day, causing disturbances in the theater. Most notoriously, J. M. Synge's *Playboy of the Western World* (1907) and Seán O'Casey's *The Plough and the Stars* (1926) caused riots because of their iconoclastic attacks on idealized cultural nationalism. Destroyed by fire in 1951, the theater was redeveloped to include a smaller auditorium (the *Peacock) and reopened in 1966. Although criticized for its conservatism at times, the Abbey continues to be the most important institution in Irish theater. In 1990, the Abbey triumphed with a production of Brian *Friel's *Dancing at Lughnasa*, which toured to great acclaim in London and New York. The best of contemporary playwrights continue to work at the Abbey, including Marina *Carr, Conor *McPherson, and Eugene O'Brien. P.J.M.

Adams, Gerry (1948–). Politician, president of *Sinn Féin (1983–present), Member of Parliament (MP) for West *Belfast. Gerry Adams was born on October 6, 1948, into a working-class *republican

Gerry Adams

family in West Belfast. Educated in local *Catholic schools, Adams joined the republican movement in 1964. When Sinn Féin split in 1969/70, he sided with the Provisional wing, and became active in the *Northern Ireland Civil Rights Association (NICRA) campaign. By early 1970, he was suspected of playing a leading role in the Ballymurphy unit of the Provisional IRA (*Irish Republican Army) in Belfast. He is credited with devising the "economic targets" bombing campaign. In 1972, Adams was interned without trial, but briefly released to participate in secret peace talks with the British government. The talks failed, but Adams reputedly became Adjutant for Belfast and important in the "middle leadership" of the IRA. He was interned again in 1973–76 and 1978, and was officially charged with membership in the IRA but was never convicted.

As a northern leadership of the IRA emerged in the late 1970s, Adams pressed for its political wing, Sinn Féin, to be more involved in electoral politics in *Northern Ireland. He consolidated his leadership role as Sinn Féin vice president during the republican prisoners' *hunger strikes of 1981, and in 1983 he became president of Sinn Féin.

A member of the United Kingdom Parliament since 1983 (except for 1992–97 when *SDLP (Social Democratic and Labour Party) representative Dr. Joe Hendron defeated him), Adams has refused to take his seat at Westminster in keeping with party policy.

Following talks with SDLP leader John *Hume (started in 1988), and overtures to the British and Irish governments, Adams helped to secure an IRA cease-fire in August 1994, which lasted until February 1996. In September 1997, after the declaration of a second IRA cease-fire in July of that year, Adams and his negotiating team joined multiparty talks to end the conflict. The resulting Belfast (or *Good Friday) Agreement, April 1998, fell well short of republican objectives, but Adams hoped it could be used as a base for further negotiations and campaigned vigorously for its acceptance. In May 1998, 95 percent of the people in the *Republic and 71 percent of those in Northern Ireland accepted the agreement. In June 1998, Adams won a seat in the new Northern Ireland Assembly. He led Sinn Féin to an electoral peak of 21.7 percent in the Westminster election in the summer of 2001, narrowly overtaking the SDLP as Northern Ireland's largest *nationalist party. In the fall of 2001, he helped to secure an IRA decommissioning of part of its arsenal and, early in 2002, spoke

Harvesting at Traditional Irish Farm, Muckross Estate, Killarney, County Kerry

openly of the need to secure the consent of a majority of the people of Northern Ireland for a united Ireland. Although he has largely been successful in unifying the republican movement behind the *peace process, Adams has not been able to prevent splits in the IRA, though they have been limited in significance. His immediate ambition, it seems, is to make Sinn Féin the largest nationalist party in Northern Ireland and a more significant force in the Republic, as well. M.M.

Aer Lingus. Ireland's national airline. In April 1936, Aer Lingus Teoranta, which was comprised of one six-seat aircraft, was registered as a private airline by the Irish government. After providing the vital *Dublin to Liverpool air link during World War II, Aer Lingus greatly expanded its fleet and services over the next two decades. Routes to numerous British and European cities were opened between 1945 and 1960 and services from Dublin and Shannon to *New York, *Boston, and *Chicago were inaugurated between 1958 and 1966. In 2000, Aer Lingus operated a fleet of thirty-eight aircraft carrying close to seven million passengers and made a profit of 79.9 million. As a consequence of the events of September 11, 2001, the airline lost 50 million dollars in 2001. Aer Lingus adapted to the worldwide fall in demand for air travel by restructuring and reducing its workforce by one-third. S.A.B.

agriculture. Ireland's *economy has traditionally been based on agriculture. Sixty-four percent of the land of Ireland (17 million acres) is used for agriculture, with forestry accounting for a further 9.4 percent in 2001. Ireland's maritime climate, with high rainfall and relatively low summer but high winter temperatures, is suitable for grass growing and animal production, but makes growing crops difficult. The percentage of grassland (80 percent) is the highest of any *European Union (EU) country. Therefore, agricultural production is dominated by livestock, with beef, dairy products, and sheep meat accounting for about three-quarters of overall production. Minor commodities include grain, sugarbeet, potatoes, pigs, and poultry. Around two-thirds of total production is exported, and access to lucrative export markets has always been a government priority.

Some of the earliest farming settlements in Europe, circa 3000 B.C., were discovered at the *Céide Fields in County *Mayo. The *Celts who arrived about 300 B.C. introduced the *brehon system of tribal land tenure, which survived up to the time of *Elizabeth I, much longer than elsewhere in Europe, where crop production favored the individual possession of land. The arrival of the *Normans in the twelfth century had no long-term impact on agricultural practices or structures. However, the *plantations in the sixteenth and seventeenth centuries rudely disrupted the old order. Not only was tribal tenure replaced by the feudal system, but ownership of land passed completely into the hands of the old *Anglo-Irish families or the new English and Scottish settlers. By the end of the eighteenth century, about 95 percent of Ireland's land was owned by settlers (who constituted less than 0.5 percent of the population), many of them absentee *landlords.

During the nineteenth century, livestock became firmly established as the preferred mode of farming because it was more profitable than tillage. A numerous tenantry, once an asset, now became a liability, leading to a sharp increase in *emigration. The *Land Act of 1885 introduced a voluntary purchase scheme to enable tenants to own their land. Land purchase was subsequently made compulsory in the first Land Act passed by the *Free State government in 1923. The owner-occupied family farm became the fundamental unit of agricultural production.

In the first five decades of independence, the Land Commission enforced a program of land purchase and redistribution to maximize the number of families working the land. However, technological progress in farming, together with rising incomes outside of agriculture, has increased the minimum size for farm viability. While the number of family farms has declined steadily from 398,000 in 1900 to 144,000 in 1999, average farm size has increased from 31.4 acres to 72.4 acres. With the growth of nonagricultural employment in rural areas, part-time farming has become common. It is now estimated that on 45 percent of farms, either the farmer and/or his or her spouse has an off-farm job.

Agriculture, traditionally the backbone of the economy, is becoming less important as Ireland's economic structure diversifies. In 1922, the agricultural sector in the Irish Free State accounted for about one-third of gross domestic product, just over half of total employment, and almost three-quarters of merchandise exports. By 2001, agriculture's share of national output had fallen to just over 3 percent, while its share of national employment was 6.5 percent.

Farmers reacted to their declining importance by lobbying hard for protection and support. They enthusiastically supported Ireland's membership in the European Economic Community (as the *EU was then called) in 1973 not only because it guaranteed market access to the high-priced EU market, but, more significantly, because the cost of supporting farm prices was transferred from the Irish to the much larger EU budget through the operation of the EU's Common Agricultural Policy (CAP).

However, the CAP itself became subject to pressures for reform on budgetary grounds. Milk quotas were introduced in 1984, and in 1992, on the proposal of Agricultural Commissioner Ray MacSharry, support prices were reduced for some commodities while farmers were compensated through increased direct payments. Direct payments now account for 57 percent of farmers' total income and this will rise in the next few years.

Agriculture has had both negative and positive environmental impacts. Fertilizer runoff contributes to the eutrophication of waterways and rising nitrate levels in groundwater. Silage effluent spillages have been responsible for killing fish. Agriculture in Ireland contributes one-third of total greenhouse gas emissions of all EU countries. On the other hand, agriculture has shaped the natural environment and produced much of Ireland's breathtaking landscape. Integrating environmental considerations into agricultural policy is a major challenge for the industry in the new millennium. Whether agriculture's future lies in being a competitive producer of food or a supplier of amenities and environmental goods is now the key question for debate. A.M.

Ahern, Bertie (1951–). Politician, *Taoiseach (prime minister), leader of *Fianna Fáil. Born in *Dublin, Ahern worked as an accountant before becoming a full-time public representative. Member of the *Dáil (Parliament) since 1977, he was minister for labour (1987–91) and minister for finance (1991–1994). Leader of Fianna Fáil since 1994, Ahern became Taoiseach in 1997. He developed a reputation as an excellent constituency worker early in his career and soon became the dominant politician in his inner-city Dublin community. He came to national prominence as minister for labour as a negotiator and mediator in labor disputes. Ahern played a major role in the development of the model of social partnership between the government and the main national interest groups, which has become the dominant policy model in Ireland since 1987 and which is credited with the rapid growth in the Irish *economy since then. He has established excellent relations with the Irish *trade union movement. His political skills were used by Fianna Fáil as they negotiated their first coalition government agreement in 1989 and also in the peace talks leading to the *Good Friday Agreement signed in *Belfast on April 10, 1998. In May 2002, Ahern led Fianna Fáil to a major victory (eighty-one seats) in a general election. J.D.

Aiken, Frank (1898–1983). Politician, government minister, IRA (*Irish Republican Army) leader. Born in County *Armagh, Aiken joined the Irish *Volunteers in 1913 and was an IRA commander during the *War of Independence. Opponent of the *Anglo-Irish Treaty of 1921, he succeeded Liam Lynch as chief of staff of the IRA in April 1923, after Lynch was shot by *Free State troops. He immediately sought an end to the *Irish Civil War, which officially ceased in May 1923. Aiken was a founding member of *Fianna Fáil and served under Éamon *de Valera and Seán *Lemass, most notably as minister for defense in 1932–45, finance 1945–48, and foreign affairs 1951–54, and again in 1957–69. P.E.

aisling. A common motif in *Celtic mythology that takes its name from the Gaelic word for a dream or a vision. From the eighteenth century onward the word was associated with a form of allegorical poetry—most commonly practiced in *Munster—in which a beautiful woman (Ireland) bemoans being forsaken by her husband in the aftermath of the Jacobean wars. The poems often ended on a positive note with hope of French, Spanish, or papal deliverance from British rule. B.D.

Allgood, Molly (1887–1952). Actress, stage name Máire O'Neill. Born in *Dublin, Molly was sent to an orphanage, along with her sister Sara *Allgood, after their father's death, and subsequently apprenticed to a dressmaker. In 1905, she joined the *Abbey Theatre Company, where, with Sara and the *Fay brothers, she developed the understated Abbey style of acting. Also in 1905, Molly became engaged to J. M. *Synge, who died four years later. She played Pegeen Mike in Synge's *The Playboy of the Western World* (1907); the play caused riots in Dublin, but subsequent performances in London were a personal triumph. In 1911, she married George Herbert Mair, and continued her successful acting career in England.

After Mair's death in 1926, she married an Abbey actor, Arthur Sinclair. With him and her sister Sara, she appeared many times in plays by Seán *O'Casey. Her later years were troubled by divorce and financial problems. J.C.E.L.

Allgood, Sara (1883–1950). Actress. Born in *Dublin, Sara and her sister Molly *Allgood were raised in an orphanage. In the first years of the century, Sara acted in plays performed by Maud *Gonne's women's *nationalist group, Inghinidhe na hÉireann (Daughters of Ireland). The stage manager of these plays, William *Fay, invited her to join the National Theatre Society in 1903. Sara acted in *Yeats's *The King's Threshold* (1903) and played Maurya in *Synge's *Riders to the Sea* (1904). With her sister Molly and the Fay brothers, she was instrumental in developing the *Abbey Theatre's acting style. Her interpretation of Maurya, modeled on her own grandmother, was praised for its naturalness and intensity of emotion. On the opening night of the Abbey Theatre in 1904, she played Mrs. Fallon in Lady *Gregory's *Spreading the News.* She joined John Hartley Manner's touring company in 1915, and married another actor, Gerald Henson, while on tour in Australia. He and their son died of influenza in 1918. Allgood returned to the Abbey in 1920 and gave memorable performances as Juno in Seán *O'Casey's *Juno and the Paycock*, and as Bessie Burgess in the London production of *The Plough and the Stars.* After an American tour she settled in Hollywood in 1940, but her transition to film acting was not successful. She died in poverty. J.C.E.L.

Alliance Party of Northern Ireland (APNI). Political party. The APNI, a moderate, cross-community party, was formed in April 1970 by activists who had campaigned for *Unionist Prime Minister Captain Terence *O'Neill in the February 1969 "Crossroads" election. Though in favor of the union with Britain, the party advocates a united community within *Northern Ireland. Largely middle-class in composition, it draws support from both *Catholics and *Protestants—the only significant party to do so. Currently aligned with the Liberal Democrat Party in Britain, the APNI, while supporting union with Britain, would accept formal links with the *Republic of Ireland. The party appears to be in long-term decline, because moderates and liberals are joining mainstream unionist parties. M.M.

Allingham, William (1824–89). Poet. Allingham was born in Ballyshannon, County *Donegal. While working as a customs officer, he frequently visited London, where he befriended many writers, including Leigh Hunt, Carlyle, the Brownings, Tennyson, and members of the Pre-Raphaelite circle. Rossetti and Millais illustrated his poetry collection *Day and Night Songs* (1854). Allingham retired to London in 1870, where he became the editor of *Fraser's Magazine.* His poetry was inspired by philosophical, social, and psychological ideas. He also published an anthology of ballads, and wrote poems about the fairy world, which profoundly influenced the young W. B. *Yeats. His most ambitious work was *Laurence Bloomfield in Ireland* (1864), a long narrative poem addressing the tensions between *landlords and tenants. J.C.E.L.

Altan. Traditional *music band. Altan was formed in 1983 by fiddler and singer Mairéad Ní Mhaonaigh of Gweedore and her husband, flute player Frankie Kennedy (1955–94). Rooted in the repertoire and style of County *Donegal, the unique, thorough integrity of Altan's many albums has made considerable impact not only in Ireland, but in folk music circles in Europe and in the United States. F.V.

American Civil War, the (1861–65). The most violent and traumatic episode in US history, resulting in some 620,000 deaths. This conflict is considered the defining moment of the American Republic, ensuring the survival of the Union and the abolition of slavery. Having predominantly settled in the urban centers of the North, Irish immigrants played an important, if often exaggerated, part in the Union victory. Nearly 150,000 of the over two million troops who served in the Federal armies, were of Irish origin. Included in these ranks was the famous Irish Brigade, commanded by the *Young Irelander Thomas Francis *Meagher. This unit consisted of three regiments recruited from *New York City's Irish population, including the celebrated "Fighting 69th," which lost more than half its men in a heroic charge at the Battle of Antietam.

However, Irish enlistment rates were below those of other immigrant groups and native-born Americans. Most likely, this was because of the antagonism of *Catholic immigrants (who mainly supported the peace faction of the Democratic Party) toward the nativist Republican Party and its pro-war, anti-slavery platform. Irish fear of competition at the bottom of the socioeconomic ladder fueled a series of anti-black "draft riots," the most infamous of which occurred in New York City in 1863. Immigrants from Ireland also contributed to the Confederate side. For example, Irish dock workers from New Orleans were a major component of the "Louisiana Tigers," while John *Mitchel, the Young Ireland radical, was an ardent supporter of the South. The war, although disruptive of *Fenian fund-raising efforts in the United States, ultimately provided a number of hardened veterans for the *nationalist cause. Most prominently, Union Captain T. J. Kelly became the leader of the Fenian Brotherhood and led the 1867 rising. J.P.

American Revolution, the (American War of Independence) (1775–83). The rebellion of thirteen British North American colonies caused by resentment over taxation and the absence of parliamentary representation. Despite a number of early setbacks, the colonists (significantly aided by France from 1778) won important victories at Saratoga in 1777 and Yorktown in 1781, culminating in the independence and the foundation of the United States in 1783. Irish *immigrants and Irish Americans, particularly *Ulster Presbyterians who constituted the largest white, non-English ethnic group in the colonies, played a central role in the Revolution. As much as one-third of the Continental army was of Irish descent, including twenty-six general officers. General Richard Montgomery, a Dublin native, commanded the American forces that invaded Canada in 1775. Continental Army Major General John Sullivan waged a devastating campaign against the Iroquois (British allies). Sullivan was the son of Limerick-born James Sullivan, the former governor of Massachusetts. Another son of Irish immigrants, Henry Knox, served as Washington's head of Artillery. After the war, Knox became the army's commander in chief and then secretary of war of the new republic. John Barry, a Wexford native, is credited as founder of the American navy. Timothy Murphy (a generation removed from Ireland) was believed to be the best shot in the Continental army. From a distance, he successfully killed two ranking British officers, thereby contributing to the American victory at Saratoga.

The Revolution deeply affected Ireland, where many Irish "patriots" clearly recognized common grievances with the American colonists. Irish reformers headed by Henry *Grattan and backed by the *Volunteer movement (local units nominally raised to defend Ireland while much of its regular garrison was engaged abroad) took advantage of the imperial crisis to extract important economic and political concessions (free trade 1779 and legislative independence 1782) from the British government. J.P.

An Claidheamh Soluis (1899–1930). The newspaper of the *Gaelic League. Its title means "The Sword of Light." The newspaper was extremely influential both culturally and politically, particularly up to the establishment of the *Irish Free State in 1922. Its more famous editors included Eoin *MacNeill and Patrick *Pearse. The newspaper had a bilingual policy of developing and supporting debate and literature in both Irish and English. A.T.

Ancient Order of Hibernians (AOH). *Catholic, *nationalist benevolent society. The Ancient Order of Hibernians was formed in *New York in 1836. In Ireland, its origins are unclear, but its roots were in the late-eighteenth-century secret peasant societies such as the *Defenders and Ribbonmen, which were formed as Catholic reaction to the *Orange Order. The AOH, which remains exclusively Catholic and male, adopted freemason-style rituals and regalia. After the *Famine, the AOH became one of the strongest Irish movements in America. Its purpose was to defend the Irish Catholic community, and it was prominent in New York during anti-Irish riots in the 1840s and 1850s, and the Orange riots of the 1870s. The order was active in Irish American politics and raised money for nationalist movements in Ireland. Its association with the Molly Maguires, a secret society among Irish miners in the Pennsylvania coal fields in the 1870s, was the subject of press hysteria, but the connection seems to have been exaggerated.

During the 1880s, *Clan na Gael dominated the American organization. In 1878, the American AOH opened membership to those of Irish descent. The Irish organization, which had become more formally organized and publically active from the 1870s, split in the 1880s, but reunited at the turn of the century as the Ancient Order of Hibernians (Board of Erin). From the 1880s, the AOH became increasingly more important in Ireland, mainly in *Ulster. After the lifting of a clerical ban (as a "secret society") in 1904, the order spread to other parts of Ireland, and AOH halls in many Irish towns date from these years.

The Belfast nationalist Joseph Devlin was the order's national president in Ireland from 1905 to 1934. Under Devlin, the AOH expanded as a political network. Membership grew from ten thousand in 1905 to sixty thousand in 1909, mainly in Ulster and the neighboring counties, as the AOH worked alongside the parliamentary nationalist movement. The renewed prospect of *home rule also prompted constitutional nationalists to join the AOH. The *Irish Parliamentary Party, led by John *Redmond, needed it as a branch network to replace its declining grass-roots organization, the United Irish League (UIL).

Because of its narrow sectarianism and its association with machine politics and jobbery, the AOH was much despised by *Sinn Féin, by some nationalist leaders, including the land agitator and MP (member of Parliament) William *O'Brien, and by *socialists like James *Connolly and James *Larkin. In *Northern Ireland, the order was closely associated with the *Nationalist Party until the 1970s. Although the AOH survives in Ireland, it has declined in recent decades and is now politically insignificant.

In America it remains widely organized, but mostly middle-class and conservative. The AOH has been at the center of controversy since the early 1990s for excluding the Irish Lesbian and Gay Organization from the New York St. Patrick's Day parade. P.D.

Andrews, John Millar (1871–1956). Prime minister of *Northern Ireland, 1940–43. Born in County *Antrim, into a business family, Andrews was MP (member of Parliament) for County *Down, 1921–29, and for Mid-Down from 1929. He was minister for labour in the Northern Ireland cabinet, 1921–37, and minister for finance, 1937–40. He served briefly as *Stormont prime minister from 1940 to 1943. His most significant achievement was to negotiate an agreement with the British exchequer to maintain the equivalent British welfare services in Northern Ireland. Failure to mobilize effectively for war led to his replacement by Basil *Brooke. He died in 1956. M.M.

Anglo-Irish, the. At its simplest level, this term denotes people, born or living in Ireland, who are of English ancestry. Traditionally, the English presence in Ireland is dated from 1170, when Dermot *MacMurrough, the deposed king of *Leinster, invited *Anglo-Norman Lord Richard fitz Gilbert (*Strongbow) to help him regain his throne. This invitation opened a veritable Pandora's box, which ultimately led to English domination of Ireland.

The Anglo-Saxon presence in Ireland is, actually, the result of a highly complex process. Both Strongbow and his overlord, *Henry II, the first King of England to claim sovereignty in Ireland, were in fact Normans. These descendants of the *Vikings had subjugated England from their French Duchy in 1066 and until the fourteenth century they remained a French-speaking ruling class in their newly acquired kingdom of England. In Ireland, Norman lords came to dominate the *Pale (an area around Dublin) and were scattered throughout much of the rest of the country where, over time, they often intermarried with the families of Gaelic chieftains, creating a hybrid culture that was often more Irish than Norman. This process of assimilation was so alarming to the English authorities that the Anglo-Norman–dominated Irish *Parliament passed the notorious Statute of *Kilkenny (1366). The statute, although ultimately doomed to failure, was a direct attempt to preserve English law, customs, and culture within the Anglo-Norman colony in Ireland. Some of its clauses banned intermarriage between English settlers and Gaelic natives and the use of the *Irish language and dress.

Historically, many of the most powerful and influential Irish families, like the Butlers and Fitzgeralds—to name only two—were descended from these so-called Anglo-Normans. With the Protestant *Reformation and *Henry VIII's establishment of a formal kingship over Ireland in the 1530s and 1540s, a new nomenclature emerged to distinguish between old, usually Catholic, families of Norman and Saxon origin and new Protestant officials and settlers from England. Thus, the respective names Old English and New English were born. The Catholic Old English sided with their Gaelic co-religionists in the *Rebellion of 1641 and the ensuing Confederate War (1641–53). After the *Cromwellian Settlement of the 1650s, the Old English ceased to be distinguished from the Gaels, and both became simply Catholic. In turn, the New English, joined by a sizable influx of Protestant settlers, became known as the Anglo-Irish. This latter nomenclature is most commonly used to denote the tiny minority (the so-called Protestant Ascendancy) drawn from the established Protestant *Church of Ireland, who owned some 90 percent of the land and dominated Ireland economically, politically, and socially in the eighteenth, nineteenth, and early twentieth centuries. Yet, it is important to remember that there were also tens of thousands of Anglo-Irish farmers, merchants, and artisans (totaling some 10 percent of the population) in the south of Ireland by 1700.

The Anglo-Irish have traditionally played a disproportionate cultural role in Irish society, particularly in the realm of *literature in English. For example, Jonathan *Swift (author of *Gulliver's Travels*), the Protestant dean of *St. Patrick's Cathedral in Dublin, was the most prominent Irish writer of the eighteenth century. More significantly, many of the writers involved in the *Irish Revival (c.1890–1910) were Anglo-Irish. Included in this movement, which centered on the *Abbey Theatre in Dublin, were such internationally renowned playwrights and authors as W. B. *Yeats, Lady *Gregory, J. M. *Synge, and, less directly, George Bernard *Shaw. Ironically, the Anglophone writers of the Irish Revival, who were reacting against a perceived English cultural imperialism, were themselves often dismissed as "West Britons" by members of the contemporaneous *Gaelic Revival who advocated a purely Irish-language literature.

Some of Ireland's greatest *nationalist leaders and politicians have been Anglo-Irish, such as Henry *Grattan, Wolfe *Tone, Robert *Emmet, Isaac *Butt, Charles Stewart *Parnell, and Erskine *Childers, to name a few. With the disestablishment of the *Church of Ireland (1869), land reform (1881, 1903), and, finally, independence (1922), the Anglo-Irish gradually shrank to the roughly 4 percent of the population of the *Republic that they are today, and the term is rarely used in a modern context. J.P.

Anglo-Irish Agreement (1985). Agreement between the Irish and British governments, signed at Hillsborough, County *Down, on November 15, 1985. Since the failure of *Sunningdale's Council of Ireland in 1973, British policy in Ireland had concentrated on security and finding common ground for an internal settlement. *Unionists preferred direct rule from London to any form of power sharing, and the influence of constitutional *nationalism waned in the absence of any real progress. Following the *hunger strikes of 1981, nationalist supporters began to desert the *Social Democratic and Labour Party (SDLP) in favor of *Sinn Féin's sterner *republicanism. Both the *Fine Gael–Labour coalition in *Dublin and *Margaret Thatcher's Conservative government in London were seriously concerned that Sinn Féin would become the majority voice of the *Catholic nationalist community. In 1985, the Anglo-Irish Agreement committed both governments to the principle that *Northern Ireland's constitutional status would not change without the consent of a majority of its people. The agreement also gave a consultative role to the government of the *Republic of Ireland in the administration of Northern Ireland.

There was some disappointment on both sides. The Irish government found its influence to be strictly secondary to Britain's perceptions of stable administration. The British were disappointed at the poor level of cooperation between the north and south on security. Republicans generally rejected the agreement but were impressed by Britain's willingness to defy unionist objections. Unionists, for their part, were frightened by the prospect of deals over their heads, and began to organize resistance to joint authority. Sinn Féin's electoral advance was checked temporarily, while loyalist paramilitaries saw an incentive to act. Nevertheless, the agreement moved both republicans and loyalists toward sowing the seeds of peace. M.M.

Anglo-Irish Treaty (1921). Agreement ending the *War of Independence. In a meeting on July 8, 1921, Éamon *de Valera and General Macready, the commander in chief of British forces in Ireland, agreed to end the *Anglo-Irish War. The truce came into effect on Monday July 11, 1921. De Valera arrived in London the following day to meet with British Prime Minister *Lloyd George, but initial negotiations failed to secure an agreement.

On September 29, Lloyd George suggested that Irish delegates come to a conference in London with a view to determine "how the association of Ireland with the British Commonwealth may be reconciled with Irish national aspirations."

De Valera sent a delegation representing *Dáil Éireann (Irish parliament), consisting of chief negotiators Arthur *Griffith, Michael *Collins, and Robert *Barton, and legal advisors Éamonn Duggan and George Gavan Duffy. Erskine *Childers also attended as nonvoting secretary. The delegates had the power to sign any agreement, but they were also confusingly told to report back to Dublin before signing anything. In what some have seen as a controversial move—that has been open to many interpretations—de Valera decided not to attend, arguing that his presence was needed in Dublin to gather support for any agreement. Some historians have argued that he did not want to take the blame in the event of a compromise solution.

Negotiations opened in London on October 11, 1921, with the British delegation led by Prime Minister Lloyd George, Winston *Churchill, Austin Chamberlain, and Lord Birkenhead. The Irish delegation had been instructed to seek recognition for the thirty-two-county Irish *Republic, which had been created by the first *Dáil in January 1919. If this failed, the delegates were told to give up some independence in return for the preservation of unity. De Valera also argued for some degree of "external association" between a united Ireland and Britain, whereby Ireland would not actually be part of the British empire, but would be closely affiliated with it.

The British, on the other hand, were adamant that Ireland should remain part of the *Commonwealth and that the demands of the *Ulster unionists be satisfied. Given these divergent positions, talks on political sovereignty and unity remained divisive, while matters such as trade, defense, and national debt were quickly resolved.

On November 2, Arthur Griffith, the leader of the Irish delegation, agreed that Ireland would remain part of the Commonwealth in return for Lloyd George's promise to persuade Ulster unionists to accept Irish unity. His efforts failed and on November 8, as an alternative solution, Lloyd George offered to establish a *Boundary Commission that would redefine the *Northern Ireland border. The British continued to reject the idea of "external association" and insisted that Ireland remain part of the British empire. Griffith reluctantly accepted the proposal and at the end of November returned to Dublin with a final draft of proposals for a treaty. On December 3, the Dáil rejected the proposals and instructed Griffith to renegotiate, without giving him specific guidelines.

Back in London, Griffith brought up the question of *partition again, but Lloyd George pointed out that they had already agreed to a Boundary Commission. He did, however, modify the *oath of allegiance and agreed that the Free State should be free to impose its own tariffs. Griffith wanted to bring these new terms back to Dublin, but Lloyd George gave him an ultimatum—they either agreed to the terms or "immediate and terrible war" would recommence. The delegates signed "the articles of agreement for a treaty" on December 6, 1921.

Under the agreement, twenty-six counties of Ireland would become the *Irish Free State, a member of the British Commonwealth of Nations, with dominion status equal to that of *Canada. A governor general would represent the British monarch and members of the Irish legislature would be required to take an oath of allegiance. If any of the six counties of Northern Ireland (*Derry, *Antrim, *Down, *Armagh, *Tyrone, *Fermanagh) decided not to become part of the Irish Free State, then a Boundary Commission would be established to adjust the border "in accordance with the wishes of the inhabitants." Britain also retained ownership of the ports of Cobh and Berehaven in County *Cork, and Lough Swilly in County *Donegal for defense purposes.

In Dublin, the debate on the treaty, which began on December 14, 1921, was emotional and divisive. De Valera rejected the treaty outright. Dominion status, which some argued gave Britain too much influence in Ireland, and the oath of allegiance took up most of the debate. There was less discussion on *partition. The treaty was ratified by the Dáil on January 7, 1922, by sixty-four votes to fifty-seven. De Valera resigned as president (to be replaced by Griffith) and led the anti-treaty faction out of the Dáil following elections in June 1922. The *Civil War commenced on June 28, 1922. P.E.

Anglo-Irish War, the (January 1919–July 1921). Campaign of guerrilla warfare against the British army and RIC (*Royal Irish Constabulary) by the *Irish Republican Army (IRA), also known as the War of Independence. On January 21, 1919, twenty-seven (of the seventy-three) *Sinn Féin elected members (who had won seats in the December 1918 general election) who were not in jail, or on the run, formed the Irish *parliament, *Dáil Éireann, and declared the creation of an independent Irish *Republic. On the same day, the South Tipperary Brigade of the *Volunteers ambushed and killed two policemen escorting explosives to a quarry at Soloheadbeg in County *Tipperary. This incident is generally seen as the start of the War of Independence. The conflict, which lasted until July 11, 1921, had three distinct phases: the IRA campaign against the RIC; the struggle between the IRA and the *Auxiliaries/*Black and Tans; the use of IRA flying columns and the search for a peaceful solution.

The Volunteers (who in August 1919 renamed themselves the *Irish Republican Army) adopted guerrilla tactics, striking quickly and fading back into the countryside. While, in theory, command lay with Cathal *Brugha, the minister for defense, the nature of guerrilla warfare made it necessary for local commanders to maintain complete control, while the Dáil was forced to endorse and take full responsibility for their actions.

Following the Soloheadbeg ambush, Cathal Brugha issued an order authorizing the shooting of soldiers and policemen and RIC barracks were targeted by the IRA as a source of weapons. In the Dáil, Éamon *de Valera proposed a motion that RIC members be "ostracized." Recruitment fell drastically, as policemen became social outcasts and the victims of intimidation. Many resigned and, in the countryside, barracks became deserted as RIC officers were transferred to larger urban centers. By the summer of 1919, over fifty policemen had been killed and during Easter 1920, the IRA, in a gesture of defiance, burned many of the abandoned barracks throughout the country.

In June 1919, de Valera, who had escaped from jail in England in April, traveled to the United States to raise funds and support for the recognition of the Irish Republic. During his absence, Michael *Collins emerged as the chief intelligence coordinator of the IRA campaign. Early in the war, he successfully established a counterintelligence network and organized a "squad" to eliminate government spies.

When the situation spiraled out of control, *Lloyd George refused to send in the army because this would have given the conflict the status of a war. Instead, five thousand former *World War I soldiers were recruited to support the RIC. They were called the Black and Tans from the colors of their uniform. Another group, the Auxiliaries, which was made up of 1,500 ex–British army officers, was formed in August 1920. The IRA's guerrilla tactics, however, proved to be unbeatable. This led to the brutal Black and Tan campaign of terror and reprisals exemplified by the murder on March 19, 1920, of Tomás *MacCurtain, lord mayor of Cork, in front of his wife and family.

As the atrocities escalated, Lloyd George attempted to find a political solution by introducing the *Government of Ireland Act, which partitioned Ireland and for which no Irish MPs (member of Parliament) of any persuasion voted when it was passed on December 23, 1920. Under this legislation, two parliaments were to be set up, one in Dublin for twenty-six of the thirty-two counties and one in Belfast for the other six. The act failed to bring peace. *Sinn Féin ignored it and the *Ulster unionists only reluctantly accepted it.

On *Bloody Sunday, November 21, 1920, eleven British agents were assassinated in Dublin by Collins's squad. In reprisal, that same afternoon the Auxiliaries fired into the crowd during a Gaelic football game in *Croke Park, killing twelve people and wounding sixty others. That night, three prisoners, Peadar Clancy, Dick McKee, and Conor Clune were also shot while (according to *Dublin Castle) "trying to escape." A week later, seventeen Auxiliaries were killed at an ambush at Kilmichael, County *Cork, and as a result, martial law was declared in Counties Cork, *Kerry, Tipperary, and *Limerick on December 10. A day later, British forces were ambushed outside Cork, and in retaliation, parts of Cork City were burned.

In December 1920, de Valera returned from the United States to find a full-scale war in progress. The IRA had perfected the tactic of the flying columns—where groups of up to thirty men operating mostly in *Munster, *Connacht, and South Ulster, would launch ambushes and surprise attacks. These men remained permanently on the run and were hidden and supported by the local population. On May 25, 1921, the IRA mounted a large-scale offensive, when they attacked and burned the Customs House in Dublin, the headquarters of British taxation and administrative services in Ireland.

By the summer of 1921, both sides realized that a political solution was essential. The war had cost the British government over twenty million pounds since 1919 and the behavior of the Black and Tans and Auxiliaries had become a great embarrassment. The IRA was short of weapons and ammunition and people were tired of the ongoing violence. On July 8, de Valera and General Macready, the commander in chief of British forces in Ireland, agreed to a ceasefire. The truce came into effect on July 11, 1921, but preliminary negotiations between de Valera and Lloyd George in London failed to secure any agreement. In October 1921, Irish delegates arrived back in London to negotiote what would become the *Anglo-Irish Treaty. P.E.

Anglo-Norman Conquest. The Normans, from northern France, conquered England in 1066.

A century later, some of their descendants in Wales and England invaded Ireland. Unlike the invasion of England, the Anglo-Normans came to Ireland by invitation.

In 1166, the deposed king of *Leinster, Dermot *MacMurrough, went to King *Henry II of England asking for help to regain his kingdom. MacMurrough had abducted the wife of Tiernan O'Rourke, a local chieftain, fourteen years previously. O'Rourke was one of the enemies who drove MacMurrough out of Ireland. Some writers have drawn the parallel to the legend of Troy and exaggerated the episode's significance in leading to the invasion. Dermot's plea for help to Henry II to restore his kingdom, however, initiated the Anglo-Norman Conquest.

With Henry's permission, Dermot recruited several hundred Anglo-Norman soldiers and their leader *Strongbow. In return, Dermot offered Strongbow the succession of his kingdom and his daughter, Aoife, in marriage. Dermot returned to Ireland in August 1167, with Norman soldiers. After Strongbow's arrival with one thousand men in August 1170, Dermot secured Leinster and the cities of Waterford and *Dublin. Dermot died in 1171. Henry II feared that Strongbow had become too powerful and might try to recover his lost earldom of Pembroke. Also, Henry wanted to avoid condemnation for the murder of Thomas à Becket at Canterbury (December 29, 1170). The pope had encouraged the king to take Ireland because the Church there had not reformed sufficiently. Henry arrived near Waterford on October 17, 1171, with four hundred ships and four thousand men and asserted lordship over his Norman subjects and several Irish kings. He returned to England in April 1172, leaving Strongbow as his representative in Ireland.

The invasion was followed by a colonization and settlement. English law and institutions were introduced—later including a *parliament, under the English crown. By the late thirteenth century, English rule was effective over two-thirds of the island. Anglo-Norman tenants settled much of Leinster and *Munster. English and Welsh landless laborers also arrived. The settlement was part of a wider population expansion and movement in northwestern Europe.

At first the Normans built wooden *castles, on artificial mounds, or mottes. Later they constructed stone castles, many of which survive today, such as those at Carrickfergus and Ballymote. The Normans developed *agriculture on the estates around their manors and founded towns, including Sligo, New Ross, and Drogheda. Some settlements, such as Shanid in Limerick, were mainly military or administrative; others, like Carlow and Kilkenny, developed as centers of commerce.

The colony expanded and was consolidated in the thirteenth century, but it was only a partial conquest. Gaelic culture survived alongside that of the settlers, and large areas remained outside English law. The colony declined in the fourteenth century, and there was a revival in the power of the Irish lords. In spite of laws against such assimilation, many settlers had adopted the culture of the native Irish. English military campaigns failed to turn the tide, and in the fifteenth century the Norman rulers concentrated on consolidating an area around Dublin known as the *Pale. In two books, A *Topography of Ireland* and *The Conquest of Ireland*, Gerald of Wales, a contemporary writer, gives a valuable account of the Anglo-Norman conquest, although he depicts the Irish as a barbarous, uncultured race. P.D.

Annals of the Four Masters, the. A compilation of annals that records the history of Ireland from early times to 1616. The work, *Annála Ríoghachta Éireann*, was written between the years

1632 and 1636 by the Franciscan brother Mícheál Ó Cléirigh with the aid of Cúchoigríche Ó Cléirigh, Cúchoigríche Ó Duibhgeannáin, and Fearfeasa Ó Maoilchonaire, who were collectively known as "the four masters." Ó Cléirigh had many enemies in the Catholic University of Louvain and the finished product was heavily criticized there for going beyond just collecting material on the lives of Irish *saints. The work is dedicated to its patron, Fearghal Ó Gadhra (a member of parliament for *Sligo). B.D.

Antrim, County. Maritime county in the extreme northeast, in the province of *Ulster, one of the six counties of *Northern Ireland. The county has an area of 1,092 square miles and a population of est. 562,216 (1996). Only twenty miles across the Irish Sea from *Scotland at its closest point, Antrim has served as a conduit linking the two *Celtic peoples for nearly two millennia. In fact, Scotland draws its very name from an Antrim-based Irish tribe, the *Scots, who expanded into the west of Caledonia from their Kingdom of Dál Riata during the fourth and fifth centuries.

County Antrim is known for the beauty of its rugged coastline. Located in the north of the county, the *Giant's Causeway is a spectacular collection of thousands of black basalt columns which were formed, geologists believe, approximately 60 million years ago. In the northeast, the world-famous green Glens of Antrim stretch inland from the sea. *Belfast, Antrim's and Northern Ireland's capital and largest city, is located in the southern part of the county.

In the late medieval and early modern periods, Antrim and the west of Scotland were linked by the Lordship of the Isles headed by the Scottish MacDonald dynasty. During the late sixteenth and throughout the seventeenth centuries, a heavy influx of Scottish settlers radically altered the religious composition of the county. By the early eighteenth century, the county had the largest *Protestant population on a percentile basis of any county in Ireland. In the 1790s, Antrim was at the forefront of the *United Irish Movement and along with neighboring *Down was one of only two Ulster counties to rise during the *Rebellion of 1798. Today, Antrim's population is mostly Protestant and *unionist. The economy of the county is mostly agricultural, with some *textile production. Belfast has many different industries, including shipbuilding. Bushmills *distillery, in the village of Bushmills, produces a famous *whiskey. J.P.

Aosdána. State-funded association of artists engaged in *literature, *music, and visual arts. Established in 1981 and administered by the *Arts Council, Aosdána aims to honor artists who have made a significant contribution to the arts and to assist members to devote their energies fully to art. Membership is confined to no more than two hundred artists of distinguished creative and original work. Members must be born in Ireland or a resident for five years. They are eligible to receive a *Cnuas*, or annuity, for five years. A maximum of five new members may be elected annually. Particular achievements are recognized through the award of *Saoi*, of which there are only five at any time. M.S.T.

Apprentice Boys. A Masonic-style organization that shares the *Orange Order's goal of *Protestant supremacy. The organization was established in 1814 in memory of apprentice boys who, in defiance of city governors, shut the gates of Derry (Londonderry) City on Catholic troops loyal to *King James II on December 7, 1688. The city subsequently withstood a Jacobite siege (known as the Siege of *Derry) from April 18 to July 31, 1689. The Apprentice Boys represent a complex tradition of heroism, defense of

O'Brien's Castle on Inisheer, Aran Islands

liberty, religious intolerance, and, more so than other loyal orders, plebeian steadfastness. The annual Apprentice Boys march in the center of Derry symbolized Protestant domination of this predominantly Catholic city. The civil rights march of October 5, 1968, challenging the Protestant monopoly of local political power, is often considered the beginning of the modern *Troubles. M.M.

Aran Islands, the. A group of three islands off the coast of County *Galway and County *Clare. The biggest of the three is Inishmore (population of 836), the smallest Inishmaan (population of 216), and the other Inisheer (population of 217). The islands get their name from the Irish word *Ára*, which means "a kidney," and by extension a ridge or a back of land. The Aran Islands are renowned because of their archaeological interest and because they have produced or inspired several important writers. *Irish is the main language of the islands and it is not surprising, therefore, that its authors should write in both Irish and English.

The most famous of these is Liam *O'Flaherty (1896–1964), who celebrates the life of the island in his short stories *Dúil* (1953), as well as in his autobiography *Shame the Devil* (1934), and in some of his novels, such as *The Black Soul* (1934). The poet Máirtín *Ó Direáin (1910–88) left Inishmore when he was eighteen years old, but the island became the central image in his poetry as a refuge from the awfulness of the modern world. Another native of the Aran Islands, Breandán Ó hEithir (1930–90), a nephew of Liam O'Flaherty, was a bilingual journalist, broadcaster, and novelist who cast a sardonic eye on Irish life in his numerous writings. Perhaps the most famous writer to explore the islands is the playwright John Millington *Synge (1871–1909). After a brief stay in Inishmore, he perfected his Irish in

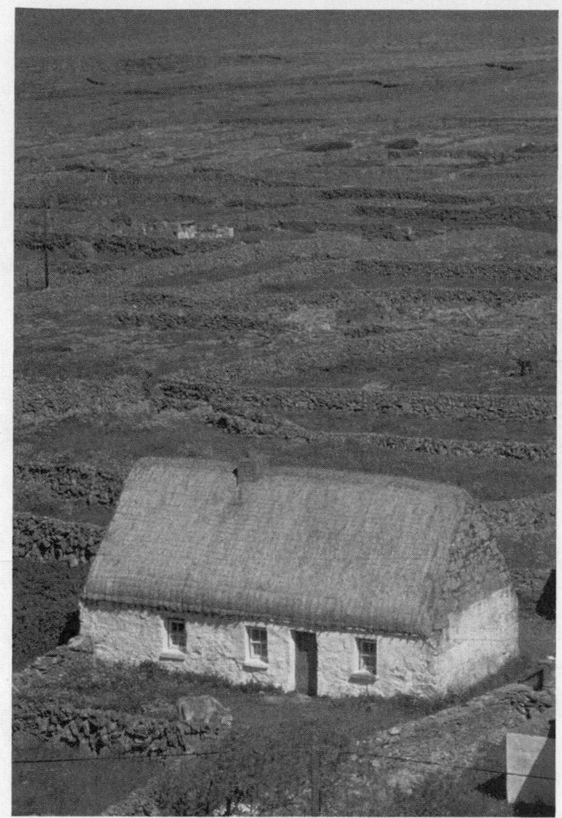

Traditional Cottage, Aran Islands

Inishmaan, and he based the strange and exotic *Hiberno-English of his plays on the rhythms, cadences, and syntax that he heard in the native language. Synge's *The Aran Islands* (1907) is a travel book that is also a piece of personal reflection and examination. Other noteworthy visitors to the islands included Samuel *Ferguson, Dr. William *Wilde, and the scholars John *O'Donovan and Eugene *O'Curry. The American filmmaker of Irish descent Robert O'Flaherty made his famous documentary film *Man of Aran* in 1934. In recent years the author and cartographer Tim Robinson (1935–) has lovingly mapped the islands as well as exhaustively written about every aspect of the landscape, history, and archaeology in *Stones of Aran* (1986 and 1995).

*Dún Aengus, perched on the high cliffs above the Atlantic Ocean, is the most prominent of several prehistoric cashels, or *hill-forts, on the islands. It is attributed in legend to the Fir Bolg, but its real age is disputed. There was certainly some settlement there as early as 800 B.C., but Dún Aengus reached its most developed form in the early *Christian period. Aran sweaters, which have become very popular, are traditionally hand-knitted from thick local wool by women on the island. According to one legend, each family used a different knitting pattern so that drowned fishermen could be identified by their sweaters. Since the opening up of the island to tourism, these sweaters have become an important business and can no longer be seen as a cottage industry. At the height of the summer season as many as two thousand visitors may come to the islands every day. A.T.

architecture. Over the centuries, Irish architecture has reflected disparate outside influences and has assimilated the styles of the many peoples who have set foot on the island's shores.

Early Neolithic builders (c.3700–2000 B.C.) constructed defensive forts and burial mounds. Some of these still survive, such as *Newgrange (c.3100 B.C.), the famous *passage-graves, and the dry-stone wall forts *Dún Aengus (Inishmore, *Aran Islands) and An Grianán Aileach (County *Donegal). Over thirty thousand *raths, enclosures surrounded by earthen embankments, still mark today's landscape.

In A.D. 432, the arrival of Christianity in Ireland brought a new architecture. Religious settlements on *Skellig Michael (County *Kerry) consisted of a basic church and a group of *beehive huts inside a walled enclosure. Gallarus Oratory (County Kerry), an isolated chamber used for single meditation, was built with inward sloping stone walls in the shape of an upturned boat. Larger monastic settlements, built between the ninth and twelfth centuries, survive at *Clonmacnoise (County *Offaly) and *Glendalough (County *Wicklow). Religious craftsmen built *high crosses, carved with biblical scenes, at these sites, and *round towers, made possible by the development of lime mortar.

Following the *Anglo-Norman invasion in 1169, Irish religious architecture adopted a Romanesque style, with carved geometric ornament around doorways and arches. From the twelfth century on, Romanesque architecture incorporated detailed exterior carvings in small churches and cathedrals, such as those at Kilkenny, Lismore, and Cashel. *Christ Church Cathedral, Dublin (c.1172), and *St. Patrick's owe more to an emerging Gothic style, whose innovative flying buttresses and rib vaults allowed vast interior spaces. Secular Norman architecture included "motte and bailey" *castles, four-storied rectangular stone towers called "keeps," and larger, fortified castles, such as *Dublin Castle, Carrickfergus Castle (County *Antrim), and King John's Castle, Limerick City (c.1200).

During the late Middle Ages (c.1400 to 1650), as the Anglo-Norman power was consolidated across the country, the construction of regional family castles and monastic settlements increased. The majority of Irish castles date from this period, including Clare (County *Kilkenny) and *Blarney (County *Cork).

Alongside the construction of larger stone buildings for the commercial and religious elite, a tradition of "vernacular" rural architecture—peasant homes, barns and agricultural sheds, and minor commercial premises—developed. Irish cottage-builders used local materials, including stone, clay, sods, grass, and straw. The ground-plan of cottages included a door opening onto a central room, which had the hearth as its social and working center, and bedrooms off to each side. The exterior was often whitewashed. Commercial premises in towns had two stories, the lower for the business and upper for the living quarters.

The period between the Battle of the *Boyne (1690) and the Act of *Union (1800) may be the high point of Irish architecture. Neo-Palladianism propounded the study of ancient Roman architecture and featured pedimented windows, tight symmetry, Doric-columned porticos, and granite materials. Sir Edward Lovett *Pearce (1698–1733) was responsible for the *Parliament House in Dublin (1722–39) and *Castletown House (c.1720s) (County *Kildare). Richard Castle (d. 1751) created a large series of country palaces in the classical style, including Westport (1731) (County *Mayo), Carton (1739) (County Kildare), and Russborough (1742) (County Wicklow). Other buildings constructed at this time in Dublin, in the Georgian style, include *Leinster House (1745), the Rotunda Hospital (1752–57), William Chambers's Marino Casino, and *James Gandon's Custom House (1781–91).

After the Act of Union, as the country declined economically and socially, architecture reflected the slump. Once-grand Georgian buildings fell into disrepair. However, some significant buildings did go up during the Victorian era, including the Italian-Renaissance-style Amiens Street Railway Station (1844) and the traditionally classical Broadstone Railway Station (1850), both in Dublin. Throughout the century, the growing confidence of *Catholicism was mirrored in the construction of a number of cathedrals, including St. Patrick's in Dundalk (1830s).

Following independence in 1922, there were no significant efforts to create an Irish style, and a modernist and international style flourished: flat, concrete, and rational. A stripped-down, bare classicism was used in several buildings during the early days of the *Free State, including the Gresham Hotel on O'Connell Street, Dublin (1925), and Cork City Hall (1935–36). Art Deco was used in cinemas, such as the Dublin (1928–29) and Cork (1931–32) Savoys. Full-blown modernism arrived in the 1930s with Desmond Fitzgerald's Dublin Airport (1937–40) and Michael *Scott's private house "Geragh" in Sandycove, Dublin (1937–39). Michael Scott created Busáras, the glass-fronted corporate headquarters of the national bus company in 1945. By the 1960s, controversial buildings in the dominant bland modern style of the era were being built on the ruins of Dublin's elegant, eighteenth-century classical architecture. Also in Dublin, Desmond O'Kelly's Liberty Hall, Ireland's first skyscraper, was finished in 1965 and the infamous tower blocks of Ballymun (in the process of being demolished) were constructed in 1966. Michael Scott, Ronald Tallon, and Reginald Walker designed modernist office blocks in the capital, including the Dublin Corporation Civic Offices at Wood Quay (1994–95). Sam Stephenson planned the Central Bank of Ireland on Dame Street (1980). By the 1990s, however, the limits of modernism had been reached. A new interest among younger architects in the eclecticism of postmodernism produced enthusiasm for inner-city renewal schemes, including preserving the old Georgian buildings, modern apartment units, livable communities, and the creation of car-free residential zones. At the forefront of these developments was the architectural collective Group '91, which masterminded the rebirth of one of Dublin's oldest and most dilapidated neighborhoods, Temple Bar.

Construction at the beginning of the twenty-first century appears to be waning, as many international companies are rethinking their commitment to Ireland. Irish architecture has been the product of local histories and international influences. A.K.

Ardagh Chalice. One of the greatest surviving masterpieces of ecclesiastical metalwork of the eighth century in Europe. It was found in 1868 near Ardagh, County *Limerick, with a smaller chalice and four brooches dating from the ninth/tenth century, by a boy hunting rabbits. Standing on a conical base and with broad handles of Late Antique inspiration, this wine chalice is made of silver, richly decorated with gold, glass, and other materials, including amber. It is also ornamented beneath the rim, around the neck, and even under the foot with a feast of filigree patterns. The chalice is on display in the *National Museum in Dublin. P.H.

Armagh, Book of. Ninth-century Irish manuscript which is the most important source for our knowledge of the life and writings of St. *Patrick. It is the only early manuscript that can be dated in the 800s with any degree of reliability. An inscription states that Ferdomnach wrote it at the behest of Torbach, who was abbott of Armagh in the years 807 and 808. This small-format book includes St. Patrick's own *Confessio*, a copy of the New Testament, and the Life of St. Martin of Tours. Its illustrations, such as the Four Evangelist symbols, are drawn in monochrome brown ink with as firm a hand as the more colorful counterparts in the *Book of Kells. It is now in the library of Trinity College, *Dublin. P.H.

Armagh, County. Inland county in the province of *Ulster, one of the six counties of *Northern Ireland. Armagh has an area of 483 square miles and a population of est. 141,585 (1996). The county is highly fertile and *agriculture is a staple of its economy. Known in song as "the orchard of Ireland," Armagh has a strong fruit-growing industry. Its hilly southern portion includes some of the most beautiful scenery in Ireland, such as the spectacular mountain Slieve Gullion. In the north, where Armagh borders Lough Neagh, lies the Lurgan valley with its industrial towns. *Linen was once a major industry, and it is still manufactured today. Throughout the county are remnants of some four hundred *raths, or ring forts, including the magnificent Navan Fort (c.700 B.C.) which was once the capital of the *pre-Christian kings of Ulster. Two miles west of the city of Armagh, this fort, known as Emhain Macha in Irish *mythology, was where King Conor Mac Nessa held court with his Red Branch Knights, whose stories feature the great hero *Cúchulainn and the tragic lover Deirdre. From the seventh century, Armagh has been the ecclesiastical center of the *Catholic Church in Ireland. This is attributed to Armagh's close association with St. *Patrick (c.400s). Written in the ninth century, the *Book of Armagh (807), portions of which contain accounts of the life of Patrick, is one of Ireland's most important early medieval monastic works.

Armagh was severely affected by the *Nine Years War (1593–1603). The devastation of the conflict was compounded by the subsequent *"Plantation of Ulster," in which Gaelic Catholic landowners had their lands confiscated and granted to English and Scottish "undertakers," who in turn replaced much of the native population with *Protestant settlers from Britain. The transfer of land ownership from Catholic to Protestant in Armagh was completed with the *Cromwellian Settlement. By 1700, almost all the land in the county was held by Protestant *landlords, with the native Catholics confined to the boggy and mountainous south. During the 1780s and 1790s as the county's population grew (Armagh was the most densely populated county in Ireland at the time), political tensions exploded into open conflict between Protestant Peep O'Day Boys and Catholic *Defenders in 1785. The *Government of Ireland Act (1920) and the *Anglo-Irish Treaty of 1921 made Armagh one of the six Ulster counties that would constitute Northern Ireland. The failure of the *Boundary Commission to attach South Armagh to the *Free State in 1925 left the almost entirely Catholic population of that region greatly dissatisfied. The sectarian demographics of the county have made Armagh one of the flashpoints of the *"Troubles." Natives of Armagh include writer George *Russell (known as AE) and poet Paul *Muldoon. J.P.

Arms Crisis of 1970. Political scandal involving *Republic of Ireland cabinet ministers. In August 1969, at the height of the *Northern Ireland conflict, as *Derry and *Belfast were swept by riots and pogroms in which loyalist mobs burned out Catholic neighborhoods, *Taoiseach (Prime Minister) Jack *Lynch implied that military force might be supplied to protect Northern *nationalists, and reiterated Irish unity as the only long-term solution. As probably intended, this brought British troops onto the streets of the North, but *republican ambitions, North and South, had been raised. Republicans in the ruling *Fianna Fáil Party believed that Lynch's words (in a national television address) had to be acted upon. Some backed covert military aid to the vulnerable nationalist areas in the North. The development of militant anti-partitionism, in parallel with long-term diplomatic strategy, was advocated to prevent the Northern Ireland issue from regaining balance. Direct aid included money to Northern defense groups, limited arms training for selected individuals, and sponsorship of traditional republican figures over the then Marxist IRA (*Irish Republican

Army) leadership. Though relatively unimportant in the crystallization and organization of the Provisional IRA, this Irish government support was important in providing a certain legitimacy for militant irredentism. The matter became public on May 6, 1970, when two Fianna Fáil ministers, Neil Blaney (agriculture and fisheries) and Charles *Haughey (finance), were dismissed by Taoiseach Jack Lynch for allegedly misappropriating government money for the purchase of arms. Charges against Blaney were dropped in July, and in October 1970, Haughey and three other defendants were acquitted of all charges. Haughey's involvement with the republican cause was supported by some sections of southern opinion. Lynch remained Fianna Fáil leader and Blaney was expelled from the party. Haughey became minister for health in Lynch's new cabinet in 1977, and after Lynch resigned in 1979, Haughey was elected leader of Fianna Fáil and subsequently served as Taoiseach. M.M.

army, Irish. The Irish army has its origins in the split among *republicans over the *Anglo-Irish Treaty of 1921. While most rank-and-file members of the IRA (*Irish Republican Army) rejected the treaty, most of the general headquarters staff accepted it. Michael *Collins, commander in chief of the new army, used the pro-treaty IRA faction to create the nucleus of the *Irish Free State army. This force, better equipped and eventually numerically superior to its anti-treaty opponents, prevailed in Ireland's bitter *Civil War (June 1922 to May 1923). The rapid demobilization of the approximately 58,000-man force after the Civil War, as well as dissatisfaction with the political direction taken by the Free State government regarding Irish unification, led to an unsuccessful mutiny by some officers in May 1924. Ever since, the Irish army has accepted without question the principle that it is subordinate to the elected government. During World War II, the poorly equipped army, which rose to a maximum strength of 41,000 in March 1941, served as a symbol of Ireland's neutrality and independence but could have done little to prevent an invasion of the country. After World War II, successive Irish governments neglected to build up an army that could deter an aggressor. Instead, the army has served an important role in aid to the civil power, especially during the *Troubles, and it has also been deployed on United Nations duty, particularly in the Congo (where nine Irish peacekeepers were killed in November 1960), Cyprus, Lebanon, and East Timor. B.G.

Arts Council, the (An Chomhairle Ealaíon). Ireland's principal organization of arts funding and advisor on arts matters. Established in 1951 and operating under the Arts Acts of 1951, 1973 and 2003, the council aims to promote and stimulate public interest in the arts. It commissions and publishes research and information, and undertakes a range of development projects, often jointly with other public sector or nongovernmental agencies. The Arts Council has twelve members and a chairman, who serve voluntarily and are appointed for five years by the minister for Arts, Sport and Tourism. The twelfth Arts Council was appointed in 2003. (Web site: *www.artscouncil.ie.*) M.C.

Arts Council of Northern Ireland, the. *Northern Ireland organization for the funding of the arts. Established in 1962, as successor to the Committee for the Encouragement of Music and the Arts (CEMA) of 1942, it became a statutory body in September 1995, consulting external advisors on the allocation of funds made available by the government and the National Lottery. Its function is to develop and improve the knowledge, appreciation, and practice of the arts in Northern Ireland and to increase public access. (Web site: *www.artscouncil-ni.org.*) M.C.

Ashe, Thomas (1885–1917). Revolutionary. Born in Lispole, County *Kerry, Ashe was a school principal by profession and member of the *Gaelic League and the *Irish Republican Brotherhood. He commanded the Fingall *Volunteers and fought against the *Royal Irish Constabulary at Ashbourne, County *Meath, during the 1916 *Easter Rising. Ashe was sentenced to death in May 1916 but his sentence was later commuted to life imprisonment. Released in August 1917, he was rearrested shortly afterward for sedition. Ashe died in *Mountjoy Prison, Dublin, while on *hunger strike for prisoner of war status. His funeral at *Glasnevin Cemetery on September 30, 1917, proved a turning point in the *republican rally, with the Volunteers wearing uniform in public for the first time since the Easter week surrender. A volley of shots was fired over the grave and an oration was delivered by Michael *Collins. P.E.

Asquith, Herbert Henry (1852–1928). British Liberal prime minister responsible for the third *home rule bill. Asquith was first elected to Parliament in 1886 and in 1892 became home secretary under William Ewart *Gladstone. In 1908, he succeeded Henry Campbell-Bannerman as prime minister. Asquith introduced the third home rule bill into the Commons in April 1912. This bill granted Ireland its own parliament with power over all internal affairs, with the exception of taxation and the police force. In addition, Ireland would continue to send 40 MPs (members of Parliament) to Westminster. The alliance between the Liberals and the *Irish Parliamentary Party ensured its passage through the Commons, but it was defeated in the House of Lords. The provisions of the 1911 Parliament Act (by which a veto in the House of Lords amounted merely to a two-year delay) meant that Asquith's home rule bill was due to become law in 1914. Considerable opposition by *Ulster unionists led to fears that Ireland was on the brink of a civil war by early 1914. The onset of *World War I, however, led to the suspension of the home rule bill until the end of the conflict. In 1915, Asquith yielded to demands for a coalition government, but in December 1916 he was forced to resign and was replaced by David *Lloyd George. This caused a catastrophic split in the Liberal Party, which went into decline after 1918. Asquith remained party leader until 1926 and became a peer in 1925. P.E.

Aughrim, Battle of (July 12, 1691). Last battle of the Williamite War, considered the bloodiest battle fought in Ireland. After the Williamite forces had taken Athlone and crossed the *Shannon on June 30, 1691, the *Jacobite forces under the French Marshal, the Marquis de St. Ruth, made a stand at Aughrim, near Ballinasloe, County *Galway. The Williamite army was led by the Dutch general, Baron van Ginkel. The Battle of Aughrim was more important than the more famous Battle of the *Boyne, fought a year earlier, in deciding Ireland's fate. As at the Boyne, the Jacobite army consisted of French and Irish troops while the Williamites had British and Continental regiments.

The Jacobites were in a good defensive position behind a marsh, but were outmaneuvered by the Williamite cavalry. Before he could organize a countermove, St. Ruth was beheaded by an enemy cannon ball. He had left no clear instructions to his subordinates, and had positioned the most daring and gifted Irish commander, Patrick *Sarsfield, at the rear. The Jacobites were defeated and routed. The fleeing army lost seven thousand. This defeat marked the end of the Jacobite cause. The Jacobites fell back upon Galway City, which, in turn, was captured by the Williamites. By this stage, many French troops had been recalled and the remaining Jacobite army was forced to make a stand at Limerick, where they were besieged. The failure of French reinforcements to arrive in time led to their surrender and the Treaty of *Limerick. T.C.

Australia, the Irish in. The Irish comprised approximately one-third of the convict and free settler emigrants to the newly established British colony of Australia. Irishmen were well represented in the *First Fleet*, the first ship of colonists from England, which arrived in New South Wales in January 1788. On board were Captain David Collins and John White, both Irishmen who held the important positions of judge advocate and chief physician, respectively, in the inaugural colonial administration. The First Fleet also contained Irish-born convicts who had been sentenced in England and their marine guards. The proportion of Irish in the colony increased rapidly from 1791 when the first transport of Irish convicts reached Australia from Cobh, County *Cork.

The mass deportation of *Defenders and *United Irishmen to the colony between 1793 and 1805 created a substantial community of experienced *republican revolutionaries whose plots and uprisings created considerable ferment in 1800. The Castle Hill Rising of March 1804 (fought at Vinegar Hill) was overwhelmingly an Irish affair, which led to the first declaration of martial law in Australia. The comparatively benign tenure of Governor Lachlan Macquarie facilitated the assimilation of the disaffected Irish after 1810. By then ex–United Irishmen William Redfern and James Meehan played vital roles in developing health care and surveying the expanding Australian colonies. As the major phase of the convict transportation to Australia drew to a close in 1853, in part spurred by Irish-Australian lobbying, the continued *emigration of Irish families maintained a strong sense of ethnic identity. Ninety thousand Irish emigrants arrived in the Australian state of New South Wales between 1836 and 1886, while numerous others went to the newer state territories of Victoria, Queensland, South Australia, Western Australia, and Tasmania. The extent and pace of the influx owed much to the discovery of gold, the availability of affordable land, and generally good employment prospects. Almost 400,000 Irish emigrants went to Australia and New Zealand between 1850 and 1921. The distinctive contribution of the Irish in Australia took many forms, not least the creation of a sizable Roman Catholic community and the adoption of a variant of *Gaelic football as a major sporting code.

Trade unions and the political fronts of the labor movement were also heavily indebted to Irish immigrants and their descendants who were well represented at every level of colonial society. Irish miners at Ballarat goldfield, Victoria, were the focal point of a highly significant and violent protest in 1854 at the Eureka Stockade. The stand against perceived administrative injustice and incompetence found an articulate figurehead in Peter Lalor, a native of County *Laois, Ireland, who subsequently became Speaker of the Victorian Assembly. In 1880, the Irish community and its supporters collected the huge sum of £95,000 for famine relief in Ireland.

The profusion of Irish cultural, religious, and political organizations mirrored that of the North

American experience. Between the 1880s and 1914, the Irish in Sydney and Melbourne offered strong moral support for *home rule in their native country. The onset of *World War I in 1914 and the repercussions of the 1916 *Easter Rising lessened Irish Australian support, although such revolutionary bodies as the *Irish Republican Brotherhood continued to maintain a presence in Australia. The percentage of Irish-born in Australia dropped after 1945 owing to a relaxation of restrictions on non-English-speaking applicants and other domestic and international factors, but the numbers increased in the 1950s and again in the 1980s. Relations between the Irish and Australians further improved in the 1990s and Australia remains a major destination for Irish visitors and emigrants. R.OD.

Auxiliaries, the. Military support for the *Royal Irish Constabulary (RIC) during the *War of Independence. Formed in July 1920, the Auxiliaries were recruited from former British army officers to combat the IRA (*Irish Republican Army). Because the British government did not recognize the conflict as a war, the Auxiliaries were made a division of the RIC. By November 1921, they were 1,900 strong. They operated independently in armed patrols striking at will. Shocked at their behavior, their commander, Brigadier General Frank Crozier, resigned. T.C.

B

Bacon, Francis (1909–92). Painter. Bacon was born in *Dublin and raised in County *Kildare, where his father, a retired British army captain, trained horses. His family moved to London in 1914, when the British army was mobilized for war, and returned to a rebellious Ireland in 1917. A witness to a turbulent time in Ireland, Bacon moved to London in 1925. He visited Berlin in 1928 and lived in Paris until 1930. Influenced by German expressionism, French surrealism, and Picasso's work, Bacon only began to paint when back in London in 1930. He produced expressionistic, distorted figurative work influenced by photography and set in surreal spaces. The inclusion of his 1933 *Crucifixion* painting (a recurring theme) in Sir Herbert Read's influential *Art Now: An Introduction of the Theory of Modern Painting and Sculpture* (1933) brought him to the attention of leading art collectors. His 1945 triptych *Three Studies for Figures at the Base of a Crucifixion*, painted in protest of World War II, established his reputation. In 1998, Mr. John Edwards, his sole heir, donated the painter's studio to the *Hugh Lane Municipal Gallery. M.C.

Balfe, Michael William (1808–70). Composer and singer. Born in *Dublin, Balfe was apprenticed to Charles Edward Horn in London in 1823. He was commissioned by La Scala in Milan to write music for the ballet *La Pérouse* in 1826. In Paris, in 1827, Balfe met the composer Gioacchino Rossini, who arranged tuition and an engagement to sing Figaro at the Théâtre des Italiens. In 1830, Balfe married the Hungarian singer Lina Rosa. He returned to London in 1833 and wrote many operas for Drury Lane, notably *The Siege of Rochelle* (1838) and *The Bohemian Girl* (1843). C.D.

Ballagh, Robert (1943–). Painter and draughtsman. Born in *Dublin, Ballagh is a member of *Aosdána. He has designed *Riverdance stage sets, logos, book jackets, postage stamps, and currency. His style is much influenced by his early architectural training and an interest in photography. The cruciform *Portrait of Noel Browne* (1985) with stones tumbling out onto the floor demonstrates Ballagh's technical skill and innovation. An organizer of the*Irish Exhibition of Living Art in the seventies, Ballagh believes in the wider social responsibility of the artist. He helped form the Association of Artists in Ireland in 1981 to improve artists' working conditions. He served on the executive committee of the UNESCO-affiliated International Association of Artists from 1983 to 1986. His international work led to paintings such as *Man Drawing a Recumbent Woman* (1984) for the Dürer Haus in Nürnberg. More recently, in works such as *The Bogman* (1997) Ballagh has painted events in his life that include imaginary landscapes and incorporate Gaelic texts and natural materials. He is vice president of the Ireland Institute and a member of Le Chéile/Together, Irish Artists Against Racism. M.C.

Banville, John (1945–) Novelist, literary editor. Born in Wexford town, Banville is best known for the tetralogy consisting of *Doctor Copernicus* (1976), *Kepler* (1981), *The Newton Letter* (1982), and *Mefisto* (1986), and a trilogy made up of *The Book of Evidence* (1989), *Ghosts* (1993), and *Athena* (1995). *The Book of Evidence* was short-listed for the Booker Prize and awarded the Guinness Peat Aviation Award in 1990. Stylistically masterful, Banville's work draws on European art, history, and literature, and has a subtle philosophical dimension. In the tetralogy, Banville explores the relationship between scientific and imaginative truth. The trilogy investigates the gap between artistic perfection and personal weakness. Other work includes the novels *Birchwood* (1973), *The Untouchable* (1997), *Shroud* (2002), and a number of plays and screenplays. For many years, Banville was literary editor of the *Irish Times* and is now that newspaper's chief literary critic. G.OB.

bardic schools. The name generally given to schools of *poetry in Ireland and *Scotland between 1200 and 1700. Although schools of poetry existed from before historic time, in the fifth century these bardic schools involved the professional training of poets (a training that sometimes took up to seven years). The schools became hereditary among certain families, particularly the Ua Dálaigh (O'Dalys) and the Ua hUiginn (O'Higgins). These families usually received patronage from a chieftain. Instruction was mainly oral, but the reading of manuscripts was also taught. The poets composed in a very formal language, which was standardized throughout the Gaelic world. The meters used were based on a complicated and subtle relationship between vowels and consonants and involved a deep and precise knowledge of assonance, rhyme, alliteration, and sound concordance. This formal language was originally based on the spoken tongue of the thirteenth century, but became remote from common speech as the living language evolved in the following centuries. Poets moved freely between Ireland and Scotland as we see in the career of Muireadhach Albanach Ó Dálaigh (c.1180–1230), for example, who worked for, or wrote poems for, patrons in *Ulster, *Connacht, *Munster, and Scotland. Most of this poetry is directly related to the patronage of a chieftain, and is therefore eulogistic, satirical, genealogical, or commemorative, but there is also a large body of religious poetry and some strikingly passionate personal poems. A.T.

Barry, Gerald (1952–). Composer. Born in Clarecastle, County *Clare, Barry, who trained in *Dublin, Amsterdam (Peter Schat), Cologne (Karlheinz Stockhausen, Mauricio Kagel), and Vienna

(Friedrich Cerha), is renowned for a highly individual style that can blend theatrical extremes of virtuosity, humor, and unexpected pathos. His first opera, *The Intelligence Park* (Almeida Festival, London, 1991), was both controversial and successful; his second, *The Triumph of Beauty and Deceit* (1995), marked a rare venture into the world of television opera. His orchestral music is renowned for its excitement and energy. Notably, his 1988 BBC Henry Wood Promenade Concerts commission, *Chevaux-de-frise* and *The Conquest of Ireland* (1995)—which set to music texts from the eponymous book by Giraldus Cambrensis—and the frenetic demands of his Second Piano Quartet (1996) are known literally to have left blood on the keyboard. M.D.

Barry, James (1741–1806). Historical painter. Barry was born in *Cork. Supported by Edmund *Burke, he was first acclaimed in 1763 for the innovative use of Irish subject matter in his painting *The Conversion by St. Patrick of the King of Cashel*. He went to London in 1764 and in 1766 to Rome, where he studied art for five years. In 1775, he was elected to the Royal Academy where he became professor of painting in 1782. His neoclassicist and republican prints, such as *The Phoenix* and *Philoctetes*, were highly prized by political radicals in Ireland. Barry worked unpaid on a series of pictures known as *The Progress of Human Culture* for the Great Room of the Society of Arts in London for many years from 1777. He wrote extensively in defense of history painting. M.C.

Barry, Sebastian (1955–). Dramatist, poet, and novelist. Born in *Dublin (the son of actress Joan O'Hara), and educated at Trinity College, Dublin, Barry is considered one of Ireland's leading young playwrights. He has written volumes of poetry, such as *The Water-Colourist* (1983) and *The Rhetorical Town* (1985), and several works of fiction for adults and for young readers, including his more recent novel *The Whereabouts of Eneas McNulty* (1998). Barry's prose is characterized by a linguistically idiosyncratic, sensuous quality. His works often reflect on Irish history through personal memory, and several of his plays purport to do so through the history of his own family, although Barry has stated that the plays are concoctions. In *Prayers of Sherkin* (1991), which is based on a true story, human kindness prevails over strict religious principles when Fanny Hawke, a member of a dwindling Quaker-like sect, decides to marry an outsider. Barry's real breakthrough as a playwright came in 1995 with the much acclaimed *The Steward of Christendom*, a moving portrayal of Thomas Dunne, the *Catholic chief superintendent of the Dublin Metropolitan Police. From his deathbed, Dunne (played brilliantly by Donal *McCann) reflects on a life torn by political allegiances in the days of James *Larkin and Michael *Collins, and a career ultimately assigned to oblivion by the *Anglo-Irish Treaty. In *Our Lady of Sligo* (1998), Barry focuses on the Irish middle class in the stifling conservatism of the postindependence era through the eyes of the main character, the alcoholic, dying Mai O'Hara (played superbly by Sinead *Cusack). *Hinterland* (2002) was controversial as some critics felt the play's plot and protagonist, Johnny Silvester, were too closely modeled on the life and person of Irish politician Charles *Haughey. In *Whistling Psyche* (2004), a 19th-century surgeon James Barry practices as a man but is really a woman. J.C.E.L.

Barton, Robert (1881–1975). *Republican politician. Born into a *Protestant family in Glendalough, County *Wicklow, Barton was a British army officer in *Dublin during the *Easter Rising of 1916. He converted to republicanism and was the *Sinn Féin minister for agriculture (1919–21) in the first *Dáil

Samuel Beckett

Éireann (Irish Parliament). Barton (a cousin of Erskine *Childers) was a member of the delegation that signed the *Anglo-Irish Treaty, but joined the anti-treaty forces in the *Civil War. After the war, he retired from political life. S.A.B.

Beckett, Samuel Barclay (1906–89). Playwright, novelist, Nobel Prize winner (1969). One of the most inventive writers of the twentieth century, Samuel Beckett revolutionized modern drama with his minimalist plays associated with the theater of the absurd. Born on April 13, 1906, in Foxrock, County *Dublin, the younger son of an affluent *Protestant quantity surveyor and an intensely religious mother, Beckett was educated at Portora Royal School, Enniskillen, County *Fermanagh. During his college years at Trinity College, Dublin, he came to love the cinema and its silent comic masters, especially Charlie Chaplin and Buster Keaton, who would inspire his work.

In 1928, Beckett moved to Paris (as a lecturer in English at L'Ecole Normale Supérieure) where he established a lasting friendship with Thomas MacGreevy, poet and later director of the *National Gallery, Dublin. In Paris, he also became the devoted disciple of his fellow Dubliner James *Joyce. Contrary to rumor, Beckett was never Joyce's secretary, but, like many of the writer's admirers, he ran errands for him, including reading out loud to the nearly blind writer.

His first publication was an essay on Joyce's *Finnegans Wake* entitled "Dante . . . Bruno. Vico.. Joyce" (1929). Beckett's first short story, "Assumption," which deliberately lacked a plot, appeared in the magazine *transition* in 1929, and in 1930 he published a long, witty, erudite, and arcane poem, *Whoroscope*. After a brief period as a lecturer in French at Trinity College, Dublin (1930–31), Beckett, penniless and plagued by ill health, lived in Germany, France, and England. His short study, *Proust* (1931), explores the breakdown of the relationship between the subject and the object, also the theme of an influential essay on contemporary poetry in Ireland, "Recent Irish Poetry," in *The Bookman* (1934). His first novel, the Joycean extravaganza *Dream of Fair to Middling Women*, written in 1932, remained unpublished until 1993. *More Pricks than Kicks* (1934), a self-consciously pedantic volume of short stories, was followed in 1938 by *Murphy*, a novel that parodies the icons of the *Irish Literary Revival. *Murphy* had been initially turned down by virtually all British and American publishers but was finally published by Routledge & Son, Ltd., in 1938. In this wonderfully funny book, Beckett invented one of his first prototypical characters—the outcast—a lone indolent, young Irish man down on his luck in London just as Beckett himself was at the time.

Beckett preferred occupied France to Ireland at peace during World War II, and became a member of the Resistance movement. Together with his friend Suzanne Dumesnil (who would later become his wife), he left Paris to avoid arrest in August 1942 and settled in Roussillon in the Vaucluse. In the three dark years they spent there, Beckett wrote *Watt*, which was published only years later, in 1953, by Merlin Press. This novel, a comic attack on rationality, contains darker tragic undertones of Beckett's war experience.

After he returned to Paris in 1945, Beckett began to write in French to divest his style of moribund literary influences. *Mercier et Camier,* written in 1946, was his first novel in French, followed by a trilogy, *Molloy* (1951), *Malone Dies* (1951), and *The Unnamable* (1953). The trilogy's fragmented narration and interior monologues reflect the theme of the split between human perception and objective reality. The vacuity of modern society is further explored in Beckett's minimalist plays, including *Waiting for Godot* (1948–49), *Endgame* (1957), *Krapp's Last Tape* (1958), and *Happy Days* (1961). *Godot*, under Roger Blin's direction, opened in Paris in 1953 to great (if not unanimous) critical acclaim, and Beckett's years of poverty and obscurity were over. In this masterpiece of the theater of the absurd, a movement that revolutionized drama, Beckett strips language and bares the human soul. Beckett's anti-heroes are marginal, barely surviving on the edges of life, in garbage dumps, ditches, gutters, lunatic asylums, searching for a meaning that remains elusive. For all the bleakness, isolation, alienation, and loneliness, there is an extraordinary element of humor, poetry, and humanity. "I can't go on, I'll go on" *(The Unnameable)* encapsulates both Beckett's and his characters' anguish and unwillingness to give up.

Beckett's later writing moves closer to silence, but its irony and endurance stops short of pessimism and despair. Plays and prose are increasingly stripped of all but the essentials of character, setting, and action. *Breath* (1969), an anti-dramatic, plotless play lasting thirty seconds, consists of a heap of rubbish, a breath, and a cry. Work for television includes *Eh Joe* (1966), *. . . but the clouds* (1976)—based on Yeats's *The Tower*—and *Ghost Trio* (1976).

He also made a film called *Film* (1963), which was premiered at the New York Film Festival in 1965 and is now considered a classic. Evident throughout Beckett's work are the skepticism and rigor of the *Anglo-Irish literary tradition and his own skeptical response to his Protestant inheritance. His distrust extends to traditional literary and dramatic forms, and to language deadened by habitual use, which ultimately became a significant thematic and formal concern. He died in 1989 and is buried in Paris. M.S.T., L.R.

beehive huts. Roughly hemispherical huts, built without mortar on the corbel principle—layers of stone placed in a circle, decreasing in circumference as they rise until closed by a single stone at the top. The best-known examples are on *Skellig Michael and on the *Dingle Peninsula in County *Kerry, but others are found on islands farther north along the coast. With few modern exceptions, these are likely to date from the early Middle Ages (A.D. c.500–1000). Sometimes explained as temporary dwellings for shepherds, beehive huts most likely served as shelters or hostels for *pilgrims. P.H.

Behan, Brendan (1923–64). Playwright and writer. Behan is famous for his political views, satire, wit, drunkenness, and storytelling. Born on February 9,

Brendan Behan

1923, in the Holles Street Hospital in *Dublin, he grew up in a working-class part of the inner city and left school at the age of fourteen. Behan had an incisive mind and was mainly taught by his father, Stephen, who read him tales by Dickens, Zola, and Galsworthy. His family also instilled in Behan his socialist views and his rebel ideals. From the age of nine, he served in a youth organization connected to the IRA (*Irish Republican Army) and in the 1930s was an IRA messenger boy.

In 1939, Behan was arrested on a sabotage mission in England and was sentenced to three years in Borstal, a reform school for boys. This experience became the impetus for one of his most famous works, the autobiographical *Borstal Boy* (1958) and its sequel, *Confessions of an Irish Rebel* (1965).

After his release, Behan returned to Ireland, but in 1942 was sentenced to fourteen years for the attempted murder of two detectives. He was released four years later under a general amnesty. After spending another month in jail in 1948 for drunk and disorderly conduct, Behan decided to leave Dublin for Paris, where he lived for two years.

Behan's first play, *The Quare Fellow*, based on his prison experiences, was first performed in 1956 and soon gained critical success. In the play, Behan attacked capital punishment and society's hypocrisy in matters of sex, politics, and religion. Other plays include *An Giall* (1958), subsequently translated and adapted by Behan and Joan Littlewood for the Theatre Workshop in London as *The Hostage* (1958). Almost completed at the time of Behan's death, *Richard's Cork Leg* was first produced by Alan Simpson as part of the 1972 Dublin Theatre Festival. Behan's plays often use song and dance, and direct addresses to the audience, which show the influence of Bertolt Brecht on his

Belfast, City Hall

writing style. By the late 1950s Behan had gained much critical attention, which ultimately led to his downfall and death. His early discipline eventually gave way to prolonged drinking bouts and self-destructive incidents. In March 1964, Behan collapsed in the Harbour Lights Pub and died on the twentieth of that month in a Dublin Hospital at the age of forty-one. T.F.

Belfast. Capital of *Northern Ireland. The name derives from the Irish, *Béal Feirsde*, meaning the "mouth of the river." In the nineteenth century, Belfast was Ireland's main industrial city and, since 1921, capital of Northern Ireland. Although a settlement had existed since the seventh century, the town was founded by Sir Arthur *Chichester in 1603 for English and *Scots settlers. It became a borough in 1613 represented by two MPs (members of Parliament) in the Irish *Parliament. In the eighteenth century, the first industries, particularly *linen, began to develop along the valley of the River Lagan.

Belfast was a *Presbyterian town with a reputation for radical politics. It supported the *American Revolution and the *1798 United Irishmen's Rebellion. The rebellion resulted in a conservative backlash and, as Belfast began to prosper after the Act of *Union, the town became more loyalist in character.

By the 1830s, Belfast was the world's main producer of linen and, after the coming of the railways in the 1840s, its harbor, Belfast Lough, became a major port. By the end of the century, the town supported a *textile industry, shipbuilding, engineering, rope manufacturing, *whiskey production, and tobacco. In 1888, it officially became a city.

The population rapidly expanded as people came from Scotland, England, and other parts of Ireland seeking work. By 1901, there were 349,180 inhabitants, most of whom were *Protestants loyal to Britain. There was, however, a significant minority of *Catholics. From the 1840s on, Belfast became the scene of violence, riots, and even sustained street warfare between these two groups. After 1886, the *Ulster Protestant opposition to *home rule led to increasing clashes with the Catholic minority. The founding of Northern Ireland in 1920 was marked by months of violence in which hundreds of Catholics were driven from their homes. The city's demographics and its segregated neighborhoods stem mainly from this time.

Belfast's politics reflected its religious makeup. Catholics were concentrated in certain areas, such as the Falls Road, and in general were poorer and employed, if at all, in nonskilled industry. They supported *nationalist candidates and had little impact on city government. Backed by the *Orange Order, *unionist politicians dominated local government and parliamentary representation. The sectarian dichotomy continues to this day.

Belfast has been a battleground during the present Northern Ireland conflict, with riots, bombings, and murders. Almost half of the fatalities and some of the worst atrocities occurred there. Due to the increase in the Catholic population, Belfast is no longer a Protestant-dominated city. In 1998, Alban Magennis of the *Social Democratic and Labour Party was elected as the first Catholic mayor, and unionist parties no longer have a majority on the city council.

In recent decades, its economic profile changed as the traditional industries, particularly textiles and shipbuilding, declined. Nevertheless, with a population around 350,000, Belfast remains the second largest city in Ireland and the dominant economic center of Northern Ireland. Prospects for further economic growth have been enhanced by the promise of peace following the *Good Friday Agreement of 1998.

Belfast sits in a bowl created by hills at the mouth of the River Lagan, which divides it in two. Ben Madigan, sometimes called Napoleon's Nose, overlooks the city to the north. Belfast is essentially a Victorian city and little of its eighteenth-century *architecture remains. The most famous building is the elaborate City Hall in Donegall Square. Most of the population live in sprawling suburbs constructed in the 1970s and 1980s. T.C.

Bell, the. Famous literary magazine (1940–54). Founded and edited by Seán *Ó Faoláin (1940–46) and Peadar O'Donnell (1946–54), the *Bell* was the leading Irish periodical of its time. Showcasing the work of established Irish writers and new talent, the journal published short stories; *poetry; literary, *theater, and *cinema criticism; and articles on important political and social issues. Ó Faoláin's editorials and essays attacked *Catholic clericalism, puritanism, *censorship, and anti-intellectualism; peasant and bourgeois conservatism; and chauvinistic Gaelic *nationalism that preserved a mythical past isolating Ireland from the realities of the present and prospects for the future. The *Bell* provided liberating intellectual light in a dark and dreary period of Irish history. L.J.MC.

Bergin, Mary (1949–). Traditional *music tin whistle player. Born of musical parents in County *Dublin, she learned to play at age nine, winning many awards during traditional music's revival in the sixties. Bergin is also the mainstay of the all-female band Dordán. Her first album *Feadóga Stáin* (1979) remains seminal. F.V.

Berkeley, George (1685–1753). Anglo-Irish philosopher, and Anglican bishop of Cloyne. Born in *Kilkenny, Berkeley attended Trinity College. By 1713, he had published his major philosophical works. He traveled in Europe, briefly settled in Rhode Island (then a British colony), and returned home in 1731. He became bishop of Cloyne in 1734. Berkeley was a staunch, though unorthodox, defender of Christianity and a brilliant critic of the newly emerging scientific worldview which, he believed, endangered Christianity by replacing traditional theistic conceptions of the universe with that of a godless universe of matter in motion. Berkeley's response was both ingenious and implausible: he denied the existence of matter. His universe contained only minds and ideas; material bodies were merely ideas organized in regular patterns by an omni-benevolent God. Berkeley also offered insightful criticisms of Newtonian calculus and gravity, published a revolutionary treatise on vision, wrote proposals for dealing with poverty, and proclaimed the medicinal virtues of tar water. Modern metaphysical idealism (the view that material reality does not exist) and scientific instrumentalism (the view that science does not explain anything but is merely a useful organizing and predictive tool) are directly traceable to Berkeley's writings. M.L.

Best, George (1946–). *Soccer player. Born in *Belfast, Best was a precocious talent who joined Manchester United at age fifteen. He became one of the first soccer superstars of his generation. Best was a key member of the Manchester United team that won the European Cup in 1968 and was named European Player of the Year. He left the club prematurely in 1973, suffering the pressures of stardom and the effects of alcohol abuse. Best never regained the consistency that rated him one of the greatest players in the world. He finished his career at an array of clubs in Britain, Ireland, and America before retiring in the early eighties. He played thirty-seven times for *Northern Ireland. F.S.

Binchy, Maeve (1940–). Journalist and best-selling fiction writer. Born in *Dublin, Binchy began her career as a schoolteacher. In 1968, she was hired to write for the *Irish Times* and continues to write columns, demonstrating her wit as well as her insights into domestic life. Her work is wide-ranging, encompassing novels, short stories, journalism, plays, and television screenplays. Binchy's first novel, *Light a Penny Candle* (1982), reveals themes common in subsequent works: relationships among friends and family, daily life in rural Ireland, individual and social tragedy, and the damaging legacy of secrets kept. Binchy's best-selling novel *Circle of Friends* (1990) was made into a popular film. This story of girlhood friends addresses issues of growing up female in Ireland, the claustrophobia of small-town life, and the economic disparities of class and religious membership that have defined the national culture. Other novels include *Echoes* (1985), *Firefly Summer* (1987), *Silver Wedding* (1988), *Glass Lake* (1994), *Evening*

Class (1997), and *Tara Road* (1998). Binchy's collections of short stories include *The Copper Beech* (1992), *The Return Journey* (1998), and *The Lilac Bus* (1984). *This Year It Will Be Different and Other Stories* (1996) is an anthology of Christmas tales. K.MI.

Birmingham Six Case (1974). Legal case of six innocent men who spent sixteen years in prison. On Thursday, November 21, 1974, twenty-one people were killed and 182 injured by bombs in two Birmingham pubs, the Mulberry Bush, and the Tavern in the Town. The bombs had been planted by an IRA (*Irish Republican Army) unit, which had failed to give a warning, allegedly due to out-of-order public phones. That night, six Irishmen were detained by the Special Branch at Heysham Ferry Port. All but one were on their way to *Belfast to attend the funeral of James McDade, an IRA man killed while trying to plant a bomb in Coventry. The six men were Robert Gerard Hunter, Patrick Joseph Hill, Noel Richard McIlkenny, William Power, John Francis Walker, and Hugh Daniel Callaghan. All, except Walker, who was from Derry, were natives of Belfast. Nearly all the men had *republican backgrounds. Forensic tests seemed to indicate that some of the men had been in contact with explosives. Only later were these tests proved unreliable. When handed over to the Birmingham police, the six men were badly beaten and subjected to considerable psychological pressure. Under duress, some of them signed confessions. On August 15, 1975, all six were convicted of murder and sentenced to life imprisonment. One appeal was dismissed in 1976, and at a second hearing in 1980, Lord Justice Denning denied appeal on the grounds that a frame-up was unthinkable. The Birmingham Six were finally released in 1991, having been found innocent after spending sixteen years in prison. This case was but one of a number of serious miscarriages of justice involving innocent IRA suspects in Britain in the past few decades, which have seriously undermined confidence and credibility in the British legal system. The cases, however, have also resulted in some very basic improvements in a judicial process whose failures are a cause of concern to other minorities in Britain, as well as the Irish. M.M.

Birr telescope. Located in Birr, County *Offaly, this was the largest telescope in the world during the nineteenth century. Also known as the "Leviathan of Parsonstown," it was built by William Parsons, the Third Earl of Rosse, in the early 1840s. When completed in 1845, the telescope contained a 72-inch mirror, mounted in a 56-foot tube, weighing over 3 tons. It was surpassed in size only in 1917 by the Hooker telescope at Mount Wilson in California. P.E.

Black and Tans. British ex-soldiers recruited to reinforce the RIC (*Royal Irish Constabulary) during the *War of Independence. The RIC was unable to respond to IRA (*Irish Republican Army) attacks, and military reinforcements were seen as essential. Because the British government would not admit that it was fighting a war, special recruits, mainly British ex-soldiers and sailors, were drafted to reinforce the RIC. Since regulation uniforms could not be supplied quickly enough, they were fitted in a mixture of RIC black jackets and army khaki trousers. Hence, they were nicknamed the Black and Tans, which also happened to be the name of a famous pack of foxhounds. Although a distinct unit, the *Auxiliaries were usually referred to as Black and Tans.

Between January 1920 and November 1921, 9,500 men had enlisted. With little or no police training, they were sent out to reinforce RIC barracks mainly in *Dublin, *Connacht, and *Munster.

The Black and Tans were notorious for their campaign of reprisals directed against civilians and property in response to IRA attacks. Originally overlooked by the authorities, this pattern of reprisals soon became official government policy. The Black and Tans gained a reputation for brutality and ruthlessness, particularly following incidents such as the burning of Cork City and the "Sack" of Balbriggan, County *Dublin. Rather than defeating the IRA, such tactics alienated people even more from the RIC and increased support for the *republicans. Such was their reputation that in popular speech the War of Independence is still often referred to as the Black and Tan War. T.C.

Blair, Tony (1953–). British Labour prime minister, 1997 to present. Two weeks after his landslide victory, Blair visited *Northern Ireland and pledged to make the *peace process a top priority for his government. He encouraged the IRA (*Irish Republican Army) to restore its cease-fire by not insisting on decommissioning of arms as a prerequisite to *Sinn Féin's involvement in official peace negotiations. Blair also set a firm April 9 (Holy Thursday) 1998 deadline for the resolution of the all-party peace talks.

As the deadline approached, Blair worked aggressively to save the peace negotiations from collapse. He spoke openly with all sides, especially with *Ulster Unionist Party leader David *Trimble, and urged Taoiseach (prime minister) Bertie *Ahern and US President Bill Clinton to remain active in the process. Blair's determined leadership was crucial to the *Good Friday Agreement.

Blair has faced difficulties in preserving the fragile peace accord. Extremists on both sides want it to fail. His ministry has struggled to resolve controversies over decommissioning, policing, Orange parades—especially Drumcree—paramilitary punishment beatings, and the IRA's links with rebels in Colombia. Through it all, however, Blair has remained committed to implementing the Good Friday Agreement. R.D.

Blarney. See **Cork, County.**

Blasket Islands, the. Group of islands off the *Dingle Peninsula. Uninhabited since 1953, the Blaskets were a mecca for linguists and anthropologists during the early years of the Gaelic, or *Irish Language Revival (1905–30). A large corpus of Gaelic autobiographies emerged from the islands in the 1930s, most notably Tomás *Ó Criomhthain's *An tOileánach* (1929), Muiris *Ó Súilleabháin's *Fiche Bliain ag Fás* (1933), and Peig *Sayers's *Peig* (1936). In recent years the ownership of the Great Blasket, the largest of the islands, has become the subject of a complex legal wrangle in which relatives of the last inhabitants successfully challenged legislation to classify the island as a national heritage park. One of the smaller islands, Inishvickillane, is owned by former *Taoiseach (prime minister) Charles *Haughey. B.D.

Bloody Friday (1972). A day of mass carnage caused by IRA (*Irish Republican Army) car bombs. In *Belfast, on Friday, July 21, 1972, within one hour twenty-six bombs exploded, two of which (one at Cavehill Road, the other at Oxford Street bus station), killed eleven people and badly injured 130. *Television chose to cover the conflict without sanitization, and the image of dismembered bodies being shoveled into bin bags induced revulsion. The IRA, which had up to then insisted that civilians must bear the collateral costs of their campaign, was itself shaken by such a visceral atrocity. They were quick to blame the authorities for not reacting with sufficient efficiency to their warnings. Much of the IRA's credibility (accumulated through relatively selective targeting, British errors such as *Bloody Sunday, and carefully timed cease-fires, and policy initiatives) was wasted. Determined to limit the IRA's capacity, and capitalizing on the crisis, the British government sent the army back into "No-Go Areas," notably the Bogside in Derry City, on July 31 (Operation Motorman). The same day, IRA no-warning bombs killed or fatally injured nine civilians in Claudy, County *Tyrone. M.M.

Bloody Sunday (I). Sunday, November 21, 1920. A day of atrocities at the peak of the *War of Independence. On this Sunday, Michael *Collins's Special Intelligence Unit, known as "the Squad," shot dead fourteen and injured five other suspected British agents operating in *Dublin. The victims, part of a spy network known as the Cairo Gang, led by Colonel Aimes and Major Bennett, had been brought from England to fight Collins and his organization. Collins chose this Sunday because there was a big GAA (*Gaelic Athletic Association) football game in *Croke Park and Dublin would be unusually crowded. The night before, the *Auxiliaries had raided Vaughan's Hotel and just missed Collins and his top men who were finalizing their plans. In another raid, two IRA (*Irish Republican Army) leaders, Peadar Clancy and Richard Kee, were captured and, along with another prisoner, Conor Clune, were tortured and shot dead on November 21, supposedly "trying to escape."

At eight o'clock in the morning, members of the Squad, together with Dublin IRA members, converged on eight different addresses. Nineteen men, some of whom may not have been agents, were roused from their sleep and shot, some in front of wives or girlfriends. Most of the assassins managed to get away, but one group was intercepted by an Auxiliary patrol and had to shoot their way out. One IRA man, Frank Teeling, was captured. By the time word was sent to Croke Park to cancel the game between *Tipperary and Dublin, it was too late. The crowds had already gathered. During the game, a contingent of Auxiliaries surrounded the stadium to search for suspects. They opened fire on the crowd with rifles and machine guns, killing twelve. They claimed later to have come under attack, but it is generally believed that this was an act of revenge for the IRA's attack that morning. T.C.

Bloody Sunday (II). Sunday, January 30, 1972. Day of atrocity in Derry City, when British soldiers opened fire on civilians. Following the introduction of *internment without trial in August 1971, the *Northern Ireland Civil Rights Association (NICRA) reactivated its campaign of mass protest demonstrations. All such marches were banned as being illegal. A demonstration was held on January 30, 1972, in Derry. Estimates of the number of marchers vary. Some observers put the number as high as twenty thousand, whereas the Widgery Report (the report of the British government inquiry into the tragedy) estimated the number at between three and five thousand. A section of the crowd rioted at the William Street British army barricade. The army ordered the First Battalion, Parachute Regiment to begin an arrest operation. At approximately 4:10 P.M., soldiers began to open fire on the marchers in the Rossville Street area. By about 4:40 P.M. the shooting ended with thirteen people dead and a further thirteen injured from gunshots, one of whom later died. The Widgery Report, released in April 1972, was rejected by the *nationalist community, and many others who were present on that day, as a cover-up.

Established in 1998, the Saville Tribunal, authorized by British Prime Minister Tony *Blair and headed by an international panel, has reopened the Bloody Sunday case to examine (among other issues) whether the soldiers came under fire first. The British soldiers claimed to have come under sustained attack by gunfire and nail bombs. None of the eyewitness accounts say they saw any guns or bombs being used. No soldiers were injured in the operation; no guns or bombs were recovered at the scene of the shooting. It seems that the elite soldiers, hyped up and expecting to make contact with the IRA (*Irish Republican Army), reacted to some innocuous signal by methodically targeting men of military age.

Bloody Sunday was the end of the civil rights movement in *Northern Ireland. There was a massive upsurge of IRA violence following the incident as large *Catholic areas in Derry and *Belfast virtually withdrew from the state, becoming "No-Go Areas" dominated by the IRA. Though Bloody Sunday had been the responsibility of the British army, the devolved *Stormont government fell victim, and was suspended on March 24, 1972. Direct rule by the United Kingdom government in London was imposed. The Saville Tribunal is expected to issue its report in 2005. M.M.

Blueshirts, the. Political organization. The Blueshirts organization was formed on February 9, 1932, as the Army Comrades' Association for ex-soldiers of the *Irish Free State army. After the *Fianna Fáil victory in a general election on February 16, 1932, *Cumann na nGaedheal supporters rushed to join the Army Comrades' Association. On February 22, 1933, Éamon *de Valera fired General Eoin *O'Duffy, who was the *Gárda commissioner. O'Duffy became the association's leader, and renamed it the National Guard. Mimicking their European counterparts, the guard adopted blue shirts as the party uniform and became known as the Blueshirts. Under O'Duffy, the Blueshirts embraced fascist ideology and paramilitary structure. After a planned march on *Dublin in August 1933 was banned by de Valera, the movement lost its momentum. In an attempt to revive its fortunes, the Blueshirts merged with Cumann na nGaedheal and the Centre Party to form a new political party, *Fine Gael (United Ireland Party), with O'Duffy as president.

However, O'Duffy was unstable and soon broke away to organize the Blueshirts as a separate organization. They formed a volunteer brigade to fight on the Fascist side in the *Spanish Civil War but had an inglorious career there. The movement enjoyed popular support for a brief period but faded into obscurity after Spain. T.C.

Blythe, Ernest (1889–1975). Politician and *Irish Free State minister. Born in Magheragall, Lisburn, County *Antrim, Blythe became a member of the *Gaelic League and the IRB (*Irish Republican Brotherhood) while working as a clerk in the civil service in *Dublin. Imprisoned during the 1916 *Easter Rising, he later supported the *Anglo-Irish Treaty and held a number of ministries (local government, 1922–23, finance, 1923–32, and vice president of the executive council, 1927–32) under *Cumann na nGaedheal. While minister for finance, he took considerable criticism for his decision to cut the old-age pension by a shilling, but he is also remembered for his support of the *Irish language and creating a state subsidy for the *Abbey National Theatre. He retired from politics in 1936 and became managing director of the Abbey Theatre from 1941 to 1967. His tenure there was considered highly controversial. P.E.

Bodley, Seóirse (1933–). Composer, conductor, lecturer, pianist. Bodley's youth in *Dublin coincided with the period when the newly formed *Radio Éireann Symphony Orchestra was introducing Irish audiences to a wide spectrum of orchestral music. His earliest work, including Music for Strings (1952), shows the influence of established European masters such as Bartók. Studies in Stuttgart (Johann Nepomuk David, composition, Hans Müller-Kray, conducting) broadened his outlook as shown in the First Symphony of 1959. He was appointed lecturer in music at University College, Dublin, in the same year. Influenced by the music and ideas he encountered at the Darmstadt Summer School, Bodley was the first Irish composer to seriously engage with the European avant-garde, as shown in the orchestral "Configurations" (1967). In the 1970s, Bodley surprised audiences with his juxtaposition of avant-garde techniques and evocations of traditional Irish *music ("A Small White Cloud Drifts Over Ireland," 1976). He has continued to produce works of both tonal and serial orientation. M.D.

Boer War, the Irish in (1899–1902). Irish fought on both sides of this British military campaign in southern Africa. The British attempted to seize control of two independent republics, Transvaal and the Orange Free State, where large deposits of gold and diamonds had been discovered. Twenty-two thousand Boers, 25,000 British troops, and 12,000 African auxiliaries died within three years, and tens of thousands were displaced and many Boer civilians perished in British concentration camps. Irish regiments in the British army suffered heavy casualties at Colenso and Spion Kop, and the sieges of Ladysmith and Mafeking. Losses sustained by the Royal Dublin Fusiliers were commemorated by a memorial in St. Stephen's Green, *Dublin, on a site originally intended for a statue of Wolfe *Tone. The activities of Irish pro-Boer commandoes led by Major John *MacBride and Arthur Lynch were acclaimed by leading Irish *nationalists, especially Arthur *Griffith whose newspaper, the *United Irishman*, helped define the *republican ideology of *Sinn Féin. The Treaty of Vereeniging ended the conflict on May 31, 1902, on favorable terms to the Boers, who went on to create the new country of South Africa. R.OD.

bogs. Seventeen percent of the land surface of Ireland is covered in bog. The word *bog* stems from the Irish word for "soft"—*bogach*. Boglands began to form in Ireland about eight thousand years ago. The peat, or turf, is composed of 95 percent water and 5 percent rotted plants, animal remains, pollen, and dust. Because of the large amount of rain that falls in parts of Ireland, much of the land is waterlogged and the micro-organisms that cause decay are unable to survive. Dead plants and animals gradually accumulate to form turf. "Blanket bog" is found in many of the counties on the western seaboard, while "raised bogs" (which are slightly higher than the rest of the countryside) are to be found in the midlands. Turf is still commonly used as a source of fuel. It has been harvested by the state company Bord na Móna since the 1930s and served as an invaluable source of alternative energy during World War II. B.D.

Bogside, the Battle of (1969). Siege of *nationalist/*Catholic neighborhood in Derry City that brought the British army into the *Northern Ireland conflict. Beginning in October 1968, when a civil rights demonstration was attacked (October 5) by the *Royal Ulster Constabulary (RUC) in Derry City center, tensions escalated. Twice, in January and April 1969, RUC incursions into the Catholic Bogside area led to intensive rioting and police brutality.

Eavan Boland

Sectarian passions were stoked by the *Orange Order's marching season, which in Derry peaked with the *Apprentice Boys' parade past the Bogside. Rioting was anticipated, and the Derry City Defense Committee prepared to defend against the police incursions. On August 12, the Apprentice Boys' march was indeed assaulted at the Bogside's perimeter. The RUC, followed by a loyalist mob, entered the Bogside, only to be forced back. Two days of siege followed, as residents fought tear gas and armored cars with stones and petrol bombs. In the course of battle, Jack *Lynch, then *Taoiseach (prime minister), in a television address announced that "the Irish government can no longer stand by and see innocent people injured and perhaps worse." With the RUC exhausted, the *Stormont government was faced with the option of throwing the *B-Specials into the fray, or asking for direct aid from Britain. They opted for the latter and late in the afternoon of August 14, 1969, British troops entered the center of Derry. M.M.

Boland, Eavan (1944–). Poet and literary critic. Daughter of a diplomat and a painter, Boland was born in *Dublin and educated in London, New York, and Trinity College, Dublin. One of Ireland's leading contemporary poets, Boland has been at the center of debates about feminism and the role of the woman poet in the Irish canon.

Her poetry gives expression to the unremembered lives of women who are "outside history." She deals frankly with issues such as childbirth, menstruation, and masturbation, and celebrates the domestic. The collections *The War Horse* (1975) and *In Her Own Image* (1980) explore the relation between domestic and political violence. Her nine volumes of poetry include *The Journey and Other Poems* (1986), *An Origin like Water: Collected Poems* (1996), *In a Time of Violence* (1994), and *Against Love Poetry* (2001). She is author of an autobiographical study, *Object Lessons* (1995), and a pamphlet, "A Kind of Scar" (1989), about women writers' relationship with the Irish nation. Since 1996, Boland has taught at Stanford University in Palo Alto, California. M.S.T.

Boland, Gerald (1885–1973). Politician. Born in Manchester, England, to Irish parents and educated at the O'Brien Institute, *Dublin, Boland (brother of Harry) joined the Irish *Volunteers, and during the 1916 *Easter Rising, fought at Jacob's biscuit factory. He was imprisoned for his part in the rising.

Boland was a member of the *Dáil (TD; Teachta Dála—member of Parliament) for Roscommon from 1923 to 1961 and was a founder member of *Fianna Fáil in 1926. He was appointed minister for posts and telegraphs in 1933, and minister for lands in 1936. As minister for justice from 1939, Boland introduced strong measures to suppress the IRA (*Irish Republican Army), including *internment without trial, military courts, and special criminal courts. He lost his seat in 1961 but continued to work in politics as a senator until 1969. C.D.

Boland, Harry (1887–1922). *Republican. Born in *Dublin on April 27, 1887, Boland was educated at Synge Street *Christian Brothers School and at the De La Salle College, Castletown, County *Laois. He was a member of the GAA (*Gaelic Athletic Association) and a renowned *hurler, who played for Dublin in the 1908 All-Ireland Senior Championship. Boland became a member of the *Irish Republican Brotherhood in 1904 and was responsible for having Michael *Collins, his close friend, initiated into the organization in London. He was imprisoned for his role in the 1916 *Easter Rising, and after his release from prison, he helped reorganize the Irish *Volunteers and was elected secretary of *Sinn Féin in 1917. A member of the First *Dáil and part of the Irish envoy to America during the *War of Independence, Boland fell under the influence of the charismatic Éamon *de Valera. He opposed the *Anglo-Irish Treaty (1921) and worked tirelessly to prevent the *Civil War. Following its outbreak, he sided with de Valera and the republicans against the new *Free State government. Boland was shot in Skerries, County *Dublin, by a party of Free State soldiers, who had been sent by Michael Collins to arrest him. Boland died a few days later on August 1, 1922. P.E.

Boland, Kevin (1917–2001). Politician. Born in *Dublin (son of Gerald and nephew of Harry), *Boland was *Fianna Fáil TD (Teachta Dála; member of Parliament) (1957–70), minister for defense (1957–61), minister for social welfare (1961–66), and minister for local government (1966–70). He resigned from government in 1970 in sympathy with ministers Neil Blaney and Charles *Haughey, who had been dismissed by *Taoiseach (prime minister) Jack *Lynch in the *Arms Crisis. Boland founded the party Aontacht Éireann, which never won popular support. A committed *republican, he remained active in extra-parliamentary politics as a regular critic of Irish government policy on *Northern Ireland. Boland unsuccessfully challenged the constitutionality of the 1973 *Sunningdale Agreement in the Irish Supreme Court, arguing that the Irish government had no authority to recognize British sovereignty over *Northern Ireland. J.D.

Bolger, Dermot (1959–). Poet, publisher, novelist, playwright. Born in *Dublin, Bolger highlights the city's unglamorous north side in his work. As founder of Raven Arts Press, he edited a number of influential anthologies and published much distinctive new writing. His prolific output includes the prizewinning play *The Lament for Arthur Cleary* (1989) and the novel *The Journey Home* (1990). G.OB.

Boole, George (1815–64). Mathematician and logician. A shoemaker's son from Lincoln, England, Boole was self-taught and became a schoolmaster at sixteen. He was the first professor of mathematics at Queen's College, *Cork, where he taught from 1849 until his death. (Boole Hall at University College Cork was named after him.) Boole is widely regarded as the father of modern symbolic logic. Abstract descendants of Boole's algebra of logic (Boolean algebras) continue to be studied today and have useful applications in fields such as computer science and quantum theory. M.L.

Boru, Brian (Bóruma) (c.941–1014). High king of Ireland from 1002 to 1014. Born in *Munster, Brian Boru was the youngest of twelve sons of Bebinn and Cennedi, who were members of the Dál Cais tribe.

In 965, Brian's brother Mathgamain seized the throne of Munster from the Éoganacht rulers. On the death of his brother, Brian established himself as the king of Munster. He invaded Ossory in 983, and by 997 had control of South Ireland. In 1002, Brian made himself Ard-Rí (high king) of Ireland, becoming the first monarch outside the *O'Neill dynasty to claim such authority. He was described in the *Book of Armagh as the emperor of the Irish.

In his expeditions to the North in 1002 and 1005, Brian took hostages and collected tributes from local kings. Much of these monies were used to rebuild monasteries and to restore the libraries, which had been burned by the *Vikings. As his power increased, relations with some of the native lords and Norse rulers on the Irish coast deteriorated. In 1013, the Vikings of Dublin and the *Leinster Irish united against him and a decisive battle was fought at *Clontarf, near Dublin, on April 23, 1014. Brian's army annihilated the forces of the Leinster-Viking alliance, but he was hacked to death in his tent by Norsemen fleeing the battlefield. M.T.D., P.E.

Boston, the Irish in. The earliest Irish arrived in Boston in the seventeenth century, and came from the northern counties of Ireland. Because they spoke English, were *Presbyterian, and possessed marketable skills, they were accepted by the Puritans. Their support of the rebellion against the oppressive British tax policies further guaranteed their place in the life of the colony. Irish *Catholics from the southern counties of Ireland, by contrast, generally avoided Massachusetts during the colonial period because of its punitive laws against Catholic priests. During the *American Revolutionary War (1775–83), however, as a result of friendly relations with France, attitudes toward the small Catholic population became more tolerant.

During the 1820s and 1830s, attitudes changed as restrictive British land policies in Ireland caused large numbers of Catholics to leave Ireland for America. Their increasing numbers produced sporadic outbreaks of violence by native Bostonians who feared the impact of unskilled workers on the city's economy and the influence of Catholicism on their Protestant institutions. The influx of Irish Catholic *immigrants in the wake of the disastrous potato *Famine during the mid-1840s caused even greater consternation. In an effort to stop further immigration, nativists organized the American Party, also called the Know-Nothings, that swept the northern states. Because of the increasing volatility of the slavery issue, however, in 1856 the Know-Nothing candidate failed to win the presidency.

During the *American Civil War (1861–65), the Boston Irish formed two separate Irish regiments, and fought gallantly to preserve the Union. After the war, they gained a measure of social acceptance and used money from army service or war work to move out of the waterfront into nearby neighborhoods. Taking menial jobs in municipal services and public utilities, they paved the way for future generations to eventually become managers and executives in many of these same enterprises.

At the same time, the Boston Irish moved into

political positions long denied them. At the ward level, they provided their immigrant constituents with the necessities of life; at the city level they revived the Democratic Party and groomed their own candidates. In 1884, Hugh O'Brien became the first Irish-born Catholic to be elected mayor of Boston; in 1901 Patrick Collins became the second. In 1905, John F. Fitzgerald was the first Boston-born Irish Catholic to serve as mayor, and in 1914 he was succeeded by James Michael Curley, who unified the city's ethnic neighborhoods and dominated Boston politics for more than thirty years.

By the late 1940s, the decades of political and ethnic division had contributed greatly to Boston's financial breakdown and physical deterioration. With the defeat of Curley in 1949, a succession of accommodationist mayors of Irish American background, like John B. Hynes, John F. Collins, and Kevin H. White, did much to lessen traditional social and religious rivalries. They also convinced Irish political leaders to work closely with Yankee business leaders to revitalize the city's economy and launch an ambitious program of urban renewal. During the decades from 1950 to 1970, a "New Boston" emerged that set the city on a new and more progressive direction. In 1960, John F. *Kennedy, a native Bostonian, was the first and only Irish American Catholic to be elected president of the United States (1961–63). His father, Joseph Kennedy, had made a fortune on Wall Street and was ambassador to England in the 1930s. The Kennedy success story has inspired many Irish Americans. Bostonians of Irish background now assume new and more responsible positions not only in politics, religion, sports, and education, but also in law, finance, science, and the fine arts. T.H.OC.

Bothy Band, the. Hugely influential traditional-*music group, which ran from 1974–79. It drew its tunes from old repertoire, but in presentation was guided by the modern-music impetus of bouzoukist Dónal *Lunny. Its key players remain influential—Matt Molloy (*Chieftains), Tríona Ní Dhomhnaill and Mícheál Ó Domhnaill (Nightnoise), Kevin Burke (Patrick Street), and Paddy Keenan. F.V.

Boucicault, Dion (1820–90). Playwright. Born Dionysius Lardner Boursiquot in *Dublin, he became the most popular and influential playwright of his generation and was known before his death as the "Irish Shakespeare" for his prodigious production of some 150 plays. Boucicault was married three times (once bigamously) but, in spite of these affronts to Victorian sensibilities, his talent was widely admired and his plays dominated the English-speaking world.

Boucicault began his career as an actor under the stage name of Lee Moreton and worked throughout England. At age twenty, he submitted *A Lover by Proxy* to Covent Garden. Although rejected by the manager, Boucicault's next effort, *London Assurance*—a brilliant comedy about the upper classes that influenced both Oscar *Wilde and George Bernard *Shaw—was eventually accepted and opened to immediate success in 1841. Boucicault was seen as a prodigy by the London theater community. His work appeared throughout Soho and his wealth grew exponentially. Boucicault, however, generous with his money, quickly squandered his new fortune, and turned to hackwork and translating French plays to maintain his lavish lifestyle. Several unwise business agreements nearly bankrupted him, but he survived by pandering to the public's love of melodrama. Many thought that, had he not sold out, he would have been a great playwright.

During his life, Boucicault's work was performed in London, Dublin, New York, Paris, and

Australia. His plays contain sharp dialogue and are theatrically inventive spectacles, but for the most part lack genuine social analysis. Boucicault was an early champion of the royalty system and several of his plays, including *London Assurance* (1841), *The Octoroon* (1859), *The Colleen Bawn* (1860), and *The Shaughraun* (1874), are still enjoyed by audiences today. P.J.H.

Boundary Commission. Established under Article Twelve of the *Anglo-Irish Treaty of 1921, this body was to adjust the boundary between the *Irish Free State and *Northern Ireland "in accordance with the wishes of the inhabitants." The Free State government assumed that the commission would recommend the transfer of large parts of the counties *Tyrone and *Fermanagh, and smaller sections of *Armagh, *Down, and *Derry to its jurisdiction. In this scenario, Northern Ireland, reduced to four counties, would not be politically or economically viable and this would eventually lead to reunification. Due to a number of factors (including the *Civil War), the commission did not meet until November 1924. It was chaired by Richard Feetham, a South African Judge, with J. R. Fisher and Eoin *MacNeill representing Northern Ireland and the Irish Free State, respectively. Feetham ruled against the use of a plebiscite and argued that the terms of the Anglo-Irish Treaty combined with economic and geographical considerations prevented him from radically altering the border. In November 1925, a summary of the commission's final report was leaked to the *Morning Post*, a British conservative paper. It stated that the Free State was to receive parts of County Fermanagh and southern Armagh but would lose a section of East Donegal. This caused considerable embarrassment for the Free State government, which had expected to acquire at least two northern counties without the loss of any territory. W. T. *Cosgrave, leader of the Free State, concerned about political stability, favored suppressing the report (which was only released in the 1960s as a historical document). A tripartite agreement was signed in London on December 3, 1925, which revoked the powers of the Boundary Commission. The border was to remain unchanged while the provisions for the Council of Ireland were in effect abolished. Under the agreement, the Free State was also released from some of the financial commitments contained in the treaty. P.E.

Bowen, Elizabeth (1899–1973). Novelist, short story writer. Chronicler of "the Big House," Bowen is one of the last great *Anglo-Irish writers. Born in *Dublin, she inherited her estate in Doneraile, County *Cork, from an unbroken line of *Cromwellian forefathers. She published a finely written description of the mansion in *Bowen's Court* (1942) and the house appears, inter alia, in an early novel *The Last September* (1929). Her novels are full of subtle sensibility; an influence is Henry James but James updated and leavened with Irish realism as well as poetry. *The Death of the Heart* (1938) is mainly regarded as her greatest work, but *The Heat of the Day* (1949) has grittier writing, impelled by her memories of the trials and ambiguities of the Blitz during World War II. It contains an Irish section, which depicts "The Big House" in wartime gloom. A beautiful late novel *The World of Love* (1955) establishes an elegiac romantic tone. Bowen was a superb short story writer. She was also an important writer of place and travel; she published a street-by-street meditation on Rome and two intimate portraits of Dublin, *The Shelbourne Hotel* (1951) and *Seven Winters: Memoirs of a Dublin Childhood* (1942). Elizabeth Bowen has been accused of being a British spy in Ireland during the war, but this was in reality ancillary to her social life on her visits to her native country. She was an indefatigable hostess and lover, richly endowed with vision and pleasure. J.L.

boxing. A hugely popular *sport at amateur level, boxing has been declining in recent years. Local boxing clubs are found in rural towns and in working-class neighborhoods of most cities throughout Ireland. National titles are contested annually on an All-Ireland basis and champions from north and south represent Ireland at international competitions like the Olympics. The financial base is too small to support a professional circuit. Irish boxers sometimes go to the United States or Britain to turn professional, and several, including Dubliners Steve Collins and Michael Carruth, and Belfast's Wayne McCullough, have gone on to become world champions. The most famous Irish champion of recent times was featherweight Barry McGuigan, who became known as "The Clones Cyclone." His career lasted until 1989 and for some time he was based in *Belfast under the management of local promoter Barney Eastwood. F.S.

Boycott, Captain Hugh Cunningham (1832–97). English ex–army officer. Captain Boycott was appointed agent for the vast estate of Lord Erne in County *Mayo in 1879. During the *Land League's campaign for tenants'rights, as a form of social protest, Charles Stewart *Parnell urged the ostracism of anyone opposed to the reforms. In Mayo, the locals refused to work for Captain Boycott because he rejected the peasants' meager demands for fair rents and wages. The situation became so desperate that British loyalists were imported to harvest the lands under the protection of an entire army regiment. Captain Boycott's name entered the English language as a synonym for social ostracism. J.OM.

Boydell, Brian (1917–2000). Composer. Born in *Dublin, Boydell is one of the leading Irish composers of the twentieth century. He was an accomplished musician and musicologist, who wrote a number of influential works on Irish musical history. His best-known compositions include *In Memoriam Mahatma Gandhi* (1948), *Symphonic Inscapes* (1968), and *Masai Mara* (1988). A.S.

Boyle, Robert (1627–91). Irish-born physicist, founder of modern chemistry and pioneer in the use of the scientific method. Born in Lismore, County *Waterford, Boyle was the first chemist to isolate and collect a gas. In 1662, he formulated Boyle's law (under conditions of constant temperature, the pressure and volume of a gas are inversely proportional). In the area of chemistry, he noted the difference between a compound and a mixture, and argued that matter was composed of corpuscles of various sorts and sizes. P.E.

Boyne, Battle of the (July 12, 1690). Battle fought between King *James II and *William III. Actually it took place on July 1, 1690 (it became the twelfth after Britain adopted the Gregorian calendar). It is the most famous battle of this conflict because both kings were present. William of Orange wanted the British throne to give him the resources to carry on the Netherlands' war against France. After the Glorious Revolution (1688), Louis XIV of France believed that James would enter the war on his side. James II arrived in Ireland, where he was still recognized as king, with an army consisting partly of French troops. William followed him. Against advice, James made a stand at the River Boyne, near Drogheda, County *Louth. The battle was little more than a skirmish. James panicked when part of his army was outflanked by the Williamite cavalry and ordered a retreat. He himself fled to *Dublin and was soon on a boat to France, leaving his army behind. William's victory assumed a symbolic importance for *Protestant *unionists and is to this day commemorated annually by the *Orange Order. T.C.

Branagh, Kenneth (1960–). Actor, director. Born in *Belfast to a working-class family, Branagh moved with his parents to Reading, England, at the age of nine. He studied acting at the Royal Academy of Dramatic Arts (RADA) in London and, at twenty-three, joined the Royal Shakespeare Company, where he had leading roles in *Henry V* and *Romeo and Juliet*. Branagh played the title role in Graham Reid's *Billy* trilogy of TV plays (1982–84), a rare screen representation of Northern Irish *Protestantism. He soon formed his own company, the Renaissance Theatre Company, and, at twenty-nine, directed and starred in the film *Henry V* (1989), which brought him Best Actor and Best Director Oscar nominations. In 1993, he brought Shakespeare to mainstream audiences with his film adaptation of *Much Ado About Nothing* (1993). At thirty, he published his autobiography and at thirty-four directed and starred as Victor Frankenstein in the big-budget adaptation of Mary Shelley's *Frankenstein* (1994) with Robert De Niro as the monster. In 1996, Branagh wrote, directed, and starred in a lavish adaptation of *Hamlet*. Recently, he appeared in the films *Celebrity* (1998), *Wild Wild West* (1999), and *Rabbit-Proof Fence* (2002). He has stated in interviews that he feels "more Irish than English." Branagh maintains links with cultural institutions in *Northern Ireland, and in 1998 made a public appeal in favor of the referendum on the *Good Friday Agreement. H.L.

Breathnach, Breandán (1912–85). *Uilleann piper, writer, traditional *music collector. His sharp intelligence and commitment made him ideological champion of the traditional music revival. Breathnach's publications (especially the journal *Ceol*, tunebook series *Ceol Rince na hÉireann*, and text *Folk Music and Dances of Ireland*) remain landmarks. The revival of uilleann piping by Na Píobairí Uilleann, the collecting of songs by University College Dublin's Department of Irish Folklore, and the founding of the Irish Traditional Music Archive are indebted to his vision. F.V.

brehon law. Legal system of ancient Ireland. The Irish word for a judge is *breitheamh*, and it is from the genitive plural of this word, *breithiún*, that the term *brehon laws* is derived for the ancient laws of Ireland. The earliest surviving versions of these laws date from the seventh and eighth centuries A.D., and exhibit a strong Christian overlayer on older native tradition. The laws continued in practice for a long time, in large areas of Ireland, even surviving Norman and English lordship down to the seventeenth century. There is a great deal of variation in rationale and prescription within the law texts, but in general they reflect the society of their time—rural, tribal, and hierarchical. The usual method of settlement of disputes was for the offending party to pay honor-price to the victim or to the victim's relatives. Such honor-price varied according to one's social status, with the main distinction being between those of lordly rank and those freemen of the farming class. Beneath these were the unfree, tenants without surety, individuals from outside the tribe, and slaves. Social mobility was, though difficult, possible between all these classes. There were some other beneficial aspects to the laws, such as the right of *women to own property and protective clauses for children. D.Oh.

Brendan, Saint (A.D. c.500–577). Sailor, navigator, and holy man. Baptized Mobhí, he was born near Ardfert, County *Kerry, possibly before A.D. 500. His name was closely associated with a once-active pilgrimage to the summit of Mount Brandon on the *Dingle Peninsula. His renown spread across Europe in the Middle Ages through the *Navigatio Brendani*, an anonymous account written in Latin c.800, which tells of his fabulous island-hopping voyage undertaken by *currach with twelve disciples in search of the Promised Land of the Saints. Characteristics of the various islands described could suggest a route starting in Kerry, passing the *Aran Islands, and continuing to the Faroes, Iceland, Greenland, and an "Island of Grapes"—perhaps the east coast of the North American continent—before finally returning to Ireland to recount his adventures for posterity. He died in 577 at Annaghdown, County *Galway, where his sister had a convent, and was buried at *Clonfert in the same county, where a cathedral with a great Romanesque doorway now stands. P.H.

Brennan, Maeve (1917–93). Short story writer and journalist. Born in *Dublin the daughter of Ireland's first ambassador to America, Brennan lived in the United States from the age of seventeen. She worked for the *New Yorker*, but suffered from mental illness and died destitute. Her incisive stories of Dublin middle-class life are collected in *The Springs of Affection* (1997). *The Long-Winded Old Lady* (1997) is a collection of her entertaining journalism. G.OB.

brewing. See **distilling and brewing.**

Brigid, Saint (450–523). Irish *saint. Born in Faughert, she is often referred to as "the Mary of the Gaels." The most famous legend associated with Brigid tells how a local chieftain would only give her the amount of land that her cloak would cover to build a convent. Her cloak began to spread miraculously until the chieftain begged her to stop it. The area that was covered by the cloak became the site of Brigid's famous convent in *Kildare. The Cros Bhríde (St. Brigid's Cross) is still woven from rushes and placed under the rafters of houses on her feast day (the first day of February). It is reputed to bring health and good fortune to the household for the coming year. St. Brigid is regarded as a special patron of farm animals and many holy wells are dedicated to her name, some of which are said to have the power to cure sterility and blindness. B.D.

Brooke, Sir Basil (1888–1973). Politician, prime minister of *Northern Ireland (1943–63). A Tory landowner, Brooke became prime minister during World War II because he was considered the best candidate to mobilize Northern Ireland's war effort. He was so successful in this that he enjoyed British goodwill well into the 1950s. His traditional conservatism, however, frustrated the postwar generation of British politicians. The *unionist establishment, conscious that automatic British goodwill could no longer be taken for granted, eased him from office in 1963 as an embarrassing anachronism. M.M.

Brosnan, Pierce (1953–). Actor. Born in Navan, County *Meath, Brosnan moved to London in 1964, where he made his acting debut in 1976. His first movie role was in *The Long Good Friday* (1981). Television work included the detective series *Remington Steele*. He played numerous film and television roles before being cast as James Bond in *GoldenEye* (1995), which was followed by *Tomorrow Never Dies* (1997), *The World Is Not Enough* (1999), and *Die Another Day* (2002). Other movies in which Brosnan has starred include *Dante's Peak* (1997), *The Thomas*

Crown Affair (1999), and *Evelyn* (2002), which he also produced. J.C.E.L.

Brown, Christy (1932–81). Novelist and poet. Born to a working-class family in Crumlin, *Dublin, Brown was almost completely paralyzed from birth by cerebral palsy. His mother taught him to read and Dr. Robert Collis taught him movement coordination and speech. After he learned how to type using his foot, he wrote a memoir of his childhood, *My Left Foot* (1954), an insightful account of the mind of a handicapped child and working-class life in Dublin. *Down All the Days* (1970), a fictional re-creation of the same autobiographical theme, combines gritty realism with lyrical language. It is generally considered his finest work. Later novels, *A Shadow on Summer* (1973), *Wild Grow the Lilies* (1976), and *A Promising Career* (1982) are less compelling. His first volume of poetry, *Come Softly to My Wake* (1971), was a bestseller. He married Mary Carr in 1972. They bought homes in Ballyheigue, County *Kerry, and in Somerset, England. *My Left Foot* was filmed by Jim *Sheridan (1990) to much acclaim. C.D.

Browne, Noel (1915–97). Politician and medical doctor. Dr. Browne came to prominence in the 1940s as a campaigner for a national program to eradicate tuberculosis, which was rampant in Ireland at that time. He joined the political party *Clann na Poblachta in 1946 (when it was established by Seán *MacBride) and was elected to the *Dáil (Parliament) in 1948. Minister for health in the coalition government from 1948 to 1951, Browne is popularly credited with solving the tuberculosis crisis. He sought to introduce free pre- and postnatal medical services through the bill known as the "Mother and Child Scheme." This was opposed by the medical lobby supported by the *Catholic Church, which believed in limiting state involvement in social welfare and family matters. Dr. Browne's own inflexibility and the unwillingness of his colleagues to have what they saw as an unnecessary public dispute with the Catholic Church led his party leader, Seán MacBride, to demand Browne's resignation. He was reelected to the Dáil as an independent in 1951, as a *Fianna Fáil TD (Teachta Dála; member of Parliament) in 1954, and again as an independent in 1957. He founded the National Progressive Democrats in 1958, and was elected as their TD in 1961. In 1963, Browne joined the *Labour Party and was a Labour TD from 1969 to 1973. He split from Labour in 1977 and was an independent (and briefly *Socialist Labour Party) TD from 1977 to 1982. In 1990, he ran against Mary *Robinson for the Labour Party nomination in the Irish presidential election, but was heavily defeated. While his difficulties in working with others left him on the margins of political life, Browne remained a hugely popular political figure until his death. J.D.

Bruce, Edward (died 1318). Younger brother of the king of *Scotland (1306–29), Robert Bruce. Between 1306 and 1314, Robert Bruce, Scotland's greatest national hero, and Edward waged a relentless guerrilla war against the English occupying forces. This campaign culminated in the decisive Battle of Bannockburn in 1314, which was England's greatest defeat in the Middle Ages and ensured the survival of Scotland as an independent nation.

During his reign, Robert Bruce attempted to create a pan-Celtic state incorporating Ireland and Scotland, a plan that came tantalizingly close to fruition. In 1316, Edward invaded Ireland and proclaimed himself king. He allied himself with several native Irish rulers and together they won a series of victories against the *Anglo-Norman lords. Robert himself joined Edward in Ireland for a time. The defeat and death of Edward Bruce at Faughart, near Dundalk, in October 1318, ended one of the greatest what-ifs of Irish history. J.P.

Brugha, Cathal (1874–1922). *Republican revolutionary. Born in *Dublin and educated at Belvedere College, Brugha joined the *Gaelic League in 1899 and became a member of the Irish *Volunteers in 1913. During the *Easter Rising of 1916, he was second in command (under Éamonn *Ceannt) at the South Dublin Union. Between 1917 and 1919 he was chief of staff of the Irish Volunteers. Brugha was elected temporary Príomh-Aire (chief minister) at the first meeting of *Dáil Éireann (Irish Parliament) and was minister for defense until January 1922. An opponent of the *Anglo-Irish Treaty (1921), he joined the republican side during the *Civil War and was shot by government forces in Dublin on July 5, 1922. He died two days later. P.E.

Bruton, John (1947–). Politician, *Taoiseach (prime minister). Member of *Dáil Éireann (Irish Parliament) for *Meath since 1969, Bruton served in several ministries (especially finance and industry) in the coalition governments of 1973–77, 1981–1982, and 1982–1987. *Fine Gael Party leader from 1990 to 2001, he became Taoiseach in December 1994 in a three-party "rainbow coalition." During his administration, partly because of a reduced corporate tax policy, economic growth doubled, inflation and unemployment were reduced, and a budget deficit was turned into a surplus. In February 1995, he and British Prime Minister John *Major issued a Framework Document (arising from the *Downing Street Declaration of 1993) guiding *Anglo-Irish/Northern Irish relations that became a foundation stone of the *Good Friday Agreement of 1998. In 1995, his government supported a narrowly successful referendum campaign for a constitutional amendment allowing *divorce in Ireland. His term as Taoiseach ended in 1997 when an opposition coalition came to power. In 2001, Michael Noonan replaced Bruton as leader of Fine Gael. J.P.MC.

Bryce, James; First Viscount Bryce of Dechmont (1838–1922). Liberal politician and academic. While chief secretary for Ireland (1905–07), Bryce promoted schemes for devolution and the improvement of Irish university *education. As a *Belfast-born *Presbyterian, Bryce's support for *home rule was tempered by his concern for the interests of *Ulster Protestants. A regius professor of civil law at Oxford University (1870–93), Bryce published numerous studies of constitutional politics, most notably *The American Commonwealth* (1888). He was British ambassador to Washington (1907–13). S.A.B.

B-Specials. Special police unit in Northern Ireland. The *Ulster Special Constabulary, or "Specials," was formed in 1920 by the British administration to prevent anti-*republican vigilantism. There were three sections: A, B, and C. The A and C Specials, consisting of full- or part-time auxiliaries, were disbanded in 1925, but the reserve "B-Specials" were retained and deployed during the various *Irish Republican Army (IRA) campaigns in Northern Ireland. *Catholics shunned the force, and were not welcome in it. Some believe that because the B-Specials were a crass demonstration of ethnic hegemony, they alienated Catholics out of all proportion to their actions. The Specials, fired by zeal and knowledgeable of local circumstances, were effective in suppressing subversion, at least in rural areas. In *nationalist areas, the Specials were seen as a state-sponsored vigilante force, and one of the original goals of the *Northern Ireland Civil Rights Association (NICRA) was their disbandment. Their deployment in urban areas, against civilians and in front of cameras was controversial, and the use of British troops was preferred to their full mobilization in 1969. In 1970, they were replaced by a regular army/militia hybrid, the *Ulster Defense Regiment (UDR). M.M.

Burke, Edmund (1729–97). Politician, orator, political thinker. Born in *Dublin, Burke studied at Trinity College and the Middle Temple in London. Abandoning legal study for literary interests, he began editing the *Annual Register* in 1758 and in 1764 joined Samuel Johnson and Oliver *Goldsmith in London's "Literary Club." Burke married Jane Mary Nugent, the daughter of an Irish *Catholic doctor, in 1757. From 1759 to 1764 he was private secretary to William *Hamilton, chief secretary for Ireland, and in 1765 to the Marquess of Rockingham. The same year, he was elected MP (member of Parliament) for Wendover. Burke's *Thoughts on the Cause of the Present Discontents* (1770) was critical of the monarchy's control of Parliament.

A superb orator, he delivered his "Speech on American Taxation" (1774) and "Speech on Conciliation with America" (1775) in sympathy with the grievances of the American colonies. He served as MP for Bristol from 1774, and for Malton from 1780. The same year, Burke introduced a bill for economic reform to prevent royal or executive domination of Parliament through patronage. Burke was Paymaster of the Forces in Rockingham's ministry in 1782, but upon Rockingham's death, he resigned. He returned to the same post in the short-lived Fox-North coalition in 1783. From 1786 to 1788 he championed the impeachment of Warren Hastings, governor general of Bengal, for abuses by the East India Company.

In 1790 Burke published his *Reflections on the Revolution in France*, a brilliant condemnation of *republican ideas, which remains a classic statement of conservative thought. The next year, he broke with many Whig allies on the issue of *France and published his *Appeal from the New to the Old Whigs and Thoughts on the Revolution in France*. His opposition to the *French Revolution, however, did not prevent him from championing relief for Irish Catholics in his 1792 *Letters to Sir Hercules Langrishe*. After retiring from Parliament in 1794, Burke continued to criticize the French Revolution in works like *A Letter to a Noble Lord* (1796) and *Letters on a Regicide Peace* (1796). He died in 1797. J.P.MC.

Burke, Joe (1939–). Traditional *music accordionist. Born in Loughrea, County *Galway, Burke was influenced by earlier generations of Irish American musicians such as Michael *Coleman. He reflects the local style of key composer Paddy Fahy, but seminal accordionists Paddy O'Brien and Joe Cooley were also mentors. Burke has become iconic to generations of players. F.V.

Butler, Hubert (Marshall) (1900–91). Essayist and critic. Born in *Kilkenny and educated at St. John's College, Oxford, Butler was strongly committed to the cooperative movement, local affairs, and minorities' rights. A scholar and polyglot particularly interested in Eastern European affairs, he was censured for his stance on the Roman Catholic Church's role in Croatia. He campaigned for nuclear disarmament and the right to choose in the divisive abortion referendum in the 1980s. His essays are collected in *Escape from the Anthill* (1986), *Grandmother and Wolfe Tone* (1990), and *In the Land of Nod* (1996). M.S.T.

Butt, Isaac (1813–79). Member of Parliament (MP), barrister, and founder of the *home rule

Gabriel Byrne

movement. Born in Glenfin, County *Donegal, Butt was the only son of a Church of Ireland rector. Educated at Trinity College, Dublin, he was professor of political economy at the college between 1836 and 1841, and became a barrister in 1838. Butt was originally a *unionist who argued against Daniel *O'Connell's *Repeal movement. However, the appalling level of poverty within Ireland and the failure of the British government to deal with the *Famine led to his growing disillusionment with direct British rule of Ireland. As a barrister, Butt had defended *Fenian leaders and was convinced that there was a political solution to what had caused the Fenian Rebellion. In 1869, he became president of the Amnesty Association, which sought amnesty for the Fenian prisoners.

Butt founded the home rule movement by establishing the Home Government Association in 1870, and then the Home Rule League in 1873. In the general elections of 1874, Home Rule candidates won 59 seats in the House of Commons (out of a total of 103 for Ireland) and subsequently organized themselves into the *Irish Parliamentary Party (later known as the Nationalist Party), with Butt as leader. Butt's conservative nationalism envisaged a home government for Ireland within a federal system centered in Westminster. Interpreted by some as a conversion to nationalism, Butt's vision of home rule can be seen as an extension of his conservative politics. Ireland's problem could be solved only within the context of the empire and not as an independent state.

In Parliament, Butt proved to be an ineffective leader, unable to control the many elements within the party and unwilling to use radical tactics to obtain Irish reform from British Prime Minister Benjamin Disraeli. He did not support the policy of obstruction (where the rules of the House of Commons were used to obstruct day-to-day business) introduced by fellow Home Ruler Joseph Biggar, and later backed by Charles Stewart *Parnell. In 1877, Parnell replaced Butt as chairman of the Home Rule Confederation of Great Britain. In February 1879, Butt narrowly won a vote of confidence as party leader. At this stage, his health was failing, and he died on May 5, 1879. He is buried at Stranorlar, County Donegal. J.OM.

Byrne, Gabriel (1950–). Actor, producer, director, and author. Born in *Dublin and educated at University College, Dublin, Byrne began acting with the Focus Theatre. He appeared in the *RTÉ series

The Riordans and *Bracken* and has acted in a number of critically acclaimed West End and Broadway productions. His film work includes *Excalibur* (1981), *Miller's Crossing* (1990), *Into the West* (1993), *Little Women* (1994), *The Usual Suspects* (1995), and *The Man in the Iron Mask* (1998). He co-produced *In the Name of the Father* (1993) and made his directing debut with *The Lark in the Clear Air* in 1996. P.E.

Byrne, Gay (1934–). Broadcaster, entertainer, media personality. Born in *Dublin, Byrne started his broadcasting career on Irish *radio in 1958. In 1962, he began producing and hosting *The Late Late Show* for Irish *television. Originally proposed as a summer filler, this highly entertaining show has become the world's longest-running live talk show. Under Byrne, it became a forum for public discussion on social and political issues, and had a modernizing influence on contemporary Ireland. From the 1970s, he hosted a *radio show, which was also highly influencial. Recipient of many awards for broadcasting, he retired from *The Late Late Show* in 1999. P.E.

C

camogie. Outdoor field game similar to *hurling and played by women of all ages. The *Gaelic Athletic Association has actively promoted camogie by setting up Cumann Camógaíochta na nGael (The Camogie Association) in 1904. Not surprisingly, camogie is most popular in the hurling heartlands of *Munster and the counties *Kilkenny and *Galway. F.S.

Canada, the Irish in. The Irish established a notable presence in Canada during the eighteenth century, when large sections of North America were contested by the British and French governments. While individuals and small groups of Irish migrants certainly visited the future state of Canada in the early 1600s, the Anglo-French wars of the mid- to late 1700s brought much greater numbers in the uniforms of both sides. The tendency of Irish-born *emigrants to sympathize with the French perspective and the periodic enforcement of anti-*Catholic legislation ensured that large-scale Irish immigration to the Canadian colonies was discouraged prior to 1800. *Newfoundland, however, was then already heavily populated by people of Irish extraction because of long-established ties with *Waterford, *Wexford, and *Cork.

Ontario and Quebec received huge volumes of Irish immigration between the 1820s and 1860s, with a sustained and heavy flow of people arriving after the *Famine. As many as 100,000 Irish may have landed in Quebec in 1847, although the settlers moved in both directions over the US/Canadian border. An estimated 329,000 Irish immigrants entered Canada between 1841 and 1850, particularly Ontario and New Brunswick. Estate clearances in Ireland, moreover, resulted in concentrated bursts of settlement in Quebec and elsewhere in the 1850s, when approximately 19 percent of Ontarians and 6 percent of Quebec residents had been born in Ireland. Census data reveal that the four provinces comprising the Dominion of Canada in 1871 contained 24.3 percent persons of Irish ethnicity (compared with 20 percent English, 15 percent Scots, and

31 percent French), making Canada among the most Irish places in the world. This prominence was reflected in every facet of the country's political and cultural evolution. R.OD.

Canary Wharf Bombing (1996). IRA (*Irish Republican Army) bombing of London's financial district. The bomb attack in London on Friday, February 9, 1996, which killed two people, caused millions of pounds worth of damage, and ended the IRA cease-fire, which had been in force since August 31, 1994. Though IRA violence did return to *Northern Ireland, the IRA's intention was to concentrate on spectacular targets in Great Britain. Many of their plans were frustrated by efficient British intelligence operations. In 1997, the IRA cease-fire was resumed. M.M.

Carleton, William (1774–1869). Novelist and short story writer. Born in County *Tyrone to an Irish-speaking peasant family, Carleton was self-educated. His stories were published in two collections, both entitled *Traits and Stories of the Irish Peasantry* (1830, 1833). His best-known novels include *The Black Prophet* (1847) and *The Tithe Proctor* (1849), indictments of the peasants' living conditions during the Great *Famine, and *Willie Reilly and his Dear Colleen Bawn*, a popular romantic melodrama. In Carleton's distinctive narrative, spirited, often grotesque characters speak a colorful *Hiberno-English. His early rejection of *Catholicism and the politics of resistance evolved into a more sympathetic but complex relation with the peasantry. M.S.T.

Carlow, County. Ireland's second smallest county, located inland in the southeast, in the province of *Leinster. The county covers an area of 346 square miles and has a population of 45,845 (2002 census). Surrounded by mountains and hills, Carlow is mainly undulating farmland. The Blackstairs Mountains form the border with *Wexford; the highest peak is Mount Leinster (2,610 ft.). The rivers Barrow and Slaney run through the county. The county capital is Carlow, on the Barrow, in the northwest of the county. Tullow, in the north on the Slaney, is a well-known angling town.

Carlow town developed around a *Norman motte-and-bailey fort, built in 1180. The fort was succeeded by Carlow Castle, but little remains of this. The ruins of many other medieval *castles can be seen in the county. In the fourteenth century, the county was of strategic and military importance, being located on the border of the *Pale, and was the scene of much fighting between Irish chieftains and English armies. In the *Rebellion of 1798, hundreds of rebels were killed in Carlow, and a rebel leader from neighboring County Wexford, Father John Murphy, was captured and hanged in Tullow.

One of the first colleges for the training of *Catholic priests, St. Patrick's College, was opened in Carlow town in 1793. The town also has a Catholic cathedral, built in 1833. Carlow, along with Mallow, in County *Cork, is one of the two centers of Ireland's sugar industry. The country's first sugar beet factory opened in Carlow in 1926 and it still employs hundreds of workers. Today Carlow is a busy market and industrial town. Besides sugar, dairy farming and crop production are the county's main economy. Carlow's most interesting archaeological monument is the five-thousand-year-old Browne's Hill *Dolmen, a granite structure with a hundred-ton capstone, two miles east of Carlow town. The remains of a seventh-century monastic settlement and a medieval abbey can be seen at St. Mullins, on the east bank of the Barrow. P.D.

Carolan, Turloch (1670–1738). Harpist and composer. Born in County *Meath, Carolan moved with his family to County *Roscommon, where he was blinded by smallpox at age eighteen. He was educated in *harp playing courtesy of a local patron, and began a career as an itinerant musician playing in the "big" houses of Gaelic and "new" *Anglo-Irish landowners. Carolan is one of Ireland's most renowned composers of words and music. His melodies have a distinctly Irish flavor, but also show the influence of the popular Italian music of the era, notably that of Corelli. Most of Carolan's music survives and is still widely played today. Carolan's life and work is minutely documented in *Carolan—The Life, Times and Music of an Irish Harper* by Dónal O'Sullivan in 1958 (republished in 2001). F.V.

Carr, Marina. (1964–). Playwright. Born in *Dublin, Carr grew up near Tullamore, County *Offaly, in the Irish Midlands. As a student at University College, Dublin, she was involved in the Drama Society and wrote her first play, *Ullaloo*. This was followed by a Beckettian play in the absurdist mode, *Low in the Dark* (1989). Carr found her own voice with *The Mai* (1994) and *Portia Coughlan* (1996), both of which were performed at the *Peacock Theatre, and *By the Bog of Cats* (1998), which premiered at the *Abbey Theatre. The heroines in these powerful tragedies, whose themes include marital strife, murder, and incest, suffer from an excess of passion that ends in suicide. The Midlands setting of these plays, which includes the use of its flat but exotic accent, functions both as a realistic rural landscape and a mythical backdrop—what Carr has called "a crossroads between the worlds." The Druid Theatre's production of *On Raftery's Hill*, a violent play also on the theme of incest, was staged in 2000. The play *Ariel* opened at the 2002 Dublin Theatre Festival. J.C.E.L.

Carrantuohill. Ireland's highest mountain (3,414 ft./1,039m.). Situated in the MacGillycuddy's Reeks, a mountain range in County *Kerry, Carrantuohill is made up mostly of coarse-grained sandstone. The name derives from the Gaelic *Carrán Tuathaill*, meaning the reversed sickle, because its crescent of jagged rocks is facing inward rather than outward. A popular climb, it is usually approached from a rocky gully called "The Devil's Ladder." B.D.

Carrowmore. Extensive megalithic cemetery, possibly started in the fifth millennium B.C. Much depleted by stone-quarrying, it was formerly the largest known collection of megalithic tombs in Ireland or Britain. Two miles west of Sligo town, the tombs include *passage-graves and *dolmens with stone circles, some excavated by a Swedish multidisciplinary team. P.H.

Carson, Ciaran (1948–). Poet. Carson was born in *Belfast and educated at Queen's University, Belfast. The local idiom of Belfast pervades his writing. The voice of the storyteller, improvising and weaving tall tales and digressions, dominates his poems. Long lines and a combination of the colloquial and the poetic distinguish his style. A surreal, occupied cityscape is tenderly conjured in *Belfast Confetti* (1989) and *The Irish for No* (1987). The collection *Opera et Cetera* (1996) has been compared to *Muldoon's poetry because both poets reflect on the power of language to mislead. Carson has also published a novel, *Last Night's Fun* (1996), and a collection of prose reflections on the Belfast of his childhood, *The Star Factory* (1998). An ambitious seventy-seven sonnet sequence, *The Twelfth of Never* (1999) was followed by *Selected Poems* in 2001. M.S.T.

Carson, Edward (1854–1935). Politician, barrister, *Unionist leader. Born in *Dublin to a liberal family, Carson became a famous barrister who successfully defended the Marquess of Queensberry in Oscar *Wilde's libel suit (1895). He was appointed solicitor general for Ireland in 1892. The same year, Carson was elected as a Unionist MP (member of Parliament) for Dublin University (Trinity College, Dublin). The Liberal government, elected in 1906, introduced a *home rule bill for Ireland in 1912. The *Ulster Unionist Council (UUC), set up in 1905 to represent all shades of unionism in the North, invited Carson to Ulster to organize resistance to home rule. Carson's rhetoric was belligerent, because behind the scenes he was urged on by his militant Ulster-born colleagues.

As leader of the UUC, Carson was acutely aware that, while seditious language and the impressively drilled and armed *Ulster Volunteer Force (UVF), established in 1912, gave weight to *loyalist resistance, they also threatened civil disorder, which was potentially disastrous for Irish unionism's support in Britain. Carson's strategy was to make home rule for Ireland unworkable by forcing the exclusion of Ulster from its operation. Unionists formed a majority in only four of the nine Ulster counties, however, and with neither side prepared to back down, civil war in Ireland seemed imminent in 1914. *World War I intervened and Carson committed his people to the war effort, and served in the British wartime government.

Following the *Easter Rising of 1916 and the rise of *Sinn Féin, Carson rejected attempts by Irish unionists to find an all-Ireland compromise. Though an all-Ireland unionist himself, he felt honor-bound to save the loyalists in Ulster from any form of Dublin rule. Carson was pressed to accept the premiership of the new devolved government of *Northern Ireland, established in *Belfast in 1920 (ruling six of the nine counties of Ulster), but, an Irish unionist at heart, he declined in favor of James *Craig. M.M.

Cary, (Arthur) Joyce Lunel (1888–1957). Writer. Born in *Derry, Cary studied art in Edinburgh and Paris (1907–09) and law at Oxford (1909–12). He served in the Red Cross in the Balkan Wars 1912–13, joined the Nigerian Colonial Service in 1913, and fought in the Cameroons during *World War I. Cary settled in Oxford with his family in 1920 and devoted himself to writing. He is best known for *The Horse's Mouth* (1944), which is considered a classic. A savage portrayal of the antisocial nature of artistic genius, this novel (the third of a trilogy) examines the conflict between individual freedom and responsibility, a theme that runs throughout Cary's work. He also wrote four novels about Africa: *Aissa Saved* (1932), *An American Visitor* (1933), *The African Witch* (1936), and *Mister Johnson* (1939). Other notable publications include *Castle Corner* (1938), *Power in Men* (1939), and *The Case for African Freedom* (1941). His autobiographical novel, *A House of Children* (1941), which recalls childhood summers in Inishowen, County *Donegal, was awarded the James Tait Black Memorial Prize. In 1958, *The Horse's Mouth* was made into a movie directed by Ronald Neame and starring Alec Guinness. C.D.

Casement, Sir Roger (1864–1916). British diplomat, Irish revolutionary. Following a remarkable

Rock of Cashel, County Tipperary

career in the British colonial service, Roger Casement was knighted in 1911. He championed humanitarianism and opposed exploitation of native workers in such outposts of the empire as central Africa and South America. In 1913, he retired from government service and became actively involved in the burgeoning Irish *nationalist movement. Convinced that an Irish revolution needed Germany's military support, Casement went to Berlin to lobby for an arms shipment for the *Easter Rising. His return to Ireland was disastrous. In April 1916, Casement and two accomplices landed on the coast of *Kerry, put ashore by a German submarine. Casement was arrested almost immediately and charged with "high treason" for collaborating with Germany, England's enemy during *World War I. Casement's famous trial was swift, only four days. To compromise him, the government leaked his diaries, which contained graphic homosexual references. Although they were never introduced as testimony, these diaries influenced the entire trial. Casement's supporters claimed the diaries were forgeries. Today, the general consensus is that the diaries are genuine. After deliberating for one hour, the jury found him guilty of "high treason." In spite of many appeals and the sympathy garnered by his numerous supporters, Casement was hanged in August 1916. J.OM.

Cashel, Rock of. Rock rising above County *Tipperary's Golden Vale and bearing one of the most imposing collections of ecclesiastical monuments in Ireland. Originally a fortress, and allegedly where St. *Patrick baptized a king of *Munster, it was handed over to the Church in 1101 and became the seat of the province's Archdiocese. Its

Leamanach Castle, County Clare

oldest surviving building is perhaps the *round tower of circa 1100, followed by Cormac's Chapel (1124–34), Ireland's most complete stone-roofed church in the Romanesque style. The chapel, built in sandstone by Cormac Mac Carrthaigh, king of South Munster, contains the country's oldest frescoes. The roofless cathedral dates from the thirteenth century. Its western end was never completed; a fortified bishop's palace was built later in its place. The twelfth-century Cross of St. Patrick is now housed in the museum, in the fifteenth-century Hall of the Vicars' Choral at the entrance to the Rock. The cathedral was burned in 1495 and again in 1647, repaired in 1686 and again in 1729, but finally abandoned in 1749. P.H.

Castlereagh, Viscount (Robert Stewart). (1769–1822). Politician, chief secretary of Ireland (1797–1801). Born in County *Down, Castlereagh was the son of the Marquess of Londonderry, a descendant of Scottish *Presbyterian settlers, who had converted to the established *Protestant Church for political reasons. Castlereagh played a key role as chief secretary of Ireland during the period of crisis that centered on the *Rebellion of 1798. Along with his superior Lord Cornwallis (Viceroy, 1798–1801), he bore responsibility for suppressing the rising. Both men tried to bring peace to Ireland after the rebellion, but were hampered by ultraconservative members of the Protestant ascendancy on the local and national levels. Between 1799 and 1800, Castlereagh worked to bring about the Act of *Union and resigned along with Cornwallis and William Pitt when King *George III blocked *Catholic Emancipation in 1801. From 1812 until his death by suicide in 1822, Castlereagh served as the foreign secretary of Great Britain. In this capacity, he was one of the central figures at the Congress of Vienna, which dictated the terms of peace to a defeated Napoleonic *France. J.P.

castles. The Irish had started building castles before the coming of the *Normans in 1169, yet none survive that we know of. The first Norman fortifications were made of earth-ring-works and motte-and-baileys. Shortly after their arrival in Ireland, the Normans were building large stone castles such as Trim in County *Meath, which consists of a tall central tower surrounded by a somewhat later curtain wall. Trim Castle and Carrickfergus Castle in County *Antrim—the most extensive in Ireland—show the Norman barons living in the towers and the soldiers in the barracks within the wall. One type of castle that remained popular until the sixteenth century was the rectangular tower with a round bastion at each corner. The Edward *Bruce invasion of 1315–18 brought castle building to a temporary halt, and when it started again in the fifteenth century (or possibly before), the builders were not only the Normans who had "become more Irish than the Irish themselves," but in most cases the native Irish as well. However, instead of being military barracks as the Norman castles had been, these later medieval fortifications were really family residences with only a few retainers. They are, therefore, more correctly called **tower houses*, though generally they bear the name castle. Usually with three stories above a vaulted basement, they were status symbols, though often sparsely furnished inside. Blarney (County *Cork) and Bunratty (County *Clare) are among the largest of their kind; the latter, now furnished in the style of circa 1600, offers medieval banquets. Though probably over two thousand tower houses were built during the fifteenth and sixteenth centuries, only a few survive in any way intact. A handful have been restored with success, but historical records usually give little information about the families that originally built tower houses. By the early seventeenth century, a manorial style had developed with large windows allowing more gracious living among their inhabitants, who were becoming increasingly English-orientated. The *Cromwellian period saw an end to castle building in Ireland, except for those built largely in the Victorian period, which were erected to impress the neighbors (like the earlier tower houses, but without any fortifications). P.H.

Castletown House. The first and largest Palladian-style country house in Ireland, located in Celbridge, County *Kildare. The original design by Alessandro Galilei (1691–1737) influenced the architecture of *Leinster House and the White House in Washington, DC. The building was commissioned in 1722 by William Conolly (1662–1729), speaker of the Irish House of Commons, and its construction was overseen by Sir Edward Lovett *Pearce. Castletown House has been recently restored and furnished in period style. S.A.B.

Cathach, the. Ireland's oldest *manuscript, written around 600 (possibly by the hand of St. *Colm Cille). The Cathach (or "Battler") Psalter is now preserved in the *Royal Irish Academy in *Dublin. The enlarged initial letters of the Psalms were ornamented in monochrome with crosses, spirals, and fish. P.H.

Cathleen Ni Houlihan. Allegorical representation of Ireland as woman and mother derived from the Gaelic **aisling* (dream or vision) tradition. With the exile of the Gaelic chieftains and establishment of the *Anglo-Irish Ascendancy, eighteenth-century Irish *bardic poetry incorporated more explicitly political motifs. The beautiful yet unattainable fairy woman featured in traditional love poetry became an impoverished, sorrowful woman—described alternately as *sean bhean bhocht* ("poor old woman"), *Róisín Dubh* ("little dark rose"), or *Caitlin Ni Houlihan*—whose only hope is the removal of English oppression and the return of her exiled husband and/or sons. Such political yearnings were given especially vivid expression in W. B. *Yeats's and Lady *Gregory's *Cathleen Ni Houlihan* (1902). In the play, Cathleen, "the poor old woman" (originally performed by Maud *Gonne), personifies Ireland and prompts a young bridegroom to abandon his wedding plans and join the French forces of 1798 fighting for the restoration of her four green fields. E.S.M.

Catholic Emancipation Act (1829). Legislation that gave *Catholics the right to sit in *Parliament. Since the *Reformation and the passing of the

*Penal Laws (1695–1709), Catholics were excluded from political life, had limited access to *education, and were prohibited from owning property. They could not practice their religion freely without fear of harsh penalties. By the end of the eighteenth century, an ongoing campaign for full civil and political rights for Catholics had led to a series of *Relief Acts (1774, 1778, 1782), which enabled British and Irish Roman Catholics to acquire property. In addition, the Relief Act of 1793 gave Catholics the right to vote in elections, but not to sit in Parliament. Catholics continued to be barred from holding high office in the government or judiciary. Various bills that were introduced (including those by *Henry Grattan and William Conyngham Plunkett) fell short of full emancipation mostly because of the resistance of the House of Lords and King George IV.

On May 12, 1823, Daniel *O'Connell, the "Liberator," along with Richard Lalor Sheil, established the Catholic Association, which aimed to achieve full Catholic emancipation "by legal and constitutional means." Ordinary people were encouraged to join by paying a small subscription (known as "Catholic rent") of one shilling a year. Approximately four hundred thousand Catholics became members. The association held mass meetings throughout the country and mounted an organized publicity campaign to highlight Catholic grievances. In 1825, the government, alarmed at the power of the organization, suppressed it, but O'Connell formed a new organization, the New Catholic Association, and the campaign continued.

In 1828, O'Connell was elected MP (member of Parliament) for County *Clare in a landmark victory, but refused to take his seat in Parliament until the anti–Roman Catholic oath was lifted. Faced with the threat of nationwide disturbances, in 1829, Prime Minister *Wellington and Home Secretary Robert Peel advised the king to grant emancipation. Under the Roman Catholic Relief Act, which was enacted on April 13, 1829, the oaths of allegiance, supremacy, and abjuration were replaced with an oath that pledged loyalty to the crown without recognizing the monarch as the head of the Church. Catholics could now enter Parliament and sit as MPs at Westminster. They could also hold all public offices with the exception of lord chancellor, monarch, regent, lord lieutenant of Ireland, and any judicial appointment in any ecclesiastical court.

However, on February 13, 1829, a bill suppressing the Catholic Association was passed along with a disenfranchise bill which raised the franchise from the 40-shilling-freehold qualification to £10 per householder. The change drastically reduced the number of poorer voters from approximately one hundred thousand to sixteen thousand. O'Connell disagreed with this change but did not consider it grounds for rejecting the Emancipation Act. While middle-class Catholics benefited from emancipation, those members of the Catholic peasantry who lost their vote saw no betterment of their political position within society. For many, emancipation may have represented only a symbolic victory. M.T.D., P.E.

Catholic Relief Acts (1774–93). A series of acts during the late eighteenth century repealing many of the restrictions of the *Penal Laws (1695–1709). Under this discriminatory legislation, *Catholics were excluded from political life, had limited access to education, and were prohibited from owning property.

In 1760, the Catholic Committee was established by Charles O' Connor and Dr. John Curry to exert pressure on the British government for relief. Some progress was made in 1774 when Parliament passed an act allowing Catholics to take an *oath of allegiance, which did not deny the articles of their faith. The war between France and Britain, which began in 1778, convinced many British politicians that in the interests of imperial security, Catholics should receive significant relief.

In 1778, Gardiner's First Relief Act was passed, allowing Catholics to own land on a 999-year lease, and enabling them to inherit land, providing they took an oath of allegiance. In 1782, Gardiner's Second Relief Act was introduced for those Catholics who had taken the 1778 oath. This act permitted them to purchase and own freehold land, and some restrictions were lifted on the bearing of arms and on *education. After much petitioning by the Catholic Committee, Hobart's Catholic Relief Act was passed in 1793, giving the right to vote to 40-shilling-freeholders, as well as the right to bear arms and to hold some positions in civil office. However, the act failed to give Catholics what they most wanted, the right to sit in Parliament. This would change in 1829 with the *Catholic Emancipation Act. M.T.D., P.E.

Catholicism. Principal religion in the *Republic of Ireland. For over 1,500 years, the Roman Catholic Church in Ireland has occupied an exceptionally important place in the lives of the Irish people. Approximately 90 percent of the Republic of Ireland's population and about 75 percent of those living on the island are Roman Catholic. Although Catholicism's origins in Ireland preceded the arrival of St. *Patrick in the fifth century, his ministry as a bishop marked the beginnings of a serious campaign to convert the Irish people. Patrick's substantial success, and that of his successors, resulted in large part because they incorporated the pagan *Celtic practices of the day into *Christianity. For example, *Samhain, the pagan festival of the dead celebrated on November 1, became the feast days of All Saints (All Hallows) and All Souls. By the sixth century, Irish monks had established a tradition of extreme asceticism in monasteries throughout the country. Monasticism quickly became the dominant Church organization in Ireland, proving more amenable to Irish society than the more centralized episcopal model. During the Dark Ages on the European continent in the seventh and eighth centuries, monasteries such as *Glendalough and *Clonmacnoise enjoyed a golden age as repositories of Western civilization's literature and art. Monasteries sent missionaries such as St. *Colm Cille and St. *Columbanus to evangelize Europe.

The *Viking raids of 795 led to the destruction of many monasteries and to the end of the golden age. The monasteries that survived became increasingly integrated with the political and secular life of the day. By the middle of the twelfth century, the Synod of Kells established a traditional diocesan structure for Ireland consisting of twenty-six dioceses in four episcopal provinces: Armagh, Dublin, Cashel, and Tuam. The *Norman invasion later that century seriously disrupted these reforms and led to Irish-Norman warfare and disputes over ecclesiastical titles and offices. The Irish Church suffered from continued factionalism and corruption for over three centuries as the native Gaelic Irish and the Norman invaders and their descendants struggled for political control of the country.

Beginning in the mid-sixteenth century through the 1760s, the British government, with the exception of a few short years, proscribed the Catholic Church in Ireland, subjecting its clergy and laity to persecution, and confiscating its property. In the 1530s, the English and Irish *Parliaments declared *Henry VIII to be the head of, respectively, the English and Irish Churches, thus substituting royal for papal authority. Henry VIII's *Reformation establishing a new state *Protestant Church was consolidated by his daughter *Elizabeth I, who began in 1560 to impose legal penalties on those who refused to conform. When Irish Catholics supported King Charles I during the English Civil War in the 1640s, Oliver *Cromwell, the leader of the antiroyalist, parliamentary forces, reconquered Ireland and repressed the Church, massacring thousands and stripping Irish Catholics of the vast majority of their land. The persecution of Catholics ceased briefly under the Catholic King of England, *James II in the 1680s. Following his defeat at the Battle of the *Boyne in 1690 by the forces of William of *Orange and the Treaty of *Limerick the following year, a series of *Penal Laws were passed designed to exclude Catholics in matters of property, trade, politics, and religion. Bishops were deported and banned from returning to Ireland. After 1770, however, the Church began to emerge as a national institution when the British government, in the wake of Enlightenment ideas and the war with America, relaxed its enforcement of the Penal Laws to grant Irish Catholics de facto religious toleration.

During the last quarter of the eighteenth century, Catholics won partial relief from the Penal Laws, including in 1793 the right to vote. Irish bishops supported the Act of *Union (1800) between Great Britain and Ireland on the understanding that Britain would concede *Catholic Emancipation, the right of a Catholic to sit in Parliament. Emancipation languished until 1829. During this period, the Irish politician Daniel *O'Connell and the Irish bishops resisted Parliament's plan to control the appointment of Irish bishops in return for Catholic emancipation. Irish Catholics, clerical and lay alike, united under O'Connell and the bishops to win emancipation in 1829. This alliance fostered the development of an identity that was self-consciously Irish and Catholic.

The Catholic Church was severely hampered by a lack of clerical manpower exacerbated by Ireland's rising population between 1750 and 1845. The Great *Famine of the mid-1840s decimated the population, reducing it from eight to six million people through death and emigration. The reduced population, ironically, afforded the Irish Church a priest-to-people ratio that allowed the Irish pastoral mission to flourish in the second half of the nineteenth century. Under Cardinal Paul *Cullen, archbishop of Dublin from 1852 to 1878, the Irish episcopacy spearheaded a devotional revolution marked by the building of schools and churches, the expansion of parish missions and sodalities, and the reform of the Irish clergy's personal conduct and administration of the sacraments. By 1900, Irish Catholics had become the most pious Catholics in the world with close to 90 percent attending weekly Sunday Mass.

The Church also gradually gained control of the nation's *educational system and remained a vital part of the Irish political system. During the 1880s, the Church sided with Charles Stewart *Parnell on the question of land reform, but turned against him after he was named a defendant in a divorce case. Its support of the *Free State forces during the *Irish Civil War solidified the Church's political influence. The Irish *Constitution of 1937 recognized the Catholic Church as having "a special position" in Irish society. (This clause was removed from the constitution in 1973.) Catholicism had so infused Irish life that the terms *Irish* and *Catholic* had become almost interchangeable. The partition of Ireland into North and South resulted in no similar ecclesiastical division for the Catholic Church in Ireland. Discrimination against the minority Catholic population in the North originally gave rise to the civil rights movement in the late sixties and later to the *Troubles between Protestants, who are predominantly unionists, and Catholics, who are predominantly nationalists.

Through continued immigration well into the twentieth century, the Irish version of Catholicism dominated the Church throughout the English-speaking world. Irish *missionaries further extended Irish Catholic influence. Orders such as the Holy Ghost and Columban Fathers and the Sisters of Mercy were founded in the nineteenth and twentieth centuries to spread the faith to Africa, Latin America, Asia, and India. In recent years, Catholicism's hold on the Irish people has weakened in the wake of changes in the country, the reforms of the *Second Vatican Council in the 1960s, and widespread allegations of clerical sexual abuse. The Irish Church has consistently supported the *peace process for the resolution of the conflict in *Northern Ireland. M.P.C.

Cavan, County. Inland county, one of the three *Ulster counties in the *Republic of Ireland. The county, which stretches over 745 square miles, has a population of 56,416 (2002 census). Cavan town is the county capital and the cathedral center of the diocese of Kilmore. Before the English conquest, the O'Reilly clan dominated the area, which was then known as Breifni, which also includes *Leitrim.

Cavan is essentially agrarian. Throughout the county there are 365 lakes. The southern part, with its fertile, rolling hills and tidy towns, borders and resembles *Leinster. The north, rugged, mountainous, and thinly populated, blends elements of *Connacht and Ulster. The northwest parish of Killanagh in the barony of Tullyhaw, dominated by the mountain Cuilcagh (2,199 ft.), is a scenic area, still largely undiscovered by tourists. Close to the mountain's base, the *Shannon Pot, a pool fed by a spring, is the source of Ireland's longest river. Cavan is also the source of the Erne, the river that produces the lovely lake country of *Fermanagh. A few hundred yards from the Shannon Pot, in the townland of Moneygashel, are interesting early *Celtic archaeological sites—a ring fort and sweat house with instruments and ornaments of the times. Ring forts are also common in other parts of the county.

The remains of Cloghoughter Castle, on an island in Lough Oughter, offers the best example of the native Irish style of circular-tower *castles of the thirteenth to fifteenth centuries. Owen Roe *O'Neill, the leading general of the Catholic Confederation, died there in 1649. At Drumlane near Belturbet are the remains of a twelfth-century *round tower. In 1726, Jonathan *Swift wrote *Gulliver's Travels* in the home of his friend Thomas Sheridan near the town of Virginia.

Celebrated personalities with Cavan connections include: Philip Sheridan, American Civil War general; Archbishop John Charles McQuaid; Francis *Sheehy Skeffington; actor T. P. McKenna; and writers Shane Connaughton, Dermot Healy, and Tom McIntyre. Two movies, *The Playboys* (1992) and *The Run of the Country* (1995), based on Connaughton's novels, were filmed in and near the town of Redhills. William Percy *French's "Come Back Paddy Reilly to Ballyjamesduff" has become the county anthem, sung wherever Cavan people gather. A.ML., L.J.MC.

Ceannt, Éamonn (1881–1916). Revolutionary and signatory of the 1916 *Proclamation of the Irish Republic. Born in County *Galway, Ceannt worked as a clerk in the Treasury Department of Dublin Corporation. In 1900, he became a member of the *Gaelic League and in 1908 joined *Sinn Féin. Membership of the IRB (*Irish Republic Brotherhood) followed in 1913, and by 1915 he had been initiated into the Supreme Council. He was court-martialed for his role in the 1916 *Easter Rising (where he commanded the *Volunteers in the South

*Dublin Union area) and was executed in *Kilmainham Gaol on May 8, 1916. P.E.

Céide Fields, the. Archaeological site. Located on spectacular sea cliffs, near Ballycastle in County *Mayo, the Céide Fields is believed to be five thousand years old, making it the oldest enclosed landscape in Europe. Extensive excavating in the 1980s revealed an integrated farm landscape of field walls, dwellings, and numerous megalithic tombs that had been trapped in time by the growth of the surrounding *bog. The fields cover an area of twenty-four square miles. B.D.

céilí. 1. An Irish word denoting, particularly in the North, a social visit or gathering. 2. In *Scotland, it indicates music and song performance, with some dance. 3. Over all of Ireland it was adopted to denote an organized, public, traditional Irish social *dance. The first of these was held by the *Gaelic League among Irish migrants in London in 1897, based on similar Scottish assemblies. The dances were popular quadrilles and waltzes, but in the 1920s peculiarly Irish social dance-forms were created and revived for such *céilithe*, visually similar to English and Scottish "country" dances, but performed to Irish *music. Bands dedicated to these were initially described as "players" or "orchestras"; the earliest to use the term *céilí band* may have been Frank Lee in London, in 1918. Dublin piper Leo *Rowsome formed the first *céilí* band in Ireland—the *Siamsa—in 1922, and starting in 1926 Irish *radio promoted the Ballinakill, Aughrim Slopes, Moate, and Athlone *céilí* bands. With the shift in dancing out of private houses to schools and purpose built halls, *céilí* bands flourished, some becoming hugely popular. Many, like the McCuskers, played to exiles in the United States and Britain. The Gallowglass Céilí Band was professional, and most—like The Tulla which has run from 1947 until the present day—made LP recordings. Hundreds proliferated at parish and national levels up until the 1960s, and several still enjoy popularity today. F.V.

Céitinn, Seathrún (c.1580–1644). Historian and poet in Irish. Of Anglo-Norman heritage, Céitinn (sometimes anglicized as Geoffrey Keating) became the greatest historian of Gaelic Ireland. Originally, he received native *bardic education, which would later inspire a series of traditional poems. Céitinn also studied in Bordeaux and Reims after being ordained as a priest in Ireland. The several theological works he wrote in the manner of the counter-Reformation use a strong, literate colloquial prose style, new to the *Irish language. His major work is *Foras Feasa ar Éirinn*, a history of Ireland, which he composed from native sources probably between 1629 and 1634. This history was copied by scribes and poets and remained the basic text through which the Irish understood themselves for the next two hundred years. His best poetry, "Óm Sceol ar Ardmhagh Fáil" ("At the News from Fal's High Plain") and "A Bhean Lán de Stuaim" ("O Woman Full of Guile"), is passionate and intricate, combining personal anguish with a political vision. A.T.

Celtic mythology. The ancient *Celts had many local deities, but the most important were a basic divine couple responsible for the material prosperity of the tribe. The father-deity was usually associated with the sky and the mother-deity with the earth. Irish *manuscript compilations featuring these deities date from the medieval period—such as Lebor na hUidre, or *Leabhar na hUidre, (The Book of the Dun Cow) and Lebor na Nuachongbhála (known as the Book of *Leinster)—but many of the actual texts are copies from periods stretching back to as early as the seventh century A.D. There are indications that the earliest Celtic sources in Ireland used variants of widespread Indo-European names for this couple. Devos was the designation of the male sky-deity, but this name became calcified in Celto-Irish tradition as *dago-devos* ("good sky"), which survived in the form *Daghdha*. The female personification of rivers and the fertile soil also followed the Indo-European pattern, being known as *Danu*, but she was usually referred to as the Mór-Ríoghan ("great queen"). Various aspects of the material and cultural landscape were connected to these deities, and both play a leading role in the great primordial battle of Irish mythology, Cath Mhuighe Tuireadh, that was reputedly fought between two sets of deities at Moytirra in County *Sligo. In that battle, the Tuatha Dé Danann ("people of the goddess Danu") defeated the Fomhoire ("under-spirits").

Basic to much of the early mythological lore was the relationship between the dead and the living, which was reflected in the system of computing time. The dark half of the year, representing the dead, preceded the bright half, representing the living; and similarly the night preceded the day. This mutual dependency between dead and living seems to have been the teaching of the *druids, and from it flowed the notion that inspiration could come from the world of the dead and also that the setting sun in the west was entering the otherworld. Also prevalent was the notion that a bright deity, called by variants of the name Fionn (Irish for *fair* or *bright*), alternated in influence with a dark deity called Donn (Irish for *dark*).

The most dramatic deity was Lugh, who led the Tuatha Dé Danann to victory at the Battle of Moytirra. He is the Irish form of the pan-Celtic Lugus, and was the master of all skills and trades and the patron of the harvest. He is described as a prophesied youth, and he slew his tyrant-grandfather Balar, who had a scorching eye that destroyed all on which it looked. Other outstanding figures who reflect Celtic deities were the marvelously handsome Aenghus, the seer-warrior Fionn Mac Cumhaill (or Finn McCool), and the superhero *Cúchulainn. Gods of specific crafts appear in the form of the master-smith Goibhniu, the ubiquitous leech Dian Cécht, and the wondrous mariner Manannán.

Several rivers bear the nicknames of the goddess of fertility of the land, Danu or Anu. For example, the names for the rivers *Shannon and Boyne come from Sionainn ("the old one") and Bóinn ("bright cow"). Other names represented social aspects of the divine mother—most notably the warrior-queen Meadhbh ("the intoxicating one") who was originally the goddess of sovereignty. Brighid ("the highest one") was the patron of poetry and of milk, and her cult survived strongly in the devotion to her Christian namesake, St. Brighid, or St. *Brigid. The goddess could be envisaged as either young and beautiful or old and ugly. In the latter guise, she is widely represented in literature and folklore as the Cailleach Bhéarra ("hag of Beare"), who, legend claims, lived longer than anybody else ever in Ireland and put several rocks and islands in their present position in the landscape. There are also many legends concerning fairy queens who reign from palaces in great rocks and hills; these derive from the goddess-image in a more localized context. The old manuscripts, mostly the work of Christian monks, and these traditions survived easily side by side with *Christianity in Ireland. D.Oh.

Celtic Revival. See **Irish Revival.**

Celts. Speakers of a language that was predominant throughout much of central and western Europe—including Ireland—in the Iron Age. A Celtic dialect of Indo-European was developing in central Europe from around 2,000 B.C., and from the eighth century B.C. a thriving culture is evidenced from that region. More clearly identifiable as Celtic are the "Hallstatt" culture from east of the Alps in the seventh and sixth centuries B.C. and the *La Tène culture from the area between the sources of the Rhine and the Danube two centuries later. These Celtic people had been spreading westward for some time, establishing strong lordships in France (then known as Gaul) and the Iberian Peninsula. Later expansions brought groups of Celts southward into northern Italy and eastward as far as the Black Sea and even into an area of Asia Minor.

Since the sixth century B.C., Celtic groups had crossed to Britain and set up kingdoms, assimilating the indigenous people. Some claim that the Celticization of Ireland was a gradual process due to commercial contacts with Britain and Gaul, but it is difficult to explain in this way the complete substitution of Celtic for other languages in the country. It appears that, from the fourth century B.C. for the next two hundred years or so, small but compact groups of Celtic-speaking warriors from Britain landed in Ireland and established power centers, which, through a combination of military and commercial success, became dominant. The early occurrence of Celtic art styles in Ireland—such as the designs on the Turoe Stone in County *Galway, dating from the first century B.C.—supports this theory.

The basic social structure of Celtic society was established in early Ireland. A particular territory was under the control of a tribe, which held it by arms and, when necessary, by arrangements with stronger neighbors. The belief in a divine ancestor was general, but individual tribes could vary and elaborate this so as to underline their own particular identity. The general social division was into three classes: the nobility, the common people, and the bondmen, or slaves. The latter seem to have consisted generally of captives taken in war. All three classes, and the gradations of them, were linked together by an elaborate system of clientage.

From the third century A.D., the continental Celts were under increasing pressure from the Roman legions. After their communities in northern Italy, in eastern Europe, and in the Iberian Peninsula were decimated by the Romans, Gaul itself fell to Julius Caesar in a series of campaigns from 58 to 50 B.C. The destruction of continental Celtdom was completed in the succeeding generations, as Roman, Germanic, and Slavic peoples took over the Celtic areas, but dialects of the Celtic language survived in scattered areas until the fourth century A.D., or perhaps even later. Britain too was conquered by the Romans, but the Celtic speech survived strongly there until pushed from the east by the Anglo-Saxon invaders from the fifth century A.D. onward. Migrations from the southwest of Britain, meanwhile, brought a Celtic language back to the continental landmass, where it survived as Breton. Ireland alone was untouched by the Roman legions, and in this western isle a Celtic culture continued to flourish. The Celtic language developed into *Irish (sometimes called Gaelic), and in this form assimilated the culture of later *Viking, *Norman, and English settlers. By the sixteenth century, Ireland was under strict English control, and the native civilization began to break down, but the Irish language, even under continuing pressure, still survives today. D.Oh.

censorship. The Film Censorship Act of 1923 set the stage for more than four decades of Irish cultural policy. Although the *Free State *Constitution of 1922 endorsed the separation of church and state, in practice, the new government invariably followed the Church's lead on issues of morality. *Divorce and birth control were proscribed, and in 1926, the government established a Committee of Enquiry on Evil Literature, which led to the Censorship of Publications Act of 1929. This law authorized the banning of books or periodicals that were perceived as generally "indecent or obscene" or that contained discussions of—or even allusions to—issues offensive to *Catholic morality. The specific criteria of "obscenity" were determined behind closed doors by a Censorship Board, rather than in the courts. Formed in 1930, the first board consisted of five members appointed by the minister of justice and approved by the Catholic Church and academic community. The board relied on vigilant members of the public to submit books, with the offending passage(s) marked, for review. This system meant that books could be banned on the basis of one phrase taken out of context, that years could pass between a book's publication and its banning, and that some books, like James *Joyce's *Ulysses* (1922), which was immediately deemed pornographic and banned in the United States (until 1933) and England (until 1936), were never banned in Ireland. However, *Ulysses* was rarely available in Irish bookstores until 1967.

Beginning in the 1930s, censorship policies seriously affected Irish literary culture. Many of the works of a budding generation of writers were banned on moral, rather than political or ideological, grounds. While Seán *O'Faoláin's collection of short stories *Midsummer Night Madness* (1932), for instance, contained biting critiques of the physical force nationalism that had fueled the Irish revolution, it was banned for its allusions to frustrated sexual desire and adultery. The banning of Kate *O'Brien's *The Land of Spices* (1941) for a single sentence alluding to a homosexual affair became a *cause célèbre*, foreshadowing a wave of bannings in the 1940s and 1950s for depictions of sexuality. Three of Benedict *Kiely's novels, including *There Was an Ancient House* (1955), which contained a description of female nudity, were banned. Highly critical of provincial Ireland, John Broderick's *The Pilgrimage* (1961) was banned for its treatment of homosexuality. John *McGahern's second novel, *The Dark*, was banned in 1965 for its descriptions of masturbation and the author was dismissed from his job as a primary school teacher. Most of Edna *O'Brien's fiction published during the 1960s was banned for its alleged assault on Irish womanhood through portraits of grim, unhappy marriages and extramarital affairs. Rather than appeal or protest the decisions of the Censorship Board, O'Brien and many other writers simply left Ireland. The list of Irish literary exiles between the 1930s and 1960s—the most intensive period of literary censorship—includes Samuel *Beckett and Brian *Moore, whose first four novels, including *Judith Hearne* (1955)—which was later renamed *The Lonely Passion of Judith Hearne*—were banned. O'Faoláin, however, remained behind to combat censorship and Irish cultural isolationism in the journal, the **Bell*, which he edited between 1940 and 1946. Frank *O'Connor, one of O'Faoláin's most vocal allies, eventually left Ireland for the United States in 1952.

While there was no official *theater censorship in Ireland (unlike in Britain), the theater was affected by the censorship climate. In 1957 the director of the Pike Theatre, Alan Simpson, was arrested on charges of obscenity because of a reference to a contraceptive in his production of Tennessee Williams's *The Rose Tattoo*. The following year, the Dublin Theatre Festival was canceled when Seán *O'Casey and Beckett withdrew their plays in protest at the archbishop's refusal to sanction the staging of Alan McClelland's stage adaptation of James Joyce's *Ulysses*.

In 1967, the government revised the Censorship of Publications Act. A new stipulation withheld from the public any book or periodical deemed "obscene" for a period lasting no more than twelve years. Following this amendment, almost five thousand titles were made available in Ireland. Censorship, however, remained a dominant cultural force in Ireland in the 1970s and 1980s. The outbreak of the *Troubles in *Northern Ireland, beginning in 1968, culminated in close surveillance of journalistic reportage of IRA (*Irish Republican Army) activity and opinion in the press, *radio, and *television. The laws upholding media censorship began to be dismantled in 1993 when the *Downing Street Declaration announced the London and Dublin governments' decision to include the IRA and its political wing, *Sinn Féin, in a series of peace talks.

While the Health, or Family Planning, Act of 1979 ensured that the subject of contraception would no longer be prohibited, the Censorship Board turned its attention to abortion and pledged to limit Irish *women's access to information about the availability of abortions in Great Britain. Although the right to abortion in the *Republic of Ireland is still denied, two constitutional referenda were passed in 1992 securing both the right to information and the right to travel to obtain an abortion. While a Censorship Board continues to exist in the Irish Republic, its activities are significantly more limited and primarily directed toward pornography. Lee Dunne's *The Cabfather* (1975), which was the last Irish novel to be banned, was finally released in Ireland in 1988. E.S.M.

Charlton, Jack (1935–). Former Irish *soccer manager. Born in Ashington, Northumberland, in the north of England, Charlton played as center-half in England's victorious World Cup team of 1966. He was made an honorary Irish citizen in recognition of his success as manager of the Irish soccer team from 1986 to 1996. During these ten years, the *Republic of Ireland qualified for the European Championships in 1988—the first major tournament that Ireland contested in soccer. The Republic of Ireland later reached the quarter finals of the World Cup in Italy in 1990, and won a famous victory against Italy in Giants Stadium, New York, on the way to qualifying for the last sixteen of the 1994 World Cup. Charlton retired as Irish manager in 1996. B.D.

Chester Beatty Library. Library collection of manuscripts and art. The library was donated to the Irish state by Chester Beatty (1875–1968) in 1950, because he did not like the recently elected Labour government in Britain. Born in New York, Beatty made his fortune in mining and became a British subject in 1933. An avid collector, he spent his wealth on Middle Eastern and Oriental manuscripts and books, most of which are richly and elaborately decorated. The Indian miniatures are among the best in the world. As well as treasures from the world of Islam, China, and Japan, the library holds Burmese, Thai, and Tibetan manuscripts. Beatty was made an honorary Irish citizen, and was given a state funeral on his death. The library recently moved to *Dublin Castle. T.C.

Chicago, the Irish in. Chicago and its Irish grew up together. In 1837, Chicago was a frontier town when Irish workers arrived to dig the Illinois and Michigan Canal, the engineering feat that connected the Great Lakes with the Mississippi River. By 1843, Irish *immigrants were 10 percent of the city's 7,580 residents. As Irish emigration intensified during and after the Great *Famine, their ranks swelled to 18 percent of Chicago's 1860 population. However, massive numbers of European newcomers between 1870 and 1924 diversified the city's ethnic and racial mix reducing the Irish share to only 7 percent by 1890. The arrival of many African Americans and Hispanics in the twentieth century further diminished Irish demographics.

Despite their small numbers, the early arrival of the Irish in the city, combined with their political and English language skills, enabled them to make a distinctive imprint on Chicago's character and history. They shaped its politics, influenced Irish nationalism, dominated the *Catholic hierarchy and church institutions, and defined many urban neighborhoods.

Because Anglo-*Protestants from the East first settled the city, the mostly *Catholic Chicago Irish confronted the same prejudices experienced by their countrymen in *Boston, *New York, and Philadelphia. Hostility and discrimination resulted in an Irish Catholic subculture that used politics as an avenue for advancement. By the end of the nineteenth century, Irish Catholic men were prominent in City Hall and had positions of political influence in the police and fire departments and on construction projects with city contracts.

Like the Irish in other American cities, those in Chicago helped create a political machine that dominated the city's politics from the late nineteenth throughout the twentieth and into the twenty-first centuries. Since 1893, eight of the city's mayors have been Irish Catholics: John Patrick Hopkins (1893–95), Edward F. Dunne (1905–07), William E. Dever (1923–27), Edward J. Kelly (1933–47), Martin J. Kennelly (1947–55), Richard J. Daley (1955–76), Jane Byrne (1979–83), and Richard M. Daley (1989 to present). Richard J. Daley was the most powerful politician in Chicago history. He influenced the nomination of John F. *Kennedy for president in 1960 and made sure he carried the important state of Illinois. During the Democratic National Convention in 1968, Mayor Daley helped Hubert Humphrey become the Democratic presidential nominee, much to the anger of radical protesters in the streets. Although the Irish generally entered politics to enrich themselves and their supporters with city contracts and jobs, by the twentieth century their politicians had become more professional in approaching the complex problems of urban government. They also excelled in integrating other ethnic and racial groups into their political machine.

Until recently, unlike Irish politicians in other cities, those in Chicago were reluctant to use their local power to launch state or national political careers. Downstate Illinois seemed too rural, small-town, Protestant, and Republican to offer solid support for a Chicago Irish Catholic candidate.

The Irish also gave shape to a vigorous Catholic Church in Chicago. While several Irishmen served as bishops and archbishops of the Chicago Diocese, it was the neighborhood parishes that centered the daily lives of Irish Americans, at once sheltering them from nativist hostility and transforming them into modern American Catholics. Despite the conservatism that characterized Irish American Catholicism, the Chicago experience also developed a liberal dimension. Opportunities of a frontier town enlarged the vision of its people. Chicago Catholic bishops proved more tolerant of Irish *nationalists than those on the East Coast. They also championed organized labor and the New Deal, New Frontier, and Great Society social agendas. Irish leaders of Chicago Catholicism did much to harmonize the conflicts that often divided various ethnic groups, unifying both church and city. Although many Chicago Irish Catholics were hostile to the African American Great Migration to the North, some of their clergy and laity founded the Catholic Interracial Council in 1945 and made the city the headquarters for a national organization.

Chicago's Irish women became a major force in the city's teaching and nursing professions. In 1920, Archbishop Mundelein estimated that 70 percent of Chicago public school teachers were Irish.

Chicago Irish writers like Finley Peter Dunne, James T. Farrell, Kate McPhelim Cleary, and Clara E. Laughlin are known for their description of urban realism, tracing the Irish experience from Famine immigrants, through working-class hardships and discrimination, to the prosperous middle class. E.McM.

Chichester Clarke, James (1923–2000). Prime minister of *Northern Ireland, 1969–71. Chichester Clarke narrowly succeeded the liberal Terence *O'Neill in April 1969. He continued reform programs, but was forced to call on the British army in support of the *Royal Ulster Constabulary (RUC) in August 1969 after loyalist mobs burned out *Catholic areas in *Belfast and other cities. The resurgent IRA (*Irish Republican Army) militarism, which had been dormant for years, increased pressure for a tough security policy. In February 1971, Chichester Clark resigned, complaining that Britain was not providing enough troops and that *unionists expected draconian solutions. M.M.

Chichester, Arthur; Baron Chichester of Belfast (1563–1625). English soldier and administrator. For his military service during the *Nine Years War (1593–1603), Chichester was granted Belfast Castle to which he added estates in *Antrim, *Down, and Inishowen, County *Donegal. As lord deputy (1605–15), he was forced by King James I to suppress *Catholicism and disrupt the clan system by establishing Scottish colonies in Ireland. Chichester was lord treasurer of Ireland (1616–25) and his son, Arthur, was created First Earl Donegal in 1647. S.A.B.

Chieftains. The leading Irish traditional *music group. The Chieftains was formed in 1963 by *uilleann piper Paddy Moloney with some of his colleagues in Seán *Ó Riada's experimental group Ceoltóirí Chualann—fiddler Martin Fay, whistle player Seán Potts, flute and concertina player Michael Tubridy, and bodhrán player Davey Fallon. They turned professional in 1975, and today only Moloney remains of the original lineup. The present band was joined by fiddler Seán Keane in 1968, by *harpist and pianist Derek Bell (d.2002) in 1974, by flute player Matt Molloy in 1979, and by singer/bodhrán player Kevin Conneff in 1980. The Chieftains broke a trail for traditional Irish music all over the world, inspiring many other Irish groups that enjoy popularity and critical acclaim today. Their albums typically incorporate folk music from other countries, but their playing of strict Irish traditional music with the highest caliber of instrumental soloists is considered exemplary. The first of their fifty-plus albums (*Chieftains*, 1963) remains iconic and highly respected within the genre. Other albums of note include: *Bonaparte's Retreat* (1977), *The Chieftains in China* (1987), *Irish Heartbeat—With Van Morrison* (1988), and *Santiago* (1996). F.V.

Childers, Erskine Hamilton (1905–74). Son of Robert Erskine *Childers and fourth president of Ireland. Born in London, educated at Cambridge, Childers became advertisement manager of Éamon *de Valera's paper the *Irish Press* in 1931. First elected to the *Dáil (Parliament) in 1938, Childers held a number of positions under successive *Fianna Fáil governments, including Tánaiste (deputy prime minister) between 1969 and 1973. He was inau-

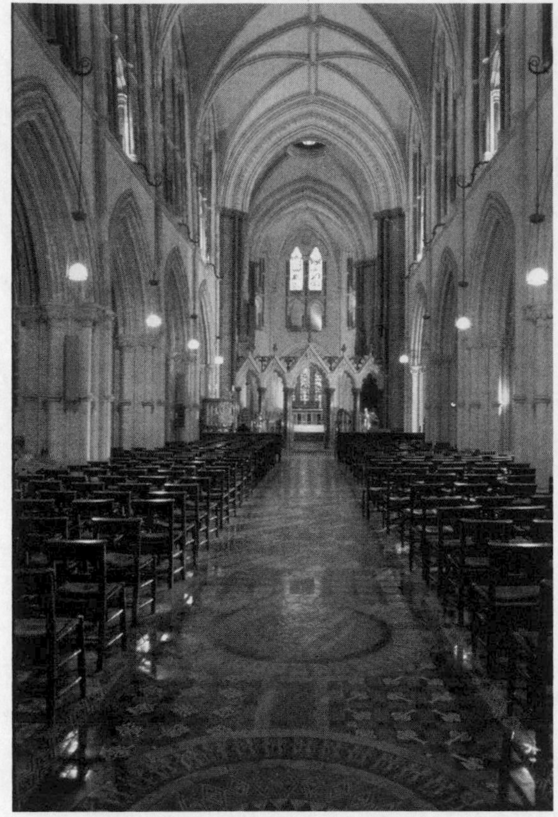

Christ Church Cathedral, interior

gurated as Irish president on June 25, 1973, and died from a heart attack while in office on November 17, 1974. P.E.

Childers, Robert Erskine (1870–1922). Author and *nationalist. Born in London, Childers was a veteran of the *Boer War and an accomplished sailor, who wrote the mystery novel *The Riddle of the Sands* in 1903. He became an advocate of *home rule and used his boat, the *Asgard*, to smuggle weapons to the Irish *Volunteers in July 1914. During *World War I, he volunteered for the Royal Navy. In 1921 he was elected to the *Dáil (Parliament). Childers was secretary of the Irish delegation to the *Anglo-Irish Treaty conference, but was opposed to the agreement as signed. He was a *republican propagandist during the *Civil War and was court-martialed for the unauthorized possession of a gun (given to him by Michael *Collins for personal protection a few months earlier). Childers was executed on November 24, 1922. P.E.

Christ Church Cathedral. The *Dublin diocesan cathedral of the *Church of Ireland. This church was founded in 1038 by King Sitric Silkenbeard in the center of *Viking Dublin. A part of the choir dates from the late twelfth century, and the nave was completed in the thirteenth. Damaged by a roof collapse in 1562, the cathedral was restored by the distiller Henry Roe in the 1870s, and recently again refurbished. Its extensive crypt reopened in 2000. P.H.

Christian Brothers, Irish. *Catholic religious teaching order. Founded in 1802 by Edmund Ignatius *Rice, the Institute of Irish Christian Brothers was dedicated to educating Ireland's impoverished youth in the catechism of the Catholic faith. Over the next seventy-five years, the Christian Brothers established 294 schools in Ireland which, by 1878, were staffed by more than four hundred brothers teaching over thirty-three thousand students ranging in age from four to seventeen. By 1838, the Brothers had separated from the government's National System of *Education, in keeping with the Irish bishops' plans to establish strictly denominational schools. In order to meet the needs of Catholic Ireland's rising middle class during the mid-nineteenth century, the Brothers expanded their curriculum to include the full array of secular subjects and established a style of strict discipline in their classrooms, which became legendary. They also formalized their teaching of the Catholic religion by emphasizing the sacraments, rituals, and devotions. This contributed to making Irish Catholics the most practicing Catholics in the world until the *Second Vatican Council. Alone among nineteenth-century Irish educators, the Brothers taught Irish history, *poetry, culture, and, after 1878, the *Irish language. This emphasis on Irish culture fostered *nationalism. The Brothers' graduates included veterans of the 1916 *Easter Rising such as Patrick *Pearse, Arthur *Griffith, and Éamon *de Valera. By the early twentieth century, the primary focus of the Brothers' ministry had shifted to the teaching of Irish *immigrants and their children in *Canada, *Australia, *New Zealand, and the United States. Recent scandals involving the physical and sexual abuse of students have diminished the prestige of the order. M.P.C.

Christianity in Ireland, early (fifth century A.D.). There are indications that small numbers of Christians were in Ireland before St. *Patrick's arrival, but most likely these were slaves and merchants from Roman Britain. There may also have been some missionaries, one of whom, called *Palladius, is actually mentioned. The mission of Patrick in the fifth century A.D. covered large areas of the north and the midlands, and he made a considerable number of converts among the lower classes and some among the nobles. By the time of his death, his missionary work, together with Christianity's consistent body of doctrine and growing prestige throughout the continent, had given widespread appeal to the new religion in Ireland.

Within a generation or two, the episcopal nature of Patrick's organization was giving way to a new system, consisting of monasteries with or without a bishop in charge. This was already becoming the trend in Britain in Patrick's time, and was particularly suitable to the Irish context. The numerous small kingdoms needed separate missionary stations, and local rulers tended to confer special parcels of land on the clerics. The monasteries grew, and by the mid-sixth century had become the prime agency for change in the country. The ascetic life of hermits added to the impetus; many of these hermits became founders of new monasteries in faraway places. The career of the celebrated Columba (called Colm *Cille in Irish) illustrates the several aspects of this development. By birth a member of the leading clan in the country, he influenced all by his personal piety. He founded monasteries in different areas, and then began a mission to the Picts of *Scotland.

So vibrant had the monastic Christianity of Ireland become by the year A.D. 664, that the Roman Church authorities had difficulty in persuading the general body of Irish monks to accept the new standard method of computing the date of Easter. The Irish Church was notable in other ways, also. Having its origins in a peaceful transition, it thrived in a context that had much continuity with native customs and beliefs. There had been some opposition, led by the *druids, but in time the saintly monks came to resemble the druids themselves in public perception. A good example of such continuity and integration of *Celtic customs and beliefs is well-worship. The druids had a cult of sacred springs, and the Christian missionaries often resorted to the same places to perform mass baptisms. Thus in Irish folk practice, the holy well remains a center of local religious practice, and miraculous cures are attributed to it. D.Oh.

Church of Ireland, the. Principal *Protestant Church in Ireland, and state church from 1560 to 1869. While the *Reformation began in Ireland under *Henry VIII, it was not until the Act of Uniformity (1560) during *Elizabeth I's reign that the monarch was officially head of the Church. All Irish people were required by law to attend Protestant services or be fined. Worship was ordained according to the Book of Common Prayer. Apart from the confiscation of ecclesiastical buildings and lands, little progress was made in imposing Protestantism on the Irish people. Because of the relative poverty of the life of a clergyman, few clerics of a high caliber were attracted to careers in the Church of Ireland, and those English clergy who did come were handicapped by a lack of knowledge of the *Irish language. While there were some efforts to found new primary and grammar schools that could have propelled evangelization, only a very few were opened. Not until Trinity College was founded in 1592 was there a national academy for the training of ministers. Even then, the mission of the Church of Ireland was mainly focused on the English-speaking, mostly newcomer population.

The character of the Church of Ireland in the early seventeenth century was shaped by the puritanism of its leadership, most notably James *Ussher, archbishop of *Armagh. Ussher emphasized the continuity of the heritage of the Church of Ireland from the earliest phase of Irish Christianity. Bishop William Bedell of Kilmore, sometime provost of Trinity, was exceptional in his dedication to preaching through the Irish language. The middle decades of the century were extremely disruptive for the organization of the Church of Ireland as the *Rebellion of 1641 badly affected many Protestant communities, and the counter-Reformation flourished under the auspices of the Catholic *Confederation of Kilkenny. Only with great difficulty were diocesan and parochial structures later reestablished. After the brief restoration of *Catholicism under *James II, the Church leadership closed ranks with the Protestant political and social ascendancy to impose rigid laws known as the *Penal Laws for the exclusion of Catholics and *Presbyterians or dissenters from the mainstream of national life. Though there were some notable exceptions in the eighteenth century such as Jonathan *Swift and William King, the quality of leadership in the Church of Ireland was not inspiring on the whole, and organization languished.

In 1800, the Churches of Ireland and England were united at the time of the Act of *Union. Challenges to Irish Protestantism came from the breakaway Methodist Church and the rise of an evangelical movement within the Church of Ireland. The Evangelicals engaged in a vigorous campaign of proselytizing among Catholics and promoted *education. The controversy over the payment of *tithes by nonmembers of the church to its clergy flared in the 1830s and was solved by a government compromise. Prime Minister William *Gladstone's government in the 1860s considered the Church of Ireland's place in Irish life to be disproportionate to its relatively small membership, and in 1869 Parliament enacted the disestablishment of the Church of Ireland and ended its endowment. Provision was, however, made for the Church's continuing mission and the payment of its clergy. A process of thorough internal reorganization ensured that, after the *partition of Ireland in 1921, the Church survived as an all-Ireland institution. C.L.

churches, early. In early Irish *Christianity, churches were built of wood or occasionally of earth—presumably small boxlike structures with corner beams *(antae)*. But the double church for monks and nuns at *Kildare, as described by St. *Brigid's seventh-century biographer Cogitosus, suggests a larger, taller building with chapels and drapes, as well as painted images. *Hisperica Famina*, another text of the same period, describes a church of massive timbers with a central altar, a western porch, and four steeples. Stone churches became more popular after A.D. 800, but wooden churches continued to be built in the twelfth century. P.H.

Churchill, Winston S. (1874–1965). British politician and prime minister, 1940–45 and 1951–55. A towering figure on the world stage, Churchill played a pivotal role in Irish history on a number of occasions during his long political career.

Though a Conservative for most of his life, Churchill defected to the Liberal Party for a time, beginning in 1904. While a Liberal, Churchill backed his party's policy of *home rule for Ireland, and supported the home rule bill of 1912. Later, when it appeared that *unionists were prepared to resort to violence to prevent home rule from going into effect, Churchill came to support the *partition of Ireland as a means of avoiding civil war. Partition was eventually legislated in Britain's *Government of Ireland Act of 1920.

Following the truce in Ireland's *War of Independence (1919–21), Churchill, as colonial secretary, was a member of the British team that negotiated the *Anglo-Irish Treaty of 1921, which created the twenty-six-county *Irish Free State as a dominion within the *Commonwealth.

Churchill had a significant impact on *Anglo-Irish relations as Britain's prime minister during World War II. As a committed imperialist, Churchill considered Ireland's proclamation of neutrality in the war an illegal act by a Commonwealth nation and was particularly incensed by Éamon *de Valera's refusal to grant the British access to the three ports reserved for the Royal Navy's use in the Anglo-Irish Treaty (ports that Churchill's predecessor Neville Chamberlain had formally turned over to the Irish government in 1938). Early in the war, Churchill was prepared to seize the ports, but he was dissuaded by military advisors, who argued that the cost of such a takeover would be greater than any gain. Even after the German threat to British security diminished later in the conflict, Churchill still considered neutrality a stain on Ireland's honor.

Despite his respect for many Irish *nationalists, Churchill's commitment to preserving the British empire prevented him from fully accepting the twenty-six counties' growing independence after 1921. T.D.

cinema. "Irish film" describes both films produced in Ireland and world cinema with Irish themes. Up to the end of the twentieth century, only about two hundred of the world's roughly two thousand films with Irish themes were Irish productions. Filmmaking, which began in Ireland in the early twentieth century, was originally dominated by North American and British companies. From the twenties through the fifties, both foreign and indigenous filmmakers helped to build a national cinema based on historical themes and set on Irish soil. Varieties of *nationalism marked films such as *The Lad from Old Ireland* (1910), *Rory O'More* (1910), *Ireland a Nation* (1914), *Willie Reilly and His Colleen Bawn* (1920), *Irish Destiny* (1926), *Man of Aran* (1934), *The Dawn* (1936), *Odd Man Out* (1947), and *Shake Hands with the Devil* (1959). Perhaps the most famous Irish film is John Ford's *The Quiet Man* (1952), a romantic comedy set in an idealized landscape. *Ryan's Daughter* (1971), directed by David Lean, was also immensely popular, and because of its spectacular cinematography of the *Kerry landscape, it was a huge boost to tourism in Ireland in the 1970s. In 1958, Seán *Lemass, then minister for industry and commerce, created Ardmore Studios, a permanent commercial facility for film production located in *Wicklow. The studios were frequently hired by both American and British producers.

Since the 1950s, an Irish documentary film genre has developed, with George Morrison, Liam O'Leary, Robert Monks, Colm O'Laoghaire, and Louis Marcus as key early figures. The organization *Gael Linn produced *Irish-language cinema newsreels, as well as the ninety-minute historical films *Mise Éire* (I Am Ireland) (1959) and *Saoirse* (Freedom) (1961). More recently, *Northern Irish independent filmmaker John T. Davis directed *Shell Shock Rock* (1978), which treats punk rock in *Northern Ireland, and *Power in the Blood* (1990), which depicts evangelism in Ireland. Britain's Channel Four commissioned videos and films for television, providing support for Irish filmmakers during the recession-ridden 1980s. Nationalist workshop collectives such as Derry Film and Video produced documentaries such as Anne Crilly's *Mother Ireland* (1988), an exploration of nationalist iconography. Desmond Bell's *The Last Storyteller?* (2002) presents the life of folklorist Seán Ó hEochaidh, while his *The Hard Road to Klondike* (1999) deals with migration.

During the 1970s and 1980s, feature filmmakers such as Thaddeus O'Sullivan (*On a Paving Stone Mounted*, 1978), Bob Quinn (*Poitin*, 1978), Cathal Black (*Pigs*, 1984), and Joe Comerford (*Reefer and the Model*, 1988), working mostly in sixteen millimeter, addressed social issues such as *economic stagnation, unemployment, *emigration, and political turmoil. Based on a newspaper story, Peter Ormrod and John Kelleher's *Eat the Peach* (1986), which explores unemployment and smuggling in a border town, achieved considerable box office success in Ireland. The first Irish Film Board (Bord Scannan na hÉireann, 1981–87), established to promote national cultural expression, funded Neil *Jordan's *Angel* (1982), the story of a jazz musician who witnesses a paramilitary shakedown and murder. Pat Murphy's films *Maeve* (1981) and *Anne Devlin* (1984) took a feminist approach to Irish nationalism. Pat O'Connor's *Cal* (1984), based on Bernard MacLaverty's novel, romanticized the *Troubles, echoing the style of earlier British and American films such as John Ford's *The Informer* (1935) and Carol Reed's *Odd Man Out* (1947). Margo Harkin's study of teen pregnancy, *Hush-a-bye Baby* (1989), and Crilly's *Mother Ireland* (1988), along with Pat Murphy's work, formed a body of film directed by *women and concerned with women's issues. By 1992, a second film board was established under the leadership of Michael D. Higgins, then minister for arts, culture, and the *Gaeltacht. The Irish Film Centre and the National Film Archive opened in *Dublin during the same year, and the magazine *Film Ireland* quickly established itself as the journal of Irish filmmaking. Flourishing around the Irish Film Centre, film festivals proliferated in cities throughout the island: Belfast, Cork, Derry, Dublin, Galway, and Limerick. A second generation of women directors includes Mary McGuckian (*Words Upon the Window Pane*, 1994; *This Is the Sea*, 1998; *Best*, 2000) and Trish McAdam (*Snakes and Ladders*, 1995).

Although commercial success has often been elusive for Irish filmmakers, in 1989, Jim *Sheridan's *My Left Foot*, based on Christy *Brown's autobiography, became the first Irish film to win Academy Awards (for best director, best actor, and best supporting actress). Sheridan's later films treat rural decline (*The Field*, 1990), the Troubles (*Some Mother's Son*, 1996—produced by Sheridan, directed by Terry George; *The Boxer*, 1997), and Irish life in the US (*In America*, 2002). In 1991, Roddy *Doyle's novel about a rock group, *The Commitments*, filmed by British director Alan Parker, achieved international success. Neil Jordan won an Oscar in 1992 for *The*

Crying Game, which remade the Troubles genre by emphasizing issues of race and sexuality. Among Jordan's fifteen films are *The Butcher Boy* (1998), adapted from Patrick *McCabe's novel, in which Jordan turns to domestic violence and insanity in a small Irish town, and *Michael Collins* (1996), a bio-epic.

Since the 1990s, when Ireland underwent extensive modernization and integration into the global economy, Irish and Irish-related filmmakers have wrestled with the economic need for Hollywood levels of distribution in order to remain competitive on the world market. However, many Irish films receive only limited distribution and short theatrical runs. British director Ken Loach's *Hidden Agenda* (1990) fictionalizes the *Stalker Affair in thriller fashion, while Paul Greengrass's *Bloody Sunday* (2002) recreates in docudrama style the events of January 30, 1972, in *Derry. Mike Newell's *Into the West* (1992) joined John Sayles's *The Secret of Roan Inish* (1994) in exploring Irish *folklore to appeal to a young audience. Alan Parker's *Angela's Ashes* (1999) capitalized on the success of Frank *McCourt's story of countermigration. *The Last September* (1999) adapts Elizabeth *Bowen's classic novel. Less popular films include Thaddeus O'Sullivan's *Nothing Personal* (1995), which joins Sheridan's *The Boxer* (1997) and Marc Evans's *Resurrection Man* (1998) in presenting a peace-process view of sectarian violence. Gerry Stembridge's *Guiltrip* (1996) is a study of domestic violence. John Boorman's *The General* (1997), Paddy Breathnach's *I Went Down* (1997) (screenplay by Conor *McPherson), and Thaddeus O'Sullivan's *Ordinary Decent Criminal* (2000) explore the criminal underground in Ireland. Scottish director Peter Mullan's controversial film *The Magdalene Sisters* (2002), set in a 1960s Magdalene Laundry (or Irish homes for unwed mothers), won the top award, the Golden Lion, at the Venice Film Festival. The chief problems facing Irish filmmaking in the early twenty-first century remain competition with Hollywood and distribution. C.H.

Civil War. See **Irish Civil War.**

Clan na Gael. Irish American revolutionary organization. Founded in *New York in 1867 by Jerome J. Collins, Clan na Gael (also called the United Brotherhood) came to dominate the Irish *republican movement in America. During the 1880s, the Clan was led by "The Triangle" of Alexander Sullivan, Michael Boland, and Denis Feeley who were committed to carrying out dynamite explosions in British cities. Clan na Gael gave *Parnell valuable assistance and support during the *Land League agitation and the campaign for Irish *home rule. Reformed in 1900 with John *Devoy as its main leader, the organization took part in preparations for the *Easter Rising of 1916 and sought to assist the German war effort against Great Britain. During the *War of Independence, Éamon *de Valera and John Devoy disagreed about the best means of securing American recognition for an Irish republic. With the long-standing connection between the Clan and the IRB (*Irish Republican Brotherhood) now severed, the organization split. One faction, under Devoy, recognized the *Anglo-Irish Treaty while another, led by Joseph McGarrity, rejected compromise and continued to support IRA (*Irish Republican Army) activity into the 1930s. Clan na Gael finally ceased activity after McGarrity's death in 1940. S.A.B.

Clancy Brothers, the. Irish folk group. The group was formed in *New York in 1959, by Tom, Pat, and Liam Clancy of County *Tipperary and Tommy Makem of County *Armagh. Their first recording was of topical and popular "rebel" ballads delivered in an upbeat, good-time style to the "folk" instruments banjo and guitar. Their style and rejection of normal stage formality created instant popularity. A performance on the *Ed Sullivan Show* led to coast-to-coast recognition in the United States. In Ireland they became a "pop" hit, and their style created a fashion that for many was an introduction to traditional *music. F.V.

Clancy, Willie (1918–73). *Uilleann piper. Born in Miltown Malbay, County *Clare, Clancy initially *step-danced and played whistle and flute. He took up the uilleann pipes after hearing traveling player Johnny Doran in 1936. Tutored by Doran and by Leo *Rowsome, and influenced by Séamus Ennis and John Potts, he won the major *Oireachtas award in 1947. Clancy established an international reputation, which drew many aficionados to his hometown each summer to hear him play. Upon his death, his onetime jocular reference to this activity as "a summer school" was taken up by teacher Muiris Ó Róchain, Séamus MacMathúna of CCÉ (*Comhaltas Ceoltóirí Éireann), and local musicians who created Scoil Samhraidh Willie Clancy (the Willie Clancy Summer School), held annually in July ever since. The festival opens in Miltown Malbay with a lecture tribute to Breandán *Breathnach, and its 1,500 students are joined by several thousand musicians and aficionados to create a unique carnival of traditional *music. F.V.

Clann na Poblachta. *Political party. Clann na Poblachta was founded in 1946 by a group of *republicans, and economic and social radicals. Led by former IRA (*Irish Republican Army) leader Seán *MacBride, the party won two out of three by-elections before its first national contest in 1948 when it won 13.2 percent of the national vote. The party helped form the first coalition government, but was fatally damaged by the split between MacBride and Noel *Browne over the controversial *health bill known as the "Mother and Child" Scheme. Clann na Poblachta never regained its initial strength and it was disbanded in 1965. J.D.

Clannad. Music group. Started in 1970 by *Donegal natives Máire, Pól, and Ciarán Brennan and cousins Pádraig and Noel Duggan, Clannad performed *Irish language songs set to arrangements of traditional tunes. Local festival success was followed by a tour of Germany, and major sound track commissions, one of which, "Robin of Sherwood," won a British Academy Award in 1984. They became influential stylists and hugely popular in Europe. "Enya" Brennan joined the group in 1979 but left in 1982 to pursue a hugely successful solo career in popular music. F.V.

Clare, County. Maritime county in the southwest of Ireland in the province of *Munster. Clare (1,332 square miles) has a population of 103,333 (2002 census). The county is surrounded by water; the Atlantic Ocean to its west; Lough Derg, the largest of the River *Shannon's lakes, on its east; Galway Bay to the north; and the Shannon estuary on its south. Clare is renowned for its spectacular and rugged beauty. A dramatic coastline runs northward from Loop Head to Ballyvaughan on the shores of Galway Bay. The Cliffs of Moher rise seven hundred feet above the Atlantic Ocean. The Burren, a geological and botanical marvel, resembling a lunar landscape, occupies a large portion of the northwestern part of the county. *Prehistoric *dolmens, such as Poulnabrone, a Neolithic burial chamber dating from 3800 B.C., rise starkly above the limestone plateau.

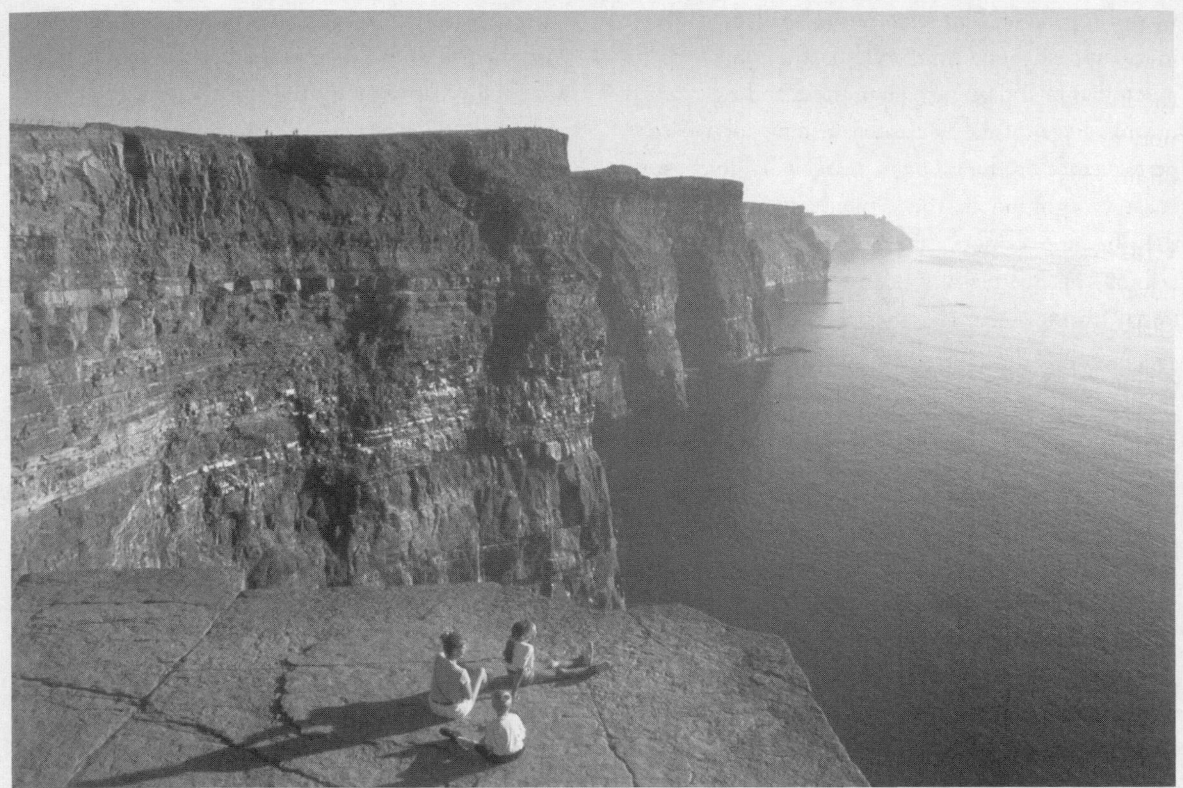

Cliffs of Moher, County Clare

Mullaghmore, a spectacular site of limestone hills, lies in the center of the Burren, close to the village of Corofin. In the eastern section of the county on the shore of Lough Derg, are the picturesque villages of Killaloe, Mountshannon, and Scarrif.

Clare has a long and rich musical tradition and is considered one of the major centers of traditional Irish *music. Tulla, Kilfenora, Kilrush, and Miltown Malbay in particular, which hosts the annual Willie *Clancy Summer School—a weeklong festival of traditional music, song, and *dance—are known for the unique Clare style of traditional Irish music. Famous musicians associated with the county include Sharon *Shannon, Junior Crehan, Tommy *Peoples, Jackie Daly, and Noel Hill.

The rich and colorful *folklore of the county includes the Biddy Early legend: a wise woman in the vicinity of the village of Feakle who reputedly could cure all manner of ailments and often ran afoul of the clergy. The writers Edna *O'Brien and Brian *Merriman are natives of the county.

Clare's economy is based on tourism, *agriculture, and some multinational industry, mostly based in Shannon International Airport.

County Clare holds a unique place in Ireland's political history. It was here that two of the country's greatest *nationalist leaders were first elected to *Parliament, Daniel *O'Connell in 1828 and Éamon *de Valera in 1917. Between the tenth and twelfth centuries, the Dál Cais dynasty, which was centered in the eastern part of Clare, reached the peak of its power under Brian Bóruma (*Boru). John Holland, the inventor of the submarine, was born in Liscannor. Ennis, the county's capital, is the first totally on-line community in the country. J.OM.

Clarke, Austin (1896–1974). Poet, dramatist, novelist, critic, and broadcaster. Born in *Dublin, Clarke was educated at University College, Dublin (UCD). He was associated with literary revivalists Douglas *Hyde, George *Russell (AE), and W. B. *Yeats, and was influenced by Standish *O'Grady and Matthew Arnold. Clarke replaced his mentor Thomas *MacDonagh as lecturer in English at UCD when MacDonagh was executed for his part in the *Easter Rising of 1916. Clarke's first publication, *The Vengeance of Fionn* (1917), an epic poem, earned him recognition and comparison with Yeats, with whom he had an uneasy relationship. The breakdown in 1919 that caused him to be hospitalized for over a year is described in the long poem *Mnemosyne Lies in Dust* (1966).

From the early twenties until 1937, Clarke worked in London as a literary journalist. Yeats nominated him in 1932 as a founding member of the *Irish Academy of Letters, which aimed to combat *censorship. Clarke's distinctive, influential experiments with Gaelic prosody are a feature of his collection *Pilgrimage and Other Poems* (1929), set in the late medieval period.

After he returned to Ireland, Clarke combined regular literary reviews in the *Irish Times* with poetry broadcasts on *Radio Éireann. In 1938 he published *Night and Morning*, whose intense, troubled poems are concerned with the loss of religious faith. The following year, he and Robert Farren founded the Dublin Verse-Speaking Society, and in 1944, the Lyric Theatre Company, which staged verse drama at the *Abbey Theatre or the *Peacock. Beginning with *The Son of Learning* (1927), Clarke wrote twenty-one verse plays. From 1955, his poetry enjoyed new audiences as he satirized church and state with Swiftian indignation and passionately defended the poor. The acclaimed *Ancient Lights* (1955) earned him the sobriquet "local complainer." In the long poems of his old age, such as *Tiresias* (1971), he turned to erotic subject matter to indicate his resistance to the pieties of his age. Two polished volumes of autobiography (*Twice Round the Black Church*, 1962, and *A Penny in the Clouds*, 1968), two critical studies, and the posthumously published *Collected Poems* (1974) show Clarke's remarkable range. He is generally regarded as one of the most accomplished Irish poets of his generation. M.S.T.

Clarke, Harry (1889–1931). Illustrator and stained glass artist. Influenced by the Art Nouveau style, Clarke, a Dubliner, is best known for his jewel-like stained glass windows found throughout Ireland, England, Scotland, and Wales. As a contributor to the Irish Arts and Craft Movement, he designed eleven highly acclaimed windows for the Honan Chapel, in the grounds of University College, *Cork. He also illustrated H. C. Andersen's *Fairy Tales* (1916) and E. A. Poe's *Tales of Mystery and Imagination* (1919). A founder of the Dublin Painters' Group in 1921, Clarke took over his father's church-decorating business in *Dublin. His *Geneva Window* with scenes from twentieth-century *Irish literature, commissioned by the Irish government in 1925 as a gift to the League of Nations, was rejected as unsuitable in 1931 and is now in the Wolfsonian Museum in Miami Beach, Florida. His final work, *The Last Judgment*, is in St. Mary's Church Newport, County *Mayo. M.C.

Romanesque doorway, Clonfert Cathedral, County Galway

Clarke, Thomas. (1857–1916) Irish *republican. After emigrating from Ireland to America in 1880, Clarke joined *Clan na Gael. In 1883 he embarked upon a dynamiting mission to England where he was arrested and sentenced to life imprisonment. On his release in 1898, Clarke went back to America but returned to *Dublin in 1907. A founder of the IRB (*Irish Republican Brotherhood) military council, he supervised preparations for the *Easter Rising of 1916. First signatory to the *Proclamation of Independence, Clarke was court-martialed and executed on May 3, 1916. S.A.B.

Clonfert Cathedral. Clonfert *Church of Ireland Cathedral in East *Galway is the burial place of the great Kerry sailor, St. *Brendan, who died in 577. Parts of the west gable, with projecting *antae* at the corners, are among the oldest surviving parts of the structure (which probably replaced an earlier wooden church around the eleventh century). Around 1200, the doorway was added. It is Ireland's most intricately ornamented Romanesque doorway, decorated with interlaced bosses, human and animal heads, as well as geometrical and floral ornaments, culminating above in a pointed gable. Carved from friable sandstone, its details are weathering badly. The cathedral became *Protestant at the *Reformation in the sixteenth century. The cathedral is on the World Monument List. P.H.

Clonmacnoise. Sixth-century monastery. One of the most important monastic ruins in Ireland, Clonmacnoise in County *Offaly was the crossroads of Ireland where the east-west thoroughfare, the Eiscir Riada, crossed the north-south-flowing *Shannon River. Around 545, St. Ciarán founded a monastery here that thrived for over a thousand years until looted by the English in 1552. Royal patronage in return for burial rights made it a rich center for arts, crafts, and the study of Irish history and *folklore.

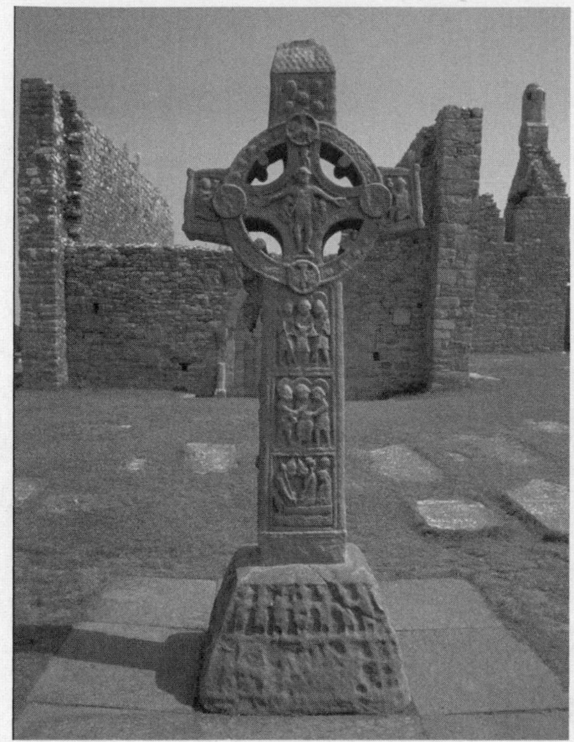

The Cross of the Scriptures, Clonmacnoise, County Offaly

Ireland's oldest all-Irish *manuscript, *Leabhar na hUidre (Book of the Dun Cow), was completed here by 1106. The surviving ruins include the country's largest pre-Norman cathedral, St. Ciarán's tomb-shrine, and two *round towers. Three *high crosses and examples of the great collection of cross-decorated memorial slabs are now housed at the site's Interpretative Center. A *Norman *castle nearby, of c.1200, guarded the river crossing, where remains of a wooden bridge of c.800 have recently been discovered. P.H.

Clontarf, Battle of (1014). Battle fought by Brian *Boru and the forces of *Munster against the *Vikings of *Dublin, the *Leinster Irish, and their Scandinavian allies. Traditionally seen as a struggle between the Irish and the Vikings for the sovereignty of Ireland, the battle was really the culmination of an internal struggle between Irish provincial rulers for the control of Ireland. The battle began at dawn on April 23 and, by that evening, Brian's forces had gained the upper hand and defeated the Leinster-Viking alliance. There were many losses on both sides. Brian himself was slain in his tent and his son Murchadh was killed on the battlefield. While the battle removed the threat of Norse domination in Ireland, it did not totally extinguish their presence or influence. Many returned to their strongholds in Dublin, *Waterford, and *Wexford, which they continued to control until the *Anglo-Norman invasion in 1169. M.T.D., P.E.

Coghlan, Éamonn. (1952–) Athlete, middle-distance runner. Born in *Dublin, Coghlan finished fourth in two successive Olympic games (1976 and 1980) but will be best remembered for his victory in the five thousand meter final at the World Championship of 1983. He set six world records at fifteen hundred meters, two thousand meters, and the mile indoors, for which he became affectionately known as "the Chairman of the Boards." B.D.

Coleman, James (1941–). Conceptual artist. Born in County *Roscommon, Coleman studied in *Dublin, Paris, London, and Milan. He represented Ireland at the Venice Biennale in 1978 and exhibited at the L' Imaginaire Irlandais show in Paris in 1996. His interactive installations use light, sound, slide, video, and live performance, making the spectator reconsider the meaning of art and its objectives. M.C.

Coleman, Michael (1891–1946). Musician. Born at Killavil, County *Sligo, an area abundant in music, Coleman is the most influential fiddle player in Irish traditional *music. In 1914, he emigrated to the United States, where he began recording in

Michael Collins

1921. The Depression interrupted his career, but he resumed recording and radio work in 1936. Coleman's albums reflect the traditional music style of Sligo and have become part of the canon of Irish traditional music. His collected recordings have been re-released on CD. F.V.

Collins, Michael (1890–1922). *Nationalist, revolutionary, *Civil War commander, government minister—Michael Collins remains one of the enduring legends of modern Irish history. During the height of the *War of Independence (1919–21), Collins was reputedly one of the most wanted men in the British empire. However, only a few months later, he would play an important role in the negotiations leading to the *Anglo-Irish Treaty and eventually the formation of the *Irish Free State.

Michael Collins was born near Clonakilty in County *Cork on October 16, 1890. The youngest of eight children, he witnessed at an early age the suffering of the Irish peasantry caused by absentee *landlords and absentee government. Ireland had not had a home government since the Act of *Union of 1800. The *Famine of the 1840s, the revolutionary *Fenians, and *Parnell's failed *home rule movement would all shape his political awareness.

After a primary education, Collins went to London in 1906 to join an older sister and to take a clerical position in the Post Office Savings Bank. An avid reader, Collins studied nationalist literature and history, and as he moved to other jobs, he learned accounting and finance, skills that he would later use in his political career.

In 1909 in London, Collins was sworn into the the *Irish Republican Brotherhood (IRB). After the outbreak of *World War I, he went to *Dublin and took part in the *Easter Rising of 1916. After one week, the rising was quelled, fifteen leaders were executed by firing squad, and many rank-and-file militants, including Collins, were jailed in Frongoch, Wales.

While in the military prison, Collins displayed the leadership qualities and dominant personality that would later distinguish him as a brilliant military and political leader. The executions raised such anti-British sentiments that the authorities stopped further executions and, in December 1916, released Collins and many of the other rebels.

Back in Ireland, Collins was appointed financial officer of *Sinn Féin, a political party committed to an independent and free Ireland. In the December 1918 general elections for the House of Commons, Collins assisted in getting a majority (73 of 105) of Sinn Féin candidates elected throughout Ireland. These candidates refused to take their seats in the House of Commons and on January 21, 1919, set up their own Parliament in Dublin, called *Dáil Éireann, with Éamon *de Valera as president.

For Britain, Ireland's declaration of independence at the first Dáil meeting was a serious crisis. Michael Collins, who was the minister of finance, organized a Dáil loan to finance the new government. As director of intelligence of the IRA (*Irish Republican Army) and the leader of the IRB, Collins was also one of the military campaign strategists in the *Anglo-Irish War of Independence. He set up an effective system of counterintelligence and coordinated a secret campaign of assassinations of pro-British *police and agents throughout Ireland. The British commissioned a special anti-terrorist unit—the notoriously ruthless *Black and Tans—to defeat Collins's campaign. Collins responded with increased guerrilla warfare. By July 1921, the British Prime Minister David *Lloyd George agreed to a truce, followed by talks with Sinn Féin's President Éamon de Valera in London.

When further talks were arranged in October 1921, in a brilliant feat of what some historians have called Machiavellian manipulation, de Valera prevailed on the "outlawed terrorist" Michael Collins to be part of the Irish delegation, while de Valera would remain in Ireland as head of the provisional government. Collins protested fiercely (he claimed not to be a politician and did not want to become a scapegoat for what could be only a treaty compromise), but eventually agreed to come out of "hiding" and travel to London, to join the rest of the Irish delegation. Led by Vice President Arthur *Griffith, minister for foreign affairs, the delegation had full plenipotentiary power from the Dáil, but, rather ambiguously, were also ordered to refer any treaty draft back to Dublin before final agreement.

Collins was to play a major role in the negotiations with the British delegation, which included the Prime Minister Lloyd George, Winston *Churchill, and Arthur Neville Chamberlain. The talks lasted from October 11 to December 6, 1921, when a compromise was reached and Articles of Agreement for a Treaty were signed. The *Anglo-Irish Treaty recognized an Irish Free State consisting of twenty-six of Ireland's thirty-two counties. The treaty (which also included a controversial *oath of allegiance to the crown) was fiercely debated in the Dáil and was accepted by a slim majority (64/57) on January 7, 1922. Collins viewed the treaty as a stepping stone to complete independence, but many accused him of selling out.

In June 1922, a few months after the anti-treaty republicans occupied the Four Courts building in Dublin, *Civil War broke out. Michael Collins, chairman of the Provisional Government and head of the Free State forces, desperately wanted an end to the violence. In late August 1922, he traveled to his home area in County Cork for an apparently routine recognizance trip. Some claim a meeting with the anti-treaty leaders was being negotiated. As Collins's convoy passed through Beal na mBláth, a sniper's bullet killed him instantly. He was only thirty-one years old. The Civil War ended in May of the following year. J.OM., L.R.

Collins, Patrick (1911–94). Painter. Born in Dromore West, County *Sligo, Collins is a semi-abstract, lyrical landscape painter whose work, in contrast to hard-edge modernism, can be described as *Celtic romanticism with an emphasis on nature and the Irish past. A member of *Aosdána, he lived in *Dublin and France and had a major retrospective in Dublin, *Cork, and *Belfast in 1982. M.C.

Colm Cille, Saint (521–597). One of Ireland's three patron *saints (together with St. *Patrick and *Brigid). Born of royal stock at Gartan, County *Donegal, St. Colm Cille (Columba in Latin) was a missionary and founder of monasteries in *Derry, Durrow, and *Iona. Tradition says that he illicitly copied a manuscript from his old teacher St. Finnian of Moville. The controversial copy Colm Cille made may be the *Cathach, the oldest surviving manuscript in Ireland. Colm Cille raised an army against the king, who had sided with Finnian and, after the Battle of Culdreimne (561), Colm Cille was banished. During his exile, he founded his most influential monastery on the island of Iona (Inner Hebrides), from where he Christianized the Picts in *Scotland. He is buried on Iona. P.H.

Colum, Padraic (1881–1972). Poet and dramatist. Born in *Longford and educated at University College, Dublin, Colum was inspired by the *Irish Revival movement while still an undergraduate. His first play, *Broken Soil*, was produced by the Irish National Theatre Society in 1903. This was followed by *The Land* (1905) and *Thomas Muskerry* (1910). Colum's plays portray the lives of small farmers and peasants, introducing a new realism to Irish Revival drama. In 1914, he and his wife emigrated to the United States, where they both taught comparative literature at Columbia University, in New York City. His first collection of poetry, *Wild Earth* (1916), displayed the dramatic lyricism for which he is famous. *Collected Poems* was published in 1953. Colum based his collections of children's stories, *At the Gateways of the Day* (1924) and *The Bright Islands* (1925), on a survey of Hawaii's native myths, legends, and folklore. His many other popular children's books include *A Boy in Eirinn* (1913), *The King of Ireland's Son* (1916), and *The Adventures of Odysseus* (1918). In 1958, he published *Our Friend James Joyce* in collaboration with his wife Mary Maguire. Colum was the last living link with *Yeats, *Synge, Lady *Gregory, and the heyday of the Irish Revival. C.D.

Columbanus, Saint (543–615). Irish monk and *saint. St. Columbanus was a trail-blazer among the Irish monks who became pilgrim-exiles to spread the word of God on the European continent. Born in 543, he studied in Bangor, County *Down, and left for *France in 591. There he founded monasteries, first at Annegray and then at Luxeuil, which added a new impetus to French monasticism. Expelled in 610, Columbanus moved to Switzerland, where he left his pupil St. Gall at a place where a famous monastery (St. Gall) later developed, before crossing the Alps to make his own final foundation at Bobbio in Northern Italy. He died there in 615. Columbanus wrote a very strict monastic rule for his monks, passionately defended his Irish viewpoint on the date of Easter against no less a person than the pope, and was a poet and brilliant letter writer in Latin. Fiery yet humble, fallible but contrite and forgiving, he was an important figure in forging a link between the classical civilization of the Mediterranean and the monastic culture of his native land. P.H.

Comhaltas Ceoltóirí Éireann (CCÉ). The major revival organization of Irish traditional *music. Founded in 1951 by musicians, including piper Leo *Rowsome, CCÉ is committed to the preservation and spread of traditional Irish music, song, and *dance. It organizes classes for Irish music education throughout the year, and competitions focused on a series of festival events called *fleadh cheoil*. The most prestigious of these is the All-Ireland Fleadh Cheoil, held annually in different towns all over Ireland. CCÉ grew rapidly, and adopted a democratic, political-style pyramid structure with local, county, and provincial branches that elect a national congress and leadership. It also has branches in Britain, Scotland, and the United States. F.V.

Commonwealth (of Nations). An association of states comprising the United Kingdom and some former British dependencies. Formally established in 1931 as an outgrowth of the British empire, the Commonwealth (including such countries as Canada, Australia, and New Zealand) acknowledges the British crown as its symbolic head. During the nineteenth and early twentieth centuries, a number of British dependencies gained dominion status, which combined a degree of practical independence with a profession of loyalty to the crown. The 1921 *Anglo-Irish Treaty gave the new *Irish Free State dominion status within the Commonwealth. The 1931 Statute of Westminster was passed by the British Parliament largely because of extensive lobbying by Irish delegates at the imperial conferences of 1926 and 1930. The statute recognized the dominions as free and equal members of the Commonwealth and acknowledged the sovereign right of each dominion to control its own domestic and foreign affairs and to establish its own diplomatic corps. Ireland's passage of the 1948 *Republic of Ireland Act marked the state's withdrawal from the Commonwealth. T.D.

Communist Party. The first Communist Party of Ireland was formed in 1921, when members of the Socialist Party of Ireland merged with the Communist International. James *Connolly's son, Roddy Connolly, led the tiny party, and the writer Liam *O'Flaherty was also a founding member. In 1924, James *Larkin's Irish Worker League replaced the party as the group affiliated to the Comintern. Larkin's son, also named James Larkin, was a leading party member. In 1928 a group of Irish communists went to Russia for political training.

In 1932, *Belfast communists successfully organized a strike of workers on relief schemes for the unemployed, uniting *Catholic and *Protestant workers. The Communist Party of Ireland, re-formed in 1933, recruited volunteers to fight on the Republican side in the *Spanish Civil War, and several party members died in Spain.

Between the 1930s and 1950s, the Church and the press were fiercely anti-communist, and at times public activity was impossible. In 1970, the communist groups in *Northern Ireland and the *Republic of Ireland reunited as a new Communist Party of Ireland. It remained closely aligned with the Soviet Union. The party's occasional election candidates have received insignificant support, but its members have been influential in *trade unions, notably in Belfast, and in various protest movements in Northern Ireland and the Republic of Ireland. The party survives, but as a force on the far left it lost out in the 1970s and 1980s to the *Workers' Party, and more recently to Trotskyist groupings such as the Socialist Party. P.D.

Confederate War (1641–53). See **Rebellion of 1641** and **Confederation of Kilkenny.**

Confederation of Kilkenny, the (1642). Assembly of Confederate *Catholics (Gaelic Irish and Old English allies) organized in 1642 to govern territory held as a result of the *Rebellion of 1641. In May 1642, the Irish Catholic clergy along with members of the Catholic nobility and prominent merchants and lawyers met at *Kilkenny to discuss means of controlling the rebellion. An alternative government for Ireland was proposed and an oath was drafted to bind together all the Catholic Confederate Allies. In October 1642, the first General Assembly of Confederate Catholics was held at Kilkenny. The assembly met annually until 1648, but it never succeeded in gaining total control of Ireland's administrative structure. The confederation itself was marked by considerable confusion and squabbling and was formally dissolved in January 1649. P.E.

Congreve, William (1670–1729). Playwright and librettist. Born in Yorkshire, England, Congreve moved to Ireland where his father was commander of the garrison in Youghal. He attended Kilkenny College and Trinity College, Dublin, and studied law in London. His literary friends included Sir Richard Steele, Alexander Pope, and Jonathan *Swift. Congreve's first play, *The Old Bachelor* (1693), was a huge success at the Theatre Royal in London. His restoration comedies, of which the best known are *Love for Love* (1695) and *The Way of the World* (1700), a comedy of manners, are masterly, witty, and subtle. Although he retired from playwriting in 1700, he collaborated in translating Molière's *Monsieur de Pourceaugnac*. M.S.T.

Conn of the Hundred Battles. Legendary figure from the Red Branch Cycle of *Celtic history. Conn was a king of Ireland, A.D. circa 177–157, son of Rechtmar, husband of Becuma. Conn discovered, by accident, the Lia Fáil (stone of destiny), which supposedly screamed under the feet of a rightful king the same number of times as he would have reigning heirs. A version of the story still survives in the "Sword in the Stone" episode of Arthurian legend. Conn's kingdom, the northern half of Ireland, was later divided into the two provinces of *Ulster and *Connacht (which derives from his name). J.MD.

Connacht. One of the four provinces of Ireland. This northwest province, which covers an area of 6,838 square miles, has a population of 464,050 (2002 census). Connacht is the least arable but one of the most beautiful provinces of Ireland. Its name derives from the Connachta, followers of *Conn of the Hundred Battles, a branch of the Venii tribe in *pre-Christian Ireland. The province consists of the counties *Roscommon, *Galway, *Mayo, *Leitrim, and *Sligo. Connacht is known for such tourist attractions as: Galway Bay, Claddagh, now part of Galway City and famous for the Claddagh ring, the Irish-speaking *Aran Islands, and *Connemara, with its famous marble, ponies, and bogs. During the *Cromwellian Settlement, the dispossessed *Catholic Irish landowners were sent to Connacht. Oliver *Cromwell is reputed to have said: "To Hell or to Connaught." J.MD.

Connemara. Area of County *Galway that is situated west of the Corrib and stretches between the townlands of Barna and Carna. One of the most scenic areas of Ireland, Connemara has a vibrant Irish-speaking community with a rich tradition of **sean-nós* singing, *dancing, and sailing. In recent years, the area has become something of a media enclave and the *Irish-language *television and *radio stations (TG4 and Raidió na Gaeltachta) as well as the *newspaper *Foinse* are all based there. South Connemara is the largest *Gaeltacht in the country. B.D.

Connolly, James (1868–1916). Labor leader, revolutionary. Connolly was born in Edinburgh into extreme poverty. His parents were Irish immigrants. An avid reader familiar with the works of Karl Marx, he learned Irish *nationalism from an uncle who was in the *Irish Republican Brotherhood. Connolly's early experiences of work and poverty turned him to *socialism. He first came to Ireland as a young soldier in the 1880s, and later, back in Edinburgh, he became involved in labor politics. In 1896, Connolly set up the Irish Socialist Republican Party in *Dublin and established and edited the *Workers' Republic*, the party's journal. His best works as a socialist journalist and pamphleteer are collected in *Labour in Irish History* (1910) and *The Reconquest of Ireland* (1915).

His socialism made little headway in Ireland and in 1903 he took his family to the United States, where he encountered other socialist thinkers, who added an international dimension to his own ideology. In 1910, Connolly returned to Dublin to run the Socialist Party of Ireland. He was also appointed the *Belfast organizer of the Irish Transport and General Workers' Union (ITGWU). He organized Belfast's dock workers and secured a pay raise for striking seamen and firemen. During the women *linen workers' unsuccessful strike of 1911, he set up the Irish Textile Workers' Union. In 1912, with James *Larkin, Connolly founded the Irish *Labour Party in association with the Irish Trade Union Congress.

During the *home rule crisis, Connolly clashed with William Walker, the leading labor *unionist in Belfast, and alienated the nationalists under Joseph Devlin because he disagreed with Devlin's reluctant acceptance of the exclusion of parts of *Ulster from home rule. His opposition to *World War I made him even more unpopular in Belfast, and he was glad to be recalled to Dublin to take over the ITGWU.

As Commandant of the *Irish Citizen Army, Connolly planned a workers' rebellion, but in January 1916, he agreed to join the Irish Republican Brotherhood's planned insurrection. During the *Easter Rising, he was with Patrick *Pearse and other leaders in the General Post Office in Dublin and was one of the signatories of the *Proclamation of the Irish Republic. Connolly was severely wounded in the fighting and after his court-martial—following the rebels' defeat—had to be tied to a chair to be executed.

He is universally recognized as a national hero even though Ireland never embraced socialism. His legacy is disputed, with both constitutional socialists and republican militants claiming him. T.C.

Connor, Jerome (1876–1943). Sculptor. Born in Annascaul, County *Kerry, Connor lived in America until his return to Ireland in 1925. His best-known works include the Robert *Emmet statue, at the National Gallery in Washington, DC, and the Lusitania Memorial, in Cobh, County *Cork. M.C.

Conor, William (1881–1968). Painter and lithographer. Born in *Belfast, Conor studied in Belfast, Paris, and London. Best known for his compassionate depictions of Belfast working people, Conor also painted landscapes and portraits. His 1932 mural on the growth and history of *Ulster is in the Ulster Museum. His work as a war artist in *World War I and II is in the Imperial War Museum, in London. He exhibited at the Paris Salon, and in London, *Dublin, Belfast, and New York. There is a collection of his work in the Ulster Museum and in the Ulster Folk Museum. M.C.

Constitution of Ireland, the. (*Bunreacht na hÉireann* in the Irish language.) The supreme law of the state. It was adopted by plebiscite in 1937 and is the successor of the Constitution of *Dáil Éireann (1919) and the Constitution of the *Irish Free State (1922). The 1919 Constitution was a brief document, adopted by the First Dáil in 1919 as part of *Sinn Féin's campaign for international recognition of Ireland's right to independence. The Free State Constitution (1922) was the first constitution of an independent Ireland but lacked popular legitimacy as the British government insisted that the provisions of the *Anglo-Irish Treaty (1921) be incorporated into the document. It was also amendable by a simple majority of the Dáil throughout its life, and forty-one of its eighty-three articles had been amended by 1937, adding to the pressure for a new constitution.

The 1937 Constitution states that all legislative, executive, and judicial powers of government "derive under God from the people." It sets out the form of government and defines the powers of the president and the two Houses (Dáil and *Seanad) of the *Oireachtas (legislature). It also defines the structure and powers of the courts, sets out the fundamental rights of citizens, and contains a number of directive principles of social policy for the general guidance of the Oireachtas. The Constitution originally described the national territory "as the whole island of Ireland, its islands and the territorial seas." In 1998, as part of the *Good Friday Agreement, the Constitution was amended to define the Irish nation as the people of the island of Ireland (and its citizens abroad). It gave up the jurisdictional claim over the area constituting *Northern Ireland and asserted the will of the Irish nation to create a united Ireland, by consent and through peaceful means.

The Constitution, which may be amended only by referendum, outlines what are considered the fundamental rights of the citizen. The definition of rights in the Constitution covers five broad headings: personal rights, the family, *education, private property, and *religion.

In addition to the personal rights specifically provided for in the words of the Constitution, the courts have held that there are other personal or "Unenumerated Rights" which "result from the Christian and democratic nature of the State," and are implicitly guaranteed by the Constitution. Citizens, and in certain cases noncitizens, have the right to apply to the courts for constitutional protection and for a ruling on whether specific legislation is constitutional.

There have been twenty-seven amendments to the Constitution since 1937. The Constitution originally provided for a three-year transition period during which amendments could be made by the Oireachtas without a referendum. This was used twice: in 1939, on the eve of World War II, to alter the provisions on a state of emergency; and in 1941, to protect emergency legislation from being declared unconstitutional by the courts. The other amendments, all carried by referenda, are:

- 3rd (1973): to permit EEC (European Economic Community) membership
- 4th (1973): to lower the voting age from twenty-one to eighteen
- 5th (1973): to remove the "special position" of the Catholic Church from the Constitution
- 6th (1979): to protect adoption from court challenges
- 7th (1979): to allow more universities representation in Seanad Éireann (This has not so far been implemented.)
- 8th (1983): to prohibit abortion, specifically to guarantee "the equal right to life of the unborn" (This was interpreted in 1992 by the Supreme Court as allowing for abortion in certain limited circumstances.)
- 9th (1984): to allow noncitizens certain voting rights
- 10th (1987): to permit the ratification of amendments to the EC (European Community) Treaties (the Single European Act)
- 11th (1992): to permit the ratification of amendments to the EC Treaties (the Maastricht Treaty on European Union or EU)
- 12th (1992): to overturn a Supreme Court judgment allowing abortion where a pregnant woman was threatening suicide (It was defeated on the same day as the 13th and 14th were passed. The numbering was not, however, altered.)
- 13th (1992): to prohibit the courts from using the anti-abortion clause (the 8th amendment) in the Constitution to restrict the right of pregnant women to travel abroad (This arose following an injunction by the High Court—though later overturned on appeal—that prevented a pregnant fourteen-year-old victim of sexual assault from traveling to the UK for an abortion.)
- 14th (1992): to prohibit the courts from using the anti-abortion clause in the Constitution to restrict the publication of material informing people about abortion services in other jurisdictions
- 15th (1995): to permit divorce legislation (The original constitution had prohibited divorce.)
- 16th (1996): to authorize the courts to refuse bail
- 17th (1997): to guarantee cabinet confidentiality
- 18th (1998): to permit the ratification of amendments to the EU Treaties (the Amsterdam Treaty)
- 19th (1998): to introduce changes in the Constitution consistent with the *Belfast Agreement
- 20th (1999): to constitutionally guarantee a system of local government
- 21st (2001): to outlaw the death penalty in any circumstances
- 23rd (2001): to allow for the ratification of the proposed International Criminal Court
- 26th (2002): to permit the ratification of the EU Treaty of Nice

- 27th (2004): to remove the automatic right to Irish citizenship of persons born in Ireland if neither of the parents is an Irish citizen or qualifies for Irish citizenship.

(There are no 22nd, 24th and 25th amendments because the referenda on those issues were rejected or withdrawn.) (Web site: *www.irlgov.ie.*) J.D.

Coole Park. Estate near Gort, County *Galway, associated with the *Irish Literary Revival. Coole Park was the home of Lady (Augusta) *Gregory, the dramatist, folklorist, and translator. She married Sir William Gregory of Coole Park, and lived there after his death in 1892. W. B. *Yeats spent frequent holidays there from 1897, and he and Lady Gregory collected folklore in the surrounding countryside. In 1919 Yeats wrote the poem "The Wild Swans at Coole," and later, "Coole Park, 1929." J. M. *Synge, Edward *Martyn, and others also frequently visited the estate.

The three-story house was built around 1770, and there are woods, a river, and a lake on the estate. In 1927, the estate was sold to the Forestry Commission, and Lady Gregory was allowed to live there until her death. The house was demolished in 1941. Today Coole Park is open to the public as a wildlife park, with an indoor exhibition. The famous "Autograph Tree" can still be seen, bearing the carved initials of Yeats, Synge, Seán *O'Casey, George Bernard *Shaw, Douglas *Hyde, George *Russell (AE), and George *Moore. P.D.

Cork, County. Ireland's largest and most southerly county, in the province of *Munster. Stretching over 2,895 square miles, the county has a population of 448,181 (2002 census), of which 123,338 live in the county capital, Cork City. The name derives from *Corcaigh*, the marshy land where St. Finbarr founded his sixth-century monastery. The rivers Lee, Bandon, and Blackwater flow eastward to divide the county into three geographical areas dominated by various mountain ranges (Caha, Miskish, Boggeragh, and Nagles), some of which reach heights of over two thousand feet. The county's coastline is heavily indented with bays (such as Bantry, Dunmanus) and fine harbors (Cork and Kinsale). Cork City is a major port for international car ferries, freight, and occasional passenger liners, while Cobh (called Queenstown until 1922) was where most nineteenth-century Irish *emigrants boarded transatlantic ships to America. Ringaskiddy in Cork harbor is an important industrial center and Middleton farther east produces famous Irish whiskies. West Cork, with its spectacular seashore and gently rolling landscape, attracts many visitors.

In early times, Cork was part of Desmuma, the south Munster territory of the Eóganacht, dominated by the MacCarthys, who resisted the *Normans in the later Middle Ages. Cork's many medieval *castles include Blarney Castle, approximately five miles from Cork City. The word *blarney* has become synonymous with good-natured banter, repartee, flattery, or cajoling talk. According to one story, it was Queen *Elizabeth I (1533–1603) who first coined the term *blarney*, meaning "flattery," in a reference to the *Anglo-Irish aristocrat the Earl of Blarney whose home was Blarney Castle. In modern times, the Irish tourist industry has mythologized Blarney Castle: the legend goes that those who kiss "the Blarney stone," a particular spot of one of Blarney's parapet walls, will be endowed with the gift of eloquence, "the gift of the gab."

Cork was planted by Elizabethan English, including the poet Edmund *Spenser (c.1552–99), who wrote most of his poetic works, notably the allegorical epic *The Faerie Queene* (1590–96), in his Kilcolman Castle. Efforts to defeat the English with Spanish aid came to naught in 1601 at the Battle of *Kinsale—a town now known as the gourmet capital of Ireland.

Cork City, the third largest city in Ireland, built "on the banks of my own lovely Lee," in the words of the county's most famous song, has various industries such as *distilling, *brewing, oil refining, and pharmaceuticals. University College, Cork (UCC), founded in 1845 as Queen's University, is now (since 1909) a major constituent college of the National University of Ireland. Cork City is also a center of the visual arts. It is home to the Crawford Gallery, the Honan Chapel, with a fine collection of church furnishings (including stained glass windows), and Fota House, with its impressive array of paintings and an arboretum. The county has produced many distinguished artists, including the painters James *Barry, Daniel *Maclise, and Patrick *Scott. Many writers were born or lived in Cork, such as: Edith Oenone *Somerville, Lennox *Robinson, Elizabeth *Bowen, Seán *Ó Faoláin, Frank *O'Connor, William *Trevor, and the poet Seán *Ó Riordáin. Other distinguished Corkonians include the composer Seán *Ó Riada, the founders of two religious orders of *nuns, Nano *Nagle and Mary Aikenhead, the *nationalist Thomas *Davis, the *Fenian John O'Mahoney, the revolutionary Michael *Collins, and Taoiseach (prime minister) Jack *Lynch. P.H.

Corkery, Daniel (1878–1964). *Nationalist writer and teacher. Born in Cork City, Corkery was educated there at the Presentation Brothers' secondary school, and at St. Patrick's College, *Dublin. After returning to Cork to teach, he became involved in the *Irish Language Revival and joined both the *Gaelic League and *Sinn Féin. With his close friends Terence *MacSwiney and Con O'Leary, Corkery founded the Cork Dramatic Society, for which he wrote plays in both the English and Irish languages. A prolific and lifelong writer, Corkery contributed to the *Leader* newspaper and wrote many excellent short stories, plays, and one of Ireland's best novels, *The Threshold of Quiet* (1917). His work consistently stressed the importance of respecting Irish traditions that he believed had been slighted and neglected by elitist elements within the *Irish Literary Revival movement. Corkery had a tremendous influence on the intellectual and literary development of some of Cork's brightest young minds, such as Seán *Ó Faoláin and Frank *O'Connor. Following the *Anglo-Irish War and the *Civil War, Corkery's ultra–*republican cultural nationalism became bitter and exclusive. He rejected most of the work of the Literary Revival, (J. M. *Synge being somewhat of an exception) as merely provincial English writing, and insisted that true *Irish literature must reflect public involvement in land, religion, and nationalism, and, hopefully, find expression in the *Irish language. These opinions pervaded his best-known books *The Hidden Ireland* (1924) and *Synge and Anglo-Irish Literature* (1931). Corkery's narrow view of Irishness attracted considerable support but alienated Ó Faoláin and O'Connor, who argued for a more inclusive definition of nationality. L.J.MC.

Corrigan-Maguire, Máiréad (1944–), Cofounder of the Peace Movement in *Northern Ireland in 1976. Born in *Belfast, Corrigan-Maguire founded the Peace Movement with Betty Williams in response to the deaths of three of her sister's children, who were killed on August 10, 1976. The children were struck by a runaway car driven by an IRA (*Irish Republican Army) volunteer who had been

W. T. Cosgrave and Mrs. Cosgrave

shot dead by the British army. The movement was later renamed the Community of Peace People. Corrigan and Williams, as representatives of the Peace Movement, received the 1976 Nobel Prize for Peace (awarded in October 1977). C.D.

Corrs, the. Music group. The Corrs are a family pop band from Dundalk, County *Louth, consisting of Andrea, Caroline, Jim, and Sharon Corr. They combine pop, folk, and *dance with traditional Irish *music and good looks. The US Ambassador to Ireland, Jean Kennedy Smith, spotted them in a small *Dublin club and invited them to play at the World Cup celebrations in Boston in 1994. This attracted the attention of Atlantic Records, and their debut album *Forgiven not Forgotten* was released in 1995. It sold over two million copies and a second album, *Talk on Corners*, was released in 1997. Their album, *In Blue*, came out in 2000, and *Borrowed Heaven* in 2004. B.D.

Cosgrave, Liam (1920–). *Fine Gael leader and *Taoiseach (prime minister). Son of W. T. *Cosgrave, the first leader of the *Irish Free State, Cosgrave was elected to the *Dáil (Parliament) in 1943. In 1955 as minister for external affairs, he supervised Ireland's entry into the *United Nations. He succeeded James *Dillon as Fine Gael leader in 1965. Cosgrave became Taoiseach and leader of a National Coalition government in 1973 and played an important role at the *Sunningdale Conference. Following the government defeat in the 1977 general election, he resigned as Fine Gael leader. He retired from politics in 1981. P.E.

Cosgrave, William Thomas (1880–1965). First president of the executive council of the *Irish Free State. Born in *Dublin, Cosgrave joined *Sinn Féin in 1905 and was elected to municipal government in Dublin in 1909. He was sentenced to death for his part in the 1916 *Easter Rising, but the sentence was commuted. A member of the First *Dáil (Parliament), he supported the *Anglo-Irish Treaty of 1921 and became chairman of the Provisional Government after the deaths of Michael *Collins and Arthur *Griffith in 1922.

From December 1922 until March 1932, he was the president of the executive council of the Irish Free State. In 1923, at the end of the *Civil War, he founded *Cumann na nGaedheal. A cautious and conservative politician, he successfully led the Free State during the Civil War, and is credited with establishing stable parliamentary democracy in Ireland.

Following defeats in the 1932 and 1933 general elections, Cumann na nGaedheal merged with the Centre Party and the *Blueshirts in 1933 to form *Fine Gael under the control of Eoin *O'Duffy. Within a year, O'Duffy resigned and Cosgrave took over as party leader until his retirement in 1944. P.E.

Costello, John A. (1891–1976). Lawyer, politician, and *Taoiseach (prime minister). Costello was born in *Dublin and took part in the *Easter Rising of 1916. From 1926 to 1932, he was attorney general of the *Irish Free State and its delegate to the League of Nations. He served as Taoiseach from 1948 to 1951, and again from 1954 to 1957 in coalition with other minority parties in what are known as the first and second interparty governments. During his first term, the *Republic of Ireland Act (1948) was passed. P.E.

Coulter, Phil (1942–). Songwriter. Born in *Derry, Coulter studied music at Queen's University, *Belfast. In London, he teamed up with Bill Martin and wrote "Puppet on a String," which won the 1967 Eurovision International Song Contest, as well as "Congratulations," which was the Eurovision runner-up in 1968. In the seventies, he produced albums with *Planxty and wrote the song "The Town I Loved So Well." Since the eighties, he has concentrated on easy-listening music and in 1997 became a visiting professor at Boston College. Major appearances include four sell-out concerts at Carnegie Hall and an outdoor performance on Capitol Hill, Washington, with the National Symphony Orchestra before an audience of six hundred thousand people. P.E.

Council of Europe. European international organization, established on May 5, 1949. Ireland was one of the ten founding member states of the Council of Europe. There are now forty-one members. Established in the aftermath of World War II, the council sought to secure peace and prosperity, through reconciliation and cooperation between states. The organization was the first to introduce enforceable human rights standards into international law, through the European Convention on Human Rights. The council created the European Court of Human Rights to enforce these standards. Today, the Council of Europe is primarily concerned with the protection of human rights, the spread of pluralist democracy, and the rule of law. It opposes discrimination against minorities, xenophobia, racism, and drug abuse, and seeks to promote Europe's cultural heritage in all its diversity. J.D.

Craig, James First Viscount Craigavon (1871–1940). Politician, prime minister of *Northern Ireland, 1921–40. Born in *Belfast to a wealthy distiller and farm owner, Craig became *Unionist MP (member of *Parliament) for East Down in 1906. During the third *home rule crisis (1911–14), he was Edward *Carson's right-hand man, enjoying a familiarity with *Ulster that Carson lacked. Craig succeeded Carson as leader of the *Ulster Unionist Party (UUP) in February 1921 and became prime minister of the new devolved government in Belfast in June 1921. To consolidate the state's security, Craig organized the almost wholly *Protestant Ulster Special Constabulary. Concerned with preserving unionist hegemony, he redrew electoral districts and abolished *proportional representation in elections to the devolved Parliament in 1929. Though he claimed that he was anxious not to egregiously oppress the *Catholic *nationalist community, he did admit in 1934 that "We are a Protestant parliament and a Protestant people." Increasingly inattentive to duties, he died in 1940 while still in office. M.M.

crannógs. Man-made, usually circular, lake islands. They consist of piles of stones as a foundation, covered by brushwood and earth, and with palisades enclosing one or more houses. Modern examples at Craggaunowen (County *Clare) and the National Heritage Park at Ferrycarrig (County *Wexford) show what crannógs would originally have looked like. Probably Bronze Age in origin, crannógs were still used in Ireland as late as the 1600s. P.H.

Croagh Patrick. Mountain in *Mayo (near Westport), where St. *Patrick is said to have fasted for forty days to obtain the right to judge the Irish people on Judgment Day. A popular annual *pilgrimage is made to the summit on the last Sunday in July, probably a Christian version of an earlier, pagan Lughnasa Festival. Prehistoric monuments and an oratory (c.490–880) have been found here. P.H.

Croke Park. The national headquarters of the *Gaelic Athletic Association (GAA), located in *Dublin's north inner city. It is named after Archbishop John Croke, first patron of the GAA, and was acquired by the association in 1911. The major games of *hurling and *Gaelic football are played there, notably the annual All-Ireland finals in September. In November 1920, on what became known as *Bloody Sunday, British forces killed twelve people during a football game between Dublin and Tipperary. The park was reconstructed in 2002 as a bowl stadium with an all seated capacity of 79,500. (Web site: *www.gaa.ie.*) K.W.

Cromwell, Oliver (1599–1658). De facto head of the English parliamentary regime in the late 1640s and, from 1653, lord protector. Cromwell landed in Ireland on August 15, 1649, and from then until his return to England on May 29, 1650, he seized the south and east of Ireland from an Irish Catholic/Royalist alliance in a lightning campaign. He was, claims Denis Murphy's *Cromwell in Ireland* (1883), "a great, bad man." "Great" in, for example, the tempo and decisiveness of his siege operations which, apart from his botched storm of Clonmel, County *Tipperary, enhanced his already formidable reputation as a military leader. "Bad" in that he was cast as the principal personification of English violence in Ireland for atrocities associated with the storming of Drogheda, County *Louth, and *Wexford. The better-documented events at Drogheda show that there was no whole-scale massacre of troops and townspeople. However, royalist troops at the Millmount surrendered, apparently, on promise of quarter and were subsequently killed.

Eyewitness testimony of Thomas Wood, a *Cromwellian soldier, suggests that an unquantifiable number of women and children were killed in and around St. Peter's Church. This severity was exceptional in the context of the English Civil Wars, though not by the grimmer standards of the Thirty Years War in central Europe. The same might be said for the killing of two thousand soldiers and civilians at Wexford and, specifically, the massacre of civilians congregated at the Bull Ring.

Cromwell might better be judged by the fact that, in contrast to his conflict with the Scots, in Ireland he was motivated by religious and ethnic hatred. He had made his unremitting hostility to *Catholicism abundantly clear: "I meddle not with any man's conscience. But if by liberty of conscience you mean liberty to exercise the mass . . . that will not be allowed of." In particular, he was driven by the conviction that Irish Catholics shared a collective blood-guilt for atrocities against *Protestant settlers in the *Rebellion of 1641 and therefore insisted on a punitive postwar settlement. This insistence prolonged (1649–53) and intensified the human suffering and destruction of the reconquest. Henry Cromwell, the son of Oliver Cromwell, served as governor in Ireland (1655–59). He tried to broaden the base of his support beyond the religious zealots and the army to encompass the "Old Protestant," or pre-1640 settler, interest. This involved veering toward an Episcopalian Church settlement and abandoning proposals of whole-scale transplantation of the Catholic Irish to *Connacht. Henry Cromwell was one of those who personified the "kingship" party that advocated a more durable and generally acceptable constitutional settlement in England and Ireland. To counter this threat, the Long Parliament, abolished by Oliver Cromwell and reinstated after his death, dismissed Henry Cromwell from the lord deputyship in June 1659. P.L.

Cromwellian Settlement, the. Confiscation of land of Irish *Catholics in retribution for the *Rebellion of 1641, laying the foundations of long-term *Protestant ascendancy. The preamble of the 1652 Act for the Settlement of Ireland disavowed any intent to extirpate "the entire nation," and the act concentrated on punishing Irish Catholic landowners according to their "respective demerits." "Delinquency" encompassed not only those landowners who held high military or civil office in the confederate Catholic and, later, royalist regimes, but also those who had simply stayed at home and paid taxes.

The scheme of forfeiture envisaged the landowner surrendering his entire estate and transplanting to the reserved part of *Connacht, chosen for its remoteness. There he would, in theory, acquire lands equivalent to a proportion (the proportion varied according to his delinquency) of his original estate. In the ensuing scramble, most landowners did not actually acquire any lands in Connacht. The beneficiaries of the confiscation were "Adventurers" who had lent money to finance the reconquest a decade before, and soldiers who received their back pay in land grants. As land was the basis of social and economic power, the Cromwellian Settlement represented a profound and irreversible disempowerment. Before the war of 1641–52, Catholics owned about 60 percent of Irish land; by the 1660s (even after limited adjustments by Charles II) they owned only about 20 percent.

Even more radical schemes of "ethnic cleansing" and mass transplantation to Connacht were seriously advocated and justified by the charge that Catholics shared a collective blood-guilt for the massacre of Protestants in the 1641 *Rebellion. The expression "To Hell or to Connacht," which has been attributed to Cromwell, summarizes his attitude to the fate of the dispossessed Irish. In the words of one of its advocates, Richard Lawrence, Ireland was, or soon would be, "an empty prepared hive to receive its swarms" of English settlers making them "equal or more considerable than the Irish." Ultimately, in the absence of sufficient immigration, the government tacitly accepted that the mass of the rural population (as opposed to those living in larger urban centers) would not be uprooted.

The Cromwellian regime smashed the institutional fabric of the Catholic Church but was notably unsuccessful in converting the Irish to Protestantism. In part this was due to sectarian divisions within Protestantism but also, apparently, through despair that Irish Catholics were unregenerate. P.L.

Cronin, Anthony (1926–). Poet, critic, and novelist. Born in Enniscorthy, County *Wexford, and educated at University College, Dublin, Cronin was appointed cultural advisor to the *Taoiseach (prime minister) Charles J. *Haughey in 1980. He created *Aosdána, an affiliation of Irish artists, in 1983. *Dead As Doornails* (1976), a memoir of the literary scene in 1950s *Dublin, has perhaps been Cronin's most successful work. His style is analytical, often ironic, always scholarly. As a columnist with the *Irish Times* (1976–80 and 1983–87), he earned a reputation as a debunker of myths and hard-hitting critic of Irish political and social affairs. A selection of his writings for the *Irish Times* newspaper was published as *An Irish Eye* (1985). Other works include *The Life of Riley* (1964), a comic novel; *The End of the Modern World* (1989) and *Relationships* (1992), both volumes of poetry; *A Question of Modernity* (1966), a critique of the work of James *Joyce; *No Laughing Matter* (1989), a biography of Flann *O'Brien; and *Samuel Beckett: The Last Modernist* (1996). C.D.

Cross of Cong. Elegant processional cross, dating from circa 1125. The cross was commissioned by the High King Turlough O'Connor to house a relic of the True Cross, which was covered by a rock crystal at the center of one side. The shaft and undulating arms are decorated with ornamental glass studs and panels bearing animal interlace typical of the Irish variant of the Scandinavian Urnes style. Arguably the finest piece of Irish twelfth-century metalwork, the cross was probably made in a *Roscommon workshop. It is now on display in the *National Museum of Ireland. P.H.

Cross, Dorothy (1956–). Installation artist and printmaker. Born in *Cork, Cross studied in Cork, Leicester, Amsterdam, and San Francisco. Using found objects and photography, she explores psychoanalytic issues of identity, gender, and authority. She represented Ireland at the Venice Biennale in 1993. M.C.

crosses, high. Tall stone crosses with decorative carving. High crosses are Ireland's greatest contribution to European sculpture of the first millennium. These crosses were erected at monasteries to edify and teach both monks and laity through biblical representations carved on many of them. High kings helped commission them from the ninth to the twelfth century. Fine examples are found at Moone (County *Kildare), Monasterboice (County *Louth), *Kells (County *Meath), *Clonmacnoise (County *Offaly) and *Cashel (County *Tipperary). P.H.

Cruise O'Brien, Conor (1917–). Diplomat, politician, and man of letters. Born in *Dublin and educated at Trinity College, Cruise O'Brien worked at the Department of External Affairs from 1944. Among his varied writings are literary criticism

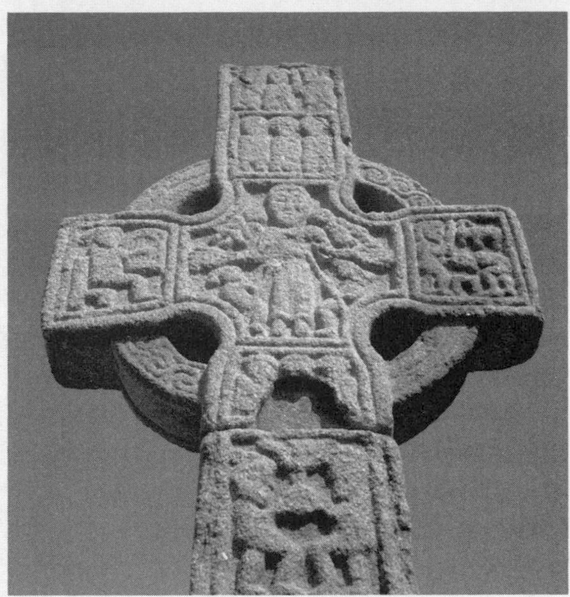

The North Cross, Castledermot, County Kildare

(often under the pseudonym Donat O'Donnell), a study of the *Parnell era, *Parnell and His Party* (1957), and an appreciative analysis of Israel and Zionism, *The Siege* (1986). From 1956 to 1961, he was a member of the Irish delegation to the *United Nations. In 1961, he was part of the UN mission in the newly independent Congo, but resigned in protest against deference to Western interests. From 1962 to 1965, he was vice chancellor of the University of Ghana and from 1965 to 1969 held a chair at New York University (where he actively agitated against American Vietnam policy). In 1969, as a member of the *Labour Party, Cruise O'Brien was elected to *Dáil Éireann (Irish Parliament) for Dublin Northeast. He was minister for posts and telegraphs in the 1973–77 coalition government. His book, *States of Ireland* (1972) appreciated the position of the *unionists and condemned *nationalist irredentism. He sat in the *Seanad (senate) for Trinity College from 1977 to 1981. His 1992 book *The Great Melody* is a sympathetic study of Edmund *Burke. His newspaper columns interpreted the recent *Northern Ireland *peace process as appeasement of *Sinn Féin and the IRA (*Irish Republican Army). In the 1990s he joined the independent UK Unionist Party. He is married to Máire *Mhac an tSaoi, the *Irish-language poet. J.P.MC.

Cúchulainn. One of the best-known Irish *mythological figures. In the legend, a smith named Culann was hosting a party for the high king of *Ulster, Conchubhar Mac Neasa. The king had forgotten to tell Culann that a boy, Setanta, would be joining them later, and Culann unleashed his famous hound to guard the house. On his arrival, Setanta was attacked by the hound, and to defend himself he threw a *sliotar*, or *hurling ball, into the dog's throat, killing it instantly. Culann was angry at the death of his favorite hound but Conchubhar decreed that Setanta would take its place, thus earning the name Cúchulainn—or Culann's hound. Cúchulainn is also famous for his single-handed defense of Ulster against the army of Maeve, queen of Connacht, which culminated in the slaying of his best friend Ferdia. He was eventually killed by his enemies when he spurned the attentions of Mór-Ríoghain, the goddess of war.

Following the publication of Standish *O'Grady's *History of Ireland: Cuculain and his Contemporaries* (1880), Cúchulainn became a symbol of heroism for many Irish nationalists and writers, including Patrick *Pearse, W. B. *Yeats, and James *Stephens. A bronze statue of Cúchulainn by Oliver *Sheppard was installed in the GPO (General Post Office) in *Dublin to commemorate the *Easter Rising. B.D.

Cullen, Cardinal Paul (1803–78). *Catholic ecclesiastic. Born in County *Kildare, Cullen served as rector in the Irish college in Rome, before being appointed archbishop of *Armagh in 1849. He was subsequently appointed archbishop of *Dublin, where he remained until his death. Cullen was a moderate *nationalist, whose main concern was to strengthen and advance the position of the Roman Catholic Church in Ireland. A staunch advocate of denominational *education, he was responsible for the Synod of Thurles's (1850) condemnation of the Queen's Colleges, which had been established as secular *universities by Sir Robert Peel in 1848. Cullen launched a devotional revolution that dramatically changed the nature of Catholicism in Ireland and throughout the diaspora. His conservative Catholicism and his commitment to centralized authority and discipline within the Church proved lastingly influential. A.S.

Cullen, Shane (1957–). Painter. Born in County *Longford, Cullen has had exhibitions in Ireland, Europe, and the United States. His *Fragments sur les Institutions Republicaines IV* reproduces the messages smuggled out of *Belfast prison by *hunger strikers in the 1980s. M.C.

Cumann na mBan. *Nationalist league of *women. Cumann na mBan (Irish for the League of Women) was set up in 1914 as a female auxiliary to the Irish *Volunteers. It absorbed Inghinidhe na hEireann (Daughters of Ireland), the women's nationalist organization founded in 1900. When the Volunteers split on whether or not to fight for Britain in *World War I later that year, the majority of Cumann na mBan members voted to side with the smaller group of volunteers who opposed fighting and whose motto was "we serve neither king nor kaiser, but Ireland." Women in Cumann na mBan were trained in first aid, signaling, dispatch riding, and other auxiliary roles, but were not allowed in combat. They served in all but one of the 1916 *Easter Rising revolutionary locales, and it was a Cumann na mBan member, Elizabeth O'Farrell, a hospital midwife, who delivered the surrender. O'Farrell, a white-collar, professional worker, was a typical Cumann member, though some factory workers were involved in Cumann na mBan as well.

After the rising, the Cumann became involved mainly in keeping the memories of the rising alive, raising money for prisoners, holding meetings and other commemorative events, and electioneering in the 1918 general election, at which *Sinn Féin won its famous victory. In the *War of Independence, 1919–21, Cumann members helped to run *Dáil (Parliament) courts and local authorities, and produced the *nationalist newspaper the *Irish Bulletin*. Most members opposed the *Anglo-Irish Treaty (1921), and at least four hundred Cumann na mBan members were imprisoned during the *Civil War. It was Cumann na mBan that conceived the Easter Lily as a commemorative symbol in 1926. In the 1930s, Cumann na mBan was active on the left wing of the *republican movement, but would never again achieve the prominence or the level of activism that it had attained in the years 1914–23. C.C.

Cumann na nGaedheal. *Political party. Launched in April 1923, Cumann na nGaedheal (Party of the Irish) formed the governments of the *Irish Free State until 1932. *Sinn Féin members who supported the *Anglo-Irish Treaty founded the party and William T. *Cosgrave, the first president of the executive council of the Free State government, became the party's first and only leader.

Cumann na nGaedheal's national organization never attracted the levels of popular participation that characterized Sinn Féin, and later, *Fianna Fáil. Its local leaders tended to be prominent businessmen, members of the professions, and large farmers.

Its popular support at elections derived largely from its achievements in setting up the new state, and fear of renewed civil war. The party consistently defended the treaty settlement and after the *Civil War introduced harsh legislation to deal with continued IRA (*Irish Republican Army) activity, including a severe Public Safety Act which followed the assassination of the party's minister for justice, Kevin *O'Higgins, in 1927.

As the party of law and order, Cumann na nGaedheal attracted the support of merchants and shopkeepers, and it was closely identified with larger farmers and the cattle trade. The export trade to Britain formed the basis of its economic policy. Although it founded several semistate companies, the party was little concerned with industrialization, and was ideologically opposed to state intervention to improve conditions for the working class or urban poor.

In the first post–Civil War general election in August 1923, Cumann na nGaedheal received 39 percent of the vote. It never surpassed this level of support. It remained in government when Fianna Fáil entered the *Dáil (Parliament) in August 1927. Fianna Fáil defeated the party in the general election of February 1932, and in the January 1933 election Cumann na nGaedheal support fell again. The party then merged with other conservative groups, the National Centre Party and the National Guard (the *Blueshirts), to form the *Fine Gael party in September 1933. P.D.

currach. Boat with light wooden frame of laths, covered formerly with leather but now with canvas and tar. Currachs are found in varying designs along the coasts of Ireland. Though the oars are narrow and featherless at the end, currachs are very fast and maneuverable, and ride high on the waves, as seen in Robert O'Flaherty's film *Man of Aran* (1934). It was probably in such a currach that St. *Brendan set off on his famous voyage. In 1976/77, Tim Severin used a large modern example with sail—the *Brendan*, now displayed at Craggaunowen, County *Clare—to show that the saint could have reached America in such a craft. (In Kerry and the southwest, the Irish word for Currach is *naomhóg* (meaning "a saint's boat"). P.H.

Curragh Mutiny, the (1914). Military protest during the *home rule crisis of 1914. When the *Ulster Volunteer Force (UVF) threatened armed resistance to home rule, the government considered deploying troops in the province. The British commander in chief in Ireland, General Sir Arthur Paget, agreed that officers from *Ulster could "disappear" during the operation, but no other officers, even those with Irish connections, were given such choice. In March 1914, at the Curragh military camp, County *Kildare, sixty cavalry officers, led by Brigadier General Hubert Gough, offered their resignations rather than "move against Ulster." The War Office refused to accept the resignations. The men were assured by the secretary of state for war and the chief of the imperial general staff that there was no intention of using troops in Ulster. Both these officials were forced to resign when the Prime Minister Herbert *Asquith rejected the assurance. However, because of fear of an army crisis, the plan was abandoned. T.C.

Cusack, Cyril James (1910–93). Actor. Born in Kentani, Kenya, Cusack arrived in Ireland as a young boy, where he played children's parts in melodramas performed by his stepfather's traveling theater company. Educated at University College, Dublin, Cusack performed in most major theaters in Ireland and Britain, including the *Abbey Theatre and the *Gate in Dublin, the Royal Shakespeare Company, and the English National Theatre. With his own theater company, which specialized in classical and Irish theater (including *Shaw, *Beckett, and *Synge), and which engaged actors like Siobhán *McKenna and Jack *MacGowran, he toured in Ireland and elsewhere. His film career began with a childhood role in *Knocknagow* in 1917 and ended in 1990 in *My Left Foot*. Other films include *Odd Man Out* (1947), *Shake Hands with the Devil* (1959), *Sacco and Vanzetti* (1974), and *True Confessions* (1981). C.D.

Cusack, Sinead (1948–). Actress. Born in Dalkey, County *Dublin, Sinead, like her younger sisters Niamh and Sorcha, followed her father Cyril *Cusack into the acting profession. She began her career at the *Abbey Theatre, Dublin, and subsequently appeared in numerous television productions and feature films, including *Hoffman* (1970) and *Stealing Beauty* (1996). However, Sinead Cusack is best known for her work as a classical actor with the Royal Shakespeare Company (RSC). Nominated for a Tony Award in 1984, she received the *Evening Standard* Award for Best Actress in 1998 for her portrayal of Mai in Sebastian *Barry's *Our Lady of Sligo* at the National Theatre in London. In 2002, she played the role of Cleopatra in the RSC production of Shakespeare's *Antony and Cleopatra*. In 1978, she married fellow actor Jeremy Irons, with whom she has two sons. S.A.B.

D

Dáil Éireann. Irish Parliament. Derived from the Old Irish word meaning an assembly, Dáil has, in modern times, been used to describe the Irish House of Representatives, that is, the lower house. The Dáil, together with the Senate, or *Seanad Éireann, and the president, make up the *Oireachtas. The first Dáil Éireann (Assembly of Ireland) was a controversial and revolutionary body, which first met in the Mansion House, Dublin, on January 21, 1919. It was convened by the *Sinn Féin party following their overwhelming victory in the historic general election of December 1918, at the end of *World War I. Sinn Féin won 73 of the 105 seats allocated at that time to Ireland in the British Parliament. In keeping with party policy since its foundation in 1905, Sinn Féin refused to take its seats at Westminster. Instead, they called an assembly of all elected Irish representatives to an All-Ireland Parliament, Dáil Éireann, and declared Ireland an independent republic.

Dáil Éireann continued to operate underground during the *War of Independence (1919–21), establishing Sinn Féin courts as alternatives to the British system, and winning the support of the people and local authorities, who gave their loyalty and revenue to the Sinn Féin minister for local government, W. T. *Cosgrave. Michael *Collins as minister for finance raised a national loan, while the *Volunteers, now known as the *Irish Republican Army (IRA) pledged to defend the republic. IRA Chief of Staff Richard *Mulcahy reported to the defense minister, Cathal *Brugha. After the *Anglo-Irish Treaty (1921), the new twenty-six-county Parliament was also called Dáil Éireann. It came together in *Leinster House on September 9, 1922, during the *Civil War, but it was boycotted by Éamon *de Valera and his Sinn Féin anti-treaty republicans, because TDs (Teachta Dála; member of Parliament) had to take an *oath of allegiance to the British monarch in order to participate. In 1926, de Valera and some of his anti-treaty supporters founded *Fianna Fáil, a new *republican party, and entered the Dáil in August 1927, maintaining the oath was merely "an empty political formula."

The roles and functions of the modern Dáil Éireann, as the elected House of Representatives of the Oireachtas are set out in the *Constitution of 1937. All citizens aged eighteen or over (the age limit was twenty-one until 1974) in the twenty-six counties are entitled to vote and to contest elections. Elections take place in multiseat constituencies (there are forty-two at present) consisting of three, four, and five seats. Each Teachta Dála or TD (member of Parliament) represents twenty to thirty thousand of the population and constituencies are redrawn at intervals of not longer than twelve years. There are currently 166 members in Dáil Éireann—up from 138 in the 1940s, and up to 50 of these are from the greater *Dublin area, in line with population trends.

TDs are elected by a system of *proportional representation that gives each citizen a single transferable vote. This system favors the smaller parties and makes single-party government difficult, but it is also very fair to minorities. The Constitution (Article 16.5.0) limits the Dáil to a maximum period of seven years, but current legislation imposes a five-year limit. The chair/speaker of the Dáil is called the Ceann Comhairle and is automatically included as a TD in any new Dáil. Under the 1937 Constitution, the Irish government is responsible to Dáil Éireann alone, and the *Taoiseach (prime minister), as head of the government must be able to command a majority of the House. The Taoiseach can dissolve the Dáil at any time by submitting his resignation, and that of the government, to the president. The president can exercise one of the few real political powers open to him/her (Article 13.2.2) and may, in his/her absolute discretion, refuse to dissolve the Dáil. If, however, the resignations are accepted, a general election will follow. The right to amend or initiate bills, in the Upper House, or Seanad Éireann, does not extend to money bills, which are exclusively the domain of the Dáil.

Dáil Éireann (and Seanad Éireann) have been televised since 1990, and the televising of committees began in 1993. The Irish Parliament remains predominantly English-speaking, although simultaneous translation services were provided over two decades ago. *Leinster House, aquired by the new *Irish Free State in 1924, has been the seat of both Dáil Éireann and Seanad Éireann ever since. N.ÓG.

dance. Dance in Ireland has been divided between participatory traditional dance and theater dance, with a few crossovers between the two. As theater dance developed in Ireland, it sought to draw on the rich heritage of traditional dance. *Riverdance is the most popular example of merging *step-dancing tradition with theatricality. *Set- and step-dancing reached their height in the nineteenth and early twentieth centuries, but received a setback with the Public Dance Halls Act of 1935, which required that all dances be licensed and operate under strict supervision, prohibiting informal dancing in private houses or in public. Today, traditional dance is largely competition-based and is overseen by the Irish Dancing Commission (An Coimisiún le Rincí Gaelacha) and the Organisation for Irish Dance (An Cómhgháil le Rincí Gaelacha). However, a revival of set-dancing in the 1980s has led to increased participation at the social level.

Performance dance developed within the theater as part of drama productions. John Ogilby (1600–76), who established the Theatre Royal, Smock Alley, in Dublin, was a dancing master who first came to Ireland to instruct the children of the lord lieutenant, the Earl of Stafford. Ogilby's dances for Smock Alley were character dances as part of plays. *Pompey* (1663) featured "an Antick dance of Gypsies," "a Military Dance," and "a Grand Masque."

Theatrical productions continued to provide the only outlet for dance performance, and it was not until William Butler *Yeats appointed Ninette de Valois (1898–1998) to establish the Abbey School of Dance that dance was affirmed outside of drama. As well as providing the dance sequences for the plays at the *Abbey Theatre, de Valois also created dance works such as "Faun" and "The Drinking Horn."

In 1947, Joan Denise Moriarty (1920–92) formed the Cork City Ballet, an amateur company that performed annually with the Cork Symphony Orchestra. Its repertoire ranged from short dances to single acts of classical repertoire to original works. Moriarty worked with Irish composers such as Aloys Fleischmann (1910–92) and visiting guest artists, such as Anton Dolin (1906–83) and Marina Svetlova (1922–). Cork City Ballet's success led to the creation of the professional Irish Theatre Ballet in 1959, which disbanded in 1964 after an unsuccessful merger with the Dublin-based National Ballet. In 1973, Moriarty formed another Cork-based company, the Irish Ballet Company, which ten years later became the Irish National Ballet. Throughout her career, Moriarty explored merging dance styles and collaborated with composer Seán* Ó Riada (1931–71), who was pioneering the use of traditional music within classical musical forms, to create *West Cork Ballet* (1961) and *Billy the Music* (1974). Her most successful work was *The Playboy of the Western World* (1977), set to music by the *Chieftains.

Dance entered cultural consciousness as the century progressed, and when a national *television network (Telefís Éireann) was launched on January 1, 1960, the opening ceremony featured a dance, set in Dublin Airport in front of a new Boeing plane. Irish Theatre Ballet appeared on national television on three occasions, and in 1966, Cork City Ballet recorded thirteen dance programs called *An Dambsa*.

The national folk theater *Siamsa Tíre was founded by Father Pat Ahern in 1974 and for many years led the way in mixing folk dance styles with theater. Dublin Contemporary Dance Theatre emerged in 1979, performing a repertory of contemporary dance. However, in 1989, the Arts Council withdrew funding to the company and to Moriarty's Irish National Ballet. Most companies now work in the contemporary idiom, and the most prominent are the Irish Modern Dance Theatre, the Dance Theatre of Ireland, Daghdha, and Coiscéim. M.S.

Darcy, Patrick (1598–1668). Politician. Born in *Galway into an Old English family, Darcy was elected MP (member of Parliament) for Navan in 1634. A gifted lawyer and skilled negotiator, he played a prominent part in the *Confederation of Kilkenny. The central contention of his treatise *An Argument Delivered* (1643) was that no legislation should have effect in Ireland without first being ratified by an Irish *parliament. This argument exercised a major influence over subsequent Irish constitutional thinkers, notably William *Molyneux, George *Berkeley, and Jonathan *Swift. A.S.

Davis, Thomas Osborne (1814–45). Writer and cultural *nationalist. Born in Mallow, County *Cork, where his father was a doctor in the British army, Davis was educated at Trinity College, Dublin, and was called to the bar in 1837. He first attracted attention in 1839 in a famous speech in Trinity to the Dublin Historical Society, in which he made a forceful case for the study of Irish history as a means of preserving Irish national identity. With Gavan *Duffy and John Blake *Dillon, Davis founded the **Nation* newspaper in 1842, which published scores of essays concerning the *Irish language, *literature, history, and *music, by a group of Romantic writers known collectively as *Young Ireland. Sincere and charismatic, Davis became the group's principal figure, emphasizing Irish cultural self-reliance and political unity. His plea that Irish writers and artists create works that would be "racy of the soil" inspired intellectuals of his generation and helped launch the *Irish Revival (also known as Celtic Revival).

In politics, Davis was a *Repealer and an admirer of Daniel *O'Connell, but the Liberator's retreat from Repeal after 1843 disappointed Davis and Young Ireland's political activists, who were impatient with, and critical of, O'Connell's constitutional methods. Religious tensions also affected his relationship with O'Connell, whose rabid *Catholic supporters attacked Davis's ecumenical spirit and support for nondenominational *university *education.

Davis died suddenly from an attack of scarlet fever in September 1845. His influence on cultural nationalists persisted long after his death. His inspirational works were continually reprinted in nationalist journals and other publications. His ballads "A Nation Once Again" and "The West's Awake" remain popular to this day. L.MB.

Davitt, Michael (1846–1906). *Nationalist, *socialist, founder of the *Land League. Davitt was born in Straide, County *Mayo, to small-tenant farmers. In 1850, his family was evicted for nonpayment of rent. They moved to England, where in 1857, at age eleven, Davitt lost his right arm in an accident while working in a cotton mill. Unable to work, he attended the local Wesleyan school and the Mechanics' Institute, where he became influenced by the ideas of the Chartist movement.

Davitt joined the *Fenians in 1865, and in May 1870, he was arrested in London on suspicion of gunrunning. He received a fifteen-year sentence and served over seven years in very difficult conditions in Dartmoor Prison before being released in December 1877.

After a brief visit to Ireland where he was appalled by the conditions of tenant farmers in County Mayo, he traveled to America to visit his family (who had moved there in 1870). In the United States, he met John *Devoy, the Fenian leader of *Clan na Gael. Along with Charles *Parnell and Devoy, Davitt was one of the architects of the "New Departure," whereby constitutional nationalists, Fenians, and land agitators agreed to work together toward achieving agrarian reform. In 1879, Davitt established the Land League with Parnell as president to end evictions and reform the system of land ownership in Ireland. Influenced by the ideas of Henry George, the American single-tax socialist, Davitt, however, distanced himself from the struggle for general agrarian reform and peasant proprietorship preferring, instead, land nationalization. This idea never gained popular support and eventually led to his falling out with Parnell.

Davitt was elected on four separate occasions to the Westminster Parliament where he sided with the anti-Parnellities. In Parliament, he campaigned tirelessly for social reform and for an end to the *Boer War.

Davitt was also a prolific journalist and writer, whose first book, *Leaves from a Prison Diary*, was published in 1885. Other works include *Within the Pale* (1903), dealing with anti-Semitism in Russia, and *The Fall of Feudalism in Ireland* (1904). In 1890, Davitt set up and edited his own socialist newspaper *Labour World*. He died in Dublin on May 30, 1906, and is buried in Straide, County Mayo. P.N., P.E.

Davitt, Michael (1950–). Poet in the *Irish language and literary activist. Davitt was the main force behind the new Irish poetry that started with the journal *Innti* in 1970. This movement superseded the Irish obsession with tradition as a closed system and tapped into the international rock and pop culture of the 1960s and 1970s. With wit and panache, Davitt organized poetry readings as if they were pop concerts. A formidable performer himself, Davitt wrote poetry that ranges from the deeply felt lyric to the funny, clever, and dramatic. His mixture of the serious and the less solemn is characteristically Irish. His collections include *Gleann ar Ghleann* (Valley on Valley; 1982) and *An Tost a Scagadh* (Silence to Sift; 1983). Translations of his work are found in *The Bright Wave (An Tonn Gheal;* 1986), *The Field Day Anthology* (1992), and *Freacnairc Mhearcair: The Oomph of Quicksilver* (2000). A.T.

Day-Lewis, Cecil (1904–72). Poet. Born in County *Laois and raised in England, Day-Lewis was educated at Oxford where he was later appointed professor of Poetry. He became poet laureate of England in 1968. With Louis *MacNeice, Sir Stephen Spender, and W. H. Auden, he was a member of the MacSpaunday group that promoted social change. Among his writings are several poetry collections, including *From Feathers to Iron* (1931), *Poems in Wartime* (1940), and *An Italian Visit* (1953); an autobiography, *The Buried Day* (1960); translations of Virgil and Valéry and, as Nicholas Blake, a series of detective novels. *The Whispering Roots* (1970) explores his complex relationship with his Irish ancestry. *The Complete Poems of C. Day-Lewis* was published in 1992. M.S.T.

Day-Lewis, Daniel (1957–). Actor. Born in London, Daniel was the second child of poet (later poet laureate) Cecil *Day-Lewis and actress Jill Balcon. Always more interested in acting than in academics, he dropped out of boarding school in his early teens and was given a small part in the film *Sunday, Bloody Sunday* (1971). He studied acting at the Bristol Old Vic, and also performed with the Royal Shakespeare Company before returning to screen acting in 1982. His first major supporting role was in *The Bounty* (1984), but it was with more prominent parts in *My Beautiful Launderette* and *A Room with a View* (both 1986) that he gained international acclaim. Known for the intensity with which he prepares his roles, Day-Lewis has played a great variety of characters, including a Czech surgeon in *The Unbearable Lightness of Being* (1988) and a cerebral palsy sufferer in *My Left Foot* (1989), based on the book by Christy *Brown, for which role he won the Academy Award for best actor. The latter movie reconnected him with his Irish roots, and he became an Irish citizen and resident. Other films in which he has starred include *The Last of the Mohicans* (1992), *In the Name of the Father* (1993), *The Age of Innocence* (1993), *The Crucible* (1996), *The Boxer* (1997), and *Gangs of New York* (2002). J.C.E.L.

Deane & Woodward. Architectural firm. Deane & Woodward, one of nineteenth-century Ireland's most influential architectural practices, bore the names of its founders Sir Thomas Deane (1792–1871) and Benjamin Woodward (1816–61). Based at first in *Cork and then in *Dublin, they designed as one of their first projects Queen's College (now University College) in Cork in 1845–49. Their work on the Museum Building in Trinity College, Dublin (1852–57) and the former Kildare Street Club (1856–61) showed the influence of Pugin and Ruskin on their designs, and led to further commissions in England: the Oxford Museum and the Crown Life Office in Blackfriars (1856–58). After Woodward's death, the Deane dynasty continued the practice for decades. P.H.

Deane, Seamus (1940–). Writer, critic. Widely regarded as one of the most influential Irish literary critics of his generation, Deane is also a distinguished poet and novelist. Born in *Derry and educated at St. Columb's College, Queen's University, Belfast, and Cambridge University, he is now professor of Irish Studies at Notre Dame University. Deane distinguished himself as a poet with the publication of *Gradual Wars* (1972) and *History Lessons* (1983). His work investigates the ways in which Irish literary and political culture can be understood as a response to the experience of colonization. Deane was a founding member of the *Field Day Theatre Company, which reenergized Irish *theater and cultural criticism in the 1980s. Although often controversial, Field Day sought to engage with the problems of contemporary Irish society and culture, particularly those precipitated by the *Northern Ireland conflict. His academic publications include: *Celtic Revivals: Essays in Modern Irish Literature* (1984), *A Short History of Irish Literature* (1986), the groundbreaking *Field Day Anthology of Irish Writing* (1991), and *Strange Country: Modernity and Nationhood in Irish Writing Since 1790* (1997). Deane has also published a novel, *Reading in the Dark* (1996), which was short-listed for the Booker Prize. P.J.M.

de Brún, Bairbre (1954–). Politician, *Northern Ireland minister for health (1999–), leading member of *Sinn Féin. De Brún was born in *Dublin and joined Sinn Féin in 1984. She is a fluent Irish speaker and was, until her election to the Northern Ireland Assembly in 1998, a teacher of French and Irish in Northern Ireland's first Irish medium secondary school. She was a leading member of the Sinn Féin negotiation team in the talks leading to the 1998 *Belfast Agreement. E.C.

De Danann. Traditional *music group. This innovative traditional band was formed in Spiddal, County *Galway, in 1974. Led by the virtuosity of fiddler Frankie Gavin and bouzouki player Alec Finn, the band has acted as a launch pad for some of Ireland's greatest singers, including Dolores Keane, Mary Black, Maura O'Connell, Eleanor Shanley, and Tommy Fleming. They have experimented with Irish American vaudeville songs ("Star Spangled Molly," 1978), black gospel music ("Half Set in Harlem," 1991), as well as covering well-known Beatles and Queen numbers. B.D.

Defenders, the. A secret society which sprang up in County *Armagh in the mid-1780s to "defend" *Catholics from sectarian attacks from the *Protestant Peep O'Day Boys. It spread through Catholic *Ulster in the 1790s, feuding with the *Orange Order, and formed an alliance with the *United Irishmen. The Defenders faded after the *Rebellion of 1798, and slowly mutated into the Ribbonmen during the first half of the nineteenth century. K.W.

Delaney, Ronnie (1935–). Irish Olympic Athlete. Born in Arklow, County *Wicklow, Delaney graduated from Villanova University, Pennsylvania. In 1954, he became the seventh athlete in history to run a mile in under four minutes. In 1956, he won the gold medal in the fifteen-hundred-meter race at the Melbourne Olympic Games, setting a new Olympic record of 3:41.2. P.E.

Democratic Unionist Party (DUP). One of the two main *Unionist political parties in *Northern Ireland. (The other is the *Ulster Unionist Party [UUP].) The DUP was formed in September 1971 by Ian *Paisley, currently its leader, and Desmond Boal, who was then member of the *Stormont Parliament for Shankill. Boal declared that the party would be "right-wing in the sense of being strong on the constitution, but to the left on social policies." The party succeeded the *Protestant Unionist Party. The DUP has participated in Northern Ireland local government elections, various local assemblies, Westminster general elections, and elections to the European Parliament. Capitalizing on discontent with the pro–*Good Friday Agreement Ulster Unionist Party, the DUP increased its vote by more than 50 percent in a Westminster general election in the Fall of 2001. With 22.5 percent of the total, it was the second largest party in Northern Ireland. The DUP in 2004 had five Westminster members of Parliament (Ian Paisley, Peter Robinson, Iris Robinson, Nigel Dodds, and Gregory Campbell) and one member of the European Parliament (Jim Allister). In 2003, the DUP became the largest single party in the Northern Ireland assembly. M.M.

Derry, County. One of the six counties in the province of *Ulster, which make up *Northern Ireland. Derry (816 square miles) has a population of est. 213,035 (1996). The county is bounded on the north by the Atlantic Ocean, and on the east and west by the Lower Bann and the river Foyle, respectively. Derry City, the county capital, was the site of a monastery founded in the sixth century by St. *Colm Cille (Columba) who, according to legend, saved the poets from being banished from Ireland. The ancient territory of Tír Eoghain (named after the son of the early Irish King Niall of the Nine Hostages) occupied most of the county, which remained Gaelic in power and culture until the *Flight of the Earls in 1607 ended Gaelic hegemony in Ulster. King James I of England granted the confiscated lands of these native chieftains to English settlers after 1609. These settlers, mostly Londoners, named the county Londonderry, and some of the smaller towns, such as Draperstown, after their trades and occupations. The English settlers were joined in the middle of the seventeenth century by dissenting *Presbyterians from *Scotland, many of whom, disappointed at not finding the religious liberty they yearned for, later left for North America. (These *Scots-Irish made up a sixth of the total population by the time of the United States' Declaration of Independence.) During the Siege of *Derry in 1689, the city, protected by its stout walls built three-quarters of a century earlier, withstood a long onslaught by *Jacobite forces. (Derry's are perhaps the last circuit of town walls to be built anywhere in Europe.) Derry had a significant naval base on the Foyle during World War II where American troops were stationed. The city was the scene of civil rights unrest in the late 1960s, which led to the *Northern Ireland conflict, or the *Troubles. The county's economy includes *textiles, farming, and light industry. The Nobel Prize–winning poet Seamus *Heaney was born in Toome, County Derry, and the well-known poet and literary critic Seamus *Deane was born in Derry City. P.H.

Derry, Siege of (1689). During the Williamite War, on April 18, 1689, Derry (Londonderry) locked out *James II with cries of "No surrender!" thus beginning the siege. Major Baker (replaced after his death by John Mitchelbourne) and Reverend Walker took over the command of the thirty thousand civilians, mostly refugees, and seven thousand troops in the city. The Jacobites lacked cannons, equipment, and troops for an attack but blockaded the city. On July 28, two ships broke through the blockade in Lough Foyle, and the siege ended July 31. In

Éamon de Valera

commemoration of the siege, the *Apprentice Boys of Derry parade annually in August. T.C.

de Valera, Éamon (1882–1975). The figure of Éamon de Valera towered over Irish politics for more than half a century, from the *Easter Rising of 1916 into the 1970s. *Nationalist, revolutionary, shrewd Machiavellian politician, fervent Irish *Catholic, *Taoiseach (prime minister), and president of Ireland, de Valera more than any other political leader shaped modern Ireland.

He was born in New York City in 1882 to *immigrant parents, Catherine Coll, an Irish domestic worker, and Juan Vivion de Valera, a Spanish sculptor. In 1885 his mother, who was widowed the previous year, sent the child to Ireland to be raised by his grandmother in the family's small cottage in Bruree, County *Limerick.

De Valera excelled in school, won a scholarship to the prestigious Blackrock College, and qualified in 1905 as a teacher of mathematics from the Royal University, Dublin.

The Ireland of his childhood was a cauldron of political turmoil—*Parnell, the *Land Wars, and *Fenianism. Increasingly attracted to the burgeoning nationalist movement, de Valera became a member of the *Gaelic League in 1908, and in 1913 joined the Irish *Volunteers, a nationalist militia.

Three years later, in the Easter Rising of 1916, de Valera commanded the defense of Boland's Mills, a strategically located factory in Dublin. He was arrested and sentenced to death along with the other leaders, but his sentence was commuted partly because of his American citizenship and partly because the executions were arousing mass sympathy for the rebels. Back in Ireland after his release from prison in 1917, de Valera enjoyed hero status as the senior surviving commander of the rising. He threw himself wholeheartedly into the campaign of the new political party *Sinn Féin and won a parliamentary seat for East *Clare in the election of June 1917.

Charismatic and politically savvy, de Valera became both president of Sinn Féin and of the Irish Volunteers, its military wing. In 1918, he was again arrested and imprisoned in Lincoln Prison in England, for his part in an alleged "German plot." The following year, he escaped with the help of Michael *Collins and Harry *Boland.

An Irish Parliament representing the thirty-two counties, the *Dáil, was convened on January 21, 1919, and declared Ireland a free and democratic republic in blatant defiance of the British government. De Valera was elected its first president. Shortly after, he went to the United States to raise money and support for Irish independence. He spent eighteen months exhaustively traveling the United States and raised five million dollars, but he alienated some *Irish American leaders and failed to gain US government recognition for the new Irish Republic.

On his return to Dublin in December 1920, de Valera was critical of some of the methods of guerrilla warfare Michael Collins had developed during the *War of Independence. In July 1921, a truce was called and de Valera went to London for discussions with *Lloyd George, the British prime minister. No progress was made but further negotiations began in October.

The *Anglo-Irish Treaty was finally negotiated in December 1921 by an Irish delegation from which de Valera was conspicuously absent. He had prevailed on Michael Collins to take part in the final treaty negotiations in London while he, de Valera, remained in Dublin to preserve unity and ensure acceptance of the final agreement. Some historians have argued that de Valera knew that the nationalist ideal of an Irish republic was not a likely outcome and in a Machiavellian move conveniently separated himself from the treaty compromise.

After a pro-treaty vote of sixty-four to fifty-seven, de Valera, who was opposed to the compromise, immediately rejected the treaty and resigned from the Dáil. In the spring of 1922, anti-treaty republicans occupied the *Four Courts building in Dublin, precipitating the *Civil War. De Valera crisscrossed Ireland during this period, arguing the case for the republic with passionate rhetoric. He was, however, criticized by some republican supporters for his "external association" theory of an independent republic within the Commonwealth. De Valera was to regain influence with the republicans only after their military leader Liam Lynch's death in 1923.

After Michael Collins's death in August 1922, the Civil War dragged on until May 1923 when the republican forces called a cease-fire.

In August 1923, de Valera was arrested while contesting the general election in Ennis, County Clare, and after his release from jail, a year later, he decided to take his place in constitutional politics. In November 1925, he failed to get Sinn Féin to recognize the new twenty-six-county *Free State Dáil, and he resigned as president. Many of his republican colleagues in Sinn Féin were outraged, but such was de Valera's power of persuasion that in 1926 he brought most of the Sinn Féin supporters into his newly founded political party, *Fianna Fáil. The new party remained abstentionist, objecting to the *oath of allegiance required by all Dáil members. However, they entered the Dáil in August 1927, reluctantly taking the oath of allegiance (de Valera's and the republicans' main objection to the *Anglo-Irish Treaty).

In the general election of September 1927, Fianna Fáil won forty-four seats and narrowly failed to form a coalition government. De Valera had reinvented himself politically, a process that would be complete in 1932 when Fianna Fáil came to power. De Valera would govern for the next sixteen years, solidifying Fianna Fáil's power and quelling any threats from the die-hard IRA (*Irish Republican Army) purists—his older colleagues from Sinn Féin—and also from the *Blueshirts. He founded the *Irish Press*, a pro–Fianna Fáil newspaper with a broad national agenda, in 1931.

In 1932, de Valera abolished the oath of allegiance, the most controversial issue of the 1921 treaty. He also refused to pay land annuity payments to Britain, causing the *Economic War. Internationally, de Valera played an important role in the League of Nations, as president of the council in 1932 and later as president of the assembly.

In 1937, de Valera drafted a new *Constitution, reflecting his conservative doctrinairism. In an ingenious political move, he extended the jurisdiction of the new constitution to cover the entire island of Ireland. Although Ireland remained neutral during World War II, the country suffered economically well into the 1950s when emigration peaked.

De Valera's greatest achievement was to create a constitutionally stable government in post-colonial Ireland, but his vision of a nationalist, self-sufficient Ireland isolated the country economically, politically, and culturally. He resigned in 1959 as Taoiseach and served two terms as president from 1959 to 1973. He died in 1975. J.OM.

de Vere, Sir Aubrey (1814–1902). Poet and author. Born in County *Limerick, de Vere was influenced by his friend William Wordsworth. An intimate of Tennyson and Robert Browning, de Vere traveled extensively in Italy (1839–44) before publishing his collection of romantic poems, *The Waldenses* (1842). In *English Misrule and Irish Misdeeds* (1848), de Vere declared his Irish sympathies and he became a Roman *Catholic in 1851. In 1854, he was appointed professor of political and social science in the Dublin Catholic University, where he developed an interest in Irish legend and history. His works include *The Legends of St. Patrick* (1872) and *Recollections* (1897). S.A.B.

Devlin, Denis (1908–59). Poet, translator, and diplomat. Devlin was born in Greenock, Scotland, and educated at Belvedere College and University College, Dublin. His and Brian Coffey's early poems were published jointly in *Poems* (1930), and Samuel *Beckett favorably reviewed his *Intercessions* (1937). Posted to the United States, he met poets Robert Penn Warren and Alan Tate who edited his *Selected Poems* (1963). A modernist poet, he wrote about the anxiety of human existence and the conflict between human beings, an impersonal god whom Devlin calls "the heavenly foreigner," and external reality. M.S.T.

Devoy, John (1842–1928). *Irish American political activist. Born in County *Kildare, John Devoy was one of the original *Fenians, and in 1866, he was imprisoned for his part in the outlawed Fenian movement. In 1871, his prison sentence was commuted in exchange for self-imposed exile to the United States. From his arrival in *New York, Devoy would immerse himself in Irish American political activism. He was one of the main architects of Irish American support for Charles Stewart *Parnell and the *Land Wars of the 1870s, the *Easter Rising of 1916, and later for Éamon *de Valera's money-raising tours in the United States. He later broke with de Valera and supported the *Anglo-Irish Treaty and the new *Free State government.

Patrick *Ford, editor of the *Irish World*, persuaded Devoy that *nationalism needed a popular cause, like the war on landlordism, to mobilize the Irish masses. In June 1879, Devoy, Parnell, future leader of the *Irish Parliamentary Party, and Michael *Davitt, a founder of the *Land League, negotiated the "New Departure," under which Irish American nationalists would support both *home rule and land reform. In 1900, Devoy became one of the leaders of *Clan na Gael, an Irish American revolutionary organization dedicated to Irish independence, and maintained close ties to the *Irish Republican Brotherhood (IRB).

Among Devoy's more adventurous exploits is the masterminding of the escape by seven Irish political prisoners from Western *Australia and their successful trip to the United States on the ship *Catalpa* in 1876. He was an early supporter of John Holland, an Irish immigrant, who designed the first underwater vessel—later called the submarine. Devoy's autobiography *Recollections of an Irish Rebel* (1929) is a firsthand account of Irish political activism in the United States. J.OM.

Dillon, Gerard (1916–71). Painter. Born in *Belfast, Dillon was a landscape and figure painter, who studied briefly at Belfast College of Art before living in London and *Dublin. Inspired by *Connemara, he produced Chagall-like surreal work with strong autobiographical content. He exhibited regularly at *Irish Exhibition of Living Art from 1943 until 1969, when he withdrew from the Belfast show in support of Northern *nationalists. M.C.

Dillon, James (1902–86). Politician, *Fine Gael leader (1959–65), and noted orator. Born into a distinguished political dynasty (son of John *Dillon), he was first elected to the *Dáil (Parliament) in 1932 and became vice president of Fine Gael in 1933 when it merged with the Centre Party. Dillon resigned from the party during World War II because he disagreed with Fine Gael's support for *neutrality. During the coalition (interparty) governments, he was minister for *agriculture, a sector he managed to rebuild following the damage of the *Economic War. In 1952, he rejoined Fine Gael and his era of leadership is seen as a period of consolidation for the party. P.E.

Dillon, John (1851–1927). Politician. Militantly anti-*landlord during the *Land War, Dillon (son of John Blake *Dillon) served four prison terms in the 1880s. He was *Irish Parliamentary Party MP (member of Parliament) for *Tipperary (1880–83) and for East *Mayo (1885–1918). After the party split in 1891 following the *O'Shea divorce case, he aligned with the anti-Parnellites. When the party reunited, in 1900, with the Parnellite John *Redmond as chairman, Dillon supported the new leader, and thereafter the two men provided effective leadership in anticipation of *home rule. On Redmond's death in 1918, Dillon became chairman. In the following general election in December 1918, *Sinn Féin crushed his party and Dillon lost his East Mayo seat to Éamon *de Valera. L.MB.

Dillon, John Blake (1816–66). Irish *nationalist politician. The son of a shopkeeper from Ballaghadereen, County *Mayo, Dillon graduated from Trinity College, Dublin, and became a lawyer in 1841. He was one of the founders of the **Nation* newspaper in 1842 and became a member of the *Repeal Association. Dillon joined the *Young Ireland movement in 1846 and led the 1848 insurgency at Killenaule, County *Tipperary. After the uprising, he escaped to the United States where he practiced law. In 1855, Dillon returned to Dublin under amnesty and became secretary to the Irish National Association in 1864. Elected as MP (member of Parliament) for County Tipperary in 1865, he opposed *Fenianism and joined British radicals in campaigning for land reform. S.A.B.

Dingle Peninsula. Peninsula in County *Kerry, jutting into the Atlantic Ocean on the southwest coast of Ireland. The town of Dingle stands near the end of the peninsula. Some of the most beautiful *Munster *Irish is spoken in the *Gaeltacht areas on the peninsula. The *Blasket Islands at its western tip produced such literary classics as *An tOileánach* (The Islandman) by Tomás *Ó Criomhthain and storytellers like Peig *Sayers. In 1579 a Spanish military

Slea Head, Dingle Peninsula

expedition was annihilated at Dún an Oir on Smerwick Harbour, and nine years later a *Spanish Armada vessel foundered off Slea Head. Many archaeological sites and *beehive huts may be associated with an ancient *pilgrimage to *Mount Brandon (3,127 feet) in honor of St. *Brendan. P.H.

distilling and brewing. Alcohol has long had a prominent and controversial place in Irish culture. Brewing and distilling have been, and continue to be, important industries in Ireland's *economy. Although neither industry was ever a large-scale direct employer, the vast network of distillers, brewers, distributors, publicans, and "spirit grocers" (there were over fourteen thousand licensed sellers of alcohol in Ireland in 1836) has formed a vital segment of the Irish middle class from the eighteenth century to the present day.

We don't know when distilling started or if, prior to the 1160s, what the Irish were distilling was something we would call *whiskey today. Production of whiskey, or *uisce beatha* (the Irish for "water of life"), probably began sometime after the eighth century when Irish missionaries brought Mediterranean distillation techniques to the British Isles. Distilling spirits from barley became more common from the twelfth century and was a ubiquitous craft industry in Ireland from the fifteenth century onward. Duties, taxes, and the licensing of retail sale of spirits, wine, and beer became an important source of revenue for the English government from the later sixteenth century, even though endemic corruption, evasion, and subversion of the same became a characteristic feature of Irish public culture for the next three centuries. Custom duties on imported spirits established from 1661, nevertheless, encouraged Irish whiskey production, and by 1765 there were 946 registered stills in Ireland, which together produced over 715,000 proof-gallons of spirit. At the same time, great quantities of illicit distillation of whiskey were produced all over the country. The industry, under steady pressure from imports, illicit distillation, and government regulation that favored larger producers, consolidated over time. Production increased steadily for most of the nineteenth century, with the exception of the 1840s, the years of Father Mathew's temperance crusade and the Great *Famine. Whiskey production became more geographically concentrated, primarily in *Dublin and *Cork. Steady consolidation in the industry continued into the twentieth century, as Irish distillers lost export ground to Scottish producers and domestic consumption leveled out. Three active distilleries remained in Ireland at the end of the twentieth century—Middleton Distillery in County Cork (where whiskeys such as Paddy, Power, Jameson, and the premium Middleton Reserve are currently distilled); Cooley Distillery in County *Louth (a twentieth-century distillery where Connemara, Locke, and other specialty whiskeys are made); and Bushmills Distillery in County *Antrim which makes varieties of the famous whiskey of the same name.

Beer, brewed in Ireland from ancient times, remained a popular drink, especially in urban areas, despite the rise in spirit consumption from the early modern period. At the end of the eighteenth century, there were hundreds of breweries in Ireland, with larger producers concentrated in Dublin and Cork and with many retail brewers throughout the country. Into the early decades of the nineteenth century, Irish brewers faced declining consumption as well as increasing competition from larger high-quality English producers, as well as from domestic spirit production and West Indian rum. However, from 1850 to 1914, Irish beer production tripled, with the *Guinness Brewery in Dublin becoming the world's largest brewer. By 1914, 40 percent of Irish beer production was exported, and beer exports made up over 3 percent of all Irish exports. Over the course of the twentieth century, the Irish brewing industry consolidated dramatically, while beer production continued to rise. *Guinness (now owned by international drinks giant Diageo) operates breweries in Dublin, Belfast, Kilkenny, and Dundalk. Cork City has two large breweries: Beamish and Crawford, producers of Beamish stout, and Lady's Well Brewery, where Murphy's stout and other beers are produced. In recent years, microbreweries and brew pubs, such as the Irish Brewing Company in County *Kildare and the Carlow Brewing Company (whose old-recipe microbrews have won international recognition), have begun to reemerge across Ireland. P.A.T.

divorce. Divorce was relatively freely available under the old *Celtic law system, but in the centuries following the *Anglo-Norman invasion, Ireland adopted the English system of law, which restricted divorce. In the nineteenth and early twentieth century, for example, each individual divorce required a separate act of the British Parliament, and was, therefore, only available to the wealthy. Divorce was totally prohibited by the first *Free State government in 1926 (as part of a *Catholic conservative policy program including censorship and a ban on contraception). Although *Northern Ireland remained part of the United Kingdom, the *Unionist government used its

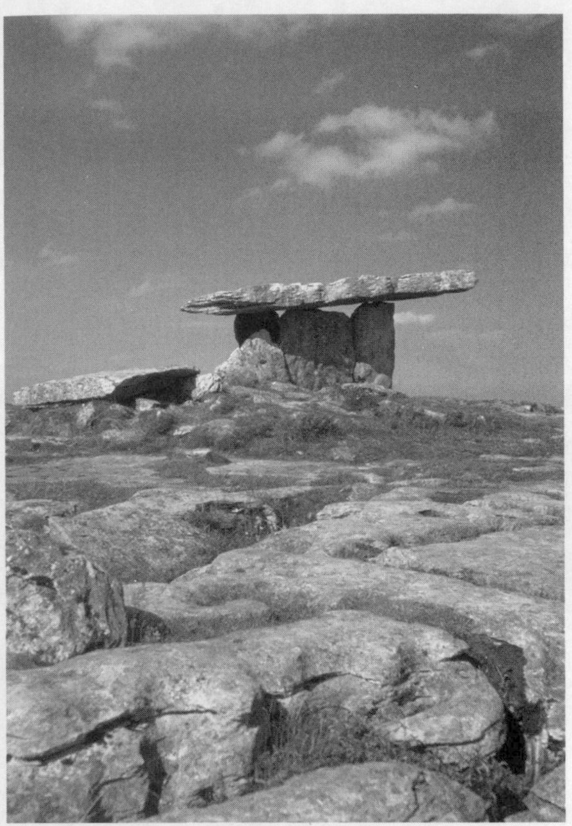

Poulnabrone Dolmen, The Burren, County Clare

devolved legislative powers to limit the liberalization of divorce legislation—even as reforms were introduced in Britain. The new Irish state's *Constitution, which was adopted by referendum in 1937, included a prohibition on divorce. During the 1970s and 1980s, in response to the growing problem of marital breakdown, the state reformed family law in such areas as custody of children, maintenance of a dependent spouse, and the division of property. However, this did not amount to a comprehensive law dealing with separation, and divorce remained banned.

The first attempt to amend the constitutional ban came in 1986, when the *Fine Gael–*Labour coalition government proposed a referendum on divorce. *Fianna Fáil officially allowed its members to campaign on either side, but a majority of the party opposed the measure. The measure was defeated with a 63.5 percent "no" vote. Subsequent analysis suggests that only one-third of the public was morally or socially opposed to the measure. However, the middle ground almost unanimously voted against it, because the government's legislative plans for the introduction of divorce were unclear, raising fears about *women's welfare entitlements and property rights in particular. In the aftermath of this defeat, comprehensive legal separation was introduced as a solution to marital breakdown. The only outstanding issue was the right to remarry. A second referendum in 1995 to remove the constitutional ban on divorce was supported by all the main political parties, but passed only by a tiny 50.3 percent majority. Following this referendum, the *Dáil (Parliament) passed appropriate legislation making divorce available in the *Republic. E.C.

Dixon, James (1887–1970). Painter. A fisherman and small farmer from Tory Island, County *Donegal, Dixon was encouraged to paint by artist Derek *Hill. The naivety of his landscape paintings, exhibited in *Belfast in 1966 and recently at the *Irish Museum of Modern Art (IMMA), is an important quality for modern painters. M.C.

Doherty, Willie (1959–). Photographer and video artist. Born in *Derry, Doherty studied in *Belfast. He worked initially in black and white, with superimposed captions on photographs of *Northern Ireland that commented upon its media representation. He moved on to color without text, and he uses video extensively—in increasingly complicated technical formats—which undermine stereotypical interpretations of the *Northern Ireland conflict. M.C.

Horse Riding on the Beach, County Donegal

dolmens. Stone Age megalithic tombs. Dolmens consist of between three and seven uprights carrying a capstone weighing up to one hundred tons, as at Browneshill, County *Carlow. These massive structures were probably erected by means of a removable ramp. Poulnabrone Dolmen, County *Clare, has been radiocarbon-dated to 3800–3200 B.C. It housed twenty-two burials. P.H.

Donegal, County. The most northerly county in Ireland and one of the three in the province of *Ulster that are part of the *Republic of Ireland. The county capital is Lifford. One of Ireland's most scenic counties, Donegal (area of 1,876 square miles) has a population of 137,383 (2002 census). The county has a spectacular two-hundred-mile coastline and its rugged interior regions are dominated by the majestic Mount Errigal. Slieve Liag in the south of the county boasts the highest sea cliffs in Europe (1, 972 feet).

The county is often referred to as Tír Chonaill or "the land of Conall." The High King Niall of the Nine Hostages who ruled between 379 to 405 carved up much of west Ulster between his two sons, Conall and Eoghan. Conall received most of Donegal while his brother Eoghan was given Tyrone (Tír Eoghain—the land of Eoghan) and Inishowen (Eoghan's island). The term *Tír Chonaill*, therefore, refers only to those parts of County Donegal outside of the Inishowen peninsula.

St. *Colm Cille has a strong association with the county. He is reputed to have been born in Gartan in 521 and is believed to have spent some time in Glencolumbcille and Tory Island.

The O'Donnell clan ruled most of Donegal until the *Flight of the Earls in 1607 shattered the dynasty's control of the county, which now became known as Donegal, or Dún na nGall—"the fort of the foreigner."

A large cottage industry has been built in the

county around tweed, especially in the towns of Ardara and Downings. Killybegs is a major fishing port and Bundoran, a popular seaside resort. Among Donegal's many tourist attractions are Glenveagh Castle and National Park and the magnificent art collection of Glebe House. The county's most important archaeological site is the Grianán of Aileach, a circular stone fort that dates back to the Iron Age and was reputed to have been the residence of various northern chieftains.

The *Annals of the Four Masters, the famous compilation of annals that records the history of Ireland from early times to 1616, was written between the years 1632 and 1636 at the Donegal Abbey, by the Franciscan brothers collectively known as "the four masters." Each year thousands of pilgrims visit Station Island in Lough Derg, known as St.*Patrick's Purgatory. A typical retreat lasts for three days and participants go without sleep or food (except for black tea and toast) and walk barefoot around the rocky island saying prayers. Much of the county is Irish speaking. B.D.

Donleavy, J. P. (1926–) Writer. Born in Brooklyn, New York, and educated at Trinity College, Dublin, Donleavy became an Irish citizen in 1967. His work is marked by wit, pessimism, and bawdiness. *The Ginger Man*, a partly autobiographical novel that evokes Donleavy's riotous student days in *Dublin, is widely acknowleged as a classic. Considered scandalous, the book was rejected by numerous publishing houses, but established a cult following after its initial 1955 publication in Paris. Donleavy and his hedonistic anti-hero Sebastian Dangerfield became known to a wider audience in the 1960s, when publishers in other countries overcame their fears about its contents. *The Ginger Man* overshadows Donleavy's subsequent work, such as *Meet My Maker the Mad Molecule* (1964), *The Saddest Summer of Samuel S* (1966), *The Beastly Beatitudes of Balthazar B* (1968), and *The Destiny of Darcy Dancer: Gentleman* (1977). M.E.

Down, County. Ireland's most easterly county, in the province of *Ulster, one of the six counties of *Northern Ireland. Down (957 square miles) has a population of est. 454,411 (1996). The name comes from the *Dún*, or fortification, which also forms part of the place-name Downpatrick, which is the county capital. The town is also named after St. *Patrick, who worked in the area in the fifth century, and died at Saul in County Down (though where he is buried is unknown). In ancient times, the county formed part of the kingdom of Ulidia, or the Ulaidh people, divided between the Dal Fiatach in eastern Down and the Uí Echach in the west of the county. *Viking settlements have left little trace, but the *Norman invasion left its mark on the county. The Norman John de Courcy, who overran the county late in the twelfth century, built *castles at Dundrum and Greencastle. Four centuries later, Down was further colonized by Scots planters who added to the racial and religious mix. Bordered by Belfast Lough on the north and the Mourne Mountains to the south (rising to a height of 2,796 feet at Slieve Donard), the county has both highlands and undulating terrain of plain and low hills. The long and lovely inlet, Strangford Lough, separates the Ards Peninsula from the main body of the county. In the inlet is Mahee Island, with its excavated early Christian monastery at Nendrum. Bordering on Strangford Lough's shores is Mount Stewart House, the eighteenth-century mansion of the Marquess of Londonderry, set in one of the finest gardens in Ireland. *Dolmens, (e.g., Legananny), castles like Dundrum, abbeys such as Inch, as well as churches old and new, dot the Down landscape. The

Ulster Folk and Transport Museum at Cultra splendidly conjures up the past of this historic county. The first canal in Britain or Ireland was built in County Down between 1731 and 1742, linking the town of Newry with Lough Neagh. The county also has majestic scenery, and attractive coastal towns and villages, including Rostrevor, Ardglass, and Strangford. Newcastle has a fine championship golf course "where the mountains of Mourne sweep down to the sea," in the words of the famous song by Percy *French. Holywood claims to be one of the first golf courses founded in Ireland. Holywood and Bangor (the site of another early monastery) are now practically suburbs of the city of *Belfast and make up a considerable proportion of the population of the northern part of the county. Distinguished natives of Down include: Sir Hans Sloane (1660–1753), founder of the British Museum; Captain Francis Crozier (1796–1848), second in command to Sir John Franklin in the ill-fated search for the northwest passage; John Butler *Yeats, artist and father of the poet W. B. *Yeats and the artist Jack B. *Yeats; and the composer Sir Hamilton *Harty. P.H.

Downing Street Declaration (December 15, 1993). Important statement by British Prime Minister John *Major and Irish *Taoiseach (prime minister) Albert *Reynolds committing both governments to the *peace process in *Northern Ireland. Talks had been going on between the British and Irish governments and four constitutional Northern Ireland political parties since 1991. The Downing Street Declaration reasserted the *Anglo-Irish Agreement's principle that Northern Ireland's status could not be changed without the consent of its people. The declaration committed the Irish government to introduce and support changes in the Irish *Constitution (specifically, the claim of sovereignty over the entire island of Ireland) and it formally asserted that the United Kingdom had no selfish, strategic, or economic interest in Northern Ireland. Finally, and perhaps most importantly, the declaration opened the way for Northern Ireland parties with paramilitary links to join negotiations if the parties committed themselves to exclusively peaceful methods and agreed to abide by the democratic process. The Downing Street Declaration is considered one of the main factors leading to the IRA's (*Irish Republican Army) historic cease-fire of August 31, 1994, which was followed by the *loyalist cease-fire of October 13. Those cease-fires eventually made it possible for *Sinn Féin and two small loyalist parties—the *Ulster Democratic Party and the *Progressive Unionist Party—to participate in the multiparty talks that concluded with the signing of the 1998 *Good Friday Agreement. T.D.

Doyle, Roddy (1958–). Novelist. Born in *Dublin, Doyle taught school in the north Dublin suburb of Kilbarrack, on which he based his "Barrytown trilogy"—*The Commitments* (1987), *The Snapper* (1990), and *The Van* (1991). These novels' depiction of life in a Dublin housing estate, the characters' resilience and irreverence, and Doyle's informal style, struck a fresh note in Irish writing. The Booker Prize–winning *Paddy Clarke Ha Ha Ha* (1993) depicts with deceptive lightness the frailty of family life and introduces the violence and frustration developed more fully in *The Woman Who Walked into Doors* (1996). Doyle's other works include the novel *A Star Called Henry* (1999) and a number of plays and screenplays. G.OB.

Drennan, William (1754–1820). *Republican, founding member of the *United Irishmen. Born into a *Belfast *Presbyterian family, Drennan studied philosophy in Glasgow and medicine in

Edinburgh. He set up a medical practice in *Belfast in 1778 and was soon drawn to the patriot politics of the *Volunteer movement, which sought parliamentary reform. By late 1791, two years after his move to Dublin, Drennan was one of the founders of the United Irishmen, closely associated with Theobald Wolfe *Tone, Thomas Addis Emmet, Dr. William McNeven, and other radicals who campaigned for the democratization of the Irish government and emancipation of *Catholics. Drennan convinced his fellow United Irishmen to adopt elements of masonic modus operandi and nomenclature. He was tried in May 1794 for publishing a seditious libel, after which he drew back from high-profile political activities. Although aloof from paramilitary republicanism, Drennan contributed prose and verse to United Irish organs and wrote the popular "Wake of William Orr" in late 1797. He avoided serious persecution during the *Rebellion (of 1798) period but was jeopardized not only by the outbreak of open conflict in May 1798 but by his subsequent closeness to the *Emmet family. Drennan retired from medicine in 1807 and returned to Belfast, where he published the *Belfast Monthly Magazine*. He died in February 1820. R.OD.

Drew, Ronnie. See **Dubliners.**

druids. The directors of religion and philosophy among the ancient *Celts. The word *druid* (Old Irish *druí*, Modern Irish *draoi*) derives from ancient Celtic dru-wid-os, meaning "one of great knowledge." Classical authors, such as Livy, Pliny, and Julius Caesar, made frequent reference to the druids of Celtic Gaul and Britain, stating that they were wise men who had supernatural knowledge, whose judgments were respected, and who oversaw various religious and social rituals. Early Irish literature shows that the institution of druidism was also well established in Ireland, the druid being considered an expert in antiquarian knowledge, in clairvoyance, and in prophesying. Druids were reputed to negotiate peace settlements between warring factions, to divine the identity of future kings by sleeping on bull hides, and to gain inspiration from the dead by sojourning near burial mounds. More fanciful accounts have them casting spells for the discovery of thieves, covering themselves with magical "cloaks of concealment," and causing storms and thunderbolts to impede the progress of hostile armies. It is obvious that the rhetoric uttered by druids was considered sacred, and they themselves were at pains to project the importance of their profession. On public occasions, they wore colorful ceremonial garments decorated by the feathers of various birds. They convened for training and ritual in quiet groves, and various traditions portray the oak, the hazel, and the rowan as trees sacred to them. There are various references to the many years spent in learning to be a druid, the teacher being an established druid with many students under his direction. D.Oh.

Dublin. Capital of the Irish *Republic and its political, economic, and cultural center. Situated on the east coast, Dublin straddles the River Liffey. The city has been immortalized in poems, novels, and plays by some of the greatest writers of the English language, including James *Joyce and Seán *O'Casey. Evidence of habitation around Dublin dates back to 5000 B.C. The *Celts developed at least two settlements near the Liffey and the city's Irish name, Baile Átha Cliath (the Town of the Hurdle Ford) refers to an ancient river crossing. During the golden age of early *Christianity, Dublin was home to several churches, monasteries, and hermit huts. In A.D. 841, the *Vikings established a settlement where the River

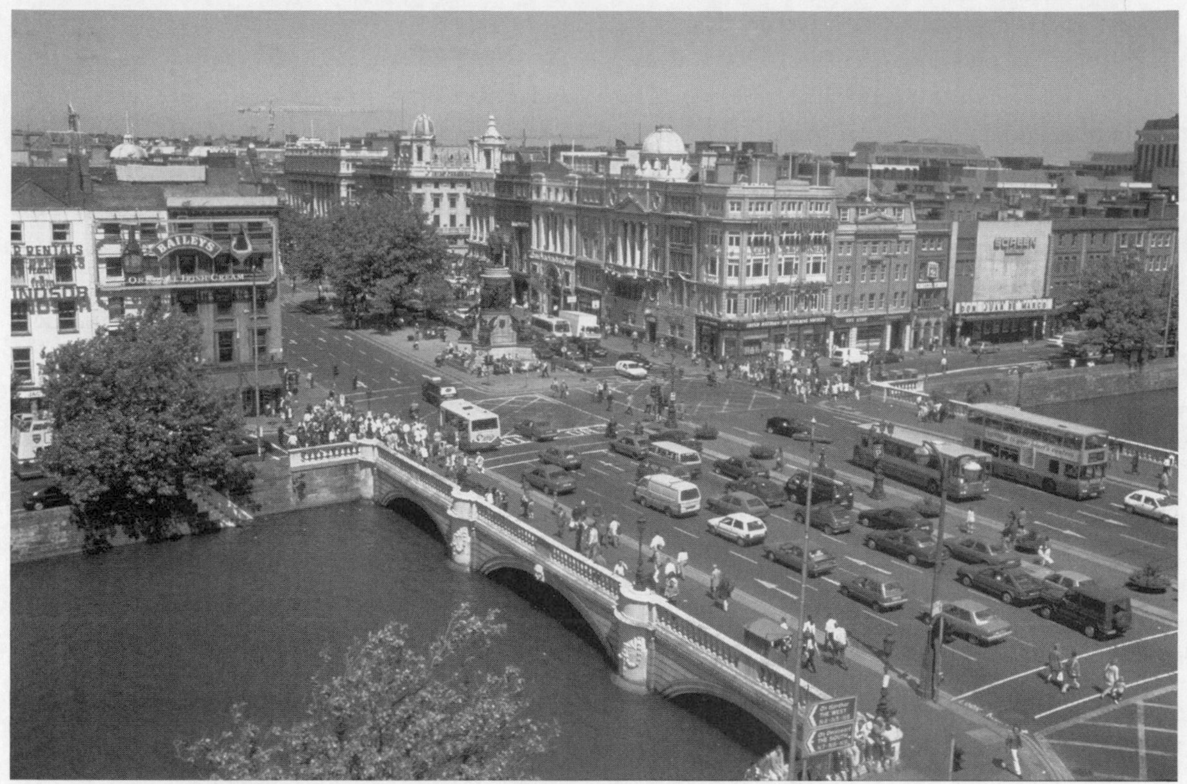

O'Connell Bridge, Dublin

Poddle joined the Liffey in an area known as Dyfflin or in Irish Dubh Linn (black pool), from which the city's name is derived. By the early tenth century, Dublin was a prosperous trading town, and after the *Anglo-Norman invasion, the city became the center of Anglo-Norman, and later English, power in Ireland.

Dublin remained a small, walled town with approximately nine thousand residents until an influx of *Protestant refugees from Europe dramatically increased its population at the end of the seventeenth century. In the eighteenth century, economic prosperity led to the development of Georgian Dublin, which became known as "the second city" in the British empire. Dublin spread beyond its old walls, developing along a gridiron pattern of squares and streets. Modern Dublin's center with the beautiful St. Stephen's Green, and the Georgian architecture of Merrion Square, Ely Place, and Fitzwilliam Square, dates from this period. After the Act of *Union (1800) and the abolishment of the Irish *Parliament, members of the ascendancy returned to England and the city fell into decline. By the end of the nineteenth century, Dublin had some of the worst slums in Europe.

In the twentieth century, Dublin was the center of labor and political unrest, from James *Larkin's protests, the Lockout of 1913, to the 1916 *Easter Rising, and the *War of Independence. The shelling of the *Four Courts in the city's center in June 1922 started the *Civil War. Between 1922 and 1932, the

*Irish Free State government, preoccupied with reestablishing law and order, was unable to deal adequately with the city's many social problems. The program of slum clearance that *Fianna Fáil started when the party came to power in 1932 was later postponed during World War II because of a shortage of building material. Thirty-four people were killed when the city was bombed by the German air force in May 1941. The 1960s and 1970s saw a renewed period of expansion. Ireland's membership of the European Economic Community (now known as the *European Union) brought an infusion of wealth and prosperity, revitalizing Dublin as a political, economic, and cultural center. Tourism became a major industry. The *Northern Ireland Conflict (the Troubles) was felt directly in Dublin on May 17, 1974, when three car bombs exploded without warning during rush hour, killing twenty-six people. The *Dublin Bombing, the biggest murder case in the Republic of Ireland, remains unsolved.

While development in the city slowed during the recession of the 1980s, the "Celtic Tiger" economy of the 1990s ushered in an era of unprecedented growth and led to the emergence of a modern cosmopolitan capital. Today, Dublin covers an area of 44.4 square miles, with a population of approximately half a million. Dublin, with one of the fastest-growing urban economies in Europe, is an international center of information technology and financial services. About 80 percent of the workforce is employed in the service sector. Twenty percent work in manufacturing—engineering, pharmaceuticals, and *brewing and distilling, most notably the *Guinness Brewery at St. James's Gate, which was founded in 1759. Prosperity has led to soaring property prices, traffic congestion, and suburban sprawl. Problems such as inner-city decay, deprivation in some suburban areas, and crime remain serious challenges.

Dublin's thriving cultural and social life boasts the world-renowned *Abbey and *Gate Theatres and perhaps the greatest conversationalists in the world. There are numerous galleries, restaurants, and over eight hundred pubs, including the Brazen Head, which claims to have been in business since 1198, and Davy Byrne's, the setting for one of the episodes of Joyce's *Ulysses*. Other attractions include *Dublin Castle, Trinity College, which was founded by *Elizabeth I in 1592 and is home to the Book of *Kells, the *Phoenix Park, one of Europe's largest parks, *Christ Church Cathedral, *St. Patrick's Cathedral, and the Dublin Writers' Museum. The city has an extraordinarily vibrant Anglo-Irish literary tradition starting with such eighteenth-century writers as Jonathan *Swift and Oliver *Goldsmith. Bram *Stoker, Oscar *Wilde, and George Bernard *Shaw were natives of the city, as was William Butler *Yeats, one of the greatest modern poets in the English language. Yeats, along with playwrights Lady *Gregory and Edward *Martyn, and novelist George *Moore, helped found the Abbey Theatre, which became famous through the plays of John Millington *Synge and Seán *O' Casey, who were also Dubliners. Every June 16, known as Bloomsday, the city celebrates the life of one of its greatest writers, James Joyce. Other twentieth-century writers associated with the city include Samuel *Beckett, Brendan *Behan, and Christy *Brown. The Dublin literary tradition continues today with writers such as Roddy *Doyle and Maeve *Binchy. P.E.

Dublin bombings (1974). *Loyalist bombings in the *Republic of Ireland. On May 17, 1974, twenty-six civilians were killed in three car bomb explosions in Dublin City center and seven in an explosion in Monaghan town. The attacks were carried out by loyalist activists from *Northern Ireland.

These related incidents represent the greatest loss of life in a single day as a result of the *Northern Ireland conflict. The Dublin government did not pursue leads as vigorously as might have been expected, fearful perhaps of the violence spilling over the border. Persistent allegations have been made of "dirty war" involvement in the atrocity by elements of the state security forces in Northern Ireland. M.M.

Dublin Castle. The center of British authority in Ireland until 1922. Dublin Castle was built by King *John of England in 1204. The original castle corresponded in extent with the present Upper Castle Yard, flanked on each corner by a great circular tower, beneath one of which—the Powder Tower—an earlier *Viking fortification was excavated. Other than these towers, much of the existing structure is the result of extensive rebuilding between 1730 and 1800, and this includes the first-floor State Apartments where Irish *presidents are inaugurated and where John F. *Kennedy was received in 1963. The castle has been recently adapted as a forum for *European Union and other meetings, and also for state tribunals. P.H.

Dublin, County. Maritime county in the province of *Leinster. Though Dublin, with 356 square miles, is ranked only thirtieth in size among the Irish counties, it is by far the most heavily populated, with 1,122,600 inhabitants (2002 census), almost a third of Ireland's total population of 3,917,336 (2002 census). The city of *Dublin, Ireland's capital and the county capital, with almost half a million inhabitants, is the administrative, financial, and cultural center of the country. It is also the center of the Irish railway network, and it contains the country's largest port. Dún Laoghaire, in south County Dublin, is also an important center for car ferry traffic between Ireland and the United Kingdom. Other prominent urban centers include the towns of Swords, Malahide, Balbriggan, and Skerries. One of the world's greatest golf links courses is in Portmarnock, in north County Dublin.

The county is bounded to the north by County *Meath, to the east by the Irish Sea, to the West by counties *Kildare and Meath, and to the south by County *Wicklow. The landscape is generally flat and low lying except in the south where the county borders the Wicklow Mountains. The main rivers include the Dodder, the Tolka, and the Liffey, which rises southwest of Dublin City in Wicklow and travels approximately fifty miles before entering the sea at Dublin Bay. The coastline stretches for over seventy miles and includes the islands of Lambay, Ireland's Eye, and St. Patrick's Island near Skerries.

Manufacturing and service industries are generally confined to the capital, while a significant fishing industry is centered in the towns of Howth and Skerries. *Agriculture remains an important, although declining, sector of the county's economy. Farms tend to be small, with cattle, barley, and potatoes the chief products. A market gardening industry is concentrated in the northern part of the county, especially around the villages of Rush and Lusk, and the area around Kinsealy. The explosion of development in the capital in the last decade has transformed the rural landscape outside the city, creating a vast low-density suburbia. The Flood Tribunal, established in 1997, has investigated charges of improper planning decisions and political corruption in land development in north County Dublin.

Human habitation in the county can be traced back to Mesolithic hunter-gatherers who dwelt in the hills to the north and south of Dublin City over six thousand years ago. The county's historical sites include: Neolithic dolmens at Woodtown; *Viking remains at Wood Quay; monastic and church buildings such as *Christ Church Cathedral, St. Mary's Abbey, St. Doulagh's Church, and St. Catherine's Well at Balgriffin; and *castles at Dalkey, Swords, and Malahide. From the twelfth to the sixteenth century, the county formed a significant part of the *Pale. During the twentieth century, Dublin City was the site of many important political and cultural movements and events, including the 1916 *Easter Rising, the birth of the *Irish Revival, and the start of the *Civil War. The county also has its own literary history: Flann *O'Brien's *The Dalkey Archive* is set in the south County Dublin picturesque seaside town of Dalkey, while the opening chapter of James *Joyce's *Ulysses* is set in a Martello tower in Sandycove, where Joyce lived with Oliver St. John *Gogarty, the inspiration for his character Buck Mulligan. P.E.

Dubliners, the. Music group. This popular ballad-group was formed in O'Donoghue's music bar in *Dublin in 1962. The original group included Barney McKenna, Luke Kelly, John Sheahan, Ciarán Bourke, and Ronnie Drew. Kelly (d. 1984) was a passionate singer, and Drew's gravelly bass became renowned. Dublin street-song was their core material, sung in local accents and set to superb arrangements with strong traditional instrumentals. F.V.

Duffy, Sir Charles Gavan (1816–1903). Politician, author, journalist. Born in County *Monaghan, Duffy was largely self-educated. In 1842, he founded the **Nation* weekly newspaper, the voice of the *Young Ireland revolutionary movement, with Thomas *Davis and John Blake *Dillon. He was in prison twice: once for sedition in 1844 and again, just before the *Rising of 1848, which he supported. Duffy started the Tenant League with James Fintan *Lalor and others in 1850 and was elected MP (member of Parliament) for New Ross in 1852. Duffy was a cofounder of the short-lived Independent Irish Party. After its collapse, he *emigrated to *Australia in 1855 and became prime minister of Victoria in 1871. From a Young Ireland revolutionary, Duffy had become a mainstream politician in the new world and was knighted in 1873. His political memoirs include *Young Ireland* (1880), *Four Years of Irish History* 1845–49 (1883), *My Life in Two Hemispheres* (1898), and *A Bird's Eye View of Irish History* (1882). C.D.

Dún Aengus. *Prehistoric stone fort. Dramatically sited above a two-hundred-foot cliff on Inishmore (*Aran Islands), Dún Aengus has multiple walls, the innermost one defended by stone stakes known as *chevaux-de-frise*. The date of construction is uncertain, but recent excavation showed human activity in the interior from about 800 B.C. onward. P.H.

Dunlop, John Boyd (1840–1921). Inventor and industrialist. Born in Dreghorn, Ayrshire, in *Scotland, Dunlop established a veterinary practice near *Belfast in 1867. He independently reinvented and pioneered the manufacture of commercially practical pneumatic rubber tires. (The first pneumatic rubber tire was patented by Robert William Thompson in 1845.) Dunlop's first design, consisting of a rubber inner tube, covered by linen tape and an outer tread of rubber, was made in 1887. The Dunlop Company began the mass production of tires in 1890 but in 1896 Dunlop sold both his patent and business for £3 million. This business, which ultimately developed into Dunlop Rubber Company, Ltd., greatly facilitated the development of motor transport. S.A.B.

Durrow, Book of. A copy of the Gospels and one of Europe's most important *manuscripts surviving from around A.D. 700. Of uncertain provenance (Ireland or Britain), the Book of Durrow was long kept at the site of the Columban Monastery at Durrow, County *Offaly, before being given to Trinity College, Dublin, in the seventeenth century. The manuscript is richly adorned with spiral and interlace ornament. P.H.

E

Easter Rising (April 24–29, 1916). Rebellion which set in motion the events that brought about the creation of an independent Irish republic. The outbreak of *World War I in August 1914 changed the course of Irish history by indefinitely postponing the *home rule bill and providing the impetus for the rising. The leader of the *Irish Parliamentary Party, John *Redmond's support of the war and the looming threat of conscription outraged an increasing number of nationalists, who came to see the war as an opportunity to separate from Britain.

The rising was originally planned by the *Irish Republican Brotherhood (IRB) in May 1915 to happen in one of three circumstances: a German invasion of Ireland, the introduction of conscription into the British army in Ireland, or if the war seemed likely to end without either of these two occurring. A group consisting of Seán *MacDiarmada, Thomas *Clarke, Patrick *Pearse, Joseph Mary *Plunkett, and Thomas *MacDonagh worked on the details of the rising. In January 1916, James *Connolly, commandant of the *Irish Citizen Army, who was planning a rising separately, was persuaded to join the nationalist cause. The plans were kept top secret within the IRB, and even the commander in chief of the Irish *Volunteers, Eoin *MacNeill, was not told. When the rising happened, almost everybody, including British intelligence, was taken by surprise.

The original plan envisaged a countrywide rebellion launched under the guise of Irish Volunteer maneuvers on Easter Sunday, April 23, 1916. However, a German ship, the *Aud*, carrying arms for the rising, was intercepted by the Royal Navy off County *Kerry and sunk on April 22, 1916. Eoin MacNeill, commander in chief of the Volunteers, canceled all maneuvers for Easter Sunday when he discovered their true purpose. On Good Friday he was talked into collaborating because he was persuaded that the government was about to arrest Volunteer leaders. On Saturday, however, aware that the government had no intention of striking and hearing of the capture of the *Aud*, he changed his mind and issued an order calling off the rebellion. The order was published on Easter Sunday in the form of an advertisement canceling all Volunteer maneuvers throughout the country for that day. This prevented most of the country from joining in the rebellion.

Nevertheless, the leaders decided to go ahead in *Dublin with whatever forces they could muster. At this stage, it was clear that the military feasibility of the rising was questionable but they believed that some gallant, symbolic gesture on behalf of Ireland's right to be a sovereign nation had to be made. They hoped that their actions and, if necessary, their sacrifice would rekindle the spirit of Irish *republicanism. On Easter Monday, April 24, about one thousand Volunteers and two hundred members of Connolly's Irish Citizen Army seized the General Post Office (GPO) and other strategic sites in Dublin. From the GPO, Pearse read out the *Proclamation of the Irish Republic, declaring Ireland a sovereign republic and announcing a provisional government. It is the first declaration of independence in history that specifically mentions *women.

Over the next two days, the British army under Sir John Maxwell, and reinforcements brought in from the *Curragh Camp, County *Kildare, *Belfast, and Athlone, surrounded rebel positions. Street fighting continued for a week during which many buildings were destroyed. British artillery and a gunboat, the *Helga*, bombarded key rebel positions, including the GPO and Liberty Hall, headquarters of Connolly's Irish Transport and General Workers Union. Although there were some sporadic incidents in *Wexford, *Galway, Ashbourne, County *Dublin, and County *Meath, there was no widespread uprising. The British sealed off Dublin and the population outside of the capital was not fully aware of what was happening. On April 29, to prevent further bloodshed, Pearse, who had been appointed first president of the Republic and head of the provisional government, surrendered. The last rebel outpost to hand over its arms was Boland's Mills under the command of Éamon *de Valera.

Sixty-four rebels had been killed, along with 132 crown forces and 230 civilians. Although initially the rising had little popular support, the British reaction to the rising provoked widespread sympathy for the rebels and their cause. The murder of Francis *Sheehy Skeffington, a well-known pacifist, the killing of civilians in North King Street by British soldiers, and the implementation of martial law antagonized most people. The execution of the leaders (Patrick Pearse, Thomas Clarke, Thomas MacDonagh, Joseph Plunkett, Edward Daly, Michael O'Hanrahan, Willie Pearse, John *MacBride, Éamonn *Ceannt, Michael Mallin, Seán Heuston, Cornelius Colbert, Seán MacDiarmada, James Connolly, and the hanging of Sir Roger *Casement) turned public opinion totally against the British and made martyrs of the executed rebels. Éamon de Valera was spared, supposedly, because he was a US citizen. The executions unleashed massive support for the republican cause and the ideal of an independent Ireland. *Sinn Féin's sweeping victory in the 1918 general election and the formation of the first *Dáil (Parliament) in January 1919 paved the way for the *War of Independence. T.C.

Economic War, the (1932–38). Economic and political dispute between the *Irish Free State and Britain. The Economic War began in 1932, when Éamon *de Valera's *Fianna Fáil government introduced legislation to abolish the *oath of allegiance to the British crown and refused to pay Britain the land annuities (repayments of British loans for land purchase). The British government retaliated by imposing duties and quotas on Irish imports, mainly on cattle and dairy produce. The Irish government responded with duties on British coal, iron, steel, and machinery.

Since almost all Irish exports were to Britain, the measures considerably damaged trade, particularly the cattle trade, but all sections of the Irish *economy were affected. The Free State government and the Fianna Fáil party, however, turned the conflict to its political advantage using rhetoric about national self-sufficiency and sacrifice in the face of a foreign oppressor. In the opposing political camp, the damage to the cattle trade was one cause of the emergence of the short-lived *Blueshirt movement.

In 1934, relations between the two countries improved with the first of three "coal-cattle" pacts. The British cabinet moved toward negotiations, which began in January 1938. In April that year, a series of agreements on trade, finance, and defense repealed most of the special duties and restrictions on imports to each country. The land annuities issue was settled for a one-time single payment of £10 million, and the Irish ports which had been retained by the British under the terms of the *Anglo-Irish Treaty were returned. P.D.

economy. For centuries before independence, Ireland had been an agrarian economy that was largely bypassed by the nineteenth century Industrial Revolution that transformed Britain and several European countries. The earlier *plantations (*Munster in the sixteenth century, *Ulster in the seventeenth) displaced the native *agricultural population in favor of a landed gentry. The land was partially returned to later generations of farm-laboring classes by a series of *land acts in the late nineteenth century. The Great *Famine in the 1840s was an economic catastrophe brought about by the potato blight and the government's failure to provide relief. Britain traditionally regarded Ireland as a source of cheap food and labor to support her rapidly expanding economy, a practice enshrined in Britain's economic policies both pre- and post-Irish independence.

Ireland gained political independence from Britain in 1922, but the fledgling Irish economy did not assume any real semblance of economic independence until the latter part of the century. Average incomes in Ireland were approximately 60 percent of those in Britain in 1913, when British living standards were among the highest in Europe. This relative situation had changed little by 1990, though, by then, British living standards had fallen well below the richer economies of mainland Europe. Through its dependence on Britain's relatively poorly performing economy, in terms of trade and labor market links, Ireland's own economic progress was arrested. The new state depended heavily on agriculture in the 1920s as a key supplier to the British market in an era of free trade but the industrial sector was almost nonexistent. The *Fianna Fáil government, which assumed power in 1932, instituted a policy of strong protectionism buttressed by high external tariff barriers, later endorsed by no less an economist than John Maynard Keynes. The objective was to develop the indigenous manufacturing base by guaranteeing exclusive access to the domestic market to home-based suppliers. The policy was inspired by the *nationalist government of the day and compounded by an *Economic War with Britain that limited access to the British market. Legislation was passed also to restrict the level of foreign ownership of Irish manufacturing firms. The manufacturing sector expanded significantly during the 1930s, with a concentration on basic industries such as food, clothing and *textiles, and wood and *furniture. However, the policy proved completely inadequate to prepare the young economy for the rigors of operating in a free trade environment in the postwar era of the 1940s and 1950s. The manufacturing sector had stagnated, inefficiencies were rampant, and output quality was poor, all of which were inevitable consequences of heavy protectionism. As Europe recovered and boomed in the 1950s, the Irish economy remained depressed. *Emigration was massive and the population was declining, while on the economic front, balance of payments crises constrained economic growth. A radically new approach was required and arrived in the shape of a strategy document, "Economic Development," prepared by T. K. *Whitaker, the then secretary of the department of finance, in 1958.

This paved the way for a radical reorientation of industrial policy toward an outward-looking economy that focused on making Ireland an attractive location for foreign direct investment (FDI) and on building up the economy for participation, eventually, in the European model of economic integration. Generous fiscal and financial incentives were used to attract overseas firms to locate in Ireland. Over a period of forty years, the industrial sector was radically transformed from being heavily dependent on the home market in highly protected, Irish-owned, inefficient firms to a modern export-oriented, largely, though not exclusively, foreign-owned and strongly competitive manufacturing sector. This transformation was not without pain as the transition to free trade that commenced in the 1960s was accelerated in the 1970s when Ireland joined the European Economic Community (1973) and many indigenous firms contracted or closed. The government also invested in building up the economy's infrastructure and its human capital through the introduction of free second-level *education in the 1960s. This led in time to a significant increase in an educated and up-skilled workforce, which proved critical to the attractiveness of Ireland as an industrial and international services center in the 1990s. The infrastructure was seriously inadequate for the needs of a modern economy (note that Ireland was classified officially as a "developing economy" in 1971) and European structural funds were vitally important in the 1990s to raise investment levels in the economy to about 30 percent of Gross Domestic Product (GDP) over a sustained period of time.

The gains to agriculture were a critical influence in encouraging Irish voters to join the European Community in 1973, though this sector has declined significantly since then and now accounts for less than 10 percent of GDP. The decision to join the *European Union (EU) (then known as the EEC) was of key long-term strategic importance to the economy and has sustained the flow of FDI from overseas firms wishing to locate their European manufacturing base in Ireland (as, for example, Dell, Apple, and Intel). Ireland enjoyed sustained economic growth from 1959 to 1973, but was severely affected by the two oil crises of the 1970s. The economy suffered from macroeconomic mismanagement during the late 1970s, when excessive spending by government severely curtailed the scope for fiscal flexibility during the depressed years of the 1980s. Government debt to GDP ratio was constantly rising and peaked at over 110 percent in 1986; average and marginal tax rates were excessive and emigration began to rise once more. The economy appeared to be unmanageable during these difficult years and at one stage the threat of International Monetary Fund (IMF) intervention was looming.

However, a period of "expansionary fiscal contraction" was initiated in 1987: government spending was severely cut, and the social partners (government, major *trade unions, and business organizations) embarked on a series of pay and tax agreements which ensured that moderate wage increases were guaranteed in exchange for generous tax concessions. Employment expanded from 1.1 million to 1.7 million from 1993 to 2000, reflecting the boom conditions of the 1990s; returned emigrants and a substantially increased female participation in the workforce contributed to this boom. The debt to GDP ratio had stabilized at 32 percent in 2003–4 and the size of government in the economy is now one of the smallest in Europe.

Today, Ireland is among the richest economies in the world and was recently ranked fifth in a league table of economies based on incomes per capita, higher than that of the UK and above the average of the European Union. This surge of economic growth since 1993 (almost 10 percent annually from 1995 to 2000) was unprecedented and the Irish economy became known as the "Celtic Tiger." Even though the standard of living improved dramatically for many Irish people, poverty levels still persist in certain sectors and locations in the country. In 2001–2002, Ireland's economy slowed down, in tandem with the international economy, though it still recorded above average GDP growth rates over 6 percent. In 2003, GDP growth slumped to 1.4 percent but rebounded in 2004, with steady employment gains. D.A.D.

Edgeworth, Maria (1767–1849). Novelist and educationalist. Born in Black Bourton, Oxfordshire, Edgeworth came to Ireland in 1782 and lived on the family estate at Edgeworthstown, County *Longford, from then until her death. Initially, she was an influential writer of children's books and of works of educational theory, but her best-known work is her first novel, *Castle Rackrent* (1800). The book, with its original use of *Hiberno-English and critique of *Anglo-Irish society, earned her an international reputation. She wrote three other novels on the challenges to Anglo-Ireland after the Act of *Union, notably *The Absentee* (1812), and several novels depicting London society in a satirical light, including *Belinda* (1801). Unlike *Castle Rackrent*, these works were substantially influenced by her father's liberal *unionism. After the publication of *Ormond* in 1817, the same year her father died, she published just two other novels, both with English settings. G.OB.

education. Ireland's long tradition of education is reflected in the country's cultural heritage. The *bardic schools of *pre-Christian Ireland helped to preserve and transmit the history of its earliest inhabitants. This system of learning, secular and oral in nature, involved the memorization of tales and myths and was central in the education of poets (**fili*) and judges (*brehons). The great monastic schools such as Clonard and *Clonmacnoise, which provided the first organized learning based on literacy in Ireland from the fifth century onward, served as a sanctuary of learning during Europe's Dark Ages. Ireland was known as *Insula Sanctorum et Doctorum*, the "Island of Saints and Scholars."

The *Protestant *Reformation ended the monastic system (the monasteries were closed), denying most *Catholics access to education. Wealthier Catholics began traveling abroad to Irish colleges, which had been established on the continent. In 1592, Trinity College was founded in Dublin to further the growth of *Protestantism and English culture in Ireland. Under the *Penal Laws, the Catholic Church was forbidden from having any role in education. In reaction, a system of hedge schools (in open fields or in primitive buildings) developed. Teachers financed by the local population taught a mixture of spelling, reading, arithmetic, and religion. During this time, Protestant evangelical groups such as the Baptist Society began establishing schools in an attempt to convert the Catholic population.

The *Catholic Relief Acts at the end of the eighteenth century allowed the widespread establishment of schools in towns and cities by religious orders such as the Irish *Christian Brothers. The Kildare Place Society, set up in 1811, provided nondenominational education and within twenty years had over 137,000 pupils attending its associated schools. In 1831, the government established the National Board of Education to organize a system of state-sponsored national primary schools, one of the first of its kind in Europe. The board had the power to cover the cost of building schools, provide schoolbooks, and contribute to teachers' salaries. Catholic and Protestant students were to be educated together for every subject with the exception of religious instruction. Despite these efforts, integration failed and, by the late 1860s, most national schools were denominational in nature. The Intermediate Education Act of 1878 introduced a common curriculum and examination system and established a Board of Commissioners to oversee the secondary schools system.

Three "Queen's Colleges" were established in 1845 in *Belfast, *Cork, and *Galway in an attempt to undermine the demand for the *repeal of the Act of *Union. These colleges were to be nonreligious with no theology faculties. They, however, failed to attract any support from the Catholic population and were labeled "godless" by the Catholic hierarchy, who in 1854 established the Catholic University in Dublin. In 1879, the British, in a fresh attempt to solve the university question, dissolved the "Queen's Colleges" and established in their place the Royal University. The Irish Universities Act, 1908, created two separate *universities: the National University of Ireland (NUI) and Queen's University. (The colleges in Galway, Cork, and Dublin became part of the National University and the College in Belfast became Queen's University.) Trinity College remained independent of these changes.

At present, there are four universities in the *Republic of Ireland: The NUI (with its constituent universities and colleges—NUI Dublin, NUI Cork, NUI Galway, NUI Maynooth, the Royal College of Surgeons, and the National College of Art and Design); the University of Dublin (Trinity College); the University of Limerick; and Dublin City University. Northern Ireland has two universities: Queen's University at Belfast and the University of Ulster with campuses in Belfast, Derry, Jordanstown, and Coleraine. In 2002/2003 the total number of students within the three sectors of education in the Irish Republic was approximately 920,274. The Department of Education and Science is responsible for the administration of primary, post primary, and special education and directs state and European support for universities and third-level colleges. State spending in education in 2004 was just over £6 billion. Nearly 50 percent of secondary school graduates advance to college and university level.

Education in *Northern Ireland is administered centrally by the Department of Education for Northern Ireland and locally by five education boards. In 2001/2002, 346,663 students were attending primary and secondary education. While the law guarantees that every school is open to all pupils regardless of religious denomination, most Catholics attend schools owned by the Catholic Church and financed by public funds, while Protestant and other non-Catholic children generally attend state schools. Integrated state schools also exist but they account for only a small percentage of enrolled students. At least 44.3 percent of students go on to higher education, the highest rate in the United Kingdom. P.M.D., P.E.

Edwards, Hilton Robert Hugh (1903–82). Actor and producer. Born in London, Edwards joined the Old Vic Theatre just before his eighteenth birthday. In 1927 he toured Ireland with Anew *McMaster's Shakespearean Company and met Micheál *MacLiammóir, with whom he formed a personal and professional partnership that would last a lifetime. Together, they became the directors of Ireland's first Irish-language theater, An Taibhdhearc, which opened in Galway in 1928. In the same year, MacLiammóir and Edwards founded the *Gate Theatre Company, which specialized in a modern, international repertoire. At the Gate, Edwards introduced innovations in production, design, and lighting, and directed over four hundred productions, acting in many of them. In the 1960s, he produced and directed several plays by Brian *Friel in *Dublin, London, and on Broadway. He directed a short film, *Road to Glenascaul* (1951), which was nominated for an Academy Award. From 1961 to 1963 he was head of drama at *RTÉ. He died in Dublin in 1982, four years after his partner. J.C.E.L.

Éire. Official (Irish) name for Ireland under the 1937 *Constitution. *Éire* is the Irish word for Ireland. In 1937, the Éamon *de Valera government replaced the 1922 Constitution with Bunreacht na hÉireann (the Constitution of Ireland), which was endorsed by the people of the *Irish Free State. Ireland was declared to be a sovereign, independent, and democratic state, and its name was changed from the Irish Free State to Éire, which was used until the *Republic of Ireland Act (passed in December 1948 but came into effect in April 1949) officially declared Ireland a republic. P.E.

Elizabeth I (1533–1603). Queen of *England (1558–1603). Elizabeth I consolidated the *Reformation in England with a new Act of Supremacy (1559) and continued the process of administrative centralization in Ireland that had begun under *Henry VIII. During her reign, the international religious and political conflicts of the Reformation and counter-Reformation caused political instability and social upheaval in Ireland. The continued *Catholicism of most of the Irish people posed a particular security dilemma for the queen and her ministers. When the pope excommunicated Elizabeth in 1570, the Old English settlers in Ireland, upon whom the crown had partly depended to maintain control, were torn between their continued faith in the Roman Church and loyalty to their queen. Increasingly, the Gaelic lords, who had also remained Catholic, looked to Spain, the most aggressive counter-Reformation power, for assistance against English dominance. Under the leadership of Hugh *O'Neill, the second Earl of Tyrone, resistance of the Gaelic lords to English impositions resulted in the *Nine Years War (1593–1603). The Irish *army and a small Spanish invasion force were defeated decisively by the English led by Lord Mountjoy at the *Battle of Kinsale, County *Cork, in 1601. In 1607, four years after Elizabeth's death, O'Neill and several other prominent Gaelic lords left Ireland for exile on the continent (an event popularly known as the *Flight of the Earls) and the old Gaelic social order came to an irrevocable end. F.B.

emigration and immigration. Over the centuries, the Irish have emigrated throughout the world. Although the Irish have departed for various reasons, the bulk of Irish emigration resulted from the effects of British political and economic domination. The English *plantations of Ireland during the sixteenth and seventeenth centuries displaced Irish *Catholics from their lands, sent thousands fleeing into political exile in Europe, and forced others into indentured servitude in the West Indies or North America. During the eighteenth century, nearly 300,000 *Scots-Irish Dissenters, most of them descendants of the *Ulster settlers, emigrated to America's frontier to escape their second-class status in Ireland.

Irish emigration from 1815 to 1914 dwarfed all earlier periods. Catholic peasants, deprived of land ownership rights and relying almost exclusively on the potato crop, suffered greatly during periods of economic depression and famine caused by crop failure. In general, the poorest and sickest emigrants, those looking for seasonal work, or seeking to retain closer ties with Ireland, crossed the Irish Sea to Great Britain. Beginning in the early nineteenth century, *Australia was a destination for Irish convicts. Throughout that century, Australia and *New Zealand attracted a core of ambitious and adventurous Irish settlers, and the occasional Irish rebel. However, the vast majority of nineteenth-century emigrants, particularly from the Great *Famine years, settled in *America, where they flooded cities from *New York to San Francisco, and soon dominated municipal politics and the Catholic Church. Many Irish during this period also went to *Canada and *Newfoundland.

After *World War I, American immigration restrictions and the Great Depression slowed the flow of Irish emigrants to the United States. After Ireland's independence, most twentieth-century Irish emigrants moved to Great Britain to seek jobs. During the 1980s and 1990s, America became a popular choice for educated and skilled young Irish immigrants seeking greater opportunities. The *Whitaker Plan and Ireland's entry into the European Economic Community (EEC, now known as the *EU) sparked an economic recovery that led to many Irish people returning from abroad during the 1970s. The Irish *economy declined again during the 1980s, only to rebound dramatically during the 1990s. Dubbed the "Celtic Tiger," this vigorous economy caused immigration to overtake emigration, and Ireland for the first time ever experienced an influx of immigrants. Some are of Irish descent but a sizable number are Eastern Europeans or Africans seeking asylum, or entering illegally. At the beginning of the twenty-first century, as the Irish economy slowed, racism and intolerance became serious problems. R.D.

Emmet, Robert (1778–1803). Revolutionary and *nationalist icon. Born in *Dublin into a highly educated *Protestant family of *Tipperary and *Kerry origins, Emmet was educated at Trinity College, Dublin, where he displayed great talent for oratory, chemistry, and mathematics. Under the influence of his brother, Thomas Addis Emmet, a founding member of the Society of *United Irishmen, the younger Emmet joined the society in December 1796. He was obliged to withdraw from Trinity College in April 1798 when suspected of sedition but remained a committed United Irishmen. Emmet was part of the Dublin leadership throughout the *Rebellion of 1798 and by January 1799 was a figure of national standing. He traveled to Scotland in the summer of 1800 to confer with associates imprisoned at Fort George before illegally going to Hamburg and Paris to petition the French government to invade Ireland. Highly active in Irish radical circles on the continent, Emmet sought support for a French-backed revolution in Ireland in the Irish communities of the Iberian Peninsula, Switzerland, Holland, and many parts of *France. He returned to Ireland in October 1802 after conferring with Napoleon and Talleyrand on the anticipated French renewal of war with Britain. Along with Thomas Russell, William Dowdall, and Philip Long, Emmet organized the remnants of the United Irishmen to assist the French in a planned rebellion or invasion. An explosion in an arms depot exposed the plot and forced Emmet to act without the French in Dublin on July 23, 1803. Violence also broke out in *Kildare, *Down, *Antrim, and County Dublin. Emmet went into hiding but was eventually apprehended by Town Major Henry Sirr in the Harold's Cross section of Dublin on August 20. Brought to trial for treason on September 19, Emmet made the most famous speech from the dock in Irish history and accepted his inevitable capital sentence with a fortitude that won him the praise of his enemies. Emmet was executed in Thomas Street, Dublin, the following day in front of a massive crowd. The circumstances of his death, youth, and tragic relationship with Sarah Curran made him a romantic figure to nineteenth-century nationalists who were largely unaware of his life as a revolutionary. R.OD.

England. England held sovereignty over Ireland from the *Anglo-Norman Conquest of 1169–71 until the creation of the *Irish Free State in 1922, with *Northern Ireland still remaining part of the United Kingdom. The long relationship between the two countries has always been a troubled one. Efforts by the English to maintain and expand their political, economic, and cultural dominance were met by continual resistance from the Irish. From 1171 until 1541, the English crown ruled over Ireland as a lordship through feudal relationships with the native Gaelic aristocracy. Despite some colonization by English settlers, who often became more Irish than the Irish themselves, effective control remained limited to the *Pale, an area around *Dublin. During the sixteenth century, the Tudor monarchs attempted to expand administrative control over Ireland and replace the traditional *brehon laws with English common law. As part of this effort, *Henry VIII was formally proclaimed "King of Ireland" in 1541. The Protestant *Reformation launched by Henry VIII had profound and traumatic consequences, because the majority of the Irish people, including most of the Old English settlers, remained faithful to the Roman *Catholic Church. After the defeat of a rebellion (the *Nine Years War, 1593–1603) led by Hugh *O'Neill and the subsequent exile of several of the most prominent Gaelic nobles (the *Flight of the Earls, 1607), the English government stepped up their policy of plantation, whereby Protestant English and Scottish settlers would consolidate England's control over its colony.

When conflict between Charles I and Parliament plunged England into civil war during the 1640s, the Irish people rose in widespread rebellion (*Rebellion of 1641) against the new settlers and formed the *Confederation of Kilkenny. After the triumph of parliamentary forces, the campaigns of Oliver *Cromwell in Ireland during 1649–50 brutally repressed both royalist and Catholic Irish. As part of the *Cromwellian Settlement, England confiscated the lands of the remaining Catholic landowners in *Leinster, *Munster, and *Ulster, with many of them being forcibly removed to *Connacht. During the "Glorious Revolution" of 1689–91, *James II, who had been deposed largely because of his uncompromising Catholicism, sought to use Ireland, with its large Catholic population, as a base to recapture the English throne. After the defeat of James's forces at the Battle of the *Boyne (1690) and the final *Jacobite stand at Limerick (1691), the British government allowed the *Protestant ascendancy of *Anglo-Irish landowners to establish political, economic, and social control over Ireland by means of extensive *Penal Laws (which discriminated against the Catholic majority) and, through the eighteenth century, to run Ireland largely as it saw fit. The Protestant ascendancy increasingly sought a degree of legislative autonomy for Ireland, and, in 1782, achieved a *parliament with substantially increased, though still limited, powers. Radical *republican ideas emerged to challenge British rule during the 1790s with the formation of the *United Irishmen. The failed, though very bloody, *Rebellion of 1798, was followed by the Act of *Union (1800), whereby Ireland became a part of the United Kingdom of Great Britain and Ireland. (*Scotland had been part of the United Kingdom since 1707.) The union provided Ireland with representation in the British House of Commons, though the country continued to be administered by an appointed lord lieutenant and chief secretary. Although all one hundred Irish MPs (members of Parliament) were initially Protestant, the *Catholic Emancipation movement (members of Parliament under the leadership of Daniel *O'Connell) achieved in 1829 the right of Catholics to sit in Parliament. During the 1840s, O'Connell launched an unsuccessful movement to *repeal the union and establish an Irish parliament (based in Dublin) that would be chosen by a democratic majority of the Irish people. For the more radical *nationalists of the conspiratorial *Irish Republican Brotherhood (IRB, founded in 1858), the inadequate response of the British government to the Great *Famine of 1845–51 underlined the need for an independent Irish republic, to be achieved by violent means if necessary. After the Famine, Irish *emigration increased to cities in England such as Liverpool, London, and Manchester. Despite facing considerable prejudice, the contribution of Irish emigrants to English society and culture has been considerable. Throughout the nineteenth century, the British government administered Ireland with a mixture of coercive and conciliatory policies: it suppressed republican rebellions in 1848 and 1867, as well as sporadic agrarian agitation, while it also funded *education and economic development programs, established local government institutions, and provided incremental measures of land reform. During the 1880s, Charles Stewart *Parnell created a disciplined Irish Party in the House of Commons that sought to achieve *home rule. After the conversion of Liberal leader William Ewart *Gladstone to this viewpoint, his party introduced unsuccessful home rule bills in 1886 and 1893. *World War I delayed implementation of a third home rule bill, which passed the House of Commons in 1914 despite *Unionist opposition. The *Easter Rising of 1916 and the subsequent emergence of *Sinn Féin as the predominant political party in Ireland led to the *Anglo-Irish War of 1919–21. Negotiations resulted in the *Anglo-Irish Treaty (1921), which founded the *Irish Free State. Home rule was, in the end, implemented only in the six northern counties that had opposed it so vehemently. Although the Free State remained initially a dominion within the British *Commonwealth, the treaty effectively ended British sovereignty over the country, except for *Northern Ireland, which still remains part of the United Kingdom. F.B.

English writers in Ireland. The *Anglo-Norman Gerald of Wales (c.1146–1223), also known as Giraldus Cambrensis, is perhaps the first English writer to undertake the task of explaining Ireland and the Irish to the civilized world. Gerald wrote: "[The Irish] are so barbarous that they cannot be said to have any culture." His two books *The History and Topography of Ireland* (1188) and *The Conquest of Ireland* (1189) remained immensely influential upon successive generations of English settlers and conquerors until the nineteenth century.

While there were a number of English-born writers in Ireland from the thirteenth through the fifteenth century who wrote in English, Norman-

French, and Latin, it was the reconquest of Ireland in the sixteenth and seventeenth centuries that gave rise to a flowering of both literary and polemical writing by new English settlers and visitors. The most famous, talented, and perhaps most influential of these was Edmund *Spenser (1552–99). Spenser's major works, including his *Amoretti and Epithalamion* (1595), as well as his great allegorical epic, *The Faerie Queene* (1590 and 1596), written at Kilcolman Castle in County *Cork, are profoundly influenced by Ireland as both a real and a symbolic place. Convinced that Gaelic culture had to be destroyed to establish civility and *Protestantism, Spenser in *A View of the Present State of Ireland* (written 1596, printed 1633) advocates a harsh military campaign for the subjugation of the Irish, "a people altogether stubborn and untamed." His prescription for the taming of Ireland's "licentious barbarism" was carried out very thoroughly by Oliver *Cromwell some fifty years later.

In the eighteenth century, there were many distinguished *Anglo-Irish writers but very few English writers of any great significance in Ireland. However, some of the greatest English writers of the nineteenth century spent time in Ireland. Anthony Trollope (1812–82) lived and worked in *Offaly and *Tipperary from 1841 to 1859, and wrote his first two novels *The Macdermots of Ballycloran* (1847) and *The Kellys and the O'Kellys* (1848) during that period. John Henry (Cardinal) *Newman (1801–90) resided in *Dublin from 1851 to 1858, during which time he delivered the lectures published as *Idea of a University*, and became the founding rector of the Catholic University of Ireland. Although Newman found his Irish sojourn difficult, it did not prevent him from making statements such as "If I were an Irishman I should be (in heart) a rebel." A fellow Oxford convert and disciple of Newman, Gerard Manley *Hopkins (1844–89) was appointed professor of classics at University College Dublin in 1884, where he wrote his final "terrible sonnets."

One of the most important nineteenth-century English writers on Ireland, John Stuart Mill (1806–73), never set foot there. Mill's many writings on Ireland, such as *The Condition of Ireland* (1846–47), *Principles of Political Economy* (1848–71) and *England and Ireland* (1868), were so sympathetic to the plight of Irish tenants that in the early 1850s, as he reports in his autobiography, leaders of "the popular party in Ireland" (probably the Tenant League) "offered to bring me into Parliament for an Irish County."

Another eminent Victorian, William Makepeace Thackeray (1811–63) published in 1843 *The Irish Sketch Book*, one of the liveliest of the many travel books written by English visitors to Ireland. This genre goes back to the seventeenth century, and includes *An Itinerary* (1617) by Fynes Moryson, who was impressed by the mildness of the winter, the greenness and fertility of the fields, and the medicinal properties of the *whiskey. The most influential traveler's account of eighteenth-century Ireland was Arthur Young's *A Tour in Ireland* (1780), which was praised by Maria *Edgeworth and later by *nationalists, and remains an important source of information about both landlords and the peasantry of the time. In the twentieth century the tradition has continued in such works as H. V. Morton's *In Search of Ireland* (1931), V. S. Pritchett's *Dublin, A Portrait* (1967), and Tim Robinson's *Stones of Aran* (1986 and 1995). In contrast to many earlier visitors, modern writers strive to resist stereotypes, whether hostile or sentimental. In the 1940s the English poet John Betjeman wrote: "The Irish are not mad and spooky and vague and dreamy, as some of them would have us think, but extremely logical. It is *we* who are the other things." J.McD.

Ennis, Séamus (1919–82). *Uilleann piper, singer, raconteur, broadcaster, and collector. Born in Finglas, *Dublin, Ennis learned from his father and local musicians to play the pipes. He collected songs for the Folklore Commission in the late 1940s, and worked on music programming with *Radio Éireann. In the 1950s, his pioneering BBC radio show "As I Roved Out" played a key part in the traditional *music revival. In later decades, he was best known for exceptional music performances. A "school" dedicated to his memory is held in North County Dublin each autumn, and a cultural center named after him was opened there in the village of Naul in 2001. F.V.

Enniskillen Bombing (1987). IRA (*Irish Republican Army) bombing in *Northern Ireland. On Sunday, November 8, 1987, eleven people—ten *Protestant civilians participating in a Remembrance Day Ceremony at the town's cenotaph and one member of the *Royal Ulster Constabulary (RUC)—were killed in a bomb attack in Enniskillen, County *Fermanagh. The attack was carried out by the IRA, who claimed that the bomb had been detonated prematurely "by mistake." Revulsion at the atrocity was widespread and it represented a landmark in public reaction against Provisional IRA militarism. For the first time, Gerry *Adams, speaking for Provisional *Sinn Féin, chided the IRA for lack of care in its operations. M.M.

Eriugena, John Scottus (c.810–c.877). Philosopher. Born and monastically educated in Ireland, Eriugena was a Greek scholar and the most productive systematic philosopher between the fifth and eleventh centuries. Between 850 and 877, he taught at the court of Charles the Bald, King of the Franks, where he was advisor to the king. During this time, he also translated Greek patristic and neoplatonist works into Latin, became embroiled in a dispute on predestination, and produced (c. 866) his systematic treatise, *De Divisione Naturae*. The book attempted the first complete rational explanation of Christianity. Its unorthodox combination of pagan pantheism with Christian theism led to its papal condemnation in 1225. M.L.

Ervine, David (1954–). *Unionist politician. Chief spokesman for the *Progressive Unionist Party (PUP), an organization with close links to the *Ulster Volunteer Force, Ervine is a member of Belfast City Council and of the *Northern Ireland Assembly. In the 1970s, Ervine served a five-year jail sentence for possession of explosives. After his release in 1980, he entered community politics. When the main *Protestant paramilitary organizations called a cease-fire in 1994, he became a highly visible media figure. Though a firm unionist, Ervine supported the *Good Friday Agreement for securing the connection with Britain. He is critical of *nationalist, particularly *republican, attempts to push the agenda of a united Ireland. However, Ervine shares something of the paramilitary worldview, and supported republican inclusion in the political process despite the IRA's (*Irish Republican Army's) ongoing activity and its stockpile of arms. (Loyalist paramilitaries, of course, behaved likewise.) His rhetoric is generally optimistic, if given to portentous epigrams, though he is quick to explain the history of loyalist violence as reflexive. M.M.

Eucharistic Congress. Large-scale Catholic assembly. Ireland's first Eucharistic Congress, convened in *Dublin in 1932, was a huge public celebration of the sacrament of the Eucharist in honor of the fifteen-hundredth anniversary of St. *Patrick's conversion of Ireland. More than one million people attended mass in *Phoenix Park, attesting to Roman *Catholicism's pervasive influence on the lives of the Irish people. The congress personified the confidence and prominence of the twentieth-century Irish Catholic Church prior to the *Second Vatican Council. M.P.C.

European Union (EU), Ireland's membership. In a 1972 referendum, the Irish electorate voted by a substantial majority to join the European Union (then the European Economic Community made up of six founding members). This was a landmark decision in a process initiated in 1959 by *Taoiseach (prime minister) Seán *Lemass and by Secretary to the Department of Finance T. K. *Whitaker to pursue a policy of *economic expansion, end Ireland's isolationist policies, and lessen its economic domination by Great Britain.

Membership of the European Union has helped Ireland achieve significant levels of economic development in the last thirty years. Ireland in 1972 was the poorest of all EU member states. It has benefited substantially from the EU budget, particularly in the form of structural funding in the 1980s and 1990s (e.g., upgrading of roads and other communication networks). Benefiting also from free trade and from the Single European Market, Ireland has been able to diversify its trade with different EU countries. In excess of 60 percent of Irish exports now go to EU countries. Its inclusion in a unified European market has been an important factor in attracting foreign (mainly US) investment in Ireland. Multinational firms such as Dell and Intel established major European centers in Ireland. As a result, Ireland's Gross Domestic Production (GDP) per capita has grown from 60 percent of the EU average in 1960 to more than 120 percent in 2000. The introduction of the euro (the single EU currency) in January 2002, in Ireland and in eleven other EU economies, was the culminating point in the process of full economic integration.

Although membership of the European Union has mostly been felt at the economic level, EU-generated law has also been responsible for significant changes in areas such as employment equality (covering equality of treatment for men and *women), safety, *health, and welfare at work. Politically, it has made Ireland less Anglocentric, more confident and open to outside influences. Ireland has both helped shape European Union policy and in turn been influenced by it. Because of a landmark Irish Supreme Court decision in the 1980s, it is necessary to have referenda in Ireland in relation to treaties associated with further European integration. While Ireland has endorsed by referenda major European legislation (in 1987, the Single European Act, which finalized the Single European Market; and in 1992, the Maastricht Treaty, which enabled the creation of the single currency, the euro), it narrowly rejected the Nice Treaty in 2001, which provided for EU enlargement to include parts of Eastern Europe. Ireland's veto of further EU expansion reflected a fear of competition and budgetary threats posed by the prospect of new members, and most importantly of threats to Irish *neutrality and fear of diminished power in a restructured union. The Irish government received a Declaration by the European Union that Ireland's traditional policy of neutrality was not affected by the treaties, before holding a second referendum on the Nice Treaty in October 2002. This was passed by a nearly two to one majority.

While EU leaders aim at making the EU (now consisting of twenty-five member states) the most competitive economy in the world by 2020, future challenges and issues include the development of a European Security and Defense Policy (ESDP), environmental change, human rights, and a wider co-operation with developing countries. Ireland's overall objectives in the EU are primarily to help protect the rights and interests of EU citizens; maintain freedom, security, and justice; promote economic prosperity; and act more effectively internationally to promote peace, security, and development. B.A.

ev+a. Annual open submission exhibition of art. Held in *Limerick since 1977, the exhibition is adjudicated by a single outside curator. A biennial participation of invited international artists alternates with colloquies on contemporary art and culture. The adjudicators are from around the world: in 2002 the curator was from Thailand and in 2001 from Sudan and the United States (Web site: *www.iol.ie/eva.*) M.C.

External Relations Act (1936). Act limiting the role of the British crown in Ireland's affairs. In December 1936, Éamon *de Valera used the abdication of Edward VIII as an opportunity to pass two pieces of related legislation. The *Constitution (Twenty-seventh Amendment) Act removed all references to the crown from the Irish Constitution, while the Executive Authority (External Relations) Act authorized the king to act on behalf of the *Irish Free State in external matters "as and when advised by the Executive Council to do so." P.E.

F

fairs. Originally, the fair was a public assembly in early Ireland. These fairs had a political and ceremonial function, particularly those in *Tara and Uisneach in *pre-Christian Ireland. The more modern fair after cultural anglicization bears only a slim resemblance to these medieval assemblies, but their echoes survive. The later fairs are related to markets, but are seasonal rather than regular. From the seventeenth century onward, rich landlords or merchants received royal grants, which allowed them to hold fairs, and charged tolls from the people who wished to sell their wares. Although regulated by English law, fairs retained much of their Irish character. Under the guise of buying and selling, much revelry took place.

Donnybrook Fair in *Dublin was suppressed in 1867 because of its riotous nature. Ballinasloe Fair in County *Galway specialized in the buying and selling of horses. Spancil Hill Fair in County *Clare was held at the end of June, and was notorious for its gatherings of *travellers. Ballindine Fair in County *Mayo was typical in that the street trade gave way to a more organized mart in the 1950s. The Two-Mile-Borris Fair in County *Tipperary only dealt in suckling pigs, but was put out of business by the Pigs and Bacon Commission in the 1940s. The highlight of the fair was a pig-guzzling competition, where bachelors had to prove their manhood by eating as many young pigs as they could within three hours. The Oul' Lammas Fair in Ballycastle in County *Antrim takes place at the end of August each year. It is now most famous because of the song (named after the fair), which includes the lines: "Did you treat your Mary Ann to the Dulse and Yellow man / at the old Lammas Fair in Ballycastle O!" Perhaps the most genuine of all the extant fairs is Puck Fair in Killorglin, County *Kerry, held every year from the tenth to the twelfth of August. A large beribboned white male goat is hoisted onto a platform and gapes bemused for three days at the revelers below. Pubs remain open all day and all night for three days. Supposedly, this ceremony of the white male goat may have a pagan origin, but it is more likely that the burghers of Kerry saw a good chance of turning some money when the chance came. A much more serious kind of fair was the Hiring Fair in East Donegal, where the children of the poor were hired out as wage slaves to the rich farmers of the lush lowlands of *Ulster and *Scotland, a practice that survived until the 1940s. A.T.

Famine, the Great Irish (1845–49). The Great Famine of the late 1840s was the worst demographic and social catastrophe in modern Irish history. The immediate cause of the calamity was the blighting of the potato crop in Ireland, in three seasons out of four, by a fungal disease—*phytophthora infestans*—to which there was no known antidote at the time. Striking first in late summer 1845, the blight destroyed one-third of that year's potato crop and three-quarters of the 1846 crop; it was less virulent in 1847, but as seed potatoes were scarce, the crop was not plentiful in "black '47." The 1848 potato crop was down almost 40 percent below average yield. By 1849 the blight was abating, but by this time Irish society had experienced a massive trauma of death, disease, and *emigration. Diseases, such as typhus, dysentery, and "relapsing fever," were even more lethal than actual starvation. An added menace was an outbreak of cholera in 1849.

Precise statistics on the "famine" calamity are difficult to establish; but the most reliable figures suggest excess mortality (i.e., famine-related deaths) of about one million, with between a million and one and a half million people estimated as having emigrated in the years 1845 to 1851. While no region or social group entirely escaped the ravages of famine and disease, the heaviest losses were experienced in the west and southwest and among children under five and adults over sixty-five years of age.

While the immediate cause of the calamity was the potato blight, the circumstances that left such a large portion of the population at risk to the failure of a single root crop were complex, and relate to very particular economic, social, and political factors operating in early-nineteenth-century Ireland. The population of Ireland had grown rapidly from the final quarter of the eighteenth century. This population growth was heavily rural-based and was encouraged by an expansion of tillage farming (driven by market demand in Britain). A growing population of rural poor in Ireland, living on small-holdings and subsistence potato plots, provided the cheap labor force for an expanding agricultural—especially tillage—sector in Ireland. While the years following the end of the Napoleonic wars in 1815 saw a slowing down in the rate of population growth in Ireland, largely due to an accelerating rise in emigration, by the early 1840s the population of Ireland was probably not far short of eight and a half million people. Some three million of this population were dependent on the potato as the staple component of their diet. This was the broad base of the Irish rural poor. For millions more of the population, the potato was an important, but not a vital, element of their diet and animal feed.

*Agriculture was the mainstay of the Irish *economy. The emergence of an industrial enclave in the northeast of the island was balanced by losses in manufacturing activity and employment in the rest of the country in the pre-Famine decades. Since the Act of *Union of 1800, Ireland was an integral part of the United Kingdom. By 1845, Ireland was fully integrated into a single free-trade economy with Britain, which by this time was the most advanced economy in the world. This very fact—that through the failure of a single root crop, massive death and suffering had been experienced in a "region" of the most developed economy in the world—fueled the anger of Irish *nationalists, both at the time and in later generations, prompting their denunciation of British rule in Ireland and their sustained demand for Irish self-government.

The response of the government in the pre-Famine decades to the problem of Irish poverty was to establish in the early 1840s a network of *workhouses—grim institutions for the custodial care of the utterly destitute. By 1845 the total capacity of the workhouse system was one hundred thousand inmates. At the height of the potato famine two years later, more than three million people would be in receipt of some form of food relief—through soup kitchens or through other channels. The workhouse system, designed to deal with "normal" Irish poverty, was overwhelmed by the scale of the Famine calamity. During the crisis years of the Irish Famine, government policy changed direction several times: from emergency grain shipments, to public works schemes, to direct food aid, and back again to the workhouses and some "outdoor relief" paid for by taxes on Irish property. The policy was excessively bureaucratic, too rigidly bound by dominant contemporary ideas of laissez-faire—inhibiting state intervention in either the labor market (wages) or the commodity market (food prices)—and, in the case of some influential members of the political and administrative elite, pervaded by a notion that this horrific check on reckless Irish population growth was ultimately "providential." Private charity—channeled largely through religious bodies of all denominations—was considerable, though not inexhaustible, and only in a small minority of instances was famine relief tainted by an excess of religious zeal in the form of proselytizing.

The Famine altered the class structure of rural Ireland, decimating the landless and cottier class. It left many landlords bankrupt and forced the sale of up to 14 percent of the land of Ireland. It altered the scale of Irish emigration, so that what had been a swelling stream of emigrants became a torrent, and a "culture of emigration" was established which was to be a feature of Irish socioeconomic life for more than a century afterward.

The population of Ireland had fallen to 6.6 million by 1851; continuing emigration would cause it to fall to 4.4 million by 1911. The nationalist political movements of Daniel *O'Connell, for *Repeal, and the *Young Irelanders were overwhelmed by the horror of the Famine. But the sense of grievance at the way in which the government had responded to the crisis was to leave later generations of Irish nationalists—both at home and throughout the Irish diaspora—with a strong determination to do whatever they could, whatever was needed, to achieve an independent Irish state. G.OT.

Farquhar, George (1677/78–1707). Dramatist. Born in *Derry and educated at Trinity College, Dublin, Farquhar abandoned an early acting career after accidentally stabbing a colleague on stage in Dublin. He moved to London, where his first two plays *Love and a Bottle* (1698) and *The Constant Couple* (1699) were well received at London's Drury Lane Theatre. As an army lieutenant, Farquhar traveled throughout England and Ireland to recruit soldiers. His play *The Recruiting Officer* (1706) draws upon these experiences. His final play, *A Beaux' Stratagem*, was a great success, but he was by then on his deathbed, possibly suffering from tuberculosis. Farquhar's genius lies in creating penetrating satire through playful and witty comedies with elaborate plots and delightfully eccentric characters. He died in poverty. C.D.

Farrell, Micheal (1940–2000). Painter. Born in Kells, County *Meath, Farrell developed from hard-edged *Celtic abstraction to engaged figurative work. He studied art in London, taught in New York and London, and represented Ireland at the Paris Biennale in 1967. Along with Gerald *Dillon and other artists, he withdrew his work in protest against treatment of *nationalists from the *Irish Exhibition of Living Art in *Northern Ireland in 1969. Excluded from *ROSC, he moved to Paris and produced work in response to events in Ireland, notably monochromes of the 1974 *Monaghan and Dublin bombings and the 1977 *Madonna Irlanda or, The Very First Real Irish Political Picture* (*Hugh Lane Municipal Gallery). His most recent projects dealt with the Great *Famine and *Bloody Sunday. M.C.

Faulkner, Brian (1921–77). Prime minister of *Northern Ireland (1971–72). A *Protestant businessman, Faulkner was educated in *Dublin and elected to the Northern Ireland Parliament as a *Unionist in 1949. As minister of home affairs (1959–63), he became known as a hard-liner in his efforts to end the *Irish Republican Army (IRA) violent border campaign. He served as commerce minister (1963–69) and minister of development (1969–71). A most capable unionist politician, Faulkner became deputy prime minister in 1966, but many believe that he undermined the leadership of Prime Minister Terence *O'Neill. Faulkner succeeded James *Chichester Clarke as prime minister in March 1971. By then, a war had developed between the IRA and the British army. In August 1971, Faulkner introduced *internment, under which hundreds of suspected IRA members were imprisoned without trial. The events of *Bloody Sunday (January 1972) and internment intensified *nationalist/*Catholic opposition to the *Stormont government. Faulkner's overtures to Catholic moderates failed, and in March 1972, Britain suspended the Northern Ireland government. Faulkner and his ministers resigned. In 1973, he helped negotiate a power-sharing Executive for Northern Ireland, and following the agreement of a Council of Ireland at *Sunningdale he became its head in January 1974. When a *loyalist general strike crippled Northern Ireland in May 1974, Faulkner resigned and the government collapsed, resulting in the reimposition of direct British rule. He was made Baron Faulkner of Downpatrick in 1976. He died following a horse-riding accident in 1977. M.M.

Fay, Frank (1871–1931). Actor. Fay was born in *Dublin and, like his brother William *Fay, was educated at Belvedere College. He founded the Dublin Dramatic School and Ormonde Dramatic Society in 1898. As drama critic for Arthur *Griffith's *United Irishman* (from 1899 to 1902), he encouraged innovation on the stage. In 1902, he directed W. B. *Yeats's *Cathleen Ni Houlihan* and AE's (George *Russell) *Deirdre*. The Irish National Dramatic Society, which he had founded with his brother in 1902, became the Irish National Theatre Society (the precursor to the *Abbey Theatre) in 1903 when they joined forces with Yeats and Lady *Gregory. Frank Fay was instrumental in building up the company and trained the actors in speech. He played Naisi in AE's *Deirdre* (1902), Cuchulain in Yeats's *On Baile's Strand* (1904), and Sean Keogh in *J. M. Synge's *The Playboy of the Western World* (1907). He left the Abbey in 1908 after a dispute with Yeats, bitterly complaining of the latter's complete ignorance of acting. With his brother Willie, he departed for the United States, but attempted several times unsuccessfully to negotiate a return to the Abbey. After his return to Dublin, the Abbey School of Acting engaged him as an elocution teacher. J.C.E.L.

Fay, William George (1872–1947). Actor and producer. Fay was born in *Dublin and, like his brother Frank *Fay, educated at Belvedere College, which he left at age sixteen to join a touring theater group. He formed his own company in 1897. He produced Alice Milligan's *Red Hugh* in 1901, which W. B. *Yeats saw. Fay coached the players for a production of Douglas *Hyde's *Casadh an t-Súgáin (The Twisting of the Rope)* in 1901, and Yeats's *Cathleen Ni Houlihan* in 1902. In the same year, William, together with his brother Frank, founded the Irish National Dramatic Society, which became the Irish National Theatre Society (precursor to the *Abbey Theatre) in 1903, after they had been joined by Yeats and Lady *Gregory. William Fay acted as stage manager for the company. As an actor, he appeared in Yeats's *The Hour-Glass* (1903). From 1904, he produced plays for the Abbey Theatre, which under his direction developed its distinctive peasant drama. With his brother and the *Allgood sisters, he created the economic acting style of the Abbey players. He married Abbey actress Brigit O'Dempsey. He was successful as Christy Mahon in J. M. *Synge's *The Playboy of the Western World*, Bartley in *Riders to the Sea*, and Martin in *The Well of the Saints*. In 1908 he resigned from the Abbey after complaints from its sponsor, Annie Horniman, and disagreements with Yeats. Joined by his brother, he went to the United States, where he produced Irish plays. After 1914, he worked in London and Birmingham. Fay played the part of Father Tom in the 1967 film *Odd Man Out*. With Catherine Carswell, he wrote *The Fays of the Abbey Theatre* (1935). J.C.E.L.

Feiritéar, Piaras (c.1600–53). Poet in the *Irish language. Feiritéar belonged to an aristocratic family in County *Kerry. His love poems were heavily influenced by the *amour courtois* traditions of continental Europe and were collected and edited by Patrick Dineen in 1903. Although he was of *Anglo-Norman descent, he sided with the native Irish in the *Rebellion of 1641, and captured Tralee Castle, which he held for ten years. He was hanged in Killarney, County Kerry, for his part in the rebellion in 1653. B.D.

Fenians. Revolutionary movement of the second half of 1800s. The Fenian Brotherhood was started in the United States in 1858 by John O'Mahony, who, like many *Irish Americans, was disillusioned with parliamentary politics in Ireland and the waning *Young Ireland movement. On St. *Patrick's Day 1858, with American backing, James *Stephens founded a secret society in *Dublin. Loosely linked with the American Fenians, the society sought the creation of an independent Irish *republic. It was so secret that, initially, it had no formal title, and was known only as the Society or Organization.

The organization eventually took the name Fenians from the branch of the movement in the United States. (The word *Fenian* refers to *Fianna, the legendary army of ancient Ireland led by Finn McCool, which performed feats of superhuman heroism while protecting *pre-Christian *Celtic Ireland from invaders and intruders both human and otherwise.) Later, the organization became known as the Brotherhood and, eventually, the *Irish Republican Brotherhood (IRB).

Stephens organized the movement in a clearly defined hierarchy with each member's knowledge of the organization confined to his own particular section. In practice, however, security was not watertight.

The movement spread throughout Ireland drawing opposition from the authorities and the *Catholic Church, which supported constitutional *nationalists. Stephens was successful in Ireland but fell out of favor with the powerful American faction. His newspaper venture, the *Irish People*, was seen as a breach of security and a means by which the movement could be infiltrated.

In 1865, the authorities, anticipating a rebellion with American backing, arrested Stephens, Jeremiah *O'Donovan Rossa, and other leaders. By 1866, the Fenians were under increased pressure to organize a rebellion. There were many splits among them. Stephens escaped from jail and fled to the United States where he briefly became head of the American organization. He was hampered, however, by a lack of resources and was replaced by *American Civil War veterans intent on rebellion as soon as possible. The American Fenians launched an unsuccessful attempt to invade *Canada in 1866.

In Ireland, the Fenians mounted a rising on March 4–5, 1867. A combination of bad weather, informers, and a highly efficient British army quickly quelled the rebellion. Many of the rebels were arrested and imprisoned. The campaign for an amnesty for Fenian prisoners and outrage at the execution of three Fenians in Manchester, England, known as the *Manchester Martyrs, aroused massive public support and gave new impetus to constitutional politics, which resulted in the *home rule movement. T.C.

Ferguson, Harry George (1884–1960). Engineer. Born in Growell, County *Down, Ferguson joined his brother's cycle-repair business in 1902. He established an engineering business in 1911, importing tractors, and later he designed his own tractor. His draught control system (patented in 1925) revolutionized farming methods by improving traction and making light inexpensive machines more effective. Ferguson joined forces with Henry Ford in the 1930s to manufacture his designs in the United States, but the partnership dissolved after a legal battle in 1947. In 1946, with British government backing, production of the Ferguson tractor was launched in Coventry. Ferguson set up his own US plant in 1948, but sold it to Massey-Harris in 1953. S.A.B.

Ferguson, Sir Samuel (1810–86). Poet and antiquarian. Born in *Belfast, Ferguson is best known for his translations from the *Irish, published in such collections as *Lays of the Western Gael* (1865) and *Congal* (1872). These works anticipated the interests of the *Irish Revival and influenced the young W. B. *Yeats. Ferguson was knighted in 1878 for reorganizing the Irish public records office, work from which his *Ogham Inscriptions in Ireland, Wales and Scotland* (1887) partly derives. G.OB.

Fermanagh, County. Inland county in the province of *Ulster, one of the six counties of *Northern Ireland. Fermanagh (648 square miles) is one of the least densely populated counties in Ireland, with a population of est. 54,033 (1996). Bordered on the east by *Monaghan and *Tyrone, on the north by *Donegal, on the west by *Leitrim, and on the south by *Cavan, Fermanagh derives its name from the Irish *Fir Manach*, meaning the tribe of Manach. The highest mountain in the county is Mount Cuilcagh (2,175 feet) on the border with Cavan. The largest lake in the county is Lough Erne and principal rivers are the Erne, the Finn, the Pettigo, and the Omna.

Until their defeat at the Battle of *Kinsale in 1601, the county was dominated by the Maguire family. Following this battle and the *Flight of the Earls, the lands formerly held by the Gaelic chieftains were confiscated and given to settlers from England and Scotland. After the *Government of Ireland Act (1920), Fermanagh came under the control of the *Northern Ireland Parliament.

Fermanagh is known for the Belleek pottery company, established in 1857, which produces a world-famous hand-painted porcelain. Tourist attractions include the Marble Arch, a natural limestone bridge near Enniskillen, and the monastic site on Devenish Island, founded by St. Molaise in the sixth century. The main industries in the county are *agriculture, fishing, forestry, and tourism. The county's capital is Enniskillen, famed as a center of *Protestant resistance to King *James II in the 1680s. One of the Irish regiments in the British army before and during *World War I was named the Enniskillen Dragoons, after this town. A.S.

Fianna. Legendary army of ancient Ireland led by Finn McCool. The Fianna (literally "soldiers") were a band of fighting men whose qualifications were quite rigid: No man could be taken into the Fianna until he knew twelve books of *poetry. He had to be put into a deep hole in the ground up to his middle while nine men would go the length of ten furrows from him and would cast their spears at him. Or he must run through the forest, pursued by other Fianna, without being harmed, upsetting his hair, or cracking a twig underfoot. The many stories of Finn and the Fianna are known as the Fianna Cycle, though the origin and dates of the various stories are spread from at least the eighth to the eighteenth centuries, in both Ireland and Scotland. J.M.D.

Fianna Fáil. *Political party. Fianna Fáil was formed in 1926 by pragmatists within the anti-*Anglo-Irish Treaty *Sinn Féin party, most notably Éamon *de Valera, who wished to engage in the political life of the new *Irish Free State. Ultimately, Fianna Fáil won the support of the vast majority of the anti-treaty public. The party was led and dominated by the personality of Éamon de Valera from its foundation until he stepped down as leader in 1959. De Valera continued to be a significant figure while serving as president, though he was almost entirely uninvolved in the day-to-day leadership of the party. Party leaders since de Valera include: Seán *Lemass (1959–66), Jack *Lynch (1966–79), Charles *Haughey (1979–92), Albert *Reynolds (1992–94), and Bertie *Ahern (1997–). Fianna Fáil has been consistently the largest party in the *Dáil (Parliament) since 1932 and has been in government 1932–48, 1951–54, 1957–73, 1977–81, February–November 1982, 1987–94, and 1997–present.

Fianna Fáil was initially organized around a radical *nationalist program, which sought to overturn those aspects of the Anglo-Irish Treaty that limited Irish sovereignty, and on a wider program of anti-partitionism and economic development. In particular, Fianna Fáil sought to abolish the *oath of allegiance to the British monarch; secure the return of those ports still occupied by the British navy; abolish the right of judicial appeal to the British Privy Council; end the payment of land annuities to Britain; and end the right of veto on legislation held by the governor general (the British monarch's representative in Ireland). All of these objectives were achieved between 1932 and 1938, but Fianna Fáil's ultimate declaration of sovereignty came with the introduction of a new (the current) *Constitution, which was adopted by referendum in 1937.

Ireland's *neutrality during World War II was supported by the other parties, but the policy was associated most strongly with Fianna Fáil and remains popular with the public, even though its real impact on the conduct of Irish *foreign policy is less clear since the ending of the Cold War.

The popularity of the party's nationalist, neutralist, and economic development policies led to sixteen uninterrupted years of Fianna Fáil government starting in 1932. This long period was interrupted only briefly from 1948 to 1951 and from 1954 to 1957, after which Fianna Fáil served another sixteen years in government until 1973.

In the 1960s, following a long period of economic development based on protectionism and *agriculture, Seán Lemass, de Valera's successor, advocated a shift toward free trade, foreign investment, and state planning. In 1972, Ireland joined the European Economic Community (now the *European Union).

Fianna Fáil returned to government in 1977 with its second-highest share of the vote ever. By 1981, the party lost power again, because of the economic crisis caused by the second oil crisis and the heightened tension in *Northern Ireland during the 1981 *hunger strikes. On their return to government in 1987, Fianna Fáil was credited with laying the ground for the rapid improvement in Ireland's economic position by negotiating the first "social partnership" agreement between government, employers, and labor unions. Since then, agreements have been renewed every three years. The party also entered its first ever coalition government (with the *Progressive Democrats) in 1989, followed by an historic Fianna Fáil /*Labour Party government between 1992 and 1994.

Fianna Fáil played a central role in the negotiation of the 1994 IRA (*Irish Republican Army) cease-fire and the 1998 *Good Friday Agreement. The public perception that Fianna Fáil could best manage the *peace process gave the party an electoral boost in the 1997 general election. In 2002, Fianna Fáil became the first government party in over thirty years to secure reelection—doing so with an increased popular vote and winning extra seats. In 2004, the party suffered a setback in local and European elections. J.D.

Field, John (1782–1837). Composer and pianist. Born in *Dublin, Field was apprentice to Muzio Clementi, owner of a piano manufacturing firm. He traveled with Clementi throughout Europe demonstrating these instruments. Field settled in St. Petersburg in 1803, where he composed most of his mature music. His work reached an artistic peak with the Nocturnes, a romantic genre he created and named, and which later inspired the work of Chopin. Field died in Moscow. S.A.B.

Field Day Theatre Company. Drama company. Founded in *Derry in 1980 by playwright Brian *Friel and actor Stephen *Rea, the Field Day Theatre Company aimed to establish Derry as a theatrical center and to initiate an intellectual movement that would redefine Irish political and cultural identity. Seamus *Deane, Seamus *Heaney, Tom Paulin, and David Hammond joined Friel and Rea on the Board of Directors. The first production, Brian Friel's *Translations* (1980), like much of the theater's subsequent work, explored questions of community, language, and identity. Other plays included Friel's *Three Sisters* (1981) and *The Communication Cord* (1982), Tom Paulin's *The Riot Act* (1984), Derek *Mahon's *High Time* (1984), Tom *Kilroy's *Double Cross* (1986), Stewart Parker's *Pentecost* (1987), Friel's *Making History* (1988), Terry Eagleton's *St. Oscar* (1989), and Seamus Heaney's *The Cure at Troy* (1990). Field Day launched a pamphlet series in 1983 with Tom Paulin's *A New Look at the Language Question*, Seamus Deane's *Civilians and Barbarians*, and Seamus Heaney's *Open Letter*. In 1988, three radical international critics—Terry Eagleton, Edward Said, and Fredric Jameson—contributed to the series. The company's largest undertaking was *The Field Day Anthology of Irish Literature* (3 vols., 1991), edited by

Seamus Deane, which presented Irish, English, and Latin texts from the earliest times to the present and included introductory essays. Two additional volumes to the anthology were published in 2002. C.D.

fili. Most easily translated as the modern word *poet*. In early and medieval society the *fili* was part of a learned class whose boundaries are not always clear. A *fili* could write praise poetry or satires for his chief and employer, but he might also be a genealogist, historian, grammarian, diplomat, advisor, storyteller, or professor of knowledge. This sense of the *fili* came to an end with the destruction of the Gaelic aristocratic polity in the early seventeenth century. A.T.

Fine Gael. Political party. Fine Gael was founded in 1933 when *Cumann na nGaedheal (an offshoot of the pro-treaty faction of *Sinn Féin) merged with the National Centre Party and the quasi-fascist *Blueshirt movement. Fine Gael was initially led by the Blueshirt's leader General Eoin *O'Duffy, but W. T. *Cosgrave became the party's leader in 1935. Thereafter the leaders were: W. T. Cosgrave (1935–44), Richard *Mulcahy (1944–59), James *Dillon (1959–65), Liam *Cosgrave (1965–77), Garret *FitzGerald (1977–87), Alan *Dukes (1987–90), John *Bruton (1990–2001), Michael *Noonan (2001–02), and Enda *Kenny (2002–present). Fine Gael has served in government on six occasions: 1948–51, 1954–57, 1973–77, 1981–Feb. 82, Nov. 1982–87, 1994–97.

The party's initial pro-treaty and conservative image was further tarnished by its relationship with the Blueshirts and it was not until 1948 that Fine Gael first entered government. Both in 1948 and 1954, Fine Gael's coalition partners rejected party leader Richard Mulcahy as *Taoiseach (prime minister) because of his hard-line security role during the *Civil War. John A. *Costello was elected Taoiseach while Mulcahy remained as Fine Gael leader. In the 1960s, Fine Gael made overtures to the *Labour Party through a new, more centrist, policy document, "The Just Society," in a bid to construct an alternative government to *Fianna Fail.

Their coalition government, with the Labour Party (1973–77), was highly unpopular as they struggled to respond to the first oil crisis of the 1970s. This government implemented very repressive internal security policies in response to the heightening conflict in *Northern Ireland and was heavily defeated in the general election of 1977.

Under a new leader, Garret FitzGerald, Fine Gael positioned itself as a liberal party on social issues and won record shares of the vote in the elections of 1981 and 1982, reaching almost 40 percent.

A series of poor election results in the 1980s and 1990s and especially in 2002 led to a growing sense of crisis. After the 2004 elections in which Fianna Fáil lost votes, Fine Gael struggled to remain the principal opposition party. J.D.

Fitzgerald, Barry (1888–1961). Actor, stage name of William Joseph Shields. Born in *Dublin and educated at Merchant Taylor's School, Fitzgerald played with the amateur Kincora Players group, and then at the *Abbey Theatre (1916–29). He took up acting full time in 1929. Fitzgerald toured the United States in 1934 and was voted the best character actor of the year by theater critics for his performance as Fluther Good in Séan *O'Casey's *The Plough and the Stars*. He played the role of Fluther again in 1936 in John Ford's film version of the play. Fitzgerald moved to Hollywood in 1937 and appeared in many films, winning an Oscar for his performance as Father

Fitzgibbon in *Going My Way* (1944). He also played in *The Quiet Man* (1952), directed in Ireland by John Ford, starring John Wayne and Maureen O'Hara. Fitzgerald returned to Ireland in 1959. C.D.

FitzGerald, Garret (1926–). Politician, leader of *Fine Gael, and *Taoiseach (prime minister). Born in *Dublin, FitzGerald worked for the Irish national airline *Aer Lingus and as a lecturer in Political Economy at University College, Dublin, before being elected to the *Dáil (Parliament) in 1969. Member of *Seanad Éireann (Senate) for Fine Gael from 1965 to 1969, he was a member of the Dáil from 1969 to 1992. He was minister for foreign affairs (1973–77), leader of Fine Gael (1977–87), and Taoiseach (June 1981–March 1982 and November 1982–March 1987). Committed to solving the *Northern Ireland conflict throughout his political career, FitzGerald was involved in the negotiations leading up to the *Sunningdale Agreement. Later, as Taoiseach, he signed the *Anglo-Irish Agreement of 1985, which gave the Irish government a formal role in the administration of Northern Ireland for the first time. FitzGerald attempted to reform social legislation in the 1980s, but his reputation was somewhat damaged by his decision to call an anti-abortion referendum in 1983 and by the rejection of legislation on *divorce in the 1986 referendum. J.D.

Fitzgerald, Lord Edward (1753–98). Chief military strategist of the *United Irishmen. Born in London into Ireland's premier titled family, the Earls of Kildare, Fitzgerald spent much of his childhood in France prior to joining the Sussex militia in 1779 under the command of his uncle, the Duke of Richmond. Following a stint in the Twenty-sixth Regiment, Fitzgerald transferred to the Nineteenth with which he fought and was wounded during the *American Revolution. On returning to Ireland, he became MP (member of Parliament) for the borough of Athy, *Kildare, due to family patronage. Tiring of political life, Fitzgerald studied at the Military College in Woolwich, England, in 1786–88, until appointed major of the Fifty-fourth Regiment in Canada. He traveled widely on the Canadian frontier, where his adventures included induction into a Native American tribe.

A lifelong Francophile, Fitzgerald went to Paris where he liaised with Thomas *Paine, a connection that led to his dismissal from the army in 1792. Fitzgerald was disaffected with constitutional politics by 1793 because of the perpetuation of anti-Catholic laws and the climate of repression during the war against France. He was a leading member of the Society of *United Irishmen from 1796, and in June of that year he traveled secretly to Paris to encourage the French government to liberate Ireland. His mission, backed by that of Wolfe *Tone, helped bring about the attempted landing of a French army in Bantry, County *Cork, in December 1796. To protest the government's counterinsurgency policy, Fitzgerald declined to stand for election in July 1797, and became instead the military leader of the revolutionary United Irishmen.

A wanted man from March 12, 1798, with a bounty of £1,000 on his head, Fitzgerald remained the most important dissident until his eventual arrest after a violent struggle in Dublin on May 19, 1798. The loss of Fitzgerald contributed to the failure of the *Rebellion (of 1798), which commenced four days later. He died in Newgate Prison on June 4 from wounds sustained in his capture. R.OD.

fitzGilbert de Clare, Richard. See **Strongbow.**

Flanagan, T. P. (1929–). Painter. Born in County *Fermanagh, Flanagan studied and taught in *Belfast. He is best known for his evocation of place, notably *Donegal *bog land, which inspired Seamus *Heaney's poem *Bogland*. A skilled draughtsman, he produces elegant and highly reflective work. M.C.

Flatley, Michael (1958–). Flute player and *step-dancer. Flatley was born in Chicago to parents from *Sligo and *Carlow. His father was the chair of the Irish Musicians Association in Chicago. Flatley studied dance at the Dennehy School and developed an award-winning Sligo flute style, which he perfected while spending vacations in his father's home in Gurteen, Michael *Coleman's native area. Flatley formed his own dance school, and often appeared with the *Chieftains. He emerged as a star soloist in *Riverdance, and later directed his own big-stage dance show, "Lord of the Dance." F.V.

Fleadh Ceoil. A weekend festival, literally the Irish for "feast of music." The name was adopted by *CCÉ (Comhaltas Ceoltóirí Éireann) for its traditional *music gatherings after 1952. It is based on competition where successful players progress from county to provincial level and then to the supreme "All-Ireland." The fleadh typically occupies all of the amenities of the host town and attracts numerous musicians, singers, and dancers who perform casually in pubs and outdoor sessions. F.V.

Flight of the Earls (September 4, 1607). A pivotal point in Irish history, when the last remaining of the Old Irish nobility fled the country. Hugh *O'Neill, Earl of Tyrone, and his followers—Rory O'Donnell, Earl of Tyrconnell, and Cúconnacht Maguire of Fermanagh—were defeated in the *Nine Years War against Queen *Elizabeth I. To ensure that the old Gaelic system was finally broken in *Ulster, the rebels had to renounce their Gaelic titles and ancestral rights, and live by English law. In return, they avoided the confiscation of their land and were pardoned.

However, English officials in Ireland tried to bring these Gaelic lords totally under English rule, if not dispossess them altogether. O'Neill and O'Donnell became involved in a secret plan with the Spanish that would have led to another rebellion. When they were summoned to *Dublin, they believed that the plot had been betrayed. Rather than face a trial and probable execution, they and their followers sailed from Rathmullen, County *Donegal, for Spain, on September 4, 1607. Their ship landed in France from where the exiles traveled to Rome. Although they probably intended to return to Ireland with Spanish troops, the earls remained in Rome until their deaths, surviving on a papal pension. Their flight is usually seen as the end of the Gaelic order in Ireland and paved the way for the *Ulster plantation. T.C.

folklore. The archive of the Irish Folklore Commission, housed at University College, Dublin, is one of the finest of its kind in the world. Because of its great variety and its surviving vibrancy, the traditional lore of Ireland has attracted much scholarly attention. Over two centuries of collecting has produced a harvest of stories, songs, *music, beliefs, customs, and other lore.

Among the most colorful genres is the native hero-lore, derived from ancient *mythology and passed down from generation to generation, often in written as well as oral form. Some of these hero-tales were in medieval vellum manuscripts, whereas others circulated in paper manuscripts of recent centuries. The adventures of Fionn Mac Cumhaill (Finn McCool) and his warrior band the *Fianna were especially popular, telling of love, intrigue, and great combats with sinister and magical foes. Less diffuse tales are told of other mythical heroes, such as Lugh, *Cúchulainn, and the legendary ideal King Cormac Mac Airt. Religious tradition has also been very influential, patron saints of the various localities being held in high regard. These *saints, historical personages from the early centuries of Irish *Christianity—such as Caoimhghin, Ciarán, and Mochua—are portrayed in legend as miracle workers who used their sacred power to banish monsters, cure illnesses, and provide food for the people in time of need.

Ireland is famous for its fairy-lore. The fairies are known in Irish as the people of the *sí*, a word which originally designated a mound or tumulus, and the Irish fairies can be connected with early beliefs of how the dead live on as a dazzling community in their burial chambers. Thousands of *raths—ancient earthenwork structures which dot the Irish landscape—are claimed to be inhabited still by the *sí*-people. This lore has been enriched by many migratory legends from the rest of Europe, with themes such as commerce between mortals and fairies, abductions, and mystical journeys to fairyland.

Versions of numerous far-flung international folktales have been current in Ireland for many centuries. The simplest of these are fanciful little tales concerning animals, ornate and highly stylized wondertales, exemplum-type religious tales, real-life romantic tales, and a wide range of short humorous anecdotes. The most popular of all these international tale-plots with Irish storytellers told of how a princess was rescued by a widow's son from the jaws of a fearsome water monster. More native in origin are the legends of historical characters and folk accounts of historical events. There are also stories concerning a variety of ghosts, revenants, and spirits. A solitary female spirit, the *bean sí* (banshee), is often heard to announce by her wailing the impending death of a member of an Irish family.

Folklore has been expressed in song, in Irish and English. In Irish, "Amhrán na mBréag" (The Song of Lies), tells of unbelievable things which the singer claims to have seen, just like a storyteller does in a tall tale. "The Cow that Ate the Piper" is a song in *Hiberno-English based on a humorous international folktale, according to which a man thinks that a cow has eaten a piper who slept in a byre, when he finds only the boots of the piper there. Songs like "Seven Drunken Nights" (popularized by Ronnie Drew and the *Dubliners) about a man returning home to find his wife in bed with another man play on another folktale theme.

A wide range of beliefs and practices are concerned with the life cycle, especially birth, marriage, and death. In the calendar cycle, four great indigenous festivals mark the beginning of the seasons. Lá Fhéile Bríde (St. *Brigid's Feast, February 1), was originally called *oímelg*, meaning "lactation." The May festival Bealtaine meant "bright fire" and marked the beginning of summer. Lughnasa, called after the god Lugh, was the harvest festival, and the November feast *Samhain, when the otherworld was believed to intervene in this world with special vigor, marked the beginning of winter. Originally, the year was divided into two halves, the dark half beginning at Samhain and the bright half at Bealtaine. Much custom centers also on Christmas, Easter, St. John's Night, and the Feast of St. Martin. D.Oh.

Ford, Patrick (1837–1913). Journalist. Ford emigrated as a child from *Galway to *Boston, where anti-Irish nativism turned him into a fervent *nationalist. His New York–based *Irish World* became the largest circulating Irish newspaper in the United

States. It combined grievances of Irish tenant farmers and Irish American laborers into attacks on agrarian and industrial capitalism. John *Devoy and Michael *Davitt embraced Ford's insistence that a campaign against *landlordism should be a key ingredient of Irish nationalism, thus producing the New Departure strategy. L.J.MC.

foreign policy. Since independence, Ireland's foreign policy has been historically dominated by two issues, *partition and *neutrality. In the 1960s, European integration became a priority for Ireland, and in 1973, Ireland joined the *European Union (EU), then known as the European Economic Community (EEC). Successive *Taoisigh (prime ministers) and ministers for foreign affairs have sought a solution to the *Northern Ireland conflict, most recently through the 1990s *peace process. In recent years, the *Republic of Ireland's foreign policy has also focused on third-world development and human rights issues. J.D.

Four Courts, the. Landmark of *Dublin's city center, located at Inns Quay on the River Liffey. Built between 1786 and 1802, the structure is a masterpiece of Georgian *architecture. Part of the building was designed by Thomas Cooley, who died before its completion. The project was then taken over by James *Gandon. The building gets its name from the four courts that traditionally made up the judicial system in Ireland: Chancery, King's Bench, Exchequer, and Common Pleas. Today the building continues to be the center of the Irish court system, housing both the High Court and the Supreme Court.

The Four Courts is best known in Irish history as the site where the first shots of the *Irish Civil War (1922–23) were fired. On the night of April 13, 1922, an *Irish Republican Army (IRA) garrison under the command of Rory O'Connor occupied the Four Courts and other prominent buildings in Dublin in defiance of the pro-treaty provisional government headed by Michael *Collins. Following the IRA kidnapping of the provisional government's deputy chief of staff, General J. J. O'Connell, on June 26, 1922, Collins ordered the Four Courts evacuated. O'Connor and his garrison ignored the order, and in the predawn hours of June 28, using artillery they had borrowed from the British, Collins's troops began shelling the Four Courts. O'Connor and his men surrendered two days later, on June 30.

In the eleven months of internecine warfare that followed, it is estimated that many more Irish *nationalists killed one another than had been killed by the British during the whole of the struggle for independence between 1916 and 1921. Thus, the Four Courts—rebuilt in the aftermath of the Civil War—can be seen, on the one hand, as a symbol of the rule of law in Ireland and, on the other, as a reminder of the chaos and fratricidal bloodshed out of which modern Ireland was born. T.D.

France. Long-term cultural, economic, religious, and political bonds have tied Ireland to France for much of the modern period. After the Treaty of *Limerick (1691), which effectively ended resistance to *William III, thousands of *Catholic soldiers (the *Wild Geese) fled to France, where they formed the first of the famous Irish Brigades. These units served with distinction in the French army through the Napoleonic era. Further Franco-Irish connections emerged in the late seventeenth century with the introduction of the *Penal Laws, which outlawed the *education of Catholics in Ireland. As a result of these acts, wealthy Irish Catholic families were forced to educate their sons on the Continent. Throughout the eighteenth century, the vast majority of Irish Catholic clergy (also banned under the penal statutes) received their training in France. Finally, trade, both legal and illicit, had been carried on with France for centuries, and Irish Catholic families were prominent in Bordeaux and Nantes. At the end of the eighteenth century, the *United Irishmen's ambassador to France, Wolfe *Tone, successfully forged an alliance with the revolutionary government. This pact nearly bore fruit when a large French fleet led by General Lazare Hoche arrived at Bantry Bay in 1796. An ill wind prevented a successful landing. A small French force under General Humbert landed in Mayo in August 1798 and scored some surprising victories prior to being overwhelmed at Ballinamuck in Longford. Irish *republicans continued to hope for French assistance until the English victory at Trafalgar effectively ended such dreams. J.P.

Free State. See **Irish Free State.**

French, William Percy (1854–1920). Songwriter and theater impresario. Born in Cloonyquin, County *Roscommon, French was educated at Trinity College, Dublin, where he graduated in 1881 with a degree in civil engineering. After working as an engineer for the Board of Works for a few years, he tried journalism, painting, and eventually songwriting. In 1891, French and Houston Collisson started a touring theatrical company, which was immediately successful. Together, they toured throughout Ireland, England, the United States, and Canada, giving concerts of songs for which Percy French wrote the lyrics and Collisson composed the music. They also wrote and produced light operas such as *The Irish Girl*. Percy French, supposedly, wrote a song about every county in Ireland. Some of these songs are so identified with the counties they represent that they have become county anthems. This is especially true of such timeless gems as the "Mountains of Mourne" (County *Down), "Come Back Paddy Reilly to Ballyjamesduff" (County *Cavan), and "Are You Right There Michael" (County *Clare.) J.OM.

French Revolution. The 1789 French Revolution inspired reformers and revolutionaries in Ireland, as in other European countries. In Ireland, the most important reform association formed in the wake of the French Revolution was the Society of *United Irishmen founded in 1791. In the early 1790s, reform clubs in *Belfast and *Dublin celebrated the anniversary of the fall of the Bastille and literature about the revolution circulated widely. Pamphlets argued for and against the revolution. Thomas *Paine's *Rights of Man* was published in seven Irish editions between 1791 and 1792. The *Northern Star* newspaper, published in Belfast, closely followed events in *France and supported the execution of the king. The revolution radicalized political reformers, who began to oppose monarchy and adopt ideas such as universal male suffrage.

In the mid-1790s, the United Irishmen formed reading societies and clubs in towns and villages. The French influence became entwined with the older *Presbyterian republican tradition and with widespread *Catholic discontent. In small towns and villages, the Catholic secret society, the *Defenders, viewed the French cause in traditional terms, as Catholic and anti-English. French symbolism was adopted in places: the "tree of liberty" was planted and pipers played the Marseillaise.

The United Irishmen corresponded with the Jacobin Society in Paris, and reported its proceedings in their publications. From 1793, the French leadership considered Ireland as a base for destabilizing England. Agents from France were arrested and tried in

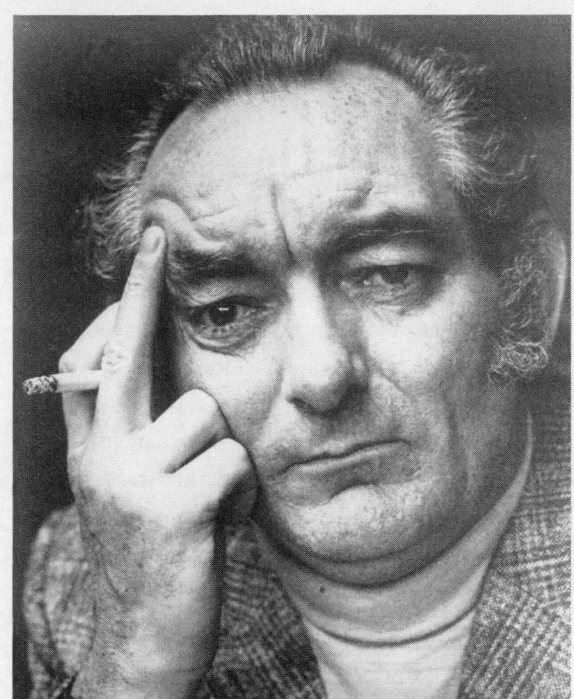

Brian Friel

Ireland in 1794–95. In May 1794, the United Irishmen were suppressed and, in 1795, they decided to seek French assistance in a rebellion. Wolfe *Tone arrived in France in February 1796. In December, Tone accompanied General Lazare Hoche's forty-three-ship fleet to Bantry Bay, County *Cork, but storms prevented a landing. During the *Rebellion of 1798 a much smaller French expedition arrived at Killala, County *Mayo, in August, but was soon defeated.

After 1798, Ireland became less and less significant to French military plans. Remnants of the republican movement still sought French help during Napoleon's reign, and individual United Irishmen remained in France until 1815. The revolution left a lasting legacy in Ireland: popular politics would contain a strong element of democratic republicanism, reinforced by the French Revolution of 1848. P.D.

Friel, Brian (1929–). Playwright. Born in County *Tyrone, Friel was educated at *Maynooth College, Kildare, and St. Joseph's College, Belfast. His early writings include short stories published in the *New Yorker* and radio plays broadcast by the BBC, among them *A Sort of Freedom* (1958) and *A Doubtful Paradise* (1962). An acute awareness of place characterizes both the stories in *The Saucer of Larks* (1962) and his plays. The *Abbey Theatre staged *The Enemy Within* in 1962. The play focuses on the inner struggle of St. Columba (*Colm Cille), torn between his patriotic love for his native Ireland and his religious calling on the island of Iona. Friel spent part of 1963 in Minneapolis learning aspects of stagecraft from Tyrone *Guthrie. His next play, *Philadelphia, Here I Come!* (1964), brought him international acclaim and enjoyed a successful run on Broadway. Its protagonist, Gar O'Donnell, is torn between his unexpressed love for his emotionally taciturn father, who runs a shop in the small *Donegal town of Ballybeg (Friel's "anytown"), and the unknown attractions of Philadelphia. Friel represents Gar's divided psyche by portraying him as two characters, "public" and "private." These early plays introduce the conflicting forces of home and exile that are pervasive in all of Friel's work. Recurring themes in his plays are the pain of loss and the inevitable necessity of change, the sacrifice, anxiety, and rare triumph associated with artistic creation, the inadequacy of language, and the roots of theater in sacred ritual.

The themes of love and disillusionment link the plays *The Loves of Cass Maguire* (1966), *Lovers* (1967), and *Crystal and Fox* (1968), while *The Mundy Scheme* (1969) bitterly lampoons political life in the Irish *Republic. *The Freedom of the City* (1973), an unusually direct reaction to political violence in *Northern Ireland, suggests that there is no single perspective on truth. *Faith Healer* (1979) consists of four contradictory monologues that leave the audience to reflect on the nature of truth and mystery.

In 1980, along with actor Stephen *Rea and others, Friel founded the *Field Day Theatre Company, established in *Derry to create a "fifth province of the imagination" that would transcend traditional sectarian and political divisions. Field Day staged plays by Tom *Kilroy, Derek *Mahon, Tom Paulin, and Friel himself. Its first production was his *Translations* (1980), set in Donegal in 1833, at a pivotal moment in Irish history as the British mapped and translated Ireland's place-names into English. *Making History* (1988), whose main protagonist is Hugh *O'Neill, scrutinizes the process of inclusion, exclusion, and manipulation by which history is written. *Dancing at Lughnasa* (1990), released as a movie in 1998, explores the atavistic forces underlying Irish society. More recent plays include *Wonderful Tennessee* (1993), *Molly Sweeney* (1995), *Give Me Your Answer, Do!* (1997), a translation of Chekhov's *Uncle Vanya* (1998), and *Performances* (2003), which continue to examine the same thematic issues from different angles. Friel's plays explore in poetic language the ways individuals and communities shape and are shaped by history, language, and myth. M.S.T., J.C.E.L.

furniture. Irish furniture—like Irish art, decorative arts, and architecture—was shaped by the island's ancient, *Celtic tradition, as well as its close proximity to Britain and the continent. Carvers and cabinetmakers, drawing from these resources, created some of the finest furniture in Europe that graced Ireland's grandest town houses, *castles, country houses, manors, and farmhouses. The vernacular furniture of the countryside, where a majority of Ireland's population lived, was simple and functional, but incorporated elements of "high style" design and displayed some of the finest Celtic carvings. Unfortunately, little if any Irish "country" furniture has survived from the period before the *Famine of the 1840s because people burned it for warmth.

Prior to the seventh century A.D., there is some material evidence of simple wooden beds, benches, and stools. High *crosses and *manuscript illuminations between the eighth and tenth centuries, such as the Book of *Kells, depict a variety of forms of varying luxury. These illustrations show that wood furniture reached high levels of artistry. It was often carved with geometric forms, spiral ornament, bands of interlacing scrolls, and animal decoration—features later defined as distinct characteristics of Irish furniture. Often the wood is painted or gilded, sometimes upholstered with leather or fabric, and seats are generally concave. Late-twentieth-century excavations in *Dublin show quality woodworking from the eleventh century onward. There is a paucity of furniture dating from the sixteenth and seventeenth centuries, a devastating period of war and strife. However, records indicate a variety of substantial, often elaborate high-style pieces: tables and cabinets; richly upholstered and embroidered chairs and stools of various types and sizes, some gilded, lacquered, or cushioned; and canopied bedsteads with fine curtains or hangings. Increasingly during this period, both furniture and styles were being imported from the continent and, especially, from England, adding to the complex task of identifying pieces as "Irish."

The eighteenth century brought, first, peace and then prosperity to Ireland and an unrivaled flowering of the decorative arts. More pieces of high-style furniture have survived from this period onward. While the patrons of the arts were generally the rich *Protestant minority who looked to Britain for furniture examples, the artists and craftsmen were almost always native Irish.

In the early 1700s, furniture of oak and walnut, as well as lacquered pieces, reflected the classical, baroque taste of Britain and the continent. By mid-century, the Irish furniture industry was thriving. As trade with the West Indies grew, mahogany became the wood of choice. At this time, the sturdy and robust characteristics that are generally associated with Irish furniture became manifest. The architectural strength of the baroque and the sensual extravagance of the rococo were seen in the central figures of aprons on tables, chairs, stools, and chests: a lion head, flowers, a shell, or a grotesque mask, festooned with carvings of foliage and birds. Table and chair legs rested on paws or claw-and-ball feet. A bulge directly above the foot, generally covered with carved hair or foliage, was a particularly Irish characteristic.

By the end of the eighteenth century, the more delicate features of the neoclassical style had reached Ireland, curtailing the general robustness of Irish design. Although nineteenth-century Irish furniture continued to reflect revival styles and tastes coming from England, such as gothic and rococo, a growing interest in an Irish national identity, especially in antiquities and cultural achievements, began to emerge. In furniture, a neo-Celtic style reflected motifs from Irish history.

Starting in the 1840s, chairs, tables, settles, and cabinets—typical Irish country furniture forms—were carved, painted, or engraved with interlaced, Celtic patterns reflecting earlier Irish craftsmanship, similar to the more elaborate, high-style examples. Although country furniture made by local craftsmen or journeymen carpenters tended to be humble and utilitarian, in many instances it was painted, sometimes elaborately, to add visual interest and hide inferior wood or joinery. It tended to be made of locally grown pine—a general term used for various softwoods such as Scots fir, larch, Norway spruce, or yellow pine. Often furniture was made with multiple uses, like the settle bed—a particularly Irish form that combines the uses of a bed and a bench.

Bog wood—ancient oak, yew, and fir trees that had lain buried and preserved in the *bogs—became widely used due to its strength and beauty. Elaborately carved suites of furniture portrayed ambitious themes from Irish history (legends, monarchs, and animals) and emblems (harps, wolfhounds, and shamrocks). Around the 1850s, a distinctive style of inlaid furniture, using motifs of historic buildings, ruins, and national symbols such as harps, roses, thistles, and shamrocks, emerged in the region of Killarney.

As mass production and, in reaction to it, the Arts and Crafts movement began to take root, first in Britain, then in Ireland, this interest in the Irish decorative history blossomed. Design from the early *Christian period was heralded as the embodiment of Irish style and character.

Today, Irish furniture—both the vernacular furniture and its high-style counterparts—is recognized as some of the finest produced in Europe. D.S.

G

Gael Linn. A major *Irish language promotion organization. Founded by Dónal Ó Móráin (1923–2001) in 1953, Gael Linn financed filmmaking (*Mise Éire,* and *Saoirse,* with soundtracks by Seán *Ó Riada), Irish-language newsreels, and children's *Gaeltacht scholarships. In 1957, it began recording traditional artists, and organized cabaret Irish music in tourist venues. Its numerous recordings promoted traditional *music in Ireland. F.V.

Gaelic Athletic Association (GAA). The main sporting organization in Ireland dedicated to the cultivation and development of the native Irish games of *hurling and *Gaelic football. Although these games existed in some form or another for hundreds of years, it was the GAA which formalized and codified the sports from its foundation in 1884. Michael Cusack (1847–1906) was the most important figure in the creation of the organization. Drawing upon the newfound enthusiasm for spectator sports, the *Irish Revival movement, local patriotism, and the exclusivist nature of other sporting organizations, the GAA flourished in its early years because of its association with the *nationalist politics of the IRB (*Irish Republican Brotherhood). Within a few years the organization was rooted in every part of the country, so that an All-Ireland Championship in hurling and football was held as early as 1887.

Hurling, a game played with sticks and a small hard light ball known as a *sliotar*, is often said to be the fastest field game in the world. Gaelic football grew out of the rough-and-tumble inter-parish brawls of the nineteenth century, and is close in appearance and style to Australian Rules football. The club is the smallest unit of the association, very often based on the parish, and the best players in these clubs are chosen to represent their counties, which vie for the title of All-Ireland champions. The All-Ireland finals are seen as the most important sporting occasions in the country, dwarfing all other events, even international *rugby and *soccer games, in terms of attendance and interest. These finals will draw close to

80,000 people to *Croke Park (Dublin), which is the main stadium and the headquarters of the association. Part of the GAA's strength derives from the fact that it is an all-Ireland thirty-two-county organization and does not recognize the border. Although for cultural and political reasons the games are played almost entirely by nationalists in the six counties of *Northern Ireland, the players are people of all social classes throughout most of the country. Gaelic football is more widespread, whereas hurling is more geographically confined. The games have developed strong local identities and regional esteem is often judged on the success of the county team. By 2004, *Cork was the most successful team in the hurling championships, and *Kerry in football.

The GAA has often been involved in political controversy because of its strong stand on national issues. For many years players were not allowed to play "foreign games," a code for rugby and soccer, and until recently members of the RUC (*Royal Ulster Constabulary) and the British army were not permitted into the organization. This had as much to do with tradition as it had with harassment of players in Northern Ireland and the occupation by the British army of some local playing fields. The games have also been very popular with Irish emigrants in the United States and in Britain, and both New York and London have entered teams in the All-Ireland Championship. Ireland plays Australia from time to time in a game of compromise football rules, and a compromise hurling game is often played with teams of Scottish shinty (a form of hurling particular to Scotland). A.T.

Gaelic football. A traditional form of football unique to Ireland based upon catching and kicking played by two teams of fifteen players each. The rules of the modern form of the game (a version of which had been played for a few hundred years) were formulated by the *Gaelic Athletic Association (GAA) in 1884. Under the auspices of the GAA, Gaelic football is now played in almost every parish in the country with competitions being organized at school, college, club, county, and provincial level. The pinnacle of the annual calendar is the Sam Maguire Cup presented to the winners of the All-Ireland final—an intercounty (thirty-two-county) football championship. The All-Ireland final is played in Dublin's *Croke Park, the GAA's national stadium, on the fourth Sunday of September each year. A capacity crowd of 79,500 attends the final and millions all over the world watch live television coverage.

In recent years, the sport has formed an alliance with a sister code, Australian Rules, resulting in an annual compromise rules series, which alternates between venues in Ireland and Australia. Although Gaelic football is still an amateur sport, this may change in future years as it strives to compete with other international field games. A game of Gaelic football lasts sixty minutes at club level and seventy minutes at senior intercounty level.

In 2004, County *Kerry held the record for the All-Ireland title, having won it thirty-one times. The record for consecutive victories is also held by Kerry, who have won it four times in a row between 1929 and 1932 and again between 1978 and 1981, together with *Wexford, who were successful from 1915 to 1918. Perhaps the most famous player was the legendary Mick O'Connell who won four All-Ireland medals with Kerry over three decades (1959, 1962, 1969, and 1970) and led them to victory in 1959. Other famous players include: Peter Canavan (Tyrone), John Joe O'Reilly (Cavan), Paidí Ó Sé (Kerry) and Mattie McDonagh (Galway). B.D.

Gaelic League (Conradh na Gaedhilge). Organization dedicated to preserving the *Irish language, founded in *Dublin in 1893. The decline of the language had reached calamitous proportions by the end of the nineteenth century. The number of Irish speakers had fallen from 320,000 in 1851 to 38,000 in 1891. Language enthusiasts insisted that radical remedial steps were required to halt the decline. Eoin *MacNeill called a meeting in Dublin on July 31, 1893, at which the new organization Conradh na Gaedhilge was set up. Douglas *Hyde was inaugurated as its first president.

The league set up language classes and had established 550 branches at home and abroad by 1908. A network of peripatetic teachers (or *timirí*) brought the language to every corner of the island and an annual Gaelic festival (An tOireachtas) was established in 1897. A weekly newspaper, **An Claidheamh Soluis*, was first published in 1899 and Patrick *Pearse was among its early editors. Though the league still exists today, its membership and influence has waned considerably. B.D.

Gaelic Revival. See **Irish Language Revival.**

Gaeltacht. A term used to describe those districts that are largely *Irish speaking. These areas are mainly in *Donegal, *Galway, and *Kerry, but there are smaller pockets in counties *Cork, *Waterford, *Mayo, and *Meath. Originally all of Ireland was a Gaeltacht, but the language began to recede from the late seventeenth century, initially from the towns and later from the rest of the country. The word *Gaeltacht* is a borrowing from Scottish Gaelic, originally meaning the Highlands and the people who lived there. When it was borrowed into Irish in the eighteenth century, it referred more to the people—the "Irishry"—than to the district. It has been used to denote an area only since the late nineteenth century.

The Gaeltacht regions do not have any separate administrative arrangements, but there is a state board Údarás na Gaeltachta (the Gaeltacht Authority) that has some economic planning and development functions. There is a radio station Raidió na Gaeltachta, which serves as a unifying force between the scattered areas and also as a national Irish-language service. In the past, the Gaeltacht, poor and marginalized, suffered from heavy *emigration. Today, prosperity and easy mobility pose different problems. Parts of the Galway Gaeltacht have been swallowed up by the urbanization of Galway City and have become extended suburbs. The romantic attraction of the west of Ireland has brought "white settlers" who care little for the native language. On the other hand, the Gaeltacht is more aware of its identity as a separate kind of place than ever before, and the lure of cultural tourism with its attendant monies has managed to slow down the inevitable conquest of English. Some of the very best *literature in Irish in the twentieth century has come from the Gaeltacht. A.T.

Gaiety Theatre. From its opening in 1871, the Gaiety has been dedicated to presenting both musical and dramatic entertainment, including *opera and ballet. The theater was conceived by John and Michael Gunn, whose family owned a music business in *Dublin's Grafton Street. The building, on King Street South, was designed by noted architect C. J. Phipps. Its interior was altered several times, in 1883, 1955, and 1984. Under the management of the Louis Elliman group (1936–65), the Gaiety became known for its home-produced Christmas pantomimes, starring Jimmy *O'Dea and Maureen

Hayfield, County Galway

Potter, and established annual seasons of the Dublin Grand Opera Society. Hilton *Edwards and Micheál *MacLiammóir began presenting plays at the theater during World War II and had great success with MacLiammóir's own *Ill Met by Moonlight* (1946) and *The Importance of Being Oscar* (1960).

Other important dramatic productions at the Gaiety include Douglas *Hyde's *Casadh an t-Súgáin (The Twisting of the Rope)* (1901) and Seán *O'Casey's *The Bishop's Bonfire* (1955). From 1965 to 1984 the theater was managed by Eamon Andrews studios. In the 1950s and 1960s, the Gaiety was the venue for Sunday night concerts with the *Radio Éireann Symphony Orchestra. In 1971 the theater hosted the Eurovision Song Contest. Once referred to by MacLiammóir as "a place of breadth and dignity," the Gaiety has staged a wide variety of entertainments, ranging from *King Lear* to *The Vagina Monologues*, and from Phil Coulter to *Carmen*. J.C.E.L.

Galway, County. Ireland's second largest county, in the province of *Connacht. Extending from the Atlantic to the River *Shannon (area of 2,374 square miles), the county has a population of 208,826 (2002 census). Galway City, the county capital, straddles the divide between the barren Irish-speaking *Connemara to the west and the fertile farmland of the east. It is a vibrant, cosmopolitan city, the site of University College, Galway, a constituent college of the National University of Ireland. It is also one of Ireland's most artistic cities, with a thriving traditional *music scene and two successful *theater companies, Macnas and the Druid Theatre. The three-week Galway Arts Festival draws large crowds in July as do the Galway Races, which take place during the first week of August. Many information technology multinationals have set up bases in the city. Traditional industries like fishing and tourism are also flourishing.

Galway City developed originally as a crossing

point on the River Corrib and was ruled by fourteen *Anglo-Norman families. It is still known today as "The City of the Tribes." During the Middle Ages, the city developed a booming trade with continental Europe, and with Spain in particular. The popular city landmarks the Spanish Arch and Lynch's Castle date from this period.

A small fishing village, the Claddagh, existed long before the city proper and had its own laws, customs, and chieftains. It is from this village that the famous Claddagh ring originates.

Beyond the Claddagh lies the popular seaside resort of Salthill, with fine Edwardian buildings blending uneasily with nightclubs and amusement arcades. Walking Salthill's famous promenade has been a popular form of recreation for city dwellers for many years.

Galway City is also the gateway to scenic areas like *Connemara, the *Aran Islands, and the Maamturk and Twelve Bens mountain ranges which lie to the west of the city. Connemara National Park covers almost eight square miles of *bogland, heath, and mountains, including much of the Twelve Bens. The granite-faced Diamond Hill is perhaps the main attraction in the park. Much of Connemara has been designated as special areas of conservation (SACs) and some traditional farming practices like harvesting turf are perceived to be under threat.

The county's most famous building is the neogothic Kylemore Abbey which was built in the 1860s and is now the monastic home of the Irish Benedictine *nuns. Galway is also the home of Ireland's only native breed of horse, the Connemara pony. Small, hardy animals, their pedigree is believed to be a cross between *Celtic horses of old and stallions that came ashore from the sunken *Spanish Armada. Originally found wild in the mountains of Connemara, they are now bred all over the world and are used particularly as riding ponies for children. Connemara marble is a unique green-colored marble used mostly for jewelry and ornate surfaces such as altars and fireplaces. It is now practically extinct. In 1919, in the first transatlantic nonstop flight starting from Newfoundland, aviators John William Alcock and Arthur Whitten Brown landed near Clifden, in the western part of the county.

Lough Corrib, world famous for angling, is situated in midcounty. The east shore of the lake is less dramatic with vast swathes of bogland and thriving market towns like Ballinasloe and Tuam. B.D.

Galway, James (1939–). Musician. An internationally renowned flautist, Galway was born in *Belfast and educated at the Royal College of Music and the Guildhall School of Music in London, and the Conservatoire National Supérieur de Musique in Paris. Galway was principal flute with the London Symphony Orchestra in 1966 and with the Royal Philharmonic Orchestra, 1967–69. He was principal solo flute with the Berlin Philharmonic Orchestra, 1969–75, where he played under Herbert von Karajan. He has pursued a solo career since and has made numerous recordings. Galway was Principal Guest Conductor of the London Mozart Players, 1999–2000. He has played at the White House and at Buckingham Palace. *James Galway: An Autobiography* was published in 1978 and the television series *James Galway's Music in Time* was aired in 1983. C.D.

Gambon, Michael (1940–). Actor. Born in *Dublin, the son of an army officer and a jeweler's daughter, Gambon moved with his family to London when he was six. His first professional acting roles were with the *Gate Theatre, Dublin, in 1962, before he joined Laurence Olivier's National Theatre the following year. He went on to appear in a number of leading roles in plays written by Alan

Ayckbourn, in particular. Gambon has regularly appeared at the Royal National Theatre and the Royal Shakespeare Company in roles including King Lear, Othello, Mark Antony, and Volpone. He was critically acclaimed for his central performance in Dennis Potter's groundbreaking TV drama, *The Singing Detective* (1986). Notable film roles include Albert Spica in *The Cook, The Thief, His Wife and Her Lover* (1989). In the 1990s, he played roles in several Irish films, including the Dublin-set comedy *A Man of No Importance* (1994); *Nothing Personal* (1995), the study of Belfast *loyalist paramilitaries; and film versions of Brian *Friel's *Dancing at Lughnasa* (1998) and Elizabeth *Bowen's *The Last September* (1999). He was knighted in 1997. H.L.

Gandon, James (1743–1823). English architect who designed much of eighteenth-century *Dublin. Born in London, Gandon was a student of the renowned architect Sir William Chambers. He established his own practice in London in 1765. Gandon won the first Gold Medal for architecture at the Royal Academy in 1769, and exhibited drawings there in 1774–80. After moving to Dublin in 1781, Gandon became the leading exponent of the neoclassical style in Ireland. He designed many of Dublin's most important public works, including the Custom House (1781–91), the east and west porticos of the Parliament House (1785–97), the *Four Courts (1786–1802), Carlisle (now O'Connell) Bridge (1794–98), and the King's Inns (1795–1808). Gandon was an original member of the *Royal Irish Academy and retired in 1808. S.A.B.

Gárda Síochána (Guardians of the Peace). Police force of the Irish *Republic. On February 22, 1922, the Civic Guard replaced the *Royal Irish Constabulary (RIC) as the national *police service of the *Irish Free State. At the same time, the Dublin Metropolitan Police (DMP), which had been established in 1836 as an unarmed, apolitical force for the capital, continued to function independently. The Civic Guard was renamed Gárda Síochána na hÉireann in August 1923, and in 1925, it merged with the DMP. Michael Staines, the first Gárda commissioner, rejected suggestions that the force would be armed, arguing that the Gárda Síochána would "succeed not by force of arms or numbers, but on their moral authority as servants of the people."

The murder of a Gárda was regarded as a capital offense until 1990, when a Criminal Justice Act abolished capital punishment from the statute books. A referendum in 2001 made capital punishment unconstitutional. Murder of a member of the force now carries a forty-year prison sentence.

Today, the Gárda Síochána is responsible for state security and for the enforcement of all criminal and traffic legislation. Besides these domestic duties, the force, along with the Irish *army, also performs peacekeeping duties overseas as part of Ireland's commitment to the *United Nations. The country is divided into six policing regions and in May 2004, there were 11,900 Gárdaí with 1,800 civilian support staff. General management and control is the responsibility of the Gárda commissioner, who is appointed by the government and is responsible to the minister for justice. P.E.

Gate Theatre. The Gate Theatre Company was founded in *Dublin in 1928 by Micheál *MacLiammóir and Hilton *Edwards. In 1930, after two seasons at the *Peacock Theatre, the company moved to its own premises, the converted Assembly Rooms of the Rotunda Buildings on Parnell Square East. From its beginnings, the Gate was dedicated to a modern, international repertoire, thus complementing the *Abbey

Theatre's focus on Irish plays. The Gate quickly became known for the high standard of its productions, which included works by Ibsen, Chekhov, and O'Neill, as well as Irish playwrights like Oscar *Wilde, Bernard *Shaw, Denis Johnston, and Mary Manning. Orson Welles and James Mason began their acting careers at the Gate Theatre. For many years after 1936, Lord Longford's theater company, Longford Productions, shared the theater with the original Edwards and MacLiammóir company, which increasingly toured abroad. In the final years of the founders' directorship, the theater went into something of a decline, but it revived with the appointment of their successor, Michael Colgan, in 1983. A new translation of Ibsen's *Peer Gynt* (which was the first play produced by the Gate Company in 1928) was commissioned from Frank *McGuinness for the theater's sixtieth anniversary in 1988. The 1991 Samuel *Beckett Festival, which presented all nineteen stage plays, met with great acclaim and toured to New York's Lincoln Center and London's Barbican. Gate premieres of Irish plays include Brian *Friel's *Molly Sweeney* (1994), and Conor *McPherson's *Dublin Carol* (2000) and *Port Authority* (2001). J.C.E.L.

Gavin, Frankie (1956–). Fiddle and flute player. Born in County *Galway, Gavin is considered one of the greatest instrumentalists in traditional *music. His band *De Danann (formed 1974) has been consistently successful and innovative. Gavin's performances with such stars as Stephan Grappelli have gained him an international reputation. F.V.

Geldof, Bob (1954–). Singer. Born in Dún Laoghaire, County *Dublin, Geldof was the founding member of the new-wave band the Boomtown Rats in 1975. Moved by the plight of starving Ethiopians in 1984, Geldof assembled a gallery of stars to record "Do They Know It's Christmas?" This evolved into Live Aid, two massive concerts that were staged simultaneously in London and Philadelphia. The concerts netted more than £50 million for famine relief and Geldof received an honorary knighthood for his humanitarian work from Queen Elizabeth II. B.D.

George I (1660–1727). King of Great Britain and Ireland (1714–27), elector of Hanover (1698–1727). By securing the *Protestant succession and establishing a "Whig ascendancy" in Great Britain and Ireland, the accession of George I was a setback for the *Catholic gentry in Ireland. His ministry's appointment of Englishmen to key positions in Ireland also alienated the Protestant ascendancy, thus provoking constitutional disputes between the Irish and British parliaments in 1719–20 and 1723–25. An experienced soldier, George I oversaw the defeat of the *Jacobites in northern Britain in 1715, but he remained unpopular in England due to his brusque manner and his indulgence of foreign favorites. S.A.B.

George II (1683–1760). King of Great Britain and Ireland (1727–60). George II was the last British monarch to lead troops into battle (at Dettingen in 1743), and his army suppressed a second *Jacobite rebellion in 1745–46. His government in Ireland extended the *Penal Laws in 1728, when Irish *Catholics were deprived of the right to vote in parliamentary elections. However, during the final years of George II's reign, the Catholic gentry reemerged as a force in Irish political life. S.A.B.

George III (1738–1820). King of Great Britain and Ireland. His long and tumultuous reign (1760–1820) witnessed the loss of the thirteen North American colonies, the *French Revolution, Napoleon, and extended periods of personal mental collapse. In Ireland, pivotal events included Henry *Grattan's successful campaigns for economic and legislative independence in 1779 and 1782 respectively, as well as the repeal of many of the anti-Catholic *Penal Laws. Yet, the failure to grant complete *Catholic Emancipation, to which the king was obstinately opposed, coupled with the recall of the reforming Lord Lieutenant Fitzwilliam, helped trigger the *Rebellion of 1798. In turn, this latter episode resulted in the Act of *Union (1800), which abolished the Irish *Parliament and established the United Kingdom of Great Britain and Ireland. J.P.

Giant's Causeway. A series of spectacular polygonal columns composed of basalt found on the north coast of County *Antrim. Geologists believe that they were formed when an ancient lava flow cooled and solidified approximately sixty million years ago during the early Tertiary period. Its name stems from a local legend that the columns were built by giants as part of a roadway to *Scotland. P.E.

Gladstone, William Ewart (1809–98). British Liberal politician and four times prime minister (1868–74, 1880–85, 1886, and 1892–94). Generally considered the most important British statesman of the second half of the nineteenth century, Gladstone had a decisive impact on Irish history. His first term as prime minister was largely focused on Irish affairs, as he declared that his primary mission was to "pacify Ireland." Two important pieces of Irish legislation were passed during the term: the 1869 Disestablishment of the *Church of Ireland Act and the 1870 *Land Act. In his second term, the 1881 *Land Act became law at the height of the *Land War (1879–82). Due to his progressive Irish policies, by the mid-1880s, Gladstone's Liberal Party generally received the support of *Parnell's *Irish Parliamentary Party. In 1885, Parnell showed the Liberals that they could not take that support for granted by using his party's decisive vote in Parliament to force Gladstone's government from office, allowing the Conservatives under Lord Salisbury to take over. Parnell's strategy paid off in December 1885, when Gladstone publicly announced that he was prepared to support *home rule for Ireland. Parnell's party once again threw its support to the Liberals, and Gladstone became prime minister for the third time in 1886. Gladstone's first home rule bill (1886) proposed a parliament in Dublin to legislate domestic matters only. The bill was defeated in the Commons and Gladstone resigned as prime minister. Gladstone's condemnation of Parnell following the *O'Shea divorce scandal in 1889 proved disastrous to the Home Rule Party, splitting it into two opposing factions. In 1893, Gladstone, again prime minister, introduced his second home rule bill, which allowed for a continued Irish presence at Westminster with its power limited to voting on Irish issues. The bill was passed in the Commons but defeated in the House of Lords. Gladstone retired a year later. P.E., T.D.

Glasnevin Cemetery. Dublin's main cemetery situated in the northside suburb of Glasnevin. The cemetery was established by Daniel *O'Connell in 1832 as a nondenominational resting-place operated by a committee. Over one million people are buried here, including Michael *Collins, Éamon *de Valera, Brendan *Behan, Peadar Kearney (who wrote the words of the Irish National Anthem), Charles Stewart *Parnell, the poet Gerard Manley *Hopkins, and Daniel O'Connell himself. The *Republic's first crematorium opened here in 1988. The chapel is by J. J. MacCarthy, and the Finglas Road gate by William Pearse, father of Patrick *Pearse. P.H.

Glendalough. Picturesque valley in the Wicklow Hills. Glendalough is—according to its name—the valley of the two lakes, but it is also the valley of two *saints. These are Kevin, a hermit who died in 618 and around whose grave a famous monastery was later built, and Laurence O'Toole, an abbot who died in 1182 and was canonized in 1226. The latter may have erected some of the Romanesque-style buildings still surviving in the valley. The *round tower, just under one hundred feet high, was restored in 1876 and is one of the best preserved in the country. The cathedral is the second largest pre-*Norman church in Ireland. Glendalough was one of Ireland's greatest places of *pilgrimages until Cardinal *Cullen banned them in 1862 because of too much "drink and debauchery." P.H.

Gogarty, Oliver St. John (1878–1957). Physician and writer. Gogarty graduated with a degree in medicine from Trinity College in his native *Dublin in 1907 and established a successful surgical practice. By the time he published his first poetry collection, *An Offering of Swans* (1923), three of his plays—on the subject of urban poverty—had already been staged by the *Abbey Theatre. Gogarty wrote both classically inspired lyrical poetry and bawdy verse. His *Collected Poems* appeared in 1951. He also wrote several novels and a series of unreliable autobiographical accounts and reminiscences, including *As I Was Going Down Sackville Street* (1937), *Tumbling in the Hay* (1939), and *It Isn't This Time of Year at All!* (1954). He moved to the United States in 1939 and died in New York in 1957. Oliver Gogarty was the model for Malachi ("Buck") Mulligan in James *Joyce's *Ulysses* (1922). J.C.E.L.

Goldsmith, Oliver (c.1730–74). Playwright, poet, novelist. Born to a *Church of Ireland clergyman in Pallas, County *Longford, and educated at Trinity College, Dublin, Edinburgh, and on the continent, Goldsmith arrived in London destitute in 1756. There, he worked as a physician, an apothecary, an editor, a musician, and a school custodian, before embarking on a literary career. His output was voluminous (more than forty volumes) and varied. Struggling to make a living, Goldsmith contributed essays, reviews, and letters to the new periodicals, and wrote histories of England (1764), Rome (1769), and Greece (1774), and biographies of Voltaire (1761) and Turloch *Carolan (1760).

Goldsmith's famous novel *The Vicar of Wakefield* (1764), (which his friend Dr. Johnson sold to rescue him from being arrested for debt) set forth some of his most enduring themes: social satire on the manners and morals of the urbane Englishman of the eighteenth century; a preference for country virtue over the corruption of the city; and a complaint against the Enclosure Laws, which turned farmland into pleasure grounds for the rich, while displacing the small farmer. Similar ideas are illustrated in his best-known poem, "The Deserted Village" (1770), based on his childhood in the village of Lissoy, in County *Westmeath. His poem, "The Traveller" (1764), which first brought him literary attention, and his *Letters of a Chinese Citizen* (1761–62) embody his ideas of the enlightened Englishman as a citizen of the world.

His plays *She Stoops to Conquer* (1773), which has become a classic, and *The Good-Natur'd Man* (1767) were produced with great success in London. This revival of the comedy of manners style was Goldsmith's response to the sentimental, or "weeping," comedies that dominated the theater at the time. A bit of a court jester, sometimes ridiculous and vain, Goldsmith was valued for his simple style and loved for his generous nature. Johnson said of him, "No man was more foolish when he had not a pen in his hand, or more wise when he had." Edmund *Burke reportedly burst into tears on hearing the news of his death. Goldsmith's and Burke's statues on either side of the main entrance of Trinity College are *Dublin landmarks. J.MD.

golf. One of Ireland's most popular sports. When *Ulster was planted in 1606, a certain Viscount Montgomery, with an ancestral home in Ayrshire, Scotland, acquired a large portion of the Ards Peninsula in County *Down. He built a school at Newtown where the scholars had "a green for recreation at goff, football and archery." This is the first mention of golf in Ireland.

It was almost three centuries later, however, before the game gained a firm foothold. In 1882, Royal Belfast, founded by Thomas Sinclair, became Ireland's first, formally constituted club. Scottish regiments of the British army played a major role in the development of golf in Ireland, establishing the Curragh Golf Club (1883), Royal Dublin (1885), and Lahinch (1892).

From these modest beginnings, the island of Ireland now boasts 405 golf clubs. The geographical term is used advisedly, because there is no political border in Irish golf. Both the men's and women's games for the country north and south are governed from Dublin, by the Golfing Union of Ireland (GUI) and the Irish Ladies Golf Union (ILGU).

Though something of a latecomer to the game, by comparison with its Scottish and English neighbors, Ireland claimed a major, pioneering role in golf administration. The GUI was launched in 1891 as the world's first national union, and the ILGU, which was instituted in 1893, claimed the same distinction for the women's game.

It is estimated that the world contains only 150 pure links courses—golf courses located on duneland linking arable land with the seashore. Ireland can boast forty of them, including such celebrated stretches as Ballybunion and Waterville in County *Kerry; Royal County Down; Portmarnock in County *Dublin; Royal Portrush in County *Antrim; Rosses Point in County *Sligo; Lahinch and the latest arrival, Doonbeg, in County *Clare. Among the major international events that the country played host to were the 1951 British Open (Royal Portrush), the only time the British Open was played in Ireland; the 1960 Canada Cup and 1991 Walker Cup (both at Portmarnock); and the 1996 Curtis Cup (at Killarney). The 2006 Ryder Cup is to be staged at the Kildare Club, twenty miles west of Dublin.

Among Ireland's leading professionals, Fred Daly won the 1947 British Open while Christy O'Connor Senior has over thirty international victories, including the World Seniors of 1977. Joe Carr, the country's leading amateur, won forty championships, including the British Amateur three times. D.G.

Gonne, Maud (1866–1953). *Nationalist and suffragette. Gonne was born in England to a wealthy British army officer. The family moved to Ireland in 1867, and when Gonne was four her mother died. Sent to France at nineteen to recuperate from tuberculosis, Gonne fell in love with Lucien Millevoye, a right-wing politician and journalist, with whom she had two children.

In 1888, Gonne returned to Ireland and threw herself into nationalist politics. In the 1890s, she led *republican protests in *Dublin, and agitated among tenant farmers in the west. She campaigned for the release of *Fenian bombers, who were imprisoned in England, and like most republicans, she supported

Maud Gonne

the *Boers in their war with England. Gonne visited France, England, Scotland, and America to lecture and collect funds. In Paris she launched the newspaper *L'Irlande Libre*, in May 1897. Arthur *Griffith and James *Connolly were important political influences. In 1900, she founded a republican and suffragist women's society, Inghinidhe na hÉireann (Daughters of Ireland).

Gonne was the great unrequited love of the poet W. B. *Yeats, whom she met in 1889. He unsuccessfully proposed marriage to her twice (in 1891 and 1916). She was the subject of many of his poems, and in 1902 she had the leading role in his play *Cathleen Ni Houlihan*. Gonne was a leading figure in the Irish National Literary Society, and like Yeats, was attracted to the occult.

Her relationship with Millevoye ended in 1899, and in 1903, in Paris, she married the republican and Boer War veteran, John *MacBride. They had a son, the future politician, Seán *MacBride, but separated soon after and MacBride returned to Ireland. She remained in Paris until 1917. MacBride was executed for his part in the 1916 *Easter Rising. On her return to Ireland, Gonne adopted his surname for the first time. She was arrested in Dublin in May 1918 for *Sinn Féin activity (the alleged "German Plot"), and she spent six months in Holloway Jail, London. She opposed the *Anglo-Irish Treaty of 1921 and was imprisoned during the *Irish Civil War. During and after the Civil War, Gonne organized the Women's Prisoners' Defense League to help republican prisoners and their families. She continued to support the republican movement and her son Seán's attempts to form a constitutional republican party. In 1938, she published a memoir of her early life, *A Servant of the Queen*. Gonne is buried in *Glasnevin Cemetery, Dublin. P.D.

Good Friday Agreement, the (1998). Agreement resulting from the *peace process in *Northern Ireland. Properly known as the 1998 Belfast Agreement, this was the culmination of multiparty talks that began January 1998 to end the *Northern Ireland conflict. A number of parties participated in the talks and largely endorsed the agreement, including *Sinn Féin, under the leadership of Gerry *Adams, but not Ian *Paisley's *Democratic Unionist Party (DUP). The substance of the agreement was worked out by David *Trimble, the leader of the *Ulster Unionist Party (UUP) and John

*Hume, the leader of the *Social Democratic and Labour Party (SDLP), in conjunction with the British Prime Minister Tony *Blair and the Irish *Taoiseach Bertie *Ahern. George Mitchell (who had compiled "The *Mitchell Report" on the situation in Northern Ireland) and US President Clinton played important roles in securing the final accord. The historic agreement was reached at around 5:00 P.M. on Good Friday, April 10, 1998. Trimble and Hume were awarded the Nobel Prize for Peace in 1999.

The complex plan was designed to balance the various interests:

East-West Relations

The British secretary of state would remain responsible for nondevolved matters—notably, security—and represent Northern Ireland in the government of the United Kingdom. Articles in the Irish *Constitution would be amended to withdraw its territorial claim (or any possible interpretations of a claim) over Northern Ireland, substituting an aspiration to Irish unity. The 1985 *Anglo-Irish Agreement was replaced by a new British-Irish Agreement, effectively restating the necessity for cooperation between the sovereign governments. A British-Irish Council would bring together delegates from the new devolved assemblies for Northern Ireland, Scotland, and Wales, the governments of the Isle of Man and the Channel Islands, and the British and Irish parliaments. The Council would meet periodically to discuss general issues.

Internal Relations

A devolved Northern Ireland Assembly and government, subordinate to London, would be established. The assembly would be based on power-sharing between representatives of the *Catholic/*nationalist and *Protestant/*unionist communities. Legislation would require either parallel consent or a weighted majority of 60 percent of the assembly's members to become law. Subcommittees, whose membership would broadly reflect party strengths, would oversee the implementation of legislation. Each government department would be headed by a minister with full executive authority. An unelected civic forum would foster a wider consensus on social and economic matters. All parties committed themselves to making their best effort to secure paramilitary disarmament. In response, British state security would be scaled down.

North-South Relations

The all-Ireland dimension would be addressed by a North-South Ministerial Council, responsible to and limited by the Northern Ireland Assembly and the Irish government. The council would seek to coordinate and harmonize transport, agriculture, education, health, environment, research, tourism, and cultural heritage.

Prisoners associated with paramilitary groups on cease-fire were to be released within two years and the *Royal Ulster Constabulary was to be reformed to encourage its acceptance by the entire community, especially the long-alienated nationalists. There were commitments to enhance the status of the *Irish language and a local, predominantly Protestant dialect, Ulster-Scots. Further measures to ensure fair employment were promised.

The agreement was approved in a Northern Ireland referendum by 71.1 percent of voters (nearly half of unionist voters opposed the accord), and by 95 percent in the Republic. After elections to the assembly, David Trimble of the UUP duly became first minister of the new devolved executive, with Séamus *Mallon of the SDLP as deputy first minister. Legislation to give effect to the Belfast Agreement became law in June 1998. Such issues as disarmament, or as it has become known decommissioning, have proved controversial and the assembly has more than once been suspended by the British government because of lack of progress on this issue. M.M.

Government of Ireland Act (1920). Legislation that set up *home rule with two separate parliaments for the North and the South of Ireland. During the *War of Independence, *Lloyd George's government decided to implement home rule with two separate parliaments, similar to the bill passed in 1914. This act was aimed at undermining *Dáil Éireann, the Parliament established by *Sinn Féin after the 1918 election, while satisfying *unionists' demands not to be ruled from Dublin. The Northern Parliament was limited to six of Ulster's nine counties. (Unionists had a majority in four of the six counties.) In subsequent elections, Sinn Féin won in the South, but refused to convene a parliament under the act and remained in Dáil Éireann. Unionists had forty of the fifty-two seats in the North and established their own parliament in *Belfast under the act, thus creating the state of *Northern Ireland and the *partition of Ireland. T.C.

Graham, Patrick (1943–). Painter. Born in Mullingar, County *Westmeath, Graham studied at the National College of Art and Design, Dublin, and is a member of *Aosdána. His neo-Expressionist technique and figurative content has been influential in the continuing reaction to formalism. M.C.

Grattan, Henry (1746–1820). Irish parliamentarian. Born in *Dublin where he was educated at Trinity College, Grattan attended the Middle Temple in London and was called to the Irish Bar in 1772. He was influenced by the nationalist politics of Henry Flood, MP (member of Parliament), who advocated the independence of the Irish House of Commons from Westminster, London. In December 1775, Grattan accepted the patronage of Whig magnate Lord Charlemont, who brought him into the Commons as a borough MP. Grattan rose quickly to prominence owing to his considerable skills as an orator and the crisis engendered by the *American Revolution. In 1778 he was closely associated with the "patriot" *Volunteer organization, which gave the pro-reform party adhering to Grattan and Flood the support of an extraparliamentary armed mass movement. This obliged Westminster to yield a large measure of legislative independence to Ireland in 1782. Grattan purchased a small estate at Tinnehinch, County *Wicklow, with a Commons grant of £50,000 and from 1790 was MP for Dublin City. Although an avid supporter of *Catholic rights and a sympathizer of the radical *United Irishmen, Grattan was falsely suspected of sedition in April 1798. His reputation was further tarnished in establishment circles during the *Rebellion of 1798, notwithstanding his temporary residence in England. An opponent of the Act of *Union, Grattan was briefly an MP in 1800 and, again, after 1804 in the Westminster Parliament. He campaigned for *Catholic Emancipation until his death in London in June 1820. R.OD.

Graves, Alfred Perceval (1846–1931). Poet and educationalist. Born in *Dublin, educated at Windermere College and Trinity College, Dublin, Graves worked initially as a schools inspector in England. His father was the *Church of Ireland bishop of Limerick. Graves published the collections *Songs of Old Ireland* in 1882 and *Songs of Erin* in 1892, both in collaboration with Sir Charles Stanford. He wrote lyrics for old Irish folk tunes derived from the collection of George *Petrie. He also wrote under the

Lady Gregory

pen name Father Prout and one of his most enduring songs is the comic ballad "Father O'Flynn." Graves was a contributor to *Punch* magazine and active in the Irish Literary Society in London. His autobiography, *To Return to All That* (1930), was written as an alternative version of the family history to that portrayed by his son, the novelist, poet, and mythologist Robert Graves (1895–1985), in *Goodbye to All That* (1929). C.D.

Graves, Robert James (1796–1853). Physician after whom Graves' Disease is named. Born in *Dublin, Graves was educated at Trinity College, Dublin, and medical schools in London, Edinburgh, and the continent. He took up a position as physician at the Meath Hospital in Dublin in 1821. He was president of the Royal College of Physicians of Ireland, 1843–44. Graves helped to found and edit the *Dublin Journal of Medical Science*. His enduring reputation rests on his *Clinical Lectures* (1843) and on his diagnosis of Graves' disease, or hyperthyroidism. His pioneering treatment of fever patients through "supportive therapy" was adopted worldwide. C.D.

Greevy, Bernadette (1940–). Mezzo-soprano. Born in *Dublin, Greevy has gained international acclaim for her performances, particularly those of works by Elgar, Mahler, and Brahms. In her early career she attracted the attention of Sir John Barbirolli, the noted conductor, who proved influential in promoting her career. She has won numerous national and international awards for her singing. A.S.

Gregory, Lady (Augusta) (1852–1932). Playwright, director, patron of the arts. Born into a landholding *Protestant family, Augusta Persse grew up in Roxborough House, County *Galway. In 1880, she married Sir William Gregory and entered the social, literary, and political circles of Europe's aristocracy. Lady Gregory is best known for her prominent role in the *Irish Literary Revival, as a playwright, director, editor, and translator. In 1896, Lady Gregory invited William Butler *Yeats to her estate *Coole Park, a gathering place for literary and political figures. Their subsequent friendship and work became the heart of the Irish Literary Revival. Lady Gregory's role as mentor and friend to Yeats and their collaborations were critical to Yeats's development as a writer.

With Yeats and J. M. *Synge, Gregory founded the Irish Literary Theatre in 1899, which in 1904 became the *Abbey Theatre. Aiming to establish an Irish national theater and to honor Irish culture, they staged works by Irish playwrights either based on folk literature or with Irish subjects. Later, Gregory was managing director of the Abbey Theatre, and wrote or translated over forty plays. A strong advocate of the *Irish language and folk literature, Gregory translated such Irish sagas as *Cuchulain of Muirthemne* (1902). Her other works include *Our Irish Theatre* (1914), *The Image and Other Plays* (1922), and *Irish Folk History Plays* (1912). Lady Gregory's political activism and literary work focused on restoring and promoting an Irish national literature, language, and cultural identity. K.MI.

Griffin, Gerald (1803–40). Novelist. Born in Limerick City, Griffin began his literary career in London in the 1820s, where he published a book of short stories. Ill health and bad luck, however, forced his return home. His best-known work is *The Collegians* (1829), based on a local murder. Significant for its depiction of the pre-*Famine Catholic middle class, it was also a popular success, inspiring Boucicault's *The Colleen Bawn* (1860) and, some believe, Theodore Dreiser's *An American Tragedy* (1925). Beset by doubts about his work, in 1838 Griffin burned his papers and entered the *Christian Brothers. G.OB.

Griffith, Arthur (1871–1922). *Nationalist leader, founder of *Sinn Féin. Born on March 31, 1871, in *Dublin, Griffith first worked as an apprentice in the printing trade and later became a journalist. In 1899, he launched the *United Irishman*, the first of a succession of newspapers he edited that called for an "Irish Ireland." Griffith's newspapers championed this ideology of cultural nationalism and political separatism, which emerged at the turn of the twentieth century and maintained that independence would be pointless if Ireland lost its cultural identity. He was also active in the *Gaelic League, a cultural nationalist organization that promoted the *Irish language and Gaelic cultural traditions, and advocated protectionist measures to encourage greater economic self-sufficiency.

In a series of articles published in 1904, *The Resurrection of Hungary: A Parallel for Ireland*, Griffith outlined a plan of constitutional change for Ireland based on the experience of the Hungarians in the Habsburg empire. According to his model of a "dual monarchy," Ireland would retain its link to the British crown and share a common foreign policy, but would otherwise govern itself. In effect, Griffith argued for a status similar to what existed before the Act of *Union (1800): domestic affairs controlled by an independent Irish parliament sitting in Dublin, but one elected by a democratic majority and not dominated by *Protestant landowners, as it had been in the eighteenth century. This new constitutional order could be achieved, Griffith argued, by a policy of "passive resistance," whereby Irish members would withdraw from the Westminster Parliament and form a new national assembly in Dublin. Griffith's "Hungarian policy" soon became known more simply as "Sinn Féin," meaning "we ourselves." On November 28, 1905, Griffith founded Sinn Féin, a political organization dedicated to promoting national political autonomy, cultural vitality, and economic self-sufficiency. The new political party unsuccessfully contested the North Leitrim parliamentary constituency in 1908.

Meanwhile, in 1906, the *United Irishman* ceased publication due to legal problems and was replaced by *Sinn Féin*, which continued to promulgate Griffith's views until its suppression by the government early in *World War I. The Sinn Féin party led by Griffith had little success until after the *Easter Rising of 1916, for which it was incorrectly held responsible because of its publicly visible radicalism.

Griffith himself did not participate in the rising because he still opposed armed force. At the party convention in 1917, Griffith relinquished leadership to Éamon *de Valera, the only surviving commander of the rising.

In the elections of 1918, Sinn Féin emerged as the strongest party in Ireland, winning 73 of 105 parliamentary seats, and proceeded to implement, in essence, Griffith's policy of withdrawing from Westminster and establishing itself in Dublin as an independent national assembly, *Dáil Éireann. This move sparked the *Anglo-Irish War, which lasted from January 1919 to July 1921. In late 1921, Griffith led a delegation (which included Michael *Collins) to London to negotiate a settlement of the conflict. The *Anglo-Irish Treaty, signed on December 6, 1921, created a twenty-six-county *Irish Free State, which was still formally under the crown and within the British *Commonwealth. Although this was consistent with Griffith's "Hungarian policy," the failure to achieve a republic for all of Ireland, and especially the mandatory *oath of allegiance to the British crown, caused an acrimonious split in the Dáil. When the treaty was narrowly ratified in January 1922, de Valera resigned as president and was replaced by Griffith. Shortly after the *Civil War erupted in June 1922, Griffith suffered a cerebral hemorrhage and died on August 12, 1922. F.B.

Guerin, Veronica (1958–96). Journalist. During her short career, Guerin won many awards for her exposés on the Irish criminal underworld. She received numerous threats and was shot in the leg in an attack on her house, before she was eventually murdered in her car in a suburb of *Dublin in 1996. Two men, connected to a Dublin criminal gang, have received life sentences for their part in her murder, but one of these convictions was overturned on appeal. The gang leader, John Gilligan, was acquitted of the charge that he had Guerin murdered but was sentenced to twenty-eight years for drug-related offenses. B.D.

Guildford Four. Notorious miscarriage of justice in England. Four innocent people spent fourteen years in prison for two Provisional IRA (*Irish Republican Army) bombings of pubs in Guildford and Woolwich, England, in 1974. The four—Carole Richardson of London, and Gerard Conlon, Patrick Armstrong, and Paul Hill, all from *Belfast—were convicted of the bombings and sentenced to life in prison in 1975 on police evidence that was later found to have been tainted: coerced and fabricated confessions; altered interrogation notes; and police perjury. Prosecutors in the case were also later found to have suppressed evidence that conflicted with the confessions.

The Guildford Four became a cause célèbre in both Britain and Ireland when a number of prominent British figures—including the Catholic archbishop of Westminster, the Anglican archbishop of Canterbury, two former home secretaries, and several retired judges—spearheaded a campaign to win their release. That campaign led British Home Secretary Douglas Hurd to order an inquiry into the case in 1989. This uncovered evidence of the conspiracy by police and prosecution, and a three-member appeals court overturned the convictions on October 19, 1989. Three of the four were immediately released. Paul Hill, who had also been sentenced to life for a murder in *Northern Ireland, was taken to Crumlin Road Prison in Belfast and released two days later after a hearing that lasted less than ten minutes. That murder conviction was also overturned later.

A 1994 British government report on the wrongful convictions found that the miscarriages of justice were the result of individual failings rather than a fault in the criminal justice system.

Gerard Conlon wrote a book on his ordeal entitled *Proved Innocent* (1990), which was later the basis of the movie *In the Name of the Father* (1993). T.D.

Guinness. Family of *brewers. In 1756 Arthur Guinness (1725–1803) established a brewery in Leixlip, County *Kildare, which he moved to *Dublin in 1759. The business grew under his son Arthur (1767–1855) and grandson Benjamin (1798–1868), who developed export markets in the United States and Europe. Sir Benjamin's sons, Arthur Edward (1840–1915), First Baron Ardilaun, and Edward Cecil (1847–1927), First Baron Iveagh, were generous benefactors to the city of Dublin. They oversaw the development of their brewery in St. James Gate, which still produces dark, creamy stout, into one of the world's largest breweries. By 1980, the family interest in the business had fallen to just 5 percent, but the company continued to expand its holdings. However, the financial takeover of Guinness by Distillers in 1986 led to a fraud trial in 1990, after which the company's former chairman was convicted for illegal manipulation of Guinness share prices. Guinness, now part of the multinational conglomerate Diageo, continues to sponsor the publication of the *Guinness Book of World Records*. S.A.B.

Guthrie, Sir Tyrone (1900–71). Dramaturge. Born in Tunbridge Wells, England, he spent his early years at Annaghmakerrig, County *Monaghan, his mother's home. Initially noted for his direction of the classical repertory at London's celebrated Old Vic Theatre, Guthrie has been internationally renowned since the 1950s. His Dublin productions included Seán *O'Casey's controversial *The Bishop's Bonfire* (1954). In 1962, he was appointed inaugural director of what became the Guthrie Theater, in Minneapolis, where Brian *Friel studied his methods. Between 1963 and 1970, Guthrie served as chancellor of Queen's University, Belfast. Annaghmakerrig House is now an artists' retreat, in accordance with his will. G.OB.

H

Hamilton, Hugh Douglas (1739–1808). Portrait painter. Born in *Dublin and trained at Dublin Society Schools, Hamilton produced small oval pastel portraits, which earned him success in London. He painted large oil portraits in Italy, where he lived for thirteen years. On his return to Ireland in 1792, Hamilton continued his career with full-length portraits in oils, most of which were of people opposed to the Act of *Union. M.C.

Hamilton, William Rowan (1805–65). Mathematician. Born in *Dublin, Hamilton was brilliant and precocious. A polyglot by age nine, he was appointed professor of astronomy at Trinity College and astronomer royal at Dunsink Observatory, even before graduating in classics and mathematics. He dabbled in poetry (discouraged by his friend Wordsworth) and philosophy (inspired by his friend Coleridge). He excelled in mathematics, where he favored highly original, abstract, general approaches. He invented quaternions (the forerunners of later noncommutative algebras) and Hamiltonian dynamics (first exploited in the 1920s by Schroedinger in his wave formulation of quantum mechanics). Unhappy in love, Hamilton struggled with alcoholism until his death. M.L.

harp, Irish. The symbolic instrument of Ireland. Its present form was established over a thousand years ago, with variations in shape being introduced up to the seventeenth century. The oldest surviving instrument, the Brian Boru harp, held in Trinity College, Dublin, dates to the fourteenth century. The older instruments were smaller and heavier, and had wire strings. From the early 1800s, they increased in size, were lighter and first used gut, then nylon strings. The old harp was associated with indigenous classical *music. Its players were meticulously trained and enjoyed considerable respect in chieftains' houses in Ireland, and abroad, particularly in *Scotland. Music composed by these early harpers still survives—most notably that of Turloch *Carolan (1670–1738), two hundred of whose tunes survive and are still available in print. Other harpists include Ruadhrí Dall Ó Catháin (his sixteenth-century tune "Give Me Your Hand" is still popular) and the Connellan brothers (from the seventeenth century).

Harping was largely extinguished along with the Gaelic order in the seventeenth and eighteenth centuries and its players and repertoire were submerged in "folk" (now called "traditional") music. The 1792 Belfast Harp Festival, a final effort to revive harping, produced hugely valuable transcriptions by Edward Bunting, still in print today. The organizations Cáirde na Cruite and the Harp Foundation maintain the popularity of the instrument today through teaching and performance. F.V.

Harris, Richard (1930–2002). Actor. Born in Limerick City, Harris was educated at Crescent College, Limerick, and at the London Academy of Music and Dramatic Art. He wanted to be a *soccer player, but during a three-year bout with tuberculosis in his late teens he turned his mind to acting. Harris made his stage debut in 1956 in Joan Littlewood's production of Brendan *Behan's *The Quare Fellow*. His first screen role was in Cyril Frankel's *Alive and Kicking* (1958). He won the Best Actor Award at Cannes and was nominated for an Oscar for his part as a *rugby player in *This Sporting Life* (1963). Other notable films include *A Man Called Horse* (1969), *Unforgiven* (1993), and *The Field* (1990), for which he was again nominated for an Oscar for best actor. His last screen role was as Albus Dumbledore in the first two Harry Potter movies in 2001/2002. Harris also had an accomplished singing career, notably in the role of King Arthur in the 1967 film version of Lerner & Loewe's musical *Camelot*, and in his recordings of the songs of Jimmy Webb. His recording of *MacArthur Park* became an international hit single in 1968. C.D.

Hartnett, Michael. See **Ó hAirtnéide, Mícheál.**

Harty, Sir Hamilton (1879–1941). Composer, conductor, pianist. Born in County *Down, Harty was a church organist from the age of twelve (Magheracoll, Belfast, Bray). He quickly established his reputation as a composer and gifted accompanist after he moved to London in his early twenties. His talent as a conductor led to his appointment in 1920 to Manchester's Hallé Orchestra, often lauded under his stewardship as the finest in Britain. After leaving Manchester in 1933, he worked mainly in London. He introduced much new music (including Mahler and Shostakovich) to British audiences, premiered Walton's First Symphony in 1934, and was a renowned interpreter of Berlioz. His arrangements of Handel's Water Music and Royal Fireworks Music were staples of the symphonic repertoire. He left many fine recordings, and his own Irish-inflected music—including an Irish Symphony (1904), concertos for violin (1908) and piano (1922), and the symphonic poem "The Children of Lir" (1938)—attracted new listeners through a series of recordings by the Ulster Orchestra in the 1980s. M.D.

Haughey, Charles J. (1925–). Politician, leader of *Fianna Fáil, *Taoiseach (prime minister). Born in County *Mayo, Haughey served as a TD (Teachta Dála; member of Parliament) from 1957 to 1992. His first ministerial post was in the Department for Justice (1961–64), where he earned a reputation as a reformer. Most notably, he introduced the Guardianship of Infants Act (1964) and the Succession Act (1965), giving wives equal legal rights with regard to the upbringing of their children and the inheritance of family property. He also effectively abolished the use of the death penalty. He served as agriculture minister (1964–66) and as a highly successful finance minister (1966–70), during which term he presided over the First Commission on the Status of *Women. He was dismissed from the government by Taoiseach Jack *Lynch and prosecuted for attempting to illegally import arms for the defense of nationalist areas in *Northern Ireland during the *Arms Crisis in 1970. Although he was found not guilty, the issue remained controversial because the extent of government involvement, including that of the Taoiseach himself, had yet to be conclusively determined. As a result of his popularity with the party grassroots, Haughey returned to government as health minister under Lynch in 1977.

In 1979, he successfully found a broadly acceptable formula for the legalization of contraception, a daunting task given the depth of public division on the issue at that time. He was elected leader of Fianna Fáil and served as Taoiseach from 1979 to 1981, February to November 1982, and from 1987 to 1992. Haughey was personally involved in 1987 in formulating the "Programme for National Recovery" between the government, *trade unions, and employers. The program heralded the modern "social partnership" model of policy making in Ireland and is generally seen as one of the reasons for the rapid economic growth in the 1990s.

A poor election result in 1989 forced Fianna Fáil to enter its first ever coalition government—with the *Progressive Democrats. Haughey was replaced as party leader in 1992. Controversy about his financial affairs has plagued him throughout his life, and since 1996 he has been subjected to a Tribunal of Inquiry regarding large corporate donations he is reported to have received during his political career. E.C.

health. Through the centuries, war and hunger brought disease. The bubonic plague epidemic of 1649–52 began in *Galway and ravaged the country, along with typhus. The famine of 1740–41 brought "famine fever"—most likely typhus—and the Napoleonic era, of apparent prosperity and intensifying poverty, was characterized by "the country disease"—dysentery—and typhus again. The first Western European cholera epidemic, in the early 1830s, did not spare Ireland, and the Great *Famine of the following decade brought famine fever, and "relapsing fever" along with mass starvation.

During the eighteenth century, a few voluntary hospitals were set up in the cities. In the early nineteenth century it was noted that, epidemics and periodic famine aside, the Irish were among the healthiest peasantry of Europe, because of their potato diet. The Famine years, 1846–49, prompted the establishment of temporary fever hospitals and laws for the medical relief of the poor. In 1851 a medical officer (dispensary doctor) was appointed for every *workhouse in the country, and people could consult him for a small fee, or for free. The several voluntary hospitals already in the cities catered mainly to the poor, and by 1861 the hospitals attached to the workhouses could take patients who were not workhouse inmates. However, before antisepsis, hospitals probably killed more people than they cured, and were important mainly for the chance they gave doctors to develop skills in the treatment of disease. *Dublin obstetricians, for example, were to become world leaders in the field. (The unusually large Irish families that persisted up to the 1960s facilitated this development.)

Health care that was brought to the people included the Jubilee and the Lady Dudley nurses, trained nurse-midwives who worked in rural areas. Set up in the years 1897–1902, these nurses were crucial in the reduction of maternal and infant mortality. Also important were the anti-tubercolosis campaign of the Women's National Health Association (1907), and the health education undertaken by the various agricultural and social organizations of this period.

People's continued good health, then as now, was more dependent upon living conditions and diet than upon medical services, however. Rural housing improved in the late nineteenth century, and remittances from *America, agricultural education, and a rising standard of living overall ensured a more varied diet for rural people. Poorer city people were at a terrible disadvantage, living in unhealthy tenements and lanes with inadequate sanitary facilities, an uncertain water supply, and no access to clean milk even when they could afford it. The housing programs of the 1930s and 1950s eventually replaced the worst of these slums with proper dwellings.

After the *Irish Free State was created in 1922, the workhouse system was abolished in the South, but it continued till 1945 in *Northern Ireland. In the Free State/*Republic, the public hospitals were poorly equipped and staffed, and it was not until the Public Health Act (1945), which established Public Health nurses, and the creation of a Department of Health two years later, that the serious public health problems of tubercolosis and typhus were seriously tackled. In 1950, the young Minister of Health Dr. Noel *Browne was forced to resign his position because of opposition from the medical profession and the *Catholic bishops to his scheme to provide free medical care for mothers and children up to the age of sixteen. In 1953, after a prolonged political battle involving the major political parties, the Catholic Church and the medical profession, a free-for-all maternal and infant health service was finally introduced. Maternal mortality, already falling since the introduction of children's allowances in 1944, fell dramatically, as it did in Northern Ireland after the introduction of the National Health Service in 1948. Infant mortality, north and south, fell definitively in the late 1950s, due to improved living conditions and medical facilities. C.C.

Healy, Timothy (1855–1931). *Nationalist politician. Born in Bandon, County *Cork, Healy worked as a barrister and journalist. As MP (member of Parliament) for *Wexford (1880–83), he became a proficient debater and an expert at parliamentary obstruction. A leading supporter of Charles Stewart *Parnell, he served as MP for *Monaghan (1883–85), South Londonderry (1885–86), and North Longford (1887–92). Healy recommended Parnell's temporary retirement after the *O'Shea divorce case and subsequently became his most bitter antagonist. Healy was anti-Parnellite MP for North Louth (1892–1910) but became estranged from the *Parliamentary Party and joined the conciliatory nationalist group "All for Ireland" League in 1910. Although a conservative, Healy developed sympathy for *Sinn Féin while MP for Northeast Cork (1910–18), and served as first governor general of the *Irish Free State (1922–28). S.A.B.

Heaney, Seamus Justin (1939–). Poet, essayist, playwright, Nobel laureate. Born into a *Catholic family, the eldest of nine children, Heaney was brought up on a small farm, "Mossbawn," between Catholic Toomebridge and *Protestant Castledawson in County *Derry. Educated at St. Columb's College in Derry

Seamus Heaney

and Queen's University, Belfast, he started teaching in the English Department at Queen's University in 1966. Heaney took part in the civil rights marches in the late 1960s. From 1970 to 1971, he was a visiting lecturer at the University of California, Berkeley.

His first collection of poems, *Death of a Naturalist* (1966), is rooted in his rural, childhood experience, which Heaney makes extraordinarily vivid through his highly sensuous language. The influences of Robert Frost, William Wordsworth, Gerard Manley *Hopkins, R. S. Thomas, and Patrick *Kavanagh are evident. The title of his second collection, *Door into the Dark* (1969), suggests both the mystical orientation and the sense of displacement and exposure that characterize much of Heaney's poetry. The preoccupation with digging, ploughing, fishing, peering down wells, probing secret recesses and dark interiors becomes an effort of cultural retrieval and restoration.

Wintering Out (1972) appeared at the height of the *Troubles, and, as the title suggests, is concerned with endurance in bleak conditions. The poetry reflects a nostalgic longing for an idealized, lost or disappearing home, transcending the ravages of history. For Heaney, P. V. Glob's book, *The Bog People* (1969), about the discovery in Danish bogs of Iron Age sacrificial victims to Nerthus, the Mother Goddess, suggested ways of understanding the contemporary conflict in *Ulster as part of a timeless continuum of ritual tribal slaughter.

In 1972, Heaney moved from Belfast to Glanmore in County *Wicklow, and was head of the English Department at Carysfort College, Dublin, between 1975 and 1981. *North* (1975) continues the attempt to define the present by exploring its relationship with the past. There are more *bog poems, and poems that use *Viking mythology to comment on the present. But, increasingly, Heaney comes to question his own aestheticizing procedures, insisting upon the stark reality of atrocity, which overwhelms and silences.

A new voice is heard in *Field-Work* (1979), where he struggles to affirm the "clear light" of imaginative freedom and transcendence. In 1980, *Preoccupations: Selected Prose 1968–1978* appeared. The following year, Heaney became visiting professor at Harvard, and, in 1984 , Boylston professor of rhetoric and poetry. His translation of the middle-Irish poem *Buile Suibhne* (*Sweeney Astray*, 1983) was published by *Field Day, the Derry theater company which he and Brian *Friel founded in 1980. For Heaney, the outcast birdman Sweeney is a figure of the displaced artist. His next collection, *Station Island* (1984), includes the Dantesque title-poem in which he encounters a series of ghosts, among them literary figures such as William *Carleton and James *Joyce, and victims of sectarian murders, who challenge him about his allegiances and his art.

In his next collection, *The Haw Lantern* (1987), the self-scrutiny is unrelenting. A series of political "parable poems" shows the influence of East European poets such as Zbigniew Herbert and Czeslaw Milosz. The central "Clearances" sonnet sequence is written out of the loss of bereavement, in memory of Heaney's mother, who died in 1984. In these poems, absence and loss are transformed through the work of memory and imagination. A second volume of essays, *The Government of the Tongue* (1988), affirms the liberating and redemptive power of art in the face of political oppression. His play *The Cure at Troy*, after *Philoctetes* by Sophocles, dramatizes questions of personal conscience, duty, and communal loyalty.

In 1989, Heaney became chair of poetry at Oxford University. A collection of his Oxford lectures entitled *The Redress of Poetry* and his translation of *Beowulf* were published in 1995, the year in which he was awarded the Nobel Prize for literature. His recent collections of poetry, *Seeing Things* (1991), *The Spirit Level* (1996), and *Electric Light* (2001), display a buoyant confidence, a relaxed visionary quality, a new lightness of touch. E.K-A.

Henry II (1133–89). King of England (1154–89). Within a year of succeeding to the English throne, Henry secured a papal letter *(Laudabiliter)* authorizing the conquest of Ireland. In 1168, he gave his consent for Dermot *MacMurrough to recruit the military assistance of Richard fitzGilbert de Clare (*"Strongbow") in his campaign to recover the kingship of *Leinster. In October 1171, Henry led a military expedition of four thousand men to Ireland, partly to avoid the full consequences of the murder of Thomas à Becket (December 29, 1170). Having secured the submission both of Strongbow and the Gaelic lords, he divided the land of Ireland into fiefs and installed a viceregent in *Dublin, thus establishing the power of the English crown in Ireland for the first time. S.A.B.

Henry VIII (1491–1547). King of England (1509–47), responsible for the *Reformation. Henry VIII was the first monarch to rule Ireland as a king rather than "lord." Since the twelfth-century *Anglo-Norman Conquest, the English monarchs had ruled Ireland and its Gaelic nobility as a "lordship" under the feudal system. Effective English control had remained largely limited to the *Pale, the area around *Dublin. After the Kildare rebellion of 1534–35, Henry sought to expand his authority. By the policy of "surrender and regrant," the Gaelic lords were obliged to surrender their ancestral lands and pledge loyalty to the king. In return for their submission, Henry VIII returned their lands (which were now held under the English law of primogeniture) and granted them English titles. In a further effort to enforce obedience, in 1541 the Irish *Parliament passed an act whereby Henry VIII became formally king of Ireland. Although he had previously supported Rome in its struggle against the *Protestantism of Martin Luther, Henry broke with Rome and decided to "reform" the Church in his kingdom when the pope refused to dissolve his marriage to Catherine of Aragon (who had failed to provide him with a male heir).

Henry VIII's *Reformation of the Church in England during the 1530s had profound consequences for the future of Ireland. The Irish aristocracy, including both the Gaelic chieftains and the "Old English" families who had settled in the country since the twelfth century, remained largely faithful to Rome, as did the masses of the Irish peasantry. After the Reformation, the English crown increasingly sought to maintain its control over Ireland by the "plantation" of loyal "new English" settlers, many of whom were actually from *Scotland. F.B.

Henry, Paul (1876–1958). Painter. Born in *Belfast, Henry painted Irish landscapes using post-impressionist techniques. He trained in Belfast and Paris and worked as an illustrator in London for ten years before going to paint on Achill Island in County *Mayo. Henry combined avant-garde techniques and traditional subject matter. His work is accessible and symbolic of political change. Henry founded the Society of Dublin Painters in 1920 to exhibit modern art. M.C.

Henry, Sam (1878–1952). Song collector. A Customs & Excise officer and a *Unionist councilor for Coleraine, County *Derry, Henry collected some one thousand songs in the North Derry/Antrim area from 1906 until his death. Half of these were published from 1923 to 1939 as "Songs of the People," a weekly column largely edited by him in the *Northern Constitution* newspaper. The "Songs of the People" both preserved old local songs and presented them for new interpretation. A 632-page book collection of songs from his columns, *Sam Henry's Songs of the People* (University of Georgia Press, 1990), makes a significant contribution to the archive of Irish traditional song. F.V.

Herzog, Chaim (1918–97). President of Israel, 1983–93. Born in *Belfast, Herzog was educated at Wesley College in *Dublin and at Cambridge and London. He was a fluent Irish speaker. Herzog enrolled in the British army in 1939, graduated from the Royal Military Academy, Sandhurst, and served with distinction in Europe in World War II. In 1947, he emigrated to Israel, and joined the Jewish underground militia, Haganah. He was appointed head of the Intelligence Department of General Staff of the Israeli Defense Force (IDF) in 1948. Herzog served as defense attaché to Washington for the IDF, 1948–50 and 1959–62, and was Israel's ambassador to Washington, 1975–78. He entered the Knesset for the Labour Party in 1981 and was elected president in 1983. C.D.

Hewitt, John (1907–87). Poet. Born in *Belfast, Hewitt remains one of the most important and influential voices in *Ulster poetry. A committed *socialist and art curator, he worked for the Belfast Museum and Art Gallery and traveled frequently to Eastern Europe. Throughout his life, he was a prolific and imaginative poet who played with language and form. Hewitt celebrated Northern regionalism while simultaneously studying what it meant to come from a community fractured by sectarianism. He edited the Northern Irish literary magazine *Lagan*, was the art critic for the *Belfast Telegraph*, and was poetry editor for *Threshold*. After working as director of the Herbert Art Gallery and Museum in Coventry, he returned to Northern Ireland in 1972 where, as writer-in-residence at Queen's University, Belfast, he received an honorary doctorate for his profound literary contributions. Hewitt is regarded as the father figure of contemporary Ulster poetry for his attempts to scrutinize the two Northern Irish communities. His work includes *Conacre* (1943), *No Rebel Word* (1948), *The Day of the Corncrake* (1969), *The Planter and the Gael* (1970, with John *Montague), and *Kites in Spring: A Belfast Boyhood* (1980). P.J.H.

Hiberno-English. Term generally describing English as it was spoken in Ireland. Sometimes known as Anglo-Irish, or Irish English, Hiberno-English originally referred to the English of the Irish country people whose speech was directly influenced by the *Irish language. When the Irish people first came into contact with English throughout the seventeenth century, they heard it through the sound system of their own language. After haltingly embracing it at first, by the late eighteenth century and early nineteenth century, they eventually reproduced a hybrid, which was either beautiful and exotic, or barbaric and ugly, depending on your point of view.

Hiberno-English differed from standard English in pronunciation, vocabulary, and syntax, each of which was heavily influenced by Irish. In pronunciation, Hiberno-English failed to reproduce a sound such as the English *th*, as it did not exist in Irish. A classic Hiberno-English speaker would say "turty tree tousand tistles and torns" or "dis, dat, dese, and dose," and roll the *r* in words such as *word* or *first*. Seventeenth-century English pronunciations have survived in Hiberno-English, such as "tay" and "say" for "tea" and "sea." Many Irish words became part of its vocabulary, such as *galore*, *smithereens*, and *kabosh*.

Many Irish authors drew inspiration from the language of the common people. In Tom *Murphy's play *A Crucial Week in the Life of a Grocer's Assistant*, one of the characters says about another: "Heeding that hussy of a clotty of a plótha of a streeleen of an ownshock of a leibidje of a girleen that's working above in the bank." The syntax is English but the words are Irish: *plótha* being a fool, *streeleen* a slut, *ownshock* a twit, and *leibidje* an idiot. As with pronunciation, there are also older strata of demotic Elizabethan English in Hiberno-English. For example, in Ireland they use *sick*, which is the Elizabethan term for "ill." The structure of the sentence in Hiberno-English was initially much dependent on Irish. Thus, curiosities such as "I am after doing it," or "I do be getting my dues" or "I bees there every day" are almost literal translations of the Irish verbs.

John Millington *Synge once seriously proposed that this mongrel speech should become the official language of the new Ireland. However, today, it is debatable whether Hiberno-English exists any longer. Most young people have an underlying desire not to speak as the country people do. While English in Ireland is spoken generally with an Irish accent, there are very few syntactical or lexicographical differences today between the English of Ireland and that of Britain. English as it is spoken in Ireland today is more influenced by American television programs and the Hollywood culture. A.T.

Hill, Derek (1916–2000). Portrait and landscape painter. Born in Southampton, England, Hill was made an honorary citizen of Ireland in 1999 for his contribution to Ireland's artistic wealth. He is best known for his atmospheric scenes of *Donegal and Tory Island. Widely traveled, he painted for a year in *Mayo and Donegal after World War II. In 1954, he bought a house in Donegal, which he filled with paintings and left to the nation in 1981. He inspired and supported the school of Tory Island painting. M.C.

hill-forts. One, two, or three concentric walls usually surrounding the summit of a hill. Too extensive for permanent fortification, the area enclosed may have served as temporary refuge or for annual folk gatherings. Most were erected in the last dozen *pre-Christian centuries. P.H.

Hoban, James (c.1762–1831). Architect of the White House, Washington, DC. Born near Callan, County *Kilkenny, Hoban studied architectural drawing in *Dublin under Thomas Ivory. He emigrated to America in 1785. He won a commission to design the State Capitol in Columbia, South Carolina, which was completed in 1791. In 1792, Hoban designed the President's House in Washington. Following the burning of the President's House by British forces in August 1814, Hoban oversaw the reconstruction (1817–29) of what henceforth would be known as the White House. Other buildings by Hoban in Washington included the Great Hotel (1793–95), the Little Hotel (1795), and the State and War Offices. C.D.

Hogan, John (1800–58). Sculptor. Born in County *Waterford, and raised and educated in *Cork, Hogan worked in the neoclassical style in Rome for over twenty years and later in Ireland. He created many funerary monuments, commemorative works, and busts of Irishmen. M.C.

Holy Cross Abbey. Cistercian abbey, founded by Dónal Mór Ó Briain in 1169. Located in County *Tipperary, the abbey gets its name from a relic of the True Cross still housed there. Rebuilt in the fifteenth century with patronage from the Butler Earls of Ormond, the monastery was suppressed during the *Reformation, but beautifully restored as a *Catholic parish church in the 1970s. P.H.

holy wells. Natural springs, found throughout Ireland and other *Celtic countries. Before Christianity, these springs were dedicated to female deities, representatives of the local earth mother deities. Holy wells are an example of how Christianity became superimposed on local pagan customs and beliefs of the *pre-Christian Celtic world. Many holy wells, according to local belief, are said to possess strange powers. Some of them are classed as healing wells, others as cursing wells, and some even combine the powers of cursing and healing. There are also wells that can make the poor rich, the unhappy happy, and the unlucky lucky. The wells are typically named for female *saints. J.MD.

home rule. Constitutional political movement in the second half of the nineteenth century, aimed at establishing an Irish *parliament. The concept was that the home rule parliament would legislate on domestic issues, while imperial matters such as finance, taxation, and *foreign policy would remain under the control of Westminster.

The home rule movement was founded by Isaac *Butt, a former *Unionist and member of Parliament (MP). Butt started questioning direct rule from Westminster as he became increasingly aware of the lack of indigenous industry and the appalling level of poverty within Ireland. A barrister who defended *Fenian rebels and president of Amnesty Association, Butt was interested in a constitutional solution to the problems which led to the Fenian rebellion.

In May 1870, Isaac Butt founded the Home Government Association to promote home rule on a federal basis. This pressure group was initially dominated by *Protestants who now saw home rule as an expression of loyalty to England and as a means of protecting both the Act of *Union and the privileged position of the ascendancy in Ireland. However, by 1873 the movement became increasingly *nationalistic and lost Protestant support. In November 1873, this organization was replaced with the Home Rule League, and fifty-nine home rulers won seats in the 1874 election, thereby establishing a sizable Home Rule party (known also as the *Irish Parliamentary Party) in Parliament. Despite this success, Butt proved to be an ineffective leader. In 1877, Charles Stewart *Parnell replaced him as chairman of the Home Rule Confederation of Great Britain. Following

Butt's death in May 1879, the leadership of the Parliamentary Party went to William Shaw.

Parnell, however, was increasingly becoming Irish nationalism's most charismatic leader, and by 1880 he had successfully replaced Shaw. In October 1882, the Irish National League was established as the new constituency organization of the Home Rule Parliamentary Party. By 1886, there were over a thousand branches throughout Ireland, responsible for funding election campaigns and contributing to MPs' salaries. Parnell at the same time organized the Parliamentary Party into a strong, closely controlled group, whose members pledged "to sit, act, and vote as one" and planned to support the political party in Westminster that offered the most concessions.

In 1885, the Conservative government attempted to win Irish support by relaxing coercion and passing the Ashbourne *Land Act of 1885. William *Gladstone, the Liberal Party leader, made no such efforts, and Parnell instructed Irish voters in Britain to vote Conservative in the November 1885 election. The results were disappointing for Parnell because, even though his party won 86 seats, it failed to hold a perfect balance of power. (The Conservatives won 249 seats and the Liberals 335.) However, after Gladstone's conversion to home rule in December 1885, Parnell decided to back the Liberals.

In April 1886, Gladstone introduced his first home rule bill. It proposed the establishment of a legislature in Dublin with control over domestic matters for the whole island. Imperial matters would still be decided by Westminster (Irish peers and MPs were excluded) and Ireland would be responsible for 15 percent of the cost of running the British empire. The bill was defeated in the Commons by thirty votes and Gladstone resigned as prime minister. The Conservatives now took office determined to undermine home rule with a policy of conciliation, known as Constructive *Unionism. This policy held that by solving Ireland's problems of poverty and land ownership, the Irish would embrace the union with Britain and abandon the quest for home rule. Parnell realized that home rule now totally depended on an alliance with the Liberals and he spent the next four years developing this relationship.

In December 1890, the *O'Shea divorce case proved disastrous for Parnell and the Home Rule party. Gladstone stated that "on moral grounds" he could no longer support Parnell. The party split into two opposing factions and was only reunited under John *Redmond in 1900.

In 1893, Gladstone introduced his second home rule bill, which allowed for a continued Irish presence at Westminster with its power limited to voting on Irish bills. The bill was passed in the Commons but was defeated in the House of Lords. The third home rule bill, introduced in 1912 by Prime Minister Herbert *Asquith, would give an Irish parliament power over all internal matters, except for taxation, and, for a time, the police, which the British government would continue to control for six years. Ireland would also continue to send forty-two MPs to Westminster under the bill. After the 1911 Parliament Act, the House of Lords no longer had veto power and could delay legislation for only two years. The home rule bill, therefore, was due to become law in 1914, but considerable opposition by *Ulster unionists placed Ireland on the brink of civil war. The onset of *World War I caused the suspension of the home rule bill until the end of the conflict. The 1916 *Easter Rising, however, completely changed the political landscape. The nationalist *Sinn Féin party increasingly gained widespread support at the expense of the Home Rule party, which was practically wiped out in the 1918 general election. During the *War of Independence, Prime Minister *Lloyd George attempted to bring peace to the country with the *Government of Ireland Act (1920), which established two home rule parliaments—one in *Belfast and one in *Dublin. The act was completely ignored in southern Ireland where it was later superseded by the *Anglo-Irish Treaty. P.E.

Hone, Evie (1894–1955). Cubist painter and stained glass designer. Born in *Dublin, Hone studied (with fellow student Mainie *Jellet) in London, and in Paris with André Lhote and Albert Gleizes. Much influenced by Irish medieval art, she worked for the stained glass workshop An Túr Gloine from 1933 to 1944 and on private commissions. Her stained glass windows can be seen in many churches in Ireland, in a few in England (including Eton College), and in Washington, DC. M.C.

Hone, Nathaniel (1718–84). Portrait painter and miniaturist. Born in *Dublin, Hone was a founding member of the Royal Academy in London in 1769. His opposition to classical Italianate painting in favor of Dutch naturalism is evident in his 1775 painting *The Pictorial Conjuror, Displaying the Whole Art of Pictorial Deception* (*National Gallery of Ireland), in which Hone satirized the British painter Joshua Reynolds. The work was rejected by the Royal Academy in 1775 and exhibited the same year by Hone in London in one of the earliest one-man exhibitions. M.C.

Hone, Nathaniel the Younger (1831–1917). Landscape painter. Born in *Dublin, Hone the Younger graduated in engineering and science from Trinity College, Dublin, in 1850. He studied painting with Thomas Couture in Paris in 1854. After seventeen years painting in Barbizon and Bourron-Marlotte, France, and eighteen months in Italy, he returned to Ireland to the family estate in Malahide. From 1876, he exhibited his paintings of the Malahide landscape regularly at the *Royal Hibernian Academy. M.C.

Hopkins, Gerard Manley (1844–89). English poet who spent the last years of his life in Ireland. Born in Stratford, Essex, Hopkins was educated at Balliol College, Oxford, where he was influenced by the Oxford movement and its leader, John Henry *Newman. Following Newman's example, he converted to Catholicism in 1866, and joined the Jesuit Order in 1868. Hopkins was ordained a priest in 1877 and ministered in parishes across England and Scotland. In 1884, he was appointed professor of Greek and Latin at University College, Dublin, where he taught until his death in 1889. On joining the Jesuit Order, Hopkins renounced poetry and burned most of his early poems. In 1875, however, the tragic death of a number of nuns on the ship the *Deutschland* inspired his first major poem, "The Wreck of the Deutschland." Hopkins continued to write poetry, mainly on religious themes but also dealing with his intense love of the beauties of nature, for the rest of his life ("The Windhover" and "Spring and Fall"). Hopkins was an intensely original poet, innovative in his use of language and metrical forms. His unhappiness in Ireland inspired the composition of his bleak late poems (mostly in 1885), known as the "Dark Sonnets," including "Carrion Comfort" and "No worst, there is none." A.S.

horse racing. One of Ireland's major sports. Records of horse racing in Ireland date from 751 when forty-six races were run with only ninety-three horses. In 2001, a total of 6,351 horses ran in 1,935 races for a total prize fund of almost $40 million. Currently over one million people attend race meetings every year. For a country of its size, Ireland's impact on international horse racing—from Australia to the United States and Hong Kong—has been remarkable.

The rules of racing are enforced by the Turf Club, a self-electing body, which was formed in the eighteenth century. The main organization of the sport, Horse Racing Ireland, formed in 2001, is made up of trainers, breeders, owners, and bookmakers. Racing in Ireland is financed by the government, which collects tax from the privately owned off-course betting shops. On-course betting includes both bookmakers and a state-run system called the Tote.

The two types of horse racing, steeplechasing (or jump racing) and flat racing, have become major attractions throughout Ireland. Steeplechasing originated in the south of Ireland, supposedly when two landowners raced their horses from one church steeple to another. Ever since, jump racing has been the more popular form, with major races such as the Irish Grand National at Fairyhouse, County *Kildare. Traditionally, Ireland has had a very strong presence and much success at the Cheltenham festival in Britain, commonly referred to as the "Olympics" of jump racing. The Irish horse Arkle, who ran in the 1960s, is reputed to be the greatest steeplechaser of all time. The legendary Irish trainer Vincent O'Brien dominated the Cheltenham races in the 1950s, winning both the Gold Cup and the Champion Hurdle three years in a row. He won England's Aintree Grand National, one of the most prestigious horse races in the world, with three different horses.

O'Brien also achieved unprecedented international success in flat racing—the more lucrative form of the sport—and helped to revolutionize the breeding industry in Ireland. In flat racing, he won the Epsom Derby six times, the Prix de l'Arc de Triomphe three times, and in 1968 the Washington International with the great Sir Ivor. Other great horses he trained include Nijinsky and Alleged. O'Brien's son-in-law, John Magnier, has built up the Coolmore Stud in County *Tipperary to be one of the most powerful breeding operations in the world and has employed Aidan O'Brien to train at Vincent O'Brien's old "Ballydoyle" stables. Magnier and Aidan O'Brien are one of the most powerful racing teams in Europe today.

Ireland's most successful trainer in terms of the number of winners is Dermot Weld, who broke the record in 2000 when saddling his 2,578th winner. Weld has also made a huge impact on international racing. He saddled Go And Go, the only European-trained winner of an American classic, at the 1990 Belmont Stakes. Three years later, Vintage Crop traveled to Australia to win the Melbourne Cup.

Irish jockeys—such as Pat Eddery and Kieren Fallon on the flat, and Tony McCoy over the jumps—dominate British racing. The best-known jockey based in Ireland is Michael Kinane, who has won ten home classics.

Some race meetings in Ireland have become legendary. The Galway Races in late July have been immortalized in songs and stories, and continue to be a huge international tourist attraction to this day. B.OC.

Horslips. The first "Celtic rock" band. Formed in 1970, Horslips capitalized on the traditional *music revival by fusing traditional melodies with rock and roll. One of its members was guitarist Declan Sinnott, who later became a noted rock musician. The band, which used mythic *Celtic heroes as motifs, heightened interest in the traditional until its demise in 1979. F.V.

Hugh Lane Municipal Gallery. Collection of almost two thousand modern and contemporary works built upon the original collection of Sir Hugh *Lane. Funded by Dublin Corporation, the Hugh Lane Gallery opened in 1933 as one of the foremost collections of modern art in Ireland. The collection is housed in Charlemont House, once the town house of James Caulfield, later First Earl of Charlemont (1728–99), and designed on classical lines by William Chambers (1723–96). The Hugh Lane Gallery offers a dynamic exhibition program that explores multimedia expression alongside historical and retrospective exhibitions of Irish work. The gallery contains the reconstructed studio of Francis *Bacon and has a lively education and outreach program. (Address: Parnell Square, Dublin 1. Web site: *www.hughlane.ie.*) M.C.

Huguenots. French *Protestants who settled in Ireland in the late seventeenth century. Huguenots had been subjected to increasing persecution in France in the seventeenth century, and when the Edict of Nantes—which had granted religious toleration—was revoked in 1685, they were expelled. By 1665, small Huguenot communities had already settled in *Dublin and *Cork. About ten thousand immigrated in the 1690s; many were veterans of the Williamite armies in the recent Irish war.

Twenty-one Huguenot communities were formed. The most notable settlement was at Portarlington, in Queen's County (now County *Laois). The Huguenots made a disproportionate contribution to Irish commercial and industrial life. Near Lisburn, County *Armagh, Huguenots, such as Samuel Crommelin (who published *Essay on Linen Manufacture in Ireland*, 1705) were part of the emerging linen trade. In Dublin, the La Touche family was prominent in banking and politics. The writer of supernatural stories, Sheridan *Le Fanu, was also of Huguenot descent. Some Huguenot congregations joined the *Church of Ireland, and the communities lost their distinct identity in the eighteenth and nineteenth centuries. Huguenot cemeteries can still be seen in Dublin and elsewhere. P.D.

Humbert, General (Jean Joseph Amable) (1767–1823). Leader of French military expedition to Ireland. On August 23, 1798, three frigates landed General Humbert and 1,070 French soldiers on the shore of Killala Bay, County *Mayo. About 1,500 Irish peasants joined him to liberate their country. Humbert's French professional and Irish ragtag army won victories before September 8 when it surrendered to superior forces at Ballinamuck, County *Longford. British victors treated the French captives with dignity and sent them home. They executed the Irish rebels. L.J.MC.

Hume, John (1937–). Politician. Born in Derry, Hume was a secondary school teacher and community activist. The outbreak of intercommunal violence in *Northern Ireland (the *Troubles) propelled him into the forefront of the *nationalist community leadership and, eventually, into a growing national and international role as one of the principal architects of the Northern Ireland *peace process. After the outbreak of violence in 1968, reacting against old-style politics, Hume became active in the Derry Citizens' Action Committee. In 1969, he became prominent in the *Northern Ireland Civil Rights Association (NICRA), founded specifically to advocate nonviolent change in Northern Ireland, without challenging its constitutional status as part of the United Kingdom. The following year, Hume became a founder of the *Social Democratic and Labour Party (SDLP), which was to take over from the old Nationalist Party as the vehicle for a more modern, articulate nationalism.

John Hume

Hume has never held executive power, with the exception of a brief period as minister for commerce in the ill-fated power-sharing Executive in Northern Ireland in 1974. However, since assuming the leadership of the SDLP in 1979 (he resigned in 2001), he has wielded immense influence in Irish politics. Hume used this influence in three key areas: to promote awareness among citizens of the *Republic of Ireland about the realities of life in Northern Ireland; to lessen the fears of Northern *unionists about their political prospects in a united Ireland; and to persuade *republican militants away from armed struggle and toward the normal democratic process. The creation by the Irish government in 1984 of the New Ireland Forum to fill the vacuum created in Northern Ireland politics by the suspension of the Northern Ireland Assembly was largely at his urging, and was at the core of his attempt to link North and South in a process aimed at removing violence from the political agenda.

In 1992, Hume took an even more dramatic initiative by engaging in secret discussions with Gerry *Adams, the *Sinn Féin leader, which eventually helped to bring about an IRA (*Irish Republican Army) cease-fire in 1997. Ironically, Hume was so successful in bringing Sinn Féin into constitutional politics, that it now rivals the SDLP as the electoral voice of Northern nationalists. Unionists have maintained a certain coolness toward Hume, even as he has tried to reassure them that the *partition of Ireland will be increasingly irrelevant in a *European Union where the emphasis is on European integration and not traditional boundaries. Under his leadership, the SDLP remained committed to a united Ireland, while at the same time accepting what is effectively a unionist veto (the "principle of consent").

Although he retired from membership of Northern Ireland's Legislative Assembly in 2001, he retained his membership both of the UK House of Commons (to which he was first elected in 1983) and of the European Parliament (to which he was first elected in 1979). Hume, who has maintained that jobs and economic growth are the best antidote to sectarianism, has played a significant role as a facilitator of substantial investment by US companies in the long-dormant but now reviving Northern Ireland economy. US President Bill Clinton—not least because of Hume's urging—played a highly significant role in the *peace process. Hume shared the Nobel Peace Prize with David *Trimble in 1998 for his essential work for peace in Northern Ireland. J.H.

hunger strikes. A form of extreme protest throughout Irish history. Hunger strikes go back to earliest times in Ireland when they were used as a means of shaming a powerful person by fasting. In the nineteenth century, *Fenian prisoners used it to protest against their conditions.

In the twentieth century, on November 25, 1917, Thomas *Ashe, who was a rebel in the *Easter Rising, 1916, died after being force-fed while on hunger strike in *Mountjoy Jail. In 1920, Terence *MacSwiney, Lord Mayor of *Cork, and ten other *republican prisoners went on hunger strike. MacSwiney, who was transferred to Brixton prison, London, died on October 25, along with two other hunger strikers. Their deaths, particularly MacSwiney's, gained massive international publicity and huge sympathy for the Irish cause. After the *Civil War in 1923, republican prisoners in Mountjoy and *Kilmainham jails went on hunger strike demanding their release. The strike ended following two deaths.

Hunger strikes continued to be used by republicans. Prisoners in the Maze (Long Kesh) began a campaign for the reinstatement of the special category or political prisoner status. Beginning in 1976, a refusal to wear prison clothes ("the blanket protest") escalated into the "dirty protest" and in 1980 into a hunger strike, which ended in confusion after the men thought mistakenly that their demands had been met. In March 1981, other republican prisoners, most notably Bobby Sands, began a hunger strike to restore special category status. At the time, the IRA (*Irish Republican Army) republican leadership did not approve of the strike, but later sanctioned it. In April, while still on hunger strike in prison, Sands was elected as MP (member of Parliament) for Fermanagh-South *Tyrone. He died May 5, 1981, the sixty-sixth day of his fast. The campaign to get the government to concede to the strikers' demands mobilized thousands. The death of a further nine hunger strikers alienated many in the nationalist community and catapulted *Sinn Féin into electoral politics. T.C.

Hunt Museum, Limerick. Museum of art and *Celtic artifacts. Art historian and connoisseur John Hunt advised many collectors, including William Randolph Hearst. Hunt and his wife, Gertrude, also assembled their own eclectic collection of objets d'art, which they left in trust to the Irish people. The collection found its permanent home in the Hunt Museum, the eighteenth-century Custom House in Limerick City, which was officially opened in 1997. The collection of two thousand items, ranging from the Stone Age to Picasso, includes a bronze horse by Leonardo da Vinci, Irish prehistoric and medieval antiquities, eighteenth-century Irish Delftware, and paintings by Renoir and Yeats. P.H.

hurling. One of the national *sports of Ireland. Less widely played than *Gaelic football (which is the other national game), hurling also attracts huge crowds, especially during the summer championship season. The game consists of two teams of fifteen players each, using a stick, which is called a hurley or *camán*, and a small leather ball, a *sliotar*. Hurling is one of the fastest field sports in the world and one of the most skillful. Codified and promoted by the *Gaelic Athletic Association (GAA), the game has existed in one form or another for over three millennia with the earliest literary reference dating the game back to 1272 B.C. The Book of *Leinster, compiled in the twelfth century, gives an account of how in 1272 B.C. the native Firbolg and the invading Tuatha De Danann, while preparing for battle, decided to stage a hurling match between the best

Hurling

players. Hurling features regularly in Irish *mythology, most famously associated with the legendary warrior *Cúchulainn, who was an acclaimed hurler.

Evolving through old Gaelic society (whose *brehon laws regulated the sport) and the *Anglo-Norman ascendancy, hurling was promoted and organized by *landlords in the seventeenth and eighteenth centuries. Contests between landowners' teams were commonplace until the agrarian agitation of the nineteenth century brought about the end of hurling in this form. Michael Cusack, one of the founders of the GAA, was a strong advocate of hurling's revival, and the game, together with Gaelic football, was at the forefront of the GAA's campaign to promote indigenous sport. Today, although hurling is played throughout Ireland, the most successful teams are in the south.

There is little top-class hurling played north of a line drawn from *Galway in the west to *Dublin in the east. As in Gaelic football, the elite competition in hurling has traditionally been organized on a provincial basis, with the climax of the season being the All-Ireland final, now played on the second Sunday in September. The history of the game has been dominated by three counties, *Cork, *Kilkenny, and *Tipperary, who between them account for two-thirds of All-Ireland title victories since the All-Ireland Championship system was established by the GAA in 1884.

In *Ulster, three counties, *Antrim, *Derry, and *Down, compete for the provincial championship, but none has won the All-Ireland. Antrim reached the final on two occasions, in 1943 and 1989. *Connacht, in the west, has only one county, Galway, which contests the hurling championship. Galway has won the All-Ireland four times. *Leinster in the east and *Munster in the south are the two leading provinces in hurling. In Dublin, the most populous county in Ireland, Gaelic football is much more popular than hurling.

Kilkenny is the second-most successful county in the history of the game—a remarkable achievement for a small county. *Wexford and *Offaly also have a tradition of hurling and both have won All-Ireland finals. Munster is regarded as the home of hurling with all six of its counties having won the All-Ireland. (*Kerry's victory was a surprise as the county concentrates on and excels in Gaelic football.) Cork and Tipperary are the leading counties in Munster hurling and their Munster finals in Thurles—regarded as the best hurling field in the country—are the stuff of legend. In 2004, Cork led with twenty-nine All-Ireland titles in hurling. Christy Ring, from Cork, is regarded by many as the greatest hurler of all time. He played on the only team to win four successive All-Ireland finals between 1941 and 1944. Other legendary players include Mick Mackey of Limerick, Eddie Keher of Kilkenny, John Doyle of Tipperary, Nicky Rackard of Wexford, and John Keane of *Waterford.

The All-Ireland final of 1931 is credited with turning hurling into a mass spectator sport. It went to two replays before Cork overcame Kilkenny, with nearly 100,000 attending the three matches. Eight years later, the same counties played in the final, with Kilkenny winning by one point in the dramatic final of 1939. It is remembered as "The Thunder and Lightning Final" because of the violent storm that broke ominously in the afternoon, the same day (September 3, 1939) that World War II began. Record crowds watched the resurgent Wexford team of the 1950s, who won All-Irelands in 1955, 1956, and 1960 and reached the finals of 1951 and 1954. The famous 1926 Cork-Tipperary Munster final in Thurles ended in turmoil due to overcrowding and encroachment on the playing field. For the rescheduled game, which drew a then-record crowd of twenty-seven thousand, and its replay, Tom Semple of the GAA—after whom the Thurles venue is now named—personally planned and oversaw the stewarding arrangements that made the occasion a great success. S.M.

Hutchinson, Billy (1959–). Politician and former *loyalist paramilitary. Born and raised in *Belfast's Shankill neighborhood, Hutchinson grew up in the middle of the *Troubles. In response to IRA (*Irish Republican Army) violence, particularly *Bloody Friday, he joined the *Ulster Volunteer Force (UVF) in 1972. In 1974, Hutchinson was sentenced to life imprisonment for the UVF-sponsored murder of two Belfast *Catholics, Michael Loughran and Edward Morgan. During his fifteen-year prison term, Hutchinson became an avid distance runner, received a social sciences degree, and developed an interest in politics. After leaving the Maze (Long Kesh) prison, Hutchinson joined the *Progressive Unionist Party (PUP) and became an active participant in the *Northern Ireland *peace process. In 1998, he earned one of the PUP's two seats in the Northern Ireland Assembly. Hutchinson is a committed *socialist and a staunch supporter of the *Good Friday Agreement. R.D.

Hyde, Douglas (1860–1949). Cultural nationalist, writer, first president of Ireland (1939–45). Born in *Sligo, son of a *Protestant minister, Hyde moved to *Roscommon and while still very young developed an interest in the *Irish language. Educated at home and then at Trinity College, Dublin, he studied arts, theology, and law. Hyde wrote numerous books on *folklore and *Irish literature, such as *Leabhar Sgéuluigheachta* (1889), *Love Songs of Connacht* (1893), *Beside the Fire* (1890), and *A Literary History of Ireland* (1899), and some poetry. His thought-provoking essay "The Necessity for De-Anglicising Ireland," which he delivered in 1890 to the National Literary Society, questioned the fashion of imitating all things English while at the same time hating the English.

A friend of W. B. *Yeats, George *Moore, Lady *Gregory, and other important writers of the *Irish Revival, Hyde wrote numerous plays, including *Casadh an t-Súgáin (The Twisting of the Rope)* (1901), a joint venture with Yeats and Lady Gregory, which was one of the first Irish-language plays to be acted in a theater.

In 1893, Hyde was elected the first president of the *Gaelic League, the major force in the revival of the Irish language. His insistence that the Gaelic League should stay out of politics led to his resignation as president in 1915. He continued with his work as professor of Irish in University College, Dublin, until 1932 and was unanimously appointed Ireland's first president in 1938. G.U.L.

Hynes, Garry (1953–). Theater director. Born in *Roscommon, Hynes founded the Druid Theatre Company in Galway in 1975 and was artistic director there until 1991. Her three-year tenure as artistic director of the *Abbey Theatre was marred by controversy and in 1995 she returned to her former position at the Druid. She directed the highly successful *Leenane Trilogy* by Martin *McDonagh, which won four Tony Awards in 1998, including one for best director. B.D.

I

Immigration. See **Emigration and Immigration.**

internment. Incarceration without trial or legal process. Internment has been used in Ireland, North and South, in every decade since *partition in 1920. The most notorious instance is part of the *Northern Ireland conflict. On August 9, 1971, to contain rising IRA (*Irish Republican Army) violence and specifically to foil a concerted bombing offensive, internment, or detention without trial, was introduced across Northern Ireland. In a series of dawn raids, 342 people, almost all *Catholics, were arrested and taken to makeshift camps. There was an immediate upsurge of violence and seventeen people were killed during the next forty-eight hours. Of these, ten were Catholic civilians who were shot dead by the British army. Internment continued until December 5, 1975. During that time, 1,981 people were detained: 1,874 were Catholic/*republican, while 107 were *Protestant/*loyalist. Seán MacStiofáin, IRA leader at the time, recalled that "the result of the internment roundup and the interrogation excesses was that the British succeeded in bringing into combat not a diminished, but a vastly reinforced republican guerrilla army."

Internment added to the sense of the IRA as an army. In Long Kesh (Maze) prison, in County *Antrim (an American air force base during World War II), all prisoners lived in "cages," compounds of four Nissen huts surrounded by barbed wire. Each of three huts (120 feet by 24 feet) would house forty men. The fourth was reserved for use as a canteen. Guards recognized IRA "officers" and all communication went through the prisoners' "Officer Commanding." Under what became known as "Special Category Status," prisoners were allowed to wear their own clothes and could freely associate at all times. The men imprisoned here organized themselves militarily. Lectures on tactics and arms were given, and there was even drilling with dummy wooden guns. In 1973, William Whitelaw, the secretary of state for Northern Ireland, also conceded this status to convicted paramilitary prisoners. Internment and Special Category Status were phased out in 1975 as part of Britain's attempt to deal with the Northern Ireland crisis as a law and order problem. M.M.

Invincibles, the. A *nationalist secret society committed to violence. Established in *Dublin in 1881, the society grew out of the revolutionary *Fenian movement. The Invincibles sought to make Ireland ungovernable by assassinating British officials. Their most notorious act was the *Phoenix Park Murders (1882), which resulted in twenty-six arrests and five executions. The society ceased to function shortly after the murders. T.C.

Iona. Scottish island in the Inner Hebrides and center of learning and piety. St. *Colm Cille, or Columba, founded a monastery here in 563. He died on the island in 597. The saint's biography was written here around 700 by his successor, Abbot Adamnan. With a strong poetic tradition, Iona kept Irish Annals up to 740, and many believe that the Book of *Kells was written there. Eighth/ninth-century high *crosses survive from the early monastery, and the restored cathedral dates from the thirteenth century. P.H.

Ireland Act, the (1949). British legislative response to the *Republic of Ireland Act (1948). In the Ireland Act enacted on June 2, 1949, Westminster recognized the secession of the *Republic of Ireland from dominion status and confirmed that *Northern Ireland was part of the United Kingdom until its own Parliament chose otherwise. It also allowed unrestricted travel between Ireland and Britain and granted British citizens' rights to Irish citizens living in the UK. P.E.

Ireton, Henry (1611–51). English politician and general. A commander of parliamentary forces during the English Civil War, Ireton married Oliver *Cromwell's daughter in 1646. In 1649, he went with Cromwell to Ireland and remained as lord deputy, capturing *Carlow, *Waterford, Duncannon (1650), and *Limerick (1651) where he died of fever. S.A.B.

Irish Academy of Letters. Modeled on the Swedish Academy that awards the Nobel Prize, the academy was founded by W. B. *Yeats in 1932 to reward achievement in letters and to organize writers to oppose literary censorship. George Bernard *Shaw was nominated its first president, Yeats its vice president. Twenty-five of Ireland's best-known writers were invited to become full founding members and a further ten associate members. All but seven (one of whom was James *Joyce) accepted. In 1933, the academy opposed the banning of Shaw's *The Black Girl in Search of God* without success. Among its awards were the Harmsworth Award for fiction, the Casement Prize for drama and verse, the O'Growney Prize for *Irish language publications, and its highest award, the Gregory Medal. Prizes were awarded irregularly and rarely between 1940 and 1969 when commercial sponsorship led to a brief revival. The academy is currently inactive but has not been dissolved. M.S.T.

Irish America. Irish Americans represent the largest portion of the Irish Diaspora. In the 1990 US census, forty-four million Americans claimed some Irish heritage. From the late seventeenth into the early nineteenth century, between a quarter- and a half-million Irish, mostly *Protestants, usually *Presbyterians, entered North America. Some *Ulster Presbyterians settled in New England and the Mid-Atlantic regions, but most chose the farmlands on the southern and northern frontiers, between Native Americans and tidewater whites. They fought on both sides in the *American Revolution. The Carnegies and Mellons date from this time. Beginning with Andrew Jackson, a number of American presidents have claimed Irish Protestant heritage, including Grover Cleveland, William McKinley, Woodrow Wilson, and, more lately, Richard Nixon, Jimmy Carter, Ronald Reagan, and Bill Clinton.

Since 1820, the vast majority of around six million Irish entering the United States have been *Catholic. Because of the Great *Famine, over a million left Ireland between 1845 and 1851, some on so-called "coffin ships." The largest portion went to the United States. Since many Americans of Ulster Presbyterian stock joined, and sometimes led, such anti-Catholic agitations as the Know-Nothing movement, claimed a British more than an Irish lineage, and defined themselves as *Scots Irish, Irish America has had a mainly Catholic image and flavor. Not until relatively recently did many American Protestants acknowledge Hibernian backgrounds.

Transitions from economically and socially limited rural Ireland, where often Irish was the vernacular, to urban America bred poverty, alienation, neuroses, crime, and broken families, exacerbating American anti-Catholic nativism.

Early Irish immigrants, mostly tenant farmers or agricultural laborers, lacked expertise to farm vast acres of rural America. Settling in cities, initially in the Northeast, they labored on docks, in mines, on riverboats, in horse barns; dug canals; and laid railroad tracks. Dangerous occupations limited male life spans. Irish Catholics tended to emigrate as singles, and, by the close of the nineteenth century, more women than men left home, taking jobs in American mills, factories or, more likely, in domestic service.

Victims of nativist bigotry themselves, many Irish Catholics, unfortunately, had little sympathy for other victims of discrimination. During the *American Civil War, Irish soldiers fought bravely on both sides. Most of those in blue did so to save the Union, not to emancipate slaves. An 1863 Draft Act provoked Irish urban riots. *New York's rampage cost over two million dollars in property damage and, more importantly, the deaths of eleven lynched African Americans, a Native American mistaken for a black, three policemen, and fifteen rioters. (Many of the police and soldiers who restored order also were Irish.) Much Irish racism stemmed from fears of losing jobs, ignorance, and an inferiority complex. Later in the century, San Francisco's Denis Kearney campaigned to keep Chinese out of the United States. In the 1960s, many Irish Americans opposed integrated housing and schooling out of the same fears. Anti-Semitism also has tarnished the Irish image, especially in the 1930s and 1940s, when a considerable number, especially in the East, became disciples of the infamous Father Charles Coughlin.

Following the Civil War, Irish America progressed economically and socially. In post-Famine Ireland, rising standards of living and an improved national school system meant that Irish immigrants now had more skills and education. New immigrants from southern and eastern Europe replaced the Irish on the lowest levels of the labor market. By the 1900s, many Irish Americans were skilled laborers, and some middle-class professionals and businessmen. A number of women became teachers and nurses.

Many Irish Americans emotionally and financially fueled militant* nationalist movements—the *Fenian movement and its counterpart in Ireland, the *Irish Republican Brotherhood (IRB), *Clan na Gael, and the *Irish Republican Army (IRA)—as well as constitutional nationalism—*home rule and the *Irish Parliamentary Party.

In the twentieth century, Irish Americans politically controlled most cities north of the Mason-Dixon line, and had significant influence in New Orleans. Tammany Hall, the headquarters of New York City's Democratic Party, was the early model of the Irish urban political machine, one that *Chicago's Richard J. Daley perfected in the 1950s, '60s, and '70s.

Often, Irish politicians were guilty of corruption, benefiting from graft and kickbacks. But on balance, Irish politics was more positive than negative. While urban reformers were more interested in morality than poverty, Irish politicians distributed food, coal, and clothing, and found jobs and paid medical and funeral expenses for impoverished constituents. Influenced by Catholic values rather than secular ideologies, Irish political machines steered the Democratic Party away from individualistic toward communal liberalism. During the 1920s, New York's multiterm governor, Al Smith, a Tammany Hall graduate, previewed much of Franklin Delano Roosevelt's New Deal agenda.

The Irish were hugely influential in the American Catholic Church, operating a vast institutional structure of primary and secondary schools, colleges, hospitals, and orphanages. Many of America's labor leaders have been Irish American: from Terence V. Powderly, the first grand master of the Knights of Labor in 1879, to Philip Murray and George Meany in the twentieth century.

After World War II, Irish America completed its difficult passage from urban ghettos to middle-class suburban neighborhoods, from insecurity to self-confidence. Because so many women were nurses and teachers and men worked for railroads, urban transport systems, local, state, and federal governments, and on police and fire departments, the Irish weathered the Depression better than most other groups. Educational benefits from the 1944 GI Bill of Rights rapidly increased Irish American economic, social, and residential mobility.

Hollywood movies in the 1930s and 1940s, with stars such as Spencer Tracy, Pat O'Brien, and Bing Crosby playing benevolent, charming Irish American priests, did much to diminish anti-Catholicism so evident after Al Smith's loss to Herbert Hoover in the 1928 presidential election.

By the 1930s, Irish politicians had gained prominence on the national stage. James J. Farley was chairman of the Democratic Party. Frank Murphy was attorney general under FDR and later served on the Supreme Court. In 1960, John F. *Kennedy's election as the first and only Catholic president of the United States symbolized the Irish Catholic success story. Other Irish American politicians have been influential and have lobbied for direct American involvement in Northern Ireland. These include Speaker of the House Thomas P. "Tip" O'Neill, Senate Majority Leader George Mitchell, and Congressman Peter King. President Bill Clinton and Senator Mitchell were instrumental in bringing about the *peace process and the 1998 *Good Friday Agreement.

Irish Americans have also been prominent in athletics, particularly in baseball, which they once dominated (Mike "King" Kelly, Ed Delahanty, Charles Comiskey, John McGraw, Connie Mack), and boxing (John L. Sullivan, "Gentleman" Jim Corbett, Jack Dempsey, Gene Tunney, Billy Conn). They have been on the forefront of American entertainment with singers (Bing Crosby, Rosemary Clooney), dancers (Gene Kelly, Ray Bolger, Donald O'Connor), comedians (Jackie Gleason, Art Carney, Fred Allen), and actors (James Cagney, Spencer Tracy, Brian Dennehy, Barbara Stanwyck, Grace Kelly, Irene Dunne). John Ford may have been America's greatest film director and Eugene O'Neill its best playwright. Along with O'Neill, F. Scott Fitzgerald, Flannery O'Connor, William Kennedy, Alice McDermott, Pete Hamill, and Tom Flanagan are among a long list of writers that indicate that there is an Irish dimension to the American literary tradition. (Flanagan's novels represent the very best in Irish historical fiction.)

With increasing assimilation throughout the twentieth century, many Irish Americans, middle class and suburban, have abandoned Democratic communalism for Republican individualism. Today, for a large number of Irish Americans, ethnicity is defined in cultural rather than religious terms. It remains to be seen whether Irish identity will survive in a pluralistic American society. L.J.MC.

Irish Architectural Archive. A collection that preserves the records of Ireland's *architectural heritage. A nonprofit organization established in 1976, the archive includes over eighty thousand Irish architectural drawings from the late seventeenth to late twentieth century and over 300,000 photographs. It also holds an extensive reference library with material on Irish architects, buildings, and styles. The archive has an active publications and outreach program. (Address: 45 Merrion Square, Dublin 2. Web site: *www.iarc.ie*.) M.C.

Irish Brigades. See **Wild Geese.**

Irish Citizen Army (ICA). A workers' militia of about 350 members. The ICA was established after excessive violence was used against workers and protesters by the Dublin Metropolitan Police during the long-running industrial dispute known as the 1913 Lockout. The Irish Citizen Army was under the auspices of the Irish Transport and General Workers Union. James *Connolly, the union's acting general secretary, became its commandant. Training was provided by former British army officer, Captain Jack Whyte. Dedicated to *socialism and Irish independence, the Citizen Army was involved in the *Easter Rising of 1916. Connolly was one of the leaders executed after the rising's defeat. T.C.

Irish Civil War (1922–23). Bloody and bitter conflict, lasting from the summer of 1922 until the spring of 1923, between factions within Irish *republicanism over the terms of the *Anglo-Irish Treaty. The treaty, which ended the *Anglo-Irish War (1919–21), established an *Irish Free State with virtual independence for twenty-six (out of thirty-two) counties of Ireland, but with dominion status within the British *Commonwealth. Many republicans especially objected to the *oath of allegiance to the crown required by the treaty of all government officials. Only a few in the *Dáil (Parliament) objected to the *partition of Ireland and the failure of the treaty to provide for a united sovereign Ireland, because most believed that the *Boundary Commission would make territorial adjustments favorable to *nationalists and that eventually the Free State would take over (in some fashion) the six northern counties. They were much more concerned with the dominion status of the Free State, which was not the full-fledged *republic for which they had fought.

Treaty proponents, including Michael *Collins, one of the negotiators, argued that the Free State was a stepping-stone on the path to a full republic. On January 7, 1922, the second Dáil approved the treaty by a narrow sixty-four to fifty-seven vote, with opponents beginning an immediate boycott of the new government. Pending the establishment of permanent institutions, sovereignty over the new Free State was shared temporarily by the Provisional Government, headed by Collins, and Arthur *Griffith, who presided over the Dáil.

The political divisions over the treaty were echoed within the *Irish Republican Army (IRA), with a majority opposed to any settlement that failed to achieve the republic for which they had fought. A final break between the Provisional Government and the strong anti-treaty faction within the IRA occurred in late March 1922. Defying a government ban, the IRA organized an army convention and established a new army executive to continue the struggle for a republic. On April 14, 1922, a group of anti-treaty forces led by Rory *O'Connor seized the *Four Courts and other buildings in *Dublin. They repudiated the civilian Provisional Government and formed a rival center of authority. Meanwhile, during the protracted efforts to overcome differences over the treaty, Collins had gained valuable time to build, with British assistance, a new Free State army.

In May 1922, Collins and Éamon *de Valera made a final effort to hold the republican movement together with an electoral pact that would create a unity government in the new Parliament to be elected in June. Arthur Griffith and other treaty supporters vigorously protested against this electoral alliance. The June elections demonstrated overwhelming backing for pro-treaty candidates, with only 36 anti-treaty representatives chosen out of a total of 128 seats. The anti-treaty group in the IRA then split into two further factions, with those in the Four Courts commanded by O'Connor advocating a resumption of the military campaign against Britain. Alarmed by the continued occupation of the Four Courts and the increasingly questionable ability of the Free State government to maintain order, the British government demanded action against the rebels and even threatened military intervention. When assassins killed the Northern Ireland *Unionist MP Sir Henry Wilson in London on June 22, the British escalated their pressure, holding the IRA faction in the Four Courts responsible. (Some historians have suggested that Collins himself probably ordered the assassination in retaliation for attacks on *Catholics in *Northern Ireland.)

On June 28, the Free State army attacked the Four Courts and, in little more than a week, the anti-treaty forces throughout Dublin had been routed. The attack on the Four Courts, however, reunified treaty opponents, including both the military forces (now referred to as "Irregulars" by the Provisional government) and politicians such as de Valera. Liam Lynch emerged as the commander of the anti-treaty militants who were strongest in the south and west of Ireland. Initially, they held *Cork and *Limerick, but the Free State army captured these strategically important cities by August. In the same month, the Free State lost two of its most important leaders. On August 10, Arthur Griffith died from a cerebral hemorrhage and, on August 22, Michael Collins was killed by an assassin's bullet in his native west Cork.

The military campaign of the anti-treaty forces suffered greatly from a lack of coordination. Guerrilla warfare fought by "flying columns" became their predominant tactic. They resorted to theft to gain supplies, alienating many from their cause. During the Civil War, the anti-treaty forces burned many of the country houses of the landed *Anglo-Irish gentry. In October 1922, the Roman Catholic bishops issued a joint pastoral, which condemned the insurgents. Under the impetus of Richard *Mulcahy, who had succeeded Collins as commander of the Free State forces, the Dáil approved a Public Safety Bill, which took effect in October 1922 and set up military courts with draconian powers. Under this emergency legislation, which included the death penalty for illegal possession of weapons, the Free State government executed seventy-seven political insurgents between November 1922 and March 1923. One of those executed was Erskine *Childers, a leading republican. In retaliation for the harsh new measures, Lynch ordered the targeting of pro-treaty members of the Dáil. After Deputy Sean Hales was assassinated on December 7, 1922, the Free State government ordered the immediate execution of Rory O'Connor, Liam Mellowes, and two other prominent leaders of the "Irregulars." During the course of the conflict, the government also interned over ten thousand rebels without trial. The uncompromising Lynch continued to overrule peace efforts as a new year of fighting began, but, in March 1923, he died in action. His successor, Frank *Aiken, suspended military operations on April 30, 1923, and de Valera began negotiations with the Free State government. Although no agreement could be reached on specific terms to end the conflict, on May 24, Aiken ordered his forces to disarm and de Valera declared that, though the legitimacy of the Free State could not be recognized by true republicans, any continuation of the military struggle would for the moment be "vain" and "unwise." The Free State government accepted this cessation of hostilities without either a negotiated peace or the complete disarmament of the rebels.

Civil War casualties, once thought to range as high as four thousand, are now estimated to be closer to one thousand. The war left the new state with significant economic burdens and caused deep psychological scars, which would cast a long shadow over Irish politics for decades to come. Beyond the disagreement about specific provisions of the treaty, the underlying issue in the Civil War involved whether the new state would have a democratic foundation. In the end, the will of the majority of the Irish people as expressed in open elections, which favored acceptance of the treaty, prevailed.

Militant republicans, who regarded any settlement short of a full republic as a betrayal of the republican ideal, would continue their struggle beyond the Civil War through the following decades into the era of the *Northern Ireland Conflict. F.B.

Irish Exhibition of Living Art (IELA). An open exhibition of modernist work. Founded in 1943 by Louis *Le Brocquy in reaction to *Royal Hibernian Academy restrictions, the exhibition was supported by Mainie *Jellett and others as a democratic alternative that presented mostly abstract work. The organizing committee was reconfigured in 1972 and a year later IELA ended. M.C.

Irish Free State (Saorstát Éireann). Official name of the twenty-six-county state that came into existence on December 6, 1922, one year after the signing of the *Anglo-Irish Treaty. Under the treaty, the state was to be a member of the *Commonwealth, with dominion status equal to that of Canada. The British monarch was to be represented by a governor-general and all members of the Irish legislature were required to take an *oath of allegiance to the British crown. The Free State legislature, or *Oireachtas, consisted of two houses, the *Dáil (Parliament) and *Seanad Éireann (Irish Senate).

A substantial anti-treaty faction led by Éamon *de Valera had bitterly opposed the Free State and its oath of allegiance to Britain, arguing for a free and independent *republic. After the treaty was ratified by a narrow margin, the dispute escalated into a bitter *Civil War in June 1922.

W. T. *Cosgrave was elected first president of the Executive Council in December 1922 at the height of the Civil War. It would be his task to establish a stable parliamentary democracy within the new state. Throughout the Civil War, the Free State government took strong measures to end the conflict, including the use of *internment without trial and execution (seventy-seven in all). Ultimately, these coercive measures and the government's superior resources helped the fledgling state to survive and in May 1923 the Civil War ended.

In August 1923, the fourth Dáil was elected with *Cumann na nGaedheal, the party founded by Cosgrave in April 1923, retaining power. De Valera's party, *Sinn Féin, refused to take the oath and participate in the new Parliament. The absence of any effective opposition greatly strengthened the power of the new government as it attempted to reestablish law and order, rebuild the Irish *economy, and assert Irish independence in foreign affairs.

In 1922, the *Gárda Síochána, an unarmed civil police force, was established. The legal system was reformed under the Courts of Justice Act (1924), which abolished both the British and Sinn Féin courts, and established District and Circuit Courts to deal with most criminal cases, and the High and Supreme Courts to adjudicate appeals and constitutional matters.

The Army Mutiny Crisis of 1924 represented a serious threat to the stability of the state. As the Free State government began to demobilize and restructure the army for a peacetime role, on March 6, 1924, officers issued a list of demands, which included an end to demobilization and a guarantee that the government intended to establish a republic. Eoin *O'Duffy, appointed supreme commander of the army to deal with the mutiny, reached a compromise agreement. By successfully quelling the mutiny, the Free State established that the army was the nonpolitical servant of the state.

In the area of economic development, the Free State government adopted a conservative policy, which was supported by banks, large farmers, and the wealthy *Anglo-Irish landlord community. *Agriculture was the most important sector of the economy, involving more than half the population, but farms remained small and inefficient. The Ardnacrusha Hydro Electric Power plant and a number of semi-state companies, including the Electricity Supply Board (ESB) and the Irish Sugar Company, were established at this time. Britain was developed as Ireland's main market, and to encourage free trade, tariffs were not widely imposed. Approximately thirteen thousand new jobs were created in industry during this period, 1922–32.

To assert its international identity, the Free State joined the *League of Nations on September 10, 1923, and created an extensive foreign diplomatic service. In 1925, a major controversy was averted when the Free State government convinced the British to suppress the *Boundary Commission's recommendations that a part of County *Donegal be ceded to *Northern Ireland (in return for parts of County *Fermanagh and County *Armagh). The Ultimate Financial Agreement between Britain and Ireland, signed on March 19, 1926, waived certain financial claims against the Free State in return for continued payments of land annuities and pensions. The agreement was never passed by the Dáil and was later repudiated by de Valera after *Fianna Fáil came to power in 1932.

The Statute of Westminster, passed in 1931 by leaders of Commonwealth countries (with the Irish representatives particularly involved), gave dominions the right to accept, annul, or amend British legislation. The statute essentially ended British involvement in the Free State's affairs.

Cosgrave's party narrowly survived a strong challenge from de Valera's new party Fianna Fáil in the general election of 1927. Kevin *O'Higgins's assassination on July 10 renewed fears of a return to violence and the government passed a Public Safety Act, banning all revolutionary societies.

The economic depression of the early 1930s and rising unemployment led to the government's defeat in the general election of 1932. Fianna Fáil with *Labour Party support formed a government. In 1937, the *Constitution of 1922 was replaced with Bunreacht na hÉireann, in which Ireland was declared a sovereign, independent, democratic state, and its name was changed to Éire (or in the English language, Ireland). P.E.

Irish Georgian Society. Ireland's *architectural heritage society. Founded in 1958 by the Honorable Desmond Guinness, the society promotes the conservation of distinguished buildings and allied arts of all periods in Ireland through education and grants, planning participation, membership, and fund-raising. The society's main achievements include the saving of such buildings as Castletown, County *Kildare; Damer House, County *Tipperary; Doneraile Court, County *Cork; Roundwood, County *Laois; Tailors Hall, *Dublin, and 13 Henrietta Street, Dublin. (Address: 74 Merrion Square, Dublin 2. Web site: *www.irish-architecture.com.*) M.C.

Irish language. *Celtic language. Irish, Welsh, Breton, Scottish Gaelic, and the extinct languages of Manx (from the Isle of Man), and Cornish (from Cornwall) form the group of Celtic languages, which share similar grammatical, phonological, syntactical, and lexicographical features. The language is historically and generally known as Irish, although some people prefer to call it "Gaelic," which is the Anglicized word for *Gaeilge*, or the Irish word for the Irish language. The most common theory put forward by linguists is that a primitive form of the Irish language arrived from the continent with Celtic invaders, colonists, or travelers some centuries before the Christian era.

Recent archaeological theory argues that the Irish language developed in Ireland over thousands of years before *Christianity, and if there was a Celtic invasion it goes much further back in time than heretofore supposed. Regardless, Irish was the only language of the country when literacy started in Ireland in the fifth and sixth centuries with the arrival of Christianity. Monks wrote it down using Latin as a model, and they transcribed Irish *mythology and sagas, often of a pagan or mythological provenance. As a result, Irish *literature is the oldest continuing vernacular literature in Western Europe. The same people who wrote the Book of *Kells (illuminated *manuscript of the Gospels) in Latin, probably also recast or composed Irish stories in the Irish language. There is a vast corpus of early Irish literature, particularly relating to religious and legal matters. These are written in Old Irish, which gave way to Middle Irish in about the ninth century.

Although the *Viking invaders disrupted commercial and religious life, they had little impact on the language itself, lending a few paltry words of commerce and of seafaring. Irish learning became more secularized from the twelfth century onward, with the responsibility for training of scholars and poets passing to families of powerful patronage. The *Anglo-Norman invasion of 1169 did little to change this pattern, except for the introduction of the English language. Although the new language had little immediate effect, it slowly took over the entire Gaelic world from the early seventeenth century onward. The Anglo-Norman aristocracy, although always described by the native Irish as *Sasanaigh*, or English, became, in the celebrated phrase, "more Irish than the Irish themselves." They wrote stories and poetry in the Irish language, became patrons of art and literature, and eventually opposed English rule.

The Statute of *Kilkenny (1366) outlawed the use of the Irish language, habits, and customs by the English who lived inside and outside the *Pale. *Henry VIII's "Act for the English order, habite, and language" of 1537 was a serious attempt to begin the Anglicization of the native Irish, but was still largely directed to those who considered themselves "the king's true subjects." The Irish language began to come under pressure only when the Irish political system was destroyed in the seventeenth century. The defeat of the Irish by the English in the *Nine Years War, in the *Cromwellian conquest and in the ultimate war of the English succession (1689–91) reduced the Irish language to one of common speech, banished from the higher domains of government, law, commerce, education, and discursive prose.

Many Irish began to turn to the English language during the eighteenth century in order to gain some power under the English system, and in the nineteenth century in order to survive. Despite this, there were probably more speakers of Irish in 1845, just before the *Famine, than ever before. But they were all poor, and the vast majority of them lived in the west and in the south of the country. Most of those who died in the Famine were Irish speakers, as were most of those who emigrated in the following decade. From the middle of the nineteenth century, Irish, by now associated with poverty, defeat, and hunger, became a minority language in its own country. At the turn of the twentieth century, the national *Irish Language Revival heralded a new life for the language, and for the first time in hundreds of years Irish speakers were given a dignity which they had been denied.

The *Gaelic League was the most important of the language organizations that spread enthusiasm for all things Irish. The *Irish Free State came into being on the basis of a cultural as well as a political revival, and, thus, it was not surprising that the new state gave proper emphasis to the language. Irish returned into domains of government, education, and thought from which it had been banished since the seventeenth century. Irish was designated an official language in the first Consititution of 1922. However, the Irish-speaking areas (the *Gaeltacht) continued to shrink, albeit at a slower pace. Irish is now one of the two official languages of Ireland and has recognition for the first time in the six counties of *Northern Ireland. It has developed a strong and vibrant literature, which is a continuation of the past. There are Irish-language newspapers, radio stations, and a television channel. Irish is taught to every schoolchild and plays a central role in much cultural activity. Although under constant and unremitting pressure from English, the day-to-day language in most of Ireland, Irish continues to flourish as the first language or the language of choice of many Irish people. A.T.

Irish Language Revival. Ongoing movement, beginning in the nineteenth century, to revive interest in, and use of, the *Irish language. The Irish Language Revival, also known as the Gaelic Revival, has its genesis in several learned societies that were founded to study antiquities in the nineteenth century. The most prominent of these were the Gaelic Society of Dublin (1807), the Archaeological Society (1840), the Celtic Society (1845), and the Ossianic Society (1853). Phillip Barron founded an Irish school in 1835 in *Waterford, and in 1862, Risteard Daltún from *Tipperary published *An Fíor-Éireannach* (Real Ireland), one of the earliest attempts at an Irish-language newspaper. Micheál Ó Lócháin from *Galway published the bilingual paper *An Gaodhal* (the *Irishman*) in *New York in 1881. New works in Irish were published by Archbishop of Tuam, John McHale, who also translated works by authors as diverse as Thomas *Moore and Homer. There was not a united movement, however, until the Society for the Preservation of the Irish Language (SPIL) was established in 1876. SPIL succeeded in having Irish included as a voluntary subject in national schools in 1878. The Gaelic Union, an offshoot of SPIL, was founded in 1879 and published the *Gaelic Journal* from 1882 onward. Dubhghlas de hÍde's (Douglas *Hyde) essay "The Necessity for De-Anglicising Ireland" decried the abandonment of the national tongue in favor of English. Essays by scholars such as Eoghan Ó Gramhnaigh and Eoin *MacNeill called on the nation to halt the decline of the language.

The founding of the *Gaelic League in 1893 was the most important single event in the revival of the language. By 1907, there were six hundred Gaelic League branches throughout Ireland. Traveling teachers were a common sight as they moved, mainly on bicycle, from one part of a county to the next, teaching both Irish and Irish history to their classes. The cultural festival the Oireachtas was founded in 1897 for native speakers and learners alike. A sense of pride was instilled in the language after years of disrespect and neglect. The Gaelic League, with its *Feiseanna* (concerts), the Oireachtas, and new periodicals such as *Fáinne an Lae* ("The Dawn of Day," 1898–1900) and **An Claidheamh Soluis* ("The Sword of Light," 1899), gave a platform to writers such as An tAthair Peadar Ó Laoghaire, Pádraig MacPiarais (Patrick *Pearse), and Pádraic *Ó Conaire, who created a new literature in Irish. Initially, many of these writers dismissed the *Irish Literary Revival of W. B. *Yeats and J. M. *Synge (which strived to create a national Irish literature in English) as a heresy and a form of British imperialism. This hard line had softened by 1905, when Pearse came to regard the Irish National Theatre as an ally rather than an enemy of the language movement.

In 1922, when part of Ireland gained independence from Britain, the Irish language was made an official language of the state. G.U.L.

Irish Literary Revival. See **Irish Revival.**

Irish Museum of Modern Art (IMMA). The main museum of modern art in Ireland. Opened in 1991 in the Royal Hospital Kilmainham under the directorship of Declan MacGonigal, the museum is directly funded by the government. The Royal Hospital was originally founded by James Butler of Kilkenny Castle (Duke of Ormonde) in 1680 as a home and hospital for aging soldiers and designed by William Robinson in 1684. Today, fully refurbished with climate-controlled galleries, the museum displays the best of Irish and international postwar art in rotating temporary exhibitions and curated shows. IMMA runs educational and community programs and helps local art organizations throughout Ireland to set up and present exhibitions and projects. The museum hosts the annual Glen Dimplex Artists Award. (Address: Kilmainham, Dublin 8. Web site: *www.modernart.ie.*) M.C.

Irish Parliament, the. See **Parliament, Irish.**

Irish Parliamentary Party. Irish *nationalist MPs (members of Parliament) in the late nineteenth and early twentieth century dedicated to *home rule. Following the general election of 1874, the Irish Parliamentary Party, a coalition of former *Repealers, Liberals, and a few former *Fenians and Conservatives, with Isaac *Butt as first chair, began its existence. Butt's hesitant leadership, inattention to duties, and pro-British imperialism antagonized Charles Stewart *Parnell and others demanding a more vigorous campaign for home rule. In 1879, William Shaw succeeded the deceased Butt. Following the 1880 general election, Parnell became chair and created a tightly disciplined party, unified in purpose and opinion, energized by the *Land War, and heavily financed by *Irish America. Playing balance of power politics in the British House of Commons, the Irish Parliamentary Party forged an alliance with *Gladstone's Liberals, resulting in significant benefits to Ireland and two home rule bills (the first lost in the House of Commons, the second in the House of Lords).

Parnell's involvement in the *O'Shea divorce scandal in 1890 split the party and Irish nationalism. In 1900, the two branches reunited under the leadership of John *Redmond, leader of the Parnellite minority. By 1914, the Irish Parliamentary Party had won the struggle for home rule but *Ulster *Unionist intransigence frustrated the victory. This disappointment, Irish casualties in *World War I, resistance to a military draft, and the popularity of the 1916 *Easter Rising martyrs led to the triumph of *Sinn Féin in the 1918 general election and, for all practical purposes, the demise of the Irish Parliamentary Party. In the Northern Ireland Parliament, the remnants of the party became the *Nationalist Party. L.J.MC.

Irish Republican Army (IRA). Paramilitary organization representing militant separatist *republicanism. Since its emergence during the *Anglo-Irish War (1919–21), the Irish Republican Army has sought to end British government in Ireland and establish an independent and unified Irish *republic by means of armed struggle. The IRA has upheld the tradition of militant republicanism that originated with the *United Irishmen in the 1790s and continued through the *Irish Republican Brotherhood (IRB) of the late nineteenth and early twentieth centuries. More specifically, the organization developed from the small faction of Irish *Volunteers that launched the *Easter Rising in 1916. Despite government suppression following the rising, the Volunteers reestablished themselves in 1917.

When *Sinn Féin became the dominant political party in the 1918 elections and established the first *Dáil Éireann (Irish Parliament) in January 1919, the Irish Volunteers, increasingly known as the Irish Republican Army, became the official military force of the emergent state. The Dáil, however, exercised limited control over the IRA and tactical decisions were largely made by local commanders.

During the *Anglo-Irish War, Michael *Collins came to the fore as the IRA's director of organization and intelligence. Despite few weapons, the organization's guerrilla strategy forced the British government to negotiate a settlement. The *Anglo-Irish Treaty (December 6, 1921) provided only dominion status for a *partitioned country (twenty-six out of thirty-two counties), rather than a full and unified republic, and also required an *oath of allegiance to the crown. These terms split the IRA into pro-treaty supporters of the new *Free State and an anti-treaty republican faction. The ensuing bitter *Civil War (1922–23) was fought between the Free State army and the IRA, referred to as the Irregulars by the new government.

In 1926, Éamon *de Valera led many of the defeated republicans into constitutional politics by forming the *Fianna Fáil party; those who did not follow de Valera and were committed to a united Ireland by armed force, remained known as the IRA. In 1932, Fianna Fáil became the governing party, and, in 1936, de Valera's government proscribed the IRA. For the next few decades, the IRA remained a fringe movement with very limited popular support. In 1939, the organization undertook a brief bombing campaign in Britain and, from 1956 to 1962, its "border campaign" targeted British military and administrative centers in *Northern Ireland. During the 1960s, its nationalist ideology became increasingly combined with socialist principles. The outbreak of "the *Troubles" in Northern Ireland in the late 1960s led to the IRA's reemergence to new prominence.

At the 1969 Army Convention, the organization split on ideological grounds into the Official and Provisional IRA. The increasingly Marxist Official IRA declared a total cease-fire in the summer of 1972 and from then on the term *IRA* has been used for the Provisionals. The IRA (now the Provisionals) launched a military campaign to end conclusively British rule in Northern Ireland. Heavy-handed incursions by the British security forces into *Catholic neighborhoods in *Belfast and the shooting of thirteen unarmed protesters on *Bloody Sunday (January 30, 1972) in *Derry reenergized the Provisional IRA. Attacks on civilian as well as military targets by IRA bombers and gunmen were countered by increasingly brutal methods by the British security forces in a seemingly endless cycle of violence.

Some of the more outrageous exploits of the IRA included the assassination of Lord Mountbatten in County *Sligo in 1979 and an explosion in Brighton, England, during the 1984 Conservative Party Conference, which nearly succeeded in killing British Prime Minister Margaret *Thatcher and other government ministers. During the *hunger strikes of 1981, a combined strategy of "the armalite and ballot box" emerged, as Sinn Féin (the IRA's political wing) contested elections in both Northern Ireland and the Irish Republic. By the early 1990s, the stalemated military campaign led some within the republican movement, including Gerry *Adams, to question the continuation of the "long war." On August 31, 1994, the IRA announced a cease-fire. Although a perceived lack of progress during negotiations with the British government led the IRA to renew its military campaign with a bombing at *Canary Wharf in London on February 9, 1996, a new *Labour government headed by Tony *Blair revived the *peace process and a new cease-fire was declared by the IRA on July 20, 1997. After difficult negotiations, Sinn Féin representatives signed the *Good Friday Agreement on April 10, 1998. Since the agreement, the "decommissioning" of weapons held by both the IRA and loyalist paramilitaries, as well as the pace of the withdrawal of British troops from Northern Ireland, have proved especially contentious. Although small groups of dissident republicans, including the "Real IRA," continue to pursue the armed conflict, most members of the IRA have now accepted constitutional methods to achieve their aim of a unified Irish Republic. F.B.

Irish Republican Brotherhood (IRB). Revolutionary *nationalist organization of the late nineteenth and early twentieth centuries, which was active in Ireland, Britain, and the United States. Inspired by revolutionary groups on the continent, James *Stephens founded the organization in *Dublin in March 1858 with the goal of achieving an Irish *republic by armed force. Its members became known as *Fenians after the legendary warriors of Irish *mythology. Although it was secret and oathbound, British agents easily infiltrated the organization. Urban workers and artisans, in particular, supported the IRB. Despite opposition from the *Catholic Church because of its revolutionary ideology, many members remained devout Catholics.

More militant members forced Stephens from the leadership in 1866 when he failed to deliver a promised armed rebellion. Partly because of informers, the subsequent rising that took place in Ireland in 1867 was easily put down by the authorities.

Meanwhile, in 1866, 1867, and 1871, Irish American Fenians, many of them veterans of the *American Civil War, launched unsuccessful attacks on British Canada. The execution of the three *Manchester Martyrs in England in November 1867, for their role in a policeman's death during an attempt to free Fenian prisoners, galvanized public sympathy in Ireland. The *home rule movement of the 1870s grew out of the Amnesty Association, founded in 1869 to free imprisoned Fenians. After his release in 1871, one former prisoner, John *Devoy, emigrated to the United States and proved to be indefatigable in promoting Irish American support for the IRB. In June 1879, Devoy negotiated a pragmatic agreement, the "New Departure," with Charles Stewart *Parnell, the leader of the *Irish Parliamentary Party (from 1880), and Michael *Davitt, a founder of the *Land League, by which the Fenians would support a unified nationalist front on both home rule and land reform. Many members of the IRB opposed this temporary alliance with constitutional nationalism.

During the 1880s, Parnell's success in building a disciplined Irish party at Westminster eclipsed the revolutionary appeal of the Fenians. The revival of the IRB from a period of dormancy began with the return to Ireland in 1907 of Thomas *Clarke, who had spent fifteen years in English prisons. The deferral of home rule by the British government in 1914 due to the beginning of *World War I provided Clarke and younger colleagues, including Seán MacDermott and Patrick *Pearse, the impetus and opportunity for radical action. Accordingly, the IRB leadership organized the *Easter Rising of 1916, in which James *Connolly's Citizen Army also participated. The formation of the *Irish Republican Army (IRA) under the leadership of Michael *Collins, an IRB member, to wage an open war against British rule from 1919 to 1921 made the conspiratorial IRB less relevant and the organization eventually dissolved in 1924. F.B.

Irish Revival. Resurgent Irish cultural movement of the nineteenth century (also known as Celtic Revival and Irish Literary Revival). By the beginning of the nineteenth century, with the *Irish language in drastic decline, societies were formed to study the riches of the native culture—such as the Gaelic Society of Dublin (1807), the Iberno-Celtic Society (1818), and the Ulster Gaelic Society (1830). Throughout the nineteenth century, a massive corpus of the old literature was edited and translated by scholars including Eugene *O'Curry, John *O'Donovan, John O'Daly, Standish Hayes O'Grady, and Whitley Stokes. European scholars were also becoming aware of the linguistic and cultural value of the Irish sources. At the same time, active forms of cultural expression emerged, such as: the *nationalist fervor of Thomas *Davis and *Young Ireland; the fresh creative voices of the poets Samuel *Ferguson and James Clarence *Mangan; and the popular folklore anthologies published by Patrick Kennedy and others. All pursued the quest for a new identity based on Gaelic sources but largely expressed through the English language.

This spirit of Irish cultural resurgence was greatly magnified by the foundation in 1884 of the *Gaelic Athletic Association to promote native games, and in 1893 of the *Gaelic League to arrest the decline of the Irish language. By the 1890s, three major literary figures had come to the forefront of this movement: the poet and dramatist W. B. *Yeats, the

Gaelic scholar and writer Douglas *Hyde, and Lady Augusta *Gregory, playwright, collector of folklore, and translator of myth. Their work would crystallize the quest for an Irish identity and spearhead the Celtic Revival. In 1897, Lady Gregory, Yeats, and others began to formulate plans for a national theater; this led to the creation of the Irish Literary Theatre (which became known as the *Abbey Theatre in 1904). The first production (in 1899) by the Irish National Theatre was Yeats's *The Countess Cathleen*, which incorporates much of the spirit of the Celtic Revival. Cathleen represented the protective female symbol of Ireland, beautiful in form and spirit, protecting her people in time of distress. Another powerful symbolic figure of the revival was the mythological hero *Cúchulainn, who single-handedly protected his people from enemy attacks. *Irish Language Revivalists who advocated a purely Irish-language literature were suspicious of the idea of writing in English and tended to dismiss *Anglo-Irish writers as irrelevant to the Irish Revival. By 1910 a specifically Irish mode of writing in English had been established, which drew its images from myth and folklore and its language from the inflections of Irish dialect speech. D.Oh.

Irish Traditional Music Archive (ITMA). A multimedia reference archive and resource center in *Dublin for Irish *music, song, and *dance. Founded in 1987, this nonprofit music center (financed by the *Arts Council) has all of *Radio Éireann's (*RTÉ) and BBC's material from the 1920s until the present, as well as manuscripts, ballad sheets, graphic images, photographs, songbooks, and tune notations. ITMA is constantly acquiring new material. All the major collections and performers are represented in its fifteen thousand printed items and ten thousand hours of sound recordings. F.V.

Irish traditional music. See **music, traditional.**

J

Jacobites. Followers of the *Catholic King *James II (1633–1701), from the Latin word for James, *Jacobus*. After the Treaty of *Limerick (1691), many Irish Jacobites emigrated to *France, where King James lived in exile. From there, they planned the restoration of the throne of England to the Stuarts, but successive attempts all failed, culminating in the Battle of Culloden (1746).

A literary Jacobite tradition (poetry celebrating the Stuarts' return to power) survived well into the eighteenth century. The Catholic Church allowed the exiled Stuarts to nominate Irish bishops until 1766. Jacobitism in Ireland was never as strong as in *Scotland, where loyalty to the Stuarts remained firm, although some Irish participated in Jacobite conspiracies in Britain and Irish soldiers in the French army fought in the 1745 Rebellion. Some contemporaries viewed Irish recruitment into France's Irish Brigade as a Jacobite threat. By the mid-eighteenth century, however, Jacobitism was in rapid decline. T.C.

James II (1633–1701). King of England and Ireland (1685–88). James II succeeded his brother Charles II in 1685, but his reign was cut short by the "Glorious Revolution." His active promotion of Roman *Catholicism offended the deep-rooted anti-Catholicism of his English and Scottish subjects. His son-in-law *William of Orange, leader of the Netherlands, invaded England and deposed him (November–December 1688) primarily to forestall an Anglo-French alliance in the looming Nine Years War (1689–97).

Richard Talbot, Earl of Tyrconnell, James's appointee as commander of the army, and later (1687) lord lieutenant, ensured that Irish Catholics controlled the administration and army in Ireland. Shortly after James's landing in Ireland (March 1689), all of the country except for *Derry and Enniskillen, County *Fermanagh, was brought under his control. While James sympathized with his fellow Catholics, he wanted to maintain Ireland's political subordination.

He very reluctantly acquiesced in the reversal of the *Cromwellian Land Settlement and the *Irish Parliament's assertion of independence from the English Parliament.

James's performance as a military commander was mixed. D'Avaux, the French envoy, identified the central weakness in James's leadership: "[H]e is much taken up with little things . . . passing over lightly those which are essential." James saw Ireland as a stepping-stone to regain Scotland and England but his Irish followers did not, by and large, share his three-kingdom preoccupation. The French, James correctly observed in his *Memoirs*, were "averse from venturing more succours than what was absolutely necessary to keep the war alive" in Ireland. James rightly rejected French advice and confronted the expeditionary force led by Marshal Schomberg in the autumn of 1689. This forced William III to lead another, larger, expedition to Ireland in 1690.

On balance, James's apparent decision to fight a delaying action at the *Boyne (July 1690) was justifiable even though the Franco-Irish army was heavily outnumbered. However, he perpetrated a gross error in switching troops from the critical river crossing at Oldbridge and suffered a psychological collapse immediately after the battle. James II was, by his later admission, "too precipitate" in embarking for France. The Battle of the Boyne was indecisive and the Irish would fight for over another year.

James spent the remainder of his life in France, lapsing into apathy and fatalism. The Irish, as evidenced by *folklore and contemporary historiography, were ambivalent about James the man, if not James the king. Even an ardently *Jacobite historian like the Abbé Mac Geoghegan could include the barbed comment, "Sire, if you possessed a hundred kingdoms, you would lose them." P.L.

Jellett, Mainie (1897–1944). Cubist painter and theorist. Born in *Dublin, Jellett studied in Dublin, London, and Paris. She learned an academic style from Walter Sickert but later developed an idealist version of cubism under the influence of Albert Gleizes. After harsh criticism of her abstract work, Jellett returned to a more figurative style that incorporated religious subject matter. She was a member of the Society of Dublin Painters and a founding member of the *Irish Exhibition of Living Art in 1943. M.C.

Jenkinson, Biddy (1929–). Pseudonym of an *Irish-language feminist poet and critic. Jenkinson has maintained her privacy and she refuses to be translated, believing that *Irish literature cannot be translated into English without loss. She has been published widely in Irish literary journals such as *Innti* and *Combar*. Her poetry collections include *Báisteadh Gintlí* (1987), *Uiscí Beatha* (1988), and *Dán na hUidhre* (1991). She published her poetic manifesto in the *Irish University Review* (spring/summer 1991). Jenkinson writes with emotional intensity about femininity, motherhood, and the woman's role in sustaining humankind's links with nature. C.D.

Jesuits. Catholic religious order, also known as the Society of Jesus. Ignatius Loyola founded the Society of Jesus in Spain in 1534. The Jesuits came to Ireland in 1542 during the reign of *Henry VIII. After the Council of Trent in 1563, the Jesuits promoted the Counter-Reformation, preserving Irish loyalty to *Catholicism during the *Protestant Reformation. Famed for their rigorous system of *education, the Jesuits opened thirteen schools, colleges, and residences in Ireland and a novitiate at Kilkenny between 1642 and 1654. After *James II's defeat at the Battle of the *Boyne in 1690, only six Jesuits remained in Ireland. The relaxation of the *Penal Laws in the mid-1700s brought a resurgence in the number of Jesuits until Pope Clement XIV, under pressure from Catholics who saw the Jesuits as overly domineering, reluctantly suppressed the order in 1773. During the order's gradual restoration between 1801 and 1814, Father Peter Kenney, the first superior of the restored order, founded the renowned College of Clongowes. Other schools opened soon after, and the Jesuit reputation for education led the Irish bishops to entrust the administration of University College, Dublin, to the Society in 1883. Jesuits also played a major role in the genesis of the new National University in 1908. During the 1960s, the *Second Vatican Council inspired Jesuits to focus on issues of social justice. M.P.C.

Jews. Although officially refused residency in 1079, a number of Jews immigrated to Ireland after the *Anglo-Norman invasion. It was an English Jew in Bristol who lent *Strongbow funds that helped finance the invasion. The Irish Jews were expelled along with the English Jews in 1290, and with the exception of a few Spanish *conversos*, there were no Jews in Ireland until the *Cromwellian Settlement.

A synagogue may have existed in *Dublin as early as 1660, a cemetery in 1717, and a new synagogue in 1762. In *Cork, a cemetery existed in 1727 and a ritual slaughterer in 1753. Jewish merchants were in *Belfast in the 1750s and a Jewish butcher in 1771. Thirty Jewish families were in Galway in 1781 and a few Jews elsewhere throughout the island. Jews, along with *Catholics, were excluded from the guilds in the eighteenth century. Legislation offering Jews citizenship was defeated in 1743. In the nineteenth century, increased persecution in Eastern Europe led to the immigration of Jews, mostly from Latvia and Lithuania, to Ireland. They settled mainly in Dublin and Cork and engaged in *furniture making, antiques, and peddling. According to census figures, there were approximately five thousand Jews in Ireland by 1911.

In the 1890s, there were anti-Jewish demonstrations in Dublin and Cork and a major anti-Jewish boycott and attack in *Limerick in 1904. This mirrored an increase in anti-Semitism on the Continent, as seen in the Dreyfus Case and the publication of *The Protocols of the Learned Elders of Zion*. Throughout the 1920s and 1930s, two Irish priests, Denis Fahey and Thomas Cahill, spread a virulent anti-Semitism premised on the Protocols and Fahey greatly influenced the infamous American anti-Semite, Father Coughlin. During the Holocaust, thousands of entry requests were denied on economic and anti-Semitic grounds. After the war, a few Jews were admitted. In the 1960s, a Dublin synagogue was set on fire. To describe modern alienation and exile, James *Joyce made the protagonist of his masterpiece *Ulysses* (1922) a Jew.

Ireland refused to recognize the existence of the State of Israel until 1963 and it was only in 1996 that the first Irish ambassador took up residence. Isaac Herzog, who was Chief Rabbi of the *Irish Free State (1921–36), became Israel's first Chief Ashkenazic Rabbi, and his son, *Chaim, who was born in Belfast, was Israel's president from 1983 to 1993. Dublin had two Jewish mayors, Robert Briscoe (1956 and 1961) and his son, Ben Briscoe (1988), and Cork had a Jewish mayor in 1977, Gerald Goldberg. Jewish life in Ireland continues today for the approximately 1,500 Jews located mainly in Dublin. G.M.W.

John, King of England (1167–1216). Third son of *Henry II, appointed Lord of Ireland, 1177.

Neil Jordan

His visit in 1185 to Ireland was disastrous. He failed to gain the support of the *Norman *landlords or local Irish kings. John became King of England in 1199, and on a second visit to Ireland in 1210, he finally stamped royal authority on the country and introduced the common law of England. However, King John's control in Ireland suffered a setback after the barons' revolt of 1212. T.C.

Johnston, Denis (1901–84). Playwright. Born in *Dublin and educated at Cambridge and Harvard, Johnston worked as a barrister in Dublin. His disillusionment with Irish *nationalism is reflected in his satirical play *The Old Lady Says "No!"* (1929). A play in the expressionist tradition, it depicts emotional experience rather than objective reality and draws on a wide range of quotations to create a pastiche effect. Like his other works, including the play *The Moon in the Yellow River* (1931), it is intellectually demanding. M.S.T.

Johnston, Jennifer (1930–). Novelist. Born in *Dublin, Johnston is best known for her spare, economical style. Her works focus on the struggle between loyalties—personal and political, public and private—which are often played out against the background of the decaying "Big House." Johnston's first novel, *The Captains and the Kings* (1972), won the *Evening Standard* First Novel Award. *The Old Jest* (1979) won the Whitbread Award and *Shadows on Our Skin* (1977) was short-listed for the Booker Prize. A collection of three novels, *The Captains and the Kings* (1972), *The Railway Station Man* (1984), and *Fool's Sanctuary* (1987) was published as *The Essential Jennifer Johnston* (2000). N.H.

Jordan, Neil (1950–). Novelist and filmmaker. Born in *Sligo, Jordan was one of the founders of the innovative Irish Writers' Cooperative, which published his first book, *Night in Tunisia* (1976), a collection of stories. A novel, *The Past* (1980) followed, but since the release of his first feature film, *Angel* (1982), he has been known mainly as a filmmaker.

His writing and directing have earned him an international reputation and a number of prestigious awards. Jordan's two best-known films are *The Crying Game* (1992) and the biographical *Michael Collins* (1996). In both, his long-term fascination with the fabrication of personality and identity is set in the context of Irish historical violence. His screenplay for *The Crying Game* won an Academy Award. Such films as *The Company of Wolves* (1984), *Mona Lisa* (1986), *The Miracle* (1991), and an adaptation of Patrick McCabe's novel *The Butcher Boy* (1997) have the intensity and psychological complexity for which Jordan has become renowned. He has also made the Hollywood films *High Spirits* (1988), *We're No Angels* (1990), *Interview with the Vampire* (1994), and *In Dreams* (1999). Jordan has published a number of screenplays, a novella, *The Dream of a Beast* (1983), and the novel *Sunrise with Sea Monster* (1995), entitled *Nightlines* in the United States. G.OB.

Joyce, James Augustine (1882–1941). Writer. No other writer has influenced twentieth-century literature as much as James Joyce. He is the ultimate modernist who revolutionized the novel with his inventive use of the stream of consciousness and verbal acrobatics.

Born on February 2, 1882, in *Dublin, James was the eldest of ten children in a relatively prosperous, middle-class, *Catholic family. Even as the family sank into poverty, largely because of his father's drinking, the young James received the best education from the *Jesuit schools Clongowes Wood and Belvedere College.

By the time Joyce enrolled at Dublin's Royal University (now University College, Dublin) in 1898, the family was living in the utmost squalor, hounded by debt collectors, evicted by landlords, constantly moving from one shabby house to another. Yet throughout this trauma, Joyce maintained an intellectual detachment, a trait he would later bring to a fine art form. An ambitious and independent-minded student, Joyce had his essay "Ibsen's New Drama" published in the *Fortnightly Review* in 1900. Ibsen sent Joyce a note in which he expressed appreciation for his insights.

After he graduated in 1902, Joyce, who was becoming known in literary circles, registered at the Royal University Medical School. However, later that year, to escape Dublin's religious and social suffocation he went to Paris, where he soon gave up medicine to write verse. There, he discovered Edouard Dujardin's French novel *Les lauriers sont coupés* (1888), which he later credited for inspiring him to use interior monologue. A year later, in 1903, Joyce returned to Dublin because his mother was dying. He would later fictionalize his own emotions of that time in *Ulysses*, where Stephen Dedalus—young Joyce's fictional alter ego—is haunted by his mother's death and plagued by feelings of guilt. During this period, Joyce taught briefly at a private school, and lived for a while in a Martello Tower with Oliver St. John *Gogarty, who appears as Buck Mulligan in *Ulysses*. On June 16, 1904, he had his first date with Nora Barnacle, with whom he would spend the rest of his life. It is this fateful day that Joyce would immortalize in his daring novel *Ulysses*. Shortly after they met, Joyce and Nora set sail for Europe. They married twenty-seven years later.

Joyce would live the rest of his life in self-imposed exile—first in Trieste, then in Rome, Paris, and Zurich—writing some of the greatest prose in the English language about the country he left behind. Throughout, he would subject his family (Nora and their two children, Giorgio and Lucia) to

James Joyce

the itinerant, impoverished lifestyle he had experienced as a child.

Joyce's first published work was *Chamber Music* (1907), a small volume of verse. *Dubliners*, his brilliant collection of short stories containing his first masterpiece "The Dead," was published in 1914, after years of legal wranglings because various publishers were afraid to print material that contained objectionable language, disrespect for religion and the crown, and references to real people and places in Dublin. Joyce would mine his life and the city of Dublin for all his books, creating scandal in his wake.

From 1904 to 1915, Joyce and his family lived in Trieste, during which time he would publish *Chamber Music*, finish *Dubliners*, revise *Stephen Hero* into *A Portrait of the Artist as a Young Man*, and begin *Ulysses*. Earning little from teaching English, Joyce was constantly on the edge of poverty but always managed to find supporters (his brother Stanislaus, Harriet Shaw Weaver, and later Sylvia Beach) to rescue him. In Trieste, he befriended Ettore Schmitz (whose pen name was Italo Svevo) and encouraged him to write his novel *Confessions of Zeno*.

Joyce's first novel *A Portrait of the Artist as a Young Man*, which had been serialized by Ezra Pound in the magazine the *Egoist*, was published only in 1916. In despair, he had once thrown the unfinished manuscript in the fireplace, but his sister who was staying with him rescued the pages from the flames. In this autobiographical novel, Joyce traces the development of the artistic sensibility and shows how the artist must escape the crippling forces of religion, family, and *nationalism. Joyce's only play, *Exiles*, was rejected by W. B. *Yeats for Dublin's *Abbey Theatre in 1915, and was staged with little success (in Munich in 1919, and in New York in 1925) until Harold Pinter's 1970 production in London. In 1915, Joyce moved with his family to Zurich and after the war to Paris, where they stayed from 1920 to 1940. Suffering from chronic eye disease and bouts of blindness, he underwent many operations throughout this period. *Ulysses* was published in Paris in 1922, on Joyce's fortieth birthday, by Sylvia Beach's bookstore Shakespeare and Company. Episodes of the book had been serialized in the *Little Review* and the *Egoist*, and the work was immediately recognized as a masterpiece by Pound, T. S. Eliot, Hemingway, and *Beckett. In this novel, Joyce experiments with formal techniques including the stream of consciousness, allowing the reader to enter the minds of his main characters, Leopold Bloom (a middle-class Dublin Jew, who stands for modern man), Stephen Dedalus, and, in the book's final episode, Bloom's wife, Molly. Structured loosely after Homer's *Odyssey*, *Ulysses* is packed with philosophical, historical, literary, and mythological allusions. *Ulysses* was banned as obscene in the United States until 1933, and in Britain until 1936. Although it was never officially banned in Ireland, it was rarely available in bookstores until 1967. Today, the novel is considered one of the great books of Western literature and has been translated into almost every language.

Joyce worked on his last book, *Finnegans Wake*, from 1923 to 1938, pushing language to its limits and creating an extravaganza of multilingual wordplay. Sections of the as yet untitled "Work in Progress" were published in avant-garde magazines, and in 1929 Joyce orchestrated the publication of a collection of essays by twelve well-known writers, including Samuel Beckett and William Carlos Williams, to respond to the objections of the work's chief critics (who included Seán *O Faoláin). By the 1930s, the years of toil, poverty, and hardship had taken their toll. Joyce's health was fragile, his daughter Lucia was mentally ill, and his son Giorgio unhappily married. As World War II loomed, *Finnegans Wake* was published in 1939, on Joyce's fifty-seventh birthday. Received with less enthusiasm than *Ulysses*, it was described as unreadable, ridiculous, and manipulative. Shortly after the outbreak of war, Joyce and Nora moved to Zurich. Joyce died there in 1941, fittingly in exile and on the move. L.R., J.OM.

Joyce, William (1906–46). Nazi propagandist and radio broadcaster. Born in New York of Irish parents, Joyce was raised in *Galway. He emigrated to England in 1922 and joined the British Union of Fascists in 1934. In 1939, he went to Germany and broadcast Nazi propaganda throughout World War II. He acquired the nickname "Lord Haw-Haw" during this period. Although a US citizen, Joyce was tried and executed for treason in England on the grounds that having once used a British passport, he was considered a British subject, and his Nazi propaganda was treason. The trial is unique in legal history. His remains were re-interred in Galway in 1976. S.A.B.

K

Kavanagh, Patrick (1904–67). Poet. Born in Inniskeen, County *Monaghan, Kavanagh was the eldest boy in a large, poor family. His formal education ended abruptly when he left school at age thirteen to help his father on the farm and in the cobbler's shop. The end of his schooling marked the beginning of a dogged, self-taught apprenticeship in poetry. Though he wrote poems and ballads from age twelve, Kavanagh's journey from local balladeer to major Irish poet was slow and painful. Discouraged from the pursuit of poetry by his practical parents, Kavanagh was eventually championed by AE (George *Russell), who published and introduced him to other writers. His first book, *Ploughman and Other Poems* (1936), was published when he was thirty-two. Three years later, Kavanagh gave up farming and went to live in *Dublin as a professional poet and literary journalist, writing for the **Bell*, *Envoy*, *Dublin Magazine*, and the *Irish Press*.

Kavanagh is admired among subsequent generations of Irish poets for his brave and original stance against the rear guard of the *Irish Literary Revival. Instead of playing the set part of country poet, Kavanagh redefined the role on his own terms, and with it, the Irish pastoral, most notably in his landmark volume *The Great Hunger* (1942), which depicted country life as harsh and spiritually unaccommodating, undermining more romantic views established by Revivalist writers. In 1960, after a fallow period lasting more than a decade, Kavanagh experienced a major poetic renewal with his buoyant canal poems in *Come Dance with Kitty Stobling*. Other works include an autobiographical novel, *The Green Fool* (1938), *A Soul for Sale* (1947), a novel, *Tarry Flynn* (1948), *Collected Poems* (1964), *Collected Prose* (1967), and a posthumously published novel, *By Night Unstarred* (1977). J.AR.

Keane, John B. (1928–2002). Writer and humorist. Born in Listowel, County *Kerry, Keane was the owner of a public house, which was the source of many of his stories. A prolific essayist and fiction writer, John B. Keane wrote many best-sellers in Ireland, including *The Gentle Art of Matchmaking and Other Important Things* (1973) and *Durango* (1992). Best known, however, for his nineteen published plays, Keane was the most popular Irish playwright working in the second half of the twentieth century and the most undervalued by the critical establishment. What became his dramatic trilogy—*Sive* (1959), *The Field* (1965), and *Big Maggie* (1969)—depicts domineering parents and harsh conditions in mid-twentieth-century rural Ireland. Keane's plays are a mix of realism, grotesquerie, and satiric wit. From 1958 onward, Keane submitted his plays to the *Abbey Theatre, but only *Hut 42* premiered there in 1962. It was not until the revival of Keane's plays in the 1980s that the national theater took his work seriously. One of Keane's best novels is *The Bodhran Makers* (1986), an elegy for a rural community dismantled by midcentury economic trouble and migration. In 1998, Keane received the coveted Gradam Medal from the National Theatre Society for exceptional contributions to Irish theater. C.H.

Keating, Geoffrey. See **Céitinn, Seathrún.**

Keating, Seán (1889–1977). Painter and teacher. Born in *Limerick, Keating was a leading pupil of William *Orpen at the Dublin Metropolitan School of Art and went on to work with him in London. Elected to the *Royal Hibernian Academy in 1919, he was a professor at the National College of Art in *Dublin from 1934 to 1954 and president of the Royal Hibernian Academy from 1948 to 1962. Although using modern techniques, Keating's work defies modernist style categories because of his use of popular *nationalist subject matter. His work often engages in a visual dialogue with the work of Orpen. M.C.

keening. A practice which was common at wakes and funerals well into the twentieth century in parts of Ireland. The word is the Anglicization of the Irish word *caoineadh*, meaning "lament." Keening consisted of a death-poem sung by *mná caointe* (or keening women) at a funeral. The poem praises the dead person and laments his or her loss. It was usually accompanied by wailing. It occasionally reached literary status as in the celebrated *Caoineadh Airt Uí Laoghaire*, or "Lament for Art O'Leary," by Eibhlín Dhubh *Ní Chonaill. A.T.

Kells, Book of. Northwestern Europe's most famous *manuscript, containing illuminated copies of the Gospels, from circa 800. The Book of Kells was preserved in the Columban monastery at Kells, in County *Meath, until 1653. Set up in the ninth century by monks from Iona, the monastery at Kells became the head of all the Columban monasteries. The Book of Kells was stolen from the monastery at Kells in 1007, but rediscovered—minus its cover—some time afterward. Iona is currently viewed as the most likely place of origin, but the book remained in Kells until the seventeenth century, when it was given to Trinity College, Dublin, where it is still preserved. The manuscript was written and illuminated by three or more hands. Its most intricate and miniscule-scale ornament of spiral, interlace, animal, and key pattern decoration, as well as its portraits of Christ, Evangelists, and the Mother and Child, make this book a marvel of inventiveness and exuberant color. One element, lapis lazuli, had been imported from as far away as Afghanistan. P.H.

Kelly, Michael (1762–1826). Tenor, composer, manager, publisher. Born in *Dublin, Kelly was the earliest Irish tenor of international note. He created the roles of Don Curzio and Don Basilio in the first performance of Mozart's *Nozze di Figaro* at the Burgtheater in Vienna on May 1, 1786. His operatic career began in his native Dublin and took him to major centers in Europe, where he worked with Gluck and Mozart. He settled in London in 1787, where he performed in opera, composed for the stage, was a stage manager and music publisher, and even set himself up as a wine merchant, a venture that led him to bankruptcy in 1811. His lively *Reminiscences*, ghost-written by Theodore Hook and published in 1826, are an important firsthand source, detailing the musical scene of his time. He was praised for his musicianship, acting skills, and vocal technique, but the actual quality of his voice was said to be "wanting in sweetness."M.D.

Kennedy, John Fitzgerald (1917–63). Thirty-fifth president of the United States (1961–63). The descendant of *Famine-era emigrants from County *Wexford, Kennedy was the first (and to date only) Roman Catholic to be elected president of the United States. Millions of *Irish Americans saw Kennedy's election in 1960 as the culmination of their community's triumph over poverty and discrimination in American society. Despite Kennedy's personal interest in Irish affairs, official American policy toward Ireland, particularly on the issue of *partition, remained unchanged during his tenure in office. This was due mainly to the United States' "special relationship" with Britain as part of American Cold War strategy. Nevertheless, on an emotional and symbolic level, his presidency was significant in Irish history, as many Irish people considered his rise to power emblematic of the diaspora's success. Kennedy's visit to Ireland in the summer of 1963 was met with tremendous popular enthusiasm. Likewise, his assassination in Dallas, Texas, the following November, was a source of national sorrow. T.D.

Kennelly, Brendan (1936–). Poet, dramatist, critic, and professor of modern literature at Trinity College, Dublin. Born in County *Kerry, Kennelly has published over twenty books of poetry and has won the AE Memorial Prize. In his best-known poetic works—*Cromwell*, *The Book of Judas*, and *Poetry My Arse*—he gives a voice to the marginalized and the outcast. He has also published two novels, *The Crooked Cross* and *The Florentines*, and dramatic adaptations of Sophocles' *Antigone* and Euripides' *Medea*. Kennelly has edited many anthologies, including *The Penguin Book of Irish Verse*. P.E.

Kerry, County. Coastal county in the southwest of Ireland, in the province of *Munster. Kerry, covering an area of 1,855 square miles, has a population of 132,424 (2002 census). Kerry is bordered by *Cork and *Limerick to the east and by the Atlantic Ocean to the west. Known as "the Kingdom," the county is one of the most scenic counties in Ireland and has distinctly diverse regions. The north is mostly lowland, much of it good dairy-farming country, with scattered *bogs. The south and west are mountainous, and sheep farming is the main land use. There is some fishing in the west, Dingle being the main fishing port. The coastline is rocky, with several sandy beaches, and many islands. Ireland's highest mountain, *Carrantuohill (3,414 feet), is in the Macgillycuddy's Reeks range in the southern part of the county.

Kerry's mountains, coastline, and the famous lakes of *Killarney make it one of Ireland's main tourist destinations. The Ring of Kerry is a famous circular drive around the spectacular Iveragh Peninsula, stretching from Killorglin to Kenmare. Other attractions include Ross Castle and Muckross House, both near Killarney; Derrynane House—once the home of Daniel *O'Connell; the annual

Muckross House, Killarney National Park, County Kerry

Puck *Fair, held every August in the town of Killorglin; and the jagged *Skellig Islands, where monks established a settlement in the seventh century. The county has a great many archaeological sites and monuments. Many are concentrated on the *Dingle Peninsula, and the county's only complete *round tower is in the north at Rattoo, near Ballyduff.

Kerry has never had much industry besides farming. The county capital, Tralee, is a busy market town, with a few factories and a nearby port at Fenit. Killarney, a smaller town, which has long depended on the tourist industry, is the seat of the Catholic bishop of Kerry and has a mid-nineteenth-century cathedral. Listowel, in north Kerry, is a market town. Since the *Famine, Kerry has had one of Ireland's highest *emigration rates to the United States.

The southern part of the county was little affected by the Norman and English settlements, though this only partly explains Kerry's distinct political history. The county was one of the main centers of the *Land War of the 1880s, and many violent incidents occurred there during the *War of Independence. During the *Civil War, the county was the last place where the *Free State army established its authority. Free State executions and massacres in the war's last days left a lasting political bitterness in the county, and strong support for *republicanism endures today.

Kerry is known for its *Gaelic football teams, which have been the country's most successful, and also for its literary tradition. The great Gaelic poets, Aodhagán *Ó Rathaille (1670–1729) and Eoghan Rua *Ó Súilleabháin (1748–84) were born in east Kerry in the Sliabh Luachra district. The *Blasket Islands produced several works of *literature in Irish, based on oral storytelling. These have been translated, including the classic autobiography *An tOileánach* (*The Islandman*) (1929) by Tomás *Ó Criomhthain (O'Crohan). Twentieth-century writers from north Kerry include Maurice Walsh, the *Abbey playwright George Fitzmaurice, and more recently the writers Bryan *MacMahon and John B. *Keane, and the poet Brendan *Kennelly. P.D.

Kickham, Charles J[oseph] (1828–82). Novelist and political activist. Born in Mullinahone, County *Tipperary, Kickham was coeditor of the Fenian newspaper the *Irish People*. In 1865, he was arrested and sentenced to fourteen years in prison for treason. He served four years before being released due to ill health. Kickham is best remembered for *Knocknagow* (1879), a loving depiction of rural life, which is one of the most popular of all Irish novels. G.OB.

Kiely, Benedict (1919–). Writer, journalist. Born in Dromore, County *Tyrone, and educated in Omagh and University College, Dublin, Kiely is a novelist, short story writer, literary critic, journalist, broadcaster, and essayist. In his first book, *Counties of Contention: A Study of the Origins and Implications of the Partition of Ireland* (1945), Kiely expresses a political consciousness that recurs in the first of his ten novels, *Land Without Stars* (1947), and his last two—*Proxopera* (1977) and *Nothing Happens in Carmincross* (1985). In his four volumes of short stories, his mature novels, memoirs, and travel writing, Kiely, like a traditional oral storyteller (*seanchaí*), combines whimsical fantasy and a wide-ranging, playful, often nostalgic reference to Irish lore and song lyrics, with shrewd realistic observation. He is well known also for his literary criticism, principally *Poor Scholar: A Study of the Works and Days of William Carleton* (1947) and *Modern Irish Fiction—A Critique* (1950). J.McD.

Kildare, County. Inland county in the province of *Leinster, in the eastern part of Ireland. Kildare, covering 654 square miles, has a population of 163,995 (2002 census). Kildare derives its name from the Irish language *Cill Dara*, "the church of the oak tree," a reference to a monastery near Kildare town which, it was claimed, was founded by St. *Brigid. The county's principal geographic features are: the Bog of Allen, a vast expanse of low-lying moorlike land that stretches over most of Ireland's midland counties; and the flat plain of the Curragh, which covers over one thousand acres and is six miles long and two miles wide. Kildare is the main center for *horse racing and also for horse breeding in Ireland. Besides the racetrack at the Curragh, race meetings are also regularly held at Naas, the county capital, and Punchestown. Since 1855, the Curragh has also been a principal army base in Ireland. The main rivers in the county are the Liffey, the Barrow, and the Boyne. The Grand and Royal canals also run through the county.

From the late fourteenth century to the early sixteenth century, the Fitzgeralds, an *Anglo-Norman family, dominated the county. Occupying a strategic position between the *Pale and the territories controlled by the Gaelic lords, the Fitzgerald family had

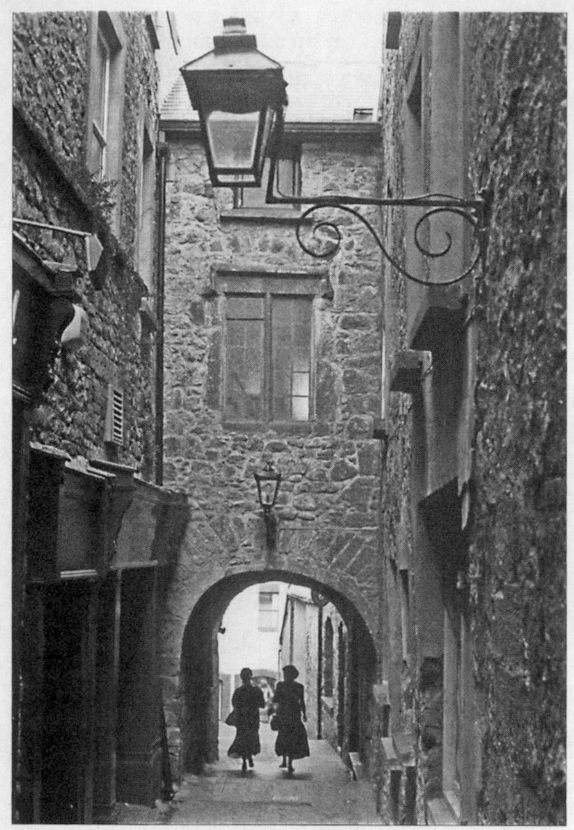

Kilkenny medieval city

a strong bargaining position with the English crown. In return for their protection of the Pale, they were granted substantial local autonomy. This dominance was ended by the execution of "Silken" Thomas Fitzgerald following his failed revolt in 1535.

County Kildare is noted for its rich pastureland, which is particularly suited to the fattening of cattle for the Dublin market and for export outside Ireland. Tillage farming is also carried on in parts of the county.

Kildare is also home to two of the most celebrated Catholic educational institutions in Ireland: Clongowes Wood College near Clane, where James *Joyce attended boarding school and which he immortalized in *A Portrait of the Artist as a Young Man*; and St. Patrick's College, *Maynooth, originally founded in 1795 as a seminary for Catholic priests. One of the major tourist attractions in the county is *Castletown House, the first and largest Palladian-style country house in Ireland, located near Celbridge. The town of Prosperous lent its name to Christy *Moore's first album, which is generally acknowledged as a classic. A.S.

Kilkenny, County. Inland county in the province of *Leinster. Stretching over 800 square miles, Kilkenny is a medium-sized county, with a population of 80,421 (2002 census). Geographically, the county is varied: the elevated Castlecomer plateau to the north, the Slieveardagh hills in the west and the hills in the south and east contrast with two low-lying valleys in the center and east of the county. Through the two valleys flow the rivers Nore and Barrow which, like the sides of the letter V, join up at the bottom before flowing into the Celtic Sea below New Ross. The Barrow, which flows through Muine Bheag (Bagenalstown) and Graignamanagh (with its splendidly restored Cistercian abbey), forms the western boundary with *Carlow, while the Suir above *Waterford partially defines the county's southern boundary.

Kilkenny has an illustrious history: the Statute of *Kilkenny (1366) prohibited *Anglo-Normans from assimilating into Gaelic culture, and the *Confederation of Kilkenny, an Assembly of Confederate Catholics (Gaelic Irish and Old English allies) held annual meetings here from 1642 to 1649. The county and city of Kilkenny preserve the atmosphere of its medieval past. The county has a number of interesting and picturesque towns and villages but the crowning jewel is the city of Kilkenny itself, known affectionately as "the Marble City," from the fossil-rich limestone that surrounds it, and which was used in many of its buildings. The cathedral and Kilkenny Castle are perhaps the most famous of these. The thirteenth-century cathedral is dedicated to St. Canice, or Cainnech, after whom (*Cill Chainnigh*, the Church of Canice) the city and county are named. The castle, founded by William the Marshal in 1192, was bought in 1391 by the Butlers, who were great benefactors to the county for centuries, and who handed the castle over to the state in 1967. Since then, Kilkenny Castle, along with its fine nineteenth-century art gallery, has been open to the public.

Kilkenny City is synonymous with high-quality design and craftsmanship. The *Kilkenny Design Workshops, set up in 1963 by the Irish Export Board, made the city into a center for innovative crafts, where many young artisans developed their skills in jewelry, pottery, weaving, and *textile design. Famous natives of county Kilkenny include the philosopher George *Berkeley; the sculptor Christopher Hewetson; Edmund Ignatius *Rice, founder of the *Irish Christian Brothers; the architect James *Hoban who designed and built the White House in Washington; the scholar and editor John *O'Donovan; the painter Tony *O'Malley; and the writer Thomas *Kilroy. The Kilkenny Arts Festival, which takes place annually in August, attracts international writers and artists. P.H.

Kilkenny, Statute of (1366). A series of reactionary laws enacted by the Irish *Parliament to quell the increasing assimilation of the *Anglo-Norman population into the Gaelic culture. Because the Normans were becoming "more Irish than the Irish themselves," the statute required that only English be spoken, English law followed, and English dress and manners observed. Intermarriage between the native Irish and Anglo-Norman population was also prohibited. T.C.

Kilkenny Design Workshops. The workshops were established at Kilkenny Castle by the Irish government in 1963 to develop design innovation for established Irish craft-based industries such as silversmithing, ceramics, *furniture, weaving, and *textile design. The craft workers, many of whom were British, German, and Scandinavian, quickly developed an outstanding reputation for graphic, industrial, and craft design. The Design Workshops were closed down in 1988, but many of the craft workers established their own workshops in Kilkenny. S.A.B.

Kilmainham Gaol. Famous prison in Dublin. Opened in 1796, Kilmainham Gaol was an ordinary prison, which also housed political prisoners such as the *United Irishmen, *Young Irelanders, and Charles Stewart *Parnell. Leaders of the *Easter Rising were executed here. During the *Irish Civil War, *republicans were also imprisoned and executed in Kilmainham until its closure in 1924. It was turned into a museum in 1966. T.C.

Kilroy, Thomas (1934–). Playwright and academic. Born in Callan, County *Kilkenny, and educated at University College, Dublin, Kilroy taught at various universities in the United States and in Ireland. His plays include *The Death and Resurrection of Mr. Roche* (1968), which addresses questions of sexual orientation, *Tea and Sex and Shakespeare* (1976), *Talbot's Box* (1977), about the personal struggle and suffering of Dublin working-class ascetic Matt Talbot, and *Double Cross* (1986), which explores the wartime careers of two Irishmen, Brendan Bracken,

*Churchill's minister of information, and William *Joyce, who broadcast Nazi propaganda as "Lord Haw-Haw." *The Madame MacAdam Travelling Theatre* (1991), a theatrically imaginative, but poorly received, critique of 1940s ideology, was produced by *Field Day. In 1997 the *Abbey Theatre staged Kilroy's *The Secret Fall of Constance Wilde*, in which Oscar *Wilde's wife confronts her husband's double life and her own mixed emotions. Kilroy is concerned with the nature of solitude and the relationship of the outcast to the stagnant Irish society from which he has withdrawn. He became a director of Field Day Theatre Company in 1988. His historical novel, *The Big Chapel* (1971), won the Guardian prize for fiction. C.D., J.C.E.L.

Kinsale, Battle of (December 25, 1601). Last battle of the *Nine Years War. A Spanish force, which landed at Kinsale, County *Cork, to help the Irish, was besieged by an English army under Lord Mountjoy. Hugh *O'Neill and his ally Red Hugh *O'Donnell took their forces in an epic march south from their *Ulster stronghold to assist the Spanish. The English became trapped between the Irish forces and the town. However, an attempt to relieve Kinsale ended in disaster when the Spanish failed to advance from the town and the ill-trained and ill-equipped Irish were routed by the English. The Spanish withdrew a week later. T.C.

Kinsella, Thomas (1928–). Poet. Born in *Dublin and educated at University College, Dublin, Thomas Kinsella worked for several decades in the civil service. Frequently described as the Irish T. S. Eliot, Kinsella became the most influential harbinger of modernism in Irish *poetry. Struggling out from the oppressive "double shadow of Yeats and English verse," he constructed his identity as a poet caught between the tensions and paradoxes of the dual Irish tradition—Gaelic and English. As his work evolved, he abandoned his early lyricism in favor of the fragmented interconnectedness of his late series of longer poems and sequences.

Most influential among Kinsella's poetry collections were *Another September* (1958), *Downstream* (1962), *Nightwalker* (1968), and *Butcher's Dozen* (1972). A prolific translator from the Irish (*The Táin*, 1969, and *An Duanaire—Poems of the Dispossessed*, 1981), Kinsella also edited *The New Oxford Book of Irish Verse* (1986). In 1995, he published an historical overview of Irish poetry, *The Dual Tradition: An Essay on Poetry and Politics*. J.AR.

Kitchener, Horatio Herbert; First Earl Kitchener of Khartoum and of Broome (1850–1916). British military commander. Born in Ballylongford, County *Kerry, Kitchener enjoyed a distinguished military career in Africa and India. As commander of the Egyptian army, he conquered Sudan (1896–99) and was subsequently commander in chief of British forces in South Africa (1900–02). As secretary for war (1914–16), Kitchener rapidly expanded Britain's small professional army into a mass volunteer force of three million men. He died when HMS *Hampshire* was sunk en route to Russia in June 1916. S.A.B.

Knowth. *Passage-grave in County *Meath. Along with *Newgrange and Dowth, Knowth forms a great Neolithic cemetery on a ridge of hills north of the Boyne river, some miles upstream from Drogheda, County *Louth. It dates from around 3000 B.C., making it older than the Pyramids. Knowth has two separate tombs back-to-back within a large earthen mound—one corbeled, like that in Newgrange, the other flat-roofed. Because of fallen stones, public access to the burial chambers is not feasible, but visitors can see the beautifully decorated stones on the outside of the mound, and also reconstructed "satellite" tombs around its periphery. Access is through the Brú na Bóinne Interpretative Center on the south bank of the Boyne. P.H.

L

Labour Party, the. *Political party. The Labour Party was formed in 1912, but had only a minimal organizational existence before the foundation of the *Irish Free State. Since 1922, Labour has seen itself as the political party of the *trade union movement. In practice, however, the Labour Party had a difficult relationship with the trade unions. Though part of the European social democratic tradition, Labour has had a low level of support. Its inability to form a government on its own has reduced Labour's position in Ireland to that of a minority party and Labour has had to make many compromises as part of coalition governments with much larger conservative parties. Its leaders have been: Thomas Johnson (1918–27), T. J. O'Connell (1927–32), William Norton (1932–60), Brendan Corish (1960–77), Frank Cluskey (1977–81), Michael O'Leary (1981–82), Dick Spring (1982–97), Ruairi Quinn (1997–2002), and Pat Rabbitte (2002 to present).

In the first election with (near) universal suffrage, in 1918, Labour stood aside to give *Sinn Féin a free run to highlight popular support for independence. This decision certainly weakened Labour in a crucial period of its development. Serving as the opposition while anti-treaty Sinn Féin boycotted the new Parliament from 1922 to 1926, Labour aligned itself with *Fianna Fáil in the 1932 general election, identifying with that party's more *republican stance and its policy to end payment of land annuities to Britain. Splits and personality clashes in the *trade union movement often spilled over into the Labour Party, and the party itself actually split in 1943. Labour remained a largely conservative force during this period; its position to the "left" of Irish politics was modified by its large rural vote and the conservative policies of the trade union leadership.

In the post–World War II period, Labour's only way of holding political office was to form coalition governments with *Fine Gael (and other small parties) in 1948–51 and 1954–57. Labour moved to the left in the late 1960s, reflecting the political mood of the time. Their 1969 election result was, however, very disappointing and though they formed a coalition government with Fine Gael in 1973, it was from a position of relative weakness. The unpopularity of that government and its conservative economic policy in response to the oil crisis led to deep splits in the party. Labour served in government with Fine Gael again from 1981 to February 1982, and November 1982 to 1987. The splits in the party, between radicals and conservatives, were now very bitter and Labour was under severe electoral pressure from the left-wing Workers Party, especially in *Dublin and other urban centers. Labour's relationship with trade unions also reached a low point at this time. The unions criticized Labour's compromises in government and sought to influence public policy directly, rather than rely on the Labour Party.

A period in opposition allowed Labour to reestablish some credibility. In the general elections of 1992, Labour achieved its highest-ever vote, 19.3 percent—mostly new middle-class supporters who deserted Fine Gael and Fianna Fáil and voters unhappy with the government's performance. The decision to enter government with Fianna Fáil was bitterly opposed by some of the party leaders' closest advisors. Labour withdrew from this government in December 1994, in a clash with Fianna Fáil leader Albert *Reynolds, and negotiated a new coalition deal with Fine Gael—based on a program similar to that which they had had with Fianna Fáil. However, the change of government halfway through a Dáil (Parliament) (the first change of government without an election) was not popular and Labour was perceived to be arrogant and aloof in power. In the 1997 election, Labour's vote fell to just over 10 percent. The party's performance in 2002 was also a major disappointment as it failed to benefit by a shift to the left by a significant number of voters. Labour's vote fell by 2 percent while both the popular vote and number of seats won by Sinn Féin, the Green Party, small left parties, and protest candidates increased. J.D.

lace. See **textiles.**

Lalor, James Fintan (1807–49). Land reform agitator, revolutionary. Born at Tinakill, County *Laois, and educated at Carlow Lay College, Lalor became involved in agrarian reform in the 1840s. In a series of letters to the **Nation* in 1847, he proposed rent strikes and joint resistance to eviction. He took charge of the newspaper the *Irish Felon*, successor to the suppressed *United Irishman* following the arrest of John *Mitchel and John Martin. Lalor was arrested after the failed *Young Ireland rising in July 1848 and released fatally ill in November 1849. His influence in his own lifetime was limited, but his declaration in the *Nation* in 1847 that "the entire ownership of Ireland, moral and material . . . is vested of right in the people of Ireland" had enduring appeal to later radical leaders such as Michael *Davitt, James *Connolly, Patrick *Pearse, and Arthur *Griffith. C.D.

Lambeg drum. A handmade cylindrical drum, about three feet in diameter. Made from goatskin over an oak frame, the drum is played with canes. The first recorded use was in the eighteenth century. Associated with *Orange Order bands, Lambeg drums were used by different organizations, including the *Ancient Order of Hibernians. The decline of other band traditions means that the Lambeg drum is almost an exclusively Orange instrument today and features in a number of Orange Order events, including drumming competitions. T.C.

Lambay Island. Large island off the North *Dublin coast where St. *Colm Cille is said to have founded a church, of which no trace remains. Recent excavations have shown that the island was inhabited as far back as the Stone Age, when flint and stone for axes were quarried. Roman remains were uncovered not far from the harbor in 1927, suggesting the presence of traders or settlers from Britain in the first centuries after Christ. The island is privately owned, and not accessible to the public. P.H.

Land Act of 1870, the (the Landlord and Tenant [Ireland] Act). The first of a series of land acts passed between 1870 and 1909 that would radically change the relationship between *landlord and tenant and would alter the nature of land tenure in Ireland. After becoming prime minister in 1868, William *Gladstone, as part of his policy "to pacify Ireland," advocated a fairer relationship between landlord and tenant. His 1870 Act gave legal recognition to the *Ulster Custom (customary rights in Ulster that protected tenants from eviction—as long as they paid their rent—and allowed them to sell their farms) in the parts of Ireland where it had existed. Elsewhere, tenants were to be compensated for improvements made to farms and eviction for causes other than the nonpayment of rent. The Bright Clause within the act allowed tenants who wished to purchase their holdings to borrow two-thirds of the purchase price. While in no way radical, the act had huge symbolic significance in the sense that seemingly absolute landlord rights were now being questioned for the first time. P.E.

Land Act of 1881, the (the Land Law [Ireland] Act). William *Gladstone's second land act passed at the height of the *Land War. The act established the principle of dual ownership between *landlord and tenant. It granted all tenants (except those in arrears or leaseholders) the three Fs—fair rent, free sale, and fixity of tenure—for which the *Land League under the leadership of Michael *Davitt and Charles Stewart *Parnell had campaigned so vigorously since 1879. Rents were to be set by a *Land Commission and fixed for fifteen years, and tenants who wished to purchase their land could borrow 75 percent of the purchase price from the government. P.E.

Land Act of 1885, the (the Purchase of Land [Ireland] Act). Important Conservative act dealing with tenant proprietorship—also known as the Ashbourne Act. As part of Lord Salisbury's Conservative government's policy of Constructive *Unionism ("killing *home rule with kindness"), the act provided £5 million to allow tenants to borrow the entire purchase price of their holdings. Repayments were to be made over forty-nine years at 4 percent interest. Within three years, twenty-five thousand tenants purchased land and amending acts between 1887 and 1889 provided further funds for the scheme. In 1891, the Balfour Land Act set aside £33 million in government bonds to aid in tenant purchase, and established the Congested Districts Board to provide relief for distressed areas of the country. P.E.

Land Act of 1903, the (the Irish Land Act). One of the last in a series of land acts reforming land ownership in Ireland. This act (commonly known as the Wyndham Land Act) expanded on previous land legislation by providing £100 million in loans for land purchase. Repayments were to be made over sixty-nine years at 3.5 percent interest. The act, however, did not compel landlords to sell, although those who sold their entire estates were rewarded with a 12 percent bonus. This act, along with the 1909 Birrell Land Act (passed by the

Liberal government under Herbert *Asquith), effectively ended the transfer of land tenure begun in 1870. P.E.

Land Commission. Quasi-judicial body established to enforce the terms of William *Gladstone's *Land Act of 1881. The act, passed at the height of the *Land War, authorized the Land Commission to set fair rents that would be fixed for fifteen years. The commission could also purchase estates and make loans to tenants who wished to own their land. The commission was seen as an arbitrator whose work had a stabilizing influence following the recent turmoil of the Land War. Later acts (1903 and 1923) expanded its functions to include redistribution of land. P.E.

Land League, the. Agrarian protest organization that agitated for land reform during the Land War of 1879–82. The economic crisis of 1878–79 threatened Ireland's rural population with a disaster comparable to the Great *Famine. Following successful mass meetings at Irishtown and Westport, County *Mayo, in April and June, 1879, the Irish National Land League was formed in *Dublin, on October 21, by Michael *Davitt. Charles Stewart *Parnell, then a rising star in the *Home Rule party, agreed to act as president. The Land League vowed to ameliorate the drastic plight of the Irish peasantry by fighting against unjust rents and evictions and for tenant ownership.

Now for the first time *landlords faced an organized tenant class in what became one of the greatest mass movements in Irish history. The league advocated nonviolence, preferring, instead, the more effective methods of mass meetings and social ostracism, or boycotting. However, assaults on landlords and their agents, intimidation, and damage to property became widespread, and the Gladstone government quickly passed the Protection of Persons and Property Act in 1881.

The Land League vigorously campaigned for the three Fs—fair rent, free sale, and fixity of tenure—and Gladstone's 1881 *Land Act, a milestone in land legislation, granted these demands to most tenants. (The 130,000 tenants in arrears and 150,000 leaseholders were, however, excluded from the act.)

Parnell could neither accept nor reject the act without losing some degree of support. If he rejected the act, his moderate supporters would desert him, but on the other hand, acceptance of the act would alienate his more militant followers, including the *Fenians who demanded more radical reforms. His solution was to abstain from voting for the legislation in Parliament and to condemn the act when it was passed.

In October 1881, Parnell was arrested for making a provocative speech in *Wexford and imprisoned in *Kilmainham Gaol. From prison, Parnell issued a "No Rent Manifesto" and the authorities responded by suppressing the league on October 20, 1881.

Parnell was released in May 1882 under the terms of the Kilmainham Treaty: he promised to restore law and order in the country, and the government, in return, would relax coercion and extend the 1881 Land Act to include those previously omitted. Following his release, Parnell refused to revive the Land League and dismantled the Ladies Land League. He now considered the land question to be solved and began concentrating solely on the issue of national self-government. Davitt, the league's chief architect, one of whose main objectives was land nationalization, remained dissatisfied and disillusioned with Parnell. T.OCon., P.E.

Land War, the. See **Land League, the.**

landlords. Landlords in Ireland were a direct consequence of the *plantations and land confiscations of the sixteenth and seventeenth centuries. Most landlords were of Scottish or English descent and their acquisition of land had come at the expense of the native Irish and Old English. The English system of renting land to tenants was copied, but while this worked well in England, it proved very divisive in Ireland. Landlords here represented not only a different economic class and separate culture, but also a conquering, imperial presence. Increasing agrarian agitation marked the nineteenth century, and a series of *land acts passed between 1870 and 1909 radically altered the relationship between landlord and tenant so that by the turn of the twentieth century tenant proprietorship had become a reality. P.E.

Lane, Sir Hugh Percy (1875–1915). Art dealer and collector. Lane is best known for establishing *Dublin's Municipal Gallery of Modern Art in 1908, albeit in temporary accommodation. Born in *Cork, Lane trained as a painting restorer and art dealer in London, but returned to Ireland regularly to visit his aunt, Lady *Gregory. He commissioned John Butler *Yeats in 1901 to paint portraits of leading Irish citizens and organized an exhibition of Old Masters at the *Royal Hibernian Academy in 1902. A collection of Irish paintings he assembled for display at the St. Louis World Fair in 1903 was shown instead in London in 1904. After an unsuccessful campaign for a new permanent gallery of modern art on a bridge over the river in Dublin, he withdrew his gift of pictures from the Municipal Gallery and later bequeathed them to the National Gallery in London. He was director of the *National Gallery of Ireland from 1914, while continuing to live and work in London as an art dealer. After his death on the *Lusitania*, a codicil to his will bequeathing his French impressionist paintings to the City of Dublin was refused recognition by British courts. The Lane Bequest is at present still divided, with thirty-one paintings in the *Hugh Lane Municipal Gallery, Dublin, and the eight remaining paintings rotating every six years between London and Dublin. M.C.

Laois, County. Midland county in the province of *Leinster. Laois (covering 664 square miles) has a population of 58,732 (2002 census). Dominated by an expanse of agricultural land, the county is bound to the east by the Castlecomer plateau and the River Barrow, to the northwest by the Slieve Bloom Mountains, and to the west by the River Nore. Portlaoise, the county capital, is situated near the Rock of Dunamase, a natural outcrop topped by a fortress belonging to the twelfth-century king of Leinster, Dermot *MacMurrough. The town has one of Ireland's top security prisons. Other main market towns include Portarlington, Mountmellick, Abbeyleix, and Mountrath. Abbeyleix is designated a Heritage Town and is one of the finest examples of a planned-estate town in Ireland.

There are over one thousand historical sites and monuments in the county, some dating back over six thousand years. These include: *pre-Christian settlement at the Heath near Portlaoise; the fifth-century monastery founded by St. Comdhan at Killeshin; Norman and medieval *castles such as Ballaghmore Castle near Borris-in-Ossory and Lea Castle east of Portarlington; and Emo Court, a large neoclassical estate house, which was begun about 1790 by James *Gandon.

After the arrival of the Normans, the territory of the county was divided among seven clans. Following the fall of the Fitzgeralds of Kildare in 1534, the

O'Moores (and O'Connors of *Offaly) became sworn enemies of the English government and began raiding the *Pale. During the reign of King Edward VI, both families were driven from their land and under the reign of Queen Mary, Laois became known as Queens County and the town of Portlaoise was established as the Fort of Maryborough. British *plantation failed in the sixteenth century due to bad planning and fierce Gaelic resistance. The eighteenth century, however, was a period of colonial consolidation, with Maryborough growing as an administrative center. The population was halved from 159,930 (1841) to 73,124 (1881) because of the *Famine. In 1920, Maryborough became Portlaoise and the county was renamed Laois at the end of the *War of Independence. During the twentieth century, the county underwent considerable *economic development, based on industrialization and the modernization of *agriculture. Today, nearly half of the county's workforce is engaged in services, 15 percent in industry, and 22 percent in agriculture. P.E.

Larkin, James (1876–1947). *Trade union leader, politician. Born in Liverpool to Irish parents, Larkin was a dock worker who embraced *socialism. In 1907, he was sent to *Belfast to organize the National Union of Dock Labourers. A charismatic leader, Larkin reinvigorated the dockers' union and tried to reduce sectarian divisions. After an employers' lockout, he organized a dockers' and carters' strike which lasted from May to November 1907. The strike was supported in other towns and even the RIC (*Royal Irish Constabulary) mutinied in sympathy. Troops were brought in, and after two deaths during a riot, the union's leadership called off the strike.

Convinced that Ireland needed its own labor movement, Larkin helped to found the Irish Transport and General Workers Union (ITGWU) in 1909. Along with James *Connolly, he established the Irish *Labour Party with the support of the Irish Congress of Trade Unions in 1912. He led the workers during the Dublin Lockout of 1913, which brought him into conflict with employers and some *Catholic Church leaders.

Disillusioned, he went to the United States in 1914. In 1919, he was charged with criminal anarchy for his involvement with the fledgling American *Communist Party, and after a three-week trial, he was sentenced to five to ten years imprisonment. Through the intervention of liberal Democrat *New York Governor Alfred E. Smith, Larkin was released from prison in 1923. He returned to Ireland, where the trade union movement was now one hundred thousand strong and under new leadership. Unable to play a dominant role, Larkin broke away and followed his own militant path. He joined the Labour Party and was elected as a TD (Teachta Dála; member of Parliament) in 1943, which led to a split with the ITGWU. Larkin's legacy is the development of organized trade unionism in Ireland. T.C.

Larne Gun Running (1914). *Unionist arms smuggling event. Alarmed at the introduction of a *home rule bill, *Ulster unionists formed the *Ulster Volunteer Force (UVF). In order to arm the UVF, on April 24–25, 1914, twenty-five thousand rifles and three million rounds of ammunition were smuggled by boat from Germany by F. H. Crawford into Larne, County *Antrim. The boats were met by units of the UVF and the arms were distributed throughout Ulster. The *police did not interfere. The arms' military value was questionable, but the political significance was immense. It put pressure on the British government and led *nationalists to arm themselves. T.C.

La Tène. The art style of the *Celts, named after a site in Switzerland. Consisting of curvilinear and trumpet patterns, spirals, palmettes, and other motifs derived from Greek designs, La Tène art developed in central Europe and reached Ireland sometime after 300 B.C. Fine examples are found on the Turoe Stone (County *Galway), and the Broighter torc in the National Museum. La Tène is one of the basic styles in early *Christian Irish art. P.H.

Lavery, John (1856–1941). Portrait painter. Born in *Belfast, Lavery was trained in Scotland and France, and influenced by Bastien-Lepage, Whistler, and Velázquez. His painting of Queen Victoria's state visit to Glasgow in 1888 brought many portrait commissions. He lived in London and was knighted in 1918 for his work as a war artist. He is mainly represented at the *Hugh Lane Municipal Gallery, where his painting of Michael *Collins lying in state, *Love of Ireland*, 1922, can be viewed. The *National Gallery of Ireland and *Ulster Museum hold many of his works, including portraits of his wife, Lady Hazel Lavery. She was the model for the figure on the original Irish £1 note, which Lavery designed. M.C.

Lavin, Mary (1912–96). Writer. Born in Massachusetts, US, Lavin returned to Ireland at the age of ten. Her first collection of short stories, *Tales from Bective Bridge*, was published in 1942. Although she also wrote novels, including *The House in Clewe Street* (1945) and *Mary O'Grady* (1950), it was as a short story writer that she was most acclaimed. These stories, including the collections *The Long Age and Other Stories* (1944) and *In the Middle of the Fields* (1967), are largely concerned with the intimate lives of middle-class Irish families, often her own family and friends. Many of her stories appeared in the *New Yorker*, as did those of her friend Frank *O'Connor. Her fiction shows her acute powers of observation and keen insights into human nature. A.S.

law and the legal system. The law in Ireland is a common law system derived from English law. Since independence in 1922, Ireland's legal system has developed its own framework and most recently has been influenced by the laws of the *European Union (EU).

In ancient times, when Ireland was made up of a system of tribal families and provincial chiefs, a sophisticated indigenous system of *brehon law developed. This system was based on custom, and the law was administered by judges who were called brehons. The oldest remaining brehon texts are from the seventh and eighth centuries, which show a pronounced Christian influence on the older brehon code. The origin of modern Ireland's legal system dates to the *Anglo-Norman invasion in 1169. Common law had been established in England by the Normans after their conquest of England in 1066. In 1171, King *Henry II landed in *Waterford and formed the King's Council to administer English law in Ireland in his absence. Originally, the council consisted of two departments, the Exchequer, headed by the treasurer, and the Chancery, headed by the chancellor, the king's chief advisor. In 1216, the Magna Carta was issued in Ireland. English common law began to prevail in Ireland from 1331, when King Edward III issued a writ giving the people of Ireland the same status at law as the English. As in England and Wales, judges traveled to different parts of Ireland to administer the king's law. In the beginning, these judges applied local customary laws, as the brehons had, but over time a uniform system emerged.

As the common law system developed, rules became rigid, and this "Black Letter" law system, emphasizing procedure over substance, often led to unfairness. Many petitioned the king to use his prerogative power to remedy unfair legal results, giving rise to the Law of Equity. The Courts of Equity worked on a basis of fairness and rivaled the Common Law Courts. In 1615, the king decreed that in a case of conflict between the two systems, equity should prevail. A system of precedent also developed, whereby previous decisions became binding on future decisions of the courts. Eventually, the two systems fused and the current Irish court system was established by the Judicature (Ireland) Act of 1877. Equity still prevails over the common law.

After the Act of *Union (1800) dissolved the native Irish *Parliament, all Irish laws were enacted from Westminster in London. The *Anglo-Irish Treaty (1921) established the *Irish Free State, which had legislative independence from Britain. The new Irish court system now had dominion status, with an ultimate appeal to the Privy Council in London (or the House of Lords, the highest court of appeal in England for the *Commonwealth countries). The Irish Free State adopted a Constitution in 1922, but the existing law remained in full force and effect, unless changed by the Constitution. The 1922 Constitution prescribed a tripartite separation of powers to the executive, the legislature, and the judiciary. The Executive Council, a cabinet elected by the legislature, consisted of the king of England and the two houses of the *Oireachtas (Parliament), the *Dáil (House of Representatives), and the *Seanad (Senate).

The Irish *Constitution of 1937 defined a new legal order. Ireland became a *republic in all but name and this document now forms the basis of Ireland's legal system. Like the 1922 document, the Constitution of 1937 outlined the principal institutions of state and certain fundamental individual rights. The 1937 Constitution revised the courts system: it designated the Supreme Court and High Court as the highest constitutional courts in Ireland, and also recognized courts of "Local and Limited Jurisdiction."

Today, law in Ireland is divided into civil and criminal areas. Civil law deals with private relationships and the settling of disputes between civilians, and between individuals and the state. The responsibility is on the injured party to initiate proceedings. Criminal law deals with public wrong. The office of the Director of Public Prosecutions generally prosecutes these cases on behalf of the state and victims are not directly involved in the process except as witnesses. As in other common law countries, an accused person is presumed innocent until proven guilty beyond reasonable doubt.

The Irish courts are divided into four major divisions. In civil cases smaller claims are dealt with by the District Court, larger claims by the Circuit Court, and the High Court has unlimited jurisdiction. The Supreme Court is the ultimate court of appeal.

In criminal law, the District Court deals with summary offenses (misdemeanors) with the power of sentence up to two years imprisonment. The Circuit Court deals with indictable offenses (felonies), except murder and rape, which are heard by the Central Criminal Court. The Circuit Court and the Central Criminal Court are conducted before judge and jury. Appeals are dealt with by the Court of Criminal Appeal, or, when a point of law is involved, by the Supreme Court. There is also a Special Criminal Court for terrorist offenses, which has no jury.

The Supreme Court consists of a chief justice and eight judges. Cases are decided by a panel of three or five judges. The Supreme Court has a consultative as well as an appellate jurisdiction. The president may refer proposed legislation to the Supreme Court to test that legislation's constitutionality and the High Court and Circuit Court may consult the Supreme Court on a point of law that may arise throughout a trial.

The legal profession in Ireland consists of solicitors and barristers, a division inherited from the English system. In most cases, a person must first consult a solicitor for legal advice. Generally, barristers are not permitted to deal directly with the public. Usually, solicitors deal with noncontentious work such as the transfer of property, the making of wills, the administration of estates, the formation of companies, and the preparation of cases for court. Solicitors advocate in the District Court and to a growing extent in the Circuit and High Court. Barristers specialize in litigation and usually concentrate in a specific area. They generally practice in the Circuit Court, High Court, and Supreme Court. Barristers continue to wear wigs and gowns in court, although this mandatory requirement was abolished in 1995. In 2000, Ireland had 5,500 solicitors and 1,300 barristers, a dramatic increase over the past twenty years. To become a solicitor or barrister in Ireland one studies law at university for three to four years as an undergraduate. University law graduates interested in becoming barristers or solicitors engage in a training program of approximately three years involving both practical experience and academic work (either at the Honourable Society of Kings Inns or the Law Society of Ireland, respectively). A non–law graduate can independently prepare for entrance exams to the Law Society of Ireland to become a solicitor, or attend a Diploma Course organized by the Honourable Society of Kings Inns to become a barrister. T.O.C.

Leabhar na hUidhre. The oldest surviving *manuscript written entirely in Irish. It gets its name "The Book of the Dun Cow" because, in the late Middle Ages, its vellum was thought to have come from a grayish-brown cow owned by St. Ciarán, the sixth-century founder of the monastery at *Clonmacnoise, County *Offaly. Most of the manuscript was written there by two monks, one of whom was killed in 1106. It contains the oldest copy of the famous epic *Tain Bó Cuailnge (The Cattle Raid of Cooley)*, and other stories from the Ulster Cycle of Tales (e.g., *The Destruction of Da Derga's Hostel*), as well as historical and religious tracts. Used as a ransom payment for a prince in 1359, it is now in the library of the *Royal Irish Academy. P.H.

Le Brocquy, Louis (1916–). Painter. Le Brocquy, probably Ireland's most distinguished living painter, was born in *Dublin. He studied chemistry before studying art in European museums, where he was especially impressed by the precision of tonal values of Spanish painting. In 1943, a year after the *Royal Hibernian Academy rejected his painting *The Spanish Shawl*, Le Brocquy helped organize the *Irish Exhibition of Living Art (IELA). His cubist-influenced *Travelling People*, 1946, and *Tinkers Resting*, 1946 (Tate Gallery) preceded a series of gray isolated figures as in *The Family*, 1951 (*National Gallery of Ireland), which won a major award at the Venice Biennale in 1956. He moved to London in 1946 and to France in 1958, where he began to produce white torso paintings. Le Brocquy's interest in Polynesian and *Celtic head cults, combined with his early employment as a scientific illustrator, helped produce an obsessive series of human heads. From 1964, he painted images of anonymous ancestral heads, such as *Reconstructed Head of an Irish Martyr*, 1967 (Smithsonian Institution), which developed in 1975 to monochromatic images of heads of writers and painters such as W. B. *Yeats, Samuel *Beckett, James *Joyce, and Francis *Bacon, among others. Le Brocquy has also painted watercolor landscapes, illustrated books, and designed tapestries, and he is widely represented in public and private collections. Since 1996, he has returned to painting more corporal images. In 2000, he returned to live and work in Ireland. M.C.

Lecky, William Edward (1838–1903). Historian. A graduate of Trinity College, Dublin, Lecky carried out extensive research in Irish archives for his monumental *History of England in the Eighteenth Century*. The last five volumes were devoted to Ireland and refuted James Anthony Froude's negative analysis of Irish culture and society. As Liberal *Unionist MP (member of Parliament) for Dublin University (1895–1902), Lecky supported the establishment of a *Catholic *university in Ireland but was firmly opposed to *home rule. He was awarded the Order of Merit in 1902. S.A.B.

Ledwidge, Francis (1887–1917). Poet. Born in Slane, County *Meath, and educated at the local national school, Ledwidge worked as a miner and road maker. His early poems appeared in the *Drogheda Independent* and gained the attention of Lord Dunsany, who organized the publication of his first collection, *Songs of the Fields* (1915). Ledwidge joined the British army at the outbreak of *World War I. He survived the Gallipoli landing but was killed in Flanders in 1917. *Complete Poems* was published in 1919. Ledwidge's tragic life experiences—a failed romance, the trauma of World War I, and the execution of friends and fellow poets after the *Easter Rising of 1916—added to the melancholy of his poetry, which remained centered on the immediate beauty of the local and the pastoral. C.D.

Le Fanu, (Joseph) Sheridan (1814–73). Novelist and short story writer. Born in *Dublin and descended both from *Huguenot stock and the family of Richard Brinsley *Sheridan, Le Fanu is best known for his ghost stories and Gothic novels. His most famous novel is *Uncle Silas* (1865), but his international reputation is based on such stories as "Green Tea" (1869) and "Carmilla" (1872). James *Joyce draws on Le Fanu's *The House by the Churchyard* (1863) in *Finnegans Wake*. G.OB.

Leinster. One of the four provinces of Ireland. The province, which covers an area of 7,645 square miles, has a population of 2,105, 449 (2002 census). Leinster consists of the counties *Carlow, *Dublin, *Kildare, *Kilkenny, *Laois, *Longford, *Louth, *Meath, *Offaly, *Westmeath, *Wexford, and *Wicklow. The name derives from *Laighan*, which in ancient Ireland was the territory of the Laigini, a powerful tribe in *pre-Christian Ireland. In the twelfth century, the Leinster King Dermot *MacMurrough sought help from the English King *Henry II to regain his kingship, initiating the *Anglo-Norman Conquest. Ireland's capital, the city of *Dublin, is on the Irish Sea, in the eastern part of the province. J.OM.

Leinster, Book of. One of the three great collections (including *Leabhar na hUihre [The Book of the Dun Cow] and MS. Rawlinson B.502, the latter in the Bodleian Library in Oxford) of Old Irish poems, tales, histories, and genealogies of kings and *saints. Housed in the Library of Trinity College, Dublin, the Book of Leinster (or Lebor na Nuachongbhála) was compiled or transcribed by a bishop of Kildare at the behest of Dermot *MacMurrough's tutor in the mid-twelfth century. P.H.

Leinster House. Palladian mansion. Designed by Richard Cassels (1690–1751) in 1745 for James FitzGerald, Earl of Kildare (1722–73), this mansion stimulated the development of Merrion Square as the center of fashionable society in *Dublin. Its design is thought to have influenced Irish architect James *Hoban, who designed the White House in Washington DC. The mansion was bought by the *Royal Dublin Society in 1815 and then purchased by the Irish government in 1925 to accommodate both houses of the Irish *Parliament (the *Dáil and the *Seanad). Leinster House remains the center of Irish government and provides a focal point for several of Ireland's cultural institutions. S.A.B.

Leitrim, County. Maritime county in the province of *Connacht. Leitrim, with an area of 613 square miles, has the smallest population, 25,815 (as per 2002 census, which shows the first increase in the county's population since record keeping began). Historically, the reason for so few inhabitants was that the county's poorly drained land forced many to leave in search of a better living elsewhere. Because of this, the county's landscape, which is divided into two separate sections north and south of Lough Allen, remains unspoiled and majestic. The name comes from *Liath Druim*, the gray ridge, suggesting the hilly terrain that takes up much of the county. Interspersed, however, are a number of coarse angling lakes (Melvin, Macnean, Allen, and Gill), which it shares with *Roscommon, *Fermanagh, and *Sligo.

Traditionally, Leitrim was the territory of the O'Rourkes of Breifne, but the areas around the eastern end of Lough Gill were taken over by the English Jacobean planters in the early seventeenth century. An English settler built Parke's Castle around 1620 on Lough Gill. Excavations in the 1980s showed this to be the site of the home of Brian, one of the last O'Rourke chieftains.

Leitrim has the shortest coastline of any Irish maritime county, a mere three miles near Tullaghan, where it is wedged in between Sligo and *Donegal. Its main boating activity is based in the fine inland marina at Carrick-on-Shannon, the county capital. Leitrim's second major town is Manorhamilton. Dromahair has a seventeenth-century *castle and the fine Franciscan friary of Creevelea, one of the last houses of the order to be founded before the *Reformation. The accomplished stained glass artist Wilhelmina Geddes (1887–1955) was a native of Drumreilly, and the writer most associated with the county is John *McGahern who, though born in *Dublin, has made his home on a farm near Fenagh. P.H.

Lemass, Seán (1899–1971). Irish revolutionary, politician, and *Taoiseach (prime minister), 1959–66. Born in *Dublin, Lemass joined the Irish *Volunteers at the age of fifteen and served under Éamon *de Valera during the *Easter Rising of 1916. He would become one of de Valera's lifelong supporters. In the *Irish War of Independence (1919–21), Lemass was an officer in the *Irish Republican Army (IRA) but spent much of the conflict in prison. During the *Irish Civil War, he followed de Valera into the *republican anti-treaty camp. In 1924, he was elected *Sinn Féin TD (Teachta Dála; member of Parliament) for South Dublin but refused to take his seat in the *Free State Dáil (in keeping with his party's policy of abstentionism).

When de Valera broke with Sinn Féin in 1926, Lemass helped him found the *Fianna Fáil party. The following year, Lemass entered the Dáil, and in 1932, when Fianna Fáil took power, Lemass became de Valera's minister for industry and commerce. He held that position until 1940, when he became minister for supplies, an important and powerful post, considering the wartime shortages facing neutral Ireland during World War II.

Though the youngest minister in the first

Fianna Fáil government, Lemass became one of the most influential and was chosen as de Valera's Tánaiste (deputy prime minister) in 1945–48, 1951–54, and again in 1957–59. When de Valera resigned as Taoiseach and leader of Fianna Fáil to run for president of Ireland in 1959, Lemass succeeded him in both positions.

As Taoiseach, one of Lemass's chief goals was to modernize Ireland's economy. Under his leadership, Fianna Fáil abandoned its traditional protectionism and adopted free trade policies. This more outward-looking approach to Irish policymaking is illustrated by two of Lemass's best-known initiatives: Ireland's bid for membership in the European Economic Community (EEC)—now the *European Union—in 1961; and his 1965 meetings with *Northern Ireland's Prime Minister Terence *O'Neill (the first such meetings any Irish head of government had held with his Northern counterpart since 1925). Although Ireland's initial EEC application was unsuccessful, the country's eventual entry into the community in 1973 is often credited to Lemass's overhaul of the Irish *economy during the 1960s. Due largely to his promotion of economic planning and trade liberalization, Irish economic growth during the decade was phenomenal: the standard of living rose by 50 percent, which helped lead to a population increase of one hundred thousand between 1961 and 1971, the highest growth level recorded since the state was founded. Lemass's pragmatic leadership and the success of the economy during his years in power also helped modernize Irish politics, as the nation's *political parties began to focus increasingly on economic and social issues and to place less emphasis on Civil War antagonisms.

Due to deteriorating health, Lemass resigned as Taoiseach and Fianna Fáil leader in 1966. He was succeeded by Jack *Lynch. T.D.

Leonard, Hugh (1926–). Playwright, pseudonym of John Keyes Byrne. Born in Dalkey, County *Dublin, and educated at Presentation College, Dún Laoghaire, Leonard worked for the *Land Commission, 1945–59. Later, he worked as script editor for Granada Television and the *Abbey Theatre. The play *Da* (1973), a portrayal of an uneasy son and father relationship, is arguably his masterpiece and has enjoyed many revivals. It received a Tony Award in 1978 and was filmed in 1988 by Matt Clark, starring Martin Sheen. *A Life* (1980), a play that developed the autobiographical theme of *Da*, was also produced on Broadway. Other plays, such as *The Patrick Pearse Motel* (1971) and *Suburb of Babylon* (1983), satirized contemporary Irish life. Television scripts include *Strumpet City* (1979), *The Irish RM* (1985), *Troubles* (1987), and *Parnell and the Englishwoman* (1988). Leonard has also written two volumes of autobiography, a memoir, *Rover and Other Cats* (1990), and three novels, *The Off-shore Island* (1993), *Parnell and the Englishwoman* (1993), and *A Wild People* (2002). C.D.

limerick. A short, humorous, and often nonsensical verse of five lines that have a particular pattern of rhyme (*aabba*) and rhythm. Lines 1, 2, and 5 are of three feet and rhyme, and lines 3 and 4 are of two feet and rhyme. The rhythm is anapestic. Generally, a person or situation is being lampooned, often in a bawdy or irreverent way. How this poetic form originated and how it came to be named after *Limerick, the city and county in Ireland, remains a mystery. Local lore has it that the eighteenth-century Irish poet and Limerick native Andreas McGrath composed in this five-line meter, which was based on an ancient Irish verse form. Another theory is that the limerick was first invented in the eighteenth century by a Limerick student at Trinity College who composed these witty ditties in classical Greek and Latin

King John's Castle, Limerick City

to poke fun at his fellow students and teachers. The practice became a fad on campus and eventually limericks were being composed in English also. The limerick is also said to have originated from a folk song in which the refrain is "Will you come up to Limerick?" as each listener contributed an impromptu verse. Supposedly, in the eighteenth century, members of the Irish Brigade returning from France brought back this song. Edward Lear popularized this form of light verse with the publication of his *Book of Nonsense* in 1846. L.R., J.OM.

Limerick, County. Inland county in the province of *Munster. The county, 1,064 square miles, has a population of 175,529 (2002 census). Very fertile areas of the county, especially in the east and center, are part of the "Golden Vale," where dairy farming thrives. The *Shannon forms the northern border of County Limerick for a total of forty-eight miles, almost until the river reaches the Atlantic Ocean. The Shannon was a commercial waterway used by travelers and traders, who probably brought the many gold objects dating from the Late Bronze Age, around 700 B.C., that have been discovered throughout the county.

Cnoc Fírinne and the Knockainey hills are ancient sites once associated with the *Celtic otherworld. The Benedictine Abbey of Glenstal on the slopes of the Slieve Felim hills is one of the most vibrant spiritual centers in Ireland today. Limerick City is the largest urban area in the midwestern region, with a population of 54,058. The *Vikings founded Limerick City in a sheltered position at the top of the Shannon estuary in 922 and were conquered in 967 by the O'Brien King of Munster, Brian *Boru and his brother. In the thirteenth century, Limerick City fell to the *Anglo-Normans. The Normans also expelled the O'Donovan chieftains southward to *Cork and *Kerry, allowing the Norman FitzGeralds to take over the lands west of the city, where they built *castles at Adare, Carrigogunnel, Askeaton, Shanid, Glin, and Newcastle West. Limerick has more surviving examples of ceremonial halls (in some of these castles) than any other county. In 1691, Limerick City was under siege and witnessed the culmination of the campaign of King *William of Orange to end the Stuart monarchy. King *James II had fled to *France after the Battle of the *Boyne a year before, and the Treaty of *Limerick in 1691 marked the end of *Catholic Ireland's alliance with the *Jacobean cause.

In the eighteenth century, the Croom area of the river Maigue became a center for poets writing in Gaelic including, among others, the Clare-born Brian *Merriman, who wrote the *Midnight Court*. English-language authors associated with Limerick include Gerald *Griffin, Kate *O'Brien, Frank *McCourt, poet Aubrey *de Vere, and his bilingual successor Michael *Hartnett. Artists include Dermod O'Brien and Seán *Keating. The *Hunt Museum in Limerick City has one of the finest art collections anywhere in the country and Limerick boasts one of the best art colleges in Ireland.

The University of Limerick, with a heavy emphasis on *technology, has had significant impact on the city's economic and cultural life. The famous Ardagh Chalice, now in the *National Museum in Dublin, was found in County Limerick, not far south of Foynes. The latter, which served as a transatlantic seaplane base in the 1930s and 1940s, is still a small but busy port. Adare is a particularly picturesque village with thatched cottages and a Tudor-style manor house (now a hotel). The *Young Irelander William Smith *O'Brien, and various members of the O'Malley clan, are among the best-known political names associated with Limerick history. Éamon *de Valera, though born in *New York, spent his childhood in Bruree, a village in the southern part of the county. Limerick City was famous for its hams and those famous five-line verses (*limericks), sometimes nonsensical but always funny, whose origin and connection with Limerick, city or county, has yet to be satisfactorily explained. P.H.

Limerick, Treaty of (October 3, 1691). Treaty ending the Williamite War. Signed by the *Jacobite and Williamite commanders at the end of the Siege of Limerick, the treaty ended the war between *James II and *William III. In exchange for surrendering, the Jacobites were granted free passage for themselves and their families to France. Those who remained were granted limited rights (similar to those enjoyed by *Catholics under Charles II). The *Protestants who dominated *Parliament in *Dublin, however, reneged on these concessions, and soon began to enact the *Penal Laws. The *Wild Geese felt betrayed and took as their battle cry, "Remember Limerick and the treachery of the English." T.C.

Linehan, Rosaleen (1937–). Actress. Born in *Dublin, Linehan studied at University College, Dublin, and first became known as a comedienne in revues and on *radio and *television. Her diverse career includes performances in plays by George Bernard *Shaw, Oscar *Wilde, Seán *O'Casey, Oliver *Goldsmith, and Shakespeare. In 1989, she was nominated for a Tony Award for her performance on Broadway in Brian *Friel's *Dancing at Lughnasa*. Her one-woman show *Mother of All the Behans* played in England, Scotland, France, and New York. In 1997, she gave a memorable performance as Winnie in Samuel *Beckett's *Happy Days* at the Lincoln Center Festival. Other roles include Lady Bracknell in Wilde's *The Importance of Being Earnest* at the *Abbey Theatre, Mommo in Tom *Murphy's *Bailegangaire* at the Royal Court Theatre, Madam Arcati in Noel Coward's *Blithe Spirit* at the Guthrie Theater in Minneapolis, and Mary Tyrone in Eugene O'Neill's *Long Day's Journey into Night* at the *Gate Theatre. She has also appeared in many movies, including the film of *Happy Days*. L.R.

linen. See **textiles.**

literature in English. The beginning of Irish literature in English is often dated to the sixteenth century when the Tudor re-conquest of Ireland brought about a flowering of writing in English. However, a number of English works survive from the Middle Ages. Friar Michael of *Kildare (born c.1280) is the first known English-language poet in Ireland. He is included in an important collection of Irish material known as Harley 913 (c.1330). The collection also contains the celebrated anonymous *Hiberno-English burlesque fantasy *The Land of Cokaygne*. One of the most interesting and self-conscious users of an "Old English" form of the language in the Elizabethan age was Richard Stanihurst (1547–1618), who contributed a section on Ireland to Holinshed's *Chronicles* (1577) and translated the first four books of Virgil's *Aeneid* (1582).

The term *Anglo-Irish* to describe literature in Ireland, while controversial, carries a special significance in the eighteenth and nineteenth centuries, not only because until the early twentieth century most Irish writers of English were of ascendancy background, but also because many of them dealt with the colonial experience of divided identity. Many of the most distinguished "English" writers of the eighteenth century were in fact either of Irish birth or lived a significant part of their lives in Ireland. Of these, Jonathan *Swift (1667–1745) and Oliver *Goldsmith (1728–74) are the best known. Swift's "savage indignation" at the grossness of "that animal called man" in his great satires *A Tale of a Tub* and *Gulliver's Travels* reflects his experience of being caught between two identities as well as his rage at the gross injustice of English treatment of both the native and Anglo-Irish. However, to adapt the Duke of Wellington's notorious retort to the suggestion that his Irish birth made him an Irishman ("being born in a stable does not make one a horse"), being born in Ireland does not necessarily make one an Irish writer. Many of those who were born there—such as Sir Richard Steele (1672–1729), George *Farquhar (1677–1707), and Laurence *Sterne (1713–68)—show little detectable influence of Ireland in their art. Conversely, neither Richard Edgeworth (1744–1817) nor his daughter Maria *Edgeworth (1767–1849) were born in Ireland, but Maria is universally regarded as a major Irish writer. While her *Castle Rackrent* (1800) is by no means the first Irish novel, as is often claimed, it is the first to rank among the finest European novels of its time. *The History of Jack Connor* (1752) by William Chaigneau (1709–81) was the first novel to address the question of Irish identity, and it was followed by numerous novels by Thomas Amory (c.1691–1788), Henry Brooke (1703–83), Charles Johnstone (1719–1800), Frances Sheridan (1724–66), and many others. The first half of the nineteenth century produced a large body of Irish fiction, including works by Lady *Morgan (1775–1859), William *Carleton (1794–1869), Gerald *Griffin (1803–40), and Sheridan *Le Fanu (1814–73).

Everything that changed the Western world between 1776 and the 1830s also changed Ireland and Irish culture: revolutionary *republicanism, *nationalism, romanticism, the beginning of industrialism. Specifically, the *Rebellion of 1798, and the new forms of political consciousness brought by it, together with the effects of the Act of *Union, created

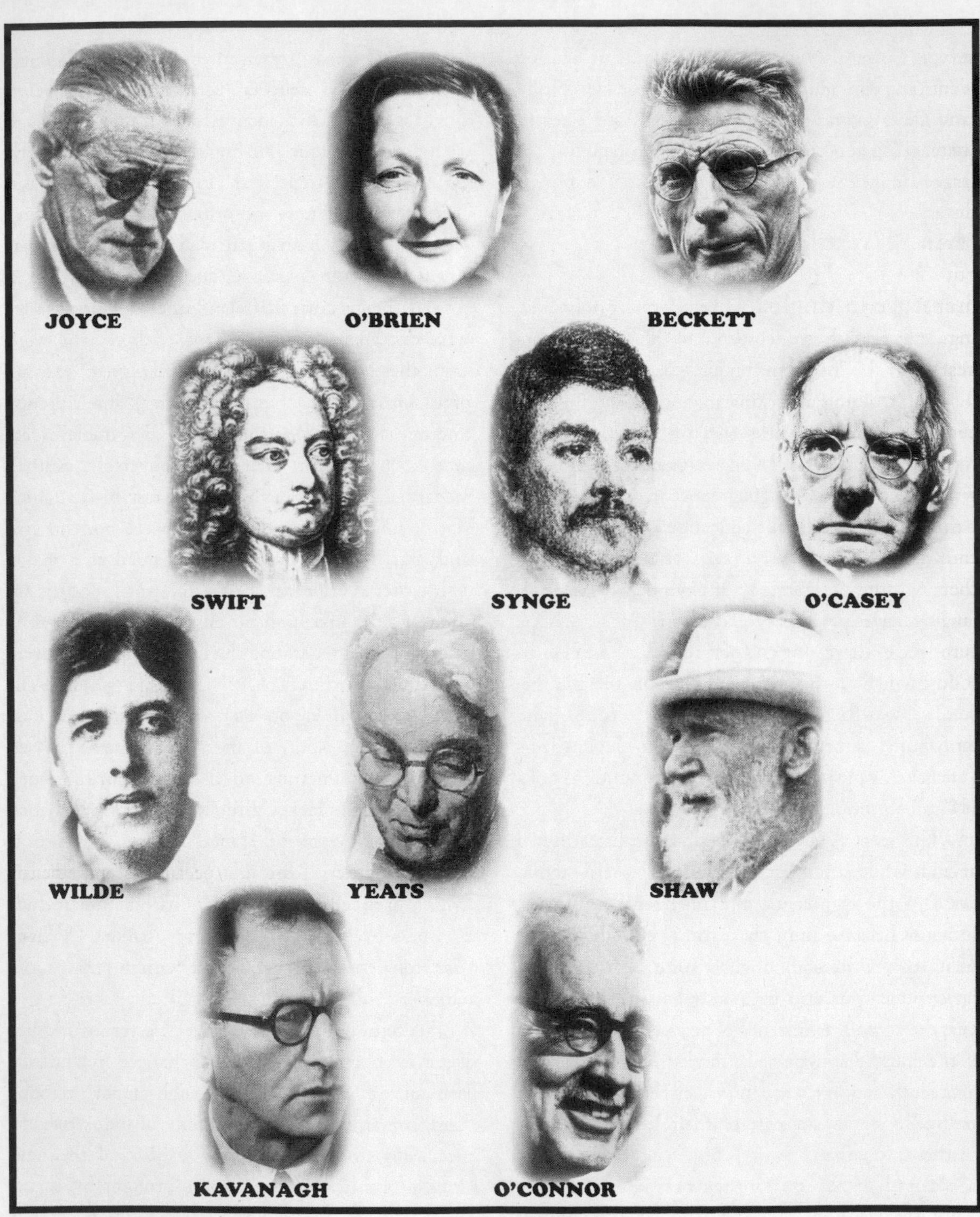

From the Literary Map of Ireland (Tourism Ireland)

new and sharper divisions and competing senses of identity. Sentimental and romantic images of Ireland's past, especially in the poetry and songs of Irish writer Thomas *Moore (1779–1852), appealed to a large European audience. Later writers and critics distanced themselves from "the sweetest lyrist of [Ireland's] saddest wrong" as Shelley called him, but Moore's *The Irish Melodies* and *National Airs* remained immensely influential on Irish culture, writing, and political consciousness for over a hundred years.

The chief literary enterprise of the nineteenth century, "inventing Ireland," is primarily attributed to the *Literary Revival, which began in the 1890s, with W. B. *Yeats (1865–1939) playing a prominent part. A cultural revival had, however, started much earlier. Beginning in the late eighteenth century, there was a concerted effort to preserve the *Irish language and *music, and to rediscover Irish literature, history, and *folklore. Yeats acknowledged his indebtedness to many of these precursors, especially to Carleton, James Clarence *Mangan (1803–49), Sir Samuel *Ferguson (1810–86), and Douglas *Hyde (1860–49). By the time Lady Augusta *Gregory (1852–1932), John Millington *Synge (1871–1909), and others helped Yeats launch the Irish Literary Theatre (which became the *Abbey Theatre in 1904), there were many competing and overlapping forms of Irish nationalism in place, some focused on political self-determination, some on cultural renewal, and some on the restoration of the Irish language. Although Patrick *Kavanagh's dismissal of the Literary Revival as "a thoroughgoing English-bred lie" is unfair, the revival was overwhelmingly Anglo-Irish in personnel and taste, and had a tense relationship with more *Catholic and politically singleminded movements such as *Sinn Féin. During the late nineteenth and early twentieth century, novels such as *Knocknagow* by Charles *Kickham (1828–82), and those of Canon Patrick Sheehan (1852–1913), which addressed political and social themes from nationalist and Catholic perspectives, enjoyed a large popular readership both within Ireland and among Irish emigrants.

As in the eighteenth century, many Anglo-Irish writers *emigrated to London, and some of the chief figures in late-nineteenth-century English literature were Irish-born, notably Oscar *Wilde (1856–1900) and George Bernard *Shaw (1856–1950), who not only continued the tradition of Irish dominance in drama that had started in the early eighteenth century, but were consciously Irish in maintaining a critical perspective on English culture. Another Irish figure in the London literary scene was novelist Bram *Stoker (1847–1912). Stoker, who was Henry Irving's theatrical agent, is best known for his famous novel *Dracula* (1897), which is deeply indebted to the tradition of Irish Gothic fiction, especially to Le Fanu's vampire tale "Carmilla" (1872). One of the most popular, prolific, and influential figures in nineteenth-century *theater was Dion *Boucicault (1820–90), whose Irish plays (especially *The Colleen Bawn*, 1860), were immensely successful not only in Ireland, but in London and America.

The Literary Revival, especially as embodied in the work of Yeats and Synge, has continued to enjoy esteem and influence until the present, but, since Irish independence in 1922, literature in English can hardly be called "Anglo-Irish." There is, however, a distinguished subcurrent of Anglo-Irish writing, which includes the novelists Elizabeth *Bowen (1900–73), Molly Keane (1905–96), and William *Trevor (b. 1928), the great playwright Samuel *Beckett, the poet Richard Murphy (b. 1927), and the essayist Hubert *Butler (1900–90). The main tradition of twentieth-century Irish literature derives from the extraordinary work of James *Joyce (1882–1941), and from the 1920s until the 1960s constituted a kind of loyal opposition to the dominant *Catholic puritanism and philistinism of the Irish *Free State (later the *Republic of Ireland). The leading writers in this period were Liam *O'Flaherty (1896–1984), Seán *Ó Faoláin, (1900–90), Frank *O'Connor (1903–66), Patrick Kavanagh (1904–67), Flann *O'Brien (1911–66), Brendan *Behan (1923–64), and outstanding women such as Kate *O'Brien (1897–1974), Mary *Lavin (1912–96), and Edna *O'Brien (b. 1930).

The past thirty years have seen the flowering of a very diverse body of literature both in the Republic and in *Northern Ireland. While there are many exceptions to the generalization, those from the South increasingly tend (somewhat in the spirit of Joyce), to see themselves as citizens of the international republic of letters, while those in the North are understandably concerned with the *Troubles and with conflicting forms of Irish identity. Ireland has four Nobel Prize winners for literature (George Bernard Shaw, W. B. Yeats, Samuel Beckett, and Seamus *Heaney). The remarkable number of internationally acclaimed living poets (Thomas *Kinsella, John *Montague, Eavan *Boland, Paul *Muldoon, and Seamus Heaney), dramatists (Brian *Friel, Tom *Murphy, and Sebastian *Barry), and writers of fiction (John *Banville, John *McGahern, Roddy *Doyle) enables contemporary Ireland to exert an influence on the world far in excess of its size or political power. J.McD.

literature in Irish. Composition of literary material, particularly myth, saga, and poetry goes back to the *prehistoric period in Irish, making Irish literature the oldest continuing tradition in Western Europe. Many of the sagas and some of the poetry reflect a society that can be dated to the first or second centuries B.C. *Christianity brought literacy in Latin and Roman script in the middle of the fifth century. Literature in Irish has its written beginnings in the monasteries that fostered the golden age of Irish art. Apart from a few poems and jottings which may be dated to the sixth century, the earliest extant material we have are lyric poems written by Irish monks on the margin of manuscripts in the eighth century. These are simple, intense, and passionate. Certainly older, but written down somewhat later, are the great heroic stories of kings and gods. The most famous of these is the **Táin Bó Cuailgne* (The Cattle Raid of Cooley)—the story of a jealous queen and two bulls, and *Cúchulainn—which is often seen as the Irish epic. It is remarkable that the most significant of this early literature is in prose, even though the **fili* is often seen as a continuation of the *druid and possessing magical powers. The *Viking invasions destroyed a lot of the monasteries and by the twelfth century Irish literature had come under the patronage of secular families. These families supported the *bardic poets and their schools and helped compile and preserve the great manuscript books in which most of the medieval literature has survived. The most famous of these books are **Leabhar na hUidhre* (The Book of the Dun Cow), and The Book of *Leinster.

A greater European influence can be detected after the Norman colonization. The common stock of romantic tales took root and helped to shape the traditional Irish stories of the *Fianna. The tradition of *amour courtois* was developed among the aristocracy and eventually made its way into the folk tradition. Works of European literature were translated into Irish. The great rupture in this literature takes place as a result of the English conquest in the early seventeenth century, although, paradoxically, some of the greatest poetry and most powerful prose grew out of the struggle. Dáibhí *Ó Bruadair's (1625–98) life and poetry reflect the story of his times and kind: a life begun with patronage and ended in poverty. Seathrún *Céitinn's *Foras Feasa ar Éirinn (A Basis of Knowledge About Ireland)* is a compendium of Irish history, written in the 1630s, which inspired Irish people for two hundred years. But the destruction of the aristocracy also exposed a literature of the common people. The eighteenth century, in particular, was a century of song-poetry, composed by the impoverished and cherished by the destitute. Although often painful and lamenting as in the poetry of Aodhagán *Ó Rathaille (c.1670–1729), or rhetorically political as in the songs of Seán Clárach Mac Domhnaill (1691–1754), this song-poetry includes such lively compositions as Brian *Merriman's *Cúirt an Mheán Oíche (The Midnight Court,* 1780).

Prose had been reduced to a trickle by the nineteenth century and the language went into serious decline after the *Famine. The *Irish Revival of the 1880s and the *Gaelic League, however, had as one of their aims the revitalization and modernization of literature in Irish. As a result, the twentieth century has been one of the richest of all. The novel was born, the short story escaped from *folklore, poetry reinvented itself, drama appeared from nowhere, and seriously intellectual discursive prose appeared for the first time since the seventeenth century. In fact, for all its longevity as a tradition, there has been more writing in Irish in the twentieth century than in all other centuries put together. Perhaps the most significant author was Máirtín *Ó Cadhain (1906–70), whose novels and short stories married traditional language of a most developed kind with a modern and wild sensibility. In poetry, Seán *Ó Ríordáin (1916–77) used his own personal investigations as the basis of his finely wrought and often scary lyricism. At the beginning of the twenty-first century, contemporary writing in Irish is vibrant. A.T.

Lloyd George, David (1863–1945). British politician, British prime minister (1916–22). One of the most important figures in British politics in the early twentieth century, Lloyd George had a profound impact on Irish history. Born in Wales, Lloyd George emerged from humble circumstances to become a dynamic figure in British politics. As MP (member of Parliament) for Caernarfon Boroughs (1890–1945), he championed Welsh causes and as chancellor of the Exchequer greatly improved social welfare services. Prime minister from 1916 to 1922, Lloyd George led Britain through *World War I and the Paris peace negotiations. In 1917, he established the Irish Convention to seek a settlement of the political crisis in Ireland. He was, however, condemned by Liberal opinion in Britain for his apparent approval of "official reprisals" against suspected *republicans by the British army and *"Black and Tan" police, which intensified the violence and brutality of the *Anglo-Irish conflict during 1920 and 1921. Nevertheless, Lloyd George successfully negotiated the *Anglo-Irish Treaty which ended the *War of Independence and led to the creation of the *Irish Free State. He was forced to resign as prime minister in October 1922 in part because of Conservative dissatisfaction with the terms of the Anglo-Irish Treaty. In 1945, he was made an earl (First Earl Lloyd George of Dwyfor). Lloyd George is the author of several books, including *War Memoirs* (6 vols., 1933–36). S.A.B.

Turf Cutting, County Longford

Longford, County. Inland county in the province of *Leinster. After Leitrim, the landlocked county of Longford (421 square miles) is the second-least populated county in Ireland, with 31,127 inhabitants (2002 census). Primarily *agricultural, the county has some light industry and *textile production. The reputation of being a flat midland county is not really justified. The western part, bordering the River *Shannon, is certainly low-lying, but to the east of Longford town, the land is higher, reaching 912 feet at Carn Clonhugh. A much lower hill, Slieve Calry, is identified with the Brí-Leith of ancient Irish *mythology, residence of Midir of the Tuatha Dé Danann tribe. At the foot of Slieve Calry is the village of Ardagh, where there is an old church dedicated to St. Mel, Longford's patron *saint, and where Oliver *Goldsmith is said to have mistaken a convent for an inn, an event recalled in his play *She Stoops to Conquer*. Goldsmith (1728–74) was supposedly born at Pallas, not far from Ballymahon. A younger contemporary was Richard Lovell Edgeworth (1744–1817), author and inventor after whom the village of Edgeworthstown (also known as Mostrim) was called. He was also father of Maria *Edgeworth (1767–1849) who, though born in England, spent most of her life in County Longford, where she wrote *Castle Rackrent* (1800) and corresponded with her friend Sir Walter Scott. Other writers from Longford include Leo Casey, author of songs and ballads, and the poet Padraic *Colum.

In early times, Longford's leading family was the O'Farrells, lords of Annaly, who defended the county against Norman invaders. A fine example of motte and bailey, erected by Hugh de Lacy in the twelfth century, overlooks the town of Granard. Other ancient monuments include the fine, but little-known, *dolmen at Aghnacliff, and the Cistercian abbey of Abbeylara. During the *Rebellion of 1798, a combined French and Irish force was defeated by the British under Lord Cornwallis at Ballinamuck. Longford's best-known modern politician is Albert *Reynolds (who was born in County *Roscommon), the *Republic's *Taoiseach (prime minister) from 1992 to 1994. P.H.

Longley, Michael (1939–). Poet. Born in *Belfast to English parents, Longley was educated at Trinity College, Dublin. Along with Seamus *Heaney, he is associated with the Northern Group founded in Belfast by Philip Hobsbaum, and is one of the few poets of his generation who stayed in Belfast throughout the *Troubles. Known for his exquisitely crafted nature poems, Longley has also written some of the best political poems of his generation. Longley's themes and subjects reflect his background in classics. *No Continuing City* (1969), his first book, depicts home both as a place of brutal violence and reunited family. Political violence intrudes on its fragile civility. However, rural *Mayo provides an alternative setting for meditation. The collections *Gorse Fires* (1991) and *The Weather in Japan* (2000) integrate the personal, communal, and universal, but approach the *Northern Irish troubles obliquely, in order to show how they disrupt domestic, private life. *Tuppenny Stung*, a short autobiography, appeared in 1994. M.S.T.

Lough Derg Pilgrimage. Catholic *pilgrimage. Long regarded as the most difficult pilgrimage in Christendom, this journey to St. *Patrick's Purgatory, or Station Island, in County *Donegal, continues to take place between June 1 and August 15 each year. Today, the pilgrims spend three days on the island and perform a series of penances, including vigils and fasting. A widely popular religious practice before the Great *Famine (1845–51), the pilgrimage was transformed during the Irish devotional revolution (1850–75), which condemned indigenous religious practices in an effort to normalize Irish *Catholicism. In their tourist handbook of 1853, *Connemara and the West of Ireland*, Mr. and Mrs. Samuel Carter Hall reassured readers that the pilgrimage to Lough Derg and "similar evil customs" were dying out. E.S.M.

Louth, County. Maritime county in the province of *Leinster. Ireland's smallest county, only 318 square miles, Louth is, however, more heavily populated (101,802; 2002 census) than other larger counties because it has the major towns of Drogheda and Dundalk near both its northern and southern extremities. These two towns together account for just over half the county's population. The most strikingly beautiful part of the county is the Cooley Peninsula, which looks across the border with *Northern Ireland to the majestic Mourne Mountains in County *Down. On the peninsula are the active port of Greenore, a small *whiskey *distillery, and the historic town of Carlingford (renowned for its oysters). The Cooley Peninsula is most famous for the legendary epic **Táin Bó Cuailnge* (The Cattle Raid of Cooley), which chronicles Queen Maeve of *Connacht's attempts to carry off a prized bull from Cooley so that her herd could equal that of her husband's. To the west of Dundalk is a standing stone that tradition associates with the death of *Cúchulainn, the hero of the *Táin Bó Cuailnge*.

The county's southern border is the river Boyne, scene of the fateful Battle of the *Boyne (1690), in which King *William of Orange defeated the forces of King *James II and changed the course of Irish history. More than three centuries earlier, the Scottish King Edward *Bruce's invasion of the county cost him his life at Faughart, where he is buried. Faughart is also the acknowledged birthplace of St. *Brigid, Ireland's foremost female *saint. The high *crosses at Monasterboice are among the most impressive and best preserved in Ireland. In Mellifont, the Cistercians founded their first Irish monastery in the twelfth century. The Church of St. Peter in Drogheda houses the head of Ireland's only canonized martyr, St. Oliver *Plunkett.

Louth, at one time on the cusp of Gaelic Ireland and the English-dominated *Pale, has some fine *castles and *tower houses including Carlingford Castle, Castle Roche, and Roodstown. St. Laurence's Gate in Drogheda is a symbol of the strength of this once-fortified town on the river Boyne. Nearby, a viaduct over the river constructed for the Dublin-Belfast railway line was regarded as the great engineering feat of mid-nineteenth-century Ireland. On the northern side of the estuary is Beaulieu, dating from the 1700s, one of the first country houses in Ireland to be built without fortifications. An Grianán, the vibrant home of the Irish Countrywomen's Association, is north of Drogheda. Notable figures from Louth include: the painter Nano Reid, architect Michael *Scott, and the economist T. K. *Whitaker. P.H.

Lover, Samuel (1797–1868). Novelist, songwriter, and painter. Born in *Dublin, Lover established himself as a miniaturist and marine painter. He published *Legends and Stories of Ireland* (1831) with his own illustrations. In 1835, Lover moved to London, where he published the stage-Irish novels *Rory O'Moore* (1837) and *Handy Andy: A Tale of Irish Life* (1842). He devised a successful stage show entitled *Irish Evenings*, which featured his own songs and sketches, and toured England and the United States. He wrote over three hundred Irish songs in all. Samuel Lover was the grandfather of Victor Herbert (1859–1924), the celebrated Dublin-born cellist and writer of Broadway musicals. C.D.

Loyalists. People who support the continued existence of Northern Ireland as part of Britain. See **Unionism.**

Lunny, Dónal (1947–). Musician and producer. Lunny is a bouzouki, guitar, and bodhrán player, composer, arranger, and producer. He popularized the modern "Irish bouzouki." Lunny experimented with different instruments as accompaniment in Irish *music and championed the style of "pitching" of notes on the bodhrán. He has been an influential figure in all modern presentations of traditional music ranging from his pop band Emmet Spiceland (1960s), to *Planxty (1972–75), *Bothy Band (1974–79), Moving Hearts (1981–84), solo work with rock and traditional musicians, and the "trad-rock" band Coolfin (1998–99). F.V.

Lusitania (May 7, 1915). *World War I maritime tragedy. The Cunard Liner *Lusitania* was sunk in 1915 by a German submarine, off Kinsale, County *Cork, with the loss of 1,198 people, including 128 Americans. Fearing that further incidents would incite the United States into entering the war, Germany temporarily ceased its campaign of unrestricted warfare in the Atlantic. P.E.

Lynch, Jack (1917–99). Politician, *Taoiseach (prime minister), leader of *Fianna Fáil. Born in Cork City, Lynch worked as a civil servant and as a barrister. He was also an extremely skilled *hurler who won eight All-Ireland medals with Cork. Member of the *Dáil (Parliament) from 1948 to 1981, a government minister from 1957 to 1966, Lynch was Taoiseach from 1966 to 1973, and again from 1977 to 1979. He was leader of Fianna Fáil from 1966–79, having been selected as a compromise at a time when the party was bitterly divided between supporters of Charles *Haughey and George Colley. Initially, Lynch was perceived as a weaker political force, overshadowed by these two great rivals. In the early years of the *Northern Ireland conflict, 1968–70, he was severely tested, but his position within the party was strengthened when he dismissed Charles Haughey and Neil Blaney from the cabinet, for alleged gun-running to Northern *nationalists, during the *Arms Crisis in 1970. He was a hugely popular political leader and, in the 1977 general election, led Fianna Fáil to its largest victory since 1938. Haughey replaced Lynch as leader of Fianna Fáil two years later after a series of by-election defeats. J.D.

M

MacBride, Major John (1865–1916). Politician, revolutionary. Born in County *Mayo, MacBride was active in *republican circles in the west of Ireland before emigrating to South Africa in 1896. While there, he organized the *Irish Brigade, which fought on the Boer side in the *Boer War. After the war, MacBride settled in France, where he married Maud *Gonne. The couple had one son, Seán *MacBride, who founded Amnesty International. On his return to Ireland, MacBride resumed his republican activities, and served on the Supreme Council of the IRB (*Irish Republican Brotherhood). He took part in the *Easter Rising of 1916, and was executed along with the other leaders in May 1916. A.S.

MacBride, Seán (1904–88). IRA (*Irish Republican Army) leader, politician, Nobel Peace Prize winner. Born in Paris, Seán was the son of John *MacBride (who was executed for his part in the *Easter Rising of 1916) and *republican activist Maud *Gonne MacBride. He was a member of the IRA in the *War of Independence, took the anti-treaty side in the *Civil War and remained active in the IRA until the enactment of the 1937 *Constitution (serving from 1936 to 1937 as its chief of staff). MacBride formed *Clann na Poblachta in 1946. He was elected to the *Dáil (Parliament) from 1948 to 1957, and was minister for external affairs between 1948 and 1951. A founding member of Amnesty International, MacBride was a barrister, who specialized in human rights cases. He was UN Commissioner for Namibia in Africa from 1973 to 1976. In 1974, MacBride was awarded the Nobel Peace Prize, as chairman of Amnesty International. In later years, he was a constant critic of the British government's human rights record in *Northern Ireland. J.D.

MacDiarmada, Seán (1884–1916). Revolutionary. Born at Kiltyclogher, County *Leitrim, MacDiarmada moved to *Belfast in 1902, where he joined the *Irish Republican Brotherhood (IRB) in

1906. He was crippled in 1912 by an attack of poliomyelitis. In 1915, MacDiarmada became a member of the military council of the IRB. He fought at the GPO (General Post Office) in *Dublin during the *Easter Rising in 1916 and was one of the seven signatories of the *Proclamation of the Irish Republic. He was executed on May 12, 1916. C.D.

MacDonagh, Thomas (1878–1916). Poet and revolutionary. Born in Cloughjordan, County *Tipperary, and educated at Rockwell College, Cashel, MacDonagh lectured in English literature at University College, Dublin. In 1908, he helped Patrick *Pearse open St. Enda's School in *Dublin. He joined the Irish *Volunteers in 1913 and the *Irish Republican Brotherhood in 1915. MacDonagh was a signatory of the *Proclamation of the Irish Republic issued at the beginning of the *Easter Rising in 1916 and was in command of Jacob's factory in Dublin during the weeklong fight. He was executed on May 3, 1916. His volumes of poetry, inspired by his deep Catholicism and the *Irish Literary Revival movement, include *Through the Ivory Gate* (1903), *Lyrical Poems* (1913), and *Poetical Works* (1916). A play, *When the Dawn Is Come*, was produced by the *Abbey Theatre in 1908. MacDonagh's most significant work is *Literature in Ireland*, a book of essays (published posthumously in July 1916) in which he proposed the existence of an "Irish Mode" of literature that applied the distinctive rhythms and patterns of Gaelic to *Hiberno-English speech and writing. C.D.

MacGonigal, Maurice (1900–79). Landscape and portrait painter. Born in *Dublin, MacGonigal was a pupil of William *Orpen. He went on to teach at the Dublin Metropolitan School of Art and National College of Art, Dublin, where, along with Seán *Keating, he continued Orpen's formal academic tradition. He exhibited his paintings often at the *Royal Hibernian Academy, where he was president from 1962 to 1977. M.C.

MacGowan, Shane (1957–). Singer. Born in London of Irish parents, MacGowan was the founding member of the Irish punk band the Pogues. Hits include the duet with Kirsty MacColl "Fairytale of New York" (1987). Their most famous album was *Rum, Sodomy and the Lash* (1985), which includes such perennial favorites as "A Pair of Brown Eyes" and "Dirty Old Town." He has been heavily influenced by the writings and the hedonistic lifestyle of Brendan *Behan. MacGowan is regarded as one of the most accomplished lyricists in modern rock music. He broke with the Pogues in the mid-nineties to set up a new band called the Popes. B.D.

MacGowran, Jack (1918–73). Actor. MacGowran was born in *Dublin and educated by the *Christian Brothers. He worked as a clerk in an insurance office but turned to acting in the early 1940s. He played at the *Gate and *Abbey Theatres, and in 1950 joined the Radio Éireann Repertory Company. John Ford brought him to Hollywood to act in *The Quiet Man* (1952). After his return to Ireland, MacGowran formed his own theater company, the Dublin Globe Theatre. In 1954, he moved to London, where he worked for television and acted successfully in the West End. Around this time, he became interested in the works of Samuel *Beckett, and would eventually be one of Beckett's most respected interpreters. Beckett wrote the radio play *Embers* (1959), which won the Prix Italia, and *Eh, Joe* (1966), a short piece for television, for him. Mac-

Gowran also had notable performances in the plays of Seán *O'Casey. MacGowran's film work includes *Darby O'Gill and the Little People* (1959), *The Fearless Vampire Killers* (1967), and *The Exorcist* (1973). In 1971 he received the New York Critics' "Actor of the Year" Award for his brilliant performance in *Beginning to End*, a one-man show based on material from Beckett plays. He died in New York in 1973. J.C.E.L.

Macken, Walter (1915–67). Novelist, actor, playwright. Born in *Galway, where he is fondly remembered, Macken wrote his first story at the age of twelve and left school at seventeen to join the Galway theater An Taibhdhearc. There he acted, directed, built sets, and wrote plays in Irish. During the 1940s and 1950s, Macken acted at the *Abbey Theatre and appeared in a number of movies. In 1948, he played the lead role on Broadway in M. J. Molloy's *The King of Friday's Men*. Macken's own play *Home Is the Hero* (1953) was made into a movie in 1959, with Macken himself in one of the lead roles. The film was nominated for a Golden Bear Award at the Berlin Film Festival. Macken also wrote the film script for Brendan *Behan's *The Quare Fellow*.

A prolific and best-selling author, Macken wrote with passion and drama about ordinary people struggling in extraordinary circumstances. His works are often set in or around Galway, and reflect *Catholic and *nationalist values. His numerous historical novels include the trilogy: *Seek the Fair Land* (1959), a treatment of the *Cromwellian migrations; *The Silent People* (1962), about the Irish *Famine; and *The Scorching Wind* (1964), which follows two brothers through the bitter struggles of the *War of Independence and the *Civil War. *Rain on the Wind* (1950), a romance set in Galway, is probably his most popular novel, while Macken himself favored *I Am Alone* (1949), which was banned upon publication. He died suddenly in 1967, a year after his appointment as artistic director of the Abbey Theatre. J.C.E.L.

MacLiammóir, Micheál (1899–1978). Dramatist, actor, writer. MacLiammóir, man of the theater, wit, and conversationalist, was the talking piece of the city of *Dublin for sixty years. For many of these, Madame Jammet offered him lunch in her famous restaurant. Born in England as Alfred Willmore, he lived in Dublin since he was a young man and became the most prominent Irish actor of his day. In the late twenties, he met his life partner Hilton *Edwards, with whom he founded the Irish-language theater An Taibhdhearc in Galway, and the renowned *Gate Theatre (1928) in Dublin. He gave the young Orson Welles his first acting job at the Gate Theatre, launching him on a brilliant and famous career.

MacLiammóir was more Irish than Oscar *Wilde, on whom he modeled his style and wit. His most lucrative performance as an actor was his one-man show *The Importance of Being Oscar*, which he published as a book in 1963. He was an elegant and serious writer in both Irish and English; among his most delightful publications were *Put Money in Thy Purse: The Filming of Orson Welles's Othello* (1952) and *Each Actor on His Ass* (1961). MacLiammóir had an almost esoteric sense of camp. For him living was theater and theater an opportunity for provocation and lyricism. He was a king of many parts in his adopted country. J.L.

Maclise, Daniel (1806–70). Painter. Born in *Cork, Maclise became a member of the Royal

Academy in 1840. He was known for painting entertaining Irish themes and for illustrating caricatures of Irish life. His use of antiquarian detail and large scale is most evident in the 1854 romantic history painting *The Marriage of *Strongbow and Aoife* in the *National Gallery, Dublin. M.C.

MacMahon, Bryan (1909–98). Short story writer, novelist, and playwright. MacMahon was born in Listowel, County *Kerry, where he worked for over forty years as a schoolteacher and headmaster. In the 1940s, he contributed poems and stories to the **Bell*. A collection of short stories entitled *The Lion Tamer* (1948) was followed in 1952 by a novel, *Children of the Rainbow*. MacMahon closely observes rural village life, with a passionate awareness that this way of life is fast disappearing. Due to his enthusiasm, the voices in his stories are at times overinsistent. His best-known play, *The Honey-Spike*, was produced at the *Abbey Theatre in 1961; rewritten as a novel in 1967, it depicts the travails of a young *traveller couple expecting a child, and displays MacMahon's knowledge of Shelta, the travellers' language. In 1966 his pageant commemorating the *Easter Rising of 1916 was staged by the *Gaelic Athletic Association at *Croke Park. MacMahon had a strong interest in the *Irish language and *folklore and translated the autobiography of Peig *Sayers (1974). He was one of the driving forces behind the Listowel Writers Week. MacMahon's autobiography, *The Master*, was published in 1992. J.C.E.L.

MacMahon, Tony (1939–). Musician and television producer. MacMahon is an accordionist, television producer, and ideologue within traditional *music. Born in Ennis, County *Clare, he was inspired as a child by the playing of accordionist Joe Cooley and piper Felix Doran. With Séamus *Ennis, MacMahon developed a formidable interpretation of slow airs. During his twenty-six years of television work with *RTÉ , he increased music popularity with the programs *Aisling Geal*, *Ag Déanamh Ceol*, *The Long Note*, *The Pure Drop*, and *Come West Along the Road*. F.V.

MacManus, Terence Bellew (1823–60). Irish *nationalist. A native of County *Fermanagh, MacManus established a successful shipping agency in Liverpool. He joined the *Repeal Association and *Young Ireland and was transported to Tasmania for his part in the uprising of 1848. He escaped to the United States in 1852 and died in poverty in San Francisco. His funeral in *Dublin in 1861 gained national attention for the *Irish Republican Brotherhood. S.A.B.

MacMathuna, Ciarán (1925–). Collector and radio presenter of traditional *music programs. His name is synonymous with the traditional music revival. In contrast to earlier broadcasts' emphasis on **céilí* bands, MacMathuna promoted the solo voices, the music of little-known people and small places, bringing such styles as *Clare, East *Galway, and *Sligo to national attention. His major shows, *Ceolta Tíre* and *Job of Journeywork*, ran for some fifteen years. F.V.

MacMurrough, Dermot (Diarmait MacMurchada) (d. 1171). King of *Leinster. In the struggle for the high kingship of Ireland, Dermot was defeated by Rory *O'Connor, high king of Ireland. After Dermot abducted the wife of O'Rourke, a local chieftain, O'Rourke deposed him and took his lands. Dermot fled to England in 1166 and sought the help of *Henry II, who gave Dermot a letter of permission to recruit mercenaries. In 1167, Dermot returned to Ireland with Norman, Flemish and Welsh mercenaries. His most important recruit among the Normans in Wales was Richard fitz-Gilbert de Clare, nicknamed *Strongbow. In return for his aid, Strongbow was promised the kingship of Leinster after Dermot's death and Dermot's daughter, Aoife, in marriage. Strongbow invaded Ireland in 1170 and soon most of Leinster was under Norman control. By the time of Dermot's death, the *Norman Conquest was well under way. To the Irish, Dermot was known as *Diarmait na nGall* (Dermot of the Foreigners) and he is generally seen as having initiated the Anglo-Norman Conquest of Ireland. T.C.

MacNeice, Louis (1907–63). Poet. Born in *Belfast and raised in Carrickfergus, County *Antrim, where his father was an Anglican clergyman, MacNeice was sent to English schools from the age of ten. He attended Marlborough College and later Merton College, Oxford, where his contemporaries included W. H. Auden, Stephen Spender, and Cecil *Day-Lewis. In 1940, after a decade of university lecturing, he joined the BBC where he worked as a writer and producer for twenty years.

MacNeice's tendency toward irony, pessimism, and classical learning, as well as his considerable lyric gift, were already apparent in his 1929 debut, *Blind Fireworks*. On his return from the *Spanish Civil War in 1936, he became linked with Auden and to the English school of left-leaning 1930s poets. His most ambitious work from this period is *Autumn Journal* (1939), a verse-journal in twenty-four cantos that brought together a broad panorama of autobiography, history, and the politics of Ireland, Britain, and Europe. MacNeice cut loose from the thirties poets with *Springboard* (1945) and *Holes in the Sky* (1948), and later *Ten Burnt Offerings* (1952) and *Solstices* (1961). He also wrote radio plays and translations, including *The Agamemnon of Aeschylus* (1936). His unfinished autobiography, *The Strings are False*, was published in 1965. J.AR.

MacNeill, Eoin (1867–1945). Historian and politician. Born in Glenarm, County *Antrim, MacNeill was vice president of the *Gaelic League, professor of early Irish history at University College, Dublin, and chief of staff of the Irish *Volunteers. In 1914, he opposed John *Redmond's plea to the Irish Volunteers to support the British in the war, prompting Redmond to found the rival National Volunteers. On the eve of the *Easter Rising of 1916, MacNeill issued a countermand order calling off the Irish Volunteer participation in the rebellion. Member of *Dáil Éireann (Irish Parliament) and minster for education (1922–25), he was also the *Free State member of the *Boundary Commission (1924–25). He withheld his signature from its final report and resigned, insisting that the commission had misinterpreted its mandate. J.P.MC.

MacSwiney, Terence (1879–1920). Politician. Born in Cork City, MacSwiney was a founding member of the Cork Dramatic Society, for which he wrote a number of plays, including *The Revolutionist*. In 1913, he played a prominent role in the foundation of the Cork *Volunteers. He complied with Eoin *MacNeill's order calling off the *Easter Rising of 1916, and was responsible for persuading Kerry Volunteers not to join the rising. In 1919, MacSwiney refused to take his seat in the British Parliament and instead joined the first *Dáil (Irish Parliament) as *Sinn Féin representative for West Cork. In March 1920, he became lord mayor of Cork City, but in August of that year, at the height of the *War of

Independence, he was arrested on charges of sedition. MacSwiney went on *hunger strike, drawing worldwide attention to the cause of Irish *nationalism. On October 24, 1920, he died in Brixton prison, after seventy-four days on hunger strike. His funeral was one of the largest ever held in Cork City. A.S.

Maguire, Brian (1951–). Painter. Born in *Dublin, Maguire uses an expressionist style to comment on sociological and political alienation of contemporary life. He is one of the most successful of the new Irish expressionists. M.C.

Maher, Alice (1956–). Painter and sculptor. Born in *Tipperary, Maher studied in *Limerick, *Cork, *Belfast, and San Francisco. Using painting and sculpture, she parodies and reverses traditional themes and associations to discomfort the viewer in surrealist fashion. M.C.

Mahon, Derek (1941–). Poet, verse dramatist, critic, and scriptwriter. Mahon was born in *Belfast and educated at Trinity College, Dublin. He is one of a renowned generation of Northern Irish poets that emerged in the 1960s, including Michael *Longley and Seamus *Heaney. A brilliant master of forms from an early age, Mahon is a mandarin poet, whose literary influences include fellow skeptical *Protestant writers Louis *MacNeice and Samuel *Beckett. Admired for their technical elegance and perfect-pitch lyricism, the poems of *Night Crossing* (1968), *Lives* (1972), *The Snow Party* (1975), and *Courtyards in Delft* (1981) are austere and fastidious: few, but precise details, a limited palette of color, controlled tone and unyielding landscape. Early on, Mahon experimented with epistolary verse, which became his primary form after 1986. *The Hudson Letter* (1995) and *The Yellow Book* (1997) adopt a contemporary conversational idiom and experiment with a longer, more flexible line. Other publications include *Collected Poems* (1999), *Journalism* (1996), verse plays such as *Racine's Phaedra* (1996), and his verse translation, *Words in the Air: A Selection of Poems by Philippe Jaccottet* (1998). M.S.T.

Major, John (1941–). British prime minister, 1990–97. Major succeeded Margaret *Thatcher as Conservative Party leader and prime minister and initiated the 1990–92 Brooke-Mayhew talks with the main *nationalist and *unionist parties in *Northern Ireland. Between 1990 and 1994, he approved secret negotiations between the British government and *Sinn Féin and signed the *Downing Street Declaration (1993), which opened the door for paramilitary organizations' political wings to enter all-party negotiations if they committed themselves to exclusively peaceful methods and agreed to abide by the democratic process. Despite ongoing negotiations with Sinn Féin, Major expressed outrage when the US government granted Sinn Féin leader Gerry *Adams a visa to the United States in January 1994. Adams's US visit was followed by an IRA (*Irish Republican Army) cease-fire that began in August 1994.

By demanding IRA arms decommissioning before he would include Sinn Féin in official peace negotiations, Major missed the opportunity for a permanent peace in Northern Ireland during his tenure. The IRA, furious that Major had trumpeted decommissioning to satisfy unionists, ended their cease-fire in February 1996 by bombing *Canary Wharf in east London. Thus, although Major played an instrumental role in moving the *peace process forward, the *Good Friday Agreement came only after the election of Tony *Blair's Labour government in 1997. R.D.

Mallon, Séamus (1936–). Politician. Born in Markethill, County *Armagh, the son of a headmaster and a nurse, Mallon was a teacher. After becoming involved in the civil rights movement, he helped form the *Social Democratic and Labour Party (SDLP). Mallon was committed to peaceful *republican *nationalism, and his election to the deputy leadership of the SDLP in the late 1970s signaled the eclipse of that party's *socialist wing. In 1981, he was nominated to the Irish *Senate by the then *Taoiseach (prime minister) Charles J. *Haughey and in 1982 to the eventually abortive Northern Ireland Assembly. While his leader, John *Hume, concentrated on influencing international public opinion and the British and Irish governments, Mallon often took the lead in intraparty negotiations within *Northern Ireland. Following the *Good Friday Agreement, he was appointed deputy first minister to David *Trimble in the Northern Ireland Assembly. When John Hume resigned the leadership of the SDLP in 2001, however, Mallon vacated his public positions (as deputy first minister and deputy leader of the SDLP) to make way for a younger generation. M.M.

Manahan, Anna (1924–). Actress. Born in *Waterford, Manahan studied under Ria Mooney at the Gaiety School of Acting, and played with the *Edwards/*MacLiammóir Company at the *Gate. Highlights in a remarkable career include roles in the notorious 1957 Pike Theatre production of *The Rose Tattoo*, which led to the arrest of its director, Alan Simpson, on charges of obscenity; *Big Maggie*, written for Manahan by John B. *Keane; and Brian *Friel's *Lovers*, for which she received her first Tony nomination in 1968. Manahan has also appeared in such movies as *Hear My Song* (1991) and *A Man of No Importance* (1994). Her role as the widow Mag in the box-office hit *The Beauty Queen of Leenane* by Martin *McDonagh won her a Tony Award in 1998. B.D.

Manchester Martyrs (November 23, 1867). Execution of William O'Meara Allen, Michael Larkin, and William O'Brien. In September 1867, two leading *Fenians, Thomas Kelly and Timothy Deasy, were arrested in Manchester on suspicion of terrorism. An attempt to free them led to the death of a police officer, Sergeant Brett. Twenty-nine arrests were made and Allen, Larkin, and O'Brien were convicted and executed for the killing. Their execution produced a great wave of sympathy for the "Manchester Martyrs." The alleged last words of the executed men, "God Save Ireland," were later made into a song by T. D. Sullivan. P.E.

Mangan, James Clarence (1803–49). Poet and translator. Born in *Dublin, Mangan grew up in poverty but received an education through a charitable priest and learned several European languages. He worked at the Ordnance Survey Office from 1833 to 1839, where he associated with the scholars George *Petrie, John *O'Donovan, and Eugene *O'Curry. These scholars provided Mangan with translations of Old Irish poems that he recreated into his own peculiar style of English. His works include the two-volume *Anthologia Germanica*, comprising translations of modern German poetry, and *Poets and Poetry of Munster* (1849, posthumously). Some of his finest poetry was written in 1846 in response to the spread of the *Famine and published in the **Nation* newspaper. These lyrical ballads, composed in a haunting style, include "Dark Rosaleen," "A Vision of Connaught in the

Constance Markievicz

XIII Century," and "Sarsfield." Addicted to opium and alcohol, always flamboyantly attired, yet destitute and depressive, Mangan had all the characteristics of the romantic genius. He died of cholera, weakened by malnutrition. He was relatively unknown in his lifetime but is now recognized as the leading Irish poet of the mid-nineteenth century. C.D.

manuscripts, illuminated. The "Island of Saints and Scholars" was famous for its manuscripts, a number of which were painted in monastic scriptoria. The oldest decorated example is the *Cathach of circa 600, followed by the Book of *Durrow around a century later, and reaching its zenith in the Book of *Kells of circa 800 (the latter two possibly written in Ireland). The Abbey Library of St. Gall in Switzerland has an important collection of Irish illuminated manuscripts of roughly the same period. Others are scattered in libraries around Europe. Illuminated manuscripts of later periods include the twelfth-century Book of *Leinster (Library of Trinity College, Dublin), which also contains important historical material. P.H.

Markievicz, Constance Gore-Booth, Countess (1868–1927). *Republican, revolutionary, politician. Born Constance Gore-Booth in London, Markievicz was brought back by her family to their Irish estate at Lissadell House, County *Sligo, shortly after her birth. She studied painting in London and Paris and in 1900 married a Ukranian-Polish count, Casimir Markievicz, who was also a painter. The marriage failed, and in 1903 she settled in *Dublin, where she was associated with the *Gaelic League and leading figures in the *Abbey Theatre.

In 1908 Markievicz joined *Sinn Féin, and a year later she founded Na Fianna, a republican-led militaristic boy-scout organization. She joined Maud *Gonne's Inghinidhe na hÉireann (Daughters of Ireland) and contributed to suffragette and *nationalist newspapers. During the Dublin lockout of 1913, Markievicz assisted James *Larkin and the Dublin workers' families, and in 1914 she became an officer in the *Irish Citizen Army, prompting the resignation of its secretary, Seán *O'Casey.

She fought in the *Easter Rising of 1916 and was sentenced to death along with the other leaders. Her sentence was commuted to penal servitude for life and she was released in 1917. In 1918, Markievicz was elected as a Sinn Féin MP—the first woman to be elected to the British House of Commons. In keeping with Sinn Féin's policy of abstention, she refused to take her seat in the British Parliament. She was minister for labour in the first *Dáil (Irish Parliament). Markievicz vehemently opposed the *Anglo-Irish Treaty and supported the republican side in the *Irish Civil War. She was arrested in December 1923 for campaigning for the release of republican prisoners, and went on *hunger strike. In 1926, she joined *Fianna Fáil, and in June 1927 was reelected to the Dáil. She died a month later. P.D.

Martyn, Edward (1859–1923). Playwright. Martyn was born into a Catholic *landlord family in County *Galway and educated at Beaumont and Oxford. He was a bachelor, a devout Catholic, a fluent Irish speaker, president of *Sinn Féin (1905–08), cofounder of Feis Ceoil (the National Music Festival), and devotee of ecclestiastical music and art. With W. B. *Yeats and Lady *Gregory, he founded the Irish Literary Theatre (1899) that evolved into the *Abbey Theatre. His preference for the drama of ideas led him to cofound, with Thomas *MacDonagh and Joseph Mary *Plunkett, the Theatre of Ireland in 1906. His plays include *The Heather Field* (1899) and *The Tale of a Town* (1902). M.S.T.

Maturin, Charles (Robert) (1780–1824). Novelist. Maturin was born in *Dublin, educated at Trinity College, Dublin, and ordained in 1803. The landscape of the west of Ireland and Maturin's interest in Irish affairs inspired *The Milesian Chief* (1812), first published under the pseudonym Dennis Jasper Murphy. *Bertram* (1816) is a successfully staged tragedy in blank verse. *Melmoth the Wanderer* (1820), a powerful novel, is his most enduring work. Its plot and narrative form are complex, and the settings are typically Gothic or exotic. Among its themes are madness, persecution, religious mania, and unrequited passion. M.S.T.

Maynooth, St. Patrick's College. National Seminary of Ireland and later a college of the National University. Founded in 1795 by an act of Parliament, the Royal College of St. Patrick's at Maynooth (known colloquially as Maynooth) has been the principal seminary for the training of secular priests in Ireland for more than two hundred years. During this time, more than ten thousand men have been ordained, a remarkable average of fifty per year. In order to replace the seminaries that were lost on the Continent after the French Revolution, the Irish bishops in 1795 pressured the British government to create a seminary. Maynooth established the bishops as an influential political force in Ireland. Stability came slowly to Maynooth; six presidents served there in its first eighteen years. In 1845, the government increased its annual grant and, by 1853, over half of the priests serving in Ireland were Maynooth graduates. These men reformed the *Catholic Church between 1850 and 1900, consolidating a devotional revolution that made Irish Catholics the most pious in the world. St. Patrick's became a Pontifical University in 1896 and its College of Arts and Sciences became associated with the National University in 1910. Lay students entered Maynooth in the 1970s. In 1997, the College of Arts and Sciences and the Pontifical University, including the seminary, separated. Today the much smaller seminary is attempting to adapt to changes in contemporary Ireland. Most of Ireland's leading ecclesiastics were educated at Maynooth, including Eugene O'Growney, early editor of the *Gaelic League's *Gaelic Journal*, and William Walsh, archbishop of Dublin, 1885–1921. M.P.C.

Mayo, County. Maritime county in the province of *Connacht in the west of Ireland. The third largest county in Ireland (2,156 square miles), Mayo

Mary McAleese

has a population of 117,428 (2002 census). It is bordered on the east by *Sligo and *Roscommon, and on the south by *Galway. While the central part of the county contains some of the most fertile land in Connacht, the eastern and western regions are largely barren. Most of the county's population lives in this central area, in towns such as Castlebar, the county capital, Ballina, and Westport. The latter is a picturesque, lively town, which was planned by an English architect, James Wyatt, in the eighteenth century. Achill Island in the northwest of the county (connected by a causeway) is known for its dramatic scenery, well described in Heinrich Böll's book *Irish Journal*. The barony of Erris in the west of the county contains the largest blanket *bog in Ireland. The most famous mountain in Mayo is *Croagh Patrick, a site closely associated with St. *Patrick and one of the most enduring pilgrimage sites in Ireland. In the village of Knock, in 1879, some local people claimed to have seen an apparition of the Virgin Mary, and the town has been known as a holy place ever since. The *Céide Fields on the north coast of Mayo is a noted archaeological site, where the remains of a human settlement, including stone walls, field patterns, houses, and megalithic tombs, some five thousand years old, were preserved by the blanket bog.

The population of the county has never recovered from the *Famine. From a peak of 388,817 in 1841, it had declined to 117,428 in the 2002 census. In the sixteenth century, Grace *O'Malley, or Granuaile, a member of a prominent local family, won considerable notoriety for smuggling, piracy, and resistance to the English. Michael *Davitt, the *Land League leader, was born in Straide and the National Land League was first established at a meeting in Daly's Hotel in Castlebar on August 16, 1879. Captain *Boycott, whose name has become a word in the English language, was a landlord's agent at the height of the *Land War in the county. Mary *Robinson, the respected former Irish president, was also born in the county. Mayo is a largely agricultural county, although fishing and tourism are of increasing importance to the local economy. A.S.

McAleese, Mary (1951–). President of Ireland, law professor, journalist, and civil rights activist. Born in *Belfast into a *Catholic family, McAleese grew up in a *Protestant area, near Ardoyne. The family was forced to move in the early 1970s when their home was machine-gunned and they were advised for their own safety not to return. In another sectarian attack, her deaf brother was badly beaten.

McAleese succeeded Mary *Robinson as Reid Professor of criminal law at Trinity College in 1975 and in 1979 joined *RTÉ as a journalist. She was involved in campaigns for prisoners' rights, gay rights, and the ordination of women as Catholic priests, but opposed abortion. In 1987, her appointment as director of Queen's University's Institute of Professional Legal Studies met with intense *Unionist opposition. In 1994, she was appointed pro-vice-chancellor of the university, the first Catholic woman to reach such a position. Selected as the *Fianna Fáil candidate for the 1997 presidential election (in preference to former *Taoiseach [prime minister] Albert *Reynolds), McAleese was elected with 58.7 percent of the popular vote, the largest percentage vote for any presidential candidate to date, surpassing even Éamon *de Valera's first election. J.D.

McAliskey, Bernadette Devlin (1947–). *Nationalist, *socialist, politician. Born into a poor *Catholic nationalist family in Cookstown, County *Tyrone, McAliskey won a scholarship to Queen's University, Belfast. She became involved with the *People's Democracy student civil rights organization, which was established in the aftermath of an infamous RUC (*Royal Ulster Constabulary) attack on a Derry demonstration in October 1968. A socialist *republican, McAliskey campaigned as the "Unity Candidate" acceptable to both republicans and traditional nationalists, in a by-election to the Westminster seat of mid-Ulster in April 1969. On a massive anti-Unionist turnout, she was elected at the age of twenty-two as the youngest member of the United Kingdom Parliament, which she electrified with a dramatic and undiplomatic maiden speech.

During the Battle of *Bogside in August 1969, McAliskey urged resistance to RUC incursion, and was later sentenced to six months imprisonment for riotous behavior. Her increasingly radical stance alienated moderate Catholics and she lost her seat in 1974. In February 1981, McAliskey (her married name) was seriously injured in an attempt on her life when loyalist gunmen entered her home. The same year, she played a leading role in the National H-Block Committee established to support the demands of the *hunger strikers. She rejected the *Good Friday Agreement as an unacceptable betrayal of republican principles. M.M.

McCabe, Eugene (1930–). Writer. Born in Glasgow, McCabe returned to Ireland at a young age. His first major play, *The King of the Castle* (1964), provoked considerable controversy for its unflinchingly realistic portrayal of Irish rural life. The most important of his later works are the trilogy of plays for television on the *Northern Ireland crisis, *Victims* (1976), one part of which was published that year as a short novel with the same title, and the novel, *Death and Nightingales* (1992), which deals with political and domestic violence in late-nineteenth-century Ireland. A.S.

McCabe, Patrick (1955–). Writer. Born in Clones, County *Monaghan, McCabe trained as a teacher in *Dublin. He has an economical writing style, rich in local idiom and frequently tinged with the macabre. *The Butcher Boy*, which was shortlisted for the Booker Prize in 1992, is undoubtedly his masterpiece and is regarded as one of the best Irish novels of the twentieth century. The *film *The Butcher Boy*, cowritten with Neil *Jordan, was received with great acclaim in 1998. The book was also made into a play called *Frank Pig Says Hello*. Other novels include *Music on Clinton Street* (1986), *Carn* (1989), *The Dead School* (1994), *Breakfast on Pluto* (1998),

Mondo Desperado (1999), and *Emerald Germs of Ireland* (2000). He has also written many plays and adapted some of his novels for the stage. B.D.

McCann, Donal (1943–99). Actor. Born in *Dublin, McCann is widely regarded as one of the greatest modern Irish actors. He appeared in numerous films and television programs, but his greatest performances were on the stage, especially in the widely acclaimed roles in Sebastian *Barry's *The Steward of Christendom* (1995) and Brian *Friel's *Faith Healer* (1979). McCann battled with alcoholism and depression for most of his life. At his best, McCann had a charisma and force unequaled by any other Irish actor of recent times. He won major critical praise for his brilliantly controlled performance in John Huston's film *The Dead* (1987). A.S.

McClure, Robert John Le Mesurier (1807–73). Explorer. Born in *Wexford and educated at Eton and Sandhurst, McClure joined the British navy in 1824 and served in the Arctic expeditions of 1836 and 1848. In 1850, he was second-in-command on an expedition to find the missing Arctic explorer Sir John Franklin. McClure discovered Baring's Island, penetrated the Barrow Strait, and discovered the Northwest Passage. He returned to England in 1854 and was knighted. McClure later served in the China Seas. He published his Arctic adventures, *Voyages*, in 1884. C.D.

McCormack, John (1884–1945). Operatic and concert tenor. Regarded as one of the greatest singers of the twentieth century, McCormack was born in Athlone, County *Westmeath, and educated at the Marist Fathers School in Athlone and at Summerhill College, *Sligo. In 1902, at Feis Ceoil (the National Music Festival), he won a gold medal in the tenor competition and the following year, he traveled to Italy to study under Vincenzo Sabatini. McCormack made his operatic debut in 1907 at Covent Garden, London, in *Cavalleria Rusticana*. By 1909, he was singing opera in Chicago and Boston and with the New York Metropolitan Opera Company. Following a tour of Australia in 1911, he began a successful career on the concert stage. McCormack became an American citizen in 1919 and was made a papal count in 1928 in recognition of his services to Catholic charities. P.E.

McCormick, F. J. (1889–1947). Actor. Stage name of Peter Judge. Judge was born in Skerries, County *Dublin, the son of a *brewery manager. During a brief career in the civil service in London and Dublin, he took part in amateur dramatics and adopted a stage name. In 1918, he joined the *Abbey Theatre Company, where he was taught elocution by Frank *Fay. McCormick appeared in over five hundred plays, most notably in those by Seán *O'Casey. He brilliantly created the role of Joxer Daly in O'Casey's *Juno and the Paycock* (1924), opposite an equally brilliant Barry *Fitzgerald as Captain Boyle. Eileen Crowe played the part of Mary Boyle, and she and McCormick were married in 1925. He was cast as Jack Clitheroe in O'Casey's *The Plough and the Stars* (1926). When riots broke out in the Abbey Theatre during the opening week of the play, McCormick attempted to quiet the audience by saying, "Don't blame the actors. We didn't write this play." The actor and O'Casey had been close friends, but the remark led to a rift that never healed. McCormick toured the United States five times and received numerous offers, but never wanted to leave the Abbey. He played several film roles, including the part of Shell in Carol Reed's *Odd Man Out* (1947). J.C.E.L.

John McGahern

McCourt, Frank (1930–). Writer. Born in Brooklyn, New York, McCourt was taken back to Ireland as a child, at the height of the Depression. At nineteen he returned to New York, where he became a high school teacher. *Angela's Ashes*, his funny and poignant memoir of an impoverished *Limerick childhood, published in 1996, won a Pulitzer Prize, sold millions of copies around the world, and was made into a movie by Alan Parker. A sequel *'Tis*, was published in 1999. M.E.

McDonagh, Martin (1970–). Playwright. Born in London, the son of Irish immigrants, McDonagh grew up in England. However, the family regularly visited Ireland on summer vacations, inspiring McDonagh to write about the isolation of Irish rural life. His first darkly comic trilogy of plays, the *Leenane Trilogy* (*The Beauty Queen of Leenane*, *A Skull in Connemara*, and *The Lonesome West*), set in the west of Ireland, rapidly won international acclaim after their initial productions at the Druid Theatre in *Galway in 1996–97. The plays went on to be major successes in London and on Broadway. McDonagh's play *The Cripple of Inishmaan*, the first of a projected *Aran Trilogy*, was first performed at the National Theatre in London in 1997. It was followed in 2001 by *The Lieutenant of Inishmore*, a bloody farce satirizing Irish terrorists. The play was turned down by several theaters and eventually staged by the RSC at The Other Place, Stratford-upon-Avon. Inspired as much by television soaps and movies as by playwrights like J. M. *Synge, Tom *Murphy, and David Mamet, McDonagh's work characteristically juxtaposes melodrama, comedy, and violence. A.S.

McGahern, John (1934–). Novelist and short story writer. Born in *Dublin, McGahern grew up in Cootehall, County *Roscommon, where his father was a police sergeant and his mother a schoolteacher. He qualified as a teacher at St. Patrick's College, Drumcondra, and later studied at University College, Dublin.

McGahern's first novel, *The Barracks*, the dark, intensely moving story of a police sergeant's wife who is dying of breast cancer, was published in 1963. His second novel, *The Dark* (1965), was banned under the Censorship of Publications Act and McGahern was dismissed from his teaching position in Clontarf, Dublin, without official explanation. Written in an unusual mix of third, second, and first person narrative, the novel depicts stages in the relationship between an adolescent boy and his difficult, widowed father. Effectively barred from teaching in Ireland, McGahern lived in England, Spain, and the United States before settling in County *Leitrim in 1974, where he still lives on a farm. His novels *The Leavetaking* (1974, revised version 1984) and *The Pornographer* (1979) chronicle this period in his life. Primarily a novelist, McGahern has published four books of short stories, *Nightlines* (1970), *Getting Through* (1978), *High Ground* (1985), and *Collected Stories* (1992). The story "Korea" was made into a movie by Cathal Black in 1995.

Frequently set in the northern midlands, McGahern's novels are dark, fiercely lyrical portrayals of the isolation and claustrophobia of rural Ireland. Recurring themes are the tensions within the family, fear of poverty and starvation, the repression of emotions and sexuality, and the struggle to choose between ambition and security, set within the ritual cycle of the farming seasons and the church calendar. McGahern's meticulous prose style—the result of much cutting and paring—is honed to a fine art in *Among Women* (1990), whose protagonist, Michael Moran, is loved by the women in his family regardless of his difficult temperament. The novel was shortlisted for the Booker Prize. *By the Lake* (2002, entitled *That They May Face the Rising Sun* in the British edition) is a broader but loving portrayal of a year in the life of a rural community. While the earlier novels *The Barracks* and *The Dark* have more raw intensity, *Among Women* and *By the Lake* show a profound understanding of human nature. J.C.E.L.

McGuckian, Medbh (1950–). Poet. McGuckian was born in *Belfast and educated at Queen's University, Belfast. Her radically innovative poetry emerged in the eighties and was labeled postmodernist by critics. McGuckian's poems, which strive to map female identity and states of mind, are playful, enigmatic, and often elusive, written in a fluid, highly associative, expansive style. Dominant images include hearth and garden, but traditional metaphors such as germination, light, and water are given new resonance. Collections include *The Flower Master* (1982), *On Ballycastle Beach* (1988), *Selected Poems* (1997), and *Shelmalier* (1998). She has translated Nuala *Ní Dhomhnaill's poetry into English. M.S.T.

McGuinness, Frank (1953–). Playwright. Born in Buncrana, County *Donegal, McGuinness is one of Ireland's leading contemporary playwrights. His first play, *Factory Girls* (1982), is a sympathetic portrayal of the lives of working-class women in his native Donegal. He is best known for his award-winning play *Observe the Sons of Ulster Marching Towards the Somme* (1985), an empathetic study of *loyalist involvement in *World War I. His other plays include: *Carthaginians* (1987), a dramatic meditation on the impact of sectarian violence on the citizens of Derry set in a graveyard; *Someone Who'll Watch Over Me* (1992), inspired by the hostage takings in Beirut, which was a major success on Broadway and in London; and *Mutabilitie* (1997), a dense play set in sixteenth-century Ireland. McGuinness's plays are bold explorations of issues relating to gender, class, religion, and politics. He has also written adaptations of classic European plays, and screenplays for film and television. A.S.

McGuinness, Martin (1950–). *Republican, *Sinn Féin politician. Born into a *Catholic family in *Derry, McGuinness was drawn to republican activities in the wake of the civil rights movement (*Northern Ireland Civil Rights Association; NICRA). By 1972, he was the second in command in the Provisional IRA (*Irish Republican Army) in Derry.

McGuinness was capable, dedicated, and ruthless, and in a meritocratic IRA, whose older leadership was depleted by continual arrests, he advanced quickly. He was part of an IRA delegation that met with Secretary of State William Whitelaw in July 1972. Subsequently, he rose to the national leadership of the IRA, and allegedly served as chief of staff periodically. Nevertheless, he served little time in jail, and his close and stable family life was not seriously disrupted. McGuinness provided a militant cover for Gerry *Adams's drift toward constitutional politics in the late 1980s. He was personally committed to the *peace process, though he pursued tactical use of armed struggle to strengthen the republican hand up to the IRA cease-fire of 1996. He has served as *Sinn Féin's chief negotiator since 1990. After the *Good Friday Agreement, McGuinness was elected as Sinn Féin MP (member of Parliament) for mid-Ulster and appointed minister of education in the Northern Ireland Assembly. M.M.

McKenna, Siobhán (1923–86). Actress. Born in *Belfast and raised as an Irish speaker, McKenna was educated at University College, Galway. She acted in An Taibhdhearc, the *Irish-language theater in Galway, and joined the *Abbey Theatre in 1944, where she acted with F. J. *McCormick and Cyril *Cusack. Among her most memorable roles were Pegeen Mike in *Synge's *The Playboy of the Western World* (which she played for the first time in 1951) and *Shaw's *Saint Joan*. She first played the part of Joan in her own Irish translation at the Taibhdhearc, where she modeled her performance on her mother, a woman of remarkable faith. She later won international acclaim for the role in productions in London in 1954 and on Broadway in 1956. *Here Are Ladies* (1970), a one-woman show, was a huge hit in London and the United States. She appeared in eight films, notably *Dr. Zhivago* (1965). C.D.

McMaster, Anew (1894–1962). Actor, manager. Born in *Monaghan, McMaster made his acting debut in 1911 with Fred Terry's company. In 1925 he founded his own touring company (he was actor, manager, and director) to bring Shakespearean plays to the Irish provinces. Revered in rural Ireland, McMaster also took his company on tours of the Near East and Australia. While his own acting style was in the grand manner of an older tradition that was rapidly going out of fashion, his Shakespearean Company served as a training ground for a number of innovative actors and directors. Micheál *MacLiammóir (whose sister McMaster married) met his future partner Hilton *Edwards while touring with McMaster. Harold Pinter spent two years with the company and subsequently praised McMaster's magnificent performances as Othello. Later in his career, McMaster had successful seasons at the *Abbey Theatre in Dublin with actors such as Sir Frank Benson and Mrs. Patrick Campbell. J.C.E.L.

McPherson, Conor (1972–). Playwright. Born in *Dublin, McPherson first made his mark at the Dublin Theatre Festival in the early nineties. His work deals mostly with the underbelly of Irish society. The best-known plays include *This Lime Tree Bower* (1995), which played at the Bush Theatre, London, and *The Weir* (1997), a box-office hit on Broadway. His quirky film *I Went Down* (1997) won the Best Screenplay Award at the San Sebastian Festival. He also wrote the screenplay for the movie *Saltwater*. B.D.

Meagher, Thomas Francis (1823–67). Politician. Born in County *Waterford, Meagher was active in the *Repeal association in the early 1840s. Closely associated with other *Young Ireland leaders like John *Mitchel and Charles Gavan *Duffy, he ultimately grew disillusioned with the conciliatory policies pursued by Daniel *O'Connell. One of the founders of the Irish Confederation, the organization established in 1847 by the Young Ireland leaders opposed to O'Connell, Meagher was sentenced to transportation to Tasmania for his part in the *rebellion of 1848. He escaped to America, where he worked as a journalist. Meagher fought on the Union side in the *American Civil War, and reached the rank of Brigadier General. From 1865 to his death, he served as secretary of the Montana Territory. His fiery oratory won him the nickname of "Meagher of the sword." A.S.

Meath, County. Maritime county in the province of *Leinster in the eastern part of Ireland. The county, covering an area of 904 square miles, has a population of 133,936 (2002 census). Bordered on the east by *Dublin and the Irish Sea, on the north by *Louth, *Monaghan, and *Cavan, on the west by *Westmeath, and on the south by *Offaly and *Kildare, Meath is known as "the Royal County" because the high kings of Ireland were believed to have been crowned at the Hill of *Tara. The county derives its name from the Irish *midhe*, meaning "middle," the name of the fifth province in early *Christian Ireland, which was dominated by the southern branch of the *O'Neill family. This included lands now in counties Meath, Westmeath, Cavan, and *Longford. The boundaries of the present-day county were formed in the twelfth century, when King *Henry II granted these lands to Hugh de Lacy.

The land is generally flat, apart from the hills of Loughcrew in the west of the county. The principal rivers in the county are the Boyne and the Blackwater. The Battle of the *Boyne, one of the turning points in Irish history, was fought at Oldcastle in July 1690. Major archaeological attractions include the megalithic *passage-graves at *Newgrange and *Knowth, which are believed to have been built around 3200 B.C. The main towns in the county are Navan, the county capital, Trim, and Kells, which is well known for its association with the celebrated Book of *Kells. It is believed that most of the book was written and illustrated in *Scotland, probably at the monastic settlement at Iona, before it was brought to Kells for its protection in the ninth century. The manuscript was kept in the monastery until 1541, and since 1661 it has been held by Trinity College, Dublin. County Meath is noted for its rich grasslands, ideal for raising cattle. A.S.

Mellifont, the Treaty of (1603). Treaty ending the *Nine Years War. After the Battle of *Kinsale, Hugh *O'Neill surrendered to Lord Mountjoy not knowing that Queen *Elizabeth I had died. The terms were favorable to O'Neill. He was pardoned for taking part in the war, and remained an earl, retaining ownership of his lands. T.C.

Merriman, Brian (c.1749–1805). Poet in the *Irish language. Author of one great masterpiece, *Cúirt an Mheán Oíche*, or *The Midnight Court*, Merriman was born in County *Clare and was a teacher of mathematics. He died in Limerick City. His great poem of more than one thousand lines in perfect rhyming couplets describes how the women of Ireland bring the men to court for their neglect and sexual cowardice. It is a rambunctious, hilarious, and dramatic poem. Scholars are divided as to whether there is a personal or even a political "message" in the poem. Merriman is poking fun at the human condition and providing great entertainment while doing so. A.T.

Mhac an tSaoi, Máire (1922–). Poet and scholar. Daughter of the politician Seán MacEntee, and married to the writer Conor *Cruise O'Brien, Mhac an tSaoi was educated at University College, *Dublin, and the Sorbonne, Paris. She became a lawyer in 1944 and served in the Department of Foreign Affairs abroad from 1947 to 1962. Her poetry combines traditional forms and meters with a contemporary idiom. Her intimate knowledge of Gaelic literature enriches her frank and unsentimental poetry. Among her themes are the pain of loss, women's sexuality, and the roles thrust upon them. Mhac an tSaoi was highly influential on the generation of women poets that followed her, including Eavan *Boland and Nuala *Ní Dhomhnaill. Collections of poetry include *Margadh na Saoire* (1956), *An Cion go dtí Seo* (1987), and *Trasládáil* (1997). M.S.T.

Middleton, Colin (1910–83). Painter. Born in *Belfast, Middleton worked as a damask designer and then studied art. He experimented with many modernist styles of European painting while still prioritizing content. Middleton exhibited regularly at the *Irish Exhibition of Living Art and produced an important body of modernist work. M.C.

missionaries, Irish. Irish priests, brothers, and *nuns commissioned to spread the *Catholic faith in foreign countries. The roots of Irish missionary activity extend back to the sixth century and the age of Irish monasticism when Irish monks traveled to Europe to spread the gospel. Modern Irish missions date from the early 1800s when the Irish *Christian Brothers opened schools in England. Later, they expanded their ministry to the United States. John Hand founded All Hallows College in *Dublin in 1842 as a seminary to train Irish men to serve as diocesan priests exclusively in foreign dioceses. Hundreds of All Hallows priests staffed parishes, especially in America. During the same period, Catholic religious teaching orders began to send members overseas and new orders were instituted specifically to establish foreign missions.

The Presentation Sisters, founded in Ireland in 1775, established a mission to Calcutta in 1841. The Sisters of Mercy, established in 1831 by Catherine Elizabeth McAuley, extended their mission during the 1840s to the United Kingdom, Australia, Canada and, under the leadership of Mary Frances Xavier Warde, to the United States. The White Fathers began a mission to Africa in 1860. The African mission eventually numbered almost half of all Irish missionaries in its ranks. In the twentieth century, new orders such as the Columban Fathers (1916) were founded and grew rapidly until the *Second Vatican Council. The Irish foreign missions grew as part of Ireland's devotional revolution and played a critical role in the development of Irish Catholicism as a worldwide phenomenon. M.P.C.

Mitchel, John (1815–75). Politician, revolutionary, writer. Raised in Newry, County *Down, and educated at Trinity College, Dublin, Mitchel was a lawyer by profession. He joined the *Young Ireland group, and wrote the life of Hugh *O'Neill for their "Library of Ireland" series. After Thomas *Davis's death, Mitchel became editor of the **Nation*, and a full-time writer and national figure. The Great *Famine deeply affected him, and in his book *The Last Conquest of Ireland*, he blamed Britain and the *landlord system for the devastation caused by the Famine.

Mitchel called for an active, and if necessary violent, campaign to end British rule in Ireland. His colleagues thought him too militant and he formed his own paper, the *United Irishman*, in February 1848. A few months later, he was tried for the new crime of treason felony and sentenced to fourteen years *transportation to *Australia. His *Jail Journal* is a classic of prison literature. Mitchell escaped from Australia to America in 1853, and his wife and children followed him there. He earned a living as a journalist and was actively involved in *Irish American politics, particularly in the *Fenian movement. During the *American Civil War, Mitchel supported the Confederate South. He returned to Ireland to run as an abstentionist candidate for Westminster. Disqualified from Parliament because he was an escaped convict, he was elected a second time as an MP (member of Parliament) for *Tipperary, but died soon after on March 20, 1875. T.C.

Mitchell Report. Central document in the *Northern Ireland *peace process. On November 28, 1995, the British and Irish governments established an International Body to examine the decommissioning of illegal arms, one of the primary obstacles to peace negotiations involving all of Northern Ireland's political parties. The International Body, chaired by former US Senator George Mitchell, issued its report on January 22, 1996. The report accepted that Northern Ireland's paramilitary groups need not decommission any arms prior to all-party negotiations, but it set out six principles to which all parties must adhere in order to move the peace process forward. These six principles, which came to be known as the "Mitchell principles," involved a "total and absolute commitment": 1) to democratic and exclusively peaceful means of resolving political issues; 2) to total disarmament of paramilitary organizations; 3) to verification of disarmament by an independent commission; 4) to renounce the use of force or the threat thereof to influence all-party negotiations; 5) to agree to abide by the terms of any agreement reached in all-party negotiations and to resort to democratic and exclusively peaceful methods in trying to alter any aspect of such an agreement; 6) to urge that "punishment" killings and beatings be stopped and to take steps to prevent them.

When the peace negotiations began on June 10, 1996, all the political parties present had to make a clear commitment to the Mitchell principles in order to participate. Because the IRA (*Irish Republican Army) had called off its 1994 cease-fire in February 1996, *Sinn Féin did not meet the requirements for participation in the June talks. The resumption of the IRA cease-fire in July 1997, however, allowed Sinn Féin to enter the negotiations on September 9, 1997. T.D.

Moloney, Mick (1944–). Singer, banjo player, researcher, and writer. Born in County *Galway, Moloney was involved in the 1960s "folk" movement in *Dublin, particularly in the seminal group the Johnstons. In the United States since 1973, he has established a distinguished career as the leading scholar of Irish *music. His Green Fields of America ensemble of musicians and dancers represented the strength of, and gave muscle and status to, Irish American music. Moloney has written extensively on Irish music and has contributed to some sixty recordings, broadcasting, and film work. In 1977, he founded the Folklife Center in Philadelphia and in 1999 he received a National Endowment for the Arts Award. F.V.

Molyneux, William (1656–98). Political writer and scientist. As surveyor general and chief engineer (1684–88, and 1691–98), Molyneux was responsible for supervising military and civil construction in Ireland. A founder of the Dublin Philosophical Society (1683–1708), he published many important works on optics and mathematics. Molyneux was elected MP (member of Parliament) for Trinity College, Dublin (1692–98). His most influential book, *The Case of Ireland's Being Bound by Acts of Parliament in England Stated* (1698), critically examined Ireland's constitutional status and questioned the English Parliament's claim to authority over the Irish *Parliament. Molyneux used the "natural right" ideas of his friend John Locke to argue that because there was a contract between ruler and ruled, legitimate government was dependent upon securing the consent of those governed. By denouncing taxation without consent and legislation without representation as unnatural, Molyneux sought to demonstrate that Ireland was bound only by the laws enacted by its own Parliament. S.A.B.

Monaghan, County. Inland county, one of the three counties of the province of *Ulster in the *Republic of Ireland. Monaghan (500 square miles) has a population of 52,772 (2002 census). Its name is derived from the Irish *Muineachān*, "the place of the shrubs." The county is bordered on the east by *Louth and *Armagh, on the north by *Tyrone, on the west by *Fermanagh and *Cavan, and on the south by *Meath. The principal rivers in the county are the Finn and the Blackwater. The Slievebeagh Mountains along the northwest border of the county separate it from Tyrone. Among the principal lakes in the county are Lough Erne, Lough Eaglish, Lough Muckno, and Glaslough.

Monaghan was dominated by the MacMahon family until the execution of Aodh Rua MacMahon in October 1590. The county was subsequently divided between the remaining native chieftains and a small number of English settlers. This so-called "native plantation" was largely successful in introducing English land-owning systems into the county. It also meant, that unlike other Ulster counties, Monaghan was not part of the "Ulster *Plantation." The county remained predominantly *Catholic in population; in 1901, for example, its population was 74 percent Roman Catholic, with the remainder being divided almost equally between Anglicans and *Presbyterians. After *partition, the county was incorporated into the *Irish Free State. The principal towns in the county are Monaghan town, the county capital, Clones, and Castleblayney. The experience of poor small farmers in Monaghan in the early years of the independent Irish state is powerfully captured in works like *Tarry Flynn* and *The Great Hunger* by the Inniskeen-born poet Patrick *Kavanagh. Charles Gavan *Duffy (1816–1903), a *nationalist leader who became prime minister of Victoria, in Australia, was born in Monaghan. A.S.

Montague, John (1929–). Poet. Montague was born in New York of Irish parents, but sent back to Ireland at an early age to live with relatives. He grew up in County *Tyrone and was educated at University College, Dublin, and Yale. His poetry explores the conflicts and continuity in the lives of individuals and their communities, and the manner in which the past shapes the present. *Death of a Chieftain* appeared in 1964. The resentment and anger about family matters and *Ulster politics in the poems of *The Rough Field* (1972), *A Slow Dance* (1975), and *The Dead Kingdom* (1984) give way to a long-suffering but celebratory tone in *Mount Eagle* (1988). Montague is skeptical about the narrow cultural and *nationalist ideals that dominated the early decades of the *Irish Free State. His best love poems, such as "All Legendary Obstacles," are intense, spare, and technically adroit. His other publications include *The*

Christy Moore

Figure in the Cave and Other Essays (1989), *Collected Poems* (1995), *Love Present and Other Stories* (1997), and *Smashing the Piano* (1999). M.S.T.

Moore, Brian (1921–99). Novelist. Born in *Belfast, Moore is *Northern Ireland's best-known novelist. At the outbreak of World War II, he joined the Air Raid Precautions Unit, and later described some of his experiences during the bombardment of Belfast in his novel *The Emperor of Ice-Cream* (1965). From 1943, Moore worked for the British government in North Africa, Naples, and Marseilles. After the war, he moved to Canada, where he worked as a newspaper reporter. He became a Canadian citizen in 1953. He moved to the United States in 1959 and settled in California. A prolific, popular writer and excellent storyteller, Moore addresses such modern Irish preoccupations as exile, identity, *nationalism, and the *Catholic faith. Among his best-known novels are *The Lonely Passion of Judith Hearne* (1955), set in Belfast (which was originally banned in Ireland); *The Great Victorian Collection* (1975), which mixes realism with surreal elements; and *Black Robe* (1985), set in seventeenth-century Canada. Several of his novels have been made into films. G.OB.

Moore, Christy (1945–). Singer, songwriter, musician, and social activist. One of Ireland's most popular entertainers, Christy Moore was born in Newbridge, County *Kildare, into a musical and politically conscious family. Strongly influenced by the folk music revival in the United States in the late fifties and sixties, Moore sought out the almost extinct pure traditional Irish *music. His early album *Prosperous* (1970) is a natural blend of American folk song influence and Irish traditional sounds such as *uilleann pipes and tin whistle. This classic album contributed to the revival of Irish traditional music. Moore's own songs are characterized by their humorous and satirical comments on Irish culture and politics. He was also the driving force behind the bands *Planxty and Moving Hearts. J.OM.

Moore, George (1852–1933). Novelist. Born at Moore Hall, Ballyglass, County *Mayo, Moore studied art in Paris before turning to fiction. Novels such as *Esther Waters* (1894), considered scandalous in their day, introduced a modern, European dimension to Irish fiction. An autobiographical trilogy, *Hail and Farewell* (1911–14), is a notorious account of his involvement in the *Irish Revival. He also published an influential collection of stories, *The Untilled Field* (1903). From 1911 until his death, Moore lived in London. G.OB.

Moore, Thomas (1779–1852). Poet and lyricist. Born in *Dublin to a *Catholic merchant family, Thomas Moore published more than forty volumes, mostly of verse and song. Educated at Trinity College, Dublin, and at the Inner Temple in London, he never practiced law but instead turned to writing. Moore contributed *nationalist pieces to his friend Robert *Emmet's journal the *United Irishman*. After first publishing a translation of the Greek poet Anacreon (1800), and other volumes of poetry, in 1808 Moore published the first two volumes of his most famous work—*Irish Melodies* (it had grown to eight volumes by 1834). Though many of the songs are openly nationalistic, treating such issues as sedition, violence, Lord Edward *Fitzgerald, and the martyred Robert Emmet, they were a great success with English audiences, due in part to Moore's insistence on singing them himself with great passion in London drawing room society.

Ireland, betrayed and misruled, remained the main theme of most of Moore's lengthy career. In patriotic times, Moore was considered "Ireland's National Bard," and in revisionist days, a trivial and sentimental rhymer. His other works on Irish history include: *Memoirs of Captain Rock, the Celebrated Irish Chieftain* (1824) and a four-volume *History of Ireland* (1835–46), as well as a *Life of Lord Edward* [Fitzgerald] (1831). His oriental romance, *Lallah Rookh*, earned him an unusual £3,000 advance in 1817, along with critical success. In 1848, he collected his numerous books of poetry on nationalistic, political, philosophical, and religious subjects into ten volumes.

Moore is also famous for his friendship with Lord Byron. The two poets met in 1811 and Moore became Byron's literary executor and custodian of Byron's memoirs upon the latter's death in 1824. Moore burned the surely scandalous memoirs at the request of Byron's widow (and half sister) and in 1830 published his own edited collection, *Letters and Journals of Lord Byron, with Notices of his Life* in two volumes. Today he is oddly neglected by literary critics but his songs (such as "The Harp that Once," "Let Erin Remember," and "The Minstrel Boy") remain enormously popular and are considered classics of Irish cultural nationalism. J.MD.

Morgan, Lady (1783–1859). Novelist. Born Sydney Owenson in *Dublin, the daughter of an actor, she first gained attention as a singer and harpist. Her compositions *Twelve Original Hibernian Melodies* (1805) anticipated Thomas *Moore's melodies and made her a celebrity. She is best known for novels that helped to shape romantic conceptions of Ireland, particularly *The Wild Irish Girl* (1806), but also *The O'Briens and the O'Flaherties* (1827). Invited to become a member of the Marquis of Abercorn's household, she married the house surgeon in 1812. She also wrote books on France and Italy. In 1837, she left Dublin for London, where she later died. G.OB.

Morris, Locky (1960–). Conceptual artist and sculptor. Born in *Derry, Morris studied sculpture in *Belfast and Manchester. His identification with local conditions can be seen in a piece of sculpture on emigration commissioned by Derry City Council and situated outside its offices. M.C.

Morrison, Van (1945–). Songwriter, musician. Born in *Belfast, Van Morrison grew up in a musical household. His father was a lover of jazz, blues, and spirituals. As a teenager, Morrison wrote many songs and started a rock and roll band, called THEM. Encouraged to go to London during the mid-sixties, the band was enormously successful in the UK and had two top ten hits, "Here Comes the Night" and

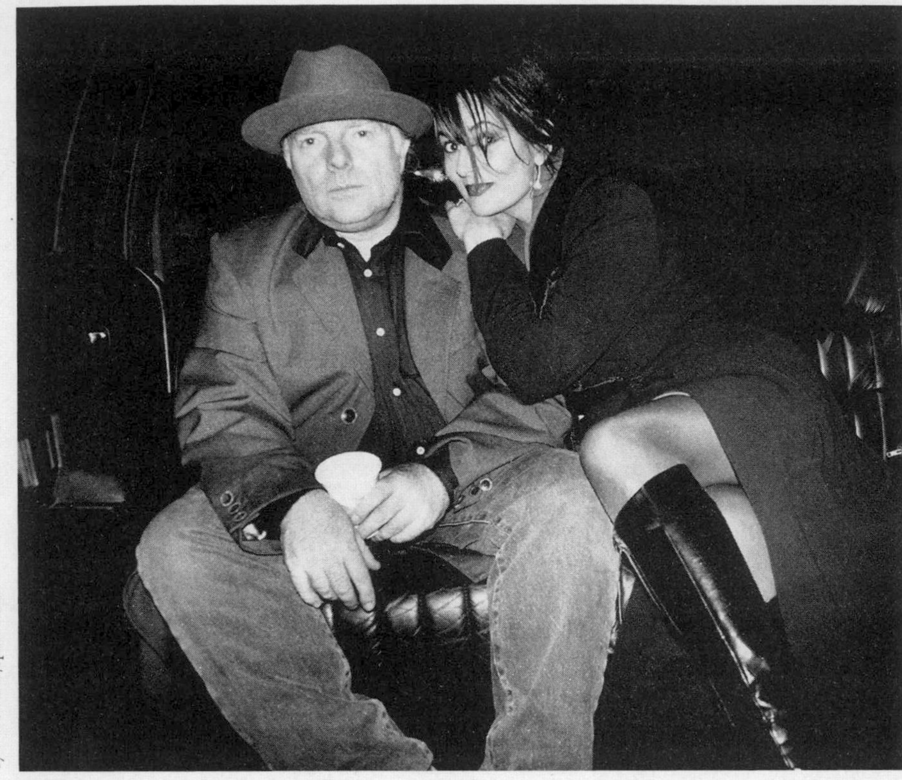

by + ©BP Fallon/bpfallon.com

Van Morrison and Michelle Rocca

"Gloria," both written by Morrison and both still recognized as rock classics. It was the heyday of sixties British rock and roll in "Swinging London," at the time the home of the Beatles, the Rolling Stones, Eric Clapton, and David Bowie. The commercialism and manipulation of the record industry proved too much for the young Morrison and he left London in 1967. He did not record again until 1969, when his album *Astral Weeks* was released. Recorded in the United States, it was universally recognized as one of the greatest albums of rock and roll. A string of classics followed. He pushed his own creative limits, combining jazz and blues influences and eventually returning to his Irish roots to record a unique album with the *Chieftains, *Celtic Heartbeat* (1987). J.OM.

Mountjoy Jail. Prison dating from 1850. This *Dublin jail has housed many thousands of inmates in its history, ranging from petty thieves to notorious murderers and famous figures in Irish history. Several of the Invincibles, a militant nationalist group, were executed in the jail for the *Phoenix Park murders in 1883. Brendan *Behan's experiences as a prisoner in Mountjoy were described in his play *The Quare Fellow* (1954). After the *Easter Rising of 1916, a *hunger strike was mounted by *republican prisoners which culminated in the death of Thomas *Ashe in September 1917. On October 14, 2001, ten *Volunteers, who had been tried and executed in the jail by British military court-martial in 1920–21, were honored with a state funeral and the remains of nine of them were re-interred in Glasnevin Cemetery, Dublin. Now a medium-security prison with a capacity of 670, Mountjoy is the main prison in the Irish *Republic for adult males. S.A.B.

Mulcahy, General Richard (1886–1971). *Irish Free State minister and *Fine Gael leader. Mulcahy was born in *Waterford and educated at Mount Sion *Christian Brothers School and later at Thurles. He was a member of the *Gaelic League and the Irish *Volunteers, and was interned for his role in the *Easter Rising of 1916. Upon his release, he was appointed director of training of the Volunteers and later its chief of staff. A member of the first *Dáil (Parliament) and supporter of the *Anglo-Irish Treaty (1921), he succeeded Michael *Collins as commander of the military forces of the Provisional Government during the *Civil War. He served as minister for defense under the *Cumann na nGaedheal government but resigned over the *Army Mutiny. A TD (Teachta Dála; member of Parliament) for *Dublin and *Tipperary, he became leader of Fine Gael following the resignation of W. T. *Cosgrave in June 1944. Mulcahy served as minister for education during the interparty governments before retiring from politics in 1961. P.E.

Muldoon, Paul (1951–). Poet, playwright, essayist. Muldoon was born into a *Catholic family in Portadown, County *Armagh, and grew up near a village called The Moy. He was educated at St. Patrick's College, Armagh, and at Queen's University, Belfast, where Seamus *Heaney was his tutor. After university, he worked for the BBC in *Northern Ireland as a radio and television producer.

Muldoon's poetry, with its suspicion of systems, myths, and visions, its notions of fluid identity, and its constant awareness of alternative possibilities, has been significantly influenced by Louis *MacNeice. In his early collections, *New Weather* (1973), *Mules* (1977), *Why Brownlee Left* (1980), and *Quoof* (1983), Muldoon writes on themes of hybridity and border crossing between diverse histories, languages, and cultures. "The More a Man Has the More a Man Wants," a sequence of forty-nine sonnets based on the Trickster cycle of the Winnebago Indians, parodies the traditional quest journey. These poems destabilize the sense of place and time, delight in elaborate digressions and verbal pyrotechnics, and dramatize an ironic negotiation between the poet's native attachments and his cosmopolitan literary and historical sensibility.

Since 1990, Muldoon has taught at Princeton University. The work after *Quoof* (his last book before leaving Ireland) elaborates the idea of departure and metamorphosis. The long title poem of *Madoc* (1990) explores interconnection and "mixed marriage"—between old and new worlds, fact and fiction, nationalism and imperialism, poetry and politics, and different kinds of discourse. The parenthetical titles of the individual poems are the names of philosophers, but "Madoc—a Mystery" resists any coherent philosophical outlook or belief.

The Annals of Chile (1994) contains the moving lament, "Incantata," on the death of his lover, the painter Mary Farl Powers, while "Yarrow," an elegy for his mother, closes the volume. In *Hay* (1998) Muldoon continues to demonstrate his formal ingenuity with examples of the ghazal, pantoum, haiku, villanelle, and sestina. The volume includes imitations of other Irish poets such as W. B. *Yeats and Michael *Longley, poems on the *Troubles, and the ambitious "The Bangle (Slight Return)," a series of thirty sonnets, moving between the Australian outback, Virgil, and a Parisian restaurant.

In 1998, he became the Clarendon Lecturer at Oxford University. His Clarendon lectures, an idiosyncratic review of Irish literary history, were published under the title *To Ireland, I* (2000). He has also published a play, *Six Honest Serving Men* (1995), a libretto, *The Shining Brow* (1993), two books for children, and translations from the Irish. Muldoon was awarded the Pulitzer Prize in 2003. E.K-A.

mummers. Participants in mumming, a costumed, masked ritual related to Christmas. This ritual dates to medieval times and survives in the East and North of Ireland. Mumming has associated rhymed verse, part originally of folk plays with legendary and historical heroes such as St. *Patrick, Brian *Boru, or Daniel *O'Connell, and may also involve music. F.V.

Munster. One of the four provinces of Ireland. The province, which covers 9,526 square miles, has a population of 1,101,266 (2002 census). Munster consists of the counties *Clare, *Cork, *Kerry, *Limerick, *Tipperary, and *Waterford. The name derives from Muma, an ancient kingdom in the south of Ireland, which was later divided into Deas Mumhan (Desmond), south Munster, and Tua Mumhan (Thomond), north Munster. The province has some of Ireland's most beautiful scenery, including the rugged coastlines of counties Clare, Cork, and Kerry, the Lakes of Killarney, and the Burren. The famous Battle of *Kinsale (in County Cork) in 1601 ended the *Nine Years War rebellion of the *Ulster Irish chieftains and effectively abolished the old Gaelic order. J.OM.

murals, Belfast wall. Political wall paintings. Belfast has a long tradition of *loyalist murals. The first one, painted around 1908, depicted the Battle of the *Boyne in 1690, when Protestant King *William III defeated Catholic King *James II. The murals were—and for the most part still are—painted on July 12, to commemorate the Battle of the Boyne. Unlike the old murals, the new ones are more intentionally anti-nationalist and anti-Catholic. The sinister images are threatening, and are meant to be.

The emergence of murals on the *nationalist side dates from the *hunger strikes. In the spring and summer of 1981, hundreds of murals were painted by *republicans. From the very beginning, republican murals portrayed the "armed struggle" (unlike the loyalist murals). This was less so in the 1990s as the *peace process unfolded. M.M.

Murphy, Thomas (Bernard) (1935–). Playwright. Born in Tuam, County *Galway, the youngest of ten children, Murphy left school at fifteen and trained as a fitter-welder, and later as a vocational teacher. In his spare time, he took part in amateur dramatics. His first play, *On the Outside*, jointly written with his friend Noel O'Donoghue, won the manuscript prize at the All-Ireland Amateur Drama Competition in 1957. *The Iron Men*, which won script competitions and was revised as *A Whistle in the Dark*, was scathingly rejected by the *Abbey Theatre's managing director, Ernest *Blythe. Often compared to Harold Pinter's *The Homecoming*, which it predates, the play was staged in London, where several reviewers misunderstood the play's violent characters as accurate depictions of all Irishmen. Murphy lived in England between 1962 and 1970. Irish productions of the powerful and tragic *Famine* (1968) and the psychological fairy tale *The Morning*

After Optimism (1971) were well received, but *The Orphans* (1968) was a failure. *The Sanctuary Lamp* (1975) was successful but controversial because it expressed disillusionment with organized religion. Murphy was disappointed by the critical response to *The Blue Macushla* (1980), a play based on the idiom of gangster movies, but three subsequent plays, *The Gigli Concert* (1983), *Conversations on a Homecoming* (1985), and *Bailegangaire* (Town Without Laughter) (1985), (with Siobhán *McKenna as Mommo in her final, brilliant performance) were highly acclaimed and cemented his reputation as one of the foremost playwrights of his generation.

Characterized by what Brian *Friel has called the "pure theatricality" of their language, Murphy's plays focus on social, institutional, familial, and personal breakdown against the backdrop of a changing Ireland. The characters in these plays are on a quest to overcome tragedy and despair; their attainment of spiritual wholeness often involves a leap of faith. With *Too Late for Logic* (1989), Murphy seemed to be looking for new directions. In 1994 he published a novel, *The Seduction of Morality*. A play based on its themes and characters, *The Wake* (1998), was well received, as was *The House* (2000). In October 2001 the Abbey Theatre celebrated Tom Murphy's career with a season of six of his plays. J.C.E.L.

music, classical. The *harp as the national symbol attests to the importance of music in Irish life. The instrument is found on Irish coins and official documents, such as passports. Not a great deal is known of the early history of music in Ireland. Much material held in churches was lost through the ages, and the tradition of the *bardic harpers, professional performers in the employ of the Irish nobility, was oral. The first harp festival was held in *Belfast in 1792, when the tradition had suffered nearly two centuries of decline. The music survives only in transcriptions of the style of the time, by the *Armagh organist, Edward Bunting.

*St. Patrick's Cathedral in *Dublin established a choir in 1432. A pair of organs was acquired in 1471 by *Christ Church Cathedral, where two English madrigal composers, John Farmer (from 1595 to 1599) and Thomas Bateson (from 1608 to 1630), served as organists. Bateson was the first music graduate of the University of Dublin (Trinity College) in 1615, and the city acquired its first theater in Werburgh Street, in 1638.

In the eighteenth century, Dublin, then the second city in the British empire, entered what has been called a "golden age" of music. British and European musicians came to Dublin, and some of them settled there, including Johann Sigismund Kusser (1660–1727), a pupil of the great Lully, composer to Louis XIV, and the Italian composer Francesco Geminiani (1687–1762), one of the great violin virtuosos of his day. The greatest musical event in eighteenth-century Ireland was the premiere of Handel's *Messiah* on April 13, 1742, in Mr. Neale's Great Musick Hall, Fishamble Street, Dublin. An audience of seven hundred was able to fit in the hall because ladies' hoops and gentlemen's swords were prohibited. The best-known Irish composer to emerge in the eighteenth century was John *Field (1782–1837), known as the inventor of the nocturne, and an important influence on Chopin and on composers in Russia, where he spent most of his life. Field's limpid style and easy melodic filigree were much admired (Liszt prepared an edition of the Nocturnes). The music of the *Cork-born composer, pianist, and organist, Philip Cogan (c.1748–1833), who was Thomas *Moore's teacher, is still performed.

Many of the more gifted Irish musicians of the nineteenth century chose to leave Ireland, where the patronage and social glitter of the eighteenth century had faded after the Act of *Union (1800). Dublin-born Michael *Balfe (1808–70) and *Waterford-born William Vincent Wallace (1812–65) were among the most successful composers of English opera in the nineteenth century, and their two most popular works, *The Bohemian Girl* and *Maritana*, were recorded in recent years. Hamilton *Harty (1879–1941) and Charles Villiers *Stanford (1852–1924), the most important Irish composers of the early twentieth century, also worked mainly abroad. However, musicians also came to Ireland from Europe. Pianist and composer Michele Esposito (1855–1929), who trained in Naples, came to the Royal Irish Academy of Music (RIAM) in 1882. The RIAM, which was founded in 1848, was the main music school in Dublin, and in 1890 launched a Dublin Municipal School of Music for the working classes, which survives today as the DIT Conservatory of Music and Drama. Würzburg-trained Heinrich Bewerunge (1862–1923) taught chant and organ at St. Patrick's College, *Maynooth, from 1888. Munich-born Aloys Fleischmann (1910–92), whose father had been cathedral organist in Cork from 1888, was appointed professor of music at University College, Cork, at the age of twenty-four. Fleischmann, Frederick May (1911–85), and Brian *Boydell (1917–2000) were the most important figures in the first generation of modern Irish composers.

The national broadcasting service, *Radio Éireann, formed a symphony orchestra in 1947, but in general the young Irish state did not greatly encourage or support classical music for many years. A national concert hall was not opened until 1981. A national conservatory and opera company have not yet been established. Composers like Gerald *Barry (1952–), Ian Wilson (1964–), Donnacha Dennehy (1970–), and Jennifer Walshe (1974–) have won international attention, as have many Irish performers. Recently, an infrastructure of institutions has been created, including most importantly, the Music Network, a national music development organization (supported by the *Arts Council since 1986) that promotes and fosters the careers of Irish musicians at home and abroad. M.D.

music, popular. Following the establishment of Ireland's national *radio service, which started broadcasting on January 1, 1926, Irish *dance and traditional *music, which up to then had been notably regional, became nationally available. After World War II, Ireland, like Britain, came increasingly under the influence of American music and culture. On the radio people listened to the big band music of the swing era, such as Glenn Miller, and in ballrooms throughout Ireland people danced to this music. In Dublin's Theatre Royal, meanwhile, big band performers such as Stan Kenton and Count Basie played to enthusiastic audiences. People could also tune in to the BBC and the American Forces Network (AFN) and hear all varieties of American music, from big band, to jazz, and the emerging rock and roll of the 1950s. Elvis Presley galvanized and sometimes appalled the Irish population (as much as the American and European). From the mid-1950s, pockets of rock and roll sedition emerged, and by the late 1950s and the early 1960s, pop charts became an essential phenomenon on the radio. European-based radio stations such as Radio Luxembourg broadcast far more pop-oriented music than Irish radio.

Replacing the big bands, the show bands came into being in Ireland to compensate for the lack of live appearances by American and other international stars who could be heard only on the radio. From the late fifties into the early seventies, show bands performed the pop hits of the day in dance halls all over Ireland. While there was discipline, rigor, and style in their execution of the pop tunes of the day, show bands performed little, if any, original material. Through the 1960s, as Ireland changed socially and economically, up to seven hundred bands toured the length and breadth of the country, including the Clipper Carlton, the Royal Showband, the Miami, and the Dixies, which achieved almost cult status. Some of Ireland's internationally known rock stars got their start in show bands, most notably Van *Morrison (1945–) with the Monarchs, and Rory Gallagher (1949–95) with the Fontana Showband. Unlike most other bands of the time, these two show bands interspersed obscure rhythm and blues songs with familiar pop chart tunes. In 1963 in Belfast, Morrison founded the rock group THEM, which was successful in the British charts until it broke up in 1966. Morrison's 1968 album *Astral Weeks* is highly regarded as one of the most important rock records of all time. Gallagher, meanwhile, formed Taste in 1965. This band split up in 1970, but by that time Gallagher was viewed as a bona fide electric guitar hero. Even after his untimely death in 1995, he is rightly regarded as one of the finest exponents of the electric guitar.

In the 1970s, Irish pop started to make it into the British charts with the folk group the *Dubliners, Celtic rock band *Horslips, singer/songwriter Gilbert O' Sullivan (1946–), and rock band Thin Lizzy. The latter's front man and main songwriter, Phil Lynott (1951–86), is regarded as one of hard rock music's most gentle, romantic lyric writers. Two emerging Irish rock bands in the late 1970s that were inspired by Thin Lizzy were the Boomtown Rats and *U2. The former, after several successful years, imploded in 1982 and its leader Bob *Geldof (1954–) went on to develop Live Aid in 1985. U2 is one of the most successful rock bands in the world. Through a mixture of shrewd marketing, an inordinate level of self-belief, and a back catalogue of remarkably resilient pop/rock songs, U2 has remained at the top of the industry for over two decades. While they remain a guiding light for Irish rock, few Irish bands have followed in their footsteps and none has come close to their success.

From the 1980s and 1990s onward, however, many Irish pop and rock bands have succeeded in topping charts internationally: the Undertones, Chris de Burgh (1947–), the Pogues, Sinéad *O'Connor (1966–), Enya (1961–), the Cranberries, the Saw Doctors, Boyzone, the *Corrs, Boyzone's former lead singer Ronan Keating (1977–), Westlife (an unashamed pop band that has become the only act to reach number one with their first seven releases), Samantha Mumba (1982–), Divine Comedy, and Ash. T.C-L.

music, traditional. The indigenous music of Ireland. Mostly "folk" music, it was created and performed locally for the entertainment and ritual usage of the plain people. The bulk of its repertoire dates to the nineteenth and the eighteenth centuries. However, traditional music also incorporates the music and ethos of the classical court musicians, the *harpists, whose art was submerged into folk music with the destruction of the Gaelic order after the sixteenth century. This stream of higher artistic consciousness was carried on in classic *uilleann pipe music and in fiddle music, and today is expressed on all instruments. The term *traditional* has been favored among players since circa 1900, implying a synergy of artistic pedigree, political awareness, and musical integrity.

Traditional music at its broadest incorporates

Henry Benagh and Jackie Daly at the Crosses of Annagh, County Clare

instrumental music (some tunes linked to specific dances), song in Irish and English (some melodies are played as instrumentals), and social and performance dancing. Its repertoire is largely of the island, closely tied to Gaelic music in Scotland, and, particularly in song, owing much to older English ballads. This amalgam includes tunes from ancient to modern that have been passed on in a largely oral process over several hundred years. Less-favored pieces fell into disuse, preferred items underwent change according to personal taste, misinterpretation, or memory lapse, compounding a slowly changing core of tunes and song which remain universally recognized and played. Printed sources from the mid-1800s onward retained once-forgotten items, making possible their reassessment and reincorporation into the oral process. Beginning in the early 1900s, recorded music preserved actual personal styles of playing, and led to a national style on a particular instrument (for example, in fiddle music *Coleman's became the standard). Since the introduction of cassette technology in the late 1960s, there has been even greater fluidity in movement of styles and repertories. Today three thousand CDs of traditional Irish music are available between Ireland, Britain, and the United States.

Instruments

Traditional music is played on the *harp, the *uilleann pipes, fiddle (violin), concert flute (wooden, open-hole model), chromatic (button) accordion, melodeon, concertina, tin whistle, and banjo. Snare drum was originally used as rhythmic percussion (in **céilí* bands), but since the 1960s the bodhrán (single-sided frame drum) has achieved huge popularity. Accompaniment initially involved piano on early 1900s recordings, but today is largely done on guitar and an Irish version of bouzouki. Other instruments used include keyboards, mandolin, harmonica, spoons, and bones—in all, thirty-seven different types of instruments.

The Music

The oldest forms of traditional music are the slow airs and marches, some dating to the sixteenth century. The jig, *dance music in 6/8, 12/8, and 9/8 time, is referenced first in the 1670s. The reel in 4/4 time came from Scotland in the late 1700s, the hornpipe also in 4/4 time came from England in the same period, and the polka in 2/4 time, the mazurka in 3/4 time, and the waltz from Europe in the mid-1800s. These tunes, after entering Irish music, acquired various Irish regional accents and styles, which render them utterly distinct from the originals. This trend continues up to the present, with popular tunes being borrowed from other cultures, and ultimately becoming acculturated by subtle change of timing and rhythmic emphasis. *Donegal, for instance, has a repertory of 4/4-time Scottish strathspeys locally known as "highlands."

Regional Styles

While all styles were originally locally based, the music has five major styles with a variety of articulation, repertoire, instrument, and context. The different styles involve combinations of basic playing techniques—use of bow in fiddle, of wind in flutes and concertinas, and so forth, basic note decoration, tempo, and rhythm. Originally (and still) geographically associated, these are now also widely disseminated by recordings and their adoption is a matter of personal taste or choice. All are defined on fiddle. The five major styles are: Donegal (fiddle based, subtle decoration, emphatic bow use, Scottish influence), *Sligo (fast tempo, highly ornamented), East *Galway (minor keys, variable modality, melody centered, slow tempo), *Clare (slower tempo, melody centered, selective decoration), and Sliabh Luachra (North *Cork/*Kerry, using polkas and 12/8 "slide" jigs, rhythm-dominant, fiddle based). On flute, a *Leitrim style (breathy, rhythmic) and a *Roscommon (florid ornament) are prominent, while on uilleann pipes regional styles have given way to individual styles because of the lack of local players.

Song

The major song styles are *sean-nós in the *Irish language, *Ulster ballad style, "old" ballads in English, a more standardized, widespread *a cappella* ballad style in the English language with regional variants, and a popular ballad style with accompaniment. Major distinctive styles within Irish-language song are found in South Ulster, in West Donegal, Connemara, Kerry, and Ring (County *Waterford).

Collectors

Despite the existence of an oral tradition, the work of nineteenth-century idealists in committing the repertoire and lyrics of Irish music to print has been both invaluable and influential. Edward Bunting compiled the first major collection of instrumental music in 1796. Other collectors include: George *Petrie, Patrick Weston Joyce, Henry Hudson, James Goodman, Francis O'Neill, Frank Roche, and Breandán *Breathnach for instrumental music; and Charlotte Brooke, Eugene *O'Curry, Maighréad Ní Annagáin & Séamus Clandillon, Sam Henry, Joseph Ranson, and Séamus Ennis for song. The Department of Irish Folklore at University College, Dublin, has also contributed to the preservation of Irish music.

Revival

Traditional music was carried in the tailspin of the *Irish Language Revival at the end of the nineteenth century. Traditional song was seen as a vehicle for language, and dance as a social bonder. When, in the wake of the 1935 Public Dance Halls Act, and in response to social change, Irish social dancing moved to specialized halls, ensembles capable of providing the necessary repertoire and volume (*céilí* bands) were formed. By the late 1950s, the majority of dancing in Ireland was to modern music provided by show bands and traditional music was rarely performed. In 1951 a group of dedicated players, backed by Irish Americans who knew and loved Irish music from the recordings of a couple of generations of Irish immigrants, formed an organization to revive traditional music, called *Comhaltas Ceoltóirí Éireann (CCE). Spearheading the revival around the same time, Ciarán *MacMathuna was promoting solo instrumental performance on the*radio and the classical composer Seán *Ó Riada was experimenting with different forms of indigenous music. In 1968, Breandán Breathnach's Na Píobairí Uilleann body was formed to promote uilleann piping. Such organizations as the Irish World Music Centre (IWMC) (a postgraduate study facility with an ethnomusicological overview and a special interest in Irish traditional music at University of *Limerick), the *Irish Traditional Music Archive (1987), and the harpists group Cáirde na Cruite (1960), and various summer schools and competitions have contributed significantly to the flourishing of traditional music today. F.V.

Mythology. See **Celtic mythology.**

N

Nagle, Nano (1718–84). Foundress of the Presentation Sisters Order of Nuns. Nagle came from a *Catholic landowning background, and ran several schools for poor children in *Cork City, from the 1750s. In 1776, she set up the Sisters of the Charitable Instruction of the Sacred Heart of Jesus in Cork. The first of the socially active female congregations in Ireland, it was formally recognized, in 1802, as the Presentation Sisters, and spread rapidly to become one of the largest and most widely distributed Roman Catholic female congregations in the world. C.C.

***Nation*, the.** Weekly *nationalist newspaper. Founded in 1842 by Thomas *Davis, John *Dillon, and Charles Gavan *Duffy, the *Nation* served as the chief vehicle for the dissemination of the *Young Ireland movement's views. Though the ideas expressed in the paper were varied, the *Nation* provided the most thoroughgoing expression of Irish cultural nationalism between its founding and 1897, when it ceased publication. Many of its writers, including such important political and literary figures as John *Mitchel, Thomas Francis *Meagher, William *Carleton, and James Clarence *Mangan, urged the Irish people to resist British domination, extolled the qualities of early Celtic culture, and celebrated the contributions of Ireland's Gaelic heritage to world civilization. In keeping with its nationalist ethos, the newspaper promoted the revival and preservation of the *Irish language. T.D.

National Archives. The official archives of the Irish government. Established in 1988, the National Archives are an amalgamation of the Public Record Office of Ireland (founded 1867) and the State Paper Office (founded 1702). Located at Bishop Street in *Dublin, the archives hold the records of Irish government departments, the courts and other state agencies, the Church of Ireland, and documents from private sources. Most records date from the nineteenth and twentieth centuries and are open to inspection by members of the public. (Address: Bishop Street, Dublin 8. Web site: *www.nationalarchives.ie.*) S.A.B.

National Botanic Gardens. Gardens founded by the *Royal Dublin Society in 1795 to serve the scientific and agricultural communities of Ireland. Dr. Walter Wade, who laid out the grounds, introduced exotic plants from around the world. The Botanic Gardens were placed under government control in 1877 and now cover fifty acres on the river Tolka at Glasnevin, a suburb of *Dublin. They contain a wonderfully large plant collection of more than twenty-thousand species, herbaceous borders, a rose garden, a rockery, an arboretum and pond, as well as Burren areas. The recently restored Curvilinear Range of Glasshouses (constructed 1843–69) are a fine example of the work of the Dublin iron-master Richard Turner, who also designed the Glasshouse at Kew Gardens (England). A new education and visitor center opened in September 2000 and the gardens continue to serve scientific functions and delight visitors of all ages. S.A.B.

National Gallery of Ireland, the. Inaugurated in 1864, the gallery houses the national collection of Irish art from the late sixteenth century to the mid-twentieth century, as well as a collection of European master paintings from the fourteenth to the twentieth centuries. Among the most important eighteenth-century painters on display are Nathaniel *Hone the Elder, George Barrett, and Thomas Roberts. The nineteenth-century collection has excellent examples of the group known as the Irish Impressionists (Nathaniel *Hone the Younger, Walter *Osborne, and Sarah Purser). The sculpture collection from the seventeenth to the nineteenth century includes many Irish portrait busts. The building was adapted from Lanyon's original plan by Francis Fowke. A new Millennium Wing designed by Benson and Forsyth houses Irish *painting and *sculpture galleries. The work of Sir William *Orpen, Paul *Henry, Mainie *Jellett, and Louis Le *Brocquy can be viewed in the new wing.

An education program arranged around exhibition themes provides constant lectures and tours. A center for the study of Irish art, a Yeats Archive, a multimedia facility, and a national portrait collection are also planned. (Address: Merrion Square West, Dublin 2. Web site: *www.nationalgallery.ie.*) M.C.

National League, the. Constituency organization of the *Irish Parliamentary Party. Following the 1882 Kilmainham Treaty, Charles Stewart *Parnell considered the land question to be solved and turned his attention to national self-government, or *home rule. On October 17, 1882, the Irish National League was established in *Dublin to aid in the constitutional struggle for home rule. While Parnell was the driving force behind the organization, its constitution was drawn up by Timothy Harrington and T. M. *Healy. The league, in theory, was to be governed by a committee of forty-eight members but, in reality, power always remained in the hands of the Parliamentary Party. By 1886, there were over a thousand branches nationwide, each responsible for financing election campaigns and MPs' (members of Parliament) salaries. The league continued this essential function until the Home Rule party split in 1890. P.E.

National Library of Ireland. Ireland's national library dedicated to the collection and preservation of materials of Irish interest. The National Library was established in 1877, being founded upon the library of the *Royal Dublin Society. Originally located in *Leinster House, the library moved to its present building on Kildare Street in 1890. The National Library's collections consist of close to one million books and extensive files of *newspapers, prints, drawings, maps, and *photographs. Important documents housed at the library include Giraldus Cambrensis's twelfth-century accounts of the topography and conquest of Ireland (*Topographia Hiberniae* and *Expugnatio Hibernica*) and the Ormond deeds, a major source for the medieval history of Ireland. The collection of manuscripts contains 1,200 Gaelic manuscripts, including the fourteenth-century Book of Magauran, and the papers of famous Irish writers (such as W. B. *Yeats and Séan *O'Casey) and political personalities (such as John *Redmond and Roger *Casement). The Genealogical Office, which originated in 1552 as the Office of Arms, was incorporated into the library in 1943. The National Library's Photographic Archive opened in Temple Bar in 1998. A genealogical advisory service for family historians is currently available for personal callers to the library. (Address: National Library of Ireland, Kildare Street, Dublin 2. National Photographic Archive, Meeting House Square, Temple Bar, Dublin 2. Genealogical Office, 2 Kildare Street, Dublin 2. Web site: *www.nli.ie.*) S.A.B.

National Museum of Ireland. Ireland's national museum consists of collections of archaeology, history, decorative arts, and natural history. Established in 1877, the National Museum acquired the scientific collections of the *Royal Dublin Society, which now form the basis of the Natural History Museum. In the 1890s, the museum also received the *Royal Irish Academy's collection of antiquities and it continues to preserve the natural and cultural material heritage of Ireland. Archaeological and historical collections are displayed at the National Museum, on Kildare Street. They include a collection of weapons, tools, and artifacts from the *Viking burial grounds at Kilmainham and Islandbridge, the largest such collection outside Scandinavia. The archaeological collection also contains the National Treasury, with outstanding examples of Celtic and medieval art such as the *Tara Brooch, the *Ardagh Chalice, and the *Cross of Cong. The Broighter Hoard is a treasure of gold objects (*La Tène–style torc or neckband, a miniature sailing boat with oars, a bowl, and two necklaces) dating from around the last century B.C., which were found at Broighter, County *Derry, in 1896. Also, displayed here is the Derrynaflan Hoard, which consists of liturgical church metalwork, comprising a chalice, a paten with support, and a strainer, all covered by a large bronze basin. The hoard was discovered in 1980, on the bog-island of Derrynaflan, County *Tipperary. The high-quality die-stamped ornament and enameled studs of the paten and stand would argue for an eighth-century date for both of them, whereas the stylized filigree of the chalice would suggest a date for it in the following century.

The museum's collection of croziers (wooden staffs, often enshrined in metal, used by Irish abbots from the eighth to the twelfth century) and reliquaries is unique in Europe, and includes decorative examples from *Clonmacnoise, County *Offaly, and Lismore, County *Waterford. The Natural History Museum on Merrion Street holds an extensive collection of zoology and the National Museum in Collins Barracks exhibits decorative arts, history, and folklore. (Address: National Museum of Ireland, Archaeology and History, Kildare Street, Dublin 2. National Museum of Ireland, Decorative Arts and History, Collins Barracks, Benburb Street, Dublin 7. National Museum of Ireland, Natural History, Merrion Street, Dublin 2. Web site: *www.museum.ie.*) S.A.B., P.H.

Nationalism. Irish nationalism emerged as an ideology during the late eighteenth century. Since then, two distinct, though interrelated traditions have developed: constitutional nationalism, which has sought to achieve substantial political autonomy by working through the existing parliamentary system, and "physical force" nationalism, which has sought a complete separation from British rule by means of armed revolt. There are also cultural nationalists who have sought to preserve the indigenous Gaelic cultural traditions, particularly the *Irish language.

The constitutional and "physical force" traditions have never been mutually exclusive. Many gains have been achieved by the constitutional movement only because of an implicit threat of mass violence and proponents of "physical force" have at times adopted parliamentary means to achieve their own strategic objectives. Generally, the constitutionalists have regarded the achievement of an independent Irish state as a gradual process and have been willing to accept less than complete autonomy. By contrast, the "physical force" movement has insisted on the immediate achievement of an Irish Republic. Cultural nationalists, meanwhile, have argued that the achievement of any degree of political autonomy would be meaningless if the "soul" of the nation—its language and cultural traditions—was lost.

Inspired by the republicanism of the *French Revolution, the *Society of United Irishmen was founded in Belfast in October 1791. It called on Irishmen of all religious denominations to overthrow British rule. The unsuccessful *Rebellion of 1798, however, exacerbated sectarian divisions and led to the Act of *Union and formal political union with Britain in 1800. Although nonsectarianism has ever since remained a guiding principle of Irish nationalism and many of its leaders have been Protestants, Irish nationalism has drawn its support largely from among Catholics. This occurred because British identity was avowedly Protestant and the British state overtly discriminated against Catholics.

In the 1820s, the first significant constitutional nationalist movement emerged, led by Daniel *O'Connell. Using grassroots organization of the Irish peasantry, the *Catholic Emancipation movement achieved the right of Catholics to sit in the British Parliament in 1829. Catholic priests actively participated in the movement, part of an increasingly close relationship between *Catholicism and nationalism. A similar constitutional movement led by O'Connell during the 1840s to *repeal the Act of Union failed. Meanwhile, a group of younger men known as *Young Ireland, which included Thomas *Davis, called for more forceful measures. Davis, in particular, placed great emphasis on cultural revival and the preservation of the *Irish language. Even before an abortive rising in 1848 during the Great *Famine, however, many of Young Ireland's leaders had been arrested.

Following the catastrophe of the Famine, which many nationalists blamed on British misgovernment, Irish *emigrants to America played an increasingly prominent role in supporting and funding Irish nationalist organizations, including the secret, oath-bound *Irish Republican Brotherhood (IRB), founded in 1858. The *Fenians, as its members were popularly known, attempted a rebellion in 1867, but it proved to be an ill-organized fiasco. In the late 1870s, Fenians joined constitutionalists in a "New Departure" to achieve fair terms of land tenure for Irish tenant farmers. In the 1880s, agrarian agitation and constitutional protest resulted in the emergence of a disciplined Irish party in the British Parliament led by Charles Stewart *Parnell. Dedicated to achieving *home rule for Ireland, the so-called *Irish Parliamentary Party frequently held the balance of power at Westminster.

In 1890, Parnell fell from power due to personal scandal, and, during the following decade, nationalist energies shifted to the cultural sphere, where such organizations as the *Gaelic League, founded in 1893, promoted the Irish language and the revival of the native culture. During the first decade of the twentieth century, political nationalism reemerged through both a revived Parliamentary Party led by John *Redmond, which put home rule back on the agenda at Westminster, as well as new "advanced" nationalist organizations, such as Arthur *Griffith's *Sinn Féin, founded in 1905, which sought a combination of political autonomy, cultural revival, and economic self-sufficiency. When resistance from *unionists in *Ulster blocked autonomy for all thirty-two counties and *World War I delayed implementation of home rule, a revived Irish Republican Brotherhood staged the *Easter Rising of 1916. Although the rising was brutally repressed and fifteen of its leaders were executed, a transformed Sinn Féin emerged after the war as the strongest political formation in Ireland and led the struggle for independence between 1919 and 1921. Under the *Anglo-Irish Treaty negotiated in December 1921, twenty-six counties became a self-governing dominion, though still formally under the crown. However, the *Constitution of 1937 made the twenty-six counties a republic in everything but name, and, in 1948, the government officially proclaimed the *Republic of Ireland. The goal of a republic consisting of the entire island of Ireland remains elusive and Northern Ireland's six counties remain part of the United Kingdom. During the *Troubles in *Northern Ireland, which began in 1968, the traditional divisions within Irish nationalism have been recapitulated, with the *Social Democratic and Labour Party (SDLP) representing the constitutionalist approach, and Sinn Féin, which is indissolubly, if indefinably, linked to the *Irish Republican Army, representing the "physical force" tradition. Under the leadership of Gerry *Adams, Sinn Féin renounced violence and turned to constitutional politics. The party was involved in the negotiations leading to the *Good Friday Agreement and its members now participate in the new institutions created by the agreement. A dissident group of republicans rejected the Good Friday Agreement and still adhere to the "physical force" tradition of nationalism. F.B.

Nationalist Party of Northern Ireland. Name given to the nationalist MPs (members of Parliament) in the *Northern Ireland Parliament. The Nationalist Party was not a proper party but a collection of local groups and organizations united mainly in their opposition to *unionism and characterized by *Catholicism. The party dominated politics in the Catholic community until the advent of the *civil rights movement in 1968. After Seán *Lemass's visit to *Stormont, Eddie McAteer, the leading Nationalist MP, was persuaded to become the leader of the opposition, in effect recognizing the Northern Parliament's legitimacy. The party would soon be eclipsed by the *Social Democratic and Labour Party (SDLP) as the *Troubles progressed. T.C.

Neeson, Liam (1952–). Actor. Born in Ballymena, County *Antrim, Neeson was an amateur boxer before taking up the theater. The director John Boorman cast him in *Excalibur* (1981) after seeing him at the *Abbey Theatre in *Dublin. His debut on Broadway was in *Anna Christie* in 1993, which won him comparisons with Marlon Brando and a Tony nomination. In 2002, he starred on Broadway in Arthur Miller's *The Crucible* to great acclaim. He received an Oscar nomination for the leading role in Steven Spielberg's *Schindler's List* (1993). Neeson

Liam Neeson

starred in Neil *Jordan's 1996 bio-epic *Michael Collins* and in such films as *Suspect* (1987), *Husbands and Wives* (1992), *Rob Roy* (1995), and *Star Wars: The Phantom Menace* (1999). M.E.

neutrality. Principle of Irish *foreign policy since World War II. The roots of Irish neutrality go back to the *War of Independence (1919–21), when Irish *republicans argued that the policy would allow an independent Ireland to respect legitimate British security interests without itself being drawn into a war involving the United Kingdom. Despite Irish aspirations, however, the *Anglo-Irish Treaty of 1921 granted Britain the use of three Irish ports (Berehaven, Cobh, and Lough Swilly) and such other facilities as might be needed in time of war, effectively making Irish neutrality unfeasible.

The situation changed in 1938, when British Prime Minister Neville Chamberlain, following negotiations with Éamon *de Valera, agreed to give the Irish government unconditional control of the treaty ports, in return for Ireland's pledge that no foreign power could use Irish territory as a base of attack on Britain. When World War II began in September 1939, Ireland announced that it would remain neutral. Over the following six years, de Valera's government kept Ireland out of the war, despite often bitter criticism from Britain and the United States. (Partly to defuse this criticism, de Valera secretly authorized informal military and intelligence cooperation with the Allies.) Ireland continued to remain neutral after the war. In 1949, the Irish coalition government then in power declined to join NATO, citing *partition as a reason for not participating in an alliance involving Britain. In recent years, suggestions that increasing inter-European cooperation should include a military component have sparked renewed debate in Ireland over the precise nature of Irish neutrality. T.D.

Newfoundland, the Irish in. The Irish became established in Newfoundland because of the annual cod-fishing expeditions to the territory from the west coast of England and the south coast of Ireland. While intermittent contact with Newfoundland was not unknown prior to the seventeenth century, Irish ships, traders, and fishermen were regularly in what became Canadian waters from the 1670s.

*Waterford was then a major staging and provisioning port for English fleets heading to Newfoundland. Together with *Wexford and *Cork, Waterford provided the bulk of the Irish population that eventually overwintered and settled in Newfoundland. By

Detail in Newgrange, Neolithic Passage Grave, County Meath

the 1770s, around five thousand men and one hundred ships left Irish ports annually for seasonal work in Newfoundland and several permanent communities were established there. Anglo-French conflict and bouts of anti-*Catholic persecution failed to reverse the trend of Irish migration and in 1784 the British authorities tolerated the first Catholic mission in *Canada. In 1800, *United Irishmen within Newfoundland's garrison attempted an anti-British revolt which testified to the strength of connections between the colony and their native country. Approximately half the Newfoundland population was of Irish birth or extraction by 1836, a proportion sustained into modern times. The distinctive features of this community included the retention of regional accents from Ireland's southern maritime counties and the survival of the *Irish language and traditions in Newfoundland, or what they called *Talamh an Éisc*, "the land of the fish." R.OD.

Newgrange. *Passage-grave in the Boyne Valley, in County *Meath. Newgrange is Ireland's most famous prehistoric monument, built about five hundred years before the Pyramids, and a millennium before Stonehenge. Under a large mound some 280 feet in diameter and 36 feet high, a 66-foot-long passage leads to a burial chamber 20 feet high. The grave is renowned for the rising sun shining into it for seventeen minutes as it climbs over the horizon at the winter solstice a few days before Christmas. Accessible from the chamber are three burial niches, two with stone basins (possibly for cremated bone). The beautifully carved stone at the entrance, others in the tomb chamber, as well as some of the ninety-seven large recumbent slabs forming the mound's kerb, are decorated with a variety of geometrical designs, including the triple spiral unique to Newgrange. Enclosing this Stone Age mound are twelve out of the original thirty-eight upright boulders which once formed a Bronze Age circle around

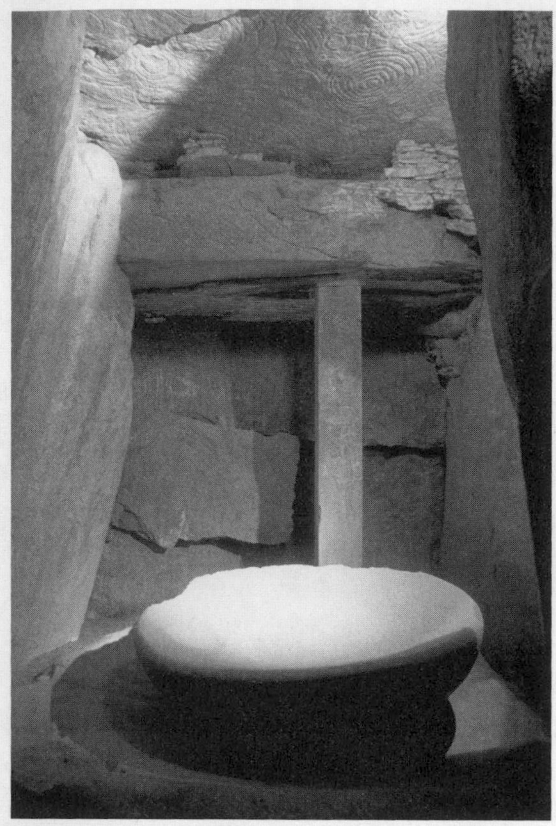

Interior of Newgrange, Neolithic Passage Grave, County Meath

it. Newgrange is accessible only through the Brú na Bóinne Interpretative Center on the south side of the Boyne. P.H.

Newman, John Henry (1801–90). English educator and cardinal. Newman was the first rector of Dublin Catholic University. Educated at Trinity College, Oxford, he became vicar of St. Mary's, Oxford, in 1828. After traveling widely in southern Europe, Newman began his *Tracts for the Times* (1833) and in 1835 joined the "Oxford movement," an attempt to revitalize the Church of England by reviving certain Roman Catholic doctrines and rituals. In 1837, Newman published a defense of Anglo-Catholicism, *Romanism and Popular Protestantism*. He converted to Roman Catholicism and was ordained a priest in 1846. Newman established oratories at Birmingham (1847) and London (1850). He reinvigorated Catholic *education in Ireland and served as the rector of Dublin Catholic University (1854–58). He was made a cardinal in 1879. S.A.B.

newspapers. More than 150 titles are published in Ireland each week, between daily, weekly, and provincial papers. Traditionally, there has been a clear distinction in the political affiliations of the major newspapers. The *Irish Independent*, which was founded by William Martin Murphy in 1905, supported *Fine Gael while the *Irish Press*, which was set up by Éamon *de Valera in 1931, was a vehicle of the *Fianna Fáil party. The *Irish Times*, established in 1859, catered to the *Protestant minority and the urban middle class, but in the 1960s it became more liberal.

These lines of political demarcation have become less evident in recent years. The *Irish Press* ceased production in 1995 after decades of financial and industrial strife. The *Irish Independent* broke with traditional affinities in the general election of 1997, when it urged its readers to vote against the government of the day, of which Fine Gael was the dominant party.

The *Irish Times* is regarded as Ireland's premier newspaper. It places particular emphasis on free thinking, with columnists such as Fintan O'Toole, Mary Holland (d. 2003), Vincent Browne, and John Waters carrying on the tradition of Flann *O'Brien and John Healy. Geraldine Kennedy became the first woman editor of the *Irish Times* in 2002. Its Web site, *www.Ireland.com,* is a fine example of electronic publishing.

In recent years, the *Cork Examiner* has been reinvented as a national newspaper—the *Irish Examiner*—which competes with the *Irish Independent* for the middlebrow market. Irish editions of British tabloids—the *Star*, the *Sun*, and the *Irish Mirror*—have also made great inroads into the market in recent years.

In the North, the ethos of the main newspapers is still determined along political and sectarian grounds. The *Irish News* is bought mostly by nationalists while the *Newsletter* and the *Belfast Telegraph* are seen to have *unionist leanings. The Sunday newspapers in the *Republic are also divided along these lines, though not as rigidly. The *Sunday Business Post* and *Ireland On Sunday* are nationalistic in their outlook while the *Sunday Independent* professes to reach out to the unionist community. The Irish edition of the *Sunday Times* might have some claim to be the first all-Ireland newspaper, with healthy sales among both communities, North and South. The *Sunday Tribune* has built up a considerable reputation for investigative journalism and exposés on political sleaze, while the Irish-language weekly *Foinse* is a bright and breezy publication combining national news with regional issues and a particular emphasis on the *Gaeltacht areas. The *Evening Herald*, which is part of the Independent Group, is Ireland's bestselling evening paper. (Web sites: *www.irishexaminer.com*; *www.independent.ie*; *www.sunday-times.co.uk*; *www.irelandonsunday.com*; *www.sbpost.ie*; *www.news-letter.co.uk*; *www.tribune.ie*; *www.belfasttelegraph.co.uk*; *www.foinse.ie*; *www.irishnews.com*.) B.D.

New York, the Irish in. New York City has been home to the Irish for three centuries. Beginning in the 1600s and through the 1700s, most of the Irish entering New York were *Ulster *Protestants with farming and mercantile backgrounds. In 1830, Irish *immigrants numbered about 20 percent of New York City's population. By the middle of the nineteenth century, however, economic, social, and political pressures in Ireland forced greater numbers, especially *Catholics, to emigrate. The *Famine accelerated this exodus, driving 848,000 men, women, and children to New York between 1847 and 1851. This unprecedented onslaught of destitute, ill, and unskilled immigrants burdened the city with its first social service crisis, resulting in the creation of institutions such as the Emigrant Savings Bank, an Emigrant Commission, and the first Immigration Station at Castle Garden. Their arrival also stretched the limits of existing institutions like the Almshouse Department, the Lunatic Asylum, Bellevue Hospital, and the House of Refugees. For the next fifty years, the flow of Irish continued despite improved economic, social, and political conditions in Ireland. This altered the profile of the typical Irish immigrant to single Catholics in their twenties, more than half female.

Irish immigrants became productive citizens, finding work mostly as domestics, day laborers, teachers, and civil servants. In 1873, John Holland, a former *Christian Brother, arrived in New York. He designed and launched the first submarine in 1878 in Paterson, New Jersey. In 1858, the Irishman John O'Mahoney established the *Fenian Brotherhood in New York. John *Devoy, the *Fenian rebel, came to New York in 1871 and went on to become an editor and journalist. Éamon *de Valera, one of modern Ireland's greatest politicians and statesmen, was born in Manhattan in 1882 to an immigrant mother who sent him back to Ireland when he was two and a half years old to be raised by her family in County *Limerick. Many famous Irish figures made New York their home, from Thomas Addis Emmet, who became attorney general of New York (1812–13), to the great Irish tenor, John *McCormack.

The Irish left indelible marks on New York's Catholic Church and politics. Under the leadership of Archbishop John Hughes, a native of County *Tyrone, and a succession of Irish and Irish American bishops, priests, and *nuns, the Catholic Church grew from a minor denomination with two churches in 1820 to a major institution with sixty by 1860. The Church also established St. Vincent's Hospital (1849), the New York Foundling Hospital (1870), St. Patrick's Cathedral (1879), and many other schools, hospitals, and orphanages.

One of the darker, more complex episodes of the Irish experience in New York was the 1863 Draft Riots. Angered by unfair conscription laws ($300 could buy an exemption), primarily Irish mobs rioted for four days, causing more than $2 million in damage, the deaths of three policeman, fifteen rioters, and eleven lynched African Americans, before police and soldiers, many of them Irish, restored order. The violence reflected fear and frustration in the Irish community with anti-Irish discrimination, Irish fatalities in the war, and the prospect of competing with freed slaves for jobs.

Beginning with "Honest" John Kelly, who took charge of Tammany in 1871, the Irish, one-third of the population in 1880, dominated city politics for more than seventy years years.Tammany Hall was the headquarters of the Democratic Party in New York City and would become synonymous with Irish machine politics tinged with corruption and "graft." In 1918, Tammany-backed Al Smith, son of Irish immigrants, won the first of four elections for governor of New York and in 1928 became the first-ever Catholic to run for president. William O'Dwyer, who emigrated from County *Mayo with his brother Paul (later a famous human rights activist), was the city's only Irish-born mayor (1946–50) of the century.

The Depression and World War II slowed emigration from Ireland. Following the war, as their economic status improved, many of the Irish moved out of city neighborhoods and jobs. In 1950, first- and second-generation Irish represented less than 6 percent of the city population. Two waves of immigrants between 1945 and 1960, and again between the early '80s and '90s, led to a healthy resurgence of Irish immigrants in the city, bringing such talent as the *Clancy Brothers and Tommy Makem, Milo *O'Shea, and Frank *McCourt.

The St. Patrick's Day parade, the symbol of the Irish in New York since 1766, remains a show of political unity, ethnic pride, and a forum for issues and controversy in the community. In the twenty-first century, the Irish are still immigrating to New York, despite Ireland's unprecedented economic prosperity. L.D.A.

New Zealand, the Irish in. The Irish emigrated to the British colony of New Zealand from the late eighteenth century and ultimately formed a sizable minority within the white population of the islands. Irish-born sailors participated in James Cook's Pacific voyages in the 1770s and the establishment of a penal colony in New South Wales (Australia) in January 1788 increased the Irish contact with New Zealand. Irish soldiers in the British military were well represented in New Zealand garrisons after 1847 and the post-*Famine exodus led to the migration of thousands of free settlers to the southern hemisphere. Emigrants from the province of *Munster were particularly drawn to New Zealand, as were men and women from the nine counties of *Ulster. By the 1860s, when the discovery of gold increased the drawing power of the country, approximately 18 percent of New Zealand's population was of Irish stock and the proportion was considerably higher in Westland. The tendency of Irish women to marry outside their cultural circle accounted for significant intermarriage with Scots and English families. William Ferguson Massey of *Derry became premier of New Zealand in 1891 and fellow Ulsterman John Ballance of *Antrim attained the office in 1912. Thomas Bracken, a native of County *Monaghan, composed the national anthem of New Zealand, "God Save New Zealand." Irish New Zealanders played a large role in labor politics and a recent premier, Jim Bolger, is the son of *Wexford immigrants. R.OD.

Ní Cathasaigh, Máire (1956–). Harpist. Born into a music family in Bandon, County *Cork, Ní Cathasaigh learned the instrument from age eleven, and went on to win all major awards. She was the first *harp player to teach at *Comhaltas Ceoltóirí Éireann's annual Scoil Éigse. As a professional player, Ní Cathasaigh bridges the old harp-playing traditions and modern-day traditional Irish *music. She has interpreted the harp music of Turloch *Carolan extensively, and her droning technique for the performance of *dance music has been hugely influential. F.V.

Ní Chonaill, Eibhlín Dhubh (c.1743–c.1801). Poet in the *Irish language. A widow (and Daniel *O'Connell's aunt), Ní Chonaill is famous for her one literary composition—"Caoineadh Airt Uí Laoghaire" ("The Lament for Art O'Leary"). This lament, or *keen or death poem, is considered one of the greatest poems written in Ireland or Britain in the eighteenth century. Composed on the murder of her husband by the forces of the British crown in 1773, this lament is a passionate outburst of love, of loss, and of horror against fate, narrow-mindedness, and misfortune, and against *Protestantism and England's rule of law. A.T.

Ní Chuilleanáin, Eiléan (1942–). Poet and lecturer. Born in *Cork, Ní Chuilleanáin was educated at University College, Cork, and Oxford. She teaches medieval and Renaissance English at Trinity College, Dublin. Ní Chuilleanáin's central theme, developed over successive volumes, is the emergence of female subjectivity from historical images of confinement—towers, nunneries, statuary, veils. Her poetry is notable for its incisive intelligence, its sustained and striking images, its wealth of careful detail, and its sensitive evocations of women's experiences in history and myth. Among her collections are *Acts and Monuments* (1972), *The Rose-Geranium* (1981), *The Magdalene Sermon* (1989), and *The Brazen Serpent* (1994). M.S.T.

Ní Dhomhnaill, Nuala (1952–). *Irish-language poet and critic. Born in Lancashire, England, to Irish-speaking parents, Ní Dhomhnaill was raised in County *Tipperary but spent long periods in the Irish-speaking district of *Kerry. She was educated at University College, Cork, and lived for some years in Turkey. Ní Dhomhnaill holds a key position as both a senior woman poet and a leading Irish-language poet. Her poetry is written exclusively in the Irish language, but is widely translated into English by well-known Irish poets. She collaborated with poet Micheál *Ó hAirtnéide to produce the bilingual *Selected Poems/Rogha Dánta* (1988) and with Paul *Muldoon in *The Astrakhan Cloak* (1991). Ciaran *Carson, Seamus *Heaney, Michael *Longley, and Muldoon are among the translators of *Pharaoh's Daughter* (1991), and Medbh *McGuckian and Eiléan *Ní Chuilleanáin translated *The Water Horse: Poems in Irish* (1999). Collections in the Irish language include *An Dealg Droighin* (The Blackthorn Brooch) (1981) and *Féar Suaithinseach* (Miraculous Grass) (1984). Much of her imagery is drawn from the *Munster folk tradition she encountered in Kerry and from *Catholic symbols. A poem such as "The Fairy Hitch Hiker" is typical in that it combines a contemporary, humorous idiom, sophisticated technique, and a feminist social awareness. M.S.T.

Ní Ghráda, Máiréad (1896–1971). Dramatist. Ní Ghráda was a prolific writer of short plays, which were both experimental and popular. She is primarily known for *An Triail* (The Trial), first performed in *Dublin in 1964. The play caused a stir at the time as it dealt with the plight of a young unmarried mother and her abandonment by lover, family, and society. *An Triail* is still regularly produced. A.T.

Nine Years War, the (April 1593–March 1603). *Ulster rebellion against Queen *Elizabeth I. Between 1593 and 1603, reacting against growing interference by the English administration in land issues in Ulster, Hugh *O'Neill of Tyrone and Red Hugh *O'Donnell of Tyrconnell led a rebellion against the crown, known as the Nine Years War. King Phillip II of Spain sent troops to assist the Irish. Arriving in Kinsale, County *Cork, in September 1601, the Spanish forces were quickly besieged by an English army led by Lord Mountjoy. Rebel forces from Ulster moved south to relieve the Spaniards, but in the Battle of *Kinsale, on Christmas Eve, 1601, the combined Irish and Spanish forces were defeated.

In March 1603, the Treaty of *Mellifont formally ended the rebellion. The new English king, *James I, wanted to ensure that the old Gaelic system was broken in Ulster in particular and so under the treaty, the rebels had to give up their Gaelic titles and ancestral rights and live by English law. In return, they avoided the confiscation of their land and were given a pardon.

The *Flight of the Earls occurred four years later when O'Neill and over ninety other Ulster chiefs, dissatisfied with their new positions and fearing future retaliation, sailed for the continent. P.E.

Norman invasion. See **Anglo-Norman Conquest.**

North Strand Bombings (May 31, 1941). Bombings of parts of *Dublin during World War II. The Luftwaffe bombed parts of the city, leaving thirty-four dead, ninety injured, and three hundred houses destroyed. The North Strand was worst hit but bombs also landed on South Circular Road, Terenure, and Sandycove. At the time, the Irish government believed that British interference in German wireless signals, the so-called "beam," had put the Luftwaffe planes off course. Recent research, however, indicates that the bombing was deliberate, a warning to the Irish government to remain neutral. After the war, Germany accepted responsibility and paid £327,000 in compensation to the Irish state. T.C.

Northern Ireland. Constituent part of the United Kingdom since 1920. Northern Ireland has a population of 1,685,267 (2001 census). Made up of the six *Ulster counties, *Antrim, *Armagh, *Down, *Fermanagh, *Londonderry, and *Tyrone, Northern Ireland was created by the *Government of Ireland Act (1920), through which Britain tried to disengage from Ireland. Britain assumed that the two *home rule administrations created by the act would eventually become one through the proposed Council of Ireland. The *Anglo-Irish Treaty of December 1921 and the subsequent Free State Act (1922) left Northern Ireland as per the Government of Ireland Act: six counties of Ulster that guaranteed a *unionist majority, even though the new state could not deliver political consensus from its minority (39 percent) nationalist population. The powers of Parliament and government (from the mid-1930s centered in Stormont Castle and known as *Stormont) were constitutionally modeled on Westminster, but remained limited and, particularly in financial matters, dependent on London. With *Civil War in the South and an IRA (*Irish Republican Army) campaign within its borders, the new state's birth was accompanied by constitutional, political, and economic uncertainties and insecurities. This experience would influence the Northern government's expectations of, and attitudes toward, respectively, governments in Dublin, Great Britain, and the *Catholic/nationalist minority within its borders. A *Protestant state for a Protestant people in the North stood as counterbalance to the Catholic state for a Catholic people that was the *Irish Free State.

While it initially intended to accommodate the Catholic minority (e.g., one-third of posts in the police were reserved for Catholics, although they were never taken up), discrimination against nationalists became endemic. In the early twenties, in particular, the state used the *Royal Ulster Constabulary to serve both as police and in a military capacity to suppress *republican insurrection, which in turn reinforced nationalist alienation from the state. More than ever, religious identities became political identities. Catholic noncooperation and Dublin's hostile rhetoric only confirmed unionists' perceptions that nationalists wanted to destroy their state. Socially, the period between the two world wars saw the consolidation of two mutually hostile groups. This was a time fraught with economic difficulties: high unemployment, an increasing population, a decline in the staple industries of shipbuilding, *linen, and *agriculture, and, compared to Britain, a poor standard in all areas of public service.

Northern Ireland, however, benefited from World War II. The southern Irish state's (*Éire) *neutrality made the North an essential part in the British war effort. Its agriculture was modernized, its government strengthened; its economy improved overall and with it came general prosperity. Britain promised and delivered parity of social services for the postwar period. The *Ireland Act (1949) confirmed the constitutional position of Northern Ireland, reassuring Unionist governments. Britain's financial aid allowed Northern Ireland to move economically and in terms of social policy well ahead of the *Republic. While unionists had primarily hoped to consolidate their position within their own constituencies through the adoption of these policies, nationalists benefited at least as much—given their overrepresentation in the disadvantaged sections of society—particularly in areas of health and education. This helped to loosen their allegiance to Dublin and made them more willing to accept the Northern state on a day-to-day basis. By the second half of the fifties, some Catholic middle-class groups were beginning to reject the *Nationalist Party's abstentionist and ineffective approach and to debate a fuller integration of the minority population into the state.

The sixties saw an increased growth in confidence among the Catholic middle classes. This coincided with Prime Minister Terence *O'Neill's administration's policies of economic planning and modernization, in which, it was hoped, Catholics might participate and thus accept the state. Civil rights groups emerged demanding equal status for all citizens of Northern Ireland. This began to alienate the conservative section of unionism, and soon counterdemonstrations were mounted. By the late sixties, politics had moved onto the streets and made Prime Minister O'Neill's standing within his own party increasingly difficult. As rioting and attacks by, and against, the police multiplied, the Unionist governments from 1969 to 1972 tried to stem the tide by granting most of the civil rights demands. But it was too late: the revival of latent violent sectarianism had made Northern Ireland ungovernable. The most recent *Troubles would last for almost thirty years. In 1972, Stormont was dissolved and direct rule of Northern Ireland from Westminster was implemented.

During the following fifteen years, British governments attempted by various means to create a political middle ground in which the liberal wings of unionism and nationalism could work together and end paramilitary violence. This proved impossible to achieve, not least because of the nature of direct rule itself, which made regional politicians powerless and focused all attention on Britain. Ultimately, paramilitary violence (by such groups as the IRA, INLA [Irish National Liberation Army], the *UVF [Ulster Volunteer Force], and the *UDA [Ulster Defense Assocation]) was accepted as a defensive necessity by each side. Both nationalism and unionism had split into more moderate and radical factions. The *Anglo-Irish Agreement of 1985 was Britain's last attempt at creating a consensus of the middle ground, now with active support from Dublin, which up to then had offered very little but hostile rhetoric. Dublin's involvement was unacceptable to unionists, thus dooming hopes that the agreement would lead to a cessation of violence.

The emergence of *Sinn Féin, the political wing of the IRA, as a political party in the wake of the *hunger strikes, probably encouraged a U-turn in British politics in Northern Ireland. With the interest and support of the Dublin government, it seemed feasible to work from the outside in: if the paramilitaries of both sides could be persuaded to substitute politics for the armed struggle, a way forward might be found. This was enthusiastically supported by John *Hume's SDLP (Social Democratic and Labour Party), but initially met with hostility from unionists. Only after David *Trimble became leader of the *Ulster Unionist Party was progress made. Trimble eventually realized that there was no way back to a unionist Stormont government and compromises in the form of power-sharing would have to be made. After long negotiations, the *Good Friday Agreement was signed in 1998 and a new form of devolved government began, based on "parity of esteem" for both traditions. To accommodate the difficulties of governing Northern Ireland, the agreement institutionalized sectarianism: no legislation can be passed without a majority percentage from each of the sectarian sides supporting it. The Good Friday Agreement faced many obstacles: decommissioning of arms, continuing sectarian violence on the streets, and radical splinter paramilitaries on both sides. During the first years of the new century, the new Northern Ireland Assembly survived shakily, under pressure in particular from the substantial section of unionists who were unwilling to accept cooperation with Sinn Féin. S.W.

Northern Ireland Civil Rights Association (NICRA). Civil rights community organization. Formed in January 1967, NICRA was inspired particularly by the campaigns of Martin Luther King in the United States. The association's organization was modeled on the British National Council for Civil Liberties. The founding committee, which represented a spectrum embracing left-wing, radical, and liberal *unionist and *nationalist opinion, included Noel Harris, Conn McCluskey, Fred Heatley, Jack Bennett, Michael Dolley, Kevin Agnew, John Quinn, Paddy Devlin, Terence O'Brien, and Robin Cole. Its aim was to reform, not overthrow, *Northern Ireland. NICRA's basic demands were "one man, one vote" in local elections, an end to gerrymandering, outlawing discrimination, and reform of the security apparatus (the disbandment of the *B-Specials and the repeal of the Special Powers Act). Like civil rights organizations in the United States, NICRA organized marches to publicize its case. The first march was on August 24, 1968, in Dungannon, County *Tyrone, to protest discrimination in housing allocation practiced by the Unionist-controlled local council. The march, which was attended by four thousand people, attracted media attention. The next march, on October 5, 1968, in *Derry, was attended by a large crowd, including the *Nationalist leader, Eddie McAteer, and other *Stormont MPs (members of Parliament). McAteer and Westminster MP Gerry Fitt were both injured when the *RUC (Royal Ulster Constabulary) attacked the marchers with batons. This violence is seen as the beginning of the *Troubles. NICRA brought public attention to bear on Northern Ireland and put pressure on the British government to introduce reforms. A series of protests and demonstrations followed. The unionist authorities viewed NICRA as a front for the IRA (*Irish Republican Army) and resisted NICRA's demands for reform. The RUC responded violently to its demonstrations and the UVF (*Ulster Volunteer Force) planted bombs in order to destabilize the region. NICRA was eventually overshadowed by the outbreak of communal violence and paramilitary campaigns. T.C.

Northern Ireland conflict (1968–97). *Northern Ireland was created by the *Government of Ireland Act in 1920 under pressure from *Ulster unionists who threatened war if included in an all-Ireland parliament. *Nationalists never accepted its legitimacy and have continually sought reunification with the rest of the island. Northern Ireland has not enjoyed one decade without violence or paramilitary campaigns since its formation.

The most recent conflict, called the *Troubles, was sparked by the unionist authorities' violent reaction to the protest marches of NICRA (*Northern Ireland Civil Rights Association). The unionist government believed that NICRA was a front for the IRA (*Irish Republican Army), although an independent investigation subsequently refuted this. The RUC (*Royal Ulster Constabulary) attacked NICRA's peaceful protests and widespread rioting resulted. The *Ulster Volunteer Force (UVF), a *loyalist paramilitary organization, planted a series of bombs in 1969, which it tried to blame on the IRA, hoping that the reforming Prime Minister Terence *O'Neill would be replaced with a hard-line unionist. As violence spread in 1970, British troops were brought in, initially to relieve the RUC and protect *Catholic areas from attack. Walls, known as "Peace Lines," were erected between Catholic and *Protestant areas in *Belfast to keep rioting factions apart.

The attacks on nationalist districts resulted in a revival of the IRA, which had been inactive since the early 1960s. The renewed IRA soon split over tactics. The Provisionals emerged as the stronger faction and conducted a military campaign against the *Stormont government and the security forces. The other faction, the Officials, carried on for a few years before giving up violence in favor of left-wing politics. On the loyalist side, the UVF was joined by the *Ulster Defense Association (UDA) in a campaign of random assassinations of Catholics.

On August 9, 1971, the government of Northern Ireland introduced *internment without trial. On January 30, 1972, which became known as

*Bloody Sunday, British soldiers shot dead thirteen civilians in *Derry during a mass demonstration against internment without trial. In response to this tragedy, the IRA escalated its campaign. Recruitment to loyalist groups increased after *Bloody Friday, March 4, 1972, when IRA bombs killed eleven in Belfast. The intense violence—180 people were killed in 1971 and 496 in 1972—convinced the British to suspend the local parliament and appoint a secretary of state to govern the region directly from London. An attempt to bring peace by the formation of a power-sharing government in 1974 was brought down by a loyalist strike. The violence continued despite sporadic attempts at finding a political settlement. The IRA continued its activities in the North and in Britain, while loyalist paramilitary groups, often in collusion with the security forces, maintained their attacks on Catholics.

In 1979, Margaret *Thatcher became the British prime minister. She was determined to defeat the IRA. Thatcher took a hard line when IRA prisoners in Long Kesh (Maze) went on *hunger strike, demanding the restoration of political status. Ten prisoners died on hunger strike, including Bobby Sands, who had been elected MP (member of Parliament) for *Fermanagh/South Tyrone before his death.

Sands's election to Parliament and *Sinn Féin's public campaign on behalf of the hunger strikers showed Sinn Féin's growing political influence. The 1985 *Anglo-Irish Agreement, in which the British and Irish governments agreed to consult on Northern Ireland issues in an attempt to end the violence, provoked, however, a unionist backlash. The IRA continued its campaign of violence despite public revulsion at actions such as the *Enniskillen bombing in 1987, which killed nineteen people.

The arrival of John *Major as prime minister in 1990 opened the way for renewed talks. The groundwork had been laid by negotiations between John *Hume and Gerry *Adams. Tortuous discussions between Dublin and London led to a framework document for negotiations involving all political parties and both governments. This led to the signing of the *Downing Street Declaration on December 15, 1993, in which the British and Irish governments agreed that it was a matter for the Irish people, North and South, to decide the future of the island. On August 31, 1994, the IRA—and shortly after, the loyalist groups—declared a cease-fire. However, the negotiations broke down and the IRA resumed military activities in February 1996.

After general elections in Ireland and Britain, in which Bertie *Ahern became *Taoiseach (prime minister) and Tony *Blair prime minister, talks began again. In July 1997, the IRA reinstated its cease-fire and in September of that year Sinn Féin became a full participant in the negotiations. This time around, with the active involvement of Ahern, Blair, US President Bill Clinton, and Senator George Mitchell, who was the US Special Envoy to Northern Ireland, an agreement was reached on Good Friday 1998, known as the *Good Friday Agreement.

Although endorsed by the people of Ireland, the agreement is still not fully implemented. Dissident republicans opposed to it planted a bomb in *Omagh, County *Tyrone, in 1998, killing twenty-nine people. The IRA began decommissioning its arsenal in October 2001. Loyalist paramilitaries continue to attack Catholics. The *UDA dissolved its political wing and came out against the agreement. Sectarian attacks and communal violence in flashpoints, like north *Belfast, continue. Over 3,600 people have died in the conflict. T.C.

Nuns. In the twelfth and thirteenth centuries, there were Augustinian, Cistercian, and Franciscan nuns.

The *Reformation and the counter-Reformation brought change, not only in the suppression of the religious life, but in the tightened regulations governing nuns. There were only nine convents in Ireland in 1731, belonging to the Poor Clares, the Carmelites, and the Dominicans. The major increase in the number of nuns in Ireland occurred in the early nineteenth century, though the first of the modern, socially active congregations, the Presentation, was effectively established by Nano *Nagle in Cork in 1776. The Irish Sisters of Charity followed in 1815, the Loreto in 1821, and the Sisters of Mercy in 1828. Congregations such as the Sacred Heart, the Sisters of St. Louis, and the Ursulines came in from abroad. Most nuns worked with the poor in schools, asylums, hospitals, orphanages, hostels, evening classes, and (for those allowed to go outside the convent) sick visitation. Some orders ran fee-paying boarding schools, which were preparing pupils for university entrance examinations by the late nineteenth century. The number of nuns multiplied by eight between 1851 and 1911, and continued to grow until well into the twentieth century. Nuns alone made up 4.6 percent of the female workforce in 1961.

The religious life offered *women challenging work, and often considerable authority, in a democratic community. The convent also gave middle-class women independence of day-to-day male authority. Convent entrants were, mostly, middle-class women in their early to mid-twenties, who brought a dowry with them. Many sisters, cousins, or friends seem to have entered convents at the same time, and nieces followed aunts into the religious life. Dowry-less girls, from artisan or small-farming backgrounds, entered the convent as lay sisters. These sisters, like lay brothers in orders of priests, did the domestic work and could not aspire to positions of authority in the house. The distinction that marked off lay sisters from other nuns was abolished by the *Second Vatican Council in the 1960s.

By the early twentieth century, nuns were very important agents of the state, as national teachers, industrial school and reformatory managers, and *workhouse nurses. This reinforced their considerable social authority and status. Numbers of recruits to the religious life remained high, up to the 1970s, by which stage Irish nuns had established flourishing convents on all five continents. C.C.

O

oath of allegiance. Pledge of loyalty by members of the Irish *Dáil (Parliament) to the British crown, required between 1922 and 1933. The *Anglo-Irish Treaty of December 1921, which conferred dominion status on the new *Irish Free State, included a provision stipulating that future members of the state's Parliament would be obliged to take an oath swearing that they would be "faithful to H. M. King George V, his heirs and successors by law in virtue of the common citizenship of Ireland with Great Britain."

Such an oath was unacceptable to many *republicans in Ireland and was the focus of much of the treaty debate in the *Dáil in January 1922. Led by Éamon *de Valera, opponents of the treaty argued that the acceptance of dominion status would represent a betrayal of the *republic and that the oath of allegiance to the crown would perpetuate British colonialism in Ireland. In the end, the Dáil ratified the treaty sixty-four to fifty-seven. Continued republican opposition to the treaty settlement culminated in the *Irish Civil War (1922–23) between the Free State and IRA (*Irish Republican Army) forces. The fledgling Free State survived the Civil War, which ended in May 1923. De Valera and his followers in the *Sinn Féin party refused to recognize the Free State as a legitimate political entity and, for the first years of the state's existence, refused to take Dáil seats to which they were elected, due primarily to their aversion to the oath. By 1925, however, de Valera had grown frustrated with the political impotence of this abstentionist policy. He therefore broke with Sinn Féin that year and in 1926 created the *Fianna Fáil party. The following year, de Valera took the oath and led his followers into the Dáil, insisting that the oath was an empty political formula that he and other Fianna Fáil members could take "without being involved, or without involving their nation, in obligations of loyalty to the English crown."

In March 1932, de Valera formed the first Fianna Fáil government in the history of the state. Within days of taking office, he began dismantling

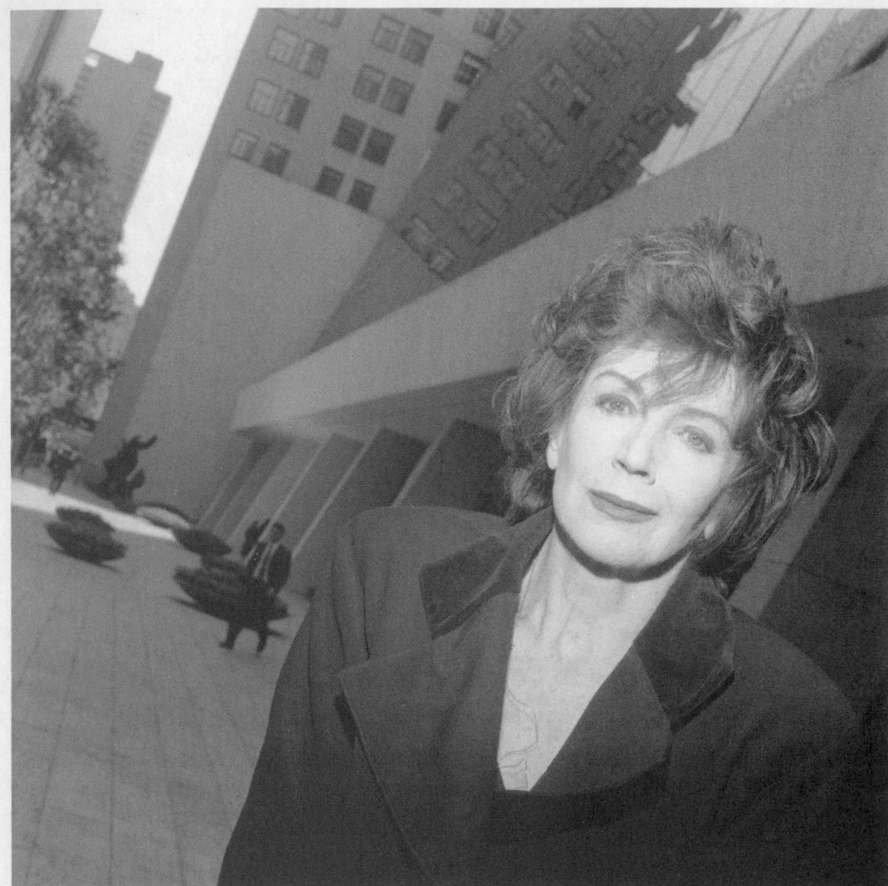

Edna O'Brien

the provisions of the Anglo-Irish Treaty. In May 1932, the Dáil passed a bill removing the oath, but it was delayed in the *Seanad (Senate) and not abolished until after another general election in May 1933, in which de Valera's party won an overall majority. T.D.

O'Brien, Edna (1934–). Novelist and short story writer. Born in Tuamgraney, County *Clare, O'Brien moved to England in 1959 where she has spent her entire writing career. She first came to prominence with *The Country Girls' Trilogy* (reissued in 1986 with an epilogue)—*The Country Girls* (1960), *The Lonely Girl* (1962, reissued in 1964 as *The Girl With Green Eyes*), and *Girls in Their Married Bliss* (1963). These novels have a strong autobiographical undercurrent, and their candor about female sexuality and the patriarchal structure of Irish life was considered scandalous. The books were banned by the *Censorship of Publications Board until 1975. In novels such as *August Is a Wicked Month* (1964) and *Casualties of Peace* (1966), O'Brien examines the fates of isolated, abandoned women living lives of emotional impoverishment in fashionable and exotic locales. In these works, O'Brien draws on her familiarity with the international film community during the 1960s and early 1970s, and her rather bleak opinion of its superficiality.

Although O'Brien lives in England, her fiction has a predominantly Irish focus. In *A Pagan Place* (1971), she returns to the County Clare landscape of the trilogy. Just as outspoken as the earlier work, the book is more psychologically sophisticated. This Irish setting is also particularly prominent in the collections of short stories *The Love Object* (1968) and *Returning* (1982), reflecting the recurring themes of home and homemaking throughout her work. The novel *Time and Tide* (1992) explores another of her perennial subjects, motherhood, in the context of contemporary issues and events. Such later works as *House of Splendid Isolation* (1994) and *Down by the River* (1996) address such taboo topics as the Provisional IRA (*Irish Republican Army) and incest. O'Brien's nonfiction includes *Mother Ireland* (1976), *Arabian Knights* (1977), and *James Joyce* (1999), whose influence she has frequently acknowledged. *In the Forest* (2002) is a controversial novel based on a series of murders in County Clare that shocked Ireland. G.OB.

O'Brien, Flann (pen name of Brian O'Nolan), (1911–66). Writer. Born in County *Tyrone and raised in *Dublin, O'Brien was educated at University College, Dublin. While still a student, he wrote reviews and pamphlets (including some bawdy ones in Old Irish) under the first of many pen names, Brother Barnabas. Later, he wrote under the name Myles na Gopaleen. James *Joyce praised his first novel, *At Swim-Two-Birds* (1939), as "a really funny book." Also described as an anti-novel, *At Swim-Two-Birds* is a wild parody of Irish myth, popular culture, and classical education, several of whose fictional characters come to life to plague their author. The book did not sell well partially because of the war, but it has since become a classic. His next book, *The Third Policeman*, was completed in 1940 but rejected by publishers and eventually published in 1967. His satirical and playful column "Cruiskeen Lawn" in the *Irish Times* delighted readers for twenty-six years. The column featured wordplay; jokes in Irish and Latin; and merciless satire of vernacular speech, journalism, and cliché. The novel *An Béal Bocht* (1941) gained immediate popularity among the *Irish language enthusiasts whom it satirized, but attracted critical attention only when it was published in English under the title *The Poor Mouth* (1964). Three plays by O'Brien were staged unsuccessfully in 1943, *Faustus Kelly*, *The Insect Play*, and *Thirst*. Other works include the novels *The Hard Life* (1961), *The Dalkey Archive* (1964), and *Slattery's Sago Saga*, which was incomplete at the time of his death. Flann O'Brien's fiction is characterized by self-reference, demolition of literary convention and pretension, and a linguistic inventiveness that rivals *Beckett and Joyce. M.S.T.

O'Brien, Kate (1897–1974). Novelist, dramatist, and essayist. O'Brien was born in *Limerick and educated at University College, Dublin. The success of her play *Distinguished Villa* (1926) led her to write full-time, and her first novel, *Without My Cloak* (1931), was enthusiastically received. Subsequent novels deal with the conflict between individuals' desire to be free and moral and social constraints. O'Brien's style is intense and realist, and her typical central characters are convincing feminists and *Catholics. *Mary Lavelle* (1936) was banned, as was *The Land of Spices* (1941), because of one offending sentence. *That Lady* (1946) explores the relationship between Spain's Philip and Ana de Mendoza. *Farewell Spain* (1957) and *My Ireland* (1962) are highly distinctive travel books and *Teresa of Avila* (1951) is a study of the Spanish saint. M.S.T.

O'Brien, William Smith (1803–64). *Nationalist politician. Born in Dromoland, County *Clare, O'Brien came from a *Protestant landowning family. As Tory MP (member of Parliament) for Ennis (1828–31), he campaigned for *Catholic Emancipation and improvements to poor relief and *education in Ireland. While MP for County *Limerick (1835–49), he joined the *Repeal Association but in 1846 broke with Daniel *O'Connell and joined the Irish Confederation. Sentenced to death in 1848 for leading the *Young Ireland insurrection, O'Brien was reprieved and transported to Tasmania. Pardoned in 1854, he returned to Ireland but took no further part in politics. S.A.B.

Ó Bruadair, Dáibhí (1625–98). Poet in the *Irish language. Born in County *Cork, Ó Bruadair spent most of his life in County *Limerick. He received training in a *bardic school and was particularly fond of the *Dán Díreach* (classical syllabic verse). His poems, *Duanaire Dháibhidh Uí Bhruadair*, were collected and edited by S. C. MacErlean in 1910. They chart the declining status of the poet with the upheaval of the old Gaelic order that resulted from *Cromwell's reign of terror and the Treaty of *Limerick. B.D.

O'Byrne, Fiach MacHugh (c.1544–97). Powerful chieftain of sixteenth-century Ireland. A native of Ballinacor in the mountainous Glenmalure district of County *Wicklow, O'Byrne, with his military acumen and resources, posed a major threat to the Anglo inhabitants and administrators of County *Dublin. The inability of the Elizabethan invaders to neutralize O'Byrne resulted in his being pardoned by the crown in February 1573. On August 25, 1580, a major punitive expedition of English forces under Lord Deputy Grey de Wilton into O'Byrne's stronghold of Glenmalure was virtually annihilated. This defeat of the English forces inspired survivor Edmund *Spenser to write *The Faerie Queen* and obliged the English Queen *Elizabeth to pardon O'Byrne in 1581. Renewed efforts to capture him in March 1594 led to the temporary loss of his Ballinacor home to English occupation until late 1596. O'Byrne, who had forged strong links with the influential *Ulster *O'Neill and O'Donnell families, was eventually trapped and summarily executed on May 8, 1597. R.OD.

Ó Cadhain, Máirtín (1906–70). Writer in Irish, scholar, language activist. Ó Cadhain is considered the foremost Irish prose-writer of the mid-twentieth century. A native speaker, who received no secondary education but finished his career as professor of Irish in Trinity College, Dublin, Ó Cadhain is author of short stories ranging from the anti-romantic rural to the postmodern fantastic. He is best known for his novel *Cré na Cille* (Graveyard Earth), a story in which all the characters are dead but who speak the most lively and vibrant vernacular while savaging and excoriating one another. A.T.

O'Casey, Seán (1880–1964). Dramatist. Born in *Dublin (as John Casey) into a poor *Protestant family, O'Casey had to support himself with manual labor well into his forties. Poverty, his father's early death, and an eye ailment disrupted his education, and only through remarkable resilience would O'Casey overcome these obstacles and become one of Ireland's most important dramatists. His six-volume autobiography, beginning with *I Knock at the Door* (1939) and finishing with *Sunset and Evening Star* (1954), offers an animated record of his difficult childhood and adulthood.

O'Casey's writing career began not in belles-

Seán O'Casey

lettres but in politics, with his first book, *The Story of the Irish Citizen Army* (1919), which exposes O'Casey's *socialist beliefs, to which he remained faithful the rest of his life. His character sketches of labor and *nationalist figures such as Jim *Larkin, James *Connolly, and the Countess *Markievicz foreshadow the dramatist O'Casey was to become. Between 1920 and 1923, the *Abbey Theatre rejected four of his plays, but he was encouraged to continue writing by Lady *Gregory, W. B. *Yeats, and Lennox *Robinson.

Never fully a part of the *nationalist movement, O'Casey demythologizes in his major plays key events of the nationalist struggle—the *Easter Rising, the *War of Independence, and the *Irish Civil War. *The Shadow of a Gunman*, which had a brief premiere in April 1923 at the end of the Abbey's season, casts a critical look at Ireland's War of Independence (1919–21) by depicting its devastating impact on Dublin's slum dwellers. The play enjoyed a successful run when the Abbey reopened in the fall and was a success in Britain and the United States a few years later. In 1924, *Juno and the Paycock*, considered O'Casey's masterpiece, proved immediately popular, and continues to be produced in Ireland and elsewhere. One of O'Casey's most entertaining works, the play presents the Irish Civil War (1922–23) as a series of selfish and irresponsible tirades between feuding parties. *The Plough and the Stars*, which dramatizes the 1916 Easter Rising, had a rocky start at the Abbey in 1926, when nationalists interrupted the show on the fourth night to protest O'Casey's representation of the heroes of the rising. Like *Juno and the Paycock*, the play exposes Ireland's nationalists as misguided and conceited, and their rebellion as a license for the mob to wreck and loot.

The success of these plays (known as the Dublin trilogy) gave the Abbey the financial lift it badly needed. Although the theater supported O'Casey during the weeklong disturbances aroused by *The Plough and the Stars*, Yeats rejected in 1928 O'Casey's next play, *The Silver Tassie* (1929), an experimental play with surrealist scenes of *World War I. O'Casey was embittered by the Abbey's decision and decided to live permanently in England where he had moved in 1926.

The Dublin trilogy's unsympathetic rendering of Irish nationalist politics underwent quiet revision in some of O'Casey's middle plays, *The Star Turns Red* (1940), *Red Roses for Me* (1943), *Purple Dust* (1945), and *Oak Leaves and Lavender* (1947). In *Purple Dust*, for instance, O'Casey appears conciliatory toward the Irish nationalist tradition when he targets English colonialism as a force victimizing the native peasantry. O'Casey's later expressionist plays, *Cock-*

a-Doodle Dandy (1949), *The Bishop's Bonfire* (1955), *The Drums of Father Ned* (1959), and *Behind the Green Curtains* (1962), consolidated his reputation as an innovative dramatist, but brought him little financial success.

O'Casey was involved much of his life in confrontations with his Irish contemporaries. In 1926, O'Casey engaged in a public debate with the prominent nationalist and feminist agitator Hanna *Sheehy Skeffington, who harshly criticized *The Plough and the Stars*. Another quarrel in 1958 proved equally dramatic when the Dublin Theatre Festival censored Alan McClelland's dramatization of James *Joyce's *Ulysses*. O'Casey and Samuel *Beckett withdrew their own plays in protest, and O'Casey further banned for five years all productions of his plays in Ireland. S.M.M.

Ó Conaire, Pádraig (1882–1928). Writer in the *Irish language. Born in *Galway, Pádraig Ó Conaire was in the vanguard of the Gaelic Revival (*Irish Language Revival) in the early years of the twentieth century and is often credited with launching Gaelic literature into a modern era. He was greatly influenced by French and Russian literature, and his collection of short stories *Scothscéalta* (Best Stories; 1956) is often compared to the works of Maupassant. He was one of the first Gaelic writers to examine themes that dealt with life outside the rural *Gaeltacht areas. His expressionist novel *Deoraíocht* (Exile; 1910), for example, explores the misfortunes of an Irish cripple in London and stemmed from his own period of exile there. Though regarded by many as the first professional Gaelic writer, it is thought that he earned no more than £700 in total from his work. He had a severe drinking problem and died destitute in 1928. B.D.

O'Connell, Daniel (1775–1847). Lawyer and politician. Born in Carhan, County *Kerry, O'Connell was raised in Derrynane by his uncle, a *Catholic landowner. He attended school in France, where the excesses of the *French Revolution fostered his lifelong abhorrence of violence. His commitment to nonviolence was later reinforced by the savagery of the *Rising of 1798, which in his view resulted in the further repression of Irish Catholics.

O'Connell studied law at Lincoln Inns in London between 1794 and 1796 and was called to the Irish Bar in 1798. He joined the Munster Circuit and, with his knowledge of the *Irish language and insight into the character of the people, he built up a large law practice. He was brilliant in rebuttal, in cross-examining witnesses, and in convincing juries of the merits of his clients' cases, particularly when defending individuals charged with violent offenses during the *tithe war (1830–38). Physically imposing, O'Connell projected a public image that embodied a chieftain's pride and a hero's strength. He married his cousin, Mary O'Connell, in 1802; they had eight children during a long and happy marriage.

O'Connell's first political appearance came in 1800, when he opposed the Act of *Union. When *Catholic Emancipation did not follow the passage of the act, he joined the campaign for civil rights for Catholics. In 1824 O'Connell transformed Irish political life by forming the Catholic Association. To finance the organization he instituted the "Catholic Rent," a penny per month collected after Mass by the clergy. This alliance with the *Catholic Church created a nationwide political movement. O'Connell then forced the emancipation issue forward in 1828 by standing for election for Clare, at a time when Catholics were excluded from Parliament. A master of political theater that both entertained and educated his audiences, O'Connell organized massive meetings across the country. He won an overwhelming victory against the government candidate, and the entire country waited to see if he would be allowed to take his seat. Government ministers, fearing an uprising, conceded Catholic Emancipation in April 1829. O'Connell, known thereafter as "the Liberator," emerged as the unrivaled leader of the Irish nation. His masterly use of the implied threat of violence to wring reform from the government became one of his principal political weapons.

O'Connell, who was not a republican, respected the institutions of British government, including Parliament and the monarchy. However, he was determined, as an Irishman and a Catholic, to bring about the *repeal of the Act of Union and the reestablishment of a parliament in Ireland. He gave up his law practice to devote himself to politics. A special collection called the "O'Connell Tribute" was made annually to compensate him for sacrificing his legal fees.

After the general election of 1832, O'Connell became the leader of thirty-nine Irish MPs (members of Parliament) who had pledged to fight for repeal. O'Connell and his fellow MPs cooperated with the Whigs to promote reform, and in 1835, when his party held the balance of power in the House of Commons, the O'Connellites and the Whigs formalized this alliance in the Litchfield House Compact. This agreement brought about the administrative reform of *Dublin Castle and the alteration of the method of paying *tithes, a much hated tax on the produce of land paid to support the *Protestant Church of Ireland by non-Church members and Catholic tenant farmers.

In 1841, O'Connell was elected lord mayor of Dublin, the first Catholic to hold that office in 150 years. He upheld the laissez-faire economic doctrines of Adam Smith and Benthamite utilitarianism. O'Connell also earned a European-wide reputation as a political radical. He supported national liberation movements, parliamentary reform, Jewish emancipation, and the abolition of slavery. When the Tories took power in 1841, O'Connell revived the repeal campaign, which he believed could be won through the constitutional means of nonviolent mass agitation. Subscriptions to his Repeal Association, through the "Repeal Rent," approached £50,000. He organized so-called "monster meetings" attended by many thousands of people. The authorities became concerned with the intimidating size of the crowds and the potential for violence. After a reputed three-quarters of a million people assembled on the Hill of *Tara in 1843, the government decided to prohibit the next meeting, scheduled at *Clontarf. O'Connell, unwilling to risk bloodshed, canceled the meeting, but he was arrested, charged with conspiracy, sentenced to a year's imprisonment, and fined. He spent three months in prison before a successful appeal was made to the House of Lords. He was devastated both emotionally and physically by the experience of the trial and the imprisonment. His health failing, he continued to speak out for repeal, but without effect. O'Connell's last speech in the House of Commons, in 1847, told of the suffering generated by the *Famine. He died in Genoa en route to Rome. According to his wishes, his heart was sent on to Rome, and his body was returned to Ireland for burial. O'Connell's reputation for securing Catholic Emancipation through constitutional agitation was diminished in some nationalists' eyes by his failure to win repeal through the same means. His legacy among later generations of Irish nationalists, however, lay in the creation of an enduring model of constitutional politics based on strong leadership, party organization, and institutional support from the Catholic Church. L.MB.

O'Connor, Frank (1903–66). Short story writer. Born Michael O'Donovan in *Cork City, O'Connor is considered one of the masters of the short story. His experiences during the *War of Independence provided the basis for his first collection, *Guests of the Nation* (1930), the title story of which is among his best-known works. His *Collected Stories* (1981) includes such masterpieces as: "My Oedipus Complex" and "First Confession," which draw on his impoverished childhood; "The Long Road to Ummera" and "The Majesty of the Law," set in traditional rural Ireland; and "The Mad Lomasneys" and "A Set of Variations," which depict the urban *Catholic lower middle class of O'Connor's youth. A recurring theme is independence, and these stories portray the spectrum of difficulties and compromises constituting the moral landscape of the newly created *Irish Free State. Told in a conversational style, with a wry sense of humor and compassion, these realistic stories capture the humanity of ordinary Irish people.

Some of his work reflects the influence of one of his schoolteachers, Daniel *Corkery. Early in his career, O'Connor worked as a librarian. Later, he was a director of the *Abbey Theatre, for which he wrote plays, and where he worked closely with W. B. *Yeats. Like many of his contemporaries, O'Connor had some of his work banned, including his translation of the risqué eighteenth-century Irish poem *The Midnight Court* (1946). O'Connor also wrote in many other literary forms, including poetry, novels—*The Saint and Mary Kate* (1932) and *Dutch Interior* (1940)—biography, and literary criticism. Among these are the autobiographical *An Only Child* (1961) and *My Father's Son* (1968); *Kings, Lords and Commoners* (1959), his translations of early Irish poetry; *The Lonely Voice* (1964), a critical study of the short story; and *The Backward Look* (1967), a history of Irish *literature. His travel books, confined to Ireland, are vehicles for his sharp criticisms of the state of the nation, particularly with regard to the maintenance of its *architectural heritage. O'Connor also wrote a good deal of outspoken journalism. During the 1950s, he was based largely in the United States, where he taught at Harvard, Northwestern, and Stanford and was a regular contributor to the *New Yorker*. He returned to Ireland in 1961. G.OB.

O'Connor, James Arthur (c.1792–1841). Landscape painter. Born in *Dublin, O'Connor was based in London from 1822. His early topographical paintings were followed by romantic and picturesque representations of idealized Irish scenes. M.C.

O'Connor, John (1947–). Pianist. Born in *Dublin and educated in Dublin and Vienna, O'Connor is particularly noted for his performances of works by Beethoven and Mozart. He has also championed the works of the Irish composer, John *Field. O'Connor has recorded widely and is professor of piano at the Royal Irish Academy. A.S.

O'Connor, Rory (d. 1198). King. Rory O'Connor succeeded his father Turlough as king of Connacht in 1156 and became high king of Ireland ten years later. He had more power than any Irish king before him, especially after he had successfully expelled Dermot *MacMurrough from his *Leinster kingdom. O'Connor was set to rule over a united Ireland, but MacMurrough's invitation to the Normans in 1169 to come and help restore him to his Leinster kingdom initiated the *Anglo-Norman invasion. The Treaty of Windsor in 1175 forced Rory to accept an Ireland divided between the Irish and the Normans and he returned to being king of Connacht only, subject to the overlordship of King *Henry II of

by + ©BP Fallon/bpfallon.com

Sinéad O'Connor and Shane MacGowan

England. The Normans largely ignored the treaty, and Rory was deposed in 1186. He died twelve years later at Cong Abbey, County *Mayo, and was buried at *Clonmacnoise, County *Offaly. P.H.

O'Connor, Sinéad (1966–). Singer. Born in *Dublin, O'Connor achieved some success with her debut album *The Lion and the Cobra* (1987), but it was her version of Prince's "Nothing Compares 2 U" (1990) that propelled her to celebrity status. The single topped the charts in seventeen countries. O'Connor has spoken openly about her troubled childhood. She caused intense controversy when she tore up a picture of the pope on the American television show *Saturday Night Live* in 1992 and when she refused to allow the American national anthem to be played at one of her concerts in 1990. O'Connor was ordained as a priest in the dissident Irish Orthodox Catholic and Apostolic Church in 1999 and changed her name to Mother Bernadette Maria. B.D.

O'Connor, Thomas Power (1848–1929). Journalist and politician. Born in Athlone, County *Westmeath, and educated at Queen's College, Galway, O'Connor (popularly known as "Tay Pay") was *nationalist MP (member of Parliament) for Galway (1880–85) and Liverpool's Scotland division (1885–1929). "Tay Pay" chronicled Irish parliamentary life in newspapers such as *T.P.'s Weekly* and published books, including *The Parnell Movement* (1886) and *Memoirs of an Old Parliamentarian* (1929). A well-loved figure at Westminster, O'Connor became the first president of the UK Board of Film Censors in 1917. S.A.B.

O'Conor, Roderic (1860–1940). Landscape, portrait, and still-life painter. Born in *Roscommon, O'Conor studied art in *Dublin and Antwerp and lived in France from 1886. Influenced by Gauguin and van Gogh, his Brittany landscapes and peasant portraits show his move from postimpressionism to expressionism and his distinctive use of Fauvist stripes of pure color. M.C.

Ó Criomhthain, Tomás (1856–1937). *Irish language writer of the *Blasket Islands. Born on the Blasket Islands, Ó Criomhthain taught himself to read and to write Irish as an adult, having been deprived of his native language by the Anglicized education system. A visiting schoolteacher persuaded him to write his life story on the model of works by Maxim Gorky and Pierre Loti. His book *An tOileánach* (*The Islandman;* 1929), ostensibly an autobiography, is also an objective description of Blasket Island life. "It is as cold as the rock from which it was hewn, as sharp as the wind from the Atlantic, and as objective as a hawk on the wing." He also wrote poetry in unbroken lines. A.T.

O'Curry, Eugene (1796–1862). Professor, archaeologist, and translator. He worked with John *O'Donovan in the Ordnance Survey of Ireland and as a cataloger in the *Royal Irish Academy and British Museum. O'Curry became the first professor of Irish history and archaeology in the Catholic University of Ireland. His collection of lectures, *The Manners and Customs of the Ancient Irish*, remains an authoritative text to this day. P.H.

O'Dea, James (Jimmy) Augustine (1899–1965). Comedian. Born in *Dublin, O'Dea studied to be an optician in Edinburgh, but became interested in amateur theater, and in 1927 formed a partnership with producer and scriptwriter Harry O'Donovan. Gentle, sad-eyed, and short-legged, O'Dea gained international renown as one of the great comedians of his era. He created a gallery of Dublin characters, the most famous of which was Biddy Mulligan, "The Pride of the Coombe." A master of comedic timing, O'Dea starred in annual pantomimes at Dublin's Royal and Gaiety Theatres for nearly forty years. He also performed in *The Irish Half-Hour,* which was broadcast on BBC radio during World War II, and appeared in a number of films, including *Darby O'Gill and the Little People* (1959) (as king of the fairies). O'Dea influenced many younger comedians like Maureen Potter, who appeared with him in television comedies during his final years. J.C.E.L.

Ó Direáin, Máirtín (1910–88). Poet in Irish. Born on Inishmore, in the *Aran Islands, Ó Direáin is widely recognized as the begetter of modern Irish poetry. He published his first collection, *Coinnle Geala* (*Bright Candles;* 1942), out of his own pocket, and continued to compose prolifically until his death. His early poetry is sentimental, but he later developed a hard edge and a noble voice. A.T.

O'Doherty, Brian (1934–). Conceptual artist. Born in County *Roscommon, O'Doherty has from 1969 exhibited his work under the name of Patrick Ireland, in protest against British military presence in *Northern Ireland. Educated in *Dublin, he lives and works in New York as artist and professor of art. M.C.

O'Donnell, (Red) Hugh (c.1571–1602). One of the last great Gaelic chieftains and a key rebel leader in the *Nine Years War. Also known as Red Hugh O' Donnell, he was the son of Sir Hugh O'Donnell, the lord of Tír Conaill. As a teenager, he was kidnapped by the English Lord Deputy Sir John Perrott who feared the growing threat to the British government posed by the O'Donnell family. He was held prisoner in *Dublin Castle, before escaping in 1592. In May 1592, he became chief of the O'Donnells. Between 1593 and 1603, in a reaction against growing interference by the English administration in land issues in *Ulster, O'Donnell and Hugh *O'Neill of *Tyrone led a rebellion against the crown, known as the Nine Years War. King Philip II of Spain sent troops to assist the Irish rebels. Arriving in Kinsale in September 1601, the Spanish forces were quickly besieged by an English army led by Lord Mountjoy. O'Donnell and O'Neill marched south, to relieve the Spaniards, but in the battle of *Kinsale, on Christmas Eve, 1601, the combined Irish and Spanish forces were defeated. O'Donnell was sent to Spain for further help. He was received by King Philip II, who promised additional forces for the Irish rebels. O'Donnell, however, fell ill at Simancas and died there in September 1602. P.E.

O'Donovan, John (1809–61). Antiquarian, scholar, and historian. John O'Donovan documented ancient Ireland in the letters that he wrote for the Ordnance Survey. He also edited many old texts for the Irish Archaeological Society. His crowning achievement was his seven-volume edition of The *Annals of the Four Masters (1848–51). P.H.

O'Donovan Rossa, Jeremiah (1831–1915). *Republican. Born in Rosscarbery, County *Cork, O'Donovan founded the Phoenix National and Literary Society in 1856. After being imprisoned for *Fenian activities (1865–71), he went to America where, as a leader of the Fenian Brotherhood, he organized a "skirmishing fund" for a war against Britain. His newspaper, the *United Irishman*, was outspoken in its support for the Fenian "dynamite campaign" (1881–85) in England. O'Donovan Rossa died in New York and his funeral in *Dublin was the occasion for a famous graveside oration by Patrick *Pearse. S.A.B.

O'Duffy, Eoin (1892–1944). *Fine Gael and *Blueshirt leader. Born in County *Monaghan, O'Duffy was appointed deputy chief of staff of the IRA (*Irish Republican Army) during the *War of Independence. A supporter of the *Anglo-Irish Treaty, he became commissioner of the *Gárda Síochána in 1922 and was also chief of staff of the army. When he was dismissed in February 1933 by Éamon *de Valera, he became the leader of the *Blueshirts (Army Comrades Association), a quasi-fascist organization. He was also the first leader of Fine Gael but resigned from the party in September 1934. In 1936, O'Duffy organized the Irish Brigade to fight for Franco in the *Spanish Civil War. P.E.

O'Faolain, Julia (1932–). Writer. Born in London, Julia O'Faolain is the daughter of Irish writer Seán *Ó Faoláin. A fiction writer, translator, and language teacher, O'Faolain explores a wide variety of political, historical, and religious themes, with particular attention to women's experiences. In Irish and foreign settings, O'Faolain's characters grapple with the mores and expectations of church and state. *No Country for Young Men*, a Booker Prize finalist in 1980, reveals the effects of the Irish political landscape on three generations of a family involved in the republican struggle.

Other fiction includes *We Might See Sights and Other Stories* (1968), *Man in the Cellar* (1974), *Women in the Wall* (1975), *Daughters of Passion* (1982), *The Obedient Wife* (1982), and *The Irish Signorina* (1984), as well as translations under the name Julia Martines. O'Faolain also edited a collection of essays, *Not in God's Image: Women in History from the Greeks to the Victorians* (1973). K.MI.

O'Faolain, Nuala (1946–). Journalist and novelist. Born in *Dublin, O'Faolain lectured in literature at University College, Dublin, and was a tele-

Seán Ó Faoláin

vision and radio producer for the BBC and *RTÉ. Beginning in the 1980s, she produced three groundbreaking series on women for RTÉ: *Women Talking*, *The Women's Programme*, and *Plain Tales*. She is an award-winning opinion columnist for the *Irish Times*.

O'Faolain's memoir *Are You Somebody? The Accidental Memoir of a Dublin Woman* (1996), which was a best-seller in both Ireland and the United States, deals frankly with sex, family, and alcoholism in Ireland since the 1950s. Her memoir courageously documents her struggle to define herself outside of the traditional gender role she was expected to fulfill. In 2001, she published her first novel, *My Dream of You*, and in 2003 another memoir, *Almost There*. N.H.

Ó Faoláin, Seán (1900–91). Short story writer, editor, intellectual. Born John Whelan in Cork City, where Daniel *Corkery was an early mentor, he assumed the Irish form of his name in 1918. Educated at University College, Cork, where he received an MA in both Irish and English, he was a Commonwealth Fellow at Harvard from 1926 to 1929. His experiences as publicity director on the *republican side during the *War of Independence and the *Civil War form the basis of a number of stories in his first collection, *Midsummer Night's Madness* (1932). More stories followed during the 1930s, as well as three novels—*A Nest of Simple Folk* (1934), *Bird Alone* (1936), and *Come Back to Erin* (1940). The most noteworthy novel, *Bird Alone*, was banned by the Irish censors. Its protagonist's conflicts with Church and society typify the stifling atmosphere that prevailed in Ireland in the first half of the twentieth century. During the 1930s, Ó Faoláin started exploring the Irish historical legacy in his biography of Daniel *O'Connell, *King of the Beggars* (1938), and later in a controversial travel book, *An Irish Journey* (1940), in *The Great O'Neill* (1942), a biography of Hugh *O'Neill, and in *The Irish* (1947).

In 1941, Ó Faoláin founded the *Bell*, the most important literary and cultural periodical to appear since the establishment of an independent Ireland. Liberal in outlook and defiant in tone, it criticized Irish society's theocratic and autocratic tendencies. Ó Faoláin resigned the editorship in 1946 and devoted himself to the short story, producing such incisive stories as "Lovers of the Lake," "Up the Bare Stairs," and "The Woman Who Married Clark Gable." In these stories, passion conflicts with society's mores. His *Collected Stories* (1983) includes stories with an international flavor such as "Foreign Affairs" and "The Faithless Wife." He also published an autobiography, *Vive Moi!* (1965), and a final novel, *And Again?* (1979). His revision of *Vive Moi!* (1993) was more personally revealing. During the 1950s, Ó Faoláin taught at Princeton, Northwestern, and Boston College. Among his other works are two travel books on Italy and several works of criticism, notably *The Vanishing Hero* (1956), a study of the modern novel. G.OB.

Offaly, County. Inland county in the province of *Leinster. The county has 772 square miles and a population of 63,702 (2002 census). "In a quiet water'd land stands Saint Kieran's city fair" are the poetic words used by the Offaly poet T. W. Rolleston (1857–1920) to describe *Clonmacnoise, the monastic jewel in Offaly. One of the country's most important centers of craftsmanship and learning in the medieval period, Clonmacnoise produced a wealth of *manuscripts, annals, and high *crosses. The "water'd land" refers to its location beside the *Shannon, which forms the county's western boundary with *Galway and *Roscommon. The eighteenth-century Grand Canal divides the county north and south. The Boyne River bounds the eastern part of the county near Edenderry. In the south, the Slieve Bloom Mountains rise to a height of 1,733 feet. But most of the county is made up of the lowlands around the Shannon and extensive turf-*bog, where some of Ireland's oldest settlement remains dating from around 7000 B.C. were discovered at Lough Boora.

The county capital, Tullamore, is famous for its Tullamore Dew Irish *whiskey and Irish Mist liqueur. Birr, an elegant town, is renowned for its giant *Birr telescope of 1845, with which the Third Earl of Rosse (1800–67) discovered spiral nebulae. Birr Castle demesne now houses the famous telescope and also has gardens and a science center. A monastery, founded by St. *Colm Cille (or Columba) at Durrow near Tullamore, was the source of the famous seventh-century Book of *Durrow, now one of the greatest treasures in the Library of Trinity College, Dublin. During the *plantation of English settlers under Mary Tudor in 1556, the county was renamed King's County after Mary's husband, King Philip II of Spain. One famous piece of art preserved in Offaly is the beautiful twelfth-century metalwork shrine of St. Manchan in Boher parish church. A pair of fine Romanesque churches at Rahan date from the same period. Aspects of nineteenth-century life in Offaly are preserved in some of the novels of Anthony Trollope (1815–82), written when he was postmaster in the town of Banagher. The county's economy consists of *agriculture and turf production by the state-owned company Bord na Móna. P.H.

O'Flaherty, Liam (1896–1984). Writer. Born on Inishmore, the largest of the *Aran Islands, O'Flaherty briefly studied for the priesthood at Rockwell College, County *Tipperary, before joining the Irish Guards Regiment. He was discharged in 1917 and thereafter suffered from nervous exhaustion. He married writer Margaret Barrington in 1926. Becoming disillusioned with the radical politics he had championed in 1921, he roamed Ireland, England, Europe, and the Americas throughout the late twenties. His first novel was *Thy Neighbour's Wife* (1923). Dostoyevski's influence is evident in the bleakness of *The Informer* (1925)—which was successfully adapted for cinema—*Mr. Gilhooley* (1926), and *The Assassin* (1928). *Famine* (1937), *Land* (1946), and *Insurrection* (1950) form a trilogy on Irish nationalism. He was a founding member of the *Irish

Ogham Stone, Dingle Peninsula, County Kerry

Academy of Letters, and several of his novels, including *The Black Soul* (1924), were banned. O'Flaherty brings the traditional storyteller's art to his most successful short stories in both English and Irish. The narrative voice in the collections *Spring Sowing* (1924) and *Dúil* (1954) is oral, vigorous, and lyrical. *Two Years* (1930) and *Shame the Devil* (1934) are autobiographical volumes. M.S.T.

O'Flynn, Críostóir (1927–). Writer in Irish and English. Born in Limerick City, O'Flynn is a rhetorical but extremely readable autobiographer in both *There Is an Isle: A Limerick Boyhood* (1998) and *Consplawkus* (1999). The latter is a diatribe against the bureaucracy of Ernest *Blythe's directorship of the *Abbey Theatre, *Irish language politics, and the inept clerical control of the state educational system. O'Flynn possesses an enrapturing dry style, redolent with comic detail. His collection *Sanctuary Island* (1971) contains remarkable short stories. O'Flynn is an exuberant poet; his intense regionalism is exemplified by "Summer in Kilkee" (1984), which is centered around the famous hostelry of the brothers Scott. His work in Irish includes the fantasy-like *Learairí Lios an Phúca* (Sketches of the Devil's Fort; 1968) and the collection of poems *O Fhás go hAois* (From Growth to Age; 1969). Three of his plays in Irish were running at the same time in 1968: *Is É A Dúirt Polonius* (So Said Polonius), *Cóta Bán Chríost* (produced in English as *The Order of Melchizedek*), and *Aggiornamento*. Above all, O'Flynn adheres to the strict discipline of the good storyteller. J.L.

Ogham. Oldest written form of the *Irish language. Notches in groups of one to five, on, diagonally across, or on either side of a central line, form letters of a twenty-letter alphabet. (The alphabet has nineteen letters but there is also a symbol for *ng*, which makes up the twentieth "letter.") Ogham inscriptions from the third to the eighth centuries A.D. are found on memorial stones in Ireland's southern maritime counties, mostly in *Cork and *Kerry. P.H.

O'Grady, Standish James (1846–1928). Writer. Born in Castletown Berehaven, County *Cork, and educated in classics at Trinity College, Dublin, O'Grady popularized the ancient Irish saga material, which had been collected and translated by antiquarians and scholars during the first half of the nineteenth century. His two-volume *History of Ireland* (*The Heroic Period*, 1878, and *Cuculainn and His Contemporaries*, 1880) featured the legendary *Ulster hero, *Cúchulainn, and inspired the cultural *nationalism of the *Irish Literary Revival as well as the *Gaelic League. O'Grady himself, however, was a staunch *unionist with aristocratic interests. He portrayed Cúchulainn as a conservative hero who honored tradition and prevented the need for revolution in ancient Ireland. Like Samuel *Ferguson before him, O'Grady hoped to convince the *Anglo-Irish *landlords that the salvation of the faltering ascendancy lay in embracing the Gaelic past, which could heal the breach between the *Protestant elite and *Catholic majority. This in turn would create a sense of cultural identity fully compatible with the union.

The sense of optimism that pervaded his *History of Ireland*, however, was short-lived. In his attacks on the *home rule bill of 1886, Toryism, and Irish democracy, O'Grady condemned Irish landlords for neglecting their responsibilities as the country's natural leaders. In 1900, he founded the weekly periodical, *All-Ireland Review*, in one last effort to spur the slumbering aristocracy into opposing the threats of the blossoming Irish nationalism and democracy. Disillusioned by the increasingly nationalist public culture that emerged in the wake of the *Easter Rising of 1916, O'Grady left Ireland permanently in 1918 and died on the Isle of Wight in 1928. E.S.M.

Ó hAirtnéide, Mícheál (1941–99). Poet. Born in County *Limerick, Ó hAirtnéide (who published in English as Michael Hartnett) worked in various jobs, but mostly lived on his writings. Author of more than thirty books of poetry in English and Irish, and of translations, he appeared to abandon the writing of English in favor of Irish in the mid-1970s with his collection *A Farewell to English* (1974). He continued, however, to write in both. His original poetry, the best of which is brought together in *Selected and New Poems* (1994), can range from the tender to the rhetorical. These styles are also reflected in his brilliant translations of the seventeenth-century Irish poets Dáibhí *Ó Bruadair, Pádraigín Haicéad, and Aodhagán *Ó Rathaille. A.T.

O'Higgins, Kevin (1892–1927). Politician. Born in Stradbally, County *Laois, O'Higgins was a member of the first *Dáil (Parliament) in 1919. An articulate supporter of the *Anglo-Irish Treaty, he became minister for home affairs (later retitled justice) in the * Free State government in 1922. A vigorous opponent of the anti-treaty faction during and after the *Civil War, he initiated controversial emergency legislation (internment without trial) and empowered the judiciary rather than the military to carry out these laws. O'Higgins also developed an unarmed national police force, the *Gárda Síochána, and purged militant *republican sympathizers from the Free State army during the Army Mutiny Crisis of March 1924. He advanced unpopular Intoxicating Liquor legislation in 1924 and 1927, curbing the operating hours and numbers of drinking establishments in Ireland. In 1925, he played a decisive role in the controversial *Boundary Commission negotiations. He advanced the autonomy of the Irish Free State within the British *Commonwealth. He was sensitive to Northern *unionists, who, he believed, would be persuaded toward unification by collaboration rather than by threats or demands. On June 10, 1927, he was assassinated by three IRA (*Irish Republican Army) members. J.P.MC.

Oireachtas. Ireland's National Parliament and legislature. The Oireachtas consists of the *president (*an tUachtarán*) and two Houses: a House of Representatives elected by popular vote (*Dáil Éireann) and a Senate (*Seanad Éireann) made up of six members elected by graduates of the older universities, forty-three elected by members of local authorities, and eleven nominated by the incoming *Taoiseach (prime minister) after a general election. The functions and powers of the Oireachtas are set out in the *Constitution. Legislation must be passed by the Dáil and Seanad and signed by the president. The Dáil, which is also known as the Parliament, however, has the power to override Seanad objections and amendments by a simple majority. The president does not have a veto and is obliged to sign bills passed by the Dáil and Seanad, unless he or she decides to send the bill to the Supreme Court to test its constitutionality, or, if at the request of a majority of the Seanad and at least one-third of the Dáil, the president calls a referendum on the bill. This second provision has never been used. J.D.

O'Kelly, Alanna (1955–). Conceptual artist. O'Kelly studied in *Galway, *Dublin, and London. Her work is about the position of the female in the contemporary environment. She uses many different media including performance. M.C.

O'Kelly, Aloysius C. (1850–c. 1935). Painter. Born in *Dublin, O'Kelly studied painting in Paris. He developed his realistic style in Brittany, Ireland, North Africa, England, and America and exhibited widely. His images for the *Illustrated London News* were collected by Vincent van Gogh. He often concealed his identity, age, and movements, possibly due to his *nationalist activities, and on occasion he exhibited under the pseudonym "Arthur Oakley." M.C.

O'Leary, John (1830–1907). *Fenian leader. In 1848, while a student at Trinity College, Dublin, O'Leary was briefly imprisoned for taking part in a raid on police in his native county of *Tipperary. A contributor to the **Nation*, he visited America on behalf of the *Irish Republican Brotherhood in 1859. Back in Dublin, O'Leary was an editor of the Fenian newspaper the *Irish People* (1863–65). He was imprisoned for nine years (1865–74) for Fenian activities, after which he lived in exile in Paris, where he continued to participate in *republican politics. In 1885, he returned to Dublin where he became prominent in literary society and influenced W. B. *Yeats, whose poem "September 1913" contains the lines "Romantic Ireland's dead and gone / It's with O'Leary in the grave." S.A.B.

Omagh Bombing (August 1998). Real IRA (a dissident group of the *Irish Republican Army) bombing in *Northern Ireland. On Saturday, August 15, 1998, a car bomb tore through the town center in Omagh, County *Tyrone. The blast killed 29 people and injured 220 others. The massacre, which occurred months after the *Good Friday Agreement, was the largest loss of life in a single incident in Northern Ireland during the current *Troubles. A warning call was placed forty minutes before the blast, but the caller's directions apparently caused people to be moved closer to the bomb-laden vehicle. The Real IRA claimed responsibility for the bombing. This dissident *republican group wanted to undermine the *peace process and the *Good Friday Agreement. The incident caused almost unanimous revulsion and hardened in many the resolve for peace.

The *RUC (Royal Ulster Constabulary) Chief Constable Ronnie Flanagan created a special task force to investigate the bombing. Recently, the Northern Ireland Police Ombudsman Nuala O'Loan has harshly criticized Flanagan and the RUC for failing to prevent the bombing despite two prior warnings about plans to attack Omagh, and for the task force's flawed investigation. R.D.

O'Malley, Donogh (1921–68). Politician. Born in *Limerick, O'Malley was elected to the *Dáil (Parliament) in 1954. A leading figure in the modernizing wing of *Fianna Fáil in the 1960s, he was minister for health from 1965 to 1966 and minister for education from 1966 to 1968. His most lasting achievement was the abolition of fees for secondary *education and the introduction of financial aid for *university education. His promising political career was abruptly ended by his death in 1968. A.S.

O'Malley, Ernie (1897–1957). Revolutionary and writer. Born in Castlebar, County *Mayo, O'Malley studied medicine at University College, Dublin, and after the 1916 *Easter Rising, joined the *Gaelic League and the *Irish Republican Army (IRA). He traveled throughout Ireland organizing the IRA structure and was wounded several times. Captured and tortured in 1920, O'Malley escaped from *Kilmainham Gaol in 1921. He opposed the 1921 *Anglo-Irish Treaty and helped lead the antitreaty occupation of the *Four Courts in April 1922. He escaped, went on to organize *republican forces in *Ulster and *Leinster, but was captured and imprisoned in November 1922 while critically wounded. When released in 1924, still weak from wounds and effects of a *hunger strike, O'Malley traveled through Europe by foot absorbing the culture and studying Renaissance painting in museums. He went to America in 1928 with Frank *Aiken to raise funds for the Irish Press. O'Malley stayed there for seven years traveling and writing, and returned to Ireland in 1935 and married American sculptor Helen Hooker. The publication of his first volume of autobiography, *On Another Man's Wound* (1936, published in the United States as *Army Without Banners*), covering the years 1916–21 brought him literary acclaim. He wrote many articles about Ireland and the arts and collected modern paintings. M.C.

O'Malley, Grace (c.1530–c.1603). Female chieftain of the O'Malley clan, also known as Granuaile. Born in County *Mayo, Grace was the daughter of Owen O'Malley, chieftain of the seafaring O'Malley clan during the turbulent era of *Henry VIII's conquest of Ireland. Grace O'Malley has become a legend for her daring exploits as a pirate queen and warrior who resisted the English. According to one legend, her nickname Granuaile derives from "Grainne Mhaol" or "bald Grace" because once she cut her hair in order to look like a boy so that she could accompany her father on a sea voyage. Her name more likely derives from "Grainne Umhaill" after her father's territories (Umhall). She was married twice but her independence and reputation as a warrior are legendary. At the height of her power, Grace had twenty ships and raided many English merchant ships. In 1577 she was caught and imprisoned, but arranged her own release. One famous story recounts how when Grace went to London to petition for her son's release and her lands (as a widow she had no rights), Queen *Elizabeth I granted Grace a pardon and a pension. Another legend tells of how, when she was refused hospitality at Howth Castle, outside *Dublin, she kidnapped the son of the Earl of Howth. The ransom she requested was that an extra place be always set at the banquet table, a tradition maintained to this day. J.OM.

O'Malley, Tony (1913–2003). Expressionist landscape painter. O'Malley worked in St. Ives, Cornwall, from 1959 and painted in County *Kilkenny where he was born. He was a member of *Aosdána. His flat, modernist works are inspired by nature and history. M.C.

O'Neill dynasty. Powerful Gaelic dynasty, based in *Ulster. The O'Neill dynasty was descended from Niall Glundúb, an Irish high king of the tenth century. Niall of the Nine Hostages (Niall Naoighiallach) is the legendary ancestor of the O'Neills. The "nine hostages" refer to his raids in the fifth century, described in ninth-century texts. The O'Neills began to assert great influence in Ulster from the late twelfth century onward. The dynasty comprised many branches, the most important of which was the Tyrone line. The heads of this branch (who bore the title Uí Néill) exerted great authority in the north of Ireland throughout the late Middle Ages, commanding the allegiance of several other Irish families. However, there was intense rivalry between the Tyrone O'Neills and other branches, most notably with the O'Neills of Clandeboye. This lasted into the early 1600s, sometimes leading to military conflict. The O'Donnells of Tír Conaill (*Donegal) were also fierce rivals of the O'Neills.

The last truly Gaelic chief of this dynasty was Hugh *O'Neill, who was "Uí Néill" from 1593. Hugh, like his predecessors, strongly resisted the spread of English power in Ulster. He was the most prominent military commander of what was the final stand by Gaelic Ireland against England, the *Nine Years War (1594–1603). After defeat at the Battle of *Kinsale (1601), in County *Cork, O'Neill fled Ireland in 1607 (known as the *Flight of the Earls).

The O'Neills, however, continued to be prominent in Irish affairs. In the mid-1600s, for instance, Sir Phelim O'Neill and Owen Roe *O'Neill played a major part in the *Rebellion of 1641 and the wars waged by the *Confederation of Kilkenny throughout the 1640s. Other members of the dynasty were to gain prominence as soldiers and statesmen on continental Europe. In particular, some members of the family entered into the Spanish nobility.

Today, the O'Neill clan association, which was established in the 1980s, has as its clan leader a Spanish nobleman, Don Carlos O'Neill, the Twelfth Marquess de La Granja, Fifth Marquess Del Norte, and Conde de Benagiar. J.C.

O'Neill, Francis (1848–1936). Musician, collector, and writer. Born in West *Cork, O'Neill went to sea at age sixteen, and after extraordinary exploits came to join the Chicago police in 1873, becoming chief of police in 1901. He was a flute player, fiddler, and piper. President of the Chicago Irish Music Club, he collected tunes from immigrant Irish musicians, and read voluminously about indigenous Irish *music. His most important books are the seminal collection of 1850 tunes *The Music of Ireland* (1903) and the hugely popular *The Dance Music of Ireland*. Other works include the theoretical book *Irish Folk Music—A Fascinating Hobby* (1910), and the widely used *Irish Minstrels and Musicians* (1913). F.V.

O'Neill, Hugh (1550–1616). Second earl of Tyrone, last "Uí Neill" (head of the *O'Neill dynasty). Born in Dungannon, after his father's death, O'Neill was brought up in England by Sir Henry Sidney, former English lord deputy of Ireland. He was sent back to Ireland in 1568 in an attempt to increase the English crown's influence in *Ulster. O'Neill initially proved a loyal servant of the crown, and commanded a horse troop within the English forces that suppressed the Desmond Rebellion in *Munster in 1569. He first aroused English suspicions of his loyalty in 1588, when he sheltered survivors of the *Spanish Armada. In 1591 he aided the escape of Red Hugh *O'Donnell from *Dublin Castle. In 1595, one year after the other Gaelic lords of Ulster, including Red Hugh O'Donnell, had rebelled against the English crown (the so-called *Nine Years War), he was inaugurated as "the Uí Néill" according to Gaelic Irish political tradition. He was subsequently proclaimed a traitor by the crown and, with encouragement from Spain, he joined the rebellion of the Ulster Gaelic lords. In 1598 he won a notable victory over the English at the Battle of the Yellow Ford. The following year, he outwitted the English commander, the Earl of Essex, by getting him to agree to a cease-fire that *Elizabeth I did not want, which contributed to Essex's downfall. The next English commander to face O'Neill, Lord Mountjoy, was more successful against the Ulster lords, using the effective tactic of destroying their resources.

In September 1601, Spanish aid for the Irish arrived at Kinsale, County *Cork, on the south coast of Ireland. In December 1601, on Christmas Eve, O'Neill along with his main ally, Red Hugh O'Donnell, suffered defeat in the Battle of *Kinsale at the hands of Mountjoy. This effectively marked the end of the Nine Years War, though a peace treaty between the Ulster lords and the crown was not signed until 1603, at *Mellifont, County *Louth. This treaty was considered to be too lenient by many within the crown administration, however, and O'Neill and the other rebels were constantly harassed by the Dublin government during the subsequent years. This led to their flight to continental Europe in September 1607, (the so-called *Flight of the Earls). Hugh O'Neill died in exile, in Rome, in 1616. J.C.

O'Neill, Máire. See **Allgood, Molly.**

O'Neill, Owen Roe (c.1599–1649). Leading military commander of the *Confederation of Kilkenny during the Confederate Wars and nephew of Hugh *O'Neill. Owen Roe spent his early years in continental Europe in the Spanish military service in Flanders (present-day Belgium). He returned to Ireland one year after the outbreak of the *Rebellion of 1641, becoming the commander of the Confederation of Kilkenny's *Ulster army. This brought him into conflict with Scottish forces, which had been sent to protect Scottish settlers in Ulster. In 1646, he defeated the Scots at the Battle of Benburb, County *Tyrone. However, political divisions within the Confederation of Kilkenny prevented him from taking full advantage of this victory. O'Neill was closely associated with the political faction led by Archbishop Rinuccini, the papal Nuncio, causing the rival pro-Ormondist faction to declare him a traitor in 1648. In early 1649, he reached a cease-fire agreement with the pro-Cromwellian forces in Ulster. He died in November 1649, before he could come into conflict with Oliver *Cromwell's army, which had landed in Ireland the previous August. J.C.

O'Neill, Terence Marne (1914–90). Politician, prime minister of *Northern Ireland from 1963 to 1969. O'Neill spent most of his first thirty years outside Northern Ireland and he never internalized its passions. His meeting with Seán *Lemass, prime minister of the *Republic, in 1965 caused a sensation, but O'Neill preferred inclusive rhetoric to substantive civil rights reform. At the outbreak of the *Troubles in 1968, O'Neill attempted to secure broad cross-community support in the February 1969 "Crossroads Election." He failed and was forced to resign by *unionist antipathy. His legacy was a

Terence O'Neill

unionism shaken out of its complacency and bitterly divided. M.M.

opera in Ireland. Until recently, opera in Ireland was dominated by the works of Italian composers, and a handful of the more popular nineteenth-century German and French standards. The first Italian opera heard in Ireland was *La Cascina*, a *burletta* (or light comic opera) by Giuseppe Scolari, performed by the Amici family touring company in *Dublin in January 1761. In 1777, Dubliners heard their first full-length Italian opera, Gazzaniga's *L'isola d'Alcina*, and a month later, Piccinni's *La buona figliuola*. Michael *Kelly, the Dublin-born tenor who would later create the roles of Basilio and Curzio in Mozart's *Le nozze di Figaro*, appeared as a boy singer in the Piccinni opera. Mozart's *Così fan tutte* was first performed in Dublin, at Crow Street, in 1811, and *Figaro* and *Don Giovanni* in September 1819. During the late eighteenth and early nineteenth centuries, Italian operas were produced in Dublin at irregular intervals, especially in the years 1781, 1782, 1808, 1811, and 1819. There were also occasional productions of English opera, as well as Italian and French works sung in English translation.

The four-thousand-seat Theatre Royal in Hawkins Street, which opened in 1821, presented operas of the Italian *ottocento* composers Rossini, Donizetti, and Bellini, and later Verdi. A series of spectacular Italian opera seasons featuring the world's best singers (including Grisi, Viardot, Lind, Patti, Mario, Rubini, and Lablache) continued almost every year until the theater was destroyed by fire in February 1880.

Although the rebuilt Royal had a successful performance of Wagner's *Der Ring des Nibelungen* cycle in 1913, the center of operatic activity in Dublin after 1880 was the considerably smaller *Gaiety Theatre. Up to the outbreak of World War II, touring companies performed operas at the Gaiety and in provincial centers, usually in English translations. The Carl Rosa Opera Company, which first performed at the Gaiety in 1875, presented the Irish premieres of Puccini's *La Bohème*, *Tosca*, and *Madama Butterfly*, as well as operas by the Italian *verismo* composers.

The earliest and still best-known Irish-born opera composer is Michael William *Balfe (1808–70), who wrote some thirty operas in English, Italian, and French. His most important operas include *The Siege of Rochelle* (1835), *The Bohemian Girl* (1843), and *The Rose of Castille* (1857). *Waterford-born William Vincent Wallace is best remembered for his opera *Maritana* (1845). Charles Villiers *Stanford (1852–1924) wrote ten operas, including *Seamus O'Brien* (1896) and *The Travelling Companion* (post. 1925), which were generally better received in Germany than in Britain and Ireland. Most of these Irish operas had their premieres in London. Victor Herbert (1859–1924), who was born in Dublin and educated in Germany, composed all of his more than fifty stage works, mostly operettas and Broadway musicals, in the United States. His only serious opera, *Natoma* (Philadelphia, 1911), featured John *McCormack in the leading tenor role. Ireland's most important contemporary composer is Gerald *Barry (1952–). Two of his works, *The Intelligence Park* and *The Triumph of Beauty and Deceit*, have won critical success at British contemporary opera festivals.

After 1945, opera in Ireland was supported by voluntary organizations, enthusiastic groups who put on short seasons in *Belfast, *Cork, *Limerick, *Galway, and smaller provincial centers with amateur choruses, ad hoc orchestras, and hired-in professional principals. The most important one, the Dublin Grand Opera Society, by the mid-fifties, had an annual opera season of seven weeks, usually in original languages, with major principals and conductors from Ireland, Britain, and mainland Europe, and the Radio Éireann Symphony Orchestra.

Wexford Festival Opera, founded in 1951 with a policy of staging unfamiliar repertory, has become world-renowned. Three new productions play to packed houses every October. Opera Ireland (formerly the Dublin Grand Opera Society) mounts four new productions from the mainstream international repertoire, in two weeklong seasons. The Anna Livia International Opera Festival gives two works during late summer, while the Opera Theatre Company (OTC) tours regularly and sometimes commissions and performs works by contemporary composers. Today, all of these companies are professional organizations.

Famous Irish singers include Michael Kelly in the eighteenth century, Limerick-born soprano Catherine Hayes (1818–61), tenors John O'Sullivan (1878–1955) from Cork and John McCormack (1884–1945) from Athlone, and *Mayo soprano Margaret Sheridan (1889–1958). More recently, sopranos Heather Harper from Belfast and Suzanne Murphy from Limerick, and Dublin mezzo-soprano Ann Murray have established international reputations. J.A.

Orange Order, the. *Loyalist political organization. The Orange Order grew out of a *Protestant secret society, the Peep O'Day Boys, which fought with the Catholic *Defenders, over land in *Ulster in the 1790s. Following a victory over the Defenders in September 1795, the Peep O'Day Boys formed the Orange Order. Named after *William III, Prince of Orange, victor of the Battle of the *Boyne, the organization sought to defend the monarchy and the Protestant ascendancy.

The *French Revolution had radicalized Irish politics and the landed-gentry class believed that the Orange Order could counteract the revolutionary Society of *United Irishmen. Under *landlord patronage, the order became synonymous with reactionary politics. It spread throughout Ireland, and in March 1798 the Grand Lodge of Ireland was formed to coordinate the 470 Orange lodges throughout the country. The *Yeomanry (part-time militia) was dominated by Orangemen, and when the United Irishmen's *Rebellion broke out in 1798, the Yeomanry quashed the rebellion and persecuted the rebels.

Although the Orange Order initially opposed

the Act of *Union (1800) because William *Pitt, the British prime minister, had promised *Catholic Emancipation, Irish Protestants flourished under the union. The Orange Order became the union's staunchest defender, and membership spread throughout the British Isles, with support at the highest levels of government. The king's brother, the Duke of Cumberland, was the order's Grand Master. Its marches, however, were often accompanied by violence and its politics were extreme. A parliamentary commission condemned the order as a threat to political stability and at the Duke's urging, it was dissolved. Individual lodges continued to exist and in 1846 the order was revived, this time without gentry support. It was strongest in Ulster and its activities continued to be marked by violence. After incidents such as Dolly's Brae in which several people were killed, the Party Processions Act outlawed marches. With its mix of Protestantism and opposition to *home rule, the order remained popular and William Johnston in the 1870s galvanized it as the respectable voice of the landed gentry against the radical *Land League. With renewed aristocratic patronage, the order united landlords and ordinary Protestants in a new dynamic *unionism.

The Orange Order was the driving force of the *Ulster Unionist Party and the UVF (*Ulster Volunteer Force), providing the geographic and organizational framework on which both operated. After *partition in 1920, the order's processions of men in orange sashes and bowler hats, parading behind banners and bands, personified *Northern Ireland. Almost all unionist politicians, and every prime minister, and the vast majority of the RUC (*Royal Ulster Constabulary), have been Orangemen. Its hundreds of annual marches have been demonstrations of Protestant strength and warnings to the Catholic minority. Its biggest event, held annually on July 12, commemorates the Battle of the *Boyne. As these marches go through or pass by Catholic areas, the order has been accused of heightening tension during the Northern Ireland conflict. Riots often follow. Local residents' opposition to them in recent years has increased, most notably in Drumcree, Portadown, County *Armagh, where since 1995, the march, or its banning, has often resulted in violence, involving loyalist paramilitaries and the British army. T.C.

Ó Rathaille, Aodhagán (c.1670–1729) Poet. Ó Rathaille is generally seen as one of the finest poets in the *Irish language between the seventeenth and the twentieth centuries. His main themes are the dispossession of the Irish nobility, the hope of a Jacobite return, and his own fall from grace and status as a poet. His life was a struggle to maintain or to attain patronage. The MacCarthys were his native masters, but they were dispossessed by the Anglicized Brownes who cared little for his, or for any, art. Although his early poems are often conventional, he is best remembered for his passionate outpourings of anger in the work of his middle and late period. His "Valentine Brown" is a savage attack on the upstart who has taken his master's lands, although it is tempered by a kind of haughty pity that characterizes much of his best poems. Ó Rathaille is one of the first and finest writers of **aisling*, or vision poetry, in which the poet dreams of a return of a savior—usually one of the Stuarts—who will bring Ireland to her former glory. The most authoritative collection of his poetry is *Dánta Aodhagáin Uí Rathaille* (Poems of Aodhagán Ó Rathaille) published for the Irish Texts Society in 1911. He has been well served in translation by Frank *O'Connor and Michael *Hartnett. A.T.

O'Reilly, John Boyle (1844–90). *Fenian and journalist. A native of County *Meath, O'Reilly lived in England before returning to Ireland to join the *Irish Republican Brotherhood (IRB). After enlisting in the British army in order to recruit soldiers for the Fenians, O'Reilly was arrested and transported to Western Australia. He escaped to the United States in 1868 and became a supporter of *Clan Na Gael. In 1870, he joined the staff of the *Boston Pilot* and later became its owner/editor. In 1876, O'Reilly helped to organize the rescue of Fenian convicts from Australia aboard the *Catalpa*. O'Reilly also wrote novels (*Moondyne*, 1880, and *In Bohemia*, 1886) and edited *The Poetry and Songs of Ireland* (1889). S.A.B.

Ó Riada, Seán (1931–71). Musician, composer, arranger. Born in County *Cork to parents full of cultural idealism, Ó Riada learned classical violin, piano, and music theory from the age of seven. He studied music at University College, Cork (UCC), and joined Radio Éireann as a music director in 1953 for two years. He played in Paris before returning to do arrangements for the Radio Éireann Light Orchestra and Radio Éireann Singers. He became interested in the traditional *music revival, and developed a theater score for Bryan *MacMahon's play *The Honey Spike*. The musicians who performed the score formed his ensemble Ceoltóirí Chualann. In the 1960s, this group presented music on the weekly *radio shows *Reacaireacht an Riadaigh* (O Riada's Recording Session) and *Fleadh Cheoil an Raidió* (Radio Music Festival), which were hugely popular and influential.

Appointed as a lecturer in music at University College, Cork, in 1963, Ó Riada moved to Cúil Aodha, County Cork, where he continued composing and formed a choir, Coir Chúil Aodha (now run by his son Peadar). He made some seven hundred arrangements for his traditional group, 25 orchestral arrangements of Irish tunes, and 120 choral arrangements of Irish songs. His influential radio lecture series *Our Musical Heritage* was published as a book. His music scores for George Morrison's films *Mise Éire* (1959) and *Saoirse* (1961), which used traditional melody in an orchestral format, are groundbreaking, as was his score for the film of *The Playboy of the Western World* (1962). With his ensemble Ceoltóirí Chualann, Ó Riada made a huge impact on traditional music. His jazz-style arrangements forced the recognition of traditional music as a valid artistic expression, inspiring and influencing a generation of musicians. F.V.

Ó Ríordáin, Seán (1916–77). Poet in Irish. Ó Ríordáin is generally recognized as the best of the postwar poets. His work is characterized by a constant wrestling between tradition and modernity, and by an even greater struggle of a conscience torn by the Catholic scruples of his time, particularly in his first collection, *Eireaball Spideoige* (Robin's Tail; 1952). He was wracked by ill health all his life and the tenousness of existence is explored in his finest collection, *Brosna* (Firesticks; 1964). Despite this darkness, Ó Ríordáin's poetry also contains a quirky humor and exciting wordplay (as in the poem "Siollabadh," which captures the rhythms of a busy hospital ward). In his weekly column in the *Irish Times* from the late-sixties to the mid-seventies, he explored social, political, and literary themes in a distinctive prose style. A.T.

Orpen, William (Newenham Montague) (1878–1931). Portrait painter, teacher, and war artist. Born in Stillorgan, County *Dublin, Orpen won many prizes as a student at the Dublin Metropolitan and the London Slade Schools of Art. In London, influenced by the work of French artists Chardin and Watteau and Dutch artist Rembrandt above all, he exhibited regularly from 1899 with the New English Art Club (NEAC). Works of that period such as *The Mirror,* 1900 (Tate Gallery, London), and *The Portrait of Augustus John*, 1900 (National Portrait Gallery, London), show influences of Whistler. From 1903 to 1905, he ran the Chelsea School of Art with Augustus John. While working as a portrait artist in London, Orpen taught regularly at the Dublin Metropolitan School, from 1902 to 1914, where he exerted much influence on Irish painters such as Seán *Keating, Leo *Whelan, and Patrick *Tuohy.

In 1907, he continued the series of portraits of famous contemporary Irishmen which John B. *Yeats had started for *Hugh Lane's collection. Orpen's *Homage to Manet*, 1909 (Manchester City Art Galleries), depicts stalwarts of the New English Art Club who rejected the teaching of the Royal Academy in favor of the realism of impressionism. Exhibited at the NEAC, the painting is an admission of the influence of Manet. Before leaving Ireland to become Official War Artist in France from 1917 to 1918 and Official Artist of the Paris Peace Conference in 1919, Orpen did three noncommissioned paintings—*Sowing New Seed,* 1913 (Adelaide Art Gallery, Australia), *The Western Wedding*, 1914 (location unknown), and *The Holy Well*, 1916 (*National Gallery of Ireland). These paintings mediate the conflict between the traditional and the modern by the representation of the Irish landscape and established symbols of Irishness. M.C.

Osborne, Walter F. (1859–1903). Genre and portrait painter. Born in *Dublin, Osborne studied in Dublin and Antwerp. His work developed from careful paintings of continental and English rural villages and cottage gardens to charming impressionistic paintings of Dublin. M.C.

Ó Searcaigh, Cathal (1958–). Poet in *Irish. Born in the *Donegal *Gaeltacht, Ó Searcaigh has written extensively about a sense of place and the loneliness of exile. Much of his writing deals with homosexual love. He has published seven collections of poetry: *Miontragóid Chathrach* (A Small City Tragedy; 1975), *Tuirlingt* (Landing; 1978; with Gabriel Rosenstock), *Súile Shuibhne* (Sweeney's Eyes; 1987), *Homecoming/An Bealach 'na Bhaile* (1993), *Na Buachaillí Bána* (The White Boys; 1996), *Out in the Open* (1997). *Ag Tnúth leis an tSolas* (Longing for Light; 2000) contains the best of his previous collections along with a volume of new poems. His work has been translated into many languages. B.D.

O'Shea, Katharine (Kitty) (1845–1921). Mistress and later wife of Charles Stewart *Parnell. Born in Essex, England, she married Captain William Henry O'Shea in 1867. The marriage failed, and in 1880, her relationship with Parnell began. Captain O' Shea remained quiet about the affair, hoping to gain from an inheritance that Katharine expected from her wealthy aunt, Mrs. Benjamin Woods. However, when the aunt died in May 1889, the inheritance was contested and Katherine was unable to give Captain O'Shea his settlement of £20,000. He filed for divorce and in November 1890, Parnell was named as a co-respondent. The scandal that followed ruined his political career and split the *Home Rule party. Katharine married Parnell in June 1891. Four months after his death, she disappeared from public life. T.OCon., P.E.

O'Shea, Milo (1926–). Actor. As a schoolboy in his native *Dublin, O'Shea played small parts for the *Edwards/*MacLiammóir Company. At age nineteen, after acting with a touring company and taking lessons at Ria Mooney's Gaiety School of Acting, he joined the Dublin Players' Theatre. In the early 1950s he toured the United States and Canada, and on his return to Ireland appeared in a variety of plays, musicals, pantomimes, and revues. The part of Leopold Bloom in Joseph Strick's movie *Ulysses* (1967), based on the book by James *Joyce, brought him international recognition and led to appearances on Broadway (where he made his debut in *Staircase* in 1968) and film roles, including in Franco Zeffirelli's *Romeo and Juliet* (1968). Other movies include *Barbarella* (1968), *The Verdict* (1981), *The Matchmaker* (1997), and *The Butcher Boy* (1998). O'Shea has also acted for television, notably with Anna *Manahan in the series *Me Mammy*, written by Hugh *Leonard. More recently he has appeared on the sitcom *Frasier*. He lives in New York. J.C.E.L.

Ó Siadhail, Mícheál (1947–). Poet and linguist. Born in *Dublin, O'Siadhail was educated at Trinity College, Dublin, and the University of Oslo. A member of *Aosdána and formerly professor at the Dublin Institute for Advanced Studies, he published works on linguistic studies, such as *Córas Fuaimeanna na Gaeilge: na Canúinti agus an Caighdeán* (Sound System of Gaelic: The Dialects and the Standard; 1975) and *Téarmaí Tógála agus Tís as Inis Meáin* (Building and Housing Terms from Inishmaan) (1978), and Irish and English poetry collections, including *An Bhliain Bhisigh* (The Leap Year; 1978), *Hail! Madam Jazz* (1992), and *A Fragile City* (1995). His verse treats the precarious position of human beings on the edges of the dominant culture but its tone is often optimistic. M.S.T.

Ossian. Legendary Gaelic bard. Ossian is said to have associated with the third-century warriors at the court of *Tara and to have related their exploits to St. *Patrick. In 1762–63, the Scottish writer James Macpherson (1736–96) published translations of two epic poems recounting the exploits of the legendary Irish hero Fionn Mac Cumhaill, (or Finn McCool) (as Fingal) which he attributed to Ossian. The publication of these poems made Ossian's name familiar throughout Europe but provoked a literary controversy over the work's authenticity. S.A.B.

Ó Súilleabháin, Diarmuid (1932–85). Novelist in the Irish language. Ó Súilleabháin is part of the first wave of modernist novelists in Irish who abandoned plodding social realism and went straight for the imagination. Although his experimentalism was untempered by any sense of linear narrative, his novels, particularly *Dianmhuilte Dé* (The Hardmills of God; 1964) and *Caoin Tú Féin* (Weep for Yourself; 1967), were read with enthusiasm in the 1960s and 1970s. His most accomplished novel is *An Uain Bheo* (The Time Alive; 1968), which exposes the seamy side of power. A.T.

Ó Súilleabháin, Eoghan Rua (1748–84). Poet in *Irish. Ó Súilleabháin is colloquially known as "Eoghan of the sweet mouth" because of the musicality of his poetry. His poetry became renowned throughout *Munster because it was set to popular tunes. Ó Súilleabháin entered folklore as a type of the clever and verbally witty word spinner. "Im Leabaidh Aréir" (In Bed Last Night) may be his finest example of word music unencumbered by sense, whereas "Ceo Draíochta" (Magical Mist) is an almost perfect *aisling composed at a time when that genre had lost much of its force. His wandering life finds expression in his wandering style. He is the greatest Irish poet who ever lived who had little to say. A.T.

Ó Súilleabháin, Muiris (1904–50). Writer, autobiographer. His autobiography *Fiche Blian ag Fás* (*Twenty Years a'Growing*; 1933) is one of the three classics of the Blasket autobiographies. Translated by George Thomson and by Moya Llewelyn Davies in 1933, this book describes the author's youth on the *Blasket Island, his leaving of the island, and his induction into the *Gárda Síochána, or Irish *police force. Bordering on sentimentality, his autobiography brought a lightheartedness to rural writing that had been missing until then. A.T.

O'Sullivan, Seán (1906–64). Portrait painter and graphic artist. Born in *Dublin, O'Sullivan studied in Dublin, London, and Paris. He exhibited many works, mostly portraits and some landscape paintings, at the *Royal Hibernian Academy for almost forty years. He designed stamps, provided book illustrations, and made posthumous drawings of the 1916 *Easter Rising leaders. The *National Gallery of Ireland has a collection of his drawings of prominent Irishmen and women and the *Abbey Theatre has a collection of his portrait paintings. M.C.

O'Sullivan Sonia (1969–). Athlete. Born in Cobh, County *Cork, Sonia O'Sullivan, a middle- and long-distance runner, is considered Ireland's greatest female athlete. She was favored to win two gold medals at the Atlanta Olympics in 1996 but failed to finish the five-thousand meter final (due to illness) and did not qualify for the fifteen-hundred final. O'Sullivan, however, went on to win an Olympic silver medal in the five-thousand meter at the Sydney Olympics in 2000. She also won a silver medal in the fifteen-hundred-meter at the World Championships in 1993 and a gold medal in the three-thousand meter at the European Championships of 1994. She was also World Student Games champion at fifteen-hundred- and two-thousand-meter in 1991. Sonia created history in 1998 by winning both the long and short course events at the World Cross-Country Championships in Marrakesh. B.D.

O'Toole, Peter (1932–). Actor. Born in *Connemara and raised in Leeds, England, O'Toole was part of the wave of provincial actors and dramatists who broke the elitist stranglehold on the London stage in the 1950s. In 1962, he won international stardom and the first of seven Oscar nominations for the title role in David Lean's *Lawrence of Arabia*. Other signature performances include his roles in *Becket* (1964), *The Lion in Winter* (1968), *Goodbye Mr. Chips* (1967), and *The Ruling Class* (1972). In 2003, O'Toole was awarded an honorary Oscar. M.E.

Ó Tuairisc, Eoghan (1919–82). Writer. Ó Tuairisc was born in Ballinasloe, County *Galway. His first novel, *Murder in Three Moves* (1960), was a thriller, but he is best known for his work in Irish. His historical novel *L'Attaque* (1962), which deals with the French invasion of Ireland in 1798, is a classic of the genre. *Dé Luain* (Monday; 1966) is a blow-by-blow account of elements of the 1916 *Easter Rising while "Aifreann na Marbh" (Mass for the Dead), his poetic tribute to the victims of Hiroshima, was published in his collection *Lux Aeterna* (1964). B.D.

Ó Tuama, Seán (1926–). Scholar in the *Irish language, dramatist, and poet. Ó Tuama is one of the few professors of Irish in modern times who championed the importance of literature and opposed the desiccated tradition of Germanic philology prevalent for most of the century. He inspired a generation of Irish poets and literary scholars. A stylist in prose and poetry, Ó Tuama established a tradition of literary drama almost single-handedly. His selected poems are published in a bilingual edition *Rogha Dánta / Death in the Land of Youth* (1997), and his literary essays in *Repossessions: Selected Essays on the Irish Literary Heritage* (1995). A.T.

P

Paine, Thomas (1737–1809). English radical political thinker. Paine was a radical pamphleteer who influenced republican thinking in North America, France, and Ireland in the 1780s and 1790s. Born in Thetford, England, into a Quaker family, Paine became interested in the French Enlightenment as a young man. Paine's hugely popular *Common Sense* appeared in January 1776, the same year that the thirteen colonies in America declared independence. The book highlighted the lack of civil liberties in the British empire. Paine met George Washington in America before moving to Paris in 1789, where he associated with progressive liberals from Ireland, Britain, and all parts of continental Europe. Paine's *The Rights of Man*, part one, was printed in early 1791, and was widely pirated in Ireland where the debate over Edmund *Burke's denunciation of the *French Revolution created a huge controversy. Paine mixed in the same Parisian circles as Irish radicals Lord Edward *Fitzgerald and Henry and John Sheares and was made an honorary *United Irishman. His *Age of Reason* was viewed by some in 1796 as a step back from earlier political extremism but he remained one of the most admired and notorious men of his times. He died in New York in 1809. R.OD.

painting. The earliest known painting in Ireland is found on megalithic pottery. The abstraction and decoration of megalithic carvings and medieval *manuscripts continue to influence Irish painting today.

Easel paintings, mostly portraits, survive in Ireland only from the late seventeenth century. Limited patronage and shortage of schools sent Irish artists to London, leaving major landowners to employ visiting portrait painters. Garret Morphey's (c.1650–1716) *Caryll, 3rd Viscount Molyneux of Maryborough*, c.1700, is an early example of Irish portraiture. James Latham (1696–1747) from County *Tipperary and Philip Hussey (1713–83) from *Cork followed.

The establishment of the Royal Dublin Society's

Schools in 1745 improved the state of painting after a period of economic stagnation. Robert West (d. 1770) trained many important painters in his own school in *Dublin and taught figure drawing at the Dublin Society School.

James *Barry (1741–1806) won the support of Edmund *Burke with *The Baptism of the King of Cashel by St. Patrick*, 1763, the earliest painting of an Irish subject, and went on to champion neoclassical ideals, history painting, and *republicanism, which led eventually to his expulsion from the London Royal Academy. Nathaniel *Hone the Elder (1718–84) continued Irish rebellion against the academy in 1775 when he satirized Sir Joshua Reynolds's taste for the Old Masters.

On his return to Ireland from Florence in 1791, Dublin-born Hugh Douglas *Hamilton (1740–1808), an ex-pupil of Robert West at the Society's School, complained of having to paint portraits such as *Lieutenant Richard Mansergh St. George*, 1796–98 (*National Gallery of Ireland). *Cupid and Psyche in the Nuptial Bower* (National Gallery of Ireland) is an example of the type of painting he preferred to paint. It was exhibited in Dublin in 1801 to great acclaim.

Eighteenth-century landscapes of tourist attractions by pupils of the Dublin Society Schools followed conventions of the sublime while paintings of *Anglo-Irish estates in the nineteenth century differed little from those of English properties in their picturesque depiction of poverty and the exclusion of agrarian unrest.

In 1846, Thomas *Davis called for Irish artists to paint national historical subjects and universal themes. In response, romantic history painting such as Daniel *Maclise's *The Marriage of *Strongbow and Aoife*, 1854 (National Gallery of Ireland) made full use of decorative effects unearthed by antiquarian research.

In 1872, *Hone the Younger's (1831–1917) modern yet realist treatment of Irish landscape he learned in Paris inspired Hugh *Lane to assemble a national collection. The subject matter of Irish impressionist painting of the late nineteenth century was much simpler than that of earlier history painting with landscape painting remaining popular.

William *Orpen (1878–1931), famous for his portrait painting and his work as war artist, renounced academy conventions in the series *Sowing New Seed*, 1913 (Adelaide Art Gallery), *The Western Wedding*, 1914 (location unknown), and *The Holy Well*, 1916 (National Gallery of Ireland) with his use of marble medium and flat opaque colors. The use of unconventional nudes, political criticism, and caricatures of Irish stereotypes in these three paintings acknowledged a growing awareness of national cultural identity.

Orpen's pupil Seán *Keating (1889–1977) challenged the establishment with heroic images of rebellion. Paintings such as his *Men of the West*, 1917 (Hugh Lane Municipal Gallery), reached a wider Irish audience. Keating's teaching at the Metropolitan School of Art in Dublin established a new Irish formal academic orthodoxy and Mainie *Jellett's (1897–1944) early idealist cubist paintings of the same period met with fierce opposition.

Landscape painting straddled the divide. Decoratively avant-garde and postimpressionist, the landscape paintings of Paul *Henry (1876–1958), seen as representations of patriotic feeling, answered demands for a national art. The emergence of Jack *Yeats's expressionist work in the 1920s perfected the combination of modern techniques and accessible subject matter. His *Communicating with Prisoners*,

1924, and *The Island Funeral*, 1923 (*Sligo County Museum and Art Gallery), portrayed the significance of historical and social events and earned Yeats the title of "national painter."

The *Irish Exhibition of Living Art (IELA), established in 1943 as a showcase for modernist works, opened the way for technical experimentation. Individual expression was emphasized, often at the expense of social engagement with the subject. Gradually, however, the meaning of modern works prevailed over technique as witnessed in work based on feminist subjectivity and in New Expressionism. Political unrest in *Northern Ireland has encouraged artists to interpret events and to abandon elitist objectivity but this is often dismissed as propaganda. M.C.

Paisley, Ian (1926–). Evangelical leader and *unionist politician in *Northern Ireland. Born in County *Armagh, Paisley followed his father into the clergy and was ordained a Presbyterian minister in 1946. In 1951, however, he founded his own church, the Free Presbyterian Church of Ulster. In the 1950s, he attracted notoriety by sheltering a young female convert from her Catholic parents and for his strident anti–Roman Catholicism. In the 1960s, during the liberal premiership of Terence *O'Neill, Paisley agitated against perceived unionist conciliation to *nationalism. He argued that the *Catholic Church wished to see Northern Ireland subsumed into a Catholic dominated all-Ireland republic. Only a minority subscribed to Paisley's entire analysis, but he found wide and growing support as a rampart against hasty concessions. On the other hand, his relative extremism (though he consistently condemned *loyalist terrorism) embarrassed many secular unionists and confirmed nationalist and *republican prejudices regarding Protestant and unionist sectarianism.

Paisley was jailed in 1966 and again in 1969 for leading demonstrations that sparked disorder. He won Terence O'Neill's former *Stormont seat in Bannside in 1970 and the Westminster seat for North *Antrim the same year. In 1971 he merged his Protestant Unionist Party with the Ulster *Democratic Unionist Party (DUP) under the leadership of the hard-line, but secular, Desmond Boal. Paisley supported the loyalist workers' strike that brought the collapse of the *Sunningdale administration in 1974. By the late 1970s, he had outstripped rivals on the unionist right, and had become the principal competitor to the *Ulster Unionist Party (UUP) for the loyalist vote. Paisley cooperated with the UUP against the *Anglo-Irish Agreement of 1985, and opposed the 1998 *Good Friday Agreement. He has won election to the European Parliament several times and was elected to the Northern Ireland Assembly in 1999. M.M.

Palatines. *Protestant refugees from the Rhineland. After arriving in England in 1709, three thousand of the Palatines were sent on to Ireland. Most of them settled in counties *Limerick and *Wexford, though smaller communities were also established in counties *Cork and *Dublin. These religious refugees maintained a distinctive religious and cultural identity throughout the eighteenth century, many of them embracing early Methodism. However, their numbers declined through *emigration and the Palatines had ceased to exist as a separate group before the end of the nineteenth century. S.A.B.

Pale, the. The part of Ireland under English rule in the medieval period. Usually called the English

Pale, the name is said to derive from an old word for *fence* or *wall*. The term was coined at Calais, France, an Anglo-Norman stronghold. In Ireland, the Pale stretched from *Wexford in the south to Carrickfergus in the north. For most of its existence, the Pale consisted approximately of the counties of *Dublin, *Louth, *Meath, and *Kildare. The first written mention of the Pale is in a statute of 1495 by *Poynings' Parliament which calls for ditches to be made around the English Pale.

The area inside the Pale was firmly under Dublin rule and the social organization was closer to that of England. Those living "beyond the Pale" were the native Irish, regarded as rebels, or the descendants of the original *Norman invaders who had become Gaelicized. Despite the name, it is doubtful if the Pale was enclosed by a fence. There may have been some fences and ditches, but it was a more fluid frontier marked by *castles and other fortifications. The Pale ceased to exist as a geographical entity by the seventeenth century after the defeat of the Gaelic order. T.C.

Palladius. Bishop and contemporary of St. *Patrick. Palladius was sent to Ireland by Pope Celestine to minister among "the Irish who believed in Christ" in 431. This is the first absolute date in Irish history. Starting on the east coast, his mission has been largely overshadowed by, and subsumed into, that of St. Patrick, though his groundbreaking work made him equally deserving of the title *saint. P.H.

Parliament, Irish (1692–1800). Introduced into Ireland in the thirteenth century by *Anglo-Norman officials, the medieval Irish Parliament began as an administrative convenience for crown officers and continued to be such for the next four hundred years. The activities of the Irish Parliament were directed by the king's representatives in *Dublin Castle. Rarely if ever throughout its medieval and early modern history did the Irish Parliament act as a check on royal authority or pretend to represent interests other than those of English colonists settled in the country. Occasionally, during periods of protracted civil strife in *England, such as the fifteenth-century Wars of the Roses, an English political faction would capture the government of Ireland and then use the Irish Parliament to try and legitimize its claims to power in England.

Continuing political and religious conflict in Ireland during the sixteenth and early seventeenth century made meetings of the Irish Parliament infrequent and irregular. Until the reign of *William III (1688–1702), the Irish Parliament had rarely functioned as a regular working instrument of government. At that time, a group of Irish *Protestant leaders determined that the recurrent cycles of *rebellion, suppression, and confiscation that had plagued the country for most of the previous two centuries had to end. They persuaded themselves that the only way the future security and prosperity of their community could be ensured was to suppress the *Catholic majority of the country and establish some form of institutionalized protection against misguided interference in their affairs by the English government. They did so by transforming a largely ineffective and occasionally meeting Irish Parliament into an exclusively Protestant assembly with regularly scheduled sessions. Once in place, this new transformed Irish Parliament managed the suppression, disenfranchisement, and dispossession of the Catholic majority quickly and effectively, but was never able to achieve for itself the level of independence and control over its own affairs comparable to that enjoyed by the Parliament of England.

The new Irish Parliament at its first meeting in

1692, and thereafter, consisted of a House of Lords and a House of Commons. Admission to the House of Lords was by hereditary right or by Episcopal appointment. In any session, there were about 140 peers and bishops called to sit in the Upper House, but less than half were regular attendees. The House of Commons consisted of three hundred members elected from thirty-two county constituencies, 117 boroughs, and the university. Though the Irish Parliament professed to represent the people of Ireland, only a small fraction of the country's Protestant inhabitants (about one thousand families) were qualified to sit in the House of Commons or even vote for its members.

The two basic laws regulating the authority of the Irish Parliament were *Poynings' Law (1494) and the Dependency Act (1720). The first prevented the Irish Parliament from meeting without permission from the king and his English privy council, and required approval in advance of all business to be undertaken by it. The second prohibited the Irish House of Lords from hearing appeals from Irish courts and declared the right of the English Parliament to make laws that were binding in Ireland.

Thus legally constrained, Irish Protestant politicians developed techniques and a political style that succeeded until the last decade of the eighteenth century. They regularly bewildered and challenged the English noblemen sent to govern them, guided the country through the harsh realities of famine and war, while managing to keep the Catholics relatively quiescent and excluded from the political process.

Fearing that the security of Protestant property would be much diminished by the withdrawal of English troops from Ireland to fight in the *American Revolution (or War of Independence) and forced by the English government to give concessions to Catholics, Irish Protestant leaders took matters into their own hands. They responded to the military vacuum in the country by raising corps of volunteers at their own expense to defend the coasts and preserve law and order in both urban and rural areas. At the same time, under the leadership of Henry *Grattan and Henry Flood in the Irish Parliament, a majority in that body pressed for greater independence from English political concerns and more control over their own affairs. In the so-called constitutional revolution of 1782, they managed to repeal the Dependency Act and obtained a renunciation of the English Parliament's right to make laws for Ireland.

The *French Revolution and war with France brought great changes and political strife to Ireland, culminating in unsuccessful rebellions and a defeated small French invasion in 1798. Convinced that Ireland could be better managed through direct rule than by governing through the Irish Parliament, the English Prime Minister William Pitt forced passage of the Act of *Union in 1800, which abolished the Irish Parliament, gave Ireland one hundred representatives in the British Parliament, and established a new system of governing the country that lasted for 120 years. R.B.

Parliament House. Former home of the *Irish Parliament. The first purpose-built Parliament building in the world, Parliament House was designed by Edward Lovett *Pearce and constructed in College Green, *Dublin, between 1729 and 1739. The original building was characterized by the huge colonnades of its central portico, graced with Edward Smyth's statues symbolizing Wisdom, Justice, and Liberty. After the Irish Parliament acquired a greater degree of independence and control over Irish affairs, Parliament House was extended, with substantial east and west porticos being added by James *Gandon and Richard Parke between 1785 and 1797. The

Charles Stewart Parnell

building continued to accommodate both houses of the Irish Parliament until the Act of *Union (1800), when it was sold to its present owner, the Bank of Ireland, and subsequently modified by Francis Johnston (1760–1829). The former House of Commons is now a banking hall while Pearce's original chamber of the House of Lords remains largely intact and is open to the public. S.A.B.

Parnell, Anna (1852–1911). *Nationalist and land agitator. A sister of Charles Stewart *Parnell, Anna organized famine relief during the agricultural depression of the late 1870s and established the Ladies Land League in 1881. In 1907 she wrote *The Tale of a Great Sham*, an intensely critical account of the *Land League agitation. Anna questioned her brother's commitment to the rent strike initiated by the "No Rent Manifesto" shortly after his arrest in October 1881. She believed that, if the strike had been strictly enforced, it would have brought benefits to the poorest and most indebted of Ireland's farmers. Anna subsequently lived in retirement in England and died in a drowning accident at Ilfracombe. S.A.B.

Parnell, Charles Stewart (1846–91). Politician, *home rule leader. One of the most important figures in modern Irish history, Parnell dominated Ireland's political landscape in the last quarter of the nineteenth century. Immortalized in the writings of James *Joyce, idealized by Irish *nationalists at home and abroad, and finally condemned and betrayed by some of his most ardent supporters and admirers, Parnell was known as "the uncrowned king of Ireland." Along with Daniel *O'Connell and Éamon *de Valera, he is considered one of the great leaders of Irish nationalism.

Parnell was born in County *Wicklow into a *landlord *Anglo-Irish family, although his mother was American. Educated at Cambridge, he was elected member of Parliament (MP) for *Meath in 1875. An avid Home Rule MP from the beginning, Parnell joined Isaac *Butt's home rule coalition and embraced Joseph Biggar's tactical obstructionist policy in Parliament to focus attention on Ireland's quest for a home government. Throughout the 1870s, Parnell's reputation as a leading nationalist continued to grow and in 1880 he became the *Irish Parliamentary Party leader.

While home rule was of the utmost importance, land reform had become the most pressing political issue. Land agitation and agrarian violence had been recurring problems throughout Irish history and by the late 1870s a series of failed harvests and an almost feudal land use system had brought rural Ireland to the brink of another *famine. Michael *Davitt had mobilized tenant farmers in County *Mayo and founded the *Land League in 1879 to bring about land reform.

Parnell accepted the role of president of the league in 1880—a shrewd tactical move. He combined in one personality the two great dreams of the overwhelming majority of the Irish people: home rule government and land reform. The *Land War that followed elevated Parnell to the pinnacle of his career. The agrarian protests—withholding of rents, boycotting, and obstruction of evictions—were highly successful. Parnell walked a fine line between constitutional agitation and violent revolution, all the while maintaining a pivotal role in the balance of power between the major British political parties, Liberals and Conservatives, both of whom often needed his support to form a majority government in the 1880s.

A major source of support for Parnell came from American *Fenians and the *Clan na Gael organization. An agreement known as the New Departure between *Irish America and the Irish Land League recognized the land issue as indispensable to the pursuit of national independence.

In 1881, the Land League was declared illegal and its leaders, including Parnell, were arrested, further inflaming the violence of the Land War. The following year, Parnell was released under the terms of the Kilmainham Treaty, in which he agreed to abandon violence and support land reform legislation.

By the mid-1880s, because of Parnell's support, the Liberals held power and home rule for Ireland and land reform made some progress in the House of Commons. However, the 1886 home rule bill was defeated when some of the Liberal Party broke from Prime Minister William *Gladstone and supported the Conservatives.

In 1887, when a series of letters linking him to the *Phoenix Park Murders of 1882 were proved to be forgeries, Parnell was elevated even further in the mainstream political world of British politics and Irish nationalism. However, the tide would soon turn as Parnell's personal life began to cloud his public achievements. In 1890, Captain William O'Shea named Parnell in a divorce action against his wife Katharine *O'Shea. Parnell offered no defense, effectively admitting Mrs. O'Shea's adultery and his own part in it. The Liberal Party leader, Gladstone, whom Parnell had supported in the House of Commons, demanded Parnell's resignation as the leader of the Irish Parliamentary Party. The Irish party itself split over Parnell's leadership and, when the *Catholic Church denounced Parnell on moral grounds, the great leader's career was effectively over.

Parnell died shortly after in 1891 following an excruciatingly strenuous election campaign. He was forty-five years old. J.OM.

Parnell, Fanny (1849–82). Sister of Charles Stewart *Parnell. While politically less radical than her sister *Anna, she played a key role in the establishment of the New York Ladies Land League in 1880. She is particularly well known for her newspaper contributions dealing with Irish issues as well as her poetry. P.E.

partition. The division of Ireland following the 1920 *Government of Ireland Act. The act partitioned Ireland, creating the six-county state of *Northern Ireland, which remained part of the United Kingdom, and led to the creation of the *Irish Free State in 1922, following the *Anglo-Irish Treaty.

In the decade prior to the outbreak of *World War I, the partition of Ireland had gained increasing support, despite the early opposition of some *Unionist leaders, like Edward *Carson, for whom abandoning the Irish *Protestants who lived outside the part of Ulster that became Northern Ireland was unacceptable. With the seemingly imminent implementation of the *home rule bill of 1912, however, pragmatism prevailed. In Ulster (the only region in Ireland with a substantial unionist population), unionists, who were almost exclusively Protestant and believed that "home rule was Rome rule," began to fight for the exclusion of the entire province of Ulster from home rule. However, since five of Ulster's nine counties had *nationalist majorities in 1914, some Unionist leaders, such as Andrew Bonar Law, James *Craig, and Lord Lansdowne, began to contemplate a political configuration that would assure Protestant ascendancy in Ulster. John *Redmond, leader of the *Irish Parliamentary Party, would not consent to partition because the home rule legislation was due to become law in 1914 and Redmond envisioned a thirty-two-county political entity. When British Prime Minister Herbert *Asquith attempted to negotiate the issue, Redmond responded with his own partition compromise.

Essentially, Redmond wanted the British government to allow the citizens of the nine Ulster counties to decide by plebiscite whether they wished to become part of a home rule Ireland. He further insisted that two Ulster cities, Newry in County *Down, and Derry in County *Londonderry (both with large Catholic majorities in counties almost certain to reject home rule) would also be given the plebiscite option. Redmond also demanded that any constituency that voted for exclusion from home rule could only remain apart from the rest of Ireland for a period of six years. Unionists threatened Asquith's Liberal Government with civil war rather than agree to such terms. The crisis was resolved for the moment with the outbreak of *World War I in Europe. Redmond responded by urging Irish nationalists to support Britain against Germany, in return for which, he believed, Ireland would surely be rewarded with home rule at the war's conclusion.

In 1916, Unionists accepted Prime Minister *Lloyd George's invitation to join his coalition government. Irish nationalists, in keeping with the party's policy of abstaining from any British executive, declined cabinet positions, thereby giving the Unionists the opportunity to become an uncontested lobby in the development of the British government's Irish policy. New elections were held in December 1918 when the war ended. Having unreservedly supported the war, Redmond's Irish Parliamentary Party lost the support and confidence of a majority of Irish people following the executions of the leaders of the *Easter Rising of 1916 and the government's attempt to conscript Irish citizens in 1918. The party was totally eclipsed by the *Sinn Féin republican nationalists who refused to take their seats in the Westminster Parliament and, in January 1919, convened the first *Dáil (Irish Parliament) and declared themselves the Provisional Government of the *Republic of Ireland.

Frustrated in its attempt to negotiate a home rule plan satisfactory to both nationalists and unionists, the British government passed the Government of Ireland Act (1920), which established a parliament near *Belfast, for the six-county jurisdiction now sought by the unionists, and a home rule parliament in Dublin for the remaining twenty-six counties. The Ulster counties of *Donegal, *Cavan, and *Monaghan were excluded from the proposed new entity of Northern Ireland because of their Catholic majorities. The remaining six counties, *Antrim,

*Armagh, Down, *Fermanagh, Londonderry, and *Tyrone, were thought to represent a geographical region that would be sufficiently large to be economically viable, and to be so selectively populated to assure unionist control. However, while unionists would comprise two-thirds of the population in this territory, nationalists would still represent a significant element. Two of the six counties, Fermanagh and Tyrone, had slight Catholic majorities, while South Down, South Armagh, and West Derry were predominantly Catholic. James Craig, the first prime minister of Northern Ireland, declared that state to be a Protestant nation for a Protestant people. The *Anglo-Irish Treaty of 1921 resulted in partition and established the *Boundary Commission, which the Irish delegation hoped would eventually lead to a united Ireland.

The *oath of allegiance to the British monarch, and not partition, was the primary issue in the *Civil War (which was fought between those advocating a republic and those accepting the Free State status) because most people thought that the Boundary Commission would eventually resolve the partition issue in favor of Irish nationalists. For fifty years—from 1922 when the government of Northern Ireland was officially inaugurated, until 1972 when the British government suspended the devolved powers of the *Stormont (Northern Ireland) Parliament—the six-county province functioned as a quasi-independent region of the United Kingdom. Throughout this period, there were often intense conflicts between nationalists and unionists, sometimes on the order of full-blown pogroms, which convulsed both communities. Despite the rhetorical attacks of Irish nationalists in the Dublin Parliament protesting the violence against Catholics in the North during the 1920s and 1930s, partition became a grudgingly accepted reality of life in Ireland.

World War II had an enduring impact upon the Irish population on both sides of the border. The economically frugal but otherwise peaceful life in the South (which had remained neutral during the war) contrasted sharply with the devastating aerial bombardment that impacted nationalist and unionist communities in the North. The partition of Ireland was rendered ever more permanent by these distinctly different experiences on either side of the border. Throughout the 1950s and early 1960s, nationalists in Northern Ireland became increasingly more accepting of their separation from the Republic of Ireland because of their participation in the British welfare system. What Catholics were denied, however, was access to equal opportunities with Protestants and the culture of discrimination prompted the oppressed minority to seek greater freedom within the United Kingdom rather than pursue the forlorn hope of national unification. The civil rights movement of the late 1960s precipitated the *Troubles that would endure for the next thirty years. The *Good Friday Agreement of 1998, which established a power-sharing assembly, affirmed that there will be no change in the status of Northern Ireland without the consent of the majority of its population (which, according to the 2001 census, was approximately 53 to 44 percent unionists to nationalists). Meanwhile, partition remains an enduring fact of life on the island of Ireland. T.F.H.

passage-graves. Megalithic tombs of around the fourth and third millennium B.C. Often located on a hilltop, the graves have a covered passage leading to a tomb at the center of a mound. Those in the Boyne Valley—notably *Newgrange and *Knowth—and Loughcrew, County *Meath, are the most decorated. Other passage-graves are found at *Carrowmore, County Sligo, and Dowth, County *Meath. P.H.

Patrick, Saint (c.389–c.461). Patron *saint and apostle of Ireland, generally credited with bringing Christianity to the country. Since there is little or no source material from the fifth century, what we know about Patrick's life comes from two of his own writings: *The Confession*, written late in his life as a defense of his Irish mission, and the *Epistola*, a letter to the British King Coroticus denouncing the treatment of captured Irish Christians. In his writings, Patrick comes across as a humble man, well-read in Scripture, fearing and glorifying God. The rest of what we know about Saint Patrick comes from secondary sources, many contained in the early-ninth-century Book of *Armagh, now preserved in the Library of Trinity College, Dublin. The life of Saint Patrick by Muirchú and the notes by Tirechan in the Book of Armagh originate from the late seventh century, and are based on traditions, written and oral, from approximately two hundred years after the saint's lifetime.

Patrick was born in Bannavem Taberniae (probably in southwestern Roman Britain). His father, Calpurnius, was a deacon of the Church. At the age of sixteen, Patrick was captured by Irish raiders and taken to Ireland where he was sold as a slave to Milchu, a chieftain in Dalriada (part of County *Antrim). Here, he tended flocks of sheep in the valley of the Braid and on the slopes of Slemish Mountain.

According to *The Confession*, during his captivity, his thoughts turned to God and he spent many solitary hours praying. After six years, he escaped and returned home, where he claims that in a dream, he heard the "voices of the Irish" calling for his return. Patrick took this as a sign that God wanted him to become a missionary. He was ordained in circa 417 after studying in Gaul, and on the death of *Palladius, he was appointed bishop of the Irish (by Pope Celestine I, according to some authors).

In 432, Patrick began his mission in Ireland, where he preached the word of the gospel, baptizing and confirming people, mostly in the north, in the area around the former capital of Ulaidh, Emhain Macha. He established his main church nearby at Ard Macha (now *Armagh) and to this day Armagh is the capital of the Irish Churches—both *Catholic and *Protestant.

Some church scholars cast doubt on various legends about him (that he spent forty days on top of *Croagh Patrick, County *Mayo, in imitation of the biblical Moses). Also, some dispute that Patrick was the first person known to have converted the Irish to Christianity, arguing that Palladius, sent by Pope Celestine in 431, preceded him.

By the start of the eighth century, Patrick had become a legendary figure. Two legends in particular are commonly known: that he drove the snakes out of Ireland, and that he used the shamrock (which has become one of Ireland's symbols) to explain the concept of the Holy Trinity.

His reputation as a baptizer and wonder-worker was spread widely in Europe in the thirteenth century with the story of his life as told in *The Golden Legend* of Jacobus de Voragine. His cult was very popular in Europe in the eighteenth century and in the nineteenth century, his renown spread with the Irish immigration to America, where his feast day, March 17, is celebrated with huge street parades in the major cities. The first parade in America took place in Boston in 1737. Presently, the largest parade in the world takes place on New York City's Fifth Avenue, with an annual participation of over two hundred thousand people.

It is believed that Patrick died in County *Down and is buried at Downpatrick, where many come on pilgrimages. P.H., P.E.

Patterson, Frank (1938–2000). Tenor. Born in Clonmel, County *Tipperary, Patterson is internationally renowned for his recordings of inspirational songs and Irish ballads. He recorded thirty-six albums and performed at Radio City Music Hall, in New York, on the steps of the Capitol in Washington DC, and in the *Phoenix Park *Dublin, before 1.3 million people during the visit of Pope John Paul II to Ireland. P.E.

peace process, the. Negotiations to resolve the *Northern Ireland conflict (the Troubles). The 1985 *Anglo-Irish Agreement created a foundation for the peace process, and by the early 1990s, a "three strand" approach, involving three key relationships, had emerged: first, between the communities in Northern Ireland; second, between Northern Ireland and the Irish *Republic; and third, between the Irish Republic and the United Kingdom. Between 1988 and 1993, John *Hume, leader of the *Social Democratic and Labour Party (SDLP), held a series of intermittent talks with Gerry *Adams, leader of *Sinn Féin, seeking to bring the *republican movement into constitutional politics. The British government publicly confirmed in November 1993 that it had engaged in secret talks with the republican movement. In December 1993, John *Major, the British prime minister, and Albert *Reynolds, the Irish *Taoiseach (prime minister), announced the *Downing Street Declaration, whereby the British government affirmed that it had "no selfish strategic or economic interest" in Northern Ireland and that the territory's future should be determined by its own people. US President Bill Clinton played a significant role in encouraging the peace process, and in January 1994, despite considerable opposition, a visa was issued to Gerry Adams, to allow the republican leader to speak in the United States for the first time.

The *Irish Republican Army (IRA) announced a cease-fire on August 31 of the same year, and cease-fires by *loyalist paramilitary organizations followed in October. During the next eighteen months, negotiations stalled over the issue of "decommissioning" (the term used for disarming of paramilitaries). The British government and the *unionist parties insisted that the IRA begin to disarm as a precondition to the participation of Sinn Féin in the peace talks. The republicans countered that disarmament could only occur in the context of an overall settlement. In January 1996, an international commission on decommissioning, chaired by former US Senator George Mitchell, issued the *Mitchell Report recommending that all-party peace talks and paramilitary decommissioning take place simultaneously. When the British government continued to insist on decommissioning prior to talks, the IRA ended its cease-fire with a bombing at *Canary Wharf in London on February 9, 1996. Although Sinn Féin was now excluded, talks continued between the London and *Dublin governments and the other Northern Ireland parties. In 1997, Tony *Blair, the new Labour prime minister, revived the peace process and the IRA declared a new cease-fire on July 20, 1997. Sinn Féin rejoined the ongoing multiparty talks, over which George Mitchell presided as independent chairman, in September 1997. Continuing to insist on prior decommissioning, the *Democratic Unionist Party (DUP), headed by Ian *Paisley, declined to participate. On April 10, 1998, these talks achieved a comprehensive settlement known as the *Good Friday Agreement. All signatories agreed that a united Ireland could only be created by a majority vote of the people of Northern Ireland. For its part, the Irish

Republic agreed to amend the territorial claim in its *Constitution to reflect this principle of consent. The agreement mandated the establishment of a Northern Ireland Assembly, in which representatives from unionist and nationalist parties would share power. In the all-Ireland referendum of May 22, 1998, the Irish people demonstrated overwhelming support for the Good Friday Agreement. In the Republic, 94.4 percent voted yes and only 5.6 percent voted no. In Northern Ireland, 71 percent voted yes and 29 percent voted no, though public opinion polls suggested that the margin of support was narrow among unionist voters.

The implementation of the Good Friday Agreement was hampered by continued acts of violence by paramilitaries, including some of those purportedly on cease-fire, and intransigent positions by the political parties on the decommissioning issue. In early May 1998, a group of dissident republicans (which became known as the "Real IRA") announced that it would continue the armed struggle. On August 15, 1998, the Real IRA claimed responsibility for the *Omagh Bombing, in County *Tyrone, which killed twenty-nine people, the single highest death toll from any one incident during the Troubles. After a public outcry, the Real IRA announced a suspension of military action on August 18, followed by a "complete cessation" on September 7. On June 25, 1998, representatives were elected to the new Northern Ireland Assembly and on July 1, David *Trimble of the *Ulster Unionist Party, was chosen as first minister designate. Séamus *Mallon of the SDLP, was chosen as deputy first minister designate. The Northern Ireland Assembly convened for the first time on September 14, 1998, but Trimble and his party refused to form an Executive that included representatives of Sinn Féin until the IRA began to decommission its weapons. After protracted negotiations, mostly concerning the decommissioning issue, and a "review" of the agreement by George Mitchell, the parties finally agreed to institute the ten-person power-sharing Executive on November 29, 1999. At midnight on December 1, British direct rule over Northern Ireland ended and the new institutions created by the Good Friday Agreement went into operation. The institutions have been suspended a number of times, due to distrust on both sides of the political divide, but the peace process has prevented a return to the widespread violence of the Troubles. F.B.

Peacock Theatre, the. With the *Abbey Theatre, the Peacock Theatre constitutes the National Theatre of Ireland, which is dedicated to the promotion, development, and presentation of the repertoire of Irish dramatic literature. In 1924, the Irish National Theatre was granted an annual subsidy by the newly established *Irish Free State. It used the first such subsidy to establish the Peacock. The theater is currently situated in a studio space beneath the foyer of the Abbey Theatre building on Lower Abbey Street. The Peacock presents new plays by young writers and directors and established playwrights. Plays that have premiered at the theater include Frank *McGuinness's *Observe the Sons of Ulster Marching Towards the Somme* (1985), Sebastian *Barry's *Boss Grady's Boys* (1988), and Dermot *Bolger's *Blinded by the Light* (1990). S.A.B.

Pearce, Edward Lovett (c.1699–1733). Architect. Pearce was the first great Irish architect, responsible for introducing the Palladian style to Ireland. The *Parliament House (now Bank of Ireland) in College Green, *Dublin, is his masterpiece (1729–39). Pearce also designed notable country houses such as Bellamont Forest, in County *Cavan, and Cashel Palace, in County *Tipperary (now a hotel). He was a member of Parliament and was appointed surveyor general in 1729. P.H.

Pearse, Patrick (Pádraig MacPiarais)

(1879–1916). Poet, educator, and revolutionary. Born at 27 Great Brunswick Street, *Dublin, Pearse was educated by the *Christian Brothers and later studied law at the Royal University. At age seventeen, he established the New Ireland Society to promote Irish *poetry and in 1895 he became a member of the *Gaelic League. His writings in the Irish language appeared in the league's weekly journal, **An Claidheamh Soluis*, and between 1903 and 1909, he was that journal's editor. In 1908, he founded St. Enda's College, an Irish-language alternative to the state-run school system.

A supporter of *home rule, Pearse, however, believed that the British government would fail to deliver self-government in the face of *unionist opposition and that Irish autonomy could only be achieved through force. In November 1913, he joined the Irish *Volunteers and was later sworn into the *Irish Republican Brotherhood. Pearse's lecture tour of the United States between February and May 1914 was a turning point. His speeches to Irish Americans, anxious for revolution in Ireland, became increasingly filled with violent rhetoric. He returned to Ireland as a radical *nationalist and in July 1914 became a member of the Supreme Council of the IRB. Following his oration at the funeral of *O'Donovan Rossa in 1915, he was admitted into the IRB Military Council.

Pearse was instrumental in planning the *Easter Rising of 1916. Even though he and the other members of the military council knew the rising was doomed, they believed in sacrificing their lives in order to ignite the cause of nationalism. Commander in chief and president of the Provisional Government, he led a column of rebels to the General Post Office, where he read aloud the *Proclamation of the Irish *Republic, which he had drafted. The rebellion was quickly crushed, and Pearse was court-martialed and executed by firing squad in *Kilmainham Gaol on May 3, 1916.

Pearse's republican idealism proved enormously influential during the *War of Independence and in the early years of the *Irish Free State. He remains a controversial figure: an iconic republican hero to many, but criticized by others for his idea of martyrdom to the nationalist tradition. P.E.

Penal Laws. Series of anti-*Catholic discriminatory legislation from the late seventeenth and early eighteenth century. Also known as Popery Laws, these laws were introduced to restrict Catholic worship, exclude Catholics from political life, limit their access to *education, and prohibit them from owning property. The first two statutes, an Act for the Better Securing (of) the Government, and an Act to Restrain Foreign Education, were passed in 1695. Under their terms, Catholics were barred from keeping weapons, prohibited from having their children educated abroad, and forbidden from teaching or running schools in Ireland. In 1697, the Banishment Act ordered all Catholic bishops and regular clergy (i.e., priests from religious orders) to leave the country by May 1, 1698, under penalty of transportation for life. Any who returned faced being hanged, drawn, and quartered. Under the 1704 Registration Act, all secular (diocesan) priests had to be registered. Every parish was allowed to have one registered priest who could not be replaced upon their death. An Act to Prevent the Further Growth of Popery, passed in 1704, prevented Catholics from purchasing land and taking leases for greater than thirty-one years. These provisions were strengthened by a further act in

1709, which entitled *Protestants to take over land that had been purchased by Catholics in property transactions prohibited under prior penal legislation. Other laws deprived Catholics of particular rights, including barring them from public office, preventing them from practicing law, and excluding them from joining the army or navy. Intermarriage between Catholics and Protestants was also forbidden. In 1728, Catholics who had been excluded from Parliament since 1691 lost the right to vote.

Traditionally, the Penal Laws were viewed as an attack on the entire Catholic population and its religion. Some historians suggest, however, that the Penal Laws were primarily designed to prevent Catholics from threatening the economic and political power of the Protestant ascendancy. The laws against the practice of the Catholic religion were applied only during periods of political unrest and the Catholic Church (provided it was discreet) was allowed to minister to its flock in fields and in Mass houses without much difficulty. In reaction to the ban on education, a system of hedge schools (in open fields or in primitive buildings) developed where Catholic teachers, financed by the local population, taught a mixture of spelling, reading, arithmetic, and religion. The laws concerning land and the professions were strictly enforced and while ordinary Catholics did suffer, it was mostly the Catholic aristocracy and landed gentry that were victimized. By 1778, less than 5 percent of Irish land remained in Catholic hands. In 1760, the Catholic Committee was established to exert pressure on the British government for relief and the Penal Laws were eventually nullified by the *Catholic Relief Acts (1774–93) and the *Catholic Emancipation Act (1829). P.E.

Peoples, Tommy (1948–). Musician/fiddler from East *Donegal. Peoples learned to play at age seven, and eventually moved to *Dublin where he was a leading session player in the renowned O'Donoghue's bar. He moved to *Clare in 1970, and joined the *Bothy Band briefly. He has played locally in Clare for many years. His album *The Quiet Glen* won an *RTÉ Traditional Musician of the Year Award in 1998. F.V.

People's Democracy (PD). Student civil rights organization. Formed on October 9, 1968, by students at Queen's University, *Belfast, following *Royal Ulster Constabulary (RUC) violence in *Derry, the organization called for peaceful but unremitting agitation to win civil rights reform. Its most famous member was Bernadette Devlin *McAliskey, who later became a member of Parliament. As traditional political allegiances asserted themselves throughout *Northern Ireland, and left-wing ideologues wrested control of the People's Democracy, the movement was eclipsed. M.M.

Petrie, George (1790–1866). Artist and antiquarian, often honored with the title of "founder of Irish archaeology." He worked with Eugene *O'Curry and John *O'Donovan in the Ordnance Survey during the 1830s, and is best known for his work on *round towers, published by the *Royal Irish Academy in 1845. It dismissed many fanciful notions about these structures and placed the towers firmly within the Christian context of the early Irish monasteries. A talented watercolorist, tireless antiquarian, and collector of ancient Irish airs, he was elected president of the *Royal Hibernian Academy of Arts in 1857. P.H.

Petty, William, Sir (1623–87). English political economist, the first to conduct detailed surveys of Ireland. Born in Hampshire, Petty studied in Europe and was appointed Oxford professor of anatomy in 1651. As physician general to *Cromwell's army in Ireland, he was enlisted to execute the "Down Survey" (1654–59), the first large-scale scientific survey of Ireland. Assisted by a team of one thousand men, Petty supervised the production of detailed maps of land forfeited to *Cromwellian settlers, for which he was awarded an estate in *Kerry. An original member of the Royal Society (1660), Petty published numerous socioeconomic studies, including *The Political Anatomy of Ireland* (1691). S.A.B.

Phoenix Park (Dublin). The world's largest enclosed urban park. Covering 1,752 acres on the northwest of Dublin, Phoenix Park was originally a royal deerpark. Áras an Uachtaráin, the president's residence (formerly the Viceregal Lodge) is in the park, as well as the official residence of the US ambassador. Within the park is the third oldest zoo in the world (after London and Paris), which was established in 1830. T.C.

Phoenix Park Murders, the (May 6, 1882). Violent incident during the *Land War. W. E. Forster, in protest against British Prime Minister William *Gladstone's Kilmainham deal with Charles Stewart *Parnell, resigned as chief secretary of Ireland. His replacement, Lord Frederick Cavendish, was assassinated along with T. H. Burke, the undersecretary, while walking in the Phoenix Park, by the *Invincibles, a secret organization. Gladstone imposed further coercive measures in Ireland, and Parnell, denouncing the murders, threatened to resign from Parliament. In April 1887, the *London Times* published a letter (later proved to be a forgery) implicating Parnell in the murders. P.E.

photography. Photography in Ireland began with the pioneering work of *Belfast engraver Francis Stewart Beatty in the use of "Talbotype" and daguerreotype processes during 1840 and 1841. English businessman Richard Beard is widely believed to have established the first commercial photographic studio in Ireland at the Rotunda in *Dublin, in October 1841. With the invention of the faster and simpler "wet plate" process in 1851, both professional and amateur photography spread throughout Ireland. Urban and rural scenes were recorded by Thomas J. Wynne and his sons, who ran thriving photographic businesses and news agencies in Castlebar, Loughrea, *Tipperary, and Portarlington. Provincial life was also photographed by A. H. Poole in *Waterford and R. J. Welch in *Ulster. Commerce was clearly a driving force in the expansion of photography in Ireland. The number of portrait studios grew dramatically after the introduction of photographic calling-cards ("cartes-de-visite") in 1861. There were more than sixty studios in Dublin's "photographic mile" which ran through Grafton, Westmoreland, and Sackville (now O'Connell) Streets. The introduction of "dry plate" photography in the 1860s made cameras more transportable and facilitated the development of professional landscape photography. A leading entrepreneur in this field was William Lawrence, who established a shop in Sackville Street in 1865. Robert French photographed architecture, historic sites, and topographical views for Lawrence's business, which sold his work as postcards and prints. Their huge catalogue of Irish landscape photography was acquired by the *National Library of Ireland in 1943. Eason & Son of Dublin and Valentine & Sons of Dundee generated similar collections (also acquired by the National Library) to cater for the postcard trade. Technical innovations made in Ireland include

Thomas Grubb's experiments in stereoscopic techniques in the 1860s and the pioneering work in color photography by Professor John Joly of Trinity College, Dublin, in the 1890s.

Recreational photography became increasingly popular among the landed gentry and aristocracy, who recorded various aspects of daily life on their estates. An early pioneer was Francis E. Curry, land agent at the Duke of Devonshire's Lismore Estate in County *Waterford. Leading exponents of the art included many women, such as the Countess of Rosse and Lady Augusta Dillon of Clonbrock, County *Galway. Technical breakthroughs made by George Eastman in the United States between 1870 and 1890, most particularly his development of roll film and the Kodak box camera, further popularized amateur photography in Ireland. Clubs and associations were formed, the most eminent being the Photographic Society of Ireland (1858–1954). Improvements to printing processes meant that photographic images were more widely used in Irish *newspapers and books. Journalistic photography captured many important documentary images. The Dublin firm Keogh Brothers recorded many incidents during pivotal events such as the *Easter Rising and the *War of Independence, and their pictures constitute a valuable record of the struggle for Irish independence. Newspapers also recorded notable people, places, and events associated with Irish *theater, literature, and the arts, as well as commerce and industry. The visual history of Ireland has been well preserved. The National Photographic Archive in Dublin is the largest repository of Irish photographic prints and negatives in the world. It holds three hundred thousand photographs in one hundred discrete collections and groupings, which illustrate diverse aspects of Irish life between the 1860s and 1990s. Both amateur and professional photographers continue to advance the art of photography in contemporary Ireland, with projects such as the "Gallery of Photography" in Dublin attracting public funding and support. S.A.B.

pilgrimage. A religious activity practiced in Ireland at least as early as the seventh century. Traditional pilgrimage sites include *Glendalough, *Lough Derg, *Croagh Patrick, the *Dingle Peninsula, and *Clonmacnoise. Knock, where the Virgin is said to have appeared in 1879, is one of the most popular places of pilgrimage today. P.H.

pirates. There were several pirates with Irish connections, the two most famous of them women. Anne Bonny (c.1700) was the bastard child of a Cork lawyer and the family maid, who sailed first to Carolina, where she escaped from a weak husband to take up with pirates. Disguising herself as a man, she had a brief and unusual career before being tried and sentenced to be hanged for piracy in Jamaica. Pregnant, her sentence was delayed until the delivery of the baby, after which she disappeared. Gráinne (Grace) *O'Malley (c. 1530–c. 1603) assumed control of the family domains on the Atlantic coast of *Mayo on her husband's death. Her ships harassed the British fleets on the west coast of Ireland until her arrest by Sir Richard Bingham in 1586. She was ultimately spared and even had an audience with Queen *Elizabeth I in London, where she is said to have assumed regal equality with the English monarch and insisted on speaking only in Irish. J.MD.

plantations. Sixteenth- and seventeenth-century campaign by successive English monarchs and Parliament to recolonize Ireland by confiscating land from disloyal subjects and replacing (or "planting") them with English and Scottish settlers. These settlers would provide centers of English culture (and from the 1580s *Protestantism), which would bring about the Anglicization of the country. This in turn would prevent Ireland from being used by continental powers as a base to usurp English power.

The first plantations, one in *Laois-*Offaly in the 1550s under Queen Mary, and the other in *Munster under Queen *Elizabeth I in the 1580s, failed due to a combination of bad planning and fierce Gaelic resistance. Following the *Flight of the Earls in 1607, a more ambitious and systematic era of plantation was initiated. Under the *Ulster Plantation, the *Cromwellian Settlement, and the Williamite Plantation, by the 1690s over 80 percent of the productive land in Ireland was confiscated from the Gaelic Irish and Old English and transferred to English and Scottish settlers.

The arrival of these colonists had long-term social and political implications for the history of the country. New plantation towns such as Enniskillen, County *Fermanagh, and Bandon, County *Cork, were built and new farming methods were introduced with arable farming replacing native cattle rearing. The growing of flax also became widespread and laid the basis for the later *Ulster *linen industry. Significantly, the plantations also created the *landlord class who differed from their tenants in religion, language, culture, and wealth. Ireland became a country of two separate societies, with the native Irish resentful and suspicious of the settlers, who were seen as a conquering, imperial presence. P.E.

Planxty. Musical group. Planxty was formed in 1972 from a group of musicians who had played with Christy *Moore on his classic album *Prosperous*. The original lineup reads like a who's who in Irish traditional *music, consisting of singer and guitarist Christy Moore, piper Liam Óg O'Flynn, mandolin player Andy Irvine, and bouzouki player Dónal *Lunny. Moore was replaced in 1974 by Paul Brady. The group split in 1975 but re-formed three years later with the original lineup. Planxty brought an innovative approach to traditional music with Andy Irvine in particular experimenting with eastern European influences. Moore and Lunny went on to form the backbone of the traditional rock band Moving Hearts. In 2004, Planxty re-formed for a series of concerts to great acclaim. B.D.

Plunkett, Horace Curzon (1854–1932). Proponent of agricultural cooperation and politician. Born into an aristocratic family in County *Meath, Plunkett was educated at Oxford University and from 1879 to 1889 was a rancher in Wyoming, US. On his return to Ireland in 1889, he launched the cooperative Irish Agricultural Organization Society. He was appointed first vice president of the Department of *Agriculture and Technical Instruction in 1899. Plunkett was a *Unionist MP (member of Parliament) (1892–1900) who later became a supporter of *home rule. He worked unsuccessfully as chairman of the Irish Convention (1917–18) and after 1919 through his Irish Dominion League to keep Ireland united and within the *Commonwealth. L.MB.

Plunkett, James (1920–2003). Novelist, playwright. Born in *Dublin, Plunkett (pseudonym of James Plunkett Kelly), was educated at Synge Street Secondary School and the College of Music. He worked as a clerk for the Dublin Gas Company and later became an official of the Workers' Union of Ireland. Plunkett joined the national *radio station (Radio Éireann) in the 1950s and later moved to its *television wing (*RTÉ) to work as a producer. Plunkett is probably best known for his two sweeping historical novels, *Strumpet City* (1969) and

Farewell Companions (1977), which portray Dublin life during the first half of the twentieth century and such historical figures as James *Larkin, the *trade union leader. Other works include the plays *Homecoming* (1954), *Farewell Harper* (1956), and *Big Jim* (1955), and the collections of short stories, *The Eagles and the Trumpets* (1954), *The Trusting and the Maimed* (1955), and *Collected Stories* (1977). P.E.

Plunkett, Joseph Mary (1887–1916). Revolutionary, poet. Born in *Dublin, the son of George Noble Plunkett, Plunkett published a volume of poetry in 1911 and was one of the founders of the Irish Theatre in 1914. A prominent member of the Irish *Volunteers, Plunkett assisted Roger *Casement in importing German arms into Ireland in 1915. As a member of the Military Council of the IRB (*Irish Republican Brotherhood), he was centrally involved in the planning of the *Easter Rising (1916). One of the signatories of the *Proclamation of the Irish Republic, Plunkett was executed for his part in the rising on May 4, 1916. He married Grace Gifford, his fiancée, shortly before his execution. A.S.

Plunkett, Oliver (1629–81). *Catholic archbishop. Born in County *Meath of Old English descent, Plunkett was appointed archbishop of *Armagh in 1669. Plunkett had relatively good relations with the *Dublin Castle authorities until the introduction of anti-Catholic legislation in 1673 forced him to go into hiding. In 1679, in reaction to the Popish Plot (an alleged English Catholic conspiracy to assassinate Charles II), he was arrested and accused of attempting to instigate a French invasion of Ireland. After an initial trial in Ireland collapsed, Plunkett's case was transferred to England where he was found guilty of treason even though many, including Charles II, believed him to be innocent. Plunkett was hanged, drawn, and quartered in 1681. The most celebrated Irish victim of official anti-Catholicism, Plunkett was canonized in 1975. A.S.

poetry. The oldest Irish poetry was composed and transmitted orally in *Irish. It consisted of rhythmical alliterative verse, mainly in praise of kings and heroes. The word for a poet, **fili*, meant "seer," indicating the prophetic role of the poet. The *filid* were the custodians of traditional lore and were highly trained in the metrical conventions of Irish verse. It was not until the arrival of *Christianity in the fifth century that poetry was written down. Christianity coexisted with traditional pagan practices, and the *filid* continued to enjoy their privileged place in society. Christian monasteries became centers of learning and, as well as copying sacred texts, the monks compiled ancient myths and tales, which were told in a mixture of verse and prose in both Latin and Irish. These texts included tales of the gods of pagan Ireland, and of heroes like *Cúchulainn and *Fionn Mac Cumhaill (Finn McCool). Poems from this period associated with the *Fenian tradition were later collected in a number of separate volumes, including *Duanaire Finn* (Lays of Finn) (1626–27) and *Leabhar na Feínne* (Book of the Fianna) (1872). Monks also composed short lyrics, which were notable for their delicacy and precision, their metrical intricacy and vivid imagery.

*Bardic schools flourished from the late sixth to the seventeenth century. The period between the *Anglo-Norman invasion in 1169 and 1600 is usually referred to as the bardic or classical period of Irish poetry, because the form changed very little during that time. Bardic poetry, emanating from schools established by learned families, chronicled the conservative society of the time. It was a highly formalized poetry, written for courtly patrons, and included courtly love poetry, which was brought to Ireland by the Normans, and poems on the lore of places called *dinnseanchas*.

After the collapse of the Gaelic aristocracy under English Tudor and Jacobean colonialism, the Irish language and Gaelic culture were suppressed. The work of poets such as Dáibhí *Ó Bruadair (1625–98) and Aodhagán *Ó Rathaille (1675–1729) reflect the anguish of dispossession. Ó Rathaille's "Gile na Gile" ("Brightness of Brightness") is a prototype of the **aisling*, a political dream-vision in which a beautiful young woman personifying Ireland appears to the poet and complains of her captivity by an idiot. The blind poet/musician Anthony *Raftery (1779–1835) was a poet of the people who composed poems and songs reflecting his subversive political views, his support for rural agitation, and his hatred of *Protestantism. The two most renowned Irish-language poems of the eighteenth century are Brian *Merriman's bawdy satire *Cuirt an Mheán-Oíche* (*The Midnight Court*; c.1780), which attacked the men of Ireland who refused to give up their freedom and accept the responsibilities of marriage, and Eibhlín Dhubh *Ní Chonaill's *Caoineadh Airt Uí Laoghaire* (*Lament for Art O'Leary*), on the death of her husband, a victim of the *Penal Laws.

During the nineteenth century, and especially after the *Famine, the Irish language further declined, but the English-language literature from the late eighteenth century reflected a growing sense of Irish national identity. Charlotte Brooke's anthology in English translation, *Reliques of Irish Poetry* (1789), and Edward Bunting's *A General Collection of Ancient Irish Music* (1796) contributed to the rising *nationalism. Between 1808 and 1834, the poet Thomas *Moore (1779–1852) published ten volumes of his *Irish Melodies*, which contain highly popular, sentimental lyrics such as "The Harp that Once" and "O Breathe Not His Name" (on Robert *Emmet's speech from the dock) that were set to traditional Irish airs. Two other notable nineteenth-century writers who celebrated a glorious and distinctively Irish heroic past were James Clarence *Mangan (1803–49), renowned for his versions of "Róisín Dubh" ("My Dark Rosaleen") and "O'Hussey's Ode to the Maguire," and Sir Samuel *Ferguson (1810–86), best known for poems such as "The Tain-Quest" and "The Burial of King Cormac."

In the latter part of the nineteenth century, Irish writers continued to recapture the Gaelic past and to write a distinctively Irish literature in the English language. This interest in reviving the native tradition of Ireland was underpinned by an idea of Celticism emanating from English romanticism: the wild and imaginative Celtic temperament as opposed to Anglo-Saxon practical common sense. Matthew Arnold's *On the Study of Celtic Literature* (1867) was a formative influence on the *Irish Literary Revival (1890–1922), even though Arnold intended his contrast between *Celt and Anglo-Saxon as justification for colonialism. Other precursors of the revival were William *Allingham (1824–89), who wrote poems about local places and local lore, and Douglas *Hyde (1860–1949), who published *Love Songs of Connaught* (1893), a collection of English translations of Irish folk songs.

The major figure of the Irish Renaissance of the last decade of the nineteenth century and the first decades of the twentieth century was W. B. *Yeats (1865–1939), whose early career was greatly influenced by the work of Mangan, Ferguson, and Allingham. Yeats's early poetry draws on Irish myth and *folklore and on Irish ballad forms. His collection of writings on the supernatural, *The Celtic Twilight* (1893), gave its name to a type of romantic, melancholy poetry popular among Yeats's imitators. As he became more involved in public affairs—president of the Irish National Dramatic Society (1902), director of the *Abbey Theatre (1904)—Yeats developed a more modern, less decorative style. Well-known poems from this middle period are "The Second Coming," "Sailing to Byzantium," and "Leda and the Swan." The poetry of the last phase of Yeats's career focuses defiantly on the ravages of old age, history, and his own life and poetic career, which he assesses in "The Circus Animals' Desertion."

Other poets associated with Yeats and the revival include George *Russell, also known as AE (1867–1935), Oliver St. John *Gogarty (1878–1957), Padraic *Colum (1881–1972), and James *Stephens (1882–1950). Against this group, another group of poets stressed modernity and internationalism rather than Irishness: Samuel *Beckett (1906–89), Thomas MacGreevy (1893–1967), Brian Coffey (1905–95), and Denis *Devlin (1908–59).

Reacting against Yeats's revivalism and nationalism, Patrick *Kavanagh (1904–67) affirmed the value of the parochial and the way the local place can stand for the world. The rural vision of John *Montague (1929–) and Seamus *Heaney (1939–) is deeply indebted to Kavanagh's sense of place. The *Ulster Protestant planter myth of John *Hewitt (1907–87) also emphasizes the value of rootedness in affirming identity. By contrast, Louis *MacNeice (1907–63) is "an example of uprootability," a "tourist in his own country," a celebrant of plurality and hybridity. MacNeice's poetics of displacement has had a marked influence on succeeding northern poets such as Michael *Longley (1939–), Derek *Mahon (1941–), Paul *Muldoon (1951–), Ciaran *Carson (1948–), and on southern poets such as Brendan *Kennelly (1936–) and Paul *Durcan (1944–), who have all been involved in a radical rewriting of the sense of home and identity. Irish poetry since the 1970s has also seen the emergence of significant women's voices: from the south, Eiléan *Ní Chuilleanáin (1942–) who specializes in a disturbing realism, Eavan *Boland (1944–) who has explored the position of women in Irish national tradition, and Nuala *Ní Dhomhnaill (1952–) who combines Gaelic, feminist, and modernist perspectives; and, from the north, Medbh *McGuckian (1950–) who has been hailed as an exponent of "the woman's sentence." E.K-A.

police. Ireland's first uniformed, professional police force was set up in *Dublin in 1786. One of its successors, the Dublin Metropolitan Police (established in 1836) was absorbed into the *Gárda Síochána (the police force of the *Irish Free State formed in 1922) in 1925. Throughout the nineteenth century, a number of police forces were created in Ireland by successive British governments. Robert Peel, chief secretary for Ireland (1812–18), established a paramilitary, cavalry constabulary, the Peace Preservation Force, which served in several Irish counties from 1814 to 1836. These were the first policemen to be nicknamed "Peelers," a term used to this day in parts of Ireland. In 1836, the Peace Preservation Force was absorbed into the Irish Constabulary.

This force, formed in 1822 and renamed the *Royal Irish Constabulary (RIC) in 1867, played an active role in monitoring and suppressing *nationalist movements and agrarian agitation. Recruited largely from the Irish small-farming class, this armed force was often unpopular in its hundred-year history. After bearing the brunt of the IRA's (*Irish Republican Army) campaign during the *War of Independence, the RIC was disbanded in 1922 and replaced by the *Royal Ulster Constabulary (RUC) in

*Northern Ireland and the Gárda Síochána in the Irish Free State. The armed, largely Protestant RUC was perceived as a sectarian and *unionist force by Northern Ireland *Catholics and suffered heavy casualties at the hands of *republican paramilitaries during the *Troubles. The RUC has recently been reformed as the Police Service of Northern Ireland. In contrast to the RUC's troubled history, the unarmed Gárda Síochána quickly integrated into society in the South. B.G.

political parties. The Irish political party system has shifted since independence between a multiparty system dominated by two large parties and what has been called a two and a half party system—*Fianna Fáil, *Fine Gael, and a very small *Labour Party. The periods 1922–27, 1943–61, and 1987 to the present might be considered multiparty.

Characterizing the major political parties in an international context has often led to a confusing use of labels. The two major parties Fianna Fáil and Fine Gael, polling between 65 percent and 80 percent collectively, are relatively conservative compared to the European Social Democratic tradition but both, especially Fianna Fáil, have a populist cross-class appeal.

Since the 1990s, the party system has become more fragmented. Fianna Fáil as the largest party has captured the center, with an average support base of around 40 percent, and has formed governments of the center-left (with Labour) and center-right (with the *Progressive Democrats).

As the traditional *Civil War divisions between Fianna Fáil and Fine Gael have diminished, Fine Gael has struggled to find an identity other than being anti–Fianna Fáil and has not won a general election since 1982.

The Labour Party has traditionally played the role of third party. Its average level of support at around 11 percent is very low by West European social democrat standards. The party is often divided between those who prioritize serving in government (almost inevitably with FG) and those who advocate a Labour left-leaning government.

*Sinn Féin is the only party to organize on an all-Ireland basis. The party offers a mix of militant nationalism and left of center radicalism. Since the 1994 IRA (*Irish Republican Army) cease-fire, it has rapidly grown to become the largest nationalist party in *Northern Ireland and the fourth largest party in the *Republic.

The Progressive Democrats, a typically European right of center liberal party, is the most conservative Irish party on economic matters but relatively liberal on social issues.

The Green Party, a typical European ecology-based party, is small but has developed a strong parliamentary presence both in the *Dáil (Irish Parliament) and the European Parliament.

The *Socialist Party has had a single deputy in the Dáil since 1997. It is well to the left of the Labour Party and, though small, has a strong campaigning presence in parts of *Dublin. J.D.

Poor Laws. Nineteenth-century poverty relief legislation. The Poor Law Act (1838) divided Ireland into 130 poor law districts (or unions), each with a *workhouse where those who required aid had to live. Entry was at the discretion of the local poor law guardians and financing came mostly from a tax levied on local landowners. During the *Famine, the Poor Law Extension Act allowed the granting of discretionary relief outside of the workhouse. The legislation was formally abolished by the *Irish Free State in the 1920s and in *Northern Ireland in 1946. P.E.

Power, Albert G. (1881–1945). Sculptor. Born in *Dublin, Power was a pupil of Oliver *Sheppard and John Hughes at the Metropolitan School, Dublin. Power produced many privately commissioned portrait busts. In 1922, he was commissioned by the government to make posthumous portrait busts of Arthur *Griffith and Michael *Collins. His work is in many public buildings and churches in Ireland, including the Cathedral of Christ the King, Mullingar, and Cavan Cathedral. His modeled head of the dying Terence *MacSwiney in the Cork Public Museum and the 1798 Pikeman Memorial at Tralee, County *Kerry, are among his best-known works. A regular contributor to the *Royal Hibernian Academy from 1906, Power was regarded as the major Irish sculptor by 1940. M.C.

Poynings' Law (1492). A law requiring royal approval before the Irish *Parliament could be summoned. Introduced by Henry VII's Lord Deputy Edward Poynings, Poynings' Law also mandated that all legislation initiated by the Dublin Parliament required the prior assent of the monarch and privy council in London. Although the original intent of the law was to curb the power of independent subjects such as the Earls of Kildare, eventually Poynings' Law subordinated the Irish Parliament to its English counterpart. The statutory subservience of the Irish Parliament became increasingly unacceptable to "patriots" during the course of the eighteenth century. Poynings' Law was substantially modified in Ireland's favor by the Reform Act of 1782 and made irrelevant by the Act of *Union (1800). J.P.

Praeger, Robert Lloyd (1865–1953). Naturalist. Born in Holywood, County *Down, and educated in *Belfast, Praeger was appointed librarian of the *Royal Irish Academy in 1903. During 1909–11, he conducted an intensive and innovative survey of Clare Island, County *Mayo, and later helped to found the journal the *Irish Naturalist*. Praeger was librarian of the *National Library of Ireland (1920–24) and his works include *The Way That I Went* (1937) and *The Natural History of Ireland* (1950). S.A.B.

pre-Christian Ireland (c.7000 B.C.–c. A.D. 432). Lack of contemporaneous sources leaves us with little knowledge of the sociopolitical system of ancient Ireland. By analyzing the legendary history as found in later sources, a tentative reconstruction can be made. The *Celtic and Celticized groups had dominance in all areas of Ireland by the second century B.C. Their assimilation with earlier communities had given rise to the tribes known as Iverni ("land-people"). A strong new group from Britain, called Lagini ("spear-men"), however, extended their power in Ireland from eastern coastal areas. In succeeding generations of further migrations from Britain, culminating in refugees from the Roman legions in the first century A.D., the Lagini strengthened their position. Another powerful group, the Venii ("tribesmen"), probably originating in southwestern Britain and northwestern Gaul, came to ascendance in the south of Ireland. The Venii, moving northward from the southern coast, pushed the Ivernian tribes to the west.

In or about the fourth century A.D., the Lagini seized the ancient ritual center of *Tara (in County *Meath) from the Ivernian tribe of Lugunii, but within a century the Lagini were driven south from Tara by the Venii. Having taken control of the rich and strategic plain of *Meath, the Venii moved northward against the strongest of the Ivernian tribes, the Uluti ("bearded men"), whose ritual center was

Isomnis (later Emhain Macha in County *Armagh). At the dawn of the fifth century A.D., therefore, the most powerful groups in the country were the Uluti (by then known as Ulaidh), the Lagini (then Laighin), and two groups of the Venii (those known as *Connachta in the north midlands and those known as Eoghanacht in *Munster). Other groups of Iverni (then Érainn) still controlled some territories, especially toward the western seaboard.

The Connachta were by now the strongest group in Ireland, and to gain both wealth and prestige they undertook raids on western Britain, seizing booty and captives. Their celebrated king in the fifth century, Niall Naoighiallach (Niall of the Nine Hostages), was in fact the son of a famous Connachta raider-king and of a British slave-woman. The reign of Niall saw the two most significant events in pre-Christian Ireland: the capture of the boy *Patrick (the future *saint and patron of Ireland) in a huge raid on the British coast, and the taking of Emhain Macha from the Ulaidh by the Connachta.

The culture which prevailed in Ireland up to the coming of Christianity was basically *Celtic in its outlines and—just as its language reflected a quite old variant of Celtic—the customs of Ireland seem to have been more antiquated than those of neighboring countries. Whereas the Celts abroad had developed systems that gave increased influence to the nobility in the affairs of the kings, in Ireland the kings were still holy rulers. A king was considered the intermediary between his people and otherworld powers; his inauguration reflected this with elaborate rituals, and his life was circumvented by taboos. These ideas permeated all social life. There were probably well in excess of a hundred local kings in Ireland, each ruling over his own territory but linked in confederations with the over-kings who ruled the major clans and their satellites. The *druids, who played a major role in public ceremonies, were an important adjunct to royal power. D.Oh.

prehistoric Ireland. *The Stone Age* was the period of man's first known appearance in Ireland as a hunter-gatherer, c. 8000 B.C. Around the fourth millennium B.C., farming communities emerged who lived in wooden houses and built megalithic tombs of stone. Stone was also the predominant material used for tools and weapons. The period was succeeded by the Bronze Age before 2000 B.C.

The Bronze Age was a period from the late third millennium to c.500 B.C., when bronze was the predominant material used for tools and weapons. At this time, however, a considerable amount of gold was used for neck ornaments such as lunulae and gorgets. Preceded by a short-lived Copper Age, the Bronze Age witnessed widespread trade along Europe's Atlantic coasts, massive production of axes and swords and, toward its end (c. 700 B.C.), bronze vessels and trumpets bespeaking riches. Burials were largely in single graves, often under low barrows and, to about 1200 B.C., often accompanied by decorative food vessels and urns (for cremated bone). Metal extraction and agriculture were widely practiced, but deteriorating weather conditions saw the development of *bogs (which were to cover one-sixth of Ireland) and the rise of *hill-forts. Cooking places known as *fulachta fiadha* also came into use at the time.

The Iron Age followed the Bronze Age around 500 B.C., and is named after the material favored at the time for implements and weapons. It saw the introduction of the *La Tène art style of the continental *Celts and the widespread use of the earliest known form of the Irish language. The scattered population may have lived in *raths and *crannógs, occasionally resorting to *hill-forts. Contacts were maintained with the late Roman Empire, and one piratical raid on Roman Britain brought a young St. *Patrick to Ireland as a slave. The Iron Age way of life continued into the medieval period. P.H.

Prendergast, Kathy (1958–). Artist. Using a wide range of media and the techniques of mapmaking, Prendergast often employs the theme of her own body's geography. Born in *Dublin, she studied at the National College of Art, Dublin, and Royal College of Art, London. In 1995, Prendergast represented Ireland at the Venice Biennale and was awarded the prize for outstanding young artist. M.C.

Presbyterians. Members of the *Protestant Church of *Scotland who flooded into the north of Ireland throughout the seventeenth century. Although the *Plantation of Ulster (1609–25) is usually perceived as the key period of Presbyterian settlement in Ireland, Scottish immigration peaked in the last third of the century with as many as ten thousand arriving each year in the 1690s. Despite the prominent role Presbyterians played in preserving Protestant Ireland during the Williamite War of 1688–91, they were reduced to second-class status by the *Penal Laws of 1704. By the latter part of the eighteenth century, the rapidly expanding commercial center of *Belfast had become the de facto economic and cultural capital of Irish Presbyterianism. Presbyterian radicalism and animosity toward the *Anglo-Irish ascendancy led to the founding of the Society of *United Irishmen in Belfast in 1791. The movement was brutally crushed in the *Rebellion of 1798. Yet many Presbyterians remained liberal until the Liberal Party under *Gladstone came to support *home rule in the 1880s. From this point onward, the vast majority of Presbyterians have been ardent *loyalists. Although Presbyterian numbers in the Irish *Republic are tiny, in *Northern Ireland they constitute the largest denomination in the Protestant community. J.P.

presidents of Ireland (Uachtaráin na hÉireann). Although Éamon *de Valera was formally elected "Príomh-Aire" (chief minister) of the *Sinn Féin cabinet in the first *Dáil Éireann (Irish Parliament) in 1919, it was decided for public relations reasons in connection with his trip to America in that year to refer to him generally as "President of the Irish Republic," while seeking international recognition. It was claimed that he occupied a somewhat similar position to the president of the United States as the father of the nation. Great play was also made of de Valera's status as "President of the Irish Republic" at the time of the *Civil War (1922–23), by the defeated *republican forces. But the term *president of Ireland*, or *Uachtarán na hÉireann*, in the modern period refers to the office established by Article Twelve of the *Constitution of 1937.

The president is elected by direct vote of the people for a seven-year term. At the end of a first term, the president may nominate him- or herself for a second seven-year term, but he or she is eligible for reelection once only. Candidates must be at least thirty-five years of age and Irish citizens. If only one candidate is nominated he or she can be declared elected without proceeding to a ballot in an election. The president cannot hold any other office or position and shall not be a member of either House of the *Oireachtas.

The president may not leave the state while in office, save with the consent of the government. A president may be impeached for stated misbehavior by either House of the Oireachtas and, if the charge is sustained, may be removed by a two-thirds vote of both Houses. The president, on the nomination of Dáil Éireann, appoints the *Taoiseach (prime minister) and, on the nomination of the Taoiseach (with previous Dáil approval), appoints the members of the government.

Most of the president's powers and functions are symbolic but the president may "in his absolute discretion refuse to dissolve Dáil Éireann on the advice of a Taoiseach, who has ceased to retain the support of a majority of Dáil Éireann" (Article 13.2.2). The president is empowered (in Article 26.1.1), after consultation with the Council of State, to refer a bill that has been passed by the Oireachtas to the Supreme Court for a decision on the question as to whether such bill or any part of it is unconstitutional. The supreme command of the Defense Forces is vested in the president and all commissioned officers of the Defense Forces hold their commissions from the president (Article 13).

The first president under the new Constitution of 1937 was Douglas *Hyde (Dubhghlas de hÍde) (1860–1949), who held office for the first seven-year term from 1938 to 1945 without any election being held. Hyde was succeeded in 1945 by Seán T. Ó Ceallaigh (1882–1966). Ó Ceallaigh continued for a second seven-year term as president without an election. In 1959, he was succeeded by his old mentor, Éamon de Valera (1882–1975), then aged seventy-seven and almost totally blind. De Valera was re-elected for a second term in 1966. In 1973, he was succeeded by Erskine H. *Childers (1905–74), the second *Protestant to hold the office. When President Childers died of a heart attack in November 1974—the first and only president to die in office—he was succeeded by Cearbhall Ó Dálaigh (1911–78), a former chief justice who was, at the time, a judge of the European Court. Ó Dálaigh came into conflict with the then *Fine Gael/*Labour government specifically because of his decision to refer Emergency Legislation to the Supreme Court in the autumn of 1976. He resigned in protest to protect the dignity and independence of the office in an unprecedented constitutional crisis.

Ó Dálaigh was succeeded by Patrick J. Hillery (1923–), a County *Clare career politician with Fianna Fáil who, as foreign minister, had negotiated Ireland's entry into the EEC (European Economic Community; now the *European Union) in 1972, and then became Ireland's first EEC Commissioner (for Social Affairs) in 1973. Hillery continued for a second term in 1983, by common consent. The election of Professor Mary *Robinson (1944–) in November 1990 marked a significant development in Irish presidential politics, not only because she was the first woman to hold the office but also because she was effectively the first non–Fianna Fáil nominee for the presidency to win it. Ms. Robinson resigned the presidency a few weeks before her seven-year term expired in 1997, to take up a position as UN Human Rights Commissioner in Geneva. She was succeeded by another legal academic, Professor Mary *McAleese, of Queen's University in *Belfast. Ms. McAleese won the election by the largest majority of any presidential winner to date. N.ÓG.

Proclamation of the Irish Republic. Formal declaration of an independent Irish *Republic at the beginning of the 1916 *Easter Rising. Drafted and read aloud outside the General Post Office by Patrick *Pearse on Easter Monday 1916, the proclamation announced the establishment of a provisional government and called the people of Ireland to arms. It explained the role of the *Irish Republican Brotherhood, the *Irish Citizen Army, and the Irish *Volunteers in the rebellion. British rule in Ireland was rejected as illegitimate, and the Irish Republic was proclaimed as a "Sovereign Independent State." Expressing advanced egalitarian ideas, the document guaranteed "religious and civil liberty, equal rights and equal opportunities" to all citizens and a future national assembly, "elected by the suffrages of all her men and women." The completed document was signed by all seven members of the Military Council of the IRB—Patrick Pearse, Thomas *Clarke, James *Connolly, Seán *MacDiarmada, Éamonn *Ceannt, Thomas *MacDonagh, and Joseph *Plunkett—and a thousand copies were printed in Liberty Hall on Easter Sunday. P.E.

Progressive Democrats (PD). Political party. The Progressive Democrats was founded in 1985 by Des O'Malley after his expulsion from *Fianna Fáil. O'Malley focused his initial policy program on three key issues, neo-liberal economics, liberal social policy, and a less rigid stance on *Northern Ireland than Fianna Fáil. The party polled 11 percent in its first general election (1987) but has since struggled around 5 percent. The Progressive Democrats formed a coalition government with Fianna Fáil in 1989, in 1997, and in 2002. Mary Harney became leader in 1993. J.D.

Progressive Unionist Party of Northern Ireland (PUP). Political party. Formed in 1979, the PUP became prominent during the 1990s representing militant *loyalists, most notably the *Ulster Volunteer Force (UVF) during the *peace process. The party attracted roughly 3 percent of the popular vote at the height of its popularity. M.M.

Proportional Representation (PR). Voting system. The *Republic of Ireland uses PR by means of the Single Transferable Vote (STV) with multimember constituencies (districts) for all elections except the president. PR is used in *Northern Ireland for local council elections, European Parliament elections, and for the Northern Ireland Assembly, but not for elections to the British House of Commons. The system allows voters to vote for every candidate contesting a specific election by marking their preferences as 1, 2, 3, etc., on their ballots. To win outright, a candidate needs a certain percentage (a quota) of first-preference votes (25 percent plus 1 in 3-seat constituencies, 20 percent plus 1 in a 4-seat, etc.). If no candidate reaches the quota after the votes are counted, then the candidate with fewest first-preference votes is eliminated and his or her first-preference votes are distributed proportionately to the other candidates who were given second preference on the eliminated candidate's ballots. This system continues until one candidate reaches the required quota of votes and is elected. If a candidate gets more votes than the quota, once they are deemed elected their "surplus" votes are also distributed to try and ensure that no vote is "wasted." Despite the fact that district sizes are relatively small (between three and five seats), PR in the Irish context produces a reasonably representative parliament. The larger parties on average get about 3 percent more seats than they would under a purely proportional vote system, *Labour gets about 1 percent fewer seats, and the smaller parties are much more underrepresented. J.D.

Protestant Reformation. See **Reformation in Ireland.**

Protestants. *Henry VIII's *Reformation did not initially affect Catholic worship in Ireland. By contrast with England, where there was already a large group of followers of the continental reformers Luther and Zwingli, in Ireland very few of the indigenous population were Protestants by the time Edward VI succeeded his father *Henry VIII as king of England. During Edward's short reign (1547–53), Protestantism was officially introduced in Ireland, but made little progress. Not until the *Elizabethan religious settlement of 1560 (Acts of Supremacy and Uniformity) was a stable Protestant regime established. From then on, the *Church of Ireland was Protestant, in line with the moderate reform of the English church, and the entire population was bound by law to adopt the new religion. The campaign of evangelization was lackluster, however, and the native Protestant coterie remained small. The majority of the Protestant community in late-sixteenth-century Ireland comprised newcomers from England who were officials, soldiers, and planters. Little effort was made to communicate the Protestant doctrines through the language and culture of the majority of the Irish population.

With the foundation of Trinity College in 1592 a more systematic Protestant campaign began in Ireland, but by then the majority of the island's population was committed to the *Catholicism of the counter-Reformation. In response to their minority position, Protestants in Ireland developed their own distinctive mentality. Not only were the articles of the Church of Ireland more puritan or radical than the English counterpart, but such prominent figures as James Ussher, the Church of Ireland archbishop of *Armagh, propounded that the Protestant religion was the true successor to the pristine *Christianity of the era of St. *Patrick in Ireland. The arrival of substantial numbers of Scottish Presbyterians as settlers in the *Ulster Plantation of the early seventeenth century consolidated Protestantism in Ireland.

The turmoil of the 1640s steeled the resolve of Irish Protestants to withstand challenges to their political and social position and forged greater self-identity among the *Presbyterians. After the *Cromwellian Settlement of the 1650s, a consolidated Protestant community emerged. The older and newer Protestants merged to become the politically and economically privileged class, while Catholics and dissenting Protestants, mainly Presbyterians, were excluded from power and position. After the victory of the Protestant *William of Orange over the forces of the Catholic King *James II, the *Penal Laws further consolidated and protected Protestantism.

Protestants showed little inclination to convert Catholics and dissenters. In the eighteenth century, Irish Protestants such as Jonathan *Swift, Oliver *Goldsmith, William and Thomas *Molyneux, George *Berkeley, and Edmund *Burke made significant contributions to *literature, philosophy, *science, and political thought. Among the Protestant political ascendancy, a strong movement for Irish legislative independence reached its climax in *Grattan's Parliament of 1782.

The Presbyterian community experienced various difficulties caused by internal factionalism, but the gradual relaxing of the religious and social restrictions benefited them as well as Catholics. Methodism, which came to Ireland in the mid-eighteenth century, achieved impressive growth as an Anglican reform movement, but the following century formed its separate Protestant Church.

The earlier nineteenth century was marked by a revitalization of the Protestant churches and an attempt to convert Catholics in a movement known as "the second Reformation." The proselytism proved a relative failure, but heightened sectarian tensions at a time when the Catholic Church itself was undergoing what has been called a "devotional revolution." The payment of *tithes by Catholics and

Presbyterians to the Church of Ireland caused huge resentment culminating in a tithe war, which effectively ended the tithes system in the 1830s. By the mid-nineteenth century, the Protestant population had declined and the political turmoil in Ireland convinced Prime Minister William *Gladstone to introduce a bill for the disestablishment and disendowment of the Church of Ireland in 1869. Nevertheless, a more coherent Protestantism emerged into the twentieth century. The term *Protestants* now referred to those of the reformed faiths, and not just to Anglicans. Presbyterians and Anglicans were brought closer by their shared experience of evangelical education and preaching in the nineteenth century. Politically, this heightened sense of Protestant identity was influential in the growth of *unionism. After *partition, Protestants found themselves in very different milieux, north and south. While the political force of Protestantism has been extremely significant in the north, its influence in the south has been less so. The growth of the ecumenical movement in the later twentieth century has been very important for relations within the family of Protestant faiths, and between them and the Catholic Church. C.L.

Q

Quakers. *Protestant sect. Quakers first arrived in Ireland during the 1650s as members of *Cromwell's armies. They had emerged in England as a radical Protestant sect during the civil war. Formerly known as the Society of Friends, the sect was reorganized by George Fox in 1669. The Quakers' pacifism and belief in social equality made them prominent in several nineteenth-century reform movements and their Central Relief Committee (1846–49) played a vital role in providing humanitarian aid during the Great *Famine. S.A.B.

R

radio. The *Irish Civil War delayed the establishment of an indigenous radio service until January 1, 1926. The Dublin Broadcasting Station (known as "2RN") was established as a state-run public service, financed by license fees and advertising revenues, and housed within the Department of Posts and Telegraphs.

Despite a chronic shortage of funds, inadequate facilities, and transmission hours, 2RN's first director, Séamus Clandillon, and his small staff sought to preserve and promote Ireland's cultural heritage. Their regular programming included traditional *music performances, *Irish-language lessons, children's shows, domestic and farming instruction, as well as weather, news, and other service bulletins. In August of its first year, the service broadcast live coverage of the All-Ireland *hurling final between *Galway and *Kilkenny. Later live broadcasts of sports events, especially sports commentaries by the legendary Micheál Ó Hehir, greatly increased interest in the new medium. Religious broadcasts, such as the weeklong coverage of the *Eucharistic Congress of 1932 held in *Dublin, which allowed the pope's voice to be heard in Ireland for the first time, showed radio's potential for mass communication. Efforts to make radio more widely available (i.e., to improve reception) in rural Ireland included the operation of a second station in *Cork from 1927 to 1930 and the establishment of a high-power transmitter at Athlone, County *Westmeath, in February 1933.

On the eve of World War II, approximately one in four families in the *Irish Free State held radio licenses, and for many tuning in to their favorite programs on Radio Éireann (as the service was called from 1937 until its merger with television in 1966) was compulsive listening. The most beloved of these was the quiz show *Question Time*, hosted by popular emcees such as Joe Linnane. Its successor, *Take the Floor*, a program on Irish *dance music with the Gárda *Céilí Band that lasted nearly twenty-five years, owed its popularity to the storytelling abilities of host Din Joe (Denis Fitzgibbon).

After World War II, *Taoiseach (prime minister) Éamon *de Valera, the politician who most capitalized on radio's political power, revived a plan for a shortwave service to bolster national defense and communicate with Irish *emigrants abroad. The change of government in 1948 ended construction on the new high-power station at Athlone, but Radio Éireann's resources had already been doubled. Among the most significant improvements in the service were the addition of a full-time repertory company, the Radio Éireann Players, directed by Roibeárd Ó Faracháin, and the development of new programs aimed at reconnecting the *Republic to the outside world and stimulating intellectual debate, such as *World Affairs* and the *Thomas Davis Lectures*.

High-quality radio reception became available throughout the country in the 1960s, and in the 1970s Irish radio, now part of Radio Telefís Éireann (*RTÉ), addressed social issues, including women's rights. RTÉ also set up Raidió na Gaeltachta, an Irish-language station, in 1972. The network's political scope and coverage of events in *Northern Ireland was, however, circumscribed by Section 31, a government ban against reporting on proscribed organizations such as the *Irish Republican Army (IRA). On the music front, pirate radio stations such as Radio Caroline became increasingly popular among listeners, especially youth, tired of traditional radio. In the late 1970s, RTÉ responded by launching a pop music station, Radio 2, and undertaking community radio broadcasts from mobile studios, but this did not diminish interest in the pirate stations. In the late 1980s, commercial radio was legalized in the Republic and RTÉ radio now competes directly with numerous commercial and local community stations throughout the country. E.M.

Raftery, Anthony (1779–1835). Poet. Born in County *Mayo, Raftery became blind at an early age and spent most of his life in the East *Galway area. He was often described as a folk-poet, but this does not do justice to the sophistication of his best work. He wrote vicious political poetry, which gave vent to the feelings of the oppressed pre-*Famine poor. He also wrote tender love poetry and penned celebrations or laments on local events. In "Eanach Dhúin," he recounts the drowning of nearly twenty people in Lough Corrib in 1828 when a sheep put a hole in the rotten bottom of a boat. His celebrated "Máire Ní Eidhin" is a more conventional love song praising a local beauty. Many of these songs are still sung today. He had immense influence on the later *Literary Revival, particularly on Douglas *Hyde and Lady *Gregory. A.T.

Raleigh, Sir Walter. (1552–1618). English adventurer and explorer. After organizing several unsuccessful expeditions to colonize North America (1584–87), Raleigh was granted a huge estate in *Munster composed of land confiscated by the English crown following the second Desmond rebellion (1579–83). On this land, he undertook to plant English settlers, but he sold the estate in 1602. The next year, Raleigh was imprisoned on suspicion of conspiring against King James I, and, following an unsuccessful expedition to South America in 1616, he was executed. Raleigh is widely credited with introducing the potato and tobacco to Europe. S.A.B.

rath. A circular area surrounded by one, two, or three circular embankments with a ditch outside—sometimes called a *lios*. Inside stood one or two houses, the home of a well-off farmer of early medieval Ireland. Built largely between A.D. 500

and 1000, raths once numbered between thirty and fifty thousand. While according to *folklore, the fairies—whose forts they were thought to have been—protected them for generations, modern agricultural development is destroying them at an ever-increasing rate. They are often called ring-forts, which is somewhat of a misnomer, as they would rarely if ever have been strong enough to defend. P.H.

Rathcroghan. Ancient royal site on the plains of County *Roscommon. Many prehistoric and early medieval earthen monuments (mounds and *raths) were found here. According to legend, Rathcroghan was the seat of King Ailill and Queen Maeve of *Connacht, whose pillow talk led to the old Irish epic, **Táin Bó Cuailnge* (The Cattle Raid of Cooley). The limestone cave, Oweynagat (Cat's Cave), with two *Ogham stones, was thought to have been an entrance to the underworld. P.H.

Rea, Stephen (1948–). Actor. Born into a *Protestant family in *Belfast, Rea has worked extensively on the stage in Dublin, London, and New York. In 1993, he won a Tony Award for his role in *Someone Who'll Watch Over Me* by Frank *McGuinness on Broadway. In 1980, together with playwright Brian *Friel, he founded the *Field Day Theatre Company in Ireland. Rea, who has a distinct understated acting style, has starred in many of director Neil *Jordan's movies, including *Angel* (1982), *The Crying Game* (1992)—for which he earned an Oscar nomination—*Michael Collins* (1996), *The Butcher Boy* (1997), and *The End of the Affair* (1999). In 1983, he married Dolours Price, who was convicted for her part in the 1973 bombing of the Old Bailey Court building in London. She was released after serving eight years in prison. M.E.

Rebellion of 1641. Gaelic Irish and Old English revolt (also known as the Confederate War) during the reign of King Charles I. In 1641, the native Irish in *Ulster used the conflict between Charles I and the English Parliament to retake land that had been confiscated from them during the *Ulster Plantation. Under the leadership of the Irish chieftain Rory O'More, a rebellion was planned for October 23, 1641. Plans to take *Dublin Castle were betrayed, but the rebels led by Sir Phelim O'Neill succeeded in taking control of Ulster. The native Irish rebels next marched south toward Dublin. They laid siege to Drogheda in November 1641 and joined in an alliance with the Old English lords of the *Pale to form a Confederate *Catholic army. An oath was taken to defend the Catholic faith and the rights of the crown, and by the autumn of 1642, the rebels controlled all the country, except for Dublin, a handful of towns, and the Scottish areas of Ulster.

An assembly known as the *Confederation of Kilkenny was organized in 1642 to govern rebel-held territory. The alliance between the Gaelic Irish and Old English was, however, marked by considerable confusion and squabbling. The Old English lords had been reluctant allies from the outset and had joined the rebellion only out of fears that a parliamentarian victory in England would usher in a new phase of plantation in Ireland. They were anxious for an early settlement to the conflict that ensured toleration for their religion and the promise that their lands would not be confiscated. The native Irish had already lost their territory and were prepared to fight to the end for the return of their land and the restoration of *Catholicism to its pre-*Reformation status. These differences in objectives widened as the war progressed. In June 1646, the Confederates under Owen Roe *O'Neill won a major battle at

Benburb, but the rebels failed to take advantage of the victory. The Catholic Confederation was formally dissolved under the terms of the Second Ormond Peace in 1649. Following the execution of King Charles I in January 1649, Oliver *Cromwell led a force to Ireland to deal with what he believed was a Catholic religious uprising, and within three years all Irish resistance had been crushed. P.E.

Rebellion of 1798. Major uprising considered one of the most violent events in Irish history. By the second half of the eighteenth century, middle-class resentment among *Leinster Catholics and *Ulster *Presbyterians had reached a critical point because of their ongoing exclusion from political participation on religious grounds. This exclusion was particularly offensive in light of the middle class's increasing numbers and wealth. Influenced by the ideals of the Enlightenment and the *American Revolution, the Irish middle class found the political discrimination increasingly intolerable.

Inspired by the events of the *French Revolution, modern Irish *Republicanism was born in *Belfast and *Dublin in 1791 with the foundation of the Society of *United Irishmen. The organization sought the radical reform of Parliament and complete *Catholic Emancipation. Within a few years, the United Irishmen had grown to several hundred thousand members. In 1795, one of the movement's founding fathers, Wolfe *Tone, traveled to Paris to persuade the French that Ireland was ready to support an invasion. Early in 1798, the movement's leadership decided to risk an indigenous rising without French assistance. The preparations were, perhaps fatally, disrupted by the arrest of most of the Leinster leadership at Oliver Bond's house in Dublin on March 12, 1798. Nonetheless, plans for a major insurrection proceeded.

The republicans' seizure of the mail coaches from Dublin to the provinces signaled the onset of the rebellion on May 23, 1798. The linchpin of the rebel plan was a coup de main directed at the capital, supported by risings in the surrounding counties. An unfortuitous leak of information quashed the planned attack on the capital, effectively dooming the insurrection. In the province of Leinster, the risings of *Carlow, *Kildare, *Meath, and *Wicklow were quickly crushed. Only in *Wexford did the rebels meet with success. They managed to take most of the county, but failed to carry the rebellion north and west. On June 21, 1798, the decisive battle of the Wexford campaign was fought at *Vinegar Hill and the republican army was routed. It is at this point (the brief, if underrated, risings in *Antrim and *Down having been put down in early June) that the Rebellion of 1798 is traditionally considered to have ended. Yet, rebel armies remained in the field until mid-July (while a belated, small-scale French landing in Mayo was overwhelmed in September) and, in fact, organized resistance continued in all four provinces until 1803. Thirty thousand died in what is considered the bloodiest Irish rebellion in history. J.P.

rebellions. See **risings and rebellions.**

Redmond, John Edward (1856–1918). Politician. Born in County *Wexford, Redmond was educated at Trinity College and entered *Parliament in 1881. He represented Waterford City in Westminster from 1891 until his death in 1918. After the split following the *O'Shea divorce case in 1891, Redmond led the *Parnellites. When the *Irish Parliamentary Party reunited in 1900, he became its chairman.

Redmond was a skillful political tactician. He

participated in the *Land Conference (1902) which precipitated the *Land Act of 1903, effectively ending *landlordism. He also negotiated legislation that established the National University (1908). His party's votes helped to lay the foundation of the British welfare state and to reform the House of Lords. In 1912 Redmond secured the introduction of the third *home rule bill, which was suspended at the onset of *World War I in 1914.

Redmond immediately pledged *nationalist support for the war effort. He believed that common sacrifice among Irishmen would convince *Ulster *unionists of nationalist loyalty to the empire. The threat that the British would introduce conscription in Ireland frustrated his attempts to increase voluntary recruitment among Irish nationalists, and his support for the war turned out to be a major political miscalculation. Militant *republicans worked throughout the war to subvert his leadership. The *Easter Rising of 1916 shattered Redmond's political world. He had tacitly accepted temporary *partition of some parts of Ulster, and his attempt in the Irish Convention (1917–18) to secure home rule made little headway when he suddenly died, his reputation with contemporaries seriously damaged. L.MB.

Referendum of 1998. The 1998 *Good Friday Agreement provided for referenda to be held in Ireland, North and South, on May 22, 1998, to ratify the agreement and to make the necessary changes to the Irish *Constitution. The response in the *Republic of Ireland to the agreement was very positive as both *nationalist parties in *Northern Ireland and all the major Southern parties called for a "yes" vote. The "yes" vote of 94.4 percent reflected the consensus in the campaign. In Northern Ireland there were in reality two separate referendum campaigns. Within the nationalist community, the campaign, like that in the South, reflected the widespread support for the agreement. In contrast, within the *unionist community there was a bitter campaign, beginning from the moment the agreement was finalized. The "no" lobby included not only those who had opposed the talks process but also a faction within the pro-agreement *Ulster Unionist Party. Those unionists who supported the deal promoted it in a very generalized way, as a hope for peace, and criticized those unionists who opposed the agreement of living in the past and of failing to offer a viable alternative. Unionist opponents of the deal were, however, the ones to set the agenda for the public debate. They argued that aspects of the agreement were so detrimental to their position that unionists should not support it even if it did in parts meet some unionist demands. The agreement was ultimately passed with 71 percent support in the North, but with a very marginal majority within the unionist community. J.D.

Reformation (Protestant) in Ireland, the. Failing to obtain a papal annulment of his marriage with Catherine of Aragon so that he could take another bride, produce a male heir, and secure the continuity of the Tudor monarchy, *Henry VIII, in 1534, broke with Rome. Both the English and Irish Parliaments endorsed the king's religious rebellion, declaring him head of the Church in both islands. Less attached to Rome than English coreligionists, Old English feudal lords, descendants of *Normans who first arrived in twelfth-century Ireland, and Gaelic chiefs easily accepted the new state religion. Like the governing class in other parts of Europe, they believed that public acceptance of the prince's religion fostered public order and tranquillity. In addition, the transfer of spiritual leadership from pope to king did not alter the day-to-day worship of the faithful. While Henry confiscated the wealth and property of monasteries, retaining much of the spoils for the royal treasury and parceling out the remainder to loyal followers among feudal lords and Gaelic chiefs, his rejection of papal supremacy did not replace traditional *Catholic rites and rituals.

The many cultural, political, religious, and social consequences of Henry's break with Rome did not become apparent until the reigns of his son, Edward VI (1547–53), and daughter, *Elizabeth I (1558–1603), when the established church in Ireland gradually became theologically, and, to a large extent, liturgically *Protestant. For the Irish majority, especially its Gaelic component, these efforts to make them truly Protestant were a more pernicious form of colonialism than previous English military and political adventures in their country. By planting Scottish *Presbyterians in *Ulster, James I (1603–25), Elizabeth's successor, diversified Irish Protestant sectarianism and intensified religious tensions. From the late fifteenth until the close of the eighteenth century, Irish rebels at various times called on Catholic powers on the continent, Spain, and, later, *France, to assist their resistance to English rule. Failed seventeenth-century Irish insurrections, aspects of the English Civil Wars between Parliament and Stuart kings and France's Louis XIV and his enemies, diminished Catholic political power, social influence, and property. Oliver *Cromwell's brutal retaliation against the Irish Catholic *Rebellion of 1641 dispossessed many Catholics of their possessions. Anti-Catholic *Penal Laws that followed King *William III's 1688 victory over King *James II stripped Catholics of remaining civil, political, and religious liberties and most of their remaining lands.

The Protestant Reformation fragmented Ireland into exclusive cultural communities, erecting impenetrable barriers against assimilation. Reacting to British imposed limitations on Irish sovereignty and trade, eighteenth-century Irish Protestants developed a local patriotism, expanded the authority of their Parliament, and eliminated economic restrictions. Some *Anglo-Irish Protestants and Ulster Presbyterians created the Society of *United Irishmen. Influenced by the *French Revolution, it tried but failed in 1798 to create an Irish republic. But following the Act of *Union (1800), the vast majority of Protestants and Presbyterians abandoned an Irish for a British identity, vigorously opposing what was overwhelmingly an Irish Catholic *nationalism.

Protestant conquerors in Ireland had little respect for the "crude and rude" natives, and consequently they not only failed to convert them to their religion, Protestantism, but also alienated them socially and politically. The Old English and the native Irish became welded into one cultural nation loyal to Catholicism. In the nineteenth century, Daniel *O'Connell expanded that Catholic-rooted cultural identity into a political nationalism that eventually resulted in a twenty-six-county Irish Republic. L.J.MC.

religion in Ireland. Religion has been a powerful social and cultural force in Ireland since the earliest times. *Pre-Christian religion was strong enough to persist in many parts of the country long after the arrival of St. *Patrick and other missionaries. Patrick began the campaign of conversion of the Irish in the fifth century, and within three hundred years a structured church was established throughout the island, with allegiance to Rome. The Irish *Catholic Church's dynamism in the seventh and eighth centuries was such that it produced many missionaries who evangelized in western and central Europe, while at home there was an efflorescence of Christian art and learning. Later, the *Viking raids on Ireland may have contributed to religious dislocation in the short term, but the Scandinavian settlers eventually became Christianized and made a significant religio-cultural contribution. By the twelfth century there was an identification of the Christian Church with the centers of political power at local and regional levels.

Religious reform entered late-medieval Ireland from abroad. The influence of the various orders of monks, *nuns, and friars, many brought in under the auspices of the *Anglo-Normans, was significant. In return for the grant of the lordship of the island from the pope, the Norman kings beginning with *Henry II undertook to foster the interests of the Catholic Church in Ireland. A system of smaller parishes based on manors developed in areas under Norman influence, while in the Gaelic regions the hereditary clerical class, very closely tied to the ruling elites, continued to dominate the more amorphous parish units. Within this framework of fractured ecclesiastical jurisdiction, a rich and variegated religious life subsisted among laity and clergy, surviving well into the post-*Reformation period.

By the seventeenth century, following the Reformation, alternative systems of worship in the Anglican and Catholic churches had developed. While relations between the denominations were equable enough, at times of turmoil such as the 1640s and the 1650s sectarian strife was inevitable. By the time of the Restoration, the consolidation of church identities, which had been evolving during the previous hundred years, was complete. Within the broad Protestant movement in Ireland, sects that were called "dissenting" emerged. The Irish followers of Calvin became organized into worshiping units and communities, mostly in *Ulster. Their need for a separate organization had not been as pressing in the earlier seventeenth century, because Calvinist ethos had dominated the Church of Ireland, but now that the established church had lost its Puritanism, circumstances had changed. Even though *Presbyterianism was a minority religion (in comparison to the mainstream Church of Ireland and the Roman Catholic Church), its strong social and community base would sustain it throughout the trials of the eighteenth century. The *Penal Laws of the eighteenth century aimed at suppressing the political and social power of the Catholics and dissenters but not necessarily their religious identities. Besides the Presbyterians and the *Quakers, other religious denominations developed in Ireland, including smaller sects such as the *Huguenots (also Calvinist) and the *Palatines, who sought refuge from oppression on the Continent. Methodism grew impressively from the mid-eighteenth century to become a major Protestant sect. The broad Protestant movement in Ireland also includes separate worshiping communities of Lutherans, Baptists, and Evangelicals. *Jews have had a continuous presence in Ireland since the Middle Ages. More recently there are members of nonaligned religions such as the Baha'i faith, Jehovah's Witnesses, and Mormonism in Ireland. Followers of Greek Orthodoxy and Islam have been expanding in numbers since the late twentieth century. Despite improved interchurch relations since the *Second Vatican Council, traditional religious divisions have flared up from the beginning of the *Troubles (1969) in *Northern Ireland, giving rise to ongoing sectarian violence. C.L.

Repeal. Movement to repeal the Act of *Union (1800) and restore a national *parliament in Ireland. Daniel *O'Connell saw Repeal of the union as the ultimate goal of the modern Irish *nationalism he had constructed during the *Catholic Emancipation struggle. Although he never specified what Repeal entailed, O'Connell's agenda indicated a democratic constituency, voting by secret ballot, electing an Irish parliament that would accept the British monarchy and enact legislation protecting civil liberties, and the separation of church and state.

In 1843, O'Connell melded anti-*tithe fury and temperance movement enthusiasm into a massive agitation to repeal the union. Although he did not attract the same degree of support from bishops, priests, and lawyers that he had for Catholic Emancipation, O'Connell did enlist the talents of *Young Ireland and their newspaper, the **Nation*, an articulate voice for cultural nationalism.

Throughout the country on Sunday afternoons, hundreds of thousands listened to O'Connell's promise that by year's end, Sir Robert Peel, the British prime minister, would concede Repeal rather than face the possibility of physical force. But Peel, who had granted Catholic Emancipation to preserve the union, had no intention of dismantling it. He flooded Ireland with troops and the authorities banned O'Connell's Monster Meeting scheduled for Clontarf on October 8, 1843. To avoid violence O'Connell called off the meeting.

Repeal fervor persuaded Peel to initiate legislation to woo Irish Catholic clerical and middle-class support for the union. However, O'Connell's maneuvering and the *Famine aborted many of his reforms. After O'Connell's death, Repeal faded in the face of physical force *republicanism and *home rule nationalism. L.J.MC.

Republic of Ireland. While the symbols of king and empire found no place in Bunreacht na hÉireann (*Constitution of Ireland) 1937, neither did the term *republic*. The term had sacrosanct connotations for Irish revolutionaries who believed that the "Irish Republic" was baptized in the blood of the 1916 *Easter Rising martyrs and made imperishable through the sacrifices of the volunteers in the *War of Independence (1919–21) before being "betrayed" in 1922. Éamon *de Valera had no doubt that the changes to the *Anglo-Irish Treaty his government had brought about between 1932 and 1936 had made the twenty-six-county state a "de facto" republic. He was aware, however, that the revered term could be proclaimed only in a unified thirty-two-county context. He also naively believed that avoiding "republic" in the Constitution showed regard for *Ulster *unionist sensitivity.

Under de Valera's *External Relations Act (ERA) of 1936, the British monarch as head of the *Commonwealth was "authorized" to act on behalf of the state in international affairs, in such matters as "the appointment of diplomatic and consular representatives and the conclusion of international agreements . . . as and when advised by the Executive Council to do so." This ingenious, if equivocal, constitutional position exposed de Valera to the taunts of his political opponents. Challenged in the *Dáil (Parliament) (July 17, 1945) about the status of the state, he stoutly maintained that it "possesses every characteristic mark by which a republic can be distinguished or recognized." He supported his argument by quoting the definition of "republic" from various dictionaries and encyclopedias. However, this characteristically pedantic exposition did not end public confusion on the issue and provoked derisive references to "the dictionary republic."

In February 1948, a *Fine Gael–led coalition under John A. *Costello replaced the de Valera administration. Two parties in the coalition, *Clann na Poblachta—composed of erstwhile militant *republicans under Séan *MacBride—and *Labour, were likely to support the repeal of the ERA. But the apparently sudden conversion of Fine Gael, traditionally a strong Commonwealth party, to that view was surprising. Costello fervently hoped that a clear-cut constitutional position, ending the "inaccuracies and infirmities" of the ERA, would satisfy national honor, placate intransigent republicans, and finally "take the gun out of politics."

At a press conference on September 7, 1948, during a visit to Canada, Costello confirmed that his government would repeal the ERA and secede from the British Commonwealth. This seemingly arbitrary development, so far from home and without regard to diplomatic protocol, caused quite a stir. There was controversy for a long time as to whether the move reflected preexisting cabinet policy or was an impulsive action on the part of the *Taoiseach (prime minister).

The *Republic of Ireland (ROI) Bill was introduced in the Dáil in November 1948. Its purpose was to repeal the ERA, to declare that the description of the state should be the Republic of Ireland, and to enable the president to exercise the prerogatives of a head of state in the area of foreign relations. This meant that the state had a more clearly defined position, internationally.

Initially, the British government was irritated by Costello's unilateral move, but the view eventually prevailed that the Irish should remain a "nonforeign" people. In arriving at this decision (a welcome one for the Irish community in Britain), the British were influenced by the Commonwealth voices of Australia, Canada, and New Zealand. The British and Irish governments safeguarded through legislation the rights of their respective citizens in each other's countries. Existing trade preferences were maintained and Irish affairs continued to be handled by the Commonwealth Relations office.

The ROI Act served to reinforce *partition. Ulster unionists, raising the rallying cry that *Northern Ireland was in danger, gained seats in the 1949 general election. More importantly, the British Parliament passed the Ireland Act of 1949 as a response to the ROI Act. It guaranteed that Northern Ireland would not cease to be part of the United Kingdom "without the consent of the Parliament of Northern Ireland." The Ireland Act provoked much noisy but ineffective anti-partition rhetoric in the South.

The ceremonial flourishes that marked the inauguration of the Republic of Ireland, on the symbolic date of Easter Monday 1949, were somewhat diminished by the absence of *Fianna Fáil from the celebrations. Die-hard republicans, who still did not recognize the legitimacy of the state, contemptuously dismissed the notion of a twenty-six-county republic. There were further criticisms that the ROI Act was unnecessary, fruitless, and precipitate—entrenching the Ulster unionists in their position, destroying a possible bridge (Commonwealth membership) to unity, leaving the gun in politics, and resulting in a futile and frustrating anti-partition campaign.

While republics such as India regarded their status as compatible with continuing membership of an increasingly flexible Commonwealth, perhaps the painfully close relationship with Britain made Irish nationalists feel that even a tenuous constitutional link suggested subordination. Consequently, the adoption of unambiguous and formal sovereignty was imperative.

Post-1949, while the *description* of the state was the "Republic of Ireland," the constitutionally unchanged *name* of the state remained "*Éire, or in the English language, Ireland" (Art. 4). Many Northerners still referred to the defunct "Free State." Unionists and British politicians and journalists persisted in using the term *Éire* for the twenty-six-county state.

Irish citizens in general were slow to incorporate the description "Republic" into everyday usage. Ideology apart, it sounded awkward or pretentious. People preferred "the South" or "the twenty-six counties" or simply "the country." Ambiguously, "Ireland" is still commonly used to denote the twenty-six-county state, as well as the whole island. In recent years, the acronym ROI has crept into commercial usage (after the pattern of UK). For most Irish people, however, the primary connotation of the "Republic of Ireland" is that of the state's international *soccer team. It should be noted that, prior to 1949, "republican" was synonymous with being a separatist, whereas in subsequent decades it has come to mean a militant supporter of a united Ireland.

Thus, various issues of nomenclature have arisen from the 1949 legislation. But the enactment of the "Republic of Ireland" was essentially cosmetic, ushering in no change in society or the economy. J.A.M.

Republic of Ireland Act (1948). Legislation by which the twenty-six-county Irish state was declared a republic, independent of the British *Commonwealth. After the 1948 general election, a group of five parties formed the first coalition (interparty) government under *Taoiseach (prime minister) John A. *Costello, a member of *Fine Gael. During a formal visit to Canada by Costello in September 1948, protocol difficulties highlighted Ireland's confusing constitutional position internationally. While the 1937 *Constitution had given the country all the semblance of a republic and the *External Relations Act had associated the country with the Commonwealth, the British government held that the relationship established in the *Anglo-Irish Treaty of 1921 remained unchanged. On September 7, Costello announced his intention to clarify these issues by taking *Éire out of the British Commonwealth and declaring it a fully independent republic.

The Republic of Ireland Bill was introduced into the *Dáil (Parliament) in November 1948 and was passed with the support of the *Fianna Fáil opposition on December 21. The act repealed the Executive Authority (*External Relations) Act of 1936 and declared the name of the state to be the Republic of Ireland. It also transferred to the president all the functions relating to external relations that had been carried out by the crown. The act came into force on Easter Monday, April 18, 1949. P.E.

Republicanism. Dominant political philosophy underlying militant Irish *nationalism. Irish republicans traditionally trace the origins of their political philosophy to the era of the *French Revolution and, in particular, to the *United Irish movement and its leader Wolfe *Tone. The United Irish movement, under the influence of the revolutionary ideas coming from *France and with some minimal French assistance, sought to organize an armed uprising in 1798. The *Rebellion of 1798 was unsuccessful but was historically important in establishing a nonsectarian radical current in Irish nationalism, which sought to unite *Catholic, *Protestant, and Dissenter around a program of Irish independence from Britain. The term *Irish republican*, also originating from this date, has suggested a willingness to use force to achieve an independent united Irish republic.

There was always a more conservative and often exclusively Catholic current in Irish nationalism, and republican organizations have used Catholic imagery and symbolism in their writing. However, Irish republicanism had also had a more radical and secular current. During the first half of the nineteenth century, in the aftermath of the failed Rebellion of 1798 and the passing of the Act of *Union (1800),

Catholic nationalism was the stronger force in Ireland, focused in particular on Daniel *O'Connell's campaign for *Catholic Emancipation. After the Great *Famine of the 1840s, the *Irish Republican Brotherhood (IRB, also known as the *Fenians) was formed in 1858 as a secret organization. It launched an ineffective rising in 1867 and a bombing campaign in England. The IRB also worked by infiltrating other nationalist organizations such as the *Gaelic Athletic Association (GAA) and the *Gaelic League. As Ireland moved into a more radical era in the early twentieth century, with the Irish and nationalist *Literary Revival, the new labor movement and the *women's suffrage campaign, the IRB became more active particularly within *Sinn Féin and the *Volunteer movement. It was instrumental in launching the *Easter Rising of 1916 and the *War of Independence in 1919.

Even though the split in Sinn Féin and the IRA (*Irish Republican Army) over the *Anglo-Irish Treaty in 1921 is often analyzed as a split within the republican strand of politics, it can be more accurately seen as a return to the long-term division between republicanism and more conservative nationalism—a split which had been briefly hidden by the unique Sinn Féin alliance from 1917 to 1921.

After *partition, these two strands of conservative nationalism and radical (and often armed) republicanism were the key competitors for nationalist support in *Northern Ireland. In the South, the lines were less clear. *Fianna Fáil split from anti-treaty Sinn Féin, leaving a largely marginalized party behind. Fianna Fáil used the subtitle "The Republican Party," and initially pursued a radical program. They also, however, reflected and absorbed the conservative Catholic ethos of the new state—abandoning the traditional commitment to secularism.

The modern meaning of republicanism in Irish society entered public debate to a limited extent in the 1980s when some politicians used the term to justify the introduction of a series of socially liberal and occasionally controversial laws, on contraception, gay rights, *divorce, and abortion information. In this instance, the term *republicanism* was used in a purely secular sense, to emphasize the separation of church and state within the Republic of Ireland and was not focused on the question of partition. However, this ideological use was largely rhetorical and disappeared when the liberalizing agenda (apart from abortion) was largely achieved in the 1990s.

The most significant contemporary debate on republicanism revolves around the conflict and *peace process in Northern Ireland. Sinn Féin has, following the IRA cease-fire of 1994, sought to reestablish republicanism as the dominant strand of Irish nationalism, but without the use of force to achieve its aims. The party's vote in Northern Ireland increased dramatically after the IRA cease-fire and, for the first time, in June 2001 Sinn Féin won the support of a majority of nationalists in Northern Ireland. In the Republic of Ireland, Sinn Féin has increased its support from a very small base and offers a more left-wing, more strongly nationalist, and more secular policy package than the mainstream parties. J.D.

Restoration, the. The reestablishment of the monarchy in Britain and Ireland, in 1660. The term is often used to refer to the reign of the restored King, Charles II (1660–85), and the first three years of the reign of *James II (1685–89). Irish Catholics hoped that the Restoration would lead to the reversal of many aspects of *Cromwell's rule, especially the *Cromwellian Land Settlement, which had greatly reduced the amount of property Catholics controlled. Charles II could not afford to alienate *Protestant opinion in Britain or Ireland, however,

Albert Reynolds

and thus under the Irish Acts of Settlement (1662) and Explanation (1665), this settlement was left, with some exceptions, as it was. By 1685, Catholics owned only about 20 percent of the land, compared with the approximately 60 percent in 1641. Other features of Cromwell's administration that were retained in the Restoration era in Ireland included a large military establishment, taxation innovations (e.g., the introduction of Customs and Excise), and the discontinuation of outmoded feudal courts, such as the Court of Wards and Liveries. Generally, Charles II's reign was a peaceful, reasonably prosperous period, with the only notable period of religious persecution occurring at the end of the 1670s. By 1685 the population of Ireland was close to two million. J.C.

Reynolds, Albert (1932–). Politician, leader of *Fianna Fáil, and *Taoiseach (prime minister), 1992–94. Born in County *Roscommon, Reynolds had a successful entrepreneurial career, and in 1974 he became involved in electoral politics, winning a seat on *Longford County Council. In 1977, he was elected Fianna Fáil TD (Teachta Dála; member of Parliament) for Longford. In the *Dáil (Parliament), he became a supporter of Charles J. *Haughey. When Haughey became Fianna Fáil leader and Taoiseach in 1979, Reynolds was appointed minister for posts and telegraphs and for transport and power. In later Haughey cabinets, he would serve as minister for industry and commerce (1987–88) and for finance (1988–91).

Reynolds resigned as finance minister in November 1991, following a break with Haughey over revelations of questionable business deals in which the latter had been implicated. When Haughey resigned due to those scandals in February 1992, Reynolds took over as leader of Fianna Fáil and as Taoiseach in the Fianna Fáil–*Progressive Democrat coalition government. In his early days as Taoiseach, Reynolds's image as a simple, decent man helped him restore the country's faith in government. In November, however, political wrangling between the coalition partners led to the collapse of the government, and Reynolds called a general election. That election resulted in the loss of several Dáil seats for Fianna Fáil while the *Labour Party doubled its representation. After long negotiations, those two parties formed a new coalition government, and Reynolds continued as Taoiseach.

The coalition faced difficulties in getting its domestic policies passed into law. However, Reynolds and his Tánaiste (deputy prime minister) Dick Spring, the leader of the Labour Party, were instrumental in furthering the *Northern Ireland *peace process. Some of the most dramatic steps in the process took place during his tenure as Taoiseach, and his active involvement in the peace process is Reynolds's greatest contribution to the course of Irish history. Most notably, Reynolds's good working relationship with British Prime Minister John *Major resulted in the two leaders' *Downing Street Declaration of December 1993, which opened the way for *Sinn Féin to join the Northern Ireland peace talks. The declaration led to the historic *republican and *loyalist cease-fires of 1994.

In November 1994, tensions surrounding a controversial appointment to Ireland's High Court forced Reynolds to resign his position, but he continued to serve as acting Taoiseach until December. Many worried that, without his leadership, the peace process might falter, but his successor, *Fine Gael leader John *Bruton, kept the process on track. T.D.

Rice, Edmund Ignatius (1762–1844). Founder of the Irish *Christian Brothers. Born near Callan, County *Kilkenny, Rice became a merchant in *Waterford in 1779. Following his wife's death, he was drawn to religious life. From his own resources he founded a free school for poor boys in Waterford, and soon a network of these schools was set up in Ireland and England. In 1820, the pope formally approved Rice's religious community as an order of *Christian Brothers. Rice devoted the rest of his life to developing the schools in which a Catholic ethos pervaded the whole teaching program. He was beatified by the Catholic Church in 1996. C.L.

risings and rebellions. Perhaps in no other country has the role of rebellion played so central a part in the development of a national identity. Often distorted by myth, the persistent theme has been that of the native Irish resisting Anglo-Saxon invasion and conquest. Modern examples date from the failed Geraldine Rising (1534–35), which featured a formidable alliance of Gaelic and *Anglo-Norman lords headed by "Silken Thomas" Fitzgerald resisting *Henry VIII's efforts to impose direct rule on Ireland. Other doomed rebellions against London's centralizing efforts were led by the Desmond branch of the Fitzgeralds in *Munster 1569–73 and 1579–83. The rising of the *Ulster lords under Hugh *O'Neill resulted in the *Nine Years War (1593–1603) and the later *Flight of the Earls 1607, which effectively ended Gaelic resistance to English direct rule. Subsequently, large numbers of English and Scottish *Protestants were "planted" on the lands confiscated from the defeated northern lords. A new era of resistance in which *religion merged with politics was ushered in with the *Rebellion of 1641 and the subsequent *Confederate War (1641–53). An alliance of *Anglo-Irish and Gaelic Catholics nominally supporting Charles I against a Puritan Parliament succeeded in controlling much of Ireland before being brutally suppressed by *Cromwell between 1650 and 1653. Widespread confiscations and the further settlement of Protestant tenants followed. Modern Irish *republicanism was born in the 1790s with the formation of the Society of *United Irishmen. The group, which was influenced by the enlightenment and advocated secular and democratic *nationalism, organized the

*Rebellion of 1798, the single bloodiest event in Irish history (thirty thousand dead). Smaller-scale republican risings by Robert *Emmet in 1803, *Young Ireland in 1848, and the *Fenians in 1867 were easily quashed. The linear descendants of the Fenians, the *Irish Republican Brotherhood (IRB), took advantage of Britain's distraction with *World War I to rise in *Dublin on Easter Monday, 1916 (the *Easter Rising). Although the republicans were compelled to surrender within a week, the execution of the principal leaders, including Patrick *Pearse and James *Connolly, dramatically swung public opinion in favor of revolutionary separatism. The final act came in the *Anglo-Irish War for independence (1919–21), in which Michael *Collins's genius for unorthodox warfare convinced the British that a negotiated peace was preferable to continued fighting, despite their superiority in numbers and firepower. J.P.

Riverdance. Internationally renowned show of traditional Irish *music and *dance. Riverdance integrated traditional and modern music, choral singing, and Irish dancing in a spectacular manner. With music and lyrics written by Bill Whelan and produced by Moya Doherty and directed by John McColgan, the show was originally an interval act for the 1994 Eurovision Song Contest. The initial piece was expanded and opened as a two-hour show at the Point Theatre in *Dublin in February 1995 and made international stars of step-dancers Michael *Flatley and Jean Butler. The show has since divided into several touring groups and has played to millions of people worldwide. P.E.

Roberts, Thomas Sautelle (1760–1826). Painter. Born in *Waterford, Roberts studied at the Dublin Society Schools. In 1778, he took up the name and profession of his dead brother Thomas, probably completed his brother's unfinished paintings, and went on to become the best-known Irish romantic landscape painter of the period. He was a founding member of the *Royal Hibernian Academy. M.C.

Robinson, Lennox (1886–1958). Playwright and theater director. Robinson was born in Douglas, County *Cork. His first play, *The Clancy Name*, appeared at the *Abbey Theatre in 1908. As the Abbey's producer and manager (1909–14 and 1919–23), Robinson was responsible for opening the *Peacock Theatre. His trendsetting plays, such as *The Round Table* (1922) and *Portrait* (1926), influenced other early-twentieth-century Irish dramatists. In the 1930s, Robinson worked in the United States and later edited *Lady Gregory's Journals 1916–1930* (1946) and *The Oxford Book of Irish Verse* (1956). S.A.B.

Robinson, Mary (1944–). President of Ireland, constitutional lawyer, UN High Commissioner for Human Rights. Between 1969 and 1975, Robinson was a professor of law in Trinity College, *Dublin, and was involved in many high-profile constitutional cases in the area of human rights, especially on women's rights. She was also a member of *Seanad Éireann representing Trinity College from 1969 to 1989. Robinson campaigned unsuccessfully as a *Labour Party candidate for the *Dáil (Parliament) in the 1977 and 1981 general elections. She resigned from the party in 1985 in protest against *unionist exclusion from negotiations on the *Anglo-Irish Agreement (1985). Although she never rejoined the Labour Party, she was Labour's nominee in the

Mary Robinson

Irish presidential election of 1990. Robinson, elected as the country's first woman president, greatly increased the profile of the presidency. Her controversial visits to *Northern Ireland, including a brief meeting with *Sinn Féin leader Gerry *Adams in 1993 (at a time when the Irish government would not meet him), created tension with Labour Party leader Dick Spring. She resigned from the presidency eleven weeks early to become the UN High Commissioner for Human Rights (UNHCHR). Robinson developed a very high international profile for the UN's work on human rights but felt frustrated at the limited funds available to her office. She withdrew a threat to resign only when the UN secretary general promised to improve funding and staffing at the UNHCHR. In September 2002, Robinson relinquished her UN post to work with another human rights organization. J.D.

Roche, Kevin (1922–). Architect. Born in *Dublin and educated at University College, Dublin, Roche is considered Ireland's most famous expatriot architect. After graduation, he entered Michael *Scott's growing practice, which promoted international-style architecture. Roche left Dublin, went to London, and then to Chicago, where he earned a postgraduate degree in architecture at the Illinois Institute of Technology. Working in Eero Saarinen's firm (noted for the TWA terminal at Kennedy Airport and the Gateway Arch in St. Louis), Roche designed such sleek, modern, commercial premises as the Ford Foundation headquarters, New York (1968); the Knights of Columbus Building, New Haven (1968); United Nations Plaza, New York (1969–75); and the Oakland Museum, California (1961–68). A.K.

Roche, Stephen (1959–). Cyclist. Born in *Dublin, Roche won cycling's three biggest races in 1987—the Tour de France, the World Championship, and the Giro d'Italia. Roche excelled as an amateur, winning the Rás Tailtean, Ireland's premier cycling event, in 1979. He also won the coveted Paris-Nice race in his first year as a professional in 1981. B.D.

ROSC. Exhibition society. Founded in 1967, ROSC showed contemporary international work alongside new and old Irish works of art every four years until 1988. Organized by the architect Michael *Scott with the advice of American curator James

Johnson Sweeney, the first two shows were hung by painter Cecil King. Difficulties in choosing the 1984 Irish selection signaled a growing tension between international modernism and a more localized expressionism. This, plus limited funding and the establishment of the *Irish Museum of Modern Art, led to its dissolution. M.C.

Roscommon, County. Inland county in the province of *Connacht. Comprising 983 square miles, the county has a population of 53,803 (2002 census). The economy of the county is *agriculture, primarily cattle. Its many market towns include Boyle, Strokestown, Castlerea, Elphin, and the largest, the county capital, Roscommon town. Roscommon is the Anglicized form of Ros Comain, "the wood of Coman," referring to the site of the monastery of the early *saint, Coman. Enclosed on the south, west, and north by counties *Galway, *Mayo, and *Sligo, County Roscommon forms an extensive, low, and rather flat plateau, broken at its northern end by the Curlew Mountains that rise to 863 feet. Its eastern border is Lough Ree, one of the River *Shannon's largest lakes.

The plains of Roscommon were the heart of ancient Ireland. Here lies *Rathcroghan, where the legendary Queen Maeve lived with her consort Ailill and from where she launched her cattle raid on Cooley in County *Louth, as told in the great Irish epic **Táin Bó Cuailnge* (The Cattle Raid of Cooley). The nearby Carnfree was the inauguration place of the ancient kings of Connacht, including Ireland's last high king, Rory *O'Connor. Clonalis House, near Castlerea, displays the O'Connor family heirlooms. The *Normans built significant *castles at Rinndoon on Lough Ree, Ballintober, and Roscommon town. The county's finest ecclesiastical monument is the great Cistercian abbey in Boyle, built between 1161 and 1220. The abbey lies beside a small river, which drains into Lough Key, one of Ireland's most beautiful lakes. Roscommon was badly affected by the *Famine of the 1840s, and a Famine Museum in Strokestown dramatically tells the story of the county's plight. Distinguished natives of Roscommon include Sir William *Wilde, great polymath and father of Oscar; Dr. Douglas *Hyde, poet and first president of Ireland; and Percy *French, a poet and songwriter. Kilronan is the burial place of Turloch *Carolan (1670–1738), blind *harpist and reputed composer of the melody to which "The Star-Spangled Banner" is sung. P.H.

Rosenstock, Gabriel (1949–). Poet in the *Irish language and translator. Rosenstock is author of more than eighty books, including original poetry, translations, children's literature, haikus, plays, novels, and short stories. His original poetry is marked by a sympathy for the marginalized and the unusual. The best of these are selected in *Rogha Rosenstock* (1994). He has translated from German, Spanish, and Flemish, and has added the smell of the earth and the taste of what might have been in his translations into Irish of the poetry of Seamus *Heaney. A.T.

round towers. Pencil-like towers with conical caps, reaching up to one hundred feet. Built between 950 and 1238, sixty-five are known from early monastic sites, their Old Irish name *cloigtheach* suggesting their use as bell towers. But the normal positioning of the door about ten feet above ground has led to much speculation about their use as refuges, hermits' towers, beacons, or monastic treasuries. P.H.

Rowsome, Leo (1903–70). Musician. Rowsome was an *uilleann piper, pipemaker, and *music

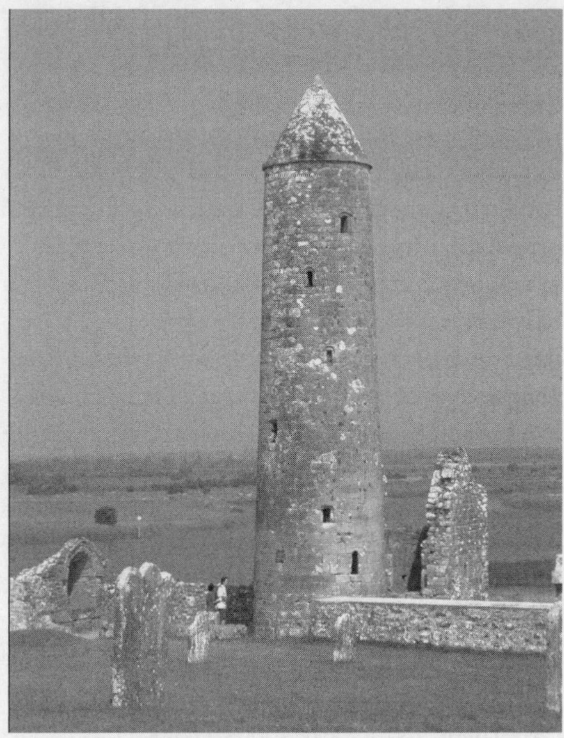

Round Tower, Clonmacnoise, County Offaly

revivalist. The third generation of pipers (his own father was a pipemaker), Rowsome formed one of the earliest *céilí* bands in 1922, revived the Dublin Pipers' Club in 1936, and was a founder of *Comhaltas Ceoltóirí Éireann in 1951. An award-winning piper, he played internationally and taught at the Dublin School of Music. His 1936 textbook on piping is still in use today, and his recordings, now on CD, remain classics. F.V.

Royal Dublin Society (RDS). Organization for the promotion of arts and sciences. One of the oldest bodies of its kind in the world, this organization originated in 1731 and became the Royal Dublin Society in 1820. It aimed to improve agricultural and manufacturing techniques by carrying out research, encouraging industries, and promoting the arts and sciences. In 1877, Parliament transferred responsibility for several of the society's activities to the state and several Irish cultural institutions owe their origins to the RDS, including the *National Botanic Gardens, the *National Library, and the *National Museum. The society received a special grant with which it purchased land at Ballsbridge for equestrian and social events. The RDS complex presently comprises ten multipurpose exhibition halls which host sporting events, concerts, and conferences. (Address: Merrion Road, Ballsbridge, Dublin 4. Web site: *www.rds.ie.*) S.A.B.

Royal Hibernian Academy of Arts. Founded in *Dublin in 1823, the academy holds an annual exhibition of carefully selected artists' works, which is one of the highlights of the Dublin social scene. It also holds separate artists' exhibitions throughout the year. Its premises were destroyed by fire in 1916, but its new home in the Gallagher Gallery (Ely Place) enhances any work it displays. (Address: 15 Ely Place, Dublin 2. Web site: *www.royalhibernianacademy.com.*) P.H.

Royal Irish Academy (RIA). The premier learned institution in Ireland. Founded in *Dublin in 1785, the RIA houses an important collection of Irish *manuscripts, including the *Cathach, and publishes *Proceedings* in the natural sciences and humanities, as well as other journals and monographs. (Address: 19 Dawson Street, Dublin 2. Web site: *www.ria.ie.*) P.H.

Royal Irish Academy of Music. From its beginnings in *Dublin in 1848, the academy has strived to improve and develop musical performance and teaching in Ireland. It also played a role in founding the Municipal School of Music, which it administered from 1895 to 1910. Since 1898 the academy has operated a nationwide examination system, which now examines thirty thousand students annually. In December 1998, a new Traditional Irish Music Examination syllabus was officially launched by the president of Ireland, Mary *McAleese. (Address: 36–39 Westland Row, Dublin 2. Web site: *www.riam.ie*.) S.A.B.

Royal Irish Constabulary (RIC). The main Irish *police force in the nineteenth and early twentieth centuries. In 1822, the chief secretary of Ireland, Henry Goulburn, established a paramilitary police force which was responsible for preventing and detecting crime throughout most of Ireland. Originally known as the County Constabulary, it was organized on a provincial basis and constituted the first professional, national police in the United Kingdom. In 1836, the force was reorganized as the Irish Constabulary. Housed in hundreds of barracks throughout the country, the constabulary became the "eyes and ears" of the *Dublin Castle authorities, providing them with an intimate knowledge of the state of law and order, including the activities of illegal secret societies. In 1867, the Irish Constabulary was the main body responsible for the suppression of the *Fenian rebellion, for which it received the epithet "Royal." Its loyalty was further demonstrated during the *Land War, when the RIC constituted the authorities' main weapon against the *Land League and the National League. During the *War of Independence, the *Irish Republican Army (IRA) killed hundreds of members of the force in its campaign against British rule. The RIC was disbanded in 1922 and replaced by the *Gárda Síochána in the *Irish Free State and the *Royal Ulster Constabulary in *Northern Ireland. B.G.

Royal Ulster Constabulary (RUC). The *Northern Ireland *police force from 1922 to 2001. Approximately 93 percent of the officers of the RUC were *Protestant. Since the *Northern Ireland conflict (the Troubles), the force has been continually criticized by the *nationalist community. During the period 1969 to 1975, the British army had primacy in security matters and the RUC was relegated to a relatively minor role in combating the IRA (*Irish Republican Army). The force was extremely unpopular with nationalists and, due to reforms following the Hunt Report of 1969, considerably weakened by the stress of reorganization. Beginning in 1975, a greatly expanded (from about 3,000 to about 8,500 with nearly 5,000 "reserves") and heavily militarized RUC gradually resumed the main responsibility for security. The force was criticized for its brutal interrogations of IRA suspects, especially in the late 1970s and for operating a *shoot-to-kill policy in the early 1980s. In the early 1990s, collusion with *loyalist paramilitaries—which some explained as the result of rank-and-file indiscipline and secret intelligence operations—came to light. The RUC lost 301 members during the Troubles since 1969 and were responsible for the deaths of (approximately) fifty-two people; of these, thirty were civilians, mostly *Catholics. Following the signing of the *Good Friday Agreement in 1998, a commission was established to make recommendations on the future of the RUC. The Report of the Commission, the Patten Report, was published on September 9, 1999, and made 175 recommendations, including a total overhaul of the force. In 2001, the RUC was disbanded and replaced by the Police Service of Northern Ireland (PSNI). M.M.

RTÉ. Irish National Public Service Broadcasting Organization. Radio Telefís Éireann is a statutory

Rugby

corporation that provides a comprehensive service on *radio (since 1926) and on *television (since 1961), as well as a large range of ancillary services. Under the terms of the Broadcasting Act, 1960, and subsequent legislation, RTÉ policy is guided by a government-appointed committee (the RTÉ Authority). The day-to-day running of RTÉ is the responsibility of the Executive Board, which reports to the RTÉ Authority. S.A.B.

rugby. A popular outdoor field game that originated in England. Students from English public schools introduced rugby football (from which American football evolved) to Ireland and set up the first club at Dublin University in 1854. The game consists of two teams of fifteen players. Rugby grew in popularity and various organizations merged in 1879 to form the Irish Rugby Football Union (IRFU), which administers the game nationally. The club game is popular around Dublin and throughout mid-*Ulster, but many regard *Limerick as rugby's spiritual home in Ireland.

Ireland competes annually in a Six Nations Championship, along with England, Scotland, Wales, France, and Italy. A World Cup tournament takes place every four years. Rugby was traditionally played as an amateur sport, but the game in Ireland, following the trend in other countries, has become more commercialized with top international players now turning professional. Some of the great names of Irish rugby include Jackie Kyle, Jack McCarthy, Tom Kiernan, Willie John MacBride, and Ollie Campbell. Even with many extra matches being played today, Mike Gibson's record of sixty-nine international appearances for Ireland still stands. F.S.

Russell, George (William); AE (1867–1935). Writer, mystic, and social reformer. Russell was born in County *Armagh and educated at the Metropolitan School of Art, Dublin. A member of the Irish Theosophical movement and the Hermeneutic Society, he also supported the cooperative movement and edited its journal, *The Irish Homestead*, and later, *The Irish Statesman*. Vice president of the Irish National Theatre Society, he resigned after clashing with its president, W. B. *Yeats. In 1916 he published essays and editorials outlining his spiritualism and pacifist *nationalism in *The National Being* (1916). His visions are described in the essays of *The Candle of Vision* (1918), and his novel *The Avatars* (1932) evokes the excitement of theosophists awaiting a new deity.

AE supported young writers generously and enjoyed modest success as a watercolorist. He refused a nomination to the *Irish Free State *Senate and in 1932 settled in England, disillusioned with Ireland.
M.S.T.

S

saints. People of outstanding holiness venerated by the *Catholic Church. The early Christian era produced outstanding exemplars of sanctity, most notably St. *Patrick, the apostle of Ireland, St. *Brigid, the foundress of *Kildare, St. *Colm Cille, the founder of monasteries in Ireland and at Iona in Scotland, and St. *Columbanus, the great missionary to continental Europe. In addition, substantial numbers of holy people were popularly acclaimed as saints. Medieval hagiographies celebrated both the lives of the famous and the locally venerated who were the subject of devotion and dedications.

A fallow period for outstanding sanctity seems to have coincided with (though not necessarily caused by) the *Viking raids on Ireland. Significantly, the first Irish saints to be proclaimed by official papal canonization, Saints Malachy and Lawrence O'Toole, both twelfth-century figures, were closely associated with reform of decayed ecclesiastical institutions. During the Irish counter-*Reformation, there was a new vogue for hagiography in which the lives of early Irish saints were presented as models of devotion and fortitude. Contemporaneously there emerged the cults of dozens of men and women who were regarded as having died for their Catholic beliefs in the *rebellions of the period, and their lives were written up in the seventeenth-century martyrologies. In 1975, Oliver *Plunkett, archbishop of *Armagh, who was executed in 1681, was the first Irish saint to be canonized in modern times, and more recently, seventeen Irish martyrs of the sixteenth and seventeenth centuries were beatified in 1992. Currently, many are promoting the causes for the canonization of other martyrs, as well as more modern Irish exemplars of charity and piety such as Edmund *Rice and Matt *Talbot. C.L.

Samhain. *Celtic festival of the dead. The Irish word for *November* or *winter*, and literally meaning "summer's end," Samhain marked the beginning of winter. Originally, the year was divided into two halves, the dark half beginning at Samhain and the bright half at Bealtaine. The November feast Samhain was when the otherworld was thought to intervene in this world. In *Christianity (which has appropriated much pagan *mythology), this pagan Celtic festival of the dead, celebrated on November eve, became the feast days of All Saints (All Hallows) and All Souls. *Samhain* was the title of an occasional journal associated with the Irish Literary Theatre in the first decade of the twentieth century. W. B. *Yeats launched *Samhain* in October 1901 to coincide with the third and final season of the Irish Literary Theatre. It contained the text of Douglas *Hyde's *Irish-language play *Casadh an t-Súgáin* (*The Twisting of the Rope*), as well as reflective essays by Yeats, George *Moore, and Lady *Gregory on the future of *theater in Ireland. Subsequent issues reveal the tension between Yeats's aesthetic mission to create a poetic, avant-garde drama rooted in Irish mythology and many of his colleagues' desire for a realist, thoroughly national, drama celebrating the virtues of the native peasantry. E.S.M.

Saor Éire. Left-wing republican group. Formed in the 1930s, as a breakaway group from the IRA (*Irish Republican Army), Saor Éire emerged in the 1960s after the IRA had ended its border campaign in 1962. It has had a shadowy existence and played little part in the *Northern Ireland conflict, despite claims to the contrary. T.C.

Sarsfield, Patrick(1655–93). *Jacobite military leader. Born into a gentry family in County *Kildare of both *Norman and Gaelic descent, Sarsfield served in France from 1675 to 1677. When *James II adopted a policy of promoting Catholics in his army, Sarsfield became a leading commander in Ireland and captured *Connacht for the Jacobite cause. An excellent cavalry commander, Sarsfield was, however, not fully appreciated by the French commanders who came to Ireland with James II. His omission from the command structure at the Battle of *Aughrim is generally seen as contributing to the Jacobite defeat. He came to prominence following Aughrim and his capture of the Williamite gun train at Ballyneety, County *Limerick, led to the defeat of the first siege of *Limerick. Sars-field played a key role in defending the city and later in negotiating the Treaty of *Limerick. In exile, he became a *maréchal de camp* in French service, and was killed at the Battle of Landen (in Flanders) in 1693. T.C.

Saunderson, Edward (1837–1906). *Unionist politician. Saunderson was the Liberal Party's member of Parliament (MP) at Westminster for his home county of *Cavan, between 1865 and 1874. Disillusioned with William *Gladstone, he gravitated toward the *Orange Order and the Tory Party. As MP for North *Armagh (1885–1906), he led the *Ulster unionist faction of the Tory Party and saw the defeat of two *home rule bills. In time, his loyalty to *landlordism came to be seen as an anachronism, but he is still remembered as one of the founders of Ulster unionism. M.M.

Sayers, Peig (1873–1958). Storyteller. Sayers was born in Dunguin, County *Kerry, and married a Blasket Islander. Celebrated for her autobiography *Peig* (1936), which begins by saying she has one leg in the grave, Sayers presents a life that is hard but in which the people are happy in their closeness to God. Her autobiography is a valuable social document describing the life of island women at the time. Its principal beauty is in its language, which is clear, precise, and poetic, exactly mirroring the speech of its author. Her stories were collected by folklorists and are an excellent example of the kinds of narrative common to women. A.T.

science and technology. Ireland is more noted for its letters, which represent a distinctively Irish culture, than it is for its sciences, which developed in tandem with the evolution of modern science throughout Europe. Nevertheless, the list of prominent scientists who were either born or pursued careers in Ireland is impressive, as are the scientific contributions they made. In the seventeenth century, the list includes William *Molyneux (1656–98) and Robert *Boyle (1627–91), founder of the Royal Society, father of chemistry, discoverer of Boyle's Law, and principal proponent of the new mechanical, corpuscular science based on the experimental method.

Unlike their Anglican-educated, amateur, and theoretically inclined precursors, the most prominent Irish scientists of the eighteenth century were Dissenters or *Catholics educated on the Continent (because of the *Penal Laws), professional, and inclined toward the practical sciences, especially chemistry with its rich applications to the *brewing, *distilling, mining, pharmaceutical, *textile, and vintage industries. Joseph Black (1782–99), the son of Belfast Scottish Dissenters and professor of chemistry at Edinburgh, discovered "fixed air" (carbon dioxide), the specific heat of substances, and the latent heat of fusion. Richard Kirwan (1733–1812) was the discoverer of chlorine bleaching and principal defender of phlogiston theory against Lavoisier's new oxygen theory. Bryan Higgins (1737–1818) founded a school of practical chemistry in fashionable Soho, where his lectures were attended by such luminaries as Benjamin Franklin, Edward Gibbon, Samuel Johnson, and Joseph Priestley. He spent time in Russia (as chemist at the court of Catherine the Great) and Jamaica (as consultant to sugar and rum manufacturers). His patents included cement, oil lamp fuel, soda and mineral water, beer, and a warm-air heating system. His nephew, William Higgins (1762–1825), had an acrimonious priority dispute with John Dalton, each claiming credit for the discovery of the atomic theory of chemistry.

As in the rest of Europe throughout the eighteenth and nineteenth centuries, science in Ireland became professionalized and institutionalized. Scientific bodies like the Dublin Philosophical Society (1684), the *Royal Dublin Society (1731), and the *Royal Irish Academy (1785) provided forums for scientists to meet and journals to disseminate their ideas. Trinity College's curriculum in mathematics and natural philosophy, modeled on the French methods of Laplace and Lagrange, was one of the most progressive in Europe. New professorships in engineering and other applied sciences were established. The newly formed Queen's Colleges at *Belfast, *Cork, and *Galway attracted top scientists and mathematicians to Ireland. Ten of the top thirty Victorian physicists were Irish-born, including: George Francis Fitzgerald (1851–1901), who independently invented the Lorentz-Fitzgerald contraction, subsequently incorporated by Einstein into his theory of Special Relativity; George Gabriel Stokes (1819–1903), the foremost Victorian theorist of hydrodynamics and elasticity; William Rowan *Hamilton (1805–65), the best mathematician of the era; and Lord Kelvin (1824–1907), the preeminent Victorian physicist who pioneered the mechanical theory of heat, masterminded the laying of the first transatlantic telegraph cable, and invented a host of scientific instruments.

The Victorian period in Ireland also produced

remarkable technological innovations: Nicholas Callan (1799–1864) invented the induction coil (1836); Charles Parsons (1854–1931) invented the steam turbine (1884) and designed the first steam turbine powered ship, the *Turbinia* (1897), whose blueprint was quickly adopted for all major shipping. Thomas Grubb (1800–78) and his son, Howard (1844–1931), were the premier designers and builders of large telescopes in the world. Most remarkable, however, was the *Birr telescope, designed and built in Ireland in 1845 by William Parsons (1800–67), the father of Charles. With its mammoth seventy-two-inch reflecting mirror, it was the largest telescope in the world until the Mt. Wilson telescope was constructed in 1917 in the United States. With it, Parsons was the first to observe the spiral structure of nebulae and identify them as distinct galaxies.

The most prominent Irish scientist of the twentieth century was the physicist E. T. S. *Walton (1903–95), who won the Nobel Prize for his pioneering work in nuclear physics. John Joly (1857–1933) pioneered radiation treatment for cancer. Erwin Schroedinger, the founder of quantum wave mechanics, became a naturalized citizen after fleeing Nazi-occupied Austria and spent the years 1940 to 1956 at the Dublin Institute for Advanced Studies (DIAS) founded by Éamon *de Valera in 1940. John L. Synge (1897–1995), the nephew of J. M. *Synge and world-renowned relativity theorist and mathematician, was also at DIAS. The engineer Harry *Ferguson (1864–1960) revolutionized *agriculture with his redesign of the lightweight tractor. In 1945, Kathleen Lonsdale (1903–71), who worked on X-ray crystallography and showed that the benzene ring was flat, became the first woman fellow of the Royal Society, the society her compatriot Boyle helped found in 1660.

In the twenty-first century, Ireland continues to be an international center of scientific and technological research and development. Most of the foremost global giants in the computer industry (including Adobe, Compaq, Dell, IBM, Intel, and Microsoft) have major operations there. In 2000, Ireland became the largest net exporter of software in the world. M.L.

Scotland. Constituent part of the United Kingdom. A tremendous cross-fertilization of people, culture, and ideas has continued between Ireland and Scotland from the early *Christian era to the present. In fact, the name Scotland is derived from the Scots, a northern Irish tribal grouping, who expanded into the west of Caledonia from their kingdom of Dál Riata by the fifth century. Under the Gaelic-speaking Scots Mac Alpin dynasty, *Celtic Picts, Britons, and Scots merged with the Germanic Angles of the southeast to form the Kingdom of Scotland between the ninth and eleventh centuries. Irish missionaries, most prominently *Colm Cille (St. Columba), converted much of Scotland to Christianity in the sixth century from their monastic center on the isle of Iona.

Scottish migration has played a prominent role in the development of Ireland. Edward *Bruce, the brother of the famed Scottish King Robert Bruce, invaded Ireland in 1315 and nearly established a unified Scottish-Irish state at the expense of the *Anglo-Norman Plantagenets. Scottish mercenaries (Gallowglasses) were the backbone of the military structures maintained by many northern Irish lords throughout the late medieval and early modern periods. Ultimately, the greatest Scottish impact on Ireland came in the form of long-term migration during the seventeenth century. This heavy influx of Scottish, largely *Presbyterian, settlers in *Ulster radically altered the religious composition of the northern province. The notorious, officially sanctioned *Ulster Plantation (1609–25) displaced many native Irish landholders, but peaceful Scottish immigration had both preceded and continued long after these dates. In counties *Antrim and *Down, Scots came to constitute the population's absolute majority. There were also major settlements in *Derry, *Armagh, *Tyrone, and *Donegal. Although Presbyterians were at the forefront of secular republican nationalism in the 1790s, by the mid- to late nineteenth century, they had largely become loyalists. In the present day, the descendants of Scottish settlers comprise the majority of the northern Irish *Protestant community. J.P.

Scots-Irish. A term describing *Ulster *Presbyterians who migrated to the British North American colonies in the seventeenth and eighteenth centuries. By 1775, they constituted the largest white ethnic minority in the colonies. Politically radical, the Scots-Irish played a major role in the *American Revolution. Known for their fierce independence, this group settled mostly on the frontiers. Thirteen American presidents, including Andrew Jackson and Woodrow Wilson, were descended from the Ulster Scots. In the nineteenth century, the term was adopted by many *Protestant Irish Americans to differentiate themselves from the new waves of *Catholic *immigrants arriving from Ireland. J.P.

Scott, Michael (1905–88). Architect. Born in Drogheda, County *Louth, Scott is considered by many the most important architect of twentieth-century Ireland. He studied at the Dublin Metropolitan School of Art and was an architect's apprentice before joining the Office of Public Works. In 1927, he started his own practice, initially designing several modern structures for the *Irish Free State, including hospitals at Tullamore (1934–37) and Portlaoise (1933–36). In 1937, Scott brought Walter Gropius to *Dublin, and, from then on, concentrated on promoting modernism in Ireland. Scott's buildings include his own home, "Geragh," at Sandycove, Dublin (1937–38), the Irish Pavilion for the New York World's Fair (1939), Donnybrook Bus Garage (1952), Busáras (1944–53), and the *Abbey Theatre (1958–66). Scott's modernist style is now considered controversial (some say inhumane and cold), but his work is still highly regarded internationally and at home. A.K.

Scott, Patrick (1921–). Painter, designer, and graphic artist. Born in Kilbrittan, County *Cork, Scott was a member of the modernist White Stag Group in the 1940s. His painting, under the influence of architectural training and Japanese art, has evolved into formal geometric images using white and gold leaf on linen. He also works in tapestry, carpets, mosaics, and furniture. He represented Ireland at the Venice Biennale in 1960 and was involved with *ROSC and *Kilkenny Design Workshops. M.C.

Scott, William (1913–89). Painter. Born in Scotland, Scott grew up in County *Fermanagh and studied art in *Belfast and London. His flat modernist treatment of still-life borders on an abstract formalism softened and made more accessible by its painterly qualities. M.C.

Scully, Sean (1945–). Painter. A native of *Dublin, Scully was influenced by the work of Mark Rothko and Bridget Riley. He now works in Barcelona, London, and New York. Since the late sixties, horizontal and vertical stripes arranged to create monumental structures have been the sole formal motif of his painting. A member of *Aosdána, he has

Details on Muiredach's Cross, County Louth

been a visiting lecturer at National College of Art and Design, Dublin. M.C.

sculpture. A tradition of sculpture has existed in Ireland since earliest times, mostly in connection with *architecture, tombs, and free-standing crosses of the early *Christian period. Church building declined with the coming of the Black Death in the mid-thirteenth century, but the fifteenth century saw a revival in the use of stone carving, mainly for the sides of box tombs.

The Dublin Society Schools, set up in 1740, facilitated the training of sculptors. During the relative political stability of the Georgian period, many superb buildings were constructed. Sculptors were employed to add decorative features to exteriors and interiors. Some of the best work is by Edward Smyth (1749–1812) on the façade of the Custom House in *Dublin (1781). His carvings are richly animated with a variety of textures. John Henry Foley (1818–74), one of a number of sculptors who sought work in England, established himself as a leading portrait sculptor and was one of eight artists chosen to work on the Memorial to Prince Albert. John *Hogan (1800–58), who lived in Rome for a few years, is renowned for the quality of his religious sculpture and his classical subject matter.

In the first half of the twentieth century, sculptors like Albert *Power (1881–1945) continued in the artistic tradition of the late nineteenth century. His near contemporary Oliver *Sheppard (1865–1941) was much influenced by Art Nouveau, while the public monuments of Andrew O'Connor (1874–1941) recall the artistic expression of Rodin. In the building boom that began in the sixties, minimalist sculpture was commissioned for public buildings. Since then, the use of geometric shapes in wood, steel, or aluminum has created exciting visual effects. Many of these works are by talented women artists including Gerda Fromel (1931–75) and Eilis O'Connell (1953–). Today sculpture has broadened to include performance art and body sculpture, and the traditional means of expression are being left behind. S.B-L.

Seanad Éireann (Senate). Upper House of the *Oireachtas, Ireland's legislature. When the British government partitioned Ireland under the *Government of Ireland Act (1920), provision was made for a second consultative chamber in both *Dublin and *Belfast. When, following the *Anglo-Irish Treaty (1921), a twenty-six-county *Free State was established within the British empire in 1922, provision was made for a similar senate. The Northern Senate together with the *Stormont Assembly in Belfast made up the government of *Northern Ireland. It was finally abolished in 1972, when the British government instituted direct rule of Northern Ireland from Westminister. The Senate of Northern Ireland has not been restored.

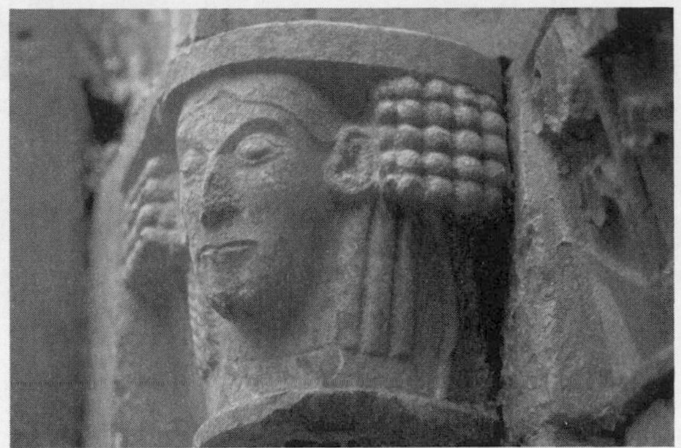

Detail in Corcomroe Abbey, County Clare

The powers of the Irish Free State Senate were limited, though it gained a reputation for lively debate throughout the 1920s. However, after Éamon *de Valera came to power as head of the new *Fianna Fáil government in 1932, his attempt to abolish the *oath of allegiance which all elected members of the Irish legislature were required to take, was frustrated by the Senate. After a sudden Dáil (Parliament) election in January 1933, where the oath was a major issue, de Valera, who gained an overall majority for the first time, abolished the Senate. However, when de Valera then proposed the *Constitution of 1937, he included a senate, Seanad Éireann, as an Upper House of the Oireachtas.

Today's Senate (Seanad Éireann) consists of sixty members. Forty-three are elected from five vocational panels (representing culture and education, agriculture, labor, industry and commerce, and public administration), by the members of the main local authorities, along with members of the incoming Dáil and the outgoing Senate. Six are elected by graduates of the two older universities, three from the National University (NUI) and three from Dublin University (Trinity College), while the remaining eleven are nominated by the new *Taoiseach (prime minister). In theory, the Senate does not recognize party political affiliations, but the nature of the electorate that votes for the forty-three Senators and the fact that the Taoiseach can nominate eleven members in a house of sixty seats usually means that the government has a comfortable majority. The Senate's main business is to review legislation sent to it by the Dáil. But it can also initiate nonfinancial legislation and, on occasions, has played a significant role in delaying controversial legislation that the Dáil has passed. N.ÓG.

sean-nós singing. Sean-nós (or "old style") is used to denote the unaccompanied song tradition in Irish or Scots Gaelic. The style is most prevalent in the *Gaeltacht areas (particularly *Connemara) and there are distinct regional differences. The compressed vocal range of the Connemara singers, for instance, contrasts with the less ornamented style of *Donegal.

Theories vary as to the origins of sean-nós. Professor Seán *Ó Tuama traces a connection with *amour courtois* and speculates that the models for popular Irish folk songs were established after the *Norman invasion. Filmmaker Bob Quinn believes that Ireland's maritime culture may have exposed it to stylistic influences from Spain and North Africa, which were under Islamic rule for seven hundred years. Sean-nós singing is currently experiencing something of a revival, the yearly highlight being the Corn Uí Riada competition which takes place during the Oireachtas festival. Organized by the *Gaelic League, the festival is a celebration of the arts among the Irish-speaking communities and includes musical, singing, and literary competitions. B.D.

Second Vatican Council (1962). Ecumenical Council of the Roman Catholic Church. Pope John XXIII convened the Second Vatican Council in 1962 to reform church teaching, discipline, and liturgical practice in order to bring the church into dialogue with the modern world. The council was a triumph for Irish *Catholicism in the sense that many of the bishops attending, not only from Ireland but from the United States, Australia, and other parts of the world, were either Irish or of Irish descent. However, the council's implementation in Ireland led many Irish Catholics away from traditional devotions and practices. A new model of Catholicism developed that emphasized religious freedom, ecumenism, and liturgical renewal in lieu of popular devotions. The reforms renewed the religious commitment of many Catholics, but caused controversy among those who still embraced a more traditional Catholicism. M.P.C.

set-dancing. A social *dance form (literally a set of quadrilles) involving nineteenth-century French choreography using Irish "steps"—and performed to Irish traditional music (jig, reel, polka, and hornpipe). An earlier version, the cotillion, was hugely popular in Ireland since the 1770s. The quadrille form spread from Europe as a dance fashion after 1816. "Sets" of quadrilles had different names and foot patterning, often connected to place. They are grouped according to type, the "first set" typified by the Plain (Clare) Set and the Fermanagh Quadrille set. The "second set" is the Lancer Quadrilles, and the "third set"of quadrilles is known as the Caledonian. Set-dance was condemned by the *Gaelic League as un-Irish, but was revived to huge popularity after the 1970s by pioneering independent dance teachers as well as by *Comhaltas Ceoltóirí Éireann and the *Gaelic Athletic Association. F.V.

Shannon, Sharon (1968–). Musician. Born in County *Clare, Shannon plays the accordion and fiddle and is considered one of Ireland's most dynamic young traditional musicians. Taught by Frank Custy of Toonagh, she began playing at an early age. While at college in *Cork, she started playing professionally. Shannon was part of the band Arcady, but it was with the popular Waterboys that she gained an international reputation. In the 1990s, she embarked on a solo career and played internationally with her own support bands. Her taste in music includes the broader Irish/Celtic world, with Cajun, Cape Breton, American country, and such influences. F.V.

Shannon, River. The longest river in Ireland or Britain. The Shannon rises in the Shannon Pot in County *Cavan, forms an estuary west of Limerick City, and flows into the Atlantic at Loop Head, County *Clare. Its total length is 214 miles. Formerly an important north-south traffic artery, it is now used mainly for pleasure cruising and is linked with the Erne system through the Ballinamore-Ballyconnell Canal. In its course, the Shannon feeds three important lakes (Allen, Ree and Derg). In 1926–30, water was diverted from the river to create the country's first major hydroelectric scheme at Ardnacrusha, County Clare. P.H.

Shaw, Fiona (1958–). Actress. Born in *Cork, Shaw graduated with a BA in philosophy from University College, Cork, before entering the Royal Academy of Dramatic Art (RADA) in London. Her rapid rise in the London theater world, and the rarity of her appearances on the Irish stage, led many to describe her incorrectly as a British, rather than Irish, actress. Shaw is widely acclaimed as one of the most talented and intellectually rigorous actors of her generation. Her theater credits at the Royal National Theatre include: Julia in Richard

George Bernard Shaw

Brinsley *Sheridan's *The Rivals*, Shen Te Shui Ta in Bertolt Brecht's *The Good Person of Szechuan*, the title role in *Richard II*, the stage version of Muriel Spark's *The Prime of Miss Jean Brodie*, and Euripides' *Electra*, and Rosalind in *As You Like It*. She has won a number of awards, including three Laurence Olivier Awards for best actress and two London Critics Awards. She received a New York Critics Award for her performance in the BBC film version of T. S. Eliot's *The Waste Land*. Notable film credits include roles in two important Irish films, *My Left Foot* (1987) and *The Butcher Boy* (1997). She has also taken lighter roles in such big-budget films as *Three Men and a Little Lady* (1990) and *Harry Potter and the Sorcerer's Stone* (2001). In 2002, she played Medea in the *Abbey Theatre production of Euripides' classic, which received rave reviews in London and New York. H.L.

Shaw, George Bernard (1856–1950). Playwright and man of letters, Nobel laureate. Born in *Dublin, Shaw was the son of an unsuccessful grain merchant with a drinking problem, and an artistic mother. Early on, Shaw developed an interest in literature, music, and art, influenced by his mother and her friend George Vandeleur Lee, a singing teacher with whom the Shaws shared a house. After leaving school at age fifteen, Shaw worked for a number of years as a clerk, and unsuccessfully submitted short articles to newspapers and magazines.

In 1876 Shaw joined his mother in London, where, unemployed, he wrote five novels in an outmoded style, none of which were successful. In 1884 he joined the Fabian Society, a utopian movement designed to achieve a socialist society by peaceful means. For the Fabians, Shaw wrote political and economic treatises, edited *Fabian Essays* (1889), and was one of their most popular speakers.

Between 1885 and 1898, Shaw established a reputation as an art and music critic (he championed Wagner and published *The Perfect Wagnerite* in 1898). He also wrote incisive theater criticism for the *Saturday Review*. At the suggestion of William Archer, the first English translator of Henrik Ibsen, Shaw began writing plays inspired by Ibsen's social criticism. An expanded version of a lecture on Ibsen, *The Quintessence of Ibsenism*, appeared in 1891. Shaw's play *Widowers' Houses*, in which he addresses middle-class hypocrisy and economic exploitation, was produced in 1892. Other plays of this early period, including *Mrs. Warren's Profession* (1894), on the theme of prostitution, and *Arms and the Man* (1894), a satirical look at the military establishment, were published in two volumes as *Plays Pleasant* and *Plays Unpleasant* (1898). Shaw married Charlotte Payne-Townshend in 1898.

Shaw's plays—invariably accompanied by extensive and argumentative introductions—indicted the institutions of society rather than the questionable actions of individuals, which he saw as the effect rather than the cause of social ills. His work is characterized by provocative wit and by the polemical nature of his dramatic dialogues. Shaw's reputation as a dramatist was established internationally with *Man and Superman* (1903), in which he developed his "religion" of Creative Evolution, a belief in a force that seeks to elevate mankind to a more evolved existence. *Pygmalion* (1912), the story of flower girl Eliza Doolittle's transformation into a society lady under the tutelage of professor Henry Higgins, illustrates Shaw's lifelong interest in the spelling and pronunciation of the English language. The play was the basis for the musical *My Fair Lady* (1956), later made into a popular movie.

Shaw was horrified at Britain's involvement in *World War I, a sentiment expressed in *Heartbreak House* (1917). A prolific writer (he wrote fifty-three plays), Shaw increasingly experimented with form and subject matter. The five-part science-fiction cycle *Back to Methuselah* (1921) further developed his theories about the "Life Force." *Saint Joan* (1924), often considered Shaw's masterpiece, depicts the trial of Joan of Arc as a struggle between honest forthrightness and hypocritical opportunism. Shaw received the Nobel Prize for literature in 1925. (He is one of four Irish writers to have won the prize.) His last full-length play, *In Good King Charles's Golden Days*, appeared in 1939. Shaw died at ninety-four, at his home in Ayot St. Lawrence, Hertfordshire. J.C.E.L.

Sheehy Skeffington, Francis (1878–1916). *Socialist, pacifist, journalist, and writer. Sheehy Skeffington (husband of *Hanna Sheehy Skeffington) was a committed suffragist and a supporter of *women's emancipation. He was active as a campaigner for women's suffrage and edited the suffrage paper the *Irish Citizen*. He joined the *Irish Citizen Army, but left as it moved from being a workers' defense organization to being an armed revolutionary group. Sheehy Skeffington opposed the use of force in the *Easter Rising of 1916, but went on the streets to prevent looting, so that it would not be used as "black propaganda" against the *Volunteer movement. He was arrested by a British army patrol and summarily executed. Following public outrage, the British officer who ordered Sheehy Skeffington's execution was later court-martialed. E.C.

Sheehy Skeffington, Hanna (1877–1946). Feminist, suffragist, and *nationalist. Hanna Sheehy Skeffington (wife of Francis *Sheehy Skeffington) was a prominent feminist campaigner who founded the Irish Women's Franchise League in 1908. In 1904, she joined the United Irish League (a support group for the *Irish Parliamentary Party) and the newly formed Socialist Party of Ireland. She broke with the Irish Party in 1912 on the issue of votes for *women. Sheehy Skeffington lectured extensively in the United States in support of the *republican cause after the 1916 *Easter Rising. She joined *Sinn Féin in 1918 as a member of the party Executive. She took the anti-treaty side in the *Civil War and joined *Fianna Fáil on its formation in 1926 as a member of its first Executive. Sheehy Skeffington left Fianna Fáil when its TDs (Teachtaí Dála; members of Parliament) took the *oath of allegiance to enter the *Dáil (Parliament) in 1927 but remained active in republican and feminist politics until her death. E.C.

Jim Sheridan

Sheela Na Gig. A stone carving of a nude female exposing her vulva. Allegedly from the Irish Síle na gCíoch, (Sheela of the breasts), or Síle ina Giob (Sheela on her Hunkers), such carvings have been interpreted variously as fertility figures, Celtic goddesses, or as objects to ward off evil. Generally of poor quality, these carvings are found on churches and *castles between A.D. 1200 and 1600. P.H.

Sheppard, Oliver (1865–1941). Sculptor. Born in County *Tyrone, Sheppard studied in *Dublin and London and taught at the Dublin Metropolitan School of Art. Influenced by Rodin, he used traditional modeling technique to achieve a naturalistic effect. He is best known for his 1798 memorials at *Wexford and Enniscorthy and his *Death of Cuchulainn* (1911), which later served as a 1916 *Easter Rising commemoration in the General Post Office, Dublin. M.C.

Sheridan, Jim (1949–). Filmmaker. One of Ireland's leading directors, Sheridan grew up on *Dublin's Northside in a working-class family (described in his brother Peter Sheridan's 1999 memoir, *44: Dublin Made Me*). Sheridan was educated at University College, Dublin, and the Abbey School of Acting. In 1977, the two brothers founded Dublin's Project Theatre Company, an alternative to Ireland's National Theatre, and supported the early work of actors such as Gabriel *Byrne and Liam *Neeson. Artistic director for New York's Irish Arts Center theater from 1982 to 1987, Sheridan returned to Ireland in 1988 to work on the movie version of Christy *Brown's autobiographical *My Left Foot* (1989). Sheridan cowrote the script with Shane Connaughton and directed the film, which won the first Oscars ever (Daniel *Day-Lewis, best actor, and Brenda Fricker, best actress) for an Irish film. Sheridan's adaptation of John B. *Keane's classic Irish drama *The Field* (1990), featuring Richard *Harris as a small farmer fighting for land against a wealthy Irish American, was followed by a trio of movies about the *Troubles. The seven-times Oscar nominated *In the Name of the Father* (1993), coscripted by Terry George, is based on Gerry Conlon's autobiographical narrative of his 1974 arrest, trial, and, wrongful imprisonment as one of the so-called *Guildford Four. Sheridan and George later cowrote *Some Mother's Son* (1996), a story about the 1981 *hunger strikes in Long Kesh (Maze) prison that stars Helen Mirren and Fionnula Flanagan. *The Boxer* (1997), starring Daniel Day-Lewis and Emily Watson, melodramatically examines love across the barricades in a divided *Belfast. Sheridan acted in Mary McGuckian's 1994 film *Words Upon the Window Pane*, wrote the screenplay for Mike Newell's mystical story about the Irish *travellers, *Into the West* (1992), and coproduced Anjelica Huston's *Agnes Brown* (1999). In 1993, with Arthur Lappin, Sheridan created Hell's Kitchen, a Dublin-based production company that continues to develop both indigenous talent and a wide range of international commercial collaborations. His film *In America* (2002) describes Irish life in the United States. C.H.

Sheridan, Richard Brinsley (1751–1816). Playwright and politician. Born in *Dublin, Sheridan first won fame with his comic play *The Rivals* (1775), which features the enduring character of Mrs. Malaprop, whose misuse of words inspired the term *malapropism*. Subsequent plays such as *The School for Scandal* (1777) and *The Critic* (1779) enhanced his reputation as a writer of comedy and a brilliant wit. In 1778, Sheridan purchased the Drury Lane Theatre, which he subsequently managed until it was destroyed by fire in 1809. Sheridan was first elected MP (member of Parliament) for Stafford in 1780. One of the most brilliant orators in the House of Commons, Sheridan was a close friend of Charles James Fox and a consistent supporter of the radical element within the Whig Party. He held a number of government offices, including the post of undersecretary for foreign affairs (1782) and treasurer of the navy (1806–7). Sheridan's later years were marked by financial problems, culminating in his arrest for debt in 1813. A.S.

shoot-to-kill. Controversial anti-terrorist policy of the security forces in *Northern Ireland. On November 11, 1982, three unarmed men were shot dead by members of a special RUC (*Royal Ulster Constabulary) anti-terrorist unit just outside Lurgan, County *Armagh. Less than two weeks later, on November 24, 1982, two youths were shot—one killed and the other seriously wounded—by the same unit in a hay shed also just outside Lurgan. Three weeks after that, on December 12, 1982, two more unarmed men were shot dead, yet again by a member of the same special unit, this time in Armagh City. Initially the shootings were investigated by the RUC. However, suspicions of a cover-up led, in May 1984, to an independent inquiry conducted by John Stalker, Deputy Chief Constable of Greater Manchester. In September 1985, Stalker delivered a highly critical interim report, recommending the prosecution of eleven RUC officers. He alleged that there was an RUC shoot-to-kill policy and an attempt to cover it up. The RUC became increasingly truculent and refused to hand over the tapes of an MI5 bug hidden at the site of one of the killings. On May 28, 1986, Stalker was relieved of his duties when rumors were raised about his association with criminal elements in Manchester. Colin Sampson, chief constable of West Yorkshire, was asked to conduct an inquiry into all allegations concerning Stalker. Sampson also took over the shoot-to-kill inquiry. Sampson largely exonerated Stalker, but after reinstatement to his post in the Greater Manchester Police, Stalker retired in March 1987. In early 1988, the British government acknowledged that the Stalker/Sampson inquiry in Northern Ireland had produced prima facie evidence of a conspiracy to pervert the course of justice by RUC men, but announced that, for reasons of national security, no criminal proceedings would take place. M.M.

Siamsa Tíre. The national folk theater of Ireland based in Tralee, County *Kerry. Started by Father Pat Ahern in 1974, the theater combines drama with traditional *music. In association with Tralee Institute of Technology, it offers a degree program in drama teaching and traditional music performance courses. F.V.

Sinn Féin. *Political party. Founded in 1905 by Arthur *Griffith as a *nationalist party, Sinn Féin remained marginal to the growing *Volunteer movement until after the 1916 *Easter Rising. In 1917, it was effectively re-formed as a *republican party and quickly became the militant nationalist opposition to the moderate nationalist (*home rule) *Irish Parliamentary Party. In the 1918 British general election, Sinn Féin won 73 of the 105 seats and in the territory of what would become the *Free State, 70 out of 75. The elected Sinn Féin candidates refused to take their seats in Westminster and instead established their own parliament in *Dublin—the first *Dáil Éireann—on January 21, 1919. Sinn Féin split on the issue of the *Anglo-Irish Treaty in 1922, with pro-treaty Sinn Féin renaming itself *Cumann na nGaedheal. Anti-treaty Sinn Féin split in 1926 with the majority joining Éamon *de Valera's newly formed *Fianna Fáil. Sinn Féin remained largely in the political margins until 1968, though they did win four seats in the Irish general election of 1957, at the start of the IRA (*Irish Republican Army) "Border Campaign."

As the civil rights campaign in *Northern Ireland heightened expectations of change and brought a repressive response from the *Unionist government, Sinn Féin saw a new opportunity for growth. The party, however, split on the issue of whether to recognize and take seats in the parliaments in Dublin, Belfast, and London. The majority, labeled "official" Sinn Féin, moved to a more reformist position, supported a cease-fire by the "official IRA," and eventually renamed themselves the Workers Party, abandoning nationalism altogether. The minority faction in 1969, "Provisional Sinn Féin," grew rapidly as a grassroots political force and was eventually the only party to use the name Sinn Féin.

Sinn Féin was a minor part of the republican campaign against British rule in Northern Ireland in the 1970s, with the IRA clearly the dominant organization. After the *hunger strikes of 1981, with the election of IRA hunger striker Bobby Sands to the British Parliament, Sinn Féin was drawn into serious electoral politics, receiving, on average, the support of 40 percent of the nationalist community. Gerry *Adams was elected to the British Parliament (but did not take his seat) in 1983 and became president of the party that autumn. Fearful that Sinn Féin, with its close links to the IRA, would become the dominant nationalist party in Northern Ireland, the British and Irish governments signed the *Anglo-Irish Agreement of 1985, to demonstrate the capacity of constitutional politics to deliver reform and to marginalize Sinn Féin.

In the late 1980s, the Sinn Féin leadership recognized that the combination of its electoral support and an IRA campaign (largely though not fully contained by the British army and *Royal Ulster Constabulary) could not break the political stalemate. Neither was any progress being made in talks between moderate nationalists, unionists, and the two governments. A series of secret talks, initially between Gerry Adams and the *Social Democratic and Labour Party (SDLP) leader John *Hume, and later involving representatives of the Irish government, eventually led to an IRA cease-fire in August 1994. In the post-cease-fire period, and especially after the *Good Friday agreement (1998) (which Sinn Féin endorsed), the party made considerable political progress, increasing support at each election until it had become the main nationalist

Skellig Michael, County Kerry

party in Northern Ireland by June 2001. The party's support is built on a continuing radical republican position, combined with a left-wing economic program and a very serious commitment to community politics. Sinn Féin also began to build a significant level of support in the *Republic, having their first TD (Teachta Dála; member of Parliament) in many years elected to the Dáil in 1997, and increasing their number of TDs to five in 2002. In 2004, the party won two seats (one in the Republic and one in Northern Ireland) in the European Parliament. J.D.

Skellig Michael. Island in the Atlantic, seven miles off the *Kerry coast. Skellig Michael was a monastery and place of *pilgrimage first mentioned in 823. Difficult to land on, it has six *beehive huts with square interiors, two oratories (all built in the corbel technique), a cemetery, a hermitage, and a lighthouse. P.H.

Sligo, County. Maritime county in the province of *Connacht in the west of Ireland. Sligo, covering an area of 709 square miles, has a population of 58,178 (2002 census). Bordered on the east by *Leitrim, on the west and south by *Mayo, and on the southeast by *Roscommon, Sligo is famous for its natural beauty. The county's most celebrated natural sites include the mountains Ben Bulben, at the foot of which the poet William Butler *Yeats is buried in Drumcliff churchyard, and Knocknarea, which is claimed to be the burial place of the mythic Queen Maeve of the legend **Táin Bó Cuailnge* (The Cattle Raid of Cooley). In the west of the county lie the Ox Mountains and in the southeast the Curlews. Principal rivers are the Sligo, the Arrow, the Owenmore, and the Esk, and lakes include Lough Gill, Lough Arrow, and Lough Colt. The name Sligo itself is derived from the Irish *Sligeach*, meaning river of shells. It is believed to refer to the large number of shellfish in Sligo Bay.

Until the seventeenth century, the county was dominated by the O'Connor family. The poet W. B. Yeats, who spent part of his childhood in his grandfather's substantial home in Sligo, was greatly influenced by the county's stunning landscape and its *folklore. Important archaeological sites include the *passage-graves at *Carrowmore and Carrowkeel and a monastic site at Inishmurray, which was founded in the sixth century. Rosses Point, just outside Sligo town, has a famous *golf links course. The main towns in the county are Sligo town, the county capital, Collooney, Ballymote, and Tubbercurry. The county enjoys a reputation for traditional Irish *music, and the distinct Sligo style is exemplified in the recordings of Michael *Coleman. Coney Island lies in the bay off Sligo town; the name was also given to a a famous section of Brooklyn in New York City. A.S.

Smith de Bruin, Michelle (1969–). Swimmer. Born in Rathcoole, County *Dublin, she made sporting history when she won one bronze and three gold medals at the Atlanta Olympics in 1996. She received a four-year competitive ban in 1998 for tampering with the results of a random drug test. She has always protested her innocence. B.D.

soccer. An immensely popular sport both nationally and internationally. The Irish Football Association (IFA) was formed in *Belfast in 1880. Following the *partition of Ireland, the game's organizing body was divided into two administrations, the IFA for *Northern Ireland and the *Dublin-based Football Association of Ireland (FAI) for the *Irish Free State. Ireland's first international game was a 1926 friendly, noncompetitive appearance against Italy in Turin.

Despite a smaller population to choose from, Northern Ireland enjoyed greater success abroad, qualifying for three World Cups (Sweden, 1958; Spain, 1982; and Mexico, 1986). The *Republic of Ireland finally reached the World Cup in Italy in 1990, and then in the United States in 1994 and in Japan/South Korea in 2002.

The IFA and FAI each run semiprofessional leagues for Irish soccer clubs. Linfield is the most successful Northern club while Shamrock Rovers leads the honors list in the Republic. However, both leagues have declined in popularity since the 1960s and the vast majority of top Irish soccer players now pursue their professional careers in England.

Belfast's George *Best is Ireland's best-known soccer player. Pat Jennings from Newry, County *Down, is internationally recognized as one of the most outstanding goalkeepers. Other major players include Liam Brady, Paul McGrath, John Giles, Noel Cantwell, Charlie Hurley, and Roy Keane. F.S.

Social Democratic and Labour Party (SDLP). Until recently, the largest of the *nationalist parties in *Northern Ireland. The SDLP was formed on August 21, 1970, from a coalition of nationalists, *socialists, and anti-*unionists at a time of escalating violence. Its first leader was the socialist

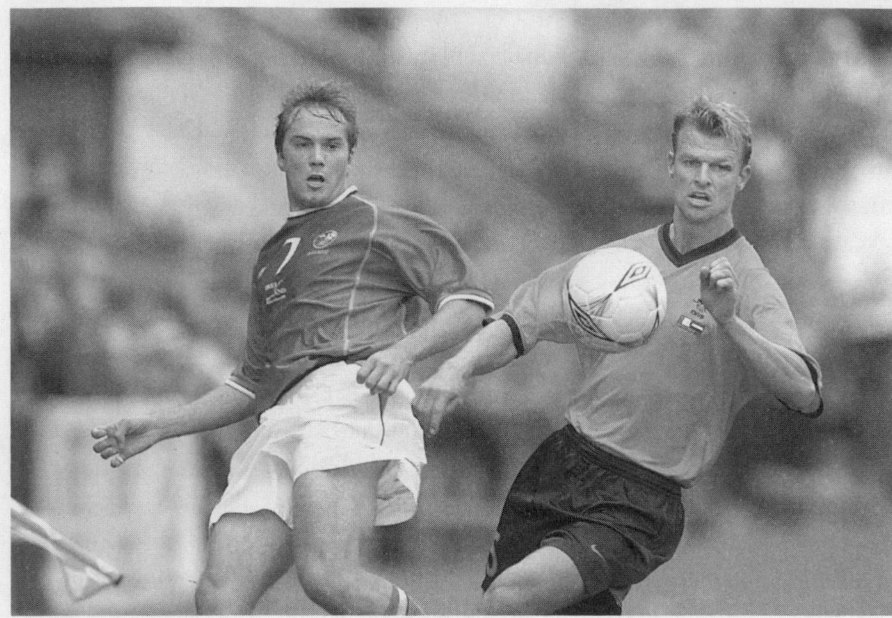

Soccer

Belfast politician Gerry Fitt. The party initially absorbed much of the traditional *Nationalist Party support. It claimed to focus on social and economic issues and advocated eventual Irish unity by agreement. In 1971, under pressure from *Sinn Féin, the SDLP withdrew from the local *Stormont Parliament in protest at British army repression and later *internment without trial. In September 1972, the party proposed a form of joint sovereignty by the British and Irish governments for Northern Ireland. After constitutional negotiations, the SDLP became part of the historic power-sharing Executive, which lasted from January to May 1974. The party was gravely disappointed when the power-sharing Executive collapsed because of a loyalist strike. The SDLP hardened its nationalist position and its socialist founders, including Gerry Fitt, drifted away disillusioned.

In 1979, John *Hume replaced Fitt as party leader. Despite Sinn Féin's increased involvement in electoral politics during the 1981 *hunger strikes, the SDLP retained its position as the leading nationalist party in Northern Ireland. Newly confident, the SDLP took part in the New Ireland Forum in the 1980s, which sought to reconsider nationalist grievances and attitudes. The party's candidates Séamus *Mallon and Eddie McGrady won seats in the British Parliament in 1986 and 1987, respectively. Beginning in 1988, John Hume initiated a secret and controversial series of talks with Gerry *Adams, president of Sinn Féin and MP (member of Parliament) for West *Belfast, in an attempt to persuade the republican movement that politics could prove more fruitful than violence. Despite initial failure, dialogue was resumed in 1993 following the *Downing Street Declaration (December 1993). These talks would prove essential to the success of the *peace process and the *Good Friday Agreement.

Of all the political parties, the SDLP was probably most pleased with the 1998 Good Friday Agreement. The agreement's emphasis on power-sharing and North-South cooperation were particularly satisfying to the party because they reflected the long-held aspirations of its nationalist constituency. Ironically, however, by drawing republicanism from violence, the SDLP helped make Sinn Féin a potent threat to its domination of the nationalist electorate. In 2001, Sinn Féin outstripped the SDLP in electoral support and John Hume resigned as leader. The party receives about 22 percent of the Northern Ireland vote in elections and its support comes predominantly from middle-class and working-class Catholics. M.M.

socialism. For over a century, socialism has been a minority force on the fringe of Irish politics. In 1896, James *Connolly formed the Irish Socialist Republican Party, and later he organized the Socialist Party of Ireland. Although the Socialists Connolly and James *Larkin were prominent in the labor movement before *World War I, socialism did not emerge as a significant political force.

Socialists took part in strikes and *soviets between 1918 and 1922, but even then remained marginal. The *Labour Party soon dropped its early socialist rhetoric. In the twenties and thirties, the *Communist Party gained little support. In 1934, left-wing IRA (*Irish Republican Army) members, led by the Socialist Peadar *O'Donnell, joined with Communists in the short-lived Republican Congress. Increasing *Catholic Church hostility toward socialism (from the 1930s) and cold war propaganda (from the 1950s) created a hostile climate for such politics.

The Workers' Party, adhering to Stalinism, emerged from the 1970 IRA split and won some *Dáil (Parliament) seats in the 1980s. With the collapse of the Soviet Union, leading Workers' Party members formed a social democratic party, Democratic Left, and then merged with the Labour Party. The Labour Party, despite its 1969 slogan "the seventies will be socialist," has never adhered to ideological socialism. Today, a Trotskyist party, the Socialist Party, has one TD (Teachta Dála; member of Parliament) in the Dáil, Joe Higgins.

Ireland has one of Europe's weakest socialist movements. In *Northern Ireland, which was the industrial base of the island, socialists faced the obstacles of sectarianism and the ongoing *nationalist/*unionist conflict. Until recently, the *Republic of Ireland had a weak industrial proletariat; but more significantly, workers felt no need for socialism. They supported populist nationalist parties—first *Sinn Féin and then *Fianna Fáil—which absorbed working-class protest by offering reforms and waving the green flag. P.D.

Somerville and Ross. (Pen names for Edith Somerville, 1858–1949, and Violet Martin, 1862–1915). Novelists. Cousins and members of an Anglo-Irish family, Somerville and Ross coauthored many popular novels which portrayed the life of the rural gentry in Ireland. Their best-known works include *The Real Charlotte* (1894) and *Some Experiences of an Irish R.M.* (1899). S.A.B.

song, English-language. Introduced to Ireland after the twelfth century, it became particularly popular from the seventeenth century onward. After the demise of the *Irish language following the Great *Famine in the mid-nineteenth century, English-language song became widespread. Ancient English ballads still survived up to the 1960s in the mouths of traveling singers such as John Reilly. Other forms of English-language song include: the interface macaronic song (with mixed Irish and English-language lyrics); the political-allegorical

*Jacobite song; the florid, Gaelic-idiom "hedge-schoolmaster" song; the *Ulster ballad city-specific or "street" styles; regional traditions (particularly distinctive in *Wexford and *Clare); political song; emigration song; Napoleonic song; sporting songs; place-praise song; satirical and comic song; popular nineteenth-century music-hall song; and Irish American song. Modern ballad styles have been created by the *Clancy Brothers, the *Dubliners, and others who combine theatrical performance with traditional type melody. F.V.

soviets. Term applied in Ireland to workers' councils, workplace seizures, and local general strikes in the years 1918–22. Most soviets involved the Irish Transport and General Workers' Union (ITGWU). During a wave of strikes for wage increases, the Irish labor movement widely employed Bolshevik rhetoric and symbols, including the red flag. While workers' socialist intentions should not be exaggerated, labor's awareness of its own strength peaked in these years.

In May 1920, workers seized thirteen creameries in County *Limerick, and raised the red flag over the central factory at Knocklong where *Socialist ITGWU organizers directed the "Knocklong soviet." At Arigna, County *Roscommon, coal miners seized mines and operated them for two months. Elsewhere, flour mills, gasworks, and factories were taken over. Workers also took direct action in support of the national cause during the *War of Independence (1919–21). For example, the "Limerick soviet" of April 1919 was a nine-day general strike in the city against British militarism. During a national strike for the release of *republican prisoners in April 1920, *trade union councils, often calling themselves *soviets,* took over the administration of many towns. From 1921, an economic slump led employers to reduce wages, forcing workers on the defensive. About eighty soviets occurred in 1922, mostly in *Munster. But the labor movement was weakening, and the *Free State army assisted employers and farmers in ending the occupations. P.D.

Spanish Armada (Sept.–Oct. 1588). Failed naval expedition of Philip II of Spain to conquer England. It turned to disaster through bad weather and English counterattack. Possibly more than twenty ships foundered on Irish coasts from *Antrim to *Kerry. The treasures from one—the *Girona*—are displayed in the *Ulster Museum in *Belfast. Only in rare instances did the Irish offer help or refuge to the Spanish survivors. Some places in Ireland are particularly identified with the Spanish Armada, such as the village of Spanish Point in County *Clare, near which several of the Armada's ships were wrecked during a fierce storm. P.H.

Spanish Civil War (1936–39). Ireland's political left and right saw the Civil War in Spain as an opportunity to revive their political fortunes. Left-wing and *republican activists followed Frank Ryan to serve with the International Brigades. Eoin *O'Duffy, hoping to regain his popularity by defending *Catholicism, took six hundred *Blueshirts to fight for Franco. T.C.

Spenser, Edmund (1552–99). English poet and administrator. Born in London, Spenser was secretary to the Lord Deputy Grey in Ireland in 1580. In 1588, he acquired an estate at Kilcolman Castle, County *Cork, where he wrote most of his poetic works, notably the allegorical epic *The Faerie Queene* (1590–96). Spenser's writing is profoundly influenced by his Irish experience. He depicts the mountains and rivers around Kilcolman as an Edenic pastoral landscape in *Colin Clouts Come Home Againe*

(1591), in Book 6 of *The Faerie Queene*, and in *Cantos of Mutabilitie* (published posthumously in 1609). In contrast, he repeatedly attacks Irish culture and society as inimical to law, civility, and love of goodness, and espouses the view that the Irish "must be altogether subdued . . . by the sword, for all [their] evils must first be cut away with a strong hand before any good can be planted." He argues this view at length in *A View of the Present State of Ireland* (written 1596, printed 1633), and gives it vehement poetic expression in *The Faerie Queene*, Book 5. Kilcolman was destroyed during the *O'Neill rebellion in 1598, and Spenser fled to London where he died in poverty. J.MD.

sport. Sport has always been an essential part of Irish life. *Hurling has been played in Ireland since *pre-Christian *Celtic times and as far back as 1272 B.C. Since its inception in 1884, the *Gaelic Athletic Association (GAA) has built an infrastructure for the indigenous sports, hurling and *Gaelic football, and provided recreation and leisure facilities for vast numbers of the population. International sporting events, such as the World Cup tournaments in *soccer and *rugby, the Olympic Games, and the Tour de France cycling race, have become for Irish people a means of expressing their national identity. Levels of public funding for sport, however, have traditionally been low. This has been countered by the GAA's organizational success and the voluntary efforts of countless coaches across a wide range of sports. Established in 1987, the National Lottery, which funds sports and the arts, and the economic prosperity of the 1990s have given sport in Ireland a much needed financial boost.

Although inevitably influenced by the evolution of organized sport in Britain, sport in Ireland hasn't been as thoroughly reliant on elite education. This is largely because one of the GAA's original missions was to wrest control of sport and athletics from the existing socially elite administration as part of its revival of the national games of hurling and Gaelic football. Soccer and rugby have traditionally based their seasons on the academic year, reflecting the importance of universities and secondary schools to those sports. The GAA promoted Gaelic football and hurling as summer pursuits. While Gaelic games were stronger in rural areas, soccer was associated with British garrisons, generally in cities or big towns, where it was played by soldiers and gradually developed a base in these urban areas. Until it became a professional sport in the 1990s, rugby was largely based in the universities and private, middle-class schools. Because it was played overwhelmingly by the professional classes, rugby in Ireland was a reluctant convert to professionalism.

The *partition of Ireland in the 1920s created difficulties for soccer and athletics. Eventually soccer administration was split between the Football Association of Ireland (FAI) in the *Republic, and Irish Football Association (IFA) in *Northern Ireland. The refusal of the National Athletic and Cycling Association of Ireland (NACAI) to cede control of athletics in Northern Ireland led to recognition disputes at the Olympic Games in 1936 and 1948.

Young Irish athletes have traditionally relied on US college scholarships. Many of the top Irish track and field performers of the past fifty years, including Eamonn Coughlan, Ronnie *Delaney, Marcus O'Sullivan, Niall Cusack, Sonia *O'Sullivan, and John Treacy, have benefited from their training in the United States.

Water sports of all kinds are found throughout Ireland. Sailing is popular in coastal areas, particularly *Dublin and *Cork, and the rivers and lakes are home to Irish rowing. The Irish Amateur

Rowing Union celebrated its centenary in 1999, but the sport has been established in Ireland for much longer with Irish clubs competing at the Henley regatta in England since the 1870s. Swimming became popular, especially since the success of Michelle *Smith de Bruin at the Atlanta Olympics of 1996. (In 1998, Smith de Bruin was accused of tampering with a drug test and banned from competition for four years. She has always protested her innocence.)

Field hockey, especially women's hockey, is a favorite sport played in many schools. The 1994 Women's World Cup of field hockey was held in Dublin. Similarly, basketball, with a semiprofessional league in both the men's and women's game, has been an established sport in Ireland since the 1950s. Women's Gaelic football is the fastest-growing sport in the country, with crowds of over twenty thousand attending its All-Ireland senior finals. The longer-established sport of *camogie (women's hurling) is also widely played. Regional sports include road bowling, played principally in County Cork in the south of Ireland and County *Armagh in the north, and rounders—a little-known version of baseball that is actually one of the GAA's four national games, along with Gaelic football, hurling, and handball. *Golf is one of the most popular leisure sports in the country. Boxing, especially at the amateur level, has had a big following in contemporary Ireland.

Ireland as an independent nation, represented by Dr. Pat O'Callaghan in hammer-throwing, won its first Olympic gold medal in 1928, at the Amsterdam Olympic Games. O'Callaghan won another gold medal in hammer-throwing in Los Angeles, in 1932, the same year that Robert Tisdall won the gold medal in the four-hundred-meters hurdles. Other Irish Olympic medalists include: John McNally (silver medal, 1952, boxing), Ronnie Delaney (gold medal, 1956, fifteen hundred meters), Fred Tiedt (silver medal, 1956, boxing), Tony Byrne, Freddie Gilroy, and John Caldwell (bronze medals, 1956, boxing), Jim McCourt (bronze medal, 1964, boxing), Hugh Russell (bronze medal, 1980, boxing), David Wilkins and Jamie Wilkinson (silver medals, 1980, yachting), John Treacy (silver medal, 1984, marathon), Michael Carruth (gold medal, 1992, boxing), Michelle Smith de Bruin (three gold medals, 1996, swimming), and Cian O'Connor (gold medal, 2004, individual show-jumping. S.M.

St. Patrick's Cathedral. One of Dublin's two *Protestant cathedrals and the national cathedral of the *Church of Ireland. St. Patrick's, built on a site where St. *Patrick is said to have baptized the pagan Irish, began as a college of priests, and became a cathedral around 1220. The largest church in medieval Ireland, it was built in a harmonious early English Gothic style, and consecrated in 1254. Between 1832 and 1904, the *Guinness family financed its extensive restoration, which succeeded in leaving much of the medieval fabric intact. Its most famous dean from 1713 to 1745 was Jonathan *Swift, author of *Gulliver's Travels*, who is buried in the cathedral. P.H.

Stalker affair. See **shoot-to-kill.**

Stanford, Sir Charles Villiers (1852–1924). Composer, academic, conductor. Born into a distinguished *Dublin legal family, Stanford wrote the first of his seven symphonies at the age of twenty-four, was appointed professor of composition at the Royal College of Music in London at thirty-one, and professor of music at Cambridge four years later. His operas and orchestral works were performed in Europe and the United States by leading musicians (including Richter, Bülow, Kreisler, Mahler, and Mengelberg) and he was one of the most influential teachers in Britain. His nine operas are now neglected, but his choral music is highly prized—his Anglican church music is still in use—and his six Irish Rhapsodies (1902–23) and Irish Symphony (1887) show his traditional orchestral mastery at its best. M.D.

step-dancing. A performance genre of *dance by males and females largely focused on foot and leg movements. Its aesthetics and features make it distinct from such forms as the English "clog" dance. Step-dancing is performed either solo or in groups, mostly to set tunes of the reel, jig, and hornpipe variety. It also uses the treble reel, slip jig, single jig, and light jig. Generally step-dancing takes place within a competition or display framework. It has been taught in seasonal and weekend "schools" since the 1920s using a code of rules set mostly by An Coimisiún le Rincí Gaelacha (Commission on Irish Dancing). Older forms of step-dancing, known as *sean-nós dance, have survived mostly in the Irish-speaking *Connemara area of County *Galway. F.V.

Stephens, James (1882–1950) Writer. Born in a *Dublin slum, Stephens published his first poems in Arthur *Griffith's *Sinn Féin.* With the encouragement of George W. *Russell and W. B. *Yeats, he published his first volume of poetry, *Insurrections* (1909), and the highly colored and lyrical novels *The Charwoman's Daughter* and *The Crock of Gold* (1912). While registrar of the National Gallery, Stephens wrote a *nationalist account of the *Easter Rising, *The Insurrection in Dublin* (1916), and a collection of poems celebrating Irish themes, *Reincarnations* (1918). He subsequently lived in Paris and London, where he broadcast verse and stories for the BBC. S.A.B.

Sterne, Laurence (1713–68). Novelist. Born in Clonmel, County *Tipperary, Sterne spent part of his childhood in Ireland. His mother was Irish, his father an English soldier. Sterne is best known for his novel *Tristram Shandy* (published in a series of volumes between 1759 and 1767). Its loose narrative structure influenced many later writers, including James *Joyce. The novel also reflected Sterne's comic gifts and delight in wordplay. The best-known of his other writings is *A Sentimental Journey* (1768), an episodic and impressionistic account of a tour of France and Italy that he made in 1765. A.S.

Stoker, Bram (Abraham) (1847–1911). Novelist. Born in *Dublin and educated at Trinity College, Dublin, Stoker married Florence Balcombe, one-time fiancée of Oscar *Wilde. He entered the civil service in Dublin and wrote a standard reference book, *Duties of Clerks of Petty Sessions in Ireland.* He managed the career of his close friend, successful actor Henry Irving, until Irving's death in 1905, recording the experience in *Personal Reminiscences of Henry Irving* (1906). His first novel, *The Snake's Pass* (1891), is set in Ireland. His reputation stands on *Dracula* (1897), a complex vampiric novel, which has enjoyed popular and cult success and has spawned several films, including Murnau's *Nosferatu* (1922) and Coppola's *Dracula Love Never Dies* (1992). M.S.T.

Stormont. Parliament building of *Northern Ireland. The term is widely used to describe the *Unionist government of Northern Ireland from 1921 to 1972. During this period only one party—the *Ulster Unionist Party—ever served in government. In a sharply divided society, and with *nationalists in a clear minority, unionists were guaranteed that they would win every election. Despite their local majority, unionist policy was framed in an atmosphere of insecurity, often referred to as a siege mentality. Unionists look back on this period with nostalgia. In comparison with the period of recent conflict, the Stormont era was, for unionists, a period of relative peace, when they had at least apparent control over their destiny. For nationalists, however, the period was characterized as intensely discriminatory, often summed up by the phrase that Stormont was a "Protestant Parliament for a Protestant people," although the nationalist community made up more than one-third of the population.

The scale of nationalist alienation can perhaps best be summarized by the demands of the *Northern Ireland Civil Rights Association in the late 1960s—universal franchise, the end of gerrymandering, and an end to discrimination in employment practices, housing, and policing. The Unionist government initially refused to consider any reform, banned civil rights protests, and used the *police to harass marchers. Reform was ultimately forced upon the Unionist government by the scale of the protests, but when it did come it was "too little and too late." It was also combined with a continuing highly repressive security policy, culminating in the introduction of *internment without trial of alleged IRA (*Irish Republican Army) members (many of whom were civil rights protestors or innocent nationalists) in August 1971. The Unionist government had lost control of the situation by early 1972 and, when they refused to allow the British government to take direct responsibility for security matters, the British government suspended the Parliament and government in Northern Ireland and transferred all its powers to London, thus ending the Stormont period. J.D.

Strongbow (c.1130–76). Colloquial name for Richard fitzGilbert de Clare, the Cambro-Norman nobleman whose arrival in Ireland in 1170 marks the beginning of the *Anglo-Norman Conquest. Strongbow succeeded his father as earl of Pembroke in 1148, but his support of the pretender Stephen led to his estates being confiscated by *Henry II, the Norman king of England. In 1168, Dermot *MacMurrough, the exiled king of *Leinster, recruited Strongbow (with Henry II's consent) to fight for him in Ireland. In return, MacMurrough offered the earl his daughter Aoife (Eva) in marriage and succession to the kingship of Leinster.

Strongbow arrived in Ireland in August 1170 with about one thousand foot soldiers and two hundred knights. This force quickly took *Waterford, and on August 23, 1170, Strongbow married Dermot's daughter. After a series of battles, much of the eastern part of the country, including *Dublin, was under Norman control. Following Dermot's death in May 1171, Strongbow became lord of Leinster.

On the surface, the Normans in Ireland were acting on behalf of Henry II, but there were suspicions that Strongbow was planning to establish an independent kingdom. Henry, concerned, traveled to Ireland in 1171, and landed in Waterford on October 17 with a formidable force of four thousand men, including five hundred knights. He placed his own men in charge of the coastal cities, but after receiving Strongbow's declarations of loyalty, Henry confirmed him as ruler of Leinster.

Strongbow in a further attempt to prove his loyalty to the king, fought for Henry in Normandy in 1173–74, and returned to Ireland as the king's governor and was rewarded with the restoration of Waterford, *Wexford, and Dublin. He was, however, to be engaged in almost continuous fighting against the native Irish until his death in 1176. P.E.

Stuart, Francis (1908–2000). Novelist. Born in Townsville, Australia, Stuart was reared in County *Antrim. While still a teenager, he married Iseult, daughter of Maud *Gonne. He was interned for his participation in the *Irish Civil War. Stuart's first book was a collection of poems, *We Have Kept the Faith* (1924). Numerous prewar novels, notably *Pigeon Irish* (1932) and *Try the Sky* (1933), project the revolutionary romanticism of his formative years. In 1939, he accepted a position lecturing in Berlin, and made radio broadcasts to Ireland from there on behalf of the Axis powers. Postwar experiences of dislocation and rejection inspired later novels such as *Redemption* (1949) and *Black List Section H* (1971). Stuart returned to Ireland in 1957, where he became a controversial and influential presence. G.OB.

Sunningdale Agreement (1973). Agreement to implement the first power-sharing government in *Northern Ireland. In November 1973, three parties, the *Ulster Unionist Party (UUP), the *Social Democratic and Labour Party (SDLP), and the Alliance Party, agreed to form a power-sharing Executive to govern Northern Ireland. The "Irish Dimension"—i.e., North-South links—had yet to be sorted out, and to this end, in December 1973, the parties met at Sunningdale, a civil service training center in Britain. A "Council of Ireland" to regulate the North-South links was agreed upon. This was to include a council of ministers, in which both the Irish government and the Belfast Executive would be represented equally, and which would have an "executive and harmonizing" function. The new coalition took office on January 1, 1974. The power-sharing experiment worked well enough, but the Sunningdale Agreement proved altogether contentious. In February 1974, a United Kingdom general election was called and unionist anti-Sunningdale parties won eleven of the twelve Northern Ireland seats, gaining 51.1 percent of the votes. In May 1974, loyalist violence and a general strike in protest against the power-sharing Executive toppled the entire arrangement. Direct rule from London was reintroduced. The *Good Friday Agreement of 1998, reinstituting power sharing and the Irish dimension, has been called "Sunningdale for slow learners." M.M.

Swift, Jonathan (1667–1745). Writer. Born in *Dublin, Swift attended Kilkenny School, along with future playwright William *Congreve. When the Catholic King *James II invaded Ireland, political uncertainty drove Swift to England, where he worked as secretary to retired diplomat Sir William Temple. A year after his return to Ireland in 1694, he was ordained in the Anglican Church and in 1702 he received a doctorate in divinity from Trinity College, Dublin. An outspoken and witty man, he had little time for Deists, Freemasons, Catholics, or nonconformists and, due in part to his formidable intelligence, was subsequently given the prestigious deanship of *St. Patrick's Cathedral in 1713. Swift never married, but had long friendships with two women. One was Esther Johnson, whom he met in England and referred to as "Stella." She was younger than Swift, and little is known about their relationship except that he educated her, they wrote to each other often, and clearly enjoyed each other's company. Swift also had a friendship with Esther Vanhomrigh, whom he later named "Vanessa."

Widely regarded for such satiric works as *A Tale of a Tub*, *The Battle of the Books*, and *The Mechanical Operation of the Spirit*—all of which were published in 1704—Swift is most familiar as the author of *Gulliver's Travels*. First printed anonymously in 1726, this fictional travelogue, consisting of four parts that chronicle the adventures of Lemuel Gulliver, caused a sensation. A radical and daring narrative, the first printing became a best-seller. To protect Swift from potential political backlash, the publisher altered the original manuscript. Unhappy with these changes, Swift eventually had it reprinted nine years later the way it was originally written. *Gulliver's Travels* is considered a masterpiece. In this ingenious critique of society, Swift delivers subtle attacks against such institutions as government and church, and against the savagery of humankind. The voyage to Lilliput (where Gulliver is perceived as a giant and tied down by a swarm of tiny Lilliputians) has become part of popular culture.

Swift was also a gifted satirist who wrote numerous political articles. Many of these, written anonymously, inflamed local politicians. Under the pseudonym of "Marcus Brutus, Drapier," Swift repeatedly called for a *boycott of British goods and, although many readers knew the real identity of the famous rabble-rouser, Swift was never reported to the authorities. His most famous satiric tract is *A Modest Proposal*, which appeared in 1729 and advocated that eating babies would solve not only problems of overpopulation, but would also solve chronic malnutrition among the poor.

At the end of his life, Swift suffered from what was thought to be bouts of madness but was in fact Ménière's syndrome, which affects the inner ear, causes deafness, nausea, and a sense of dizziness. Swift contracted this disorder in his early twenties and, as he aged, the symptoms worsened. In 1742, his friends declared him of unsound mind. He died three years later and was buried next to Stella in the graveyard of St. Patrick's Cathedral. His entire fortune was used to establish a mental institution. An immensely complicated and dynamic figure, Jonathan Swift remains one of the most important writers in the English language. P.J.H.

Swift, Patrick (1927–83). Neo-realist portrait and landscape painter. Swift studied in *Dublin and Paris, and in the 1960s in London he founded *X: A Literary Magazine* with Anthony *Cronin. He wrote criticism under the pseudonym of James Mahon. M.C.

Synge, John Millington (1871–1909). Playwright. J. M. Synge is considered the most significant playwright of the *Irish Revival and one of the most important Irish playwrights of the twentieth century. Born in *Dublin, Synge, like many of the leading figures of the Irish Revival, came from a comfortable *Anglo-Irish ascendancy background. He became increasingly alienated from his class while developing an interest in Irish national culture. Having read Darwin at an early age, the young Synge renounced the evangelical *Protestantism of his family and became interested in the wonders of the natural world. He was educated at Trinity College, Dublin, and his study there of *Irish language and *literature would have a profound effect on his subsequent literary development. After graduation, he was drawn to mainland Europe, where he spent several years studying and writing. In 1896, he met W. B. *Yeats in Paris who advised him to go to the *Aran Islands to seek artistic inspiration. Synge's time on Aran constituted a turning point for the budding writer. Here he chose to live among the people and to learn to speak Irish as the islanders spoke it. Attracted to the unconventional lifestyle that he encountered on Aran, Synge also developed an interest in the lore and folktales of local storytellers. Many of these tales are collected in his fascinating account of his time on the islands, *The Aran Islands* (1907), which blends autobiography, travel writing, and folklore.

By 1902, Synge had turned to writing plays for

J. M. Synge

the emerging Irish *theater movement. He created a folk drama that was based on the stories he had gathered in his travels around Ireland and that was beholden to the rhythms and cadences of Gaelic speech. His plays are distinctive for their exuberant use of the English language as it is spoken in Ireland. His discovery of the literary potential of *Hiberno-English stands as one of his lasting achievements. Although it was fashionable for *nationalist writers to idealize the Irish peasantry at this time, Synge pledged that he would reflect the realities of rural Ireland "warts and all." Consequently, his plays caused controversy when they were first produced. The first play to be performed, *The Shadow of the Glen* (1903), which explores the subject of a loveless marriage, caused a heated row because the play's heroine leaves her husband to run away with a vagrant. *The Playboy of the Western World* (1907) caused even more outrage. This play, in which the hero is acclaimed for telling a story of how he murdered his father, caused a full-scale riot in the *Abbey Theatre when it was first produced. Audience members who had come to expect idealized versions of Irishness blamed Synge for defaming the image of the nation. Other plays include: *Riders to the Sea* (1904)—widely regarded as an almost perfect one-act tragedy—*The Well of the Saints* (1905), *The Tinker's Wedding* (1907), and the posthumously produced *Deirdre of the Sorrows* (1910). Synge was struck down by Hodgkin's disease in 1909. P.J.M.

Tailtinn Games. Annual festival of athletic contests in Old Ireland. The *rath of Tailtinn is situated near the Blackwater River, midway between Navan and Kells in County *Meath. One of the residences of the high king, Tailtinn takes its name from the ancient form of the place-name Tailtiu (meaning "valuable site"). It was the chief cultic site of the god Lugh, patron of the harvest, who was said to have introduced ball games, chess, and *horse racing to Ireland. A great assembly was held in autumn each year at Tailtinn, with games and athletic contests as the major attraction. This assembly continued until the Middle Ages. D.Oh.

Táin Bó Cuailnge (The Cattle Raid of Cooley). The most celebrated hero-tale of Ireland. The tale seems to have grown out of the dim memory of a war between the Ulaidh people of Emhain Macha (in County *Armagh) and the Connachta clan of *Tara (in County *Meath). Legends of this and related matters were strung together by the poets for the Gaelic chieftains of east *Ulster in the seventh century A.D., but in its full form the story was the compilation of authors some centuries later. The principal versions are in *Leabhar na hUidhre (The Book of the Dun Cow), The Yellow Book of Lecan, and The *Book of Leinster. The Táin tells of how Maeve (or Meadhbh), queen of the province of *Connacht in the west, wished to have a bull equal to the great white bull owned by her husband. She therefore invaded Ulster to seize the brown bull of Cooley (on the southeastern boundary of Ulster). The Ulstermen were stricken by an old curse in this hour of need, debilitating them, and only the young champion *Cúchulainn could take the field on their behalf. Cúchulainn performed prodigious feats, keeping Maeve's army at bay, and when the curse wore off the Ulster warriors routed Maeve's forces. A melodramatic high point has Cúchulainn killing his best friend, Fear Diadh, in single combat. The epic ends with the clash of the two bulls, the brown bull of Cooley rending asunder his opponent, the white bull, in a frightful contest. D.Oh.

Three Taoisigh: Seán Lemass, Jack Lynch, Charles J. Haughey

Talbot, Matt (1856–1925). Ascetic. Talbot, a *Dublin laborer and alcoholic, resolved upon a life of abstinence and piety after reading the works of St. Augustine in 1884. Considered highly eccentric even by the standards of Irish Catholic asceticism, he practiced strict penitential exercises in which he wore chains around his body and slept on a plank bed. Talbot led a campaign against alcohol and its vices mostly aimed at the poor working class of inner-city Dublin. A bridge on the River Liffey was dedicated to Talbot in 1978 and his cause for beatification is now well advanced. S.A.B.

Tandy, James Napper (1740–1803). Revolutionary *nationalist. Born in *Dublin, Tandy was prominent in radical circles from the late 1770s onward. One of the founding members of the *United Irishmen, he was the first secretary of its Dublin branch. Fearing arrest, he went to America in 1793, and then in 1797 to France. A year later, Tandy led an unsuccessful expedition of French troops, which landed on the Donegal coast. After this failure, he fled Ireland and was captured in Hamburg. Although sentenced to death at a trial held in Lifford, County *Donegal, he was not executed (due to intervention by Napoleon), but instead deported to France in 1802, where he died a year later. A.S.

Taoiseach. Prime minister of Ireland. The term *Taoiseach* (an Irish word that means "chief" or "head of the clan") originates from the 1937 *Constitution. The Taoiseach has considerable political power compared with other European prime ministers. The Taoiseach appoints other cabinet members, the attorney general, and junior ministers. The Taoiseach also nominates eleven members of the *Seanad (Senate). Most importantly, the Taoiseach can call a general election at any time (provided he or she has not lost the confidence of the *Dáil [Parliament]). In addition to constitutional powers, the Taoiseach chairs government meetings and controls the cabinet agenda. Irish prime ministers before 1937 were known as the president of the executive council. The following is a list of Taoisigh:

William T. *Cosgrave (*Cumann na nGaedheal), President of Executive Council, 1922–32
Éamon *de Valera (*Fianna Fáil), President of Executive Council, 1932–37, Taoiseach, 1937–48; 1951–54; 1957–59
John A. *Costello (*Fine Gael), 1948–51; 1954–57
Seán *Lemass (Fianna Fáil), 1959–66
Jack *Lynch (Fianna Fáil), 1966–73; 1977–79

Liam *Cosgrave (Fine Gael), 1973–77
Charles J. *Haughey (Fianna Fáil), 1979–81; March–December 1982; 1987–92
Garret *FitzGerald (Fine Gael), 1981–February 1982; 1982–87
Albert *Reynolds (Fianna Fáil), 1992–94
John *Bruton (Fine Gael), 1994–97
Bertie *Ahern (Fianna Fáil), 1997–present

Tara. The symbolic seat and coronation site of early medieval Ireland's high kings (though not their permanent residence). Located in County *Meath, this site includes a stone pillar—the Lia Fáil, or Stone of Destiny—and an earthen mound known as the Mound of the Hostages, together with many other earthworks. Many generations of the royal *O'Neill (Uí Néill) dynasty fought over this seat of power in their quest to restore the old Irish monarchy. In the nineteenth century, Tara was used to invoke the glories of ancient Ireland by Daniel *O'Connell, who held a Monster Meeting here in 1843 during the campaign to *Repeal the Act of *Union. P.H.

Tara Brooch. Ireland's most superbly crafted piece of jewelry, dating from the eighth century. The brooch was found at Bettystown, County *Meath, and given the name *Tara* by a commercially minded jeweler. It is now in the *National Museum in Dublin. The brooch's exquisite minuscule spiral, animal, and interlace designs are made of bronze, gold, amber, glass, silver, and copper. P.H.

television. The *Republic of Ireland's indigenous television service began on December 31, 1961, and developed in competition with the British Broadcasting Corporation and Ulster Television, whose signals had for several years reached parts of Ireland. Telefís Éireann, renamed Radio Telefís Éireann (*RTÉ) in 1966 after it merged with Radio Éireann, was set up as a government-controlled network, funded by license fees and advertising revenues.

Beginning in the early 1960s, television quickly became a major catalyst of social change. By importing programs from other cultures, Telefís Éireann familiarized Irish citizens with foreign values and images, and encouraged them to scrutinize their own assumptions and convictions. The service also employed foreigners and returned émigrés because, in the early 1960s, there were very few resident Irish citizens with training in television broadcasting.

Gay *Byrne's talk show *The Late Late Show*, launched in 1962, pioneered what might be termed "confrontational television." It regularly challenged the views of conservative politicians and church leaders, and greatly liberalized public discourse on such taboo topics as sex and contraception. Byrne's studio audience often participated, and the unpredictable and spontaneous nature of the show attracted viewers throughout the nation.

RTÉ's drama serials also addressed social problems. Although not subversive, the network's first hit, *Tolka Row* (1964–68), dealt with crises such as alcoholism and unemployment in a working-class *Dublin family. Uniquely Irish in content, such serials modeled their formats on Anglo-American shows. The long-running soap opera *The Riordans* (1965–79) took the serial drama out of the studio, making unprecedented use of outdoor location work.

Whereas foreign television broadcasts successfully alerted the international community to the escalation of violence in *Northern Ireland in the late 1960s and early 1970s, RTÉ was not able to cover, let alone illuminate, the conflict for its viewers. In 1971, Gerry Collins, then minister of posts and telegraphs, reissued Section 31 of the 1960 Broadcasting Act, which prohibited the broadcast of any matter engaging "the aims or activities" of paramilitary organizations. (This ban was lifted in 1994.) In 1972, when RTÉ tried to circumvent this blatant form of censorship by showing mute footage of IRA (*Irish Republican Army) members, the government dismissed the entire RTÉ governing body.

RTÉ has nevertheless maintained a high-quality national service, especially in serial drama, news, and current affairs. Recently it has been criticized for its dearth of serious dramas—single plays, miniseries, and serials. By 1980, the percentage of Irish programs had fallen to 30 percent because importing programs was often cheaper than making them in Ireland. Some media critics have urged greater state financial support for indigenous television.

While there is no privatized alternative to the national network in the Republic, RTÉ has never enjoyed a monopoly due to competition from foreign broadcasting companies. In addition to RTÉ's three channels (RTÉ 1, Network 2, Teilifís na Gaeilge) and the independent TV3 station (launched in 1998), most people watch on cable and satellite channels programs from the United States, Great Britain, and, increasingly in the past decade, from Australia. E.M.

textiles. Woolen and linen textiles have been manufactured in Ireland from *pre-Christian times, while Irish lace became famous in the 1800s.

Sheep rearing is one of Ireland's main *economies, especially in the mountainous areas of the country and in places with poorer soil. After the *Anglo-Norman invasion, large-scale wool production began, particularly within abbeys. The southeast was the most important area of production, and much of the output was exported. Cloaks of coarse cloth and frieze were the most widely produced woolen commodities, and England was a major market. During the 1600s, regulations to ensure that Irish wool went exclusively to England were passed, culminating in the 1699 Woollen Act, which effectively ended Ireland's export trade to any other country.

Contemporaneously, flax, the raw material for linen, was grown extensively throughout Ireland. Fibers from this plant are woven into linen cloth, bleached, and dyed to produce the finished textile. In the 1700s, an influx of skilled settlers, strong British demand, and encouragement from *landlords and government, combined to make linen Ireland's major industry. The area of heaviest linen production—both coarse and fine—was *Ulster, though coarse-linen manufacture was common throughout Ireland until the 1840s. At this time linen weaving took place mainly within individual cottages, with bleaching and dying in specialized bleach yards. From the 1820s onward, English competition and falling domestic demand caused both coarse-linen manufacturing and cottage-based weaving to decline. In nineteenth-century Ulster, however, due to a lack of foreign competition, continuing international demand, and the mechanization of production within factories, fine-linen manufacture continued to expand, making a major contribution to the province's industrialization. By the mid-1800s, *Belfast was the fine-linen capital of the world, with a global reputation for quality. In the face of growing competition from artificial textiles, however, the fine-linen industry declined from the early 1900s onward, though it did not die out.

Despite the impact of the 1699 Woollen Act, domestic demand ensured that the wool industry remained important in the 1700s, with coarse woolen cloth also being manufactured on a cottage industry basis. Likewise, fine woolen cloth manufacturing developed in major towns in the 1700s, especially *Dublin. Competition from British exports caused this industry to die away from the late 1700s. The same pressures began to affect cottage-based coarse woolen cloth manufacturing in the nineteenth century, though it still managed to survive in many parts into the late 1800s, notably on the west coast. The latter half of this century also saw major developments in factory-based woolen cloth manufacturing. This sector grew significantly, due to concentration on niche products, such as blarney tweed.

Meanwhile, lacemaking, brought from France in the 1700s, became an important craft in many parts of the country in the mid-1800s. Limerick lace, the most famous style of Irish lace, was first produced at Mount Kennet, County *Limerick, in 1829. Strictly speaking, this is not true lace, but rather an embroidered machine-made net, which was first introduced into Ireland by an English entrepreneur.

Lace production as a whole grew greatly in the mid-1800s, mainly because a number of individuals and groups, particularly *nuns, wished to provide some measure of *Famine relief. Lacemaking also helped to offset the financial losses of some households after the decline of the coarse-linen industry. *Women were central to this handicraft, and their earnings were important to their standing within Irish society. At the end of the nineteenth century, the Congested Districts Board and the Department of Agriculture established classes to improve the quality of Irish lace.

The production of lace, wool, and fine-linen goods continues in Ireland today, and these Irish textiles have become world-renowned. J.C.

Thatcher, Margaret (1925–). British Conservative prime minister, 1979–90. Known as the "Iron Lady" because of her intransigent conservative politics, Thatcher continually clashed with *republicans, nationalists, and unionists in *Northern Ireland. She refused to recognize the H-Block prisoners' political status during their 1980 *hunger strike. However, the same year, she held a high-level meeting with *Taoiseach (prime minister) Charles *Haughey at *Dublin Castle that seemingly acknowledged the Irish government's place in Northern Ireland affairs. When the hunger strikes resumed in 1981, Thatcher remained opposed to the strikers' demands, even after Bobby Sands's election to Parliament, and the death of Sands and nine other hunger strikers. In October 1984, Thatcher barely survived a Provisional IRA (*Irish Republican Army) assassination attempt during the Conservative Party's annual conference in Brighton. A month later, she firmly rejected the New Ireland Forum's (a meeting of constitutional nationalists) solutions to the Northern Ireland crisis in her infamous "out, out, out" speech: a united Ireland, a federal structure consisting of the Irish *Republic and Northern Ireland, and joint rule by Dublin and London—were all out of the question. Pressed by US President Ronald Reagan to maintain dialogue with constitutional nationalists, however, Thatcher signed the *Anglo-Irish Agreement in November 1985. The agreement, which gave the Irish government a direct consultative role in Northern Ireland for the first time, infuriated unionists. Ultimately, Thatcher was reviled by republicans, resented by nationalists, and distrusted by unionists. R.D.

theater. The Irish dramatic tradition goes back to at least the fourteenth century, with the performance of miracle plays and pageants. During the Renaissance, most plays were produced privately in great houses, but around 1635, a theater was built in Werburgh Street, *Dublin. It closed in 1640. In 1662, English dramatist John Fletcher's *Wit Without Money* was the first play to be performed at the newly opened Smock Alley Theatre. Shakespeare was a favorite, but there were few productions of contemporary plays. The Smock Alley Theatre closed in 1689, during *William of Orange's campaign in Ireland, but it reopened in 1692.

A theater opened in Aungier Street in 1734. Around this time, Dublin theaters introduced changes in performance, including more elaborate stage machinery. Thomas Sheridan became manager of Smock Alley in 1745 and made reforms that professionalized the theater business and curtailed rowdy audience behavior. A former Smock Alley actor, Spranger Barry opened a theater in Crowe Street, Dublin, in 1760, for which *Donegal-born Charles Macklin, who was already successful in London, wrote his first Irish play, *The True-Born Irishman*. Dublin theater companies began touring other cities on a more frequent basis. In *Cork, the Theatre Royal had opened its doors in 1736, followed in 1770 by similar venues in *Belfast and *Limerick.

In 1784, Robert Owenson (Lady *Morgan's father) opened the Fishamble Street Theatre in Dublin. Dedicated to staging patriotic plays, he gave theater a more Irish flavor. The Crowe Street Theatre was demolished and replaced in 1821 by the Theatre Royal in Hawkins Street. The Queen's Royal Theatre opened in 1844. Thus far, the Irish theater world produced few Irish playwrights, but this changed with the arrival in Dublin in 1861 of Dion *Boucicault, who by then had already had a successful career in London and New York. Boucicault added an Irish setting and characters to traditional sentimental comedy. His play *The Colleen Bawn* received its Irish premiere at Hawkins Street in 1861. In 1884 the Queen's Royal Theatre declared itself the "home of Irish drama" with productions of political melodramas like Hubert O'Grady's *The Fenian* (1888) and J. W. Whitbread's *Wolfe Tone* (1898). In Dublin, the *Gaiety Theatre opened in 1871, followed by the Star of Erin Music Hall (now the Olympia Theatre) in 1879. In 1880, the Theatre Royal burned down. In Belfast, the magnificent Grand Opera House opened in 1895. At the turn of the twentieth century, the Irish drama scene became increasingly international, with visiting performances by the likes of Sarah Bernhardt, and touring productions of Maeterlinck, Ibsen, and Sudermann.

In 1897 W. B. *Yeats, Lady *Gregory, and Edward *Martyn established a national theater, the Irish Literary Theatre, dedicated to staging Irish plays. Its first performance, in 1899, was Yeats's *The Countess Cathleen*. In 1903, the Irish Literary Theatre joined forces with Frank and William *Fay to form the National Dramatic Society. Annie Horniman sponsored the purchase of buildings for the National Dramatic Society in Abbey Street, and the *Abbey Theatre opened on December 27, 1904, with performances of plays by Yeats and Lady Gregory. The Fay brothers, who had previous experience as actors and directors, would significantly influence the development of the Abbey Company's understated acting style. Also in 1904, Bulmer Hobson and Lewis Purcell founded the *Ulster Literary Theatre, which would develop plays that reflected the defining characteristics of northern Irish society. The Abbey's staging of J. M. *Synge's *The Playboy of the Western World* in 1907 caused a riot when the audience objected to what it perceived as the play's disparaging depiction of the west of Ireland. In 1910, Miss Horniman withdrew her support, and from then on the

Abbey increasingly staged rural comedies, much to Yeats's chagrin. In 1925 the Abbey was granted an annual government subsidy, establishing its position as the national theater.

Also in 1925, at a time when traveling companies were fast disappearing, Anew *McMaster set up his own touring company to bring Shakespeare to the Irish provinces. Two of its members, Micheál *MacLiammóir and Hilton *Edwards, became the directors of Ireland's first Irish-language theater, An Taibhdhearc, which opened in *Galway in 1928. In the same year, the partners started the *Gate Theatre company, which staged a groundbreaking production of Oscar *Wilde's *Salomé*. The Gate Theatre, which acquired a venue in the Rotunda Buildings on Parnell Square, Dublin, in 1930, was dedicated to a modern, international repertoire. Early productions included Eugene O'Neill's *The Hairy Ape* and Strindberg's *Simoom*.

Seán *O'Casey's politicized social melodrama dominated the Abbey stage in the early 1920s, including *The Shadow of a Gunman* (1923), *Juno and the Paycock* (1924), and *The Plough and the Stars* (1926). The depiction of the heroes of the *Easter Rising in the latter play led to protests during its opening run. Yeats wrote some of his best dramas in his later years, including *Purgatory* (1938), but he was troubled by the mainstream direction taken by the Abbey, an approach furthered by Ernest *Blythe, the Abbey's managing director from 1941 to 1967. The Abbey Theatre burned down in 1951, and was rebuilt in 1966.

The Amateur Dramatic Association (founded in 1932) and its many member organizations became a rich breeding ground for local talent, many of whom became professional actors. Amateur standards were high, and the first competitive All-Ireland Drama Festival was held in Athlone in 1953. Professional theater, which had become less exciting, did have some notable moments, especially when Samuel *Beckett's *Waiting for Godot* received its English-language premiere at the Pike Theatre, Dublin, in 1955. In 1957 the Pike's director, Alan Simpson, was arrested when a production of Tennessee Williams's *The Rose Tattoo* led to charges of obscenity. The following year, the fledgling Dublin Theatre Festival was canceled when O'Casey withdrew his play *The Drums of Father Ned*, because the archbishop of Dublin refused to sanction the staging of Alan McClelland's *Bloomsday*, an adaptation of James *Joyce's *Ulysses*.

The 1960s, an era of economic and social renewal, also heralded a new era in the theater, which saw a plethora of new talent, including playwrights like John B. *Keane, Brian *Friel, Tom *Murphy, and Thomas *Kilroy. Memorable Dublin premieres include Friel's *Philadelphia, Here I Come!* at the Gaiety Theatre in 1964, and Kilroy's *The Death and Resurrection of Mr. Roche* (1968). The innovative Druid Theatre was founded in *Galway in 1975 by Garry *Hynes, Marie Mullen, and Mick Lally. In 1980, Brian Friel and actor Stephen *Rea staged the first play of their *Field Day Theatre Company, which was dedicated to creating a "fifth province of the imagination" that would overcome set ways of political and sectarian thinking. The play, Friel's *Translations*, was performed, to universal acclaim, in the Guildhall in Derry, with a cast including Ray McAnally and Liam *Neeson. Over the years, Irish theater has produced many celebrated, often internationally acclaimed actors, including Barry *Fitzgerald, F. J. *McCormick, Siobhán *McKenna, Cyril *Cusack, and Donal *McCann. Since the 1980s, established playwrights such as Friel and Murphy have been joined by younger talent, including Frank *McGuinness, Sebastian *Barry, Marina *Carr, Conor *McPherson, and Martin *McDonagh. Irish theater since the 1980s has been characterized by increasing diversification and fragmentation, with numerous new theater groups and small theaters being founded all over the country. J.C.E.L.

Tipperary, County. Inland county in the province of *Munster. The county, divided for administrative purposes into North and South Ridings, covers 1,662 square miles and has a population of 140,281 (2002 census). Tipperary became known worldwide through the *World War I song "It's a Long Way to Tipperary." The county has a varied and beautiful landscape, ranging from the Golden Vale, to the Knockmealdown and Galtee Mountains. The legendary peaks Galtymore (3,018 feet) and Slievenamon (2,364 feet) are immortalized in song and story. Tipperary is agriculturally one of the richest counties in Ireland, with an active dairy industry centered in the fertile plain known as the Golden Vale. Rising dramatically out of this rich landscape, the Rock of *Cashel consists of a *round tower, Cormac's Chapel (twelfth century), and a Gothic cathedral, all perched on what was once the seat of the MacCarthy (MacCarrthaigh) kings of Munster. The county has a wealth of important historic monuments, with *castles at Cahir, Nenagh, Roscrea, and Carrick-on-Suir, and the abbeys of Holy Cross and Lorrha. In 1980, the Derrynaflan hoard, a treasure of early medieval metalwork, was discovered. Medieval *high crosses can be seen at Ahenny, near the *Kilkenny border.

Tipperary consists of a number of small to medium-sized prosperous towns, including Clonmel, the county capital, Thurles, where the *Gaelic Athletic Association (GAA) was established in 1884, and Tipperary town—from the Irish name *Tiobraid Árann*, "well of Ara." Natives of Tipperary include the *Fenian John *O'Leary; Gaelic poet Geoffrey *Keating; Laurence *Sterne, author of *Tristram Shandy* (who was born in Clonmel); and the novelist and Fenian Charles *Kickham. P.H.

***Titanic*.** White Star liner built by Harland and Wolff in *Belfast, which sank in the most famous maritime disaster. On April 10, 1912, the ship embarked on its maiden voyage from Southampton, England, bound for Cherbourg, France, Queenstown (Cobh), Ireland, and New York. At Queenstown, 123 Irish passengers boarded the *Titanic*. Of these, 113 were third-class passengers, aged between seventeen and twenty-five, from poor rural backgrounds, intent on beginning a new life in the United States. Just before midnight on April 14, the *Titanic* struck an iceberg about ninety-five miles south of the Grand Banks of Newfoundland. Between 1,503 and 1,517 of the 2,224 people on board perished. Of the passengers who boarded at Queenstown, only 44 survived. The wreck of the liner was located by a joint French–United States expedition in 1985. P.E.

tithes. A traditional medieval payment (10 percent of the produce of the land) levied on farmers for the support of the clergy. Tithes were first imposed in the twelfth century. After the establishment of the *Protestant *Church of Ireland in 1537, such payments were used by the new church. From the seventeenth century, members of the *Catholic majority, as well as *Presbyterians, were required to support the minority clergy. This taxation bred tremendous animosity among the roughly 90 percent of the population who were not members of the established church. By the second half of the eighteenth century, pasture lands were no longer tithable because of a resolution passed by the Irish *Parliament. The change in policy placed the tithe burden entirely on tillage lands. Compounding the problem was the fact that the clergy increasingly leased their rights of collection to brutally efficient "tithe farmers." Coupled with a rapidly growing population and corresponding increase in rents, the situation became intolerable for much of the peasantry. Resentment over tithes and other agrarian issues resulted in the appearance of secret societies in the 1760s. Overt resistance to such payments crested in the Tithe War (1830–33). In 1838, tithes were directly incorporated into rents ending the worst of the hostilities. The final removal of tithe payments came with the disestablishment of the Church of Ireland in 1869. J.P.

Titley, Alan (1947–). Writer in the Irish language. Born in *Cork, Titley has written several novels and collections of short stories in Irish, as well as a play, *Tagann Godot* (Godot Comes). *An Fear Dána* (The Daring Man; 1993), which is based on the ramblings of medieval poet Muireadhach Albanach Ó Dálaigh, is one of the finest historical novels written in Irish. He also published a definitive critique of the Gaelic novel (*An tÚrscéal Gaeilge;* 1991) and two collections of fables. A comic fabulist, Titley's prose is notable for his prodigious punning and wordplay. B.D.

Tóibín, Colm (1955–). Novelist and journalist. Born in Enniscorthy, County *Wexford, Tóibín gives a resonant depiction of a changing Ireland in such novels as *The Heather Blazing* (1992). Subsequent novels, notably *The Blackwater Lightship* (1999), focus on homosexuality, making Tóibín Ireland's leading gay novelist. *The Master* (2004), a novel based on the life of Henry James, received critical acclaim. A prominent cultural commentator, he has written nonfiction books, including *The Sign of the Cross* (1994). G.OB.

Tone, Theobald Wolfe (1763–98). Founder of the *United Irishmen. Born in *Dublin and educated at Trinity College, Dublin, and the Middle Temple, London, Tone was called to the Irish Bar in 1789. A talented polemicist, he began examining the status of his native country in the British empire. His 1790 anti-government pamphlet entitled "A review of the conduct of administration addressed to the electors and free people of Ireland" brought him to the attention of the Whig Club, a pro-reform association of intellectuals and politicians who admired Henry *Grattan. Although he disapproved of the moderation of the Whig Club, Tone participated in their activities and came under the influence of the radical MP (member of Parliament) Sir Lawrence Parsons. The latter helped Tone refine his theories about the negative role of Westminster in Irish affairs, even though the repeal of *Poynings' Law in 1782 had somewhat ameliorated the situation. After parting with the Whig Club, Tone gravitated toward a group that included Thomas Russell, an ex–army officer, Dr. William *Drennan, a *Belfast medical practitioner based in Dublin, and barrister Thomas Addis Emmet, who were anxious to exploit the opportunity for political reform in the aftermath of the *French Revolution.

Political debates sparked by the publication of Thomas *Paine's *Rights of Man* in February 1791 convinced Tone that Ireland required total separation from Britain in order to democratize the country. In 1791, Tone wrote an address to celebrants of the anniversary of the French Revolution in which he claimed it was necessary "to break the connection with England, the never-failing source of all our political evils" by "substituting the common name of Irishman, in place of the denominations of Protestant, Catholic and Dissenter." Tone reassured a skeptical element within *Presbyterian radicalism in

1791 with a brilliant polemic, "An argument on behalf of the Catholics of Ireland," in which he argued that *Catholicism was waning and that Irish Catholics were open to political alliances with other groups. This vision distinguished Tone as the key figure in the creation of the Irish *republican tradition.

Tone's organizational and propaganda skills were essential to the founding of the Society of United Irishmen in Belfast and Dublin in October/November 1791, a legal and largely middle-class association pledged to bring about an independent Irish republic. The United Irishmen sought out and ultimately absorbed kindred political societies and in early 1792 Tone accepted the secretaryship of the Catholic Committee (a national organization that sent delegates to a Catholic Convention in Dublin in December 1792). The disappointing *Catholic Relief Act of 1793 and the harsh tenor of the accompanying debates indicated to Tone that Parliament was incapable of implementing *Catholic Emancipation. The declaration of war on *France made it extremely difficult for the United Irishmen to advance their perspective. Prohibitions on public assemblies, armed bodies, and seditious publications effectively ruled out any repeat of the successes enjoyed by the *Volunteers in the early 1780s. In April 1794, Tone was offered French military assistance and from that time the United Irishmen were an avowedly revolutionary organization. However, the government discovered the overture, and the subsequent arrest of French emissary Reverend William Jackson implicated Tone in treason. The Jackson case offered the pretext of proscribing the United Irishmen, and those members who continued to meet did so under threat of *transportation. Tone was permitted to exile himself in America, and, before departing for Philadelphia from Belfast in June 1795, he and his leading associates in Dublin and Belfast remodeled the United Irishmen as a paramilitary organization. The *Defenders, a violent and sprawling anti-government movement, which drew inspiration from France, were merged with the United Irishmen.

Tone sailed to France on January 1, 1796, and successfully petitioned the French government to invade Ireland. A large army reached Bantry Bay, *Cork, in December but was unable to land because of severe weather. Tone had accompanied the French and, while bitterly disappointed, did not give up hope that his allies would try again. A small expeditionary force under General *Humbert landed in Killala, County *Mayo, in late August 1798 when the premature uprising of the United Irishmen was waning. They were contained within a month. Tone participated in a further French effort, which came to grief off the Derry coast on October 12, 1798. He was placed under arrest in Buncrana, County *Donegal, and tried for treason in the Royal Barracks, Dublin, on November 10. It is believed that Tone inflicted a mortal throat wound in Newgate prison the following day to protest the decision to hang him as a traitor rather than execute him as a uniformed officer in the French army. He died from this wound on November 19, and was buried in Bodenstown, County *Kildare, where his life and legacy is annually commemorated by various Irish republican parties. R.OD.

tower houses. Tall, often four- or five-story, *castles erected in the fifteenth, sixteenth, and early seventeenth centuries. Affluent Irish landowners built these tower houses as defenses, status symbols, and homes for their families and retainers. Sparsely furnished within, the houses sometimes had an outer protective wall. P.H.

trade unions. Irish trade unions originated in guilds and illegal workmen's associations in the eighteenth and early nineteenth centuries. Each skilled trade formed its own society, and many then joined British-based unions. In the 1890s, Irish railway workers and dockers also joined British unions. Later, Irish-based national unions emerged. James *Larkin's Irish Transport and General Workers' Union (ITGWU), founded in 1909, organized laborers, dockers, and transport workers, and launched several major strikes, culminating in the great Dublin Lockout of 1913.

In 1894, an Irish Trade Union Congress (ITUC) was formed, and Larkin and other radicals dominated the leadership from 1911. Larkin and James *Connolly hoped to build one big union as a step toward *socialism. In 1914, after the Dublin workers' defeat, Larkin left for America, and Connolly was executed as a leader of the 1916 *Easter Rising.

Wartime conditions caused unions to expand dramatically between 1917 and 1921. The ITGWU, now led by William O'Brien, increased from 5,000 members in 1916 to over 120,000 in 1920, with hundreds of branches all over the country. The southern unions supported the national struggle, and there were countless wage strikes, and short-lived *soviets. White-collar unions also expanded and joined the mainstream labor movement.

Economic depression and unemployment caused union membership to fall steeply in the 1920s. When Larkin returned from America in 1923, he clashed with the ITGWU's new leaders; from 1924 he led a breakaway Workers' Union of Ireland (WUI). The feud between Larkin and O'Brien continued through the thirties and forties, sapping the labor movement's energies. Rivalry also occurred as British and Irish unions competed for the diminishing membership.

During World War II, the *Fianna Fáil government's policy of dealing only with the larger Irish unions, and continuing rivalry between O'Brien and Larkin, caused the ITUC to split, but the unions reunited in 1959 in the Irish Congress of Trade Unions (ICTU). In 1945, the ITUC had established its *Northern Ireland Committee, which campaigned in defense of jobs and, since the 1970s, organized public demonstrations against sectarian violence.

In 1990, the ITGWU and the WUI merged to form the Services Industrial Professional and Technical Union (SIPTU), now Ireland's largest union, with over 200,000 members. It has branches throughout the south and in Northern Ireland, where British-based unions are strong. Today, in the island as a whole, sixty-five unions are attached to the ICTU, with over 680,000 members. Since the 1980s, southern unions have entered a series of national pay deals with governments and employers.

In the *Republic, union membership (as a proportion of employees) fell in the 1990s. This happened as jobs in technology and services increased, employers' attitudes toward unions hardened, and the state no longer encouraged companies to recognize or bargain with unions. The decline was mainly in the private sector. While unions face many challenges today, actual membership in the Republic is at its highest ever, at 561,800, and the Irish union movement remains one of the strongest in Europe. P.D.

transportation. The transport of convicted criminals overseas to British colonies. Transportation became a regular punishment in Ireland after the Transportation Act of 1717 was used to send some convicted criminals overseas. Neither execution nor imprisonment was deemed appropriate for these convicts and by 1789, approximately fifteen thousand Irish men, women, and children had been dispatched to plantations in the thirteen continental North American colonies. Most went to Virginia, Maryland, and Pennsylvania, but some ended up in the Carolinas, Connecticut, and Massachusetts, either as plantation workers or as indentured servants. Convicts were required to serve their employers for set periods before being emancipated and free to either settle in the colonies or return home.

The outbreak of the *American War of Independence in 1775 closed colonial ports to British and Irish shipping for eight years and created a crisis in the criminal justice system as convicts filled prisons and hulks. During this time, the illegal transportation of Irish felons to Maryland, *Newfoundland, and the Bahamas precipitated a series of diplomatic incidents which compelled the British government to include the Irish in the Botany Bay scheme, the first use of *Australia as a penal colony. The penal colony founded in Port Jackson, New South Wales (Australia), in January 1788, was initially intended for the sole use of convicts sentenced in Britain, but in 1791 Irish convicts were also sent to Australia (on the Queen) as part of the Third Fleet. At least forty-eight thousand Irish convicts were transported to Australian penal colonies by 1853 and small numbers of political prisoners were sent to Western Australia in 1868.

From 1840, when transportation to New South Wales ceased, Van Diemen's Land (Tasmania) was the destination of virtually all Irish convicts until 1853. Many of them had been tried during the *Famine years and were not regarded by the authorities as hardened recidivists. *United Irishmen and *Defenders, who comprised a sizable number of Irish transportees between 1793 and 1806, mounted a series of armed challenges to the colonial administration in 1800 and 1804. Members of the revolutionary *Young Ireland and *Fenian movements were also exiled in Australia. Some of them integrated into colonial society while others, such as John Boyle *O'Reilly and Thomas Francis *Meagher, escaped to America. R.OD.

travellers. Irish gypsies. There are an estimated twenty-five thousand travellers living in Ireland. It is commonly believed that they are the descendants of *Famine victims or of those dispossessed during *Cromwellian times. Though their ranks may well have swollen during these upheavals, neither theory is now thought to hold much weight. There is plenty of historical evidence to show that travellers existed in Ireland prior to these events. The surnames Tynkler and Tynker began to appear in the twelfth century and the Acte for Tynkers and Peddlars was issued in 1551. In 1834, the Royal Commission on the *Poor Laws made a clear distinction between "ordinary beggars" and "wandering tynkers." (The word "tinker" was used interchangeably with "traveller" or "gypsy.") It would appear therefore that Ireland, in common with most other European countries, had an indigenous community of traveling tradesmen and tinsmiths from medieval times.

Though Irish travellers have a similar lifestyle to European gypsies or Romanies and share a history of persecution, they are not believed to belong to the same ethnic group. Some historians believe that there were commercial nomads in Europe—independent of the Romanies—who migrated from India through Persia between the fifth and thirteenth centuries, and that they have survived today as distinct ethnic groups. Irish travellers are thought to belong to this group.

One of the defining characteristics of Irish traveller culture is nomadism. Though some travellers have settled in houses, many still take to the road. With the advent of social welfare payments in the

1950s, travellers started to gravitate toward the large urban areas. This led to efforts by the state to assimilate them into mainstream Irish settled society. Though well intentioned, the state considered "nomadism" as a deviancy rather than an integral part of traveller culture. The Commission on Itinerancy (1963), for example, suggested that all efforts directed at improving the lot of travellers "must always have as their aim the eventual absorption of the itinerants into the general community."

The 1995 *Report of the Task Force on the Travelling Community* put much emphasis on the accommodation issue, recommending the construction of 3,100 living units, ranging from halting bays, transient sites, and group housing schemes. All local authorities have subsequently adopted a five-year traveller accommodation plan.

In his book *The Secret Languages of Ireland* (Cambridge University Press: 1937), R.A.S. Macalister compiled hundreds of words of the travellers' language, known as "Travellers' Cant." Much of the vocabulary consisted of inverted Irish words and Macalister concluded that Cant was like a secret code designed to exclude members of the settled community. Although its syntactic structure is solidly based on English, a lot of the vocabulary clearly stems from Irish. This has led scholars to believe that it may have developed about 350 years ago when its original speakers would have been bilingual.

Successive studies have shown that the Irish traveller community is still among the most marginalized and disadvantaged in the country. Infant mortality among travellers is more than twice the national average and only 1 percent reach the age of sixty-five. Only a handful have graduated from third-level institutions and fewer than a thousand transfer to post-primary schools. More than 24 percent of travellers live on unofficial halting sites and on the side of the road, and often have no access to running water, toilets, refuse collection, or electricity.

The most common surnames among travellers are Connors, Ward, Maugham, O'Brien, and McDonagh. B.D.

Trevor, William (1928–). Novelist and short story writer. Born William Trevor Cox in Mitchelstown, County *Cork, Trevor was educated at Trinity College, Dublin. He has lived in England since 1953, and a good deal of his work addresses his experiences there. His early novels, notably *The Old Boys* (1965), highlight the foibles, cruelties, and delusions of the English middle classes. He continues to revisit the eccentric domestic interiors of the Home Counties in such novels as *Elizabeth Alone* (1973) and *Death in Summer* (1998), but he has increasingly focused on Irish themes, particularly in his short stories. The novel *Fools of Fortune* (1983) is his most substantial statement on the violence of Irish history. Trevor uses the family to portray Irish history's destructiveness. He elaborately delineates the devastating effects of politics on personal lives. Decline is another recurring Trevor subject, whether it is the dwindling of the *Protestant minority in the *Republic of Ireland, as in "Reading Turgenev" (in *Two Lives*, 1991), or a more general air of private loss and lack of emotional fulfillment, as in the title story of his collection, *The Ballroom of Romance* (1972). Trevor has adapted his overall sense of the misfit and the incompatible to represent Anglo-Irish relations in such works as the title story of his collection *The News from Ireland* (1986), the novels *Felicia's Journey* (1994) and *The Story of Lucy Gault* (2002). He has also written two works of nonfiction, *A Writer's Ireland* (1984) and *Excursions in the Real World* (1993). Trevor's many awards include that of Honorary Commander of the British Empire for services to literature. G.OB.

David Trimble and George Mitchell

Trimble, David (1944–). Politician. Born on October 15, 1944, Trimble was educated at Bangor Grammar School and at Queen's University, *Belfast, where he read law and later lectured. In the early 1970s, Trimble was associated with the Vanguard, an organization that straddled constitutional *unionist politics and paramilitary *loyalism. Though Trimble repudiated violence, he worked to develop populist agitation against the temporizing unionist leadership, and played an important role in the successful loyalist strike against *Sunningdale in 1974. He did much to provide intellectual ballast for intransigent unionism.

After the Sunningdale Executive fell, Trimble was expelled from the United Ulster Unionist Council, a coalition of parties opposed to Sunningdale, because he favored "voluntary coalition" with the *Social Democratic and Labour Party (SDLP). Even in his militant phase, Trimble was not averse to dialogue.

Trimble helped fellow loyalists on the fringe produce a policy document—*Ulster can Survive Unfettered*—advocating an independent *Northern Ireland. Such a state would seek cross-border cooperation as an equal with the *Republic and, an idea Trimble resurrected (in diluted form) in the *Good Friday Agreement, a Community of the British Isles. In 1987 he presented to the Ulster Clubs (a movement established in 1987 to oppose the *Anglo-Irish Agreement) a document advocating dominion status for "Ulster."

Trimble had joined the *Ulster Unionist Party in 1978, though his application was approved by only 103 votes to 100. Nevertheless, by trading upon his hard-line reputation, he won the leadership of the UUP in 1995, after the seventy-five-year-old James *Molyneaux had resigned. The same year he had notoriously marched in triumph with Ian *Paisley in an *Orange parade through the predominantly Catholic Garvaghy Road in Portadown.

Throughout the *peace process negotiations, Trimble believed that the *republican movement intended to place such pressure on the unionists that they would walk away from the talks. Determined to avoid a "green settlement" (favoring the *nationalists) imposed by the British and Irish governments, he trenchantly criticized nationalist maneuvers, but stayed in the all-party talks. The result was the *Good Friday Agreement of 1998. Though he lost votes to anti-agreement unionists, Trimble, as leader of the single largest party, became first minister of the new devolved government in the *Northern Ireland Assembly. Determined to push on with unfinished business, principally forcing the IRA (*Irish Republican Army) to decommission weapons, in November 2000, he banned *Sinn Féin ministers from participating in the North-South bodies until the IRA gave up arms. In the summer of 2001, he resigned as first minister in protest at the IRA's failure to act. The agreement was saved, and Trimble reelected, when the IRA conceded a token decommissioning in the fall of 2001. However, in 2002–2003, the Northern Ireland Assembly was again suspended.

Trimble is a pragmatist with considerable intellect and vision. His unionism draws upon an impressively eclectic range of intellectual influences, including Edmund *Burke and modern constitutional concepts of sovereignty borrowed from Canada, Australia, and New Zealand. He envisages the development of an "Ulster patriotism" no longer based upon religious cleavages, but rather grounded in a pluralist conception of a devolved United Kingdom. M.M.

Troubles, the. See **Northern Ireland conflict.**

Tuatha. Term for approximately 150 small independent kingdoms within Gaelic Ireland, each ruled by a local king, or Rí. Tuatha were populated by four classes of people: the king and royal family, or derbfine, the nobles, the freemen, and the unfree. Under *brehon law, the Rí was elected by the freemen. Since claimants could include sons, grandsons, and great-grandsons of kings, wars of succession were common. To prevent such wars, a successor or Tánaiste was often chosen during the king's lifetime. P.E.

Tuohy, Patrick (1894–1930). Painter. Born in *Dublin, Tuohy studied art at St. Enda's under William Pearse and at Dublin Metropolitan School of Art under William *Orpen. He was an accomplished portrait painter of such celebrated figures as James *Joyce, Richard *Mulcahy, James *Stephens, and George *Russell. He taught at the Dublin Metropolitan School of Art from 1920 and exhibited regularly at the *Royal Hibernian Academy until his departure to New York in 1927. He exhibited there in 1929. M.C.

Tyrone, County. Inland county in the province of *Ulster, one of the six counties of *Northern Ireland. Covering an area of 1,260 square miles, Tyrone has a population of est. 152,827 (1996). The county's economy is mainly agricultural with some *textile production. Tyrone comes from the Irish *Tír Eoghain*, the land of Eoin, who was a son of Niall of the Nine Hostages, the fifth-century ancestor of the Uí Néill (*O'Neill) dynasty. One of their great scions was Owen Roe *O'Neill, who defeated the English General Monroe at the Battle of Benburb, in County Tyrone, in 1646. A little farther to the north, a famous convention took place at

Dungannon in February of 1782, at which *Protestant *Volunteers asserted Ireland's claim to independence and free trade, and demanded the relaxation of the *Penal Laws.

A reconstruction of Tyrone's past can be seen in both the Heritage Park, at Gortin Glen, and in the Ulster-American Folk Park outside Omagh. Important urban centers include Dungannon, Omagh, the scene of a horrific dissident IRA (*Irish Republican Army) bombing in 1998 (known as the *Omagh Bombing), Cookstown, and Strabane, birthplace of Brian O'Nolan (1912–66), known also as Flann *O'Brien and Myles na Gopaleen. Strabane was also the birthplace of John Dunlop (1747–1812), who printed the first copies of the American Declaration of Independence, and Dergalt, nearby, was the birthplace of American President Woodrow Wilson's grandfather. Tyrone's landscape varies from the two-thousand-foot-high Sperrin Mountains (where gold may have been panned four thousand years ago), to the lowlands around Lough Neagh, Ireland's largest lake. On its shores stands the "Old Cross of Ardboe" (ninth/tenth century), one of Ireland's most venerable monuments. Famous natives include William *Carleton, author of *Traits and Stories of the Irish Peasantry*; man of letters Benedict *Kiely; sculptor Oliver *Sheppard; and Bernadette Devlin *McAliskey, the youngest ever member of the House of Commons. P.H.

U

uilleann pipes. A bellows-blown bagpipe peculiar to Ireland, which evolved from earlier Irish pipes most likely in the mid-seventeenth or early eighteenth century. A key feature is a versatile melody-producing chanter which covers two full octaves. It also has three accompanying drones tuned to the chanter's lowest note (tenor, baritone, and bass) and, also a unique feature, additional melody pipes (usually three—tenor, baritone, and bass), which extend the lower range of the instrument to G below middle C. Called "regulators," these additional pipes are used in harmonic, melodic, or vamping ways and use double (oboe-style) reeds. The pipe's chanter also has a double reed which, with the dry air that the bellows supplies, can be easily "overblown" to yield the second octave; the drones use "single" reeds. Its modern, popular concert form was evolved in Philadelphia during the 1870s to 1890s by the Drogheda-born Taylor brothers. F.V.

Ulster. Northern province, which is divided between the *Republic of Ireland and *Northern Ireland. Six of Ulster's nine counties—*Antrim, *Armagh, *Down, *Derry, *Fermanagh, and *Tyrone—have made up Northern Ireland since the *Government of Ireland Act (1920). The other three counties—*Cavan, *Donegal, and *Monaghan—are part of the Republic of Ireland. The name derives from the Uluti, a tribe in *pre-Christian Ireland. The term *Ulster* is often used interchangeably with Northern Ireland, even though the province includes the three counties of the Republic of Ireland. In the fifteenth and sixteenth centuries, Ulster was a stronghold of Irish resistance (mostly by the *O'Neill and O'Donnell clans) to the spread of English power. *Belfast, the capital of Northern Ireland, is located in the southern part of County Antrim. The province has the island's largest lake—Lough Neagh—and the unique rock formation known as the *Giant's Causeway. J.OM.

Ulster Defense Association (UDA). *Loyalist paramilitary group. Formed in September 1971 from a number of loyalist vigilante groups (principally the Shankill Defense Association), the UDA was, and remains, the largest loyalist paramilitary group in *Northern Ireland. From the imposition of direct rule in March 1972, the UDA participated in an assassination campaign against Catholic civilians. The UDA sought to "punish" support for the IRA (*Irish Republican Army) in Catholic areas, and to warn the British government of the loyalist capacity for atrocity in the event of a "sell-out to *nationalism." The association reached a peak in 1974, when it played an important role in the strike that brought down the *Sunningdale Agreement. With fluctuating degrees of intensity, UDA violence continued throughout the *Troubles, killing hundreds. At first the UDA backed the *Good Friday Agreement, particularly as it led to the release of its prisoners. However, support for the agreement gradually dissipated as the UDA witnessed apparent *republican political gains. M.M.

Ulster Defense Regiment (UDR). British army unit. A locally recruited regiment of the British army, the UDR was formed on April 1, 1970, to replace the *B-Specials (Ulster Special Constabulary). The UDR was merged with the Royal Irish Rangers in July 1992. The UDR initially attracted *Catholic membership of 18 percent, but this figure fell to 3 percent. There has been collusion between loyalist paramilitaries and some UDR members. During its existence, the UDR lost 197 serving members and 47 former members, killed mainly by the IRA (*Irish Republican Army). The UDR killed two members of the IRA and six Catholic civilians. M.M.

Ulster Democratic Party (UDP). Political party. The UDP was formed in 1989 from the Ulster Loyalist Democratic Party, which had been set up by the *Ulster Defense Association (UDA) in 1981. The UDP seeks to present itself as a distinct and separate organization from the UDA, much in the same fashion as *Sinn Féin sees its relationship with the IRA (*Irish Republican Army). The poor electoral showing of the party has reduced its political leverage on the loyalist paramilitants. M.M.

Ulster Museum. *Northern Ireland's principal museum. Located in *Belfast, the museum displays artifacts relating to the history and heritage of *Ulster. The collection of the Belfast Natural History Society (which was first displayed in 1831) was incorporated into the Belfast Museum and Art Gallery in the 1890s. The museum came to its present location in the city's *Botanic Gardens in 1929 and was later renamed the Ulster Museum. A major extension was opened in 1972. (Address: Botanic Gardens, Belfast BT9 5AB. Web site: *www.ulstermuseum.org.uk.*) S.A.B.

Ulster Plantation, the. Seventeenth-century colonization of *Ulster by English and Scottish settlers. In March 1603, the Treaty of *Mellifont ended the *Nine Years War against England. To avoid the confiscation of their lands, the rebels had to renounce their Gaelic titles and ancestral rights and live by English law. However, in what is known as the *Flight of the Earls, *O'Neill and over ninety other Ulster chieftains sailed for the Continent in September 1607. This flight was considered treason and the British government confiscated all their lands. Approximately four million acres in six counties (*Donegal, *Derry, *Tyrone, *Fermanagh, *Armagh, and *Cavan) mapped out in a survey were now to be colonized. The confiscated territory was divided into estates of 1,000, 1,500, and 2,000 acres. The estates were distributed to three groups: English and Scottish Undertakers, who undertook to bring settlers to Ireland; Servitors, who were being rewarded for service to the crown in Ireland; and Irish "of good merit," whom the British trusted. Any remaining land was to be set aside for the established Church, Trinity College, and the building of towns and six free schools. Rents for the English and Scottish planters were low, but settlers were expected to build fortified enclosures or bawns.

Despite extensive planning, problems with the *plantation quickly developed. Not enough Undertakers arrived, while some began taking Irish tenants illegally. The scheme did not succeed in establishing purely English-Scottish settlements because the native population was never fully removed. Despite these setbacks, by 1640, over forty thousand English and mostly Scottish settlers had arrived. Even though the *Rebellion of 1641 showed that the Ulster Irish still had the capacity to wage war, the plantation by that stage was too well developed to be totally overthrown. The arrival of these colonists led to a social and political revolution that was to have long-term implications for the history of Ulster. P.E.

Ulster Unionist Party, the (UUP). Political party. The Ulster Unionist Party grew out of the Irish and British *unionism of the nineteenth century. In 1904/05, the Ulster Unionist Council (UUC) was set up in protest against British Prime Minster Arthur J. Balfour's perceived *home rule policies in Ireland. When the UUP emerged as a semi-independent party after *partition, the UUC became and remained its ruling body. The UUC consists of delegates from all the constituent parts of the party (e.g., women, *Orange men and women, youths, students, the actual local constituency organizations, etc.). These delegates elect the leadership of the UUP and determine its policies. (In this they are probably the most democratically organized party). The party's main rationale had been the prevention of home rule, but after the *Government of Ireland Act (1920) and the *Anglo-Irish Treaty of 1921 had ironically bestowed a version of home rule on *Northern Ireland, the UUP felt compelled to defend the union with Great Britain not only against a perceived hostile southern state, but also against Irish *nationalism within its own jurisdiction. It was, and remained, the largest party in Northern Ireland, which it governed from 1921 to 1972. Until the 1960s, the UUP was led by a landed social elite distant from its rank and file, but its policies comprised a populist agenda that addressed the attitudes, prejudices, and expectations of its constituency. In the tradition of nineteenth-century British parties, it was a coalition of interests embracing left-to-right policies with the common aim of maintaining the union with Britain and its Parliament at *Stormont.

The relative prosperity of the 1960s allowed the liberal wing within the party to grow, and Prime Minister Terence *O'Neill used Catholic-friendly rhetoric in the hope of encouraging nationalist acceptance of the state. This, combined with the growing self-confidence of the Catholic middle classes and the civil rights movement, alienated the conservative wing of the party. With O'Neill's fall and the subsequent imposition of direct rule from London in 1972, the UUP found itself weakened and removed from government. Unless willing to engage in some form of power sharing with the constitutional nationalists, the *Social Democratic and Labour Party (SDLP), the UUP was bound to stay in the wilderness. A first attempt, Brian *Faulkner's power-sharing Executive of 1974 failed, however, under pressure from a constituency not willing to compromise with nationalists.

Throughout the following twenty-five years, the major policy issue for the party was whether or not a compromise with constitutional nationalism was possible. Its opposition to the *Anglo-Irish Agreement of 1985 showed the difficulties the party faced, which were increased when subsequent British governments changed their policy in Northern Ireland by encouraging *republican political participation. It was only in 1997, under its new leader (from 1995), David *Trimble, that the party was willing to enter negotiations with *Sinn Féin. A year later, the UUC endorsed the *Good Friday Agreement and the UUP joined a power-sharing government that included constitutional as well as republican nationalists. Over the coming years the party remained split as to the benefits of the new arrangements, which appeared to many to offer political benefits to nationalists at the expense of unionists. In the early years of the new century, it was becoming clear that the *Democratic Unionist Party (DUP), a much more radical unionist party, could overtake Trimble's unionism. S.W.

Ulster Volunteer Force (UVF). *Loyalist paramilitary organization. Originally formed in 1912 to resist *home rule, the Ulster Volunteer Force was revived in 1966 by loyalists to oppose attempts by the *Belfast and *Dublin governments to improve North-South relations. As the *Northern Ireland conflict (the Troubles) erupted in the early 1970s, the UVF embarked on an intensive campaign of assassination of *nationalists and was responsible for some of the most infamous killings of the Troubles, including the *Dublin and *Monaghan Bombings. In the Miami Showband killings, three members of a southern music group were killed in a gun and bomb attack by a UVF gang which included two *Ulster Defense Regiment soldiers. The Shankill Butchers, an infamously violent UVF gang, brutally attacked innocent Catholic civilians in the 1970s and were convicted of nineteen murders and over a hundred other offenses.

The UVF has made a number of attempts to organize a political party (the Volunteer Political Party in 1974), but there were long periods when the organization saw its role as purely military and left politics to the mainstream *unionist parties. The formation of the *Progressive Unionist Party (PUP) in 1979 was a reemergence of open political activity for the UVF, but that party remained marginal until after the 1994 cease-fires.

As a paramilitary organization, the UVF was always smaller, more disciplined, and more centrally controlled than its main rival the *Ulster Defense Association (UDA), which had a reputation for drug dealing, extortion, and personal enrichment. In later years, the UVF has been involved in some of the most brutal attacks on nationalist civilians in Northern Ireland, such as the pub shootings in Loughinisland in 1994, when six people were killed while watching a World Cup *soccer match on television. Following the 1994 cease-fire, the Portadown-based organization led by Billy Wright opposed the UVF leadership. Wright was eventually expelled from the UVF and ordered to leave Northern Ireland. (He was killed by the Irish National Liberation Army in the Maze prison on December 27, 1997.) While there have been breaches of the UVF cease-fire, the organization has been much more disciplined than the UDA. The PUP have made some political inroads, having two members elected to the Assembly in 1998 and maintaining a reasonably high media profile. Consequently, the UVF has remained positive toward the *peace process, despite the ultimate rejection of the process by the UDA. J.D.

Union, Act of (1800). The law that created the United Kingdom of Great Britain and Ireland. After the *Rebellion of 1798, the British Prime Minister William Pitt decided to abolish the Dublin *Parliament and introduce direct rule from London. The act, which was passed by both the Irish and British Parliaments, came into effect on January 1, 1801. Under the union, Ireland was represented at Westminster by one hundred members of Parliament (MPs), and in the House of Lords by four bishops and twenty-eight lords chosen from the Irish peerage. The union meant common citizenship for the two islands, the same legal, tax, and trading systems, and a new state Church of England and Ireland. Ireland would have to contribute two seventeenths of United Kingdom Expenditure.

Initially many opposed the union: merchants who feared English competition, patriots loyal to the national Parliament, and the *Orange Order that believed the union would end Protestant ascendancy because Pitt had promised full *Catholic Emancipation in order to win Catholic support. Catholic bishops and others welcomed the union and the new era of stability it promised.

The bill was first introduced in January 1799 and was rejected in the Irish Parliament by 111 votes to 106. Following this defeat, anti-union office-holders were replaced with supporters. The government won over MPs and peers with promotions and titles, and compensated corrupt borough patrons who would lose influence under the union. When the bill was reintroduced a year later, there was a large pro-union majority.

Protestants did well under the union and, in time, became its strongest supporters. However, the British government's failure to deliver Catholic Emancipation and continuing social problems led Irish Catholics to seek the act's *repeal. But all attempts to gain even a modest measure of *home rule failed for over a century and the Act of Union remained in effect until the *Government of Ireland Act (1920) and the *Anglo-Irish Treaty (1921). T.C.

unionism. Political philosophy that advocates the union of *Northern Ireland with Great Britain. Founded in 1886, unionism was initially a loose collection of unionist associations spread throughout Ireland, united in opposition against *home rule, or self-government for the island of Ireland. The unionist movement changed British politics, which until then mainly consisted of rivalry between the Conservative and Liberal Parties. Unionists allied themselves with the Conservatives in opposition to the pro–home rule Liberals, and their combined strength in the House of Commons kept the Liberals out of power from 1886 to 1906. To this day, the formal title of the British Conservative Party remains the "Conservative and Unionist Party."

In the north of Ireland, where it was concentrated, unionism had roots going back to the late eighteenth century. One of unionism's most important constituent elements, the *Orange Order (which still nominates a substantial part of the Unionist Party's ruling council) had been founded in 1795 following an attack by a *Catholic group on a *Protestant inn in County *Armagh.

After 1906, home rule was back on the political agenda, and as Britain moved inexorably toward granting a measure of self-government to the rebellious island, unionism became, in effect, a rebellion within a rebellion. Unionists were determined to resist home rule by force of arms if necessary, even if this meant military opposition to the government of the state with which it wished to remain united. By 1912, a total of some 447,000 people (Northern Ireland had approximately 500,000 adult Protestants) signed the so-called *Ulster Covenant, by which they swore, among other things, to use "all means which may be found necessary to defeat the present conspiracy to set up a home rule Parliament in Ireland."

Under unionist pressure, Prime Minister *Lloyd George passed the *Government of Ireland Act (1920), thereby establishing the state of Northern Ireland. In 1921, under the *Anglo-Irish Treaty, the *Irish Free State (later to become the independent *Republic of Ireland), was created consisting of twenty-six counties. The largely autonomous region of Northern Ireland as provided in the Government of Ireland Act continued to remain an integral part of the United Kingdom. This statelet (which had its own Parliament) embodied six of the nine counties of the province of Ulster and was specifically constructed to ensure that unionists would have a guaranteed electoral majority for the indefinite future.

Political unionism was now confined to Northern Ireland, where it had an effective monopoly of state power, including control over security. For the following half a century, it exercised this power under the shadow, as unionism saw it, of two distinct threats: one from Northern Ireland's dissident *nationalist minority, the other from the irredentism (rarely if ever backed up by practical action) ritually displayed by successive governments of the new state in Dublin. This, in turn, produced a regime in Northern Ireland characterized by subtle and not-so-subtle erosion of the civil rights of the nationalist minority, harsh security policies, and by an endemically sectarian administration.

Unionism united Protestants of all social classes in opposition to the perceived threat of rule by the island's overwhelming Catholic majority. This outward unity, however, concealed rather than eradicated class tensions. Working-class Protestants, in particular, were tempted by *socialist solutions to political problems, leading to the emergence of splinter groups among unionism in the 1920s. The Northern Ireland government's abolition of the proportional voting system in 1929 checked this trend. Another threat to the hegemony of unionism arose in the mid-1930s, when harsh economic conditions provoked anti-government joint hunger marches by Catholic and Protestant working-class men. Unionist leaders, however, deflected this political threat with well-worn anti-nationalist rhetoric.

From 1940 to 1963, unionism was an implacable, immovable political force, both to the nationalist minority and to the British Parliament, which had effectively washed its hands of responsibility for the gerrymandering and discrimination which had become hallmarks of the *Stormont administration. The IRA (*Irish Republican Army) heightened unionists' fears by mounting a sporadic and largely ineffective campaign of attacks on Northern Ireland security installations between 1956 and 1962. In the latter year, however, Captain Terence *O'Neill became prime minister of Northern Ireland with a mildly reformist agenda and, in 1965, made well-intentioned but sometimes gauche attempts to create better relationships with nationalists within Northern Ireland and, across the border, with the Republic. O'Neill was prompted partly by a desire to attract industrial entrepreneurs to the region, especially from the United States. These moves, however, created fresh tensions within unionism. Liberal unionism, most firmly entrenched among the middle classes, embraced the idea, albeit with some initial hesitation and caution. The emergence of the Reverend Ian *Paisley's brand of independent unionism provoked ungovernable tensions within unionism generally, and contributed to O'Neill's loss of office in 1969. Paisley's creation of the *Democratic Unionist Party (DUP) in 1971 was a religiously inspired, formal rejection of mainstream unionism. Since then, the DUP has become a powerful force within unionism, continually threatening its older parent and influencing its political agenda. Extreme unionism, or loyalism as it is more generally described, is characterized by its willingness to resort to armed force, and has spawned a number of paramilitary organizations. Other factions, such as the *Progressive Unionist Party (PUP) and the Ulster Popular Unionist Party, are left-leaning working-class splinter groups. These parties' relationship with paramilitaries mirrors the relationship between *Sinn Féin and the IRA, the major difference being that loyalist paramilitaries have been less susceptible to political influence or control than their republican contemporaries.

This process of splintering within unionism, aided by the reintroduction of a proportional electoral system, has allowed for the representation of most of the variegated forms of unionism within the *peace process and, more importantly, within the new Legislative Assembly. These groups, with their strong social bases, distrust the traditional middle-class leadership of unionism to the point that, without relinquishing their traditional constitutional allegiance to Britain, on occasion they find themselves sharing at least part of a political agenda with working-class nationalists in Sinn Féin and similar organizations. In this, as in some other respects, the future of unionism may be markedly different from its past. J.H.

United Irishmen, the Society of. Organization that pioneered the politics and agenda of Irish *republicanism from its inception in October 1791. The United Irishmen were a product of the political environment in Ireland in the years following the *American War of Independence and the *French Revolution of 1789. Many Irish liberals argued that the democratic rights effected by force of arms in America and France should be extended to the people of Ireland where an elite comprising less than 3 percent of the population had total control of the government. An exceptionally narrow franchise, weighted toward large property owners and from which Catholics and *Presbyterians were all but excluded, was increasingly regarded in progressive Irish circles as unjust. The pioneering republican coterie of Theobald Wolfe *Tone, William *Drennan, Thomas Addis Emmet, Thomas Russell, and Samuel Neilson, whose political ideas drew on the most promising international precedents and the diffused legacy of the Enlightenment, founded the Society of United Irishmen in *Belfast and *Dublin in October/November 1791. Using the *Northern Star* and other radical organs, the United Irishmen sought to mobilize popular opinion through print and thereby exert pressure on government to instigate far-reaching reforms.

After the outbreak of war with France in February 1793, the organization was banned in April 1794 when proof of seditious contact with the French government was uncovered in Dublin. On May 10, 1795, the United Irishmen were effectively revived using a model constitution for an organizationally sophisticated paramilitary organization intended to function as auxiliaries to their invading French allies. The Jacobin and violent *Defenders were quickly subsumed into the United Irishmen's superstructure and a major recruitment drive was mounted after December 1796 when a French army came within sight of the *Cork coast but did not disembark. Refinements were made to the modus operandi of the United Irishmen in August 1797, but it proved necessary to mount a unilateral *Rebellion on May 23–24, 1798, owing to severe losses of personnel and equipment under martial law. Early setbacks in Dublin and unexpected communications problems turned a potentially decisive revolution of up to three hundred thousand United Irishmen into a partial and ad hoc effort in various zones. Lack of coordination between the provinces, inadequate leadership, and the chronic imbalance of firepower between the insurgents and crown forces produced a string of heavy defeats and Pyrrhic victories for the rebels. Nonetheless, several important wins by the rebels, most notably in *Wexford, contributed to the extreme seriousness with which the rebellion was regarded in Dublin and then in London. It required the transfer of the bulk of available military forces in Britain and the extension of a liberal amnesty program to contain and then demobilize the rebel armies. Rebels held out in several sectors until the end of 1803, and the chronic disaffection of the Irish population was a critical consideration in effecting legislative union with Britain in 1800. R.OD.

United Nations (UN). Ireland joined the UN in 1955 as part of an agreement between the United States and the Soviet Union on new members. Ireland has served three times on the UN Security Council, in 1962, 1981–82, and from 2001 to 2003. The Nuclear Non-Proliferation Treaty originated in an Irish initiative at the UN General Assembly in 1958 and Ireland was the first to ratify the treaty. The Irish Defense Forces have been a major contributor to UN peacekeeping and peacemaking missions, with a significant proportion of the forces deployed on UN missions at any time. J.D.

universities. Following two failed attempts to found a native university in Ireland in the fourteenth century, Trinity College, the sole college of the University of *Dublin, was established with the city's assistance in 1592. Trinity was modeled on the residential colleges of the universities of Oxford and Cambridge. In spite of an early effort to encourage the teaching of the *Irish language, Trinity remained a bastion of the New English *Protestant establishment in Ireland and much of the college's revenues came from its extensive landholdings. The Anglican constitution of the university was firmly established by Chancellor William Laud during the 1630s. Roman *Catholics and Protestant Dissenters were formally excluded from the University of Dublin until 1793, and religious tests for some fellowships survived until 1873.

The academic reputation of the University of Dublin fluctuated during the seventeenth and eighteenth centuries. However, the "Debating Club" founded at Trinity by Edmund *Burke in 1747 provided a forum for undergraduates to discuss political issues. The club proved to be a seedbed for radical ideas and its members included the revolutionary leaders Wolfe *Tone and Robert *Emmet, who was expelled from the college in 1798. The number of Catholic students attending Trinity rose steadily during the early nineteenth century. Catholics accounted for almost one in ten of the student body in 1830, but their numbers declined thereafter. Both

Trinity College, Long Room, Old Library

Protestant and Catholic students of Trinity College, such as Thomas *Davis and John *O'Leary, became prominent Irish *nationalists during the nineteenth century. However, the university remained a stronghold of the *Anglo-Irish establishment and elected *Unionist MPs (members of Parliament) to Parliament until 1922. Trinity College acquired a reputation as an important center for the study of medicine and produced many leading scholars in the fields of classics and history, including J. P. Mahaffy (1839–1919) and J. B. Bury (1861–1927).

Because of Trinity's discrimination against Catholics and Protestant Dissenters, several *Presbyterian academies were established in the north of Ireland, including the Belfast Academical Institution (1814) and Magee College in *Derry (1865). During the seventeenth and eighteenth centuries, Roman Catholic students were forced to attend seminaries known as "Irish colleges" in *France and Spain. After a number of these colleges were closed by the revolutionary regime in France, William Pitt encouraged the Irish Parliament to establish a seminary in Ireland. St. Patrick's College, founded in *Maynooth in 1795, was state-funded until 1871. It served primarily as a seminary for clerical students but also provided higher education for lay students until 1817. Its creation stimulated the foundation of diocesan seminaries throughout Ireland.

After *Catholic Emancipation in 1829, the "Irish university question" became a highly charged political issue as middle-class Catholics sought equal access to university education. Sir Robert Peel's decision to substantially increase the annual grant to Maynooth in 1845 aroused considerable anti-Catholic sentiment in Great Britain and Ireland. That same year, Parliament created three "Queen's Colleges" in *Belfast, *Cork, and *Galway. They opened to students in 1849 and were linked together in 1850 to form the Queen's University of Ireland. The university offered students low fees and vocationally orientated curricula and was designed to meet the Catholic demand for higher education. However, the institution's secular constitution was criticized by both Daniel *O'Connell and the Catholic Church. A papal rescript issued in 1847 condemned the Queen's Colleges and proposed the foundation of an autonomous Catholic university modeled on Louvain. In 1851, John Henry *Newman was appointed first rector of the Catholic University, which opened in Dublin in 1854. The new institution was, however, underfunded and failed largely because it was not empowered to award its own degrees.

In 1873, Prime Minister William *Gladstone's ambitious scheme to create a single university for Ireland consisting of the Dublin, Queen's, and Catholic universities was decisively rejected by all sides. Nevertheless, in 1879 the University Education (Ireland) Act established an examining body, the Royal University (1882), which was empowered to grant degrees to any students who passed its examinations. This scheme allowed Catholic students, whose attendance at Trinity College was later restricted by a ban imposed by the Catholic Church (1944), to graduate from their own colleges. The government made a further concession to Catholic students in 1908 when it established two new universities. The National University of Ireland (NUI) was a federal institution consisting of the Catholic University, known since 1883 as University College, Dublin (UCD), and the Queen's Colleges in Cork and Galway. Maynooth was recognized by the NUI in 1910 and became a full constituent college in 1967. The remaining Queen's College was reestablished as the Queen's University of Belfast. While the NUI was in theory a nondenominational body, the Catholic hierarchy was given a major role in governing its colleges. The NUI played an important part in educating a Catholic professional class in Ireland, and the staff and students of UCD, such as Thomas Kettle, Francis *Sheehy Skeffington, and James *Joyce, were particularly influential in Irish cultural and political life. The early twentieth century also saw Irish *women establish themselves within the universities. Since 1882, the Royal University had awarded degrees to female students including Hanna *Sheehy Skeffington. Women were first admitted to Trinity College in 1904 and the vibrant atmosphere at UCD encouraged the emergence of a new generation of feminist campaigners.

After *partition, university education in *Northern Ireland centered upon the Queen's University of Belfast. After World War II, improved funding enabled increasing numbers of Catholic students to attend the university and by the 1960s, Queen's had become an important center of the civil rights movement. During 1965 to 1968, the New University of *Ulster was created. Controversy ensued when *Stormont decided to situate the campus in the *unionist stronghold of Coleraine rather than in the more populous and largely nationalist city of Derry. Public protest at this decision was mobilized by a new generation of national figures including John *Hume. In 1984, the multicampus University of Ulster was created by merging the New University with the Ulster Polytechnic and the Ulster College of Art.

As higher education expanded in the *Republic of Ireland during the 1960s, the rivalry between, and perception of, Trinity College and UCD as Protestant and Catholic colleges declined significantly. The Catholic Church lifted its ban on Catholics attending Trinity in 1970 and most of the students currently attending Trinity, Queen's, and the New University of Ulster are Roman Catholics. Nevertheless, government schemes to merge the two institutions were unsuccessful. As the number of full-time students in the Republic rose from 19,000 in 1966 to 115,000 in 2001, reform of the university system became necessary. National Institutes of Higher Education were established in *Limerick (1970) and Dublin (1976) and both became universities in 1989. In 1997, the Universities Act redefined the constitution of the NUI and gave its four constituent colleges in Dublin, Cork, Galway, and Maynooth a greater degree of administrative independence. S.A.B.

urbanization. Ireland has been a predominantly rural society. The original inhabitants of the island and, later, the *Celts were nomadic. Monastic sites became important population centers in the age of *Christianity, but they were not cities as presently defined. The origin of towns in Ireland begins with the arrival of the *Vikings in the late eighth century, who founded the cities of *Limerick, *Dublin, and *Waterford. The original towns were trading centers for the Norse. After the *Anglo-Norman Conquest in 1169, the Normans built *castles. The Church, which up to then had been monastic-centered, became diocesan-based and controlled by bishops. Whereas the Church organized people in parishes or small villages, the commercialization of *agriculture under British dominance led to the establishment of towns as trading centers. Towns, however, remained small with a few notable exceptions because Ireland's agrarian-based *economy did not need large urban centers for industrial production. In the nineteenth century Irish population growth continued to be concentrated in rural areas until the *Famine. After the Famine, the population of Ireland stabilized based on high levels of *emigration, decreasing the demographic pressure for urban growth. By the time of independence in 1922, less than a third of Ireland's population lived in urban areas. Throughout the twentieth century, the mechanization of agriculture production caused the rural population to decline, so that by the 1990s only about 40 percent of the population lived in rural areas. This is a remarkably high number, considering Ireland's recent dramatic economic growth. Because of Ireland's small size, the urbanization of Ireland has resulted in almost 40 percent of the Irish population living in and around Dublin, making it one of the most capital-concentrated countries in the *EU, with the exception of Greece.

There are several reasons for the slow pace of urbanization. First, Ireland never experienced the industrial revolution and the majority of its workforce did not work in industry. In most other European countries, the industrialization of the workforce in the nineteenth century propelled urbanization. Ireland has made a transition from an agrarian economy to a service-oriented economy in the latter half of the twentieth century. Today, approximately two-thirds of the Irish workforce is in the service sector, and less than 6 percent is engaged in agriculture and related activities. Secondly, the Irish people generally prefer living in the countryside rather than in Dublin and other cities. The pace of life, county and local loyalties, as well as a lower cost of living, make life in small towns and villages much more attractive. Thirdly, the Irish government actively promotes economic growth and job creation in nonurban areas and subsidizes agriculture. While urbanization has been comparatively slow in Ireland, recent projections by the Central Statistics Office in Dublin suggest a continuing decline in the rural population, especially in the Midlands, while the major cities of

Bono, lead singer with U2

Dublin, Cork, Limerick, and Galway will continue to grow rapidly. Urbanization is accelerating and changing the character of Irish society. T.W.

Ussher, James (1581–1656). Anglican archbishop of *Armagh, scholar, and theologian. Born in *Dublin, he was ordained in 1601 and was professor of theological controversies and twice vice chancellor at Trinity College, Dublin, between 1607 and 1621. He became bishop of *Meath in 1621 and archbishop of Armagh in 1625. His most famous work, *Annals of the World* (published between 1650 and 1654), used his chronology of the Old Testament to date the creation of the universe to 4004 B.C. His extensive library is now in the possession of Trinity College, Dublin. P.E.

U2. Rock band. Consisting of Bono (Paul Hewson, b. 1960), The Edge (David Evans, b. 1961), Adam Clayton (b. 1960), and Larry Mullen, Jr. (b. 1961), U2 is one of the most successful rock bands of all time. Formed in 1976 while its original five then-teenage members were students at Mount Temple Comprehensive School in *Dublin, the band was initially known as Feedback and then as the Hype. The current lineup became known as U2 in 1978. Their first full-length album, *Boy*, was released on Island Records in 1980, to critical acclaim. What distinguishes U2 are the intelligent, spiritual, politically and socially aware lyrics and the band's unique sound. Since the early 1980s, the band has attracted a huge following and in 1985 *Rolling Stone* magazine branded them "Band of the '80s." Stellar performances at the 1985 Live Aid concert and Amnesty International's 1986 Conspiracy of Hope tour were followed by the album *The Joshua Tree* (1987), which became an international hit. In 1988, the band released *Rattle and Hum*, a concert film and album, to mixed reviews. The 1990s were a time of musical experimentation for U2, to varying degrees of success in terms of sales, critics, and fans. Their 2000 release *All That You Can't Leave Behind* was hailed as a critical success, winning seven Grammy Awards. Bono continues to work tirelessly for humanitarian causes such as the cancellation of Third World countries' debt and the elimination of land mines. N.H.

Victoria, Queen (1819–1901). Queen of Great Britain and Ireland (1837–1901), Empress of India (1876–1901). Queen Victoria made the first of four visits to Ireland in May 1849, bestowing the name of Queenstown upon Cobh, County *Cork. She was criticized for ignoring the plight of her Irish subjects during the Great *Famine. The Queen supported the public funding of the Roman *Catholic seminary at *Maynooth (1845) and disapproved of the violent public reaction against the Vatican's revival of territorial titles for Roman Catholic bishops in England (1851). After the death of her husband, Prince Albert, in 1861, she played a significant role in domestic politics. She disapproved of the disestablishment of the *Church of Ireland (1871), but recognized its inevitability and endeavored to minimize opposition to the measure in the House of Lords. She was strongly opposed to *Gladstone's Irish *home rule bills (1886 and 1893). In April 1900, Victoria visited Ireland for the last time to encourage army recruitment for the *Boer War. S.A.B.

Vikings. Norsemen, largely from western Norway, who made raids on Ireland from 795 onward. The Vikings founded the first Irish cities, such as *Dublin, *Limerick, *Wexford, and *Waterford, after 840. Their frequent raids on Irish monasteries gave them a reputation of being uncivilized barbarians. However, by bringing home looted treasures and later burying them in graves in Scandinavia, they preserved important Irish metalwork fragments that might otherwise have perished, and which are now preserved in museums in Bergen, Oslo, Stockholm, and elsewhere. Recent research suggests that the Vikings had a complex and dynamic culture.

The Vikings often made strategic alliances with Irish kings, intermarried with the native population, and many became Christian by the year 1000. Great traders, they taught the Irish much about commerce and boat building, at which they excelled. Contrary to popular tradition, the Viking influence began to decline before the Battle of *Clontarf in 1014. P.H.

Vinegar Hill, Battle of (County *Wexford; June 21, 1798). One of the turning points of the *Rebellion of 1798 in which the *United Irishmen attempted to establish an Irish republic with French military assistance. By mid-May 1798, the United Irishmen decided to mount an insurrection on May 23 without awaiting the French. A string of victories in Wexford marked that county as the most successful rebel sector and led to the mobilization of large insurgent armies. At Vinegar Hill camp, which towered over the town of Enniscorthy, Reverend Philip Roche ordered all Wexford rebel groups to mass there on June 21, but only a proportion came before the government forces attacked. The military focused their counterattack on Enniscorthy and used almost ten thousand men backed by artillery to drive the rebels from Vinegar Hill. While losses were comparatively slight owing to a gap in the army's cordon through which the vast majority of rebels escaped, the strategic initiative passed decisively to the government. Wexford quickly became untenable as a theater for the rebels and the rebellion waned in the eastern counties outside the Wicklow mountains. R.OD.

Volunteers, the. Militia force organized in Ireland during the *American War of Independence to protect Ireland from an opportunist attack from *France. Uniformed units of infantry, cavalry, and artillery, frequently formed by lesser gentry and magistrates at their own expense, offered nominal service to the Irish *Parliament at College Green, *Dublin, for the duration of the war. While predominantly *Protestant in membership and overwhelmingly so at officer level, many units made ostentatious overtures to Catholic recruits in 1777–78 to signal their support for the "Patriot" reform agenda of Henry Flood and Henry *Grattan, which sought to free Irish legislation from the Westminster system. A series of conventions or rallies, most notably that held at Dungannon, Tyrone, in 1782, issued pro-reform resolutions which identified the Volunteers as a de facto armed wing of the Grattanites. It rapidly became apparent that the Irish Patriots and the Volunteers in particular were perhaps not only capable, but possibly willing, to emulate the achievements of the rebellious American colonists with whom they sympathized. Veiled threats of violence by the Volunteers obliged Westminster to concede a measure of legislative independence to the Dublin Parliament in 1782. After Ireland had a largely sovereign Parliament, Grattan rejected violent coercion pressures and the Volunteers faded away. But later the Society of *United Irishmen posed a serious threat of revolution. Alarmed, *Dublin Castle imposed tight control of the *Yeomanry raised in 1796. At the same time, army headquarters strictly supervised the full-time Irish militia, which had enlisted for the duration of the French War and served as infantry alongside the regular army mustered in 1793.

The term was also used for the Irish Volunteers, which was formed in 1913 and later became the *Irish Republican Army. R.OD.

Wall, Mervyn (pseudonym for Eugene Welply) (1908–97). Writer, playwright. Born in *Dublin, Wall presents in his novels and plays a sardonic view of the alliance of priests, shopkeepers, and farmers dominating post-treaty (*Anglo-Irish Treaty) Irish life. In the novels *The Unfortunate Fursey* (1946) and *The Return of Fursey* (1948), he uses the adventures and misfortunes of a speech-impaired early medieval monk to satirize twentieth-century puritan, *Catholic Ireland. Wall's beautifully crafted 1952 novel, *Leaves for the Burning*, is a most insightful literary look at 1940s and early 1950s Ireland. After many years in the civil service, Wall became secretary (1957–73) and director (1973–75) of the Irish Arts Council, where he championed Irish *literature, *theater, and the visual and *musical arts. L.J.MC.

Walton, E[rnest] T. S. (1903–95) Physicist and Nobel laureate. Born in Dungarvan, County *Waterford, Walton spent most of his life at Trinity College, Dublin, as student, fellow, and physics professor. From 1927 to 1934, he was a member of Rutherford's nuclear physics research group at the Cavendish Laboratory. In 1932, he and John Cockcroft bombarded lithium nuclei with protons accelerated to high energies, caused the nuclei to disintegrate, and identified the products as helium nuclei. They thus achieved the alchemists' dream of transforming one substance into another and launched accelerator-based experimental nuclear physics. In 1951, they received the Nobel Prize for physics. M.L.

War of Independence. See **Anglo-Irish War, the.**

Waterford, County. Maritime county in the province of *Munster. Covering 716 square miles, Waterford has a population of 101,518 (2002 census). The county is bounded on the north by the River Suir, on the east by Waterford Harbour, and on the south by the Celtic Sea. The Knockmealdown (2,609 feet) and the Comeragh/Monavallagh mountains on its western boundary provide dramatic scenery. Waterford has many megalithic tombs, including Harristown near the fishing port of Dunmore East. Tramore (with one of the longest beaches in Ireland) and Dunmore East are the county's most popular summer resorts. Ardmore has an elegant twelfth-century *round tower and cathedral, built on a site founded by St. Declan, one of the four *saints reputed to have been in Ireland before St. *Patrick. Waterford was the ancient territory known as the Decies (Déise), some of whose people crossed the Irish Sea and settled in Wales in the fifth century. The area around Ring (An Rinn) is an Irish-speaking, or *Gaeltacht, area. The name Waterford derives from the ninth-century *Viking name for the harbor—Vethrafjörthr in old Norse. Its Irish name is Port Láirge. The city's most prominent monument is Reginald's Tower on the Quays, which local tradition dates to 1003.

Since 1783, Waterford has been a center for glassmaking and its handcrafted *Waterford Crystal ranks among the most famous in the world. Other industries in the county are dairy farming and crop production, electronics, and pharmaceuticals. Although Waterford City's population of 44,564 makes up almost half of the county's total, the county capital is the much smaller town of Dungarvan. Waterford City has an annual Light *Opera Festival. Natives of the county include the great actor Tyrone Power (1797–1841), great-grandfather of the Hollywood swashbuckling actor of the same name; the theatrical producer Sir Tyrone *Guthrie; and Robert *Boyle, father of modern chemistry. P.H.

Waterford Crystal. World-famous crystal. The Waterford Glasshouse was founded by George and William Penrose in 1783. Over several generations, this family perfected the art of mixing minerals and glass to produce brilliant yet durable crystal ware. In 1851, the Penroses' crystal won several prizes at the Great Exhibition in London, but heavy export taxes forced their factory to close. The production of Waterford Crystal was revived in 1947 and it was relaunched on the world market in 1951. In the early 1960s a larger glassworks was built and by 1980 Waterford Crystal was the world's largest producer of handcrafted crystal. S.A.B.

wedge tombs. The last type of megalithic tomb. These wedge-shaped graves were erected largely during the early Bronze Age, before and after 2000 B.C. Some, particularly in West *Cork (Altar and Lahardane Mór) may have been associated with early copper miners. Consisting of a long, gallery-like burial chamber facing westward, and sometimes preceded by a portico, many were probably originally covered by a mound. P.H.

Wellesley, Arthur; Duke of Wellington (1769–1852). Politician and military leader. Born in *Dublin, Wellington always denied his Irishness and is reputed to have said: "If one is born in a stable, one is not necessarily a horse." He began his military career in India and became Britain's leading general against Napoleon, finally defeating him at Waterloo, in Belgium, in 1815. He was chief secretary for Ireland from 1807 to 1809. A hero after the Napoleonic War, Wellington became prime minister and in 1829 he oversaw the passing of *Catholic Emancipation. T.C.

Wentworth, Thomas (1593–1641). English statesman and lord deputy of Ireland (1632–40). Wentworth reestablished royal authority in Ireland

and reformed the system of government, building for himself a large official residence in Jigginstown, County *Kildare. However, Wentworth's despotic style of government alienated both Old and New English landowners. As chief advisor to King Charles I, Wentworth (made the earl of Strafford in January 1640), raised funds from the Irish *Parliament for the king's wars against the Scottish Covenanters (1639 and 1640). However, Wentworth's ruthless and unpopular use of the law to confiscate lands from English settlers in Ireland coincided with a widespread belief that he intended to use an Irish army to crush parliamentary opposition to the king. Consequently, he was impeached by the English Parliament and put on trial in March 1641. Wentworth mounted a sturdy defense against these charges but he was found guilty and was executed on May 12, 1641. Portraits of Wentworth include *Thomas Wentworth and his Secretary, Sir Phillip Mainwaring* by Anthony van Dyck (c.1634). S.A.B.

Wesley, John (1703–91). Evangelist who established Methodism in Ireland. Born in Epworth, Lincolnshire, John Wesley was educated in Oxford where he and his brother Charles founded a "methodist" society in 1729. In 1739, he began "field preaching" in Bristol and formally established Methodism. Wesley first visited Ireland in 1747 and by the time of his death, fifteen thousand Irish members had joined Methodist societies. By 1901 there were sixty-two thousand Methodists in Ireland, making them the country's third-largest *Protestant denomination. S.A.B.

Westmeath, County. Inland county in the province of *Leinster. The county has an area of 710 square miles and a population of 72,027 (2002 census). The old royal kingdom of Mide became part of the de Lacy earldom of Meath during the twelfth- and thirteenth-century *Anglo-Norman Conquest of Ireland. In the sixteenth century, Meath was subdivided into East Meath and West Meath, the latter retaining its name, while the former is now simply County *Meath. Westmeath is a gentle, pastoral county with livestock and dairy farming the principal economy. The county capital, Mullingar, has a population of around twelve thousand. Athlone, on the River *Shannon, is a larger town with an urban district council and a rich history. It was besieged more than three times during the course of the seventeenth century, most famously in June 1690 when Williamite forces overcame the *Jacobites in what was the largest bombardment in Irish history. Athlone is the birthplace of renowned tenor John *McCormack and the novelist John Broderick (1927–89). To the northwest of the town lies Lissoy, where Oliver *Goldsmith went to school and which is normally identified with the "Sweet Auburn" of his famous poem *The Deserted Village*.

The center of ancient Ireland was at Uisneach, east of Ballymore. The county is now bisected by the early-nineteenth century Royal Canal, which connects the Shannon with *Dublin City. Eskers, wormlike earthworks formed by glaciers millions of years ago, are found throughout the county. Fore is famous for its Seven Wonders (1. monastery in a *bog; 2. the mill without a race; 3. the water that flows uphill; 4. the tree that won't burn; 5. the water that won't boil; 6. the anchorite in a stone; 7. the stone raised by St. Feichin's prayer), some associated with St. Feichin who founded a monastery here in the seventh century. Other attractions in the county include Belvedere House, a mansion dating from the mid-eighteenth century, and Ballinlough Gardens.

Tullynally *Castle is the home of the Pakenham family, earls of Longford. (Edward Pakenham, Lord Longford, was a playwright and director of the *Gate Theatre.) The novelist J. P. *Donleavy has lived in the county for many years. P.H.

Wexford, County. Maritime county in the province of *Leinster. Often referred to as "the sunny southeast" of Ireland, Wexford (913 square miles) has a population of 116, 543 (2002 census). Its terrain falls gradually southeastward from the Blackstairs Mountains (2,409 feet) to the low-lying countryside around the county's capital, also called Wexford. The origin of its name is Norse, as the town was founded by the *Vikings in the ninth century. But the agriculturally rich county had, of course, been settled thousands of years before that. Beg Eire, on the opposite bank of Wexford harbor, was founded by St. Ibar, who may have been in Ireland before St. *Patrick. Close by are the Wexford Slobs, an extensive wildfowl reserve. The Normans first landed in Ireland at Baginbun in Wexford in 1169, initiating the *Anglo-Norman Conquest. South Wexford has fine *tower houses, built by the Norman invaders. In the baronies of Bargy and Forth, the most ancient English speech was preserved in a dialect known as Yola, until around 1850. County Wexford was one of the few places where the *Rebellion of 1798 actually took place under the leadership of Father John Murphy. The disastrous battle on *Vinegar Hill outside Enniscorthy ended the rebellion in Wexford.

The county is well endowed with historic monuments, including the great medieval Cistercian abbeys of Dunbrody and Tintern, the Norman church in New Ross, and the *castle, *churches, and high *crosses at Ferns, seat of Dermot *MacMurrough, who first invited the Normans to Ireland. Wexford's past is imaginatively re-created at the National Heritage Park at Ferrycarrig on the Slaney estuary. Kilmore Quay, with its picturesque thatched houses, looks out onto Saltee Islands, one of the great gannet colonies of northwestern Europe. The port of Rosslare offers links with Wales and France by car ferries, which ply routes that have brought people and ideas to Ireland since the Stone Age. In Wexford town, a fine statue by the American sculptor Wheeler Williams commemorates Wexford-born Commodore John Barry (1745–1803), father of the American navy. The internationally renowned *Wexford Opera Festival, held annually since 1951 in October/November, is devoted to the staging of rarely heard *operas. Notable natives of the county include the painter Francis Danby (1793–1861) and the novelist John *Banville. The famous English architect A. W. Pugin (1812–52) designed a number of churches in county Wexford, including the cathedral at Enniscorthy. The John F. *Kennedy Arboretum near New Ross commemorates the American president, whose ancestors came from nearby Dunganstown. P.H.

Wexford Festival. *Opera festival. Since it was founded by Dr. Thomas Walsh in 1951, the annual Wexford Festival has presented productions of rare opera at the tiny, atmospheric Theatre Royal. The festival now includes forty daytime events and eighteen evening performances of three major opera productions, each of them unique to the festival. Over the years, Wexford has displayed the talents of many young singers who went on to achieve international success, such as Dame Janet Baker, Sir Geraint Evans, and Fiorenza Cossotto. (Web site: *www.wexfordopera.com*.) S.A.B.

Whelan, Leo (1892–1956). Portrait and genre painter. Born in *Dublin, Whelan was considered one of William *Orpen's finest pupils at the Dublin Metropolitan School of Art. He exhibited regularly at the *Royal Hibernian Academy from 1911. Whelan taught at the Royal Hibernian Academy schools and was elected to the academy in 1924. Reproductions of his portraits of *saints were widely circulated. His portraits of leading statesmen and dignitaries can be viewed at the *Ulster, *Cork, and *Hugh Lane galleries. M.C.

whiskey. The whiskey that most of the world drinks is spelled without the *e*, as in Scotch whisky. But Irish whiskey once dominated the world market. Besides the spelling of the word, the main difference between Scotch and Irish is that Scotch features malted, or germinated, barley, and Irish uses a wide variety of grains including both malted and unmalted barleys. Other crucial differences include the tendency for the Scottish product to blend various whiskeys and for the Irish to distill multiple times. We do not know when or where the first whiskey was distilled, although it seems to have been a *Celt who did it. The earliest written references are a 1494 record from *Scotland and a 1556 Irish law. Whiskey, however, was drunk far earlier than this. English soldiers under *Henry II allegedly brought whiskey back home with them from Ireland in 1174. Legend further has it that in the early Middle Ages, traveling Catholic clerics imported *distilling technology directly or indirectly from the Middle East. The etymology of the word *whiskey* (from the Irish language *uisce beatha*, meaning "water of life") indicates a Celtic origin.

The golden age of whiskey-making in Ireland lasted from the 1600s, when massive amounts of the liquor were consumed on both sides of the Irish Sea (Queen *Elizabeth I was a great fan) through the middle of the nineteenth century, when the world fell in love with Scotland's new, smoother, blended whiskies. Previously, Irish whiskey had been favored over Scotch and was the main beneficiary of the phylloxera epidemic that devastated French vineyards in 1872. With brandy unavailable, the drinking nations adopted whiskey and soda as their evening drink. The 1600s saw the first tax on Irish whiskey and, consequently, the first poteen (pronounced "potcheen"), or moonshine, whiskey. Poteen is still made in Ireland today.

After a long fallow period, the 1980s and 1990s have seen a tremendous upsurge in both quality and variety in Irish whiskies. Principal brands of Irish whiskey today include Bushmills, Jameson, Power, Paddy, Connemara, Locke's, Tullamore Dew, and Middleton Reserve. T.G.

Whitaker, T[homas] K[enneth] (1916–). Economist, public servant. Born in 1916, T. K. Whitaker was the preeminent economist of the *Republic of Ireland. As secretary of the Department of Finance (1956–69), he was pivotal in charting a new economic course, which he outlined in a government document, "Economic Development" (1958). Whitaker advocated abandonment of protectionism in favor of competitive participation in world trade. He was instrumental in arranging the historic meeting between *Taoiseach (prime minister) Seán *Lemass and Prime Minister of Northern Ireland Terence *O'Neill in 1965. Whitaker was governor of the Central Bank between 1969 and 1976, and subsequently served in the Irish senate. His public service continued after his retirement from the Central Bank: as chairman of the Constitution Review Group in the

1990s, chancellor of the National University of Ireland from 1976 to 1996, and chairman of Bord na Gaeilge, the Irish Folklore Council, and the Salmon Research Agency. F.OM.

Whiteboys. Agrarian secret society. Active in *Munster in the mid-eighteenth century, the Whiteboys protested against evictions, high rents, and *tithes. The name comes from the white smocks they wore as a uniform. Seen as a major threat to the social order, "Whiteboys" became a term used to describe any group of agrarian protestors. T.C.

Wicklow, County. Maritime county in the province of *Leinster. The county, covering an area of 782 square miles, has a population of 114,719 (2002 census). Bordered to the north by County *Dublin, Wicklow is divided by a central range of mountains, the highest of which is Lugnaquilla at 3,070 feet above sea level, Ireland's second-highest mountain after *Carrauntuohill (3,414 feet) in County *Kerry. The Wicklow mountains were used as refuge points by rebels from the time of the O'Byrnes in the late sixteenth century to the time of Michael Dwyer and Joseph Holt after the *Rebellion of 1798. These mountains impeded communications between the various regions of the county. This isolation was the main reason why the county was not formed as an administrative unit until 1606.

The principal rivers in the county are the Liffey and the Slaney. Wicklow, known as the garden of Ireland, has been a center for regional tourism since the early nineteenth century, principally for attractions like the monastic site at *Glendalough and the impressive gardens and waterfall at Powerscourt. Charles Stewart *Parnell, the most important Irish *nationalist leader in the second half of the nineteenth century, was born at Avondale House, near Rathdrum. His family owned an estate there of 3,800 acres. The celebrated art collection of Sir Alfred Beit is housed at Russborough House, near Bray. The principal towns in the county are Arklow, Bray, Greystones, and Wicklow, the county capital. A.S.

Wild Geese (Irish Brigades). Popular name given to those who left Ireland after the Treaty of *Limerick. Under the treaty, Irish regiments were allowed to enter French service. The Irish Brigade of the French army is the most famous, but there were also Irish regiments in the Hapsburg empire and Spain. It is estimated that up to three hundred thousand Irishmen served in European armies in the eighteenth century. To the *Protestant ascendancy, the Irish Brigades were a *Catholic army in exile, proof of the *Jacobite threat. Their exploits were followed eagerly at home. The brigade in *France fought together only once as a unit in 1745, at the Battle of Fontenoy, during the War of the Austrian Succession. The brigade played a decisive part in France's victory over the British and their allies. In the nineteenth century, various units of Irishmen in foreign armies were known—usually unofficially—as Irish brigades. These units fought for Napoleon, in the South American wars of liberation, for the papacy, and in the *American Civil War. In the twentieth century, the name was applied to those who fought in the *Boer War and to Eoin *O'Duffy's Catholic volunteers in Spain. T.C.

Wilde, Lady Jane Francesca (1826–96). Poet and folklorist; mother of Oscar *Wilde. A native of County *Wexford, Jane Elgee was influenced by the *nationalist poetry of Richard D'Alton Williams, which was published in the **Nation*. She also contributed to the *Nation* under the pen name "Speranza." Elgee married renowned physician Sir

Oscar Wilde

William *Wilde in 1851. Her works include the poem "The Famine Year" (1871) and the nationalist-inspired prose collection *Ancient Legends of Ireland* (1887). S.A.B.

Wilde, Oscar (1854–1900). Playwright. Wit, raconteur, poet, and brilliant speaker, Wilde is one of the great dramatists of the English language. He was born in *Dublin, the son of Sir William *Wilde, a famous surgeon, and Lady *Wilde, an eccentric, *nationalist poet. As a student at Trinity College, Dublin, and Magdalen College, Oxford, where he excelled in classics, Wilde was strongly influenced by the aestheticism of Ruskin and Pater. He moved to London in 1879 and embarked on a career as a writer, lecturer, and critic. His publications from this period include *The Happy Prince and Other Tales* (1888), and *Lord Arthur Savile's Crime and Other Stories* (1891), which includes "The Canterville Ghost," often considered his best story.

Wilde cultivated his reputation as a dandy and wit. The satirical magazine *Punch* caricatured him as the adorer of white lilies, while Gilbert and Sullivan's *opera *Patience* made fun of him in the figure of Bunthorne. Arriving in New York for his very successful lecture tour of the United States in 1882, he quipped to a Customs' officer, "I have nothing to declare but my genius." An outrageous and extravagant aesthete, Wilde confessed in one of his witticisms, "I can resist everything, except temptation." He married Constance Lloyd in 1884. They had two sons, Cyril (1885) and Vyvyan (1886). The latter, under the adopted name of Vyvyan Holland, wrote the history of his family in *Son of Oscar Wilde* (1954). In 1887 (until 1889), Wilde became editor of a women's magazine in London, *The Woman's World*, for which he wrote literary notes and articles on fashion.

Wilde is known chiefly for his plays, masterpieces in the genre of the comedy of manners: *Lady Windermere's Fan* (1891), *The Importance of Being Earnest* (1895), and *An Ideal Husband* (1895). Never before had the hypocrisy of London's high society been satirized with such hilarity. A planned London production of Wilde's biblical play *Salomé* (with Sarah Bernhardt) was censored in 1893, but the play was performed in Paris in 1896. Published in 1891, Wilde's controversial novel *The Picture of Dorian Gray*, whose beautiful, hedonistic protagonist miraculously retains his youth while his portrait increasingly exhibits signs of decay, was described as "filthy," "dangerous," and "brilliant."

At the height of his fame in the mid-1890s, Wilde's public affair with Lord Alfred Douglas, the son of the Marquess of Queensberry (who invented the rules of modern boxing), created a scandal and led to Wilde's ill-fated decision to sue the Marquess for libel. The legal proceedings that followed would become legendary and lead to Wilde's downfall. Prosecuted for, and convicted of, homosexuality, he was sentenced to prison in 1898 and served two years in Reading Gaol. A modified version of a letter written to Douglas during the final months of his incarceration was published in 1905 under the title *De Profundis*. Wilde's final work is the moving if uneven poem *The Ballad of Reading Gaol* (1898). After his release, Wilde moved to France and died in Paris in 1900, a broken and lonely man. J.OM., L.R., J.C.E.L.

Wilde, Sir William (1815–76). Surgeon, father of Oscar *Wilde. Wilde was also an archaeologist, ethnologist, antiquarian, biographer, statistician, naturalist, topographer, historian, and folklorist. From 1855 to 1876, this remarkable nineteenth-century polymath lived at No.1 Merrion Square, *Dublin, where a plaque commemorates him. His wife, Lady *Wilde, was a *nationalist and a poet, who wrote under the name Speranza. P.H.

William III, Prince of Orange (1650–1702). King of England (1688–1702), leader of the Netherlands. William of Orange invaded England in 1688 and deposed *James II, his uncle and father-in-law, in order to secure naval and financial resources for his ongoing war (the War of the Grand Alliance, 1689–97) with Louis XIV, the "Sun King" of France. He also sought to preempt any Anglo-French alliance. This so-called "Glorious Revolution" shifted the balance of constitutional power decisively from the monarch toward Parliament, but for William III it was a necessary means to a larger end—defeating France. James II fled to France and, in March 1689, landed in Ireland with a view to using it as a stepping-stone to regain his other two kingdoms, Scotland and England. Later that year, a Williamite army of fourteen thousand men landed in *Ulster, led by the elderly Duke of Schomberg. His instructions were to march on *Dublin without delay and destroy the Jacobite forces opposing him. However, Schomberg failed dismally to end the Irish campaign in the autumn of 1689 thereby forcing William to intervene in person. Having to go to Ireland was, as he explained apologetically to one of his Allies, "a terrible mortification," but ". . . If I can reduce that kingdom quickly, I shall then have my hands free to act with so much more vigour against the common enemy."

However, William did not "reduce that kingdom quickly": he failed to encircle and prevent the retreat of the much smaller Franco-Irish army at the Battle of the *Boyne (July 12, 1690), though James II's flight made it a propaganda triumph which counteracted simultaneous defeats on land (Fleurus) and sea (Beachy Head). Deluded, perhaps, by his own propaganda, William of Orange demanded more-or-less unconditional surrender after the Battle of the Boyne. The Finglas Declaration promised pardon to "the meaner sort" but did not offer guarantees of property and religious freedom. This severity was mistaken because it stiffened Irish resistance and ensured that the Boyne would not be a decisive victory.

After an unduly long delay, William of Orange decided to attack *Limerick. This was a key to the Irish defensive line along the *Shannon River. His assault (August, 27, 1690) was repulsed and his forces suffered heavy losses. William was forced to call off the siege because of increasingly wet weather and a shortage of gunpowder. He returned to England shortly afterward. The war would not end until October 1691, when the Treaty of *Limerick offered improved peace terms to the Irish and the Finglas Declaration was disregarded.

William of Orange's commemoration as an Irish *Protestant folk hero in the eighteenth century owes much to the simple fact that he personified definitive Irish Protestant victory after the uncertainty of the seventeenth century. Moreover, his repeated and unflinching exposure to danger at the Boyne, notably when struck on the shoulder by an artillery shot, conspicuously exemplified the forbearance in battle that contemporaries most admired. "He may not have always won" admitted a *Huguenot biographer, "but he always deserved to win." The *Orange Order, founded in 1795, revived and popularized the cult of William III. The annual Battle of the Boyne parades on "the twelfth" of July affirm its continuing potency and appeal to *Northern Ireland's Protestants. P.L.

witchcraft. The belief in magic was common in ancient Ireland as in other countries, but Gaelic Ireland was little influenced by the demonization of magic, which was widespread in medieval Europe. In Irish tradition, the devil remained a mischievous character who could be outwitted by clever individuals. Accusations of sinister collusion with the devil, leading to witchcraft trials, seem to have occurred only in *Norman and English settlements. One such case concerned Dame Alice Kyteler, a wealthy lady who was accused of witchcraft in *Kilkenny in 1324 by the Norman Bishop Richard de Ledrede. Her maidservant was burned at the stake, but Dame Alice herself escaped to England. Another celebrated case occurred at a Puritan colony in Youghal, County *Cork, in 1661, when an old woman called Florence Newton was accused of bewitching several of the local residents. The verdict is unknown, but the evidence offered was of a standard nature—that of inveigling people into her power by pretensions of affection, and causing them to vomit up many kinds of strange objects. In another case, at Island Magee in Country *Antrim in 1710, seven women were accused of causing the death of a widow and of bewitching a young girl. They were found guilty in court after quite selective evidence was offered by the prosecution, and were jailed for a year and pilloried.

In more recent generations, some old festival rituals have become confused with malicious practices. This is particularly so in the case of the May Festival. It was customary to collect the dew from the fields and to sprinkle the crops after sundown on May Eve for good luck. Such practices, especially when carried out surreptitiously, have attracted suspicion, and certain individuals are thought to magically steal the good fortune of their neighbors. The practice is usually known as *pishoguery*, from the Irish word *piseog* meaning "superstition." It is based on the notion that only a limited amount of prosperity is available, and that for one person to gain another must lose. Abstract feelings tend to be given physical form in traditional belief; thus, it is often held that people can be magically harmed by the envious feelings of others or by malicious comments.

Other beliefs and practices, sometimes confused with witchcraft by outsiders, reflect concerns about the relationship between human society and the fairies, and between the world of the living and the world of the dead. It was thought, for instance, that the fairies could inflict sickness on people, and even "abduct" individuals and replace them with fairy beings. Various means were employed to banish such "changelings" and recover the "real" person, sometimes with tragic results. As late as 1895, this happened to a young woman called Bridget Cleary, whose husband caused her death by submitting her to such ordeals, including burning. People who were noted for healing, and who used arcane practices in this regard, were regarded as being "wise" and their influence was generally beneficial. The most famous such "wise woman" was Biddy Early from Feakle in County *Clare in the nineteenth century. D.Oh.

women. Under *brehon law, women had certain property and marital rights, and women were accepted, though not often, as heads of lordships. Irish abbesses, like their European counterparts, had extensive ecclesiastical authority. However, this power and independence applied mainly to rich and powerful women. Little is known about the lives of women at the humbler levels of society. The political and religious changes of the sixteenth and seventeenth centuries, brought about by English law, removed women's property rights. The *Reformation suppressed religious houses, and the counter-Reformation brought in new and stricter regulations for *nuns. Eighteenth-century middle- and upper-class women were expected to take an interest in politics, and many did, particularly in the revolutionary generation of the 1780s and 1790s.Women often ran commercial and craft enterprises. Working-class and small-farming women's home-based *textile and garment work gave them a measure of economic independence from the 1790s, though the poverty and vulnerability of this class is illustrated by the dramatic decline in their number in the calamitous decade of the 1840s.

Home-based textile and manufacture, however, continued to be important in some areas up to the early twentieth century. The farm woman, involved in all aspects of farm work, controlled poultry and dairying up to the mid-twentieth century. Most shopkeepers' womenfolk would have had hands-on involvement with the family business, and the widowed female shopkeeper, like the widowed female farmer, was a familiar and authoritative figure. Paid work for unskilled or uneducated women was, however, quite scarce. In the north the textile and garment industry employed females in factories and mills from the mid-nineteenth century. In other parts of Ireland, however, apart from some factory work in the major cities, the only work these women could hope to find was in domestic or institutional service. *Emigration to North America or *Australia was, therefore, an attractive option for Irish women. Not only was the number of women who emigrated roughly equal to that of men (unusual for Europe at the time), but almost all Irish women who emigrated did so with friends, or peers, rather than under family/male protection.

For women from lower, middle, and skilled working-class backgrounds whose parents could afford to let them stay on at school into their teens, the mid-nineteenth century was a time of economic opportunity. They could work as national (primary) teachers, prison officers, nurses, trained midwives, or, by the end of the century, post office clerks or telegraphists/telephonists.

There were no bars to hiring married women, though informal ones might have operated in some offices. Upper-middle-class girls who attended fee-paying superior schools could take the Intermediate Certficate School-Leaving Examination from 1878, when it was established on a basis of strict gender equality. Women were admitted to most Irish *universities in the 1880s.

In the opening decade of the twentieth century, women became involved in *nationalism, *unionism, the labor movement, and the suffrage movement. The *Proclamation of the *Easter Rising of 1916 addressed men and women as equal citizens, and promised equal citizenship. Women participated in the rising and were particularly important in the propaganda and support work thereafter. *Ulster unionism, while it had a much bigger women's auxiliary movement than nationalism, had no commitment to gender equality, and no high-profile women. Irish women voted for the first time in 1918 when the Representation of the People Act in the UK granted the vote for the first time to all men over twenty-one and all women of certain property qualifications over thirty. The first woman elected to the House of Commons was Constance *Markievicz; as a *Sinn Féin member, she did not take her seat, but became minister for Labour in the First *Dáil (Parliament), in Dublin in 1919. Women played a strong administrative role in the new state set up by the first Dáil during the *War of Independence, 1919–21. After the *Anglo-Irish Treaty (1921), most of the high-profile women—Markievicz, Mary McSwiney, Hanna *Sheehy Skeffington—took the anti-treaty side. An exception among the famous women was Jennie Wyse Power, veteran of the Ladies Land League (1879–82) and of all the struggles since then, who took the pro-treaty side and was a strong defender of women's rights in the *Free State Senate. The 1922 Constitution of the Irish Free State granted equal citizenship to women and men, without qualifications of any kind.

Once granted, political equality was never rescinded, and women sat in both houses of the *Oireachtas (legislature). Women's citizenship came under attack in a number of ways, however. They were "exempted" from jury duty in 1927, and the 1937 *Constitution seemed to imply a synonymity between women and motherhood—ironic, in view of the falling marriage rate. Employment bars against married women in teaching and the public service were introduced 1928–32, and the number of women in industrial employment was cut down in 1936. Sex-specific labor legislation affected lower-middle and working-class women, leaving the wealthier women professionals—doctors, solicitors, barristers, accountants, and public representatives—untouched. Birth control was totally banned by 1936. *Divorce was unconstitutional.

From 1940 until about 1960, tens of thousands of Irish women and girls emigrated, this time to Britain, to plentiful, well-paid work and training. Thousands of women deserted domestic service, to the oft-expressed chagrin of upper-middle-class women. Life was also changing for women who did not emigrate. Many women chose financial independence over marriage, prompting alarm at population decline. The employment bar on married women as national teachers was lifted in 1958 partly to encourage marriage. Women who stayed on the land began to demand electricity and indoor plumbing, and membership of the Irish Countrywomen's Association soared in the 1950s and 1960s. Meanwhile a free-for-all maternity *health care system, introduced in Northern Ireland in 1948 and in the *Republic in 1953, caused an already-declining maternal mortality rate to fall even further. Family allowances, introduced in both administrations in the mid-1940s, improved women's nutrition. The economic recovery of the 1960s saw industrial work opening up for women, while the introduction of free secondary education in 1966 in the Republic (it had been introduced in Northern Ireland with the Butler Act in 1948) gave opportunities to a new generation of Irish girls. Female participation in every area of economic life rose significantly from the 1970s, keeping pace with their higher profile in public life. The feminist movement of the early 1970s led to the establishment of a Council for the Status of Women in 1973. Groups such as Irishwomen United, AIM, Cherish, the Women's Political Association, and other organizations improved women's legal, occupational, economic, and social position. Reforms such as the removal of the marriage bar on public servants, the introduction of paid maternity leave, improvement of women's family law status, support for unmarried mothers and deserted wives, access to contraception, and other reforms—all came in the 1970s and 1980s. C.C.

Wood's Half-Pence Controversy (1722–25). Political scandal. This controversy arose over the granting of a patent to produce copper coin for Ireland to William Wood, an English manufacturer. The patent had been issued without the consent of the Irish *Parliament, which passed resolutions condemning the measure. It was rumored in Ireland that Wood had acquired the patent through King *George I's mistress, the Duchess of Kendal. The controversy inspired the famous series of pamphlets, *Drapier's Letters* (1724–25), by Jonathan *Swift. Ultimately, a combined campaign of political and popular protest led to the rescinding of the patent in 1725. While much of the hostility to the new coinage was based on the fear that it would debase the Irish currency, it also served to highlight popular hostility to what was perceived as English misgovernment of Ireland. A.S.

wool. See **textiles.**

Workers' Party. Political party. The Workers' Party evolved from the left-wing Official *Irish Republican Army, which declared a unilateral ceasefire in 1972. The party suffered a serious split in 1992 when leading members set up a rival organization, Democratic Left, which has since merged with the *Labour Party. The Workers' Party support in *Northern Ireland has also withered away. M.M.

workhouse. Institutions established to provide poor relief. The *Poor Law Act, 1838, divided Ireland into 130 poor law districts (unions), each with a workhouse. Entry for those who required aid was at the discretion of the local poor law guardians and financing came mostly from a poor-rate collected from local landowners. The buildings were of a standardized design, drawn up by George Wilkinson, an English architect. In general, conditions were deliberately harsh and degrading in order to discourage the poor from using them. During the *Famine, thousands of destitute people flocked to these institutions, causing an accommodation crisis. In reaction, the government established temporary soup kitchens and introduced a system of out-relief under the 1847 Poor Law Extension Act. The workhouse system was formally abolished by the *Free State government in the 1920s and in *Northern Ireland in 1946. P.E.

World War I. The Great War, which claimed ten million lives in Europe, played a pivotal role in the creation of an independent Ireland. Some two hundred thousand Irishmen served in the British army during the war, with tens of thousands of casualties. The list of Irish regiments that fought in France includes the largely Catholic Connaught Rangers, Dublin Fusiliers, and Munster Fusiliers. Similarly, the Thirty-sixth Division, which enlisted in block form from the loyalist *Ulster Volunteer Force, was decimated on the first day of the Battle of the Somme (July 1, 1916) after having advanced, in the face of withering German fire, farther than any other British army unit.

At the onset of hostilities, John *Redmond and his *Irish Parliamentary Party successfully traded their support for the imperial war effort in exchange for Parliament's passage of the *Home Rule Act (September 1914). However, home rule was suspended for the duration of the conflict and the war ultimately doomed constitutional *nationalism. The radical *republicans of the *Irish Republican Brotherhood (IRB) took advantage of Britain's distraction with World War I to rise in Dublin on Easter Monday, 1916, in what is known as the *Easter Rising. Although the rebels were compelled to surrender within a week, the execution of the principal leaders, including Patrick *Pearse and James *Connolly, dramatically swung public opinion in favor of independence. By 1918, *Sinn Féin, partially as a result of London's attempts to extend conscription to Ireland, had supplanted Redmond's Irish Parliamentary Party as the largest single party in the country. In fact, for Ireland, the *Anglo-Irish War (1919–21) was the final act of World War I. J.P.

wren-boys. Midwinter revelers in traditional Ireland. It is customary throughout most of Ireland for groups to travel in disguise from house to house on St. Stephen's Day, December 26, playing music and singing songs. They chant a verse claiming to have killed a wren and seeking money for its funeral. In former times, the dead body of a wren was carried on top of a little pole or branch of holly. There is evidence for such a "wren-hunt" from the Middle Ages in Ireland and in parts of Britain and France, and it may be that the custom originated in prehistoric times with a ritual to banish the spirit of winter, envisaged as the tiny bird. D.Oh.

Y

Yeats, Anne (1919–2001). Painter and lithographer. A committee member and regular exhibitor of the *Irish Exhibition of Living Art (IELA), Anne Yeats was the daughter of the poet and niece of the painter Jack Butler *Yeats. Born in *Dublin, she studied at the *Royal Hibernian Academy school and worked as a designer and painter of sets at various theaters, including the *Abbey Theatre. She eventually took up painting full-time and later moved on to lithography and monotypes. She helped revive the Cuala Press in 1969. M.C.

Yeats, Jack B. (1871–1957). Painter. The best-known Irish painter of the twentieth century, Jack B. Yeats was born in London and influenced greatly by his childhood years spent with maternal grandparents in County *Sligo. He was the younger brother of the poet William Butler *Yeats. Jack B. Yeats attended art schools in London and worked as a magazine, book, and poster illustrator in England before producing watercolors of Devon and the West of Ireland. Yeats also edited and illustrated traditional ballads and wrote prose, novels, and plays. He traveled with John *Synge around *Connemara in 1904, providing illustrations for the writer's articles for the *Guardian* newspaper, and in 1907 advised Synge on costumes for *The Playboy of the Western World*. In 1910, he moved to *Dublin and painted in oils for the first time. His landscapes, dominated by dramatic characters, were often used as book illustrations. American John Quinn collected his work and helped Yeats exhibit his paintings at the Armory Show in New York in 1913, and many times after in America. Elected to the *Royal Hibernian Academy in 1917, he began to use color in the 1920s as an emotional form of expression often in work that was based on memory. He captured the subjective world of individuals and their natural dignity in relation to each other and their environment. His sensitive portrayal of national events such as *The Funeral of Harry Boland*, 1922 (Sligo County Museum and Art Gallery), and *Death for Only One*, 1927 (private collection), captured the new note of intensity in Irish life and earned him the title of Ireland's first national painter. *Going to Wolfe Tone's Grave*, 1929, demonstrates his ability to capture memory directly with passionate authority. He published three plays in 1933, as well as reminiscences and articles, and wrote four novels: *Sailing, Sailing Swiftly* (1933), *The Amaranthers* (1936), *The Charmed Life* (1938), and *The Careless Flower* (1947). The National Gallery in London hosted a retrospective exhibition of his paintings in 1942. A loan exhibition was held in Dublin in 1945 and at the Tate Gallery London in 1948 and a retrospective exhibition traveled to American cities in 1951–52. M.C.

Yeats, John Butler (1839–1922). Portrait painter and writer. Father of the famous painter Jack and the poet William, Yeats was born in County *Down and studied law at Trinity College, Dublin. His determination to be a painter prevented him from practicing law and kept the family impoverished, but provided them with an appreciation of intellectual independence. Seeking portrait commissions, he and his family moved back and forth from London to Dublin. He was elected to the *Royal Hibernian Academy in 1892, and at his exhibition with Nathaniel *Hone in 1901 he came to the attention of American collector John Quinn. Before settling in New York in 1909, he painted many portraits of leading figures in the Irish artistic and literary world, some of which were commissioned by Hugh *Lane. In America he lectured on art, wrote magazine articles and memoirs, painted and sketched portraits, and gave public readings of the poetry of his son William. A selection of his letters made by Ezra Pound (*Passages from the Letters of J.B. Yeats*) was published in 1917 and Cuala Press published his *Early Memoirs* in 1923. M.C.

Yeats, William Butler. (1865–1939). Poet, playwright, Nobel laureate. Widely reckoned the greatest English-language poet of the twentieth century, Yeats was born in *Dublin on June 13, 1865, the first child of John Butler *Yeats and Susan Pollexfen Yeats. His childhood and youth were spent in London, Dublin, and in *Sligo, where his mother's family, originally from Devonshire, had settled and prospered in the nineteenth century. John Butler Yeats, scion of a *Protestant family that came to Ireland in the seventeenth century, was heir to lands in County *Kildare that made him an *Anglo-Irish gentleman but did not supply an adequate income. He had abandoned a promising career in the law for the insecure profession of artist and portrait painter in which he never achieved financial success. The poet grew up in an atmosphere of bohemian indifference to money values and of genteel poverty alleviated by sojourns in his grandfather's substantial home in Sligo, where he developed his profound love of the Irish countryside and its folk.

Yeats's young manhood in London, where his family took up residence in 1887, was marked by an urgent need to establish himself as poet and man of letters and by his burgeoning interest in magic and occult knowledge. Around this time, he became increasingly committed to Irish *republican *nationalism to which he had been introduced by the old *Fenian John *O'Leary in 1885. He was also hopelessly in love with his poetic muse, the nationalist firebrand and beauty Maud *Gonne, who spurned his romantic and marital advances.

Yeats's early reputation as a romantic and symbolist poet who exploited Irish mythic and national material was established by *The Wanderings of Oisin* (1889), *Poems* (1895), and *The Wind among the Reeds* (1899).

In 1899, along with Lady Augusta *Gregory and

William Butler Yeats

others, Yeats started the Irish Literary Theatre, the precursor of the *Abbey Theatre that opened in 1904. He gave much of his energy to the theater in the first decade of the twentieth century, escaping each summer from his home in London and the theater in Dublin, to the comforts of Lady Gregory's Galway home, *Coole Park. It was not until the publication of *Responsibilities* (1914) that he moved away from the romantic poetry of dreams and mythology and established his reputation as a poet of modernity. In this austere and harsh volume, Yeats registered his bitter alienation from an Ireland whose philistine reaction to John Millington *Synge's *The Playboy of the Western World* had hastened, Yeats believed, its author's premature death, and from the city of Dublin whose citizens scorned great art.

Yeats spent the *World War I years of 1914–18 in Sussex and London. He was deeply distressed and moved—in a way that he was not by the vast slaughter of the Great War—by the *Easter Rising in Dublin in April 1916, which drew from him the troubled elegy and peroration "Easter 1916," with its memorable refrain "A terrible beauty is born." From the war years came many of the poems gathered in the most ample collection he had published since 1899, *The Wild Swans at Coole* (1917, 1919). It was also during the war years that he began his dramatic experiments with the Japanese Noh theater.

Yeats married in 1917. His young bride Georgie Hyde-Lees brought him domestic security and her talents as a medium made the first five years of their marriage an extraordinary spiritualist experiment. From her spirit communications Yeats assembled a body of psychological and historical doctrine published as *A Vision* (1925, 1937). This material stimulated the poet to address a disturbed period of revolution and civil war in Europe and Ireland in highly charged dramatic verse. The collaboration of poet and medium bore particular fruit in what is regarded by many as Yeats's finest single volume of poetry, *The Tower* (1928).

Yeats served as a senator in the *Parliament of the *Irish Free State from 1922 until 1928. He was awarded the Nobel Prize for literature in 1923. Yet honors and advancing years did not diminish his creativity or his imaginative engagement with the destiny of his country. In the 1930s he blamed the crude democracy of a leveling age ("the filthy modern tide") for the puritan zeal with which the new Irish state sought to impose Catholic social values, and he increasingly represented himself as a self-consciously *Anglo-Irish poet, a poet of Swiftian, savage indignation. He also allowed himself moments of bawdy sexuality in his verse and struck wildly intemperate social attitudes. *The Winding Stair and Other Poems* (1933) combined Anglo-Irish hauteur and distaste for modernity with lyric celebration of bodily experience.

A tragic note is struck in Yeats's late poetry, when ill health and impending death made him seek the warmer climes of southern Europe for extended periods. As the continent was riven by extreme social philosophies, Yeats reacted with a mixture of rage, dark premonition, and the "tragic joy" he sought to express in his most ambitious late work. His posthumously published *Last Poems and Plays* (1939) is a chilling testament of a poet *in extremis*. Yeats died in the south of France on January 28, 1939, where he was buried. He was reinterred in Drumcliff churchyard, County Sligo, in 1948, the resting place he had chosen for himself in his poem "Under Ben Bulben."

Yeats's oeuvre includes experimental drama, fiction, autobiography, and criticism, but it is in the indisputable power of his poetry that he makes his claim on posterity. T.B.

Yeomanry, the. Volunteer civilian militia. Formed in September/October 1796 to assist the authorities in the event of French invasion, the Yeomanry was responsible with policing local areas if the regular military forces were called away to repel invaders. In regions where martial law was declared between 1797 and 1803, the uniformed yeomen were placed on "permanent duty," housed at government expense in barracks, subjected to military command, and given patrolling and guard duties. Yeomen proved useful auxiliaries to the military during the *Rebellion of 1798, when they participated in several pitched battles with insurgents. R.OD.

Young Ireland. *Nationalist group of the 1840s. In October 1842, several idealistic young Irishmen, including Thomas *Davis, Charles Gavan *Duffy, and John Blake *Dillon, founded a newspaper in *Dublin, the **Nation*, which advocated both political autonomy and cultural revival for a nonsectarian Ireland. This circle became known as "Young Ireland" by reference to Giuseppi Mazzini's "Young Italy" organization. Davis, who died at thirty in 1845, emphasized the need to preserve the *Irish language and create a new national literature. Initially, the "Young Irelanders" allied themselves with Daniel *O'Connell's *Repeal movement. As some Young Ireland leaders were *Protestants firmly committed to a nonsectarian national identity, however, the group objected to the close ties that O'Connell's movement had developed with the *Catholic Church. Even more serious differences emerged over O'Connell's pragmatic and nonviolent strategy, and, in July 1846, "Young Ireland" withdrew from the Repeal movement. In January 1847, two of the most influential Young Ireland personalities, John *Mitchel and Thomas Francis *Meagher, founded the Irish Confederation in opposition to O'Connell's Repeal Association. The confederation, which soon established clubs throughout Ireland and Britain, formed a militantly revolutionary and *republican rival to O'Connell's constitutional movement. In July 1848 during the Great *Famine, William Smith *O'Brien led an unsuccessful *rebellion in County *Tipperary. In its aftermath, most leaders of Young Ireland fled abroad or were *transported to penal colonies in *Australia. The movement's legacy for later nationalists included a willingness to use physical force to achieve its goals and an emphasis on cultural revival as a vital aspect of nationalism. F.B.

Z

Zozimus (1794–1846). Nickname for Michael Moran, a blind *Dublin storyteller. Born in the Liberties section of Dublin, Zozimus lost his sight as a child following a short illness. Described by some as Ireland's nineteenth-century Homer, he had an exceptional memory for stories and songs, and a prodigious talent for composition and recitation. His nickname came about because of his fondness for reciting the story of Zozimus, a bishop who administered the Holy Sacraments to St. Mary of Egypt in the fifth century. P.E.

Chronology of Irish History

B.C.

c. 7000	Evidence of Ireland's earliest people, Mesolithic hunter-gatherers, at Mount Sandel, County *Derry.
3500–3000	Arrival of Neolithic farmers in Ireland. Construction of megalithic tombs.
2500	Construction of the *passage-grave at *Newgrange, County *Meath.
2000–1800	Bronze Age begins in Ireland.
c. 500–150	The *Celts (iron-using farmers and warriors from central and western mainland Europe) arrive in Ireland.

A.D.

c. 130–80	Ptolemy's *Geography* contains a map of Ireland and a list of Irish rivers, settlements, and tribes.
300–450	Irish raiders plunder Roman Britain.
c. 377–405	Niall of the Nine Hostages, high king of Ireland.
431	Pope Celestine I (422–32) appoints *Palladius as the first bishop to Ireland.
432	St. *Patrick begins his mission in Ireland.
c. 490	St. Enda sets up the first Irish monastery on the *Aran Islands.
493	Traditional date for the death of St. Patrick (17 March).

Sixth century — Start of the Golden Age of Irish Monasticism.

547 — Monastery of *Clonmacnoise founded by St. Ciarán.

563 — St. *Colm Cille establishes a monastery on Iona.

795 — *Viking raids on Ireland begin with an attack on the monastery on Lambay Island.

841 — The future city of *Dublin is established by Vikings on the River Liffey.

914–22 — Viking settlements established at *Waterford, *Wexford, and *Limerick.

1002 — Brian *Boru becomes high king of Ireland.

1014 — Battle of *Clontarf. Brian Boru defeats the Vikings of Dublin and their *Leinster allies. After the battle, Boru is slain by a fleeing Norseman.

1152 — Synod of Kells. Diocesan organization of the Irish Church.

1155 — A proposed invasion of Ireland by the Norman King *Henry II is sanctioned by Pope Adrian IV in the papal bull *Laudabiliter*.

1166 — Rory *O'Connor becomes the last high king of Ireland. Dermot *MacMurrough, king of Leinster, is defeated in battle by O'Connor and goes to England and France to seek assistance from Henry II. Dermot obtains permission from Henry II to enlist the services of Norman knights in Wales and England.

1167 — MacMurrough returns to Ireland with Norman, Flemish, and Welsh mercenaries.

1169 — The *Norman invasion of Ireland begins when a large force arrives at Bannow Bay, County *Wexford.

1170 — *Strongbow (Richard fitzGilbert de Clare) lands with an army near *Waterford and takes the city. He marries Aoife, daughter of Dermot MacMurrough.

1171 — Dermot MacMurrough dies and is succeeded by Strongbow. Henry II lands in Ireland near Waterford with four hundred ships and a large army. He receives submission from his Norman lords, native kings, and the entire Irish clergy at Cashel.

1175 — Treaty of Windsor: in return for a declaration of loyalty to Henry II, Rory O'Connor is recognized as king of *Connacht.

1177 — Prince John (Henry II's son) becomes Lord of Ireland.

1210 — King John arrives in Ireland, establishes English common law and government.

1250 — Normans control most of the south of Ireland, as well as parts of eastern *Ulster.

Fourteenth century	Gaelic resurgence throughout Ireland.
1315–18	Edward *Bruce, the brother of Robert Bruce, King of *Scotland, invades Ireland and attempts unsuccessfully to overthrow the Anglo-Normans.
1348	The first Irish cases of Black Death in Howth and Balbriggan, near Dublin.
1366	A Parliament in *Kilkenny passes the *Statute of Kilkenny, forbidding English settlers in Ireland from adopting native customs.
Fifteenth century	Area under English control shrinks to the *Pale—counties Dublin, *Meath, *Kildare, and *Louth.
1494	*Poynings' Law enacted at Drogheda. Irish *Parliament to convene only with the permission of the king of England. All legislation needs royal approval.
1535	Rebellion of Silken Thomas is crushed by Lord Grey's army.
1536–37	Protestant *Reformation begins in Ireland with the establishment of the *Church of Ireland and the dissolution of Irish monasteries.
1540	*Henry VIII begins his policy of Surrender and Regrant. Native and Old English lords are granted titles in return for submission to the king's sovereignty and English law.
1541	Henry VIII declared king of Ireland by the Irish Parliament.
1550–57	*Plantation of *Offaly and *Laois.
1561–67	*Rebellion of Shane O'Neill.
1569–83	Two Desmond rebellions are crushed.
1586	Plantation of *Munster.
1588	Spanish Armada is destroyed in storms off the West Coast of Ireland.
1592	Trinity College, Dublin, is established.
1593–1603	The *Nine Years War rebellion by Hugh *O'Neill and Red Hugh *O'Donnell against the crown.
1601	The Battle of *Kinsale. O'Neill, O'Donnell, and their Spanish allies are defeated by Lord Deputy Mountjoy.
1603	The Treaty of *Mellifont brings the Nine Years War to an end.
1607	The *Flight of the Earls. Hugh O'Neill, Earl of Tyrone, and Red Hugh O'Donnell, Earl of Tyrconnell, along with ninety other Irish chiefs flee to the continent.
1609	The *Plantation of Ulster.
1641–49	The *Rebellion of 1641 begins the Confederate Wars—Rebellion of Ulster Irish and Old English Lords of the Pale against the crown.

1649 Oliver *Cromwell arrives in Ireland.

1652 *Cromwellian land settlement commences.

1685 *James II accedes to the English throne.

1688 James II deposed as king of England.

1689 *William of Orange becomes king of England and the Williamite campaign in Ireland begins.
James II lands at Kinsale. The Siege of *Derry.

1690 Battle of the *Boyne. James II and Irish forces defeated by William of Orange. First siege of *Limerick.

1691 Battle of *Aughrim. The bloodiest battle in Irish History—Irish and French allies of James II defeated by William of Orange.
Second siege of Limerick.
The Treaty of Limerick ends the Williamite war in Ireland.
Williamite land confiscations.

1695–1709 *Penal Laws enacted against *Catholics.

1713 Jonathan *Swift becomes Dean of *St. Patrick's Cathedral.

1742 World premiere of Handel's *Messiah* in Dublin.

1791 Society of *United Irishmen founded in *Belfast and Dublin.

1795 *Orange Order formed.

1796 French invading fleet arrives at Bantry Bay with Wolfe *Tone.

1798 United Irishmen rebellion in Wexford, *Antrim, and *Down crushed. French fleet which arrives in Mayo is defeated at Ballinamuck (Sept. 8), County *Longford. Wolfe Tone is arrested and commits suicide in prison.

1800 The Act of *Union passed, creating the United Kingdom of Great Britain and Ireland.

1803 Attempted rebellion in Dublin by Robert *Emmet.

1823 Catholic Association founded to campaign for *Catholic Emancipation.

1828 Daniel *O'Connell elected to the Westminster House of Commons for County *Clare.

1829 Catholic Emancipation Act allows Catholics to enter Parliament and hold civil and military office.

1840 Repeal Association founded to campaign against the Act of Union.

1842 The **Nation* *newspaper founded by Thomas *Davis, John Blake *Dillon, and Charles Gavan *Duffy.

1843 Mass Repeal Association meeting at *Clontarf, County Dublin, canceled by O'Connell following government ban.

1845–49 The Great *Famine. Potato blight causes starvation and mass *emigration.

1847 Daniel O'Connell dies in Genoa, Italy.

1848 Rebellion led by the radical wing of the *Young Ireland movement fails.

1854 Catholic University of Ireland founded in Dublin.

1858 *Irish Republican Brotherhood (IRB) founded in Dublin by James *Stephens.

1859 *Fenian Brotherhood founded in *New York by John O'Mahony.

1867 Fenian Rebellion fails.
*Clan na Gael founded in New York.

1868 William *Gladstone elected British prime minister.

1869 Gladstone disestablishes the Church of Ireland.

1870 *Home Government Association started by Isaac *Butt.
Gladstone's First *Land Act is passed.

1873 Isaac Butt founds the Home Rule League.

1874 Fifty-nine Home Rule candidates elected to Parliament in general election.

1875 Charles Stewart *Parnell elected MP for Meath.

1876–78 Obstructionism used by some Home Rule MPs led by Joseph Biggar in Parliament.

1878 New Departure—parliamentarians, agrarian reformers, and *nationalist revolutionaries agree to seek land reform and a settlement of the national question.

1879–82 The Land War.

1879 Irish National Land League founded in Dublin.

1881 Gladstone's Second Land Act passed.
The Land League is suppressed and Parnell imprisoned in *Kilmainham Gaol.

1882 Parnell released under the terms of the Kilmainham Treaty.
Land War ends.
*Phoenix Park Murders.

1884 *Gaelic Athletic Association (GAA) established in Thurles, County *Tipperary.

1885 Ashbourne Land Act is passed.

1886 First home rule bill defeated in the House of Commons.

1889	Parnell named as co-respondent in *O'Shea divorce case.
1890	Home Rule party splits over Parnell's involvement in O'Shea divorce case.
1891	Death of Parnell. Balfour Land Act is passed.
1893	Gladstone's Second home rule bill defeated in the House of Lords. The *Gaelic League founded by Douglas *Hyde.
1898	Local Government Act establishes County and Urban councils.
1899	Irish Literary Theatre (precursor to the *Abbey Theatre) established in Dublin.
1900	Home Rule party reunited under the leadership of John *Redmond.
1903	Wyndham Land Act passed.
1904	The Abbey Theatre is founded in Dublin.
1905	*Sinn Féin founded by Arthur *Griffith.
1909	Birrell Land Act enacted.
1912	Third home rule bill introduced into Parliament. Ulster Solemn League and Covenant pledges resistance to home rule by *unionists. Irish *Labour Party founded. **Titanic*, which was built in Belfast, sinks.
1913	*Ulster Volunteer Force (UVF), *Irish Citizen Army, and Irish *Volunteers founded. Lockout of workers under James *Larkin in Dublin.
1914	Outbreak of *World War I. John Redmond supports British war effort.
1915	*Lusitania* sunk by German U-boat off the Irish coast.
1916	*Easter Rising, on Easter Monday, April 24. Executions of fifteen leaders, May 3–12.
1918	Sinn Féin wins a majority of seats in the general election in Ireland.
1919	Sinn Féin MPs abstain from British Parliament and form first *Dáil (Parliament) in Dublin.
1919–21	*Anglo-Irish War.
1920	*Government of Ireland Act establishes two Irish Parliaments (in Dublin and Belfast). *Black and Tans arrive in Ireland. *Bloody Sunday (November 21): British forces open fire on crowd in *Croke Park in retaliation for assassinations of British agents.
1921	*Anglo-Irish Treaty signed in London.
1922	The *Irish Free State is created. *Ulysses*, by James *Joyce, is published in Paris.

1922–23 *Civil War between Free State forces and anti-treaty Republicans.

1922 Arthur Griffith dies on August 12. Michael *Collins killed on August 22. Erskine *Childers executed.

1922–32 William T. *Cosgrave becomes the first head of government (President of the Executive Council) of the Irish Free State.

1923 W. B. *Yeats awarded the Nobel Prize for literature.

1925 *Boundary Commission disbanded. Border between the Irish Free State and *Northern Ireland remains as set out in the Anglo-Irish Treaty.

1926 *Fianna Fáil party founded by Éamon *de Valera. George Bernard *Shaw is awarded the Nobel Prize for literature.

1931 The Statute of Westminster passed.

1932–48 Éamon de Valera serves as President of the Executive Council and (after the 1937 constitution) *Taoiseach (prime minister).

1933 *Fine Gael founded.

1937 A new *Constitution (Bunreacht na hÉireann) approved by referendum. Name of country changes from the Irish Free State to *Éire (in Irish), or Ireland.

1938 Economic War with Britain (begun in 1932) ends.

1938–45 Douglas Hyde is the first president of Ireland.

1939 Outbreak of World War II (known in Ireland as the Emergency). Ireland remains neutral.

1941 Dublin and Belfast bombed by the German air force.

1945–59 Seán T. Ó Ceallaigh is president of Ireland.

1948–51 John A. *Costello is Taoiseach.

1948 Ireland declared a Republic (*Republic of Ireland Act).

1949 Ireland Act passed at Westminster.

1951 E.T.S. *Walton shares Nobel Prize for physics.

1951–54 Éamon de Valera is Taoiseach.

1954–57 John A. Costello is Taoiseach.

1955 Ireland becomes a member of the *United Nations.

1957–59 Éamon de Valera is Taoiseach.

1959–66 Seán *Lemass is Taoiseach.

1959–73 Éamon de Valera is president of Ireland.

1961 *Television service is established in the Republic of Ireland.

1963 John F. *Kennedy visits Ireland.

1966–73 Jack *Lynch is Taoiseach.

1967 Civil Rights Association established in Northern Ireland (*NICRA) to campaign for equal rights for the Catholic Community.

1968 Civil rights demonstrators clash with police in Northern Ireland.

1969 Commencement of the *Troubles in Northern Ireland—British troops sent to Northern Ireland. Samuel *Beckett awarded Nobel Prize for literature.

1970 The IRA splits into Provisional and Official wings.

1971 *Internment without trial introduced in Northern Ireland.

1972 *Bloody Sunday: thirteen unarmed civilians are shot dead by the British army in Derry.
Northern Ireland *Stormont Parliament abolished. Direct rule of Northern Ireland from London.

1973–77 Liam *Cosgrave is Taoiseach.

1973 Ireland becomes a member of the European Economic Community (EEC).
Erskine *Childers is president of Ireland; he dies in office in November 1974.

1974 *Dublin-*Monaghan bombings. Seán *MacBride is awarded the Nobel Peace Prize.

1974–76 Cearbhall Ó Dálaigh is the fifth president of Ireland.

1976–90 Patrick Hillery is the sixth president of Ireland.

1976 Máiréad Maguire *Corrigan and Betty Williams are awarded the Nobel Peace Prize.

1977–79 Jack Lynch is Taoiseach.

1979 The IRA assassinate Lord Mountbatten and three relatives at Mullaghmore, County *Sligo. On the same day (August 27), eighteen British soldiers are ambushed and killed at Warrenpoint, County Down.
Pope John Paul II visits Ireland.

1979–81 Charles J. *Haughey is Taoiseach. He holds the office again briefly between February and November 1982.

1981 *Hunger strikes by republican prisoners in Long Kesh (Maze), including Bobby *Sands, MP.

1981–Feb. 1982 Garret *FitzGerald is Taoiseach.
Nov. 1982–87

1985 *Anglo-Irish Agreement signed.

1987 IRA bombing in Enniskillen kills eleven civilians.

1987–92 Charles J. Haughey is Taoiseach.

1990s Decade of the Celtic Tiger economy.

1990–97 Mary *Robinson is first woman president of Ireland.

1992–94 Albert *Reynolds is Taoiseach.

1993 Single European Act binds Ireland closer to the European Union.
*Downing Street Declaration begins the Northern Ireland *peace process.

1994 The IRA announce a complete cessation of military operations. Loyalist paramilitaries follow suit. In December the British government holds its first public talks with Sinn Féin.

1995 Framework document for all-party negotiations launched by Dublin and London governments. David *Trimble elected leader of the *Ulster Unionist party.
Seamus *Heaney is awarded the Nobel Prize for literature.

1994–97 John *Bruton is Taoiseach.

1996 IRA cease-fire ends but resumes a year later.
*Mitchell Report published.

1997–2002 Bertie *Ahern is Taoiseach. He continues as Taoiseach for a second term following general elections in May 2002.

1997 Mary *McAleese becomes the eighth president of Ireland.

1998 The *Good Friday Agreement is signed.
Northern Ireland Assembly established.
David Trimble and John *Hume awarded Nobel Peace Prize.
Bombing in *Omagh by dissident IRA group kills twenty-nine.

2000 Northern Assembly suspended in February over the issue of weapons decommissioning by the IRA. It reconvenes in May 2000.

2001 Irish voters reject the Treaty of Nice.

2002 The Republic of Ireland adopts the euro as its currency.
Treaty of Nice ratified in a second referendum.
Northern Ireland Executive suspended.

2004 Ireland held the presidency of the EU from January to June.

Acknowledgments

We are deeply indebted to our General Editorial Advisor Lawrence J. McCaffrey and our Editorial Consultant José Lanters for their extraordinary help. Their immense knowledge and patience were invaluable. Special thanks for editorial suggestions and fact checking to Nollaig Ó Gadhra and for editorial assistance in the art category to Sighle Breathnach-Lynch. For helping to shape the list of entries, we want to thank: Terence Brown, Sighle Breathnach-Lynch, Peter Harbison, Declan Kiberd, José Lanters, Joe Lee, Lawrence J. McCaffrey, and Kevin Whelan. We are very grateful for their comments to Patrick J. Egan, Troy Davis, Frank Biletz, Jody AllenRandolph, and Hugh Linehan. Our thanks to all our contributors.

A special thanks to David Mattingly for graphics and technical computer assistance.

We also want to thank photographer B. P. Fallon, Catherine Gale at Tourism Ireland, Debbie McGoldrick at the *Irish Voice*, Peter Thursfield at the *Irish Times*, Ciaran O'Reilly and Charlotte Moore of the Irish Repertory Theater (New York), and Niall Rynne for their generous help with photographs.

Photo Credits

We gratefully acknowledge the following for permission to reproduce photographs listed on the pages below:

+ ©*BP Fallon/bpFallon.com:* 272, 307

+ ©*BP Fallon/bpFallon.com, from BP Fallon's book* U2 Faraway So Close*:* 430

The Irish Times: 39, 92, 190, 263, 303, 310, 318, 368, 375, 392, 404

The Irish Voice: 2, 30, 50, 82, 153, 167, 170, 179, 188, 212, 214, 286, 300, 371, 387, 401, 416, 439, 449

Christy Moore, ©Jill Furmanovsky: 270

Áras an Uachtaráin: 260

Lelia Ruckenstein: 278

Northern Ireland Tourist Board: 31

Tourism Ireland: xi, 3, 16, 17, 57, 58, 71, 78, 80, 81, 97, 112, 114, 115, 119, 160, 220, 222, 239, 242 (from the Literary Map of Ireland), 246, 287, 288, 312, 373, 382, 383, 390, 427

Every effort has been made to establish the sources of all the photographs used and acknowledgment has been given. Should a source not have been acknowledged, we take this opportunity to apologize for such an oversight and we will make the necessary correction at the first opportunity.

Photo Credits

Cover Illustrations

Front Cover

First row, from left: Bewley's Oriental Cafe, Grafton St.; Detail in Newgrange; DART train at Killiney Bay, County Dublin; Ayesha Castle and garden, Killiney, County Dublin; the Olympia Theatre, Dublin

Second row, from left: Read's Cutlers—Dublin's Oldest Shop (1670); River Liffey, Dublin; Fireworks over Derry; Cross of Clogher, Monaghan County Museum; John Cleeres, a Kilkenny pub

Third row, from left: Maud Gonne; Ross Castle, Killarney, County Kerry; Michael Collins; Lakeside flora, Killarney, County Kerry; Oscar Wilde

Fourth row, from left: James Joyce; Muckross House and Garden, Killarney, County Kerry; Interior of St. Columb's Cathedral; Puffin Island, County Kerry; Adare Village Detail, County Limerick

Fifth row, from left: Kilkenny Castle and River Nore, Kilkenny; Irish girl; Valentia Island, County Kerry; Christ Church Cathedral, the nave; W. B. Yeats

Sixth row, from left: Charles Stewart Parnell; Traditional cottage, Aran Islands; Johnstown Castle and Gardens; Mary Robinson; St. Finbarr's Cathedral and River Lee

Spine

From top: Custom House and International Financial Services Centre; Muiredach's Cross, Monasterboice, County Louth; River Liffey, Dublin; Kilkenny Castle and River Nore, Kilkenny

Back Cover
Top row, from left: Morrissey's pub in Abbeyleix, County Laois; Interior of St. Columb's Cathedral; Edna O'Brien; Drombeg Stone Circle Glandore, County Cork; Ayesha Castle and garden, Killiney, County Dublin

Bottom row, from left: O'Connell Bridge, O'Connell Street and River Liffey; Holy Cross Cistercian Abbey, County Kilkenny; The Geraldine Experience, Tralee, County Kerry; Birr Castle Gardens, County Offaly; Adare Village detail, County Limerick

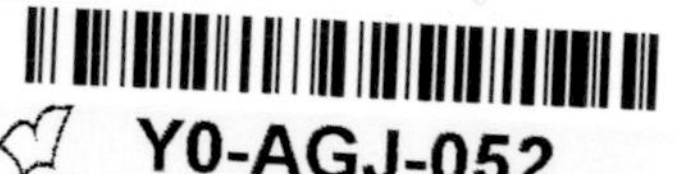

INTERVENTIONS INFIRMIÈRES

- NE PAS CONFONDRE DIFLUCAN (FLUCONAZOLE) AVEC DIPRIVAN (PROPOFOL).

PO: Bien agiter la suspension orale avant de l'administrer.

- Des noms de médicaments à « NE PAS CONFONDRE ».

- Les mentions **GÉR.** et **PÉD.**, quant à elles, attirent l'attention sur les précautions à prendre en cas d'utilisation chez les personnes âgées et les enfants.
- Les mentions **ALLAITEMENT** et **OBST.** permettent de connaître la conduite à tenir pendant l'allaitement et la grossesse.

Précautions et mises en garde: Insuffisance cardiaque compensée (risque de décompensation) ■ Insuffisance rénale ou hépatique (réduire la dose si la Cl_{Cr} < 50 mL/min/1,73 m²) ■ **GÉR.**: sensibilité accrue aux bêtabloquants; il est recommandé de réduire la dose initiale ■ Thyrotoxicose (l'acébutolol peut en masquer les symptômes) ■ Diabète (l'agent peut masquer les symptômes d'hypoglycémie) ■ **OBST., ALLAITEMENT, PÉD.**: L'innocuité du médicament n'a pas été établie; rares cas de bradycardie néonatale, d'hypotension, d'hypoglycémie et de dépression respiratoire ■ Antécédents de réactions allergiques graves (risque d'augmenter l'intensité des réactions) ■ Maladie respiratoire bronchospastique.

TOXICITÉ ET SURDOSAGE: Les concentrations sanguines thérapeutiques se situent entre 0,2 et 1 µg/mL. Il faut mesurer fréquemment les creux des concentrations plasmatiques pendant la période d'adaptation posologique chez les patients souffrant d'une maladie rénale ou hépatique grave ou chez ceux souffrant d'insuffisance cardiaque et d'insuffisance rénale modérée.

- Des sections sur la toxicité et le surdosage.

- Des médicaments qu'il ne faut pas écraser ou mâcher.

PO: ADMINISTRER LE DICLOFÉNAC APRÈS LES REPAS, AVEC DES ALIMENTS OU AVEC DES ANTIACIDES CONTENANT DE L'ALUMINIUM OU DU MAGNÉSIUM POUR DIMINUER L'IRRITATION GASTRIQUE. Le patient peut prendre les deux premières doses à jeun pour un début d'action plus rapide. IL NE FAUT PAS ÉCRASER NI MÂCHER LES COMPRIMÉS À ENROBAGE ENTÉRIQUE OU À LIBÉRATION PROLONGÉE.

Cefprozil

- **PO (adultes et enfants ≥ 13 ans)**: *La plupart des infections* – de 250 à 500 mg, toutes les 12 heures ou 500 mg, toutes les 24 heures, selon l'infection.
- **PO (enfants de 6 mois à 12 ans)**: *Otite moyenne* – 15 mg/kg, toutes les 12 heures.
- **PO (enfants de 2 à 12 ans)**: *Infections des voies respiratoires supérieures* – de 7,5 à 15 mg/kg, toutes les 12 heures. Posologie quotidienne maximale: 1 g. *Infections de la peau et des tissus mous* – 20 mg/kg toutes les 24 heures. Posologie quotidienne maximale: 1 g.
- ***INSUFFISANCE RÉNALE***
  PO (ADULTES): $Cl_{CR} \leq 30$ *mL/MIN* – LA MOITIÉ DE LA DOSE HABITUELLE, TOUTES LES 12 OU 24 HEURES.

- On trouve des **remarques spéciales concernant la posologie chez le plus large éventail de patients possible:** adultes, personnes âgées, enfants, nouveau-nés, patients souffrant d'insuffisance hépatique ou rénale.

Et bien plus...

Un guide
constamment à jour grâce au ***Compagnon Web!***

Deux fois par an (en août et en janvier), des monographies sont ajoutées et d'autres sont modifiées.

Entrez dans le Compagnon Web et ajoutez votre nom à notre liste de diffusion afin d'être avisé par courriel lorsque des mises à jour seront effectuées.

Voici comment accéder au Compagnon Web du *Guide des médicaments*:

Étape 1 : Allez à l'adresse www.erpi.com/deglin.cw

Étape 2 : Lorsqu'ils seront demandés, entrez le nom d'usager et le mot de passe ci-dessous :

Nom d'usager	cw20322
Mot de passe	ce65cg

Étape 3 : Suivez les instructions à l'écran

Assistance technique : tech@erpi.com

PRISE EN CHARGE RAPIDE DES RÉACTIONS ANAPHYLACTIQUES

1. **Arrêter l'administration du médicament en cause.** (Arrêter l'administration par voie intraveineuse ou par voie intramusculaire ou sous-cutanée et poser un garrot).

2. **Maintenir la perméabilité des voies respiratoires.** En cas de détresse respiratoire grave, il peut s'avérer nécessaire d'administrer de l'aminophylline ou d'autres bronchodilatateurs.

3. **Administrer de l'*adrénaline.***

   SC, IM (adultes): De 0,3 à 0,5 mg (solution 1:1 000); on peut répéter l'administration de cette dose toutes les 15 à 20 minutes.

   SC, IM (enfants): 0,01 mg/kg/dose (solution 1:1 000); on peut répéter l'administration de cette dose toutes les 15 à 20 minutes.

   IV (adultes): 0,1 mg (solution 1:10 000), pendant 5 minutes; on peut répéter l'administration de cette dose toutes les 15 minutes *ou* perfuser de 1 à 4 µg/min.

   IV (enfants): 0,01 mg/kg/dose (solution 1:10 000) pendant 5 minutes; on peut répéter l'administration de cette dose toutes les 30 minutes ou perfuser de 0,1 à 1,0 µg/kg/min.

4. **Administrer des *antihistaminiques.*** Ces agents peuvent prévenir la récurrence ou diminuer l'intensité de la réaction.

   diphenhydramine (Benadryl)

   IM, IV (adultes): De 50 à 100 mg en une seule dose; on peut administrer ensuite 5 mg/kg/jour en doses fractionnées ou 50 mg, toutes 6 heures, pendant un jour ou deux.

   IM, IV (enfants): 5 mg/kg/jour en doses fractionnées, toutes les 6 à 8 heures (ne pas dépasser 300 mg/jour). On peut administrer par la suite l'agent par voie orale pendant un jour ou deux.

   cimétidine (Tagamet)

   IV (adultes): 300 mg, toutes les 6 heures.

   IV (enfants): De 25 à 30 mg/kg/jour en 6 doses fractionnées.

5. **Suivre de près la pression artérielle.** Au besoin, administrer des liquides et/ou des vasopresseurs. Les patients sous bêtabloquants peuvent résister aux effets des vasopresseurs.

6. **Administrer des *corticostéroïdes.*** (Ces agents peuvent diminuer l'intensité de la réaction.)

   hydrocortisone (Solu-Cortef)

   IV (adultes et enfants): De 100 à 1 000 mg. On peut administrer par la suite 7 mg/kg/jour par voie IV ou par voie orale, pendant un jour ou deux.

7. **Inscrire la réaction** dans le dossier du patient. Lui recommander de porter constamment sur lui une pièce d'identité où cette réaction est mentionnée (ou faire cette recommandation à ses proches).

GUIDE DES MÉDICAMENTS

3e édition

Judith Hopfer Deglin
April Hazard Vallerand

Adaptation française

Éric Beaudoin, B.Pharm., M.Sc.
Annie Langlais, B.Pharm., M.Sc.
Hugo Laplante, B.Pharm., M.Sc.
Isabelle Marceau, B.Pharm., M.Sc.
Simon Ouellet, B.Pharm., M.Sc.
Karine Pelletier, B.Pharm., M.Sc.

Avec la collaboration de
Caroline Groleau, Dt.P., M.Sc., nutritionniste

Sous la direction de Hugo Laplante

Éric Beaudoin, Hugo Laplante et Isabelle Marceau
www.erpi.com/deglin.cw

ÉDITIONS DU RENOUVEAU PÉDAGOGIQUE INC.

5757, RUE CYPIHOT, SAINT-LAURENT (QUÉBEC) H4S 1R3
TÉLÉPHONE : 514 334-2690 TÉLÉCOPIEUR : 514 334-4720
erpidlm@erpi.com www.erpi.com

Les auteurs et l'éditeur ont tout fait, dans la mesure du possible, pour que les renseignements sur les médicaments ainsi que les posologies mentionnées soient justes et conformes aux recommandations des fabricants et aux monographies canadiennes en vigueur au moment de la publication de cet ouvrage. Cependant, étant donné l'évolution rapide des connaissances en pharmacologie, il est recommandé de consulter la notice contenue à l'intérieur du conditionnement avant d'administrer un médicament afin de vérifier la posologie conseillée, les contre-indications, la mise en garde et les précautions. Cela est particulièrement important en ce qui concerne les nouveaux médicaments, les médicaments peu utilisés et les médicaments très toxiques. Par ailleurs, les renseignements mentionnés ne peuvent être considérés comme absolus ou universels. On ne saurait trop insister sur le fait que le traitement médicamenteux doit tenir compte des particularités de chaque patient. Les auteurs, les traducteurs et l'éditeur ne pourraient être tenus responsables des erreurs glissées par inadvertance dans la publication et des conséquences, quelles qu'elles soient, qui pourraient résulter de l'utilisation des renseignements contenus dans cet ouvrage.

L'éditeur tient à remercier Nathalie Archambault et Sylvie Delorme, ainsi que leur équipe, pour le travail qu'elles ont effectué lors de la publication de la deuxième édition.

Direction, développement de produits: Sylvain Giroux
Supervision éditoriale: Sylvie Chapleau et Christiane Desjardins
Traduction: Véra Pollak et Sylvie Beaupré, Isabelle Laporte, Josée Vidal
Révision linguistique: Véra Pollak
Correction d'épreuves: Marie-Claude Rochon et Dominique Johnson
Direction artistique: Hélène Cousineau
Supervision de la production: Muriel Normand
Édition électronique: Info GL
Conception de la couverture: Martin Tremblay

Dans cet ouvrage, le générique masculin est utilisé sans aucune discrimination et uniquement pour alléger le texte.

Cet ouvrage est une version française de la dixième édition de *Davis's Drug Guide for Nurses* de Judith Hopfer Deglin et April Hazard Vallerand, publiée et vendue à travers le monde avec l'autorisation de F.A. Davis.

Dépôt légal – Bibliothèque et Archives nationales du Québec, 2008
Dépôt légal – Bibliothèque et Archives Canada, 2008
Imprimé au Canada

ISBN 978-2-7613-2294-2

567890 IG 12
20430 ABCD VO-7

AVANT-PROPOS

La version française de ce guide a été entièrement revue et adaptée au contexte canadien. Les indications qui y paraissent sont basées sur les monographies canadiennes officielles. D'autres indications, qui n'ont pas encore été officiellement approuvées au Canada, apparaissent sous le titre « Usages non approuvés ». Les noms commerciaux canadiens les plus courants sont mentionnés sous le nom générique, sauf si le médicament en question n'est pas commercialisé au Canada.

Les contre-indications ainsi que les voies d'administration et posologies ont également été revues à la lumière des informations indiquées dans les monographies canadiennes officielles. Toutefois, lorsqu'un médicament n'est pas commercialisé au Canada, nous avons laissé la posologie inscrite dans la version anglaise du présent guide.

Les présentations mentionnées sont celles qu'on trouve sur le marché canadien et les unités de mesure sont celles qui correspondent au système international d'unités (SI).

Hugo Laplante

TABLE DES MATIÈRES

COMMENT UTILISER LE *GUIDE DES MÉDICAMENTS*

Le *Guide des médicaments* donne des renseignements détaillés de dernière heure sur les médicaments sous la forme de monographies axées sur les soins infirmiers. Il comporte également un grand nombre de données additionnelles présentées dans 21 annexes, tout comme des renseignements sur plus de 50 classes de médicaments. Dans tout cet ouvrage, nous accordons, comme par le passé, une attention particulière à l'administration sans danger des produits pharmaceutiques et ajoutons des nouvelles informations sur les soins destinés à des patients vulnérables: enfants, personnes âgées, femmes enceintes et allaitantes. Vous trouverez ces informations dans les monographies, sous de nouvelles sous-rubriques, à savoir: **PÉD.**, **GÉR.**, **OBST.**, **ALLAITEMENT**. Ce *Guide* vise à vous aider à améliorer vos compétences d'évaluation et de mise en œuvre des traitements médicamenteux. Dans les paragraphes ci-dessous, nous décrivons la présentation du *Guide des médicaments* et expliquons comment vous pourrez trouver rapidement les informations dont vous avez besoin.

Sections sur l'usage sans danger des médicaments

Le *Guide* commence par quatre sections intitulées « Les erreurs de médication: comment améliorer la pratique et la sécurité des patients », « Les réactions indésirables aux médicaments », « Consignes posologiques pour les cas particuliers » et « Sensibilisation du patient à l'usage sans danger des médicaments ». Ces sections expliquent les moyens permettant d'utiliser les médicaments sans danger, en évitant les erreurs les plus courantes. Le texte sur les erreurs de médication vous familiarisera avec les erreurs qui découlent des différents systèmes engagés dans l'administration des médicaments et de certaines situations cliniques. On y propose des méthodes pratiques permettant au professionnel de la santé de les éviter ou de les corriger. Il renseigne également sur des médicaments (dont les monographies portent la mention « *Alerte clinique* ») qui risquent plus que les autres de porter préjudice aux patients. Le texte sur les réactions indésirables explique les différents types d'effets secondaires et réactions indésirables et propose des pistes permettant de les déceler et de les prendre en charge. Celui sur les consignes posologiques dans les cas particuliers recense des populations, comme les nouveau-nés et les insuffisants rénaux, chez lesquelles il faut faire des adaptations posologiques attentives afin d'assurer une issue optimale des traitements. Enfin, le texte sur la sensibilisation du patient à l'usage sans danger des médicaments fait le point sur les principaux sujets auxquels l'infirmière doit sensibiliser le patient et ses proches.

En plus de ces textes sur l'usage sans danger des produits pharmaceutiques, vous trouverez d'autres données essentielles mises en évidence dans les monographies. Vous pourrez ainsi repérer rapidement des informations utiles et comprendre comment adapter les soins infirmiers, notamment l'évaluation de la situation, les interventions et l'enseignement au patient et à ses proches, pour assurer une issue optimale des traitements.

Classification

Cette section présente les principales classes de médicaments. On y fournit une brève description de chacune d'entre elles, avec la liste des médicaments répertoriés et la page où se trouve leur monographie détaillée. Les classes sont présentées par ordre alphabétique.

MONOGRAPHIES

Voici les renseignements fournis pour chaque médicament:

Mention « Alerte clinique »

Certains médicaments, comme ceux utilisés dans le cadre d'une chimiothérapie, les anticoagulants ou les insulines, risquent, plus que d'autres, d'entraîner des réactions indésirables, parfois très graves. L'*Institute for Safe Medication Practices* les classe sous la rubrique « Alerte clinique ». Dans le *Guide des médicaments*, chacun de ces agents est repéré à l'aide de la mention « **ALERTE CLINIQUE** », placée dans le haut de l'en-tête de sa monographie. Ainsi, les professionnels de la santé chargés de l'administration de ces médicaments sont avertis du risque que peut comporter leur utilisation. On trouve la même mention dans d'autres parties de la monographie également, afin d'assurer l'administration sans danger du médicament en question.

Nom générique et noms commerciaux

Le nom générique apparaît en premier. Il est suivi des noms commerciaux canadiens les plus fréquents, classés par ordre alphabétique. Le nom générique, ou dénomination commune du médicament, est le nom adopté d'un commun accord par les organismes de réglementation pharmaceutique. Dans de nombreux établissements, les médicaments sont classés selon leur nom générique. Le lecteur qui ne connaît pas le nom générique d'un médicament trouvera dans l'index la liste des dénominations communes, des noms commerciaux et des classifications.

Classification

Dans le *Guide des médicaments,* les agents pharmacologiques, tout comme les produits naturels, sont classés d'après les maladies qu'ils servent à traiter et cette classification est affichée dans l'en-tête de chaque monographie. Elle correspond à celle donnée dans la section intitulée « Classification » (page C1), où sont décrites les classes les plus connues ou importantes.

Grossesse – catégorie

La Direction générale des produits de santé et des aliments (DGPSA) n'ayant pas publié de règles concernant l'administration des médicaments pendant la grossesse, nous utilisons les catégories établies par la Food and Drug Administration (FDA) des États-Unis. À l'annexe D, nous expliquons plus en détail la signification de ces catégories (A, B, C, D et X), qui permettent à l'infirmière d'évaluer les risques auxquels est exposé le fœtus lorsque le médicament est administré à une femme enceinte ou à une femme qui peut le devenir.

Indications

Les indications qui paraissent dans le guide sont basées sur les monographies canadiennes officielles. Les principaux usages qui n'ont pas encore été officiellement approuvés au Canada apparaissent sous le titre **Usages non approuvés**.

Mécanisme d'action

Le mode d'action connu ou présumé par lequel le médicament produit l'effet thérapeutique souhaité est expliqué brièvement sous cette rubrique.

Pharmacocinétique

Les données présentées ici portent sur le cheminement du médicament après son administration, à travers les étapes suivantes :

Absorption : C'est l'ensemble des mécanismes qui permettent au médicament de pénétrer dans la circulation générale. Ainsi, si seulement une petite fraction de la dose est absorbée après l'administration par voie orale (biodisponibilité réduite), il faut une dose beaucoup plus élevée que par voie parentérale. Le médicament peut également être absorbé et atteindre la circulation générale par voie topique, transdermique, intramusculaire, sous-cutanée, rectale et ophtalmique. La biodisponibilité d'un médicament administré par voie intraveineuse est de 100 %.

Distribution : Après leur absorption, les médicaments se répartissent, parfois de manière spécifique, dans les différents tissus et liquides organiques. Il est important de tenir compte de ce facteur lorsqu'on choisit un médicament plutôt qu'un autre. Par exemple, les antibiotiques doivent pénétrer dans le système nerveux central lors du traitement de la méningite, ou encore on doit éviter d'administrer un médicament qui traverse la barrière placentaire pendant la grossesse ou qui s'accumule dans le lait maternel pendant l'allaitement. Pendant la distribution, plusieurs médicaments se lient à des récepteurs spécifiques et exercent ainsi leur effet pharmacologique.

Métabolisme et excrétion: Après qu'il a exercé l'effet souhaité, le médicament est éliminé de l'organisme, soit par transformation hépatique en composés inactifs (métabolisme et biotransformation) qui sont ensuite excrétés par les reins, soit par élimination rénale à l'état inchangé. En outre, certains médicaments peuvent être éliminés par d'autres voies, soit l'excrétion biliaire, la transpiration, les fèces et la respiration. Si un certain médicament subit un métabolisme hépatique important, il faudrait probablement en diminuer les doses chez les patients qui souffrent d'une maladie hépatique grave. Par contre, si le rein constitue le principal organe excréteur, on doit ajuster la posologie en cas d'insuffisance rénale. Dans le cas des médicaments éliminés par les reins, la clairance de la créatinine (Cl_{Cr}), calculée au moyen de formules mathématiques (voir l'annexe E), permet de quantifier la fonction rénale et d'adapter la dose en conséquence. On devrait également ajuster la dose ou les intervalles posologiques chez les très jeunes enfants (prématurés et nouveau-nés) et les personnes âgées de plus de 60 ans, chez qui l'excrétion rénale et le métabolisme hépatique sont réduits.

Demi-vie: La demi-vie d'un médicament est le temps nécessaire pour que sa concentration diminue de 50 %. Les demi-vies indiquées dans ce *Guide* correspondent à celles qu'on note chez les patients ayant une fonction rénale ou hépatique normale. On précise également les maladies qui pourraient modifier la demi-vie.

Profil temps-action: Grâce aux données fournies sous cette rubrique, l'infirmière peut connaître le début d'action du médicament, son effet maximal (pic) et sa durée d'action, et mieux planifier ainsi le schéma posologique. Cette section est présentée sous forme de tableau, selon la voie d'administration, de façon à rendre compte des différences auxquelles on peut s'attendre si l'on choisit une voie plutôt qu'une autre.

Contre-indications, précautions et mises en garde

On présente ici les cas où l'on devrait éviter l'administration du médicament et envisager des solutions de rechange. En général, la plupart des médicaments sont contre-indiqués pendant la grossesse ou l'allaitement, à moins que les avantages éventuels ne dépassent les risques auxquels sont exposés la mère ou son enfant (comme c'est le cas des anticonvulsivants et des antihypertenseurs). Les contre-indications peuvent être absolues (le médicament ne doit absolument pas être administré) ou relatives (dans certaines circonstances cliniques, on peut administrer le médicament avec prudence). La section des précautions et mises en garde porte sur les maladies ou les circonstances cliniques où l'administration du médicament peut comporter des risques particuliers ou encore celles qui dictent une modification de la posologie. On y indique aussi les additifs qui pourraient être dangereux chez les patients qui ne les tolèrent pas (par exemple, l'alcool, les bisulfites, l'alcool benzylique ou la tartrazine).

Réactions indésirables et effets secondaires

Les réactions indésirables et les effets secondaires sont classés par système, de la tête aux pieds, chaque fois que cela est possible. Comme on ne peut évidemment pas mentionner toutes les réactions déclarées, ce sont les plus importantes qui sont signalées ici. Les réactions indésirables ou les effets secondaires qui mettent la vie en danger sont indiqués en PETITES MAJUSCULES et ceux qui se manifestent le plus souvent sont soulignés. En général, les effets soulignés ont une incidence de 10 % ou plus; les autres surviennent chez moins de 10 %, mais chez plus de

1 % des patients. Même si les réactions mettant la vie en danger peuvent être rares (incidence de moins de 1 %), elles sont incluses en raison de leur importance. Les abréviations suivantes sont utilisées:

SNC: Système nerveux central
ORLO: Yeux, oreilles, nez, gorge
Resp.: Système respiratoire
CV: Système cardiovasculaire
GI: Système gastro-intestinal
GU: Système génito-urinaire
End.: Système endocrinien
HÉ: Équilibre hydroélectrolytique
Tég.: Système tégumentaire
Hémat.: Système hématologique
Métab.: Métabolisme
Loc.: Système locomoteur
SN: Système nerveux
Locaux: Effets locaux
Divers: Effets divers

Interactions

Plus le nombre de médicaments qu'un patient reçoit augmente, plus le risque d'interactions entre les divers agents est grand. On énumère ici les interactions médicamenteuses les plus importantes en précisant leurs effets, ainsi que les principales interactions entre les médicaments et les aliments et entre les médicaments et les produits naturels. On présente également des recommandations permettant d'éviter ou de réduire ces interactions.

Voies d'administration et posologie

On trouve sous cette rubrique les voies d'administration et les posologies recommandées dans les monographies canadiennes chez les adultes, les enfants et les groupes d'âge particuliers, ainsi que chez les insuffisants rénaux et hépatiques, s'il y a lieu. Les unités de mesure des doses correspondent à celles qui sont prescrites le plus souvent (par exemple, la posologie de la pénicilline G est donnée en unités plutôt qu'en milligrammes).

Présentation

On indique ici les teneurs et concentrations des diverses formes pharmaceutiques commercialisées au Canada. Ces renseignements sont utiles pour choisir le schéma le plus pratique (moins de comprimés ou de capsules, plus petits volumes d'injection) ou la forme la plus appropriée (suppositoires, concentrés oraux, comprimés retard ou à libération prolongée). On précise si les médicaments sont vendus sur ordonnance ([Pr]), s'ils sont en vente libre ([VL]), s'il s'agit de drogues contrôlées ([C]), de stupéfiants (narcotiques) ([N]) ou de benzodiazépines et autres substances ciblées ([T\C]). Certains médicaments ne nécessitent pas d'ordonnance, mais leur distribution est sous le contrôle direct du pharmacien ([Phc]). Le lecteur pourra consulter l'annexe B pour connaître la classification officielle des substances contrôlées. On indique également, le cas échéant, les saveurs des préparations liquides et des comprimés à mâcher dans le but d'améliorer l'observance thérapeutique chez les enfants.

Soins infirmiers

Grâce aux données qu'elle trouve sous les différentes rubriques de cette section, l'infirmière peut appliquer la démarche des soins infirmiers à la pharmacothérapie en suivant les étapes liées à l'administration des médicaments.

Évaluation de la situation: Se trouvent ici les renseignements concernant les antécédents et l'état physique du patient dont l'infirmière doit tenir compte avant de lui administrer le médicament et pendant toute la durée du traitement. Ils incluent des directives générales ainsi que des observations particulières aux diverses indications du médicament. Sous la rubrique *Tests de laboratoire*, l'infirmière trouve les résultats des tests de laboratoire qu'elle doit vérifier attentivement, mais aussi la façon dont le médicament peut influer sur ces résultats. Sous la rubrique *Toxicité et surdosage,* sont précisés les concentrations sériques thérapeutiques, les signes et les symptômes de toxicité ainsi que l'antidote et le traitement qui conviennent en cas de toxicité ou de surdosage.

Diagnostics infirmiers possibles: Il s'agit des diagnostics infirmiers approuvés par NANDA International. On indique ici les deux ou trois principaux diagnostics qui peuvent s'appliquer à la situation du patient qui reçoit le médicament en question. À la suite de chaque diagnostic, la rubrique à laquelle le diagnostic se rapporte est indiquée entre parenthèses, par exemple «Risque d'infection (Indications, Effets secondaires)». La liste complète des diagnostics infirmiers approuvés par NANDA se trouve à l'annexe P.

Interventions infirmières: On trouve sous cette rubrique des consignes particulières d'administration. On commence par indiquer les précautions à prendre au sujet des médicaments qui font l'objet d'une «**ALERTE CLINIQUE**» afin d'éviter les erreurs d'administration des médicaments dangereux à cause de leur nature même. Les informations fournies à cet égard portent notamment sur des confusions possibles à cause d'une similitude des noms ou des présentations. Les confusions possibles des noms ou des présentations sont inscrites en PETITES MAJUSCULES. Dans cette section, on trouve également des renseignements sur la voie d'administration. Ainsi, pour la voie orale (PO), on indique quand administrer le médicament, si les comprimés peuvent être écrasés ou si les capsules peuvent être ouvertes et si le médicament doit être administré à jeun, avec des aliments ou autrement. Pour la voie intraveineuse (IV) (*Intraveineuse directe, Perfusion intermittente* et *Perfusion continue*), on fournit des détails concernant la reconstitution du médicament et sa dilution, le débit auquel il faut l'administrer (*Vitesse d'administration*), ainsi que la stabilité des préparations. On présente également les *Associations compatibles et incompatibles dans la même seringue*, ce genre de compatibilité se limitant habituellement à 15 minutes après le mélange, les *Compatibilités et incompatibilités (tubulure en Y)*, valables aussi pour une tubulure à trois voies, les *Compatibilités et incompatibilités en addition au soluté*, qui se limitent habituellement à 24 heures, et les *Compatibilités et incompatibilités dans une même solution*. Les données sur la compatibilité sont tirées de *Handbook of Injectable Drugs* de Trissel (voir la bibliographie, p. 1312). Veuillez noter que les informations sur les compatibilités sont données à titre indicatif seulement, car les différentes compatibilités peuvent varier selon les concentrations des médicaments et les diluants utilisés.

Enseignement au patient et à ses proches: Les renseignements que l'infirmière devrait transmettre au patient et à ses proches comprennent, par exemple, les effets secondaires à signaler à un professionnel de la santé, les mesures à prendre pour réduire les réactions indésirables, certains détails concernant l'administration du médicament ainsi que l'importance des examens de suivi. L'infirmière devrait également consulter les rubriques *Réactions indésirables et effets secondaires*, *Interactions médicamenteuses* et *Interventions infirmières* pour établir un plan d'enseignement plus complet.

Vérification de l'efficacité thérapeutique: Cette section renferme les critères permettant de déterminer si le traitement médicamenteux a donné les résultats escomptés.

ABRÉVIATIONS USUELLES

L'emploi de certaines de ces abréviations est critiqué. Voir la section sur les erreurs de médication (pages XV à XXII).

AC	avant les repas (*ante cibum*)
ACTH	adrénocorticotrophine (hormone adrénocorticotrope)
ACP	analgésie contrôlée par le patient
ADH	hormone antidiurétique
ADN	acide désoxyribonucléique
AINS	anti-inflammatoire non stéroïdien
ALT	alanine aminotransférase
ARN	acide ribonucléique
Asp	acide aspartique
AST	aspartate aminotransférase
ATP	adénosine triphosphate
AV	auriculoventriculaire
AVC	accident vasculaire cérébral
BID	deux fois par jour (*bis in die*)
bpm	battements par minute
BUN	urée
C	drogue contrôlée
cc	centimètre cube
Cl_{Cr}	clairance de la créatinine
cm	centimètre
CPK ou CK	créatine phosphokinase
CV	cardiovasculaire
D5%E	dextrose à 5 % dans l'eau
DIE ou ID	une fois par jour
dL	décilitre
ECA	enzyme de conversion de l'angiotensine
ÉCG	électrocardiogramme
ÉEG	électroencéphalogramme
End.	système endocrinien
É.-U.	États-Unis
FA	fibrillation auriculaire
fL	femtolitre (10^{-15} L)
FSC	formule sanguine complète
FSH	hormone folliculostimulante (*follicle stimulating hormone*)
FPS	facteur de protection solaire (pour les filtres et écrans solaires)
FV	fibrillation ventriculaire
g	gramme
GGT	gammaglutamyl transpeptidase
GI	système gastro-intestinal
GMPc	guanosine monophosphate cyclique
G-6-PD	glucose-6-phosphate déshydrogénase
GU	système génito-urinaire
h	heure
HbA_{1c}	hémoglobine glycosylée
HBP	hyperplasie bénigne de la prostate

HDL	lipoprotéines de haute densité
HÉ	équilibre hydroélectrolytique
Hémat.	système hématologique
HS	au coucher (*hora somni*)
ICT	ischémie cérébrale transitoire
ID ou DIE	une fois par jour
IECA	inhibiteur de l'enzyme de conversion de l'angiotensine
IM	intramusculaire ou infarctus du myocarde ou insuffisance mitrale (selon le contexte)
IMAO	inhibiteur de la monoamine-oxydase
IMC	indice de masse corporelle (kg/m^2)
IR	intrarectal
IRC	insuffisance rénale chronique
IRM	imagerie par résonance magnétique
ISRS	inhibiteur sélectif du recaptage de la sérotonine
IT	intrathécal
IV	intraveineux
J	joule
kg	kilogramme
L	litre
LDH ou LD	lactate déshydrogénase
LDL	lipoprotéines de faible densité
LH	hormone lutéinisante (*luteinizing hormone*) ou lutéinostimuline
LH-RH	hormone de libération de la lutéostimuline
Loc.	système locomoteur
LP	libération prolongée
MAO	monoamine-oxydase
mÉq	milliéquivalent
Métab.	métabolisme
µg, mcg	microgramme (10^{-6} g)
mg	milligramme (10^{-3} g)
min	minute
mL	millilitre
mmol	millimole
µmol	micromole (10^{-6} mol)
µm	micromètre
N	narcotique (opioïde ou stupéfiant)
Na	sodium
NaCl	chlorure de sodium
NaCl 0,9 %	chlorure de sodium à 0,9 %, soluté salin, salin normal
ng	nanogramme (10^{-6} g)
nmol	nanomole
NPO	rien par la bouche (*nil per os*)
ORLO	yeux, oreilles, nez, gorge
OD	dans l'œil droit (*oculus dexter*)
OS	dans l'œil gauche (*oculus sinister*)
OU	dans les deux yeux (*oculi unitas*)
PC	après les repas (*post cibum*)
PO	voie orale (*per os*)
Pr	médicament d'ordonnance
pg	picogramme (10^{-12} g)

PRN	au besoin (*pro re nata*)
PT	temps de prothrombine
PVC	pression veineuse centrale
QID	quatre fois par jour (*quater in die*)
Resp.	système respiratoire
RGO	reflux gastro-œsophagien
RI	réaction indésirable
RNI	rapport normalisé international
SC	sous-cutané
SL	sublingual
s	seconde
Sida	syndrome d'immunodéficience acquise
SNA	système nerveux autonome
SNC	système nerveux central
STAT	immédiatement
supp.	suppositoire
T\C	substances ciblées (benzodiazépines et autres)
TCA	temps de céphaline activée
TDM	tomodensitométrie
Tég.	système tégumentaire
TDAH	trouble déficitaire de l'attention avec hyperactivité
TID	trois fois par jour (*ter in die*)
TOC	trouble obsessionnel compulsif
TSVP	tachycardie supraventriculaire paroxystique
TT	temps de thrombine
TV	tachycardie ventriculaire
TVP	thrombose veineuse profonde
U	unité
UI	unité internationale
Vag.	vaginal
VHS	virus de l'herpès simplex
VIH	virus de l'immunodéficience humaine
VL	en vente libre
VLDL	lipoprotéines de très faible densité

LES ERREURS DE MÉDICATION : COMMENT AMÉLIORER LA PRATIQUE ET LA SÉCURITÉ DES PATIENTS

Personne ne conteste le fait que, années après années, les erreurs de médication sont responsables de milliers de réactions indésirables et décès qu'on aurait pu prévenir. Les infirmières, les médecins, les pharmaciens, les organismes de défense de la sécurité des patients, la Food and Drug Administration des États-Unis et la Direction générale de la protection de la santé du Canada, ainsi que l'industrie pharmaceutique et d'autres intervenants ont la responsabilité de déterminer les raisons pour lesquelles des erreurs de médication se produisent et d'élaborer des stratégies en vue d'en réduire le nombre.

En 1999, l'*Institute of Medicine* (IoM) publiait: *To Err is Human: Building a Safer Health System*. Dans ce rapport, on avançait que même d'excellents professionnels de la santé pouvaient commettre des erreurs de médication, que de nombreux processus intervenant dans le système d'utilisation des médicaments donnaient lieu à des erreurs et que d'autres facteurs, notamment l'étiquetage et le conditionnement, y contribuaient également. Par ailleurs, l'IoM, ainsi que d'autres organismes, comme l'*United States Pharmacopeia* (USP) et l'*Institute for Safe Medication Practices* (ISMP), demandaient qu'on modifie les systèmes susceptibles de donner lieu à des erreurs, de façon à y inclure des processus plus adéquats, tenant compte de la faillibilité des êtres humains qui les utilisent. Cette initiative permet actuellement de modifier la façon dont l'industrie des soins de santé aborde les erreurs de médication : au lieu de chercher un bouc émissaire, elle considère maintenant qu'il s'agit d'un problème qui découle du système tout entier[1].

Le *National Coordinating Council for Medication Error Reporting and Prevention* (NCC-MERP) a élaboré une définition des erreurs de médication qui illustre ce changement de point de vue, rend compte de son envergure et élargit le débat :

> « Une erreur de médication est un accident évitable, entraînant l'utilisation inappropriée d'un médicament ou portant préjudice à un patient, lorsque l'administration incombe à un professionnel de la santé, à un consommateur ou au patient lui-même. De tels accidents peuvent être liés à la pratique de la profession, aux produits de soins, aux procédés et aux systèmes, notamment la prescription, la communication des consignes, l'étiquetage et le conditionnement des produits, la nomenclature, la composition du produit, son mode de délivrance, sa distribution, son administration, son utilisation, ou encore une surveillance ou un enseignement insuffisants[2]. »

En vertu de cette définition, les facteurs humains font partie intégrante du système d'utilisation des médicaments. Par exemple, une infirmière ou un pharmacien qui a besoin de dobutamine peut machinalement prendre du plateau sur lequel ce médicament est conservé habituellement la dopamine, tout simplement parce que, dans la précipitation, il n'a lu que « do » et « amine ». Le travail dans un milieu où l'on est constamment dérangé, où l'on est à court de personnel, où l'on exige de longues heures de présence, où règne une culture qui prône la perfection et qui décourage toute remise en question, est un autre exemple de la façon dont le facteur humain et les conditions de travail contribuent aux erreurs de médication.

Le but de l'élaboration d'un système d'utilisation des médicaments, qu'il concerne une seule personne ou un centre hospitalier tout entier, est de déterminer les facteurs qui peuvent générer des erreurs et de trouver des moyens de protection qui réduisent au minimum tout risque à ce chapitre. On peut aborder ce processus en étudiant les médicaments ou les pratiques qui ont donné lieu par le passé à des erreurs graves.

En cas d'erreur

Il est essentiel de consigner aux dossiers les erreurs de tous genres, même si elles n'ont pas porté préjudice au patient. Lorsqu'on documente une erreur, il faut rédiger les observations de façon à aider à l'évaluation du problème et à proposer des mesures préventives, plutôt qu'à chercher à punir la personne qui a commis l'erreur.

Dans un effort de compilation des données entourant les circonstances qui contribuent aux erreurs de médication, l'Association des hôpitaux du Québec a élaboré un formulaire intitulé « Rapport d'incident/accident », qui sert à recueillir, à analyser et à diffuser les renseignements. Nous encourageons fortement les infirmières à remplir ce formulaire (reproduit à l'annexe O) ou tout autre formulaire en vigueur dans leur établissement.

Alertes cliniques

Certains médicaments, en raison d'un indice thérapeutique étroit ou de leur nature toxique, exposent le patient à un risque élevé d'accidents graves ou de décès, s'ils sont mal prescrits, préparés, stockés, délivrés ou administrés, ou encore si leurs effets ne sont pas adéquatement surveillés. Même si ces médicaments ne donnent pas nécessairement lieu à des erreurs plus fréquentes, leur administration doit s'accompagner d'une prudence extrême, à cause des conséquences graves et parfois mortelles qu'une erreur à cet égard peut entraîner. Dans ce *Guide des médicaments*, la mention « **ALERTE CLINIQUE** » précède le nom de ce type d'agents, afin de mettre en garde le professionnel de la santé contre sa dangerosité et de l'inciter à prendre encore plus de précautions que d'habitude. Un grand nombre de ces médicaments sont couramment destinés à la population générale ou fréquemment utilisés dans les cas d'urgence. La *Joint Commission of Accreditation of Healthcare Organizations* (JCAHO) surveille l'administration des cinq types de médicaments faisant l'objet d'une alerte clinique qui sont prescrits le plus souvent, soit les insulines, les opioïdes et les narcotiques, les concentrés de potassium injectables (chlorure ou phosphate), les anticoagulants intraveineux (comme l'héparine) et les solutions de chlorure de sodium d'une teneur supérieure à 0,9 %. On trouve au tableau 1 la liste des médicaments qui se trouvent dans le *Guide* et qui font l'objet d'une alerte clinique. Pour plus de détails sur ces médicaments, on peut aussi visiter le site de l'*Institute for Safe Medication Practices*, à l'adresse www.ismp.org.

Causes des erreurs de médication

L'objectif d'une pharmacothérapie optimale est la prise du bon médicament, par le bon patient, à la bonne dose, par la bonne voie d'administration, au bon moment et pour la bonne indication. Ce processus comporte un énorme potentiel d'erreur tout au long de ses différentes étapes: la prescription (par les médecins et autres prescripteurs), la transcription (par une secrétaire ou une infirmière), l'exécution de l'ordonnance (par les pharmaciens) et l'administration (par les infirmières).

On a repéré un grand nombre de facteurs qui peuvent contribuer aux erreurs de médication ou être la cause qui sous-tend de telles erreurs: par exemple, communication défaillante, mauvaises pratiques de distribution, erreurs de calcul des doses, problèmes liés au conditionnement ou aux dispositifs de mesure, mauvaise administration et enseignement insuffisant au patient et à ses proches[3].

Communication défaillante. Une communication défaillante est la cause d'un grand nombre d'erreurs commises au moment de la prescription et bien que ce soit le prescripteur qui communique les consignes à ce moment-là, les infirmières, les préposés et les pharmaciens qui les interprètent sont également engagés dans le processus de communication.

- **Consignes transmises verbalement ou rédigées d'une écriture illisible.** Une écriture illisible donne souvent lieu à des erreurs d'interprétation, notamment en ce qui concerne le médicament à administrer, la voie et la fréquence d'administration et la posologie. Les ordonnances communiquées verbalement ou par téléphone peuvent, elles aussi, donner lieu à une interprétation erronée.

- **Médicaments dont les noms se ressemblent ou se prononcent de façon semblable.** On confond souvent deux médicaments dont le nom s'écrit ou se prononce de façon semblable. Le métoprolol et le misoprostol ou Nizoral et Neoral en sont des exemples. Dans la *United States Pharmacopoeia*, on retrouve plus de 700 médicaments qui se ressemblent dans leur aspect ou dont le nom se prononce de façon presque identique. La confusion est encore plus grande lorsque les intervalles posologiques et la fréquence des administrations des deux médicaments sont similaires.
- **Utilisation fautive des zéros dans les nombres décimaux.** Des surdoses massives, correspondant parfois à des doses décuplées, ont souvent été dues à l'absence d'un zéro avant la virgule décimale (,2 mg au lieu de 0,2 mg) ou à l'ajout d'un zéro inutile après la virgule, par exemple 2,0 mg, au lieu de 2 mg. Elles peuvent également résulter d'une écriture négligée ou d'une ordonnance rédigée sur du papier ligné ou portant des marques, rendant la virgule illisible (d'où le risque de lire 31 g au lieu de 3,1 g). Ce même type d'erreurs peut conduire à l'administration d'une dose insuffisante et empêcher le patient de bénéficier de l'effet souhaitable d'un médicament, qui pourrait, peut-être, lui sauver la vie.
- **Expression des doses en unités de poids d'apothicaire (grains, drams) ou en unités de stock (ampoules, fioles, comprimés) au lieu d'unités du système international (grammes, milligrammes, millimoles).** Les anciennes unités de poids d'apothicaire sont mal connues et leur abréviation donne lieu à des confusions avec d'autres unités de mesure. Il faut abandonner l'utilisation de ces anciennes unités. Des erreurs sont également commises si on utilise des unités posologiques au lieu d'unités du SI. Par exemple, une ordonnance qui indique 2 comprimés, 1½ fiole ou 2 ampoules peut donner lieu à un surdosage ou à l'administration d'une dose insuffisante, lorsque le médicament prescrit a plusieurs teneurs.
- **Abréviations mal comprises.** Il est facile de mal interpréter une abréviation, notamment lorsqu'elle précise la dose, donnant ainsi lieu à l'administration d'une posologie erronée du bon médicament. Par exemple, un « U » écrit à la main, en majuscule ou en minuscule, pour exprimer des unités, a déjà été pris pour un zéro (0), et de ce fait au lieu d'administrer « 10u » d'insuline, on en a administré 100 unités. L'abréviation latine « QOD », signifiant un jour sur deux, peut être lue « QID » (quatre fois par jour). Voir au tableau 2 la liste des abréviations entraînant de la confusion et des solutions de rechange plus sûres.
- **Ordonnances ambiguës ou incomplètes.** Les ordonnances qui ne précisent pas clairement la dose, la voie d'administration, la fréquence des administrations ou l'indication ne communiquent pas tous les renseignements nécessaires et donnent lieu à des interprétations erronées.

Mauvaises pratiques de distribution. Parmi ces pratiques, citons les mauvaises conditions de conservation (par exemple, la conservation de produits ayant un aspect similaire l'un à côté de l'autre). La délivrance de médicaments dans des formats réservés à la pharmacie à la place des formats destinés à l'utilisation dans les unités de soins peut également donner lieu à des erreurs, tout comme la délivrance des médicaments par des techniciens, lorsque le pharmacien n'est pas sur les lieux.

Mauvais calcul des doses. Le mauvais calcul des doses est l'une des principales sources d'erreurs de médication. Par ailleurs, dans le cas de nombreux médicaments, il faut adapter la dose en cas d'insuffisance rénale ou hépatique ou en fonction de l'âge du patient, de sa taille et de son poids ou de la quantité de tissu adipeux (par exemple, en présence d'obésité). Des formules de calcul compliquées des posologies sont fréquemment des sources d'erreurs. Souvent, les populations vulnérables, comme les prématurés, les enfants, les personnes âgées ou celles souffrant de maladies sous-jacentes graves, sont exposées au risque le plus élevé dans ce cas.

Conditionnements et méthodes de délivrance des médicaments. Des erreurs surviennent fréquemment lorsque les conditionnements sont semblables ou mal conçus. Les laboratoires pharmaceutiques peuvent utiliser le même type de conditionnement pour différentes préparations ou ne pas indiquer clairement les différentes concentrations ou teneurs d'un même médicament. Le lettrage, la taille de la police, la couleur et la méthode d'emballage peuvent rendre un médicament facilement reconnaissable ou, au contraire, méconnaissable.

Les dispositifs de délivrance des médicaments, comme les pompes à perfusion et les instruments qui règlent la vitesse d'administration, peuvent également être des sources d'erreurs. L'absence de méthodes de protection contre un écoulement irrégulier ou une pompe à perfusion mal programmée font partie des problèmes qu'on rencontre lorsque les systèmes de délivrance ne sont pas soigneusement réglés.

Administration incorrecte des médicaments. Les médicaments peuvent être incorrectement administrés à plusieurs égards, par exemple lorsqu'on les administre aux patients auxquels ils ne sont pas destinés ou par une voie d'administration incorrecte, lorsqu'on saute des doses ou lorsqu'on les prépare de façon inappropriée.

Enseignement insuffisant au patient et à ses proches. Pour favoriser l'utilisation sans danger des médicaments en milieu hospitalier et à domicile, il faut informer adéquatement le patient. Le patient averti peut se rendre compte si un changement est intervenu dans sa médication et peut poser des questions au professionnel de la santé qui l'administre. Dans un même ordre d'idées, de nombreux facteurs donnant lieu à des erreurs de médication, par exemple des consignes ambiguës, le manque de connaissances de la pharmacothérapie ou des conditionnements qui prêtent à confusion, peuvent toucher autant le patient que son soignant, ce qui renforce le besoin de séances rigoureuses de sensibilisation. Un enseignement approprié au patient favorise également l'observance du traitement, l'un des principaux facteurs qui déterminent un bon usage des médicaments.

Stratégies de prévention

Étant donné que les systèmes d'utilisation des médicaments sont complexes et comportent de nombreuses étapes et un investissement humain important, ils sont responsables de nombreuses erreurs. De leur côté, les infirmières peuvent aider à en réduire la fréquence en mettant en place les stratégies suivantes:

- Demander des éclaircissements dans le cas de toute ordonnance qui n'est pas évidente et parfaitement lisible. Demander au prescripteur de rédiger ses ordonnances en caractères d'imprimerie.
- Ne pas accepter des ordonnances qui contiennent l'abréviation « u » pour les unités. Bien se faire expliquer la posologie et demander au prescripteur d'écrire le mot « unités » en toutes lettres.
- Demander des éclaircissements lorsque le nom du médicament ou la fréquence d'administration sont abrégés, par exemple, QD, QOD et QID. Proposer au prescripteur d'abandonner les abréviations latines en faveur d'une fréquence d'administration exprimée clairement (par exemple, une fois par jour, un jour sur deux ou quatre fois par jour).
- Ne pas accepter une ordonnance sur laquelle la posologie est exprimée sous forme d'unités posologiques ou de poids au lieu d'unités du SI. Demander des éclaircissements lorsque l'ordonnance indique la dose en nombre d'ampoules, de fioles ou de comprimés (par exemple, « calcium, 1 fiole » ou « adrénaline, 1 seringue »).
- Les erreurs liées à la virgule décimale peuvent être difficiles à déceler. Remettre l'ordonnance en question lorsqu'on soupçonne que la virgule décimale manque ou lorsque la dose est exprimée en plus de trois unités.
- Si la dose prescrite est exprimée en un nombre excessif de prises ou en de très petites fractions d'une dose, revoir la posologie, faire vérifier l'ordonnance d'origine et les calculs

par un autre professionnel de la santé, et demander au prescripteur de reconfirmer la posologie.

- Dans le cas des ordonnances verbales, demander au prescripteur d'épeler le nom du médicament et la posologie pour éviter toute erreur de compréhension auditive, par exemple, «Cerebyx», au lieu de «Celebrex» ou «dix» au lieu de «six». Relire l'ordonnance au prescripteur après l'avoir inscrite dans les dossiers. Confirmer l'indication et la documenter pour améliorer davantage la communication.
- Demander des éclaircissements lorsque le poids n'est pas exprimé en unités du SI et lorsque la fréquence ou la voie d'administration prêtent à confusion.
- Vérifier la transcription effectuée par l'infirmière ou d'autres professionnels par rapport à l'ordonnance d'origine. S'assurer que des initiales ou des marques sur le papier ne cachent pas les indications portées sur l'ordonnance d'origine.
- Ne pas administrer à un patient un médicament destiné à une autre personne, car ainsi le pharmacien ne peut pas procéder à la contre-vérification de l'ordonnance.
- Toujours vérifier le nom du patient inscrit sur son bracelet, avant de lui administrer des médicaments. S'adresser à lui par son nom n'est pas un moyen suffisant de l'identifier.
- Utiliser les horaires d'administration standard en vigueur dans l'établissement pour réduire le risque d'omettre des doses.
- S'assurer qu'on connaît parfaitement le mode d'emploi du dispositif d'administration avant de l'utiliser, qu'il s'agisse d'une pompe à perfusion, d'un inhalateur ou d'un timbre transdermique.
- Dans le cas des médicaments faisant l'objet d'une alerte clinique, demander à un autre professionnel de la santé de vérifier l'ordonnance d'origine, le calcul des doses et le réglage de la pompe à perfusion.
- Garder à l'esprit le fait que les inscriptions portées sur les boîtes, les fioles, les ampoules, les seringues préremplies ou sur tout autre conditionnement dans lequel le médicament est conservé peuvent prêter à confusion. S'assurer de bien distinguer les médicaments les uns des autres, ainsi que le nombre de milligrammes par millilitre (mg/mL) par rapport au nombre total de milligrammes contenu dans le conditionnement. Des surdoses massives ont déjà été administrées en présumant que le nombre de milligrammes par millilitre (mg/mL) indiqué sur la fiole ou l'ampoule était le nombre total de milligrammes (mg) contenu dans la fiole ou l'ampoule. Bien lire l'étiquette lorsqu'on reçoit le médicament, avant de le préparer ou de le verser et après avoir accompli ces opérations.
- Enseigner au patient la façon de prendre le médicament. Lui transmettre les consignes verbalement et par écrit et lui demander de répéter les principaux points à retenir. Voir la section «Sensibilisation du patient à l'usage sans danger des médicaments» à la page XXXIV.

Comme nous l'avons expliqué auparavant, les erreurs découlent de problèmes inhérents au système d'utilisation des médicaments et on ne peut pas toutes les éliminer même si chacun des groupes de professionnels de la santé se montre extrêmement vigilant. Une nouvelle conception du système ne peut se passer du leadership de l'administration et de tous les services concernés. Les établissements de soins devraient prendre les mesures suivantes lorsqu'ils cherchent à prévenir les erreurs de médication:

- Ne pas fournir aux services les médicaments dangereux ou faisant l'objet d'une alerte clinique en gros format. Si on ne peut pas faire autrement, essayer d'en réduire le nombre et de standardiser les concentrations et les formes de médicaments dont le personnel peut disposer.

- Former des comités chargés des problèmes d'innocuité.
- Se doter d'un système informatique d'inscription des ordonnances par les médecins pour réduire le nombre d'ordonnances rédigées à la main. Prévoir des liens vers les tests de laboratoire et les données pertinentes sur les allergies et les traitements médicamenteux.
- Recourir à la technologie des codes à barres pour s'assurer que le bon médicament est administré au bon patient.
- Élaborer des politiques qui découragent toute pratique de prescription pouvant donner lieu à des erreurs, telle que l'utilisation inappropriée des ordonnances verbales, l'utilisation de symboles posologiques ou d'abréviations prêtant à confusion.
- Élaborer des politiques qui encouragent une meilleure communication des informations médicales, comme l'inscription sur l'ordonnance du nom du médicament en caractères d'imprimerie, de son indication, de son nom commercial et de son nom générique.
- S'assurer que la charge de travail du personnel infirmier et des pharmaciens est raisonnable et leur fournir un espace de travail qui leur convient.
- Limiter le nombre de concentrations des médicaments faisant l'objet d'une alerte clinique dont le personnel peut disposer.
- Fournir des tableaux de concentrations et de vitesses d'administration standard.
- Rendre accessible un matériel de référence mis à jour, autant par le personnel de la pharmacie que par celui des unités de soins.
- Opter pour une culture qui ne cherche pas à blâmer quiconque lorsque des erreurs de médication se produisent, mais qui essaie plutôt d'en trouver la cause profonde.
- Encourager le personnel à participer au programme de signalement des erreurs de l'établissement.

RÉFÉRENCES

1. Kohn, LT, JM Corrigan et MS Donaldson (dir.) (1999). *To Err is Human: Building a Safer Health System*, Washington, DC: National Academy Press.

2. National Coordinating Council for Medication Error Reporting and Prevention, disponible à www.nccmerp.org/aboutMedErrors.html.

3. Cohen MR (1999). *Medication Errors: Causes, Prevention, Risk Management*, Sudbury: Jones et Bartlett, éditeurs.

4. Branowicki P *et al.* (2003). Improving complex medication systems: an interdisciplinary approach, *J. Nurs. Adm.*, avril, 33 (4): 199-200.

5. Burke KG (2005). Executive summary: the state of the science on safe medication administration symposium, *J. Infus. Nurs.*, mars–avril, 28 (suppl. 2): 4-9.

6. McPhillips HA *et al.* (2005). Potential medication dosing errors in outpatient pediatrics, *Pediatr.*, décembre, 147 (6): 727-8.

Tableau 1: Médicaments faisant l'objet d'une alerte clinique inscrits dans le *Guide*

adrénaline	daunorubicine	hydromorphone	paclitaxel
alemtuzumab	digoxine	idarubicine	paclitaxel lié à l'albumine
alfentanil	dobutamine	imatinib	pancuronium
amiodarone	docétaxel	insulines	pentazocine
asparaginase	dopamine	irinotécan	potassium, suppléments de
bléomycine	doxorubicine	labétalol	propoxyphène
busulfan	épirubicine	lidocaïne	propranolol
butorphanol	eptifibatide	magnésium, sulfate de (IV)	sodium, chlorure de
calcium, sels de	esmolol	mépéridine	sufentanil
capécitabine	étoposide	méthadone	sulfonylurées
carboplatine	fentanyl (voie parentérale)	méthotrexate	thrombolytiques
carmustine	fentanyl (voie transdermique)	métoprolol	tirofiban
chloral, hydrate de	fluorouracile	midazolam	topotécan
cisplatine	gemcitabine	milrinone	trastuzumab
codéine	héparine	morphine	vinblastine
colchicine	héparines de faible poids moléculaire/héparinoïdes	nalbuphine	vincristine
cyclophosphamide		nelfinavir	vinorelbine
cytarabine	hydrocodone	oxycodone	warfarine

Tableau 2: Abréviations et symboles entraînant des erreurs de médication

Abréviation/symbole	Signification	Erreur courante	Recommandation
AZT	Zidovudine	Azathioprine	Écrire le nom du médicament en toutes lettres
CPZ	Compazine (prochlorpérazine)	chlorpromazine	Écrire le nom du médicament en toutes lettres
HCl	acide chlorhydrique	KCl (chlorure de potassium)	Écrire le nom du médicament en toutes lettres
HCT	hydrocortisone	hydrochlorothiazide	Écrire le nom du médicament en toutes lettres
$MgSO_4$*	sulfate de magnésium	sulfate de morphine	Écrire le nom du médicament en toutes lettres
MS, MSO_4*	sulfate de morphine	sulfate de magnésium	Écrire le nom du médicament en toutes lettres
MTX	méthotrexate	mitoxantrone	Écrire le nom du médicament en toutes lettres
Nitro drip (goutte-à-goutte)	nitroprusside	nitroglycérine	Écrire le nom du médicament en toutes lettres
Norflox	norfloxacine	norflex	Écrire le nom du médicament en toutes lettres
PCA (ACP)	procaïnamide	analgésie contrôlée par le patient	Écrire le nom du médicament en toutes lettres
mcg	microgramme	mg (milligramme)	Écrire µg
/ (barre oblique)	« par »	1 (chiffre)	Écrire « par »
+	le signe +	4 (chiffre)	Demander d'épeler
Zéro **après** la virgule décimale (p. ex., 1,0 mg)*	1 mg	10 mg	NE JAMAIS METTRE un zéro après la virgule
Pas de zéro **avant** la virgule décimale (p. ex., .1 mg)*	0,1 mg	1 mg	TOUJOURS METTRE un zéro avant la virgule
u ou U*	unités	0 (zéro), 4 (quatre) ou cc	Écrire « unité » en toutes lettres
U.I.	unité internationale	IV ou 0,1	Écrire « unité » en toutes lettres
q.d. ou Q.D.*	tous les jours	q.i.d. (4 fois par jour)	Écrire en toutes lettres
q.o.d. ou Q.O.D.*	tous les deux jours	q.i.d. (4 fois par jour) ou qd (tous les jours)	Écrire en toutes lettres

* Sur la liste des abréviations de la JCAHO, sous la rubrique « ne pas utiliser ».

Tableau 2: Abréviations et symboles entraînant des erreurs de médication (suite)

Abréviation/symbole	Signification	Erreur courante	Recommandation
SC, SQ, sub q†	sous-cutané	SL (sublingual)	Écrire en toutes lettres
AD, AS, AU†	oreille droite, oreille gauche, chaque oreille	OD, OS, OU (œil droit, œil gauche, chaque œil)	Écrire en toutes lettres
OD, OS, OU	œil droit, œil gauche, chaque œil	AD, AS, AU (oreille droite, oreille gauche, chaque oreille)	Écrire en toutes lettres
cc†	centimètres cubes	U (unités)	Utiliser mL
@	à	2	Écrire « à »
&	et	2	Écrire « et »
+	« plus » ou « et »	4	Écrire « et »
°	heure	zéro (toutes les 1° pris pour toutes les 10)	Écrire h ou heures
Nom du médicament et dose écrits sans espace (p. ex., Indéral40 mg)	Indéral 40 mg	Indéral 140 mg	Laisser un espace entre le nom du médicament, la dose et l'unité de mesure

† Sur la liste des abréviations de la JCAHO, sous la rubrique « usage déconseillé ».

Adapté d'après *The Institute for the Safe Medication Practices Safety Alert*, vol. 8, nº 24, 27 novembre 2003.

LES RÉACTIONS INDÉSIRABLES AUX MÉDICAMENTS

Une *réaction indésirable à un médicament* est une réaction imprévue, non souhaitée ou excessive, qui peut entraîner:

- une gêne ou un malaise de léger à intense, de durée brève ou prolongée;
- des lésions graves ou des invalidités passagères ou permanentes;
- l'hospitalisation, la nécessité de passer à des soins d'un niveau plus élevé ou un séjour prolongé en établissement hospitalier;
- le décès.

Les réactions indésirables peuvent être regroupées en deux grandes catégories. La première comprend les réactions prévisibles, qui découlent des effets pharmacologiques primaires ou secondaires du médicament. Les réactions liées à la dose et les interactions médicament-médicament sont des exemples de ces réactions. La deuxième catégorie comprend les réactions imprévisibles. Celles-ci ne sont pas associées à la dose et ne découlent pas des effets pharmacologiques primaires ou secondaires du médicament. Les réactions idiosyncrasiques et les réactions d'hypersensibilité sont des exemples de réactions de ce type.

Le fait de bien connaître les réactions indésirables peut protéger le patient de problèmes ultérieurs au moment où il doit recevoir le même médicament ou un médicament doté de propriétés chimiques ou pharmacologiques similaires. Avant d'administrer des médicaments, particulièrement pour la première fois, il est important de prendre connaissance des réactions indésirables les plus fréquentes (soulignées dans la section **Réactions indésirables et effets secondaires** de chaque monographie). Dès leur apparition, l'infirmière devrait être au fait des mesures qu'elle doit prendre et de leur séquence. En plus des réactions courantes, elle devrait également connaître les réactions plus rares mais ayant des conséquences plus graves (en PETITES MAJUSCULES dans la section **Réactions indésirables et effets secondaires** de chaque monographie). Ces réactions peuvent exiger une intervention immédiate, au moment où elles surviennent, ou une préparation préalable à l'administration pour parer à toute éventualité.

Dépistage d'une réaction indésirable aux médicaments

On devrait soupçonner une réaction indésirable chaque fois que survient un changement dans l'état d'un patient qui ne peut être interprété comme une réponse thérapeutique au médicament administré, particulièrement au début de l'administration d'un nouvel agent. Bien qu'une maladie concomitante ou en évolution puisse également expliquer l'apparition ou l'aggravation des symptômes, les réactions indésirables et les effets secondaires devraient toujours être envisagés parmi les causes possibles. Comme toujours, la surveillance de la réponse du patient à un traitement et une évaluation continue sont des étapes importantes de la démarche de soins infirmiers. Il faut apprendre à reconnaître les manifestations qui évoquent une réaction indésirable à un médicament. Il s'agit, entre autres, des suivantes:

- rash;
- modification de la fréquence respiratoire, de la fréquence cardiaque, de la pression artérielle ou de l'état mental;
- convulsions;
- anaphylaxie;
- diarrhée;
- fièvre.

N'importe lequel de ces symptômes peut évoquer une réaction indésirable à un médicament et doit être rapidement documenté, afin qu'on puisse démarrer les interventions qui s'imposent.

Une intervention rapide peut empêcher qu'une réaction légère ne se transforme en un problème de santé grave. Les autres mesures que l'équipe soignante doit prendre au moment où elle dépiste et prend en charge des réactions indésirables aux médicaments sont les suivantes:

1. Vérifier si le médicament prescrit a été celui qui a été administré et réellement celui qui était destiné au patient en question;
2. Vérifier si le médicament a été administré à la dose correcte et par la bonne voie;
3. Établir la chronologie des événements: heure de l'administration et heure à laquelle les symptômes se sont installés;
4. Arrêter l'administration du médicament en cause et suivre l'état du patient pour voir si l'effet négatif se maintient (arrêt du traitement);
5. Recommencer l'administration du médicament, le cas échéant, et suivre de près les réactions indésirables (reprise du traitement).

Réactions liées à la dose (réactions de toxicité)

En général, les réactions liées à la dose signifient que celle-ci est excessive. Ce genre de réaction peut avoir des causes évidentes, par exemple:

- On n'a pas pris en considération la taille du patient (patient cachectique, âgé ou débilité);
- On n'a pas évalué la distribution du médicament (certains médicaments pénètrent mal dans les tissus adipeux);
- On a calculé la dose en fonction du poids véritable plutôt que du poids idéal du patient (erreur qui peut entraîner une toxicité);
- On n'a pas évalué les capacités d'élimination ou de métabolisme du patient (qui peut être très jeune ou très âgé, ou qui peut souffrir d'insuffisance rénale ou hépatique due à une maladie sous-jacente);
- On n'a pas déterminé l'effet des médicaments pris en concomitance (déplacement de certains médicaments en raison d'une liaison aux mêmes protéines plasmatiques);
- On n'a pas tenu compte de la sensibilité accrue du patient due à une maladie sous-jacente (les patients souffrant d'hypothyroïdie sont plus sensibles aux effets de la digoxine).

Les médicaments ayant un indice thérapeutique étroit (comme la digoxine, les aminosides, les antiépileptiques) ou ceux qui dictent une surveillance étroite ou des tests de laboratoire (comme les anticoagulants et les agents néphrotoxiques) sont fréquemment responsables de réactions indésirables liées à la dose. La majorité du temps, il faut tout d'abord cesser temporairement l'administration du médicament, puis en réduire la dose ou augmenter l'intervalle posologique, selon le cas. Dans certains cas, les effets toxiques doivent être traités par un autre agent (par exemple, Digibind, en cas d'intoxication à la digoxine ou la protamine, en cas de saignements liés à l'héparine).

Quelques mesures sont déterminantes pour assurer une prise en charge qui n'expose pas le patient à des risques et pour prévenir les réactions liées à la dose:

- La surveillance en temps opportun des concentrations sanguines du médicament;
- Une révision de la pharmacothérapie lorsqu'on ajoute au régime thérapeutique courant de nouveaux médicaments qui peuvent modifier les concentrations sanguines de ceux que le patient prend déjà;
- Des vérifications fréquentes des paramètres des tests de laboratoire.

On devrait aussi informer les patients que, malgré la survenue d'une réaction, ils peuvent continuer de recevoir le médicament en question. Il faut dissiper dans l'esprit du patient l'idée qu'il est « allergique » au médicament. Il est important de préciser le fait que la réaction est liée à la dose, parce qu'ainsi on n'écarte pas la possibilité de recourir au médicament en question et on précise davantage les paramètres du patient qui pourraient aider à déterminer la dose d'autres médicaments.

Effets secondaires

Les effets secondaires sont généralement des symptômes consécutifs à l'administration d'un médicament qui ne sont pas liés à son action souhaitée ou escomptée. Même s'ils sont indésirables et peuvent être gênants, les effets secondaires surviennent à la prise de doses habituelles assez souvent pour que les patients soient mis au courant du risque et de la conduite à tenir le cas échéant.

Certains effets secondaires sont si minimes qu'il n'est pas nécessaire de cesser l'administration du médicament qui les a induits. On peut donner l'exemple des céphalées qui accompagnent habituellement l'administration de la nitroglycérine ; lors d'un traitement prolongé, cette réaction se dissipe et elle peut être traitée au départ par de l'acétaminophène. D'autres effets secondaires demandent une modification de la dose, l'ajout d'un autre agent ou l'arrêt de la médication, selon la réponse du patient ou la gravité de sa réaction. Ainsi, certains antihypertenseurs peuvent entraîner l'impuissance ; si le patient juge cet effet inacceptable, on devrait chercher une autre option pharmacologique. Les analgésiques opioïdes entraînent souvent la constipation ; cependant, l'ajout de laxatifs au schéma thérapeutique peut corriger ce problème ou le prévenir. L'apparition du syndrome malin des neuroleptiques, une réaction pouvant mettre la vie du patient en danger, qui peut être associé au traitement par des antipsychotiques, exige l'abandon du médicament en cause.

La documentation des effets secondaires devrait inclure le nom de l'agent en question et le moment où les effets surviennent. Elle contribuera ainsi à éviter toute nouvelle administration du médicament si l'effet secondaire est grave ou à renseigner le patient si le médicament doit lui être administré de nouveau.

Réactions idiosyncrasiques

Les réactions idiosyncrasiques sont sans rapport avec la dose, et leur apparition est imprévisible et sporadique. Elles peuvent se manifester de nombreuses façons différentes, incluant la fièvre, la dyscrasie sanguine, des effets cardiovasculaires ou des modifications de l'état mental. Le temps qui s'écoule entre le début du traitement et l'apparition du problème est parfois le seul indice qui lie le médicament au symptôme.

Ces réactions sont problématiques pour de nombreuses raisons. La première est que la réaction peut ou non se reproduire lors d'une deuxième exposition du patient au même médicament. De toute évidence, la décision d'administrer de nouveau le médicament dépend de la nécessité de poursuivre le traitement et de l'existence de solutions de rechange. On doit également se demander si la réaction est susceptible de se produire lors de l'administration de médicaments similaires. Cette décision doit être prise en fonction de chaque cas individuel. Certaines réactions idiosyncrasiques s'expliquent par des différences génétiques dans les enzymes qui métabolisent les médicaments.

Il est très important de bien renseigner le patient, qui doit comprendre la nature imprévisible de telles réactions. Le patient doit également comprendre que le médecin qui a prescrit le médicament a pris en considération les bienfaits potentiels de ce traitement et les a comparés aux risques qu'il comporte. La survenue d'une réaction idiosyncrasique n'écarte pas la possibilité de poursuivre le traitement par des agents similaires, mais on doit la documenter afin de pouvoir en tenir compte lors de la planification des schémas thérapeutiques suivants.

Réactions d'hypersensibilité

En général, les réactions d'hypersensibilité sont de nature allergique et impliquent une exposition préalable à l'agent. Les manifestations d'hypersensibilité vont des éruptions cutanées (rash) de tous types jusqu'à la néphrite, la pneumonite, l'anémie hémolytique et des manifestations d'anaphylaxie pouvant mettre la vie du patient en danger. Les médicaments à base de protéines (comme les vaccins ou les enzymes) sont plus susceptibles d'induire des réactions d'hypersensibilité lors d'expositions ultérieures.

Dans de nombreux cas, la formation d'anticorps intervient dans le processus. Lorsque ces réactions surviennent, on doit prendre en considération le risque de sensibilité croisée. Le meilleur exemple est l'hypersensibilité à la pénicilline. Si le patient a des antécédents de réaction à la pénicilline, on peut s'attendre à ce qu'il manifeste des réactions similaires à d'autres anti-infectieux, comme d'autres pénicillines ou des céphalosporines. C'est pour cette raison qu'il est très important de documenter les réactions d'hypersensibilité. On devrait éviter par la suite de prescrire des agents similaires ou, s'ils sont nécessaires, on devrait administrer un prétraitement (par des antihistaminiques ou des corticostéroïdes) ou un traitement de désensibilisation.

Interactions médicamenteuses : réactions qui surviennent lors de l'ajout d'un deuxième agent (ou de plusieurs autres) au schéma thérapeutique

Ces interactions se produisent lorsque les propriétés pharmacocinétiques ou pharmacodynamiques d'un médicament modifient celles d'un autre. Lorsqu'il y a interaction, les propriétés pharmacocinétiques d'un médicament peuvent entraîner des modifications de la concentration sanguine d'un autre et modifier la réponse de l'organisme à l'un ou l'autre agent ou aux deux. Par exemple, un médicament bloquera les enzymes qui métabolisent un deuxième médicament. Alors, la concentration du deuxième médicament peut s'élever et devenir toxique ou entraîner des réactions indésirables. Les interactions pharmacodynamiques découlent des effets souhaitables et secondaires connus des médicaments. Par exemple, deux médicaments ayant des effets thérapeutiques similaires peuvent agir en synergie. Ainsi, on parle d'interactions pharmacodynamiques dans le cas des effets anticoagulants accrus qui se produisent lorsque la warfarine et l'aspirine sont administrées en concomitance et dans le cas de la dépression accrue du SNC à la suite de l'administration de deux médicaments ayant des effets dépresseurs du SNC, qui potentialisent réciproquement leurs effets.

Si une interaction médicamenteuse survient ou est soupçonnée, on devrait évaluer le besoin de continuer d'administrer les deux agents et de changer la dose ou le médicament utilisé. Le fait de documenter ces réactions pourrait aider à prévenir leur récurrence.

Certaines classes de médicaments sont plus susceptibles d'entraîner des interactions médicamenteuses graves, et les patients qui reçoivent ces agents devraient être surveillés de près. De plus, il est utile de conseiller à ces patients d'être vigilants lors de l'ajout de nouveaux médicaments à leur régime et de toujours consulter un médecin ou un pharmacien avant de prendre des médicaments en vente libre ou des produits naturels. Certaines classes de médicaments sont davantage susceptibles d'entraîner des interactions médicamenteuses plus préjudiciables, raison pour laquelle les patients qui en reçoivent doivent faire l'objet d'une surveillance attentive. Parmi ces classes de médicaments, citons les anticoagulants, les anti-inflammatoires non stéroïdiens (AINS), les inhibiteurs de la MAO, les antihypertenseurs, les antiépileptiques et les antirétroviraux. Par ailleurs, certains médicaments en particulier, comme la théophylline, le lithium et la digoxine, peuvent provoquer des réactions indésirables graves.

Prévention

À la suite des pressions exercées par les consommateurs et les autorités, les établissements de soins ont élaboré des programmes qui visent à réduire les réactions indésirables évitables. En milieu hospitalier, les systèmes informatiques peuvent renseigner rapidement sur l'âge, la taille et le poids du patient, sur sa clairance de la créatinine ou sur sa concentration sérique de créatinine et alerter le médecin si la dose prescrite ne convient pas en raison de l'un de ces paramètres.

En consultations externes, des stratégies destinées à accroître les connaissances du patient sur son traitement médicamenteux et à faciliter ses communications avec les infirmières et les pharmaciens peuvent également aider à prévenir les réactions indésirables aux médicaments. Les ordinateurs de nombreuses pharmacies sont programmés de façon à afficher les limites des doses et à permettre la vérification des interactions médicamenteuses pour aider le pharmacien au moment où celui-ci exécute une commande.

De telles stratégies, bien qu'utiles, ne remplacent pas une prise consciencieuse des antécédents du patient, une évaluation attentive et une surveillance constante. Le prescripteur doit connaître tous les antécédents pharmaceutiques du patient (tous les médicaments d'ordonnance et en vente libre qu'il prend, tous les effets secondaires et réactions indésirables qu'il a subis, ses allergies et toutes les autres données physiques pertinentes). Il est de la responsabilité du prescripteur de revoir ces données en même temps que les valeurs de laboratoire et toutes les autres variables qui peuvent modifier la réponse individuelle à un médicament donné.

Personne ne s'attend à ce que les médecins se souviennent de toutes les données pertinentes au moment où ils prescrivent un médicament. En réalité, en se fiant à la mémoire, on risque de commettre de nombreuses erreurs, et les praticiens doivent avoir accès aux ressources disponibles pour vérifier les interactions médicamenteuses chaque fois qu'ils ajoutent un nouveau médicament à la pharmacothérapie d'un patient. Il incombe aux professionnels de la santé de s'appuyer sur des résultats probants plutôt que sur leur mémoire lorsqu'ils prescrivent, délivrent ou administrent un médicament ou lorsqu'ils surveillent l'état du patient afin de réduire la fréquence des réactions indésirables évitables.

Programme MedEffet de Santé Canada

Pour suivre et évaluer l'incidence des réactions indésirables, Santé Canada dirige le programme MedEffet. Santé Canada se charge, par l'intermédiaire du Programme canadien de surveillance des effets indésirables des médicaments, de recueillir et d'évaluer les déclarations d'effets indésirables concernant les produits de santé suivants, vendus au Canada : produits pharmaceutiques, produits biologiques (y compris les dérivés plasmatiques ainsi que les vaccins thérapeutiques et diagnostiques), produits de santé naturels et produits radiopharmaceutiques. En vertu de ce programme, les professionnels de la santé et les consommateurs peuvent signaler des réactions indésirables à des médicaments ou des défauts des produits pharmaceutiques, appareils médicaux, produits nutritionnels particuliers ou autres articles dont Santé Canada réglemente l'utilisation.

Il faut signaler ces problèmes, même si le lien de cause à effet n'est pas évident ou si l'on ne dispose pas de tous les détails. Le formulaire de déclaration peut être trouvé à l'adresse www.hc-sc.gc.ca/dhp-mps/medeff/report-declaration/index_f.html et à l'annexe O. Des formulaires distincts existent pour les vaccins et pour signaler des incidents relatifs à des instruments médicaux. On peut aussi télécopier sans frais ces rapports à Santé Canada en composant le 1 866 678-6789 ou signaler des effets indésirables par téléphone, sans frais, au 1 866 234-2345.

Les infirmières partagent avec les autres professionnels de la santé la responsabilité de signaler les réactions indésirables en vertu du programme MedEffet, afin qu'on puisse analyser toutes les données importantes en vue d'améliorer les soins aux patients.

CONSIGNES POSOLOGIQUES POUR LES CAS PARTICULIERS

La plupart des médicaments doivent être administrés dans les limites d'une plage posologique. Toutefois, il existe de nombreux cas où la dose moyenne est toxique ou inefficace. Nous indiquons ici plusieurs circonstances où il faut envisager des ajustements particuliers pour que le traitement procure l'effet escompté. Ces directives sont générales, mais elles devraient permettre à l'infirmière de mieux évaluer les paramètres individuels. Lorsqu'elle se trouve devant un cas particulier, l'infirmière devrait examiner attentivement les doses prescrites et prévenir, selon le cas, le médecin ou un autre professionnel de la santé, afin qu'ils puissent recommander les ajustements qui s'imposent. De nombreuses situations cliniques changent au fil du temps (insuffisance rénale ou hépatique, taille, âge), ce qui dicte une réévaluation de la posologie à intervalles réguliers.

Enfants

La majorité des médicaments administrés aux enfants ne sont pas officiellement approuvés chez cette population. Leur usage chez les enfants n'est toutefois pas inapproprié ; il n'a seulement pas fait l'objet d'études chez ce groupe de patients. Ce manque d'information peut mener à des réactions indésirables ou même à une issue fatale. Pour cette raison, les autorités de réglementation exigent maintenant des données sur une administration sans danger chez les enfants pour les nouveaux médicaments qui pourraient être utilisés en pédiatrie.

C'est essentiellement en raison de leur petite taille que l'on doit ajuster la posologie chez les enfants. La plupart des doses des médicaments destinés à cette population sont indiquées en fonction du poids, en milligrammes par kilogramme (mg/kg) ou en fonction de la surface corporelle en milligrammes par mètre carré (mg/m^2). La surface corporelle est déterminée à l'aide des nomogrammes qu'on trouve à l'annexe F ou des formules présentées à l'annexe E.

Dans le cas du nouveau-né et de l'enfant prématuré, des adaptations supplémentaires s'imposent en raison de leur immaturité physiologique. Chez ce groupe, l'absorption après l'administration par voie orale peut être incomplète ou modifiée à cause de variations dans le pH gastrique ou dans la motilité gastro-intestinale ; la distribution peut être modifiée à cause de variations dans l'équilibre hydrique, alors que le métabolisme et l'excrétion peuvent être retardés étant donné que le foie et les reins ne sont pas encore totalement développés. Pour assurer un traitement médicamenteux optimal chez l'enfant prématuré ou le nouveau-né, il faut faire des ajustements fréquents de la posologie qui tiennent compte de la maturation de ces organes. Les changements rapides de poids qui caractérisent ce groupe d'âge dictent, eux aussi, des ajustements additionnels.

L'infirmière devrait tenir compte d'autres variables également. La voie d'administration pour laquelle on opte chez les enfants dépend souvent de la gravité de la maladie. Il faut prendre en considération le niveau de développement de l'enfant et sa capacité de compréhension. Le jeune enfant pourrait redouter les injections intraveineuses ou intramusculaires et les parents pourraient aussi avoir des inquiétudes à l'égard de ce type d'administration. L'infirmière doit alors donner les explications nécessaires à l'enfant et aux parents, et les réconforter. Il faut choisir avec attention les points d'injection sous-cutanée et intramusculaire chez ce groupe d'âge, afin de prévenir les lésions des nerfs ou des tissus.

Personnes âgées

Chez les personnes qui ont plus de 60 à 65 ans, la pharmacocinétique des médicaments change. L'absorption du médicament peut être retardée par suite d'une motilité gastro-intestinale réduite (à cause de l'âge ou d'autres médicaments que la personne âgée doit prendre en concomitance) ou de la congestion passive des vaisseaux sanguins abdominaux qui caractérise, par exemple, l'insuffisance cardiaque. La distribution du médicament peut être modifiée en raison des faibles concentrations de protéines plasmatiques, particulièrement chez les patients qui souffrent de malnutrition. En présence d'une concentration réduite des protéines plasmatiques, une plus grande quantité de médicament reste libre (ne se lie pas) et, pour cette raison, son effet sera accru; certains médicaments administrés à la dose habituelle pourraient alors être toxiques. Comme le métabolisme hépatique et l'excrétion rénale ralentissent avec l'âge, les médicaments peuvent avoir un effet excessif et prolongé. La physiologie de l'organisme change également avec l'âge: il y a augmentation des tissus adipeux et diminution des muscles squelettiques et de la quantité totale d'eau contenue dans l'organisme; habituellement, la taille et le poids diminuent également.

Toutes ces variables changent avec l'âge, souvent de façon imprévisible. Il faut donc diminuer les doses initiales de la plupart des médicaments et les adapter prudemment, selon la réponse clinique, car la sensibilité des patients âgés aux effets indésirables est souvent accrue. La posologie qui était adéquate chez le patient robuste, âgé d'une cinquantaine d'années, peut s'avérer souvent trop élevée chez le même patient 20 ou 30 ans plus tard.

Il faut également tenir compte du fait que la plupart des personnes âgées prennent un grand nombre de médicaments. Plus le nombre de médicaments est grand, plus il y a de risques qu'un médicament modifie ou entrave les effets des autres (interactions médicamenteuses).

Les schémas posologiques devraient être simplifiés, étant donné que la plupart des personnes âgées prennent plusieurs médicaments à la fois. Il faudrait déterminer le moment de l'administration en veillant à ce que le patient n'ait pas à interrompre ses activités plusieurs fois par jour pour prendre ses médicaments. L'administration d'associations médicamenteuses à des doses fixes peut simplifier le traitement.

Au moment d'expliquer les schémas posologiques aux personnes âgées, l'infirmière devrait se rappeler que les troubles de l'ouïe sont courants chez ce groupe de patients. Les patients peuvent hésiter à révéler cette information et l'observance du traitement peut s'en trouver réduite. Les consignes verbales et écrites devraient également être transmises dans la langue que les patients comprennent le mieux et en utilisant une terminologie adaptée à leur compréhension.

Patients en âge de procréer

De façon générale, les femmes enceintes devraient éviter de prendre des médicaments. Lorsque l'administration d'un médicament donné est nécessaire, on doit tenir compte des risques auxquels sont exposés la mère et le fœtus. Le placenta, autrefois considéré comme une barrière protectrice, n'est en fait qu'une simple membrane qui protège le fœtus uniquement contre des molécules très volumineuses. Cette membrane assure le transport passif et actif des médicaments. Le fœtus est particulièrement vulnérable au cours du premier et du dernier trimestre. Au cours du premier trimestre, les organes vitaux se forment. Pendant cette étape de la grossesse, la prise de médicaments potentiellement nuisibles (agents pouvant avoir des effets tératogènes) risque d'entraîner des malformations chez le fœtus ou de provoquer un avortement. Malhcurcusement, c'est l'étape de la grossesse où la femme ignore souvent son état. Par conséquent, il serait sage d'informer toutes les femmes en âge de procréer des risques auxquels le fœtus est exposé. Au cours du troisième trimestre, et particulièrement vers la fin de la grossesse, les médicaments administrés à la mère, et qui traversent le placenta, pourraient ne pas être métabolisés et excrétés de façon adéquate par l'organisme du fœtus. Lorsque les médicaments sont administrés juste avant l'accouchement, ils peuvent s'accumuler dans l'organisme du fœtus et l'intoxiquer après la naissance, puisque le placenta ne contribue plus à l'excrétion du médicament.

On ne peut pas ignorer le fait que certains médicaments altèrent la qualité et la quantité des spermatozoïdes. Il faudrait informer de ce risque les futurs pères qui prennent ce genre d'agents.

Parfois, pour préserver la santé de la mère et pour protéger le fœtus, il faut administrer certains médicaments tout au long de la grossesse, par exemple aux patientes épileptiques ou hypertcnducs.

Dans ce cas, il faut choisir le médicament le plus sûr et l'administrer aux doses les plus faibles qui restent efficaces. À cause des modifications éventuelles de l'effet des médicaments pendant la grossesse, on doit ajuster la posologie pendant toute cette période, et même après l'accouchement. Dans le cas des toxicomanes et des alcooliques, l'effet des médicaments pose des problèmes particuliers pendant la grossesse. En effet, les nouveau-nés dont les mères sont alcooliques ou toxicomanes (abus de sédatifs, comprenant les benzodiazépines, l'héroïne ou la cocaïne) peuvent avoir un poids inférieur à la normale, manifester des réactions de sevrage après la naissance et connaître un retard de croissance. L'évaluation attentive des données relatives aux antécédents devrait mettre en garde l'infirmière contre ces risques.

Maladies rénales

Les reins sont les principaux organes excréteurs. L'adaptation des doses selon la fonction rénale de chaque patient est donc une façon de prévenir des réactions indésirables. Certains médicaments sont excrétés seulement après avoir été métabolisés ou après avoir subi une biotransformation hépatique, alors que d'autres peuvent être éliminés tels quels par les reins. Il ne faut pas oublier que la fonction rénale est insuffisamment développée chez l'enfant prématuré, et qu'elle est diminuée chez la personne âgée. Pour ajuster correctement les doses chez les patients qui souffrent d'insuffisance rénale, on doit connaître la gravité de l'atteinte et déterminer le pourcentage de médicament qui est éliminé par les reins. Le degré d'atteinte peut être établi par des tests de laboratoire, dont le plus courant est celui qui détermine la clairance de la créatinine, ou peut être évalué approximativement à l'aide de calculs (voir l'annexe E). Le pourcentage de médicament excrété par les reins peut être déterminé à partir de divers paramètres pharmacocinétiques. En outre, pour que la posologie soit la plus efficace possible, on peut mesurer les concentrations sanguines de médicament chez chaque patient et apporter les modifications qui s'imposent. On procède souvent à ce genre d'ajustement dans le cas de la digoxine et des aminosides.

Maladies hépatiques

Le foie est le principal organe où a lieu le métabolisme des médicaments. Pour la plupart des médicaments, il s'agit d'une étape d'inactivation. Les métabolites inactifs sont par la suite excrétés par les reins. Habituellement, lors de ce processus de transformation, le médicament qui est relativement liposoluble devient plus hydrosoluble.

Il est plus difficile de déterminer l'état de la fonction hépatique que celui de la fonction rénale. On ne peut donc pas prévoir la posologie uniquement d'après les tests de laboratoire chez le patient souffrant d'insuffisance hépatique. Par ailleurs, même si la fonction hépatique est très fortement diminuée, le métabolisme du médicament peut être adéquat.

Chez le patient qui souffre d'un ictère grave ou qui présente des concentrations très faibles de protéines sériques (particulièrement d'albumine), le métabolisme des médicaments peut poser des problèmes. En cas de maladie hépatique avancée, l'absorption des médicaments peut également être altérée à cause de la congestion du système porte. Les faibles concentrations de protéines sériques peuvent également modifier la quantité de médicament qui peut être liée. Si une moindre quantité de médicament se lie aux protéines, une quantité accrue de médicament reste libre et peut exercer des effets pharmacologiques. La théophylline, les diurétiques et les sédatifs qui sont métabolisés par le foie font partie des médicaments dont la posologie doit être ajustée très attentivement chez les patients souffrant de maladie hépatique. L'usage de certains promédicaments, dont l'activation a lieu dans le foie (comme le sulindac ou le cyclophosphamide), devrait être évité chez les patients qui présentent un dysfonctionnement hépatique prononcé.

Insuffisance cardiaque

Il faut également modifier la posologie des agents administrés aux patients souffrant d'insuffisance cardiaque, car, dans leur cas, l'absorption des médicaments peut être entravée à cause de la congestion passive des vaisseaux sanguins qui alimentent le tractus gastro-intestinal. Du fait de cette congestion passive, le transport du médicament jusqu'au foie ainsi que son métabolisme sont ralentis. En outre, la fonction rénale peut être atteinte : l'élimination du médicament est alors retardée, et son effet, prolongé. Un grand nombre de patients qui souffrent d'insuffisance cardiaque sont d'autant plus vulnérables qu'ils sont âgés. Chez les patients qui souffrent d'insuffisance cardiaque manifeste, il faut réduire la posologie des médicaments qui sont surtout métabolisés par le foie ou excrétés par les reins.

Taille et poids

Dans la plupart des cas, la posologie du médicament doit être ajustée selon le poids corporel total. Certains médicaments (par exemple, la digoxine et les aminosides) pénètrent difficilement dans les tissus adipeux et, si on les administre à un patient obèse, il faut en déterminer la posologie selon le poids idéal ou selon une estimation du poids maigre. On peut calculer les doses à partir de tableaux de poids souhaitables ou à partir d'une formule permettant de déterminer le poids maigre, lorsque la taille et le poids du patient sont connus (voir l'annexe E). Sans ce type d'ajustement, les risques de toxicité sont considérables.

La taille corporelle devrait également être évaluée chez les patients très maigres. Chez les personnes âgées, les alcooliques, les personnes atteintes du sida, de cancer ou de toute autre maladie chronique et débilitante en phase terminale, il faut porter une attention toute particulière à la posologie, dont le calcul peut être fondé sur celle qu'on administre à l'adulte ayant un poids normal (70 kg). De même, on devrait considérer une modification de la posologie chez les patients amputés.

Transport du médicament à son lieu d'action

Pour que le traitement donne les résultats escomptés, il faut que le médicament atteigne le lieu où il doit exercer son action. Dans le meilleur des cas, le médicament n'aura qu'un effet minime sur les autres tissus ou organes. Par exemple, les préparations topiques, destinées au traitement des maladies cutanées, sont la plupart du temps faiblement absorbées. Dans le cas de la plupart des maladies, cependant, cette voie d'administration n'est ni possible ni pratique. On doit parfois emprunter des voies d'administration inhabituelles pour assurer la présence du médicament à son lieu d'action. Chez les patients souffrant de méningite bactérienne, par exemple, l'administration de médicaments par voie parentérale ne peut pas toujours assurer des concentrations suffisamment élevées dans le liquide céphalorachidien. On doit parfois administrer le médicament par voie intrathécale et, en même temps, par voie parentérale, comme dans le cas des aminosides. L'œil constitue également une barrière relativement imperméable à de nombreux médicaments. Afin qu'ils puissent la traverser, il faut qu'on les administre par instillation ou par injection locale.

Dans certains cas, l'absorption locale étant entravée, le médicament ne peut pas exercer l'effet général escompté. Chez les patients en état de choc ou présentant une irrigation tissulaire réduite attribuable à une autre cause, il est possible que le médicament ne soit pas absorbé dans la circulation générale à partir des points d'injection sous-cutanée ou intramusculaire.

Interactions médicamenteuses

Il peut également être nécessaire d'ajuster la posologie lorsque le patient prend plusieurs médicaments en concomitance. Les médicaments qui se lient fortement aux protéines plasmatiques, comme la warfarine et la phénytoïne, peuvent être déplacés par d'autres médicaments ayant cette même propriété. Lorsque ce phénomène se produit, le médicament qui a été déplacé devient plus actif étant donné que c'est toujours la forme libre qui est active.

Certains agents, comme la cimétidine et le ritonavir, diminuent la capacité du foie de métaboliser d'autres médicaments. Il faut parfois réduire la posologie des médicaments fortement métabolisés par le foie qui sont administrés en concomitance. Par ailleurs, certains agents, comme le phénobarbital, la carbamazépine et la rifampine, peuvent accélérer le métabolisme hépatique des médicaments; il faut alors en augmenter la dose.

Les médicaments qui modifient fortement le pH de l'urine peuvent affecter l'élimination d'autres substances dont l'excrétion dépend du pH. L'alcalinisation de l'urine accélère l'excrétion des médicaments acides. L'acidification de l'urine augmente la réabsorption des médicaments acides, ce qui en prolonge et en intensifie l'action. Par contre, les médicaments qui acidifient l'urine accélèrent l'excrétion des médicaments alcalins. Par exemple, on administre du bicarbonate de sodium en cas de surdosage par l'aspirine, car l'alcalinisation de l'urine favorise l'excrétion rénale de l'acide acétylsalicylique.

Certains médicaments modifient l'activité des enzymes qui interviennent dans le métabolisme d'autres agents. L'allopurinol inhibe l'enzyme qui participe à la production de l'acide urique, mais il inhibe également le métabolisme de la 6-mercaptopurine (inactivation), ce qui en augmente grandement la toxicité. Il faut, par conséquent, réduire considérablement la posologie de la mercaptopurine lorsqu'elle est administrée en même temps que l'allopurinol.

De nombreux produits naturels exposent le patient au même risque d'interactions.

Présentation (formes pharmaceutiques)

La forme de la préparation pose souvent des problèmes à l'infirmière. Certains médicaments ne sont pas offerts sous forme de solution ou de comprimés à croquer. Le pharmacien doit alors préparer la forme pharmaceutique demandée pour un patient en particulier. D'autres fois, pour que le patient reste fidèle à son traitement, il faut camoufler le goût ou l'aspect du médicament en le mélangeant à des aliments ou à une boisson. Enfin, certaines formes pharmaceutiques, comme les préparations en aérosol pour inhalation, ne conviennent pas toujours à de très jeunes enfants, car leur administration nécessite de leur part une collaboration qu'ils sont incapables de fournir.

Avant de modifier la forme pharmaceutique (réduire en poudre les comprimés ou ouvrir les capsules) ou d'utiliser une voie d'administration pour laquelle elle n'est pas prévue, il faut s'assurer que l'effet et l'innocuité du médicament ne changeront pas. En général, il est déconseillé de réduire en poudre les préparations à libération lente ou prolongée ou d'ouvrir les capsules contenant des granules, car on risque de raccourcir la durée d'action et d'intensifier l'effet du médicament. D'autres présentations (comme les préparations à saupoudrer) doivent au contraire être ouvertes. Les comprimés à enrobage entérique ne doivent pas être écrasés, car cet enrobage protège l'estomac de leurs effets irritants ou protège les médicaments des effets de l'acide gastrique. Si une préparation doit être réduite en poudre, on peut mélanger la poudre avec de la compote de fruits ou de la nourriture en purée ou avec une petite quantité d'eau afin de faciliter son administration au patient. Si on fait un tel mélange, il doit être ingéré immédiatement.

Facteurs ambiants

La fumée de cigarette peut accélérer le métabolisme des médicaments par les enzymes hépatiques. Il faut donc administrer des doses plus importantes de certains médicaments métabolisés par le foie aux patients qui fument et même, parfois, aux patients qui sont tout simplement exposés à la fumée de cigarette. L'effet du tabac sur le métabolisme des médicaments peut persister pendant plusieurs mois après que la personne a cessé de fumer.

Aliments

La présence de certains aliments dans l'appareil gastro-intestinal peut également modifier le sort de certains médicaments. Le calcium alimentaire, que l'on trouve en grande concentration dans les produits laitiers, se lie aux tétracyclines et aux fluoroquinolones (chélation) et en empêche l'absorption. De nombreux antibiotiques sont mieux absorbés s'ils sont administrés à jeun. Les aliments riches en pyridoxine (vitamine B_6) peuvent inhiber l'effet antiparkinsonien de la lévodopa (effet qu'on peut contrecarrer par l'administration concomitante de carbidopa). Les aliments qui peuvent modifier le pH de l'urine sont également susceptibles d'entraver l'excrétion des médicaments, ce qui en augmente ou en diminue l'efficacité. Puisqu'il n'existe pas de directives générales à cet égard, il est prudent de vérifier si des problèmes d'interaction existent et s'ils peuvent expliquer l'échec du traitement, puis d'effectuer les adaptations de posologie qui s'imposent.

Résumé

La posologie moyenne d'un médicament est calculée en fonction du patient moyen. Toutefois, chaque patient constitue un cas particulier, car le cheminement du médicament après son administration est chaque fois différent. Il faut donc tenir compte des données exposées ici pour pouvoir planifier un traitement médicamenteux qui soit adapté au patient et qui permette d'obtenir les résultats escomptés tout en réduisant au minimum le risque de toxicité.

SENSIBILISATION DU PATIENT À L'USAGE SANS DANGER DES MÉDICAMENTS

La recherche a démontré que les patients doivent être renseignés sur plusieurs volets de la pharmacothérapie, quel que soit le médicament qu'ils prennent. Un patient et des proches bien informés peuvent prévenir les erreurs de médication commises par le personnel hospitalier et sont moins susceptibles de faire des erreurs lors d'un traitement à domicile. La sensibilisation du patient à cet égard favorise également l'observance du traitement médicamenteux.

Avant de s'engager dans l'enseignement, il faut toujours évaluer les connaissances actuelles du patient, en lui demandant s'il connaît le médicament en question, la façon de le prendre chez lui, les précautions ou le suivi nécessaires et toute autre question reliée à cet agent en particulier. Il faut adapter l'enseignement selon le niveau de connaissances du patient et selon d'autres facteurs comme sa volonté d'apprendre, les obstacles environnementaux et sociaux à l'apprentissage et à l'observance du traitement ainsi que des facteurs culturels. L'enseignement doit porter sur les points suivants :

1. **Nom générique (ou dénomination commune) et nom commercial (ou nom de marque).** Le patient devrait connaître le nom commercial et le nom générique de chacun des médicaments qu'il prend pour deux raisons. Premièrement, cela l'aide à reconnaître son médicament en cas de substitution du produit de marque par sa version générique. Deuxièmement, cela prévient toute confusion d'ordre auditif au moment de la prise des antécédents pharmacologiques ou de leur inscription dans le dossier du patient. C'est le cas lorsqu'on prononce Celebrex, mais qu'on entend ou qu'on veut dire Cerebyx.

2. **But du médicament.** Les patients ont le droit de connaître les bienfaits thérapeutiques du médicament qui leur a été prescrit, mais aussi les conséquences d'une prise irrégulière, information qui pourrait améliorer l'observance du traitement. Par exemple, le patient pourrait mieux accepter de prendre un antihypertenseur si on lui explique qu'en abaissant sa pression artérielle, ce médicament l'aide à prévenir une crise cardiaque, la maladie rénale ou un accident vasculaire cérébral, au lieu de se contenter de lui dire qu'il abaissera tout simplement sa pression artérielle.

3. **Posologie et mode d'emploi du médicament.** Pour tirer profit de son médicament, et pour éviter des réactions indésirables et d'autres issues défavorables, le patient doit connaître les quantités à prendre ainsi que l'heure des prises. Il faut lui indiquer la posologie en unités de poids du SI (à savoir, nombre de milligrammes ou de grammes) plutôt qu'en unités posologiques (nombre de comprimés) ou en unités de volume (nombre de cuillérées à thé). Il faut également l'informer du moment opportun des prises, par exemple à jeun ou avec des aliments, au coucher, ou avec ou sans autres médicaments. Si possible, il faudrait aider le patient à intégrer les prises dans son propre horaire, afin que cela ne représente pas pour lui une tâche ardue ou facile à oublier.

4. **Doses sautées.** Il faut toujours expliquer au patient la marche à suivre si, pour une raison ou une autre, il a sauté une dose. Certains patients ont signalé qu'ils avaient pris, plus tard, une dose double pour remplacer la dose qu'ils n'ont pas pu prendre au moment habituel, s'exposant ainsi au risque d'effets secondaires et de réactions indésirables.

5. **Durée du traitement.** Il arrive souvent que le patient cesse de prendre son médicament lorsqu'il se sent mieux ou lorsqu'il ne perçoit pas l'avantage du traitement. Dans le cas des traitements de très long cours, ou même à vie, il faut rappeler au patient que le médicament l'aide à maintenir le niveau courant de bien-être. Dans le cas des traitements à court terme, il faut par ailleurs lui préciser qu'il doit prendre toute la quantité de médicament qui lui a été prescrite, même s'il se sent mieux. Dans le cas de certains médicaments dont on ne peut

interrompre brusquement la prise, il faut informer le patient qu'il doit toujours consulter un professionnel de la santé avant d'arrêter le traitement.

6. **Effets secondaires légers et marche à suivre s'ils surviennent.** Il faut prévenir le patient que tous les médicaments peuvent avoir des effets secondaires. Il doit en connaître les plus fréquents et savoir quoi faire pour les prendre en charge. Un patient averti sera moins susceptible d'arrêter de prendre son médicament à cause d'un effet secondaire léger, qui pourrait être évité.
7. **Effets secondaires graves et marche à suivre s'ils surviennent.** Le patient doit être informé du risque d'effets secondaires graves. Il doit connaître les signes et les symptômes associés aux effets secondaires graves et savoir qu'il doit prévenir immédiatement le médecin ou l'infirmière s'ils se manifestent. Il faut expliquer au patient qu'il doit communiquer avec le professionnel de la santé avant l'heure de la prise de la dose suivante, sans présumer que le médicament en question est responsable des symptômes et décider d'arrêter prématurément le traitement de son propre chef.
8. **Médicaments à éviter.** Les interactions médicamenteuses peuvent atténuer ou potentialiser les effets de chacun des médicaments pris en concomitance ou provoquer des réactions indésirables mettant en jeu le pronostic vital, comme des arythmies cardiaques, l'hépatite, l'insuffisance rénale ou des hémorragies. Le patient et ses proches doivent connaître les médicaments à éviter, y compris les agents en vente libre et les produits naturels.
9. **Aliments à éviter et autres précautions à prendre.** Les interactions entre les médicaments et les aliments sont fréquentes et leurs conséquences sont similaires à celles des interactions médicamenteuses. Les interactions médicament-environnement ne sont pas rares non plus pendant certains traitements médicamenteux; elles causent par exemple des réactions cutanées graves à la suite d'une exposition prolongée au soleil. Dans le même ordre d'idées, le patient doit être informé des activités à éviter si, par exemple, le médicament qu'il prend risque de diminuer sa vigilance ou sa coordination.
10. **Conservation des médicaments.** Les médicaments doivent être conservés de manière appropriée pour que leur puissance soit maintenue. La plupart des médicaments doivent être gardés à l'abri de la chaleur et de l'humidité, donc il faut éviter de les placer dans l'armoire de pharmacie de la salle de bains. De plus, il est possible de prévenir les mélanges malencontreux en adoptant de sages pratiques de rangement, par exemple en conservant les médicaments de deux membres de la famille dans des endroits distincts. Il faut aussi veiller à ce que les médicaments se trouvent hors de la portée des enfants et des animaux. Par ailleurs, il faut expliquer au patient la manière dont il doit conserver ses médicaments et lui demander quelles sont ses façons habituelles de les ranger.
11. **Soins de suivi.** Toute personne qui prend des médicaments doit être suivie de près; c'est la seule façon de déterminer si le médicament prescrit lui convient et est efficace. Dans le cas de nombreux traitements médicamenteux, il faut faire des tests effractifs et non effractifs pour évaluer les concentrations sanguines, la fonction hépatique ou rénale, l'hématopoïèse ou d'autres effets sur différents systèmes de l'organisme. Grâce à une évaluation suivie, on peut adapter la posologie, changer de médicament ou arrêter un traitement, si besoin est.
12. **Médicaments et produits à ne pas prendre.** On doit mettre en garde le patient contre la consommation de médicaments périmés ou de médicaments prescrits à une autre personne, tout comme contre l'automédication avec des agents qu'il n'utilisait plus depuis un certain temps, même s'ils ne sont pas périmés. On doit aussi lui recommander de garder sur lui la liste des médicaments qu'il prend et, le cas échéant, de demander au professionnel de la santé si un médicament nouvellement prescrit est censé en remplacer un autre d'usage courant.

Pendant les séances d'enseignement, on doit encourager le patient et ses proches à poser des questions. Grâce à des explications plus poussées, à la suite de leurs questions, on peut vérifier leur compréhension et déceler les points qu'il faut approfondir. Il est aussi utile de faire répéter au patient les explications qui lui ont été données et de l'inviter à faire lui-même la démonstration d'un mode d'application ou d'une technique d'administration.

On doit également souligner l'importance des traitements concomitants. La médication ne constitue souvent qu'un volet du traitement. Il est toujours utile de revoir avec le patient et ses proches les autres mesures permettant d'améliorer ou de maintenir la santé. Il faut aussi toujours tenir compte du contexte culturel dans lequel on transmet des informations sur la santé et adapter le plan de traitement en conséquence: par exemple, s'assurer des services d'un interprète du même sexe que le patient ou planifier l'heure des prises du médicament pour éviter tout conflit avec certains rituels ou traditions.

Enfin, il faut remettre au patient des consignes écrites dans un langage simple et facile à comprendre. Il ne faut jamais oublier que les professionnels de la santé rédigent souvent leurs informations à un niveau qui correspond à la quatrième année du secondaire, alors que le patient moyen qui les lit a un niveau de compréhension qui correspond à une cinquième année du primaire. Il faut, par ailleurs, recommander au patient de garder les consignes écrites pour pouvoir les relire plus tard, chez lui, lorsqu'il sera moins stressé et connaîtra les difficultés pratiques auxquelles il doit faire face, compte tenu de son plan de traitement.

CLASSIFICATION

Nous présentons dans cette section les caractéristiques générales des principales classes de médicaments. Pour obtenir des informations plus détaillées et plus précises, prière de consulter la monographie de chacun des médicaments.

AGENTS ANTI-ALZHEIMER

INDICATIONS

Traitement de la maladie d'Alzheimer.

MÉCANISME D'ACTION

Tous les agents, à l'exception de la mémantine, augmentent la quantité d'acétylcholine dans le SNC en inhibant la cholinestérase ■ Aucun des médicaments commercialisés à ce jour ne peut arrêter l'évolution de la démence de type Alzheimer. Les agents qu'on trouve actuellement sur le marché peuvent cependant améliorer la fonction cognitive ou ralentir sa détérioration et, de ce fait, améliorer la qualité de vie.

CONTRE-INDICATIONS, PRÉCAUTIONS ET MISES EN GARDE

Contre-indications: Hypersensibilité.

Précautions et mises en garde: La prudence est de mise chez les patients ayant des antécédents de maladie du sinus ou d'autres anomalies de conduction cardiaque de type supraventriculaires (en raison des risques de bradycardie) ■ Les effets cholinergiques des inhibiteurs de la cholinestérase peuvent entraîner des réactions indésirables gastro-intestinales (nausées, vomissements, diarrhée, anorexie, perte de poids) et augmenter la sécrétion d'acide gastrique, provoquant des saignements gastro-intestinaux, particulièrement au cours d'un traitement concomitant par des AINS ■ Les autres effets cholinergiques sont notamment la rétention urinaire, des convulsions ou le bronchospasme.

INTERACTIONS (inhibiteurs de la cholinestérase)

Effets additifs lors de l'administration concomitante d'autres **médicaments ayant des propriétés cholinergiques** ■ Risque d'intensification des effets des **myorelaxants de type succinylcholine** pendant une anesthésie ■ Risque de diminution des effets thérapeutiques des **anticholinergiques**.

SOINS INFIRMIERS

ÉVALUATION DE LA SITUATION

- Évaluer la fonction cognitive (mémoire, attention, raisonnement, langage, capacité de mener à bien des tâches simples) tout au long du traitement.
- Suivre de près les nausées, les vomissements, l'anorexie et la perte de poids. Prévenir le médecin si ces effets secondaires se manifestent.

DIAGNOSTICS INFIRMIERS POSSIBLES

- Opérations de la pensée perturbées (Indications).
- Alimentation déficiente (Enseignement au patient et à ses proches).
- Connaissances insuffisantes sur la maladie et sur le traitement médicamenteux (Enseignement au patient et à ses proches).

ENSEIGNEMENT AU PATIENT ET À SES PROCHES

- Expliquer au patient et à son soignant qu'il faut prendre ce type de médicaments en respectant rigoureusement les recommandations du médecin.
- Prévenir le patient et son soignant qu'ils doivent informer un professionnel de la santé en cas de nausées, de vomissements, d'anorexie ou de perte de poids.

VÉRIFICATION DE L'EFFICACITÉ THÉRAPEUTIQUE

L'efficacité du traitement peut être démontrée par: l'amélioration passagère ou le ralentissement de la diminution de la fonction cognitive (mémoire, attention, raisonnement, langage, capacité de mener à bien des tâches simples), chez les patients atteints de la maladie d'Alzheimer.

AGENTS ANTI-ALZHEIMER INCLUS DANS LE *GUIDE*

AGENTS ANTIOBÉSITÉ

INDICATIONS

Prise en charge de l'obésité exogène dans le cadre d'une intervention globale comprenant une diète hypocalorique ■ Ces agents sont particulièrement utiles en présence d'autres facteurs de risque, notamment l'hypertension, le diabète ou les dyslipidémies.

MÉCANISME D'ACTION

La sibutramine est un anorexigène qui diminue l'appétit par son effet sur le SNC ■ L'orlistat est un inhibiteur de la lipase qui diminue l'absorption des graisses alimentaires.

CONTRE-INDICATIONS, PRÉCAUTIONS ET MISES EN GARDE

Contre-indications: Tous ces agents sont déconseillés pendant la grossesse et l'allaitement ■ La sibutramine est contre-indiquée en présence de maladies hépatique ou rénale graves, d'hypertension non maîtrisée, d'insuffisance cardiaque diagnostiquée ou de maladie cardiovasculaire ■ L'orlistat est contre-indiqué en présence de malabsorption chronique.

Précautions et mises en garde: La sibutramine devrait être administrée avec prudence chez les patients ayant des antécédents de convulsions, chez ceux présentant un glaucome par fermeture de l'angle ainsi que chez les personnes âgées.

INTERACTIONS

Risque d'effets additifs lors de l'administration concomitante de sibutramine et de **stimulants du SNC**, de certains **suppresseurs des céphalées vasculaires**, d'**inhibiteurs de la MAO** et de certains **opioïdes** (éviter l'administration concomitante) ■ L'orlistat réduit l'absorption de certaines **vitamines liposolubles** et du **bêtacarotène**.

SOINS INFIRMIERS

ÉVALUATION DE LA SITUATION

- Mesurer le poids et noter l'apport alimentaire du patient avant le traitement et à intervalles réguliers pendant toute sa durée. Adapter les posologies des médicaments pris en concomitance (antihypertenseurs, antidiabétiques, hypolipémiants), selon les besoins.

DIAGNOSTICS INFIRMIERS POSSIBLES

- Image corporelle perturbée (Indications).
- Alimentation excessive (Indications).
- Connaissances insuffisantes sur la maladie et sur le traitement médicamenteux (Enseignement au patient et à ses proches).

ENSEIGNEMENT AU PATIENT ET À SES PROCHES

- Expliquer au patient qu'il est utile d'associer une activité physique régulière, autorisée par le médecin, au traitement et à la diétothérapie.

VÉRIFICATION DE L'EFFICACITÉ THÉRAPEUTIQUE

L'efficacité du traitement peut être démontrée par: une perte de poids lente et constante, si le traitement s'accompagne d'une diète hypocalorique.

AGENTS ANTIOBÉSITÉ INCLUS DANS LE *GUIDE*

orlistat, 895
sibutramine, 1103

AGENTS UTILISÉS DANS LE TRAITEMENT DE L'IMPUISSANCE

INDICATIONS

Traitement du dysfonctionnement érectile.

MÉCANISME D'ACTION

Le sildénafil, le tadalafil et le vardénafil inhibent l'enzyme qui inactive le GMP cyclique; ce dernier entraîne le relâchement des muscles lisses des corps caverneux, ce qui intensifie l'afflux de sang dans le pénis et renforce l'érection qui s'ensuit. L'alprostadil est une prostaglandine qui agit localement pour relâcher les muscles lisses trabéculaires et pour dilater les artères caverneuses.

CONTRE-INDICATIONS, PRÉCAUTIONS ET MISES EN GARDE

Contre-indications: Hypersensibilité ■ *Sildénafil, tadalafil et vardénafil* – Administration concomitante de dérivés nitrés (nitroglycérine, isosorbide) ■ *Alprostadil* – Présence d'un implant pénien ou d'une anomalie structurale ou pathologique du pénis ■ Affection qui pourrait prédisposer au priapisme (anémie drépanocytaire, myélome multiple, leucémie, etc.).
Précautions et mises en garde: *Sildénafil, tadalafil et vardénafil* – Maladie cardiovasculaire grave sous-jacente, malformation anatomique du pénis, maladies associées au priapisme et aux troubles de saignement, ulcère gastroduodénal en évolution (la prudence est de mise) ■ *Alprostadil* – Anomalies de la coagulation (la prudence est de mise).

INTERACTIONS

La **cimétidine**, l'**érythromycine**, la **clarithromycine**, le **kétoconazole**, le **nelfinavir**, l'**indinavir**, le **ritonavir** et l'**itraconazole** peuvent élever les concentrations sanguines du sildénafil, du tadalafil et du vardénafil ■ Risque accru d'hypotension grave lorsque le sildénafil, le tadalafil ou le vardénafil sont utilisés avec des **dérivés nitrés** (l'administration concomitante est donc contre-indiquée).

SOINS INFIRMIERS

ÉVALUATION DE LA SITUATION

- Déterminer le degré de dysfonctionnement érectile avant l'administration du médicament. Le sildénafil, le tadalafil et le vardénafil n'ont aucun effet en l'absence d'une stimulation sexuelle.
- Écarter la présence de troubles vasculaires et de lésions aux corps caverneux avant d'administrer l'alprostadil, car ce médicament est inefficace en ce cas.

DIAGNOSTICS INFIRMIERS POSSIBLES

- Dysfonctionnement sexuel (Indications).
- Connaissances insuffisantes sur le traitement médicamenteux (Enseignement au patient et à ses proches).

INTERVENTIONS INFIRMIÈRES

- Le sildénafil, le tadalafil et le vardénafil sont administrés par voie orale. La dose doit habituellement être administrée de 30 à 60 minutes avant les rapports sexuels. Le début et la durée d'action varient selon l'agent utilisé.
- L'alprostadil est administré par voie intracaverneuse ou transurétrale. Lorsqu'il est administré par voie intracaverneuse, il doit être injecté dans la face dorsolatérale du tiers proximal du pénis en évitant les veines visibles. Alterner les points d'injection d'un côté et de l'autre. La dose est déterminée dans le cabinet du médecin.

ENSEIGNEMENT AU PATIENT ET À SES PROCHES

- Expliquer au patient qu'il doit prendre le sildénafil, le tadalafil ou le vardénafil de 30 à 60 minutes avant les rapports sexuels et pas plus de 1 fois par jour.
- Avertir le patient que l'utilisation du sildénafil, du tadalafil ou du vardénafil chez les femmes n'a pas été approuvée.
- Mettre en garde le patient contre la prise concomitante de sildénafil, de tadalafil et de vardénafil et de dérivés nitrés.
- Expliquer au patient sous traitement par l'alprostadil qu'il ne doit prendre cet agent qu'une seule fois en 24 heures et jamais plus de 3 fois par semaine, en respectant un intervalle d'au moins 24 heures entre 2 injections par voie intracaverneuse, et de ne pas s'en servir plus de 2 fois en 24 heures par voie transurétrale.
- Avertir le patient que le priapisme (érection prolongée durant plus de 60 minutes) est dangereux et que, le cas échéant, il doit consulter immédiatement un médecin. Si le priapisme n'est pas traité, il y a risque de lésions permanentes irréversibles.
- Expliquer au patient que les médicaments qui traitent le dysfonctionnement érectile ne le protègent pas contre les infections transmissibles sexuellement. Lui conseiller de prendre les mesures nécessaires pour se protéger contre les infections transmissibles sexuellement et l'infection par le VIH.

VÉRIFICATION DE L'EFFICACITÉ THÉRAPEUTIQUE

L'efficacité du traitement peut être démontrée par: une érection suffisante pour permettre à l'homme de s'engager dans des rapports sexuels sans manifestation d'effets indésirables.

AGENTS UTILISÉS DANS LE TRAITEMENT DE L'IMPUISSANCE INCLUS DANS LE *GUIDE*

AGENTS UTILISÉS DANS LE TRAITEMENT DES CÉPHALÉES VASCULAIRES

INDICATIONS

Traitement de courte durée des céphalées vasculaires (migraines, céphalées vasculaires de Horton, variantes migraineuses). On administre d'autres agents en prophylaxie, comme certains bêtabloquants et bloqueurs des canaux calciques pour prévenir les céphalées vasculaires récurrentes.

MÉCANISME D'ACTION

Les dérivés de l'ergot (ergotamine, dihydroergotamine) stimulent directement les récepteurs alpha-adrénergiques et sérotoninergiques, ce qui entraîne une vasoconstriction des muscles vasculaires lisses ■ Les agonistes de la sérotonine 5-HT_1 entraînent aussi la vasoconstriction ■ Dans le cas du composé de butalbital, le butalbital exerce un effet sédatif et l'aspirine soulage la douleur.

CONTRE-INDICATIONS, PRÉCAUTIONS ET MISES EN GARDE

Contre-indications: Les dérivés de l'ergot et les agonistes sérotoninergiques sont déconseillés chez les patients souffrant de maladie cardiovasculaire ou qui ont de tels antécédents ■ Les composés de butalbital sont contre-indiqués en présence d'hypersensibilité à l'un de leurs ingrédients, de porphyrie, d'ulcère gastro-intestinal et de surdosage à l'alcool, aux hypnotiques, aux analgésiques ou aux médicaments psychotropes, ou en cas d'intoxication à l'une de ces substances.

Précautions et mises en garde: On doit administrer ces médicaments avec prudence aux patients ayant des antécédents de maladie cardiovasculaire ou qui sont exposés au risque d'en souffrir ■ Les composés de butalbital doivent être administrés avec prudence dans les cas suivants: coma, dépression préexistante du SNC, prédisposition à la dépression respiratoire.

INTERACTIONS

Éviter l'administration de **dérivés de l'ergot** et d'**agonistes de la sérotonine** pendant un même intervalle de 24 heures ■ Consulter la monographie de chaque médicament.

SOINS INFIRMIERS

ÉVALUATION DE LA SITUATION

Déterminer le siège, l'intensité et la durée de la douleur ainsi que les symptômes connexes (photophobie, phonophobie, nausées, vomissements) durant les crises de migraine.

DIAGNOSTICS INFIRMIERS POSSIBLES

- Douleur aiguë (Indications).
- Connaissances insuffisantes sur le traitement médicamenteux (Enseignement au patient et à ses proches).

INTERVENTIONS INFIRMIÈRES

- Le médicament devrait être administré dès le premier signe de céphalée imminente.

ENSEIGNEMENT AU PATIENT ET À SES PROCHES

- Expliquer au patient que le médicament ne devrait être utilisé que lors des crises de migraine. Il est destiné au soulagement de ces crises, mais non à leur prévention ni à la réduction de leur fréquence.
- Informer le patient que le fait de se reposer dans une pièce sombre après avoir pris le médicament pourrait l'aider à soulager davantage la douleur.
- Prévenir le patient que les agents de cette classe peuvent provoquer de la somnolence ou des étourdissements. Lui conseiller de ne pas conduire et d'éviter les activités qui exigent sa vigilance jusqu'à ce qu'on ait la certitude que le médicament qui lui a été prescrit n'entraîne pas ces effets chez lui.
- Recommander au patient de ne pas boire d'alcool, puisque cette substance peut aggraver les céphalées.
- Après un traitement prolongé avec un composé de butalbital, interrompre l'administration graduellement pour prévenir les symptômes de sevrage.

VÉRIFICATION DE L'EFFICACITÉ THÉRAPEUTIQUE

L'efficacité du traitement peut être démontrée par: le soulagement de la douleur provoquée par les crises de migraine.

AGENTS UTILISÉS DANS LE TRAITEMENT DES CÉPHALÉES VASCULAIRES INCLUS DANS LE *GUIDE*

agonistes de la sérotonine 5-HT$_1$
almotriptan, 27
élétriptan, 27
naratriptan, 27
rizatriptan, 27
sumatriptan, 27
zolmitriptan, 27

dérivés de l'ergot
dihydroergotamine, 434
ergotamine, 434

divers
butalbital, composés de, 171

AGENTS UTILISÉS PENDANT LA GROSSESSE ET L'ALLAITEMENT

INDICATIONS

Les médicaments utilisés au cours du travail et de l'accouchement sont notamment les agents tocolytiques et ocytociques. Les agents tocolytiques inhibent l'activité des muscles utérins afin de prévenir l'accouchement prématuré. Les agents ocytociques stimulent les muscles utérins dans le but de déclencher le travail, de le stimuler ou de le renforcer; on les utilise également comme des adjuvants au traitement de l'avortement incomplet ou inévitable et pour réprimer l'hémorragie post-partum.

MÉCANISME D'ACTION

Les agents tocolytiques (qui ne sont pas traités dans le *Guide*) incluent les agents bêtasympathomimétiques (ritodrine) et le sulfate de magnésium ■ Les agents bêtasympathomimétiques relâchent les muscles lisses de l'utérus en se fixant aux récepteurs bêta$_2$ ■ Les agents ocytociques (prostaglandines et oxytocine synthétique) stimulent les contractions des muscles lisses de l'utérus.

CONTRE-INDICATIONS, PRÉCAUTIONS ET MISES EN GARDE

Contre-indications: *Agents bêtasympathomimétiques* – Antécédents de maladie cardiaque, rénale ou hépatique; migraines, hyperthyroïdie, asthme ou hypertension. *Oxytocine* – Hypersensibilité ou accouchement prévu par césarienne. *Alcaloïdes de l'ergot* – Hypersensibilité, insuffisance hépatique et rénale, hypertension et maladie cardiovasculaire. Ne pas utiliser ces agents pour déclencher le travail de l'accouchement. *Dinoprostone* – Hypersensibilité. L'usage du gel ou de l'insertion vaginale est déconseillé lorsqu'il faut éviter des contractions utérines prolongées (p. ex., en cas d'antécédents de césarienne ou de chirurgie utérine).

Précautions et mises en garde: *Oxytocine* – Première et deuxième phases du travail, en présence de maladie cardiovasculaire, d'hypertension et de maladie rénale (la prudence est de mise) ■ *Agents bêtasympathomimétiques* – Diabète (la prudence est de mise) ■ *Dinoprostone* – Tissus utérins cicatriciels ■ asthme ■ hypotension ■ maladie cardiaque ■ troubles surrénaliens ■ anémie ■ ictère ■ diabète ■ glaucome ■ maladie pulmonaire, rénale ou hépatique ■ multiparité (jusqu'à 5 grossesses à terme).

INTERACTIONS

Oxytocine: Risque d'hypertension grave lorsque l'oxytocine est administrée après des **vasopresseurs** ■ L'anesthésie simultanée par le **cyclopropane** peut entraîner une hypotension excessive.

SOINS INFIRMIERS

ÉVALUATION DE LA SITUATION

- Déterminer la fréquence, la durée et la force des contractions ainsi que le tonus utérin au repos. On peut administrer des opioïdes pour soulager les douleurs utérines.
- Mesurer la température, le pouls et la pression artérielle à intervalles réguliers pendant toute la durée du traitement pour déceler tout signe de maturation du col ou d'avortement.

DIAGNOSTICS INFIRMIERS POSSIBLES

- Connaissances insuffisantes sur le traitement médicamenteux (Enseignement au patient et à ses proches).

INTERVENTIONS INFIRMIÈRES

- Administrer l'immunoglobuline Rh_0 (D) dans le muscle deltoïde de 3 à 72 heures après l'accouchement, la fausse couche, l'avortement ou la transfusion.
- Placer l'insertion vaginale transversalement dans le cul-de-sac postérieur du vagin, immédiatement après l'avoir retiré de son emballage d'aluminium. Consulter la monographie de la dinoprostone pour en connaître le mode d'emploi.
- Déterminer le degré d'effacement du col avant d'utiliser le gel. Ne pas le déposer au-delà de l'orifice cervical. Suivre les directives du fabricant concernant l'administration.
- Pour éviter tout risque d'absorption par la peau, porter des gants lors de la manipulation du gel. En cas de contact avec la peau, se laver les mains immédiatement.

ENSEIGNEMENT AU PATIENT ET À SES PROCHES

- Expliquer à la patiente le but de la maturation du col, de l'administration des agents abortifs ainsi que la nécessité de se soumettre à des examens vaginaux. Lui recommander de prévenir un professionnel de la santé si les contractions se prolongent.
- Assurer un soutien moral tout au long du traitement.

- Recommander à la patiente qui prend un agent abortif de signaler immédiatement à un professionnel de la santé la fièvre et les frissons, les pertes vaginales nauséabondes, la douleur abdominale basse ou l'intensification des saignements.

VÉRIFICATION DE L'EFFICACITÉ THÉRAPEUTIQUE

L'efficacité du traitement peut être démontrée par: l'avortement complet ■ la maturation du col et le déclenchement du travail ■ la prévention de l'accouchement prématuré.

AGENTS UTILISÉS PENDANT LA GROSSESSE ET L'ALLAITEMENT INCLUS DANS LE *GUIDE*

abortifs
dinoprostone, 360

ocytociques
dinoprostone, 360
ergonovine, 432
oxytocine, 912

divers
immunoglobuline Rh_0(D), 604

ANALGÉSIQUES NON OPIOÏDES

INDICATIONS

Acétaminophène et salicylates: Soulagement de la douleur légère à modérée, abaissement de la fièvre ■ **Phénazopyridine**: Traitement des douleurs touchant les voies urinaires seulement ■ **Capsaïcine**: traitement topique de divers syndromes douloureux ■ **Tramadol**: Traitement de la douleur modérée à modérément grave ■ **Chlorzoxazone**: Complément pharmaceutique au repos, à la physiothérapie et à d'autres mesures visant le soulagement du spasme musculaire associé aux maladies musculosquelettiques aiguës douloureuses.

MÉCANISME D'ACTION

La plupart des analgésiques non opioïdes inhibent la synthèse des prostaglandines en périphérie (effet analgésique) et au centre (effet antipyrétique) ■ Consulter la monographie de chaque médicament pour connaître le mécanisme d'action exact.

CONTRE-INDICATIONS, PRÉCAUTIONS ET MISES EN GARDE

Contre-indications: Risque d'hypersensibilité et de réactions de sensibilité croisée avec les AINS. *Chlorzoxazone* – porphyrie, troubles hépatiques. *Capsaïcine* – hypersensibilité à la capsaïcine ou aux piments forts ■ Usage près des yeux, sur une lésion ouverte ou sur une peau écorchée.

Précautions et mises en garde: Maladie hépatique ou rénale, alcoolisme chronique ou abus d'alcool, malnutrition ■ Le tramadol est doté de propriétés entraînant une dépression du SNC ■ La chlorzoxazone doit être utilisée avec prudence chez les patients souffrant d'une maladie cardiovasculaire sous-jacente ou d'insuffisance rénale.

INTERACTIONS

L'administration concomitante prolongée d'**acétaminophène** et d'**AINS** peut augmenter le risque de réactions rénales indésirables ■ L'administration prolongée de doses élevées d'acétaminophène en concomitance avec la **warfarine** peut accroître le risque de saignement ■ Effets hépatotoxiques additifs lors de la prise concomitante d'autres **substances hépatotoxiques** incluant l'**alcool** ■

La chlorzoxazone exerce un effet additif sur la dépression du SNC lors d'un usage concomitant d'autres **dépresseurs du SNC** (**alcool**, **hypnosédatifs**, **antidépresseurs**).

SOINS INFIRMIERS

ÉVALUATION DE LA SITUATION

- Les patients souffrant d'asthme, d'allergies et de polypes nasaux ou qui sont allergiques à la tartrazine, sont davantage prédisposés à des réactions d'hypersensibilité.

Douleur: Évaluer la douleur et l'amplitude du mouvement des articulations et noter le type de douleur, son siège et son intensité, avant l'administration du médicament et au moment de son plein effet (voir « Profil temps-action » dans chacune des monographies).

Fièvre: Prendre la température et noter les signes connexes suivants: diaphorèse, tachycardie, malaise, frissons.

Tests de laboratoire: Obtenir les résultats des tests des fonctions hépatique, hématologique et rénale à intervalles réguliers, tout au long d'un traitement prolongé à des doses élevées. L'aspirine allonge le temps de saignement en raison de l'inhibition de l'agrégation plaquettaire et, à des doses élevées, peut allonger le temps de prothrombine. Mesurer l'hématocrite à intervalles réguliers pendant toute la durée d'un traitement prolongé à doses élevées afin de déceler une hémorragie gastro-intestinale.

DIAGNOSTICS INFIRMIERS POSSIBLES

- Douleur aiguë (Indications).
- Risque de température corporelle anormale (Indications).
- Connaissances insuffisantes sur le traitement médicamenteux (Enseignement au patient et à ses proches).

INTERVENTIONS INFIRMIÈRES

PO: Administrer l'aspirine avec des aliments ou après les repas ou encore en même temps qu'un antiacide pour réduire l'irritation gastrique.

ENSEIGNEMENT AU PATIENT ET À SES PROCHES

- Expliquer au patient qu'il doit prendre l'aspirine avec un grand verre d'eau et rester en position verticale pendant 15 à 30 minutes après l'avoir prise.
- Les adultes ne devraient pas prendre de l'acétaminophène pendant plus de 10 jours, et les enfants, pendant plus de 5 jours, sauf recommandation médicale contraire. Lors d'un traitement d'association de courte durée par l'acétaminophène et l'aspirine ou un AINS, il ne faut pas dépasser les doses quotidiennes recommandées pour chacun des médicaments.
- Inciter le patient à ne pas consommer d'alcool en même temps que ces médicaments afin de réduire le risque d'irritation gastrique; 3 verres ou plus d'alcool par jour peuvent augmenter le risque d'hémorragie digestive en cas de prise d'aspirine ou d'AINS. Recommander au patient de ne pas prendre en concomitance de l'acétaminophène, de l'aspirine ou des AINS pendant plus de quelques jours, sauf recommandation médicale contraire, afin de prévenir la néphropathie induite par les analgésiques.
- Recommander au patient qui suit un traitement prolongé et qui doit subir une intervention chirurgicale d'avertir le professionnel de la santé qu'il suit un traitement par ce type de médicament. Il peut s'avérer nécessaire d'interrompre le traitement par l'aspirine avant une chirurgie.
- Conseiller au patient qui prend de la chlorzoxazone d'éviter de boire de l'alcool ou de prendre d'autres dépresseurs du SNC en même temps que ce médicament.

VÉRIFICATION DE L'EFFICACITÉ THÉRAPEUTIQUE

L'efficacité du traitement peut être démontrée par: le soulagement de la douleur légère à modérée ■ la baisse de la fièvre.

ANALGÉSIQUES NON OPIOÏDES INCLUS DANS LE *GUIDE*

anti-inflammatoires non stéroïdiens (AINS)
Voir la liste des médicaments dans cette classe.

salicylates
aspirine (acide acétylsalicylique), 111

divers
acétaminophène, 7
capsaïcine, 187
chlorzoxazone, 284
phénazopyridine, 956

ANALGÉSIQUES OPIOÏDES

INDICATIONS

Soulagement de la douleur modérée à grave ■ **Alfentanil, fentanyl et sufentanil**: Médicaments d'appoint lors d'une anesthésie générale.

MÉCANISME D'ACTION

Liaison aux récepteurs opioïdes du SNC. Il en résulte une modification de la perception de la douleur et de la réaction aux stimuli douloureux et une dépression généralisée du SNC.

CONTRE-INDICATIONS, PRÉCAUTIONS ET MISES EN GARDE

Contre-indications: Hypersensibilité à chacun de ces agents.

Précautions et mises en garde: Douleurs abdominales non diagnostiquées ■ Trouble ou traumatisme crânien ■ Maladie hépatique ■ Antécédents d'abus d'opioïdes ■ Administrer initialement de plus faibles doses aux personnes âgées et aux sujets souffrant de maladies respiratoires ■ Le traitement prolongé peut entraîner une tolérance et le besoin de recourir à des doses plus élevées pour soulager la douleur ■ Risque de dépendance psychologique ou physique.

INTERACTIONS

Dépression additive du SNC et du système respiratoire lors de l'usage concomitant d'**alcool**, d'**antihistaminiques**, de **phénothiazines**, de **barbituriques**, d'**antidépresseurs**, d'**hypnosédatifs** et d'autres **opioïdes** ■ L'administration d'**analgésiques opioïdes agonistes/antagonistes (nalbuphine**, **butorphanol**, **pentazocine)** peut diminuer l'analgésie et/ou déclencher des symptômes de sevrage chez les patients présentant une dépendance physique aux analgésiques opioïdes ■ Risque de réactions graves (particulièrement dans le cas de la mépéridine) lors de l'administration d'**IMAO** ou de **procarbazine** durant les 14 jours précédents.

SOINS INFIRMIERS

ÉVALUATION DE LA SITUATION

- Déterminer le type de douleur, son siège et son intensité, avant l'administration du médicament et au moment de son plein effet. Lorsqu'on majore la dose d'un opioïde, on devrait l'augmenter de 25 à 50 % jusqu'à ce qu'on note une réduction de 50 % de la douleur, selon l'évaluation qu'en fait le patient sur une échelle numérique ou visuelle ou jusqu'à ce que le patient signale un soulagement adéquat de la douleur. On peut administrer sans danger une dose de plus au moment du pic de l'effet, si la dose précédente s'est avérée inefficace et si les effets secondaires sont minimes. Chez les patients ayant besoin de doses plus élevées d'opioïdes agonistes/antagonistes, on devrait opter pour un opioïde agoniste. Les opioïdes agonistes/antagonistes ne sont pas recommandés en administration prolongée ni en traitement de première intention en cas de douleurs aiguës ou de douleurs dues au cancer.

- Utiliser un tableau d'équivalences de doses (voir l'annexe A) lorsqu'on doit changer de voie d'administration ou opter pour un autre type d'opioïde. Les doses orales et parentérales ne sont pas équivalentes.
- Évaluer l'état de conscience et mesurer la pression artérielle, le pouls et la fréquence respiratoire avant le traitement et à intervalles réguliers tout au long de l'administration de ce type de médicaments. Si la fréquence respiratoire est ≤10/min, évaluer le degré de sédation. Une stimulation physique peut s'avérer suffisante pour prévenir une hypoventilation importante. Il peut s'avérer nécessaire de réduire la dose de 25 à 50 %. La somnolence initiale disparaît au fil du traitement.
- Déterminer les antécédents de réactions aux analgésiques. En raison de leurs propriétés antagonistes, les opioïdes agonistes/antagonistes peuvent déclencher des symptômes de sevrage (vomissements, agitation, crampes abdominales, élévation de la pression artérielle et de la température) chez les patients présentant une dépendance physique aux opioïdes.
- L'usage prolongé peut entraîner une dépendance physique et psychologique ainsi qu'une tolérance aux effets du médicament, mais cela ne doit pas empêcher le patient de recevoir une quantité suffisante d'analgésiques. La dépendance psychologique est rare chez la plupart des patients qui reçoivent des analgésiques opioïdes pour soulager la douleur. Lors d'un traitement prolongé, il faut parfois administrer des doses de plus en plus élevées pour soulager la douleur.
- Examiner la fonction intestinale du patient à intervalles réguliers. La consommation accrue de liquides et d'aliments riches en fibres et la prise de laxatifs permettent de réduire les effets constipants de ces médicaments. Sauf contre-indication, des laxatifs stimulants devraient être administrés de façon systématique si le traitement par un opioïde dure plus de 2 ou 3 jours.
- Effectuer le bilan quotidien des ingesta et des excreta. En cas d'écarts importants, rester à l'affût de la rétention urinaire et en avertir un médecin ou un autre professionnel de la santé.

Toxicité et surdosage: S'il est nécessaire d'administrer un antagoniste opioïde pour renverser la dépression respiratoire ou le coma, l'antidote est la naloxone (Narcan). Diluer l'ampoule de naloxone à 0,4 mg dans 10 mL de solution de NaCl 0,9 % et administrer 0,5 mL (0,02 mg) par voie IV directe, toutes les 2 minutes. Dans le cas des enfants et des patients pesant moins de 40 kg, diluer 0,1 mg de naloxone dans 10 mL de solution de NaCl 0,9 % pour obtenir une concentration de 10 µg/mL et administrer 0,5 µg/kg, toutes les 2 minutes. Les doses peuvent varier fortement selon l'état du patient. Consulter la monographie pour obtenir plus d'informations. Adapter la dose pour prévenir les symptômes de sevrage, les convulsions et la douleur intense. L'administration ultérieure de doses supplémentaires pourra s'avérer nécessaire, selon l'opioïde en cause et sa durée d'action.

DIAGNOSTICS INFIRMIERS POSSIBLES

- Douleur aiguë (Indications).
- Trouble de la perception visuelle et auditive (Effets secondaires).
- Risque d'accident (Effets secondaires).
- Connaissances insuffisantes sur le traitement médicamenteux (Enseignement au patient et à ses proches).

INTERVENTIONS INFIRMIÈRES

- Ne pas confondre la morphine avec l'hydromorphone ou la mépéridine et porter une attention particulière aux différentes concentrations disponibles ; des erreurs ont mené à une issue fatale.
- Pour augmenter l'effet analgésique du médicament, avant de l'administrer, expliquer au patient sa valeur thérapeutique.
- Les doses administrées selon un horaire fixe peuvent être plus efficaces que celles administrées sur demande (au besoin). L'analgésique s'avère plus efficace s'il est administré avant que la douleur ne devienne intense.
- L'association avec des analgésiques non opioïdes peut entraîner des effets analgésiques additifs et permettre d'administrer des doses plus faibles.
- Après un traitement prolongé, interrompre l'administration graduellement pour prévenir les symptômes de sevrage.

ENSEIGNEMENT AU PATIENT ET À SES PROCHES

- Expliquer au patient ce qu'on entend par administration sur demande et à quel moment il doit réclamer l'analgésique.
- Expliquer au patient les propriétés pharmacocinétiques (début, durée de l'effet, etc.) des différentes préparations disponibles (action brève, action prolongée pendant 12 ou 24 heures, timbre transdermique, injection, etc.).
- Prévenir le patient que les agents de cette classe peuvent provoquer de la somnolence et des étourdissements. Lui recommander de demander de l'aide lorsqu'il se déplace et lorsqu'il veut fumer. Lui conseiller de ne pas conduire et d'éviter les activités qui exigent sa vigilance jusqu'à ce qu'on ait la certitude que le médicament qui lui a été prescrit n'entraîne pas ces effets chez lui.
- Recommander au patient de changer lentement de position pour diminuer le risque d'hypotension orthostatique.
- Inciter le patient à ne pas boire d'alcool et à ne pas prendre d'autres dépresseurs du SNC en même temps que ce type de médicament.
- Conseiller au patient de se tourner dans le lit, de tousser et de faire des exercices de respiration profonde toutes les 2 heures pour prévenir l'atélectasie.

VÉRIFICATION DE L'EFFICACITÉ THÉRAPEUTIQUE

L'efficacité du traitement peut être démontrée par: la diminution de l'intensité de la douleur sans modification importante de l'état de conscience ou de l'état respiratoire.

ANALGÉSIQUES OPIOÏDES INCLUS DANS LE *GUIDE*

agonistes
alfentanil, 40
codéine, 266
fentanyl (voie parentérale), 471
fentanyl (voie transdermique), 474
hydrocodone, 572
hydromorphone, 575
mépéridine, 752
méthadone, 763
morphine, 819
oxycodone, 909
propoxyphène, 1025
sufentanil, 1130
tramadol, 1210

agonistes/antagonistes
butorphanol, 173
nalbuphine, 830
pentazocine, 947

ANESTHÉSIQUES ET ADJUVANTS ANESTHÉSIQUES

INDICATIONS

On utilise les anesthésiques (à action générale, locale ou régionale) pour induire l'anesthésie au cours d'une intervention chirurgicale, d'un accouchement, d'un procédé diagnostique ou dentaire et d'autres traitements ■ On administre l'anesthésie générale par voie parentérale ou par inhalation afin d'induire une dépression du SNC par stades progressifs et réversibles ■ Les anesthésiques locaux (par voie topique ou en injection) induisent l'anesthésie dans de petits territoires circonscrits ■ Les anesthésiques régionaux couvrent des territoires plus étendus (rachianesthésie ou anesthésie épidurale) ■ Les adjuvants anesthésiques (anxiolytiques et hypnosédatifs, agents anticholinergiques, analgésiques opioïdes, bloqueurs neuromusculaires) sont administrés avant, pendant ou après une intervention chirurgicale pour intensifier l'effet des anesthésiques.

MÉCANISME D'ACTION

Les anesthésiques locaux exercent une inhibition réversible du passage des ions à travers les membranes neuronales, empêchant ainsi le déclenchement et la transmission des influx nerveux normaux ■ Les adjuvants anesthésiques (alfentanil, fentanyl et sufentanil) se lient aux récepteurs opioïdes du SNC modifiant ainsi la perception de la douleur et la réaction à celle-ci et entraînent une dépression du SNC ■ Le mécanisme d'action du propofol est inconnu, mais on sait qu'il exerce un effet hypnotique de courte durée et induit l'amnésie. Il ne possède aucune propriété analgésique.

CONTRE-INDICATIONS, PRÉCAUTIONS ET MISES EN GARDE

Contre-indications: Hypersensibilité et risque d'hypersensibilité croisée.

Précautions et mises en garde: Maladie hépatique ■ Maladie cardiaque ■ Hyperthyroïdie ■ Dépression respiratoire ■ Choc ou bloc cardiaque ■ **OBST., ALLAITEMENT**: La prudence est de mise, car l'innocuité de ces agents n'a pas été établie.

INTERACTIONS

Dépression additive du SNC lors de l'administration concomitante d'autres **dépresseurs du SNC** ■ Dépression et toxicité cardiaques additives lors de l'administration concomitante de **phénytoïne**, de **quinidine**, de **procaïnamide** ou de **propranolol**.

SOINS INFIRMIERS

ÉVALUATION DE LA SITUATION

- Déterminer le degré d'engourdissement de la région à anesthésier.
- Avant d'utiliser les anesthésiques par voie topique, il faut déceler la présence d'une éventuelle lésion. Appliquer seulement sur une peau intacte.
- Lors de l'utilisation du timbre de lidocaïne/prilocaïne, évaluer l'effet anesthésique sur la surface d'application après le retrait du timbre et avant l'intervention.
- Rester à l'affût des signes de toxicité générale, d'hypotension orthostatique et de déficit sensoriel et moteur non souhaité lors de l'administration d'agents épiduraux locaux.
- Lors de l'utilisation d'un agent à action générale (propofol), mesurer le pouls et la pression artérielle et suivre de près la fonction respiratoire et le niveau de conscience du patient, tout au long de l'administration du médicament et après le traitement.
- Consulter l'annexe N pour connaître la méthode d'administration des produits ophtalmiques.

DIAGNOSTICS INFIRMIERS POSSIBLES

- Douleur aiguë (Indications).
- Mobilité physique réduite (Réactions indésirables).
- Mode de respiration inefficace (Réactions indésirables).
- Connaissances insuffisantes sur le traitement médicamenteux (Enseignement au patient et à ses proches).

INTERVENTIONS INFIRMIÈRES

Infiltration locale: La lidocaïne peut être administrée en concomitance avec l'adrénaline pour réduire l'absorption par voie générale et pour prolonger l'anesthésie locale.

Lidocaïne/prilocaïne: Appliquer une couche épaisse de médicament sur la région à anesthésier et couvrir d'un pansement occlusif au moins 1 heure avant le début de l'intervention.

Médicaments épiduraux: La dose est adaptée selon la réponse du patient jusqu'à ce qu'on ait obtenu le degré d'anesthésie souhaité.

Propofol: La dose de propofol doit être adaptée selon la réponse du patient. Le propofol n'exerce aucun effet sur le seuil de la douleur. On devrait toujours assurer une analgésie appropriée lorsque le propofol est administré lors des interventions chirurgicales. Bien agiter la solution avant de l'administrer par voie IV et utiliser une technique aseptique rigoureuse lors de l'administration.

ENSEIGNEMENT AU PATIENT ET À SES PROCHES

Bloc ou infiltration locale: Recommander au patient de prévenir un professionnel de la santé dès qu'il ressent la moindre douleur.

Lidocaïne/prilocaïne: Expliquer au patient ou à ses parents l'objectif du traitement par la crème et le pansement occlusif.

Médicaments épiduraux: Recommander au patient de signaler à l'infirmière tout signe de toxicité générale.

Propofol: Expliquer au patient que ce médicament entraînera une perte de la mémoire et, de ce fait, ses souvenirs de l'intervention seront estompés. Lui recommander d'éviter de boire de l'alcool et de prendre d'autres dépresseurs du SNC dans les 24 heures qui suivent l'administration du médicament. Lui conseiller également de ne pas conduire et d'éviter les activités qui exigent sa vigilance pendant les 24 heures qui suivent l'administration de ce médicament.

VÉRIFICATION DE L'EFFICACITÉ THÉRAPEUTIQUE

L'efficacité du traitement peut être démontrée par: l'inhibition complète de la sensation de douleur *(infiltration locale et médicaments épiduraux)* ▪ l'anesthésie de la surface sur laquelle le produit est appliqué *(lidocaïne/prilocaïne)* ▪ l'induction et le maintien de l'anesthésie; l'amnésie *(propofol)*.

ANESTHÉSIQUES ET ADJUVANTS ANESTHÉSIQUES INCLUS DANS LE *GUIDE*

à action générale
alfentanil, 40
fentanyl (voie parentérale), 471
propofol, 1022
sufentanil, 1130

épiduraux à action locale
bupivacaïne, 90
ropivacaïne, 90

usage ophtalmique
proparacaïne, 1355
tétracaïne, 1355

topiques (anesthésie des muqueuses)
lidocaïne, 704
lidocaïne/prilocaïne, 706

ANTIANÉMIQUES

INDICATIONS

Prévention et traitement des anémies.

MÉCANISME D'ACTION

Le fer (fer dextran, fer saccharose, fumarate ferreux, gluconate ferreux, sulfate ferreux) est nécessaire à la synthèse de l'hémoglobine, laquelle est utilisée pour le transport de l'oxygène vers les cellules ■ La cyanocobalamine et l'hydroxocobalamine (vitamine B_{12}), ainsi que l'acide folique sont des vitamines hydrosolubles nécessaires à la production de globules rouges ■ La darbépoétine et l'époétine stimulent la production de globules rouges ■ La nandrolone stimule la production de l'érythropoïétine.

CONTRE-INDICATIONS, PRÉCAUTIONS ET MISES EN GARDE

Contre-indications: Anémies non diagnostiquées ■ Hémochromatose ■ Hémosidérose ■ Anémie hémolytique (fer) ■ Hypertension non maîtrisée (darbépoétine, époétine).
Précautions et mises en garde: Le fer par voie parentérale (fer dextran, fer saccharose) doit être administré avec prudence aux patients ayant des antécédents d'allergie ou de réactions d'hypersensibilité.

INTERACTIONS

Le fer administré par voie orale peut diminuer l'absorption des **tétracyclines**, des **fluoroquinolones** ou de la **pénicillamine** ■ La **vitamine E** peut entraver la réponse au traitement par le fer ■ La **phénytoïne** et les autres **anticonvulsivants** peuvent augmenter les besoins en acide folique ■ La réponse à la vitamine B_{12}, à l'acide folique ou au fer peut être retardée par le **chloramphénicol** ■ La darbépoétine et l'époétine peuvent augmenter les besoins en **héparine** au cours de l'hémodialyse.

SOINS INFIRMIERS

ÉVALUATION DE LA SITUATION

- Évaluer l'état nutritionnel du patient et ses antécédents diététiques pour déterminer les causes possibles de l'anémie et ses besoins d'apprentissage à cet égard.

DIAGNOSTICS INFIRMIERS POSSIBLES

- Intolérance à l'activité (Indications).
- Alimentation déficiente (Indications).
- Connaissances insuffisantes sur la maladie et sur le traitement médicamenteux (Enseignement au patient et à ses proches).

INTERVENTIONS INFIRMIÈRES

- Le fer est présenté en association avec de nombreuses vitamines et de nombreux minéraux (voir l'annexe U).

ENSEIGNEMENT AU PATIENT ET À SES PROCHES

- Encourager le patient à observer les recommandations diététiques du professionnel de la santé. Lui expliquer que la meilleure source de vitamines et de minéraux est un régime alimentaire équilibré contenant des aliments des quatre principaux groupes.

- Prévenir le patient qui s'autoadministre des vitamines et des minéraux qu'il ne faut pas dépasser l'apport quotidien recommandé. L'efficacité des doses massives pour traiter diverses maladies n'a pas été confirmée, et elles peuvent provoquer des effets indésirables.

VÉRIFICATION DE L'EFFICACITÉ THÉRAPEUTIQUE

L'efficacité du traitement peut être démontrée par: la résolution de l'anémie.

ANTIANÉMIQUES INCLUS DANS LE *GUIDE*

ANTIANGINEUX

INDICATIONS

Les dérivés nitrés sont utilisés pour traiter et prévenir les crises d'angine. Seuls les dérivés nitrés (administrés par voie sublinguale, par voie linguale en pulvérisateur ou par voie IV) peuvent être utilisés dans le traitement des crises aiguës d'angine de poitrine ■ Les bloqueurs des canaux calciques et les bêtabloquants sont utilisés en prophylaxie, lors du traitement prolongé de l'angine.

MÉCANISME D'ACTION

Plusieurs groupes différents de médicaments sont destinés au traitement de l'angine de poitrine ■ Les dérivés nitrés (dinitrate d'isosorbide, mononitrate d'isosorbide et nitroglycérine) sont conditionnés en pulvérisateur pour administration linguale ou sont présentés sous forme de comprimés sublinguaux, de solutions parentérales, de timbres cutanés et de préparations orales à libération prolongée ■ Les dérivés nitrés dilatent les coronaires et entraînent une vasodilatation systémique (diminution de la précharge). ■ Les bloqueurs des canaux calciques dilatent les coronaires (certains ralentissent également la fréquence cardiaque) ■ Les bêtabloquants réduisent la consommation d'oxygène du myocarde en ralentissant la fréquence cardiaque ■ On peut associer deux ou même plusieurs agents, si on cherche à diminuer les effets secondaires ou les réactions indésirables.

CONTRE-INDICATIONS, PRÉCAUTIONS ET MISES EN GARDE

Contre-indications: Hypersensibilité ■ Éviter l'administration de bêtabloquants et de bloqueurs des canaux calciques en présence d'un bloc cardiaque de stade avancé, d'un choc cardiogénique ou d'une insuffisance cardiaque non traitée.

Précautions et mises en garde: L'administration de bêtabloquants aux patients souffrant de diabète ou de maladie pulmonaire doit s'accompagner de prudence.

INTERACTIONS

Les dérivés nitrés, les bloqueurs des canaux calciques et les bêtabloquants peuvent induire de l'hypotension lors de l'administration simultanée d'autres **antihypertenseurs** ou lors de l'ingestion de quantités importantes d'**alcool** ■ Le vérapamil, le diltiazem et les bêtabloquants peuvent exercer des effets dépresseurs additifs sur le myocarde lors de l'administration simultanée d'autres **agents qui modifient la fonction cardiaque** ■ Le vérapamil est associé à de nombreuses autres interactions médicamenteuses importantes.

SOINS INFIRMIERS

ÉVALUATION DE LA SITUATION

- Déterminer le siège, la durée et l'intensité des douleurs angineuses et les facteurs qui les déclenchent.
- Mesurer la pression artérielle et le pouls à intervalles réguliers pendant toute la durée du traitement.

DIAGNOSTICS INFIRMIERS POSSIBLES

- Douleur aiguë (Indications).
- Irrigation tissulaire inefficace (Indications).
- Connaissances insuffisantes sur le traitement médicamenteux (Enseignement au patient et à ses proches).

INTERVENTIONS INFIRMIÈRES

- Ces médicaments sont présentés sous diverses formes. Consulter la monographie de chaque médicament pour obtenir des renseignements sur la méthode d'administration.

ENSEIGNEMENT AU PATIENT ET À SES PROCHES

- Expliquer au patient qui prend simultanément des dérivés nitrés et des médicaments destinés au traitement prophylactique de l'angine qu'il doit continuer de suivre ces 2 traitements en même temps, en respectant la prescription du médecin, et qu'il doit prendre la nitroglycérine par voie sublinguale, selon les besoins, en cas de crise d'angine.
- Demander au patient de prévenir immédiatement un professionnel de la santé si les douleurs thoraciques persistent ou s'aggravent après le traitement ou si elles sont accompagnées de diaphorèse, d'essoufflement ou de céphalées graves et persistantes.
- Conseiller au patient de changer lentement de position pour réduire le risque d'hypotension orthostatique.
- Recommander au patient d'éviter de boire de l'alcool pendant qu'il prend ces médicaments.

VÉRIFICATION DE L'EFFICACITÉ THÉRAPEUTIQUE

L'efficacité du traitement peut être démontrée par: la diminution de la fréquence et de la gravité des crises d'angine ■ l'augmentation de la tolérance à l'effort.

ANTIANGINEUX INCLUS DANS LE *GUIDE*

CLASSIFICATION

ANTIARYTHMIQUES

INDICATIONS

Suppression des arythmies cardiaques.

MÉCANISME D'ACTION

Ces médicaments corrigent les arythmies cardiaques par divers mécanismes, selon la classe d'agents utilisée. L'objectif thérapeutique est de diminuer les symptômes et d'augmenter le rendement hémodynamique ▪ Le choix du médicament dépend de l'étiologie des arythmies et des caractéristiques de chaque patient ▪ Avant d'amorcer la pharmacothérapie, il faut corriger, dans la mesure du possible, la cause de l'arythmie (par exemple, troubles électrolytiques, médicaments) ▪ Les principaux antiarythmiques sont généralement classés selon leurs effets sur les tissus qui assurent la conduction cardiaque (voir le tableau ci-dessous) ▪ On utilise également comme antiarythmiques l'adénosine, l'atropine et la digoxine.

MÉCANISME D'ACTION DES PRINCIPAUX ANTIARYTHMIQUES

Classe	Médicament	Mécanisme
IA	disopyramide, procaïnamide, quinidine	Dépression de la conductance du sodium, prolongation de la période réfractaire efficace et de la durée du potentiel d'action, diminution de la capacité de réponse de la membrane.
IB	fosphénytoïne, lidocaïne, mexilétine, phénytoïne	Augmentation de la conductance du potassium, raccourcissement de la période réfractaire efficace et de la durée du potentiel d'action.
IC	flécaïnide, propafénone	Ralentissement prononcé de la conduction, dépression marquée de la phase 0.
II	acébutolol, esmolol, métoprolol, propranolol	Interférence avec la conductance du sodium, dépression de la membrane cellulaire, diminution de l'automaticité, prolongation de la période réfractaire efficace du nœud A-V, inhibition d'une activité sympathique excessive.
III	amiodarone, dofétilide, ibutilide, sotalol	Interférence avec la noradrénaline, prolongation de la durée du potentiel d'action et de la période réfractaire efficace.
IV	diltiazem, vérapamil	Prolongation de la période réfractaire efficace du nœud A-V, inhibition des canaux calciques.

CONTRE-INDICATIONS, PRÉCAUTIONS ET MISES EN GARDE

Contre-indications: Très différentes, selon l'agent administré. Consulter la monographie de chaque médicament.

Précautions et mises en garde: Très différentes, selon l'agent administré ▪ Chez les personnes âgées et chez les patients souffrant d'insuffisance rénale ou hépatique, il faut adapter la posologie en fonction du médicament administré ▪ On doit évaluer les causes qu'il est possible de corriger (troubles électrolytiques, toxicité médicamenteuse) ▪ Consulter la monographie de chaque médicament.

INTERACTIONS

Très différentes, selon l'agent administré. Consulter la monographie de chaque médicament.

SOINS INFIRMIERS

ÉVALUATION DE LA SITUATION

- Surveiller l'ÉCG et mesurer le pouls et la pression artérielle tout au long de l'administration par voie IV et à intervalles réguliers pendant le traitement par voie orale.

DIAGNOSTICS INFIRMIERS POSSIBLES

- Débit cardiaque diminué (Indications).
- Connaissances insuffisantes sur le traitement médicamenteux (Enseignement au patient et à ses proches).

INTERVENTIONS INFIRMIÈRES

- Mesurer le pouls à l'apex du cœur avant d'administrer le médicament par voie orale. Si la fréquence cardiaque est inférieure à 50 bpm, ne pas administrer l'agent et en informer le médecin ou un autre professionnel de la santé.
- Administrer les médicaments par voie orale avec un grand verre d'eau. La plupart des préparations à libération prolongée doivent être avalées telles quelles. Recommander au patient de ne pas briser, réduire en poudre ni croquer les comprimés et de ne pas ouvrir les capsules, à moins d'avoir reçu des consignes claires à ce sujet.

ENSEIGNEMENT AU PATIENT ET À SES PROCHES

- Expliquer au patient qu'il doit prendre le médicament par voie orale, à intervalles réguliers, en respectant rigoureusement la posologie recommandée, même s'il se sent mieux.
- Montrer au patient ou à ses proches comment prendre le pouls. Recommander au patient de contacter un professionnel de la santé si la fréquence ou le rythme du pouls change.
- Conseiller au patient de consulter un professionnel de la santé avant de prendre un médicament en vente libre.
- Conseiller au patient de toujours porter sur lui une pièce d'identité où sont inscrits son problème de santé et son traitement médicamenteux.
- Insister sur l'importance des examens de suivi permettant d'évaluer les bienfaits du traitement.

VÉRIFICATION DE L'EFFICACITÉ THÉRAPEUTIQUE

L'efficacité du traitement peut être démontrée par: la réduction des arythmies cardiaques sans que des effets nocifs se manifestent.

ANTIARYTHMIQUES INCLUS DANS LE *GUIDE*

CLASSIFICATION

ANTIASTHMATIQUES

INDICATIONS

Prise en charge des épisodes aigus et chroniques réversibles de bronchoconstriction. Le but du traitement est de maîtriser les crises aiguës (maîtrise à court terme) et de diminuer la fréquence et la gravité des crises futures (maîtrise à long terme). Le choix des modalités de traitement dépend des besoins constants d'agents qu'il faut administrer à court terme.

MÉCANISME D'ACTION

Les bronchodilatateurs adrénergiques et les inhibiteurs de la phosphodiestérase élèvent les concentrations intracellulaires d'adénosine monophosphate cyclique (AMPc) ; les agents adrénergiques augmentent la production de cette substance et les inhibiteurs diminuent sa décomposition. Des concentrations accrues d'AMPc entraînent une bronchodilatation ■ Les corticostéroïdes diminuent l'inflammation des voies aériennes ■ Les antagonistes des récepteurs des leucotriènes et les stabilisateurs des mastocytes diminuent la libération de substances qui provoquent le bronchospasme.

CONTRE-INDICATIONS, PRÉCAUTIONS ET MISES EN GARDE

Contre-indications: Ne pas utiliser en cas de crise aiguë d'asthme des corticostéroïdes en inhalation, des agents adrénergiques à action prolongée (sauf le formotérol), des stabilisateurs des mastocytes, des antagonistes des récepteurs des leucotriènes ou des anticorps monoclonaux.

Précautions et mises en garde: Administrer avec prudence les bronchodilatateurs adrénergiques en présence de maladie cardiovasculaire ■ **OBST., ALLAITEMENT, PÉD.**: Éviter l'usage prolongé de corticostéroïdes par voie générale chez les enfants, tout comme chez les femmes enceintes et allaitantes ■ Il y a risque de déséquilibre glycémique chez les patients diabétiques qui suivent une corticothérapie ■ Ne jamais interrompre une corticothérapie brusquement.

INTERACTIONS

Les bronchodilatateurs adrénergiques et les inhibiteurs de la phosphodiestérase, administrés en même temps que d'autres **agents adrénergiques**, peuvent exercer des effets additifs sur le SNC ou sur le système cardiovasculaire ■ La **cimétidine** élève les concentrations de théophylline et le risque de toxicité ■ Les corticostéroïdes peuvent diminuer l'effet des **antidiabétiques** ■ Les corticostéroïdes peuvent provoquer une hypokaliémie, et cet effet peut être additif en cas d'administration simultanée de **diurétiques hypokaliémiants** ■ Les corticostéroïdes peuvent élever le risque de toxicité par la **digoxine**.

SOINS INFIRMIERS

ÉVALUATION DE LA SITUATION

- Ausculter les bruits pulmonaires et évaluer la fonction respiratoire avant le traitement et à intervalles réguliers pendant toute sa durée.
- Évaluer l'état cardiovasculaire des patients qui prennent des bronchodilatateurs adrénergiques. Rester à l'affût des modifications électrocardiographiques et des douleurs thoraciques.

DIAGNOSTICS INFIRMIERS POSSIBLES

- Dégagement inefficace des voies respiratoires (Indications).

- Connaissances insuffisantes sur la maladie et sur le traitement médicamenteux (Enseignement au patient et à ses proches).
- Non-observance du traitement médicamenteux (Enseignement au patient et à ses proches).

ENSEIGNEMENT AU PATIENT ET À SES PROCHES

- Recommander au patient de prendre les antiasthmatiques en suivant rigoureusement les recommandations du médecin. Le prévenir qu'il ne faut pas prendre une plus grande quantité que celle qui lui a été prescrite ni arrêter le traitement sans prévenir un professionnel de la santé au préalable.
- Conseiller au patient d'arrêter de fumer et d'éviter les autres irritants respiratoires.
- Montrer au patient l'usage approprié de l'aérosol doseur et des autres dispositifs servant à l'administration de ces médicaments (voir l'annexe G).
- Recommander au patient de prévenir un professionnel de la santé si la dose habituelle de médicament ne produit pas les résultats escomptés, si les symptômes s'aggravent après le traitement ou si des effets toxiques se manifestent.
- Prévenir le patient qui prend des bronchodilatateurs et des médicaments en inhalation qu'il faut commencer par les bronchodilatateurs et attendre 5 minutes avant de prendre les autres médicaments, sauf si le médecin l'a recommandé autrement.

VÉRIFICATION DE L'EFFICACITÉ THÉRAPEUTIQUE

L'efficacité du traitement peut être démontrée par: la prévention et la diminution des symptômes d'asthme.

ANTIASTHMATIQUES INCLUS DANS LE *GUIDE*

bronchodilatateurs
adrénaline, 23
aminophylline, 159
formotérol, 520
oxtriphylline, 159
salbutamol, 1087
salmétérol, 1089
terbutaline, 1160
théophylline, 159

corticostéroïdes
béclométhasone, 278
bétaméthasone, 284
budésonide, 278, 284
ciclésonide, 278
cortisone, 284
dexaméthasone, 284
fluticasone, 278
hydrocortisone, 284
méthylprednisolone, 284
prednisolone, 284
prednisone, 284
triamcinolone, 284

antagonistes des récepteurs des leucotriènes
montélukast, 817
zafirlukast, 1273

stabilisateurs des mastocytes
cromolyn, 1122

anticorps monoclonal
omalizumab, 886

ANTIBIOTIQUES

INDICATIONS

Traitement et prophylaxie de diverses infections bactériennes ■ Consulter la monographie de chaque médicament pour en connaître le spectre d'action et les indications ■ Dans le cas de certaines infections, une intervention chirurgicale et un traitement de soutien peuvent également s'imposer.

MÉCANISME D'ACTION

Les antibiotiques peuvent détruire les bactéries pathogènes sensibles (effet bactéricide) ou en inhiber la prolifération (effet bactériostatique). Ils n'ont aucun effet sur les virus et les champignons ■ Les antibiotiques sont divisés en plusieurs catégories selon la similitude de leurs structures chimiques et de leur spectre antimicrobien.

CONTRE-INDICATIONS, PRÉCAUTIONS ET MISES EN GARDE

Contre-indications: Antécédents d'hypersensibilité à l'un des médicaments ■ Risque de réactions de sensibilité croisée en cas d'administration de substances semblables.

Précautions et mises en garde: Pour rendre le traitement aussi efficace que possible, il est souhaitable d'analyser les cultures et d'effectuer les antibiogrammes ■ Chez les patients souffrant d'insuffisance hépatique ou rénale, une modification de la posologie peut être nécessaire ■ **OBST., ALLAITEMENT**: L'administration pendant la grossesse et l'allaitement doit s'accompagner de prudence ■ L'administration prolongée et inopportune d'antibiotiques ayant un large spectre peut provoquer une surinfection par des champignons ou des bactéries résistantes.

INTERACTIONS

Les **pénicillines** et les **aminosides** s'inactivent réciproquement sur le plan chimique; il faut, par conséquent, éviter de les mélanger en solution ■ Les **macrolides** peuvent diminuer le métabolisme hépatique d'autres médicaments ■ Le **probénécide** élève les concentrations sériques des pénicillines et des céphalosporines ■ Certains **antibiotiques qui se lient fortement aux protéines**, comme les **sulfamides**, peuvent déplacer d'autres médicaments dotés de cette propriété ou être déplacés par eux. Consulter la monographie de chaque médicament ■ Les antiacides (**aluminium** et **magnésium**), le **calcium**, le **sous-salicylate de bismuth**, les **sels de fer**, le **sucralfate** et les **sels de zinc** réduisent l'absorption des fluoroquinolones et des tétracyclines.

SOINS INFIRMIERS

ÉVALUATION DE LA SITUATION

- Suivre de près les signes et les symptômes d'infection avant l'administration du médicament et pendant toute la durée du traitement.
- Interroger les patients, particulièrement ceux qui doivent recevoir des pénicillines, des céphalosporines ou des sulfamides, sur leurs antécédents d'hypersensibilité.
- Prélever des échantillons pour l'analyse des cultures et les antibiogrammes avant le début du traitement. On peut administrer la première dose avant de recevoir les résultats de ces analyses.

DIAGNOSTICS INFIRMIERS POSSIBLES

- Risque d'infection (Indications).
- Connaissances insuffisantes sur le traitement médicamenteux (Enseignement au patient et à ses proches).
- Non-observance du traitement médicamenteux (Enseignement au patient et à ses proches).

INTERVENTIONS INFIRMIÈRES

- La plupart des antibiotiques doivent être administrés à intervalles réguliers afin d'assurer le maintien de concentrations sériques thérapeutiques.

ENSEIGNEMENT AU PATIENT ET À SES PROCHES

- Expliquer au patient qu'il doit prendre toute la quantité de médicament qui lui a été prescrite, à intervalles réguliers, même s'il se sent mieux.
- Recommander au patient de signaler à un professionnel de la santé les allergies et les signes de surinfection suivants: excroissances noires et pileuses sur la langue, démangeaisons ou écoulements vaginaux, selles molles ou nauséabondes.
- Conseiller au patient d'informer un professionnel de la santé de l'apparition de la fièvre et de la diarrhée, particulièrement si les selles contiennent du pus, du sang ou du mucus. Lui recommander de ne pas traiter la diarrhée sans avoir consulté un professionnel de la santé au préalable.
- Conseiller au patient de consulter un professionnel de la santé si les symptômes persistent.

VÉRIFICATION DE L'EFFICACITÉ THÉRAPEUTIQUE

L'efficacité du traitement peut être démontrée par: la disparition des signes et des symptômes d'infection. Le temps de résolution dépend du microorganisme infectant et du siège de l'infection.

ANTIBIOTIQUES INCLUS DANS LE *GUIDE*

tétracyclines
doxycycline, 1167
minocycline, 1167
tétracycline, 1167
divers
clindamycine, 246
éthambutol, 453
isoniazide, 659
linézolide, 710
métronidazole, 790
mupirocine, 823
nitrofurantoïne, 861
pyrazinamide, 1037
quinupristine/dalfopristine, 1053
rifabutine, 1066
rifampine, 1068
télithromycine, 1149
tigécycline, 1188
triméthoprime, 1223
vancomycine, 1238

ANTICHOLINERGIQUES

INDICATIONS

Atropine: Bradyarythmies ■ **Scopolamine**: Nausées et vomissements provoqués par le mal des transports et le vertige ■ L'atropine et la scopolamine sont également des mydriatiques ■ **Propanthéline** et **glycopyrrolate**: Diminution des sécrétions gastriques et augmentation du tonus du sphincter œsophagien ■ **Oxybutynine** et **toltérodine**: Traitement des symptômes urinaires pouvant être associés à une vessie neurogène, p. ex., mictions fréquentes, mictions impérieuses, nycturie, incontinence urinaire, dysurie.

MÉCANISME D'ACTION

Inhibition compétitive de l'effet de l'acétylcholine ■ En plus, les anticholinergiques présentés dans le *Guide* ont des effets antimuscariniques, puisqu'ils inhibent l'action de l'acétylcholine aux sites innervés par les nerfs cholinergiques postganglionnaires.

CONTRE-INDICATIONS, PRÉCAUTIONS ET MISES EN GARDE

Contre-indications: Hypersensibilité ■ Glaucome à angle fermé ■ Hémorragie grave ■ Tachycardie (provoquée par la thyrotoxicose ou l'insuffisance cardiaque) ■ Myasthénie grave.
Précautions et mises en garde: **GÉR., PÉD.**: Les personnes âgées et les enfants sont davantage prédisposés à des réactions indésirables ■ Administrer avec prudence aux patients souffrant de troubles des voies urinaires, aux patients qui présentent un risque d'obstruction du tractus gastro-intestinal et à ceux souffrant de maladies rénale, cardiaque, hépatique ou pulmonaire chroniques.

INTERACTIONS

Effets anticholinergiques additifs, p. ex., sécheresse de la bouche (xérostomie), sécheresse des yeux (xérophtalmie), vision trouble, constipation, lors de l'administration d'autres **agents ayant des effets anticholinergiques**, dont les **antihistaminiques**, les **antidépresseurs**, la **quinidine** et le **disopyramide** ■ Ces agents peuvent modifier l'absorption gastro-intestinale d'autres médicaments en inhibant la motilité gastrique et en prolongeant le transit intestinal ■ Les **antiacides** peuvent diminuer l'absorption des anticholinergiques.

SOINS INFIRMIERS

ÉVALUATION DE LA SITUATION

- Mesurer les signes vitaux et examiner l'ÉCG fréquemment pendant l'administration par voie IV. Signaler rapidement au médecin toute modification importante de la fréquence

cardiaque ou de la pression artérielle, tout comme l'angine et l'aggravation des extrasystoles ventriculaires.
- Effectuer le bilan des ingesta et des excreta chez les personnes âgées ou chez les patients ayant subi une intervention chirurgicale; les anticholinergiques peuvent provoquer une rétention urinaire.
- Suivre de près les signes de distension abdominale et ausculter les bruits intestinaux. La constipation peut devenir un problème. L'augmentation de l'apport de liquides et d'aliments riches en fibres peut aider à la soulager.
- Suivre à intervalles réguliers, pendant toute la durée du traitement, les mictions impérieuses ou fréquentes et l'incontinence urinaire par besoin impérieux.

DIAGNOSTICS INFIRMIERS POSSIBLES

- Débit cardiaque diminué (Indications).
- Atteinte à l'intégrité de la muqueuse buccale (Effets secondaires).
- Constipation (Effets secondaires).
- Élimination urinaire altérée (Indications).

INTERVENTIONS INFIRMIÈRES

- Les timbres transdermiques de scopolamine doivent être appliqués au moins 4 heures avant les déplacements susceptibles d'entraîner le mal des transports.

PO: Administrer les doses orales d'atropine, de glycopyrrolate, de propanthéline ou de scopolamine 30 minutes avant les repas.

ENSEIGNEMENT AU PATIENT ET À SES PROCHES

- Conseiller au patient de se rincer fréquemment la bouche, de consommer de la gomme à mâcher ou des bonbons sans sucre et de pratiquer une bonne hygiène buccale pour soulager la sécheresse de la bouche.
- Prévenir le patient que les anticholinergiques peuvent provoquer de la somnolence. Lui conseiller de ne pas conduire et d'éviter les autres activités qui exigent sa vigilance jusqu'à ce qu'on ait la certitude que le médicament n'entraîne pas cet effet chez lui.

Usage ophtalmique: Prévenir le patient que les préparations ophtalmiques peuvent rendre passagèrement la vision trouble et entraver la capacité d'apprécier les distances. Lui conseiller de porter des verres fumés pour se protéger de la lumière vive.

VÉRIFICATION DE L'EFFICACITÉ THÉRAPEUTIQUE

L'efficacité du traitement peut être démontrée par: l'augmentation de la fréquence cardiaque ■ la diminution des nausées et des vomissements provoqués par le mal des transports ou le vertige ■ la sécheresse de la bouche (xérostomie) ■ la dilatation des pupilles ■ la diminution de la motilité gastro-intestinale ■ la résolution des symptômes de la maladie de Parkinson ■ le soulagement du spasme de la vessie et des symptômes connexes (mictions fréquentes ou impérieuses, nycturie et incontinence urinaire) chez les patients présentant une vessie neurogène.

ANTICHOLINERGIQUES INCLUS DANS LE *GUIDE*

ANTICOAGULANTS

INDICATIONS

Prévention et traitement des thromboembolies, comprenant la thrombose veineuse profonde, l'embolie pulmonaire et la fibrillation auriculaire ■ Traitement de l'angine instable ou de l'infarctus du myocarde sans onde Q, associé à la prise d'antiplaquettaires et/ou de thrombolytiques.

MÉCANISME D'ACTION

Ces agents préviennent la formation et la prolifération des caillots sanguins, sans pour autant pouvoir dissoudre les caillots existants ■ Les deux types d'anticoagulants administrés le plus souvent sont les héparines, par voie parentérale, et la warfarine, par voie orale ■ On amorce habituellement le traitement avec une héparine non fractionnée ou une héparine de faible poids moléculaire (HFPM), en raison de son début d'action rapide. Comme les effets anticoagulants de la warfarine ne se manifestent qu'après plusieurs jours, ce médicament est administré en traitement d'entretien ■ Si la thromboembolie est grave, le traitement à l'héparine peut être précédé par un traitement thrombolytique (alteplase, retéplase, streptokinase ou ténectéplase) ■ On utilise de faibles doses d'héparine non fractionnée, d'héparine à faible poids moléculaire (HFPM) ou de fondaparinux pour prévenir la thrombose veineuse profonde après certaines interventions chirurgicales ■ Les héparines sont aussi utilisées dans certaines circonstances où l'alitement prolongé augmente le risque de thromboembolie ■ Le danaparoïde, l'argatroban et la lépirudine sont surtout utilisés chez les patients souffrant d'une thrombopénie induite par l'héparine (TIH), accompagnée ou non d'épisodes thrombolytiques, ainsi que chez ceux qui ont des antécédents bien documentés de TIH ■ Le fondaparinux est un nouvel anticoagulant qui peut être utilisé dans plusieurs indications comme le traitement et la prévention de la thrombose veineuse profonde et le traitement de l'angine instable et de l'infarctus du myocarde.

CONTRE-INDICATIONS, PRÉCAUTIONS ET MISES EN GARDE

Contre-indications: Troubles de coagulation sous-jacents ■ Ulcère gastro-intestinal ■ Intervention chirurgicale récente ■ Hémorragie active ■ **OBST.:** L'administration de warfarine aux femmes enceintes est contre-indiquée ■ Antécédents de thrombopénie à la suite d'un traitement par une héparine (héparine, HFPM).

Précautions et mises en garde: L'administration d'un anticoagulant aux patients qui présentent un risque de saignement doit s'accompagner de prudence ■ L'héparine ne traverse pas la barrière placentaire ■ L'héparine et les agents apparentés devraient être utilisés avec prudence chez les patients qui reçoivent une analgésie épidurale ou rachidienne ■ Insuffisance rénale (HFPM, fondaparinux).

INTERACTIONS

La warfarine se lie fortement aux protéines et peut déplacer d'autres **médicaments dotés de cette propriété** ou être déplacée par eux. Les interactions qui en résultent dépendent du médicament qui a été déplacé ■ Les saignements peuvent être aggravés par l'**aspirine**, les autres **antiplaquettaires** et les **AINS** ■ Plusieurs autres interactions médicamenteuses peuvent se produire dans le cas de la warfarine en raison de son métabolisme par les cytochromes P450.

SOINS INFIRMIERS

ÉVALUATION DE LA SITUATION

- Rechercher les signes de saignement et d'hémorragie (saignement des gencives et du nez; contusions inhabituelles; selles noires, goudronneuses; hématurie, chute de l'hématocrite ou de la pression artérielle; présence de sang dans les selles ou les échantillons prélevés par aspiration nasogastrique).

- Rechercher les signes et les symptômes qui révèlent l'apparition ou l'aggravation de la thrombose. Les symptômes dépendent du territoire touché.

Tests de laboratoire:

- Noter à intervalles fréquents le temps de céphaline activée (TCA) pendant le traitement à l'héparine administrée à pleine dose et le rapport normalisé international (RNI) pendant le traitement à la warfarine, ainsi que l'hématocrite et la numération plaquettaire.
- Surveiller le temps de saignement tout au long du traitement antiplaquettaire. L'allongement du temps de saignement, dépendant de la dose et du temps écoulé depuis l'administration, est prévisible.

Toxicité et surdosage: En cas de surdosage ou d'une anticoagulation qu'il faut renverser sans délai, l'antidote des héparines est le sulfate de protamine, et celui de la warfarine, la vitamine K (phytonadione). En cas d'hémorragie grave provoquée par la warfarine, l'administration de sang complet ou de plasma peut également s'avérer nécessaire en raison du délai d'action de la vitamine K.

DIAGNOSTICS INFIRMIERS POSSIBLES

- Irrigation tissulaire inefficace (Indications).
- Risque d'accident (Effets secondaires).
- Connaissances insuffisantes sur le traitement médicamenteux (Enseignement au patient et à ses proches).

INTERVENTIONS INFIRMIÈRES

- Signaler à tous les membres de l'équipe de soins que le patient suit un traitement anticoagulant. Appliquer une pression sur les points d'injection et de ponction veineuse pour éviter le saignement ou la formation d'un hématome. Éviter les injections intramusculaires.
- Lors des perfusions continues, administrer la solution par une pompe à perfusion afin de s'assurer que le patient reçoit la dose exacte.

ENSEIGNEMENT AU PATIENT ET À SES PROCHES

- Recommander au patient d'éviter les activités pendant lesquelles il pourrait se blesser, d'utiliser une brosse à dents à poils doux et un rasoir électrique et de signaler immédiatement à un professionnel de la santé les saignements ou les contusions inhabituels.
- Conseiller au patient de consulter un professionnel de la santé avant de prendre des médicaments en vente libre ou des produits naturels, particulièrement ceux qui contiennent de l'aspirine, des AINS ou de l'alcool.
- Passer en revue avec le patient qui prend de la warfarine les aliments riches en vitamine K (voir l'annexe J). Lui expliquer qu'il devrait consommer les aliments de ce type en quantité limitée, en tout temps, étant donné que la vitamine K contrecarre l'effet de la warfarine. L'avertir que si sa consommation de tels aliments varie fortement, il y a risque de fluctuations dans le rapport normalisé international.
- Expliquer au patient qu'il est important de se soumettre fréquemment à des tests permettant de mesurer l'effet de l'anticoagulation.
- Conseiller au patient de porter constamment sur lui une pièce d'identité où est inscrit son traitement médicamenteux et d'informer tous les membres de l'équipe de soins qu'il suit un traitement anticoagulant, avant de se soumettre à des examens diagnostiques, à un quelconque traitement ou à une intervention chirurgicale.

VÉRIFICATION DE L'EFFICACITÉ THÉRAPEUTIQUE

L'efficacité du traitement peut être démontrée par: la prévention et le traitement d'une coagulation indésirable et de ses séquelles ■ la prévention des AVC chez les patients atteints de fibrillation auriculaire ■ la diminution du décès par maladie cardiovasculaire en cas d'angine instable et d'infarctus du myocarde.

ANTICOAGULANTS INCLUS DANS LE *GUIDE*

argatroban, 107
bivalirudine, 152
fondaparinux sodique, 518
héparine, 557
lépirudine, 690
warfarine, 1270

héparines de faible poids moléculaire
daltéparine, 561
danaparoïde, 561
énoxaparine, 561
nadroparine, 561
tinzaparine, 561

ANTICONVULSIVANTS

INDICATIONS

Les anticonvulsivants sont utilisés pour réduire la fréquence et la gravité des crises épileptiques. Certains d'entre eux sont administrés par voie parentérale pour un traitement immédiat des crises ■ Il n'est pas rare qu'on prescrive plus d'un anticonvulsivant pour une maîtrise à long terme de l'épilepsie ■ Le suivi des concentrations sériques de certains médicaments assure une surveillance adéquate.

MÉCANISME D'ACTION

Les anticonvulsivants englobent un grand nombre d'agents capables d'inhiber les décharges neuronales anormales du SNC, qui pourraient entraîner des crises convulsives ■ Selon le groupe auquel ils appartiennent, ces agents peuvent prévenir la propagation de l'activité convulsive, déprimer le centre moteur du cortex, élever le seuil de convulsion ou modifier les concentrations de neurotransmetteurs. Consulter la monographie de chaque médicament.

PRINCIPALES CLASSES D'ANTICONVULSIVANTS: MÉDICAMENTS ET INDICATIONS

CLASSE	MÉDICAMENT	TYPE DE CRISE
Barbituriques	pentobarbital	Traitement d'urgence de certains états convulsifs associés au tétanos, à l'état de mal épileptique et aux réactions toxiques à la strychnine ou aux anesthésiques locaux.
	phénobarbital	Crises tonicocloniques généralisées complexes, crises partielles, état de mal épileptique.
	primidone	Traitement des crises généralisées et tonicocloniques et des crises épileptiques focales ou partielles à sémiologie complexe.
Benzodiazépines	clonazépam	Prophylaxie: petit mal, petit mal variant (syndrome de Lennox-Gastaut), crises akinétiques, crises myocloniques.
	clorazépate	Crises épileptiques partielles (usage non approuvé).
	diazépam (voie IV)	État de mal épileptique, y compris les crises graves et récurrentes.
	lorazépam (voie IV)	État de mal épileptique.
Hydantoïnes	fosphénytoïne	Traitement parentéral à court terme des crises épileptiques, traitement/prévention des convulsions pendant une neurochirurgie.
	phénytoïne	Crises tonicocloniques, crises épileptiques partielles à symptomatologie complexe.
Valproates	acide valproïque, divalproex sodique, valproate sodique	Crises tonicocloniques. Absences à symptomatologie simple ou complexe.

CLASSE	MÉDICAMENT	TYPE DE CRISE
Divers	carbamazépine	Crises tonicocloniques, crises partielles à symptomatologie complexe, crises mixtes.
	gabapentine	Traitement adjuvant.
	lamotrigine	Traitement d'appoint chez les adultes atteints d'épilepsie dont l'état n'est pas maîtrisé de façon satisfaisante par les traitements classiques.
		En monothérapie chez les adultes, après l'arrêt du traitement par les antiépileptiques administrés en concomitance.
		Traitement d'appoint chez les enfants et les adultes présentant des crises épileptiques associées au syndrome de Lennox-Gastaut.
	lévétiracétam	Traitement d'appoint chez les patients épileptiques dont les crises ne sont pas convenablement maîtrisées par les traitements classiques.
	magnésium, sulfate de	Éclampsie ou pré-éclampsie graves.
	oxcarbazépine	Monothérapie ou traitement d'appoint des crises partielles chez les adultes.
		Traitement d'appoint des crises partielles chez les enfants âgés de 6 à 16 ans.
	topiramate	Traitement adjuvant des crises partielles ou épileptiques tonicocloniques primaires généralisées.

CONTRE-INDICATIONS, PRÉCAUTIONS ET MISES EN GARDE

Contre-indications: Très différentes selon l'agent administré. Consulter la monographie de chaque médicament.

Précautions et mises en garde: Maladie hépatique ou rénale grave (administrer ces agents avec prudence dans ce cas). Chez les patients atteints d'une telle maladie, une adaptation de la posologie peut s'imposer ■ **OBST., ALLAITEMENT**: Choisir soigneusement les agents à administrer pendant la grossesse et l'allaitement. Risque de syndrome fœtal dû à l'hydantoïne, si la mère a reçu de la phénytoïne au cours de la grossesse.

INTERACTIONS

Les barbituriques stimulent le métabolisme d'autres **médicaments métabolisés par le foie** et en diminuent l'efficacité ■ Les hydantoïnes se lient très fortement aux protéines et peuvent déplacer les autres **médicaments dotés de cette propriété** ou être déplacées par eux ■ La lamotrigine et le topiramate peuvent interagir avec plusieurs autres **anticonvulsivants**. On trouve plus de détails sur les interactions spécifiques dans la monographie de chaque médicament ■ De nombreux médicaments, dont les **antidépresseurs tricycliques** et les **phénothiazines**, peuvent abaisser le seuil de convulsion et diminuer l'efficacité des anticonvulsivants.

SOINS INFIRMIERS

ÉVALUATION DE LA SITUATION

- Déterminer le siège, la durée et les caractéristiques des crises.

TOXICITÉ ET SURDOSAGE: Suivre de près les concentrations sériques de médicament pendant toute la durée du traitement anticonvulsivant, particulièrement lors de l'ajout ou de l'abandon d'autres agents.

DIAGNOSTICS INFIRMIERS POSSIBLES

- Risque d'accident (Indications, Effets secondaires).
- Connaissances insuffisantes sur le traitement médicamenteux (Enseignement au patient et à ses proches).

INTERVENTIONS INFIRMIÈRES

- Administrer les anticonvulsivants aux posologies recommandées. Le sevrage brusque peut déclencher l'état de mal épileptique.
- Prendre les mesures qui s'imposent en cas de crise.

ENSEIGNEMENT AU PATIENT ET À SES PROCHES

- Expliquer au patient qu'il doit prendre le médicament tous les jours, en respectant rigoureusement la posologie recommandée.
- Prévenir le patient que ces médicaments peuvent provoquer de la somnolence. Lui conseiller de ne pas conduire et d'éviter les activités qui exigent sa vigilance jusqu'à ce qu'on ait la certitude que le médicament qui lui a été prescrit n'entraîne pas cet effet chez lui. Lui expliquer qu'il ne pourra reprendre la conduite automobile que si le médecin lui en donne l'autorisation, une fois que les crises auront été stabilisées.
- Recommander au patient de ne pas boire d'alcool et de ne pas prendre d'autres dépresseurs du SNC en même temps que ces médicaments.
- Conseiller au patient de porter constamment sur lui une pièce d'identité où sont inscrits son problème de santé et son traitement médicamenteux.

VÉRIFICATION DE L'EFFICACITÉ THÉRAPEUTIQUE

L'efficacité du traitement peut être démontrée par: la diminution de la fréquence ou la suppression des crises, sans sédation excessive.

ANTICONVULSIVANTS INCLUS DANS LE *GUIDE*

barbituriques
pentobarbital, 950
phénobarbital, 957
primidone, 999

benzodiazépines
clonazépam, 253
clorazépate, 259
diazépam, 339
lorazépam, 721

hydantoïnes
fosphénytoïne, 961
phénytoïne, 961

valproates
acide valproïque, 1235
divalproex sodique, 1235
valproate sodique, 1236

divers
carbamazépine, 188
gabapentine, 532
lamotrigine, 683
lévétiracétam, 699
magnésium, sulfate de, 731
oxcarbazépine, 905
topiramate, 1204

ANTIDÉPRESSEURS

INDICATIONS

Traitement des diverses formes de dépression endogène, souvent en association avec la psychothérapie ▪ Les autres indications comprennent: le traitement de l'anxiété (doxépine) ▪ le traitement de l'anxiété généralisée (escitalopram, paroxétine et venlafaxine) ▪ l'énurésie (imipramine) ▪ la douleur chronique (amitriptyline, doxépine, imipramine, nortriptyline et trazodone [usage non approuvé]) ▪ l'abandon de la cigarette (bupropion) ▪ la boulimie (fluoxétine) ▪ le trouble obsessionnel-compulsif (clomipramine, fluoxétine, fluvoxamine, paroxétine et sertraline) ▪ le trouble panique (fluoxétine [usage non approuvé], paroxétine, sertraline et venlafaxine) ▪ la phobie sociale (paroxétine et venlafaxine) ■ le prurit (doxépine [usage non approuvé]) ■ l'anorexie (fluoxétine [usage non approuvé]) ■ le trouble déficitaire de l'attention avec hyperactivité (TDAH) (fluoxétine [usage non approuvé]) ■ la fibromyalgie (fluoxétine [usage non approuvé]) ■ l'obésité (fluoxétine [usage non approuvé]) ■ le syndrome prémenstruel (fluoxétine [usage non approuvé], paroxétine et venlafaxine [usage non approuvé]) ■ le phénomène de Raynaud (fluoxétine [usage non approuvé]) ■ Prophylaxie des céphalées de Horton et des migraines (imipramine [usage non approuvé]) ■ Traitement de l'état de stress post-traumatique (paroxétine) ■ Traitement de l'insomnie (trazodone [usage non approuvé]).

MÉCANISME D'ACTION

L'effet antidépresseur de ces médicaments est vraisemblablement attribuable à la prévention du recaptage de la dopamine, de la noradrénaline ou de la sérotonine (selon l'agent) par les neurones présynaptiques, ce qui entraîne une accumulation de ces neurotransmetteurs ■ Les deux principales classes d'antidépresseurs sont les antidépresseurs tricycliques et les inhibiteurs sélectifs du recaptage de la sérotonine (ISRS) ■ La plupart des antidépresseurs tricycliques sont dotés de propriétés anticholinergiques et sédatives importantes, ce qui explique bon nombre de leurs effets secondaires (amitriptyline, clomipramine, doxépine, imipramine, nortriptyline) ■ Les ISRS sont particulièrement susceptibles d'induire l'insomnie (fluoxétine, fluvoxamine, paroxétine et sertraline).

CONTRE-INDICATIONS, PRÉCAUTIONS ET MISES EN GARDE

Contre-indications: Hypersensibilité ■ L'administration de ces agents est déconseillée en présence d'un glaucome à angle fermé ■ Administration déconseillée pendant la grossesse et l'allaitement et immédiatement après un infarctus du myocarde.

Précautions et mises en garde: Administrer ce type de médicament avec prudence aux personnes âgées et aux patients souffrant de maladie cardiovasculaire ■ Les hommes âgés souffrant d'hyperplasie de la prostate peuvent être davantage prédisposés à la rétention urinaire ■ Les effets secondaires anticholinergiques, p. ex., sécheresse des yeux (xérophtalmie), sécheresse de la bouche (xérostomie), vision trouble et constipation, peuvent dicter la modification de la posologie ou l'abandon du traitement ■ La posologie doit être ajustée lentement; la réponse thérapeutique peut commencer à se manifester de 2 à 4 semaines après le début du traitement ■ Ces médicaments, et particulièrement le bupropion, peuvent abaisser le seuil de convulsion.

INTERACTIONS

Antidépresseurs tricycliques: Ces médicaments peuvent provoquer de l'hypertension, de la tachycardie et des convulsions lors de l'administration concomitante d'**IMAO** ■ Ils peuvent prévenir la réponse thérapeutique à certains **antihypertenseurs** ■ Effets additifs sur la dépression du système nerveux central, lors de l'administration simultanée d'autres **dépresseurs du SNC** ■ L'activité sympathomimétique peut être intensifiée lors de l'administration concomitante d'autres **sympathomimétiques** ■ Effets anticholinergiques additifs lors de l'administration simultanée d'autres **médicaments dotés de telles propriétés** ■ **IMAO:** Une crise hypertensive peut être déclenchée par l'administration simultanée d'**amphétamines**, de **méthyldopa**, de **lévodopa**, de **dopamine**, d'**adrénaline**, de **noradrénaline**, de **désipramine**, d'**imipramine**, de réserpine ou de vasoconstricteurs ■ Les aliments contenant de la **tyramine** peuvent aussi déclencher une crise hypertensive ■ Risque d'hypertension ou d'hypotension, de coma, de convulsions et de décès lors de l'administration simultanée de la **mépéridine** ou d'autres **analgésiques opioïdes** ■ Risques additifs d'hypotension lors de l'administration concomitante d'**antihypertenseurs** ou d'une **rachianesthésie** ■ Risques additifs d'hypoglycémie lors de l'administration simultanée d'**insuline** ou d'**hypoglycémiants oraux** ■ **Fluoxétine, fluvoxamine, bupropion, citalopram, escitalopram, paroxétine, sertraline ou venlafaxine:** Ne pas les administrer en association avec des **IMAO**

ou dans les semaines suivant un traitement par ces agents (voir la monographie de chaque médicament) ▪ Le risque de réactions indésirables peut être accru par le **rizatriptan**, l'**élétriptan**, le **naratriptan**, le **sumatriptan** ou le **zolmitriptan**.

SOINS INFIRMIERS

ÉVALUATION DE LA SITUATION

- Observer l'état de conscience et l'affect du patient. Déceler les tendances suicidaires, particulièrement au début du traitement. Réduire la quantité de médicament dont le patient peut disposer.

TOXICITÉ ET SURDOSAGE: La consommation d'aliments contenant de la tyramine lors d'un traitement par les IMAO peut déclencher une crise hypertensive. Les symptômes comprennent des douleurs thoraciques, des céphalées graves, la raideur de la nuque, des nausées et des vomissements, la photosensibilité et la dilatation des pupilles. Traitement: phentolamine par voie IV.

DIAGNOSTICS INFIRMIERS POSSIBLES

- Stratégies d'adaptation inefficaces (Indications).
- Risque d'accident (Effets secondaires).
- Connaissances insuffisantes sur le traitement médicamenteux (Enseignement au patient et à ses proches).

INTERVENTIONS INFIRMIÈRES

- Administrer les médicaments qui entraînent la sédation au coucher, pour éviter une somnolence diurne excessive, et les médicaments qui entraînent l'insomnie (fluoxétine, fluvoxamine, paroxétine, sertraline, IMAO), dans la matinée.

ENSEIGNEMENT AU PATIENT ET À SES PROCHES

- Recommander au patient d'éviter de boire de l'alcool et de prendre des dépresseurs du SNC en même temps que ces médicaments. Inciter le patient qui reçoit des IMAO à ne pas prendre de médicaments en vente libre et à ne pas consommer des aliments et des boissons qui contiennent de la tyramine (voir l'annexe J) pendant le traitement et pendant au moins 2 semaines après l'arrêt de la médication, pour éviter les risques de crise hypertensive. Conseiller au patient de signaler immédiatement à un professionnel de la santé tout symptôme qui peut évoquer une crise hypertensive.
- Prévenir le patient que les antidépresseurs peuvent provoquer des étourdissements ou de la somnolence. Lui conseiller de ne pas conduire et d'éviter les activités qui exigent sa vigilance jusqu'à ce qu'on ait la certitude que le médicament n'entraîne pas ces effets chez lui.
- Conseiller au patient de changer lentement de position afin de réduire le risque d'hypotension orthostatique.
- Recommander au patient de signaler à un professionnel de la santé les symptômes suivants: sécheresse de la bouche, rétention urinaire, constipation. Lui expliquer qu'il peut soulager la sécheresse de la bouche en se rinçant souvent la bouche, en pratiquant une bonne hygiène orale et en consommant des bonbons ou de la gomme à mâcher sans sucre. Lui expliquer également que pour prévenir la constipation, il doit consommer plus de liquides et d'aliments riches en fibres et faire régulièrement de l'exercice.
- Recommander au patient qui doit suivre un traitement ou subir une intervention chirurgicale de prévenir le professionnel de la santé qu'il suit un traitement médicamenteux. Il faut habituellement arrêter le traitement aux IMAO au moins 2 semaines avant l'administration d'agents anesthésiques.

- Expliquer au patient l'importance de la psychothérapie et des examens de suivi permettant de déterminer les bienfaits du traitement.

VÉRIFICATION DE L'EFFICACITÉ THÉRAPEUTIQUE

L'efficacité du traitement peut être démontrée par: la résolution de l'état dépressif ▪ l'apaisement de l'anxiété ▪ la maîtrise de l'énurésie chez les enfants > 5 ans ▪ le soulagement de la douleur chronique d'origine neurologique ▪ la maîtrise du trouble panique, de la phobie sociale, de la boulimie et du trouble obsessionnel-compulsif ▪ l'abandon de la cigarette.

ANTIDÉPRESSEURS INCLUS DANS LE *GUIDE*

inhibiteurs de la monoamine-oxydase (IMAO)
phénelzine, 616
tranylcypromine, 616

inhibiteurs sélectifs du recaptage de la sérotonine (ISRS)
citalopram, 241
escitalopram, 442
fluoxétine, 505
fluvoxamine, 516
paroxétine, 926
sertraline, 1099

tricycliques
amitriptyline, 65
clomipramine, 250
doxépine, 398
imipramine, 601
nortriptyline, 869

divers
bupropion, 164
mirtazapine, 806
trazodone, 1214
venlafaxine, 1243

ANTIDIABÉTIQUES

INDICATIONS

On administre l'insuline dans le traitement du diabète de type 1. On peut également l'administrer pour traiter le diabète de type 2, lorsque la diétothérapie et le traitement par un agent oral ne réussissent pas à équilibrer adéquatement la glycémie ▪ Le choix de la préparation d'insuline (action très rapide, action rapide, action intermédiaire ou action prolongée) dépend du degré de maîtrise souhaité, des fluctuations quotidiennes de la glycémie et des réactions préalables ▪ Les préparations orales sont principalement administrées aux patients atteints de diabète de type 2 ▪ L'administration des médicaments par voie orale n'est justifiée que si la diétothérapie et l'exercice physique n'équilibrent pas la glycémie ▪ Certains agents oraux peuvent être administrés en même temps que l'insuline.

MÉCANISME D'ACTION

L'insuline, hormone produite par le pancréas, abaisse la glycémie en augmentant le transport du glucose vers les cellules et en favorisant la transformation du glucose en glycogène. Elle favorise également la transformation des acides aminés en protéines dans le tissu musculaire, stimule la formation des triglycérides et inhibe la libération d'acides gras libres ▪ Les sulfonylurées et les méglitinides abaissent la glycémie, en stimulant la sécrétion endogène d'insuline par les cellules bêta du pancréas ▪ Les sulfonylurées, en traitement à long terme, et la metformine augmentent la sensibilité à l'insuline au niveau des sites des récepteurs intracellulaires ▪ La metformine diminue la production de glucose par le foie et son absorption par les intestins ▪ Les hypoglycémiants oraux ne doivent être administrés que si la fonction pancréatique est intacte ■ L'acarbose retarde et réduit l'absorption du glucose ■ Les thiazolidinediones (pioglitazone et rosiglitazone) améliorent la sensibilité à l'insuline par un effet agoniste au niveau des sites récepteurs, jouant un rôle dans la réactivité de l'insuline et la production et l'utilisation du glucose qui s'ensuit. Cet effet ne peut se manifester qu'en présence d'insuline.

CONTRE-INDICATIONS, PRÉCAUTIONS ET MISES EN GARDE

Contre-indications: *Insuline* – Hypoglycémie ■ *Sulfonylurées* – Hypersensibilité (une sensibilité croisée peut se produire lors de l'administration d'autres sulfonylurées ou sulfamides), hypoglycémie, diabète de type 1, coma diabétique ou acidocétose, éviter l'administration de ces médicaments aux patients souffrant de dysfonctionnement grave des reins, du foie et de la thyroïde ou d'autres dysfonctionnements des glandes endocrines, **OBST., ALLAITEMENT**: Ne pas administrer ces médicaments aux femmes enceintes ou à celles qui allaitent ■ *Metformine* – Hypersensibilité, diabète de type 1, acidose métabolique et antécédents d'acidocétose ou d'acidose lactique, insuffisance rénale, études radiographiques concomitantes nécessitant l'administration IV d'une substance de contraste iodée (interrompre temporairement l'administration de la metformine), grossesse ■ *Méglitinides* – Hypersensibilité, grossesse ou allaitement, acidocétose diabétique avec ou sans coma, diabète de type 1 ■ *Acarbose* – Hypersensibilité, acidocétose diabétique, maladies inflammatoires de l'intestin ou autre maladie intestinale chronique qui entravent l'absorption ou qui prédisposent à l'occlusion intestinale ■ *Thiazolidinediones* – Hypersensibilité, insuffisance hépatique grave, insuffisance cardiaque aiguë.

Précautions et mises en garde: *Insuline* – L'infection, le stress ou les modifications d'ordre diététique peuvent modifier les besoins en insuline ■ *Sulfonylurées* – **GÉR.**: Administrer ces agents avec prudence aux personnes âgées; une réduction de la posologie peut être nécessaire, l'infection, le stress ou les modifications diététiques peuvent modifier les besoins en hypoglycémiants, faire preuve de prudence lors de l'administration de ces agents chez les patients ayant des antécédents de maladie cardiovasculaire ■ *Metformine* – La metformine peut provoquer une acidose lactique, **GÉR.**: Faire preuve de prudence lors de l'administration de ce médicament aux patients âgés ou débilités; il est parfois nécessaire de diminuer la dose ■ *Acarbose* – L'infection, le stress ou les modifications diététiques peuvent modifier les besoins en hypoglycémiants ■ *Méglitinides* – Insuffisance hépatique ■ *Thiazolidinediones* – Œdème.

INTERACTIONS

Insuline: Effets hypoglycémiants additifs lors de l'administration concomitante d'**hypoglycémiants oraux** ■ **Hypoglycémiants oraux**: L'**alcool**, pris en même temps que certains de ces agents, peut entraîner une réaction similaire à la réaction au disulfirame ■ L'**alcool**, les **corticostéroïdes**, la **rifampine**, le **glucagon** et les **diurétiques thiazidiques** peuvent diminuer l'efficacité de ces médicaments ■ Les **stéroïdes anabolisants**, le **chloramphénicol**, les **IMAO**, la plupart des **anti-inflammatoires non stéroïdiens** et les **salicylates** peuvent en augmenter l'effet hypoglycémiant ■ Les **bêtabloquants** peuvent provoquer une hypoglycémie et en masquer les signes et les symptômes ■ **Metformine**: L'administration d'une **substance de contraste à base d'iode** ou une consommation excessive ou prolongée d'**alcool** peuvent élever le risque d'acidose lactique.

SOINS INFIRMIERS

ÉVALUATION DE LA SITUATION

- Suivre de près les signes et les symptômes d'hypoglycémie.
- Les thiazolidinediones, la metformine et l'acarbose ne provoquent pas d'hypoglycémie lorsqu'ils sont administrés seuls, mais peuvent intensifier l'effet hypoglycémiant des autres agents hypoglycémiants.

- Chez les patients dont la glycémie a été bien équilibrée par la metformine, mais qui manifestent une maladie ou dont les épreuves de laboratoire révèlent des anomalies, on devrait rechercher des signes d'acidocétose ou d'acidose lactique. Noter les taux d'électrolytes sériques, les corps cétoniques, la glycémie et, au besoin, le pH sanguin, les concentrations de lactate, de pyruvate et de metformine. Si l'une de ces formes d'acidose est présente, cesser immédiatement l'administration de la metformine et traiter l'acidose.

Tests de laboratoire: Il faudrait suivre de près les taux de glucose sérique et d'hémoglobine glyquée à intervalles réguliers tout au long du traitement afin d'en déterminer les bienfaits.

DIAGNOSTICS INFIRMIERS POSSIBLES

- Alimentation excessive (Indications).
- Connaissances insuffisantes sur le traitement médicamenteux (Enseignement au patient et à ses proches).
- Non-observance du traitement médicamenteux (Enseignement au patient et à ses proches).

INTERVENTIONS INFIRMIÈRES

- Administrer l'insuline selon une échelle aux patients dont la glycémie est équilibrée, mais qui sont soumis à un stress, qui ont de la fièvre, qui souffrent de traumatismes ou d'infection ou qui doivent subir une intervention chirurgicale. En présence d'un épisode aigu, cesser l'administration de metformine; ne la reprendre qu'une fois que l'épisode a été maîtrisé.
- Chez les patients qui passent des doses quotidiennes d'insuline aux hypoglycémiants oraux, la substitution doit se faire parfois graduellement.

Insuline: Il existe différents types d'insuline. Vérifier le type, la dose et la date de péremption de l'insuline en présence d'un autre professionnel de la santé. Ne pas substituer une insuline à une autre sans l'ordre explicite du médecin. Utiliser toujours une seringue à insuline pour prélever la dose.

ENSEIGNEMENT AU PATIENT ET À SES PROCHES

- Expliquer au patient que les antidiabétiques équilibrent l'hyperglycémie, mais ne guérissent pas le diabète. Le traitement est de longue durée.
- Expliquer au patient les signes d'hypoglycémie et d'hyperglycémie. En cas d'hypoglycémie, recommander au patient de prendre un verre de jus d'orange, ou 2 ou 3 cuillères à thé de sucre, de miel ou de sirop de maïs dans de l'eau (les patients sous acarbose doivent prendre du glucose, et non du sucre ordinaire) et d'en informer immédiatement un professionnel de la santé.
- Inciter le patient à suivre la diétothérapie, la pharmacothérapie et le programme d'exercices prescrits afin de prévenir les épisodes d'hypoglycémie ou d'hyperglycémie.
- Enseigner au patient la méthode de mesure de la glycémie et de la cétonémie.
- Recommander au patient de signaler à un professionnel de la santé les nausées, les vomissements et la fièvre, et de le prévenir s'il est incapable de suivre son régime alimentaire habituel ou si sa glycémie n'est pas équilibrée.
- Inciter le patient à toujours avoir sur lui du sucre ou une forme de glucose et à porter en tout temps un bracelet d'identité où est inscrit son traitement médicamenteux.
- Pendant la grossesse, on recommande d'équilibrer la glycémie par l'insuline. Conseiller à la patiente d'utiliser une méthode contraceptive autre que les contraceptifs oraux et d'informer sans délai le médecin si elle pense être enceinte ou si elle souhaite le devenir.

Insuline: Faire une démonstration de la technique d'auto-injection et informer le patient du type d'insuline qu'il doit utiliser ainsi que des fournitures médicales dont il doit se munir (seringue et stylo-cartouche). Lui expliquer comment conserver l'insuline et comment mettre au rebut les seringues. Lui expliquer aussi qu'il est important de ne pas changer de marque d'insuline ou de seringue. Lui montrer comment choisir les points d'injection et comment en effectuer la rotation. Insister sur la nécessité d'observer rigoureusement le traitement.

Sulfonylurées: Prévenir le patient que la consommation simultanée d'alcool peut entraîner une réaction semblable à la réaction au disulfirame (crampes abdominales, nausées, bouffées vasomotrices, céphalées et hypoglycémie).

Metformine: Mettre en garde le patient contre le risque d'acidose lactique et lui expliquer qu'il pourrait être nécessaire d'arrêter le traitement par cet agent en cas d'infection grave, de déshydratation ou de diarrhée grave ou persistante, ou si des tests médicaux ou une intervention chirurgicale s'imposent.

Thiazolidinediones: Conseiller au patient d'informer un professionnel de la santé si des signes de dysfonctionnement hépatique (nausées, vomissements, douleurs abdominales, fatigue, anorexie, urines foncées, jaunisse) ou d'insuffisance cardiaque (œdème, difficultés respiratoires, gain de poids rapide) se manifestent.

VÉRIFICATION DE L'EFFICACITÉ THÉRAPEUTIQUE

L'efficacité du traitement peut être démontrée par: la maîtrise de la glycémie sans épisodes d'hypoglycémie ou d'hyperglycémie.

ANTIDIABÉTIQUES INCLUS DANS LE *GUIDE*

ANTIDIARRHÉIQUES

INDICATIONS

Soulagement de la diarrhée aiguë et chronique non spécifique et suppression des symptômes.

MÉCANISME D'ACTION

Le diphénoxylate avec de l'atropine et le lopéramide ralentissent la motilité intestinale et le péristaltisme ■ Le sous-salicylate de bismuth modifie le contenu en liquides des selles ■ Le polycarbophile est un antidiarrhéique qui capte l'eau contenue dans la lumière de l'intestin, favorisant ainsi l'élimination de selles bien formées ■ L'octréotide est surtout administré en cas de diarrhée associée à des tumeurs gastro-intestinales endocrines ■ La cholestyramine est utilisée pour le traitement symptomatique de la diarrhée induite par les acides biliaires.

CONTRE-INDICATIONS, PRÉCAUTIONS ET MISES EN GARDE

Contre-indications: Antécédents d'hypersensibilité ■ Douleurs abdominales graves, d'étiologie inconnue, particulièrement lorsqu'elles s'accompagnent de fièvre ■ *Cholestyramine* - Obstruction biliaire totale ■ phénylcétonurie (certains produits contiennent de l'aspartame).

Précautions et mises en garde: Administrer ces agents avec prudence aux patients souffrant de maladie intestinale inflammatoire ou de maladie hépatique grave ■ **OBST., ALLAITEMENT**: L'innocuité des antidiarrhéiques n'a pas été établie (diphénoxylate avec atropine et lopéramide) ■ L'octréotide peut aggraver la cholécystopathie ■ *Cholestyramine* - **PÉD.**: Risque d'obstruction intestinale; des décès ont été signalés.

INTERACTIONS

L'octréotide peut modifier la réponse à l'**insuline** ou aux **hypoglycémiants oraux** ■ La cholestyramine peut diminuer l'absorption et les effets de plusieurs **médicaments administrés par voie orale**.

SOINS INFIRMIERS

ÉVALUATION DE LA SITUATION

- Observer la fréquence et la consistance des selles et ausculter les bruits intestinaux, avant l'administration du médicament et pendant toute la durée du traitement.
- Effectuer le bilan hydroélectrolytique et observer l'élasticité de la peau pour déceler les signes de déshydratation.

DIAGNOSTICS INFIRMIERS POSSIBLES

- Diarrhée (Indications).
- Constipation (Effets secondaires).
- Connaissances insuffisantes sur le traitement médicamenteux (Enseignement au patient et à ses proches).

INTERVENTIONS INFIRMIÈRES

- Bien mélanger les préparations liquides avant de les administrer.

ENSEIGNEMENT AU PATIENT ET À SES PROCHES

- Recommander au patient de communiquer avec un professionnel de la santé si la diarrhée persiste, et de lui signaler les symptômes suivants: fièvre, douleurs abdominales, palpitations.

VÉRIFICATION DE L'EFFICACITÉ THÉRAPEUTIQUE

L'efficacité du traitement peut être démontrée par: la diminution de la diarrhée.

ANTIDIARRHÉIQUES INCLUS DANS LE *GUIDE*

CLASSIFICATION

ANTIDOTES

INDICATIONS

Voir le tableau ci-dessous.

MÉCANISME D'ACTION

Les antidotes sont utilisés dans le traitement du surdosage accidentel ou intentionnel par des médicaments ou des substances toxiques. L'objectif du traitement par un antidote est de diminuer les complications systémiques du surdosage tout en assurant le maintien des fonctions vitales. Un examen attentif des antécédents du patient permettra de déterminer le type de traitement, le choix du médicament et la dose à administrer ■ Certains antidotes permettent d'évacuer la substance nocive avant son absorption par voie générale ou d'en accélérer l'élimination (charbon activé), alors que d'autres agissent de façon plus spécifique. On doit, dans ce cas, avoir des données plus précises quant au type et à la quantité de substance nocive ingérée.

SUBSTANCES TOXIQUES ET ANTIDOTES SPÉCIFIQUES

Substance toxique	Antidote
acétaminophène	acétylcystéine
anticholinestérases	atropine
benzodiazépines	flumazénil
cyclophosphamide	mesna
digoxine, digitoxine	fragments d'anticorps spécifiques de la digoxine [Fab (ovins)]
doxorubicine	dexrazoxane
héparine	protamine, sulfate de
fer	déféroxamine
plomb	succimer
méthotrexate	leucovorine calcique
opioïdes (analgésiques), héroïne	naloxone
warfarine	phytonadione (vitamine K1)

CONTRE-INDICATIONS, PRÉCAUTIONS ET MISES EN GARDE

Contre-indications: Consulter la monographie de chaque médicament.

Précautions et mises en garde: Consulter la monographie de chaque médicament.

INTERACTIONS

Consulter la monographie de chaque médicament.

SOINS INFIRMIERS

ÉVALUATION DE LA SITUATION

- Se renseigner sur le type de médicament ou de substance toxique ingéré et sur le moment de l'ingestion.
- Consulter les références, un centre anti-poisons ou le médecin pour connaître les symptômes de toxicité de la substance ingérée et son antidote. Prendre les signes vitaux, observer de près les systèmes touchés et examiner attentivement les concentrations sériques.
- Déceler les idées suicidaires et prendre les mesures nécessaires pour empêcher une tentative de suicide, le cas échéant.

DIAGNOSTICS INFIRMIERS POSSIBLES

- Stratégies d'adaptation inefficaces (Indications).
- Risque d'intoxication (Enseignement au patient et à ses proches).
- Connaissances insuffisantes sur le traitement médicamenteux (Enseignement au patient et à ses proches).

INTERVENTIONS INFIRMIÈRES

- On peut administrer les antidotes pendant qu'on essaie de faire vomir le patient, qu'on effectue l'aspiration et le lavage gastriques, qu'on administre des cathartiques et des substances qui modifient le pH de l'urine, et qu'on prend les mesures de soutien nécessaires pour combattre les effets respiratoires et cardiaques du surdosage ou de l'intoxication.

ENSEIGNEMENT AU PATIENT ET À SES PROCHES

- Expliquer les risques d'empoisonnement à domicile, les méthodes de prévention et la nécessité de consulter un centre anti-poisons, un médecin ou le personnel d'un service des urgences avant d'administrer du sirop d'ipéca. Insister sur la nécessité d'apporter au service des urgences un échantillon de la substance ingérée afin qu'on puisse en déterminer la nature. Insister également sur le fait qu'il faut garder tous les médicaments et substances dangereuses hors de la portée des enfants.

VÉRIFICATION DE L'EFFICACITÉ THÉRAPEUTIQUE

L'efficacité du traitement peut être démontrée par: la prévention ou la suppression des effets secondaires toxiques de la substance ingérée.

ANTIDOTES INCLUS DANS LE *GUIDE*

ANTIÉMÉTIQUES

INDICATIONS

Les phénothiazines, le dolasétron, le granisétron, l'halopéridol, le métoclopramide et l'ondansétron sont utilisés pour traiter les nausées et les vomissements de diverses causes, comprenant les interventions chirurgicales, l'anesthésie, la chimiothérapie anticancéreuse et la radiothérapie ▪ Le dimenhydrinate, la scopolamine et la méclizine sont utilisés principalement pour la prévention et le traitement du mal des transports ▪ Le dropéridol est utilisé pour diminuer les nausées et les vomissements consécutifs à une intervention chirurgicale ou en présence de nausées réfractaires (usage non approuvé).

MÉCANISME D'ACTION

Les phénothiazines inhibent les nausées et les vomissements en agissant sur la zone gâchette chémoréceptrice. Le dimenhydrinate, la scopolamine et la méclizine diminuent surtout les nausées engendrées par le mal des transports. Le métoclopramide diminue les nausées et les vomissements en accélérant la vidange gastrique et en agissant sur la zone gâchette chémoréceptrice. Le dolasétron, le granisétron et l'ondansétron bloquent les effets de la sérotonine. Le dropéridol modifie les effets de la dopamine dans le SNC.

CONTRE-INDICATIONS, PRÉCAUTIONS ET MISES EN GARDE

Contre-indications: Antécédents d'hypersensibilité.

Précautions et mises en garde: **PÉD.**: Administrer les phénothiazines avec prudence aux enfants qui peuvent souffrir d'une maladie virale ■ **OBST.**: Choisir soigneusement les agents destinés aux femmes enceintes (l'innocuité de ces agents pendant la grossesse n'a pas été établie) ■ Utiliser avec prudence chez les patients exposés au risque de présenter un intervalle QT allongé.

INTERACTIONS

Effets additifs sur la dépression du système nerveux central lors de l'administration simultanée d'autres **dépresseurs du SNC**, y compris les **antidépresseurs**, les **antihistaminiques**, les **analgésiques opioïdes** et les **hypnosédatifs** ■ Les phénothiazines peuvent provoquer l'hypotension lors de l'administration simultanée d'**antihypertenseurs** et de **dérivés nitrés** ou lors de l'ingestion de quantités importantes d'**alcool**.

SOINS INFIRMIERS

ÉVALUATION DE LA SITUATION

- Suivre de près les nausées et les vomissements, ausculter les bruits intestinaux et observer les douleurs abdominales, avant et après l'administration de l'antiémétique.
- Évaluer le degré d'hydratation du patient ainsi que les ingesta et les excreta. Chez les patients souffrant de nausées et de vomissements graves, il faut parfois administrer des liquides par voie IV en même temps que l'antiémétique.

DIAGNOSTICS INFIRMIERS POSSIBLES

- Déficit de volume liquidien (Indications).
- Alimentation déficiente (Indications).
- Risque d'accident (Effets secondaires).

INTERVENTIONS INFIRMIÈRES

- Lors d'une administration prophylactique, suivre le mode d'emploi de chaque médicament de façon à ce que son effet maximal puisse s'exercer au moment où l'on prévoit l'apparition des nausées.
- On devrait cesser le traitement par les phénothiazines 48 heures avant la myélographie et attendre 24 heures avant de le reprendre, étant donné que ces agents abaissent le seuil de convulsions.

ENSEIGNEMENT AU PATIENT ET À SES PROCHES

- Expliquer au patient et à ses proches les mesures habituelles qui permettent de diminuer les nausées: commencer par prendre quelques gorgées de liquides, consommer des repas légers, pauvres en matières grasses, pratiquer une bonne hygiène buccale et éliminer les stimuli nocifs du milieu ambiant.
- Prévenir le patient que l'administration des antiémétiques peut entraîner de la somnolence. L'encourager à demander de l'aide lors de ses déplacements. Lui conseiller de ne pas

conduire et d'éviter les activités exigeant sa vigilance jusqu'à ce qu'on ait la certitude que le médicament n'entraîne pas cet effet chez lui.

- Conseiller au patient de changer lentement de position pour réduire le risque d'hypotension orthostatique.

VÉRIFICATION DE L'EFFICACITÉ THÉRAPEUTIQUE

L'efficacité du traitement peut être démontrée par: la prévention ou la diminution des nausées et des vomissements.

ANTIÉMÉTIQUES INCLUS DANS LE *GUIDE*

antagonistes de la sérotonine (5-HT$_3$)
dolasétron, 390
granisétron, 550
ondansétron, 890

anticholinergique
scopolamine, 1094

antihistaminiques
dimenhydrinate, 358
diphenhydramine, 362
méclizine, 739

phénothiazines
chlorpromazine, 230
méthotriméprazine, 774
prochlorpérazine, 1008
prométhazine, 1016
trifluopérazine, 1218

divers
aprépitant, 105
dropéridol, 406
halopéridol, 554
métoclopramide, 782

ANTIFONGIQUES

INDICATIONS

Traitement des infections fongiques ■ Les infections de la peau ou des muqueuses peuvent être traitées avec des préparations topiques ou vaginales ■ Pour traiter les infections profondes ou généralisées, il faut administrer une préparation par voie orale ou parentérale ■ Les nouvelles préparations parentérales d'amphotéricine sont conditionnées selon un procédé d'encapsulation lipidique, visant à diminuer la toxicité.

MÉCANISME D'ACTION

Les antifongiques détruisent les champignons sensibles (effet fongicide) ou en inhibent la prolifération (effet fongistatique), en modifiant la perméabilité de la membrane des cellules fongiques ou la synthèse des protéines à l'intérieur même de la cellule.

CONTRE-INDICATIONS, PRÉCAUTIONS ET MISES EN GARDE

Contre-indications: Antécédents d'hypersensibilité.

Précautions et mises en garde: Étant donné que la plupart des antifongiques à action systémique peuvent exercer des effets indésirables sur la fonction médullaire, il faut les administrer avec prudence aux patients dont la réserve médullaire est réduite ■ L'amphotéricine B provoque souvent une insuffisance rénale ■ On devrait adapter la posologie du fluconazole chez les insuffisants rénaux ■ Chez les patients séropositifs (VIH), les réactions indésirables au fluconazole peuvent être plus importantes.

INTERACTIONS

Très différentes, selon l'antifongique administré. Consulter la monographie de chaque médicament.

SOINS INFIRMIERS

ÉVALUATION DE LA SITUATION

- Suivre de près les signes d'infection. Observer les muqueuses et les territoires cutanés atteints avant l'administration de l'antifongique et pendant toute la durée du traitement. Une aggravation de l'irritation de la peau peut indiquer la nécessité d'arrêter la médication.

DIAGNOSTICS INFIRMIERS POSSIBLES

- Risque d'infection (Indications).
- Atteinte à l'intégrité de la peau (Indications).
- Connaissances insuffisantes sur le traitement médicamenteux (Enseignement au patient et à ses proches).

INTERVENTIONS INFIRMIÈRES

- Les antifongiques sont présentés sous diverses formes. Consulter la monographie de chaque médicament pour en déterminer la méthode d'administration.

Antifongiques topiques: Avant d'appliquer le médicament, se renseigner auprès du médecin ou d'un autre professionnel de la santé sur la méthode de nettoyage qu'il préconise. Porter des gants au cours de l'application. Ne pas appliquer de pansements occlusifs, sauf si le médecin ou un autre professionnel de la santé le recommande expressément.

ENSEIGNEMENT AU PATIENT ET À SES PROCHES

- Expliquer au patient la méthode d'administration de l'agent prescrit.
- Conseiller au patient de mener à terme son traitement, en respectant scrupuleusement la posologie prescrite, même s'il se sent mieux.
- Recommander au patient de prévenir un professionnel de la santé si l'irritation de la peau s'aggrave ou si aucune réponse thérapeutique ne se manifeste.

VÉRIFICATION DE L'EFFICACITÉ THÉRAPEUTIQUE

L'efficacité du traitement peut être démontrée par: la résolution des signes et des symptômes de l'infection. Le délai de guérison dépend du microorganisme infectant et du siège de l'infection. En cas d'infections fongiques profondes, le traitement doit parfois se prolonger pendant plusieurs semaines ou mois. Les infections fongiques récurrentes peuvent être le signe d'une maladie grave, intéressant l'organisme entier.

ANTIFONGIQUES INCLUS DANS LE *GUIDE*

par voie générale

topiques

vaginaux

ANTIHISTAMINIQUES

INDICATIONS

Soulagement des symptômes associés aux allergies, y compris la rhinite, l'urticaire et l'œdème angioneurotique ■ Traitement d'appoint des réactions anaphylactiques ■ Traitement d'appoint d'affections allergiques incluant la rhinite et l'asthme (stabilisateurs des mastocytes) ■ Prévention des bronchospasmes induits par des facteurs déclenchants connus: l'effort, l'air froid, les allergènes et les polluants atmosphériques (stabilisateurs des mastocytes) ■ Certains antihistaminiques sont utilisés dans le traitement du mal des transports (dimenhydrinate et méclizine), de l'insomnie (diphenhydramine), des réactions de type parkinsonien (diphenhydramine) et d'autres affections non allergiques.

MÉCANISME D'ACTION

Les antihistaminiques bloquent les effets de l'histamine au site des récepteurs H_1 ■ Ils n'inhibent pas la libération de l'histamine, la production d'anticorps ni les réactions antigène-anticorps ■ Les stabilisateurs des mastocytes, quant à eux, préviennent la libération de l'histamine et de la SRS-A des mastocytes sensibilisés ■ La plupart des antihistaminiques sont dotés de propriétés anticholinergiques. Ils peuvent rendre la vision trouble et provoquer la constipation, la sécheresse des yeux (xérophtalmie) et la sécheresse de la bouche (xérostomie) ■ Un grand nombre d'antihistaminiques peuvent provoquer la sédation. Les stabilisateurs des mastocytes n'entraînent pas ces effets indésirables ■ Certaines phénothiazines sont dotées de fortes propriétés antihistaminiques (hydroxyzine et prométhazine).

CONTRE-INDICATIONS, PRÉCAUTIONS ET MISES EN GARDE

Contre-indications: Hypersensibilité ■ Glaucome à angle fermé (sauf pour les stabilisateurs des mastocytes) ■ **PÉD.**: Ne pas administrer ces agents aux nouveau-nés ni aux enfants prématurés ■ Crises aiguës d'asthme (stabilisateurs des mastocytes).

Précautions et mises en garde: **GÉR.**: Les personnes âgées peuvent être plus sensibles aux effets anticholinergiques indésirables des antihistaminiques ■ Administrer ces agents avec prudence aux patients qui souffrent d'obstruction du pylore, d'hyperplasie bénigne de la prostate, d'hyperthyroïdie, de maladie cardiovasculaire ou de maladie hépatique grave ■ **OBST., ALLAITEMENT**: Administrer avec prudence aux femmes enceintes et à celles qui allaitent.

INTERACTIONS

Effets sédatifs additifs lors de la prise simultanée d'autres **dépresseurs du SNC**, dont l'**alcool**, les **antidépresseurs**, les **analgésiques opioïdes** et les **hypnosédatifs** ■ Les stabilisateurs des mastocytes ne causent pas de sédation ■ Les **IMAO** prolongent et accentuent les propriétés anticholinergiques des antihistaminiques.

SOINS INFIRMIERS

ÉVALUATION DE LA SITUATION

- Suivre de près les symptômes d'allergie (rhinite, conjonctivite et urticaire) avant l'administration du médicament et à intervalles réguliers pendant toute la durée du traitement.
- Mesurer le pouls et la pression artérielle avant d'amorcer le traitement et tout au long de l'administration par voie IV.

- Ausculter les murmures vésiculaires et noter les caractéristiques des sécrétions bronchiques. Maintenir l'apport de liquides entre 1 500 et 2 000 mL par jour pour diminuer la viscosité des sécrétions.
- Chez les patients asthmatiques, examiner les résultats des tests de la fonction pulmonaire avant d'amorcer le traitement avec les stabilisateurs des mastocytes par inhalation.
- Noter le murmure vésiculaire et la fonction respiratoire avant le début du traitement et à intervalles réguliers pendant toute sa durée (stabilisateurs des mastocytes par inhalation).

Traitement des nausées et vomissements: Noter l'intensité des nausées ainsi que la fréquence et la gravité des vomissements.

Traitement de l'anxiété: Évaluer l'état mental, l'humeur et le comportement du patient.

Traitement du prurit: Noter les caractéristiques et le siège du prurit, ainsi que l'étendue de la région cutanée atteinte.

DIAGNOSTICS INFIRMIERS POSSIBLES

- Dégagement inefficace des voies respiratoires (Indications).
- Risque d'accident (Réactions indésirables).
- Connaissances insuffisantes sur le traitement médicamenteux (Enseignement au patient et à ses proches).

INTERVENTIONS INFIRMIÈRES

- Prophylaxie du mal des transports: administrer au moins 30 minutes et, de préférence, de 1 à 2 heures avant que le patient ne soit exposé aux facteurs qui peuvent déclencher le mal des transports.
- Lors d'une administration concomitante d'analgésiques opioïdes (hydroxyzine, prométhazine), surveiller attentivement les déplacements du patient pour éviter les accidents dus à une sédation accrue.

ENSEIGNEMENT AU PATIENT ET À SES PROCHES

- Prévenir le patient que le médicament peut provoquer de la somnolence. Lui conseiller de ne pas conduire et d'éviter les activités qui exigent sa vigilance jusqu'à ce qu'on ait la certitude que le médicament n'entraîne pas cet effet chez lui.
- Mettre en garde le patient contre la consommation d'alcool ou d'autres dépresseurs du SNC.
- Conseiller au patient de pratiquer une bonne hygiène buccale, de se rincer la bouche fréquemment avec de l'eau et de consommer de la gomme à mâcher ou des bonbons sans sucre pour diminuer la sécheresse de la bouche.
- Demander au patient de prévenir un professionnel de la santé si les symptômes persistent.

VÉRIFICATION DE L'EFFICACITÉ THÉRAPEUTIQUE

L'efficacité du traitement peut être démontrée par: la diminution des symptômes allergiques ▪ la prévention ou la diminution de la gravité des nausées et des vomissements ▪ la diminution de l'anxiété ▪ le soulagement du prurit ▪ la sédation si l'on recherche un effet hypnosédatif.

ANTIHISTAMINIQUES INCLUS DANS LE *GUIDE*

ANTIHYPERTENSEURS

INDICATIONS

Traitement de l'hypertension de diverses étiologies et surtout de l'hypertension essentielle ■ Les médicaments administrés par voie parentérale sont destinés au traitement des urgences hypertensives ■ Le traitement par voie orale devrait être amorcé aussitôt que possible et adapté à chaque cas particulier pour favoriser l'observance du traitement prolongé ■ On amorce le traitement par les antihypertenseurs ayant les effets secondaires les plus faibles. Si ce traitement ne donne pas les résultats escomptés, afin de normaliser la pression artérielle, on doit ajouter au régime thérapeutique des médicaments plus puissants, ayant des effets secondaires différents, et provoquant le moins de réactions indésirables possible.

MÉCANISME D'ACTION

Les antihypertenseurs, en tant que classe thérapeutique, sont utilisés pour normaliser la pression artérielle (pression diastolique inférieure à 90 mm Hg et pression systolique inférieure à 140 mm Hg) ou pour la ramener à la valeur la plus basse tolérée ■ Le but de tout traitement antihypertenseur est de prévenir la lésion des organes cibles ■ Les antihypertenseurs sont divisés en divers groupes selon leur lieu d'action, à savoir, les antagonistes alpha-adrénergiques à action périphérique, les agonistes alpha-adrénergiques à action centrale, les bêtabloquants, les vasodilatateurs, les inhibiteurs de l'enzyme de conversion de l'angiotensine (IECA), les antagonistes des récepteurs de l'angiotensine II, les bloqueurs des canaux calciques et les diurétiques ■ Les urgences hypertensives peuvent être traitées par voie parentérale par le nitroprussiate, le labétalol ou l'énalaprilate.

CONTRE-INDICATIONS, PRÉCAUTIONS ET MISES EN GARDE

Contre-indications: Hypersensibilité à l'un des médicaments. Consulter la monographie de chaque antihypertenseur.

Précautions et mises en garde: **OBST., ALLAITEMENT**: Choisir attentivement les médicaments à administrer aux femmes enceintes ou à celles qui allaitent tout comme aux patients recevant des dérivés digitaliques ■ Ne pas administrer au cours de la grossesse des IECA ou des antagonistes des récepteurs de l'angiotensine II ■ Les agonistes alpha-adrénergiques et les bêtabloquants ne devraient être administrés qu'aux patients qui suivront fidèlement le traitement, car le sevrage brusque peut provoquer une élévation rapide et exagérée de la pression artérielle (phénomène de rebond) ■ Les diurétiques thiazidiques peuvent augmenter les besoins en insuline ou en hypoglycémiants oraux et dicter certaines modifications diététiques chez les patients souffrant de diabète ■ Les vasodilatateurs peuvent provoquer une tachycardie, s'ils sont administrés seuls; on les administre généralement en association avec des bêtabloquants ■ Certains antihypertenseurs entraînent une rétention hydrosodée. On les administre habituellement en association avec un diurétique.

INTERACTIONS

Un grand nombre de médicaments, comme les **antihistaminiques**, les **AINS**, les **bronchodilatateurs sympathomimétiques**, les **décongestionnants**, les **anorexigènes**, les **antidépresseurs** et les **IMAO**, peuvent neutraliser l'efficacité thérapeutique des antihypertenseurs ■ L'hypokaliémie induite par les diurétiques peut augmenter les risques de toxicité **digitalique** ■ L'administration de **suppléments de potassium** et de **diurétiques épargneurs de potassium** en même temps que les IECA ou les antagonistes des récepteurs de l'angiotensine II peut provoquer une hyperkaliémie.

SOINS INFIRMIERS

ÉVALUATION DE LA SITUATION

- Mesurer souvent la pression artérielle et le pouls pendant la période d'adaptation de la posologie et à intervalles réguliers pendant toute la durée du traitement.
- Effectuer le bilan quotidien des ingesta et des excreta et noter le poids du patient tous les jours.
- Vérifier la fréquence du renouvellement des ordonnances pour s'assurer que le patient observe son traitement.

DIAGNOSTICS INFIRMIERS POSSIBLES

- Irrigation tissulaire inefficace (Indications).
- Connaissances insuffisantes sur le traitement médicamenteux (Enseignement au patient et à ses proches).
- Non-observance du traitement médicamenteux (Enseignement au patient et à ses proches).

INTERVENTIONS INFIRMIÈRES

- Pour favoriser l'observance du traitement, de nombreux antihypertenseurs sont présentés sous forme d'associations médicamenteuses.

ENSEIGNEMENT AU PATIENT ET À SES PROCHES

- Expliquer au patient qu'il doit continuer à prendre le médicament même s'il se sent bien. Le prévenir que le sevrage brusque peut déclencher une hypertension rebond et que le médicament stabilise la pression artérielle, mais ne guérit pas l'hypertension.
- Inciter le patient à suivre d'autres mesures de réduction de l'hypertension: perdre du poids, réduire sa consommation de sel, faire régulièrement de l'exercice, cesser de fumer, boire de l'alcool avec modération et diminuer le stress.
- Expliquer au patient et à ses proches comment mesurer la pression artérielle. Leur demander de prendre la pression artérielle 1 fois par semaine et leur recommander de signaler au médecin tout changement important.
- Recommander au patient de changer lentement de position pour prévenir le risque d'hypotension orthostatique. Prévenir le patient que l'effort ou la chaleur peuvent intensifier les effets hypotenseurs du médicament.
- Conseiller au patient de consulter un professionnel de la santé avant de prendre un médicament en vente libre, et particulièrement des médicaments contre le rhume.
- Recommander au patient qui doit suivre un traitement ou subir une intervention chirurgicale de prévenir le professionnel de la santé qu'il suit un traitement antihypertenseur.
- Recommander à la patiente qui prend des IECA ou des antagonistes des récepteurs de l'angiotensine II de contacter un professionnel de la santé si elle pense être enceinte ou si elle souhaite le devenir.
- Expliquer au patient qu'il est important de se soumettre à des examens de suivi permettant d'évaluer les bienfaits du traitement.

VÉRIFICATION DE L'EFFICACITÉ THÉRAPEUTIQUE

L'efficacité du traitement peut être démontrée par: la baisse de la pression artérielle.

ANTIHYPERTENSEURS INCLUS DANS LE *GUIDE*

agonistes alpha-adrénergiques à action centrale
clonidine, 255
méthyldopa, 777

antagonistes alpha-adrénergiques à action périphérique
doxazosine, 396
phentolamine, 960
prazosine, 995
térazosine, 1156

antagonistes des récepteurs de l'angiotensine II
Pour connaître les médicaments de cette classe, prière de consulter la section des monographies.

bêtabloquants
acébutolol, 5
aténolol, 117
bisoprolol, 149
carvédilol, 197
esmolol, 444
labétalol, 676
métoprolol, 787
nadolol, 826
pindolol, 973
propranolol, 1027
timolol, 1190

bloqueurs des canaux calciques
amlodipine, 68
diltiazem, 355
félodipine, 466
nifédipine, 855
vérapamil, 1245

diurétiques de l'anse
Pour connaître la liste des médicaments de cette classe, prière de consulter la section des monographies.

diurétiques épargneurs de potassium
Pour connaître la liste des médicaments de cette classe, prière de consulter la section des monographies.

diurétiques thiazidiques
Pour connaître la liste des médicaments de cette classe, prière de consulter la section des monographies.
indapamide, 606

inhibiteurs de l'enzyme de conversion de l'angiotensine (IECA)
Pour connaître la liste des médicaments de cette classe, prière de consulter la section des monographies.

vasodilatateurs
hydralazine, 570
minoxidil, 804
nitroprusside, 866

ANTI-INFLAMMATOIRES NON STÉROÏDIENS (AINS)

INDICATIONS

Traitement des douleurs légères à modérées, de la fièvre et de diverses maladies inflammatoires, telles que la polyarthrite rhumatoïde et l'arthrose ■ AINS pour usage ophtalmique: diminution de l'inflammation oculaire postopératoire, inhibition du myosis périopératoire et réduction de l'inflammation attribuable à des allergies.

MÉCANISME D'ACTION

Les AINS sont dotés de propriétés analgésiques, antipyrétiques et anti-inflammatoires. Les effets analgésiques et anti-inflammatoires sont dus à l'inhibition de la synthèse des prostaglandines. L'effet antipyrétique est attribuable à la vasodilatation et à l'inhibition de la synthèse des prostaglandines au niveau du SNC ■ Les inhibiteurs de la cyclo-oxygénase-2 (célécoxib) semblent provoquer moins de saignements gastro-intestinaux.

CONTRE-INDICATIONS, PRÉCAUTIONS ET MISES EN GARDE

Contre-indications: Hypersensibilité à l'aspirine ou à un AINS quel qu'il soit ■ Risque de réactions de sensibilité croisée.

Précautions et mises en garde: Maladie cardiovasculaire ou facteurs de risque de maladies cardiovasculaires (risque accru de complications coronariennes, d'infarctus du myocarde ou d'accidents vasculaires cérébraux, surtout lors d'un usage prolongé) ■ Utiliser avec prudence chez les patients ayant des antécédents de saignements, d'hémorragie digestive et de maladies hépatique, rénale ou cardiovasculaire graves ■ **Obst.**: L'innocuité de ces médicaments pendant la grossesse n'a pas été établie. L'administration devrait donc être évitée pendant la deuxième moitié de la grossesse.

INTERACTIONS

Risque accru de saignement lors de l'administration concomitante d'AINS et d'**anticoagulants oraux**, d'**agents thrombolytiques**, d'**agents antiplaquettaires**, de **certaines céphalosporines** ou d'**acide valproïque** ■ L'utilisation prolongée de ces agents en même temps que l'aspirine peut entraîner des effets secondaires gastro-intestinaux accrus et une efficacité réduite ■ Les AINS peuvent également diminuer la réponse aux **diurétiques** ou aux **antihypertenseurs** ■ L'ibuprofène diminue les effets cardioprotecteurs de l'**aspirine à faible dose** ■ Les inhibiteurs de la cyclo-oxygénase-2 ne semblent pas diminuer les effets cardioprotecteurs de l'aspirine à faible dose.

SOINS INFIRMIERS

ÉVALUATION DE LA SITUATION

- Les patients souffrant d'asthme, d'allergies et de polypes nasaux ou qui sont allergiques à la tartrazine sont davantage prédisposés à des réactions d'hypersensibilité.

Douleur: Évaluer l'amplitude du mouvement des articulations et noter le type de douleur, son siège et son intensité, avant l'administration du médicament et au pic de l'effet.
Fièvre: Prendre la température et noter les signes connexes suivants: diaphorèse, tachycardie, malaise, frissons.
Tests de laboratoire: La plupart des AINS allongent le temps de saignement en raison de l'inhibition de l'agrégation plaquettaire et, à des doses élevées, peuvent allonger le temps de prothrombine. Mesurer l'hématocrite à intervalles réguliers pendant toute la durée d'un traitement prolongé à doses élevées afin de déceler une hémorragie gastro-intestinale.

DIAGNOSTICS INFIRMIERS POSSIBLES

- Douleur aiguë (Indications).
- Risque de température corporelle anormale (Indications).
- Connaissances insuffisantes sur le traitement médicamenteux (Enseignement au patient et à ses proches).

INTERVENTIONS INFIRMIÈRES

PO: Administrer les AINS avec des aliments ou après les repas ou encore en même temps qu'un antiacide pour réduire l'irritation gastrique.

ENSEIGNEMENT AU PATIENT ET À SES PROCHES

- Expliquer au patient qu'il doit prendre les AINS avec un grand verre d'eau et rester en position verticale pendant 15 à 30 minutes après l'avoir pris.
- Inciter le patient à ne pas consommer d'alcool en même temps que ces médicaments afin de réduire le risque d'irritation gastrique; 3 verres ou plus d'alcool par jour peuvent augmenter le risque d'hémorragie digestive lors de la prise d'aspirine ou d'AINS. Recommander au patient de ne pas prendre en même temps de l'acétaminophène, de l'aspirine ou des AINS pendant plus de quelques jours, sauf recommandation médicale contraire, afin de prévenir la néphropathie induite par les analgésiques.

- Recommander au patient qui suit un traitement prolongé et qui doit subir une intervention chirurgicale d'avertir le professionnel de la santé qu'il suit un traitement par ce type de médicament. Il peut s'avérer nécessaire d'interrompre le traitement par l'AINS avant une chirurgie.

VÉRIFICATION DE L'EFFICACITÉ THÉRAPEUTIQUE

L'efficacité du traitement peut être démontrée par: le soulagement de la douleur légère à modérée ■ la baisse de la fièvre.

ANTI-INFLAMMATOIRES NON STÉROÏDIENS INCLUS DANS LE *GUIDE*

aspirine (acide acétylsalicylique), 111
célécoxib, 201
diclofénac, 342
étodolac, 457
flurbiprofène, 512
ibuprofène, 587
indométhacine, 610
kétoprofène, 671
kétorolac, 673
méloxicam, 744
nabumétone, 825
naproxène, 836
naproxène sodique, 836
oxaprozine, 901
piroxicam, 981
sulindac, 1138
tolmétine, 1201

pour usage ophtalmique
diclofénac, 1358
kétorolac, 1358

ANTINÉOPLASIQUES

INDICATIONS

Traitement de diverses tumeurs solides, lymphomes et leucémies ■ Certains antinéoplasiques sont également utilisés dans le traitement de certaines maladies auto-immunes comme la polyarthrite rhumatoïde (cyclophosphamide [usage non approuvé], méthotrexate) ■ On les administre souvent sous forme d'association médicamenteuse pour réduire la toxicité de chacun des agents et pour intensifier la réponse thérapeutique ■ La chimiothérapie peut être associée à d'autres modes de traitement, comme les interventions chirurgicales et la radiothérapie ■ Les posologies varient grandement selon la gravité de la maladie, les autres médicaments administrés et l'état du patient ■ Certaines préparations nouvelles (doxorubicine), encapsulées dans une membrane lipidique, sont moins toxiques.

MÉCANISME D'ACTION

Les mécanismes d'action des antinéoplasiques sont très différents (voir le tableau ci-dessous). Le plus souvent, ces médicaments modifient la synthèse ou la fonction de l'ADN. Cependant, leur effet peut ne pas se limiter aux cellules néoplasiques seules.

MÉCANISME D'ACTION DE DIVERS ANTINÉOPLASIQUES

Mécanisme d'action	Agents		Effet sur le cycle cellulaire
Les **agents hormonaux inhibiteurs de l'aromatase** inhibent l'enzyme responsable de la formation des œstrogènes.	anastrazole létrozole		Sans objet.
Les **alcaloïdes extraits de la pervenche** entravent la mitose.	vinblastine vincristine	vinorelbine	Effet spécifique sur la phase M du cycle cellulaire (mitose).
Les **alkylants** entraînent la formation d'une liaison entre deux chaînes d'ADN.	busulfan carboplatine carmustine chlorambucil cisplatine cyclophosphamide	ifosfamide méchloréthamine melphalan oxaliplatin témozolomide	Effet non spécifique.

MÉCANISME D'ACTION	AGENTS		EFFET SUR LE CYCLE CELLULAIRE
Les **anthracyclines** entravent la synthèse de l'ADN et de l'ARN.	daunorubicine doxorubicine	épirubicine idarubicine	Effet non spécifique.
Les **antibiotiques antitumoraux** entravent la synthèse de l'ADN et de l'ARN.	bléomycine mitomycine	mitoxantrone	Effet non spécifique (sauf pour la bléomycine).
Les **antimétabolites** entravent la synthèse de l'ADN et des protéines.	capécitabine cytarabine fluorouracile gemcitabine	hydroxyurée méthotrexate pemetrexed	Effet spécifique qui s'exerce surtout au cours de la phase S de la synthèse de l'ADN.
Les **dérivés de la podophyllotoxine** inhibent la topoisomérase II.	étoposide		Effet spécifique sur une phase du cycle cellulaire.
Les **enzymes** provoquent la déplétion de l'asparagine.	asparaginase pégaspargase		Effet spécifique sur une phase du cycle cellulaire.
Les **inhibiteurs enzymatiques** inhibent la topoisomérase I.	irinotécan topotécan		Effet spécifique sur une phase du cycle cellulaire.
Les **hormones de synthèse** et les **bloqueurs des œstrogèneset de la testostérone** modifient l'équilibre hormonal dans les tumeurs sensibles.	bicalutamide flutamide goséréline leuprolide médroxyprogestérone	mégestrol nilutamide tamoxifène torémifène	Inconnu.
Les **immunomodulateurs** modulent la réponse immunitaire.	aldesleukine alentuzumab bevacizumab interféron	rituximab thalidomide trastuzumab	Inconnu.
Les **taxoïdes** interrompent l'interphase et la mitose.	docétaxel paclitaxel		Effet spécifique sur une phase du cycle cellulaire.
Les **inhibiteurs de l'activation des kinases** interfèrent avec la prolifération et la survie des cellules cancéreuses.	gefitinib imatinib		Inconnu.
Mécanismes divers.	altrétamine procarbazine		Inconnu.

CONTRE-INDICATIONS, PRÉCAUTIONS ET MISES EN GARDE

Contre-indications: Antécédents d'hypersensibilité; consulter la monographie de chaque médicament.

Précautions et mises en garde: Administrer ces agents avec prudence en présence d'une infection, d'une diminution de la réserve médullaire ou d'une autre maladie débilitante ■ Il faut également les administrer avec prudence aux patients qui suivent une radiothérapie et aux patientes en âge de procréer ■ Consulter la monographie de chaque médicament.

INTERACTIONS

L'**allopurinol** diminue le métabolisme de la mercaptopurine ■ La toxicité par le méthotrexate peut être aggravée par d'autres **médicaments néphrotoxiques** ou par de fortes doses d'**aspirine** ou d'**AINS** ■ Effet additif sur la dépression de la moelle osseuse ■ Consulter la monographie de chaque médicament.

SOINS INFIRMIERS

ÉVALUATION DE LA SITUATION

- Surveiller les signes d'aplasie médullaire. Suivre de près les saignements (saignement des gencives, ecchymoses, pétéchies, présence de sang dans les selles, dans l'urine et dans les vomissements). En cas de thrombopénie, éviter les injections IM et la prise de température par voie rectale. Appliquer une pression sur les points de ponction veineuse pendant 10 minutes. Évaluer les signes d'infection en présence de neutropénie. Une anémie peut survenir. Rechercher les signes de fatigue accrue, de dyspnée et d'hypotension orthostatique.

- Effectuer le bilan des ingesta et des excreta, noter l'appétit du patient et son apport nutritionnel. On peut administrer des antiémétiques en prophylaxie. La modification de l'alimentation en fonction des aliments que le patient tolère peut permettre de maintenir l'équilibre hydroélectrolytique et une nutrition adéquate.
- Évaluer avec soin les points d'injection IV et s'assurer du bon fonctionnement du matériel de perfusion. Arrêter immédiatement la perfusion en cas de douleur, d'érythème qui se forme le long de la veine ou d'infiltration. L'infiltration de certains médicaments peut provoquer l'ulcération et la nécrose des tissus.
- Suivre de près les symptômes de goutte (concentrations accrues d'acide urique, douleurs articulaires et œdème). Encourager le patient à boire au moins 2 000 mL de liquide par jour, si son état le permet. On peut administrer de l'allopurinol pour diminuer les concentrations d'acide urique. Le médecin peut recommander l'alcalinisation de l'urine pour favoriser l'excrétion d'acide urique.

DIAGNOSTICS INFIRMIERS POSSIBLES

- Risque d'infection (Effets secondaires).
- Alimentation déficiente (Réactions indésirables).
- Connaissances insuffisantes sur le traitement médicamenteux (Enseignement au patient et à ses proches).

INTERVENTIONS INFIRMIÈRES

- Préparer les solutions à injecter sous une hotte à flux laminaire. Porter des gants, une blouse et un masque pendant la manipulation de ces médicaments. Mettre au rebut le matériel dans les contenants réservés à cette fin (voir à l'annexe H les directives destinées au personnel qui administre des antinéoplasiques).
- Vérifier soigneusement la dose à administrer. On a signalé des décès à la suite d'erreurs de posologie.

ENSEIGNEMENT AU PATIENT ET À SES PROCHES

- Expliquer au patient qu'il doit éviter les foules et les personnes contagieuses. Lui recommander de signaler immédiatement à un professionnel de la santé tout symptôme d'infection.
- Recommander au patient de signaler les saignements inhabituels. Lui expliquer les précautions à prendre en cas de thrombopénie.
- Prévenir le patient que ces médicaments peuvent diminuer la fonction gonadique; lui conseiller cependant de continuer à prendre des mesures de contraception, car la plupart de ces médicaments sont dotés de propriétés tératogènes. Recommander à la patiente d'informer immédiatement un professionnel de la santé si elle pense être enceinte.
- Expliquer au patient qu'il risque de perdre ses cheveux. Explorer avec lui les stratégies lui permettant de s'adapter à ce changement.
- Recommander au patient d'observer ses muqueuses buccales à la recherche de signes d'érythème et d'ulcération. Si une ulcération se manifeste, conseiller au patient de remplacer la brosse à dents par une brosse-éponge et de se rincer la bouche avec de l'eau après avoir bu ou mangé. On peut administrer des agents topiques si la douleur l'empêche de manger. La douleur associée à la stomatite peut dicter le traitement par des analgésiques opioïdes.

- Expliquer au patient qu'il ne doit pas se faire vacciner sans recommandation expresse d'un professionnel de la santé. Les antinéoplasiques peuvent réduire la réponse des anticorps et augmenter le risque de réactions indésirables.
- Expliquer au patient la nécessité des examens de suivi et d'examens diagnostiques fréquents.

VÉRIFICATION DE L'EFFICACITÉ THÉRAPEUTIQUE

L'efficacité du traitement peut être démontrée par: la diminution de la taille et de l'étendue de la tumeur ■ l'amélioration de l'hématopoïèse chez les patients souffrant de leucémie.

ANTINÉOPLASIQUES INCLUS DANS LE *GUIDE*

ANTIPARKINSONIENS

INDICATIONS

Traitement de la maladie de Parkinson de diverses étiologies, dont les maladies dégénératives, l'intoxication, les infections, les cancers ou les troubles d'origine médicamenteuse.

MÉCANISME D'ACTION

Le traitement médicamenteux du syndrome parkinsonien et des autres dyskinésies vise à rétablir l'équilibre naturel de deux neurotransmetteurs importants du SNC, l'acétylcholine et la dopamine. Ce déséquilibre correspond à un déficit en dopamine qui entraîne une activité cholinergique excessive. Les médicaments utilisés sont des anticholinergiques (benztropine et trihexyphénidyle) et des agonistes des récepteurs dopaminergiques (bromocriptine, lévodopa, pergolide, etc.) ■ On trouve également parmi ces médicaments les inhibiteurs de la cathécol-O-méthyl-transférase (entacapone) et l'inhibiteur sélectif (type B) de la monoamine-oxydase (sélégiline) ■ Le pramipexole et le ropinirole sont deux agonistes de la dopamine qui ne sont pas dérivés de l'ergot de seigle ■ L'entacapone inhibe l'enzyme qui décompose la dopamine. De ce fait, les effets de celle-ci sont intensifiés ■ La cabergoline inhibe la sécrétion de la prolactine par une action dopaminergique de type agoniste ■ La sélégiline inactive la monoamine-oxydase en se liant à elle de façon irréversible aux sites de type B. Cette inactivation entraîne une élévation des concentrations de dopamine dans le SNC.

CONTRE-INDICATIONS, PRÉCAUTIONS ET MISES EN GARDE

Contre-indications: Glaucome à angle fermé (l'administration d'anticholinergiques est déconseillée) ■ La sélégiline est contre-indiquée si le patient reçoit un traitement concomitant par la mépéridine ou par un analgésique opioïde (risque de réactions d'issue fatale).

Précautions et mises en garde: Chez les patients qui souffrent de cardiopathie grave, d'obstruction du pylore ou d'hypertrophie de la prostate, l'administration de plusieurs de ces agents doit s'accompagner de prudence ■ *Sélégiline* – L'administration de doses supérieures à 10 mg/jour entraîne un risque accru de réactions hypertensives si le patient consomme en même temps des aliments contenant de la tyramine ou s'il prend certains médicaments.

INTERACTIONS

La **pyridoxine**, les **IMAO**, les **benzodiazépines**, la **phénytoïne**, les **phénothiazines** et l'**halopéridol** peuvent neutraliser les effets de la lévodopa (effet antagoniste) ■ Les **antagonistes de la dopamine** (**phénothiazines**, **métoclopramide**) peuvent réduire l'efficacité des agonistes de la dopamine ■ L'administration concomitante de **mépéridine** ou d'autres **analgésiques opioïdes** et de la sélégiline peut provoquer une réaction d'issue fatale (excitation, transpiration, rigidité, hypertension ou hypotension et coma).

SOINS INFIRMIERS

ÉVALUATION DE LA SITUATION

- Suivre de près, avant l'administration du médicament et pendant toute la durée du traitement, les symptômes parkinsoniens et extrapyramidaux suivants: akinésie, rigidité, tremblements, mouvements d'émiettement, faciès figé, démarche traînante, spasmes musculaires, mouvements de torsion et bouche ouverte laissant s'échapper la salive (sialorrhée). À cause des fluctuations dans les réactions aux médicaments (effet *on-off*), les symptômes peuvent apparaître ou disparaître soudainement.

- Mesurer la pression artérielle à intervalles fréquents, pendant toute la durée du traitement. Inciter le patient à demeurer en position couchée lors de l'administration de la première dose de bromocriptine et pendant plusieurs heures par la suite, à cause du risque d'hypotension grave.

DIAGNOSTICS INFIRMIERS POSSIBLES

- Mobilité physique réduite (Indications).
- Risque d'accident (Indications).
- Connaissances insuffisantes sur le traitement médicamenteux (Enseignement au patient et à ses proches).

INTERVENTIONS INFIRMIÈRES

- Association de carbidopa et de lévodopa ou de bensérazide et de lévodopa: les chiffres qui suivent le nom de chaque médicament correspondent à la teneur respective en milligrammes.

ENSEIGNEMENT AU PATIENT ET À SES PROCHES

- Prévenir le patient que ces agents peut provoquer de la somnolence ou des étourdissements. Lui conseiller de ne pas conduire et d'éviter les activités qui exigent sa vigilance jusqu'à ce qu'on ait la certitude que le médicament qui lui a été prescrit n'entraîne pas ces effets chez lui.
- Conseiller au patient de changer lentement de position afin de réduire le risque d'hypotension orthostatique.
- Conseiller au patient de se rincer fréquemment la bouche, de pratiquer une bonne hygiène buccale et de consommer de la gomme ou des bonbons sans sucre pour soulager la sécheresse de la bouche. Lui recommander de prévenir un professionnel de la santé si la sécheresse de la bouche persiste. (On pourrait lui prescrire des substituts de salive.) Lui recommander également de consulter un professionnel de la santé si la sécheresse de la bouche gêne le port des prothèses dentaires.
- Conseiller au patient de consulter le médecin ou le pharmacien avant de prendre un médicament en vente libre, particulièrement un médicament contre le rhume, et avant de consommer des boissons alcoolisées. Prévenir le patient qui prend de la lévodopa que les multivitamines lui sont déconseillées. La vitamine B_6 (pyridoxine) peut contrecarrer l'effet de la lévodopa.
- Prévenir le patient que le médicament peut diminuer la sécrétion de sueur et que la chaleur pourrait l'incommoder. Lui conseiller de rester dans une pièce climatisée par temps chaud.
- Recommander au patient de faire de l'exercice et de consommer plus d'aliments riches en fibres et plus de liquides pour réduire les effets constipants du médicament.
- Recommander au patient de signaler à un professionnel de la santé les symptômes suivants: confusion, rash, rétention urinaire, constipation grave, modification de la vision, ainsi que l'aggravation des symptômes parkinsoniens.
- Expliquer au patient qui prend de la sélégiline et à ses proches les signes et les symptômes d'une crise hypertensive déclenchée par les IMAO (céphalées graves, douleurs thoraciques, nausées, vomissements, photosensibilité, pupilles dilatées). Conseiller au patient de signaler immédiatement à un professionnel de la santé les céphalées graves ou tout autre symptôme inhabituel.

VÉRIFICATION DE L'EFFICACITÉ THÉRAPEUTIQUE

L'efficacité du traitement peut être démontrée par: la disparition des signes et des symptômes parkinsoniens ■ la résolution des symptômes extrapyramidaux induits par les médicaments.

ANTIPARKINSONIENS INCLUS DANS LE *GUIDE*

agonistes de la dopamine
bromocriptine, 156
bensérazide/lévodopa, 701
cabergoline, 177
carbidopa/lévodopa, 701
lévodopa, 701
pramipexole, 993
ropinirole, 1082

anticholinergiques
benztropine, 138
procyclidine, 1012
trihexyphénidyle, 1221

inhibiteur de la cathécol-O-méthyltransférase
entacapone, 420

inhibiteur sélectif (type B) de la monoamine-oxydase
sélégiline, 1096

autres
amantadine, 52

ANTIPLAQUETTAIRES

INDICATIONS

Les agents antiplaquettaires sont utilisés dans le traitement et la prévention des épisodes thromboemboliques, tels que l'accident vasculaire cérébral et l'infarctus du myocarde.

MÉCANISME D'ACTION

Inhibition de l'agrégation plaquettaire et prolongation du temps de saignement ■ L'aspirine, le clopidogrel, le dipyridamole et la ticlopidine sont utilisés dans la prévention des infarctus du myocarde ou des accidents vasculaires cérébraux ■ L'abciximab, l'eptifibatide et le tirofiban sont utilisés dans le traitement de divers syndromes coronariens aigus et lors des interventions coronariennes percutanées. Ces agents ont été administrés de façon concomitante ou séquentielle avec des agents anticoagulants et thrombolytiques.

CONTRE-INDICATIONS, PRÉCAUTIONS ET MISES EN GARDE

Contre-indications: Hypersensibilité ■ Ulcère ■ Hémorragie ■ Chirurgie récente.
Précautions et mises en garde: Patients présentant un risque de saignement (traumatisme, intervention chirurgicale) ■ Antécédents d'hémorragie digestive ou d'ulcère ■ **OBST., ALLAITEMENT, PÉD.**: L'innocuité de ces agents n'a pas été établie.

INTERACTIONS

Risque accru de saignements lors de l'administration concomitante d'**AINS**, d'**héparine**, d'**agents thrombolytiques** ou de **warfarine**.

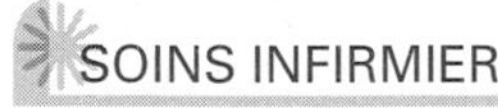

SOINS INFIRMIERS

ÉVALUATION DE LA SITUATION

- Rester à l'affût des signes de saignement et d'hémorragie (saignement des gencives, épistaxis, formation inhabituelle d'ecchymoses, selles noires et goudronneuses, hématurie, chute de l'hématocrite ou de la pression artérielle, présence de sang occulte dans les selles, dans l'urine ou dans les produits d'aspiration nasogastrique).
- Examiner le patient pour déceler tout signe de thrombose additionnelle ou accrue. Les symptômes dépendront de la région touchée.
- Observer le patient prenant des agents antiplaquettaires à intervalles réguliers pendant toute la durée du traitement, à la recherche des symptômes d'accident vasculaire cérébral, de maladie vasculaire périphérique ou d'infarctus du myocarde.

Tests de laboratoire:

- Mesurer, à intervalles fréquents au cours du traitement, le temps de céphaline activée (TCA), lors du traitement par l'héparine à pleine dose, le temps de prothrombine (PT) ou le rapport normalisé international (RNI), lors du traitement par la warfarine ainsi que l'hématocrite et les autres facteurs de coagulation pour les deux types de traitement.
- Noter le temps de saignement pendant toute la durée du traitement antiplaquettaire. On prévoit un temps de saignement prolongé qui dépend de la dose et du temps écoulé depuis l'administration.

DIAGNOSTICS INFIRMIERS POSSIBLES

- Irrigation tissulaire inefficace (Indications).
- Risque d'accident (Effets secondaires).
- Connaissances insuffisantes sur le traitement médicamenteux (Enseignement au patient et à ses proches).

INTERVENTIONS INFIRMIÈRES

- Informer tout le personnel soignant que ces patients suivent un traitement antiplaquettaire. Il faut appliquer une pression sur les points de ponction veineuse et sur les points d'injection pour prévenir l'hémorragie ou la formation d'un hématome.
- Utiliser une pompe à perfusion lors des perfusions continues pour s'assurer que le patient reçoit la dose appropriée.

ENSEIGNEMENT AU PATIENT ET À SES PROCHES

- Recommander au patient d'éviter les activités qui pourraient entraîner des blessures, d'utiliser une brosse à dents à poils doux et un rasoir électrique et de signaler immédiatement à un professionnel de la santé tout saignement ou ecchymose inhabituels.
- Conseiller au patient de consulter un professionnel de la santé avant de prendre un médicament en vente libre, particulièrement des préparations renfermant de l'aspirine, des AINS ou de l'alcool.

VÉRIFICATION DE L'EFFICACITÉ THÉRAPEUTIQUE

L'efficacité du traitement peut être démontrée par: la prévention d'une coagulation non souhaitée et de ses séquelles sans signes d'hémorragie ■ la prévention des accidents vasculaires cérébraux, des infarctus du myocarde et des décès par atteinte vasculaire chez les patients à risque.

ANTIPLAQUETTAIRES INCLUS DANS LE *GUIDE*

aspirine (acide acétylsalicylique), 111
clopidogrel, 257
dipyridamole, 367
eptifibatide, 430
ticlopidine, 1186
tirofiban, 1197

ANTIPSYCHOTIQUES

INDICATIONS

Traitement des psychoses aiguës et chroniques, particulièrement lorsqu'elles s'accompagnent d'une activité psychomotrice accrue ■ L'usage de la clozapine est réservé au traitement de la schizophrénie réfractaire aux interventions classiques ■ Certains antipsychotiques sont également dotés de propriétés antihistaminiques ou antiémétiques ■ La chlorpromazine est également utilisée dans le traitement du hoquet incoercible.

MÉCANISME D'ACTION

Les antipsychotiques bloquent les récepteurs dopaminergiques du cerveau et inhibent la libération de la dopamine et son cycle de reconstitution (*turnover*) ■ Ils sont également dotés de propriétés anticholinergiques et ils bloquent les récepteurs alpha-adrénergiques ■ Les principaux antipsychotiques sont des phénothiazines, sauf l'halopéridol, qui est une butyrophénone, et la clozapine, l'olanzapine, la quétiapine et la rispéridone, qui font partie des agents divers. Les nouveaux agents, comme l'olanzapine, la quétiapine et la rispéridone peuvent entraîner moins de réactions indésirables ■ Les phénothiazines n'entraînent pas toutes le même degré de sédation (la chlorpromazine et la thioridazine provoquent la sédation la plus forte) ni les mêmes effets extrapyramidaux (la prochlorpérazine et la trifluopérazine provoquent les effets les plus marqués) ou anticholinergiques (la chlorpromazine induit les effets les plus marqués).

CONTRE-INDICATIONS, PRÉCAUTIONS ET MISES EN GARDE

Contre-indications: Hypersensibilité ■ Risque de réactions de sensibilité croisée entre les phénothiazines ■ Ne pas administrer ces agents aux patients qui présentent un glaucome à angle fermé ni aux patients atteints d'une dépression du SNC.

Précautions et mises en garde: OBST., ALLAITEMENT: L'innocuité de ces médicaments pendant la grossesse et l'allaitement n'a pas été établie ■ Administrer ces médicaments avec prudence aux patients souffrant de maladie cardiaque symptomatique ■ Pendant le traitement par ces médicaments, les patients devraient éviter les températures extrêmes ■ Administrer les antipsychotiques avec prudence aux patients gravement malades ou débilités, aux patients diabétiques et à ceux souffrant d'insuffisance respiratoire, d'hyperplasie de la prostate ou d'obstruction intestinale ■ Ces médicaments peuvent abaisser le seuil de convulsion ■ La clozapine peut entraîner l'agranulocytose ■ La plupart des agents peuvent induire le syndrome malin des neuroleptiques ■ Ces médicaments ne devraient pas être utilisés systématiquement pour traiter l'anxiété ou l'agitation qui n'est pas reliée à une psychose.

INTERACTIONS

Risque d'effets hypotenseurs additifs lors de la prise concomitante d'**antihypertenseurs**, de **dérivés nitrés** ou d'**alcool** ■ Les **antiacides** peuvent diminuer l'absorption des antipsychotiques ■ Le **phénobarbital** peut en accélérer le métabolisme et en diminuer l'efficacité ■ Effets additifs sur la dépression du système nerveux central lors de l'administration concomitante d'autres **dépresseurs du SNC** dont l'**alcool**, les **antihistaminiques**, les **antidépresseurs**, les **analgésiques opioïdes** ou les **hypnosédatifs** ■ Le **lithium** peut diminuer les concentrations sanguines des phénothiazines ainsi que leur efficacité ■ Les antipsychotiques peuvent réduire la réponse à la **lévodopa** ■ L'administration concomitante d'**agents antithyroïdiens** peut augmenter les risques d'agranulocytose.

SOINS INFIRMIERS

ÉVALUATION DE LA SITUATION

- Noter l'état de conscience du patient (orientation, humeur, comportement), avant l'administration du médicament et à intervalles réguliers tout au long du traitement.
- Mesurer la pression artérielle (en position assise, debout et couchée) ainsi que le pouls et la fréquence respiratoire, avant l'administration du médicament et à intervalles fréquents pendant la période d'ajustement de la posologie.
- Observer attentivement le patient pendant qu'il prend le médicament pour s'assurer qu'il l'a bien avalé.

- Suivre de près l'apparition de l'akathisie (agitation ou désir de bouger continuellement) et de symptômes extrapyramidaux, de symptômes parkinsoniens (difficulté d'élocution ou de déglutition, perte d'équilibre, mouvements d'émiettement, faciès figé, démarche traînante, rigidité, tremblements) et de symptômes dystoniques (spasmes musculaires, torsions, secousses musculaires, incapacité de bouger les yeux, faiblesse des bras ou des jambes), tous les 2 mois pendant la durée du traitement et de 8 à 12 semaines après qu'il a pris fin. Les effets parkinsoniens sont plus courants chez les personnes âgées, et les symptômes dystoniques, chez les jeunes patients. Informer immédiatement un professionnel de la santé de l'apparition de ces symptômes; il peut s'avérer nécessaire de réduire la dose ou d'abandonner le traitement. Le médecin peut recommander l'administration de trihexyphénidyle ou de diphenhydramine pour maîtriser ces symptômes.
- Suivre de près l'apparition des symptômes suivants de dyskinésie tardive: mouvements rythmiques et incontrôlés de la bouche, du visage et des membres; émission de bruits secs avec les lèvres, moue; gonflement des joues; mastication incontrôlée; mouvements rapides de la langue. Signaler immédiatement à un professionnel de la santé ces symptômes, qui peuvent être irréversibles.
- Rester à l'affût des symptômes suivants du syndrome malin des neuroleptiques: fièvre, détresse respiratoire, tachycardie, convulsions, diaphorèse, hypertension ou hypotension, pâleur, fatigue, forte rigidité musculaire, perte de contrôle de la vessie. Informer immédiatement un professionnel de la santé de l'apparition de ces symptômes.

DIAGNOSTICS INFIRMIERS POSSIBLES

- Opérations de la pensée perturbées (Indications).
- Connaissances insuffisantes sur le traitement médicamenteux (Enseignement au patient et à ses proches).
- Non-observance du traitement médicamenteux (Enseignement au patient et à ses proches).

INTERVENTIONS INFIRMIÈRES

- Éviter les éclaboussures des solutions sur les mains, étant donné les risques de dermatite de contact.
- Interrompre le traitement aux phénothiazines, 48 heures avant une myélographie, et ne le reprendre que 24 heures plus tard, car ces médicaments abaissent le seuil de convulsion.

PO:

- Administrer ces médicaments avec des aliments, du lait ou un grand verre d'eau afin de diminuer l'irritation gastrique.
- Diluer la plupart des concentrés oraux dans 120 mL d'eau distillée ou d'eau courante acidifiée ou de jus de fruits, juste avant de les administrer.

ENSEIGNEMENT AU PATIENT ET À SES PROCHES

- Expliquer au patient qu'il doit respecter rigoureusement la posologie recommandée. L'avertir qu'il ne doit jamais sauter de dose ni remplacer une dose manquée par une double dose. Le sevrage brusque peut provoquer une gastrite, des nausées, des vomissements, des étourdissements, des céphalées, de la tachycardie et de l'insomnie.
- Recommander au patient de rester couché pendant au moins 30 minutes après l'administration parentérale du médicament afin d'en réduire les effets hypotenseurs.
- Recommander au patient de changer lentement de position afin de réduire le risque d'hypotension orthostatique.
- Prévenir le patient que les antipsychotiques peuvent provoquer de la somnolence. Lui conseiller de ne pas conduire et d'éviter les activités qui exigent sa vigilance jusqu'à ce qu'on ait la certitude que le médicament n'entraîne pas cet effet chez lui.

- Mettre en garde le patient contre la consommation d'alcool ou d'autres dépresseurs du SNC en même temps qu'un antipsychotique.
- Recommander au patient d'utiliser un écran solaire et de porter des vêtements protecteurs lors des expositions au soleil pour prévenir les réactions de photosensibilité. Lui recommander également d'éviter les températures extrêmes, car ces médicaments altèrent la thermorégulation.
- Recommander au patient de faire de l'exercice et de consommer plus d'aliments riches en fibres et plus de liquides pour réduire les effets constipants du médicament.
- Conseiller au patient de se rincer fréquemment la bouche, de pratiquer une bonne hygiène buccale et de consommer de la gomme ou des bonbons sans sucre pour soulager la sécheresse de la bouche.
- Recommander au patient qui doit suivre un autre traitement ou subir une intervention chirurgicale d'avertir le professionnel de la santé qu'il suit un traitement avec un agent de cette classe.
- Expliquer au patient l'importance des examens réguliers de suivi et de la psychothérapie, le cas échéant.

VÉRIFICATION DE L'EFFICACITÉ THÉRAPEUTIQUE

L'efficacité du traitement peut être démontrée par: la diminution de l'excitation et un moindre recours à des comportements paranoïdes ou au repli sur soi ▪ le soulagement des nausées et des vomissements ▪ la disparition du hoquet incoercible.

ANTIPSYCHOTIQUES INCLUS DANS LE *GUIDE*

butyrophénones
dropéridol, 406
halopéridol, 554

phénothiazines
chlorpromazine, 230
fluphénazine, 508
méthotriméprazine, 774
prochlorpérazine, 1008
trifluopérazine, 1218

divers
clozapine, 263
loxapine, 723
olanzapine, 882
quétiapine, 1045
rispéridone, 1072

ANTIPYRÉTIQUES

INDICATIONS

Abaissement de la fièvre de diverses étiologies: infection ▪ inflammation ▪ néoplasmes.

MÉCANISME D'ACTION

Les antipyrétiques abaissent la fièvre en modifiant la thermorégulation du système nerveux central et en inhibant en périphérie l'activité des prostaglandines ▪ Plusieurs antipyrétiques affectent la fonction plaquettaire. Parmi ceux-ci, l'aspirine a l'effet le plus marqué sur la fonction plaquettaire lorsqu'on la compare à l'ibuprofène et au kétoprofène.

CONTRE-INDICATIONS, PRÉCAUTIONS ET MISES EN GARDE

Contre-indications: Ne pas administrer de l'aspirine ou de l'indométhacine aux patients souffrant de maladies hémorragiques (le risque de saignement est moindre lors de l'administration d'autres anti-inflammatoires non stéroïdiens [AINS]) ■ **Péd.**: Éviter d'administrer de l'aspirine aux enfants et aux adolescents.

Précautions et mises en garde: L'administration d'AINS doit s'accompagner d'une très grande prudence chez les patients souffrant d'ulcère et ne doit se faire que sous supervision médicale ■ Éviter l'administration prolongée de fortes doses d'acétaminophène ■ Éviter d'administrer des AINS en cas d'insuffisance rénale modérée à grave.

INTERACTIONS

Les doses élevées d'aspirine peuvent déplacer d'autres **médicaments qui se lient fortement aux protéines** ■ L'administration simultanée d'**aspirine**, d'autres **AINS** ou de **corticostéroïdes** a des effets irritants additifs sur le tractus gastro-intestinal ■ L'aspirine et les autres AINS peuvent augmenter les risques d'hémorragie lorsqu'ils sont administrés en même temps que d'autres **agents qui affectent l'hémostase** (**anticoagulants**, **thrombolytiques** et **certains antinéoplasiques**).

SOINS INFIRMIERS

ÉVALUATION DE LA SITUATION

- Mesurer la température; suivre de près les symptômes connexes suivants: diaphorèse, tachycardie et malaise.

DIAGNOSTICS INFIRMIERS POSSIBLES

- Risque de température corporelle anormale (Indications).
- Connaissances insuffisantes sur le traitement médicamenteux (Enseignement au patient et à ses proches).

INTERVENTIONS INFIRMIÈRES

- Administrer l'agent avec des aliments ou des antiacides pour réduire l'irritation gastro-intestinale (AINS).
- Présentation: préparations orales, préparations rectales et associations avec d'autres médicaments.

ENSEIGNEMENT AU PATIENT ET À SES PROCHES

- Recommander au patient de consulter un professionnel de la santé si la fièvre ne diminue pas lors de la prise de doses habituelles, si la température est supérieure à 39,5 °C ou si la fièvre dure plus de 3 jours.
- Les centres épidémiologiques mettent en garde contre l'administration de l'aspirine aux enfants et aux adolescents souffrant de varicelle, de maladies pseudogrippales ou de maladies virales, en raison du risque d'apparition du syndrome de Reye.

VÉRIFICATION DE L'EFFICACITÉ THÉRAPEUTIQUE

L'efficacité du traitement peut être démontrée par: la diminution de la fièvre.

ANTIPYRÉTIQUES INCLUS DANS LE *GUIDE*

ANTIRÉTROVIRAUX

INDICATIONS

Le but du traitement antirétroviral dans la prise en charge de l'infection par le VIH est l'augmentation du nombre de lymphocytes CD4 et la diminution de la charge virale. Le succès thérapeutique se traduit généralement par un ralentissement de l'évolution de la maladie, une amélioration de la qualité de vie et une diminution du risque d'infections opportunistes ■ L'usage périnatal de ces agents permet de prévenir la transmission du virus au fœtus ■ On recommande un traitement prophylactique par des antirétroviraux à la suite d'une exposition accidentelle au virus.

MÉCANISME D'ACTION

En raison de l'émergence rapide d'une résistance et des effets toxiques des différents agents, l'infection par le VIH est presque toujours traitée au moyen d'une polythérapie. Le choix des agents et la posologie recommandée dépendent des effets toxiques de chaque agent, des maladies sous-jacentes, des traitements médicamenteux concomitants et de la gravité de la maladie. On utilise diverses associations pouvant inclure jusqu'à quatre agents administrés simultanément.

CONTRE-INDICATIONS, PRÉCAUTIONS ET MISES EN GARDE

Contre-indications: Hypersensibilité. Puisque les effets toxiques de ces agents sont très différents, consulter la monographie de chaque médicament pour obtenir de plus amples renseignements à ce sujet.

Précautions et mises en garde: En présence d'une insuffisance rénale, il faut adapter la posologie de bon nombre de ces agents ■ Les inhibiteurs de la protéase peuvent induire l'hyperglycémie et devraient être utilisés avec prudence chez les diabétiques ■ Certains antirétroviraux peuvent exposer les hémophiles à un risque de saignement ■ Consulter la monographie de chaque médicament pour obtenir de plus amples renseignements à ce sujet.

INTERACTIONS

On note de nombreuses interactions importantes. Les antirétroviraux sont affectés par les médicaments qui modifient le métabolisme; certains agents modifient eux-mêmes le métabolisme. Voir la monographie de chaque médicament.

SOINS INFIRMIERS

ÉVALUATION DE LA SITUATION

- Observer étroitement le patient pour déceler tout changement dans la gravité des symptômes de l'infection par le VIH et l'apparition des symptômes d'infections opportunistes tout au long du traitement.

Tests de laboratoire: Surveiller la charge virale et la numération des lymphocytes CD4, avant l'administration initiale du traitement et à intervalles réguliers pendant toute sa durée.

DIAGNOSTICS INFIRMIERS POSSIBLES

- Risque d'infection (Indications).
- Connaissances insuffisantes sur le traitement médicamenteux (Enseignement au patient et à ses proches).
- Non-observance du traitement médicamenteux (Enseignement au patient et à ses proches).

INTERVENTIONS INFIRMIÈRES

- Administrer les doses à intervalles réguliers.

ENSEIGNEMENT AU PATIENT ET À SES PROCHES

- Inciter le patient à respecter rigoureusement la posologie recommandée et à prendre le médicament à intervalles réguliers, même s'il doit interrompre son sommeil. Insister sur le fait qu'il est important d'observer ce traitement, de ne pas prendre une quantité plus grande de médicament que celle qui a été prescrite et de ne pas abandonner le traitement sans consulter un professionnel de la santé au préalable. Prévenir le patient que s'il n'a pu prendre le médicament au moment habituel, il doit le prendre dès que possible à moins que ce ne soit presque l'heure prévue pour la dose suivante. Lui conseiller de ne jamais remplacer une dose manquée par une double dose. Informer le patient qu'on ne connaît pas les effets à long terme de ces médicaments.
- Expliquer au patient qu'il ne faut pas donner d'antirétroviraux à une autre personne.
- Expliquer au patient que les antirétroviraux ne guérissent pas le sida et qu'ils ne réduisent pas le risque de transmission du VIH à d'autres personnes par les rapports sexuels ou par la contamination du sang. Inciter le patient à utiliser un condom lors des rapports sexuels, à éviter le partage d'aiguilles et les dons de sang, afin de prévenir la transmission du virus du sida.
- Recommander au patient d'éviter de prendre des médicaments sur ordonnance ou en vente libre ou des produits naturels sans consulter au préalable un professionnel de la santé.
- Insister sur le fait qu'il est important de se soumettre à intervalles réguliers à des examens de suivi et à des analyses de sang permettant de déceler les effets secondaires et les bienfaits du traitement.

VÉRIFICATION DE L'EFFICACITÉ THÉRAPEUTIQUE

L'efficacité du traitement peut être démontrée par: la diminution de la charge virale et l'augmentation du nombre de lymphocytes CD4 chez les patients infectés par le VIH ▪ le ralentissement de l'évolution de l'infection par le VIH et la diminution du risque d'infections opportunistes.

ANTIRÉTROVIRAUX INCLUS DANS LE *GUIDE*

inhibiteurs de la protéase (IP)
amprénavir, 84
atazanavir, 114
fosamprénavir, 523
indinavir, 608
lopinavir/ritonavir, 716
nelfinavir, 841
ritonavir, 1075
saquinavir, 1091
tipranavir, 1194

inhibiteurs non nucléosidiques de la transcriptase inverse (INNTI)
délavirdine, 324
éfavirenz, 413
névirapine, 846

inhibiteurs nucléosidiques de la transcriptase inverse (INTI)
abacavir, 1
didanosine, 347
emtricitabine, 415
lamivudine, 680
stavudine, 1124
ténofovir disoproxil, 1154
zidovudine, 1275

inhibiteurs de la fusion du VIH-1
enfuvirtide, 417

ANTIRHUMATISMAUX

INDICATIONS

Les antirhumatismaux aident à prendre en charge les symptômes de la polyarthrite rhumatoïde (douleur, tuméfaction) et, dans les cas plus graves, à ralentir la destruction des articulations et à en préserver le fonctionnement ■ On administre les AINS et l'aspirine pour traiter des symptômes comme la douleur et la tuméfaction, afin de préserver la capacité de mouvement et d'améliorer la qualité de vie du patient ■ On réserve les corticostéroïdes aux cas plus graves qui s'accompagnent de douleur et de tuméfaction, surtout en raison de leurs effets secondaires accrus, particulièrement lors d'un usage prolongé. On peut aussi les administrer pour soulager les douleurs au cours d'une poussée aiguë de la maladie. Ni les AINS ni les corticostéroïdes ne peuvent prévenir l'évolution de la maladie ou la destruction des articulations ■ Les agents antirhumatismaux modificateurs de la maladie (ou AARMM) ralentissent l'évolution de la polyarthrite rhumatoïde et la destruction des articulations. On réserve les AARMM aux cas graves en raison de leur toxicité. Parfois, plusieurs mois de traitement peuvent s'écouler avant que les bienfaits des AARMM puissent être notés et maintenus. Des réactions indésirables graves et fréquentes peuvent dicter l'abandon du traitement, malgré ses bienfaits initiaux.

MÉCANISME D'ACTION

Les AINS et les corticostéroïdes ont des propriétés anti-inflammatoires puissantes. L'effet des AARMM s'exerce par différents mécanismes d'action (voir la monographie de chacun des agents). Cependant, la plupart d'entre eux suppriment la réponse auto-immune qui semble responsable de la destruction des articulations.

CONTRE-INDICATIONS, PRÉCAUTIONS ET MISES EN GARDE

Contre-indications: Hypersensibilité ■ Ne pas administrer des AINS aux patients allergiques à l'aspirine ■ Ne pas administrer des corticostéroïdes en présence d'infections évolutives non traitées.

Précautions et mises en garde: Administrer les AINS et les corticostéroïdes avec prudence aux patients ayant des antécédents de saignements GI ■ Administrer les corticostéroïdes avec prudence aux patients diabétiques ■ Un grand nombre d'AARMM ont des propriétés immunosuppressives; leur usage est déconseillé lorsque la suppression de la réponse immunitaire expose le patient à des risques graves, comme en cas d'infections évolutives, de cancer et de diabète non maîtrisé.

INTERACTIONS

Les AINS peuvent diminuer la réponse aux **diurétiques** et aux **antihypertenseurs** ■ Les corticostéroïdes peuvent élever l'hypokaliémie provoquée par d'autres médicaments et accroître le risque de toxicité par la **digoxine** ■ Les AARMM, administrés en même temps que d'autres **immunosuppresseurs**, peuvent accroître le risque de suppression grave du système immunitaire.

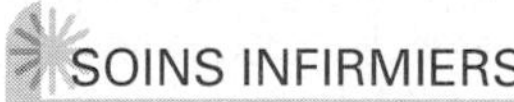

SOINS INFIRMIERS

ÉVALUATION DE LA SITUATION

■ Évaluer tous les mois la douleur, la tuméfaction et l'amplitude du mouvement articulaire.

DIAGNOSTICS INFIRMIERS POSSIBLES

■ Douleur chronique (Indications).

- Connaissances insuffisantes sur la maladie et sur le traitement médicamenteux (Enseignement au patient et à ses proches).

INTERVENTIONS INFIRMIÈRES

- Il faut administrer la plupart des agents à intervalles réguliers pour qu'on puisse bénéficier de leur plein effet.

ENSEIGNEMENT AU PATIENT ET À SES PROCHES

- Recommander au patient de prévenir un professionnel de la santé s'il ne note pas d'amélioration après quelques jours.

VÉRIFICATION DE L'EFFICACITÉ THÉRAPEUTIQUE

L'efficacité du traitement peut être démontrée par: l'amélioration des signes et des symptômes de polyarthrite rhumatoïde.

ANTIRHUMATISMAUX INCLUS DANS LE *GUIDE*

AARMM
adalimumab, 19
anakinra, 86
étanercept, 451
hydroxychloroquine, 579
infliximab, 613
léflunomide, 687
méthotrexate, 770
pénicillamine, 938
sulfasalazine, 1132

AINS
célécoxib, 201
flurbiprofène, 512
ibuprofène, 587
indométhacine, 610
kétoprofène, 671
nabumétone, 825
oxaprozine, 901
piroxicam, 981
sulindac, 1138
tolmétine, 1201

corticostéroïdes
bétaméthasone, 284
cortisone, 284
dexaméthasone, 284
hydrocortisone, 284
méthylprednisolone, 284
prednisolone, 284
prednisone, 284
triamcinolone, 284

divers
cyclosporine, 298

ANTITHYROÏDIENS

INDICATIONS

Traitement de l'hyperthyroïdie de diverses causes (maladie de Graves, goitre multinodulaire, thyroïdite et crise thyrotoxique) ■ Préparation du patient à la thyroïdectomie ■ Ces médicaments sont également indiqués lorsque la thyroïdectomie est déconseillée ■ On administre parfois des bêtabloquants (comme le propranolol) en association avec des antithyroïdiens pour maîtriser les symptômes d'hyperthyroïdie (tachycardie et tremblements), mais ces médicaments n'ont pas d'effet sur la fonction thyroïdienne.

MÉCANISME D'ACTION

Ces médicaments inhibent la synthèse des hormones thyroïdiennes.

CONTRE-INDICATIONS, PRÉCAUTIONS ET MISES EN GARDE

Contre-indications: Hypersensibilité ■ Antécédents d'aplasie médullaire.

Précautions et mises en garde: Administrer le méthimazole et le propylthiouracile avec prudence aux patients dont la réserve médullaire est diminuée.

INTERACTIONS

Le **lithium** et l'**amiodarone** peuvent induire des anomalies thyroïdiennes et entraver la réaction au traitement antithyroïdien ■ Les **phénothiazines** peuvent augmenter le risque d'agranulocytose.

SOINS INFIRMIERS

ÉVALUATION DE LA SITUATION

- Suivre de près les symptômes d'hyperthyroïdie ou de thyrotoxicose: tachycardie, palpitations, nervosité, insomnie, fièvre, diaphorèse, intolérance à la chaleur, tremblements, perte de poids, diarrhée.
- Suivre de près l'apparition de symptômes d'hypothyroïdie: intolérance au froid, constipation, peau sèche, céphalées, apragmatisme, fatigue ou faiblesse. Un ajustement de la posologie peut être nécessaire.
- Suivre de près les éruptions cutanées ou l'œdème des ganglions lymphatiques du cou, symptômes qui peuvent dicter l'arrêt du traitement.
- Étudier les résultats des tests de la fonction thyroïdienne avant l'administration du médicament et pendant toute la durée du traitement.

Iodures: Suivre de près les signes et les symptômes d'iodisme (goût métallique, stomatite, lésions cutanées, symptômes de rhume, irritation gastro-intestinale grave) ou d'anaphylaxie. Signaler immédiatement ces symptômes au médecin.

DIAGNOSTICS INFIRMIERS POSSIBLES

- Connaissances insuffisantes sur le traitement médicamenteux (Enseignement au patient et à ses proches).

INTERVENTIONS INFIRMIÈRES

- Servir les solutions d'iodure dans un grand verre de jus de fruits, d'eau ou de lait. Administrer la préparation après les repas pour réduire l'irritation gastro-intestinale.

ENSEIGNEMENT AU PATIENT ET À SES PROCHES

- Expliquer au patient qu'il doit respecter rigoureusement la posologie recommandée et l'avertir qu'une dose manquée peut déclencher l'hyperthyroïdie.
- Conseiller au patient de demander à un professionnel de la santé quels sont les aliments riches en iode qu'il peut consommer (sel iodé, crustacés, chou, chou frisé, navets).
- Recommander au patient de porter sur lui en tout temps un bracelet d'identité où sont inscrits son problème de santé et son traitement et de prévenir le professionnel de la santé qu'il suit un traitement médicamenteux avant de se soumettre à un autre traitement ou à une intervention chirurgicale.
- Expliquer au patient l'importance des examens réguliers permettant d'évaluer les bienfaits du traitement et de déceler les effets secondaires du médicament.

VÉRIFICATION DE L'EFFICACITÉ THÉRAPEUTIQUE

L'efficacité du traitement peut être démontrée par: la diminution de la gravité des symptômes d'hyperthyroïdie ■ la réduction de la vascularité et de la friabilité de la glande thyroïde pour préparer le patient à une intervention chirurgicale ■ la protection de la thyroïde en cas de radiothérapie d'urgence.

ANTITHYROÏDIENS INCLUS DANS LE *GUIDE*

ANTITUBERCULEUX

INDICATIONS

Traitement et prévention de la tuberculose et des maladies provoquées par d'autres mycobactéries, incluant le complexe *Mycobacterium avium* (MAC), présent surtout chez les patients infectés par le VIH ■ On administre des associations médicamenteuses dans le traitement de la tuberculose évolutive pour enrayer rapidement l'infection et pour retarder ou prévenir l'apparition de souches résistantes. Dans certains cas particuliers, la posologie peut être intermittente (2 fois par semaine) ■ La streptomycine est également dotée de propriétés antituberculeuses ■ L'azithromycine et la clarithromycine, deux antibiotiques, sont utiles dans la prévention et le traitement de l'infection à MAC ■ La rifampine est utilisée en prophylaxie de la méningite méningococcique et de l'infection à *Hæmophilus influenzæ* de type B.

MÉCANISME D'ACTION

Ces médicaments tuent les bactéries *Mycobacterium tuberculosis* (effet tuberculocide) ou en inhibent la prolifération (effet tuberculostatique) ■ Il faut traiter le patient avec une association de deux ou de plusieurs agents, à moins que le médicament ne soit administré en prophylaxie (isoniazide).

CONTRE-INDICATIONS, PRÉCAUTIONS ET MISES EN GARDE

Contre-indications: Hypersensibilité ■ Maladie hépatique grave.

Précautions et mises en garde: Administrer ces médicaments avec prudence aux patients ayant des antécédents de maladie hépatique, aux personnes âgées et aux patients débilités ■ Le traitement à l'éthambutol dicte un suivi ophtalmique ■ **OBST., ALLAITEMENT**: L'innocuité de ces médicaments pendant la grossesse et l'allaitement n'a pas été établie, bien que certains agents aient été utilisés sans que des effets indésirables se manifestent chez le fœtus. L'observance du traitement est essentielle.

INTERACTIONS

L'isoniazide inhibe le métabolisme de la **phénytoïne** ■ La rifampine diminue de façon marquée les concentrations de **saquinavir** (association déconseillée).

SOINS INFIRMIERS

ÉVALUATION DE LA SITUATION

- Examiner les résultats des tests de dépistage de *Mycobacterium* ou les antibiogrammes avant l'administration du médicament et à intervalles réguliers tout au long du traitement, pour déceler une éventuelle résistance.
- Ausculter le murmure vésiculaire et noter les caractéristiques et la quantité des expectorations à intervalles réguliers tout au long du traitement.

DIAGNOSTICS INFIRMIERS POSSIBLES

- Risque d'infection (Indications).
- Connaissances insuffisantes sur le traitement médicamenteux (Enseignement au patient et à ses proches).
- Non-observance du traitement médicamenteux (Enseignement au patient et à ses proches).

INTERVENTIONS INFIRMIÈRES

- Si une irritation gastrique survient, on peut administrer la plupart des médicaments avec des aliments ou un antiacide.

ENSEIGNEMENT AU PATIENT ET À SES PROCHES

- Expliquer au patient qu'il est important de poursuivre le traitement même après la disparition des symptômes.
- Insister sur l'importance des examens réguliers de suivi permettant d'évaluer les bienfaits du traitement et de déceler les effets secondaires du médicament.
- Prévenir le patient que la rifampine peut faire virer la couleur de la salive, des expectorations, de la sueur, des larmes, de l'urine et des selles au rouge orangé ou au rouge-brun et modifier la couleur des verres de contact de façon permanente.

VÉRIFICATION DE L'EFFICACITÉ THÉRAPEUTIQUE

L'efficacité du traitement peut être déterminée par: la résolution des signes et des symptômes de tuberculose ■ des résultats négatifs aux analyses des cultures des expectorations.

ANTITUBERCULEUX INCLUS DANS LE *GUIDE*

éthambutol, 453
isoniazide, 659
pyrazinamide, 1037
pyrazinamide/isoniazide/rifampine, 1037
rifampine, 1068

ANTITUSSIFS

INDICATIONS

Soulagement symptomatique de la toux de diverses étiologies, y compris de la toux provoquée par les infections virales des voies respiratoires supérieures ■ L'usage prolongé des antitussifs est déconseillé.

MÉCANISME D'ACTION

Les antitussifs (codéine, dextrométhorphane, hydrocodone) suppriment la toux par une action centrale ■ La toux productive ne doit être supprimée que dans la mesure où elle perturbe le sommeil ou les activités de la vie quotidienne ■ Les liquides, consommés en grande quantité, restent probablement les meilleurs expectorants, étant donné qu'ils diminuent la viscosité des sécrétions, ce qui en facilite l'expulsion.

CONTRE-INDICATIONS, PRÉCAUTIONS ET MISES EN GARDE

Contre-indications: Hypersensibilité.

Précautions et mises en garde: Péd.: Administrer ces agents avec prudence aux enfants ■ On ne doit pas les utiliser pendant des périodes prolongées, sauf sur recommandation du médecin ou d'un autre professionnel de la santé.

INTERACTIONS

Les antitussifs à action centrale, administrés en même temps que des **dépresseurs du SNC**, peuvent exercer des effets dépresseurs additifs sur le SNC.

SOINS INFIRMIERS

ÉVALUATION DE LA SITUATION

- Noter la fréquence et la nature de la toux, ausculter le murmure vésiculaire et noter la quantité et le type d'expectorations.

DIAGNOSTICS INFIRMIERS POSSIBLES

- Dégagement inefficace des voies respiratoires (Indications).
- Connaissances insuffisantes sur le traitement médicamenteux (Enseignement au patient et à ses proches).

INTERVENTIONS INFIRMIÈRES

- Sauf contre-indication, maintenir l'apport quotidien de liquides entre 1 500 et 2 000 mL pour diminuer la viscosité des sécrétions bronchiques.

ENSEIGNEMENT AU PATIENT ET À SES PROCHES

- Expliquer au patient les méthodes lui permettant de tousser efficacement; lui conseiller de s'asseoir et de prendre plusieurs respirations profondes avant de tousser.
- Expliquer au patient qu'il peut calmer la toux en évitant les agents irritants (fumée de cigarette, autres fumées, poussière). Lui conseiller d'humidifier l'air de la pièce, de prendre des gorgées fréquentes d'eau et de sucer des bonbons durs sans sucre pour diminuer la fréquence des accès de toux sèche irritante.
- Recommander au patient d'éviter de boire de l'alcool et de ne pas prendre des dépresseurs du SNC en même temps que ces médicaments.
- Prévenir le patient que ces médicaments peuvent provoquer des étourdissements ou de la somnolence. Lui conseiller de ne pas conduire et d'éviter les activités qui exigent sa vigilance jusqu'à ce qu'on ait la certitude que le médicament n'entraîne pas ces effets chez lui.
- Recommander au patient de prévenir le médecin si la toux persiste au-delà de 1 semaine ou si elle s'accompagne de fièvre, de douleurs thoraciques, de céphalées persistantes ou de rash.

VÉRIFICATION DE L'EFFICACITÉ THÉRAPEUTIQUE

L'efficacité du traitement peut être démontrée par: la diminution de la fréquence et de l'intensité de la toux, sans suppression du réflexe tussigène.

ANTITUSSIFS INCLUS DANS LE *GUIDE*

codéine, 266
dextrométhorphane, 337
diphenhydramine, 362
hydrocodone, 572

ANTIULCÉREUX

INDICATIONS

Traitement et prophylaxie de l'ulcère gastroduodénal et des maladies caractérisées par une hypersécrétion gastrique, comme le syndrome de Zollinger-Ellison. Pour traiter le reflux gastro-œsophagien, on utilise également des antagonistes des récepteurs H_2 de l'histamine et des inhibiteurs de la pompe à protons.

MÉCANISME D'ACTION

Étant donné que la grande majorité des ulcères gastroduodénaux ont pour origine une infection du tractus gastro-intestinal due à *Helicobacter pylori*, l'éradication de cette bactérie réduit les symptômes et la récurrence. Les antibiotiques qui sont très efficaces contre ce microorganisme sont l'amoxicilline, la clarithromycine, le métronidazole et la tétracycline. Le bismuth exerce également des effets antibiotiques contre *H. pylori*. Les schémas thérapeutiques associent habituellement un antagoniste des récepteurs H_2 de l'histamine ou un inhibiteur de la pompe à protons à deux antibiotiques avec ou sans bismuth, à prendre pendant 7 à 14 jours.

EXEMPLES DE SCHÉMAS THÉRAPEUTIQUES VISANT L'ÉRADICATION DE *H. PYLORI*

Schéma	Posologie
oméprazole	20 mg, 2 fois par jour, pendant 1 à 2 semaines
clarithromycine	500 mg, 2 fois par jour, pendant 1 à 2 semaines
amoxicilline	1 000 mg, 2 fois par jour, pendant 1 à 2 semaines
oméprazole	20 mg, 2 fois par jour, pendant 1 à 2 semaines
clarithromycine	250 mg, 2 fois par jour, pendant 1 à 2 semaines
métronidazole	500 mg, 2 fois par jour, pendant 1 à 2 semaines
pantoprazole	40 mg, 2 fois par jour, pendant 1 à 2 semaines
clarithromycine	500 mg, 2 fois par jour, pendant 1 à 2 semaines
amoxicilline	1 000 mg, 2 fois par jour, pendant 1 à 2 semaines
pantoprazole	40 mg, 2 fois par jour, pendant 1 à 2 semaines
clarithromycine	500 mg, 2 fois par jour, pendant 1 à 2 semaines
métronidazole	500 mg, 2 fois par jour, pendant 1 à 2 semaines
ésoméprazole	20 mg, 2 fois par jour, pendant 1 à 2 semaines
clarithromycine	500 mg, 2 fois par jour, pendant 1 à 2 semaines
amoxicilline	1 000 mg, 2 fois par jour, pendant 1 à 2 semaines
rabéprazole	20 mg, 2 fois par jour, pendant 1 à 2 semaines
clarithromycine	500 mg, 2 fois par jour, pendant 1 à 2 semaines
amoxicilline	1 000 mg, 2 fois par jour, pendant 1 à 2 semaines
ranitidine, citrate de bismuth	400 mg, 2 fois par jour, pendant 4 semaines
clarithromycine	500 mg, 3 fois par jour, pendant 2 semaines
métronidazole	250 mg, 4 fois par jour (aux repas et au coucher), pendant 2 semaines
tétracycline	500 mg, 4 fois par jour (aux repas et au coucher), pendant 2 semaines
bismuth, sous-salicylate de	525 mg, 4 fois par jour (aux repas et au coucher), pendant 2 semaines
lansoprazole	30 mg, 1 fois par jour, pendant 2 semaines
clarithromycine	500 mg, 2 fois par jour, pendant 2 semaines
amoxicilline	1 000 mg, 2 fois par jour, pendant 2 semaines
lansoprazole	30 mg, 1 fois par jour, pendant 2 semaines
amoxicilline	1 000 mg, 3 fois par jour, pendant 2 semaines

Les autres médicaments utilisés dans le traitement des ulcères gastroduodénaux visent à neutraliser l'acide gastrique (antiacides), à réduire la sécrétion d'acide (antagonistes des récepteurs H_2 de l'histamine, inhibiteurs de la pompe à protons, misoprostol) ou à protéger la surface de l'ulcère contre d'autres lésions (misoprostol, sucralfate) ■ Les antagonistes des récepteurs H_2 de l'histamine entraînent une inhibition compétitive de l'activité de l'histamine au niveau des récepteurs H_2, situés surtout dans les cellules pariétales gastriques, ce qui provoque l'inhibition de la sécrétion d'acide gastrique ■ Le misoprostol réduit la sécrétion d'acide gastrique et augmente la production de mucus protecteur ■ Les inhibiteurs de la pompe à protons empêchent la libération des ions hydrogène dans la lumière gastrique.

CONTRE-INDICATIONS, PRÉCAUTIONS ET MISES EN GARDE

Contre-indications: Hypersensibilité.

Précautions et mises en garde: **GÉR.:** On recommande de réduire la posologie de la plupart des antagonistes des récepteurs H_2 de l'histamine chez les patients souffrant d'insuffisance rénale et chez les personnes âgées ■ Les antiacides à base de magnésium devraient être utilisés avec prudence chez les insuffisants rénaux, tout comme le misoprostol chez les femmes en âge de procréer.

INTERACTIONS

Les antiacides renfermant du calcium et du magnésium diminuent l'absorption de la **tétracycline** et des **fluoroquinolones** ■ La cimétidine inhibe le métabolisme hépatique de plusieurs médicaments, ce qui peut augmenter les risques de toxicité par la **warfarine**, les **antidépresseurs tricycliques**, la **théophylline**, le **métoprolol**, la **phénytoïne**, le **propranolol** ou la **lidocaïne** ■ L'oméprazole diminue le métabolisme de la **phénytoïne**, du **diazépam** et de la **warfarine** ■ Tous les agents qui élèvent le pH gastrique diminuent l'absorption du **kétoconazole**.

SOINS INFIRMIERS

ÉVALUATION DE LA SITUATION

- Suivre de près la douleur épigastrique ou abdominale et la présence de sang occulte ou franc dans les selles, les vomissements et les échantillons prélevés par aspiration gastrique.

Antiacides: Rester à l'affût des brûlures d'estomac et de l'indigestion; déterminer l'emplacement, la durée et les caractéristiques de la douleur gastrique ainsi que les facteurs qui les déclenchent.

Antagonistes des récepteurs H_2 de l'histamine: Observer étroitement les personnes âgées et les patients gravement malades, pour déceler les signes de confusion et en prévenir immédiatement le médecin ou un autre professionnel de la santé.

Misoprostol: Dans les 2 semaines précédant le début du traitement, faire passer un test sérique de grossesse aux patientes en âge de procréer. On amorce habituellement le traitement le 2e ou le 3e jour du cycle menstruel, si le test de grossesse est négatif.

Tests de laboratoire:

- Les antagonistes des récepteurs H_2 de l'histamine contrecarrent les effets de la pentagastrine et de l'histamine lors du test de sécrétion de l'acidité gastrique. Ne pas administrer ces agents dans les 24 heures qui précèdent cette analyse.
- Le traitement peut entraîner des résultats faussement négatifs aux tests cutanés effectués au moyen d'extraits d'allergènes. Ne pas administrer ces médicaments pendant les 24 heures qui précèdent ce test.

DIAGNOSTICS INFIRMIERS POSSIBLES

- Douleur aiguë (Indications).
- Connaissances insuffisantes sur le traitement médicamenteux (Enseignement au patient et à ses proches).

INTERVENTIONS INFIRMIÈRES

Antiacides:

- Les antiacides entraînent la dissolution et l'absorption prématurées des comprimés entérosolubles et peuvent entraver l'absorption des autres médicaments pris par voie orale. Si ces derniers sont administrés en même temps que des antiacides, prévoir au moins 1 heure d'intervalle entre les deux administrations.

- Bien agiter les préparations liquides avant de les verser. Après l'administration du médicament, faire boire au patient un grand verre d'eau pour s'assurer que le médicament pénètre dans l'estomac. Les présentations sous forme de liquide et de poudre sont considérées comme plus efficaces que les comprimés à croquer.
- Les comprimés à croquer doivent être bien mâchés avant d'être avalés. Le patient doit ensuite boire un demi-verre d'eau.
- Administrer le médicament 1 heure et 3 heures après les repas et à l'heure du coucher pour obtenir un effet antiacide maximal.

Misoprostol: Administrer cet agent avec des aliments et à l'heure du coucher pour réduire la gravité de la diarrhée.

Pantoprazole, rabéprazole, oméprazole, esoméprazole et lansoprazole:

- Administrer ces agents avant les repas, de préférence le matin. Les capsules et les comprimés doivent être avalés tels quels, sans être ouverts, broyés ou mâchés.
- Ces agents peuvent être pris en même temps que des antiacides.

Sucralfate: Administrer à jeun, 1 heure avant les repas et à l'heure du coucher. Prévenir le patient qu'il ne faut pas broyer ou mâcher les comprimés. Bien agiter la suspension avant de l'administrer. En cas d'administration nasogastrique, consulter un pharmacien, étant donné qu'en raison de ses propriétés de liaison aux protéines, le sucralfate peut entraîner la formation d'un bézoard, si on l'administre en même temps qu'une alimentation entérale ou d'autres médicaments.

ENSEIGNEMENT AU PATIENT ET À SES PROCHES

- Expliquer au patient qu'il doit respecter rigoureusement la posologie recommandée et qu'il doit continuer à prendre le médicament même s'il se sent mieux. S'il n'a pu le prendre au moment habituel, il doit le prendre dès que possible à moins que ce ne soit presque l'heure prévue pour la dose suivante. Lui conseiller de ne jamais remplacer une dose manquée par une double dose.
- Conseiller au patient de ne pas boire d'alcool, de ne pas prendre des préparations contenant de l'aspirine ou des AINS et de ne pas consommer des aliments qui peuvent aggraver l'irritation gastro-intestinale.
- Recommander au patient de prévenir rapidement le médecin ou un autre professionnel de la santé si ses selles deviennent noires ou goudronneuses.
- Expliquer au patient que l'abandon de la cigarette peut aider à prévenir la récurrence des ulcères gastroduodénaux.

Antiacides: Inciter le patient à consulter un professionnel de la santé s'il doit prendre des antiacides pendant plus de 2 semaines ou si le problème récidive. Lui recommander de consulter également un professionnel de la santé si la douleur n'est pas soulagée ou si les symptômes suivants de saignements gastro-intestinaux se manifestent: selles noires ou goudronneuses et vomissements ayant l'aspect du marc de café.

Misoprostol:

- Insister sur le fait qu'il peut être dangereux de donner ce médicament à une autre personne.
- Prévenir la patiente que le misoprostol peut provoquer des fausses couches. Il faut informer de cet effet verbalement et par écrit toute femme en âge de procréer et lui recommander de prendre des mesures de contraception pendant toute la durée du traitement. Si on soupçonne une grossesse, il faut arrêter de prendre le misoprostol et prévenir immédiatement un professionnel de la santé.

Sucralfate:

- Recommander au patient de poursuivre le traitement pendant 4 à 8 semaines, même s'il se sent mieux, pour assurer la guérison complète de l'ulcère.

- Recommander au patient d'augmenter sa consommation de liquides et d'aliments riches en fibres et de faire de l'exercice pour essayer de prévenir la constipation induite par le médicament.

VÉRIFICATION DE L'EFFICACITÉ THÉRAPEUTIQUE

L'efficacité du traitement peut être démontrée par: la diminution des douleurs et de l'irritation gastro-intestinales ■ la prévention des saignements ou de l'irritation gastriques. La guérison des ulcères duodénaux peut être confirmée par un examen radiologique ou l'endoscopie. Après l'épisode initial, il faut poursuivre le traitement par les antagonistes des récepteurs H_2 de l'histamine pendant au moins 6 semaines ■ la diminution des symptômes de reflux gastro-œsophagien ■ l'augmentation du pH des sécrétions gastriques (antiacides) ■ la prévention des ulcères gastriques chez les patients recevant un traitement prolongé par des AINS (misoprostol seulement).

ANTIULCÉREUX INCLUS DANS LE *GUIDE*

ANTIVIRAUX

INDICATIONS

L'acyclovir, le famciclovir et le valacyclovir sont utilisés pour le traitement des infections par le virus de l'herpès ■ L'acyclovir est également utilisé pour traiter la varicelle ■ Le zanamivir et l'oseltamivir sont principalement utilisés pour le traitement des infections par le virus de l'influenza de type A ■ Le cidofovir, le ganciclovir, le valganciclovir et le foscarnet sont destinés au traitement de la rétinite à cytomégalovirus ■ La ribavirine en inhalation est utilisée chez les nourrissons et les jeunes enfants pour le traitement des infections graves des voies respiratoires inférieures dues au virus respiratoire syncytial ■ La ribavirine par voie orale est utilisée en association avec l'interféron alpha-2b pour le traitement des patients souffrant d'hépatite C chronique qui n'ont pas répondu aux traitements antérieurs ■ La trifluridine ophtalmique est indiquée pour le traitement de la kératoconjonctivite primaire et de la kératite épithéliale récurrente causées par les virus de l'herpès simplex de types 1 et 2.

MÉCANISME D'ACTION

La plupart des agents inhibent la réplication virale.

CONTRE-INDICATIONS, PRÉCAUTIONS ET MISES EN GARDE

Contre-indications: Antécédents d'hypersensibilité.

Précautions et mises en garde: En présence d'une insuffisance rénale, il faut adapter la posologie de tous ces médicaments, sauf du zanamivir ■ L'acyclovir peut parfois provoquer une insuffisance rénale et une toxicité du SNC ■ Le foscarnet augmente le risque de convulsions.

INTERACTIONS

Risque de toxicité du SNC et de néphrotoxicité additives, si l'acyclovir est administré en même temps que d'autres **médicaments qui provoquent des réactions indésirables similaires**.

SOINS INFIRMIERS

ÉVALUATION DE LA SITUATION

- Suivre de près les signes et les symptômes d'infection avant l'administration du médicament et pendant toute la durée du traitement.

Préparations ophtalmiques: Examiner les lésions oculaires avant l'administration de la préparation et quotidiennement pendant toute la durée du traitement.

Préparations topiques: Examiner les lésions avant l'application de la préparation et quotidiennement pendant toute la durée du traitement.

DIAGNOSTICS INFIRMIERS POSSIBLES

- Risque d'infection (Indications).
- Atteinte à l'intégrité de la peau (Indications).
- Connaissances insuffisantes sur le traitement médicamenteux (Enseignement au patient et à ses proches).

INTERVENTIONS INFIRMIÈRES

- La plupart des antiviraux à action générale doivent être administrés 24 heures sur 24 pour maintenir des concentrations thérapeutiques de médicament dans le sang.

ENSEIGNEMENT AU PATIENT ET À SES PROCHES

- Expliquer au patient qu'il doit prendre son médicament 24 heures sur 24, pendant toute la durée du traitement, même s'il se sent mieux.
- Prévenir le patient que les antiviraux et les antirétroviraux ne réduisent pas le risque de transmission du virus. Des précautions doivent être prises pour éviter la transmission du virus à d'autres personnes.
- Montrer au patient comment utiliser les préparations topiques et ophtalmiques.
- Recommander au patient de prévenir un professionnel de la santé si les symptômes ne s'améliorent pas.

VÉRIFICATION DE L'EFFICACITÉ THÉRAPEUTIQUE

L'efficacité du traitement peut être démontrée par: la prévention ou la résolution des signes et des symptômes d'infection virale. Le temps de guérison dépend du microorganisme infectant et du siège de l'infection.

ANTIVIRAUX INCLUS DANS LE *GUIDE*

ANXIOLYTIQUES ET HYPNOSÉDATIFS

INDICATIONS

Anxiolytiques et sédatifs: Traitement des troubles de l'anxiété . On les administre également pour assurer une sédation préopératoire. **Hypnotiques**: Traitement de l'insomnie ■ Certains agents ont des effets anticonvulsivants (clorazépate, diazépam, phénobarbital), d'autres sont des relaxants des muscles squelettiques (diazépam). On les utilise comme médicaments d'appoint pour traiter les symptômes du sevrage alcoolique (chlordiazépoxide, clorazépate, diazépam, oxazépam), comme adjuvants des anesthésiques à action générale (dropéridol) et comme amnésiques (midazolam, diazépam).

MÉCANISME D'ACTION

Dépression généralisée du SNC ■ Risque de tolérance lors d'un usage prolongé et de dépendance physique et psychologique ■ Ces agents n'ont pas de propriétés analgésiques.

CONTRE-INDICATIONS, PRÉCAUTIONS ET MISES EN GARDE

Contre-indications: Hypersensibilité ■ Coma ou dépression préexistante du SNC ■ Douleurs intenses, non maîtrisées ■ Grossesse ou allaitement.

Précautions et mises en garde: Dysfonctionnement hépatique, insuffisance rénale grave ou maladie pulmonaire grave sous-jacente (la prudence est de mise) ■ Idées suicidaires ou antécédents de tentatives de suicide ou de toxicomanie ■ L'administration d'hypnotiques devrait être de courte durée ■ **GÉR.**: Les personnes âgées peuvent être plus sensibles aux effets des dépresseurs du SNC (une réduction de la dose initiale peut s'avérer nécessaire).

INTERACTIONS

Dépression additive du SNC lors de l'usage concomitant d'**alcool**, d'**antihistaminiques**, d'**antidépresseurs**, d'**analgésiques opioïdes** ou de **phénothiazines** ■ Les barbituriques déclenchent la libération d'enzymes hépatiques qui métabolisent les médicaments et peuvent diminuer l'efficacité des **agents métabolisés par le foie** ■ Éviter l'administration concomitante d'**IMAO**.

SOINS INFIRMIERS

ÉVALUATION DE LA SITUATION

- Mesurer la pression artérielle, le pouls et la fréquence respiratoire à intervalles fréquents pendant toute la durée de l'administration par voie IV.

- Le traitement prolongé à des doses élevées peut entraîner une dépendance psychologique ou physique. Limiter la quantité de médicament dont peut disposer le patient, particulièrement s'il est déprimé ou suicidaire ou s'il a des antécédents de toxicomanie.

Insomnie: Déterminer les habitudes de sommeil, avant le traitement et à intervalles réguliers pendant toute sa durée.

Anxiété: Noter le degré d'anxiété et de sédation (ataxie, étourdissements, troubles d'élocution), avant le traitement et à intervalles réguliers pendant toute sa durée.

Convulsions: Observer et consigner dans le dossier l'intensité, la durée et les caractéristiques des convulsions. Prendre les précautions qui s'imposent en cas de crise.

Spasmes musculaires: Suivre de près les spasmes musculaires, déterminer la douleur qui les accompagne et les limites des mouvements, avant l'administration du médicament et pendant toute la durée du traitement.

Sevrage alcoolique: En cas de sevrage alcoolique, suivre de près les tremblements, l'agitation, le délire et les hallucinations. Protéger le patient contre les accidents.

DIAGNOSTICS INFIRMIERS POSSIBLES

- Habitudes de sommeil perturbées (Indications).
- Risque d'accident (Effets secondaires).
- Connaissances insuffisantes sur le traitement médicamenteux (Enseignement au patient et à ses proches).

INTERVENTIONS INFIRMIÈRES

- Après l'administration de doses hypnotiques, suivre de près le patient lors de ses déplacements et des transferts. Lui retirer les cigarettes. Remonter les ridelles du lit, garder le lit en position basse et placer la sonnette d'appel à portée de la main.

ENSEIGNEMENT AU PATIENT ET À SES PROCHES

- Expliquer au patient qu'il est important de préparer un cadre propice au sommeil: la pièce doit être sombre et calme; la nicotine et la caféine sont à proscrire. Le prévenir qu'il ne doit pas augmenter la dose si elle devient moins efficace après quelques semaines, sans consulter au préalable un professionnel de la santé. Un retrait graduel du médicament peut s'avérer nécessaire pour prévenir les réactions de sevrage provoquées par un traitement prolongé.
- Prévenir le patient que ce type de médicament peut provoquer de la somnolence diurne. Lui conseiller de ne pas conduire et d'éviter les activités qui exigent sa vigilance jusqu'à ce qu'on ait la certitude que le médicament qui lui a été prescrit n'entraîne pas cet effet chez lui.
- Recommander au patient d'éviter de boire de l'alcool et de prendre d'autres dépresseurs du SNC en même temps que ces médicaments.
- Conseiller à la patiente de prévenir un professionnel de la santé si elle pense être enceinte ou si elle souhaite le devenir.

VÉRIFICATION DE L'EFFICACITÉ THÉRAPEUTIQUE

L'efficacité du traitement peut être démontrée par: l'amélioration du sommeil ■ la diminution de l'anxiété ■ la maîtrise des convulsions ■ la diminution des spasmes musculaires ■ la diminution des tremblements ■ une idéation plus rationnelle lors du traitement des symptômes du sevrage alcoolique.

ANXIOLYTIQUES ET HYPNOSÉDATIFS INCLUS DANS LE *GUIDE*

BÊTABLOQUANTS

INDICATIONS

Traitement de l'hypertension, de l'angine de poitrine, des tachyarythmies, de la sténose subaortique hypertrophique ■ Prophylaxie des migraines ■ Prévention de l'infarctus du myocarde ■ Traitement du glaucome (usage ophtalmique) ■ Traitement de l'insuffisance cardiaque (carvédilol).

MÉCANISME D'ACTION

Les bêtabloquants entrent en compétition avec les neurotransmetteurs adrénergiques (sympathiques) pour occuper les sites des récepteurs adrénergiques. Les sites des récepteurs adrénergiques bêta$_1$ sont surtout situés dans le cœur, et leur stimulation entraîne une élévation de la fréquence cardiaque, de la contractilité et de la conduction AV. Les récepteurs adrénergiques bêta$_2$ se retrouvent surtout dans le muscle lisse bronchique et vasculaire ainsi que dans l'utérus. La stimulation de ces récepteurs entraîne la vasodilatation, la bronchodilatation et la relaxation de l'utérus. Le blocage de ces récepteurs contrecarre les effets des neurotransmetteurs. Les bêtabloquants peuvent avoir une affinité relativement sélective pour les récepteurs bêta$_1$ (acébutolol, aténolol, esmolol et métoprolol) ou être relativement non sélectifs (carvédilol, labétalol, nadolol, pindolol, propranolol, sotalol et timolol), bloquant à la fois les récepteurs bêta$_1$ et bêta$_2$ ■ Le carvédilol et le labétalol exercent en plus des effets alphabloquants ■ L'acébutolol, le carvédilol et le pindolol sont pourvus d'une activité sympathomimétique intrinsèque (ASI), grâce à laquelle ces agents peuvent provoquer moins de bradycardie que les autres ■ Les bêtabloquants destinés à l'usage ophtalmique diminuent la production d'humeur aqueuse.

CONTRE-INDICATIONS, PRÉCAUTIONS ET MISES EN GARDE

Contre-indications: Insuffisance cardiaque non compensée (la plupart des bêtabloquants), bronchospasme aigu, certaines formes de cardiopathie valvulaire, bradyarythmies et bloc cardiaque. **Précautions et mises en garde: OBST., ALLAITEMENT**: Administrer avec prudence chez les femmes enceintes ou allaitantes (risque de bradycardie et d'hypoglycémie fœtales) ■ La prudence est de mise en présence de toutes les formes de maladie pulmonaire ou d'une insuffisance cardiaque compensée sous-jacente (la plupart des agents) ■ Administrer avec prudence en présence de diabète et de maladie hépatique grave ■ Ne pas interrompre brusquement le traitement par les bêtabloquants.

INTERACTIONS

Risque de dépression du myocarde et de bradycardie additive lors de l'usage concomitant d'autres agents ayant ces effets (**digoxine** et certains **antiarythmiques**) ▪ Les bêtabloquants peuvent contrecarrer les effets thérapeutiques des **bronchodilatateurs** ▪ Ces agents peuvent modifier les besoins en **insuline** ou en **hypoglycémiants** chez les patients diabétiques ▪ La **cimétidine** peut ralentir le métabolisme de certains bêtabloquants et en accroître les effets.

SOINS INFIRMIERS

ÉVALUATION DE LA SITUATION

- Mesurer à intervalles fréquents la pression artérielle et le pouls pendant la période d'adaptation de la posologie et à intervalles réguliers pendant toute la durée du traitement.
- Mesurer les ingesta et les excreta et peser le patient tous les jours. Rester à l'affût des signes et des symptômes d'insuffisance cardiaque (râles et crépitations, gain pondéral, œdème périphérique, distension jugulaire).

Angine: Évaluer la fréquence et la gravité des épisodes de douleurs thoraciques à intervalles réguliers tout au long du traitement.

Prophylaxie de la migraine: Évaluer la fréquence et la gravité des migraines à intervalles réguliers tout au long du traitement.

DIAGNOSTICS INFIRMIERS POSSIBLES

- Irrigation tissulaire inefficace (Indications).
- Connaissances insuffisantes sur la maladie et sur le traitement médicamenteux (Enseignement au patient et à ses proches).
- Non-observance du traitement médicamenteux (Enseignement au patient et à ses proches).

INTERVENTIONS INFIRMIÈRES

- Prendre le pouls apical avant d'administrer le médicament. Si la fréquence cardiaque est inférieure à 50 battements/min ou si des arythmies se manifestent, ne pas administrer l'agent et en prévenir le médecin.

ENSEIGNEMENT AU PATIENT ET À SES PROCHES

Renseignements généraux: Recommander au patient de continuer de prendre ses médicaments même s'il se sent mieux. Un arrêt brusque du traitement peut provoquer des arythmies mettant en jeu le pronostic vital, de l'hypertension ou une ischémie du myocarde. Expliquer au patient que les bêtabloquants permettent de normaliser la pression artérielle, mais ne guérissent pas l'hypertension.

- Encourager le patient à prendre des mesures supplémentaires pour abaisser sa pression artérielle (perdre du poids, réduire sa consommation de sel, faire de l'exercice régulièrement, renoncer au tabac, consommer de l'alcool avec modération et maîtriser son stress).
- Montrer au patient et à ses proches comment mesurer la pression artérielle. Leur recommander de mesurer la pression toutes les semaines et d'informer le professionnel de la santé de tout changement notable.
- Conseiller au patient de changer lentement de position pour réduire le risque d'hypotension orthostatique. Le prévenir que l'effort par temps chaud intensifie les effets hypotenseurs des bêtabloquants.
- Recommander au patient de consulter un professionnel de la santé avant de prendre des médicaments en vente libre, particulièrement des agents contre le rhume, ou des produits naturels.

- Expliquer au patient que les bêtabloquants peuvent le rendre plus sensible au froid.
- Inciter le patient diabétique à suivre de près sa glycémie, particulièrement en présence de fatigue, de faiblesse, de malaise ou d'irritabilité.
- Recommander au patient de prévenir le chirurgien ou le dentiste qu'il suit un traitement par des bêtabloquants, avant de se soumettre à un traitement ou à une intervention chirurgicale.
- Conseiller au patient de toujours porter sur lui une pièce d'identité sur laquelle sont inscrits sa maladie et son traitement médicamenteux.
- Insister sur l'importance des examens de suivi permettant de vérifier les progrès du traitement.

Usage ophtalmique: Montrer au patient le mode d'administration approprié des préparations ophtalmiques.

VÉRIFICATION DE L'EFFICACITÉ THÉRAPEUTIQUE

L'efficacité du traitement peut être vérifiée par: la baisse de la pression artérielle ■ la diminution de la fréquence et de l'intensité des crises d'angine ■ la réduction des arythmies ■ la prévention des récurrences des infarctus du myocarde ■ la prévention des migraines ■ la diminution des tremblements ■ la baisse de la pression intraoculaire.

BÊTABLOQUANTS INCLUS DANS LE *GUIDE*

bêtabloquants (non sélectifs)
carvédilol, 197
labétalol, 676
nadolol, 826
pindolol, 973
propranolol, 1027
sotalol, 1119
timolol, 1190

bêtabloquants (sélectifs)
acébutolol, 5
aténolol, 177
bisoprolol, 149
esmolol, 444
métoprolol, 787

bêtabloquants (usage ophtalmique)
bétaxolol, 1359
lévobunolol, 1359
timolol, 1360

BLOQUEURS DES CANAUX CALCIQUES

INDICATIONS

Traitement de l'hypertension (amlodipine, diltiazem, félodipine, nifédipine, vérapamil) ■ Traitement et prophylaxie de l'angine de poitrine ou des spasmes coronariens (amlodipine, diltiazem, nifédipine, vérapamil) ■ Le diltiazem et le vérapamil sont également utilisés comme antiarythmiques ■ Traitement d'appoint de l'hémorragie subarachnoïdienne (nimodipine).

MÉCANISME D'ACTION

Blocage de l'entrée du calcium dans les cellules du muscle lisse vasculaire et du myocarde ■ Dilatation des artères coronariennes, que le myocarde soit normal ou ischémique, et inhibition des spasmes coronariens ■ Le diltiazem et le vérapamil diminuent la conduction AV ■ La nimodipine a un effet relativement sélectif sur les vaisseaux sanguins du cerveau.

CONTRE-INDICATIONS, PRÉCAUTIONS ET MISES EN GARDE

Contre-indications: Hypersensibilité ■ Bradycardie, bloc cardiaque du 2e ou du 3e degré ou insuffisance cardiaque non compensée (diltiazem et vérapamil).

Précautions et mises en garde: OBST., ALLAITEMENT: L'innocuité de ces agents n'a pas été établie ■ Administrer avec prudence chez les patients atteints de maladie hépatique ou d'arythmies difficiles à maîtriser.

INTERACTIONS

Dépression additive du myocarde lors de l'administration simultanée de **bêtabloquants** et de **disopyramide** (diltiazem et vérapamil) ■ L'efficacité des bloqueurs des canaux calciques peut être diminuée lors de la prise concomitante de **phénytoïne** et de **phénobarbital** et accrue lors d'un traitement concomitant au **propranolol** ou à la **cimétidine** ■ Le vérapamil et le diltiazem peuvent accroître les concentrations sériques de **digoxine** et provoquer une toxicité.

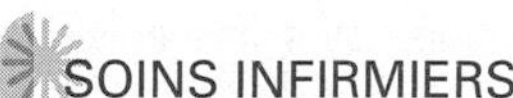

SOINS INFIRMIERS

ÉVALUATION DE LA SITUATION

- Mesurer la pression artérielle et le pouls à intervalles fréquents au cours de la période d'adaptation posologique et à intervalles réguliers pendant toute la durée du traitement.
- Mesurer les ingesta et les excreta et peser le patient tous les jours. Rester à l'affût des signes et des symptômes d'insuffisance cardiaque (râles et crépitations, gain pondéral, œdème périphérique, distension des jugulaires).

Angine: Évaluer la fréquence et la gravité des épisodes de douleurs thoraciques à intervalles réguliers tout au long du traitement.

Arythmies: Suivre continuellement le tracé électrocardiographique au cours du traitement IV et à intervalles réguliers pendant le traitement de long cours par le diltiazem et le vérapamil.

Hémorragies subarachnoïdiennes: Évaluer l'état neurologique (niveau de conscience, mouvements) avant le traitement par la nimodipine et à intervalles réguliers pendant toute sa durée.

DIAGNOSTICS INFIRMIERS POSSIBLES

- Irrigation tissulaire inefficace (Indications).
- Douleur aiguë (Indications).
- Connaissances insuffisantes sur la maladie et sur le traitement médicamenteux (Enseignement au patient et à ses proches).

INTERVENTIONS INFIRMIÈRES

- On peut administrer ces agents sans égard aux repas.
- Ne pas ouvrir, briser ou croquer les capsules ou les comprimés à libération prolongée.

ENSEIGNEMENT AU PATIENT ET À SES PROCHES

- Encourager le patient à continuer de prendre le médicament même s'il se sent bien.
- Conseiller au patient de changer lentement de position pour réduire le risque d'hypotension orthostatique. Le prévenir que l'effort par temps chaud intensifie les effets hypotenseurs de ces agents.
- Expliquer au patient qu'il est important de maintenir une bonne hygiène buccale et de se soumettre à des soins fréquents d'hygiène dentaire pour prévenir la sensibilité, le saignement et l'hyperplasie des gencives (développement anormal des tissus gingivaux).
- Recommander au patient de consulter un professionnel de la santé avant de prendre des médicaments en vente libre, particulièrement des agents contre le rhume, ou des produits naturels.
- Recommander au patient de prévenir le chirurgien ou le dentiste qu'il suit un traitement par ces agents, avant de se soumettre à un traitement ou à une intervention chirurgicale.

- Conseiller au patient de toujours porter sur lui une pièce d'identité sur laquelle sont inscrits sa maladie et son traitement médicamenteux.
- Insister sur l'importance des examens de suivi permettant de vérifier les progrès du traitement.

Angine: Expliquer au patient qui prend en même temps des dérivés nitrés qu'il doit continuer de prendre les deux médicaments, en respectant rigoureusement les recommandations du médecin et de prendre de la nitroglycérine sublinguale, selon les besoins, en cas de crise d'angine. Lui recommander de prévenir un professionnel de la santé si la douleur thoracique s'aggrave ou si elle n'est pas soulagée par le traitement, ou si elle s'accompagne de diaphorèse ou d'essoufflements, ou encore si des maux de tête persistants surviennent. Lui recommander également de s'informer auprès d'un professionnel de la santé des précautions à prendre par rapport à l'exercice avant de se soumettre à un effort physique.

Hypertension: Encourager le patient à prendre des mesures supplémentaires pour abaisser sa pression artérielle (perdre du poids, réduire sa consommation de sel, faire de l'exercice régulièrement, renoncer au tabac, consommer de l'alcool avec modération et maîtriser sons stress). Lui expliquer que ces agents aident à normaliser la pression artérielle, mais ne guérissent pas l'hypertension.

VÉRIFICATION DE L'EFFICACITÉ THÉRAPEUTIQUE

L'efficacité du traitement peut être démontrée par: la baisse de la pression artérielle ■ la diminution de la fréquence et de la gravité des crises d'angine ■ la diminution du besoin de recourir au traitement par des dérivés nitrés ■ l'augmentation de la tolérance à l'effort et du sentiment de bien-être ■ la suppression et la prévention des tachyarythmies supraventriculaires ■ l'amélioration du déficit neurologique dû au vasospasme à la suite d'une hémorragie subarachnoïdienne.

BLOQUEURS DES CANAUX CALCIQUES INCLUS DANS LE *GUIDE*

amlodipine, 68
diltiazem, 355
félodipine, 466
nifédipine, 855
nimodipine, 859
vérapamil, 1245

BRONCHODILATATEURS

INDICATIONS

Traitement de l'obstruction réversible des voies respiratoires attribuable à l'asthme ou à la bronchopneumopathie chronique obstructive ■ Les lignes directrices concernant le traitement de l'asthme recommandent que les agonistes bêta-adrénergiques à action rapide, administrés par inhalation (sauf le salmétérol), soient réservés au traitement immédiat des bronchospasmes; l'usage répété ou prolongé indique le besoin de recourir à des agents additionnels destinés au traitement prolongé, comme les corticostéroïdes pris par inhalation, les stabilisants mastocytaires, les bronchodilatateurs à action prolongée (les agonistes bêta-adrénergiques ou la théophylline par voie orale) et les antagonistes des récepteurs des leucotriènes (montélukast, zafirlukast).

MÉCANISME D'ACTION

Les agonistes bêta-adrénergiques (adrénaline, formotérol, orciprénaline, salbutamol, salmétérol et terbutaline) entraînent la bronchodilatation en stimulant la production de l'adénosine monophosphate cyclique (AMPc). ■ En raison du début d'action rapide de ces médicaments, on peut les utiliser dans le traitement des crises aiguës, sauf le salmétérol, dont le début d'action est retardé ■ Les inhibiteurs de la phosphodiestérase (aminophylline, oxtriphylline et théophylline) inhibent la décomposition de l'AMPc ■ L'ipratropium et le tiotropium sont des agents anticholinergiques qui entraînent la bronchodilatation en bloquant l'action de l'acétylcholine dans les voies respiratoires ■ Le montélukast et le zafirlukast sont des antagonistes des récepteurs des leucotriènes. Les leucotriènes sont des constituants de la substance SRD-A, qui pourrait être l'une des causes des bronchospasmes.

CONTRE-INDICATIONS, PRÉCAUTIONS ET MISES EN GARDE

Contre-indications: Hypersensibilité aux ingrédients actifs ou aux agents pulseurs qui entrent dans la composition de la préparation ■ Éviter l'administration de ces médicaments en cas d'arythmies cardiaques rebelles.

Précautions et mises en garde: Administrer ces agents avec prudence aux patients souffrant de diabète, de maladie cardiovasculaire ou d'hyperthyroïdie.

INTERACTIONS

Les **bêtabloquants**, administrés simultanément, peuvent neutraliser l'efficacité de ces médicaments ■ Effets sympathomimétiques additifs lors de l'administration concomitante d'autres **agents adrénergiques** (qui agissent sur le système sympathique), y compris les **vasopresseurs** et les **décongestionnants** ■ Les effets cardiovasculaires peuvent être potentialisés par les **antidépresseurs** et les **IMAO**.

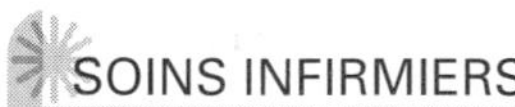

SOINS INFIRMIERS

ÉVALUATION DE LA SITUATION

- Mesurer la pression artérielle et le pouls, ausculter la respiration et le murmure vésiculaire, noter les caractéristiques des sécrétions, avant l'administration du médicament et pendant toute la durée du traitement.
- Relever les modifications électrocardiographiques et suivre de près les douleurs thoraciques chez les patients ayant des antécédents de troubles cardiovasculaires.

DIAGNOSTICS INFIRMIERS POSSIBLES

- Dégagement inefficace des voies respiratoires (Indications).
- Intolérance à l'activité (Indications).
- Connaissances insuffisantes sur le traitement médicamenteux (Enseignement au patient et à ses proches).

INTERVENTIONS INFIRMIÈRES

- Administrer ces agents 24 heures sur 24 pour maintenir des concentrations thérapeutiques dans le sang.

ENSEIGNEMENT AU PATIENT ET À SES PROCHES

- Expliquer au patient qu'il est important de prendre uniquement la dose prescrite, aux intervalles de temps prescrits.
- Recommander au patient de boire suffisamment de liquides (2 000 mL par jour, au minimum), à moins de contre-indication médicale, pour diminuer la viscosité des sécrétions des voies respiratoires.
- Conseiller au patient de consulter un professionnel de la santé avant de prendre un médicament en vente libre contre la toux, le rhume ou les difficultés respiratoires et de consommer le moins possible d'aliments ou de boissons contenant des xanthines (boissons à base de cola, de café et de chocolat), étant donné les risques accrus d'arythmies et d'effets secondaires.

- Conseiller au patient de cesser de fumer et d'éviter les autres agents qui irritent les voies respiratoires.
- Montrer au patient comment utiliser les aérosols doseurs (voir l'annexe G).
- Conseiller au patient d'informer sans délai un professionnel de la santé si la dose habituelle de médicament ne produit pas les résultats escomptés, si les symptômes s'aggravent après le traitement ou si des effets toxiques surviennent.
- Expliquer au patient qui prend des bronchodilatateurs en même temps que d'autres médicaments par inhalation qu'il doit commencer par le bronchodilatateur et attendre 5 minutes avant de prendre l'autre médicament, sauf si le professionnel de la santé le lui recommande autrement.

VÉRIFICATION DE L'EFFICACITÉ THÉRAPEUTIQUE

L'efficacité du traitement peut être démontrée par: la diminution des bronchospasmes ■ une respiration plus facile.

BRONCHODILATATEURS INCLUS DANS LE *GUIDE*

agonistes bêta-adrénergiques
adrénaline, 23
formotérol, 520
orciprénaline, 894
salbutamol, 1087
salmétérol, 1089
terbutaline, 1160

antagonistes des récepteurs des leucotriènes
montélukast, 817
zafirlukast, 1273

anticholinergique
ipratropium, 654
tiotropium, 1193

inhibiteurs de la phosphodiestérase (xanthines)
aminophylline, 159
oxtriphylline, 159
théophylline, 159

CORTICOSTÉROÏDES

INDICATIONS

Traitement de substitution (dose de 20 mg d'hydrocortisone ou l'équivalent) en cas d'insuffisance corticosurrénalienne ■ Les doses élevées sont habituellement utilisées pour leurs propriétés anti-inflammatoires, immunosuppressives ou antinéoplasiques ■ Traitement d'appoint dans de nombreux cas dont l'hypercalcémie et les maladies auto-immunes ■ Les corticostéroïdes topiques sont utilisés dans le traitement de diverses maladies allergiques ou inflammatoires ■ Les corticostéroïdes par inhalation sont administrés dans le traitement d'entretien des maladies réversibles des voies respiratoires (asthme) ■ Les corticostéroïdes administrés par voie intranasale ou ophtalmique sont utilisés dans le traitement des maladies allergiques et inflammatoires chroniques.

MÉCANISME D'ACTION

Tous les agents ont de nombreux effets métaboliques intenses en plus d'entraîner une suppression de l'inflammation et une modification de la réponse immunitaire normale ■ Ils existent sous plusieurs formes pharmaceutiques, incluant les préparations orales, topiques ou injectables et celles administrées par inhalation ■ L'utilisation prolongée de grandes quantités d'agents topiques ou de ceux administrés par inhalation peut entraîner l'absorption par voie générale et la suppression de la fonction des surrénales.

CONTRE-INDICATIONS, PRÉCAUTIONS ET MISES EN GARDE

Contre-indications: Infections graves (sauf en présence de certaines formes de méningite) ■ Ne pas administrer de vaccins à virus vivants aux patients recevant de plus fortes doses.
Précautions et mises en garde: Suppression des surrénales en cas de traitement prolongé ■ Ne pas arrêter le traitement brusquement ■ En période de stress (intervention chirurgicale, infections), il peut s'avérer nécessaire d'administrer des doses supplémentaires ■ **OBST., ALLAITEMENT**: L'innocuité du médicament n'a pas été établie ■ **PÉD.**: Le traitement prolongé entraîne le ralentissement de la croissance ■ Ces médicaments peuvent masquer les signes d'infection. Administrer la plus faible dose pendant le moins de temps possible. En cas de traitement prolongé, il est préférable d'administrer ce type de médicament 1 jour sur 2.

INTERACTIONS

Effets hypokaliémiques additifs lors de l'administration concomitante d'**amphotéricine B**, de **diurétiques épargneurs de potassium**, de **pipéracilline** ou de **ticarcilline** ■ l'hypokaliémie peut augmenter le risque de toxicité **digitalique** ■ Le traitement par des corticostéroïdes peut augmenter les besoins en **insuline** ou en **hypoglycémiants oraux** ■ La **phénytoïne**, le **phénobarbital** et la **rifampine** accélèrent le métabolisme et peuvent diminuer l'efficacité des corticostéroïdes ■ Les **contraceptifs oraux** peuvent inhiber le métabolisme des corticostéroïdes ■ La **cholestyramine** et le **colestipol** peuvent diminuer l'absorption de ces agents.

SOINS INFIRMIERS

ÉVALUATION DE LA SITUATION

- Ces médicaments sont indiqués dans le traitement de nombreuses maladies. Évaluer les systèmes touchés avant le traitement et à intervalles réguliers pendant toute sa durée.
- Avant le traitement et à intervalles réguliers pendant toute sa durée, surveiller l'apparition des signes suivants d'insuffisance surrénalienne: hypotension, perte de poids, faiblesse, nausées, vomissements, anorexie, léthargie, confusion, agitation.
- Noter à intervalles réguliers la croissance chez les enfants.

DIAGNOSTICS INFIRMIERS POSSIBLES

- Risque d'infection (Effets secondaires).
- Connaissances insuffisantes sur le traitement médicamenteux (Enseignement au patient et à ses proches).
- Image corporelle perturbée (Effets secondaires).

INTERVENTIONS INFIRMIÈRES

- Si le médicament doit être pris tous les jours ou tous les deux jours, administrer la dose le matin pour faire coïncider la prise avec les sécrétions naturelles de cortisol.

PO: Administrer le médicament avec des aliments pour réduire l'irritation gastrique.

ENSEIGNEMENT AU PATIENT ET À SES PROCHES

- Conseiller au patient de respecter rigoureusement la posologie recommandée. Lui expliquer que le sevrage brusque peut entraîner des symptômes d'insuffisance surrénalienne, qui peuvent mettre sa vie en danger.
- Inciter le patient suivant un traitement prolongé à adopter un régime riche en protéines, en calcium et en potassium et pauvre en sodium et en glucides.

- Expliquer au patient que ces médicaments ont des effets immunosuppresseurs et qu'ils peuvent masquer les symptômes d'infection. Lui conseiller d'éviter tout contact avec des personnes contagieuses et de signaler immédiatement à un professionnel de la santé tout signe d'infection. Conseiller au patient de ne pas se faire vacciner avant d'avoir consulté un professionnel de la santé au préalable.
- Prévenir le patient que le traitement pourrait affecter son image corporelle. Explorer avec lui les stratégies d'adaptation auxquelles il pourrait recourir.
- Conseiller au patient de toujours porter sur lui une pièce d'identité où sont inscrits son problème de santé et son traitement médicamenteux pour parer à toute urgence dans le cas où il serait incapable de communiquer ses antécédents médicaux.

VÉRIFICATION DE L'EFFICACITÉ THÉRAPEUTIQUE

L'efficacité du traitement peut être démontrée par: la suppression des réponses inflammatoire et immunitaire en présence de maladies auto-immunes, de réactions allergiques ou de greffes d'organes ▪ la maîtrise des symptômes d'insuffisance surrénalienne grâce au traitement de substitution ▪ la disparition de l'inflammation, du prurit ou d'autres troubles dermatologiques.

CORTICOSTÉROÏDES INCLUS DANS LE *GUIDE*

DIURÉTIQUES

INDICATIONS

Les diurétiques thiazidiques et les diurétiques de l'anse sont administrés seuls ou en association pour traiter l'hypertension ou l'œdème dû à l'insuffisance cardiaque ou à d'autres causes ▪ Les diurétiques épargneurs de potassium ont de faibles propriétés diurétiques et antihypertensives; ils sont surtout administrés pour empêcher l'élimination de potassium chez les patients recevant des diurétiques thiazidiques ou des diurétiques de l'anse ■ Les diurétiques osmotiques sont souvent utilisés dans le traitement de l'œdème cérébral.

MÉCANISME D'ACTION

Les diurétiques améliorent la diurèse de certains électrolytes et de l'eau en modifiant le mécanisme de sécrétion et de réabsorption des tubules rénaux ■ Les médicaments couramment administrés font partie des classes suivantes: diurétiques thiazidiques et dérivés ayant une structure proche (chlorthalidone, hydrochlorothiazide, indapamide et métolazone), diurétiques de l'anse (bumétanide et furosémide), diurétiques épargneurs de potassium (amiloride, spironolactone et triamtérène), diurétiques osmotiques (mannitol). Les mécanismes varient d'un médicament à l'autre.

CONTRE-INDICATIONS, PRÉCAUTIONS ET MISES EN GARDE

Contre-indications: Hypersensibilité ■ Risque de réactions de sensibilité croisée lors de l'administration de sulfamides.

Précautions et mises en garde: Administrer ces médicaments avec prudence aux patients souffrant de maladie rénale ou hépatique ■ **OBST., ALLAITEMENT**: L'innocuité des diurétiques n'a pas été établie.

INTERACTIONS

Effets additifs sur l'hypokaliémie lors de l'administration simultanée de **corticostéroïdes**, d'**amphotéricine B**, de **pipéracilline** ou de **ticarcilline** ■ L'hypokaliémie augmente la toxicité des **dérivés digitaliques** ■ Les diurétiques kaliurétiques diminuent l'excrétion du **lithium** et peuvent provoquer une toxicité ■ Effets additifs sur l'hypotension lors de l'administration simultanée d'autres **antihypertenseurs** ou de **dérivés nitrés** ■ Les diurétiques épargneurs de potassium peuvent provoquer l'hyperkaliémie, s'ils sont administrés en même temps que des **suppléments de potassium** ou des **inhibiteurs de l'enzyme de conversion de l'angiotensine (IECA)**.

SOINS INFIRMIERS

ÉVALUATION DE LA SITUATION

- Suivre de près l'équilibre hydrique pendant toute la durée du traitement. Noter tous les jours le poids du patient, effectuer le bilan quotidien des ingesta et des excreta, déterminer l'étendue et le siège de l'œdème, ausculter le murmure vésiculaire et examiner l'intégrité de la peau et des muqueuses.
- Suivre de près les signes et les symptômes suivants: anorexie, faiblesse musculaire, engourdissements, picotements, paresthésie, confusion et soif incoercible. Prévenir le médecin ou un autre professionnel de la santé dès l'apparition de ces signes de déséquilibre électrolytique.

Hypertension: Mesurer la pression artérielle et le pouls avant et pendant l'administration. Vérifier la fréquence du renouvellement des ordonnances pour s'assurer que le patient est fidèle au traitement antihypertenseur.

Pression intracrânienne accrue: Déterminer l'état neurologique et mesurer la pression intracrânienne des patients qui reçoivent des diurétiques osmotiques pour réduire l'œdème cérébral.

Pression intraoculaire accrue: Suivre de près les douleurs oculaires persistantes ou accrues ou la diminution de l'acuité visuelle.

Tests de laboratoire:

- Noter les concentrations d'électrolytes (particulièrement de potassium), d'urée et d'acide urique sérique ainsi que la glycémie, avant l'administration du diurétique et à intervalles réguliers tout au long du traitement.
- Les diurétiques thiazidiques peuvent élever les concentrations sanguines de cholestérol, de lipoprotéines de faible densité (LDL) et de triglycérides.

DIAGNOSTICS INFIRMIERS POSSIBLES

- Excès de volume liquidien (Indications).
- Connaissances insuffisantes sur le traitement médicamenteux (Enseignement au patient et à ses proches).
- Non-observance du traitement médicamenteux (Enseignement au patient et à ses proches).

INTERVENTIONS INFIRMIÈRES

- Administrer les diurétiques par voie orale le matin pour prévenir l'interruption du cycle du sommeil.
- De nombreux diurétiques sont disponibles en association avec des antihypertenseurs ou des diurétiques épargneurs de potassium.

ENSEIGNEMENT AU PATIENT ET À SES PROCHES

- Expliquer au patient qu'il doit respecter rigoureusement la posologie recommandée. Conseiller au patient sous traitement antihypertenseur de continuer à prendre le médicament même s'il se sent mieux. Ces agents aident à maîtriser la pression artérielle, mais ne guérissent pas l'hypertension.
- Conseiller au patient de changer lentement de position pour réduire le risque d'hypotension orthostatique. Le prévenir que la consommation d'alcool, l'effort par temps chaud ou la station debout pendant de longues périodes peuvent aggraver l'hypotension orthostatique durant ce traitement.
- Conseiller au patient de demander à un professionnel de la santé quelles sont les recommandations concernant la consommation de potassium d'origine alimentaire.
- Demander au patient de se peser toutes les semaines et de signaler tout changement de poids important.
- Recommander au patient d'utiliser un écran solaire et de porter des vêtements de protection pour prévenir les réactions de photosensibilité.
- Conseiller au patient de consulter un professionnel de la santé avant de prendre un médicament en vente libre en même temps qu'un diurétique.
- Recommander au patient qui doit suivre un traitement dentaire ou subir une intervention chirurgicale d'avertir le dentiste ou le médecin qu'il suit ce traitement médicamenteux.
- Recommander au patient de signaler immédiatement à un professionnel de la santé les symptômes suivants: faiblesse musculaire, crampes, nausées, étourdissements, engourdissements ou picotements au niveau des membres.
- Expliquer au patient l'importance des examens de suivi réguliers.

Hypertension:

- Inciter le patient à prendre d'autres mesures de réduction de l'hypertension, comme perdre du poids, faire régulièrement de l'exercice, réduire sa consommation de sel, diminuer le stress, boire de l'alcool avec modération et cesser de fumer.
- Montrer au patient souffrant d'hypertension comment mesurer sa pression artérielle et lui recommander de prendre cette mesure toutes les semaines.

VÉRIFICATION DE L'EFFICACITÉ THÉRAPEUTIQUE

L'efficacité du traitement peut être démontrée par: la baisse de la pression artérielle ■ l'augmentation du débit urinaire ■ la réduction de l'œdème ■ la baisse de la pression intracrânienne ■ la prévention de l'hypokaliémie chez les patients prenant des diurétiques ■ la diminution de l'hypersécrétion d'aldostérone ■ la baisse de la pression intraoculaire.

DIURÉTIQUES INCLUS DANS LE *GUIDE*

de l'anse
bumétanide, 371
furosémide, 371

épargneurs de potassium
amiloride, 375
spironolactone, 375
triamtérène, 375

inhibiteurs de l'anhydrase carbonique
acétazolamide, 619
méthazolamide, 619

osmotique
mannitol, 733

thiazidiques et dérivés ayant une structure proche
chlorthalidone, 378
hydrochlorothiazide, 378
indapamide, 606
métolazone, 785

HORMONES

INDICATIONS

Traitement des maladies de carence et des troubles déficitaires, notamment le diabète (insuline), le diabète insipide (desmoprésine), l'hypothyroïdie (hormones thyroïdiennes) et la ménopause (œstrogènes et œstrogènes/progestatifs) ■ Les œstrogènes et la progestérone sont utilisés à titre de contraceptifs en différentes associations et séquences ■ On peut également utiliser des hormones dans le traitement des tumeurs hormonosensibles (androgènes, œstrogènes) et dans d'autres cas particuliers. Voir les monographies des différents agents.

MÉCANISME D'ACTION

Ces agents sont des substances naturelles et synthétiques ayant des effets spécifiques sur les tissus cibles. Leurs effets sont très différents, selon l'agent en cause et les tissus qu'ils ciblent.

CONTRE-INDICATIONS, PRÉCAUTIONS ET MISES EN GARDE

Contre-indications: Les contre-indications dépendent de chacun des agents; voir les monographies.
Précautions et mises en garde: Les précautions à prendre dépendent de chacun des agents; voir les monographies.

INTERACTIONS

Les interactions dépendent de chacun des agents; voir les monographies.

SOINS INFIRMIERS

ÉVALUATION DE LA SITUATION

■ Suivre de près le patient pour déterminer les symptômes de carence ou d'excès hormonal.
Hormones sexuelles: Suivre à intervalles réguliers tout au long du traitement la pression artérielle et les résultats des tests de la fonction hépatique.

DIAGNOSTICS INFIRMIERS POSSIBLES

- Dysfonctionnement sexuel (Indications).
- Image corporelle perturbée (Indications, Effets secondaires).
- Connaissances insuffisantes sur la maladie et sur le traitement médicamenteux (Enseignement au patient et à ses proches).

INTERVENTIONS INFIRMIÈRES

Hormones sexuelles: Au cours de l'hospitalisation, continuer d'administrer les hormones selon le schéma posologique que le patient suivait auparavant.

ENSEIGNEMENT AU PATIENT ET À SES PROCHES

- Expliquer au patient le schéma posologique (informer la patiente qui prend des hormones femelles de la possibilité d'hémorragies de retrait).
- Insister sur l'importance des examens de suivi permettant de déterminer l'efficacité du traitement, de s'assurer du développement approprié des enfants et de dépister rapidement les effets secondaires possibles.

Hormones sexuelles femelles: Recommander à la patiente de signaler à un professionnel de la santé les signes et les symptômes de rétention hydrique, de maladie thromboembolique, de dépression ou de dysfonctionnement hépatique.

VÉRIFICATION DE L'EFFICACITÉ THÉRAPEUTIQUE

L'efficacité du traitement peut être démontrée par: la résolution des symptômes cliniques de déséquilibres hormonaux, notamment des symptômes de ménopause ■ la contraception ■ la correction des déséquilibres hydriques et électrolytiques ■ l'arrêt de la propagation des cancers métastatiques avancés du sein et de la prostate ■ le ralentissement de l'évolution de l'ostéoporose postménopausique.

HORMONES INCLUSES DANS LE *GUIDE*

HYPOLIPIDÉMIANTS

INDICATIONS

Traitement d'appoint dans le cadre d'un programme global comprenant également la diétothérapie et l'exercice, visant à abaisser les concentrations des lipides sanguins, pour essayer de réduire par cette voie la morbidité et la mortalité attribuables à la maladie cardiovasculaire athéroscléreuse et à ses séquelles.

MÉCANISME D'ACTION

Les inhibiteurs de l'HMG-CoA réductase (atorvastatine, fluvastatine, lovastatine, pravastatine, rosuvastatine, simvastatine) inhibent une enzyme qui intervient dans la synthèse du cholestérol ▪ Les chélateurs des acides biliaires (cholestyramine, colestipol) se lient au cholestérol dans le tractus gastro-intestinal ▪ La niacine, l'ézétimibe, le fénofibrate et le gemfibrozil agissent par d'autres mécanismes (consulter la monographie de chaque médicament).

CONTRE-INDICATIONS, PRÉCAUTIONS ET MISES EN GARDE

Contre-indications: Hypersensibilité.

Précautions et mises en garde: OBST., ALLAITEMENT, PÉD.: L'innocuité de ces médicaments chez les femmes enceintes ou chez celles qui allaitent et chez les enfants n'a pas été établie ▪ Consulter la monographie de chaque médicament ▪ Il est conseillé d'essayer dans un premier temps d'abaisser les taux des lipides sanguins par la diétothérapie, pendant 2 ou 3 mois, avant d'amorcer un traitement médicamenteux.

INTERACTIONS

Les chélateurs des acides biliaires (cholestyramine et colestipol) peuvent lier les **vitamines liposolubles (A, D, E et K)** et empêcher l'absorption de certains médicaments au niveau du tractus gastro-intestinal ▪ L'administration concomitante de **niacine**, d'**érythromycine**, de **gemfibrozil**, de **fénofibrate** et de **cyclosporine** augmente le risque de myopathie induite par les inhibiteurs de l'HMG-CoA réductase.

SOINS INFIRMIERS

ÉVALUATION DE LA SITUATION

- Recueillir des données sur les habitudes alimentaires du patient, notamment sur sa consommation de matières grasses et d'alcool.

Tests de laboratoire:

- Vérifier les concentrations de cholestérol et de triglycérides avant l'administration de l'agent et à intervalles réguliers pendant toute la durée du traitement. Ne pas administrer ces agents en cas d'élévation paradoxale des concentrations de cholestérol.

- Vérifier les résultats des tests de la fonction hépatique avant le traitement et à intervalles réguliers pendant toute sa durée. Certains hypolipidémiants peuvent élever les concentrations enzymatiques.

DIAGNOSTICS INFIRMIERS POSSIBLES

- Connaissances insuffisantes sur le traitement médicamenteux (Enseignement au patient et à ses proches).
- Non-observance du traitement médicamenteux (Enseignement au patient et à ses proches).

INTERVENTIONS INFIRMIÈRES

- Consulter la monographie de chaque médicament pour déterminer s'il faut l'administrer avec des aliments ou en dehors des repas.

ENSEIGNEMENT AU PATIENT ET À SES PROCHES

- Expliquer au patient que le traitement médicamenteux ne peut être efficace que s'il suit en même temps un régime alimentaire pauvre en matières grasses, en cholestérol et en glucides, s'il évite de boire de l'alcool, s'il fait de l'exercice et s'il cesse de fumer.

VÉRIFICATION DE L'EFFICACITÉ THÉRAPEUTIQUE

L'efficacité du traitement peut être démontrée par: la baisse des concentrations sériques de triglycérides et de cholestérol-LDL (lipoprotéines de basse densité) et l'élévation des concentrations de cholestérol-HDL (lipoprotéines de haute densité). Il faut habituellement réévaluer le traitement si aucune réponse clinique ne se manifeste après 3 mois.

HYPOLIPIDÉMIANTS INCLUS DANS LE *GUIDE*

chélateurs des acides biliaires
cholestyramine, 218
colestipol, 218

inhibiteurs de l'HMG-CoA réductase
Pour connaître les médicaments de cette classe, prière de consulter la section des monographies.

divers
ézétimibe, 462
fénofibrate, 469
gemfibrozil, 541
niacine, niacinamide, 849

IMMUNOSUPPRESSEURS

INDICATIONS

Azathioprine, basiliximab, cyclosporine, daclizumab, mycophénolate, sirolimus et tacrolimus: Traitement d'association avec des glucocorticoïdes dans la prévention des réactions de rejet d'une greffe ■ **Azathioprine, cyclosporine et méthotrexate**: Traitement de maladies auto-immunes spécifiques (p. ex., syndrome néphrotique de l'enfance et polyarthrite rhumatoïde grave).

MÉCANISME D'ACTION

Inhibition des réponses immunitaires à médiation cellulaire par différents mécanismes ■ En plus de l'azathioprine et de la cyclosporine, qui sont principalement utilisées pour leurs propriétés d'immunomodulation, le cyclophosphamide et le méthotrexate sont utilisés pour supprimer les réponses immunitaires dans le cas de certaines maladies (syndrome néphrotique de l'enfance et polyarthrite rhumatoïde grave) ■ Le basiliximab et le daclizumab sont des anticorps monoclonaux ■ Le mofétilmycophénolate bloque la prolifération des lymphocytes T et B ■ Le sirolimus et le tacrolimus inhibent l'activation des lymphocytes T. Le sirolimus inhibe aussi la prolifération des lymphocytes T et la production d'anticorps.

CONTRE-INDICATIONS, PRÉCAUTIONS ET MISES EN GARDE

Contre-indications: Hypersensibilité au médicament ou à l'excipient.

Précautions et mises en garde: Infections ■ **OBST., ALLAITEMENT:** L'innocuité de ces agents n'a pas été établie.

INTERACTIONS

L'**allopurinol** inhibe le métabolisme de l'azathioprine ■ Les **médicaments qui modifient le métabolisme hépatique** peuvent aussi modifier l'effet de la cyclosporine, du sirolimus et du tacrolimus ■ Risque de toxicité additive du méthotrexate lors de l'administration concomitante d'autres **médicaments néphrotoxiques**, de doses élevées d'**aspirine** ou d'**AINS** ■ On a signalé plusieurs interactions avec la cyclosporine, le sirolimus, le mofétilmycophénolate ou le tacrolimus et d'**autres médicaments** ou certains **aliments** ■ Consulter la monographie de chaque médicament.

SOINS INFIRMIERS

ÉVALUATION DE LA SITUATION

- Rester à l'affût des signes suivants d'infection: altération des signes vitaux, aspect des crachats, mictions douloureuses, pollakiurie, diarrhée, accroissement du nombre de leucocytes. Prévenir immédiatement le médecin ou un autre professionnel de la santé si ces symptômes se manifestent.

Prévention du rejet d'une greffe: Suivre de près, pendant toute la durée du traitement, les symptômes de rejet d'organe.

Tests de laboratoire: Noter la numération globulaire et la formule leucocytaire pendant toute la durée du traitement.

DIAGNOSTICS INFIRMIERS POSSIBLES

- Risque d'infection (Effets secondaires).
- Connaissances insuffisantes sur le traitement médicamenteux (Enseignement au patient et à ses proches).

INTERVENTIONS INFIRMIÈRES

- Le patient ayant subi une transplantation doit être isolé des membres du personnel et des visiteurs qui pourraient être contagieux.
- Maintenir l'isolement de protection, selon le protocole de l'établissement.

ENSEIGNEMENT AU PATIENT ET À SES PROCHES

- Expliquer au patient qu'il doit suivre ce traitement toute sa vie durant pour prévenir le rejet de l'organe transplanté. Passer en revue les symptômes de rejet d'un organe greffé et insister sur le fait qu'il faut prévenir un professionnel de la santé dès que ces symptômes apparaissent.
- Recommander au patient d'éviter les personnes contagieuses et celles qui ont récemment reçu le vaccin Salk inactivé (antipoliomyélitique) par voie orale. Le prévenir qu'il ne doit pas se faire vacciner sans avoir consulté au préalable un professionnel de la santé.
- Insister sur l'importance des examens de suivi et des tests de laboratoire.

VÉRIFICATION DE L'EFFICACITÉ THÉRAPEUTIQUE

L'efficacité du traitement peut être démontrée par: la prévention ou la résolution des symptômes associés aux réactions de rejet des greffes ou la diminution des symptômes de maladies auto-immunes.

IMMUNOSUPPRESSEURS INCLUS DANS LE *GUIDE*

INOTROPES ET CARDIOTONIQUES

INDICATIONS

Traitement de courte durée de l'insuffisance cardiaque ou de la décompensation cardiaque rebelle au traitement habituel par des dérivés digitaliques, des diurétiques ou des vasodilatateurs ■ Administration au cours d'une chirurgie cardiaque.

MÉCANISME D'ACTION

Élévation du débit cardiaque, principalement par des effets directs sur le myocarde et par certains effets vasculaires périphériques ■ La milrinone augmente la contractilité cardiaque par inhibition de l'enzyme adénosine monophosphate cyclique (AMP_c)-phosphodiestérase, ce qui élève les concentrations d'AMP_c intracellulaire.

CONTRE-INDICATIONS, PRÉCAUTIONS ET MISES EN GARDE

Contre-indications: Hypersensibilité ■ Patients souffrant de cardiomyopathie hypertrophique (usage déconseillé).

Précautions et mises en garde: **OBST., ALLAITEMENT, PÉD.**: L'innocuité de ces médicaments n'a pas été établie.

INTERACTIONS

Les **agents qui provoquent l'hypokaliémie, l'hypomagnésémie ou l'hypercalcémie** augmentent le risque de toxicité digitalique ■ Risque de bradycardie additive lors de l'administration concomitante de **bêtabloquants** et de dérivés digitaliques ■ La **quinidine** élève les concentrations sériques de digoxine.

SOINS INFIRMIERS

ÉVALUATION DE LA SITUATION

- Mesurer la pression artérielle, le pouls et la fréquence respiratoire avant le traitement et pendant toute sa durée.
- Effectuer le bilan quotidien des ingesta et des excreta et peser le patient tous les jours. Observer le patient, pendant toute la durée du traitement, pour déterminer la présence des signes et des symptômes suivants d'insuffisance cardiaque: œdème périphérique, râles et crépitations, dyspnée, gain pondéral, turgescence des jugulaires.
- Avant d'administrer la dose d'attaque initiale, déterminer si le patient a déjà pris des préparations digitaliques au cours des 2 à 3 semaines précédentes.

Tests de laboratoire: Examiner à intervalles réguliers pendant toute la durée du traitement les concentrations des électrolytes sériques, particulièrement de potassium, de magnésium et de calcium, ainsi que les résultats des tests des fonctions rénale et hépatique.
Toxicité et surdosage: Chez les patients prenant des dérivés digitaliques, on devrait mesurer à intervalles réguliers les concentrations sériques de ces médicaments.

DIAGNOSTICS INFIRMIERS POSSIBLES

- Débit cardiaque diminué (Indications).
- Connaissances insuffisantes sur le traitement médicamenteux (Enseignement au patient et à ses proches).

INTERVENTIONS INFIRMIÈRES

- Corriger l'hypokaliémie avant d'administrer la milrinone ou la digoxine.
- Corriger l'hypovolémie par des agents qui augmentent le volume plasmatique avant d'administrer ces agents.

ENSEIGNEMENT AU PATIENT ET À SES PROCHES

- Conseiller au patient de prévenir un professionnel de la santé si les symptômes ne diminuent pas ou s'ils s'aggravent.
- Recommander au patient de prévenir immédiatement l'infirmière en cas de douleur ou de gêne au point de ponction au cours de l'administration par voie IV.

VÉRIFICATION DE L'EFFICACITÉ THÉRAPEUTIQUE

L'efficacité du traitement peut être démontrée par: l'élévation du débit cardiaque ▪ la réduction de la gravité de l'insuffisance cardiaque ▪ l'augmentation du débit urinaire.

INOTROPES ET CARDIOTONIQUES INCLUS DANS LE *GUIDE*

digoxine, 350
dobutamine, 380
dopamine, 394
milrinone, 802

LAXATIFS

INDICATIONS

Traitement ou prévention de la constipation ou préparation des intestins à la radiologie ou à l'endoscopie.

MÉCANISME D'ACTION

Les laxatifs entraînent 1 ou plusieurs défécations par jour ▪ Il existe plusieurs types de laxatifs: les laxatifs stimulants (bisacodyl, séné), les laxatifs salins (sels de magnésium et phosphates), les laxatifs émollients (docusate), les agents de masse (polycarbophile et psyllium), les laxatifs osmotiques (lactulose, polyéthylène glycol avec électrolytes) et les lubrifiants (huile minérale) ▪ L'augmentation de l'apport de liquides, l'exercice et la consommation accrue d'aliments riches en fibres permettent également de soulager la constipation chronique.

CONTRE-INDICATIONS, PRÉCAUTIONS ET MISES EN GARDE

Contre-indications: Hypersensibilité ▪ Douleurs abdominales persistantes, nausées ou vomissements d'étiologie inconnue, particulièrement s'ils s'accompagnent de fièvre ou d'autres signes d'abdomen aigu.

Précautions et mises en garde: L'utilisation excessive ou prolongée de laxatifs peut entraîner la dépendance ■ **PÉD.**: Ne pas administrer ces médicaments aux enfants, sauf si le médecin ou un autre professionnel de la santé le recommande.

INTERACTIONS

En théorie, les laxatifs peuvent diminuer l'absorption des autres **médicaments administrés par voie orale** en accélérant le transit intestinal ■ L'huile minérale diminue l'absorption des **vitamines liposolubles (A, D, E et K)**. L'administration concomitante de docusate et d'huile minérale est contre-indiquée.

SOINS INFIRMIERS

ÉVALUATION DE LA SITUATION

- Noter la présence d'une distension abdominale, ausculter les bruits intestinaux, observer les habitudes normales d'élimination.
- Noter la couleur, la consistance et la quantité des selles produites.

DIAGNOSTICS INFIRMIERS POSSIBLES

- Constipation (Indications).
- Connaissances insuffisantes sur le traitement médicamenteux (Enseignement au patient et à ses proches).

INTERVENTIONS INFIRMIÈRES

- On peut administrer de nombreux laxatifs au coucher pour que l'élimination intestinale ait lieu le lendemain matin.
- L'administration des médicaments par voie orale à jeun produit habituellement des résultats plus rapides.
- DEMANDER AU PATIENT DE NE PAS ÉCRASER NI CROQUER LES COMPRIMÉS À DÉLITEMENT ENTÉRIQUE; lui conseiller plutôt de les prendre avec un grand verre d'eau ou de jus.
- Parfois, les laxatifs émollients et les agents de masse n'entraînent pas d'élimination intestinale avant plusieurs jours.

ENSEIGNEMENT AU PATIENT ET À SES PROCHES

- Prévenir le patient (sauf s'il souffre de lésion de la moelle épinière) que les laxatifs ne sont destinés qu'à un traitement de courte durée. Lui expliquer que le traitement prolongé peut entraîner un déséquilibre électrolytique et la dépendance.
- Inciter le patient à boire plus de liquides pendant le traitement, à moins de contre-indication médicale, (au minimum, de 1 500 à 2 000 mL par jour) pour prévenir la déshydratation.
- Recommander au patient de prendre d'autres mesures qui favorisent l'élimination intestinale: boire plus de liquides, manger plus d'aliments riches en fibres, faire de l'exercice. Expliquer au patient que chaque personne a ses propres habitudes d'élimination et qu'il est tout aussi normal de déféquer 3 fois par jour que 3 fois par semaine.
- Recommander au patient souffrant de maladie cardiaque d'éviter les efforts de défécation (manœuvre de Valsalva).
- Prévenir le patient que les laxatifs sont déconseillés si la constipation s'accompagne de douleurs abdominales, de fièvre, de nausées et de vomissements.

VÉRIFICATION DE L'EFFICACITÉ THÉRAPEUTIQUE

L'efficacité du traitement peut être démontrée par: l'émission de selles molles et bien moulées ■ l'évacuation des résidus alimentaires du côlon.

LAXATIFS INCLUS DANS LE *GUIDE*

agents de masse
polycarbophile, 983
psyllium, 1036

émollient
docusate, 386

lubrifiant
huile minérale, 568

osmotiques
lactulose, 679
polyéthylène glycol/électrolytes, 984

salins
phosphate/biphosphate, 966
sels de magnésium, 727

stimulants
bisacodyl, 146
séné, sennosides, 1098

MÉDICAMENTS OPHTALMIQUES

Voir l'annexe N.

MINÉRAUX ET ÉLECTROLYTES

INDICATIONS

Électrolytes: Prévention ou traitement des déséquilibres hydroélectrolytiques et maintien de l'équilibre acidobasique et de la pression osmotique ■ **Minéraux**: Prévention ou traitement des carences en oligoéléments.

MÉCANISME D'ACTION

Électrolytes: Éléments essentiels à l'homéostasie. Le maintien des concentrations d'électrolytes dans les limites normales est indispensable à de nombreuses fonctions physiologiques, telles que les fonctions cardiaque, nerveuse et musculaire, la croissance et la stabilité osseuses, etc. ■ **Minéraux**: Éléments nécessaires à une croissance et à des fonctions normales; ils jouent le rôle de cofacteurs dans les réactions enzymatiques et de facteurs stabilisants dans la synthèse de l'hémoglobine et des protéines ainsi que dans de nombreux autres processus physiologiques.

CONTRE-INDICATIONS, PRÉCAUTIONS ET MISES EN GARDE

Contre-indications: Cas où l'administration pourrait entraîner des concentrations excessives ■ Présence de facteurs de risque de rétention hydrique.

Précautions et mises en garde: Maladies où des déséquilibres électrolytiques sont fréquents, p. ex., maladie hépatique ou rénale, troubles surrénaliens ou hypophysaires et diabète.

INTERACTIONS

Consulter la monographie de chaque agent.

SOINS INFIRMIERS

ÉVALUATION DE LA SITUATION

- Observer le patient avec attention pour déceler tout signe d'excès ou de carence électrolytique. Vérifier les résultats des tests de laboratoire avant le traitement et à intervalles réguliers pendant toute sa durée.

DIAGNOSTICS INFIRMIERS POSSIBLES

- Alimentation déficiente (Indications).
- Connaissances insuffisantes sur le traitement médicamenteux (Enseignement au patient et à ses proches).

INTERVENTIONS INFIRMIÈRES

CHLORURE DE POTASSIUM: N'ADMINISTRER LA PRÉPARATION PARENTÉRALE DE CHLORURE DE POTASSIUM QU'APRÈS DILUTION.

ENSEIGNEMENT AU PATIENT ET À SES PROCHES

- Passer en revue avec le patient atteint d'un déséquilibre électrolytique chronique les modifications qu'il doit apporter à son alimentation.

VÉRIFICATION DE L'EFFICACITÉ THÉRAPEUTIQUE

L'efficacité du traitement peut être démontrée par: le rétablissement des concentrations sériques normales d'électrolytes et la disparition des symptômes cliniques de déséquilibres électrolytiques ■ la modification du pH ou de la composition de l'urine, prévenant ainsi la formation de calculs rénaux.

MINÉRAUX ET ÉLECTROLYTES INCLUS DANS LE *GUIDE*

suppléments de calcium
acétate de calcium, 180
carbonate de calcium, 180
chlorure de calcium, 180
citrate de calcium, 180
gluconate de calcium, 181

suppléments de fer
fer dextran, 477
fer saccharose, 477
fumarate ferreux, 477
gluconate ferreux, 477
sulfate ferreux, 477

suppléments de magnésium
sels de magnésium (voie orale), 727
sulfate de magnésium, 731

suppléments de phosphate
phosphate de potassium, 987
phosphate de potassium monobasique, 987
phosphate de sodium, 1116

suppléments de potassium
acétate de potassium, 989
bicarbonate de potassium/citrate de potassium, 998
chlorure de potassium, 990
citrate de potassium, 990
gluconate de potassium, 990

divers
bicarbonate de sodium, 1110
chlorure de sodium, 1112
citrate de sodium et acide citrique, 1114
sulfate de zinc, 1278

PRODUITS NATURELS

INDICATIONS

On utilise ces agents pour traiter un grand nombre de troubles. Ce sont des produits en vente libre et les consommateurs peuvent choisir parmi un grand nombre de marques.

MÉCANISME D'ACTION

L'utilisation de ces produits se fonde sur des témoignages et des preuves souvent empiriques. Santé Canada exerce peu de contrôle sur ces agents et, actuellement, leur teneur n'est pas véritablement standardisée.

CONTRE-INDICATIONS, PRÉCAUTIONS ET MISES EN GARDE

Contre-indications: Hypersensibilité. La plupart de ces agents sont extraits de plantes et peuvent contenir un grand nombre d'impuretés.
Précautions et mises en garde: Il faut prévenir tous les patients, mais particulièrement les personnes âgées, les enfants et les femmes enceintes et allaitantes, que l'utilisation de ces agents les expose aux mêmes genres de risques que les médicaments d'ordonnance. Les patients atteints d'une maladie chronique grave doivent consulter un professionnel de la santé avant de prendre l'un de ces agents.

INTERACTIONS

Ces agents peuvent interagir avec les médicaments d'ordonnance et peuvent prévenir ou exacerber un effet thérapeutique souhaitable ■ Le **millepertuis** et le **kava-kava** exposent aux risques les plus élevés d'interactions graves.

SOINS INFIRMIERS

ÉVALUATION DE LA SITUATION

- Suivre de près le trouble contre lequel le patient prend l'agent en question.

DIAGNOSTICS INFIRMIERS POSSIBLES

- Connaissances insuffisantes sur la maladie et sur le traitement médicamenteux (Enseignement au patient et à ses proches).

ENSEIGNEMENT AU PATIENT ET À SES PROCHES

- Interroger le patient sur la raison pour laquelle il prend ce genre d'agent.
- Informer le patient des effets secondaires et des interactions connues avec d'autres médicaments.

VÉRIFICATION DE L'EFFICACITÉ THÉRAPEUTIQUE

L'efficacité thérapeutique peut être démontrée par: l'amélioration du trouble contre lequel l'agent est utilisé.

PRODUITS NATURELS INCLUS DANS LE *GUIDE*

RÉGULATEURS DU MÉTABOLISME OSSEUX

INDICATIONS

Les régulateurs du métabolisme osseux sont tout d'abord destinés au traitement et à la prévention de l'ostéoporose chez les femmes ménopausées ■ Les autres indications sont: traitement de l'ostéoporose chez l'homme ■ traitement et prévention de l'ostéoporose d'autres causes, dont la corticothérapie ■ traitement de la maladie osseuse de Paget ■ prise en charge de l'hypercalcémie.

MÉCANISME D'ACTION

Les biphosphonates (alendronate, étidronate, pamidronate, risédronate et acide zolédronique) inhibent la résorption osseuse par inhibition de l'activité des ostéoclastes ■ Le raloxifène se lie aux récepteurs des œstrogènes et il produit sur les os des effets qui ressemblent à ceux des œstrogènes, notamment la diminution de la résorption osseuse et le ralentissement du renouvellement des ostéocytes ■ La calcitonine est une hormone qui inhibe l'activité des ostéoclastes ■ Le tériparatide est un analogue de la parathormone qui stimule l'activité des ostéoblastes et accélère la formation osseuse.

CONTRE-INDICATIONS, PRÉCAUTIONS ET MISES EN GARDE

Contre-indications: Hypersensibilité ■ Hypocalcémie (biphosphonates) ■ Hypercalcémie (tériparatide) ■ Femmes en âge de procréer ■ Antécédents de thromboembolie (raloxifène).
Précautions et mises en garde: La prudence est de mise chez les patients insuffisants rénaux ■ L'utilisation de certains agents en présence d'insuffisance rénale de modérée à grave devrait être évitée.

INTERACTIONS

Les **suppléments de calcium** diminuent l'absorption des biphosphonates; espacer les prises d'au moins 2 heures ■ L'**aspirine** peut accroître les effets gastro-intestinaux de l'alendronate ■ La **cholestyramine** diminue l'absorption du raloxifène.

SOINS INFIRMIERS

ÉVALUATION DE LA SITUATION

- Évaluer le patient à la recherche d'une faible densité osseuse, avant le traitement et à intervalles réguliers pendant toute sa durée.
- Rester à l'affût des symptômes de la maladie de Paget (douleurs osseuses, céphalées, diminution de l'acuité visuelle et auditive, augmentation de la taille du crâne).

Tests de laboratoire:

- Suivre les concentrations sériques de calcium chez les patients atteints d'ostéoporose.

- Suivre de près les concentrations de phosphatase alcaline chez les patients atteints de la maladie de Paget.

DIAGNOSTICS INFIRMIERS POSSIBLES

- Risque d'accident (Indications).
- Connaissances insuffisantes sur la maladie et sur le traitement médicamenteux (Enseignement au patient et à ses proches).

ENSEIGNEMENT AU PATIENT ET À SES PROCHES

- Inciter le patient à prendre ce type de médicaments en respectant rigoureusement les recommandations du médecin.
- Encourager le patient à faire régulièrement de l'exercice et à modifier les comportements qui augmentent le risque d'ostéoporose.

VÉRIFICATION DE L'EFFICACITÉ THÉRAPEUTIQUE

L'efficacité du traitement peut être démontrée par: la prévention ou le ralentissement de l'évolution de l'ostéoporose chez les femmes ménopausées ■ le ralentissement de l'évolution de la maladie de Paget.

RÉGULATEURS DU MÉTABOLISME OSSEUX INCLUS DANS LE *GUIDE*

biphosphonates
alendronate, 38
étidronate, 455
pamidronate, 919
risédronate, 1070

modulateur sélectif des récepteurs des œstrogènes
raloxifène, 1057

hormones
calcitonine, 178
tériparatide, 1162

RELAXANTS MUSCULOSQUELETTIQUES

INDICATIONS

Les deux principales indications de ces agents sont la spasticité associée aux lésions de la moelle épinière ou aux maladies médullaires (baclofène et dantrolène) et le traitement d'appoint des symptômes des maladies musculosquelettiques douloureuses aiguës (chlorzoxazone, cyclobenzaprine, diazépam, méthocarbamol et orphénadrine) ■ Le dantrolène par voie IV est également administré pour traiter et prévenir l'hyperthermie maligne, alors que la voie orale est utilisée en prévention de ce trouble.

MÉCANISME D'ACTION

Ces agents exercent un effet central (baclofène, chlorzoxazone, cyclobenzaprine, diazépam, méthocarbamol et orphénadrine) ou un effet direct (dantrolène).

CONTRE-INDICATIONS, PRÉCAUTIONS ET MISES EN GARDE

Contre-indications: Le dantrolène par voie orale est contre-indiqué lorsque la spasticité permet au patient de maintenir son équilibre et sa position ■ L'orphénadrine est contre-indiquée, entre autres, en cas d'ulcère gastroduodénal sténosant, d'hypertrophie de la prostate, de glaucome, de cardiospasme et de myasthénie grave.

Précautions et mises en garde: OBST., ALLAITEMENT: L'innocuité de ces médicaments n'a pas été établie ■ Administrer avec prudence aux patients ayant des antécédents de maladie hépatique

- Le baclofène doit être utilisé avec prudence lorsque la spasticité permet au patient de maintenir son équilibre et sa position.

INTERACTIONS

Effets additifs sur la dépression du système nerveux central lors de la prise simultanée d'autres **dépresseurs du SNC**, incluant l'**alcool**, les **antihistaminiques**, les **antidépresseurs**, les **analgésiques opioïdes** et les **hypnosédatifs**.

SOINS INFIRMIERS

ÉVALUATION DE LA SITUATION

- Noter l'intensité de la douleur, mesurer le degré de rigidité musculaire et l'amplitude des mouvements avant l'administration du médicament et à intervalles réguliers tout au long du traitement.

DIAGNOSTICS INFIRMIERS POSSIBLES

- Douleur aiguë (Indications).
- Mobilité physique réduite (Indications).
- Risque d'accident (Effets secondaires).

INTERVENTIONS INFIRMIÈRES

- Prendre les mesures de sécurité qui s'imposent. Suivre de près les déplacements et le transfert du patient.

ENSEIGNEMENT AU PATIENT ET À SES PROCHES

- Encourager le patient à suivre les autres traitements prescrits pour soulager les spasmes musculaires: repos, physiothérapie, application de chaleur.
- Prévenir le patient que ces agents peuvent provoquer de la somnolence. Lui conseiller de ne pas conduire et d'éviter les activités qui exigent sa vigilance jusqu'à ce qu'on ait la certitude que le médicament qui lui a été prescrit n'entraîne pas cet effet chez lui.
- Conseiller au patient de ne pas boire d'alcool et de ne pas prendre d'autres dépresseurs du SNC en même temps que ces médicaments.

VÉRIFICATION DE L'EFFICACITÉ THÉRAPEUTIQUE

L'efficacité du traitement peut être démontrée par: la diminution de l'intensité des douleurs musculosquelettiques ▪ la diminution de la spasticité musculaire ▪ l'augmentation de l'amplitude des mouvements ▪ la prévention ou la diminution de la fièvre et de la rigidité squelettique en cas d'hyperthermie maligne.

RELAXANTS MUSCULOSQUELETTIQUES INCLUS DANS LE *GUIDE*

STIMULANTS DU SYSTÈME NERVEUX CENTRAL (SNC)

INDICATIONS

Traitement d'appoint du trouble déficitaire de l'attention accompagné d'hyperactivité ■ Traitement de la narcolepsie.

MÉCANISME D'ACTION

Stimulation du SNC entraînant la prolongation de la durée de la concentration en cas de trouble déficitaire de l'attention accompagné d'hyperactivité ■ Augmentation de l'activité motrice et de la vigilance et diminution de la fatigue chez les patients narcoleptiques.

CONTRE-INDICATIONS, PRÉCAUTIONS ET MISES EN GARDE

Contre-indications: Hypersensibilité ■ Grossesse ou allaitement ■ Maladie psychiatrique, toxicomanie, pharmacodépendance ■ Glaucome ■ Maladie cardiovasculaire grave.
Précautions et mises en garde: Maladie cardiovasculaire ■ Hypertension ■ Diabète ■ Troubles convulsifs ■ Usage continu (risque de dépendance psychologique ou physique)

INTERACTIONS

Effets sympathomimétiques additifs lors de l'administration concomitante d'autres **agents adrénergiques** ■ L'usage simultané d'**IMAO** peut déclencher une crise hypertensive ■ Les **médicaments qui rendent l'urine alcaline** (**bicarbonate de sodium**, **acétazolamide**) diminuent l'excrétion et intensifient les effets des amphétamines ■ Les **médicaments qui rendent l'urine acide** (**chlorure d'ammonium**, **doses importantes d'acide ascorbique**) intensifient l'excrétion et diminuent les effets des amphétamines ■ Les **phénothiazines** peuvent diminuer les effets de ces agents ■ Le méthylphénidate peut diminuer le métabolisme et augmenter les effets d'**autres médicaments** (**warfarine**, **anticonvulsivants** et **antidépresseurs tricycliques**).

SOINS INFIRMIERS

ÉVALUATION DE LA SITUATION

- Mesurer la pression artérielle, le pouls et la fréquence respiratoire avant l'administration et à intervalles réguliers pendant toute la durée du traitement.
- En présence de trouble déficitaire de l'attention accompagné d'hyperactivité, peser le patient 2 fois par semaine et prévenir le médecin s'il y a perte de poids importante. Mesurer la taille de l'enfant à intervalles réguliers et informer le médecin en cas d'arrêt de la croissance.
- Chez les patients atteints de narcolepsie, observer la fréquence des épisodes de narcolepsie et les consigner dans les dossiers.
- Noter la durée de l'attention, les tics moteurs ou verbaux, la maîtrise des impulsions et les interactions avec autrui chez les enfants atteints de trouble déficitaire de l'attention accompagné d'hyperactivité.
- Les stimulants du SNC peuvent provoquer un faux sentiment d'euphorie et de bien-être. Observer le patient et l'inciter à se reposer.
- L'usage de ces agents comporte des risques élevés de dépendance et d'abus. La tolérance survient rapidement; ne pas augmenter la dose.

DIAGNOSTICS INFIRMIERS POSSIBLES

- Opérations de la pensée perturbées (Effets secondaires).
- Habitudes de sommeil perturbées (Effets secondaires).
- Connaissances insuffisantes sur le traitement médicamenteux (Enseignement au patient et à ses proches).

INTERVENTIONS INFIRMIÈRES

- Administrer la plus faible dose possible.
- Les comprimés à libération prolongée devraient être avalés tels quels sans être brisés, écrasés ou croqués.

Trouble déficitaire de l'attention accompagné d'hyperactivité: Lorsque les symptômes du trouble déficitaire de l'attention accompagné d'hyperactivité sont maîtrisés, on peut réduire la dose ou interrompre le traitement durant l'été. On peut aussi administrer le médicament les 5 jours d'école seulement et en arrêter la prise pendant la fin de semaine ou les jours de congé.
Narcolepsie: Observer et documenter la fréquence des épisodes.

ENSEIGNEMENT AU PATIENT ET À SES PROCHES

- Recommander au patient de prendre le médicament au moins 6 heures avant l'heure du coucher afin de prévenir les troubles du sommeil.
- Expliquer au patient qu'il peut soulager la sécheresse de la bouche en se rinçant souvent la bouche avec de l'eau et en consommant de la gomme ou des bonbons sans sucre.
- Conseiller au patient d'éviter de consommer des boissons à base de caféine.
- Prévenir le patient que ce type de médicament peut altérer sa capacité de jugement et provoquer des étourdissements ou une vision trouble. Lui conseiller de ne pas conduire et d'éviter les activités qui exigent sa vigilance.
- Recommander au patient de prévenir un professionnel de la santé si les symptômes de nervosité, d'agitation, d'insomnie, d'anorexie ou de sécheresse de la bouche s'aggravent.
- Informer le patient que le médecin peut prescrire des arrêts temporaires de la médication lui permettant d'évaluer les bienfaits du traitement et de diminuer le risque de dépendance.
- Recommander au patient de se peser 2 fois par semaine et de signaler à un professionnel de la santé toute perte de poids.
- Conseiller aux parents d'un enfant atteint d'un trouble déficitaire de l'attention accompagné d'hyperactivité d'informer l'infirmière de l'école du traitement que suit leur enfant.

VÉRIFICATION DE L'EFFICACITÉ THÉRAPEUTIQUE

L'efficacité du traitement peut être démontrée par: un effet calmant associé à une moindre hyperactivité et à une durée prolongée de l'attention chez les enfants souffrant d'un trouble déficitaire de l'attention accompagné d'hyperactivité ▪ la diminution de la fréquence des symptômes narcoleptiques.

STIMULANTS DU SYSTÈME NERVEUX CENTRAL INCLUS DANS LE *GUIDE*

THROMBOLYTIQUES

Voir la monographie «Thrombolytiques».

VACCINS ET AGENTS IMMUNISANTS

INDICATIONS

Les immunoglobulines confèrent une immunité passive aux maladies infectieuses, en permettant à l'organisme de développer des anticorps. Les vaccins et les anatoxines contenant des antigènes bactériens ou viraux favorisent la synthèse endogène d'anticorps.

MÉCANISME D'ACTION

L'immunité conférée par les immunoglobulines se développe rapidement, mais elle est de courte durée (jusqu'à 3 mois). L'immunisation active par des vaccins ou des anatoxines entraîne une immunité prolongée (de plusieurs années).

CONTRE-INDICATIONS, PRÉCAUTIONS ET MISES EN GARDE

Contre-indications: Hypersensibilité aux ingrédients actifs, aux agents de conservation ou aux autres additifs ■ Certains agents contiennent du thimérosal, de la néomycine ou des protéines d'œuf.

Précautions et mises en garde: Patients souffrant de troubles de la coagulation graves (injections IM) ■ Patients prenant des médicaments anticoagulants.

INTERACTIONS

Diminution de la réponse des anticorps aux vaccins/anatoxines et risque accru de réactions indésirables chez les patients sous traitement par des **antinéoplasiques** ou des **immunosuppresseurs** ou chez ceux sous **radiothérapie**.

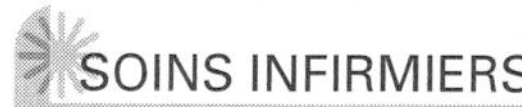

SOINS INFIRMIERS

ÉVALUATION DE LA SITUATION

- Établir les antécédents de vaccination et d'hypersensibilité.

DIAGNOSTICS INFIRMIERS POSSIBLES

- Risque d'infection (Indications).
- Connaissances insuffisantes sur la maladie et sur le traitement médicamenteux (Enseignement au patient et à ses proches).

INTERVENTIONS INFIRMIÈRES

- Certains vaccins peuvent être administrés en même temps alors qu'un certain délai peut être nécessaire pour d'autres. Toujours vérifier le Protocole d'immunisation du Québec (PIQ) avant d'administrer un vaccin.

ENSEIGNEMENT AU PATIENT ET À SES PROCHES

- Informer le patient et ses parents des effets secondaires possibles de la vaccination et leur demander de signaler au professionnel de la santé les réactions suivantes: fièvre de plus 39,4 °C, difficultés respiratoires, urticaire, démangeaisons, tuméfaction des yeux, du visage et de l'intérieur du nez, fatigue et faiblesse fortes et soudaines, convulsions.
- Revoir le calendrier de vaccination avec les parents. Insister sur le fait qu'il est important de prendre en note les vaccins administrés et les dates d'administration.

VÉRIFICATION DE L'EFFICACITÉ THÉRAPEUTIQUE

L'efficacité du traitement peut être démontrée par: la prévention des maladies par immunité active.

VACCINS ET AGENTS IMMUNISANTS INCLUS DANS LE *GUIDE*

immunoglobulines

immunoglobuline Rh_0(D), 604

vaccin

vaccin recombinant quadrivalent contre le virus du papillome humain (types 6, 11, 16 et 18), 1230

VITAMINES

INDICATIONS

Prévention et traitement des carences vitaminiques ■ Suppléments nutritionnels permettant d'équilibrer divers troubles du métabolisme ■ Vitamine K: consulter la monographie.

MÉCANISME D'ACTION

Les vitamines font partie des systèmes enzymatiques qui servent de catalyseur à un grand nombre de réactions métaboliques ■ Elles sont indispensables à l'homéostasie ■ Les vitamines hydrosolubles (vitamines B et C) sont rarement toxiques ■ Les vitamines liposolubles (vitamines A, D, E et K) peuvent s'accumuler dans les tissus et provoquer une intoxication.

CONTRE-INDICATIONS, PRÉCAUTIONS ET MISES EN GARDE

Contre-indications: Hypersensibilité aux additifs, aux agents de conservation ou aux colorants.
Précautions et mises en garde: Adapter la posologie pour prévenir la toxicité, particulièrement dans le cas des vitamines liposolubles.

INTERACTIONS

La pyridoxine, administrée à doses élevées, peut contrecarrer l'efficacité de la **lévodopa** ■ La **cholestyramine**, le **colestipol** et l'**huile minérale** diminuent l'absorption des vitamines liposolubles.

SOINS INFIRMIERS

ÉVALUATION DE LA SITUATION

- Suivre de près les signes de carence vitaminique avant l'administration de l'agent et à intervalles réguliers pendant tout le traitement.
- Effectuer le bilan nutritionnel du patient en recueillant des données sur son alimentation des 24 dernières heures. Déterminer la fréquence à laquelle il consomme des aliments riches en vitamines.

DIAGNOSTICS INFIRMIERS POSSIBLES

- Alimentation déficiente (Indications).
- Connaissances insuffisantes sur le traitement médicamenteux (Enseignement au patient et à ses proches).

INTERVENTIONS INFIRMIÈRES

- Étant donné qu'il est rare qu'une seule carence vitaminique soit présente, on administre le plus souvent des associations de plusieurs vitamines.

ENSEIGNEMENT AU PATIENT ET À SES PROCHES

- Encourager le patient à respecter rigoureusement les recommandations diététiques du médecin ou d'un autre professionnel de la santé. Lui expliquer que la meilleure source de vitamines est une alimentation équilibrée. Lui recommander de suivre un régime comprenant des aliments provenant des quatre principaux groupes alimentaires.
- Recommander au patient qui pratique l'automédication par des suppléments vitaminiques de ne pas dépasser les apports quotidiens recommandés d'éléments nutritifs (voir l'annexe K).

Les doses massives ne se sont pas avérées efficaces pour traiter les divers problèmes de santé ; elles peuvent par contre provoquer des effets secondaires et une toxicité.

VÉRIFICATION DE L'EFFICACITÉ THÉRAPEUTIQUE

L'efficacité du traitement peut être démontrée par: la prévention ou la diminution des symptômes de carence vitaminique.

VITAMINES INCLUSES DANS LE *GUIDE*

CLASSIFICATION

AAS,
voir Aspirine

ABACAVIR
Ziagen

CLASSIFICATION:
Antirétroviral (inhibiteur nucléosidique de la transcriptase inverse)

Grossesse – catégorie C

INDICATIONS
Traitement de l'infection par le VIH en association avec d'autres antirétroviraux.

MÉCANISME D'ACTION
Transformation intracellulaire en triphosphate de carbovir, le métabolite actif. Le triphosphate de carbovir inhibe l'activité de la transcriptase inverse du VIH-1, ce qui met un terme à la croissance de l'ADN viral. ***Effets thérapeutiques:*** Ralentissement de l'évolution de l'infection par le VIH et de l'apparition de ses complications ■ Augmentation du nombre de CD4 et diminution de la charge virale.

PHARMACOCINÉTIQUE
Absorption: Rapide et bonne (biodisponibilité à 83 %).
Distribution: L'agent se répartit dans le compartiment extravasculaire et rapidement dans les érythrocytes.
Métabolisme et excrétion: Métabolisme majoritairement hépatique; 1,2 % est excrété à l'état inchangé dans l'urine.
Demi-vie: 1,5 heure.

Profil temps-action

	DÉBUT D'ACTION	PIC	DURÉE
PO	inconnu	1 – 1,5 h	inconnue

CONTRE-INDICATIONS, PRÉCAUTIONS ET MISES EN GARDE
Contre-indications: Hypersensibilité (la reprise du traitement risque de mener à une issue fatale) ■ Insuffisance hépatique modérée ou grave.
Précautions et mises en garde: Obésité, femmes, prise prolongée d'inhibiteur nucléosidique (il peut s'agir de facteurs de risque d'acidose lactique ou d'hépatomégalie) ■ **OBST., ALLAITEMENT**: Grossesse (l'innocuité de l'agent n'a pas été établie), allaitement (l'allaitement est déconseillé chez les patientes infectées par le VIH) ■ **PÉD.**: Enfants < 3 mois (l'innocuité de l'agent n'a pas été établie).

RÉACTIONS INDÉSIRABLES ET EFFETS SECONDAIRES
SNC: céphalées, insomnie fatigue, fièvre.
GI: HÉPATOTOXICITÉ, diarrhée, nausées, vomissements, douleurs abdominales, anorexie.
Tég.: rash.
HÉ: ACIDOSE LACTIQUE.
Loc.: myalgies.
Divers: RÉACTIONS D'HYPERSENSIBILITÉ, modification de la distribution du tissu adipeux, syndrome de reconstitution immunitaire.

INTERACTIONS
Médicament-médicament: L'**alcool** élève les taux sanguins d'abacavir ■ L'agent peut accélérer le métabolisme de la **méthadone** chez certains patients; il peut s'avérer nécessaire d'accroître la posologie de la méthadone.

VOIES D'ADMINISTRATION ET POSOLOGIE
- **PO (adultes > 18 ans)**: 300 mg, 2 fois par jour ou 600 mg, 1 fois par jour, en association avec d'autres agents antirétroviraux. La posologie uniquotidienne (600 mg, 1 fois par jour) peut entraîner des réactions d'hypersensibilité graves plus fréquentes.
- **PO (adolescents de 12 à 18 ans)**: 300 mg, 2 fois par jour.
- **PO (enfants âgés de 3 mois à 12 ans)**: 8 mg/kg, 2 fois par jour (ne pas dépasser 300 mg, 2 fois par jour).

ATTEINTE HÉPATIQUE LÉGÈRE AVEC CIRRHOSE DIAGNOSTIQUÉE
- **PO (ADULTES)**: *SCORE DE CHILD-PUGH DE 5 À 6*: 200 mg, 2 FOIS PAR JOUR.

PRÉSENTATION
Comprimés: 300 mg[Pr] ■ **Solution orale (aromatisée à la fraise ou à la banane)**: 20 mg/mL[Pr] en flacons de 240 mL ■ **En association avec**: lamivudine (Kivexa[Pr]), lamivudine et zidovudine (Trizivir[Pr]). Voir l'annexe U.

SOINS INFIRMIERS

ÉVALUATION DE LA SITUATION
- Suivre de près le patient tout au long du traitement à la recherche de changements dans la gravité des symptômes de l'infection par le VIH et de symptômes d'infections opportunistes.
- RESTER À L'AFFÛT DES SIGNES DE RÉACTIONS D'HYPERSENSIBILITÉ (FIÈVRE, RASH; RÉACTIONS GI – NAUSÉES, VOMISSEMENTS, DIARRHÉE, DOULEURS ABDOMINALES; RÉACTIONS CONSTITUTIONNELLES –

MALAISES, FATIGUE, DOULEURS ; RÉACTIONS RESPIRATOIRES – DYSPNÉE, TOUX, PHARYNGITE ET RÉSULTATS ANORMAUX DE LA RADIOGRAPHIE PULMONAIRE [PRINCIPALEMENT DES INFILTRATS POUVANT ÊTRE LOCALISÉS]).

- L'AGENT PEUT AUSSI ÉLEVER LES RÉSULTATS DES TESTS DE LA FONCTION HÉPATIQUE ET LES CONCENTRATIONS DE CRÉATINE PHOSPHOKINASE ET DE CRÉATININE, ET PROVOQUER UNE LYMPHOPÉNIE. ARRÊTER LE TRAITEMENT PAR L'ABACAVIR DÈS L'APPARITION DES PREMIERS SIGNES DE RÉACTION D'HYPERSENSIBILITÉ. NE PAS LE REPRENDRE PAR LA SUITE ; DES SYMPTÔMES PLUS GRAVES PEUVENT SURVENIR DANS LES HEURES QUI SUIVENT, PARMI LESQUELS CITONS UNE HYPOTENSION QUI PEUT METTRE EN JEU LE PRONOSTIC VITAL ET ENTRAÎNER LE DÉCÈS. LES SYMPTÔMES DISPARAISSENT HABITUELLEMENT À L'ARRÊT DU TRAITEMENT.
- L'ABACAVIR PEUT PROVOQUER UNE ACIDOSE LACTIQUE ET UNE HÉPATOMÉGALIE GRAVE AVEC STÉATOSE. RESTER À L'AFFÛT DES SIGNES SUIVANTS : ÉLÉVATION DES TAUX DE LACTATE SÉRIQUE ET D'ENZYMES HÉPATIQUES, HYPERTROPHIE DU FOIE RÉVÉLÉE PAR PALPATION. IL FAUT ABANDONNER LE TRAITEMENT SI L'ON DÉCÈLE L'APPARITION DE SIGNES CLINIQUES OU BIOCHIMIQUES.
- Si une patiente enceinte est exposée à des antirétroviraux, l'inscrire dans le registre des femmes exposées aux antirétroviraux pendant leur grossesse, en composant le 1-800-258-4263.

Tests de laboratoire :

- Suivre à intervalles réguliers tout au long du traitement la charge virale et la numération des CD4.
- L'agent peut élever la glycémie et les taux sériques de triglycérides.

DIAGNOSTICS INFIRMIERS POSSIBLES

- Risque d'infection (Indications).
- Non-observance du traitement médicamenteux (Enseignement au patient et à ses proches).

INTERVENTIONS INFIRMIÈRES

PO : On peut prendre l'abacavir avec ou sans aliments. La solution orale peut être gardée à la température ambiante ou peut être réfrigérée ; ne pas la congeler.

ENSEIGNEMENT AU PATIENT ET À SES PROCHES

- Insister sur le fait qu'il est important de prendre l'abacavir en respectant rigoureusement les recommandations du médecin. L'abacavir doit toujours être pris en association avec d'autres antirétroviraux. Expliquer au patient qu'il ne doit pas prendre plus que la quantité prescrite ni arrêter le traitement sans consulter un professionnel de la santé au préalable. Le prévenir qu'il doit prendre toute dose oubliée dès qu'il s'en souvient et reprendre ensuite l'horaire habituel, sans jamais remplacer une dose manquée par une double dose.
- Expliquer au patient qu'il ne doit pas donner de l'abacavir à d'autres personnes.
- Prévenir le patient que l'abacavir ne guérit pas l'infection par le VIH ni ne prévient les infections associées ou opportunistes. L'abacavir ne réduit pas le risque de transmission du VIH à d'autres personnes par les rapports sexuels ou par la contamination du sang. Inciter le patient à utiliser un condom et à éviter le partage d'aiguilles ou les dons de sang pour prévenir la propagation du VIH. Prévenir le patient que les effets à long terme de ce médicament sont pour le moment inconnus.
- METTRE EN GARDE LE PATIENT CONTRE LE RISQUE DE RÉACTIONS D'HYPERSENSIBILITÉ QUI PEUVENT ÊTRE MORTELLES. LUI RECOMMANDER D'ARRÊTER DE PRENDRE L'ABACAVIR ET DE PRÉVENIR UN PROFESSIONNEL DE LA SANTÉ SI DES RÉACTIONS D'HYPERSENSIBILITÉ SE MANIFESTENT. IL FAUT LUI REMETTRE LE FEUILLET D'INFORMATIONS DESTINÉ AUX PATIENTS À CHAQUE RENOUVELLEMENT D'ORDONNANCE ET LUI RECOMMANDER DE LE RELIRE CHAQUE FOIS. REMETTRE AUSSI AU PATIENT UNE CARTE DE MISE EN GARDE RÉSUMANT LES SYMPTÔMES D'HYPERSENSIBILITÉ À L'ABACAVIR LORS DE CHAQUE RENOUVELLEMENT D'ORDONNANCE ET LUI RECOMMANDER DE LA PORTER TOUJOURS SUR LUI.
- RECOMMANDER AU PATIENT DE PRÉVENIR UN PROFESSIONNEL DE LA SANTÉ IMMÉDIATEMENT, SI DES SIGNES D'ACIDOSE LACTIQUE (FATIGUE OU FAIBLESSE, DOULEURS MUSCULAIRES INHABITUELLES, DIFFICULTÉS RESPIRATOIRES, DOULEURS D'ESTOMAC AVEC DES NAUSÉES ET DES VOMISSEMENTS, SENSATION DE FROID, SURTOUT AU NIVEAU DES EXTRÉMITÉS, ÉTOURDISSEMENTS OU BATTEMENTS CARDIAQUES RAPIDES ET IRRÉGULIERS) OU D'HÉPATOTOXICITÉ (JAUNISSEMENT DE LA PEAU OU DU BLANC DES YEUX, URINE DE COULEUR FONCÉE, SELLES DE COULEUR PÂLE, PERTE D'APPÉTIT PENDANT PLUSIEURS JOURS DE SUITE, NAUSÉES OU DOULEURS ABDOMINALES) SE MANIFESTENT. Ces symptômes peuvent se présenter plus fréquemment chez les sujets de sexe féminin, les personnes obèses ou celles qui prennent des médicaments comme l'abacavir pendant un laps de temps prolongé.
- Prévenir le patient que le traitement antirétroviral l'expose au risque de redistribution ou d'accumulation de tissus adipeux dont les causes et les consé-

quences à long terme sur la santé sont pour le moment inconnues.

- Insister sur l'importance des examens réguliers de suivi et des numérations globulaires permettant d'évaluer les progrès du traitement et de surveiller les effets secondaires.

VÉRIFICATION DE L'EFFICACITÉ THÉRAPEUTIQUE

L'efficacité du traitement peut être démontrée par: le ralentissement de l'évolution de l'infection par le VIH et la diminution du risque d'infections opportunistes chez les patients infectés ■ la diminution de la charge virale et l'augmentation du nombre de CD4. ✳

ACARBOSE

Glucobay

CLASSIFICATION:

Antidiabétique (inhibiteur des alpha-glucosidases)

Grossesse – catégorie B

INDICATIONS

Traitement en monothérapie pour équilibrer la glycémie chez les patients atteints de diabète de type 2 dont l'état n'est pas convenablement maîtrisé par le régime alimentaire seul et l'activité physique ou en association, lorsqu'un sulfamide hypoglycémiant, la metformine ou l'insuline, administrés seuls, ne parviennent pas à équilibrer adéquatement la glycémie.

MÉCANISME D'ACTION

Abaissement de la glycémie par inhibition de l'activité des enzymes alpha-glucosidases dans la bordure en brosse de l'intestin grêle. Cette inhibition retarde et réduit l'absorption du glucose. ***Effets thérapeutiques:*** Abaissement de la glycémie, et particulièrement de la glycémie postprandiale chez les patients diabétiques.

PHARMACOCINÉTIQUE

Absorption: Moins de 2 %; l'effet est principalement local (dans le tractus GI).

Distribution: Inconnue.

Métabolisme et excrétion: Métabolisme majoritairement GI. La faible portion absorbée est excrétée par les reins.

Demi-vie: 2 heures.

Profil temps-action (effet sur la glycémie)

	DÉBUT D'ACTION	PIC	DURÉE
PO	inconnu	1 h	inconnu

CONTRE-INDICATIONS, PRÉCAUTIONS ET MISES EN GARDE

Contre-indications: Hypersensibilité ■ Acidocétose diabétique ■ Affections intestinales inflammatoires ■ Ulcère colique ■ Occlusion intestinale partielle ou prédisposition aux occlusions intestinales ■ Clairance de la créatinine < 25 mL/min.

Précautions et mises en garde: Élévation des transaminases sériques ■ Correction de l'hypoglycémie (utiliser du glucose dont l'absorption n'est pas inhibée par l'acarbose) ■ **PÉD.:** L'innocuité et l'efficacité de l'acarbose chez les patients de moins de 18 ans n'ont pas été établies ■ **OBST., ALLAITEMENT:** L'innocuité de l'acarbose n'a pas été établie.

RÉACTIONS INDÉSIRABLES ET EFFETS SECONDAIRES

GI: <u>douleurs abdominales</u>, <u>diarrhée</u>, <u>flatulence</u>, élévation des taux des transaminases.

INTERACTIONS

Médicament-médicament: Les **diurétiques thiazidiques** et les **diurétiques de l'anse**, les **corticostéroïdes**, les **phénothiazines**, les **préparations thyroïdiennes**, les **œstrogènes conjugués**, les **progestatifs**, les **contraceptifs hormonaux**, la **phénytoïne**, la **niacine**, les **sympathomimétiques**, les **bloqueurs des canaux calciques** et l'**isoniazide** peuvent élever la glycémie chez les patients diabétiques et rendre difficile l'équilibrage de la glycémie ■ Les effets de l'acarbose sont atténués par les **adsorbants intestinaux**, notamment le **charbon activé** et les **préparations d'enzymes digestives (amylase, pancréatine)**; éviter l'usage concomitant ■ L'agent intensifie l'effet des **hypoglycémiants à base de sulfonylurée** ■ Risque de diminution de l'absorption de la **digoxine**; une adaptation de la posologie peut s'imposer.

Médicament-produits naturels: La **glucosamine** peut entraver l'équilibrage de la glycémie ■ Le **chrome** et la **coenzyme Q-10** peuvent intensifier les effets hypoglycémiants de l'acarbose.

VOIES D'ADMINISTRATION ET POSOLOGIE

- **PO (adultes):** *Dose initiale* – 50 mg, 1 fois par jour; augmenter la dose à raison de 50 mg/jour toutes les 1 à 2 semaines selon la réponse au traitement et la tolérance du patient, jusqu'à l'atteinte de la dose de

A

50 mg, 3 fois par jour; la posologie est ensuite adaptée toutes les 4 à 8 semaines (intervalle posologique – de 50 à 100 mg, 3 fois par jour).

PRÉSENTATION

Comprimés: 50 mg^{Pr}, 100 mg^{Pr}.

SOINS INFIRMIERS

ÉVALUATION DE LA SITUATION

- Rester à l'affût des signes et des symptômes d'hypoglycémie (transpiration, faim, faiblesse, étourdissements, tremblements, tachycardie, anxiété), particulièrement chez les patients qui prennent en concomitance d'autres hypoglycémiants oraux.

Tests de laboratoire:

- Suivre de près les concentrations de glucose sérique et d'hémoglobine glyquée à intervalles réguliers pendant toute la durée du traitement pour évaluer l'efficacité de l'agent.
- Suivre les concentrations d'AST et d'ALT tous les 3 mois pendant la première année et à intervalles réguliers par la suite. Des concentrations élevées peuvent nécessiter une réduction de la dose ou l'arrêt du traitement par l'acarbose. Ces élévations se produisent plus souvent chez les patients qui prennent plus de 300 mg par jour et chez les femmes. Après l'arrêt du traitement, les concentrations reviennent habituellement à la normale, sans autres signes de lésions hépatiques.

TOXICITÉ ET SURDOSAGE: Les symptômes de surdosage sont une aggravation transitoire des flatulences, de la diarrhée et de la gêne abdominale. L'acarbose seul ne provoque pas d'hypoglycémie; toutefois les autres hypoglycémiants administrés en concomitance peuvent entraîner une hypoglycémie devant être traitée.

DIAGNOSTICS INFIRMIERS POSSIBLES

- Alimentation excessive (Indications).
- Non-observance du traitement médicamenteux (Enseignement au patient et à ses proches).

INTERVENTIONS INFIRMIÈRES

- Les patients prenant des antidiabétiques, qui sont exposés au stress, à la fièvre, à un traumatisme, à une infection ou à une intervention chirurgicale, peuvent avoir besoin d'insuline.
- L'agent ne provoque pas d'hypoglycémie s'il est pris pendant une période de jeûne, mais il peut augmenter les effets hypoglycémiants des autres agents hypoglycémiants.
- **PO:** Administrer avec la première bouchée de chaque repas, 3 fois par jour.

ENSEIGNEMENT AU PATIENT ET À SES PROCHES

- Conseiller au patient de prendre l'acarbose tous les jours à la même heure. S'il a oublié de prendre une dose et qu'il a fini de manger, lui recommander de sauter la dose en question et de prendre la dose suivante avec le repas suivant. L'avertir qu'il ne faut jamais remplacer une dose manquée par une double dose.
- Expliquer au patient que l'acarbose aide à équilibrer la glycémie, mais qu'il ne guérit pas le diabète. Le traitement est de long cours.
- Sensibiliser le patient aux signes d'hypoglycémie et d'hyperglycémie (vision trouble, étourdissements, sécheresse de la bouche, rougeur et sécheresse de la peau, haleine fruitée, augmentation du nombre de mictions, présence de corps cétoniques dans l'urine, perte d'appétit, maux de ventre, nausées ou vomissements, fatigue, respirations rapides et profondes, soif inhabituelle, perte de conscience). En cas d'hypoglycémie, conseiller au patient de prendre du glucose par voie orale (comprimés ou gel liquide) plutôt que du sucre (l'acarbose bloque l'absorption du sucre) et d'en prévenir un professionnel de la santé.
- Encourager le patient à suivre rigoureusement sa diétothérapie et sa pharmacothérapie et de faire de l'exercice régulièrement afin de prévenir les épisodes d'hypoglycémie ou d'hyperglycémie.
- Enseigner au patient les techniques de mesure de la glycémie et des cétones urinaires. L'inciter à les mesurer souvent pendant les périodes de stress ou de maladie et à prévenir un professionnel de la santé en cas de changements importants.
- Mettre en garde le patient contre l'usage d'autres médicaments ou de produits naturels sans avoir consulté un professionnel de la santé au préalable.
- Conseiller au patient qui doit se soumettre à un traitement ou à une intervention chirurgicale d'informer tous les professionnels de la santé qu'il suit un traitement avec ce médicament.
- Conseiller au patient de toujours porter sur lui une forme de glucose à prendre par voie orale et un bracelet d'identité sur lequel sont inscrits sa maladie et son traitement médicamenteux.
- Insister sur l'importance des examens réguliers de suivi.

VÉRIFICATION DE L'EFFICACITÉ THÉRAPEUTIQUE

L'efficacité du traitement peut être démontrée par: l'équilibrage de la glycémie sans survenue d'épisodes d'hypoglycémie ou d'hyperglycémie. ✳

ACÉBUTOLOL

Apo-Acébutolol, Gen-Acébutolol, Monitan, Novo-Acébutolol, Nu-Acébutolol, Rhotral, Sectral

CLASSIFICATION:

Antiarythmique (classe II), antihypertenseur (bêtabloquant), antiangineux

Grossesse – catégories B (1er trimestre) et D (2e et 3e trimestres)

INDICATIONS

Traitement de l'hypertension en monothérapie ou en association ▪ Traitement à long terme des patients qui souffrent d'angine de poitrine due à l'ischémie du myocarde. **Usages non approuvés**: Prophylaxie de l'infarctus du myocarde ▪ Traitement des tachyarythmies ventriculaires, du syndrome du prolapsus valvulaire mitral et de l'insuffisance cardiaque hypertrophique ▪ Traitement des manifestations physiques de l'anxiété et de la thyrotoxicose ▪ Traitement des tremblements.

MÉCANISME D'ACTION

Blocage des récepteurs bêta$_1$-adrénergiques (du myocarde), sans affecter habituellement les sites des récepteurs bêta$_2$ (pulmonaires, vasculaires ou utérins) ▪ Légère activité sympathomimétique intrinsèque. ***Effets thérapeutiques:*** Diminution de la fréquence cardiaque ▪ Diminution de la conduction du nœud AV ▪ Abaissement de la pression artérielle.

PHARMACOCINÉTIQUE

Absorption: Bonne (PO), mais premier passage hépatique important.

Distribution: Minime pénétration au SNC. L'agent traverse la barrière placentaire et passe en petites quantités dans le lait maternel.

Métabolisme et excrétion: Métabolisme hépatique, transformation principalement en diacétolol, métabolite pharmacologiquement actif (bêtabloquant). Excrétion rénale (de 30 à 40 %), fécale (56 %) et biliaire (de 3 à 8 %).

Demi-vie: De 3 à 4 heures (diacétolol: de 8 à 13 heures).

Profil temps-action (effet sur la pression artérielle)

	DÉBUT D'ACTION	PIC	DURÉE
PO	1 - 1,5 h	2 - 8 h	12 - 24 h

CONTRE-INDICATIONS, PRÉCAUTIONS ET MISES EN GARDE

Contre-indications: Insuffisance cardiaque non compensée ▪ Insuffisance ventriculaire droite, consécutive à une hypertension pulmonaire ▪ Œdème pulmonaire ▪ Choc cardiogénique ▪ Bradycardie sinusale ou bloc auriculoventriculaire des 2e et 3e degrés ▪ Anesthésie par des produits entraînant une dépression du myocarde (éther).

Précautions et mises en garde: Insuffisance cardiaque compensée (risque de décompensation) ▪ Insuffisance rénale ou hépatique (réduire la dose si la $Cl_{Cr} < 50$ mL/min/1,73 m^2) ▪ **GÉR.**: sensibilité accrue aux bêtabloquants; il est recommandé de réduire la dose initiale ▪ Thyrotoxicose (l'acébutolol peut en masquer les symptômes) ▪ Diabète (l'agent peut masquer les symptômes d'hypoglycémie) ▪ **OBST., ALLAITEMENT, PÉD.**: L'innocuité du médicament n'a pas été établie; rares cas de bradycardie néonatale, d'hypotension, d'hypoglycémie et de dépression respiratoire ▪ Antécédents de réactions allergiques graves (risque d'augmenter l'intensité des réactions) ▪ Maladie respiratoire bronchospastique.

RÉACTIONS INDÉSIRABLES ET EFFETS SECONDAIRES

SNC: fatigue, faiblesse, anxiété, dépression, étourdissements, somnolence, insomnie, perte de mémoire, nervosité, cauchemars.

ORLO: vision trouble, congestion nasale.

Resp.: bronchospasme, respiration sifflante.

CV: BRADYCARDIE, INSUFFISANCE CARDIAQUE, ŒDÈME PULMONAIRE, hypotension, vasoconstriction périphérique.

GI: constipation, diarrhée, nausées, vomissements.

GU: impuissance, baisse de la libido, mictions fréquentes.

Tég.: rash.

End.: hyperglycémie, hypoglycémie.

Loc.: douleurs articulaires, arthralgie.

Divers: lupus érythémateux induit par le médicament.

INTERACTIONS

Médicament-médicament: L'**anesthésie générale**, le **diltiazem** et le **vérapamil** peuvent exercer un effet additif sur la dépression du myocarde ▪ L'utilisation concomitante de **digoxine** peut exercer un effet sur la bradycardie ▪ Risque d'effets hypotenseurs additifs lors de

A

la prise d'**antihypertenseurs** et de **dérivés nitrés** ainsi que de l'ingestion de quantités importantes d'**alcool** ▪ L'administration concomitante d'**adrénaline** peut entraîner une stimulation alpha-adrénergique excessive ▪ L'acébutolol peut masquer les symptômes de l'hypoglycémie induite par l'**insuline** ou d'autres **hypoglycémiants oraux**, et en prolonger aussi la durée.

VOIES D'ADMINISTRATION ET POSOLOGIE

Hypertension

- **PO (adultes)**: *Dose initiale* – 100 mg, 2 fois par jour. *Dose d'entretien* – de 400 à 800 mg par jour. Lorsqu'une dose quotidienne de 400 mg ou moins permet d'obtenir une réponse satisfaisante, il est possible d'administrer la dose quotidienne totale en 1 seule fois, le matin. Une dose quotidienne supérieure à 400 mg doit être divisée en 2 prises égales.
- **PO (personnes âgées)**: La biodisponibilité est doublée chez ces patients; on pourrait donc leur administrer des doses d'entretien plus faibles.

Angine de poitrine

- **PO (adultes)**: *Dose initiale* – 200 mg, 2 fois par jour. *Dose d'entretien* – de 200 à 600 mg par jour, en 2 prises.
- **PO (personnes âgées)**: La biodisponibilité est doublée chez ces patients; on pourrait donc leur administrer des doses d'entretien plus faibles.

INSUFFISANCE RÉNALE

- **PO (ADULTES)**: SI LA Cl_{CR} < 50 mL/MIN/1,73 m^2, ADMINISTRER 50 % DE LA DOSE HABITUELLE. SI LA Cl_{CR} < 25 mL/MIN/1,73 m^2, ADMINISTRER 25 % DE LA DOSE HABITUELLE.

PRÉSENTATION (version générique disponible)

Comprimés: 100 mg[Pr], 200 mg[Pr], 400 mg[Pr].

SOINS INFIRMIERS

ÉVALUATION DE LA SITUATION

- Mesurer fréquemment la pression artérielle et le pouls et suivre l'ÉCG pendant la période d'adaptation posologique et à intervalles réguliers pendant toute la durée du traitement.
- Effectuer le bilan quotidien des ingesta et des excreta, et noter le poids du patient tous les jours. OBSERVER RÉGULIÈREMENT LE PATIENT POUR DÉCELER DES SIGNES ET DES SYMPTÔMES D'INSUFFISANCE CARDIAQUE (dyspnée, râles ou crépitations, gain pondéral, œdème périphérique, turgescence des jugulaires).

Tests de laboratoire:

- Ce médicament peut entraîner l'élévation des concentrations sériques d'urée, de lipoprotéines, de potassium, de triglycérides et d'acide urique.
- Il peut entraîner une élévation des concentrations sériques de phosphatase alcaline, de LDH, d'AST et d'ALT.
- Il peut provoquer une élévation de la glycémie.

DIAGNOSTICS INFIRMIERS POSSIBLES

- Débit cardiaque diminué (Effets secondaires).
- Connaissances insuffisantes sur le traitement médicamenteux (Enseignement au patient et à ses proches).
- Non-observance du traitement médicamenteux (Enseignement au patient et à ses proches).

INTERVENTIONS INFIRMIÈRES

- MESURER LE POULS À L'APEX DU CŒUR AVANT D'ADMINISTRER LE MÉDICAMENT. S'il est inférieur à 50 battements par minute ou s'il y a arythmie, ne pas administrer l'acébutolol et en avertir le médecin ou un autre professionnel de la santé.
- Administrer le médicament à jeun ou avec des aliments.

ENSEIGNEMENT AU PATIENT ET À SES PROCHES

- Conseiller au patient de respecter rigoureusement la posologie recommandée et de prendre le médicament à la même heure tous les jours même s'il se sent bien; l'avertir qu'il ne doit jamais sauter de dose ni remplacer une dose manquée par une double dose. S'il n'a pu prendre le médicament au moment habituel, il doit le prendre aussitôt que possible, mais au moins 4 heures avant l'heure prévue pour la dose suivante. Un sevrage brusque peut provoquer des arythmies mettant la vie en danger, l'hypertension ou l'ischémie du myocarde.
- Conseiller au patient d'avoir une réserve suffisante de médicament pour les fins de semaine, les congés et les vacances. Lui conseiller aussi de conserver une ordonnance dans son portefeuille pour parer à toute urgence.
- Enseigner au patient et à ses proches les techniques de mesure du pouls et de la pression artérielle. Leur recommander de mesurer le pouls tous les jours et la pression artérielle 2 fois par semaine. Leur recommander également de signaler à un professionnel de la santé tout changement important.
- Prévenir le patient que l'acébutolol peut parfois provoquer des étourdissements. Lui conseiller de ne pas conduire et d'éviter les activités qui exigent sa vigilance jusqu'à ce qu'on ait la certitude que le médicament n'entraîne pas cet effet chez lui.

- Prévenir le patient que le médicament peut le rendre plus sensible au froid.
- Conseiller au patient de consulter un professionnel de la santé avant de prendre un médicament en vente libre, particulièrement des préparations contre le rhume, ou des produits naturels en même temps que l'acébutolol.
- Recommander au patient diabétique de mesurer sa glycémie, particulièrement lorsqu'il se sent fatigué, faible ou irritable ou lorsqu'il ressent un malaise. L'acébutolol peut masquer la tachycardie ou les changements de pression artérielle, signes d'hypoglycémie. Cependant, il n'inhibe pas les étourdissements et les sueurs qui peuvent survenir, et qui sont des signes d'hypoglycémie.
- Recommander au patient de signaler à un professionnel de la santé les symptômes suivants: ralentissement du pouls, difficultés respiratoires, respiration sifflante, mains et pieds froids, étourdissements, sensation de tête légère, confusion, dépression, rash, fièvre, maux de gorge, saignements inhabituels ou ecchymoses.
- Conseiller au patient de signaler au professionnel de la santé qu'il prend de l'acébutolol, avant de se soumettre à une intervention chirurgicale ou à un nouveau traitement.
- Conseiller au patient de porter sur lui en tout temps une fiche où sont inscrits son problème de santé et son traitement médicamenteux.

Hypertension: Encourager le patient à prendre des mesures non pharmacologiques pour favoriser la maîtrise de l'hypertension: perdre du poids, réduire la consommation de sel, diminuer le stress, faire régulièrement de l'exercice, boire de l'alcool avec modération et cesser de fumer. L'acébutolol stabilise la pression artérielle, mais ne guérit pas l'hypertension.

VÉRIFICATION DE L'EFFICACITÉ THÉRAPEUTIQUE

L'efficacité du traitement peut être démontrée par: la baisse de la pression artérielle et de la fréquence cardiaque ■ la diminution de la fréquence des douleurs angineuses.

ACÉTAMINOPHÈNE

Abenol, Apo-Acetaminophen, Atasol, Novogesic, Tempra, Tylenol

CLASSIFICATION:

Antipyrétique, analgésique non opioïde

Grossesse – catégorie B

INDICATIONS

Douleur légère à modérée ■ Fièvre.

MÉCANISME D'ACTION

Inhibition de la synthèse des prostaglandines qui pourraient être des médiateurs de la douleur et de la fièvre, surtout au niveau du SNC ■ Aucune propriété anti-inflammatoire notable ni effets toxiques gastro-intestinaux. ***Effets thérapeutiques:*** Analgésie ■ Antipyrèse.

PHARMACOCINÉTIQUE

Absorption: Bonne (PO). Variable (IR).

Distribution: Le médicament se répartit dans tout l'organisme. Il traverse la barrière placentaire et passe dans le lait maternel.

Métabolisme et excrétion: Métabolisme hépatique de l'ordre de 85 à 95 %. En cas de surdosage, les métabolites peuvent être toxiques. Les métabolites sont excrétés par les reins.

Demi-vie: Nouveau-nés: de 2 à 5 heures; adultes: de 1 à 3 heures.

Profil temps-action (effet analgésique et antipyrétique)

	Début d'action	Pic	Durée
PO	0,5 - 1 h	1 - 3 h	3 - 8 h†
IR	0,5 - 1 h	1 - 3 h	3 - 4 h

† Varie selon la dose.

CONTRE-INDICATIONS, PRÉCAUTIONS ET MISES EN GARDE

Contre-indications: Antécédents d'hypersensibilité à l'acétaminophène ■ Les produits contenant de l'alcool, de l'aspartame, de la saccharine, du sucre ou de la tartrazine (FD&C 5) sont déconseillés chez les patients intolérants ou allergiques à ces ingrédients.

Précautions et mises en garde: Maladie hépatique ou rénale (les doses recommandées en usage prolongé doivent être plus faibles) ■ Abus ou consommation prolongée de doses massives d'alcool ■ Malnutrition.

RÉACTIONS INDÉSIRABLES ET EFFETS SECONDAIRES

GI: INSUFFISANCE HÉPATIQUE, HÉPATOTOXICITÉ (surdosage).

GU: insuffisance rénale (doses élevées/usage prolongé).

Hémat.: neutropénie, pancytopénie, leucopénie.

Tég.: rash, urticaire.

INTERACTIONS

Médicament-médicament: L'administration prolongée de doses élevées (> 2 g/jour) d'acétaminophène avec la

warfarine peut accroître le risque de saignement (il faut surveiller régulièrement le temps de prothrombine et s'assurer que le RNI ne témoigne pas d'une dose suprathérapeutique. ▪ Effets hépatotoxiques additifs lors de l'administration concomitante d'autres **substances hépatotoxiques**, incluant l'**alcool** ▪ L'administration concomitante de **diflunisal**, d'**isoniazide**, de **rifampicine**, de **rifabutine**, de **phénytoïne**, de **barbituriques** et de **carbamazépine** peut accroître le risque de lésions du foie induites par l'acétaminophène (restreindre l'automédication) ▪ La **cholestyramine** et le **colestipol** diminuent l'absorption de l'acétaminophène et en réduisent l'efficacité (espacer les prises de ces médicaments de 2 heures) ▪ Le **propranolol** diminue le métabolisme de l'acétaminophène et peut en intensifier l'effet ▪ L'effet de la **lamotrigine** et de la **zidovudine** peut être diminué.

VOIES D'ADMINISTRATION ET POSOLOGIE

Formes posologiques à libération immédiate (par voie orale ou rectale)

- **Adultes:** De 325 à 650 mg, toutes les 4 à 6 heures (dose maximale: 4 g en 24 heures).
- **Enfants:** De 10 à 15 mg/kg, toutes les 4 à 6 heures (dose maximale: 65 mg/kg/24 heures). Ne pas administrer plus de 5 doses en l'espace de 24 heures à des enfants de moins de 12 ans, sans en prévenir au préalable le médecin ou un autre professionnel de la santé.

PRÉSENTATION (version générique disponible)

Comprimés à croquer (aromatisés aux fruits, à la «gomme balloune» ou aux raisins): 80 mg[VL], 160 mg[VL] ▪ **Comprimés:** 160 mg[VL], 325 mg[VL], 500 mg[VL] ▪ **Comprimés à libération retard: (Tylenol, caplets longue durée):** 650 mg[VL] ▪ **Solution (aromatisée aux fruits et aux raisins):** 80 mg/mL[VL], 80 mg/5 mL[VL], 160 mg/5 mL[VL], 16 mg/mL[VL], 32 mg/mL[VL] ▪ **Élixir (aromatisé aux raisins et à la cerise):** 160 mg/5 mL[VL], 80 mg/mL[VL], 32 mg/mL[VL] ▪ **Suspension:** 32 mg/mL[VL], 80 mg/mL[VL], 160 mg/5 mL[VL] ▪ **Sirop:** 16 mg/mL[VL], 32 mg/mL[VL], 80 mg/5 mL[VL], 160 mg/5 mL[VL] ▪ **Suppositoires:** 120 mg[VL], 325 mg[VL], 650 mg[VL] ▪ **Gelcaps:** 500 mg[VL] ▪ **En association avec:** bon nombre d'autres médicaments (avec codéine: Empracet; avec oxycodone: Percocet; etc.).

SOINS INFIRMIERS

ÉVALUATION DE LA SITUATION

- Avant d'administrer l'acétaminophène, il faut évaluer l'état général du patient et connaître sa consommation d'alcool. Les patients qui souffrent de malnutrition ou les alcooliques sont exposés à un risque plus élevé d'hépatotoxicité, si le traitement par ce médicament, aux doses habituelles, se prolonge.
- Évaluer la quantité, le type de médicament ainsi que la fréquence des prises chez les patients ayant recours à l'automédication, particulièrement à l'aide de médicaments en vente libre. L'utilisation prolongée d'acétaminophène en monothérapie ou en association avec des salicylates ou des AINS augmente le risque de toxicité rénale. Lorsqu'on doit prendre en concomitance, pendant une courte période, l'acétaminophène avec des salicylates, on ne devrait pas dépasser la dose recommandée pour chacun de ces médicaments, administrés séparément.

Douleur: Déterminer le type de douleur, son siège et son intensité, avant l'administration du médicament et de 30 à 60 minutes après.

Fièvre: Mesurer la température du patient; rester à l'affût des signes associés à la fièvre (diaphorèse, tachycardie et malaises).

Tests de laboratoire:

- Noter les résultats des analyses de sang et l'état de la fonction hépatique et rénale à des intervalles réguliers, tout au long d'un traitement prolongé à des doses élevées.
- L'acétaminophène peut fausser à la baisse la mesure de la glycémie par la méthode glucose-oxydase/peroxydase, mais non par la méthode hexokinase/glucose-6-phosphate-déshydrogénase. Le médicament peut aussi fausser à la hausse les mesures prises avec certains instruments; consulter le guide d'utilisation du fabricant.
- Des concentrations accrues de bilirubine, de LDH, d'AST et d'ALT ainsi que l'allongement du temps de prothrombine peuvent être des indices d'hépatotoxicité.

TOXICITÉ ET SURDOSAGE: En cas de surdosage, administrer comme antidote de l'**acétylcystéine** (Mucomyst).

DIAGNOSTICS INFIRMIERS POSSIBLES

- Douleur aiguë (Indications).
- Risque de température corporelle anormale (Indications).
- Connaissances insuffisantes sur le traitement médicamenteux (Enseignement au patient et à ses proches).

INTERVENTIONS INFIRMIÈRES

- Lorsque l'acétaminophène est administré en association avec un analgésique opioïde, il ne faut pas dépasser la dose quotidienne recommandée d'acétaminophène.

PO:

- Administrer le médicament avec un grand verre d'eau.
- On peut prendre le médicament à jeun ou avec des aliments.

ENSEIGNEMENT AU PATIENT ET À SES PROCHES

- Conseiller au patient de suivre rigoureusement la posologie recommandée et de ne pas dépasser la dose prescrite. L'ACÉTAMINOPHÈNE EN TRAITEMENT PROLONGÉ À DES DOSES ÉLEVÉES PEUT PROVOQUER DES LÉSIONS HÉPATIQUES GRAVES ET PERMANENTES. Les adultes ne devraient pas prendre de l'acétaminophène pendant plus de 10 jours, et les enfants, pendant plus de 5 jours, sauf recommandation médicale contraire. Lors d'un traitement d'association de courte durée d'acétaminophène avec un salicylate ou un AINS, ne pas dépasser les doses quotidiennes recommandées pour chacun des médicaments, pris séparément.
- Inciter le patient à ne pas consommer d'alcool (3 verres ou plus par jour augmentent le risque de lésions hépatiques), s'il prend plus de 1 ou 2 doses d'acétaminophène à l'occasion. Lui expliquer qu'il ne doit pas prendre de l'acétaminophène en même temps que des salicylates ou des AINS, pendant plus de quelques jours, sauf recommandation médicale contraire.

PÉD.: RECOMMANDER AUX PARENTS OU AUX SOIGNANTS DE VÉRIFIER LES CONCENTRATIONS DES PRÉPARATIONS LIQUIDES, CAR DE GRAVES LÉSIONS HÉPATIQUES SONT SURVENUES À CAUSE D'ERREURS DE POSOLOGIE. CONSEILLER LES PARENTS OU LES SOIGNANTS SUR L'UTILISATION DE LA PRÉPARATION ET DE LA DOSE APPROPRIÉES CHEZ L'ENFANT (EN FONCTION DE SON POIDS ET DE SON ÂGE), ET LEUR MONTRER COMMENT MESURER CORRECTEMENT LES DOSES.

- Informer le patient diabétique que l'acétaminophène peut fausser les mesures de la glycémie. Lui conseiller de consulter un professionnel de la santé s'il remarque des changements.
- Conseiller au patient de vérifier les ingrédients des médicaments en vente libre. L'avertir qu'il ne doit pas prendre plusieurs produits contenant de l'acétaminophène à la fois, pour prévenir la toxicité hépatique.
- Inciter le patient à consulter un professionnel de la santé si la douleur ou la fièvre ne sont pas soulagées par les doses habituelles de ce médicament ou encore si la fièvre s'élève au-dessus de 39,5 °C (103 °F) ou si elle persiste pendant plus de 3 jours.

VÉRIFICATION DE L'EFFICACITÉ THÉRAPEUTIQUE

L'efficacité du traitement peut être démontrée par: le soulagement de la douleur légère à modérée ■ la baisse de la fièvre. ✳

ACÉTAZOLAMIDE,

voir Inhibiteurs de l'anhydrase carbonique

ACÉTYLCYSTÉINE

Mucomyst, Parvolex

CLASSIFICATION:

Antidote (surdosage par l'acétaminophène), mucolytique

Grossesse – catégorie B

INDICATIONS

PO, IV: Traitement d'urgence (dans les 24 heures) du surdosage à l'acétaminophène exposant le patient à un risque d'hépatotoxicité ■ **Inhalation:** Mucolytique: traitement adjuvant des affections caractérisées par des sécrétions visqueuses et épaisses. **Usages non approuvés: PO, IV:** Prévention des néphropathies chez les patients à risque lors d'examens radiologiques avec injection de produits de contraste iodés.

MÉCANISME D'ACTION

PO, IV: Diminution de l'accumulation des métabolites hépatotoxiques en cas de surdosage par l'acétaminophène ■ **Inhalation:** Liquéfaction des sécrétions bronchiques favorisant ainsi leur mobilisation et leur expectoration. ***Effets thérapeutiques:* PO ou IV:** Prévention des lésions hépatiques induites par un surdosage par l'acétaminophène ■ **Inhalation:** Diminution de la viscosité des sécrétions bronchiques.

PHARMACOCINÉTIQUE

Absorption: Faible biodisponibilité (PO). Effet local (inhalation); les fractions résiduelles peuvent être absorbées à partir de l'épithélium pulmonaire.

Distribution: Inconnue.

Liaison aux protéines: 50 %, après administration de la dose.

Métabolisme et excrétion: Métabolisme hépatique. Excrétion rénale (30 %).

Demi-vie: 5,6 heures.

A

Profil temps-action

	Début d'action	Pic	Durée
PO (antidote)	inconnu	inconnu	4 h
Inhalation (mucolytique)	1 min	5 - 10 min	courte

CONTRE-INDICATIONS, PRÉCAUTIONS ET MISES EN GARDE

Contre-indications: Hypersensibilité à l'acétylcystéine.

Précautions et mises en garde: Insuffisance respiratoire grave ou asthme ■ Personnes âgées ou patients débilités ■ Encéphalopathie résultant de lésions hépatiques ■ Antécédents d'hémorragie gastro-intestinale (voie orale seulement) ■ **Obst., allaitement**: L'innocuité du médicament n'a pas été établie.

RÉACTIONS INDÉSIRABLES ET EFFETS SECONDAIRES

SNC: somnolence.

ORLO: rhinorrhée.

Resp.: bronchospasme, toux, dyspnée, augmentation des sécrétions.

CV: hypertension, hypotension (IV), vasodilatation (IV).

GI: nausées, vomissements, stomatite.

Tég.: transpiration, urticaire, érythème, prurit.

Divers: frissons, fièvre, œdème de Quincke, RÉACTIONS D'HYPERSENSIBILITÉ ET ANAPHYLAXIE (IV).

INTERACTIONS

Médicament-médicament: Le **charbon activé** peut adsorber l'acétylcystéine lorsque celle-ci est administrée par voie orale et en diminuer l'efficacité.

VOIES D'ADMINISTRATION ET POSOLOGIE

Surdosage par l'acétaminophène

- **PO (adultes et enfants)**: Initialement, 140 mg/kg, ensuite, 70 mg/kg toutes les 4 heures, jusqu'à concurrence de 17 doses supplémentaires.
- **IV (adultes et enfants)**: Initialement, 150 mg/kg, perfusés en 15 minutes, puis 50 mg/kg, perfusés en 4 heures, et 100 mg/kg, perfusés en 16 heures.

Mucolytique

- **Inhalation (adultes et enfants)**: *Nébulisation (masque facial appareil buccal, trachéostomie)* – dose habituelle: de 3 à 5 mL de la solution à 20 %, 3 ou 4 fois par jour (écart posologique habituel: de 1 à 10 mL de la solution à 20 %, toutes les 2 à 6 heures); *nébulisation (tente ou croupette)* – volume de solution à 10 % ou à 20 % permettant de produire une buée très dense; *instillation directe* – 1 ou 2 mL de la solution à 10 % ou à 20 %, toutes les heures; *instillation intratrachéale par trachéotomie* – 1 ou 2 mL de la solution à 10 % ou à 20 %, toutes les 1 à 4 heures.

Prévention des néphropathies

- **PO (adultes)**: 600 mg, à toutes les 12 heures. La veille et la journée même de l'examen radiologique.

PRÉSENTATION (version générique disponible)

Solution: solution à 20 % dans des fioles de 10 et de 30 mL[VL].

SOINS INFIRMIERS

ÉVALUATION DE LA SITUATION

Antidote en cas de surdosage par l'acétaminophène:

- Déterminer l'heure de l'ingestion ainsi que le type et la quantité d'acétaminophène ingérés. Évaluer les concentrations plasmatiques d'acétaminophène. Les concentrations initiales doivent être établies au moins 4 heures après l'ingestion de l'acétaminophène. Il peut être difficile d'interpréter les concentrations plasmatiques exactes par suite de l'ingestion d'une préparation à libération prolongée. Amorcer le traitement sans attendre les résultats des analyses.
- Suivre de près les concentrations d'AST, d'ALT et de bilirubine ainsi que le temps de prothrombine, toutes les 24 heures pendant 96 heures, chez les patients présentant des concentrations plasmatiques d'acétaminophène qui évoquent un risque d'hépatotoxicité.
- Surveiller les fonctions cardiaque et rénale (créatinine, urée), la glycémie et les électrolytes. Maintenir l'équilibre hydroélectrolytique, corriger l'hypoglycémie et administrer de la vitamine K_1 ou du plasma frais congelé ou encore un concentré de facteur de coagulation, si le ratio du temps de prothrombine ou le RNI dépassent 1,5 ou 3, respectivement.
- Déceler la présence de nausées, de vomissements ou d'urticaire. En informer le médecin, le cas échéant.

Mucolytique: Afin de déterminer l'efficacité du médicament, suivre de près la fonction respiratoire (murmure vésiculaire, dyspnée), et noter la couleur, la quantité et la consistance des sécrétions avant le traitement et immédiatement après.

DIAGNOSTICS INFIRMIERS POSSIBLES

- Risque de violence envers soi (Indications).
- Dégagement inefficace des voies respiratoires (Indications).

- Connaissances insuffisantes sur le traitement médicamenteux (Enseignement au patient et à ses proches).

INTERVENTIONS INFIRMIÈRES

- Après ouverture de la fiole, la solution peut virer au violet pâle, sans que cela modifie la puissance du médicament. Réfrigérer les fioles ouvertes et jeter les portions inutilisées après 96 heures.
- Une réaction se produit au contact du médicament avec du caoutchouc et des métaux (fer, nickel, cuivre); éviter tout contact avec ces matériaux.

PO - Surdosage par l'acétaminophène: Il faut d'abord vider l'estomac par lavage ou en provoquant des vomissements. Afin d'améliorer le goût du médicament et d'en faciliter l'administration par voie orale, diluer la solution à 20 % dans une boisson à base de cola, dans de l'eau ou dans du jus jusqu'à l'obtention d'une concentration finale de 1:3, chez les patients dont le poids ne dépasse pas 20 kg, ou dans une quantité de diluant suffisante pour obtenir une solution à 5 %, chez les patients de plus de 20 kg. Si le patient est incapable d'avaler, lui administrer le médicament par une sonde duodénale. Si le patient vomit la dose d'attaque ou les doses d'entretien dans l'heure qui suit l'administration, administrer une nouvelle dose.

IV - Surdosage par l'acétaminophène: Les dilutions recommandées doivent être préparées avec du D5%E, selon les proportions recommandées par le fabricant. Les fioles d'acétylcystéine pour injection IV doivent être considérées comme des doses unitaires. Les solutions doivent être préparées extemporanément et n'être injectées que dans le laps de temps stipulé.

Inhalation - Mucolytique:

- Inciter le patient à consommer suffisamment de liquides (de 2 000 à 3 000 mL par jour) pour diminuer la viscosité des sécrétions.
- *Nébulisation* - On peut diluer la solution à 20 % dans une solution de NaCl 0, 9 % pour injection ou pour inhalation ou dans de l'eau stérile pour injection ou pour inhalation. On peut administrer le médicament par nébulisation ou instiller de 1 à 2 mL directement dans les voies respiratoires. Au cours de l'administration, lorsqu'une fraction de 25 % du médicament reste dans le nébuliseur, la diluer avec une quantité égale de NaCl 0,9 % ou d'eau stérile.
- Après administration du médicament, le volume des sécrétions bronchiques liquéfiées peut augmenter. Lors du traitement administré aux patients qui sont incapables de dégager adéquatement leurs voies aériennes, garder à portée de la main le matériel de succion nécessaire.
- Si un bronchospasme survient pendant le traitement, arrêter l'administration du médicament et demander à un professionnel de la santé si l'on peut ajouter un bronchodilatateur à la pharmacothérapie. Pour prévenir les bronchospasmes chez les patients atteints d'asthme ou d'une maladie des voies aériennes hyperréactives, il faudrait administrer un bronchodilatateur avant le traitement par l'acétylcystéine.
- Rincer la bouche du patient et lui laver le visage après le traitement, car le médicament laisse des résidus collants.

ENSEIGNEMENT AU PATIENT ET À SES PROCHES

Surdosage par l'acétaminophène: Expliquer au patient le but du traitement.

Inhalation:

- Avant le traitement par aérosol, demander au patient de tousser fortement pour dégager ses voies respiratoires.
- Prévenir le patient que l'odeur désagréable de ce médicament s'estompe au fur et à mesure que le traitement avance.

VÉRIFICATION DE L'EFFICACITÉ THÉRAPEUTIQUE

L'efficacité du traitement peut être démontrée par: la diminution des concentrations d'acétaminophène ■ l'arrêt de l'évolution de l'atteinte hépatique en cas de traitement du surdosage par l'acétaminophène ■ la diminution de la dyspnée et la disparition du murmure vésiculaire lorsque le médicament est utilisé comme mucolytique. ✳

ACIDE 5-AMINOSALICYLIQUE,

voir Mésalamine

ACIDE ACÉTYLSALICYLIQUE,

voir Aspirine

ACIDE ASCORBIQUE

Apo-C, Ester-C, Vita-C, Vitamine C

CLASSIFICATION:

Vitamine C (hydrosoluble)

Grossesse - catégorie C

A

INDICATIONS

Traitement et prévention des carences en vitamine C (scorbut) ■ Un apport supplémentaire est nécessaire en présence de certaines maladies gastro-intestinales dictant une nutrition parentérale totale prolongée ou chez les patients soumis à des hémodialyses répétées ■ Les besoins en vitamine C peuvent augmenter dans les cas suivants: grossesse ■ allaitement ■ stress ■ hyperthyroïdie ■ traumatisme ■ brûlures ■ très jeune âge.

MÉCANISME D'ACTION

Élément essentiel à la formation du collagène et à la réparation des tissus ■ Effets sur la formation de l'hémoglobine, la maturation des érythrocytes et certaines réactions immunologiques et biochimiques de l'organisme. ***Effets thérapeutiques:*** Supplément lors de carences ■ Supplément en présence de besoins accrus.

PHARMACOCINÉTIQUE

Absorption: Active (PO), par le biais d'un processus saturable.

Distribution: Tout l'organisme; l'agent traverse la barrière placentaire et passe dans le lait maternel.

Métabolisme et excrétion: Transformation en composés excrétés par les reins.

Demi-vie: Inconnue.

Profil temps-action

	Début d'action	Pic	Durée
PO, IM, IV, SC	2 jours – 3 semaines	inconnu	inconnue

CONTRE-INDICATIONS, PRÉCAUTIONS ET MISES EN GARDE

Contre-indications: Hypersensibilité à la tartrazine (certaines préparations contiennent cette substance ou du colorant FD&C jaune n° 5; voir les directives du fabricant).

Précautions et mises en garde: Calculs rénaux récurrents ■ **Obst.**: Éviter l'usage prolongé à des doses élevées.

RÉACTIONS INDÉSIRABLES ET EFFETS SECONDAIRES

SNC: étourdissements, fatigue, céphalées, insomnie.

GI: crampes, diarrhée, brûlures épigastriques, nausées, vomissements.

GU: calculs rénaux.

Tég.: rougeurs.

Hémat.: thrombose veineuse profonde, hémolyse (en cas de déficit en glucose-6-phosphate-déshydrogénase), drépanocytose.

Locaux: douleurs au point d'injection SC ou IM.

INTERACTIONS

Médicament-médicament: En cas d'acidification de l'urine, l'excrétion de la **mexilétine**, des **amphétamines** ou des **antidépresseurs tricycliques** peut être accrue, et les effets de ces médicaments, diminués ■ Les doses élevées d'acide ascorbique (> 10 g par jour) peuvent diminuer la réponse à la **warfarine** ■ La vitamine C, administrée en concomitance avec la **déféroxamine**, augmente la toxicité du fer.

VOIES D'ADMINISTRATION ET POSOLOGIE

- **PO, IM (adultes)**: *Scorbut* – 500 mg par jour, pendant au moins 14 jours.
- **PO**: *Prévention d'une carence* – de 50 à 100 mg par jour.
- **PO, IM (enfants)**: *Scorbut* – de 100 à 300 mg par jour, pendant au moins 14 jours. **PO**: *Prévention d'une carence* – de 30 à 45 mg par jour.
- **IV (adultes et enfants)**: *Prévention d'une carence* – posologie à établir selon les besoins.

PRÉSENTATION (version générique disponible)

Nombreuses présentations: comprimés, comprimés à croquer, comprimés à libération retard, capsules à libération retard, solution pour injection ■ **Différentes teneurs**: 100, 250, 500, 1 000 mg, etc. ■ **En association avec**: autres vitamines et minéraux dans des préparations multivitaminiques.

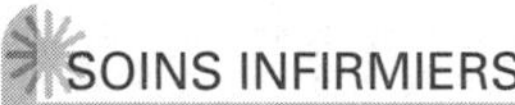

SOINS INFIRMIERS

ÉVALUATION DE LA SITUATION

Carence en vitamine C: Avant l'administration de la vitamine C et pendant toute la durée du traitement, rester à l'affût des signes suivants de carence: développement anormal des os et des dents, gingivite, saignements des gencives et déchaussement des dents.

Tests de laboratoire:

- Les doses élevées d'acide ascorbique (> 10 fois l'apport quotidien recommandé) peuvent entraîner des résultats faussement négatifs aux tests de dépistage du sang occulte dans les selles.
- L'acide ascorbique peut diminuer les concentrations sériques de bilirubine et augmenter les concentrations urinaires d'oxalate, d'urate et de cystéine.

DIAGNOSTICS INFIRMIERS POSSIBLES

- Alimentation déficiente (Indications).

- Connaissances insuffisantes sur l'alimentation et sur le traitement médicamenteux (Enseignement au patient et à ses proches).

INTERVENTIONS INFIRMIÈRES

- L'acide ascorbique fait souvent partie d'une multivitaminothérapie, car une alimentation inadéquate entraîne souvent la carence de plusieurs vitamines.
- La pression à l'intérieur des ampoules peut être accrue à la température ambiante; enrouler une gaine de protection autour de l'ampoule avant de la casser.

PO: Les capsules et les comprimés à libération retard doivent être avalés tels quels, sans les écraser, les mâcher ou les croquer; on peut mélanger le contenu des capsules avec de la gelée ou de la confiture. Les comprimés à croquer doivent être bien mâchés ou écrasés avant d'être avalés. On peut boire les solutions destinées à la voie orale directement ou les mélanger avec du jus de fruits, des céréales ou d'autres aliments.

IM: Cette voie d'administration est la voie parentérale de prédilection.

Perfusion continue: Diluer l'acide ascorbique dans une grande quantité de D5%E, de D10%E, de NaCl 0,9 % ou de NaCl 0,45 %, ou dans une solution de lactate de Ringer ou une solution de Ringer ou encore dans une solution combinée de dextrose/soluté salin ou de dextrose/solution de Ringer. Consulter les directives de chaque fabricant avant de reconstituer la préparation. ***Vitesse de perfusion***: Perfusion lente.

Association compatible dans la même seringue: métoclopramide.

Associations incompatibles dans la même seringue: céphazoline ■ doxapram.

Compatibilité en addition au soluté: amikacine ■ calcium, chlorure de ■ calcium, gluceptate de ■ calcium, gluconate de ■ céphalothine ■ chloramphénicol ■ chlorpromazine ■ colistiméthate ■ cyanocobalamine ■ diphenhydramine ■ héparine ■ kanamycine ■ méthicilline ■ méthyldopa ■ pénicilline G potassique ■ polymyxine B ■ prednisolone ■ procaïne ■ prochlorpérazine ■ prométhazine ■ vérapamil.

Incompatibilité en addition au soluté: bléomycine ■ céphapirine ■ nafcilline ■ sodium, bicarbonate de ■ warfarine.

ENSEIGNEMENT AU PATIENT ET À SES PROCHES

Conseiller au patient de respecter rigoureusement la posologie recommandée et de ne pas dépasser les doses prescrites. Les excès peuvent entraîner de la diarrhée et la formation de calculs urinaires. Si le patient a oublié de prendre une dose, il peut la sauter et reprendre ensuite son horaire habituel.

Carence en vitamine C:

- Encourager le patient à suivre les recommandations diététiques du professionnel de la santé. Lui expliquer que la meilleure source de vitamines est une alimentation bien équilibrée.
- Informer le patient que les aliments riches en acide ascorbique sont les agrumes, les tomates, les fraises, le cantaloup et les poivrons crus. Lui expliquer qu'il y a une déperdition d'acide ascorbique si les aliments frais sont gardés pendant plusieurs jours, mais non s'ils sont surgelés. La déperdition est également rapide si les aliments sont séchés, salés ou cuits.
- Prévenir le patient qui pratique l'automédication par des suppléments vitaminiques qu'il ne doit pas dépasser la dose quotidienne recommandée (voir l'annexe K). L'efficacité des mégadoses de vitamines dans le traitement de divers problèmes de santé n'a pas été prouvée. Par contre, de telles doses peuvent entraîner des effets secondaires. Le sevrage brusque, après l'administration de doses importantes d'acide ascorbique, peut provoquer une carence rebond.

VÉRIFICATION DE L'EFFICACITÉ THÉRAPEUTIQUE

L'efficacité du traitement peut être démontrée par: la diminution des symptômes de carence en acide ascorbique. ✳

ACIDE FOLINIQUE,

voir Leucovorine calcique

ACIDE FOLIQUE

Synonyme: folate

Acide Folique, Apo-Folic, Folvite, Novo-Folacid

CLASSIFICATION:

Vitamine B (traitement de l'anémie)

Grossesse – catégorie A (C à des doses supérieures aux doses recommandées)

INDICATIONS

Prévention et traitement des anémies mégaloblastiques et macrocytaires ■ Administration au cours de la grossesse pour favoriser le développement normal du fœtus et prévenir les malformations du tube neural ■ Traitement de la sprue tropicale ■ Prévention de la toxicité du méthotrexate.

A

MÉCANISME D'ACTION

Élément indispensable à la synthèse des protéines et au fonctionnement des érythrocytes. Stimulation de la formation des globules rouges et blancs et des plaquettes. Élément essentiel au développement du fœtus.
Effets thérapeutiques: Rétablissement et maintien d'une hématopoïèse normale.

PHARMACOCINÉTIQUE

Absorption: Bonne (PO, IM et SC).
Distribution: La moitié de la réserve de ce médicament se retrouve dans le foie. Il traverse la barrière placentaire et passe dans le lait maternel.
Liaison aux protéines: Importante.
Métabolisme et excrétion: Métabolisme hépatique et plasmatique, transformation en acide tétrahydrofolique, le métabolite actif. Excrétion rénale.
Demi-vie: Inconnue.

Profil temps-action
(augmentation de la numérotation réticulocytaire)

	DÉBUT D'ACTION	PIC	DURÉE
PO, IM, SC, IV	3 - 5 jours	5 - 10 jours	inconnue

CONTRE-INDICATIONS, PRÉCAUTIONS ET MISES EN GARDE

Contre-indications: Anémie pernicieuse non corrigée (les lésions neurologiques évolueront malgré la correction des anomalies hématologiques) ■ **PÉD.:** Nouveau-nés (ne pas administrer les préparations contenant de l'alcool benzylique).
Précautions et mises en garde: Anémie non diagnostiquée.

RÉACTIONS INDÉSIRABLES ET EFFETS SECONDAIRES

Tég.: rash.
SNC: (à fortes doses: ≥ 15 mg/jour): modification du sommeil, irritabilité, malaise, confusion.
Divers: fièvre.

INTERACTIONS

Médicament-médicament: La **pyriméthamine**, le **méthotrexate**, le **trimétroprime** et le **triamtérène** peuvent entraîner une carence en folates ■ Les **sulfamides** (incluant la **sulfasalazine**), les **antiacides** et la **cholestyramine** diminuent l'absorption de l'acide folique ■ Les **œstrogènes**, la **phénytoïne**, les **barbituriques**, la **primidone**, la **carbamazépine** ou les **glucocorticoïdes** augmentent les besoins en acide folique. ■ L'acide folique peut diminuer les concentrations sériques de la **phénytoïne**.

VOIES D'ADMINISTRATION ET POSOLOGIE

Dose thérapeutique

- **PO, IM, IV, SC (adultes et enfants ≥ 11 ans):** *Traitement de la carence* – de 0,25 à 1 mg, 1 fois par jour. *Sprue tropicale* – de 3 à 15 mg, 1 fois par jour. *Prévention de la toxicité du méthotrexate* – de 0,4 à 1 mg, 1 fois par jour.
- **PO, IM, IV, SC (enfants > 1 an):** *Traitement de la carence* – 1 mg, 1 fois par jour.
- **PO, IM, IV, SC (nourrissons ≤ 1 an):** *Traitement de la carence* – 15 µg/kg/dose, 1 fois par jour, ou 50 µg, 1 fois par jour.

Dose d'entretien

- **PO, IM, IV, SC (adultes et enfants ≥ 4 ans):** 0,4 mg, 1 fois par jour.
- **PO, IM, IV, SC (enfants < 4 ans):** Jusqu'à 0,3 mg, 1 fois par jour.
- **PO, IM, IV, SC (nourrissons ≤ 1 an):** 0,1 mg, 1 fois par jour.
- **PO, IM, IV, SC (adultes, femmes enceintes ou allaitantes):** 0,4 mg, 1 fois par jour. *Prophylaxie de la malformation du tube neural* – 0,4 mg, 1 fois par jour, pendant 10 à 12 semaines après la dernière menstruation. *Antécédents de grossesse compliquée par une malformation du tube neural* – 4 mg, 1 fois par jour. *Femmes à risque* – de 1 à 4 mg, 1 fois par jour; poursuivre le traitement pendant 10 à 12 semaines après la dernière menstruation.

PRÉSENTATION (version générique disponible)

Comprimés: 0,4 mg^{VL}, 0,8 mg^{VL}, 1 mg^{VL}, 5 mg^{Pr} ■ **Solution pour injection:** 5 mg/mL^{Pr} ■ **En association avec:** autres vitamines et minéraux sous forme de multivitamines^{VL}.

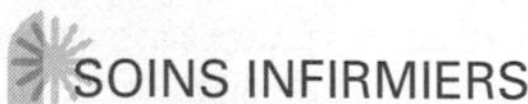

SOINS INFIRMIERS

ÉVALUATION DE LA SITUATION

- Observer le patient avant le traitement et à intervalles réguliers pendant toute sa durée à la recherche des signes suivants d'anémie mégaloblastique: fatigue, faiblesse, dyspnée.

Tests de laboratoire:

- Noter les concentrations plasmatiques d'acide folique, les concentrations d'hémoglobine, l'hématocrite et la numération réticulocytaire avant le traitement et à intervalles réguliers pendant toute sa durée.
- L'acide folique, administré continuellement à dose élevée, peut entraîner la diminution des concentrations sériques de vitamine B.

DIAGNOSTICS INFIRMIERS POSSIBLES

- Alimentation déficiente (Indications).
- Intolérance à l'activité (Indications).
- Connaissances insuffisantes sur le traitement médicamenteux (Enseignement au patient et à ses proches).

INTERVENTIONS INFIRMIÈRES

- NE PAS CONFONDRE L'ACIDE FOLIQUE ET L'ACIDE FOLINIQUE (LEUCOVORINE CALCIQUE).
- On administre habituellement l'acide folique en association avec d'autres vitamines, car il est rare que le patient ne présente que ce seul type d'avitaminose.
- Lorsque l'administration par voie orale est impossible, l'acide folique peut être administré par voie SC, par voie IM profonde ou par voie IV (voie parentérale de choix lorsque l'administration par voie orale est impossible).

IV: La couleur de la solution varie de jaune à orange.

IV directe: Administrer à un débit de 5 mg pendant au moins 1 minute.

Perfusion continue (méthode d'administration à privilégier): On peut ajouter l'acide folique à une solution destinée à l'alimentation parentérale. Consulter les directives de chaque fabricant avant de reconstituer la préparation.

Compatibilité (tubulure en Y): famotidine.

Compatibilité en addition au soluté: D20%E.

Incompatibilité en addition au soluté: D50%E ■ calcium, gluconate de.

ENSEIGNEMENT AU PATIENT ET À SES PROCHES

- Conseiller au patient de respecter rigoureusement les recommandations diététiques du professionnel de la santé. Lui expliquer que la meilleure source de vitamines est une alimentation bien équilibrée, contenant des aliments provenant des 4 principaux groupes. Si le médecin essaie de diagnostiquer la carence en acide folique, sans écarter l'anémie pernicieuse, il prescrira un régime pauvre en vitamine B et en folate.
- Les aliments riches en acide folique comprennent les légumes, les fruits et les abats; l'acide folique contenu dans les aliments est détruit par la chaleur.
- Prévenir le patient qui pratique l'automédication par des suppléments vitaminiques qu'il ne doit pas dépasser la dose quotidienne recommandée (voir l'annexe K). L'efficacité des mégadoses de vitamines dans le traitement de divers problèmes de santé n'a pas été prouvée. Par contre, de telles doses peuvent entraîner des effets secondaires.
- Expliquer au patient que l'acide folique peut rendre l'urine d'un jaune plus foncé.
- Conseiller au patient de signaler à un professionnel de la santé le rash qui peut être un signe d'hypersensibilité.
- Insister sur l'importance des examens de suivi permettant d'évaluer les bienfaits du traitement.

VÉRIFICATION DE L'EFFICACITÉ THÉRAPEUTIQUE

L'efficacité du traitement peut être démontrée par: la réticulocytose se manifestant de 2 à 5 jours après le début du traitement ■ la résolution des symptômes d'anémie mégaloblastique. ✳

ACIDE NICOTINIQUE,
voir Niacine

ACIDE VALPROÏQUE,
voir Valproates

ACYCLOVIR

Apo-Acyclovir, Gen-Acyclovir, Nu-Acyclovir, Zovirax

CLASSIFICATION:

Antiviral (analogue des purines)

Grossesse – catégorie B

INDICATIONS

PO: Traitement des primo-infections et prophylaxie des infections génitales herpétiques récurrentes (6 épisodes ou plus par année) ■ Traitement de la phase aiguë des lésions cutanées localisées du zona et de la varicelle ■ **IV**: Traitement des épisodes initiaux (primo-infections) graves d'herpès simplex chez les patients non immunodéprimés ■ Traitement des infections muqueuses ou cutanées provoquées par l'herpès simplex ou des infections provoquées par l'herpès zoster chez les patients immunodéprimés ■ **Usage topique**: *Crème ou onguent* – traitement des primo-infections génitales d'herpès simplex ■ *Onguent* – chez les patients immunodéprimés, traitement des infections cutanées du virus herpès simplex qui ne mettent pas leur vie en danger.

MÉCANISME D'ACTION

Inhibition de la synthèse de l'ADN viral. ***Effets thérapeutiques:*** Inhibition de la réplication virale, diminution de l'excrétion du virus et accélération du temps de cicatrisation des lésions.

A

PHARMACOCINÉTIQUE

Absorption: De 15 à 30 % (PO).

Distribution: Le médicament se répartit dans tout l'organisme. La concentration dans le liquide céphalorachidien correspond à 50 % de la concentration plasmatique. L'acyclovir traverse la barrière placentaire et passe dans le lait maternel.

Liaison aux protéines: De 9 à 33 %.

Métabolisme et excrétion: Élimination majoritairement rénale (90 %) à l'état inchangé; la fraction restante est métabolisée par le foie.

Demi-vie: De 2,1 à 3,5 heures (prolongée en cas d'insuffisance rénale).

Profil temps-action

	Début d'action	Pic	Durée
PO	inconnu	1,5 – 2,5 h	4 h
IV	rapide	fin de la perfusion	8 h

CONTRE-INDICATIONS, PRÉCAUTIONS ET MISES EN GARDE

Contre-indications: Hypersensibilité à l'acyclovir ou au valacyclovir ou à un autre ingrédient de la préparation.

Précautions et mises en garde: Graves anomalies neurologiques, hépatiques, pulmonaires et hydroélectrolytiques préexistantes ■ Patients recevant de fortes doses par voie orale ou IV (maintenir une hydratation adéquate) ■ Utilisation concomitante de médicaments pouvant être néphrotoxiques ■ Insuffisance rénale (réduire la dose si la Cl_{Cr} < 50 mL/min) ■ **Gér.**: Tenir compte de la diminution de la fonction rénale chez cette population ■ Patients obèses (établir la dose d'après le poids idéal) ■ **Obst., allaitement**: L'innocuité du médicament n'a pas été établie ■ **Péd.**: Enfants âgés de moins de 2 ans (l'innocuité du médicament n'a pas été établie).

RÉACTIONS INDÉSIRABLES ET EFFETS SECONDAIRES

SNC: CONVULSIONS, étourdissements, céphalées, hallucinations, tremblements.

GI: diarrhée, nausées, vomissements, douleurs abdominales, anorexie, hyperbilirubinémie, élévation des enzymes hépatiques.

GU: INSUFFISANCE RÉNALE, cristallurie, hématurie.

Tég.: acné, urticaire, rash, sécrétion de sueur inhabituelle, syndrome de Stevens-Johnson.

End.: modifications du cycle menstruel.

Hémat.: PURPURA THROMBOPÉNIQUE THROMBOTIQUE, SYNDROME HÉMOLYTIQUE ET URÉMIQUE (doses élevées chez les patients immunodéprimés).

Locaux: douleur, phlébite, irritation locale.

Loc.: douleurs articulaires.

Divers: polydipsie.

INTERACTIONS

Médicament-médicament: Le **probénécide** et la **cimétidine** élèvent les concentrations sanguines d'acyclovir ■ L'acyclovir peut élever les concentrations plasmatiques de la **théophylline** et, par conséquence, le risque d'effets secondaires; il peut s'avérer nécessaire d'adapter la dose de théophylline ■ L'acyclovir peut diminuer les concentrations plasmatiques et l'efficacité de l'**acide valproïque** et des **hydantoïnes** ■ L'utilisation concomitante d'autres **médicaments néphrotoxiques** augmente le risque d'effets rénaux indésirables ■ La **zidovudine** ainsi que le **méthotrexate par voie intrathécale** augmentent le risque d'effets secondaires sur le SNC.

VOIES D'ADMINISTRATION ET POSOLOGIE

Infection herpétique génitale primaire

- **PO (adultes)**: 200 mg, toutes les 4 heures, 5 fois par jour, pour un total de 1 g/jour pendant 10 jours.
- **IV (adultes)**: 5 mg/kg, toutes les 8 heures, pendant 7 jours.
- **IV (enfants de 2 à 12 ans)**: 250 mg/m^2, toutes les 8 heures, pendant 7 jours.
- **Usage topique (adultes)**: Appliquer un ruban de 1,25 cm d'onguent ou de crème à 5 % par 10 cm^2 de peau, de 4 à 6 fois par jour, pendant un maximum de 10 jours.

Traitement suppressif prolongé des infections génitales herpétiques récurrentes

- **PO (adultes)**: 400 mg, 2 fois par jour *ou* 200 mg, de 3 à 5 fois par jour, pendant 12 mois au maximum.

Traitement intermittent des infections génitales herpétiques récurrentes

- **PO (adultes)**: 200 mg, toutes les 4 heures, pendant que le patient est éveillé (5 fois par jour), pendant 5 jours; amorcer le traitement dès l'apparition des symptômes.

Zona aigu

- **PO (adultes)**: 800 mg, toutes les 4 heures, pendant que le patient est éveillé (5 fois par jour), pendant 7 à 10 jours. Amorcer le traitement dans les 72 heures (idéalement en moins de 48 heures) suivant l'apparition des lésions.

Varicelle

- **PO (adultes)**: 20 mg/kg (au maximum, 800 mg/dose), 4 fois par jour, pendant 5 jours. Amorcer le traitement dans les 24 heures suivant l'apparition des éruptions cutanées.

Infections mucocutanées provoquées par l'herpès simplex chez les patients immunodéprimés

- **IV (adultes)**: 5 mg/kg, toutes les 8 heures, pendant 7 jours.

- **IV (enfants de 2 à 12 ans)**: 250 mg/m², toutes les 8 heures, pendant 7 jours.
- **Usage topique (adultes)**: Un ruban de 1,25 cm d'onguent ou de crème à 5 % par 10 cm² de peau, de 4 à 6 fois par jour, pendant un maximum de 10 jours.

Infections provoquées par le virus zona-varicelle chez les patients immunodéprimés

- **IV (adultes)**: 10 mg/kg, toutes les 8 heures, pendant 7 jours.
- **IV (enfants de 2 à 12 ans)**: 500 mg/m², toutes les 8 heures, pendant 7 jours.

INSUFFISANCE RÉNALE

- **IV (ADULTES ET ENFANTS)**: *CL_{CR} > 50 mL/MIN/1,73 m²*: 100 % DE LA DOSE TOUTES LES 8 HEURES; *CL_{CR} DE 25 À 50 mL/MIN/1,73 m²*: 100 % DE LA DOSE TOUTES LES 12 HEURES; *CL_{CR} DE 10 À 25 mL/MIN/1,73 m²*: 100 % DE LA DOSE TOUTES LES 24 HEURES; *CL_{CR} DE 0 À 10 mL/MIN/1,73 m²*: 50 % DE LA DOSE, TOUTES LES 24 À 48 HEURES.
- **PO (ADULTES)**: ADAPTER LES DOSES SELON LE TABLEAU SUIVANT:

RÉGIME POSOLOGIQUE NORMAL	CLAIRANCE DE LA CRÉATININE (mL/MIN/1,73 m²)	RÉGIME POSOLOGIQUE ADAPTÉ — DOSE (mg)	INTERVALLE ENTRE LES DOSES (HEURES)
200 mg, toutes les 4 heures	> 10	200	toutes les 4 heures, 5 fois/jour
	0 – 10	200	toutes les 12 heures
400 mg, toutes les 12 heures	> 10	400	toutes les 12 heures
	0 – 10	200	toutes les 12 heures
800 mg, toutes les 4 heures	> 25	800	toutes les 4 heures, 5 fois/jour
	10 – 25	800	toutes les 8 heures
	0 – 10	800	toutes les 12 heures

PRÉSENTATION
(version générique disponible)

Comprimés: 200 mg^Pr^, 400 mg^Pr^, 800 mg^Pr^ ■ **Suspension orale**: 200 mg/5 mL^Pr^ ■ **Solution pour injection**: 25 mg/mL^Pr^ (fioles de 20 mL); 50 mg/mL^Pr^ (fioles de 10 et de 20 mL) ■ **Poudre pour injection**: fioles de 500 et de 1 000 mg^Pr^ ■ **Crème topique**: 5 %^Pr^ ■ **Onguent topique**: 5 %^Pr^.

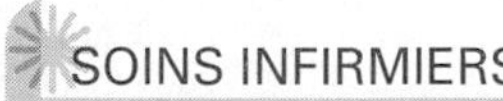

SOINS INFIRMIERS

ÉVALUATION DE LA SITUATION

- Examiner les lésions avant le début du traitement et quotidiennement pendant toute sa durée.
- Examiner l'état neurologique des patients souffrant d'encéphalite herpétique.

Tests de laboratoire: Noter les concentrations sériques d'urée et de créatinine ainsi que la clairance de la créatinine avant et pendant le traitement. Des concentrations sériques accrues de créatinine et d'urée ou une clairance diminuée de la créatinine peuvent être des indices d'insuffisance rénale.

DIAGNOSTICS INFIRMIERS POSSIBLES

- Risque d'atteinte à l'intégrité de la peau (Indications).
- Risque de contagion (Enseignement au patient et à ses proches).
- Connaissances insuffisantes sur l'évolution de la maladie et sur le traitement médicamenteux (Enseignement au patient et à ses proches).

INTERVENTIONS INFIRMIÈRES

- Il faut commencer le traitement à l'acyclovir dès l'apparition des symptômes d'herpès simplex, dans les 72 heures (idéalement dans les 48 heures) suivant une flambée de zona et dans les 24 heures suivant les éruptions cutanées de varicelle.

PO:

- On peut prendre l'acyclovir à jeun ou avec des aliments; l'administrer avec un grand verre d'eau.
- Bien agiter la suspension orale avant de l'administrer.
- Pour prévenir la cristallurie chez les patients prenant une dose orale élevée, il faut maintenir une hydratation suffisante (de 2 000 à 3 000 mL/jour).

IV:

- Pour prévenir la cristallurie, il faut maintenir une hydratation suffisante (de 2 000 à 3 000 mL/jour), particulièrement au cours des 2 premières heures qui suivent la perfusion IV.
- Observer le point de perfusion pour déceler les signes de phlébite. Pour la prévenir, assurer la rotation des points de perfusion.
- L'acyclovir pour injection ne doit pas être administré par voies topique, IM, SC ou PO ni dans les yeux.

Perfusion intermittente: Reconstituer le contenu d'une fiole de 500 mg ou de 1 g avec 10 mL ou 20 mL, respectivement, d'eau stérile pour injection sans agent de conservation pour obtenir une concentration de 50 mg/mL. Ne pas reconstituer avec de l'eau bactériostatique contenant de l'alcool benzylique ou des parabènes. Bien agiter pour dissoudre tout le médicament. Il existe également une forme de solution prémélangée qui doit, elle aussi, être diluée.

Solutions pour perfusion IV: solution de D5%E pour injection, de D5%E/NaCl 0,9 % pour injection, de D5%E/NaCl 0,2 % pour injection, de Ringer pour injection, de NaCl 0,9 % pour injection, de lactate de Ringer pour injection. Des concentrations supérieures à 10 mg/mL ne sont pas recommandées. Utiliser la solution reconstituée dans les 12 heures qui suivent sa

A

préparation. La solution destinée à la perfusion doit être utilisée dans les 24 heures qui suivent sa dilution. La réfrigération entraîne la formation de précipités qui se dissolvent à la température ambiante. Consulter les directives de chaque fabricant avant de reconstituer la préparation.

Vitesse d'administration: Administrer à l'aide d'une pompe à perfusion pendant au moins 1 heure afin de réduire le risque de lésion rénale.

Compatibilité (tubulure en Y): allopurinol ▪ amikacine ▪ ampicilline ▪ céfamandole ▪ céfazoline ▪ céfonicide ▪ céfopérazone ▪ céfotaxime ▪ céfoxitine ▪ ceftazidime ▪ ceftizoxime ▪ ceftriaxone ▪ céfuroxime ▪ céphapirine ▪ chloramphénicol ▪ cimétidine ▪ clindamycine ▪ dexaméthasone sodique, phosphate de ▪ dimenhydrinate ▪ diphenhydramine ▪ doxycycline ▪ érythromycine, lactobionate d' ▪ famotidine ▪ filgrastrim ▪ fluconazole ▪ gallium, nitrate de ▪ gentamicine ▪ granisétron ▪ héparine ▪ hydrocortisone sodique, succinate d' ▪ hydromorphone ▪ imipénem/cilastatine ▪ lorazépam ▪ magnésium, sulfate de ▪ melphalan ▪ méthylprednisolone sodique, succinate de ▪ métoclopramide ▪ métronidazole ▪ multivitamines pour perfusion ▪ nafcilline ▪ oxacilline ▪ paclitaxel ▪ pénicilline G potassique ▪ pentobarbital ▪ perphénazine ▪ pipéracilline ▪ potassium, chlorure de ▪ propofol ▪ ranitidine ▪ sodium, bicarbonate de ▪ tacrolimus ▪ téniposide ▪ théophylline ▪ thiotépa ▪ ticarcilline ▪ tobramycine ▪ timéthroprime/sulfaméthoxazole ▪ vancomycine ▪ zidovudine.

Incompatibilité (tubulure en Y): amifostine ▪ aztréonam ▪ céfépime ▪ dobutamine ▪ dopamine ▪ fludarabine ▪ foscarnet ▪ idarubicine ▪ ondansétron ▪ pipéracilline/tazobactam ▪ sargramostim ▪ vinorelbine.

Compatibilité en addition au soluté: fluconazole.

Incompatibilité en addition au soluté: produits du sang ▪ solutions qui contiennent des protéines.

Usage topique: Appliquer sur les lésions cutanées seulement; ne pas administrer dans les yeux.

ENSEIGNEMENT AU PATIENT ET À SES PROCHES

- Inciter le patient à suivre rigoureusement la posologie recommandée pendant toute la durée du traitement. S'il n'a pu prendre le médicament au moment habituel, il doit le prendre le plus rapidement possible sauf si c'est presque l'heure prévue pour la dose suivante. Avertir le patient qu'il ne faut jamais remplacer une dose manquée par une dose double. L'acyclovir ne doit pas être utilisé plus fréquemment ni plus longtemps qu'il n'a été prescrit.
- Signaler au patient que l'application concomitante de crèmes, de lotions et d'onguents en vente libre peut retarder la guérison et provoquer la dissémination des lésions.
- Prévenir le patient que l'acyclovir ne guérit pas l'infection par le virus, étant donné que celui-ci reste à l'état latent dans les ganglions. Le médicament ne prévient pas, non plus, la transmission de l'infection à d'autres personnes.
- Inciter le patient souffrant d'herpès génital à utiliser des préservatifs pendant les rapports sexuels et à éviter les rapports sexuels pendant que les lésions sont présentes.
- Prévenir le patient qu'il doit consulter un professionnel de la santé si les symptômes ne sont pas soulagés après un traitement topique d'une durée de 7 jours ou si l'acyclovir par voie orale ne diminue pas la fréquence ou la gravité des récurrences. Chez les patients immunodéprimés, la formation de croûtes recouvrant les lésions peut prendre plus de temps, habituellement 2 semaines.
- Prévenir les patientes qui souffrent d'herpès génital qu'elles devraient se soumettre tous les ans à un test de Papanicolaou, étant donné qu'elles sont davantage prédisposées au cancer du col.

Usage topique:

- Expliquer au patient qu'il doit appliquer l'onguent ou la crème toutes les 3 heures, 6 fois par jour, pendant 7 jours. Un ruban d'onguent ou de crème de 1,25 cm recouvre environ 10 cm^2 de peau. Utiliser un doigtier ou un gant lors de l'application de l'onguent ou de la crème afin d'éviter la contamination d'autres parties du corps ou la transmission de l'infection à d'autres personnes. Garder les parties atteintes propres et sèches. Pour prévenir l'irritation, recommander au patient de porter des vêtements amples.
- Expliquer au patient qu'il doit éviter le contact du médicament avec l'œil ou la région périoculaire. Lui demander de signaler sans délai à un professionnel de la santé tous les symptômes oculaires inexpliqués, étant donné qu'une infection oculaire par le virus de l'herpès simplex peut mener à la cécité.

VÉRIFICATION DE L'EFFICACITÉ THÉRAPEUTIQUE

L'efficacité du traitement peut être démontrée par: la formation de croûtes et la cicatrisation des lésions cutanées ▪ la diminution de la fréquence et de la gravité des récurrences ▪ le raccourcissement du délai de cicatrisation complète des lésions provoquées par le zona et le soulagement de la douleur ▪ la diminution de la gravité de la varicelle.

ADALIMUMAB

Humira

CLASSIFICATION:

Agent antirhumatismal modificateur de la maladie [AARMM] (anticorps monoclonal)

Grossesse – catégorie B

INDICATIONS

Traitement de la polyarthrite rhumatoïde de modérément à fortement évolutive, en monothérapie ou en association avec le méthotrexate ou un AARMM ■ Atténuation des signes et des symptômes d'arthrite évolutive chez l'adulte atteint de rhumatisme psoriasique (on peut l'utiliser en association avec le méthotrexate chez les patients qui n'ont pas répondu de façon satisfaisante au traitement par le méthotrexate seul) ■ Atténuation des signes et des symptômes de la maladie chez les patients atteints de spondylarthrite ankylosante évolutive qui n'ont pas répondu de façon satisfaisante à un traitement classique.

MÉCANISME D'ACTION

L'adalimumab est un anticorps monoclonal humain recombinant, qui bloque l'action du facteur humain de nécrose tumorale (TNFalpha) en se liant à ce dernier, empêchant ainsi son interaction avec les récepteurs. Il provoque également la lyse des cellules qui expriment le TNF à leur surface. Le TNF est une cytokine naturelle qui participe aux réactions inflammatoires et immunitaires normales. On trouve des taux anormalement élevés de TNF dans le liquide synovial des patients atteints de polyarthrite rhumatoïde, de rhumatisme psoriasique et de spondylarthrite ankylosante; cette élévation joue un rôle important dans le dérèglement du processus inflammatoire et la destruction des articulations caractéristiques de ces maladies. L'adalimumab module aussi les réponses biologiques déclenchées ou régulées par le TNF. ***Effets thérapeutiques:*** Diminution des signes et symptômes, induction d'une réponse clinique et d'une rémission clinique importantes, arrêt de l'évolution des lésions structurelles de la polyarthrite rhumatoïde et amélioration des capacités physiques et du fonctionnement des patients ■ Diminution des signes et des symptômes du rhumatisme psoriasique ou de la spondylarthrite ankylosante.

PHARMACOCINÉTIQUE

Absorption: Bonne (SC). Biodisponibilité à 64 %.

Distribution: Concentration dans le liquide synovial entre 31 et 96 % des concentrations plasmatiques. On ignore si le médicament passe dans le lait maternel.

Métabolisme et excrétion: Inconnus. Le métabolisme et l'excrétion devraient être similaires à ceux d'autres molécules d'IgG.

Demi-vie: Environ 2 semaines (de 10 à 20 jours).

Profil temps-action

(amélioration clinique – polyarthrite rhumatoïde)

	DÉBUT D'ACTION	PIC	DURÉE
SC	24 h – 1 semaine†	moins de 3 mois‡	2 semaines§

† Données pour la voie IV.

‡ Temps nécessaire pour atteindre une amélioration clinique maximale après l'administration de doses hebdomadaires répétées.

§ Après l'arrêt du traitement.

CONTRE-INDICATIONS, PRÉCAUTIONS ET MISES EN GARDE

Contre-indications: Hypersensibilité ■ Infections graves, comme la septicémie, la tuberculose et les infections opportunistes ■ Infections évolutives, chroniques ou localisées dont une tuberculose évolutive ou latente (l'infection doit être maîtrisée avant de commencer le traitement) ■ Administration concomitante d'anakinra.

Précautions et mises en garde: Infection (arrêter le traitement si une infection grave se développe) ■ Affection démyélinisante du système nerveux central, préexistante ou de survenue récente ■ Traitement immunosuppresseur concomitant ■ Cancer (risque accru de lymphome) ■ Formation d'autoanticorps (risque d'apparition du syndrome pseudolupique) ■ Risque de réactions allergiques et d'anaphylaxie ■ Allergie au latex (le capuchon de l'aiguille de la seringue renferme du latex) ■ Vaccins à virus vivants (ne pas administrer avec l'adalimumab) ■ Antécédents d'hépatite B ■ Antécédents d'anomalies hématologiques notables ■ Insuffisance cardiaque congestive ■ Insuffisance rénale ■ Insuffisance hépatique ■ **OBST.**: N'administrer ce médicament aux femmes enceintes qu'en cas d'absolue nécessité ■ **ALLAITEMENT**: L'innocuité du médicament n'a pas été établie ■ **PÉD.**: L'innocuité et l'efficacité du médicament n'ont pas été établies ■ **GÉR.**: Risque accru d'infections et de cancers chez cette population.

RÉACTIONS INDÉSIRABLES ET EFFETS SECONDAIRES

SNC: céphalées, fatigue, étourdissements.

Resp.: bronchospasme, dyspnée, aggravation de la toux, infections des voies respiratoires supérieures, sinusite, bronchite, rhinite, PNEUMONIE.

CV: hypertension artérielle, insuffisance cardiaque congestive.

GI: nausées, diarrhée, douleurs abdominales.

GU: infections des voies urinaires, hématurie.

A

Tég.: éruptions cutanées, prurit, alopécie, zona.
Hémat.: neutropénie, thrombopénie, pancytopénie.
Métab.: hypercholestérolémie, hyperlipidémie.
Loc.: douleurs dorsales.
SN: paresthésies, exacerbation des maladies démyélinisantes préexistantes (comme la sclérose en plaques).
Locaux: douleurs et réactions au point d'injection.
Divers: réactions allergiques dont l'ANAPHYLAXIE, infections graves (comme la TUBERCULOSE), CANCERS (principalement lymphomes), syndrome pseudogrippal, anomalies des résultats des tests de laboratoire, infections par l'herpès simplex.

INTERACTIONS

Médicament-médicament: L'**anakinra** ne doit pas être administré avec un agent anti-TNF comme l'adalimumab en raison du risque accru d'infections graves, sans que cette association apporte des bienfaits cliniques additionnels ■ Ne pas administrer de **vaccins vivants** chez les patients traités par l'adalimumab.

VOIES D'ADMINISTRATION ET POSOLOGIE

- **SC (adultes)**: 40 mg, toutes les 2 semaines. On peut administrer cette dose toutes les semaines chez les patients qui reçoivent l'adalimumab en monothérapie et chez lesquels la réponse diminue si le médicament est administré toutes les 2 semaines.
- Dans le traitement de la polyarthrite rhumatoïde et du rhumatisme psoriasique, selon les données actuelles, on obtient habituellement une réponse clinique en l'espace de 12 semaines de traitement. Il faut reconsidérer soigneusement le bien-fondé de la poursuite du traitement chez le patient qui ne répond pas au traitement après ce délai.

PRÉSENTATION

Solution pour injection: seringues préremplies de 40 mg/0,8 mL[Pr].

SOINS INFIRMIERS

ÉVALUATION DE LA SITUATION

- Déterminer l'amplitude des mouvements articulaires et la gravité de la tuméfaction des articulations ainsi que l'intensité de la douleur au niveau des articulations atteintes, avant le traitement et à intervalles réguliers pendant toute sa durée.
- RESTER À L'AFFÛT DES SIGNES ET DES SYMPTÔMES D'INFECTION (FIÈVRE, DYSPNÉE, SYMPTÔMES PSEUDOGRIPPAUX, MICTIONS DOULOUREUSES OU FRÉQUENTES, ROUGEURS OU ENFLURES AU NIVEAU D'UNE PLAIE) AVANT D'INJECTER LE MÉDICAMENT. L'ADALIMUMAB EST CONTRE-INDIQUÉ CHEZ LES PATIENTS PRÉSENTANT UNE INFECTION ACTIVE. LA SURVENUE D'UNE NOUVELLE INFECTION CHEZ UN PATIENT DOIT ÊTRE SUIVIE DE PRÈS; LES INFECTIONS LES PLUS FRÉQUENTES SONT LES INFECTIONS DES VOIES RESPIRATOIRES SUPÉRIEURES, LES BRONCHITES ET LES INFECTIONS DES VOIES URINAIRES. LES INFECTIONS CHEZ LES PATIENTS SOUS ADALIMUMAB PEUVENT ÊTRE MORTELLES, SURTOUT SI CES PATIENTS REÇOIVENT DES IMMUNOSUPPRESSEURS.
- Rester à l'affût des réactions suivantes au point d'injection: érythème, démangeaisons, saignement, douleur ou enflure. Dans la plupart des cas, ces réactions sont bénignes. L'érythème devrait disparaître en quelques jours. L'application d'une compresse à l'eau froide aide à diminuer la douleur et l'enflure.
- Déterminer si le patient est allergique au latex. Le capuchon de l'aiguille de la seringue renferme du latex et ne devrait pas être manipulé par une personne allergique à cette substance.
- Suivre de près les signes d'anaphylaxie (urticaire, dyspnée, œdème facial) après l'administration d'une dose d'adalimumab. Garder à portée de la main les médicaments (antihistaminiques, corticostéroïdes, adrénaline) et le matériel de réanimation nécessaires pour parer à toute réaction grave. Cesser immédiatement l'administration de l'adalimumab en présence d'anaphylaxie ou de réactions allergiques graves.
- Faire un test à la tuberculine pour détecter une tuberculose latente avant de commencer le traitement par l'adalimumab. On doit traiter la tuberculose latente avant de commencer le traitement.

Tests de laboratoire: L'adalimumab peut provoquer des troubles hématologiques.

DIAGNOSTICS INFIRMIERS POSSIBLES

- Mobilité physique réduite (Indications).
- Douleur aiguë (Indications).
- Risque d'infection (Réactions indésirables).
- Connaissances insuffisantes sur le traitement médicamenteux (Enseignement au patient et à ses proches).

INTERVENTIONS INFIRMIÈRES

- L'administration de la première dose d'adalimumab doit se faire sous la surveillance d'un professionnel de la santé.
- Le patient qui reçoit un traitement par l'adalimumab devrait continuer de prendre des AARMM (sauf des anti-TNF), le cas échéant.

- Le capuchon de l'aiguille contient du caoutchouc sec (latex) ; il ne devrait donc pas être manipulé par des personnes allergiques à cette substance.
- Avant l'injection, il faut examiner la solution dans la seringue préremplie afin de détecter la présence de particules en suspension ou un changement de couleur. Ne pas l'administrer si elle contient des particules ou a changé de couleur. Comme Humira[MD] ne contient aucun agent de conservation, il faut également jeter tout médicament restant dans la seringue après l'administration.

SC: L'adalimumab peut être injecté dans la région abdominale ou dans les cuisses. Dans la région abdominale, éviter d'injecter à moins de 5 cm du nombril. Il faut changer de point d'injection lors de l'administration de chaque nouvelle dose et ne jamais injecter le produit dans une partie du corps où la peau est sensible, meurtrie, rouge ou indurée.

- Ne pas agiter la seringue. Conserver le produit au réfrigérateur (entre 2 °C et 8 °C).
- Jeter les aiguilles et les seringues souillées en respectant les méthodes habituelles de sécurité.

ENSEIGNEMENT AU PATIENT ET À SES PROCHES

- Expliquer au patient qu'il doit respecter rigoureusement la posologie recommandée. S'il n'a pu prendre le médicament au moment habituel, il doit le prendre aussitôt que possible à moins que ce ne soit presque le moment prévu pour la dose suivante. Le prévenir qu'il ne doit jamais remplacer une dose manquée par une double dose. Le traitement peut durer plusieurs mois et même plusieurs années. Conseiller également au patient de ne pas arrêter le traitement avant d'avoir consulté un professionnel de la santé.
- Enseigner au patient la technique d'autoadministration et lui montrer comment conserver et mettre au rebut le matériel. La première injection doit être administrée sous la surveillance d'un professionnel de la santé. Fournir au patient un contenant imperforable pour la mise au rebut du matériel usagé.
- Recommander au patient de ne pas recevoir de vaccin à virus vivants durant le traitement.
- Expliquer au patient qu'il peut prendre simultanément le méthotrexate, un analgésique, un AINS, des glucocorticoïdes et des salicylates. Lui recommander de toujours consulter un professionnel de la santé avant de prendre tout autre médicament.
- RECOMMANDER AU PATIENT DE SIGNALER À UN PROFESSIONNEL DE LA SANTÉ TOUT SIGNE D'INFECTION, AINSI QU'UN ÉRYTHÈME GRAVE, L'ENFLURE DU VISAGE OU LA DIFFICULTÉ À RESPIRER. L'ARRÊT DU TRAITEMENT POURRAIT S'IMPOSER EN CAS D'INFECTIONS GRAVES.
- Prévenir le patient qu'avant tout nouveau traitement ou avant une intervention chirurgicale, il doit informer le professionnel de la santé qu'il suit ce traitement médicamenteux.

VÉRIFICATION DE L'EFFICACITÉ THÉRAPEUTIQUE

L'efficacité du traitement peut être démontrée par: la diminution des signes et des symptômes, l'induction d'une réponse et d'une rémission cliniques importantes, l'arrêt de l'évolution des lésions structurelles de la polyarthrite rhumatoïde et l'amélioration des capacités physiques fonctionnelles ■ la diminution des signes et des symptômes du rhumatisme psoriasique ou de la spondylarthrite ankylosante. ✳

ADÉNOSINE

Adenocard

CLASSIFICATION:

Antiarythmique

Grossesse – catégorie C

INDICATIONS

Conversion des tachycardies paroxystiques supraventriculaires en rythme sinusal normal lorsque les manœuvres vagales échouent ■ Médicament d'appoint pouvant aider au diagnostic des tachycardies supraventriculaires complexes en présence d'ondes larges ou étroites.

MÉCANISME D'ACTION

Rétablissement du rythme sinusal normal en bloquant les voies de réentrée à travers le nœud AV ■ Ralentissement de la conduction à travers le nœud AV ■ Vasodilatation des artères coronaires. ***Effets thérapeutiques:*** Rétablissement du rythme sinusal normal.

PHARMACOCINÉTIQUE

Absorption: Complète (IV).

Distribution: L'adénosine est captée par les érythrocytes et l'endothélium vasculaire.

Métabolisme et excrétion: Transformation rapide en inosine et en monophosphate d'adénosine.

Demi-vie: Moins de 10 secondes.

Profil temps-action (effet antiarythmique)

	DÉBUT D'ACTION	PIC	DURÉE
IV	immédiat	inconnu	1 – 2 min

A

CONTRE-INDICATIONS, PRÉCAUTIONS ET MISES EN GARDE

Contre-indications: Hypersensibilité ■ Bloc AV du 2e ou du 3e degré, maladie du sinus ou bradycardie symptomatique, sauf en présence d'un stimulateur cardiaque artificiel qui fonctionne adéquatement.

Précautions et mises en garde: Antécédents d'asthme (risque de bronchospasme) ■ Angine instable ■ Grossesse et allaitement ■ Enfants ■ Usage sous monitorage cardiaque approprié seulement.

RÉACTIONS INDÉSIRABLES ET EFFETS SECONDAIRES

SNC: appréhension, étourdissements, céphalées, sensation d'oppression dans la tête, sensation de tête légère.

ORLO: vision trouble, sensation de serrement dans la gorge.

Resp.: essoufflements, oppression thoracique, hyperventilation.

CV: bouffées vasomotrices, arythmies transitoires, douleurs thoraciques, hypotension, palpitations.

GI: goût métallique, nausées.

Tég.: sensation de brûlure, rougeur du visage, transpiration.

Loc.: douleurs à la nuque et dorsalgie.

SN: engourdissements, picotements.

Divers: sensation de lourdeur dans les bras, sensation d'oppression dans l'aine.

INTERACTIONS

Médicament-médicament: La **carbamazépine** peut accroître le risque de bloc cardiaque ■ Le **dipyridamole** potentialise les effets de l'adénosine (il est recommandé de diminuer la dose d'adénosine) ■ Les effets de l'adénosine peuvent être diminués par la **théophylline** ou la **caféine** (des doses plus élevées d'adénosine pourraient s'avérer nécessaires) ■ L'administration concomitante de **digoxine** et de **vérapamil** peut accroître le risque de fibrillation ventriculaire.

VOIES D'ADMINISTRATION ET POSOLOGIE

- **IV (adultes et enfants > 50 kg):** *Antiarythmique* – 6 mg par bolus IV rapide, administré en 1 ou 2 secondes; en l'absence de résultats, répéter l'administration 1 ou 2 minutes plus tard en injectant rapidement un bolus de 12 mg. Cette dose peut être répétée (ne pas dépasser 12 mg par dose).
- **IV (enfants < 50 kg):** *Antiarythmique* – de 0,05 à 0,1 mg/kg par bolus IV rapide, administré en 1 ou 2 secondes; cette dose peut être répétée 1 ou 2 minutes plus tard. En cas de réponse insuffisante, on peut augmenter la dose de 0,05 ou de 0,1 mg/kg jusqu'au rétablissement du rythme sinusal ou jusqu'à l'atteinte de la dose maximale, soit de 0,3 mg/kg.

PRÉSENTATION

Solution pour injection: fioles unidose de 6 mg/2 mL[Pr]; seringues préremplies de 2 et de 4 mL[Pr], dosées à 3 mg/mL.

SOINS INFIRMIERS

ÉVALUATION DE LA SITUATION

- Mesurer souvent la fréquence cardiaque (toutes les 15 secondes), suivre de près l'ÉCG tout au long du traitement. Une courte période transitoire de bloc cardiaque du 1er, du 2e ou du 3e degré ou une pause cardiaque peut survenir après l'injection; habituellement, ce phénomène disparaît rapidement en raison de la courte durée de l'effet de l'adénosine. Une fois que le rythme sinusal est rétabli, des arythmies transitoires (contractions ventriculaires prématurées, contractions auriculaires prématurées, tachycardie sinusale, bradycardie sinusale, extrasystoles, bloc du nœud AV) peuvent se manifester, mais elles ne durent généralement que quelques secondes.
- Mesurer la pression artérielle tout au long du traitement.
- Suivre de près l'état de la respiration (murmure vésiculaire et fréquence respiratoire) après l'administration. Un bronchospasme peut se manifester chez les patients ayant des antécédents d'asthme.

DIAGNOSTICS INFIRMIERS POSSIBLES

- Débit cardiaque diminué (Indications).
- Connaissances insuffisantes sur le traitement médicamenteux (Enseignement au patient et à ses proches).

INTERVENTIONS INFIRMIÈRES

- Si l'adénosine est réfrigérée, des cristaux peuvent se former; pour les dissoudre, laisser reposer le médicament à la température ambiante. Il ne faut utiliser que les solutions transparentes. Jeter toute portion inutilisée.

IV directe: Administrer la solution sans la diluer.

Vitesse d'administration: Administrer en 1 ou 2 secondes par voie IV directe ou dans une tubulure IV proximale. Poursuivre avec un rinçage rapide au soluté pour s'assurer que le médicament injecté pénètre dans la circulation générale. Une administration lente risque d'élever la fréquence cardiaque en réponse à la vasodilatation.

Compatibilité (tubulure en Y): thallium-201.

ENSEIGNEMENT AU PATIENT ET À SES PROCHES

- Conseiller au patient de changer lentement de position pour réduire l'hypotension orthostatique. Des doses supérieures à 12 mg diminuent la pression artérielle en réduisant la résistance vasculaire périphérique.
- Recommander au patient de signaler à un professionnel de la santé les symptômes suivants : rougeur du visage, essoufflement, étourdissements.

VÉRIFICATION DE L'EFFICACITÉ THÉRAPEUTIQUE

L'efficacité du traitement peut être démontrée par: la conversion des tachycardies supraventriculaires en rythme sinusal normal. ✳

ALERTE CLINIQUE

ADRÉNALINE

Synonyme: épinéphrine

adrénaline

Adrenalin, Épinéphrine, EpiPen, EpiPen Jr., Twinject

adrénaline racémique

S-2, Vaponefrin

***CLASSIFICATION*:**

Bronchodilatateur (agoniste bêta-adrénergique), vasopresseur, sympathomimétique

Grossesse – catégorie C

Pour l'usage ophtalmique, voir l'annexe N.

INDICATIONS

SC, IV, inhalation: Soulagement passager des crises aiguës d'asthme ou des bronchospasmes ■ **Voies SC, IM, IV**: Soulagement des réactions d'hypersensibilité ■ **Voies IV, intracardiaque, endotrachéale, intraosseuse** (dans le cadre des lignes directrices de la réanimation cardiorespiratoire avancée (ACLS) ou de la réanimation cardiorespiratoire avancée pédiatrique (PALS) : Traitement de l'arrêt cardiaque ■ **Traitement local, rachidien**: Médicament d'appoint pour circonscrire ou prolonger l'effet d'un anesthésique.

MÉCANISME D'ACTION

Accumulation de l'adénosine monophosphate cyclique (AMPc) au niveau des sites des récepteurs bêta-adrénergiques ■ Effet qui s'exerce au niveau des sites des récepteurs bêta-adrénergiques cardiaques et pulmonaires ■ Effets bronchodilatateurs ■ Effets vasoconstricteurs dus à des propriétés alpha-adrénergiques agonistes ■ Inhibition de la libération des médiateurs responsables des réactions immédiates d'hypersensibilité, situés dans les mastocytes. ***Effets thérapeutiques:*** Bronchodilatation ■ Maintien de la fréquence cardiaque et de la pression artérielle ■ Localisation et prolongation de l'effet de l'anesthésique local ou rachidien.

PHARMACOCINÉTIQUE

Absorption: Bonne (SC) ; une certaine absorption peut se produire lors de l'inhalation répétée de doses élevées.

Distribution: L'adrénaline ne traverse pas la barrière hématoencéphalique, mais elle traverse la barrière placentaire et passe dans le lait maternel.

Métabolisme et excrétion: L'effet du médicament est rapidement aboli après métabolisme et captage par les terminaisons nerveuses.

Demi-vie: Inconnue.

Profil temps-action (bronchodilatation)

	DÉBUT D'ACTION	PIC	DURÉE
Inhalation	3 - 5 min	inconnu	1 - 3 h
SC	6 - 12 min	20 min	< 1 - 4 h
IM	6 - 12 min	inconnu	< 1 - 4 h
IV	rapide	20 min	20 - 30 min

CONTRE-INDICATIONS, PRÉCAUTIONS ET MISES EN GARDE

Contre-indications: Hypersensibilité aux amines adrénergiques ■ Glaucome à angle fermé ■ Choc survenant lors d'une anesthésie générale par un hydrocarbure halogéné ou du cyclopropane ■ Dilatation cardiaque et insuffisance coronarienne ■ Anesthésie locale de certaines régions du corps (doigts et orteils) en raison du danger de nécrose ■ Travail de l'accouchement ■ Personnes atteintes d'une lésion cérébrale organique ■ Patients prenant des IMAO.

Précautions et mises en garde: Hyperthyroïdie ■ Glaucome (sauf pour les préparations destinées à l'usage ophtalmique) ■ **GÉR.**: Réduire la dose chez les personnes âgées ■ Grossesse (près du terme), allaitement ■ Usage excessif pouvant mener à la tolérance et à un bronchospasme paradoxal (inhalateur) ■ Antécédents d'hypersensibilité ou d'intolérance aux bisulfites ou aux fluorocarbures (contenus dans certaines préparations pour inhalation) ■ Maladie cardiovasculaire, hypertension et diabète.

A

RÉACTIONS INDÉSIRABLES ET EFFETS SECONDAIRES

SNC: nervosité, agitation, tremblements, céphalées, insomnie.
Resp.: bronchospasme paradoxal (usage abusif des inhalateurs).
CV: angine, arythmies, hypertension, tachycardie.
GI: nausées, vomissements.
End.: hyperglycémie.

INTERACTIONS

Médicament-médicament: L'utilisation concomitante d'autres **agents adrénergiques (sympathomimétiques)** intensifie les effets secondaires adrénergiques de l'adrénaline ■ L'usage concomitant d'**IMAO** peut déclencher une crise hypertensive ■ Les **bêtabloquants** peuvent abolir l'effet thérapeutique de l'adrénaline ■ Les effets de l'adrénaline peuvent être potentialisés par les **antidépresseurs tricycliques**.
Médicament-produits naturels: La teneur en caféine de certaines plantes (**noix de kola, guarana, maté, thé, café**) peut accentuer l'effet stimulant de l'adrénaline.

VOIES D'ADMINISTRATION ET POSOLOGIE

- **SC, IM (adultes)**: *Réactions d'hypersensibilité et asthme* - de 0,1 à 0,5 mg (une dose unique ne doit pas dépasser 1 mg); on peut répéter l'administration de cette dose toutes les 10 à 15 minutes en cas de choc anaphylactique ou toutes les 20 minutes à toutes les 4 heures en cas d'asthme.
- **SC, IM (enfants)**: *Réactions d'hypersensibilité et asthme* - 0,01 mg/kg ou 0,3 mg/m² (une dose unique ne doit pas dépasser 0,5 mg); on peut répéter l'administration de cette dose à 2 reprises, espacées de 15 minutes, si besoin est, puis toutes les 4 heures, selon la gravité de l'affection et la réponse du patient.
- **IV (adultes)**: *Anaphylaxie grave* - de 0,1 à 0,25 mg, toutes les 5 à 15 minutes. *Réanimation cardiorespiratoire* - 1 mg; on peut répéter l'administration de cette dose, toutes les 3 à 5 minutes. *Bradycardie* - de 2 à 10 µg/min.
- **IV (enfants)**: *Anaphylaxie grave* - 0,1 mg (dose plus faible chez les jeunes enfants); on peut ensuite administrer 0,1 µg/kg/min en perfusion continue (la dose peut être majorée jusqu'à un maximum de 1,5 µg/kg/min). *Réanimation cardiorespiratoire* - 0,01 mg/kg; on peut répéter l'administration de cette dose toutes les 3 à 5 minutes. Les doses élevées (de 0,1 à 0,2 mg/kg) sont rarement indiquées par la voie IV. On peut également envisager l'administration par voie intraosseuse. Si la voie endotrachéale est envisagée, diluer les doses de 0,1 à 0,2 mg/kg dans un volume de 3 à 5 mL de soluté normal salin et faire suivre par plusieurs ventilations à pression positive.
- **IV (nouveau-nés)**: *Réanimation cardiorespiratoire* - de 0,01 à 0,03 mg/kg, on peut répéter l'administration de cette dose toutes les 5 minutes.
- **Inhalation (adultes et enfants ≥ 12 ans)**: *Solution pour nébulisation* - par nébuliseur portatif: diluer 0,5 mL d'une solution à 2,25 % dans 2 à 4 mL d'eau stérile ou de sérum physiologique et placer la préparation dans le nébuliseur. La dose doit être administrée au moyen d'un masque, en 10 à 15 minutes. Espacer les doses de 4 heures.
- **Voie intracardiaque (adultes)**: De 0,3 à 0,5 mg.
- **IM (enfants)**: ≤ 30 kg: 0,15 mg (Epipen Jr.); > 30 kg: 0,3 mg (Epipen).
- **Voie endotrachéale (adultes)**: *Réanimation cardiorespiratoire* - de 2 à 2,5 mg.
- **Voie endotrachéale (nouveau-nés)**: De 0,01 à 0,03 mg/kg.

PRÉSENTATION

Solution pour inhalation: 2,25 %[Pr] ■ **Solution pour injection**: 0,1 mg/mL (1:10 000)[Pr], 1 mg/mL (1:1000) [Pr] ■ **Auto-injecteur**: 0,15 mg[Pr], 0,3 mg[Pr].

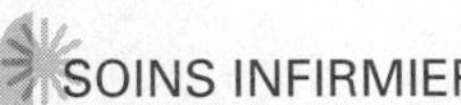

SOINS INFIRMIERS

ÉVALUATION DE LA SITUATION

Bronchodilatateur:

- Ausculter le murmure vésiculaire, déterminer le mode respiratoire, mesurer le pouls et la pression artérielle, avant l'administration du médicament et lorsque les concentrations atteignent un pic. Noter la quantité, la couleur et les caractéristiques des expectorations. Informer le médecin ou un autre professionnel de la santé de toute anomalie.
- Noter les résultats des tests de l'exploration fonctionnelle pulmonaire, avant le début du traitement et à intervalles réguliers pendant toute sa durée, pour déterminer l'efficacité du médicament.
- Suivre de près l'apparition d'un bronchospasme paradoxal (respiration sifflante). S'il survient, arrêter l'administration du médicament et prévenir immédiatement le médecin ou un autre professionnel de la santé.
- Observer les signes de tolérance à l'effet du médicament et de bronchospasme rebond.
- Observer le patient à la recherche des réactions d'hypersensibilité suivantes: rash, urticaire, œdème du visage, des lèvres ou des paupières. Si une telle

réaction se manifeste, interrompre le traitement et en informer immédiatement le médecin ou un autre professionnel de la santé.

Vasopresseur:

- Mesurer la pression artérielle et le pouls et suivre de près l'ÉCG et la fréquence respiratoire à intervalles fréquents pendant toute la durée de l'administration IV. Il faut assurer une surveillance continue par ÉCG et noter les paramètres hémodynamiques et la diurèse pendant toute la durée de l'administration IV.
- Suivre de près le patient pour déceler les douleurs thoraciques, les arythmies, une fréquence cardiaque > 110 battements par minute ou l'hypertension. Demander au médecin de préciser les valeurs du pouls, de la pression artérielle et de l'ÉCG qu'il préconise pour savoir quand adapter la dose ou arrêter le traitement, le cas échéant.

État de choc: Noter le volume sanguin. Avant d'administrer l'adrénaline par voie IV, il faut corriger l'hypovolémie.

Tests de laboratoire:

- Le médicament administré par nébuliseur ou à des doses supérieures à celles recommandées peut entraîner une baisse passagère des concentrations de potassium.
- L'adrénaline peut entraîner l'élévation de la glycémie et des concentrations sériques d'acide lactique.

TOXICITÉ ET SURDOSAGE:

- Les symptômes de surdosage sont une agitation persistante, des douleurs ou une gêne thoraciques, une baisse de la pression artérielle, des étourdissements, l'hyperglycémie, l'hypokaliémie, des convulsions, des tachyarythmies, des tremblements persistants et des vomissements.
- Le traitement du surdosage inclut l'arrêt de l'administration du bronchodilatateur adrénergique ou de tout autre agoniste bêta-adrénergique et sympathomimétique et l'amorce d'un traitement de soutien visant le soulagement des symptômes. Les bêtabloquants cardiosélectifs doivent être utilisés avec prudence, car ils peuvent induire des bronchospasmes.

DIAGNOSTICS INFIRMIERS POSSIBLES

- Dégagement inefficace des voies respiratoires (Indications).
- Irrigation tissulaire inefficace (Indications).
- Connaissances insuffisantes sur le traitement médicamenteux (Enseignement au patient et à ses proches).

INTERVENTIONS INFIRMIÈRES

ALERTE CLINIQUE: VÉRIFIER ATTENTIVEMENT LA DOSE, LA CONCENTRATION ET LA VOIE D'ADMINISTRATION AVANT DE COMMENCER LE TRAITEMENT. ON A SIGNALÉ DES DÉCÈS À CAUSE DE CE TYPE D'ERREURS. LES DILUTIONS DEVRAIENT ÊTRE EFFECTUÉES PAR UN PHARMACIEN. LES DOSES IV DEVRAIENT ÊTRE PRESCRITES EN TERMES DE MILLIGRAMMES ET NON D'AMPOULES, DE CONCENTRATION OU DE VOLUME. AVANT L'ADMINISTRATION, IL EST RECOMMANDÉ DE FAIRE VÉRIFIER L'ORDONNANCE D'ORIGINE, LE CALCUL DES DOSES ET LA PROGRAMMATION DE LA POMPE VOLUMÉTRIQUE PAR UN AUTRE PROFESSIONNEL DE LA SANTÉ.

- Il faut administrer le médicament dès les premières manifestations du bronchospasme.
- Utiliser pour l'injection par voie SC une seringue à tuberculine munie d'une aiguille de 1,25 cm et de calibre 26 afin de s'assurer que l'on administre la quantité appropriée de médicament.
- Un usage prolongé ou excessif peut mener à la tolérance des effets du médicament. Pour rétablir l'efficacité de l'agent, on devrait en interrompre l'administration pendant quelques jours et la reprendre par la suite.
- Ne pas utiliser de solution de couleur rosâtre ou brunâtre ni celle qui contient un précipité.
- En cas de choc anaphylactique, on doit restaurer le volume sanguin en même temps qu'on administre l'adrénaline. On peut administrer des antihistaminiques et des glucocorticoïdes en concomitance.

SC, IM: Le médicament peut provoquer l'irritation des tissus. Assurer la rotation des points d'injection afin de prévenir la nécrose tissulaire. Bien masser les points d'injection après l'administration afin de stimuler l'absorption du médicament et de diminuer la vasoconstriction locale. Éviter l'administration IM dans le muscle fessier.

IV: Diluer à raison de 1 mg (1 mL) d'une solution de 1:1000 dans au moins 10 mL de solution de NaCl 0,9 % pour injection pour obtenir une solution de 1:10 000. Jeter toute portion inutilisée dans les 24 heures qui suivent la préparation.

IV directe: Administrer à raison de 1 mg pendant au moins 1 minute; on peut accélérer le débit lors des tentatives de réanimation cardiaque.

Perfusion intermittente: En cas de choc anaphylactique grave, on peut administrer la dose de 0,1 à 0,25 mg toutes les 5 à 15 minutes.

Vitesse d'administration: Administrer en 5 à 10 minutes.

Perfusion continue: Pour le traitement d'entretien, on peut diluer de nouveau la solution dans 500 mL de solution de D5%E ou de D10%E, de NaCl 0,9 %, de

A

D5% dans du soluté NaCl, dans une solution de Ringer ou de lactate de Ringer. Administrer la solution par une tubulure en Y à l'aide d'une pompe à perfusion afin de s'assurer que le patient reçoit la dose exacte.

Vitesse d'administration: Administrer à un débit de 1 à 4 μg/min.

Consulter les directives de chaque fabricant avant de reconstituer la préparation.

Associations compatibles dans la même seringue: doxapram ■ héparine ■ milrinone.

Compatibilité (tubulure en Y): atracurium ■ calcium, chlorure de ■ calcium, gluconate de ■ cisatracurium ■ diltiazem ■ dobutamine ■ dopamine ■ famotidine ■ fentanyl ■ furosémide ■ héparine ■ hydrocortisone sodique, succinate d' ■ hydromorphone ■ labétalol ■ lorazépam ■ midazolam ■ milrinone ■ morphine ■ nitroglycérine ■ noradrénaline ■ pancuronium ■ phytonadione ■ potassium, chlorure de ■ propofol ■ ranitidine ■ rémifentanil ■ vécuronium ■ vitamines du groupe B avec C ■ warfarine.

Incompatibilité (tubulure en Y): ampicilline ■ thiopental.

Compatibilité en addition au soluté: cimétidine ■ ranitidine.

Incompatibilité en addition au soluté: aminophylline ■ sodium, bicarbonate de.

Inhalation:

- Lorsqu'on administre la solution d'adrénaline par inhalation, il faut déposer 0,5 mL de la solution de base à 2,25 % dans le réservoir du nébuliseur.
- Avant d'utiliser la solution d'adrénaline racémique à 2,25 % par inhalation dans un nébuliseur/respirateur, il faut la diluer.

Voie endotrachéale: Si le patient a été intubé, on peut injecter l'adrénaline directement dans l'arbre bronchique par le tube endotrachéal. Effectuer 5 insufflations rapides; administrer de 2 à 2,5 mg d'adrénaline diluée dans 10 mL de NaCl 0,9 % directement dans le tube, faire suivre de 5 autres insufflations rapides.

ENSEIGNEMENT AU PATIENT ET À SES PROCHES

- Conseiller au patient de respecter rigoureusement la posologie recommandée. Lorsque les doses doivent être prises à une heure précise, s'il n'a pu prendre une dose à l'heure prévue, il devra la prendre le plus rapidement possible et espacer les doses restantes de façon à pouvoir les prendre à intervalles réguliers. Le prévenir qu'il ne doit jamais remplacer une dose manquée par une double dose. Expliquer au patient qu'il ne doit pas dépasser la dose recommandée, car il s'expose au risque d'effets nocifs, de bronchospasme paradoxal ou d'une baisse de l'efficacité du médicament.
- Conseiller au patient de prévenir immédiatement un professionnel de la santé si les essoufflements ne sont pas soulagés par le médicament ou s'ils s'accompagnent de diaphorèse, d'étourdissements, de palpitations ou de douleurs thoraciques.
- Recommander au patient de consulter un professionnel de la santé avant de prendre un médicament en vente libre et d'éviter de boire de l'alcool durant le traitement avec ce médicament. Mettre en garde le patient contre l'usage du tabac et d'autres agents irritants des voies respiratoires.

Auto-injecteur: Montrer au patient comment utiliser l'auto-injecteur lors d'une réaction anaphylactique: retirer le bouchon de sécurité de couleur grise, placer l'embout noir sur la cuisse, perpendiculairement à celle-ci, pousser fortement dans la cuisse jusqu'à ce que l'auto-injecteur se mette en fonction, le maintenir en place pendant plusieurs secondes, le retirer et le mettre au rebut de manière appropriée. Masser le point d'injection pendant 10 secondes. **PÉD.:** Expliquer aux parents ou aux soignants les signes et les symptômes d'anaphylaxie, ainsi que l'utilisation sans danger de l'auto-injecteur, et leur conseiller de conduire l'enfant à l'hôpital le plus rapidement possible en cas de crise. Leur recommander d'enseigner à l'enfant la méthode de traitement de ses allergies, la bonne utilisation de l'auto-injecteur et les mesures à prendre si une crise d'allergie survient. Si l'enfant est trop jeune pour utiliser un auto-injecteur et s'il ne peut être surveillé pendant un certain laps de temps, conseiller aux parents de confier l'utilisation de l'auto-injecteur à un adulte responsable qu'ils auraient mis au courant des allergies de l'enfant.

VÉRIFICATION DE L'EFFICACITÉ THÉRAPEUTIQUE

L'efficacité du traitement peut être démontrée par: la prévention ou le soulagement du bronchospasme ■ une respiration moins laborieuse ■ la baisse de la fréquence des crises aiguës d'asthme chez les patients atteints d'asthme chronique ■ la prévention des crises d'asthme induites par l'effort ■ la résolution des signes et des symptômes d'anaphylaxie ■ l'augmentation de la fréquence et du débit cardiaques lorsque l'adrénaline est administrée en réanimation cardiaque ■ la hausse de la pression artérielle lorsque l'adrénaline est utilisée comme vasopresseur ■ la localisation de l'effet de l'anesthésique local.

AGONISTES DE LA SÉROTONINE 5-HT_1

almotriptan
Axert
élétriptan
Relpax
naratriptan
Amerge
rizatriptan
Maxalt, Maxalt RPD
sumatriptan
Imitrex
zolmitriptan
Zomig, Zomig Rapimelt

CLASSIFICATION:
Traitement des céphalées vasculaires (agoniste de la sérotonine)

Grossesse – catégorie C

INDICATIONS

Traitement de courte durée des crises migraineuses avec ou sans aura chez l'adulte ■ Usage déconseillé en traitement de fond (prophylactique) de la migraine et de la migraine hémiplégique, ophtalmoplégique et basilaire. L'innocuité et l'efficacité de ces agents dans le traitement des céphalées de Horton n'ont pas été établies.

MÉCANISME D'ACTION

Activité agoniste sélective au niveau de sites récepteurs sérotoninergiques spécifiques (5-HT_1). Première hypothèse: l'activation de ces récepteurs, situés dans les vaisseaux sanguins intracrâniens dont ceux des anastomoses artérioveineuses, entraînerait une vasoconstriction. Deuxième hypothèse: l'activation de ces récepteurs, situés sur les terminaisons des projections sensitives du trijumeau, aurait pour effet d'inhiber la libération de neuropeptides pro-inflammatoires. ***Effets thérapeutiques:*** Soulagement des crises aiguës de migraine.

PHARMACOCINÉTIQUE

Absorption: *Almotriptan* – bonne (PO). Biodisponibilité à 70 %. *Élétriptan* – Rapide et efficace. Biodisponibilité d'environ 50 %. *Naratriptan* – 70 % (PO). *Rizatriptan* – complète (PO), mais le médicament subit un métabolisme de premier passage entraînant une biodisponibilité de 45 %. *Sumatriptan* – 97 % (SC); incomplète (PO); de grandes quantités subissent un métabolisme hépatique important, d'où une faible biodisponibilité (14 %); bonne (voie intranasale). *Zolmitriptan* – biodisponibilité à 40 % (PO et voie intranasale).

Distribution: *Almotriptan* – inconnue. *Élétriptan* – le médicament passe dans le lait maternel. *Naratriptan* – inconnue. *Rizatriptan* – inconnue. *Sumatriptan* – le médicament ne traverse pas la barrière hématoencéphalique. Le reste de la distribution est inconnu. *Zolmitriptan* – inconnue.

Liaison aux protéines: *Almotriptan* – 35 %. *Élétriptan* – environ 85 %. *Naratriptan* – 29 %. *Rizatriptan* – 14 %. *Sumatriptan, zolmitriptan* – 25 %.

Métabolisme et excrétion: *Almotriptan* – métabolisme à 27 % par la monoamine-oxydase et à 12 % par le système enzymatique du cytochrome P450. 40 % est excrété sous forme inchangée dans l'urine, 13 % est excrété dans les selles, sous forme inchangée et sous forme métabolisée. *Élétriptan* – métabolisme majoritairement hépatique par l'intermédiaire de l'isoenzyme 3A4 du cytochrome P450. *Naratriptan* – 60 % est excrété à l'état inchangé dans l'urine; 30 % est métabolisé par le foie. *Rizatriptan* – métabolisme majoritairement attribuable à la monoamine-oxydase-A (MAO-A); une petite partie est transformée en un composé actif et 14 % est excrété à l'état inchangé dans l'urine. *Sumatriptan* – Métabolisme hépatique à 80 %. *Zolmitriptan* – Métabolisme majoritairement hépatique; une fraction est transformée en métabolites plus actifs que le zolmitriptan. 8 % est excrété sous forme inchangée dans l'urine.

Demi-vie: *Almotriptan* – de 3 à 4 heures. *Élétriptan* – environ 4 heures. *Naratriptan* – 6 heures (prolongée en présence d'insuffisance rénale). *Rizatriptan* – de 2 à 3 heures. *Sumatriptan* – 2 heures. *Zolmitriptan* – 3 heures (le zolmitriptan et les métabolites actifs).

Profil temps-action (soulagement de la migraine)

	DÉBUT D'ACTION	PIC	DURÉE
Almotriptan PO	inconnu	1 – 3 h	inconnue
Élétriptan PO	60 – 120 min	1 – 3 h	jusqu'à 24 h
Naratriptan PO	inconnu	2 – 3 h†	inconnue
Rizatriptan PO	30 min	1 – 1,5 h	inconnue
Sumatriptan PO	en l'espace de 30 min	2 – 4 h	jusqu'à 24 h
Sumatriptan SC	10 – 15 min	jusqu'à 2 h	jusqu'à 24 h
Sumatriptan intranasal	en l'espace de 15 min	2 h	inconnue
Zolmitriptan PO	inconnu	1,5 – 3 h	inconnue
Zolmitriptan intranasal	inconnu	3 h	inconnue

† De 3 à 4 heures pendant une crise migraineuse.

A

CONTRE-INDICATIONS, PRÉCAUTIONS ET MISES EN GARDE

Contre-indications: Antécédents de signes ou de symptômes de syndrome ischémique cardiaque (p. ex., angine de poitrine, infarctus du myocarde, ischémie myocardique asymptomatique), de syndrome vasculaire cérébral (p. ex., accident vasculaire cérébral [AVC], accident ischémique transitoire) ou périphérique (p. ex., colite ischémique et syndrome de Raynaud), de valvulopathie ou d'arythmies (surtout tachycardie) ■ Maladie cardiovasculaire sous-jacente notable (p. ex., athérosclérose, cardiopathie congénitale) ■ Hypertension artérielle grave ou non maîtrisée ■ Prise d'un autre agoniste des récepteurs de la 5-HT$_1$ ou d'un agent contenant de l'ergotamine ou un dérivé de l'ergot, comme la dihydroergotamine ou le méthysergide, dans les 24 heures précédant ou suivant l'administration ■ Migraine hémiplégique, ophtalmoplégique ou basilaire ■ Atteinte hépatique grave ■ Traitement par un IMAO en concomitance ou dans les 2 semaines suivant l'arrêt du traitement par un tel agent ■ Hypersensibilité connue au médicament, à l'un de ses composants ou à d'autres agonistes sérotoninergiques (5-HT$_1$) ■ *Élétriptan* – prise d'un inhibiteur du CYP3A4 dans les 72 heures précédant ou suivant l'administration (p. ex., kétoconazole, fluconazole, itraconazole, néfazodone, clarithromycine, érythromycine, ritonavir et nelfinavir) ■ *Naratriptan* – insuffisance rénale grave (Cl_{Cr} < 15 mL/ min) ■ *Rizatriptan* – phénylcétonurie (les cachets ultrafondants renferment de l'aspartame) ■ *Zolmitriptan* – syndrome de Wolff-Parkinson-White symptomatique ou autres arythmies associées à des voies de conduction accessoires.

Précautions et mises en garde: Insuffisance hépatique légère à modérée ■ Insuffisance rénale (élévation de la pression artérielle chez certains patients; amorcer le traitement avec une dose plus faible) ■ **OBST., ALLAITEMENT**: L'innocuité de ces agents n'a pas été établie ■ **PÉD.**: Enfants et adolescents < 18 ans (l'innocuité et l'efficacité de ces agents n'ont pas été établies) ■ **GÉR.**: L'innocuité et l'efficacité de ces agents n'ont pas été établies chez les personnes > 65 ans ■ *Almotriptan* – insuffisance hépatique (administrer une dose plus faible) ■ *Élétriptan* – **GÉR.**: Plus fortes élévations de la pression artérielle et allongement de la demi-vie; amorcer le traitement avec une dose plus faible ■ *Naratriptan* – insuffisance rénale ou hépatique légère ou modérée (la dose ne devrait pas dépasser 2,5 mg/24 heures; la dose initiale devrait être réduite) ■ *Rizatriptan* – insuffisance rénale grave, particulièrement chez les patients dialysés; insuffisance hépatique modérée ■ *Sumatriptan* – insuffisance hépatique légère ou modérée (une dose de 25 mg peut être envisagée) ■ *Zolmitriptan* – insuffisance hépatique (administrer une dose plus faible).

EXTRÊME PRUDENCE: SOUPÇON DE CORONAROPATHIE NON DIAGNOSTIQUÉE EN RAISON DE CERTAINS FACTEURS DE RISQUE, COMME L'HYPERTENSION ARTÉRIELLE, L'HYPERCHOLESTÉROLÉMIE, LE TABAGISME, L'OBÉSITÉ, LE DIABÈTE, DE LOURDS ANTÉCÉDENTS FAMILIAUX DE CORONAROPATHIE, LA MÉNOPAUSE CHIRURGICALE OU NATURELLE ET HOMMES ÂGÉS DE PLUS DE 40 ANS. UTILISER SEULEMENT SI L'ÉTAT CARDIOVASCULAIRE A ÉTÉ ÉVALUÉ, SI LE MÉDICAMENT SEMBLE SANS DANGER ET SI LA PREMIÈRE DOSE EST ADMINISTRÉE SOUS SURVEILLANCE.

RÉACTIONS INDÉSIRABLES ET EFFETS SECONDAIRES

SNC: étourdissements, somnolence, céphalées, fatigue, vertiges.

Resp.: pharyngite.

CV: ANGIOSPASME CORONARIEN, ISCHÉMIE PASSAGÈRE DU MYOCARDE, INFARCTUS DU MYOCARDE, TACHYCARDIE VENTRICULAIRE, FIBRILLATION VENTRICULAIRE, sensation désagréable au niveau du thorax, du cou, de la gorge, de la mâchoire et des membres supérieurs (p. ex., oppression, lourdeur, chaleur, douleur, paresthésie, engourdissements), ÉLÉVATION MARQUÉE DE LA PRESSION ARTÉRIELLE (POUVANT ALLER JUSQU'À UNE CRISE HYPERTENSIVE), palpitations.

GI: nausées, diarrhée, douleurs et malaises abdominaux, vomissements, hyposalivation.

Tég.: transpiration, prurit, éruption cutanée, urticaire, sensation de brûlure, de chaleur ou de froid.

Loc.: faiblesse et fatigue musculaires, douleurs musculaires; *sumatriptan* – réactions au point d'injection.

SN: hypertonie, paresthésie.

Divers: asthénie, RÉACTIONS ALLERGIQUES PARFOIS GRAVES.

INTERACTIONS

Médicament-médicament: Les agonistes de la sérotonine 5-HT$_1$ et l'**ergotamine** ou une substance apparentée (comme la **dihydroergotamine [DHE]** ou le **méthysergide**) doivent être administrés à au moins 24 heures d'intervalle en raison d'un risque accru de réactions angiospastiques prolongées en cas d'usage concomitant ■ Ne pas administrer d'autres **agonistes de la sérotonine 5-HT$_1$** dans un intervalle de moins de 24 heures ■ La prudence est de mise lors de la prise concomitante d'autres **médicaments sérotoninergiques** incluant les **ISRS** (**citalopram**, **fluoxétine**, **fluvoxamine**, **paroxétine**, **sertraline**), les **antidépresseurs tricycliques** et la **sibutramine**, étant donné le risque de faiblesse, d'hyperréflexie et d'incoordination (symptômes du syndrome sérotoninergique) ■ *Almotriptan* – les **inhibiteurs puissants du CYP3A4** (p. ex., **kétoco-**

nazole, **itraconazole**, **érythromycine**, **ritonavir**) peuvent élever les concentrations et la toxicité du médicament ■ *Élétriptan* – ne pas administrer dans les 72 heures précédant ou suivant l'usage d'un **inhibiteur du CYP3A4** (p. ex., **kétoconazole**, **itraconazole**, **néfazodone**, **clarithromycine**, **érythromycine**, **ritonavir**, **nelfinavir**, **vérapamil**) ■ *Naratriptan* – l'usage du tabac (**nicotine**) accélère le métabolisme; les **contraceptifs oraux** augmentent les concentrations plasmatiques et l'effet ■ *Rizatriptan* – les **IMAO** élèvent les concentrations sanguines du rizatriptan et augmentent la gravité des réactions indésirables (l'usage d'un IMAO en concomitance ou dans les 2 semaines qui suivent l'arrêt du traitement par un tel agent est contre-indiqué); le **propranolol** élève les concentrations sanguines de rizatriptan et augmente le risque de réactions indésirables (il est recommandé de réduire la dose) ■ *Zolmitriptan* – l'administration concomitante d'un **IMAO** élève les concentrations sanguines de zolmitriptan et le risque de toxicité (ne pas administrer dans les deux semaines suivant l'administration d'un IMAO); les **contraceptifs oraux** peuvent élever les concentrations sanguines du zolmitriptan; la **cimétidine** et les autres **inhibiteurs du CYP1A2** peuvent prolonger la demi-vie du zolmitriptan et de ses métabolites.

Médicament-produits naturels: L'usage concomitant de **millepertuis** ou de **S-adénosylméthionine (SAMe)** peut accroître le risque d'effets secondaires sérotoninergiques, incluant le syndrome sérotoninergique.

VOIES D'ADMINISTRATION ET POSOLOGIE

Almotriptan

- **PO (adultes)**: De 6,25 à 12,5 mg. Si la céphalée migraineuse récidive ou si le patient n'a obtenu qu'un soulagement partiel après la première dose, on peut répéter l'administration de cette dose après 2 heures (ne pas dépasser 2 doses/24 heures; ne pas administrer plus de 4 traitements par mois).
- ***INSUFFISANCE HÉPATIQUE OU RÉNALE***

  PO (ADULTES): DÉBUTER À 6,25 mg ET NE PAS DÉPASSER 12,5 mg/24 HEURES.

Élétriptan

- **PO (adultes)**: 20 ou 40 mg, selon les besoins du patient et sa réponse au traitement. En cas de récurrence ou si le patient n'a obtenu qu'un soulagement partiel après la première dose de 20 mg, on peut répéter l'administration de cette dose 1 fois, après au moins 2 heures. Si la dose initiale était de 40 mg, la prise d'une seconde dose n'est pas recommandée, la dose quotidienne maximale étant de 40 mg. L'innocuité du traitement de plus de 3 céphalées en moyenne en 30 jours n'a pas été établie.
- ***INSUFFISANCE HÉPATIQUE***

  PO (ADULTES): *LÉGÈRE OU MODÉRÉE* – IL N'EST PAS NÉCESSAIRE DE MODIFIER LA DOSE. *GRAVE* – NE PAS ADMINISTRER.
- ***INSUFFISANCE RÉNALE***

  PO (ADULTES): CHEZ CERTAINS PATIENTS, ON A OBSERVÉ UNE ÉLÉVATION DE LA PRESSION ARTÉRIELLE. LA PRUDENCE EST DONC DE MISE LORS DE L'ADMINISTRATION D'UNE DOSE QUOTIDIENNE DE PLUS DE 20 mg.

Naratriptan

- **PO (adultes)**: De 1 à 2,5 mg. Si la céphalée migraineuse récidive ou si le patient n'a obtenu qu'un soulagement partiel après la première dose, on peut répéter l'administration de cette dose après 4 heures (ne pas dépasser 5 mg/24 heures; ne pas administrer plus de 4 traitements par mois).
- ***INSUFFISANCE HÉPATIQUE OU RÉNALE LÉGÈRE OU MODÉRÉE***

  PO (ADULTES): DÉBUTER À 1 mg ET NE PAS DÉPASSER 2 mg/24 HEURES.

Rizatriptan

- **PO (adultes)**: De 5 à 10 mg; on peut répéter l'administration de cette dose 2 heures plus tard; ne pas dépasser 20 mg/24 heures. La dose est la même pour les deux types de comprimés.
- ***INSUFFISANCE RÉNALE, INSUFFISANCE HÉPATIQUE MODÉRÉE, PATIENT RECEVANT DU PROPRANOLOL***

  PO (ADULTES): 5 mg; ON PEUT RÉPÉTER L'ADMINISTRATION DE CETTE DOSE 2 HEURES PLUS TARD; NE PAS DÉPASSER 10 mg/24 HEURES. LA DOSE EST LA MÊME POUR LES DEUX TYPES DE COMPRIMÉS.

Sumatriptan

- **PO (adultes)**: 25, 50 ou 100 mg, selon les besoins du patient et sa réponse au traitement (des doses de 50 ou de 100 mg peuvent être plus efficaces qu'une dose de 25 mg). On peut répéter l'administration de cette dose 1 fois après 2 heures (ne pas dépasser 200 mg/24 heures ni 100 mg en 1 seule prise).
- **SC (adultes)**: 6 mg; on peut répéter l'administration de cette dose 1 fois après 1 heure (ne pas dépasser 12 mg/24 heures).
- **Voie intranasale (adultes)**: 1 dose unique de 5 ou de 20 mg dans 1 seule narine; on peut répéter l'administration de cette dose 1 fois après 2 heures (ne pas dépasser 40 mg/24 heures).
- ***INSUFFISANCE HÉPATIQUE LÉGÈRE À MODÉRÉE***

  PO (ADULTES): ENVISAGER L'ADMINISTRATION DE 1 DOSE DE 25 mg.

Zolmitriptan

- **PO (adultes)**: Initialement, 2,5 mg ou moins; si les symptômes de migraine récidivent, on peut répéter l'administration de cette dose après 2 heures (ne

A

pas dépasser 10 mg/24 heures). L'innocuité du médicament n'a pas été établie lorsqu'on l'utilise pour le traitement de plus de 3 crises par mois. La dose est la même pour les deux types de comprimés.
- **Voie intranasale (adultes)**: Initialement, 2,5 mg; si les symptômes de migraine récidivent, on peut répéter l'administration de cette dose après 2 heures (ne pas dépasser 10 mg/24 heures).

PRÉSENTATION

- **Almotriptan**
  Comprimés: 6,25 mg^{Pr}, 12,5 mg^{Pr}.
- **Élétriptan**
  Comprimés: 20 mg^{Pr}, 40 mg^{Pr}.
- **Naratriptan**
  Comprimés: 1 mg^{Pr}, 2,5 mg^{Pr}.
- **Rizatriptan**
  Comprimés: 5 mg^{Pr}, 10 mg^{Pr} ■ **Cachets ultrafondants (Maxalt RPD)**: 5 mg^{Pr}, 10 mg^{Pr}.
- **Sumatriptan**
  Comprimés: 25 mg^{Pr}, 50 mg^{Pr}, 100 mg^{Pr} ■ **Solution pour injection**: 6 mg/seringue préremplie de 0,5 mL^{Pr}, trousse de départ contenant 2 seringues préremplies, un mode d'emploi et un auto-injecteur^{Pr}, 0,6 mg/fiole de 0,5 mL^{Pr} (présentation à l'usage exclusif des hôpitaux et des médecins) ■ **Vaporisateur nasal**: 5 mg^{Pr}, 20 mg^{Pr}.
- **Zolmitriptan**
  Comprimés: 2,5 mg^{Pr} ■ **Comprimés fondants (Zomig Rapimelt)**: 2,5 mg^{Pr} ■ **Vaporisateur nasal**: 2,5 mg^{Pr}, 5 mg^{Pr}.

SOINS INFIRMIERS

ÉVALUATION DE LA SITUATION

- Durant la crise migraineuse, évaluer le siège, l'intensité et la durée des douleurs ainsi que les symptômes associés (photophobie, phonophobie, nausées, vomissements).
- LORS DE L'ADMINISTRATION DE LA PREMIÈRE DOSE, OBSERVER ATTENTIVEMENT LES PATIENTS QUI PEUVENT SOUFFRIR DE CORONAROPATHIE, NOTAMMENT LES FEMMES MÉNOPAUSÉES, LES HOMMES DE PLUS DE 40 ANS, LES PATIENTS AYANT DES FACTEURS DE RISQUE DE CORONAROPATHIE COMME L'HYPERTENSION, L'HYPERCHOLESTÉROLÉMIE, L'OBÉSITÉ, LE DIABÈTE, L'USAGE DU TABAC OU DES ANTÉCÉDENTS FAMILIAUX DE TELS FACTEURS DE RISQUE. MESURER LA PRESSION ARTÉRIELLE AVANT L'ADMINISTRATION ET À INTERVALLES RÉGULIERS PENDANT LES HEURES SUIVANTES. EN CAS D'ANGINE, SUIVRE LE TRACÉ DE L'ÉCG POUR DÉCELER TOUT CHANGEMENT DE NATURE ISCHÉMIQUE.

DIAGNOSTICS INFIRMIERS POSSIBLES

- Douleur aiguë (Indications).
- Connaissances insuffisantes sur le traitement médicamenteux (Enseignement au patient et à ses proches).

INTERVENTIONS INFIRMIÈRES

- Les comprimés devraient être avalés tels quels avec de l'eau.
- Administrer dès les premiers signes de migraine, bien qu'on puisse prendre les comprimés en tout temps après le début de la crise.

Comprimés fondants: Les comprimés fondants doivent être conservés dans leur emballage jusqu'au moment de l'utilisation. Pour retirer un comprimé de la plaquette alvéolaire, il ne faut pas le pousser à travers la pellicule, mais plutôt soulever celle-ci, sortir le cachet avec les doigts (qui doivent être secs) et le placer sur la langue. Il se dissoudra rapidement et sera avalé avec la salive. Il n'est pas nécessaire de prendre ce type de comprimé avec du liquide.

Voie intranasale: Demander au patient de se moucher avant l'administration. Retirer le bouchon du vaporisateur nasal. Tenir le vaporisateur à la verticale. Demander au patient de se boucher une narine et d'incliner légèrement la tête vers l'arrière. Introduire le vaporisateur dans la narine opposée et appuyer sur le déclencheur.

Sumatriptan

- LES COMPRIMÉS DOIVENT ÊTRE AVALÉS TELS QUELS, SANS LES ÉCRASER, LES CASSER OU LES MÂCHER. Ils sont enrobés afin de prévenir le contact avec leur contenu, qui a un goût désagréable, pouvant occasionner des nausées et des vomissements.
- **SC**: Administrer en une seule injection juste sous la peau (face externe de la cuisse ou du bras).

Zolmitriptan

- La dose initiale est de 2,5 mg. Il est possible de scinder le comprimé pour administrer une dose plus faible.

ENSEIGNEMENT AU PATIENT ET À SES PROCHES

- Informer le patient que les agonistes de la sérotonine 5-HT$_1$ doivent être utilisés seulement lors des crises de migraine. Ces médicaments sont destinés au soulagement des crises, mais non à leur prévention ni à la réduction de leur nombre.
- Recommander au patient de prendre l'agoniste de la sérotonine 5-HT$_1$ aussitôt que les symptômes

de migraine apparaissent; cependant, le médicament peut être administré à tout moment pendant la crise. Si le patient n'obtient pas de soulagement après une première dose, la prise d'une seconde dose durant le même accès migraineux ne procurera pas de bienfait additionnel.

Si les symptômes de migraine récidivent, le patient peut prendre une deuxième dose.

Almotriptan

- Expliquer au patient qu'il doit espacer les doses d'au moins 2 heures et qu'il ne doit pas prendre plus de 2 comprimés en 24 heures. Le prévenir qu'il ne doit pas prendre ce médicament plus de 4 fois par mois pour traiter les céphalées.

Élétriptan

- Recommander au patient d'attendre au moins 2 heures entre les doses et de ne pas prendre plus de 40 mg en 24 heures. Le prévenir qu'il ne doit pas prendre ce médicament plus de 3 fois par mois pour traiter les céphalées.

Naratriptan

- Expliquer au patient qu'il doit espacer les doses d'au moins 4 heures et qu'il ne doit pas prendre plus de 2 comprimés en 24 heures. Le prévenir qu'il ne doit pas prendre ce médicament plus de 4 fois par mois pour traiter les céphalées.

Rizatriptan

- Expliquer au patient qu'il doit espacer les doses d'au moins 2 heures et qu'il ne doit pas prendre plus de 20 mg en 24 heures.

Sumatriptan

- On peut répéter l'administration par voie orale 1 fois après 2 heures (ne pas dépasser 200 mg en 24 heures et 100 mg en 1 seule prise).
- Attendre au moins 1 heure entre les doses SC et ne pas administrer plus de 2 injections en 24 heures.
- On peut répéter l'administration par voie intranasale 1 fois après 2 heures (ne pas dépasser 40 mg en 24 heures).

Zolmitriptan

- Expliquer au patient qu'il doit espacer les doses d'au moins 2 heures et qu'il ne doit pas prendre plus de 10 mg en 24 heures.
- Recommander au patient de ne pas prendre un agoniste de la sérotonine 5-HT$_1$ dans les 24 heures qui suivent ou qui précèdent l'utilisation d'un autre médicament pour traiter les céphalées vasculaires.
- Inciter le patient à rester couché dans une pièce sombre après la prise d'un agoniste de la sérotonine 5-HT$_1$ afin de favoriser davantage le soulagement de la migraine.
- Déconseiller à la patiente de prendre un agoniste de la sérotonine 5-HT$_1$ si elle est enceinte, croit l'être ou prévoit le devenir. Une contraception adéquate est de rigueur pendant le traitement.
- RECOMMANDER AU PATIENT DE CONSULTER UN PROFESSIONNEL DE LA SANTÉ AVANT DE PRENDRE UNE NOUVELLE DOSE D'UN AGONISTE DE LA SÉROTONINE 5-HT$_1$ S'IL RESSENT DES DOULEURS OU UNE OPPRESSION AU NIVEAU DE LA POITRINE, DU COU, DE LA GORGE, DE LA MÂCHOIRE OU DES BRAS. SI LA DOULEUR EST GRAVE ET NE DISPARAÎT PAS, LUI CONSEILLER DE COMMUNIQUER IMMÉDIATEMENT AVEC UN PROFESSIONNEL DE LA SANTÉ. EN CAS DE PICOTEMENTS, D'UNE SENSATION DE CHALEUR, DE LOURDEUR OU D'OPPRESSION, DE BOUFFÉES VASOMOTRICES OU DE FATIGUE, LE PATIENT DOIT PRÉVENIR UN PROFESSIONNEL DE LA SANTÉ.
- En cas d'essoufflement, de respiration sifflante, d'une sensation pulsatile au niveau du cœur, d'œdème des paupières, du visage ou des lèvres, de rash ou d'urticaire, recommander au patient de consulter immédiatement un professionnel de la santé et de ne pas prendre de doses additionnelles d'un agoniste de la sérotonine 5-HT$_1$ sans son autorisation.
- Conseiller au patient de consulter un professionnel de la santé si la dose habituelle ne parvient pas à soulager trois migraines consécutives ou si la fréquence ou la gravité des migraines augmente.
- Prévenir le patient que les agonistes de la sérotonine 5-HT$_1$ peuvent provoquer de la somnolence ou des étourdissements. Lui conseiller de ne pas conduire et d'éviter les activités qui exigent sa vigilance jusqu'à ce qu'on ait la certitude que ce type de médicament n'entraîne pas ces effets chez lui.
- Conseiller au patient d'éviter de prendre de l'alcool en même temps qu'un agoniste de la sérotonine 5-HT$_1$, car l'alcool aggrave les migraines.
- Conseiller au patient de s'informer auprès d'un professionnel de la santé avant de prendre tout autre médicament vendu avec ou sans ordonnance, y compris les produits naturels, en raison des interactions médicamenteuses graves qui peuvent survenir.

Voie intranasale: Montrer au patient la bonne méthode d'administration par voie intranasale. Le dispositif à dose unitaire est prêt à l'emploi et ne doit pas être amorcé avant l'usage. La dose habituelle est de 1 seule vaporisation dans 1 seule narine.

Sumatriptan SC

- Enseigner au patient comment charger l'auto-injecteur, comment s'administrer la préparation et comment mettre au rebut l'auto-injecteur. Lui recommander de lire le livret d'information fourni dans

A

l'emballage du produit et lui expliquer qu'il peut se procurer une cassette vidéo sur l'utilisation du sumatriptan auprès du fabricant.

- Expliquer au patient que la douleur ou la rougeur au point d'injection dure habituellement moins de 1 heure.

VÉRIFICATION DE L'EFFICACITÉ THÉRAPEUTIQUE

L'efficacité du traitement peut être démontrée par: le soulagement de la douleur migraineuse.

ALBUMINE (HUMAINE)

Albuminar, Albumine sérique normale (humaine), Albutein, Buminate, Humanalbin, Plasbumin

CLASSIFICATION:

Agent d'expansion volumique (succédané du plasma/dérivé sanguin)

Grossesse - catégorie C

INDICATIONS

Expansion du volume plasmatique et maintien du débit cardiaque dans des circonstances où on assiste à des pertes de volume, comme le choc, l'hémorragie et les brûlures ■ Remplacement temporaire de l'albumine en présence de maladies associées à des concentrations faibles de protéines plasmatiques, comme le syndrome néphrotique ou la maladie hépatique terminale, entraînant une réduction de l'œdème qui en découle.

MÉCANISME D'ACTION

Production d'une pression colloïdale oncotique, grâce à laquelle les liquides des tissus extravasculaires peuvent retourner au compartiment intravasculaire. L'administration concurrente des cristalloïdes appropriés s'impose. ***Effets thérapeutiques:*** Augmentation du volume de liquides intravasculaires.

PHARMACOCINÉTIQUE

Absorption: Complète (IV).

Distribution: L'albumine reste confinée dans le compartiment intravasculaire, à moins que la perméabilité capillaire ne soit accrue.

Métabolisme et excrétion: L'albumine est probablement décomposée par le foie.

Demi-vie: De 2 à 3 semaines.

Profil temps-action (effet oncotique)

	DÉBUT D'ACTION	PIC	DURÉE
IV	15 - 30 min	inconnu	inconnue

CONTRE-INDICATIONS, PRÉCAUTIONS ET MISES EN GARDE

Contre-indications: Réactions allergiques à l'albumine ■ Anémie grave ■ Insuffisance cardiaque ■ Volume intravasculaire normal ou accru.

Précautions et mises en garde: Maladie hépatique ou rénale grave ■ Déshydratation (l'administration de liquides supplémentaires peut s'avérer nécessaire).

RÉACTIONS INDÉSIRABLES ET EFFETS SECONDAIRES

SNC: céphalées.

CV: ŒDÈME PULMONAIRE, surcharge liquidienne, hypertension, hypotension, tachycardie.

GI: salivation accrue, nausées, vomissements.

Tég.: rash, urticaire.

Loc.: douleurs lombaires.

Divers: frissons, fièvre, bouffées vasomotrices.

INTERACTIONS

Médicament-médicament: Aucune interaction notable.

VOIE D'ADMINISTRATION ET POSOLOGIE

La posologie est fortement individualisée et dépend de la maladie qu'il faut traiter.

Choc hypovolémique - albumine à 5 %

- **IV (adultes):** 500 mL; on peut répéter cette dose en l'espace de 30 minutes.
- **IV (enfants):** 50 mL.
- **IV (nourrissons et nouveau-nés):** De 10 à 20 mL/kg, sous forme de solution à 5 %.

Hypoprotéinémie - albumine à 25 %

- **IV (adultes):** De 50 à 75 g.
- **IV (enfants):** 25 g.

Néphrose aiguë - albumine à 25 %

- **IV (adultes):** De 100 à 200 mL.

PRÉSENTATION

Solution pour injection: 5 %^{Pr}, 25 %^{Pr}.

SOINS INFIRMIERS

ÉVALUATION DE LA SITUATION

- Suivre de près les signes vitaux, la PVC et les ingesta et les excreta, avant le traitement et à intervalles fréquents pendant toute sa durée. En cas de fièvre, de tachycardie ou d'hypotension, arrêter la perfusion et en prévenir le médecin sans tarder. Il peut s'avérer nécessaire d'administrer des antihistaminiques pour supprimer la réaction d'hypersensibilité. L'hypotension peut aussi être provoquée par une perfusion trop rapide. On peut administrer l'albumine sans égard au groupe sanguin du patient.

- Rester à l'affût des signes de surcharge vasculaire (élévation de la PVC, râles ou crépitations, dyspnée, hypertension, distension des jugulaires) pendant et après l'administration.

Interventions chirurgicales: Rester à l'affût d'une hémorragie plus forte après l'administration en raison de l'élévation de la pression sanguine et du volume de sang circulant. L'albumine ne contient pas de facteurs de coagulation.

Tests de laboratoire:

- Les concentrations d'albumine sérique devraient s'élever lors du traitement par l'albumine.
- Suivre de près les concentrations sériques de sodium, lesquelles pourraient s'élever.
- La perfusion d'albumine sérique normale peut entraîner de fausses élévations des concentrations de phosphatase alcaline.
- HÉMORRAGIE: SUIVRE DE PRÈS LES CONCENTRATIONS D'HÉMOGLOBINE ET L'HÉMATOCRITE. CES VALEURS PEUVENT DIMINUER À CAUSE DE L'HÉMODILUTION.

DIAGNOSTICS INFIRMIERS POSSIBLES

- Débit cardiaque diminué (Indications).
- Déficit de volume liquidien (Indications).
- Excès de volume liquidien (Effets secondaires).

INTERVENTIONS INFIRMIÈRES

- Administrer selon les recommandations du fabricant. Employer uniquement une aiguille de calibre 16 pour perforer le bouchon des flacons de 20 mL et plus. On peut administrer l'albumine par les tubulures pour pompe volumétrique. Inscrire le numéro de lot dans le dossier du patient.
- La solution doit être de couleur ambre clair. L'albumine à 25 % a 5 fois la valeur osmotique du plasma. Ne pas administrer de solutions qui ont changé de couleur ou qui contiennent des particules. Chaque litre d'albumine sérique normale contient de 130 à 160 mmol de sodium et le flacon ne porte plus l'étiquette albumine «pauvre en sel».
- L'administration de quantités importantes d'albumine sérique normale devrait parfois s'accompagner de la transfusion de sang entier afin de prévenir l'anémie. Si l'on doit administrer plus de 1 000 mL d'albumine sérique normale à 5 % ou si une hémorragie survient, il peut s'avérer nécessaire de transfuser du sang entier ou un culot globulaire. Suivre de près l'hydratation et la maintenir par l'administration de liquides additionnels.

Perfusion intermittente: Administrer l'albumine sérique normale à 5 % sans la diluer. On peut administrer l'albumine sérique normale à 25 % sans la diluer ou la diluer dans une solution de NaCl 0,9 %, de D5%E ou de lactate de sodium pour injection; ne pas diluer dans de l'eau stérile ordinaire. La perfusion peut se terminer en 4 heures.

Vitesse d'administration: La vitesse d'administration est déterminée par la concentration de solution, le volume sanguin, l'indication et la réponse du patient. Chez les patients dont le volume sanguin est normal, la vitesse d'administration des solutions à 5 % et à 25 % ne devrait pas dépasser de 2 à 4 mL/min et 1 mL/min, respectivement. Chez l'enfant, la vitesse d'administration est habituellement de 25 à 50 % de la vitesse utilisée chez l'adulte.

Choc hypovolémique: L'albumine sérique à 5 % ou à 25 % peut être administrée aussi rapidement que le patient peut le tolérer; l'administration peut être répétée de 15 à 30 minutes plus tard, si nécessaire.

Brûlures: Au cours des 24 premières heures, la vitesse d'administration doit être réglée de façon à maintenir les concentrations d'albumine plasmatique à 2,5 g/100 mL ou celles des protéines plasmatiques totales à 5,2 g/100 mL.

Hypoprotéinémie: L'albumine sérique normale à 25 % est la solution qu'il faudrait privilégier en raison de sa concentration accrue de protéines. La vitesse d'administration ne devrait pas dépasser les 2 ou 3 mL/min pour la solution à 25 % ou les 5 à 10 mL/min pour celle à 5 %, afin de prévenir la surcharge circulatoire ou l'œdème pulmonaire. Ce traitement entraîne une élévation passagère des protéines plasmatiques jusqu'au moment où l'hypoprotéinémie est corrigée.

Compatibilité (tubulure en Y): diltiazem.

Incompatibilité (tubulure en Y): vancomycine ■ vérapamil.

Compatibilité en addition au soluté: solution de NaCl 0,9 % ■ solution de D5%E ■ solution de D5%/NaCl 0,9 % ■ solution de D5%/NaCl 0,45 % ■ solution de lactate de sodium $^{1}/_{6}$ M ■ solution de D5%/LR ■ solution de LR.

ENSEIGNEMENT AU PATIENT ET À SES PROCHES

- Expliquer au patient le but de la perfusion de cette solution.
- Inciter le patient à signaler les signes et les symptômes d'une réaction d'hypersensibilité.

VÉRIFICATION DE L'EFFICACITÉ THÉRAPEUTIQUE

L'efficacité du traitement peut être démontrée par: l'élévation de la pression et du volume du sang lorsque l'albumine est utilisée pour traiter des chocs et des brûlures ■ l'élévation du débit urinaire, qui témoigne de la sortie des liquides des tissus extravasculaires ■ l'élévation des concentrations de protéines plasmatiques en cas d'hypoprotéinémie.

ALBUTÉROL,
voir Salbutamol

ALDESLEUKINE
Proleukin

CLASSIFICATION:
Modulateur de la réponse biologique (antinéoplasique, analogue de l'interleukine-2 humaine)

Grossesse – catégorie C

INDICATIONS
Adénocarcinome rénal métastatique de l'adulte ■ Mélanome malin métastatique de l'adulte.

MÉCANISME D'ACTION
Augmentation de l'immunité cellulaire (caractérisée par la lymphocytose et l'éosinophilie), de la production de cytokines (incluant le facteur de nécrose tumorale, l'interleukine-1 et l'interféron gamma) et inhibition de la croissance de la tumeur. ***Effets thérapeutiques:*** Inhibition de la croissance tumorale.

PHARMACOCINÉTIQUE
Absorption: Biodisponibilité à 100 % (IV).
Distribution: Distribution rapide dans les espaces intravasculaires et extracellulaires. Distribution importante dans le foie, les reins, les poumons et la rate.
Métabolisme et excrétion: Lors du métabolisme, transformation en acides aminés par les cellules des tubules rénaux.
Demi-vie: 85 minutes.

Profil temps-action
(régression de la tumeur après le premier cycle)

	DÉBUT D'ACTION	PIC	DURÉE
IV	4 semaines	inconnu	jusqu'à 12 mois

CONTRE-INDICATIONS, PRÉCAUTIONS ET MISES EN GARDE
Contre-indications: Hypersensibilité à l'interleukine-2 ou à tout autre composant du produit ■ Antécédents de maladie cardiaque ou pulmonaire, corroborés par des résultats anormaux à l'épreuve d'effort au thallium ou aux tests de la fonction respiratoire ■ Antécédents des réactions suivantes, manifestées lors de cycles antérieurs par l'aldesleukine: tachycardie ventriculaire soutenue (≥ 5 battements) ■ troubles du rythme cardiaque non maîtrisés ■ angine ou infarctus du myocarde confirmés par des modifications de l'ÉCG ■ problèmes respiratoires dictant l'intubation pendant plus de 72 heures ■ tamponnade péricardique ■ toxicité rénale dictant plus de 72 heures de dialyse ■ psychose ou coma se prolongeant au-delà de 48 heures ■ crises convulsives difficiles à maîtriser ■ perforation ou ischémie de l'intestin ■ hémorragie gastro-intestinale nécessitant une intervention chirurgicale ■ Allogreffe d'organe (risque accru de rejet).
Précautions et mises en garde: Risque de sensibilité croisée avec les protéines dérivées de *Escherichia coli* ■ Antécédents de maladie cardiovasculaire, respiratoire, hépatique ou rénale ■ Antécédents de convulsions ou présence soupçonnée de métastases au niveau du SNC (aggravation des symptômes et risque de convulsions) ■ Patientes en âge de procréer ■ **OBST., ALLAITEMENT:** L'innocuité du médicament n'a pas été établie ■ **PÉD.:** L'innocuité du médicament n'a pas été établie chez les enfants de moins de 18 ans ■ Maladie auto-immune.

RÉACTIONS INDÉSIRABLES ET EFFETS SECONDAIRES
Resp.: APNÉE, INSUFFISANCE RESPIRATOIRE, dyspnée, congestion pulmonaire, œdème pulmonaire, hémoptysie, épanchement pleural, pneumothorax, tachypnée, respiration sifflante.
CV: ARRÊT CARDIAQUE, INSUFFISANCE CARDIAQUE, INFARCTUS DU MYOCARDE, ACCIDENT VASCULAIRE CÉRÉBRAL, arythmies, hypotension, tachycardie, ischémie myocardique, épanchement péricardique, thrombose.
GI: PERFORATION INTESTINALE, diarrhée, jaunisse, nausées, stomatite, vomissements, ascite, hépatomégalie.
GU: oligurie/anurie, protéinurie, dysurie, hématurie, insuffisance rénale.
Tég.: DERMATITE EXFOLIATIVE, prurit, eczéma exfoliatif.
HÉ: acidose, hypocalcémie, hypokaliémie, hypomagnésémie, hypophosphatémie, alcalose, hyperkaliémie, hyperuricémie, hyponatrémie.
SNC: confusion, somnolence, anxiété, vertiges.
Hémat.: anémie, troubles de la coagulation, leucopénie, thrombopénie, éosinophilie, leucocytose.
Divers: SYNDROME DE FUITE CAPILLAIRE, frissons, fièvre, gain pondéral, perte pondérale, infection.

INTERACTIONS
Médicament-médicament: L'administration concomitante de **glucocorticoïdes** diminue l'efficacité antinéo-

plasique. Éviter le traitement d'association ■ Une hypotension additive peut survenir lors de l'administration concomitante d'**antihypertenseurs** ■ L'administration concomitante d'**agents cardiotoxiques**, **hépatotoxiques**, **myélotoxiques** ou **néphrotoxiques** augmente le risque de toxicité au niveau de ces organes ■ L'aldesleukine peut agir au niveau du système nerveux central. Par conséquent, des interactions peuvent se produire après l'administration concomitante de **médicaments psychotropes** ■ Après l'administration concomitante d'**interféron alpha** et d'aldesleukine, on a observé l'exacerbation ou l'apparition de nombreuses maladies auto-immunes et inflammatoires.

VOIES D'ADMINISTRATION ET POSOLOGIE

- **IV (adultes)**: 1 dose de 600 000 UI/kg (0,037 mg/kg) en perfusion IV de 15 minutes, toutes les 8 heures, pour 14 doses. Le cycle est répété 1 fois, après un repos de 9 jours, jusqu'à concurrence de 28 doses au total, si elles sont tolérées. Après une période de repos de 7 semaines, on devrait évaluer l'état des patients qui ont bien répondu au traitement pour déterminer s'ils peuvent se soumettre à des cycles additionnels.

PRÉSENTATION

Flacons: 22 millions UI[Pr] (1,3 mg) sous forme de poudre lyophilisée.

SOINS INFIRMIERS

ÉVALUATION DE LA SITUATION

- Surveiller l'ÉCG pendant toute la durée de la perfusion. Avant d'amorcer le traitement, il faut évaluer la fonction cardiaque par une épreuve d'effort au thallium, entre autres. Les arythmies supraventriculaires peuvent répondre au traitement par la digoxine ou le vérapamil et disparaissent habituellement après la fin du traitement.
- Mesurer les signes vitaux au moins 1 fois par jour pendant toute la durée du traitement. La fièvre, les frissons, la rigidité et les malaises surviennent habituellement dans les heures qui suivent le début du traitement. Afin d'abaisser la fièvre, administrer de l'acétaminophène et un AINS, comme l'indométhacine, avant d'amorcer le traitement par l'aldesleukine. On peut administrer de la mépéridine pour enrayer la raideur qui accompagne la fièvre.
- Observer les signes du SYNDROME DE FUITE CAPILLAIRE (hypotension, hypovolémie, œdème, ascite, épanchements pleuraux). Ce phénomène se manifeste d'abord par une chute de la pression artérielle dans les 2 à 12 heures qui suivent le début de l'administration. Si la pression artérielle baisse en dessous de 90 mm Hg, il est recommandé de surveiller constamment l'ÉCG et la pression veineuse centrale et de mesurer les signes vitaux toutes les heures.
- Évaluer fréquemment la fonction respiratoire et la saturation en oxygène. Il faut noter les résultats des tests de la fonction pulmonaire, incluant la gazométrie du sang artériel et des radiographies pulmonaires, avant le traitement et à intervalles réguliers pendant toute sa durée. La toxicité pulmonaire (insuffisance respiratoire, tachypnée, respiration sifflante) et les infiltrats pulmonaires, qui peuvent devenir manifestes vers le 4e jour de traitement, disparaissent habituellement dans les quelques semaines qui suivent la fin du traitement. EN CAS D'INSUFFISANCE RESPIRATOIRE, L'INTUBATION DU PATIENT PEUT S'AVÉRER NÉCESSAIRE.
- Peser le patient tous les jours. Le gain pondéral durant le traitement peut dépasser 10 % du poids initial. La perte de ce gain pondéral par diurèse peut prendre jusqu'à 1 à 2 semaines après la fin du traitement.
- Surveiller tout changement de l'état mental. Interrompre l'administration en présence de léthargie ou de somnolence modérée à grave. On a déjà utilisé de faibles doses d'halopéridol pour traiter les modifications invalidantes de l'état mental.
- Rester à l'affût des signes d'infection, particulièrement de septicémie et d'endocardite bactérienne. On peut administrer en prophylaxie une antibiothérapie efficace contre *Staphylococcus aureus* aux patients qui reçoivent l'agent par une tubulure centrale. Toute infection intercurrente doit être traitée vigoureusement. L'aldesleukine altère la fonction leucocytaire.
- Déceler les signes d'anémie (fatigue accrue, dyspnée, hypotension orthostatique) et d'hémorragie (saignements des gencives, ecchymoses, pétéchies, présence de sang dans les selles, dans l'urine et dans les vomissements). On peut administrer de la ranitidine ou de la cimétidine en traitement prophylactique de l'irritation et des hémorragies gastro-intestinales. Une transfusion de globules rouges et/ou de plaquettes peut s'avérer nécessaire.
- Effectuer le bilan des ingesta et des excreta. En présence de stomatite, il peut être nécessaire d'amorcer une diète liquide ou l'alimentation par voie parentérale. Les nausées, les vomissements et la diarrhée surviennent chez la plupart des patients et peuvent entraîner l'hypokaliémie et l'acidose. On peut administrer des antiémétiques et des antidiarrhéiques,

A

selon les besoins. Ces traitements sont habituellement arrêtés 12 heures après l'administration de la dernière dose d'aldesleukine.

- Examiner la peau tous les jours afin de déceler la présence de rash ou d'ampoules. Le cas échéant, en informer le médecin. LA DERMATITE EXFOLIATIVE PEUT MENER À UNE ISSUE FATALE.

Tests de laboratoire:

- Noter la numération globulaire, la formule leucocytaire, la numération plaquettaire, la chimie sanguine incluant les électrolytes et l'état des fonctions hépatique et rénale, avant le traitement et tous les jours pendant toute sa durée. Le médicament peut entraîner une élévation des concentrations de bilirubine, d'urée, de créatinine sérique, de transaminases et de phosphatase alcaline. Il peut provoquer l'anémie, la thrombopénie, l'hypomagnésémie, l'acidose, l'hypocalcémie, l'hypophosphatémie, l'hypokaliémie, l'hyperuricémie, l'hypoalbuminémie et l'hypoprotéinémie.
- Suivre de près la fonction thyroïdienne à intervalles réguliers pendant toute la durée du traitement.

DIAGNOSTICS INFIRMIERS POSSIBLES

- Risque d'infection (Réactions indésirables).
- Connaissances insuffisantes sur le traitement médicamenteux (Enseignement au patient et à ses proches).

INTERVENTIONS INFIRMIÈRES

- Le traitement par l'aldesleukine ne devrait être entrepris que dans les centres hospitaliers dotés d'une unité de soins intensifs.
- NE PAS CONFONDRE LEUKERAN (CHLORAMBUCIL) ET PROLEUKIN (ALDESLEUKINE).

Perfusion intermittente:

- Reconstituer le contenu de chaque flacon avec 1,2 mL d'eau stérile pour injection pour obtenir une concentration de 18 millions UI (1,1 mg)/mL. Lors de la reconstitution, on devrait diriger l'eau stérile vers la paroi du flacon et le remuer délicatement pour empêcher la formation de mousse. Ne pas agiter. La solution devrait être transparente, d'incolore à légèrement jaunâtre. Administrer dans les 48 heures suivant la reconstitution. Jeter toute portion inutilisée. Consulter les directives de chaque fabricant avant de reconstituer.
- Diluer la dose reconstituée dans 50 mL de D5%E. Ne pas reconstituer ni diluer dans de l'eau bactériostatique pour injection, dans une solution de NaCl 0,9 % ou dans de l'albumine.
- Ne pas administrer l'aldesleukine par des tubulures munies de filtres.

Vitesse d'administration: Perfuser la dose en 15 minutes.
Compatibilité (tubulure en Y): amphotéricine B ▪ calcium, gluconate de ▪ diphenhydramine ▪ dopamine ▪ fluconazole ▪ foscarnet ▪ héparine ▪ magnésium, sulfate de ▪ métoclopramide ▪ ondansétron ▪ potassium, chlorure de ▪ ranitidine ▪ thiéthylpérazine ▪ triméthoprime/sulfaméthoxazole.
Incompatibilité (tubulure en Y): ganciclovir ▪ lorazépam ▪ pentamidine ▪ prochlorpérazine ▪ prométhazine.
Incompatibilité en addition au soluté: Ne pas mélanger avec d'autres médicaments.

ENSEIGNEMENT AU PATIENT ET À SES PROCHES

- Recommander au patient de signaler à un professionnel de la santé les symptômes suivants: dyspnée, maux de gorge, fièvre, frissons, jaunissement de la peau, saignements ou ecchymoses inhabituels, fatigue. Conseiller au patient d'éviter les foules et les personnes contagieuses. Lui recommander d'utiliser une brosse à dents à poils doux et un rasoir électrique et de prendre garde aux chutes. Le prévenir qu'il ne faut pas consommer de boissons alcoolisées ni prendre d'AINS ou de médicaments à base d'aspirine, étant donné que ces agents peuvent déclencher une hémorragie gastro-intestinale.
- Informer le patient que les troubles visuels, qui sont réversibles, se manifestent habituellement peu de temps après l'administration de l'aldesleukine et peuvent persister pendant plusieurs semaines.
- Inciter la patiente à utiliser pendant toute la durée du traitement une méthode de contraception non hormonale.

VÉRIFICATION DE L'EFFICACITÉ THÉRAPEUTIQUE

L'efficacité du traitement peut être démontrée par: la diminution de la tumeur ou le ralentissement de la propagation du cancer. ✳

ALERTE CLINIQUE

ALEMTUZUMAB

MABCampath

CLASSIFICATION:

Antinéoplasique (anticorps monoclonal)

Grossesse - catégorie C

INDICATIONS

Traitement de la leucémie lymphocytaire chronique à cellules B, chez des patients traités antérieurement par des agents alkylants et chez qui le traitement par la fludarabine s'est soldé par un échec.

MÉCANISME D'ACTION

Liaison à l'antigène CD52 situé à la surface des lymphocytes B et T et d'autres globules blancs, ce qui entraîne leur lyse. ***Effets thérapeutiques:*** Lyse des cellules leucémiques avec amélioration possible des paramètres hématologiques.

PHARMACOCINÉTIQUE

Absorption: Biodisponibilité à 100 % (IV).
Distribution: Inconnue. L'agent se répartit dans les tissus lymphoïdes, la moelle osseuse et la peau.
Métabolisme et excrétion: Inconnus. Élimination non linéaire.
Demi-vie: 11 heures après la première dose, 6 jours après 12 semaines.

Profil temps-action

	DÉBUT D'ACTION	PIC	DURÉE
IV	inconnu	2 - 4 mois†	7 - 11 mois‡

† Temps médian jusqu'à l'obtention d'une réponse.
‡ Durée de la réponse.

CONTRE-INDICATIONS, PRÉCAUTIONS ET MISES EN GARDE

Contre-indications: Hypersensibilité ■ Infections généralisées ■ Immunodéficience sous-jacente, dont l'infection par le VIH ■ Affection maligne secondaire évolutive.
Précautions et mises en garde: **PÉD.**: L'innocuité de l'agent n'a pas été établie ■ **OBST.**: Grossesse et allaitement.

RÉACTIONS INDÉSIRABLES ET EFFETS SECONDAIRES

SNC: dépression, étourdissements, somnolence, fatigue, céphalées, faiblesse.
Resp.: bronchospasme, toux, dyspnée.
CV: hypertension, hypotension, tachycardie.
GI: douleurs abdominales, anorexie, constipation, stomatite, nausées, vomissements, diarrhée.
Tég.: rash, transpiration.
HÉ: œdème.
Hémat.: NEUTROPÉNIE, PANCYTOPÉNIE/HYPOPLASIE MÉDULLAIRE, anémie, lymphopénie, thrombopénie.
Loc.: douleurs lombaires, douleurs osseuses.
Divers: complications reliées à la perfusion, fièvre, infections, septicémie.

INTERACTIONS

Médicament-médicament: Dépression additive de la moelle osseuse lors de l'administration d'autres **antinéoplasiques** ou d'une **radiothérapie** ■ Risque de diminution de la réponse des anticorps aux **vaccins à virus vivants** et risque de réactions indésirables accrues à ces vaccins.

VOIES D'ADMINISTRATION ET POSOLOGIE

- **IV (adultes)**: 3 mg/jour, initialement; selon la tolérance, porter la dose à 10 mg/jour et ensuite à 30 mg/jour, 3 fois par semaine (1 jour sur 2: p. ex., lundi, mercredi et vendredi), pendant 12 semaines au maximum; ne pas dépasser 30 mg par dose ou 90 mg/semaine.

PRÉSENTATION

Solution pour injection (dilution additionnelle nécessaire): 30 mg/3 mL[Pr] en ampoules à usage unique.

SOINS INFIRMIERS

ÉVALUATION DE LA SITUATION

- Rester à l'affût des réactions pendant la perfusion (hypotension, frisson solennel, fièvre, essoufflement, bronchospasme, frissons, rash). Administrer au patient un antihistaminique oral et de l'acétaminophène, 30 minutes avant la dose initiale, avant l'augmentation des doses ou lorsque les circonstances cliniques l'exigent. Mesurer très attentivement la pression artérielle et suivre de près les symptômes d'hypotension, particulièrement chez les patients atteints de cardiopathie ischémique. Pour prévenir et traiter les réactions liées à la perfusion, on a administré des antihistaminiques, de l'acétaminophène, des antiémétiques, de la mépéridine et des corticostéroïdes et on a augmenté les doses par paliers. Commencer le traitement à la dose la plus faible, qu'on augmentera graduellement. Si le traitement est interrompu pendant au moins 7 jours, le recommencer en augmentant la dose par paliers.
- On recommande un traitement prophylactique anti-infectieux et antiviral jusqu'à 2 mois au moins après la fin du traitement ou jusqu'à ce que le nombre de CD4 se rétablisse à $\geq 0,2 \times 10^9$/L.

Tests de laboratoire:

- Vérifier les numérations globulaires et plaquettaires toutes les semaines, tout au long du traitement, et à des intervalles plus fréquents, si l'anémie, la neutropénie ou la thrombopénie s'aggravent. Dès que le nombre absolu de polynucléaires neutrophiles (NAN) est, pour une première fois, inférieur à $0,25 \times 10^9$/L ou que le nombre de plaquettes est inférieur à 25×10^9/L, interrompre le traitement par l'alemtuzumab. Lorsque le NAN remonte à plus de

A

$0,5 \times 10^9$/L et le nombre de plaquettes à plus de 50×10^9/L, reprendre le traitement à la même dose. Si 7 jours ou plus s'écoulent jusqu'à la reprise du traitement, commencer par une dose de 3 mg, qu'on portera à 10 mg et ensuite à 30 mg, selon la tolérance du patient. Si, pour une deuxième fois, le NAN redescend à moins de $0,25 \times 10^9$/L ou le nombre de plaquettes à moins de 25×10^9/L, interrompre le traitement par l'alemtuzumab. Lorsque le NAN remonte à plus de $0,5 \times 10^9$/L et le nombre de plaquettes à plus de 50×10^9/L, reprendre le traitement à une dose de 10 mg. Si 7 jours ou plus s'écoulent jusqu'à la reprise du traitement, commencer par une dose de 3 mg, qu'on portera à 10 mg seulement. Si, pour une troisième fois, le NAN redescend à moins de $0,25 \times 10^9$/L ou le nombre de plaquettes à moins de 25×10^9/L, arrêter complètement le traitement par l'alemtuzumab. Chez les patients qui avaient en début de traitement un NAN inférieur à $0,5 \times 10^9$/L ou un nombre de plaquettes inférieur à 25×10^9/L, interrompre le traitement lorsque le NAN ou le nombre de plaquettes diminuent de 50 % par rapport aux valeurs initiales. On reprend le traitement lorsque les valeurs initiales se rétablissent. Si 7 jours ou plus s'écoulent jusqu'à la reprise du traitement, commencer par une dose de 3 mg, qu'on portera à 10 mg, puis à 30 mg, selon la tolérance.

- Évaluer le nombre de CD4 après le traitement, jusqu'au moment où le nombre de cellules se rétablit à $\geq 0,2 \times 10^9$/L.

DIAGNOSTICS INFIRMIERS POSSIBLES

- Risque d'infection (Effets secondaires).
- Risque d'accident (Réactions indésirables).

INTERVENTIONS INFIRMIÈRES

Alerte clinique: Des décès sont survenus lors de certaines chimiothérapies. Avant d'administrer l'agent, clarifier tous les points ambigus. Vérifier la limite des doses unitaires et quotidiennes ainsi que la dose à administrer pendant le traitement. Demander à un autre professionnel de la santé de vérifier une fois de plus l'ordonnance d'origine, les calculs et le réglage de la pompe à perfusion. L'alemtuzumab ne doit être administré que sous la surveillance d'un médecin expérimenté dans le traitement antinéoplasique.

- N'administrer que par voie IV. Inspecter la solution pour déceler des particules ou un changement de couleur. Ne pas administrer de solutions qui contiennent des particules ou qui ont changé de couleur.

Perfusion intermittente: Retirer dans la seringue la quantité nécessaire de solution. Avant la dilution, la filtrer par un filtre stérile de 5 µm ayant une faible capacité de liaison aux protéines et qui n'est pas susceptible de libérer des fibres. Injecter dans 100 mL de NaCl 0,9 % ou de D5%E. Renverser délicatement le sac pour en mélanger le contenu. Mettre au rebut la seringue et le produit inutilisé selon les consignes de l'établissement. Utiliser dans les 8 heures qui suivent la dilution. Conserver à la température ambiante ou au réfrigérateur, à l'abri de la lumière.

Vitesse d'administration: Administrer en 2 heures.

Incompatibilité (tubulure en Y): On ne dispose d'aucune donnée sur les mélanges avec d'autres solutions et médicaments. Ne pas ajouter à d'autres solutions ou médicaments et ne pas les perfuser simultanément.

ENSEIGNEMENT AU PATIENT ET À SES PROCHES

- Expliquer au patient et à ses proches le but du traitement par l'alemtuzumab.
- Mettre en garde le patient contre la vaccination par des virus vivants, car l'alemtuzumab peut supprimer les réactions immunitaires.

VÉRIFICATION DE L'EFFICACITÉ THÉRAPEUTIQUE

L'efficacité du traitement peut être démontrée par: l'amélioration des paramètres hématologiques des patients atteints de leucémie lymphocytaire chronique à cellules B. ✳

ALENDRONATE

Fosamax, Gen-Alendronate, Novo-Alendronate, Apo-Alendronate

CLASSIFICATION:

Régulateur du métabolisme osseux (bisphosphonate)

Grossesse – catégorie C

INDICATIONS

Traitement et prévention de l'ostéoporose postménopausique et prévention de l'ostéoporose chez les femmes ménopausées à risque ■ Traitement de l'ostéoporose chez l'homme ■ Traitement de la maladie osseuse de Paget ■ Traitement de l'ostéoporose induite par les corticostéroïdes chez les hommes et les femmes.

MÉCANISME D'ACTION

Inhibition de la résorption osseuse par l'inhibition de l'activité des ostéoclastes. ***Effets thérapeutiques:*** Inhibition de l'évolution de l'ostéoporose, accompagnée d'une baisse du nombre de fractures ■ Ralentissement de l'évolution de la maladie osseuse de Paget.

PHARMACOCINÉTIQUE

Absorption: Faible (de 0,6 à 0,8 %) (PO).
Distribution: Le médicament se distribue temporairement dans les tissus mous avant d'atteindre les os.
Métabolisme et excrétion: Excrétion urinaire.
Demi-vie: 10 ans (signe probable de la libération du médicament par le squelette).
Profil temps-action (inhibition de la résorption osseuse)

	Début d'action	Pic	Durée
PO	1 mois	3 - 6 mois	3 semaines - 7 mois†

† Après l'arrêt de l'administration d'alendronate.

CONTRE-INDICATIONS, PRÉCAUTIONS ET MISES EN GARDE

Contre-indications: Anomalies œsophagiennes retardant la vidange de l'œsophage (sténose ou achalasie) ■ Incapacité de rester debout ou assis, le dos droit, durant au moins 30 minutes ■ Insuffisance rénale (Cl_{Cr} < 35 mL/min).
Précautions et mises en garde: Troubles gastro-intestinaux évolutifs (dysphagie, maladie de l'œsophage, gastrite, duodénite, ulcères) ■ Antécédents d'hypocalcémie ou carence en vitamine D ■ **Obst.**: Grossesse ou allaitement.

RÉACTIONS INDÉSIRABLES ET EFFETS SECONDAIRES

SNC: céphalées.
ORLO: vision brouillée, conjonctivites, inflammation/douleur oculaire.
GI: distension abdominale, douleurs abdominales, régurgitations acides, constipation, diarrhée, dyspepsie, dysphagie, ulcère de l'œsophage, flatulence, gastrite, nausées, altération du goût, vomissements.
Tég.: érythème, photosensibilité, rash.
Loc.: douleurs musculosquelettiques.

INTERACTIONS

Médicament-médicament: L'administration concomitante de **suppléments calciques**, d'**antiacides** et d'autres **médicaments administrés par voie orale** diminue l'absorption de l'alendronate ■ Les doses supérieures à 10 mg/ jour augmentent le risque de réactions gastro-intestinales lorsqu'elles sont administrées en concomitance avec les **AINS**.
Médicament-aliments: Les **aliments** diminuent nettement l'absorption de l'alendronate ■ **La caféine (café, thé, cola)**, l'**eau minérale** et le **jus d'orange** en diminuent également l'absorption.

VOIES D'ADMINISTRATION ET POSOLOGIE

- **PO (adultes)**: *Traitement de l'ostéoporose* – 10 mg, 1 fois par jour, ou 70 mg, 1 fois par semaine. *Prévention de l'ostéoporose* – 5 mg, 1 fois par jour. *Maladie osseuse de Paget* – 40 mg, 1 fois par jour, pendant 6 mois. On peut envisager la reprise du traitement en cas de rechute. *Traitement de l'ostéoporose induite par les corticostéroïdes chez les hommes et les femmes* – 5 mg, 1 fois par jour. *Traitement de l'ostéoporose induite par les corticostéroïdes chez les femmes ménopausées qui ne suivent pas d'œstrogénothérapie* – 10 mg, 1 fois par jour.

PRÉSENTATION

Comprimés: 5 mg[Pr], 10 mg[Pr], 40 mg[Pr], 70 mg[Pr] ■ **Solution orale**: 70 mg/75 mL[Pr].

SOINS INFIRMIERS

ÉVALUATION DE LA SITUATION

Ostéoporose: Évaluer l'état du patient pour déceler une masse osseuse faible, avant le traitement et à intervalles réguliers pendant toute sa durée.
Maladie osseuse de Paget: Rester à l'affût des symptômes de la maladie osseuse de Paget (douleur aux os, céphalées, baisse de l'acuité visuelle et auditive, augmentation de la taille du crâne).

Tests de laboratoire:

- *Ostéoporose:* Évaluer les concentrations sériques de calcium avant le traitement et à intervalles réguliers pendant toute sa durée. Il faut traiter l'hypocalcémie et les carences en vitamine D avant d'amorcer le traitement par l'alendronate. Le médicament peut entraîner une faible élévation passagère des concentrations de calcium et de phosphate.
- *Maladie osseuse de Paget:* Noter les concentrations de phosphatase alcaline avant le traitement et à intervalles réguliers pendant toute sa durée. L'alendronate est indiqué chez les patients présentant des concentrations de phosphatase alcaline deux fois supérieures à la limite normale.

DIAGNOSTICS INFIRMIERS POSSIBLES

- Risque d'accident (Indications).
- Connaissances insuffisantes sur le traitement médicamenteux (Enseignement au patient et à ses proches).

INTERVENTIONS INFIRMIÈRES

- NE PAS CONFONDRE FOMASAX (ALENDRONATE) ET FLOMAX (TAMSULOSIN).

A

Comprimés: Administrer le matin, à la première heure, avec un grand verre d'eau (de 200 à 250 mL), 30 minutes avant la prise d'autres médicaments, de boissons ou d'aliments.

Solution orale: Administrer le matin, à la première heure, avec un minimum de 60 mL (¼ de tasse) d'eau, 30 minutes avant la prise d'autres médicaments, de boissons ou d'aliments.

ENSEIGNEMENT AU PATIENT ET À SES PROCHES

- Expliquer au patient qu'il est important de prendre le médicament exactement comme il lui a été prescrit, le matin, à la première heure, 30 minutes avant de prendre d'autres médicaments, des boissons ou des aliments. On peut améliorer l'absorption du médicament si on attend plus de 30 minutes. Il faut prendre l'alendronate avec un grand verre d'eau (l'eau minérale, le jus d'orange, le café et les autres boissons en réduisent l'absorption). Si le patient oublie de prendre une dose, il doit la sauter et reprendre le traitement le lendemain matin; il ne doit pas doubler la dose ni la prendre plus tard dans la journée. Le prévenir qu'il ne doit pas arrêter le traitement sans consulter un professionnel de la santé au préalable.
- Conseiller au patient de rester debout pendant les 30 minutes qui suivent la prise de la dose afin de faciliter le passage du médicament vers l'estomac et de diminuer le risque d'irritation de l'œsophage.
- Recommander au patient de suivre un régime équilibré et de consulter un professionnel de la santé concernant le besoin de prendre un supplément de calcium ou de vitamine D.
- Encourager le patient à faire régulièrement de l'exercice et à modifier les comportements qui accroissent le risque d'ostéoporose (cesser de fumer, réduire la consommation d'alcool).
- Conseiller au patient d'utiliser un écran solaire et des vêtements protecteurs pour prévenir les réactions de photosensibilité.
- Lui recommander de prévenir un professionnel de la santé en cas de vision brouillée, de douleurs ou d'inflammation oculaire.
- Recommander à la patiente d'informer un professionnel de la santé si elle pense être enceinte ou désire le devenir ou, encore, si elle allaite.

VÉRIFICATION DE L'EFFICACITÉ THÉRAPEUTIQUE

L'efficacité du traitement peut être démontrée par: la prévention de l'ostéoporose ou le ralentissement de son évolution chez les femmes ménopausées ■ la diminution des signes et des symptômes d'ostéoporose chez les hommes ■ le ralentissement de l'évolution de la maladie de Paget ■ la diminution des signes et des symptômes d'ostéoporose induite par les corticostéroïdes. ✳

ALFACALCIDOL,
voir Vitamine D (composés de)

ALERTE CLINIQUE

ALFENTANIL

Alfenta

CLASSIFICATION:

Analgésique opioïde (agoniste), adjuvant anesthésique (à action générale)

Grossesse – catégorie C et D (usage prolongé ou doses élevées prises près du terme)

INDICATIONS

Adjuvant analgésique administré en doses successives pour maintenir l'anesthésie par une association à base de barbituriques, de protoxyde d'azote et d'oxygène lors des interventions chirurgicales de courte durée ■ Adjuvant analgésique d'un agent d'induction barbiturique lors des interventions chirurgicales de courte durée ■ Analgésie par perfusion continue, en association avec du protoxyde d'azote et de l'oxygène pendant le maintien de l'anesthésie générale ■ Administration en perfusion continue, comme analgésique et inhibiteur de la fonction respiratoire, pour aider le patient à s'adapter au respirateur et pour faciliter l'acceptation de la sonde endotrachéale ■ Administration en bolus, en plus de la perfusion continue, comme analgésique supplémentaire pendant les interventions douloureuses brèves.

MÉCANISME D'ACTION

Liaison aux récepteurs des opioïdes du SNC modifiant la réaction à la douleur et sa perception, et entraînant une dépression généralisée du système nerveux central. ***Effets thérapeutiques:*** Soulagement de la douleur modérée à grave ■ Anesthésie.

PHARMACOCINÉTIQUE

Absorption: Complète (IV).

Distribution: L'alfentanil pénètre difficilement dans les tissus adipeux. Il traverse la barrière placentaire et passe dans le lait maternel.

Métabolisme et excrétion: Métabolisme majoritairement hépatique (à plus de 95 %).
Demi-vie: De 60 à 120 minutes.
Profil temps-action (analgésie et dépression respiratoire)

	DÉBUT D'ACTION	PIC	DURÉE
IV	immédiat	1 - 1,5 min	5 - 10 min

CONTRE-INDICATIONS, PRÉCAUTIONS ET MISES EN GARDE

Contre-indications: Hypersensibilité ■ Intolérance connue.
Précautions et mises en garde: Personnes âgées ■ Patients débilités ou très malades ■ Diabète ■ Maladies pulmonaire ou hépatique graves ■ Tumeur du SNC ■ Pression intracrânienne accrue ■ Traumatisme crânien ■ Insuffisance surrénalienne ■ Douleur abdominale non diagnostiquée ■ Hypothyroïdisme ■ Alcoolisme ■ Maladie cardiaque ■ OBST., ALLAITEMENT, PÉD. (enfants de moins de 12 ans): L'innocuité du médicament n'a pas été établie.

RÉACTIONS INDÉSIRABLES ET EFFETS SECONDAIRES

SNC: étourdissements, somnolence.
ORLO: vision trouble.
CV: bradycardie, tachycardie, hypotension, hypertension, arythmies.
Resp.: apnée, DÉPRESSION RESPIRATOIRE.
GI: nausées, vomissements.
Loc.: rigidité des muscles thoraciques, rigidité des muscles squelettiques.

INTERACTIONS

Médicament-médicament: Dépression additive du SNC et du système respiratoire lors de l'usage concomitant d'**alcool**, d'**antihistaminiques**, de **phénothiazines**, de **barbituriques**, d'**antidépresseurs tricycliques**, d'**hypnosédatifs** et d'**autres opioïdes** ■ Éviter l'administration d'**IMAO** pendant les 14 jours qui précèdent le traitement avec ce médicament ■ Les **inhibiteurs du CYP3A4** (comme la **cimétidine**, le **kétoconazole**, le **fluconazole**, l'**itraconazole**, la **néfazodone**, la **clarithromycine**, l'**érythromycine**, le **ritonavir** et le **nelfinavir**) peuvent inhiber le métabolisme de l'alfentanil et retarder le réveil ■ Les **benzodiazépines**, administrées en concomitance, peuvent augmenter le risque d'hypotension ■ Les **analgésiques opioïdes agonistes/antagonistes** (**nalbuphine**, **butorphanol**, **pentazocine**) peuvent diminuer l'analgésie et/ou déclencher des symptômes de sevrage chez les patients présentant une dépendance physique aux analgésiques opioïdes.

VOIES D'ADMINISTRATION ET POSOLOGIE

Injection par doses successives (durée de l'anesthésie ≤ 30 minutes)

- ***Période d'induction* - IV (adultes)**: De 5 à 20 µg/kg.
- ***Période d'entretien* - IV (adultes)**: 2,5 µg/kg par doses successives (dose totale: de 5 à 40 µg/kg).

Injection par doses successives (durée de l'anesthésie de 30 à 60 minutes)

- ***Période d'induction* - IV (adultes)**: De 20 à 50 µg/kg.
- ***Période d'entretien* - IV (adultes)**: De 5 à 15 µg/kg par doses successives (jusqu'à une dose totale de 75 µg/kg).

Perfusion continue (durée de l'anesthésie > 45 minutes)

- ***Induction* - IV (adultes)**: De 50 à 75 µg/kg.
- ***Dose d'entretien* - IV (adultes)**: De 0,5 à 1,5 µg/kg/min. Si l'effet de l'anesthésie commence à s'épuiser ou si certains changements des signes vitaux indiquent un stress chirurgical, on peut augmenter la vitesse de perfusion pour la passer à 1,5 µg/kg/min ou administrer jusqu'à 3 bolus de 7 µg/kg en 5 à 10 minutes. En l'absence de ces changements, on abaissera la vitesse de perfusion jusqu'au minimum efficace.

Anesthésie sous ventilation mécanique dans l'unité de soins intensifs

- ***Induction* - IV (adultes)**: De 0 à 50 µg/kg.
- ***Dose d'entretien* - IV (adultes)**: De 0,2 à 2,0 µg/kg/min.
- ***Bolus supplémentaires:*** De 10 à 20 µg/kg, au besoin.

PRÉSENTATION

Solution pour injection: 500 µg/mL[N], ampoules et fioles de 2 mL.

SOINS INFIRMIERS

ÉVALUATION DE LA SITUATION

- SUIVRE DE PRÈS LES SIGNES VITAUX, PARTICULIÈREMENT LA FONCTION RESPIRATOIRE ET L'ÉCG DURANT ET APRÈS L'ADMINISTRATION. SIGNALER IMMÉDIATEMENT AU MÉDECIN TOUTE MODIFICATION IMPORTANTE.

Tests de laboratoire: Le médicament peut élever les concentrations sériques d'amylase et de lipase.

TOXICITÉ ET SURDOSAGE: Les symptômes de toxicité comprennent la dépression respiratoire, l'hypotension, les arythmies, la bradycardie et l'asystolie. On peut renverser la dépression respiratoire avec de la naloxone. La bradycardie peut être traitée avec de l'atropine.

A

DIAGNOSTICS INFIRMIERS POSSIBLES

- Douleur aiguë (Indications).
- Mode de respiration inefficace (Réactions indésirables).
- Risque d'accident (Effets secondaires).

INTERVENTIONS INFIRMIÈRES

Alerte clinique: DES SURDOSES ACCIDENTELLES D'ANALGÉSIQUES OPIOÏDES ONT CAUSÉ DES DÉCÈS. AVANT D'ADMINISTRER L'AGENT, CLARIFIER TOUS LES POINTS AMBIGUS ET FAIRE VÉRIFIER L'ORDONNANCE D'ORIGINE ET LE CALCUL DES DOSES PAR UN AUTRE PROFESSIONNEL DE LA SANTÉ.

- NE PAS CONFONDRE L'ALFENTANIL, LE FENTANYL ET LE SUFENTANIL.
- On peut administrer des benzodiazépines avant d'administrer l'alfentanil pour réduire la dose nécessaire à l'induction et la durée de la perte de conscience. Cette association peut accroître le risque d'hypotension.
- La durée d'action de l'alfentanil est brève. Pour soulager les douleurs postopératoires, il faudrait amorcer le traitement analgésique dès le début de la période de réveil.

Alerte clinique: AU COURS DE L'ADMINISTRATION DE L'ALFENTANIL, GARDER À PORTÉE DE LA MAIN UN ANTAGONISTE DES OPIOÏDES, DE L'OXYGÈNE ET LES APPAREILS DE RÉANIMATION. L'ALFENTANIL NE DOIT ÊTRE ADMINISTRÉ PAR VOIE IV QUE DANS UN MILIEU OÙ L'ANESTHÉSIE EST SURVEILLÉE DE PRÈS (SALLE D'OPÉRATION, UNITÉ DE SOINS INTENSIFS) ET OÙ L'ON DISPOSE D'APPAREILS DE MAINTIEN DES FONCTIONS VITALES. L'ADMINISTRATION EST RÉSERVÉE AU PERSONNEL DÛMENT FORMÉ EN RÉANIMATION ET EN PRISE EN CHARGE DES URGENCES EN CAS DE TROUBLES RESPIRATOIRES.

IV directe: Lors de l'administration de petits volumes, utiliser une seringue à tuberculine pour s'assurer qu'on donne la dose exacte.

Vitesse d'administration: L'injection doit prendre de 90 secondes à 3 minutes. L'administration IV lente peut réduire la fréquence et la gravité de la rigidité musculaire, de la bradycardie ou de l'hypotension. Pour diminuer la rigidité musculaire, on peut administrer simultanément des agents de blocage neuromusculaire.

Perfusion continue:

- Pour administrer en perfusion continue, diluer jusqu'à une concentration de 25 à 80 μg/mL (20 mL d'alfentanil dans 230 mL de diluant donnent une solution de 40 μg/mL) dans une solution de NaCl 0,9 %, de D5%E, de D5%/NaCl 0,9 % ou de lactate de Ringer.
- Arrêter la perfusion IV au moins 10 à 15 minutes avant la fin de l'intervention chirurgicale.

ENSEIGNEMENT AU PATIENT ET À SES PROCHES

- Avant l'intervention chirurgicale, expliquer au patient le mode d'administration des agents anesthésiques et les sensations auxquelles il doit s'attendre.
- Expliquer au patient que l'alfentanil peut provoquer de la somnolence et des étourdissements. Lui recommander de demander de l'aide lorsqu'il doit se déplacer et lorsqu'il veut fumer.
- Recommander au patient de changer de position lentement pour réduire les risques d'hypotension orthostatique.
- Prévenir le patient ayant subi une intervention chirurgicale dans le service de consultations externes, qu'il ne doit pas prendre d'alcool ni d'autres dépresseurs du SNC dans les 24 heures qui suivent l'administration de l'alfentanil.

VÉRIFICATION DE L'EFFICACITÉ THÉRAPEUTIQUE

L'efficacité du traitement peut être démontrée par: une sensation générale d'apaisement ■ la diminution de l'activité motrice ■ l'analgésie profonde.

ALFUZOSINE

Xatral

CLASSIFICATION:

Antagoniste sélectif des récepteurs alpha$_1$-adrénergiques de la prostate

Grossesse – catégorie X

INDICATIONS

Traitement des signes et des symptômes de l'hyperplasie bénigne de la prostate ■ Traitement adjuvant de la rétention urinaire aiguë.

MÉCANISME D'ACTION

Diminution des contractions des muscles lisses de la capsule prostatique et du col de la vessie par liaison préférentielle aux récepteurs alpha$_1$-adrénergiques. ***Effets thérapeutiques:*** Diminution des symptômes d'hyperplasie prostatique (mictions impérieuses, retard à la miction, nycturie) ■ Augmentation du débit urinaire.

A

PHARMACOCINÉTIQUE

Absorption: 49 % (PO). La biodisponibilité de l'alfuzosine prise à jeun étant réduite, il est recommandé de prendre ce médicament après un repas, afin d'obtenir un profil pharmacocinétique constant.

Distribution: Liquides extracellulaires (volume de distribution de 2,5 L/kg).

Liaison aux protéines: L'alfuzosine se lie moyennement aux protéines plasmatiques; la fraction libre est de 13,3 %. Elle se lie à l'albumine et aux alpha$_1$-glycoprotéines avec une affinité de 68,2 % et de 52,5 %, respectivement.

Métabolisme et excrétion: Métabolisme majoritairement hépatique, sous l'influence des isoenzymes 3A4 du cytochrome P450, par trois voies métaboliques, soit oxydation, O-déméthylation et N-désalkylation. Une fraction de 11 % seulement est excrétée sous forme inchangée dans l'urine. Les métabolites, qui sont tous inactifs, sont excrétés dans l'urine (de 15 à 30 %) et dans les selles (de 75 à 91 %).

Demi-vie: De 4,8 à 10,1 heures, selon l'âge du patient.

Profil temps-action (augmentation du débit urinaire)

	DÉBUT D'ACTION	PIC	DURÉE
PO	quelques heures	8 h	24 h

CONTRE-INDICATIONS, PRÉCAUTIONS ET MISES EN GARDE

Contre-indications: Hypersensibilité connue ■ Insuffisance hépatique modérée ou grave (les taux sanguins d'alfuzosine augmentent) ■ Utilisation en association avec d'autres antagonistes alpha$_1$-adrénergiques ■ Femmes ■ Grossesse ■ Allaitement ■ Enfants.

Précautions et mises en garde: Carcinome de la prostate ■ Insuffisance coronarienne ■ Hypersensibilité connue aux antagonistes alpha$_1$-adrénergiques ■ Insuffisance hépatique légère ■ Insuffisance rénale terminale (les effets n'ont pas été évalués) ■ Hypotension orthostatique symptomatique ou antécédents d'une forte réaction hypotensive à la suite de l'administration d'un autre antagoniste alpha$_1$-adrénergique.

RÉACTIONS INDÉSIRABLES ET EFFETS SECONDAIRES

SNC: céphalées, sensations vertigineuses, sédation.

CV: hypotension ou hypotension orthostatique, syncope.

GI: dyspepsie, nausées, constipation, douleurs abdominales.

GU: impuissance.

Loc.: lombalgies, douleurs articulaires.

ORLO: infection des voies respiratoires supérieures, bronchite, symptômes pseudogrippaux.

INTERACTIONS

Médicament-médicament: Les concentrations sanguines d'alfuzosine et ses effets peuvent être accrus par les **médicaments inhibant l'isoenzyme 3A4 du cytochrome P450** (**diltiazem**, **kétoconazole**, etc.) ■ L'usage concomitant d'**aténolol** ou de **diltiazem** est possible, mais il faut tenir compte de leur effet additif sur la pression artérielle et suivre de près le patient ■ Risque accru d'hypotension lors de l'administration concomitante d'**antihypertenseurs** ou d'autres **adrénolytiques à action périphérique** (**doxazosine**, **prazosine**, **térazosine**, **tamsulosine**); en éviter l'usage concomitant.

VOIES D'ADMINISTRATION ET POSOLOGIE

- **PO (adultes)**: 10 mg, 1 fois par jour, tous les jours, après le même repas. Il faut avaler le comprimé entier, sans le croquer, le mâcher ni l'écraser.

PRÉSENTATION

Comprimés à libération prolongée: 10 mg[Pr].

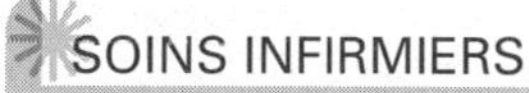

SOINS INFIRMIERS

ÉVALUATION DE LA SITUATION

- Suivre de près le patient, avant le traitement et à intervalles réguliers pendant toute sa durée, pour déceler l'apparition des symptômes suivants d'hyperplasie bénigne de la prostate: retard de la miction, sensation d'évacuation incomplète de la vessie, interruption du jet, puissance du jet et quantités d'urine éliminées insuffisantes, fuites postmictionnelles, effort à la miction, dysurie, mictions impérieuses.
- Après l'administration de la première dose d'alfuzosine, observer le patient pour déceler des signes d'hypotension et la syncope. Mesurer la pression artérielle en position debout et couchée ainsi que la fréquence cardiaque à intervalles réguliers pendant toute la durée du traitement. Ces effets peuvent apparaître peu de temps après la première dose et, occasionnellement, par la suite. Si ces effets se manifestaient, prendre les mesures qui s'imposent pour prévenir les accidents.

DIAGNOSTICS INFIRMIERS POSSIBLES

- Risque d'accident (Effets secondaires).
- Élimination urinaire altérée (Indications).

A

- Connaissances insuffisantes sur le traitement médicamenteux (Enseignement au patient et à ses proches).

INTERVENTIONS INFIRMIÈRES

- NE PAS CONFONDRE XATRAL (ALFUSOSINE) ET XANAX (ALPRAZOLAM).
- Administrer la dose quotidienne, 30 minutes après le même repas de la journée. LES COMPRIMÉS DOIVENT ÊTRE AVALÉS ENTIERS. ILS NE DOIVENT PAS ÊTRE CROQUÉS, MACHÉS OU ÉCRASÉS NI RÉDUITS EN POUDRE.

ENSEIGNEMENT AU PATIENT ET À SES PROCHES

- Expliquer au patient qu'il doit prendre l'alfuzosine tous les jours, à la même heure, après le même repas, même s'il se sent mieux. S'il n'a pu prendre le médicament au moment habituel, il doit le prendre aussitôt que possible, à moins que ce ne soit presque l'heure prévue pour la dose suivante. Le prévenir qu'il ne doit jamais remplacer une dose manquée par une double dose.
- Prévenir le patient que l'alfuzosine peut provoquer de la somnolence et des étourdissements. Lui conseiller de ne pas conduire et d'éviter les activités qui exigent sa vigilance jusqu'à ce qu'on ait la certitude que le médicament n'entraîne pas ces effets chez lui.
- Recommander au patient de changer lentement de position pour diminuer le risque d'hypotension orthostatique et de sensations vertigineuses, surtout en début de traitement. Conseiller au patient de prévenir un professionnel de la santé si ces effets surviennent fréquemment ou s'ils deviennent incommodants.
- Conseiller au patient de consulter un professionnel de la santé avant de prendre un médicament en vente libre contre la toux, le rhume ou les allergies.
- Insister sur l'importance des examens de suivi permettant d'évaluer les bienfaits du traitement.
- Recommander au patient qui doit suivre un autre traitement ou subir une intervention chirurgicale d'avertir le professionnel de la santé qu'il suit un traitement par ce médicament.

VÉRIFICATION DE L'EFFICACITÉ THÉRAPEUTIQUE

L'efficacité du traitement peut être démontrée par: la diminution des symptômes urinaires associés à l'hyperplasie bénigne de la prostate. ✻

ALLOPURINOL

Alloprin, Apo-Allopurinol, Novo-Purol, Zyloprim

CLASSIFICATION:

Traitement de la goutte (inhibiteur de la xanthine-oxydase)

Grossesse – catégorie C

INDICATIONS

Traitement de la goutte ■ Prophylaxie des lithiases rénales calciques ■ Prévention de la néphropathie urique au cours d'un traitement intensif des maladies néoplasiques.

MÉCANISME D'ACTION

Inhibition de la production d'acide urique. ***Effets thérapeutiques:*** Diminution des concentrations sériques et urinaires d'acide urique.

PHARMACOCINÉTIQUE

Absorption: 80 % (PO).

Distribution: Tous les liquides corporels.

Métabolisme et excrétion: Transformation lors du métabolisme en oxypurinol, un métabolite actif; 12 % excrété sous forme inchangée, et 76 %, sous forme d'oxypurinol.

Demi-vie: De 2 à 3 heures (oxypurinol, 24 heures).

Profil temps-action (effet hypo-uricémique)

	DÉBUT D'ACTION	PIC	DURÉE†
PO	2 - 3 jours	1 - 3 semaines	1 - 2 semaines

† Après l'arrêt du traitement par l'allopurinol.

CONTRE-INDICATIONS, PRÉCAUTIONS ET MISES EN GARDE

Contre-indications: Hypersensibilité ■ **PÉD.**: Sauf les enfants qui présentent une hyperuricémie consécutive au traitement intensif d'une maladie néoplasique.

Précautions et mises en garde: Crises aiguës de goutte ■ Insuffisance rénale (réduire la dose si la Cl_{Cr} < 20 mL/min) ■ Insuffisance rénale ou hépatique (interrompre le traitement si les troubles hépatiques ou rénaux s'aggravent) ■ Déshydratation (assurer une hydratation adéquate) ■ Grossesse ■ **ALLAITEMENT**: L'allopurinol et l'oxypurinol passent dans le lait maternel. En général, on considère l'allopurinol compatible avec l'allaitement ■ Risque d'éruptions cutanées suivies parfois de réactions d'hypersensibilité plus graves; arrêter le traitement dès les premières manifestations. S'il n'y a pas d'autre traitement possible, envisager la désensibilisation dans le cas des patients qui présentent une réaction cutanée à l'allopurinol.

RÉACTIONS INDÉSIRABLES ET EFFETS SECONDAIRES

SNC: somnolence.
GI: diarrhée, hépatite, nausées, vomissements.
GU: insuffisance rénale.
Tég.: rash, urticaire.
Hémat.: aplasie médullaire.
Divers: réactions d'hypersensibilité.

INTERACTIONS

Médicament-médicament: L'administration concomitante de **mercaptopurine** ou d'**azathioprine** intensifie les effets médullodépresseurs de ces médicaments. Une réduction de la dose de ces médicaments est nécessaire ▪ L'administration concomitante d'**ampicilline** ou d'**amoxicilline** augmente le risque de rash ▪ L'administration concomitante d'**hypoglycémiants oraux** ou de **warfarine** augmente les effets de ces médicaments ▪ L'administration concomitante de **diurétiques thiazidiques** ou d'**inhibiteurs de l'enzyme de conversion de l'angiotensine (IECA)** augmente les risques de réactions d'hypersensibilité ▪ L'administration de fortes doses d'allopurinol peut accroître le risque de toxicité associée à la **théophylline** ▪ L'administration concomitante d'**antiacides à base d'hydroxyde d'aluminium** peut réduire l'absorption de l'allopurinol dans le tractus gastro-intestinal. On conseille d'administrer l'allopurinol au moins 3 heures avant l'antiacide ▪ L'**alcool** peut diminuer l'effet uricosurique de l'allopurinol.

VOIES D'ADMINISTRATION ET POSOLOGIE

Traitement de la goutte

- **PO (adultes)**: *Dose initiale* – 100 mg/jour; augmenter la dose à intervalles hebdomadaires selon les concentrations sériques d'acide urique (ne pas dépasser 800 mg/jour). Les doses de plus de 300 mg/jour doivent être fractionnées. *Dose d'entretien* – de 100 à 200 mg, 2 ou 3 fois par jour. Les doses de 300 mg ou moins peuvent être administrées 1 fois par jour.

Prophylaxie des lithiases rénales calciques

- **PO (adultes)**: De 100 à 300 mg par jour en une seule dose ou en doses fractionnées.

Prévention de la néphropathie urique au cours d'un traitement intensif des maladies néoplasiques

- **PO (adultes et enfants > 10 ans)**: De 600 à 800 mg/jour en doses fractionnées. Amorcer le traitement de 12 heures à 3 jours avant le début de la chimiothérapie ou de la radiothérapie.
- **PO (enfants ≤ 10 ans)**: 10 mg/kg/jour en 2 ou 3 doses fractionnées; au maximum, 800 mg par jour.

INSUFFISANCE RÉNALE

- **PO (ADULTES)**: *CL_{CR} DE 10 À 20 mL/MIN*: 200 mg/JOUR; *CL_{CR} < 10 mL/MIN*: 100 mg/JOUR.

PRÉSENTATION (version générique disponible)

Comprimés: 100 mg[Pr], 200 mg[Pr], 300 mg[Pr].

SOINS INFIRMIERS

ÉVALUATION DE LA SITUATION

- Effectuer le bilan quotidien des ingesta et des excreta. En présence d'insuffisance rénale, le médicament peut s'accumuler dans les tissus et exercer des effets toxiques. Assurer une consommation suffisante de liquides (de 2 500 à 3 000 mL par jour, au minimum) pour réduire le risque de formation de calculs rénaux.
- Rester à l'affût d'un rash ou de tout signe de réactions d'hypersensibilité graves. Arrêter immédiatement l'administration de l'allopurinol en présence de rash. Il faut abandonner le traitement définitivement si la réaction est grave. On peut reprendre le traitement à une plus faible dose (50 mg/jour; majorer la dose très graduellement) après la disparition d'une réaction qui a été légère. En cas de récurrence du rash, abandonner définitivement le traitement.

Goutte: Suivre de près la douleur et l'enflure des articulations. L'ajout de colchicine ou d'un AINS est nécessaire pour contrer une crise aiguë. L'administration prophylactique de colchicine ou d'un AINS devrait se faire en concomitance pendant les 3 à 6 premiers mois de traitement, car la fréquence des crises aiguës de goutte peut augmenter en début de traitement.

Tests de laboratoire:

- Les concentrations urinaires et sériques d'acide urique commencent habituellement à diminuer 2 ou 3 jours après le début du traitement par voie orale.
- Noter la glycémie chez les patients qui reçoivent des hypoglycémiants oraux. Chez ces patients, l'allopurinol peut déclencher une hypoglycémie.
- Noter les résultats des analyses de sang ainsi que ceux des tests des fonctions rénale et hépatique, avant l'administration initiale et à intervalles réguliers tout au long du traitement, particulièrement durant les premiers mois. L'allopurinol peut entraîner l'élévation des concentrations sériques de phosphatase alcaline, de bilirubine, d'AST et d'ALT. Un

A

hémogramme faisant état d'une diminution du nombre de globules sanguins ou de plaquettes peut être un signe d'aplasie médullaire. Des concentrations sériques élevées d'urée et de créatinine ainsi que la diminution la Cl_{Cr} peuvent être des indices de toxicité rénale, qui est habituellement renversée à l'arrêt du traitement.

DIAGNOSTICS INFIRMIERS POSSIBLES

- Douleur aiguë (Indications).
- Connaissances insuffisantes sur le traitement médicamenteux (Enseignement au patient et à ses proches).

INTERVENTIONS INFIRMIÈRES

- L'allopurinol peut être administré avec du lait ou des aliments pour réduire l'irritation gastrique. Dans le cas des patients ayant des difficultés de déglutition, on peut écraser le comprimé et l'administrer avec des liquides ou le mélanger à la nourriture.

ENSEIGNEMENT AU PATIENT ET À SES PROCHES

- Expliquer au patient qu'il doit suivre rigoureusement la posologie recommandée. S'il a oublié de prendre le médicament au moment habituel, il doit le prendre aussitôt que possible. Si le médecin a prescrit une dose uniquotidienne, il ne faut pas prendre la dose manquée le jour suivant. Si le médicament est pris plusieurs fois par jour, on peut augmenter la dose suivante, jusqu'à un maximum de 300 mg.
- Expliquer au patient qu'il doit continuer de prendre l'allopurinol en association avec un AINS ou la colchicine pendant une crise aiguë de goutte. L'allopurinol aide à prévenir les crises de goutte, mais ne les soulage pas.
- Le médecin peut prescrire un régime alimentaire alcalin. L'acidification de l'urine avec des doses élevées de vitamine C ou d'autres acides peut augmenter le risque de formation de calculs rénaux (voir l'annexe J). Prévenir le patient qu'il doit augmenter sa consommation de liquides.
- Prévenir le patient que l'allopurinol peut parfois provoquer la somnolence. Lui conseiller de ne pas conduire et d'éviter les activités qui exigent sa vigilance jusqu'à ce qu'on ait la certitude que le médicament n'entraîne pas cet effet chez lui.
- Conseiller au patient de signaler rapidement à un professionnel de la santé tout nouveau rash ou tout symptôme de grippe (frissons, fièvre, douleurs musculaires, nausées ou vomissements) accompagnant un rash ou survenant peu après son apparition; ces réactions pourraient être des signes d'hypersensibilité.
- Prévenir le patient que les quantités importantes d'alcool augmentent les concentrations d'acide urique et peuvent diminuer l'efficacité de l'allopurinol.
- Insister sur l'importance d'un suivi médical permettant de déterminer l'efficacité du médicament et ses effets secondaires.

VÉRIFICATION DE L'EFFICACITÉ THÉRAPEUTIQUE

L'efficacité du traitement peut être démontrée par: la diminution des concentrations sériques et urinaires d'acide urique. L'amélioration pourrait ne pas être notable avant 2 à 6 semaines chez les patients atteints de goutte. ✳

ALMOTRIPTAN,

voir Agonistes de la sérotonine 5-HT_1

ALPRAZOLAM

Apo-Alpraz, Gen-Alprazolam, Novo-Alprazol, Nu-Alpraz, Xanax, Xanax TS

CLASSIFICATION:

Anxiolytique, antipanique (benzodiazépine)

Grossesse – catégorie D

INDICATIONS

Traitement de l'anxiété ▪ Traitement du trouble panique, avec ou sans agoraphobie. **Usages non approuvés:** Traitement des symptômes du syndrome prémenstruel (SPM) ▪ Traitement de l'insomnie ▪ Traitement des tremblements.

MÉCANISME D'ACTION

Effet anxiolytique à plusieurs niveaux du SNC ▪ Risque de dépression du SNC ▪ Effets probablement attribuables à l'acide gamma-aminobutyrique (GABA), un neurotransmetteur inhibiteur. ***Effets thérapeutiques:*** Soulagement de l'anxiété.

PHARMACOCINÉTIQUE

Absorption: Bonne (PO – 90 %).

Distribution: L'agent se répartit dans tout l'organisme et traverse la barrière hématoencéphalique. Il traverse probablement la barrière placentaire et passe dans le lait maternel. L'accumulation est minime.

Métabolisme et excrétion: Métabolisme hépatique, transformation en un métabolite actif qui est par la suite métabolisé rapidement. Excrétion rénale sous forme inchangée ou de métabolites.

Demi-vie: 11 heures en moyenne (écart de 6 à 27 heures).

Profil temps-action (effet anxiolytique)

	Début d'action	Pic	Durée
PO	1 - 2 h	1 - 2 h	jusqu'à 24 h

CONTRE-INDICATIONS, PRÉCAUTIONS ET MISES EN GARDE

Contre-indications: Hypersensibilité à l'alprazolam ou à d'autres benzodiazépines ■ Glaucome à angle fermé ■ Myasthénie grave.

Précautions et mises en garde: Insuffisance hépatique (réduire la dose) ■ Insuffisance rénale (réduire la dose) ■ Sevrage brusque déconseillé ■ Patients suicidaires ou ayant des antécédents de toxicomanie ■ **Gér.**: Il est recommandé de réduire la dose chez les personnes âgées ou débilitées ■ **Obst.**: L'innocuité du médicament n'a pas été établie; l'usage prolongé pendant la grossesse peut entraîner des symptômes de sevrage chez le nouveau-né ■ **Allaitement**: Le médicament passe dans le lait maternel, il y a donc risque d'accumulation chez le nouveau-né.

RÉACTIONS INDÉSIRABLES ET EFFETS SECONDAIRES

SNC: étourdissements, somnolence, léthargie, confusion, sensation de tête légère, céphalées, dépression, excitation paradoxale.

ORLO: vision trouble.

GI: constipation, diarrhée, nausées, vomissements.

Tég.: rash.

Divers: dépendance physique, dépendance psychologique, tolérance aux effets du médicament.

INTERACTIONS

Médicament-médicament: L'usage concomitant d'**alcool**, d'**antidépresseurs**, d'autres **benzodiazépines**, d'**antihistaminiques** et d'**analgésiques opioïdes** entraîne une dépression accrue du SNC ■ La **cimétidine**, la **clarithromycine**, les **contraceptifs oraux**, le **disulfiram**, l'**érythromycine**, la **fluoxétine**, la **fluvoxamine**, l'**isoniazide**, l'**itraconazole**, le **kétoconazole**, le **métoprolol**, le **propoxyphène**, le **propranolol**, la **télithromycine** ou l'**acide valproïque** peuvent ralentir le métabolisme de l'alprazolam et en accroître les effets ■ L'alprazolam peut diminuer l'efficacité de la **lévodopa** ■ La **rifampine,** la **carbamazépine** ou les **barbituriques** peuvent accélérer le métabolisme de l'alprazolam et en diminuer l'efficacité ■ La **théophylline** peut diminuer les effets sédatifs de l'alprazolam.

Médicament-aliments: L'ingestion concomitante de **jus de pamplemousse** augmente les concentrations sanguines du médicament.

Médicament-produits naturels: Risque de dépression accrue du SNC lors de la consommation concomitante de **kava**, de **valériane** et de **camomille**.

VOIES D'ADMINISTRATION ET POSOLOGIE

Anxiété

- **PO (adultes)**: 0,25 mg, 2 ou 3 fois par jour; augmenter par paliers de 0,25 mg selon la réponse. La dose d'entretien ne doit pas dépasser 3 mg par jour.
- **PO (personnes âgées ou débilitées)**: Initialement, 0,125 mg, 2 ou 3 fois par jour; augmenter la posologie graduellement selon la tolérance et la réponse du patient.

INSUFFISANCE RÉNALE OU HÉPATIQUE

- **PO (ADULTES)**: DE 0,125 À 0,25 MG, 2 OU 3 FOIS PAR JOUR; AUGMENTER LA POSOLOGIE GRADUELLEMENT SELON LA TOLÉRANCE ET LA RÉPONSE DU PATIENT.

Crises de panique

- **PO (adultes)**: De 0,5 mg à 1 mg, au coucher, ou 0,5 mg, 3 fois par jour; augmenter par paliers de maximum 1 mg, tous les 3 à 4 jours, selon la réponse. La dose d'entretien ne doit pas dépasser 10 mg par jour.

PRÉSENTATION

Comprimés: 0,25 mg[T\C], 0,5 mg[T\C], 1 mg[T\C], 2 mg[T\C].

SOINS INFIRMIERS

ÉVALUATION DE LA SITUATION

- Déterminer le degré d'anxiété et ses manifestations ainsi que l'état de conscience avant le traitement et à intervalles réguliers pendant toute sa durée.
- Suivre de près les symptômes suivants: somnolence, sensation de tête légère et étourdissements. Ces symptômes disparaissent habituellement avec le temps. Réduire la dose s'ils persistent.

Gér.: Déterminer les effets au niveau du SNC et le risque de chutes. Prendre des mesures de prévention des chutes.

- Le traitement prolongé à des doses élevées peut entraîner une dépendance psychologique ou physique. Le risque est plus élevé chez les patients qui reçoivent plus de 4 mg/jour. Réduire la quantité du médicament dont le patient peut disposer.

Tests de laboratoire: Noter la numération globulaire et les résultats des tests des fonctions rénale et hépatique à intervalles réguliers au cours d'un traitement prolongé. Le médicament peut entraîner une diminution de l'hématocrite et la neutropénie.

DIAGNOSTICS INFIRMIERS POSSIBLES

- Anxiété (Indications).
- Risque d'accident (Effets secondaires).
- Connaissances insuffisantes sur le traitement médicamenteux (Enseignement au patient et à ses proches).

INTERVENTIONS INFIRMIÈRES

- NE PAS CONFONDRE XANAX (ALPRAZOLAM), ZANTAC (RANITIDINE) ET XATRAL (ALFUZOSINE).
- En cas d'anxiété se manifestant tôt le matin ou entre les prises, la même dose quotidienne totale devrait être divisée et administrée à des intervalles plus fréquents.
- En présence de réactions gastro-intestinales indésirables, le médicament peut être administré avec des aliments.
- Si le patient a des difficultés de déglutition, on peut écraser les comprimés et les administrer avec des aliments ou des liquides.

ENSEIGNEMENT AU PATIENT ET À SES PROCHES

- Expliquer au patient qu'il doit respecter rigoureusement la posologie recommandée; l'avertir qu'il ne doit jamais sauter une dose, ni remplacer une dose manquée par une double dose. S'il n'a pu prendre le médicament au moment habituel, il doit le prendre en l'espace de 1 heure; sinon, il doit sauter cette dose et revenir à l'horaire habituel. Si le médicament s'avère moins efficace après quelques semaines, lui conseiller de prévenir un professionnel de la santé sans augmenter lui-même les doses. Le sevrage brusque peut provoquer la transpiration, des vomissements, des crampes musculaires, des tremblements et des convulsions.
- Prévenir le patient que l'alprazolam peut provoquer de la somnolence ou des étourdissements. Lui conseiller de ne pas conduire et d'éviter les activités qui exigent sa vigilance jusqu'à ce qu'on ait la certitude que le médicament n'entraîne pas ces effets chez lui. **GÉR.**: Expliquer au patient et à ses proches les mesures à prendre pour diminuer le risque de chutes à domicile.
- Prévenir le patient qu'il ne doit pas consommer d'alcool ni prendre des dépresseurs du SNC en même temps que ce médicament. Lui conseiller de consulter un professionnel de la santé avant de prendre un médicament d'ordonnance, en vente libre ou un produit naturel en même temps que l'alprazolam.

VÉRIFICATION DE L'EFFICACITÉ THÉRAPEUTIQUE

L'efficacité du traitement peut être démontrée par: la diminution de la sensation d'anxiété ▪ une capacité accrue d'adaptation ▪ la diminution de la fréquence et de la gravité des crises de panique; après une période prolongée sans crise de panique, le bien-fondé du traitement devrait être réévalué.

ALTEPLASE,

voir Thrombolytiques

ALTRÉTAMINE

Hexalen

CLASSIFICATION:

Antinéoplasique

Grossesse – catégorie D

INDICATIONS

Monothérapie du cancer ovarien rebelle au traitement par d'autres agents.

MÉCANISME D'ACTION

Mécanisme inconnu, mais qui semble arrêter la synthèse de l'ADN et de l'ARN. La molécule mère n'est probablement pas active. ***Effets thérapeutiques:*** Destruction des cellules à réplication rapide et, particulièrement, des cellules malignes.

PHARMACOCINÉTIQUE

Absorption: Bonne (PO).

Distribution: Concentrations élevées dans le foie, les reins et l'intestin grêle. Faible pénétration dans le cerveau.

Métabolisme et excrétion: Métabolisme majoritairement hépatique et transformation en composés dotés d'effets antinéoplasiques.

Demi-vie: De 4,7 à 10,2 heures.

Profil temps-action
(effet sur la numération globulaire)

	DÉBUT D'ACTION	PIC	DURÉE
PO	inconnu	3 – 4 semaines	6 semaines

CONTRE-INDICATIONS, PRÉCAUTIONS ET MISES EN GARDE

Contre-indications: Hypersensibilité ▪ Myélosuppression importante (leucopénie, thrombopénie, anémie) ▪ Toxicité neurologique grave.

Précautions et mises en garde: Maladies neurologiques préexistantes ▪ Femmes en âge de procréer ▪ **OBST., ALLAITEMENT:** Cesser le traitement à l'altrétamine ▪ Infections ▪ Aplasie médullaire ▪ Autres maladies chroniques débilitantes ▪ **PÉD.:** L'innocuité du médicament n'a pas été établie.

RÉACTIONS INDÉSIRABLES ET EFFETS SECONDAIRES

SNC: CONVULSIONS, fatigue, ataxie, vertige, diminution de l'état de conscience.
GI: nausées, vomissements, anorexie, toxicité hépatique.
GU: suppression de la fonction des gonades, toxicité rénale.
Tég.: alopécie, prurit, rash.
Hémat.: anémie, leucopénie, thrombopénie.
SN: neuropathie périphérique.

INTERACTIONS

Médicament-médicament: L'administration concomitante d'**IMAO** peut déclencher une hypotension orthostatique ▪ Le médicament peut diminuer la réponse immunitaire et augmenter le risque de réactions indésirables dues aux **vaccins à virus vivants** ▪ Une aplasie médullaire additive peut survenir lors de l'administration concomitante d'autres **agents antinéoplasiques** ou d'une **radiothérapie** ▪ La **cimétidine** augmente les concentrations sanguines du médicament et le risque de toxicité.

VOIES D'ADMINISTRATION ET POSOLOGIE

- **PO (adultes):** *En monothérapie* – 260 mg/m^2/jour en 3 ou 4 prises, pour les cycles de 14 à 21 jours. On recommande une période sans médicament de 7 à 14 jours entre les cycles. En présence d'effets indésirables importants, réduire la posologie ou interrompre temporairement l'administration du médicament.

PRÉSENTATION

Gélules: 50 mg[Pr].

SOINS INFIRMIERS

ÉVALUATION DE LA SITUATION

- Des nausées et des vomissements peuvent survenir. Cependant, une tolérance à ces effets peut être notée après plusieurs semaines de traitement. Pour contrer ces réactions, on peut administrer des antiémétiques ou réduire la dose d'altrétamine. Dans de rares cas, il faut arrêter le traitement. Noter la quantité de vomissures et prévenir le médecin si elle est supérieure à celle indiquée dans les directives concernant la prévention de la déshydratation.
- Tout au long du traitement, rester à l'affût des signes d'aplasie médullaire. Bien que la patiente soit souvent asymptomatique, les symptômes peuvent être les suivants: anémie (fatigue inhabituelle), leucopénie (fièvre, frissons, maux de gorge, toux ou raucité de la voix, douleurs lombaires ou latérales basses, mictions difficiles ou douloureuses) et thrombopénie (saignement des gencives, formation d'ecchymoses, pétéchies, présence de sang dans les selles, l'urine et les vomissures). Signaler ces symptômes au médecin.
- Éviter les injections IM et la prise de la température rectale. Appliquer une pression sur les points de ponction veineuse pendant 10 minutes.
- Observer les signes suivants de neurotoxicité, incluant les effets sur le SNC (anxiété, maladresse, confusion, étourdissements, dépression, faiblesse, convulsions), et de neuropathie périphérique (engourdissements, picotements, paresthésie), avant le début de chaque cycle de traitement et à intervalles réguliers pendant toute sa durée. La neuropathie périphérique est habituellement réversible après l'arrêt du traitement; l'administration concomitante de pyridoxine permet de réduire les effets neurotoxiques de l'altrétamine, mais le traitement d'association est déconseillé en raison du risque de diminuer l'efficacité du traitement. Si la neurotoxicité persiste après la réduction de la dose, il faut interrompre le traitement.

Tests de laboratoire: Noter le nombre de globules sanguins et de plaquettes, avant chaque cycle de traitement, mensuellement ou selon l'état clinique de la patiente. Pendant une cure de 21 jours, la leucopénie et la thrombopénie atteignent leur nadir au bout de 3 à 4 semaines, mais elles reviennent à la normale en l'espace de 6 semaines. Les nadirs sont atteints en l'espace de 6 à 8 semaines à la suite d'un traitement continu. Interrompre l'administration pendant 14 jours ou plus et reprendre le traitement à 200 mg/m^2/jour dans les cas suivants: intolérance gastro-intestinale rebelle au traitement habituel, nombre de leucocytes $< 2{,}0 \times 10^9$/L, de granulocytes $< 1{,}0 \times 10^9$/L et de plaquettes $< 75 \times 10^9$/L, ou neurotoxicité évolutive.

DIAGNOSTICS INFIRMIERS POSSIBLES

- Risque d'infection (Réactions indésirables).
- Risque d'accident (Effets secondaires).
- Connaissances insuffisantes sur le traitement médicamenteux (Enseignement au patient et à ses proches).

A

INTERVENTIONS INFIRMIÈRES

- Administrer le médicament après les repas et au coucher pour réduire les nausées et les vomissements.

ENSEIGNEMENT AU PATIENT ET À SES PROCHES

- Recommander à la patiente de signaler rapidement à un professionnel de la santé les symptômes suivants: fièvre, maux de gorge, signes d'infection, saignements des gencives, formation d'ecchymoses, pétéchies, présence de sang dans les selles, l'urine ou les vomissures, fatigue accrue, dyspnée ou hypotension orthostatique. Conseiller à la patiente d'éviter les foules et les personnes contagieuses. Lui recommander d'utiliser une brosse à dents à poils doux et un rasoir électrique, et de prendre garde aux chutes. La prévenir qu'il ne faut pas consommer de boissons alcoolisées ni prendre de médicaments à base d'aspirine ou d'AINS, étant donné que ces substances peuvent déclencher une hémorragie gastro-intestinale.
- Informer la patiente qu'elle doit prévenir le médecin en cas d'engourdissements ou de picotements au niveau des membres.
- Prévenir la patiente qu'elle ne doit pas se faire vacciner sans avoir consulté au préalable un professionnel de la santé.
- Inciter la patiente à prendre des mesures de contraception.
- Souligner le besoin de se soumettre à intervalles réguliers à des tests de laboratoire permettant de déceler les effets secondaires du médicament.

VÉRIFICATION DE L'EFFICACITÉ THÉRAPEUTIQUE

L'efficacité du traitement peut être démontrée par: la diminution de la tumeur ou le ralentissement de la propagation de la maladie. ✳

ALUMINIUM, HYDROXYDE D'

Alugel, Alu-Tab, Amphojel, Basaljel, Gaviscon

CLASSIFICATION:

Antiulcéreux (antiacide), agent gastro-intestinal de fixation du phosphate

Grossesse – catégorie inconnue

Voir aussi Magnésium et aluminium, sels de

INDICATIONS

Diminution des concentrations de phosphate chez les patients souffrant d'insuffisance rénale chronique (Basaljel) ■ Traitement symptomatique de l'hyperchlorhydrie reliée aux troubles suivants: ulcères gastroduodénaux, gastrite, œsophagite de reflux, brûlures d'estomac, indigestion.

MÉCANISME D'ACTION

Liaison au phosphate dans le tractus gastro-intestinal ■ Neutralisation de l'acide gastrique et inactivation de la pepsine. ***Effets thérapeutiques:*** Diminution des concentrations sériques de phosphate ■ Guérison des ulcères et diminution de la douleur provoquée par les ulcères ou l'hyperacidité gastrique ■ Puisque ce médicament provoque la constipation, son usage en monothérapie des maladies ulcéreuses devrait être limité ■ L'hydroxyde d'aluminium est souvent présenté en association avec des composés contenant du magnésium.

PHARMACOCINÉTIQUE

Absorption: Lors d'un usage prolongé, de petites quantités d'aluminium sont absorbées par voie systémique.

Distribution: Lorsqu'il y a absorption systémique, l'hydroxyde d'aluminium est largement distribué dans les tissus, traverse la barrière placentaire et est excrété dans le lait maternel. Lors d'un usage prolongé, l'aluminium se concentre dans le SNC.

Métabolisme et excrétion: Excrétion majoritairement fécale. Les petites quantités absorbées sont excrétées par les reins.

Demi-vie: Inconnue.

Profil temps-action

(effet hypophosphatémiant et effet antiacide)

	Début d'action	Pic	Durée
PO†	plusieurs heures – jours	plusieurs jours – semaines	plusieurs jours
PO‡	15 – 30 min	30 min	30 min – 3 h

† Effet hypophosphatémiant.
‡ Effet antiacide.

CONTRE-INDICATIONS, PRÉCAUTIONS ET MISES EN GARDE

Contre-indications: Patients débilités ■ Dysfonctionnement rénal ■ Idiosyncrasie à l'hydroxyde d'aluminium ou au sucrose (Basaljel) ■ Traitement antiacide de routine (Basaljel) ■ Douleurs abdominales intenses de cause inconnue.

Précautions et mises en garde: Hypercalcémie ■ Hypophosphatémie ■ **Obst.**: Bien que l'innocuité de ce médicament ne soit pas remise en question, le traitement prolongé avec des doses élevées est à éviter.

RÉACTIONS INDÉSIRABLES ET EFFETS SECONDAIRES

GI: constipation.
HÉ: hypophosphatémie.

INTERACTIONS

Médicament-médicament: L'absorption des **tétracyclines**, de la **chlorpromazine**, des **sels ferreux**, de l'**isoniazide**, de la **digoxine** ou des **fluoroquinolones** peut être diminuée lors d'un traitement concomitant ■ L'agent peut diminuer les concentrations sanguines de **salicylates** ■ Les concentrations de **quinidine**, de **mexilétine** et d'**amphétamine** peuvent être accrues si la quantité d'antiacide ingérée est suffisante pour élever le pH de l'urine.

VOIES D'ADMINISTRATION ET POSOLOGIE

Agent hypophosphatémiant

- **PO (adultes)**: De 1 à 6 g/jour, selon la phosphatémie.

Antiacide

- **PO (adultes)**: 1 comprimé (600 mg) ou 10 mL (640 mg), 5 ou 6 fois par jour, entre les repas et au coucher.

PRÉSENTATION (version générique disponible)

Capsules: 500 mg^{VL} ■ **Comprimés**: 600 mg^{VL} ■ **Suspension**: 300 mg/5 mL^{VL}, 320 mg/5 mL^{VL} ■ **En association avec**: magnésium, carbonate de calcium, siméthicone, acide alginique.

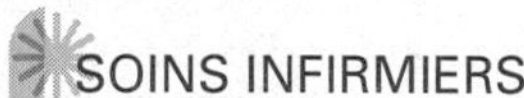

SOINS INFIRMIERS

ÉVALUATION DE LA SITUATION

- Déterminer l'emplacement, la durée et les caractéristiques de la douleur gastrique ainsi que les facteurs qui la déclenchent.

Tests de laboratoire:

- Pendant un traitement prolongé avec l'hydroxyde d'aluminium, vérifier à intervalles réguliers les concentrations sériques de calcium et de phosphate.
- L'agent peut augmenter les concentrations sériques de gastrine et diminuer les concentrations sériques de phosphate.
- Lors du traitement des maladies ulcéreuses graves, rechercher le sang occulte dans les selles et les vomissures par la méthode au gaïac et noter le pH des sécrétions gastriques.

DIAGNOSTICS INFIRMIERS POSSIBLES

- Douleur aiguë (Indications).
- Constipation (Réactions indésirables).
- Connaissances insuffisantes sur le traitement médicamenteux (Enseignement au patient et à ses proches).

INTERVENTIONS INFIRMIÈRES

- Les antiacides entraînent la dissolution et l'absorption prématurées des comprimés à enrobage entérique et peuvent entraver l'absorption d'autres médicaments administrés par voie orale. Espacer d'au moins 1 ou 2 heures les prises d'hydroxyde d'aluminium et des autres médicaments par voie orale.
- Demander au patient de bien croquer les comprimés avant de les avaler afin de les empêcher d'atteindre l'intestin grêle sous forme non dissoute. Lui demander ensuite de boire un verre d'eau.
- Bien agiter les préparations liquides avant de les verser. Pour s'assurer du passage du médicament dans l'estomac, demander au patient de boire de l'eau après l'avoir pris.
- Les préparations sous forme liquide sont considérées comme plus efficaces que les comprimés.

Agent hypophosphatémiant: Faire boire au patient un verre d'eau ou de jus de fruits après lui avoir administré le médicament.

Antiacide:

- On peut administrer le médicament en association avec des antiacides contenant du magnésium pour réduire le risque de constipation, sauf chez les patients souffrant d'insuffisance rénale. Administrer 1 et 3 heures après les repas et au coucher pour obtenir un effet antiacide maximal.
- Pour le traitement de l'ulcère gastroduodénal, on peut administrer l'hydroxyde d'aluminium toutes les 1 ou 2 heures, en respectant le sommeil du patient; on peut également le diluer dans 2 ou 3 parties d'eau et l'administrer par sonde gastrique, toutes les 30 minutes, pendant 12 heures ou plus par jour. Le médecin peut demander de faire clamper la sonde nasogastrique après l'administration du médicament.
- En présence d'une œsophagite par reflux, administrer 15 mL, de 20 à 40 minutes après les repas et au coucher.

ENSEIGNEMENT AU PATIENT ET À SES PROCHES

- Conseiller au patient de suivre rigoureusement la posologie recommandée. S'il a oublié de prendre une dose, il doit la prendre aussitôt que possible, à moins que ce ne soit presque l'heure prévue pour la

A

dose suivante; il ne faut jamais remplacer une dose manquée par une double dose.

- Conseiller au patient d'espacer d'au moins 1 ou 2 heures la prise d'hydroxyde d'aluminium et des autres médicaments et de ne pas changer cette pratique sans avoir consulté au préalable un professionnel de la santé.
- Conseiller au patient de vérifier sur l'étiquette la teneur en sodium de l'agent. Les patients souffrant d'insuffisance cardiaque ou d'hypertension et ceux qui doivent suivre un régime hyposodé ne devraient prendre que les préparations à faible teneur en sodium.
- Prévenir le patient que l'hydroxyde d'aluminium peut avoir des effets constipants.

Agent hypophosphatémiant: Expliquer au patient qui prend de l'hydroxyde d'aluminium pour traiter l'hyperphosphatémie qu'il doit suivre un régime alimentaire à faible teneur en phosphate.

Antiacide: Prévenir le patient qu'il doit consulter un professionnel de la santé: s'il doit prendre des antiacides pendant plus de 2 semaines pour traiter des troubles récurrents, s'il prend d'autres médicaments, si la douleur n'est pas soulagée ou si des symptômes de saignement gastrique (selles goudronneuses noires, vomissures ayant l'aspect du marc de café) se manifestent.

VÉRIFICATION DE L'EFFICACITÉ THÉRAPEUTIQUE

L'efficacité du traitement peut être démontrée par: la diminution des concentrations sériques de phosphate ▪ le soulagement de la douleur et de l'irritation gastrointestinales ▪ l'augmentation du pH des sécrétions gastriques. Puisqu'il n'y a pas de lien entre la disparition des symptômes d'ulcère gastroduodénal et la cicatrisation de l'ulcère, il faut poursuivre l'administration des antiacides pendant au moins 4 à 6 semaines après la disparition de tous les symptômes.

AMANTADINE

Dom-Amantadine, Endantadine, Gen-Amantadine, PMS-Amantadine, Symmetrel

CLASSIFICATION:

Antiparkinsonien, antiviral

Grossesse – catégorie C

INDICATIONS

Traitement initial et d'appoint des symptômes de la maladie de Parkinson ▪ Traitement à court terme des symptômes extrapyramidaux d'origine médicamenteuse ▪ Prophylaxie et traitement des infections par le virus grippal de type A.

MÉCANISME D'ACTION

Potentialisation des effets de la dopamine dans le SNC ▪ Prévention de la pénétration du virus grippal de type A dans les cellules hôtes. ***Effets thérapeutiques:*** Soulagement des symptômes parkinsoniens ▪ Prévention et diminution des symptômes de l'infection par le virus grippal de type A.

PHARMACOCINÉTIQUE

Absorption: Bonne (PO).

Distribution: L'agent se répartit dans divers tissus et liquides physiologiques. Il traverse la barrière hématoencéphalique et passe dans le lait maternel.

Métabolisme et excrétion: Excrétion sous forme inchangée dans l'urine.

Demi-vie: 24 heures.

Profil temps-action (effet antiparkinsonien)

	DÉBUT D'ACTION	PIC	DURÉE
PO	dans les 48 h	jusqu'à 2 semaines	inconnue

CONTRE-INDICATIONS, PRÉCAUTIONS ET MISES EN GARDE

Contre-indications: Hypersensibilité.

Précautions et mises en garde: Troubles convulsifs ▪ Maladies hépatiques ▪ Des tentatives de suicide et des idées suicidaires ont été notées chez des patients avec ou sans antécédents de maladie psychiatrique ▪ Insuffisance cardiaque et œdème périphérique ▪ Éviter l'arrêt brusque du traitement par l'amantadine, car certains patients atteints du syndrome de Parkinson ont manifesté une crise de parkinsonisme ▪ Une diminution de la dose d'amantadine ou l'interruption du traitement peut entraîner la survenue du syndrome neuroleptique malin (rare) ▪ Insuffisance rénale (réduire les doses ou allonger l'intervalle posologique, si la $Cl_{Cr} \leq 80$ mL/min) ▪ Personnes âgées ▪ Hypotension orthostatique ▪ **OBST., ALLAITEMENT:** L'innocuité de l'agent n'a pas été établie.

RÉACTIONS INDÉSIRABLES ET EFFETS SECONDAIRES

SNC: ataxie, étourdissements, insomnie, anxiété, confusion, dépression, somnolence, psychose, convulsions.

ORLO: vision trouble, sécheresse de la bouche (xérostomie).

Resp.: dyspnée.

CV: hypotension, insuffisance cardiaque, œdème.

GI: nausées.

GU: rétention urinaire.

Tég.: marbrures, livedo réticulaire, rash.

Hémat.: leucopénie, neutropénie.

INTERACTIONS

Médicament-médicament: L'administration concomitante d'**antihistaminiques**, de **phénothiazines**, de **quinidine**, de **disopyramide** et d'**antidépresseurs tricycliques** peut intensifier les effets anticholinergiques (sécheresse de la bouche, vision trouble, constipation) ▪ Risque accru d'effets indésirables sur le SNC lors de la consommation concomitante d'**alcool** ▪ Risque accru de stimulation du SNC lors de l'administration d'autres **stimulants du SNC**.

VOIES D'ADMINISTRATION ET POSOLOGIE

Maladie de Parkinson

- **PO (adultes)**: 100 mg, 1 ou 2 fois par jour (jusqu'à concurrence de 300 mg/jour).

Symptômes extrapyramidaux d'origine médicamenteuse

- **PO (adultes)**: 100 mg, 2 fois par jour (jusqu'à concurrence de 300 mg/jour).

Infection par le virus grippal de type A

- **PO (adultes < 65 ans et enfants > 12 ans)**: 200 mg/jour en une seule dose, ou 100 mg, 2 fois par jour.
- **PO (adultes ≥ 65 ans)**: 100 mg, 1 fois par jour.
- **PO (enfants de 9 à 12 ans)**: 100 mg, 2 fois par jour.
- **PO (enfants de 1 à 9 ans)**: De 4,5 à 9,0 mg/kg/jour (sans dépasser 150 mg/jour). La dose quotidienne, donnée sous forme de sirop, doit être fractionnée en 2 ou 3 portions égales.

INSUFFISANCE RÉNALE

- **PO (ADULTES)**: *CL_{CR} DE 60 À 79 mL/MIN*: DOSES QUOTIDIENNES DE 100 ET DE 200 mg EN ALTERNANCE; *CL_{CR} DE 40 À 59 mL/MIN*: 100 mg, 1 FOIS PAR JOUR; *CL_{CR} DE 30 À 39 mL/MIN*: 200 mg, 2 FOIS/SEMAINE; *CL_{CR} DE 20 À 29 mL/MIN*: 100 mg, 3 FOIS/SEMAINE; *CL_{CR} DE 10 À 19 mL/MIN*: DOSES HEBDOMADAIRES DE 100 ET DE 200 mg EN ALTERNANCE; *PATIENTS HÉMODIALYSÉS*: 200 mg, TOUS LES 7 JOURS.

PRÉSENTATION (version générique disponible)

Capsules: 100 mg[Pr] ▪ **Sirop**: 50 mg/5 mL[Pr].

SOINS INFIRMIERS

ÉVALUATION DE LA SITUATION

- Mesurer la pression artérielle à intervalles réguliers. Rester à l'affût de l'hypotension orthostatique induite par le médicament.
- Suivre de près les ingesta et les excreta chez les personnes âgées. L'agent peut provoquer une rétention urinaire. Signaler tout écart notable ou la distention de la vessie.
- Suivre les signes vitaux et l'état mental à intervalles réguliers au cours des premiers jours des adaptations posologiques chez les patients prenant plus de 200 mg par jour; le risque d'effets secondaires est accru.
- Rester à l'affût des signes d'insuffisance cardiaque (œdème périphérique, gain de poids, dyspnée, râles et crépitations, distension des jugulaires), particulièrement chez les patients qui suivent un traitement de long cours ou qui ont des antécédents d'insuffisance cardiaque.
- Rester à l'affût de l'apparition de marbrures rouges et diffuses sur la peau (livedo réticulaire), particulièrement sur les membres inférieurs ou lors de l'exposition à des températures froides. Elles disparaissent malgré la poursuite du traitement, mais peuvent ne se résorber complètement que de 2 à 12 semaines après qu'il a pris fin.

Maladie de Parkinson: Noter l'akinésie, la rigidité, les tremblements et les troubles de la démarche avant le traitement et pendant toute sa durée.

Prophylaxie ou traitement de la grippe: Suivre de près l'état respiratoire (fréquence, bruits, expectorations) et mesurer la température à intervalles réguliers. En cas d'apparition de symptômes, un traitement de soutien est indiqué.

TOXICITÉ ET SURDOSAGE: Les symptômes de toxicité sont notamment ceux qui découlent de la stimulation du SNC (confusion, changements d'humeur, tremblements, convulsions, arythmies et hypotension). On ne connaît pas d'antidote spécifique, bien qu'on ait déjà utilisé la physostigmine pour renverser les effets sur le SNC.

DIAGNOSTICS INFIRMIERS POSSIBLES

- Mobilité physique réduite (Indications).
- Risque d'infection (Indications).

INTERVENTIONS INFIRMIÈRES

- NE PAS CONFONDRE L'AMANTADINE AVEC LA RANITIDINE.

A

PO: Ne pas administrer la dernière dose du médicament à l'heure du coucher; risque d'insomnie chez certains patients.

- Administrer l'amantadine en doses fractionnées pour tenter de réduire ses effets sur le SNC.
- Chez les patients éprouvant des difficultés de déglutition, mélanger le contenu des capsules avec des aliments ou des liquides.

Prophylaxie antivirale: Commencer le traitement en prévision d'une exposition ou dès que possible après que celle-ci s'est produite et le continuer pendant au moins 10 jours après l'exposition. La période d'infectiosité commence juste avant l'apparition des symptômes et dure 1 semaine. Si le vaccin n'est pas accessible ou s'il est contre-indiqué, on peut administrer l'amantadine pendant une période allant jusqu'à 90 jours afin de protéger le patient contre les expositions répétées.

- On peut administrer l'agent avec le vaccin contre le virus grippal de type A inactivé jusqu'à l'apparition de la réponse des anticorps protecteurs. Administrer pendant les 2 à 3 semaines qui suivent la vaccination.

Traitement antiviral: Administrer le médicament dès que possible après l'apparition des symptômes et continuer le traitement pendant les 24 à 48 heures qui suivent leur disparition.

ENSEIGNEMENT AU PATIENT ET À SES PROCHES

- Expliquer au patient qu'il doit respecter rigoureusement la posologie recommandée, sans sauter de dose ni remplacer une dose manquée par une double dose. Si une dose a été oubliée, ne pas la prendre dans les 4 heures qui précèdent la dose suivante.
- Prévenir le patient que le médicament peut provoquer des étourdissements ou une vision trouble. Recommander au patient de ne pas conduire et d'éviter toute autre activité qui exige sa vigilance jusqu'à ce qu'on ait la certitude que le médicament n'entraîne pas ces effets chez lui.
- Recommander au patient de changer lentement de position pour prévenir l'hypotension orthostatique.
- Conseiller au patient souffrant de sécheresse de la bouche de se rincer fréquemment la bouche, de pratiquer une bonne hygiène buccale et de consommer de la gomme à mâcher ou des bonbons sans sucre. Si ce symptôme persiste pendant plus de 2 semaines, lui recommander de consulter un professionnel de la santé.
- Recommander au patient de ne pas consommer des boissons alcoolisées et de consulter un professionnel de la santé avant de prendre des médicaments en vente libre, et particulièrement des médicaments contre le rhume.
- Conseiller au patient de prévenir un professionnel de la santé en cas de confusion, de sautes d'humeur, de difficultés de miction, d'œdème et d'essoufflement ou si les symptômes de la maladie de Parkinson s'aggravent.

Antiviral: Recommander au patient et aux membres de sa famille de prévenir chaque professionnel de la santé qui s'occupe du patient que celui-ci prend de l'amantadine en prophylaxie. Si le médicament est pris en traitement de l'infection, informer également un professionnel si les symptômes ne s'améliorent pas.

Maladie de Parkinson: Prévenir le patient que les pleins bienfaits du médicament pourraient ne pas être manifestes avant 2 semaines de traitement. Lui recommander d'informer un professionnel de la santé si le médicament perd graduellement de son effet. Le traitement par l'amantadine doit être diminué graduellement; l'arrêt brusque peut déclencher une crise de parkinsonisme.

VÉRIFICATION DE L'EFFICACITÉ THÉRAPEUTIQUE

L'efficacité du traitement peut être démontrée par: la diminution de l'akinésie et de la rigidité; le plein effet thérapeutique peut ne pas être manifeste avant 2 semaines de traitement ■ l'absence ou la réduction des symptômes de l'infection par le virus grippal de type A. ✳

AMCINONIDE,

voir Corticostéroïdes (topiques)

AMIFOSTINE

Éthyol

CLASSIFICATION:

Agent cytoprotecteur

Grossesse – catégorie C

INDICATIONS

Agent cytoprotecteur contre les effets toxiques rénaux cumulatifs associés au cisplatine et contre les effets hématologiques associés au cyclophosphamide et aux antinéoplasiques à base de platine, chez les patients présentant des tumeurs solides avancées, d'origine non germinale ■ Diminution de l'incidence de la sécheresse de la bouche (xérostomie) modérée à grave, chez les patients qui reçoivent une radiothérapie postopératoire comme traitement contre le cancer du cou et de la tête et chez lesquels la zone de radiation englobe une bonne partie des glandes parotides.

MÉCANISME D'ACTION

La phosphatase alcaline transforme le médicament dans les tissus en un composé thiol libre qui se fixe aux métabolites nuisibles du cisplatine et aux molécules réactives d'oxygène générées par la radiothérapie, et qui les détoxifie. ***Effets thérapeutiques:*** Réduction des effets toxiques rénaux du cisplatine ■ Diminution de la sécheresse de la bouche (xérostomie) induite par la radiothérapie contre le cancer du cou et de la tête.

PHARMACOCINÉTIQUE

Absorption: Biodisponibilité à 100 % (IV).
Distribution: Inconnue.
Métabolisme et excrétion: Élimination rapide du plasma et transformation par la phosphatase alcaline au niveau des tissus en composés cytoprotecteurs.
Demi-vie: 8 minutes.

Profil temps-action

	Début d'action	Pic	Durée
IV	inconnu	inconnu	inconnue

CONTRE-INDICATIONS, PRÉCAUTIONS ET MISES EN GARDE

Contre-indications: Hypersensibilité connue aux composés aminothiol ■ Réactions cutanées.
Précautions et mises en garde: Personnes âgées ou patients souffrant d'une maladie cardiovasculaire ou vasculaire cérébrale (risque accru de réactions indésirables) ■ Prise d'antihypertenseurs dans les 24 heures précédant l'administration ■ **Obst., Péd.:** L'innocuité du médicament n'a pas été établie ■ Hypotension ou déshydratation ■ **Allaitement:** Il est recommandé d'interrompre l'allaitement ■ Traitement antinéoplasique concomitant d'autres tumeurs (particulièrement des cancers d'origine germinale).

RÉACTIONS INDÉSIRABLES ET EFFETS SECONDAIRES

SNC: étourdissements, somnolence, perte de conscience.
ORLO: éternuements.
CV: hypotension.
GI: hoquet, nausées, vomissements.
Tég.: bouffées vasomotrices.
HÉ: hypocalcémie.
Divers: réactions allergiques, incluant l'ANAPHYLAXIE, l'ÉRYTHÈME MULTIFORME, le SYNDROME DE STEVENS-JOHNSON, l'ÉRYTHRODERMIE BULLEUSE AVEC ÉPIDERMOLYSE, la TOXIDERMIE et la DERMATITE EXFOLIATIVE (risque accru en cas de radiothérapie concomitante), frissons.

INTERACTIONS

Médicament-médicament: L'administration concomitante d'**antihypertenseurs** peut accroître le risque d'hypotension.

VOIES D'ADMINISTRATION ET POSOLOGIE

Diminution des effets toxiques rénaux cumulatifs associés au cisplatine et des effets hématologiques associés au cyclophosphamide et aux antinéoplasiques à base de platine

- **IV (adultes):** 910 mg/m², 1 fois par jour, dans les 30 minutes qui précèdent la chimiothérapie. Si le patient ne tolère pas la pleine dose, il faudrait réduire les doses ultérieures pour les passer à 740 mg/m².

Diminution de la xérostomie secondaire à une radiothérapie postopératoire du cou et de la tête

- **IV (adultes):** 200 mg/m², 1 fois par jour, de 15 à 30 minutes avant la radiothérapie.

PRÉSENTATION

Poudre lyophilisée stérile: 500 mg/fiole[Pr].

SOINS INFIRMIERS

ÉVALUATION DE LA SITUATION

- Mesurer la pression artérielle avant la perfusion et toutes les 5 minutes pendant toute sa durée. L'administration d'antihypertenseurs devrait être suspendue 24 heures avant l'administration de l'amifostine. En cas d'hypotension importante dictant l'arrêt du traitement, installer le patient en position de Trendelenburg et administrer une perfusion de NaCl 0,9 % par une tubulure de perfusion séparée. Si la pression artérielle revient à la normale en 5 minutes et si le patient est asymptomatique, on peut reprendre la perfusion pour lui administrer le reste de la dose.
- Évaluer l'état de l'hydratation avant l'administration de l'agent. Corriger la déshydratation avant d'amorcer le traitement. Puisque les nausées et les vomissements sont fréquents et qu'ils peuvent être graves, il faut administrer des agents antiémétiques, tels que la dexaméthasone à 20 mg, par voie IV, et un antiémétique antagoniste de la sérotonine (ondansétron, dolasétron, granisétron), avant la perfusion de l'amifostine. Continuer de suivre de près l'état de l'hydratation.
- Rester à l'affût des signes et des symptômes d'anaphylaxie, tels que le rash, le prurit, l'œdème laryngé

et la respiration sifflante. En présence de l'une de ces manifestations, cesser le traitement et prévenir immédiatement le médecin ou un autre professionnel de la santé. Garder de l'adrénaline, un antihistaminique et du matériel de réanimation à portée de main pour parer à toute réaction anaphylactique.

Xérostomie: Suivre de près les symptômes de xérostomie (sécheresse et douleurs buccales) à intervalles réguliers durant le traitement.

Tests de laboratoire: L'amifostine peut entraîner l'hypocalcémie; noter les concentrations sériques de calcium avant le traitement et à intervalles réguliers pendant toute sa durée. Il peut s'avérer nécessaire d'administrer des suppléments de calcium.

DIAGNOSTICS INFIRMIERS POSSIBLES

- Risque d'accident (Indications).
- Connaissances insuffisantes sur le traitement médicamenteux (Enseignement au patient et à ses proches).

INTERVENTIONS INFIRMIÈRES

Perfusion intermittente: Reconstituer la poudre avec 9,7 mL d'une solution stérile de NaCl 0,9 %. Diluer avec une quantité supplémentaire de solution de NaCl 0,9 % pour obtenir une concentration se situant entre 5 et 40 mg/mL. Ne pas administrer une solution qui a changé de couleur ou qui contient des particules. La solution est stable pendant 6 heures à la température ambiante ou jusqu'à 24 heures au réfrigérateur. Consulter les directives de chaque fabricant avant de reconstituer la préparation.

Vitesse d'administration: *Prévention de la toxicité rénale* – Administrer la perfusion en 15 minutes, dans les 30 minutes qui précèdent la chimiothérapie. Des perfusions de plus longue durée semblent être moins bien tolérées. *Xérostomie* – Administrer la perfusion en 3 minutes, dans les 15 à 30 minutes qui précèdent la radiothérapie.

Compatibilité (tubulure en Y): amikacine ■ aminophylline ■ ampicilline ■ ampicilline/sulbactam ■ aztréonam ■ bléomycine ■ bumétanide ■ buprénorphine ■ butorphanol ■ calcium, gluconate de ■ carboplatine ■ carmustine ■ céfazoline ■ céfonicide ■ céfotaxime ■ céfotétane ■ céfoxitine ■ ceftazidime ■ ceftizoxime ■ ceftriaxone ■ céfuroxime ■ cimétidine ■ ciprofloxacine ■ clindamycine ■ cyclophosphamide ■ cytarabine ■ dacarbazine ■ dactinomycine ■ daunorubicine ■ dexaméthasone ■ diphenhydramine ■ dobutamine ■ dopamine ■ doxorubicine ■ doxycycline ■ dropéridol ■ énalaprilate ■ étoposide ■ famotidine ■ floxuridine ■ fluconazole ■ fludarabine ■ fluorouracile ■ furosémide ■ gallium, nitrate de ■ gentamicine ■ halopéridol ■ héparine ■ hydrocortisone ■ hydromorphone ■ idarubicine ■ ifosfamide ■ imipénem/cilastatine ■ leucovorine ■ lorazépam ■ magnésium, sulfate de ■ mannitol ■ méchloréthamine ■ mépéridine ■ mesna ■ méthotrexate ■ méthylprednisolone ■ métoclopramide ■ métronidazole ■ mezlocilline ■ mitomycine ■ mitoxantrone ■ morphine ■ nalbuphine ■ nétilmicine ■ ondansétron ■ pipéracilline ■ plicamycine ■ potassium, chlorure de ■ prométhazine ■ ranitidine ■ sodium, bicarbonate de ■ streptozocine ■ téniposide ■ thiotépa ■ ticarcilline ■ ticarcilline/clavulanate ■ tobramycine ■ triméthoprime/sulfaméthoxazole ■ trimétrexate ■ vancomycine ■ vinblastine ■ vincristine ■ zidovudine.

Incompatibilité (tubulure en Y): amphotéricine B ■ céfopérazone ■ cisplatine ■ miconazole ■ minocycline ■ prochlorpérazine.

Incompatibilité en addition au soluté: Ne pas mélanger à d'autres solutions ou médicaments.

ENSEIGNEMENT AU PATIENT ET À SES PROCHES

- Expliquer au patient le but de la perfusion de l'amifostine.
- Informer le patient que l'amifostine peut entraîner les effets suivants: hypotension, nausées, vomissements, bouffées vasomotrices, frissons, étourdissements, somnolence, hoquets et éternuements.

VÉRIFICATION DE L'EFFICACITÉ THÉRAPEUTIQUE

L'efficacité du traitement peut être démontrée par: la prévention de la toxicité rénale associée à une administration répétée de cisplatine ■ la diminution de la toxicité hématologique causée par le cyclophosphamide ou par des antinéoplasiques à base de platine ■ la diminution de la sécheresse de la bouche (xérostomie) induite par la radiothérapie administrée contre le cancer du cou et de la tête. ✳

AMIKACINE,
Voir Aminosides

AMILORIDE,
voir Diurétiques (épargneurs de potassium)

AMINOPHYLLINE,
voir Bronchodilatateurs (xanthines)

AMINOSIDES

amikacine
Amikin

gentamicine†
Garamycin, Gentamicine, Septotal

néomycine

streptomycine
Streptomycine

tobramycine†
Nebcin, TOBI, Tobrex

CLASSIFICATION:
Antibiotiques (aminosides)

Grossesse – catégories C (amikacine, gentamicine, tobramycine) et D (streptomycine)

† Pour l'usage ophtalmique, voir l'annexe N.

INDICATIONS

Amikacine, gentamicine et tobramycine: Traitement des infections suivantes dues aux bactéries sensibles: septicémie, infections urinaires, infections des voies respiratoires, infections des os et des tissus mous, y compris la péritonite et les brûlures, et des infections dues aux staphylocoques, lorsque les pénicillines ou les autres médicaments moins toxiques sont contre-indiqués ▪ **Streptomycine**: En association avec d'autres agents pour traiter la tuberculose ▪ En association avec d'autres agents pour traiter la tularémie, la peste et la brucellose ▪ **Néomycine par voie topique en association avec d'autres agents**: Traitement des infections dermatologiques et traitement prophylactique des brûlures, greffes de peau et autres lésions cutanées ▪ **Tobramycine par inhalation**: Traitement de la fibrose kystique compliquée par des infections pulmonaires chroniques imputables à *Pseudomonas æruginosa* ▪ **Préparation topique et ophtalmique de gentamicine et de tobramycine**: Traitement des infections localisées dues à des microorganismes sensibles ▪ **Gentamicine par voie IM, IV**: Agent administré dans le cadre du traitement prophylactique de l'endocardite bactérienne (voir l'annexe M). **Usages non approuvés: Amikacine, streptomycine**: En association avec d'autres agents pour traiter les infections complexes dues à *Mycobacterium avium.*

MÉCANISME D'ACTION

Inhibition de la synthèse des protéines bactériennes au niveau de la sous-unité 30S du ribosome. ***Effets thérapeutiques:*** Effet bactéricide. **Spectre d'action**: La plupart des aminosides exercent un effet contre: *P. æruginosa* ▪ *Klebsiella* ▪ *Escherichia coli* ▪ *Proteus* ▪ *Providencia* ▪ *Serratia* ▪ *Acinetobacter* ▪ *Enterobacter* ▪ *Salmonella* ▪ *Citrobacter* ▪ les staphylocoques ▪ Traitement des infections à entérocoques, en association avec une pénicilline ou la vancomycine ▪ La streptomycine et l'amikacine sont également actives contre *Mycobacterium.*

PHARMACOCINÉTIQUE

Absorption: Bonne (IM); complète (IV); faible (inhalation).

Distribution: Les aminosides se répartissent dans tous les liquides extracellulaires; ils traversent la barrière placentaire et se retrouvent en petites quantités dans le lait maternel. La pénétration dans le liquide céphalorachidien est faible.

Métabolisme et excrétion: Excrétion majoritairement rénale (> 90 %).

Demi-vie: De 2 à 4 heures (prolongée en cas d'insuffisance rénale).

Profil temps-action (concentrations sanguines†)

	DÉBUT D'ACTION	PIC	DURÉE
IM	rapide	30 – 90 min	inconnue
IV	rapide	15 – 30 min‡	inconnue

† Pour tous les aminosides administrés par voie parentérale.
‡ Le pic après distribution se produit 30 minutes après la fin d'une perfusion de 30 minutes et 15 minutes après la fin d'une perfusion de 1 heure.

CONTRE-INDICATIONS, PRÉCAUTIONS ET MISES EN GARDE

Contre-indications: Hypersensibilité ▪ Intolérance aux bisulfites (la plupart des produits parentéraux contiennent ces substances; leur administration devrait être évitée chez ce type de patients) ▪ **PÉD.**: Ne pas administrer aux nouveau-nés les préparations renfermant de l'alcool benzylique ▪ Risque de réactions d'hypersensibilité croisée avec les autres aminosides ▪ **OBST.**: Risque de surdité congénitale ▪ *Streptomycine* – Antécédents d'effets ototoxiques.

Précautions et mises en garde: Insuffisance rénale (des adaptations posologiques sont nécessaires; le suivi des concentrations sanguines est utile pour prévenir l'ototoxicité et la néphrotoxicité) ▪ Troubles auditifs ▪ **GÉR.**: Risque accru de toxicités otique et rénale en raison de l'insuffisance rénale liée au vieillissement ▪ Maladies neuromusculaires, telle la myasthénie grave ▪ Patients obèses (la dose doit être calculée selon le poids corporel idéal) ▪ **PÉD.**: Enfants prématurés et nouveau-nés (risque accru de blocage neuromusculaire; difficulté à

A

évaluer les fonctions auditive et vestibulaire; fonction rénale n'ayant pas atteint la pleine maturité) ■ **ALLAITEMENT**: L'innocuité du médicament n'a pas été établie.

RÉACTIONS INDÉSIRABLES ET EFFETS SECONDAIRES

ORLO: ototoxicité (vestibulaire et cochléaire).

Resp.: bronchospasme (administration en inhalation).

GU: néphrotoxicité.

HÉ: hypomagnésémie.

Loc.: paralysie musculaire (à des doses élevées administrées par voie parentérale).

Divers: altération de la voix (administration en inhalation), réactions d'hypersensibilité.

INTERACTIONS

Médicament-médicament: Risque de paralysie respiratoire après inhalation d'**anesthésiques,** administration de **bloqueurs neuromusculaires** ou injection de **toxine botulinique** ■ Risque accru de néphrotoxicité et d'ototoxicité lors de l'administration concomitante de **diurétiques de l'anse** et d'**acide éthacrinique** ■ L'administration d'autres **médicaments néphrotoxiques** (comme l'**amphotéricine B**, la **cisplatine**, la **cyclosporine**, la **vancomycine**) peut augmenter le risque de toxicité rénale.

VOIES D'ADMINISTRATION ET POSOLOGIE

Amikacine

- **IM, IV (adultes et enfants)**: 5 mg/kg, toutes les 8 heures, ou 7,5 mg/kg, toutes les 12 heures. *Posologie uniquotidienne* (usage non approuvé) – de 15 à 20 mg/kg, toutes les 24 heures.
- **IM, IV (nourrissons)**: 5 mg/kg, toutes les 8 heures, ou 7,5 mg/kg, toutes les 12 heures.
- **IM, IV (nouveau-nés)**: 5 mg/kg, toutes les 8 heures, ou 7,5 mg/kg, toutes les 12 heures. *Prématurés* – 7,5 mg/kg, toutes les 12 heures.
- ***INSUFFISANCE RÉNALE***

  IM, IV (ADULTES): 7,5 mg/kg; LES DOSES ET LES INTERVALLES ULTÉRIEURS SONT DÉTERMINÉS D'APRÈS L'ÉVALUATION DE LA FONCTION RÉNALE ET DES CONCENTRATIONS SANGUINES.

Gentamicine

On utilise de nombreux régimes thérapeutiques; la plupart nécessitent des adaptations posologiques d'après l'évaluation de la fonction rénale et des concentrations sanguines. Pour le traitement prophylactique de l'endocardite bactérienne, voir l'annexe M.

- **IM, IV (adultes)**: De 1 à 2 mg/kg, toutes les 8 heures (jusqu'à 5 mg/kg/jour en 3 doses fractionnées). *Posologie uniquotidienne* (usage non approuvé) – de 5 à 7 mg/kg, toutes les 24 heures.
- **IM, IV (enfants)**: De 2 à 2,5 mg/kg, toutes les 8 heures.
- **IM, IV (nourrissons et nouveau-nés > 1 semaine)**: 2,5 mg/kg, toutes les 8 à 12 heures.
- **IM, IV (nourrissons et nouveau-nés ≤ 1 semaine)**: 2,5 mg/kg, toutes les 12 heures.
- **IM, IV (nouveau-nés prématurés)**: 2,5 mg/kg, toutes les 18 à 24 heures.
- ***INSUFFISANCE RÉNALE***

  IM, IV (ADULTES): DOSE INITIALE DE 1 À 1,7 mg/kg; LES DOSES ET LES INTERVALLES ULTÉRIEURS SONT DÉTERMINÉS D'APRÈS L'ÉVALUATION DE LA FONCTION RÉNALE ET DES CONCENTRATIONS SANGUINES.
- **Usage topique (adultes et enfants)**: Appliquer la crème ou l'onguent 3 ou 4 fois par jour.

Néomycine

- **Usage topique (adultes et enfants)**: Appliquer la préparation topique de 1 à 5 fois par jour.

Streptomycine

- **IM (adultes)**: *Tuberculose* – dose initiale: 1 g/jour ou 15 mg/kg/jour; réduire à 1 g ou 25 mg/kg/jour, 2 ou 3 fois par semaine dès que l'état clinique du patient le permet, une fois que la maladie est maîtrisée. *Personnes âgées* – 10 mg/kg/jour; ne pas dépasser 750 mg par jour. *Autres infections* – de 1 à 4 g par jour.
- **IM (enfants)**: De 20 à 40 mg/kg/jour (ne pas dépasser 1 g/jour).
- ***INSUFFISANCE RÉNALE***

  IM (ADULTES): DOSE INITIALE DE 1 g; LES DOSES ULTÉRIEURES SONT DÉTERMINÉES D'APRÈS L'ÉVALUATION DE LA FONCTION RÉNALE ET DES CONCENTRATIONS SANGUINES.

Tobramycine

On utilise de nombreux régimes thérapeutiques; la plupart nécessitent des adaptations posologiques d'après l'évaluation de la fonction rénale et des concentrations sanguines.

- **IM, IV (adultes)**: De 1 à 2 mg/kg, toutes les 8 heures (jusqu'à 10 mg/kg/jour chez les patients souffrant de fibrose kystique). *Infections mettant la vie du patient en danger* – jusqu'à 5 mg/kg/jour en 3 ou 4 doses fractionnées, toutes les 6 ou 8 heures. *Posologie uniquotidienne* (usage non approuvé) – de 5 à 7 mg/kg, toutes les 24 heures.
- **IM, IV (enfants et nourrissons plus âgés)**: De 6 à 7,5 mg/kg/jour en 3 ou 4 doses fractionnées, toutes les 6 ou 8 heures, jusqu'à concurrence de 10 mg/kg/jour, chez les patients souffrant de fibrose kystique (on

utilise divers intervalles posologiques: on peut administrer les doses toutes les 4 heures ainsi que toutes les 24 heures, selon l'état clinique du patient).

- **IM, IV (nourrissons < 1 semaine):** Jusqu'à 4 mg/kg/jour en 2 doses fractionnées, toutes les 12 heures.
- ***INSUFFISANCE RÉNALE***
  IM, IV (ADULTES): DOSE INITIALE DE 1 À 1,5 mg/kg; LES DOSES ULTÉRIEURES SONT DÉTERMINÉES D'APRÈS L'ÉVALUATION DE LA FONCTION RÉNALE ET DES CONCENTRATIONS SANGUINES.
- **Inhalation (adultes et enfants > 6 ans):** 300 mg, 2 fois par jour, pendant 28 jours; prévoir une période de 28 jours sans médication, puis recommencer un nouveau cycle de 28 jours.

PRÉSENTATION

- **Amikacine**
  Solution pour injection: 250 mg/mL[Pr], en fioles de 2 mL.
- **Gentamicine (version générique disponible)**
  Solution pour injection: 10 mg/mL[Pr], en fioles de 2 mL; 40 mg/mL[Pr], en fioles de 2 et de 20 mL ■ **Solution prémélangée pour injection:** 60 mg/50 mL[Pr], 80 mg/50 mL[Pr], 80 mg/100 mL[Pr], 100 mg/100 mL[Pr], 120 mg/100 mL[Pr] ■ **Crème topique:** 0,1 %[Pr] ■ **Onguent topique:** 0,1 %[Pr] ■ **Gouttes ophtalmiques:** 0,3 %[Pr] ■ **Pommade ophtalmique:** 0,3 %[Pr] ■ **Gouttes otiques:** 0,3 %[Pr] ■ **Billes de polyméthylméthacrylate pour implantation chirurgicale (Septotal):** 4,5 mg/bille (chaînes de 10, 30 ou 60 billes).
- **Néomycine**
  Ce médicament seul n'est pas commercialisé au Canada ■ **En association avec:** autres antibiotiques topiques ou corticostéroïdes topiques pour traiter les infections de la peau, des oreilles et des yeux.
- **Streptomycine**
  Solution pour injection: 1 g[Pr].
- **Tobramycine (version générique disponible)**
  Solution pour injection: 10 mg/mL[Pr], en fioles de 2 mL, 40 mg/mL[Pr], en fioles de 2 mL et de 1,2 g[Pr] ■ **Solution pour nébuliseur:** 300 mg/5 mL[Pr], en ampoules de 5 mL ■ **Solution ophtalmique:** 0,3 %[Pr] ■ **Onguent ophtalmique:** 0,3 %[Pr].

SOINS INFIRMIERS

ÉVALUATION DE LA SITUATION

- Au début du traitement et pendant toute sa durée, suivre de près les signes suivants d'infection: altération des signes vitaux, aspect de la plaie, des crachats, de l'urine et des selles, accroissement du nombre de leucocytes.
- Prélever des échantillons pour les cultures et les antibiogrammes avant le début du traitement. La première dose peut être administrée avant que les résultats soient connus.
- Mesurer par audiogramme la fonction auditive avant l'administration initiale et tout au long du traitement. La perte de l'ouïe se situe habituellement au niveau des sons à haute fréquence. Un diagnostic et une intervention rapides sont essentiels pour prévenir la surdité permanente. Rester à l'affût des symptômes suivants de dysfonctionnement vestibulaire: vertiges, ataxie, nausées, vomissements. Ce dysfonctionnement de la huitième paire de nerfs crâniens est associé à la persistance de concentrations élevées d'aminosides. On devrait donc arrêter le traitement en présence d'acouphènes ou d'une perte auditive subjective.
- Effectuer le bilan quotidien des ingesta et des excreta et peser le patient tous les jours pour évaluer son hydratation et sa fonction rénale.
- Observer le patient à la recherche des signes suivants de surinfection: fièvre, infection des voies respiratoires supérieures, démangeaisons ou pertes vaginales, malaise accru, diarrhée. Signaler ces réactions au médecin ou à un autre professionnel de la santé.

Tests de laboratoire:

- Suivre de près la fonction rénale en notant les résultats des analyses d'urine, la densité de l'urine, les concentrations sériques d'urée et de créatinine ainsi que la clairance de la créatinine, avant l'administration initiale du médicament et tout au long du traitement.
- Les aminosides peuvent entraîner une élévation des concentrations d'urée, d'AST, d'ALT, de phosphatase alcaline sérique, de bilirubine, de créatinine et de LDH.
- Les aminosides peuvent diminuer les concentrations sériques de calcium, de magnésium, de sodium et de potassium.

TOXICITÉ ET SURDOSAGE: Noter les concentrations sériques de médicament à intervalles réguliers pendant toute la durée du traitement. Pour interpréter correctement les résultats, il est important de bien choisir le moment où l'on examine les concentrations sériques. Pour déterminer les pics, prélever un échantillon de sang 1 heure après l'injection par voie IM ou 30 minutes après la fin d'une perfusion IV de 30 minutes. Pour déterminer les creux, prélever l'échantillon juste avant l'administration de la dose suivante. Les pics acceptables pour l'**amikacine** ne devraient pas dépasser 35 µg/mL; les

A

creux ne devraient pas dépasser 5 µg/mL. Les pics acceptables pour la **gentamicine** et la **tobramycine** ne devraient pas dépasser de 10 à 12 µg/mL; les creux ne devraient pas dépasser de 1 à 2 µg/mL. *Ces valeurs de pics et de creux ne s'appliquent pas lorsqu'on utilise une posologie uniquotidienne.* Les pics acceptables pour la **streptomycine** ne devraient pas dépasser 25 µg/mL; les creux ne devraient pas dépasser 5 µg/mL.

DIAGNOSTICS INFIRMIERS POSSIBLES

- Risque d'infection (Indications).
- Trouble de la perception sensorielle auditive (Effets secondaires).
- Connaissances insuffisantes sur le traitement médicamenteux (Enseignement au patient et à ses proches).

INTERVENTIONS INFIRMIÈRES

- Sauf en cas de contre-indication, assurer une bonne hydratation (de 1 500 à 2 000 mL de liquides par jour) pendant toute la durée du traitement.

IM: Injecter profondément dans une masse musculaire bien développée. Assurer la rotation des points de ponction.

IV: LES AMINOSIDES SONT INCOMPATIBLES AVEC LES PÉNICILLINES ET LES CÉPHALOSPORINES. IL FAUT DONC RINCER LA TUBULURE ENTRE L'ADMINISTRATION DES DEUX MÉDICAMENTS.

Amikacine

Perfusion intermittente: Diluer chaque dose d'amikacine dans 100 à 250 mL de solution de D5%E, de NaCl 0,9 %, de D5%/NaCl 0,9 %, de D5%/NaCl 0,45 % ou de lactate de Ringer. La solution peut être jaune pâle sans qu'elle perde de son efficacité. Elle est stable pendant 24 heures à la température ambiante. Consulter les directives de chaque fabricant avant de reconstituer la préparation.

Vitesse d'administration: Administrer en perfusion pendant 30 à 60 minutes (de 1 à 2 heures dans le cas des nourrissons).

Associations incompatibles dans la même seringue: héparine.

Compatibilité (tubulure en Y): acyclovir ■ amifostine ■ amiodarone ■ aztréonam ■ cyclophosphamide ■ dexaméthasone ■ diltiazem ■ énalaprilate ■ esmolol ■ filgrastim ■ fluconazole ■ fludarabine ■ foscarnet ■ furosémide ■ granisétron ■ idarubicine ■ labétalol ■ lorazépam ■ magnésium ■ melphalan ■ midazolam ■ morphine ■ ondansétron ■ paclitaxel ■ perphénazine ■ sargramostim ■ téniposide ■ thiotépa ■ vinorelbine ■ warfarine ■ zidovudine.

Incompatibilité (tubulure en Y): allopurinol sodique ■ amidon ■ amphotéricine B ■ azythromycine ■ propofol.

Incompatibilité en addition au soluté: Le fabricant recommande de ne pas faire de mélanges.

Gentamicine

Perfusion intermittente: Diluer chaque dose de gentamicine dans 50 à 200 mL de solution de D5%E, de NaCl 0,9 % ou de lactate de Ringer. Le médicament est aussi présenté en solution pour injection prête à être administrée par une tubulure en Y. Ne pas utiliser la solution si elle a changé de couleur et si elle renferme un précipité. Consulter les directives de chaque fabricant avant de reconstituer la préparation.

Vitesse d'administration: Administrer lentement la perfusion pendant 30 à 60 minutes. Chez les enfants, le volume de diluant peut être réduit, mais devrait être suffisant pour faire durer la perfusion de 30 à 60 minutes.

Associations incompatibles dans la même seringue: ampicilline ■ héparine.

Compatibilité (tubulure en Y): acyclovir ■ amifostine ■ amiodarone ■ atracurium ■ aztréonam ■ ciprofloxacine ■ cyclophosphamide ■ cytarabine ■ diltiazem ■ énalaprilate ■ esmolol ■ famotidine ■ fluconazole ■ fludarabine ■ foscarnet ■ granisétron ■ hydromorphone ■ insuline ■ labétalol ■ lorazépam ■ magnésium ■ melphalan ■ mépéridine ■ méropénem ■ midazolam ■ morphine ■ multivitamines ■ ondansétron ■ paclitaxel ■ pancuronium ■ perphénazine ■ sargramostim ■ tacrolimus ■ téniposide ■ théophylline ■ thiotépa ■ tolazoline ■ vécuronium ■ vinorelbine ■ vitamines du complexe B avec C ■ zidovudine.

Incompatibilité (tubulure en Y): amidon ■ allopurinol ■ amphotéricine B ■ azithromycine ■ furosémide ■ héparine ■ idarubicine ■ indométhacine ■ warfarine.

Compatibilité en addition au soluté: atracurium ■ aztréonam ■ bléomycine ■ cimétidine ■ ciprofloxacine ■ métronidazole ■ ofloxacine ■ ranitidine.

Incompatibilité en addition au soluté: amphotéricine B ■ héparine.

Tobramycine

Perfusion intermittente: Diluer chaque dose de tobramycine dans 50 à 100 mL de D5%E, de D5%/NaCl 0,9 %, de NaCl 0,9 %, de solution de Ringer ou de solution de lactate de Ringer. Diluer dans un volume proportionnellement plus petit si on administre la tobramycine à des enfants. La solution est stable pendant 24 heures à la température ambiante et pendant 96 heures au réfrigérateur. Le médicament est aussi présenté en solution pour injection prête à être administrée par une tubulure en Y. Consulter les directives de chaque fabricant avant de reconstituer la préparation.

Vitesse d'administration: Perfuser lentement pendant 30 à 60 minutes chez les adultes et les enfants.

Associations incompatibles dans la même seringue: clindamycine ■ héparine.
Compatibilité (tubulure en Y): acyclovir ■ amifostine ■ amiodarone ■ aztréonam ■ ciprofloxacine ■ cyclophosphamide ■ diltiazem ■ énalaprilate ■ esmolol ■ filgrastim ■ fluconazole ■ fludarabine ■ foscarnet ■ furosémide ■ granisétron ■ hydromorphone ■ insuline ■ labétalol ■ magnésium, sulfate de ■ melphalan ■ méperidine ■ midazolam ■ morphine ■ perphénazine ■ tacrolimus ■ téniposide ■ thiotépa ■ tolazoline ■ vinorelbine ■ zidovudine.
Incompatibilité (tubulure en Y): amidon ■ amphotéricine B ■ azithromycine ■ héparine ■ indométhacine ■ propofol ■ sargramostim.
Incompatibilité en addition au soluté: Le fabricant recommande d'administrer le médicament séparément et de ne pas faire de mélanges.
Usage topique: Nettoyer la peau avant l'application. Porter des gants pendant l'application.

ENSEIGNEMENT AU PATIENT ET À SES PROCHES

- Conseiller au patient de signaler à un professionnel de la santé les signes d'hypersensibilité, les acouphènes, les vertiges, la surdité, le rash, les étourdissements ou les mictions difficiles.
- Sauf en cas de contre-indication, insister sur le fait qu'il est important de boire beaucoup de liquides.
- Expliquer au patient ayant des antécédents de cardiopathie rhumatismale ou ayant subi un remplacement valvulaire l'importance de la prophylaxie antimicrobienne avant une intervention dentaire ou médicale effractive.

Usage topique: Expliquer au patient qu'il doit nettoyer délicatement la peau affectée et l'assécher par tapotements. Il doit ensuite appliquer une mince couche de crème ou d'onguent et ne recouvrir d'un pansement occlusif que si un professionnel de la santé l'a recommandé. Le patient devrait examiner sa peau et informer un professionnel de la santé si une irritation se manifeste ou si l'infection s'aggrave.
Inhalation: Recommander au patient de faire une inhalation 2 fois par jour en espaçant, dans la mesure du possible, les doses d'environ 12 heures, mais jamais de moins de 6 heures. Il doit inhaler le médicament pendant 10 à 15 minutes, à l'aide du nébuliseur réutilisable PARI LC PLUS, muni d'un compresseur *DeVilbiss Pulmo-Aide*. Lui préciser qu'il ne doit pas mélanger l'agent avec la dornase alpha dans le nébuliseur. Conseiller au patient qui suit plusieurs traitements de prendre les autres médicaments en premier et la tobramycine en dernier. On peut réduire le bronchospasme induit par la tobramycine si elle est administrée après les bronchodilatateurs. Conseiller au patient de s'asseoir ou de se tenir debout pendant l'inhalation et de respirer normalement par la pièce buccale du nébuliseur. Un pince-nez pourrait aider le patient à respirer par la bouche.

VÉRIFICATION DE L'EFFICACITÉ THÉRAPEUTIQUE

L'efficacité du traitement peut être démontrée par: la résolution des signes et des symptômes d'infection; s'il n'y a pas d'amélioration dans les 3 à 5 jours suivant le début du traitement, il faudrait remettre de nouveaux prélèvements en culture ■ la prophylaxie de l'endocardite bactérienne. ✳

ALERTE CLINIQUE

AMIODARONE

Cordarone, Cordarone I.V., Gen-Amiodarone, Novo-Amiodarone, PMS-Amiodarone, Ratio-Amiodarone

CLASSIFICATION:
Antiarythmique (classe III)

Grossesse – catégorie D

INDICATIONS

Traitement de la fibrillation ventriculaire confirmée, pouvant mener à une issue fatale, à récidives fréquentes, et de la tachycardie ventriculaire avec instabilité hémodynamique chez les patients réfractaires à tout autre traitement. **Usages non approuvés**: Contrôle de la réponse ventriculaire dans les tachyarythmies supraventriculaires en phase aiguë, incluant la fibrillation auriculaire récente. Traitement de la fibrillation ventriculaire et de la tachycardie ventriculaire sans pouls dans le cadre des lignes directrices de la réanimation cardiorespiratoire avancée (ACLS) ou de la réanimation cardiorespiratoire avancée pédiatrique (PALS).

MÉCANISME D'ACTION

Prolongation du potentiel d'action et de la période réfractaire ■ Inhibition de la stimulation adrénergique ■ Ralentissement du rythme sinusal, allongement des intervalles PR et QT et diminution de la résistance vasculaire périphérique (vasodilatation). ***Effets thérapeutiques:*** Suppression des arythmies.

PHARMACOCINÉTIQUE

Absorption: Complète (IV); de 35 à 65 % (PO).
Distribution: Le médicament se répartit et s'accumule lentement dans la plupart des tissus. Il atteint des

A

concentrations élevées dans les tissus adipeux, les muscles, le foie, les poumons et la rate. Il traverse la barrière placentaire et passe dans le lait maternel.

Liaison aux protéines: 96 %.

Métabolisme et excrétion: Métabolisme hépatique, excrétion dans la bile. L'excrétion rénale est minime. Un métabolite exerce une activité antiarythmique.

Demi-vie: De 13 à 107 jours.

Profil temps-action
(suppression des arythmies ventriculaires)

	DÉBUT D'ACTION	PIC	DURÉE
PO	2 - 3 jours (jusqu'à 2 - 3 mois)	3 - 7 h	plusieurs semaines - mois
IV	2 h	3 - 7 h	inconnue

CONTRE-INDICATIONS, PRÉCAUTIONS ET MISES EN GARDE

Contre-indications: Dysfonctionnement marqué du nœud sinusal ■ Bloc AV du 2e et du 3e degré ■ Bradycardie (en l'absence d'un stimulateur cardiaque, le médicament a déjà provoqué des syncopes) ■ Choc cardiogénique ■ Hypersensibilité ■ **PÉD.:** L'amiodarone injectable contenant de l'alcool benzylique comme agent de conservation ne devrait pas être utilisé chez le nouveau-né (< 1 mois).

Précautions et mises en garde: Antécédents d'insuffisance cardiaque ■ Troubles thyroïdiens ■ Maladie pulmonaire ou hépatique grave ■ **PÉD.:** L'innocuité du médicament n'a pas été établie ■ **OBST.:** Grossesse et allaitement ■ Risque d'allongement de l'intervalle QTc pouvant se manifester par une torsade de pointes.

RÉACTIONS INDÉSIRABLES ET EFFETS SECONDAIRES

SNC: troubles cognitifs, troubles de la vigilance, étourdissements, fatigue, malaise, céphalées, insomnie.

ORLO: microdépôts cornéens, altération de l'odorat, xérophtalmie, névrite optique et neuropathie oculaire, photophobie.

Resp.: SYNDROME DE DÉTRESSE RESPIRATOIRE, FIBROSE PULMONAIRE.

CV: INSUFFISANCE CARDIAQUE CONGESTIVE, EXACERBATION DES ARYTHMIES, bradycardie, hypotension.

GI: ALTÉRATION DE LA FONCTION HÉPATIQUE, anorexie, constipation, nausées, vomissements, douleurs abdominales, altération du goût.

GU: baisse de la libido, épididymite.

Tég.: NÉCROLYSE ÉPIDERMIQUE TOXIQUE, photosensibilité, coloration bleue de la peau.

End.: hypothyroïdie, hyperthyroïdie.

SN: ataxie, mouvements involontaires, paresthésie, neuropathie périphérique, perte de coordination, tremblements.

INTERACTIONS

Médicament-médicament: Les **fluoroquinolones,** les **macrolides** et les **antifongiques azoles,** administrés en concomitance, peuvent accroître le risque d'allongement de l'intervalle QT_c ■ L'amiodarone élève les concentrations sanguines de **digoxine** et peut entraîner une toxicité (diminuer la dose de digoxine de 50 %) ■ L'amiodarone élève les concentrations sanguines des autres **antiarythmiques de classe I** (**quinidine**, **procaïnamide**, **lidocaïne** ou **flécaïnide**) et peut entraîner une toxicité (diminuer la dose des autres agents de 30 à 50 %) ■ L'amiodarone élève les concentrations de **cyclosporine**, de **dextrométhorphane**, de **méthotrexate**, de **phénytoïne** et de **théophylline** ■ La **phénytoïne** diminue les concentrations sanguines d'amiodarone ■ L'amiodarone intensifie l'activité de la **warfarine** (diminuer la dose de la warfarine de 33 à 50 %) ■ Lors de l'administration concomitante de **bêtabloquants** ou de **bloqueurs des canaux calciques**, le risque de bradycardie, d'arrêt sinusal ou de bloc AV est accru ■ La **cholestyramine** peut diminuer les concentrations sanguines d'amiodarone ■ La **cimétidine** et le **ritonavir** élèvent les concentrations sanguines d'amiodarone ■ Le risque de dépression myocardique est accru lors de l'administration d'**anesthésiques par inhalation (halogénés)**.

Médicament-aliments: Le **jus de pamplemousse** inhibe la biotransformation de l'amiodarone administrée par voie orale dans la muqueuse intestinale, ce qui provoque l'élévation des taux plasmatiques pouvant entraîner des effets toxiques. Éviter la consommation pendant le traitement par l'amiodarone.

Médicament-produits naturels: Le **millepertuis** est un inducteur des enzymes qui métabolisent l'amiodarone, d'où le risque de diminution de ses concentrations sériques et de son efficacité; éviter la consommation concomitante.

VOIES D'ADMINISTRATION ET POSOLOGIE

Arythmies ventriculaires

- **PO (adultes):** De 800 à 1 600 mg/jour en 1 ou 2 doses, pendant 1 à 3 semaines; puis, de 600 à 800 mg/jour en 1 ou 2 doses, pendant 1 mois, et, enfin, de 200 à 400 mg/jour (parfois 600 mg) comme dose d'entretien.
- **IV (adultes):** Perfusion de 150 mg en 10 minutes, suivie de 360 mg pendant les 6 heures suivantes et, ensuite, de 540 mg pendant les 18 heures suivantes. Continuer la perfusion à un débit de 0,5 mg/min

jusqu'à ce que l'on puisse amorcer le traitement par voie orale. En cas d'un nouvel épisode d'arythmie, administrer une faible dose de 150 mg en perfusion pendant 10 minutes; on peut, cependant, accélérer la vitesse de la perfusion d'entretien. *Passage de la voie IV à la voie orale* - si la perfusion IV a été administrée pendant moins de 1 semaine, la dose initiale devrait être de 800 à 1 600 mg/jour; si elle a été administrée pendant 1 à 3 semaines, la dose initiale devrait être de 600 à 800 mg/jour; si elle a duré plus de 3 semaines, la dose initiale devrait être de 400 mg/jour.

Fibrillation ventriculaire/tachycardie ventriculaire sans pouls

- **IV (adultes)**: 300 mg par bolus IV rapide (dilué dans 20 mL de dextrose à 5 %).

PRÉSENTATION (version générique disponible)

Comprimés: 200 mg[Pr] ▪ **Solution pour injection**: 50 mg/mL, en ampoules de 3 mL[Pr].

SOINS INFIRMIERS

ÉVALUATION DE LA SITUATION

- SUIVRE DE PRÈS L'ÉCG au cours du traitement par voie IV et au début du traitement par voie orale. Mesurer le rythme et la fréquence cardiaques tout au long du traitement. Les anomalies électrocardiographiques suivantes peuvent se produire: allongement des intervalles PR, léger élargissement des espaces QRS, réduction de l'amplitude des ondes T avec élargissement et bifurcation, et apparition d'ondes U. L'allongement des intervalles QT peut traduire une aggravation de l'arythmie, il faut donc suivre de près ce signe pendant le traitement IV. Signaler sans délai au médecin l'apparition de la bradycardie ou l'aggravation des arythmies. Chez les patients recevant un traitement IV, il peut s'avérer nécessaire de ralentir la vitesse de perfusion, d'arrêter la perfusion ou d'installer temporairement un stimulateur cardiaque.
- OBSERVER L'APPARITION DES SIGNES SUIVANTS DE TOXICITÉ PULMONAIRE: râles et crépitations, diminution des bruits respiratoires, frottement pleural, fatigue, dyspnée, toux, douleur pleurale, fièvre. On recommande une radiographie pulmonaire et des tests de la fonction pulmonaire avant de commencer le traitement. Tout au long du traitement, effectuer une radiographie pulmonaire tous les 3 à 6 mois, afin de déceler la présence d'une atteinte interstitielle diffuse ou d'un infiltrat alvéolaire. Pour poser un diagnostic, on peut aussi recourir à la bronchoscopie ou à la scintigraphie au gallium. Ces symptômes sont habituellement réversibles après l'arrêt du traitement, mais quelques décès sont survenus.

IV:

- SUIVRE DE PRÈS LES SIGNES ET LES SYMPTÔMES DU SYNDROME DE DÉTRESSE RESPIRATOIRE pendant toute la durée du traitement. Signaler immédiatement au médecin tout signe de dyspnée ou de tachypnée ainsi que les râles et les crépitations. On peut observer sur la radiographie pulmonaire la présence d'infiltrats pulmonaires diffus bilatéraux.
- Mesurer fréquemment la pression artérielle. L'hypotension survient habituellement au cours des premières heures de traitement et elle est reliée à la vitesse de perfusion. En cas d'hypotension, ralentir la vitesse de perfusion.

PO:

- Demander au patient de se soumettre à des examens ophtalmiques avant le traitement et, à intervalles réguliers, pendant toute sa durée ou si les symptômes visuels suivants se manifestent: photophobie, halos autour des lumières, acuité visuelle réduite. Le traitement peut entraîner une cécité permanente.
- Surveiller les signes de dysfonctionnement de la thyroïde, particulièrement au cours du traitement initial. La léthargie, le gain de poids, l'œdème des mains, des pieds et de la région périorbitale ainsi qu'une peau pâle et froide évoquent l'hypothyroïdie. Dans ce cas, une diminution des doses ou l'arrêt du traitement et l'administration d'une hormonothérapie thyroïdienne substitutive peuvent s'imposer. La tachycardie, la perte de poids, la nervosité, la sensibilité à la chaleur, l'insomnie et une peau chaude, rouge et moite évoquent l'hyperthyroïdie; ces symptômes peuvent dicter l'arrêt du traitement et l'administration d'agents antithyroïdiens.

Tests de laboratoire:

- INTERPRÉTER LES RÉSULTATS DES TESTS DE LA FONCTION HÉPATIQUE ET THYROÏDIENNE, AVANT LE TRAITEMENT ET À INTERVALLES RÉGULIERS PENDANT TOUTE SA DURÉE. Les effets du médicament persistent longtemps après l'arrêt du traitement. Les altérations de la fonction thyroïdienne sont fréquentes, mais le dysfonctionnement thyroïdien clinique est rare.
- NOTER LES CONCENTRATIONS D'AST, D'ALT ET DE PHOSPHATASE ALCALINE, À INTERVALLES RÉGULIERS, TOUT AU LONG DU TRAITEMENT, PARTICULIÈREMENT CHEZ LES PATIENTS RECEVANT DES DOSES D'ENTRETIEN ÉLEVÉES. ON DEVRAIT RÉDUIRE LA DOSE SI LES RÉSULTATS DES TESTS DE LA FONCTION HÉPATIQUE

A

SONT 3 FOIS PLUS ÉLEVÉS QUE LA NORMALE OU SI UNE HÉPATOMÉGALIE SURVIENT. CHEZ LES PATIENTS PRÉSENTANT DES CONCENTRATIONS INITIALES ÉLEVÉES, ON DEVRAIT RÉDUIRE LA DOSE, SI LES RÉSULTATS DES TESTS DE LA FONCTION HÉPATIQUE ONT DOUBLÉ.

- L'amiodarone peut entraîner des élévations asymptomatiques du titre des anticorps antinucléaires.

DIAGNOSTICS INFIRMIERS POSSIBLES

- Débit cardiaque diminué (Indications).
- Échanges gazeux perturbés (Effets secondaires).
- Connaissances insuffisantes sur le traitement médicamenteux (Enseignement au patient et à ses proches).

INTERVENTIONS INFIRMIÈRES

Alerte clinique: LES MÉDICAMENTS INTRAVEINEUX VASOACTIFS PEUVENT ÊTRE DANGEREUX; ON A SIGNALÉ DES ERREURS AYANT PARFOIS MENÉ À UNE ISSUE FATALE LORS DE L'ADMINISTRATION DE L'AMIODARONE. AVANT L'ADMINISTRATION, IL EST RECOMMANDÉ DE DEMANDER À UN AUTRE PROFESSIONNEL DE LA SANTÉ DE VÉRIFIER L'ORDONNANCE D'ORIGINE, LE CALCUL DES DOSES ET LE RÉGLAGE DE LA POMPE VOLUMÉTRIQUE. PENDANT LE TRAITEMENT IV ET AU DÉBUT DU TRAITEMENT PAR VOIE ORALE, LES PATIENTS DOIVENT ÊTRE HOSPITALISÉS ET SUIVIS DE PRÈS. LE TRAITEMENT IV DEVRAIT ÊTRE ADMINISTRÉ SEULEMENT PAR DES MÉDECINS AYANT DE L'EXPÉRIENCE DANS LE TRAITEMENT DES ARYTHMIES QUI METTENT EN JEU LE PRONOSTIC VITAL.

- L'hypokaliémie et l'hypomagnésémie peuvent diminuer l'efficacité de l'amiodarone ou provoquer des arythmies additionnelles. Il faut donc les corriger avant le début du traitement.
- Aider le patient pendant qu'il se déplace afin de prévenir les chutes attribuables aux troubles neurologiques. La neurotoxicité (ataxie, faiblesse des muscles proximaux, picotements ou engourdissements au niveau des doigts ou des orteils, mouvements involontaires, tremblements) est courante lors du traitement initial, mais elle peut aussi survenir une semaine ou plusieurs mois après le début du traitement et persister pendant plus de 1 an après l'arrêt de la médication. Une réduction de la dose est donc recommandée.
- Suivre de près l'état du patient, surtout dans le cas du patient âgé, lors du passage de la voie IV à la voie orale.

PO: En présence d'intolérance gastro-intestinale, administrer le médicament avec des aliments ou en doses fractionnées.

IV:

- Administrer à l'aide d'une pompe volumétrique; la taille des gouttes peut être réduite, d'où le risque d'administration d'une dose insuffisante lorsqu'on emploie un appareil de perfusion à comptegouttes.
- Dans le cas des perfusions qui durent plus de 1 heure, on ne devrait pas dépasser une concentration de 2 mg/mL, à moins qu'on ne les administre par un cathéter veineux central.
- Utiliser un filtre durant la perfusion.
- Pour des perfusions qui durent plus de 2 heures, le médicament doit être conditionné dans des flacons de verre ou de polyoléfine pour prévenir l'adsorption. Toutefois, on doit utiliser une tubulure de polychlorure de vinyle (PVC) au cours de l'administration, car les recommandations concernant les concentrations et les vitesses de perfusion sont faites en fonction de ce type de tubulure.

Perfusion intermittente: La dose initiale recommandée de 1 050 mg doit être administrée au cours des 24 premières heures de traitement, selon le schéma posologique suivant:

- **Première étape**

  Ajouter 3 mL (150 mg) d'amiodarone à 100 mL de solution de D5%E pour obtenir une concentration de 1,5 mg/mL.

  Vitesse d'administration: Administrer rapidement en 10 minutes.
- **Deuxième étape**

  Ajouter 18 mL (900 mg) d'amiodarone à 500 mL de solution de D5%E pour obtenir une concentration de 1,8 mg/mL.

  Vitesse d'administration: Administrer lentement 360 mg pendant les 6 heures suivantes, à une vitesse de 1 mg/min.
- **Troisième étape**

  Administrer le reste de la solution destinée à la première étape de la perfusion.

  Vitesse d'administration: Administrer 540 mg pendant les 18 heures restantes, à une vitesse de 0,5 mg/min.

Perfusion continue: Après les 24 premières heures, on peut poursuivre la perfusion à une concentration de 1 à 6 mg/mL. Administrer les concentrations > 2 mg/mL par un cathéter veineux central. Consulter les directives de chaque fabricant avant de reconstituer la préparation.

Vitesse d'administration: Administrer à la vitesse de la perfusion d'entretien de 0,5 mg/min (720 mg/24 h). On peut accélérer la perfusion pour obtenir une suppression efficace des arythmies, mais on ne devrait pas dépasser 30 mg/min.

Perfusions d'appoint: En cas d'épisodes soudains de fibrillation ventriculaire ou de tachycardie ventriculaire s'accompagnant d'une instabilité hémodynamique, administrer 150 mg d'amiodarone dilués dans 100 mL d'une solution de D5%E.

Vitesse d'administration: Administrer pendant 10 minutes pour réduire l'hypotension.

Compatibilité (tubulure en Y): amikacine ▪ clindamycine ▪ dobutamine ▪ dopamine ▪ doxycycline ▪ érythromycine, lactobionate d' ▪ esmolol ▪ gentamicine ▪ insuline ▪ isoprotérénol ▪ labétalol ▪ lidocaïne ▪ métaraminol ▪ métronidazole ▪ midazolam ▪ morphine ▪ nitroglycérine ▪ noradrénaline ▪ pénicilline G potassique ▪ phentolamine ▪ phényléphrine ▪ potassium, chlorure de ▪ procaïnamide ▪ tobramycine ▪ vancomycine.

Incompatibilité (tubulure en Y): aminophylline ▪ céfamandole ▪ céfazoline ▪ héparine ▪ mezlocilline ▪ sodium, bicarbonate de.

Incompatibilité en addition au soluté: aminophylline ▪ céfamandole ▪ céfazoline ▪ héparine ▪ mezlocilline ▪ sodium, bicarbonate de.

ENSEIGNEMENT AU PATIENT ET À SES PROCHES

- Expliquer au patient qu'il doit respecter rigoureusement la posologie recommandée. S'il n'a pu prendre le médicament au moment habituel, il doit sauter cette dose. L'inciter à prévenir un professionnel de la santé s'il a sauté plus de 2 doses.
- Prévenir le patient qu'il doit éviter de boire du jus de pamplemousse durant le traitement.
- Informer le patient que les effets secondaires peuvent n'apparaître que plusieurs jours, semaines, voire années, après le début du traitement et qu'ils peuvent persister pendant plusieurs mois après l'arrêt de la médication.
- Montrer au patient comment mesurer son pouls. Lui conseiller de prendre son pouls tous les jours et de signaler à un professionnel de la santé toute anomalie.
- Expliquer au patient que des réactions de photosensibilité peuvent se produire s'il se tient près d'une fenêtre ensoleillée, s'il porte des vêtements trop légers ou s'il utilise un écran solaire qui ne le protège pas totalement. Lui recommander de porter des vêtements de protection et d'appliquer un écran solaire total pendant le traitement et jusqu'à 4 mois après l'arrêt de la médication. En cas de réaction de photosensibilité, une réduction de la dose peut s'avérer utile.
- Expliquer au patient que la coloration bleuâtre que peuvent prendre son visage, son cou et ses bras est un effet secondaire possible du médicament lors d'un traitement prolongé. Ces symptômes sont réversibles et disparaissent en l'espace de plusieurs mois. Lui conseiller de signaler ce symptôme à un professionnel de la santé.
- Recommander aux patients de sexe masculin de signaler à un professionnel de la santé tout signe d'épididymite (douleurs et œdème au niveau du scrotum). Dans ce cas, il peut s'avérer nécessaire de réduire la dose.
- Conseiller au patient d'informer le professionnel de la santé de son traitement médicamenteux avant de se soumettre à une intervention chirurgicale ou à un autre traitement.
- Expliquer au patient qu'il doit se soumettre à des examens médicaux réguliers, incluant les radiographies pulmonaires et les tests de la fonction pulmonaire, effectués tous les 3 à 6 mois, et à des examens ophtalmiques, 6 mois après le début du traitement et, tous les ans, par la suite.

VÉRIFICATION DE L'EFFICACITÉ THÉRAPEUTIQUE

L'efficacité du traitement peut être démontrée par: la suppression des arythmies ventriculaires qui mettent en danger la vie du patient. Les effets indésirables peuvent ne disparaître qu'au bout de 4 mois.

AMITRIPTYLINE

Apo-Amitriptyline, Elavil, Levate, Novo-Tryptin, PMS-Amitriptyline

CLASSIFICATION:

Antidépresseur (tricyclique)

Grossesse – catégorie C (risque durant le 3e trimestre; voir «Précautions et mises en garde»

INDICATIONS

Traitement de la dépression, souvent en association avec une psychothérapie. **Usages non approuvés:** Traitement des divers syndromes douloureux chroniques.

MÉCANISME D'ACTION

Potentialisation des effets de la sérotonine et de la noradrénaline au niveau du SNC ▪ L'amitriptyline est dotée de propriétés anticholinergiques importantes. ***Effets thérapeutiques:*** Effet antidépresseur.

A

PHARMACOCINÉTIQUE

Absorption: Bonne (PO).

Distribution: Répartition dans tout l'organisme.

Liaison aux protéines: 95 %.

Métabolisme et excrétion: Métabolisme majoritairement hépatique. Certains métabolites exercent des effets antidépresseurs. L'amitriptyline subit plusieurs cycles entérohépatiques et est sécrétée dans les sucs gastriques. Elle semble traverser la barrière placentaire et passer dans le lait maternel.

Demi-vie: De 10 à 50 heures.

Profil temps-action (effet antidépresseur)

	DÉBUT D'ACTION	PIC	DURÉE
PO	2 – 3 semaines (jusqu'à 30 jours)	2 – 6 semaines	plusieurs jours ou semaines

CONTRE-INDICATIONS, PRÉCAUTIONS ET MISES EN GARDE

Contre-indications: Hypersensibilité ■ Administration en association avec un IMAO (prévoir 14 jours entre l'arrêt de l'IMAO et le début de l'administration d'amitriptyline et vice versa) ■ Phase aiguë de rétablissement après un infarctus du myocarde.

Précautions et mises en garde: Suivre de près les idées suicidaires chez tous les patients recevant ce médicament ■ Troubles bipolaires (l'emploi d'antidépresseurs durant la phase dépressive d'un trouble bipolaire peut déclencher un épisode hypomaniaque ou maniaque) ■ Risque d'arythmies cardiaques transitoires chez les patients prenant en concomitance un médicament destiné au traitement des troubles thyroïdiens ou souffrant d'hyperthyroïdie ■ **GÉR.**: Risque accru de réactions indésirables ■ Maladie cardiovasculaire préexistante ■ Hyperplasie bénigne de la prostate (risque accru de rétention urinaire) ■ Antécédents de convulsions (le seuil de crise peut être abaissé) ■ Glaucome à angle fermé ■ **OBST.**: Il n'existe pas d'études appropriées chez la femme enceinte; n'administrer au cours de la grossesse que si les bienfaits éventuels pour la femme enceinte l'emportent sur les risques possibles auxquels est exposé le fœtus. Il y a des risques de complications après l'accouchement chez les nouveau-nés lorsque la mère a pris ce médicament durant le 3e trimestre ■ **ALLAITEMENT**: Risque de sédation chez le nourrisson ■ **PÉD.**: Administrer avec précautions et sous étroite surveillance. Usage déconseillé chez les enfants de moins de 12 ans (l'innocuité de l'agent n'a pas été établie).

RÉACTIONS INDÉSIRABLES ET EFFETS SECONDAIRES

SNC: léthargie, sédation.

ORLO: vision trouble, xérophtalmie, sécheresse de la bouche (xérostomie).

CV: ARYTHMIES, hypotension, modifications de l'ÉCG.

GI: constipation, hépatite, iléus paralytique.

GU: rétention urinaire.

Tég.: photosensibilité.

End.: modifications de la glycémie, gynécomastie.

Hémat.: dyscrasie sanguine.

Divers: gain d'appétit, gain de poids.

INTERACTIONS

Médicament-médicament: L'amitriptyline est métabolisée dans le foie par l'**enzyme 2D6 du cytochrome P450**, et ses effets peuvent être modifiés par les **médicaments qui sont aussi métabolisés par cette enzyme**, incluant d'autres **antidépresseurs**, les **phénothiazines**, la **carbamazépine**, les **antiarythmiques de classe 1C**, dont la **propafénone**, et le **flécaïnide**. Lors de l'administration concomitante de ces agents et de l'amitriptyline, il peut s'avérer nécessaire de réduire la dose de l'un ou l'autre de ces deux médicaments ou des deux à la fois ■ L'usage concomitant d'autres médicaments qui inhibent l'activité de cette enzyme, incluant la **cimétidine**, la **quinidine**, l'**amiodarone** et le **ritonavir**, peut accroître les effets de l'amitriptyline ■ L'amitriptyline peut provoquer l'hypotension, la tachycardie et des réactions qui peuvent être mortelles lors de l'administration concomitante d'**IMAO** (éviter l'administration conjointe; interrompre le traitement 2 semaines avant d'administrer l'amitriptyline) ■ Il faudrait éviter l'usage concomitant d'**antidépresseurs du type ISRS**, car ils peuvent entraîner une toxicité accrue (le traitement par la **fluoxétine** doit être interrompu 5 semaines avant de commencer l'administration de l'amitriptyline) ■ L'amitriptyline peut inhiber la réponse thérapeutique à la **guanéthidine** ■ L'usage concomitant d'amitriptyline et de **clonidine** peut provoquer une crise hypertensive; il faudrait donc éviter d'administrer ces deux agents en même temps ■ L'administration concomitante d'amitriptyline et de **lévodopa** peut retarder et diminuer l'absorption de cette dernière ou provoquer l'hypertension ■ Les concentrations sanguines du médicament et ses effets peuvent être diminués par les **rifamycines** (**rifampine**, **rifapentine** et **rifabutine**) ■ L'usage concomitant de **moxifloxacine** augmente le risque de réactions cardiovasculaires indésirables ■ Effet dépresseur additif sur le SNC, lors de l'usage concomitant d'autres **dépresseurs du système nerveux central**, incluant l'**alcool**, les **antihistaminiques**, la **clonidine**, les **opioïdes** et les **hypnosédatifs** ■ Les **barbituriques** peuvent modifier les concentrations sanguines de l'amitriptyline et ses effets ■ Les effets secondaires peuvent être additifs lors de l'administration concomitante d'autres **agents dotés de propriétés adrénergiques et anticholinergiques** ■ Les **phénothiazines** et les **contraceptifs oraux** augmentent les concentrations d'amitriptyline et peuvent entraîner une toxicité ■ L'amitriptyline peut potentialiser l'effet vasopresseur de la **noradrénaline** et augmenter les effets cardiovasculaires des **agents sympathomimétiques** ■ L'utilisation concomitante de **lithium** peut accroître le risque de neurotoxicité, en particulier chez les personnes âgées ■ L'utilisation concomitante de **lévothyroxine** peut augmenter les effets secondaires cardiovasculaires ■ La **nicotine** peut accélérer le métabolisme du médicament et en diminuer les effets.

Médicament-produits naturels: Le **millepertuis** peut diminuer les concentrations et l'efficacité de l'amitriptyline ■ La consommation concomitante de **kava**, de **valériane** ou de **camomille** peut intensifier l'effet dépresseur sur le SNC ■ Le **datura** et le **scopolia** augmentent les effets secondaires cholinergiques.

VOIES D'ADMINISTRATION ET POSOLOGIE

- **PO (adultes)**: 75 mg/jour en doses fractionnées; on peut augmenter cette dose jusqu'à 150 mg/jour *ou* de 50 à 100 mg, au coucher, dose qu'on peut augmenter par paliers de 25 à 50 mg, jusqu'à concurrence de 150 mg (chez les patients hospitalisés, on peut commencer le traitement par une dose de 100 mg/jour et l'augmenter jusqu'à une dose quotidienne totale de 300 mg).
- **PO (adolescents)**: Initialement, 10 mg, 3 fois par jour, et 20 mg, au coucher; puis augmenter la dose graduellement jusqu'à concurrence de 100 mg/jour en une seule prise, au coucher, ou en prises fractionnées.
- **PO (personnes âgées)**: Initialement, de 10 à 25 mg au coucher. Augmenter la posologie par paliers de 10 à 25 mg/jour, à intervalles de 1 semaine, jusqu'à concurrence de 150 mg/jour.

PRÉSENTATION

Comprimés: 10 mg[Pr], 25 mg[Pr], 50 mg[Pr], 75 mg[Pr] ■ **En association avec**: perphénazine: Apo-Peram[Pr], Etrafon[Pr], PMS-Levazine[Pr].

SOINS INFIRMIERS

ÉVALUATION DE LA SITUATION

- Mesurer la pression artérielle et le pouls avant l'administration du médicament et en début de traitement. Signaler au médecin ou à un autre professionnel de la santé les chutes de pression artérielle (de 10 à 20 mm Hg) ou l'élévation soudaine de la fréquence du pouls. LES PATIENTS RECEVANT DES DOSES ÉLEVÉES OU AYANT DES ANTÉCÉDENTS DE MALADIE CARDIOVASCULAIRE DEVRAIENT SE SOUMETTRE À UN ÉCG AVANT LE TRAITEMENT ET À INTERVALLES RÉGULIERS PENDANT TOUTE SA DURÉE.
- Les personnes âgées qui commencent un traitement par l'amitriptyline sont exposées à un risque plus élevé de chutes; amorcer le traitement avec une faible dose et suivre de près l'état du patient (faiblesse et sédation).

Dépression: Suivre de près l'état mental du patient et son affect. Rester à l'affût des tendances suicidaires, particulièrement au début du traitement. Limiter la quantité de médicament dont le patient peut disposer.

Douleur: Évaluer l'intensité, le type et le siège de la douleur à intervalles réguliers tout au long du traitement. Les effets du médicament peuvent ne se manifester qu'après plusieurs semaines.

Tests de laboratoire: Noter les résultats de la numération et la formule leucocytaire, les résultats des tests de la fonction hépatique et la glycémie avant le traitement et à intervalles réguliers pendant toute sa durée. Le médicament peut entraîner une élévation des concentrations de bilirubine sérique et de phosphatase alcaline ainsi qu'une aplasie médullaire. La glycémie peut être accrue ou réduite.

DIAGNOSTICS INFIRMIERS POSSIBLES

- Stratégies d'adaptation inefficaces (Indications).
- Risque d'accident (Effets secondaires).
- Connaissances insuffisantes sur le traitement médicamenteux (Enseignement au patient et à ses proches).

INTERVENTIONS INFIRMIÈRES

- NE PAS CONFONDRE ELAVIL (AMITRIPTYLINE) ET ORUVAIL (KÉTOPROPHÈNE).
- Les majorations des doses devraient s'effectuer au coucher en raison du risque de sédation. L'adaptation posologique est un processus lent, qui peut prendre plusieurs semaines ou mois. L'effet sédatif peut être apparent avant que l'effet antidépresseur ne puisse être observé.

PO: Administrer le médicament au moment des repas ou immédiatement après pour réduire l'irritation gastrique. On peut écraser les comprimés et les administrer avec des aliments ou des liquides.

ENSEIGNEMENT AU PATIENT ET À SES PROCHES

- Expliquer au patient qu'il doit respecter rigoureusement la posologie recommandée. S'il n'a pu prendre le médicament au moment habituel, il doit le prendre aussitôt que possible à moins que ce ne soit presque l'heure prévue pour la dose suivante. Si le patient prend le médicament 1 fois par jour, au coucher, il ne devrait pas prendre la dose manquée le lendemain matin en raison du risque d'effets secondaires. Prévenir le patient que les effets du médicament peuvent ne pas se manifester avant au moins 2 semaines. L'arrêt brusque du traitement peut provoquer des nausées, des vomissements, la diarrhée, des céphalées, des troubles du sommeil s'accompagnant de rêves saisissants et d'irritabilité.

- Prévenir le patient que l'amitriptyline peut parfois provoquer de la somnolence et rendre la vision trouble. Lui conseiller de ne pas conduire et d'éviter les activités qui exigent sa vigilance jusqu'à ce qu'on ait la certitude que le médicament n'entraîne pas ces effets chez lui.
- Prévenir le patient que l'hypotension orthostatique, la sédation et la confusion sont des effets courants de l'amitriptyline au cours de l'étape initiale du traitement, particulièrement chez les personnes âgées. Protéger le patient contre les chutes et lui recommander de changer lentement de position.
- Recommander au patient de ne pas boire d'alcool et de ne pas prendre d'autres médicaments dépresseurs du SNC pendant toute la durée du traitement et pendant les 3 à 7 jours qui suivent l'arrêt de la médication.
- Conseiller au patient de prévenir un professionnel de la santé en cas de rétention urinaire, de sécheresse de la bouche ou de constipation persistante. Lui expliquer que les bonbons ou la gomme à mâcher sans sucre peuvent diminuer la sécheresse de la bouche et qu'une consommation accrue de liquides et d'aliments riches en fibres peut prévenir la constipation. Si ces symptômes persistent, une réduction de la dose ou l'arrêt du traitement pourraient s'avérer nécessaires. Lui conseiller de consulter un professionnel de la santé si la sécheresse de la bouche persiste pendant plus de 2 semaines.
- Recommander au patient d'utiliser un écran solaire et des vêtements protecteurs afin de prévenir les réactions de photosensibilité.
- Inciter le patient à surveiller son alimentation, car le médicament peut lui donner plus d'appétit, ce qui risque d'entraîner un gain de poids indésirable.
- Conseiller à la patiente de prévenir un professionnel de la santé si elle pense être enceinte ou désire le devenir ou, encore, si elle allaite.
- Prévenir le patient qu'avant tout nouveau traitement ou avant une intervention chirurgicale, il doit informer le professionnel de la santé qu'il suit ce traitement médicamenteux. Il est possible qu'on lui recommande d'interrompre ce traitement avant une chirurgie.
- Informer le patient que le traitement de la dépression est habituellement long et qu'il devrait le prolonger pendant au moins 3 mois pour prévenir les rechutes. Insister sur l'importance d'un suivi régulier permettant de déterminer les bienfaits du traitement et de déceler les effets secondaires.

VÉRIFICATION DE L'EFFICACITÉ THÉRAPEUTIQUE

L'efficacité du traitement peut être démontrée par: un sentiment de mieux-être ▪ un regain d'intérêt pour l'entourage ▪ un gain d'appétit ▪ un regain d'énergie ▪ l'amélioration du sommeil ▪ la diminution des symptômes douloureux chroniques. Les pleins effets thérapeutiques pourraient ne se manifester que de 2 à 6 semaines après le début du traitement. ✳

AMLODIPINE

Norvasc

CLASSIFICATION:

Antihypertenseur, antiangineux (bloqueur des canaux calciques)

Grossesse – catégorie C

INDICATIONS

En monothérapie ou en association avec d'autres agents dans le traitement de l'hypertension et de l'angine chronique stable.

MÉCANISME D'ACTION

Inhibition du transport du calcium dans les cellules musculaires lisses vasculaires et myocardiques, entraînant une inhibition du couplage excitation-contraction et de la contraction qui suit. ***Effets thérapeutiques:*** Vasodilatation artérielle périphérique entraînant une chute de la pression artérielle ▪ Vasodilatation coronarienne se traduisant par une diminution de la fréquence et de la gravité des crises d'angine.

PHARMACOCINÉTIQUE

Absorption: Bonne (PO – de 64 à 90 %).

Distribution: Le médicament traverse probablement la barrière placentaire.

Liaison aux protéines: De 95 à 98 %.

Métabolisme et excrétion: Métabolisme hépatique. Excrétion majoritairement rénale sous forme de métabolites inactifs.

Demi-vie: De 30 à 50 heures (prolongée chez les patients âgés et les insuffisants hépatiques).

Profil temps-action (effets cardiovasculaires)

	Début d'action	Pic	Durée
PO	1-2 h	6-12 h	24 h

CONTRE-INDICATIONS, PRÉCAUTIONS ET MISES EN GARDE

Contre-indications: Hypersensibilité (risque de sensibilité croisée) ■ Pression artérielle systolique < 90 mm Hg.

Précautions et mises en garde: Insuffisance hépatique grave (réduire la dose) ■ **Gér.**: Sensibilité accrue aux effets hypotenseurs chez les personnes âgées; il est recommandé de réduire la dose initiale ■ Sténose aortique ■ Insuffisance cardiaque ■ **Obst., allaitement, Péd.**: L'innocuité de l'agent n'a pas été établie pendant la grossesse et l'allaitement ni chez les enfants.

RÉACTIONS INDÉSIRABLES ET EFFETS SECONDAIRES

SNC: céphalées, étourdissements, fatigue.

CV: œdème périphérique, tachycardie, hypotension, palpitations, hypotension orthostatique.

GI: hyperplasie gingivale, nausées.

Tég.: bouffées vasomotrices.

INTERACTIONS

Médicament-médicament: Une hypotension additive peut survenir lors de l'administration concomitante de **fentanyl**, d'autres **agents antihypertenseurs**, de **dérivés nitrés** et de **quinidine** ou d'une consommation excessive d'**alcool** ■ Risque de diminution des effets antihypertenseurs lors de l'usage concomitant d'**anti-inflammatoires non stéroïdiens.**

VOIES D'ADMINISTRATION ET POSOLOGIE

- **PO (adultes)**: *Dose initiale* – 5 mg, 1 fois par jour; augmenter la dose, selon la réponse au traitement et la tolérance du patient (jusqu'à 10 mg/jour).
- **PO (patients âgés ou insuffisants rénaux)**: *Dose initiale* – de 2,5 à 5 mg, 1 fois par jour; augmenter graduellement la dose, si besoin est, selon la réponse au traitement et la tolérance du patient (jusqu'à 10 mg, 1 fois par jour).
- **PO (enfants de 6 à 17 ans)**: De 2,5 à 5 mg, 1 fois par jour (dose maximale: 5 mg, 1 fois par jour).

Insuffisance hépatique

- **PO (ADULTES)**: *DOSE INITIALE* – 2,5 mg, 1 FOIS PAR JOUR; AUGMENTER LA DOSE GRADUELLEMENT, SELON LA RÉPONSE AU TRAITEMENT ET LA TOLÉRANCE DU PATIENT (JUSQU'À 10 mg, 1 FOIS PAR JOUR).

PRÉSENTATION

Comprimés: 5 mgPr, 10 mgPr ■ **En association avec**: atorvastatine (CaduetPr).

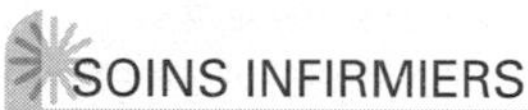

SOINS INFIRMIERS

ÉVALUATION DE LA SITUATION

- Mesurer la pression artérielle et le pouls avant le traitement, pendant la période d'adaptation posologique et à intervalles réguliers pendant toute la durée du traitement. Effectuer des ÉCG à intervalles réguliers au cours d'un traitement prolongé.
- Effectuer le bilan quotidien des ingesta et des excreta et peser le patient tous les jours. Rester à l'affût des signes d'insuffisance cardiaque (œdème périphérique, râles ou crépitations, dyspnée, gain de poids, turgescence de la veine jugulaire).

Angine: Déterminer le siège, la durée et l'intensité de la douleur angineuse ainsi que les facteurs qui la déclenchent.

Tests de laboratoire: Les concentrations totales de calcium sérique ne sont pas affectées par les bloqueurs des canaux calciques.

DIAGNOSTICS INFIRMIERS POSSIBLES

- Irrigation tissulaire inefficace (Indications).
- Douleur aiguë (Indications).
- Connaissances insuffisantes sur le traitement médicamenteux (Enseignement au patient et à ses proches).

INTERVENTIONS INFIRMIÈRES

- L'amlodipine peut être administrée sans égard aux repas.

ENSEIGNEMENT AU PATIENT ET À SES PROCHES

- Expliquer au patient qu'il doit respecter rigoureusement la posologie recommandée, même s'il se sent mieux. S'il n'a pu prendre le médicament au moment habituel, il doit le prendre aussitôt que possible à moins que ce ne soit presque l'heure prévue pour la dose suivante. Le prévenir qu'il ne doit jamais remplacer une dose manquée par une double dose. Le traitement peut être interrompu graduellement.

A

- Enseigner au patient comment prendre correctement son pouls. Lui conseiller de communiquer avec un professionnel de la santé si la fréquence cardiaque est < 50 bpm.
- Recommander au patient de changer lentement de position pour réduire le risque d'hypotension orthostatique.
- Prévenir le patient que l'amlodipine peut provoquer des étourdissements.
- Expliquer au patient qu'il est important de pratiquer une bonne hygiène buccale et de consulter fréquemment le dentiste pour faire nettoyer ses dents afin de prévenir la sensibilité et le saignement des gencives et une hyperplasie gingivale (hypertrophie des gencives).
- Expliquer au patient qu'il doit éviter de consommer de l'alcool et de prendre des médicaments en vente libre, particulièrement des médicaments contre le rhume, ou des produits naturels sans avoir consulté au préalable un professionnel de la santé.
- Recommander au patient de signaler à un professionnel de la santé les symptômes suivants: battements cardiaques irréguliers, dyspnée, œdème des mains et des pieds, étourdissements prononcés, nausées, constipation, hypotension ou céphalées graves ou persistantes.
- Conseiller au patient de porter des vêtements de protection et d'utiliser un écran solaire pour prévenir les réactions de photosensibilité.
- Conseiller au patient d'informer le professionnel de la santé des médicaments qu'il prend avant de se soumettre à une intervention chirurgicale ou à un nouveau traitement.

Angine:

- Recommander au patient qui suit un traitement en association avec un dérivé nitré ou un bêtabloquant de continuer à prendre les 2 médicaments selon la posologie recommandée, et d'utiliser la nitroglycérine sublinguale, au besoin, en cas de crises d'angine.
- Conseiller au patient de prévenir un professionnel de la santé si les douleurs thoraciques ne diminuent pas ou si elles s'aggravent après le traitement et si elles s'accompagnent de diaphorèse ou si des essoufflements ou des céphalées graves et persistantes se manifestent.
- Inciter le patient à discuter avec un professionnel de la santé des restrictions à respecter sur le plan de l'effort avant de faire de l'exercice.

Hypertension:

- Encourager le patient à appliquer d'autres mesures visant à stabiliser la pression artérielle (perdre du poids, suivre un régime alimentaire hyposodé, cesser de fumer, consommer de l'alcool avec modération, faire régulièrement de l'exercice, gérer le stress). Le prévenir que le médicament stabilise la pression artérielle, mais ne guérit pas l'hypertension.
- Expliquer au patient et à ses proches comment prendre la pression artérielle. Leur recommander de la mesurer toutes les semaines et de signaler tout changement important à un professionnel de la santé.

VÉRIFICATION DE L'EFFICACITÉ THÉRAPEUTIQUE

L'efficacité du traitement peut être démontrée par: une baisse de la pression artérielle ▪ une diminution de la fréquence et de la gravité des crises d'angine ▪ un moindre recours à des dérivés nitrés ▪ une augmentation de la tolérance à l'effort et un sentiment de mieux-être. ✳

AMOXICILLINE

Amoxil, Apo-Amoxi, Gen-Amoxicillin, Lin-Amox, Novamoxin, Nu-Amoxi, Pro-Amox, Riva-Amoxicillin, Schein-Amoxicillin

CLASSIFICATION:

Antibiotique (pénicilline)

Grossesse – catégorie B

INDICATIONS

Traitement des infections suivantes: otite moyenne ▪ sinusite ▪ infections des voies respiratoires ▪ infections génito-urinaires ▪ Prophylaxie de l'endocardite ▪ Traitement de l'ulcère gastroduodénal dû à *Helicobacter pylori* (en association avec d'autres agents) ▪ Traitement de la maladie de Lyme ▪ Traitement de la fièvre typhoïde.

MÉCANISME D'ACTION

Liaison à la paroi de la cellule bactérienne entraînant la destruction de la cellule. ***Effets thérapeutiques:*** Effet bactéricide; spectre plus large que celui de la pénicilline. **Spectre d'action:** L'amoxicilline est active contre: les streptocoques ▪ les pneumocoques ▪ les entérocoques ▪ *Hæmophilus influenzæ* ▪ *Escherichia coli* ▪ *Proteus mirabilis* ▪ *Neisseria meningitidis* ▪ *Shigella* ▪ *Chlamydia trachomatis* ▪ *Salmonella* ▪ *Borrelia burgdorferi* ▪ *Helicobacter pylori*. Certains de ces microorganismes ont le pouvoir de produire des bêta-lactamases qui confèrent aux bactéries une résistance à l'amoxicilline (voir amoxicilline/clavulanate).

PHARMACOCINÉTIQUE

Absorption: Bonne (de 75 à 90 %) (PO). L'amoxicilline résiste mieux à l'inactivation par les acides que les autres pénicillines.
Distribution: Le médicament diffuse rapidement dans la plupart des tissus et liquides corporels. La pénétration dans le liquide céphalorachidien est accrue en présence d'une inflammation des méninges. L'amoxicilline traverse la barrière placentaire et passe en petites quantités dans le lait maternel.
Métabolisme et excrétion: Excrétion urinaire à l'état inchangé (70 %); métabolisme hépatique (30 %).
Demi-vie: Nouveau-nés: 3,7 heures; enfants: de 1 à 2 heures; adultes: de 0,7 à 1,4 heure.

Profil temps-action (concentrations sanguines)

	DÉBUT D'ACTION	PIC	DURÉE
PO	30 min	1 - 2 h	8 - 12 h

CONTRE-INDICATIONS, PRÉCAUTIONS ET MISES EN GARDE

Contre-indications: Hypersensibilité à la pénicilline.
Précautions et mises en garde: Insuffisance rénale grave (réduire la dose si la Cl_{Cr} < 30 mL/min) ■ Mononucléose infectieuse (incidence accrue de rash) ■ Antécédents d'hypersensibilité aux céphalosporines ■ **OBST.**: L'utilisation durant la grossesse ou l'allaitement ne comporte pas de risque pour le nouveau-né.

RÉACTIONS INDÉSIRABLES ET EFFETS SECONDAIRES

SNC: CONVULSIONS (doses élevées).
GI: COLITE PSEUDOMEMBRANEUSE, diarrhée, nausées, vomissements, élévation des enzymes hépatiques.
GU: candidose vaginale.
Tég.: rash, urticaire.
Hémat.: dyscrasie sanguine.
Divers: réactions allergiques incluant l'ANAPHYLAXIE et la MALADIE SÉRIQUE, surinfection.

INTERACTIONS

Médicament-médicament: Le **probénécide** diminue l'excrétion rénale et augmente les concentrations sanguines d'amoxicilline. Une association médicamenteuse est parfois utilisée à cette fin ■ L'amoxicilline peut potentialiser les effets de la **warfarine** ■ Le traitement concomitant par l'**allopurinol** augmente le risque de rash ■ L'amoxicilline peut diminuer l'efficacité des **contraceptifs oraux** ■ L'amoxicilline peut diminuer l'élimination du **méthotrexate** et en élever de ce fait les concentrations sériques, ce qui peut accroître le risque de toxicité.

VOIES D'ADMINISTRATION ET POSOLOGIE

La plupart des infections

- **PO (adultes)**: De 250 à 500 mg, toutes les 8 heures.
- **PO (enfants > 3 mois)**: De 25 à 50 mg/kg/jour, en doses fractionnées, toutes les 8 heures. La posologie peut être portée jusqu'à 80 à 90 mg/kg/jour; administrer en doses fractionnées, toutes les 8 heures, en présence d'otite moyenne aiguë à *S. pneumoniæ* résistant à l'amoxicilline (au maximum, 4 g par jour).
- **PO (enfants < 3 mois)**: De 20 à 30 mg/kg/jour, en doses fractionnées, toutes les 12 heures.

Infections dues à H. pylori

- **PO (adultes)**: *Trithérapie* – 1 000 mg d'amoxicilline, 2 fois par jour, avec 30 mg de lansoprazole, 2 fois par jour, et 500 mg de clarithromycine, 2 fois par jour, pendant 7 à 14 jours *ou* 1 000 mg d'amoxicilline, 2 fois par jour, avec 20 mg d'oméprazole, 2 fois par jour, et 500 mg de clarithromycine, 2 fois par jour, pendant 7 à 14 jours *ou* 1 000 mg d'amoxicilline, 2 fois par jour, avec 20 mg d'esoméprazole, 2 fois par jour, et 500 mg de clarithromycine, 2 fois par jour, pendant 7 jours.

Prophylaxie de l'endocardite

- **PO (adultes)**: 2 g, 1 heure avant l'intervention.
- **PO (enfants)**: 50 mg/kg (jusqu'à 2 g), 1 heure avant l'intervention.

INSUFFISANCE RÉNALE

- **PO (ADULTES)**: CL_{CR} *DE 10 À 50 mL/MIN* – ADMINISTRER TOUTES LES 8 À 12 HEURES.
- **PO (ADULTES)**: CL_{CR} *< 10 mL/MIN* – ADMINISTRER TOUTES LES 12 À 24 HEURES.

PRÉSENTATION (version générique disponible)

Comprimés à croquer: 125 mg[Pr], 250 mg[Pr] ■ **Capsules**: 250 mg[Pr], 500 mg[Pr] ■ **Suspension orale**: 125 mg/5 mL[Pr], 250 mg/5 mL[Pr] (préparations sans sucre ou légères disponibles) ■ **En association avec**: clarithromycine et lansoprazole dans des plaquettes alvéolées (Hp-PAC[Pr]); clarithromycine et oméprazole (Losec 1-2-3 A[Pr]), clarithromycine et esoméprazole (Nexium 1-2-3 A[Pr]), acide clavulanique (Clavulin[Pr]).

A

SOINS INFIRMIERS

ÉVALUATION DE LA SITUATION

- Au début du traitement et pendant toute sa durée, rester à l'affût des signes suivants d'infection: altération des signes vitaux, aspect de la plaie, des crachats, de l'urine et des selles, accroissement du nombre de globules blancs.
- Recueillir les antécédents du patient avant d'amorcer le traitement afin de déterminer ses réactions antérieures à une pénicilline ou à une céphalosporine. Même les personnes n'ayant jamais manifesté de sensibilité à la pénicilline peuvent manifester une réaction allergique.
- SUIVRE DE PRÈS LES SIGNES ET LES SYMPTÔMES SUIVANTS D'ANAPHYLAXIE: RASH, PRURIT, ŒDÈME LARYNGÉ, RESPIRATION SIFFLANTE. SIGNALER IMMÉDIATEMENT CES SYMPTÔMES AU MÉDECIN OU À UN AUTRE PROFESSIONNEL DE LA SANTÉ.
- Prélever des échantillons pour les cultures et les antibiogrammes avant le début du traitement. La première dose peut être administrée avant que les résultats soient connus.
- SUIVRE DE PRÈS LA FONCTION INTESTINALE. ON DEVRAIT SIGNALER RAPIDEMENT À UN PROFESSIONNEL DE LA SANTÉ LES SYMPTÔMES SUIVANTS DE COLITE PSEUDOMEMBRANEUSE: DIARRHÉE, CRAMPES ABDOMINALES, FIÈVRE ET SELLES SANGLANTES. UNE COLITE PSEUDOMEMBRANEUSE PEUT APPARAÎTRE PLUSIEURS SEMAINES APRÈS L'ARRÊT DU TRAITEMENT.

Tests de laboratoire:

- Le médicament peut entraîner l'élévation des concentrations sériques de phosphatase alcaline, de LDH, d'AST et d'ALT.
- Le médicament peut entraîner des résultats faussement positifs au test de Coombs direct.

DIAGNOSTICS INFIRMIERS POSSIBLES

- Risque d'infection (Indications, Effets secondaires).
- Connaissances insuffisantes sur le traitement médicamenteux (Enseignement au patient et à ses proches).
- Non-observance du traitement médicamenteux (Enseignement au patient et à ses proches).

INTERVENTIONS INFIRMIÈRES

- Administrer le médicament à intervalles réguliers, sans égard aux repas. On peut l'administrer avec des aliments pour diminuer les effets secondaires gastro-intestinaux. On peut vider le contenu des capsules et l'avaler avec du liquide. Les comprimés à croquer doivent être écrasés ou croqués et mâchés avant d'être avalés avec du liquide.
- Bien mélanger la suspension orale avant de l'administrer. La suspension peut être administrée telle quelle ou mélangée avec une préparation pour nourrissons, du lait, du jus de fruits, de l'eau ou du *ginger ale* (boisson gazeuse). Administrer immédiatement après l'avoir mélangée. Jeter la suspension reconstituée et réfrigérée après 10 à 14 jours (consulter les directives de chaque fabricant).

ENSEIGNEMENT AU PATIENT ET À SES PROCHES

- Expliquer au patient qu'il doit prendre le médicament à intervalles réguliers et qu'il doit finir toute la quantité qui lui a été prescrite, même s'il se sent mieux. Insister sur le fait qu'il peut être dangereux de donner ce médicament à une autre personne.
- Recommander à la patiente qui prend des contraceptifs oraux d'utiliser tout au long du traitement par l'amoxicilline et jusqu'aux règles suivantes une méthode de contraception non hormonale différente ou supplémentaire.
- Conseiller au patient de signaler à un professionnel de la santé tout signe de surinfection (excroissance pileuse sur la langue, pertes et démangeaisons vaginales, selles molles ou nauséabondes) ou d'allergie.
- CONSEILLER AU PATIENT DE PRÉVENIR IMMÉDIATEMENT UN PROFESSIONNEL DE LA SANTÉ EN CAS DE DIARRHÉE, DE CRAMPES ABDOMINALES, DE FIÈVRE, DE SELLES SANGLANTES, et de ne prendre aucun agent antidiarrhéique avant de consulter un professionnel de la santé.
- Recommander au patient de prévenir un professionnel de la santé si les symptômes ne s'améliorent pas.
- Expliquer au patient ayant des antécédents de rhumatisme cardiaque ou de remplacement valvulaire qu'il est important de suivre un traitement antimicrobien prophylactique avant de se soumettre à une intervention médicale ou dentaire effractive (voir l'annexe M).

PÉD.: Enseigner aux parents ou aux soignants la façon adéquate de calculer et de mesurer les doses. Insister sur le fait qu'il est important d'utiliser les mesures recommandées par le pharmacien et non les mesures de cuisine.

VÉRIFICATION DE L'EFFICACITÉ THÉRAPEUTIQUE

L'efficacité du traitement peut être démontrée par: la disparition des signes et des symptômes d'infection; le temps de résolution dépend du microorganisme infectant et du siège de l'infection ■ la prévention de l'endocardite ■ l'éradication de *H. pylori* avec disparition des symptômes d'ulcère.

AMOXICILLINE/ CLAVULANATE

Apo-Amoxi Clav, Clavulin, Clavulin bid, Novo-Clavamoxin, Ratio-Aclavulanate

CLASSIFICATION:

Antibiotique (pénicilline/inhibiteur des bêtalactamases)

Grossesse – catégorie B

INDICATIONS

Traitement d'un grand nombre d'infections comprenant: les infections de la peau et des tissus mous ▪ l'otite moyenne ▪ la sinusite ▪ les infections des voies respiratoires supérieures et inférieures ▪ les infections urinaires.

MÉCANISME D'ACTION

Liaison à la paroi de la cellule bactérienne entraînant la destruction de la cellule; le spectre d'action de l'amoxicilline est plus large que celui de la pénicilline. L'association avec le clavulanate augmente la résistance à l'action des bêtalactamases, enzymes produites par les bactéries qui sont capables d'inactiver certaines pénicillines. ***Effets thérapeutiques:*** Effet bactéricide contre les bactéries sensibles. **Spectre d'action**: L'amoxicilline avec clavulanate est active contre: les streptocoques ▪ les pneumocoques ▪ les entérocoques ▪ *Hæmophilus influenzæ* ▪ *Escherichia coli* ▪ *Proteus mirabilis* ▪ *Neisseria meningitidis* ▪ *Neisseria gonorrhϾ* ▪ *Staphylococcus aureus* ▪ *Klebsiella pneumoniæ* ▪ *Shigella* ▪ *Salmonella* ▪ *Moraxella catarrhalis*.

PHARMACOCINÉTIQUE

Absorption: Bonne à partir du duodénum (de 75 à 90 %). Le médicament résiste mieux à l'inactivation par les acides que les autres pénicillines.

Distribution: Répartition rapide dans la plupart des tissus et liquides corporels. La pénétration dans le liquide céphalorachidien est accrue en présence d'une inflammation des méninges. L'amoxicilline avec clavulanate traverse la barrière placentaire et pénètre en petites quantités dans le lait maternel.

Métabolisme et excrétion: Excrétion urinaire à l'état inchangé (70 %); métabolisme hépatique (30 %).

Demi-vie: De 1 à 1,3 heure.

Profil temps-action (concentrations sanguines)

	DÉBUT D'ACTION	PIC	DURÉE
PO	30 min	1 - 2 h	8 - 12 h

CONTRE-INDICATIONS, PRÉCAUTIONS ET MISES EN GARDE

Contre-indications: Hypersensibilité à la pénicilline ▪ Hypersensibilité au clavulanate ▪ Hypersensibilité aux céphalosporines ▪ Mononucléose infectieuse ▪ Hépatotoxicité reliée au produit ▪ **OBST.**: Risque accru d'entérocolite ulcéronécrosante du nouveau-né. Éviter l'usage de ce médicament, à moins que le médecin ne le considère comme essentiel.

Précautions et mises en garde: Insuffisance rénale grave (réduire la dose) ▪ Insuffisance hépatique (administrer avec prudence; suivre de près la fonction hépatique).

RÉACTIONS INDÉSIRABLES ET EFFETS SECONDAIRES

SNC: CONVULSIONS (doses élevées).

GI: COLITE PSEUDOMEMBRANEUSE, diarrhée, dysfonctionnement hépatique, nausées, vomissements.

GU: candidose vaginale.

Tég.: rash, urticaire.

Hémat.: dyscrasie sanguine.

Divers: réactions allergiques incluant l'ANAPHYLAXIE et la MALADIE SÉRIQUE, surinfection.

INTERACTIONS

Médicament-médicament: Le **probénécide** diminue l'excrétion rénale et augmente les concentrations sanguines d'amoxicilline; une association médicamenteuse est parfois utilisée à cette fin ▪ L'association de l'amoxicilline avec le clavulanate peut potentialiser les effets de la **warfarine** ▪ Un traitement concomitant par l'**allopurinol** augmente le risque de rash ▪ Le médicament peut diminuer l'efficacité des **contraceptifs oraux**.

Médicament-aliments: L'absorption est diminuée si le médicament est pris avec un **repas riche en matières grasses**.

VOIES D'ADMINISTRATION ET POSOLOGIE

Les doses sont données en mg d'amoxicilline.

La plupart des infections

- **PO (adultes et enfants > 38 kg)**: *Comprimés* – 500 mg, toutes les 12 heures, *ou* 250 mg, toutes les 8 heures. *Suspension* – 500 mg de la préparation à 125 mg/5 mL ou à 250 mg/5 mL, toutes les 12 heures.

Infections graves et infections respiratoires

- **PO (adultes et enfants > 38 kg)**: 875 mg, toutes les 12 heures, *ou* 500 mg, toutes les 8 heures.

A

Otite moyenne, sinusite, infections des voies respiratoires inférieures, infections graves

- **PO (enfants ≥ 3 mois):** *Suspension de 200 mg/5 mL ou de 400 mg/5 mL* - 22,5 mg/kg, toutes les 12 heures; *suspension de 125 mg/5 mL ou de 250 mg/5 mL* - 13,3 mg/kg, toutes les 8 heures.

Infections légères à modérées

- **PO (enfants ≥ 3 mois):** *Suspension de 200 mg/5 mL ou de 400 mg/5 mL* - 12,5 mg/kg, toutes les 12 heures; *suspension de 125 mg/5 mL ou de 250 mg/5 mL* - 6,6 mg/kg, toutes les 8 heures.
- **PO (enfants < 3 mois):** 15 mg/kg, toutes les 12 heures (on recommande la suspension de 125 mg/5 mL).

INSUFFISANCE RÉNALE

- **PO (ADULTES):** *CL_{CR} DE 10 À 50 mL/MIN* - ADMINISTRER TOUTES LES 8 À 12 HEURES.
- **PO (ADULTES):** *CL_{CR} < 10 mL/MIN* - ADMINISTRER TOUTES LES 12 À 24 HEURES.

PRÉSENTATION

Comprimés: 250 mg d'amoxicilline avec 125 mg d'acide clavulanique[Pr], 500 mg d'amoxicilline avec 125 mg de clavulanate[Pr], 875 mg d'amoxicilline avec 125 mg de clavulanate[Pr] ■ **Suspension orale (125 mg/5 mL et 250 mg/5 mL; 200 mg/5 mL et 400 mg/5 mL):** 125 mg d'amoxicilline avec 31,25 mg d'acide clavulanique/5 mL[Pr], 200 mg d'amoxicilline avec 28,5 mg d'acide clavulanique/5 mL[Pr], 250 mg d'amoxicilline avec 62,5 mg de clavulanate/5 mL[Pr], 400 mg d'amoxicilline avec 57 mg d'acide clavulanique/5 mL[Pr].

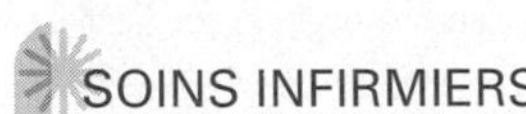

SOINS INFIRMIERS

ÉVALUATION DE LA SITUATION

- Au début du traitement et pendant toute sa durée, rester à l'affût des signes suivants d'infection: altération des signes vitaux, aspect de la plaie, des crachats, de l'urine et des selles, accroissement du nombre de globules blancs.
- Recueillir les antécédents du patient avant d'amorcer le traitement afin de déterminer ses réactions antérieures à une pénicilline ou à une céphalosporine. Même les personnes n'ayant jamais manifesté de sensibilité à la pénicilline peuvent manifester une réaction allergique.
- SUIVRE DE PRÈS LES SIGNES ET LES SYMPTÔMES SUIVANTS D'ANAPHYLAXIE: RASH, PRURIT, ŒDÈME LARYNGÉ, RESPIRATION SIFFLANTE. SIGNALER IMMÉDIATEMENT CES SYMPTÔMES AU MÉDECIN OU À UN AUTRE PROFESSIONNEL DE LA SANTÉ.
- Prélever les échantillons pour les cultures et les antibiogrammes avant le début du traitement. La première dose peut être administrée avant que les résultats soient connus.
- SUIVRE DE PRÈS LA FONCTION INTESTINALE. ON DEVRAIT SIGNALER RAPIDEMENT À UN PROFESSIONNEL DE LA SANTÉ LES SYMPTÔMES SUIVANTS DE COLITE PSEUDOMEMBRANEUSE: DIARRHÉE, CRAMPES ABDOMINALES, FIÈVRE ET SELLES SANGLANTES. UNE COLITE PSEUDOMEMBRANEUSE PEUT APPARAÎTRE PLUSIEURS SEMAINES APRÈS L'ARRÊT DU TRAITEMENT.

Tests de laboratoire:

- Le médicament peut entraîner l'élévation des concentrations sériques de phosphatase alcaline, de LDH, d'AST et d'ALT. Les hommes âgés et les patients recevant un traitement prolongé sont exposés à un risque accru de dysfonctionnement hépatique.
- Le médicament peut entraîner des résultats faussement positifs au test de Coombs direct.

DIAGNOSTICS INFIRMIERS POSSIBLES

- Risque d'infection (Indications, Effets secondaires).
- Connaissances insuffisantes sur le traitement médicamenteux (Enseignement au patient et à ses proches).
- Non-observance du traitement médicamenteux (Enseignement au patient et à ses proches).

INTERVENTIONS INFIRMIÈRES

- Administrer le médicament à intervalles réguliers, sans égard aux repas. On peut l'administrer avec des aliments pour diminuer les effets secondaires gastro-intestinaux. Bien mélanger la suspension orale avant de l'administrer. Jeter la suspension reconstituée et réfrigérée après 10 jours (125 mg/5 mL et 250 mg/5 mL) ou après 7 jours (200 mg/5 mL et 400 mg/5 mL). (Consulter les directives de chaque fabricant.)
- Deux comprimés à 250 mg et un comprimé à 500 mg ne sont pas bioéquivalents, même s'ils contiennent la même quantité d'acide clavulanique. Ne jamais remplacer un comprimé de 500 mg par deux comprimés de 250 mg.
- Les suspensions de 125 mg/5 mL et de 250 mg/5 mL (ratio amoxicilline/acide clavulanique de 4/1) ainsi que celles de 200 mg/5 mL et de 400 mg/5 mL (ratio amoxicilline/acide clavulanique de 7/1) ne sont pas interchangeables.

PÉD.: Il est recommandé d'administrer aux enfants < 3 mois la solution orale de 125 mg/5 mL.

ENSEIGNEMENT AU PATIENT ET À SES PROCHES

- Expliquer au patient qu'il doit prendre le médicament à intervalles réguliers et qu'il doit finir toute la quantité qui lui a été prescrite, même s'il se sent mieux. Insister sur le fait qu'il peut être dangereux de donner ce médicament à une autre personne.
- Recommander à la patiente qui prend des contraceptifs oraux d'utiliser au cours du traitement par l'amoxicilline et jusqu'aux règles suivantes une méthode de contraception non hormonale supplémentaire parallèlement aux contraceptifs oraux.
- Conseiller au patient de signaler tout signe de surinfection (excroissance pileuse sur la langue, pertes et démangeaisons vaginales, selles molles ou nauséabondes) ou d'allergie.
- CONSEILLER AU PATIENT DE PRÉVENIR IMMÉDIATEMENT UN PROFESSIONNEL DE LA SANTÉ EN CAS DE DIARRHÉE, DE CRAMPES ABDOMINALES, DE FIÈVRE, DE SELLES SANGLANTES et de ne prendre aucun agent antidiarrhéique avant de consulter un professionnel de la santé.
- Recommander au patient de prévenir un professionnel de la santé si les symptômes ne s'améliorent pas ou si les nausées et vomissements persistent même lorsque le médicament est pris avec des aliments.

PÉD.: Enseigner aux parents ou aux soignants la façon adéquate de calculer et de mesurer les doses. Insister sur le fait qu'il est important d'utiliser les mesures recommandées par le pharmacien et non les mesures de cuisine.

VÉRIFICATION DE L'EFFICACITÉ THÉRAPEUTIQUE

L'efficacité du traitement peut être démontrée par: la disparition des signes et des symptômes d'infection. Le temps de résolution dépend du microorganisme infectant et du siège de l'infection. ✳

AMPHÉTAMINES, SELS MIXTES D'

Adderall XR

CLASSIFICATION:

Stimulant du système nerveux central

Tableau II

Grossesse – catégorie C

INDICATIONS

Traitement des troubles déficitaires de l'attention avec hyperactivité.

MÉCANISME D'ACTION

Libération de la noradrénaline des terminaisons nerveuses. Les effets pharmacologiques sont les suivants: stimulation du SNC et de la respiration ■ vasoconstriction ■ mydriase (dilatation de la pupille). ***Effets thérapeutiques:*** Prolongation de la capacité de concentration en présence de troubles déficitaires de l'attention.

PHARMACOCINÉTIQUE

Absorption: Bonne (PO).

Distribution: Répartition dans tous les tissus; on en trouve des concentrations élevées dans le cerveau et le liquide céphalorachidien. Les amphétamines traversent la barrière placentaire et passent dans le lait maternel.

Métabolisme et excrétion: Faible métabolisme hépatique. L'excrétion urinaire dépend du pH urinaire. L'urine alcaline favorise la réabsorption du médicament et en prolonge les effets.

Demi-vie: Enfants (de 6 à 12 ans): de 9 à 11 heures; adultes: de 10 à 13 heures (selon le pH urinaire).

Profil temps-action (stimulation du SNC)

	DÉBUT D'ACTION	PIC	DURÉE
PO	0,5 – 1 h	7 h (gélules)	inconnue

CONTRE-INDICATIONS, PRÉCAUTIONS ET MISES EN GARDE

Contre-indications: Hypersensibilité ■ Grossesse et allaitement ■ États d'hyperexcitabilité, dont l'hyperthyroïdie ■ Personnalités psychotiques ■ Tendances suicidaires ou homicides ■ Glaucome ■ Anomalies cardiaques structurales (risque accru de mort soudaine) ■ Maladie cardiovasculaire ■ Antécédents de toxicomanie (l'usage abusif peut entraîner de graves problèmes cardiovasculaires ou la mort soudaine) ■ Usage concomitant ou récent (< 14 jours) d'IMAO ■ Hypertension modérée à grave.

Précautions et mises en garde: Diabète ■ **GÉR.**: L'innocuité de l'agent n'a pas été établie ■ Maladie de la Tourette (risque d'exacerbation des tics).

RÉACTIONS INDÉSIRABLES ET EFFETS SECONDAIRES

SNC: <u>hyperactivité</u>, <u>insomnie</u>, irritabilité, <u>agitation</u>, <u>tremblements</u>, étourdissements, céphalées.

CV: <u>palpitations</u>, <u>tachycardie</u>, cardiomyopathie (effets accrus lors d'un usage prolongé ou de l'administration de doses élevées), hypertension, hypotension.

A

GI: anorexie, constipation, crampes, diarrhée, sécheresse de la bouche (xérostomie), goût métallique, nausées, vomissements.
GU: impuissance, augmentation de la libido.
Tég.: urticaire.
End.: inhibition de la croissance (lors d'un usage prolongé chez les enfants).
Divers: dépendance psychologique.

INTERACTIONS

Médicament-médicament: L'UTILISATION CONCOMITANTE D'**IMAO** OU DE **MÉPÉRIDINE** PEUT ENTRAÎNER UNE CRISE HYPERTENSIVE ■ Intensification des effets adrénergiques lors de l'usage concomitant d'autres **agents adrénergiques** ou de **préparations thyroïdiennes** ■ Les **médicaments qui rendent l'urine alcaline** (**bicarbonate de sodium**, **acétazolamide**) diminuent l'excrétion et intensifient les effets des amphétamines ■ Les **médicaments qui rendent l'urine acide** (**chlorure d'ammonium**, doses importantes d'**acide ascorbique**) intensifient l'excrétion et diminuent les effets des amphétamines ■ Risque accru d'hypertension et de bradycardie lors de l'usage concomitant de **bêtabloquants** ■ Risque accru d'arythmies lors de l'usage concomitant de **digoxine** ■ Les **antidépresseurs tricycliques** peuvent intensifier les effets des amphétamines et accroître les risques d'arythmie, d'hypertension ou d'hyperpyrexie.
Médicament-produits naturels: La prise concomitante de **millepertuis** peut accroître le risque d'effets secondaires graves (éviter l'usage concomitant).
Médicament-aliments: Les **aliments qui rendent l'urine alcaline** (**jus de fruits**) peuvent intensifier les effets des amphétamines.

VOIES D'ADMINISTRATION ET POSOLOGIE

La dose traduit la teneur totale en amphétamines (amphétamine + dextroamphétamine).

- **PO (adultes ou enfants > 13 ans)**: Initialement, 10 mg, 1 fois par jour; par la suite, la dose quotidienne peut être majorée par tranches de 5 à 10 mg par semaine (jusqu'à une dose maximale de 30 mg).
- **PO (enfants ≥ 6 ans)**: Initialement, de 5 à 10 mg/jour, 1 fois par jour; par la suite, la dose quotidienne peut être majorée par tranches de 5 à 10 mg par semaine (jusqu'à une dose maximale de 30 mg).

PRÉSENTATION

La dose traduit la teneur totale en amphétamines (amphétamine + dextroamphétamine).
Gélules: 5 mg^{C}, 10 mg^{C}, 15 mg^{C}, 20 mg^{C}, 25 mg^{C}, 30 mg^{C}.

SOINS INFIRMIERS

ÉVALUATION DE LA SITUATION

- Mesurer la pression artérielle, le pouls et la fréquence respiratoire avant le traitement et à intervalles réguliers pendant toute sa durée.
- Le médicament peut provoquer un faux sentiment d'euphorie et de bien-être. Prévoir de fréquentes périodes de repos et observer le patient à la recherche d'une dépression rebond qui risque de survenir lorsque les effets du médicament se sont épuisés.
- L'usage du médicament comporte des risques élevés de dépendance et d'abus. La tolérance est rapide; ne pas augmenter la dose.
- **Trouble déficitaire de l'attention**: Mesurer le poids 2 fois par semaine et prévenir le médecin en cas de perte importante. **PÉD.**: Mesurer la taille des enfants à intervalles réguliers; prévenir le médecin en cas d'arrêt de la croissance.
- Noter la durée de la capacité de maintenir l'attention, la capacité de maîtriser les impulsions, les tics moteurs ou verbaux et les interactions de l'enfant avec autrui.

Tests de laboratoire:

- Le médicament peut modifier les résultats du dosage des concentrations urinaires de corticostéroïdes.
- Il peut élever les concentrations plasmatiques de corticostéroïdes, surtout le soir.

DIAGNOSTICS INFIRMIERS POSSIBLES

- Opérations de la pensée perturbées (Effets secondaires).

INTERVENTIONS INFIRMIÈRES

- NE PAS CONFONDRE ADDERALL (DEXTROAMPHÉTAMINE) ET INDÉRAL (PROPRANOLOL).

PO: Utiliser la dose la plus faible efficace.

- On peut prendre l'agent avec ou sans aliments.
- Les gélules à libération prolongée peuvent être avalées telles quelles; on peut aussi les ouvrir et en saupoudrer le contenu sur de la compote de pommes; avaler le mélange sans mâcher. La compote de pommes doit être consommée immédiatement; ne pas la conserver. Ne pas fractionner le contenu des gélules; le prendre en entier. Les gélules ne doivent pas être mâchées ou écrasées.

PÉD.: Lorsque les symptômes sont maîtrisés, il est possible de réduire la dose ou d'arrêter le traitement au cours des mois d'été ou d'administrer le médicament les jours d'école seulement (en prévoyant un arrêt temporaire de la médication pendant les fins de semaine ou les vacances scolaires).

ENSEIGNEMENT AU PATIENT ET À SES PROCHES

- Conseiller au patient de suivre rigoureusement la posologie recommandée. S'il n'a pu prendre le médicament au moment habituel, il devrait prendre la dose manquée dès que possible, sans jamais doubler les doses, ni les modifier sans consulter le médecin au préalable. Il est recommandé de ne pas prendre la dose en après-midi, en raison du risque d'insomnie. L'arrêt brusque du traitement par des doses élevées peut provoquer une fatigue extrême et la dépression.
- Expliquer au patient qu'il peut diminuer la sécheresse de la bouche induite par le médicament en se rinçant fréquemment la bouche avec de l'eau ou en consommant de la gomme à mâcher et des bonbons sans sucre.
- Conseiller au patient de limiter sa consommation de caféine.
- Prévenir le patient que le médicament peut altérer sa capacité de jugement. Lui conseiller d'être prudent lorsqu'il conduit ou lorsqu'il s'engage dans des activités qui exigent sa vigilance.
- Informer le patient que le médecin peut prescrire des arrêts temporaires de la médication lui permettant d'évaluer les bienfaits du traitement et de diminuer le risque de dépendance.

PÉD.: Prévoir un arrêt temporaire de la médication chaque année afin de réévaluer les symptômes et le traitement. La posologie changera à mesure que l'enfant vieillit, en raison de certaines modifications pharmacocinétiques, comme le ralentissement du métabolisme hépatique.

- Conseiller au patient de prévenir le médecin si la nervosité, l'agitation, l'insomnie, les étourdissements, l'anorexie ou la sécheresse buccale s'aggravent.

PÉD.: Si les pertes d'appétit ou de poids posent problème, conseiller aux parents de servir à l'enfant des repas hypercaloriques lorsque les concentrations de médicament sont basses (au petit-déjeuner ou au coucher).

VÉRIFICATION DE L'EFFICACITÉ THÉRAPEUTIQUE

L'efficacité du traitement peut être démontrée par: la prolongation de la capacité de se concentrer. ✳

AMPHOTÉRICINE B, DÉSOXYCHOLATE D'

Fungizone

AMPHOTÉRICINE B, COMPLEXE LIPIDIQUE D'

Abelcet

AMPHOTÉRICINE B LIPOSOMIQUE

AmBisome

CLASSIFICATION:
Antifongique

Grossesse – catégorie B

INDICATIONS

IV: Traitement des infections fongiques manifestes, évolutives, qui risquent d'être mortelles ■ **Amphotéricine B liposomique**: Traitement des infections générales ou disséminées dues à *Candida, Aspergillus* ou *Cryptococcus,* chez les patients réfractaires ou intolérants au traitement à l'amphotéricine B classique ou chez les insuffisants rénaux ■ Traitement des méningites à *Cryptococcus* chez des patients infectés par le VIH ■ Traitement empirique des infections mycologiques présumées chez les patients neutropéniques fébriles ■ **Complexe lipidique d'amphotéricine B**: Traitement des infections fongiques envahissantes chez les patients résistants ou intolérants au traitement par l'amphotéricine B classique ■ **Autres voies**: orale, topique, irrigation vésicale, administration par aérosol dans les yeux ou dans les oreilles. **Usages non approuvés: Amphotéricine B liposomique**: Traitement de la leishmaniose viscérale.

MÉCANISME D'ACTION

Liaison à la membrane de la cellule fongique favorisant l'écoulement du contenu cellulaire ■ La toxicité (particulièrement, les réactions aiguës reliées à la perfusion et la néphrotoxicité) est moindre si on administre des préparations lipidiques. ***Effets thérapeutiques:*** Action fongistatique. **Spectre d'action**: L'amphotéricine B est active contre: *Aspergillus* ■ *Blastomyces* ■ *Candida* ■ *Coccidioides* ■ *Cryptococcus* ■ *Hystoplasma* ■ *Leishmania* ■ les champignons responsables de la mucomycose.

PHARMACOCINÉTIQUE

Absorption: Nulle (PO). Les préparations topiques sont peu absorbées.

Distribution: Répartition dans les tissus et les liquides corporels. De faibles quantités pénètrent dans le liquide céphalorachidien.

A

Métabolisme et excrétion: L'élimination est très lente. On peut déceler le médicament dans l'urine jusqu'à 7 semaines après l'arrêt du traitement.

Demi-vie: *Deux phases* – la première est de 24 à 48 heures, et la deuxième, de 15 jours. *Amphotéricine B liposomique* – 174 heures; *complexe lipidique* – 170 heures.

Profil temps-action

	DÉBUT D'ACTION	PIC	DURÉE
IV	rapide	fin de la perfusion	24 h

CONTRE-INDICATIONS, PRÉCAUTIONS ET MISES EN GARDE

Contre-indications: Hypersensibilité.

Précautions et mises en garde: Insuffisance rénale ou anomalies électrolytiques ■ Patients recevant en même temps des transfusions de leucocytes (risque accru de toxicité pulmonaire avec le complexe lipidique seulement) ■ Risque de réactions anaphylactiques ■ **OBST.**: Il existe des précédents d'usage sans danger ■ Allaitement ■ **PÉD.**: Enfants < 1 mois (l'efficacité et l'innocuité de l'agent n'ont pas été établies).

RÉACTIONS INDÉSIRABLES ET EFFETS SECONDAIRES

SNC: céphalées, étourdissements, tremblements.
Resp.: dyspnée, hypoxie, respiration sifflante.
CV: hypotension, arythmies.
GI: diarrhée, nausées, vomissements, douleurs abdominales, abdomen dilaté.
GU: néphrotoxicité, hématurie.
HÉ: hypokaliémie, hypomagnésémie.
Hémat.: anémie, dyscrasie sanguine.
Locaux: phlébite.
Loc.: arthralgie, myalgie.
SN: neuropathie périphérique.
Divers: RÉACTIONS D'HYPERSENSIBILITÉ, frissons, fièvre, réactions aiguës reliées à la perfusion.

INTERACTIONS

Médicament-médicament: Risque accru de toxicité rénale, de bronchospasme et d'hypotension lors de l'administration concomitante d'**agents antinéoplasiques** ■ L'usage concomitant de **corticostéroïdes** ou de **corticotrophine** augmente le risque d'hypokaliémie et de dysfonctionnement cardiaque ■ L'administration simultanée de **zidovudine** peut accroître le risque de myélotoxicité et de néphrotoxicité ■ L'administration concomitante de **médicaments néphrotoxiques**, comme la **cyclosporine** et les **aminosides**, augmente le risque de néphrotoxicité ■ L'association avec la **flucytosine** accentue l'activité antifongique, mais peut augmenter le risque de toxicité induite par la flucytosine ■ L'association avec des **agents antifongiques de type azole** peut induire une résistance ■ Risque accru de néphrotoxicité lors de l'administration d'autres **agents néphrotoxiques** ■ Les **diurétiques thiazidiques** peuvent potentialiser l'hypokaliémie ■ L'hypokaliémie due à l'amphotéricine augmente le risque de toxicité **digitalique** ■ L'hypokaliémie peut accentuer les effets curariformes des **myorelaxants**.

VOIES D'ADMINISTRATION ET POSOLOGIE

La dose à administrer et la durée du traitement dépendent de la nature de l'infection à traiter.

Désoxycholate d'amphotéricine B (Fungizone)

- **IV (adultes):** *Dose initiale* – 0,25 mg/kg; augmenter lentement les doses quotidiennes jusqu'à 1 mg/kg, selon la tolérance du patient (certaines infections peuvent dicter l'administration de 1,5 mg/kg lorsque le médicament est administré tous les 2 jours).

Complexe lipidique d'amphotéricine B (Abelcet)

- **IV (adultes et enfants):** 5 mg/kg/jour.

Amphotéricine B liposomique (AmBisome)

- **IV (adultes et enfants):** *Mycoses générales – dose initiale* – 3 mg/kg/jour, qu'on augmente graduellement jusqu'à 5 mg/kg/jour, au besoin. *Méningite à* Cryptococcus *chez les patients infectés par le VIH* – 3 mg/kg/jour, qu'on augmente graduellement jusqu'à 6 mg/kg/jour, au besoin.

PRÉSENTATION

- **Désoxycholate d'amphotéricine B**
  Poudre pour injection: fioles de 50 mg^{Pr}.
- **Complexe lipidique d'amphotéricine B**
  Suspension pour injection: 100 mg, en fioles de 20 mL^{Pr}.
- **Amphotéricine B liposomique**
  Poudre pour injection: fioles de 50 mg^{Pr}.

SOINS INFIRMIERS

ÉVALUATION DE LA SITUATION

- Au cours de la dose test et des deux premières heures qui suivent le début de la perfusion de chaque dose, rester à l'affût des symptômes suivants: fièvre, frissons, céphalées, anorexie, nausées ou vomissements. L'administration préalable d'agents antipyrétiques, de corticostéroïdes, d'antihistaminiques, de mépéridine et d'antiémétiques et le maintien de l'équilibre sodique peuvent diminuer ces réactions. La réaction fébrile disparaît habituellement dans les 4 heures qui suivent la fin de la perfusion.

- Observer fréquemment le point d'injection pour déceler des signes de thrombophlébite ou les fuites. Le médicament irrite fortement les tissus. L'ajout d'héparine à la solution IV peut diminuer le risque de thrombophlébite.
- NOTER LES SIGNES VITAUX TOUTES LES 15 À 30 MINUTES DURANT LA DOSE TEST ET TOUTES LES 30 MINUTES AU COURS DES 2 À 4 HEURES QUI SUIVENT L'ADMINISTRATION. On a déjà administré de la mépéridine et du dantrolène pour prévenir et pour traiter les frissons intenses. Évaluer l'état des voies respiratoires (murmure vésiculaire, dyspnée) tous les jours. Prévenir le médecin de tout changement. En cas de détresse respiratoire, arrêter immédiatement la perfusion, car il y a risque d'anaphylaxie. Le matériel de réanimation cardiopulmonaire devrait toujours être à portée de la main.
- Effectuer le bilan quotidien des ingesta et des excreta et peser le patient tous les jours. Une hydratation adéquate (de 2 000 à 3 000 mL/jour) peut réduire le risque de néphrotoxicité.

Tests de laboratoire: VÉRIFIER TOUTES LES SEMAINES LES RÉSULTATS DE LA NUMÉRATION GLOBULAIRE ET DE LA NUMÉRATION PLAQUETTAIRE. MESURER UN JOUR SUR DEUX LES CONCENTRATIONS D'URÉE ET DE CRÉATININE SÉRIQUE PENDANT LES MAJORATIONS DES DOSES, PUIS, 2 FOIS PAR SEMAINE; MESURER LES CONCENTRATIONS DE POTASSIUM ET DE MAGNÉSIUM, 2 FOIS PAR SEMAINE. UNE HYPOKALIÉMIE MORTELLE PEUT SURVENIR APRÈS L'ADMINISTRATION DE CHAQUE DOSE. Si les concentrations d'urée dépassent 14 mmol/L ou si celles de créatinine sérique dépassent 273 µmol/L, on devrait réduire la dose ou arrêter l'administration jusqu'à ce que la fonction rénale s'améliore. Le médicament peut diminuer les concentrations d'hémoglobine et de magnésium, ainsi que l'hématocrite.

DIAGNOSTICS INFIRMIERS POSSIBLES

- Risque d'infection (Indications).
- Connaissances insuffisantes sur le traitement médicamenteux (Enseignement au patient et à ses proches).

INTERVENTIONS INFIRMIÈRES

- NE PAS CONFONDRE LE DÉSOXYCHOLATE D'AMPHOTÉRICINE B (FUNGIZONE), LE COMPLEXE LIPIDIQUE D'AMPHOTÉRICINE B (ABELCET) ET L'AMPHOTÉRICINE B LIPOSOMIQUE (AMBISOME), CAR ILS NE SONT PAS INTERCHANGEABLES.
- Ce médicament devrait être administré par voie IV seulement aux patients hospitalisés ou à ceux qui se trouvent sous une étroite surveillance. On doit confirmer le diagnostic avant de commencer l'administration.

Désoxycholate d'amphotéricine B

IV: Reconstituer le contenu d'une fiole de 50 mg avec 10 mL d'eau stérile pour injection sans agents bactériostatiques. La concentration obtenue sera de 5 mg/mL. Bien mélanger la solution jusqu'à ce qu'elle devienne transparente. Diluer de nouveau chaque mg avec au maximum 10 mL de solution de D5%E (pH > 4,2) pour obtenir une concentration de 100 µg (0,1 mg)/mL. Ne pas utiliser d'autres diluants. Éviter d'utiliser une solution contenant un précipité. Utiliser une aiguille de calibre 20; changer d'aiguille à chaque étape de la dilution. Porter des gants au cours de la manipulation de ce médicament. Conserver le médicament à l'abri de la lumière. La solution reconstituée est stable pendant 24 heures à température ambiante et pendant une semaine au réfrigérateur. Consulter les directives du fabricant avant de reconstituer la préparation.

Dose test: Administrer 1 mg dans 20 mL d'une solution de D5%E en 20 à 30 minutes afin de déterminer la tolérance du patient. Lorsque le traitement est interrompu pendant plus de 7 jours, il faut le reprendre en administrant la dose la plus faible. Si le patient présente une infection grave menaçant sa vie, la dose test peut être omise.

Perfusion intermittente: Administrer de préférence par une tubulure centrale. Si on administre par une tubulure périphérique, changer l'emplacement de l'aiguille lors de l'administration de chaque dose pour éviter la phlébite. Si on utilise un filtre intégré, le diamètre moyen des pores ne devrait pas être inférieur à 1 micron. Une brève exposition à la lumière (8 heures) ne modifie pas la puissance du médicament.

Vitesse d'administration: Administrer lentement par une pompe à perfusion pendant 2 à 6 heures.

Association compatible dans la même seringue: héparine.

Compatibilité (tubulure en Y): aldesleukine ■ diltiazem ■ famotidine ■ tacrolimus ■ téniposide ■ thiotépa ■ zidovudine.

Incompatibilité (tubulure en Y): allopurinol sodique ■ amifostine ■ aztréonam ■ énalaprilate ■ filgrastim ■ fluconazole ■ fludarabine ■ foscarnet ■ granisétron ■ melphalan ■ méropenem ■ ondansétron ■ paclitaxel ■ pipéracilline/tazobactam ■ propofol ■ vinorelbine.

Compatibilité en addition au soluté: héparine ■ hydrocortisone ■ sodium, bicarbonate de.

Incompatibilité en addition au soluté: calcium, chlorure de ■ calcium, gluconate de ■ cimétidine ■ diphenhydramine ■ potassium, chlorure de ■ ranitidine.

Incompatibilité avec des solutions: solution de lactate de Ringer pour injection ■ solutions salées.

Complexe lipidique d'amphotéricine B

IV: Préparer la solution juste avant de l'administrer. Secouer délicatement la fiole jusqu'à ce que le sédiment jaune soit dissous. Retirer la dose nécessaire avec une aiguille de calibre 18. Remplacer l'aiguille de la seringue remplie de complexe lipidique d'amphotéricine B par l'aiguille à filtre de 5 microns fournie. On peut utiliser une même aiguille à filtre pour filtrer le contenu d'un maximum de 4 fioles de 100 mg ou de 8 fioles de 50 mg. Introduire l'aiguille à filtre dans un sac IV contenant une solution de D5%E et vider le contenu de la seringue dans le sac pour obtenir une concentration de 1 mg/mL (2 mg/mL pour les enfants ou les patients qui ne peuvent tolérer de gros volumes de liquides). Ne pas utiliser des mélanges contenant des particules étrangères. Les fioles sont destinées à un usage unique; jeter toute quantité inutilisée. Réfrigérer la solution après dilution. Elle peut être conservée au réfrigérateur pendant 48 heures au maximum et pendant 6 heures supplémentaires à la température ambiante. Consulter les directives du fabricant avant de reconstituer la préparation.

Perfusion intermittente: Ne pas utiliser de filtre intégré.

Vitesse d'administration: Administrer à une vitesse de 2,5 mg/kg/h par une pompe à perfusion. Si le temps de perfusion dépasse 2 heures, mélanger le contenu toutes les 2 heures en agitant le sac.

Incompatibilité (tubulure en Y): Rincer la tubulure IV avant la perfusion avec une solution de D5%E ou utiliser une tubulure séparée.

Incompatibilité en addition au soluté: électrolytes.

Incompatibilité avec des solutions: solutions salées.

Préparation topique (usage non approuvé): Enfiler des gants; appliquer la préparation topique généreusement et frotter pour bien la faire pénétrer. Bien agiter la lotion avant de l'appliquer. Ne pas recouvrir de pansements occlusifs. Cesser le traitement si les lésions s'aggravent ou si des signes d'hypersensibilité apparaissent.

Amphotéricine B liposomique

Perfusion intermittente: Pour reconstituer la solution, ajouter 12 mL d'eau stérile sans agent bactériostatique à une fiole de 50 mg pour obtenir une concentration de 4 mg/mL. Secouer immédiatement la fiole avec vigueur, pendant au moins 30 secondes, jusqu'à ce toutes les particules soient complètement dispersées. Retirer le volume nécessaire à la dilution. À l'aide d'une seringue munie d'un filtre de 5 microns, diluer la préparation dans une solution de D5%E pour obtenir une concentration de 0,5 à 2 mg/mL. La solution reconstituée est stable pendant 24 heures au réfrigérateur. La solution diluée devrait être utilisée dans les 6 heures qui suivent la dilution. Consulter les directives du fabricant avant de reconstituer la préparation.

Vitesse d'administration: Perfuser en 60 à 120 minutes. Si le patient éprouve un malaise pendant la perfusion, on peut en prolonger la durée. Elle peut être administrée par un filtre intégré dont le diamètre des pores est d'au moins 1 micron.

Incompatibilité (tubulure en Y): Si la solution est administrée par une tubulure déjà en place, la rincer avec une solution de D5%E avant la perfusion ou utiliser une tubulure séparée.

Incompatibilité avec des solutions: Ne pas diluer ni mélanger avec des solutions salées, d'autres médicaments ou une solution contenant un agent bactériostatique.

ENSEIGNEMENT AU PATIENT ET À SES PROCHES

- Expliquer au patient le besoin de recourir à un traitement prolongé par voie IV ou par voie topique.

PO: Conseiller au patient de faire rouler le médicament dans la bouche aussi longtemps que possible avant de l'avaler.

IV: Informer le patient des effets secondaires possibles et du risque de douleur au point d'injection IV. En cas d'effets secondaires, lui conseiller de les signaler à un professionnel de la santé.

Soins à domicile: Expliquer au membre de la famille ou au soignant la méthode de dilution, la vitesse d'administration, le mode d'administration du médicament et l'entretien approprié du matériel IV.

Usage topique: Prévenir le patient que la préparation topique peut tacher les vêtements. La crème ou la lotion peut être enlevée avec du savon et de l'eau tiède, et l'onguent, avec un liquide nettoyant.

VÉRIFICATION DE L'EFFICACITÉ THÉRAPEUTIQUE

L'efficacité du traitement peut être démontrée par: la disparition des signes et des symptômes d'infection. Pour éviter les rechutes, il peut s'avérer nécessaire d'administrer le traitement pendant plusieurs semaines et même pendant plusieurs mois. ✳

AMPICILLINE

Ampicin, Novo-Ampicillin, Nu-Ampi, Pro-Ampi

CLASSIFICATION:

Antibiotique (pénicilline)

Grossesse - catégorie B

INDICATIONS

Traitement des infections suivantes dues à des microorganismes sensibles à Gram négatif et à Gram positif:

otite moyenne ■ sinusite ■ infections respiratoires ■ infections génito-urinaires ■ infections gastro-intestinales ■ méningite bactérienne ■ septicémie ■ endocardite ■ prophylaxie de l'endocardite bactérienne. **Usages non approuvés**: Prévention de l'infection chez certaines patientes exposées à un risque élevé qui doivent subir une césarienne ■ Infections de la peau et de ses annexes, infections des tissus mous ■ Prophylaxie de l'endocardite.

MÉCANISME D'ACTION

Liaison à la paroi de la cellule bactérienne entraînant la destruction de la cellule. ***Effets thérapeutiques:*** Effet bactéricide; spectre plus large que celui de la pénicilline. **Spectre d'action**: L'ampicilline est active contre: les streptocoques ■ les pneumocoques ■ les entérocoques ■ *Hæmophilus influenzæ* non producteur de pénicillinase ■ *Escherichia coli* ■ *Proteus mirabilis* ■ *Staphylococcus epidermidis* ■ *Neisseria meningitidis* ■ *Neisseria gonorrhϾ* ■ *Shigella* ■ *Salmonella.*

PHARMACOCINÉTIQUE

Absorption: De 30 à 50 % (PO).

Distribution: Répartition rapide dans les tissus et liquides corporels. La pénétration dans le liquide céphalorachidien est accrue en présence d'une inflammation des méninges. L'ampicilline traverse la barrière placentaire et passe en petites quantités dans le lait maternel.

Métabolisme et excrétion: Métabolisme hépatique variable (entre 12 et 50 %). Excrétion rénale variable (de 25 à 60 % [PO] et de 50 à 85 % [IM]).

Demi-vie: Nouveau-nés: de 1,7 à 4 heures; enfants et adultes: de 1 à 1,5 heure (prolongée en cas d'insuffisance rénale).

Profil temps-action (concentrations sériques)

	DÉBUT D'ACTION	PIC	DURÉE
PO	rapide	1,5 - 2 h	4 - 6 h
IM	rapide	1 h	4 - 6 h
IV	rapide	fin de la perfusion	4 - 6 h

CONTRE-INDICATIONS, PRÉCAUTIONS ET MISES EN GARDE

Contre-indications: Hypersensibilité aux pénicillines ou aux céphalosporines.

Précautions et mises en garde: Insuffisance rénale (réduction de la dose nécessaire si la Cl_{Cr} < 50 mL/min) ■ Mononucléose infectieuse, leucémie lymphoïde aiguë et infection au cytomégalovirus (incidence accrue de rash) ■ **OBST.**: Sans risque pour le fœtus ■ **ALLAITEMENT**: Bien que cet antibiotique soit généralement considéré comme sûr, de faibles quantités peuvent passer dans le lait maternel. Le nourrisson risque une altération de la flore intestinale, la diarrhée et une réaction d'hypersensibilité.

RÉACTIONS INDÉSIRABLES ET EFFETS SECONDAIRES

SNC: CONVULSIONS (doses élevées).

GI: COLITE PSEUDOMEMBRANEUSE, diarrhée, nausées, vomissements

Tég.: rash, urticaire.

Hémat.: dyscrasie sanguine.

Divers: réactions allergiques incluant l'ANAPHYLAXIE et la MALADIE SÉRIQUE, surinfection.

INTERACTIONS

Médicament-médicament: Le **probénécide** diminue l'excrétion rénale et augmente les concentrations sanguines d'ampicilline. Une association médicamenteuse est parfois utilisée à cette fin ■ Des doses élevées d'ampicilline peuvent accroître le risque de saignements lors de l'usage concomitant de **warfarine** ■ L'incidence de rash est plus élevée lors de l'administration concomitante d'**allopurinol** ■ L'ampicilline peut diminuer l'efficacité des **contraceptifs hormonaux**.

VOIES D'ADMINISTRATION ET POSOLOGIE

Infections des oreilles, du nez, de la gorge et des voies respiratoires

- **PO, IM, IV (adultes)**: 250 mg, toutes les 6 heures.
- **IM, IV (enfants > 1 mois)**: De 25 à 50 mg/kg/jour, en doses fractionnées, toutes les 6 heures.
- **IM, IV (enfants < 1 mois)**: *≤ 7 jours – ≤ 2 kg:* 50 mg/kg/jour, en doses fractionnées, toutes les 12 heures; *> 2 kg:* 75 mg/kg/jour, en doses fractionnées, toutes les 8 heures; *> 7 jours – < 1,2 kg:* 50 mg/kg/jour, en doses fractionnées, toutes les 12 heures; *1,2-2 kg:* 75 mg/kg/jour, en doses fractionnées, toutes les 8 heures; *> 2 kg:* 100 mg/kg/jour, en doses fractionnées, toutes les 6 heures. (La dose maximale ne doit pas dépasser la dose recommandée chez l'adulte.)

Infections GI/GU

- **PO, IM, IV (adultes)**: 500 mg, toutes les 6 heures (administrer des doses plus élevées pour traiter les infections plus graves ou chroniques).
- **PO (enfants > 1 mois)**: *Infection GI*: De 50 à 100 mg/kg/jour, en doses fractionnées, toutes les 6 heures (au maximum, 4 g par jour).
- **IM, IV (enfants > 1 mois)**: *Infection GU:* De 100 à 200 mg/kg/jour, en doses fractionnées, toutes les 6 heures.

A

- **IM, IV (enfants < 1 mois)**: ≤ *7 jours* – ≤ *2 kg*: 50 mg/kg/jour, en doses fractionnées, toutes les 12 heures; > *2 kg*: 75 mg/kg/jour, en doses fractionnées, toutes les 8 heures; > *7 jours* – < *1,2 kg*: 50 mg/kg/jour, en doses fractionnées, toutes les 12 heures; *1,2–2 kg*: 75 mg/kg/jour, en doses fractionnées, toutes les 8 heures; > *2 kg*: 100 mg/kg/jour, en doses fractionnées, toutes les 6 heures. (La dose maximale ne doit pas dépasser la dose recommandée chez l'adulte.)

Méningite

- **IM, IV (adultes)**: De 8 à 14 g par jour, en doses fractionnées, toutes les 3 ou 4 heures.
- **IM, IV (enfants > 1 mois)**: De 200 à 400 mg/kg/jour, en doses fractionnées, toutes les 6 heures (au maximum, 12 g par jour).
- **IM, IV (enfants < 1 mois)**: ≤*7 jours* – ≤*2kg*: 100 mg/kg/jour, en doses fractionnées, toutes les 12 heures; > *2 kg*: 150 mg/kg/jour, en doses fractionnées, toutes les 8 heures; > *7 jours* – < *1,2 kg*: 100 mg/kg/jour, en doses fractionnées, toutes les 12 heures; *1,2–2 kg*: 150 mg/kg/jour, en doses fractionnées, toutes les 8 heures; > *2 kg*: 200 mg/kg/jour, en doses fractionnées, toutes les 6 heures. (La dose maximale ne doit pas dépasser la dose recommandée chez l'adulte.)

Septicémie

- **IM, IV (adultes)**: De 8 à 14 g par jour, en doses fractionnées, toutes les 3 ou 4 heures.
- **IM, IV (enfants > 1 mois)**: De 100 à 200 mg/kg/jour, en doses fractionnées, toutes les 6 heures (au maximum, 12 g par jour).
- **IM, IV (enfants < 1 mois)**: ≤*7 jours* – ≤ *2 kg*: 50 mg/kg/jour, en doses fractionnées, toutes les 12 heures; > *2 kg*: 75 mg/kg/jour, en doses fractionnées, toutes les 8 heures; > *7 jours* – < *1,2 kg*: 50 mg/kg/jour, en doses fractionnées, toutes les 12 heures; *1,2–2 kg*: 75 mg/kg/jour, en doses fractionnées, toutes les 8 heures; > *2 kg*: 100 mg/kg/jour, en doses fractionnées, toutes les 6 heures. (La dose maximale ne doit pas dépasser la dose recommandée chez l'adulte.)

Prévention de l'endocardite

- **IM, IV (adultes)**: 2 g en 1 dose, 30 minutes avant l'intervention.
- **IM, IV (enfants > 1 mois)**: 50 mg/kg en 1 dose, 30 minutes avant l'intervention.

Traitement de l'endocardite

- **IV (adultes)**: 12 g par jour, en doses fractionnées, toutes les 4 heures.

INSUFFISANCE RÉNALE

- **ADULTES**: CL_{CR} *DE 10 À 50 mL/MIN* – ADMINISTRER TOUTES LES 6 À 12 HEURES.
- **ADULTES**: CL_{CR} < *10 mL/MIN* – ADMINISTRER TOUTES LES 12 À 24 HEURES.

PRÉSENTATION

Capsules: 250 mg[Pr], 500 mg[Pr] ■ **Suspension orale (parfum de cerise sauvage)**: 125 mg/5 mL[Pr], 250 mg/5 mL[Pr] ■ **Solution pour injection**: fioles à 250 mg[Pr], 500 mg, 1 et 2 g[Pr].

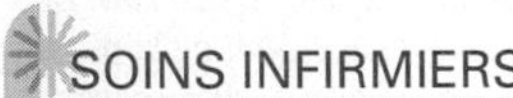

SOINS INFIRMIERS

ÉVALUATION DE LA SITUATION

- Au début du traitement et pendant toute sa durée, rester à l'affût des signes suivants d'infection: altération des signes vitaux, aspect de la plaie, des crachats, de l'urine et des selles, accroissement du nombre de leucocytes.
- Recueillir les antécédents du patient avant d'amorcer le traitement afin de déterminer ses réactions antérieures à une pénicilline ou à une céphalosporine. Même les personnes n'ayant jamais manifesté de sensibilité à la pénicilline peuvent manifester une réaction allergique.
- Prélever des échantillons pour les cultures et les antibiogrammes avant le début du traitement. La première dose peut être administrée avant que les résultats soient connus.
- SUIVRE DE PRÈS LES SIGNES ET LES SYMPTÔMES SUIVANTS D'ANAPHYLAXIE: rash, prurit, œdème laryngé, respiration sifflante. Interrompre l'administration du médicament et signaler immédiatement ces symptômes au médecin ou à un autre professionnel de la santé. Garder à portée de la main de l'adrénaline, un antihistaminique et le matériel de réanimation pour parer à une réaction anaphylactique.
- Évaluer l'état de la peau à la recherche d'un rash induit par l'ampicilline, qui se présente sous la forme d'une éruption non allergique, maculaire ou maculopapulaire, légèrement prurigineuse, d'un rouge mat.

Tests de laboratoire:

- Le médicament peut entraîner l'élévation des concentrations sériques d'AST et d'ALT.
- Le médicament peut provoquer des diminutions passagères des concentrations d'œstradiol, d'œstriol conjugué total, d'œstriol-glucuronide ou d'œstrone conjuguée chez les femmes enceintes.

- Le médicament peut entraîner des résultats faussement positifs au test de Coombs direct.
- Le médicament peut entraîner des résultats faussement positifs au test de glucose urinaire.

DIAGNOSTICS INFIRMIERS POSSIBLES

- Risque d'infection (Indications, Effets secondaires).
- Connaissances insuffisantes sur le traitement médicamenteux (Enseignement au patient et à ses proches).
- Non-observance du traitement médicamenteux (Enseignement au patient et à ses proches).

INTERVENTIONS INFIRMIÈRES

- Réserver l'administration par voie IM ou IV aux infections modérément graves ou graves ou chez les patients incapables de prendre le médicament par voie orale. Substituer à ces voies la voie orale aussitôt que possible.

PO: Administrer le médicament à intervalles réguliers. Il doit être pris à jeun, avec un grand verre d'eau, au moins 1 heure avant ou 2 heures après les repas. On peut vider le contenu des capsules dans un verre d'eau. La suspension orale reconstituée garde son efficacité pendant 21 jours au réfrigérateur. Consulter les directives de chaque fabricant. L'association avec le probénécide devrait être utilisée immédiatement après la reconstitution de la solution.

IM: Reconstituer les préparations IM et IV en ajoutant de 0,9 à 1,9 mL à une fiole de 250 mg, de 1,2 à 1,8 mL à une fiole de 500 mg, de 2,4 à 7,4 mL à une fiole de 1 g et 6,8 mL à une fiole de 2 g. Consulter les directives de chaque fabricant avant de reconstituer la préparation.

IV directe: Ajouter le volume d'eau stérile pour injection recommandé par le fabricant et rediluer de façon à obtenir une concentration de 50 mg/mL.

Vitesse d'administration: Les doses de 125 à 500 mg peuvent être administrées en perfusion pendant 3 à 5 minutes (vitesse maximale, 100 mg/min), dans l'heure qui suit la reconstitution. Une administration rapide peut provoquer des convulsions.

Perfusion intermittente: Diluer dans 50 mL ou plus de solution de NaCl 0,9 %, de D5%E, de D5%/NaCl 0,45 % ou de lactate de Ringer, jusqu'à l'obtention d'une concentration maximale de 30 mg/mL et administrer en 4 heures (la solution est plus stable si elle contient du NaCl).

Vitesse d'administration: Administrer les doses (de 1 à 2 g) en perfusion pendant 30 minutes.

Associations compatibles dans la même seringue: chloramphénicol ■ héparine ■ procaïne.

Associations incompatibles dans la même seringue: érythromycine, lactobionate d' ■ gentamicine ■ kanamycine ■ métoclopramide.

Compatibilité (tubulure en Y): acyclovir ■ allopurinol sodique ■ amifostine ■ aztréonam ■ cyclophosphamide ■ énalaprilate ■ esmolol ■ famotidine ■ filgrastim ■ fludarabine ■ foscarnet ■ granisétron ■ héparine ■ insuline régulière ■ labétalol ■ magnésium, sulfate de ■ melphalan ■ mépéridine ■ morphine ■ multivitamines ■ ofloxacine ■ perphénazine ■ phytonadione ■ potassium, chlorure de ■ propofol ■ tacrolimus ■ téniposide ■ théophylline ■ thiotépa ■ tolazoline ■ vitamines du complexe B avec C.

Incompatibilité (tubulure en Y): adrénaline ■ fluconazole ■ hydralazine ■ midazolam ■ ondansétron ■ sargramostim ■ vérapamil ■ vinorelbine ■ Si les aminosides et les pénicillines doivent être administrés en concomitance, choisir des points de ponction différents et espacer les injections de 1 heure.

Incompatibilité en addition au soluté: amikacine ■ gentamicine ■ kanamycine ■ tobramycine.

ENSEIGNEMENT AU PATIENT ET À SES PROCHES

- Expliquer au patient qu'il doit prendre le médicament à intervalles réguliers et qu'il doit finir toute la quantité qui lui a été prescrite, même s'il se sent mieux. Insister sur le fait qu'il peut être dangereux de donner ce médicament à une autre personne.

PÉD.: Informer les parents et les soignants qu'il ne faut pas conserver ce médicament en vue d'un usage futur ou du traitement d'un autre type d'infection.

- Conseiller au patient de signaler à un professionnel de la santé les signes de surinfection (excroissance pileuse sur la langue, pertes et démangeaisons vaginales, selles molles ou nauséabondes) et les allergies.
- Recommander à la patiente qui prend un contraceptif oral de recourir à un moyen de contraception non hormonal différent ou supplémentaire durant le traitement par l'ampicilline et jusqu'aux prochaines règles.
- RECOMMANDER AU PATIENT DE COMMUNIQUER AVEC UN PROFESSIONNEL DE LA SANTÉ EN CAS DE FIÈVRE ET DE DIARRHÉE, PARTICULIÈREMENT EN PRÉSENCE DE SANG, DE PUS OU DE MUCUS DANS LES SELLES. LUI CONSEILLER DE NE PAS TRAITER LA DIARRHÉE SANS AVOIR CONSULTÉ UN PROFESSIONNEL DE LA SANTÉ. CES SYMPTÔMES PEUVENT SE MANIFESTER MÊME PLUSIEURS SEMAINES APRÈS L'ARRÊT DU TRAITEMENT.
- Recommander au patient de prévenir un professionnel de la santé si les symptômes ne s'améliorent pas.
- Expliquer au patient ayant des antécédents de rhumatisme cardiaque ou de remplacement valvulaire qu'il est important de suivre un traitement antimicrobien prophylactique avant de se soumettre à une

intervention médicale ou dentaire effractive (voir l'annexe M).

ALLAITEMENT: Les faibles quantités d'ampicilline qui passent dans le lait maternel peuvent altérer la flore intestinale et causer une réaction d'hypersensibilité chez le nourrisson. Expliquer à la patiente qu'il faut surveiller l'apparition de ce type de réactions et discuter avec un médecin de la possibilité d'interrompre temporairement l'allaitement durant le traitement antibiotique.

VÉRIFICATION DE L'EFFICACITÉ THÉRAPEUTIQUE

L'efficacité du traitement peut être démontrée par: la disparition des signes et des symptômes d'infection. Le temps de résolution complète dépend du microorganisme infectant et du siège de l'infection ■ la prophylaxie de l'endocardite.

AMPRÉNAVIR

Agenerase

CLASSIFICATION:

Antirétroviral (inhibiteur de la protéase)

Grossesse – catégorie C

INDICATIONS

Traitement des infections par le VIH en association avec d'autres agents antirétroviraux chez les patients qui ont déjà pris un inhibiteur de la protéase.

MÉCANISME D'ACTION

Inhibition des effets de la protéase du VIH et prévention du clivage des polyprotéines virales. ***Effets thérapeutiques:*** Augmentation du nombre de cellules CD4 et diminution de la charge virale, ce qui ralentit l'évolution du VIH et de ses complications.

PHARMACOCINÉTIQUE

Absorption: Rapide (PO). Les repas riches en matières grasses réduisent l'absorption de l'amprénavir. La biodisponibilité de l'amprénavir en solution buvable est de 14 % inférieure à celle de l'amprénavir sous forme de capsules.

Liaison aux protéines: 90 %.

Distribution: L'amprénavir se distribue largement dans l'organisme.

Métabolisme et excrétion: Métabolisme majoritairement hépatique; moins de 3 % est excrété à l'état inchangé par les reins.

Demi-vie: De 7,1 à 10,6 heures.

Profil temps-action

	DÉBUT D'ACTION	PIC	DURÉE
PO	rapide	1-2 h	8-12 h

CONTRE-INDICATIONS, PRÉCAUTIONS ET MISES EN GARDE

Contre-indications: Hypersensibilité cliniquement importante à l'un des ingrédients des formulations ■ Administration concomitante de cisapride, de diazépam, de dihydroergotamine, d'ergotamine, de flurazépam, de midazolam, de pimozide et de triazolam (risque de toxicité grave pouvant mener à une issue fatale) ■ Administration concomitante de rifampine ■ *Solution buvable (à cause du risque de toxicité attribuable à la forte teneur en propylène glycol)*: nourrissons, enfants de moins de 4 ans, femmes enceintes, insuffisance rénale, insuffisance hépatique, administration concomitante de disulfirame ou de métronidazole.

Précautions et mises en garde: Nombreuses interactions médicamenteuses ■ Hypersensibilité aux sulfamides ■ Insuffisance hépatique (réduire la dose) ■ Hémophilie (risque accru de saignements) ■ Diabète (risque d'aggravation de l'hyperglycémie) ■ **OBST., ALLAITEMENT**: L'innocuité du médicament n'a pas été établie; il est déconseillé aux patientes infectées par le VIH d'allaiter ■ Administration concomitante de vitamine E.

EXTRÊME PRUDENCE: ADMINISTRATION CONCOMITANTE D'AMIODARONE, DE LIDOCAÏNE PAR VOIE PARENTÉRALE, D'ANTIDÉPRESSEURS TRICYCLIQUES OU DE QUINIDINE (RISQUE D'INTERACTIONS MÉDICAMENTEUSES POUVANT METTRE LA VIE DU PATIENT EN DANGER).

RÉACTIONS INDÉSIRABLES ET EFFETS SECONDAIRES

SNC: dépression, troubles de l'humeur.

GI: diarrhée, nausées, altération du goût, vomissements, paresthésies péribuccales.

Tég.: rash.

End.: hyperglycémie.

Métab.: hyperlipidémie, modification de la distribution des tissus adipeux.

Divers: syndrome de reconstitution immunitaire.

INTERACTIONS

Médicament-médicament: L'amprénavir étant la forme active du **fosamprénavir**, ces deux médicaments ne doivent pas être administrés en concomitance en raison de l'absence d'effets bénéfiques et de l'augmentation du risque de toxicité ■ L'amprénavir est métabolisé par le **CYP3A4**; il inhibe également ce système enzymatique ■ L'administration concomitante de **midazolam**, de **triazolam**, de **dihydroergotamine**, d'**ergotamine** et de **cisapride** entraîne une élévation des concentrations sanguines et du risque de toxicité de ces médicaments; l'administration concomitante est contre-indiquée ■ L'administration concomitante d'**amiodarone**, de **lidocaïne (par voie parentérale)**, de **quinidine**, d'**antidépresseurs tricycliques** et de **warfarine** entraîne une élévation des concentrations sanguines et du risque de toxicité de ces médicaments; une observation étroite des patients s'impose ■ Élévation marquée des concentrations sanguines de **rifabutine**; diminuer la dose de rifabutine d'au moins 50 % en cas d'administration concomitante ■ L'administration concomitante d'**atorvastatine**, de **lovastatine**, de **pravastatine**, de **simvastatine**, d'**érythromycine**, de **dapsone**, d'**itraconazole**, d'**alprazolam**, de **diazépam**, de **flurazépam**, de **diltiazem**, de **nifédipine**, de **nimodipine**, de **clozapine**, de **carbamazépine**, de **loratadine** et de **pimozide** peut entraîner une élévation des concentrations sanguines et du risque de toxicité de ces médicaments (commencer le traitement par une dose plus faible et faire un suivi étroit) ■ L'administration concomitante de **sildénafil**, de **tadalafil** ou de **vardénafil** augmente le risque de priapisme, d'hypotension et de troubles de la vue (suivre de près l'état du patient et administrer des doses beaucoup plus faibles) ■ La **rifampine** abaisse considérablement les concentrations sanguines et l'efficacité de l'amprénavir; l'administration concomitante de ces deux médicaments est contre-indiquée ■ Le **phénobarbital**, la **phénytoïne**, la **carbamazépine**, l'**éfavirenz** et la **névirapine** abaissent les concentrations de l'amprénavir et peuvent réduire son effet antirétroviral (une adaptation de la dose d'amprénavir peut être nécessaire) ■ Le médicament peut modifier les effets des **contraceptifs hormonaux** ■ La **cimétidine** et le **ritonavir** peuvent élever les concentrations d'amprénavir ■ Les **antiacides** et la **didanosine** (en raison du tampon qu'elle contient) peuvent réduire l'absorption de l'amprénavir (espacer les administrations de 1 heure) ■ Le propylène glycol contenu dans la solution d'amprénavir et l'alcool contenu dans la **solution de ritonavir** entrent en compétition pour la même voie métabolique, ce qui peut causer une accumulation d'un des véhicules (éviter l'usage concomitant des deux solutions).

Médicament-aliments: Risque de diminution de l'absorption du médicament si le patient prend un **repas riche en matières grasses**.

Médicament-produits naturels: L'usage concomitant du **millepertuis** peut entraîner la diminution des concentrations sanguines et de l'efficacité de l'amprénavir, associée à l'émergence d'une résistance virale.

VOIES D'ADMINISTRATION ET POSOLOGIE

- **PO (adultes, adolescents > 12 ans):** 1 200 mg (8 capsules de 150 mg), 2 fois par jour, en association avec d'autres agents antirétroviraux, à part le ritonavir. La dose recommandée est de 600 mg d'amprénavir et de 100 mg de ritonavir, 2 fois par jour, lorsqu'on administre ces deux médicaments en association en plus d'autres antirétroviraux.
- **Patients incapables d'avaler les capsules:** 22,5 mg (1,5 mL)/kg, 2 fois par jour ou 17 mg (1,1 mL)/kg, 3 fois par jour, en association avec d'autres antirétroviraux, jusqu'à concurrence de 2 800 mg par jour.

Insuffisance hépatique

- **PO (adultes):** *Score de Child-Pugh de 5 à 8:* capsules: 450 mg, 2 fois par jour; solution buvable: 513 mg (34 mL), 2 fois par jour en association avec d'autres agents antirétroviraux; *score de Child-Pugh de 9 à 12:* capsules: 300 mg, 2 fois par jour; solution buvable: 342 mg (23 mL), 2 fois par jour en association avec d'autres agents antirétroviraux.

PRÉSENTATION

Les capsules et la solution buvable renferment une quantité de vitamine E qui dépasse l'apport quotidien recommandé.

Capsules: 50 mg[Pr], 150 mg[Pr] ■ **Solution buvable (parfum de raisin, de «gomme balloune», de menthe poivrée):** 15 mg/mL[Pr].

SOINS INFIRMIERS

ÉVALUATION DE LA SITUATION

- Suivre de près le patient pour déceler tout changement dans la gravité des symptômes associés au VIH; rester à l'affût des symptômes d'infections opportunistes pendant toute la durée du traitement.
- Déceler les signes d'allergie aux sulfamides. Risque de sensibilité croisée.
- Suivre de près le patient pour déceler les réactions cutanées tout au long du traitement. Ces réactions peuvent être graves et même mortelles. Cesser le traitement en cas de réactions graves ou de rash modéré s'accompagnant de symptômes généraux.
- Si une patiente enceinte est exposée à des antirétroviraux, l'inscrire dans le registre des femmes exposées aux antirétroviraux pendant leur grossesse, en composant le 1-800 258-4263.

A

Tests de laboratoire: Noter la charge virale et le nombre de cellules CD4 à intervalles réguliers tout au long du traitement. Le médicament peut élever la glycémie, la cholestérolémie et les taux de triglycérides.

DIAGNOSTICS INFIRMIERS POSSIBLES

- Risque d'infection (Indications).
- Connaissances insuffisantes sur la maladie et sur le traitement médicamenteux (Enseignement au patient et à ses proches).
- Non-observance du traitement médicamenteux (Enseignement au patient et à ses proches).

INTERVENTIONS INFIRMIÈRES

- Administrer les antiacides ou la didanosine au moins 1 heure avant ou après l'amprénavir.

PO:

- Le médicament peut être administré avec ou sans aliments. Éviter de servir au patient des repas riches en matières grasses qui pourraient réduire l'absorption de l'amprénavir. Les capsules et la solution buvable peuvent être conservées à la température ambiante; ne pas réfrigérer ni congeler la préparation.
- La solution buvable et les capsules ne sont pas interchangeables mg pour mg.

ENSEIGNEMENT AU PATIENT ET À SES PROCHES

- Expliquer au patient qu'il doit respecter rigoureusement la posologie recommandée. Le médicament doit toujours être administré en association avec d'autres agents antirétroviraux. Prévenir le patient qu'il ne doit pas dépasser la dose qui lui a été prescrite et qu'il ne doit pas arrêter le traitement sans avoir consulté un professionnel de la santé. S'il n'a pas pu prendre une dose, il doit la prendre aussitôt que possible dans les 4 heures suivant l'heure prévue, puis reprendre l'horaire habituel. Si plus de 4 heures se sont écoulées, il doit sauter cette dose et prendre la dose suivante à l'heure prévue, sans jamais remplacer une dose manquée par une double dose.
- Expliquer au patient qu'il ne doit pas donner de l'amprénavir à une autre personne.
- Expliquer au patient que l'amprénavir ne guérit pas le sida, n'empêche pas l'apparition d'infections associées ou opportunistes et ne réduit pas le risque de transmission du VIH à d'autres personnes par les rapports sexuels ou par la contamination du sang. Inciter le patient à utiliser un condom et à éviter le partage d'aiguilles ou les dons de sang afin de prévenir la propagation du VIH. Informer le patient que les effets à longue échéance de l'amprénavir sont encore inconnus.
- Prévenir le patient que le traitement antirétroviral l'expose au risque de redistribution ou d'accumulation de tissus adipeux dont les causes et les conséquences à long terme sur la santé sont pour le moment inconnues.
- Conseiller au patient d'informer tous les professionnels de la santé de tous les médicaments qu'il prend et de les consulter avant de prendre un médicament sur ordonnance ou en vente libre en raison du risque d'interactions médicamenteuses graves. Il doit éviter de prendre des suppléments de vitamine E tout au long du traitement par l'amprénavir.
- L'amprénavir peut réduire l'efficacité des contraceptifs oraux; conseiller à la patiente d'utiliser un autre moyen de contraception non hormonal pendant toute la durée du traitement.
- Recommander au patient de signaler à un professionnel de la santé si des nausées, des vomissements, de la diarrhée ou un rash surviennent durant le traitement.
- Insister sur le fait qu'il est important de se soumettre à intervalles réguliers à des examens de suivi et à des analyses de sang permettant de déterminer les bienfaits du médicament et d'en déceler les effets secondaires.

VÉRIFICATION DE L'EFFICACITÉ THÉRAPEUTIQUE

L'efficacité du traitement peut être démontrée par: le ralentissement de l'évolution de l'infection par le VIH et la diminution de la fréquence des infections opportunistes chez les patients infectés ■ la diminution de la charge virale et l'augmentation du nombre de cellules CD4.

ANAKINRA

Kineret

CLASSIFICATION:

Agent antirhumatismal modificateur de la maladie [AARMM] (antagoniste de l'interleukine-1)

Grossesse – catégorie B

INDICATIONS

En monothérapie ou en association avec d'autres AARMM (sauf des anti-TNF) pour réduire les signes et les symptômes reliés à la polyarthrite rhumatoïde (PAR) évolutive chez les patients qui n'ont pas bien répondu au traitement par d'autres AARMM. L'anakinra peut être administré en concomitance avec le méthotrexate ▪ Inhibition de l'évolution des lésions structurelles en freinant les érosions et la dégradation du cartilage chez les patients qui présentent une polyarthrite rhumatoïde évolutive malgré un traitement par des doses stables de méthotrexate.

MÉCANISME D'ACTION

Liaison au récepteur de l'interleukine-1 de type 1 (IL-1R1), entraînant son inactivation. L'IL-1R1 est l'un des médiateurs de la réponse inflammatoire. ***Effets thérapeutiques:*** Diminution de l'inflammation et ralentissement de l'évolution de la PAR.

PHARMACOCINÉTIQUE

Absorption: 95 % (SC). Le pic des concentrations plasmatiques survient de 3 à 7 heures après l'injection sous-cutanée.

Distribution: Le médicament se retrouve en plus grande concentration au niveau des articulations enflammées. On ne sait pas s'il passe dans le lait maternel.

Métabolisme et excrétion: Excrétion sous forme inchangée dans l'urine à 80 %.

Demi-vie: De 4 à 6 heures.

Profil temps-action (amélioration des signes et des symptômes cliniques de la PAR)

	Début d'action	Pic	Durée
SC	1 - 3 semaines	inconnu	inconnue

CONTRE-INDICATIONS, PRÉCAUTIONS ET MISES EN GARDE

Contre-indications: Hypersensibilité à l'anakinra ou aux protéines dérivées de *E. coli* ▪ Infection active (risque d'exacerbation) ▪ Utilisation concomitante d'agents inhibant le TNF (p. ex., étanercept, infliximab, adalimumab).

Précautions et mises en garde: Infection (cesser le traitement si une infection grave se développe) ▪ Patients immunosupprimés ou atteints d'infections chroniques ▪ **Gér.**: Risque plus élevé d'infections ▪ Insuffisance rénale grave (Cl_{Cr} < 30 mL/min) ou aggravation d'une néphropathie existante ▪ Maladie hépatique ▪ **Obst.**: L'innocuité du médicament n'a pas été établie; utiliser l'anakinra seulement si les avantages potentiels pour la femme enceinte justifient le risque auquel est exposé le fœtus ▪ **Allaitement**: L'innocuité du médicament n'a pas été établie ▪ **Péd.**: L'innocuité et l'efficacité du médicament n'ont pas été établies ▪ Patients souffrant d'asthme (plus susceptibles de contracter une infection grave).

RÉACTIONS INDÉSIRABLES ET EFFETS SECONDAIRES

SNC: céphalées, fatigue.
ORLO: sinusite.
Resp.: infections des voies respiratoires, symptômes pseudogrippaux.
GI: nausées, douleurs abdominales, diarrhée.
Hémat.: neutropénie.
Locaux: réactions au point d'injection (érythème, ecchymoses, prurit, inflammation, douleur).
Loc.: arthralgie.
Divers: INFECTIONS, réactions d'hypersensibilités (rares).

INTERACTIONS

Médicament-médicament: L'usage concomitant d'**étanercept**, d'**adalimumab** ou d'**infliximab** augmente le risque d'infections graves. Cette association n'est pas recommandée ▪ L'anakinra peut réduire la production d'anticorps déclenchée par l'administration d'un **vaccin** et accroître le risque de réactions indésirables; ne pas administrer en concomitance des **vaccins à virus vivants**.

VOIES D'ADMINISTRATION ET POSOLOGIE

Traitement de la PAR évolutive

- **SC (adultes)**: 100 mg, 1 fois par jour.

Insuffisance rénale

- **SC (adultes)**: Aucune recommandation précise, mais la clairance plasmatique de l'anakinra est réduite de 70 à 75 % en présence d'une atteinte rénale grave (Cl_{CR} < 30 mL/min). Le médecin peut décider de n'administrer que 100 mg, tous les 2 jours.

Insuffisance hépatique

- **SC (adultes)**: On ne possède aucune donnée à cet égard.

PRÉSENTATION

Solution pour injection: 100 mg/0,67 mL[Pr] (seringues préremplies à usage unique).

SOINS INFIRMIERS

ÉVALUATION DE LA SITUATION

- Déterminer l'amplitude des mouvements articulaires et la gravité de la tuméfaction des articulations ainsi que l'intensité de la douleur au niveau des articulations atteintes, avant le traitement et à intervalles réguliers pendant toute sa durée.
- Rester à l'affût des réactions suivantes au point d'injection: érythème, douleur, démangeaisons, œdème.

A

- Rester à l'affût des signes et des symptômes d'infection (fièvre, augmentation du nombre de globules blancs) avant le traitement et à intervalles réguliers pendant toute sa durée. L'anakinra ne devrait pas être administré aux patients qui présentent une infection active et le traitement devrait être arrêté en cas d'infection grave ou de septicémie.
- Lors de la première injection d'anakinra, rester à l'affût des réactions d'hypersensibilité: urticaire, dyspnée, hypotension. Arrêter l'administration si des réactions graves se manifestent. Garder à portée de la main les médicaments (antihistaminiques, acétaminophène, corticostéroïdes, adrénaline) et le matériel de réanimation nécessaires pour parer à toute réaction grave.

Tests de laboratoire:

- Effectuer un décompte des polynucléaires neutrophiles avant d'amorcer le traitement, tous les mois pendant les 3 premiers mois et, ensuite, après 6, 9 et 12 mois de traitement, afin de déceler les signes d'anomalies hématologiques qui peuvent mener à une issue fatale. Arrêter d'administrer ce médicament si on constate une aplasie médullaire.
- Noter les concentrations sériques de protéine-C réactive, le taux de sédimentation ainsi que le facteur rhumatoïde à intervalles réguliers durant un traitement prolongé.

Toxicité et surdosage: L'analyse des concentrations plasmatiques d'anakinra n'est pas utile. Il faut cependant effectuer le décompte des polynucléaires neutrophiles. Rester à l'affût des signes et des symptômes de toxicité, tels que la fièvre, les malaises gastro-intestinaux ou l'éruption cutanée.

DIAGNOSTICS INFIRMIERS POSSIBLES

- Mobilité physique réduite (Indications).
- Douleur aiguë (Indications).
- Connaissances insuffisantes sur le traitement médicamenteux (Enseignement au patient et à ses proches).

INTERVENTIONS INFIRMIÈRES

- L'administration d'une dose plus élevée que celle recommandée n'améliore pas les résultats.

SC:

- Administrer le médicament tous les jours, à la même heure. Ne pas administrer une solution qui a changé de couleur ou qui contient des particules. L'anakinra est conditionné en seringues préremplies à usage unique.
- L'anakinra doit être injecté dans la face postérieure du bras, dans la portion située entre le coude et l'épaule, dans l'abdomen ou dans le haut des cuisses.
- Il faut conserver l'anakinra au réfrigérateur (entre 2 °C et 8 °C). Il peut rester à la température ambiante pendant un maximum de 24 heures.

ENSEIGNEMENT AU PATIENT ET À SES PROCHES

- Enseigner au patient la technique d'autoadministration et lui montrer comment conserver le produit et mettre au rebut le matériel. La première injection doit être administrée sous la supervision d'un professionnel de la santé. Fournir au patient un contenant spécial (imperforable) pour la mise au rebut du matériel usagé.
- Expliquer au patient que l'anakinra s'administre par voie sous-cutanée, à raison de 1 injection par jour. Il devrait essayer d'administrer le médicament tous les jours à la même heure. S'il n'a pu s'injecter le médicament au moment habituel, il doit le faire aussitôt que possible. Si l'heure de la dose suivante est proche, sauter la dose manquée et s'injecter la dose suivante comme prévu.
- Expliquer au patient qu'il doit utiliser une nouvelle seringue préremplie ainsi qu'une aiguille neuve pour l'administration de chaque dose de médicament. Jeter les seringues et les aiguilles utilisées dans le contenant destiné à la récupération du matériel souillé. Garder ce contenant hors de la portée des enfants ou des animaux.
- Conseiller au patient de conserver l'anakinra au réfrigérateur (entre 2 °C et 8 °C). Ne pas congeler ni secouer le médicament.
- Recommander au patient d'alterner les points d'injection à chaque administration. Les endroits recommandés pour l'injection sont: a) la partie postérieure du bras, dans la portion située entre le coude et l'épaule, b) l'abdomen (sauf le nombril et la taille) et c) le haut des cuisses.
- Conseiller au patient de signaler immédiatement à un professionnel de la santé les symptômes suivants: fièvre, maux de gorge, aphtes buccaux, frissons, toux productive, problèmes au niveau des articulations (douleurs, chaleur, rougeurs, enflure), douleurs à la poitrine, souffle court, réactions allergiques (difficultés respiratoires, démangeaisons, sensation de serrement au niveau de la poitrine).
- Expliquer au patient les signes et les symptômes d'une réaction d'hypersensibilité ou d'une autre réaction indésirable possible. Lui conseiller de consulter immédiatement un professionnel de la santé s'ils se manifestent.
- Conseiller à la patiente d'utiliser une méthode contraceptive pendant toute la durée du traitement par l'anakinra. Avant d'envisager une grossesse, la

patiente devrait discuter avec son médecin des risques pour le fœtus par rapport aux bienfaits du traitement pour la mère.

- Recommander au patient de toujours demander conseil à un pharmacien ou à un médecin avant de prendre un médicament en vente libre, des vitamines ou des produits naturels.
- Recommander au patient de communiquer avec son médecin avant de recevoir un vaccin contre la grippe ou tout autre type de vaccin. Les vaccins peuvent ne pas être aussi efficaces pendant un traitement par l'anakinra.
- Recommander au patient qui doit suivre un traitement ou subir une intervention chirurgicale de prévenir le professionnel de la santé qu'il prend de l'anakinra.
- Insister sur l'importance des examens diagnostiques de suivi permettant de déceler les effets secondaires du médicament.
- Expliquer au patient qu'il peut prendre du méthotrexate, un analgésique, un AINS, des corticostéroïdes et des salicylates en concomitance avec l'anakinra.

Polyarthrite rhumatoïde: Conseiller au patient de porter sur lui en tout temps un bracelet d'identité où sont inscrits son problème de santé et son traitement médicamenteux.

VÉRIFICATION DE L'EFFICACITÉ THÉRAPEUTIQUE

L'efficacité du traitement peut être démontrée par: la diminution des signes et des symptômes cliniques et le ralentissement de l'évolution de la PAR. ✳

ANASTRAZOLE

Arimidex

CLASSIFICATION:

Antinéoplasique (agent hormonal – inhibiteur non stéroïdien de l'aromatase)

Grossesse – catégorie D

INDICATIONS

Traitement du cancer du sein d'un stade avancé chez les femmes ménopausées ▪ Traitement adjuvant du cancer du sein précoce à récepteurs hormonaux positifs chez les femmes ménopausées.

MÉCANISME D'ACTION

Inhibition de l'enzyme aromatase, qui est partiellement responsable de la transformation des précurseurs des œstrogènes. ***Effets thérapeutiques:*** Abaissement des concentrations d'œstrogènes circulants, ce qui pourrait arrêter l'évolution des tumeurs sensibles aux œstrogènes.

PHARMACOCINÉTIQUE

Absorption: De 83 à 85 % (PO).

Distribution: Inconnue.

Métabolisme et excrétion: Métabolisme majoritairement hépatique (85 %); faible excrétion rénale (11 %).

Demi-vie: 50 heures.

Profil temps-action
(abaissement des concentrations sériques d'œstradiol)

	DÉBUT D'ACTION	PIC	DURÉE
PO	dans les 24 h	14 jours	6 jours†

† Après l'arrêt du traitement.

CONTRE-INDICATIONS, PRÉCAUTIONS ET MISES EN GARDE

Contre-indications: OBST., ALLAITEMENT: Hypersensibilité au médicament ou à un de ses ingrédients.

Précautions et mises en garde: Femmes en âge de procréer (l'innocuité et l'efficacité du médicament n'ont pas été établies) ▪ PÉD.: L'innocuité du médicament n'a pas été établie ▪ Insuffisance hépatique ou rénale graves ▪ Femmes atteintes d'ostéoporose ou à risque élevé d'en souffrir.

RÉACTIONS INDÉSIRABLES ET EFFETS SECONDAIRES

SNC: céphalées, faiblesse, étourdissements.

ORLO: pharyngite.

Resp.: dyspnée, toux accrue.

CV: œdème périphérique.

GI: nausées, douleurs abdominales, anorexie, constipation, diarrhée, sécheresse de la bouche (xérostomie), vomissements.

GU: douleurs pelviennes, saignements vaginaux, sécheresse vaginale.

Tég.: rash, troubles mucocutanés, transpiration.

Métab.: gain pondéral.

Loc.: douleurs au dos, douleurs aux os.

SN: paresthésie.

Divers: réactions allergiques (incluant l'ŒDÈME DE QUINCKE, l'urticaire et l'ANAPHYLAXIE), bouffées vasomotrices, douleurs.

INTERACTIONS

Médicament-médicament: Aucune interaction notable.

VOIES D'ADMINISTRATION ET POSOLOGIE

- **PO (adultes)**: 1 mg par jour.

PRÉSENTATION

Comprimés: 1 mg[Pr].

SOINS INFIRMIERS

ÉVALUATION DE LA SITUATION

- Suivre la patiente à intervalles réguliers, pendant toute la durée du traitement, pour évaluer l'intensité de la douleur et pour déceler les autres effets secondaires.

Tests de laboratoire: Le médicament peut entraîner une élévation des concentrations de GGT, d'AST, d'ALT, de phosphatase alcaline, de cholestérol total et de cholestérol LDL.

DIAGNOSTICS INFIRMIERS POSSIBLES

- Douleur aiguë (Effets secondaires).
- Connaissances insuffisantes sur le traitement médicamenteux (Enseignement au patient et à ses proches).

INTERVENTIONS INFIRMIÈRES

- Choisir d'administrer le médicament à jeun ou avec de la nourriture et s'en tenir à ce choix.

ENSEIGNEMENT AU PATIENT ET À SES PROCHES

- Recommander à la patiente de prendre le médicament exactement comme il lui a été prescrit.
- Indiquer à la patiente les réactions indésirables possibles et lui conseiller de communiquer avec un professionnel de la santé si ces réactions l'incommodent.
- Expliquer à la patiente que des saignements vaginaux peuvent survenir au cours des premières semaines qui suivent le passage à cette hormonothérapie. Lui préciser cependant que les saignements prolongés doivent être évalués.
- Prévenir la patiente qu'elle doit signaler l'intensification des douleurs afin qu'un traitement puisse être amorcé.

VÉRIFICATION DE L'EFFICACITÉ THÉRAPEUTIQUE

L'efficacité du traitement peut être démontrée par: le ralentissement de l'évolution de la maladie chez les femmes atteintes d'un cancer du sein d'un stade avancé ▪ l'absence de récidive de la maladie chez les femmes qui reçoivent l'anastrozole comme traitement adjuvant d'un cancer du sein précoce.

ANESTHÉSIQUES ÉPIDURAUX À ACTION LOCALE

bupivacaïne

Bupivacaine, Marcaine, Sensorcaine

ropivacaïne

Naropin

CLASSIFICATION:

Anesthésiques et adjuvants anesthésiques (épiduraux à action locale)

Grossesse – catégorie C

INDICATIONS

Anesthésie et analgésie locales ou régionales par bloc épidural.

MÉCANISME D'ACTION

Les anesthésiques locaux inhibent le déclenchement et la transmission des influx nerveux en modifiant l'influx de sodium et la sortie de potassium au niveau des neurones, ce qui entraîne le ralentissement ou l'arrêt de la transmission de la douleur. L'administration péridurale entraîne un effet au niveau des racines des nerfs rachidiens dans le territoire adjacent au point d'injection. Le cathéter doit être placé aussi près que possible des dermatomes (territoires cutanés innervés par un seul nerf rachidien ou par un groupe de nerfs rachidiens), ce qui donne un blocage permettant de répandre l'analgésie dans le territoire douloureux de la manière la plus efficace possible. ***Effets thérapeutiques:*** Diminution de la douleur; les faibles doses exercent un effet minimal sur les fonctions sensorielle et motrice; les doses élevées peuvent produire un blocage moteur complet. L'installation d'un cathéter permet de circonscrire cet effet.

PHARMACOCINÉTIQUE

Absorption: Absorption par voie générale à la suite de l'administration péridurale, mais la quantité absorbée dépend de la dose administrée.

Distribution: Les agents sont liposolubles, ce qui les maintient de façon spécifique dans l'espace épidural et limite leur absorption par voie générale. En cas d'ab-

sorption par voie générale, ces agents se répartissent dans tout l'organisme et traversent la barrière placentaire.
Métabolisme et excrétion: Les petites quantités qui pourraient entrer dans la circulation générale sont surtout métabolisées par le foie. Puisque seules de petites quantités sont éliminées par les reins, l'état de la fonction rénale n'est pas un facteur important à considérer.
Demi-vie: *Bupivacaïne* – 5 heures (après administration péridurale); *ropivacaïne* – 3 heures (après administration péridurale).

Profil temps-action (analgésie)

	DÉBUT D'ACTION	PIC	DURÉE
Voie péridurale	5 - 20 min	inconnu	jusqu'à 6 h†

† Durée de l'anesthésie par blocage nerveux.

CONTRE-INDICATIONS, PRÉCAUTIONS ET MISES EN GARDE

Contre-indications: Hypersensibilité, risque de sensibilité croisée avec d'autres anesthésiques locaux de type amide (lidocaïne, mépivacaïne, prilocaïne) ■ Anesthésie obstétricale par bloc paracervical ■ Inflammation ou infection près du point d'injection ■ Anesthésie par voie IV régionale (bloc de Bier, phléboanesthésie) ■ Hypotension marquée, comme en cas de choc cardiogénique et de choc hypovolémique ■ Usage rachidien sauf certaines exceptions.
Précautions et mises en garde: Usage concomitant d'autres anesthésiques locaux ■ Maladie hépatique ■ Administration concomitante d'anticoagulants (incluant de faibles doses d'héparine et d'héparine de faible poids moléculaire/héparinoïdes) – risque accru de formation d'un hématome épidural ou rachidien ■ **PÉD.**: L'innocuité de ces agents n'a pas été établie ■ Antécédents d'intolérance aux bisulfites (la bupivacaïne renferme des bisulfites et ne devrait pas être administrée aux patients qui ne les tolèrent pas).

RÉACTIONS INDÉSIRABLES ET EFFETS SECONDAIRES

Surtout signalés lors du traitement de la douleur.
SNC: CONVULSIONS, céphalées, irritabilité, ralentissement de l'élocution, contractions musculaires.
ORLO: acouphènes.
CV: COLLAPSUS CARDIOVASCULAIRE, arythmies, bradycardie, hypotension.
GI: goût métallique.
GU: rétention urinaire.
Tég.: prurit.
HÉ: acidose.
SN: picotements et engourdissement péribuccaux.
Divers: réactions allergiques, fièvre.

INTERACTIONS

Médicament-médicament: Risque de toxicité additive lors de l'administration concomitante d'autres **anesthésiques locaux de type amide**, dont la **lidocaïne**, la **mépivacaïne** et la **prilocaïne**.

VOIES D'ADMINISTRATION ET POSOLOGIE

La posologie des anesthésiques locaux, utilisés par voie épidurale, est plutôt complexe et dépend de plusieurs facteurs; il est important de se référer aux ouvrages spécialisés dans le domaine pour connaître la posologie exacte qu'il faut administrer lors de chacune des interventions particulières de blocage épidural. La posologie donnée ci-dessous ne représente qu'un résumé très succinct.

Bupivacaïne

- **Voie péridurale (adultes):** *Blocage moteur de partiel à intermédiaire* – jusqu'à un maximum de 25 à 50 mg/dose; *blocage moteur d'intermédiaire à complet* – jusqu'à un maximum de 50 à 100 mg/dose; *blocage moteur complet* – jusqu'à un maximum de 75 à 150 mg/dose.

Ropivacaïne

- **Voie péridurale (adultes):** *Soulagement de la douleur aiguë par bloc péridural au niveau lombaire – par injections intermittentes:* de 20 à 30 mg; – *par perfusion continue:* de 12 à 28 mg/h. *Anesthésie chirurgicale par bloc péridural au niveau lombaire* – de 75 à 200 mg selon l'intervention.

PRÉSENTATION

- **Bupivacaïne**
  Solutions pour injection: 0,25 %^Pr^, 0,5 %^Pr^, 0,75 %^Pr^ ■ **En association avec:** adrénaline^Pr^.
- **Ropivacaïne**
  Solutions pour injection: 0,2 %^Pr^, 0,5 %^Pr^, 0,75 %^Pr^, 1 %^Pr^.

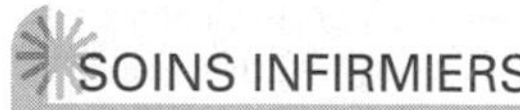

SOINS INFIRMIERS

ÉVALUATION DE LA SITUATION

TOXICITÉ ET SURDOSAGE: Observer le patient à chaque quart de travail pour déceler les signes suivants de toxicité générale: picotements et engourdissement péribuccaux, acouphènes, goût métallique, ralentissement de l'élocution, irritabilité, contractions musculaires, convulsions, dysrythmies cardiaques. Le cas échéant, les signaler à l'anesthésiste. Le traitement inclut le retrait des analgésiques locaux de la solution analgésique.

A

Hypotension orthostatique: Mesurer la fréquence cardiaque et la pression artérielle, incluant la pression orthostatique, avant de permettre au patient de se lever et les vérifier régulièrement jusqu'à ce qu'on ait stabilisé la dose ou que l'on se soit assuré que l'hypotension ne pose plus de problème. Une légère hypotension est courante puisque l'effet de l'anesthésique provoque le blocage des fibres nerveuses du système nerveux sympathique, ce qui entraîne une vasodilatation. Une hypotension et une bradycardie graves peuvent survenir, particulièrement lorsque le patient se lève ou lorsqu'on majore la dose de façon notable ou qu'on administre le médicament sous forme de bolus. Le traitement de l'hypotension rebelle peut inclure l'hydratation, le ralentissement de la vitesse de perfusion et/ou le retrait de l'anesthésique local de la solution analgésique.

Déficit moteur ou sensoriel indésirable:

- Lorsqu'on ajoute de faibles doses d'anesthésiques locaux à des opioïdes administrés par voie péridurale pour traiter la douleur, on cherche à obtenir l'analgésie et non l'anesthésie. Le patient devrait pouvoir se déplacer si son état le permet; l'analgésie péridurale ne devrait pas l'empêcher de poursuivre cette activité importante du processus de guérison. Toutefois, de nombreux facteurs, dont l'emplacement du cathéter, la dose d'anesthésique et la variabilité de la réponse, peuvent entraîner des déficits moteurs et sensoriels indésirables. La douleur est la première sensation à disparaître, suivie de la sensibilité thermique, du toucher, de la proprioception et du tonus des muscles squelettiques.
- À chaque quart de travail, observer le patient afin de déceler tout signe de déficit sensoriel. Lui demander d'indiquer les territoires cutanés où il ressent une sensation de picotement ou d'engourdissement (la sensation de picotement et d'engourdissement au point d'incision est normale).
- Suivre de près le patient à la recherche des signes de déficit moteur. Lui demander de plier les genoux et de soulever ses fesses du matelas. La plupart des patients peuvent le faire sans difficulté. Établir la capacité du patient de porter un poids. Aider le patient lorsqu'il se déplace. Informer l'anesthésiste de tout déficit moteur et sensoriel indésirable.
- Les déficits moteurs et sensoriels peuvent souvent être corrigés par une intervention simple. Par exemple, un changement de position peut permettre de soulager une perte de sensation passagère au niveau de l'un des membres. On traite souvent une légère faiblesse des muscles des membres en ralentissant la vitesse de perfusion et en maintenant le patient au lit jusqu'à la disparition de cette faiblesse. Il est parfois nécessaire de retirer l'anesthésique local de la solution analgésique, par exemple, en présence de signes de toxicité attribuables à l'analgésique local ou en cas d'échec du traitement simple des déficits moteurs et sensoriels.

DIAGNOSTICS INFIRMIERS POSSIBLES

- Douleur aiguë (Indications).
- Mobilité physique réduite (Réactions indésirables).
- Connaissances insuffisantes sur le traitement médicamenteux (Enseignement au patient et à ses proches).

INTERVENTIONS INFIRMIÈRES

- Consulter la section « Voies d'administration et posologie ».

ENSEIGNEMENT AU PATIENT ET À SES PROCHES

- Conseiller au patient de prévenir l'infirmière s'il note des signes ou des symptômes de toxicité générale.
- Recommander au patient de demander de l'aide lorsqu'il se déplace jusqu'à ce que l'on se soit assuré qu'il ne manifeste pas d'hypotension orthostatique et de déficits moteurs.

VÉRIFICATION DE L'EFFICACITÉ THÉRAPEUTIQUE

L'efficacité du traitement peut être démontrée par: la diminution de la douleur postopératoire sans déficits moteurs ou sensoriels.

ANTAGONISTES DES RÉCEPTEURS DE L'ANGIOTENSINE II

candésartan
Atacand

éprosartan
Teveten

irbesartan
Avapro

losartan
Cozaar

telmisartan
Micardis

valsartan
Diovan

CLASSIFICATION:
Antihypertenseurs (antagonistes des récepteurs de l'angiotensine II)
Grossesse – catégories C (1er trimestre) et D (2e et 3e trimestres)

INDICATIONS

Traitement de l'hypertension en monothérapie ou en association avec d'autres agents ▪ Traitement de l'insuffisance cardiaque lorsqu'un IECA n'est pas toléré ou est contre-indiqué (candésartan) ▪ Traitement de l'insuffisance cardiaque après un infarctus lorsqu'un IECA n'est pas toléré ou est contre-indiqué (valsartan) ▪ Traitement des patients hypertendus souffrant de diabète de type 2 et de néphropathie afin de ralentir l'évolution de la néphropathie (irbesartan et losartan).

MÉCANISME D'ACTION

Inhibition des effets vasoconstricteurs et de sécrétion d'aldostérone de l'angiotensine II par blocage sélectif de la liaison de l'angiotensine II aux récepteurs de type 1 (AT_1), présents dans de nombreux tissus dont ceux des muscles lisses vasculaires et des surrénales. ***Effets thérapeutiques:*** Abaissement de la pression artérielle ▪ Diminution du nombre d'hospitalisations chez les insuffisants cardiaques (candésartan et valsartan) ▪ Ralentissement de l'évolution de la néphropathie diabétique (irbesartan et losartan).

PHARMACOCINÉTIQUE

Absorption: *Candésartan* – le cilexétil de candésartan est transformé en candésartan dans le tractus gastro-intestinal au cours de l'absorption; biodisponibilité à 15 %; *éprosartan* – biodisponibilité à 13 %; *irbesartan* – biodisponibilité de 60 à 80 %; *losartan* – bonne absorption, mais métabolisme hépatique de premier passage important entraînant une biodisponibilité à 33 %; *telmisartan* – biodisponibilité de 42 à 58 % (accrue chez les insuffisants hépatiques); *valsartan* – biodisponibilité à 25 %.

Distribution: Inconnue; *candésartan* – une faible quantité traverse la barrière hématoencéphalique.

Métabolisme et excrétion: *Candésartan* – léger métabolisme hépatique; excrétion majoritairement rénale et fécale (par la bile) sous forme inchangée. *Éprosartan* – excrétion rénale et fécale (par la bile) (sous forme inchangée). *Irbesartan* – léger métabolisme hépatique; excrétion majoritairement biliaire, une petite fraction est éliminée sous forme inchangée par les reins. *Losartan* – important métabolisme hépatique de premier passage; 14 % est transformé en métabolite actif; 4 % du médicament est excrété sous forme inchangée par les reins; 6 % du métabolite actif est excrété sous forme inchangée par les reins; on note également une faible élimination biliaire. *Telmisartan* – faible métabolisme hépatique (11 %); excrétion principalement sous forme inchangée dans les fèces par excrétion biliaire. *Valsartan* – faible métabolisme hépatique (20 %); excrétion majoritairement fécale (par la bile).

Demi-vie: *Candésartan* – 9 heures; *éprosartan* – de 5 à 9 heures; *irbesartan* – de 11 à 15 heures; *losartan* – 2 heures (de 6 à 9 heures dans le cas du métabolite actif); *telmisartan* – 24 heures; *valsartan* – 6 heures.

Profil temps-action (effet antihypertenseur†)

	DÉBUT D'ACTION	PIC	DURÉE
Candésartan	2 – 4 h	6 – 8 h	24 h
Éprosartan	1 – 2 h	inconnu	24 h
Irbesartan	dans les 2 h	3 – 14 h	24 h
Losartan	dans les 2 h	6 h	24 h
Telmisartan	dans les 3 h	inconnu	24 h
Valsartan	dans les 2 h	4 – 6 h	24 h

† La réponse maximale au traitement peut prendre jusqu'à 2 ou 3 semaines.

CONTRE-INDICATIONS, PRÉCAUTIONS ET MISES EN GARDE

Contre-indications: Hypersensibilité.

Précautions et mises en garde: Patients présentant une déplétion volémique ou une déplétion sodée ou patients recevant des doses élevées de diurétiques (corriger ces déficits avant d'amorcer le traitement ou commencer le traitement à de plus faibles doses) ▪ Sténose aortique ▪ Patients de race noire (le médicament pourrait ne pas être aussi efficace en monothérapie; l'ajout d'autres agents pourrait s'avérer nécessaire) ▪ Hyperkaliémie ▪ Insuffisance rénale attribuable à l'insuffisance cardiaque ou à une néphropathie primaire (risque d'aggravation de l'insuffisance rénale) ▪ Troubles biliaires obstructifs ou insuffisance hépatique (il est recommandé d'abaisser la dose initiale d'éprosartan, de losartan, de telmisartan ou de valsartan) ▪ **OBST., ALLAITEMENT**: L'innocuité du médicament n'a pas été établie chez la femme enceinte, en âge de procréer ou qui allaite ▪ **PÉD.**: L'innocuité du médicament n'a pas été établie chez les enfants < 18 ans.

RÉACTIONS INDÉSIRABLES ET EFFETS SECONDAIRES

SNC: étourdissements, fatigue, céphalées.

CV: hypotension.

GI: diarrhée, hépatite induite par le médicament.

GU: ALTÉRATION DE LA FONCTION RÉNALE.

HÉ: hyperkaliémie.

INTERACTIONS

Médicament-médicament: Les **AINS** peuvent diminuer les effets antihypertenseurs de ces médicaments ▪ L'administration concomitante d'autres **antihypertenseurs** et de **diurétiques** entraîne des effets antihypertenseurs additifs ▪ L'administration concomitante de **diurétiques** (administrer une plus faible dose initiale) et de **dérivés nitrés** peut accroître le risque d'hypotension ▪ L'administration concomitante de **diurétiques épargneurs de potassium** ou de **suppléments de potassium** augmente le risque d'hyperkaliémie ▪ Les antagonistes des récepteurs de l'angiotensine II augmentent les concentrations sériques de **lithium**; le suivi des concentrations sériques est recommandé.

VOIES D'ADMINISTRATION ET POSOLOGIE

Candésartan

Hypertension

- **PO (adultes)**: *En monothérapie - dose initiale* - 16 mg, 1 fois par jour (écart posologique: de 8 à 32 mg, 1 fois par jour). *Patients sous diurétiques ou présentant une déplétion volémique* - commencer le traitement à une dose plus faible.

Insuffisance cardiaque

- **PO (adultes)**: *Dose initiale* - 4 mg, 1 fois par jour; doubler la dose à intervalle de 2 semaines, selon la tolérance du patient (dose cible: 32 mg, 1 fois par jour).

INSUFFISANCE RÉNALE

- **PO (ADULTES)**: COMMENCER LE TRAITEMENT À UNE DOSE PLUS FAIBLE.

Éprosartan

Hypertension

- **PO (adultes)**: *Dose initiale* - 600 mg, 1 fois par jour; on peut porter la dose jusqu'à 800 mg par jour, administrée en 1 ou 2 prises (écart posologique: de 400 à 800 mg, en 1 ou 2 prises).
- **PO (patients âgés)**: *Dose initiale* - 400 mg, 1 fois par jour.

INSUFFISANCE RÉNALE ET HÉPATIQUE

- **PO (ADULTES)**: *DOSE INITIALE* - 400 mg, 1 FOIS PAR JOUR.

Irbesartan

Hypertension

- **PO (adultes)**: *Dose initiale* - 150 mg, 1 fois par jour; on peut porter la dose jusqu'à 300 mg, 1 fois par jour. *Patients sous diurétiques, présentant une déplétion volémique ou patients hémodialysés - dose initiale* - 75 mg, 1 fois par jour.

Néphropathie diabétique

- **PO (adultes)**: *Dose initiale* - 150 mg, 1 fois par jour; on peut porter la dose jusqu'à 300 mg, 1 fois par jour (dose cible: 300 mg, 1 fois par jour).

Losartan

Hypertension

- **PO (adultes)**: *Dose initiale* - 50 mg, 1 fois par jour; on peut porter la dose jusqu'à 100 mg par jour, administrée en 1 ou 2 prises (écart posologique: de 25 à 100 mg, en 1 ou 2 prises). *Patients sous diurétiques ou présentant une déplétion volémique - dose initiale* - 25 mg, 1 fois par jour; augmenter selon la tolérance du patient.

Néphropathie diabétique

- **PO (adultes)**: *Dose initiale* - 50 mg, 1 fois par jour; on peut porter la dose jusqu'à 100 mg par jour, administrée en 1 ou 2 prises (écart posologique: de 25 à 100 mg, en 1 ou 2 prises).

INSUFFISANCE HÉPATIQUE

- **PO (ADULTES)**: *DOSE INITIALE* - 25 mg, 1 FOIS PAR JOUR; AUGMENTER SELON LA TOLÉRANCE DU PATIENT.

Telmisartan

Hypertension

- **PO (adultes)**: *Dose initiale* - 80 mg, 1 fois par jour (écart posologique: de 40 à 80 mg, 1 fois par jour).

INSUFFISANCE HÉPATIQUE

- **PO (ADULTES)**: *DOSE INITIALE* - 40 mg, 1 FOIS PAR JOUR.

Valsartan

Hypertension

- **PO (adultes)**: *Dose initiale* - 80 mg, 1 fois par jour; on peut porter la dose jusqu'à 160 mg, 1 fois par jour. *Patients sous diurétiques ou présentant une déplétion volémique* - commencer le traitement à une dose plus faible.

Insuffisance cardiaque après infarctus

- **PO (adultes)**: *Dose initiale* - 20 mg, 2 fois par jour; doubler la dose à intervalle de 2 semaines, selon la tolérance du patient (dose cible: 160 mg, 2 fois par jour).

PRÉSENTATION

- **Candésartan**

  Comprimés: 4 mg[Pr], 8 mg[Pr], 16 mg[Pr] ▪ **En association avec**: hydrochlorothiazide (Atacand Plus[Pr]).
- **Éprosartan**

  Comprimés: 400 mg[Pr], 600 mg[Pr] ▪ **En association avec**: hydrochlorothiazide (Teveten Plus[Pr]).

- **Irbesartan**
  Comprimés: 75 mgPr, 150 mgPr, 300 mgPr ■ **En association avec**: hydrochlorothiazide (AvalidePr).
- **Losartan**
  Comprimés: 25 mgPr, 50 mgPr, 100 mgPr ■ **En association avec**: hydrochlorothiazide (HyzaarPr).
- **Telmisartan**
  Comprimés: 40 mgPr, 80 mgPr ■ **En association avec**: hydrochlorothiazide (Micardis PlusPr).
- **Valsartan**
  Capsules: 80 mgPr, 160 mgPr ■ **Comprimés**: 40 mgPr, 80 mgPr, 160 mgPr, 320 mgPr ■ **En association avec**: hydrochlorothiazide (Diovan-HCTPr).

SOINS INFIRMIERS

ÉVALUATION DE LA SITUATION

- Mesurer le pouls et la pression artérielle (en position couchée, debout et assise), à intervalles réguliers, pendant toute la durée du traitement.
- Vérifier la fréquence du renouvellement des ordonnances afin de déterminer l'observance du traitement.
- Rester à l'affût des signes d'œdème de Quincke (dyspnée, œdème facial). Ces médicaments peuvent provoquer rarement un œdème de Quincke; cette réaction est plus courante chez les patients qui ont manifesté cet effet lors d'un traitement par les inhibiteurs de l'ECA.

Insuffisance cardiaque: Effectuer le bilan quotidien des ingesta et des excreta et peser le patient tous les jours. Rester à l'affût des signes d'insuffisance cardiaque (œdème périphérique, râles ou crépitations, dyspnée, gain de poids, turgescence des jugulaires).

Tests de laboratoire:

- Noter les concentrations de créatinine sérique et de protéines urinaires chez les patients traités en raison d'une néphropathie diabétique.
- Ces médicaments peuvent entraîner, dans de rares cas, une élévation des concentrations d'urée et de créatinine sérique.
- Ces médicaments peuvent provoquer une élévation des concentrations sériques de bilirubine.
- Ils peuvent parfois entraîner l'hyperkaliémie.
- Ils peuvent entraîner une élévation des concentrations d'ALT et d'AST.
- Ils peuvent entraîner une légère diminution des concentrations d'hémoglobine et de l'hématocrite.
- Le losartan peut entraîner une diminution des concentrations sanguines d'acide urique.

DIAGNOSTICS INFIRMIERS POSSIBLES

- Risque d'accident (Réactions indésirables).
- Connaissances insuffisantes sur le traitement médicamenteux (Enseignement au patient et à ses proches).
- Non-observance du traitement médicamenteux (Enseignement au patient et à ses proches).

INTERVENTIONS INFIRMIÈRES

- Dans la mesure du possible, il faut corriger la déplétion volémique avant d'amorcer le traitement.
- Ces médicaments peuvent être administrés sans égard aux repas.

ENSEIGNEMENT AU PATIENT ET À SES PROCHES

- Conseiller au patient de respecter rigoureusement la posologie recommandée et de continuer à prendre le médicament même s'il se sent bien. S'il n'a pas pu prendre le médicament au moment habituel, il doit le prendre aussitôt que possible à moins qu'il ne soit presque l'heure de prendre la dose suivante; l'avertir qu'il ne doit jamais remplacer une dose manquée par une double dose. Le prévenir que ce médicament stabilise la pression artérielle mais ne guérit pas l'hypertension. Recommander au patient de prendre le médicament à la même heure tous les jours. Il est conseillé de réduire graduellement la dose avant de cesser le traitement.
- Inciter le patient à appliquer d'autres mesures pour maîtriser l'hypertension: perdre du poids, adopter un régime alimentaire hyposodé, cesser de fumer, boire de l'alcool avec modération, faire de l'exercice régulièrement et diminuer le stress.
- Expliquer au patient et à ses proches comment mesurer la pression artérielle. Leur demander de la mesurer au moins 1 fois par semaine et de signaler au médecin ou à un autre professionnel de la santé tout changement important.
- Conseiller au patient de changer de position lentement afin de réduire le risque d'hypotension orthostatique. Lui expliquer que la consommation d'alcool, la position debout pendant une période prolongée, l'effort ou la chaleur peuvent augmenter le risque d'hypotension orthostatique.
- Inciter la patiente en âge de procréer à utiliser une méthode de contraception et à informer un professionnel de la santé si elle pense être enceinte ou désire le devenir.
- Prévenir le patient que ce médicament peut parfois provoquer des étourdissements.
- Conseiller au patient de consulter un professionnel de la santé avant de prendre un médicament en

vente libre contre la toux, le rhume ou les allergies ou tout autre médicament, quel qu'il soit.

- Conseiller au patient d'informer le professionnel de la santé des médicaments qu'il prend avant de se soumettre à une intervention chirurgicale ou à un nouveau traitement.
- Insister sur l'importance des examens de suivi permettant d'évaluer l'efficacité du traitement.

VÉRIFICATION DE L'EFFICACITÉ THÉRAPEUTIQUE

L'efficacité du traitement peut être démontrée par: la baisse de la pression artérielle sans manifestation de réactions indésirables excessives ▪ la diminution du nombre d'hospitalisations chez les patients atteints d'insuffisance cardiaque ▪ le ralentissement de l'évolution de la néphropathie diabétique. ✳

ANTAGONISTES DES RÉCEPTEURS H_2 DE L'HISTAMINE

cimétidine
Apo-Cimetidine, Novo-Cimetine, Nu-Cimet, Tagamet

famotidine
Acid Control, Maalox H_2 Acid Controller, Pepcid, Pepcid AC, Ulcidine

nizatidine
Apo-Nizatidine, Axid, Gen-Nizatidine, PMS-Nizatidine

ranitidine
Acid Reducer, Apo-Ranitidine, Nu-Ranit, Zantac, Zantac 75

CLASSIFICATION:
Antiulcéreux

Grossesse – catégorie B

INDICATIONS

Traitement de courte durée de l'ulcère duodénal en poussée active et de l'ulcère gastrique bénin ▪ Prophylaxie de l'ulcère duodénal ou gastrique (doses peu élevées) ▪ Traitement du reflux gastro-œsophagien ▪ **Cimétidine:** Traitement et prévention des brûlures d'estomac, de l'acidité gastrique et des aigreurs d'estomac (préparations en vente libre) ▪ **Cimétidine, ranitidine:** Traitement de l'hypergastrinémie (comme le syndrome de Zollinger-Ellison) ▪ Traitement et prévention des symptômes gastro-intestinaux associés à l'usage des AINS ▪ **Ranitidine:** Prophylaxie des hémorragies gastro-intestinales par ulcération due au stress chez les grands malades et des hémorragies récidivantes des ulcères hémorragiques, prophylaxie du syndrome de Mendelson ▪ **Famotidine IV:** traitement de certains patients hospitalisés atteints d'hypersécrétion gastrique ou d'ulcères réfractaires. **Usages non approuvés:** Pneumonie de déglutition ▪ Prévention de l'inactivation, par l'acidité, des enzymes pancréatiques de substitution administrées aux patients souffrant d'insuffisance pancréatique ▪ Traitement de l'urticaire ▪ **Cimétidine:** Prévention et traitement de l'hémorragie digestive haute, induite par le stress, chez les patients très malades.

MÉCANISME D'ACTION

Inhibition de l'activité de l'histamine au niveau des récepteurs H_2 situés pour leur majorité dans les cellules pariétales de l'estomac, ce qui se traduit par l'inhibition de la sécrétion d'acide gastrique. ***Effets thérapeutiques:*** Cicatrisation et prophylaxie des ulcères ▪ Réduction des symptômes de reflux gastro-œsophagien ▪ Diminution de la sécrétion d'acide gastrique.

PHARMACOCINÉTIQUE

Absorption: *Cimétidine* – bonne (PO); *famotidine* – de 40 à 45 % (PO); *nizatidine* – de 70 à 95 % (PO); *ranitidine* – 50 % (PO) et de 90 à 100 % (IM).
Distribution: Tous les agents pénètrent dans le lait maternel et dans le liquide céphalorachidien.
Métabolisme et excrétion: *Cimétidine* – environ 50 % de la dose administrée par voie orale est métabolisé par le foie; le reste est éliminé sous forme inchangée par les reins. *Famotidine* – jusqu'à 70 % est éliminé sous forme inchangée par les reins, le reste est métabolisé par le foie. *Nizatidine* – 60 % est éliminé sous forme inchangée par les reins; un certain métabolisme hépatique intervient; au moins un métabolite est actif. *Ranitidine* – métabolisme hépatique; excrétion sous forme inchangée par les reins (30 % PO); de 70 à 80 % est éliminé dans le cas de l'administration parentérale.
Demi-vie: *Cimétidine* – 2 heures; *famotidine* – de 2,5 à 3,5 heures; *nizatidine* – 1,6 heure; *ranitidine* – de 1,7 à 3 heures (toutes ces demi-vies sont prolongées en cas d'insuffisance rénale).

Profil temps-action

	DÉBUT D'ACTION	PIC	DURÉE
Cimétidine PO	30 min	45 – 90 min	4 – 8 h
Famotidine PO	en l'espace de 60 min	1 – 4 h	6 – 12 h
Famotidine IV	en l'espace de 60 min	0,5 – 3 h	8 – 15 h
Nizatidine PO	inconnu	inconnu	8 – 12 h
Ranitidine PO	inconnu	1 – 3 h	8 – 12 h
Ranitidine IM	inconnu	15 min	8 – 12 h
Ranitidine IV	inconnu	15 min	8 – 12 h

CONTRE-INDICATIONS, PRÉCAUTIONS ET MISES EN GARDE

Contre-indications: Hypersensibilité ■ Risque de réactions de sensibilité croisée ■ Intolérance à l'alcool (certaines préparations orales en contiennent et ne devraient pas être administrées aux patients qui ne le tolèrent pas) ■ Porphyrie (ranitidine seulement) ■ Certaines préparations contiennent de l'aspartame; ne pas les administrer aux patients souffrant de phénylcétonurie.

Précautions et mises en garde: Insuffisance rénale (prédisposition accrue aux effets indésirables sur le SNC; on recommande de prolonger l'écart posologique de la *cimétidine*, si la Cl_{Cr} < 50 mL/min; de la *famotidine*, si la Cl_{Cr} < 50 mL/min; de la *nizatidine*, si la Cl_{Cr} < 50 mL/min et de la *ranitidine*, si la Cl_{Cr} < 50 mL/min ■ **GÉR.**: Prédisposition accrue aux effets indésirables sur le SNC; on recommande de réduire la dose ■ Insuffisance hépatique (diminuer la dose en raison du risque de confusion) ■ **OBST.**: L'innocuité de ces médicaments n'a pas été établie ■ Allaitement.

RÉACTIONS INDÉSIRABLES ET EFFETS SECONDAIRES

SNC: confusion, étourdissements, somnolence, hallucinations, céphalées.
CV: ARYTHMIES.
GI: dysgueusie, constipation, diarrhée, hépatite (nizatidine, cimétidine), nausées.
GU: diminution du nombre de spermatozoïdes, impuissance.
End.: gynécomastie.
Hémat.: AGRANULOCYTOSE, ANÉMIE APLASIQUE, anémie, neutropénie, thrombocytopénie.
Locaux: douleurs au point d'injection IM.
Divers: réactions d'hypersensibilité, vasculite.

INTERACTIONS

Médicament-médicament: La cimétidine inhibe les enzymes participant au métabolisme hépatique de plusieurs médicaments, ce qui peut entraîner une augmentation des concentrations sanguines et de la toxicité des agents suivants: **amiodarone**, **antidépresseurs tricycliques**, certaines **benzodiazépines** (particulièrement **chlordiazépoxide**, **diazépam** et **midazolam**), certains **bêtabloquants** (**labétalol**, **métoprolol**, **propranolol**, **pindolol**), **carbamazépine**, **chloroquine**, **citalopram**, **clozapine**, **lidocaïne**, **metformine**, **nifédipine**, **pentoxifylline**, **phénytoïne**, **quinidine**, **quinine**, **sulfonylurées**, **tacrine**, **théophylline** et **warfarine**; la famotidine, la nizatidine et la ranitidine ont un effet bien moindre sur le métabolisme des autres médicaments ■ Les effets de la **succinylcholine**, du **flécaïnide**, du **procaïnamide**, de la **carmustine** et du **fluorouracile** sont accrus par la cimétidine ■ La nizatidine diminue les concentrations plasmatiques de l'**atazanavir** et la biodisponibilité du **céfuroxime axétil** (espacer la prise de ces médicaments) ■ Tous les agents réduisent l'absorption du **kétoconazole** et de l'**itraconazole** ■ Les **antiacides** et le **sucralfate** réduisent l'absorption de tous les agents ■ La **clarithromycine** accroît les concentrations de ranitidine.

VOIES D'ADMINISTRATION ET POSOLOGIE

Cimétidine

- **PO (adultes)**: *Traitement de courte durée des crises d'ulcère* – 300 mg, 4 fois par jour; ou 800 mg au coucher; ou de 400 à 600 mg, 2 fois par jour (ne pas dépasser 2,4 g par jour). *Prophylaxie de l'ulcère duodénal ou gastrique* – 300 mg, 2 fois par jour, ou 400 mg au coucher. *Traitement des lésions et des symptômes dus aux AINS* – 800 mg par jour, en 1 dose ou en 2 doses fractionnées. *Prophylaxie des lésions et des symptômes dus aux AINS* – 400 mg, au coucher. *Reflux gastro-œsophagien* – de 800 à 1 200 mg par jour, en doses fractionnées. *Maladies caractérisées par une hypersécrétion gastrique* – 300 mg, toutes les 6 heures (on a déjà utilisé jusqu'à 12 g par jour). *Pyrosis et hyperchlorhydrie occasionnels* – 200 mg, 1 ou 2 fois par jour.
- **PO (enfants de 0 à 4 semaines)**: De 5 à 10 mg/kg par jour, en doses fractionnées, toutes les 8 à 12 heures.
- **PO (enfants de 1 mois à 1 an)**: De 10 à 20 mg/kg par jour, en doses fractionnées, toutes les 6 à 12 heures.
- **PO (enfants de 1 à 12 ans)**: De 20 à 40 mg/kg par jour, en doses fractionnées, toutes les 6 heures.
  La dose maximale chez l'enfant ne doit pas dépasser celle recommandée chez l'adulte. On dispose de peu de données concernant la posologie recommandée chez l'enfant. N'administrer qu'en présence d'une fonction rénale normale.
- ***INSUFFISANCE RÉNALE***
  PO (ADULTES): *CL_{CR} DE 10 À 50 mL/MIN* – DIMINUER LA DOSE DE 50 %; *CL_{CR} < 10 mL/MIN* – DIMINUER LA DOSE DE 75 %.

Famotidine

- **PO (adultes)**: *Traitement de courte durée des crises d'ulcère* – 40 mg par jour, au coucher, ou 20 mg, 2 fois par jour, pendant un maximum de 8 semaines. *Prophylaxie de l'ulcère duodénal* – 20 mg, 1 fois par jour, au coucher. *Reflux gastro-œsophagien* – 20 mg, 2 fois par jour, et jusqu'à 40 mg, 2 fois par jour. *Maladies caractérisées par une hypersécrétion gastrique* – initialement 20 mg, toutes les 6 heures, jusqu'à 200 mg, toutes les 6 heures.

A

Préparations en vente libre – 10 mg pour le soulagement des symptômes ; en cas d'usage prophylactique, 15 minutes avant la consommation d'aliments ou de boissons provoquant des brûlures d'estomac (ne pas dépasser 20 mg en 24 heures, pendant un maximum de 2 semaines).

- **IV (adultes) :** Patients hospitalisés atteints de maladies liées à une hypersécrétion gastrique ou d'ulcères réfractaires – 20 mg, toutes les 12 heures.
- ***INSUFFISANCE RÉNALE***

  PO (ADULTES) : *CL_{CR} < 50 mL/MIN* – RÉDUIRE DE MOITIÉ LA DOSE OU AUGMENTER L'INTERVALLE ENTRE LES DOSES JUSQU'À 36 À 48 HEURES EN FONCTION DE LA RÉPONSE CLINIQUE.

Nizatidine

- **PO (adultes) :** *Traitement de courte durée des crises d'ulcère* – 300 mg, 1 fois par jour, au coucher, ou 150 mg, 2 fois par jour. *Prophylaxie de l'ulcère duodénal* – 150 mg, 1 fois par jour, au coucher. *Reflux gastro-œsophagien* – 150 mg, 2 fois par jour.
- **PO (enfants < 12 ans) :** *Reflux gastro-œsophagien* – 150 mg, 2 fois par jour.
- **PO (enfants ≥ 12 ans) :** *Reflux gastro-œsophagien* – de 5 à 10 mg/kg par jour, en doses fractionnées, 2 fois par jour. Ne pas dépasser 300 mg par jour.
- ***INSUFFISANCE RÉNALE***

  PO (ADULTES) : *TRAITEMENT DE COURTE DURÉE DES CRISES D'ULCÈRE – CL_{CR} DE 20 À 50 mL/MIN* – 150 mg, 1 FOIS PAR JOUR ; *CL_{CR} < 20 mL/MIN* – 150 mg, TOUS LES 2 JOURS. *PROPHYLAXIE DE L'ULCÈRE DUODÉNAL – CL_{CR} DE 20 À 50 mL/MIN* – 150 mg, TOUS LES 2 JOURS ; *CL_{CR} < 20 mL/MIN* – 150 mg, TOUS LES 3 JOURS.

Ranitidine

- **PO (adultes) :** *Traitement de courte durée des crises d'ulcère* – 150 mg, 2 fois par jour, ou 300 mg, 1 fois par jour, au coucher. *Prophylaxie de l'ulcère duodénal* – 150 mg, 1 fois par jour, au coucher. *Reflux gastro-œsophagien* – 150 mg, 2 fois par jour. *Œsophagite érosive* – initialement, 150 mg, 4 fois par jour, puis 150 mg, 2 fois par jour, en traitement d'entretien. *Maladies caractérisées par une hypersécrétion gastrique* – initialement, 150 mg, 3 fois par jour ; on a déjà utilisé jusqu'à 6 g par jour. *Traitement et prévention des lésions et des symptômes dus aux AINS* – 150 mg, 2 fois par jour. *Prophylaxie du syndrome de Mendelson :* 150 mg, le soir précédant l'induction de l'anesthésie ; cependant, 150 mg 2 heures avant l'induction de l'anesthésie sont également efficaces. *Prophylaxie du syndrome de Mendelson chez les patientes qui choisissent d'accoucher sous anesthésie :* 150 mg, toutes les 6 heures *Préparations en vente libre* – 75 mg, en cas de symptômes (jusqu'à 2 fois par jour).
- **IV, IM (adultes) :** 50 mg, toutes les 6 à 8 heures (ne pas dépasser 400 mg par jour) ■ *Prophylaxie du syndrome de Mendelson :* 50 mg, de 45 à 60 minutes avant l'induction de l'anesthésie générale. *Perfusion IV continue* – de 0,125 mg à 0,250 mg/kg/h.
- ***INSUFFISANCE RÉNALE***

  PO (ADULTES) : *CL_{CR} < 50 mL/MIN* – 150 mg, TOUTES LES 24 HEURES ; CETTE DOSE PEUT ÊTRE MAJORÉE JUSQU'À 150 mg, TOUTES LES 12 HEURES OU PLUS FRÉQUEMMENT, AU BESOIN ; IL PEUT S'AVÉRER NÉCESSAIRE DE RÉDUIRE DAVANTAGE LA DOSE EN CAS D'INSUFFISANCE HÉPATIQUE CONCOMITANTE.

PRÉSENTATION

- **Cimétidine**

  Comprimés : 200 mg[Pr], 300 mg[Pr], 400 mg[Pr], 600 mg[Pr], 800 mg[Pr] ■ **Préparation orale :** 300 mg/5 mL[Pr].
- **Famotidine**

  Comprimés : 10 mg[VL], 20 mg[Pr], 40 mg[Pr] ■ **Comprimés à croquer avec aspartame :** 10 mg[VL] ■ **Solution pour injection :** 10 mg/mL[Pr].
- **Nizatidine**

  Capsules : 150 mg[Pr], 300 mg[Pr].
- **Ranitidine**

  Comprimés : 75 mg[VL], 150 mg[Pr], 300 mg[Pr] ■ **Sirop :** 15 mg/mL[Pr] ■ **Solution pour injection :** 25 mg/mL[Pr].

SOINS INFIRMIERS

ÉVALUATION DE LA SITUATION

- Suivre de près la douleur épigastrique ou abdominale et la présence de sang occulte ou franc dans les selles, les vomissures et les échantillons prélevés par aspiration gastrique.

GÉR. : Observer les personnes âgées et les patients débilités pour déceler les signes de confusion. Prévenir immédiatement le médecin s'ils se manifestent.

Tests de laboratoire :

- FAIRE LE SUIVI DE LA NUMÉRATION GLOBULAIRE ET DE LA FORMULE LEUCOCYTAIRE À INTERVALLES RÉGULIERS, PENDANT TOUTE LA DURÉE DU TRAITEMENT.
- Les effets de ces agents s'opposent à ceux de la pentagastrine et de l'histamine lors de l'analyse de l'acidité gastrique. Ne pas administrer ces agents dans les 24 heures qui précèdent cette analyse.

- Ces agents peuvent entraîner des résultats faussement négatifs aux tests cutanés effectués au moyen d'extraits d'allergène. Ne pas administrer ces agents pendant les 24 heures qui précèdent ce test.
- Ces agents peuvent entraîner une élévation des concentrations sériques de transaminases et de créatinine.
- La *nizatidine* peut entraîner l'élévation des concentrations de phosphatase alcaline ou des résultats faussement positifs lors de la recherche d'urobilinogène.
- La *ranitidine* peut entraîner des résultats faussement négatifs au dosage des protéines urinaires; effectuer le test avec de l'acide sulfosalicylique.

DIAGNOSTICS INFIRMIERS POSSIBLES

- Douleur aiguë (Indications).
- Connaissances insuffisantes sur le traitement médicamenteux (Enseignement au patient et à ses proches).

INTERVENTIONS INFIRMIÈRES

PO:

- Si l'on administre en même temps des antiacides ou du sucralfate pour soulager la douleur, ne pas administrer les antiacides dans les 30 à 60 minutes qui suivent la prise de l'antagoniste des récepteurs H_2 de l'histamine; administrer le sucralfate, 2 heures après l'administration des antagonistes des récepteurs H_2 de l'histamine; ces agents peuvent réduire l'absorption des antagonistes des récepteurs H_2 de l'histamine.
- Administrer les antagonistes des récepteurs H_2 de l'histamine aux repas ou immédiatement après et au coucher pour en prolonger l'effet.
- Les doses administrées 1 fois par jour devraient être prises au coucher pour en prolonger l'effet.
- Les comprimés de cimétidine dégagent une odeur particulière.
- Agiter la suspension orale avant de l'administrer. Jeter toute portion inutilisée après 30 jours.
- Retirer *les granules ou les comprimés effervescents de ranitidine* du papier d'aluminium et les dissoudre dans 175 à 250 mL d'eau avant de faire boire la préparation au patient.

Famotidine

IV directe: Diluer 2 mL (10 mg/mL de solution) dans 5 ou 10 mL de solution de NaCl 0,9 % pour injection. Consulter les directives de chaque fabricant avant de reconstituer la préparation.

Vitesse d'administration: Administrer la préparation à une vitesse maximale de 10 mg/min. L'administration rapide peut entraîner de l'hypotension.

Perfusion intermittente: Diluer à raison de 20 mg dans 100 mL de solution de NaCl 0,9 % ou de D5%E pour obtenir une concentration de 0,2 mg/mL. La solution diluée est stable pendant 48 heures à la température ambiante. Ne pas administrer la solution si elle change de couleur ou si elle renferme un précipité. Consulter les directives de chaque fabricant avant de reconstituer la préparation.

Vitesse d'administration: Administrer la préparation en 15 à 30 minutes.

Compatibilité (tubulure en Y): acide folique ■ adrénaline ■ amifostine ■ aminophylline ■ ampicilline ■ ampicilline/sulbactam ■ amrinone ■ atropine ■ aztréonam ■ brétyllium ■ calcium, gluconate de ■ céfazoline ■ céfopérazone ■ céfotaxime ■ céfotétane ■ céfoxitine ■ ceftazidime ■ ceftizoxime ■ céfuroxime ■ céphalothine ■ céphapirine ■ cisatracurium ■ cisplatine ■ cyclophosphamide ■ cytarabine ■ dexaméthasone ■ dextran 40 ■ digoxine ■ dobutamine ■ dopamine ■ doxorubicine ■ doxorubicine liposomale ■ énalaprilate ■ érythromycine, lactobionate d' ■ esmolol ■ filgrastim ■ fluconazole ■ fludarabine ■ furosémide ■ gentamicine ■ halopéridol ■ héparine ■ hydrocortisone sodique, succinate d' ■ imipénem/cilastatine ■ insuline ■ isoprotérénol ■ labétalol ■ lidocaïne ■ magnésium, sulfate de ■ melphalan ■ mépéridine ■ méthylprednisolone ■ métoclopramide ■ mezlocilline ■ midazolam ■ morphine ■ nafcilline ■ nitroglycérine ■ nitroprusside ■ noradrénaline ■ ondansétron ■ oxacilline ■ paclitaxel ■ perphénazine ■ phényléphrine ■ phénytoïne ■ phytonadione ■ pipéracilline ■ potassium, chlorure de ■ potassium, phosphate de ■ procaïnamide ■ rémifentanil ■ sargramostim ■ sodium, bicarbonate de ■ téniposide ■ théophylline ■ thiamine ■ thiotépa ■ ticarcilline ■ ticarcilline/clavulanate ■ vérapamil ■ vinorelbine.

Incompatibilité (tubulure en Y): amphotéricine B, cholestéryle d' ■ céfépime ■ pipéracilline/tazobactam.

Ranitidine

IV directe: Diluer à raison de 50 mg dans 20 mL de solution de NaCl 0,9 % ou de D5%E pour injection. Consulter les directives de chaque fabricant avant de reconstituer la préparation.

Vitesse d'administration: Administrer la préparation en au moins 5 minutes. L'administration rapide peut provoquer de la bradycardie, de l'hypotension et des arythmies.

Perfusion intermittente: Diluer à raison de 50 mg dans 100 mL de solution de NaCl 0,9 % ou de D5%E. La solution diluée est stable pendant 48 heures à la température ambiante. Ne pas administrer la solution si elle change de couleur ou si elle renferme un précipité.

Consulter les directives de chaque fabricant avant de reconstituer la préparation.

Vitesse d'administration: Administrer la préparation en 15 à 20 minutes.

Perfusion continue: Diluer la ranitidine dans une solution de D5%E pour obtenir une concentration de 150 mg/250 mL (ne pas dépasser 2,5 mg/mL dans le cas des patients souffrant du syndrome de Zollinger-Ellison). Consulter les directives de chaque fabricant avant de reconstituer la préparation.

Vitesse d'administration: Administrer à un débit de 6,25 mg/h. Chez les patients souffrant du syndrome de Zollinger-Ellison, amorcer la perfusion à un débit de 1 mg/kg/h. Si la sécrétion d'acide gastrique est supérieure à 10 mmol/h ou si les symptômes réapparaissent après 4 heures, augmenter la dose par paliers de 0,5 mg/kg/h, jusqu'à un maximum de 2,5 mg/kg/h et mesurer de nouveau les sécrétions d'acide gastrique.

Associations compatibles dans la même seringue: atropine ■ cyclizine ■ dexaméthasone ■ dimenhydrinate ■ diphenhydramine ■ fentanyl ■ glycopyrrolate ■ hydromorphone ■ mépéridine ■ métoclopramide ■ morphine ■ nalbuphine ■ oxymorphone ■ pentazocine ■ perphénazine ■ prochlorpérazine ■ prométhazine ■ scopolamine ■ thiéthylpérazine.

Associations incompatibles dans la même seringue: hydroxyzine ■ méthotriméprazine ■ midazolam ■ pentobarbital ■ phénobarbital.

Compatibilité (tubulure en Y): acyclovir ■ aldesleukine ■ amifostine ■ aminophylline ■ atracurium ■ aztréonam ■ brétyllium ■ céfépime ■ cefmétazole ■ ceftazidime ■ ciprofloxacine ■ cisatracurium ■ cisplatine ■ cyclophosphamide ■ cytarabine ■ diltiazem ■ dobutamine ■ dopamine ■ doxorubicine ■ doxorubicine liposomale ■ énalaprilate ■ esmolol ■ filgrastim ■ fluconazole ■ fludarabine ■ foscarnet ■ gallium ■ granisétron ■ héparine ■ hydromorphone ■ idarubicine ■ labétalol ■ lorazépam ■ melphalan ■ mépéridine ■ méthotrexate ■ midazolam ■ milrinone ■ morphine ■ nitroglycérine ■ ondansétron ■ paclitaxel ■ pancuronium ■ pipéracilline ■ pipéracilline/tazobactam ■ procaïnamide ■ rémifentanil ■ sargramostim ■ tacrolimus ■ téniposide ■ thiotépa ■ vécuronium ■ vinorelbine ■ warfarine ■ zidovudine.

Compatibilité en addition au soluté: amikacine ■ amphotéricine B, cholestéryle d' ■ chloramphénicol ■ doxycycline ■ furosémide ■ gentamicine ■ héparine ■ insuline régulière ■ lidocaïne ■ pénicilline G sodique ■ potassium, chlorure de ■ ticarcilline ■ tobramycine ■ vancomycine.

Incompatibilité en addition au soluté: amphotéricine B ■ clindamycine.

ENSEIGNEMENT AU PATIENT ET À SES PROCHES

- Expliquer au patient qu'il doit respecter rigoureusement la posologie recommandée et continuer à prendre son médicament même s'il se sent mieux. S'il n'a pas pu prendre le médicament au moment habituel, il doit le prendre aussitôt que possible, à moins que ce ne soit presque l'heure prévue pour la dose suivante. L'avertir qu'il ne doit jamais remplacer une dose manquée par une double dose.
- Conseiller au patient qui prend une préparation en vente libre de ne pas prendre la dose maximale de façon continue pendant plus de 2 semaines sans consulter un professionnel de la santé. Lui recommander de consulter également un professionnel de la santé en cas de difficultés de déglutition ou de douleurs abdominales persistantes.
- Expliquer au patient que le tabac entrave l'effet de ces agents. L'encourager à cesser de fumer ou, au moins, à ne pas fumer après la prise de la dernière dose de la journée.
- Prévenir le patient que ces agents peuvent provoquer de la somnolence ou des étourdissements. Lui conseiller de ne pas conduire et d'éviter les activités qui exigent sa vigilance jusqu'à ce qu'on ait la certitude que le médicament n'entraîne pas ces effets chez lui.
- Conseiller au patient d'éviter de boire de l'alcool, de prendre des préparations contenant de l'aspirine ou des AINS ou de consommer des aliments qui peuvent aggraver l'irritation gastrique.
- Conseiller au patient d'augmenter sa consommation de liquides et d'aliments riches en fibres et de faire de l'exercice pour réduire la constipation.
- Recommander au patient de signaler rapidement à un professionnel de la santé les symptômes suivants: selles noires ou goudronneuses, fièvre, maux de gorge, diarrhée, étourdissements, rash, confusion ou hallucinations.

VÉRIFICATION DE L'EFFICACITÉ THÉRAPEUTIQUE

L'efficacité du traitement peut être démontrée par: la diminution des douleurs abdominales ■ la prévention et le traitement de l'irritation ou de l'hémorragie gastrique; la cicatrisation des ulcères duodénaux peut être révélée par les radiographies ou l'endoscopie; il faut poursuivre le traitement de l'ulcère pendant au moins 6 semaines, mais généralement pendant un maximum de 8 semaines ■ la diminution des symptômes du reflux gastro-œsophagien ■ le traitement des brûlures d'estomac, de l'acidité gastrique et des aigreurs d'estomac (préparations en vente libre). ✳

ANTIFONGIQUES TOPIQUES

ciclopirox
Loprox, Penlac, Stieprox

clotrimazole
Canesten, Clotrimaderm, Myclo-Derm, Neo-Zol

éconazole
Ecostatin

kétoconazole
Nizoral

miconazole
Micatin, Micozole, Monistat-Derm

nystatine
Candistatin, Mycostatin, Nadostine, Nilstat, Nyaderm

terbinafine
Lamisil

tolnaftate
Absorbine Jr. antifongique liquide, Dr. Scholl's Pied d'athlète poudre, poudre aérosol et gel, Pitrex, Tinactin, Ting, Zeasorb AF

CLASSIFICATION:
Antifongiques (topiques)

Grossesse – catégories B (ciclopirox, clotrimazole, terbinafine), C (éconazole, kétoconazole, miconazole, nystatine) et inconnue (tolnaftate)

INDICATIONS

Traitement de diverses infections fongiques cutanées dont la candidose cutanée, le *tinea pedis* (pied d'athlète), le *tinea cruris*, le *tinea corporis* (teigne), et le pityriasis versicolor ■ **Clotrimazole**: Traitement de l'érythème fessier infecté par *Candida albicans* ■ **Ciclopirox (vernis à ongles)**: Traitement de l'onychomycose ■ **Ciclopirox (shampooing) et kétoconazole (crème et shampooing)**: Traitement de la dermatite séborrhéique ■ **Kétoconazole (shampooing)**: Traitement et prévention par voie topique du pityriasis capitis.

MÉCANISME D'ACTION

Le clotrimazole, l'éconazole, le kétoconazole, le miconazole et la nystatine agissent sur la synthèse de la paroi de la cellule fongique, favorisant la libération du contenu intracellulaire. ***Effets thérapeutiques:*** Effet fongicide ou fongistatique, selon l'agent et la concentration utilisés, entraînant la diminution des symptômes d'infection fongique.

PHARMACOCINÉTIQUE

Absorption: Nulle ou minime si la peau est intacte.
Distribution: Inconnue (voie topique). L'action est surtout locale.
Métabolisme et excrétion: Inconnus (application locale).
Demi-vie: *Ciclopirox* – 1,7 heure; *miconazole* – 24,1 heures (terminale).

Profil temps-action
(disparition des symptômes et cicatrisation des lésions)

	DÉBUT D'ACTION	PIC	DURÉE
Ciclopirox	en 1 semaine	inconnu	12 h
Clotrimazole	en 1 semaine	inconnu	12 h
Miconazole	2 – 3 jours	2 semaines	12 – 24 h

CONTRE-INDICATIONS, PRÉCAUTIONS ET MISES EN GARDE

Contre-indications: Hypersensibilité aux ingrédients actifs, aux additifs, aux agents de conservation ou aux excipients ■ Certains agents renfermant de l'alcool ou des bisulfites, il ne faut pas les administrer aux patients présentant une intolérance à ces ingrédients.
Précautions et mises en garde: Infections des ongles et du cuir chevelu (un traitement additionnel, par voie générale, pourrait être de mise) ■ Usage ophtalmique déconseillé ■ **OBST., ALLAITEMENT**: L'innocuité de ces agents n'a pas été établie ■ **PÉD.**: Enfants < 10 ans (ciclopirox); enfants < 12 ans (kétoconazole shampooing); enfants < 2 ans (miconazole et tolnaftate); enfants < 18 ans (terbinafine).

RÉACTIONS INDÉSIRABLES ET EFFETS SECONDAIRES

Locales: brûlures, démangeaisons, réactions locales d'hypersensibilité, rougeurs, douleur cuisante.

INTERACTIONS

Médicament-médicament: Si une quantité suffisante de kétoconazole est absorbée par la peau, plusieurs interactions médicamenteuses peuvent survenir. Consulter la monographie du kétoconazole (voie générale).

VOIES D'ADMINISTRATION ET POSOLOGIE

Ciclopirox

- **Usage topique (adultes)**: Appliquer la crème ou la lotion, 2 fois par jour, pendant 2 à 4 semaines, selon les indications. Pour traiter les pellicules, utiliser le shampooing 2 ou 3 fois par semaine ou aussi souvent que nécessaire. Pour traiter la dermatite séborrhéique, utiliser le shampooing 3 fois par semaine ou aussi souvent que nécessaire. Pour traiter l'onychomycose, appliquer le vernis à ongles sur tous les

A

ongles infectés 1 fois par jour, à l'aide du pinceau applicateur, de préférence au coucher ou 8 heures avant de se laver.

Clotrimazole

- **Usage topique (adultes):** Appliquer la crème ou la solution, 2 fois par jour, pendant 1 à 4 semaines.
- **Usage topique (enfants):** Pour le traitement de l'érythème fessier, appliquer la crème 2 fois par jour, au moment des changements de couche. Ne pas utiliser pendant plus de 14 jours.

Éconazole

- **Usage topique (adultes):** Appliquer la crème 2 fois par jour. Le traitement doit être poursuivi pendant 2 à 4 semaines.

Kétoconazole

- **Usage topique (adultes):** Appliquer la crème 1 fois par jour, pour traiter les candidoses cutanées. Dans les cas les plus résistants, la posologie peut être portée à 4 fois par jour. La durée du traitement varie de 2 à 6 semaines en fonction de l'indication. Pour traiter la dermite séborrhéique, appliquer la crème 2 fois par jour, pendant 4 semaines. Pour traiter les pellicules, utiliser le shampooing 2 fois par semaine (en espaçant les traitements de 3 jours), pendant 2 à 4 semaines, puis par intermittence. Pour prévenir les pellicules, utiliser le shampooing 1 fois, toutes les 1 à 2 semaines.

Miconazole

- **Usage topique (adultes):** Appliquer la crème ou le produit en aérosol, 2 fois par jour, pendant 2 à 4 semaines.

Nystatine

- **Usage topique (adultes et enfants):** Appliquer la crème, l'onguent ou la poudre, 1 à 4 fois par jour, jusqu'à la guérison complète.

Terbinafine

- **Usage topique (adultes):** Appliquer la crème ou le produit en aérosol 1 ou 2 fois par jour. Le traitement doit être poursuivi pendant 1 à 2 semaines.

Tolnaftate

- **Usage topique (adultes):** Appliquer l'agent 2 fois par jour, pendant 2 à 3 semaines.

PRÉSENTATION

- **Ciclopirox**
  Crème: 1 %[Pr] ■ **Lotion:** 1 %[Pr] ■ **Shampooing:** 1,5 %[Pr] ■ **Vernis à ongles:** 80 mg/g[Pr].
- **Clotrimazole**
  Crème: 1 %[VL] ■ **Solution:** 1 %[VL] ■ **En association avec:** dipropionate de bétaméthasone (Lotridem)[Pr].
- **Éconazole**
  Crème: 1 %[Pr].
- **Kétoconazole**
  Crème: 2 %[Pr] ■ **Shampooing:** 2 %[VL].
- **Miconazole**
  Crème: 2 %[VL] ■ **Aérosol:** 2 %[VL].
- **Nystatine**
  Crème: 100 000 unités/g[VL] ■ **Onguent:** 100 000 unités/g[VL] ■ **Poudre:** 100 000 unités/g[VL] ■ **En association avec:** triamcinolone/gramicidine/néomycine (Kenacomb, Viaderm-K.C., Triacomb)[Pr].
- **Terbinafine**
  Crème: 1 %[Pr] ■ **Vaporisateur:** 1 %[Pr].
- **Tolnaftate**
  Crème: 1 %[VL] ■ **Solution:** 1 %[VL] ■ **Gel:** 1 %[VL] ■ **Poudre:** 1 %[VL] ■ **Poudre en aérosol:** 1 %[VL] ■ **Liquide en aérosol:** 1 %[VL].

SOINS INFIRMIERS

ÉVALUATION DE LA SITUATION

- Observer les territoires cutanés et muqueux atteints avant l'administration et à intervalles réguliers pendant toute la durée du traitement. Une irritation cutanée accrue peut dicter l'arrêt du traitement.

DIAGNOSTICS INFIRMIERS POSSIBLES

- Risque d'atteinte à l'intégrité de la peau (Indications).
- Risque d'infection (Indications).
- Connaissances insuffisantes sur le traitement médicamenteux (Enseignement au patient et à ses proches).

INTERVENTIONS INFIRMIÈRES

- Avant d'appliquer le médicament, se renseigner auprès du médecin ou d'un autre professionnel de la santé sur la méthode de nettoyage préconisée.
- Le choix du véhicule dépend de l'usage auquel on destine le médicament. Les onguents, les crèmes et les liquides sont surtout utilisés en traitement de première intention. On choisira habituellement la lotion pour traiter les régions intertrigineuses. Si on choisit la crème, il faut l'appliquer avec modération pour éviter la macération de la peau. Les poudres sont habituellement utilisées comme traitement d'appoint, mais on peut aussi y recourir en première intention, en présence d'infections bénignes.

Usage topique: Appliquer une petite quantité pour couvrir complètement la région affectée. Ne pas utiliser de pansements occlusifs sauf recommandation contraire du médecin ou d'un autre professionnel de la santé.

Vernis à ongles: Éviter le contact avec la peau autre que celle qui entoure immédiatement l'ongle traité. Éviter tout contact avec les yeux et les muqueuses. Le patient doit: 1) enlever le vernis tous les 7 jours à l'aide d'alcool isopropylique et effectuer une taille hebdomadaire et 2) se soumettre à l'élimination mensuelle des parties libres de l'ongle infecté par un professionnel de la santé. Il faut compter jusqu'à 6 mois de traitement avant de constater une amélioration; le traitement peut parfois se poursuivre pendant 48 semaines avant une guérison totale.

Shampooing – ciclopirox ou kétoconazole: Bien mouiller les cheveux et le cuir chevelu avec de l'eau. Appliquer suffisamment de shampooing pour produire une mousse permettant de laver le cuir chevelu et les cheveux. Masser délicatement le cuir chevelu pendant environ 1 minute. Bien rincer les cheveux avec de l'eau chaude. Répéter l'opération en laissant le shampooing sur les cheveux pendant 3 minutes. Après le deuxième shampooing, rincer et sécher les cheveux avec une serviette ou à l'air chaud. Utiliser le shampooing 2 fois par semaine, pendant 4 semaines, en espaçant les applications d'au moins 3 jours. Utiliser ensuite de façon intermittente, selon les besoins, pour maintenir la santé du cuir chevelu.

ENSEIGNEMENT AU PATIENT ET À SES PROCHES

- Expliquer au patient qu'il doit utiliser ces médicaments, en respectant rigoureusement les recommandations, même s'il constate une amélioration de son état. Insister sur le fait qu'il faut éviter tout contact avec les yeux.
- Prévenir le patient que certains produits peuvent tacher les tissus, la peau et les cheveux. Lui recommander de lire les mentions portées sur l'étiquette. Les tissus tachés avec les crèmes ou les lotions peuvent être lavés à la main, avec du savon et de l'eau chaude. Pour faire disparaître les taches d'onguent, on peut habituellement recourir aux solutions nettoyantes ordinaires.
- Recommander au patient atteint du pied d'athlète de porter des chaussures qui ne serrent pas les pieds et qui laissent respirer la peau. Lui conseiller de changer de souliers et de bas au moins 1 fois par jour.
- Conseiller au patient de prévenir un professionnel de la santé si l'irritation de la peau s'aggrave ou s'il ne remarque aucune réponse au traitement.

Vernis à ongles: Enlever le vernis à ongles à l'aide d'un tampon imbibé d'alcool à friction, 1 fois par semaine (tous les 7 jours). Enlever ensuite la plus grande partie possible des ongles atteints avec des ciseaux, un coupe-ongles ou une lime à ongles. Ne pas utiliser de vernis à ongles non médicamenteux sur les ongles traités. Prévenir un professionnel de la santé si la région traitée présente des signes d'irritation: rougeurs, démangeaisons, sensation de brûlure, phlyctènes, tuméfaction et suintement.

VÉRIFICATION DE L'EFFICACITÉ THÉRAPEUTIQUE

L'efficacité du traitement peut être démontrée par: une diminution de l'irritation de la peau et la guérison de l'infection. Les premiers signes de résolution des symptômes peuvent se manifester en l'espace de 2 ou de 3 jours. En cas de candidose, de *tinea cruris* et de *tinea corporis*, la réponse au traitement peut ne pas se manifester avant 2 semaines, et en cas de *tinea pedis*, elle peut prendre 3 ou 4 semaines. Les infections fongiques récurrentes peuvent être un signe de maladie systémique. ✳

ANTIFONGIQUES VAGINAUX

Butoconazole
Gynazole•1

clotrimazole
Canesten, Clotrimaderm, Neo-Zol

miconazole
Miconazole, Micozole, Monazole 7, Monistat

nystatine
Mycostatin, Nilstat, Nyaderm

terconazole
Terazol

CLASSIFICATION:
Antifongiques (vaginaux)

Grossesse – catégories B (clotrimazole), C (butoconazole, miconazole, nystatine, terconazole)

INDICATIONS

Traitement local de la candidose vulvovaginale.

MÉCANISME D'ACTION

Altération de la membrane de la cellule fongique entraînant la libération du contenu intracellulaire. Aucun effet sur les bactéries. ***Effets thérapeutiques:*** Inhibition de la prolifération des souches sensibles de *Candida* et destruction de ces agents pathogènes, entraînant la diminution des symptômes suivants de vulvovaginite: sensation de brûlure, démangeaisons et écoulements vaginaux.

A

PHARMACOCINÉTIQUE

Absorption: Faible (*nystatine* et *miconazole*); *butoconazole* – 5,5 %; *clotrimazole* – de 3 à 10 %; *terconazole* – de 5 à 15 % (voie intravaginale).

Distribution: Inconnue. L'action est surtout locale.

Métabolisme et excrétion: De petites quantités de *clotrimazole* sont absorbées et rapidement métabolisées.

Demi-vie: *Miconazole* – de 20 à 25 heures (administration par voie parentérale).

Profil temps-action

	DÉBUT D'ACTION	PIC	DURÉE
Tous les agents	rapide	inconnu	24 h

CONTRE-INDICATIONS, PRÉCAUTIONS ET MISES EN GARDE

Contre-indications: Hypersensibilité aux ingrédients actifs, aux additifs ou aux agents de conservation ■ **OBST.:** Le butoconazole est contre-indiqué au cours du 1er trimestre de grossesse ■ Les préparations de butoconazole, de miconazole et de terconazole peuvent altérer les propriétés du latex ou des produits en caoutchouc comme les condoms ou les diaphragmes; l'utilisation de ces articles n'est donc pas recommandée pendant les 72 heures suivant le traitement par ces médicaments ■ Ces produits ne sont pas indiqués pour l'usage ophtalmique.

Précautions et mises en garde: Infections vulvovaginales récurrentes dues aux levures ■ Allaitement ■ **PÉD.:** L'innocuité et l'efficacité de ces médicaments n'ont pas été établies.

RÉACTIONS INDÉSIRABLES ET EFFETS SECONDAIRES

SNC: *terconazole et miconazole* – céphalées.

Locales: irritation, sensibilisation, brûlures vulvovaginales.

Divers: réactions d'hypersensibilité; *terconazole* – douleurs dans tout le corps.

INTERACTIONS

Médicament-médicament: L'utilisation concomitante de miconazole et de **warfarine** peut entraîner une augmentation du risque de saignements (un suivi adéquat est recommandé).

VOIES D'ADMINISTRATION ET POSOLOGIE

Butoconazole

- **Préparation vaginale (adultes et adolescentes):** *Crème vaginale* – le contenu d'un applicateur à dose unique.

Clotrimazole

- **Préparation vaginale (adultes et adolescentes):** *Comprimés vaginaux* – 200 mg, au coucher, pendant 3 jours, *ou* une seule dose de 500 mg (1 comprimé vaginal de 500 mg), au coucher. *Crème vaginale* – le contenu d'un applicateur, au coucher; la durée du traitement varie selon le produit.

Miconazole

- **Préparation vaginale (adultes et adolescentes):** *Ovules vaginaux* – 1 seule dose de 1 200 mg (ovule de 1 200 mg), au coucher, ou 1 ovule de 400 mg, au coucher, pendant 3 jours. *Suppositoires vaginaux* – 100 mg, au coucher, pendant 7 jours. *Crème vaginale* – le contenu d'un applicateur, au coucher, pendant 7 jours. Les Duopak renferment les ovules ou les suppositoires et la crème; la crème est indiquée pour soulager les démangeaisons externes.

Nystatine

- **Préparation vaginale (adultes et adolescentes):** *Crème vaginale* – le contenu d'un applicateur (4 g: 100 000 unités) 1 ou 2 fois par jour, pendant 2 semaines. *Comprimés vaginaux* – 100 000 unités (1 comprimé) 1 ou 2 fois par jour, pendant 2 semaines.

Terconazole

- **Préparation vaginale (adultes et adolescentes):** *Crème vaginale* – le contenu d'un applicateur (5 g) de crème à 0,4 %, au coucher, pendant 7 jours ou le contenu d'un applicateur (5 g) de crème à 0,8 %, au coucher, pendant 3 jours. *Ovules vaginaux* – 1 ovule (80 mg), au coucher, pendant 3 jours.

PRÉSENTATION

- **Butoconazole**
  Crème vaginale: 2 %Pr.
- **Clotrimazole (version générique disponible)**
  Comprimés vaginaux: 200 mgVL, 500 mgVL ■ **Crème vaginale:** 1 %VL, 2 %VL, 10 %VL ■ **En association avec:** Combi-Pak: crème ou comprimés vaginaux et un tube de crème de clotrimazole à 1 % pour application externeVL.
- **Miconazole (version générique disponible)**
  Crème vaginale: 2 %VL, 4 %VL ■ **Ovules vaginaux:** 400 mgVL, 1 200 mgVL ■ **Suppositoires vaginaux:** 100 mgVL ■ **En association avec:** Duopak – ovules ou suppositoires vaginaux et un tube de crème de miconazole à 2 % pour application externeVL.
- **Nystatine (version générique disponible)**
  Comprimés vaginaux: 100 00 unitésPr ■ **Crème vaginale:** 25 000 unités/gPr.
- **Terconazole**
  Crème vaginale: 0,4 %Pr, 0,8 %Pr ■ **Ovules vaginaux:** 80 mgPr ■ **En association avec:** Duopak – 3 ovules à

80 mg et un tube de crème vaginale pour application externe à 0,8 %[Pr].

SOINS INFIRMIERS

ÉVALUATION DE LA SITUATION

- Observer les territoires atteints de la peau et des muqueuses avant l'administration du médicament et à intervalles réguliers pendant toute la durée du traitement. Une irritation cutanée accrue peut dicter l'arrêt du traitement.

DIAGNOSTICS INFIRMIERS POSSIBLES

- Risque d'infection (Indications).
- Risque d'atteinte à l'intégrité de la peau (Indications).
- Connaissances insuffisantes sur le traitement médicamenteux (Enseignement au patient et à ses proches).

INTERVENTIONS INFIRMIÈRES

- Avant d'administrer le médicament, se renseigner auprès du médecin ou d'un autre professionnel de la santé sur la méthode de nettoyage préconisée. Le médecin peut prescrire à la patiente de prendre des bains de siège et des douches vaginales pendant qu'elle suit ce traitement.

Préparation vaginale: Les applicateurs sont fournis avec les agents destinés à l'administration par voie intravaginale.

ENSEIGNEMENT AU PATIENT ET À SES PROCHES

- Expliquer à la patiente qu'elle doit utiliser toute la quantité de médicament prescrite, même si elle se sent mieux. La prévenir qu'elle doit continuer le traitement pendant la menstruation.
- Montrer à la patiente comment utiliser l'applicateur. Lui recommander d'introduire la préparation profondément dans le vagin, au coucher, et de rester ensuite étendue pendant au moins 30 minutes. Lui conseiller d'utiliser des serviettes hygiéniques pour ne pas tacher les vêtements ou la literie.
- Recommander à la patiente de demander à un professionnel de la santé si elle peut prendre des douches vaginales et avoir des rapports sexuels pendant le traitement. Les préparations vaginales peuvent provoquer une légère irritation cutanée chez le partenaire. Conseiller à la patiente d'éviter les rapports sexuels pendant le traitement ou de s'assurer que son partenaire porte un condom. Certains produits peuvent altérer les propriétés des préservatifs en latex.
- Conseiller à la patiente de prévenir un professionnel de la santé si l'irritation cutanée s'aggrave ou si elle ne remarque aucune réponse au traitement. Un deuxième traitement pourrait être nécessaire si les symptômes persistent.

VÉRIFICATION DE L'EFFICACITÉ THÉRAPEUTIQUE

L'efficacité du traitement peut être démontrée par: une diminution de l'irritation cutanée et de la gêne vaginale. La réponse thérapeutique se manifeste habituellement après 1 semaine. Le diagnostic devrait être reconfirmé par des frottis ou par une mise en culture avant de commencer un deuxième traitement, afin d'écarter la présence d'autres microorganismes associés aux vulvovaginites. Les infections vaginales récurrentes peuvent être un signe de maladie systémique.

APRÉPITANT

Emend

CLASSIFICATION:

Antiémétique (antagoniste des neurokinines)

Grossesse – catégorie B

INDICATIONS

Prévention des nausées et des vomissements aigus et tardifs, provoqués par des agents chimiothérapeutiques fortement émétisants (en association avec un antagoniste de la sérotonine et la dexaméthasone) ■ Prévention des nausées et des vomissements chez les femmes, causés par des agents chimiothérapeutiques modérément émétisants comprenant le cyclophosphamide et une anthracycline (en association avec un antagoniste de la sérotonine et la dexaméthasone).

MÉCANISME D'ACTION

Antagoniste sélectif des récepteurs de la neurokinine 1 (NK_1) de la substance P dans le cerveau. ***Effets thérapeutiques:*** Diminution des nausées et vomissements provoqués par la chimiothérapie ■ Augmentation des effets antiémétiques de la dexaméthasone et des antagonistes des récepteurs $5\text{-}HT_3$.

PHARMACOCINÉTIQUE

Absorption: De 60 à 65 % (PO).

Distribution: L'agent traverse la barrière hémato-encéphalique; le reste de sa distribution est inconnu.

A

Métabolisme et excrétion: Métabolisme principalement hépatique (par le système enzymatique du CYP3A4); excrétion non rénale.

Demi-vie: De 9 à 13 heures.

Profil temps-action (effet antiémétique)

	DÉBUT D'ACTION	PIC	DURÉE
PO	1 heure	4 heures†	24 heures

† Concentrations sanguines.

CONTRE-INDICATIONS, PRÉCAUTIONS ET MISES EN GARDE

Contre-indications: Hypersensibilité ■ Usage concomitant de pimozide ou de cisapride (risque de réactions cardiovasculaires pouvant mener à une issue fatale).

Précautions et mises en garde: Usage concomitant de tout autre agent métabolisé par le CYP3A4 (voir les interactions médicament-médicament) ■ **OBST.**: N'utiliser qu'en cas de besoin indiscutable ■ **PÉD.**: L'innocuité de l'agent n'a pas été établie ■ Allaitement.

RÉACTIONS INDÉSIRABLES ET EFFETS SECONDAIRES

CV: étourdissements, fatigue, faiblesse.

GI: diarrhée.

Divers: hoquets.

INTERACTIONS

Médicament-médicament: L'aprépitant inhibe et induit le système enzymatique CYP3A4 et il est métabolisé par lui. L'usage concomitant d'autres **médicaments métabolisés par le CYP3A4** peut entraîner une intoxication par ces agents, notamment les suivants: **docétaxel**, **paclitaxel**, **étoposide**, **irinotécan**, **ifosfamide**, **imatinib**, **vinorelbine**, **vinblastine**, **vincristine**, **midazolam**, **triazolam** et **alprazolam**; l'usage concomitant doit s'accompagner de prudence ■ Les **médicaments qui inhibent fortement le système enzymatique CYP3A4** (p. ex., le **kétoconazole**, l'**itraconazole**, la **clarithromycine**, le **ritonavir**, le **nelfinavir** et le **diltiazem**), administrés en concomitance, peuvent élever les concentrations sanguines et intensifier les effets de l'aprépitant ■ Les **médicaments qui induisent le système enzymatique CYP3A4**, notamment la **rifampine**, la **carbamazépine** et la **phénytoïne**, administrés en concomitance, peuvent diminuer les concentrations sanguines et les effets de l'aprépitant ■ L'agent élève les concentrations sanguines et intensifie les effets de la **dexaméthasone** (réduire la dose de 50 %); on observe un effet similaire dans le cas de la **méthylprednisolone** (réduire la dose par voie IV de 25 % et celle par voie orale de 50 % lors d'un usage concomitant) ■ L'agent induit le système enzymatique CYP2C9 ■ L'aprépitant peut diminuer les effets de la **warfarine** (on recommande une surveillance attentive pendant 2 semaines), des **contraceptifs oraux** (utiliser une autre méthode contraceptive), du **tolbutamide** et de la **phénytoïne**.

VOIES D'ADMINISTRATION ET POSOLOGIE

- **PO (adultes):** *Chimiothérapie fortement émétisante* – 125 mg, 1 heure avant la chimiothérapie, ensuite 80 mg, 1 fois par jour, pendant 2 jours (en administration concomitante avec la dexaméthasone, à 12 mg par voie orale, 30 minutes avant la chimiothérapie, ensuite 8 mg, 1 fois par jour, pendant 3 jours, et avec l'ondansétron, à 32 mg par voie IV, 30 minutes avant la chimiothérapie). *Chimiothérapie modérément émétisante* – 125 mg, 1 heure avant la chimiothérapie, ensuite 80 mg, 1 fois par jour, pendant 2 jours (en administration concomitante avec la dexaméthasone, à 12 mg par voie orale, 30 minutes avant la chimiothérapie, et avec l'ondansétron, à 8 mg par voie orale, de 30 à 60 minutes avant la chimiothérapie et à 8 mg, par voie orale, 8 heures après la première dose).

PRÉSENTATION

Capsules: 80 mg[Pr], 125 mg[Pr].

SOINS INFIRMIERS

ÉVALUATION DE LA SITUATION

- Évaluer les nausées, les vomissements, l'appétit, les bruits intestinaux et les douleurs intestinales, avant et après l'administration.
- Suivre de près l'hydratation, l'état nutritionnel, les ingesta et les excreta. Chez les patients qui souffrent de nausées et de vomissements graves, envisager l'administration de liquides par voie IV en plus d'antiémétiques.

***Tests de laboratoire*:**

- Chez les patients qui suivent un traitement prolongé à la warfarine, suivre de près l'état de la coagulation pendant les 2 semaines qui suivent l'administration de l'aprépitant, et particulièrement au cours des 7 à 10 premiers jours.
- L'agent peut entraîner des élévations légères et transitoires des concentrations d'AST et d'ALT.

DIAGNOSTICS INFIRMIERS POSSIBLES

- Risque de déficit de volume liquidien (Indications).
- Risque d'alimentation déficiente (Indications).

INTERVENTIONS INFIRMIÈRES

- L'aprépitant est administré dans le cadre d'un régime qui comprend un corticostéroïde et un antagoniste des récepteurs 5-HT_3 (voir « Voies d'administration et posologie »).

PO: Administrer l'aprépitant tous les jours, pendant 3 jours. *Premier jour* - administrer 125 mg, 1 heure avant la chimiothérapie. *Deuxième et troisième jours* - administrer 80 mg, 1 fois, le matin. On peut administrer la dose avec ou sans aliments.

ENSEIGNEMENT AU PATIENT ET À SES PROCHES

- Inciter le patient à prendre l'aprépitant en suivant rigoureusement les recommandations du médecin. Lui conseiller de lire la notice du conditionnement avant de commencer le traitement et de la relire chaque fois qu'il renouvelle son ordonnance.
- Recommander au patient de consulter un professionnel de la santé avant de prendre d'autres médicaments d'ordonnance ou en vente libre ou des produits à base d'herbes médicinales en même temps que ce médicament.
- Prévenir la patiente que l'aprépitant peut diminuer l'efficacité des contraceptifs oraux. Lui conseiller d'opter pour une autre méthode contraceptive non hormonale.
- Conseiller au patient et à ses proches de prendre des mesures d'ordre général pour diminuer les nausées (commencer par de petites gorgées de liquides et par de petits repas sans matières grasses; pratiquer une bonne hygiène buccale, retirer les stimuli nocifs du milieu environnant).

VÉRIFICATION DE L'EFFICACITÉ THÉRAPEUTIQUE

L'efficacité du traitement peut être démontrée par: la diminution des nausées et des vomissements provoqués par la chimiothérapie. ✳

ARGATROBAN

Argatroban

CLASSIFICATION:

Anticoagulant (inhibiteur de la thrombine)

Grossesse – catégorie B

INDICATIONS

Prophylaxie ou traitement de la thrombose chez les patients présentant une thrombopénie induite par l'héparine.

MÉCANISME D'ACTION

Inhibition de la thrombine par liaison à ses sites récepteurs. L'inhibition de la thrombine prévient ▪ l'activation des facteurs V, VIII et XIII ▪ la transformation du fibrinogène en fibrine ▪ l'adhérence et l'agrégation plaquettaires. ***Effets thérapeutiques:*** Réduction de la formation et de la propagation des thrombus, ainsi que des complications de la thrombose (emboles, syndrome postphlébitique).

PHARMACOCINÉTIQUE

Absorption: Biodisponibilité à 100 % (IV).

Distribution: Inconnue.

Métabolisme et excrétion: Métabolisme majoritairement hépatique; élimination principalement par excrétion biliaire, 16 % est excrété sous forme inchangée dans l'urine, et 14 %, inchangée dans les fèces.

Demi-vie: De 39 à 51 min (prolongée en cas d'insuffisance hépatique).

Profil temps-action (effet anticoagulant)

	DÉBUT D'ACTION	PIC	DURÉE
IV	immédiat	1-3 h	2-4 h

CONTRE-INDICATIONS, PRÉCAUTIONS ET MISES EN GARDE

Contre-indications: Saignements majeurs ▪ Hypersensibilité ▪ Allaitement.

Précautions et mises en garde: Insuffisance hépatique (diminuer la vitesse de la perfusion initiale et ajuster la dose avec prudence) ▪ **PÉD.**: Enfants de moins de 18 ans (l'innocuité de l'agent n'a pas été établie) ▪ **OBST.**: Grossesse (n'utiliser qu'en cas de besoin indiscutable).

RÉACTIONS INDÉSIRALBES ET EFFETS SECONDAIRES

CV: hypotension.

GI: diarrhée, nausées, vomissements.

Hémat.: SAIGNEMENTS.

Divers: réactions allergiques, dont l'ANAPHYLAXIE, fièvre.

INTERACTIONS

Médicament-médicament: Le risque de saignements peut être accru lors de l'administration concomitante d'**agents antiplaquettaires**, de **thrombolytiques** ou d'autres **anticoagulants** ▪ L'usage concomitant de **warfarine** élève le RNI plus que la warfarine seule. Le lien entre le RNI et le risque de saignement n'est donc plus valide (suivre de près le RNI).

Médicament-produits naturels: Risque accru de saignement lors de la consommation concomitante des produits naturels suivants: **anis**, **arnica**, **camomille**, **clou**

de girofle, **grande camomille**, **ail**, **gingembre**, **ginkgo**, **panax ginseng** et autres.

VOIES D'ADMINISTRATION ET POSOLOGIE

- **IV (adultes)**: 2 µg/kg/min, sous forme de perfusion continue; régler la vitesse d'administration selon le temps de céphaline activée, jusqu'à un maximum de 10 µg/kg/min.

INSUFFISANCE HÉPATIQUE

- **IV (ADULTES)**: 0,5 µg/kg/MIN, SOUS FORME DE PERFUSION CONTINUE; RÉGLER LA VITESSE DE PERFUSION D'APRÈS LE TEMPS DE CÉPHALINE ACTIVÉE.

PRÉSENTATION

Solution pour injection: 250 mg/fiole de 2,5 mL.

SOINS INFIRMIERS

ÉVALUATION DE LA SITUATION

- SUIVRE LES SIGNES VITAUX À INTERVALLES RÉGULIERS TOUT AU LONG DU TRAITEMENT. UNE CHUTE INEXPLIQUÉE DE LA PRESSION ARTÉRIELLE PEUT ÊTRE UN SIGNE D'HÉMORRAGIE. RESTER À L'AFFÛT DES SAIGNEMENTS. RÉDUIRE LE RECOURS AUX PONCTIONS ARTÉRIELLES OU VEINEUSES, AUX INJECTIONS IM, AUX SONDES URINAIRES, À L'INTUBATION NASOTRACHÉALE ET NASOGASTRIQUE. ÉVITER LES POINTS D'ACCÈS IV NON COMPRESSIBLES. RESTER À L'AFFÛT DE LA PRÉSENCE DE SANG DANS L'URINE, DES DOULEURS LOMBAIRES, DES DOULEURS OU DES BRÛLURES À LA MICTION. SI LE SAIGNEMENT NE PEUT ÊTRE ARRÊTÉ PAR PRESSION, DIMINUER LA DOSE OU CESSER L'ADMINISTRATION DE L'ARGATROBAN IMMÉDIATEMENT.
- RESTER À L'AFFÛT DES SIGNES D'ANAPHYLAXIE (RASH, TOUX, DYSPNÉE) TOUT AU LONG DU TRAITEMENT.

Tests de laboratoire:

- Surveiller le temps de céphaline activée, avant le début de la perfusion continue, 2 heures après l'avoir démarrée et à intervalles réguliers pendant toute sa durée pour s'assurer qu'il reste dans la plage thérapeutique.
- Noter les concentrations d'hémoglobine, l'hématocrite et le nombre de plaquettes avant le traitement par l'argatroban et à intervalles réguliers pendant toute sa durée. L'agent peut faire chuter les concentrations d'hémoglobine et l'hématocrite. Une chute inexplicable de l'hématocrite peut indiquer la présence d'une hémorragie.
- L'administration d'argatroban en même temps que de doses multiples de warfarine peut prolonger le temps de prothrombine et modifier le rapport normalisé international (RNI), bien qu'on n'observe pas une augmentation plus grande de l'activité du facteur X_a dépendant de la vitamine K que n'entraîne la warfarine seule. Surveiller le RNI quotidiennement tout au long du traitement concomitant. Répéter la mesure du RNI de 4 à 6 heures après avoir arrêté l'administration de l'argatroban. Si la valeur est inférieure à la valeur thérapeutique souhaitée, reprendre le traitement à l'argatroban et le poursuivre jusqu'à l'atteinte de l'intervalle thérapeutique souhaité pour la warfarine seule. Pour obtenir le RNI pour la warfarine seule lorsque la dose d'argatroban est > 2 µg/kg/min, il faut réduire passagèrement cette dernière jusqu'à 2 µg/kg/min. On peut ensuite obtenir le RNI pour le traitement combiné, de 4 à 6 heures après que la dose d'argatroban a été diminuée.

TOXICITÉ ET SURDOSAGE: On ne connaît pas l'antidote spécifique de l'argatroban. En cas de surdosage, arrêter d'administrer le médicament. Les paramètres de l'anticoagulation retournent habituellement aux valeurs initiales dans les 2 à 4 heures qui suivent l'arrêt du traitement.

DIAGNOSTICS INFIRMIERS POSSIBLES

- Irrigation tissulaire inefficace (Indications).

INTERVENTIONS INFIRMIÈRES

- Arrêter l'administration de tous les anticoagulants par voie parentérale avant de commencer le traitement par l'argatroban. L'anticoagulothérapie par voie orale peut être démarrée avec une dose d'entretien de warfarine; ne pas administrer de dose de charge. Arrêter d'administrer l'argatroban lorsque le RNI pour le traitement combiné est > 4.
- La solution est transparente, légèrement visqueuse et d'incolore à jaune pâle. Ne pas administrer de solutions troubles ou qui contiennent des particules. Jeter toute portion inutilisée.

Perfusion continue: Diluer chaque fiole de 2,5 mL d'argatroban dans 250 mL de NaCl 0,9 %, de D5%E, ou de solution de lactate de Ringer pour obtenir une concentration de 1 mg/mL. Mélanger en inversant le sac à répétition pendant 1 minute. La solution peut être légèrement trouble, mais elle se rétablit pendant le mélange. La solution est stable pendant 48 heures, si elle est réfrigérée et à l'abri de la lumière.

Vitesse d'administration: La vitesse d'administration dépend du poids du patient. Administrer à une vitesse de 2 µg/kg/min. Adapter la vitesse d'administration une fois que l'état d'équilibre a été atteint (de 1 à 3 heures) et jusqu'à ce que le temps de céphaline activée à l'état d'équilibre soit à 1,5 à 3 fois la valeur initiale (ne pas dépasser 100 secondes).

Incompatibilité (tubulure en Y): Ne pas mélanger avec d'autres médicaments.

ENSEIGNEMENT AU PATIENT ET À SES PROCHES

- Expliquer au patient la raison de l'administration de l'argatroban.
- RECOMMANDER AU PATIENT DE PRÉVENIR UN PROFESSIONNEL DE LA SANTÉ IMMÉDIATEMENT S'IL OBSERVE UN SAIGNEMENT.

VÉRIFICATION DE L'EFFICACITÉ THÉRAPEUTIQUE

L'efficacité du traitement peut être démontrée par: la diminution de la formation de thrombus et de leur propagation ▪ la diminution des complications de la thrombose (emboles, syndrome postphlébitique).

ASA,
voir Aspirine

ALERTE CLINIQUE

ASPARAGINASE

Kidrolase

CLASSIFICATION:
Antinéoplasique (enzyme)

Grossesse – catégorie C

INDICATIONS

Traitement d'induction de la rémission chez les patients atteints de leucémie lymphoblastique aiguë.

MÉCANISME D'ACTION

Catalyseur de la transformation de l'asparagine (un acide aminé) en acide aspartique et en ammoniac ▪ Déplétion de l'asparagine dans les cellules leucémiques. ***Effets thérapeutiques:*** Destruction des cellules leucémiques.

PHARMACOCINÉTIQUE

Absorption: IM – concentrations plasmatiques de 50 % plus faibles qu'en cas d'administration IV.

Distribution: L'agent demeure dans le compartiment intravasculaire après administration IV; le volume de distribution est plus grand après administration IM; faible pénétration dans le liquide céphalorachidien.

Métabolisme et excrétion: Séquestration lente dans le système réticuloendothélial.

Demi-vie: *IV* – de 8 à 30 heures; *IM* – de 39 à 49 heures.

Profil temps-action (déplétion de l'asparagine)

	DÉBUT D'ACTION	PIC†	DURÉE
IM	immédiat	14 – 24 h	23 – 33 jours
IV	immédiat	inconnu	23 – 33 jours

† Concentrations plasmatiques d'asparaginase.

CONTRE-INDICATIONS, PRÉCAUTIONS ET MISES EN GARDE

Contre-indications: Hypersensibilité ▪ Insuffisance hépatique ▪ Pancréatite ▪ Grossesse ou allaitement ▪ Vaccination récente contre la fièvre jaune ▪ Prise de phénytoïne.

Précautions et mises en garde: Antécédents de réactions d'hypersensibilité ▪ Néphropathie ou maladie pancréatique ▪ Dépression du SNC ▪ Anomalies de coagulation ▪ Maladies chroniques débilitantes ▪ Patientes en âge de procréer ▪ Diabète.

RÉACTIONS INDÉSIRABLES ET EFFETS SECONDAIRES

SNC: CONVULSIONS, agitation, coma, confusion, dépression, étourdissements, fatigue, hallucinations, céphalées, irritabilité, somnolence.

GI: nausées, vomissements, anorexie, crampes, hépatotoxicité, pancréatite, perte de poids.

GU: insuffisance rénale.

Tég.: rash, urticaire.

End.: hyperglycémie, diminution de la fonction des gonades.

Hémat.: anomalies de coagulation, hypoplasie médullaire transitoire.

Métab.: élévation des concentrations d'ammoniac sérique, hyperuricémie, hypercholestérolémie, hypertriglycéridémie.

Divers: réactions d'hypersensibilité incluant l'ANAPHYLAXIE.

INTERACTIONS

Médicament-médicament: L'asparaginase peut contrecarrer l'effet antinéoplasique du **méthotrexate,** si elle est administrée avant celui-ci, ou augmenter son effet si elle est administrée après ▪ Le médicament peut augmenter l'hépatotoxicité induite par d'autres **médicaments hépatotoxiques** ▪ L'administration intraveineuse simultanée d'asparaginase et de **vincristine** ou de **prednisone** ou une administration qui précède immédiatement celle de ces deux médicaments peut aggraver la neurotoxicité et l'hyperglycémie ▪ L'administration de l'asparaginase peut modifier la réponse aux **vaccins à virus vivants** (diminution de la réponse des anticorps, risque accru de réactions indésirables)

A

■ Diminution de l'absorption gastro-intestinale de **phénytoïne**, ce qui peut entraîner des convulsions ■ L'utilisation concomitante d'**immunosuppresseurs** peut entraîner une immunosuppression excessive.

VOIES D'ADMINISTRATION ET POSOLOGIE

D'autres schémas thérapeutiques peuvent aussi être utilisés.

Monothérapie de la leucémie lymphoblastique aiguë

- **IV, IM (adultes)**: Administrer dans la tubulure de perfusion en marche d'un soluté glucosé isotonique ou d'un soluté physiologique ne contenant pas d'agent de conservation. La dose recommandée est de 200 à 1 000 UI/kg/jour pendant 28 jours consécutifs (il s'agit de la méthode habituelle la moins susceptible de provoquer des effets secondaires). Après cette période, si l'on a obtenu une rémission complète, on passe au traitement d'entretien, sinon le traitement d'induction peut être poursuivi pendant 14 jours supplémentaires. L'asparaginase peut aussi être administrée de façon intermittente, à raison de 3 injections par semaine, soit une de 400 UI/kg, les lundis et les mercredis, et une de 600 UI/kg, les vendredis, pendant 4 semaines. Dans ce cas, il faudrait préférer la voie IM.

Polychimiothérapie de la leucémie

- **IV, IM (adultes)**: Lorsque l'asparaginase est administrée dans le cadre d'une polychimiothérapie, les doses utilisées sont les mêmes. Le choix des doses est en fonction des circonstances particulières à chaque cas.
- **IV (enfants)**: 1 000 UI/kg/jour, 1 fois par jour, pendant 10 jours, à commencer le 22e jour du cycle, en association avec la vincristine et la prednisone (*usage non approuvé*).
- **IM (enfants)**: 6 000 UI/m^2/jour, 1 fois par jour, les 4e, 7e, 10e, 13e, 16e, 19e, 22e, 25e et 28e jours du cycle, en association avec la vincristine et la prednisone (*usage non approuvé*).

PRÉSENTATION

Flacons de poudre lyophilisée: contenant 10 000 UI de L-asparaginase^{Pr}.

SOINS INFIRMIERS

ÉVALUATION DE LA SITUATION

- Suivre de près les signes vitaux avant l'administration de l'asparaginase et à intervalles fréquents pendant toute la durée du traitement. Prévenir le médecin si de la fièvre ou des frissons se manifestent.
- Effectuer le bilan des ingesta et des excreta. Signaler au médecin tout écart important. Si son état le permet, recommander au patient de boire de 2 000 à 3 000 mL de liquides par jour pour favoriser l'excrétion d'acide urique. Le médecin peut prescrire de l'allopurinol ou un agent alcalinisant de l'urine pour prévenir la formation de calculs d'urate.
- RESTER À L'AFFÛT DES RÉACTIONS D'HYPERSENSIBILITÉ SUIVANTES: urticaire, diaphorèse, boursouflure du visage, douleurs articulaires, hypotension, bronchospasme. Garder de l'adrénaline et le matériel de réanimation à portée de la main. Des réactions peuvent survenir jusqu'à 2 heures après l'administration du médicament.
- Évaluer l'intensité des nausées et des vomissements ainsi que l'appétit du patient. Peser le patient toutes les semaines. Un antiémétique peut être administré avant le traitement.
- Observer l'affect et les signes neurologiques. Signaler au médecin la dépression, la somnolence ou les hallucinations. Ces symptômes disparaissent habituellement en l'espace de 2 ou de 3 jours après l'arrêt du traitement.

Tests de laboratoire:

- Examiner la numération globulaire avant le traitement et à intervalles réguliers pendant toute sa durée. Le médicament peut modifier les résultats des tests de la coagulation. Les temps de prothrombine et de céphaline peuvent s'allonger et le nombre de plaquettes peut être augmenté. Le médicament peut élever les concentrations d'urée.
- L'hépatotoxicité peut se traduire par une élévation des concentrations d'AST, d'ALT, de phosphatase alcaline, de bilirubine ou de cholestérol. Les résultats de tests de la fonction hépatique se normalisent habituellement après le traitement. Le médicament peut provoquer une pancréatite; suivre de près l'élévation des concentrations d'amylase ou de glucose.
- Évaluer la glycémie pendant toute la durée du traitement. Le médicament peut provoquer une hyperglycémie, qu'on peut traiter en administrant des liquides et de l'insuline. L'hyperglycémie peut mener à une issue fatale.
- Le médicament peut élever les concentrations sériques et urinaires d'acide urique.
- L'asparaginase peut modifier les résultats des tests de la fonction thyroïdienne.

DIAGNOSTICS INFIRMIERS POSSIBLES

- Risque d'accident (Effets secondaires).
- Risque d'infection (Effets secondaires).
- Connaissances insuffisantes sur le traitement médicamenteux (Enseignement au patient et à ses proches).

INTERVENTIONS INFIRMIÈRES

- NE PAS CONFONDRE L'ASPARAGINASE ET LA PEGASPARGASE

ALERTE CLINIQUE: DES DÉCÈS SONT SURVENUS LORS DE CERTAINES CHIMIOTHÉRAPIES. AVANT D'ADMINISTRER L'AGENT, CLARIFIER TOUS LES POINTS AMBIGUS. VÉRIFIER LA LIMITE DES DOSES UNITAIRES ET QUOTIDIENNES AINSI QUE LA DOSE À ADMINISTRER PENDANT LE TRAITEMENT. DEMANDER À UN AUTRE PROFESSIONNEL DE LA SANTÉ DE VÉRIFIER UNE FOIS DE PLUS L'ORDONNANCE D'ORIGINE, LES CALCULS ET LE RÉGLAGE DE LA POMPE À PERFUSION.

- Les solutions doivent être préparées sous une hotte à flux laminaire. Porter des gants, une blouse et un masque pendant qu'on manipule ce médicament. Jeter le matériel utilisé dans les contenants réservés à cet usage (voir l'annexe H).
- En cas de coagulopathie, appliquer une pression sur les points de ponction veineuse; éviter les injections IM.

Vitesse d'administration: Reconstituer la fiole avec 4 mL d'eau stérile pour injection. Administrer par une tubulure en Y à écoulement rapide, par laquelle on fait passer une solution de D5%E ou de NaCl 0,9 %, pendant au moins 30 minutes. Maintenir la voie IV pendant 2 heures après l'administration de la dose. Consulter les directives du fabricant avant de reconstituer la préparation.

Compatibilité (tubulure en Y): méthotrexate ■ sodium, bicarbonate de.

Incompatibilité en addition au soluté: Aucune donnée disponible. Ne pas mélanger la solution à d'autres médicaments.

ENSEIGNEMENT AU PATIENT ET À SES PROCHES

- Demander au patient de signaler à un professionnel de la santé les symptômes suivants: douleurs abdominales, nausées et vomissements graves, jaunisse, fièvre, frissons, maux de gorge, saignement ou formation d'ecchymoses, soif ou mictions excessives, aphtes. Recommander au patient d'éviter les foules et les personnes contagieuses. Lui conseiller d'utiliser une brosse à dents à poils doux et un rasoir électrique et de prendre garde aux chutes. Recommander également au patient d'éviter de consommer des boissons alcoolisées et de ne pas prendre de médicaments contenant de l'aspirine ou des AINS en raison du risque d'hémorragie gastrique.
- Expliquer à la patiente qu'elle doit prendre des mesures contraceptives en raison des effets tératogènes de l'asparaginase.
- Prévenir le patient qu'il ne doit recevoir aucun vaccin sans consulter au préalable un professionnel de la santé. Informer les parents que le traitement peut modifier le calendrier de vaccination.
- Expliquer au patient qu'il doit se soumettre à intervalles réguliers à des tests de laboratoire permettant de suivre l'apparition d'effets secondaires.

VÉRIFICATION DE L'EFFICACITÉ THÉRAPEUTIQUE

L'efficacité du traitement peut être démontrée par: l'amélioration de l'hématopoïèse chez les patients souffrant de leucémie. ✳

ASPIRINE

Synonymes: acide acétylsalicylique, AAS, ASA

Apo-ASA, Asadol, Asaphen, Aspirin, Entrophen, MSD-AAS, Novasen, PMS-ASA, Rivasa

CLASSIFICATION:

Agent antiplaquettaire, antipyrétique, analgésique non opioïde, anti-inflammatoire non stéroïdien, salicylate

Grossesse – catégories C et D (3e trimestre si la dose est plus élevée que celle administrée en prévention)

INDICATIONS

Soulagement de l'inflammation et de la douleur légère à modérée ■ Soulagement de la migraine et des symptômes associés ■ Abaissement de la fièvre ■ Réduction du risque de mortalité dans le traitement de l'infarctus du myocarde (IM) aigu confirmé ou suspecté ■ Prévention primaire d'un IM non fatal ■ Prévention secondaire chez les patients ayant subi un IM et chez ceux atteints d'angine instable ■ Prévention secondaire de l'ischémie cérébrale transitoire (ICT) et de l'AVC athérothrombotique ■ Prévention secondaire de l'ICT chez les patients ayant subi une endartériectomie carotidienne ■ Antiplaquettaire chez les patients en hémodialyse porteurs d'une canule artérioveineuse en caoutchouc de silicone ■ **Usages non approuvés:** Péricardite aiguë ■ Fièvre rhumatismale ■ Maladie de Kawasaki.

MÉCANISME D'ACTION

Effet analgésique et réduction de l'inflammation et de la fièvre par inhibition de la production de prostaglandines par la cyclo-oxygénase (COX) ■ Diminution de l'agrégation plaquettaire. ***Effets thérapeutiques:*** Analgésie ■ Suppression de l'inflammation ■ Réduction de la fièvre ■ Diminution de l'incidence des ICT, AVC et IM.

A

PHARMACOCINÉTIQUE

Absorption: Bonne (PO); l'absorption des préparations entérosolubles peut s'avérer incertaine; lente et variable (IR).

Distribution: L'aspirine se répartit rapidement dans tout l'organisme. Elle traverse la barrière placentaire et passe dans le lait maternel.

Métabolisme et excrétion: Métabolisme hépatique important, avec transformation en métabolites actifs qui sont aussi métabolisés par le foie; les métabolites inactifs sont excrétés par les reins. La quantité excrétée à l'état inchangé par les reins dépend du pH de l'urine; au fur et à mesure que le pH augmente, la quantité excrétée à l'état inchangé augmente d'une base de 1 à 3 % jusqu'à concurrence de 80 %.

Demi-vie: *Aspirine* – de 15 à 20 minutes; *métabolites actifs* – de 2 à 3 heures pour les faibles doses; jusqu'à 15 à 30 heures pour les doses plus élevées, en raison de la saturation du métabolisme hépatique.

Profil temps-action (analgésie/abaissement de la fièvre)

	DÉBUT D'ACTION	PIC	DURÉE†
PO	5 - 30 min	1 - 2 h	4 - 6 h
PO - CE‡	30 - 120 min	6 - 8 h	inconnue
IR	1 - 2 h	3 - 5 h	7 h

† L'effet antiplaquettaire étant irréversible, il dépend de la durée de vie des plaquettes.

‡ CE = comprimés entérosolubles.

CONTRE-INDICATIONS, PRÉCAUTIONS ET MISES EN GARDE

Contre-indications: Hypersensibilité (bronchospasmes, urticaire généralisée, œdème angioneurotique, rhinite grave, œdème laryngé ou état de choc) à l'aspirine, aux autres salicylates, aux AINS ou à la tartrazine (un colorant jaune) ■ Ulcère gastroduodénal actif.

Précautions et mises en garde: **PÉD.**: ENFANTS OU ADOLESCENTS ATTEINTS DE GRIPPE, DE VARICELLE OU D'UNE AUTRE INFECTION VIRALE (RISQUE ACCRU D'APPARITION DU SYNDROME DE REYE) ■ Antécédents d'hémorragie digestive ou d'ulcère ■ Consommation excessive d'alcool et alcoolisme ■ Insuffisance rénale ■ Maladie hépatique grave ■ Anémie ■ Asthme ou états allergiques ■ **GÉR.**: Risque accru de réactions indésirables; sensibilité accrue aux concentrations toxiques ■ **OBST.**: L'aspirine peut entraîner des effets indésirables chez le fœtus et la mère et, en général, leur administration devrait être évitée pendant la grossesse, particulièrement au cours du 3e trimestre ■ **ALLAITEMENT**: L'innocuité du médicament n'a pas été établie ■ Troubles hémorragiques, thrombopénie ou hypoprothrombinémie ■ En cas de chirurgie non urgente, on doit envisager l'arrêt du traitement au moins 7 jours avant l'intervention pour que l'effet du médicament ait le temps de se dissiper.

RÉACTIONS INDÉSIRABLES ET EFFETS SECONDAIRES

ORLO: perte auditive, acouphènes.

GI: HÉMORRAGIE DIGESTIVE, ulcère gastroduodénal, dyspepsie, troubles épigastriques, brûlures d'estomac, nausées, douleurs abdominales, anorexie, hépatotoxicité, vomissements.

Hémat.: anémie, hémolyse, thrombopénie, prolongation du temps de saignement.

Divers: saignements, réactions allergiques incluant l'ANAPHYLAXIE et l'ŒDÈME LARYNGÉ, œdème pulmonaire non cardiogénique.

INTERACTIONS

Médicament-médicament: L'aspirine augmente le risque de saignement si elle est administrée en même temps que la **warfarine**, l'**héparine**, les **agents apparentés à l'héparine**, les **agents thrombolytiques**, l'**abciximab**, la **ticlopidine**, le **clopidogrel**, le **tirofiban** ou l'**eptifibatide**, bien que ces agents soient souvent utilisés sans danger en association et en séquence ■ L'**ibuprofène** peut contrecarrer les effets antiplaquettaires de l'aspirine (administrer l'ibuprofène au moins 8 heures avant ou 2 heures après) ■ L'aspirine peut élever le risque de saignement si elle est administrée en même temps que l'**acide valproïque** ■ L'aspirine peut intensifier l'activité ou augmenter les concentrations de la **phénytoïne**, du **méthotrexate**, de l'**acide valproïque** et des **sulfonylurées** ■ Elle peut contrecarrer les effets bénéfiques du **probénécide** ou de la **sulfinpyrazone** ■ Les **corticostéroïdes**, administrés en concomitance, peuvent diminuer les concentrations sériques d'aspirine et augmentent le risque d'irritation gastro-intestinale ■ Les **agents qui acidifient l'urine** intensifient la réabsorption de l'aspirine et peuvent en augmenter les concentrations sériques ■ Les **agents qui alcalinisent l'urine,** ou les **antiacides** consommés en grandes quantités, favorisent l'excrétion de l'aspirine et en diminuent les concentrations sériques ■ L'aspirine peut diminuer la réponse thérapeutique aux **diurétiques**, à certains **antihypertenseurs** ou à certains **anti-inflammatoires non stéroïdiens** ■ Risque accru d'irritation gastro-intestinale lors de l'administration concomitante d'**anti-inflammatoires non stéroïdiens** ■ Risque accru d'ototoxicité lors de l'administration concomitante de **vancomycine**.

Médicament-produits naturels: Risque accru de saignement lors de la consommation concomitante d'**ail**, d'**anis**, d'**arnica**, de **camomille**, de **clou de girofle**, de

fenugrec, de **grande camomille**, de **gingembre**, de **ginkgo**, de **ginseng** et d'**autres produits**.
Médicament-aliments: Les **aliments qui acidifient l'urine** (voir l'annexe J) peuvent élever les concentrations sériques d'aspirine. Les **aliments qui alcalinisent l'urine** (voir l'annexe J) peuvent diminuer les concentrations sériques d'aspirine.

VOIES D'ADMINISTRATION ET POSOLOGIE

Soulagement de la douleur et de la fièvre
- **PO, IR (adultes)**: De 325 à 650 mg, de 4 à 6 fois par jour.
- **PO, IR (enfants de 2 à 11 ans)**: De 10 à 15 mg/kg, toutes les 4 à 6 heures, selon les besoins, jusqu'à un maximum de 65 mg/kg/jour. LES AUTORITÉS COMPÉTENTES DÉCONSEILLENT L'ADMINISTRATION D'ASPIRINE AUX ENFANTS ET AUX ADOLESCENTS ATTEINTS DE GRIPPE, DE VARICELLE OU D'UNE AUTRE INFECTION VIRALE.

Soulagement de la migraine et des symptômes associés
- **PO (adultes)**: 1 000 mg dès l'apparition de la douleur ou des symptômes.

Diminution de l'inflammation
- **PO (adultes)**: *Initialement* – de 2,4 à 3,6 g par jour, en 4 à 6 doses fractionnées; *traitement d'entretien* – de 3,6 à 5,4 g par jour, en 4 à 6 doses fractionnées.
- **PO (enfants)**: De 60 à 100 mg/kg/jour, en doses fractionnées.

Traitement d'un IM aigu confirmé ou suspecté
- **PO (adultes)**: De 160 à 325 mg, immédiatement (pour être rapidement absorbés, les comprimés doivent être mâchés ou écrasés), puis poursuivre avec la dose indiquée en prévention secondaire.

Prévention primaire d'un IM sans issue fatale
- **PO (adultes)**: De 75 à 325 mg par jour.

Prévention secondaire après un IM ou en présence d'angine instable
- **PO (adultes)**: De 75 à 325 mg par jour, à vie.

Prévention secondaire de l'ICT ou de l'AVC
- **PO (adultes)**: De 50 à 325 mg par jour, à vie.

Prévention secondaire de l'ICT chez les patients ayant subi une endartériectomie carotidienne
- **PO (adultes)**: De 81 à 325 mg par jour, à commencer avant l'intervention et à poursuivre à vie.

PRÉSENTATION

Comprimés: 80 mg^VL^, 325 mg^VL^, 500 mg^VL^ ■ **Comprimés à croquer**: 80 mg^VL^ ■ **Comprimés entérosolubles (libération retard)**: 80 mg^VL^, 81 mg^VL^, 325 mg^VL^, 500 mg^VL^, 650 mg^VL^ ■ **Suppositoires**: 150 mg^VL^, 650 mg^VL^ ■ **En association avec**: antihistaminiques, caféine, décongestionnants, antitussifs^VL^ et opioïdes^Pr^.

SOINS INFIRMIERS

ÉVALUATION DE LA SITUATION

- LES PATIENTS SOUFFRANT D'ASTHME, D'ALLERGIES OU DE POLYPES NASAUX ET CEUX QUI SONT ALLERGIQUES À LA TARTRAZINE SONT DAVANTAGE PRÉDISPOSÉS AUX RÉACTIONS D'HYPERSENSIBILITÉ À L'ASPIRINE.

Douleur: Suivre de près la douleur et l'amplitude des mouvements; noter le type de douleur, son siège et son intensité, avant l'administration du médicament et au moment de l'effet maximal (voir « Profil temps-action »).
Fièvre: Mesurer la température et noter les signes associés à la fièvre (diaphorèse, tachycardie, malaise, frissons).

Tests de laboratoire:
- Noter les résultats des tests de la fonction hépatique avant le traitement antirhumatismal et si des symptômes d'hépatotoxicité se manifestent, plus particulièrement chez les patients (surtout les enfants) qui souffrent de rhumatisme articulaire aigu, de lupus érythémateux disséminé, d'arthrite juvénile ou d'une maladie hépatique préexistante. L'aspirine peut élever les concentrations sériques d'AST, d'ALT et de phosphatase alcaline, particulièrement lorsque les concentrations plasmatiques dépassent 25 mg/100 mL. Ces concentrations peuvent revenir aux valeurs normales malgré la poursuite du traitement ou si la dose est réduite. Si des anomalies graves ou une maladie hépatique active se manifestent, cesser l'administration du médicament et l'utiliser avec prudence à l'avenir.
- Déterminer les concentrations sériques d'aspirine à intervalles réguliers lors du traitement prolongé par des doses élevées pour déterminer la dose appropriée, son innocuité et son efficacité, particulièrement chez les enfants souffrant de la maladie de Kawasaki.
- L'aspirine peut modifier les taux sériques d'acide urique et les taux urinaires d'acide vanilmandélique (VMA), les taux de protiréline induite par la thyréostimuline (TSH) et les taux urinaires d'acide hydroxy-indolacétique, ainsi que les résultats de la scintigraphie thyroïdienne.
- L'aspirine peut entraîner une baisse des concentrations sériques de potassium et de cholestérol.
- L'aspirine prolonge le temps de saignement pendant 4 à 7 jours et, administrée à des doses élevées, elle

peut prolonger le temps de prothrombine. Lors du traitement prolongé par des doses élevées, mesurer l'hématocrite à intervalles réguliers afin de déceler les saignements au niveau des voies digestives.

Toxicité et surdosage: Suivre de près les acouphènes, les céphalées, l'hyperventilation, l'agitation, la confusion mentale, la léthargie, la diarrhée et la transpiration. Si ces symptômes se manifestent, cesser l'administration de l'aspirine et prévenir immédiatement le médecin ou un autre professionnel de la santé.

DIAGNOSTICS INFIRMIERS POSSIBLES

- Douleur aiguë (Indications).
- Mobilité physique réduite (Indications).
- Connaissances insuffisantes sur le traitement médicamenteux (Enseignement au patient et à ses proches).

INTERVENTIONS INFIRMIÈRES

- Utiliser la dose minimale efficace pendant le laps de temps le plus court possible.
- En cas de chirurgie non urgente, on doit envisager l'arrêt du traitement au moins 7 jours avant l'intervention pour que l'effet du médicament ait le temps de se dissiper.

PO:

- Afin de réduire l'irritation gastrique, administrer l'aspirine après les repas ou avec des aliments ou un antiacide. Les aliments ralentissent l'absorption du médicament, mais ne réduisent pas la quantité totale absorbée.
- Il ne faut pas croquer ni mâcher les comprimés entérosolubles, ni prendre d'antiacide en l'espace de 1 ou 2 heures après la prise d'un tel comprimé.
- On peut mâcher les comprimés à croquer, les dissoudre dans du liquide ou les avaler tels quels.

ENSEIGNEMENT AU PATIENT ET À SES PROCHES

- Conseiller au patient de prendre l'aspirine avec un grand verre d'eau et de ne pas se coucher pendant les 15 à 30 minutes qui suivent.
- Recommander au patient de signaler la présence d'acouphènes, de saignements inhabituels des gencives, d'ecchymoses, de selles noires et goudronneuses, ou de fièvre persistant pendant plus de 3 jours.
- Prévenir le patient qu'il doit éviter de boire de l'alcool s'il prend de l'aspirine, afin de prévenir l'irritation gastrique. Lui expliquer que s'il prend 3 verres d'alcool ou plus par jour pendant ce traitement, il peut accroître le risque d'hémorragie digestive. Le prévenir également qu'il ne peut prendre en concomitance de l'acétaminophène ou des AINS que pendant quelques jours, à moins qu'un professionnel de la santé ne l'ait recommandé, en raison du risque de néphropathie attribuable aux analgésiques.
- Recommander au patient qui reçoit un traitement prolongé et qui doit subir une intervention chirurgicale d'avertir le professionnel de la santé qu'il suit un traitement par l'aspirine. Il peut être nécessaire de cesser l'administration de l'aspirine 1 semaine avant l'intervention chirurgicale.
- LES AUTORITÉS COMPÉTENTES METTENT EN GARDE LA POPULATION CONTRE L'ADMINISTRATION DE L'ASPIRINE À DES ENFANTS OU À DES ADOLESCENTS (< 18 ANS) SOUFFRANT DE VARICELLE, D'AFFECTIONS VIRALES OU DE SYNDROME GRIPPAL, EN RAISON DU RISQUE D'APPARITION DU SYNDROME DE REYE.

Ischémies cérébrales transitoires ou infarctus du myocarde: Prévenir le patient qui reçoit l'aspirine en traitement prophylactique qu'il doit respecter rigoureusement la posologie recommandée. Il n'a pas été constaté que l'augmentation de la dose entraînait des bienfaits additionnels.

VÉRIFICATION DE L'EFFICACITÉ THÉRAPEUTIQUE

L'efficacité du traitement peut être démontrée par: le soulagement de la douleur légère à modérée ■ l'amélioration de la mobilité des articulations; les pleins effets peuvent ne se manifester qu'après 2 ou 3 semaines ■ la baisse de la fièvre ■ la prévention des ICT et des AVC ■ la prévention de l'infarctus du myocarde. ✳

ATAZANAVIR

Reyataz

CLASSIFICATION:

Antirétroviral (inhibiteur de la protéase)

Grossesse – catégorie B

INDICATIONS

Infection par le VIH (en association avec d'autres antirétroviraux). **Usages non approuvés:** En association avec d'autre antirétroviraux, prophylaxie après l'exposition accidentelle au VIH.

MÉCANISME D'ACTION

Inhibition de la protéase du VIH, prévenant la maturation des virions. ***Effets thérapeutiques:*** Augmentation du nombre de cellules CD4 et diminution de la charge virale, ce qui ralentit l'évolution du VIH et de ses complications.

PHARMACOCINÉTIQUE

Absorption: Rapide (accrue si le médicament est pris avec des aliments).

Distribution: L'agent pénètre dans le liquide céphalorachidien et dans le sperme.

Métabolisme et excrétion: 80 % est métabolisé (CYP3A); 13 % est excrété sous forme inchangée dans l'urine.

Demi-vie: 7 heures.

Profil temps-action

	Début d'action	Pic	Durée
PO	rapide	2,5 h	24 h

CONTRE-INDICATIONS, PRÉCAUTIONS ET MISES EN GARDE

Contre-indications: Hypersensibilité ■ Insuffisance hépatique grave ■ Usage concomitant de cisapride, d'ergotamine, d'ergonovine, de dihydroergotamine, de lovastatine, de méthylergonovine, de midazolam, d'oméprazole, de pimozide, de quinidine, de simvastatine et de triazolam (risque de toxicité pouvant mettre la vie en péril) ■ **Péd.**: Nourrissons âgés de moins de 3 mois (risque accru de kernictère).

Précautions et mises en garde: Nombreuses interactions médicamenteuses ■ Insuffisance hépatique de légère à modérée ■ Atteinte préexistante du système de conduction (bloc AV de premier degré marqué ou bloc AV de deuxième ou de troisième degré) ou usage concomitant d'autres médicaments qui allongent l'intervalle PR (en particulier ceux métabolisés par la voie du cytochrome CYP3A4, dont le vérapamil et le diltiazem) ■ Diabète ■ Hémophilie (risque accru de saignements) ■ **Obst.**: N'utiliser qu'en cas de besoin incontestable ■ **Allaitement**: L'allaitement au sein est déconseillé aux patientes infectées par le VIH.

RÉACTIONS INDÉSIRABLES ET EFFETS SECONDAIRES

En administration concomitante avec d'autres antirétroviraux.

SNC: céphalées, dépression, étourdissements, insomnie.

CV: allongement de l'intervalle PR.

GI: nausées, douleurs abdominales, élévation des concentrations de bilirubine, diarrhée, jaunisse, vomissements, élévation des concentrations de transaminases.

Tég.: rash.

End.: hyperglycémie.

Métab.: modification de la distribution des tissus adipeux.

Loc.: myalgie.

Divers: fièvre, syndrome de reconstitution immunitaire.

INTERACTIONS

Médicament-médicament: L'atazanavir est un inhibiteur des systèmes enzymatiques **CYP3A4** et **UGT1A1**. C'est aussi un substrat du **CYP3A4** ■ L'AGENT ÉLÈVE DES CONCENTRATIONS D'**ERGOTAMINE**, D'**ERGONOVINE**, DE **DIHYDROERGOTAMINE**, DE **MÉTHYLERGONOVINE**, DE **MIDAZOLAM**, DE **PIMOZIDE**, DE **TRIAZOLAM**, DE **LOVASTATINE**, DE **SIMVASTATINE**; L'USAGE CONCOMITANT PEUT ENTRAÎNER UNE TOXICITÉ DU SNC, AINSI QU'UNE TOXICITÉ CARDIOVASCULAIRE OU MUSCULOSQUELETTIQUE POUVANT METTRE LA VIE EN DANGER; IL EST DONC CONTRE-INDIQUÉ ■ L'atazanavir peut entraver le métabolisme de l'**irinotécan**, ce qui entraîne l'accroissement de ses effets toxiques ■ L'absorption et les concentrations peuvent être diminuées par les **inhibiteurs de la pompe à protons,** ce qui favorise l'émergence d'une résistance virale ■ L'absorption et les concentrations peuvent être diminuées par les **antagonistes des récepteurs H_2 de l'histamine**, ce qui favorise l'émergence d'une résistance virale; administrer l'atazanavir au moins 2 heures avant ou 10 heures après ■ Les **antiacides** ou les **médicaments tamponnés** diminuent l'absorption; administrer l'atazanavir 2 heures avant ou 1 heure après ■ Les concentrations sont considérablement diminuées par la **rifampine** (risque d'émergence d'une résistance virale, éviter l'usage concomitant) ■ Le traitement en association avec le **ténofovir** peut diminuer la réponse virologique et mener à l'émergence d'une résistance (on doit ajouter 100 mg de **ritonavir** pour élever les concentrations sanguines et réduire la dose d'atazanavir à 300 mg/jour); l'atazanavir augmente les concentrations du **ténofovir**, ce qui peut accentuer les effets indésirables associés à cet agent (faire un suivi plus étroit) ■ L'administration concomitante d'**indinavir** peut accroître le risque d'hyperbilirubinémie et il faut l'éviter ■ L'administration concomitante de comprimés tamponnés de **didanosine** réduit l'absorption et les concentrations; administrer l'atazanavir avec des aliments, 2 heures avant ou 1 heure après la didanosine ■ L'**éfavirenz** diminue les concentrations d'atazanavir et peut favoriser l'émergence d'une résistance (on doit ajouter 100 mg de **ritonavir** pour élever les concentrations sanguines et réduire la dose d'atazanavir à 300 mg/jour) ■ L'agent accroît les concentrations de **saquinavir** ■ Les concentrations d'atazanavir sont élevées par le **ritonavir**; réduire la dose d'atazanavir à 300 mg/jour ■ La **névirapine** peut diminuer les concentrations; éviter

A

l'usage concomitant ■ L'agent élève les concentrations de **lidocaïne**, d'**amiodarone** ou de **quinidine**; on recommande de surveiller les concentrations sanguines ■ Risque accru de saignement avec la **warfarine**: surveiller le RNI ■ Élévation des concentrations sanguines d'**antidépresseurs tricycliques**; on recommande de surveiller les concentrations sanguines ■ Élévation des concentrations de **trazodone**; diminuer la dose de cette dernière ■ L'agent élève les concentrations de **rifabutine**; diminuer la dose de rifabutine de 75 % ■ L'agent élève les concentrations de **diltiazem**, de **félodipine**, de **nifédipine** et de **vérapamil** et de leurs métabolites actifs, le cas échéant; on recommande de diminuer la dose de ces agents de 50 % et de suivre de près l'état du patient ■ Le **ritonavir** élève les concentrations de **fluticasone**; envisager une solution de rechange lorsque l'atazanavir est utilisé avec le ritonavir ■ Diminution des concentrations de **voriconazole** lorsque l'atazanavir est administré avec le ritonavir; éviter l'usage concomitant ■ Le **voriconazole** peut aussi élever les concentrations d'atazanavir (lorsque ce dernier est administré sans ritonavir) ■ Élévation des concentrations de **kétoconazole** ou d'**itraconazole** lorsque l'atazanavir est administré avec le ritonavir ■ Élévation des concentrations de **sildénafil**, de **vardénafil** et de **tadalafil** et augmentation possible de leurs effets indésirables, notamment l'hypotension, l'altération de la vue et le priapisme; faire preuve de prudence et diminuer la dose de **sildénafil** à 25 mg toutes les 48 heures; diminuer la dose de **vardénafil** à 2,5 mg toutes les 72 heures; diminuer la dose de **tadalafil** à 10 mg toutes les 72 heures ■ Risque accru de myopathie lors de l'usage concomitant d'**atorvastatine** ■ Élévation des concentrations de **cyclosporine**, de **sirolimus** et de **tacrolimus**; surveiller les concentrations sanguines de l'immunosuppresseur ■ Élévation des concentrations de **clarithromycine**; diminuer les doses de clarithromycine de 50 % ou envisager une solution de rechange ■ L'agent peut augmenter les doses de certains **œstrogènes** qui entrent dans la composition des **contraceptifs hormonaux**; opter pour une autre méthode de contraception non hormonale ■ Éviter l'usage concomitant d'autres **médicaments qui allongent l'intervalle PR**.

Médicament-produits naturels: La consommation concomitante de **millepertuis** peut entraîner la diminution des concentrations sanguines et de l'efficacité de l'atazanavir, associée à l'émergence d'une résistance virale.

VOIES D'ADMINISTRATION ET POSOLOGIE

- **PO (adultes)**: 400 mg, 1 fois par jour avec des aliments ■ *Avec le ritonavir* – 300 mg, 1 fois par jour, avec du ritonavir à 100 mg, 1 fois par jour avec des aliments ■ *Avec l'éfavirenz* – atazanavir à 300 mg avec du ritonavir à 100 mg et de l'éfavirenz à 600 mg (chacun des agents, 1 fois par jour avec des aliments) ■ *Avec le ténofovir* – atazanavir à 300 mg avec du ritonavir à 100 mg et du ténofovir à 300 mg (chacun des agents, 1 fois par jour avec des aliments).

Insuffisance hépatique modérée (classe B de Child-Pugh)

- **PO (adultes)**: 300 mg, 1 fois par jour.

PRÉSENTATION

Capsules: 150 mg^Pr^, 200 mg^Pr^.

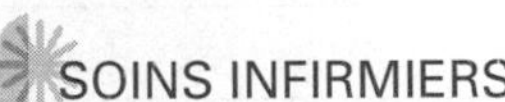

SOINS INFIRMIERS

ÉVALUATION DE LA SITUATION

- Rester à l'affût de l'aggravation des symptômes de l'infection par le VIH et des symptômes d'infections opportunistes tout au long du traitement.
- L'agent peut aussi entraîner l'élévation des valeurs du bilan hépatique, des concentrations de créatine kinase ou de glucose, et provoquer une neutropénie.
- Rester à l'affût du rash qui peut apparaître dans les 8 premières semaines de traitement. Il disparaît habituellement dans les 2 semaines, sans qu'on ait besoin de modifier le traitement.
- Si une patiente enceinte est exposée à des antirétroviraux, l'inscrire dans le registre des femmes exposées aux antirétroviraux pendant leur grossesse, en composant le 1-800-258-4263.

Tests de laboratoire:

- Suivre la charge virale et la numération des CD4 à intervalles réguliers tout au long du traitement.
- L'atazanavir peut élever les concentrations sériques d'amylase et de lipase.
- L'agent peut élever les taux d'enzymes hépatiques.
- L'agent peut élever les concentrations de créatine kinase.
- L'agent peut diminuer les concentrations d'hémoglobine et le nombre de polynucléaires neutrophiles et de plaquettes.
- L'agent peut élever les taux de bilirubine non conjuguée; effet réversible à l'arrêt du traitement.

DIAGNOSTICS INFIRMIERS POSSIBLES

- Risque d'infection (Indications).
- Non-observance du traitement médicamenteux (Enseignement au patient et à ses proches).

INTERVENTIONS INFIRMIÈRES

PO: Administrer tous les jours avec des aliments pour accroître l'absorption. Les capsules doivent être avalées telles quelles; ne pas les ouvrir.

- Lorsqu'on administre l'atazanavir avec le ritonavir et l'éfavirenz, les administrer en tant que dose quotidienne unique avec des aliments. Ne pas administrer l'agent avec l'éfavirenz sans administrer également du ritonavir.
- Si l'agent est administré avec le ritonavir et le ténofovir, les administrer en tant que dose quotidienne unique avec des aliments. Ne pas administrer l'agent avec le ténofovir sans administrer également du ritonavir.
- Lorsque l'atazanavir est administré avec la préparation tamponnée de didanosine, l'administrer avec des aliments, 2 heures avant ou 1 heure après la didanosine.

ENSEIGNEMENT AU PATIENT ET À SES PROCHES

- Insister sur le fait qu'il est important de prendre l'atazanavir avec des aliments, comme il est recommandé. Inciter le patient à lire les renseignements destinés au patient qu'on lui remet avec le médicament à chaque renouvellement d'ordonnance. L'atazanavir doit toujours être pris en association avec d'autres antirétroviraux. Expliquer au patient qu'il ne doit pas prendre plus que la quantité prescrite ni arrêter le traitement sans consulter un professionnel de la santé au préalable. Le prévenir qu'il doit prendre toute dose oubliée aussitôt que possible et reprendre ensuite l'horaire habituel. Lui préciser cependant qu'il ne doit pas prendre le médicament dans les 6 heures qui précèdent la dose suivante; sauter plutôt cette dose et prendre la dose suivante à l'heurc habituelle. Le prévenir qu'il ne faut jamais remplacer une dose manquée par une double dose.
- Expliquer au patient qu'il ne doit pas donner de l'atazanavir à d'autres personnes.
- Prévenir le patient que l'atazanavir ne guérit par l'infection par le VIH ni ne prévient les infections associées ou opportunistes. L'atazanavir ne réduit pas le risque de transmission du VIH à d'autres personnes par les rapports sexuels ou par la contamination du sang. Inciter le patient à utiliser un condom et à éviter le partage d'aiguilles ou les dons de sang pour prévenir la propagation du VIH.
- Recommander au patient de consulter un professionnel de la santé avant de prendre d'autres médicaments d'ordonnance, des médicaments en vente libre ou des produits à base de plantes médicinales, et en particulier du millepertuis; les interactions peuvent mener à une issue fatale.
- Conseiller à la patiente qui prend des contraceptifs hormonaux d'utiliser une autre méthode contraceptive non hormonale.
- Prévenir le patient que l'agent peut provoquer des étourdissements. Lui conseiller de prévenir un professionnel de la santé si ce symptôme se manifeste et d'éviter de conduire ou de s'engager dans d'autres activités qui exigent sa vigilance jusqu'à ce qu'on ait la certitude que le médicament n'entraîne pas cet effet chez lui.
- Recommander au patient de prévenir un professionnel de la santé en cas de jaunissement des yeux ou de la peau, de modification de la fréquence cardiaque ou d'hyperglycémie.
- Prévenir le patient que le traitement antirétroviral l'expose au risque de redistribution ou d'accumulation de tissus adipeux dont les causes et les conséquences à long terme sur la santé sont pour le moment inconnues.
- Recommander à la patiente d'informer un professionnel de la santé si elle pense être enceinte ou désire le devenir ou, encore, si elle allaite.
- Insister sur l'importance des examens réguliers de suivi et des numérations globulaires permettant d'évaluer les progrès du traitement et de surveiller les effets secondaires.

VÉRIFICATION DE L'EFFICACITÉ THÉRAPEUTIQUE

L'efficacité du traitement peut être démontrée par: le ralentissement de l'évolution de l'infection par le VIH et la diminution du risque d'infections opportunistes chez les patients infectés ■ la diminution de la charge virale et l'augmentation du nombre de CD4. ✳

ATÉNOLOL

Apo-Aténolol, Gen-Aténolol, Novo-Aténol, Nu-Aténol, PMS-Aténolol, Ratio-Aténolol, Riva-Aténolol, Tenormin

CLASSIFICATION:

Antiangineux, antihypertenseur (bêtabloquant)

Grossesse – catégorie D

INDICATIONS

Hypertension ■ Angine de poitrine. **Usages non approuvés**: Prévention des décès chez les patients ayant subi un infarctus du myocarde.

A

MÉCANISME D'ACTION

Blocage de la stimulation des récepteurs bêta$_1$ adrénergiques (myocardiques). Habituellement, les doses thérapeutiques n'affectent pas les récepteurs bêta$_2$ (pulmonaires, vasculaires ou utérins). ***Effets thérapeutiques:*** Abaissement de la pression artérielle et ralentissement de la fréquence cardiaque ■ Réduction de la fréquence des crises d'angine de poitrine ■ Prévention de l'infarctus du myocarde.

PHARMACOCINÉTIQUE

Absorption: De 50 à 60 % (PO).

Distribution: Faible pénétration du SNC. L'aténolol traverse la barrière placentaire et passe dans le lait maternel.

Métabolisme et excrétion: Excrétion rénale de 40 à 50 % à l'état inchangé. Le reste est excrété dans les fèces sous forme de médicament non absorbé.

Demi-vie: De 6 à 9 heures.

Profil temps-action (effets cardiovasculaires)

	DÉBUT D'ACTION	PIC	DURÉE
PO	1 h	2 – 4 h	24 h

CONTRE-INDICATIONS, PRÉCAUTIONS ET MISES EN GARDE

Contre-indications: Insuffisance cardiaque congestive décompensée ■ Œdème pulmonaire ■ Choc cardiogénique ■ Bradycardie sinusale ou bloc AV du 2e et 3e degré ■ Maladie du sinus ■ Insuffisance ventriculaire droite attribuable à l'hypertension pulmonaire ■ Hypotension ■ Maladies artérielles périphériques graves ■ Anesthésie au moyen d'agents dépresseurs du myocarde ■ Phéochromocytome en l'absence de blocage des récepteurs alpha ■ Acidose métabolique ■ Hypersensibilité.

Précautions et mises en garde: Insuffisance rénale (réduire la dose si la $Cl_{Cr} \leq 35$ mL/min) ■ **GÉR.**: Sensibilité accrue aux bêtabloquants; il est recommandé de réduire la dose initiale chez les personnes âgées ■ Insuffisance cardiaque congestive compensée ■ Bloc AV de 1er degré ■ Maladie pulmonaire bronchospastique (dont l'asthme; la sélectivité pour les récepteurs bêta peut disparaître lors de l'administration de doses élevées) ■ Diabète (le médicament peut masquer les symptômes d'hypoglycémie) ■ Thyrotoxicose (le médicament peut en masquer les symptômes) ■ Antécédents de réactions allergiques graves (les réactions peuvent être aggravées) ■ **OBST., ALLAITEMENT, PÉD.**: L'innocuité du médicament n'a pas été établie pendant la grossesse ou l'allaitement ni chez les enfants; il traverse la barrière placentaire et peut provoquer une bradycardie, de l'hypotension, de l'hypoglycémie ou une dépression respiratoire chez le fœtus ou le nouveau-né.

RÉACTIONS INDÉSIRABLES ET EFFETS SECONDAIRES

SNC: fatigue, faiblesse, anxiété, dépression, étourdissements, somnolence, insomnie, perte de mémoire, modifications de l'état mental, nervosité, cauchemars.

ORLO: vision trouble, enchifrènement.

Resp.: bronchospasme, respiration sifflante.

CV: BRADYCARDIE, INSUFFISANCE CARDIAQUE, ŒDÈME PULMONAIRE, hypotension, vasoconstriction périphérique.

GI: constipation, diarrhée, anomalies de la fonction hépatique, nausées, vomissements.

GU: impuissance, baisse de la libido, mictions fréquentes.

Tég.: rash.

End.: hyperglycémie, hypoglycémie.

Loc.: arthralgie, douleurs lombaires, douleurs articulaires.

Divers: lupus érythémateux induit par le médicament.

INTERACTIONS

Médicament-médicament: Les **anesthésiques généraux**, le **diltiazem** et le **vérapamil** peuvent exercer des effets additifs sur la dépression du myocarde ■ Risque accru de bradycardie lors de l'administration concomitante de **digoxine** ■ Les **antihypertenseurs** ou les **dérivés nitrés** ainsi que l'ingestion rapide de grandes quantités d'**alcool** peuvent entraîner des effets hypotenseurs additifs ■ L'usage concomitant d'**amphétamines**, de **cocaïne**, d'**éphédrine**, d'**adrénaline**, de **noradrénaline**, de **phényléphrine** ou de **pseudoéphédrine** peut provoquer une stimulation des récepteurs alpha-adrénergiques excessive (hypertension excessive, bradycardie) ■ L'administration concomitante de **bloqueurs des canaux calciques ayant des effets inotropes négatifs** (**diltiazem** et **vérapamil**) peut entraîner une prolongation de la conduction SA et AV, ce qui risque de provoquer une hypotension grave, une bradycardie ou une insuffisance cardiaque ■ Le médicament peut exacerber l'hypertension réactionnelle pouvant résulter du retrait de la **clonidine** ■ L'administration concomitante de **thyroxine** peut diminuer l'efficacité de l'aténolol ■ L'aténolol peut diminuer l'efficacité de l'**insuline** ou des **hypoglycémiants oraux** (il peut être nécessaire de modifier la dose) ■ L'aténolol peut réduire l'efficacité de la **théophylline** ■ Le médicament peut diminuer les effets cardiovasculaires bénéfiques sur les récepteurs bêta$_1$ de la **dopamine** et de la **dobutamine** ■ Administrer le médicament avec prudence dans les 14 jours qui suivent un traitement par un **IMAO** (risque d'hypertension).

VOIES D'ADMINISTRATION ET POSOLOGIE

- **PO (adultes)**: *Antiangineux* – 50 mg, 1 fois par jour; après 1 semaine, on peut augmenter la dose jusqu'à concurrence de 100 mg, administré en 1 ou 2 prises (dose maximale: 200 mg, en 1 ou 2 prises). *Antihypertenseur* – de 25 à 50 mg, 1 fois par jour; après 2 semaines, on peut augmenter la dose jusqu'à 50 - 100 mg, 1 fois par jour (dose maximale: 100 mg, 1 fois par jour).

Insuffisance rénale

- **PO (adultes)**: *CL_{CR} de 15 à 35 mL/min* – ne pas dépasser 50 mg par jour; *CL_{CR} < 15 mL/min* – ne pas dépasser 50 mg tous les 2 jours.

PRÉSENTATION (version générique disponible)

Comprimés: 25 mg[Pr], 50 mg[Pr], 100 mg[Pr] ▪ **En association avec**: chlorthalidone (Tenoretic[Pr]).

SOINS INFIRMIERS

ÉVALUATION DE LA SITUATION

- Mesurer la pression artérielle et le pouls et suivre l'ÉCG à intervalles fréquents pendant toute la période d'adaptation posologique et, à intervalles réguliers, pendant toute la durée du traitement.
- Effectuer le bilan quotidien des ingesta et des excreta; peser le patient tous les jours. Rester à l'affût des signes et des symptômes suivants d'insuffisance cardiaque: dyspnée, râles ou crépitations, gain pondéral, œdème périphérique, turgescence des jugulaires.

Angine: Évaluer la fréquence et les caractéristiques des crises d'angine à intervalles réguliers pendant toute la durée du traitement.

Tests de laboratoire:

- L'aténolol peut élever les concentrations sériques d'urée, de lipoprotéines, du potassium, de triglycérides et d'acide urique.
- L'aténolol peut élever la glycémie.

Toxicité et surdosage: Suivre de près les patients recevant des bêtabloquants afin de déceler les signes suivants de surdosage: bradycardie, étourdissements graves ou évanouissements, somnolence prononcée, dyspnée, ongles ou paumes des mains bleutés, convulsions. Prévenir immédiatement le médecin si ces signes se manifestent.

DIAGNOSTICS INFIRMIERS POSSIBLES

- Débit cardiaque diminué (Effets secondaires).
- Connaissances insuffisantes sur le traitement médicamenteux (Enseignement au patient et à ses proches).
- Non-observance du traitement médicamenteux (Enseignement au patient et à ses proches).

INTERVENTIONS INFIRMIÈRES

- Mesurer le pouls à l'apex du cœur avant d'administrer le médicament. S'il est inférieur à 50 battements par minute ou si des arythmies se produisent, ne pas administrer l'aténolol et en informer le médecin ou un autre professionnel de la santé.

ENSEIGNEMENT AU PATIENT ET À SES PROCHES

- Prévenir le patient qu'il doit prendre l'aténolol tous les jours au même moment de la journée, même s'il se sent bien. L'avertir qu'il ne doit jamais sauter de dose ni remplacer une dose manquée par une double dose. S'il n'a pu prendre son médicament au moment habituel, il doit le prendre aussitôt que possible, mais au moins 8 heures avant l'heure prévue pour la dose suivante. Un sevrage brusque peut provoquer des arythmies mortelles, de l'hypertension ou une ischémie du myocarde.
- Conseiller au patient d'avoir une réserve suffisante de médicament pour les fins de semaine, les congés et les vacances. Lui conseiller également de conserver une ordonnance dans son portefeuille pour parer à toute urgence.
- Expliquer au patient et à ses proches comment prendre le pouls et la pression artérielle. Leur demander de mesurer le pouls tous les jours et la pression artérielle 2 fois par semaine. Leur recommander de signaler tout changement important à un professionnel de la santé.
- Prévenir le patient que l'aténolol peut parfois provoquer des étourdissements. Lui conseiller de ne pas conduire et d'éviter les activités qui exigent sa vigilance jusqu'à ce qu'on ait la certitude que le médicament n'entraîne pas cet effet chez lui.
- Conseiller au patient de changer lentement de position pour réduire le risque d'hypotension orthostatique.
- Prévenir le patient que le médicament peut le rendre plus sensible au froid.
- Conseiller au patient de consulter un professionnel de la santé avant de prendre des médicaments en vente libre, particulièrement des préparations contre le rhume, ou des produits naturels en même temps que l'aténolol.

A

- Recommander au patient diabétique de suivre sa glycémie de près, particulièrement lorsqu'il se sent fatigué, faible ou irritable ou lorsqu'il ressent un malaise. La transpiration est un signe d'hypoglycémie qui n'est pas masqué par l'aténolol.
- Recommander au patient de signaler à un professionnel de la santé les symptômes suivants: ralentissement du pouls, difficultés respiratoires, respiration sifflante, mains et pieds froids, étourdissements, sensation de tête légère, confusion, dépression, rash, fièvre, maux de gorge, saignements inhabituels ou ecchymoses.
- Conseiller au patient d'informer le professionnel de la santé des médicaments qu'il prend avant de se soumettre à une intervention chirurgicale ou à un nouveau traitement.
- Conseiller au patient de porter sur lui en tout temps un bracelet d'identité où sont inscrits ses problèmes de santé et sa médication.

Hypertension: Prévenir le patient qu'il doit continuer à appliquer les autres mesures non pharmacologiques de réduction de l'hypertension: perdre du poids, réduire sa consommation de sel, diminuer le stress, faire régulièrement de l'exercice, boire avec modération et cesser de fumer. L'aténolol stabilise la pression artérielle, mais ne guérit pas l'hypertension.

VÉRIFICATION DE L'EFFICACITÉ THÉRAPEUTIQUE

L'efficacité du traitement peut être démontrée par: la baisse de la pression artérielle ■ la réduction de la fréquence des crises d'angine ■ la prévention des infarctus du myocarde. ✳

ATOMOXÉTINE

Strattera

CLASSIFICATION:

Inhibiteur sélectif du recaptage de la noradrénaline

Grossesse – catégorie C

INDICATIONS

Traitement du trouble déficitaire de l'attention avec hyperactivité (TDAH) chez l'enfant de 6 ans ou plus, l'adolescent et l'adulte.

MÉCANISME D'ACTION

Inhibition sélective du recaptage de la noradrénaline. ***Effets thérapeutiques:*** Diminution des symptômes d'hyperactivité-impulsivité et des symptômes d'inattention ■ Amélioration du fonctionnement et de la qualité de vie.

PHARMACOCINÉTIQUE

Absorption: Bonne (PO).

Distribution: Liquides corporels.

Liaison aux protéines: 98 %.

Métabolisme et excrétion: Métabolisme majoritairement hépatique (principalement par l'intermédiaire du CYP2D6). Excrétion majoritairement urinaire et, dans une moindre mesure, fécale.

Demi-vie: 5 heures (métaboliseurs rapides) ou 21,6 heures (métaboliseurs lents).

Profil temps-action (stimulation du SNC)

	Début d'action	Pic	Durée
PO	inconnu	1 – 2 h (T_{max})	12 – 24 h

CONTRE-INDICATIONS, PRÉCAUTIONS ET MISES EN GARDE

Contre-indications: Hypersensibilité ■ Usage concomitant ou récent (moins de 14 jours) d'IMAO ■ Glaucome à angle fermé ■ Hypertension modérée à grave ■ Maladie cardiovasculaire symptomatique ■ Artériosclérose avancée ■ Hyperthyroïdie non maîtrisée.

Précautions et mises en garde: Atteinte hépatique grave ■ Tendances suicidaires (risque accru d'idées suicidaires en début de traitement ou lors de l'adaptation des doses; le risque semble plus élevé chez les enfants ou les adolescents) ■ Antécédents de maladie cardiovasculaire ou vasculaire cérébrale ■ Risque accru d'effets secondaires cardiovasculaires en cas d'usage concomitant de salbutamol ou de vasopresseurs ■ Hypertension, tachycardie, syndrome congénital du QT long ■ **GÉR., PÉD.**: Personnes âgées > 65 ans et enfants âgés < 6 ans (l'innocuité et l'efficacité du médicament n'ont pas été établies) ■ **OBST., ALLAITEMENT**: L'innocuité du médicament n'a pas été établie.

RÉACTIONS INDÉSIRABLES ET EFFETS SECONDAIRES

SNC: somnolence, céphalées, agressivité, irritabilité, insomnie, étourdissements, fatigue ou léthargie, sédation, dépression ou humeur dépressive.

CV: hypertension, palpitations, tachycardie, hypotension orthostatique, ALLONGEMENT DU SEGMENT QT À L'ÉCG.

GI: vomissements, douleurs abdominales, perte d'appétit, dyspepsie, nausées, constipation, sécheresse de la bouche (xérostomie), LÉSIONS HÉPATIQUES.

GU: rétention urinaire, retard de la miction. *Adultes*: dysménorrhée, absence ou trouble d'éjaculation, impuissance, diminution de la libido.

Tég.: éruptions cutanées, urticaire.

End.: *Enfants*: diminution de la croissance et du gain pondéral.

Divers: réactions d'hypersensibilité, ŒDÈME ANGIONEUROTIQUE.

INTERACTIONS

Médicament-médicament: Chez une fraction de la population (7 % des personnes de race blanche et 2 % des personnes de race noire), le métabolisme des médicaments par l'intermédiaire du CYP2D6 est lent. Chez ces personnes, l'activité de cette voie enzymatique est réduite, ce qui entraîne des concentrations plasmatiques plus élevées et une élimination plus lente de l'atomoxétine comparativement aux personnes chez qui l'activité est normale (métaboliseurs rapides) ■ La coadministration de **médicaments qui inhibent le CYP2D6** (**fluoxétine**, **paroxétine**, **quinidine**) donne lieu à une augmentation substantielle des concentrations plasmatiques d'atomoxétine; une adaptation posologique peut être nécessaire ■ L'usage concomitant ou rapproché d'**IMAO** et d'autres **médicaments qui modifient les concentrations des monoamines dans le cerveau** a donné lieu à des réactions graves et parfois mortelles ■ La prudence est de mise lors de l'administration d'un autre médicament qui agit sur la **noradrénaline** à cause du risque d'effets pharmacologiques additifs ou synergiques ■ La prudence est de mise lors de l'administration de **salbutamol** ou d'autres **vasopresseurs**, car il y a risque d'élévation de la fréquence cardiaque et de la pression artérielle surtout au début d'une administration concomitante.

VOIES D'ADMINISTRATION ET POSOLOGIE

L'atomoxétine peut être administrée soit en une dose quotidienne unique, le matin, soit en doses fractionnées, le matin et en fin d'après-midi ou en début de soirée.

- **PO (enfants > 6 ans et adolescents < 70 kg)**: *Dose initiale* – 0,5 mg/kg/jour, à maintenir pendant un minimum de 10 jours. Ensuite, on peut administrer la dose intermédiaire (0,8 mg/kg/jour), qui doit également être maintenue pendant un minimum de 10 jours. Selon la réponse clinique et la tolérance du patient au médicament, on peut augmenter cette dose pour la porter à 1,2 mg/kg/jour. (Ne pas dépasser la dose quotidienne totale maximale de 1,4 mg/kg ou 100 mg, soit la plus faible de ces doses.)

Doses recommandées – augmentations par paliers, selon le poids et les capsules disponibles

POIDS	DOSE INITIALE (ENVIRON 0,5 mg/kg/JOUR)	DOSE INTERMÉDIAIRE (ENVIRON 0,8 mg/kg/JOUR)	DOSE ÉLEVÉE (ENVIRON 1,2 mg/kg/JOUR)
20 – 29 kg	10 mg	18 mg	25 mg
30 – 44 kg	18 mg	25 mg	40 mg
45 – 64 kg	25 mg	40 mg	60 mg
65 – 70 kg	40 mg	60 mg	80 mg

- **PO (enfants et adolescents > 70 kg et adultes)**: *Dose initiale* – 40 mg par jour. Maintenir cette dose initiale pendant un minimum de 10 jours. Ensuite, on peut administrer la dose intermédiaire (60 mg par jour), qui doit également être maintenue pendant un minimum de 10 jours. Selon la réponse clinique et la tolérance du patient, on peut porter cette dose à 80 mg par jour. Après 2 à 4 semaines de plus, on peut augmenter la dose jusqu'à concurrence de 100 mg par jour. (Ne pas dépasser la dose quotidienne totale maximale de 100 mg.)

INSUFFISANCE HÉPATIQUE

- EN CAS D'INSUFFISANCE HÉPATIQUE *MODÉRÉE (CLASSE B DE CHILD-PUGH)*, LES DOSES INITIALES ET CIBLES DOIVENT ÊTRE RÉDUITES À 50 % DE LA DOSE NORMALE. EN CAS D'INSUFFISANCE HÉPATIQUE *GRAVE (CLASSE C DE CHILD-PUGH)*, LES DOSES INITIALES ET CIBLES DOIVENT ÊTRE RÉDUITES À 25 % DE LA DOSE NORMALE.

Prise concomitante d'un inhibiteur puissant du 2D6 (fluoxétine, paroxétine, quinidine): Les doses de départ sont les mêmes mais l'augmentation des doses devra se faire à des intervalles de 14 jours, au minimum, et à condition que la dose précédente soit bien tolérée.

PRÉSENTATION

Capsules: 10 mg[Pr], 18 mg[Pr], 25 mg[Pr], 40 mg[Pr] et 60 mg[Pr].

SOINS INFIRMIERS

ÉVALUATION DE LA SITUATION

- Mesurer la pression artérielle et le pouls avant l'administration, après les majorations de la dose et à intervalles réguliers pendant toute la durée du traitement.
- Suivre de près la croissance, en mesurant la taille et le poids de l'enfant qui suit un traitement prolongé.
- Noter la durée de l'attention, la maîtrise des impulsions et les interactions de l'enfant avec autrui. On peut interrompre le traitement pendant un certain

A

temps afin de déterminer si les symptômes sont suffisamment graves pour en justifier la poursuite.

Tests de laboratoire: Mesurer les concentrations d'enzymes hépatiques (AST, ALT) et de bilirubine, dès les premiers signes ou symptômes de dysfonctionnement hépatique (prurit, urine foncée, peau ou yeux de couleur jaunâtre, douleurs au niveau de la partie supérieure droite de l'abdomen, vomissements, jaunisse ou symptômes de type grippal inexpliqués). Ne pas recommencer le traitement à l'atomoxétine chez un patient atteint d'ictère ou manifestant un signe de dysfonctionnement hépatique.

DIAGNOSTICS INFIRMIERS POSSIBLES

- Opérations de la pensée perturbées (Effets secondaires).
- Connaissances insuffisantes sur le traitement médicamenteux (Enseignement au patient et à ses proches).

INTERVENTIONS INFIRMIÈRES

- Administrer le médicament avec ou sans aliments.

ENSEIGNEMENT AU PATIENT ET À SES PROCHES

- Conseiller au patient de suivre rigoureusement la posologie recommandée. S'il n'a pu prendre le médicament au moment habituel, il devrait prendre les autres doses de la journée en les espaçant également, sans jamais doubler les doses et sans dépasser la dose quotidienne totale. Insister sur le fait qu'il ne faut pas modifier la posologie sans consulter un professionnel de la santé.
- En général, les symptômes du TDAH commencent à diminuer en l'espace de 1 à 4 semaines après le début du traitement.
- Conseiller au patient d'informer son médecin et son pharmacien de tous les médicaments qu'il prend ou prévoit prendre, y compris les médicaments vendus sans ordonnance, les suppléments alimentaires et les plantes médicinales.
- Recommander au patient de se peser régulièrement et de signaler à un professionnel de la santé toute perte de poids.
- Prévenir le patient que l'atomoxétine peut provoquer des étourdissements ou de la somnolence. Lui conseiller de ne pas conduire et d'éviter les activités qui exigent sa vigilance jusqu'à ce qu'on ait la certitude que le médicament n'entraîne pas ces effets chez lui.
- Recommander au patient de signaler à un professionnel de la santé la nervosité, l'insomnie et les palpitations.
- Conseiller au patient de consulter un professionnel de la santé avant de prendre un médicament en vente libre, un supplément alimentaire ou un produit naturel.
- Recommander au patient de signaler immédiatement à un professionnel de la santé tout signe ou symptôme de dysfonctionnement hépatique (prurit, urine foncée, peau ou yeux de couleur jaunâtre, douleurs au niveau de la partie supérieure droite de l'abdomen, vomissements, jaunisse ou symptômes de type grippal inexpliqués), ainsi que le rash ou la fièvre.
- Informer le patient que si le médecin décide de prescrire un traitement prolongé, il devrait réévaluer l'utilité de la médication à intervalles réguliers.
- Insister sur l'importance des examens réguliers de suivi permettant d'évaluer les bienfaits du traitement.
- Prévenir le patient qu'il n'est pas nécessaire de diminuer graduellement la dose d'atomoxétine avant d'arrêter le traitement.
- Recommander à la patiente de prévenir un professionnel de la santé si elle pense être enceinte ou si elle désire le devenir ou, encore, si elle allaite.
- Conseiller aux parents d'informer l'infirmière de l'école du traitement que suit leur enfant.

VÉRIFICATION DE L'EFFICACITÉ THÉRAPEUTIQUE

L'efficacité du traitement peut être démontrée par: la prolongation de la durée de l'attention et l'amélioration des interactions sociales en présence du trouble déficitaire de l'attention avec hyperactivité. ✳

ATORVASTATINE,

voir Inhibiteurs de l'HMG-CoA réductase

ATOVAQUONE

Mepron

CLASSIFICATION:

Anti-infectieux (antiprotozoaire)

Grossesse – catégorie C

INDICATIONS

Traitement de la pneumonie légère à modérée due à *Pneumocystis carinii* chez les patients qui ne peuvent tolérer l'association de triméthoprime et de sulfaméthoxazole (TMP-SMX).

A

MÉCANISME D'ACTION

Inhibition de l'action des enzymes nécessaires à la synthèse de l'acide nucléique et de l'adénosine triphosphate (ATP) chez les protozoaires. ***Effets thérapeutiques:*** Activité antiprotozoaire dirigée contre *Pneumocystis carinii*.

PHARMACOCINÉTIQUE

Absorption: Relativement faible, mais considérablement accrue en présence d'aliments, particulièrement de matières grasses.
Distribution: Pénétration dans le liquide céphalorachidien à de très faibles concentrations (moins de 1 % des concentrations plasmatiques).
Liaison aux protéines: > 99,9 %.
Métabolisme et excrétion: L'agent subit plusieurs cycles entérohépatiques et est éliminé dans les fèces.
Demi-vie: De 2,2 à 2,9 jours.

Profil temps-action (concentrations sanguines)

	DÉBUT D'ACTION	PIC†	DURÉE
PO	inconnu	1 - 8 h 24 - 96 h	12 h

† L'existence de 2 pics est attribuable au fait que l'agent subit plusieurs cycles entérohépatiques.

CONTRE-INDICATIONS, PRÉCAUTIONS ET MISES EN GARDE

Contre-indications: Hypersensibilité.
Précautions et mises en garde: Troubles gastro-intestinaux (l'absorption peut être moindre) ■ **OBST., ALLAITEMENT, PÉD.:** L'innocuité du médicament n'a pas été établie ■ Insuffisance hépatique, rénale ou cardiaque (une modification de la posologie peut s'avérer nécessaire).

RÉACTIONS INDÉSIRABLES ET EFFETS SECONDAIRES

SNC: céphalées, insomnie, faiblesse, étourdissements.
Resp.: toux.
GI: nausées, diarrhée, vomissements, douleurs abdominales, résultats anormaux aux tests de la fonction hépatique, anorexie, goût anormal.
Tég.: rash, prurit.
Divers: fièvre.

INTERACTIONS

Médicament-médicament: Interaction possible avec les **médicaments qui se lient fortement aux protéines plasmatiques**, mais l'atovaquone ne semble pas interagir avec la phénytoïne.
Médicament-aliments: Les **aliments** favorisent l'absorption de l'atovaquone.

VOIES D'ADMINISTRATION ET POSOLOGIE

- **PO (adultes):** 750 mg, 2 fois par jour, avec des aliments, pendant 21 jours.

PRÉSENTATION

Suspensions: 750 mg/5 mL[Pr] ■ **En association avec:** proguanil (Malarone[Pr]).

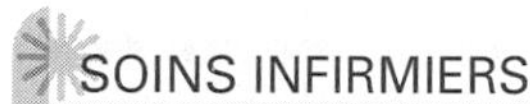

SOINS INFIRMIERS

ÉVALUATION DE LA SITUATION

- Au début du traitement et pendant toute sa durée, suivre de près les signes suivants de pneumonie due à *Pneumocystis carinii*: altération des signes vitaux, murmure vésiculaire, aspect des crachats, accroissement du nombre de globules blancs.
- Prélever des échantillons pour les cultures avant le début du traitement. On peut administrer la première dose avant que les résultats soient connus.

Tests de laboratoire:

- Noter les résultats des tests des fonctions hématologique et hépatique. L'atovaquone peut entraîner l'anémie et la neutropénie. Elle peut également entraîner une élévation des concentrations sériques d'AST, d'ALT et de phosphatase alcaline.
- Noter les concentrations d'électrolytes, car l'atovaquone peut entraîner l'hyponatrémie.
- L'atovaquone peut modifier la glycémie. Suivre de près les patients diabétiques.

DIAGNOSTICS INFIRMIERS POSSIBLES

- Risque d'infection (Indications).
- Connaissances insuffisantes sur le traitement médicamenteux (Enseignement au patient et à ses proches).

INTERVENTIONS INFIRMIÈRES

- Administrer le médicament 2 fois par jour, avec des aliments, pendant 21 jours.

ENSEIGNEMENT AU PATIENT ET À SES PROCHES

- Expliquer au patient qu'il doit respecter rigoureusement la posologie recommandée. Insister sur la nécessité de prendre l'atovaquone avec des aliments, particulièrement avec des aliments riches en matières grasses. Si le médicament est pris sans aliments, les concentrations plasmatiques peuvent être diminuées et l'efficacité réduite.
- Recommander au patient de prévenir un professionnel de la santé si un rash survient.

VÉRIFICATION DE L'EFFICACITÉ THÉRAPEUTIQUE

L'efficacité du traitement peut être démontrée par: la disparition des signes et des symptômes de pneumonie due à *Pneumocystis carinii*. ✻

ATROPINE

Atropine

CLASSIFICATION:

Antiarythmique, antidote, anticholinergique (antimuscarinique), parasympatholytique

Grossesse – catégorie C

Pour l'usage ophtalmique, voir l'annexe N.

INDICATIONS

En administration préopératoire, pour diminuer les sécrétions excessives des voies respiratoires et de la bouche ■ Traitement de la bradycardie sinusale et du bloc cardiaque ■ Durant la réanimation cardiopulmonaire: traitement de l'asystolie et de l'activité électrique lente sans contraction ■ Traitement de l'empoisonnement par des anticholinestérasiques (insecticides organophosphorés). **Usages non approuvés:** Renversement des effets muscariniques indésirables des agents anticholinestérasiques (néostigmine, physostigmine ou pyridostigmine ■ Antidote en cas d'intoxications attribuables à la muscarine (présente dans certains champignons comme l'*Amanita muscaria*).

MÉCANISME D'ACTION

Inhibition de l'effet de l'acétylcholine aux sites des récepteurs postganglionnaires situés dans: les muscles lisses ■ les glandes exocrines ■ le système nerveux central (activité antimuscarinique) ■ Les faibles doses diminuent: la sécrétion de sueur ■ la salivation ■ les sécrétions des voies respiratoires ■ Les doses moyennes entraînent: la mydriase (dilatation des pupilles) ■ la cycloplégie (paralysie de l'accommodation visuelle) ■ l'élévation de la fréquence cardiaque ■ Les doses élevées diminuent la motilité du tractus gastro-intestinal et des voies génito-urinaires. ***Effets thérapeutiques:*** Élévation de la fréquence cardiaque ■ Diminution des sécrétions du tractus gastro-intestinal et des voies respiratoires ■ Renversement des effets de la muscarine ■ Effets spasmolytiques possibles sur les voies biliaire et génito-urinaire.

PHARMACOCINÉTIQUE

Absorption: Bonne (PO, SC ou IM).

Distribution: Le médicament traverse rapidement la barrière hématoencéphalique. Il traverse la barrière placentaire et passe dans le lait maternel.

Métabolisme et excrétion: Métabolisme majoritairement hépatique; de 30 à 50 % est excrété sous forme inchangée par les reins.

Demi-vie: De 13 à 38 heures.

Profil temps-action (inhibition de la salivation)

	DÉBUT D'ACTION	PIC	DURÉE
PO	30 min	30 - 60 min	4 - 6 h
IM, SC	rapide	15 - 50 min	4 - 6 h
IV	immédiat	2 - 4 min	4 - 6 h

CONTRE-INDICATIONS, PRÉCAUTIONS ET MISES EN GARDE

Contre-indications: Hypersensibilité ■ Glaucome à angle fermé ■ Sténose pylorique (sauf aux doses habituellement utilisées en préanesthésie) ■ Hyperplasie de la prostate (sauf aux doses habituellement utilisées en préanesthésie) ■ Hémorragie aiguë ■ Maladie gastro-intestinale obstructive ■ Iléus paralytique ■ Tachycardie ■ Thyrotoxicose.

Précautions et mises en garde: Personnes âgées de plus de 40 ans et très jeunes enfants (prédisposition accrue aux réactions indésirables) ■ Infections intra-abdominales ■ Maladies rénale, hépatique, pulmonaire ou cardiaque chroniques ■ **OBST., ALLAITEMENT:** L'innocuité du médicament n'a pas été établie ■ **PÉD.:** Enfants atteints de paralysie spastique ou de lésions cérébrales; enfants atteints du syndrome de Down (prédisposition accrue aux effets cardiaques et à la mydriase).

RÉACTIONS INDÉSIRABLES ET EFFETS SECONDAIRES

SNC: somnolence, confusion, fièvre.

ORLO: vision trouble, cycloplégie, photophobie, sécheresse des yeux (xérophtalmie), mydriase.

CV: tachycardie, palpitations.

GI: sécheresse de la bouche (xérostomie), constipation.

GU: retard de la miction avec effort pour uriner, rétention urinaire, impuissance.

Tég.: bouffées vasomotrices, peau chaude et sèche, diminution de la sécrétion de sueur.

INTERACTIONS

Médicament-médicament: Effets anticholinergiques additifs lors de l'administration d'autres **composés anticholinergiques**, notamment les **antihistaminiques**, les **antidépresseurs tricycliques**, la **quinidine** et le **diso-**

pyramide ■ Les anticholinergiques peuvent modifier l'absorption d'autres **médicaments administrés par voie orale** en ralentissant la motilité du tractus gastro-intestinal ■ Les **antiacides** diminuent l'absorption des anticholinergiques ■ L'atropine peut aggraver les lésions de la muqueuse gastro-intestinale chez les patients qui prennent des **comprimés de chlorure de potassium par voie orale**.

VOIES D'ADMINISTRATION ET POSOLOGIE

Préanesthésie (pour diminuer la salivation et les sécrétions)

- **IM, SC (adultes)**: De 0,2 à 0,6 mg, de 30 à 60 minutes avant l'intervention.
- **IM, SC (nourrissons et enfants)**: De 0,01 à 0,02 mg/kg/dose, de 30 à 60 minutes avant l'intervention chirurgicale. Dose minimale: 0,1 mg/dose; dose maximale: 0,6 mg/dose.

Bradycardie

- **IV (adultes)**: De 0,4 à 1 mg, on peut répéter l'administration de cette dose toutes les 5 minutes, jusqu'à une dose maximale de 2 mg. *Pendant la réanimation cardiopulmonaire:* de 0,5 à 1 mg, toutes les 3 à 5 minutes, jusqu'à un total de 0,03 à 0,04 mg/kg.
- **IV (nourrissons et enfants)**: 0,02 mg/kg/dose. Dose minimale: 0,1 mg. Dose unique maximale: enfants: 0,5 mg; adolescents: 1 mg. Répéter l'administration après 5 minutes, au besoin, jusqu'à l'atteinte d'une dose maximale cumulative de 1 mg chez les enfants et de 2 mg chez les adolescents.
- **Voie endotrachéale (nourrissons et enfants)**: Utiliser la dose IV et diluer avant l'administration.

Empoisonnement par les insecticides organophosphorés

- **IM, IV (adultes)**: De 1 à 2 mg; répéter l'administration toutes les 5 à 60 minutes jusqu'à la disparition des symptômes muscariniques ou jusqu'à l'apparition de signes de surdosage atropinique. On peut administrer initialement de 2 à 6 mg dans les cas graves et répéter l'administration de cette dose toutes les 5 à 60 minutes. Poursuivre l'administration jusqu'à ce que l'état du patient soit nettement satisfaisant et qu'il le demeure, ce qui peut parfois se prolonger pendant 2 jours ou plus. On peut administrer de la pralidoxime simultanément.
- **IV (nourrissons et enfants)**: De 0,02 à 0,05 mg/kg, toutes les 10 à 20 minutes jusqu'à l'apparition des effets de l'atropine (p. ex., tachycardie, mydriase, fièvre), puis poursuivre toutes les 1 à 4 heures pendant au moins 24 heures.

PRÉSENTATION (version générique disponible)

Solution pour injection: 0,1 mg/mL[Pr], 0,3 mg/mL[Pr], 0,4 mg/mL[Pr], 0,6 mg/mL[Pr], 1 mg/mL[Pr] ■ **En association avec**: diphénoxylate[Pr], hyoscyamine[Pr] ■ **Gouttes et onguent pour usage ophtalmique**: voir l'annexe N.

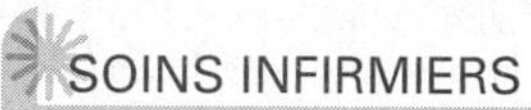

SOINS INFIRMIERS

ÉVALUATION DE LA SITUATION

- Suivre les signes vitaux et l'ÉCG à intervalles fréquents, pendant toute la durée du traitement par voie IV. Signaler immédiatement au médecin toute modification importante de la fréquence cardiaque ou de la pression artérielle ainsi que l'aggravation des extrasystoles ventriculaires ou de l'angine.
- Effectuer le bilan quotidien des ingesta et des excreta chez les personnes âgées ou chez les patients ayant subi une intervention chirurgicale, car l'atropine peut provoquer de la rétention urinaire.
- Observer le patient à intervalles réguliers à la recherche de signes de distension abdominale et ausculter les bruits intestinaux. Si la constipation devient gênante, augmenter la consommation de liquides et ajouter au régime des aliments riches en fibres pour soulager les effets constipants de l'atropine.

Toxicité et surdosage: En cas de surdosage, administrer de la physostigmine comme antidote.

DIAGNOSTICS INFIRMIERS POSSIBLES

- Débit cardiaque diminué (Indications).
- Atteinte à l'intégrité de la muqueuse buccale (Effets secondaires).
- Constipation (Effets secondaires).

INTERVENTIONS INFIRMIÈRES

IM: Une forte rougeur du visage et du tronc peut se produire de 15 à 20 minutes après l'administration IM. En pédiatrie, cette réaction, qui n'est pas nocive, porte le nom de « rougeur atropinique ».

IV directe: Administrer l'atropine par voie IV sans la diluer ou la diluer avec 10 mL d'eau stérile. Consulter les directives de chaque fabricant avant d'administrer la préparation.

Vitesse d'administration: Administrer à un débit de 0,6 mg/min. Ne pas ajouter l'atropine à des solutions IV. Injecter par une tubulure en Y ou par un robinet à trois voies. Administrée par voie IV à des doses inférieures à 0,4 mg ou pendant plus de 1 minute, l'atropine peut provoquer une bradycardie paradoxale qui disparaît habituellement en l'espace de 2 minutes environ.

Voie endotrachéale: Diluer avec du NaCl 0,9 % et faire suivre de 1 mL de NaCl 0,9 % et de plusieurs ventilations à pression positive.

Associations compatibles dans la même seringue: butorphanol ■ chlorpromazine ■ cimétidine ■ dimenhydrinate ■ diphenhydramine ■ dropéridol ■ fentanyl ■ glycopyrrolate ■ héparine ■ hydromorphone ■ hydroxyzine ■ mépéridine ■ métoclopramide ■ midazolam ■ milrinone ■ morphine ■ nalbuphine ■ pentazocine ■ perphénazine ■ prochlorpérazine ■ promazine ■ prométhazine ■ ranitidine ■ scopolamine ■ sufentanil.

Compatibilité (tubulure en Y): amrinone ■ étomidate ■ famotidine ■ héparine ■ hydrocortisone sodique, succinate d' ■ méropénem ■ nafcilline ■ potassium, chlorure de ■ sufentanil ■ vitamines du complexe B avec C.

Incompatibilité (tubulure en Y): thiopental.

ENSEIGNEMENT AU PATIENT ET À SES PROCHES

- Expliquer au patient qu'il doit respecter rigoureusement la posologie recommandée. S'il n'a pu prendre le médicament au moment habituel, il doit le prendre dès que possible à moins que ce ne soit presque l'heure prévue pour la dose suivante. Le prévenir qu'il ne doit jamais remplacer une dose manquée par une double dose.
- Prévenir le patient que l'atropine peut provoquer de la somnolence. Lui recommander de ne pas conduire et d'éviter les autres activités qui exigent sa vigilance jusqu'à ce qu'on ait la certitude que le médicament n'entraîne pas cet effet chez lui.
- Expliquer au patient que pour soulager la sécheresse de la bouche, il devrait se rincer fréquemment la bouche, consommer des bonbons ou de la gomme à mâcher sans sucre et pratiquer une bonne hygiène buccale.
- Prévenir le patient que l'atropine peut altérer la thermorégulation et qu'il y a risque de coup de chaleur s'il poursuit des activités physiques vigoureuses dans un milieu surchauffé.

PÉD.: Informer les parents ou les soignants que l'atropine peut causer de la fièvre et leur recommander de consulter un professionnel de la santé avant de l'administrer à un enfant fiévreux.

- Conseiller au patient de consulter un professionnel de la santé avant de prendre un médicament en vente libre en même temps que l'atropine.

GÉR.: Informer le patient qui souffre d'hyperplasie bénigne de la prostate que l'atropine peut provoquer de la rétention urinaire et un retard de la miction avec effort pour uriner. Lui recommander de signaler à un professionnel de la santé toute modification du jet de la miction.

VÉRIFICATION DE L'EFFICACITÉ THÉRAPEUTIQUE

L'efficacité du traitement peut être démontrée par: l'accélération de la fréquence cardiaque ■ la sécheresse de la bouche (xérostomie) ■ le renversement des effets muscariniques. ✱

AZATADINE

Optimine

CLASSIFICATION:

Antihistaminique

Grossesse – catégorie B

INDICATIONS

Soulagement des symptômes d'allergie (rhinite, pollinose [rhume des foins], urticaire, œdème angioneurotique, eczéma, piqûres d'insectes, prurit, réactions sériques et médicamenteuses, dermographisme, réactions anaphylactiques, etc.), provoqués par la libération d'histamine.

MÉCANISME D'ACTION

Blocage des effets de l'histamine au niveau des récepteurs H_1 et inhibition de la libération d'histamine par les cellules; le médicament ne se lie pas à l'histamine ni ne l'inactive. Il possède des propriétés antisérotoninergiques, anticholinergiques et sédatives. ***Effets thérapeutiques:*** Diminution des symptômes associés aux excès d'histamine (éternuements, rhinorrhée, prurit nasal et oculaire, yeux larmoyants et rouges).

PHARMACOCINÉTIQUE

Absorption: Bonne (PO).

Distribution: Le médicament traverse probablement la barrière placentaire.

Métabolisme et excrétion: Métabolisme majoritairement hépatique. 20 % excrété à l'état inchangé par les reins.

Demi-vie: 12 heures.

Profil temps-action (effet antihistaminique)

	DÉBUT D'ACTION	PIC	DURÉE
PO	15 - 60 min	4 h	12 h

CONTRE-INDICATIONS, PRÉCAUTIONS ET MISES EN GARDE

Contre-indications: Hypersensibilité ■ Traitement des symptômes des affections des voies respiratoires inférieures ■ Traitement concomitant par un IMAO et pendant les 10 jours suivant l'arrêt de ce traitement.

Précautions et mises en garde: Glaucome à angle fermé ■ Ulcère gastroduodénal sténosant ■ Obstruction pyloroduodénale ■ Hyperplasie bénigne de la prostate ■ Obstruction du col de la vessie ■ Maladie cardiovasculaire ■ Élévation de la pression intraoculaire ■ Maladie hépatique ■ **GÉR.:** Plus grande prédisposition aux réactions indésirables ■ Hyperthyroïdie ■ Hypertension ■ Asthme bronchique ■ **OBST., PÉD.:** Grossesse ou enfants < 6 ans (l'innocuité du médicament n'a pas été établie).

RÉACTIONS INDÉSIRABLES ET EFFETS SECONDAIRES

SNC: étourdissements, sédation, excitation, céphalées, convulsions.

ORLO: acouphènes, vision trouble, congestion nasale.

Resp.: sécrétions bronchiques épaissies, respiration sifflante.

CV: hypertension, arythmies, oppression thoracique, hypotension, palpitations, tachycardie.

GI: douleurs épigastriques, anorexie, constipation, diarrhée, sécheresse de la bouche (xérostomie), vomissements.

GU: apparition précoce des règles, retard de la miction avec effort pour uriner, rétention urinaire.

Tég.: transpiration.

Hémat.: AGRANULOCYTOSE, anémie, thrombopénie.

INTERACTIONS

Médicament-médicament: Effets additifs sur la dépression du SNC lors de l'usage concomitant d'autres **dépresseurs du SNC** comprenant l'**alcool**, les **barbituriques**, les **antidépresseurs tricycliques**, les **analgésiques opioïdes** et les **hypnosédatifs** ■ Les **IMAO** intensifient et prolongent les effets anticholinergiques des antihistaminiques. Une hypotension grave peut survenir.

VOIES D'ADMINISTRATION ET POSOLOGIE

- **PO (adultes et enfants > 12 ans):** De 1 à 2 mg, toutes les 12 heures.
- **PO (enfants < 12 ans):** De 0,5 à 1 mg, 2 fois par jour.

PRÉSENTATION

Comprimés: 1 mg[Pr] ■ **En association avec:** pseudoéphédrine (Trinalin[Pr]).

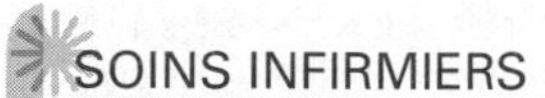

SOINS INFIRMIERS

ÉVALUATION DE LA SITUATION

- Avant le traitement et à intervalles réguliers pendant toute sa durée, rester à l'affût des symptômes suivants d'allergie: rhinite, conjonctivite, urticaire.
- Ausculter le murmure vésiculaire et déterminer les caractéristiques des sécrétions bronchiques. Maintenir l'apport liquidien entre 1 500 et 2 000 mL par jour pour diminuer la viscosité des sécrétions.

Tests de laboratoire: L'azatadine peut entraîner des résultats faussement négatifs aux épreuves de sensibilité cutanée. Interrompre l'administration des antihistaminiques au moins 4 jours avant ces tests.

DIAGNOSTICS INFIRMIERS POSSIBLES

- Dégagement inefficace des voies respiratoires (Indications).
- Risque d'accident (Effets secondaires).
- Connaissances insuffisantes sur le traitement médicamenteux (Enseignement au patient et à ses proches).

INTERVENTIONS INFIRMIÈRES

- Administrer les comprimés avec des aliments ou du lait pour diminuer l'irritation gastro-intestinale.

ENSEIGNEMENT AU PATIENT ET À SES PROCHES

- Prévenir le patient qu'il doit respecter rigoureusement la posologie recommandée. S'il n'a pu prendre le médicament au moment habituel, il doit le prendre dès que possible à moins que ce ne soit presque l'heure prévue pour la dose suivante. Le prévenir qu'il ne doit jamais remplacer une dose manquée par une double dose.
- Prévenir le patient que l'azatadine peut provoquer de la somnolence. Lui recommander de ne pas conduire et d'éviter les autres activités qui exigent sa vigilance jusqu'à ce qu'on ait la certitude que le médicament n'entraîne pas cet effet chez lui.
- Recommander au patient d'éviter de boire de l'alcool ou de prendre d'autres dépresseurs du SNC en même temps que ce médicament.
- Expliquer au patient que pour aider à soulager la sécheresse de la bouche, il doit se rincer fréquemment la bouche, consommer des bonbons ou de la gomme à mâcher sans sucre et pratiquer une bonne hygiène buccale. Lui recommander de consulter le dentiste si la sécheresse de la bouche persiste pendant plus de 2 semaines.

GÉR.: Les personnes âgées sont prédisposées à l'hypotension orthostatique. Leur conseiller de changer lentement de position.

- Recommander au patient de consulter un professionnel de la santé si les symptômes persistent.

VÉRIFICATION DE L'EFFICACITÉ THÉRAPEUTIQUE

L'efficacité du traitement peut être démontrée par: la diminution des symptômes d'allergie.

AZATHIOPRINE

Apo-Azathioprine, Gen-Azathioprine, Imuran, Novo-Azathioprine

CLASSIFICATION:

Immunosuppresseur (antagoniste des purines)

Grossesse – catégorie D

INDICATIONS

Traitement d'appoint pour prévenir le rejet de l'allogreffe rénale ■ Traitement des poussées érosives graves de la polyarthrite rhumatoïde chronique, réfractaire à un traitement plus traditionnel. **Usages non approuvés:** Traitement de la maladie de Crohn.

MÉCANISME D'ACTION

Effet antagoniste sur le métabolisme des purines entraînant l'inhibition de la synthèse de l'ADN et de l'ARN. ***Effets thérapeutiques:*** Suppression de l'immunité à médiation cellulaire et inhibition de la formation d'anticorps.

PHARMACOCINÉTIQUE

Absorption: Rapide (PO).

Distribution: Le médicament traverse la barrière placentaire et passe à de faibles concentrations dans le lait maternel.

Métabolisme et excrétion: Transformation en mercaptopurine, qui subit par la suite un nouveau métabolisme. Excrétion rénale minime à l'état inchangé.

Demi-vie: 3 heures.

Profil temps-action

(effet anti-inflammatoire/immunosuppresseur)

	DÉBUT D'ACTION	PIC	DURÉE
PO (anti-inflammatoire)	6 – 8 semaines	12 semaines	inconnue
IV (immunosuppresseur)	plusieurs jours – semaines	inconnu	plusieurs jours – semaines

CONTRE-INDICATIONS, PRÉCAUTIONS ET MISES EN GARDE

Contre-indications: Hypersensibilité ■ **OBST., PÉD.**: Traitement de la polyarthrite rhumatoïde ■ Les patients atteints de polyarthrite rhumatoïde ayant déjà pris des agents alkylants peuvent être exposés à des risques très élevés de néoplasie s'ils sont traités par l'azathioprine.

Précautions et mises en garde: Infections ■ Tumeurs malignes ■ Aplasie médullaire ■ Radiothérapie antérieure ou concomitante ■ Usage concomitant de mycophénolate ■ Autres maladies chroniques débilitantes ■ Insuffisance rénale grave ou oligurie (sensibilité accrue) ■ Patientes en âge de procréer ■ **OBST., ALLAITEMENT:** Effets mutagènes et cancérigènes.

RÉACTIONS INDÉSIRABLES ET EFFETS SECONDAIRES

ORLO: rétinopathie.

Resp.: œdème pulmonaire.

GI: <u>anorexie</u>, <u>hépatotoxicité</u>, <u>nausées</u>, <u>vomissements</u>, diarrhée, mucosite, pancréatite.

Tég.: alopécie, rash.

Hémat.: <u>anémie</u>, <u>leucopénie</u>, <u>pancytopénie</u>, <u>thrombopénie</u>.

Loc.: arthralgie.

Divers: MALADIE SÉRIQUE, <u>frissons</u>, <u>fièvre</u>, néoplasie, phénomène de Raynaud.

INTERACTIONS

Médicament-médicament: Effets myélodépressifs additifs lors de l'administration concomitante d'**antinéoplasiques**, de **cyclosporine** ou d'**agents myélodépresseurs** ■ L'**allopurinol** inhibe le métabolisme de l'azathioprine, ce qui en augmente la toxicité. Lors d'un traitement concomitant par l'allopurinol, il faudrait diminuer la dose d'azathioprine de 25 à 33 % ■ L'administration de l'azathioprine peut diminuer la réponse des anticorps aux **vaccins à virus vivants** et accroître le risque de réactions indésirables.

Médicament-produits naturels: La consommation concomitante d'**échinacée** ou de **mélatonine** peut entraver l'effet immunosuppresseur de l'azathioprine.

VOIES D'ADMINISTRATION ET POSOLOGIE

Prévention du rejet d'allogreffe rénale

- **PO, IV (adultes et enfants):** Initialement, de 3 à 5 mg/kg par jour; dose d'entretien: de 1 à 3 mg/kg par jour.

Polyarthrite rhumatoïde

- **PO (adultes):** 1 mg/kg par jour, pendant 6 à 8 semaines; augmenter la dose de 0,5 mg/kg par jour, toutes les 4 semaines, jusqu'au moment où une réponse se manifeste ou jusqu'à concurrence de 2,5 mg/kg par jour, puis réduire la dose de 0,5 mg/kg par jour, toutes les 4 à 8 semaines jusqu'à l'atteinte de la plus faible dose efficace.

PRÉSENTATION (version générique disponible)

Comprimés: 50 mg[Pr] ■ **Injection**: fioles de 50 mg[Pr].

SOINS INFIRMIERS

ÉVALUATION DE LA SITUATION

- Pendant toute la durée du traitement, rester à l'affût des signes suivants d'infection: altération des signes vitaux, aspect des crachats, de l'urine et des selles, accroissement du nombre de leucocytes.
- Effectuer le bilan quotidien des ingesta et des excreta et peser le patient tous les jours. La diminution du débit urinaire peut entraîner une toxicité reliée à ce médicament.

Polyarthrite rhumatoïde: Avant le traitement et à intervalles réguliers pendant toute sa durée, évaluer l'amplitude des mouvements articulaires, l'enflure, la douleur et la force des articulations atteintes, ainsi que la capacité du patient de poursuivre diverses activités de la vie quotidienne.

Tests de laboratoire:

- Examiner les résultats des tests des fonctions rénale, hépatique et hématologique, avant l'administration initiale et, ensuite, hebdomadairement, pendant le premier mois de traitement, deux fois par mois, pendant les 2 ou 3 mois qui suivent et tous les mois par la suite, pendant toute la durée du traitement.
- Prévenir le médecin si le nombre de leucocytes est inférieur à 3×10^9/L ou si le nombre de plaquettes est inférieur à 100×10^9/L; dans ce cas, une réduction de la dose ou une interruption passagère du traitement pourrait s'imposer.
- La diminution de la concentration d'hémoglobine peut indiquer la présence d'une hypoplasie médullaire.
- L'hépatotoxicité peut se traduire par une augmentation des concentrations de phosphatase alcaline, de bilirubine, d'AST, d'ALT et d'amylase. Cet effet survient habituellement dans les 6 mois suivant la greffe; il se manifeste rarement dans les cas de polyarthrite rhumatoïde et il est réversible à l'arrêt du traitement par l'azathioprine.
- Le médicament peut diminuer les concentrations sériques et urinaires d'acide urique et les concentrations plasmatiques d'albumine.

DIAGNOSTICS INFIRMIERS POSSIBLES

- Risque d'infection (Indications).
- Connaissances insuffisantes sur le traitement médicamenteux (Enseignement au patient et à ses proches).

INTERVENTIONS INFIRMIÈRES

- NE PAS CONFONDRE IMURAN (AZATHIOPRINE) ET IMDUR (MONONITRATE D'ISOSORBIDE).
- Le patient ayant subi une transplantation doit être isolé des membres du personnel et des visiteurs qui pourraient être contagieux. Maintenir l'isolement de protection, selon les besoins.

PO: Pour réduire les nausées, administrer le médicament avec ou après les repas ou en doses fractionnées.

IV:

- Reconstituer la dose de 50 mg avec 5 mL d'eau stérile pour injection. Agiter délicatement la fiole jusqu'à dissolution complète. Les solutions reconstituées peuvent être administrées jusqu'à 24 heures après la préparation. Consulter les directives de chaque fabricant avant de reconstituer la préparation.
- Il faut préparer la solution sous une hotte à flux laminaire. Porter des gants, une blouse et un masque pendant la manipulation du médicament. Jeter le matériel utilisé dans les contenants réservés à cet usage (voir l'annexe H).

Perfusion intermittente: On peut effectuer une dilution supplémentaire dans 50 mL de solution de NaCl 0,9 % ou de NaCl 0,45 % ou dans une solution de D5%E. Ne pas mélanger avec d'autres médicaments.

Vitesse d'administration: La perfusion dure habituellement de 30 à 60 minutes; sa durée pourra cependant varier de 5 minutes à 8 heures.

ENSEIGNEMENT AU PATIENT ET À SES PROCHES

- Conseiller au patient de prendre l'azathioprine en respectant rigoureusement la posologie recommandée. Expliquer au patient qui doit prendre une seule dose par jour que, s'il a oublié de prendre son médicament une journée, il doit sauter cette dose. S'il prend le médicament plusieurs fois par jour, il doit le prendre le plus rapidement possible ou doubler la dose suivante. Lui recommander de prévenir un professionnel de la santé s'il a sauté plus d'une dose ou si des vomissements surviennent rapidement après qu'il a pris le médicament. L'informer qu'il ne doit pas abandonner le traitement sans avoir consulté un professionnel de la santé au préalable.

A

- Recommander au patient de signaler sans tarder à un professionnel de la santé une fatigue ou une faiblesse inhabituelles, la toux ou la raucité de la voix, la fièvre ou les frissons, les douleurs lombaires ou aux flancs, les mictions douloureuses ou difficiles, la diarrhée grave, les selles noires ou goudronneuses, la présence de sang dans les urines ou le rejet de l'organe transplanté.
- Expliquer au patient qu'il doit suivre ce traitement toute sa vie durant pour prévenir le rejet de l'organe transplanté.
- Conseiller au patient de consulter un professionnel de la santé avant de prendre un médicament en vente libre ou un produit naturel ou avant de se faire vacciner pendant qu'il suit ce traitement.
- Expliquer au patient qu'il doit éviter tout contact avec des personnes contagieuses ou avec celles ayant reçu depuis peu un vaccin par voie orale contre le virus de la polio.
- Prévenir la patiente que le médicament peut être doté de propriétés tératogènes. Lui conseiller de prendre des mesures contraceptives pendant toute la durée du traitement et pendant au moins 4 mois après l'arrêt de la médication.
- Insister sur l'importance des examens médicaux de suivi et des tests de laboratoire.

Polyarthrite rhumatoïde: Prévenir le patient qu'un traitement concomitant avec des salicylates, des anti-inflammatoires non stéroïdiens ou des corticostéroïdes pourrait s'avérer nécessaire. Lui recommander de continuer de faire de l'exercice et de se reposer suffisamment. Lui expliquer que les lésions articulaires ne peuvent être guéries; le but du traitement est de ralentir ou d'arrêter l'évolution de la maladie.

VÉRIFICATION DE L'EFFICACITÉ THÉRAPEUTIQUE

L'efficacité du traitement peut être démontrée par: la prévention du rejet de l'organe transplanté ■ la diminution de la rigidité, de la douleur et de l'enflure des articulations affectées en 6 à 8 semaines, en cas de polyarthrite rhumatoïde. Si aucune amélioration ne se manifeste après 12 semaines, il faut arrêter le traitement. ✳

AZITHROMYCINE

Zithromax, Z-Pak, Novo-Azithromycin, Ratio-Azithromycin, Sandoz Azithromycin, CO Azithromycin, PMS-Azithromycin

CLASSIFICATION:

Antibiotique (macrolide)

Grossesse – catégorie B

INDICATIONS

Traitement des infections suivantes dues aux microorganismes sensibles ■ *Adultes:* infections des voies respiratoires supérieures, incluant la pharyngite et l'amygdalite dues aux streptocoques ■ infections des voies respiratoires inférieures, y compris la bronchite et la pneumonie ■ infections de la peau et de ses annexes ■ urétrite non gonococcique, cervicite, gonorrhée et chancre mou ■ Prévention des infections disséminées à *Mycobacterium avium intracellulare* (MAI), chez les patients atteints d'une infection au VIH d'un stade avancé ■ *Enfants*: otite moyenne aiguë ■ pharyngite et amygdalite ■ pneumonie extrahospitalière. **Usages non approuvés**: Prévention de l'endocardite bactérienne.

MÉCANISME D'ACTION

Inhibition de la synthèse des protéines au niveau de la sous-unité 50S des ribosomes bactériens. ***Effets thérapeutiques:*** Effet bactériostatique contre les bactéries sensibles. **Spectre d'action**: Le médicament est efficace contre les bactéries aérobies à Gram positif suivantes: *Staphylococcus aureus* ■ *Streptococcus pneumoniæ* ■ *Streptococcus pyogenes (du groupe A)* ■ L'azithromycine est efficace contre les bactéries aérobies à Gram négatif suivantes: *Hæmophilus influenzæ* ■ *Moraxella catarrhalis* ■ *Neisseria gonorrhϾ* ■ Le médicament est aussi efficace contre: *Mycoplasma* ■ *Legionella* ■ *Chlamydia trachomatis* ■ *Ureaplasma urealyticum* ■ *Borrelia burgdorferi* ■ *M. avium* ■ Il n'est pas efficace contre *S. aureus* résistant à la méthicilline.

PHARMACOCINÉTIQUE

Absorption: 40 % (PO). Biodisponibilité à 100 % (IV).

Distribution: Tissus et liquides corporels. Les concentrations intracellulaires et tissulaires sont plus élevées que les concentrations sériques; les concentrations dans le liquide céphalorachidien sont faibles.

Métabolisme et excrétion: Excrétion sous forme inchangée dans la bile; 4,5 % excrété sous forme inchangée dans l'urine.

Demi-vie: De 11 à 14 heures, après l'administration d'une dose unique; 68 heures, après l'administration de plusieurs doses.

Profil temps-action (concentrations sériques)

	DÉBUT D'ACTION	PIC	DURÉE
PO	rapide	2,5 – 3,2 h	24 h
IV	rapide	fin de la perfusion	24 h

A

CONTRE-INDICATIONS, PRÉCAUTIONS ET MISES EN GARDE

Contre-indications: Hypersensibilité à l'azithromycine, à l'érythromycine ou à tout autre macrolide.

Précautions et mises en garde: Insuffisance hépatique grave (il peut être nécessaire d'adapter la posologie) ■ Insuffisance rénale sévère (Cl_{Cr} < 10 ml/min) ■ Grossesse et allaitement ■ **PÉD.**: enfants < 2 ans en cas de pharyngite ou d'amygdalite, enfants < 6 mois en cas d'otite moyenne et de pneumonie extrahospitalière (l'innocuité du médicament n'a pas été établie).

RÉACTIONS INDÉSIRABLES ET EFFETS SECONDAIRES

SNC: étourdissements, somnolence, fatigue, céphalée.

CV: douleurs thoraciques, palpitations, allongement de l'intervalle QT.

GI: COLITE PSEUDOMEMBRANEUSE, douleurs abdominales, diarrhée, nausées, jaunisse cholestatique, élévation des enzymes hépatiques, dyspepsie, flatulences, méléna, candidose orale.

GU: néphrite, vaginite.

ORLO: ototoxicité.

Tég.: photosensibilité, rash, syndrome de Stevens-Johnson.

End.: hyperglycémie.

HÉ: hyperkaliémie.

Divers: ŒDÈME DE QUINCKE.

INTERACTIONS

Médicament-médicament: L'administration concomitante d'**antiacides renfermant de l'aluminium et du magnésium** réduit les concentrations sériques de pointe de l'azithromycine ■ Le médicament peut accroître les concentrations sériques de **pimozide** ou de **carbamazépine** et le risque de toxicité qui y est associé ■ L'azithromycine peut augmenter l'effet de la **warfarine** ■ Le **nelfinavir** élève les concentrations sériques de pointe de l'azithromycine ■ Les **antibiotiques de la classe des macrolides** élèvent les concentrations sériques et l'effet de la **digoxine**, de la **théophylline**, de l'**ergotamine**, de la **dihydroergotamine**, du **triazolam**, de la **cyclosporine**, du **tacrolimus** et de la **phénytoïne**. Il est donc recommandé de suivre de près les concentrations lors d'un usage concomitant.

VOIES D'ADMINISTRATION ET POSOLOGIE

La plupart des infections des voies respiratoires et de la peau

- **PO (adultes):** 500 mg le premier jour, puis 250 mg par jour pendant 4 jours (la dose totale est de 1,5 g).

Surinfection bronchique chez un patient atteint de bronchopneumopathie chronique obstructive

- **PO (adultes):** 500 mg, toutes les 24 heures, pendant 3 jours, ou 500 mg le premier jour, puis 250 mg par jour, pendant 4 jours.

Pneumonie extrahospitalière

- **IV, PO (adultes):** 500 mg IV, toutes les 24 heures, pendant au moins 2 jours, puis 500 mg PO, toutes les 24 heures, pour une durée totale de traitement de 7 à 10 jours.

Infection génitale haute

- **IV, PO (adultes):** 500 mg IV, toutes les 24 heures, pendant 1 jour au moins, puis 250 mg PO, toutes les 24 heures, pour une durée totale de traitement de 7 jours.

Urétrite ou cervicite non gonococcique, chancre mou, chlamydia

- **PO (adultes):** 1 seule dose de 1 g.

Gonorrhée

- **PO (adultes):** 1 seule dose de 2 g.

Prévention des infections disséminées à* Mycobacterium avium intracellulare *(MAI)

- **PO (adultes):** 1,2 g, 1 fois par semaine (en monothérapie ou en association avec la rifabutine).

Otite moyenne aiguë

- **PO (enfants):** 30 mg/kg en une seule dose (au maximum, 1 500 mg) ou 10 mg/kg (au maximum, 500 mg) toutes les 24 heures, pendant 3 jours ou 10 mg/kg (au maximum, 500 mg), le premier jour, puis 5 mg/kg (au maximum, 250 mg), toutes les 24 heures, pendant 4 jours.

Pneumonie extrahospitalière

- **PO (enfants):** 10 mg/kg (au maximum, 500 mg), le premier jour, puis 5 mg/kg (au maximum, 250 mg), toutes les 24 heures, pendant 4 jours.

Pharyngite et amygdalite

- **PO (enfants):** 12 mg/kg (au maximum, 500 mg) toutes les 24 heures, pendant 5 jours.

PRÉSENTATION

Comprimés: 250 mg^{Pr}, 600 mg^{Pr} ■ **Suspension orale (parfum de cerise):** 100 mg/5 mL^{Pr} en flacons de 15 mL, 200 mg/5 mL^{Pr} en flacons de 15 et de 22,5 mL ■ **Poudre pour injection:** 500 mg^{Pr}.

SOINS INFIRMIERS

ÉVALUATION DE LA SITUATION

- Au début du traitement et pendant toute sa durée, rester à l'affût des signes suivants d'infection:

A

altération des signes vitaux, aspect de la plaie, des crachats, de l'urine et des selles, accroissement du nombre de leucocytes.

- Prélever des échantillons pour les cultures et les antibiogrammes avant le début du traitement. La première dose peut être administrée avant que les résultats soient connus.
- OBSERVER LE PATIENT À LA RECHERCHE DES SIGNES ET DES SYMPTÔMES SUIVANTS D'ANAPHYLAXIE: RASH, PRURIT, ŒDÈME LARYNGÉ, RESPIRATION SIFFLANTE. SIGNALER IMMÉDIATEMENT CES RÉACTIONS AU MÉDECIN OU À UN AUTRE PROFESSIONNEL DE LA SANTÉ.

Tests de laboratoire:

- L'azithromycine peut entraîner une élévation des concentrations sériques de bilirubine, d'AST, d'ALT, de LDH et de phosphatase alcaline.
- Le médicament peut entraîner une élévation des concentrations de créatine phosphokinase, de potassium, d'urée, de créatinine et de la glycémie; il peut aussi allonger le temps de prothrombine.
- L'azithromycine peut parfois réduire le nombre de leucocytes et de plaquettes.

DIAGNOSTICS INFIRMIERS POSSIBLES

- Risque d'infection (Indications, Effets secondaires).
- Connaissances insuffisantes sur le traitement médicamenteux (Enseignement au patient et à ses proches).
- Non-observance du traitement médicamenteux (Enseignement au patient et à ses proches).

INTERVENTIONS INFIRMIÈRES

- NE PAS CONFONDRE L'AZITHROMYCINE ET L'ÉRYTHROMYCINE.

PO: Administrer l'azithromycine sans égard aux repas.

Perfusion intermittente: Reconstituer le contenu d'une fiole de 500 mg avec 4,8 mL d'eau stérile pour injection et bien agiter jusqu'à ce que la poudre soit dissoute, pour obtenir une concentration de 100 mg/mL. Puisque l'azithromycine est conditionnée sous vide, il faut utiliser une seringue standard de 5 mL pour s'assurer qu'on ajoute la quantité exacte d'eau stérile, soit 4,8 mL. Ne pas administrer la solution si elle contient des particules. Diluer davantage la solution en transvidant 5 mL de la solution à 100 mg/mL dans 250 ou 500 mL de solution de NaCl 0,9 % ou de NaCl 0,45 %, de D5%E, de lactate de Ringer, de D5%/NaCl 0,45 % ou de D5%/solution de lactate de Ringer, pour obtenir une concentration de 2 mg/mL ou de 1 mg/mL, respectivement. La solution est stable pendant 24 heures à la température ambiante ou pendant 3 jours au réfrigérateur. Consulter les directives de chaque fabricant avant de reconstituer la préparation.

Vitesse d'administration: Administrer la solution à 1 mg/mL en 3 heures ou la solution à 2 mg/mL en 1 heure. Ne pas administrer en bolus.

ENSEIGNEMENT AU PATIENT ET À SES PROCHES

- Expliquer au patient qu'il est important de respecter la posologie recommandée et de suivre le traitement jusqu'à la fin, même s'il se sent mieux. S'il n'a pu prendre le médicament au moment habituel, il doit le prendre aussitôt que possible à moins que ce ne soit presque l'heure prévue pour la dose suivante. Le prévenir qu'il ne doit jamais remplacer une dose manquée par une double dose. Lui expliquer qu'il peut être dangereux de donner ce médicament à une autre personne.
- Recommander au patient de ne pas prendre l'azithromycine avec des antiacides.
- Prévenir le patient que l'azithromycine peut parfois provoquer de la somnolence et des étourdissements. Lui conseiller de ne pas conduire et d'éviter les activités qui exigent sa vigilance jusqu'à ce qu'on ait la certitude que le médicament n'entraîne pas ces effets chez lui.
- Conseiller au patient d'utiliser un écran solaire et de porter des vêtements protecteurs pour prévenir les réactions de photosensibilité.
- Conseiller au patient de signaler à un professionnel de la santé les douleurs thoraciques, les palpitations, le jaunissement de la peau ou des yeux, ou les signes suivants de surinfection: excroissance pileuse sur la langue, pertes et démangeaisons vaginales, selles molles ou nauséabondes.
- INCITER LE PATIENT À PRÉVENIR LE PROFESSIONNEL DE LA SANTÉ EN CAS DE FIÈVRE ET DE DIARRHÉE, PARTICULIÈREMENT SI SES SELLES CONTIENNENT DU SANG, DU PUS OU DU MUCUS. RECOMMANDER AU PATIENT DE NE PAS TRAITER LA DIARRHÉE AVANT D'AVOIR CONSULTÉ UN PROFESSIONNEL DE LA SANTÉ.
- Prévenir la patiente qu'elle doit informer le médecin si elle pense être enceinte ou désire le devenir.
- Informer le patient traité en raison d'une urétrite ou d'une cervicite non gonococcique que les partenaires sexuels doivent aussi être traités.
- Conseiller aux parents, aux soignants ou au patient de prévenir un professionnel de la santé si aucune amélioration des symptômes n'est notée.

PÉD.: Informer les parents ou les soignants que l'azithromycine est généralement bien tolérée par les enfants. Les effets secondaires les plus communs sont la diarrhée légère et le rash. Inciter les parents à prévenir un professionnel de la santé si ces réactions surviennent.

VÉRIFICATION DE L'EFFICACITÉ THÉRAPEUTIQUE

L'efficacité du traitement peut être démontrée par: La disparition des signes et des symptômes d'infection. Le temps de résolution dépend du microorganisme infectant et du siège de l'infection. ✳

AZT,

voir Zidovudine

B

BACLOFÈNE

Apo-Baclofen, Baclofen, Dom-Baclofen, Gen-Baclofen, Lioresal, Med-Baclofen, Novo-Baclofen, Nu-Baclofen, PMS-Baclofen

CLASSIFICATION:

Relaxant musculosquelettique (à action centrale), antispastique

Grossesse – catégorie C

INDICATIONS

PO: Traitement de la spasticité réversible, attribuable à la sclérose en plaques ou aux lésions de la moelle épinière ■ **IT**: Traitement de la spasticité grave provenant de lésions de la moelle épinière ou due à la sclérose en plaques. **Usages non approuvés**: Soulagement des douleurs provoquées par la névralgie du trijumeau.

MÉCANISME D'ACTION

Inhibition des réflexes au niveau de la moelle épinière. ***Effets thérapeutiques:*** Soulagement de la spasticité musculaire; amélioration possible de la fonction intestinale et vésicale.

PHARMACOCINÉTIQUE

Absorption: Bonne (PO).

Distribution: Le baclofène se répartit dans tout l'organisme et traverse la barrière placentaire.

Métabolisme et excrétion: Excrétion majoritairement rénale sous forme inchangée (de 70 à 80 %).

Demi-vie: De 2,5 à 4 heures.

Profil temps-action (effet sur la spasticité)

	DÉBUT D'ACTION	PIC	DURÉE
PO	plusieurs heures – semaines	inconnu	inconnue
IT	0,5 – 1 h	4 h	4 – 8 h

CONTRE-INDICATIONS, PRÉCAUTIONS ET MISES EN GARDE

Contre-indication: Hypersensibilité.

Précautions et mises en garde: Patients chez lesquels la spasticité permet de maintenir la posture et l'équilibre ■ Épilepsie (le médicament peut abaisser le seuil des convulsions) ■ **GÉR.**: Les personnes âgées sont plus sensibles aux effets secondaires sur le SNC ■ Insuffisance rénale (une réduction de la dose peut s'avérer nécessaire) ■ **OBST., ALLAITEMENT, PÉD.**: L'innocuité du médicament n'a pas été établie.

RÉACTIONS INDÉSIRABLES ET EFFETS SECONDAIRES

SNC: CONVULSIONS (IT), étourdissements, somnolence, fatigue, faiblesse, confusion, dépression, céphalées, insomnie.

ORLO: congestion nasale, acouphènes.

CV: œdème, hypotension.

GI: nausées, constipation.

GU: mictions fréquentes.

Tég.: prurit, éruptions cutanées.

Métab.: hyperglycémie, gain pondéral.

SN: ataxie.

Divers: réactions d'hypersensibilité, sudation excessive.

INTERACTIONS

Médicament-médicament: Effets additifs sur la dépression du SNC, lors de l'usage concomitant d'autres **dépresseurs du SNC** dont l'**alcool**, les **antihistaminiques**, les **analgésiques opioïdes** et les **hypnosédatifs** ■ L'administration simultanée d'**IMAO** peut aggraver la dépression du SNC ou l'hypotension.

Médicament-produits naturels: Risque accru de dépression du SNC lors de la consommation concomitante de **kava**, de **valériane** et de **camomillle.**

VOIES D'ADMINISTRATION ET POSOLOGIE

- **PO (adultes)**: 5 mg, 3 fois par jour. On peut augmenter la dose tous les 3 jours, à raison de 5 mg par dose, jusqu'à un maximum de 80 mg par jour (la dose quotidienne totale peut également être administrée en prises fractionnées, 4 fois par jour).
- **IT (adultes)**: *Traitement d'entretien* – chez la plupart des patients, de 300 à 800 µg par jour, en perfusion intrathécale; la dose est déterminée par la réponse obtenue au cours de l'épreuve de sélection.

PRÉSENTATION (version générique disponible)

Comprimés: 10 mg^Pr^, 20 mg^Pr^ ■ **Solution pour injection par voie intrathécale**: 50 µg/1 mL, 10 mg/20 mL (500 µg/mL)^Pr^, 10 mg/5 mL (2 000 µg/mL)^Pr^.

SOINS INFIRMIERS

ÉVALUATION DE LA SITUATION

- Noter le degré de spasticité musculaire avant le début du traitement et à intervalles réguliers pendant toute sa durée.
- Rester à l'affût des symptômes suivants: somnolence, étourdissements, ataxie. Une modification de la dose peut soulager ces symptômes.

IT: Suivre de près l'état du patient lors de l'administration de la dose-test et pendant la période d'adaptation posologique. Garder à portée de la main le matériel de réanimation nécessaire pour parer à des effets secondaires intolérables ou qui mettent la vie du patient en danger.

Tests de laboratoire: Le médicament peut entraîner l'élévation de la glycémie et des concentrations sériques de phosphatase alcaline, d'AST et d'ALT.

DIAGNOSTICS INFIRMIERS POSSIBLES

- Mobilité physique réduite (Indications).
- Risque d'accident (Réactions indésirables).
- Connaissances insuffisantes sur le traitement médicamenteux (Enseignement au patient et à ses proches).

INTERVENTIONS INFIRMIÈRES

PO: Le médicament peut être administré avec du lait ou avec des aliments pour réduire l'irritation gastrique.

IT: *Pour l'épreuve de sélection*, la dose-test initiale habituelle est de 25 µg ou de 50 µg. Elle devrait être administrée pendant au moins 1 minute. Suivre de près l'état du patient pour déceler une diminution importante du tonus musculaire, ainsi que de la fréquence et de la gravité des spasmes. Si la réponse n'est pas adéquate, on peut administrer, à 24 heures d'intervalle, 2 doses-test supplémentaires de 75 µg/1,5 mL et de 100 µg/2 mL, respectivement. Les patients qui ne répondent pas adéquatement à ces doses ne devraient pas recevoir de traitement prolongé par voie intrathécale.

- L'adaptation posologique dans le cas d'une administration par pompe IT implantable devrait se fonder sur la réponse du patient. Si, après la majoration de la dose, la réponse n'est pas notable, il faut vérifier le fonctionnement de la pompe et la perméabilité du cathéter.

ENSEIGNEMENT AU PATIENT ET À SES PROCHES

- Expliquer au patient qu'il doit respecter rigoureusement la posologie recommandée. S'il n'a pas pu prendre le médicament au moment habituel, il doit le prendre dans l'heure qui suit; le prévenir qu'il ne doit jamais remplacer une dose manquée par une double dose. Mettre en garde le patient contre l'arrêt brusque du traitement en raison du risque de réactions de sevrage aiguës: hallucinations, spasticité accrue, convulsions, modifications de l'état mental, agitation. Le traitement par le baclofène devrait être abandonné graduellement au cours d'une période d'au moins 2 semaines.
- Prévenir le patient que le baclofène peut parfois provoquer de la somnolence et des étourdissements; lui conseiller de ne pas conduire et d'éviter les activités qui exigent sa vigilance jusqu'à ce qu'on ait la certitude que le médicament n'entraîne pas ces effets chez lui.
- Conseiller au patient de changer de position lentement afin de réduire le risque d'hypotension orthostatique.
- Avertir le patient qu'il ne doit pas consommer d'alcool ou de dépresseurs du SNC en même temps qu'il prend ce médicament.
- Recommander au patient de prévenir un professionnel de la santé si les symptômes suivants persistent: besoin urgent et fréquent d'uriner, mictions douloureuses, constipation, nausées, céphalées, insomnie, acouphènes, dépression ou confusion. L'informer qu'il doit signaler rapidement à un professionnel de la santé les signes et les symptômes suivants d'hypersensibilité: rash, démangeaisons.

VÉRIFICATION DE L'EFFICACITÉ THÉRAPEUTIQUE

L'efficacité du traitement peut être démontrée par: la diminution de la spasticité musculaire et de la douleur musculosquelettique connexe, accompagnée d'une capacité accrue de mener à bien les activités de la vie quotidienne ▪ le soulagement de la douleur chez le patient souffrant de névralgie du trijumeau. Parfois, le plein effet du traitement peut ne se manifester qu'après plusieurs semaines. ✳

BASILIXIMAB

Simulect

CLASSIFICATION:

Immunosuppresseur (anticorps monoclonal)

Grossesse – catégorie B

INDICATIONS

Prévention des réactions aiguës de rejet chez les patients subissant une greffe de rein; ce médicament doit être administré en association avec des corticostéroïdes et la cyclosporine.

MÉCANISME D'ACTION

Liaison aux sites des récepteurs spécifiques de l'interleukine-2 (IL-2), qui se trouvent sur les lymphocytes T activés, et blocage de ces sites. ***Effets thérapeutiques:*** Prévention des réactions aiguës de rejet après une greffe rénale.

B

PHARMACOCINÉTIQUE

Absorption: Biodisponibilité à 100 % (IV).
Distribution: Inconnue.
Métabolisme et excrétion: Inconnus.
Demi-vie: 7,2 jours.
Profil temps-action (effet sur la fonction immunitaire)

	DÉBUT D'ACTION	PIC	DURÉE
IV	2 h	inconnu	36 jours

CONTRE-INDICATIONS, PRÉCAUTIONS ET MISES EN GARDE

Contre-indications: Hypersensibilité.
Précautions et mises en garde: Femmes en âge de procréer ■ **GÉR., OBST., ALLAITEMENT, PÉD.**: Administration déconseillée.

RÉACTIONS INDÉSIRABLES ET EFFETS SECONDAIRES

(chez les patients recevant des corticostéroïdes et de la cyclosporine en plus du basiliximab)
SNC: étourdissements, céphalées, insomnie, faiblesse.
ORLO: vision anormale, formation de cataractes.
Resp.: toux.
CV: INSUFFISANCE CARDIAQUE, œdème, hypertension, angine, arythmies, hypotension.
GI: hémorragie gastro-intestinale, douleurs abdominales, constipation, diarrhée, dyspepsie, candidose, nausées, vomissements, hyperplasie gingivale, stomatite.
Tég.: acné, complications des plaies, hypertrichose, prurit.
End.: hyperglycémie, hypoglycémie.
HÉ: acidose, hypercholestérolémie, hyperkaliémie, hyperuricémie, hypocalcémie, hypokaliémie, hypophosphatémie.
Hémat.: hémorragie, anomalies de la coagulation.
Loc.: douleurs dorsales, douleurs aux jambes.
SN: tremblements, neuropathie, paresthésie.
Divers: infections, gain pondéral, frissons, réactions d'hypersensibilité incluant l'ANAPHYLAXIE et le syndrome de libération de cytokines.

INTERACTIONS

Médicament-médicament: Effets immunosuppresseurs additifs lors de l'administration concomitante d'autres **agents immunosuppresseurs**.
Médicament-produits naturels: La consommation concomitante d'**échinacée** ou de **mélatonine** peut entraver l'effet immunosuppresseur du basiliximab.

VOIES D'ADMINISTRATION ET POSOLOGIE

- **IV (adultes)**: 20 mg, administrés au cours des 2 heures qui précèdent la transplantation; répéter l'administration 4 jours après la transplantation. La deuxième dose ne devrait pas être administrée en présence de complications ou en cas de perte du greffon.
- **IV (enfants 2 à 15 ans)**: 12 mg/m^2, jusqu'à concurrence de 20 mg, administrés au cours des 2 heures qui précèdent la transplantation; répéter l'administration 4 jours après la transplantation. La deuxième dose ne devrait pas être administrée en présence de complications ou en cas de perte du greffon.

PRÉSENTATION

Poudre à reconstituer: 20 mg/fiole[Pr].

SOINS INFIRMIERS

ÉVALUATION DE LA SITUATION

- LORS DE L'ADMINISTRATION DE CHAQUE DOSE, OBSERVER LE PATIENT À LA RECHERCHE DES SIGNES DE RÉACTIONS ANAPHYLACTIQUES OU DE RÉACTIONS D'HYPERSENSIBILITÉ (HYPOTENSION, TACHYCARDIE, INSUFFISANCE CARDIAQUE, DYSPNÉE, RESPIRATION SIFFLANTE, BRONCHOSPASME, ŒDÈME PULMONAIRE, INSUFFISANCE RESPIRATOIRE, URTICAIRE, RASH, PRURIT, ÉTERNUEMENTS). CES SYMPTÔMES APPARAISSENT HABITUELLEMENT EN 24 HEURES. GARDER À PORTÉE DE LA MAIN LE MATÉRIEL DE RÉANIMATION NÉCESSAIRE POUR PARER À TOUTE URGENCE. SI UNE RÉACTION D'HYPERSENSIBILITÉ GRAVE SURVIENT, IL FAUDRAIT ARRÊTER DÉFINITIVEMENT LE TRAITEMENT PAR LE BASILIXIMAC. CHEZ LES PATIENTS AYANT DÉJÀ REÇU DU BASILIXIMAB, LA REPRISE DU TRAITEMENT PAR CET AGENT DOIT S'ACCOMPAGNER DE PRUDENCE.
- Observer le patient à la recherche des signes suivants d'infection: fièvre, frissons, rash, maux de gorge, écoulements purulents, dysurie. Prévenir immédiatement le médecin si ces symptômes se manifestent, car ils peuvent dicter l'arrêt du traitement.

Tests de laboratoire:

- L'agent peut entraîner une élévation ou une diminution de la concentration d'hémoglobine, de l'hématocrite, de la glycémie et des concentrations de potassium et de calcium.
- Il peut élever les taux sériques de cholestérol.
- Il peut entraîner une élévation des concentrations d'urée, de créatinine sérique et d'acide urique.
- Il peut diminuer les concentrations sériques de magnésium et de phosphate ainsi que le nombre de plaquettes.

DIAGNOSTICS INFIRMIERS POSSIBLES

- Risque d'infection (Réactions indésirables).
- Connaissances insuffisantes sur le traitement médicamenteux (Enseignement au patient et à ses proches).

INTERVENTIONS INFIRMIÈRES

- Le basiliximab est habituellement administré en concomitance avec la cyclosporine et des corticostéroïdes.

Perfusion intermittente: Reconstituer avec 5 mL d'eau stérile pour injection. Agiter délicatement pour dissoudre la poudre.

IV directe: Après avoir reconstitué la préparation, on peut l'administrer sans la diluer davantage. L'administration IV directe peut entraîner des nausées, des vomissements et des réactions locales (douleurs).

Perfusion intermittente: Diluer de nouveau avec 50 mL de solution de NaCl 0,9 % ou de D5%E. Retourner le sac pour bien mélanger le contenu, sans l'agiter, pour éviter la formation de mousse. La solution doit être transparente jusqu'à opalescente, et incolore; ne pas administrer une solution qui a changé de couleur ou qui contient des particules. Jeter toute portion inutilisée. Administrer la préparation dans les 4 heures qui suivent sa reconstitution. On peut la garder au réfrigérateur pendant une période allant jusqu'à 24 heures. Jeter ensuite toute portion qui n'a pas été utilisée. Consulter les directives de chaque fabricant avant de reconstituer la préparation.

Vitesse d'administration: Perfuser la préparation en 20 à 30 minutes par une voie périphérique ou centrale.

Compatibilité: Ne pas mélanger avec d'autres médicaments; ne pas administrer par une tubulure IV par laquelle s'écoulent d'autres médicaments.

ENSEIGNEMENT AU PATIENT ET À SES PROCHES

- Expliquer au patient le rôle thérapeutique de ce médicament. Le prévenir qu'après le traitement par le basiliximab, il devra se soumettre aux autres traitements immunosuppresseurs et les poursuivre pendant toute sa vie.
- Prévenir le patient que le basiliximab peut provoquer des étourdissements. Lui conseiller de ne pas conduire et d'éviter les activités qui exigent sa vigilance jusqu'à ce qu'on ait la certitude que le médicament n'entraîne pas cet effet chez lui.
- Conseiller au patient d'éviter les foules et les personnes contagieuses, car ce médicament supprime la réponse immunitaire.

VÉRIFICATION DE L'EFFICACITÉ THÉRAPEUTIQUE

L'efficacité du traitement peut être démontrée par: la prévention des réactions aiguës de rejet chez les patients qui subissent une greffe de rein. ✳

BÉCAPLERMINE

Regranex

CLASSIFICATION:

Agent dermatologique (facteur de croissance favorisant la cicatrisation)

Grossesse – catégorie C

INDICATIONS

Cicatrisation des ulcères de pleine épaisseur des membres inférieurs chez les patients diabétiques.

MÉCANISME D'ACTION

Activité semblable à celle du facteur de croissance des plaquettes sanguines humaines, qui entraîne une stimulation de la chimiotaxie des cellules jouant un rôle dans la cicatrisation des plaies et la stimulation de la formation de tissus de granulation. ***Effets thérapeutiques:*** Accélération de la cicatrisation.

PHARMACOCINÉTIQUE

Absorption: Négligeable (application topique).
Distribution: Effet local seulement.
Métabolisme et excrétion: Inconnus.
Demi-vie: Inconnue.
Profil temps-action (cicatrisation des ulcères)

	DÉBUT D'ACTION	PIC	DURÉE
Usage topique	en l'espace de 10 semaines	inconnu	inconnue

CONTRE-INDICATIONS, PRÉCAUTIONS ET MISES EN GARDE

Contre-indications: Néoplasie connue au niveau des régions où la préparation est appliquée ■ Hypersensibilité connue aux parabènes, au metacrésol ou à tout autre ingrédient du produit.

Précautions et mises en garde: **OBST., ALLAITEMENT, PÉD.:** L'innocuité du médicament n'a pas été établie pendant la grossesse, l'allaitement et chez les enfants < 18 ans ■ Cancer.

RÉACTIONS INDÉSIRABLES ET EFFETS SECONDAIRES

Tég.: rash érythémateux à l'endroit où l'agent est appliqué.

B

INTERACTIONS

Médicament-médicament: Aucune connue ■ Ne pas appliquer sur l'ulcère en même temps que d'autres médicaments topiques.

VOIES D'ADMINISTRATION ET POSOLOGIE

- **Usage topique (adultes):** Appliquer une couche mince et uniforme sur toutes les régions atteintes, 1 fois par jour, jusqu'à ce qu'elles soient complètement cicatrisées.

PRÉSENTATION

Gel: 100 µg/g (0,01 %), en tubes de 15 g[Pr].

SOINS INFIRMIERS

ÉVALUATION DE LA SITUATION

Évaluer la taille et la couleur de l'ulcère, la consistance des écoulements et l'état de la peau environnante, toutes les semaines ou 2 fois par semaine.

DIAGNOSTICS INFIRMIERS POSSIBLES

- Atteinte à l'intégrité des tissus (Indications).
- Connaissances insuffisantes sur le traitement médicamenteux (Enseignement au patient et à ses proches).

INTERVENTIONS INFIRMIÈRES

- À l'aide d'un applicateur propre (p. ex., un abaisse-langue ou un bâtonnet ouaté), appliquer une couche mince et uniforme de bécaplermine, 1 fois par jour, sur toutes les régions atteintes. Recouvrir ensuite chaque région traitée d'un pansement non adhésif, qui maintient un milieu humide, propice à la cicatrisation. Avant l'application suivante, nettoyer délicatement la plaie à l'aide d'une solution physiologique pour enlever le résidu de gel. Répéter le traitement tous les jours.
- Conserver le gel au réfrigérateur; ne pas congeler. Ne pas utiliser le gel après la date de péremption inscrite sur le repli du tube.

ENSEIGNEMENT AU PATIENT ET À SES PROCHES

- Montrer au patient la technique appropriée d'application: se laver les mains avant d'appliquer le gel et utiliser un bâtonnet ouaté ou un abaisse-langue pour en faciliter l'application. Le bout du tube ne devrait entrer en contact ni avec la plaie ni avec une autre surface; bien refermer le tube après usage. Faire sortir la quantité de gel sur une surface propre, solide et non absorbante (par exemple, un morceau de papier ciré). Répandre le gel à l'aide du bâtonnet ouaté ou de l'abaisse-langue sur la surface de la plaie en une couche mince et uniforme. Recouvrir d'un pansement de gaze humidifié avec une solution physiologique. Avant l'application suivante, nettoyer délicatement la plaie à l'aide d'une solution physiologique pour enlever le résidu de gel.
- Expliquer au patient que le tube doit être conservé au réfrigérateur et qu'il ne doit pas congeler la préparation.
- Prévenir le patient que l'application d'une couche très épaisse de gel n'accélère pas la cicatrisation. S'il n'a pas pu appliquer le gel à l'heure habituelle, il devrait le faire aussitôt que possible. S'il oublie de l'appliquer pendant une journée, il devrait reprendre le lendemain l'horaire habituel sans jamais remplacer une dose manquée par une double dose.
- Insister sur l'importance des soins rigoureux des plaies et d'un programme visant la mise au repos des membres inférieurs.

VÉRIFICATION DE L'EFFICACITÉ THÉRAPEUTIQUE

L'efficacité du traitement peut être démontrée par: l'accélération de la cicatrisation des plaies. Si la taille de la plaie ne diminue pas de 30 % dans les 10 semaines qui suivent le début du traitement ou si la guérison n'est pas complète en l'espace de 20 semaines, il faudrait décider s'il y a lieu de poursuivre le traitement.

BÉCLOMÉTHASONE,

voir Corticostéroïdes (inhalation) et Corticostéroïdes (voie intranasale)

BÉNAZÉPRIL,

voir Inhibiteurs de l'enzyme de conversion de l'angiotensine (IECA)

BENSÉRAZIDE,

voir Lévodopa

BENZTROPINE

Apo-Benztropine, Cogentin, PMS-Benztropine

CLASSIFICATION:

Antiparkinsonien (anticholinergique)

Grossesse – catégorie C

B

INDICATIONS

Traitement d'appoint de toutes les formes de la maladie de Parkinson et des troubles extrapyramidaux d'origine médicamenteuse.

MÉCANISME D'ACTION

Blocage de l'activité cholinergique dans le SNC, en partie responsable des symptômes de la maladie de Parkinson ▪ Rétablissement de l'équilibre naturel des neurotransmetteurs du SNC. ***Effets thérapeutiques:*** Diminution de la rigidité et des tremblements.

PHARMACOCINÉTIQUE

Absorption: Bonne (PO et IM).
Distribution: Inconnue.
Métabolisme et excrétion: Inconnus.
Demi-vie: Inconnue.

Profil temps-action (activité antidyskinétique)

	DÉBUT D'ACTION	PIC	DURÉE
PO	1 – 2 h	plusieurs jours	24 h
IM, IV	quelques minutes	inconnu	24 h

CONTRE-INDICATIONS, PRÉCAUTIONS ET MISES EN GARDE

Contre-indications: Hypersensibilité ▪ Enfants âgés < 3 ans ▪ Glaucome à angle fermé ▪ Colite ulcéreuse ▪ Dyskinésie tardive.
Précautions et mises en garde: **GÉR.:** Risque accru de réactions indésirables ▪ Hyperplasie de la prostate ▪ Troubles convulsifs ▪ Arythmies ▪ **OBST., ALLAITEMENT:** L'innocuité du médicament n'a pas été établie ▪ **PÉD.:** Enfants > 3 ans (risque de réactions indésirables) ▪ Risque d'anhidrose et d'hyperthermie mortelles (éviter les activités qui augmentent le risque d'hyperthermie) ▪ Ulcère gastrique ou reflux gastro-œsophagien.

RÉACTIONS INDÉSIRABLES ET EFFETS SECONDAIRES

SNC: confusion, dépression, étourdissements, hallucinations, céphalées, sédation, faiblesse.
ORLO: vision trouble, xérophtalmie, mydriase.
CV: arythmies, hypotension, palpitations, tachycardie.
GI: constipation, sécheresse de la bouche (xérostomie), iléus, nausées.
GU: retard de la miction, rétention urinaire.
Divers: diminution de la sécrétion de sueur.

INTERACTIONS

Médicament-médicament: Effets anticholinergiques additifs lors de l'administration concomitante de **médicaments dotés de propriétés anticholinergiques**, tels que les **antihistaminiques**, les **phénothiazines**, la **quinidine**, le **disopyramide** et les **antidépresseurs tricycliques** ▪ La benztropine contrecarre les effets cholinergiques du **béthanécol** ▪ Les **antiacides** et les **antidiarrhéiques** peuvent diminuer l'absorption de la benztropine ▪ Risque d'intensification des effets secondaires de l'**amantadine** ▪ La benztropine peut accentuer les effets dépressifs de certaines substances sur le SNC, dont l'**alcool**, les **antiépileptiques**, les **barbituriques**, les **IMAO**, les **analgésiques opioïdes**, les **phénothiazines** et les **antidépresseurs tricycliques** ▪ La benztropine peut en théorie entraver l'action du **donépézil** et d'autres **inhibiteurs de la cholinestérase à action centrale,** et vice versa.
Médicament-produits naturels: Effets anticholinergiques accrus lors de la consommation concomitante de **stramoine parfumée,** de **datura** et de **scopolia**.

VOIES D'ADMINISTRATION ET POSOLOGIE

Parkinsonisme

- **PO (adultes):** De 0,5 à 1 mg, au coucher, puis augmenter la dose par paliers de 0,5 mg, à intervalles de 5 ou 6 jours, au besoin. La dose complète peut être donnée au coucher ou en prises fractionnées, de 2 à 4 fois par jour (écart posologique de 0,5 à 6 mg/jour).

Réactions dystoniques aiguës

- **IM, IV (adultes):** De 1 à 2 mg, puis de 1 à 2 mg par voie orale, 2 fois par jour.
- **IM, IV (enfants > 3 ans):** De 0,02 à 0,05 mg/kg/jour, 1 ou 2 fois par jour.

Effets extrapyramidaux induits par les médicaments

- **PO, IM, IV (adultes):** De 1 à 4 mg/jour, en 1 ou 2 prises. Cette posologie doit être adaptée aux besoins de chaque patient (1 ou 2 mg, 2 ou 3 fois par jour; utilisation par voie orale possible à cette posologie).

PRÉSENTATION (version générique disponible)

Comprimés: 0,5 mg^{Pr}, 1 mg^{Pr}, 2 mg^{Pr} ▪ **Solution orale:** 0,4mg/mL^{Pr} ▪ **Solution pour injection:** 1 mg/mL^{Pr}, en flacons de 2 mL.

SOINS INFIRMIERS

ÉVALUATION DE LA SITUATION

- Observer le patient avant le traitement et pendant toute sa durée, à la recherche de symptômes parkinsoniens et extrapyramidaux tels que: agitation ou akathisie, rigidité, tremblements, mouvements d'émiettement, faciès figé, démarche traînante, spasmes musculaires, mouvements de torsion, troubles d'élocution ou de déglutition, perte d'équilibre.

- Noter quotidiennement la fréquence des selles. Suivre de près la constipation, la douleur et la distension abdominales ou l'absence de bruits intestinaux.
- Effectuer le bilan quotidien des ingesta et des excreta et observer le patient à la recherche des signes suivants de rétention urinaire: dysurie, distension abdominale, élimination peu fréquente de petites quantités d'urine, incontinence par regorgement.
- Chez les patients souffrant de maladie mentale, le risque d'exacerbation des symptômes de leur maladie est accru au début du traitement par la benztropine. Interrompre l'administration du médicament et prévenir le médecin ou un autre professionnel de la santé si des changements de comportement importants se produisent.

IM, IV: Mesurer attentivement le pouls et la pression artérielle et demander au patient de garder le lit pendant l'heure qui suit l'administration du médicament. Lui conseiller de changer lentement de position afin de réduire le risque d'hypotension orthostatique.

DIAGNOSTICS INFIRMIERS POSSIBLES

- Mobilité physique réduite (Indications).
- Risque d'accident (Indications).
- Connaissances insuffisantes sur le traitement médicamenteux (Enseignement au patient et à ses proches).

INTERVENTIONS INFIRMIÈRES

PO: Administrer la benztropine avec des aliments ou immédiatement après les repas afin de réduire l'irritation gastrique. Si le patient éprouve des difficultés de déglutition, on peut écraser les comprimés et les administrer avec des aliments.

IM: Ce médicament n'est administré par voie parentérale que dans les cas de réactions dystoniques.

IV directe: La voie IV est rarement utilisée, car les effets se manifestent aussi rapidement lors de l'administration par voie IM.

Vitesse d'administration: Administrer la préparation à un débit de 1 mg/min.

Association compatible dans la même seringue: métoclopramide.

Compatibilité (tubulure en Y): fluconazole ■ tacrolimus.

ENSEIGNEMENT AU PATIENT ET À SES PROCHES

- Conseiller au patient de respecter rigoureusement la posologie recommandée. S'il n'a pu prendre le médicament au moment habituel, il doit le prendre dès que possible, mais pas plus tard que 2 heures avant l'heure prévue pour la dose suivante. Avant d'arrêter le traitement par la benztropine, on doit diminuer graduellement la dose pour prévenir les réactions suivantes de sevrage: anxiété, tachycardie, insomnie, réapparition des symptômes parkinsoniens ou extrapyramidaux.
- Prévenir le patient que la benztropine peut parfois provoquer de la somnolence ou des étourdissements. Lui conseiller de ne pas conduire et d'éviter les activités qui exigent sa vigilance jusqu'à ce qu'on ait la certitude que le médicament n'entraîne pas ces effets chez lui.
- Conseiller au patient de se rincer fréquemment la bouche, de pratiquer une bonne hygiène buccale et de consommer de la gomme à mâcher ou des bonbons sans sucre pour diminuer la sécheresse de la bouche. Lui recommander de consulter un professionnel de la santé si la sécheresse de la bouche persiste (des substituts de salive pourraient lui être prescrits). Lui recommander également de prévenir le dentiste si la sécheresse de la bouche l'empêche de porter sa prothèse dentaire.
- Conseiller au patient de changer lentement de position afin de réduire le risque d'hypotension orthostatique.
- Recommander au patient de signaler à un professionnel de la santé les symptômes suivants: mictions difficiles, constipation, douleurs abdominales, battements cardiaques rapides ou très forts, confusion, douleurs oculaires ou rash.
- Conseiller au patient de consulter un professionnel de la santé avant de prendre un médicament en vente libre, particulièrement des préparations contre le rhume, et d'éviter de consommer des boissons alcoolisées.
- Prévenir le patient que ce médicament peut diminuer la sécrétion de la sueur et qu'il y a risque d'hyperthermie par temps chaud. Lui conseiller de prévenir un professionnel de la santé s'il lui est impossible de rester dans une pièce climatisée par temps chaud.
- Conseiller au patient de ne pas prendre des antiacides ou des antidiarrhéiques dans l'heure ou dans les 2 heures qui suivent la prise de ce médicament.
- Insister sur l'importance des examens de suivi réguliers.

VÉRIFICATION DE L'EFFICACITÉ THÉRAPEUTIQUE

L'efficacité du traitement peut être démontrée par: la diminution des tremblements et de la rigidité et l'amélioration de la démarche et de l'équilibre. Les effets thérapeutiques se manifestent habituellement dans les 2 ou 3 jours qui suivent le début du traitement.

BÉTAHISTINE

Serc

CLASSIFICATION:
Antivertigineux

Grossesse – catégorie inconnue

INDICATIONS

Atténuation des accès de vertiges récurrents liés au syndrome de Ménière.

MÉCANISME D'ACTION

Agoniste des récepteurs H_1 de l'histamine, dont l'activité au niveau de ce récepteur équivaut à 0,07 fois celle de l'histamine ■ La bétahistine, contrairement à l'histamine, est virtuellement inactive au niveau du récepteur H_2. ***Effets thérapeutiques:*** Diminution des accès de vertiges récurrents liés au syndrome de Ménière.

PHARMACOCINÉTIQUE

Absorption: Rapide et complète.
Distribution: On ignore si la bétahistine passe dans le lait maternel.
Liaison aux protéines: Inconnue.
Métabolisme et excrétion: Le médicament est rapidement métabolisé dans le foie et transformé en au moins 2 métabolites, dont un métabolite principal. Il est excrété dans l'urine. La plus grande partie de la dose de bétahistine est excrétée dans l'urine sous forme de métabolites dans les 3 jours qui suivent l'administration par voie orale.
Demi-vie: 3,5 heures.

Profil temps-action

	DÉBUT D'ACTION	PIC	DURÉE
PO	inconnu	inconnu	inconnue

CONTRE-INDICATIONS, PRÉCAUTIONS ET MISES EN GARDE

Contre-indications: Hypersensibilité ■ Phéochromocytome ■ Ulcère gastroduodénal actif ou ancien.
Précautions et mises en garde: Asthme bronchique ■ **OBST., ALLAITEMENT:** L'innocuité du médicament n'a pas été établie ■ **PÉD.:** Ce médicament n'est pas recommandé chez les enfants.

RÉACTIONS INDÉSIRABLES ET EFFETS SECONDAIRES

SNC: céphalées, somnolence (rare).
CV: extrasystoles ventriculaires (un cas).
GI: troubles gastriques, nausées.
Tég.: éruptions cutanées, urticaire, démangeaisons.
Resp.: réactions d'hypersensibilité, notamment d'anaphylaxie.

INTERACTIONS

Médicament-médicament: Aucune interaction cliniquement significative.

VOIES D'ADMINISTRATION ET POSOLOGIE

- **PO (adultes):** De 24 à 48 mg par jour, en doses fractionnées, soit 24 mg, 2 fois par jour, ou de 8 à 16 mg, 3 fois par jour, avec des aliments.

PRÉSENTATION

Comprimés: 16 mg[Pr], 24 mg[Pr].

SOINS INFIRMIERS

ÉVALUATION DE LA SITUATION

- Observer les accès de vertiges récurrents avant le traitement et à intervalles réguliers pendant toute sa durée.

DIAGNOSTICS INFIRMIERS POSSIBLES

- Connaissances insuffisantes sur le traitement médicamenteux (Enseignement au patient et à ses proches).

INTERVENTIONS INFIRMIÈRES

- Administrer la bétahistine avec des aliments pour diminuer les effets gastro-intestinaux.

ENSEIGNEMENT AU PATIENT ET À SES PROCHES

- Conseiller au patient de respecter rigoureusement la posologie recommandée. S'il n'a pu prendre le médicament au moment habituel, il doit le faire dès que possible à moins que ce ne soit presque l'heure prévue pour la dose suivante. Le prévenir qu'il ne doit jamais remplacer une dose manquée par une double dose.
- Prévenir le patient que le médicament cause peu ou pas d'effets indésirables chez la plupart des gens. Toutefois, il peut en occasionner chez certains. Les effets indésirables qui se produisent tendent à être généralement bénins et ne durent pas longtemps.

B

Les principaux effets indésirables signalés ont été des éruptions cutanées de divers types, de l'urticaire et des démangeaisons. La bétahistine peut aussi provoquer des maux d'estomac, des nausées et des maux de tête.

- Conseiller à la patiente d'informer immédiatement un professionnel de la santé si elle croit être enceinte ou souhaite le devenir ou, encore, si elle allaite.

VÉRIFICATION DE L'EFFICACITÉ THÉRAPEUTIQUE

L'efficacité du traitement peut être démontrée par: l'atténuation des accès de vertiges récurrents. ✳

BÉTAMÉTHASONE,

voir Corticostéroïdes (topiques) et Corticostéroïdes (voie générale)

BÉTHANÉCHOL

Duvoid, PMS-Béthanechol, Urecholine

CLASSIFICATION:

Cholinergique, parasympathomimétique

Grossesse – catégorie C

INDICATIONS

Traitement de la rétention urinaire non obstructive postpartum ou en période postopératoire ▪ Traitement de la rétention urinaire entraînée par une vessie neurogène. **Usages non approuvés**: Adjuvant du traitement du reflux gastro-œsophagien avec pyrosis, réfractaire au traitement classique.

MÉCANISME D'ACTION

Stimulation des récepteurs cholinergiques. Les effets du médicament comprennent: la contraction de la vessie ▪ l'augmentation de la fréquence des rythmes péristaltiques urétéraux ▪ l'augmentation du tonus et du péristaltisme du tractus gastro-intestinal ▪ l'augmentation de la pression du sphincter œsophagien inférieur ▪ l'augmentation des sécrétions gastriques. ***Effets thérapeutiques:*** Vidange de la vessie.

PHARMACOCINÉTIQUE

Absorption: Faible (PO).

Distribution: Le médicament ne traverse pas la barrière hématoencéphalique.

Métabolisme et excrétion: Inconnus.

Demi-vie: Inconnue.

Profil temps-action

(réponse au niveau des muscles de la vessie)

	DÉBUT D'ACTION	PIC	DURÉE
PO	30 – 90 min	1 h	6 h

CONTRE-INDICATIONS, PRÉCAUTIONS ET MISES EN GARDE

Contre-indications: Hypersensibilité ▪ Obstruction mécanique des voies gastro-intestinales ou génito-urinaires ▪ Asthme bronchique latent ou évolutif ▪ Ulcère gastroduodénal ▪ Bradycardie marquée ou hypotension ▪ Instabilité vasomotrice ▪ Coronaropathie ▪ Épilepsie ▪ Hyperthyroïdie ▪ Syndrome parkinsonien ▪ **OBST., ALLAITEMENT**: L'innocuité du médicament n'a pas été établie.

Précautions et mises en garde: Sensibilité aux agents cholinergiques ou à leurs effets ▪ **PÉD.**: L'innocuité du médicament n'a pas été établie.

RÉACTIONS INDÉSIRABLES ET EFFETS SECONDAIRES

SNC: céphalées, malaises.

ORLO: larmoiement, myosis.

Resp.: bronchospasme.

CV: BLOC CARDIAQUE, SYNCOPE ACCOMPAGNÉE D'ARRÊT CARDIAQUE, bradycardie, hypotension.

GI: gêne abdominale, diarrhée, nausées, salivation, vomissements.

GU: mictions impérieuses.

Divers: bouffées vasomotrices, transpiration, hypothermie.

INTERACTIONS

Médicament-médicament: La **quinidine** et le **procaïnamide** peuvent contrecarrer les effets cholinergiques du béthanéchol ▪ Le béthanéchol peut exercer des effets cholinergiques additifs lors de l'administration simultanée d'**inhibiteurs de la cholinestérase** ▪ L'administration concomitante d'**agents ganglioplégiques** peut entraîner une hypotension grave ▪ L'administration simultanée de **bloqueurs neuromusculaires du type dépolarisant** est déconseillée ▪ L'efficacité du béthanéchol est diminuée lors de l'administration concomitante d'**agents anticholinergiques**.

VOIES D'ADMINISTRATION ET POSOLOGIE

- **PO (adultes)**: De 10 à 50 mg, 3 ou 4 fois par jour. Pour déterminer la dose efficace, on peut administrer de 5 à 10 mg toutes les heures, jusqu'à l'obtention d'une réponse ou jusqu'à concurrence d'une dose maximale de 50 mg.

PRÉSENTATION (version générique disponible)

Comprimés: 10 mg^{Pr}, 25 mg^{Pr}, 50 mg^{Pr}.

SOINS INFIRMIERS

ÉVALUATION DE LA SITUATION

- Effectuer le bilan quotidien des ingesta et des excreta. Palper l'abdomen pour déterminer si la vessie est distendue. Prévenir le médecin ou un autre professionnel de la santé si le médicament ne soulage pas les symptômes de la maladie pour laquelle il a été prescrit. On peut prescrire le cathétérisme pour analyser l'urine résiduelle postmictionnelle.

Tests de laboratoire: Le médicament peut entraîner l'élévation des concentrations sériques d'AST, d'amylase et de lipase.

Toxicité et surdosage: Observer le patient à la recherche des signes et des symptômes suivants de toxicité médicamenteuse: transpiration, bouffées vasomotrices, crampes abdominales, nausées, salivation. En cas de surdosage, l'atropine fait partie du traitement (antidote spécifique).

DIAGNOSTICS INFIRMIERS POSSIBLES

- Élimination urinaire altérée (Indications).
- Connaissances insuffisantes sur le traitement médicamenteux (Enseignement au patient et à ses proches).

INTERVENTIONS INFIRMIÈRES

- Il est d'usage d'administrer une dose-test avant le traitement d'entretien pour déterminer la dose minimale efficace.
- Administrer le médicament à jeun, 1 heure avant ou 2 heures après les repas, afin de prévenir les nausées et les vomissements.

ENSEIGNEMENT AU PATIENT ET À SES PROCHES

- Conseiller au patient de respecter rigoureusement la posologie recommandée. S'il n'a pas pu prendre le médicament au moment habituel, il doit le prendre dans les 2 heures qui suivent; sinon, il doit reprendre son horaire habituel. Le prévenir qu'il ne doit jamais remplacer une dose manquée par une double dose.
- Conseiller au patient de changer lentement de position afin de réduire le risque d'hypotension orthostatique.
- Inciter le patient à signaler à un professionnel de la santé les symptômes suivants: gêne abdominale, salivation, transpiration ou bouffées vasomotrices.

VÉRIFICATION DE L'EFFICACITÉ THÉRAPEUTIQUE

L'efficacité du traitement peut être démontrée par: l'amélioration du tonus et du fonctionnement de la vessie ■ la diminution du pyrosis.

BÉVACIZUMAB

Avastin

CLASSIFICATION:

Antinéoplasique (anticorps monoclonal)

Grossesse – catégorie C

INDICATIONS

Carcinome métastatique du côlon et du rectum (avec du 5–fluorouracile par voie IV).

MÉCANISME D'ACTION

Anticorps monoclonal qui se lie au facteur de croissance de l'épithélium vasculaire (VEGF), prévenant sa liaison aux récepteurs de l'endothélium vasculaire. Le VEGF favorise la prolifération de l'endothélium et la formation de nouveaux vaisseaux sanguins. ***Effets thérapeutiques:*** Ralentissement de la propagation des métastases et de la croissance des microvaisseaux.

PHARMACOCINÉTIQUE

Absorption: Biodisponibilité à 100 % (IV).

Distribution: Inconnue.

Métabolisme et excrétion: Inconnus.

Demi-vie: 20 jours (de 11 à 50 jours).

Profil temps-action

	Début d'action	Pic	Durée
IV	rapide	fin de la perfusion	14 jours

CONTRE-INDICATIONS, PRÉCAUTIONS ET MISES EN GARDE

Contre-indications: Hypersensibilité à un ingrédient de l'agent, aux anticorps recombinants humains ou humanisés ou à tout produit à base de cellules ovariennes de hamster chinois ■ Métastases non traitées du système nerveux central.

B

Précautions et mises en garde: GÉR.: Risque accru de réactions indésirables graves, notamment de complications artérielles thromboemboliques, chez les patients > 65 ans ■ Maladie cardiovasculaire ■ **PÉD.:** L'innocuité de l'agent n'a pas été établie ■ Hémoptysie récente ou autre épisode de saignement récent grave ■ 28 premiers jours après une intervention chirurgicale majeure ■ **OBST.:** Grossesse et allaitement.

RÉACTIONS INDÉSIRABLES ET EFFETS SECONDAIRES

CV: COMPLICATIONS ARTÉRIELLES THROMBOEMBOLIQUES, INSUFFISANCE CARDIAQUE, hypertension, hypotension.
Resp.: HÉMOPTYSIE.
GI: PERFORATION GI.
GU: syndrome néphrotique, protéinurie.
Hémat.: SAIGNEMENTS, leucopénie.
Divers: DÉHISCENCE DES PLAIES, cicatrisation retardée des plaies, réactions à la perfusion.

INTERACTIONS

Médicament-médicament: Élévation des concentrations de SN 38 (le métabolite actif de l'**irinotécan**); la signification de cette interaction est inconnue. La dose d'irinotécan doit être diminuée en cas d'effets indésirables importants.

VOIES D'ADMINISTRATION ET POSOLOGIE

- **IV (adultes):** 5 mg/kg en perfusion tous les 14 jours.

PRÉSENTATION

Solution pour injection: fioles de 100 mg[Pr] et fioles de 400 mg[Pr] à une concentration de 25 mg/mL.

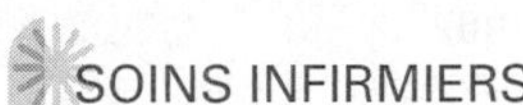

SOINS INFIRMIERS

ÉVALUATION DE LA SITUATION

- RESTER À L'AFFÛT DES SIGNES DE PERFORATION GI (DOULEURS ABDOMINALES, AVEC CONSTIPATION ET VOMISSEMENTS) ET DE LA DÉHISCENCE DES PLAIES, TOUT AU LONG DU TRAITEMENT; L'ARRÊT DU TRAITEMENT POURRAIT S'IMPOSER.
- RECHERCHER LES SIGNES D'HÉMORRAGIE (ÉPISTAXIS, HÉMOPTYSIE, SAIGNEMENTS) ET LES COMPLICATIONS THROMBOEMBOLIQUES (AVC, INFARCTUS DU MYOCARDE, THROMBOSE VEINEUSE PROFONDE) TOUT AU LONG DU TRAITEMENT; L'ARRÊT DU TRAITEMENT POURRAIT S'IMPOSER.
- Mesurer la pression artérielle toutes les 2 ou 3 semaines pendant toute la durée du traitement. Interrompre passagèrement le traitement pendant un épisode d'hypertension grave, rebelle à toute pharmacothérapie; l'arrêter définitivement en cas de crise hypertensive.
- Rester à l'affût des réactions à la perfusion (stridor, respiration sifflante) pendant toute la durée du traitement.
- RECHERCHER LES SIGNES D'INSUFFISANCE CARDIAQUE (DYSPNÉE, ŒDÈME PÉRIPHÉRIQUE, RÂLES ET CRÉPITATIONS, distension des jugulaires) tout au long du traitement.

Tests de laboratoire:

- Suivre de près les analyses d'urine en série pendant toute la durée du traitement pour dépister la protéinurie. Chez les patients dont le résultat de l'analyse des urines par immersion de bâtonnets est de 2+ ou plus, mesurer la protéinurie par une collecte des urines de 24 heures.
- L'agent peut provoquer une leucopénie, une thrombopénie, une hypokaliémie et une élévation des concentrations de bilirubine sérique.

DIAGNOSTICS INFIRMIERS POSSIBLES

- Irrigation tissulaire inefficace (Réactions indésirables).

INTERVENTIONS INFIRMIÈRES

- Ne pas administrer pendant au moins 28 jours après une intervention chirurgicale majeure; l'incision doit être complètement cicatrisée, car ce médicament retarde la cicatrisation des plaies.

Perfusion intermittente: Retirer de la fiole la quantité de bévacizumab nécessaire pour une dose de 5 mg/kg et la diluer dans un volume total de 100 mL de NaCl 0,9 %. Ne pas secouer. Jeter toute portion inutilisée. Ne pas administrer une solution qui a changé de couleur ou qui contient des particules. La solution est stable pendant 8 heures si elle est réfrigérée.

Vitesse d'administration: Administrer la dose initiale en 90 minutes. Si elle est bien tolérée, la deuxième perfusion peut être administrée en 60 minutes. Si elle est également bien tolérée, toutes les perfusions ultérieures peuvent être administrées en 30 minutes. **Ne pas administrer par IV directe ou en bolus.**

Incompatibilité en addition au soluté: Ne pas mélanger à une solution de dextrose ni administrer en même temps que ce type de solution.

ENSEIGNEMENT AU PATIENT ET À SES PROCHES

- Expliquer au patient le but de ce traitement.
- Inciter le patient à signaler immédiatement à un professionnel de la santé tout signe de saignement.

VÉRIFICATION DE L'EFFICACITÉ THÉRAPEUTIQUE

L'efficacité du traitement peut être démontrée par: le ralentissement de la propagation des métastases et de la croissance de microvaisseaux.

BICALUTAMIDE

Casodex, Novo-Bicalutamide, PMS-Bicalutamide, Ratio-Bicalutamide, Sandoz Bicalutamide

CLASSIFICATION:

Antinéoplasique (antiandrogène non stéroïdien)

Grossesse – catégorie X

INDICATIONS

Traitement d'association avec un analogue de la LH-RH ou avec la castration chirurgicale dans le traitement du cancer de la prostate avec métastases (stade D2).

MÉCANISME D'ACTION

Inhibition des effets des hormones androgènes au niveau cellulaire. ***Effets thérapeutiques:*** Ralentissement de la propagation du cancer de la prostate.

PHARMACOCINÉTIQUE

Absorption: Bonne (PO).
Distribution: Inconnue.
Liaison aux protéines: 96 %.
Métabolisme et excrétion: Métabolisme majoritairement hépatique.
Demi-vie: 5,8 jours.

Profil temps-action

	DÉBUT D'ACTION	PIC	DURÉE
PO	inconnu	31,3 h	inconnue

CONTRE-INDICATIONS, PRÉCAUTIONS ET MISES EN GARDE

Contre-indications: Hypersensibilité ▪ Femmes ▪ Enfants ▪ Patients atteints d'un cancer de la prostate localisé.

Précautions et mises en garde: Insuffisance hépatique modérée à grave ▪ Patients en âge de procréer.

RÉACTIONS INDÉSIRABLES ET EFFETS SECONDAIRES

SNC: faiblesse, étourdissements, céphalées, insomnie.
Resp.: dyspnée.
CV: douleurs thoraciques, hypertension, œdème périphérique.
GI: constipation, diarrhée, nausées, douleurs abdominales, élévations des concentrations des enzymes hépatiques, vomissements.
GU: hématurie, impuissance, incontinence, nycturie, infections urinaires.
Tég.: alopécie, rash, transpiration.
End.: mastalgie, gynécomastie.
Hémat.: anémie.
Métab.: hyperglycémie, perte pondérale.
Loc.: douleurs lombaires, douleurs pelviennes, douleurs osseuses.
SN: paresthésie.
Divers: douleurs généralisées, bouffées vasomotrices, syndrome pseudogrippal, infections.

INTERACTIONS

Médicament-médicament: Le bicalutamide peut accentuer l'effet de la **warfarine**.

VOIES D'ADMINISTRATION ET POSOLOGIE

- **PO (adultes):** 50 mg, 1 fois par jour (administrer en concomitance avec un analogue de la LH-RH ou après une castration chirurgicale).

PRÉSENTATION

Comprimés: 50 mg[Pr].

SOINS INFIRMIERS

ÉVALUATION DE LA SITUATION

Suivre l'état du patient pour déceler les effets gastrointestinaux indésirables. La diarrhée est la raison la plus fréquente d'abandon du traitement.

Tests de laboratoire:

- Mesurer à intervalles réguliers les concentrations sériques d'antigène prostatique spécifique (APS), pour déterminer l'efficacité du traitement. Si les concentrations d'antigène s'élèvent, évaluer l'évolution de la maladie. Il peut s'avérer nécessaire d'administrer à intervalles réguliers un analogue de la LH-RH sans le bicalutamide.
- Effectuer un test de la fonction hépatique avant le traitement et à intervalles réguliers pendant toute sa durée. Le bicalutamide peut entraîner une élévation des concentrations de phosphatase alcaline sérique, d'AST, d'ALT et de bilirubine. Si les concentrations de transaminases augmentent à des niveaux 2 fois supérieurs à la normale, il faudrait interrompre le traitement par le bicalutamide; les concentrations reviennent habituellement à la normale après l'arrêt du traitement.

B

- Le bicalutamide peut entraîner l'élévation des concentrations d'urée et de créatinine sérique et la diminution des concentrations d'hémoglobine et du nombre de globules blancs.

DIAGNOSTICS INFIRMIERS POSSIBLES

- Diarrhée (Réactions indésirables).
- Connaissances insuffisantes sur le traitement médicamenteux (Enseignement au patient et à ses proches).

INTERVENTIONS INFIRMIÈRES

- Amorcer le traitement par le bicalutamide en même temps que celui par un analogue de la LH-RH.
- Le médicament peut être administré le matin ou le soir, sans égard aux repas.

ENSEIGNEMENT AU PATIENT ET À SES PROCHES

- Expliquer au patient qu'il doit respecter rigoureusement la posologie recommandée et qu'il doit prendre le bicalutamide à la même heure, tous les jours. Le prévenir qu'il ne doit pas interrompre le traitement sans avoir consulté au préalable un professionnel de la santé.
- Prévenir le patient qu'il ne doit pas prendre d'autres médicaments sans avoir consulté au préalable un professionnel de la santé.
- Recommander au patient de signaler à un professionnel de la santé toute diarrhée grave ou persistante.
- Insister sur le fait qu'il est important de se soumettre régulièrement à des examens de suivi et à des analyses sanguines permettant de déterminer l'évolution de la maladie et de déceler les effets secondaires.

VÉRIFICATION DE L'EFFICACITÉ THÉRAPEUTIQUE

L'efficacité du traitement peut être démontrée par: le ralentissement de la propagation du cancer de la prostate. ✳

BIPHOSPHATE,
voir Phosphate

BISACODYL

Alophen, Apo-Bisacodyl, Bisacolax, Dulcolax, Petites pilules Carter's, PMS-Bisacodyl, Soflax

CLASSIFICATION:
Laxatif (stimulant)

Grossesse – catégorie inconnue

INDICATIONS

Traitement de la constipation occasionnelle ■ Évacuation intestinale avant un examen radiologique, un examen diagnostique (coloscopie) ou une intervention chirurgicale ■ Sous supervision médicale, dans les cas où la défécation doit être facilitée.

MÉCANISME D'ACTION

Stimulation du péristaltisme ■ Modification du transport des liquides et des électrolytes favorisant l'accumulation de liquides dans le côlon. ***Effets thérapeutiques:*** Évacuation des matières accumulées dans le côlon.

PHARMACOCINÉTIQUE

Absorption: Variable (PO), minime (IR). Le médicament agit au niveau du côlon seulement.
Distribution: De petites quantités de métabolites passent dans le lait maternel.
Métabolisme et excrétion: Les petites quantités absorbées sont métabolisées par le foie.
Demi-vie: Inconnue.

Profil temps-action
(évacuation des matières accumulées dans le côlon)

	Début d'action	Pic	Durée
PO	6 – 12 h	inconnu	inconnue
IR	15 – 60 min	inconnu	inconnue

CONTRE-INDICATIONS, PRÉCAUTIONS ET MISES EN GARDE

Contre-indications: Hypersensibilité ■ Occlusion intestinale ■ Abdomen chirurgical aigu, p. ex., appendicite aiguë ■ Infection inflammatoire intestinale aiguë ■ Déshydratation importante.
Précautions et mises en garde: Maladie cardiovasculaire grave ■ Douleurs abdominales ■ Nausées ou vomissements (particulièrement lorsqu'ils s'accompagnent de fièvre) ■ Fissures anales ou rectales ■ Doses élevées ou traitement prolongé (risque d'accoutumance) ■ Risque accru d'hépatotoxicité (les produits renfermant de l'acide tannique ne doivent pas être utilisés en lave-

ments à répétition) ■ **Obst., allaitement**: N'administrer que sur la recommandation du médecin.

RÉACTIONS INDÉSIRABLES ET EFFETS SECONDAIRES

GI: crampes abdominales, nausées, diarrhée, brûlures rectales.
HÉ: hypokaliémie (administration prolongée).
Loc.: faiblesse musculaire (administration prolongée).
Divers: entéropathie exsudative, tétanie (administration prolongée).

INTERACTIONS

Médicament-médicament: Les **antiacides**, les **antagonistes des récepteurs H_2 de l'histamine** et les **inhibiteurs de la pompe à protons** peuvent dissoudre l'enrobage entérique des comprimés et provoquer de l'irritation gastrique ■ Le bisacodyl peut réduire l'absorption d'autres **médicaments administrés par voie orale** en raison d'une motilité accrue et d'un transit intestinal réduit.
Médicament-aliments: Le **lait** peut dissoudre l'enrobage entérique des comprimés et provoquer de l'irritation gastrique.

VOIES D'ADMINISTRATION ET POSOLOGIE

Constipation

- **PO (adultes et enfants > 12 ans)**: De 5 à 15 mg, au coucher ou le matin, avant le déjeuner, afin de produire une défécation environ 8 heures plus tard.
- **PO (enfants de 6 à 12 ans)**: 5 mg, au coucher ou le matin, avant le déjeuner, afin de produire une défécation environ 8 heures plus tard.
- **IR (adultes et enfants > 12 ans)**: Un suppositoire à 10 mg ou le contenu d'un microlavement, pour produire, en général, une défécation en 30 minutes.
- **IR (enfants de 6 à 12 ans)**: Un suppositoire à 5 mg ou la moitié du contenu d'un microlavement, pour produire, en général, une défécation en 30 minutes.

Interventions diagnostiques ou préopératoires

- **PO, IR (adultes)**: De 10 à 20 mg, au coucher, et un suppositoire à 10 mg ou un microlavement, le lendemain matin.
- **PO, IR (enfants de 6 à 12 ans)**: Un comprimé à 5 mg, au coucher, et un suppositoire à 5 mg ou la moitié d'un microlavement, le lendemain matin.

PRÉSENTATION (version générique disponible)

Comprimés: 5 mg[VL] ■ **Comprimés à enrobage entérique**: 5 mg[VL] ■ **Suppositoires**: 5 mg[VL], 10 mg[VL] ■ **Microlavement**: 10 mg/5 mL[VL] ■ **En association avec**: docusate sodique (Gentlax-S[VL]), citrate de magnésium (Royvac Bowel Evacuant kit[VL]).

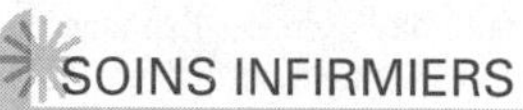

SOINS INFIRMIERS

ÉVALUATION DE LA SITUATION

- Déterminer le degré de distension abdominale, ausculter les bruits intestinaux, noter les habitudes normales d'élimination.
- Noter la couleur, la consistance et la quantité des selles.

DIAGNOSTICS INFIRMIERS POSSIBLES

- Constipation (Indications).
- Connaissances insuffisantes sur le traitement médicamenteux (Enseignement au patient et à ses proches).

INTERVENTIONS INFIRMIÈRES

- Administrer le médicament au coucher pour favoriser la défécation le lendemain matin.

PO:

- Les préparations orales, administrées à jeun, produisent des résultats plus rapides.
- IL NE FAUT PAS ÉCRASER NI CROQUER LES COMPRIMÉS À ENROBAGE ENTÉRIQUE. Demander au patient de les avaler avec un grand verre d'eau ou de jus.
- Si le patient a pris du lait ou des antiacides, éviter d'administrer la préparation orale dans l'heure qui suit, car le comprimé risque d'être prématurément dissous, ce qui peut entraîner une irritation gastrique ou duodénale.

IR: Administrer le suppositoire ou le lavement au moment où l'élimination est souhaitée. Lubrifier le suppositoire avec de l'eau ou un lubrifiant hydrosoluble avant de l'administrer. Inciter le patient à retenir le suppositoire ou le lavement pendant 15 à 30 minutes avant d'évacuer les selles.

ENSEIGNEMENT AU PATIENT ET À SES PROCHES

- Prévenir le patient que les laxatifs ne sont destinés qu'à un traitement de courte durée (sauf dans le cas du patient souffrant de lésions de la moelle épinière). Lui expliquer que le traitement prolongé peut entraîner un déséquilibre électrolytique et l'accoutumance.
- Recommander au patient d'augmenter sa consommation de liquides pendant le traitement et de boire de 1 500 à 2 000 mL de liquide par jour au minimum (si aucune restriction hydrique n'est prescrite) pour prévenir la déshydratation.

B

- Recommander au patient de prendre d'autres mesures qui favorisent la défécation: augmenter la consommation d'aliments riches en fibres, boire plus de liquides, faire de l'exercice. Expliquer au patient que chaque personne a ses propres habitudes d'élimination et qu'il est tout aussi normal de déféquer 3 fois par jour que 3 fois par semaine.
- Recommander au patient souffrant de maladie cardiaque d'éviter les efforts de défécation (manœuvre de Valsalva).
- Prévenir le patient que le bisacodyl est déconseillé si la constipation s'accompagne de douleurs abdominales, de fièvre, de nausées ou de vomissements.

VÉRIFICATION DE L'EFFICACITÉ THÉRAPEUTIQUE

L'efficacité du traitement peut être démontrée par: l'émission de selles molles et moulées, lorsque le bisacodyl est administré en traitement de la constipation ■ l'évacuation des matières accumulées dans le côlon chez le patient qui doit subir un examen radiologique, un examen diagnostique (coloscopie) ou une intervention chirurgicale. ✳

BISMUTH, SOUS-SALICYLATE DE

Bismed, Bismuth, Pepto-Bismol, Personnel bismuth

CLASSIFICATION:

Antidiarrhéique, antiacide

Grossesse – catégorie C

INDICATIONS

Traitement d'appoint de la diarrhée légère à modérée ■ Traitement des nausées, des crampes abdominales, des brûlures d'estomac et de l'indigestion qui peuvent accompagner les maladies diarrhéiques ■ Traitement de la diarrhée du voyageur chez l'adulte (due à *Escherichia coli* entérotoxigène). **Usages non approuvés:** En association avec des antibiotiques dans le traitement de l'ulcère dû à *Helicobacter pylori* ■ Prévention de la diarrhée du voyageur.

MÉCANISME D'ACTION

Effet favorable sur l'absorption intestinale de liquides et d'électrolytes ■ Diminution de la synthèse des prostaglandines intestinales. ***Effets thérapeutiques:*** Soulagement de la diarrhée.

PHARMACOCINÉTIQUE

Absorption: Le bismuth n'est pas absorbé; le salicylate séparé du composé mère est absorbé à > 90 % depuis l'intestin grêle.

Distribution: Le salicylate traverse la barrière placentaire et passe dans le lait maternel. Il est fortement lié à l'albumine.

Métabolisme et excrétion: Le bismuth est excrété à l'état inchangé dans les fèces. Le salicylate est fortement métabolisé par le foie.

Demi-vie: Salicylate – de 2 à 3 heures, dans le cas des doses faibles; de 15 à 30 heures, dans le cas de doses plus élevées.

Profil temps-action
(soulagement de la diarrhée et d'autres symptômes GI)

	DÉBUT D'ACTION	PIC	DURÉE
PO	en 24 h	inconnu	inconnue

CONTRE-INDICATIONS, PRÉCAUTIONS ET MISES EN GARDE

Contre-indications: **GÉR.:** Personnes âgées souffrant de fécalome ■ **PÉD.:** Enfants ou adolescents atteints de varicelle ou de syndrome pseudogrippal ou qui sont en convalescence (en raison du contenu en salicylate) ■ Hypersensibilité à l'aspirine (acide acétylsalicylique); risque de sensibilité croisée avec les AINS ou l'essence de *wintergreen.*

Précautions et mises en garde: Nourrissons, personnes âgées ou patients débilités (risque de formation d'un fécalome) ■ Examen radiologique du tractus gastro-intestinal (le bismuth est opaque aux rayons X) ■ Diabète ■ Goutte ■ **OBST.:** Grossesse ou allaitement (l'innocuité du médicament n'a pas été établie; éviter l'administration prolongée de doses élevées).

RÉACTIONS INDÉSIRABLES ET EFFETS SECONDAIRES

GI: constipation, selles gris-noir, fécalome.

INTERACTIONS

Médicament-médicament: L'administration simultanée d'**aspirine** peut exacerber les signes de toxicité par les salicylates ■ Le sous-salicylate de bismuth peut diminuer l'absorption de la **tétracycline** ■ Le médicament peut modifier l'efficacité du **probénécide** (doses élevées).

VOIES D'ADMINISTRATION ET POSOLOGIE

- **PO (adultes):** 2 comprimés ou 30 mL; on peut répéter l'administration toutes les 30 à 60 minutes, jusqu'à concurrence de 8 doses en 24 heures.

- **PO (enfants de 9 à 12 ans)**: 1 comprimé ou 15 mL; on peut répéter l'administration toutes les 30 à 60 minutes, jusqu'à concurrence de 8 doses en 24 heures.
- **PO (enfants de 6 à 9 ans)**: 10 mL; on peut répéter l'administration toutes les 30 à 60 minutes, jusqu'à concurrence de 8 doses en 24 heures.
- **PO (enfants de 3 à 6 ans)**: 5 mL; on peut répéter l'administration toutes les 30 à 60 minutes, jusqu'à concurrence de 8 doses en 24 heures.
- **PO (enfants < 3 ans)**: Sur recommandation du médecin seulement.

PRÉSENTATION (version générique disponible)

Comprimés: 262 mg[VL] ■ **Comprimés à croquer**: 262 mg[VL] (renferment du carbonate de calcium à 308 mg, à 350 mg ou à 675 mg) ■ **Suspension liquide**: 17,6 mg/mL[VL], 35,2 mg/mL[VL] ■ **En association avec**: Pectin/Phenyl salicylate (Watkins settelz[VL]).

SOINS INFIRMIERS

ÉVALUATION DE LA SITUATION

Diarrhée:

- Observer la fréquence et la consistance des selles, noter la présence des nausées et de l'indigestion et ausculter les bruits intestinaux avant l'administration initiale et pendant toute la durée du traitement.
- Effectuer le bilan hydroélectrolytique et observer la turgescence de la peau à la recherche de signes de déshydratation en cas de diarrhée prolongée.

Ulcère: Rester à l'affût des douleurs épigastriques ou abdominales; déceler la présence de sang apparent ou occulte dans les selles, les vomissements ou les liquides d'aspiration gastrique.

Tests de laboratoire:

- L'administration prolongée de doses élevées peut entraîner des concentrations d'acide urique faussement élevées lors du test colorimétrique.
- Le médicament peut modifier les résultats de l'examen radiologique du tractus gastro-intestinal.
- Il peut entraîner des résultats anormaux aux tests de dosage de la phosphatase alcaline, de l'AST ou de l'ALT.
- Il peut abaisser les concentrations de potassium et de thyroxines sériques T3 et T4.
- Les doses plus élevées de salicylates peuvent également prolonger le temps de prothrombine.
- Pour en savoir plus sur les épreuves diagnostiques et biochimiques qui peuvent être modifiées par le contenu de salicylate, consulter la monographie des salicylates.

DIAGNOSTICS INFIRMIERS POSSIBLES

- Diarrhée (Indications).
- Constipation (Effets secondaires).
- Connaissances insuffisantes sur le traitement médicamenteux (Enseignement au patient et à ses proches).

INTERVENTIONS INFIRMIÈRES

- Bien agiter la préparation liquide avant de l'administrer. Les comprimés à croquer peuvent être mâchés ou dissous avant d'être avalés.

ENSEIGNEMENT AU PATIENT ET À SES PROCHES

- Conseiller au patient de respecter rigoureusement la posologie recommandée.
- Expliquer au patient que le médicament peut colorer passagèrement ses selles et sa langue en gris-noir.
- Prévenir le patient que ce médicament contient de l'aspirine et qu'il doit cesser de prendre le sous-salicylate de bismuth en même temps que des produits à base d'acide acétylsalicylique en cas d'acouphènes.

Diarrhée:

- Conseiller au patient de prévenir un professionnel de la santé si la diarrhée persiste pendant plus de 2 jours ou si elle s'accompagne d'une forte fièvre.
- Prévenir le patient que les centres épidémiologiques mettent en garde contre l'administration de préparations de salicylates aux enfants ou aux adolescents souffrant de varicelle, de maladie virale ou de syndrome pseudogrippal étant donné le risque d'apparition du syndrome de Reye.

VÉRIFICATION DE L'EFFICACITÉ THÉRAPEUTIQUE

L'efficacité du traitement peut être démontrée par: la diminution de la diarrhée ■ la diminution des symptômes d'indigestion.

BISOPROLOL

Apo-Bisoprolol, Monocor, Novo-Bisoprolol, Sandoz-Bisoprolol

CLASSIFICATION:

Antihypertenseur (bêtabloquant)

Grossesse – catégories C (1er trimestre) et D (2e et 3e trimestres)

B

INDICATIONS

Traitement de l'hypertension légère à modérée.

MÉCANISME D'ACTION

Blocage de la stimulation des récepteurs bêta$_1$-adrénergiques (myocardiques). Habituellement, aucun effet sur les récepteurs bêta$_2$-adrénergiques (pulmonaires, vasculaires, utérins). ***Effets thérapeutiques:*** Abaissement de la pression artérielle et de la fréquence cardiaque.

PHARMACOCINÉTIQUE

Absorption: Bonne (PO); biodisponibilité > 80 %.

Distribution: Inconnue.

Métabolisme et excrétion: Environ 20 % subit un métabolisme hépatique de premier passage; 50 % est excrété inchangé par les reins; le reste est excrété par les reins sous forme de métabolites inactifs; < 2 % se retrouve dans les fèces.

Demi-vie: De 9 à 12 heures.

Profil temps-action (effet antihypertenseur)

	DÉBUT D'ACTION	PIC	DURÉE
PO	inconnu	1-4 h	24 h

CONTRE-INDICATIONS, PRÉCAUTIONS ET MISES EN GARDE

Contre-indications: Insuffisance cardiaque congestive décompensée ■ Choc cardiogénique ■ Bradycardie sinusale ou bloc A-V du 2e et 3e degré ■ Insuffisance ventriculaire droite attribuable à l'hypertension pulmonaire.

Précautions et mises en garde: Insuffisance cardiaque compensée ■ Insuffisance rénale (on recommande de réduire la dose) ■ Insuffisance hépatique (on recommande de réduire la dose) ■ **GÉR.**: Sensibilité accrue aux bêtabloquants; il est recommandé de réduire la dose initiale ■ Maladie pulmonaire bronchospastique (incluant l'asthme; cette sélectivité pour les récepteurs bêta$_1$ peut disparaître aux doses plus élevées); dans la mesure du possible, en éviter l'usage ■ Diabète (le médicament peut masquer les signes d'hypoglycémie) ■ Thyrotoxicose (le médicament peut en masquer les symptômes) ■ Antécédents de réactions allergiques graves (l'intensité des réactions peut être accrue) ■ **OBST., ALLAITEMENT, PÉD.**: L'innocuité du médicament n'a pas été établie pendant la grossesse ou l'allaitement et chez les enfants; l'agent traverse la barrière placentaire et peut entraîner la bradycardie, l'hypotension, l'hypoglycémie ou la dépression respiratoire chez le fœtus ou le nouveau-né.

RÉACTIONS INDÉSIRABLES ET EFFETS SECONDAIRES

SNC: fatigue, faiblesse, anxiété, dépression, étourdissements, somnolence, insomnie, perte de mémoire, modifications de l'état mental, nervosité, cauchemars.

ORLO: vision trouble, congestion nasale.

Resp.: bronchospasme, respiration sifflante.

CV: BRADYCARDIE, INSUFFISANCE CARDIAQUE, ŒDÈME PULMONAIRE, hypotension, vasoconstriction périphérique.

GI: constipation, diarrhée, dysfonctionnement hépatique, nausées, vomissements.

GU: impuissance, baisse de la libido, mictions fréquentes.

Tég.: rash.

End.: hyperglycémie, hypoglycémie.

Loc.: arthralgie, douleurs lombaires, douleurs articulaires.

Divers: lupus érythémateux induit par le médicament.

INTERACTIONS

Médicament-médicament: Les **anesthésiques généraux**, le **diltiazem** et le **vérapamil** peuvent exercer des effets additifs sur la dépression myocardique ■ Risque accru de bradycardie lors de l'administration de **digoxine** ■ La consommation de grandes quantités d'**alcool** pendant un court laps de temps ou l'administration concomitante d'autres **antihypertenseurs** ou de **dérivés nitrés** peut provoquer des effets hypotenseurs additifs ■ L'usage concomitant d'**amphétamines**, de **cocaïne**, d'**éphédrine**, d'**adrénaline**, de **noradrénaline**, de **phényléphrine** ou de **pseudoéphédrine** peut entraîner une stimulation alpha-adrénergique excessive (hypertension excessive, bradycardie) ■ L'administration concomitante d'**hormones thyroïdiennes** peut diminuer l'efficacité du médicament ■ Le médicament peut entraver les effets de l'**insuline** ou des **hypoglycémiants oraux** (une adaptation de la dose peut s'avérer nécessaire) ■ Le bisoprolol peut réduire l'efficacité de la **théophylline** ■ Le médicament peut diminuer les effets cardiovasculaires bénéfiques sur les récepteurs bêta$_1$ de la **dopamine** ou de la **dobutamine** ■ Risque d'hypertension lors de l'administration concomitante d'un **IMAO**; administrer le bisoprolol avec prudence dans les 14 jours qui suivent ou qui précèdent ce traitement.

VOIES D'ADMINISTRATION ET POSOLOGIE

- **PO (adultes)**: 5 mg, 1 fois par jour; on peut augmenter la dose jusqu'à 10 mg, 1 fois par jour (écart posologique de 2,5 à 20 mg par jour).

Insuffisance rénale et insuffisance hépatique

- **PO (adultes)**: *CL_{CR} < 40 mL/min – dose initiale:* 5 mg, 1 fois par jour; augmenter la dose avec prudence.

PRÉSENTATION

Comprimés: 5 mg[Pr], 10 mg[Pr].

SOINS INFIRMIERS

ÉVALUATION DE LA SITUATION

- Mesurer la pression artérielle et le pouls, suivre de près l'ÉCG à intervalles fréquents tout au long de la période d'adaptation posologique et à intervalles réguliers, pendant toute la durée du traitement.
- Effectuer le bilan quotidien des ingesta et des excreta; peser le patient tous les jours. Rester à l'affût des signes et des symptômes suivants d'insuffisance cardiaque: dyspnée, râles ou crépitations, gain pondéral, œdème périphérique, turgescence des jugulaires.
- Suivre de près la fréquence du renouvellement des ordonnances afin de déterminer si l'observance du traitement est satisfaisante.

Tests de laboratoire:

- L'agent peut élever les taux d'urée et les concentrations sériques de lipoprotéines, de potassium, de triglycérides et d'acide urique.
- L'agent peut élever la glycémie.

DIAGNOSTICS INFIRMIERS POSSIBLES

- Débit cardiaque diminué (Effets secondaires).
- Connaissances insuffisantes sur le traitement médicamenteux (Enseignement au patient et à ses proches).
- Non-observance du traitement médicamenteux (Enseignement au patient et à ses proches).

INTERVENTIONS INFIRMIÈRES

- Mesurer le pouls à l'apex du cœur avant d'administrer le médicament. S'il est < 50 bpm ou si des arythmies se manifestent, ne pas administrer le médicament et prévenir le médecin ou un professionnel de la santé.
- Le médicament peut être administré sans égard aux repas.

ENSEIGNEMENT AU PATIENT ET À SES PROCHES

- Conseiller au patient de suivre rigoureusement la posologie recommandée et de prendre le médicament à des heures fixes, tous les jours, même s'il se sent mieux; l'avertir qu'il ne doit jamais sauter de dose, ni remplacer une dose manquée par une double dose. S'il n'a pu prendre le médicament au moment habituel, il doit le prendre aussitôt que possible, à moins qu'il ne soit presque l'heure prévue pour la dose suivante. Le sevrage brusque peut provoquer des arythmies menaçantes pour la vie, de l'hypertension ou l'ischémie du myocarde.
- Enseigner au patient et à ses proches la méthode de mesure du pouls et de la pression artérielle. Leur recommander de noter le pouls tous les jours et la pression artérielle, 2 fois par semaine, et de signaler tout changement important à un professionnel de la santé.
- Prévenir le patient que le bisoprolol peut parfois provoquer de la somnolence.
- Recommander au patient de changer lentement de position pour réduire le risque d'hypotension orthostatique.
- Expliquer au patient qu'il doit éviter de prendre en même temps des médicaments en vente libre, particulièrement des préparations contre le rhume ou des produits naturels, sans avoir consulté au préalable un professionnel de la santé. Le prévenir qu'il devrait également éviter de consommer des quantités excessives de café, de thé ou de boissons de type cola.
- Recommander au patient diabétique de suivre de près sa glycémie, particulièrement en cas de faiblesse, de malaise, d'irritabilité ou de fatigue. Cependant, le bisoprolol ne bloque pas la transpiration et les étourdissements qui sont des signes d'hypoglycémie.
- Recommander au patient de signaler à un professionnel de la santé les symptômes suivants: ralentissement du pouls, difficultés respiratoires, respiration sifflante, mains et pieds froids, étourdissements, sensation de tête légère, confusion, dépression, rash, fièvre, maux de gorge, saignements ou ecchymoses inhabituels.
- Conseiller au patient d'informer tous les professionnels de la santé de son traitement médicamenteux avant de se soumettre à une intervention chirurgicale ou à un autre traitement.
- Conseiller au patient de porter sur lui en tout temps une pièce d'identité où sont inscrits son problème de santé et son traitement.

B

Hypertension: Inciter le patient à appliquer des mesures non pharmacologiques pour favoriser l'abaissement de la pression artérielle: perdre du poids, consommer moins de sel, diminuer le stress, faire régulièrement de l'exercice, boire de l'alcool avec modération et cesser de fumer. Le prévenir que le médicament stabilise la pression artérielle, mais ne guérit pas l'hypertension.

VÉRIFICATION DE L'EFFICACITÉ THÉRAPEUTIQUE

L'efficacité du traitement peut être démontrée par: l'abaissement de la pression artérielle.

BIVALIRUDINE

Angiomax

CLASSIFICATION:

Anticoagulant (inhibiteur de la thrombine)

Grossesse – catégorie B

INDICATIONS

Anticoagulothérapie chez les patients soumis à une intervention coronarienne percutanée (ICP) ■ Patients soumis à une ICP, atteints d'une thrombopénie induite par l'héparine ou à risque pour ce trouble ■ L'innocuité et l'efficacité n'ont pas été établies chez les patients souffrant de syndrome coronarien aigu qui n'ont pas subi d'ICP.

MÉCANISME D'ACTION

Inhibition spécifique et réversible de la thrombine par liaison à ses sites récepteurs. L'inhibition de la thrombine prévient: l'activation des facteurs V, VIII et XIII ■ la transformation du fibrinogène en fibrine ■ l'adhérence et l'agrégation plaquettaires. ***Effets thérapeutiques:*** Diminution des complications ischémiques chez les patients soumis à une ICP (décès, IM, besoin urgent de recourir à des procédés de revascularisation).

PHARMACOCINÉTIQUE

Absorption: Biodisponibilité à 100 % (IV).

Distribution: Inconnue.

Métabolisme et excrétion: L'élimination du plasma se fait par des mécanismes rénaux combinés à une dégradation protéolytique.

Demi-vie: 25 min (prolongée en cas d'insuffisance rénale).

Profil temps-action (effet anticoagulant)

	DÉBUT D'ACTION	PIC	DURÉE
IV	immédiat	inconnu	1-2 h

CONTRE-INDICATIONS, PRÉCAUTIONS ET MISES EN GARDE

Contre-indications: Hypersensibilité ■ Hémorragie active impossible à réprimer ■ Troubles majeurs de coagulation sanguine ■ Ulcère gastrique ou duodénal grave ■ Hémorragie cérébrale ■ Traumatisme cérébrospinal grave ■ Endocardite bactérienne ■ Hypertension grave non maîtrisée ■ Rétinopathie diabétique ou hémorragique ■ Anesthésie rachidienne ou épidurale proximales.

Précautions et mises en garde: Présence de toute maladie associée à un risque accru de saignements ■ Usage concomitant d'autres inhibiteurs de l'agrégation plaquettaire (l'innocuité de l'agent n'a pas été établie) ■ Brachythérapie (l'efficacité de l'agent n'a pas été établie) ■ Insuffisance rénale (il est recommandé de réduire la vitesse de la perfusion si la Cl_{Cr} < 60 mL/min) ■ **OBST., PÉD.**: Allaitement ou enfants (l'innocuité de l'agent n'a pas été établie); grossesse (n'administrer qu'en cas de besoin incontestable) ■ **GÉR.**: On a signalé une incidence accrue des hémorragies.

RÉACTIONS INDÉSIRABLES ET EFFETS SECONDAIRES

SNC: céphalées, anxiété, insomnie, nervosité.

CV: hypotension, bradycardie, hypertension.

GI: nausées, douleurs abdominales, dyspepsie, vomissements.

Hémat.: SAIGNEMENTS.

Locaux: douleurs au point d'injection.

Loc.: douleurs dorsales.

Divers: douleurs, fièvre, douleurs pelviennes.

INTERACTIONS

Médicament-médicament: Risque accru de saignements en cas d'usage concomitant d'**abciximab**, de **tirofiban**, d'**eptifibatide**, d'**héparine**, d'**héparine à faible poids moléculaire** ou d'**héparinoïdes**, de **clopidogrel**, de **ticlopidine**, de **thrombolytiques**, de **warfarine** ou de tout autre **médicament qui inhibe la coagulation**.

Médicament-produits naturels: Risque accru de saignements en cas de consommation concomitante d'**arnica**, de **camomille**, de **clou de girofle**, de **dong quai**, de **grande camomille**, d'**ail**, de **gingembre**, de **ginkgo**, de **ginseng** et **autres**.

VOIES D'ADMINISTRATION ET POSOLOGIE

- **IV (adultes):** De 0,75 à 1 mg/kg, sous forme d'injection en bolus, suivie d'une perfusion de 4 heures, à une vitesse de 1,7 à 2,5 mg/kg/h. Cette perfusion peut être suivie par une autre de 0,2 mg/kg/h, qui peut durer jusqu'à 20 heures. Le traitement doit être commencé avant l'ICP et administré en association avec de l'aspirine.

Insuffisance rénale

- **IV (adultes):** *Cl_{CR} de 30 à 59 mL/min* – Réduire la vitesse de perfusion à 1,75 mg/kg/h; *Cl_{CR} de 10 à 29 mL/min* – Réduire la vitesse de perfusion à 1 mg/kg/h. *Patients ayant besoin de dialyse (hors dialyse)* – Réduire la vitesse de perfusion à 0,25 mg/kg/h. Le temps de coagulation activée doit être mesuré chez tous les insuffisants rénaux.

PRÉSENTATION

Poudre pour injection (à reconstituer): 250 mg/fiole[Pr].

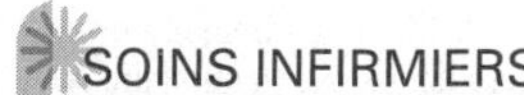

SOINS INFIRMIERS

ÉVALUATION DE LA SITUATION

- Rester à l'affût des saignements. Les plus fréquents sont les suintements des points d'accès artériel nécessaires au cathétérisme cardiaque. Réduire le recours aux ponctions artérielles ou veineuses, aux injections IM, aux sondes urinaires, à l'intubation nasotrachéale et nasogastrique. Éviter les points d'accès IV non compressibles. Si le saignement ne peut être arrêté par pression, cesser l'administration de la bivalirudine immédiatement.
- Prendre les signes vitaux. L'agent peut provoquer la bradycardie, l'hypertension ou l'hypotension. Une chute inexpliquée de la pression artérielle peut être un indice d'hémorragie.
- ***Tests de laboratoire:*** Noter les concentrations d'hémoglobine, l'hématocrite et le nombre de plaquettes avant le traitement par la bivalirudine et à intervalles réguliers pendant toute sa durée. L'agent peut faire chuter les concentrations d'hémoglobine et l'hématocrite. Une chute inexpliquée de l'hématocrite peut être un indice d'hémorragie.
- Mesurer le TCA à intervalles réguliers chez les insuffisants rénaux.

DIAGNOSTICS INFIRMIERS POSSIBLES

- Irrigation tissulaire inefficace (Indications).

INTERVENTIONS INFIRMIÈRES

- Administrer la perfusion juste avant l'ICP, en association avec de l'aspirine, à raison de 300 à 325 mg/jour. Ne pas administrer par voie IM.
- Ne pas administrer des solutions qui ont changé de couleur ou qui contiennent des particules. Jeter toute portion inutilisée. La solution doit être transparente à légèrement opalescente, d'incolore à jaune pâle.

IV directe et perfusion en 4 heures: Diluer avec 5 mL d'eau stérile pour injection par dose de 250 mg de bivalirudine et tourner la fiole jusqu'à dissolution complète de son contenu. Diluer de nouveau dans 50 mL de D5E ou de NaCl 0,9 % pour obtenir une concentration de 5 mg/mL. La fiole dont le contenu a été reconstitué est stable pendant 24 heures si elle est réfrigérée. La solution diluée à 5 mg/mL est stable pendant 24 heures à température ambiante. Consulter les directives de chaque fabricant avant de reconstituer la préparation.
Vitesse d'administration: Administrer la dose initiale en bolus; faire suivre par une perfusion en 4 heures, à une vitesse de 1,7 à 2,5 mg/kg/h.

Perfusion additionnelle allant jusqu'à 20 heures: Diluer en ajoutant 5 mL d'eau stérile pour injection par dose de 250 mg de bivalirudine et tourner la fiole jusqu'à dissolution complète de son contenu. Diluer de nouveau le contenu de la fiole dans 500 mL de D5E ou de NaCl 0,9 % pour obtenir une concentration de 0,5 mg/mL. La solution diluée à 0,5 mg/mL est stable pendant 24 heures à la température ambiante. Consulter les directives de chaque fabricant avant de reconstituer la préparation.
Vitesse d'administration: Après la perfusion en 4 heures, on peut en administrer une autre, si besoin est, à une vitesse de 0,2 mg/kg/h, pendant un laps de temps pouvant aller jusqu'à 20 heures.

Compatibilité (tubulure en Y): abciximab ▪ adrénaline ▪ alfentanil ▪ amikacine ▪ aminophylline ▪ ampicilline ▪ ampicilline/sulbactam ▪ azithromycine ▪ aztréonam ▪ bumétanide ▪ butorphanol ▪ calcium, gluconate de ▪ céfazoline ▪ céfépime ▪ céfotaxime ▪ céfoxitine ▪ ceftazidime ▪ ceftriaxone ▪ céfuroxime ▪ cimétidine ▪ ciprofloxacine ▪ clindamycine ▪ dexaméthasone sodique, phosphate de ▪ digoxine ▪ diltiazem ▪ diphenhydramine ▪ dobutamine ▪ dopamine ▪ doxycycline ▪ dropéridol ▪ énalaprilate ▪ éphédrine ▪ époprosténol ▪ eptifibatide ▪ érythromycine ▪ esmolol ▪ famotidine ▪ fentanyl ▪ fluconazole ▪ furosémide ▪ gentamicine ▪ halopéridol ▪ héparine ▪ hydrocortisone ▪ hydromorphone ▪ inamrinone ▪ isoprotérénol ▪ labétalol ▪ lévofloxacine ▪ lidocaïne ▪ lorazépam ▪ magnésium, sulfate de ▪ mannitol ▪ mépéridine ▪ méthylprednisolone ▪ métoclopramide ▪ métronidazole ▪ midazolam

B

■ milrinone ■ morphine ■ nalbuphine ■ nitroglycérine ■ nitroprusside ■ noradrénaline ■ ofloxacine ■ phényléphrine ■ piperacilline ■ piperacilline/tazobactam ■ potassium, chlorure de ■ procaïnamide ■ prométhazine ■ ranitidine ■ sodium, bicarbonate de ■ sufentanil ■ théophylline ■ thiopental ■ ticarcilline ■ ticarcilline/clavulanate ■ tirofiban ■ tobramycine ■ triméthoprime/sulfaméthoxazole ■ vérapamil ■ warfarine.

Incompatibilité (tubulure en Y): alteplase ■ amiodarone ■ amphotéricine B ■ chlorpromazine ■ diazépam ■ rétéplase ■ streptokinase ■ vancomycine. Administrer par une tubulure séparée, sans mélanger avec d'autres médicaments.

ENSEIGNEMENT AU PATIENT ET À SES PROCHES

- Expliquer au patient le but de ce traitement.
- Inciter le patient à signaler immédiatement à un professionnel de la santé tout signe de saignement.

VÉRIFICATION DE L'EFFICACITÉ THÉRAPEUTIQUE

L'efficacité du traitement peut être démontrée par: la diminution des complications ischémiques chez les patients soumis à une ICP (décès, IM ou besoin urgent de recourir à une intervention de revascularisation). ✳

ALERTE CLINIQUE

BLÉOMYCINE

Blenoxane

CLASSIFICATION:

Antinéoplasique (antibiotique antitumoral)

Grossesse – catégorie D

INDICATIONS

Traitement des cancers suivants: lymphome ■ épithélioma malpighien ■ cancer des testicules (choriocarcinome, carcinome embryonnaire, tératocarcinome) ■ Traitement et prévention des récurrences des épanchements pleuraux malins (administration intrapleurale) ■ Autres tumeurs malignes: réponse favorable dans certains cas de cancer du rein et de sarcome des tissus mous.

MÉCANISME D'ACTION

Inhibition de la synthèse de l'ADN et de l'ARN. ***Effets thérapeutiques:*** Élimination des cellules à réplication rapide, particulièrement des cellules malignes.

PHARMACOCINÉTIQUE

Absorption: Bonne (IM et SC). L'agent est également absorbé à la suite de l'administration intrapleurale et intrapéritonéale.

Distribution: Le médicament se répartit dans tout l'organisme et se concentre dans la peau, les poumons, le péritoine, les reins et le système lymphatique.

Métabolisme et excrétion: De 60 à 70 % du médicament est excrété à l'état inchangé par les reins.

Demi-vie: 2 heures (prolongée en cas d'insuffisance rénale).

Profil temps-action (réponse tumorale)

	DÉBUT D'ACTION	PIC	DURÉE
IM, IV, SC	2 – 3 semaines	inconnu	inconnue

CONTRE-INDICATIONS, PRÉCAUTIONS ET MISES EN GARDE

Contre-indications: Hypersensibilité.

Précautions et mises en garde: Insuffisance rénale (réduire la dose si la Cl_{Cr} est < 40 mL/min) ■ Insuffisance pulmonaire ■ Maladie débilitante chronique non maligne ■ **GÉR.**: Risque accru de toxicité pulmonaire et de diminution de la fonction rénale ■ Femmes en âge de procréer ■ Grossesse ou allaitement.

RÉACTIONS INDÉSIRABLES ET EFFETS SECONDAIRES

SNC: comportement agressif, désorientation, faiblesse.

Resp.: FIBROSE PULMONAIRE, pneumopathie inflammatoire.

CV: hypotension, vasoconstriction périphérique.

GI: anorexie, nausées, stomatite, vomissements, toxicité hépatique.

Tég.: hyperpigmentation, toxicité mucocutanée, alopécie, érythème, rash, urticaire, vésication.

Hémat.: anémie, leucopénie, thrombopénie.

Locaux: douleur au siège de la tumeur, phlébite au point d'injection IV.

Métab.: perte de poids.

Divers: RÉACTIONS IDIOSYNCRASIQUES, RÉACTIONS ANAPHYLACTIQUES, frissons, fièvre.

INTERACTIONS

Médicament-médicament: La **radiothérapie** et les autres **agents antinéoplasiques**, administrés en concomitance, peuvent accroître la toxicité hématologique ■ L'administration concomitante de **cisplatine** diminue l'élimination de la bléomycine et peut en augmenter la toxicité ■ L'administration en concomitance d'autres **agents antinéoplasiques** ou d'une **radiothérapie** thoracique peut augmenter le risque de toxicité pulmonaire

■ L'**anesthésie générale** augmente le risque de toxicité pulmonaire ■ Risque accru d'apparition du syndrome de Raynaud, si la bléomycine est administrée en association avec la **vinblastine**.

VOIES D'ADMINISTRATION ET POSOLOGIE

Les patients souffrant de lymphome devraient recevoir initialement 2 doses-test de 2 unités ou moins.

- **IV, IM, SC (adultes et enfants)**: Initialement, de 0,25 à 0,5 unités/kg (de 10 à 20 unités/m^2), 1 ou 2 fois par semaine. Si la réponse est satisfaisante, on peut administrer des doses d'entretien plus faibles (1 unité par jour ou 5 unités par semaine par voie IV ou IM).
- **Voie intrapleurale (adultes)**: 60 unités, instillées par une tubulure qu'on laissera en place pendant 4 heures; la retirer par la suite.

PRÉSENTATION

Solution pour injection: 15 unités/fiole[Pr].

SOINS INFIRMIERS

ÉVALUATION DE LA SITUATION

- Mesurer les signes vitaux avant le traitement et à intervalles fréquents pendant toute sa durée.
- Suivre de près la fièvre et les frissons qui peuvent se manifester de 3 à 6 heures après l'administration de la bléomycine et durer de 4 à 12 heures.
- OBSERVER LE PATIENT À LA RECHERCHE DE RÉACTIONS ANAPHYLACTIQUES (FIÈVRE, FRISSONS, HYPOTENSION, RESPIRATION SIFFLANTE) ET IDIOSYNCRASIQUES (CONFUSION, HYPOTENSION, FIÈVRE, FRISSONS, RESPIRATION SIFFLANTE). Garder les médicaments et le matériel de réanimation à portée de la main. Les patients souffrant de lymphome sont particulièrement prédisposés à des réactions idiosyncrasiques qui peuvent se manifester immédiatement ou plusieurs heures après le traitement, habituellement après l'administration de la première ou de la deuxième dose.
- Suivre de près la fonction respiratoire pour déceler la dyspnée, les râles ou les crépitations. Des radiographies pulmonaires devraient être effectuées avant le traitement et à intervalles réguliers pendant toute sa durée. La toxicité pulmonaire survient principalement chez les personnes âgées (de 70 ans ou plus) ayant reçu une dose supérieure ou égale à 400 unités ou, à des doses plus faibles, chez les patients ayant également reçu d'autres agents antinéoplasiques ou ayant subi une radiothérapie thoracique. Cette toxicité peut se manifester de 4 à 10 semaines après la fin du traitement. En cas de toxicité pulmonaire, arrêter définitivement le traitement par la bléomycine.
- Suivre de près les nausées, les vomissements et l'appétit du patient. Le peser toutes les semaines. Modifier l'alimentation selon sa tolérance. On peut administrer un antiémétique avant le traitement.

Tests de laboratoire:

- NOTER LA NUMÉRATION GLOBULAIRE AVANT LE TRAITEMENT ET À INTERVALLES RÉGULIERS PENDANT TOUTE SA DURÉE. LA BLÉOMYCINE PEUT PROVOQUER LA THROMBOPÉNIE ET LA LEUCOPÉNIE (LE NADIR EST ATTEINT APRÈS 12 JOURS; LES VALEURS INITIALES SE RÉTABLISSENT VERS LE 17e JOUR).
- Noter l'état des fonctions rénale et hépatique avant le traitement et à intervalles réguliers pendant toute sa durée.

DIAGNOSTICS INFIRMIERS POSSIBLES

- Risque d'accident (Effets secondaires).
- Image corporelle perturbée (Effets secondaires).
- Connaissances insuffisantes sur le traitement médicamenteux (Enseignement au patient et à ses proches).

INTERVENTIONS INFIRMIÈRES

ALERTE CLINIQUE: DES DÉCÈS SONT SURVENUS LORS DE CERTAINES CHIMIOTHÉRAPIES. AVANT D'ADMINISTRER L'AGENT, CLARIFIER TOUS LES POINTS AMBIGUS. VÉRIFIER LA LIMITE DES DOSES UNITAIRES ET QUOTIDIENNES AINSI QUE LA DOSE À ADMINISTRER PENDANT LE TRAITEMENT. DEMANDER À UN AUTRE PROFESSIONNEL DE LA SANTÉ DE VÉRIFIER UNE FOIS DE PLUS L'ORDONNANCE D'ORIGINE, LES CALCULS ET LE RÉGLAGE DE LA POMPE À PERFUSION.

- Préparer les solutions sous une hotte à flux laminaire. Porter des vêtements protecteurs, des gants et un masque pendant la manipulation de ce médicament. Mettre au rebut le matériel dans les contenants réservés à cet usage (voir l'annexe H).
- Les patients souffrant de lymphome devraient recevoir une dose-test de 1 ou de 2 unités, de 2 à 4 heures avant le début du traitement. Suivre de près ces patients pour déceler les réactions anaphylactiques. Certains patients peuvent présenter une réaction au traitement même s'ils n'ont pas réagi à la dose-test.
- Un prétraitement par l'acétaminophène, des corticostéroïdes et la diphenhydramine peut diminuer la fièvre induite par le médicament et le risque d'anaphylaxie.
- La solution reconstituée est stable pendant 48 heures si elle est réfrigérée. Consulter les directives de

B

chaque fabricant avant de reconstituer la préparation.

IM, SC: Diluer le contenu de la fiole avec 1 à 5 mL d'eau stérile pour injection, de solution de NaCl 0,9 % ou d'eau bactériostatique pour injection. Ne pas reconstituer la solution destinée aux nouveau-nés avec des diluants contenant de l'alcool benzylique.

IV directe: Reconstituer le contenu d'une fiole de 15 unités avec au moins 5 mL de solution de NaCl 0,9 %.

Vitesse d'administration: Administrer le médicament lentement pendant 10 minutes.

Associations compatibles dans la même seringue: cisplatine ▪ cyclophosphamide ▪ doxorubicine ▪ dropéridol ▪ fluorouracile ▪ furosémide ▪ héparine ▪ leucovorine calcique ▪ méthotrexate ▪ métoclopramide ▪ mitomycine ▪ vinblastine ▪ vincristine.

Compatibilité (tubulure en Y): allopurinol ▪ amifostine ▪ aztréonam ▪ céfépime ▪ cisplatine ▪ cyclophosphamide ▪ doxorubicine ▪ dropéridol ▪ filgrastim ▪ fludarabine ▪ fluorouracile ▪ granisétron ▪ héparine ▪ leucovorine calcique ▪ melphalan ▪ méthotrexate ▪ métoclopramide ▪ mitomycine ▪ ondansétron ▪ paclitaxel ▪ péracilline/tazobactam ▪ sargramostim ▪ téniposide ▪ thiotépa ▪ vinblastine ▪ vincristine ▪ vinorelbine.

Voie intrapleurale:

- Dissoudre 60 unités dans 50 à 100 mL d'une solution de NaCl 0,9 %.
- Le médecin peut administrer le médicament par une sonde introduite par thoracotomie. Aider le patient à se placer dans la position recommandée.

ENSEIGNEMENT AU PATIENT ET À SES PROCHES

- Conseiller au patient de signaler à un professionnel de la santé les symptômes suivants: fièvre, frissons, respiration sifflante, évanouissements, diaphorèse, essoufflements, nausées et vomissements prolongés ou aphtes buccaux.
- Inciter le patient à ne pas fumer pour ne pas aggraver la toxicité pulmonaire.
- Expliquer au patient que la toxicité cutanée peut se manifester sous forme d'hypersensibilité de la peau ou d'hyperpigmentation (particulièrement dans les plis cutanés et les régions irritées), de rash et d'épaississement de la peau.
- Recommander au patient d'examiner ses muqueuses buccales pour déceler l'érythème et les aphtes. En cas d'aphtes, lui conseiller de remplacer la brosse à dents par une brosse-éponge et de se rincer la bouche avec de l'eau après avoir bu ou mangé. L'administration d'analgésiques opioïdes peut s'avérer nécessaire si les douleurs empêchent le patient de manger.
- Expliquer au patient qu'il risque de perdre ses cheveux. Explorer avec lui les stratégies lui permettant de s'adapter à ce changement.
- Inciter la patiente à prendre des mesures contraceptives.
- Expliquer au patient qu'il ne doit pas se faire vacciner sans recommandation expresse d'un professionnel de la santé.
- Insister sur la nécessité de se soumettre à des tests de laboratoire réguliers permettant de déceler les effets secondaires du médicament.

VÉRIFICATION DE L'EFFICACITÉ THÉRAPEUTIQUE

L'efficacité du traitement peut être démontrée par: la diminution de la taille de la tumeur sans signe d'hypersensibilité ni de toxicité pulmonaire. ✳

BROMOCRIPTINE

Apo-Bromocriptine, Dom-Bromocriptine, Parlodel, PMS-Bromocriptine

CLASSIFICATION:

Antiparkinsonien (agoniste de la dopamine), inhibiteur de la prolactine, inhibiteur de l'hormone de croissance en présence d'acromégalie

Grossesse – catégorie B

INDICATIONS

Adjuvant de la lévodopa dans le traitement de la maladie de Parkinson ▪ Galactorrhée avec ou sans aménorrhée imputable à une hyperprolactinémie ▪ Troubles du cycle menstruel prolactinodépendants et stérilité (p. ex., insuffisance ovulatoire, phase lutéale courte) ▪ Hypogonadisme masculin prolactinodépendant ▪ Traitement de l'acromégalie en monothérapie ou en traitement d'appoint ▪ Traitement des adénomes à prolactine. **Usages non approuvés**: Traitement du syndrome malin des neuroleptiques.

MÉCANISME D'ACTION

Agoniste de la dopamine, par stimulation directe des récepteurs dopaminergiques situés dans le SNC ▪ Inhibition de la libération et de la synthèse de la prolactine par action directe sur les cellules sécrétrices de l'antéhypophyse. ***Effets thérapeutiques:*** Soulagement de la rigidité et des tremblements qui caractérisent la maladie de Parkinson ▪ Rétablissement de la fécondité chez les femmes souffrant d'hyperprolactinémie ▪

Diminution des sécrétions de somatotrophine en cas d'acromégalie.

PHARMACOCINÉTIQUE

Absorption: Faible (30 % PO).
Distribution: Inconnue.
Métabolisme et excrétion: Métabolisme hépatique.
Demi-vie: Biphasique – phase initiale, de 4 à 4,5 heures, phase terminale, de 45 à 50 heures.

Profil temps-action (suppression des divers paramètres)

	Début d'action	Pic	Durée
PO†	30 - 90 min	1 - 2 h	8 - 12 h
PO‡	2 h	8 h	24 h
PO§	1 - 2 h	4 - 8 semaines¶	4 - 8 h

† Effet sur les symptômes parkinsoniens.
‡ Effet sur les concentrations sériques de prolactine.
§ Effet sur la somatotrophine.
¶ Pendant un traitement prolongé.

CONTRE-INDICATIONS, PRÉCAUTIONS ET MISES EN GARDE

Contre-indications: Hypersensibilité à la bromocriptine, aux alcaloïdes de l'ergot de seigle ou aux bisulfites ■ Hypertension non maîtrisée, troubles hypertensifs gravidiques (comme l'éclampsie), hypertension du post-partum et de la période puerpérale ■ Maladie cardiovasculaire ou maladie vasculaire périphérique graves ■ Antécédents de troubles psychiques graves.
Précautions et mises en garde: Cardiopathie ■ Troubles mentaux ■ Risque de rétablissement de la fécondité (des mesures contraceptives supplémentaires sont conseillées si une grossesse n'est pas souhaitée) ■ Insuffisance rénale ou hépatique grave (l'innocuité et l'efficacité du médicament n'ont pas été établies) ■ Risque d'hypotension ou d'hypotension orthostatique; la prudence est de mise lors de l'utilisation de ce médicament en association avec des médicaments hypotenseurs ■ Grossesse et enfants < 15 ans (l'innocuité du médicament n'a pas été établie) ■ Allaitement.

RÉACTIONS INDÉSIRABLES ET EFFETS SECONDAIRES

SNC: <u>étourdissements</u>, confusion, somnolence, hallucinations, céphalées, insomnie, cauchemars.
ORLO: sensation de brûlure oculaire, congestion nasale, troubles visuels.
Resp.: épanchement pleural, infiltrats pulmonaires.
CV: infarctus du myocarde, <u>hypotension</u>.
GI: <u>nausées</u>, douleurs abdominales, anorexie, sécheresse de la bouche (xérostomie), goût métallique, vomissements.
Tég.: urticaire.
Loc.: crampes dans les jambes.
Divers: angiospasme digital (acromégalie seulement).

B

INTERACTIONS

Médicament-médicament: Effets hypotenseurs additifs, lors de l'administration concomitante d'**antihypertenseurs** ■ Effets dépressifs additifs sur le SNC, lors de l'administration concomitante d'**antihistaminiques**, d'**analgésiques opioïdes** et d'**hypnosédatifs** ou lors de l'ingestion d'**alcool** ■ L'utilisation concomitante d'**antibiotiques macrolides** ou d'**octréotide** peut augmenter les concentrations plasmatiques de bromocriptine ■ La **dompéridone** peut s'opposer à l'effet thérapeutique de la bromocriptine ■ Effets neurologiques additifs lors de l'administration concomitante de **lévodopa** ■ Les effets de la bromocriptine sur les concentrations de prolactine peuvent être contrecarrés par les **phénothiazines**, l'**halopéridol**, la **méthyldopa**, les **antidépresseurs tricycliques** et la **réserpine**.

VOIES D'ADMINISTRATION ET POSOLOGIE

La bromocriptine doit toujours être prise avec des aliments. Suivant l'indication, il est recommandé d'administrer la première dose au coucher, avec des aliments, pour déterminer si le patient tolère le médicament.

Syndrome parkinsonien

- **PO (adultes)**: 1,25 mg, 1 ou 2 fois par jour; on peut augmenter la dose par paliers de 2,5 mg par jour, à intervalles de 2 à 4 semaines. La dose maximale recommandée par le fabricant est de 40 mg par jour. Il pourrait être nécessaire de diminuer graduellement la dose de lévodopa.

Galactorrhée avec ou sans aménorrhée imputable à une hyperprolactinémie

- **PO (adultes)**: De 1,25 à 2,5 mg au coucher, avec des aliments, pour déterminer si la patiente tolère le médicament. On doit ensuite augmenter graduellement la dose après 2 ou 3 jours pour la porter à 2,5 mg, 2 fois/jour, à prendre pendant les repas. Au besoin, on peut administrer 2,5 mg, 3 fois/jour.

Troubles du cycle menstruel prolactinodépendants et infertilité

- **PO (adultes)**: De 1,25 à 2,5 mg au coucher, avec des aliments, pour déterminer si la patiente tolère le médicament. Augmenter la dose graduellement après 2 ou 3 jours pour la porter à 1 comprimé, 2 fois/jour, à prendre pendant les repas. Au besoin, on peut administrer 2,5 mg, 3 fois/jour.

Hypogonadisme masculin prolactinodépendant

- **PO (adultes)**: De 1,25 à 2,5 mg au coucher avec des aliments, pour déterminer si le patient tolère le

B

médicament. Augmenter la dose graduellement après 2 ou 3 jours pour atteindre 2,5 mg, 2 fois/jour, à prendre pendant les repas. Au besoin, on peut administrer 2,5 mg, 3 fois/jour.

Acromégalie

- **PO (adultes)**: De 1,25 à 2,5 mg au coucher, avec des aliments, pour déterminer si le patient tolère le médicament. Suivant la réponse du patient, on doit ensuite augmenter graduellement la dose pendant 2 à 4 semaines pour atteindre de 10 à 20 mg par jour, à prendre pendant les repas. Il est recommandé de répartir une dose quotidienne de 20 mg en 4 prises égales.

Adénomes hypophysaires à prolactine

- **PO (adultes)**: 1,25 mg, 2 ou 3 fois par jour; on peut augmenter graduellement la dose pendant plusieurs semaines (écart posologique: de 2,5 à 20 mg/jour).

PRÉSENTATION (version générique disponible)

Comprimés: 2,5 mg^Pr ▪ **Gélules**: 5 mg^Pr.

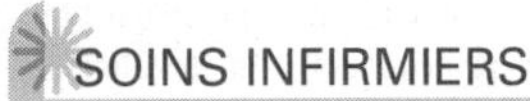

SOINS INFIRMIERS

ÉVALUATION DE LA SITUATION

- Rester à l'affût d'une allergie aux dérivés de l'ergot de seigle.
- Mesurer la pression artérielle avant le traitement et à intervalles réguliers pendant toute sa durée. Inciter le patient à rester couché au cours de l'administration de la première dose de bromocriptine et plusieurs heures après, en raison du risque d'hypotension grave. Suivre rigoureusement les déplacements et les transferts du patient pendant le traitement initial pour prévenir les accidents dus à l'hypotension.

Maladie de Parkinson: Observer le patient, avant le traitement et pendant toute sa durée, à la recherche des symptômes parkinsoniens suivants: agitation ou désir incessant de bouger, rigidité, tremblements, mouvements d'émiettement, faciès figé, démarche traînante, spasmes musculaires, mouvements de torsion, troubles d'élocution ou de déglutition, perte d'équilibre.

Acromégalie: On devrait effectuer des examens physiques à intervalles réguliers, pendant toute la durée du traitement, qui devraient englober la mesure de la taille de l'annulaire, de l'épaisseur du coussinet plantaire et du volume des tissus mous.

Hyperprolactinémie: On devrait évaluer la selle turcique, par tomodensitométrie (scanographie) ou par résonance magnétique nucléaire (RMN), avant le traitement et annuellement, par la suite.

Syndrome malin des neuroleptiques: Rester à l'affût des symptômes suivants: fièvre, détresse respiratoire, tachycardie, convulsions, diaphorèse, hypertension, hypotension, pâleur, fatigue.

Tests de laboratoire:

- Le médicament peut entraîner l'élévation de l'urée et des concentrations sériques d'ALT, d'AST, de créatine-kinase, de phosphatase alcaline et d'acide urique. Ces élévations sont habituellement passagères et n'ont aucun effet sur le plan clinique.
- *Stérilité chez la femme:* Mesurer, avant d'amorcer le traitement, les concentrations sériques de prolactine et évaluer le fonctionnement de l'hypophyse antérieure. Suivre de près l'ovulation tout au long du traitement.
- *Acromégalie:* Mesurer à intervalles réguliers tout au long du traitement les concentrations sériques de somatotrophine et du facteur de croissance analogue à l'insuline (IGF).
- *Hyperprolactinémie:* Pour déterminer l'efficacité du traitement, évaluer mensuellement les concentrations sériques de prolactine au cours du traitement initial, et, semestriellement, pendant le traitement d'entretien.

DIAGNOSTICS INFIRMIERS POSSIBLES

- Mobilité physique réduite (Indications).
- Risque d'accident (Indications, Effets secondaires).
- Connaissances insuffisantes sur le traitement médicamenteux (Enseignement au patient et à ses proches).

INTERVENTIONS INFIRMIÈRES

Directives générales: En traitement de la maladie de Parkinson, le médicament est souvent administré avec la lévodopa ou avec une association de carbidopa et de lévodopa.

PO: Administrer le médicament avec des aliments ou du lait afin de réduire l'irritation gastrique. Le patient peut croquer les comprimés s'il éprouve des difficultés de déglutition. Pour réduire les nausées, administrer le médicament au coucher.

ENSEIGNEMENT AU PATIENT ET À SES PROCHES

- Inciter le patient à suivre rigoureusement la posologie recommandée. S'il n'a pu prendre le médicament au moment habituel, il doit le prendre au moins 4 heures avant l'heure prévue pour la dose suivante; sinon il doit sauter cette dose. Le prévenir qu'il ne doit pas remplacer une dose manquée par une double dose.

- Prévenir le patient que la bromocriptine peut provoquer de la somnolence et des étourdissements. Lui conseiller de ne pas conduire et d'éviter les activités qui exigent sa vigilance jusqu'à ce qu'on ait la certitude que le médicament n'entraîne pas ces effets chez lui.
- Mettre en garde le patient contre la consommation concomitante d'alcool pendant le traitement.
- Conseiller au patient de prévenir immédiatement un professionnel de la santé si les signes suivants d'infarctus du myocarde se manifestent: douleurs thoraciques intenses, évanouissements, accélération de la fréquence cardiaque, sécrétion accrue de sueur, nausées et vomissements graves ou continus, nervosité, essoufflements, faiblesse, ou si les essoufflements s'aggravent, car le traitement prolongé peut augmenter le risque de formation d'infiltrats pulmonaires et d'épanchement pleural.
- Recommander à la patiente de s'informer auprès d'un professionnel de la santé au sujet d'une méthode de contraception non hormonale. L'inciter à prévenir immédiatement un professionnel de la santé si elle pense être enceinte.
- Insister sur l'importance des examens réguliers de suivi permettant de déterminer l'efficacité du traitement et de déceler les effets secondaires.

Stérilité: Conseiller à la patiente qui suit un traitement contre la stérilité de prendre tous les jours sa température basale afin de déterminer le moment de l'ovulation.

Tumeurs hypophysaires: Conseiller au patient qui reçoit la bromocriptine pour le traitement d'une tumeur hypophysaire de prévenir immédiatement un professionnel de la santé s'il note les signes suivants d'augmentation de la masse tumorale: vision trouble, céphalées soudaines, nausées graves et vomissements.

VÉRIFICATION DE L'EFFICACITÉ THÉRAPEUTIQUE

L'efficacité du traitement peut être démontrée par: la diminution des tremblements, de la rigidité et de la bradykinésie chez les patients atteints de la maladie de Parkinson ▪ l'amélioration de l'équilibre et de la démarche chez les patients atteints de la maladie de Parkinson ▪ la diminution de la galactorrhée chez les patientes souffrant d'hyperprolactinémie ▪ le rétablissement de cycles menstruels normaux et de la fécondité (chez les patientes souffrant d'aménorrhée et de galactorrhée, les règles reviennent habituellement dans les 6 à 8 semaines et la galactorrhée disparaît dans les 8 à 12 semaines qui suivent le début du traitement) ▪ la diminution des concentrations sériques de somatotrophine chez les patients atteints d'acromégalie ▪ la diminution des symptômes qui caractérisent le syndrome malin des neuroleptiques. ✳

BRONCHODILATATEURS (XANTHINES)

aminophylline
Phyllocontin

oxtriphylline
Apo-Oxtriphylline, Choledyl, PMS-Oxtriphylline

théophylline
Apo-Theo LA, Novo-Theophyl SR, Theolair, Uniphyl

CLASSIFICATION:
Bronchodilatateurs (xanthines)

Grossesse – catégories C

INDICATIONS

Traitement symptomatique de la bronchoconstriction réversible associée à l'asthme bronchique, à la bronchopneumonie chronique obstructive (BPCO), à la bronchite chronique et aux troubles bronchospastiques connexes. **Usages non approuvés**: Myocardiotonique et analeptique respiratoire pour traiter l'apnée du nouveau-né.

MÉCANISME D'ACTION

Inhibition de la phosphodiestérase, ce qui mène à des concentrations élevées d'adénosine monophosphate cyclique (AMPc) dans les tissus. Les concentrations élevées d'AMPc entraînent: la bronchodilatation ▪ la stimulation du SNC ▪ des effets inotropes et chronotropes positifs ▪ la diurèse ▪ des sécrétions d'acide gastrique ▪ L'aminophylline est un sel de théophylline; après être administrée, elle libère de la théophylline libre. ***Effets thérapeutiques:*** Bronchodilatation.

PHARMACOCINÉTIQUE

Absorption: Après l'administration, l'aminophylline et l'oxtriphylline libèrent de la théophylline. *Aminophylline* – bonne (PO); l'absorption des préparations à libération prolongée est lente mais complète. *Oxtriphylline* – bonne (PO). *Théophylline* – bonne (PO); l'absorption des préparations à libération prolongée est lente mais complète.

Distribution: *Aminophylline* et *oxtriphylline* – ces 2 médicaments se répartissent dans tout l'organisme sous forme de théophylline; ils traversent la barrière placentaire et on les retrouve dans le lait maternel à une concentration correspondant à 70 % des concentrations plasmatiques; ils ne se déposent pas dans les tissus adipeux. *Théophylline* – le médicament se répartit dans tout l'organisme; il traverse la barrière placentaire et on le retrouve dans le lait maternel à une concentration correspondant à 70 % des concentrations plasmatiques; il ne se dépose pas dans les tissus adipeux.

Métabolisme et excrétion: *Aminophylline, oxtriphylline* et *théophylline* – l'aminophylline et l'oxtriphylline sont transformées en théophylline; la théophylline est majoritairement métabolisée par le foie (90 %) et transformée en caféine, qui peut s'accumuler chez les nouveau-nés; les métabolites sont excrétés par les reins; 10 % excrété à l'état inchangé par les reins.

Demi-vie: *Théophylline* – de 3 à 13 heures (prolongée chez les personnes > 60 ans, les nouveau-nés et les patients souffrant d'insuffisance cardiaque ou de maladie hépatique; écourtée chez les fumeurs et les enfants).

Profil temps-action (bronchodilatation)

	DÉBUT D'ACTION†	PIC	DURÉE
Aminophylline PO	15 - 60 min	1 - 2 h	6 - 8 h
Aminophylline à libération prolongée, PO	inconnu	4 - 7 h	8 - 12 h
Aminophylline IV	rapide	fin de la perfusion	6 - 8 h
Oxtriphylline PO – préparations liquides	inconnu	1 h	inconnue
Oxtriphylline PO – comprimés	15 - 60 min	5 h	6 - 8 h
Théophylline PO	rapide	1 - 2 h	6 h
Théophylline à libération prolongée, PO	retardé	4 - 8 h	8 - 24 h
Théophylline IV	rapide	fin de la perfusion	6 - 8 h

† Dans la mesure où une dose d'attaque a été administrée et les concentrations sanguines à l'état d'équilibre ont été atteintes.

CONTRE-INDICATIONS, PRÉCAUTIONS ET MISES EN GARDE

Contre-indications: Arythmies non maîtrisées ■ Hypersensibilité aux xanthines ■ Maladie évolutive ou symptomatique des artères coronaires (lorsque le médecin estime qu'une stimulation cardiaque pourrait nuire au patient) ■ **PÉD.**: Enfants < 10 ans (oxtriphylline).

Précautions et mises en garde: **GÉR.**: Il est recommandé de réduire la dose chez les personnes âgées > 60 ans ■ Insuffisance cardiaque ou maladie hépatique (réduire la dose) ■ Patients obèses (la dose devrait être calculée selon le poids corporel idéal) ■ **OBST.**: Il existe des précédents d'usage sans augmentation du risque de malformations fœtales ■ Ulcère gastroduodénal.

RÉACTIONS INDÉSIRABLES ET EFFETS SECONDAIRES

SNC: CONVULSIONS, anxiété, céphalées, insomnie.
CV: ARYTHMIES, tachycardie, angine, palpitations.
GI: nausées, vomissements, anorexie, crampes.
SN: tremblements.

INTERACTIONS

Médicament-médicament: Les **amines sympathomimétiques**, administrées en concomitance, exercent des effets secondaires additifs sur l'appareil cardiovasculaire et le SNC ■ Les xanthines peuvent diminuer l'effet thérapeutique du **lithium** ■ La **nicotine** (cigarettes, gomme, timbre transdermique), les **amines sympathomimétiques**, les **barbituriques**, la **névirapine**, la **phénytoïne**, le **kétoconazole,** la **rifampine** et le **ritonavir** peuvent accélérer le métabolisme des xanthines et en diminuer l'efficacité ■ L'**érythromycine**, les **bêtabloquants**, les **bloqueurs des canaux calciques**, la **clarithromycine**, la **cimétidine**, le **vaccin antigrippal**, les **contraceptifs oraux**, les **corticostéroïdes**, le **disulfirame**, la **fluvoxamine**, les **interférons**, le **méthotrexate**, la **méxilétine**, le **thiabendazole**, certaines **fluoroquinolones** et des doses élevées d'**allopurinol** ralentissent le métabolisme des xanthines et peuvent entraîner une toxicité ■ L'administration concomitante d'**halothane** augmente le risque d'arythmies ■ L'**isoniazide**, la **carbamazépine** et les **diurétiques de l'anse** peuvent augmenter ou diminuer les concentrations de théophylline.

Médicament-aliments: La consommation régulière et excessive d'**aliments grillés sur le charbon de bois** peut diminuer l'efficacité des bronchodilatateurs ■ La consommation excessive d'**aliments** ou de **boissons** (**cola**, **café**, **chocolat**) **à base de xanthines** peut augmenter le risque d'effets secondaires au niveau de l'appareil cardiovasculaire ou du SNC.

Médicament-produits naturels: Les **produits à base de caféine** (**noix de cola**, **guarana**, **yerba maté**, **thé**, **café**) peuvent élever les concentrations sériques des xanthines et le risque d'effets secondaires au niveau de l'appareil cardiovasculaire ou du SNC ■ Le **millepertuis** diminue les concentrations sériques et l'efficacité des xanthines.

VOIES D'ADMINISTRATION ET POSOLOGIE

La posologie des bronchodilatateurs doit être déterminée d'après les concentrations sériques de théophylline. La dose d'attaque devrait être diminuée ou éliminée si une préparation à la théophylline a été administrée dans les 24 heures précédentes. L'aminophylline est composée de 85 % de théophylline, et l'oxtriphylline, de 65 %. Les produits à libération prolongée (à libération lente) peuvent être administrés toutes les 8 à 24 heures.

Aminophylline/théophylline

La posologie habituelle chez l'adulte se situe entre 400 et 900 mg par jour; la dose quotidienne totale peut être fractionnée et administrée, dans le cas de la préparation à libération prolongée, toutes les 12 à 24 heures. Les doses sont exprimées en mg de théophylline.

- **PO (adultes non fumeurs)**: *Dose initiale* – 400 mg/jour, en 3 ou 4 prises, à intervalles de 6 à 8 heures; *dose d'entretien* – de 10 à 14 mg/kg/jour ou 900 mg/jour.
- **PO (enfants de 12 à 16 ans ou jeunes adultes fumeurs)**: *Dose initiale* – 16 mg/kg/jour (au maximum: 400 mg/jour), en 3 ou 4 prises, à intervalles de 6 à 8 heures; *dose d'entretien* – de 13 à 18 mg/kg/jour, en 3 ou 4 prises à intervalles de 6 à 8 heures (au maximum: 900 mg/jour).
- **PO (enfants de 9 à 12 ans)**: *Dose initiale* – 16 mg/kg/jour (au maximum: 400 mg/jour), en 3 ou 4 prises, à intervalles de 6 à 8 heures; *dose d'entretien* – 16 mg/kg/jour, en 3 ou 4 prises, à intervalles de 6 à 8 heures (au maximum: 800 mg/jour).
- **PO (enfants de 1 à 9 ans)**: *Dose initiale* – 16 mg/kg/jour (au maximum: 400 mg/jour), en 3 ou 4 prises, à intervalles de 6 à 8 heures; *dose d'entretien* – de 20 à 24 mg/kg/jour, en 3 ou 4 prises, à intervalles de 6 à 8 heures.
- **IV (adultes non fumeurs)**: *Dose d'attaque* – 5 mg/kg, suivie d'une perfusion d'entretien, administrée à une vitesse de 0,6 mg/kg/h.
- **IV (adultes souffrant d'insuffisance cardiaque ou d'insuffisance hépatique)**: *Dose d'attaque* – 5 mg/kg, suivie d'une perfusion d'entretien, administrée à une vitesse de 0,21 mg/kg/h.
- **IV (personnes âgées et adultes présentant un cœur pulmonaire)**: *Dose d'attaque* – 5 mg/kg, suivie d'une perfusion d'entretien, administrée à une vitesse de 0,21 mg/kg/h.
- **IV (enfants de 9 à 12 ans ou jeunes adultes fumeurs)**: 5 mg/kg, suivie d'une perfusion d'entretien, administrée à une vitesse de 0,77 mg/kg/h.
- **IV (enfants de 1 an à 9 ans)**: 5 mg/kg, suivie d'une perfusion d'entretien, administrée à une vitesse de 0,85 à 1 mg/kg/h.
- **IV (enfants de 6 mois à 1 an)**: 5 mg/kg, suivie d'une perfusion d'entretien, administrée à une vitesse de 0,5 à 0,6 mg/kg/h.
- **IV (nouveau-nés de 6 semaines à 6 mois)**: 5 mg/kg, suivie d'une perfusion d'entretien, administrée à une vitesse de 0,43 mg/kg/h.
- **IV (nouveau-nés < 6 semaines)**: 5 mg/kg, suivie d'une perfusion d'entretien, administrée à une vitesse de 0,17 mg/kg/h.

Oxtriphylline

- **PO (adultes)**: *Dose initiale* – 200 mg (128 mg de théophylline), 4 fois par jour; *dose d'entretien* – de 800 à 1 200 mg (de 512 à 768 mg de théophylline), toutes les 6 à 8 heures.
- **PO (enfants de 10 à 14 ans)**: *Dose initiale* – de 100 à 200 mg (de 64 à 128 mg de théophylline), toutes les 6 à 8 heures, adapter selon les concentrations sanguines (dose moyenne: de 10 à 20 mg/kg/jour).

PRÉSENTATION

- **Aminophylline (version générique disponible)**
  Comprimés à libération prolongée: 225 mg^Pr^, 350 mg^Pr^ ■ **Solution pour injection**: 25 mg/mL^Pr^.
- **Oxtriphylline**
  Comprimés: 100 mg^Pr^, 200 mg^Pr^ et 300 mg^Pr^ ■ **Élixir**: 100 mg/5 mL^Pr^ ■ **En association avec**: guaifénésine (Choledyl^Pr^Expectorant).
- **Théophylline (version générique disponible)**
  Ce médicament est disponible en comprimés à libération prolongée, en sirop, en élixir, en solution pour injection de teneurs diverses. Voir la monographie de chacun des produits.

SOINS INFIRMIERS

ÉVALUATION DE LA SITUATION

- Mesurer la pression artérielle et le pouls, examiner la fonction respiratoire (fréquence des respirations, murmure vésiculaire, utilisation des muscles accessoires) avant le traitement et pendant toute sa durée. S'assurer que l'oxygénothérapie a été correctement amorcée en cas de crises d'asthme aiguës.
- Effectuer le bilan des ingesta et des excreta pour déceler une augmentation de la diurèse ou une surcharge liquidienne.
- CHEZ LES PATIENTS AYANT DES ANTÉCÉDENTS DE TROUBLES CARDIOVASCULAIRES, SUIVRE DE PRÈS LES DOULEURS THORACIQUES ET LES MODIFICATIONS DE L'ÉCG (CONTRACTIONS AURICULAIRES PRÉMATURÉES, TACHYCARDIE SUPRAVENTRICULAIRE, EXTRASYSTOLES VENTRICULAIRES, TACHYCARDIE VENTRICULAIRE). GARDER À PORTÉE DE LA MAIN LE MATÉRIEL DE RÉANIMATION.
- Suivre de près les résultats des tests de la fonction pulmonaire, avant le traitement et à intervalles réguliers pendant toute sa durée, afin de vérifier si le médicament agit efficacement chez les patients

B

souffrant de bronchite chronique ou d'emphysème.

Tests de laboratoire: Noter les concentrations des gaz du sang artériel, l'équilibre acidobasique et hydroélectrolytique chez les patients recevant le traitement par voie parentérale ou lorsque l'état du patient le dicte.

TOXICITÉ ET SURDOSAGE:

- Suivre les concentrations sériques de médicament à intervalles réguliers, particulièrement chez les patients ayant besoin de doses élevées ou d'un traitement intensif prolongé. Prélever un échantillon de sérum au moment du pic de l'absorption. On devrait noter les concentrations de pointe de 15 à 30 minutes après l'administration par voie IV de la dose d'attaque, de 12 à 24 heures après le début d'une perfusion continue, de 1 à 2 heures après l'administration des préparations à libération immédiate et de 4 à 12 heures après l'administration des préparations à libération prolongée. Les concentrations plasmatiques thérapeutiques se situent habituellement entre 55 et 110 μmol/L. La consommation de caféine peut entraîner une fausse élévation des concentrations sériques de théophylline.
- Suivre de près les symptômes suivants de toxicité médicamenteuse: anorexie, nausées, vomissements, crampes d'estomac, diarrhée, confusion, céphalées, agitation, bouffées vasomotrices, mictions fréquentes, insomnie, tachycardie, arythmies, convulsions. Si ces symptômes se manifestent, en informer sans délai le médecin ou un autre professionnel de la santé. La tachycardie, les arythmies ventriculaires ou les convulsions peuvent être les premiers signes de toxicité.

DIAGNOSTICS INFIRMIERS POSSIBLES

- Dégagement inefficace des voies respiratoires (Indications).
- Intolérance à l'activité (Indications).
- Connaissances insuffisantes sur le traitement médicamenteux (Enseignement au patient et à ses proches).

INTERVENTIONS INFIRMIÈRES

- Administrer le bronchodilatateur 24 heures sur 24, afin de maintenir des concentrations thérapeutiques dans le plasma. Les doses uniquotidiennes (Uniphyl^Pr) devraient être administrées en soirée.
- Ne pas réfrigérer les élixirs, les solutions, les sirops ou les suspensions, car des cristaux peuvent se former. Ces derniers devraient se dissoudre lorsque le liquide est réchauffé à la température ambiante.
- Attendre au moins de 4 à 6 heures après l'arrêt du traitement IV avant d'administrer la préparation orale à libération immédiate. Administrer la première dose de la préparation PO à libération prolongée au moment où l'on arrête le traitement IV.

PO: Administrer les préparations orales avec des aliments ou un grand verre d'eau pour réduire l'irritation gastro-intestinale. Les aliments ralentissent l'absorption du médicament, mais ne réduisent pas la quantité totale absorbée. Pour accélérer l'absorption du bronchodilatateur, on peut l'administrer 1 heure avant ou 2 heures après les repas. **PÉD.**: Utiliser un récipient gradué pour mesurer avec précision les doses de préparation liquide. LES COMPRIMÉS DOIVENT ÊTRE AVALÉS TELS QUELS; LES COMPRIMÉS À ENROBAGE ENTÉRIQUE OU À LIBÉRATION PROLONGÉE NE DOIVENT PAS ÊTRE ÉCRASÉS, CROQUÉS OU MÂCHÉS (LES COMPRIMÉS À LIBÉRATION PROLONGÉE SÉCABLES PEUVENT ÊTRE BRISÉS).

Aminophylline

IV: Le médicament peut être dilué dans une solution de D5%E, de D10%E, de D20%E, de NaCl 0,9 %, de NaCl 0,45 %, de D5%E/NaCl 0,9 %, de D5%E/NaCl 0,45 %, de D5%E/NaCl 0,25 % ou de solution de lactate de Ringer. La solution est stable pendant 48 heures à température ambiante. Consulter les directives du fabricant avant de diluer la préparation. ■ Ne pas administrer une solution qui a changé de couleur ou qui contient des précipités. Rincer la tubulure IV principale avant l'administration du médicament. ■ En cas d'extravasation, injecter localement de la procaïne à 1 % et appliquer de la chaleur afin de soulager la douleur et de favoriser la vasodilatation.

Dose d'attaque: Administrer cette dose pendant 20 à 30 minutes.

Vitesse d'administration: Ne pas dépasser un débit de 20 à 25 mg/min ou de 0,36 mg/kg/min chez les enfants. Administrer par une pompe à perfusion pour s'assurer que le patient reçoit la dose exacte. Une administration rapide peut entraîner les symptômes suivants: douleurs thoraciques, étourdissements, hypotension, tachypnée, bouffées vasomotrices, arythmies, réactions à la solution ou à la méthode d'administration utilisées (frissons, fièvre, rougeur, douleurs ou œdème au point d'injection).

Perfusion continue: La dose d'attaque est habituellement administrée dans un petit volume, suivie d'une perfusion continue, dans un plus grand volume.

Vitesse d'administration: Voir la section «Voies d'administration et posologie».

Associations compatibles dans la même seringue: héparine ■ métoclopramide.

Associations incompatibles dans la même seringue: doxapram.

Compatibilité (tubulure en Y): allopurinol ■ amifostine ■ amrinone ■ aztréonam ■ ceftazidime ■ cimétidine ■ cladribine ■ énalaprilate ■ esmolol ■ famotidine ■ filgrastim ■ fluconazole ■ fludarabine ■ foscarnet ■ gallium, nitrate de ■ granisétron ■ labétalol ■ melphalan ■ méropénem ■ morphine ■ netilmicine ■ paclitaxel ■ pancuronium ■ pipéracilline/tazobactam ■ potassium, chlorure de ■ propofol ■ ranitidine ■ sargramostim ■ tacrolimus ■ téniposide ■ thiotépa ■ tolazoline ■ vécuronium ■ vitamines du complexe B avec C.

Incompatibilité (tubulure en Y): amiodarone ■ ciprofloxacine ■ dobutamine ■ hydralazine ■ ondansétron ■ vinorelbine.

Incompatibilité en addition au soluté: Les additions au soluté ne sont pas recommandées en raison des adaptations posologiques fréquemment nécessaires et des incompatibilités.

Théophylline

Perfusion continue: La solution de théophylline et de dextrose à 5 %, destinée à l'administration IV, est emballée dans une surenveloppe étanche. Sortir le sac de l'emballage juste avant l'administration et le comprimer pour s'assurer qu'il ne fuit pas. Jeter toute solution qui n'est pas transparente. Consulter les directives du fabricant avant d'utiliser la préparation.

Dose d'attaque: Administrer cette dose pendant 20 à 30 minutes. Si le patient a reçu une autre forme de théophylline avant la dose d'attaque, il faut mesurer les concentrations sériques de médicament au préalable et réduire proportionnellement la dose d'attaque.

Vitesse d'administration: Ne pas dépasser un débit de 20 à 25 mg/min. Une administration rapide peut entraîner les symptômes suivants: douleurs thoraciques, étourdissements, hypotension, tachypnée, bouffées vasomotrices, arythmies, réactions à la solution ou à la méthode d'administration utilisée (frissons, fièvre, rougeur, douleurs ou œdème au point d'injection). La vitesse de perfusion peut être augmentée après 12 heures. Administrer par une pompe à perfusion pour s'assurer que le patient reçoit la dose exacte. Suivre continuellement l'ÉCG en raison des risques de tachyarythmies.

Compatibilité (tubulure en Y): acyclovir ■ ampicilline ■ ampicilline/sulbactam ■ aztréonam ■ céfazoline ■ céfotétane ■ ceftazidime ■ ceftriaxone ■ cimétidine ■ clindamycine ■ dexaméthasone ■ diltiazem ■ dobutamine ■ dopamine ■ doxycycline ■ érythromycine, lactobionate d' ■ famotidine ■ fluconazole ■ gentamicine ■ halopéridol ■ héparine ■ hydrocortisone sodique, succinate d' ■ lidocaïne ■ méthyldopa ■ méthylprednisolone sodique, succinate d' ■ métronidazole ■ midazolam ■ nafcilline ■ nitroglycérine ■ nitroprusside ■ pénicilline G potassique ■ pipéracilline ■ potassium, chlorure de ■ ranitidine ■ ticarcilline ■ ticarcilline/clavulanate ■ tobramycine ■ vancomycine.

Incompatibilité (tubulure en Y): heta-starch ■ phénytoïne.

Incompatibilité en addition au soluté: Les additions au soluté ne sont pas recommandées en raison des ajustements posologiques fréquemment nécessaires et des incompatibilités.

B

ENSEIGNEMENT AU PATIENT ET À SES PROCHES

- Expliquer au patient qu'il est important de ne prendre que la dose qui lui a été prescrite, aux heures prescrites. S'il n'a pu prendre le médicament au moment habituel, il doit le prendre dès que possible à moins que ce ne soit presque l'heure prévue pour la dose suivante.
- Inciter le patient à boire suffisamment de liquides (2 000 mL par jour, au minimum) pour diminuer la viscosité des sécrétions des voies respiratoires.
- Conseiller au patient de consulter un professionnel de la santé avant de prendre un médicament en vente libre pour traiter la toux, le rhume ou les difficultés respiratoires, en même temps que la théophylline. Ces médicaments peuvent intensifier les effets secondaires des bronchodilatateurs et déclencher des arythmies.
- Inciter le patient à ne pas fumer. Lui recommander d'informer un professionnel de la santé si l'usage qu'il fait du tabac change, car, dans un tel cas, il faudrait éventuellement modifier la posologie des bronchodilatateurs.
- Conseiller au patient de réduire sa consommation d'aliments ou de boissons à base de xanthines (cola, café, chocolat) et de ne pas manger tous les jours des aliments grillés sur le charbon de bois.
- Recommander au patient de ne pas changer de marque de médicament sans consulter un professionnel de la santé au préalable.
- Recommander au patient de prévenir immédiatement un professionnel de la santé si la dose habituelle de médicament ne produit pas les résultats escomptés, si les symptômes s'aggravent après le traitement ou si des effets toxiques se manifestent.
- Expliquer au patient qu'il est important d'effectuer un dosage des concentrations sériques à intervalles de 6 à 12 mois.

VÉRIFICATION DE L'EFFICACITÉ THÉRAPEUTIQUE

L'efficacité du traitement peut être démontrée par: une respiration plus facile ■ le dégagement des champs pulmonaires, vérifiable par auscultation ■ la stimulation du myocarde et des voies respiratoires, en cas d'apnée du nouveau-né.

B

BUDÉSONIDE,
voir Corticostéroïdes (inhalation), Corticostéroïdes (voie générale) et Corticostéroïdes (voie intranasale)

BUMÉTANIDE,
voir Diurétiques (de l'anse)

BUPIVACAÏNE,
voir Anesthésiques épiduraux à action locale

BUPROPION
Wellbutrin SR, Wellbutrin XL, Zyban

CLASSIFICATION:
Antidépresseur, aide antitabagique

Grossesse – catégorie B (risque durant le 3e trimestre; voir «Précautions et mises en garde»)

INDICATIONS
Soulagement symptomatique de la dépression (Wellbutrin) ■ Aide antitabagique, conjointement avec une modification du comportement (Zyban).

MÉCANISME D'ACTION
Diminution du recaptage de la dopamine par les neurones du SNC ■ Diminution du recaptage de la sérotonine et de la noradrénaline (action moindre que celle des antidépresseurs tricycliques). ***Effets thérapeutiques:*** Diminution des symptômes de dépression ■ Diminution de l'envie de fumer.

PHARMACOCINÉTIQUE
Absorption: Bonne (PO).

Distribution: Inconnue.

Métabolisme et excrétion: Métabolisme majoritairement hépatique. Une fraction du médicament est transformée en métabolites actifs.

Demi-vie: 14 heures (les métabolites actifs peuvent avoir une demi-vie plus longue).

Profil temps-action (effet antidépresseur)

	DÉBUT D'ACTION	PIC	DURÉE
PO	1 – 3 semaines	inconnu	inconnue

CONTRE-INDICATIONS, PRÉCAUTIONS ET MISES EN GARDE
Contre-indications: Hypersensibilité au bupropion ou à d'autres ingrédients de la préparation ■ Antécédents de convulsions, de boulimie et d'anorexie mentale ■ Administration concomitante de tout autre médicament contenant du bupropion ■ Traitement concomitant par les IMAO (attendre 14 jours entre l'arrêt de la prise de l'IMAO et le début du traitement par le bupropion, et vice versa) ■ Sevrage éthylique abrupt ou retrait soudain des benzodiazépines ou d'autres sédatifs.

Précautions et mises en garde: Antécédents de traumatisme crânien ■ Insuffisance rénale ou hépatique (il est recommandé de réduire la dose) ■ Infarctus du myocarde récent ■ La surveillance des idées suicidaires est conseillée chez tous les patients prenant ce médicament ■ **ADULTES ET ENFANTS**: Risque d'effets indésirables de type agitation grave, parallèlement à des blessures infligées à soi-même ou aux autres ■ **GÉR.**: Risque accru d'accumulation médicamenteuse; sensibilité accrue aux effets du médicament. Il est conseillé de commencer le traitement avec la plus faible dose recommandée (100 mg/jour) ■ État cardiovasculaire instable ■ **OBST.**: On n'a pas mené d'études adéquates chez la femme enceinte. N'administrer au cours de la grossesse que si les bienfaits éventuels l'emportent sur les risques possibles ■ Risques de complication après l'accouchement chez les nouveau-nés, lorsque la mère a pris ce médicament durant le 3e trimestre ■ **ALLAITEMENT**: Risque de réactions indésirables graves chez les nouveau-nés; la mère doit décider soit de cesser l'allaitement soit de cesser la prise du médicament, compte tenu de l'importance du médicament pour elle ■ **PÉD.**: L'innocuité et l'efficacité n'ont pas été établies. Risque possible de changements comportementaux et émotifs, dont l'automutilation.

RÉACTIONS INDÉSIRABLES ET EFFETS SECONDAIRES
SNC: CONVULSIONS, agitation, céphalées, insomnie, manie, psychoses.

GI: sécheresse de la bouche (xérostomie), nausées, vomissements, modification de l'appétit, gain de poids, perte de poids.

Tég.: photosensibilité.

End.: hyperglycémie, hypoglycémie, syndrome d'antidiurèse inappropriée.
SN: tremblements.

INTERACTIONS

Médicament-médicament: L'administration concomitante de **lévodopa**, d'**amantadine** ou d'un **IMAO** peut accroître le risque de réactions indésirables ▪ L'administration concomitante de **phénothiazines**, d'**antidépresseurs**, de **théophylline**, de **corticostéroïdes**, de **stimulants** ou d'**anorexigènes en vente libre**, ou le sevrage des **benzodiazépines** ou de l'**alcool** ou de tout autre **médicament abaissant le seuil convulsif** peuvent accroître le risque de convulsions ▪ L'administration concomitante de la **carbamazépine** peut diminuer les concentrations plasmatiques, et donc l'efficacité du bupropion ▪ L'administration concomitante de **nicotine** peut augmenter les risques d'hypertension artérielle ▪ L'administration concomitante de **médicaments métabolisés par l'isoenzyme CYP2D6** (**ISRS**, **antidépresseurs tricycliques**, certains **bêtabloquants**, **antiarythmiques** et **antipsychotiques**, par exemple) peut augmenter les risques de toxicité de ces agents.

VOIES D'ADMINISTRATION ET POSOLOGIE

PO (adultes):

- *Dépression – Comprimé SR:* la posologie initiale est de 100 à 150 mg/jour, jusqu'à un maximum de 300 mg/jour. Augmenter la dose à intervalles d'au moins 1 semaine. Les doses uniques de bupropion SR ne doivent pas dépasser 150 mg afin de réduire les risques de convulsions. Les doses supérieures à 150 mg de comprimé SR doivent être fractionnées en deux prises et les espacer d'au moins 8 heures. *Comprimé XL:* La posologie initiale est de 150 mg, 1 fois par jour. La dose peut être augmentée jusqu'à concurrence de 300 mg, 1 fois par jour. Augmenter la dose après au moins 1 semaine.
- *Abandon du tabagisme* – 150 mg, 1 fois par jour, pendant 3 jours; puis, 150 mg, 2 fois par jour, pendant 7 à 12 semaines (il faut espacer les doses d'au moins 8 heures).

PRÉSENTATION

Comprimés à libération prolongée SR: 100 mg^{Pr}, 150 mg^{Pr}.
Comprimés à libération prolongée XL: 150 mg^{Pr}, 300 mg^{Pr}.
Comprimés à libération prolongée (Zyban): 150 mg^{Pr}.

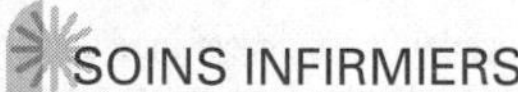

SOINS INFIRMIERS

ÉVALUATION DE LA SITUATION

- Suivre de près les changements d'humeur. Signaler au médecin ou à un autre professionnel de la santé l'aggravation de l'anxiété, de l'agitation ou de l'insomnie.
- Surveiller les tendances suicidaires, particulièrement en début de traitement. Réduire la quantité de médicament dont le patient peut disposer.

Tests de laboratoire: Suivre de près la fonction hépatique et rénale chez les patients présentant une insuffisance rénale ou hépatique pour prévenir l'intensification des effets secondaires.

DIAGNOSTICS INFIRMIERS POSSIBLES

- Stratégies d'adaptation inefficaces (Indications).
- Connaissances insuffisantes sur le traitement médicamenteux (Enseignement au patient et à ses proches).

INTERVENTIONS INFIRMIÈRES

- NE PAS CONFONDRE LE BUPROPION ET LA BUSPIRONE. NE PAS ADMINISTRER LE BUPROPION (WELLBUTRIN) ET ZYBAN CHEZ LE MÊME PATIENT, CAR CES DEUX MÉDICAMENTS CONTIENNENT LE MÊME INGRÉDIENT.
- ADMINISTRER LES DOSES QUOTIDIENNES À INTERVALLES ÉGAUX AFIN DE RÉDUIRE LES RISQUES DE CONVULSIONS. UNE DOSE SUPÉRIEURE À 450 mg/JOUR AUGMENTE DE 4 FOIS LE RISQUE DE CONVULSIONS.
- Initialement, on peut administrer le bupropion en association avec des sédatifs pour réduire l'agitation. Après la première semaine, l'administration de sédatifs peut habituellement être arrêtée.
- Pour diminuer l'insomnie, ne pas administrer le médicament au coucher.
- Pour réduire l'irritation gastrique, on peut administrer le bupropion avec des aliments.
- Le patient peut utiliser des timbres à la nicotine en même temps qu'il prend le bupropion.
- LES COMPRIMÉS À LIBÉRATION PROLONGÉE DOIVENT ÊTRE AVALÉS TELS QUELS, SANS LES COUPER, LES ÉCRASER OU LES MÂCHER.

ENSEIGNEMENT AU PATIENT ET À SES PROCHES

- Conseiller au patient de respecter rigoureusement la posologie recommandée. Lorsque le médicament lui est prescrit pour le traitement de la dépression, s'il n'a pas pu prendre une dose au moment habituel, il doit la prendre aussitôt que possible et espacer les autres doses de la journée à intervalles égaux d'au moins 8 heures. Lorsqu'il prend le médicament pour arrêter de fumer, il doit sauter la dose manquée. Lui recommander de ne jamais prendre une double dose ni une dose plus grande que celle qui

B

B

lui a été prescrite. Les pleins effets du médicament peuvent ne se manifester qu'après 4 semaines ou même davantage. Conseiller au patient de ne pas cesser le traitement avant d'avoir consulté un professionnel de la santé. Il peut s'avérer nécessaire de réduire graduellement la dose avant d'arrêter le traitement.

- Prévenir le patient que le bupropion peut altérer sa capacité de jugement ainsi que ses capacités motrices et cognitives. Lui recommander de ne pas conduire et d'éviter les activités qui exigent sa vigilance jusqu'à ce qu'on ait la certitude que le médicament n'entraîne pas ces effets chez lui.
- Conseiller au patient d'éviter la consommation d'alcool pendant le traitement et de consulter un professionnel de la santé avant de prendre d'autres médicaments en même temps que le bupropion.
- Expliquer au patient qu'il peut soulager la sécheresse de la bouche en se rinçant souvent la bouche, en pratiquant une bonne hygiène buccale et en consommant des bonbons ou de la gomme à mâcher sans sucre. Si la sécheresse de la bouche persiste pendant plus de 2 semaines, lui recommander de consulter un professionnel de la santé qui pourrait lui prescrire des substituts de salive.
- Conseiller au patient de signaler à un professionnel de la santé si un rash ou d'autres effets indésirables se manifestent.
- Recommander au patient d'utiliser un écran solaire et des vêtements protecteurs afin de prévenir les réactions de photosensibilité.
- Conseiller à la patiente de prévenir le professionnel de la santé si elle prévoit devenir enceinte ou si elle pense l'être.
- Recommander au patient qui doit suivre un autre traitement ou subir une intervention chirurgicale de prévenir le professionnel de la santé qu'il suit un traitement avec ce médicament.
- Expliquer au patient l'importance des examens de suivi qui permettent de déterminer les bienfaits du traitement. Encourager le patient à s'engager dans une psychothérapie.

Renoncement au tabac: Expliquer au patient qu'il devrait cesser de fumer au cours de la deuxième semaine de traitement pour que les effets du bupropion puissent s'installer et pour maximiser ses chances d'abandonner l'usage du tabac.

VÉRIFICATION DE L'EFFICACITÉ THÉRAPEUTIQUE

L'efficacité du traitement peut être démontrée par: une sensation de mieux-être ■ un regain d'intérêt à l'égard de l'entourage; pour contrer les épisodes aigus de dépression, il faut parfois poursuivre le traitement pendant plusieurs mois ■ l'abandon de la cigarette. ✳

BUSPIRONE

Apo-Buspirone, BuSpar, Gen-Buspirone, Novo-Buspirone, PMS-Buspirone

CLASSIFICATION:
Anxiolytique

Grossesse – catégorie B

INDICATIONS

Traitement symptomatique de courte durée de l'anxiété chez les patients souffrant d'anxiété généralisée (l'efficacité du médicament, utilisé pendant > 4 semaines, n'a pas été établie).

MÉCANISME D'ACTION

Liaison aux récepteurs sérotoninergiques et dopaminergiques du cerveau ■ Accélération du métabolisme cérébral de la noradrénaline. ***Effets thérapeutiques***: Apaisement de l'anxiété.

PHARMACOCINÉTIQUE

Absorption: Le médicament est absorbé rapidement, mais subit un effet de premier passage hépatique important, d'où une biodisponibilité absolue d'environ 4 %.
Distribution: Inconnue.
Liaison aux protéines: 95 %.
Métabolisme et excrétion: Fort métabolisme hépatique (CYP3A4). De 20 à 40 % excrété dans les fèces et de 30 à 60 % excrété dans les urines.
Demi-vie: De 2 à 3 heures.

Profil temps-action (apaisement de l'anxiété)

	DÉBUT D'ACTION	PIC	DURÉE
PO	7 – 10 jours	3 – 4 semaines	inconnue

CONTRE-INDICATIONS, PRÉCAUTIONS ET MISES EN GARDE

Contre-indications: Hypersensibilité à la buspirone ou à l'un des ingrédients inactifs ■ Insuffisance hépatique ou rénale grave.
Précautions et mises en garde: Patients recevant d'autres anxiolytiques (l'administration des autres agents devrait être arrêtée graduellement afin de prévenir les symptômes de sevrage ou l'anxiété rebond) ■ Patients recevant d'autres agents psychoactifs ■ Troubles convulsifs ■ **OBST., ALLAITEMENT, PÉD.**: L'innocuité du médicament

n'a pas été établie chez les femmes enceintes ou qui allaitent ni chez les enfants < 18 ans.

RÉACTIONS INDÉSIRABLES ET EFFETS SECONDAIRES

SNC: étourdissements, somnolence, excitation, fatigue, céphalées, insomnie, agitation, faiblesse, modifications de la personnalité.

ORLO: vision trouble, congestion nasale, maux de gorge, acouphènes, altération du goût ou de l'odorat, conjonctivite.

Resp.: congestion thoracique, hyperventilation, essoufflements.

CV: douleurs thoraciques, palpitations, tachycardie, hypertension, hypotension, syncope.

GI: nausées, douleurs abdominales, constipation, diarrhée, sécheresse de la bouche (xérostomie), vomissements.

GU: modification de la libido, dysurie, mictions fréquentes, retard de la miction.

Tég.: rash, chute des cheveux (alopécie), phlyctènes, peau sèche, apparition d'ecchymoses au moindre traumatisme, œdème, rougeurs du visage, prurit.

End.: troubles du cycle menstruel.

Loc.: myalgie.

SN: manque de coordination, engourdissements, paresthésie, tremblements.

Divers: peau moite et froide, transpiration, fièvre.

INTERACTIONS

Médicament-médicament: Risque d'hypertension lors de l'administration concomitante d'**IMAO** ▪ La buspirone peut augmenter le risque d'apparition des effets hépatiques induits par la **trazodone** ▪ L'utilisation concomitante d'**érythromycine**, de **kétoconazole**, d'**itraconazole**, de **ritonavir** et d'autres **inhibiteurs du CYP3A4** élève les concentrations sanguines de buspirone; il peut s'avérer nécessaire de réduire la dose ▪ L'utilisation concomitante de **rifampine**, de **dexaméthasone**, de **phénytoïne**, de **phénobarbital**, de **carbamazépine** et d'autres **inducteurs du CYP3A4** diminue les concentrations sanguines de buspirone; il peut s'avérer nécessaire d'ajuster la dose ▪ La consommation d'**alcool** est déconseillée.

Médicament-aliments: L'ingestion concomitante de **jus de pamplemousse** augmente les concentrations sanguines du médicament; éviter la consommation de grandes quantités de jus de pamplemousse.

Médicament-produits naturels: Le **kava**, la **valériane** et la **camomille** peuvent accentuer la dépression du SNC.

VOIES D'ADMINISTRATION ET POSOLOGIE

- **PO (adultes)**: 5 mg, 2 ou 3 fois par jour; augmenter la dose par paliers de 5 mg, tous les 2 ou 3 jours, selon les besoins (ne pas dépasser 45 mg par jour, ou, pour les personnes âgées, 30 mg par jour, pendant 4 semaines). La dose habituelle est de 20 à 30 mg par jour, en prises fractionnées.

PRÉSENTATION

Comprimés: 5 mg[Pr], 10 mg[Pr].

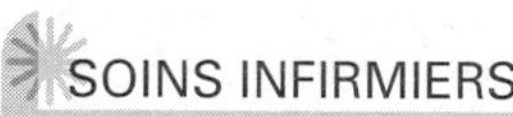

SOINS INFIRMIERS

ÉVALUATION DE LA SITUATION

- Déterminer le degré d'anxiété et la fréquence de ses manifestations, avant le traitement et à intervalles réguliers pendant toute sa durée.
- La buspirone ne semble pas entraîner de dépendance physique ou psychologique ni de tolérance. Toutefois, chez le patient ayant des antécédents de toxicomanie ou de pharmacodépendance, il faudrait surveiller l'accoutumance ou la tolérance aux effets du médicament et limiter la quantité de médicament dont il peut disposer.

DIAGNOSTICS INFIRMIERS POSSIBLES

- Anxiété (Indications).
- Risque d'accident (Effets secondaires).
- Connaissances insuffisantes sur le traitement médicamenteux (Enseignement au patient et à ses proches).

INTERVENTIONS INFIRMIÈRES

- NE PAS CONFONDRE LA BUSPIRONE AVEC LE BUPROPION.
- Lorsque l'on substitue la buspirone à un autre anxiolytique, il faut diminuer graduellement les doses de ce dernier, car la buspirone ne peut pas prévenir les symptômes de sevrage.
- Afin de réduire les risques d'irritation gastrique, administrer la buspirone avec des aliments, lesquels ralentissent l'absorption du médicament, mais ne réduisent pas la quantité totale absorbée.

ENSEIGNEMENT AU PATIENT ET À SES PROCHES

- Inciter le patient à respecter rigoureusement la posologie recommandée. S'il n'a pu prendre le médicament au moment habituel, il doit le prendre aussitôt que possible, à moins que ce ne soit presque l'heure prévue pour la dose suivante. Le prévenir

B

qu'il ne faut jamais remplacer une dose manquée par une double dose. Insister sur le fait qu'il ne faut pas prendre une dose plus importante que celle qui a été prescrite.

- Expliquer au patient que la buspirone peut provoquer des étourdissements ou de la somnolence. Lui conseiller de ne pas conduire ou d'éviter les activités qui exigent sa vigilance jusqu'à ce qu'on ait la certitude que le médicament n'entraîne pas ces effets chez lui.
- Recommander au patient de ne pas boire d'alcool et de ne pas prendre d'autres dépresseurs du SNC en même temps que la buspirone.
- Conseiller au patient de consulter un professionnel de la santé avant de prendre un médicament en vente libre ou un produit naturel en même temps que la buspirone.
- Conseiller au patient de signaler à un professionnel de la santé tout mouvement anormal persistant, tel que la dystonie, l'agitation motrice, les mouvements involontaires des muscles cervicaux ou faciaux.
- Inciter la patiente à communiquer avec un professionnel de la santé si elle pense être enceinte.
- Insister sur l'importance des examens de suivi permettant d'évaluer les bienfaits du traitement.

VÉRIFICATION DE L'EFFICACITÉ THÉRAPEUTIQUE

L'efficacité du traitement peut être démontrée par: une sensation de mieux-être ■ la diminution de la sensation subjective d'anxiété. On peut observer une certaine amélioration après 7 à 10 jours. Les résultats optimaux peuvent ne se manifester qu'après 3 à 4 semaines de traitement. La buspirone est habituellement administrée en traitement de courte durée (de 3 à 4 semaines). Si elle est prescrite en traitement prolongé, son efficacité doit être évaluée à intervalles réguliers. ✳

ALERTE CLINIQUE

BUSULFAN

Busulfex, Myleran

CLASSIFICATION:

Antinéoplasique (alkylant)

Grossesse – catégorie D

INDICATIONS

PO: Traitement de la leucémie granulocytaire chronique en vue d'obtenir une rémission ■ **IV:** En association avec d'autres agents antinéoplasiques ou la radiothérapie comme traitement de préparation à la transplantation de cellules souches hématopoïétiques, notamment dans le cadre du traitement de la leucémie lymphoblastique, non lymphocitaire ou myéloïde, ainsi que dans celui du lymphome, du myélome multiple, de la maladie de Hodgkin, du syndrome myélodysplasique, du cancer du sein et de l'ovaire et de plusieurs maladies génétiques.

MÉCANISME D'ACTION

Blocage des fonctions de l'acide nucléique et de la synthèse protéique (effet non spécifique sur le cycle cellulaire). ***Effets thérapeutiques:*** Destruction des cellules à croissance rapide, particulièrement des cellules malignes.

PHARMACOCINÉTIQUE

Absorption: Rapide (PO). La biodisponibilité présente des variations intra-individuelles importantes (de 22 à 120 %).

Distribution: À fortes doses, le busulfan pénètre dans le liquide céphalorachidien.

Métabolisme et excrétion: Fort métabolisme hépatique.

Demi-vie: 2,5 heures.

Profil temps-action (effet sur les numérations globulaires)

	DÉBUT D'ACTION	PIC	DURÉE
PO	1 - 2 semaines	plusieurs semaines	jusqu'à 1 mois†
IV	7 - 10 jours	11 - 30 jours	24 - 54 jours‡

† Le rétablissement complet peut prendre jusqu'à 20 mois.
‡ Après l'administration de la dernière dose.

CONTRE-INDICATIONS, PRÉCAUTIONS ET MISES EN GARDE

Contre-indications: Hypersensibilité au médicament ou à ses excipients ■ Absence de réponse à des cures antérieures de busulfan ■ Diminution du nombre de polynucléaires neutrophiles ou de plaquettes.

Précautions et mises en garde: Infections actives ■ Aplasie médullaire ■ Patients obèses (la dose est calculée en fonction du poids corporel idéal) ■ Autres maladies chroniques débilitantes ■ Patientes en âge de procréer, grossesse et allaitement ■ Prise concomitante d'itraconazole ■ Insuffisance hépatique.

RÉACTIONS INDÉSIRABLES ET EFFETS SECONDAIRES

L'incidence et la gravité des réactions indésirables et des effets secondaires sont accrues lors de l'administration par voie IV.

SNC: *PO et IV* – CONVULSIONS ■ *IV* – HÉMORRAGIE CÉRÉBRALE, COMA, anxiété, confusion, dépression,

étourdissements, céphalées, encéphalopathie, modifications de l'état mental, faiblesse.
ORLO: *PO* – cataractes ■ *IV* – épistaxis, pharyngite, maladies touchant l'oreille.
Resp.: *PO* – FIBROSE PULMONAIRE ■ *IV* – dyspnée, hémorragie alvéolaire, asthme, atélectasie, toux, hémoptysie, hypoxie, épanchement pleural, pneumonie, rhinite, sinusite.
CV: *PO et IV* – MALADIE HÉPATIQUE VÉNO-OBSTRUCTIVE (fréquence accrue en cas de transplantation allogénique) ■ *PO* – TAMPONNADE CARDIAQUE (EN PRÉSENCE DE DOSES ÉLEVÉES DE CYCLOPHOSPHAMIDE) ■ *IV* – douleurs thoraciques, hypotension, tachycardie, thrombose, arythmies, fibrillation auriculaire, cardiomégalie, modifications de l'ÉCG, œdème, bloc cardiaque, hypertension, insuffisance cardiaque gauche, épanchement péricardique, extrasystoles ventriculaires.
GI: *PO* – hépatite induite par le médicament, nausées, vomissements, varices œsophagiennes (en association avec la thioguanine) ■ *IV* – élévation des concentrations de bilirubine sérique, distension abdominale, anorexie, constipation, diarrhée, sécheresse de la bouche (xérostomie), hématémèse, nausées, gêne rectale, vomissements, douleurs abdominales, dyspepsie, hépatomégalie, pancréatite, stomatite.
GU: oligurie, dysurie, hématurie.
Tég.: *PO* – démangeaisons, rash, acné, alopécie, érythème noueux, dermatite exfoliative, hyperpigmentation ■ *IV* – alopécie, rash, prurit.
End.: *PO* – stérilité, gynécomastie.
HÉ: hypokaliémie, hypomagnésémie, hypophosphatémie.
Hémat.: APLASIE MÉDULLAIRE.
Locaux: *IV* – inflammation et douleurs au point d'injection, thrombose au point d'injection.
Métab.: *PO et IV* – hyperuricémie ■ *IV* – hyperglycémie.
Loc.: arthralgie, myalgie, douleurs lombaires.
Divers: réactions allergiques, frissons, fièvre, infections.

INTERACTIONS

Médicament-médicament: L'usage concomitant ou préalable (dans les 72 heures qui précèdent) d'**acétaminophène** peut diminuer l'élimination du busulfan et augmenter le risque de toxicité ■ L'administration concomitante de doses élevées de **cyclophosphamide** chez les patients thalassémiques peut entraîner une tamponnade cardiaque ■ L'usage concomitant de **phénytoïne** diminue les concentrations sanguines de busulfan réduisant ainsi son efficacité ■ L'**itraconazole**, administré en concomitance, élève les concentrations sanguines de busulfan, augmentant ainsi sa toxicité ■ Un traitement continu et prolongé par la **thioguanine**, administrée en concomitance, peut augmenter le risque de toxicité hépatique ■ La **radiothérapie** ou d'autres **agents antinéoplasiques**, administrés simultanément, peuvent aggraver l'aplasie médullaire et les effets toxiques pulmonaires ■ Le busulfan peut diminuer la réponse aux **vaccins à virus vivants** et accroître le risque de réactions indésirables.

VOIES D'ADMINISTRATION ET POSOLOGIE

Outre les suivants, de nombreux autres traitements sont utilisés. Voir les protocoles en vigueur pour déterminer les doses les plus récentes administrées.

- **PO (adultes)**: *Traitement d'induction* – initialement, 1,8 mg/m²/jour ou 0,06 mg/kg/jour, jusqu'à ce qu'on note une amélioration sur les plans hématologique et clinique. La dose maximale quotidienne est de 4 mg. *Traitement d'entretien* – de 1 à 3 mg par jour.
- **PO (enfants)**: *Traitement d'induction* – initialement, de 1,8 à 4,6 mg/m²/jour ou de 0,06 à 0,12 mg/kg/jour, jusqu'à ce qu'on note une amélioration sur les plans hématologique et clinique. *Traitement d'entretien* – adapter la dose pour maintenir le nombre de globules blancs entre 15 et 20 × 10^9/L (*usage non approuvé*).
- **IV (adultes)**: 0,8 mg/kg, toutes les 6 heures, pendant 4 jours consécutifs, jusqu'à concurrence de 16 doses. La dose est calculée selon le poids corporel idéal ou le poids réel, selon la valeur la plus basse; chez les patients obèses, la dose devrait être calculée selon le poids corporel idéal. Le busulfan doit être administré au moyen d'un cathéter central, en perfusion d'une durée de 2 heures. On l'administre en concomitance avec le cyclophosphamide.

PRÉSENTATION

Comprimés: 2 mg[Pr] ■ **Solution pour injection**: 6 mg/mL, en ampoules de 10 mL (60 mg)[Pr].

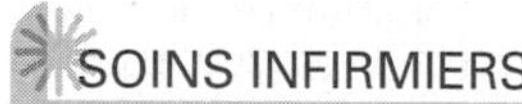

SOINS INFIRMIERS

ÉVALUATION DE LA SITUATION

ALERTE CLINIQUE: OBSERVER LES SIGNES D'APLASIE MÉDULLAIRE. SUIVRE DE PRÈS LES SIGNES ET LES SYMPTÔMES DE SAIGNEMENTS: GENCIVES QUI SAIGNENT, FORMATION D'ECCHYMOSES, PÉTÉCHIES, PRÉSENCE DE SANG OCCULTE DANS LES SELLES, DANS L'URINE ET DANS LES VOMISSEMENTS. ÉVITER LES INJECTIONS PAR VOIE IM ET LA PRISE DE LA TEMPÉRATURE RECTALE. EXERCER UNE PRESSION SUR TOUS LES POINTS DE PONCTION VEINEUSE PENDANT AU MOINS 10 MINUTES.

B

EN PRÉSENCE D'UNE NEUTROPÉNIE, RESTER À L'AFFÛT DES SIGNES SUIVANTS D'INFECTION : FIÈVRE, FRISSONS, MAUX DE GORGE, TOUX, ENROUEMENT, DOULEURS AU DOS OU AUX FLANCS, MICTIONS DIFFICILES OU DOULOUREUSES. UNE ANÉMIE PEUT SURVENIR. OBSERVER LE PATIENT POUR DÉCELER UNE FATIGUE ACCRUE, LA DYSPNÉE ET L'HYPOTENSION ORTHOSTATIQUE. SI CES SYMPTÔMES SE MANIFESTENT, EN INFORMER LE MÉDECIN.

- Effectuer le bilan quotidien des ingesta et des excreta et peser le patient tous les jours. Prévenir le médecin si des modifications importantes des valeurs totales surviennent.
- Observer le patient à la recherche des symptômes suivants de goutte : concentration accrue d'acide urique, douleurs articulaires, douleurs au dos ou aux flancs, œdème des pieds et du bas des jambes. Inciter le patient à boire au moins 2 litres de liquide par jour si son état le permet. On peut administrer de l'allopurinol pour diminuer les concentrations d'acide urique. Le médecin peut prescrire l'alcalinisation de l'urine pour augmenter l'excrétion de l'acide urique.
- OBSERVER LE PATIENT, À INTERVALLES RÉGULIERS PENDANT ET APRÈS LE TRAITEMENT, POUR DÉCELER LES SIGNES SUIVANTS DE FIBROSE PULMONAIRE : FIÈVRE, TOUX, ESSOUFFLEMENTS. INTERROMPRE LE TRAITEMENT DÈS LE PREMIER SIGNE DE FIBROSE PULMONAIRE QUI SE MANIFESTE HABITUELLEMENT DE 8 MOIS À 10 ANS (4 ANS EN MOYENNE) APRÈS LE DÉBUT DU TRAITEMENT.

IV :

- ADMINISTRER UN PRÉTRAITEMENT PAR LA PHÉNYTOÏNE AVANT L'ADMINISTRATION IV AFIN DE RÉDUIRE LE RISQUE DE CONVULSIONS.
- Des agents antiémétiques devraient être administrés avant l'administration IV et à intervalles fixes pendant toute la durée du traitement par voie IV.

Tests de laboratoire :

- SUIVRE DE PRÈS LES NUMÉRATIONS GLOBULAIRE ET PLAQUETTAIRE AINSI QUE LA FORMULE LEUCOCYTAIRE AVANT L'ADMINISTRATION INITIALE ET TOUTES LES SEMAINES, TOUT AU LONG DU TRAITEMENT. Le nadir de la leucopénie se produit en 11 à 30 jours. Les valeurs se rétablissent habituellement en l'espace de 24 à 54 jours. Si le nombre de plaquettes est < 150 × 10⁹/L, prendre les mesures qui s'imposent en cas de thrombopénie. L'aplasie médullaire peut être grave et graduelle ; le rétablissement survient en l'espace de 1 mois à 2 ans après l'arrêt du traitement.
- Mesurer les concentrations sériques d'ALT, de bilirubine, de phosphatase alcaline et d'acide urique avant le traitement et à intervalles réguliers pendant toute sa durée. Le busulfan peut entraîner l'élévation des concentrations d'acide urique.
- Le busulfan peut entraîner des résultats faussement positifs aux études cytologiques des tissus des seins, de la vessie, du col et des poumons.

DIAGNOSTICS INFIRMIERS POSSIBLES

- Image corporelle perturbée (Indications).
- Risque d'accident (Effets secondaires).
- Risque d'infection (Effets secondaires).

INTERVENTIONS INFIRMIÈRES

ALERTE CLINIQUE : DES DÉCÈS SONT SURVENUS LORS DE CERTAINES CHIMIOTHÉRAPIES. AVANT D'ADMINISTRER L'AGENT, CLARIFIER TOUS LES POINTS AMBIGUS. VÉRIFIER LA LIMITE DES DOSES UNITAIRES ET QUOTIDIENNES AINSI QUE LA DOSE À ADMINISTRER PENDANT LE TRAITEMENT. DEMANDER À UN AUTRE PROFESSIONNEL DE LA SANTÉ DE VÉRIFIER UNE FOIS DE PLUS L'ORDONNANCE D'ORIGINE, LES CALCULS ET LE RÉGLAGE DE LA POMPE À PERFUSION.

PO : Administrer le busulfan à la même heure chaque jour. Il faut le prendre à jeun pour réduire les nausées et les vomissements.

IV : Préparer les solutions destinées à l'administration IV sous une hotte à flux laminaire. Porter des vêtements protecteurs, des gants et un masque pendant la manipulation de ce médicament. Mettre au rebut le matériel servant à l'administration IV dans les contenants réservés à cet usage (voir l'annexe H).

Perfusion intermittente : Diluer le busulfan dans 10 fois son volume d'une solution de NaCl 0,9 % ou de D5%E, pour obtenir une concentration finale d'cnviron 0,5 mg/mL. Pour prélever le busulfan de l'ampoule, utiliser une aiguille avec filtre de 5 μm, aspirer le volume à prélever, retirer l'aiguille et le filtre, remplacer l'aiguille de la seringue par une autre et injecter le busulfan dans le diluant. Utiliser seulement les filtres fournis avec le médicament. Ajouter toujours le busulfan au diluant et non le diluant au busulfan. La préparation diluée avec de la solution de NaCl 0,9 % ou de D5%E est stable pendant 8 heures à la température ambiante et celle diluée avec de la solution de NaCl 0,9 % est stable pendant 12 heures, si elle est gardée au réfrigérateur. L'administration doit être terminée dans ce laps de temps.

Vitesse d'administration : Administrer la préparation par un cathéter veineux central en 2 heures, toutes les 6 heures, pendant 4 jours, pour un total de 16 doses. Utiliser une pompe à perfusion pour s'assurer qu'on a administré toute la dose en 2 heures.

Incompatibilité (tubulure en Y): Ne pas administrer le busulfan avec d'autres solutions. Rincer le cathéter avec de la solution de NaCl 0,9 % ou de D5%E, avant et après l'administration.

ENSEIGNEMENT AU PATIENT ET À SES PROCHES

- Encourager le patient à suivre rigoureusement la posologie recommandée et à prendre le médicament à la même heure chaque jour, même si les nausées et les vomissements deviennent gênants. Lui conseiller d'informer un professionnel de la santé si les vomissements se produisent peu de temps après la prise de la dose. S'il n'a pas pu prendre une dose, il ne doit pas la reprendre. Le prévenir qu'il ne doit jamais remplacer une dose manquée par une double dose.
- Recommander au patient de signaler à un professionnel de la santé la fièvre, les maux de gorge, les signes d'infection, les douleurs au dos ou aux flancs, les mictions difficiles ou douloureuses, les ulcérations dans la bouche ou sur les lèvres, les frissons, la dyspnée, une toux persistante, les saignements des gencives, la formation d'ecchymoses, les pétéchies ou la présence de sang dans les urines, les selles ou les vomissements. Lui conseiller d'utiliser une brosse à dents à poils doux et un rasoir électrique. Mettre en garde le patient contre la consommation de boissons alcoolisées, de produits contenant de l'aspirine ou d'anti-inflammatoires non stéroïdiens.
- Expliquer au patient qu'il doit éviter les foules et les personnes contagieuses. Lui recommander de signaler immédiatement à un professionnel de la santé tout symptôme d'infection.
- Expliquer au patient qu'il risque de perdre ses cheveux. Explorer avec lui les stratégies lui permettant de s'adapter à ce changement.
- Expliquer à la patiente la nécessité d'utiliser des méthodes de contraception pendant le traitement. Il faut prendre des mesures contraceptives même si l'aménorrhée survient.
- Expliquer au patient qu'il ne doit pas se faire vacciner sans recommandation expresse d'un professionnel de la santé.
- Recommander au patient de signaler à un professionnel de la santé les signes et les symptômes suivants: saignements inhabituels, formation d'ecchymoses, douleurs lombaires, gastriques ou articulaires.
- Conseiller au patient qui suit un traitement prolongé de signaler immédiatement à un professionnel de la santé la toux, les essoufflements et la fièvre ou de le prévenir si sa peau devient plus foncée et si la diarrhée, les étourdissements, la fatigue, l'anorexie, la confusion ou les nausées et les vomissements s'aggravent.
- Prévenir le patient que le traitement par le busulfan accroît le risque d'apparition d'un deuxième cancer.

VÉRIFICATION DE L'EFFICACITÉ THÉRAPEUTIQUE

L'efficacité du traitement peut être démontrée par: la diminution du nombre de leucocytes jusqu'aux limites normales ▪ la diminution des sécrétions nocturnes de sueur ▪ un gain d'appétit ▪ une sensation de mieux-être. On reprend le traitement lorsque le nombre de leucocytes atteint 50 × 10^9/L. ✳

BUTALBITAL, COMPOSÉS DE

butalbital, AAS, caféine†
Fiorinal, Tecnal, Trianal

butalbital, AAS, caféine, codéine†
Fiorinal-C1/4, Fiorinal-C1/2, Tecnal-C1/4, Tecnal-C1/2, Trianal-C1/4, Trianal-C1/2

CLASSIFICATION:
Analgésiques, sédatifs

Grossesse – catégories C et D (en usage prolongé ou à dose élevée près du terme)

† Les renseignements sur l'aspirine contenue dans ces composés se trouvent dans la monographie de l'aspirine. Ceux sur la codéine se trouvent dans la monographie de la codéine.

INDICATIONS

Soulagement des céphalées de tension (ou par contraction musculaire) et lorsqu'une sédation et une action analgésique simultanées sont nécessaires, p. ex., céphalées de tension, céphalées mixtes, douleur et tension menstruelles ainsi que douleur et tension du post-partum.

MÉCANISME D'ACTION

Soulagement de la douleur par l'ingrédient analgésique (aspirine); effet sédatif exercé par l'ingrédient barbiturique (butalbital); la caféine contenue dans certains composés aurait un effet bénéfique en cas de céphalées vasculaires. ***Effets thérapeutiques:*** Diminution de l'intensité de la douleur s'accompagnant d'une certaine sédation.

B

PHARMACOCINÉTIQUE

Absorption: Bonne (PO).

Distribution: L'agent se répartit dans tout l'organisme, il traverse la barrière placentaire et passe dans le lait maternel.

Métabolisme et excrétion: Métabolisme majoritairement hépatique.

Demi-vie: 35 heures.

Profil temps-action (effet analgésique)

	Début d'action	Pic	Durée
PO	15 - 30 min	1 - 2 h	2 - 6 h

CONTRE-INDICATIONS, PRÉCAUTIONS ET MISES EN GARDE

Contre-indications: Hypersensibilité à l'un des ingrédients de ces composés ■ Porphyrie ■ Ulcère gastro-intestinal ou toute autre lésion gastro-intestinale ■ Surdosage à l'alcool, aux hypnotiques, aux analgésiques ou aux médicaments psychotropes ou intoxication par l'une de ces substances ■ Diathèse hémorragique ■ Syndrome des polypes nasaux, œdème et réactivité bronchospastique à l'aspirine ou à d'autres AINS.

Précautions et mises en garde: Coma ou dépression du SNC préexistante ■ Prédisposition à la dépression respiratoire ■ Douleurs intenses qu'on ne peut maîtriser ■ Insuffisance hépatique ou rénale grave ■ Maladie cardiovasculaire grave (caféine à éviter) ■ Troubles de la coagulation ■ Blessure à la tête ou hypertension intracrânienne ■ Hypothyroïdie ■ Rétrécissement de l'urètre ou hyperplasie de la prostate ■ Maladie d'Addison ■ Grossesse ou allaitement ■ Tendances suicidaires ou antécédents de toxicomanie ou de pharmacodépendance ■ Consommation excessive d'alcool ou alcoolisme (précautions en ce qui concerne l'usage d'aspirine) ■ **Gér.**: Risque accru d'effets indésirables chez les personnes âgées (réduire la dose) ■ Usage réservé à un traitement de courte durée ■ **Péd.**: L'innocuité du médicament n'a pas été établie ■ Syndrome de Reye (éviter l'aspirine chez les enfants, adolescents ou jeunes adultes qui ont la grippe, la varicelle ou un autre infection virale) ■ Risque de pharmacodépendance et d'abus.

RÉACTIONS INDÉSIRABLES ET EFFETS SECONDAIRES

SNC: <u>somnolence</u>, <u>sensation de tête légère</u>, délire, dépression, excitation, céphalées (lors d'un usage prolongé), insomnie, irritabilité, léthargie, nervosité, vertiges.

Resp.: dépression respiratoire.

CV: *caféine* – palpitations, tachycardie.

GI: *caféine* – constipation, diarrhée, épigastralgie, brûlures d'estomac, nausées, vomissements.

Tég.: dermatite, rash.

Divers: réactions d'hypersensibilité incluant l'ŒDÈME ANGIONEUROTIQUE et la MALADIE SÉRIQUE, dépendance physique, dépendance psychologique, tolérance aux effets du médicament.

INTERACTIONS

Médicament-médicament: Effets dépressifs additifs sur le SNC, lors de l'usage concomitant d'autres **dépresseurs du SNC**, tels l'**alcool**, les **antihistaminiques**, les **antidépresseurs**, les **analgésiques opioïdes** et les **hypnosédatifs** ■ Les **IMAO** peuvent intensifier les effets du butalbital sur le SNC ■ Induction du métabolisme hépatique et diminution de l'efficacité d'autres médicaments dont les **contraceptifs oraux**, la **félodipine**, la **nifédipine**, l'**acébutolol**, le **propranolol**, le **métoprolol**, la **doxycycline**, les **corticostéroïdes**, les **antidépresseurs tricycliques**, les **phénothiazines**, la **méthadone**, la **carbamazépine** et la **quinidine** ■ Le médicament peut diminuer l'efficacité des **agents uricosuriques**, tels que le **probénécide** et le **sulfinpyrazone**, administrés dans le traitement de la goutte ■ Le médicament peut augmenter la toxicité hématologique du **6-mercaptopurine** et du **méthotrexate** ■ Le médicament peut modifier l'effet de la **warfarine** (surveiller le RNI) ■ Le médicament, pris à des doses supérieures aux doses maximales recommandées, peut potentialiser l'effet des **hypoglycémiants oraux** et de l'**insuline** et causer une hypoglycémie.

Médicament-produits naturels: Le **millepertuis** peut entraîner une diminution des concentrations et donc de l'effet du butalbital ■ Effets dépresseurs additifs sur le SNC lors de la consommation concomitante de **kava**, de **valériane**, de **scutellaire**, de **camomille** et de **houblon**.

VOIES D'ADMINISTRATION ET POSOLOGIE

- **PO (adultes)**: 1 ou 2 capsules ou comprimés (de 50 à 100 mg de butalbital), suivis de 1 capsule ou de 1 comprimé, toutes les 3 à 4 heures, selon les besoins, jusqu'à 6 comprimés ou capsules par jour ou suivre les recommandations du médecin.

PRÉSENTATION

Comprimés et capsules: en association avec aspirine et caféine[C] ■ **Capsules**: en association avec aspirine, caféine et codéine[N]; voir l'annexe U.

SOINS INFIRMIERS

ÉVALUATION DE LA SITUATION

- Déterminer le type, le siège et l'intensité de la douleur avant et 60 minutes après l'administration du médicament.
- L'usage prolongé de cet agent peut entraîner une dépendance physique et psychologique ainsi qu'une tolérance aux effets du médicament, mais cela ne doit pas empêcher le patient de recevoir une quantité suffisante d'analgésique. La dépendance psychologique est rare chez la plupart des patients qui reçoivent des préparations de butalbital pour des raisons médicales.
- Évaluer la fréquence d'usage. Un usage fréquent et prolongé peut entraîner des céphalées quotidiennes chez les personnes prédisposées aux céphalées en raison d'une dépendance physique à la caféine et aux autres composés. Les céphalées chroniques dues à une surmédication (appelées céphalées rebond) sont difficiles à traiter et peuvent nécessiter l'hospitalisation du patient afin qu'il reçoive un traitement ou un médicament prophylactique.

DIAGNOSTICS INFIRMIERS POSSIBLES

- Douleur aiguë (Indications).
- Risque d'accident (Effets secondaires).
- Connaissances insuffisantes sur le traitement médicamenteux (Enseignement au patient et à ses proches).

INTERVENTIONS INFIRMIÈRES

- Pour augmenter l'effet analgésique de ce médicament, avant de l'administrer, en expliquer au patient la valeur thérapeutique.
- Après un traitement prolongé, interrompre l'administration graduellement pour prévenir les symptômes de sevrage.

PO: Administrer avec des aliments, du lait ou un grand verre d'eau afin de réduire l'irritation gastrique.

ENSEIGNEMENT AU PATIENT ET À SES PROCHES

- Conseiller au patient de respecter rigoureusement la posologie recommandée. Lui recommander de ne pas augmenter la dose en raison du risque d'accoutumance au butalbital. Si le médicament semble moins efficace après quelques semaines, il faut consulter un professionnel de la santé. Prévenir le patient que l'administration prolongée d'aspirine peut entraîner des lésions rénales et que les doses d'aspirine qui entrent dans la composition des préparations de butalbital ne devraient pas dépasser les doses maximales quotidiennes recommandées.
- Recommander au patient souffrant de céphalées vasculaires de prendre le médicament dès le premier signe de douleur. Lui conseiller également de se coucher dans une pièce sombre et calme. Le prévenir que si on lui a prescrit un médicament en prophylaxie, il doit continuer de le prendre.
- Prévenir le patient que les composés de butalbital peuvent provoquer de la somnolence ou des étourdissements. Lui conseiller de ne pas conduire et d'éviter les activités qui exigent sa vigilance jusqu'à ce qu'on ait la certitude que le médicament n'entraîne pas ces effets chez lui.
- Recommander au patient de ne pas boire d'alcool et de ne pas prendre d'autres dépresseurs du SNC en même temps que ce médicament.
- Recommander à la patiente d'utiliser une méthode de contraception supplémentaire non hormonale pendant la prise de composés de butalbital.

VÉRIFICATION DE L'EFFICACITÉ THÉRAPEUTIQUE

L'efficacité du traitement peut être démontrée par: la diminution de l'intensité de la douleur sans modification importante de l'état de conscience.

BUTOCONAZOLE,
voir Antifongiques vaginaux

ALERTE CLINIQUE

BUTORPHANOL

Apo-Butorphanol, PMS-Butorphanol, Stadol NS

CLASSIFICATION:
Analgésique opioïde (agoniste-antagoniste)

Grossesse – catégorie C

INDICATIONS

Soulagement de la douleur modérée à grave (l'efficacité du médicament, administré pendant plus de 3 jours, n'a pas été établie).

MÉCANISME D'ACTION

Liaison aux récepteurs des opioïdes du SNC ■ Modification de la perception de la douleur et de la réaction aux stimuli douloureux avec une dépression généralisée du SNC ■ Propriétés antagonistes partielles qui peuvent entraîner des symptômes de sevrage aux opioïdes en cas de pharmacodépendance physique. ***Effets thérapeutiques:*** Diminution de l'intensité de la douleur.

PHARMACOCINÉTIQUE

Absorption: Bonne à partir des muqueuses nasales.

Distribution: L'agent traverse la barrière placentaire et passe dans le lait maternel.

Métabolisme et excrétion: Métabolisme presque entièrement hépatique. De 11 à 14 % est excrété dans les fèces. Des quantités infimes sont excrétées par les reins.

Demi-vie: De 4 à 6 heures.

Profil temps-action (effet analgésique)

	DÉBUT D'ACTION	PIC	DURÉE
Voie intranasale	en 15 - 30 min	1 - 2 h	3 - 6 h

CONTRE-INDICATIONS, PRÉCAUTIONS ET MISES EN GARDE

Contre-indications: Hypersensibilité au butorphanol ou à l'un des ingrédients de la préparation.

Précautions et mises en garde: Traumatisme crânien ■ Pression intracrânienne accrue ■ Maladies rénale, hépatique ou pulmonaire graves (initialement, prolonger l'intervalle entre les prises jusqu'à 6 à 8 heures en présence d'insuffisance hépatique ou rénale) ■ Hypothyroïdie ■ Insuffisance surrénalienne ■ Alcoolisme ■ **GÉR.:** (ou patients débilités): Réduire la dose habituelle de 50 %; initialement, doubler l'intervalle posologique habituel ■ Douleurs abdominales non diagnostiquées ■ Hypertrophie de la prostate ■ **OBST., ALLAITEMENT, PÉD.** (< 18 ans): L'innocuité du médicament n'a pas été établie ■ Personnes présentant une dépendance physique aux opioïdes (risque accru de symptômes de sevrage).

RÉACTIONS INDÉSIRABLES ET EFFETS SECONDAIRES

SNC: confusion, dysphorie, hallucinations, sédation, euphorie, sensation de flottement, céphalées, rêves bizarres.

ORLO: vision trouble, diplopie, myosis (doses élevées).

Resp.: DÉPRESSION RESPIRATOIRE.

CV: hypertension, hypotension, palpitations.

GI: nausées, constipation, sécheresse de la bouche (xérostomie), iléus, vomissements.

GU: rétention urinaire.

Tég.: transpiration, sensation de peau moite et froide.

Divers: dépendance physique, dépendance psychologique, tolérance aux effets du médicament.

INTERACTIONS

Médicament-médicament: LE BUTORPHANOL DOIT ÊTRE ADMINISTRÉ AVEC UNE EXTRÊME PRUDENCE AUX PATIENTS RECEVANT DES **IMAO** (IL PEUT ENTRAÎNER DES RÉACTIONS GRAVES ET MÊME MORTELLES; RÉDUIRE LA DOSE INITIALE DE BUTORPHANOL À 25 % DE LA DOSE HABITUELLE) ■ Dépression additive du SNC et du système respiratoire lors de l'usage concomitant d'**alcool**, d'**antihistaminiques**, de **phénothiazines**, de **barbituriques**, d'**antidépresseurs**, d'**hypnosédatifs** et d'autres **opioïdes** ■ La prise de ce médicament peut déclencher des symptômes de sevrage chez les patients qui présentent une dépendance physique aux **opioïdes** ■ Le butorphanol peut diminuer les effets des **opioïdes** administrés en concomitance.

Médicament-produits naturels: Effets dépresseurs additifs sur le SNC lors de la consommation concomitante de **kava**, de **valériane**, de **scutellaire**, de **camomille** et de **houblon**.

VOIES D'ADMINISTRATION ET POSOLOGIE

- **Voie intranasale (adultes):** Initialement, 1 mg (une vaporisation dans une narine). Si la douleur n'est pas adéquatement soulagée dans les 60 à 90 minutes qui suivent, on peut administrer une dose supplémentaire de 1 mg. La posologie et la séquence d'administration initiales peuvent être répétées 3 ou 4 heures plus tard, selon les besoins. Si la douleur est intense et si le patient demeure en position couchée, on peut administrer initialement une dose de 2 mg (une vaporisation dans chaque narine). Dans ce cas, il ne faudrait pas administrer de dose supplémentaire pendant 3 ou 4 heures. La dose maximale est de 16 mg/jour.
- **Voie intranasale (personnes âgées):** Initialement, 1 mg (une vaporisation dans une narine). On peut administrer une dose supplémentaire de 90 à 120 minutes plus tard. Espacer les doses ultérieures d'au moins 6 heures.

INSUFFISANCE RÉNALE GRAVE (Cl_{CR} < 30 mL/MIN)

- **VOIE INTRANASALE (ADULTES):** L'INTERVALLE POSOLOGIQUE INITIAL DEVRAIT ÊTRE DE 6 À 8 HEURES, JUSQU'À CE QUE LES CARACTÉRISTIQUES DE LA RÉPONSE DU PATIENT SOIENT CONNUES. DÉTERMINER LES DOSES ULTÉRIEURES D'APRÈS LA RÉPONSE DU PATIENT PLUTÔT QUE D'OPTER POUR UNE ADMINISTRATION SELON UN HORAIRE FIXE.

INSUFFISANCE HÉPATIQUE

- **VOIE INTRANASALE (ADULTES):** L'INTERVALLE POSOLOGIQUE INITIAL DEVRAIT ÊTRE DE 6 À 12 HEURES, JUSQU'À CE QUE LES CARACTÉRISTIQUES DE LA RÉPONSE DU PATIENT SOIENT CONNUES. DÉTERMINER

LES DOSES ULTÉRIEURES D'APRÈS LA RÉPONSE DU PATIENT PLUTÔT QUE D'OPTER POUR UNE ADMINISTRATION SELON UN HORAIRE FIXE.

PRÉSENTATION

Solution pour vaporisation intranasale: 10 mg/mL – flacons de 2,5 mL avec vaporisateur-doseur (le flacon de 2,5 mL donne 14 ou 15 doses en moyenne; 1 mg/vaporisation)[C].

SOINS INFIRMIERS

ÉVALUATION DE LA SITUATION

- Noter le type, le siège et l'intensité de la douleur, avant l'administration du médicament, et de 60 à 90 minutes après l'administration par voie intranasale. Chez les patients ayant besoin de doses supérieures à 4 mg, on peut substituer au butorphanol un opioïde agoniste. Le butorphanol n'est pas recommandé en traitement prolongé ou en traitement de première intention des douleurs aiguës ou de celles dues au cancer.
- On devrait utiliser un tableau d'équivalences (voir l'annexe A) lorsqu'on change de voie d'administration ou de type d'opioïde.
- Mesurer la pression artérielle et le pouls et évaluer la fonction respiratoire avant l'administration du médicament et à intervalles réguliers pendant toute la durée du traitement. Si la fréquence respiratoire est < 10 respirations/minute, évaluer le niveau de sédation. Il peut s'avérer nécessaire de diminuer la dose de 25 à 50 %. Lorsqu'on augmente la dose du médicament, la dépression respiratoire ne s'aggrave pas, mais elle dure plus longtemps.
- Déterminer les antécédents de prises d'analgésiques du patient. En raison de ses propriétés antagonistes, le médicament peut induire chez les patients présentant une dépendance physique aux analgésiques opioïdes les symptômes suivants de sevrage: vomissements, agitation, crampes abdominales, pression artérielle accrue et fièvre.
- Bien que le risque de dépendance au butorphanol soit plus faible que dans le cas des autres opioïdes, l'administration prolongée de cet agent peut entraîner une pharmacodépendance physique et psychologique ainsi qu'une tolérance aux effets du médicament, ce qui ne doit pas empêcher le patient de recevoir une quantité suffisante d'analgésique. La dépendance psychologique est rare chez la plupart des patients qui reçoivent le butorphanol pour soulager la douleur. Si une tolérance aux effets du médicament se développe, il faudrait alors envisager l'administration d'un autre agoniste opioïde pour soulager la douleur.

Tests de laboratoire: Le médicament peut entraîner l'élévation des concentrations sériques d'amylase et de lipase.

TOXICITÉ ET SURDOSAGE: En cas de surdosage, la dépression respiratoire ou le coma peut être renversé par la naloxone (Narcan), qui est l'antidote du butorphanol. Diluer le contenu d'une ampoule à 0,4 mg de naloxone dans 10 mL d'une solution de NaCl 0,9 % et administrer 0,5 mL (0,02 mg) par bolus IV direct, toutes les 2 minutes. Chez les enfants et les patients pesant moins de 40 kg, diluer 0,1 mg de naloxone dans 10 mL de NaCl 0,9 % pour obtenir une concentration de 10 µg/mL et administrer 0,5 µg/kg, toutes les 1 à 2 minutes. Ajuster la dose pour éviter les symptômes de sevrage, les convulsions et les douleurs intenses.

DIAGNOSTICS INFIRMIERS POSSIBLES

- Douleur aiguë (Indications).
- Risque d'accident (Effets secondaires).
- Trouble de la perception sensorielle (visuelle, auditive) (Effets secondaires).
- Connaissances insuffisantes sur le traitement médicamenteux (Enseignement au patient et à ses proches).

INTERVENTIONS INFIRMIÈRES

- **ALERTE CLINIQUE**: DES SURDOSES ACCIDENTELLES D'ANALGÉSIQUES OPIOÏDES ONT CAUSÉ DES DÉCÈS. AVANT L'ADMINISTRATION, CLARIFIER TOUTE AMBIGUÏTÉ DES ORDONNANCES ET FAIRE VÉRIFIER L'ORDONNANCE D'ORIGINE ET LES CALCULS DES DOSES PAR UN AUTRE PROFESSIONNEL DE LA SANTÉ.
- NE PAS CONFONDRE STADOL ET HALDOL.
- Pour augmenter l'effet analgésique du butorphanol, expliquer au patient la valeur thérapeutique de ce médicament, avant de l'administrer.
- L'analgésie s'avère plus efficace si le médicament est administré avant que la douleur ne devienne intense.
- Les analgésiques non opioïdes, administrés simultanément, peuvent exercer des effets analgésiques additifs, ce qui permet de diminuer les doses d'opioïde.

Voie intranasale: Administrer une vaporisation dans une narine.

ENSEIGNEMENT AU PATIENT ET À SES PROCHES

- Expliquer au patient ce qu'on entend par administration au besoin et à quel moment il doit demander un analgésique.

B

- Prévenir le patient que le butorphanol peut provoquer de la somnolence ou des étourdissements. Lui recommander de demander de l'aide lorsqu'il se déplace et lui conseiller de ne pas conduire et d'éviter les activités qui exigent sa vigilance jusqu'à ce qu'on ait la certitude que le médicament n'entraîne pas ces effets chez lui.
- Recommander au patient de se tourner dans le lit, de tousser et de faire des exercices de respiration profonde toutes les 2 heures pour prévenir l'atélectasie.
- Recommander au patient de changer lentement de position pour diminuer le risque d'hypotension orthostatique.
- Mettre en garde le patient contre l'usage concomitant d'alcool ou d'autres dépresseurs du SNC.
- Conseiller au patient de pratiquer une bonne hygiène buccale, de se rincer la bouche fréquemment et de consommer de la gomme ou des bonbons sans sucre pour diminuer la sécheresse de la bouche.

Vaporisation intranasale:
- Expliquer au patient comment utiliser le vaporisateur nasal. Lui recommander de consulter la notice de conditionnement pour connaître le mode d'emploi détaillé. Lui expliquer qu'il doit replacer la pince de protection et le capuchon après usage et ranger le vaporisateur-doseur dans son contenant, gardé hors de la portée des enfants. Prévenir le patient que le médicament ne devrait pas être utilisé par une autre personne que celle à laquelle il a été prescrit. L'informer qu'il doit mettre au rebut le médicament inutilisé dès qu'il ne s'en sert plus. Pour ce faire, il doit dévisser le bouchon, rincer le flacon en pompant de l'eau à l'intérieur et jeter le contenant à la poubelle.
- Expliquer au patient que si une dose de 2 mg (2 vaporisations) lui est prescrite, il doit administrer une vaporisation dans chaque narine. Prévenir le patient que le butorphanol peut entraîner des étourdissements et de la dysphorie. Lui conseiller de rester couché après avoir pris une dose de 2 mg jusqu'à ce que sa réponse au médicament soit connue.

VÉRIFICATION DE L'EFFICACITÉ THÉRAPEUTIQUE

L'efficacité du traitement peut être démontrée par: la diminution de l'intensité de la douleur sans altération importante de l'état de conscience ni de la fonction respiratoire.

CABERGOLINE

Dostinex

CLASSIFICATION:

Antihyperprolactinémique (agoniste de la dopamine)

Grossesse – catégorie B

INDICATIONS

Traitement de l'hyperprolactinémie (idiopathique ou hypophysaire) ▪ Inhibition de la lactation physiologique.

MÉCANISME D'ACTION

Inhibition de la sécrétion de prolactine par une action dopaminergique de type agoniste. ***Effets thérapeutiques:*** Diminution de la sécrétion de prolactine.

PHARMACOCINÉTIQUE

Absorption: Bonne (PO); premier passage hépatique important.

Distribution: Tous les tissus, mais accumulation dans l'hypophyse.

Métabolisme et excrétion: Fort métabolisme hépatique; une fraction inférieure à 4 % est excrétée à l'état inchangé par les reins.

Demi-vie: De 63 à 69 heures.

Profil temps-action

(effet sur la concentration sérique de prolactine)

	DÉBUT D'ACTION	PIC	DURÉE
PO	inconnu	4 semaines	inconnue

CONTRE-INDICATIONS, PRÉCAUTIONS ET MISES EN GARDE

Contre-indications: Hypersensibilité à la cabergoline ou aux alcaloïdes de l'ergot ▪ Hypertension non maîtrisée.

Précautions et mises en garde: Grossesse ou allaitement ▪ Insuffisance hépatique ▪ Insuffisance rénale ▪ Risque d'hypotension ou d'hypotension orthostatique (la prudence est de mise lors de l'administration de ce médicament en association avec des antihypertenseurs) ▪ Antécédents de maladie cardiovasculaire ▪ Syndrome de Raynaud ▪ Antécédents d'ulcère gastroduodénal ou d'hémorragie digestive ▪ Antécédents de maladie mentale grave, en particulier de maladie psychotique ▪ **PÉD.**: L'innocuité de l'agent n'a pas été établie.

RÉACTIONS INDÉSIRABLES ET EFFETS SECONDAIRES

SNC: <u>étourdissements</u>, <u>céphalées</u>, dépression, somnolence, fatigue, nervosité, vertiges, faiblesse.

ORLO: vision anormale.

CV: hypotension orthostatique.

GI: <u>constipation</u>, <u>nausées</u>, douleurs abdominales, dyspepsie, vomissements.

GU: dysménorrhée.

End.: douleurs mammaires.

Métab.: bouffées vasomotrices.

SN: paresthésie.

INTERACTIONS

Médicament-médicament: Risque accru d'hypotension lors de l'administration concomitante d'**agents antihypertenseurs** ▪ L'efficacité de l'agent peut être réduite par les **phénothiazines**, les **butyrophénones** (**halopéridol**), les **thioxanthènes** ou le **métoclopramide** (éviter l'usage concomitant) ▪ Malgré l'absence de preuve concluante d'interaction entre la cabergoline et d'autres **alcaloïdes de l'ergot**, l'utilisation concomitante de ces médicaments durant un traitement de longue durée par la cabergoline est déconseillée ▪ La cabergoline ne devrait pas être administrée avec des **antibiotiques macrolides** (comme l'**érythromycine**) en raison du risque de biodisponibilité systémique et d'effets indésirables accrus.

VOIES D'ADMINISTRATION ET POSOLOGIE

- **PO (adultes)**: *Hyperprolactinémie* – initialement, 0,5 mg par semaine (en 1 ou 2 prises); la dose peut être majorée par paliers de 0,5 mg/semaine, à des intervalles de 4 semaines, jusqu'à 1 mg, 2 fois par semaine. *Inhibition de la lactation physiologique* – 1 mg en une seule prise, dose qui devrait être administrée le premier jour du postpartum.

PRÉSENTATION

Comprimés: 0,5 mg^{Pr}.

SOINS INFIRMIERS

ÉVALUATION DE LA SITUATION

Mesurer la pression artérielle avant l'administration du médicament et à intervalles fréquents pendant le traitement initial. Des doses initiales supérieures à 1 mg peuvent provoquer une hypotension orthostatique. Faire preuve de prudence lors de l'administration concomitante d'autres médicaments qui abaissent la pression artérielle. Surveiller attentivement les déplacements et les transferts du patient pendant la période initiale d'adaptation de la posologie pour éviter les accidents dus à l'hypotension.

Tests de laboratoire: On devrait mesurer les concentrations sériques de prolactine tous les mois, jusqu'à ce qu'elles reviennent aux valeurs normales (< 20 µg/L chez les femmes et < 15 µg/L chez les hommes).

C

DIAGNOSTICS INFIRMIERS POSSIBLES

- Risque d'accident (Effets secondaires).
- Connaissances insuffisantes sur le traitement médicamenteux (Enseignement au patient et à ses proches).

INTERVENTIONS INFIRMIÈRES

Cet agent peut être pris avec ou sans aliments.

ENSEIGNEMENT AU PATIENT ET À SES PROCHES

- Recommander au patient de respecter rigoureusement la posologie recommandée. S'il n'a pu prendre le médicament au moment habituel, il doit le prendre aussitôt que possible, le lendemain ou le surlendemain. S'il ne l'a pas pris jusqu'au jour où il doit prendre la dose suivante, il ne doit pas doubler la dose. Lui conseiller de prévenir un professionnel de la santé s'il souffre de nausées.
- Prévenir le patient que la cabergoline peut provoquer de la somnolence et des étourdissements. Lui conseiller de ne pas conduire et d'éviter les activités qui exigent sa vigilance jusqu'à ce qu'on ait la certitude que le médicament n'entraîne pas ces effets chez lui.
- Recommander au patient de changer lentement de position pour prévenir le risque d'hypotension orthostatique.
- Recommander au patient d'éviter de boire de l'alcool pendant qu'il prend ce médicament.
- Conseiller à la patiente d'utiliser une méthode contraceptive non hormonale et de prévenir un professionnel de la santé sans délai si elle prévoit devenir enceinte ou si elle pense l'être.
- Recommander au patient qui prend la cabergoline pour traiter une tumeur hypophysaire d'informer immédiatement un professionnel de la santé si les signes suivants qui évoquent l'accroissement de la taille de la tumeur se manifestent: vision trouble, céphalées soudaines, fortes nausées et vomissements.
- Insister sur l'importance des examens de suivi réguliers permettant d'évaluer l'efficacité du traitement et de surveiller les effets secondaires.

VÉRIFICATION DE L'EFFICACITÉ THÉRAPEUTIQUE

L'efficacité du traitement peut être démontrée par: la diminution de la galactorrhée chez les patients souffrant d'hyperprolactinémie ■ On peut abandonner le traitement à la cabergoline si les taux sériques normaux de prolactine se maintiennent pendant plus de 6 mois. On devrait mesurer ces taux à intervalles réguliers pour déterminer s'il est nécessaire de reprendre le traitement par la cabergoline. ✳

CALCITONINE (SAUMON)

Calcimar, Caltine, Miacalcin NS, Apo-Calcitonin, Sandoz-Calcitonin NS

CLASSIFICATION:

Hormones de régularisation du calcium et du phosphore: traitement de l'hypercalcémie, traitement de la maladie de Paget

Grossesse – catégorie C

INDICATIONS

IM, SC: Traitement de la maladie osseuse de Paget ■ Traitement d'appoint de l'hypercalcémie ■ **Voie intranasale:** Traitement de l'ostéoporose postménopausique. **Usages non approuvés:** Douleurs osseuses.

MÉCANISME D'ACTION

Diminution de la concentration de calcium sérique par un effet direct sur les os, les reins et le tractus gastro-intestinal ■ Activation de l'excrétion rénale du calcium. ***Effets thérapeutiques:*** Inhibition de la résorption osseuse accélérée ■ Diminution des concentrations de calcium sérique.

PHARMACOCINÉTIQUE

Absorption: Complète (IM et SC); rapide à partir des muqueuses nasales; écart de 3 % par rapport à l'administration parentérale.

Distribution: Inconnue.

Métabolisme et excrétion: Métabolisme rapide dans les reins, le sang et les tissus.

Demi-vie: De 70 à 90 minutes.

Profil temps-action (effets thérapeutiques)

	DÉBUT D'ACTION	PIC	DURÉE
IM, SC†	inconnu	2 h	6 – 8 h
Voie intranasale‡	rapide	31 – 39 min	inconnue

† Effet sur la concentration sérique de calcium; en présence de maladie de Paget, pour que l'effet sur la phosphatase alcaline et l'hydroxyproline urinaire soit notable, il faut compter de 6 à 24 mois de traitement.

‡ Concentration sérique de calcitonine.

CONTRE-INDICATIONS, PRÉCAUTIONS ET MISES EN GARDE

Contre-indications: Hypersensibilité aux protéines de saumon ou aux diluants de gélatine.

Précautions et mises en garde: **OBST.**: Grossesse et allaitement (l'usage de cet agent est déconseillé) ▪ **PÉD.**: L'innocuité de cet agent n'a pas été établie.

RÉACTIONS INDÉSIRABLES ET EFFETS SECONDAIRES

SNC: céphalées.

ORLO: *voie nasale seulement* – épistaxis, irritation nasale, rhinite.

GI: *IM, SC* – nausées, vomissements, goût inusité, diarrhée.

GU: *IM, SC* – mictions fréquentes.

Tég.: rash.

Locaux: réactions au point d'injection.

Loc.: *voie nasale* – arthralgie, douleurs lombaires.

Divers: réactions allergiques incluant l'ANAPHYLAXIE, rougeur du visage, enflure, picotements et sensibilité au niveau des mains.

INTERACTIONS

Médicament-médicament: Un traitement antérieur par un biphosphonate, comme l'**étidronate**, l'**alendronate** et le **pamidronate**, peut réduire la réponse à la calcitonine.

VOIES D'ADMINISTRATION ET POSOLOGIE

Ostéoporose postménopausique

- **Voie intranasale (adultes):** 200 UI par jour.

Maladie de Paget

IM, SC (adultes): Initialement, 100 UI par jour; ensuite, environ 50 UI par jour ou de 50 à 100 UI, 3 fois par semaine comme dose d'entretien.

Hypercalcémie

- **IM, SC (adultes):** 4 UI/kg, toutes les 12 heures; on peut augmenter la dose après 1 ou 2 jours jusqu'à concurrence de 8 UI/kg, toutes les 12 heures. Si besoin est, après 2 jours de plus, on peut aller jusqu'à 8 UI/kg, toutes les 6 heures.

PRÉSENTATION

Solution pour injection: 100 UI/mL[Pr], 200 UI/mL[Pr] ▪ **Vaporisateur nasal:** 200 UI/vaporisation[Pr].

SOINS INFIRMIERS

ÉVALUATION DE LA SITUATION

- RESTER À L'AFFÛT DES SIGNES SUIVANTS D'HYPERSENSIBILITÉ: RASH, FIÈVRE, ÉRUPTIONS URTICARIENNES, ANAPHYLAXIE, MALADIE SÉRIQUE. GARDER DE L'ADRÉNALINE, DES ANTIHISTAMINIQUES ET DE L'OXYGÈNE À PORTÉE DE LA MAIN POUR PARER À UNE ÉVENTUELLE RÉACTION ANAPHYLACTIQUE.
- Au cours de l'administration des premières doses de calcitonine, rechercher les signes suivants de tétanie hypocalcémique: nervosité, irritabilité, paresthésie, soubresauts musculaires, spasmes tétaniques, convulsions. Garder à portée de la main du calcium destiné à l'administration par voie parentérale (p. ex., gluconate de calcium), pour parer à cette éventualité.
- **Voie intranasale:** Évaluer à intervalles réguliers pendant toute la durée du traitement la muqueuse nasale, la cloison, les cornets ainsi que les vaisseaux sanguins nasaux.

Tests de laboratoire:

- Noter à intervalles réguliers pendant toute la durée du traitement, les concentrations sériques de phosphatase alcaline et de calcium. Ces concentrations devraient se normaliser dans les quelques mois qui suivent le début du traitement.
- Suivre à intervalles réguliers l'hydroxyproline urinaire (24 heures) chez les patients souffrant de la maladie de Paget.

DIAGNOSTICS INFIRMIERS POSSIBLES

- Douleur aiguë (Indications).
- Risque d'accident (Indications, Effets secondaires).
- Connaissances insuffisantes sur le traitement médicamenteux (Enseignement au patient et à ses proches).

INTERVENTIONS INFIRMIÈRES

- Avant le début du traitement, déterminer la sensibilité à la calcitonine de saumon, en administrant par voie intradermique une dose d'épreuve (1 UI) dans la face intérieure de l'avant-bras. Pour préparer une dose d'épreuve, faire une dilution de 10 UI/mL, en prélevant 0,05 mL (10 UI) d'une solution à 200 UI/mL ou 0,1 mL (10 UI) d'une solution à 100 UI/mL dans une seringue à tuberculine que l'on remplira jusqu'à concurrence de 1 mL avec une solution de NaCl 0,9 % pour injection. Bien mélanger et jeter 0,9 mL. Administrer 0,1 mL (1 UI) et observer le point d'injection pendant 15 minutes. La présence d'un érythème plus que léger ou d'une papule signifie que le patient est allergique à ce médicament.
- Garder la solution au réfrigérateur.

IM, SC:

- Observer le point d'injection pour déceler la rougeur, l'enflure ou la douleur. Assurer la rotation des points d'injection. La voie SC est la voie d'administration privilégiée. Administrer par voie IM si la dose est supérieure à 2 mL. Utiliser plusieurs points d'injection pour diminuer le risque de réaction inflammatoire.

- Ne pas administrer la solution si elle a changé de couleur ou si elle renferme des particules.

ENSEIGNEMENT AU PATIENT ET À SES PROCHES

- Conseiller au patient de respecter rigoureusement la posologie recommandée. S'il n'a pu prendre le médicament au moment habituel et si le médecin lui a prescrit 2 doses par jour, il ne doit s'autoadministrer l'injection que dans les 2 heures qui suivent l'heure habituelle. Si le médecin lui a prescrit une seule dose par jour, il ne doit s'autoadministrer la dose manquée que le jour même. S'il doit s'autoadministrer le médicament tous les 2 jours, il doit s'injecter la dose manquée dès que possible et reprendre ensuite le programme recommandé d'un jour sur deux. Si le médecin lui a prescrit 1 dose, 3 fois par semaine (lundi, mercredi, vendredi), il doit prendre la dose manquée le lendemain et reporter chaque injection d'une journée; il doit ensuite reprendre l'horaire habituel la semaine suivante. Le prévenir qu'il ne faut jamais remplacer une dose manquée par une double dose.
- Faire la démonstration de la méthode d'autoadministration de l'injection.
- Recommander au patient de signaler rapidement à un professionnel de la santé toute réaction allergique et les signes suivants d'hypercalcémie récidivante: douleur profonde des os ou du flanc, calculs rénaux, anorexie, nausées, vomissements, soif, léthargie.
- Expliquer au patient que les bouffées vasomotrices et la sensation de chaleur qu'il risque d'éprouver après l'injection sont passagères et ne durent habituellement qu'environ 1 heure.
- Expliquer au patient que les nausées qui se manifestent après l'injection ont tendance à diminuer avec le temps, même s'il poursuit le traitement.
- Recommander au patient de ne consommer des aliments à faible teneur en calcium que si un professionnel de la santé lui a prescrit un tel régime (voir l'annexe J). Les femmes souffrant d'ostéoporose postménopausique devraient consommer des aliments riches en calcium et en vitamine D.

Ostéoporose: Expliquer au patient qui reçoit de la calcitonine pour le traitement de l'ostéoporose que l'exercice semble arrêter, voire même renverser, le processus de résorption osseuse. Lui recommander de demander à un professionnel de la santé, avant de s'engager dans un programme d'exercices, s'il lui faut restreindre ses activités physiques.

Voie intranasale:

- Montrer au patient comment utiliser le vaporisateur nasal. Lors de la première utilisation seulement, il faut d'abord activer la pompe en la tenant droite et en ramenant les ailerons blancs vers le flacon (suivre les recommandations du fabricant). La pompe est prête à l'emploi lorsque la fenêtre qui se trouve dans le bas passe au vert. Après l'activation, introduire l'embout fermement dans la narine, en gardant la tête droite, puis actionner la pompe. Une marque rouge qui apparaît dans la fenêtre du compteur indique que le flacon est vide.
- Une fois ouvert, le flacon vaporisateur doit être conservé à la température ambiante, et son contenu doit être utilisé en l'espace de 4 semaines au maximum.
- Recommander au patient de signaler à un professionnel de la santé une irritation nasale importante.

VÉRIFICATION DE L'EFFICACITÉ THÉRAPEUTIQUE

L'efficacité du traitement peut être démontrée par: la diminution des concentrations sériques de calcium ■ la diminution des douleurs osseuses ■ le ralentissement de l'évolution de l'ostéoporose postménopausique. Une amélioration marquée de la densité osseuse peut être observée dès le premier mois de traitement. ✳

CALCITRIOL,

voir Vitamine D (composés de)

ALERTE CLINIQUE

CALCIUM, SELS DE

acétate de calcium (25 % de Ca ou 6,3 mmol/g)
Acétate de calcium

carbonate de calcium (40 % de Ca ou 10 mmol/g)
Apo-Cal, Calci-forte, Calcite, Cal-citrus, Calcium Rougier, Calcium Sandoz, Cal-Plus, Calsan, Caltrate, Neo-Cal, Nu-Cal, Os-Cal, Tums, Tums E-X, Viactiv

chlorure de calcium (27 % de Ca ou 6,8 mmol/g)
Calciject, Chlorure de calcium

citrate de calcium (21 % de Ca ou 5,3 mmol/g)
Citracal, Citrate de calcium

gluconate de calcium (9 % de Ca ou 2,25 mmol/g)
Gluconate de calcium

CLASSIFICATION:
Minéraux et électrolytes (suppléments de calcium)

Grossesse – catégories C (acétate de calcium, chlorure de calcium, injections de gluconate de calcium) et inconnue (carbonate de calcium, citrate de calcium)

INDICATIONS

PO, IV: Traitement et prévention de l'hypocalcémie ■ Tétanie ■ **PO:** Traitement préventif d'appoint de l'ostéoporose postménopausique ■ Hypoparathyroïdie ■ Pseudohypoparathyroïdie ■ Ostéomalacie ■ Hypocalcémie secondaire à un traitement anticonvulsivant ■ **IV:** Traitement d'urgence de l'hyperkaliémie et de l'hypermagnésémie et traitement d'appoint en cas d'arrêt cardiaque (chlorure de calcium, gluconate de calcium) ■ Traitement d'appoint dans un certain nombre de cas comme les morsures ou les piqûres d'insectes, les réactions allergiques comme l'urticaire ou l'œdème angioneurotique, le surdosage au sulfate de magnésium, la colique saturnine ■ **Carbonate de calcium:** Usage possible à titre d'antiacide ■ **Acétate et carbonate de calcium:** Maîtrise de l'hyperphosphatémie en présence d'une néphropathie terminale.

MÉCANISME D'ACTION

Élément essentiel pour le fonctionnement du système nerveux et de l'appareil locomoteur ■ Maintien de la perméabilité des membranes cellulaires et des capillaires ■ Activation de la transmission des influx nerveux et de la contraction des muscles squelettiques et cardiaques et des muscles lisses ■ Élément essentiel pour la formation osseuse et la coagulation du sang. ***Effets thérapeutiques:*** Substitution du calcium en cas de carence ■ Maîtrise de l'hyperphosphatémie en présence de néphropathie terminale, sans que l'absorption de l'aluminium (acétate de calcium et carbonate de calcium) en soit accrue.

PHARMACOCINÉTIQUE

Absorption: *PO* – l'apport en vitamine D doit être suffisant pour qu'il y ait absorption. *IV* – biodisponibilité à 100 % (IV).

Distribution: Rapide dans le liquide extracellulaire. Le médicament traverse la barrière placentaire et passe dans le lait maternel.

Métabolisme et excrétion: L'excrétion est surtout fécale; 20 % est éliminé par les reins.

Demi-vie: Inconnue.

Profil temps-action (effet sur le taux de calcium sérique)

	DÉBUT D'ACTION	PIC	DURÉE
PO	inconnu	inconnu	inconnue
IV	immédiat	immédiat	0,5 – 2 h

CONTRE-INDICATIONS, PRÉCAUTIONS ET MISES EN GARDE

Contre-indications: Hypercalcémie ■ Fibrillation ventriculaire ■ Cardiopathie grave ■ Néphropathie ■ Hypercalciurie ■ Perte de calcium due à l'immobilisation.

Précautions et mises en garde: Patients recevant des dérivés digitaliques ■ Insuffisance respiratoire grave ■ Maladie rénale ■ Calculs rénaux ■ Maladie cardiaque.

RÉACTIONS INDÉSIRABLES ET EFFETS SECONDAIRES

SNC: syncope (voie IV seulement), picotements.

CV: ARRÊT CARDIAQUE (voie IV seulement), arythmies, bradycardie.

GI: constipation, nausées, vomissements.

GU: calculs, hypercalciurie.

Locaux: phlébite (voie IV seulement).

INTERACTIONS

Médicament-médicament: L'hypercalcémie augmente le risque de toxicité par les **dérivés digitaliques** ■ L'utilisation prolongée de calcium avec des **antiacides** peut induire, en présence d'une insuffisance rénale, le syndrome du lait et des alcalins (syndrome de Burnett) ■ La prise par voie orale de ces préparations de calcium diminue l'absorption des **tétracyclines**, des **fluoroquinolones**, de la **phénytoïne** et des **sels de fer**, administrés par voie orale ■ Les préparations à base de calcium, prises en quantités excessives, peuvent diminuer les effets des **bloqueurs des canaux calciques** ■ Ces agents diminuent l'absorption de l'**étidronate**, du **risedronate** et de l'**alendronate** (ne pas prendre ces médicaments dans les 2 heures précédant ou suivant la prise de suppléments de calcium) ■ Les suppléments de calcium peuvent diminuer l'efficacité de l'**aténolol** ■ L'usage concomitant de **diurétiques thiazidiques** peut induire une hypercalcémie ■ Les sels de calcium peuvent diminuer la capacité du **sulfonate de polystyrène sodique** de réduire les taux de potassium sérique.

Médicament-aliments: Les **produits céréaliers**, les **épinards** ou la **rhubarbe** peuvent diminuer l'absorption des suppléments de calcium ■ L'acétate de calcium ne devrait pas être administré en même temps que d'autres **suppléments de calcium**.

C

VOIES D'ADMINISTRATION ET POSOLOGIE

Les doses sont indiquées en mg, en g ou en mmol de calcium. 1 g de chlorure de calcium = 270 mg (6,7 mmol) de calcium élémentaire. 1 g de gluconate de calcium = 90 mg (2,25 mmol) de calcium élémentaire.

- **PO (adultes)**: *Prévention de l'hypocalcémie, traitement des carences, ostéoporose* – de 1 à 1,5 g/jour. *Antiacide* – de 0,5 à 1,5 g, selon les besoins (carbonate de calcium seulement). *Hyperphosphatémie en présence d'une néphropathie terminale (acétate de calcium et carbonate de calcium)* – quantité nécessaire pour normaliser les taux sériques de phosphate et de calcium. La posologie habituelle correspond à environ 500 à 700 mg de calcium élémentaire pris à chaque repas.
- **PO (enfants)**: *Supplément* – de 45 à 65 mg/kg/jour.
- **PO (nourrissons)**: *Hypocalcémie du nourrisson* – de 50 à 150 mg/kg (ne pas dépasser 1 g).
- **IV (adultes)**: *Traitement d'urgence de l'hypocalcémie, réanimation cardiaque* – de 3,5 à 7 mmol. *Tétanie hypocalcémique* – de 2,25 à 8 mmol; répéter l'administration 1 fois par jour jusqu'à ce que les symptômes soient maîtrisés. *Hyperkaliémie avec cardiotoxicité* – de 1,25 à 7 mmol; répéter, au besoin, après 1 ou 2 minutes. *Hypermagnésémie* – 2,5 à 5 mmol; répéter en fonction de la réponse obtenue.
- **IV (enfants)**: *Traitement d'urgence de l'hypocalcémie* – de 0,5 à 3,5 mmol. *Tétanie hypocalcémique* – de 0,25 à 0,7 mmol/kg, 3 ou 4 fois par jour.
- **IV (nourissons)**: *Traitement d'urgence de l'hypocalcémie* – < 0,5 mmol. *Tétanie hypocalcémique* – 1,2 mmol/kg/jour en doses fractionnées.

PRÉSENTATION
(version générique disponible)

- **Carbonate de calcium**
  Consulter les monographies de chaque fabricant pour connaître les différentes préparations offertes.
- **Chlorure de calcium**
  Solution pour injection: 10 % (0,7 mmol/mL)[Pr].
- **Gluconate de calcium**
  Comprimés: 500 mg (45 mg de Ca)[VL], 650 mg (58,5 mg de Ca)[VL], 975 mg (87,75 mg de Ca)[VL], 1 g (90 mg de Ca)[VL] ■ **Solution pour injection**: 10 % (0,23 mmol/mL)[Pr].

Les sels de calcium sont présentés sous de nombreuses formes pharmaceutiques: comprimés (ordinaires, à croquer, effervescents, etc.), capsules, liquide, poudre et solution pour injection de teneurs. Consulter la monographie du fabricant pour plus de détails.

SOINS INFIRMIERS

ÉVALUATION DE LA SITUATION

Supplément de calcium ou traitement de supplémentation calcique:

- Rester à l'affût des signes suivants d'hypocalcémie: paresthésie, soubresauts musculaires, laryngospasme, coliques, arythmies cardiaques et signe de Chvostek ou de Trousseau. En signaler l'apparition au médecin ou à un autre professionnel de la santé. Pour protéger les patients qui manifestent des symptômes d'hypocalcémie, remonter et rembourrer les ridelles du lit; garder le lit en position basse.
- MESURER SOUVENT LA PRESSION ARTÉRIELLE ET LE POULS; SUIVRE L'ÉCG PENDANT TOUTE LA DURÉE DU TRAITEMENT PAR VOIE PARENTÉRALE. LE MÉDICAMENT PEUT INDUIRE LA VASODILATATION ET, PAR VOIE DE CONSÉQUENCE, L'HYPOTENSION, LA BRADYCARDIE, DES ARYTHMIES ET L'ARRÊT CARDIAQUE. UNE ÉLÉVATION PASSAGÈRE DE LA PRESSION ARTÉRIELLE PEUT SURVENIR DURANT L'ADMINISTRATION PAR VOIE IV, PARTICULIÈREMENT CHEZ LES PATIENTS ÂGÉS OU HYPERTENDUS.
- Vérifier la perméabilité de la tubulure IV. L'extravasation peut provoquer la cellulite, la nécrose et la desquamation tissulaire.
- Suivre de près le patient prenant des dérivés digitaliques pour déceler les signes de toxicité digitalique.

Antiacide: Lorsqu'on administre le médicament en tant qu'antiacide, rester à l'affût des symptômes suivants: pyrosis, indigestion, douleurs abdominales. Inspecter l'abdomen; ausculter les bruits intestinaux.

Tests de laboratoire:

- Examiner les concentrations sériques de calcium ou de calcium ionisé, de chlorure, de sodium, de potassium, de magnésium, d'albumine et d'hormone parathyroïdienne (PTH), avant l'administration de ces agents et à intervalles réguliers pendant toute la durée du traitement de l'hypocalcémie.
- En cas d'administration prolongée ou excessive, l'agent peut entraîner une baisse des concentrations sériques de phosphate. Dans le traitement de l'hyperphosphatémie chez les patients souffrant d'insuffisance rénale, suivre les concentrations de phosphate.

TOXICITÉ ET SURDOSAGE: Suivre de près le patient pour déceler l'apparition des symptômes suivants d'hypercalcémie: nausées, vomissements, anorexie, soif, constipation grave, iléus paralytique et bradycardie. Signaler immédiatement au médecin ces symptômes.

DIAGNOSTICS INFIRMIERS POSSIBLES

- Alimentation déficiente (Indications).
- Risque d'accident relié à l'ostéoporose et au déséquilibre électrolytique (Indications).
- Connaissances insuffisantes sur le traitement médicamenteux (Enseignement au patient et à ses proches).

INTERVENTIONS INFIRMIÈRES

Alerte clinique: Des erreurs dans l'administration du calcium intraveineux sont survenues à cause d'une confusion entre les différents sels prescrits. Les doses en milligrammes de chlorure de calcium, de gluconate de calcium et de gluceptate de calcium ne sont pas équivalentes; éviter de substituer ces agents l'un à l'autre. On peut généralement trouver sur le chariot de réanimation du chlorure de calcium et du gluconate de calcium. Le médecin doit préciser la forme de calcium qu'il souhaite administrer. Les doses devraient être exprimées en mmol.

- Ne pas confondre Os-Cal (carbonate de calcium) avec Asacol (mésalamine).
- En cas d'arrêt cardiaque, l'administration de chlorure de calcium est maintenant réservée aux patients souffrant d'hyperkaliémie et d'hypocalcémie ou intoxiqués par les bloqueurs des canaux calciques.

PO: Administrer les sels de calcium avec les repas pour en augmenter l'absorption. Demander au patient de bien mâcher les comprimés à croquer avant de les avaler. Dissoudre les comprimés effervescents dans un verre d'eau. Demander au patient de boire un grand verre d'eau après avoir pris une dose par voie orale, sauf s'il s'agit de carbonate de calcium utilisé comme chélateur de phosphore lors d'une dialyse rénale. Dans le traitement de l'hyperphosphatémie, administrer les suppléments de calcium avec les repas.

IM: Dans les situations d'urgence, on peut administrer le gluconate de calcium par voie IM si les veines sont inaccessibles. Chez l'enfant, n'administrer l'injection que dans la cuisse. Chez l'adulte, n'administrer l'injection que dans le muscle fessier. Ne pas administrer le chlorure de calcium par voie IM.

IV:

- Réchauffer les solutions IV à la température du corps et les administrer par une aiguille de petit diamètre dans une grosse veine pour diminuer les risques de phlébite. Ne pas administrer la préparation dans une veine du cuir chevelu. L'injection peut provoquer une sensation de brûlure, une vasodilatation périphérique et une chute de la pression artérielle. Demander au patient de rester couché pendant 30 à 60 minutes après l'administration IV. Consulter les directives de chaque fabricant avant d'administrer la préparation.
- En cas d'infiltration, arrêter l'administration IV. On peut surélever la région atteinte ou appliquer de la chaleur et infiltrer localement un soluté ordinaire, du chlorhydrate de procaïne à 1 % ou de l'hyaluronidase.
- **Alerte clinique:** Administrer la solution lentement. Des concentrations élevées peuvent provoquer l'arrêt cardiaque. L'administration rapide peut provoquer des picotements, une sensation de chaleur ou un goût métallique. Arrêter la perfusion si ces symptômes se manifestent et la reprendre à un débit plus lent lorsqu'ils disparaissent.
- La solution doit être transparente. Ne pas l'utiliser si des cristaux se sont formés.

Chlorure de calcium

IV directe: On peut administrer le chlorure de calcium sans dilution préalable par injection IV directe.

Perfusion intermittente ou continue: On peut diluer le chlorure de calcium dans une solution de D5%E ou de D10%E, dans une solution de NaCl 0,9 %, dans une solution de D5% et de NaCl 0,25 %, 0,45 % ou 0,9 % ou dans une solution de D5% et de lactate de Ringer.

Vitesse d'administration: Le débit maximal chez l'adulte est de 0,35 à 0,75 mmol/min (de 0,5 à 1 mL de solution à 10 %); chez les enfants, il est de 0,5 mL/min. Consulter les directives de chaque fabricant avant d'administrer la préparation.

Association compatible dans la même seringue: milrinone.

Compatibilité (tubulure en Y): amrinone ▪ dobutamine ▪ adrénaline ▪ esmolol ▪ morphine ▪ paclitaxel.

Incompatibilité (tubulure en Y): propofol ▪ sodium, bicarbonate de.

Gluconate de calcium

IV directe: Administrer lentement par injection IV directe.

Vitesse d'administration: Le débit maximal chez l'adulte est de 1,5 mL à la minute (de 0,35 à 0,75 mmol/min). Consulter les directives de chaque fabricant avant d'administrer la préparation.

Perfusion continue: On peut effectuer une dilution supplémentaire dans 1 000 mL de solution de D5%E, D10%E ou D20%E, de solution de D5%/NaCl 0,9 %, de solution de NaCl 0,9 %, de solution de D5% et de lactate de Ringer ou de lactate de Ringer.

Vitesse d'administration: Le débit maximal chez l'adulte est de 200 mg/min pendant 12 à 24 heures. Consulter les directives de chaque fabricant avant d'administrer la préparation.

Association incompatible dans la même seringue: métoclopramide.

C

Compatibilité (tubulure en Y): adrénaline ■ aldesleukine ■ allopurinol ■ amifostine ■ aztréonam ■ céfazoline ■ céfépime ■ ciprofloxacine ■ cladribine ■ dobutamine ■ énalaprilate ■ famotidine ■ filgrastim ■ granisétron ■ labétol ■ melphalan ■ méropenem ■ midazolam ■ nétilmicine ■ pipéracilline/tazobactam ■ potassium, chlorure de ■ prochlorpérazine, édisylate de ■ propofol ■ sargramostim ■ tacrolimus ■ téniposide ■ thiotépa ■ tolazoline ■ vinorelbine ■ vitamine du complexe B avec C.

Incompatibilité (tubulure en Y): fluconazole ■ indométhacine.

ENSEIGNEMENT AU PATIENT ET À SES PROCHES

- Recommander au patient de ne pas prendre de comprimés à délitement entérique 1 heure avant de prendre le carbonate de calcium ou 1 heure après l'avoir pris étant donné le risque de dissolution prématurée de ces comprimés.
- Expliquer au patient qu'il ne doit pas prendre de préparations de calcium en même temps que des aliments riches en acide oxalique (épinards, rhubarbe), en acide phytique (son, produits céréaliers) ou en phosphore (lait ou produits laitiers). Lui expliquer que s'il prend ces suppléments en même temps que des produits laitiers, il s'expose au risque d'apparition du syndrome du lait et des alcalins (syndrome de Burnett) dont les symptômes sont les nausées, les vomissements, la confusion et les céphalées. Conseiller au patient d'attendre de 1 à 2 heures avant de prendre d'autres médicaments ou de les prendre de 1 à 2 heures avant les préparations de calcium, si possible.
- Conseiller au patient qui suit un traitement par le calcium de prendre dès que possible toute dose qu'il a omis de s'autoadministrer au moment habituel et de reprendre par la suite l'horaire habituel.
- Prévenir le patient que le carbonate de calcium peut provoquer la constipation. Lui expliquer les méthodes permettant de la prévenir: augmenter la consommation de liquides et d'aliments riches en fibres et faire de l'exercice. Lui recommander également de consulter le médecin à propos de l'utilisation de laxatifs. Une constipation grave peut être un signe de toxicité.
- Conseiller au patient d'éviter l'usage excessif du tabac ou la consommation excessive de boissons contenant de l'alcool ou de la caféine.

Supplément de calcium: Encourager le patient à consommer des aliments riches en vitamine D (voir l'annexe J).

Ostéoporose: Expliquer au patient que l'exercice semble arrêter, voire même renverser, la résorption osseuse. Lui recommander toutefois de s'informer auprès d'un professionnel de la santé s'il faut restreindre ses activités physiques, avant de s'engager dans un programme d'exercices.

VÉRIFICATION DE L'EFFICACITÉ THÉRAPEUTIQUE

L'efficacité du traitement peut être démontrée par: l'élévation des concentrations sériques de calcium ■ la diminution des signes et des symptômes d'hypocalcémie ■ la suppression de l'indigestion ■ la normalisation de l'hyperphosphatémie chez les patients souffrant d'insuffisance rénale (acétate et carbonate de calcium). ✳

CANDÉSARTAN,

voir Antagonistes des récepteurs de l'angiotensine II

ALERTE CLINIQUE

CAPÉCITABINE

Xeloda

CLASSIFICATION:

Antinéoplasique (antimétabolite)

Grossesse – catégorie D

INDICATIONS

En monothérapie: traitement du cancer du sein avancé ou métastatique après échec d'un traitement classique par un taxane (à moins de contre-indication clinique au traitement par un taxane) ■ Traitement adjuvant du cancer du côlon de stade III (stade C selon la classification de Dukes) ■ Traitement de première ligne du cancer colorectal métastatique ■ En association avec le docétaxel: traitement du cancer du sein avancé ou métastatique après échec d'un traitement contenant une anthracycline.

MÉCANISME D'ACTION

La capécitabine se transforme dans les tissus en 5-fluorouracile, qui inhibe la synthèse de l'ADN et de l'ARN en empêchant la production de thymidine ■ Certaines tumeurs peuvent présenter des concentrations plus fortes de l'enzyme responsable de la dernière étape de la transformation en 5-fluorouracile (5-FU). ***Effets thérapeutiques:*** Destruction des cellules à réplication rapide, particulièrement des cellules malignes.

PHARMACOCINÉTIQUE

Absorption: Bonne (PO).

Distribution: Inconnue.

Métabolisme et excrétion: Métabolisme tissulaire et hépatique; excrétion majoritairement rénale sous forme de métabolites inactifs.

Demi-vie: 45 minutes.

Profil temps-action

	DÉBUT D'ACTION	PIC	DURÉE
PO	inconnu†	1,5 h (5-FU : 2 h)‡	inconnue

† L'effet antinéoplasique se manifeste à la 6e semaine.
‡ Les concentrations de 5-FU atteignent un pic après 2 heures.

CONTRE-INDICATIONS, PRÉCAUTIONS ET MISES EN GARDE

Contre-indications: Hypersensibilité à la capécitabine, à tout autre ingrédient du médicament ou au 5-fluorouracile ■ Insuffisance rénale grave (Cl_{Cr} < 30 mL/min) ■ Déficit connu en dihydropyrimidine-déshydrogénase (enzyme qui métabolise le 5-FU le transformant en métabolites non toxiques).

Précautions et mises en garde: **GÉR.**: Risque accru de diarrhée grave chez les patients > 80 ans; risque accru d'effets indésirables lors de l'administration en association avec le docétaxel; risque accru de saignements lors de la prise d'anticoagulants oraux ■ Insuffisance hépatique ou rénale (administrer 75 % de la dose de départ si la Cl_{Cr} est entre 30 et 50 mL/min) ■ Coronaropathie ■ **OBST.**: Grossesse et allaitement ■ **PÉD.**: Enfants de moins de 18 ans (l'innocuité de l'agent n'a pas été établie).

RÉACTIONS INDÉSIRABLES ET EFFETS SECONDAIRES

SNC: fatigue, céphalées, étourdissements, insomnie.

ORLO: irritation oculaire, épistaxis, rhinorrhée.

CV: œdème, douleurs rétrosternales.

GI: DIARRHÉE, ENTÉROCOLITE NÉCROSANTE, douleurs abdominales, anorexie, constipation, dysgueusie, hyperbilirubinémie, nausées, stomatite, vomissements, dyspepsie, sécheresse de la bouche (xérostomie).

Tég.: dermatite, dysesthésie érythémateuse palmoplantaire, maladies des ongles, alopécie, érythème, rash.

HÉ: déshydratation.

Hémat.: anémie, leucopénie, thrombopénie.

Loc.: arthralgie, myalgie.

SN: neuropathie périphérique.

Resp.: toux, dyspnée.

Divers: fièvre.

INTERACTIONS

Médicament-médicament: La prise concomitante de **leucovorine** accroît la toxicité de cet agent ■ Les **antiacides** peuvent accroître l'absorption de la capécitabine ■ LA **WARFARINE** PEUT AUGMENTER LE RISQUE DE SAIGNEMENTS (SURVEILLER FRÉQUEMMENT LE RNI) ■ La capécitabine peut élever les concentrations sanguines et la toxicité de la **phénytoïne** (la diminution des doses de phénytoïne peut être nécessaire).

Médicament-aliments: Les **aliments** diminuent l'absorption de la capécitabine. Il faut tout de même l'administrer à la fin d'un repas.

VOIES D'ADMINISTRATION ET POSOLOGIE

- **PO (adultes)**: 2 500 mg/m^2/jour en 2 doses fractionnées, à 12 heures d'intervalle, pendant 14 jours, suivis d'une période sans médication de 7 jours; la capécitabine est administrée en cures de 3 semaines.

INSUFFISANCE RÉNALE

PO (ADULTES DONT LA Cl_{CR} EST ENTRE 30 ET 50 mL/MIN): ADMINISTRER EN DOSE INITIALE 75 % DE LA DOSE HABITUELLE.

PRÉSENTATION

Comprimés: 150 mg[Pr], 500 mg[Pr].

SOINS INFIRMIERS

ÉVALUATION DE LA SITUATION

- EXAMINER LES MUQUEUSES, NOTER LE NOMBRE ET LA CONSISTANCE DES SELLES ET LA FRÉQUENCE DES VOMISSEMENTS. Rester à l'affût des signes suivants d'infection: fièvre, frissons, mal de gorge, toux, enrouement, douleurs lombaires ou aux flancs, mictions difficiles ou douloureuses. Suivre de près les saignements: saignement des gencives, formation d'ecchymoses, pétéchies, présence de sang occulte dans les selles, l'urine et les vomissements. Éviter les injections IM et la prise de la température rectale. Appliquer une pression sur les points de ponction veineuse pendant 10 minutes. Une anémie peut survenir. Suivre de près les signes de fatigue accrue, de dyspnée et d'hypotension orthostatique.
- **ALERTE CLINIQUE**: PRÉVENIR LE MÉDECIN SI LES SYMPTÔMES SUIVANTS DE TOXICITÉ SE MANIFESTENT: STOMATITE, VOMISSEMENTS IMPOSSIBLES À MAÎTRISER, DIARRHÉE, FIÈVRE; IL PEUT S'AVÉRER NÉCESSAIRE D'ABANDONNER LE TRAITEMENT OU DE DIMINUER LA DOSE DE MÉDICAMENT. ON DEVRAIT SURVEILLER DE PRÈS LES PATIENTS QUI PRÉSENTENT UNE DIARRHÉE GRAVE ET LEUR ADMINISTRER UN TRAITEMENT DE

C

REMPLACEMENT HYDROÉLECTROLYTIQUE EN CAS DE DÉSHYDRATATION.

- Vérifier la présence de dysesthésie érythémateuse palmoplantaire (syndrome d'enflure douloureuse des mains et des pieds). Les symptômes sont notamment l'engourdissement, la dysesthésie ou la paresthésie, les picotements, l'enflure douloureuse ou indolore, l'érythème, la desquamation, la formation de phlyctènes et des douleurs intenses.

Tests de laboratoire: Évaluer les fonctions hépatique (concentrations sériques de phosphatase alcaline, d'AST, d'ALT et de bilirubine), rénale et hématopoïétique (hématocrite, concentration d'hémoglobine, nombre de leucocytes et de thrombocytes) avant l'administration de l'agent et à intervalles réguliers pendant toute la durée du traitement. La capécitabine peut mener à une leucopénie, à une anémie et à une thrombopénie. La leucopénie peut dicter l'abandon du traitement. Le traitement devrait être interrompu si les concentrations sériques de bilirubine atteignent ou dépassent 1,5 fois la limite supérieure de la normale; le traitement peut être repris une fois que les concentrations de bilirubine sont revenues à la normale.

Tests de laboratoire: **ALERTE CLINIQUE**: SURVEILLER LE RNI À INTERVALLES FRÉQUENTS CHEZ LES PATIENTS RECEVANT DE LA WARFARINE POUR EN ADAPTER LA DOSE SELON LES BESOINS. LA FRÉQUENCE DES SAIGNEMENTS PEUT S'ACCROÎTRE DANS LES JOURS QUI SUIVENT LE DÉBUT DU TRAITEMENT À LA CAPÉCITABINE ET JUSQU'À UN MOIS APRÈS QU'IL A PRIS FIN. LE RISQUE EST PLUS GRAND CHEZ LES PATIENTS DE PLUS DE 60 ANS.

DIAGNOSTICS INFIRMIERS POSSIBLES

- Risque d'infection (Indications).
- Alimentation déficiente (Effets secondaires).
- Connaissances insuffisantes sur le traitement médicamenteux (Enseignement au patient et à ses proches).

INTERVENTIONS INFIRMIÈRES

- **ALERTE CLINIQUE**: DES DÉCÈS SONT SURVENUS LORS DE CERTAINES CHIMIOTHÉRAPIES. AVANT D'ADMINISTRER L'AGENT, CLARIFIER TOUS LES POINTS AMBIGUS. VÉRIFIER LA LIMITE DES DOSES UNITAIRES ET QUOTIDIENNES AINSI QUE LA DOSE À ADMINISTRER PENDANT LE TRAITEMENT. DEMANDER À UN DEUXIÈME PROFESSIONNEL DE LA SANTÉ DE VÉRIFIER UNE FOIS DE PLUS L'ORDONNANCE D'ORIGINE, LES CALCULS ET LE RÉGLAGE DE LA POMPE À PERFUSION. NE PAS CONFONDRE LA CAPÉCITABINE (XELODA) ET L'ORLISTAT (XENICAL).
- On doit adapter la posologie en fonction des effets toxiques. Si on réduit la dose en raison d'une toxicité, on ne doit pas la majorer par la suite. Consulter les recommandations du fabricant.
- Administrer le médicament avec des aliments à la fin d'un repas, toutes les 12 heures pendant 2 semaines et observer une période de 1 semaine sans médication. Les comprimés devraient être pris avec de l'eau.

ENSEIGNEMENT AU PATIENT ET À SES PROCHES

- Conseiller au patient de prendre le médicament toutes les 12 heures, à la fin d'un repas, avec de l'eau, en suivant rigoureusement les recommandations du médecin. S'il n'a pu prendre une dose au moment habituel, il ne doit pas doubler la dose suivante, mais plutôt reprendre l'horaire habituel.
- RENSEIGNER LE PATIENT SUR LES EFFETS SECONDAIRES LES PLUS COURANTS. LUI RECOMMANDER DE PRÉVENIR IMMÉDIATEMENT LE MÉDECIN SI L'UN DES SYMPTÔMES SUIVANTS SE MANIFESTE: DIARRHÉE (PLUS DE 4 DÉFÉCATIONS PENDANT LA JOURNÉE OU 1 OU PLUSIEURS DIARRHÉES NOCTURNES), VOMISSEMENTS (PLUS DE 1 FOIS EN 24 HEURES), NAUSÉES (PERTE D'APPÉTIT ET DIMINUTION MARQUÉE DE LA CONSOMMATION QUOTIDIENNE D'ALIMENTS), STOMATITE (DOULEURS, ROUGEURS, ENFLURE OU APHTES DANS LA BOUCHE), SYNDROME D'ENFLURE DOULOUREUSE DES MAINS ET DES PIEDS (DOULEURS, ENFLURE OU ROUGEUR AU NIVEAU DES MAINS OU DES PIEDS), FIÈVRE ET INFECTION (TEMPÉRATURE ≥ 38 °C OU AUTRES SIGNES D'INFECTION).
- Recommander au patient d'informer un professionnel de la santé s'il prend de l'acide folique.
- Demander au patient d'informer un professionnel de la santé si les symptômes suivants se manifestent: fièvre, frissons, mal de gorge, signes d'infection, jaunissement de la peau ou des yeux, douleurs abdominales, douleurs articulaires ou lombaires; enflure des pieds ou des jambes, saignement des gencives, formation d'ecchymoses, pétéchies ou présence de sang dans l'urine, les selles ou les vomissements. Lui conseiller d'éviter les foules et les personnes contagieuses. Lui recommander d'utiliser une brosse à dents à poils doux et un rasoir électrique et d'éviter de consommer des boissons alcoolisées ou de prendre des produits contenant de l'aspirine ou des AINS.
- Recommander au patient de se rincer la bouche avec de l'eau après avoir mangé et bu et d'éviter d'utiliser de la soie dentaire afin de réduire le risque de stomatite. Lui expliquer que les gargarismes à la lidocaïne visqueuse peuvent l'aider si la douleur buccale l'empêche de s'alimenter. La douleur asso-

ciée à la stomatite peut dicter un traitement par des analgésiques opioïdes.

- Rappeler à la patiente qu'elle doit utiliser une méthode de contraception fiable pendant toute la durée du traitement.
- Insister sur l'importance des tests de laboratoire à intervalles réguliers permettant de suivre de près l'efficacité du traitement et les effets secondaires.

VÉRIFICATION DE L'EFFICACITÉ THÉRAPEUTIQUE

L'efficacité du traitement peut être démontrée par: la régression de la tumeur.

CAPSAÏCINE

Antiphlogistine Rub A-535 Capsaicin, Capsaïcine, Zoderm, Zostrix, Zostrix-HP

CLASSIFICATION:
Analgésique non opioïde (topique)

Grossesse – catégorie inconnue

INDICATIONS

Traitement temporaire de la douleur associée à la polyarthrite rhumatoïde ou à l'arthrose ■ Traitement de la névralgie postherpétique ou de la neuropathie diabétique. **Usages non approuvés:** Traitement du syndrome de douleur consécutif à la mastectomie ■ Traitement de l'algodystrophie sympathique réflexe.

MÉCANISME D'ACTION

Déplétion ou prévention de l'accumulation d'une substance chimique (la substance P) qui transmet les impulsions douloureuses des nerfs périphériques au SNC. ***Effets thérapeutiques:*** Soulagement de la douleur.

PHARMACOCINÉTIQUE

Absorption: Inconnue.

Distribution: Inconnue.

Métabolisme et excrétion: Inconnus.

Demi-vie: Inconnue.

Profil temps-action (analgésie)

	DÉBUT D'ACTION	PIC	DURÉE
Voie topique	1 - 2 semaines	2 - 4 semaines†	inconnue

† Pouvant prendre jusqu'à 6 semaines en cas de névralgies de la tête et du cou.

CONTRE-INDICATIONS, PRÉCAUTIONS ET MISES EN GARDE

Contre-indications: Hypersensibilité à la capsaïcine ou aux piments forts ■ Usage près des yeux, sur une lésion ouverte ou sur une peau éraflée.

Précautions et mises en garde: Grossesse, allaitement ou enfants de moins de 2 ans (l'innocuité du médicament n'a pas été établie).

RÉACTIONS INDÉSIRABLES ET EFFETS SECONDAIRES

Resp.: toux.

Tég.: sensation passagère de brûlure.

INTERACTIONS

Médicament-médicament: Aucune interaction importante.

VOIES D'ADMINISTRATION ET POSOLOGIE

- **Application topique (adultes et enfants âgés d'au moins 2 ans):** Appliquer sur les régions affectées 3 ou 4 fois par jour, au maximum.

PRÉSENTATION

Crème: 0,025 %^{VL}, 0,05 %^{VL}, 0,075 %^{VL} ■ **Gel:** 0,025 %^{VL}, 0,05 %^{VL} ■ **Lotion:** 0,025 %^{VL}.

SOINS INFIRMIERS

ÉVALUATION DE LA SITUATION

Déterminer l'intensité et le siège de la douleur avant l'administration et à intervalles réguliers pendant toute la durée du traitement.

DIAGNOSTICS INFIRMIERS POSSIBLES

- Douleur chronique (Indications).
- Connaissances insuffisantes sur le traitement médicamenteux (Enseignement au patient et à ses proches).
- Non-observance du traitement médicamenteux (Enseignement au patient et à ses proches).

INTERVENTIONS INFIRMIÈRES

- Appliquer sur les régions affectées 3 ou 4 fois par jour, au maximum. Éviter le contact avec les yeux; ne pas appliquer sur une peau éraflée ou irritée. Ne pas serrer le pansement.
- On peut appliquer de la lidocaïne topique au cours des 2 premières semaines de traitement pour réduire la gêne initiale.

C

ENSEIGNEMENT AU PATIENT ET À SES PROCHES

- Faire une démonstration de la méthode d'application. Faire pénétrer la crème dans la région affectée jusqu'à son absorption complète ou presque complète. Pour appliquer la capsaïcine, il faut porter des gants ou se laver les mains immédiatement après. Expliquer au patient souffrant d'arthrite que s'il applique la capsaïcine sur les mains, il ne doit pas se les laver pendant au moins 30 minutes après l'application.
- Expliquer au patient qui n'a pas pu appliquer une dose au moment habituel qu'il doit le faire aussitôt que possible, à moins que ce ne soit presque l'heure prévue pour l'application suivante. La capsaïcine soulage la douleur à condition d'être utilisée régulièrement.
- Prévenir le patient qu'il peut ressentir une sensation passagère de brûlure lors de l'application, particulièrement s'il utilise la préparation moins de 3 ou de 4 fois par jour. Cette sensation de brûlure disparaît habituellement après quelques jours, mais peut persister pendant 2 à 4 semaines ou plus. La sensation est intensifiée par la chaleur, la transpiration, les bains chauds, l'humidité et le port de vêtements. Sa fréquence et son intensité diminuent habituellement au fil du traitement. On n'obtiendra pas de diminution de la sensation de brûlure en réduisant le nombre de doses; de plus, l'effet analgésique sera amoindri et la sensation de brûlure pourrait durer plus longtemps.
- En cas de contact avec les yeux, recommander au patient de se rincer à l'eau. Si la capsaïcine entre en contact avec d'autres parties sensibles, il faut rincer à l'eau tiède, mais non chaude, et au savon.
- Conseiller au patient atteint d'herpès zoster (zona) d'attendre la guérison complète des lésions avant d'appliquer la crème de capsaïcine.
- Recommander au patient d'arrêter le traitement et de prévenir un professionnel de la santé si la douleur persiste pendant plus de 1 mois, si elle s'intensifie ou si des signes d'infection apparaissent.

VÉRIFICATION DE L'EFFICACITÉ THÉRAPEUTIQUE

L'efficacité du traitement peut être démontrée par: la diminution de la douleur associée à: la neuropathie postherpétique ■ la neuropathie diabétique ■ la polyarthrite rhumatoïde ■ l'arthrose. Le soulagement de la douleur survient généralement en l'espace de 1 à 2 semaines en présence d'arthrite, de 2 à 4 semaines en présence de névralgies et de 4 à 6 semaines en présence de névralgies intéressant la tête et la nuque. ✳

CAPTOPRIL,

voir Inhibiteurs de l'enzyme de conversion de l'angiotensine (IECA)

CARBAMAZÉPINE

Apo-Carbamazepine, Carbamazepine, Gen-Carbamazepine CR, Novo-Carbamaz, Nu-Carbamazepine, PMS-Carbamazepine, Taro-Carbamazepine, Tegretol

CLASSIFICATION:

Anticonvulsivant, traitement de la névralgie du trijumeau, antimaniaque

Grossesse – catégorie D

INDICATIONS

Prophylaxie des crises tonicocloniques, des crises mixtes et des crises partielles avec symptomatologie complexe ■ Soulagement de la douleur provoquée par la névralgie du trijumeau ■ Traitement de la manie aiguë et prophylaxie des troubles bipolaires (maniacodépressifs). **Usages non approuvés:** Autres formes de douleurs névralgiques.

MÉCANISME D'ACTION

Diminution de la transmission synaptique dans le SNC par l'action sur les canaux sodiques des neurones. ***Effets thérapeutiques:*** Prévention des crises convulsives ■ Soulagement de la douleur provoquée par la névralgie du trijumeau.

PHARMACOCINÉTIQUE

Absorption: Lente mais complète. Les pics et les creux des concentrations de la suspension surviennent plus tôt et sont plus importants.

Distribution: Le médicament se répartit rapidement dans tout l'organisme et traverse la barrière hématoencéphalique. Il traverse rapidement la barrière placentaire et pénètre dans le lait maternel à fortes concentrations.

Métabolisme et excrétion: Fort métabolisme hépatique; le métabolite époxyde a une action anticonvulsivante et antinévralgique.

Demi-vie: *Carbamazépine* – dose unique: de 25 à 65 heures, traitement prolongé: de 8 à 29 heures; *époxyde* – de 5 à 8 heures.

Profil temps-action (effet anticonvulsivant)

	Début d'action	Pic	Durée
PO	2-4 jours	2-12 h†	inconnue

† L'effet antidouleur s'installe en l'espace de 8 à 72 heures.

CONTRE-INDICATIONS, PRÉCAUTIONS ET MISES EN GARDE

Contre-indications: Hypersensibilité à la carbamazépine, aux ingrédients inactifs ou aux antidépresseurs tricycliques ▪ Aplasie médullaire ▪ Bloc AV ▪ Maladie hépatique ▪ Porphyrie aiguë intermittente ou maladie du sang importante.

Précautions et mises en garde: Maladie cardiaque ▪ **Gér.**: Hyperplasie bénigne de la prostate ▪ Pression intraoculaire accrue ▪ **Obst.**: Grossesse (utiliser cet agent seulement si les bienfaits possibles l'emportent sur les risques pour le fœtus; dans ce cas, il est recommandé de prendre un supplément de vitamine K au cours des dernières semaines de la grossesse) ▪ Allaitement.

RÉACTIONS INDÉSIRABLES ET EFFETS SECONDAIRES

SNC: ataxie, somnolence, fatigue, psychose, vertiges.
ORLO: vision trouble, opacité de la cornée.
Resp.: pneumopathie.
CV: insuffisance cardiaque, hypertension, hypotension, syncope.
GI: hépatite.
GU: retard de la miction, rétention d'urine.
Tég.: photosensibilité, rash, urticaire.
End.: syndrome d'antidiurèse inappropriée.
Hémat.: AGRANULOCYTOSE, ANÉMIE APLASIQUE, THROMBOPÉNIE, éosinophilie, leucopénie.
Divers: frissons, fièvre, lymphadénopathie.

INTERACTIONS

Médicament-médicament: La carbamazépine réduit les concentrations des médicaments suivants et peut en diminuer l'efficacité: **corticostéroïdes**, **doxycycline**, **felbamate**, **quinidine**, **warfarine**, **contraceptifs oraux**, **barbituriques**, **cyclosporine**, **benzodiazépines**, **théophylline**, **lamotrigine**, **acide valproïque**, **bupropion** et **halopéridol** ▪ Le **danazol** élève les concentrations sanguines de carbamazépine (éviter l'administration concomitante dans la mesure du possible) ▪ Les **IMAO** (pris dans les 14 jours qui précèdent ou qui suivent l'administration de la carbamazépine) peuvent provoquer l'hyperpyrexie, l'hypertension, des convulsions et la mort ▪ Le **vérapamil**, le **diltiazem**, le **propoxyphène**, l'**érythromycine**, la **clarithromycine**, les **inhibiteurs sélectifs du recaptage de la sérotonine (ISRS)** et la **cimétidine** élèvent les concentrations sanguines de carbamazépine et peuvent provoquer une toxicité ▪ La carbamazépine peut augmenter le risque d'hépatotoxicité lié à l'**isoniazide** ▪ Le **felbamate** diminue les concentrations de carbamazépine, mais augmente les concentrations du métabolite actif ▪ La carbamazépine peut réduire l'efficacité de l'**acétaminophène** et augmenter le risque de toxicité par cet agent ▪ La carbamazépine peut augmenter le risque de toxicité du SNC associé au **lithium** ▪ La carbamazépine peut accroître la durée d'action des **curarisants non dépolarisants**.

VOIES D'ADMINISTRATION ET POSOLOGIE

- **PO (adultes):** *Anticonvulsivant* – de 100 à 200 mg, 1 ou 2 fois par jour (comprimés) ou 100 mg, 4 fois par jour (suspension); augmenter par paliers de 200 mg par jour, tous les 7 jours, jusqu'à l'atteinte des concentrations thérapeutiques (l'écart posologique se situe entre 800 et 1 200 mg par jour en doses fractionnées, administrées toutes les 6 à 8 heures); ne pas dépasser 1 g par jour chez les adolescents âgés de 12 à 15 ans. Les comprimés à libération prolongée (CR) sont administrés 2 fois par jour. *Antinévralgique* – 100 mg, 2 fois par jour (comprimés) ou 50 mg, 4 fois par jour (suspension); augmenter par paliers de 200 mg au maximum jusqu'au moment où la douleur est soulagée. Administrer ensuite une dose d'entretien de 200 à 1 200 mg par jour, en prises fractionnées (écart habituel: de 200 à 800 mg par jour). *Traitement de la manie aiguë et prophylaxie des troubles bipolaires* – monothérapie: la dose initiale doit être faible, soit de 200 à 400 mg par jour, en prises fractionnées. En cas de manie aiguë, on peut toutefois amorcer le traitement avec des doses de 400 à 600 mg par jour. Augmenter graduellement cette dose jusqu'à la maîtrise des symptômes ou jusqu'à concurrence de 1 600 mg par jour. *Traitement d'association avec le lithium ou les neuroleptiques* – on commence le traitement à une dose plus faible, soit de 100 à 200 mg par jour (jusqu'à un maximum de 800 mg par jour). Les taux plasmatiques se révèlent rarement utiles pour permettre de déterminer le traitement approprié des troubles bipolaires.
- **PO (enfants de 6 à 12 ans):** De 100 mg à 200 mg, 1 ou 2 fois par jour (comprimés) ou 50 mg, 4 fois par jour (suspension); augmenter par paliers de 100 mg, à des intervalles de 1 semaine jusqu'à l'atteinte des concentrations thérapeutiques (écart habituel: de 400 à 800 mg par jour; ne pas dépasser 1 g par jour). Les comprimés à libération prolongée (CR) doivent être administrés 2 fois par jour.

C

PRÉSENTATION (version générique disponible)

Comprimés: 200 mg[Pr] ■ **Comprimés à croquer**: 100 mg[Pr], 200 mg[Pr] ■ **Comprimés à libération prolongée**: 200 mg[Pr], 400 mg[Pr] ■ **Suspension orale (parfum citron-vanille)**: 100 mg/5 mL[Pr].

SOINS INFIRMIERS

ÉVALUATION DE LA SITUATION

Convulsions: Déterminer la fréquence, le siège, la durée et les caractéristiques des convulsions.

Névralgie du trijumeau: Suivre de près la douleur faciale (siège, intensité, durée). Demander au patient d'observer les stimuli qui peuvent déclencher la douleur (aliments chauds ou froids, draps, toucher).

Maladie affective bipolaire: Suivre l'humeur du patient, ses idées de grandeur et ses comportements en général.

Tests de laboratoire:

- EXAMINER TOUTES LES SEMAINES, AU COURS DES 2 PREMIERS MOIS, ET TOUS LES ANS PAR LA SUITE, LA NUMÉRATION GLOBULAIRE COMPRENANT LA NUMÉRATION PLAQUETTAIRE ET RÉTICULOCYTAIRE AINSI QUE LES CONCENTRATIONS SÉRIQUES DE FER, POUR DÉCELER LES SIGNES D'ANOMALIES HÉMATOLOGIQUES QUI PEUVENT MENER À UNE ISSUE FATALE. ARRÊTER D'ADMINISTRER CE MÉDICAMENT SI ON CONSTATE UNE APLASIE MÉDULLAIRE.
- Il faut effectuer à intervalles réguliers des tests de la fonction hépatique, des analyses des urines ainsi que le dosage de l'urée. Le médicament peut élever les concentrations d'AST, d'ALT, de phosphatase alcaline sérique, de bilirubine, d'urée ainsi que la protéinurie et la glycosurie.
- Noter les concentrations sériques de calcium ionisé tous les 6 mois ou si la fréquence des convulsions augmente. La fonction thyroïdienne et les concentrations sériques de calcium ionisé peuvent diminuer; l'hypocalcémie abaisse le seuil épileptogène.
- Suivre de près l'ÉCG et les concentrations d'électrolytes sériques avant l'administration de l'agent et à intervalles réguliers pendant toute la durée du traitement. La carbamazépine peut provoquer une hyponatrémie.
- La carbamazépine peut parfois augmenter les concentrations sériques de cholestérol, de lipoprotéines de haute densité et de triglycérides.
- La carbamazépine peut entraîner des résultats faussement négatifs aux tests de grossesse par le dosage de la gonadotrophine chorionique humaine.

Toxicité et surdosage: Vérifier les concentrations sériques à intervalles réguliers pendant toute la durée du traitement. Les concentrations thérapeutiques se situent entre 34 et 51 µmol/L, lorsque la carbamazépine est administrée en monothérapie.

DIAGNOSTICS INFIRMIERS POSSIBLES

- Risque d'accident (Indications, Effets secondaires).
- Douleur chronique (Indications).
- Connaissances insuffisantes sur le traitement médicamenteux (Enseignement au patient et à ses proches).

INTERVENTIONS INFIRMIÈRES

- Prendre les précautions qui s'imposent en cas de convulsions.
- Administrer le médicament avec des aliments pour diminuer l'irritation gastrique. On peut écraser les comprimés si le patient éprouve des difficultés de déglutition. CEPENDANT, IL NE FAUT PAS ÉCRASER NI CROQUER LES COMPRIMÉS À LIBÉRATION PROLONGÉE.
- Ne pas administrer la suspension en même temps que d'autres médicaments liquides ou des diluants; le mélange se transforme en une pâte caoutchouteuse orange.

ENSEIGNEMENT AU PATIENT ET À SES PROCHES

- Expliquer au patient qu'il doit prendre la carbamazépine tous les jours, en respectant rigoureusement la posologie recommandée. S'il n'a pu prendre le médicament au moment habituel, il doit le prendre aussitôt que possible, mais non pas juste avant l'heure prévue pour la dose suivante. Il ne faut jamais remplacer une dose manquée par une double dose. Lui recommander de prévenir le médecin s'il n'a pas pu prendre plus d'une dose de suite. Le sevrage doit être graduel, afin de prévenir les convulsions.
- Prévenir le patient que la carbamazépine peut provoquer des étourdissements et de la somnolence. Lui conseiller de ne pas conduire et d'éviter les activités qui exigent sa vigilance jusqu'à ce qu'on ait la certitude que le médicament n'entraîne pas ces effets chez lui.
- CONSEILLER AU PATIENT DE SIGNALER IMMÉDIATEMENT À UN PROFESSIONNEL DE LA SANTÉ LES SYMPTÔMES SUIVANTS: FIÈVRE, MAUX DE GORGE, APHTES BUCCAUX, APPARITION D'ECCHYMOSES AU MOINDRE TRAUMATISME, PÉTÉCHIES, SAIGNEMENTS INHABITUELS, DOULEURS ABDOMINALES, FRISSONS, RASH, SELLES DE COULEUR PÂLE, URINE DE COULEUR FONCÉE OU JAUNISSE.

- Recommander au patient d'éviter de boire de l'alcool et de prendre des dépresseurs du SNC en même temps que la carbamazépine.
- Inciter le patient à utiliser un écran solaire et à porter des vêtements protecteurs pour prévenir les réactions de photosensibilité.
- Expliquer au patient qu'il peut réduire la sécheresse buccale en se rinçant souvent la bouche, en pratiquant une bonne hygiène buccale et en consommant des bonbons et de la gomme à mâcher sans sucre. Il peut également utiliser des substituts de salive. Lui recommander de consulter le dentiste si la sécheresse de la bouche persiste au-delà de 2 semaines.
- Conseiller à la patiente d'utiliser pendant le traitement à la carbamazépine une méthode contraceptive non hormonale.
- Recommander au patient qui doit suivre un traitement ou subir une intervention chirurgicale d'avertir le professionnel de la santé qu'il suit un traitement par ce médicament.
- Insister sur l'importance des examens diagnostiques de suivi et des examens ophtalmologiques permettant de déceler les effets secondaires du médicament.

Crises épileptiques: Conseiller au patient de porter sur lui en tout temps un bracelet d'identité où sont inscrits son problème de santé et son traitement médicamenteux.

VÉRIFICATION DE L'EFFICACITÉ THÉRAPEUTIQUE

L'efficacité du traitement peut être démontrée par: l'absence des convulsions ou la réduction de leur fréquence ■ la diminution de la douleur névralgique du trijumeau; réévaluer tous les 3 mois l'état des patients souffrant de névralgie du trijumeau qui n'éprouvent pas de douleurs, pour déterminer la dose minimale efficace. ✳

CARBIDOPA,
voir Lévodopa

ALERTE CLINIQUE

CARBOPLATINE

Carboplatine, Paraplatin-AQ

CLASSIFICATION:
Antinéoplasique (alkylant)

Grossesse – catégorie D

INDICATIONS

Traitement du cancer des ovaires avancé d'origine épithéliale.

MÉCANISME D'ACTION

Inhibition de la synthèse de l'ADN par la production de ponts intercaténaires dans l'ADN des cellules mères (action non spécifique sur le cycle cellulaire). ***Effets thérapeutiques***: Destruction des cellules à réplication rapide et, particulièrement, des cellules malignes.

PHARMACOCINÉTIQUE

Absorption: Biodisponibilité à 100 % (IV).

Distribution: Inconnue.

Liaison aux protéines: Le platine se lie aux protéines plasmatiques de manière irréversible.

Métabolisme et excrétion: Excrétion majoritairement rénale.

Demi-vie: *Carboplatine* – de 2,6 à 5,9 heures (prolongée en présence d'une insuffisance rénale); *platine* – 5 jours.

Profil temps-action (effet sur la numération globulaire)

	Début d'action	Pic	Durée
IV	inconnu	21 jours	28 jours

CONTRE-INDICATIONS, PRÉCAUTIONS ET MISES EN GARDE

Contre-indications: Hypersensibilité au carboplatine, au cisplatine ou au mannitol ■ Insuffisance rénale grave ■ Aplasie médullaire grave ■ Tumeurs hémorragiques.

Précautions et mises en garde: Surdité ■ Anomalies électrolytiques ■ Insuffisance rénale (il est recommandé de diminuer la dose si la Cl_{Cr} < 60 mL/min) ■ Infection active ■ Aplasie médullaire (il est recommandé de réduire la dose) ■ Autres maladies chroniques débilitantes ■ **Gér.**: Risque accru de thrombopénie. Tenir compte de la fonction rénale dans le choix de la dose ■ **Péd.**: L'innocuité du carboplatine n'a pas été établie ■ **Obst.**: Grossesse, allaitement, patientes en âge de procréer.

RÉACTIONS INDÉSIRABLES ET EFFETS SECONDAIRES

SNC: faiblesse.

ORLO: ototoxicité.

GI: douleurs abdominales, nausées, vomissements, constipation, diarrhée, hépatite, stomatite.

GU: suppression de la fonction des gonades, néphrotoxicité.

Tég.: alopécie, rash.

C

HÉ: hypocalcémie, hypokaliémie, hypomagnésémie, hyponatrémie.
Hémat.: ANÉMIE, LEUCOPÉNIE, THROMBOPÉNIE.
Métab.: hyperuricémie.
SN: neuropathie périphérique.
Divers: réactions d'hypersensibilité, incluant l'ANAPHYLAXIE.

INTERACTIONS

Médicament-médicament: Effets additifs sur la néphrotoxicité et l'ototoxicité lors de l'administration concomitante d'autres **médicaments néphrotoxiques** et **ototoxiques** (**aminosides**, **diurétiques de l'anse**) ■ Effets additifs sur l'aplasie médullaire lors de l'administration concomitante d'autres **médicaments qui dépriment la moelle osseuse** ou d'une **radiothérapie** ■ Le carboplatine peut réduire la réponse des anticorps aux **vaccins à virus vivants** et augmenter le risque de réactions indésirables.

VOIES D'ADMINISTRATION ET POSOLOGIE

On utilise également d'autres régimes posologiques.

- **IV (adultes)**: *Traitement initial* – 400 mg/m^2 en une seule dose, par perfusion IV de 15 à 60 minutes, qu'on peut répéter à des intervalles de 4 semaines, selon la réponse.

INSUFFISANCE RÉNALE

- **IV (ADULTES)**: *CL_{CR} DE 41 À 59 mL/MIN* – DOSE INITIALE DE 250 mg/m^2; *CL_{CR} DE 16 À 40 mL/MIN* – DOSE INITIALE DE 200 mg/m^2.

PRÉSENTATION

Solution pour injection: fioles de 50 mg[Pr], de 150 mg[Pr], de 450 mg[Pr] et de 600 mg[Pr].

SOINS INFIRMIERS

ÉVALUATION DE LA SITUATION

- Suivre de près les nausées et les vomissements. Des nausées et des vomissements se produisent souvent de 6 à 12 heures après le traitement (de 1 à 4 heures dans le cas de l'administration de la solution aqueuse) et peuvent persister pendant 24 heures. Pour les prévenir, on peut administrer des antiémétiques. Adapter le régime alimentaire selon la tolérance de la patiente pour maintenir l'équilibre hydroélectrolytique et pour assurer un apport nutritionnel suffisant. Des nausées ou des vomissements graves peuvent dicter l'arrêt du traitement.
- Observer la patiente à la recherche de symptômes de neurotoxicité, tels que les paresthésies des mains et des pieds, l'aréflexie, la diminution de la proprioception et des sensations vibratoires. Cesser le traitement dès que les premiers symptômes de neuropathie se manifestent. Les symptômes peuvent évoluer même si le traitement est arrêté. La neurotoxicité peut être irréversible.
- OBSERVER ÉTROITEMENT LA PATIENTE POUR DÉCELER LA SURVENUE D'UNE APLASIE MÉDULLAIRE. Suivre de près les saignements: saignement des gencives, formation d'ecchymoses, pétéchies, présence de sang occulte dans les selles, l'urine et les vomissements. Éviter les injections IM et la prise de la température rectale si la numération plaquettaire est basse. Appliquer une pression sur les points de ponction veineuse pendant 10 minutes. Évaluer les signes d'infection en présence d'une neutropénie. Une anémie peut survenir et être cumulative; des transfusions sont souvent nécessaires. Suivre de près les signes de fatigue accrue, de dyspnée et d'hypotension orthostatique.
- SUIVRE DE PRÈS LA PATIENTE À LA RECHERCHE DES SIGNES SUIVANTS D'ANAPHYLAXIE: RASH, URTICAIRE, PRURIT, ŒDÈME FACIAL, RESPIRATION SIFFLANTE, TACHYCARDIE, HYPOTENSION. ARRÊTER L'ADMINISTRATION DU MÉDICAMENT IMMÉDIATEMENT ET EN PRÉVENIR LE MÉDECIN. GARDER À LA PORTÉE DE LA MAIN DE L'ADRÉNALINE ET LE MATÉRIEL DE RÉANIMATION.
- On recommande de soumettre la patiente à un test audiométrique avant de démarrer le traitement et pendant toute sa durée, si on soupçonne la présence d'une ototoxicité. L'ototoxicité se manifeste par des acouphènes et une diminution de l'audition des hautes fréquences (unilatérale ou bilatérale). Elle devient plus fréquente et plus grave après l'administration de plusieurs doses. L'ototoxicité est plus prononcée chez les enfants.

Tests de laboratoire:

- NOTER LA NUMÉRATION GLOBULAIRE, LA FORMULE LEUCOCYTAIRE ET LES RÉSULTATS DES EXAMENS DE COAGULATION AVANT L'ADMINISTRATION ET À INTERVALLES RÉGULIERS PENDANT TOUT LE TRAITEMENT. Les nadirs de la thrombopénie, de la leucopénie et de l'anémie se produisent entre le 18e et le 23e jour et se rétablissent dans les 39 jours suivant l'administration d'une dose unique. Le nadir de la numération granulocytaire survient habituellement dans les 21 à 28 jours et se rétablit dans les 35 jours. Interrompre l'administration des doses ultérieures jusqu'au moment où le nombre de polynucléaires neutrophiles est supérieur à 2×10^9/L, et celui des plaquettes, supérieur à 100×10^9/L.

- Déterminer l'état de la fonction rénale avant le début du traitement et avant chaque cure de carboplatine. Le médicament peut entraîner une élévation des concentrations d'urée et des concentrations sériques de créatinine et une diminution de la clairance de la créatinine. La néphropathie est cumulative et elle peut être aggravée lors de l'administration concomitante d'aminosides. La fonction rénale doit revenir à la normale avant l'administration de chaque dose.
- Noter les résultats des tests de la fonction hépatique avant l'administration du carboplatine et à intervalles réguliers tout au long du traitement. Le médicament peut élever les concentrations sériques de bilirubine, de phosphatase alcaline et d'AST.
- Mesurer les électrolytes sériques avant de commencer le traitement, avant l'administration de chaque dose ultérieure et tout au long du traitement. Le carboplatine peut abaisser les concentrations sériques de potassium, de calcium, de magnésium et de sodium.
- Une hyperuricémie peut survenir, habituellement de 3 à 5 jours après l'administration du carboplatine. On peut administrer de l'allopurinol pour diminuer les concentrations sanguines d'acide urique.
- Il y a risque d'élévation des concentrations sériques d'amylase.

DIAGNOSTICS INFIRMIERS POSSIBLES

- Risque d'infection (Réactions indésirables).
- Risque d'accident (Effets secondaires).
- Connaissances insuffisantes sur le traitement médicamenteux (Enseignement au patient et à ses proches).

INTERVENTIONS INFIRMIÈRES

ALERTE CLINIQUE: DES DÉCÈS SONT SURVENUS LORS DE CERTAINES CHIMIOTHÉRAPIES. AVANT D'ADMINISTRER L'AGENT, CLARIFIER TOUS LES POINTS AMBIGUS. VÉRIFIER LA LIMITE DES DOSES UNITAIRES ET QUOTIDIENNES AINSI QUE LA DOSE À ADMINISTRER PENDANT LE TRAITEMENT. DEMANDER À UN DEUXIÈME PROFESSIONNEL DE LA SANTÉ DE VÉRIFIER UNE FOIS DE PLUS L'ORDONNANCE D'ORIGINE, LES CALCULS ET LE RÉGLAGE DE LA POMPE À PERFUSION.

ALERTE CLINIQUE: NE PAS CONFONDRE LE CARBOPLATINE ET LE CISPLATINE. NE PAS CONFONDRE PARAPLATIN (CARBOPLATINE) ET PLATINOL (CISPLATINE).

ALERTE CLINIQUE: LE CARBOPLATINE DEVRAIT ÊTRE ADMINISTRÉ EN MILIEU CONTRÔLÉ, SOUS LA SUPERVISION D'UN MÉDECIN EXPÉRIMENTÉ DANS LA CHIMIOTHÉRAPIE DU CANCER.

- Ne pas utiliser d'aiguilles ou de matériel en aluminium au cours de la préparation ou de l'administration, étant donné que l'aluminium produit une réaction au contact du médicament (précipité noir).
- Préparer les solutions sous une hotte à flux laminaire vertical de type biologique de classe II. Porter des gants, un vêtement protecteur et un masque pendant la manipulation de ce médicament. Jeter le matériel dans les contenants réservés à la mise au rebut (voir l'annexe H).

Perfusion intermittente:

- La solution de 10 mg/mL peut être diluée avec une solution de D5%E ou de NaCl 0,9 %, jusqu'à l'obtention d'une concentration de 0,5 mg/mL. La solution est stable pendant 8 heures à la température ambiante ou pendant 24 heures au réfrigérateur. Consulter les directives de chaque fabricant avant de diluer la préparation.

Vitesse d'administration: Administrer la perfusion en 15 à 60 minutes.

Compatibilité (tubulure en Y): allopurinol ■ amifostine ■ aztréonam ■ céfépime ■ cladribine ■ filgrastim ■ fludarabine ■ granisétron ■ melphalan ■ ondansétron ■ paclitaxel ■ pipéracilline/tazobactam ■ propofol ■ sargramostim ■ téniposide ■ thiotépa ■ vinorelbine.

ENSEIGNEMENT AU PATIENT ET À SES PROCHES

- RECOMMANDER À LA PATIENTE DE SIGNALER RAPIDEMENT À UN PROFESSIONNEL DE LA SANTÉ LA FIÈVRE, LES FRISSONS, LES MAUX DE GORGE, LES SIGNES D'INFECTION, LES DOULEURS LOMBAIRES OU AUX FLANCS, LES MICTIONS DIFFICILES OU DOULOUREUSES, LE SAIGNEMENT DES GENCIVES, LA FORMATION D'ECCHYMOSES, LES PÉTÉCHIES, LA PRÉSENCE DE SANG DANS LES SELLES, L'URINE OU LES VOMISSEMENTS, UNE FATIGUE ACCRUE, LA DYSPNÉE OU L'HYPOTENSION ORTHOSTATIQUE.
- Expliquer à la patiente qu'elle doit éviter les foules et les personnes contagieuses. Lui recommander d'utiliser une brosse à dents à poils doux et un rasoir électrique et la mettre en garde contre les chutes. Prévenir la patiente qu'elle ne doit pas consommer de boissons alcoolisées ni prendre de médicaments contenant de l'acide acétylsalicylique ou d'AINS, car ces substances peuvent déclencher une hémorragie digestive.
- Recommander à la patiente de signaler rapidement à un professionnel de la santé les symptômes suivants: engourdissement ou picotements au niveau des membres ou du visage, diminution de la coordination motrice, diminution de l'ouïe ou acouphènes,

C

enflure inhabituelle ou gain pondéral. Le risque d'ototoxicité, de neurotoxicité et de néphrotoxicité est moindre que lorsque l'on administre du cisplatine.

- Recommander à la patiente de ne pas se faire vacciner sans recommandation expresse du médecin et d'éviter les personnes qui ont reçu un vaccin antipoliomyélitique par voie orale au cours des derniers mois.
- Conseiller à la patiente de prendre des mesures contraceptives (si elle n'est pas devenue stérile à la suite d'un traitement chirurgical ou d'une radiothérapie).
- Recommander à la patiente d'inspecter ses muqueuses buccales à la recherche d'érythème ou d'aphtes. En cas d'aphtes, l'inciter à en informer le médecin, à se rincer la bouche avec de l'eau après avoir mangé et à utiliser une brosse-éponge pour se brosser les dents. La douleur buccale peut dicter un traitement par des analgésiques opioïdes.
- Informer la patiente qu'elle est exposée à un faible risque de perdre ses cheveux. Explorer avec elle les stratégies lui permettant de s'adapter à ce changement.
- Expliquer à la patiente qu'elle doit se soumettre à des examens diagnostiques et biochimiques à intervalles réguliers pour qu'on puisse surveiller les effets secondaires du médicament.

VÉRIFICATION DE L'EFFICACITÉ THÉRAPEUTIQUE

L'efficacité du traitement peut être démontrée par: la diminution de la taille ou de la propagation de la tumeur ovarienne. ✳

ALERTE CLINIQUE

CARMUSTINE

BiCNU, Gliadel

CLASSIFICATION:

Antinéoplasique (alkylant)

Grossesse – catégorie D

INDICATIONS

Adjuvant à la chirurgie et à la radiothérapie ou en association avec d'autres agents chimiothérapeutiques pour traiter les néoplasmes suivants: tumeurs du cerveau ■ myélome multiple ■ maladie de Hodgkin ■ lymphomes malins ■ mélanome malin (forme disséminée) ■ cancer du tractus gastro-intestinal.

MÉCANISME D'ACTION

Inhibition de la synthèse de l'ADN et de l'ARN (quelle que soit l'étape du cycle cellulaire). ***Effets thérapeutiques:*** Destruction des cellules à réplication rapide, particulièrement des cellules malignes.

PHARMACOCINÉTIQUE

Absorption: Biodisponibilité à 100 % (IV); 70 % du polymère contenant la carmustine (Gliadel) se décompose après 3 semaines.

Distribution: Préparation très liposoluble, qui pénètre rapidement dans le liquide céphalorachidien et passe dans le lait maternel. Après l'implantation intracavitaire de Gliadel, la distribution est inconnue.

Métabolisme et excrétion: Métabolisme rapide; certains métabolites exercent une activité antinéoplasique.

Demi-vie: De 15 à 30 minutes.

Profil temps-action (effet sur la numération plaquettaire)

	DÉBUT D'ACTION	PIC	DURÉE
IV	plusieurs jours	4 – 5 semaines	6 semaines

CONTRE-INDICATIONS, PRÉCAUTIONS ET MISES EN GARDE

Contre-indications: Hypersensibilité.

Précautions et mises en garde: Infections ■ Aplasie médullaire ■ **GÉR.**: Tenir compte de la diminution du poids corporel reliée à l'âge, des fonctions rénale, hépatique et cardiovasculaire, des autres médicaments que prend le patient et des maladies chroniques concomitantes ■ Insuffisance rénale, hépatique ou pulmonaire ■ Autres maladies chroniques débilitantes ■ **OBST., ALLAITEMENT**: Patientes en âge de procréer ■ **PÉD.**: Enfants de moins de 18 ans.

RÉACTIONS INDÉSIRABLES ET EFFETS SECONDAIRES

Resp.: FIBROSE PULMONAIRE, infiltrats pulmonaires.

GI: <u>hépatotoxicité</u>, <u>nausées</u>, <u>vomissements</u>, anorexie, diarrhée, œsophagite.

GU: insuffisance rénale.

Tég.: alopécie.

Hémat.: LEUCOPÉNIE, THROMBOPÉNIE, anémie.

Locaux: douleur et hyperémie au point d'injection IV.

INTERACTIONS

Médicament-médicament: Effets additifs sur l'aplasie médullaire lors de l'administration concomitante d'autres **antinéoplasiques** ou d'une **radiothérapie** ■ L'usage du **tabac** augmente le risque de toxicité pulmonaire ■ L'agent peut diminuer la réponse des anticorps aux **vaccins à virus vivants** et augmenter le risque de réactions indésirables ■ La **cimétidine** peut accroître l'aplasie médullaire entraînée par la carmustine.

VOIES D'ADMINISTRATION ET POSOLOGIE

- **IV (adultes et enfants)**: 200 mg/m^2 en une seule dose, toutes les 6 semaines; on peut administrer cette dose en une seule fois ou la fractionner en injections quotidiennes: 100 mg/m^2 par jour, pendant 2 jours, toutes les 6 semaines ou 40 mg/m^2 par jour, pendant 5 jours, toutes les 6 semaines (USAGE NON APPROUVÉ CHEZ LES ENFANTS).
- **Implant intracavitaire (adultes)**: Jusqu'à 61,6 mg (8 implants) placés dans la cavité créée durant la résection chirurgicale d'une tumeur cérébrale.

PRÉSENTATION

Poudre pour injection: fioles de 100 mg^{Pr} ■ **implant intracavitaire**: 7,7 mg^{Pr}.

SOINS INFIRMIERS

ÉVALUATION DE LA SITUATION

- Prendre les signes vitaux avant l'administration initiale et à intervalles fréquents pendant toute la durée du traitement.
- OBSERVER ÉTROITEMENT LE PATIENT POUR DÉCELER L'APPARITION D'UNE APLASIE MÉDULLAIRE. Suivre de près les saignements: saignement des gencives, formation d'ecchymoses, pétéchies, présence de sang occulte dans les selles, l'urine et les vomissements. Éviter les injections IM et la prise de la température rectale si la numération plaquettaire est basse. Appliquer une pression sur les points de ponction veineuse pendant 10 minutes. Rester à l'affût des signes d'infection en présence d'une neutropénie. Une anémie peut survenir; suivre de près les signes de fatigue accrue, de dyspnée et d'hypotension orthostatique.
- SUIVRE DE PRÈS LA FONCTION RESPIRATOIRE POUR DÉCELER L'APPARITION DE LA DYSPNÉE OU DE LA TOUX. UNE TOXICITÉ PULMONAIRE SE PRODUIT HABITUELLEMENT LORS DE L'ACCUMULATION DE DOSES ÉLEVÉES OU À LA SUITE DE PLUSIEURS CYCLES DE TRAITEMENT, MAIS PEUT ÉGALEMENT SE MANIFESTER APRÈS 1 OU 2 CYCLES PENDANT LESQUELS ON A ADMINISTRÉ DE FAIBLES DOSES. LES SYMPTÔMES PEUVENT APPARAÎTRE RAPIDEMENT OU GRADUELLEMENT; LES LÉSIONS PEUVENT ÊTRE RÉVERSIBLES OU NON. UNE FIBROSE PULMONAIRE TARDIVE PEUT SE MANIFESTER PLUSIEURS ANNÉES APRÈS LE TRAITEMENT. PRÉVENIR IMMÉDIATEMENT LE MÉDECIN SI CES SYMPTÔMES SE MANIFESTENT.
- Observer de près le point d'injection IV. La carmustine irrite les tissus. Recommander au patient de prévenir l'infirmière dès qu'il ressent une douleur au point d'injection IV. Arrêter immédiatement l'administration en cas d'infiltration. On peut appliquer de la glace sur le point d'injection. Le médicament peut entraîner une hyperpigmentation de la peau sur le trajet de la veine.
- Effectuer le bilan quotidien des ingesta et des excreta. Observer l'appétit du patient ainsi que sa consommation d'aliments. Rester à l'affût des nausées et des vomissements qui peuvent survenir dans les 2 heures suivant l'administration et persister pendant 4 à 6 heures. L'administration d'un antiémétique avant le traitement et à intervalles réguliers pendant toute sa durée ainsi que la modification du régime alimentaire selon les aliments que le patient peut tolérer peuvent favoriser le maintien de l'équilibre hydroélectrolytique et de l'état nutritionnel.

Tests de laboratoire:

- NOTER LA NUMÉRATION GLOBULAIRE, LA FORMULE LEUCOCYTAIRE ET LA NUMÉRATION PLAQUETTAIRE AVANT L'ADMINISTRATION INITIALE ET À INTERVALLES RÉGULIERS PENDANT TOUT LE TRAITEMENT. LE NADIR DE LA THROMBOPÉNIE SE PRODUIT EN L'ESPACE DE 4 À 5 SEMAINES, ET CELUI DE LA LEUCOPÉNIE, EN L'ESPACE DE 5 À 6 SEMAINES. LE RÉTABLISSEMENT SURVIENT HABITUELLEMENT EN L'ESPACE DE 6 À 7 SEMAINES, MAIS POURRAIT PRENDRE JUSQU'À 10 À 12 SEMAINES EN CAS DE TRAITEMENT PROLONGÉ. ARRÊTER L'ADMINISTRATION ET PRÉVENIR LE MÉDECIN SI LE NOMBRE DE PLAQUETTES EST INFÉRIEUR À 100×10^9/L, ET CELUI DES LEUCOCYTES, INFÉRIEUR À 4×10^9/L. L'ANÉMIE EST HABITUELLEMENT LÉGÈRE.
- Vérifier les concentrations sériques de bilirubine, d'AST, d'ALT et de LDH avant l'administration initiale et à intervalles réguliers pendant toute la durée du traitement. La carmustine peut entraîner une élévation légère et réversible des concentrations d'AST, de phosphatase alcaline et de bilirubine.
- Noter les concentrations d'urée, de créatinine sérique et d'acide urique avant l'administration initiale et à intervalles réguliers tout au long du traitement. Prévenir le médecin si la concentration d'urée est élevée.

DIAGNOSTICS INFIRMIERS POSSIBLES

- Risque d'accident (Effets secondaires).
- Altération de l'image corporelle (Effets secondaires).
- Connaissances insuffisantes sur le traitement médicamenteux (Enseignement au patient et à ses proches).

C

INTERVENTIONS INFIRMIÈRES

ALERTE CLINIQUE: DES DÉCÈS SONT SURVENUS LORS DE CERTAINES CHIMIOTHÉRAPIES. AVANT D'ADMINISTRER L'AGENT, CLARIFIER TOUS LES POINTS AMBIGUS. VÉRIFIER LA LIMITE DES DOSES UNITAIRES ET QUOTIDIENNES AINSI QUE LA DOSE À ADMINISTRER PENDANT LE TRAITEMENT. DEMANDER À UN DEUXIÈME PROFESSIONNEL DE LA SANTÉ DE VÉRIFIER UNE FOIS DE PLUS L'ORDONNANCE D'ORIGINE, LES CALCULS ET LE RÉGLAGE DE LA POMPE À PERFUSION.

- Préparer les solutions sous une hotte à flux laminaire. Porter des gants, un vêtement protecteur et un masque pendant la manipulation de ce médicament. Jeter le matériel utilisé dans les contenants réservés à la mise au rebut. Le contact du médicament avec la peau peut provoquer une hyperpigmentation passagère (voir l'annexe H).

Perfusion intermittente:

- Reconstituer le contenu de la fiole à 100 mg dans 3 mL d'alcool éthylique absolu fourni comme diluant. Diluer cette solution avec 27 mL d'eau stérile pour injection, afin d'obtenir une concentration de 3,3 mg/mL. Effectuer une dilution supplémentaire dans un contenant en verre avec 500 mL de solution de D5%E ou de NaCl 0,9 %.
- La solution est transparente et d'incolore à jaune pâle. Ne pas utiliser les fioles renfermant une pellicule huileuse, qui est un indice de décomposition. Les solutions reconstituées sont stables pendant 24 heures si elles sont réfrigérées et protégées de la lumière. Les solutions ne contiennent pas d'agents de conservation et elles sont destinées à un usage unique. Consulter les directives de chaque fabricant avant de reconstituer la préparation.
- On peut rincer la tubulure IV avec 5 à 10 mL de solution de NaCl 0,9 %, avant et après la perfusion de la carmustine, afin de réduire l'irritation au point d'injection.

Vitesse d'administration: Administrer la dose en 1 à 2 heures. Une perfusion rapide peut provoquer des douleurs locales, des brûlures au point d'injection et des rougeurs de la peau. La rougeur du visage apparaît en l'espace de 2 heures et peut persister pendant 4 heures.

Compatibilité (tubulure en Y): amifostine ▪ aztréonam ▪ céfépime ▪ filgrastim ▪ fludarabine ▪ granisétron ▪ melphalan ▪ ondansétron ▪ pipéracilline/tazobactam ▪ sargramostim ▪ téniposide ▪ thiotépa ▪ vinorelbine.

Incompatibilité en addition au soluté: allopurinol ▪ sodium, bicarbonate de.

ENSEIGNEMENT AU PATIENT ET À SES PROCHES

- RECOMMANDER AU PATIENT DE SIGNALER À UN PROFESSIONNEL DE LA SANTÉ LA FIÈVRE, LES FRISSONS, LES MAUX DE GORGE, LES SIGNES D'INFECTION, LES DOULEURS LOMBAIRES OU AUX FLANCS, LES MICTIONS DIFFICILES OU DOULOUREUSES, LE SAIGNEMENT DES GENCIVES, LA FORMATION D'ECCHYMOSES, LES PÉTÉCHIES, LA PRÉSENCE DE SANG DANS LES SELLES, L'URINE OU LES VOMISSEMENTS. Lui expliquer qu'il doit éviter les foules et les personnes contagieuses. Lui recommander d'utiliser une brosse à dents à poils doux et un rasoir électrique. Prévenir le patient qu'il ne doit pas consommer de boissons alcoolisées ni prendre de médicaments contenant de l'acide acétylsalicylique ou d'AINS.
- INCITER LE PATIENT À PRÉVENIR UN PROFESSIONNEL DE LA SANTÉ EN CAS D'ESSOUFFLEMENT OU D'UNE EXACERBATION DE LA TOUX. LUI RECOMMANDER DE NE PAS FUMER ÉTANT DONNÉ QUE LES FUMEURS SONT DAVANTAGE PRÉDISPOSÉS À LA TOXICITÉ PULMONAIRE.
- Recommander au patient d'inspecter ses muqueuses buccales à la recherche d'érythème ou d'aphtes. En cas d'aphtes, lui recommander de se rincer la bouche avec de l'eau après avoir mangé et d'utiliser une brosse-éponge pour se brosser les dents. La stomatite peut nécessiter un traitement par des analgésiques opioïdes.
- Informer le patient qu'il risque de perdre ses cheveux. Explorer avec lui les stratégies lui permettant de s'adapter à ce changement.
- Expliquer à la patiente pourquoi elle doit prendre des mesures contraceptives.
- Conseiller au patient de ne pas se faire vacciner sans recommandation expresse du médecin.
- Expliquer au patient qu'il doit se soumettre à des tests de laboratoire à intervalles réguliers pour qu'on puisse déceler les effets secondaires du médicament.

VÉRIFICATION DE L'EFFICACITÉ THÉRAPEUTIQUE

L'efficacité du traitement peut être démontrée par: la diminution de la taille des tumeurs et le ralentissement de la prolifération tumorale ▪ l'amélioration des paramètres sanguins en présence de cancers hématologiques. ✳

CARVÉDILOL

Apo-Carvédilol, Coreg, PMS-Carvédilol, Ran-carvédilol, Ratio-Carvédilol

CLASSIFICATION:

Antihypertenseur (bêtabloquant), traitement de l'insuffisance cardiaque

Grossesse – catégories C (1er trimestre) et D (2e et 3e trimestres)

INDICATIONS

Traitement de l'insuffisance cardiaque légère, modérée ou grave (due à l'ischémie ou à la cardiomyopathie), en association avec un diurétique et un inhibiteur de l'ECA, avec ou sans digoxine. **Usages non approuvés:** Traitement de l'hypertension.

MÉCANISME D'ACTION

Inhibition de la stimulation des récepteurs bêta$_1$-adrénergiques (myocardiques) ou bêta$_2$-adrénergiques (pulmonaires, vasculaires ou utérins) ■ Le carvédilol bloque également les récepteurs alpha$_1$-adrénergiques, ce qui peut entraîner l'hypotension orthostatique. ***Effets thérapeutiques:*** Amélioration de la fraction d'éjection ventriculaire gauche, ralentissement de l'évolution de l'insuffisance cardiaque et diminution de la mortalité et du nombre d'hospitalisations ■ Abaissement de la fréquence cardiaque et de la pression artérielle.

PHARMACOCINÉTIQUE

Absorption: Le médicament est bien absorbé mais subit un effet de premier passage hépatique important, d'où une biodisponibilité absolue de 25 à 35 %. La nourriture ralentit l'absorption, mais ne diminue pas la quantité absorbée.

Distribution: Inconnue. L'agent traverse la barrière placentaire.

Liaison aux protéines: 98 %.

Métabolisme et excrétion: Métabolisme important. Excrétion majoritairement dans les fèces par la bile sous forme de métabolites. Une fraction inférieure à 2 % est excrétée à l'état inchangé par les reins.

Demi-vie: De 7 à 10 heures.

Profil temps-action (effets cardiovasculaires)

	DÉBUT D'ACTION	PIC	DURÉE
PO	en l'espace de 1 h	1 – 2 h	12 h

CONTRE-INDICATIONS, PRÉCAUTIONS ET MISES EN GARDE

Contre-indications: Hypersensibilité connue au produit ou à l'un de ses composants ■ Insuffisance cardiaque non compensée ■ Asthme bronchique ou affection bronchospastique ■ Bloc auriculoventriculaire de 2e ou de 3e degré ou maladie du sinus (à moins qu'un pacemaker permanent ne soit en place) ■ Œdème pulmonaire ■ Choc cardiogénique ■ Bradycardie sévère ■ Insuffisance hépatique grave ■ Hypotension sévère ■ Cardiopathie valvulaire obstructive primaire ■ Incapacité mentale (maladie d'Alzheimer, alcoolisme, toxicomanie), sauf si le patient est surveillé de près par un soignant compétent.

Précautions et mises en garde: Insuffisance rénale ■ Insuffisance hépatique ■ **GÉR.:** Sensibilité accrue aux bêtabloquants chez les personnes âgées; il est recommandé de réduire la dose initiale ■ Diabète (le médicament peut masquer les symptômes d'hypoglycémie) ■ Thyrotoxicose (le médicament peut en masquer les symptômes) ■ Maladie vasculaire périphérique ■ Antécédents de réactions allergiques graves (risque d'augmenter l'intensité des réactions) ■ **OBST., ALLAITEMENT, PÉD.:** L'innocuité du médicament n'a pas été établie chez les femmes enceintes ou qui allaitent (risque de bradycardie, d'hypotension, d'hypoglycémie ou de dépression respiratoire chez le fœtus ou le nouveau-né) ni chez les enfants ■ Phéochromocytome.

RÉACTIONS INDÉSIRABLES ET EFFETS SECONDAIRES

SNC: étourdissements, fatigue, faiblesse, anxiété, dépression, somnolence, insomnie, perte de la mémoire, modification de l'état mental, nervosité, cauchemars.
ORLO: vision trouble, xérophtalmie, congestion nasale.
Resp.: bronchospasme, respiration sifflante.
CV: BRADYCARDIE, INSUFFISANCE CARDIAQUE, ŒDÈME PULMONAIRE, hypotension orthostatique, vasoconstriction périphérique.
GI: diarrhée, constipation, nausées.
GU: impuissance, diminution de la libido.
Tég.: prurit, rash.
End.: hyperglycémie, hypoglycémie.
Loc.: arthralgie, douleurs lombaires, crampes musculaires.
SN: paresthésie.
Divers: lupus érythémateux induit par le médicament.

INTERACTIONS

Médicament-médicament: Les **anesthésiques généraux**, la **phénytoïne par voie parentérale**, le **diltiazem** et le **vérapamil**, administrés simultanément, peuvent entraîner une dépression myocardique additive ■ La

digoxine, administrée simultanément, peut entraîner des effets bradycardiques additifs ■ Risque d'effets hypotenseurs additifs lors de l'administration concomitante d'autres **antihypertenseurs** et de **dérivés nitrés** ou de l'ingestion rapide de quantités importantes d'**alcool** ■ L'usage concomitant de la **clonidine** augmente l'hypotension et la bradycardie ■ Possibilité d'exacerbation du phénomène de sevrage à la **clonidine** ■ Les **hormones thyroïdiennes**, administrées simultanément, peuvent diminuer l'efficacité du médicament ■ Le carvédilol peut modifier l'efficacité des **insulines** ou des **hypoglycémiants oraux** (une adaptation de la posologie peut s'avérer nécessaire) ■ Le carvédilol peut réduire l'efficacité de la **théophylline** ■ Le carvédilol peut contrecarrer les effets bénéfiques sur les récepteurs bêta$_1$ cardiaques de la **dopamine** ou de la **dobutamine** ■ Le carvédilol doit être utilisé avec prudence dans les 14 jours suivant ou précédant le traitement par un **IMAO** (risque d'hypertension) ■ La **cimétidine** peut accroître la toxicité du carvédilol ■ L'usage concomitant d'**AINS** peut réduire l'effet antihypertenseur de l'agent ■ La **rifampine** peut réduire l'efficacité du carvédilol ■ Le carvédilol peut élever les concentrations sériques de **digoxine** ■ Le carvédilol peut augmenter les concentrations sériques de **cyclosporine** (une adaptation de la posologie peut s'avérer nécessaire selon les dosages sanguins).

VOIES D'ADMINISTRATION ET POSOLOGIE

- **PO (adultes)**: *Insuffisance cardiaque* – 3,125 mg, 2 fois par jour, pendant 2 semaines; on peut passer graduellement à une dose de 6,25 mg, 2 fois par jour. On peut doubler la dose toutes les 2 semaines, selon la tolérance du patient; il ne faut pas dépasser 25 mg, 2 fois par jour.

PRÉSENTATION

Comprimés: 3,125 mg^{Pr}, 6,25 mg^{Pr}, 12,5 mg^{Pr}, 25 mg^{Pr}.

SOINS INFIRMIERS

ÉVALUATION DE LA SITUATION

- MESURER LA PRESSION ARTÉRIELLE ET LE POULS À INTERVALLES FRÉQUENTS AU COURS DE LA PÉRIODE D'ADAPTATION DE LA POSOLOGIE, ET À INTERVALLES RÉGULIERS, PENDANT TOUTE LA DURÉE DU TRAITEMENT. Si le patient est resté couché, le suivre de près au moment où il se lève en raison du risque d'hypotension orthostatique.
- EFFECTUER LE BILAN QUOTIDIEN DES INGESTA ET DES EXCRETA ET PESER LE PATIENT TOUS LES JOURS. SUIVRE DE PRÈS L'APPARITION DES SIGNES SUIVANTS DE SURCHARGE LIQUIDIENNE: ŒDÈME PÉRIPHÉRIQUE, DYSPNÉE, RÂLES ET CRÉPITATIONS, FATIGUE, GAIN PONDÉRAL, TURGESCENCE DES JUGULAIRES. ON PEUT OBSERVER UNE AGGRAVATION DES SYMPTÔMES LORS DU TRAITEMENT INITIAL DE L'INSUFFISANCE CARDIAQUE.

Insuffisance cardiaque: Vérifier la fréquence du renouvellement des ordonnances pour évaluer l'observance du traitement.

Tests de laboratoire:

- Le carvédilol peut élever les concentrations sériques de lipoprotéines, ainsi que les concentrations d'urée, de potassium, de triglycérides et d'acide urique.
- Le carvédilol peut élever la glycémie.

TOXICITÉ ET SURDOSAGE: Suivre de près les patients recevant des bêtabloquants, à la recherche de signes de surdosage: bradycardie, étourdissements graves ou évanouissements, somnolence importante, dyspnée, bleuissement des ongles ou des paumes, convulsions. Prévenir immédiatement le médecin si ces signes apparaissent.

DIAGNOSTICS INFIRMIERS POSSIBLES

- Débit cardiaque diminué (Effets secondaires).
- Connaissances insuffisantes sur le traitement médicamenteux (Enseignement au patient et à ses proches).
- Non-observance du traitement médicamenteux (Enseignement au patient et à ses proches).

INTERVENTIONS INFIRMIÈRES

- L'abandon du traitement concomitant par la clonidine devrait se faire graduellement. On doit abandonner d'abord le bêtabloquant et, après plusieurs jours, la clonidine.
- Prendre le pouls à l'apex du cœur avant d'administrer le médicament. Si le pouls est inférieur à 50 battements par minute ou si une arythmie survient, ne pas administrer le médicament et prévenir le médecin.
- Administrer le médicament sans égard aux aliments.

ENSEIGNEMENT AU PATIENT ET À SES PROCHES

- Expliquer au patient qu'il doit respecter rigoureusement la posologie recommandée et continuer à prendre le médicament même s'il se sent bien. L'avertir qu'il ne doit jamais sauter de dose ni remplacer une dose manquée par une double dose. S'il n'a pu prendre le médicament au moment habituel, il doit le prendre aussitôt que possible, mais au moins 4 heures avant l'heure prévue pour la dose suivante. UN SEVRAGE BRUSQUE PEUT PROVOQUER DES ARYTHMIES MORTELLES, DE L'HYPERTENSION OU L'ISCHÉMIE DU MYOCARDE.

- Recommander au patient de prévoir une quantité suffisante de médicament pour les fins de semaine, les congés et les vacances. Lui conseiller de conserver une ordonnance dans son portefeuille pour parer aux urgences.
- EXPLIQUER AU PATIENT ET À SES PROCHES COMMENT PRENDRE LE POULS ET LA PRESSION ARTÉRIELLE. Leur demander de mesurer le pouls tous les jours et la pression artérielle 2 fois par semaine. Recommander au patient d'informer le médecin si le pouls est inférieur à 50 battements par minute ou si sa pression artérielle change considérablement.
- Prévenir le patient que le médicament peut parfois provoquer des étourdissements.
- Recommander au patient de changer de position lentement pour réduire le risque d'hypotension orthostatique, particulièrement au début du traitement ou lorsque la dose est majorée.
- Prévenir le patient que le médicament peut le rendre plus sensible au froid.
- Conseiller au patient de consulter un professionnel de la santé avant de prendre un médicament en vente libre, particulièrement des préparations contre le rhume ou un produit naturel en même temps que le carvédilol.
- Recommander au patient diabétique de mesurer minutieusement sa glycémie, particulièrement lorsqu'il se sent fatigué, faible ou irritable ou lorsqu'il ressent un malaise. Le médicament peut masquer certains signes d'hypoglycémie, bien que des étourdissements et la transpiration puissent survenir malgré tout.
- Recommander au patient de signaler au médecin les symptômes suivants: ralentissement du pouls, difficultés respiratoires, respiration sifflante, mains et pieds froids, étourdissements, confusion, état dépressif, rash, fièvre, maux de gorge, saignements inhabituels ou formation d'ecchymoses.
- Recommander au patient qui doit suivre un autre traitement ou subir une intervention chirurgicale d'avertir le professionnel de la santé qu'il suit un traitement par ce médicament.
- Conseiller au patient de porter sur lui en tout temps une pièce d'identité où sont inscrits son problème de santé et son traitement médicamenteux.

VÉRIFICATION DE L'EFFICACITÉ THÉRAPEUTIQUE

L'efficacité du traitement peut être démontrée par: la diminution de la gravité de l'insuffisance cardiaque. ✳

C

CASPOFONGINE

Cancidas

CLASSIFICATION:

Antifongique (échinocandine)

Grossesse - catégorie C

INDICATIONS

Aspergillose invasive chez les patients qui ne répondent pas à d'autres traitements ou qui ne les tolèrent pas ■ Candidose invasive (candidémie, abcès intraabdominaux, péritonite, infections de la cavité pleurale; les effets de l'agent dans le traitement de l'endocardite, de l'ostéomyélite et de la méningite dues à *Candida* n'ont pas été étudiés) ■ Candidose œsophagienne ■ Traitement empirique des infections fongiques soupçonnées chez des patients neutropéniques fébriles.

MÉCANISME D'ACTION

Inhibition de la synthèse du β(1, 3)-D-glucan, composant nécessaire de la paroi de la cellule fongique. ***Effets thérapeutiques:*** Destruction des champignons sensibles.

PHARMACOCINÉTIQUE

Absorption: Biodisponibilité à 100 % (IV).

Distribution: Tous les tissus.

Liaison aux protéines: 97 %.

Métabolisme et excrétion: Métabolisme lent et important; < 1,5 % excrété sous forme inchangée dans l'urine.

Demi-vie: Polyphasique: *phase* α – de 1 à 2 h; *phase* β – de 9 à 11 h; *phase* γ – de 40 à 50 h.

Profil temps-action

	DÉBUT D'ACTION	PIC	DURÉE
IV	inconnu	fin de la perfusion	24 h

CONTRE-INDICATIONS, PRÉCAUTIONS ET MISES EN GARDE

Contre-indications: Hypersensibilité.

Précautions et mises en garde: Usage concomitant de cyclosporine (risque d'élévation des résultats des tests de la fonction hépatique) ■ Insuffisance hépatique modérée (il est recommandé de diminuer la dose d'entretien) ■ Insuffisance hépatique grave (l'innocuité du médicament n'a pas été établie) ■ **PÉD.**: Enfants < 18 ans (l'innocuité de l'agent n'a pas été établie) ■ **OBST., ALLAITEMENT**: L'innocuité de l'agent n'a pas été établie ■ **GÉR.**: Personnes âgées ≥ 65 ans (risque de sensibilité accrue aux effets du médicament).

C

RÉACTIONS INDÉSIRABLES ET EFFETS SECONDAIRES

SNC: céphalées.
Resp.: dyspnée.
CV: tachycardie.
GI: diarrhée, nausées, vomissements.
Tég.: bouffées vasomotrices, transpiration.
Locaux: irritation de la veine au point d'injection.
Divers: réactions allergiques comprenant l'ANAPHYLAXIE, fièvre, frissons.

INTERACTIONS

Médicament-médicament: L'usage concomitant de la **cyclosporine** est déconseillé en raison d'un risque accru de toxicité hépatique ■ L'agent peut diminuer les concentrations sanguines et les effets du **tacrolimus** ■ Les concentrations sanguines et l'efficacité de l'agent peuvent être réduites par la **rifampine**; porter la dose d'entretien à 70 mg (chez les patients dont la fonction hépatique est normale) ■ Les concentrations sanguines et l'efficacité peuvent aussi être réduites par l'**éfavirenz**, le **nelfinavir**, la **névirapine**, la **phénytoïne**, le **dexaméthasone** ou la **carbamazépine**; envisager la possibilité de porter la dose d'entretien à 70 mg chez les patients dont la réponse clinique est insuffisante.

VOIES D'ADMINISTRATION ET POSOLOGIE

Aspergillose invasive et traitement empirique des patients neutropéniques fébriles

- **IV (adultes)**: Dose d'attaque (1er jour): 70 mg, suivie d'une dose d'entretien de 50 mg par jour; la durée du traitement est déterminée par les circonstances cliniques et la réponse du patient. On peut maintenir la dose quotidienne à 70 mg chez les patients qui ne semblent pas répondre au traitement, mais qui tolèrent bien le médicament.

Candidose invasive

- **IV (adultes)**: Dose d'attaque (1er jour): 70 mg, suivie d'une dose d'entretien de 50 mg par jour; la durée du traitement est déterminée par les circonstances cliniques et la réponse du patient.

Candidose œsophagienne

- **IV (adultes)**: 50 mg par jour; la durée du traitement est déterminée par les circonstances cliniques et la réponse du patient.

INSUFFISANCE HÉPATIQUE MODÉRÉE (STADE 7 À 9 DE CHILD-PUGH)

- **IV (ADULTES)**: 35 mg PAR JOUR; CEPENDANT, LORSQUE C'EST INDIQUÉ, ON DOIT QUAND MÊME ADMINISTRER UNE DOSE D'ATTAQUE DE 70 mg LE PREMIER JOUR. LA DURÉE DU TRAITEMENT EST DÉTERMINÉE PAR LES CIRCONSTANCES CLINIQUES ET LA RÉPONSE DU PATIENT.

PRÉSENTATION

Poudre pour injection: 50 mg[Pr], 70 mg[Pr].

SOINS INFIRMIERS

ÉVALUATION DE LA SITUATION

- Rester à l'affût des signes et des symptômes d'infections fongiques, avant le traitement et à intervalles réguliers pendant toute sa durée.
- Rechercher les signes d'anaphylaxie (rash, dyspnée, stridor) tout au long du traitement.

Tests de laboratoire: L'agent peut élever les concentrations sériques de phosphatase alcaline sérique, d'AST, d'ALT, d'éosinophiles, ainsi que les taux de protéines urinaires et le nombre d'érythrocytes. Il peut aussi abaisser les concentrations sériques de potassium et d'hémoglobine, l'hématocrite et le nombre de leucocytes.

DIAGNOSTICS INFIRMIERS POSSIBLES

- Risque d'infection (Indications).

INTERVENTIONS INFIRMIÈRES

Perfusion intermittente:

- Dissoudre complètement la poudre blanche. Mélanger délicatement jusqu'à l'obtention d'une solution transparente. Ne pas utiliser une solution trouble, qui a changé de couleur ou qui contient un précipité. La solution reconstituée peut être conservée jusqu'à 1 heure entre 15 et 25 °C.
- Pour préparer une dose de 70 mg ou de 50 mg, attendre que la fiole réfrigérée soit à la température ambiante. Ajouter par voie aseptique 10,5 mL de NaCl 0,9 %, d'eau stérile ou d'eau bactériostatique à la fiole de 70 mg ou de 50 mg. On peut conserver la solution pendant 1 heure au plus à la température ambiante. Transvaser 10 mL de la solution de 70 mg ou de 50 mg dans le sac pour administration IV contenant 250 mL de NaCl 0,9 %, 0,45 % ou 0,225 % ou de LR, pour obtenir une concentration de 0,28 mg/mL ou de 0,20 mg/mL, respectivement. La solution diluée est stable pendant 24 heures à température ambiante ou pendant 48 heures au réfrigérateur.

- Si on ne dispose que de la fiole de 50 mg, pour préparer une dose à 70 mg, transvaser au total 14 mL de deux fioles de 50 mg dans 250 mL de NaCl 0,9 %, 0,45 % ou 0,225 % ou de LR.
- Si le médecin prescrit un volume réduit, on peut préparer la dose à 50 mg en ajoutant 10 mL de solution reconstituée à 100 mL de NaCl 0,9 %, 0,45 % ou 0,225 % ou de LR pour obtenir une concentration de 0,47 mg/mL.
- Pour préparer une dose à 35 mg destinée à des insuffisants hépatiques, reconstituer le contenu d'une fiole de 50 mg. Transvaser 7 mL dans 250 mL ou, si c'est médicalement conseillé, dans 100 mL de NaCl 0,9 %, 0,45 % ou 0,225 % ou de LR pour obtenir une concentration de 0,14 mg/mL ou de 0,34 mg/mL, respectivement.
- Consulter les directives du fabricant avant de reconstituer la préparation.

Vitesse d'administration: Administrer par perfusion lente pendant 1 heure environ.

Incompatibilité (tubulure en Y): Ne pas utiliser de diluants contenant de dextrose. Ne pas mélanger la caspofongine à d'autres médicaments ni la perfuser par la même tubulure.

ENSEIGNEMENT AU PATIENT ET À SES PROCHES

- Expliquer le but du traitement au patient et à ses proches.

VÉRIFICATION DE L'EFFICACITÉ THÉRAPEUTIQUE

L'efficacité du traitement peut être démontrée par: la diminution des signes et des symptômes d'infection fongique. La durée du traitement est déterminée par la gravité de la maladie sous-jacente, le rétablissement de la réponse immunitaire et la réponse clinique. ✳

CÉFACLOR,
voir Céphalosporines de la deuxième génération

CÉFADROXIL,
voir Céphalosporines de la première génération

CÉFAZOLINE,
voir Céphalosporines de la première génération

CÉFÉPIME,
voir Céphalosporines de la troisième génération

CÉFIXIME,
voir Céphalosporines de la troisième génération

CÉFOTAXIME,
voir Céphalosporines de la troisième génération

CÉFOXITINE,
voir Céphalosporines de la deuxième génération

CEFPROZIL,
voir Céphalosporines de la deuxième génération

CEFTAZIDIME,
voir Céphalosporines de la troisième génération

CEFTRIAXONE,
voir Céphalosporines de la troisième génération

CÉFUROXIME,
voir Céphalosporines de la deuxième génération

CÉLÉCOXIB

Celebrex

CLASSIFICATION:

Anti-inflammatoire non stéroïdien, analgésique non opioïde

Grossesse – catégorie D (1er et 3e trimestres); catégorie B (2e trimestre)

C

INDICATIONS

Soulagement des signes et des symptômes d'arthrose ▪ Soulagement des signes et des symptômes de polyarthrite rhumatoïde chez l'adulte ▪ Soulagement de la douleur aiguë modérée ou grave. **Usages non approuvés:** Réduction du nombre de polyadénomes colorectaux associés à la polypose adénomateuse familiale, comme adjuvant aux soins habituels (surveillance endoscopique, chirurgie).

MÉCANISME D'ACTION

Inhibition de la cyclo-oxygénase-2 (COX-2), enzyme nécessaire à la synthèse des prostaglandines ▪ Propriétés analgésiques, anti-inflammatoires et antipyrétiques. ***Effets thérapeutiques:*** Diminution de la douleur et de l'inflammation dues à l'arthrite ▪ Diminution du nombre de polypes colorectaux ▪ Diminution de la douleur.

PHARMACOCINÉTIQUE

Absorption: Biodisponibilité inconnue.
Distribution: Le médicament se lie à 97 % aux protéines plasmatiques et se répartit dans la plupart des tissus.
Métabolisme et excrétion: Métabolisme majoritairement hépatique; moins de 3 % excrété à l'état inchangé dans l'urine et les fèces.
Demi-vie: 11 heures.

Profil temps-action (soulagement de la douleur)

	Début d'action	Pic	Durée
PO	24 - 48 h	inconnu	12 - 24 h

CONTRE-INDICATIONS, PRÉCAUTIONS ET MISES EN GARDE

Contre-indications: Hypersensibilité ▪ Antécédents de réactions de type allergique aux sulfamides ▪ Usage concomitant d'autres AINS ▪ Antécédents d'asthme, d'urticaire ou de réactions de type allergique à l'aspirine ou aux autres AINS, incluant la triade de réactions provoquées par l'AAS (asthme, polype nasal, réactions graves d'hypersensibilité) ▪ Néphropathie avancée ▪ Contexte périopératoire en cas de pontage aortocoronarien ▪ Ulcère gastrique, duodénal ou gastroduodénal en poussée évolutive ▪ Maladie intestinale inflammatoire ▪ **OBST.:** 3e trimestre (le médicament peut entraîner l'obturation prématurée du canal artériel) ▪ **ALLAITEMENT:** Risque d'effets indésirables graves chez le nourrisson.

Précautions et mises en garde: Maladie cardiovasculaire ou facteurs de risque de maladies cardiovasculaires (risque accru de complications coronariennes, d'infarctus du myocarde ou d'accidents vasculaires cérébraux, surtout lors d'un usage prolongé) ▪ Traitement concomitant par des glucocorticoïdes ou des anticoagulants; traitement prolongé par des AINS, usage du tabac, alcoolisme, patients âgés ou en mauvaise santé (risque accru d'hémorragie digestive) ▪ Néphropathie, insuffisance cardiaque ou dysfonctionnement hépatique préexistants, traitement concomitant par un diurétique ou un inhibiteur de l'ECA (risque accru d'insuffisance rénale) ▪ Hypertension ou rétention liquidienne ▪ Déshydratation grave (corriger les déficits avant d'administrer le médicament) ▪ Asthme préexistant ▪ **OBST., PÉD.:** L'innocuité du médicament n'a pas été établie, son usage n'est pas recommandé en fin de grossesse.

EXTRÊME PRUDENCE: ANTÉCÉDENTS D'ULCÈRE OU D'HÉMORRAGIE DIGESTIVE.

RÉACTIONS INDÉSIRABLES ET EFFETS SECONDAIRES

SNC: étourdissements, céphalées, insomnie.
CV: œdème
GI: HÉMORRAGIE DIGESTIVE, douleurs abdominales, diarrhée, dyspepsie, flatulences, nausées.
Tég.: DERMATITE EXFOLIATIVE, SYNDROME DE STEVENS-JOHNSON, ÉPIDERMOLYSE NÉCROSANTE SUBAIGUË, rash.

INTERACTIONS

Médicament-médicament: Risque d'interactions importantes en cas d'administration concomitante d'autres **médicaments qui inhibent le système enzymatique CYP450 2C9** ▪ Le célécoxib peut réduire l'efficacité des **inhibiteurs de l'ECA**, des **diurétiques thiazidiques** et du **furosémide** ▪ Bien que le célécoxib puisse être pris en même temps que l'**aspirine**, cette association peut augmenter le risque d'hémorragie digestive ▪ Le **fluconazole** élève les concentrations sanguines de célécoxib (une réduction de la posologie est recommandée) ▪ Risque de saignements si le médicament est administré en même temps que la **warfarine** ▪ Le célécoxib peut élever les concentrations sériques de **lithium**.

VOIES D'ADMINISTRATION ET POSOLOGIE

- **PO (adultes):** *Arthrose* – 200 mg par jour, en une seule dose ou 100 mg, 2 fois par jour. *Polyarthrite rhumatoïde* – posologie de départ: 100 mg, 2 fois par jour; on peut augmenter la dose jusqu'à 200 mg, 2 fois par jour. *Douleur aiguë* – 400 mg en une seule dose, le premier jour, puis 200 mg, 1 fois par jour. On peut conseiller au patient de prendre une dose additionnelle de 200 mg par jour, au besoin. *Polypose adénomateuse familiale* – 400 mg, 2 fois par jour (usage non approuvé).

PRÉSENTATION

Capsules: 100 mg^{Pr}, 200 mg^{Pr}.

SOINS INFIRMIERS

ÉVALUATION DE LA SITUATION

- LES PATIENTS SOUFFRANT D'ASTHME, D'ALLERGIE INDUITE PAR L'ASPIRINE ET DE POLYPES NASAUX SONT DAVANTAGE PRÉDISPOSÉS À DES RÉACTIONS D'HYPERSENSIBILITÉ. SUIVRE DE PRÈS LA RHINITE, L'ASTHME ET L'URTICAIRE.
- Suivre de près l'amplitude des mouvements, le degré d'enflure et la douleur au niveau des articulations touchées, avant l'administration du médicament et à intervalles réguliers tout au long du traitement.
- Déterminer si le patient est allergique aux sulfamides, à l'aspirine ou aux AINS. Les patients allergiques ne devraient pas recevoir de célécoxib.

Tests de laboratoire:

- Le célécoxib peut élever les concentrations d'AST et d'ALT.
- Le célécoxib peut induire une hypophosphatémie et une élévation des concentrations d'urée.

DIAGNOSTICS INFIRMIERS POSSIBLES

- Mobilité physique réduite (Indications).
- Douleur aiguë (Indications).
- Connaissances insuffisantes sur le traitement médicamenteux (Enseignement au patient et à ses proches).

INTERVENTIONS INFIRMIÈRES

- NE PAS CONFONDRE CET AGENT AVEC CELEXA (CITALOPRAM) OU AVEC CEREBYX (FOSPHÉNYTOÏNE).
- Le médicament peut être administré sans égard aux aliments.

ENSEIGNEMENT AU PATIENT ET À SES PROCHES

- Conseiller au patient de respecter rigoureusement la posologie recommandée et de ne pas dépasser la dose qui lui a été prescrite. Les doses accrues ne semblent pas accroître l'efficacité du médicament.
- RECOMMANDER AU PATIENT DE PRÉVENIR UN PROFESSIONNEL DE LA SANTÉ SANS TARDER EN CAS DE SIGNES OU DE SYMPTÔMES DE TOXICITÉ GASTRO-INTESTINALE (DOULEURS ABDOMINALES, SELLES NOIRÂTRES), DE RASH CUTANÉ, DE GAIN DE POIDS INEXPLIQUÉ OU D'ŒDÈME. Lui conseiller de cesser de prendre le célécoxib et de prévenir le médecin si les signes et les symptômes suivants d'hépatotoxicité se manifestent: nausées, fatigue, léthargie, prurit, jaunisse, sensibilité au niveau du quadrant supérieur droit de l'abdomen, symptômes pseudogrippaux.
- Conseiller à la patiente de prévenir le médecin sans délai si elle prévoit devenir enceinte ou si elle pense l'être.
- Recommander aux patients souffrant de polypose adénomateuse familiale de continuer à se soumettre aux interventions de surveillance habituelles.

VÉRIFICATION DE L'EFFICACITÉ THÉRAPEUTIQUE

L'efficacité du traitement peut être démontrée par: la réduction de la douleur articulaire chez les patients souffrant d'arthrose ■ la réduction de la douleur, de la sensibilité et de l'enflure des articulations chez les patients souffrant de polyarthrite rhumatoïde ■ la diminution du nombre de polypes chez les patients atteints de polypose adénomateuse familiale.

CÉPHALEXINE,

voir Céphalosporines de la première génération

CÉPHALOSPORINES DE LA PREMIÈRE GÉNÉRATION

céfadroxil

Apo-Céfadroxil, Duricef, Novo-Céfadroxil

céfazoline

Ancef, Kefzol

céphalexine

Apo-Cephalex, Keflex, Novo-Lexin, Nu-Cephalex

CLASSIFICATION:

Antibiotiques (céphalosporines de la première génération)

Grossesse – catégorie B

INDICATIONS

Traitement des infections suivantes dues à des microorganismes sensibles: infections de la peau et des tissus mous, incluant les lésions entraînées par des brûlures ■ infections des voies respiratoires ■ infections des voies urinaires ■ pharyngoamygdalite aiguë due aux streptocoques bêtahémolytiques du groupe A ■ **Céfazoline et céphalexine:** Infections des os et des articulations ■ **Céfazoline:** Prophylaxie périopératoire ■

Septicémie ■ Ces antibiotiques ne conviennent pas au traitement de la méningite.

MÉCANISME D'ACTION

C

Liaison à la membrane de la paroi de la cellule bactérienne, entraînant la destruction de la bactérie. ***Effets thérapeutiques:*** Action bactéricide contre les bactéries sensibles. **Spectre d'action**: Agent efficace contre de nombreux cocci à Gram positif dont: *Streptococcus pneumoniæ* ■ streptocoques bêtahémolytiques du groupe A ■ staphylocoques produisant de la pénicillinase ■ Aucun effet sur les microorganismes suivants: staphylocoques résistant à la méthicilline ■ *Bacteroides fragilis* ■ entérocoques ■ Effet limité contre certains bacilles à Gram négatif, incluant: *Klebsiella pneumoniæ* ■ *Proteus mirabilis* ■ *Escherichia coli.*

PHARMACOCINÉTIQUE

Absorption: *Céfadroxil* et *céphalexine* – bonne (PO); *céfazoline* – bonne(IM).

Distribution: Tout l'organisme. Toutes les céphalosporines de la première génération traversent la barrière placentaire et passent dans le lait maternel à faible concentration. La pénétration dans le liquide céphalorachidien est minimale.

Liaison aux protéines: *Céfadroxil* – 20 %; *céfazoline* – de 74 à 86 %; *céphalexine* – 10 %.

Métabolisme et excrétion: Excrétion majoritairement rénale à l'état inchangé.

Demi-vie: *Céfadroxil* – de 1,3 à 1,5 heure; *céfazoline* – de 1,5 à 2 heures; *céphalexine* – de 0,5 à 1,2 heure (toutes ces demi-vies sont prolongées en cas d'insuffisance rénale).

Profil temps-action

	DÉBUT D'ACTION	PIC	DURÉE
Céfadroxil PO	rapide	1,5 - 2 h	12 - 24 h
Céfazoline IM	rapide	1 - 2 h	6 - 12 h
Céfazoline IV	rapide	fin de la perfusion	6 - 12 h
Céphalexine PO	rapide	1 h	6 - 12 h

CONTRE-INDICATIONS, PRÉCAUTIONS ET MISES EN GARDE

Contre-indications: Hypersensibilité aux céphalosporines ■ Réactions graves d'hypersensibilité aux pénicillines (une réaction de sensibilité croisée peut survenir chez 10 % des patients ayant des antécédents d'allergie à la pénicilline).

Précautions et mises en garde: Sensibilité à la pénicilline (risque de réaction croisée) ■ Insuffisance rénale (on recommande de réduire la dose ou d'accroître l'intervalle posologique du *céfadroxil*, si la Cl_{Cr} < 50 mL/min, de la *céfazoline*, si la Cl_{Cr} < 50 mL/min, de la *céphalexine*, si la Cl_{Cr} < 40 mL/min) ■ Antécédents de maladie gastro-intestinale, particulièrement de colite ■ **GÉR.**: Il peut s'avérer nécessaire d'adapter la posologie en fonction de la détérioration de la fonction rénale, liée à l'âge ■ **OBST.**: Grossesse ou allaitement (la demi-vie est plus courte et les concentrations sanguines sont plus basses pendant la grossesse; on note cependant des précédents d'usage sans apparition d'effets nocifs).

RÉACTIONS INDÉSIRABLES ET EFFETS SECONDAIRES

SNC: CONVULSIONS (doses élevées), céphalées.

GI: COLITE PSEUDOMEMBRANEUSE, diarrhée, nausées, vomissements, crampes.

GU: vaginite, candidose génitale, néphrite interstitielle.

Tég.: rash, urticaire.

Hémat.: dyscrasie sanguine, neutropénie, thrombopénie, anémie hémolytique.

Locaux: douleur au point d'injection IM, phlébite au point d'injection IV.

Divers: réactions allergiques, incluant l'ANAPHYLAXIE, la MALADIE SÉRIQUE, le SYNDROME DE STEVENS-JOHNSON et la NÉCROLYSE ÉPIDERMIQUE TOXIQUE, surinfection.

INTERACTIONS

Médicament-médicament: Le **probénécide** diminue l'excrétion et élève les concentrations sanguines des céphalosporines excrétées par voie rénale ■ Risque accru de néphrotoxicité lors de l'administration concomitante d'autres **médicaments néphrotoxiques**.

VOIES D'ADMINISTRATION ET POSOLOGIE

Céfadroxil

- **PO (adultes)**: *Pharyngite et amygdalite dues aux streptocoques bêtahémolytiques du groupe A* – 500 mg, toutes les 12 heures, ou 1 g, toutes les 24 heures, pendant 10 jours. *Infections de la peau et des tissus mous* – 1 g, toutes les 24 heures. *Infections des voies urinaires* – de 500 mg à 1 g, toutes les 12 heures, ou de 1 à 2 g, toutes les 24 heures. *Infections des voies respiratoires inférieures* – de 0,5 à 1 g, toutes les 12 heures.
- **PO (enfants ≥ 6 semaines)**: *Pharyngoamygdalite due aux streptocoques bêtahémolytiques du groupe A* – 15 mg/kg, toutes les 12 heures, pendant 10 jours. *Infections de la peau et des tissus mous* – 15 mg/kg, toutes les 12 heures, ou 30 mg/kg, toutes les 24 heures. *Infections des voies urinaires* – 15 mg/kg, toutes les 12 heures.

- *INSUFFISANCE RÉNALE*
  PO (ADULTES): DOSE INITIALE DE 1 g, PUIS ADAPTER SELON LA CLAIRANCE DE LA CRÉATININE: *Cl_{CR} DE 25 À 50 mL/MIN* – 500 mg, TOUTES LES 12 HEURES; *Cl_{CR} DE 10 À 25 mL/MIN* – 500 mg, TOUTES LES 24 HEURES; *Cl_{CR} DE 0 À 10 mL/MIN* – 500 mg, TOUTES LES 36 HEURES.

Céfazoline

- **IM, IV (adultes)**: *La plupart des infections* – de 500 mg à 2 g, toutes les 6 à 8 heures. *Prophylaxie périopératoire* – de 1 à 2 g, de 30 à 60 minutes avant l'incision, puis 1 g, toutes les 8 heures, pendant 24 heures après la chirurgie.
- **IM, IV (enfants et nourrissons > 1 mois)**: De 25 à 50 mg/kg/jour en 3 ou 4 doses égales. La dose peut être augmentée jusqu'à 100 mg/kg/jour dans le cas des infections graves.
- *INSUFFISANCE RÉNALE*
  IM, IV (ADULTES): *Cl_{CR} DE 10 À 50 mL/MIN* – ADMINISTRER TOUTES LES 12 HEURES; *Cl_{CR} < 10 mL/MIN* – ADMINISTRER TOUTES LES 24 HEURES.

Céphalexine

- **PO (adultes)**: *La plupart des infections* – de 250 à 500 mg, toutes les 6 heures. *Cystite, infections de la peau et des tissus mous, pharyngite streptococcique* – 500 mg, toutes les 12 heures.
- **PO (enfants)**: de 25 à 50 mg/kg/jour, en doses fractionnées, toutes les 6 heures (au maximum: 4 g/jour).
- *INSUFFISANCE RÉNALE*
  PO (ADULTES): *Cl_{CR} DE 10 À 40 mL/MIN* – ADMINISTRER TOUTES LES 8 À 12 HEURES; *Cl_{CR} < 10 mL/MIN* – ADMINISTRER TOUTES LES 12 À 24 HEURES.

PRÉSENTATION

- **Céfadroxil** (version générique disponible)
  Capsules: 500 mg^Pr^.
- **Céfazoline** (version générique disponible)
  Poudre pour injection: 500 mg^Pr^, 1 g^Pr^, 10 g^Pr^.
- **Céphalexine** (version générique disponible)
  Capsules: 250 mg^Pr^, 500 mg^Pr^ ■ **Comprimés**: 250 mg^Pr^, 500 mg^Pr^ ■ **Suspension orale**: 125 mg/5 mL^Pr^, 250 mg/5 mL^Pr^.

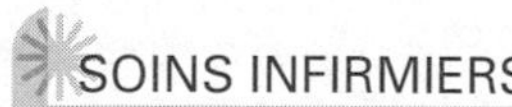

SOINS INFIRMIERS

ÉVALUATION DE LA SITUATION

- Au début du traitement et pendant toute sa durée, rester à l'affût des signes suivants d'infection: altération des signes vitaux; aspect de la plaie, des crachats, de l'urine et des selles; accroissement du nombre de leucocytes.
- Avant d'amorcer le traitement, recueillir les antécédents du patient afin de déterminer ses réactions antérieures à une pénicilline ou à une céphalosporine. Même les personnes n'ayant jamais manifesté de sensibilité aux pénicillines peuvent présenter une réaction allergique.
- Prélever des échantillons pour les cultures et les antibiogrammes avant le début du traitement. La première dose peut être administrée avant que les résultats soient connus.
- RESTER À L'AFFÛT DES SIGNES ET DES SYMPTÔMES SUIVANTS D'ANAPHYLAXIE: RASH, PRURIT, ŒDÈME LARYNGÉ, RESPIRATION SIFFLANTE. SI CES RÉACTIONS SE MANIFESTENT, ARRÊTER L'ADMINISTRATION DU MÉDICAMENT ET AVERTIR IMMÉDIATEMENT LE MÉDECIN. GARDER À PORTÉE DE LA MAIN DE L'ADRÉNALINE, UN ANTIHISTAMINIQUE ET LE MATÉRIEL DE RÉANIMATION POUR PARER À UNE ÉVENTUELLE RÉACTION ANAPHYLACTIQUE.
- Déterminer si le patient présente une insuffisance rénale et adapter la dose en conséquence.

Tests de laboratoire:

- Les céphalosporines de la première génération peuvent entraîner des résultats faussement positifs au test de Coombs chez les patients recevant de fortes doses ou chez les nouveau-nés dont les mères ont reçu une céphalosporine avant l'accouchement.
- Les céphalosporines de la première génération peuvent entraîner l'élévation des concentrations sériques d'AST, d'ALT, de phosphatase alcaline, de bilirubine, de LDH, d'urée et de créatinine.
- Les céphalosporines de la première génération peuvent entraîner rarement les effets suivants: leucopénie, neutropénie, agranulocytose, thrombopénie, éosinophilie, lymphocytose et thrombocytose.

DIAGNOSTICS INFIRMIERS POSSIBLES

- Risque d'infection (Indications, Effets secondaires).
- Diarrhée (Réactions indésirables).
- Connaissances insuffisantes sur le traitement médicamenteux (Enseignement au patient et à ses proches).

INTERVENTIONS INFIRMIÈRES

PO: Administrer ces antibiotiques à intervalles réguliers, sans égard aux repas. En cas d'irritation gastrique, les administrer avec des aliments. Bien agiter la suspension orale avant de l'administrer. La suspension orale reconstituée de céphalexine est stable pendant 14 jours si elle est gardée au réfrigérateur.

IM: Reconstituer les doses destinées à l'administration par voie IM en diluant le contenu de la fiole dans de l'eau stérile, de l'eau bactériostatique pour injection ou une solution de NaCl 0,9 % pour injection. Consulter les directives de chaque fabricant avant de reconstituer la préparation. Injecter en profondeur dans une masse musculaire bien développée; bien masser.

C

IV:

- Observer fréquemment le point d'injection pour déceler les signes suivants de thrombophlébite: douleur, rougeur, enflure. Changer de point d'injection toutes les 48 à 72 heures afin de prévenir la phlébite.
- Ne pas utiliser de solutions troubles ou contenant un précipité.
- En cas d'administration concomitante d'aminosides, rincer la tubulure avant d'administrer le deuxième médicament, car les aminosides et les céphalosporines ne sont pas compatibles.
- **PÉD. (nouveau-nés)**: ne pas utiliser de préparations contenant de l'alcool benzylique.

Céfazoline

Perfusion intermittente: La solution reconstituée de 500 mg ou de 1 g peut être diluée dans 50 à 100 mL de NaCl 0,9 %, de D5%E, de D5%/NaCl 0,45 % ou de D5%/NaCl 0,9 %, de D5%E dans une solution de lactate de Ringer ou d'une solution de lactate de Ringer. La solution est stable pendant 24 heures à la température ambiante et pendant 96 heures au réfrigérateur.

Vitesse d'administration: La perfusion doit durer de 10 à 60 minutes.

IV directe: Diluer 1 g dans au moins 10 mL d'eau stérile pour injection. Consulter les directives de chaque fabricant avant de reconstituer la préparation.

Vitesse d'administration: Administrer lentement, en 3 à 5 minutes.

Associations compatibles dans la même seringue: héparine ■ vitamines du complexe B avec C.

Associations incompatibles dans la même seringue: acide ascorbique, injection d' ■ cimétidine ■ lidocaïne.

Compatibilité (tubulure en Y): acyclovir ■ allopurinol ■ amifostine ■ atracurium ■ aztréonam ■ calcium, gluconate de ■ cyclophosphamide ■ diltiazem ■ énalaprilate ■ esmolol ■ famotidine ■ filgrastim ■ fluconazole ■ fludarabine ■ foscarnet ■ gallium, nitrate de ■ granisétron ■ héparine ■ insuline ■ labétolol ■ lidocaïne ■ magnésium, sulfate de ■ melphalan ■ mépéridine ■ midazolam ■ morphine ■ multivitamines ■ ondansétron ■ pancuronium ■ perphénazine ■ propofol ■ sargramostim ■ tacrolimus ■ téniposide ■ théophylline ■ thiotépa ■ vécuronium ■ vitamines du complexe B avec C ■ warfarine.

Incompatibilité (tubulure en Y): idarubicine ■ pentamidine ■ vinorelbine.

ENSEIGNEMENT AU PATIENT ET À SES PROCHES

- Expliquer au patient qu'il doit prendre le médicament à intervalles réguliers et qu'il doit utiliser toute la quantité qui lui a été prescrite, même s'il se sent mieux. S'il n'a pu prendre le médicament au moment habituel, il doit le prendre aussitôt que possible, mais non pas juste avant l'heure prévue pour la dose suivante. Il ne faut jamais doubler la dose. Recommander au patient de mesurer les doses de suspension à l'aide d'un récipient gradué. Insister sur le fait qu'il peut être dangereux de donner ce médicament à une autre personne.
- Conseiller au patient de signaler les réactions allergiques et les signes suivants de surinfection: excroissance pileuse sur la langue, démangeaisons ou pertes vaginales, selles molles ou nauséabondes.
- RECOMMANDER AU PATIENT DE COMMUNIQUER AVEC UN PROFESSIONNEL DE LA SANTÉ EN CAS DE FIÈVRE OU DE DIARRHÉE, PARTICULIÈREMENT SI SES SELLES RENFERMENT DU SANG, DU PUS OU DU MUCUS. CONSEILLER AU PATIENT DE NE PAS TRAITER LA DIARRHÉE SANS CONSULTER AU PRÉALABLE UN PROFESSIONNEL DE LA SANTÉ.

VÉRIFICATION DE L'EFFICACITÉ THÉRAPEUTIQUE

L'efficacité du traitement peut être démontrée par: la disparition des signes et des symptômes d'infection; le temps de résolution dépend du microorganisme infectant et du siège de l'infection ■ la réduction de l'incidence des infections en cas d'usage prophylactique. ✳

CÉPHALOSPORINES DE LA DEUXIÈME GÉNÉRATION

céfaclor

Apo-Cefaclor, Ceclor, Novo-Cefaclor

céfoxitine

Mefoxin

cefprozil

Cefzil

céfuroxime

Apo-Cefuroxime, Ceftin, Kefurox, Ratio-Cefuroxime, Zinacef

CLASSIFICATION:

Antibiotiques (céphalosporines de la deuxième génération)

Grossesse – catégorie B

INDICATIONS

Traitement des infections suivantes: infections des voies respiratoires ■ infections de la peau et des tissus mous ■ infections des voies urinaires ■ **Céfoxitine, céfuroxime**: Infections des os et des articulations ■ **Céfoxitine**: Infections gynécologiques ■ infections intra-abdominales ■ septicémie ■ **Céfuroxime**: Gonorrhée, méningite ■ **Céfaclor, cefprozil**: Otite moyenne ■ **Céfoxitine, céfuroxime**: Prophylaxie périopératoire.

MÉCANISME D'ACTION

Liaison à la membrane de la paroi de la cellule bactérienne, entraînant la destruction de la bactérie. ***Effets thérapeutiques:*** Action bactéricide contre les bactéries sensibles. **Spectre d'action**: Effet similaire à celui des céphalosporines de la première génération, mais l'effet contre plusieurs autres agents pathogènes à Gram négatif est accru, le spectre d'action englobant les microorganismes suivants: *Hæmophilus influenzæ* ■ *Escherichia coli* ■ *Klebsiella pneumoniæ* ■ *Proteus* ■ *Moraxella catarrhalis* ■ La céfoxitine est efficace contre *Bacteroides fragilis* ■ Le céfuroxime est efficace contre *Neisseria meningitidis* et *Neisseria gonorrhœæ* (incluant les souches produisant de la pénicillinase) ■ Aucun effet contre les staphylocoques résistant à la méthicilline ou les entérocoques.

PHARMACOCINÉTIQUE

Absorption: Bonne (IM). *Céfaclor, cefprozil, céfuroxime* – bonne (PO).

Distribution: Tout l'organisme. Le céfuroxime pénètre suffisamment dans le liquide céphalorachidien pour traiter adéquatement la méningite. Toutes les céphalosporines de la deuxième génération traversent la barrière placentaire et passent dans le lait maternel à faible concentration.

Métabolisme et excrétion: Excrétion majoritairement rénale à l'état inchangé.

Demi-vie: *Céfaclor* – de 35 à 54 minutes; *céfoxitine* – de 40 à 60 minutes; *cefprozil* – 90 minutes; *céfuroxime* – 80 minutes (toutes ces demi-vies sont prolongées en cas d'insuffisance rénale).

Profil temps-action

	DÉBUT D'ACTION	PIC	DURÉE
Céfaclor PO	rapide	30 – 60 min	6 – 12 h
Céfoxitine IM	rapide	30 min	4 – 8 h
Céfoxitine IV	rapide	fin de la perfusion	4 – 8 h
Cefprozil PO	inconnu	1 – 2 h	12 – 24 h
Céfuroxime PO	inconnu	2 h	8 – 12 h
Céfuroxime IM	rapide	30 – 40 min	6 – 12 h
Céfuroxime IV	rapide	fin de la perfusion	6 – 12 h

CONTRE-INDICATIONS, PRÉCAUTIONS ET MISES EN GARDE

Contre-indications: Hypersensibilité aux céphalosporines ■ Réactions graves d'hypersensibilité aux pénicillines (une réaction de sensibilité croisée peut survenir chez 10 % des patients ayant des antécédents d'allergie à la pénicilline).

Précautions et mises en garde: Sensibilité à la pénicilline (risque de réaction croisée) ■ Insuffisance rénale (on recommande de réduire la dose ou d'accroître l'intervalle posologique du *céfaclor*, si la Cl_{Cr} < 50 mL/min, de la *céfoxitine*, si la Cl_{Cr} < 50 mL/min, du *cefprozil*, si la Cl_{Cr} < 30 mL/min, du *céfuroxime*, si la Cl_{Cr} < 20 mL/min) ■ Patients âgés, émaciés ou atteints d'une maladie débilitante (on doit parfois administrer un supplément de vitamine K pour prévenir les saignements) ■ Antécédents de maladie gastro-intestinale, particulièrement la colite ■ Patients atteints de phénylcétonurie (certains produits contiennent de l'aspartame et sont déconseillés dans leur cas) ■ **GÉR.**: Il peut s'avérer nécessaire d'adapter la posologie en fonction de la détérioration de la fonction rénale, liée à l'âge ■ **OBST.**: Grossesse ou allaitement (précédents d'usage sans apparition d'effets secondaires).

RÉACTIONS INDÉSIRABLES ET EFFETS SECONDAIRES

SNC: CONVULSIONS (doses élevées), céphalées.

GI: COLITE PSEUDO-MEMBRANEUSE, diarrhée, nausées, vomissements, crampes.

GU: vaginite, candidose génitale, néphrite interstitielle (céfaclor).

Tég.: rash, urticaire.

Hémat.: dyscrasie sanguine, neutropénie, thrombopénie, anémie hémolytique.

Locaux: douleur au point d'injection IM, phlébite au point d'injection IV.

Divers: réactions allergiques, incluant l'ANAPHYLAXIE, la MALADIE SÉRIQUE, le SYNDROME DE STEVENS-JOHNSON et la NÉCROLYSE ÉPIDERMIQUE TOXIQUE, surinfection.

INTERACTIONS

Médicament-médicament: Le **probénécide** diminue l'excrétion et accroît les concentrations sanguines des céphalosporines de la deuxième génération ■ Risque accru de néphrotoxicité lors de l'administration concomitante d'autres **médicaments néphrotoxiques**.

VOIES D'ADMINISTRATION ET POSOLOGIE

Céfaclor

- **PO (adultes)**: De 250 à 500 mg, toutes les 8 à 12 heures (les infections plus graves ou celles dues à des microorganismes moins sensibles peuvent dicter l'administration de doses plus élevées). Posologie quotidienne maximale recommandée: 2 g.

- **PO (enfants > 1 mois)**: 20 mg/kg/jour en doses fractionnées, toutes les 8 à 12 heures. *Infections plus graves, otite moyenne* – 40 mg/kg/jour, en doses fractionnées, toutes les 8 à 12 heures. Dose quotidienne maximale: 2 g/jour.
- ***INSUFFISANCE RÉNALE***

  PO (ADULTES): *CL_{CR} DE 10 À 50 mL/MIN* – 50 À 100 % DE LA DOSE HABITUELLE; *CL_{CR} < 10 mL/MIN* – 50 % DE LA DOSE HABITUELLE.

Céfoxitine

- **IM, IV (adultes)**: *La plupart des infections* – de 1 à 2 g, toutes les 6 à 8 heures. *Infections graves* – 1 g, toutes les 4 heures, ou 2 g, toutes les 6 à 8 heures. *Infections mettant la vie du patient en danger* – 2 g, toutes les 4 heures, ou 3 g, toutes les 6 heures. *Prophylaxie périopératoire* – 2 g, dans les 30 à 60 minutes précédant l'incision; ensuite, 2 g, toutes les 6 heures pendant 24 heures. Dose maximale: 12 g/jour.
- **IV (prématurés pesant > 1 500 g)**: De 20 à 40 mg/kg, toutes les 12 heures.
- **IV (nouveau-nés et nourrissons < 7 jours)**: De 20 à 40 mg/kg, toutes les 12 heures.
- **IV (nouveau-nés de 7 jours à 1 mois)**: De 20 à 40 mg/kg, toutes les 8 heures.
- **IM, IV (enfants > 1 mois)**: De 20 à 40 mg/kg, toutes les 6 à 8 heures.
- Chez les nourrissons et les enfants atteints d'une infection grave, *la posologie quotidienne totale peut être augmentée jusqu'à 200 mg/kg, sans toutefois dépasser 12 g.*
- ***INSUFFISANCE RÉNALE***

  IM, IV (ADULTES): *CL_{CR} DE 30 À 50 mL/MIN* – DE 1 À 2 g, TOUTES LES 8 À 12 HEURES; *CL_{CR} DE 10 À 29 mL/MIN* – DE 1 À 2 g, TOUTES LES 12 À 24 HEURES; *CL_{CR} DE 5 À 9 mL/MIN* – DE 0,5 À 1 g, TOUTES LES 12 À 24 HEURES; *CL_{CR} < 5 mL/MIN* – DE 0,5 À 1 g, TOUTES LES 24 À 48 HEURES.

Cefprozil

- **PO (adultes et enfants ≥ 13 ans)**: *La plupart des infections* – de 250 à 500 mg, toutes les 12 heures ou 500 mg, toutes les 24 heures, selon l'infection.
- **PO (enfants de 6 mois à 12 ans)**: *Otite moyenne* – 15 mg/kg, toutes les 12 heures.
- **PO (enfants de 2 à 12 ans)**: *Infections des voies respiratoires supérieures* – de 7,5 à 15 mg/kg, toutes les 12 heures. Posologie quotidienne maximale: 1 g. *Infections de la peau et des tissus mous* – 20 mg/kg toutes les 24 heures. Posologie quotidienne maximale: 1 g.
- ***INSUFFISANCE RÉNALE***

  PO (ADULTES): *CL_{CR} ≤ 30 mL/MIN* – LA MOITIÉ DE LA DOSE HABITUELLE, TOUTES LES 12 OU 24 HEURES.

Céfuroxime

- **PO (adultes et enfants ≥ 12 ans)**: *La plupart des infections* – de 250 à 500 mg, toutes les 12 heures. *Gonorrhée* – 1 g, en une seule dose. Les comprimés ne sont pas recommandés chez les enfants de moins de 12 ans.
- **PO (enfants de 3 mois à 11 ans)**: *Otite moyenne, infections cutanées* – 15 mg/kg, toutes les 12 heures (suspension orale – dose maximale: 1 g/jour). *Pharyngoamygdalite* – 10 mg/kg, toutes les 12 heures (suspension orale – dose maximale: 500 mg/jour).
- **IM, IV (adultes et enfants ≥ 12 ans)**: *La plupart des infections* – 750 mg (IV), toutes les 8 heures. *Infections graves mettant en danger la vie du patient et infections osseuses et articulaires* – 1,5 g, toutes les 8 heures. *Méningite bactérienne* – 3 g (IV), toutes les 8 heures. *Gonorrhée* – 1,5 g (IM dans 2 points d'injection différents), en même temps que 1 g de probénécide par voie orale. *Prophylaxie périopératoire* – 1,5 g (IV), immédiatement avant l'intervention; s'il s'agit d'une longue intervention, une dose supplémentaire de 750 mg peut être administrée par voie IM ou IV à la 8e et à la 16e heure. *Interventions chirurgicales à cœur ouvert* – 1,5 g (IV), au moment de l'induction de l'anesthésie et, par la suite, toutes les 12 heures, pendant 48 heures.
- **IM, IV (enfants et nourrissons > 1 mois et < 12 ans)**: De 30 à 100 mg/kg/jour, répartis en 3 ou 4 injections égales. Une dose quotidienne de 60 mg/kg/jour convient au traitement de la plupart des infections. *Infections osseuses et articulaires* – de 70 à 150 mg/kg, toutes les 8 heures par voie IV. *Méningite bactérienne* – de 200 à 240 mg/kg/jour, répartis en 3 ou 4 doses égales par voie IV.
- **IM, IV (nouveau-nés < 1 mois)**: (ATTENTION ! LA DEMI-VIE PEUT ÊTRE DE 3 À 5 FOIS PLUS LONGUE QUE CHEZ L'ADULTE.) *La plupart des infections* – de 30 à 100 mg/kg/jour, répartis en 2 ou 3 doses égales. *Méningite bactérienne* – 100 mg/kg/jour, répartis en 2 ou 3 doses égales.
- ***INSUFFISANCE RÉNALE***

  IM (ADULTES): *CL_{CR} DE 10 À 20 mL/MIN* – 750 mg, TOUTES LES 12 HEURES; *CL_{CR} < 10 mL/MIN* – 750 mg, TOUTES LES 24 HEURES.

PRÉSENTATION

- **Céfaclor** (version générique disponible)
  Capsules: 250 mg[Pr], 500 mg[Pr] ■ **Suspension orale (parfum de fraise)**: 125 mg/5 mL[Pr], 250 mg/5 mL[Pr], 375 mg/5 mL[Pr].
- **Céfoxitine**
  Poudre pour injection: 1 g[Pr], 2 g[Pr], 10 g[Pr].
- **Cefprozil**
  Comprimés: 250 mg[Pr], 500 mg[Pr] ■ **Suspension orale (parfum de «gomme balloune»)**: 125 mg/5 mL[Pr], 250 mg/5 mL[Pr].
- **Céfuroxime**
  Comprimés: 250 mg[Pr], 500 mg[Pr] ■ **Suspension orale (parfum de fruits)**: 125 mg/5 mL[Pr] ■ **Poudre pour injection**: 750 mg[Pr], 1,5 g[Pr], 7,5 g[Pr].

SOINS INFIRMIERS

ÉVALUATION DE LA SITUATION

- Au début du traitement et pendant toute sa durée, rester à l'affût des signes suivants d'infection: altération des signes vitaux; aspect de la plaie, des crachats, de l'urine et des selles; accroissement du nombre de leucocytes.
- Avant d'amorcer le traitement, recueillir les antécédents du patient afin de déterminer ses réactions antérieures à une pénicilline ou à une céphalosporine. Même les personnes n'ayant jamais manifesté de sensibilité aux pénicillines peuvent présenter une réaction allergique.
- Prélever des échantillons pour les cultures et les antibiogrammes avant le début du traitement. La première dose peut être administrée avant que les résultats soient connus.
- RESTER À L'AFFÛT DES SIGNES ET DES SYMPTÔMES SUIVANTS D'ANAPHYLAXIE: RASH, PRURIT, ŒDÈME LARYNGÉ, RESPIRATION SIFFLANTE. SI CES RÉACTIONS SE MANIFESTENT, ARRÊTER L'ADMINISTRATION DU MÉDICAMENT ET AVERTIR IMMÉDIATEMENT LE MÉDECIN. GARDER À PORTÉE DE LA MAIN DE L'ADRÉNALINE, UN ANTIHISTAMINIQUE ET LE MATÉRIEL DE RÉANIMATION POUR PARER À UNE ÉVENTUELLE RÉACTION ANAPHYLACTIQUE.
- Déterminer si le patient présente une insuffisance rénale et adapter la dose en conséquence.

Tests de laboratoire:

- Les céphalosporines de la deuxième génération peuvent entraîner des résultats faussement positifs au test de Coombs chez les patients recevant de fortes doses ou chez les nouveau-nés dont les mères ont reçu une céphalosporine avant l'accouchement.
- Le *céfuroxime* peut également entraîner des résultats faussement négatifs lors du dosage de la glycémie par le ferricyanure. Pour effectuer ce dosage, recourir plutôt à la méthode enzymatique ou par la hexokinase.
- Les céphalosporines de la deuxième génération peuvent entraîner l'élévation des concentrations sériques d'AST, d'ALT, de phosphatase alcaline, de bilirubine, de LDH, d'urée et de créatinine.
- Ne pas prélever de sang dans les 2 heures suivant l'administration de la *céfoxitine*, car les concentrations de créatinine dans le sang et dans les urines pourraient être faussement élevées.
- Les céphalosporines de la deuxième génération peuvent entraîner rarement les effets suivants: leucopénie, neutropénie, agranulocytose, thrombopénie, éosinophilie, lymphocytose et thrombocytose.

DIAGNOSTICS INFIRMIERS POSSIBLES

- Risque d'infection (Indications, Effets secondaires).
- Diarrhée (Réactions indésirables).
- Connaissances insuffisantes sur le traitement médicamenteux (Enseignement au patient et à ses proches).

INTERVENTIONS INFIRMIÈRES

PO:

- Administrer ces antibiotiques à intervalles réguliers, sans égard aux repas. En cas d'irritation gastrique, les administrer avec des aliments. Bien agiter la suspension orale avant de l'administrer.
- Les comprimés de *céfuroxime* doivent être avalés tels quels, sans être écrasés. Les comprimés écrasés ont un goût amer prononcé et persistant. Les comprimés peuvent être pris sans égard aux repas. Le médicament est toutefois mieux absorbé s'il est pris avec des aliments. La suspension doit être prise avec des aliments. On doit bien l'agiter avant de l'administrer. Les comprimés et la suspension ne sont pas interchangeables (lors d'études comparatives de biodisponibilité chez l'adulte sain, la suspension et les comprimés ne se sont pas révélés bioéquivalents).
- Après reconstitution, les suspensions de *céfaclor* et de *cefprozil* sont stables pendant 14 jours si elles sont réfrigérées; la suspension de *céfuroxime* est stable pendant 10 jours si elle est réfrigérée.

IM: Reconstituer les doses destinées à l'administration par voie IM en diluant le contenu de la fiole dans de l'eau stérile ou de l'eau bactériostatique pour injection ou dans une solution de NaCl 0,9 % pour injection. Le contenu de la fiole peut aussi être dilué avec de la lidocaïne sans adrénaline pour réduire la douleur au point d'injection. Consulter les directives de chaque fabricant avant de reconstituer la préparation. Injecter la préparation en profondeur, dans une masse musculaire bien développée; bien masser.

C

IV:

- Changer de point d'injection toutes les 48 à 72 heures afin de prévenir la phlébite. Observer fréquemment le point d'injection pour déceler les signes de thrombophlébite (douleur, rougeur, enflure).
- En cas d'administration concomitante d'aminosides, rincer la tubulure avant d'administrer le deuxième médicament, car les aminosides et les céphalosporines ne sont pas compatibles.
- **PÉD. (nouveau-nés):** Ne pas utiliser de préparations contenant de l'alcool benzylique.

IV directe: Diluer 1 g dans au moins 10 mL d'eau stérile pour injection. Consulter les directives de chaque fabricant avant de reconstituer la préparation.

Vitesse d'administration: Administrer lentement, en 3 à 5 minutes.

Céfoxitine

Perfusion intermittente: La solution reconstituée peut être diluée de nouveau dans 50 à 100 mL de solution de D5%E, de NaCl 0,9 %, de D5%/NaCl 0,45 %, de D5%/NaCl 0,9 %, de D5%E dans une solution de lactate de Ringer, de solution de Ringer ou de solution de lactate de Ringer. La solution est stable pendant 24 heures à la température ambiante et pendant 7 jours au réfrigérateur. La poudre peut devenir plus foncée, mais cela n'affecte en rien la puissance de l'antibiotique. Consulter les directives de chaque fabricant avant de reconstituer la préparation.

Vitesse d'administration: La perfusion doit durer de 10 à 60 minutes.

Perfusion continue: On peut aussi diluer la préparation dans 500 à 1 000 mL de solution pour l'administrer en perfusion continue.

Association compatible dans la même seringue: héparine.

Incompatibilité (tubulure en Y): Le fabricant recommande d'arrêter l'administration d'autres solutions IV pendant la perfusion.

Céfuroxime

Perfusion intermittente: La solution reconstituée peut être diluée de nouveau dans 50 à 100 mL de NaCl 0,9 %, de D5%E ou de D5%/NaCl 0,45 % ou de D5%/NaCl 0,9 %. La solution est stable pendant 24 heures à la température ambiante et pendant 7 jours au réfrigérateur.

Vitesse d'administration: La perfusion doit durer de 15 à 60 minutes.

Perfusion continue: On peut aussi diluer la préparation dans 500 à 1 000 mL de solution et l'administrer en perfusion continue.

Compatibilité (tubulure en Y): acyclovir ■ amifostine ■ atracurium ■ cyclophosphamide ■ diltiazem ■ famotidine ■ fludarabine ■ foscarnet ■ granisétron ■ hydromorphone ■ melphalan ■ mépéridine ■ morphine ■ ondansétron ■ pancuronium ■ perphénazine ■ propofol ■ sargramostim ■ tacrolimus ■ téniposide ■ thiotépa ■ vécuronium.

Incompatibilité (tubulure en Y): filgrastim ■ fluconazole ■ midazolam ■ vinorelbine. Le fabricant recommande d'arrêter l'administration d'autres solutions IV pendant l'administration du céfuroxime par une tubulure en Y.

ENSEIGNEMENT AU PATIENT ET À SES PROCHES

- Expliquer au patient qu'il doit prendre le médicament à intervalles réguliers, et qu'il doit utiliser toute la quantité qui lui a été prescrite, même s'il se sent mieux. S'il n'a pu prendre le médicament au moment habituel, il doit le prendre aussitôt que possible, mais non pas juste avant l'heure prévue pour la dose suivante. Il ne faut jamais doubler la dose. Insister sur le fait qu'il peut être dangereux de donner ce médicament à une autre personne.
- Conseiller au patient de signaler les réactions allergiques et les signes suivants de surinfection: excroissance pileuse sur la langue, démangeaisons ou pertes vaginales, selles molles ou nauséabondes.
- RECOMMANDER AU PATIENT DE COMMUNIQUER AVEC UN PROFESSIONNEL DE LA SANTÉ EN CAS DE FIÈVRE OU DE DIARRHÉE, PARTICULIÈREMENT SI SES SELLES RENFERMENT DU SANG, DU PUS OU DU MUCUS. CONSEILLER AU PATIENT DE NE PAS TRAITER LA DIARRHÉE SANS CONSULTER AU PRÉALABLE UN PROFESSIONNEL DE LA SANTÉ.

VÉRIFICATION DE L'EFFICACITÉ THÉRAPEUTIQUE

L'efficacité du traitement peut être démontrée par: la disparition des signes et des symptômes d'infection; le temps de résolution dépend du microorganisme infectant et du siège de l'infection ■ la réduction de l'incidence des infections en cas d'usage prophylactique. ✷

CÉPHALOSPORINES DE LA TROISIÈME GÉNÉRATION

céfépime

Maxipime

céfixime
Suprax
céfotaxime
Claforan
ceftazidime
Fortaz
ceftriaxone
Rocephin
CLASSIFICATION:
Antibiotiques (céphalosporines de la troisième génération)
Grossesse – catégorie B

INDICATIONS

Traitement des infections suivantes: infections de la peau et des tissus mous (sauf céfixime) ■ infections des voies urinaires ■ infections des voies respiratoires ■ infections intra-abdominales (sauf céfixime) ■ septicémie (sauf céfixime) ■ **Céfotaxime, ceftazidime, ceftriaxone**: Méningite ■ **Céfépime**: Traitement empirique des patients atteints de neutropénie fébrile ■ **Céfixime**: Otite moyenne ■ **Céfotaxime**: Infections gynécologiques ■ **Céfotaxime, ceftriaxone**: Prophylaxie périopératoire ■ **Céfixime, céfotaxime, ceftriaxone**: Gonorrhée ■ **Ceftriaxone, ceftazidime**: Infections des os et des articulations. **Usages non approuvés**: **Céfotaxime, ceftriaxone** – maladie de Lyme.

MÉCANISME D'ACTION

Liaison à la membrane de la paroi de la cellule bactérienne, entraînant la destruction de la bactérie. ***Effets thérapeutiques:*** Action bactéricide contre les bactéries sensibles. **Spectre d'action**: Effet similaire à celui des céphalosporines de la deuxième génération; cependant, l'effet contre les staphylocoques est moins fort, mais celui contre les bactéries à Gram négatif est accru, le spectre d'action englobant même les microorganismes qui résistent aux céphalosporines de la première et de la deuxième génération ■ Action marquée contre les microorganismes suivants: *Enterobacter* ■ *Hæmophilus influenzæ* ■ *Escherichia coli* ■ *Klebsiella pneumoniæ* ■ *Neisseria* ■ *Proteus* ■ *Providencia* ■ *Serratia* ■ *Moraxella catarrhalis* ■ Certains agents ont un effet accru contre: *Pseudomonas æruginosa* (ceftazidime, céfépime) ■ *Borrelia burgdorferi* (céfotaxime, ceftriaxone) ■ Tous les agents exercent une action modérée contre certaines bactéries anaérobies ■ La céfixime n'est pas efficace contre *S. aureus*.

PHARMACOCINÉTIQUE

Absorption: Bonne (IM). *Céfixime* – bonne (PO) (la céfixime en suspension entraîne des concentrations sanguines de 20 à 25 % plus élevées que les comprimés).
Distribution: Ces antibiotiques se répartissent dans tout l'organisme. Toutes les céphalosporines de la troisième génération traversent la barrière placentaire et passent dans le lait maternel à faible concentration. Elles pénètrent davantage dans le liquide céphalorachidien que les céphalosporines de la première et de la deuxième génération.
Métabolisme et excrétion: *Céfépime, ceftazidime* – > 85 % est excrété dans l'urine. *Céfixime* – 50 % est excrété à l'état inchangé dans l'urine, et 10 %, dans la bile. *Ceftriaxone, céfotaxime* – agents métabolisés partiellement et excrétés partiellement dans l'urine.
Demi-vie: *Céfépime* – 120 minutes; *céfixime* – de 180 à 240 minutes; *céfotaxime* – 60 minutes; *ceftazidime* – de 114 à 120 minutes; *ceftriaxone* – de 348 à 522 minutes (toutes ces demi-vies, à l'exception de celles de la *ceftriaxone*, sont prolongées en cas d'insuffisance rénale).

Profil temps-action

	Début d'action	Pic	Durée
Céfépime IM	rapide	1 – 2 h	12 h
Céfépime IV	rapide	fin de la perfusion	12 h
Céfixime PO	rapide	2 - 6 h	24 h
Céfotaxime IM	rapide	0,5 h	4 – 12 h
Céfotaxime IV	rapide	fin de la perfusion	4 – 12 h
Ceftazidime IM	rapide	1 h	6 – 12 h
Ceftazidime IV	rapide	fin de la perfusion	6 – 12 h
Ceftriaxone IM	rapide	1 – 2 h	12 – 24 h
Ceftriaxone IV	rapide	fin de la perfusion	12 – 24 h

CONTRE-INDICATIONS, PRÉCAUTIONS ET MISES EN GARDE

Contre-indications: Hypersensibilité aux céphalosporines ■ Réactions graves d'hypersensibilité aux pénicillines ou aux autres bêta-lactamines.
Précautions et mises en garde: Insuffisance rénale (on recommande de réduire la dose ou d'accroître l'intervalle posologique de la *céfépime* si la Cl_{Cr} < 50 mL/min, de la *céfixime*, si la Cl_{Cr} < 40 mL/min, du *céfotaxime*, si la Cl_{Cr} < 20 mL/min, de la *ceftazidime*, si la Cl_{Cr} < 50 mL/min ■ Insuffisances hépatique et rénale graves (on recommande de réduire la dose ou d'accroître l'intervalle posologique de la *ceftriaxone*) ■ Antécédents de maladie gastro-intestinale, particulièrement la colite ■ **Gér.**: Il peut s'avérer nécessaire d'adapter la posologie en fonction de la détérioration de la fonction

C

rénale, liée à l'âge ■ Patients âgés, émaciés ou atteints d'une maladie débilitante (on doit parfois administrer un supplément de vitamine K pour prévenir les saignements) ■ **OBST.**: Grossesse ou allaitement (précédents d'usage sans apparition d'effets secondaires) ■ Patients ayant déjà manifesté des réactions allergiques, particulièrement aux médicaments ■ **PÉD.**: La *ceftriaxone* peut déloger la bilirubine de l'albumine sérique (faire preuve de prudence chez les nouveau-nés hyperbilirubinémiques, surtout s'il s'agit de prématurés) ■ *Céfotaxime* – patients devant suivre un régime hyposodé ou ayant une prédisposition à l'œdème (la solution injectable contient 42,8 mg de sodium/g de céfotaxime) ■ *Ceftriaxone* – troubles de la vésicule biliaire.

RÉACTIONS INDÉSIRABLES ET EFFETS SECONDAIRES

SNC: CONVULSIONS (doses élevées), céphalées.
GI: COLITE PSEUDOMEMBRANEUSE, diarrhée, nausées, vomissements, crampes, pseudolithiase (ceftriaxone).
GU: vaginite, candidose génitale.
Tég.: rash, urticaire.
Hémat.: dyscrasie sanguine, neutropénie, thrombopénie, anémie hémolytique, éosinophilie.
Locaux: douleur au point d'injection IM, phlébite au point d'injection IV.
Divers: réactions allergiques, incluant l'ANAPHYLAXIE, la MALADIE SÉRIQUE, le SYNDROME DE STEVENS-JOHNSON et la NÉCROLYSE ÉPIDERMIQUE TOXIQUE, surinfection.

INTERACTIONS

Médicament-médicament: Le **probénécide** diminue l'excrétion et accroît les concentrations sanguines de la céfixime et du céfotaxime ■ L'usage concomitant de **diurétiques de l'anse** ou d'**agents néphrotoxiques**, incluant les **aminosides**, peut accroître le risque de néphrotoxicité.

VOIES D'ADMINISTRATION ET POSOLOGIE

Céfépime

- **IM (adultes)**: *Infections légères à modérées* – de 0,5 à 1 g, toutes les 12 heures.
- **IV (adultes et enfants > 12 ans)**: *Infections légères à modérées* – de 0,5 à 1 g, toutes les 12 heures. *Infections graves* – 2 g, toutes les 12 heures. *Traitement empirique chez des patients neutropéniques fébriles* – 2 g, toutes les 8 heures.
- **IV (enfants de 2 mois à 12 ans, jusqu'à 40 kg)**: *Traitement empirique de la neutropénie fébrile* – 50 mg/kg, toutes les 8 heures. *Pneumonie, infections urinaires, infections de la peau et des tissus mous* – 50 mg/kg, toutes les 12 heures. Chez les enfants dont le poids > 40 kg, on doit suivre les recommandations posologiques qui s'appliquent chez les adultes. Chez les patients âgés de plus de 12 ans dont le poids < 40 kg, on doit suivre les recommandations posologiques s'appliquant aux enfants pesant 40 kg ou moins. Dose maximale chez les enfants: 2 g, toutes les 8 heures.
- ***INSUFFISANCE RÉNALE***

  IM, IV (ADULTES): CL_{CR} *DE 30 À 50 mL/MIN* – DE 1 À 2 g, TOUTES LES 24 HEURES, OU 2 g, TOUTES LES 8 HEURES LORS DU TRAITEMENT EMPIRIQUE DE LA NEUTROPÉNIE FÉBRILE; CL_{CR} *DE 11 À 29 mL/MIN* – DE 0,5 À 1 g, TOUTES LES 24 HEURES, OU 2 g, TOUTES LES 24 HEURES LORS DU TRAITEMENT EMPIRIQUE DE LA NEUTROPÉNIE FÉBRILE; CL_{CR} *< 11 mL/MIN* – DE 250 À 500 mg, TOUTES LES 24 HEURES, OU 1 g, TOUTES LES 24 HEURES LORS DU TRAITEMENT EMPIRIQUE DE LA NEUTROPÉNIE FÉBRILE.

Céfixime

- **PO (adultes et enfants > 12 ans ou > 50 kg)**: *La plupart des infections* – 400 mg, toutes les 24 heures. *Infections urinaires et gonorrhée* – 400 mg, en une seule dose.
- **PO (enfants > 6 mois)**: 8 mg/kg, toutes les 24 heures, ou 4 mg/kg, toutes les 12 heures (pour traiter l'otite moyenne, administrer la suspension seulement).
- ***INSUFFISANCE RÉNALE***

  PO (ADULTES): CL_{CR} *DE 20 À 40 mL/MIN* – 75 % DE LA DOSE STANDARD; CL_{CR} *< 20 mL/MIN* – 50 % DE LA DOSE STANDARD.

Céfotaxime

- **IM, IV (adultes et enfants > 50 kg)**: *La plupart des infections* – 1 g, toutes les 12 heures. *Infections graves* – de 1 à 2 g, toutes les 6 à 8 heures. *Infections mettant en danger la vie du patient* – 2 g par voie IV, toutes les 4 heures. Posologie quotidienne maximale: 12 g. *Gonorrhée* – 1 g par voie IM, en une seule dose. *Prophylaxie périopératoire* – 1 g, de 30 à 90 minutes avant la première incision. Dans le cas d'une intervention chirurgicale de longue durée, des doses additionnelles de 1 g peuvent être administrées pendant l'opération, toutes les 1,5 à 2 heures. La dose prophylactique totale ne doit pas dépasser 6 g au cours d'une période de 12 heures.
- **IM, IV (enfants > 1 mois et < 12 ans)**: Enfants de moins de 50 kg: de 50 à 100 mg/kg/jour, fractionné en 4 à 6 doses égales, ou jusqu'à 180 mg/kg/jour dans le cas d'infections graves. Posologie quotidienne maximale: 12 g. Chez les enfants pesant 50 kg et plus, on devrait administrer la posologie recommandée chez l'adulte.
- **IV (nouveau-nés de 1 à 4 semaines)**: 50 mg/kg, toutes les 8 heures.

- **IV (nouveau-nés < 1 semaine):** 50 mg/kg, toutes les 12 heures.
- ***INSUFFISANCE RÉNALE***
  IM, IV (ADULTES): *CL_{CR} < 20 mL/MIN* – RÉDUIRE LA DOSE DE 50 %.

Ceftazidime

- **IM, IV (adultes):** *La plupart des infections* – de 500 mg à 2 g, toutes les 8 à 12 heures. *Pneumonie et infections des tissus mous* – de 500 mg à 1 g, toutes les 8 heures. *Infections des os* – 2 g, toutes les 12 heures par voie IV. *Infections graves et mettant la vie du patient en danger* – 2 g, toutes les 8 heures par voie IV. *Infections des voies urinaires compliquées* – 500 mg, toutes les 8 à 12 heures. *Infections des voies urinaires non compliquées* – 250 mg, toutes les 12 heures. On recommande de ne pas dépasser 3 g par jour chez les patients âgés, gravement malades, car chez eux la clairance rénale est diminuée.
- **IV (enfants > 1 mois à 12 ans):** De 25 à 50 mg/kg, toutes les 8 à 12 heures, au maximum: 6 g/jour.
- **IV (nouveau-nés):** De 25 à 50 mg/kg, toutes 12 heures.
- ***INSUFFISANCE RÉNALE***
  IM, IV (ADULTES): *CL_{CR} DE 31 À 50 mL/MIN* – DE 1 À 1,5 g, TOUTES LES 12 HEURES; *CL_{CR} DE 16 À 30 mL/MIN* – DE 1 À 1,5 g, TOUTES LES 24 HEURES; *CL_{CR} DE 6 À 15 mL/MIN* – DE 500 À 750 mg, TOUTES LES 24 HEURES; *CL_{CR} < 6 mL/MIN* – DE 500 À 750 mg, TOUTES LES 48 HEURES.

Ceftriaxone

- **IM, IV (adultes et enfants > 50 kg):** *La plupart des infections* – de 0,5 à 1 g, toutes les 12 heures, ou de 1 à 2 g, toutes les 24 heures. *Gonorrhée* – 250 mg par voie IM, en une seule dose. *Méningite* – 2 g, toutes les 12 heures. *Prophylaxie périopératoire* - 1 g, de 0,5 à 2 heures avant la première incision. Dose maximale: 4 g/jour.
- **IM, IV (enfants de 1 mois à 12 ans):** *La plupart des infections* – de 25 à 37,5 mg/kg, toutes les 12 heures. *Méningite* – 50 mg/kg, toutes les 12 heures. Dose maximum: 2 g/jour. Si le poids est de 50 kg ou plus, utiliser la posologie pour adultes.

PRÉSENTATION

- **Céfépime**
  Poudre pour injection: fioles à 1 g^{Pr} et à 2 g^{Pr}.
- **Céfixime**
  Comprimés: 400 mg^{Pr} ■ **Suspension orale (parfum de fraise):** 100 mg/5 mL^{Pr}.
- **Céfotaxime**
  Poudre pour injection: 500 mg^{Pr}, 1 g^{Pr}, 2 g^{Pr}.
- **Ceftazidime**
  Poudre pour injection: 1 g^{Pr}, 2 g^{Pr}, 6 g^{Pr}.
- **Ceftriaxone**
  Poudre pour injection: 250 mg^{Pr}, 1 g^{Pr}, 2 g^{Pr}, 10 g^{Pr}.

SOINS INFIRMIERS

ÉVALUATION DE LA SITUATION

- Au début du traitement et pendant toute sa durée, rester à l'affût des signes suivants d'infection: altération des signes vitaux; aspect de la plaie, des crachats, de l'urine et des selles; accroissement du nombre de leucocytes.
- Avant d'amorcer le traitement, recueillir les antécédents du patient afin de déterminer ses réactions antérieures à une pénicilline ou à une céphalosporine. Même les personnes n'ayant jamais manifesté de sensibilité aux pénicillines peuvent présenter une réaction allergique.
- Prélever des échantillons pour les cultures et les antibiogrammes avant le début du traitement. La première dose peut être administrée avant que les résultats soient connus.
- RESTER À L'AFFÛT DES SIGNES ET DES SYMPTÔMES SUIVANTS D'ANAPHYLAXIE: RASH, PRURIT, ŒDÈME LARYNGÉ, RESPIRATION SIFFLANTE. SI CES RÉACTIONS SE MANIFESTENT, ARRÊTER L'ADMINISTRATION DU MÉDICAMENT ET AVERTIR IMMÉDIATEMENT LE MÉDECIN. GARDER À PORTÉE DE LA MAIN DE L'ADRÉNALINE, UN ANTIHISTAMINIQUE ET LE MATÉRIEL DE RÉANIMATION POUR PARER À UNE ÉVENTUELLE RÉACTION ANAPHYLACTIQUE.
- *Céfotaxime* – Effectuer le bilan quotidien des ingesta et des excreta et peser le patient tous les jours, particulièrement s'il doit suivre un régime hyposodé. Une dose de 1 g de céfotaxime injectable contient 48,2 mg de sodium.

Tests de laboratoire:

- Les céphalosporines de la troisième génération peuvent entraîner des résultats faussement positifs au test de Coombs chez les patients recevant de fortes doses ou chez les nouveau-nés dont les mères ont reçu une céphalosporine avant l'accouchement.
- Les céphalosporines de la troisième génération peuvent entraîner l'élévation des concentrations sériques d'AST, d'ALT, de phosphatase alcaline, de bilirubine, de LDH, d'urée et de créatinine.
- Les céphalosporines de la troisième génération peuvent entraîner rarement les effets suivants: leucopénie, neutropénie, agranulocytose, thrombopénie, éosinophilie, lymphocytose et thrombocytose.

DIAGNOSTICS INFIRMIERS POSSIBLES

- Risque d'infection (Indications, Effets secondaires).
- Diarrhée (Réactions indésirables).
- Connaissances insuffisantes sur le traitement médicamenteux (Enseignement au patient et à ses proches).

INTERVENTIONS INFIRMIÈRES

PO: Administrer ces antibiotiques à intervalles réguliers, sans égard aux repas. En cas d'irritation gastrique, les administrer avec des aliments. Bien agiter la suspension orale avant de l'administrer. Les comprimés de *céfixime* peuvent être écrasés et dissous dans de l'eau. Après l'administration, rincer le verre avec un peu d'eau et la faire boire au patient pour s'assurer qu'il a reçu toute la dose. Les comprimés et la suspension ne sont pas bioéquivalents. Après avoir été mélangée, la suspension de *céfixime* peut être conservée 14 jours à la température ambiante ou au réfrigérateur. Jeter toute portion inutilisée après 14 jours.

IM: Reconstituer les doses destinées à l'administration par voie IM en diluant le contenu de la fiole dans de l'eau stérile ou de l'eau bactériostatique pour injection ou dans une solution de NaCl 0,9 % pour injection. La poudre peut aussi être diluée avec de la lidocaïne pour réduire la douleur au point d'injection. Consulter les directives de chaque fabricant avant de reconstituer la préparation. Injecter la préparation en profondeur dans une masse musculaire bien développée; bien masser.

IV:

- Observer fréquemment le point d'injection pour déceler les signes de phlébite (douleur, rougeur, enflure). Changer de point d'injection toutes les 48 à 72 heures afin de prévenir la phlébite.
- En cas d'administration concomitante d'aminosides, rincer la tubulure avant d'administrer le deuxième médicament, car les aminosides et les céphalosporines ne sont pas compatibles.
- Consulter les directives de chaque fabricant avant de reconstituer la préparation.
- **PÉD. (nouveau-nés):** Ne pas utiliser de préparations contenant de l'alcool benzylique.

IV directe: Diluer chaque gramme dans au moins 10 mL d'eau stérile pour injection.

Vitesse d'administration: Administrer lentement, en 3 à 5 minutes.

Céfépime

Perfusion intermittente: Diluer le médicament de façon à obtenir des concentrations de 1 à 40 mg/mL, dans 50 à 100 mL de NaCl 0,9 %, de D5%E ou D10%E, de solution de lactate de sodium 1/6 M, de solution de D5%/NaCl 0,9 %, de D5% dans une solution de lactate de Ringer, de D5% dans du Normosol-R ou de solution de D5% dans du Normosol-M pour injection. La solution est stable pendant 24 heures à la température ambiante et pendant 7 jours au réfrigérateur.

Vitesse d'administration: La perfusion doit durer 30 minutes.

Compatibilité (tubulure en Y): bléomycine ▪ bumétanide ▪ butorphanol ▪ calcium, gluconate de ▪ carboplatine ▪ carmustine ▪ cyclophosphamide ▪ cytarabine ▪ dactinomycine ▪ dexaméthasone sodique, phosphate de ▪ fluconazole ▪ fludarabine ▪ fluorouracile ▪ furosémide ▪ granisétron ▪ hydrocortisone sodique, phosphate d' ▪ hydrocortisone sodique, succinate d' ▪ hydromorphone ▪ imipénem/cilastatine ▪ leucovorine ▪ lorazépam ▪ melphalan ▪ mesna ▪ méthotrexate ▪ méthylprednisolone sodique, succinate de ▪ métronidazole ▪ paclitaxel ▪ pipéracilline/tazobactam ▪ ranitidine ▪ sargramostim ▪ sodium, bicarbonate de ▪ thiotépa ▪ ticarcilline-clavulanate ▪ triméthoprim/sulfaméthoxazole ▪ zidovudine.

Incompatibilité (tubulure en Y): acyclovir ▪ amphotéricine B ▪ chlordiazépoxide ▪ chlorpromazine ▪ cimétidine ▪ ciprofloxacine ▪ cisplatine ▪ dacarbazine ▪ daunorubicine ▪ diazépam ▪ diphenhydramine ▪ dobutamine ▪ dopamine ▪ doxorubicine ▪ dropéridol ▪ énalaprilate ▪ étoposide ▪ famotidine ▪ filgrastim ▪ floxuridine ▪ gallium, nitrate de ▪ ganciclovir ▪ halopéridol ▪ idarubicine ▪ ifosfamide ▪ magnésium, sulfate de ▪ mannitol ▪ méchloréthamine ▪ mépéridine ▪ métoclopramide ▪ mitomycine ▪ mitoxantrone ▪ morphine ▪ nalbuphine ▪ ofloxacine ▪ ondansétron ▪ plicamycine ▪ prochlorpérazine ▪ prométhazine ▪ streptozocine ▪ vancomycine ▪ vinblastine ▪ vincristine.

Céfotaxime

Perfusion intermittente: La solution reconstituée peut être diluée de nouveau dans 50 à 100 mL de solution de D5%E, de solution de lactate de Ringer, de D5%/NaCl 0,45 % ou de D5%/NaCl 0,9 % ou de solution de NaCl 0,9 %. La couleur de la solution peut varier de jaune pâle à ambre. La solution est stable pendant 24 heures à la température ambiante et pendant 5 jours au réfrigérateur. Consulter les directives de chaque fabricant avant de reconstituer la préparation.

Vitesse d'administration: La perfusion intermittente doit durer de 20 à 30 minutes.

Associations compatibles dans la même seringue: héparine ▪ ofloxacine.

Compatibilité (tubulure en Y): acyclovir ▪ amifostine ▪ cyclophosphamide ▪ diltiazem ▪ famotidine ▪ fludarabine ▪ granisétron ▪ hydromorphone ▪ lorazépam ▪ magnésium, sulfate de ▪ melphalan ▪ mépéridine ▪ midazolam ▪ morphine ▪ ondansétron ▪ perphénazine

■ propofol ■ sargramostim ■ téniposide ■ thiotépa ■ tolazoline ■ vinorelbine.

Incompatibilité (tubulure en Y): amidon ■ allopurinol ■ filgrastim ■ fluconazole ■ pentamidine.

Ceftazidime

Perfusion intermittente: La solution reconstituée peut être diluée de nouveau dans 50 à 100 mL de NaCl 0,9 %, de D5%E, de D5%/NaCl 0,45 %, de D5%/NaCl 0,9 % ou de solution de lactate de Ringer. Pendant la dilution, le gaz carbonique qui se forme dans la fiole produit une pression positive; il faut libérer le gaz de la fiole après la dissolution de son contenu. La couleur de la solution peut varier de jaune à ambre; la solution peut prendre une couleur plus foncée sans que la puissance du médicament soit altérée. La solution est stable pendant 24 heures à la température ambiante et pendant 7 jours au réfrigérateur. Consulter les directives de chaque fabricant avant de reconstituer la préparation.

Vitesse d'administration: La perfusion doit durer de 15 à 30 minutes.

Compatibilité (tubulure en Y): acyclovir ■ amifostine ■ aminophylline ■ ciprofloxacine ■ diltiazem ■ énalaprilate ■ esmolol ■ famotidine ■ filgrastim ■ fludarabine ■ foscarnet ■ gallium, nitrate de ■ granisétron ■ héparine ■ hydromorphone ■ labétalol ■ melphalan ■ mépéridine ■ morphine ■ ondansétron ■ paclitaxel ■ propofol ■ ranitidine ■ tacrolimus ■ téniposide ■ théophylline ■ thiotépa ■ vinorelbine ■ zidovudine.

Incompatibilité (tubulure en Y): fluconazole ■ idarubicine ■ midazolam ■ pentamidine.

Ceftriaxone

Perfusion intermittente: Reconstituer le contenu d'une fiole de 250 mg, de 1 g ou de 2 g avec, respectivement, 2,4 mL, 9,6 mL ou 19,2 mL d'eau stérile pour injection ou de solution de NaCl 0,9 % ou de D5%E pour obtenir une concentration de 100 mg/mL. On peut diluer de nouveau la solution dans 50 à 100 mL de NaCl 0,9 %, de D5%E, de D5%/NaCl 0,45 % ou de solution de lactate de Ringer. La couleur de la solution reconstituée peut varier de jaune pâle à ambre. La solution est stable pendant 3 jours à la température ambiante. Consulter les directives de chaque fabricant avant de reconstituer la préparation.

Vitesse d'administration: La perfusion doit durer de 15 à 30 minutes, chez l'adulte, et de 10 à 30 minutes, chez le nourrisson ou l'enfant.

Compatibilité (tubulure en Y): acyclovir ■ amifostine ■ diltiazem ■ fludarabine ■ foscarnet ■ gallium, nitrate de ■ granisétron ■ héparine ■ melphalan ■ mépéridine ■ méthotrexate ■ morphine ■ paclitaxel ■ propofol ■ sargramostim ■ sodium, bicarbonate de ■ tacrolimus ■ téniposide ■ théophylline ■ thiotépa ■ zidovudine.

Incompatibilité (tubulure en Y): filgrastim ■ fluconazole ■ labétalol ■ pentamidine ■ vancomycine ■ vinorelbine.

C

ENSEIGNEMENT AU PATIENT ET À SES PROCHES

- Expliquer au patient qu'il doit prendre le médicament à intervalles réguliers et qu'il doit utiliser toute la quantité qui lui a été prescrite, même s'il se sent mieux. S'il n'a pu prendre le médicament au moment habituel, il doit le prendre aussitôt que possible, mais non pas juste avant l'heure prévue pour la dose suivante. Il ne faut jamais doubler la dose. Insister sur le fait qu'il peut être dangereux de donner ce médicament à une autre personne.
- Conseiller au patient de signaler les réactions allergiques et les signes suivants de surinfection: excroissance pileuse sur la langue, démangeaisons ou pertes vaginales, selles molles ou nauséabondes.
- RECOMMANDER AU PATIENT DE COMMUNIQUER AVEC UN PROFESSIONNEL DE LA SANTÉ EN CAS DE FIÈVRE OU DE DIARRHÉE, PARTICULIÈREMENT SI SES SELLES RENFERMENT DU SANG, DU PUS OU DU MUCUS. CONSEILLER AU PATIENT DE NE PAS TRAITER LA DIARRHÉE SANS CONSULTER AU PRÉALABLE UN PROFESSIONNEL DE LA SANTÉ.

VÉRIFICATION DE L'EFFICACITÉ THÉRAPEUTIQUE

L'efficacité du traitement peut être démontrée par: la disparition des signes et des symptômes d'infection; le temps de résolution dépend du microorganisme infectant et du siège de l'infection ■ la réduction de l'incidence des infections en cas d'usage prophylactique. ✳

CÉTIRIZINE

Apo-Cétirizine, Allergy-Relief, Aller-Relief, Reactine

CLASSIFICATION:

Antihistaminique (inhibiteur des récepteurs H_1 de l'histamine)

Grossesse – catégorie B

INDICATIONS

Soulagement des symptômes d'allergie attribuables à la libération d'histamine, dont: la rhinite allergique saisonnière et apériodique ■ l'urticaire chronique.

C

MÉCANISME D'ACTION

Inhibition des effets de l'histamine au niveau des récepteurs H_1; l'agent ne se lie pas à l'histamine ni ne l'inactive ■ Les effets anticholinergiques sont minimes et les effets sédatifs sont liés à la dose. ***Effets thérapeutiques:*** Diminution des symptômes associés à un excès d'histamine: éternuements, rhinorrhée, larmoiements, rougeurs oculaires, prurit.

PHARMACOCINÉTIQUE

Absorption: Bonne (PO).
Distribution: Inconnue.
Métabolisme et excrétion: Faible métabolisme hépatique. Excrétion rénale à l'état inchangé (60 %).
Demi-vie: 8 heures (réduite chez les enfants, prolongée chez les insuffisants rénaux).

Profil temps-action (effet antihistaminique)

	DÉBUT D'ACTION	PIC	DURÉE
PO	30 min	4 – 8 h	24 h

CONTRE-INDICATIONS, PRÉCAUTIONS ET MISES EN GARDE

Contre-indications: Hypersensibilité à la cétirizine ou à sa molécule mère, l'hydroxyzine ■ Insuffisance rénale grave ($Cl_{Cr} \leq 10$ mL/min).
Précautions et mises en garde: Insuffisance hépatique ou rénale ■ **GÉR.:** Commencer par une dose plus faible ■ **OBST.:** Ce médicament est déconseillé chez les femmes enceintes, sauf avis médical contraire ■ **ALLAITEMENT:** Ce médicament est déconseillé pendant l'allaitement, sauf avis médical contraire ■ **PÉD.:** L'innocuité du médicament n'a pas été établie chez les enfants < 2 ans.

RÉACTIONS INDÉSIRABLES ET EFFETS SECONDAIRES

SNC: étourdissements, somnolence, fatigue.
ORLO: pharyngite.
GI: sécheresse de la bouche (xérostomie).

INTERACTIONS

Médicament-médicament: Effets additifs sur la dépression du SNC lors de l'usage concomitant d'**alcool**, d'**opioïdes** et d'**hypnosédatifs**.

VOIES D'ADMINISTRATION ET POSOLOGIE

- **PO (enfants > 12 ans et adultes):** De 5 à 10 mg, 1 fois par jour selon la gravité des symptômes. La dose peut être portée à 20 mg/jour selon l'évolution des symptômes.
- **PO (enfants de 6 à 12 ans):** 10 mg, 1 fois par jour, ou 5 mg, 2 fois par jour.
- **PO (enfants de 2 à 6 ans):** 2,5 mg, 2 fois par jour, ou 5 mg, 1 fois par jour.
- **PO (personnes âgées):** La dose de départ recommandée est de 5 mg, 1 fois par jour.

INSUFFISANCE RÉNALE

- **PO (ADULTES):** *CL_{CR} DE 11 À 31 mL/MIN* – 5 mg/JOUR; *CL_{CR} < 11 mL/MIN* – NE PAS ADMINISTRER CE MÉDICAMENT.

INSUFFISANCE HÉPATIQUE

- **PO (ADULTES):** 5 mg/JOUR.

PRÉSENTATION

Comprimés: 5 mg^{VL}, 10 mg^{VL}, 20 mg^{Pr} ■ **Sirop (parfum de banane-raisin):** 5 mg/5 mL^{VL} ■ **En association avec:** pseudoéphédrine (Reactine Allergie et Sinus)^{VL}.

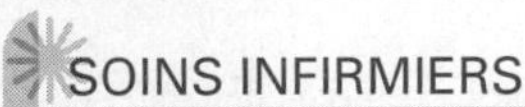

SOINS INFIRMIERS

ÉVALUATION DE LA SITUATION

- Avant l'administration initiale et à intervalles réguliers pendant toute la durée du traitement, rester à l'affût des symptômes suivants d'allergie: rhinite, conjonctivite et urticaire.
- Ausculter le murmure vésiculaire et noter les caractéristiques des sécrétions bronchiques. Maintenir l'apport de liquides entre 1 500 et 2 000 mL par jour pour diminuer la viscosité des sécrétions.

Tests de laboratoire: Le médicament peut entraîner des résultats faussement négatifs aux tests d'allergie cutanés.

DIAGNOSTICS INFIRMIERS POSSIBLES

- Dégagement inefficace des voies respiratoires (Indications).
- Risque d'accident (Réactions indésirables).
- Connaissances insuffisantes sur le traitement médicamenteux (Enseignement au patient et à ses proches).

INTERVENTIONS INFIRMIÈRES

- Administrer le médicament 1 fois par jour, sans égard aux repas.

ENSEIGNEMENT AU PATIENT ET À SES PROCHES

- Expliquer au patient qu'il doit respecter rigoureusement la posologie recommandée.
- Prévenir le patient que la cétirizine peut provoquer des étourdissements et de la somnolence. Lui

conseiller de ne pas conduire et d'éviter les activités qui exigent sa vigilance jusqu'à ce qu'on ait la certitude que le médicament n'entraîne pas ces effets chez lui.

- Mettre en garde le patient contre la consommation d'alcool ou d'autres dépresseurs du SNC en même temps que ce médicament.
- Conseiller au patient de pratiquer une bonne hygiène buccale, de se rincer la bouche avec de l'eau, de mâcher de la gomme ou de sucer des bonbons sans sucre pour diminuer la sécheresse de la bouche. Lui recommander de consulter un professionnel de la santé si la sécheresse de la bouche persiste pendant plus de 2 semaines.
- Demander au patient de prévenir un professionnel de la santé en cas d'étourdissements ou si les symptômes allergiques persistent.

VÉRIFICATION DE L'EFFICACITÉ THÉRAPEUTIQUE

L'efficacité du traitement peut être démontrée par: la diminution des symptômes allergiques.

CHARBON ACTIVÉ

Charac-50, Charac-25, Charactol-50, Charactol-25, Charcodote, Charcodote Aqueux, Charcodote pédiatrique, Charcodote pédiatrique aqueux, Charcodote TFS-50, Charcodote TFS-25

CLASSIFICATION:
Antidote (absorbant)

Grossesse – catégorie inconnue

INDICATIONS

Traitement d'urgence de l'empoisonnement par de nombreuses substances absorbées par voie orale, après induction de vomissements et lavage gastrique. Cependant, le charbon activé est inefficace en cas d'ingestion d'acides et de bases caustiques ou corrosifs, d'éthanol, de méthanol, de chlorure de sodium, de plomb, de lithium, de sels de fer, d'acide borique et d'autres acides minéraux.

MÉCANISME D'ACTION

Liaison des médicaments et des substances chimiques qui se trouvent dans le tractus gastro-intestinal. ***Effets thérapeutiques:*** Diminution de l'absorption intestinale des médicaments ou des substances chimiques, en cas de surdosage.

PHARMACOCINÉTIQUE

Absorption: Nulle.
Distribution: Nulle.
Métabolisme et excrétion: Excrétion à l'état inchangé dans les fèces.
Demi-vie: Inconnue.

Profil temps-action (antidote)

	DÉBUT D'ACTION	PIC	DURÉE
PO	en quelques minutes	inconnu	4 - 12 h

CONTRE-INDICATIONS, PRÉCAUTIONS ET MISES EN GARDE

Contre-indications: Ne pas administrer si les voies respiratoires du patient ne sont pas protégées (p. ex., diminution du niveau de conscience en l'absence d'intubation trachéale) ■ Ingestion d'une substance caustique ou de distillats de pétrole purs ■ L'administration de doses multiples de charbon activé est contre-indiquée en présence d'obstruction intestinale ou de signes de diminution du péristaltisme (p. ex., diminution des bruits intestinaux, distension abdominale et iléus).

Précautions et mises en garde: Empoisonnement dû aux cyanures, à l'éthanol, au méthanol, aux solvants organiques, aux acides minéraux ou au fer ■ Examen endoscopique (difficulté d'interprétation des résultats) ■ **PÉD.:** Les préparations commerciales qui contiennent du sorbitol doivent être utilisées avec prudence chez les enfants. Suivre de près le bilan hydroélectrolytique et n'administrer qu'une seule dose.

RÉACTIONS INDÉSIRABLES ET EFFETS SECONDAIRES

GI: selles noires, constipation, diarrhée, vomissements.

INTERACTIONS

Médicament-médicament: Le charbon adsorbe les **autres médicaments**, dont le **sirop d'ipéca**, la **digoxine** et le **mycophénolate mofétil**, ce qui empêche leur absorption par voie systémique à partir du tractus gastro-intestinal et peut diminuer leur efficacité.

VOIES D'ADMINISTRATION ET POSOLOGIE

- **PO (adultes):** De 25 à 100 g ou 10 fois la quantité de substance toxique ingérée, si elle est connue; cependant, de nombreux médecins considèrent que la dose de 50 g est la dose minimale chez l'adulte. La dose peut être administrée de nouveau si le médecin le recommande.
- **PO (enfants):** 1 mg/kg; la dose peut être administrée de nouveau si le médecin le recommande.

PRÉSENTATION (version générique disponible)

Suspension orale (diluée avec de l'eau ou du sorbitol): 50 g/250 mL^{VL}, 25 g/125 mL^{VL} ▪ **Également disponible sous forme de poudre ou de comprimés.**

C

SOINS INFIRMIERS

ÉVALUATION DE LA SITUATION

- Examiner l'état neurologique du patient et administrer le médicament seulement lorsque celui-ci est éveillé (à moins que ses voies respiratoires soient protégées).
- Établir le type de médicament ou de poison ingéré ainsi que l'heure de l'ingestion.
- Consulter les ouvrages de référence, les centres antipoison ou le médecin pour connaître les symptômes de toxicité induits par les agents ingérés.
- Mesurer la pression artérielle, le pouls, le débit urinaire, et suivre l'état respiratoire et neurologique du patient, compte tenu des réactions que l'agent toxique en question peut provoquer. Prévenir le médecin si les symptômes persistent ou s'aggravent.

Tests de laboratoire: L'administration prolongée de cet agent peut entraver l'absorption de nutriments essentiels, ce qui peut entraîner une réduction des concentrations de minéraux ou d'électrolytes.

DIAGNOSTICS INFIRMIERS POSSIBLES

- Risque de violence envers soi (Indications).
- Risque d'accident (Indications).

INTERVENTIONS INFIRMIÈRES

- L'efficacité du charbon activé est plus grande s'il est administré dans les 60 minutes qui suivent l'ingestion du médicament ou du poison ayant provoqué l'intoxication. Pour réduire l'absorption ultérieure des médicaments éliminés par voie entérohépatique, on peut répéter l'administration du charbon activé. Si on administre au patient du sirop d'ipéca, lui en faire boire d'abord et attendre qu'il ait fini de vomir avant de lui administrer du charbon activé.
- Ne pas administrer le charbon activé en comprimés ou en capsules pour traiter l'empoisonnement.
- Mélanger la dose avec 180 à 240 mL d'eau et administrer la solution (lorsqu'on utilise la poudre de charbon activé). Ne pas administrer le charbon activé avec des produits laitiers (lait, crème glacée ou sorbet). On peut ajouter de l'eau pour diluer davantage la solution s'il faut l'administrer par sonde nasogastrique.
- Bien agiter la suspension orale pendant 1 minute avant de l'administrer.
- L'ingestion rapide peut provoquer des vomissements. Si le patient vomit peu de temps après avoir ingéré du charbon activé, demander au médecin si l'on peut administrer une nouvelle dose.
- Ne pas administrer d'autres médicaments par voie orale pendant les 2 heures qui précèdent ou qui suivent l'administration du charbon activé.
- La solution de charbon activé provoque la constipation; le médecin peut prescrire un laxatif pour accélérer l'élimination du médicament. Cette mesure pourrait ne pas être nécessaire avec les produits renfermant du sorbitol.

ENSEIGNEMENT AU PATIENT ET À SES PROCHES

- Prévenir le patient que ses selles deviendront noires.
- Expliquer au patient les méthodes de prévention de l'empoisonnement. Avant de prendre le charbon activé, il faut s'informer auprès d'un centre antipoison, du médecin ou du personnel du service des urgences. Il faut aussi apporter un échantillon de la substance ingérée au service des urgences afin qu'on puisse en déterminer la nature.

VÉRIFICATION DE L'EFFICACITÉ THÉRAPEUTIQUE

L'efficacité du traitement peut être démontrée par: la prévention ou la suppression des effets toxiques de l'agent ingéré. ✳

CHÉLATEURS DES ACIDES BILIAIRES

cholestyramine

PMS-Cholestyramine, PMS-Cholestyramine léger, Questran

colestipol

Colestid

CLASSIFICATION:

Hypolipidémiants, antidiarrhéique (pour la cholestyramine seulement)

Grossesse – catégorie B

INDICATIONS

Traitement adjuvant de l'hypercholestérolémie primaire ▪ **Cholestyramine:** Soulagement du prurit induit par des concentrations élevées d'acides biliaires et traitement symptomatique de la diarrhée induite par un excès d'acides biliaires fécaux, dû au syndrome de l'intestin court.

MÉCANISME D'ACTION

Liaison aux acides biliaires du tractus gastro-intestinal, formant un complexe insoluble, ce qui entraîne une élimination accrue du cholestérol. ***Effets thérapeutiques:*** Diminution des concentrations plasmatiques de cholestérol et de lipoprotéines de basse densité (LDL) ■ Réduction de la diarrhée ■ Réduction du prurit.

PHARMACOCINÉTIQUE

Absorption: Nulle (le médicament agit dans le tractus gastro-intestinal).
Distribution: Aucune.
Métabolisme et excrétion: Liaison aux acides biliaires formant un complexe insoluble, qui est éliminé dans les fèces.
Demi-vie: Inconnue.

Profil temps-action (effet hypocholestérolémiant)

	DÉBUT D'ACTION	PIC	DURÉE
Cholestyramine	24 – 48 h	1 - 3 semaines	2 - 4 semaines
Colestipol	24 – 48 h	1 mois	1 mois

CONTRE-INDICATIONS, PRÉCAUTIONS ET MISES EN GARDE

Contre-indications: Hypersensibilité ■ Obstruction biliaire complète.
Précautions et mises en garde: Antécédents de constipation ■ Phénylcétonurie (certains produits contiennent de l'aspartame; il faudrait en éviter l'administration chez les patients qui sont atteints de ce trouble).
EXTRÊME PRUDENCE: PÉD.: RISQUE D'OBSTRUCTION INTESTINALE; DES DÉCÈS ONT ÉTÉ SIGNALÉS.

RÉACTIONS INDÉSIRABLES ET EFFETS SECONDAIRES

ORLO: irritation de langue.
GI: gêne abdominale, constipation, nausées, fécalome, flatulence, hémorroïdes, irritation périanale, stéatorrhée, vomissements.
Tég.: irritation, rash.
HÉ: acidose hyperchlorémique.
Métab.: carence en vitamines A, D et K.

INTERACTIONS

Médicament-médicament: Les chélateurs des acides biliaires peuvent diminuer l'absorption et les effets des médicaments suivants administrés par voie orale: **acétaminophène, AINS, amiodarone, céphalosporines, clindamycine, clofibrate, dérivés digitaliques, ézétimibe, agents destinés à une hormonothérapie thyroïdienne substitutive, diurétiques, gemfibrozil, glipizide, corticostéroïdes, imipramine, léflunomide, mycophénolate, méthotrexate, méthyldopa, métronidazole, niacine, pénicilline, phénytoïne, phosphates, propranolol, tétracyclines, tolbutamide, ursodiol, vitamines liposolubles (A, D, E et K)** et **warfarine** ■ Ces agents peuvent aussi diminuer l'absorption d'autres **médicaments administrés par voie orale**.

C

VOIES D'ADMINISTRATION ET POSOLOGIE

Cholestyramine

- **PO (adultes):** 4 g, de 1 à 6 fois par jour (toujours commencer le traitement par une seule dose quotidienne).

Colestipol

- **PO (adultes):** *Granules et granules orange* – 5 g, 1 ou 2 fois par jour; on peut augmenter la dose par paliers de 5 g, tous les 1 à 2 mois, jusqu'à concurrence de 30 g par jour. *Comprimés* – 2 g, 1 ou 2 fois par jour; on peut augmenter la dose par paliers de 2 g, tous les 1 à 2 mois, jusqu'à concurrence de 16 g par jour.

PRÉSENTATION

- **Cholestyramine, Questran léger ou saveur d'orange (version générique disponible)**
  Poudre pour suspension orale avec aspartame (Questran léger, version générique): 4 g de cholestyramine par sachet ou cuillerée[Pr] ■ **Poudre pour suspension orale avec aspartame (Questran saveur orange, version générique):** 4 g de cholestyramine par sachet ou cuillerée[Pr] ■ **Poudre pour suspension orale (Questran, version générique):** 4 g de cholestyramine par sachet ou cuillerée[Pr].
- **Colestipol**
  Granules pour suspension (non parfumés): 5 g par sachet ou cuillerée[Pr] ■ **Granules pour suspension avec aspartame (parfum d'orange):** 5 g par sachet ou cuillerée[Pr] ■ **Comprimés:** 1 g[Pr].

SOINS INFIRMIERS

ÉVALUATION DE LA SITUATION

Hypercholestérolémie: Recueillir des données sur l'alimentation du patient, notamment sur sa consommation de matières grasses.
Prurit: Déterminer la gravité des démangeaisons et de l'atteinte à l'intégrité de la peau. On peut réduire la dose lorsque le prurit disparaît.
Diarrhée: Évaluer la fréquence, la quantité et la consistance des selles.

C

Tests de laboratoire:

- Vérifier les concentrations sériques de cholestérol et de triglycérides avant l'administration initiale, fréquemment au cours des premiers mois et à intervalles réguliers pendant toute la durée du traitement. Cesser l'administration du médicament en cas d'élévation paradoxale des concentrations de cholestérol.
- Ces médicaments peuvent élever les concentrations d'AST, d'ALT, de phosphore, de chlorure et de phosphatase alcaline et diminuer les concentrations sériques de calcium, de sodium et de potassium.
- Ils peuvent également prolonger les temps de prothrombine.

DIAGNOSTICS INFIRMIERS POSSIBLES

- Constipation (Effets secondaires).
- Connaissances insuffisantes sur le régime alimentaire et le traitement médicamenteux (Enseignement au patient et à ses proches).
- Non-observance du traitement médicamenteux (Enseignement au patient et à ses proches).

INTERVENTIONS INFIRMIÈRES

- Le médecin peut prescrire en cas de traitement prolongé des vitamines liposolubles (A, D, E, K) et de l'acide folique, en préparation parentérale ou hydrosoluble.
- Administrer le médicament avant les repas.
- Les cuillères qui servent à mesurer les diverses préparations en poudre ne sont pas interchangeables.
- Les autres médicaments doivent être pris 1 heure avant ou de 4 à 6 heures après les chélateurs des acides biliaires.
- LES COMPRIMÉS DE COLESTIPOL DOIVENT ÊTRE AVALÉS EN ENTIER; IL NE FAUT PAS LES COUPER, LES ÉCRASER OU LES MÂCHER.

ENSEIGNEMENT AU PATIENT ET À SES PROCHES

- Expliquer au patient qu'il doit respecter rigoureusement la posologie recommandée; l'avertir qu'il ne doit jamais sauter de dose, ni remplacer une dose manquée par une double dose.
- Recommander au patient de prendre le médicament avant les repas. Conseiller au patient qui prend de la cholestyramine de la mélanger avec environ 150 mL d'eau, de lait, de jus de fruits ou d'autres boissons non gazéifiées et de secouer vigoureusement le mélange. Conseiller au patient qui prend le colestipol de le mélanger dans un grand verre avec de l'eau, du jus de fruits ou une boisson gazéifiée, de brasser délicatement le mélange et de rincer le verre avec une petite quantité de liquide supplémentaire de façon à s'assurer qu'il a pris toute la dose. Lui préciser qu'il peut aussi mélanger le colestipol avec des soupes très liquides, des céréales ou des préparations de pulpes de fruits (compote de pommes, purée d'ananas). Avant de mélanger, laisser la poudre reposer sur le liquide pour l'hydrater pendant 1 ou 2 minutes. Prévenir le patient qu'il ne doit pas prendre le médicament à l'état sec. Lui expliquer que les variations de couleur ne modifient pas la stabilité de la cholestyramine.
- Expliquer au patient que, pendant ce traitement, il doit aussi observer certaines restrictions alimentaires (réduire sa consommation de matières grasses, de cholestérol, de glucides et d'alcool), suivre un programme d'exercices et arrêter de fumer.
- Prévenir le patient qu'il risque de souffrir de constipation. Pour réduire les effets constipants de ce médicament, il devrait augmenter sa consommation de liquides et de fibres alimentaires, faire de l'exercice et prendre des laxatifs émollients ou d'un autre type. Recommander au patient de prévenir un professionnel de la santé si la constipation, les nausées, la flatulence et les brûlures d'estomac persistent ou si ses selles deviennent mousseuses et nauséabondes.
- Conseiller au patient de signaler au médecin la présence de saignements ou d'ecchymoses inhabituels, de pétéchies ou de selles noires ou goudronneuses. L'administration de vitamine K peut s'avérer nécessaire.

VÉRIFICATION DE L'EFFICACITÉ THÉRAPEUTIQUE

L'efficacité du traitement peut être démontrée par: la baisse des concentrations sériques de cholestérol lié aux lipoprotéines de basse densité (LDL); on arrête habituellement le traitement si la réponse clinique après trois mois de traitement reste faible ■ la diminution de la gravité du prurit; le soulagement survient habituellement dans les 1 à 3 semaines qui suivent le début du traitement ■ la réduction de la fréquence et de la gravité de la diarrhée. ✳

ALERTE CLINIQUE

CHLORAL, HYDRATE DE

Apo-Chloral Hydrate, Chloral Hydrate Odan, PMS-Chloral Hydrate

CLASSIFICATION:

Sédatif et hypnotique

Grossesse – catégorie C

INDICATIONS

Sédation et induction du sommeil pendant une brève période (il se produit souvent une tolérance à ces effets après 2 semaines de traitement) ■ Avant une intervention chirurgicale ou autres interventions pour soulager l'anxiété ou produire une sédation ou le sommeil sans déprimer la respiration ou le réflexe de la toux (adjuvant à l'anesthésie).

MÉCANISME D'ACTION

Transformation lors du métabolisme en trichloroéthanol, qui est l'ingrédient actif. L'hydrate de chloral est doté de propriétés de dépression généralisée du SNC. ***Effets thérapeutiques:*** Sédation ou induction du sommeil.

PHARMACOCINÉTIQUE

Absorption: Bonne (PO ou IR).

Distribution: L'agent se répartit dans tout l'organisme. Il traverse la barrière placentaire et passe à faible concentration dans le lait maternel.

Métabolisme et excrétion: Lors du métabolisme hépatique, l'hydrate de chloral se transforme en trichloroéthanol, le métabolite actif. Le trichloroéthanol est métabolisé, à son tour, par le foie et les reins en composés inactifs. Ce métabolite est ensuite éliminé dans l'urine et la bile.

Demi-vie: *Trichloroéthanol* – nouveau-nés: de 8,5 à 66 heures; enfants: 10 heures; adultes: de 8 à 11 heures.

Profil temps-action (sédation)

	DÉBUT D'ACTION	PIC	DURÉE
PO	30 min	1 h	4-8 h
IR	0,5-1 h	1 h	4-8 h

CONTRE-INDICATIONS, PRÉCAUTIONS ET MISES EN GARDE

Contre-indications: Hypersensibilité ou réaction idiosyncrasique à l'hydrate de chloral ■ Insuffisance rénale grave ■ Insuffisance hépatique grave.

Précautions et mises en garde: Abus et pharmacodépendance: l'hydrate de chloral ne devrait être utilisé que pendant de courtes périodes, généralement de 2 à 7 jours à la fois. L'utilisation prolongée d'hydrate de chloral peut entraîner une tolérance et une dépendance physique ou psychologique ■ Cardiopathie grave (risque d'arythmies et d'hypotension en cas d'administration de doses importantes) ■ **OBST., ALLAITEMENT**: L'innocuité du médicament n'a pas été démontrée chez les femmes enceintes (le médicament traverse la barrière placentaire; l'emploi prolongé pendant la grossesse peut entraîner des symptômes de sevrage chez le nouveau-né); le médicament est excrété dans le lait maternel (son utilisation pendant l'allaitement peut entraîner de la somnolence chez le nourrisson) ■ Œsophagite, gastrite ou ulcère ■ Rectite ou colite (administration par voie rectale) ■ Comportement suicidaire ou antécédents de toxicomanie ■ **GÉR.**: Il est recommandé de réduire la dose chez les personnes âgées ou débilitées ■ **PÉD.**: Il faut calculer les doses attentivement et faire preuve de prudence lors de l'administration du produit; suivre de près les effets dépresseurs sur la respiration ou sur le SNC ■ Coma ou dépression préexistante du SNC.

C

RÉACTIONS INDÉSIRABLES ET EFFETS SECONDAIRES

SNC: <u>sédation excessive</u>, désorientation, étourdissements, sensation de tête légère, céphalées, incoordination, irritabilité, excitation paradoxale (enfants).

Resp.: dépression respiratoire.

GI: <u>diarrhée</u>, <u>nausées</u>, <u>vomissements</u>, flatulence.

Tég.: rash.

Divers: <u>tolérance à l'effet du médicament</u>, dépendance physique, dépendance psychologique.

INTERACTIONS

Médicament-médicament: Effets additifs sur la dépression du SNC lors de l'usage concomitant d'autres **dépresseurs du SNC**, incluant l'**alcool**, les **antihistaminiques**, les **antidépresseurs**, les **hypnosédatifs** et les **analgésiques opioïdes** ■ L'hydrate de chloral peut potentialiser l'effet de la **warfarine** ■ Administré dans les 24 heures qui suivent un traitement par voie IV au **furosémide**, l'hydrate de chloral peut entraîner la diaphorèse, des fluctuations de la pression artérielle et des bouffées vasomotrices ■ Risque d'accélérer le métabolisme et de diminuer l'effet de la **phénytoïne** ■ Risque d'augmenter la toxicité de l'**ifosfamide** et du **cyclophosphamide**.

Médicament-produits naturels: Le **kava**, le **houblon**, la **scutellaire**, la **valériane** et la **camomille** peuvent accentuer la dépression du SNC.

VOIES D'ADMINISTRATION ET POSOLOGIE

Les doses orales et rectales sont équivalentes. On peut administrer la dose par voie rectale sous forme de lavement de rétention, en dissolvant le liquide dans de l'huile de coton ou de l'huile d'olive ou encore dans un excipient de polyéthylène glycol hydrophile.

- **PO (adultes)**: *Hypnotique* – de 500 à 1 000 mg, de 15 à 30 minutes avant le coucher. *Sédation préopératoire* – de 500 mg à 1 000 mg, 30 minutes avant l'intervention. *Sédation diurne* – 250 mg, 3 fois par jour après les repas; maximum 2 000 mg/jour.

- **PO (patients âgés)**: *Hypnotique* – 250 mg, de 15 à 30 minutes avant le coucher.
- **PO (enfants)**: *Hypnotique* – 50 mg/kg au coucher. Ne pas dépasser 1 000 mg par dose. *Sédation* – 25 mg/kg par jour, en 3 ou 4 doses fractionnées, après les repas. Ne pas dépasser 500 mg/dose. *Sédation préopératoire* – de 25 à 50 mg/kg, 30 minutes avant l'intervention. On peut administrer une demi-dose 30 minutes plus tard. Ne pas administrer plus de 1 000 mg en une seule dose.

PRÉSENTATION

Capsules: 500 mg[Pr] ■ **Sirop**: 500 mg/5 mL[Pr].

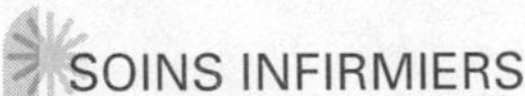

SOINS INFIRMIERS

ÉVALUATION DE LA SITUATION

- Évaluer l'état de conscience, les habitudes de sommeil et le risque de pharmacodépendance avant d'administrer le médicament. Un traitement prolongé peut entraîner une dépendance physique et psychologique. Limiter la quantité de médicament dont le patient peut disposer.
- Évaluer le niveau de vigilance au moment où l'effet atteint son pic. Prévenir le médecin en l'absence d'une sédation satisfaisante ou si des réactions paradoxales surviennent.

Tests de laboratoire: L'hydrate de chloral peut fausser les résultats du dosage des 17-hydroxycorticostéroïdes et des catécholamines urinaires.

DIAGNOSTICS INFIRMIERS POSSIBLES

- Habitudes de sommeil perturbées (Indications).
- Anxiété (Indications).
- Risque d'accident (Effets secondaires).

INTERVENTIONS INFIRMIÈRES

ALERTE CLINIQUE: PÉD.: RESTER À L'AFFÛT DES EFFETS DÉPRESSEURS SUR LA RESPIRATION OU LE SNC. DES DÉCÈS ASSOCIÉS À L'EMPLOI DE L'HYDRATE DE CHLORAL À TITRE DE SÉDATIF AVANT DES EXAMENS DIAGNOSTIQUES OU THÉRAPEUTIQUES ONT ÉTÉ SIGNALÉS, SURTOUT EN PÉDIATRIE. DE PLUS, IL FAUT FAIRE PREUVE DE PRUDENCE DANS LE CALCUL ET L'ADMINISTRATION DE LA DOSE ADÉQUATE. ACCEPTER SEULEMENT LES ORDONNANCES RÉDIGÉES EN MILLIGRAMMES (ET NON EN VOLUME [CUILLÉRÉES À THÉ] OU EN CONCENTRATION). L'ADMINISTRATION DE CE MÉDICAMENT DEVRAIT ÊTRE RÉSERVÉE AUX PROFESSIONNELS DE LA SANTÉ SPÉCIALISÉS DU CENTRE HOSPITALIER. LORSQUE L'HYDRATE DE CHLORAL EST UTILISÉ À TITRE DE SÉDATIF AVANT UNE INTERVENTION, IL FAUT L'ADMINISTRER DANS LE CENTRE OÙ L'INTERVENTION DOIT AVOIR LIEU. COMME LA DEMI-VIE DES MÉTABOLITES DE L'HYDRATE DE CHLORAL EST LONGUE, L'ADMINISTRATION RÉPÉTÉE DE CE MÉDICAMENT PEUT PRODUIRE UNE ACCUMULATION DE MÉTABOLITES ET PROVOQUER UNE DÉPRESSION EXCESSIVE DU SNC. LE PERSONNEL SOIGNANT DOIT DONC SURVEILLER LE DEGRÉ DE SÉDATION ET NE PAS DÉPASSER LA DOSE PRESCRITE. ON DOIT SURVEILLER LE PATIENT JUSQU'À CE QUE SON ÉTAT DE CONSCIENCE LUI PERMETTE DE QUITTER LES LIEUX.

- Avant le traitement, atténuer les stimulations venant de l'extérieur et améliorer le confort du patient pour accroître l'efficacité du médicament.
- Prévenir les accidents. Remonter les ridelles du lit. Aider le patient lorsqu'il se déplace. Retirer les cigarettes lors de l'administration de doses hypnotiques.
- Il faut avaler les capsules telles quelles avec un grand verre d'eau ou de jus pour réduire l'irritation gastrique. Demander au patient de ne pas les mâcher. Diluer le sirop dans un demi-verre d'eau ou de jus.

ENSEIGNEMENT AU PATIENT ET À SES PROCHES

- Conseiller au patient de prendre l'hydrate de chloral en suivant rigoureusement la posologie recommandée. S'il n'a pas pu prendre le médicament au moment habituel, il devrait sauter cette dose; il ne faut jamais remplacer une dose manquée par une double dose. Le sevrage abrupt, après un traitement de 2 semaines ou plus, peut entraîner l'excitation du SNC, des tremblements, de l'anxiété, des hallucinations et le délire.
- Prévenir le patient que l'hydrate de chloral entraîne de la somnolence et des étourdissements. Lui conseiller de ne pas conduire et d'éviter les activités qui exigent sa vigilance jusqu'à ce qu'on ait la certitude que le médicament n'entraîne pas ces effets chez lui.
- Prévenir le patient que la consommation concomitante d'alcool peut entraîner un effet additif se traduisant par de la tachycardie, de la vasodilatation, des bouffées vasomotrices, des céphalées, de l'hypotension et par une dépression marquée du SNC. Lui conseiller d'éviter de boire de l'alcool et de prendre des dépresseurs du SNC en même temps que l'hydrate de chloral.
- Conseiller au patient d'arrêter le traitement et de prévenir le médecin si les symptômes suivants se manifestent: rash, étourdissements, irritabilité, altération des opérations de la pensée, céphalées ou incoordination motrice.

C

VÉRIFICATION DE L'EFFICACITÉ THÉRAPEUTIQUE

L'efficacité du traitement peut être démontrée par: la sédation ▪ l'amélioration du sommeil.

CHLORAMBUCIL

Leukeran

CLASSIFICATION:
Antinéoplasique (alkylant)

Grossesse – catégorie D

INDICATIONS

Traitement de la leucémie lymphoblastique chronique, des lymphomes malins et de la maladie de Hodgkin.

MÉCANISME D'ACTION

Inhibition de la synthèse des protéines cellulaires (effet non spécifique sur le cycle cellulaire). ***Effets thérapeutiques:*** Destruction des cellules à réplication rapide, particulièrement des cellules malignes.

PHARMACOCINÉTIQUE

Absorption: Rapide et totale (PO).
Distribution: Le médicament traverse la barrière placentaire.
Liaison aux protéines: 99 %.
Métabolisme et excrétion: Métabolisme majoritairement hépatique.
Demi-vie: 1,5 heure.

Profil temps-action (effet sur la numération leucocytaire)

	DÉBUT D'ACTION	PIC	DURÉE
PO	7 - 14 jours	7 - 14 jours	14 - 28 jours

CONTRE-INDICATIONS, PRÉCAUTIONS ET MISES EN GARDE

Contre-indications: Hypersensibilité (risque d'allergie croisée avec les autres agents alkylants) ▪ Radiothérapie (ne pas administrer le médicament dans les 4 semaines qui suivent la fin d'un traitement).

Précautions et mises en garde: Infection ▪ Toute autre maladie chronique débilitante ▪ **GÉR.:** Plus grande sensibilité aux effets du médicament ▪ **OBST.:** Patientes en âge de procréer; en cas de grossesse, retarder le traitement le plus longtemps possible, au moins jusqu'à la fin du 1er trimestre ▪ **ALLAITEMENT:** Antécédents de résistance au chlorambucil ▪ **PÉD.:** L'efficacité et l'innocuité du médicament n'ont pas été établies.

RÉACTIONS INDÉSIRABLES ET EFFETS SECONDAIRES

Resp.: fibrose pulmonaire.
GI: nausées, stomatite (rare), vomissements, hépatotoxicité.
GU: diminution du nombre de spermatozoïdes, stérilité.
Tég.: alopécie (rare), dermatite, rash.
Hémat.: LEUCOPÉNIE, anémie, thrombopénie.
Métab.: hyperuricémie.
Divers: réactions allergiques, risque de formation de tumeurs secondaires.

INTERACTIONS

Médicament-médicament: Les **agents dépresseurs de la moelle osseuse** (**antinéoplasiques**) ou les **immunosuppresseurs** peuvent entraîner une aplasie médullaire additive ▪ Le médicament peut réduire la réponse des anticorps aux **vaccins à virus vivants** et augmenter le risque de réactions indésirables.

VOIES D'ADMINISTRATION ET POSOLOGIE

- **PO (adultes):** *Leucémie lymphoblastique chronique* – 0,15 mg/kg/jour, jusqu'à ce que la numération leucocytaire soit de 10×10^9/L. On peut reprendre le traitement 4 semaines après la fin du premier cycle à une dose de 0,1 mg/kg/jour. *Lymphome non hodgkinien* – (monothérapie) de 0,1 à 0,2 mg/kg/jour, pendant 4 à 8 semaines ▪ *Maladie de Hodgkin* – (monothérapie) 0,2 mg/kg/jour, pendant 4 à 8 semaines.
- **PO (enfants):** De 0,1 à 0,2 mg/kg/jour (4,5 mg/m^2/jour), en une seule ou en plusieurs doses, pendant 3 à 6 semaines pour l'induction d'une rémission *(usage non approuvé: l'innocuité du chlorambucil n'a pas été établie chez les enfants)*.

PRÉSENTATION

Comprimés: 2 mg^{Pr}.

SOINS INFIRMIERS

ÉVALUATION DE LA SITUATION

- SUIVRE DE PRÈS LE PATIENT POUR DÉCELER L'APPARITION D'UNE DÉPRESSION MÉDULLAIRE. Rester à l'affût des saignements: saignement des gencives, formation d'ecchymoses, pétéchies, présence de sang occulte dans les selles, l'urine et les vomissements. Éviter les injections IM et la prise de la température rectale, si la numération plaquettaire est basse. Appliquer une pression sur les points de ponction veineuse pendant 10 minutes. Évaluer les signes d'infection en présence d'une neutropénie. Une anémie peut survenir; suivre de près les signes de fatigue accrue, de dyspnée et d'hypotension orthostatique.

C

- Effectuer le bilan quotidien des ingesta et des excreta et peser le patient tous les jours. Prévenir le médecin de tout écart important entre les valeurs totales.
- Observer les symptômes suivants de goutte: concentration accrue d'acide urique, douleurs articulaires et œdème. Inciter le patient à boire au moins 2 litres de liquide par jour si son état le permet. On peut administrer de l'allopurinol pour diminuer les concentrations d'acide urique. Le médecin peut recommander l'alcalinisation de l'urine pour augmenter l'excrétion de l'acide urique.

Tests de laboratoire:

- Examiner la numération globulaire et la formule leucocytaire avant le début du traitement et hebdomadairement pendant toute sa durée. Prévenir le médecin si le nombre de granulocytes diminue considérablement. La leucopénie survient habituellement vers la troisième semaine de traitement et persiste pendant une semaine ou deux après un traitement de courte durée. Le nadir de la leucopénie se produit entre le 7e et le 14e jour suivant l'administration d'une seule dose élevée; les concentrations se rétablissant de 2 à 3 semaines plus tard. Le nombre de polynucléaires neutrophiles peut diminuer pendant les 10 jours qui suivent la prise de la dernière dose. Noter les numérations plaquettaires pendant toute la durée du traitement. La thrombopénie survient habituellement vers la 3e semaine de traitement et se maintient pendant 1 semaine ou 2 après un traitement de courte durée. Le nadir de la thrombopénie se produit 1 semaine ou 2 après l'administration d'une seule dose; les concentrations se rétablissent de 2 à 3 semaines plus tard. Prendre les mesures nécessaires en cas de thrombopénie, si le nombre de plaquettes est inférieur à 150×10^9/L.
- Noter les résultats des tests de la fonction hépatique et les concentrations d'urée, de créatinine et d'acide urique avant le traitement et à intervalles réguliers pendant toute sa durée. Le médicament peut entraîner l'élévation des concentrations d'ALT et de phosphatase alcaline, ce qui peut être un signe d'hépatotoxicité.

DIAGNOSTICS INFIRMIERS POSSIBLES

- Risque d'accident (Effets secondaires).
- Risque d'infection (Effets secondaires).
- Connaissances insuffisantes sur le traitement médicamenteux (Enseignement au patient et à ses proches).

INTERVENTIONS INFIRMIÈRES

- NE PAS CONFONDRE LEUKÉRAN (CHLORAMBUCIL) ET LA LEUCOVORINE (ACIDE FOLINIQUE).
- Administrer le médicament 1 heure avant ou 2 heures après les repas. Le pharmacien peut préparer une suspension lorsque le patient éprouve des difficultés de déglutition.

ENSEIGNEMENT AU PATIENT ET À SES PROCHES

- Expliquer au patient qu'il doit suivre rigoureusement la posologie recommandée même si les nausées et les vomissements le gênent considérablement. Lui recommander de demander des conseils à un professionnel de la santé si les vomissements surviennent peu de temps après la prise du médicament. Prévenir le patient que s'il n'a pu prendre le médicament au moment habituel, il doit le prendre aussitôt que possible dans la même journée, dans le cas d'un traitement uniquotidien. S'il doit prendre le médicament en doses fractionnées, il doit le prendre aussitôt que possible à moins que ce ne soit presque l'heure prévue pour la dose suivante. Il ne faut jamais remplacer une dose manquée par une double dose.
- Recommander au patient de signaler les saignements inhabituels. Lui expliquer les mesures à prendre en cas de thrombopénie: utiliser une brosse à dents à poils souples et un rasoir électrique; prendre garde aux chutes; ne pas boire d'alcool ni prendre des médicaments contenant de l'acide acétylsalicylique (aspirine) ou des AINS étant donné le risque de saignements gastriques.
- Expliquer au patient qu'il doit éviter les foules et les personnes contagieuses. Lui recommander de signaler immédiatement au médecin le rash ou les symptômes suivants d'infection: fièvre, maux de gorge, frissons, toux, enrouement, douleurs lombaires ou aux flancs, mictions difficiles ou douloureuses.
- Recommander au patient d'observer ses muqueuses buccales à la recherche de rougeurs ou d'aphtes. En cas d'aphtes, lui conseiller de remplacer la brosse à dents par une brosse-éponge et de se rincer la bouche avec de l'eau après avoir bu ou mangé. La douleur associée à la stomatite peut dicter un traitement par des analgésiques opioïdes.
- Conseiller au patient qui suit un traitement prolongé de signaler immédiatement au médecin la toux, les essoufflements et la fièvre.

- Recommander au patient de prévenir le médecin si les nausées et les vomissements persistent. Le médecin peut lui prescrire un antiémétique, bien que ces effets secondaires durent en général moins de 24 heures et qu'ils semblent s'atténuer malgré la poursuite du traitement.
- Expliquer au patient qu'il est exposé à un faible risque de perdre ses cheveux. Explorer avec lui les méthodes lui permettant de s'adapter à ce changement.
- Prévenir le patient que le chlorambucil peut provoquer une suppression irréversible de la fonction des gonades; lui conseiller cependant de continuer à prendre des mesures de contraception. Recommander à la patiente d'informer le médecin sans délai si elle pense être enceinte.
- Expliquer au patient qu'il ne doit pas se faire vacciner sans recommandation expresse du médecin.

VÉRIFICATION DE L'EFFICACITÉ THÉRAPEUTIQUE

L'efficacité du traitement peut être démontrée par: l'amélioration des paramètres hématopoïétiques en cas de leucémie ▪ la diminution de la taille de la tumeur et le ralentissement de la propagation des métastases. Les effets thérapeutiques de ce médicament sont habituellement manifestes vers la troisième semaine de traitement.

CHLORDIAZÉPOXIDE

Apo-Chlordiazepoxide, Chlordiazépoxide

CLASSIFICATION:

Anxiolytique et hypnosédatif (benzodiazépine)

Grossesse – catégorie D

INDICATIONS

Traitement d'appoint de l'anxiété ▪ Traitement d'appoint de l'insomnie d'origine tensionnelle ▪ Traitement des symptômes du sevrage alcoolique.

MÉCANISME D'ACTION

Effet anxiolytique à de nombreux niveaux du SNC ▪ Dépression du SNC, probablement par la potentialisation des effets de l'acide gamma-aminobutyrique (GABA), un neurotransmetteur inhibiteur. ***Effets thérapeutiques:*** Sédation ▪ Soulagement de l'anxiété.

PHARMACOCINÉTIQUE

Absorption: Bonne (PO).

Distribution: Tout l'organisme; le chlordiazépoxide traverse la barrière hématoencéphalique et placentaire et passe dans le lait maternel.

Métabolisme et excrétion: Fort métabolisme hépatique. Certains produits du métabolisme dépriment le SNC.

Demi-vie: De 5 à 30 heures.

Profil temps-action (sédation)

	DÉBUT D'ACTION	PIC	DURÉE
PO	1 - 2 h	0,5 - 4 h	jusqu'à 24 h

CONTRE-INDICATIONS, PRÉCAUTIONS ET MISES EN GARDE

Contre-indications: Hypersensibilité connue au médicament ou à d'autres benzodiazépines (allergie croisée) ▪ Glaucome à angle fermé ▪ Myasthénie grave.

Précautions et mises en garde: Altération de la fonction hépatique ▪ Insuffisance respiratoire grave ou apnée du sommeil ▪ Insuffisance rénale grave ▪ Comportement suicidaire ou antécédents de toxicomanie ou de pharmacodépendance ▪ **GÉR.:** Il est recommandé de réduire la dose chez les personnes âgées ou débilitées ▪ Coma ou dépression préexistante du SNC ▪ **OBST.:** Le médicament traverse la barrière placentaire et peut s'accumuler dans l'organisme du fœtus ▪ **ALLAITEMENT:** Le médicament est excrété dans le lait maternel et peut s'accumuler dans l'organisme du nourrisson ▪ **PÉD.:** L'innocuité du médicament n'a pas été établie chez les enfants âgés ≤ 6 ans.

RÉACTIONS INDÉSIRABLES ET EFFETS SECONDAIRES

SNC: étourdissements, somnolence, sensation de tête légère, céphalées, dépression, excitation paradoxale.

ORLO: vision trouble.

GI: constipation, diarrhée, nausées, vomissements.

Tég.: rash.

Divers: dépendance physique, dépendance psychologique, tolérance à l'effet du médicament.

INTERACTIONS

Médicament-médicament: Effets additifs sur la dépression du SNC lors de l'usage concomitant d'**alcool**, d'**antidépresseurs**, d'**antihistaminiques** et d'**analgésiques opiacés** ▪ La **cimétidine**, les **contraceptifs oraux**, le **disulfirame**, la **fluoxétine**, l'**isoniazide**, le **kétoconazole**, le **métoprolol**, le **propoxyphène**, le **propanolol** ou l'**acide valproïque** peuvent intensifier les effets du chlordiazépoxide ▪ Le chlordiazépoxide peut réduire l'efficacité de la **lévodopa** ▪ La **rifampine** et les **barbituriques** peuvent diminuer l'efficacité du chlordiazépoxide ■ Les effets sédatifs du chlordiazépoxide peuvent être réduits par la **théophylline**.

Médicament-produits naturels: Le **kava**, le **houblon**, la **scutellaire**, la **valériane** et la **camomille** peuvent accentuer la dépression du SNC.

C

VOIES D'ADMINISTRATION ET POSOLOGIE

- **PO (adultes)**: *Anxiété* – de 5 à 25 mg, de 2 à 4 fois par jour. *Sevrage alcoolique* – de 50 à 100 mg; répéter l'administration jusqu'à ce que l'agitation soit apaisée (300 mg par jour, au maximum).
- **PO (patients âgés ou débilités)**: *Anxiété* – dose initiale de 5 mg, de 2 à 4 fois par jour, qu'on peut majorer selon les besoins.
- **PO (enfants > 6 ans)**: *Anxiété* – 5 mg, de 2 à 4 fois par jour, jusqu'à 10 mg, 3 fois par jour.

PRÉSENTATION (version générique disponible)

Capsules: 5 mg$^{T\backslash C}$, 10 mg$^{T\backslash C}$, 25 mg$^{T\backslash C}$ ■ **En association avec**: clidinium (Apo-Chlorax, Librax, Pro-Chlorax)$^{T\backslash C}$.

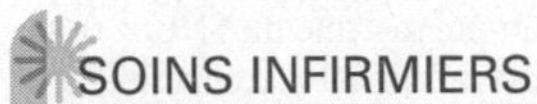

SOINS INFIRMIERS

ÉVALUATION DE LA SITUATION

- Noter le degré d'anxiété et de sédation (ataxie, étourdissements et trouble de l'élocution) à intervalles réguliers pendant toute la durée du traitement.

GÉR.: Évaluer le risque de chutes et mettre en place des mesures préventives.

- Le traitement prolongé avec des doses élevées peut entraîner une dépendance psychologique ou physique. Limiter la quantité de médicament dont le patient peut disposer.

Sevrage alcoolique: Surveiller l'apparition des symptômes suivants: tremblements, agitation, délire et hallucinations. Protéger le patient contre les accidents.

Tests de laboratoire:

- Chez les patients suivant un traitement prolongé, effectuer à intervalles réguliers une numération globulaire et des tests de la fonction hépatique. Le médicament peut entraîner l'élévation des concentrations de bilirubine, d'AST et d'ALT.
- Le chlordiazépoxide peut fausser les résultats du dosage des 17-cétostéroïdes et des 17-stéroïdes cétogènes urinaires. Il peut réduire la réponse aux épreuves par la métyrapone et le captage par la thyroïde des isotopes ^{123}I et ^{131}I.

DIAGNOSTICS INFIRMIERS POSSIBLES

- Anxiété (Indications).
- Risque d'accident (Effets secondaires).
- Connaissances insuffisantes sur le traitement médicamenteux (Enseignement au patient et à ses proches).

INTERVENTIONS INFIRMIÈRES

- NE PAS CONFONDRE LIBRIUM (CHLORDIAZÉPOXIDE) AVEC LIBRAX (CHLORDIAZÉPOXIDE/CLIDINIUM).

PO: Administrer le médicament après les repas ou avec du lait pour réduire l'irritation gastro-intestinale.

ENSEIGNEMENT AU PATIENT ET À SES PROCHES

- Conseiller au patient de prendre le médicament en respectant rigoureusement la posologie recommandée. L'inciter à consulter le médecin si le médicament est moins efficace après quelques semaines, sans qu'il augmente la dose de sa propre initiative. Après un traitement prolongé, le retrait du médicament doit se faire graduellement. L'arrêt brusque du traitement peut entraîner les symptômes de sevrage suivants: insomnie, irritation, nervosité, tremblements.
- Prévenir le patient que le chlordiazépoxide peut provoquer de la somnolence ou des étourdissements. Lui conseiller de ne pas conduire et d'éviter les activités qui exigent sa vigilance jusqu'à ce qu'on ait la certitude que le médicament n'entraîne pas ces effets chez lui.

GÉR.: Enseigner au patient âgé et à ses proches les mesures préventives pour réduire le risque de chutes.

- Recommander au patient d'éviter de boire de l'alcool ou de prendre des dépresseurs du SNC en même temps que cet agent.
- Conseiller au patient de consulter un professionnel de la santé avant de prendre un médicament en vente libre ou un produit naturel en même temps que le chlordiazépoxide.
- Conseiller à la patiente de prévenir le médecin si elle prévoit devenir enceinte ou si elle pense l'être.

VÉRIFICATION DE L'EFFICACITÉ THÉRAPEUTIQUE

L'efficacité du traitement peut être démontrée par: la diminution du sentiment d'anxiété ■ une meilleure capacité d'adaptation ■ la diminution des tremblements et un enchaînement des idées plus logique lors du traitement des symptômes du sevrage alcoolique.

CHLOROQUINE

Aralen, Novo-Chloroquine

CLASSIFICATION:

Anti-infectieux (antipaludéen)

Grossesse – catégorie C

INDICATIONS

Traitement suppressif des crises aiguës de paludisme (malaria) ■ Traitement de l'amibiase extra-intestinale (hépatique). **Usages non approuvés**: Traitement de la polyarthrite rhumatoïde grave et du lupus érythémateux disséminé.

MÉCANISME D'ACTION

Inhibition de la synthèse protéique des microorganismes sensibles par inhibition de la polymérase de l'ADN et de l'ARN. ***Effets thérapeutiques:*** Destruction des plasmodies qui provoquent le paludisme ■ Élimination de l'amibiase.

PHARMACOCINÉTIQUE

Absorption: Près de 90 % (PO).

Distribution: L'agent se répartit dans tout l'organisme et atteint de fortes concentrations tissulaires. Il traverse la barrière placentaire et passe dans le lait maternel.

Métabolisme et excrétion: Métabolisme hépatique (30 %). Le métabolite exerce aussi un effet antiplasmodial. Excrétion rénale à l'état inchangé (70 %).

Demi-vie: De 72 à 120 heures.

Profil temps-action (effet antipaludique)

	DÉBUT D'ACTION	PIC	DURÉE
PO	rapide	1 - 2 h	plusieurs jours - semaines

CONTRE-INDICATIONS, PRÉCAUTIONS ET MISES EN GARDE

Contre-indications: Hypersensibilité au médicament ■ Hypersensibilité aux dérivés de 4-aminoquinoline (hydroxychloroquine) ■ Lésions oculaires provoquées par la chloroquine ou les dérivés de 4-aminoquinoline.

Précautions et mises en garde: Maladie hépatique ■ Alcoolisme ■ Traitement par des médicaments hépatotoxiques ■ Psoriasis ■ Insuffisance en G-6-PD ■ Aplasie médullaire ■ Grossesse.

RÉACTIONS INDÉSIRABLES ET EFFETS SECONDAIRES

SNC: céphalées, fatigue, nervosité, anxiété, irritation, modification de la personnalité, confusion, CONVULSIONS, étourdissements.

ORLO: troubles visuels, kératite, rétinopathie, ototoxicité.

CV: hypotension, modifications de l'ÉCG.

GI: gêne épigastrique, anorexie, nausées, vomissements, crampes abdominales, diarrhée.

GU: urine de couleur jaune rouille ou brune.

Tég.: modifications de la pigmentation, alopécie, prurit, photosensibilité, éruptions cutanées, dermatoses.

Hémat.: leucopénie, thrombopénie, agranulocytose, ANÉMIE APLASIQUE.

SN: névrite périphérique, neuromyopathie.

INTERACTIONS

Médicament-médicament: L'administration concomitante d'autres **agents hépatotoxiques** peut accroître le risque d'hépatotoxicité ■ La **pénicillamine** augmente le risque de toxicité hématologique ■ L'administration concomitante d'**agents dotés de propriétés toxidermiques** peut accroître le risque de toxidermie ■ L'administration concomitante d'un **vaccin antirabique** obtenu sur des cellules diploïdes humaines peut réduire le titrage des anticorps de la rage ■ Les **acidifiants urinaires** peuvent accroître l'excrétion urinaire de la chloroquine et en réduire l'efficacité.

Médicament-aliments: Les **aliments qui acidifient l'urine** (voir l'annexe J) peuvent augmenter l'excrétion du médicament et en diminuer l'efficacité.

VOIES D'ADMINISTRATION ET POSOLOGIE

Paludisme (traitement suppressif)

- **PO (adultes)**: 500 mg (300 mg de base), 1 fois par semaine. Il faudrait commencer le traitement 2 semaines avant d'entrer dans la région impaludée et le poursuivre pendant 8 semaines après l'avoir quittée.
- **PO (enfants)**: 5 mg de base/kg, 1 fois par semaine. Il faudrait commencer le traitement 2 semaines avant d'entrer dans la région impaludée et le poursuivre pendant 8 semaines après l'avoir quittée. Dose maximale: 500 mg (300 mg de base) par jour, sans égard au poids.

Paludisme (crise aiguë)

- **PO (adultes)**: Initialement 1 g (600 mg de base), suivi de 500 mg (300 mg de base), de 6 à 8 heures plus tard et d'une dose supplémentaire de 500 mg (300 mg de base) pendant 2 jours consécutifs. Dose totale: 2,5 g de phosphate de chloroquine ou 1,5 g de base en 3 jours.
- **PO (nourrissons et enfants)**: Une dose représentant 25 mg de base/kg est administrée en 3 jours comme suit: *première dose* – 10 mg de base/kg (mais sans dépasser 600 mg de base en une seule dose); *deuxième dose* – 5 mg de base/kg (mais sans

dépasser 300 mg de base en une seule dose), 6 heures après la première dose; *troisième dose* – 5 mg de base/kg, 18 heures après la deuxième dose; *quatrième dose* – 5 mg de base/kg, 24 heures après la troisième dose.

C

Amibiase extra-intestinale

- **PO (adultes)**: 1 g (600 mg de base), 1 fois par jour pendant 2 jours, puis 500 mg (300 mg de base), 1 fois par jour pendant au moins 2 à 3 semaines.

PRÉSENTATION

Comprimés: 250 mg[Pr] (équivalant à 150 mg de chloroquine base).

SOINS INFIRMIERS

ÉVALUATION DE LA SITUATION

- Recueillir des données sur les symptômes qui se sont manifestés avant l'administration du médicament.
- Évaluer le réflexe tendineux régulièrement afin de déceler toute faiblesse musculaire. Parfois, il faut arrêter le traitement si celle-ci se manifeste.

Paludisme ou amibiase: Observer quotidiennement l'amélioration des signes et des symptômes de la maladie pendant toute la durée du traitement.

Tests de laboratoire: Examiner régulièrement les numérations globulaire et plaquettaire pendant toute la durée du traitement. Le nombre de leucocytes et de plaquettes peut chuter.

DIAGNOSTICS INFIRMIERS POSSIBLES

- Risque d'infection (Indications).
- Connaissances insuffisantes sur le traitement médicamenteux (Enseignement au patient et à ses proches).

INTERVENTIONS INFIRMIÈRES

- Dans le cas d'un traitement prophylactique de la malaria, la prise de la chloroquine doit commencer 2 semaines avant l'exposition anticipée et se poursuivre pendant les 8 semaines qui suivent le jour où on quitte la région impaludée.
- Administrer le médicament avec du lait ou des aliments afin de réduire les troubles gastro-intestinaux.
- Dans le cas des patients qui éprouvent des difficultés de déglutition, on peut écraser les comprimés et introduire la poudre dans des capsules vides. Le pharmacien peut aussi préparer une suspension.

ENSEIGNEMENT AU PATIENT ET À SES PROCHES

- Expliquer au patient qu'il doit respecter rigoureusement la posologie recommandée et continuer à prendre le médicament même s'il se sent mieux. S'il n'a pas pu prendre le médicament au moment habituel, il doit le prendre aussitôt que possible. Par ailleurs, s'il doit prendre le médicament plusieurs fois par jour, il doit prendre la dose oubliée dans l'heure suivant le moment habituel ou sauter cette dose. Il ne faut jamais remplacer une dose manquée par une double dose.
- Dans le cas où le médicament est pris en prophylaxie, il faut déterminer les moyens de réduire l'exposition aux moustiques: utiliser un insectifuge, porter des chemises à manches longues et des pantalons, se protéger par une moustiquaire.
- Prévenir le patient que la chloroquine peut provoquer des étourdissements et de la somnolence. Lui conseiller de ne pas conduire et d'éviter les activités qui exigent sa vigilance jusqu'à ce qu'on ait la certitude que le médicament n'entraîne pas ces effets chez lui.
- Recommander au patient d'éviter de boire de l'alcool pendant qu'il prend de la chloroquine.
- Prévenir le patient qu'il doit garder la chloroquine hors de la portée des enfants. On a signalé des décès d'enfants après l'ingestion de 3 ou de 4 comprimés.
- Expliquer au patient recevant un traitement de longue durée à doses élevées l'importance d'un suivi ophtalmique régulier. L'informer que le risque de lésions oculaires peut être réduit par le port de verres fumés lorsque la lumière est vive. Lui conseiller de porter des vêtements protecteurs et d'utiliser un écran solaire pour réduire le risque de dermatoses.
- Prévenir le patient que la chloroquine peut rendre l'urine de couleur rouille ou brune.
- Recommander au patient de signaler immédiatement à un professionnel de la santé les symptômes suivants: maux de gorge, fièvre, saignements ou ecchymoses inhabituels, vision trouble, difficultés de lecture, modifications de la vue, acouphènes, troubles auditifs, modifications de l'état de conscience ou faiblesse musculaire. La plupart de ces réactions indésirables sont reliées à la dose.

VÉRIFICATION DE L'EFFICACITÉ THÉRAPEUTIQUE

L'efficacité du traitement peut être démontrée par: la prévention ou la diminution des signes et des symptômes de paludisme ▪ l'amélioration des signes et des symptômes d'amibiase.

CHLORPHÉNIRAMINE

Chlor-Tripolon, Novo-Pheniram

CLASSIFICATION:

Antihistaminique

Grossesse – catégorie B

INDICATIONS

Soulagement des symptômes d'allergie attribuables à la libération de l'histamine, dont: les rhinites allergiques ■ les dermatoses allergiques ■ Traitement des allergies graves ou des réactions d'hypersensibilité incluant les réactions aux médicaments et l'œdème angioneurotique (de Quincke).

MÉCANISME D'ACTION

Inhibition des effets de l'histamine au niveau des récepteurs H_1; l'agent ne se lie pas à l'histamine, ni ne l'inactive ■ Effets anticholinergiques. ***Effets thérapeutiques:*** Diminution des symptômes associés à un excès d'histamine: éternuements, rhinorrhée, prurit nasal et oculaire, larmoiements et rougeurs oculaires.

PHARMACOCINÉTIQUE

Absorption: Bonne (PO).

Distribution: Tout l'organisme. Une très faible quantité est excrétée dans le lait maternel. L'agent traverse la barrière hématoencéphalique.

Métabolisme et excrétion: Métabolisme majoritairement hépatique.

Demi-vie: De 12 à 15 heures.

Profil temps-action (effet antihistaminique)

	DÉBUT D'ACTION	PIC	DURÉE
PO	15 – 30 min	6 h	4 – 12 h
PO-LP†	inconnu	Inconnu	8 – 24 h

† LP = libération prolongée.

CONTRE-INDICATIONS, PRÉCAUTIONS ET MISES EN GARDE

Contre-indications: Hypersensibilité ■ Traitement concomitant par un IMAO ■ **PÉD.**: Nouveau-nés ou prématurés.

Précautions et mises en garde: Glaucome à angle fermé ■ Ulcère gastroduodénal sténosé ■ Obstruction pyloroduodénale ■ Hyperplasie de la prostate ■ Obstruction du col de la vessie ■ Maladie cardiovasculaire (y compris l'hypertension) ■ Hyperthyroïdie ■ Maladie hépatique ■ **GÉR.**: Plus grand risque de réactions indésirables anticholinergiques ■ **OBST.**: L'innocuité du médicament n'a pas été établie ■ Crise aiguë d'asthme ■ **ALLAITEMENT**: L'innocuité du médicament n'a pas été établie ■ **PÉD.**: L'innocuité du médicament n'a pas été établie chez les enfants < 2 ans. L'innocuité des comprimés à libération prolongée n'a pas été établie chez les enfants < 12 ans ■ Intolérance connue à l'alcool (certaines présentations liquides).

C

RÉACTIONS INDÉSIRABLES ET EFFETS SECONDAIRES

SNC: somnolence, étourdissements, excitation (enfants).

ORLO: vision trouble.

CV: arythmies, hypotension, palpitations.

GI: sécheresse de la bouche (xérostomie), constipation, occlusion intestinale.

GU: rétention urinaire, retard de la miction avec effort pour uriner.

INTERACTIONS

Médicament-médicament: Effets additifs sur la dépression du SNC lors de l'usage concomitant d'autres **dépresseurs du SNC**, dont l'**alcool**, les **analgésiques opioïdes** et les **hypnosédatifs** ■ Les **IMAO** prolongent et accentuent les propriétés anticholinergiques des antihistaminiques (risque d'hypotension grave) ■ Effets anticholinergiques additifs lors de l'administration concomitante de **médicaments dotés de propriétés anticholinergiques**, notamment les **antidépresseurs**, l'**atropine**, l'**halopéridol**, les **phénothiazines**, la **quinidine** et le **disopyramide**.

VOIES D'ADMINISTRATION ET POSOLOGIE

- **PO (adultes et enfants > 12 ans)**: *Comprimés* – 4 mg, toutes les 4 à 6 heures; *Comprimés à libération prolongée* – 12 mg, toutes les 12 heures (ne pas dépasser 24 mg par jour); *Sirop* – de 2,5 à 5 mg (de 5 à 10 mL), toutes les 6 à 8 heures.
- **PO (enfants de 6 à 12 ans)**: *Comprimés* – 2 mg, toutes les 6 à 8 heures. *Sirop* – de 1,25 à 2,5 mg (de 2,5 à 5 mL), toutes les 6 à 8 heures.

PRÉSENTATION (version générique disponible)

Comprimés: 4 mg[VL] ■ **Comprimés à libération prolongée**: 12 mg[VL] ■ **Sirop**: 2,5 mg/5 mL[VL] ■ **En association avec**: divers décongestionnants[Pr, VL].

SOINS INFIRMIERS

ÉVALUATION DE LA SITUATION

C

- Avant l'administration initiale et à intervalles réguliers pendant toute la durée du traitement, rester à l'affût des symptômes suivants d'allergie : rhinite, conjonctivite et urticaire.

GÉR. : Rester à l'affût des effets secondaires anticholinergiques suivants chez les patients âgés : délire, confusion aiguë, étourdissements, xérostomie, vision trouble, rétention urinaire, constipation, tachycardie.

- Ausculter le murmure vésiculaire et noter les caractéristiques des sécrétions bronchiques. Maintenir l'apport de liquides entre 1 500 et 2 000 mL par jour pour diminuer la viscosité des sécrétions.

Tests de laboratoire : Le médicament peut inhiber les réactions positives aux épreuves de sensibilité cutanée ou en réduire l'intensité ; arrêter le traitement 48 heures avant d'effectuer ces épreuves.

DIAGNOSTICS INFIRMIERS POSSIBLES

- Dégagement inefficace des voies respiratoires (Indications).
- Risque d'accident (Réactions indésirables).
- Connaissances insuffisantes sur le traitement médicamenteux (Enseignement au patient et à ses proches).

INTERVENTIONS INFIRMIÈRES

PO : Administrer le médicament avec des aliments ou du lait afin de réduire l'irritation gastro-intestinale. LES COMPRIMÉS À LIBÉRATION PROLONGÉE DOIVENT ÊTRE AVALÉS TELS QUELS, SANS ÊTRE ÉCRASÉS, COUPÉS OU MÂCHÉS.

ENSEIGNEMENT AU PATIENT ET À SES PROCHES

- Expliquer au patient qu'il doit respecter rigoureusement la posologie recommandée.

GÉR. : Expliquer au patient âgé et à sa famille comment reconnaître les effets secondaires anticholinergiques. Leur conseiller de prévenir un professionnel de la santé si ces effets persistent.

- Prévenir le patient que le médicament peut provoquer de la somnolence. Lui conseiller de ne pas conduire et d'éviter les activités qui exigent sa vigilance jusqu'à ce qu'on ait la certitude que le médicament n'entraîne pas cet effet chez lui.
- Mettre en garde le patient contre la consommation d'alcool ou d'autres dépresseurs du SNC en même temps que ce médicament.
- Conseiller au patient de pratiquer une bonne hygiène buccale, de se rincer la bouche avec de l'eau, de mâcher de la gomme ou de sucer des bonbons sans sucre pour diminuer la sécheresse de la bouche.
- Demander au patient de prévenir un professionnel de la santé si les symptômes persistent.

VÉRIFICATION DE L'EFFICACITÉ THÉRAPEUTIQUE

L'efficacité du traitement peut être démontrée par : la diminution des symptômes allergiques.

CHLORPROMAZINE

Novo-Chlorpromazine

CLASSIFICATION :

Antiémétique, antipsychotique (phénothiazine)

Grossesse – catégorie C

INDICATIONS

Traitement des troubles psychotiques ■ Prévention et traitement des nausées et des vomissements ■ Traitement de la porphyrie aiguë intermittente ■ Traitement d'appoint du tétanos ■ Soulagement du hoquet incoercible. **Usages non approuvés** : Traitement des céphalées vasculaires.

MÉCANISME D'ACTION

Modification des effets de la dopamine sur le SNC ■ Action anticholinergique et alpha-adrénolytique marquée. ***Effets thérapeutiques :*** Diminution des signes et des symptômes de psychose ■ Soulagement des nausées et des vomissements ; maîtrise du hoquet incoercible ■ Diminution des symptômes de porphyrie.

PHARMACOCINÉTIQUE

Absorption : Variable (comprimés), meilleures (PO – préparations liquides), bonne (IM).

Distribution : Tout l'organisme ; on en trouve de fortes concentrations dans le SNC. La chlorpromazine traverse la barrière placentaire et pénètre dans le lait maternel.

Liaison aux protéines : ≥ 90 %.

Métabolisme et excrétion : Fort métabolisme par le foie et la muqueuse gastro-intestinale. Substrat du CYP 2D6 et 3A4. Certains métabolites sont actifs.

Demi-vie : 30 heures.

Profil temps-action
(effets antipsychotiques, antiémétiques et sédatifs)

	Début d'action	Pic	Durée
PO	30 - 60 min	inconnu	4 - 6 h
IM	inconnu	inconnu	4 - 8 h
IV	rapide	inconnu	inconnue

CONTRE-INDICATIONS, PRÉCAUTIONS ET MISES EN GARDE

Contre-indications: Hypersensibilité ■ Risque de sensibilité croisée avec d'autres phénothiazines ■ Coma ■ Dépression grave du SNC induite par la prise de dépresseurs du SNC ■ Dyscrasie ou aplasie médullaire ■ Lésion de l'hypothalamus soupçonnée ou avérée (risque de réactions d'hyperthermie, avec des températures pouvant atteindre 40 °C; quelquefois ces réactions peuvent ne se manifester que 14 à 16 heures après l'administration du médicament) ■ Glaucome à angle fermé ■ Maladie hépatique ou cardiovasculaire grave.

Précautions et mises en garde: Gér.: Il est recommandé de réduire la dose initiale chez les personnes âgées ou débilitées ■ Diabète ■ Maladie respiratoire ■ Hyperplasie de la prostate ■ Tumeurs du SNC ■ Épilepsie ■ Occlusion intestinale ■ **Obst., Allaitement:** L'innocuité du médicament n'a pas été établie ■ Traitement concomitant par le pimozide.

RÉACTIONS INDÉSIRABLES ET EFFETS SECONDAIRES

SNC: SYNDROME MALIN DES NEUROLEPTIQUES, <u>sédation</u>, réactions extrapyramidales, dyskinésie tardive.

ORLO: <u>vision trouble</u>, <u>xérophtalmie</u>, opacité du cristallin.

CV: <u>hypotension</u> (surtout voies IM et IV), tachycardie.

GI: <u>constipation</u>, <u>sécheresse de la bouche (xérostomie)</u>, anorexie, hépatite, occlusion intestinale.

GU: rétention urinaire.

Tég.: <u>photosensibilité</u>, modification de la pigmentation, rash.

End.: galactorrhée.

Hémat.: AGRANULOCYTOSE, leucopénie.

Métab.: hyperthermie.

Divers: réactions allergiques.

INTERACTIONS

Médicament-médicament: L'usage concomitant de **pimozide** augmente le risque de réactions cardiovasculaires pouvant être graves ■ La chlorpromazine peut élever les concentrations sériques de **phénytoïne** ■ La chlorpromazine diminue l'effet vasopresseur de la **noradrénaline** et élimine la bradycardie ■ La chlorpromazine contrecarre la vasoconstriction périphérique induite par l'**adrénaline** et peut renverser certains de ses effets ■ La chlorpromazine peut réduire l'élimination de l'**acide valproïque** et en accroître les effets ■ La chlorpromazine peut réduire les effets pharmacologiques de l'**amphétamine** et des **substances apparentées** ■ La chlorpromazine peut réduire l'efficacité de la **bromocriptine** ■ La chlorpromazine peut élever les concentrations sériques des **antidépresseurs tricycliques** et en accroître les effets ■ Les **antiacides** ou les **antidiarrhéiques adsorbants** peuvent réduire l'adsorption de la chlorpromazine; les administrer 1 heure avant ou 2 heures après celle-ci ■ Le **charbon activé** réduit l'absorption de la chlorpromazine ■ Risque accru d'effets anticholinergiques lors de l'administration concomitante d'**antihistaminiques**, d'**antidépresseurs tricycliques**, de **quinidine** ou de **disopyramide** ■ La prémédication par la chlorpromazine augmente le risque d'excitation neuromusculaire et d'hypotension lors d'une anesthésie ultérieure par les **barbituriques** ■ Les **barbituriques** peuvent intensifier le métabolisme de la chlorpromazine et en réduire l'efficacité ■ La chlorpromazine peut réduire les concentrations sanguines des **barbituriques** ■ Effets additifs sur l'hypotension lors de l'administration concomitante d'**antihypertenseurs** ■ Effets additifs sur la dépression du SNC lors de l'usage concomitant d'**alcool**, d'**antidépresseurs**, d'**antihistaminiques**, d'**IMAO**, d'**analgésiques opiacés**, d'**hypnosédatifs** ou d'**anesthésiques généraux** ■ L'administration concomitante de **lithium** peut induire la désorientation, la perte de connaissance ou des symptômes extrapyramidaux ■ L'administration concomitante de **mépéridine** peut entraîner une sédation excessive et l'hypotension ■ L'administration concomitante de **propranolol** augmente les concentrations sériques des deux médicaments ■ Les **inhibiteurs du CYP 2D6/3A4** peuvent augmenter les concentrations, les effets thérapeutiques et la toxicité de la chlorpromazine. Parmi ces médicaments, citons: l'**amiodarone**, le **célécoxib**, la **chloroquine**, la **cimétidine**, la **clarithromycine**, l'**érythromycine**, la **fluoxétine**, l'**itraconazole**, le **kétoconazole**, la **méthadone**, le **métronidazole**, la **paroxétine**, la **quinidine** et le **ritonavir** ■ Les **inducteurs du CYP 2D6/3A4** peuvent diminuer l'efficacité de la chlorpromazine (p. ex., la **carbamazépine**, le **phénobarbital** et la **phénytoïne**).

Médicament-produits naturels: L'usage concomitant de **kava**, de **valériane**, de **camomille**, de **houblon** ou de **toque** peut augmenter les effets dépresseurs sur le SNC ■ L'usage concomitant de **datura** ou de **scopolia** peut amplifier les effets indésirables anticholinergiques.

C

VOIES D'ADMINISTRATION ET POSOLOGIE

- **PO (adultes):** *Troubles psychotiques* – dose initiale: de 25 à 75 mg par jour, en 2 à 4 doses fractionnées. On peut augmenter la dose de 20 à 50 mg, 2 fois par semaine. La dose quotidienne maximale est de 1 g. *Porphyrie aiguë intermittente* – de 25 à 50 mg, 3 ou 4 fois par jour. *Hoquet* – de 25 à 50 mg, 3 ou 4 fois par jour. Si le hoquet n'est pas maîtrisé après 2 ou 3 jours, on peut administrer de 25 à 50 mg par voie IM. *Nausées et vomissements* – de 10 à 25 mg, toutes les 4 heures, selon les besoins.
- **PO (enfants):** De 0,5 à 1 mg/kg, toutes les 4 à 6 heures, selon les besoins. Dose maximale: 40 mg par jour, si le poids de l'enfant est < 22,7 kg, et 75 mg par jour, si le poids de l'enfant se situe entre 22,7 et 45,5 kg.
- **IM (adultes):** *Troubles psychotiques* – 25 mg, pouvant être suivis de doses de 25 à 50 mg, 1 heure plus tard; augmenter cette dose jusqu'à un maximum de 400 mg, toutes les 4 à 6 heures, au besoin. *Porphyrie aiguë intermittente* – 25 mg, 3 ou 4 fois par jour. *Traitement d'appoint du tétanos* – de 25 à 50 mg, 3 ou 4 fois par jour. La dose peut aussi être administrée par voie IV. *Hoquet* – de 25 à 50 mg, 3 ou 4 fois par jour. *Nausées et vomissements* – de 25 à 50 mg, toutes les 3 à 4 heures.
- **IM (enfants > 6 mois):** *Traitement d'appoint du tétanos* – 0,55 mg/kg, 3 ou 4 fois par jour, par voie IM ou IV. La dose quotidienne maximale chez l'enfant pesant moins de 22,7 kg est de 40 mg/jour; si le poids se situe entre 22,7 et 45,5 kg, la dose quotidienne maximale est de 75 mg. *Soulagement des nausées et des vomissements* – de 0,5 à 1 mg/kg, toutes les 6 à 8 heures, selon les besoins.

PRÉSENTATION (version générique disponible)

Comprimés: 10 mg[Pr], 25 mg[Pr], 50 mg[Pr], 100 mg[Pr], 200 mg[Pr] ■ **Solution pour injection:** 25 mg/mL[Pr].

SOINS INFIRMIERS

ÉVALUATION DE LA SITUATION

- Évaluer l'état de conscience du patient (orientation, humeur, comportement) avant l'administration initiale et à intervalles réguliers pendant toute la durée du traitement.
- Mesurer la pression artérielle (en position assise, debout et couchée), le pouls et la fréquence respiratoire avant l'administration initiale et à intervalles fréquents pendant la période d'adaptation de la posologie.
- Observer le patient attentivement lorsqu'on lui administre le médicament pour s'assurer qu'il l'a bien avalé.
- Noter la consommation de liquides et l'élimination intestinale. Accroître l'apport en liquide et en aliments riches en fibres pour réduire la constipation.
- Suivre le patient pour déceler l'apparition d'une akathisie (agitation ou besoin de bouger continuellement) et de symptômes extrapyramidaux (*symptômes parkinsoniens:* difficulté d'élocution ou de déglutition, perte d'équilibre, mouvements d'émiettement, faciès figé, démarche traînante, rigidité, tremblements; *symptômes dystoniques:* spasmes musculaires, torsions, secousses musculaires, incapacité de bouger les yeux, faiblesse des bras ou des jambes), tous les 2 mois pendant toute la durée du traitement et de 8 à 12 semaines après qu'il a pris fin. Prévenir le médecin ou un autre professionnel de la santé dès que ces symptômes apparaissent; il peut s'avérer nécessaire de réduire la dose ou d'abandonner le traitement. Le médecin peut recommander l'administration de trihexyphénidyle ou de diphenhydramine pour maîtriser ces symptômes.
- Rester à l'affût des symptômes de dyskinésie tardive (mouvements rythmiques et incontrôlables de la bouche, du visage et des membres; émission de bruits secs avec les lèvres ou la langue; gonflement des joues; mouvements masticatoires incontrôlables; mouvements rapides de la langue). Signaler immédiatement au médecin ces symptômes, qui peuvent être irréversibles.
- SUIVRE DE PRÈS L'APPARITION DES SYMPTÔMES SUIVANTS DU SYNDROME MALIN DES NEUROLEPTIQUES: FIÈVRE, DÉTRESSE RESPIRATOIRE, TACHYCARDIE, CONVULSIONS, DIAPHORÈSE, HYPERTENSION OU HYPOTENSION, PÂLEUR, FATIGUE, RIGIDITÉ MUSCULAIRE MARQUÉE, PERTE DE CONTRÔLE DE LA VESSIE. INFORMER IMMÉDIATEMENT LE MÉDECIN DE LA PRÉSENCE DE CES SYMPTÔMES.

Sédation préopératoire: Évaluer le degré d'anxiété avant et après l'administration du médicament.

Céphalées vasculaires: Évaluer le type, le siège, l'intensité et la durée de la douleur et des symptômes afférents.

Tests de laboratoire: NOTER À INTERVALLES RÉGULIERS LA NUMÉRATION GLOBULAIRE ET LA FORMULE LEUCOCYTAIRE, AINSI QUE LES RÉSULTATS DES TESTS DE LA FONCTION HÉPATIQUE ET DES EXAMENS OCULAIRES. LE MÉDICAMENT PEUT PROVOQUER UNE DIMINUTION DE L'HÉMATOCRITE ET DES CONCENTRATIONS D'HÉMOGLOBINE, DE LEUCOCYTES, DE GRANULOCYTES ET DE PLAQUETTES. IL PEUT ENTRAÎNER L'ÉLÉVATION DES CONCENTRATIONS DE BILIRUBINE, D'AST, D'ALT ET DE PHOSPHATASE ALCALINE. UNE AGRANULOCYTOSE PEUT

SE MANIFESTER DE 4 À 10 SEMAINES APRÈS LE DÉBUT DU TRAITEMENT, LAQUELLE DISPARAÎT DE 1 À 2 SEMAINES APRÈS QU'IL A PRIS FIN. ELLE PEUT RÉAPPARAÎTRE À LA REPRISE DU TRAITEMENT. Les anomalies des tests de la fonction hépatique peuvent dicter l'abandon du traitement. La chlorpromazine peut entraîner des résultats faussement positifs ou négatifs aux tests de grossesse et des résultats faussement négatifs au dosage de la bilirubine urinaire.

DIAGNOSTICS INFIRMIERS POSSIBLES

- Opérations de la pensée perturbées (Indications).
- Connaissances insuffisantes sur le traitement médicamenteux (Enseignement au patient et à ses proches).
- Non-observance du traitement médicamenteux (Enseignement au patient et à ses proches).

INTERVENTIONS INFIRMIÈRES

- NE PAS CONFONDRE LA CHLORPROMAZINE AVEC LE CHLORPROPAMIDE OU LA PROCHLORPÉRAZINE.
- Recommander au patient de rester couché pendant au moins 30 minutes après l'administration parentérale afin de réduire les effets hypotenseurs de la chlorpromazine.
- Éviter les éclaboussures sur les mains, étant donné les risques de dermatite de contact.
- Interrompre le traitement aux phénothiazines 48 heures avant une myélographie au métrizamide et ne le reprendre que 24 heures plus tard, car ces médicaments abaissent le seuil de convulsion.

Hoquet: On doit administrer le traitement par voie orale. Si le hoquet persiste pendant 2 ou 3 jours, on peut administrer une injection par voie IM, suivie d'une perfusion IV.

PO: Administrer le médicament avec des aliments, du lait ou un grand verre d'eau afin de diminuer l'irritation gastrique. Les comprimés peuvent être broyés. Diluer les gouttes, juste avant de les administrer, dans 120 mL de café, de thé, de jus de tomate ou de fruit, de lait, d'eau, de soupe ou de boissons gazeuses.

IM: Ne pas injecter par voie SC. Administrer lentement et en profondeur dans un muscle bien développé. On peut diluer l'agent dans une solution de NaCl 0,9 % ou de procaïne à 2 %. Même si la solution prend une couleur jaune citron, sa puissance n'est en rien altérée. Ne pas administrer la solution si elle a fortement changé de couleur ou si elle renferme un précipité. Consulter les directives de chaque fabricant avant de reconstituer la préparation.

IV directe: Diluer dans une solution de NaCl 0,9 % pour obtenir une concentration maximale de 1 mg/mL. Consulter les directives de chaque fabricant avant de reconstituer la préparation.

Vitesse d'administration: Administrer lentement, à un débit d'au moins 1 mg/min (adultes) ou d'au moins 0,5 mg/min (enfants).

Perfusion continue: On peut diluer de 25 à 50 mg de solution dans 500 à 1 000 mL de D5%E ou D10%E, de NaCl 0,45 % ou 0,9 %, de solution de Ringer ou de lactate de Ringer ou de D5%E dans une solution de Ringer ou de dextrose dans une solution de lactate de Ringer. Consulter les directives de chaque fabricant avant de reconstituer la préparation.

Associations compatibles dans la même seringue: atropine ■ benztropine ■ butorphanol ■ diphenhydramine ■ doxapram ■ dropéridol ■ fentanyl ■ glycopyrrolate ■ hydromorphone ■ hydroxyzine ■ mépéridine ■ métoclopramide ■ midazolam ■ morphine ■ pentazocine ■ scopolamine.

Associations incompatibles dans la même seringue: cimétidine ■ dimenhydrinate ■ héparine ■ pentobarbital ■ thiopental.

Compatibilité (tubulure en Y): cisplatine ■ cladribine ■ cyclophosphamide ■ cytarabine ■ doxorubicine ■ famotidine ■ filgrastim ■ fluconazole ■ granisétron ■ héparine ■ hydrocortisone sodique, succinate d' ■ ondansétron ■ potassium, chlorure de ■ propofol ■ téniposide ■ thiotépa ■ vinorelbine ■ vitamines du complexe B avec C.

Incompatibilité (tubulure en Y): allopurinol ■ amifostine ■ aztréonam ■ céfépime ■ fludarabine ■ melphalan ■ méthotrexate ■ paclitaxel ■ pipéracilline/tazobactam ■ sargramostim.

ENSEIGNEMENT AU PATIENT ET À SES PROCHES

- Expliquer au patient qu'il doit respecter rigoureusement la posologie recommandée; l'avertir qu'il ne doit jamais sauter de dose ni remplacer une dose manquée par une double dose. L'inciter à prendre la dose oubliée en l'espace de 1 heure ou à l'omettre, puis à revenir à son horaire habituel. Le sevrage brusque peut provoquer une gastrite, des nausées, des vomissements, des étourdissements, des céphalées, de la tachycardie et de l'insomnie.
- Informer le patient qu'il risque de manifester des symptômes extrapyramidaux ou une dyskinésie tardive. Lui recommander de signaler immédiatement ces symptômes au médecin.
- Recommander au patient de changer lentement de position afin de réduire le risque d'hypotension orthostatique.
- Prévenir le patient que la chlorpromazine peut provoquer de la somnolence. Lui conseiller de ne pas

conduire et d'éviter les activités qui exigent sa vigilance jusqu'à ce qu'on ait la certitude que le médicament n'entraîne pas cet effet chez lui.

- Mettre en garde le patient contre la consommation d'alcool ou d'autres dépresseurs du SNC avec ce médicament.
- Recommander au patient d'utiliser un écran solaire et de porter des vêtements protecteurs lors des expositions au soleil, car, sur les surfaces exposées, la couleur de la pigmentation peut changer temporairement (allant de jaune brun au mauve gris). Lui recommander également d'éviter les températures extrêmes, les exercices vigoureux, les sorties par temps chaud, les douches ou les bains chauds, car ce médicament altère la thermorégulation.
- Conseiller au patient de se rincer fréquemment la bouche, de pratiquer une bonne hygiène buccale et de consommer de la gomme ou des bonbons sans sucre pour soulager la sécheresse de la bouche. Lui recommander de consulter un médecin ou un dentiste si la sécheresse de la bouche persiste pendant plus de 2 semaines.
- Expliquer au patient qu'il ne doit pas prendre la chlorpromazine dans les 2 heures suivant la prise d'antiacides ou d'antidiarrhéiques.
- Informer le patient que la chlorpromazine peut rendre l'urine rose ou rouge brun.
- Recommander au patient qui doit suivre un traitement dentaire ou subir une intervention chirurgicale d'avertir le professionnel de la santé qu'il suit un traitement par ce médicament.
- Informer le patient qu'il doit prévenir sans délai un professionnel de la santé en cas de maux de gorge, de fièvre, de saignements ou d'ecchymoses inhabituels, de rash, de faiblesse, de tremblements, de troubles de la vue, d'urine de couleur foncée ou de selles grises.
- Insister sur l'importance des examens réguliers de suivi et de la psychothérapie, le cas échéant.

VÉRIFICATION DE L'EFFICACITÉ THÉRAPEUTIQUE

L'efficacité du traitement peut être démontrée par: la diminution de l'excitation et un moindre recours au comportement paranoïde ou au repli sur soi; les effets thérapeutiques peuvent ne pas se manifester avant 7 à 8 semaines ■ le soulagement des nausées et des vomissements ■ le soulagement du hoquet ■ la sédation préopératoire ■ le soulagement des symptômes de porphyrie ■ le soulagement des céphalées vasculaires. ✳

CHLORPROPAMIDE,

voir Hypoglycémiants (oraux)

CHLORTHALIDONE,

voir Diurétiques (thiazidiques)

CHLORZOXAZONE

Acetazone Forte, Parafon Forte, Tylenol Douleurs Musculaires

CLASSIFICATION:

Relaxant musculosquelettique (à action centrale), analgésique

Grossesse – catégorie C

INDICATIONS

Adjuvant thérapeutique au repos, à la physiothérapie et à d'autres mesures pour soulager les malaises associés à des troubles musculosquelettiques aigus et douloureux.

MÉCANISME D'ACTION

Relaxation des muscles squelettiques, probablement grâce à des propriétés sédatives. ***Effets thérapeutiques:*** Relaxation des muscles squelettiques et diminution de la douleur.

PHARMACOCINÉTIQUE

Absorption: Complète (PO).

Distribution: Inconnue.

Métabolisme et excrétion: Métabolisme majoritairement hépatique; moins de 1 % est excrété à l'état inchangé dans l'urine.

Demi-vie: 1,1 heure.

Profil temps-action (relaxation des muscles squelettiques)

	DÉBUT D'ACTION	PIC	DURÉE
PO	en l'espace de 1 h	1 – 2 h	3 – 4 h

CONTRE-INDICATIONS, PRÉCAUTIONS ET MISES EN GARDE

Contre-indications: Hypersensibilité ■ Porphyrie ■ Troubles hépatiques.

Précautions et mises en garde: Maladie cardiovasculaire sous-jacente ■ Insuffisance rénale ■ **OBST., ALLAITEMENT,**

PÉD.: L'innocuité du médicament n'a pas été établie ■ **GÉR.**: Piètre tolérance à cause des effets anticholinergiques.

RÉACTIONS INDÉSIRABLES ET EFFETS SECONDAIRES

SNC: étourdissements, somnolence.
GI: SAIGNEMENTS GASTRO-INTESTINAUX, constipation, diarrhée, brûlures d'estomac, nausées, vomissements.
Tég.: dermatite allergique.
Divers: réactions allergiques, incluant l'ŒDÈME DE QUINCKE.

INTERACTIONS

Médicament-médicament: La chlorzoxazone exerce un effet additif sur la dépression du SNC lors de l'usage concomitant d'autres **dépresseurs du SNC**, comprenant l'**alcool**, les **antihistaminiques**, les **antidépresseurs**, les **analgésiques opioïdes** et les **hypnosédatifs**.
Médicament-produits naturels: Le **kava**, la **valériane**, la **scutellaire**, la **camomille** et le **houblon**, consommés en concomitance, peuvent accentuer la dépression du SNC.

VOIES D'ADMINISTRATION ET POSOLOGIE

PO (adultes et enfants > 12 ans): 500 mg, 4 fois par jour. Dose maximale quotidienne: 2 g.

PRÉSENTATION (version générique disponible)

Comprimés: 250 mg[Pr] en association avec 300 mg d'acétaminophène par comprimé.

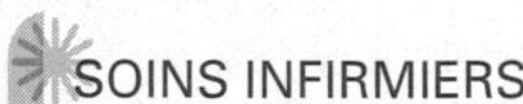

SOINS INFIRMIERS

ÉVALUATION DE LA SITUATION

- Noter l'intensité de la douleur, le degré de rigidité des muscles et l'amplitude des mouvements avant l'administration du médicament et à intervalles réguliers pendant toute la durée du traitement.

GÉR.: Rester à l'affût des effets anticholinergiques (somnolence et fatigue).

DIAGNOSTICS INFIRMIERS POSSIBLES

- Douleur aiguë (Indications).
- Mobilité physique réduite (Indications).
- Risque d'accident (Effets secondaires).

INTERVENTIONS INFIRMIÈRES

- Administrer la chlorzoxazone avec les repas pour réduire l'irritation gastrique. Les comprimés peuvent être écrasés et mélangés à des aliments ou à des liquides pour en faciliter l'administration.

ENSEIGNEMENT AU PATIENT ET À SES PROCHES

- Conseiller au patient de respecter rigoureusement la posologie recommandée. S'il n'a pu prendre le médicament au moment habituel, il doit le prendre dans l'heure qui suit. Sinon, il doit sauter cette dose et reprendre son horaire habituel. Le prévenir qu'il ne faut jamais remplacer une dose manquée par une double dose.
- Prévenir le patient que la chlorzoxazone peut provoquer des étourdissements ou de la somnolence. Lui conseiller de ne pas conduire et d'éviter les activités qui exigent sa vigilance jusqu'à ce qu'on ait la certitude que le médicament n'entraîne pas ces effets chez lui.
- Conseiller au patient d'éviter de boire de l'alcool et de prendre d'autres dépresseurs du SNC en même temps que ce médicament.
- Si la constipation pose problème, informer le patient que l'augmentation de la consommation de liquides et d'aliments riches en fibres et la prise de laxatifs émollients peuvent la soulager.

VÉRIFICATION DE L'EFFICACITÉ THÉRAPEUTIQUE

L'efficacité du traitement peut être démontrée par: le soulagement des spasmes musculaires associés aux maladies musculosquelettiques aiguës.

CHOLÉCALCIFÉROL (VITAMINE D_3),

voir Vitamine D (composés de)

CHOLESTYRAMINE,

voir Chélateurs des acides biliaires

CICLÉSONIDE,

voir Corticostéroïdes (inhalation)

CICLOPIROX,

voir Antifongiques topiques

C

CIDOFOVIR

Ce médicament n'est pas commercialisé au Canada. Disponible par l'intermédiaire du Programme d'accès spécial de Santé Canada

CLASSIFICATION:
Antiviral

Grossesse – catégorie C

INDICATIONS

Usages non approuvés: Traitement de la rétinite provoquée par le cytomégalovirus (CMV) chez les patients infectés par le VIH (en association avec le probénécide).

MÉCANISME D'ACTION

Suppression de la réplication du CMV par inhibition de la synthèse de l'ADN viral. ***Effets thérapeutiques:*** Ralentissement de l'évolution de la rétinite provoquée par le CMV; le cidofovir n'entraîne pas nécessairement la guérison.

PHARMACOCINÉTIQUE

Absorption: Biodisponibilité à 100 % (IV).
Distribution: Inconnue.
Métabolisme et excrétion: Excrétion majoritairement rénale à l'état inchangé.
Demi-vie: Inconnue.

Profil temps-action

	DÉBUT D'ACTION	PIC	DURÉE
IV	rapide	fin de la perfusion	inconnue

CONTRE-INDICATIONS, PRÉCAUTIONS ET MISES EN GARDE

Contre-indications: Hypersensibilité au cidofovir, au probénécide ou aux sulfamides ■ Créatinine sérique > 130 mmol/L; Cl_{Cr} ≤ 55 mL/min ou protéinurie ≥ 1 g/L (protéinurie ≥ 2 +) ■ Usage concomitant de médicaments néphrotoxiques (arrêter l'administration de ces médicaments 7 jours avant le début du traitement par le cidofovir) ■ Administration intraoculaire.
Précautions et mises en garde: OBST., PÉD.: L'innocuité du médicament n'a pas été établie ■ **ALLAITEMENT:** L'allaitement est déconseillé aux patientes séropositives ■ Risque d'abaissement de la pression intraoculaire qui peut être associé à une diminution de l'acuité visuelle ■ Risque de toxicité rénale ■ Risque de toxicité hématologique (neutropénie).
EXTRÊME PRUDENCE: TOUTE MALADIE OU TOUT MÉDICAMENT QUI AUGMENTE LE RISQUE DE DÉSHYDRATATION.

RÉACTIONS INDÉSIRABLES ET EFFETS SECONDAIRES

SNC: céphalées, faiblesse.
ORLO: diminution de la pression intraoculaire, baisse de l'acuité auditive, iritis, hypotonie oculaire, uvéite.
Resp.: dyspnée, pneumonie.
GI: DYSFONCTIONNEMENT HÉPATIQUE, PANCRÉATITE, douleurs abdominales, nausées, vomissements, anorexie, diarrhée.
GU: NÉPHROTOXICITÉ, protéinurie, syndrome de Toni-Fanconi.
Tég.: alopécie, rash.
HÉ: diminution des concentrations sériques de bicarbonate.
Hémat.: neutropénie, anémie.
Métab.: ACIDOSE MÉTABOLIQUE.
Divers: frissons, fièvre, infection.

INTERACTIONS

Médicament-médicament: Le risque de néphrotoxicité est accru lors de l'administration concomitante d'autres **médicaments néphrotoxiques** dont les **aminosides**, l'**amphotéricine B**, le **foscarnet,** la **vancomycine** et les **AINS** et elle devrait donc être évitée; attendre 7 jours après avoir administré d'autres agents néphrotoxiques ■ Le **probénécide**, qui doit être pris simultanément, peut interagir avec plusieurs médicaments dont l'**acétaminophène**, l'**acyclovir**, les **inhibiteurs de l'ECA**, les **barbituriques**, les **benzodiazépines**, le **bumétanide**, le **méthotrexate**, la **famotidine**, le **furosémide**, les **AINS**, la **théophylline** et la **zidovudine**.

VOIES D'ADMINISTRATION ET POSOLOGIE

- **IV (adultes):** 5 mg/kg, 1 fois par semaine, pendant 2 semaines, puis 5 mg/kg, toutes les 2 semaines (le cidofovir doit être administré en concomitance avec le probénécide).

INSUFFISANCE RÉNALE

- **IV (ADULTES):** *CRÉATININE SÉRIQUE DE 26 À 35 mmol/L SUPÉRIEURE AUX VALEURS DE BASE:* DIMINUER LA DOSE JUSQU'À 3 mg/kg; ARRÊTER LE TRAITEMENT SI CETTE ÉLÉVATION EST ≥ 44 mmol/L.

PRÉSENTATION

Ce médicament n'est pas commercialisé au Canada.
Solution pour injection: 75 mg/mL (fiole de 5 mL).

SOINS INFIRMIERS

ÉVALUATION DE LA SITUATION

- Suivre de près la vision afin de déceler l'évolution de la rétinite provoquée par le CMV. Surveiller à intervalles réguliers les symptômes oculaires, la pression intraoculaire et l'acuité visuelle.

- La prise d'antiémétiques et l'administration du médicament après un repas peuvent réduire les nausées et les vomissements associés au probénécide. En cas de réactions allergiques à l'association avec le probénécide, on devrait envisager une prémédication par des antihistaminiques ou de l'acétaminophène.
- Prendre les signes vitaux à intervalles réguliers. Le cidofovir peut provoquer de la fièvre, de l'hypotension et la tachycardie. Suivre de près les patients pour déceler les signes et symptômes précoces d'infection.

Tests de laboratoire:

- DANS LES 48 HEURES PRÉCÉDANT L'ADMINISTRATION DE CHAQUE DOSE ET TOUT AU LONG DU TRAITEMENT AU CIDOFOVIR, ON DOIT ÉVALUER LA FONCTION RÉNALE EN MESURANT LES CONCENTRATIONS SÉRIQUES DE CRÉATININE ET LA PROTÉINURIE. EN CAS DE PROTÉINURIE, HYDRATER LE PATIENT PAR VOIE IV ET RÉPÉTER LE DOSAGE DES PROTÉINES URINAIRES. SI LA FONCTION RÉNALE SE DÉTÉRIORE, ON DEVRAIT ENVISAGER UNE MODIFICATION DE LA DOSE OU L'ABANDON TEMPORAIRE DU TRAITEMENT.
- Noter la numération leucocytaire avant l'administration de chaque dose. Il y a risque de granulopénie.
- LE CIDOFOVIR PEUT PROVOQUER L'HYPERGLYCÉMIE, L'HYPERLIPIDÉMIE, L'HYPOCALCÉMIE, L'HYPOKALIÉMIE ET L'ÉLÉVATION DES CONCENTRATIONS SÉRIQUES DE PHOSPHATASE ALCALINE, D'AST ET D'ALT.

DIAGNOSTICS INFIRMIERS POSSIBLES

- Risque d'infection (Indications).
- Connaissances insuffisantes sur le traitement médicamenteux (Enseignement au patient et à ses proches).

INTERVENTIONS INFIRMIÈRES

- Le traitement par le cidofovir doit s'accompagner de l'administration de probénécide et d'une hydratation préalable du patient afin de réduire la toxicité rénale. On doit administrer 2 g de *probénécide* par voie orale 3 heures avant la perfusion par le cidofovir, puis administrer 1 g de plus, 2 heures et 8 heures après la fin de la perfusion. On doit *hydrater le patient* 1 ou 2 heures avant le traitement par le cidofovir en lui administrant 1 litre de NaCl 0,9 %. On recommande d'administrer un deuxième litre, en 1 à 3 heures, pendant le traitement par le cidofovir ou après celui-ci.
- Chez les patients qui ont reçu un médicament néphrotoxique dont le foscarnet, l'amphotéricine B, un aminoside, un AINS ou la pentamidine par voie IV, on doit attendre au moins 7 jours avant d'administrer le cidofovir.

Perfusion intermittente: Diluer dans 100 mL de NaCl 0,9 %. La solution est stable pendant 24 heures au réfrigérateur. Laisser la solution réfrigérée revenir à la température ambiante avant de l'administrer. Consulter les directives de chaque fabricant avant de reconstituer la préparation.

Vitesse d'administration: La perfusion doit durer 1 heure.

Incompatibilité en addition au soluté: Puisqu'on ne dispose d'aucune donnée à ce sujet, ne pas mélanger cet agent à d'autres solutions ou médicaments.

ENSEIGNEMENT AU PATIENT ET À SES PROCHES

- Expliquer au patient que le cidofovir ne guérit pas la rétinite à CMV et qu'elle peut continuer d'évoluer pendant et après le traitement.
- Informer le patient qu'il peut continuer de suivre son traitement antirétroviral. Cependant, il faudrait interrompre passagèrement le traitement par la zidovudine ou réduire de moitié la dose de ce médicament les jours du traitement par le cidofovir, en raison des effets du probénécide sur la zidovudine.
- INFORMER LE PATIENT DU RISQUE DE NÉPHROTOXICITÉ ASSOCIÉ AU TRAITEMENT PAR LE CIDOFOVIR. SOULIGNER L'IMPORTANCE DES EXAMENS DE SUIVI DE LA FONCTION RÉNALE.
- Informer la patiente des effets tératogènes possibles du cidofovir. Les femmes devraient utiliser une méthode de contraception tout au long du traitement et jusqu'à 1 mois après qu'il a pris fin. Les hommes devraient utiliser une barrière contraceptive pendant le traitement et jusqu'à 3 mois après qu'il a pris fin.
- Parler avec le patient du risque de perdre ses cheveux. Explorer avec lui les stratégies lui permettant de s'adapter à ce changement.
- Recommander au patient de passer les examens ophtalmologiques de routine après le traitement par le cidofovir.

VÉRIFICATION DE L'EFFICACITÉ THÉRAPEUTIQUE

L'efficacité du traitement peut être démontrée par: la diminution des symptômes et l'arrêt de l'évolution de la rétinite à CMV chez les patients infectés par le VIH. ✳

CILASTATINE,

voir Imipénem/cilastatine

CILAZAPRIL,
voir Inhibiteurs de l'enzyme de conversion de l'angiotensine (IECA)

C

CIMÉTIDINE,
voir Antagonistes des récepteurs H_2 de l'histamine

CIPROFLOXACINE,
voir Fluoroquinolones

ALERTE CLINIQUE

CISPLATINE
Cisplatine

CLASSIFICATION:
Antinéoplasique (alkylant)

Grossesse – catégorie D

INDICATIONS

En monothérapie ou en association (avec d'autres antinéoplasiques, la chirurgie ou la radiothérapie) dans les cas suivants: cancer métastatique des testicules et des ovaires ■ cancer avancé de la vessie ■ cancer de la tête et du cou ■ cancer cervical ■ cancer des poumons ■ cancer de l'œsophage ■ autres tumeurs.

MÉCANISME D'ACTION

Inhibition de la synthèse de l'ADN produisant des ponts intercaténaires dans l'ADN des cellules mères (effet indépendant du cycle cellulaire). ***Effets thérapeutiques:*** Destruction des cellules à réplication rapide et particulièrement des cellules malignes.

PHARMACOCINÉTIQUE

Absorption: Biodisponibilité à 100 % (IV).

Distribution: Le médicament se répartit dans la plupart des tissus; le platinium est encore présent dans les tissus pendant plusieurs mois après le traitement. Le médicament passe dans le lait maternel.

Métabolisme et excrétion: Excrétion majoritairement rénale.

Demi-vie: *Platinium* – de 30 à 100 heures.

Profil temps-action (effet sur la numération globulaire)

	DÉBUT D'ACTION	PIC	DURÉE
IV	inconnu	18 – 23 jours	39 jours

CONTRE-INDICATIONS, PRÉCAUTIONS ET MISES EN GARDE

Contre-indications: Hypersensibilité au cisplatine ou à d'autres composés renfermant du platine ■ Patients présentant une insuffisance rénale ou une surdité partielle à moins que le médecin et le patient jugent que les bienfaits possibles du traitement dépassent les risques ■ Aplasie médullaire.

Précautions et mises en garde: Surdité ■ Insuffisance rénale (réduire la dose) ■ Insuffisance cardiaque ■ Anomalies électrolytiques ■ Infection active ■ Maladies chroniques débilitantes ■ **OBST.**: Patientes en âge de procréer ■ Grossesse ou allaitement ■ **GÉR.**: Risque accru de néphrotoxicité et de neuropathie périphérique.

RÉACTIONS INDÉSIRABLES ET EFFETS SECONDAIRES

SNC: CONVULSIONS, malaises, faiblesse.

ORLO: ototoxicité, acouphènes, névrite optique.

GI: nausées intenses, vomissements, diarrhée, hépatotoxicité.

GU: néphrotoxicité, stérilité.

Tég.: alopécie.

HÉ: hypocalcémie, hypokaliémie, hypomagnésémie.

Hémat.: LEUCOPÉNIE, THROMBOPÉNIE, anémie.

Locaux: phlébite au point d'injection IV.

Métab.: hyperuricémie.

SN: neuropathie périphérique.

Divers: réactions anaphylactoïdes.

INTERACTIONS

Médicament-médicament: Effets néphrotoxiques et ototoxiques additifs lors de l'administration concomitante d'autres **médicaments néphrotoxiques** et **ototoxiques** (**aminosides**, **diurétiques de l'anse**) ■ Risque accru d'hypokaliémie et d'hypomagnésémie lors de l'administration concomitante de **diurétiques de l'anse** et d'**amphotéricine B** ■ Le cisplatine peut réduire les concentrations de **phénytoïne** ■ Effets additifs sur l'aplasie médullaire lors de l'administration concomitante d'autres **antinéoplasiques** ou d'une **radiothérapie** ■ Le médicament peut réduire la réponse des anticorps aux **vaccins à virus vivants** et augmenter le risque de réactions indésirables.

VOIES D'ADMINISTRATION ET POSOLOGIE

D'autres régimes posologiques sont aussi utilisés. La posologie peut être réduite en fonction de la chimiothérapie et de la radiothérapie déjà administrées.

- **IV (adultes)**: *Cancer métastatique des testicules* – 20 mg/m², pendant 5 jours. *Cancer métastatique des ovaires* – de 50 à 100 mg/m² en une seule dose, toutes les 3 ou 4 semaines, en association avec d'autres agents, ou 100 mg/m², toutes les 4 semaines, en monothérapie. *Cancer avancé de la vessie* – de 50 à 70 mg/m², toutes les 3 ou 4 semaines, en monothérapie.
- **IV (enfants)**: La posologie n'a pas été clairement établie. *Ostéosarcomes/neuroblastomes*: 90 mg/m², toutes les 3 semaines, ou 30 mg/m², toutes les semaines. *Tumeurs cérébrales récurrentes:* 60 mg/m², 1 fois par jour, pendant 2 jours, toutes les 3 ou 4 semaines.

PRÉSENTATION

Solution pour injection: 1 mg/mL, en fioles de 10 mg^Pr, 50 mg^Pr et 100 mg^Pr.

SOINS INFIRMIERS

ÉVALUATION DE LA SITUATION

- Mesurer la pression artérielle, le pouls, la fréquence respiratoire et la température à intervalles réguliers pendant l'administration du médicament. Informer le médecin de tout changement marqué.
- Effectuer le bilan des ingesta et des excreta et noter la densité de l'urine à intervalles réguliers pendant toute la durée du traitement. Prévenir le médecin dès que des écarts entre les valeurs totales surviennent. Afin de réduire le risque de toxicité rénale, maintenir une diurèse d'au moins 100 mL/h pendant les 4 heures qui précèdent le début de l'administration et pendant au moins 24 heures par la suite.
- Si son état le permet, encourager le patient à boire de 2 000 à 3 000 mL de liquides par jour pour favoriser l'excrétion d'acide urique. On peut administrer de l'allopurinol et un agent d'alcalinisation de l'urine pour prévenir la néphropathie.
- Vérifier fréquemment la perméabilité de la tubulure IV. L'extravasation de cisplatine peut provoquer une ulcération grave et la nécrose des tissus. En cas d'extravasation d'une grande quantité de solution très concentrée de cisplatine, mélanger 1,6 mL de thiosulfate sodique à 25 % avec 8,4 mL d'eau stérile et injecter de 1 à 4 mL (1 mL/mL de liquide extravasé) par la tubulure ou le cathéter en place. Injecter par voie SC si l'aiguille a été retirée. Le thiosulfate sodique inactive le cisplatine.
- Des nausées et des vomissements graves et prolongés peuvent survenir dans les 4 heures qui suivent le traitement; les vomissements peuvent persister pendant 24 heures. Administrer des antiémétiques par voie parentérale de 30 à 45 minutes avant le début du traitement et à intervalles réguliers pendant les 24 heures qui suivent. Noter la quantité de vomissures et prévenir le médecin ou un autre professionnel de la santé si elle dépasse celle dictée par les directives concernant la prévention de la déshydratation. Les nausées et l'anorexie peuvent persister pendant 1 semaine.
- RESTER À L'AFFÛT D'UNE DÉPRESSION MÉDULLAIRE. Suivre de près les saignements: saignement des gencives, formation d'ecchymoses, pétéchies, présence de sang occulte dans les selles, l'urine et les vomissures. Éviter les injections IM et la prise de température rectale si la numération plaquettaire est basse. Appliquer une pression sur les points de ponction veineuse pendant 10 minutes. En présence d'une neutropénie, rester à l'affût des signes d'infection. Une anémie peut survenir. Suivre de près les signes de fatigue accrue, de dyspnée et d'hypotension orthostatique.
- SUIVRE DE PRÈS LE PATIENT À LA RECHERCHE DES SIGNES SUIVANTS D'ANAPHYLAXIE: ŒDÈME FACIAL, RESPIRATION SIFFLANTE, ÉTOURDISSEMENTS, ÉVANOUISSEMENTS, TACHYCARDIE, HYPOTENSION. ARRÊTER L'ADMINISTRATION DU MÉDICAMENT IMMÉDIATEMENT ET EN PRÉVENIR LE MÉDECIN. GARDER À PORTÉE DE LA MAIN DE L'ADRÉNALINE ET LE MATÉRIEL DE RÉANIMATION.
- Le médicament peut entraîner une ototoxicité et une neurotoxicité. Observer étroitement le patient pour déceler les étourdissements, les acouphènes, la surdité, la perte de la coordination, l'agueusie ou la sensation de picotement dans les membres ou d'engourdissement des mains et des pieds. Ces symptômes peuvent être irréversibles. En informer immédiatement le médecin ou un autre professionnel de la santé. On recommande de soumettre le patient à un test audiométrique avant de démarrer le traitement et avant d'administrer chaque dose. La perte de l'acuité auditive est plus fréquente chez les enfants et porte d'abord sur les sons aigus; elle peut être unilatérale ou bilatérale.
- S'assurer que le patient ne reçoit pas une surdose de cisplatine. Des doses de plus de 100 mg/m²/cycle toutes les 3 ou 4 semaines sont rarement utilisées.

Bien distinguer la dose quotidienne de la dose totale par cycle. L'administration répétée de fortes doses entraîne des crampes musculaires (contractions musculaires involontaires, douloureuses, localisées, d'apparition rapide et de courte durée); elles sont habituellement associées à une neuropathie périphérique avancée.

Tests de laboratoire:

- NOTER LA NUMÉRATION GLOBULAIRE, LA FORMULE LEUCOCYTAIRE ET LA NUMÉRATION PLAQUETTAIRE AVANT L'ADMINISTRATION ET À INTERVALLES RÉGULIERS PENDANT TOUTE LA DURÉE DU TRAITEMENT. LES NADIRS DE LA LEUCOPÉNIE, DE LA THROMBOPÉNIE ET DE L'ANÉMIE SE PRODUISENT DANS LES 18 À 23 JOURS ET SE RÉTABLISSENT DANS LES 39 JOURS SUIVANT L'ADMINISTRATION DE LA PREMIÈRE DOSE. INTERROMPRE L'ADMINISTRATION DES DOSES ULTÉRIEURES JUSQU'AU MOMENT OÙ LE NOMBRE DE GLOBULES BLANCS EST SUPÉRIEUR À 4×10^9/L, ET CELUI DES PLAQUETTES, À 100×10^9/L.
- Noter les concentrations d'urée et de créatinine sérique et la clairance de la créatinine avant le début du traitement et avant chaque cycle pour déceler la néphrotoxicité. Le médicament peut entraîner une élévation des concentrations d'urée et de créatinine et une réduction des concentrations de calcium, de magnésium, de phosphate, de sodium et de potassium, qui surviennent habituellement durant la deuxième semaine qui suit l'administration de la dose. Ne pas administrer de doses additionnelles avant que la concentration d'urée ne descende au-dessous de 8,92 mmol/L, et celle de créatinine sérique, au-dessous de 133 µmol/L. Le médicament peut accroître les concentrations d'acide urique, qui atteignent habituellement un pic de 3 à 5 jours après l'administration d'une dose.
- Le médicament peut élever passagèrement les concentrations sériques de bilirubine et d'AST.
- Le cisplatine peut entraîner des résultats faussement positifs au test de Coombs.

DIAGNOSTICS INFIRMIERS POSSIBLES

- Risque d'infection (Réactions indésirables).
- Risque d'accident (Effets secondaires).
- Connaissances insuffisantes sur le traitement médicamenteux (Enseignement au patient et à ses proches).

INTERVENTIONS INFIRMIÈRES

ALERTE CLINIQUE: DES DÉCÈS SONT SURVENUS LORS DE CERTAINES CHIMIOTHÉRAPIES. AVANT D'ADMINISTRER L'AGENT, CLARIFIER TOUS LES POINTS AMBIGUS. VÉRIFIER LA LIMITE DES DOSES UNITAIRES ET QUOTIDIENNES AINSI QUE LA DOSE À ADMINISTRER PENDANT LE TRAITEMENT. DEMANDER À UN DEUXIÈME PROFESSIONNEL DE LA SANTÉ DE VÉRIFIER UNE FOIS DE PLUS L'ORDONNANCE D'ORIGINE, LES CALCULS ET LE RÉGLAGE DE LA POMPE À PERFUSION.

- NE PAS CONFONDRE LE CISPLATINE ET LE CARBOPLATINE. POUR ÉVITER TOUTE CONFUSION, LES ORDONNANCES DEVRAIENT INDIQUER LES NOMS GÉNÉRIQUE ET COMMERCIAL. ADMINISTRER SOUS LA SUPERVISION D'UN MÉDECIN EXPÉRIMENTÉ DANS L'UTILISATION DES ANTINÉOPLASIQUES.
- Hydrater le patient avec au moins 1 à 2 litres de liquide par voie IV, de 8 à 12 heures avant d'amorcer le traitement par le cisplatine. On peut administrer de l'amifostine pour réduire la néphrotoxicité.
- Ne pas utiliser d'aiguilles ou de matériel en aluminium au cours de la préparation de la solution ou de son administration. Par suite d'une réaction chimique entre l'aluminium et le cisplatine, il se forme un précipité noir ou brun qui rend le médicament inefficace.
- Ne pas réfrigérer.
- Préparer les solutions sous une hotte à flux laminaire. Porter des gants, un vêtement protecteur et un masque pendant la manipulation de ce médicament. Si la poudre ou la solution entre en contact avec la peau ou les muqueuses, nettoyer la région à fond avec de l'eau et du savon. Jeter le matériel dans les contenants réservés à la mise au rebut (voir l'annexe H).

Perfusion intermittente:

- Ne pas réfrigérer pour éviter la formation de cristaux. La solution devrait être transparente et incolore; ne pas l'utiliser si elle est trouble ou si elle contient un précipité. Consulter les directives de chaque fabricant avant de reconstituer la préparation.
- On recommande de diluer l'agent dans 2 L de D5%E/NaCl 0,3 % ou D5%E/NaCl 0,45 % renfermant 37,5 g de mannitol.

Vitesse d'administration: Administrer la solution en 6 à 8 heures.

Perfusion continue: Le cisplatine a déjà été administré en perfusion continue pendant une période allant de 24 heures à 5 jours; grâce à cette méthode, les nausées et les vomissements ont diminué.

ALERTE CLINIQUE: DEMANDER AU MÉDECIN SI LA DOSE QU'IL RECOMMANDE EST CUMULATIVE OU QUOTIDIENNE; UNE ERREUR POURRAIT AVOIR DES CONSÉQUENCES FATALES.

Associations compatibles dans la même seringue: bléomycine ▪ cyclophosphamide ▪ doxapram ▪ doxorubicine ▪ dropéridol ▪ fluorouracile ▪ furosémide ▪ héparine

■ leucovorine calcique ■ méthotrexate ■ métoclopramide ■ mitomycine ■ vinblastine ■ vincristine.

Compatibilité (tubulure en Y): allopurinol ■ aztréonam ■ bléomycine ■ chlorpromazine ■ cladribine ■ cyclophosphamide ■ dexaméthasone ■ diphenhydramine ■ doxorubicine ■ dropéridol ■ famotidine ■ filgrastim ■ fludarabine ■ fluorouracile ■ furosémide ■ ganciclovir ■ granisétron ■ héparine ■ hydromorphone ■ leucovorine calcique ■ lorazépam ■ melphalan ■ méthotrexate ■ méthylprednisolone ■ métoclopramide ■ mitomycine ■ morphine ■ ondansétron ■ paclitaxel ■ prochlorpérazine, édisylate de ■ prométhazine ■ propofol ■ ranitidine ■ sargramostim ■ téniposide ■ vinblastine ■ vincristine ■ vinorelbine.

Incompatibilité (tubulure en Y): amifostine ■ céfépime ■ gallium, nitrate de ■ pipéracilline/tazobactam ■ thiotépa.

Compatibilité en addition au soluté: étoposide ■ floxuridine ■ ifosfamide ■ leucovorine calcique ■ magnésium, sulfate de ■ mannitol ■ ondansétron ■ solution de NaCl 0,9 % ■ solution de D5%E/NaCl 0,9 %.

Incompatibilité en addition au soluté: fluorouracile ■ mesna ■ sodium, bicarbonate de ■ thiotépa.

ENSEIGNEMENT AU PATIENT ET À SES PROCHES

- Inciter le patient à signaler immédiatement la douleur au point d'injection.
- Recommander au patient de signaler rapidement à un professionnel de la santé la fièvre, les frissons, la toux, l'enrouement, les maux de gorge, les signes d'infection, les douleurs lombaires ou aux flancs, les mictions difficiles ou douloureuses, le saignement des gencives, la formation d'ecchymoses, les pétéchies, la présence de sang dans les selles, l'urine ou les vomissements, une fatigue accrue, la dyspnée ou l'hypotension orthostatique. Expliquer au patient qu'il doit éviter les foules et les personnes contagieuses. Lui recommander d'utiliser une brosse à dents à poils doux et un rasoir électrique et le mettre en garde contre les chutes. Prévenir le patient qu'il ne doit pas consommer de boissons alcoolisées ni prendre de médicaments contenant de l'acide acétylsalicylique ou des AINS, car ces substances peuvent déclencher une hémorragie digestive.
- Recommander au patient de signaler rapidement au médecin les symptômes suivants: engourdissement ou picotements au niveau des membres ou du visage, perte de l'ouïe ou acouphènes, enflure inhabituelle ou douleurs articulaires.
- Recommander au patient de ne pas se faire vacciner sans la recommandation expresse du médecin.
- Expliquer à la patiente qu'elle doit prendre des mesures contraceptives, même si le cisplatine peut entraîner la stérilité.
- Conseiller au patient de se soumettre à intervalles réguliers à des examens diagnostiques permettant de suivre de près les effets secondaires du médicament.

VÉRIFICATION DE L'EFFICACITÉ THÉRAPEUTIQUE

L'efficacité du traitement peut être démontrée par: la diminution de la taille de la tumeur et le ralentissement de la propagation des métastases. Le traitement ne doit être administré que toutes les 3 ou 4 semaines et seulement si les valeurs de laboratoire s'inscrivent dans les limites acceptables et si le patient ne manifeste pas de signes d'ototoxicité ou d'autres réactions graves. ✳

CITALOPRAM

Apo-Citalopram, Celexa, Novo-Citalopram, PHL-Citalopram

CLASSIFICATION:

Antidépresseur (inhibiteur sélectif du recaptage de la sérotonine [ISRS])

Grossesse – catégorie C (risque durant le 3e trimestre; voir « Précautions et mises en garde »)

INDICATIONS

Soulagement des symptômes de la dépression, souvent en association avec la psychothérapie.

MÉCANISME D'ACTION

Inhibition sélective du recaptage de la sérotonine dans le SNC. ***Effets thérapeutiques:*** Effet antidépresseur.

PHARMACOCINÉTIQUE

Absorption: 80 % (PO).

Distribution: Le citalopram passe dans le lait maternel.

Métabolisme et excrétion: Fort métabolisme hépatique (10 %, par les enzymes CYP 3A4 et 2C19); excrétion à l'état inchangé dans l'urine.

Demi-vie: 35 heures.

Profil temps-action (effet antidépresseur)

	DÉBUT D'ACTION	PIC	DURÉE
PO	1 – 4 semaines	inconnu	inconnue

C

CONTRE-INDICATIONS, PRÉCAUTIONS ET MISES EN GARDE

Contre-indications: Hypersensibilité au citalopram ou aux excipients du médicament ■ Traitement concomitant par un IMAO (prévoir 14 jours entre l'arrêt de l'administration l'IMAO et le début de l'administration du citalopram, et vice versa) ■ Traitement concomitant par le pimozide.

Précautions et mises en garde: Antécédents de manie ■ Antécédents de troubles épileptiques ■ La surveillance des idées suicidaires est indiquée chez tous les patients recevant ce médicament ■ Maladie ou état qui risque de modifier le métabolisme ou la réponse hémodynamique ■ Insuffisance hépatique (la prudence est de mise; réduire la dose maximale) ■ Risque d'effets indésirables de type agitation grave, parallèlement à des blessures infligées à soi-même ou aux autres ■ Insuffisance rénale grave ■ **GÉR.**: Risque accru d'accumulation médicamenteuse et d'effets secondaires; il est recommandé d'utiliser une dose plus faible ■ **OBST.**: Il n'existe pas d'études adéquates menées chez la femme enceinte. N'administrer au cours de la grossesse que si les bienfaits éventuels pour la femme enceinte l'emportent sur les risques possibles pour le fœtus ■ Risque de complication chez le nouveau-né lorsque la mère a pris ce médicament durant le 3e trimestre ■ **ALLAITEMENT**: Risque de réactions indésirables graves chez le nouveau-né; il faut décider soit de cesser l'allaitement, soit de cesser la prise du médicament, compte tenu de l'importance du médicament pour la mère ■ **PÉD.**: L'innocuité et l'efficacité de l'agent n'ont pas été établies ■ Éviter de mettre fin abruptement au traitement, en raison du risque de symptômes de sevrage ■ Risque d'hyponatrémie et de syndrome de sécrétion inappropriée d'hormone antidiurétique (SIADH) surtout chez les femmes âgées.

RÉACTIONS INDÉSIRABLES ET EFFETS SECONDAIRES

SNC: apathie, confusion, somnolence, insomnie, faiblesse, agitation, amnésie, anxiété, baisse de la libido, étourdissements, fatigue, difficultés de concentration, dépression accrue, migraines, céphalées, tentative de suicide.

ORLO: accommodation anormale.

Resp.: toux.

CV: hypotension orthostatique, tachycardie.

GI: douleurs abdominales, anorexie, diarrhée, sécheresse de la bouche (xérostomie), dyspepsie, flatulence, ptyalisme, nausées, dysgueusie, gain d'appétit, vomissements.

GU: aménorrhée, dysménorrhée, retard de l'éjaculation, impuissance, polyurie.

Tég.: sécrétion excessive de sueur, photosensibilité, prurit, rash.

Métab.: perte pondérale, gain pondéral.

Loc.: arthralgie, myalgie.

SN: tremblements, paresthésie.

Divers: fièvre, bâillements.

INTERACTIONS

Médicament-médicament: LE CITALOPRAM PEUT PROVOQUER DES RÉACTIONS GRAVES, POUVANT ÊTRE D'ISSUE FATALE, EN CAS D'ADMINISTRATION CONCOMITANTE D'**IMAO**; PRÉVOIR AU MOINS 14 JOURS ENTRE LA PRISE DU CITALOPRAM ET CELLE D'UN IMAO ■ LA PRISE CONCOMITANTE DE **PIMOZIDE** EST CONTRE-INDIQUÉE EN RAISON DU RISQUE D'ALLONGEMENT DE L'INTERVALLE QT_C ■ La prise simultanée d'autres **médicaments à action centrale** (incluant l'**alcool**, les **antihistaminiques**, les **analgésiques opioïdes** et les **hypnosédatifs**) doit s'accompagner de prudence; l'usage concomitant d'**alcool** n'est pas recommandé ■ La **cimétidine** augmente les concentrations sanguines de citalopram ■ Le **lithium** peut potentialiser les effets sérotoninergiques du citalopram (l'usage concomitant devrait faire l'objet d'une surveillance étroite) ■ Le **kétoconazole**, l'**itraconazole**, l'**érythromycine** et l'**oméprazole** peuvent élever les concentrations sanguines de citalopram ■ La **carbamazépine** peut réduire les concentrations sanguines de ce médicament ■ Le citalopram peut élever les concentrations sanguines de **métoprolol** ■ L'administration concomitante d'**antidépresseurs tricycliques** devrait être surveillée étroitement en raison de la modification des paramètres pharmacocinétiques et des effets imprévisibles sur le recaptage de la sérotonine et de la noradrénaline ■ Risque accru d'effets secondaires (faiblesse, hyperréflectivité, incoordination) lors de l'administration concomitante d'**agonistes 5-HT$_1$** utilisés en traitement des migraines.

Médicament-produits naturels: La consommation concomitante de **millepertuis** ou de **SAMe** augmente le risque d'effets secondaires sérotoninergiques, incluant le syndrome sérotoninergique.

VOIES D'ADMINISTRATION ET POSOLOGIE

- **PO (adultes)**: Initialement, 20 mg, 1 fois par jour; on peut majorer cette dose par paliers de 20 mg par jour, à intervalles hebdomadaires, jusqu'à un maximum de 60 mg par jour.
- **PO (personnes âgées)**: La dose recommandée est de 20 mg, 1 fois par jour; certains patients peuvent répondre à une dose de 10 mg par jour. La dose peut être portée à 40 mg par jour si le patient tolère bien cette dose.

Insuffisance hépatique

- **PO (adultes)**: Initialement, 20 mg, 1 fois par jour; on peut majorer cette dose jusqu'à 30 mg par jour, seulement chez les patients n'ayant pas répondu aux doses inférieures.

PRÉSENTATION

Comprimés: 10 mg[Pr], 20 mg[Pr], 40 mg[Pr].

ÉVALUATION DE LA SITUATION

- Suivre les changements d'humeur tout au long du traitement.
- Rester à l'affût des idées suicidaires, particulièrement au début du traitement. Limiter la quantité de médicament dont le patient peut disposer.

DIAGNOSTICS INFIRMIERS POSSIBLES

- Stratégies d'adaptation inefficaces (Indications).
- Risque d'accident (Effets secondaires).
- Connaissances insuffisantes sur le traitement médicamenteux (Enseignement au patient et à ses proches).

INTERVENTIONS INFIRMIÈRES

- Ne pas confondre Celexa (citalopram) avec Celebrex (célécoxib), avec Cerebyx (fosphénytoïne) ou avec Zyprexa (olanzapine).
- Administrer en une seule dose, le matin ou le soir, sans égard aux repas.

ENSEIGNEMENT AU PATIENT ET À SES PROCHES

- Conseiller au patient de respecter rigoureusement la posologie recommandée.
- Prévenir le patient que le citalopram peut altérer sa capacité de jugement et peut provoquer de la somnolence, des étourdissements et une vision trouble. Lui recommander de ne pas conduire et d'éviter les activités qui exigent sa vigilance jusqu'à ce qu'on ait la certitude que le médicament n'entraîne pas ces effets chez lui.
- Conseiller au patient d'éviter la consommation d'alcool ou la prise d'autres dépresseurs du SNC pendant le traitement et de consulter un professionnel de la santé avant de prendre d'autres médicaments en même temps que le citalopram.
- Conseiller au patient de changer lentement de position pour éviter les étourdissements.
- Conseiller au patient d'utiliser un écran solaire et de porter des vêtements protecteurs pour prévenir les réactions de photosensibilité.
- Expliquer au patient qu'il peut soulager la sécheresse de la bouche en se rinçant souvent la bouche, en pratiquant une bonne hygiène buccale et en consommant des bonbons ou de la gomme à mâcher sans sucre. Si la sécheresse de la bouche persiste pendant plus de 2 semaines, lui recommander de consulter le médecin ou le dentiste qui pourra lui prescrire des substituts de salive.
- Conseiller à la patiente de prévenir le médecin si elle souhaite devenir enceinte ou si elle pense l'être ou encore si elle prévoit allaiter.
- Signaler au patient que le citalopram ne doit pas être pris pendant au moins 14 jours après la fin du traitement par un IMAO et qu'on doit attendre au moins 14 jours après l'arrêt du traitement par le citalopram avant d'amorcer celui par un IMAO.
- Insister sur l'importance des examens de suivi permettant de déterminer les bienfaits du traitement. Encourager le patient à s'engager dans une psychothérapie, le cas échéant.

VÉRIFICATION DE L'EFFICACITÉ THÉRAPEUTIQUE

L'efficacité du traitement peut être démontrée par: une sensation de mieux-être ■ un regain d'intérêt pour l'entourage; les effets antidépresseurs peuvent ne pas se manifester avant 1 à 4 semaines.

CLARITHROMYCINE

Biaxin, Biaxin BID, Biaxin XL

CLASSIFICATION:

Antibiotique (macrolide)

Grossesse – catégorie C

INDICATIONS

Traitement des infections suivantes: infections des voies respiratoires supérieures, incluant la pharyngite et la sinusite streptococciques ■ infections des voies respiratoires inférieures, incluant la bronchite et la pneumonie ■ infections légères de la peau et des structures cutanées ■ Traitement (en association avec d'autres antimycobactériens) et prévention des infections disséminées à MAC (complexe *Mycobacterium avium*) ■ Traitement des infections suivantes chez les enfants: otite moyenne ■ sinusite ■ pharyngite ■ infections de la peau et des structures cutanées ■ Traitement (en association avec d'autres médicaments) de l'ulcère duodénal dû à *Helicobacter pylori.* **Usages non approuvés**: Prophylaxie de l'endocardite.

MÉCANISME D'ACTION

Inhibition de la synthèse des protéines par fixation au ribosome bactérien 50S. ***Effets thérapeutiques:*** Action bactériostatique contre les bactéries sensibles. **Spectre d'action**: Action contre les microorganismes aérobies à Gram positif suivants: *Staphylococcus aureus* ■ *Streptococcus pneumoniæ* ■ *Streptococcus pyogenes* (streptocoques du groupe A) ■ Action contre les microorganismes aérobies à Gram négatif suivants: *Hæmophilus influenzæ* ■ *Moraxella catarrhalis* ■ La clarithromycine est également active contre: *Mycoplasma* ■ *Legionella* ■ *H. pylori* ■ *M. avium* ■ La clarithromycine n'a pas d'effet sur *S. aureus* résistant à la méthicilline.

PHARMACOCINÉTIQUE

Absorption: Rapide (PO) (50 %).

Distribution: Tous les tissus et les liquides de l'organisme. Les concentrations tissulaires peuvent être plus élevées que les concentrations sériques.

Métabolisme et excrétion: Substrat et inhibiteur du CYP 3A4. De 10 à 15 % du médicament est transformé pendant le métabolisme hépatique en 14-hydroxy-clarithromycine, métabolite exerçant un effet anti-infectieux. De 20 à 30 % du médicament est excrété à l'état inchangé dans l'urine.

Demi-vie: Dose de 250 mg: de 3 à 4 heures; dose de 500 mg: de 5 à 7 heures.

Profil temps-action (concentrations sériques)

	DÉBUT D'ACTION	PIC	DURÉE
PO	inconnu	2 h	12 h
PO-XL	inconnu	4 h	24 h

CONTRE-INDICATIONS, PRÉCAUTIONS ET MISES EN GARDE

Contre-indications: Hypersensibilité à la clarithromycine, à l'érythromycine ou à d'autres antibiotiques macrolides ■ Traitement concomitant par l'astémizole, la terfénadine, le cisapride, le pimozide, l'ergotamine ou la dihydroergotamine ■ **OBST.**: Éviter l'usage (surtout au cours du 1er trimestre) à moins qu'il n'existe aucune solution de rechange.

Précautions et mises en garde: Insuffisance rénale ou hépatique grave (réduire la dose si la Cl_{Cr} < 30 mL/min) ■ Allaitement.

RÉACTIONS INDÉSIRABLES ET EFFETS SECONDAIRES

SNC: céphalées.

CV: ARYTHMIES VENTRICULAIRES.

GI: COLITE PSEUDOMEMBRANEUSE, douleur et gêne abdominale, altération du goût, diarrhée, dyspepsie, nausées.

INTERACTIONS

Médicament-médicament: La clarithromycine est un inhibiteur du **CYP 3A4**. Les concentrations sanguines des **agents métabolisés par ce système** vont augmenter, ce qui entraîne un risque de toxicité ■ LA CLARITHROMYCINE PEUT ACCROÎTRE LE RISQUE D'ARYTHMIE CHEZ LES PATIENTS QUI SUIVENT SIMULTANÉMENT UN TRAITEMENT PAR L'**ASTÉMIZOLE**, LA **TERFÉNADINE**, LE **CISAPRIDE**, LE **PIMOZIDE**, L'**ERGOTAMINE** OU LA **DIHYDROERGOTAMINE**. L'ADMINISTRATION CONCOMITANTE EST CONTRE-INDIQUÉE ■ Des effets similaires peuvent survenir lors de l'utilisation concomitante d'autres **antiarythmiques**. Faire un ÉCG pour déceler un éventuel allongement de l'intervalle QT ■ Risque d'élévation des concentrations sériques et risque accru de toxicité lors de l'administration concomitante de **carbamazépine**, de **digoxine**, de **cyclosporine**, de **buspirone**, de **disopyramide**, de **felodipine**, d'**oméprazole**, de **tacrolimus**, d'**alcaloïdes de l'ergot** ou de **théophylline** ■ La clarithromycine élève les concentrations des **inhibiteurs de l'HMG-CoA réductase** et peut accroître le risque de rhabdomyolyse ■ Risque d'intensification des effets de la **warfarine** et du **sildénafil** ■ La clarithromycine peut diminuer les effets de la **zidovudine** ■ La **délaverdine** et le **fluconazole** augmentent les concentrations sanguines de clarithromycine ■ La **rifampicine** et la **rifabutine** peuvent diminuer les concentrations sanguines de clarithromycine.

VOIES D'ADMINISTRATION ET POSOLOGIE

- **PO (adultes)**: **Biaxin BID**: *Voies respiratoires supérieures (pharyngite et amygdalite)* – de 250 à 500 mg, toutes les 12 heures. *Infections sans complications de la peau et des structures cutanées* – 250 mg, toutes les 12 heures. *Voies respiratoires inférieures (surinfection bactérienne, bronchite chronique et pneumonie)* – de 250 à 500 mg, toutes les 12 heures. *Sinusite maxillaire aiguë* – 500 mg, toutes les 12 heures. *Infection disséminée à MAC: prophylaxie* – 500 mg, toutes les 12 heures; *traitement* – 500 mg, toutes les 12 heures, en association avec d'autres antimycobactériens (éthambutol, clofazimine, rifampine). *Infection à* H. pylori – 500 mg, 2 fois par jour (en association avec l'oméprazole, l'esoméprazole ou le lansoprazole et l'amoxicil-

line); 250 mg, 2 fois par jour (en association avec l'oméprazole et le métronidazole).
Biaxin XL: *Sinusite maxillaire aiguë, surinfection bactérienne de la bronchite chronique et de la pneumonie extrahospitalières* – 1 000 mg, toutes les 24 heures.

- **PO (enfants)**: *La plupart des infections* – 7,5 mg/kg, toutes les 12 heures (ne pas dépasser 1 000 mg par jour).

INSUFFISANCE RÉNALE

- **PO (ADULTES)**: *CL_{CR} < 30 mL/MIN* – 250 mg, 1 FOIS PAR JOUR, OU 250 mg, 2 FOIS PAR JOUR, DANS LE CAS D'INFECTIONS PLUS GRAVES. ON NE DOIT PAS POURSUIVRE LE TRAITEMENT AU-DELÀ DE 14 JOURS CHEZ CES PATIENTS.
- **PO (ENFANTS)**: *CL_{CR} < 30 mL/MIN* – LA POSOLOGIE DOIT ÊTRE RÉDUITE DE MOITIÉ, SOIT JUSQU'À UN MAXIMUM DE 250 mg, 1 FOIS PAR JOUR, OU DE 250 mg, 2 FOIS PAR JOUR, DANS LE CAS D'INFECTIONS PLUS GRAVES. ON NE DOIT PAS POURSUIVRE LE TRAITEMENT AU-DELÀ DE 14 JOURS.

PRÉSENTATION

Comprimés: 250 mg^{Pr}, 500 mg^{Pr} ■ **Comprimés à libération prolongée**: 500 mg^{Pr} ■ **Suspension orale (punch aux fruits)**: 125 mg/5 mL^{Pr}, en flacons de 55, 105 et 150 mL; 250 mg/5 mL^{Pr}, en flacons de 105 mL ■ **En association avec**: amoxicilline et lansoprazole (HP-PAC^{Pr}), amoxicilline et oméprazole (Losec 1-2-3 A^{Pr}), métronidazole et oméprazole (Losec 1-2-3 M^{Pr}), amoxicilline et esoméprazole (Nexium 1-2-3 A^{Pr}).

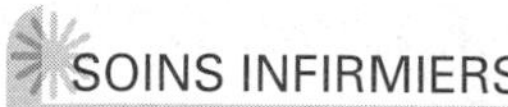

SOINS INFIRMIERS

ÉVALUATION DE LA SITUATION

- Au début du traitement et pendant toute sa durée, rester à l'affût des signes suivants d'infection: altération des signes vitaux; aspect de la plaie, des crachats, de l'urine et des selles; accroissement du nombre de leucocytes.
- Prélever des échantillons pour les cultures et les antibiogrammes avant le début du traitement. La première dose peut être administrée avant que les résultats soient connus.

Ulcères: Évaluer la présence de douleurs épigastriques ou abdominales et la présence de sang visible ou occulte dans les selles, les vomissures ou le liquide d'aspiration gastrique.

Tests de laboratoire:

- La clarithromycine peut rarement entraîner une élévation des concentrations sériques d'AST, d'ALT et de phosphatase alcaline.
- Le médicament peut parfois entraîner une élévation des concentrations d'urée.

DIAGNOSTICS INFIRMIERS POSSIBLES

- Risque d'infection (Indications).
- Connaissances insuffisantes sur le traitement médicamenteux (Enseignement au patient et à ses proches).
- Non-observance du traitement médicamenteux (Enseignement au patient et à ses proches).

INTERVENTIONS INFIRMIÈRES

- Administrer le médicament à intervalles réguliers, sans égard aux repas. Les aliments ralentissent l'absorption du médicament, mais ne modifient pas la quantité absorbée.
- Les comprimés XL doivent être administrés avec de la nourriture. Ils doivent être pris tels quels, sans être brisés, écrasés ou croqués.
- Bien agiter la suspension avant de l'administrer et la conserver à la température ambiante.
- Administrer la clarithromycine et la zidovudine à au moins 4 heures d'intervalle.

ENSEIGNEMENT AU PATIENT ET À SES PROCHES

- Expliquer au patient qu'il doit prendre le médicament à intervalles réguliers, et qu'il doit utiliser toute la quantité qui lui a été prescrite, même s'il se sent mieux. S'il n'a pu prendre le médicament au moment habituel, il doit le prendre aussitôt que possible, mais non pas juste avant l'heure prévue pour la dose suivante. Il ne faut jamais remplacer une dose manquée par une double dose. Insister sur le fait qu'il peut être dangereux de donner ce médicament à une autre personne.
- Conseiller au patient de signaler au médecin les signes suivants de surinfection: excroissance pileuse sur la langue, démangeaisons ou pertes vaginales, selles molles ou nauséabondes.
- RECOMMANDER AU PATIENT DE COMMUNIQUER AVEC LE MÉDECIN EN CAS DE FIÈVRE OU DE DIARRHÉE, PARTICULIÈREMENT SI SES SELLES RENFERMENT DU SANG, DU PUS OU DU MUCUS. LUI CONSEILLER DE NE PAS TRAITER LA DIARRHÉE SANS CONSULTER AU PRÉALABLE UN PROFESSIONNEL DE LA SANTÉ.
- Recommander au patient qui suit un traitement concomitant par la zidovudine de prendre la clarithromycine et la zidovudine à au moins 4 heures d'intervalle.
- Recommander à la patiente d'informer le médecin si elle pense être enceinte ou si elle souhaite le devenir.

- Inciter le patient à prévenir un professionnel de la santé si les symptômes ne diminuent pas en l'espace de quelques jours.

VÉRIFICATION DE L'EFFICACITÉ THÉRAPEUTIQUE

L'efficacité du traitement peut être démontrée par: la disparition des signes et des symptômes d'infection; le temps de résolution dépend du microorganisme infectant et du siège de l'infection ▪ le soulagement de la douleur provoquée par l'ulcère ▪ la prophylaxie de l'endocardite.

CLAVULANATE,

voir Amoxicilline/Clavulanate et Ticarcilline

CLINDAMYCINE

Apo-Clindamycine, Clindets, Clinda-T, Dalacin C, Dalacin T, Gen-Clindamycine, Novo-Clindamycine, Ratio-Clindamycine

CLASSIFICATION:
Antibiotique

Grossesse – catégorie B

INDICATIONS

PO, IM, IV: Traitement des infections suivantes: infections de la peau et des tissus mous ▪ infections des voies respiratoires inférieures ▪ septicémie ▪ infections intra-abdominales ▪ infections gynécologiques ▪ infections osseuses et articulaires ▪ prophylaxie de l'endocardite bactérienne chez les patients allergiques à la pénicilline ▪ En association avec la primaquine pour le traitement de la pneumonie à *P. carinii* chez les patients atteints du sida qui ne tolèrent pas le traitement classique ou qui n'y répondent pas ▪ **Préparation topique:** Acné vulgaire ▪ **Préparation vaginale:** Vaginose bactérienne. **Usages non approuvés: PO, IM, IV** – Traitement de la toxoplasmose du SNC et de la babésiose.

MÉCANISME D'ACTION

Inhibition de la synthèse protéique au niveau de la sous-unité 50S du ribosome des bactéries sensibles. ***Effets thérapeutiques:*** Action bactéricide ou bactériostatique, selon la sensibilité des microorganismes et la concentration du médicament. **Spectre d'action:** Action contre la plupart des bactéries anaérobies, telles que les espèces *Bacteroides*, *Peptostreptococcus*, les streptocoques anaérobies, les espèces *Clostridium* et les streptocoques microaérophiles ▪ les bactéries aérobies à Gram positif (staphylocoques, y compris les staphylocoques producteurs de pénicillinase, les streptocoques et les pneumocoques, mais pas les entérocoques) ▪ Action notable contre les bactéries anaérobies qui causent la vaginose bactérienne, incluant *Bacteroides fragilis*, *Gardnerella vaginalis*, *Mobiluncus* (toutes les espèces), *Mycoplasma hominis* et *Corynebacterium* ▪ La clindamycine est également active contre *P. carinii* et *Toxoplasma gondii*.

PHARMACOCINÉTIQUE

Absorption: Bonne (PO et IM); minime (voie topique ou vaginale).
Distribution: Tout l'organisme. La clindamycine traverse faiblement la barrière hématoencéphalique. Elle traverse la barrière placentaire et passe dans le lait maternel.
Liaison aux protéines: 90 %.
Métabolisme et excrétion: Métabolisme majoritairement hépatique.
Demi-vie: De 2 à 3 heures.

Profil temps-action

	Début d'action	Pic	Durée
PO	rapide	45 min	6 – 8 h
IM	rapide	1,3 h	6 – 8 h
IV	rapide	fin de la perfusion	6 – 8 h

CONTRE-INDICATIONS, PRÉCAUTIONS ET MISES EN GARDE

Contre-indications: Hypersensibilité à la clindamycine ou à la lincomycine.
Précautions et mises en garde: Antécédents d'iléite régionale ou de rectocolite hémorragique ou antécédents de colite après une antibiothérapie ▪ **Allaitement:** L'innocuité du médicament administré par voie générale ou topique n'a pas été établie ▪ Diarrhée en cours de traitement (le cas échéant, interrompre l'antibiothérapie) ▪ Grossesse ▪ Insuffisance hépatique grave ▪ Diarrhée ▪ Intolérance connue à l'alcool (solution topique, suspension) ▪ **Péd.:** Nourrissons âgés de moins de 30 jours (la forme injectable contient de l'alcool benzylique, qui a été associé à un « syndrome de halètement » mortel chez les nouveau-nés).

RÉACTIONS INDÉSIRABLES ET EFFETS SECONDAIRES

SNC: étourdissements, céphalées, vertiges.
CV: arythmies, hypotension.

GI: COLITE PSEUDOMEMBRANEUSE, diarrhée, goût amer (voie IV seulement), nausées, vomissements.
Tég.: rash.
Locaux: phlébite au point d'injection IV.

INTERACTIONS

Médicament-médicament: Le **kaolin/pectine** peut réduire l'absorption gastro-intestinale de la clindamycine ■ La clindamycine peut intensifier l'effet des **agents de blocage neuromusculaire** ■ Effet bactéricide antagoniste, si la clindamycine et l'**érythromycine** sont administrées en concomitance (éviter l'administration concomitante) ■ **Préparation topique**: L'administration concomitante d'**agents irritants**, **abrasifs** ou **exfoliants** peut accentuer l'irritation.

VOIES D'ADMINISTRATION ET POSOLOGIE

- **PO (adultes)**: *La plupart des infections* – de 150 à 450 mg, toutes les 6 heures. *Pneumonie à* P. carinii – de 300 à 450 mg, toutes les 6 heures, en association avec 15 à 30 mg de primaquine par jour, pendant 21 jours. *Prophylaxie de l'endocardite bactérienne* – 300 mg, 1 heure avant l'intervention, et 150 mg, 6 heures après la dose initiale.
- **PO (enfants > 1 mois)**: De 8 à 16 mg/kg par jour, en 3 ou 4 doses égales; on peut augmenter la dose jusqu'à 16 à 20 mg/kg par jour, en 3 ou 4 doses égales, selon la gravité de l'infection. *Prophylaxie de l'endocardite* – 10 mg/ kg, 1 heure avant l'intervention (ne pas dépasser la dose recommandée chez l'adulte), et 5 mg/kg, 6 heures après la dose initiale.
- **IM, IV (adultes)**: *La plupart des infections* – de 2 400 à 2 700 mg répartis en 2, 3 ou 4 doses égales. Les infections moins compliquées peuvent répondre à des posologies de 1 200 à 1 800 mg par jour, répartis en 3 ou 4 doses égales (on a utilisé des doses IV allant jusqu'à 4,8 g par jour; des doses IM uniques, supérieures à 600 mg, ne sont pas recommandées). *Pneumonie à* P. carinii – de 600 à 900 mg par voie IV, toutes les 6 heures, ou 900 mg, toutes les 8 heures, en association avec la primaquine par voie orale, à une dose quotidienne de 15 à 30 mg, pendant 21 jours.
- **IM, IV (enfants > 1 mois)**: De 20 à 40 mg/kg par jour, répartis en 3 ou 4 doses égales.
- **IM, IV (nourrissons < 1 mois)**: De 10 à 20 mg/kg par jour, répartis en 3 ou 4 doses égales. La dose la plus faible peut s'avérer suffisante chez des prématurés de petit poids de naissance.
- **Préparation vaginale (adultes)**: Le contenu de 1 applicateur (5 g) par jour, pendant 7 jours.
- **Préparation topique (adultes)**: *Solution* – appliquer 2 fois par jour.

PRÉSENTATION
(version générique disponible)

Capsules: 150 mg[Pr], 300 mg[Pr] ■ **Suspension orale**: 75 mg/5 mL[Pr] ■ **Solution pour injection**: 150 mg/mL[Pr] ■ **Préparation topique**: solution à 1 %[Pr] ■ **Crème vaginale**: crème à 2 %[Pr] ■ **En association avec**: peroxyde de benzoyle (BenzaClin[Pr], Clindoxyl[Pr]). Voir l'annexe U.

C

SOINS INFIRMIERS

ÉVALUATION DE LA SITUATION

- Au début du traitement et pendant toute sa durée, rester à l'affût des signes suivants d'infection: altération des signes vitaux; aspect de la plaie, des crachats, de l'urine et des selles; accroissement du nombre de leucocytes.
- Prélever des échantillons pour les cultures et les antibiogrammes avant le début du traitement. Les premières doses peuvent être administrées avant que les résultats soient connus.
- OBSERVER L'ÉLIMINATION INTESTINALE. LA DIARRHÉE, LES CRAMPES ABDOMINALES, LA FIÈVRE ET LA PRÉSENCE DE SANG DANS LES SELLES SONT DES SIGNES DE COLITE PSEUDOMEMBRANEUSE INDUITE PAR LE MÉDICAMENT. EN INFORMER IMMÉDIATEMENT UN PROFESSIONNEL DE LA SANTÉ. CES SYMPTÔMES PEUVENT SURVENIR MÊME PLUSIEURS SEMAINES APRÈS L'ARRÊT DU TRAITEMENT.
- Rester à l'affût des signes suivants d'hypersensibilité: rash, urticaire.

Tests de laboratoire:

- Noter la numération globulaire; la clindamycine peut entraîner une diminution passagère du nombre de leucocytes, d'éosinophiles et de plaquettes.
- Le médicament peut entraîner l'élévation des concentrations de phosphatase alcaline, de bilirubine, de créatine kinase, d'AST et d'ALT.

DIAGNOSTICS INFIRMIERS POSSIBLES

- Risque d'infection (Indications).
- Diarrhée (Effets secondaires).
- Connaissances insuffisantes sur le traitement médicamenteux (Enseignement au patient et à ses proches).

INTERVENTIONS INFIRMIÈRES

PO: Administrer la clindamycine avec un grand verre d'eau. Le médicament peut être pris aux repas. Bien agiter la préparation liquide. Ne pas conserver au réfrigérateur. La solution est stable pendant 14 jours à la température ambiante.

C

IM: Ne pas administrer plus de 600 mg en une seule injection IM.

Perfusion intermittente: Ne pas administrer par voie IV en bolus non dilué. Diluer 300 ou 600 mg de solution destinée à l'administration IV dans au moins 50 mL, et 900 ou 1 200 mg, dans au moins 100 mL de solution de D5%E, de D5%E/NaCl 0,45 % ou D5%E/NaCl 0,9 %, de D5%E dans une solution de Ringer pour injection, de solution de NaCl 0,9 % ou d'une solution de lactate de Ringer pour injection. La solution est stable pendant 24 heures à la température ambiante. Consulter les directives de chaque fabricant avant de reconstituer la préparation.

Vitesse d'administration: Administrer chaque dose de 300 mg en au moins 10 minutes. Le débit de la perfusion ne doit pas dépasser 30 mg/min. Ne pas administrer plus de 1 200 mg en une seule perfusion de 1 heure.

Perfusion continue: On peut d'abord administrer le médicament en une seule perfusion rapide (dose d'attaque), suivie d'une perfusion IV continue.

Vitesse d'administration: Administrer le médicament à raison de 10 à 20 mg/min pendant 30 minutes, puis de 0,75 à 1,25 mg/min.

Associations compatibles dans la même seringue: amikacine ▪ aztréonam ▪ gentamicine ▪ héparine.

Association incompatible dans la même seringue: tobramycine.

Compatibilité (tubulure en Y): amifostine ▪ amiodarone ▪ aztréonam ▪ cyclophosphamide ▪ diltiazem ▪ énalaprilate ▪ esmolol ▪ fludarabine ▪ foscarnet ▪ granisétron ▪ héparine ▪ hydromorphone ▪ labétalol ▪ magnésium, sulfate de ▪ melphalan ▪ mépéridine ▪ midazolam ▪ morphine ▪ multivitamines ▪ ondansétron ▪ perphénazine ▪ pipéracilline/tazobactam ▪ propofol ▪ sargramostim ▪ tacrolimus ▪ téniposide ▪ théophylline ▪ thiotépa ▪ vinorelbine ▪ zidovudine.

Incompatibilité (tubulure en Y): filgrastim ▪ fluconazole ▪ idarubicine.

Préparation vaginale: Les applicateurs sont contenus dans le conditionnement de la préparation vaginale. Lorsqu'on traite la vaginose bactérienne, il n'est habituellement pas nécessaire de traiter simultanément le conjoint.

Préparation topique:

- Éviter tout contact avec les yeux, les muqueuses et les plaies ouvertes. En cas de contact accidentel, rincer abondamment la partie atteinte à l'eau froide.
- Nettoyer les régions touchées avec de l'eau chaude et du savon, rincer et assécher délicatement avant l'application. Appliquer sur toute la région affectée.

ENSEIGNEMENT AU PATIENT ET À SES PROCHES

- Expliquer au patient qu'il doit prendre le médicament à intervalles réguliers, et qu'il doit prendre toute la quantité qui lui a été prescrite, même s'il se sent mieux. S'il n'a pu prendre le médicament au moment prévu, il doit le prendre aussitôt que possible, mais non pas juste avant l'heure prévue pour la dose suivante. Il ne faut jamais remplacer une dose manquée par une double dose. Insister sur le fait qu'il peut être dangereux de donner ce médicament à une autre personne.
- RECOMMANDER AU PATIENT D'INFORMER IMMÉDIATEMENT UN PROFESSIONNEL DE LA SANTÉ SI LES SYMPTÔMES SUIVANTS SE MANIFESTENT: DIARRHÉE, CRAMPES ABDOMINALES, FIÈVRE OU PRÉSENCE DE SANG DANS LES SELLES. LUI CONSEILLER DE NE PAS UTILISER D'ANTIDIARRHÉIQUES SANS AVOIR CONSULTÉ AU PRÉALABLE UN PROFESSIONNEL DE LA SANTÉ.
- Conseiller au patient de signaler les signes suivants de surinfection: excroissance pileuse sur la langue, démangeaisons ou pertes vaginales ou anales.
- Inciter le patient à prévenir le médecin si les symptômes ne s'améliorent pas en l'espace de quelques jours.
- Expliquer au patient ayant des antécédents de cardiopathie rhumatismale ou ayant subi une chirurgie de remplacement valvulaire qu'il est important de suivre un traitement antimicrobien prophylactique avant de se soumettre à une intervention médicale ou dentaire effractive (voir l'annexe M).

IV: Prévenir le patient que le goût amer qu'il peut ressentir au cours de l'administration par voie IV ne comporte aucun danger particulier.

Préparation vaginale:

- Expliquer à la patiente comment utiliser l'applicateur vaginal. Lui recommander de l'introduire profondément dans le vagin, de se traiter à l'heure du coucher et de rester étendue pendant au moins 30 minutes après. Lui conseiller d'utiliser une serviette hygiénique pour ne pas tacher les vêtements ou les draps. Lui préciser qu'elle doit continuer le traitement pendant ses règles.
- Conseiller à la patiente d'éviter les rapports sexuels vaginaux pendant le traitement.
- Mettre la patiente en garde contre le fait que l'huile minérale contenue dans la crème de clindamycine peut rendre moins efficaces les dispositifs contraceptifs en latex ou en caoutchouc. Ces produits ne devraient pas être utilisés dans les 72 heures suivant l'administration de la crème vaginale.

Préparation topique:

- Expliquer au patient que la solution de clindamycine destinée à l'administration topique est inflammable (le véhicule étant l'alcool isopropylique). Insister sur le fait qu'il ne faut pas appliquer la préparation pendant qu'on fume ni en se tenant près d'une flamme ou d'une source de chaleur.
- Conseiller au patient d'informer un professionnel de la santé si sa peau se dessèche excessivement.
- Recommander au patient d'attendre 30 minutes après avoir lavé ou rasé la surface à traiter avant d'appliquer la préparation.

VÉRIFICATION DE L'EFFICACITÉ THÉRAPEUTIQUE

L'efficacité du traitement peut être démontrée par: la disparition des signes et des symptômes d'infection; le temps de résolution dépend du microorganisme infectant et du siège de l'infection ■ la prophylaxie de l'endocardite ■ l'amélioration des lésions acnéiques; une amélioration devrait être notable dans les 6 semaines suivant le début du traitement, mais les pleins avantages du médicament pourraient ne pas être manifestes avant 8 à 12 semaines. ✳

CLOBÉTASOL,

voir Corticostéroïdes (topiques)

CLOBÉTASONE,

voir Corticostéroïdes (topiques)

CLOMIPHÈNE

Clomid, Serophene

CLASSIFICATION:

Hormone (stimulation de l'ovulation)

Grossesse – catégorie X

INDICATIONS

Stimulation de l'ovulation chez les femmes qui n'ovulent pas et qui désirent devenir enceintes, dont le partenaire produit un sperme approprié, dont les systèmes ovarien, hypothalamique et hypophysaire peuvent permettre la conception et dont la sécrétion d'œstrogènes est appropriée. Les obstacles à la grossesse doivent être écartés ou traités de façon appropriée avant le début du traitement.

MÉCANISME D'ACTION

Stimulation de la libération des gonadotrophines hypophysaires, de l'hormone folliculostimulante et de l'hormone lutéinisante, entraînant l'ovulation et la formation du corps jaune. ***Effets thérapeutiques:*** Stimulation de l'ovulation.

PHARMACOCINÉTIQUE

Absorption: Bonne (PO).

Distribution: Inconnue.

Métabolisme et excrétion: Le médicament semble être métabolisé par le foie et traverser un cycle entérohépatique; il est ensuite éliminé par la bile. Environ 50 % est excrété dans les fèces.

Demi-vie: 5 jours.

Profil temps-action (ovulation)

	DÉBUT D'ACTION	PIC	DURÉE
PO	6 – 12 jours	inconnu	inconnue

CONTRE-INDICATIONS, PRÉCAUTIONS ET MISES EN GARDE

Contre-indications: Hypersensibilité ■ Maladie hépatique évolutive ou antérieure ■ Kyste de l'ovaire ■ Fibromes utérins ■ Dépression mentale ■ Thrombophlébite ■ Tumeur hormonodépendante ■ Pertes sanguines anormales ■ Grossesse.

Précautions et mises en garde: Sensibilité connue aux gonadotrophines hypophysaires ■ Polykystose ovarienne ■ ALLAITEMENT: Le clomiphène peut diminuer la production de lait.

RÉACTIONS INDÉSIRABLES ET EFFETS SECONDAIRES

SNC: nervosité, agitation, céphalées, insomnie, sensation de tête légère, fatigue.

ORLO: vision brouillée, scotome, photophobie, troubles visuels.

CV: rougeurs, bouffées vasomotrices.

GI: distension, ballonnements, douleurs abdominales, nausées, vomissements, gain d'appétit.

GU: mictions fréquentes, augmentation du volume urinaire.

Tég.: rash, urticaire, dermatite allergique, alopécie réversible.

End.: hypertrophie des ovaires, formation de kystes, sensibilité mammaire, grossesses plurigémellaires.

Métab.: gain pondéral.

INTERACTIONS

Médicament-médicament: Aucune interaction notable.

C

VOIES D'ADMINISTRATION ET POSOLOGIE

- **PO (adultes)**: 50 mg par jour, pendant 5 jours; en l'absence d'ovulation, entreprendre un deuxième traitement, 30 jours après le premier, à raison de 100 mg par jour, pendant 5 jours. On peut soumettre la patiente à un maximum de 3 traitements.

PRÉSENTATION

Comprimés: 50 mg^Pr^.

SOINS INFIRMIERS

ÉVALUATION DE LA SITUATION

- Il faut effectuer un examen pelvien avant d'amorcer le traitement afin de déterminer la taille des ovaires.
- Chez les patientes plus âgées, il est recommandé de pratiquer une biopsie de l'endomètre avant l'administration du clomiphène afin d'écarter les doutes quant à la présence d'un cancer de l'endomètre.
- Effectuer les examens de la fonction hépatique avant le début du traitement.

Tests de laboratoire:

- Afin de déterminer si le clomiphène induit l'ovulation, on peut avoir recours aux tests suivants: dosage de l'excrétion des œstrogènes, études histologiques de l'endomètre lors de la phase lutéale, dosage des concentrations sériques de progestérone et excrétion urinaire de prégnandiol.
- Un test de grossesse devrait être effectué avant le début du traitement par le clomiphène.
- Le médicament peut entraîner l'élévation des concentrations sériques de thyroxine et de globuline fixant la thyroxine.

DIAGNOSTICS INFIRMIERS POSSIBLES

Connaissances insuffisantes sur le traitement médicamenteux (Enseignement au patient et à ses proches).

INTERVENTIONS INFIRMIÈRES

- Le traitement par le clomiphène commence habituellement le 5e jour du cycle menstruel.

ENSEIGNEMENT AU PATIENT ET À SES PROCHES

- Inciter la patiente à prendre le clomiphène tous les jours, à la même heure. Si elle n'a pu prendre le médicament au moment habituel, elle doit le prendre dès que possible. Elle doit doubler la dose s'il est l'heure de prendre la dose suivante. Lui conseiller de prévenir un professionnel de la santé si elle n'a pu prendre plusieurs doses de suite.
- Inciter la patiente à s'engager dans des rapports sexuels un jour sur deux, en commençant 48 heures avant le début du traitement.
- Montrer à la patiente comment prendre sa température basale. La température basale doit être notée tous les jours, avant le traitement et pendant toute sa durée. Insister sur le fait qu'il est important d'observer tous les aspects du traitement.
- Renseigner la patiente, avant le traitement, de la possibilité d'une grossesse plurigémellaire (triplés, quadruplés et quintuplés).
- Le clomiphène peut entraîner des troubles de la vue ou des étourdissements. Conseiller à la patiente de ne pas conduire et d'éviter les activités qui exigent sa vigilance jusqu'à ce qu'on ait la certitude que le médicament n'entraîne pas ces effets chez elle.
- Recommander à la patiente d'informer un professionnel de la santé immédiatement si elle pense être enceinte. Le clomiphène est contre-indiqué en cas de grossesse.
- Expliquer à la patiente l'importance des examens ophtalmologiques permettant de déceler tout signe de toxicité oculaire si le traitement est administré pendant plus de 1 an.
- Conseiller à la patiente de signaler immédiatement à un professionnel de la santé les ballonnements, les douleurs gastriques ou pelviennes, la vision trouble, la jaunisse, les bouffées vasomotrices persistantes, la sensibilité mammaire, les céphalées ou les nausées et les vomissements.
- Insister sur l'importance d'un suivi médical étroit pendant toute la durée du traitement.

VÉRIFICATION DE L'EFFICACITÉ THÉRAPEUTIQUE

L'efficacité du traitement peut être démontrée par: l'ovulation, attestée par l'excrétion d'œstrogènes, la courbe thermique biphasique, l'excrétion urinaire de prégnandiol à des concentrations correspondant à la phase postovulatoire et les modifications histologiques de l'endomètre. Faute d'une grossesse après 3 traitements au clomiphène, il faut remettre en question le diagnostic.

CLOMIPRAMINE

Anafranil, Apo-Clomipramine, Dom-Clomipramine, Gen-Clomipramine, Novo-Clopamine

CLASSIFICATION:

Antidépresseur (tricyclique), antiobsessionnel

Grossesse – catégorie C (risque durant le 3e trimestre; voir «Précautions et mises en garde»)

INDICATIONS

Traitement de la dépression ▪ Traitement des obsessions et des compulsions chez les patients qui souffrent de troubles obsessionnels-compulsifs (TOC).

MÉCANISME D'ACTION

Potentialisation des effets de la sérotonine et de la noradrénaline sur le SNC. La clomipramine est aussi dotée de propriétés anticholinergiques modérées. ***Effets thérapeutiques:*** Effet antidépresseur ▪ Diminution des comportements obsessionnels-compulsifs.

PHARMACOCINÉTIQUE

Absorption: Bonne (PO).
Distribution: Tout l'organisme.
Liaison aux protéines: 90 %.
Métabolisme et excrétion: Fort métabolisme hépatique. Une fraction du médicament est transformée en desméthylclomipramine, un métabolite actif. La clomipramine subit un cycle entérohépatique et est sécrétée dans les liquides gastriques.
Demi-vie: De 21 à 31 heures.

Profil temps-action (effet antiobsessionnel)

	DÉBUT D'ACTION	PIC	DURÉE
PO	4 – 10 semaines	inconnu	inconnue

CONTRE-INDICATIONS, PRÉCAUTIONS ET MISES EN GARDE

Contre-indications: Hypersensibilité ▪ Glaucome à angle fermé ▪ Début de la convalescence après un infarctus du myocarde ▪ Insuffisance cardiaque congestive aiguë ▪ Administration concomitante d'un IMAO (prévoir 14 jours entre l'arrêt du traitement par l'IMAO et le début de celui par la clomipramine et vice versa) ▪ Atteinte hépatique ou rénale ou antécédents de dyscrasie sanguine.
Précautions et mises en garde: Suivre de près les idées suicidaires chez tous les patients recevant ce médicament ▪ Antécédents de crises convulsives (le seuil convulsif peut être abaissé) ▪ Personnes âgées ▪ Antécédents de maladie cardiovasculaire ▪ Risque d'arythmies cardiaques transitoires chez des patients prenant en concomitance un médicament thyroïdien ou souffrant d'hyperthyroïdie ▪ Hyperplasie bénigne de la prostate (risque accru de rétention urinaire) ▪ Patients présentant des tumeurs médullosurrénales (risque de crise hypertensive) ▪ Éviter de mettre fin abruptement au traitement en raison du risque de symptômes de sevrage ▪ **GÉR.:** Risque accru d'accumulation médicamenteuse et d'effets secondaires; il est recommandé d'utiliser une dose plus faible ▪ **OBST., PÉD.:** Il n'existe pas d'études adéquates menées chez la femme enceinte. N'administrer au cours de la grossesse que si les bienfaits éventuels pour la femme l'emportent sur les risques possibles pour le fœtus ▪ Risque de complications chez le nouveau-né lorsque la mère a pris ce médicament durant le 3e trimestre ▪ Enfants de moins de 10 ans (l'innocuité du médicament n'a pas été établie) ▪ **ALLAITEMENT:** Risque de réactions indésirables graves chez le nouveau-né; il faut décider soit de cesser l'allaitement, soit de cesser la prise du médicament, compte tenu de l'importance du médicament pour la mère.

C

RÉACTIONS INDÉSIRABLES ET EFFETS SECONDAIRES

SNC: CONVULSIONS, léthargie, sédation, faiblesse, comportement agressif.
ORLO: vision trouble, xérophtalmie, sécheresse de la bouche (xérostomie), troubles vestibulaires.
CV: ARYTHMIES, modifications de l'ÉCG, hypotension orthostatique.
GI: constipation, nausées, vomissements, éructations.
GU: dysfonctionnement sexuel chez l'homme, rétention urinaire.
Tég.: peau sèche, photosensibilité.
End.: gynécomastie.
Hémat.: dyscrasie sanguine.
Loc.: faiblesse musculaire.
SN: réactions extrapyramidales.
Divers: hyperthermie, gain pondéral.

INTERACTIONS

Médicament-médicament: L'administration concomitante d'un **IMAO** peut entraîner l'hypotension ou la tachycardie (éviter l'administration conjointe, attendre 14 jours entre l'arrêt de la prise de l'IMAO et le début de la prise de clomipramine et vice versa) ▪ Éviter l'administration concomitante de **quinidine** (risque d'augmentation des effets secondaires de la clomipramine) ▪ La clomipramine peut entraver la réponse thérapeutique aux **antihypertenseurs**, tels que **guanéthidine**, la **clonidine** et l'**alphaméthyldopa** ▪ L'administration concomitante de **clonidine** peut provoquer une crise hypertensive (éviter l'usage simultané) ▪ Les **médicaments qui activent le système enzymatique de la mono-oxygénase hépatique** (comme les **barbituriques**, la **carbamazépine**, la **phénytoïne** et la **nicotine**) peuvent abaisser les concentrations plasmatiques de clomipramine et en réduire l'efficacité ▪ Effets additifs sur la dépression du SNC lors de l'usage concomitant d'autres **dépresseurs du SNC** dont l'**alcool**, les **antihistaminiques**, les **analgésiques opioïdes** et les **hypnosédatifs** ▪ Les effets secondaires **anticholinergiques**

C

et **adrénergiques** peuvent être additifs lors de l'administration concomitante d'autres **agents dotés de ces propriétés** ■ Les effets et la toxicité de la clomipramine peuvent être accentués par l'administration concomitante d'un **ISRS** (attendre plusieurs semaines après l'arrêt du traitement par un ISRS avant d'amorcer celui par la clomipramine; jusqu'à 5 semaines dans le cas de la fluoxétine), d'une **phénothiazine**, de la **cimétidine**, du **méthylphénidate** ou de **contraceptifs oraux**.

VOIES D'ADMINISTRATION ET POSOLOGIE

- **PO (adultes)**: *Traitement antiobsessionnel et antidépresseur* – Initialement, 25 mg par jour; augmenter la dose par paliers de 25 mg, tous les 3 ou 4 jours pour atteindre une dose de 100 ou de 150 mg par jour après 2 semaines. Par la suite, on peut augmenter graduellement la dose pendant plusieurs semaines, jusqu'à concurrence de 250 mg/jour (*TOC*) ou de 300 mg/jour (*dépression*). Une fois la dose thérapeutique atteinte, on peut administrer la dose quotidienne en une seule fois, au coucher.
- **PO (personnes âgées)**: Initialement, de 20 à 30 mg par jour, en prises fractionnées, à augmenter très graduellement, selon les besoins et la tolérance du patient.
- **PO (enfants de 10 à 17 ans)**: Initialement, 25 mg par jour; augmenter la dose par paliers de 25 mg tous les 3 ou 4 jours. Après 2 semaines, on pourra augmenter la dose jusqu'à concurrence de 100 mg ou de 150 mg par jour ou de 3 mg/kg par jour (selon la valeur qui est la plus faible). Par la suite, on pourra augmenter graduellement la dose quotidienne jusqu'à concurrence de 200 mg ou de 3 mg/kg, en choisissant toujours la plus faible des deux. Ne pas dépasser une dose quotidienne totale de 200 mg chez les enfants et les adolescents. Une fois la dose thérapeutique atteinte, on peut administrer la dose quotidienne en une seule fois, au coucher.

PRÉSENTATION

Comprimés dragéifiés: 10 mg^Pr^, 25 mg^Pr^, 50 mg^Pr^.

SOINS INFIRMIERS

ÉVALUATION DE LA SITUATION

- Examiner l'état de conscience et l'affect du patient. Noter la fréquence des comportements obsessionnels-compulsifs; déterminer jusqu'à quel point ces pensées et comportements peuvent entraver les activités quotidiennes.
- Mesurer la pression artérielle et le pouls avant et pendant le traitement initial. Informer le médecin en cas de chute de la pression artérielle (de 10 à 20 mm Hg) ou d'accélération soudaine du pouls. AVANT L'ADMINISTRATION DU MÉDICAMENT ET TOUT AU LONG DU TRAITEMENT, SURVEILLER L'ÉCG DES PATIENTS QUI PRENNENT DE FORTES DOSES OU QUI ONT DES ANTÉCÉDENTS DE MALADIE CARDIOVASCULAIRE.
- Rester à l'affût des symptômes extrapyramidaux parkinsoniens suivants: difficulté d'élocution ou de déglutition, perte d'équilibre, mouvements d'émiettement, faciès figé, démarche traînante, rigidité, tremblements. Informer immédiatement le médecin de l'apparition de ces symptômes; il peut s'avérer nécessaire de réduire la dose ou d'abandonner le traitement. On peut administrer du trihexyphénidyle ou de la diphenhydramine pour maîtriser ces symptômes.

Tests de laboratoire:

- La clomipramine peut élever ou abaisser la glycémie.
- Noter la numération globulaire et la formule leucocytaire lors d'un traitement prolongé. La clomipramine peut rarement entraîner une aplasie médullaire.
- Noter à intervalles réguliers les résultats des tests des fonctions rénale et hépatique des patients qui suivent un traitement prolongé.

DIAGNOSTICS INFIRMIERS POSSIBLES

- Stratégies d'adaptation inefficaces (comportements obsessionnels-compulsifs), reliées à la répression de l'anxiété (Indications).
- Risque d'accident (Effets secondaires).
- Connaissances insuffisantes sur le traitement médicamenteux (Enseignement au patient et à ses proches).

INTERVENTIONS INFIRMIÈRES

- Administrer le médicament aux repas ou immédiatement après afin de diminuer l'irritation gastrique. Une fois la dose thérapeutique atteinte, la dose totale peut être administrée en une seule fois, au coucher.

ENSEIGNEMENT AU PATIENT ET À SES PROCHES

- Expliquer au patient qu'il doit respecter rigoureusement la posologie recommandée. Le sevrage brusque peut provoquer des nausées, des céphalées et des malaises.
- Prévenir le patient que la clomipramine peut provoquer de la somnolence et rendre la vision trouble.

Lui conseiller de ne pas conduire et d'éviter les activités qui exigent sa vigilance jusqu'à ce qu'on ait la certitude que le médicament n'entraîne pas ces effets chez lui.

- Prévenir le patient que l'hypotension orthostatique, la sédation et la confusion sont courantes au début du traitement, particulièrement chez les personnes âgées. L'inciter à se protéger contre les chutes et à changer de position lentement.
- Mettre en garde le patient contre la consommation d'alcool ou d'autres dépresseurs du SNC pendant le traitement et de 3 à 7 jours après l'avoir arrêté.
- Recommander au patient de prévenir le médecin si la sécheresse de la bouche ou la constipation persistent ou si la rétention urinaire, des mouvements incontrôlables ou la rigidité surviennent. Lui conseiller de consommer de la gomme à mâcher ou des bonbons sans sucre afin de soulager la sécheresse de la bouche et d'augmenter sa consommation d'eau ou de fibres alimentaires afin de prévenir la constipation. Si ces symptômes persistent, il faudrait éventuellement réduire la dose de médicament ou arrêter le traitement. Lui recommander de consulter un médecin ou un dentiste si la sécheresse de la bouche persiste pendant plus de 2 semaines.
- Recommander au patient de signaler au médecin tout dysfonctionnement sexuel. Informer le patient de sexe masculin que le dysfonctionnement sexuel est courant lors du traitement par ce médicament.
- Recommander au patient d'utiliser un écran solaire et de porter des vêtements protecteurs pour prévenir les réactions de photosensibilité.
- Expliquer au patient qu'il doit surveiller son alimentation puisqu'une augmentation possible de l'appétit peut entraîner un gain pondéral.
- Recommander au patient qui doit suivre un traitement dentaire ou subir une intervention chirurgicale d'avertir le dentiste ou le médecin qu'il suit un traitement par ce médicament.
- Expliquer au patient l'importance des examens réguliers de suivi permettant d'évaluer l'efficacité du traitement et de déceler les effets secondaires.

VÉRIFICATION DE L'EFFICACITÉ THÉRAPEUTIQUE

L'efficacité du traitement peut être démontrée par: une sensation de mieux-être ■ un moindre recours à un comportement obsessionnel-compulsif. ✳

CLONAZÉPAM

Apo-Clonazépam, Clonapam, Gen-Clonazépam, Novo-Clonazépam, PMS-Clonazépam, Rhoxal-Clonazépam, Rivotril

CLASSIFICATION:

Anticonvulsivant (benzodiazépine)

Grossesse – catégorie D

INDICATIONS

Prophylaxie dans les cas suivants: Petit mal ■ Petit mal variant (syndrome de Lennox-Gastaut) ■ Crises akinésiques ■ Crises myocloniques. **Usages non approuvés:** Anxiété ■ Traitement du trouble panique avec ou sans agoraphobie ■ Insomnie ■ Névralgies ■ Sédation ■ Syndrome des jambes sans repos ■ Tremblements essentiels.

MÉCANISME D'ACTION

Effets anticonvulsivants et sédatifs sur le SNC, probablement attribuables à la stimulation des récepteurs gamma-aminobutyriques (GABA). ***Effets thérapeutiques:*** Prévention des crises convulsives.

PHARMACOCINÉTIQUE

Absorption: Bonne (PO) (> 60 %).

Distribution: L'agent traverse probablement les barrières hématoencéphalique et placentaire.

Métabolisme et excrétion: Métabolisme majoritairement hépatique.

Demi-vie: De 18 à 50 heures.

Profil temps-action (effet anticonvulsivant)

	Début d'action	Pic	Durée
PO	20 – 60 min	1 – 2 h	6 – 12 h

CONTRE-INDICATIONS, PRÉCAUTIONS ET MISES EN GARDE

Contre-indications: Hypersensibilité au clonazépam ou à d'autres benzodiazépines ■ Maladie hépatique grave ■ Glaucome à angle fermé.

Précautions et mises en garde: Maladie respiratoire chronique ■ Apnée du sommeil ■ Insuffisance rénale ■ Sevrage brusque déconseillé ■ **Obst.:** L'innocuité du médicament n'a pas été établie; l'usage prolongé pendant la grossesse peut entraîner des symptômes de sevrage chez le nouveau-né ■ **Allaitement:** Le médicament passe dans le lait maternel, risque d'accumulation chez les nouveau-nés.

C

C

RÉACTIONS INDÉSIRABLES ET EFFETS SECONDAIRES

SNC: modifications du comportement, somnolence.

ORLO: mouvements oculaires anormaux, diplopie, nystagmus.

Resp.: augmentation des sécrétions.

CV: palpitations.

GI: constipation, diarrhée, hépatite.

GU: dysurie, nycturie, rétention urinaire.

Hémat.: anémie, éosinophilie, leucopénie, thrombocytopénie.

SN: ataxie, hypotonie.

Divers: fièvre, dépendance physique, dépendance psychologique, tolérance à l'effet du médicament.

INTERACTIONS

Médicament-médicament: L'**alcool**, les **antidépresseurs**, les **antihistaminiques**, les autres **benzodiazépines** et les **analgésiques opioïdes**, administrés en concomitance, accentuent la dépression du SNC ■ La **cimétidine**, les **contraceptifs oraux**, le **disulfirame**, la **fluoxétine**, l'**isoniazide**, le **kétoconazole**, le **métoprolol**, le **propoxyphène**, le **propanolol** ou l'**acide valproïque** peuvent ralentir le métabolisme du clonazépam et en accroître l'effet ■ Le clonazépam peut diminuer l'efficacité de la **lévodopa** ■ La **rifampine** ou les **barbituriques** peuvent accélérer le métabolisme du clonazépam et en diminuer l'efficacité ■ La **théophylline** peut diminuer les effets sédatifs du clonazépam ■ Le clonazépam peut élever les concentrations sériques de **phénytoïne** ■ La **phénytoïne** peut abaisser les concentrations sériques de clonazépam.

Médicament-produits naturels: Le **kava**, la **valériane** et la **camomille** peuvent accentuer la dépression du SNC.

VOIES D'ADMINISTRATION ET POSOLOGIE

- **PO (adultes)**: 0,5 mg, 3 fois par jour; cette dose peut être augmentée par paliers de 0,5 à 1 mg, tous les 3 jours. La dose d'entretien ne doit pas dépasser 20 mg par jour.
- **PO (enfants < 10 ans ou < 30 kg)**: Initialement, de 0,01 à 0,05 mg/kg par jour, en 2 ou 3 doses également fractionnées; ne pas augmenter la dose de plus de 0,25 à 0,5 mg, tous les 3 jours, jusqu'à l'atteinte de concentrations thérapeutiques dans le sang. La dose quotidienne ne doit pas dépasser 0,2 mg/kg.

PRÉSENTATION (version générique disponible)

Comprimés: 0,25 mg$^{T\backslash C}$; 0,5 mg$^{T\backslash C}$; 1 mg$^{T\backslash C}$; 2 mg$^{T\backslash C}$.

SOINS INFIRMIERS

ÉVALUATION DE LA SITUATION

- Noter l'intensité, la durée et le siège des convulsions.
- Avant le traitement et à intervalles réguliers pendant toute sa durée, noter la gravité des manifestations d'anxiété et suivre de près l'état mental du patient.
- Rester à l'affût de la somnolence, de l'instabilité ou des gestes maladroits. Ces symptômes sont reliés à la dose et ils sont plus graves au début du traitement; ils peuvent s'affaiblir ou disparaître au cours d'un traitement prolongé.

Tests de laboratoire:

- Vérifier, à intervalles réguliers pendant toute la durée d'un traitement prolongé, la numération globulaire et les résultats des tests de la fonction hépatique. Le clonazépam peut élever les concentrations de bilirubine sérique, d'AST et d'ALT.
- Le clonazépam peut réduire le captage par la thyroïde de l'iodure de sodium et des isotopes ^{123}I et ^{131}I.

TOXICITÉ ET SURDOSAGE: Les concentrations thérapeutiques se situent entre 20 et 80 mg/mL (de 32 à 158 mmol/L), mesurées avant l'administration de la dose.

DIAGNOSTICS INFIRMIERS POSSIBLES

- Risque d'accident (Indications, Effets secondaires).
- Connaissances insuffisantes sur le traitement médicamenteux (Enseignement au patient et à ses proches).

INTERVENTIONS INFIRMIÈRES

- NE PAS CONFONDRE LE CLONAZÉPAM AVEC LE CLORAZEPATE.
- Au début du traitement ou lors des adaptations posologiques, prendre les précautions qui s'imposent en cas de convulsions.
- Administrer le médicament avec des aliments afin de réduire l'irritation gastrique. On peut écraser les comprimés si le patient éprouve des difficultés de déglutition.

ENSEIGNEMENT AU PATIENT ET À SES PROCHES

- Expliquer au patient qu'il doit respecter rigoureusement la posologie recommandée. S'il n'a pu prendre son médicament au moment habituel, il doit le prendre dans l'heure qui suit, sinon il doit sauter cette dose. Le prévenir qu'il ne doit jamais remplacer une dose manquée par une double dose.

Le sevrage brusque peut entraîner un état de mal épileptique, des tremblements, des nausées, des vomissements et des crampes musculaires et abdominales.

- Prévenir le patient que le clonazépam peut provoquer des étourdissements et de la somnolence. Lui conseiller de ne pas conduire et d'éviter les activités qui exigent sa vigilance jusqu'à ce qu'on ait la certitude que le médicament n'entraîne pas ces effets chez lui.
- Recommander au patient d'éviter de boire de l'alcool et de prendre d'autres dépresseurs du SNC en même temps que le clonazépam.
- Recommander au patient qui doit suivre un autre traitement ou subir une intervention chirurgicale de prévenir le professionnel de la santé qu'il suit un traitement par ce médicament.
- Recommander au patient et à ses proches de signaler au médecin la fatigue inhabituelle, les hémorragies, les maux de gorge, la fièvre, les selles couleur de glaise, le jaunissement de la peau ou les modifications du comportement.
- Conseiller au patient de porter constamment sur lui une pièce d'identité où sont inscrits son problème de santé et son traitement médicamenteux.
- Insister sur l'importance des examens de suivi permettant d'évaluer l'efficacité du traitement.

VÉRIFICATION DE L'EFFICACITÉ THÉRAPEUTIQUE

L'efficacité du traitement peut être démontrée par: la diminution de la fréquence ou la suppression des crises sans sédation excessive; un ajustement de la posologie peut s'avérer nécessaire après plusieurs mois de traitement. ✳

CLONIDINE

Apo-Clonidine, Catapres, Dixarit, Novo-Clonidine, Nu-Clonidine

CLASSIFICATION:

Antihypertenseur (agoniste alpha$_2$-adrénergique à action centrale), stabilisateur vasculaire (traitement des bouffées de chaleur de la ménopause)

Grossesse – catégorie C

INDICATIONS

PO: Traitement de l'hypertension ■ Soulagement des bouffées de chaleur de la ménopause. **Usages non approuvés**: Traitement du sevrage narcotique ■ Urgence hypertensive.

MÉCANISME D'ACTION

Stimulation des récepteurs alpha-adrénergiques du SNC, qui se traduit par l'inhibition du centre cardioaccélérateur et du centre vasoconstricteur ■ Inhibition de la transmission des signaux de douleur au SNC par la stimulation des récepteurs alpha-adrénergiques situés au niveau de la moelle épinière ■ Réduction de la réaction des vaisseaux sanguins périphériques aux stimuli vasoconstricteurs et vasodilatateurs. ***Effets thérapeutiques:*** Baisse de la pression artérielle ■ Diminution de la douleur ■ Diminution des bouffées de chaleur.

PHARMACOCINÉTIQUE

Absorption: Bonne (de 75 à 95 %) ou partielle (voie sublinguale).

Distribution: L'agent se répartit dans tout l'organisme et pénètre dans le SNC. Il traverse rapidement la barrière placentaire et se retrouve dans le lait maternel à forte concentration.

Métabolisme et excrétion: Métabolisme majoritairement hépatique. Excrétion rénale à l'état inchangé (de 40 à 50 %).

Demi-vie: *Plasma* – de 12 à 22 heures; *SNC* – 1,3 heure.

Profil temps-action (effet sur la pression artérielle)

	DÉBUT D'ACTION	PIC	DURÉE
PO	30 - 60 min	2 - 4 h	8 - 12 h

CONTRE-INDICATIONS, PRÉCAUTIONS ET MISES EN GARDE

Contre-indications: Hypersensibilité ■ Bradyarythmie grave ■ Déficience du nœud sinusal.

Précautions et mises en garde: Maladie cardiaque grave ou maladie vasculaire cérébrale ■ Insuffisance rénale ■ **OBST., ALLAITEMENT**: L'innocuité du médicament n'a pas été établie ■ **GÉR.**: Risque accru d'hypotension orthostatique et d'effets secondaires sur le SNC; une réduction de la dose peut s'avérer nécessaire.

RÉACTIONS INDÉSIRABLES ET EFFETS SECONDAIRES

SNC: somnolence, dépression, étourdissements, nervosité, cauchemars.

CV: bradycardie, hypotension, palpitations.

GI: sécheresse de la bouche (xérostomie), constipation, nausées, vomissements.

GU: impuissance.

Tég.: rash, transpiration.

HÉ: rétention sodique.

Métab.: gain pondéral.

Divers: syndrome de sevrage.

C

INTERACTIONS

Médicament-médicament: Sédation accrue lors de l'usage concomitant de **dépresseurs du SNC**, dont l'**alcool**, les **antihistaminiques**, les **analgésiques opiacés** et les **hypnosédatifs** ▪ Effets hypotenseurs additifs lors de l'administration concomitante d'autres **antihypertenseurs** et de **dérivés nitrés** ▪ Accentuation de la bradycardie lors de l'administration de **dépresseurs du myocarde**, dont les **bêtabloquants** ▪ Les **IMAO**, les **amphétamines**, les **bêtabloquants**, la **prazosine** ou les **antidépresseurs tricycliques** peuvent réduire l'effet antihypertenseur de la clonidine ▪ Le syndrome de sevrage peut être amplifié lors de l'abandon du traitement par les **bêtabloquants** ▪ La clonidine peut réduire l'efficacité de la **lévodopa** ▪ Risque accru de réactions cardiovasculaires indésirables lors de l'administration concomitante du **vérapamil**.

VOIES D'ADMINISTRATION ET POSOLOGIE

- **PO (adultes)**: *Hypertension (dose initiale)* – 100 µg (0,1 mg), 2 fois par jour; augmenter cette dose par paliers de 100 à 200 µg (de 0,1 à 0,2 mg) par jour, tous les 2 à 4 jours, au besoin. La *dose d'entretien habituelle* est de 200 à 600 µg (de 0,2 à 0,6 mg) par jour, en 2 ou 3 prises fractionnées. *Bouffées de chaleur de la ménopause* – 0,05 mg, 2 fois par jour. **Usages non approuvés**: *Traitement de l'urgence hypertensive* – dose d'attaque de 200 µg (0,2 mg), puis 100 µg (0,1 mg), toutes les heures, jusqu'à la stabilisation de la pression artérielle ou jusqu'à concurrence de 800 µg (0,8 mg). Amorcer ensuite le traitement d'entretien. *Sevrage narcotique* – de 300 µg (0,3 mg) à 1,2 mg par jour; on peut réduire cette dose de 50 % par jour, et l'administrer pendant 3 jours; arrêter ensuite le traitement ou diminuer la dose de 100 à 200 µg (de 0,1 à 0,2 mg) par jour.
- **PO (personnes âgées)**: Dose initiale de 100 µg (0,1 mg), administrée au coucher. Augmenter la dose selon les besoins.

PRÉSENTATION (version générique disponible)

Comprimés: 0,025 mg^Pr, 0,1 mg^Pr, 0,2 mg^Pr.

SOINS INFIRMIERS

ÉVALUATION DE LA SITUATION

- Effectuer le bilan quotidien des ingesta et des excreta et peser le patient tous les jours. Observer le patient tous les jours pour déceler la formation d'un œdème, particulièrement au début du traitement.
- Mesurer souvent la pression artérielle et le pouls pendant la période d'adaptation de la posologie et à intervalles réguliers pendant toute la durée du traitement. Signaler tout changement important.

Sevrage narcotique: Rester à l'affût des signes et des symptômes suivants de sevrage narcotique: tachycardie, fièvre, rhinorrhée, diarrhée, transpiration, nausées, vomissements, irritabilité, crampes d'estomac, frissons, pupilles excessivement dilatées, faiblesse, troubles du sommeil, chair de poule.

Tests de laboratoire:

- Le médicament peut entraîner une élévation transitoire de la glycémie.
- La clonidine peut réduire les concentrations urinaires de catécholamines et d'acide vanylmandélique; ces concentrations peuvent s'accroître en cas de sevrage abrupt.
- Le médicament peut entraîner une réponse faiblement positive au test de Coombs.

DIAGNOSTICS INFIRMIERS POSSIBLES

- Risque d'accident (Effets secondaires).
- Connaissances insuffisantes sur le traitement médicamenteux (Enseignement au patient et à ses proches).

INTERVENTIONS INFIRMIÈRES

- NE PAS CONFONDRE LA CLONIDINE AVEC LE CLONAZÉPAM.
- Suivre de près la pression artérielle.
- Administrer la dernière dose de la journée au coucher.

ENSEIGNEMENT AU PATIENT ET À SES PROCHES

- Expliquer au patient qu'il doit prendre la clonidine tous les jours, à la même heure, même s'il se sent mieux. S'il n'a pu prendre le médicament au moment habituel, il doit le prendre dès que possible. S'il n'a pu prendre plusieurs doses consécutives, lui conseiller de consulter un professionnel de la santé. Il faut arrêter tout traitement par la clonidine graduellement pendant 2 à 4 jours afin de prévenir l'hypertension rebond.
- Recommander au patient de faire des provisions suffisantes de médicament pour les fins de semaine, les congés et les vacances. Lui conseiller de garder une ordonnance dans son portefeuille pour parer à toute urgence.
- Prévenir le patient que la clonidine peut provoquer de la somnolence, effet indésirable qui diminue habituellement lors d'un usage prolongé. Lui conseiller

de ne pas conduire et d'éviter les activités qui exigent sa vigilance jusqu'à ce qu'on ait la certitude que le médicament n'entraîne pas cet effet chez lui.

- Recommander au patient de changer lentement de position pour prévenir l'hypotension orthostatique. Le prévenir que l'alcool, une station debout prolongée, l'exercice et la chaleur peuvent intensifier l'hypotension orthostatique.
- Conseiller au patient souffrant de sécheresse de la bouche de se rincer fréquemment la bouche, de pratiquer une bonne hygiène buccale et de consommer de la gomme à mâcher ou des bonbons sans sucre. Si ce symptôme persiste pendant plus de 2 semaines, lui recommander de consulter un professionnel de la santé.
- Mettre en garde le patient contre la consommation concomitante d'alcool ou d'autres dépresseurs du SNC.
- Conseiller au patient de consulter un professionnel de la santé avant de prendre un médicament en vente libre, et particulièrement des médicaments contre le rhume, la toux et les allergies.
- Recommander au patient qui doit suivre un autre traitement ou subir une intervention chirurgicale de prévenir le professionnel de la santé qu'il suit ce traitement antihypertenseur.
- Recommander au patient de prévenir un professionnel de la santé en cas de dépression, d'enflure des pieds et des membres inférieurs, de pâleur ou de froideur des doigts ou des orteils, de rêves saisissants ou de cauchemars. Ces symptômes, en particulier la dépression, peuvent dicter l'arrêt du traitement.

Hypertension:

- Inciter le patient à suivre d'autres mesures d'abaissement de l'hypertension: perdre du poids, réduire la consommation de sel, arrêter de fumer, boire de l'alcool avec modération, faire régulièrement de l'exercice et diminuer le stress. La clonidine aide à stabiliser la pression artérielle, mais ne guérit pas l'hypertension.
- Montrer au patient et à ses proches comment mesurer la pression artérielle. Leur demander de prendre la pression artérielle au moins 1 fois par semaine et leur recommander de signaler tout changement important à un professionnel de la santé.

VÉRIFICATION DE L'EFFICACITÉ THÉRAPEUTIQUE

L'efficacité du traitement peut être démontrée par: la baisse de la pression artérielle ▪ la diminution des signes et des symptômes de sevrage narcotique ▪ la diminution des bouffées de chaleur de la ménopause.

CLOPIDOGREL

Plavix

CLASSIFICATION:
Antiplaquettaire

Grossesse - catégorie B

INDICATIONS

Prévention secondaire des épisodes vasculaires ischémiques (infarctus du myocarde, accident vasculaire cérébral, décès par maladie vasculaire) chez les patients ayant des antécédents de maladie athéroscléreuse symptomatique (antécédents récents d'infarctus du myocarde, d'accident vasculaire cérébral ou de maladie vasculaire périphérique) ▪ En association avec l'aspirine: prévention secondaire précoce et à long terme des complications athérothrombotiques (infarctus du myocarde, accident vasculaire ischémique, décès d'origine cardiovasculaire ou ischémie réfractaire), chez les patients présentant un syndrome coronarien aigu sans élévation du segment ST (c.-à-d., angine de poitrine instable ou infarctus du myocarde sans onde Q). Ces bienfaits du clopidogrel ont été observés uniquement chez les patients qui recevaient de l'aspirine en concomitance, en plus des autres traitements classiques, de même que chez les patients qui faisaient l'objet d'un traitement médicamenteux ou qui avaient subi une intervention coronarienne percutanée (avec ou sans endoprothèse vasculaire) ou un pontage aortocoronarien.

MÉCANISME D'ACTION

Inhibition de l'agrégation plaquettaire par l'inhibition irréversible de la liaison de l'adénosine-diphosphate (ADP) aux récepteurs des plaquettes. ***Effets thérapeutiques:*** Diminution du nombre d'épisodes vasculaires ischémiques chez les patients à risque.

PHARMACOCINÉTIQUE

Absorption: Bonne (PO). Transformation rapide en un métabolite doté d'effets antiplaquettaires. La molécule mère n'exerce aucun effet antiplaquettaire.

Distribution: Inconnue.

Liaison aux protéines: *Clopidogrel* – 98 %; *métabolite actif* – 94 %.

Métabolisme et excrétion: Rapidement et complètement transformé par le foie en un métabolite actif, qui est ensuite éliminé à 50 % dans l'urine et à 45 % dans les fèces.

Demi-vie: 8 heures (métabolite actif).

C

Profil temps-action (effet sur la fonction plaquettaire)

	Début d'action	Pic	Durée
PO	24 h	3 - 7 jours	5 - 7 jours†

† Après l'arrêt du traitement.

CONTRE-INDICATIONS, PRÉCAUTIONS ET MISES EN GARDE

Contre-indications: Hypersensibilité ■ Hémorragie active (p. ex., ulcère gastroduodénal ou hémorragie intracrânienne) ■ Atteinte hépatique grave ou ictère cholostatique.

Précautions et mises en garde: Patients présentant un risque d'hémorragie (traumatisme, intervention chirurgicale ou diverses pathologies) ■ En cas de chirurgie non urgente, on doit envisager l'arrêt du traitement de 5 à 7 jours avant l'intervention pour que l'effet du médicament ait le temps de disparaître ■ Antécédents d'hémorragie digestive ou d'ulcère ■ Insuffisance hépatique grave ■ **OBST., ALLAITEMENT, PÉD.**: L'innocuité du médicament n'a pas été établie; n'administrer le clopidogrel chez les femmes enceintes que s'il est spécifiquement indiqué.

RÉACTIONS INDÉSIRABLES ET EFFETS SECONDAIRES

SNC: dépression, étourdissements, fatigue, céphalées.

ORLO: épistaxis.

Resp.: toux, dyspnée.

CV: douleurs thoraciques, œdème, hypertension.

GI: HÉMORRAGIE DIGESTIVE, douleurs abdominales, diarrhée, dyspepsie, gastrite.

Tég.: prurit, purpura, rash.

Hémat.: HÉMORRAGIE, NEUTROPÉNIE, PURPURA THROMBOPÉNIQUE THROMBOTIQUE.

Métab.: hypercholestérolémie.

Loc.: arthralgie, douleurs lombaires.

Divers: fièvre, réactions d'hypersensibilité.

INTERACTIONS

Médicament-médicament: L'administration concomitante d'**abciximab**, d'**eptifibatide**, de **tirofiban**, d'**aspirine**, d'**AINS**, d'**héparine**, d'**héparinoïdes**, d'**agents thrombolytiques**, de **ticlopidine** ou de **warfarine** peut accroître le risque d'hémorragie ■ Le clopidogrel peut inhiber le métabolisme de la **phénytoïne**, du **tolbutamide**, du **tamoxifène**, de la **warfarine**, de la **fluvastatine** et de nombreux **AINS** et en intensifier les effets.

Médicament-produits naturels: Risque accru de saignement lors de la consommation concomitante d'**ail**, **d'anis**, d'**arnica**, de **camomille**, de **clou de girofle**, de **fenugrec**, de **grande camomille**, de **gingembre**, de **ginkgo**, de **ginseng** et d'**autres produits**.

VOIES D'ADMINISTRATION ET POSOLOGIE

Prévention secondaire des épisodes vasculaires ischémiques

- **PO (adultes):** 75 mg, 1 fois par jour.

Syndrome coronarien aigu

- **PO (adultes):** 300 mg le premier jour, puis 75 mg 1 fois par jour (en association avec de l'aspirine, de 80 mg à 325 mg par jour).

PRÉSENTATION

Comprimés: 75 mg[Pr].

SOINS INFIRMIERS

ÉVALUATION DE LA SITUATION

- Suivre le patient à intervalles réguliers tout au long du traitement pour déceler les signes d'accident vasculaire cérébral, de maladie vasculaire périphérique et d'infarctus du myocarde.
- RESTER À L'AFFÛT DES SIGNES DE PURPURA THROMBOPÉNIQUE THROMBOTIQUE (THROMBOPÉNIE, ANÉMIE HÉMOLYTIQUE MICROANGIOPATHIQUE, SYMPTÔMES NEUROLOGIQUES, INSUFFISANCE RÉNALE, FIÈVRE). EFFET INDÉSIRABLE PEU FRÉQUENT MAIS SÉRIEUX, POUVANT SURVENIR MÊME LORS D'UN TRAITEMENT DE COURTE DURÉE (< 2 SEMAINES) ET NÉCESSITANT UN TRAITEMENT RAPIDE.

Tests de laboratoire:

- NOTER LE TEMPS DE SAIGNEMENT TOUT AU LONG DU TRAITEMENT. LE CLOPIDOGEL ALLONGE LE TEMPS DE SAIGNEMENT. CET EFFET DÉPEND DE LA DURÉE DU TRAITEMENT ET DE LA DOSE ADMINISTRÉE.
- NOTER LA NUMÉRATION GLOBULAIRE, LA FORMULE LEUCOCYTAIRE ET LA NUMÉRATION PLAQUETTAIRE À INTERVALLES RÉGULIERS TOUT AU LONG DU TRAITEMENT. LA NEUTROPÉNIE ET LA THROMBOPÉNIE PEUVENT SURVENIR, BIEN QUE RAREMENT.
- Le médicament peut élever les concentrations de bilirubine sérique, d'enzymes hépatiques, de cholestérol total, d'azote non protéique et d'acide urique.

DIAGNOSTICS INFIRMIERS POSSIBLES

- Risque d'accident (Indications, Effets secondaires).
- Connaissances insuffisantes sur le traitement médicamenteux (Enseignement au patient et à ses proches).

INTERVENTIONS INFIRMIÈRES

- En cas de chirurgie non urgente, on doit envisager l'arrêt du traitement de 5 à 7 jours avant l'intervention.
- Administrer le clopidogrel 1 fois par jour, sans égard aux repas.

ENSEIGNEMENT AU PATIENT ET À SES PROCHES

- Expliquer au patient qu'il doit respecter rigoureusement la posologie recommandée. S'il n'a pu prendre le médicament au moment habituel, il doit le prendre aussitôt que possible, mais non pas juste avant l'heure prévue pour la dose suivante. Il ne faut jamais remplacer une dose manquée par une double dose.
- RECOMMANDER AU PATIENT DE SIGNALER IMMÉDIATEMENT À UN PROFESSIONNEL DE LA SANTÉ LES SYMPTÔMES SUIVANTS : FIÈVRE, FRISSONS, MAUX DE GORGE, SAIGNEMENTS INHABITUELS OU FORMATION D'ECCHYMOSES.
- Recommander au patient qui doit suivre un nouveau traitement ou subir une intervention chirurgicale d'avertir le professionnel de la santé qu'il suit ce traitement médicamenteux.
- Conseiller au patient de consulter un professionnel de la santé avant de prendre des médicaments en vente libre contenant de l'aspirine ou un AINS.

VÉRIFICATION DE L'EFFICACITÉ THÉRAPEUTIQUE

L'efficacité du traitement peut être démontrée par: la prévention des accidents vasculaires cérébraux, des infarctus du myocarde et du décès par maladie vasculaire chez les patients exposés à un tel risque.

CLORAZÉPATE

Apo-Clorazepate, Novo-Clopate, Tranxene

CLASSIFICATION:

Anxiolytique et hypnosédatif, anticonvulsivant (benzodiazépine)

Grossesse – catégorie D

INDICATIONS

Traitement de l'anxiété ■ Traitement du sevrage alcoolique ■ Traitement des crises partielles avec symptomatologie élémentaire.

MÉCANISME D'ACTION

Effet anxiolytique et dépression du SNC à de nombreux niveaux par stimulation des récepteurs inhibiteurs du GABA ■ Relaxation des muscles squelettiques par l'inhibition des voies polysynaptiques afférentes ■ Effets anticonvulsivants, accentuation de l'inhibition présynaptique. ***Effets thérapeutiques:*** Soulagement de l'anxiété ■ Sédation ■ Prévention des crises.

PHARMACOCINÉTIQUE

Absorption: Bonne (PO) sous forme de desméthyldiazépam.

Distribution: Tout l'organisme. Le clorazépate traverse la barrière placentaire et passe dans le lait maternel.

Métabolisme et excrétion: Métabolisme hépatique. Une fraction du clorazépate est transformée en composés actifs.

Demi-vie: 48 heures

Profil temps-action (sédation)

	DÉBUT D'ACTION	PIC	DURÉE
PO	1 - 2 h	1 - 2 h	jusqu'à 24 h†

† Parfois prolongée chez les personnes âgées.

CONTRE-INDICATIONS, PRÉCAUTIONS ET MISES EN GARDE

Contre-indications: Hypersensibilité connue au médicament ou à d'autres benzodiazépines (allergie croisée) ■ Glaucome à angle fermé ■ Myasthénie grave.

Précautions et mises en garde: Altération de la fonction hépatique ■ Insuffisance respiratoire grave ou apnée du sommeil ■ Insuffisance rénale grave ■ Comportement suicidaire ou antécédents de toxicomanie ou de pharmacodépendance ■ **GÉR.:** Il est recommandé de réduire la dose chez les personnes âgées ou débilitées ■ Coma ou dépression préexistante du SNC ■ **OBST.:** Le médicament traverse la barrière placentaire et peut s'accumuler dans l'organisme du fœtus ■ **ALLAITEMENT:** Le médicament est excrété dans le lait maternel et peut s'accumuler dans l'organisme du nourrisson.

RÉACTIONS INDÉSIRABLES ET EFFETS SECONDAIRES

SNC: étourdissements, somnolence, léthargie, sensation de tête légère, céphalées, dépression mentale, excitation paradoxale.

ORLO: vision trouble.

Resp.: dépression respiratoire.

GI: constipation, diarrhée, nausées, vomissements.

Tég.: rash.

Divers: dépendance physique, dépendance psychologique, tolérance aux effets du médicament.

C

INTERACTIONS

Médicament-médicament: Effets additifs sur la dépression du SNC lors de l'usage concomitant d'**alcool**, d'**antidépresseurs**, d'**antihistaminiques** et d'**analgésiques opiacés** ■ La **cimétidine**, les **contraceptifs oraux**, le **disulfirame**, la **fluoxétine**, l'**isoniazide**, le **kétoconazole**, le **métoprolol**, le **propoxyphène**, le **propranolol** et l'**acide valproïque** peuvent diminuer le métabolisme du clorazépate et en intensifier les effets ■ Le clorazépate peut réduire l'efficacité de la **lévodopa** ■ La **rifampine** et les **barbituriques** peuvent accélérer le métabolisme du clorazépate et en diminuer l'efficacité ■ La **théophylline** peut réduire les effets sédatifs du clorazépate.

Médicament-produits naturels: Le **kava**, la **valériane** et la **camomille** peuvent accentuer la dépression du SNC.

VOIES D'ADMINISTRATION ET POSOLOGIE

- **PO (adultes):** *Anxiété* – de 7,5 à 15 mg, de 2 à 4 fois par jour, ou dose unique de 15 à 22,5 mg, au coucher. *Sevrage alcoolique* – initialement 30 mg, puis 15 mg, de 2 à 4 fois par jour, le premier jour. Réduire graduellement la dose pendant les jours suivants. *Anticonvulsivant* – 7,5 mg, 3 fois par jour; augmenter par paliers de 7,5 mg par jour, toutes les semaines (dose maximale: 90 mg par jour).
- **PO (personnes âgées ou patients débilités):** *Anxiété* – initialement 3,75 mg, 1 fois par jour, de préférence au coucher, puis augmenter la dose graduellement selon la réponse au traitement et la tolérance du patient.
- **PO (enfants de 9 à 12 ans):** *Anticonvulsivant* – initialement 7,5 mg, 2 fois par jour, puis augmenter la dose par paliers de 7,5 mg par semaine (dose maximale: 60 mg par jour).

PRÉSENTATION

Capsules: 3,75 mg^T\C^, 7,5 mg^T\C^, 15 mg^T\C^.

SOINS INFIRMIERS

ÉVALUATION DE LA SITUATION

- Suivre de près la somnolence, l'instabilité ou les gestes maladroits. Ces symptômes sont reliés à la dose et ils sont plus graves au début du traitement; ils peuvent s'affaiblir ou disparaître au cours d'un traitement prolongé.

GÉR.: Évaluer le risque de chutes et mettre en place les mesures préventives.

- Le traitement prolongé avec des doses élevées peut entraîner une dépendance psychologique ou physique. Limiter la quantité de médicament dont le patient peut disposer.

Anxiété: Noter le degré d'anxiété et ses manifestations avant le traitement et à intervalles réguliers pendant toute sa durée.

Sevrage alcoolique: Rester à l'affût des symptômes suivants: tremblements, agitation, délire et hallucinations. Protéger le patient contre les accidents.

Convulsions: Noter l'intensité, la durée et le siège des convulsions.

Tests de laboratoire:

- Chez les patients recevant un traitement prolongé, il faut noter à intervalles réguliers la numération globulaire et la fonction hépatique. Le médicament peut entraîner l'élévation des concentrations sériques de bilirubine, d'AST et d'ALT.
- Le médicament peut réduire le captage par la thyroïde de l'iodure de sodium et des isotopes ^{123}I et ^{131}I.

DIAGNOSTICS INFIRMIERS POSSIBLES

- Anxiété (Indications).
- Risque d'accident (Indications, Effets secondaires).
- Connaissances insuffisantes sur le traitement médicamenteux (Enseignement au patient et à ses proches).

INTERVENTIONS INFIRMIÈRES

- NE PAS CONFONDRE LE CLORAZÉPATE AVEC LE CLONAZÉPAM.
- Administrer le médicament avec des aliments ou une boisson pour réduire l'irritation gastrique. LES CAPSULES DOIVENT ÊTRE AVALÉES TELLES QUELLES, SANS ÊTRE OUVERTES.
- Ne pas administrer d'antiacides dans l'heure qui suit la prise du clorazépate, car son absorption pourrait être retardée.

ENSEIGNEMENT AU PATIENT ET À SES PROCHES

- Expliquer au patient qu'il doit respecter rigoureusement la posologie recommandée et qu'il ne doit ni sauter de dose ni remplacer une dose manquée par une double dose. Le sevrage brusque peut entraîner les symptômes suivants: état de mal épileptique, tremblements, nausées, vomissements, crampes musculaires et abdominales.
- Prévenir le patient que le clorazépate peut provoquer de la somnolence et des étourdissements. Lui conseiller de ne pas conduire et d'éviter les activités qui exigent sa vigilance jusqu'à ce qu'on ait la cer-

titude que le médicament n'entraîne pas ces effets chez lui.

GÉR.: Enseigner au patient âgé et à ses proches les mesures préventives pour réduire le risque de chutes.

- Recommander au patient d'éviter la consommation d'alcool ou de dépresseurs du SNC pendant le traitement au clorazépate.
- Conseiller à la patiente de prévenir immédiatement un professionnel de la santé si elle pense être enceinte.
- Recommander au patient qui doit suivre un autre traitement ou subir une intervention chirurgicale de prévenir le professionnel de la santé qu'il suit un traitement avec ce médicament.
- Recommander au patient et à ses proches de signaler à un professionnel de la santé la fatigue inhabituelle, les hémorragies, les maux de gorge, la fièvre, les selles couleur de glaise, le jaunissement de la peau ou les modifications du comportement.
- Insister sur l'importance des examens de suivi permettant de déterminer l'efficacité du traitement.

Crises épileptiques: Conseiller au patient de porter constamment sur lui une pièce d'identité où sont inscrits son problème de santé et son traitement médicamenteux.

VÉRIFICATION DE L'EFFICACITÉ THÉRAPEUTIQUE

L'efficacité du traitement peut être démontrée par: une sensation de mieux-être ■ la diminution des symptômes subjectifs d'anxiété ■ la maîtrise des symptômes aigus du sevrage alcoolique ■ la diminution ou l'arrêt des crises d'épilepsie sans sédation excessive. ✳

CLOTRIMAZOLE,

voir Antifongiques topiques et Antifongiques vaginaux

CLOXACILLINE

Apo-Cloxi, Novo-Cloxin, Nu-Cloxi, Orbenin, Riva-Cloxacillin

CLASSIFICATION:

Antibiotique (pénicilline résistante à la pénicillinase)

Grossesse – catégorie B

INDICATIONS

Traitement des infections à streptocoques bêtahémolytiques, à pneumocoques et à staphylocoques (y compris celles dues à des microorganismes produisant de la bêtalactamase). Elle n'est toutefois pas active contre les souches de staphylocoques dites résistantes à la méthicilline.

MÉCANISME D'ACTION

Liaison à la paroi de la cellule bactérienne entraînant sa destruction. Résistance à l'action de la pénicillinase, enzyme capable d'inactiver la pénicilline. ***Effets thérapeutiques:*** Action bactéricide. **Spectre d'action**: Activité contre la plupart des coccis aérobies à Gram positif, mais à un degré moindre que la pénicilline ■ Action notable contre les microorganismes suivants: souches de *Staphylococcus aureus* produisant de la pénicillinase ■ *Staphylococcus epidermis* ■ Aucun effet sur les staphylocoques résistants à la méthicilline.

PHARMACOCINÉTIQUE

Absorption: De 37 à 60 % (PO)

Distribution: Répartition importante dans l'organisme. L'agent pénètre en quantité infime dans le liquide céphalorachidien, traverse la barrière placentaire et passe dans le lait maternel.

Liaison aux protéines: 95 %.

Métabolisme et excrétion: Métabolisme hépatique faible (de 9 à 22 %). Excrétion rénale (de 30 à 45 % sous forme inchangée).

Demi-vie: De 0,5 à 1,1 heure (prolongée en cas d'insuffisance hépatique ou rénale grave ou chez les nouveau-nés).

Profil temps-action (concentrations sanguines)

	DÉBUT D'ACTION	PIC	DURÉE
PO	30 min	30 – 120 min	6 h
IV	rapide	fin de la perfusion	4 – 6 h
IM	rapide	30 min	4 – 6 h

CONTRE-INDICATIONS, PRÉCAUTIONS ET MISES EN GARDE

Contre-indications: Hypersensibilité aux pénicillines ou aux céphalosporines (risque de réactions de sensibilité croisée avec les céphalosporines).

Précautions et mises en garde: **OBST., ALLAITEMENT**: L'innocuité du médicament n'a pas été établie.

RÉACTIONS INDÉSIRABLES ET EFFETS SECONDAIRES

SNC: CONVULSIONS (doses élevées).

GI: COLITE PSEUDOMEMBRANEUSE, diarrhée, nausées, hépatite médicamenteuse, vomissements.

GU: néphrite interstitielle.

Tég.: rash, urticaire.

Hémat.: dyscrasie sanguine.

Locaux: douleur au point d'injection IM, phlébite au point d'injection IV.
Divers: réactions allergiques, incluant l'ANAPHYLAXIE et la MALADIE SÉRIQUE, surinfection.

C

INTERACTIONS

Médicament-médicament: Le **probénécide** diminue l'excrétion rénale et accroît les concentrations de cloxacilline dans le sang ■ La cloxacilline peut modifier les effets de la **warfarine**.
Médicament-aliments: Les **aliments** et les **jus acides** réduisent l'absorption de la cloxacilline.

VOIES D'ADMINISTRATION ET POSOLOGIE

- **PO (adultes)**: De 250 à 500 mg, toutes les 6 heures (dose maximale: 6 g/jour).
- **PO (enfants < 20 kg)**: De 50 à 100 mg/kg/jour en 4 doses égales, toutes les 6 heures.
- **IM, IV (adultes)**: De 1 000 à 2 000 mg, toutes les 4 à 6 heures. La dose par voie IV peut être majorée dans le cas des infections graves. La dose maximale chez l'adulte est de 12 g/jour.
- **IM, IV (enfants > 1 mois et < 20 kg)**: De 50 à 100 mg/kg/jour en 4 doses égales, toutes les 6 heures. La dose par voie IV peut être majorée dans le cas des infections graves. On peut administrer des doses de 150 à 200 mg/kg/jour en 4 doses égales, toutes les 6 heures, sans dépasser 12 g/jour.
- **PO, IV (enfants > 7 jours et ≤ 1 mois)**: 75 mg/kg/jour, toutes les 8 heures (poids < 2 kg), ou 100 mg/kg/jour, toutes les 12 heures (poids ≥ 2 kg). *Méningite* (IV seulement): 150 mg/kg/jour, toutes les 8 heures (poids < 2 kg), ou 200 mg/kg/jour, toutes les 6 heures (poids ≥ 2 kg).
- **PO, IV (enfants ≤ 7 jours)**: 50 mg/kg/jour, toutes les 12 heures (poids < 2 kg), ou 75 mg/kg/jour, toutes les 8 heures (poids ≥ 2 kg). *Méningite* (IV seulement): 100 mg/kg/jour, toutes les 12 heures (poids < 2 kg), ou 150 mg/kg/jour, toutes les 8 heures (poids ≥ 2 kg).

PRÉSENTATION
(version générique disponible)

Capsules: 250 mg^Pr, 500 mg^Pr ■ **Solution orale**: 125 mg/5 mL^Pr ■ **Poudre pour injection**: fioles de 250 mg^Pr, 500 mg^Pr, 1 g^Pr et 2 g^Pr.

SOINS INFIRMIERS

ÉVALUATION DE LA SITUATION

- Au début du traitement et pendant toute sa durée, rester à l'affût des signes suivants d'infection: altération des signes vitaux, aspect de la plaie, des crachats, de l'urine et des selles, accroissement du nombre de globules blancs.
- Recueillir les antécédents du patient avant d'amorcer le traitement afin de déterminer ses réactions antérieures à une pénicilline ou à une céphalosporine. Même les personnes n'ayant jamais manifesté de sensibilité à la pénicilline peuvent présenter une réaction allergique.
- Prélever des échantillons pour les cultures et les antibiogrammes avant le début du traitement. La première dose peut être administrée avant que les résultats soient connus.
- RESTER À L'AFFÛT DES SIGNES ET DES SYMPTÔMES SUIVANTS D'ANAPHYLAXIE: RASH, PRURIT, ŒDÈME LARYNGÉ, RESPIRATION SIFFLANTE, DOULEURS ABDOMINALES. SI CES RÉACTIONS SE MANIFESTENT, ARRÊTER L'ADMINISTRATION DU MÉDICAMENT ET PRÉVENIR IMMÉDIATEMENT LE MÉDECIN OU UN AUTRE PROFESSIONNEL DE LA SANTÉ. GARDER À PORTÉE DE LA MAIN DE L'ADRÉNALINE, UN ANTIHISTAMINIQUE ET LE MATÉRIEL DE RÉANIMATION POUR PARER À UNE ÉVENTUELLE RÉACTION ANAPHYLACTIQUE.
- Examiner les veines pour déceler les signes d'irritation et de phlébite. Changer le point d'injection IV toutes les 48 heures pour prévenir la phlébite.

Tests de laboratoire:

- La cloxacilline peut entraîner une leucopénie ou une neutropénie, particulièrement en cas de traitement prolongé ou d'insuffisance hépatique.
- La cloxacilline peut positiver le test de Coombs direct.
- La cloxacilline peut entraîner une élévation des concentrations sériques d'AST, d'ALT, de LDH et de phosphatase alcaline.

DIAGNOSTICS INFIRMIERS POSSIBLES

- Risque d'infection (Indications, Effets secondaires).
- Connaissances insuffisantes sur le traitement médicamenteux (Enseignement au patient et à ses proches).
- Non-observance du traitement médicamenteux (Enseignement au patient et à ses proches).

INTERVENTIONS INFIRMIÈRES

PO:

- Administrer la cloxacilline à intervalles réguliers, à jeun, au moins 1 heure avant les repas ou 2 heures après. Demander au patient de prendre son médicament avec un grand verre d'eau; les jus acides peuvent en réduire l'absorption.

- Utiliser un récipient gradué pour mesurer les préparations liquides. Bien agiter.
- Pour reconstituer les solutions à administrer par voie IM, ajouter 1,9 mL d'eau stérile pour injection à chaque fiole de 250 mg, et 1,7 mL, à chaque fiole de 500 mg pour obtenir une concentration de 125 et 250 mg/mL, respectivement. Pour reconstituer les solutions à administrer par voie IV, ajouter 4,9 mL d'eau stérile pour injection à chaque fiole de 250 mg, 4,8 mL, à chaque fiole de 500 mg, et 9,6 mL, à chaque fiole de 1 g pour obtenir une concentration de 50, 100 et 100 mg/mL, respectivement. Pour reconstituer les solutions à administrer par perfusion IV, ajouter 3,4 mL d'eau stérile pour injection à chaque fiole de 1 g, et 6,8 mL, à chaque fiole de 2 g, pour obtenir une concentration de 250 mg/mL. Consulter les directives de chaque fabricant avant de reconstituer la préparation.

Perfusion intermittente: Diluer dans une solution de NaCl 0,9 % ou de D5%E.

Vitesse d'administration: Administrer en 30 à 40 minutes.

ENSEIGNEMENT AU PATIENT ET À SES PROCHES

- Recommander au patient de prendre toute la quantité de médicament qui lui a été prescrite, à intervalles réguliers, même s'il se sent mieux. S'il n'a pas pu prendre le médicament au moment habituel, il doit le prendre dès que possible. Insister sur le fait qu'il peut être dangereux de donner ce médicament à une autre personne.
- Conseiller au patient de signaler à un professionnel de la santé les signes de surinfection (excroissance pileuse sur la langue, pertes et démangeaisons vaginales, selles molles ou nauséabondes) et les allergies.
- CONSEILLER AU PATIENT DE CONSULTER UN PROFESSIONNEL DE LA SANTÉ EN CAS DE FIÈVRE OU DE DIARRHÉE, PARTICULIÈREMENT SI SES SELLES RENFERMENT DU SANG, DU PUS OU DU MUCUS. LUI RECOMMANDER DE NE PAS TRAITER LA DIARRHÉE SANS AVOIR CONSULTÉ AU PRÉALABLE UN PROFESSIONNEL DE LA SANTÉ.
- Recommander au patient de prévenir un professionnel de la santé si les symptômes ne s'améliorent pas.

VÉRIFICATION DE L'EFFICACITÉ THÉRAPEUTIQUE

L'efficacité du traitement peut être démontrée par: la disparition des signes et des symptômes d'infection. Le temps de la résolution dépend du microorganisme infectant et du siège de l'infection. ✳

CLOZAPINE

Clozaril, Apo-clozapine, Gen-Clozapine

CLASSIFICATION:
Antipsychotique

Grossesse – catégorie B

INDICATIONS

Traitement des patients schizophrènes qui ne répondent pas aux antipsychotiques classiques ou qui ne peuvent pas les tolérer.

MÉCANISME D'ACTION

Liaison aux récepteurs dopaminergiques du SNC ■ Propriétés anticholinergiques et alpha-adrénolytiques ■ Effets extrapyramidaux et réactions de dyskinésie tardive moindres que dans le cas des traitements antipsychotiques classiques, mais risque élevé d'anomalies hématologiques. ***Effets thérapeutiques:*** Diminution du comportement schizophrénique.

PHARMACOCINÉTIQUE

Absorption: Bonne (PO).

Distribution: L'agent se répartit rapidement dans tout l'organisme; il traverse la barrière hématoencéphalique et la barrière placentaire.

Liaison aux protéines: 95 %.

Métabolisme et excrétion: Premier passage hépatique important.

Demi-vie: De 8 à 12 heures.

Profil temps-action (effet antipsychotique)

	DÉBUT D'ACTION	PIC	DURÉE
PO	inconnu	plusieurs semaines	4 - 12 h

CONTRE-INDICATIONS, PRÉCAUTIONS ET MISES EN GARDE

Contre-indications: Hypersensibilité ■ Aplasie médullaire ■ Allaitement ■ Dépression grave du SNC ou coma ■ Malnutrition ou maladie cardiovasculaire, hépatique ou rénale ■ Trouble épileptique non maîtrisé ■ Patients incapables de subir des prélèvements sanguins.

Précautions et mises en garde: Hyperplasie bénigne de la prostate ■ Glaucome à angle fermé ■ Diabète ■ **PÉD.**: Enfants de moins de 16 ans (l'innocuité du médicament n'a pas été établie) ■ **GÉR.**: Personnes âgées atteintes de démence (risque accru de décès).

C

RÉACTIONS INDÉSIRABLES ET EFFETS SECONDAIRES

SNC: SYNDROME MALIN DES NEUROLEPTIQUES, CONVULSIONS, étourdissements, sédation.
ORLO: troubles de la vue.
CV: MYOCARDITE, hypotension, tachycardie, modifications de l'ÉCG, hypertension.
GI: constipation, malaises abdominaux, sécheresse de la bouche (xérostomie), salivation accrue, nausées, vomissements.
Tég.: rash, transpiration.
End.: hyperglycémie.
Hémat.: AGRANULOCYTOSE, LEUCOPÉNIE.
SN: réactions extrapyramidales.
Divers: fièvre, gain pondéral.

INTERACTIONS

Médicament-médicament: Effets anticholinergiques additifs lors de l'administration concomitante d'autres **agents dotés de propriétés anticholinergiques**, dont les **antihistaminiques**, la **quinidine**, le **disopyramide** et les **antidépresseurs** ■ Les **ISRS** (particulièrement la **fluvoxamine**), administrés en concomitance, élèvent les concentrations sanguines de clozapine et le risque de toxicité ■ Effets additifs sur la dépression du SNC lors de l'usage concomitant d'**alcool**, d'**antidépresseurs**, d'**antihistaminiques**, d'**analgésiques opioïdes** ou d'**hypnosédatifs** ■ Effets hypotenseurs additifs lors de l'administration concomitante d'**antihypertenseurs** et de **dérivés nitrés** et de l'ingestion de grandes quantités d'**alcool** ■ Risque accru d'aplasie médullaire lors de l'administration concomitante d'**agents dépresseurs de la moelle osseuse** ou d'une **radiothérapie** ■ Le **lithium**, administré simultanément, peut élever le risque d'effets indésirables sur le SNC, dont celui de convulsions.
Médicament-produits naturels: Les produits contenant de la **caféine** (thé, café, boisson de type cola) peuvent accroître les concentrations sanguines et les effets secondaires de la clozapine ■ Le **millepertuis** peut diminuer les concentrations sanguines et l'efficacité de la clozapine.

VOIES D'ADMINISTRATION ET POSOLOGIE

- **PO (adultes)**: Dose initiale de 12,5 mg, 1 ou 2 fois par jour, le premier jour, puis 25 mg, 1 ou 2 fois par jour, le deuxième jour. Si le médicament est bien toléré, augmenter la dose par paliers de 25 à 50 mg par jour pendant 2 semaines pour atteindre une dose cible de 300 à 450 mg par jour. Au-dessus de ce palier, on peut augmenter la dose jusqu'à concurrence de 100 mg par jour, 1 ou 2 fois par semaine, sans dépasser 900 mg par jour.

PRÉSENTATION

Comprimés: 25 mg[Pr], 100 mg[Pr].

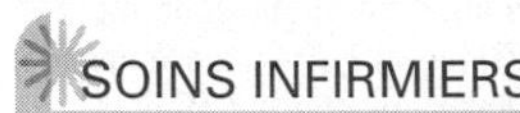

SOINS INFIRMIERS

ÉVALUATION DE LA SITUATION

- OBSERVER, AVANT LE TRAITEMENT ET À INTERVALLES RÉGULIERS PENDANT TOUTE SA DURÉE, L'ÉTAT MENTAL DU PATIENT (DÉLIRE, HALLUCINATIONS, COMPORTEMENT).
- Mesurer le pouls et la pression artérielle (en position assise, en station debout et en décubitus) avant l'administration initiale et fréquemment pendant la période initiale d'adaptation de la posologie.
- Observer attentivement le patient pendant qu'il prend le médicament pour s'assurer qu'il l'a bien avalé.
- DURANT LES PREMIERS MOIS DU TRAITEMENT, RESTER À L'AFFÛT DES SIGNES DE MYOCARDITE (FATIGUE INEXPLIQUÉE, DYSPNÉE, TACHYPNÉE, FIÈVRE, DOULEURS RÉTROSTERNALES, PALPITATIONS, SIGNES D'INSUFFISANCE CARDIAQUE, CHANGEMENTS À L'ÉCG, ARYTHMIES, TACHYCARDIE). L'ARRÊT DU TRAITEMENT DEVRAIT ÊTRE ENVISAGÉ SI CES SIGNES SURVENAIENT.
- Suivre de près le patient pour déceler l'akathisie (agitation ou besoin de bouger continuellement) et les symptômes extrapyramidaux (*symptômes parkinsoniens:* difficulté d'élocution ou de déglutition, perte de l'équilibre, mouvements d'émiettement, faciès figé, démarche traînante, rigidité, tremblements; *symptômes dystoniques:* spasmes musculaires dystoniques, torsions, secousses musculaires, incapacité de bouger les yeux, faiblesse des bras ou des jambes), tous les 2 mois pendant la durée du traitement et de 8 à 12 semaines après qu'il a pris fin. Informer immédiatement le médecin ou un autre professionnel de la santé de l'apparition de ces symptômes; il peut s'avérer nécessaire de réduire la dose ou d'abandonner le traitement. On peut administrer du trihexyphénidyle ou de la diphenhydramine pour maîtriser ces symptômes.
- Bien qu'on n'ait jamais signalé un tel effet avec la clozapine, suivre de près l'apparition de la dyskinésie tardive qui se traduit par les symptômes suivants: mouvements rythmiques des mâchoires, de la bouche, du visage et des membres; émission de bruits secs avec les lèvres, moue; gonflement des joues; mastication incontrôlée; mouvements rapides de la langue. Signaler immédiatement l'apparition de ces

symptômes, car de tels effets secondaires peuvent être irréversibles.

- Suivre la fréquence des défécations et noter la consistance des selles. Une consommation accrue de fibres alimentaires et de liquides peut aider à réduire la constipation.
- LA CLOZAPINE ABAISSE LE SEUIL DE CONVULSION. PRENDRE LES PRÉCAUTIONS DE MISE DANS LE CAS DU PATIENT AYANT DES ANTÉCÉDENTS DE TROUBLE ÉPILEPTIQUE.
- Une fièvre passagère peut se manifester, particulièrement au cours des 3 premières semaines de traitement. Elle se résorbe habituellement d'elle-même, mais elle peut parfois dicter l'arrêt du traitement. SUIVRE DE PRÈS L'APPARITION DES SYMPTÔMES SUIVANTS DU SYNDROME MALIN DES NEUROLEPTIQUES: FIÈVRE, DÉPRESSION RESPIRATOIRE, TACHYCARDIE, CONVULSIONS, DIAPHORÈSE, HYPERTENSION OU HYPOTENSION, PÂLEUR, FATIGUE. SIGNALER IMMÉDIATEMENT À UN PROFESSIONNEL DE LA SANTÉ L'APPARITION DE CES SYMPTÔMES.

Tests de laboratoire: LE TRAITEMENT NE PEUT ÊTRE AMORCÉ QUE LORSQUE LA NUMÉRATION ET LA FORMULE LEUCOCYTAIRES SONT NORMALES. CES ÉPREUVES DOIVENT ÊTRE EFFECTUÉES ENSUITE AU MOINS 1 FOIS PAR SEMAINE AU COURS DES 26 PREMIÈRES SEMAINES DE TRAITEMENT, ET AU MOINS TOUTES LES 2 SEMAINES, PAR LA SUITE, SELON L'ÉTAT CLINIQUE DU PATIENT. EN RAISON DU RISQUE D'AGRANULOCYTOSE, ON NE PEUT SE PROCURER LA CLOZAPINE QUE PAR L'INTERMÉDIAIRE D'UN RÉSEAU DE DISTRIBUTION EXIGEANT L'EXÉCUTION D'ANALYSES HÉMATOLOGIQUES TOUTES LES 1 OU 2 SEMAINES AVANT QU'ON NE REMETTE AU PATIENT LA PROVISION DE MÉDICAMENT POUR LA PÉRIODE SUIVANTE. SI LE NOMBRE DE LEUCOCYTES TOMBE AU-DESSOUS DE $2{,}0 \times 10^9$/L OU LE NOMBRE ABSOLU DE POLYNUCLÉAIRES NEUTROPHILES AU-DESSOUS DE $1{,}5 \times 10^9$/L, INTERROMPRE L'ADMINISTRATION DE LA CLOZAPINE ET RESTER À L'AFFÛT DES SIGNES ET DES SYMPTÔMES D'INFECTION.

TOXICITÉ ET SURDOSAGE:

- En cas de surdosage, il faut administrer du charbon activé et assurer un traitement de soutien. Observer le patient pendant plusieurs jours en raison du risque d'effets tardifs.
- Éviter d'administrer de l'adrénaline et ses dérivés pour traiter l'hypotension, tout comme de la quinidine et du procaïnamide pour traiter les arythmies.

DIAGNOSTICS INFIRMIERS POSSIBLES

- Risque de violence envers soi et envers les autres (Indications).
- Opérations de la pensée perturbées (Indications).
- Risque d'accident (Effets secondaires).

INTERVENTIONS INFIRMIÈRES

- Administrer les comprimés avec des aliments ou du lait pour réduire l'irritation gastrique.

ENSEIGNEMENT AU PATIENT ET À SES PROCHES

- Expliquer au patient qu'il doit respecter rigoureusement la posologie recommandée. Lorsque le traitement doit être arrêté, les patients suivant un traitement prolongé doivent être sevrés graduellement pendant une période de 1 à 2 semaines.
- Mettre en garde le patient contre le risque de symptômes extrapyramidaux. L'inciter à prévenir immédiatement un professionnel de la santé si ces symptômes se manifestent.
- Recommander au patient de changer lentement de position afin de réduire le risque d'hypotension orthostatique.
- Prévenir le patient que la clozapine peut provoquer des convulsions et de la somnolence. Lui conseiller de ne pas conduire et d'éviter les activités qui exigent sa vigilance durant le traitement à la clozapine.
- Mettre en garde le patient contre la consommation d'alcool, d'autres dépresseurs du SNC ou de médicaments en vente libre sans avoir consulté au préalable un professionnel de la santé.
- Conseiller au patient de se rincer fréquemment la bouche, de pratiquer une bonne hygiène buccale et de consommer de la gomme à mâcher ou des bonbons sans sucre pour soulager la sécheresse de la bouche.
- Recommander au patient qui doit suivre un autre traitement ou subir une intervention chirurgicale d'avertir le professionnel de la santé qu'il suit un traitement avec ce médicament.
- Conseiller au patient d'informer rapidement un professionnel de la santé de l'apparition des symptômes suivants: maux de gorge, fièvre, léthargie, faiblesse, malaises ou symptômes pseudogrippaux. Demander à la patiente d'avertir un professionnel de la santé si elle est enceinte ou désire le devenir.
- Insister sur l'importance des examens réguliers de suivi, des examens de la vue, des examens diagnostiques et de la psychothérapie.

VÉRIFICATION DE L'EFFICACITÉ THÉRAPEUTIQUE

L'efficacité du traitement peut être démontrée par: la diminution du comportement schizophrénique. ✳

C

ALERTE CLINIQUE

CODÉINE

Codéine Contin, Codéine, Ratio-Codéine

CLASSIFICATION:

Antitussif, analgésique opioïde (agoniste)

Grossesse – catégories C et D (en usage prolongé ou à doses élevées près du terme)

INDICATIONS

Traitement de la douleur légère à modérée ■ Traitement de la toux (faibles doses) ■ **Préparation à action prolongée**: Traitement de la douleur légère à modérée nécessitant l'usage prolongé d'un analgésique opioïde. **Usages non approuvés**: Traitement de la diarrhée.

MÉCANISME D'ACTION

Liaison aux récepteurs opioïdes du SNC. Modification de la perception des stimuli douloureux et de la réaction à la douleur tout en produisant une dépression généralisée du SNC ■ Réduction du réflexe de la toux ■ Diminution de la motilité du tractus gastro-intestinal. ***Effets thérapeutiques:*** Diminution de l'intensité de la douleur ■ Suppression du réflexe de la toux ■ Diminution de la diarrhée.

PHARMACOCINÉTIQUE

Absorption: 50 % (PO), 100 % (IM). Les doses par voies orale et parentérale ne sont pas équivalentes.

Distribution: Tout l'organisme. La codéine traverse la barrière placentaire et pénètre dans le lait maternel.

Métabolisme et excrétion: Métabolisme majoritairement hépatique. 10 % est transformé en morphine et de 5 à 15 % est excrété à l'état inchangé dans l'urine.

Demi-vie: De 2,5 à 4 heures.

Profil temps-action (effet analgésique)

	DÉBUT D'ACTION	PIC	DURÉE
PO	30 – 45 min	60 – 120 min	4 h
PO (comprimé à libération contrôlée)	60 min et +	3 – 4 h	12 h
IM	10 – 30 min	30 – 60 min	4 h
SC	10 – 30 min	inconnu	4 h

CONTRE-INDICATIONS, PRÉCAUTIONS ET MISES EN GARDE

Contre-indications: Hypersensibilité ■ Crise d'asthme ou autres troubles obstructifs des voies respiratoires supérieures et dépression respiratoire aiguë ■ Cœur pulmonaire ■ Alcoolisme aigu ■ Delirium tremens ■ Dépression grave du SNC ■ Troubles convulsifs ■ Abdomen aigu soupçonné ■ Traumatisme crânien ■ Pression intracrânienne accrue ■ Diarrhée due à un empoisonnement (toxine) ■ Prise concomitante d'un IMAO (ou dans les 14 jours qui suivent un tel traitement). ■ Les patients ayant une hypersensibilité ou une intolérance à l'alcool, à l'aspartame, à la saccharine, au sucre ou à la tartrazine doivent éviter les associations de médicaments contenant ces substances.

Précautions et mises en garde: ■ Maladies hépatique, rénale ou pulmonaire graves ■ Hypothyroïdie ■ Insuffisance surrénalienne ■ Alcoolisme ■ **GÉR.**: Personnes âgées ou patients débilités (réduire la dose; ces patients sont davantage exposés au risque de dépression du SNC et de constipation) ■ Douleurs abdominales non diagnostiquées ■ Hyperplasie de la prostate ■ **OBST., ALLAITEMENT**: Précédents d'utilisation pendant le travail de l'accouchement; risque de dépression respiratoire chez le nouveau-né ■ Grossesse et allaitement (éviter l'administration prolongée) ■ **PÉD.**: Nouveau-nés et enfants < 3 mois (risque accru de dépression respiratoire); nouveau-nés (éviter les préparations injectables contenant des agents de conservation et les solutions buvables contenant du benzoate de sodium, car elles peuvent causer un « syndrome de halètement » pouvant être mortel) ■ Risque de pharmacodépendance et d'abus.

RÉACTIONS INDÉSIRABLES ET EFFETS SECONDAIRES

SNC: confusion, sédation, dysphorie, euphorie, sensation de flottement, hallucinations, céphalées, rêves bizarres.

ORLO: vision trouble, diplopie, myosis.

Resp.: DÉPRESSION RESPIRATOIRE.

CV: hypotension, bradycardie.

GI: constipation, nausées, vomissements.

GU: rétention urinaire.

Tég.: rash, transpiration.

Divers: dépendance physique, dépendance psychologique, tolérance à l'effet du médicament.

INTERACTIONS

Médicament-médicament: LA CODÉINE NE DOIT PAS ÊTRE ADMINISTRÉE CHEZ DES PATIENTS RECEVANT DES **IMAO** OU LA **PROCARBAZINE**, CAR ELLE PEUT PROVOQUER DES RÉACTIONS GRAVES ET IMPRÉVISIBLES ■ Dépression additive du SNC et du système respiratoire lors de l'usage concomitant d'**alcool**, d'**antihistaminiques**, de **phénothiazines**, de **barbituriques**, d'**antidépresseurs**, d'**hypnosédatifs** et d'autres **opioïdes** ■ L'administration d'**analgésiques opioïdes agonistes/antagonistes** (**nalbuphine**, **butorphanol**, **pentazocine**) peut diminuer l'analgésie ou déclencher des symptômes de sevrage chez les patients présentant une dépendance physique aux analgésiques opioïdes.

Médicament-produits naturels: Effets dépresseurs additifs sur le SNC lors de la consommation concomitante de **kava**, de **valériane**, de **scutellaire**, de **camomille** et de **houblon**.

VOIES D'ADMINISTRATION ET POSOLOGIE

- **PO (adultes):** *Analgésique* – de 15 à 60 mg, toutes les 3 à 6 heures, selon les besoins. *Antitussif* – de 10 à 20 mg, toutes les 4 à 6 heures, selon les besoins (ne pas dépasser 120 mg par jour). *Usages non approuvés: Antidiarrhéique* – 30 mg, jusqu'à 4 fois par jour.
- **PO (enfants de 6 à 12 ans):** *Analgésique* – 0,5 mg/kg, toutes les 4 à 6 heures (jusqu'à 4 fois par jour), selon les besoins. *Antitussif* – de 5 à 10 mg, toutes les 4 à 6 heures, selon les besoins (ne pas dépasser 60 mg par jour).
- **PO (enfants de 2 à 5 ans):** *Analgésique* – 0,5 mg/kg, toutes les 4 à 6 heures (jusqu'à 4 fois par jour), selon les besoins. *Antitussif* – de 2,5 à 5 mg, toutes les 4 à 6 heures, selon les besoins (ne pas dépasser 30 mg par jour).
- **Préparation à action prolongée (PO):** *Analgésique* – Il faut calculer la dose quotidienne totale approximative de codéine à libération normale par voie orale qui devrait procurer une analgésie équivalente. On administre une dose de la préparation à action prolongée environ 25 % moindre, divisée en 2 prises égales, administrées à 12 heures d'intervalle.
- **IM, SC (adultes):** *Analgésique* – de 15 à 60 mg, toutes les 4 à 6 heures, selon les besoins.
- **IM, SC (enfants et nourrissons):** *Analgésique* – 0,5 mg/kg, toutes les 4 à 6 heures, selon les besoins.

PRÉSENTATION (version générique disponible)

Comprimés: 15 mg[N], 30 mg[N] ■ **Comprimés à libération prolongée (Codeine Contin):** 50 mg[N], 100 mg[N], 150 mg[N], 200 mg[N] ■ **Solution orale:** 5 mg/mL[N] ■ **Solution pour injection:** 30 mg/mL[N], 60 mg/mL[N] ■ **En association avec:** antihistaminiques, décongestionnants, antipyrétiques, caféine, butalbital et analgésiques non opioïdes[N]. Voir l'annexe U.

SOINS INFIRMIERS

ÉVALUATION DE LA SITUATION

- ÉVALUER L'ÉTAT DE CONSCIENCE ET MESURER LA PRESSION ARTÉRIELLE, LE POULS ET LA FRÉQUENCE RESPIRATOIRE AVANT L'ADMINISTRATION DU MÉDICAMENT ET À INTERVALLES RÉGULIERS TOUT AU LONG DU TRAITEMENT. SI LA FRÉQUENCE RESPIRATOIRE EST < 10 RESPIRATIONS PAR MINUTE, ÉVALUER LE NIVEAU DE SÉDATION. DES STIMULI PHYSIQUES PEUVENT SUFFIRE POUR PRÉVENIR UNE HYPOVENTILATION MARQUÉE. IL PEUT ÊTRE NÉCESSAIRE DE RÉDUIRE LA DOSE DE 25 À 50 %. LA SOMNOLENCE OBSERVÉE AU DÉBUT DU TRAITEMENT DIMINUERA AU COURS D'UN TRAITEMENT PROLONGÉ.

GÉR.: Évaluer les patients âgés à intervalles fréquents, car ils sont plus sensibles aux effets des analgésiques opioïdes que les adultes plus jeunes; chez eux, les effets indésirables et les complications respiratoires peuvent être plus fréquents.

PÉD.: Évaluer les enfants à intervalles fréquents, car ils sont plus sensibles aux effets des analgésiques opioïdes; chez eux, les complications respiratoires, l'excitabilité et l'agitation peuvent être plus fréquentes.

- Déterminer les habitudes d'élimination intestinale à intervalles réguliers. Pour réduire les effets constipants du médicament, augmenter l'apport de liquides et de fibres alimentaires et administrer des laxatifs. Sauf contre-indication, des laxatifs stimulants devraient être administrés systématiquement si le traitement par l'opioïde dure plus de 2 ou 3 jours.

Douleur:

- Noter le type de douleur, son siège et son intensité avant l'administration du médicament et 60 minutes (pic) après. Lors de l'adaptation de la posologie, on devrait augmenter la dose par paliers de 25 à 50 % jusqu'à ce qu'on obtienne une réduction de 50 % de la douleur sur une échelle numérique ou analogique visuelle ou jusqu'à ce que le patient signale un soulagement adéquat de la douleur. On peut administrer sans danger une dose additionnelle lorsque la concentration de médicament atteint un pic, si la dose précédente s'est avérée inefficace et si les effets secondaires ont été minimes.
- On devrait utiliser un tableau des analgésiques équivalents (voir l'annexe A) lorsqu'on change de voie d'administration ou lorsqu'on substitue un opioïde à un autre.
- L'usage prolongé peut entraîner la dépendance physique et psychologique ainsi qu'une tolérance à l'effet du médicament, mais cela ne doit pas empêcher le patient de recevoir une quantité suffisante d'analgésique. La psychodépendance est rare chez la plupart des patients qui reçoivent de la codéine pour le soulagement de la douleur. Si des doses de plus en plus élevées sont nécessaires, on devrait envisager de passer à un opioïde plus puissant.

C

Toux: Noter la fréquence et la nature de la toux, ausculter le murmure vésiculaire tout au long du traitement antitussif.

Tests de laboratoire: La codéine peut entraîner l'élévation des concentrations plasmatiques d'amylase et de lipase.

Toxicité et surdosage: Si on doit administrer un antagoniste opioïde pour renverser la dépression respiratoire ou le coma, l'antidote est la naloxone (Narcan). Diluer 0,4 mg de naloxone dans 10 mL de solution de NaCl 0,9 % et administrer 0,5 mL (0,02 mg) par bolus intraveineux direct, toutes les 2 minutes. Dans le cas des enfants et des patients pesant moins de 40 kg, diluer 0,1 mg de naloxone dans 10 mL de solution de NaCl 0,9 %, pour obtenir une concentration de 10 µg/mL et administrer 0,5 µg/kg, toutes les 2 minutes. Adapter la dose pour prévenir les symptômes de sevrage, les crises convulsives et la douleur intense.

DIAGNOSTICS INFIRMIERS POSSIBLES

- Douleur aiguë (Indications).
- Trouble de la perception visuelle et auditive (Effets secondaires).
- Risque d'accident (Effets secondaires).

INTERVENTIONS INFIRMIÈRES

Alerte clinique: Des surdoses accidentelles d'analgésiques opioïdes ont causé des décès. Évaluer l'utilisation antérieure d'analgésiques opioïdes par le patient et ses besoins courants. Avant l'administration, clarifier tous les points ambigus et faire vérifier l'ordonnance originale et le calcul des doses par un autre professionnel de la santé.

Péd.: Les erreurs dans l'administration des analgésiques opioïdes sont fréquentes dans la population pédiatrique; elles comprennent des erreurs d'interprétation, de calculs de dose et l'usage d'instruments de mesure inappropriés.

- Utiliser seulement des préparations sans agent de conservation chez les nouveau-nés et pour l'administration épidurale et intrathécale chez tous les patients.
- Expliquer au patient le rôle thérapeutique du médicament, avant de l'administrer, pour en augmenter l'effet analgésique.
- Les doses administrées selon un horaire fixe peuvent être plus efficaces que celles administrées sur demande. Le médicament s'avère plus efficace s'il est administré avant que la douleur ne devienne intense.
- Les analgésiques non opioïdes, administrés simultanément, peuvent exercer des effets analgésiques additifs, ce qui permet parfois de diminuer la dose d'opioïde.
- Après un traitement prolongé, interrompre l'administration de la codéine graduellement pour prévenir les symptômes de sevrage.
- La codéine est souvent présentée en association avec des analgésiques non opioïdes (aspirine, acétaminophène; n° 1 = 8 mg, n° 2 = 15 mg, n° 3 = 30 mg, n° 4 = 60 mg de codéine). La distribution de la codéine, seule et en association, doit respecter les exigences du Règlement sur les stupéfiants, régi par le Bureau des substances contrôlées de Santé Canada (voir l'annexe B).

PO: Administrer avec des aliments ou du lait pour réduire l'irritation gastrique.

Préparation à action prolongée: Les comprimés à libération contrôlée doivent être avalés entiers, sans être ni mâchés ni écrasés. La prise de comprimés brisés, mâchés ou écrasés pourrait entraîner la libération et l'absorption rapides d'une dose de codéine qui pourrait être mortelle. Toutes les concentrations, sauf celle de 50 mg, peuvent être fractionnées. Les demi-comprimés doivent aussi être avalés intacts.

SC, IM: Ne pas administrer la solution si elle a fortement changé de couleur ou si elle renferme un précipité.

IV directe: La codéine est habituellement administrée par voie IM ou SC, mais on l'a déjà administrée par injection IV lente.

Associations compatibles dans la même seringue: glycopyrrolate ▪ hydroxyzine.

ENSEIGNEMENT AU PATIENT ET À SES PROCHES

- Expliquer au patient ce qu'on entend par administration sur demande et à quel moment il doit réclamer l'analgésique.
- Prévenir le patient que la codéine peut provoquer des étourdissements et de la somnolence. Lui recommander de demander de l'aide lorsqu'il se déplace et lorsqu'il veut fumer. Lui conseiller de ne pas conduire et d'éviter les activités qui exigent sa vigilance jusqu'à ce qu'on ait la certitude que le médicament n'entraîne pas ces effets chez lui.
- Recommander au patient de changer lentement de position pour diminuer le risque d'hypotension orthostatique.
- Recommander au patient de ne pas boire d'alcool et de ne pas prendre d'autres dépresseurs du SNC en même temps que la codéine.
- Recommander au patient de se tourner dans le lit, de tousser et de faire des exercices de respiration

profonde toutes les 2 heures pour prévenir l'atélectasie.

- Conseiller au patient de se rincer fréquemment la bouche, de pratiquer une bonne hygiène buccale et de consommer de la gomme à mâcher ou des bonbons sans sucre pour soulager la sécheresse de la bouche.
- Insister sur l'importance de la prévention de la constipation associée à la prise d'analgésiques opioïdes.

PÉD.: ENSEIGNER AUX PARENTS OU AUX SOIGNANTS COMMENT MESURER AVEC PRÉCISION LE MÉDICAMENT EN LIQUIDE ET LEUR CONSEILLER D'UTILISER SEULEMENT LA MESURE FOURNIE.

VÉRIFICATION DE L'EFFICACITÉ THÉRAPEUTIQUE

L'efficacité du traitement peut être démontrée par: la diminution de l'intensité de la douleur sans modification importante de l'état de conscience ou de l'état respiratoire ■ la suppression de la toux ■ la maîtrise de la diarrhée. ✳

ALERTE CLINIQUE

COLCHICINE

Colchicine

CLASSIFICATION:

Antigoutteux

Grossesse – catégorie D

INDICATIONS

Traitement des accès aigus d'arthrite goutteuse (crises de goutte) (doses élevées) ■ Prévention des accès récurrents de goutte (doses faibles). **Usages non approuvés:** Traitement de la cirrhose hépatique et de la fièvre familiale méditerranéenne, de diverses amyloses, du syndrome de Behçet, de la péricardite et d'autres maladies.

MÉCANISME D'ACTION

Effets thérapeutiques: Atténuation de la douleur et de l'inflammation lors d'accès aigus de goutte ■ Prévention de la récurrence des accès de goutte.

PHARMACOCINÉTIQUE

Absorption: Bonne (PO).

Distribution: Le médicament se concentre dans les leucocytes.

Métabolisme et excrétion: Métabolisme partiellement hépatique. La colchicine subit plusieurs cycles entérohépatiques. Élimination dans les fèces. Faible excrétion urinaire.

Demi-vie: 20 minutes (plasma), 60 heures (leucocytes).

Profil temps-action (effet anti-inflammatoire)

	DÉBUT D'ACTION	PIC	DURÉE
PO	12 h	24 – 72 h	inconnue

CONTRE-INDICATIONS, PRÉCAUTIONS ET MISES EN GARDE

Contre-indications: Hypersensibilité ■ Dyscrasies sanguines ■ Insuffisance rénale (Cl_{Cr} < 10 mL/minute) ■ Insuffisance hépatique grave ■ Ulcère gastroduodénal évolutif ou maladie gastro-intestinale ■ Maladie cardiaque grave.

Précautions et mises en garde: **GÉR.**: Personnes âgées ou patients débilités (risque de toxicité cumulative) ■ Insuffisance rénale (réduire la dose si la Cl_{Cr} est < 50 mL/min) ■ **OBST., ALLAITEMENT, PÉD.**: L'innocuité du médicament n'a pas été établie.

RÉACTIONS INDÉSIRABLES ET EFFETS SECONDAIRES

GI: diarrhée, nausées, vomissements, douleurs abdominales.

GU: anurie, hématurie, lésions rénales.

Tég.: alopécie.

Hémat.: AGRANULOCYTOSE, ANÉMIE APLASIQUE, leucopénie, thrombopénie.

SN: névrite périphérique.

INTERACTIONS

Médicament-médicament: Risque accru d'aplasie médullaire lors de l'administration concomitante d'**agents dépresseurs de la moelle osseuse** ou d'une **radiothérapie** ■ L'administration concomitante d'**AINS** entraîne une augmentation des effets indésirables gastro-intestinaux et du risque d'hémorragie ■ La colchicine peut entraîner la malabsorption réversible de la **vitamine B_{12}** ■ L'association d'**alcool** et de colchicine peut augmenter la toxicité gastro-intestinale et diminuer l'efficacité du traitement, car l'alcool peut élever les taux d'acide urique ■ L'administration concomitante de **cyclosporine** peut provoquer des manifestations toxiques gastro-intestinales, hépatorénales et neuromusculaires ■ La **clarithromycine, l'érythromycine** ou d'autres **médicaments inhibant la p-glycoprotéine ou le CYP3A4**, administrés en concomitance, peuvent élever les concentrations plasmatiques de colchicine et augmenter sa toxicité.

C

VOIES D'ADMINISTRATION ET POSOLOGIE

- **PO (adultes):** *Traitement des crises aiguës de goutte* – 0,6 mg, 3 ou 4 fois par jour jusqu'au soulagement des symptômes ou jusqu'à ce que des effets indésirables gastro-intestinaux surviennent ou jusqu'à un maximum de 10 à 12 doses (risque plus élevé de toxicité); ou 1,2 mg, toutes les 12 heures, pour 3 doses au maximum. *Prophylaxie* – De 0,5 mg, de 1 à 4 fois par semaine, à 1,8 mg/jour (en 3 prises), selon la fréquence des crises. La dose habituelle est de 1 mg/jour.

INSUFFISANCE RÉNALE

- **PO (ADULTES):** *CL_{CR} DE 10 À 50 mL/MIN* – RÉDUIRE LA DOSE DE 50 %; *CL_{CR} < 10 mL/MIN* – NE PAS ADMINISTRER CE MÉDICAMENT.

INSUFFISANCE HÉPATIQUE

- **PO (ADULTES):** ADMINISTRER DE FAIBLES DOSES. SUIVRE DE PRÈS LES EFFETS INDÉSIRABLES.

PRÉSENTATION (version générique disponible)

Comprimés: 0,6 mg[Pr], 1 mg[Pr].

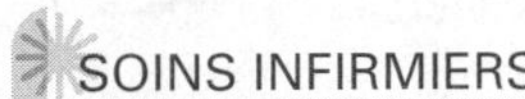

SOINS INFIRMIERS

ÉVALUATION DE LA SITUATION

- RESTER À L'AFFÛT DES SIGNES ET DES SYMPTÔMES DE TOXICITÉ SUIVANTS: FAIBLESSE, DOULEURS ABDOMINALES, NAUSÉES, VOMISSEMENTS, DIARRHÉE, DÉLIRE, CONVULSIONS, SENSATION DE SUFFOCATION, DILATATION DES PUPILLES, DIFFICULTÉS DE DÉGLUTITION, PARALYSIE ASCENDANTE, OLIGURIE. EN CAS DE TOXICITÉ, ARRÊTER LE TRAITEMENT ET PRÉVENIR IMMÉDIATEMENT LE MÉDECIN TRAITANT.
- Suivre de près les douleurs articulaires, l'enflure et la mobilité des articulations pendant toute la durée du traitement. Au début du traitement, noter la réponse thérapeutique toutes les 1 ou 2 heures.
- Effectuer le bilan des ingesta et des excreta. Inciter le patient à boire beaucoup de liquides pour favoriser un débit urinaire d'au moins 2 000 mL par jour.

Tests de laboratoire:

- NOTER LA NUMÉRATION GLOBULAIRE COMPLÈTE AU DÉBUT DU TRAITEMENT ET À INTERVALLES RÉGULIERS CHEZ LES PATIENTS SUIVANT UN TRAITEMENT DE LONGUE DURÉE; SIGNALER TOUTE MODIFICATION IMPORTANTE DE L'UN DES RÉSULTATS. LA COLCHICINE PEUT PROVOQUER UNE BAISSE DE LA NUMÉRATION PLAQUETTAIRE, LA LEUCOPÉNIE, L'ANÉMIE APLASIQUE ET L'AGRANULOCYTOSE.
- La colchicine peut entraîner l'élévation des concentrations d'AST et de phosphatase alcaline.
- Le médicament peut entraîner des résultats faussement positifs au dosage de l'hémoglobine urinaire.
- La colchicine peut fausser les résultats du dosage des 17-hydroxycorticostéroïdes dans l'urine.

TOXICITÉ ET SURDOSAGE: Observer le patient à la recherche des symptômes suivants de toxicité: faiblesse, malaises abdominaux, nausées, vomissements, diarrhée. Si ces symptômes se manifestent, arrêter le traitement et prévenir le médecin ou un autre professionnel de la santé. La diarrhée peut dicter un traitement par des opioïdes.

DIAGNOSTICS INFIRMIERS POSSIBLES

- Douleur aiguë (Indications).
- Mobilité physique réduite (Indications).
- Connaissances insuffisantes sur le traitement médicamenteux (Enseignement au patient et à ses proches).

INTERVENTIONS INFIRMIÈRES

- UN SURDOSAGE DE COLCHICINE PEUT MENER À UNE ISSUE FATALE. LA DOSE CUMULATIVE NE DEVRAIT PAS DÉPASSER 4 mg. UNE FOIS CETTE DOSE ATTEINTE, LE PATIENT DEVRAIT ARRÊTER DE PRENDRE LA COLCHICINE PENDANT 7 JOURS. CHEZ LES PATIENTS ÂGÉS ET CHEZ LES INSUFFISANTS RÉNAUX OU HÉPATIQUES, LA DOSE CUMULATIVE NE DEVRAIT PAS DÉPASSER 2 mg. UNE FOIS CETTE DOSE ATTEINTE, LE PATIENT DEVRAIT ARRÊTER DE PRENDRE LA COLCHICINE PENDANT 21 JOURS.
- Afin de réduire le risque de toxicité, on pourrait prescrire un traitement intermittent avec un arrêt de la médication de 3 jours entre les cures.
- Administrer le médicament avec des aliments pour réduire l'irritation gastrique.
- Ne pas administrer des doses additionnelles de colchicine pendant les 3 jours qui suivent le traitement d'une crise.

ENSEIGNEMENT AU PATIENT ET À SES PROCHES

- Expliquer au patient le schéma posologique. S'il n'a pas pu prendre le médicament au moment habituel, il doit le prendre aussitôt que possible à moins que ce ne soit presque l'heure prévue pour la dose suivante. Le prévenir qu'il ne faut jamais remplacer une dose manquée par une double dose.
- Recommander aux patients prenant des doses prophylactiques de ne pas les augmenter jusqu'au niveau des doses thérapeutiques lors d'un accès aigu afin de prévenir le risque de toxicité. Pour traiter les accès aigus, il faudrait prendre un AINS ou un cor-

ticostéroïde, préférablement administré par injection intrasynoviale.

- Inciter le patient à suivre les recommandations des professionnels de la santé concernant la perte de poids, le régime alimentaire et la consommation d'alcool.
- Conseiller au patient de signaler immédiatement les nausées, les vomissements, les douleurs abdominales, la diarrhée, les saignements et les ecchymoses inhabituels, les maux de gorge, la fatigue, les malaises ou le rash. Lui recommander d'interrompre le traitement si des symptômes gastriques, évocateurs de toxicité, se manifestent.
- Une intervention chirurgicale peut déclencher un accès aigu de goutte. Recommander au patient de consulter un professionnel de la santé au sujet de la prise de colchicine 3 jours avant une intervention chirurgicale ou un traitement dentaire.

VÉRIFICATION DE L'EFFICACITÉ THÉRAPEUTIQUE

L'efficacité du traitement peut être démontrée par: l'atténuation de la douleur et de l'inflammation des articulations touchées dans les 12 heures ▪ le soulagement des symptômes dans les 24 à 48 heures ▪ la prévention des accès aigus de goutte.

COLESTIPOL,

voir Chélateurs des acides biliaires

CONTRACEPTIFS HORMONAUX

contraceptifs oraux monophasiques

désogestrel/éthinylœstradiol
Marvelon, Ortho-Cept, Linessa

drospirénone/éthinylœstradiol
Yasmin

éthynodiol/éthinylœstradiol
Demulen 30

lévonorgestrel/éthinylœstradiol
Alesse, Min-Ovral

noréthindrone/éthinylœstradiol
Brevicon 0,5/35, Brevicon 1/35, Loestrin 1,5/30, Minestrin 1/20, Ortho 0,5/35, Ortho 1/35, Select 0,5/35, Select 1/35

noréthindrone/mestranol
Ortho-Novum 1/50

norgestimate/éthinylœstradiol
Cyclen

norgestrel/éthinylœstradiol
Lo-Femeral, Ovral

contraceptifs oraux biphasiques

noréthindrone/éthinylœstradiol
Ortho 10/11

contraceptifs oraux triphasiques

lévonorgestrel/éthinylœstradiol
Triphasil, Triquilar

noréthindrone/éthinylœstradiol
Ortho 7/7/7, Synphasic

norgestimate/éthinylœstradiol
Tri-Cyclen, Tri-Cyclen Lo

contraceptif oral à base de progestatif seulement

noréthindrone
Micronor

contraceptif d'urgence

lévonorgestrel
Plan B

contraceptif injectable

médroxyprogestérone
Depo-Provera

contraceptif intra-utérin

lévonorgestrel
Mirena

contraceptif en anneau vaginal

étonogestrel/éthinylœstradiol
NuvaRing

C

contraceptif transdermique

norelgestromine/éthinylœstradiol

Evra

CLASSIFICATION:

Œstrogènes, progestatifs ou contraceptifs hormonaux

Grossesse – catégorie X

INDICATIONS

Prévention de la grossesse ▪ Régulation du cycle menstruel ▪ Contraception d'urgence (certains agents) ▪ Traitement de l'acné, en cas d'échec du traitement topique, chez les femmes > 14 ans qui souhaitent prendre un contraceptif et qui n'ont aucun problème de santé (certains agents).

MÉCANISME D'ACTION

Contraceptifs oraux monophasiques: Libération d'une dose fixe d'œstrogènes et de progestatifs pendant un cycle de 21 jours. Inhibition de l'ovulation par la suppression de l'hormone folliculostimulante et de l'hormone lutéinisante. Le contraceptif peut modifier la muqueuse du col cervical et la cavité endométriale, empêchant la fécondation de l'ovule par le spermatozoïde et l'implantation de l'œuf ▪ **Contraceptifs oraux biphasiques**: Inhibition de l'ovulation par la suppression de l'hormone folliculostimulante et de l'hormone lutéinisante. Le contraceptif peut modifier la muqueuse du col cervical et la cavité endométriale, empêchant la fécondation de l'ovule par le spermatozoïde et l'implantation de l'œuf. De plus, les plus petites doses de progestatifs libérées pendant la phase 1 favorisent la prolifération de l'endomètre. Les doses plus élevées, libérées pendant la phase 2, font passer l'endomètre de la phase proliférative à la phase sécrétoire ▪ **Contraceptifs oraux triphasiques**: Inhibition de l'ovulation par la suppression de l'hormone folliculostimulante et de l'hormone lutéinisante. Le contraceptif peut modifier la muqueuse du col cervical et la cavité endométriale, empêchant la fécondation de l'ovule par le spermatozoïde et l'implantation de l'œuf. Les doses variables d'œstrogènes et de progestatifs peuvent mieux simuler les fluctuations hormonales naturelles ▪ **Contraceptifs à base de progestatifs seulement**: Mécanisme d'action inconnu. Le contraceptif peut modifier la muqueuse du col cervical et la cavité endométriale, empêchant la fécondation de l'ovule par le spermatozoïde et l'implantation de l'œuf. L'ovulation peut également être supprimée ▪ **Injection de médroxyprogestérone**: Inhibition de la sécrétion de gonadotrophines, de la maturation des follicules et de l'ovulation. Amincissement de l'endomètre ▪ **Contraceptifs d'urgence**: Inhibition de l'ovulation ou de la fécondation en modifiant le transport du spermatozoïde ou de l'ovule. Ils peuvent également empêcher l'ovule fécondé de se fixer à la paroi utérine (en modifiant l'endomètre) ▪ **Contraceptifs en anneau vaginal, timbre transdermique**: Inhibition de l'ovulation, épaississement de la glaire cervicale (qui rend plus difficile la pénétration du sperme dans l'utérus) et modification de l'endomètre (ce qui réduit la probabilité d'implantation) ▪ **Effets antiacné**: Réduction marquée de la quantité de testostérone sérique biodisponible, qui serait en partie responsable de l'apparition de l'acné, en maintenant des concentrations élevées de protéine porteuse des stéroïdes sexuels (SHBG, *sex hormone binding globulin*). ***Effets thérapeutiques:*** Prévention de la grossesse ▪ Diminution de la gravité de l'acné.

PHARMACOCINÉTIQUE

Absorption: Bonne (PO); *éthinylœstradiol* – rapide; *noréthindrone* – 65 %; *lévonorgestrel et désogestrel* – 100 %. Lente (IM). Légère (administration intra-utérine).

Distribution: Inconnue.

Liaison aux protéines: *Éthinylœstradiol* – 97-98 %.

Métabolisme et excrétion: Métabolisme majoritairement hépatique. *Éthinylœstradiol* et *noréthindrone* – premier passage hépatique important. *Désogestrel* – rapidement transformé en son métabolite actif.

Demi-vie: *Éthinylœstradiol* – de 6 à 20 heures; *lévonorgestrel* – 45 heures; *noréthindrone* – de 5 à 14 heures; *désogestrel (métabolite)* – 38 ± 20 heures; *norgestimate (métabolite)* – de 12 à 20 heures; autres: inconnue.

Profil temps-action (prévention de la grossesse)

	DÉBUT D'ACTION	PIC	DURÉE
PO	1 mois	1 mois	1 mois†
Dispositif intra-utérin	1 mois	1 mois	5 ans
Timbre transdermique	1 semaine (premier cycle)	48 h	pendant la période d'application du timbre
IM	1 mois	1 mois	3 mois

† Seulement durant le mois de la prise du contraceptif.

CONTRE-INDICATIONS, PRÉCAUTIONS ET MISES EN GARDE

Contre-indications: Épisode courant ou antécédents de thrombophlébite ou de troubles thromboemboliques, de maladie cardiovasculaire, de maladie vasculaire cérébrale, de tumeurs hépatiques ou de cholécystite ▪ Cancer du sein connu ou soupçonné ▪ Néoplasie œstrogénodépendante connue ou soupçonnée ▪ Saignement vaginal anormal d'étiologie inconnue ■ Lésion oculaire d'origine vasculaire ■ Hypersensibilité aux parabènes (solution injectable seulement) ■ **Obst.**: La femme enceinte ne doit pas prendre de contraceptifs oraux. Toutefois, s'il y a conception au cours de l'utilisation des contraceptifs oraux, aucune donnée concluante n'indique qu'il y aurait un risque pour l'enfant ■ *Administration intra-utérine seulement:* anomalies intra-utérines, endométrite post-partum, infection pelvienne nouvelle ou récidivante, infection génitale basse, saignements utérins anormaux de cause inconnue, cancer de l'utérus ou du col de l'utérus, cervicite, dysplasie cervicale, maladie hépatique, avortement septique au cours des 3 mois précédents, endocardite bactérienne, immunodéficience établie, leucémie ou autres hémopathies malignes aiguës, affection trophoblastique en présence d'une élévation des taux d'hCG.

Précautions et mises en garde: Interventions chirurgicales (selon le type d'intervention, il faut parfois interrompre l'administration de 2 à 4 semaines avant) ■ Antécédents de tabagisme ou patientes âgées de plus de 30 à 35 ans (risque accru de maladie cardiovasculaire ou de thromboembolie) ■ Présence d'autres facteurs de risque cardiovasculaire (obésité, hyperglycémie, taux lipidiques élevés, hypertension) ■ Antécédents de diabète, de maladies hémorragiques ou de céphalées ■ Allaitement ■ Patientes exposées à un risque plus élevé de cancer du sein ou du foie (certains agents) ■ **Péd.**: Ne pas utiliser avant la puberté.

Extrême prudence: PRODUITS RENFERMANT PLUS DE 50 µg D'ŒSTROGÈNES (RISQUE ACCRU DE THROMBOEMBOLIE OU D'AUTRES TROUBLES VASCULAIRES) ■ FILLETTES PRÉPUBÈRES (L'INNOCUITÉ DU MÉDICAMENT N'A PAS ÉTÉ ÉTABLIE).

RÉACTIONS INDÉSIRABLES ET EFFETS SECONDAIRES

SNC: dépression, migraines.

ORLO: intolérance aux verres de contact, névrite optique, thrombose rétinienne.

CV: HÉMORRAGIE CÉRÉBRALE, THROMBOSE CÉRÉBRALE, THROMBOSE CORONARIENNE, EMBOLIE PULMONAIRE, œdème, hypertension, maladie de Raynaud, thromboembolie, thrombophlébite.

GI: crampes abdominales, ballonnement, ictère cholostatique, cholécystite, tumeurs hépatiques, nausées, vomissements.

GU: aménorrhée, saignements intermenstruels, dysménorrhée, saignotements. *Administration intra-utérine seulement:* perforation utérine.

Tég.: chloasma, rash.

End.: hyperglycémie.

Loc.: *Médroxyprogestérone injectable seulement:* perte osseuse.

Divers: modification du poids.

INTERACTIONS

Médicament-médicament: Les **pénicillines**, l'**ampicilline**, **le chloramphénicol**, la **dihydroergotamine**, l'**huile minérale**, la **néomycine orale**, les **sulfamides**, les **barbituriques**, la **carbamazépine**, les **glucocorticoïdes (systémiques)**, la **griséofulvine**, le **modafinil**, **la phénylbutazone**, la **phénytoïne**, la **primidone**, la **rifampine**, le **topiramate**, certains **antirétroviraux inhibiteurs de la protéase** (incluant le **ritonavir**) ou les **tétracyclines**, ainsi que la consommation régulière d'**alcool**, peuvent réduire l'efficacité des contraceptifs oraux ■ Les contraceptifs oraux peuvent accroître les effets des **antidépresseurs tricycliques**, des **benzodiazépines**, des **bêtabloquants**, de la **caféine**, des **corticostéroïdes** et de la **théophylline** ou le risque de toxicité qui leur est associé ■ Risque accru de toxicité hépatique lors de l'administration concomitante de **dantrolène** (œstrogènes seulement) ■ La **carbamazépine** ou la **phénytoïne** peut diminuer l'efficacité des contraceptifs ■ Le **tabac** augmente le risque de troubles thromboemboliques (œstrogènes seulement) ■ Les contraceptifs oraux peuvent entraver les effets de la **bromocriptine** ■ Les contraceptifs oraux peuvent diminuer l'efficacité de l'**acétaminophène**, du **témazépam**, du **lorazépam**, de l'**oxazépam**, de l'**aspirine** (**acide salicylique**) ou de la **morphine** ■ *Yasmin seulement:* l'utilisation concomitante d'**AINS**, de **diurétiques épargneurs de potassium**, de **suppléments de potassium**, d'**inhibiteurs de l'enzyme de conversion de l'angiotensine**, d'**antagonistes des récepteurs de l'angiotensine II** ou d'**héparine** peut provoquer une hyperkaliémie.

Médicament-produits naturels: La consommation concomitante de **millepertuis** peut diminuer l'efficacité des contraceptifs et entraîner des saignements intermenstruels et des irrégularités du cycle menstruel ■ Risque d'élévation des taux de caféine et de ses effets indésirables, lors de la consommation concomitante de produits contenant de la **caféine** (**thé**, **café**, **cola**).

VOIES D'ADMINISTRATION ET POSOLOGIE

Contraceptifs oraux monophasiques

- **PO (adultes)**: Cycle de 21 jours: prendre le premier comprimé le premier dimanche après le début des règles (le dimanche, si les règles débutent le dimanche), puis continuer de prendre un comprimé par jour, pendant 21 jours; ne pas prendre l'agent pendant 7 jours. Reprendre ensuite le même cycle. On peut aussi commencer à prendre le contraceptif le premier jour des règles et poursuivre la prise

C

pendant 21 jours, avec un arrêt de la médication pendant 7 jours. Reprendre ensuite le même cycle. Certains distributeurs de contraceptifs destinés à une cure de 28 jours contiennent 7 comprimés de placebo. Dans ce cas, il faut prendre 1 comprimé tous les jours pour ne pas perdre l'habitude.

Contraceptifs oraux biphasiques

- **PO (adultes)**: Administration en deux phases. Pendant la première phase, de 10 jours, la dose de progestatifs est plus faible et, pendant la deuxième phase, elle est plus élevée. La dose d'œstrogènes reste constante pendant toute la période (21 jours). Arrêter la médication pendant 7 jours. Reprendre ensuite le même cycle. Certains distributeurs de contraceptifs destinés à une cure de 28 jours contiennent 7 comprimés de placebo. Dans ce cas, il faut prendre 1 comprimé tous les jours pour ne pas perdre l'habitude.

Contraceptifs oraux triphasiques

- **PO (adultes)**: La dose de progestatifs varie tout au long du cycle de 21 jours. La dose d'œstrogènes varie ou demeure la même. Arrêter la médication pendant 7 jours. Reprendre ensuite le même cycle. Certains distributeurs de contraceptifs destinés à une cure de 28 jours contiennent 7 comprimés de placebo. Dans ce cas, il faut prendre 1 comprimé tous les jours pour ne pas perdre l'habitude.

Contraceptifs oraux à base de progestatifs seulement

- **PO (adultes)**: Amorcer le traitement le premier jour des règles, et prendre tous les jours sans interruption.

Contraceptifs d'urgence

- **PO (adultes et adolescentes)**: Prendre une première dose dans les 72 heures suivant des rapports sexuels non protégés, et une dose additionnelle, 12 heures plus tard. *Plan B* – prendre un comprimé, et un deuxième, 12 heures plus tard, OU prendre 2 comprimés en une seule dose dans les 72 heures suivant un rapport sexuel non protégé; *Preven Ovral* – 2 comprimés blancs, suivis de 2 comprimés de plus, 12 heures plus tard.

Contraceptif injectable

- **IM (adultes)**: 150 mg dans les 5 premiers jours suivant le début des règles ou l'accouchement, si la patiente n'allaite pas. Si la patiente allaite, administrer 6 semaines après l'accouchement; répéter tous les 3 mois.

Acné

- **PO (adultes)**: *Alesse, Tri-Cyclen* – un comprimé par jour, pendant 21 jours, puis arrêter la médication pendant 7 jours. Reprendre ensuite le même cycle. Certains distributeurs de contraceptifs destinés à une cure de 28 jours contiennent 7 comprimés de placebo. Dans ce cas, il faut prendre 1 comprimé tous les jours pour ne pas perdre l'habitude.

Anneau intravaginal

- **Intravaginal (adultes)**: Insérer un anneau dans les premiers jours suivant le début des règles. L'anneau doit demeurer en place pendant 21 jours, puis, il faut le retirer pendant 7 jours. Reprendre ensuite le même cycle.

Timbre transdermique

- **Transdermique (adultes)**: Appliquer un timbre, 1 fois par semaine, pendant 3 semaines. Ne pas appliquer de timbre durant la 4e semaine. On peut s'attendre à un saignement de retrait durant cette période. Chaque nouveau timbre doit être appliqué le même jour de la semaine.

Contraceptif intra-utérin

- **Intra-utérin (adultes)**: Insérer un dispositif dans les 7 jours suivant le début de la menstruation. Remplacer le dispositif après 5 ans.

PRÉSENTATION

- **Contraceptifs oraux à base d'œstrogènes et de progestatifs**
  Comprimés: Généralement présentés en plaquettes-calendriers^{Pr} contenant suffisamment de comprimés actifs (21) pour un cycle complet de 28 jours. Certains distributeurs^{Pr} contiennent 7 comprimés inertes pour compléter le cycle.
- **Lévonorgestrel**
  Contraceptifs d'urgence: 2 comprimés à 0,75 mg de lévonorgestrel (Plan B)^{Pr}.
- **Médroxyprogestérone**
  Solution pour injection: 150 mg/mL^{Pr}.
- **Anneau vaginal**
  Anneau: libération de 120 µg d'étonogestrel et de 15 µg d'éthinylœstradiol ^{Pr} par jour.
- **Timbre transdermique**
  Timbres transdermiques: taux de libération moyen de 150 µg de norelgestromine et de 20 µg d'éthinylœstradiol^{Pr} par jour.
- **Dispositif intra-utérin**
  Dispositif intra-utérin: 52 mg de lévonorgestrel USP dans un réservoir cylindrique composé d'une matrice de lévonorgestrel et de polyméthylsiloxane (PDMS)^{Pr}.

SOINS INFIRMIERS

ÉVALUATION DE LA SITUATION

- Mesurer la pression artérielle avant le traitement et à intervalles réguliers pendant toute sa durée.

Acné: Surveiller les lésions cutanées avant le traitement et à intervalles réguliers pendant toute sa durée.

***Tests de laboratoire*:**

- Noter les résultats des tests de la fonction hépatique à intervalles réguliers pendant toute la durée du traitement.
- *Œstrogènes seulement:* Ces hormones peuvent entraîner l'élévation des concentrations sériques de glucose, de sodium, de triglycérides, de lipoprotéines de très haute densité (VHDL), de cholestérol total, de prothrombine et des facteurs VII, VIII, IX et X. Elles peuvent aussi entraîner la diminution des concentrations de lipoprotéines de faible densité (LDL) et d'antithrombine III ■ Ces hormones peuvent fausser l'interprétation des tests de la fonction thyroïdienne, entraîner de fausses élévations de l'agrégation plaquettaire induite par la noradrénaline et de fausses diminutions des résultats du test à la métopirone.
- *Progestatifs seulement:* Ces hormones peuvent entraîner l'élévation des concentrations de lipoprotéines de basse densité (LDL). Elles peuvent entraîner la diminution des concentrations sériques de phosphatase alcaline et de lipoprotéines de haute densité (HDL).

DIAGNOSTICS INFIRMIERS POSSIBLES

- Connaissances insuffisantes sur le traitement médicamenteux (Enseignement au patient et à ses proches).
- Non-observance du traitement médicamenteux (Enseignement au patient et à ses proches).

INTERVENTIONS INFIRMIÈRES

PO: Il est conseillé de prendre les contraceptifs oraux avec les repas ou immédiatement après, afin de réduire les nausées.

IM: Agiter vigoureusement la fiole juste avant de l'utiliser pour s'assurer que la suspension est homogène. Administrer en profondeur, dans le muscle fessier ou deltoïdien. Si plus de 14 semaines s'écoulent entre les injections, s'assurer que la patiente n'est pas enceinte avant de lui injecter le contraceptif.

- La préparation injectable peut provoquer une perte de densité minérale osseuse, surtout chez les femmes de moins de 21 ans. On devrait la réserver aux femmes chez lesquelles aucune autre méthode de contraception n'est envisageable, et ne la prescrire que pendant 2 ans au maximum. Si l'usage à long terme est inévitable, la patiente devrait prendre des suppléments de calcium et de vitamine D et se soumettre à un suivi régulier de la densité minérale osseuse.

ENSEIGNEMENT AU PATIENT ET À SES PROCHES

- Recommander à la patiente de prendre le médicament tous les jours, à la même heure. Les comprimés doivent être pris en séquence et conservés dans la plaquette d'origine.
- *Si la patiente oublie de prendre une dose*, la prévenir qu'elle doit prendre le comprimé dès que possible ou, à la rigueur, prendre 2 comprimés le lendemain, puis reprendre le schéma habituel. *Si elle oublie de prendre 2 doses consécutives*, elle doit prendre 2 comprimés par jour les 2 jours suivants, puis reprendre le schéma habituel; elle doit aussi recourir à un autre moyen de contraception pour le reste du cycle. *Si elle oublie de prendre 3 doses consécutives*, elle doit arrêter de prendre les contraceptifs et utiliser un autre moyen de contraception jusqu'au début des règles ou jusqu'à ce que le diagnostic de grossesse soit écarté; elle peut ensuite recommencer le traitement en utilisant une nouvelle plaquette. *Schéma posologique de 28 jours:* si la posologie est respectée pendant les 21 premiers jours de traitement, mais si la patiente oublie de prendre l'un des 7 comprimés suivants (placebo), elle doit prendre le premier comprimé de la nouvelle plaquette à la date prévue.
- Inciter la patiente à adopter une autre méthode contraceptive pendant les 3 premières semaines où elle démarre un traitement à base de contraceptifs oraux.
- Conseiller à la patiente de recourir à une seconde méthode de contraception pendant les cycles où elle prend des *contraceptifs oraux* en même temps que de l'ampicilline, des corticostéroïdes, de l'ampicilline, des barbituriques, de la carbamazépine, du chloramphénicol, de la dihydroergotamine, des glucocorticoïdes (systémiques), de la griséofulvine, de l'huile minérale, des inhibiteurs de la protéase, de la néomycine par voie orale, de la pénicilline V, de la phénylbutazone, de la primidone, de la rifampine, des sulfamides, des tétracyclines, du topiramate ou de l'acide valproïque.
- Expliquer à la patiente le schéma posologique et le traitement d'entretien. L'arrêt brusque de la médication peut entraîner une hémorragie de retrait.
- Si les nausées deviennent gênantes, conseiller à la patiente de consommer des aliments solides.
- RECOMMANDER À LA PATIENTE DE SIGNALER À UN PROFESSIONNEL DE LA SANTÉ LES SIGNES ET LES SYMPTÔMES DE RÉTENTION HYDRIQUE (ENFLURE DES CHEVILLES ET DES PIEDS, GAIN PONDÉRAL); DE MALADIE THROMBOEMBOLIQUE (DOULEUR, ENFLURE ET SENSIBILITÉ D'UN MEMBRE, CÉPHALÉES, DOULEURS

C

C

THORACIQUES, VISION TROUBLE); DE DÉPRESSION; DE DYSFONCTIONNEMENT HÉPATIQUE (COULEUR JAUNÂTRE DE LA PEAU OU DES YEUX, PRURIT, URINE FONCÉE, SELLES DE COULEUR PÂLE); OU LES SAIGNEMENTS VAGINAUX ANORMAUX. LA FEMME AYANT DES ANTÉCÉDENTS FAMILIAUX DE CANCER DU SEIN, DE MALADIE FIBROKYSTIQUE DU SEIN, DE MAMMOGRAPHIE ANORMALE OU DE DYSPLASIE CERVICALE DEVRAIT SE SOUMETTRE TOUS LES ANS AU DÉPISTAGE DU CANCER DU SEIN.

- Prévenir la patiente qu'elle doit arrêter de prendre le médicament si elle pense être enceinte et en informer immédiatement un professionnel de la santé.
- Mettre en garde la patiente, particulièrement si elle a plus de 35 ans, contre l'usage concomitant du tabac, car l'œstrogénothérapie peut accroître le risque de réactions indésirables graves.
- Recommander à la patiente d'utiliser un écran solaire et de porter des vêtements protecteurs pour prévenir l'hyperpigmentation de la peau.
- Rappeler à la patiente que les contraceptifs oraux ne la protègent pas contre le VIH ou contre les autres infections transmissibles sexuellement.
- Recommander à la patiente qui doit suivre un autre traitement ou subir une intervention chirurgicale d'avertir le professionnel de la santé qu'elle prend des contraceptifs.
- Insister sur l'importance d'un suivi médical régulier, incluant la prise de la pression artérielle, l'examen des seins, de l'abdomen et du pelvis et le test de Papanicolaou, tous les 6 à 12 mois.

IM: Recommander à la patiente de consommer régulièrement des produits alimentaires riches en vitamine D et en calcium pour prévenir la perte minérale osseuse.

Timbre transdermique:

- Si la patiente commence à utiliser un timbre transdermique pour la première fois, elle doit attendre le premier jour de la menstruation. Elle peut choisir de commencer par « Premier jour » ou par «Dimanche». Le jour où elle appliquera son premier timbre sera le jour 1. Le jour de changement du timbre devra être ce jour-là, chaque semaine. Si la patiente commence par « Premier jour », elle doit appliquer le premier timbre au cours des 24 premières heures de la menstruation; aucune méthode de contraception supplémentaire n'est nécessaire. Si le traitement commence après le premier jour du cycle menstruel, un contraceptif non hormonal supplémentaire (comme un condom ou un diaphragme) doit être utilisé pendant les 7 premiers jours consécutifs du premier cycle de traitement. Si la patiente commence par « Dimanche », elle doit appliquer le premier timbre le premier dimanche qui suit le début de la menstruation. Elle doit utiliser une méthode de contraception supplémentaire pendant la première semaine de son premier cycle seulement. Si la menstruation commence un dimanche, le premier timbre doit être appliqué ce jour-là; aucune méthode de contraception supplémentaire n'est nécessaire.
- Le timbre doit être appliqué sur une peau propre, sèche et intacte, sur les fesses, l'abdomen, la partie supérieure et externe du bras ou le haut du torse, à un endroit où les vêtements ajustés ne risquent pas de frotter. Il ne faut pas appliquer le timbre sur une peau rouge, irritée ou fissurée, ni le coller sur les seins.
- Il ne faut pas appliquer de maquillage, de crème, de lotion, de poudre ni de produits topiques sur la peau à l'endroit où le timbre est collé ou sera collé prochainement, pour ne pas entraver ses propriétés adhésives.
- Après avoir appliqué le timbre, il faut appuyer fermement dessus avec la paume de la main pendant 10 secondes en s'assurant que les bords adhèrent bien. On doit s'assurer tous les jours que le timbre reste bien collé.
- Lorsqu'on enlève le timbre, il faut le replier sur lui-même avant de le jeter, car il contient encore des substances actives. On doit toujours le conserver hors de la portée des enfants et des animaux domestiques et le jeter à un endroit qui leur est inaccessible.
- Le changement de timbre peut se faire à n'importe quel moment de la journée prévue pour le changement. Le nouveau timbre doit être appliqué à un endroit différent pour éviter tout risque d'irritation, bien qu'on puisse le laisser sur la même région anatomique.
- La menstruation devrait survenir durant la 4e semaine, soit durant la semaine sans timbre.
- Le cycle suivant de 4 semaines commence le jour habituel de l'application d'un nouveau timbre, le lendemain du 28e jour, quel que soit le jour du début ou de la fin de la menstruation. On ne doit en aucun cas laisser passer plus de 7 jours sans timbre entre les cycles de contraception.
- Si le timbre se décolle partiellement ou complètement et qu'il reste décollé, la libération de médicament sera insuffisante. S'il reste décollé, même partiellement, pendant moins de 24 heures, il faut essayer de le remettre au même endroit ou le remplacer par un nouveau timbre. Aucune méthode de contraception supplémentaire n'est nécessaire. S'il reste décollé pendant plus de 24 heures ou si la patiente ne sait pas exactement depuis combien de

temps le timbre s'est décollé, elle pourrait ne pas être protégée contre une grossesse. Elle doit arrêter le cycle de contraception en cours et commencer immédiatement un nouveau cycle en appliquant un nouveau timbre. Elle a maintenant un nouveau « Premier jour » et un nouveau jour de changement du timbre. Elle doit utiliser une méthode de contraception supplémentaire pendant la première semaine du nouveau cycle seulement. Il ne faut pas remettre un timbre s'il ne colle plus, s'il adhère à lui-même ou à une autre surface, si un corps étranger s'y est collé ou s'il s'est déjà décollé partiellement ou complètement auparavant. Si un timbre ne peut pas être remis, il faut en appliquer immédiatement un nouveau. Il ne faut utiliser aucun ruban adhésif ni bandage pour maintenir le timbre en place.

Si la patiente oublie de changer le timbre:

- **Au début d'un cycle de contraception (1re semaine, 1er jour):** Elle pourrait ne pas être protégée contre une grossesse. Elle doit appliquer le premier timbre de son nouveau cycle aussitôt qu'elle s'en aperçoit. Elle a maintenant un nouveau jour de changement du timbre et un nouveau « Premier jour ». Elle doit utiliser une méthode de contraception supplémentaire pendant la première semaine de son nouveau cycle.
- **Au milieu d'un cycle de contraception (2e semaine, 8e jour, ou 3e semaine, 15e jour)**

  Pendant 1 ou 2 jours (au maximum 48 heures): Elle doit appliquer immédiatement un nouveau timbre. Le timbre suivant doit être appliqué le jour habituel de changement du timbre. Aucune méthode de contraception supplémentaire n'est nécessaire.

  Pendant plus de 2 jours: Elle pourrait ne pas être protégée contre une grossesse. Elle doit arrêter le cycle de contraception en cours et commencer immédiatement un nouveau cycle de 4 semaines en appliquant un nouveau timbre. Elle a maintenant un nouveau jour de changement du timbre et un nouveau « Premier jour ». La patiente doit utiliser une méthode de contraception supplémentaire pendant une semaine.
- **À la fin du cycle de contraception:** Si la patiente oublie d'enlever son timbre, elle doit le retirer aussitôt qu'elle s'en aperçoit. Le cycle suivant doit commencer le jour habituel de changement du timbre, c'est-à-dire le lendemain du 28e jour. Aucune méthode de contraception supplémentaire n'est nécessaire.
- Inciter la patiente à adopter une autre méthode contraceptive, si nécessaire, pendant la première semaine où elle démarre un traitement par un nouveau timbre transdermique.

NuvaRing:

- *Si la patiente n'utilisait pas de contraceptif hormonal durant le dernier mois:* on compte le premier jour de la menstruation comme le « Jour 1 », et on insère NuvaRing entre le 1er et le 5e jour du cycle, même si le saignement n'a pas cessé. On doit utiliser une autre méthode contraceptive de type barrière, comme des préservatifs ou un spermicide, au cours des 7 premiers jours d'utilisation continue de l'anneau. *Après l'utilisation d'un contraceptif oral combiné (pilule anticonceptionnelle œstroprogestative):* La femme peut passer à NuvaRing à tout moment si elle a toujours utilisé correctement la méthode de contraception combinée et si elle est raisonnablement certaine qu'elle n'est pas enceinte. La période de repos (sans hormones) de la méthode antérieure ne doit jamais être prolongée au-delà de la durée recommandée. Aucun moyen de contraception supplémentaire n'est nécessaire. *Après l'utilisation d'un progestatif (pilule minidosée):* On peut arrêter l'usage de la pilule n'importe quel jour du mois et passer à NuvaRing. On peut utiliser NuvaRing le jour suivant la prise de la dernière pilule. Ne laisser passer aucun jour entre la dernière pilule et le 1er jour d'utilisation de NuvaRing. *Après l'utilisation d'un progestatif (injectable):* On peut commencer l'utilisation de NuvaRing le jour où la patiente devait normalement recevoir l'injection suivante. *Après l'utilisation d'un progestatif (stérilet):* On doit insérer NuvaRing le jour même où le stérilet est retiré. Après l'utilisation d'un progestatif sous forme de comprimés, d'anneau, d'injection ou de stérilet, on doit utiliser une méthode anticonceptionnelle complémentaire, par exemple préservatifs ou spermicide, pendant les 7 premiers jours qui suivent l'insertion de NuvaRing.
- *NuvaRing* est fourni dans un sachet refermable en aluminium. Après s'être bien lavé et séché les mains, retirer NuvaRing du sachet. Conserver le sachet afin de jeter l'anneau après son utilisation. Choisir une position confortable (couchée, accroupie ou debout avec une jambe relevée). Tenir NuvaRing entre le pouce et l'index et pincer les côtés opposés de l'anneau. Pousser doucement l'anneau plié dans le vagin. NuvaRing reste efficace quelle que soit sa position dans le vagin. La majorité des femmes ne ressentent pas la présence de l'anneau une fois qu'il a été placé dans le vagin. Si une gêne est ressentie, il est possible que l'anneau n'ait pas été introduit assez profondément dans le vagin. On doit utiliser le doigt pour pousser doucement NuvaRing plus loin dans le vagin. *Il n'y a aucun danger que NuvaRing*

soit poussé trop loin dans le vagin ou qu'il disparaisse. Après son insertion, l'anneau doit être gardé en place pendant 3 semaines.

- L'anneau doit être enlevé 3 semaines après son insertion, le même jour de la semaine où il a été inséré. Pour le retirer, introduire l'index recourbé sous le rebord avant ou saisir celui-ci entre l'index et le majeur et tirer. Placer l'anneau utilisé dans le sachet d'aluminium et le jeter. Ne pas jeter dans les toilettes. La menstruation devrait débuter 2 ou 3 jours après le retrait de l'anneau et pourrait ne pas finir avant l'insertion du suivant. Pour maintenir la protection anticonceptionnelle, un nouvel anneau doit être inséré 1 semaine après le retrait du précédent, même si les règles n'ont toujours pas commencé.
- Si NuvaRing glisse hors du vagin et qu'il est remis en place dans les 3 heures suivant sa sortie, la protection anticonceptionnelle est toujours présente. On peut rincer l'anneau avec de l'eau froide ou tiède et le réinsérer dès que possible. Si l'anneau est perdu, on doit insérer un nouvel anneau et continuer le schéma posologique de l'anneau perdu. Si NuvaRing a été plus de 3 heures hors du vagin, une méthode anticonceptionnelle complémentaire, par des préservatifs, par exemple, devra être utilisée pendant les 7 jours suivants.
- *Si NuvaRing est resté dans le vagin pendant une semaine supplémentaire ou moins (jusqu'à 4 semaines au total),* il doit être enlevé et un nouvel anneau doit être installé après un intervalle de 7 jours sans anneau. Si NuvaRing est resté en place pendant plus de 4 semaines au total, la patiente devrait effectuer un test de grossesse. Une méthode anticonceptionnelle complémentaire, de type préservatifs ou spermicide, devra être utilisée pendant les 7 jours suivants.

VÉRIFICATION DE L'EFFICACITÉ THÉRAPEUTIQUE

L'efficacité du traitement peut être démontrée par: la prévention de la grossesse ■ la régulation du cycle menstruel ■ la diminution de l'acné.

CORTICOSTÉROÏDES (INHALATION)

béclométhasone
Beclodisk, Qvar, Ratio-Béclométhasone, Vanceril

budésonide
Pulmicort, Pulmicort Nebuamp

ciclésonide
Alvesco

fluticasone
Flovent, Flovent Diskus

CLASSIFICATION:
Corticostéroïdes (par inhalation)

Grossesse – catégories B (budésonide) et C (béclométhasone et fluticasone); catégorie non établie pour le ciclésonide

INDICATIONS

Traitement d'entretien et traitement prophylactique de l'asthme ■ L'inhalation peut diminuer le besoin d'utiliser des corticostéroïdes systémiques et retarder les lésions pulmonaires qui découlent de l'asthme chronique ■ Adjuvants dans le traitement de la bronchopneumopathie chronique obstructive (BPCO) chez les patients dont le VEMS < 50 % de la valeur prédite et qui subissent des exacerbations répétées exigeant l'administration d'antibiotiques ou de corticostéroïdes par voie générale.

MÉCANISME D'ACTION

Effet anti-inflammatoire local puissant, pouvant modifier la réponse immunitaire. ***Effets thérapeutiques:*** Diminution de la fréquence et de la gravité des crises d'asthme ■ Prévention des lésions pulmonaires associées à l'asthme chronique.

PHARMACOCINÉTIQUE

Absorption: *Béclométhasone* – 20 %; *budésonide* – 39 %; *ciclésonide* – < 0,5 % (ciclésonide), < 1 % (des-ciclésonide); *fluticasone* – 30 % (aérosol), 13,5 % (poudre). Tous les agents agissent surtout localement après inhalation.

Distribution: Une fraction de 10 à 25 % de la dose inhalée sans dispositif d'espacement se dépose dans les voies respiratoires. L'usage d'un dispositif d'espacement favorise la pénétration d'une fraction plus importante de médicament dans les voies respiratoires. Tous les agents traversent la barrière placentaire et passent dans le lait maternel à faible concentration.

Liaison aux protéines: *Budésonide* – de 85 à 90 %; *ciclésonide* – 99 % (ciclésonide), 98 % (des-ciclésonide); *fluticasone* – 91 %.

Métabolisme et excrétion: *Béclométhasone* – après inhalation, le dipropionate de béclométhasone se transforme en monopropionate de béclométhasone, un métabolite actif; une fraction inférieure à 10 % est excrétée dans les fèces et dans l'urine. *Budésonide et fluticasone* – ces agents sont métabolisés par le foie après avoir été absorbés depuis les poumons. *Budésonide* – une fraction de 60 % est excrétée dans l'urine, une fraction moindre dans les fèces; *fluticasone* – une fraction inférieure à 5 % est excrétée dans l'urine et dans les fèces; *ciclésonide* – transformé en son métabolite actif, le des-ciclésonide dans les poumons; le métabolite est transformé dans le foie en métabolites inactifs qui sont éliminés dans les fèces.

Demi-vie: *Béclométhasone* – 0,5 heure; *budésonide* – de 2 à 3 heures; *ciclésonide* – 6 heures; *fluticasone* – 3,1 heures.

Profil temps-action (amélioration des symptômes)

	DÉBUT D'ACTION	PIC	DURÉE
Inhalation	24 h	1 - 4 semaines†	inconnue

† Amélioration de la fonction pulmonaire; la diminution de la réactivité des voies aériennes peut prendre plus longtemps.

CONTRE-INDICATIONS, PRÉCAUTIONS ET MISES EN GARDE

Contre-indications: Antécédents d'hypersensibilité à l'un ou l'autre des ingrédients de la préparation ■ Traitement principal d'une crise aiguë d'asthme, état de mal asthmatique, bronchectasie modérée ou grave ■ Tuberculose pulmonaire active ou quiescente, infection des voies respiratoires non traitée d'origine fongique, bactérienne ou virale.

Précautions et mises en garde: Diabète ou glaucome (doses élevées) ■ Immunosuppression sous-jacente, en raison d'une maladie ou d'un traitement concomitant (doses élevées) ■ Traitement par un corticostéroïde systémique (ne pas l'arrêter brusquement au début du traitement par inhalation; administrer des corticostéroïdes additionnels en cas de stress ou de traumatisme) ■ **OBST.:** L'innocuité chez les femmes enceintes n'a pas été établie; employer la plus petite dose nécessaire au maintien d'une maîtrise optimale des symptômes asthmatiques ■ **ALLAITEMENT:** L'innocuité chez les femmes qui allaitent n'a pas été établie; les corticostéroïdes passent dans le lait maternel ■ **PÉD.:** L'innocuité n'a pas été établie chez les enfants < 5 ans pour la béclométhasone, < 6 ans pour le budésonide (Turbuhaler), < 18 ans pour le ciclésonide ou < 12 mois pour la fluticasone.

RÉACTIONS INDÉSIRABLES ET EFFETS SECONDAIRES

SNC: *Budésonide, fluticasone* – céphalées. *Fluticasone* – agitation, dépression, fatigue, insomnie.

ORLO: dysphonie, enrouement, infections fongiques oropharyngées, cataractes. *Fluticasone* – congestion nasale, sinusite.

Resp.: bronchospasme, toux, respiration sifflante.

GI: sécheresse de la bouche (xérostomie), candidose œsophagienne. *Budésonide* – dyspepsie, gastroentérite. *Fluticasone* – nausées.

End.: suppression de la fonction surrénalienne (traitement prolongé, à doses élevées seulement), retard de croissance (enfants).

Loc.: *Budésonide* – douleurs lombaires. *Fluticasone* – douleurs musculaires.

Divers: SYNDROME DE CHURG ET STRAUSS. *Budésonide* – syndrome pseudogrippal.

INTERACTIONS

Médicament-médicament: L'**itraconazole**, le **kétoconazole**, le **ritonavir** et le **nelfinavir** ralentissent le métabolisme du budésonide, du ciclésonide et de la fluticasone et en élèvent les concentrations.

VOIES D'ADMINISTRATION ET POSOLOGIE

Béclométhasone

- **Inhalation (adultes et enfants ≥ 12 ans):** *Asthme léger* – de 50 à 100 µg, 2 fois par jour. *Asthme modéré* – de 100 à 250 µg, 2 fois par jour. *Asthme grave* – de 300 à 400 µg, 2 fois par jour.
- **Inhalation (enfants de 5 à 11 ans):** De 50 à 100 µg, 2 fois par jour.

Budésonide

- Turbuhaler

  Inhalation (adultes et enfants > 12 ans): De 400 à 2 400 µg par jour, répartis en 2 à 4 prises. Si la dose < 400 µg par jour, on peut l'administrer en une seule fois.

  Inhalation (enfants de 6 à 12 ans): De 200 à 400 µg par jour, répartis en 2 prises.
- Solution pour nébulisation

  Inhalation (adultes et enfants > 12 ans): De 1 à 2 mg, 2 fois par jour. Dans certains cas, on peut augmenter la dose davantage.

  Inhalation (enfants de 3 mois à 12 ans): De 0,25 mg à 0,5 mg, 2 fois par jour. Dans certains cas, on peut augmenter la dose pour la passer à 1 mg, 2 fois par jour.

Ciclésonide

- **Inhalation (adultes ≥ 18 ans):** La dose recommandée varie de 100 à 800 µg par jour. La dose habituelle est de 400 µg, 1 fois par jour. En cas d'asthme grave, on peut obtenir une meilleure maîtrise avec une dose quotidienne de 800 µg administrée à raison de 400 µg, 2 fois par jour.

C

Fluticasone (aérosol doseur et inhalateur de poudre sèche – Diskus)

- **Inhalation (adultes et adolescents > 16 ans)**: De 100 à 500 µg, 2 fois par jour. Dose maximale: 2 000 µg par jour.
- **Inhalation (enfants de 4 à 16 ans)**: De 50 à 100 µg, 2 fois par jour. Dans certains cas, on peut augmenter la dose pour la passer à 200 µg, 2 fois par jour.
- **Inhalation (enfants de 12 mois à 4 ans)**: 100 µg, 2 fois par jour, à l'aide d'un dispositif d'espacement.

PRÉSENTATION

- **Béclométhasone**
  Aérosol doseur: 50 ou 100 µg par inhalation, en flacons de 100 ou de 200 doses[Pr].
- **Budésonide**
  Turbuhaler: 100, 200 ou 400 µg par inhalation, en flacons de 200 doses[Pr]; 200 µg par inhalation, en flacons de 100 doses[Pr] ■ **En association avec**: formotérol (Symbicort[Pr]).
  Solution pour nébulisation: ampoule de 0,25 mg/2 mL[Pr]; 0,5 mg/2 mL[Pr] ou 1 g/2 mL[Pr].
- **Ciclésonide**
  Aérosol doseur: 100 ou 200 µg par inhalation, en flacons de 120 doses[Pr].
- **Fluticasone**
  Aérosol doseur: 50, 125 ou 250 µg par inhalation, en flacons de 60 ou de 120 doses[Pr] ■ **Inhalateur à poudre sèche (Diskus)**: 50, 100, 250 ou 500 µg par inhalation, en flacons de 60 doses[Pr] ■ **En association avec**: salméterol (Advair[Pr]).

SOINS INFIRMIERS

ÉVALUATION DE LA SITUATION

- Noter l'état de la fonction respiratoire et ausculter le murmure vésiculaire. On doit soumettre le patient à des tests de la fonction pulmonaire pendant le traitement et plusieurs mois après avoir remplacé un corticostéroïde systémique par un corticostéroïde en inhalation.
- Lorsqu'on substitue les corticostéroïdes administrés par inhalation aux corticostéroïdes systémiques, suivre de près, au cours de la période initiale du traitement et en périodes de stress, les signes suivants d'insuffisance surrénalienne: anorexie, nausées, faiblesse, fatigue, hypotension, hypoglycémie. Si ces signes se manifestent, prévenir immédiatement un professionnel de la santé, car il peut s'agir d'une réaction mettant la vie du patient en danger.
- Pendant la période d'arrêt graduel d'une corticothérapie par voie orale, suivre de près les symptômes de sevrage suivants: douleurs articulaires ou musculaires, lassitude, dépression.

Tests de laboratoire:

- Le médecin peut recommander des tests de la fonction surrénalienne à intervalles réguliers au cours du traitement prolongé afin d'évaluer le degré de suppression de l'axe hypothalamo-hypophyso-surrénalien. Les enfants et les patients prenant des doses plus fortes que celles recommandées sont exposés à un risque plus élevé de suppression de l'axe hypothalamo-hypophyso-surrénalien.
- Ces médicaments peuvent élever la glycémie et la glycosurie si l'absorption est importante.
- Suivre de près le taux de croissance des enfants; utiliser la dose la plus faible possible.

DIAGNOSTICS INFIRMIERS POSSIBLES

- Dégagement inefficace des voies respiratoires (Indications).
- Risque d'infection (Effets secondaires).
- Connaissances insuffisantes sur le traitement médicamenteux (Enseignement au patient et à ses proches).

INTERVENTIONS INFIRMIÈRES

- Une fois qu'on a obtenu l'effet clinique souhaité, on doit essayer de réduire la dose jusqu'à la dose la plus faible qui permette de maîtriser les symptômes. Réduire graduellement la dose toutes les 2 à 4 semaines, tant que l'effet souhaité est maintenu. Si les symptômes réapparaissent, on peut revenir rapidement à la dose de départ.

Inhalation: Si plus de 1 inhalation est prescrite, espacer les inhalations d'au moins 1 minute.

ENSEIGNEMENT AU PATIENT ET À SES PROCHES

- Conseiller au patient de respecter rigoureusement la posologie recommandée. S'il n'a pu prendre le médicament au moment habituel, il doit le prendre aussitôt que possible à moins que ce ne soit presque l'heure prévue pour la dose suivante. Conseiller au patient de ne pas interrompre le traitement sans consulter d'abord un professionnel de la santé; les doses doivent être réduites graduellement.
- Recommander aux patients qui utilisent des corticostéroïdes et un bronchodilatateur destiné à l'inhalation d'utiliser le bronchodilatateur en premier et d'attendre 5 minutes avant d'administrer le corticostéroïde, sauf recommandation contraire du professionnel de la santé.

- Informer le patient que les corticostéroïdes destinés à l'inhalation ne devraient pas être utilisés pour traiter une crise d'asthme aiguë, mais qu'il faut continuer de les prendre, même s'il utilise en même temps d'autres agents destinés à l'inhalation.
- Prévenir le patient qui utilise des corticostéroïdes destinés à l'inhalation pour maîtriser l'asthme qu'il pourrait avoir besoin de corticostéroïdes administrés par voie orale pour traiter les crises aiguës. Lui conseiller d'utiliser un débitmètre de pointe à intervalles réguliers pour évaluer l'état de sa fonction respiratoire.
- Recommander au patient d'éviter de fumer ou de s'exposer aux allergènes ou aux autres irritants connus des voies respiratoires.
- Conseiller au patient d'informer un professionnel de la santé s'il souffre de maux de gorge ou de douleurs dans la bouche.
- Conseiller au patient dont le traitement par des corticostéroïdes à action systémique a récemment été réduit ou interrompu de porter sur lui une pièce d'identité où est inscrit le fait qu'on doit lui administrer des doses additionnelles de corticostéroïdes à action systémique en cas de stress ou de crise d'asthme grave ne répondant pas aux bronchodilatateurs.

Aérosol-doseur, Turbuhaler, Diskus: (voir l'annexe G – Méthodes d'administration).

VÉRIFICATION DE L'EFFICACITÉ THÉRAPEUTIQUE

L'efficacité du traitement peut être démontrée par: le traitement des symptômes d'asthme chronique ■ la prévention des lésions pulmonaires associées à l'asthme chronique.

CORTICOSTÉROÏDES (TOPIQUES)

amcinonide
Cyclocort, Ratio-Amcinonide, Taro-Amcinonide

bétaméthasone
Betaderm, Betnovate, Betnovate-1/2, Celestoderm-V, Celestoderm-V/2, Diprogen, Diprolene, Diprosone, Ectosone, Pro-Lene Glycol, Propaderm, Pro-Sone, Rivasone, Ratio-Topisone, Rolene, Rosone, Taro-Rone, Topilene, Topisone, Valisone

clobétasol
Dermovate, Gen-Clobétasol, Novo-Clobétasol, PMS-Clobétasol, Ratio-Clobetasol

clobétasone
Eumovate

désonide
Desocort, PMS-Desonide, Tridesilon

désoximétasone
Topicort, Topicort doux

diflucortolone, valérate de
Nérisone

fluocinolone
Capex, Derma-Smoothe/FS, Synalar

fluocinonide
Lidemol, Lyderm, Lidex, Tiamol, Topactin

fluticasone
Cutivate

halcinonide
Halog

halobétasol
Ultravate

hydrocortisone
Barrière-HC, Cortate, Cortoderm, Dermaflex HC, Emo-Cort, Hyderm, Hydroval, Néo-HC, Prevex HC, Sarna-HC, Westcort

méthylprednisolone
Medrol

mométasone
Elocom, PMS-Mometasone, Ratio-Mometasone, Taro-Mometasone

prednicarbate
Dermatop

triamcinolone
Aristocort, Kenalog, Kenalog-Orabase

CLASSIFICATION:
Corticostéroïdes (topiques)

Grossesse – catégorie C

INDICATIONS

Traitement local des éruptions cutanées aiguës et chroniques, sensibles aux corticostéroïdes, lorsqu'on cherche à obtenir des effets anti-inflammatoires, antiallergiques et antiprurigineux.

MÉCANISME D'ACTION

Suppression de l'inflammation et de la réponse immunitaire normale. Risque de suppression de la fonction surrénalienne en cas d'absorption systémique prolongée. ***Effets thérapeutiques:*** Suppression de l'inflammation de la peau et des processus immunitaires.

PHARMACOCINÉTIQUE

C

Absorption: L'application du médicament sur de grandes surfaces, en grandes quantités et pendant une période prolongée, tout comme l'usage de pansements occlusifs, mène à une absorption systémique et à la suppression de la fonction surrénalienne.

Distribution: Le médicament reste principalement à son site d'action.

Métabolisme et excrétion: Le médicament est habituellement métabolisé au niveau de la peau; certains agents ont été modifiés pour résister au métabolisme local et pour prolonger leur effet local.

Demi-vie: *Bétaméthasone* – de 3 à 5 heures (plasma), de 36 à 54 heures (tissus); la suppression de la fonction surrénalienne dure 3,25 jours. *Dexaméthasone* – de 3 à 4,5 heures (plasma), de 36 à 54 heures (tissus); la suppression de la fonction surrénalienne dure 2,75 jours. *Hydrocortisone* – de 1,5 à 2 heures (plasma), de 8 à 12 heures (tissus); la suppression de la fonction surrénalienne dure de 1,25 à 1,5 jour. *Triamcinolone* – de 2 à plus de 5 heures (plasma), de 18 à 36 heures (tissus); la suppression de la fonction surrénalienne dure 2,25 jours.

Profil temps-action (réponse anti-inflammatoire)

	DÉBUT D'ACTION	PIC	DURÉE
Préparation topique	de plusieurs minutes à plusieurs heures	de plusieurs heures à plusieurs jours	de plusieurs heures à plusieurs jours

CONTRE-INDICATIONS, PRÉCAUTIONS ET MISES EN GARDE

Contre-indications: Hypersensibilité à l'agent ou à un de ses ingrédients ■ Infections bactériennes ou virales non traitées, ainsi qu'infections tuberculeuses et fongiques de la peau.

Précautions et mises en garde: Dysfonctionnement hépatique ■ Diabète, cataractes, glaucome ou tuberculose (l'administration de grandes quantités d'agents puissants peut aggraver la maladie) ■ Atrophie cutanée préexistante ■ **OBST., ALLAITEMENT, PÉD.**: L'usage prolongé de doses élevées peut entraîner une suppression de la fonction surrénalienne chez la mère et l'arrêt de la croissance chez l'enfant; les enfants peuvent être davantage prédisposés à la suppression de la fonction surrénalienne et à l'arrêt de la croissance ■ **GÉR.**: Chez les personnes âgées présentant une atrophie cutanée, on recommande un traitement de courte durée.

RÉACTIONS INDÉSIRABLES ET EFFETS SECONDAIRES

Tég.: dermatite de contact allergique, atrophie, sensation de brûlure, sécheresse, œdème, folliculite, réactions d'hypersensibilité, hypertrichose, hypopigmentation, irritation, macération, miliaire, dermite périorale, infection secondaire, vergetures.

Divers: suppression de la fonction surrénalienne (fortes doses en administration prolongée).

INTERACTIONS

Médicament-médicament: Aucune interaction notable.

VOIES D'ADMINISTRATION ET POSOLOGIE

- **Préparation topique (adultes)**: En application topique en une couche mince, de 1 à 4 fois par jour (selon le produit, la préparation et la maladie à traiter). Consulter la notice de conditionnement de chaque produit pour plus de détails.

PRÉSENTATION

- **Amcinonide**
  Crème: 0,1 %Pr ■ **Lotion**: 0,1 %Pr ■ **Onguent**: 0,1 %Pr.
- **Bétaméthasone (dipropionate de)**
  Crème: 0,025 %Pr, 0,05 %Pr ■ **Lotion**: 0,05 %Pr ■ **Onguent**: 0,05 %Pr.
- **Bétaméthasone (dipropionate de)/propylène glycol**
  Crème: 0,05 %Pr ■ **Lotion**: 0,05 %Pr ■ **Onguent**: 0,05 %Pr.
- **Bétaméthasone (valérate de)**
  Crème: 0,05 %Pr, 0,1 %Pr ■ **Lotion**: 0,05 %Pr, 0,1 %Pr ■ **Lotion capillaire**: 0,1 %Pr ■ **Onguent**: 0,05 %Pr, 0,1 %Pr.
- **Clobétasol**
  Crème: 0,05 %Pr ■ **Onguent**: 0,05 %Pr ■ **Lotion capillaire**: 0,05 %Pr.
- **Clobétasone (butyrate de)**
  Crème: 0,05 %Pr ■ **Onguent**: 0,05 %Pr.
- **Désonide**
  Crème: 0,05 %Pr ■ **Onguent**: 0,05 %Pr ■ **Lotion**: 0,05 %Pr.
- **Désoximétasone**
  Crème: 0,05 %Pr, 0,25 %Pr ■ **Gel**: 0,05 %Pr ■ **Onguent**: 0,25 %Pr.
- **Diflucortolone (valérate de)**
  Crème: 0,1 %Pr ■ **Onguent**: 0,1 %Pr ■ **Crème topique huileuse**: 0,1 %Pr.
- **Fluocinolone (acétonide de)**
  Crème: 0,01 %Pr, 0,025 %Pr ■ **Onguent**: 0,025 %Pr ■ **Solution topique**: 0,01 %Pr ■ **Shampooing**: 0,01 %Pr ■ **Huile topique**: 0,01 %Pr.

- **Fluocinonide**
  Crème: 0,05 %[Pr] ▪ **Gel**: 0,05 %[Pr] ▪ **Onguent**: 0,05 %[Pr].
- **Fluticasone**
  Crème: 0,05 %[Pr].
- **Halcinonide**
  Crème: 0,1 %[Pr] ▪ **Onguent**: 0,1 %[Pr] ▪ **Solution topique**: 0,1 %[Pr].
- **Halobétasol (propionate de)**
  Crème: 0,05 %[Pr] ▪ **Onguent**: 0,05 %[Pr].
- **Hydrocortisone**
  Crème: 0,5 %[VL], 1 %[Pr], 2,5 %[Pr] ▪ **Onguent**: 0,5 %[VL], 1 %[Pr] ▪ **Lotion**: 0,5 %[VL], 1 %[Pr], 2,5 %[Pr] ▪ **Solution capillaire**: 2,5 %[Pr].
- **Hydrocortisone (acétate d')**
  Crème: 0,5 %, 1 %[Pr], 2 %[Pr] ▪ **Lotion**: 1 %[Pr].
- **Hydrocortisone (valérate d')**
  Onguent: 0,2 %[Pr] ▪ **Crème**: 0,2 %[Pr].
- **Méthylprednisolone (acétate de)**
  Crème: 0,25 %[Pr].
- **Mométasone (furoate de)**
  Crème: 0,1 %[Pr] ▪ **Onguent**: 0,1 %[Pr] ▪ **Lotion**: 0,1 %[Pr].
- **Prednicarbate**
  Crème: 0,1 %[Pr] ▪ **Onguent**: 0,1 %[Pr].
- **Triamcinolone (acétonide de)**
  Crème: 0,025 %[Pr], 0,1 %[Pr], 0,5 %[Pr] ▪ **Onguent**: 0,1 %[Pr] **Pâte**: 0,1 %[Pr].

SOINS INFIRMIERS

ÉVALUATION DE LA SITUATION

- Examiner la peau affectée avant l'application de la préparation et quotidiennement pendant toute la durée du traitement. Noter le degré d'inflammation et de prurit. Prévenir le médecin ou un autre professionnel de la santé si les symptômes suivants d'infection se manifestent: douleur accrue, érythème, exsudats purulents.

Tests de laboratoire:

- En cas de traitement topique prolongé, on peut effectuer à intervalles réguliers des tests de la fonction surrénalienne pour déterminer le degré de suppression de l'axe hypothalamo-hypophyso-surrénalien. Les enfants et les patients chez lesquels le médicament a été appliqué sur une grande surface ou a été recouvert d'un pansement occlusif, ou encore chez lesquels on a utilisé des produits puissants, sont plus exposés au risque de suppression de l'axe hypothalamo-hypophyso-surrénalien.
- Le médicament peut élever la glycémie et la glycosurie en cas d'absorption importante.

DIAGNOSTICS INFIRMIERS POSSIBLES

- Risque d'atteinte à l'intégrité de la peau (Indications).
- Risque d'infection (Effets secondaires).
- Connaissances insuffisantes sur le traitement médicamenteux (Enseignement au patient et à ses proches).

INTERVENTIONS INFIRMIÈRES

- Le choix du véhicule dépend de la région atteinte et du type de lésion. Les onguents sont plus occlusifs et ils sont recommandés dans le cas des lésions sèches et squameuses. Les crèmes devraient être utilisées sur les surfaces suintantes ou intertrigineuses, où l'action occlusive des onguents pourrait entraîner la folliculite ou la macération. Les crèmes peuvent être privilégiées pour des raisons esthétiques, même si elles sont plus desséchantes que les onguents. Les gels, les aérosols, les lotions et les solutions peuvent être pratiques lorsqu'il s'agit de traiter des surfaces poilues.

Préparation topique:

- Appliquer une couche mince d'*onguent*, de *crème* ou de *gel* sur une peau propre et légèrement humide. Enfiler des gants lors de l'application. Appliquer un pansement occlusif seulement sur recommandation du médecin ou d'un autre professionnel de la santé.
- Appliquer les *lotions*, les *solutions* ou les *gels* sur les cheveux, en faisant une raie et en n'utilisant qu'une petite quantité sur la région affectée, puis masser délicatement. Ne pas nettoyer la région, ne pas la frotter et ne pas la recouvrir avant que le médicament ait séché. On peut se laver les cheveux comme d'habitude, mais non immédiatement après l'application.
- Bien agiter les *aérosols* et vaporiser la préparation à une distance de 7,5 à 15 cm de la région à traiter. Vaporiser pendant environ 2 secondes pour couvrir une région de la taille d'une main. Ne pas inhaler. En cas de vaporisation près du visage, protéger les yeux.

ENSEIGNEMENT AU PATIENT ET À SES PROCHES

- Montrer au patient comment appliquer les corticoïdes topiques. Insister sur le fait qu'il est important d'éviter tout contact avec les yeux. S'il n'a pas pu appliquer le médicament au moment habituel, il doit l'appliquer dès que possible à moins que ce ne soit presque l'heure prévue pour la dose suivante.
- Recommander au patient de respecter rigoureusement la posologie recommandée et d'éviter d'utiliser des cosmétiques, des bandages, des pansements

C

ou d'autres produits topiques sur la région traitée, sauf sur recommandation d'un professionnel de la santé.

- Conseiller aux parents des patients en bas âge de ne pas faire porter de couches ajustées ou de culottes de plastique à l'enfant traité pour l'érythème fessier ou d'autres affections dans la même région; ces vêtements agissent comme un pansement occlusif et pourraient entraîner une absorption accrue du médicament.
- Expliquer à la patiente qui est enceinte ou qui prévoit le devenir que le médicament ne devrait pas être utilisé sur une grande surface, en grandes quantités ou pendant une période prolongée.
- Recommander au patient de consulter un professionnel de la santé avant d'utiliser le médicament pour une autre forme de traitement.
- Recommander au patient de prévenir le professionnel de la santé si les symptômes de la maladie sous-jacente ressurgissent ou s'aggravent ou si des symptômes d'infection se manifestent.

VÉRIFICATION DE L'EFFICACITÉ THÉRAPEUTIQUE

L'efficacité du traitement peut être démontrée par: la résolution de l'inflammation, du prurit ou d'autres affections de la peau. ✳

CORTICOSTÉROÏDES (VOIE GÉNÉRALE)

corticostéroïdes à action brève

cortisone
Cortisone Acétate, Cortone

hydrocortisone
A-hydroCort, Cortef, Cortenema, Cortifoam, Hydrocortone, Solu-Cortef

corticostéroïdes à action intermédiaire

méthylprednisolone
Depo-Medrol, Medrol, Solu-Medrol

prednisolone†
Novo-Prednisolone, Pediapred

prednisone
Apo-Prednisone, Deltasone, Novo-Prednisone, Prednisone, Winpred

triamcinolone
Aristopan, Kenalog

corticostéroïdes à action prolongée

bétaméthasone
Betaject, Betnesol, Celestone Soluspan

budésonide
Entocort

dexaméthasone†
Alti-Dexaméthasone, Decadron, Dexaméthasone, Dexasone, PMS-Dexamethasone

CLASSIFICATION:
Corticostéroïdes (voie générale), anti-inflammatoires, immunosuppresseurs

Grossesse – catégories inconnue (méthylprednisolone), C (budésonide), D (1er trimestre) (tous les autres) et C (2e et 3e trimestres) (tous les autres)

† Pour l'usage ophtalmique, voir l'annexe N.

INDICATIONS

Cortisone, hydrocortisone: Traitement de l'insuffisance corticosurrénalienne. Usage à long terme limité dans d'autres cas, en raison des propriétés minéralocorticoïdes ▪ **Bétaméthasone, dexaméthasone, prednisolone, prednisone, méthylprednisolone, triamcinolone**: Traitement par voie générale et locale d'une grande variété de maladies incluant: les maladies inflammatoires ▪ l'asthme ▪ les allergies ▪ les troubles hématologiques ▪ les troubles endocriniens ▪ les troubles respiratoires ▪ les néoplasies ▪ les maladies auto-immunes ▪ Prévention du rejet d'organe lors d'une chirurgie de transplantation (en concomitance avec d'autres immunosuppresseurs) ▪ Certains agents conviennent à un traitement administré 1 jour sur 2 en présence de certaines maladies chroniques ▪ **Dexaméthasone**: Traitement de l'œdème cérébral ▪ Agent de diagnostic des troubles surrénaliens ▪ **Budésonide**: Traitement de la maladie de Crohn de légère à modérée. **Usages non approuvés**: Administration à court terme avant l'accouchement, chez les mères à haut risque, afin de prévenir le syndrome de détresse respiratoire chez les nouveau-nés prématurés (bétaméthasone, dexaméthasone) ▪ Thérapie complémentaire de l'hypercalcémie ▪ Traitement des lésions médullaires aiguës (méthylprednisolone) ▪

Thérapie complémentaire des nausées et des vomissements induits par la chimiothérapie ■ Traitement du croup (dexaméthasone).

MÉCANISME D'ACTION

À des doses thérapeutiques, tous les agents entraînent une suppression de l'inflammation et de la réponse immunitaire normale ■ Tous les agents ont de nombreux effets métaboliques intenses (voir « Réactions indésirables et effets secondaires ») ■ Suppression de la fonction des surrénales aux doses suivantes, administrées en traitement prolongé: *bétaméthasone* – 0,6 mg par jour; *cortisone, hydrocortisone* – 20 mg par jour; *dexaméthasone* – 0,75 mg par jour; *méthylprednisolone* – 4 mg par jour; *prednisone, prednisolone* – 5 mg par jour; *triamcinolone* – 4 mg par jour ■ **Cortisone, hydrocortisone**: remplacement du cortisol endogène en présence d'une insuffisance surrénalienne ■ **Cortisone, hydrocortisone**: puissante activité minéralocorticoïde (rétention sodique) ■ **Prednisolone, prednisone**: activité minéralocorticoïde minime ■ **Bétaméthasone, dexaméthasone, méthylprednisolone, triamcinolone**: activité minéralocorticoïde négligeable ■ **Budésonide**: effet anti-inflammatoire local dans le lumen du tractus gastro-intestinal. ***Effets thérapeutiques***: Suppression de l'inflammation et modification de la réponse immunitaire normale ■ Corticothérapie supplétive de l'insuffisance surrénalienne ■ Amélioration des symptômes et des séquelles de la maladie de Crohn.

PHARMACOCINÉTIQUE

Absorption: Bonne (PO). Les sels de phosphate sodique et de succinate sodique sont rapidement absorbés (IM). Les sels d'acétate, d'acétonide et d'hexacétonide sont absorbés lentement mais complètement (IM). L'absorption à partir d'un point d'injection (intra-articulaire, intralésionnelle) est lente mais complète. Le budésonide est rapidement inactivé après son absorption.

Distribution: Tous les agents se répartissent dans tout l'organisme, traversent la barrière placentaire et pénètrent probablement dans le lait maternel.

Métabolisme et excrétion: Métabolisme principalement hépatique (tous les agents). La *cortisone* est transformée par le foie en hydrocortisone. La *prednisone* est transformée par le foie en prednisolone, qui subit à son tour un métabolisme hépatique.

Demi-vie: *Bétaméthasone* – de 3 à 5 heures (plasma), de 36 à 54 heures (tissus); la suppression de la fonction surrénalienne dure 3,25 jours. *Budésonide* – de 2 à 3,6 heures. *Cortisone* – 0,5 heure (plasma), de 8 à 12 heures (tissus); la suppression de la fonction surrénalienne dure de 1,25 à 1,5 jour. *Dexaméthasone* – de 3 à 4,5 heures (plasma), de 36 à 54 heures (tissus); la suppression de la fonction surrénalienne dure 2,75 jours. *Hydrocortisone* – de 1,5 à 2 heures (plasma), de 8 à 12 heures (tissus); la suppression de la fonction surrénalienne dure de 1,25 à 1,5 jour. *Méthylprednisolone* – plus de 3,5 heures (plasma), de 18 à 36 heures (tissus); la suppression de la fonction surrénalienne dure de 1,25 à 1,5 jour. *Prednisolone* – de 2,1 à 3,5 heures (plasma); de 18 à 36 heures (tissus); la suppression de la fonction surrénalienne dure de 1,25 à 1,5 jour. *Prednisone* – de 3,4 à 3,8 heures (plasma), de 18 à 36 heures (tissus); la suppression de la fonction surrénalienne dure de 1,25 à 1,5 jour. *Triamcinolone* – de 2 à plus de 5 heures (plasma), de 18 à 36 heures (tissus); la suppression de la fonction surrénalienne dure 2,25 jours.

Profil temps-action (effet anti-inflammatoire)

	DÉBUT D'ACTION	PIC	DURÉE
Bétaméthasone IM (acétate/phosphate)	1 – 3 h	inconnu	1 semaine
Budésonide PO	inconnu	inconnu	inconnue
Cortisone PO	rapide	2 h	1,25 – 1,5 jour
Dexaméthasone PO	inconnu	1 – 2 h	2,75 jours
Dexaméthasone IM, IV (phosphate)	rapide	inconnu	2,75 jours
Hydrocortisone PO	inconnu	1 – 2 h	1,25 – 1,5 jour
Hydrocortisone IM (succinate)	rapide	1 h	variable
Hydrocortisone IV (succinate)	rapide	inconnu	inconnue
Méthylprednisolone PO	inconnu	1 – 2 h	1,25 – 1,5 jour
Méthylprednisolone IM (acétate)	6 – 48 h	4 – 8 jours	1 – 4 semaines
Méthylprednisolone IM, IV (succinate)	rapide	inconnu	inconnue
Prednisolone PO	inconnu	1 – 2 h	1,25 – 1,5 jour
Prednisone PO	plusieurs heures	inconnu	1,25 – 1,5 jour
Triamcinolone PO	inconnu	1 – 2 h	2,25 jours
Triamcinolone IM (acétonide)	24 – 48 h	inconnu	1 – 6 semaines

CONTRE-INDICATIONS, PRÉCAUTIONS ET MISES EN GARDE

Contre-indications: Infections actives non traitées (sauf chez les patients traités pour certaines formes de méningite) ■ Hypersensibilité à l'agent ou à ses ingrédients ■ Vaccination avec un virus vivant chez les personnes qui reçoivent une corticothérapie immunosuppressive.

Précautions et mises en garde: Traitement prolongé (suppression de la fonction surrénalienne; administrer la plus faible dose pendant le moins longtemps possible)

■ Myasthénie grave ■ Diabète ■ Ulcère gastroduodénal en poussées évolutives ■ Hypothyroïdie ■ Cirrhose ■ **PÉD.**: Le traitement prolongé entraîne le ralentissement de la croissance; administrer la plus faible dose pendant le moins longtemps possible ■ *Prématurés*: éviter d'administrer des préparations contenant de l'alcool benzylique; administrer des préparations sans agents de conservation ■ Périodes de stress (intervention chirurgicale, infections); il peut s'avérer nécessaire d'administrer des doses supplémentaires ■ Infections (fièvre, inflammation); ces médicaments peuvent en masquer les signes ■ **OBST.**: L'innocuité du médicament n'a pas été établie ■ **ALLAITEMENT**: Éviter l'usage prolongé.

RÉACTIONS INDÉSIRABLES ET EFFETS SECONDAIRES

Les réactions indésirables et les effets secondaires sont bien plus courants lors d'un traitement prolongé ou à la suite de la prise de doses élevées.

SNC: dépression, euphorie, céphalées, pression intracrânienne accrue (enfants seulement), modifications de la personnalité, psychoses, agitation.

ORLO: cataractes, pression intraoculaire accrue.

CV: hypertension.

GI: ULCÈRE GASTRODUODÉNAL, anorexie, nausées, vomissements.

Tég.: acné, ralentissement de la cicatrisation des plaies, ecchymoses, fragilité cutanée, hirsutisme, pétéchies.

End.: suppression de la fonction surrénalienne, hyperglycémie.

HÉ: rétention hydrique (fortes doses à long terme), hypokaliémie, alcalose métabolique.

Hémat.: THROMBOEMBOLIE, thrombophlébite.

Métab.: gain pondéral, perte pondérale.

Loc.: atrophie musculaire, ostéoporose, nécrose aseptique des articulations, douleurs musculaires.

Divers: aspect cushingoïde (faciès lunaire, bosse de bison), prédisposition accrue aux infections.

INTERACTIONS

Médicament-médicament: Effets hypokaliémiques additifs lors de l'administration concomitante de **diurétiques thiazidiques** ou de **diurétiques de l'anse**, d'**amphotéricine B**, de **pipéracilline** ou de **ticarcilline** ■ L'hypokaliémie peut augmenter le risque de toxicité **digitalique** ■ Le traitement par des corticostéroïdes à action générale peut augmenter les besoins en **insuline** ou en **hypoglycémiants oraux** ■ La **phénytoïne**, le **phénobarbital** et la **rifampine** accélèrent le métabolisme et peuvent diminuer l'efficacité des corticostéroïdes à action générale ■ Les **contraceptifs oraux** peuvent inhiber le métabolisme des corticostéroïdes à action générale ■ Risque accru d'effets indésirables gastro-intestinaux lors de l'administration concomitante d'**AINS** (incluant l'**aspirine**) ■ Les corticostéroïdes à action générale, aux doses et à une durée de traitement entraînant la suppression de la fonction surrénalienne, peuvent diminuer la réponse des anticorps aux **vaccins à virus vivants** et augmenter le risque de réactions indésirables ■ Les corticostéroïdes à action générale peuvent élever les concentrations plasmatiques de **cyclosporine** et de **tacrolimus** ■ Les corticostéroïdes à action générale peuvent accroître le risque de déchirure des tendons associé aux **fluoroquinolones** ■ L'administration concomitante de cortisone par voie orale, à des doses de 12,5 à 18,8 mg/m^2 par jour, peut inhiber la réponse au **somatrem** ou à la **somatropine** ■ Les **antiacides** diminuent l'absorption de la prednisone et de la dexaméthasone ■ Le **kétoconazole**, l'**itraconazole**, le **ritonavir**, l'**indinavir**, le **saquinavir** et l'**érytrhomycine** peuvent élever les concentrations plasmatiques et intensifier l'effet des corticostéroïdes à action générale ■ Les corticostéroïdes à action générale peuvent diminuer les concentrations plasmatiques et l'effet des **salicylates** et de l'**isoniazide** ■ Risque de contrecarrer l'effet des **anticholinestérases** administrées aux patients souffrant de myasthénie grave ■ Les corticostéroïdes à action générale peuvent diminuer ou intensifier l'effet des **anticoagulants oraux**.

Médicament-aliments: Le **jus de pamplemousse** peut élever les concentrations plasmatiques et l'effet de la méthylprednisolone et du budésonide.

VOIES D'ADMINISTRATION ET POSOLOGIE

Il faut se souvenir que les posologies de tous les corticostéroïdes à action générale varient d'un patient à l'autre et qu'elles doivent être individualisées selon l'affection et la réponse clinique. Dans tous les cas, dès qu'on a obtenu une réponse satisfaisante, il est important de diminuer la posologie initiale par petites doses à intervalles appropriés, jusqu'à l'atteinte de la dose efficace la plus faible possible.

Bétaméthasone

- **IM, intra-articulaire (adultes)**: De 1 à 2 mL, tous les 3 jours ou toutes les semaines, selon la maladie à traiter.
- **IM (adultes)**: *En prévention du syndrome de détresse respiratoire des nouveau-nés prématurés (femmes enceintes de 24 à 34 semaines à risque d'accouchement prématuré dans les 7 jours qui suivent):* 12 mg, à répéter 1 fois, 24 heures plus tard.

Budésonide

- **PO (adultes)**: *Maladie active:* 9 mg, 1 fois par jour, pendant un maximum de 8 semaines. *Maintien de* *la rémission:* 6 mg, 1 fois par jour. On doit prescrire la dose d'entretien la plus faible qui permet de maîtriser les symptômes.

Cortisone

- **PO (adultes):** La posologie initiale va de 10 à 300 mg par jour, selon la maladie à traiter. Chez les enfants et les nourrissons, il faut habituellement réduire la posologie recommandée; cependant, la posologie dépend plus de la gravité de la maladie que de l'âge ou du poids du patient.

Dexaméthasone

- **PO (adultes):** De 0,5 à 15 mg par jour, en 1 ou plusieurs doses, selon la maladie à traiter. Chez les enfants et les nourrissons, il faut habituellement réduire la posologie recommandée; cependant, la posologie doit être adaptée en fonction de la gravité de la maladie plutôt qu'en fonction de l'âge ou du poids du patient.
- **IV, IM (adultes):** La posologie initiale va de 0,5 à 20 mg par jour, selon la maladie à traiter.

Dexaméthasone (épreuve de freinage par la dexaméthasone)

- **PO (adultes):** 1 mg à 23 heures, ou 0,5 mg, toutes les 6 heures, pendant 48 heures.

Dexaméthasone (œdème cérébral)

- **IM, IV (adultes):** 10 mg IV, initialement, suivis de 4 mg IM, toutes les 6 heures jusqu'à ce que les symptômes se dissipent. Diminuer la dose après 2 à 4 jours et interrompre graduellement le traitement en l'espace de 5 à 7 jours.

Hydrocortisone

- **PO (adultes):** La posologie initiale va de 20 à 240 mg par jour, selon la maladie à traiter.
- **IM, IV (adultes):** De 100 à 500 mg, toutes les 2 à 6 heures, selon la réponse clinique et la maladie à traiter.

Méthylprednisolone

- **PO (adultes):** La posologie initiale va de 4 à 48 mg par jour, selon la maladie à traiter.
- **IM, IV (adultes):** *La plupart des indications: succinate sodique de méthylprednisolone* – la posologie initiale va de 10 à 250 mg, toutes les 4 à 24 heures, selon la réponse clinique et la maladie à traiter. On peut commencer le traitement par voie IV et administrer les doses ultérieures par voie IM. *États de choc: succinate sodique de méthylprednisolone* – 30 mg/kg, par voie IV, toutes les 4 à 6 heures, pendant 48 heures, au maximum.
- **IM, intra-articulaire (adultes):** *Acétate de méthylprednisolone* – La posologie varie énormément selon l'indication: de 40 à 120 mg, tous les 5, 7, 10 ou 15 jours.

Prednisolone

- **PO (adultes):** *La plupart des indications* – la posologie initiale va de 5 à 60 mg par jour, selon la maladie à traiter.
- **PO (enfants):** *La plupart des indications* – la posologie initiale va de 0,1 à 2 mg/kg par jour, selon la maladie à traiter. Administrer en 1 ou plusieurs doses.

Prednisone

- **PO (adultes):** *La plupart des indications* – la posologie initiale va de 5 à 60 mg par jour, selon la maladie à traiter.
- **PO (enfants):** *La plupart des indications* – la posologie initiale va de 1 à 2 mg/kg par jour, selon la maladie à traiter. Administrer en 1 ou plusieurs doses.

Triamcinolone

- **IM (adultes):** *Acétonide de triamcinolone* – de 2,5 mg à 60 mg, selon la maladie à traiter, la réponse du patient et la durée du soulagement obtenu.
- **IM (enfants de 6 à 12 ans):** *Acétonide de triamcinolone* – la dose initiale recommandée est de 40 mg, mais la posologie doit être adaptée en fonction de la gravité des symptômes plutôt que de l'âge ou du poids du patient.
- **Intra-articulaire (adultes):** *Acétonide de triamcinolone* – de 2,5 à 5 mg, habituellement toutes les 3 à 4 semaines, selon la réponse du patient. *Hexacétonide de triamcinolone* – de 2 à 20 mg, habituellement toutes les 3 à 4 semaines, selon la réponse du patient.

PRÉSENTATION

- **Bétaméthasone**
  Suspension pour injection (phosphate/acétate): 6 mg (total)/mL^{Pr}.
- **Cortisone**
  Comprimés: 25 mg^{Pr}.
- **Dexaméthasone**
  Comprimés: 0,5 mg^{Pr}, 0,75 mg^{Pr}, 4 mg^{Pr} ■ **Élixir:** 0,5 mg/5 mL^{Pr} ■ **Solution pour injection (phosphate sodique):** 4 mg/mL^{Pr}, 10 mg/mL^{Pr}.
- **Hydrocortisone**
  Comprimés: 10 mg^{Pr}, 20 mg^{Pr} ■ **Poudre pour injection (succinate sodique):** 100 mg^{Pr}, 250 mg^{Pr}, 500 mg^{Pr}, 1 g^{Pr}.
- **Méthylprednisolone**
  Comprimés: 4 mg^{Pr}, 16 mg^{Pr} ■ **Solution pour injection (succinate sodique):** 40 mg^{Pr}, 125 mg^{Pr}, 500 mg^{Pr}, 1 g^{Pr} ■ **Suspension pour injection (acétate):** 20 mg/mL^{Pr}, 40 mg/mL^{Pr}, 80 mg/mL^{Pr}.

- **Prednisolone**
  Solution orale: 5 mg/5 mL^Pr^.
- **Prednisone**
  Comprimés: 1 mg^Pr^, 5 mg^Pr^, 50 mg^Pr^.
- **Triamcinolone**
  Suspension pour injection (acétonide): 10 mg/mL^Pr^, 40 mg/mL^Pr^ ■ **Suspension pour injection (hexacétonide):** 20 mg/mL^Pr^.

SOINS INFIRMIERS

ÉVALUATION DE LA SITUATION

- Ces médicaments sont indiqués dans le traitement de nombreuses affections. Évaluer les systèmes et appareils touchés avant le traitement et, à intervalles réguliers, pendant toute sa durée.
- Avant le traitement et à intervalles réguliers pendant toute sa durée, rester à l'affût des signes suivants d'insuffisance surrénalienne: hypotension, perte de poids, faiblesse, nausées, vomissements, anorexie, léthargie, confusion, agitation.
- Effectuer le bilan quotidien des ingesta et des excreta et peser le patient tous les jours. Suivre de près l'apparition d'un œdème périphérique, de râles et de crépitations ou de la dyspnée ainsi qu'un gain de poids constant. Prévenir le médecin ou un autre professionnel de la santé si ces symptômes surviennent.
- Noter à intervalles réguliers la croissance chez les enfants.

Œdème cérébral: Suivre de près, tout au long du traitement, toute modification de l'état de conscience et l'apparition de céphalées.

Budésonide: Suivre à intervalles réguliers, pendant toute la durée du traitement les signes et les symptômes suivants de la maladie de Crohn: diarrhée, douleurs abdominales sous forme de crampes et rectorragie.

Tests de laboratoire:

- Noter les concentrations sériques d'électrolytes et de glucose. Les corticostéroïdes à action générale peuvent provoquer l'hyperglycémie, particulièrement chez les diabétiques, et l'hypokaliémie. Les patients qui suivent un traitement prolongé devraient se soumettre, à intervalles réguliers, à des analyses permettant de mesurer les paramètres hématologiques, les électrolytes sériques, la glycémie et la glycosurie. Les corticostéroïdes à action générale peuvent également diminuer le nombre de globules blancs ainsi que les concentrations sériques de calcium, et élever celles de sodium.
- Prévenir rapidement le médecin si on a décelé du sang occulte dans les selles par la méthode au gaïac.
- Ces médicaments peuvent accroître les concentrations sériques de cholestérol et de lipides. Ils peuvent réduire le captage par la thyroïde des isotopes ^{123}I ou ^{131}I.
- Les corticostéroïdes à action générale suppriment les réactions aux tests d'allergie cutanés.
- En cas de traitement par voie générale ou de traitement topique prolongé, le médecin peut prescrire à intervalles réguliers des tests de la fonction surrénalienne pour déterminer le degré de suppression de l'axe hypothalamo-hypophyso-surrénalien.

Épreuve de freinage par la dexaméthasone:

- Pour diagnostiquer le syndrome de Cushing: obtenir les concentrations initiales de cortisol; administrer la dexaméthasone à 23 heures, et mesurer les concentrations de cortisol à 8 heures, le lendemain. La réponse normale se traduit par une baisse de la concentration de cortisol.
- Solution de rechange: obtenir un échantillon des urines de 24 heures pour déterminer les concentrations initiales de 17-hydroxycorticostéroïdes, puis administrer la dexaméthasone pendant 48 heures. Effectuer un second dosage des 17-hydroxycorticostéroïdes dans les urines de 24 heures, 24 heures après l'administration de la dexaméthasone.

DIAGNOSTICS INFIRMIERS POSSIBLES

- Risque d'infection (Effets secondaires).
- Image corporelle perturbée (Effets secondaires).
- Connaissances insuffisantes sur le traitement médicamenteux (Enseignement au patient et à ses proches).

INTERVENTIONS INFIRMIÈRES

- NE PAS CONFONDRE LA PREDNISONE AVEC LA PREDNISOLONE, LA MÉTHYLPREDNISOLONE OU LA PRIMIDONE.
- Si le médicament doit être pris tous les 1 ou 2 jours, administrer la dose le matin pour faire coïncider la prise avec les sécrétions naturelles de cortisol.
- Pendant les périodes de stress (p. ex., avant ou après une intervention chirurgicale), il est parfois recommander d'augmenter la dose de corticostéroïdes à action générale.
- Chez les patients souffrant de la maladie de Crohn légère ou modérée, qui ne présentent pas d'insuffisance surrénalienne, on peut diminuer graduellement la dose de prednisone ou de prednisolone et ajouter le budésonide à la pharmacothérapie.

PO:

- Administrer le médicament avec des aliments pour réduire l'irritation gastrique. Ne pas administrer avec du jus de pamplemousse (budénoside ou méthylprednisolone).
- Si le patient éprouve des difficultés de déglutition, on peut écraser les comprimés et les administrer avec des aliments ou des liquides. (Consulter les recommandations du fabricant.) LES CAPSULES DE BUDÉSONIDE DOIVENT ÊTRE AVALÉES EN ENTIER; NE PAS LES ÉCRASER, LES OUVRIR NI LES MÂCHER.
- Utiliser un récipient gradué pour mesurer correctement les préparations liquides.

IM, intra-articulaire: Bien agiter la suspension avant de la prélever de la fiole. Ne pas administrer par voie IM lorsqu'il faut obtenir un effet rapide. Ne pas diluer ni mélanger avec d'autres solutions. Ne pas administrer les suspensions par voie IV.

- Pour la voie parentérale, consulter les directives du fabricant pour savoir comment reconstituer et administrer le corticostéroïde et pour obtenir des informations sur le mode de conservation.

Dexaméthasone

IV directe: Le médicament peut être administré non dilué.

Vitesse d'administration: Administrer en au moins 1 minute.

Perfusion intermittente: On peut diluer le médicament dans une solution de D5%E ou dans une solution de NaCl 0,9 %. Administrer la perfusion à la vitesse prescrite. La solution diluée devrait être utilisée dans les 24 heures qui suivent la préparation.

Dexaméthasone (phosphate sodique)

Compatibilité dans la même seringue: granisétron ■ métoclopramide ■ ranitidine ■ sufentanil.

Associations incompatibles dans la même seringue: doxapram ■ glycopyrrolate.

Compatibilité (tubulure en Y): acyclovir ■ amifostine ■ aztréonam ■ céfépime ■ cisplatine ■ cyclophosphamide ■ cytarabine ■ doxorubicine ■ famotidine ■ filgrastim ■ fluconazole ■ fludarabine ■ foscarnet ■ granisétron ■ héparine ■ lorazépam ■ melphalan ■ mépéridine ■ méthotrexate ■ morphine ■ ondansétron ■ paclitaxel ■ pipéracilline/tazobactam ■ potassium ■ sargramostim ■ sufentanil ■ tacrolimus ■ téniposide ■ thiotépa ■ vinorelbine ■ vitamines du complexe B avec C ■ zidovudine.

Incompatibilité (tubulure en Y): ciprofloxacine ■ idarubicine ■ midazolam.

Compatibilité en addition au soluté: aminophylline ■ bléomycine ■ cimétidine ■ furosémide ■ lidocaïne ■ nafcilline ■ nétilmicine ■ ondansétron ■ ranitidine.

Incompatibilité en addition au soluté: daunorubicine ■ doxorubicine ■ métaraminol ■ vancomycine.

Hydrocortisone

IV directe: Reconstituer la préparation avec la solution fournie (par exemple, Act-O-Vials) ou avec le volume d'eau stérile pour injection recommandé par le fabricant.

Vitesse d'administration: Chaque dose de 100 mg doit être administrée en 1 minute. Les doses de 500 mg ou plus doivent être perfusées en au moins 10 minutes.

Perfusion intermittente/continue: On peut ajouter la préparation à entre 50 et 1 000 mL de D5%E, à une solution de NaCl 0,9 % ou à une solution D5%E/NaCl 0,9 %. Administrer les perfusions à la vitesse prescrite. La solution diluée devrait être utilisée dans les 24 heures qui suivent la préparation.

Hydrocortisone (succinate sodique)

Compatibilité dans la même seringue: métoclopramide ■ thiopental.

Compatibilité (tubulure en Y): acyclovir■ adrénaline ■ amifostine ■ aminophylline ■ ampicilline ■ amrinone ■ atracurium ■ atropine ■ aztréonam ■ calcium, gluconate de ■ céfépime ■ céphalothine ■ céphapirine ■ chlordiazépoxide ■ chlorpromazine ■ cyanocabalamine ■ dexaméthasone ■ digoxine ■ diphenhydramine ■ dopamine ■ dropéridol ■ dropéridol/fentanyl ■ édrophonium ■ énalaprilate ■ esmolol ■ éthacrynate ■ famotidine ■ fentanyl ■ filgrastim ■ fludarabine ■ fluorouracile ■ foscarnet ■ furosémide ■ gallium, nitrate de ■ hydralazine ■ insuline ■ isoprotérénol ■ kanamycine ■ lidocaïne ■ magnésium ■ mépéridine ■ méthicilline ■ méthoxamine ■ méthylergonovine ■ minocycline ■ morphine ■ néostigmine ■ noradrénaline ■ œstrogènes conjugués ■ ondansétron ■ oxacilline ■ oxytocine ■ paclitaxel ■ pancuronium ■ pénicilline G potassique ■ pentazocine ■ phytonadione ■ pipéracilline/tazobactam ■ procaïnamide ■ prochlorpérazine, édisylate de ■ propranolol ■ pyridostigmine ■ scopolamine ■ sodium, bicarbonate de ■ succinylcholine ■ tacrolimus ■ thiotépa ■ triméthobenzamide ■ triméthaphane, camsylate de ■ vécuronium.

Incompatibilité (tubulure en Y): ciprofloxacine ■ diazépam ■ ergotamine, tartrate d' ■ idarubicine ■ phénytoïne ■ sargramostim.

Compatibilité en addition au soluté: amikacine ■ aminophylline ■ amphotéricine ■ daunorubicine ■ diphenhydramine ■ magnésium, sulfate de ■ mitoxantrone ■ potassium, chlorure de ■ vitamines du complexe B avec C.

Incompatibilité en addition au soluté: bléomycine ■ doxorubicine.

Méthylprednisolone

IV directe: Reconstituer le médicament avec la solution fournie (Act-O-Vials, Univials, fioles ADD-Vantage) ou avec le volume d'eau stérile pour injection avec ou sans agent bactériostatique recommandé par le fabricant.

Vitesse d'administration: Administrer en au moins 5 minutes. L'administration IV directe de doses > 250 mg n'est pas recommandée par le fabricant et devrait se faire par perfusion.

Perfusion intermittente/continue: On peut diluer la solution de nouveau dans une solution de D5%E, de NaCl 0,9 % ou de D5%E/NaCl 0,9 % et l'administrer sous forme de perfusion intermittente ou continue au débit prescrit. La solution peut devenir trouble après dilution.

Méthylprednisolone (succinate sodique)

Compatibilité dans la même seringue: granisétron ■ métoclopramide.

Compatibilité (tubulure en Y): acyclovir ■ amifostine ■ amrinone ■ aztréonam ■ céfépime ■ cisplatine ■ cyclophosphamide ■ cytarabine ■ doxorubicine ■ énalaprilate ■ famotidine ■ fludarabine ■ héparine ■ melphalan ■ mépéridine ■ méthotrexate ■ midazolam ■ morphine ■ pipéracilline/tazobactam ■ sodium, bicarbonate de ■ tacrolimus ■ téniposide ■ thiotépa.

Incompatibilité (tubulure en Y): ciprofloxacine ■ filgrastim ■ ondansétron ■ paclitaxel ■ sargramostim.

Compatibilité en addition au soluté: cimétidine ■ granisétron ■ héparine ■ ranitidine ■ théophylline.

ENSEIGNEMENT AU PATIENT ET À SES PROCHES

- Montrer au patient comment prendre le médicament. Lui conseiller de respecter rigoureusement la posologie prescrite. S'il n'a pu prendre le médicament au moment habituel, il doit le prendre dès que possible à moins que ce ne soit presque l'heure prévue pour la dose suivante. Le prévenir qu'il ne doit jamais remplacer une dose manquée par une double dose. Lui expliquer que l'arrêt brusque de la corticothérapie peut entraîner les symptômes suivants d'insuffisance surrénalienne: anorexie, nausées, faiblesse, fatigue, dyspnée, hypotension, hypoglycémie. Si ces réactions se manifestent, il doit en informer immédiatement le médecin, car elles peuvent mettre sa vie en danger.
- Expliquer au patient que ce médicament a des effets immunosuppresseurs et qu'il peut masquer les symptômes d'infection. Lui conseiller d'éviter tout contact avec des personnes contagieuses et de signaler immédiatement au médecin tout signe d'infection.
- Conseiller au patient de ne pas se faire vacciner avant d'avoir consulté le médecin au préalable.
- Expliquer au patient les effets secondaires possibles. LUI RECOMMANDER DE PRÉVENIR RAPIDEMENT UN PROFESSIONNEL DE LA SANTÉ EN CAS DE DOULEURS ABDOMINALES GRAVES OU DE SELLES GOUDRONNEUSES. Le prévenir qu'il devrait également signaler les symptômes suivants: œdème, gain pondéral, fatigue, douleurs osseuses, ecchymoses, lésions qui ne cicatrisent pas, troubles visuels ou modification du comportement.
- Recommander au patient qui doit suivre un autre traitement ou subir une intervention chirurgicale d'avertir le professionnel de la santé qu'il suit une corticothérapie.
- Prévenir le patient que le traitement pourrait affecter son image corporelle. Explorer avec lui les stratégies d'adaptation auxquelles il pourrait recourir.
- Conseiller au patient d'informer un professionnel de la santé si les symptômes de la maladie sousjacente ressurgissent ou s'aggravent.
- Conseiller au patient de toujours porter sur lui une pièce d'identité où sont inscrits son problème de santé et son traitement médicamenteux pour parer à toute urgence dans le cas où il serait incapable de communiquer ses antécédents médicaux.
- Insister sur la nécessité d'un suivi médical régulier permettant d'évaluer l'efficacité du médicament et ses effets secondaires possibles. Le médecin peut recommander des examens diagnostiques et des examens de la vue à intervalles réguliers.

Traitement prolongé: Inciter le patient à adopter un régime riche en protéines, en calcium et en potassium et pauvre en sodium et en hydrates de carbone (voir l'annexe J). Lui conseiller de s'abstenir de consommer de l'alcool au cours du traitement.

VÉRIFICATION DE L'EFFICACITÉ THÉRAPEUTIQUE

L'efficacité du traitement peut être démontrée par: la diminution des symptômes initiaux avec très peu d'effets secondaires systémiques ■ la suppression des réponses inflammatoire et immunitaire en présence de maladies auto-immunes, de réactions allergiques ou de néoplasies ■ la maîtrise des symptômes d'insuffisance surrénalienne ■ l'amélioration des signes et des symptômes de la maladie de Crohn, soit la diminution de la fréquence des selles liquides, la diminution des symptômes abdominaux et une sensation de mieux-être. ✳

CORTICOSTÉROÏDES (VOIE INTRANASALE)

béclométhasone
Apo-Béclométhasone AQ, Gen-Beclo AQ, Nu-Béclométhasone AQ, Ratio-Béclométhasone AQ, Rivanase AQ

budésonide
Gen-Budésonide AQ, Rhinocort Aqua, Rhinocort turbuhaler

flunisolide
Apo-Flunisolide, PMS-Flunisolide, Ratio-Flunisolide, Rhinalar

fluticasone
Flonase

mométasone
Nasonex

triamcinolone
Nasacort, Nasacort AQ

CLASSIFICATION:
Corticostéroïdes (par voie intranasale)

Grossesse – catégorie C

INDICATIONS

Traitement de la rhinite allergique saisonnière ou apériodique ne répondant pas au traitement habituel ■ Le budésonide est aussi indiqué pour traiter la rhinite non allergique et la rhinite vasomotrice. Il est aussi indiqué pour le traitement des polypes nasaux et leur prévention à la suite d'une polypectomie ■ La mométasone est également indiquée comme traitement adjuvant à l'antibiothérapie pour traiter les accès de sinusite aiguë.

MÉCANISME D'ACTION

Effet anti-inflammatoire local puissant, pouvant modifier la réponse immunitaire. ***Effets thérapeutiques:*** Diminution des symptômes de rhinite allergique ■ Diminution des polypes nasaux ■ Amélioration des symptômes de la sinusite aiguë.

PHARMACOCINÉTIQUE

Absorption: *Béclométhasone* – biodisponibilité systémique à 44 %; *budésonide* – biodisponibilité systémique à 34 % (aqueux) et 22 % (Turbuhaler); *flunisolide* – biodisponibilité systémique à 50 %; *fluticasone* – biodisponibilité systémique < 2 %; *mométasone et triamcinolone* – absorption négligeable. Par voie intranasale, ces corticostéroïdes agissent surtout localement; l'absorption systémique aux doses recommandées est minime.

Distribution: Une petite fraction des doses administrées par voie intranasale est avalée. Tous les agents traversent la barrière placentaire et passent dans le lait maternel à faible concentration.

Métabolisme et excrétion: Métabolisme hépatique fort et rapide après absorption par les muqueuses nasales.

Demi-vie: *Béclométhasone* – 3 heures; *budésonide* – 2 heures (plasma); *flunisolide* – de 1 à 2 heures; *fluticasone* – 3 heures; *mométasone* – 5,8 heures; *triamcinolone* – 4 heures (en raison de l'absorption prolongée).

Profil temps-action (diminution des symptômes)

	Début d'action	Pic	Durée
Béclométhasone	5 – 7 jours	jusqu'à 3 semaines	inconnue
Budésonide	24 h (jusqu'à 3 jours)	1 – 2 semaines	inconnue
Flunisolide	quelques jours	jusqu'à 3 semaines	inconnue
Fluticasone	quelques jours	1 – 2 semaines	inconnue
Mométasone	2 jours	1 – 2 semaines	inconnue
Triamcinolone	quelques jours	2 – 3 semaines	inconnue

CONTRE-INDICATIONS, PRÉCAUTIONS ET MISES EN GARDE

Contre-indications: Hypersensibilité ou intolérance à l'un ou l'autre des constituants des produits ■ Tuberculose active ou quiescente des voies respiratoires, ou infection bactérienne, fongique ou virale non traitée ■ **Péd.**: L'innocuité n'a pas été établie chez les enfants < 6 ans (béclométhasone, budésonide et flunisolide), et chez les enfants < 4 ans (fluticasone et triamcinolone).

Précautions et mises en garde: Infections actives non traitées ■ Immunosuppression sous-jacente (en raison d'une maladie ou d'un traitement concomitant) ■ Traitement par un corticostéroïde systémique (ne pas l'arrêter brusquement au début du traitement par voie intranasale) ■ Intervention chirurgicale ou traumatisme nasal récent (la cicatrisation de la plaie peut être retardée par l'usage d'un corticostéroïde par voie intranasale) ■ **Obst., Allaitement**: L'innocuité chez la femme enceinte ou qui allaite n'a pas été établie (un traitement prolongé ou à des doses élevées peut mener à des complications).

RÉACTIONS INDÉSIRABLES ET EFFETS SECONDAIRES

SNC: étourdissements, céphalées (incidence accrue avec le triamcinolone).

C

ORLO: perte de l'odorat (flunisolide seulement), sensation de brûlure des muqueuses nasales, irritation des muqueuses nasales, crises d'éternuements, chatouillements dans la gorge (budésonide seulement), saignement du nez.
GI: douleurs abdominales, perte du goût (flunisolide seulement), candidose œsophagienne.
End.: suppression de la fonction surrénalienne (traitement prolongé, à des doses élevées seulement).

INTERACTIONS

Médicament-médicament: Aucune interaction importante aux doses recommandées.

VOIES D'ADMINISTRATION ET POSOLOGIE

Béclométhasone

- **Préparation intranasale (adultes et enfants > 12 ans)**: 2 vaporisations dans chaque narine, 2 fois par jour (ne pas dépasser 12 vaporisations par jour).
- **Préparation intranasale (enfants de 6 à 12 ans)**: 2 vaporisations dans chaque narine, 2 fois par jour (ne pas dépasser 8 vaporisations par jour).

Budésonide

- **Préparation aqueuse intranasale (adultes et enfants > 6 ans)**: *Rhinite allergique* – 1 vaporisation dans chaque narine, 2 fois par jour, ou 2 vaporisations dans chaque narine, 1 fois par jour le matin; la dose peut être réduite graduellement toutes les 2 à 4 semaines, une fois que l'effet souhaité a été obtenu (64 µg ou 100 µg par vaporisation). *Traitement ou prévention des polypes nasaux* – 1 vaporisation dans chaque narine, 2 fois par jour (64 µg ou 100 µg par vaporisation).
- **Inhalateur de poudre sèche intranasale – Turbuhaler (adultes et enfants > 6 ans)**: *Rhinite allergique* – 2 inhalations dans chaque narine, 1 fois par jour (100 µg par inhalation). *Traitement ou prévention des polypes nasaux* – 1 vaporisation dans chaque narine, 2 fois par jour (100 µg par inhalation).

Flunisolide

- **Préparation aqueuse intranasale (adultes et enfants > 14 ans)**: 2 vaporisations dans chaque narine, 2 fois par jour; la posologie devrait être diminuée jusqu'à la dose thérapeutique la plus faible, puis le traitement interrompu dès que possible (25 µg par vaporisation; ne pas dépasser 16 vaporisations par jour).
- **Préparation aqueuse intranasale (enfants de 6 à 14 ans)**: 1 vaporisation dans chaque narine, 3 fois par jour *ou* 2 vaporisations dans chaque narine, 2 fois par jour; la posologie devrait être diminuée jusqu'à la dose thérapeutique la plus faible, puis le traitement interrompu dès que possible (25 µg par vaporisation; ne pas dépasser 8 vaporisations par jour).

Fluticasone

- **Préparation intranasale (adultes et enfants ≥ 12 ans)**: 1 ou 2 vaporisations dans chaque narine, 1 ou 2 fois par jour selon la gravité du trouble, puis réduire la posologie (50 µg par vaporisation; ne pas dépasser 4 vaporisations/narine par jour).
- **Préparation intranasale (enfants de 4 à 11 ans)**: 1 ou 2 vaporisations dans chaque narine, 1 fois par jour (50 µg par vaporisation; ne pas dépasser 2 vaporisations/narine par jour).

Mométasone

- **Préparation aqueuse intranasale (adultes et enfants ≥ 12 ans)**: *Rhinite allergique* – 1 ou 2 vaporisations dans chaque narine, 1 ou 2 fois par jour selon la gravité du trouble, puis réduire la posologie (50 µg par vaporisation; ne pas dépasser 4 vaporisations/narine par jour). *Adjuvant au traitement de la sinusite aiguë* – 2 vaporisations dans chaque narine, 2 fois par jour. Si les symptômes ne sont pas maîtrisés, on peut passer la posologie à 4 vaporisations par narine, 2 fois par jour.
- **Préparation aqueuse intranasale (enfants de 3 à 11 ans)**: 1 vaporisation dans chaque narine, 1 fois par jour (50 µg par vaporisation).

Triamcinolone

- **Préparation aqueuse et aérosol intranasal (adultes et enfants > 12 ans)**: 2 vaporisations dans chaque narine, 1 fois par jour (55 µg – préparation aqueuse/vaporisation ou 100 µg – aérosol/par vaporisation).
- **Préparation aqueuse intranasale (enfants de 4 à 12 ans)**: 1 vaporisation dans chaque narine, 1 fois par jour (55 µg par vaporisation; ne pas dépasser 2 vaporisations/narine par jour).

PRÉSENTATION

- **Béclométhasone**

  Vaporisateur nasal – préparation aqueuse: 50 µg par vaporisation, en flacons de 200 doses[Pr].
- **Budésonide**

  Vaporisateur nasal – préparation aqueuse: 64 µg par vaporisation, en flacons de 120 doses[Pr]; 100 µg par vaporisation, en flacons de 165 doses[Pr] ■ **Turbuhaler**: 100 µg par inhalation, en flacons de 200 doses[Pr].
- **Flunisolide**

  Atomiseur nasal – préparation aqueuse: 25 µg par vaporisation, en flacons de 25 mL[Pr].
- **Fluticasone**

  Vaporisateur nasal: 50 µg par vaporisation, en flacons de 120 doses[Pr].

- **Mométasone**
  Vaporisateur nasal – préparation aqueuse: 50 µg par vaporisation, en flacons de 120 doses[Pr].
- **Triamcinolone**
  Vaporisateur nasal – préparation aqueuse: 55 µg par vaporisation, en flacons de 120 doses[Pr] ■ **Aérosol nasal:** 100 µg par vaporisation, en flacons de 100 doses[Pr].

SOINS INFIRMIERS

ÉVALUATION DE LA SITUATION

- Déterminer la gravité de la congestion nasale, la quantité et la couleur des écoulements, ainsi que la fréquence des éternuements.
- Chez les patients qui suivent un traitement prolongé, on devrait mener des examens otorhinolaryngologiques à intervalles réguliers afin de déceler les signes d'infection ou d'ulcération des muqueuses et des voies nasales.

Tests de laboratoire: Le médecin peut recommander des tests de la fonction surrénalienne à intervalles réguliers au cours du traitement prolongé afin d'évaluer le degré de suppression de l'axe hypothalamo-hypophyso-surrénalien. Les enfants et les patients prenant des doses plus élevées que celles recommandées sont exposés à un risque plus élevé de suppression de l'axe hypothalamo-hypophyso-surrénalien.

DIAGNOSTICS INFIRMIERS POSSIBLES

- Dégagement inefficace des voies respiratoires (Indications).
- Risque d'infection (Effets secondaires).
- Connaissances insuffisantes sur le traitement médicamenteux (Enseignement au patient et à ses proches).

INTERVENTIONS INFIRMIÈRES

- Une fois qu'on a obtenu l'effet clinique souhaité, on doit essayer de réduire la dose jusqu'à la dose la plus faible qui permette de maîtriser les symptômes. Réduire graduellement la dose toutes les 2 à 4 semaines, tant que l'effet souhaité est maintenu. Si les symptômes réapparaissent, on peut reprendre rapidement la dose de départ.

Préparation intranasale: Si le patient doit utiliser également un décongestionnant topique, on doit l'administrer de 5 à 15 minutes avant l'administration du corticostéroïde par voie intranasale. Si le patient ne peut respirer librement par le nez, lui conseiller de se moucher délicatement avant que le médicament ne lui soit administré.

ENSEIGNEMENT AU PATIENT ET À SES PROCHES

- Conseiller au patient de respecter rigoureusement la posologie recommandée. S'il n'a pu prendre le médicament au moment habituel, il doit le prendre aussitôt que possible à moins que ce ne soit presque l'heure prévue pour la dose suivante.
- Recommander au patient de ne pas dépasser la dose quotidienne maximale de vaporisations par narine recommandée par le fabricant.
- Expliquer au patient le mode d'emploi du vaporisateur (voir l'annexe G). Bien agiter avant usage. Prévenir le patient qu'il peut ressentir un picotement passager dans le nez.
- Le flacon ne devrait pas être gardé dans un endroit froid ou humide et son contenu devrait être utilisé en l'espace de 3 mois (béclométhasone, flunisolide) ou de 6 mois après l'ouverture du sachet d'aluminium, ou selon les recommandations du fabricant.
- Inciter le patient à prévenir un professionnel de la santé si les symptômes ne diminuent pas dans le mois qui suit ou si les écoulements deviennent purulents.

VÉRIFICATION DE L'EFFICACITÉ THÉRAPEUTIQUE

L'efficacité du traitement peut être démontrée par: la résolution de la congestion nasale et la disparition des écoulements et des éternuements en cas de rhinite saisonnière ou apériodique ■ la diminution des polypes nasaux ■ l'amélioration des symptômes de la sinusite aiguë.

CORTISONE,

voir Corticostéroïdes (voie générale)

CROMOGLYCATE,

voir Stabilisateurs des mastocytes

CROMOLYN,

voir Stabilisateurs des mastocytes

CYANOCOBALAMINE,

voir Vitamine B_{12} (préparations)

C

CYCLOBENZAPRINE

Alti-Cyclobenzaprine, Apo-Cyclobenzaprine, Cyclobenzaprine-10, Flexeril, Gen-Cycloprine, Novo-Cycloprine, Nu-Cyclobenzaprine, PMS-Cyclobenzaprine, Ratio-Cyclobenzaprine, Riva-Cycloprine

CLASSIFICATION:
Relaxant musculosquelettique

Grossesse - catégorie B

INDICATIONS

Traitement adjuvant des spasmes musculaires associés aux troubles aigus et douloureux de l'appareil locomoteur. **Usages non approuvés**: Traitement de la fibromyalgie.

MÉCANISME D'ACTION

Diminution de l'activité musculaire tonique et somatique au niveau du tronc cérébral. La structure de la cyclobenzaprine ressemble à celle des antidépresseurs tricycliques. ***Effets thérapeutiques:*** Soulagement de la spasticité musculaire et de l'hyperactivité sans perte des fonctions.

PHARMACOCINÉTIQUE

Absorption: Complète (PO).
Distribution: Inconnue.
Liaison aux protéines: 93 %.
Métabolisme et excrétion: Métabolisme majoritairement hépatique.
Demi-vie: De 1 à 3 jours.

Profil temps-action (relaxation des muscles squelettiques)

	DÉBUT D'ACTION	PIC†	DURÉE
PO	1 h	4 - 6 h	12 - 24 h

† Le plein effet du traitement peut se manifester en 1 à 2 semaines.

CONTRE-INDICATIONS, PRÉCAUTIONS ET MISES EN GARDE

Contre-indications: Hypersensibilité ■ Administration d'un IMAO en concomitance ou administration de l'agent dans les 14 jours suivant le retrait des IMAO ■ Infarctus du myocarde récent ■ Troubles de la conduction ou insuffisance cardiaque ■ Arythmies ■ Bloc cardiaque ■ Hyperthyroïdie.

Précautions et mises en garde: Maladie cardiovasculaire ■ Grossesse, allaitement et enfants < 15 ans (l'innocuité du médicament n'a pas été établie) ■ **GÉR.**: Piètre tolérance des effets anticholinergiques.

RÉACTIONS INDÉSIRABLES ET EFFETS SECONDAIRES

SNC: étourdissements, somnolence, confusion, fatigue, céphalées, nervosité.
ORLO: sécheresse de la bouche (xérostomie), vision trouble.
CV: arythmies.
GI: constipation, dyspepsie, nausées, goût désagréable.
GU: rétention urinaire.

INTERACTIONS

Médicament-médicament: Effets additifs sur la dépression du SNC, lors de l'usage concomitant d'autres **dépresseurs du SNC**, dont l'**alcool**, les **antihistaminiques**, les **opiacés** et les **hypnosédatifs** ■ Effets anticholinergiques additifs lors de l'administration concomitante d'autres **médicaments ayant des propriétés anticholinergiques**, dont les **antihistaminiques**, les **antidépresseurs**, l'**atropine**, le **disopyramide** et les **phénothiazines** ■ L'administration de cyclobenzaprine pendant ou dans les 14 jours qui suivent un traitement par des **IMAO** est contre-indiquée en raison du risque de crise d'hyperthermie, de convulsions ou de mort ■ La cyclobenzaprine peut bloquer l'action du **guanadrel** ou de la **guanéthidine**.

Médicament-produits naturels: Le **kava**, la **valériane**, la **scutellaire**, la **camomille** et le **houblon**, consommés en concomitance, peuvent accentuer la dépression du SNC.

VOIES D'ADMINISTRATION ET POSOLOGIE

- **PO (adultes)**: *Troubles aigus et douloureux de l'appareil locomoteur* – 10 mg, 3 fois par jour (écart posologique entre 20 à 40 mg par jour, en 2 à 4 doses fractionnées; ne pas dépasser 60 mg par jour). Un traitement qui dure plus de 2 à 3 semaines n'est pas recommandé.

PRÉSENTATION

Comprimés: 10 mg[Pr].

SOINS INFIRMIERS

ÉVALUATION DE LA SITUATION

Déterminer l'intensité de la douleur, le degré de rigidité musculaire et l'amplitude des mouvements avant le début du traitement et à intervalles réguliers pendant toute sa durée. **GÉR.**: Rester à l'affût des effets anticholinergiques (somnolence et fatigue).

DIAGNOSTICS INFIRMIERS POSSIBLES

- Douleur aiguë (Indications).
- Mobilité physique réduite (Indications).
- Risque d'accident (Effets secondaires).

INTERVENTIONS INFIRMIÈRES

- On peut administrer le médicament avec des aliments pour réduire l'irritation gastrique.
- NE PAS CONFONDRE LA CYCLOBENZAPRINE AVEC LA CYPROHEPTADINE.

ENSEIGNEMENT AU PATIENT ET À SES PROCHES

- Expliquer au patient qu'il doit respecter rigoureusement la posologie prescrite. S'il n'a pu prendre son médicament au moment habituel, il doit le prendre dans l'heure qui suit; sinon il doit sauter cette dose et reprendre l'horaire habituel. Le prévenir qu'il ne faut jamais remplacer une dose manquée par une double dose.
- Prévenir le patient que la cyclobenzaprine peut provoquer de la somnolence, des étourdissements et une vision trouble. Lui conseiller de ne pas conduire et d'éviter les activités qui exigent sa vigilance jusqu'à ce qu'on ait la certitude que le médicament n'entraîne pas ces effets chez lui.
- Mettre en garde le patient contre la consommation d'alcool ou de dépresseurs du SNC en même temps que ce médicament.
- Si la constipation pose problème, informer le patient que l'augmentation de la consommation de liquides et d'aliments riches en fibres et la prise de laxatifs émollients peuvent corriger la situation.
- Recommander au patient de communiquer avec un professionnel de la santé si les symptômes suivants de rétention urinaire se manifestent: distension abdominale, sensation de plénitude, incontinence par regorgement, élimination de petites quantités d'urine.
- Conseiller au patient de pratiquer une bonne hygiène buccale, de se rincer fréquemment la bouche et de consommer de la gomme ou des bonbons sans sucre pour soulager la sécheresse de la bouche.

VÉRIFICATION DE L'EFFICACITÉ THÉRAPEUTIQUE

L'efficacité du traitement peut être démontrée par: le soulagement des spasmes musculaires en cas de troubles aigus de l'appareil locomoteur. Le plein effet du traitement peut ne se manifester qu'en l'espace de 1 à 2 semaines. Habituellement, le traitement dure 2 ou 3 semaines. ✳

ALERTE CLINIQUE

CYCLOPHOSPHAMIDE

Cytoxan, Procytox

CLASSIFICATION:

Antinéoplasique (alkylant)/immunosuppresseur

Grossesse – catégorie D

C

INDICATIONS

En monothérapie ou en association avec d'autres agents chimiothérapeutiques, la radiothérapie ou la chirurgie, dans le traitement des affections suivantes: maladie de Hodgkin ■ lymphome malin ■ myélome multiple ■ leucémie ■ mycose fongoïde au stade avancé ■ neuroblastome ■ cancer de l'ovaire ■ cancer du sein ■ rétinoblastome ■ cancer du poumon. **Usages non approuvés**: Polyarthrite rhumatoïde grave ou granulomatose de Wegener ■ Traitement du syndrome néphrotique pur chez l'enfant.

MÉCANISME D'ACTION

Inhibition de la réplication de l'ADN et de la transcription de l'ARN, ce qui mène en fin de compte à l'inhibition de la synthèse des protéines (action indépendante du cycle cellulaire). ***Effets thérapeutiques:*** Destruction des cellules à réplication rapide et particulièrement des cellules malignes ■ Effet immunosuppresseur à faibles doses.

PHARMACOCINÉTIQUE

Absorption: Bonne absorption de la molécule mère inactive (PO).

Distribution: Répartition dans tous les tissus. L'agent traverse faiblement la barrière hémato-encéphalique. Il traverse la barrière placentaire et passe dans le lait maternel.

Métabolisme et excrétion: Transformation en médicament actif par le foie. 30 % est excrété à l'état inchangé par les reins.

Demi-vie: De 4 à 6,5 heures.

Profil temps-action (effet sur la numération globulaire)

	DÉBUT D'ACTION	PIC	DURÉE
PO, IV	7 jours	7 - 15 jours	21 jours

CONTRE-INDICATIONS, PRÉCAUTIONS ET MISES EN GARDE

Contre-indications: Hypersensibilité au médicament ou à l'un de ses ingrédients ■ Aplasie médullaire ■ Grossesse et allaitement ■ Varicelle (infection active) ■ Zona (infection active) ■ Cystite active ■ Obstruction urinaire.

Précautions et mises en garde: Infection active ■ Autres maladies chroniques débilitantes ■ Patientes en âge de procréer ■ Dysfonctionnement rénal ou hépatique.

RÉACTIONS INDÉSIRABLES ET EFFETS SECONDAIRES

C

Resp.: FIBROSE PULMONAIRE.
CV: FIBROSE DU MYOCARDE, hypotension.
GI: anorexie, nausées, vomissements.
GU: CYSTITE HÉMORRAGIQUE, hématurie.
Tég.: alopécie.
End.: suppression de la fonction des gonades, syndrome de sécrétion inappropriée de l'hormone antidiurétique.
Hémat.: LEUCOPÉNIE, thrombopénie, anémie.
Métab.: hyperuricémie.
Divers: réactions d'hypersensibilité incluant l'ANAPHYLAXIE, néoplasmes secondaires.

INTERACTIONS

Médicament-médicament: L'administration concomitante de **phénobarbital** ou de **rifampine** peut accentuer la toxicité du cyclophosphamide ■ L'administration concomitante d'**allopurinol** ou de **diurétiques thiazidiques** peut intensifier l'aplasie médullaire ■ Le cyclophosphamide peut prolonger l'effet curarisant de la **succinylcholine** ■ Risque d'effets cardiotoxiques additifs lors de l'administration concomitante d'autres **agents cardiotoxiques** (**cytarabine**, **daunorubicine**, **doxorubicine**) ■ Le cyclophosphamide peut réduire les concentrations sériques de **digoxine** ■ Effets additifs sur l'aplasie médullaire lors de l'administration concomitante d'autres **antinéoplasiques** ou d'une **radiothérapie** ■ Le cyclophosphamide peut potentialiser les effets de la **warfarine** ■ Le cyclophosphamide peut diminuer la réponse des anticorps aux **vaccins à virus vivants** et augmenter le risque de réactions indésirables ■ Le cyclophosphamide prolonge les effets de la **cocaïne**.

VOIES D'ADMINISTRATION ET POSOLOGIE

De nombreux schémas thérapeutiques sont utilisés.

Traitement d'attaque

- **PO (adultes):** De 1 à 5 mg/kg/jour, selon la tolérance du patient.
- **PO (enfants):** De 2 à 8 mg/kg, en doses étalées sur 6 jours ou plus.
- **IV (adultes):** De 10 à 20 mg/kg/jour pendant 2 à 5 jours, selon la tolérance du patient.
- **IV (enfants):** De 2 à 8 mg/kg, en doses étalées sur 6 jours ou plus.

La dose d'attaque doit être réduite de 33 à 50 % chez les patients qui ont déjà reçu d'autres chimiothérapies ou une radiothérapie pouvant affecter la capacité fonctionnelle de la moelle osseuse, ou chez les patients souffrant d'infiltration néoplasique de la moelle osseuse.

Traitement d'entretien

- **PO (adultes):** De 1 à 5 mg/kg/jour.
- **PO (enfants):** De 2 à 5 mg/kg, 2 fois par semaine.
- **IV (adultes):** De 10 à 15 mg/kg, tous les 7 à 10 jours, ou de 3 à 5 mg/kg, 2 fois par semaine.
- **IV (enfants):** De 10 à 15 mg/kg, tous les 7 à 10 jours, ou de 30 mg/kg, toutes les 3 ou 4 semaines.

PRÉSENTATION

Comprimés: 25 mg^Pr, 50 mg^Pr ■ **Poudre lyophilisée pour injection:** 200 mg^Pr, 500 mg^Pr, 1 000 mg^Pr, 2 000 mg^Pr.

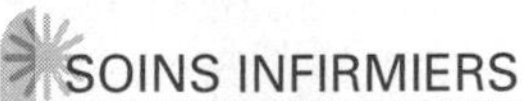

SOINS INFIRMIERS

ÉVALUATION DE LA SITUATION

- Mesurer la pression artérielle, le pouls, la fréquence respiratoire et la température à intervalles réguliers tout au long de l'administration. Informer le médecin de tout changement marqué.
- MESURER FRÉQUEMMENT LA DIURÈSE PENDANT TOUTE LA DURÉE DU TRAITEMENT. ENCOURAGER L'ADULTE À BOIRE AU MOINS 3 000 mL DE LIQUIDES PAR JOUR, ET L'ENFANT, ENTRE 1 000 ET 2 000 mL DE LIQUIDES PAR JOUR POUR RÉDUIRE LE RISQUE DE CYSTITE HÉMORRAGIQUE. ON PEUT ADMINISTRER LE MÉDICAMENT EN ASSOCIATION AVEC LE MESNA.
- DÉCELER L'APPARITION D'UNE APLASIE MÉDULLAIRE. Suivre de près les saignements: saignement des gencives, formation d'ecchymoses, pétéchies, présence de sang occulte dans les selles, l'urine et les vomissements. Éviter les injections IM et la prise de la température rectale, si la numération plaquettaire est basse. Appliquer une pression sur les points de ponction veineuse pendant 10 minutes. Surveiller les signes d'infection en présence d'une neutropénie. Une anémie peut survenir. Suivre de près une fatigue accrue, la dyspnée et l'hypotension orthostatique.
- Noter les nausées, les vomissements et l'appétit du patient. Peser le patient toutes les semaines. On peut administrer un antiémétique 30 minutes avant le médicament afin de réduire les effets gastro-intestinaux. On peut diminuer l'anorexie et la perte de poids en servant fréquemment des repas légers.
- Encourager le patient à boire de 2 000 à 3 000 mL de liquides par jour pour favoriser l'excrétion d'acide urique. Le médecin peut prescrire un agent

alcalinisant de l'urine pour prévenir la néphropathie.

- SUIVRE DE PRÈS L'ÉTAT DE LA FONCTION CARDIAQUE ET RESPIRATOIRE POUR DÉCELER LA DYSPNÉE, LES RÂLES ET LES CRÉPITATIONS, LE GAIN DE POIDS ET L'ŒDÈME. UNE TOXICITÉ PULMONAIRE PEUT SURVENIR À LA SUITE D'UN TRAITEMENT DE LONGUE DURÉE. LA CARDIOTOXICITÉ PEUT SE MANIFESTER EN DÉBUT DE TRAITEMENT ET ELLE SE CARACTÉRISE PAR DES SYMPTÔMES D'INSUFFISANCE CARDIAQUE CONGESTIVE.

Tests de laboratoire:

- NOTER LA NUMÉRATION GLOBULAIRE, LA FORMULE LEUCOCYTAIRE ET LA NUMÉRATION PLAQUETTAIRE AVANT L'ADMINISTRATION DE L'AGENT ET À INTERVALLES RÉGULIERS PENDANT TOUTE LA DURÉE DU TRAITEMENT. LE NADIR DE LA LEUCOPÉNIE SE PRODUIT DANS LES 7 À 12 JOURS, LES CONCENTRATIONS SE RÉTABLISSANT DANS LES 17 À 21 JOURS. LE NOMBRE DE LEUCOCYTES DEVRAIT SE MAINTENIR ENTRE 2,5 ET 4 × 10^9/L. LE CYCLOPHOSPHAMIDE PEUT AUSSI PROVOQUER UNE TROMBOPÉNIE (LE NADIR SURVIENT DANS LES 10 À 15 JOURS) ET, RAREMENT, L'ANÉMIE.
- Noter les concentrations d'urée, de créatinine et d'acide urique avant l'administration du médicament et à intervalles réguliers pendant toute la durée du traitement afin de déceler la toxicité rénale.
- Noter les concentrations d'ALT, d'AST, de LDH et de bilirubine sérique avant l'administration du médicament et à intervalles réguliers pendant toute la durée du traitement afin de déceler l'hépatotoxicité.
- Effectuer des analyses des urines avant d'amorcer le traitement et à intervalles réguliers par la suite afin de déceler l'hématurie ou tout changement de densité, indice du syndrome de sécrétion inappropriée de l'hormone antidiurétique (SIADH).
- Le médicament peut inhiber les réactions positives aux tests épicutanés qui décèlent les candidoses, les oreillons et les trichophytoses ainsi qu'aux tests à la tuberculine purifiée. Le cyclophosphamide peut aussi entraîner des résultats faussement positifs au test de Papanicolaou.

DIAGNOSTICS INFIRMIERS POSSIBLES

- Risque d'infection (Effets secondaires).
- Image corporelle perturbée (Effets secondaires).
- Connaissances insuffisantes sur le traitement médicamenteux (Enseignement au patient et à ses proches).

INTERVENTIONS INFIRMIÈRES

ALERTE CLINIQUE: DES DÉCÈS SONT SURVENUS LORS DE CERTAINES CHIMIOTHÉRAPIES. AVANT D'ADMINISTRER L'AGENT, CLARIFIER TOUS LES POINTS AMBIGUS. VÉRIFIER LA LIMITE DES DOSES UNITAIRES ET QUOTIDIENNES AINSI QUE LA DOSE À ADMINISTRER PENDANT LE TRAITEMENT. DEMANDER À UN DEUXIÈME PROFESSIONNEL DE LA SANTÉ DE VÉRIFIER UNE FOIS DE PLUS L'ORDONNANCE D'ORIGINE, LES CALCULS ET LE RÉGLAGE DE LA POMPE À PERFUSION.

ALERTE CLINIQUE: NE PAS CONFONDRE LE CYCLOPHOSPHAMIDE ET LA CYCLOSPORINE. NE PAS CONFONDRE CYTOXAN (CYCLOPHOSPHAMIDE) ET CYTOZAR (CYTARABINE) OU CYTOTEC (MISOPROSTOL).

PO:

- Administrer le médicament à jeun. En cas d'irritation gastrique grave, on peut administrer le médicament avec des aliments.
- On peut préparer une solution orale en diluant la poudre pour injection dans de l'élixir aromatique USP pour obtenir une concentration de 1 à 5 mg de cyclophosphamide par mL. Cette solution doit être conservée au réfrigérateur et administrée dans les 2 semaines.

IV:

- Préparer les solutions destinées à l'administration IV sous une hotte à flux laminaire. Porter des gants, un vêtement protecteur et un masque pendant la manipulation du cyclophosphamide. Mettre au rebut le matériel dans les contenants réservés à cet usage (voir l'annexe H).
- Préparer les solutions à injecter en reconstituant chaque 100 mg avec 5 mL d'eau stérile ou d'eau bactériostatique pour injection. Agiter délicatement la solution et la laisser reposer jusqu'à ce qu'elle devienne transparente. Administrer les solutions préparées sans eau bactériostatique dans les 6 heures. Les solutions préparées dans des conditions d'asepsie sont stables pendant 24 heures à la température ambiante et pendant 6 jours au réfrigérateur. Consulter les directives du fabricant concernant la reconstitution et la conservation.

IV directe: Administrer la solution reconstituée directement (ne pas l'administrer par injection directe si elle a été diluée dans l'eau stérile).

Vitesse d'administration: Administrer la solution reconstituée à un débit maximum de 100 mg/min.

Perfusion intermittente: Diluer de nouveau le médicament dans un volume allant jusqu'à 250 mL de solution de D5%E, de solution de NaCl 0,9 % ou 0,45 %, de solution de D5%E/NaCl 0,9 %, de solution de lactate de Ringer ou de solution de dextrose dans une solution de Ringer.

Compatibilité dans la même seringue: bléomycine ▪ cisplatine ▪ doxapram ▪ doxorubicine ▪ dropéridol ▪ fluorouracile ▪ furosémide ▪ héparine ▪ leucovorine

C

calcique ■ méthotrexate ■ métoclopramide ■ mitomycine ■ vinblastine ■ vincristine.

Compatibilité (tubulure en Y): amifostine ■ amikacine ■ ampicilline ■ aztréonam ■ bléomycine ■ céfamandole ■ céfazoline ■ céfépime ■ céfopérazone ■ céfotaxime ■ céfoxitine ■ céfuroxime ■ céphapirine ■ chloramphénicol ■ chlorpromazine ■ cimétidine ■ cisplatine ■ cladribine ■ clindamycine ■ dexaméthasone ■ diphenhydramine ■ doxorubicine ■ doxycycline ■ dropéridol ■ érythromycine, lactobionate d' ■ famotidine ■ filgrastim ■ fludarabine ■ fluorouracile ■ furosémide ■ gallium, nitrate de ■ ganciclovir ■ gentamicine ■ granisétron ■ héparine ■ hydromorphone ■ idarubicine ■ kanamycine ■ leucovorine calcique ■ lorazépam ■ melphalan ■ méthotrexate ■ méthylprednisone ■ métoclopramide ■ métronidazole ■ mezlocilline ■ minocycline ■ mitomycine ■ morphine ■ nafcilline ■ ondansétron ■ oxacilline ■ paclitaxel ■ pénicilline G potassique ■ pipéracilline ■ pipéracilline/tazobactam ■ prochlorpérazine ■ prométhazine ■ propofol ■ ranitidine ■ sargramostim ■ sodium, bicarbonate de ■ téniposide ■ thiotépa ■ ticarcilline ■ ticarcilline/clavulanate ■ tobramycine ■ triméthoprime/sulfaméthoxazole ■ vancomycine ■ vinblastine ■ vincristine ■ vinorelbine.

Compatibilité en addition au soluté: fluorouracile ■ méthotrexate ■ mitoxantrone ■ ondansétron.

ENSEIGNEMENT AU PATIENT ET À SES PROCHES

- Recommander au patient de prendre le médicament tôt le matin. Lui expliquer qu'il doit boire suffisamment de liquides pendant les 72 heures qui suivent le traitement et qu'il doit uriner fréquemment afin de réduire l'irritation de la vessie entraînée par les métabolites excrétés par les reins. Lui recommander de signaler immédiatement au médecin la présence d'hématurie. L'inciter à communiquer avec un professionnel de la santé s'il a oublié de prendre une dose.
- Recommander au patient de signaler rapidement à un professionnel de la santé la fièvre, les maux de gorge, les signes d'infection, les douleurs lombaires ou aux flancs, les mictions difficiles ou douloureuses, les aphtes buccaux ou sur les lèvres, le jaunissement de la peau ou des yeux, le saignement des gencives, la formation d'ecchymoses, les pétéchies; la présence de sang dans les selles, l'urine ou les vomissements; toute enflure inhabituelle, les douleurs articulaires, l'essoufflement ou la confusion. Expliquer au patient qu'il doit éviter les foules et les personnes contagieuses. Lui recommander d'utiliser une brosse à dents à poils doux et un rasoir électrique et de prendre garde aux chutes. Prévenir le patient qu'il ne doit pas boire de boissons alcoolisées ni prendre de médicaments contenant de l'aspirine ou des AINS, car ces substances peuvent déclencher une hémorragie digestive.
- Expliquer aux patients des deux sexes que ce médicament peut entraîner la stérilité, et, chez la femme, des troubles du cycle menstruel ou même l'arrêt des règles. Ce médicament est aussi tératogène. La patiente doit donc continuer de prendre des mesures contraceptives pendant au moins 4 mois après l'arrêt du traitement.
- Expliquer au patient qu'il risque de perdre ses cheveux. Explorer avec lui les stratégies lui permettant de s'adapter à ce changement. Le médicament peut aussi rendre la peau et les ongles de couleur foncée.
- Expliquer au patient qu'il ne doit pas se faire vacciner sans recommandation expresse du médecin.

VÉRIFICATION DE L'EFFICACITÉ THÉRAPEUTIQUE

L'efficacité du traitement peut être démontrée par: la diminution de la taille de la tumeur ou le ralentissement de la propagation des métastases ■ l'amélioration du bilan hématopoïétique en cas de leucémie; le traitement d'entretien est amorcé si le nombre de leucocytes se maintient entre 2,5 et 4 × 10^9/L et si aucun effet secondaire grave ne se manifeste ■ la résolution des signes et des symptômes du syndrome néphrotique chez les enfants. ✳

CYCLOSPORINE

Neoral, Sandimmune, Sandoz Cyclosporine

CLASSIFICATION:

Immunosuppresseur/antirhumatoïde (polypeptide cyclique)

Grossesse – catégorie C

INDICATIONS

PO, IV: Prévention et traitement (chez le patient ayant reçu d'autres immunosuppresseurs) du rejet du greffon à la suite d'une transplantation d'organes ou de la greffe de moelle osseuse ■ Prévention et traitement de la réaction du greffon contre l'hôte ■ **PO:** Traitement de la polyarthrite rhumatoïde grave ou du psoriasis grave ne répondant pas au traitement habituel ■ Traitement du syndrome néphrotique stéroïdodépendant ou réfractaire aux corticostéroïdes. **Usages non approu-**

vés: Traitement de la rectocolite ulcéreuse sévère ■ Traitement des maladies auto-immunes graves résistantes aux corticostéroïdes.

MÉCANISME D'ACTION

Suppression de la réponse immunitaire (cellulaire et humorale) par inhibition de l'interleukine-2, facteur nécessaire au déclenchement de l'activité des lymphocytes T. ***Effets thérapeutiques:*** Prévention des réactions de rejet ■ Ralentissement de l'évolution de la polyarthrite rhumatoïde ou du psoriasis.

PHARMACOCINÉTIQUE

Absorption: Erratique (de l'ordre de 10 à 60 %) (PO). Effet de premier passage hépatique marqué. La biodisponibilité de la micro-émulsion (Neoral) est meilleure.
Distribution: Répartition dans tout l'organisme, majoritairement dans le liquide extracellulaire et les cellules sanguines. L'agent traverse la barrière placentaire et passe dans le lait maternel.
Liaison aux protéines: 90 %.
Métabolisme et excrétion: Important métabolisme hépatique (premier passage hépatique important); excrétion dans la bile; une petite quantité est excrétée sous forme inchangée dans l'urine.
Demi-vie: *Enfants* – 7 heures; *adultes* – 19 heures.

Profil temps-action

	DÉBUT D'ACTION	PIC	DURÉE
PO	inconnu†	2 – 6 h	inconnue
IV	inconnu	fin de la perfusion	inconnue

† En cas de polyarthrite rhumatoïde, l'effet se manifeste en l'espace de 4 à 8 semaines et peut durer pendant 4 semaines après l'arrêt du traitement; en cas de psoriasis, l'effet se manifeste en l'espace de 2 à 6 semaines et dure pendant 6 semaines après l'arrêt du traitement.

CONTRE-INDICATIONS, PRÉCAUTIONS ET MISES EN GARDE

Contre-indications: Hypersensibilité à la cyclosporine ou à l'un de ses excipients, l'huile de ricin polyoxéthylée (véhicule de la solution IV) ■ **PO (Neoral)**: Patients traités pour le psoriasis ou la polyarthrite rhumatoïde présentant les troubles suivants: fonction rénale anormale, hypertension non maîtrisée, affection maligne (sauf cancer de la peau sans mélanome), infection non jugulée, immunodéficience primaire ou secondaire, à l'exception des maladies auto-immunes.
Précautions et mises en garde: Insuffisance hépatique grave (réduire la dose) ■ Insuffisance rénale (des adaptations posologiques fréquentes peuvent être nécessaires) ■ Infection active ■ **OBST., ALLAITEMENT**: Sauf lorsque les bienfaits du médicament dépassent les risques auxquels sont exposés la mère et l'enfant ■ Traitement au disulfirame ou intolérance connue à l'alcool (les préparations orales et intraveineuses renferment de l'alcool) ■ **PÉD.**: Des doses plus fortes ou plus fréquentes peuvent être nécessaires.

RÉACTIONS INDÉSIRABLES ET EFFETS SECONDAIRES

SNC: CONVULSIONS, tremblements, confusion, bouffées vasomotrices, céphalées, troubles psychiatriques.
CV: hypertension.
GI: diarrhée, hépatotoxicité, nausées, vomissements, malaises abdominaux, anorexie, pancréatite.
GU: toxicité rénale.
Tég.: hirsutisme, acné.
HÉ: hyperkaliémie, hypomagnésémie.
Hémat.: anémie, leucopénie, thrombopénie.
Métab.: hyperlipidémie, hyperuricémie.
SN: hyperesthésie, paresthésie, tremblements.
Divers: hyperplasie gingivale, réactions d'hypersensibilité, infections.

INTERACTIONS

Médicament-médicament: Augmentation des concentrations sanguines de cyclosporine et risque accru de toxicité lors de l'administration concomitante d'**amphotéricine B**, d'**aminosides**, d'**amiodarone**, d'**azithromycine**, de **clarithromycine**, de **stéroïdes anabolisants**, de certains **inhibiteurs des canaux calciques**, de **cimétidine**, de **colchicine**, de **danazol**, d'**érythromycine**, de **fluconazole**, de **fluoroquinolones**, de **kétoconazole**, d'**itraconazole**, de **métoclopramide**, de **méthotrexate**, de **miconazole**, d'**AINS**, de **melphalan** ou de **contraceptifs oraux** ■ Risque accru de néphrotoxicité lors de l'administration concomitante d'**acyclovir**, d'**amphotéricine B**, d'**aminosides**, d'**AINS**, de **triméthoprime**, de **ciprofloxacine** et de **vancomycine** ■ Effets immunosuppresseurs additifs lors de l'administration concomitante d'autres **immunosuppresseurs** (**cyclophosphamide**, **azathioprine**, **corticostéroïdes**) ■ Les **barbituriques**, la **phénytoïne**, la **rifampine**, la **rifabutine**, la **carbamazépine** ou les **sulfamides** peuvent diminuer l'effet de la cyclosporine ■ Effets hyperkaliémiques additifs lors de l'administration concomitante de **diurétiques épargneurs de potassium**, de **suppléments potassiques** ou d'**inhibiteurs de l'ECA** ■ La cyclosporine augmente les concentrations sériques de **digoxine** en entraînant ainsi un risque de toxicité (réduire la dose de digoxine de 50 %) ■ La cyclosporine prolonge l'effet des **bloqueurs neuromusculaires** ■ Le risque de crise convulsive est accru lors de l'administration concomitante d'**imipénème/cilastatine** ■ La cyclosporine peut diminuer la réponse des anticorps aux **vaccins à virus vivants** et augmenter le risque de réactions indésirables ■ Risque accru de rhabdomyolyse lors de l'administration concomitante de **statines** ■ L'administration concomitante de **tacrolimus** est déconseillée ■ L'**orlistat** peut diminuer l'absorption de cyclosporine ; éviter l'usage concomitant ■ Certains **inhibiteurs de la protéase** administrés en traitement des infections par le VIH peuvent élever les concentrations sériques de cyclosporine et en augmenter la toxicité.

Médicament-aliments: La consommation concomitante de **jus de pamplemousse** augmente l'absorption et devrait être évitée ■ Les **aliments** réduisent l'absorption des produits présentés en microémulsion (Neoral).

Médicament-produits naturels: La consommation concomitante d'**échinacée** et de **mélatonine** peut interférer avec l'immunosuppression ■ Le **millepertuis** peut diminuer les concentrations sériques de cyclosporine, ce qui peut provoquer le rejet du greffon.

VOIES D'ADMINISTRATION ET POSOLOGIE

La posologie est adaptée en fonction des concentrations sériques.

Prévention du rejet des transplantations d'organe

- **PO (adultes et enfants)**: De 10 à 15 mg/kg/jour en 2 doses fractionnées (toutes les 12 heures). Démarrer le traitement au cours des 12 heures qui précèdent la transplantation et le poursuivre pendant 1 à 2 semaines suivant la greffe. Réduire la dose graduellement en fonction de la concentration sanguine jusqu'à une posologie d'entretien de 2 à 6 mg/kg/jour, en 2 doses fractionnées. Lorsque le médicament est administré en association avec d'autres immunosuppresseurs, des doses initiales plus faibles peuvent être envisagées (par exemple, de 3 à 6 mg/kg/jour, en 2 prises fractionnées).
- **IV (adultes et enfants)**: Traitement initial de 3 à 5 mg/kg/jour, en 2 doses fractionnées (un tiers de la dose orale) pendant 2 semaines au maximum après l'intervention ; substituer la voie orale à la voie IV dès que possible.

Greffe de la moelle osseuse

- **IV (adultes et enfants)**: Démarrer le traitement le jour précédant la greffe. Il est préférable de commencer le traitement par la voie IV dans la plupart des cas, à la posologie de 3 à 5 mg/kg/jour, en 2 doses fractionnées, pendant 2 semaines au maximum après l'intervention ; substituer la voie orale à la voie IV dès que possible.
- **PO (adultes et enfants)**: Si on démarre le traitement par voie orale, la dose recommandée est de 12,5 à 15 mg/kg/jour en 2 prises, en commençant le jour précédant l'intervention. Le traitement d'entretien par voie orale est d'environ 12,5 mg/kg/jour, en 2 doses fractionnées, pendant au moins 3 mois (6 mois de préférence). Diminuer par la suite graduellement la dose pour la ramener à zéro dans un délai de 1 an suivant la transplantation.

Polyarthrite rhumatoïde

- **PO (adultes)**: 2 mg/kg/jour, en 2 doses fractionnées, pendant les 6 premières semaines de traitement. On peut augmenter la dose jusqu'à concurrence de 5 mg/kg/jour suivant la tolérance du patient. Adapter la posologie d'entretien selon la tolérance du patient.

Psoriasis grave

- **PO (adultes)**: 2 mg/kg/jour, en 2 doses fractionnées, pendant au moins 4 semaines. S'il n'y a pas d'amélioration, on peut augmenter la dose par paliers mensuels de 0,5 à 1 mg/kg/jour, jusqu'à concurrence de 5 mg/kg/jour, selon la tolérance du patient. La dose d'entretien devrait être modifiée en fonction des besoins du patient et ramenée à la plus petite dose efficace possible.

Syndrome néphrotique

- **PO (adultes)**: Si la fonction rénale est normale, commencer le traitement à 3,5 mg/kg/jour en 2 doses fractionnées, jusqu'à concurrence de 5 mg/kg/jour (posologie d'entretien).
- **PO (enfants)**: Si la fonction rénale est normale, commencer le traitement à 4,2 mg/kg/jour en 2 doses fractionnées, jusqu'à concurrence de 6 mg/kg/jour (posologie d'entretien).

Maladies auto-immunes

- **PO (adultes et enfants)**: De 1 à 3 mg/kg/jour (usage non approuvé).

PRÉSENTATION

Capsules (Sandoz): 25 mg^{Pr}, 50 mg^{Pr}, 100 mg^{Pr} ■ **Microémulsion en capsules (Neoral)**: 10 mg^{Pr}, 25 mg^{Pr}, 50 mg^{Pr}, 100 mg^{Pr} ■ **Micro-émulsion en solution orale (Neoral)**: 100 mg/mL^{Pr}, en flacons de 50 mL ■ **Solution pour injection**: 50 mg/mL, en ampoules de 1mL^{Pr} et de 5 mL^{Pr}.

SOINS INFIRMIERS

ÉVALUATION DE LA SITUATION

- Noter la créatinine sérique, effectuer le bilan quotidien des ingesta et des excreta, peser le patient chaque jour et prendre sa pression artérielle pendant toute la durée du traitement. Signaler tout changement marqué.

Prévention du rejet d'une greffe: Rester à l'affût des symptômes de rejet d'organe pendant toute la durée du traitement.

IV: Suivre continuellement pendant au moins les 30 premières minutes de chaque traitement, et à intervalles fréquents par la suite, l'apparition des signes et des symptômes suivants d'hypersensibilité: respiration sifflante, dyspnée, rougeur du visage et du cou. Lors de l'administration par voie IV, garder à portée de la main de l'oxygène, de l'adrénaline et le matériel nécessaire au traitement d'une réaction anaphylactique.

Polyarthrite rhumatoïde:

- Déterminer l'intensité de la douleur et l'amplitude des mouvements avant le début du traitement et à intervalles réguliers pendant toute sa durée.
- Avant d'amorcer le traitement, effectuer un examen physique, incluant la mesure de la pression artérielle à deux reprises afin de déterminer les chiffres tensionnels de départ. Mesurer la pression artérielle toutes les 2 semaines pendant les 3 premiers mois, puis tous les mois, si elle est stable. En cas d'hypertension, la dose devrait être réduite.

Psoriasis: Évaluer les lésions cutanées avant le début du traitement et à intervalles réguliers pendant toute sa durée.

Tests de laboratoire:

- On devrait établir les concentrations sériques de créatinine, de magnésium, de potassium, d'acide urique, de lipides, les concentrations d'urée et la numération globulaire avant le traitement, toutes les 2 semaines au début du traitement, puis tous les mois si ces valeurs demeurent stables. Une toxicité rénale peut survenir; signaler toute détérioration marquée.
- Le médicament peut entraîner l'hépatotoxicité; suivre de près l'élévation des concentrations d'AST, d'ALT, de phosphatase alcaline, d'amylase et de bilirubine.
- La cyclosporine peut entraîner l'élévation des concentrations sériques de potassium et d'acide urique et la diminution des concentrations sériques de magnésium.
- Le médicament peut entraîner l'élévation des concentrations sériques de lipides.

TOXICITÉ ET SURDOSAGE: Noter les concentrations sériques de cyclosporine à intervalles réguliers pendant toute la durée du traitement. Lors du traitement initial, on peut adapter quotidiennement la dose selon les concentrations sériques. Les lignes directrices concernant les concentrations sériques souhaitables varient selon les établissements.

DIAGNOSTICS INFIRMIERS POSSIBLES

- Risque d'infection (Effets secondaires).
- Douleur aiguë (Indications).
- Connaissances insuffisantes sur le traitement médicamenteux (Enseignement au patient et à ses proches).

INTERVENTIONS INFIRMIÈRES

- NE PAS CONFONDRE LA CYCLOSPORINE ET LE CYCLOPHOSPHAMIDE.
- On peut administrer la cyclosporine avec d'autres immunosuppresseurs. Éloigner les personnes contagieuses des patients ayant subi une greffe. Maintenir l'isolement de protection, selon les directives.
- Les micro-émulsions (Neoral) et les autres produits (Sandimmune) ne sont pas interchangeables.

PO: Prélever la solution orale à l'aide de la pipette fournie. Mélanger la solution orale avec du lait, du lait au chocolat ou du jus d'orange ou de pomme, gardés de préférence à la température ambiante. Bien mélanger et demander au patient de boire immédiatement la préparation. Utiliser un contenant en verre et le rincer avec le diluant afin de s'assurer que le patient a pris toute la dose. Administrer les doses orales avec des aliments. Après l'utilisation, essuyer la pipette sans la laver.

Perfusion intermittente: Diluer immédiatement avant l'administration 1 mL (50 mg) de concentré IV dans 20 à 100 mL de solution de D5%E ou de NaCl 0,9 % pour injection. La dilution dans une solution de D5%E est stable pendant 24 heures dans un contenant en verre. La stabilité, à la température ambiante, dans une solution de NaCl 0,9 % est de 6 heures dans un contenant en polychlorure de vinyle et de 12 heures dans un contenant en verre. Consulter les directives de chaque fabricant pour savoir comment diluer et conserver le produit.

Vitesse d'administration: La perfusion doit se faire lentement en 2 à 6 heures, à l'aide d'une pompe à perfusion.

Perfusion continue: La perfusion continue peut être administrée en 24 heures.

Compatibilité (tubulure en Y): cefmétazole ■ propofol ■ sargramostim.

Incompatibilité en addition au soluté: sulfate de magnésium.

ENSEIGNEMENT AU PATIENT ET À SES PROCHES

- Expliquer au patient qu'il doit prendre le médicament à la même heure tous les jours en respectant rigoureusement la posologie recommandée et les directives concernant la consommation d'aliments. Le prévenir qu'il ne doit pas sauter de dose ni remplacer une dose manquée par une double dose. S'il n'a pu prendre le médicament au moment habituel, il doit le prendre le plus rapidement possible dans les 12 heures qui suivent. Prévenir le patient qu'il ne doit pas abandonner le traitement sans avoir consulté le professionnel de la santé au préalable.

- Expliquer au patient qu'il doit suivre ce traitement toute sa vie durant pour prévenir le rejet de l'organe transplanté. Passer en revue les symptômes de rejet d'un organe greffé et insister sur le fait qu'il faut prévenir un professionnel de la santé dès que ces symptômes apparaissent.

PÉD.: Expliquer aux parents les effets indésirables et leur indiquer comment reconnaître l'hypertension, les infections et les problèmes rénaux. Les prévenir qu'ils doivent informer le médecin en présence de diarrhée, car celle-ci peut diminuer l'absorption de la cyclosporine et entraîner le rejet de l'organe greffé.

- Conseiller au patient d'éviter de consommer des pamplemousses et du jus de pamplemousse afin de prévenir les interactions avec la cyclosporine.
- Indiquer au patient les effets secondaires les plus courants: toxicité rénale, élévation de la pression artérielle, tremblement des mains, hirsutisme facial, hyperplasie gingivale. **PÉD.**: Conseiller aux parents d'utiliser des agents épilatoires ou de la cire si l'hirsutisme devient incommodant.
- Montrer au patient comment mesurer la pression artérielle à domicile. Lui conseiller de prévenir un professionnel de la santé s'il note les symptômes suivants: changement marqué de la pression artérielle, hématurie, mictions fréquentes, urine trouble, diminution de la diurèse, fièvre, maux de gorge, fatigue ou ecchymoses inhabituelles.
- Inciter le patient à pratiquer une bonne hygiène buccale. Une hygiène buccale méticuleuse et des soins dentaires réguliers (nettoyage des dents et détartrage tous les 3 mois) aident à réduire l'inflammation et l'hyperplasie gingivales.
- Conseiller au patient de consulter un professionnel de la santé, avant de prendre un médicament en vente libre ou de recevoir un vaccin en même temps que la cyclosporine.
- Recommander à la patiente de prévenir un professionnel de la santé si elle croit être enceinte ou si elle souhaite le devenir.
- Insister sur l'importance des tests de laboratoire de suivi.

VÉRIFICATION DE L'EFFICACITÉ THÉRAPEUTIQUE

L'efficacité du traitement peut être démontrée par: la prévention du rejet des tissus transplantés ▪ la diminution de l'intensité de la douleur ▪ l'amélioration de la mobilité articulaire ▪ le ralentissement de l'évolution du psoriasis. ✻

CYPROHEPTADINE

Periactin, PMS-Cyproheptadine, Euro-Cyproheptadine

CLASSIFICATION:

Antihistaminique

Grossesse – catégorie B

INDICATIONS

Traitement d'affections aiguës et chroniques de nature allergique et prurigineuse telles les dermites, la rhinite allergique, la conjonctivite allergique, l'urticaire chronique, y compris l'urticaire due à l'exposition au froid, etc. ▪ Stimulation de l'appétit.

MÉCANISME D'ACTION

Inhibition des effets de l'histamine au niveau de ses récepteurs; l'agent ne se lie pas à l'histamine, ni ne l'active ▪ Inhibition des effets de la sérotonine entraînant un gain d'appétit. ***Effets thérapeutiques:*** Diminution des symptômes associés à un excès d'histamine: éternuements, rhinorrhée, prurit nasal et oculaire, larmoiements et rougeurs oculaires ▪ Diminution de l'urticaire due à l'exposition au froid.

PHARMACOCINÉTIQUE

Absorption: Bonne (PO).
Distribution: Inconnue.
Métabolisme et excrétion: Fort métabolisme hépatique.
Demi-vie: Inconnue.

Profil temps-action (effet antihistaminique)

	DÉBUT D'ACTION	PIC	DURÉE
PO	15 - 60 min	1 - 2 h	8 h

CONTRE-INDICATIONS, PRÉCAUTIONS ET MISES EN GARDE

Contre-indications: Hypersensibilité ▪ Crises aiguës d'asthme ▪ Glaucome à angle fermé ▪ Prédisposition à la rétention urinaire ▪ Ulcère gastroduodénal sténosant ▪ Obstruction pyloroduodénale ▪ Hyperplasie symptomatique de la prostate ▪ Obstruction du col de la vessie ▪ Administration concomitante d'IMAO ▪ **PÉD.**: Ne pas administrer chez les nouveau-nés ou chez les prématurés ▪ **GÉR.**: Les personnes âgées et affaiblies sont plus sensibles aux effets anticholinergiques et sont davantage prédisposées aux effets secondaires ■ Allaitement ■ Ne pas administrer en cas de crise d'asthme aiguë.

Précautions et mises en garde: Maladie hépatique ■ **OBST.:** L'innocuité du médicament n'a pas été établie ■ Intolérance connue à l'alcool (sirop seulement) ■ **PÉD.:** Enfants < 2 ans (l'efficacité et l'innocuité de l'agent n'ont pas été établies) ■ Le mode d'action de la cyproheptadine est semblable à celle de l'atropine. La prudence est de mise chez les patients ayant des antécédents d'asthme bronchique, de pression intraoculaire accrue, d'hyperthyroïdisme, de maladie cardiovasculaire et d'hypertension.

RÉACTIONS INDÉSIRABLES ET EFFETS SECONDAIRES

SNC: somnolence, excitation (accrue chez les enfants).
ORLO: vision trouble.
CV: arythmies, hypotension, palpitations.
GI: sécheresse de la bouche (xérostomie), constipation.
GU: retard de la miction avec effort pour uriner, rétention urinaire.
Tég.: photosensibilité, rash.
Divers: gain pondéral.

INTERACTIONS

Médicament-médicament: Effets additifs sur la dépression du SNC lors de l'usage concomitant d'autres **dépresseurs du SNC**, dont l'**alcool**, les **opioïdes** et les **hypnosédatifs** ■ Risque accru d'effets secondaires anticholinergiques lors de l'utilisation concomitante d'autres **médicaments dotés de propriétés anticholinergiques** ■ Les **IMAO** peuvent intensifier et prolonger les effets anticholinergiques des antihistaminiques.

VOIES D'ADMINISTRATION ET POSOLOGIE

- **PO (adultes):** *Traitement des symptômes d'allergie et de prurit* – la posologie initiale est de 4 mg, 3 fois par jour (écart posologique de 4 à 20 mg par jour, en 3 doses fractionnées; ne pas dépasser 32 mg par jour). *Stimulation de l'appétit* – 4 mg, 3 fois par jour avec les repas. La durée du traitement ne devrait pas dépasser 6 mois.
- **PO (enfants de 7 à 14 ans):** *Traitement des symptômes d'allergie et de prurit* – la posologie initiale est de 2 mg, 3 ou 4 fois par jour. La posologie d'entretien habituelle est de 4 mg, 2 ou 3 fois par jour (ne pas dépasser 16 mg par jour). *Stimulation de l'appétit* – la posologie initiale est de 2 mg, 3 ou 4 fois par jour. Ne pas dépasser 12 mg par jour. La durée du traitement ne devrait pas dépasser 3 mois.
- **PO (enfants de 2 à 6 ans):** *Traitement des symptômes d'allergie et de prurit* – la posologie initiale est de 2 mg, toutes les 8 à 12 heures (ne pas dépasser 12 mg par jour). *Stimulation de l'appétit* – la posologie initiale est de 2 mg, 3 fois par jour. Ne pas dépasser 8 mg par jour. La durée du traitement ne devrait pas dépasser 3 mois.

C

PRÉSENTATION (version générique disponible)

Comprimés: 4 mg[VL] ■ **Sirop:** 2 mg/5 mL[VL].

SOINS INFIRMIERS

ÉVALUATION DE LA SITUATION

GÉR.: Rester à l'affût des effets secondaires anticholinergiques chez les patients âgés: délire, confusion aiguë, étourdissements, xérostomie, vision trouble, rétention urinaire, constipation et tachycardie.

Allergie:

- Avant l'administration initiale et à intervalles réguliers pendant toute la durée du traitement, suivre de près les symptômes suivants: rhinite, conjonctivite et urticaire.
- Ausculter le murmure vésiculaire et examiner la fonction respiratoire avant l'administration initiale et à intervalles réguliers pendant toute la durée du traitement. La cyproheptadine peut entraîner un épaississement des sécrétions bronchiques. Maintenir l'apport de liquides entre 1 500 et 2 000 mL par jour pour diminuer la viscosité des sécrétions.

Stimulant de l'appétit: Mesurer l'apport alimentaire et peser le patient à intervalles réguliers.

Tests de laboratoire:

- Le médicament peut entraîner des résultats faussement négatifs aux tests d'allergie cutanés; arrêter le traitement 72 heures avant ces tests.
- L'administration concomitante de cyproheptadine et de thyréolibérine peut entraîner une élévation des concentrations sériques d'amylase et de prolactine.

DIAGNOSTICS INFIRMIERS POSSIBLES

- Dégagement inefficace des voies respiratoires (Indications).
- Risque d'accident (Réactions indésirables).
- Connaissances insuffisantes sur le traitement médicamenteux (Enseignement au patient et à ses proches).

INTERVENTIONS INFIRMIÈRES

- NE PAS CONFONDRE LA CYPROHEPTADINE AVEC LA CYCLOBENZAPRINE.
- Administrer le médicament avec des aliments, de l'eau ou du lait afin de réduire l'irritation gastrique.

C

ENSEIGNEMENT AU PATIENT ET À SES PROCHES

- Conseiller au patient de suivre rigoureusement la posologie recommandée. S'il n'a pu prendre le médicament au moment habituel, il doit le prendre dès que possible. Le prévenir qu'il ne faut jamais remplacer une dose manquée par une double dose. Pour mesurer la quantité exacte de sirop, il faut se servir d'un récipient gradué.
- Prévenir le patient que la cyproheptadine peut provoquer de la somnolence. Lui conseiller de ne pas conduire et d'éviter les activités qui exigent sa vigilance jusqu'à ce qu'on ait la certitude que le médicament n'entraîne pas cet effet chez lui.
- Recommander au patient d'utiliser un écran solaire et de porter des vêtements protecteurs afin de prévenir les réactions de photosensibilité.
- Mettre en garde le patient contre la consommation d'alcool ou d'autres dépresseurs du SNC en même temps que ce médicament.
- Expliquer au patient que pour soulager la sécheresse de la bouche, il devrait pratiquer une bonne hygiène buccale, se rincer fréquemment la bouche et consommer de la gomme à mâcher ou des bonbons sans sucre. Recommander au patient de consulter un professionnel de la santé si la sécheresse de la bouche persiste pendant plus de 2 semaines.

GÉR.: Prévenir le patient âgé et ses proches que le médicament peut entraîner des effets secondaires anticholinergiques; leur expliquer comment les reconnaître. Leur recommander de communiquer avec un professionnel de la santé si ces effets persistent.

VÉRIFICATION DE L'EFFICACITÉ THÉRAPEUTIQUE

L'efficacité du traitement peut être démontrée par: le soulagement des symptômes allergiques ■ le soulagement de l'urticaire due à l'exposition au froid ■ un gain d'appétit.

ALERTE CLINIQUE

CYTARABINE

Cytarabine, Cytosar, Depocyt

CLASSIFICATION:
Antinéoplasique (antimétabolite)

Grossesse – catégorie D

INDICATIONS

IV: Agent essentiellement utilisé seul ou en association avec d'autres agents chimiothérapeutiques pour le traitement des leucémies et des lymphomes non hodgkiniens ■ **Voie intrathécale**: Traitement de la méningite néoplasique due à des lymphomes ou à des leucémies ■ **Voie intrathécale sous forme liposomale (Depocyt)**: Traitement de la méningite lymphomateuse.

MÉCANISME D'ACTION

Inhibition de la synthèse de l'ADN par le blocage de l'ADN-polymérase (effet spécifique sur la phase S du cycle cellulaire). ***Effets thérapeutiques:*** Destruction des cellules à réplication rapide, particulièrement des cellules malignes.

PHARMACOCINÉTIQUE

Absorption: Absorption à la suite de l'administration par voie SC, mais les concentrations sanguines sont moins élevées que lors de l'administration par voie IV; l'administration par voie intrathécale de la préparation liposomale entraîne une exposition systémique négligeable.

Distribution: La cytarabine se répartit dans tout l'organisme; les doses administrées par voie IV et SC traversent la barrière hématoencéphalique, mais en quantité insuffisante, si le médicament est administré rapidement par voie IV. L'agent traverse la barrière placentaire.

Métabolisme et excrétion: Métabolisme majoritairement hépatique; moins de 10 % est excrété à l'état inchangé par les reins. La transformation en médicament inactif dans le liquide céphalorachidien est négligeable, puisque l'enzyme responsable du métabolisme y est présente en très faibles concentrations.

Demi-vie: *IV, SC* – de 1 à 3 heures; *forme liposomale par voie intrathécale* – de 100 à 236 heures.

Profil temps-action
(IV, SC – effet sur la numération leucocytaire; préparation liposomale par voie intrathécale – concentration dans le liquide céphalorachidien)

	DÉBUT D'ACTION	PIC	DURÉE
SC, IV (1re phase)	24 h	7 - 9 jours	12 jours
SC, IV (2e phase)	15 - 24 jours	15 - 24 jours	25 - 34 jours
Voie intrathécale (liposome)	rapide	5 h	14 - 28 jours

CONTRE-INDICATIONS, PRÉCAUTIONS ET MISES EN GARDE

Contre-indications: Hypersensibilité.

Précautions et mises en garde: Maladie infectieuse active ■ Réserve médullaire réduite ■ Maladie rénale ou hépatique ■ Autres maladies chroniques débilitantes ■ Infection active des tissus méningés (voie intrathécale seulement) ■ **OBST.**: Patientes en âge de procréer, grossesse ou allaitement ■ **PÉD.**: L'innocuité chez le nourrisson n'a pas été établie.

RÉACTIONS INDÉSIRABLES ET EFFETS SECONDAIRES

SNC: dysfonctionnement du SNC (doses élevées), confusion, somnolence, céphalées.
ORLO: toxicité de la cornée (doses élevées), conjonctivite hémorragique (doses élevées).
Resp.: ŒDÈME PULMONAIRE (doses élevées).
CV: œdème.
GI: nausées, vomissements, hépatite, hépatotoxicité, ulcérations gastro-intestinales graves (doses élevées), stomatite, anorexie.
GU: incontinence urinaire.
Tég.: alopécie, rash.
End.: stérilité.
Hémat.: (toxicité accrue avec les voies IV, SC) anémie, leucopénie, thrombopénie.
Métab.: hyperuricémie.
SN: *voie intrathécale seulement* – ARACHNOÏDITE D'ORIGINE CHIMIQUE, démarche anormale.
Divers: syndrome associé à la cytarabine, fièvre, infections.

INTERACTIONS

Médicament-médicament: Interactions valables pour la cytarabine administrée par voie IV ou SC, sauf remarque contraire ■ Aplasie médullaire additive lors de l'administration concomitante d'autres **antinéoplasiques** ou d'une **radiothérapie** ■ Risque accru de cardiomyopathie lors de l'administration de doses élevées en concomitance avec le **cyclophosphamide** ■ La cytarabine peut diminuer la réponse des anticorps aux **vaccins à virus vivants** et augmenter le risque de réactions indésirables ■ La cytarabine peut diminuer l'absorption des comprimés de **digoxine** ■ La cytarabine peut réduire l'efficacité de la **gentamicine** utilisée pour traiter les infections dues à *Klebsiella pneumoniæ* ■ Le traitement récent par l'**asparaginase** peut accroître le risque de pancréatite ■ Neurotoxicité additive lors de l'administration concomitante d'**agents antinéoplasiques administrés par voie intrathécale** (voie intrathécale seulement).

VOIES D'ADMINISTRATION ET POSOLOGIE

De nombreux schémas posologiques sont utilisés.

- **IV (adultes)**: *Chimiothérapie d'induction* – En monothérapie, 200 mg/m²/jour, en perfusion continue pendant 5 jours (120 heures; dose totale de 1 000 mg/m²), toutes les 2 semaines. Il faut adapter le traitement aux paramètres hématologiques. En polythérapie, de nombreux régimes thérapeutiques sont utilisés avec différents agents antinéoplasiques, allant de 100 à 200 mg/m²/jour du 1er au 7e jour, ou du 1er au 10e jour. *Doses élevées* – 2 g/m² perfusés pendant 3 heures, toutes les 12 heures, pour 12 doses (du 1er au 6e jour), ou 3 g/m² en perfusion de 1 heure, toutes les 12 heures, pour 12 doses (du 1er au 6e jour), ou 3 g/m² en perfusion de 75 minutes, toutes les 12 heures, pour 12 doses (du 1er au 6e jour).
- **Voie intrathécale (adultes): Cytarabine liposomique pour injection (DepoCyt)**: *Méningite lymphomateuse – traitement d'induction:* 50 mg, tous les 14 jours, pour 2 doses (1re et 3e semaines); *traitement de consolidation:* 50 mg, tous les 14 jours, pour 3 doses (5e, 7e et 9e semaines), puis 1 dose supplémentaire à la 13e semaine; *phase d'entretien:* 50 mg, tous les 28 jours, pour 4 doses (17e, 21e, 25e et 29e semaines). En cas de neurotoxicité, diminuer la dose jusqu'à 25 mg. Si la neurotoxicité persiste, le traitement doit être arrêté.
- **Voie intrathécale (adultes): Cytarabine**: *Leucémie méningée* – De 5 à 75 mg/m², à une fréquence allant de 1 administration par jour pendant 4 jours à 1 administration tous les 4 jours.

PRÉSENTATION (version générique disponible)

Poudre pour injection: 100 mgPr, 500 mgPr, 1 gPr, 2 gPr ■ **Solution pour injection**: fioles de 100 mg/mL contenant 100 mgPr, 500 mgPr, 1 gPr, 2 gPr ■ **Injection liposomique à libération prolongée, pour usage intrathécal**: fiole de 50 mg/5 mLPr.

SOINS INFIRMIERS

ÉVALUATION DE LA SITUATION

- Rester à l'affût de l'apparition d'une aplasie médullaire. Suivre de près les saignements: saignement des gencives, formation d'ecchymoses, pétéchies, présence de sang occulte dans les selles, l'urine et les vomissements. Éviter les injections IM et la prise de la température rectale si la numération plaquettaire est basse. Appliquer une pression sur les points de ponction veineuse pendant 10 minutes. Évaluer les signes d'infection en présence d'une neutropénie. Une anémie peut survenir. Suivre de près la fatigue accrue, la dyspnée et l'hypotension orthostatique.
- Effectuer le bilan quotidien des ingesta et des excreta et peser le patient tous les jours. Signaler tout changement marqué.

C

- Surveiller l'apparition des symptômes suivants de goutte: élévation des concentrations d'acide urique, douleurs articulaires et œdème. Inciter le patient à boire au moins 2 litres de liquide par jour, si son état le permet. L'allopurinol et l'alcalinisation de l'urine constituent des mesures pouvant prévenir la formation de calculs d'urate.
- Évaluer l'état nutritionnel du patient. Les nausées et les vomissements peuvent survenir dans l'heure suivant l'administration de la cytarabine, surtout si la dose IV est administrée rapidement. Les nausées et les vomissements peuvent être moins intenses si le médicament est perfusé plus lentement. L'administration d'un antiémétique avant le début du traitement et à intervalles réguliers pendant toute sa durée et l'adaptation du régime alimentaire en fonction des aliments que le patient peut tolérer peuvent maintenir l'équilibre hydroélectrolytique et l'état nutritionnel.
- Déceler l'apparition du *syndrome associé à la cytarabine ou à l'ara-C*: fièvre, myalgie, douleurs osseuses, douleurs thoraciques, rash maculopapulaire, conjonctivite, malaise. Ces symptômes surviennent généralement dans les 6 à 12 heures suivant l'administration. On peut administrer des corticostéroïdes à titre prophylactique ou thérapeutique. Si le patient répond aux corticostéroïdes, poursuivre le traitement par la cytarabine et les corticostéroïdes.
- OBSERVER LE PATIENT POUR DÉCELER L'APPARITION D'UNE DÉTRESSE RESPIRATOIRE OU D'UN ŒDÈME PULMONAIRE. CES RÉACTIONS SURVIENNENT RAREMENT LORS DE L'ADMINISTRATION DE DOSES ÉLEVÉES, MAIS PEUVENT ÊTRE D'ISSUE FATALE.
- SURVEILLER LE PATIENT À LA RECHERCHE DES SIGNES SUIVANTS D'ANAPHYLAXIE: RASH, DYSPNÉE, ŒDÈME. GARDER À LA PORTÉE DE LA MAIN DE L'ADRÉNALINE, DES CORTICOSTÉROÏDES ET LE MATÉRIEL DE RÉANIMATION.

VOIE INTRATHÉCALE:

- UNE ARACHNOÏDITE D'ORIGINE CHIMIQUE, S'ACCOMPAGNANT DE NAUSÉES, DE VOMISSEMENTS, DE CÉPHALÉES, DE FIÈVRE, DE DOULEURS LOMBAIRES, DE PLÉOCYTOSE DU LIQUIDE CÉPHALORACHIDIEN, DE RAIDEURS OU DOULEURS AU NIVEAU DE LA NUQUE ET DE MÉNINGISME, EST UN EFFET SECONDAIRE POSSIBLE DE LA CYTARABINE ADMINISTRÉE PAR VOIE INTRATHÉCALE. L'ADMINISTRATION CONCOMITANTE DE DEXAMÉTHASONE PEUT RÉDUIRE L'INCIDENCE ET LA GRAVITÉ DES SYMPTÔMES.
- Rester à l'affût des signes suivants de neurotoxicité chez les patients recevant la cytarabine par voie intrathécale: myélopathie, modifications de la personnalité, dysarthrie, ataxie, confusion, somnolence, coma. En cas de neurotoxicité, réduire les doses ultérieures, puis cesser le traitement si les signes persistent. Le risque peut être accru si la cytarabine est administrée par voie intrathécale et par voie IV en l'espace de quelques jours.

Tests de laboratoire:

- Noter la numération globulaire, la formule leucocytaire et la numération plaquettaire avant l'administration initiale et à intervalles réguliers pendant toute la durée du traitement. La leucopénie commence à apparaître dans les 24 heures qui suivent l'administration. Le nadir initial survient dans les 7 à 9 jours. Une légère élévation du nombre de leucocytes précède un deuxième nadir, plus important, qui survient de 15 à 24 jours après l'administration. Le nombre de plaquettes commence à diminuer 5 jours après l'administration et le nadir survient dans les 12 à 15 jours. Le nombre de leucocytes et de thrombocytes commence habituellement à remonter 10 jours après l'atteinte des nadirs. On doit habituellement arrêter le traitement si le nombre de leucocytes est inférieur à 1×10^9/L, ou celui des plaquettes, à 50×10^9/L. On recommande de mener des examens de la moelle osseuse toutes les 2 semaines, jusqu'à la rémission.
- Noter les résultats des tests de la fonction rénale (concentrations d'urée et de créatinine) et hépatique (concentrations d'AST, d'ALT, de bilirubine, de phosphatase alcaline et de LDH), avant le traitement et à intervalles réguliers pendant toute sa durée.
- La cytarabine peut entraîner l'élévation des concentrations d'acide urique.

DIAGNOSTICS INFIRMIERS POSSIBLES

- Risque d'infection (Réactions indésirables).
- Risque d'accident (Effets secondaires).
- Connaissances insuffisantes sur le traitement médicamenteux (Enseignement au patient et à ses proches).

INTERVENTIONS INFIRMIÈRES

ALERTE CLINIQUE: DES DÉCÈS SONT SURVENUS LORS DE CERTAINES CHIMIOTHÉRAPIES. AVANT D'ADMINISTRER L'AGENT, CLARIFIER TOUS LES POINTS AMBIGUS. VÉRIFIER LA LIMITE DES DOSES UNITAIRES ET QUOTIDIENNES AINSI QUE LA DOSE À ADMINISTRER PENDANT LE TRAITEMENT. DEMANDER À UN DEUXIÈME PROFESSIONNEL DE LA SANTÉ DE VÉRIFIER UNE FOIS DE PLUS L'ORDONNANCE D'ORIGINE, LES CALCULS ET LE RÉGLAGE DE LA POMPE À PERFUSION.

ALERTE CLINIQUE: NE PAS CONFONDRE LA CYTARABINE AVEC CYTOXAN (CYCLOPHOSPHAMIDE) OU LE CYTOVENE

(GANCICLOVIR). NE PAS CONFONDRE LE TRAITEMENT À DOSES NORMALES AVEC CELUI À DOSES ÉLEVÉES. LE TRAITEMENT À DOSES ÉLEVÉES COMPORTE UN RISQUE DE DÉCÈS.

- Préparer les solutions sous une hotte à flux vertical. Porter des gants, un vêtement protecteur et un masque pendant la manipulation de la cytarabine. Mettre au rebut le matériel dans les contenants réservés à cet usage (voir l'annexe H).
- La cytarabine peut être administrée par voie SC, par IV directe, par perfusion intermittente, par perfusion IV continue ou par voie intrathécale.

SC, IV: Reconstituer le contenu d'une fiole de 100 mg avec 5 mL d'eau bactériostatique (alcool benzylique à 0,9 %) pour injection, pour obtenir une concentration de 20 mg/mL. Reconstituer le contenu d'une fiole de 500 mg avec 10 mL, pour obtenir une concentration de 50 mg/mL, et celui des fioles de 1 g et de 2 g, avec 10 et 20 mL, respectivement, pour obtenir une concentration de 100 mg/mL. La solution reconstituée est stable pendant 48 heures. Ne pas administrer la solution si elle est trouble. Consulter les directives de chaque fabricant avant de reconstituer la préparation.

IV directe: Administrer chaque dose de 100 mg par bolus intraveineux direct, en 1 à 3 minutes.

Perfusion intermittente: La solution reconstituée peut être diluée davantage dans 100 mL de solution de NaCl 0,9 % ou de D5%E. On peut également la diluer dans une solution de D10%E, de D5%E/NaCl 0,9 %, de Ringer, de lactate de Ringer ou dans du dextrose 5 % dans une solution de lactate de Ringer.

Vitesse d'administration: Administrer en l'espace de 30 minutes.

Perfusion continue: La vitesse et la concentration de la perfusion sont déterminées par le médecin dans chaque cas.

Association compatible dans la même seringue: métoclopramide.

Compatibilité (tubulure en Y): amifostine ■ aztréonam ■ céfépime ■ chlorpromazine ■ cimétidine ■ cladribine ■ dexaméthasone ■ diphenhydramine ■ dropéridol ■ famotidine ■ filgrastim ■ fludarabine ■ furosémide ■ granisétron ■ héparine ■ hydrocortisone ■ hydromorphone ■ idarubicine ■ lorazépam ■ melphalan ■ méthotrexate ■ méthylprednisolone ■ métoclopramide ■ morphine ■ ondansétron ■ paclitaxel ■ pipéracilline/tazobactam ■ prochlorpérazine ■ prométhazine ■ propofol ■ ranitidine ■ sargramostim ■ téniposide ■ thiotépa ■ vinorelbine.

Incompatibilité (tubulure en Y): gallium, nitrate de ■ ganciclovir.

Compatibilité en addition au soluté: étoposide ■ méthotrexate ■ mitoxantrone ■ potassium, chlorure de ■ prednisolone sodique, phosphate de ■ sodium, bicarbonate de ■ vincristine.

Incompatibilité en addition au soluté: fluorouracile ■ héparine ■ insuline régulière ■ nafcilline ■ oxacilline ■ pénicilline G sodique.

Voie intrathécale:

- Les patients traités par la *cytarabine liposomique* devraient recevoir une dose de dexaméthasone à 4 mg, 2 fois par jour, par voie orale ou IV, pendant 5 jours, dès le premier jour où l'on administre l'injection de cytarabine liposomique.
- Laisser la fiole se réchauffer à la température ambiante. Agiter délicatement la fiole ou la renverser pour suspendre de nouveau les particules immédiatement avant d'en retirer la suspension. La *cytarabine liposomique* est prête à l'emploi. Reconstituer la *cytarabine ordinaire* avec une solution de NaCl à 0,9 % sans agent de conservation ou du liquide rachidien autologue. Utiliser immédiatement cette préparation pour prévenir la contamination bactérienne.
- La cytarabine liposomique doit être utilisée dans les 4 heures suivant le retrait de la fiole. Jeter les portions inutilisées. Injecter directement dans le liquide céphalorachidien par l'intermédiaire du réservoir intraventriculaire ou dans la cavité lombaire. Ne pas utiliser de filtres intégrés.
- Demander au patient de rester couché pendant 1 heure après l'injection intrathécale. Rester à l'affût des réactions toxiques immédiates.

ENSEIGNEMENT AU PATIENT ET À SES PROCHES

- Inciter le patient à éviter les foules et les personnes contagieuses. Lui recommander de prévenir immédiatement un professionnel de la santé si les symptômes d'infection suivants se manifestent: fièvre, frissons, toux, enrouement, maux de gorge, douleurs lombaires ou aux flancs, mictions difficiles ou douloureuses.
- Recommander au patient de signaler tout saignement inhabituel. Lui expliquer les précautions à prendre en cas de thrombopénie: utiliser une brosse à dents à poils doux et un rasoir électrique, prendre garde aux chutes, ne pas consommer de boissons alcoolisées ni prendre de médicaments contenant de l'aspirine ou des AINS, car ces substances peuvent déclencher une hémorragie digestive.
- Recommander au patient d'examiner ses muqueuses buccales pour déceler l'érythème et les aphtes. En cas d'aphtes, lui conseiller de remplacer la brosse à dents par une brosse-éponge et de se rincer la bouche avec de l'eau après avoir bu ou mangé. La

C

stomatite peut dicter le traitement par des analgésiques opioïdes.

- Expliquer à la patiente que ce médicament peut avoir des effets tératogènes; elle doit donc prendre des mesures contraceptives tout au long du traitement et pendant au moins 4 mois après l'avoir mené à terme.
- Expliquer au patient qu'il ne doit pas se faire vacciner sans recommandation expresse d'un professionnel de la santé.
- Insister sur l'importance des tests de laboratoire à intervalles réguliers permettant de déceler les effets secondaires.

Voie intrathécale:

- Renseigner le patient sur les effets secondaires possibles (céphalées, nausées, vomissements, fièvre) et les signes précoces de neurotoxicité. Lui recommander de prévenir un professionnel de la santé si ces symptômes se manifestent.
- Expliquer au patient qu'il doit prendre de la dexaméthasone en concomitance avec la cytarabine liposomique.

VÉRIFICATION DE L'EFFICACITÉ THÉRAPEUTIQUE

L'efficacité du traitement peut être démontrée par: l'amélioration des paramètres hématologiques en cas de leucémie ■ la diminution de la taille des tumeurs et le ralentissement de la propagation des lymphomes non hodgkiniens; le traitement est administré toutes les 2 semaines jusqu'à l'obtention d'une rémission complète ou jusqu'à ce que le nombre de thrombocytes ou de leucocytes diminue en dessous des valeurs acceptables ■ la rémission de la méningite néoplasique ou lymphomateuse. ✳

D4T,
voir Stavudine

DALFOPRISTINE,
voir Quinupristine

DALTÉPARINE,
voir Héparines de faible poids moléculaire/héparinoïdes

DANAPAROÏDE (HÉPARINOÏDE),
voir Héparines de faible poids moléculaire/héparinoïdes

DANAZOL
Cyclomen

***CLASSIFICATION*:**
Hormone androgène et stéroïde anabolisant, inhibiteur de la gonadotrophine hypophysaire

Grossesse – catégorie X

INDICATIONS
Traitement de l'endométriose ■ Traitement de la maladie fibrokystique du sein ■ Traitement de courte durée de la ménorragie primaire. **Usages non approuvés:** Prophylaxie de l'œdème angioneurotique héréditaire.

MÉCANISME D'ACTION
Inhibition de la sécrétion hypophysaire des gonadotrophines se traduisant par la suppression de la fonction ovarienne. Faible effet androgène anabolisant. ***Effets thérapeutiques:*** Atrophie du tissu endométrial ectopique en cas d'endométriose ■ Réduction de la douleur et du nombre de nodules en cas de maladie fibrokystique du sein ■ Correction des anomalies biochimiques en cas d'œdème angioneurotique héréditaire.

PHARMACOCINÉTIQUE
Absorption: Bonne (PO).
Distribution: Inconnue.
Métabolisme et excrétion: Métabolisme hépatique. Excrétion rénale sous forme de métabolites.
Demi-vie: 4,5 heures.

Profil temps-action (réponse au traitement)

	DÉBUT D'ACTION	PIC	DURÉE
PO (endométriose)	quelques semaines	6 - 8 semaines	60 - 90 jours
PO (maladie fibrokystique)	1 mois	2 - 6 mois	1 an
PO (œdème angioneurotique)	inconnu	1 - 3 mois	inconnue

CONTRE-INDICATIONS, PRÉCAUTIONS ET MISES EN GARDE
Contre-indications: Hypersensibilité ■ Maladies hépatique, rénale ou cardiaque graves ■ Grossesse ou allaitement ■ Porphyrie ■ Saignements génitaux anormaux non diagnostiqués ■ Néoplasme génital ■ Tumeur androgénodépendante ■ Thrombose évolutive, maladie thromboembolique ou antécédents de tels troubles.
Précautions et mises en garde: Antécédents de maladie hépatique ■ Coronaropathie ■ Prépuberté masculine ■ Patients de sexe masculin atteints d'un cancer du sein ou de la prostate ■ Hypercalcémie.

RÉACTIONS INDÉSIRABLES ET EFFETS SECONDAIRES
SNC: labilité émotionnelle.
ORLO: voix caverneuse.
CV: œdème.
GI: hépatite (jaunisse cholestatique).
GU: aménorrhée, hyperplasie du clitoris, atrophie des testicules.
Tég.: acné, hirsutisme, peau huileuse.
End.: aménorrhée, anovulation, diminution du volume des seins (chez les femmes), diminution de la libido.
Métab.: gain de poids.

INTERACTIONS
Médicament-médicament: Le danazol peut potentialiser les effets de la **warfarine**, des **hypoglycémiants oraux**, de l'**insuline** ou des **corticostéroïdes** ■ Le médicament peut élever les concentrations de **cyclosporine** et accroître le risque de toxicité par cette dernière ■ Le danazol peut augmenter les effets de la **carbamazépine** et du **tacrolimus**.

VOIES D'ADMINISTRATION ET POSOLOGIE
- **PO (adultes et adolescentes):** *Endométriose* – de 200 à 800 mg/jour, en 2 à 4 doses fractionnées, pendant 3 à 9 mois. *Maladie fibrokystique du sein* – de 100 à 400 mg/jour, en 2 doses fractionnées, jusqu'à la disparition complète des symptômes ou pendant 6 mois. *Ménorragie primaire* – de 200 à 400 mg/jour en 2 doses fractionnées, pendant une période allant jusqu'à 6 mois.

Usage non approuvé: *Prophylaxie de l'œdème angioneurotique héréditaire* – de 100 à 200 mg, 2 ou 3 fois par jour.

PRÉSENTATION

Capsules: 50 mg^{Pr}, 100 mg^{Pr}, 200 mg^{Pr}.

SOINS INFIRMIERS

ÉVALUATION DE LA SITUATION

Endométriose: Suivre de près les douleurs endométriales avant le traitement et à intervalles réguliers pendant toute sa durée.

Maladie fibrokystique du sein: Suivre de près les douleurs, la sensibilité et les nodules mammaires avant le traitement et mensuellement pendant toute sa durée. Pour écarter le diagnostic de cancer, si les nodules persistent ou s'hypertrophient, il est recommandé d'effectuer une mammographie ou une biopsie du kyste avant le traitement et pendant toute sa durée.

Œdème héréditaire: Suivre de près l'apparition de crises d'œdème angioneurotique tout au long du traitement, particulièrement durant les périodes d'adaptation posologique.

Tests de laboratoire:

- Noter les résultats des tests de la fonction hépatique à intervalles réguliers tout au long du traitement.
- Il est recommandé d'effectuer une numération des spermatozoïdes et d'en déterminer la mobilité ainsi que le volume et la viscosité du sperme tous les 3 ou 4 mois durant le traitement de l'œdème angioneurotique héréditaire, particulièrement chez les adolescents.
- Le danazol peut modifier les résultats des tests de tolérance au glucose ou des test de la fonction thyroïdienne. Il peut également élever la glycémie et les concentrations des lipoprotéines de basse densité et diminuer les concentrations des lipoprotéines de haute densité.

DIAGNOSTICS INFIRMIERS POSSIBLES

- Dysfonctionnement sexuel (Effets secondaires).
- Image corporelle perturbée (Effets secondaires).
- Connaissances insuffisantes sur le traitement médicamenteux (Enseignement au patient et à ses proches).

INTERVENTIONS INFIRMIÈRES

- NE PAS CONFONDRE LE DANAZOL AVEC DANTRIUM.
- Chez les patientes souffrant d'endométriose ou de maladie fibrokystique du sein, le traitement doit être amorcé durant la menstruation ou être précédé par un test de grossesse. Recommander à la patiente d'informer immédiatement le médecin si elle pense être enceinte.
- Administrer le médicament avec des aliments afin de réduire l'irritation gastro-intestinale.

ENSEIGNEMENT AU PATIENT ET À SES PROCHES

- Informer le patient qu'il doit respecter rigoureusement la posologie recommandée. S'il n'a pu prendre le médicament au moment habituel, il doit le prendre dès que possible à moins qu'il ne soit presque l'heure prévue pour la dose suivante. Il ne faut jamais remplacer une dose manquée par une double dose.
- Conseiller à la patiente d'utiliser durant le traitement une méthode de contraception non hormonale. La prévenir que l'aménorrhée est un effet prévisible du danazol lors du traitement avec des doses élevées. Lui recommander de consulter un professionnel de la santé si le cycle menstruel normal ne se rétablit pas dans les 60 à 90 jours qui suivent l'arrêt du traitement ou si elle pense être enceinte.
- Recommander à la patiente de signaler à un professionnel de la santé l'apparition des effets virilisants du médicament (croissance anormale de poils sur le visage ou sur toute autre partie du corps, voix caverneuse).
- Conseiller au patient d'utiliser un écran solaire et des vêtements protecteurs pour prévenir les réactions de photosensibilité.
- Insister sur l'importance des examens médicaux réguliers permettant d'évaluer l'efficacité du traitement.

Maladie fibrokystique du sein: Montrer à la patiente la méthode appropriée d'autoexamen mensuel des seins. Lui conseiller de signaler immédiatement à un professionnel de la santé toute augmentation du volume des nodules.

VÉRIFICATION DE L'EFFICACITÉ THÉRAPEUTIQUE

L'efficacité du traitement peut être démontrée par: la diminution des symptômes d'endométriose; le traitement de l'endométriose dure habituellement de 3 à 6 mois, mais peut se prolonger jusqu'à 9 mois avant que les symptômes ne diminuent ■ le soulagement de la douleur et de la sensibilité en cas de maladie fibrokystique du sein; ces symptômes s'estompent habituellement durant le premier mois de traitement et sont complètement éliminés en 2 ou 3 mois; la disparition des nodules se produit habituellement en l'espace de 4 à 6 mois de traitement ■ la résolution des signes et des symptômes d'œdème angioneurotique héréditaire; la réponse initiale peut survenir après 1 à 3 mois de traitement. Il faudrait essayer de diminuer les doses à des intervalles de 1 à 3 mois.

DANTROLÈNE

Dantrium

CLASSIFICATION:

Relaxant musculosquelettique (à action directe); traitement de l'hyperthermie maligne

Grossesse – catégorie C

INDICATIONS

PO: Traitement de la spasticité imputable à: des lésions de la moelle épinière ■ l'apoplexie ■ la paralysie par encéphalopathie ■ la sclérose en plaques ■ Prophylaxie de l'hyperthermie maligne ■ **IV:** Traitement d'urgence de l'hyperthermie maligne. **Usages non approuvés:** Traitement du syndrome malin des neuroleptiques.

MÉCANISME D'ACTION

Action directe sur le muscle squelettique entraînant sa relaxation, grâce à la diminution de la quantité de calcium libérée du réticulum sarcoplasmique des cellules musculaires ■ Prévention du processus catabolique intense associé à l'hyperthermie maligne. ***Effets thérapeutiques:*** Réduction de la spasticité musculaire ■ Prévention de l'hyperthermie maligne.

PHARMACOCINÉTIQUE

Absorption: Faible (environ 35 %) (PO).
Distribution: Inconnue.
Métabolisme et excrétion: Métabolisme majoritairement hépatique.
Demi-vie: 8,7 heures.

Profil temps-action (effets sur la spasticité)

	Début d'action	Pic	Durée
PO	1 semaine	inconnu	6 – 12 h
IV	rapide	rapide	inconnue

CONTRE-INDICATIONS, PRÉCAUTIONS ET MISES EN GARDE

Contre-indications: Aucune contre-indication pour la préparation IV destinée au traitement de l'hyperthermie maligne ■ Cas où la spasticité permet de maintenir la posture et l'équilibre ■ Patients ayant une fonction pulmonaire déficiente ■ Maladies hépatiques évolutives, telles que l'hépatite ou la cirrhose.
Précautions et mises en garde: Maladie cardiaque ou pulmonaire ou antécédents de maladie hépatique ■ Femmes, patients > 35 ans (risque accru d'hépatotoxicité) ■ Grossesse et allaitement.

RÉACTIONS INDÉSIRABLES ET EFFETS SECONDAIRES

SNC: somnolence, faiblesse musculaire, confusion, étourdissements, céphalées, insomnie, malaises, nervosité.
ORLO: larmoiement excessif, troubles de la vue.
Resp.: épanchement pleural.
CV: modification de la pression artérielle, tachycardie.
GI: HÉPATOTOXICITÉ, diarrhée, anorexie, crampes, dysphagie, saignements GI, vomissements.
GU: cristallurie, dysurie, mictions fréquentes, impuissance, incontinence, nycturie.
Tég.: prurit, transpiration, urticaire.
Hémat.: éosinophilie.
Locaux: irritation au point d'injection IV, phlébite.
Loc.: myalgie.
Divers: frissons, sialorrhée, fièvre.

INTERACTIONS

Médicament-médicament: Dépression additive du SNC lors de la prise concomitante d'autres **dépresseurs du SNC** dont l'**alcool**, les **antihistaminiques**, les **opioïdes**, les **hypnosédatifs** et le **sulfate de magnésium** administré par voie parentérale ■ Risque accru d'hépatotoxicité lors de l'administration d'autres **agents hépatotoxiques** ou d'**œstrogènes** ■ Risque accru d'arythmies lors d'un traitement concomitant par le **vérapamil**.
Médicament-produits naturels: Le **kava**, la **valériane**, la **scutellaire**, la **camomille** et le **houblon** peuvent accentuer la dépression du SNC.

VOIES D'ADMINISTRATION ET POSOLOGIE

- **PO (adultes):** Il faut individualiser les doses et administrer, dans la mesure du possible, la posologie la plus faible permettant d'obtenir un maximum de résultats. *Spasticité* – initialement, 25 mg/jour; augmenter la dose en la faisant passer à 25 mg, 2, 3 ou 4 fois par jour. Par la suite, on peut majorer la dose de 25 mg/jour, tous les 4 à 7 jours, jusqu'à l'obtention de la réponse souhaitée ou jusqu'à l'atteinte d'une dose totale de 100 mg, 4 fois par jour. *Prophylaxie de l'hyperthermie maligne* – de 1 à 2 mg/kg, 4 fois par jour, commençant 1 ou 2 jours avant l'intervention chirurgicale; la dernière dose doit être administrée de 3 à 5 heures avant l'intervention.

Traitement suivant une crise hyperthermique – de 4 à 8 mg/kg/jour, en 4 doses fractionnées, pendant 1 à 3 jours après le traitement IV.

- **PO (enfants > 5 ans)**: *Spasticité* – 0,5 mg/kg, 2 fois par jour; augmenter la dose en la faisant passer à 0,5 mg/kg, 3 ou 4 fois par jour. Par la suite, on peut majorer la dose de 0,5 mg/kg par jour, tous les 4 à 7 jours, jusqu'à l'obtention de la réponse souhaitée ou jusqu'à l'atteinte d'une dose de 3 mg/kg, 4 fois par jour (ne pas dépasser 400 mg/jour). *Prophylaxie de l'hyperthermie maligne* – la même posologie que chez l'adulte.
- **IV (adultes et enfants)**: *Traitement de l'hyperthermie maligne* – au moins 1 mg/kg; continuer l'administration jusqu'à la diminution des symptômes ou jusqu'à l'atteinte d'une dose cumulative de 10 mg/kg. Si les symptômes récidivent, on peut répéter l'administration de cette dose.

PRÉSENTATION

Capsules: 25 mg[Pr], 100 mg[Pr] ■ **Poudre pour injection**: 20 mg/fiole[Pr].

SOINS INFIRMIERS

ÉVALUATION DE LA SITUATION

- Suivre la fonction intestinale à intervalles réguliers. En cas de diarrhée persistante, il faudrait arrêter le traitement.

Spasticité musculaire: Examiner l'appareil locomoteur et noter le degré de spasticité musculaire avant de commencer le traitement et à intervalles réguliers, par la suite, pour déterminer la réponse du patient.

Hyperthermie maligne:

- Chez le patient ayant déjà subi une intervention chirurgicale, analyser les réactions à une anesthésie préalable ainsi que les antécédents familiaux de réactions à l'anesthésie (hyperthermie maligne et décès pendant la période périopératoire).
- Examiner l'ÉCG, prendre les signes vitaux, étudier les concentrations d'électrolytes et le débit urinaire tout au long de l'administration IV, afin de déceler tout signe d'hyperthermie maligne.
- Le jour de l'administration du médicament, surveiller le patient au cours des repas, pour prévenir les troubles de déglutition et la suffocation.

Tests de laboratoire:

- SUIVRE DE PRÈS LA FONCTION HÉPATIQUE À INTERVALLES FRÉQUENTS TOUT AU LONG DU TRAITEMENT. DES RÉSULTATS ANORMAUX AUX TESTS DE LA FONCTION HÉPATIQUE (CONCENTRATIONS ÉLEVÉES D'AST, D'ALT, DE PHOSPHATASE ALCALINE, DE BILIRUBINE, DE GGT) PEUVENT DICTER L'ABANDON DU TRAITEMENT.
- Lors d'un traitement de longue durée, examiner les résultats des tests de la fonction rénale et la numération globulaire avant l'administration initiale et à intervalles réguliers, par la suite.

DIAGNOSTICS INFIRMIERS POSSIBLES

- Mobilité physique réduite (Indications).
- Douleur aiguë (Indications).
- Risque d'accident (Effets secondaires).

INTERVENTIONS INFIRMIÈRES

PO:

- NE PAS CONFONDRE DANTRIUM (DANTROLENE) AVEC LE DANAZOL.
- En cas d'irritation gastrique gênante, administrer le dantrolène avec des aliments. Pour préparer une suspension orale, ouvrir les capsules et ajouter le contenu à du jus de fruits ou à d'autres boissons. Demander au patient de boire la solution aussitôt que le mélange a été préparé.
- Dans le cas du traitement de la spasticité, la dose orale devrait être fractionnée et administrée 4 fois par jour.

IV directe: Reconstituer 20 mg avec 60 mL d'eau stérile pour injection sans agent bactériostatique afin d'obtenir une concentration de 333 µg/mL. Agiter la solution jusqu'à ce qu'elle devienne transparente. Utiliser la solution dans les 6 heures suivant sa préparation. Garder la solution diluée à l'abri d'une lumière directe. Consulter les directives de chaque fabricant avant de reconstituer la préparation.

Vitesse d'administration: Administrer chaque dose unique par IV rapide directement dans une tubulure en Y ou dans un robinet à 3 voies. Administrer aussitôt les doses suivantes selon les indications. Le médicament irrite fortement les tissus; observer fréquemment le point d'injection pour éviter l'extravasation.

Perfusion intermittente: On a déjà administré la dose prophylactique sous forme de perfusion.

Vitesse d'administration: Administrer la solution pendant 1 heure, 75 minutes avant l'induction de l'anesthésie.

ENSEIGNEMENT AU PATIENT ET À SES PROCHES

- Recommander au patient de ne pas dépasser la dose prescrite afin de réduire les risques de toxicité hépatique et les autres effets secondaires du médicament. S'il n'a pas pu prendre le médicament à l'heure habituelle, il ne doit le prendre que s'il peut le faire dans l'heure qui suit. Le prévenir qu'il ne faut jamais remplacer une dose manquée par une double dose.

- Prévenir le patient que le dantrolène peut provoquer des étourdissements, de la somnolence, des troubles visuels et de la faiblesse musculaire. Lui conseiller de ne pas conduire et d'éviter les activités qui exigent sa vigilance jusqu'à ce qu'on ait la certitude que le médicament n'entraîne pas ces effets chez lui. Après la dose IV administrée en cas d'intervention chirurgicale, les patients peuvent connaître une diminution de la force de préhension, une faiblesse au niveau des jambes, une sensation de tête légère et des difficultés de déglutition pendant une période pouvant aller jusqu'à 48 heures. Durant cette période, conseiller au patient d'éviter les activités qui exigent sa vigilance et d'être prudent lorsqu'il descend un escalier ou lorsqu'il mange.
- Avertir le patient qu'il ne doit pas consommer de l'alcool ou d'autres dépresseurs du SNC en même temps que ce médicament.
- Recommander au patient de signaler à un professionnel de la santé les symptômes suivants: rash, démangeaisons, jaunissement du blanc des yeux ou de la peau, urine foncée, selles couleur de glaise, sanguinolentes ou noires et nauséabondes, ainsi que les nausées, la faiblesse, les malaises, la fatigue ou la diarrhée persistante. Dans ces cas, il peut s'avérer nécessaire d'abandonner le traitement.
- Recommander au patient d'utiliser un écran solaire et des vêtements protecteurs afin de prévenir les réactions de photosensibilité.
- Insister sur l'importance des examens de suivi permettant de déterminer l'évolution du traitement de longue durée et des analyses sanguines permettant de déceler les effets secondaires du médicament.

Hyperthermie maligne: Conseiller au patient souffrant d'hyperthermie maligne de porter sur lui en tout temps un bracelet d'identité où est inscrit son trouble de santé.

VÉRIFICATION DE L'EFFICACITÉ THÉRAPEUTIQUE

L'efficacité du traitement peut être démontrée par: le soulagement des spasmes musculaires en cas de trouble locomoteur; parfois, l'amélioration n'est manifeste qu'après 1 semaine ou plus; en l'absence de tout signe d'amélioration après 45 jours, il faut habituellement abandonner le traitement ■ la prévention ou la réduction de la fièvre et de la rigidité musculosquelettique en cas d'hyperthermie maligne. ✳

DARBÉPOÉTINE ALFA

Aranesp

CLASSIFICATION:

Traitement de l'anémie, hormone régulatrice d'érythropoïèse

Grossesse – catégorie C

D

INDICATIONS

Traitement de l'anémie associée à l'insuffisance rénale chronique (IRC), chez les patients dialysés ou non dialysés ■ Traitement de l'anémie chez les patients présentant des tumeurs non myéloïdes, dont l'anémie est due à l'effet d'une concomitance.

MÉCANISME D'ACTION

Stimulation de l'érythropoïèse (production d'érythrocytes). ***Effets thérapeutiques:*** Maintien et même augmentation du nombre d'érythrocytes, ce qui réduit le besoin de transfusion ■ Correction de l'anémie et maintien des concentrations d'hémoglobine dans une gamme cible définie.

PHARMACOCINÉTIQUE

Absorption: Lente (SC); biodisponibilité se situant entre 30 et 50 %.

Distribution: Espaces vasculaires.

Métabolisme et excrétion: Métabolisme hépatique.

Demi-vie terminale: *SC:* de 27 à 89 heures; *IV:* 21 heures. La demi-vie terminale de la darbépoétine est environ 3 fois plus longue que celle de l'érythropoïétine humaine recombinante, en raison de sa teneur plus élevée en glucides contenant de l'acide sialique; la darbépoétine a donc une activité *in vivo* plus marquée que l'érythropoïétine quand elle est administrée par voie SC ou IV.

Profil temps-action
(élévation des concentrations d'hémoglobine)

	DÉBUT D'ACTION	PIC	DURÉE
IV, SC	2 – 6 semaines	7 – 10 semaines	inconnue

CONTRE-INDICATIONS, PRÉCAUTIONS ET MISES EN GARDE

Contre-indications: Hypersensibilité aux produits dérivés de cellules de mammifères, à l'ingrédient actif ou à l'un des autres ingrédients de la préparation (par exemple, le polysorbate 80) ■ Hypertension non maîtrisée ■ Érythroblastopénie consécutive à un traitement au moyen de toute protéine stimulant l'érythropoïèse.

D

Précautions et mises en garde: Hypertension ▪ Antécédents de convulsions ▪ **OBST., ALLAITEMENT, PÉD.:** L'innocuité pendant la grossesse ou l'allaitement et chez les enfants n'a pas été établie ▪ Patients souffrant d'une maladie coronarienne, artérielle périphérique, carotidienne ou cérébrale grave, y compris un infarctus du myocarde ou un accident vasculaire cérébral récent.

RÉACTIONS INDÉSIRABLES ET EFFETS SECONDAIRES

SNC: CONVULSIONS, céphalées, étourdissements, fatigue, faiblesse.
Resp.: toux, dyspnée, bronchite.
CV: ARYTHMIES CARDIAQUES, INSUFFISANCE CARDIAQUE GLOBALE, INFARCTUS DU MYOCARDE, ACCIDENT VASCULAIRE CÉRÉBRAL/ISCHÉMIE CÉRÉBRALE TRANSITOIRE, COMPLICATIONS THROMBOTIQUES (surtout si l'hémoglobine > 120 g/L), THROMBOSE DE L'ACCÈS VASCULAIRE (patients en hémodialyse), hypertension, hypotension, angine de poitrine et douleurs thoraciques d'origine cardiaque, œdème périphérique.
GI: douleurs abdominales, nausées, diarrhée, vomissements, constipation.
Tég.: prurit, douleurs au point d'injection.
Loc.: myalgie, arthralgie, douleurs lombaires.
Divers: fièvre, SEPTICÉMIE, symptômes pseudogrippaux, réactions allergiques.
Immunogénicité: Comme toutes les protéines thérapeutiques, Aranesp présente un potentiel d'immunogénicité. On a signalé, dans de rares cas, la présence d'une aplasie érythrocytaire (ou érythroblastopénie), associée à la présence d'anticorps antiérythropoïétine, chez des patients traités avec d'autres érythropoïétines recombinées. En raison du rapport étroit entre la darbépoétine et l'érythropoïétine endogène, une telle réponse est théoriquement possible avec Aranesp, bien qu'on ne l'ait pas observée jusqu'ici.

INTERACTIONS

Médicament-médicament: Aucune étude en bonne et due forme n'a été effectuée à cet égard.

VOIES D'ADMINISTRATION ET POSOLOGIE

Anémie due à l'insuffisance rénale chronique

- **SC, IV (adultes):** *Chez les patients n'ayant jamais reçu d'époïétine*: dose initiale – 0,45 µg/kg de poids corporel, 1 fois par semaine; on ajuste ensuite la dose selon la concentration d'hémoglobine cible (généralement un maximum de 120 g/L). Les ajustements doivent se faire à intervalle de 4 semaines. Chez certains patients, la dose peut être administrée 1 fois toutes les 2 semaines.
- **SC, IV (adultes):** *Remplacement de l'érythropoïétine humaine recombinée par Aranesp:*

DOSE HEBDOMADAIRE DE L'ANCIENNE ÉPOÉTINE ALFA (UNITÉS/SEMAINE)	DOSE HEBDOMADAIRE D'ARANESP (µg/SEMAINE)†
< 2 500	6,25
2 500 - 4 999	12,5
5 000 - 10 999	25
11 000 - 17 999	40
18 000 - 33 999	60
34 000 - 89 999	100
≥ 90 000	200

† Ajuster selon les capacités des seringues disponibles.

Anémie due à la chimiothérapie

- SC (adultes): *Dose initiale* – 2,25 µg/kg de poids corporel, 1 fois par semaine ou 500 µg, 1 fois toutes les 3 semaines; on ajuste ensuite la dose selon la concentration d'hémoglobine cible.

PRÉSENTATION

Seringues préremplies à usage unique: 10 µg/0,4 mL^Pr, 15 µg/0,38 mL^Pr, 20 µg/0,5 mL^Pr, 30 µg/0,3 mL^Pr, 40 µg/0,4 mL^Pr, 50 µg/0,5 mL^Pr, 60 µg/0,3 mL^Pr, 80 µg/0,4 mL^Pr, 100 µg /0,5 mL^Pr, 130 µg/0,4 mL^Pr, 150 µg/0,3 mL^Pr, 200 µg/0,4 mL^Pr, 250 µg/0,5 mL^Pr, 300 µg/0,6 mL^Pr, 400 µg/0,8 mL^Pr, 500 µg/1,0 mL^Pr ▪ **Fioles à usage unique:** 15 µg/1,0 mL^Pr; 25 µg/1,0 mL^Pr, 40 µg/1,0 mL^Pr, 60 µg/1,0 mL^Pr, 100 µg/1,0 mL^Pr, 200 µg/1,0 mL^Pr, 325 µg/1,0 mL^Pr, 500 µg /1,0 mL^Pr.

SOINS INFIRMIERS

ÉVALUATION DE LA SITUATION

- Mesurer la pression artérielle avant l'administration initiale et tout au long du traitement. Prévenir le médecin ou un professionnel de la santé en cas d'hypertension grave ou si la pression artérielle commence à s'élever. Un traitement antihypertenseur supplémentaire peut s'avérer nécessaire en début de traitement.
- Suivre la réponse du patient au traitement pour déceler les signes et les symptômes suivants d'anémie: fatigue, dyspnée, pâleur.
- Déterminer l'état du shunt artérioveineux (frémissements et bruits) et celui du rein artificiel au cours de l'hémodialyse. On doit parfois augmenter la dose d'héparine afin de prévenir la coagulation du sang. Suivre de près les patients souffrant d'une maladie vasculaire sous-jacente afin de déceler les signes et les symptômes d'une diminution de la circulation sanguine périphérique.

- Suivre la réaction du patient à l'injection pour déceler les signes et les symptômes d'une réaction allergique: rash, urticaire. Il faudrait arrêter l'administration de la darbépoétine si l'un des symptômes suivants survient: dyspnée, œdème laryngé.

Tests de laboratoire:

- **Bilan martial:** Noter les concentrations sériques de ferritine et de fer et le coefficient de saturation de la transferrine afin de déterminer la nécessité d'amorcer un traitement concomitant au fer. Le coefficient de saturation de la transferrine devrait être d'au moins 20 %; la ferritine devrait être d'au moins 100 µg/L.
- Noter la concentration d'hémoglobine ou l'hématocrite avant l'administration, 1 fois par semaine au cours du traitement initial, 1 fois par semaine pendant au moins 4 semaines après un ajustement de la dose et à intervalles réguliers (au moins mensuels) après qu'on a atteint la valeur cible et qu'on a déterminé la dose d'entretien. Il faudrait également noter d'autres paramètres hématopoïétiques (par exemple, la numération globulaire), avant le début du traitement et à intervalles réguliers pendant toute sa durée. En raison du temps nécessaire à l'érythropoïèse et de la demi-vie des globules rouges, il peut y avoir un intervalle de 2 à 6 semaines entre le moment de l'ajustement de la dose et un changement notable dans la concentration d'hémoglobine. On ne doit pas augmenter la dose plus de 1 fois par mois.
- Si l'hémoglobine augmente de plus de 10 g/L en l'espace de 2 semaines ou si elle atteint 120 g/L, le risque de réaction hypertensive, d'arrêt cardiaque, d'insuffisance cardiaque globale, d'infarctus du myocarde, d'accident vasculaire cérébral, de thrombose vasculaire, d'ischémie, d'œdème et de convulsions peut être accru. On doit alors diminuer la dose de 25 % et suivre les concentrations d'hémoglobine toutes les semaines, pendant 4 semaines. Si l'hémoglobine continue de s'élever et si elle est supérieure à 120 g/L, on devrait interrompre l'administration jusqu'à ce qu'elle diminue; on peut ensuite recommencer à administrer la darbépoétine à une dose réduite d'environ 25 %. Par contre, si l'hémoglobine ne s'élève pas de 10 g/L après 4 semaines de traitement et si les réserves en fer sont adéquates, on peut augmenter la dose d'Aranesp d'environ 25 %. Par la suite, on peut augmenter la dose à des intervalles de 4 semaines, jusqu'à l'obtention de la réponse souhaitée. La dose doit être adaptée pour chaque patient.
- Noter les résultats des tests de la fonction rénale et la concentration des électrolytes, car, en raison d'une sensation de mieux-être, le patient pourrait ne pas observer les autres traitements de l'insuffisance rénale, d'où un risque d'élévation des concentrations d'urée, de créatinine, d'acide urique, de phosphore et de potassium.

DIAGNOSTICS INFIRMIERS POSSIBLES

- Intolérance à l'activité (Indications).
- Connaissances insuffisantes sur le traitement médicamenteux (Enseignement au patient et à ses proches).
- Non-observance du traitement médicamenteux (Enseignement au patient et à ses proches).

INTERVENTIONS INFIRMIÈRES

- En cas d'anémie symptomatique grave, les transfusions continuent d'être nécessaires. Il faut administrer en concomitance un supplément de fer pendant toute la durée du traitement, à moins de contre-indication.
- RESTER À L'AFFÛT DES CONVULSIONS CHEZ LE PATIENT DONT L'HÉMOGLOBINE AUGMENTE TROP RAPIDEMENT, DONT L'ÉTAT NEUROLOGIQUE SE MODIFIE OU DONT LA PRESSION ARTÉRIELLE S'ÉLÈVE CONSIDÉRABLEMENT. LE RISQUE DE CONVULSIONS EST PLUS ÉLEVÉ AU COURS DES PREMIERS MOIS DE TRAITEMENT. ON RECOMMANDE DE RÉDUIRE LA DOSE D'ARANESP SI L'HÉMOGLOBINE S'ÉLÈVE DE PLUS DE 10 g/L EN 2 SEMAINES.
- Conservation: Conserver au réfrigérateur, entre 2 °C et 8 °C. Ne pas exposer au gel et ne pas agiter le produit. Garder à l'abri de la lumière. Ne pas utiliser le produit au-delà de la date de péremption indiquée sur l'étiquette.

IV directe: Administrer la solution non diluée.

Vitesse d'administration: On peut administrer le médicament par injection directe ou par bolus IV, injecté dans le point de ponction de la tubulure le plus près possible du patient ou dans la veine, lors d'une séance de dialyse.

ENSEIGNEMENT AU PATIENT ET À SES PROCHES

- Expliquer au patient l'utilité d'un traitement concomitant au fer (la production d'une quantité accrue d'érythrocytes ne peut se faire sans un apport de fer adéquat).
- Expliquer à la patiente qui est en âge de procréer que les règles et la fécondité peuvent se rétablir. Lui recommander de consulter un professionnel de la santé pour choisir une méthode de contraception appropriée.
- EXPLIQUER AU PATIENT EXPOSÉ AU RISQUE DE CONVULSIONS COMMENT PRÉVENIR LES BLESSURES.

D

LUI CONSEILLER DE NE PAS CONDUIRE ET D'ÉVITER LES ACTIVITÉS QUI EXIGENT SA VIGILANCE.

- Aider le patient à se trouver des moyens lui permettant de se souvenir qu'il doit prendre sa dose régulièrement (1 fois par semaine ou 1 fois toutes les 2 semaines). Il pourrait être facile de l'oublier. Lui conseiller de prendre la dose toujours la même journée de la semaine et de l'inscrire dans un agenda ou sur un calendrier.
- Expliquer au patient qu'il est important de garder le produit au réfrigérateur et de respecter la chaîne de froid lors du transport jusqu'à son domicile ou lorsqu'il doit apporter sa seringue à l'hôpital pour son injection. (Lui recommander d'utiliser les sacs de transport avec bloc réfrigérant, mis à la disposition des patients par le fabricant.)

Anémie due à l'insuffisance rénale chronique:

- Insister sur le fait qu'il est important d'observer les restrictions liquidiennes et alimentaires et de respecter rigoureusement le traitement médicamenteux recommandé et les rendez-vous fixés pour la dialyse. Expliquer au patient que les aliments riches en fer et pauvres en potassium sont le foie, la viande de porc, de veau et de bœuf, les pois, les œufs, le brocoli, le chou frisé, les mûres, les fraises, le jus de pomme, la pastèque, les flocons d'avoine et le pain enrichi. La darbépoétine donne une sensation de mieux-être, mais ne guérit pas la maladie rénale sous-jacente.
- On doit rappeler au patient qu'il est important de rester fidèle à son traitement antihypertenseur. Il faut surveiller de près et maîtriser la pression artérielle chez les patients recevant la darbépoétine. Il faudrait peut-être adapter le traitement antihypertenseur pendant le traitement de l'anémie.

Soins à domicile: Expliquer au patient qui est jugé apte à s'administrer la darbépoétine à domicile efficacement et sans danger la posologie, la technique d'administration et la méthode de mise au rebut du matériel. Lui remettre les renseignements destinés au patient en même temps que le médicament.

VÉRIFICATION DE L'EFFICACITÉ THÉRAPEUTIQUE

L'efficacité du traitement peut être démontrée par: l'élévation des concentrations d'hémoglobine jusqu'à un maximum de 120 g/L (la cible visée doit être adaptée pour chaque patient) et l'amélioration ultérieure des symptômes d'anémie chez les patients souffrant d'insuffisance rénale chronique. ✳

DARIFÉNACINE

Enablex

CLASSIFICATION:

Anticholinergique, antagoniste sélectif des récepteurs muscariniques M_3 (antispasmodique urinaire)

Grossesse – catégorie C

INDICATIONS

Traitement de la vessie hyperactive, terme désignant un ensemble de symptômes urinaires comprenant: les mictions fréquentes ■ les mictions impérieuses ■ la nycturie ■ l'incontinence. Il faut écarter au préalable la présence d'une infection ou d'un autre trouble manifeste.

MÉCANISME D'ACTION

Antagonisme sélectif des récepteurs cholinergiques muscariniques M_3. Ces récepteurs constituent le principal sous-type qui module la contraction musculaire de la vessie. ***Effets thérapeutiques:*** Diminution des symptômes d'une vessie hyperactive.

PHARMACOCINÉTIQUE

Absorption: Rapide et complète (PO > 98 %). Toutefois, la biodisponibilité varie entre 15 et 19 %, selon les doses, en raison du métabolisme de premier passage.
Distribution: La concentration du médicament dans le liquide céphalorachidien est négligeable, ce qui évoque une faible pénétration de la barrière hématoencéphalique.
Liaison aux protéines plasmatiques: 98 %.
Métabolisme et excrétion: Métabolisme par les isoenzymes CYP2D6 et CYP3A4 du cytochrome P450. Excrétion à 60 % dans l'urine et à 40 % dans les fèces.
Demi-vie: De 13 à 19 heures.

Profil temps-action

	DÉBUT D'ACTION	PIC	DURÉE
PO	2 semaines	inconnu	inconnue

CONTRE-INDICATIONS, PRÉCAUTIONS ET MISES EN GARDE

Contre-indications: Hypersensibilité ■ Rétention urinaire ■ Rétention gastrique ■ Glaucome à angle fermé non maîtrisé ■ Prédisposition à l'une de ces affections.
Précautions et mises en garde: Obstruction importante des voies urinaires (aggravation possible des symptômes de rétention urinaire) ■ Troubles digestifs obstructifs (p. ex., sténose du pylore), en raison du risque d'obstruction gastro-intestinale ■ Constipation grave

(2 selles ou moins par semaine) ■ Insuffisance hépatique modérée (limiter la dose à 7,5 mg par jour) ■ Insuffisance hépatique grave (usage déconseillé) ■ Insuffisance rénale grave (données insuffisantes) ■ **OBST., ALLAITEMENT**: L'innocuité du médicament n'a pas été établie ■ **PÉD.**: L'innocuité et l'efficacité du médicament n'ont pas été établies.

RÉACTIONS INDÉSIRABLES ET EFFETS SECONDAIRES

SNC: asthénie, céphalées, étourdissements.
ORLO: sécheresse oculaire, vision anormale.
CV: hypertension.
GI: constipation, sécheresse de la bouche (xérostomie), nausées, vomissements, dyspepsie, douleurs abdominales.
GU: infection des voies urinaires, RÉTENTION URINAIRE AIGUË.
Métab.: œdème périphérique, gain pondéral.
Loc.: arthralgie.
Locaux: éruptions cutanées, sécheresse de la peau, prurit.

INTERACTIONS

Médicament-médicament: La biotransformation de la darifénacine dépend essentiellement des isoenzymes CYP2D6 et CYP3A4 du cytochrome P450. Par conséquent, les **médicaments qui induisent le CYP3A4 ou qui inhibent l'un ou l'autre de ces isoenzymes** peuvent influer sur la pharmacocinétique de la darifénacine ■ Le **kétoconazole**, l'**itraconazole** et la **clarithromycine** (inhibiteurs puissants du CYP3A4) augmentent l'ampleur de l'exposition à la darifénacine; par conséquent, il faut limiter la dose quotidienne de cette dernière à 7,5 mg ■ La **cimétidine**, le **fluconazole** et l'**érythromycine** (inhibiteurs modérés du CYP3A4) ne dictent pas d'adaptation posologique de la darifénacine ■ La prudence est de mise lorsque la darifénacine est administrée en concomitance avec des **médicaments qui sont principalement métabolisés par le CYP2D6 et qui ont un index thérapeutique étroit**, tels que le **flécaïnide**, la **thioridazine** et les **antidépresseurs tricycliques** ■ La darifénacine peut entraîner une augmentation légère, mais pouvant être cliniquement notable, de l'exposition à la **digoxine** ■ Le RNI des patients traités à la **warfarine** n'a pas été notablement modifié par l'administration concomitante de darifénacine.

VOIES D'ADMINISTRATION ET POSOLOGIE

- **PO (adultes)**: 7,5 mg, 1 fois par jour. La dose peut être portée à 15 mg, 1 fois par jour, 2 semaines après le début du traitement, selon la réponse du patient.
- **INSUFFISANCE RÉNALE**: AUCUNE ADAPTATION PARTICULIÈRE DE LA POSOLOGIE N'EST NÉCESSAIRE.
- **INSUFFISANCE HÉPATIQUE**: *MODÉRÉE (STADE B DE CHILD-PUGH)* – NE PAS DÉPASSER 7,5 mg, 1 FOIS PAR JOUR; *GRAVE (STADE C DE CHILD-PUGH)* – USAGE DÉCONSEILLÉ.

PRÉSENTATION

Comprimés à libération prolongée: 7,5 mg[Pr], 15 mg[Pr].

SOINS INFIRMIERS

ÉVALUATION DE LA SITUATION

Avant le début du traitement et pendant toute sa durée, noter le mode d'élimination urinaire, faire le bilan des ingesta et des excreta et examiner l'abdomen afin de déceler la distension de la vessie. Pour évaluer les résidus postmictionnels, on peut installer une sonde. La cystométrie, permettant de diagnostiquer le type de dysfonctionnement vésical, est habituellement effectuée avant que la darifénacine ne soit prescrite.

TOXICITÉ ET SURDOSAGE: Le surdosage d'agents antimuscariniques peut provoquer des effets antimuscariniques graves. On doit administrer un traitement symptomatique sous étroite surveillance médicale, et utiliser des mesures de soutien, au besoin, le but visé étant de faire disparaître les symptômes anticholinergiques.

DIAGNOSTICS INFIRMIERS POSSIBLES

- Élimination urinaire altérée (Indications).
- Connaissances insuffisantes sur le traitement médicamenteux (Enseignement au patient et à ses proches).

INTERVENTIONS INFIRMIÈRES

- La darifénacine doit être administrée 1 fois par jour, dans la mesure du possible à la même heure, avec ou sans aliments. Les comprimés doivent être avalés entiers; on ne doit pas les croquer, les couper ou les écraser.

ENSEIGNEMENT AU PATIENT ET À SES PROCHES

- Conseiller au patient de respecter rigoureusement la posologie recommandée. S'il n'a pas pu prendre le médicament au moment habituel, il doit le prendre dès que possible, à moins que ce ne soit presque l'heure prévue pour la dose suivante.
- Conseiller au patient de se rincer fréquemment la bouche, de pratiquer une bonne hygiène buccale et

de consommer de la gomme à mâcher ou des bonbons sans sucre pour soulager la sécheresse de la bouche. Lui recommander de consulter un professionnel de la santé si la sécheresse de la bouche persiste pendant plus de 2 semaines.

- Conseiller au patient de prévenir un professionnel de la santé en cas de rétention urinaire ou de constipation persistante. Lui expliquer qu'il peut prévenir la constipation en adoptant un régime alimentaire riche en fibres, en buvant plus de liquides (si son état le permet) et en faisant de l'exercice.
- Expliquer au patient que la darifénacine peut diminuer les sécrétions de sueur. Lui recommander d'éviter les activités épuisantes par temps chaud en raison des risques d'hyperthermie.
- Insister sur la nécessité d'un suivi médical constant. On peut effectuer des cystométries à intervalles réguliers, afin d'évaluer l'efficacité du traitement et des examens ophtalmiques à intervalles réguliers, afin de déceler tout signe de glaucome, particulièrement chez les patients âgés de plus de 40 ans.
- Bien que la darifénacine n'ait pas provoqué plus fréquemment de somnolence que le placebo lors des études cliniques, conseiller au patient de ne pas conduire et d'éviter les activités qui exigent sa vigilance jusqu'à ce qu'on ait la certitude que le médicament n'entraîne pas cet effet chez lui.
- Recommander au patient de ne pas prendre de médicaments en vente libre et de ne pas commencer à prendre de nouveaux médicaments ou de cesser la prise de ceux qui lui ont été prescrits sans consulter au préalable un professionnel de la santé.

VÉRIFICATION DE L'EFFICACITÉ THÉRAPEUTIQUE

L'efficacité du traitement peut être démontrée par: le soulagement du spasme de la vessie et des symptômes connexes (mictions fréquentes, mictions impérieuses, nycturie et incontinence) chez les patients présentant une vessie hyperactive. ✳

ALERTE CLINIQUE

DAUNORUBICINE

Cérubidine

CLASSIFICATION:

Antinéoplasique (anthracycline)

Grossesse – catégorie D

INDICATIONS

En monothérapie ou en association avec d'autres antinéoplasiques dans le traitement des leucémies et de certaines autres tumeurs.

MÉCANISME D'ACTION

Formation d'un complexe avec l'ADN, ce qui inhibe la synthèse de l'ADN et de l'ARN (effets indépendants du cycle cellulaire). ***Effets thérapeutiques:*** Destruction des cellules à croissance rapide, particulièrement des cellules malignes. Ce médicament est également doté de propriétés immunosuppressives.

PHARMACOCINÉTIQUE

Absorption: Biodisponibilité à 100 % (IV).

Distribution: La daunorubicine se répartit dans tout l'organisme et traverse la barrière placentaire.

Métabolisme et excrétion: Fort métabolisme hépatique. Transformation partielle en un composé également doté d'effets antinéoplasiques (daunorubicinol). 40 % est éliminé par excrétion biliaire.

Demi-vie: *Chlorhydrate de daunorubicine* – 18,5 heures. *Daunorubicinol* – 26,7 heures.

Profil temps-action (effet sur la numération globulaire)

	DÉBUT D'ACTION	PIC	DURÉE
IV	7 – 10 jours	10 – 14 jours	21 jours

CONTRE-INDICATIONS, PRÉCAUTIONS ET MISES EN GARDE

Contre-indications: Hypersensibilité à la daunorubicine ou l'un des autres ingrédients de la préparation.

Précautions et mises en garde: Infections actives ■ Aplasie médullaire ■ **GÉR.:** Personnes âgées ou patients souffrant d'une maladie chronique débilitante (il est recommandé de réduire la dose chez les patients > 60 ans) ■ Risque de réactivation des lésions cutanées provoquées par une radiothérapie antérieure ■ Insuffisance hépatique ou rénale (il est recommandé de réduire la dose si les concentrations sériques de créatinine > 265 µmol/L ou de bilirubine > 20,5 µmol/L) ■ Patients ayant déjà reçu un traitement par des anthracyclines ou qui présentent une maladie cardiovasculaire sous-jacente (risque accru de cardiotoxicité) ■ Insuffisance cardiaque symptomatique ■ Arythmies ■ **OBST.:** Grossesse, allaitement ou patientes en âge de procréer.

RÉACTIONS INDÉSIRABLES ET EFFETS SECONDAIRES

CV: CARDIOTOXICITÉ, arythmies.

GI: nausées, vomissements, œsophagite, stomatite, hépatotoxicité.
GU: urine de couleur rouge, suppression de la fonction des gonades.
Tég.: alopécie.
Hémat.: anémie, leucopénie, thrombopénie.
Locaux: phlébite au point d'injection IV, vésication.
Métab.: hyperuricémie.
Divers: frissons, fièvre, réactions allergiques.

INTERACTIONS

Médicament-médicament: Aggravation de l'aplasie médullaire lors de l'administration concomitante d'autres **agents antinéoplasiques** ■ La daunorubicine peut diminuer la réponse immunitaire et augmenter le risque de réactions indésirables dues aux **vaccins à virus vivants** ■ Le **cyclophosphamide** administré en concomitance augmente le risque de cardiotoxicité ■ Augmentation du risque d'hépatotoxicité lors de l'administration concomitante d'autres **agents hépatotoxiques**.

VOIES D'ADMINISTRATION ET POSOLOGIE

D'autres schémas posologiques sont également utilisés. La dose cumulative ne devrait pas dépasser 25 mg/kg chez les enfants ou 900 mg/m^2 chez les adultes (450 mg/m^2, si le patient a déjà reçu une radiothérapie ou présente d'autres facteurs de risque de toxicité cardiaque).

- **IV (adultes)**

  Traitement d'attaque en monothérapie: *Leucémie lymphoblastique aiguë* – 1 mg/kg/jour (30 mg/m^2/jour), pendant 3 à 6 jours. La dose totale au cours d'un traitement d'attaque ne doit pas dépasser 20 mg/kg. *Leucémies myéloblastique, granulocytique et promyélocytique aiguë* – 2 mg/kg/jour (60 mg/m^2/jour), pendant 3 à 6 jours, plus 1 ou 2 doses supplémentaires administrées quelques jours plus tard, si besoin est. La dose totale se situe entre 3 et 22,5 mg/kg (de 90 à 600 mg/m^2).

  Traitement d'attaque en association: 1 mg/kg/injection, tous les 2 ou 3 jours, jusqu'à un total de 12 mg/kg. Si la rémission n'est pas complète, on peut poursuivre le traitement jusqu'à concurrence d'une dose maximale de 20 mg/kg au cours d'un même cycle de traitement.

  Traitement d'entretien: Utiliser de préférence d'autres antinéoplasiques. Si la moelle n'est pas complètement ablastique au cours des 4 premières semaines, on peut administrer 1 mg/kg/semaine. La dose cumulative ne devrait pas dépasser 25 mg/kg. Chez les patients résistant à tout traitement et chez lesquels une tentative d'obtenir une rémission est souhaitable, la dose totale cumulative pourrait atteindre 30 mg/kg.

  Leucémie myéloïde chronique: De 1 à 2 mg/kg/injection, tous les 1 ou 2 jours, jusqu'à l'atteinte d'une dose totale de 6 à 12 mg/kg.

- **IV (enfants > 2 ans)**: *Traitement d'association avec d'autres antinéoplasiques* – 25 mg/m^2, 1 fois par semaine. Chez les enfants de moins de 2 ans et chez ceux dont la surface corporelle est inférieure à 0,5 m^2, la dose doit être calculée en fonction du poids et non de la surface corporelle *(usage non approuvé chez les enfants)*.

D

PRÉSENTATION

- **Poudre pour injection**: 20 mg/fiole[Pr].

SOINS INFIRMIERS

ÉVALUATION DE LA SITUATION

- Mesurer les signes vitaux avant le traitement et à intervalles fréquents pendant toute sa durée.
- Suivre de près les signes d'aplasie médullaire. Rester à l'affût des saignements: saignements des gencives, formation d'ecchymoses, pétéchies, présence de sang occulte dans les selles, l'urine et les vomissures; éviter les injections IM et la prise de la température rectale si la numération plaquettaire est basse. Appliquer une pression sur les points de ponction veineuse pendant 10 minutes. Évaluer les signes d'infection en présence de neutropénie. Il y a risque d'anémie. Observer le patient pour déceler une fatigue accrue, la dyspnée et l'hypotension orthostatique.
- Observer fréquemment le point d'injection IV pour déceler l'inflammation ou l'infiltration. Recommander au patient de prévenir immédiatement l'infirmière s'il ressent des douleurs ou de l'irritation au point d'injection IV. En cas d'extravasation, arrêter immédiatement la perfusion et la reprendre dans une autre veine afin d'éviter la lésion des tissus sous-cutanés. En informer le médecin sur-le-champ. La daunorubicine est un agent vésicant. Le traitement classique inclut des injections locales de corticostéroïdes et l'application de compresses de glace.
- Effectuer le bilan des ingesta et des excreta, noter l'appétit du patient et son apport nutritionnel. Suivre de près les nausées et les vomissements qui, bien que modérés, peuvent persister pendant 24 à 48 heures. Pour essayer de maintenir l'équilibre hydroélectrolytique et l'état nutritionnel, administrer un antiémétique avant le traitement et à intervalles

réguliers, pendant toute sa durée, et modifier le régime alimentaire en fonction des aliments que le patient peut tolérer. Inciter le patient à boire de 2 000 à 3 000 mL de liquides par jour si son état le permet. L'allopurinol et l'alcalinisation de l'urine constituent des mesures pouvant prévenir la formation de calculs d'urate.

D

- RESTER À L'AFFÛT DES SIGNES DE CARDIOTOXICITÉ QUI SE MANIFESTENT PAR LES SYMPTÔMES SUIVANTS D'INSUFFISANCE CARDIAQUE: ŒDÈME PÉRIPHÉRIQUE, DYSPNÉE, RÂLES ET CRÉPITATIONS, GAIN PONDÉRAL, TURGESCENCE DES JUGULAIRES, ET QUI SURVIENNENT HABITUELLEMENT DE 1 À 6 MOIS APRÈS LE DÉBUT DU TRAITEMENT. LE MÉDECIN PEUT RECOMMANDER UNE RADIOGRAPHIE PULMONAIRE, UNE ÉCHOCARDIOGRAPHIE, UNE ÉCG ET LA DÉTERMINATION PAR ANGIOGRAPHIE ISOTOPIQUE DE LA FRACTION D'ÉJECTION, AVANT LE TRAITEMENT ET À INTERVALLES RÉGULIERS PENDANT TOUTE SA DURÉE. UNE BAISSE DE 30 % DU VOLTAGE DES COMPLEXES QRS ET LA DIMINUTION DE LA FRACTION D'ÉJECTION CONSTITUENT DES SIGNES PRÉCOCES DE CARDIOTOXICITÉ. LES PATIENTS QUI ONT REÇU DES DOSES CUMULATIVES TOTALES > 550 mg/m², QUI ONT DES ANTÉCÉDENTS DE MALADIE CARDIAQUE OU QUI ONT ÉTÉ SOUMIS À UNE RADIOTHÉRAPIE DU MÉDIASTIN SONT EXPOSÉS À UN RISQUE PLUS ÉLEVÉ DE CARDIOTOXICITÉ. CETTE CARDIOTOXICITÉ PEUT ÊTRE IRRÉVERSIBLE ET MORTELLE, MAIS ELLE RÉPOND HABITUELLEMENT À UN TRAITEMENT PRÉCOCE.

Tests de laboratoire:

- Mesurer les concentrations d'acide urique.
- Noter la numération globulaire et la formule leucocytaire avant le traitement et à intervalles réguliers, pendant toute sa durée. Le nadir des leucocytes se produit dans les 10 à 14 jours qui suivent l'administration de l'agent. Les valeurs se rétablissent habituellement dans les 21 jours qui suivent l'administration de la daunorubicine.
- Noter les concentrations d'AST, d'ALT, de LDH et de bilirubine sérique. Le médicament peut entraîner une élévation passagère des concentrations sériques de phosphatase alcaline, de bilirubine et d'AST.

DIAGNOSTICS INFIRMIERS POSSIBLES

- Risque d'infection (Réactions indésirables).
- Débit cardiaque diminué (Effets secondaires).
- Connaissances insuffisantes sur le traitement médicamenteux (Enseignement au patient et à ses proches).

INTERVENTIONS INFIRMIÈRES

- **ALERTE CLINIQUE:** DES DÉCÈS SONT SURVENUS LORS DE CERTAINES CHIMIOTHÉRAPIES. AVANT D'ADMINISTRER L'AGENT, CLARIFIER TOUS LES POINTS AMBIGUS. VÉRIFIER LA LIMITE DES DOSES UNITAIRES ET QUOTIDIENNES AINSI QUE LA DOSE À ADMINISTRER PENDANT LE TRAITEMENT. DEMANDER À UN DEUXIÈME PROFESSIONNEL DE LA SANTÉ DE VÉRIFIER UNE FOIS DE PLUS L'ORDONNANCE D'ORIGINE, LES CALCULS ET LE RÉGLAGE DE LA POMPE À PERFUSION. IL EST IMPORTANT DE NE PAS CONFONDRE LE CHLORHYDRATE DE DAUNORUBICINE (CÉRUBIDINE) AVEC LA DOXORUBICINE (ADRIAMYCIN, CAELYX, MYOCET). POUR ÉVITER TOUTE CONFUSION, LA DÉNOMINATION COMMUNE ET LE NOM COMMERCIAL DU MÉDICAMENT DEVRAIENT FIGURER TOUS DEUX SUR L'ORDONNANCE.
- Préparer les solutions sous une hotte à flux laminaire. Porter des vêtements protecteurs ainsi que des gants et un masque pendant la manipulation du médicament destiné à l'administration IV. Mettre au rebut le matériel dans les contenants réservés à cet usage (voir l'annexe H).
- Reconstituer le contenu de la fiole de 20 mg avec 4 mL d'eau stérile pour injection afin d'obtenir une concentration de 5 mg/mL. Secouer délicatement la fiole pour en dissoudre le contenu. La solution reconstituée est stable pendant 24 heures à la température ambiante et pendant 48 heures au réfrigérateur. Garder la solution à l'abri des rayons du soleil. Consulter les directives de chaque fabricant avant de reconstituer la préparation.
- Ne pas utiliser d'aiguilles en aluminium pour reconstituer ou pour injecter la daunorubicine, car l'aluminium rend la solution foncée.

IV directe: Diluer de nouveau dans 10 à 15 mL de solution de NaCl 0,9%. Administrer par injection IV directe dans une tubulure en Y d'un soluté primaire de NaCl 0,9% ou de D5%E.

Vitesse d'administration: L'administration par bolus IV doit durer au moins 2 ou 3 minutes. L'administration rapide peut provoquer des rougeurs du visage ou un érythème le long de la veine.

Perfusion intermittente: On peut effectuer une dilution supplémentaire dans 50 ou 100 mL de solution de NaCl 0,9%.

Vitesse d'administration: Injecter les 50 mL en 10 à 15 minutes ou les 100 mL en 30 à 45 minutes.

Compatibilité (tubulure en Y): amifostine ■ filgrastim ■ granisétron ■ melphalan ■ méthotrexate ■ ondansétron ■ sodium, bicarbonate de ■ téniposide ■ thiotépa ■ vinorelbine.

Incompatibilité (tubulure en Y): allopurinol ■ aztréonam ■ céfépime ■ fludarabine ■ pipéracilline/tazobactam.

Compatibilité en addition au soluté: Le fabricant ne recommande pas de mélanger la daunorubicine avec d'autres médicaments.

ENSEIGNEMENT AU PATIENT ET À SES PROCHES

- Recommander au patient de communiquer avec un professionnel de la santé si les symptômes suivants se manifestent: fièvre, frissons, maux de gorge, infection, saignements des gencives, ecchymoses, pétéchies, présence de sang dans l'urine, les selles et les vomissures. Expliquer au patient qu'il doit éviter les foules et les personnes contagieuses. Lui conseiller d'utiliser une brosse à dents à poils doux et un rasoir électrique. Le prévenir qu'il ne doit pas consommer de boissons alcoolisées ni prendre des préparations contenant de l'aspirine ou des AINS en même temps que la daunorubicine.
- Recommander au patient d'examiner ses muqueuses buccales à la recherche d'érythème et d'aphtes. En présence d'aphtes, lui conseiller de remplacer la brosse à dents par une brosse-éponge et de se rincer la bouche avec de l'eau après avoir bu ou mangé. Il peut s'avérer nécessaire d'administrer des opioïdes pour soulager les douleurs dues à la stomatite. Le risque est le plus élevé dans les 3 à 7 jours suivant l'administration de la daunorubicine.
- RECOMMANDER AU PATIENT DE PRÉVENIR IMMÉDIATEMENT UN PROFESSIONNEL DE LA SANTÉ EN CAS DE BATTEMENTS CARDIAQUES IRRÉGULIERS, D'ESSOUFFLEMENT OU D'ENFLURE DES MEMBRES INFÉRIEURS.
- Expliquer au patient qu'il risque de perdre ses cheveux. Explorer avec lui les stratégies lui permettant de s'adapter à ce changement. Les cheveux recommencent à pousser environ 5 semaines après l'arrêt du traitement.
- Prévenir le patient que la daunorubicine peut rendre l'urine rouge pendant 1 ou 2 journées après l'administration.
- Prévenir le patient que ce médicament peut provoquer une suppression irréversible de la fonction des gonades. Informer la patiente que la daunorubicine peut avoir des effets tératogènes, lui conseiller de continuer à prendre des mesures de contraception pendant toute la durée du traitement et pendant au moins 4 mois après l'avoir arrêté.
- Expliquer au patient qu'il ne doit pas se faire vacciner sans recommandation expresse d'un professionnel de la santé.
- Insister sur la nécessité des tests de laboratoire à intervalles réguliers permettant de déceler les effets secondaires du médicament.

VÉRIFICATION DE L'EFFICACITÉ THÉRAPEUTIQUE

L'efficacité du traitement peut être démontrée par: l'amélioration des paramètres hématologiques chez les patients atteints de leucémie. ✳

ddI,
voir Didanosine

DÉFÉROXAMINE

Desferal, PMS-Deferoxamine

CLASSIFICATION:

Antidote (chélateur du fer et de l'aluminium)

Grossesse – catégorie C

INDICATIONS

Traitement de l'intoxication aiguë par le fer ■ Traitement de la surcharge chronique en fer, secondaire au traitement de l'anémie par des transfusions sanguines répétées ■ Diagnostic de surcharge en aluminium ■ Traitement de la surcharge chronique en aluminium chez les insuffisants rénaux en phase terminale.

MÉCANISME D'ACTION

Chélation du fer non lié et de l'aluminium tissulaire pour former dans le plasma des complexes hydrosolubles (ferrioxamine et aluminoxamine, respectivement) qui sont facilement excrétés par les reins. ***Effets thérapeutiques:*** Élimination du surplus de fer et d'aluminium.

PHARMACOCINÉTIQUE

Absorption: Faible (PO); bonne (IM et SC).

Distribution: Le médicament semble se répartir dans tout l'organisme.

Métabolisme et excrétion: Métabolisme par les enzymes tissulaires et plasmatiques. Excrétion rénale à l'état inchangé et sous forme chélatée. 33 % du fer éliminé est excrété par la bile dans les fèces.

Demi-vie: 1 heure.

Profil temps-action
(effets sur les paramètres hématologiques)

	DÉBUT D'ACTION	PIC	DURÉE
IV	rapide	inconnu	inconnue
IM	inconnu	inconnu	inconnue
SC	inconnu	inconnu	inconnue

D

CONTRE-INDICATIONS, PRÉCAUTIONS ET MISES EN GARDE

Contre-indications: Hypersensibilité.

Précautions et mises en garde: **Péd.**: Enfants < 3 ans (l'innocuité du médicament n'a pas été établie) ▪ Maladie rénale grave ▪ Anurie ▪ Risque d'infections causées par les bactéries de souche Yersinia et de mucormycose, une infection fongique ▪ Risque d'aggravation des troubles neurologiques (crises convulsives) chez les patients atteints d'une encéphalopathie liée à l'aluminium. La déféroxamine peut également favoriser le déclenchement de la démence du dialysé ▪ **Obst.**: L'utilisation de la déféroxamine chez les femmes enceintes ou en âge de procréer devrait être évitée. Une méthode contraceptive efficace doit être adoptée avant le début du traitement, et poursuivie pendant toute sa durée et au moins 1 mois après sa fin. Toutefois, si les avantages sont supérieurs aux risques, l'agent peut être administré chez les femmes enceintes souffrant d'une intoxication aiguë par le fer, de modérée à grave ▪ **Allaitement**: L'innocuité du médicament n'a pas été établie.

RÉACTIONS INDÉSIRABLES ET EFFETS SECONDAIRES

ORLO: vision trouble, cataractes, ototoxicité.
CV: hypotension, tachycardie.
GI: douleurs abdominales, diarrhée.
GU: urine de couleur rouge.
Tég.: érythème, rougeurs du visage, urticaire.
Locaux: induration et douleurs au point d'injection.
Loc.: crampes dans les jambes.
Divers: réactions allergiques dont l'ANAPHYLAXIE, fièvre, frissons, malaise, choc par suite d'une administration IV rapide.

INTERACTIONS

Médicament-médicament: L'**acide ascorbique** peut augmenter l'efficacité de la déféroxamine, mais aussi la toxicité cardiaque du fer ▪ L'administration concomitante de **prochlorpérazine** peut entraîner une modification passagère de l'état de la conscience.

VOIES D'ADMINISTRATION ET POSOLOGIE

Intoxication aiguë par le fer

- **IV (adultes et enfants)**: La dose totale ne devra pas dépasser 80 mg/kg, jusqu'à un maximum de 6 g par 24 heures. Le débit de la perfusion varie selon la gravité de l'intoxication et ne devra pas dépasser 15 mg/kg/h. En général, la voie IV est la voie d'administration à privilégier.
- **IM (adultes et enfants)**: La dose initiale est de 90 mg/kg; administrer par la suite, 45 mg/kg à intervalles de 4 à 12 heures, jusqu'à un maximum de 6 g par 24 heures. Chez l'enfant, il ne faut pas dépasser la dose maximale de 1 g/injection, et chez l'adulte, de 2 g/injection. Suivre de près le volume de solution injectée. Chez les jeunes enfants, il faudra peut-être faire l'injection à 2 endroits différents.

Surcharge chronique en fer

- La perfusion IV est généralement plus efficace que la perfusion SC.
- **IV, SC (adultes et enfants)**: La dose quotidienne moyenne se situe entre 1 et 4 g (de 20 à 60 mg/kg, selon la quantité de fer présente dans l'organisme), administrée en perfusion pendant 12 ou 24 heures.
- **IM (adultes et enfants)**: Quand les perfusions IV et SC sont impossibles, on peut administrer la déféroxamine par voie IM; la dose d'attaque moyenne dans ce cas est de 0,5 à 1 g/jour en 1 ou 2 injections. La posologie dépend du taux individuel d'excrétion du fer.

Diagnostic de la surcharge en aluminium: 5 mg/kg en une dose unique, en perfusion IV lente à un débit ne devant pas dépasser 15 mg/kg/h à la fin de la dialyse.

Traitement de la surcharge chronique en aluminium: 5 mg/kg, 1 fois par semaine, en perfusion IV lente à un débit ne devant pas dépasser 15 mg/kg/h, durant les 60 dernières minutes de la dialyse ou après celle-ci. Si le patient est sous dialyse péritonéale ambulatoire continue ou cyclique, on administre la déféroxamine avant le dernier échange quotidien. Dans ce cas, la voie intrapéritonéale est recommandée, bien que les voies IM, SC ou IV s'avèrent tout aussi efficaces.

PRÉSENTATION

Poudre lyophilisée pour injection: 500 mg/flacon[Pr], 2 g/flacon[Pr].

SOINS INFIRMIERS

ÉVALUATION DE LA SITUATION

- En cas d'empoisonnement aigu, déterminer le type et la quantité de préparation ferrique ingérée et le moment de l'ingestion.
- Suivre l'apparition des signes suivants de toxicité par le fer: signes précoces aigus (douleurs abdominales, selles diarrhéiques sanguinolentes, vomissements) ou signes tardifs aigus (diminution de l'état de conscience, choc, acidose métabolique).
- Observer étroitement les signes vitaux, particulièrement durant l'administration par voie IV. Signaler au médecin ou à un autre professionnel de la santé l'hypotension, l'érythème, l'urticaire ou tout autre signe de réaction allergique. Garder de l'adrénaline,

un antihistaminique et le matériel de réanimation cardiorespiratoire à portée de la main pour contrer toute réaction anaphylactique.

- La déféroxamine peut provoquer une toxicité oculaire ou une ototoxicité. Signaler au médecin ou à un professionnel de la santé toute perte d'acuité visuelle ou auditive. On devrait effectuer des examens auditifs et visuels, tous les 3 mois, chez les patients qui présentent une surcharge persistante en fer.
- Mesurer quotidiennement les ingesta et les excreta et suivre de près la couleur de l'urine. Informer le médecin ou un autre professionnel de la santé si le patient est anurique. Le fer chélaté est excrété principalement par les reins; l'urine peut devenir rouge.

Tests de laboratoire:

- Noter les concentrations sériques de fer, la capacité de liaison du fer, les concentrations de ferritine et de fer urinaire, avant le traitement et à intervalles réguliers pendant toute sa durée.
- Vérifier les résultats des tests de la fonction hépatique afin de déceler des lésions dues à l'intoxication par le fer.

DIAGNOSTICS INFIRMIERS POSSIBLES

- Risque d'intoxication (Indications).
- Connaissances insuffisantes sur le traitement médicamenteux (Enseignement au patient et à ses proches).

INTERVENTIONS INFIRMIÈRES

- Reconstituer le contenu de la fiole de 500 mg avec 5 mL d'eau stérile pour injection ou en ajoutant 20 mL d'eau stérile pour injection à chaque flacon de 2 g. Dissoudre entièrement la poudre avant d'administrer la solution. La solution est stable pendant 24 heures après la reconstitution. Consulter les directives de chaque fabricant avant de reconstituer la préparation.
- Le contenu des fioles de déféroxamine peut être reconstitué avec un volume d'eau stérile plus petit, si un plus faible volume de solution reconstituée est nécessaire (p. ex., injection par voie IM). La quantité d'eau stérile nécessaire est de 2 mL pour la fiole de 500 mg et de 8 mL pour la fiole de 2 g. Consulter les directives de chaque fabricant avant de reconstituer la préparation.
- Dans les cas d'empoisonnement aigu, administrer la déféroxamine comme traitement d'appoint dans le cadre d'autres mesures thérapeutiques, telles que l'induction des vomissements, l'aspiration et le lavage gastrique avec du bicarbonate de sodium, ainsi que dans le cadre des mesures de soutien nécessaires pour combattre le choc et l'acidose métabolique.

IM: Administrer profondément dans le muscle et bien masser. Assurer la rotation des points d'injection. L'administration par voie IM peut entraîner une forte douleur passagère.

SC: Utiliser la voie SC pour traiter le patient qui présente des concentrations élevées persistantes de fer. Administrer la déféroxamine dans le tissu SC abdominal par une pompe de perfusion pendant 12 à 24 heures par traitement.

IV: Reconstituer la solution et la diluer de nouveau dans une solution de D5%E, de NaCl 0,9% ou de lactate de Ringer.

Vitesse d'administration:

- La vitesse maximale de perfusion est de 15 mg/kg/h. La perfusion rapide peut provoquer de l'hypotension, un érythème, une urticaire, une respiration sifflante, des convulsions, une tachycardie ou un choc.
- Le médicament peut être administré en même temps qu'une transfusion sanguine chez les personnes présentant des concentrations sériques élevées persistantes de fer. Administrer la déféroxamine par un point d'injection différent.

ENSEIGNEMENT AU PATIENT ET À SES PROCHES

- Insister sur le fait qu'il faut garder les préparations à base de fer, ainsi que tous les médicaments et substances dangereuses, hors de la portée des enfants.
- Rassurer le patient en lui expliquant que la couleur rouge de l'urine est prévisible et traduit l'excrétion du surplus de fer.
- Conseiller au patient de ne pas prendre de préparations à base de vitamine C sans consulter au préalable un professionnel de la santé, car la toxicité tissulaire pourrait augmenter.
- Inciter le patient qui suit un traitement prolongé à respecter les rendez-vous destinés aux examens de suivi et aux tests de laboratoire. Lui recommander également de se soumettre à un examen de la vue et de l'ouïe tous les 3 mois.

VÉRIFICATION DE L'EFFICACITÉ THÉRAPEUTIQUE

L'efficacité du traitement peut être démontrée par: le rétablissement des concentrations sériques normales de fer (de 9 à 27 µmol/L).

D

DÉLAVIRDINE

Rescriptor

CLASSIFICATION :

Antirétroviral (inhibiteur non nucléosidique de la transcriptase inverse [INNTI])

Grossesse – catégorie C

INDICATIONS

Traitement de l'infection par le VIH-1 dans le cadre de schémas thérapeutiques hautement personnalisés, chez les patients susceptibles d'être intolérants aux autres inhibiteurs non nucléosidiques de la transcriptase inverse.

MÉCANISME D'ACTION

Liaison à la transcriptase inverse inhibant ainsi la synthèse de l'ADN viral. ***Effets thérapeutiques :*** Diminution de la charge virale et augmentation du nombre de cellules CD4 ▪ Ralentissement de l'évolution de l'infection par le VIH et de l'apparition de ses complications.

PHARMACOCINÉTIQUE

Absorption : 85 % (PO) ; accrue lorsque le comprimé est dispersé dans l'eau.

Distribution : Inconnue.

Liaison aux protéines : 98 %.

Métabolisme et excrétion : Fort métabolisme hépatique ; < 5 % excrété à l'état inchangé dans l'urine.

Demi-vie : 5,8 heures.

Profil temps-action

	DÉBUT D'ACTION	PIC	DURÉE
PO	rapide	1 h	8 h

CONTRE-INDICATIONS, PRÉCAUTIONS ET MISES EN GARDE

Contre-indications : Hypersensibilité à l'un des ingrédients de la préparation ▪ Administration concomitante de dihydroergotamine, d'ergotamine, d'ergonovine, de méthylergonovine, d'alprazolam, de midazolam, de triazolam, de pimozide (risque de toxicité grave pouvant mener à une issue fatale).

Précautions et mises en garde : Nombreuses interactions médicamenteuses ▪ Dysfonctionnement hépatique ▪ Achlorhydrie (l'absorption ne peut se faire qu'en milieu acide) ▪ **OBST., ALLAITEMENT :** L'innocuité du médicament pendant la grossesse n'a pas été établie. Les patientes infectées par le VIH ne devraient pas allaiter ▪ **PÉD. :** L'innocuité et l'efficacité n'ont pas été établies chez les enfants < 16 ans ▪ Utilisation concomitante de benzodiazépines, d'antiarythmiques, de bloqueurs des canaux calciques de la famille des dihydropyridines, d'anticonvulsivants, d'inhibiteurs de l'HMG-CoA réductase, d'amphétamines, de sildénafil, de tadalafil, de vardénafil et de cisapride (risque accru d'effets indésirables graves).

RÉACTIONS INDÉSIRABLES ET EFFETS SECONDAIRES

SNC : fatigue, céphalées.

GI : diarrhée, augmentation des concentrations d'amylase et d'enzymes hépatiques, nausées, vomissements.

Tég. : rash, prurit.

Métab. : modification de la distribution du tissu adipeux.

Divers : syndrome de reconstitution immunitaire.

INTERACTIONS

Médicament-médicament : LA DÉLAVIRDINE, EN INHIBANT LE CYP 3A4, UNE ENZYME HÉPATIQUE QUI MÉTABOLISE LES MÉDICAMENTS, ÉLÈVE LES CONCENTRATIONS SANGUINES DES **HYPNOSÉDATIFS**, DES **ANTIARYTHMIQUES**, DES **BLOQUEURS DES CANAUX CALCIQUES**, DES **PRÉPARATIONS D'ALCALOÏDES DE L'ERGOT**, DU **PIMOZIDE** ET DU **CISAPRIDE**, D'OÙ RISQUE DE RÉACTIONS INDÉSIRABLES QUI PEUVENT METTRE LA VIE DU PATIENT EN DANGER (ÉVITER L'ADMINISTRATION CONCOMITANTE) ▪ L'usage concomitant de **sildénafil**, de **vardénafil** ou de **tadalafil** doit s'accompagner d'une extrême prudence, en raison du risque d'hypotension, de syncope, de changements visuels et d'érection prolongée (suivre de près l'état du patient, réduire la dose de sildénafil à 25 mg toutes les 48 heures et celle de tadalafil à 10 mg toutes les 72 heures, et éviter l'usage de vardénafil) ▪ L'administration concomitante de **clarithromycine** augmente de façon marquée les concentrations des deux agents ▪ La **fluoxétine** et le **kétoconazole** augmentent les concentrations de délavirdine ▪ L'agent élève les concentrations d'**amphétamines** ▪ Les **antiacides** diminuent l'absorption de la délavirdine (espacer l'administration de ces deux agents d'au moins 1 heure) ▪ Les **antagonistes des récepteurs H_2 de l'histamine** et les **inhibiteurs de la pompe à protons** en diminuent également l'absorption (éviter l'usage prolongé) ▪ La **rifabutine**, la **rifampine**, la **phénytoïne**, le **phénobarbital** et la **carbamazépine** abaissent les concentrations de délavirdine (en éviter l'usage concomitant) ▪ La **dexaméthasone** abaisse les concentrations de délavirdine (risque de diminution de son efficacité) ▪ Le médicament peut augmenter les concentrations de certains **contraceptifs hormonaux** (la signification clinique est

toutefois inconnue) ■ L'administration concomitante d'**atorvastatine**, de **fluvastatine**, de **lovastatine** et de **simvastatine** peut entraîner une élévation des concentrations sanguines et du risque de toxicité de ces médicaments (débuter avec une dose faible et faire un suivi étroit) ■ Il peut être nécessaire de réduire la dose de **méthadone** lorsqu'elle est administrée en concomitance avec la délavirdine ■ L'agent augmente les concentrations de **warfarine** (surveiller le RNI) ■ L'administration concomitante de **cyclosporine** ou de **tacrolimus** peut entraîner une élévation des concentrations sanguines et du risque de toxicité de ces médicaments (surveiller les concentrations sanguines des immunosuppresseurs) ■ L'agent augmente les concentrations d'**amprénavir**, d'**indinavir**, de **lopinavir**, de **nelfinavir**, de **ritonavir** et de **saquinavir** (une réduction des doses peut s'avérer nécessaire) ■ L'utilisation de délavirdine en association avec le **saquinavir** peut accroître le risque de dysfonctionnement hépatique ■ L'administration concomitante de **didanosine** diminue les concentrations des deux agents (espacer l'administration de ces deux agents de 1 heure, en raison du tampon contenu dans les comprimés de didanosine).
Médicament-produits naturels: L'usage concomitant du **millepertuis** peut diminuer les concentrations sanguines et l'efficacité du délavirdine, associées à l'émergence d'une résistance virale.

VOIES D'ADMINISTRATION ET POSOLOGIE

- **PO (adultes)**: 400 mg, 3 fois par jour.

PRÉSENTATION

Comprimés: 100 mg^{Pr}.

SOINS INFIRMIERS

ÉVALUATION DE LA SITUATION

- Observer le patient, pendant toute la durée du traitement, pour déceler une aggravation des symptômes de l'infection par le VIH et l'apparition des symptômes d'une infection opportuniste.
- Si une patiente enceinte est exposée à des antirétroviraux, l'inscrire dans le registre des femmes exposées aux antirétroviraux pendant leur grossesse, en composant le 1-800-258-4263.

Tests de laboratoire:

- Noter la charge virale et le nombre de cellules CD4, à intervalles réguliers pendant toute la durée du traitement.
- L'agent peut entraîner l'élévation des concentrations sériques d'AST et d'ALT.
- L'agent peut diminuer le nombre de polynucléaires neutrophiles.

DIAGNOSTICS INFIRMIERS POSSIBLES

- Risque d'infection (Indications).
- Connaissances insuffisantes sur le traitement médicamenteux (Enseignement au patient et à ses proches).
- Non-observance du traitement médicamenteux (Enseignement au patient et à ses proches).

INTERVENTIONS INFIRMIÈRES

- Administrer le médicament sans égard aux repas. Les comprimés doivent être avalés en entier ou dispersés dans l'eau. Pour préparer la dispersion, ajouter 4 comprimés à au moins 90 mL d'eau et laisser reposer la solution pendant quelques minutes. Il faut ensuite la mélanger jusqu'à ce qu'elle devienne homogène. La solution devrait être consommée rapidement. Il faudrait ensuite rincer le verre et faire boire au patient le résidu de médicament pour s'assurer qu'il a pris toute la dose.
- Ne pas administrer dans l'heure qui suit la prise d'antiacides ou de didanosine.
- Les patients présentant une achlorhydrie devraient prendre la délavirdine avec une boisson acide telle qu'un jus d'orange ou un jus de canneberges.

ENSEIGNEMENT AU PATIENT ET À SES PROCHES

- Expliquer au patient qu'il doit prendre la délavirdine en suivant rigoureusement les recommandations du médecin et en espaçant les prises également, tout au long de la journée. Le médicament doit toujours être administré en association avec d'autres agents antirétroviraux. Prévenir le patient qu'il ne doit pas prendre une plus grande quantité de médicament que celle qui lui a été prescrite et qu'il ne doit pas arrêter le traitement sans consulter un professionnel de la santé au préalable. S'il n'a pu prendre le médicament à l'heure prévue, il devrait le prendre aussitôt que possible, sans jamais remplacer une dose manquée par une double dose.
- Expliquer au patient qu'il doit éviter de donner ce médicament à une autre personne.
- Conseiller au patient de ne pas prendre d'autres médicaments, sur ordonnance ou en vente libre, en même temps que la délavirdine, sans consulter au préalable un professionnel de la santé.
- Prévenir le patient que la délavirdine ne guérit pas le sida et n'empêche pas l'apparition d'infections associées ou opportunistes. Lui expliquer que ce médicament ne réduit pas le risque de transmission du VIH à d'autres personnes par les rapports

sexuels ou par la contamination du sang. Inciter le patient à utiliser un condom, et à éviter le partage d'aiguilles ou les dons de sang afin de prévenir la propagation du VIH. Informer le patient que les effets à long terme de la délavirdine sont encore inconnus.

- Prévenir le patient qu'il peut se produire une redistribution ou une accumulation de graisses corporelles à la suite du traitement antirétroviral, dont les causes et les conséquences à long terme sur la santé sont actuellement inconnues.
- Insister sur le fait qu'il est important de se soumettre à intervalles réguliers à des examens de suivi et à des numérations globulaires permettant de déterminer l'évolution de l'infection et de déceler les effets secondaires.

VÉRIFICATION DE L'EFFICACITÉ THÉRAPEUTIQUE

L'efficacité du traitement peut être démontrée par: le ralentissement de l'évolution de l'infection par le VIH et la diminution du risque d'infections opportunistes chez les patients infectés ■ la réduction de la charge virale et l'augmentation du nombre de cellules CD4.

DELTA-9-TÉTRAHYDROCANNABINOL (THC)/CANNABIDIOL (CBD)

Sativex

CLASSIFICATION:

Analgésique cannabinoïde

Grossesse – catégorie inconnue, mais les recherches sur l'animal ont montré que les cannabinoïdes pourraient être associés à une toxicité en début de grossesse et qu'ils pourraient également avoir un effet négatif sur la spermatogenèse

INDICATIONS

Traitement d'appoint de la douleur neuropathique en présence de sclérose en plaques chez l'adulte.

MÉCANISME D'ACTION

Médiation de l'analgésie produite par les cannabinoïdes par l'entremise des récepteurs CB_1 se trouvant dans les voies de la douleur du cerveau et de la moelle épinière ainsi que sur les terminaisons des neurones afférents primaires du système nerveux périphérique. ***Effets thérapeutiques:*** Soulagement de la douleur neuropathique en présence de sclérose en plaques.

PHARMACOCINÉTIQUE

Absorption: Après une seule vaporisation buccale, les concentrations plasmatiques maximales de CBD et de THC sont en général atteintes en 2 à 4 heures. L'administration par voie buccale produit des concentrations sanguines de THC et d'autres cannabinoïdes plus faibles que si la fumée de cannabis était inhalée. Les concentrations sanguines résultantes sont inférieures à celles produites par l'inhalation de la même dose parce que l'absorption est plus lente, la distribution dans les tissus adipeux est rapide et une partie du THC est transformée en un métabolite psychoactif par métabolisme hépatique de premier passage.

Distribution: Les cannabinoïdes se distribuent dans tout l'organisme; ils sont fortement liposolubles et s'accumulent dans les tissus adipeux.

Liaison aux protéines: Le THC est fortement lié aux protéines plasmatiques.

Métabolisme et excrétion: Le THC et le CBD sont métabolisés dans le foie par diverses isoenzymes du cytochrome P450, notamment 2C9, 2C19, 2D6 et 3A4. Ils peuvent rester jusqu'à 4 semaines dans les tissus adipeux, puis ils sont lentement libérés dans le sang à des concentrations sous-thérapeutiques et métabolisés par les systèmes rénal et biliaire. Le THC et le CBD sont excrétés dans l'urine et les fèces.

Demi-vie: Initiale – de 1 à 2 heures; terminale – de 24 à 36 heures, voire plus longue. La libération des cannabinoïdes par les tissus adipeux explique la longue demi-vie d'élimination terminale.

Profil temps-action
(diminution de la douleur neuropathique)

	Début d'action	Pic (concentrations plasmatiques)	Durée
Vaporisation buccale	environ 30 min	2 – 4 h	inconnue

CONTRE-INDICATIONS, PRÉCAUTIONS ET MISES EN GARDE

Contre-indications: Hypersensibilité connue aux cannabinoïdes, au propylèneglycol, à l'éthanol ou à l'essence de menthe poivrée ■ Insuffisance hépatique ou rénale grave ■ Maladie cardiovasculaire grave (p. ex., cardiopathie ischémique, arythmie, hypertension insuffisamment maîtrisée ou insuffisance cardiaque grave) ■ Antécédents de schizophrénie ou de tout autre trouble psychotique ■ Enfants (< 18 ans) ■ Femmes en âge de procréer qui n'utilisent pas de méthode de contraception fiable ■ Hommes qui veulent procréer ■ Grossesse ■ Allaitement.

Précautions et mises en garde: Antécédents d'épilepsie ou de convulsions à répétition ■ Hépatopathie (cet agent contient de l'éthanol) ▪ Antécédents d'abus d'alcool ou d'autres drogues ou de dépendance à l'alcool ▪ Période périopératoire (risque de modifications légères et passagères de la pression artérielle et de la fréquence cardiaque) ▪ Prise concomitante de médicaments psychoactifs ou d'alcool (risques d'effets additifs ou synergiques sur le SNC) ▪ Personnes âgées ▪ Risque de pharmacodépendance et d'abus.

RÉACTIONS INDÉSIRABLES ET EFFETS SECONDAIRES

SNC: céphalées, humeur dépressive, dépression ou aggravation de la dépression, altération de la mémoire, fatigue, faiblesse, chutes, léthargie; **réactions évoquant une intoxication au traitement**: sensation pseudoébrieuse, baisse des performances cognitives et de la mémoire, perturbation de la faculté d'attention, étourdissements, somnolence, désorientation, dissociation, humeur euphorique, altération de la perception de la réalité, particulièrement du temps, évanouissements, réduction de la capacité de maîtriser les pulsions et les impulsions.

ORLO: vertiges.

Resp.: toux, pharyngite.

CV: tachycardie, hypotension orthostatique, syncope.

GI: sécheresse de la bouche (xérostomie), diarrhée, aphtes buccaux, irritation locale, douleurs buccales, nausées, vomissements, dysgueusie (anomalie du goût), élévation de l'ALT, soif.

Métab.: gain d'appétit.

Loc.: sensation de lourdeur.

Divers: perte d'équilibre.

INTERACTIONS

Médicament-médicament: Le THC est un faible inhibiteur des systèmes enzymatiques du cytochrome P450, CYP3A4, CYP1A2, CYP2C9 et CYP2C19. Le CBD est un inhibiteur relativement puissant de l'activité du CYP2C19 et du CYP3A4 et un inhibiteur relativement faible du CYP1A2, du CYP2C9 et du CYP2D6. Toutefois, l'association du CBD et du THC est un faible inhibiteur du CYP1A2, du CYP2C6, du CYP2D6, du CYP2C19 et du CYP3A4. Par conséquent, la prudence s'impose chez les patients qui prennent aussi des **médicaments métabolisés par les cytochromes P4502D6, 2C19, 1A2, 2C9, 2C6 et 3A4** (p. ex., **fentanyl**, **sufentanil**, **alfentanil** et **amitriptyline**). Les effets de ces médicaments pourraient être accrus ▪ Faire preuve de prudence lorsqu'on prescrit l'association THC/CBD à des patients qui prennent un **sédatif** ou un **hypnotique**, ou encore un médicament pouvant avoir des effets sédatifs, car les effets peuvent être additifs.

Médicament-aliments: L'**alcool** peut interagir avec le THC/CBD, d'où risque d'altération de la coordination, de la concentration et de la capacité de réagir rapidement.

VOIES D'ADMINISTRATION ET POSOLOGIE

- **PO (adultes)**: La dose optimale est déterminée par le patient. Elle varie fortement d'une personne à une autre. Il faut parfois compter une semaine, sinon plus, avant de pouvoir établir la dose optimale. Avant de commencer le traitement, le patient doit se familiariser avec les symptômes d'un surdosage léger, modéré ou grave par le THC. *Premier jour* – posologie maximale de 1 vaporisation, toutes les 4 heures, jusqu'à concurrence de 4 vaporisations, mais la dose peut être plus faible. *Jours suivants* – le patient peut augmenter graduellement le nombre total de vaporisations, en fonction de ses besoins et de sa tolérance. Les doses doivent être réparties également au cours de la journée. En cas de réactions indésirables inacceptables, telles que des étourdissements ou autres réactions évoquant un surdosage, le patient doit cesser de prendre le médicament jusqu'à ce que ces effets disparaissent. Certains patients peuvent continuer de prendre la même dose en augmentant l'intervalle entre les vaporisations, tandis que d'autres devront réduire la dose. Le patient doit ensuite déterminer de nouveau la posologie qu'il tolère et qui produit un soulagement convenable de la douleur. Au cours d'une étude menée auprès de patients atteints de sclérose en plaques, la dose quotidienne médiane a été de 5 vaporisations, une fois les adaptations posologiques terminées. Les données sur l'administration de plus de 12 vaporisations par jour sont limitées. Chez certains patients, le nombre de vaporisations nécessaire et toléré peut être plus élevé.

PRÉSENTATION

Vaporisateur buccal: 27 mg/mL de delta-9-tétrahydrocannabinol (THC) et 25 mg/mL de cannabidiol (CBD)[Pr]. Le flacon de 5,5 mL permet d'administrer jusqu'à 51 doses mesurées.

SOINS INFIRMIERS

ÉVALUATION DE LA SITUATION

- Noter le type, le siège et l'intensité de la douleur, avant et après chaque vaporisation buccale, jusqu'à l'atteinte de la posologie optimale pour le patient et, par la suite, à intervalles réguliers. Il faut suivre de près la douleur ainsi que les adaptations posologiques pendant le traitement initial pour déterminer si le médicament soulage le patient et si ce dernier présente des symptômes de surdosage.

- Mesurer la pression artérielle et le pouls avant et après la vaporisation buccale initiale et à intervalles réguliers, tout au long du traitement.
- L'usage prolongé peut entraîner une dépendance physique et psychologique, mais cela ne doit pas empêcher le patient de recevoir une quantité suffisante d'analgésique.

Tests de laboratoire: Aucun effet sur les résultats des essais de laboratoire. Toutefois, les cannabinoïdes peuvent se retrouver dans le plasma et dans l'urine plusieurs semaines après l'arrêt du traitement.

TOXICITÉ ET SURDOSAGE:

- Intoxication LÉGÈRE par le THC: somnolence, euphorie, accroissement de l'acuité sensorielle, altération de la perception du temps, rougeur de la conjonctive, sécheresse de la bouche (xérostomie) et tachycardie.
- Intoxication MODÉRÉE par le THC: altération de la mémoire, dépersonnalisation, altération de l'humeur, rétention urinaire et ralentissement du transit intestinal.
- Intoxication GRAVE par le THC: baisse de la coordination motrice, léthargie, troubles de l'élocution et hypotension orthostatique. Des réactions de panique peuvent survenir chez les patients anxieux, ainsi que des convulsions chez les patients qui présentent un trouble convulsif. En cas de surdosage assez grave pour causer une altération de la conscience, il faut prendre les précautions habituellement nécessaires chez un patient inconscient, soit assurer la perméabilité des voies aériennes et surveiller les signes vitaux. Si le patient manifeste des réactions dépressives ou psychotiques ou des hallucinations, il faut l'installer dans une pièce calme et le rassurer. On peut administrer une benzodiazépine en cas d'agitation extrême. En cas d'hypotension, le patient doit être placé dans la position de Trendelenburg (tête plus basse que les pieds) ou dans la position de Trendelenburg modifiée (élévation des jambes seulement) jusqu'à ce que sa pression artérielle se normalise. L'administration intraveineuse de liquides ou de vasopresseurs est rarement nécessaire. Il faut communiquer avec le centre antipoison le plus près.

DIAGNOSTICS INFIRMIERS POSSIBLES

- Douleur chronique (Indications).
- Risque d'accident (Effets secondaires).
- Connaissances insuffisantes sur le traitement médicamenteux (Enseignement au patient et à ses proches).

INTERVENTIONS INFIRMIÈRES

- Pour adapter la posologie, il faut se fier à la perception de la douleur signalée par le patient jusqu'à la survenue de l'effet analgésique.

Vaporisateur buccal: Agiter doucement le flacon avant usage, puis retirer le capuchon protecteur. Lors de l'usage initial, il faut amorcer la pompe. Pour ce faire, il faut tenir le flacon en position verticale et, en dirigeant le jet vers un papier-mouchoir, appuyer 2 ou 3 fois fermement et rapidement sur la buse jusqu'à l'obtention d'un fin brouillard. Ne pas orienter le jet vers soi ni vers des enfants, des animaux domestiques ou une flamme nue. Lors des utilisations ultérieures, il n'est pas nécessaire d'amorcer la pompe. Il suffit d'agiter doucement le flacon, puis de le tenir en position verticale et de diriger le jet vers la bouche. On doit ensuite appuyer fermement et rapidement sur la buse et vaporiser sur la muqueuse orale, sous la langue ou à l'intérieur des joues. Il est recommandé de ne pas toujours vaporiser le médicament au même endroit. Le jet ne doit jamais être dirigé vers la gorge, car une irritation pourrait s'ensuivre. Ne pas placer le flacon près d'une source de chaleur ni l'exposer au soleil.

ENSEIGNEMENT AU PATIENT ET À SES PROCHES

- Expliquer au patient comment utiliser la pompe et comment adapter et stabiliser la posologie. Préciser qu'il faut compter 1 semaine, sinon plus, avant de pouvoir établir la dose optimale. Le prévenir qu'il doit se familiariser avec les symptômes de surdosage avant de commencer le traitement.
- Prévenir le patient que le THC/CBD peut parfois provoquer des effets indésirables importants, tels des étourdissements, et ce, surtout pendant l'adaptation initiale de la posologie. La réduction de la dose ou l'interruption du traitement devrait aider à éliminer ces symptômes. Lui conseiller de ne pas conduire et d'éviter les activités qui exigent sa vigilance, son jugement ou sa coordination durant cette période.
- Prévenir le patient que cet agent induit fréquemment des irritations buccales. Lui recommander d'inspecter régulièrement sa muqueuse orale. Si la muqueuse est douloureuse ou enflammée, il ne doit pas y vaporiser le médicament. Si des lésions apparaissent ou si la douleur persiste, le traitement doit être interrompu jusqu'à ce que ces effets indésirables disparaissent.

- Expliquer au patient que, dans la majorité des cas, les effets indésirables disparaîtront d'eux-mêmes sans qu'un traitement soit nécessaire; dans certains cas, ils disparaîtront après une réduction de la dose.
- Expliquer au patient que le médicament peut provoquer la sécheresse de la bouche. Lui conseiller de consommer des bonbons ou de la gomme à mâcher sans sucre pour diminuer cet effet indésirable.
- Recommander au patient d'informer tous les professionnels de la santé qu'il prend ce type de médicament, car plusieurs autres médicaments peuvent aggraver certains effets indésirables du THC/CBD (p. ex., les sédatifs peuvent aggraver la somnolence).
- Prévenir le patient que l'alcool peut interagir avec le THC/CBD, d'où un risque d'altération de la coordination, de la concentration et de la capacité de réagir rapidement. Inciter le patient à ne pas boire d'alcool en même temps qu'il suit un traitement par ce médicament.
- Expliquer au patient que les effets de la fumée de cannabis ou des autres formes de cannabis s'ajouteraient à ceux du THC/CBD, d'où un risque d'intoxication ou d'autres effets indésirables. Inciter le patient à ne pas consommer de cannabis pendant son traitement.
- Expliquer au patient que ce traitement peut l'exposer à un risque d'abus ou de dépendance, mais que ce fait ne doit pas l'empêcher d'utiliser la dose qui soulage sa douleur sans entraîner d'effets indésirables inacceptables.
- Recommander au patient d'informer tous les professionnels de la santé de ce traitement médicamenteux avant une intervention chirurgicale. Le médicament peut produire des modifications légères et passagères de la pression artérielle et de la fréquence cardiaque. Il faut tenir compte des effets centraux et périphériques du THC/CBD en période périopératoire.
- Recommander aux femmes en âge de procréer d'utiliser une méthode de contraception fiable pendant le traitement et pendant 3 mois de plus, après qu'il a pris fin parce que des recherches sur l'animal ont montré que les cannabinoïdes pourraient exercer des effets toxiques sur le fœtus au début de la gestation et qu'ils altèrent la spermatogenèse. Les hommes qui ont une partenaire en âge de procréer doivent aussi prendre les mêmes précautions.
- Prévenir le patient qu'un rythme de 5 vaporisations par jour pendant 10 jours entraîne un changement dans le bruit que fait le vaporisateur. Il est également possible que le patient éprouve une sensation différente dans la bouche. Ces changements indiquent que le flacon est presque vide et qu'il est temps de le remplacer.
- Expliquer au patient que le flacon doit être conservé au réfrigérateur (entre 2 °C et 8 °C) s'il n'est pas ouvert; une fois qu'il est ouvert, il faut le conserver à la température ambiante (entre 15 et 25 °C) et l'utiliser dans les 28 jours.
- Insister sur l'importance des examens de suivi réguliers pouvant déterminer les effets du traitement.

D

VÉRIFICATION DE L'EFFICACITÉ THÉRAPEUTIQUE

L'efficacité du traitement peut être démontrée par: la diminution de l'intensité de la douleur, sans effets indésirables inacceptables évoquant un surdosage.

DESLORATADINE

Aerius

CLASSIFICATION:

Antihistaminique (antagoniste des récepteurs H_1 de l'histamine)

Grossesse – catégorie C

INDICATIONS

Soulagement des symptômes nasaux de la rhinite allergique (éternuements, écoulement, prurit, enchifrènement et congestion) et des autres symptômes souvent associés (prurit du palais et toux, picotement et irritation des yeux et larmoiement) ■ Soulagement des symptômes associés à l'urticaire chronique idiopathique (prurit et éruptions urticariennes).

MÉCANISME D'ACTION

Inhibition des effets de l'histamine au niveau des récepteurs H_1 périphériques. La desloratadine a des propriétés antiallergiques, antihistaminiques et anti-inflammatoires. ***Effets thérapeutiques:*** Diminution des symptômes associés à un excès d'histamine (éternuements, rhinorrhée, prurit nasal et oculaire, larmoiement et rougeurs oculaires) ■ Diminution de l'urticaire.

PHARMACOCINÉTIQUE

Absorption: Bonne (PO).

Distribution: La pénétration dans le SNC est pratiquement nulle. L'agent passe dans le lait maternel.

Liaison aux protéines: De 83 à 87 %.

Métabolisme et excrétion: Fort métabolisme hépatique et transformation en un métabolite actif, le 3-hydroxy-desloratadine. Un petit pourcentage des patients peuvent être des métabolisateurs lents. Ce médicament est ensuite glucuronoconjugué et éliminé par les reins et dans les fèces.

Demi-vie: 27 heures.

Profil temps-action (effets antihistaminiques)

	DÉBUT D'ACTION	PIC	DURÉE
PO	1,25 h (rhinite allergique saisonnière) 24 h (urticaire chronique idiopathique)	3 h	24 h

D

CONTRE-INDICATIONS, PRÉCAUTIONS ET MISES EN GARDE

Contre-indications: Hypersensibilité.

Précautions et mises en garde: Insuffisance rénale grave ■ Insuffisance hépatique grave ■ **OBST.**: L'innocuité du médicament n'a pas été établie ■ **ALLAITEMENT**: La desloratadine passe dans le lait maternel. Par conséquent, l'allaitement est déconseillé ■ **PÉD.**: On n'a pas établi l'innocuité ni l'efficacité des comprimés de desloratadine chez les enfants de moins de 12 ans, ni celles du sirop de desloratadine chez les enfants de moins de 2 ans ■ **GÉR.**: Risque d'augmentation des effets secondaires surtout si le patient âgé souffre d'insuffisance hépatique ou rénale et qu'il prend plusieurs autres médicaments.

RÉACTIONS INDÉSIRABLES ET EFFETS SECONDAIRES

SNC: céphalées, fatigue, somnolence (incidence similaire à la somnolence induite par le placebo).

GI: sécheresse de la bouche (xérostomie).

ORLO: pharyngite.

Divers: RÉACTIONS D'HYPERSENSIBILITÉ (ANAPHYLAXIE) (rares).

INTERACTIONS

Médicament-médicament: Les interactions suivantes sont susceptibles de se produire mais dans une proportion moindre que dans le cas des antihistaminiques plus sédatifs. Effets additifs sur la dépression du SNC lors de l'usage concomitant d'**alcool**, d'**antidépresseurs**, d'**opioïdes** et d'**hypnosédatifs** ■ Les **IMAO** pourraient augmenter et prolonger l'effet sédatif des antihistaminiques.

VOIES D'ADMINISTRATION ET POSOLOGIE

- **PO (comprimés et sirop) (adultes et adolescents ≥ 12 ans)**: 5 mg, 1 fois par jour.
- **PO (sirop) (enfants de 6 à 11 ans)**: 2,5 mg (5 mL) de sirop, 1 fois par jour. Ne pas administrer pendant plus de 14 jours, sauf sur les conseils d'un médecin.
- **PO (sirop) (enfants de 2 à 5 ans)**: 1,25 mg (2,5 mL) de sirop, 1 fois par jour. Ne pas administrer pendant plus de 14 jours, sauf sur les conseils d'un médecin.

PRÉSENTATION

Comprimés: 5 mg^{VL} ■ **Sirop**: 0,5 mg/mL^{VL}.

SOINS INFIRMIERS

ÉVALUATION DE LA SITUATION

- Avant l'administration initiale du médicament et à intervalles réguliers pendant toute la durée du traitement, rester à l'affût des symptômes suivants d'allergie: rhinite, conjonctivite et urticaire.
- Ausculter le murmure vésiculaire et noter les caractéristiques des sécrétions bronchiques. Maintenir l'apport de liquides entre 1 500 et 2 000 mL par jour pour diminuer la viscosité des sécrétions (à moins de contre-indication).

Tests de laboratoire: Le médicament peut entraîner des résultats faussement négatifs aux tests d'allergie cutanés.

DIAGNOSTICS INFIRMIERS POSSIBLES

- Dégagement inefficace des voies respiratoires (Indications).
- Risque d'accident (Réactions indésirables).
- Connaissances insuffisantes sur le traitement médicamenteux (Enseignement au patient et à ses proches).

INTERVENTIONS INFIRMIÈRES

- Administrer le médicament 1 fois par jour, sans égard aux repas.

PÉD.: Utiliser un dispositif de mesure calibré afin d'administrer la quantité exacte de sirop.

ENSEIGNEMENT AU PATIENT ET À SES PROCHES

- Expliquer au patient qu'il doit respecter rigoureusement la posologie recommandée. Une augmentation de la dose ou de la fréquence d'administration n'augmente pas l'efficacité du médicament, mais peut augmenter ses effets secondaires.
- Prévenir le patient que la desloratadine peut provoquer de la somnolence (incidence similaire à la somnolence induite par le placebo). Lui conseiller de ne pas conduire et d'éviter les activités qui exigent sa vigilance jusqu'à ce qu'on ait la certitude que le médicament n'entraîne pas cet effet chez lui.

- Conseiller au patient de pratiquer une bonne hygiène buccale, de se rincer la bouche avec de l'eau et de mâcher de la gomme ou de sucer des bonbons sans sucre pour diminuer la sécheresse de la bouche. Lui recommander de consulter un professionnel de la santé si la sécheresse de la bouche persiste pendant plus de 2 semaines.
- Demander au patient de prévenir un professionnel de la santé si les symptômes allergiques persistent.

VÉRIFICATION DE L'EFFICACITÉ THÉRAPEUTIQUE

L'efficacité du traitement peut être démontrée par: la diminution des symptômes allergiques.

DESMOPRESSINE

Apo-Desmopressine, DDAVP, Desmopressine, Minirin, Octostim

CLASSIFICATION:

Hormone hypothalamique et hypophysaire, analogue d'hormone antidiurétique, antihémorragique

Grossesse – catégorie B

INDICATIONS

Voie intranasale: Traitement de courte durée de l'énurésie nocturne (DDAVP), prévention des saignements chez les patients atteints d'hémophilie A ou de la maladie de von Willebrand de type 1 (Octostim) ■ **Voie intranasale, PO, SC, IM et IV:** Traitement du diabète insipide ■ **IV:** Prévention des saignements chez les patients atteints d'hémophilie A ou de la maladie de von Willebrand de type 1.

MÉCANISME D'ACTION

Analogue synthétique de la vasopressine, une hormone antidiurétique naturelle. Son principal effet est d'intensifier la réabsorption de l'eau par les reins. ***Effets thérapeutiques:*** Prévention de l'énurésie nocturne ■ Maintien d'une quantité appropriée d'eau dans l'organisme chez les patients souffrant de diabète insipide ■ Prévention de l'hémorragie chez les patients atteints de certains types d'hémophilie ou de la maladie de von Willebrand.

PHARMACOCINÉTIQUE

Absorption: 5 % (PO); de 10 à 20 % (voie intranasale).

Distribution: Peu connue. Le médicament passe dans le lait maternel.

Métabolisme et excrétion: Inconnus.

Demi-vie: 75 minutes.

Profil temps-action

(effet antidiurétique [PO, voie intranasale]; effet sur l'activité du facteur VIII [facteur antihémophilique A] [voie IV])

	DÉBUT D'ACTION	PIC	DURÉE
PO	1 h	4 – 7 h	8 – 12 h
Voie intranasale	1 h	1 – 5 h	8 – 20 h
IV	quelques min	15 – 30 min	3 h†

† De 4 à 24 heures en cas d'hémophilie A légère.

CONTRE-INDICATIONS, PRÉCAUTIONS ET MISES EN GARDE

Contre-indications: Hypersensibilité ■ Hypersensibilité au chlorobutanol (Octostim) ■ Patients souffrant de maladie de von Willebrand de type IIb ou de type plaquettaire (pseudomaladie de von Willebrand) ■ Insuffisance cardiaque ou autres affections nécessitant un traitement aux antidiurétiques.

Précautions et mises en garde: Angine de poitrine ■ Hypertension ■ **OBST., ALLAITEMENT:** L'innocuité du médicament n'a pas été établie.

RÉACTIONS INDÉSIRABLES ET EFFETS SECONDAIRES

SNC: somnolence, céphalées, apathie.

ORLO: *Voie intranasale* – congestion nasale, rhinite.

Resp.: dyspnée.

CV: hypertension, hypotension, tachycardie (fortes doses, administrées par voie IV seulement).

GI: crampes abdominales légères, nausées.

GU: douleurs vulvaires.

Tég.: bouffées vasomotrices.

HÉ: intoxication hydrique, hyponatrémie.

Locaux: phlébite au point d'injection IV.

INTERACTIONS

Médicament-médicament: Le **chlorpropamide**, le **clofibrate** ou la **carbamazépine** peuvent intensifier la réponse antidiurétique à la desmopressine ■ Le **lithium** ou la **noradrénaline** peuvent diminuer la réponse antidiurétique à la desmopressine ■ De fortes doses du médicament peuvent intensifier les effets des **agents vasopresseurs**.

VOIES D'ADMINISTRATION ET POSOLOGIE

Énurésie nocturne

- **Voie intranasale (adultes et enfants > 5 ans):** De 10 à 40 μg par jour, 1 heure avant le coucher.

Diabète insipide

- **PO (adultes et enfants)**: 100 µg (0,1 mg), 3 fois par jour, la dose maximale est de 1,2 mg par jour (400 µg, 3 fois par jour).
- **PO comprimé fondant (adultes)**: 0,06 mg sous la langue, 3 fois par jour (intervalle posologique – de 0,12 à 0,72 mg).
- **Voie intranasale (adultes)**: *Dispositif d'administration intranasale ou vaporisateur nasal* – de 10 à 40 µg (de 0,1 à 0,4 mL) par jour, en une seule dose ou en 2 ou 3 doses fractionnées.
- **Voie intranasale (enfants de 3 mois à 12 ans)**: *Dispositif d'administration intranasale ou vaporisateur nasal* – de 5 à 30 µg (de 0,05 à 0,3 mL) par jour, en une seule dose ou en 2 ou 3 doses fractionnées.
- **SC, IM, IV (adultes)**: De 1 à 4 µg (0,25 à 1 mL), 1 fois par jour.
- **SC, IM, IV (enfants)**: 0,4 µg (0,1 mL), 1 fois par jour.

Antihémorragique

- **IV (enfants > 3 mois)**: 0,3 µg/kg (dose maximale de 20 µg).
- **IV (adultes)**: 10,0 µg/m^2 (dose maximale de 20 µg).
- **Voie intranasale (adultes et enfants > 50 kg)**: 1 vaporisation (150 µg) dans chaque narine (Octostim).
- **Voie intranasale (adultes et enfants ≤ 50 kg)**: 1 vaporisation (150 µg) dans une seule narine (Octostim).

PRÉSENTATION

Comprimés: 0,1 mg^{Pr}, 0,2 mg^{Pr} ▪ **Comprimé fondant**: 0,06 mg^{Pr}, 0,12 mg^{Pr} ▪ **Vaporisateur nasal**: 10 µg/vaporisation – le flacon de 2,5 mL (0,1 mg/mL) contient 25 doses (DDAVP)^{Pr}, 150 µg/dose (1,5 mg/mL) – flacon de 2,5 mL (Octostim)^{Pr} ▪ **Dispositif d'administration intranasale – solution nasale**: fioles de 2,5 mL avec tube rhinyle calibré (0,1 mg/mL)^{Pr} ▪ **Solution pour injection**: 4 µg/mL^{Pr}, 15 µg/mL^{Pr}.

SOINS INFIRMIERS

ÉVALUATION DE LA SITUATION

- Une utilisation prolongée par voie intranasale peut entraîner une tolérance aux effets du médicament. Si le médicament est administré par voie IV plus souvent que toutes les 24 à 48 heures, il y a risque de tachyphylaxie (tolérance aiguë).

Énurésie nocturne: Noter la fréquence de l'énurésie tout au long du traitement.

Diabète insipide: Mesurer à intervalles fréquents l'osmolalité de l'urine et du plasma ainsi que le volume urinaire, pour déterminer les effets du médicament. Rester à l'affût des symptômes de déshydratation (soif excessive, dessèchement de la peau et des muqueuses, tachycardie, diminution de la turgescence de la peau). Peser le patient tous les jours et suivre de près l'apparition d'un œdème.

Hémophilie:

- Suivre les résultats des tests suivants: taux du facteur VIII de coagulation, de l'antigène du facteur VIII et du cofacteur de la ristocétine du facteur VII (facteur de von Willebrand). On peut également suivre les résultats des tests du temps de thromboplastinoformation partiel et du temps de saignement. Rester à l'affût de tout signe de saignement.
- Mesurer la pression artérielle et le pouls durant la perfusion IV.
- Effectuer le bilan quotidien des ingesta et des excreta et ajuster la consommation de liquides (particulièrement chez les enfants et les personnes âgées) afin d'éviter l'hyperhydratation chez les patients recevant la desmopressine pour le traitement de l'hémophilie.

TOXICITÉ ET SURDOSAGE:

- Les signes et les symptômes de l'intoxication hydrique sont notamment la confusion, la somnolence, les céphalées, le gain pondéral, les difficultés de miction, les convulsions et le coma.
- Pour traiter le surdosage, réduire la dose et, si les symptômes sont graves, administrer du furosémide.

DIAGNOSTICS INFIRMIERS POSSIBLES

- Déficit de volume liquidien (Indications).
- Excès de volume liquidien (Réactions indésirables).
- Connaissances insuffisantes sur le traitement médicamenteux (Enseignement au patient et à ses proches).

INTERVENTIONS INFIRMIÈRES

- L'effet antidiurétique de la desmopressine administrée par voie IV est 10 fois plus puissant que celui de la desmopressine par voie intranasale.

PO: Amorcer l'administration de la dose par voie orale 12 heures après avoir administré la dernière dose par voie intranasale. Suivre de près la réponse du patient.

Diabète insipide: On peut administrer la desmopressine par IV directe, par voie IM ou par voie SC pour tirer profit de son effet antidiurétique.

Hémophilie: Pour prévenir l'hémorragie, il faut administrer la dose parentérale de desmopressine par perfusion IV. Si elle est utilisée avant une intervention chirurgicale, elle doit être administrée 30 minutes avant l'intervention.

IV directe: Pour traiter le diabète insipide, administrer la dose en 1 minute.

Perfusion intermittente: Pour administrer une perfusion aux adultes et aux enfants dont le poids > 10 kg, diluer la dose dans 50 mL de solution de NaCl 0,9 %; pour l'administrer aux enfants < 10 kg, la diluer dans 10 mL. Consulter les directives de chaque fabricant avant de reconstituer la préparation.

Vitesse d'administration: Chez le patient hémophile, la perfusion doit se faire lentement, en 15 à 30 minutes.

Voie intranasale: Si la dose par voie intranasale est administrée avant une intervention chirurgicale, l'administrer 2 heures avant l'intervention.

ENSEIGNEMENT AU PATIENT ET À SES PROCHES

- Recommander au patient de communiquer avec un professionnel de la santé si les saignements ne sont pas réprimés ou si les symptômes suivants se manifestent: céphalées, dyspnée, brûlures d'estomac, nausées, crampes abdominales, douleurs vulvaires, congestion ou irritation nasales graves.
- Mettre en garde le patient contre la consommation d'alcool pendant le traitement par ce médicament.

Diabète insipide:

- Montrer au patient comment administrer la desmopressine par voie intranasale. Le médicament est fourni avec une pipette souple graduée (tube rhinyle gradué). Aspirer la solution dans le tube. Introduire une extrémité dans la narine, souffler dans l'autre extrémité pour déposer la solution profondément dans la cavité nasale. On peut attacher une seringue remplie d'air au tube pour administrer le médicament aux enfants, aux nourrissons ou aux patients insensibles à la douleur. Rincer le tube gradué à l'eau après utilisation.
- Avant d'utiliser le vaporisateur intranasal pour la première fois, on doit amorcer la pompe par 4 poussées. Prévenir le patient qu'il doit respecter le nombre de vaporisations recommandé sur l'étiquette, car s'il dépasse le nombre prescrit, les vaporisations suivantes pourraient ne pas délivrer des doses exactes. Lui expliquer qu'il ne doit pas transvider la solution restante dans un autre flacon.
- Si le patient n'a pu prendre le médicament au moment habituel, lui conseiller de le prendre dès que possible, à moins qu'il ne soit presque l'heure prévue pour la dose suivante. Le prévenir qu'il ne doit jamais remplacer une dose manquée par une double dose.
- Expliquer au patient que la rhinite ou l'infection des voies respiratoires supérieures peuvent diminuer l'efficacité de ce traitement. Lui conseiller de signaler à un professionnel de la santé toute augmentation de la diurèse. Une nouvelle adaptation des doses pourrait s'avérer nécessaire.
- Conseiller au patient souffrant de diabète insipide de toujours porter sur lui une pièce d'identité où sont inscrits son problème de santé et son traitement médicamenteux.

VÉRIFICATION DE L'EFFICACITÉ THÉRAPEUTIQUE

L'efficacité du traitement peut être démontrée par: la diminution de la fréquence de l'énurésie nocturne ■ la diminution du volume urinaire ■ le soulagement de la polydipsie ■ l'augmentation de l'osmolalité de l'urine ■ la prévention de l'hémorragie chez le patient hémophile. ✳

DÉSOGESTREL,

voir Contraceptifs hormonaux

DÉSONIDE,

voir Corticostéroïdes (topiques)

DÉSOXIMÉTASONE,

voir Corticostéroïdes (topiques)

DEXAMÉTHASONE,

voir Corticostéroïdes (voie générale)

DEXRAZOXANE

Zinecard

CLASSIFICATION:

Antidote (cardioprotecteur)

Grossesse – catégorie C

INDICATIONS

Diminution de l'incidence et de la gravité de la cardiomyopathie attribuable à la doxorubicine chez les femmes atteintes du cancer du sein qui ont reçu une dose cumulative de 300 mg/m^2 de doxorubicine et qui continuent leur traitement.

MÉCANISME D'ACTION

Chélation intracellulaire. ***Effets thérapeutiques:*** Diminution des effets cardiotoxiques de la doxorubicine.

PHARMACOCINÉTIQUE

Absorption: Biodisponibilité à 100 % (IV).

Distribution: Inconnue.

Métabolisme et excrétion: Faible métabolisme. 42 % est éliminé dans l'urine.

Demi-vie: De 2,1 à 2,5 heures.

Profil temps-action (effet cardioprotecteur)

	DÉBUT D'ACTION	PIC	DURÉE
IV	rapide	inconnu	inconnue

CONTRE-INDICATIONS, PRÉCAUTIONS ET MISES EN GARDE

Contre-indications: Le dexrazoxane ne doit pas être utilisé en tant qu'agent antinéoplasique.

Précautions et mises en garde: **OBST., PÉD.:** Grossesse, allaitement ou enfants (l'innocuité du médicament n'a pas été établie) ■ Tout autre type de chimiothérapie, à l'exception d'une chimiothérapie par les autres anthracyclines (agents similaires à la doxorubicine) ■ Cl_{Cr} < 40 mL/min (une diminution de la dose peut être nécessaire).

RÉACTIONS INDÉSIRABLES ET EFFETS SECONDAIRES

Hémat.: aplasie médullaire.

Locaux: douleurs au point d'injection.

INTERACTIONS

Médicament-médicament: Aggravation de l'aplasie médullaire lors de l'administration concomitante d'**agents antinéoplasiques** ou d'une **radiothérapie** ■ Le dexrazoxane peut diminuer les effets antitumoraux des chimiothérapies à base de **fluorouracile** et de **cyclophosphamide**, administrées en concomitance.

VOIES D'ADMINISTRATION ET POSOLOGIE

- **IV (adultes):** 500 mg/m^2.

INSUFFISANCE RÉNALE

- **IV (ADULTES):** CHEZ LES PATIENTES DONT LA CL_{CR} EST < 40 mL/MIN, DIMINUER LA DOSE DE 50 %.

PRÉSENTATION

Poudre pour injection: flacons de 250 mg^{Pr}, flacons de 500 mg^{Pr}.

SOINS INFIRMIERS

ÉVALUATION DE LA SITUATION

Déterminer la gravité de la cardiomyopathie (cardiomégalie visible à la radiographie, râles basilaires, bruit de galop S, dyspnée, diminution de la fraction d'éjection du ventricule gauche), avant le traitement et à intervalles réguliers pendant toute sa durée.

Tests de laboratoire: Noter à intervalles fréquents, tout au long du traitement, la numération globulaire et plaquettaire. Lors du traitement par le dexrazoxane, la thrombopénie, la leucopénie et la granulopénie attribuables à la chimiothérapie peuvent être plus graves au nadir.

DIAGNOSTICS INFIRMIERS POSSIBLES

- Débit cardiaque diminué (Indications).
- Douleur aiguë (Effets secondaires).
- Connaissances insuffisantes sur le traitement médicamenteux (Enseignement au patient et à ses proches).

INTERVENTIONS INFIRMIÈRES

- La doxorubicine devrait être administrée dans les 30 minutes qui précèdent ou dans les 15 minutes qui suivent l'administration du dexrazoxane.
- Préparer la solution sous une hotte à flux laminaire. Porter des gants, une blouse et un masque pendant la manipulation de la solution IV. Jeter le matériel IV dans les contenants réservés à cet usage (voir l'annexe H).
- Ne pas administrer les solutions qui ont changé de couleur ou qui renferment des particules. Les solutions reconstituées sont stables pendant 6 heures au réfrigérateur. Jeter toute portion inutilisée.

IV directe: Reconstituer le dexrazoxane avec la solution de lactate de sodium à 0,167 molaire (M/6) pour injection fournie afin d'obtenir une concentration de 10 mg/mL. Consulter les directives de chaque fabricant avant de reconstituer la préparation.

Vitesse d'administration: Administrer lentement par bolus IV.

Perfusion intermittente: La solution reconstituée peut également être diluée avec une solution de NaCl 0,9 % ou de D5%E, pour obtenir une concentration de 1,3 à 5,0 mg/mL. La solution est stable pendant 6 heures à la température ambiante ou au réfrigérateur. Consulter les directives du fabricant avant de diluer et d'administrer la préparation. Jeter toute solution inutilisée.

Vitesse d'administration: La solution peut être administrée par perfusion IV en 5 à 15 minutes.

Incompatibilité en addition au soluté: Ne pas mélanger à d'autres médicaments.

ENSEIGNEMENT AU PATIENT ET À SES PROCHES

- Expliquer à la patiente le but de ce traitement.
- Insister sur la nécessité d'une surveillance de la fonction cardiaque.

VÉRIFICATION DE L'EFFICACITÉ THÉRAPEUTIQUE

L'efficacité du traitement peut être démontrée par: la réduction de l'incidence et de la gravité de la cardiomyopathie associée à l'administration de la doxorubicine chez les femmes atteintes d'un cancer du sein.

DEXTROAMPHÉTAMINE

Dexedrine

CLASSIFICATION:

Stimulant du système nerveux central (SNC), sympathomimétique

Grossesse – catégorie C

INDICATIONS

Traitement d'appoint de la narcolepsie ■ Traitement d'appoint des troubles déficitaires de l'attention avec hyperactivité.

MÉCANISME D'ACTION

Stimulation du SNC par la libération de la noradrénaline des terminaisons nerveuses. Les effets pharmacologiques sont les suivants: stimulation du SNC et de la respiration ■ vasoconstriction ■ mydriase (dilatation des pupilles) ■ contraction du sphincter de la vessie. ***Effets thérapeutiques:*** Augmentation de l'activité motrice et de la vigilance et diminution de la fatigue chez les patients narcoleptiques ■ Prolongation de la capacité de se concentrer en présence de troubles déficitaires de l'attention.

PHARMACOCINÉTIQUE

Absorption: Bonne (PO).

Distribution: Tous les tissus; on trouve des concentrations élevées dans le cerveau et le liquide céphalorachidien. La dextroamphétamine traverse la barrière placentaire et passe dans le lait maternel; elle peut être embryotoxique.

Métabolisme et excrétion: Faible métabolisme hépatique. L'excrétion urinaire dépend du pH. L'urine alcaline favorise la réabsorption du médicament et en prolonge l'action.

Demi-vie: De 10 à 12 heures (6,8 heures chez les enfants).

Profil temps-action (stimulation du SNC)

	Début d'action	Pic	Durée
PO	1 - 2 h	3 h	2 - 10 h
PO - LP†	inconnu	inconnu	jusqu'à 24 h

† LP = libération prolongée.

CONTRE-INDICATIONS, PRÉCAUTIONS ET MISES EN GARDE

Contre-indications: Artériosclérose au stade avancé ■ Maladie cardiovasculaire symptomatique ■ Hypertension modérée à grave ■ Hyperthyroïdie ■ Hypersensibilité ou idiosyncrasie aux amines sympathomimétiques ■ États d'agitation ■ Antécédents de toxicomanie ■ Glaucome ■ Anxiété ■ Administration concomitante ou dans les 14 jours suivant la prise d'un IMAO (risque de crise hypertensive).

Précautions et mises en garde: Maladie cardiovasculaire ■ Hypertension ■ Diabète ■ **GÉR.:** Risque accru d'effets secondaires cardiovasculaires chez les personnes âgées ou débilitées ■ Usage continu (risque de dépendance psychologique ou d'accoutumance physique) ■ Grossesse et allaitement ■ États d'hyperexcitation comprenant l'hyperthyroïdie ■ Personnalités psychotiques ■ Tendances suicidaires ou homicides ■ Hypersensibilité à la tartrazine (éviter l'administration des agents qui contiennent cet ingrédient chez les patients hypersensibles).

RÉACTIONS INDÉSIRABLES ET EFFETS SECONDAIRES

SNC: hyperactivité, insomnie, agitation, tremblements, dépression, étourdissements, céphalées, irritabilité.

CV: palpitations, tachycardie, arythmies, hypertension.

GI: anorexie, constipation, crampes, diarrhée, sécheresse de la bouche (xérostomie), goût métallique, nausées, vomissements.

GU: impuissance, augmentation de la libido.

Tég.: urticaire.

Divers: dépendance physique, dépendance psychologique.

D

INTERACTIONS

Médicament-médicament: Effets adrénergiques additifs lors de l'administration concomitante d'autres **agents adrénergiques** ■ L'administration concomitante d'**IMAO** peut déclencher une crise hypertensive ■ L'alcalinisation de l'urine (**bicarbonate de sodium**, **acétazolamide**) prolonge l'effet de la dextroamphétamine ■ L'acidification de l'urine (**chlorure d'ammonium**, doses élevées d'**acide ascorbique**) diminue l'effet de la dextroamphétamine ■ Les **phénothiazines** peuvent diminuer l'effet de la dextroamphétamine ■ Le médicament peut contrecarrer les effets des **antihypertenseurs** ■ Les **bêtabloquants** et les **antidépresseurs tricycliques**, administrés en concomitance, augmentent le risque d'effets secondaires cardiovasculaires.

Médicament-produits naturels: Le **millepertuis** peut augmenter les effets secondaires de la dextroamphétamine. L'usage concomitant n'est pas recommandé ■ Les produits contenants de la **caféine** ou s'y apparentant (**café**, **thé**, **guarana**) peuvent intensifier les effets stimulants du médicament.

VOIES D'ADMINISTRATION ET POSOLOGIE

Les capsules Spansule doivent être administrées 1 fois par jour, et les comprimés, en doses fractionnées: la première dose, au réveil, et les autres (1 ou 2) à des intervalles de 4 à 6 heures.

Trouble déficitaire de l'attention avec hyperactivité

- **PO (enfants > 6 ans)**: 5 mg, 1 ou 2 fois par jour; augmenter la dose par paliers de 5 mg/jour à des intervalles hebdomadaires. Dans les cas exceptionnels, il peut s'avérer nécessaire d'administrer plus de 40 mg/jour. On ne devrait pas utiliser les capsules à libération prolongée en traitement initial.

Narcolepsie

La posologie se situe entre 5 et 60 mg/jour. On ne devrait pas utiliser les capsules à libération prolongée en traitement initial.

- **PO (enfants > 12 ans et adultes)**: 10 mg par jour; augmenter la dose par paliers de 10 mg/jour, à des intervalles hebdomadaires, jusqu'à l'obtention d'une réponse.
- **PO (enfants de 6 à 12 ans)**: 5 mg par jour; augmenter la dose par paliers de 5 mg/jour, à des intervalles hebdomadaires, jusqu'à l'obtention d'une réponse.

PRÉSENTATION

Comprimés: 5 mg[Pr] ■ **Capsules à libération prolongée**: 10 mg[Pr], 15 mg[Pr].

SOINS INFIRMIERS

ÉVALUATION DE LA SITUATION

- Mesurer la pression artérielle, le pouls et la fréquence respiratoire avant l'administration du médicament et à intervalles réguliers pendant toute la durée du traitement.

GÉR.: L'usage est déconseillé, étant donné le risque d'hypertension, d'angine et d'infarctus du myocarde.

Trouble déficitaire de l'attention:

- Peser le patient 2 fois par semaine. Informer le médecin de toute perte de poids importante. **PÉD.**: Mesurer à intervalles réguliers la taille de l'enfant; signaler au médecin l'inhibition de la croissance.
- Chez les enfants souffrant de trouble déficitaire de l'attention, noter la durée de la capacité à maintenir l'attention, la capacité à maîtriser les impulsions, les tics moteurs et vocaux et les interactions avec autrui.

Narcolepsie:

- Observer la fréquence des épisodes de narcolepsie et les consigner dans les dossiers.
- La dextroamphétamine peut entraîner un faux sentiment d'euphorie et de bien-être. Prévoir des repos fréquents et rester à l'affût d'une dépression rebond qui risque de survenir lorsque les effets du médicament se sont épuisés.
- L'usage de la dextroamphétamine comporte des risques élevés de dépendance et d'abus. La tolérance est rapide; ne pas augmenter la dose.

Tests de laboratoire:

- La dextroamphétamine peut modifier le résultat du dosage des concentrations urinaires de stéroïdes.
- Le médicament peut élever les concentrations plasmatiques de corticostéroïdes, surtout le soir.

DIAGNOSTICS INFIRMIERS POSSIBLES

- Opérations de la pensée perturbées (Effets secondaires).
- Connaissances insuffisantes sur le traitement médicamenteux (Enseignement au patient et à ses proches).

INTERVENTIONS INFIRMIÈRES

- Administrer la plus faible dose qui s'avère efficace.
- Les capsules à libération prolongée devraient être avalées telles quelles; il ne faut pas les briser, les écraser ni les croquer.

Trouble déficitaire de l'attention:

PÉD.: Lorsque les symptômes sont maîtrisés, il est possible de réduire la dose ou de cesser le traitement au cours des mois d'été ou d'administrer le médicament les jours d'école seulement (en prévoyant un arrêt temporaire de la médication pendant les fins de semaine ou les vacances scolaires).

ENSEIGNEMENT AU PATIENT ET À SES PROCHES

- Recommander au patient de prendre le médicament au moins 6 heures avant l'heure du coucher pour prévenir les troubles du sommeil. S'il n'a pas pu le prendre au moment habituel, lui conseiller de le prendre dès que possible, mais jusqu'à 6 heures avant l'heure du coucher. Le prévenir qu'il ne doit jamais remplacer une dose manquée par une double dose. Insister sur le fait qu'il ne doit pas modifier la posologie sans consulter un professionnel de la santé au préalable. Le sevrage brusque après un traitement à des doses élevées peut provoquer une fatigue extrême et la dépression.
- Expliquer au patient que, pour diminuer la sécheresse de la bouche induite par le médicament, il devrait se rincer fréquemment la bouche et consommer de la gomme à mâcher ou des bonbons sans sucre.
- Conseiller au patient d'éviter de consommer des quantités excessives de caféine.
- Prévenir le patient que le médicament peut altérer son jugement. Lui conseiller d'être prudent lorsqu'il conduit ou lorsqu'il s'engage dans des activités qui exigent sa vigilance.
- Recommander au patient de prévenir un professionnel de la santé si les symptômes suivants s'aggravent: nervosité, agitation, insomnie, étourdissements, anorexie, sécheresse de la bouche.
- Informer le patient que le médecin peut prescrire un arrêt temporaire de la médication permettant d'évaluer les bienfaits du traitement et de diminuer la dépendance.

VÉRIFICATION DE L'EFFICACITÉ THÉRAPEUTIQUE

L'efficacité du traitement peut être démontrée par: la prolongation de la capacité de se concentrer; le traitement devrait être interrompu et réévalué à intervalles réguliers ■ la diminution des symptômes narcoleptiques. ✳

DEXTROMÉTHORPHANE

Balminil DM, Benylin DM, Buckley's DM, Delsym, Koffex, PMS-Dextrométhorphane, Robitussin DM, Sirop DM, Sucrets pastilles contre la toux, Triaminic DM, Triaminic Thin Strips Cough, Triaminic Softchews Cough

CLASSIFICATION:

Antitussif

Grossesse – catégorie C

INDICATIONS

Soulagement symptomatique de la toux due à des infections virales mineures des voies respiratoires supérieures ou à l'inhalation d'irritants ■ Soulagement très efficace de la toux sèche non productive ■ Ingrédient qui entre souvent dans la composition des préparations en vente libre contre la toux et le rhume.

MÉCANISME D'ACTION

Suppression du réflexe tussigène grâce à un effet direct sur le centre de la toux, situé dans le bulbe rachidien. Le dextrométhorphane s'apparente aux opioïdes de par sa structure, mais il est dépourvu de propriétés analgésiques. ***Effets thérapeutiques:*** Soulagement de la toux sèche irritante.

PHARMACOCINÉTIQUE

Absorption: Le médicament est rapidement absorbé depuis le tractus gastro-intestinal. L'absorption de la préparation à libération prolongée est lente.

Distribution: Inconnue. Le médicament traverse probablement la barrière placentaire et passe dans le lait maternel.

Métabolisme et excrétion: L'agent est transformé en un métabolite actif, le dextrorphane. Le dextrométhorphane et le dextrorphane sont excrétés par les reins.

Demi-vie: Inconnue.

Profil temps-action (suppression de la toux)

	DÉBUT D'ACTION	PIC	DURÉE
PO	15 – 30 min	inconnu	3 - 6 h
PO – LP†	inconnu	inconnu	9 - 12 h

† LP = libération prolongée.

CONTRE-INDICATIONS, PRÉCAUTIONS ET MISES EN GARDE

Contre-indications: Hypersensibilité ■ Patients ayant reçu des IMAO au cours des 3 semaines précédentes ■ Les patients ayant une hypersensibilité ou une intolérance à l'alcool, à l'aspartame, à la saccharine, au sucre ou à la tartrazine doivent éviter les associations de médicaments contenant ces substances.

Précautions et mises en garde: Toux qui dure depuis plus de 1 semaine ou qui s'accompagne de fièvre, d'hémoptysie, d'éruptions cutanées, de maux de tête persistants ou d'un mal de gorge intense (il est conseillé de consulter un professionnel de la santé au préalable) ■ Patients prenant des ISRS ou d'autres médicaments ayant des effets sérotoninergiques, comme la sibutramine ■ Toux chronique productive ■ Diabète (certains produits contiennent du sucrose) ■ **Obst.**: Précédents d'utilisation sans danger ■ Allaitement et enfants < 2 ans (l'innocuité du médicament n'a pas été établie).

RÉACTIONS INDÉSIRABLES ET EFFETS SECONDAIRES

SNC: *dose élevée* – étourdissements, sédation.
GI: nausées.

INTERACTIONS

Médicament-médicament: Les **IMAO**, les **ISRS** et les autres **médicaments ayant des effets sérotoninergiques** (comme la **sibutramine**), administrés en même temps, peuvent déclencher le syndrome sérotoninergique (nausées, confusion, modifications de la pression artérielle); l'usage concomitant est déconseillé ■ Dépression additive du SNC lors de l'usage concomitant d'**antihistaminiques**, d'**alcool**, d'**antidépresseurs**, d'**hypnosédatifs** et d'**opioïdes** ■ L'**amiodarone**, la **fluoxétine** ou la **quinidine** peuvent élever les concentrations sanguines de dextrométhorphane et augmenter les réactions indésirables.

VOIES D'ADMINISTRATION ET POSOLOGIE

- **PO (adultes et enfants ≥ 12 ans)**: De 10 à 20 mg, toutes les 4 heures, ou 30 mg, toutes les 6 à 8 heures, ou 60 mg de la préparation à libération prolongée, 2 fois par jour (ne pas dépasser 120 mg par jour).
- **PO (enfants de 6 à 11 ans)**: De 5 à 10 mg, toutes les 4 heures, ou 15 mg, toutes les 6 à 8 heures, ou 30 mg de la préparation à libération prolongée, toutes les 12 heures (ne pas dépasser 60 mg par jour).
- **PO (enfants de 2 à 5 ans)**: De 2,5 à 5 mg, toutes les 4 heures, ou 7,5 mg, toutes les 6 à 8 heures, ou 15 mg de la préparation à libération prolongée, toutes les 12 heures (ne pas dépasser 30 mg par jour).

PRÉSENTATION

Pastilles: 5 mg[VL], 15 mg[VL] ■ **Bandes minces**: 7,5 mg[VL] ■ **Comprimés**: 7,5 mg[VL] ■ **Liquide**: 7,5 mg/5 mL[VL], 15 mg/5 mL[VL] ■ **Suspension à libération prolongée**: 15 mg/5 mL[VL], 30 mg/5 mL[VL] ■ **En association avec**: antihistaminiques, antipyrétiques, décongestionnants et expectorants contenus dans les préparations antitussives et les préparations contre le rhume[VL]. Voir l'annexe U.

SOINS INFIRMIERS

ÉVALUATION DE LA SITUATION

Évaluer la fréquence et la nature de la toux, ausculter le murmure vésiculaire et noter la quantité et le type d'expectorations. Sauf contre-indication, maintenir la consommation de liquides entre 1 500 et 2 000 mL par jour afin de diminuer la viscosité des sécrétions bronchiques.

DIAGNOSTICS INFIRMIERS POSSIBLES

- Dégagement inefficace des voies respiratoires (Indications).
- Connaissances insuffisantes sur le traitement médicamenteux (Enseignement au patient et à ses proches).

INTERVENTIONS INFIRMIÈRES

- NE PAS CONFONDRE BENYLIN (DEXTROMÉTHORPHANE) AVEC BENADRYL (DIPHENHYDRAMINE).
- Une dose de dextrométhorphane de 15 à 30 mg est équivalente en termes d'effet antitussif à une dose de codéine de 8 à 15 mg.
- Bien agiter la suspension orale avant de l'administrer.

ENSEIGNEMENT AU PATIENT ET À SES PROCHES

- Expliquer au patient que pour tousser efficacement il doit s'asseoir et prendre plusieurs respirations profondes avant de tousser.
- Expliquer au patient que, pour calmer la toux, il doit éviter les agents irritants comme la fumée de cigarette ou autres fumées et la poussière. Lui conseiller d'humidifier l'air de la pièce, de prendre souvent des gorgées d'eau et de sucer des bonbons durs sans sucre pour diminuer la fréquence des accès de toux sèche et irritante.
- Recommander au patient d'éviter de boire de l'alcool et de prendre d'autres dépresseurs du SNC en même temps que le dextrométhorphane; des décès sont survenus.
- Prévenir le patient que le dextrométhorphane peut parfois provoquer des étourdissements. Lui conseiller de ne pas conduire et d'éviter les activités qui

exigent sa vigilance jusqu'à ce qu'on ait la certitude que le médicament n'entraîne pas cet effet chez lui.

- Recommander au patient de prévenir un professionnel de la santé si la toux persiste au-delà de 1 semaine ou si elle s'accompagne de fièvre, de douleurs thoraciques, de céphalées persistantes ou de rash.

VÉRIFICATION DE L'EFFICACITÉ THÉRAPEUTIQUE

L'efficacité du traitement peut être démontrée par: la diminution de la fréquence et de l'intensité de la toux, sans suppression du réflexe tussigène.

DIAZÉPAM

Apo-Diazépam, Diastat, Diazemuls, Novo-Dipam, PMS-Diazépam, Valium

CLASSIFICATION:

Anticonvulsivant, anxiolytique et hypnosédatif, relaxant musculosquelettique à action centrale (benzodiazépine)

Grossesse – catégorie D

INDICATIONS

Traitement de l'anxiété ■ Relaxation des muscles squelettiques ■ Sédation préopératoire (effet anesthésique léger et amnésie antérograde) ■ Sédation avant une intervention chirurgicale (enfants) ■ Traitement de l'épilepsie ■ Traitement de l'état de mal épileptique et des convulsions non maîtrisées ■ Traitement des symptômes du sevrage alcoolique. **Usages non approuvés:** Sédation consciente ■ Traitement des convulsions fébriles ■ Traitement de l'insomnie ■ Traitement des tremblements ■ Traitement des troubles de panique.

MÉCANISME D'ACTION

Dépression du SNC, probablement par la potentialisation de l'activité neuro-inhibitrice de l'acide gamma-aminobutyrique (GABA) ■ Relaxation musculosquelettique par inhibition des voies polysynaptiques afférentes de la moelle épinière ■ Propriétés anticonvulsivantes attribuables à une inhibition présynaptique accrue. ***Effets thérapeutiques:*** Soulagement de l'anxiété ■ Sédation ■ Amnésie ■ Relaxation des muscles squelettiques ■ Suppression des crises d'épilepsie.

PHARMACOCINÉTIQUE

Absorption: Bonne (> 60 %) (PO); lente et imprévisible (IM); bonne (90 %) (IR).

Distribution: Tout l'organisme. Le diazépam traverse les barrières hématoencéphalique et placentaire et passe dans le lait maternel.

Métabolisme et excrétion: Métabolisme hépatique; certains métabolites actifs ont des effets dépresseurs du SNC. Élimination rénale sous forme de métabolites.

Demi-vie: *Nouveau-nés:* de 50 à 95 heures; *enfants (de 1 mois à 2 ans):* de 40 à 50 heures; *enfants (de 2 à 12 ans):* de 15 à 21 heures; *enfants (de 12 à 16 ans):* de 18 à 20 heures; *adultes:* de 20 à 80 heures (molécule mère); de 40 à 120 heures (métabolites actifs).

Profil temps-action (sédation)

	DÉBUT D'ACTION	PIC	DURÉE
PO	30 - 60 min	1 - 2 h	jusqu'à 24 h
IM	moins de 20 min	0,5 - 1,5 h	inconnue
IV	1 - 5 min	15 - 30 min	15 - 60 min†
IR	2 - 10 min	1 - 2 h	4 - 12 h

† En cas d'état de mal épileptique, la durée de l'effet anticonvulsivant est de 15 à 20 minutes.

CONTRE-INDICATIONS, PRÉCAUTIONS ET MISES EN GARDE

Contre-indications: Hypersensibilité au diazépam ou à d'autres benzodiazépines ■ Glaucome à angle fermé ■ Glaucome à angle ouvert non traité ■ Myasthénie grave ■ Hypersensibilité ou intolérance à l'alcool, au propylèneglycol ou à la tartrazine contenus dans certaines préparations.

Précautions et mises en garde: Coma ■ Dépression préexistante du SNC ■ Maladie respiratoire chronique ■ Dysfonctionnement hépatique ■ Insuffisance rénale grave ■ Antécédents de tentatives de suicide ou de toxicomanie ■ **GÉR.:** Les benzodiazépines à longue durée d'action provoquent une sédation prolongée (réduire la dose ou utiliser une benzodiazépine qui n'est pas considérée comme dangereuse pour cette population) ■ **OBST.:** L'innocuité du médicament n'a pas été établie; l'usage prolongé pendant la grossesse peut entraîner des symptômes de sevrage chez le nouveau-né ■ **ALLAITEMENT:** Le médicament passe dans le lait maternel, donc risque d'accumulation chez les nouveau-nés ■ **PÉD.:** Accumulation possible de métabolites chez le nouveau-né.

RÉACTIONS INDÉSIRABLES ET EFFETS SECONDAIRES

SNC: étourdissements, somnolence, léthargie, dépression, sensation de tête légère, céphalées, excitation paradoxale.

ORLO: vision trouble.

Resp.: dépression respiratoire.

CV: hypotension (voie IV seulement).
GI: constipation, diarrhée, nausées, vomissements.
Tég.: rash.
Locaux: douleurs (voie IM), phlébite (voie IV), thrombose veineuse.
Divers: dépendance physique, dépendance psychologique, tolérance aux effets du médicament.

D

INTERACTIONS

Médicament-médicament: Dépression additive du SNC lors de l'usage concomitant d'**alcool**, d'**antidépresseurs**, d'**antihistaminiques** et d'**opioïdes** ■ La **cimétidine**, la **clarithromycine**, les **contraceptifs oraux**, le **disulfirame**, l'**érythromycine**, le **fluconazole**, la **fluoxétine**, l'**isoniazide**, l'**itraconazole**, le **kétoconazole**, le **métoprolol**, le **propoxyphène**, le **propranolol** ou l'**acide valproïque** peuvent ralentir le métabolisme du diazépam et en augmenter les effets ■ Le diazépam peut diminuer l'efficacité de la **lévodopa** ■ La **rifampine** ou les **barbituriques** peuvent accélérer le métabolisme du diazépam et en diminuer l'efficacité ■ La **théophylline** peut diminuer les effets sédatifs du diazépam ■ L'**amprenavir**, le **fosamprenavir**, l'**indinavir**, le **nelfinavir**, le **ritonavir** et le **saquinavir** augmentent l'effet du diazépam.
Médicament-aliments: Le **jus de pamplemousse** pris en concomitance élève les concentrations sanguines du médicament.
Médicament-produits naturels: Le **kava**, la **valériane** et la **camomille** peuvent accentuer la dépression du SNC.

VOIES D'ADMINISTRATION ET POSOLOGIE

Anxiolytique, anticonvulsivant

- **PO, IM, IV (adultes)**: De 2 à 10 mg, de 2 à 4 fois par jour.

Administration avant une cardioversion

- **IV (adultes)**: De 5 à 15 mg, de 10 à 20 minutes avant l'intervention.

Administration avant une intervention chirurgicale

- **IM, IV (adultes)**: De 2,5 à 10 mg, de 30 minutes à 1 heure avant l'intervention.

Sédation avant une intervention

- **PO (enfants > 1 mois)**: De 0,2 à 0,3 mg/kg (au maximum, 10 mg/dose), de 45 à 60 minutes avant l'intervention.

État de mal épileptique ou épisodes convulsifs aigus

- **IV (adultes)**: Ne pas utiliser l'émulsion stérile pour injection. Doses de 5 à 10 mg; on peut répéter l'administration de cette dose toutes les 10 à 15 minutes jusqu'à concurrence de 30 mg; on peut administrer une nouvelle dose dans les 2 à 4 heures suivantes (par voie IM, si la voie IV n'est pas accessible).
- **IM, IV (enfants ≥ 5 ans)**: De 0,05 à 0,3 mg/kg/dose, administré en 3 à 5 minutes; on peut répéter l'administration de cette dose toutes les 10 à 15 minutes jusqu'à concurrence de 10 mg; on peut administrer une nouvelle dose dans les 2 à 4 heures suivantes (par voie IM, si la voie IV n'est pas accessible).
- **IM, IV (enfants de 1 mois à 5 ans)**: De 0,05 à 0,3 mg/kg/dose, administré en 3 à 5 minutes; on peut répéter l'administration de cette dose toutes les 10 à 15 minutes jusqu'à concurrence de 5 mg; on peut administrer une nouvelle dose dans les 2 à 4 heures suivantes (par voie IM, si la voie IV n'est pas accessible).
- **IV (nouveau-nés)**: De 0,1 à 0,3 mg/kg/dose, administré en 3 à 5 minutes; on peut répéter l'administration de cette dose toutes les 10 à 15 minutes jusqu'à concurrence de 2 mg.
- **IR (adultes et enfants ≥ 12 ans)**: 0,2 mg/kg; on peut répéter l'administration de cette dose de 4 à 12 heures plus tard.
- **IR (enfants de 6 à 11 ans)**: 0,3 mg/kg; on peut répéter l'administration de cette dose de 4 à 12 heures plus tard.
- **IR (enfants de 2 à 5 ans)**: 0,5 mg/kg; on peut répéter l'administration de cette dose de 4 à 12 heures plus tard.

Relaxation des muscles squelettiques

- **PO (adultes)**: De 2 à 10 mg, de 2 à 4 fois par jour.
- **PO (personnes âgées ou patients débilités)**: Initialement de 2 à 2,5 mg, 1 ou 2 fois par jour.
- **IM, IV (adultes)**: De 5 à 10 mg; on peut répéter l'administration de cette dose de 2 à 4 heures plus tard.
- **IM, IV (personnes âgées ou patients débilités)**: De 2 à 5 mg; on peut répéter l'administration de cette dose de 2 à 4 heures plus tard.

Sevrage alcoolique

- **PO (adultes)**: 10 mg, 3 ou 4 fois par jour dans les 24 premières heures; diminuer la dose jusqu'à 5 mg, 3 ou 4 fois par jour, selon les besoins.
- **IM, IV (adultes)**: 10 mg au départ, puis de 5 à 10 mg, de 3 à 4 heures plus tard, selon les besoins.

PRÉSENTATION (version générique disponible)

Comprimés: 2 mg^T\C^, 5 mg^T\C^, 10 mg^T\C^ ■ **Solution orale**: 1 mg/ml^T\C^ ■ **Solution pour injection**: 5 mg/mL (contient 10 % d'alcool et 40 % de propylèneglycol)^T\C^ ■ **Gel pour usage rectal**: 5 mg^T\C^, 10 mg^T\C^ (taille de l'embout rectal: 4,4 cm), 15 mg^T\C^ (taille de l'embout rectal: 6 cm) ■ **Émulsion stérile pour injection**: 5 mg/mL (contient des phospholipides d'œuf et d'huile de soya)^T\C^.

SOINS INFIRMIERS

ÉVALUATION DE LA SITUATION

- Mesurer la pression artérielle, le pouls et la fréquence respiratoire avant le traitement, à intervalles réguliers pendant toute sa durée et à intervalles fréquents durant le traitement par voie IV.
- Observer le point d'injection IV à intervalles fréquents durant l'administration, car le diazépam peut provoquer une phlébite ou une thrombose veineuse.

GÉR.: Déterminer les effets au niveau du SNC et le risque de chutes. Mettre en place les mesures de prévention des chutes.

- Le traitement prolongé avec des doses élevées peut entraîner une dépendance psychologique ou physique. Limiter la quantité de médicament dont le patient peut disposer. Chez les patients déprimés, rester à l'affût des tendances suicidaires.

Anxiété: Noter le degré d'anxiété et de sédation (ataxie, étourdissements, troubles d'élocution), avant le traitement et à intervalles réguliers pendant toute sa durée.

Crises d'épilepsie: Observer et consigner dans les dossiers l'intensité, la durée et les caractéristiques de la crise. La dose initiale de diazépam permet de maîtriser les crises pendant 15 à 20 minutes après l'administration. Prendre les précautions qui s'imposent dans ce cas.

Spasmes musculaires: Suivre de près les spasmes musculaires, déterminer la douleur qui les accompagne et la limite des mouvements avant l'administration du diazépam et pendant toute la durée du traitement.

Sevrage alcoolique: En cas de sevrage alcoolique, suivre de près les tremblements, l'agitation, les crises de delirium et les hallucinations. Protéger le patient contre les accidents.

Tests de laboratoire: Noter les résultats des tests de la fonction hépatique et rénale ainsi que la numération globulaire à intervalles réguliers tout au long du traitement.

DIAGNOSTICS INFIRMIERS POSSIBLES

- Anxiété (Indications).
- Mobilité physique réduite (Indications).
- Risque d'accident (Effets secondaires).

INTERVENTIONS INFIRMIÈRES

- NE PAS CONFONDRE LE DIAZÉPAM AVEC DITROPAN (OXYLRITININE).
- Demander au patient de rester au lit et l'observer étroitement pendant au moins 3 heures après l'administration du diazépam par voie parentérale.
- Si on doit administrer par voie parentérale un analgésique opioïde en même temps que le diazépam, diminuer la dose de ce dernier de $^1/_3$ et la majorer ensuite en fonction de l'effet.

PO: On peut écraser les comprimés et les administrer avec des aliments ou de l'eau si le patient éprouve des difficultés de déglutition.

IM: Les injections IM sont douloureuses et l'absorption est imprévisible. Si l'on a recours à cette voie d'administration, injecter la solution profondément dans le muscle deltoïde pour favoriser au maximum l'absorption du médicament.

IV: Garder le matériel de réanimation à portée de la main lors de l'administration du diazépam par voie IV.

IV directe: Ne pas diluer ni mélanger le diazépam à d'autres médicaments. S'il est impossible d'administrer le diazépam par intraveineuse directe, l'administrer dans une tubulure aussi près que possible du point d'injection. On ne recommande pas la perfusion continue, car les solutions IV ont tendance à précipiter et le diazépam peut être adsorbé par les sacs et les tubulures de perfusion. L'injection peut provoquer une brûlure et l'irritation veineuses. Ne pas injecter dans de petites veines.

Vitesse d'administration: Administrer lentement à un débit minimal de 5 mg/min. Chez les nourrissons et les enfants, administrer la dose totale en 3 minutes au minimum. Une administration rapide peut entraîner l'apnée, l'hypotension, la bradycardie ou l'arrêt cardiaque.

Association compatible dans la même seringue: cimétidine.

Associations incompatibles dans la même seringue: glycopyrrolate ▪ héparine ▪ nalbuphine ▪ sufentanil.

Compatibilité (tubulure en Y): cefmétazole ▪ dobutamine ▪ nafcilline ▪ sufentanil.

Incompatibilité (tubulure en Y): atracurium ▪ céfépime ▪ diltiazem ▪ fluconazole ▪ foscarnet ▪ héparine ▪ hydromorphone ▪ méropénem ▪ pancuronium ▪ potassium, chlorure de ▪ propofol ▪ vécuronium ▪ vitamines du complexe B avec C.

Émulsion stérile pour injection: Utiliser une technique aseptique rigoureuse. Ne pas diluer. L'ampoule est destinée à un usage uniservice; jeter toute portion inutilisée. Ne pas utiliser de filtres > 5 microns; le filtre limite le débit et entraîne la décomposition de l'émulsion. Administrer dans les 6 heures qui suivent l'ouverture du flacon; rincer la tubulure à la fin de l'administration.

IR:

- Ne pas répéter la dose de *Diastat* par voie rectale plus de 5 fois par mois et ne pas dépasser 1 administration, tous les 5 jours. Arrondir la dose prescrite à la dose unitaire supérieure.

D

- On a déjà administré la solution de diazépam pour injection par voie rectale. Instiller la solution par un cathéter ou une canule qui s'adapte à la seringue ou directement à partir d'une seringue de 1 mL, introduite dans le rectum jusqu'à 4 ou 5 cm. On a déjà utilisé une solution de diazépam pour injection diluée dans du propylèneglycol à 1 mg/mL.
- Ne pas diluer dans d'autres solutions, liquides IV ou médicaments.

ENSEIGNEMENT AU PATIENT ET À SES PROCHES

- Conseiller au patient de respecter rigoureusement la posologie recommandée. Le prévenir qu'il ne doit pas dépasser la dose prescrite ni augmenter la dose si elle devient moins efficace après quelques semaines, sans consulter au préalable un professionnel de la santé. Le sevrage brusque peut entraîner de l'insomnie, de l'irritabilité ou une nervosité inhabituelles ainsi que des convulsions. Insister sur le fait qu'il peut être dangereux de donner ce médicament à d'autres personnes.
- Prévenir le patient que le diazépam peut entraîner la somnolence, la maladresse ou des troubles de la marche. Lui conseiller de ne pas conduire et d'éviter les activités qui exigent sa vigilance jusqu'à ce qu'on ait la certitude que le médicament n'entraîne pas ces effets chez lui.

GÉR.: Expliquer au patient et à ses proches les mesures à prendre pour diminuer le risque de chutes à domicile.

- Recommander au patient d'éviter de boire de l'alcool et de prendre d'autres dépresseurs du SNC en même temps que le diazépam.
- Conseiller à la patiente d'informer un professionnel de la santé si elle pense être enceinte ou si elle souhaite le devenir.
- Insister sur l'importance des examens de suivi permettant d'évaluer l'efficacité du médicament.

Crises épileptiques:

- Conseiller au patient recevant un traitement anticonvulsivant de toujours porter sur lui une pièce d'identité où sont inscrits son problème de santé et son traitement médicamenteux.
- Relire attentivement avec les proches du patient le dépliant contenant le mode d'administration du gel Diastat réservé à la voie rectale, avant de l'administrer.

VÉRIFICATION DE L'EFFICACITÉ THÉRAPEUTIQUE

L'efficacité du traitement peut être démontrée par: la diminution de l'anxiété; les pleins effets anxiolytiques se manifestent après 1 à 2 semaines de traitement ■ l'amnésie à la suite d'une intervention chirurgicale ou d'un test diagnostique ■ la maîtrise des crises d'épilepsie ■ la diminution des spasmes musculaires ■ la diminution des tremblements et une idéation plus logique lors du traitement des symptômes du sevrage alcoolique.

DICLOFÉNAC

diclofénac potassique

Apo-Diclo Rapide, Novo-Difenac K, PMS-Diclofénac K, Voltaren Rapide

diclofénac sodique

Apo-Diclo, Apo-Diclo SR, Diclotec, Dom-Diclofénac, Dom-Diclofenac SR, Novo-Difenac, Novo-Difenac SR, Nu-Diclo, Nu-Diclo SR, Penta-Diclofénac, PMS-Diclofénac, PMS-Diclofénac SR, Riva-Diclofénac, Sab-Diclofénac, Taro-Diclofénac, Voltaren, Voltaren SR

diclofénac topique

Pennsaid

CLASSIFICATION:

Analgésique non opioïde, anti-inflammatoire non stéroïdien

Grossesse – catégories D (1er et 3e trimestres) et B (2e trimestre)

Pour l'usage ophtalmique, voir l'annexe N.

INDICATIONS

Traitement symptomatique des troubles inflammatoires suivants: polyarthrite rhumatoïde ■ arthrose ■ arthrose de la hanche ■ Traitement de courte durée de la douleur aiguë, d'intensité légère à modérément grave, parfois accompagnée d'inflammation ■ Traumatismes des muscles squelettiques ou des tissus mous ■ Entorses ■ Douleurs postopératoires ■ Dysménorrhée ■ **Usage topique**: Traitement des symptômes associés à l'arthrose du genou seulement.

MÉCANISME D'ACTION

Inhibition de la synthèse des prostaglandines. ***Effets thérapeutiques:*** Suppression de la douleur et de l'inflammation.

PHARMACOCINÉTIQUE

Absorption: Bonne (PO). Le diclofénac sodique est une préparation à libération retard (à enrobage entérique). Le diclofénac potassique est une préparation à libération immédiate.

Distribution: Le diclofénac traverse la barrière placentaire et passe dans le lait maternel.

Liaison aux protéines: > 99 %.
Métabolisme et excrétion: Métabolisme hépatique à > 50 %.
Demi-vie: De 1,2 à 2 heures.

Profil temps-action
(diminution de la douleur et de l'inflammation)

	DÉBUT D'ACTION	PIC	DURÉE
PO (inflammation)	de quelques jours à 1 semaine	2 semaines ou plus	inconnue
PO (douleurs)	30 min	inconnu	jusqu'à 8 h

CONTRE-INDICATIONS, PRÉCAUTIONS ET MISES EN GARDE

Contre-indications: Hypersensibilité ▪ Risque de réactions d'hypersensibilité croisée avec d'autres anti-inflammatoires non stéroïdiens incluant l'aspirine ▪ Syndrome complet ou partiel des polypes nasaux ▪ Présence d'ulcères récidivants ou d'une maladie inflammatoire évolutive ou récente du tractus gastro-intestinal (ulcère gastro-duodénal, gastrite, entérite régionale ou colite ulcéreuse) ▪ Insuffisance hépatique notable ou maladie hépatique évolutive ▪ Insuffisance rénale grave (Cl_{Cr} < 30 mL/min).
Précautions et mises en garde: Maladies cardiovasculaire, rénale ou hépatique graves ▪ Antécédents de porphyrie ▪ Patient déshydraté (risque accru d'insuffisance rénale aiguë) ▪ Antécédents d'ulcère ▪ **GÉR.**: Réduire la dose; les patients âgés peuvent être davantage prédisposés aux réactions indésirables ▪ Tendance aux saignements ou traitement anticoagulant concomitant ▪ **OBST., ALLAITEMENT, PÉD.**: L'innocuité du médicament n'a pas été établie; l'administration de cet agent n'est pas recommandée au cours de la deuxième moitié de la grossesse.

RÉACTIONS INDÉSIRABLES ET EFFETS SECONDAIRES

SNC: étourdissements, somnolence, céphalées.
CV: hypertension.
GI: HÉMORRAGIE DIGESTIVE, douleurs abdominales, dyspepsie, brûlures d'estomac, diarrhée, hépatotoxicité.
GU: insuffisance rénale aiguë, dysurie, mictions fréquentes, hématurie, néphrite, protéinurie.
Tég.: DERMATITE EXFOLIATIVE, SYNDROME DE STEVENS-JOHNSON, ÉPIDERMOLYSE NÉCROSANTE SUBAIGUË, eczéma, photosensibilité, rash.
HÉ: œdème.
Local: (application topique) dermatite de contact, peau sèche, rash.
Hémat.: allongement du temps de saignement.
Divers: réactions allergiques incluant l'ANAPHYLAXIE.

INTERACTIONS

Médicament-médicament (s'appliquent à l'administration par voie orale): L'**aspirine** peut diminuer l'efficacité du diclofénac ▪ Effets nocifs additifs sur le tractus gastro-intestinal lors de l'usage concomitant d'**aspirine**, d'autres **anti-inflammatoires non stéroïdiens**, de **colchicine**, de **corticostéroïdes** ou d'**alcool** ▪ L'usage prolongé en association avec l'**acétaminophène** peut augmenter le risque d'effets nocifs sur les reins ▪ Le diclofénac peut diminuer l'efficacité des **diurétiques**, des **antihypertenseurs**, de l'**insuline** ou des **hypoglycémiants** ▪ Le diclofénac élève les concentrations sériques de **digoxine** (adapter la posologie, au besoin) ▪ Le diclofénac peut élever les concentrations sériques de **cyclosporine**, de **lithium** ou de **méthotrexate** et le risque de toxicité associé à ces médicaments ▪ Le **probénécide** augmente le risque de toxicité associé au diclofénac ▪ Certaines **céphalosporines**, les **agents thrombolytiques**, les **agents antiplaquettaires**, l'**acide valproïque** ou les **anticoagulants**, administrés en concomitance, augmentent le risque d'hémorragie ▪ Le diclofénac augmente le risque de réactions hématologiques indésirables induites par les **antinéoplasiques** ou la **radiothérapie** ▪ L'usage concomitant de **diurétiques épargneurs de potassium** accroît le risque d'hyperkaliémie ▪ L'administration concomitante de **composés d'or** peut augmenter le risque de réactions rénales indésirables ▪ L'administration concomitante d'**anti-inflammatoires non stéroïdiens** par voie orale et topique devrait être réduite au minimum.
Médicament-produits naturels (s'appliquent à l'administration par voie orale): Risque accru de saignements lors de la prise concomitante d'**arnica,** de **camomille**, d'**ail**, de **dong quai**, de **grande camomille**, de **gingembre**, de **ginkgo biloba** et de **ginseng**.

VOIES D'ADMINISTRATION ET POSOLOGIE

Comprimés à libération immédiate et comprimés à enrobage entérique

- **PO (adultes)**: *Analgésie et traitement de la dysménorrhée* – initialement, 100 mg, puis 50 mg, 3 fois par jour, selon les besoins. *Polyarthrite rhumatoïde* – 50 mg, 3 ou 4 fois par jour; après la réponse initiale, administrer la dose la plus faible qui puisse maîtriser les symptômes (la dose d'entretien habituelle est de 25 mg, 3 fois par jour). *Arthrose* – 50 mg, 2 ou 3 fois par jour; après la réponse initiale, administrer la dose la plus faible qui puisse maîtriser les symptômes.

Comprimés à libération prolongée (SR)

- **PO (adultes)**: De 75 mg à 100 mg, 1 fois par jour. La dose quotidienne maximale est de 75 mg, 2 fois par jour.

Suppositoires

- **IR (adultes)**: On peut administrer les suppositoires à 50 ou à 100 mg en remplacement de la dernière des trois doses par voie orale de la journée. La dose quotidienne totale ne doit pas dépasser 150 mg.

Solution topique (Pennsaid)

- 40 gouttes, 4 fois par jour. Placer 10 gouttes dans la main ou directement sur le genou. Étendre uniformément sur le devant, les côtés et l'arrière du genou. Répéter l'opération jusqu'à ce qu'on ait utilisé 40 gouttes. Laisser sécher pendant plusieurs minutes. Se laver les mains après l'application.

D

PRÉSENTATION (version générique disponible)

Comprimés de diclofénac potassique à libération immédiate: 50 mg^{Pr} ■ **Comprimés de diclofénac sodique à libération retard (à enrobage entérique)**: 25 mg^{Pr}, 50 mg^{Pr} ■ **Comprimés de diclofénac sodique à libération prolongée (SR)**: 75 mg^{Pr}, 100 mg^{Pr} ■ **Suppositoires**: 50 mg^{Pr}, 100 mg^{Pr} ■ **Solution topique**: 1,5 %, 15 mL^{Pr}, 60 mL^{Pr} ■ **En association avec**: misoprostol à 200 µg (Arthrotec)^{Pr}.

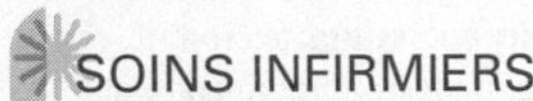

SOINS INFIRMIERS

ÉVALUATION DE LA SITUATION

- LES PATIENTS SOUFFRANT D'ASTHME, D'ALLERGIE INDUITE PAR L'ASPIRINE ET DE POLYPES NASAUX SONT DAVANTAGE PRÉDISPOSÉS À DES RÉACTIONS D'HYPERSENSIBILITÉ. SUIVRE DE PRÈS LA RHINITE, L'ASTHME ET L'URTICAIRE.

Douleurs: Suivre de près la douleur et l'amplitude des mouvements; noter le type de douleur, son siège, et son intensité, avant l'administration du diclofénac et de 30 à 60 minutes après.

Arthrite: Suivre de près les douleurs arthritiques (noter le type de douleur, son siège et son intensité) et l'amplitude des mouvements, avant l'administration du diclofénac et à intervalles réguliers pendant toute la durée du traitement.

Tests de laboratoire:

- Le diclofénac a un effet minime sur le temps de saignement et l'agrégation plaquettaire.
- Le diclofénac peut diminuer les concentrations d'hémoglobine, l'hématocrite et le nombre de leucocytes et de plaquettes.
- Vérifier les résultats des tests de la fonction hépatique dans les 8 semaines qui suivent le début du traitement par le diclofénac, puis à intervalles réguliers pendant toute sa durée. Le diclofénac peut élever les concentrations sériques de phosphatase alcaline, de LDH, d'AST et d'ALT.
- Noter les concentrations d'urée, de créatinine sérique et d'électrolytes à intervalles réguliers pendant toute la durée du traitement. Le diclofénac peut élever les concentrations sériques d'urée, de créatinine et d'électrolytes et diminuer les concentrations urinaires d'électrolytes.
- Le diclofénac peut diminuer les concentrations sériques d'acide urique et en élever les concentrations urinaires.

DIAGNOSTICS INFIRMIERS POSSIBLES

- Douleur aiguë (Indications).
- Mobilité physique réduite (Indications).
- Connaissances insuffisantes sur le traitement médicamenteux (Enseignement au patient et à ses proches).

INTERVENTIONS INFIRMIÈRES

- Des doses plus élevées que celles recommandées ne s'avèrent pas plus efficaces, mais peuvent entraîner un plus grand nombre d'effets secondaires.

PO: ADMINISTRER LE DICLOFÉNAC APRÈS LES REPAS, AVEC DES ALIMENTS OU AVEC DES ANTIACIDES CONTENANT DE L'ALUMINIUM OU DU MAGNÉSIUM POUR DIMINUER L'IRRITATION GASTRIQUE. Le patient peut prendre les deux premières doses à jeun pour un début d'action plus rapide. IL NE FAUT PAS ÉCRASER NI MÂCHER LES COMPRIMÉS À ENROBAGE ENTÉRIQUE OU À LIBÉRATION PROLONGÉE.

Solution topique: Appliquer sur une peau intacte; ne pas recouvrir la région traitée. Éviter le contact avec les yeux et les muqueuses.

Dysménorrhée: Administrer le diclofénac le plus rapidement possible dès le début des règles. Le traitement prophylactique ne s'est pas avéré efficace.

ENSEIGNEMENT AU PATIENT ET À SES PROCHES

PO:

- Conseiller au patient de prendre le diclofénac avec un grand verre d'eau et de rester en position assise pendant les 15 à 30 minutes qui suivent. S'il n'a pu prendre le médicament au moment habituel, il doit le prendre le plus rapidement possible dans les 1 à 2 heures qui suivent (s'il le prend 1 ou 2 fois par jour), ou aussitôt qu'il peut le faire, à moins qu'il ne soit presque l'heure prévue pour la dose suivante (s'il prend le médicament plus de 2 fois par jour); le prévenir qu'il ne doit jamais remplacer une dose manquée par une double dose.

- Informer le patient qu'il doit éviter de boire de l'alcool et de prendre de l'aspirine, de l'acétaminophène, d'autres anti-inflammatoires non stéroïdiens ou d'autres médicaments en vente libre en même temps que le diclofénac, sans avoir consulté au préalable un professionnel de la santé.
- Prévenir le patient que le diclofénac peut parfois provoquer de la somnolence ou des étourdissements; lui conseiller de ne pas conduire et d'éviter les activités qui exigent sa vigilance jusqu'à ce qu'on ait la certitude que le médicament n'entraîne pas ces effets chez lui.
- Conseiller au patient d'informer tous les professionnels de la santé de son traitement médicamenteux avant de se soumettre à une intervention chirurgicale ou à un autre traitement.
- Recommander au patient d'utiliser un écran solaire et des vêtements protecteurs afin de prévenir les réactions de photosensibilité.
- Recommander au patient de consulter un professionnel de la santé si les symptômes suivants se manifestent: rash, démangeaisons, troubles de la vision, acouphènes, gain pondéral, œdème, selles noires, céphalées persistantes ou syndrome pseudogrippal (frissons, fièvre, muscles endoloris, douleurs).

Solution topique: Prévenir le patient qu'il doit éviter de prendre en concomitance des anti-inflammatoires non stéroïdiens par voie orale. Lors de l'application, placer 10 gouttes dans la main ou directement sur le genou. Étendre uniformément sur le devant, les côtés et l'arrière du genou. Répéter l'opération jusqu'à ce qu'on ait utilisé 40 gouttes. Laisser sécher pendant plusieurs minutes. Se laver les mains après l'application.

VÉRIFICATION DE L'EFFICACITÉ THÉRAPEUTIQUE

L'efficacité du traitement peut être démontrée par: le soulagement de la douleur légère ou modérée ■ une mobilité accrue des articulations; les patients qui ne répondent pas à un anti-inflammatoire non stéroïdien peuvent répondre à un autre. Les effets maximaux du médicament peuvent ne se manifester qu'après 2 semaines ou plus de traitement. ✳

DICYCLOMINE

Bentylol, Formulex, Lomine, Protylol

CLASSIFICATION:

Antispasmodique (anticholinergique)

Grossesse – catégorie B

INDICATIONS

Traitement du syndrome du côlon irritable chez les patients qui ne répondent pas aux interventions habituelles (sédation/modification de l'alimentation) ■ Traitement d'appoint dans les affections gastro-intestinales organiques pour éliminer le spasme secondaire du muscle lisse (p. ex., colite, diverticulite, entérite régionale, gastrite et ulcère gastroduodénal).

D

MÉCANISME D'ACTION

La dicyclomine a un double mécanisme d'action: 1) un effet anticholinergique spécifique (effet antimuscarinique) aux sites récepteurs de l'acétylcholine (ACh); 2) un effet direct sur le muscle lisse (effet musculotrope). ***Effets thérapeutiques:*** Diminution de la motilité et du tonus GI.

PHARMACOCINÉTIQUE

Absorption: Bonne (PO et IM).
Distribution: Inconnue.
Métabolisme et excrétion: 80 % est éliminé dans l'urine et 10 %, dans les fèces.
Demi-vie: 1,8 h (phase initiale), 9-10 h (phase terminale).

Profil temps-action (effet antispasmodique)

	DÉBUT D'ACTION	PIC	DURÉE
PO, IM	inconnu	inconnu	inconnue

CONTRE-INDICATIONS, PRÉCAUTIONS ET MISES EN GARDE

Contre-indications: Hypersensibilité ■ Obstruction du tractus GI ou GU ■ Reflux gastro-œsophagien ■ Colite ulcérative grave (risque d'iléus paralytique) ■ Atonie intestinale ■ État cardiovasculaire instable ■ Glaucome ■ Myasthénie grave ■ Nourrissons < 6 mois ■ Allaitement.
Précautions et mises en garde: Température extérieure élevée (risque de prostration due à la chaleur) ■ Insuffisance hépatique ou rénale ■ Atteinte du système nerveux autonome associée à une neuropathie ■ Hyperthyroïdisme ■ Maladie cardiovasculaire (hypertension, coronaropathie, insuffisance cardiaque congestive, tachyarythmie cardiaque) ■ Hyperplasie bénigne de la prostate ■ **GÉR.**: Sensibilité accrue aux anticholinergiques ■ **OBST.**: L'innocuité du médicament n'a pas été établie.

RÉACTIONS INDÉSIRABLES ET EFFETS SECONDAIRES

SNC: confusion (accrue chez les personnes âgées), étourdissements, sensation de tête légère (voie IM seulement).

D

ORLO: vision trouble, pression intraoculaire accrue.
CV: palpitations, tachycardie.
GI: ILÉUS PARALYTIQUE, constipation, brûlures d'estomac, diminution de la salivation, sécheresse de la bouche (xérostomie), nausées, vomissements.
GU: impuissance, difficultés de miction, rétention urinaire.
Tég.: sécrétion diminuée de sueur.
End.: diminution de la lactation.
Locaux: douleurs et rougeurs au point d'injection.
Divers: réactions allergiques, comprenant l'ANAPHYLAXIE.

INTERACTIONS

Médicament-médicament: Effets anticholinergiques additifs lors de l'administration concomitante d'autres **anticholinergiques**, notamment les **antihistaminiques**, la **quinidine** et le **disopyramide** ■ Risque de modification de l'absorption d'autres **médicaments administrés par voie orale** à cause du ralentissement de la motilité du tractus GI ■ Les **antiacides** ou les **antidiarrhéiques adsorbants** diminuent l'absorption des anticholinergiques ■ Risque d'aggravation des lésions de la muqueuse GI chez les patients prenant des comprimés de **chlorure de potassium** par voie orale ■ Risque accru de réactions cardiovasculaires indésirables lors d'une anesthésie au **cyclopropane**.

VOIES D'ADMINISTRATION ET POSOLOGIE

- **PO (adultes)**: De 10 à 20 mg, 3 ou 4 fois par jour (jusqu'à concurrence de 160 mg/jour).
- **PO (enfants de 2 à 12 ans)**: 10 mg, 3 ou 4 fois par jour; adapter la posologie selon la tolérance.
- **PO (enfants de 6 mois à 2 ans)**: De 5 à 10 mg, 3 ou 4 fois par jour; adapter la posologie selon la tolérance. Ne pas excéder 40 mg/jour.
- **IM (adultes)**: 20 mg, toutes les 4 à 6 heures; adapter la posologie selon la tolérance. Ne pas excéder 80 mg/jour.

PRÉSENTATION

Comprimés: 10 mg^{Phc}, 20 mg^{Phc} ■ **Capsules**: 10 mg^{Phc} ■ **Sirop**: 10 mg/5 mL^{Phc} ■ **Solution pour injection**: 10 mg/mL^{Phc}.

SOINS INFIRMIERS

ÉVALUATION DE LA SITUATION

- Rester à l'affût des symptômes du syndrome du côlon irritable (crampes abdominales, alternance de constipation et de diarrhée, mucus dans les selles), avant le traitement et à intervalles réguliers pendant toute sa durée.
- Rechercher systématiquement la distention abdominale; ausculter les bruits intestinaux. Si la constipation pose problème, l'augmentation de la quantité de liquides et l'ajout de fibres à l'alimentation peuvent aider à soulager les effets constipants du médicament.
- Suivre de près les ingesta et les excreta, risque de rétention urinaire.

Tests de laboratoire: L'agent contrecarre les effets de la pentagastrine et de l'histamine au cours de la mesure de la sécrétion d'acide gastrique. Ne pas administrer l'agent dans les 24 heures qui précèdent ce test.

TOXICITÉ ET SURDOSAGE: Les symptômes anticholinergiques graves peuvent être renversés par la physostigmine ou la néostigmine.

DIAGNOSTICS INFIRMIERS POSSIBLES

- Douleur aiguë (Indications).
- Diarrhée (Indications).

INTERVENTIONS INFIRMIÈRES

PO: Administrer la dicyclomine de 30 minutes à 1 heure avant les repas.
IM: Suivre de près le patient après l'administration du médicament; risque de sensation de tête légère et d'irritation au point de ponction.

ENSEIGNEMENT AU PATIENT ET À SES PROCHES

- Inciter le patient à prendre la dicyclomine en suivant rigoureusement les recommandations du médecin et à ne pas dépasser la dose prescrite. S'il n'a pas pu prendre le médicament au moment habituel, il doit le prendre dès que possible, à moins que ce ne soit presque l'heure prévue pour la dose suivante.
- La dicyclomine peut provoquer des étourdissements et une vision trouble. Conseiller au patient de ne pas conduire et de ne pas s'engager dans d'autres activités qui exigent sa vigilance jusqu'à ce qu'on ait la certitude que le médicament n'entraîne pas ces effets chez lui.
- Expliquer au patient que pour soulager la sécheresse de la bouche, il doit se rincer souvent la bouche, consommer de la gomme à mâcher et des bonbons sans sucre et pratiquer une bonne hygiène buccale. Lui recommander de consulter un professionnel de la santé au sujet de l'utilisation de substituts de salive, si la sécheresse de la bouche persiste pendant plus de 2 semaines.
- Recommander au patient qui prend la dicyclomine de changer lentement de position pour réduire l'hypotension orthostatique induite par le médicament.

- Conseiller au patient d'éviter les températures extrêmes. Lui expliquer que ce médicament diminue la sécrétion de sueur et peut accroître le risque de coup de chaleur.
- Recommander au patient de consulter un professionnel de la santé avant de prendre des médicaments en vente libre pendant ce traitement.
- Conseiller au patient de prévenir immédiatement un professionnel de la santé s'il éprouve des douleurs oculaires ou une sensibilité accrue à la lumière. Lui expliquer qu'il est important de se faire examiner la vue à intervalles réguliers tout au long du traitement.

VÉRIFICATION DE L'EFFICACITÉ THÉRAPEUTIQUE

L'efficacité du traitement peut être démontrée par: la diminution des symptômes du syndrome du côlon irritable. ✳

DIDANOSINE

Synonyme: ddI

Videx, Videx EC

CLASSIFICATION:

Antirétroviral (inhibiteur nucléosidique de la transcriptase inverse)

Grossesse – catégorie B

INDICATIONS

Traitement des infections par le VIH en association avec d'autres agents antirétroviraux. **Usages non approuvés**: En association avec d'autres antirétroviraux, prophylaxie après exposition accidentelle au VIH.

MÉCANISME D'ACTION

Inhibition de la réplication virale par l'action sur la transcriptase inverse qui transcrit dans le cytoplasme l'ARN viral en ADN. La didanosine doit être transformée à l'intérieur des cellules en sa forme active par phosphorylation. ***Effets thérapeutiques:*** Augmentation du nombre de cellules CD4 et diminution de la charge virale pouvant se traduire par une réduction de l'incidence des infections opportunistes et un ralentissement de l'évolution de l'infection par le VIH.

PHARMACOCINÉTIQUE

Absorption: La didanosine se décompose rapidement dans un milieu gastrique acide. L'absorption est de 33 à 37 % grâce aux capsules entérosolubles ou aux tampons des comprimés et de la solution préparée, qui neutralisent l'acide gastrique.

Distribution: Chez l'adulte, la concentration dans le liquide céphalorachidien correspond à 21 % de la concentration plasmatique.

Métabolisme et excrétion: Métabolisme par les mêmes voies que les purines endogènes; 55 % est éliminé par les reins (18 % à l'état inchangé; l'excrétion urinaire semble moindre chez les enfants).

Demi-vie: 1,6 heure (0,8 heure chez les enfants).

Profil temps-action

	DÉBUT D'ACTION	PIC	DURÉE
PO	inconnu	0,25 – 1,5 h	12 h

CONTRE-INDICATIONS, PRÉCAUTIONS ET MISES EN GARDE

Contre-indications: Hypersensibilité.

Précautions et mises en garde: Obésité, femmes, prise prolongée d'un inhibiteur nucléosidique (il peut s'agir de facteurs de risque d'acidose lactique ou d'hépatomégalie) ■ Antécédents de goutte ■ Patients suivant un régime hyposodé (les comprimés contiennent 264,5 mg de sodium) ■ Insuffisance rénale (modifier la dose si la Cl_{Cr} < 60 mL/min; risque accru de pancréatite) ■ Antécédents de convulsions ■ Diabète ■ Phénylcétonurie (les comprimés contiennent de la phénylalanine) ■ **PÉD.**: Enfants (risque accru de pancréatite) ■ **OBST., ALLAITEMENT**: Les patientes infectées par le VIH ne devraient pas allaiter ■ Traitement concomitant par la stavudine chez des femmes enceintes (précédents d'acidose lactique d'issue fatale).

RÉACTIONS INDÉSIRABLES ET EFFETS SECONDAIRES

SNC: CONVULSIONS, céphalées, étourdissements, insomnie, léthargie, douleurs, faiblesse.

ORLO: rhinite, otalgie, épistaxis, névrite optique, hypertrophie de la glande parotide, photophobie, dépigmentation de la rétine, sialoadénite.

Resp.: toux, asthme.

CV: arythmies, œdème, hypertension, vasodilatation.

GI: INSUFFISANCE HÉPATIQUE, PANCRÉATITE, anorexie, diarrhée, anomalies de la fonction hépatique, nausées, vomissements, douleurs abdominales, constipation, sécheresse de la bouche (xérostomie), dyspepsie, flatulence, stéatose hépatique, stomatite.

GU: mictions fréquentes.

Tég.: alopécie, ecchymoses, rash.

End.: hyperglycémie.

Hémat.: granulopénie, anémie, saignements, leucopénie.

Métab.: ACIDOSE LACTIQUE, hyperlipidémie, hyperuricémie, perte de poids, modification de la distribution du tissu adipeux.
Loc.: RHABDOMYOLYSE, arthrite, myalgie.
SN: neuropathie périphérique, mauvaise coordination.
Divers: frissons, fièvre, réactions anaphylactoïdes, syndrome de reconstitution immunitaire.

D

INTERACTIONS

Médicament-médicament: L'**allopurinol** et la **ribavirine** augmentent les concentrations de didanosine et le risque de toxicité (éviter l'usage concomitant) ■ La **méthadone** réduit les concentrations de didanosine (envisager d'augmenter la dose de didanosine) ■ Le **ganciclovir** et le **ténofovir** augmentent les concentrations de didanosine (envisager de réduire la dose de didanosine) ■ Les tampons dans les comprimés et la solution préparée de didanosine diminuent l'absorption du **kétoconazole**, de l'**itraconazole**, de la **dapsone**, des **tétracyclines** et des **fluoroquinolones** (espacer l'administration d'au moins 2 heures) ■ La didanosine peut augmenter le risque de neuropathie périphérique lors de l'administration concomitante d'autres **médicaments qui induisent une neuropathie périphérique** (**isoniazide**, **phénytoïne**, **stavudine**, **éthambutol** et **autres**) ■ Risque accru de pancréatite si la didanosine est administrée en même temps que des **agents qui peuvent induire une pancréatite** (**alcool**, **diurétiques thiazidiques**, **pentamidine IV**, **tétracyclines** et **autres**) ■ Risque accru d'aplasie médullaire lors de l'administration concomitante d'autres **médicaments qui induisent une aplasie médullaire** ■ L'administration concomitante de **stavudine** augmente le risque d'acidose lactique, d'hépatotoxicité, de neuropathie périphérique et de pancréatite (éviter l'usage concomitant sauf si d'autres options ne sont pas envisageables).
Médicament-aliments: L'administration de la didanosine avec des **aliments** diminue son absorption de 50 %.

VOIES D'ADMINISTRATION ET POSOLOGIE

Lorsqu'on suit le traitement à base de comprimés, les adultes et les enfants > 1 an doivent recevoir 2 comprimés par dose pour assurer un tamponnage adéquat. Les enfants < 1 an peuvent recevoir 1 comprimé.

- **PO (adultes ≥ 60 kg)**: *Comprimés* – 200 mg, 2 fois par jour; *capsules* – 400 mg, 1 fois par jour. *Avec le ténofovir: capsules* – 250 mg, 1 fois par jour.
- **PO (adultes < 60 kg)**: *Comprimés* – 125 mg, 2 fois par jour; *capsules* – 250 mg, 1 fois par jour. *Avec le ténofovir: capsules* – 200 mg, 1 fois par jour.
- **PO (enfants de 2 semaines à < 8 mois)**: 100 mg/m^2, toutes les 12 heures.
- **PO (enfants > 8 mois)**: 120 mg/m^2, toutes les 12 heures.
- **PO (enfants, surface corporelle ≥ 0,9 m^2)**: *Comprimés* – 120 mg, toutes les 12 heures. *Poudre reconstituée réservée à l'usage pédiatrique* – 120 mg, toutes les 12 heures.
- **PO (enfants, surface corporelle de 0,6 à 0,8 m^2)**: *Comprimés* – de 70 à 100 mg, toutes les 12 heures. *Poudre reconstituée réservée à l'usage pédiatrique* – de 70 à 100 mg, toutes les 12 heures.
- **PO (enfants, surface corporelle ≤ 0,5 m^2)**: *Comprimés* – de 40 à 60 mg, toutes les 12 heures. *Poudre reconstituée réservée à l'usage pédiatrique* – de 40 à 60 mg, toutes les 12 heures.

INSUFFISANCE RÉNALE

- **PO (ADULTES > 60 kg)**: *CL_{CR} DE 30 À 59 mL/MIN – COMPRIMÉS* – 100 mg, TOUTES LES 12 HEURES; *CAPSULES* – 250 mg, TOUTES LES 24 HEURES; *CL_{CR} DE 10 À 29 mL/MIN – COMPRIMÉS* – 150 mg, TOUTES LES 24 HEURES; *CAPSULES* – 125 mg, TOUTES LES 24 HEURES; *CL_{CR} < 10 mL/MIN – COMPRIMÉS* – 100 mg, TOUTES LES 24 HEURES; *CAPSULES* – 125 mg, TOUTES LES 24 HEURES.
- **PO (ADULTES < 60 kg)**: *CL_{CR} DE 30 À 59 mL/MIN – COMPRIMÉS* – 75 mg, TOUTES LES 12 HEURES; *CAPSULES* – 125 mg, TOUTES LES 24 HEURES; *CL_{CR} DE 10 À 29 mL/MIN – COMPRIMÉS* – 100 mg, TOUTES LES 24 HEURES; *CAPSULES* – 125 mg, TOUTES LES 24 HEURES; *CL_{CR} < 10 mL/MIN – COMPRIMÉS* – 75 mg, TOUTES LES 24 HEURES; *CAPSULES* – L'ADMINISTRATION DES CAPSULES NE CONVIENT PAS À CES PATIENTS.

LA POSOLOGIE DE L'ASSOCIATION AVEC LE TÉNOFOVIR EN CAS D'INSUFFISANCE RÉNALE N'A PAS ÉTÉ ÉTABLIE.

PRÉSENTATION

Comprimés tamponnés dispersables ou mâchables: 25 mg[Pr], 100 mg[Pr], 150 mg[Pr] ■ **Poudre pour solution orale réservée à l'usage pédiatrique (à reconstituer)**: flacons de 4 g[Pr] ■ **Capsules entérosolubles (Videx EC)**: 125 mg[Pr], 200 mg[Pr], 250 mg[Pr], 400 mg[Pr].

SOINS INFIRMIERS

ÉVALUATION DE LA SITUATION

- Examiner le patient, avant et pendant toute la durée du traitement, pour déceler toute aggravation des symptômes de l'infection par le VIH ou l'apparition de symptômes d'infection opportuniste.
- Tout au long du traitement, rester à l'affût des symptômes suivants de neuropathie périphérique:

engourdissement des membres, fourmillements ou douleurs aux pieds ou aux mains. Il peut s'avérer nécessaire de réduire la dose.

- OBSERVER LE PATIENT À LA RECHERCHE DES SYMPTÔMES SUIVANTS DE PANCRÉATITE : DOULEURS ABDOMINALES, NAUSÉES, VOMISSEMENTS, CONCENTRATIONS ACCRUES D'AMYLASE, DE LIPASE OU DE TRIGLYCÉRIDES. SI LES CONCENTRATIONS D'AMYLASE DÉPASSENT DE 1,5 À 2 FOIS LA LIMITE SUPÉRIEURE DE LA NORMALE OU SI LE PATIENT MANIFESTE DES SYMPTÔMES DE PANCRÉATITE, LE TRAITEMENT PAR LA DIDANOSINE DEVRAIT ÊTRE INTERROMPU. LA PANCRÉATITE PEUT METTRE LA VIE DU PATIENT EN DANGER.
- L'AGENT PEUT PROVOQUER UNE ACIDOSE LACTIQUE ET UNE HÉPATOMÉGALIE GRAVE AVEC STÉATOSE. CES COMPLICATIONS SONT PLUS PROBABLES CHEZ LES FEMMES, LES OBÈSES ET LES PERSONNES QUI PRENNENT DES ANALOGUES NUCLÉOSIDIQUES PENDANT UN TEMPS PROLONGÉ. SUIVRE DE PRÈS LES SIGNES DE CES COMPLICATIONS (TAUX ACCRUS DE LACTATE SÉRIQUE, CONCENTRATIONS ÉLEVÉES D'ENZYMES HÉPATIQUES, HYPERTROPHIE DU FOIE DÉCELÉE À LA PALPATION). ARRÊTER LE TRAITEMENT DÈS L'APPARITION DE SIGNES CLINIQUES OU DE RÉSULTATS DE TESTS DE LABORATOIRE QUI ÉVOQUENT UN TEL PROBLÈME.
- Si une patiente enceinte est exposée à des antirétroviraux, l'inscrire dans le registre des femmes exposées aux antirétroviraux pendant leur grossesse, en composant le 1-800-258-4263.

Tests de laboratoire:

- NOTER À INTERVALLES RÉGULIERS PENDANT TOUTE LA DURÉE DU TRAITEMENT LES CONCENTRATIONS SÉRIQUES D'AMYLASE, DE LIPASE ET DE TRIGLYCÉRIDES. DES CONCENTRATIONS ÉLEVÉES PEUVENT RÉVÉLER LA PRÉSENCE D'UNE PANCRÉATITE ET DICTENT L'ARRÊT DU TRAITEMENT.
- Déterminer la charge virale et le nombre de cellules CD4, avant le traitement et à intervalles réguliers pendant toute sa durée, afin de déterminer la réponse du patient au médicament.
- Noter la numération globulaire, les résultats des tests de la fonction hépatique et les concentrations d'acide urique tout au long du traitement. La didanosine peut entraîner la leucopénie, la granulopénie, la thrombopénie et l'anémie. Elle peut également entraîner l'élévation des concentrations d'AST, d'ALT, de phosphatase alcaline, de bilirubine, d'acide urique, d'amylase, de lipase et de triglycérides. IL Y A RISQUE D'ACIDOSE LACTIQUE ET D'HÉPATOMÉGALIE GRAVE AVEC STÉATOSE, QUI PEUT ÊTRE D'ISSUE FATALE, PARTICULIÈREMENT CHEZ LES FEMMES.
- La didanosine peut entraîner l'hyperglycémie.
- Noter les concentrations sériques de potassium à intervalles réguliers. La diarrhée due au tampon peut entraîner une diminution des concentrations sériques de potassium.

D

DIAGNOSTICS INFIRMIERS POSSIBLES

- Risque d'infection (Indications, Effets secondaires).
- Risque d'accident (Effets secondaires).
- Connaissances insuffisantes sur le traitement médicamenteux (Enseignement au patient et à ses proches).

INTERVENTIONS INFIRMIÈRES

- On désigne souvent la didanosine par l'abréviation « ddI », mais le prescripteur devrait indiquer sur l'ordonnance la dénomination commune et le nom commercial pour éviter toute confusion.
- Si la solution fuit ou si la poudre se répand, essuyer la surface avec un chiffon humide ou une éponge mouillée afin d'éviter la dispersion de la poussière de médicament dans l'air. Nettoyer la surface avec de l'eau et du savon, au besoin.

PO (comprimés et solution préparée):

- Administrer le médicament toutes les 12 heures à jeun, 30 minutes avant les repas ou 2 heures après. Ne pas administrer de kétoconazole, de dapsone, de tétracyclines ou de fluoroquinolones dans les 2 heures suivant l'administration de la didanosine.
- Les comprimés doivent être bien croqués, écrasés à la main ou dispersés dans au moins 30 mL d'eau avant d'être avalés. Pour disperser la préparation, ajouter 1 ou 2 comprimés à au moins 30 mL d'eau et mélanger jusqu'à la formation d'une suspension homogène. La suspension doit être administrée immédiatement. Pour agrémenter le goût, on peut diluer une fois de plus la solution aqueuse dans 30 mL de jus de pomme clair. Mélanger et boire immédiatement toute la solution. Cette solution est stable à la température ambiante (entre 17 °C et 23 °C) pendant 1 heure.
- La solution pour usage pédiatrique est préparée par le pharmacien et reste stable pendant 30 jours au réfrigérateur. Agiter le mélange immédiatement avant de l'administrer.

PO (capsules):

- Administrer le médicament toutes les 24 heures à jeun, 1,5 heure avant les repas ou 2 heures après. Les capsules devraient être avalées telles quelles.

ENSEIGNEMENT AU PATIENT ET À SES PROCHES

- Conseiller au patient de respecter rigoureusement la posologie recommandée et de continuer de prendre la didanosine même s'il se sent mieux. Insister sur le fait qu'il ne faut pas donner ce médicament à d'autres personnes ni l'échanger contre un autre médicament.
- Prévenir le patient que la didanosine peut provoquer des étourdissements. Lui conseiller de ne pas conduire et d'éviter les activités qui exigent sa vigilance jusqu'à ce qu'on ait la certitude que le médicament n'entraîne pas cet effet chez lui.
- Informer le patient que la didanosine peut induire l'hyperglycémie. Lui conseiller de consulter un professionnel de la santé si la soif ou la faim s'intensifient, s'il note une perte de poids inexpliquée, des mictions plus fréquentes ou une fatigue accrue ou encore si sa peau devient sèche ou prurigineuse.
- Conseiller au patient de ne pas prendre d'autres médicaments en même temps que la didanosine sans consulter au préalable un professionnel de la santé.
- Conseiller au patient d'éviter les foules et les personnes contagieuses.
- Recommander au patient de signaler immédiatement à un professionnel de la santé l'engourdissement des mains ou des pieds ou les picotements dans les membres, les douleurs d'estomac, les nausées ou les vomissements.
- RECOMMANDER AU PATIENT DE PRÉVENIR UN PROFESSIONNEL DE LA SANTÉ IMMÉDIATEMENT, SI DES SIGNES D'ACIDOSE LACTIQUE (FATIGUE OU FAIBLESSE, DOULEURS MUSCULAIRES INHABITUELLES, DIFFICULTÉS RESPIRATOIRES, DOULEURS D'ESTOMAC AVEC DES NAUSÉES ET DES VOMISSEMENTS, SENSATION DE FROID, SURTOUT AU NIVEAU DES EXTRÉMITÉS, ÉTOURDISSEMENTS OU BATTEMENTS CARDIAQUES RAPIDES ET IRRÉGULIERS) OU D'HÉPATOTOXICITÉ (JAUNISSEMENT DE LA PEAU OU DU BLANC DES YEUX, URINE DE COULEUR FONCÉE, SELLES DE COULEUR PÂLE, PERTE D'APPÉTIT PENDANT PLUSIEURS JOURS DE SUITE, NAUSÉES OU DOULEURS ABDOMINALES) SE MANIFESTENT. Ces symptômes peuvent se présenter plus fréquemment chez les femmes, les obèses ou les personnes qui prennent des médicaments comme la didanosine pendant un laps de temps prolongé.
- Recommander au patient de se servir d'un condom lors des rapports sexuels et de ne pas utiliser les mêmes aiguilles qu'une autre personne afin de prévenir la transmission du VIH.
- Expliquer aux parents que l'enfant qui reçoit de la didanosine devrait passer un examen ophtalmoscopique de la rétine tous les 3 à 6 mois ou s'il y a modification de la vue, pendant toute la durée du traitement.
- Prévenir le patient que ce traitement antirétroviral l'expose à un risque de redistribution ou d'accumulation des graisses corporelles, dont les causes et les conséquences à long terme sur la santé sont actuellement inconnues.
- Insister sur l'importance des examens réguliers permettant de déceler les effets secondaires de la didanosine.

VÉRIFICATION DE L'EFFICACITÉ THÉRAPEUTIQUE

L'efficacité du traitement peut être démontrée par: la diminution de l'incidence des infections opportunistes et le ralentissement de l'évolution de l'infection par le VIH ■ la réduction de la charge virale et l'augmentation du nombre de cellules CD4. ✳

DIFLUCORTOLONE (VALÉRATE DE),
voir Corticostéroïdes (topiques)

ALERTE CLINIQUE

DIGOXINE

Apo-Digoxine, Lanoxin, PMS-Digoxine

CLASSIFICATION:

Antiarythmique, inotrope et glucoside cardiotonique

Grossesse – catégorie C

INDICATIONS

Insuffisance cardiaque ■ Tachyarythmies auriculaires: fibrillation auriculaire et flutter auriculaire, tachycardie auriculaire paroxystique (ralentissement de la fréquence ventriculaire).

MÉCANISME D'ACTION

Augmentation de la force contractile du myocarde ■ Prolongation de la période réfractaire du nœud AV ■ Diminution de la conduction par les nœuds sinusal et AV. ***Effets thérapeutiques:*** Élévation du débit cardiaque (effet inotrope positif) et ralentissement de la fréquence cardiaque (effet chronotrope négatif).

PHARMACOCINÉTIQUE

Absorption: De 60 à 85 % (PO – comprimés); de 75 à 80 % (PO – élixir); 80 % (IM, mais cette voie d'administration n'est pas recommandée, car l'injection est très douloureuse et irritante).

Distribution: Tout l'organisme. La digoxine traverse la barrière placentaire et passe dans le lait maternel.

Métabolisme et excrétion: Excrétion rénale de 50 à 70 % à l'état inchangé.

Demi-vie: De 36 à 48 heures (prolongée en cas d'insuffisance rénale).

Profil temps-action
(effet antiarythmique ou inotrope,
si une dose d'attaque a été administrée)

	DÉBUT D'ACTION	PIC	DURÉE
PO	30 - 120 min	2 - 8 h	2 - 4 jours†
IV	5 - 30 min	1 - 5 h	2 - 4 jours

† La durée d'action est celle observée chez les patients ayant une fonction rénale normale; chez les patients présentant une insuffisance rénale, elle est prolongée.

CONTRE-INDICATIONS, PRÉCAUTIONS ET MISES EN GARDE

Contre-indications: Hypersensibilité ■ Fibrillation ventriculaire.

Précautions et mises en garde: Arythmies ventriculaires non maîtrisées ■ Bloc AV ■ Sténose sous-aortique hypertrophique idiopathique ■ Péricardite constrictive ■ Anomalies électrolytiques (l'hypokaliémie, l'hypercalcémie et l'hypomagnésémie peuvent prédisposer à une intoxication digitalique) ■ **GÉR.:** Sensibilité accrue aux effets toxiques ■ Infarctus du myocarde ■ Insuffisance rénale (réduire la dose) ■ Patients obèses (la dose doit être calculée en fonction du poids idéal) ■ Intolérance connue à l'alcool (élixir seulement) ■ **OBST.:** Grossesse (bien que son innocuité n'ait pas été établie, la digoxine a été utilisée durant la grossesse sans qu'elle entraîne des réactions indésirables chez le fœtus). **ALLAITEMENT:** Les concentrations de digoxine dans le sérum et le lait maternel sont similaires. Toutefois, la dose quotidienne estimative à laquelle le nourrisson est exposé est bien inférieure à la dose d'entretien habituellement prescrite aux nourrissons et ne devrait donc avoir aucun effet pharmacologique sur l'enfant.

RÉACTIONS INDÉSIRABLES ET EFFETS SECONDAIRES

SNC: fatigue, céphalées, faiblesse.

ORLO: vision trouble, vision jaune ou verte des surfaces blanches (xanthopsie).

CV: ARYTHMIES, bradycardie, modifications de l'ÉCG, bloc AV.

GI: anorexie, nausées, vomissements, diarrhée.

End.: gynécomastie.

Hémat.: thrombopénie.

Métab.: hyperkaliémie en cas d'intoxications aiguës.

INTERACTIONS

Médicament-médicament: Les **diurétiques thiazidiques** et les **diurétiques de l'anse**, la **pipéracilline**, la **ticarcilline**, l'**amphotéricine B**, les **laxatifs** utilisés en grandes quantités et les **corticostéroïdes** peuvent augmenter le risque de toxicité en raison de leur effet hypokaliémiant ■ La **quinidine**, le **flécaïnide**, la **cyclosporine**, l'**itraconazole**, l'**indométhacine**, l'**amiodarone**, le **vérapamil**, le **diltiazem**, la **propafénone** et le **carvédilol** augmentent les concentrations sériques de digoxine et le risque de toxicité (il est recommandé de suivre de près les concentrations sériques et de réduire la dose) ■ La **spironolactone** allonge la demi-vie de la digoxine (il peut s'avérer nécessaire de réduire la dose ou d'augmenter l'écart posologique) ■ Risque de bradycardie additive lors de l'administration concomitante de **bêtabloquants** et de **bloquants des canaux calciques non dihydropiridiniques** ■ L'absorption de la digoxine est diminuée lors de l'administration concomitante d'**antiacides,** de **sucralfate**, de **charbon activé**, de **sulfasalazine**, de **métoclopramide**, de **certains antinéoplasiques** (comme la **bléomycine**, le **cyclophosphamide**, la **cytarabine**, la **doxorubicine,** la **procarbazine** et la **vincristine**), de **kaolin-pectine**, de **cholestyramine** ou de **colestipol** ■ Les **hormones thyroïdiennes** et les **antithyroïdiens** modifient les effets thérapeutiques de la digoxine selon les variations de la fonction thyroïdienne qu'ils engendrent ■ L'usage concomitant de **sympathomimétiques** peut augmenter le risque d'arythmies cardiaques ■ La **succinylcholine** peut provoquer une expulsion soudaine de potassium des cellules musculaires, ce qui peut être à l'origine d'arythmies chez les patients digitalisés ■ L'utilisation concomitante de **certains antibiotiques** (tels que les **macrolides** et les **tétracyclines**) peut augmenter la concentration sérique de digoxine dans le cas des patients chez lesquels la digoxine est inactivée dans le gros intestin par métabolisme bactérien (environ 10 % des patients).

Médicament-aliments: L'absorption de la digoxine peut être diminuée en cas de consommation concomitante d'**aliments riches en fibres**. Administrer la digoxine 1 heure avant ou 2 heures après ces aliments.

Médicament-produits naturels: L'**extrait d'aloès par voie orale**, pris en même temps que la digoxine, peut entraîner une diarrhée excessive avec perte de potassium, ce qui peut augmenter le risque de toxicité ■ La toxicité cardiaque peut être accrue par la prise concomitante de produits à base d'**aubépine** ■ Les effets diurétiques de l'extrait de **réglisse** peuvent entraîner l'hypokaliémie et accroître le risque de toxicité associé à la digoxine ■ La **quinine** peut élever les concentrations sériques de digoxine et fausser les résultats du dosage de cet agent ■ Le **ginseng** peut augmenter les concentrations sériques de digoxine ■ Le **millepertuis** peut diminuer les concentrations sanguines et l'efficacité de la digoxine.

VOIES D'ADMINISTRATION ET POSOLOGIE

Pour obtenir un effet rapide, administrer une dose d'attaque plus importante ou une dose de « digitalisation », en plusieurs prises fractionnées pendant 12 à 24 heures. On doit calculer les doses en fonction du poids maigre du patient. Les doses d'entretien doivent être déterminées d'après l'état de la fonction rénale. Toutes les doses doivent être ajustées d'après la réponse du patient. En règle générale, les doses destinées à la réduction des arythmies auriculaires sont plus fortes que celles nécessaires pour obtenir un effet inotrope.

- **IV (adultes et enfants > 10 ans)**: *Dose de digitalisation* – de 8 à 12 µg/kg; administrer initialement la moitié de cette dose, et le reste, en doses fractionnées, à intervalles de 6 à 8 heures.
- **IV (enfants de 5 à 10 ans)**: *Dose de digitalisation* – de 15 à 30 µg/kg; administrer initialement la moitié de cette dose, et le reste, en doses fractionnées, à intervalles de 6 à 8 heures.
- **IV (enfants de 2 à 5 ans)**: *Dose de digitalisation* – de 25 à 35 µg/kg; administrer initialement la moitié de cette dose, et le reste, en doses fractionnées, à intervalles de 6 à 8 heures.
- **IV (enfants de 1 à 24 mois)**: *Dose de digitalisation* – de 30 à 50 µg/kg; administrer initialement la moitié de cette dose, et le reste, en doses fractionnées, à intervalles de 6 à 8 heures.
- **IV (nourrissons nés à terme)**: *Dose de digitalisation* – de 20 à 30 µg/kg; administrer initialement la moitié de cette dose, et le reste, en doses fractionnées, à intervalles de 6 à 8 heures.
- **IV (nourrissons prématurés)**: *Dose de digitalisation* – de 15 à 25 µg/kg; administrer initialement la moitié de cette dose, et le reste, en doses fractionnées, à intervalles de 6 à 8 heures.
- **PO (adultes)**: *Dose de digitalisation* – de 0,75 à 1,25 mg; administrer initialement la moitié de cette dose, et le reste, en doses fractionnées, à intervalles de 6 à 8 heures. *Dose d'entretien* – de 0,063 à 0,5 mg/jour en comprimés selon le poids maigre du patient, l'état de sa fonction rénale et les concentrations sériques.
- **PO (personnes âgées)**: La dose quotidienne ne doit pas dépasser 0,125 mg, sauf si on traite une fibrillation auriculaire.
- **PO (enfants > 10 ans)**: *Dose de digitalisation* – de 10 à 15 µg/kg; administrer initialement la moitié de cette dose, et le reste, en doses fractionnées, à intervalles de 6 à 8 heures. *Dose d'entretien* – de 3 à 5 µg/kg par jour, 1 fois par jour.
- **PO (enfants de 5 à 10 ans)**: *Dose de digitalisation* – de 20 à 35 µg/kg; administrer initialement la moitié de cette dose, et le reste, en doses fractionnées, à intervalles de 6 à 8 heures. *Dose d'entretien* – de 7 à 10 µg/kg par jour, en 2 prises.
- **PO (enfants de 2 à 5 ans)**: *Dose de digitalisation* – de 30 à 40 µg/kg; administrer initialement la moitié de cette dose, et le reste, en doses fractionnées, à intervalles de 6 à 8 heures. *Dose d'entretien* – de 10 à 15 µg/kg par jour, en 2 prises.
- **PO (enfants de 1 à 24 mois)**: *Dose de digitalisation* – de 35 à 60 µg/kg; administrer initialement la moitié de cette dose, et le reste, en doses fractionnées, à intervalles de 6 à 8 heures. *Dose d'entretien* – de 25 à 35 % de la dose de digitalisation, en 2 prises.
- **PO (nourrissons nés à terme)**: *Dose de digitalisation* – de 25 à 35 µg/kg; administrer initialement la moitié de cette dose, et le reste, en doses fractionnées, à intervalles de 6 à 8 heures. *Dose d'entretien* – de 25 à 35 % de la dose de digitalisation, en 2 prises.
- **PO (nourrissons prématurés)**: *Dose de digitalisation* – de 20 à 30 µg/kg; administrer initialement la moitié de cette dose, et le reste, en doses fractionnées, à intervalles de 6 à 8 heures. *Dose d'entretien* – de 20 à 30 % de la dose de digitalisation, en 2 prises.

PRÉSENTATION

Comprimés: 0,0625 mg[Pr], 0,125 mg[Pr], 0,25 mg[Pr] ■ **Élixir, usage pédiatrique**: 0,05 mg/mL[Pr] ■ **Solution pour injection**: 0,25 mg/mL[Pr] ■ **Solution pour injection, usage pédiatrique**: 0,05 mg/mL[Pr].

SOINS INFIRMIERS

ÉVALUATION DE LA SITUATION

- Mesurer le pouls à l'apex pendant 60 secondes avant d'administrer le médicament. Si la fréquence du pouls est < 60 battements par minute chez l'adulte, < 70 battements par minute chez l'enfant ou < 90 battements par minute chez le nourrisson, ne pas administrer la digoxine et en informer le médecin. Prévenir rapidement le médecin ou un autre professionnel de la santé de toute modification importante de la fréquence, du rythme ou de la qualité du pouls.

PÉD.: La fréquence cardiaque varie selon l'âge de l'enfant. Demander au médecin quelle est la fréquence cardiaque à partir de laquelle il ne faut pas administrer la digoxine.

- Mesurer la pression artérielle à intervalles réguliers lorsque la digoxine est administrée par voie IV.

- SUIVRE L'ÉCG TOUT AU LONG DE L'ADMINISTRATION PAR VOIE IV ET À INTERVALLES RÉGULIERS PENDANT TOUTE LA DURÉE DU TRAITEMENT. PRÉVENIR LE MÉDECIN OU UN AUTRE PROFESSIONNEL DE LA SANTÉ EN CAS DE BRADYCARDIE OU DE NOUVELLES ARYTHMIES.
- Observer le point d'injection IV à la recherche de rougeur ou d'infiltration; l'extravasation peut entraîner l'irritation des tissus et la formation d'une escarre.
- Effectuer le bilan quotidien des ingesta et des excreta et peser le patient tous les jours. Déceler l'œdème périphérique et ausculter les poumons pendant toute la durée du traitement, à la recherche de râles ou de crépitations.
- Avant d'administrer la dose d'attaque initiale, déterminer si le patient a pris des préparations digitaliques au cours des 2 à 3 semaines précédentes.

GÉR.: La digoxine a été associée à un risque plus élevé de chutes chez les personnes âgées. Évaluer le risque de chutes et prendre les mesures de prévention propres à l'établissement.

Tests de laboratoire: Examiner à intervalles réguliers, pendant toute la durée du traitement, les concentrations des électrolytes sériques (particulièrement de potassium, de magnésium et de calcium), ainsi que les résultats des tests des fonctions rénale et hépatique. Si le patient est hypokaliémique, en informer le médecin ou un autre professionnel de la santé avant d'administrer la digoxine. L'hypokaliémie, l'hypomagnésémie ou l'hypercalcémie peuvent prédisposer le patient à une intoxication digitalique.

PÉD.: Les nouveau-nés peuvent présenter des concentrations sériques de digoxine faussement élevées à cause d'une substance naturelle contenue dans leur organisme, similaire du point de vue chimique à la digoxine.

GÉR.: Les personnes âgées peuvent présenter des signes d'intoxication à la digoxine même lorsque les concentrations sériques sont dans les limites normales; rester à l'affût des symptômes cliniques de toxicité, même lorsque les concentrations sériques sont normales.

TOXICITÉ ET SURDOSAGE:

- Les concentrations sériques thérapeutiques de digoxine se situent entre 0,5 et 2,0 nmol/L. Pour être valides, les concentrations sériques de digoxine doivent être mesurées au moins 6 à 8 heures après l'administration de la dose, bien qu'on mesure habituellement ces concentrations immédiatement avant d'administrer la dose suivante.
- Les bactéries qui se trouvent dans le tractus GI peuvent métaboliser une quantité importante de digoxine avant son absorption. Les patients qui reçoivent un antibiotique qui tue ces bactéries intestinales (comme l'érythromycine ou la tétracycline) peuvent être intoxiqués par leurs doses habituelles de digoxine.

GÉR.: Les personnes âgées risquent davantage de subir les effets toxiques de la digoxine à cause d'une clairance rénale réduite due au vieillissement; cette réduction de la clairance peut se manifester même lorsque les concentrations sériques de créatinine sont normales. Les besoins en digoxine des personnes âgées peuvent changer et une dose qui était auparavant thérapeutique peut devenir toxique.

- Rester à l'affût des signes et des symptômes d'intoxication. Chez les adultes et les enfants plus âgés, les premiers signes d'intoxication sont habituellement les douleurs abdominales, l'anorexie, les nausées, les vomissements, les troubles visuels, la bradycardie et d'autres arythmies. Chez les nourrissons et les jeunes enfants, les premiers symptômes de surdosage sont habituellement les arythmies cardiaques. En présence de ces symptômes, ne pas administrer la digoxine et prévenir immédiatement le médecin ou un autre professionnel de la santé.
- Si les signes d'intoxication ne sont pas graves, il peut être suffisant d'arrêter le traitement par la digoxine.
- En présence d'hypokaliémie et d'une fonction rénale normale, on peut administrer des sels de potassium. Ne pas en administrer en présence d'hyperkaliémie ou de bloc cardiaque.
- Il faut aussi corriger tous les autres déséquilibres électrolytiques.
- On peut essayer de corriger les arythmies attribuables à la toxicité digitalique en administrant les agents suivants: lidocaïne, procaïnamide, quinidine, propranolol ou phénytoïne. Une stimulation ventriculaire temporaire peut s'avérer utile en présence d'un bloc cardiaque avancé.
- Le traitement des arythmies pouvant mettre la vie du patient en danger peut inclure l'administration de fragments d'anticorps spécifiques de la digoxine Fab (Digibind), qui se lient à la digoxine dans le sang. Ce complexe est ensuite excrété par les reins.

DIAGNOSTICS INFIRMIERS POSSIBLES

- Débit cardiaque diminué (Indications).
- Connaissances insuffisantes sur le traitement médicamenteux (Enseignement au patient et à ses proches).

INTERVENTIONS INFIRMIÈRES

ALERTE CLINIQUE: LA DIGOXINE A UN INDEX THÉRAPEUTIQUE ÉTROIT. PARMI LES ERREURS MÉDICAMENTEUSES

ASSOCIÉES À LA DIGOXINE, CITONS DES ERREURS DE CALCUL DES DOSES PÉDIATRIQUES ET UN SUIVI INSUFFISANT DES CONCENTRATIONS SÉRIQUES. FAIRE VÉRIFIER L'ORDONNANCE D'ORIGINE ET LE CALCUL DES DOSES PAR UN AUTRE PROFESSIONNEL DE LA SANTÉ. FAIRE LE SUIVI DES CONCENTRATIONS SÉRIQUES.

- Pour obtenir une digitalisation rapide, on doit administrer une dose initiale de digoxine plus élevée que la dose d'entretien. On peut administrer en traitement initial entre 25 et 50 % de la dose totale de digitalisation. Administrer le reste de la dose totale de digitalisation en fractions de 25 %, à intervalles de 6 à 8 heures.
- Lorsqu'on substitue la forme orale à la forme destinée à l'administration parentérale, il faut adapter les doses en raison des variations pharmacocinétiques de la quantité de digoxine absorbée. Une dose de 100 µg (0,1 mg) de digoxine pour injection équivaut à 125 µg (0,125 mg) de digoxine en comprimé ou à 125 µg (0,125 mg) en élixir.

PO: Les préparations orales peuvent être administrées sans égard aux repas. Si le patient éprouve des difficultés de déglutition, on peut écraser les comprimés et les administrer avec des aliments ou des liquides. Utiliser un récipient gradué pour mesurer les préparations liquides.

IM: L'administration IM n'est habituellement pas recommandée, car elle est très douloureuse. Injecter profondément dans le muscle fessier et bien masser pour réduire les réactions locales douloureuses. Ne pas administrer plus de 2 mL de digoxine par point d'injection IM.

IV directe: On peut administrer les doses par voie IV sans diluer le médicament ou en le diluant à raison de 1 mL par 4 mL d'eau stérile, de solution de NaCl 0,9 %, de solution de D5%E ou de solution de lactate de Ringer pour injection. Si on utilise moins de diluant, la solution peut précipiter. Administrer immédiatement la solution diluée. Ne pas utiliser la solution qui a changé de couleur ou qui contient un précipité.

Vitesse d'administration: Administrer chacune des doses par injection dans une tubulure en Y en au moins 5 minutes.

Associations compatibles dans la même seringue: héparine ▪ milrinone.

Compatibilité (tubulure en Y): ciprofloxacine ▪ diltiazem ▪ famotidine ▪ mépéridine ▪ méropenem ▪ milrinone ▪ morphine ▪ potassium, chlorure de ▪ propofol ▪ tacrolimus ▪ vitamines du complexe B avec C.

Incompatibilité (tubulure en Y): fluconazole ▪ foscarnet.

Incompatibilité en addition au soluté: Le fabricant recommande de ne pas mélanger la digoxine à d'autres médicaments.

ENSEIGNEMENT AU PATIENT ET À SES PROCHES

- Expliquer au patient qu'il doit respecter rigoureusement la posologie recommandée et qu'il doit prendre la digoxine à la même heure chaque jour. S'il n'a pu prendre le médicament au moment habituel, il doit le prendre en l'espace de 12 heures; sinon lui conseiller de ne pas le prendre du tout ce jour-là. Le prévenir qu'il ne doit jamais remplacer une dose manquée par une double dose. Lui recommander de consulter un professionnel de la santé s'il n'a pas pris le médicament pendant 2 jours ou plus. Prévenir le patient qu'il ne doit pas arrêter le traitement sans avoir consulté au préalable un professionnel de la santé.
- Montrer au patient comment prendre son pouls et lui recommander de communiquer avec un professionnel de la santé avant de prendre la digoxine si la fréquence du pouls est inférieure à 50 ou supérieure à 100 battements par minute.

PÉD.: Expliquer aux parents ou aux soignants que des changements dans la fréquence cardiaque, particulièrement la bradycardie, sont parmi les premiers signes de toxicité à la digoxine chez les enfants. Leur montrer comment prendre le pouls apical. Leur recommander de prévenir un professionnel de la santé avant d'administrer la dose si la fréquence cardiaque n'est pas dans l'intervalle qui leur a été recommandé.

- Expliquer les signes et les symptômes de toxicité digitalique au patient et à ses proches. Recommander au patient de prévenir immédiatement un professionnel de la santé si des symptômes de toxicité digitalique ou d'insuffisance cardiaque se manifestent. Expliquer au patient que ces symptômes peuvent être pris pour des symptômes de rhume ou de grippe.
- Recommander au patient de laisser les comprimés de digoxine dans leur emballage d'origine. Étant donné qu'ils ressemblent fortement à d'autres comprimés, il est facile de se tromper.
- Insister sur le fait qu'il peut être dangereux de donner ce médicament à d'autres personnes.
- Conseiller au patient de consulter un professionnel de la santé avant de prendre des médicaments en vente libre ou des produits naturels en même temps que la digoxine. Le prévenir qu'il ne doit pas prendre d'antiacides ou d'antidiarrhéiques dans les 2 heures qui suivent la prise de la digoxine.
- Conseiller au patient d'informer le professionnel de la santé de son traitement médicamenteux avant de se soumettre à un autre traitement.

- Conseiller au patient de toujours porter sur lui une pièce d'identité où sont inscrits ses problèmes de santé et son traitement médicamenteux.

GÉR.: Expliquer aux personnes âgées et à leur proches les mesures de prévention des chutes.

ALERTE CLINIQUE: INSISTER SUR L'IMPORTANCE DES EXAMENS DE SUIVI PERMETTANT D'ÉVALUER L'EFFICACITÉ DU MÉDICAMENT ET DE DÉCELER LES SIGNES D'INTOXICATION.

PÉD.: ENSEIGNER AUX PARENTS OU AUX SOIGNANTS COMMENT MESURER AVEC PRÉCISION LE MÉDICAMENT SOUS FORME LIQUIDE.

VÉRIFICATION DE L'EFFICACITÉ THÉRAPEUTIQUE

L'efficacité du traitement peut être démontrée par: la réduction de la gravité de l'insuffisance cardiaque ▪ l'augmentation du débit cardiaque ▪ la diminution de la réponse ventriculaire en présence de tachyarythmies auriculaires ▪ l'interruption de la tachycardie auriculaire paroxystique. ✳

DIHYDROERGOTAMINE,

voir Ergotamine

DILTIAZEM

Apo-Diltiaz/SR/CD, Cardizem/Cardizem CD, Gen-Diltiazem, Novo-Diltazem/CD, Novo-Diltiazem HCL ER, Nu-Diltiaz/CD, Ratio-Diltiazem CD, Tiazac/Tiazac XC

CLASSIFICATION:

Antiangineux, antiarythmique (classe IV), antihypertenseur (bloqueur des canaux calciques)

Grossesse – catégorie C

INDICATIONS

Traitement de: l'hypertension ▪ l'angine chronique stable ▪ l'angine vasospastique (comprimés ordinaires seulement) ▪ (IV seulement) Prise en charge des tachyarythmies supraventriculaires et d'une fréquence ventriculaire rapide, en présence de flutter ou de fibrillation auriculaire. **Usages non approuvés**: Traitement de la maladie de Raynaud.

MÉCANISME D'ACTION

Inhibition de la pénétration des ions calcium dans les cellules des muscles lisses vasculaires et myocardiques, ce qui entraîne l'inhibition du couplage excitation-contraction et de la contraction qui en découle. ***Effets thérapeutiques:*** Vasodilatation systémique entraînant une chute de la pression artérielle ▪ Vasodilatation coronarienne se traduisant par une diminution de la fréquence et de la gravité des crises d'angine ▪ Suppression des arythmies.

PHARMACOCINÉTIQUE

Absorption: Bonne (PO), mais premier passage hépatique important.

Distribution: Inconnue.

Liaison aux protéines: De 70 à 80 %.

Métabolisme et excrétion: Métabolisme majoritairement hépatique (CYP3A4).

Demi-vie: De 3,5 à 9 heures.

Profil temps-action

	DÉBUT D'ACTION	PIC	DURÉE
PO	30 - 60 min	2 - 3 h	6 - 8 h
PO - SR	inconnu	inconnu	12 h
PO - CD, ER	2 h	10 - 14 h	jusqu'à 24 h
IV	2 - 5 min	2 - 4 h	inconnue

CONTRE-INDICATIONS, PRÉCAUTIONS ET MISES EN GARDE

Contre-indications: Hypersensibilité ▪ Syndrome de dysfonctionnement sinusal (sauf en présence d'un stimulateur cardiaque) ▪ Bloc AV du 2e et du 3e degré (sauf en présence d'un stimulateur cardiaque) ▪ Pression artérielle < 90 mm Hg ▪ Infarctus du myocarde avec insuffisance ventriculaire gauche se manifestant par une congestion pulmonaire ▪ **OBST.**: Femmes enceintes ou en âge de procréer (risque accru de malformation chez l'animal).

Précautions et mises en garde: Insuffisance hépatique grave (il est recommandé de réduire la dose de la plupart de ces agents) ▪ Insuffisance cardiaque congestive ▪ **GÉR.**: Il est recommandé de réduire la dose et de ralentir la vitesse de perfusion IV; risque accru d'hypotension ▪ Insuffisance rénale grave ▪ Antécédents d'arythmies ventriculaires graves ou d'insuffisance cardiaque ▪ **ALLAITEMENT**: Le médicament passe dans le lait maternel ▪ **PÉD.**: L'innocuité du médicament chez les enfants n'a pas été établie.

RÉACTIONS INDÉSIRABLES ET EFFETS SECONDAIRES

SNC: rêves bizarres, anxiété, confusion, étourdissements, somnolence, céphalées, nervosité, troubles psychiatriques, faiblesse.

ORLO: vision trouble, trouble d'équilibre, épistaxis, acouphènes.

Resp.: toux, dyspnée.

D

CV: ARYTHMIES, INSUFFISANCE CARDIAQUE, <u>œdème périphérique</u>, bradycardie, douleurs thoraciques, hypotension, palpitations, syncope, tachycardie.

GI: résultats anormaux aux tests de la fonction hépatique, anorexie, constipation, diarrhée, sécheresse de la bouche (xérostomie), dysgueusie, dyspepsie, nausées, vomissements.

GU: dysurie, nycturie, polyurie, dysfonctionnement sexuel, mictions fréquentes.

Tég.: dermatite, érythème polymorphe, bouffées vasomotrices, sécrétion accrue de sueur, photosensibilité, prurit, urticaire, rash.

End.: gynécomastie, hyperglycémie.

Hémat.: anémie, leucopénie, thrombopénie.

Métab.: gain pondéral.

Loc.: raideurs articulaires, crampes musculaires.

SN: paresthésie, tremblements.

Divers: SYNDROME DE STEVENS-JOHNSON, hyperplasie gingivale.

INTERACTIONS

Médicament-médicament: Risque d'hypotension additive lors de l'administration concomitante de **fentanyl**, d'autres **antihypertenseurs**, de **dérivés nitrés** et de **quinidine** ou lors d'une consommation excessive d'**alcool** ▪ Les effets antihypertenseurs peuvent être réduits lors de l'usage concomitant d'**anti-inflammatoires non stéroïdiens** ▪ Le diltiazem peut élever les concentrations sériques de **digoxine** ▪ Risque accru de bradycardie, d'anomalies de la conduction ou d'insuffisance cardiaque lors de l'administration concomitante de **bêtabloquants**, de **digoxine**, de **disopyramide** ou de **phénytoïne** ▪ Le **phénobarbital**, la **phénytoïne** et la **rifampine** peuvent accélérer le métabolisme du diltiazem et en diminuer l'efficacité ▪ Le diltiazem peut diminuer le métabolisme de la **cyclosporine**, de la **quinidine** ou de la **carbamazépine** et augmenter le risque de toxicité.

VOIES D'ADMINISTRATION ET POSOLOGIE

- **PO (adultes)**: *Comprimés ordinaires* – de 30 à 90 mg, 3 ou 4 fois par jour. *Capsules SR* – de 60 à 120 mg, 2 fois par jour. *Capsules CD ou ER* – de 180 à 240 mg, 1 fois par jour (jusqu'à concurrence de 360 mg/jour).
- **IV (adultes)**: 0,25 mg/kg; on peut répéter l'administration d'une dose de 0,35 mg/kg, 15 minutes plus tard; on peut poursuivre l'administration en perfusion continue, à 10 mg/h (écart posologique: de 5 à 15 mg/h), pendant une période pouvant aller jusqu'à 24 heures.

PRÉSENTATION
(version générique disponible)

Comprimés ordinaires: 30 mg[Pr], 60 mg[Pr] ▪ **Capsules à libération prolongée SR**: 60 mg[Pr], 90 mg[Pr], 120 mg[Pr] ▪ **Capsules à libération prolongée CD ou ER**: 120 mg[Pr], 180 mg[Pr], 240 mg[Pr], 300 mg[Pr], 360 mg[Pr] ▪ **Solution pour injection**: 5 mg/mL, en fioles de 5 mL[Pr] ou de 10 mL[Pr].

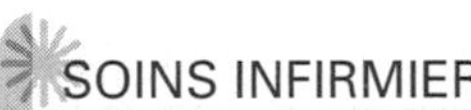

SOINS INFIRMIERS

ÉVALUATION DE LA SITUATION

- Mesurer la pression artérielle et le pouls, avant le début du traitement, au cours de l'adaptation de la posologie et à intervalles réguliers pendant toute la durée du traitement. Suivre l'ÉCG à intervalles réguliers pendant toute la durée du traitement prolongé. Le diltiazem peut entraîner l'allongement des intervalles PR.
- Effectuer le bilan quotidien des ingesta et des excreta et peser le patient tous les jours. RESTER À L'AFFÛT DES SIGNES D'INSUFFISANCE CARDIAQUE (ŒDÈME PÉRIPHÉRIQUE, RÂLES OU CRÉPITATIONS, DYSPNÉE, GAIN PONDÉRAL, TURGESCENCE DES JUGULAIRES).
- Chez les patients recevant de la digoxine en même temps qu'un bloqueur des canaux calciques, examiner régulièrement les concentrations sériques de la digoxine et suivre de près les signes et les symptômes de toxicité digitalique.

Angine: Déterminer le siège, la durée et l'intensité de la douleur angineuse, ainsi que les facteurs qui la déclenchent.

Arythmies: SUIVRE L'ÉCG TOUT AU LONG DE L'ADMINISTRATION. SIGNALER SANS TARDER AU MÉDECIN LA BRADYCARDIE OU UNE HYPOTENSION PROLONGÉE. GARDER À PORTÉE DE LA MAIN LE MATÉRIEL ET LES MÉDICAMENTS PERMETTANT D'ADMINISTRER DES SOINS D'URGENCE. MESURER LA PRESSION ARTÉRIELLE ET LE POULS AVANT LE TRAITEMENT ET À INTERVALLES FRÉQUENTS DURANT L'ADMINISTRATION.

Tests de laboratoire:

- Les concentrations totales de calcium sérique ne sont pas modifiées par les bloqueurs des canaux calciques.
- Noter, à intervalles réguliers, les concentrations sériques de potassium. L'hypokaliémie augmente le risque d'arythmies et devrait être traitée.
- Examiner, à intervalles réguliers, les résultats des tests des fonctions hépatique et rénale chez les patients qui suivent un traitement prolongé. Après plusieurs jours de traitement, les concentrations des

enzymes hépatiques peuvent augmenter; elles reviennent à la normale après l'arrêt du traitement.

DIAGNOSTICS INFIRMIERS POSSIBLES

- Douleur aiguë (Indications).
- Débit cardiaque diminué (Réactions indésirables).
- Connaissances insuffisantes sur le traitement médicamenteux (Enseignement au patient et à ses proches).

INTERVENTIONS INFIRMIÈRES

PO:

- Le diltiazem peut être administré sans égard aux repas. On peut l'administrer avec des aliments si l'irritation gastrique devient gênante.
- IL NE FAUT PAS ÉCRASER, BRISER NI MÂCHER LES COMPRIMÉS OU LES CAPSULES À LIBÉRATION RETARD. Il est normal de retrouver dans les selles des capsules vides; elles n'ont pas d'effet nuisible. On peut écraser les comprimés ordinaires et les mélanger à des aliments ou à des liquides avant de les administrer aux patients qui éprouvent des difficultés de déglutition.

IV directe:

- On peut administrer la solution de diltiazem non diluée.
- ***Vitesse d'administration:*** Administrer chaque dose sous forme de bolus IV en l'espace de 2 minutes.

Perfusion continue:

- Diluer 125 mg (25 mL) dans 100 mL, 250 mg (50 mL) dans 250 mL, ou 250 mg (50 mL) dans 500 mL d'une solution de NaCl 0,9%, de D5%E ou de D5%/NaCl 0,45%, pour obtenir des concentrations de 1 mg/mL, de 0,83 mg/mL ou de 0,45 mg/mL, respectivement. La solution est stable pendant 24 heures à la température ambiante ou au réfrigérateur.
- ***Vitesse d'administration:*** La perfusion initiale devrait être administrée à une vitesse de 10 mg/h. On peut l'augmenter par paliers de 5 mg/h, jusqu'à 15 mg/h si une réduction plus grande du débit cardiaque est nécessaire. Certains patients peuvent répondre à un débit de 5 mg/h. La perfusion peut être poursuivie pendant 24 heures.

Compatibilité (tubulure en Y): adrénaline ■ albumine ■ amikacine ■ amphotéricine B, désoxycholate d' ■ aztréonam ■ brétylium ■ bumétanide ■ céfazoline ■ céfotaxime ■ céfotétane ■ céfoxitine ■ ceftazidime ■ ceftriaxone ■ céfuroxime ■ cimétidine ■ ciprofloxacine ■ clindamycine ■ digoxine ■ dobutamine ■ dopamine ■ doxycycline ■ érythromycine, lactobionate d' ■ esmolol ■ fentanyl ■ fluconazole ■ gentamicine ■ hydromorphone ■ imipénem/cilastatine ■ labétalol ■ lidocaïne ■ lorazépam ■ mépéridine ■ métoclopramide ■ métronidazole ■ midazolam ■ milrinone ■ morphine ■ multivitamines ■ nitroprusside ■ nitroglycérine ■ noradrénaline ■ oxacilline ■ pénicilline G potassique ■ pentamidine ■ pipéracilline ■ potassium, chlorure de ■ potassium, phosphate de ■ ranitidine ■ théophylline ■ ticarcilline ■ ticarcilline/clavulanate ■ tobramycine ■ triméthoprime/sulfaméthoxazole ■ vancomycine ■ vécuronium.

Incompatibilité (tubulure en Y): acétazolamide ■ acyclovir ■ aminophylline ■ ampicilline ■ ampicilline/sulbactam ■ céfamandole ■ céfopérazone ■ diazépam ■ furosémide ■ hydrocortisone sodique, succinate d' ■ mezlocilline ■ nafcilline ■ phénytoïne ■ rifampicine ■ thiopental.

D

ENSEIGNEMENT AU PATIENT ET À SES PROCHES

- Conseiller au patient de suivre rigoureusement la posologie recommandée même s'il se sent bien. S'il n'a pu prendre le médicament au moment habituel, il doit le prendre aussitôt que possible, à moins que ce ne soit presque l'heure prévue pour la dose suivante. Le prévenir qu'il ne doit jamais remplacer une dose manquée par une double dose. Avant d'arrêter le traitement au diltiazem, il faudrait probablement diminuer la dose graduellement.
- Montrer au patient comment mesurer son pouls. Lui conseiller de communiquer avec un professionnel de la santé si sa fréquence cardiaque est < 50 battements par minute.
- Recommander au patient de changer lentement de position pour réduire le risque d'hypotension orthostatique.
- Expliquer au patient qu'il est important de pratiquer une bonne hygiène buccale et de voir régulièrement le dentiste pour se faire nettoyer les dents afin de prévenir la sensibilité et le saignement des gencives ainsi qu'une hyperplasie gingivale (hypertrophie des gencives).
- Conseiller au patient d'éviter de boire de l'alcool et de consulter un professionnel de la santé avant de prendre des médicaments en vente libre, surtout des préparations contre le rhume, en même temps que le diltiazem.
- Recommander au patient de communiquer avec un professionnel de la santé si les symptômes suivants se manifestent: battements cardiaques irréguliers, dyspnée, enflure des mains et des pieds, étourdissements prononcés, nausées, constipation, hypotension ou céphalées graves ou persistantes.

D

- Recommander au patient d'utiliser un écran solaire et de porter des vêtements protecteurs afin de prévenir les réactions de photosensibilité.

Angine:

- Inciter le patient qui suit simultanément un traitement par des dérivés nitrés ou par un bêtabloquant à continuer de prendre les deux médicaments selon les recommandations du médecin et à utiliser de la nitroglycérine sublinguale, selon les besoins, en cas de crise d'angine.
- Recommander au patient de prévenir un professionnel de la santé si les douleurs thoraciques ne sont pas soulagées par le traitement, si elles s'aggravent ou si elles s'accompagnent de diaphorèse, ou encore si des essoufflements ou des céphalées graves persistantes se manifestent.
- Conseiller au patient de s'informer auprès d'un professionnel de la santé des restrictions à respecter sur le plan de l'effort avant de s'engager dans un programme d'exercices.

Hypertension:

- Encourager le patient à prendre d'autres mesures permettant de maîtriser l'hypertension (perdre du poids, suivre un régime hyposodé, cesser de fumer, consommer de l'alcool avec modération, faire régulièrement de l'exercice, gérer le stress). Le prévenir que le médicament stabilise la pression artérielle, mais ne guérit pas l'hypertension.
- Montrer au patient et à ses proches comment prendre la pression artérielle. Leur recommander de la mesurer toutes les semaines et de signaler tout changement important à un professionnel de la santé.

VÉRIFICATION DE L'EFFICACITÉ THÉRAPEUTIQUE

L'efficacité du traitement peut être démontrée par: une baisse de la pression artérielle ■ une diminution de la fréquence et de la gravité des crises d'angine ■ un moindre recours à des dérivés nitrés ■ une meilleure tolérance à l'effort et un sentiment de mieux-être ■ la suppression et la prévention des tachyarythmies auriculaires. ✳

DIMENHYDRINATE

Anti-Nausée dimenhydrinate, Apo-Dimenhydrinate, Dinate, Gravol, Nauseatol, Novo-Dimenate, PMS-Dimenhydrinate

CLASSIFICATION:
Antiémétique/antihistaminique/antivertige

Grossesse – catégorie B

INDICATIONS

Prévention et soulagement des nausées, des vomissements et des vertiges qui accompagnent le mal des transports ■ Prévention et soulagement de la maladie des rayons, des nausées et des vomissements postopératoires et d'origine médicamenteuse ■ Soulagement symptomatique des nausées et des vertiges dus au syndrome de Ménière et à d'autres troubles labyrinthiques.

MÉCANISME D'ACTION

Inhibition de la stimulation vestibulaire ■ Dépression du SNC et propriétés anticholinergiques, antihistaminiques et antiémétiques. ***Effets thérapeutiques:*** Diminution de la stimulation vestibulaire, ce qui peut prévenir le mal des transports.

PHARMACOCINÉTIQUE

Absorption: Bonne absorption (PO ou IM).

Distribution: Le médicament traverse probablement la barrière placentaire et passe dans le lait maternel.

Métabolisme et excrétion: Métabolisme hépatique.

Demi-vie: Inconnue.

Profil temps-action
(effet sur le mal des transports, effet antiémétique)

	Début d'action	Pic	Durée
PO	15 - 60 min	1 - 2 h	3 - 6 h
IR	30 - 45 min	inconnu	6 - 12 h
IM	20 - 30 min	1 - 2 h	3 - 6 h
IV	rapide	inconnu	3 - 6 h

CONTRE-INDICATIONS, PRÉCAUTIONS ET MISES EN GARDE

Contre-indications: Hypersensibilité ■ Glaucome ■ Maladie pulmonaire chronique ■ Difficulté à uriner due à l'hyperplasie de la prostate.

Précautions et mises en garde: Troubles convulsifs ■ Intolérance à l'alcool et à la tartrazine (ne pas administrer les préparations qui contiennent ces ingrédients chez ce type de patients) ■ Grossesse et allaitement ■ Glaucome à angle étroit.

RÉACTIONS INDÉSIRABLES ET EFFETS SECONDAIRES

SNC: somnolence, étourdissements, céphalées, excitation paradoxale (enfants).

ORLO: vision trouble, acouphènes.

CV: hypotension, palpitations.

GI: anorexie, constipation, diarrhée, sécheresse de la bouche (xérostomie).

GU: dysurie, mictions fréquentes.
Tég.: photosensibilité.
Locaux: douleur au point d'injection IM.

INTERACTIONS

Médicament-médicament: Effets additifs sur la dépression du SNC lors de l'usage concomitant d'autres **antihistaminiques**, d'**alcool**, d'**opioïdes** et d'**hypnosédatifs** ■ Le dimenhydrinate peut masquer les signes ou les symptômes d'ototoxicité chez les patients recevant des **médicaments ototoxiques** (**aminosides**, **acide éthacrynique**) ■ Propriétés anticholinergiques additives lors de l'administration concomitante d'**antidépresseurs tricycliques**, de **quinidine** ou de **disopyramide** ■ Les **IMAO** accentuent et prolongent les effets anticholinergiques des antihistaminiques.

VOIES D'ADMINISTRATION ET POSOLOGIE

- **PO (adultes)**: *Comprimés à libération rapide* – de 50 à 100 mg, toutes les 4 heures (ne pas dépasser 400 mg/jour), au besoin. *Capsules à libération prolongée* – 1 ou 2 capsules de 75 mg, toutes les 8 heures, au besoin (ne pas dépasser 5 capsules en 24 heures).
- **PO (enfants de 6 à 12 ans)**: De 25 à 50 mg, toutes les 6 à 8 heures, au besoin (ne pas dépasser 150 mg/jour).
- **PO (enfants de 2 à 6 ans)**: De 15 à 25 mg, toutes les 6 à 8 heures, au besoin (ne pas dépasser 75 mg/jour).
- **IR (adultes)**: De 50 à 100 mg, toutes les 6 à 8 heures, au besoin.
- **IR (enfants de 8 à 12 ans)**: De 25 à 50 mg, toutes les 8 à 12 heures, au besoin.
- **IR (enfants de 6 à 8 ans)**: De 12,5 à 25 mg, toutes les 8 à 12 heures, au besoin.
- **IR (enfants de 2 à 6 ans)**: De 12,5 à 25 mg, 1 fois par jour (n'administrer des doses additionnelles que sur recommandation du médecin).
- **IM, IV (adultes)**: 50 mg, toutes les 4 heures, selon les besoins.
- **IM (enfants de 6 à 8 ans)**: De 12,5 mg à 25 mg, 2 ou 3 fois par jour.
- **IM (enfants de 8 à 12 ans)**: De 25 mg à 50 mg, 2 ou 3 fois par jour.
- **IM (enfants > 12 ans)**: 50 mg, 2 ou 3 fois par jour.

PRÉSENTATION (version générique disponible)

Comprimés: 15 mg[Phc], 25 mg[Phc], 50 mg[Phc] ■ **Comprimés à croquer**: 15,50 mg[Phc] ■ **Capsules à libération prolongée**: 75 mg[Phc] ■ **Liquide**: 15 mg/5 mL[Phc] ■ **Suppositoires**: 25 mg[Phc], 50 mg[Phc], 100 mg[Phc] ■ **Solution pour injection**: 10 mg/mL[Phc], 50 mg/mL[Phc] (plusieurs concentrations et présentations disponibles) ■ **En association avec**: caféine et ergotamine (Gravergol[Pr]).

SOINS INFIRMIERS

D

ÉVALUATION DE LA SITUATION

- Suivre de près les nausées et les vomissements, ausculter les bruits intestinaux et observer les douleurs abdominales avant et après l'administration du médicament. Le dimenhydrinate peut masquer les signes d'abdomen aigu.
- Effectuer le bilan quotidien des ingesta et des excreta et mesurer la quantité de vomissures. Rester à l'affût des signes de déshydratation (soif excessive, peau et muqueuses sèches, tachycardie, augmentation de la densité de l'urine, diminution de la turgescence de la peau).

Tests de laboratoire: Le dimenhydrinate entraîne des résultats faussement négatifs aux tests cutanés allergologiques; arrêter le traitement 72 heures avant ces tests.

DIAGNOSTICS INFIRMIERS POSSIBLES

- Déficit de volume liquidien (Indications).
- Alimentation déficiente (Indications).
- Risque d'accident (Effets secondaires).

INTERVENTIONS INFIRMIÈRES

- Pour la prophylaxie du mal des transports, administrer au moins 30 minutes et, de préférence, 1 ou 2 heures avant que le patient ne se trouve dans une situation où le mal des transports peut survenir.

PO: Utiliser un récipient gradué pour mesurer la dose de solution.

IM: Injecter dans une masse musculaire bien développée; bien masser.

IV directe: Diluer 50 mg de dimenhydrinate dans 10 mL de solution de NaCl 0,9% pour injection. Consulter les directives de chaque fabricant avant de diluer la préparation.

Vitesse d'administration: Injecter en 2 minutes.

Associations compatibles dans la même seringue: atropine ■ dropéridol ■ fentanyl ■ héparine ■ hydromorphone ■ mépéridine ■ métoclopromide ■ morphine ■ pentazocine ■ perphénazine ■ ranitidine ■ scopolamine.

Associations incompatibles dans la même seringue: butorphanol ■ glycopyrrolate ■ midazolam ■ pentobarbital ■ thiopental.

Compatibilité (tubulure en Y): acyclovir.

Incompatibilité (tubulure en Y): aminophylline ■ héparine ■ hydrocortisone sodique, succinate d' ■ phénobarbital

■ phénytoïne ■ prednisolone ■ prochlorpérazine, édisylate de ■ promazine ■ prométhazine.
Compatibilité en addition au soluté: D5%E, NaCl 0,45 %, NaCl 0,9 %, solution de Ringer, solution de lactate de Ringer, association de dextrose et de soluté salin physiologique ou de dextrose et de solution de Ringer.

D

ENSEIGNEMENT AU PATIENT ET À SES PROCHES

- Prévenir le patient que le dimenhydrinate peut provoquer de la somnolence. Lui conseiller de ne pas conduire et d'éviter les activités qui exigent sa vigilance jusqu'à ce qu'on ait la certitude que le médicament n'entraîne pas cet effet chez lui.
- Informer le patient que le dimenhydrinate peut rendre la bouche sèche. Lui conseiller de pratiquer une bonne hygiène buccale, de se rincer la bouche fréquemment avec de l'eau et de consommer de la gomme à mâcher ou des bonbons sans sucre pour diminuer cet effet.
- Mettre en garde le patient contre la consommation d'alcool ou d'autres dépresseurs du SNC en même temps que le dimenhydrinate.
- Recommander au patient d'utiliser un écran solaire et des vêtements protecteurs afin de prévenir les réactions de photosensibilité.

VÉRIFICATION DE L'EFFICACITÉ THÉRAPEUTIQUE

L'efficacité du traitement peut être démontrée par: la prévention ou la diminution de la gravité des nausées et des vomissements, des vertiges ou du mal des transports. ✳

DINOPROSTONE

Cervidil, Prepidil, Prostin E_2

CLASSIFICATION:

Agent utilisé pendant la grossesse pour déclencher le travail, agent favorisant la maturation du col (prostaglandine)

Grossesse – catégorie C

INDICATIONS

Préparation ou maturation du col pendant une grossesse à terme ou près du terme, lorsqu'il est indiqué de déclencher le travail de l'accouchement.

MÉCANISME D'ACTION

Induction de contractions utérines similaires à celles du travail de l'accouchement à terme par stimulation directe du myomètre (effet ocytocique) ■ « Maturation du col » incluant le ramollissement, l'effacement et la dilatation ■ Stimulation des cellules des muscles lisses gastro-intestinaux. ***Effets thérapeutiques:*** Déclenchement du travail de l'accouchement ■ Évacuation du fœtus.

PHARMACOCINÉTIQUE

Absorption: Rapide.
Distribution: Inconnue. L'effet est surtout local.
Métabolisme et excrétion: La dinoprostone est métabolisée par les enzymes des tissus des poumons, des reins, de la rate et du foie.
Demi-vie: Inconnue.

Profil temps-action (maturation du col)

	Début d'action	Pic	Durée
Gel	rapide	30 – 45 min	inconnue
Insertion	rapide	inconnu	12 h
Comprimés	rapide	inconnu	inconnue

CONTRE-INDICATIONS, PRÉCAUTIONS ET MISES EN GARDE

Contre-indications: Hypersensibilité aux prostaglandines ou aux adjuvants présents dans le produit ■ L'usage du gel ou de l'insertion vaginale est déconseillé lorsqu'il faut éviter des contractions utérines prolongées, par exemple: antécédents de césarienne ou de chirurgie utérine ■ disproportion céphalopelvienne ■ accouchement traumatique ou difficile ■ multiparité (≥ 6 grossesses à terme) ■ utérus hyperactif ou hypertonique ■ souffrance fœtale (si l'accouchement n'est pas imminent) ■ hémorragie vaginale inexpliquée ■ *placenta prævia* ■ *vasa prævia* ■ herpès génital en poussée évolutive ■ urgence obstétrique dictant une intervention chirurgicale ■ accouchement par voie vaginale contre-indiqué ■ Salpingite aiguë ou rupture des membranes ■ Traitement ocytocique concomitant (après avoir retiré l'insertion vaginale, attendre 30 minutes avant d'administrer l'ocytocine) ■ Surdistention de l'utérus (grossesse multiple) ■ Épilepsie ■ Présentation fœtale anormale.
Précautions et mises en garde: Tissus utérins cicatriciels ■ Asthme ■ Hypotension ■ Maladie cardiaque ■ Troubles surrénaliens ■ Anémie ■ Ictère ■ Diabète ■ Glaucome ■ Maladie pulmonaire, rénale ou hépatique ■ Multiparité (jusqu'à 5 grossesses à terme).

RÉACTIONS INDÉSIRABLES ET EFFETS SECONDAIRES

Gel endocervical, insertion vaginale

GU: contractions utérines anormales, sensation de chaleur dans le vagin.

Loc.: douleurs lombaires.
Divers: fièvre.

Comprimés
GI: nausées, vomissements, diarrhée.

INTERACTIONS

Médicament-médicament: La dinoprostone intensifie les effets des autres **ocytociques**.

VOIES D'ADMINISTRATION ET POSOLOGIE

Maturation du col

- **Préparation vaginale (adultes)**: *Gel endocervical* – de 0,5 à 2 mg (selon le type de gel utilisé). *Insertion vaginale* – 10 mg. Retirer dès l'amorce du travail ou dans les 12 heures suivant l'insertion.
- **Préparation orale (adultes)**: Initialement, 0,5 mg (1 comprimé); répéter 1 heure plus tard. Toutes les doses ultérieures doivent être administrées à intervalles de 1 heure, si besoin est. Dose unique maximale: 1,5 mg.

PRÉSENTATION

Gel endocervical (Prepidil): 0,5 mg de dinoprostone dans 3 g de gel, dans une seringue préremplie, munie d'une sonde[Pr] ■ **Insertion vaginale (Cervidil)**: 10 mg[Pr] ■ **Gel endocervical (Prostin E2 Vaginal)**: 1 ou 2 mg de dinoprostone dans 3 g de gel, dans une seringue préremplie[Pr] ■ **Comprimés oraux (Prostin E2)**: 0,5 mg.

SOINS INFIRMIERS

ÉVALUATION DE LA SITUATION

Abortif:

- Déterminer la fréquence, la durée et la force des contractions ainsi que le tonus utérin au repos. On peut administrer des opioïdes pour soulager les douleurs utérines.
- Mesurer la température, le pouls et la pression artérielle à intervalles réguliers tout au long du traitement. La fièvre induite par la dinoprostone (élévation de plus de 1,1 °C) se manifeste habituellement dans les 15 à 45 minutes qui suivent l'introduction de l'ovule. La température se normalise de 2 à 6 heures après l'arrêt du traitement ou le retrait de l'ovule du vagin.
- AUSCULTER LE MURMURE VÉSICULAIRE. LA RESPIRATION SIFFLANTE ET L'OPPRESSION THORACIQUE PEUVENT ÊTRE DES INDICES D'UNE RÉACTION D'HYPERSENSIBILITÉ.
- Chez les patientes ayant reçu un ovule vaginal, suivre de près les nausées, les vomissements et la diarrhée. Les vomissements et la diarrhée sont fréquents. Le médecin peut prescrire une prémédication par un antiémétique et un antidiarrhéique.
- Évaluer la quantité et le type de pertes vaginales. Prévenir immédiatement le médecin ou un autre professionnel de la santé si les symptômes suivants d'hémorragie se manifestent: saignements accrus, hypotension, pâleur, tachycardie.

Maturation du col: Suivre continuellement, pendant toute la durée du traitement, l'activité utérine, l'état du fœtus ainsi que le degré de dilatation et d'effacement du col. Déceler l'hypertonie, la contractilité utérine soutenue et la détresse fœtale. On devrait retirer l'insertion vaginale au début de la période active du travail.

DIAGNOSTICS INFIRMIERS POSSIBLES

Connaissances insuffisantes sur le traitement médicamenteux (Enseignement au patient et à ses proches).

INTERVENTIONS INFIRMIÈRES

Abortif:

- Juste avant d'utiliser l'ovule, le laisser réchauffer à la température ambiante.
- Pour éviter tout risque d'absorption par la peau, porter des gants lors de la manipulation de l'ovule sans son emballage.
- Recommander à la patiente de rester en position couchée pendant les 10 minutes qui suivent l'introduction de l'ovule, après quoi elle peut se lever.

Insertion vaginale:

- Placer l'insertion vaginale transversalement dans le cul-de-sac postérieur du vagin, immédiatement après l'avoir retirée de son emballage d'aluminium. Il n'est pas nécessaire de la réchauffer ni de l'introduire par une technique stérile. N'utiliser l'insertion vaginale que si elle est munie d'un cordon de retrait. N'utiliser qu'une quantité minimale de lubrifiant hydrosoluble pour l'introduire; éviter d'en utiliser trop pour ne pas retarder la libération de la dinoprostone. La patiente devrait rester en position couchée pendant les 2 heures qui suivent l'introduction de cet agent, après quoi elle peut se lever.
- L'insertion vaginale libère 0,3 mg de dinoprostone à l'heure, pendant 12 heures. La retirer au début du travail, avant l'amniotomie ou après 12 heures.
- On ne devrait pas administrer l'ocytocine pendant que l'insertion est en place ou dans les 30 minutes qui suivent son retrait du vagin.

Gel endocervical:

- Déterminer le degré d'effacement du col avant d'introduire la sonde endocervicale. Ne pas l'administrer au-dessus du niveau de l'orifice interne. Utiliser une sonde endocervicale de 20 mm si le col n'est

pas effacé, et une sonde de 10 mm, s'il est effacé à 50 %.
- Administrer le gel de dinoprostone de façon à éviter tout contact avec la peau. Bien se laver les mains avec du savon et de l'eau après l'administration du gel.
- Laisser réchauffer le gel à la température ambiante, juste avant de l'administrer. Ne pas le réchauffer artificiellement (en bain-marie, aux micro-ondes). Retirer le cachet détachable de l'extrémité de la seringue, puis le capuchon protecteur et introduire l'embout dans le piston du cylindre de la seringue. Retirer la sonde de son emballage par une technique aseptique. Attacher solidement l'embout de la sonde à l'embout de la seringue; un «clic» prouve que la sonde est bien en place. Avant d'administrer la préparation, remplir la sonde de gel stérile en poussant le piston pour évacuer l'air. Le gel est stable pendant 24 mois au réfrigérateur.
- Installer la patiente en décubitus dorsal et, à l'aide d'un spéculum, exposer le col pour qu'il soit bien visible. En utilisant une méthode aseptique, introduire la sonde contenant le gel dans la cavité du col. Administrer le gel en poussant délicatement sur le piston de la seringue, puis retirer la sonde. Ne pas essayer d'administrer la petite quantité de gel qui reste dans la seringue. N'utiliser la même seringue que chez une seule patiente; après utilisation, mettre au rebut la seringue, la sonde et le gel inutilisé.
- La patiente doit rester en position couchée pendant 15 à 30 minutes après l'administration pour prévenir l'écoulement du gel.
- On peut administrer l'ocytocine de 6 à 12 heures après avoir obtenu la réponse souhaitée au traitement par la dinoprostone. Si, après avoir administré la dose initiale de dinoprostone, on n'obtient aucune réponse au niveau utérin ou cervical, on peut administrer une nouvelle dose, 6 heures plus tard.

ENSEIGNEMENT AU PATIENT ET À SES PROCHES

Expliquer à la patiente le but du traitement et des examens vaginaux.

Abortif:
- Recommander à la patiente de signaler immédiatement à un professionnel de la santé la fièvre et les frissons, les pertes vaginales nauséabondes, la douleur abdominale basse ou l'intensification des saignements.
- Assurer un soutien moral tout au long du traitement.

Maturation du col:
- Prévenir la patiente qu'elle peut ressentir une sensation de chaleur dans le vagin au cours du traitement.
- Recommander à la patiente de prévenir un professionnel de la santé si les contractions deviennent plus longues.

VÉRIFICATION DE L'EFFICACITÉ THÉRAPEUTIQUE

L'efficacité du traitement peut être démontrée par: l'avortement complet; l'administration continue pendant plus de deux jours n'est habituellement pas recommandée ■ la dilatation du col et le déclenchement du travail de l'accouchement. ✳

DIPHENHYDRAMINE

Allerdryl, Allernix, Benadryl, Dormex, Dormiphen, Nytol, PMS-Diphenhydramine, Sominex, Unisom

CLASSIFICATION:

Antihistaminique, hypnosédatif, antiémétique, antitussif et anxiolytique

Grossesse – catégorie B

INDICATIONS

Soulagement des symptômes allergiques entraînés par la libération d'histamine incluant l'anaphylaxie, les rhinites allergiques saisonnières et apériodiques, les dermatoses allergiques ■ Sédation nocturne légère ■ Prévention du mal des transports ■ Réduction des nausées et vomissements postopératoires ou des nausées causées par une néoplasie ou un traitement antinéoplasique ■ Traitement de la toux (sirop seulement) ■ **Usage topique**: Soulagement passager des démangeaisons dues ■ à des piqûres d'insectes ■ au contact avec l'herbe à puces (sumac grimpant), le sumac lustré ou le sumac de l'Ouest (chêne vénéneux) ■ aux coups de soleil légers ■ aux irritations légères de la peau. **Usages non approuvés**: Maladie de Parkinson et réactions dystoniques d'origine médicamenteuse.

MÉCANISME D'ACTION

Blocage des effets de l'histamine au niveau des récepteurs H_1; l'agent ne se fixe pas à l'histamine ni ne l'inactive ■ Dépression du SNC et effets anticholinergiques. ***Effets thérapeutiques:*** Soulagement des symptômes associés à un surplus d'histamine (éternuements, rhinorrhée, prurit nasal et oculaire, larmoiement et rougeur des yeux, urticaire) ■ Soulagement des réactions dystoniques aiguës ▪ Prévention du mal des transports ▪ Soulagement de la toux ▪ Soulagement des nausées et des vomissements ▪ Soulagement des démangeaisons.

PHARMACOCINÉTIQUE

Absorption: Bonne (PO et IM). Absorption systémique (voie topique).

Distribution: L'agent se répartit dans tout l'organisme, traverse la barrière placentaire et passe dans le lait maternel.

Métabolisme et excrétion: Métabolisme hépatique à 95 %.

Demi-vie: De 2,4 à 7 heures.

Profil temps-action (effets antihistaminiques)

	DÉBUT D'ACTION	PIC	DURÉE
PO	15 - 60 min	2 - 4 h	4 - 8 h
IM	20 - 30 min	2 - 4 h	4 - 8 h
IV	rapide	inconnu	4 - 8 h

CONTRE-INDICATIONS, PRÉCAUTIONS ET MISES EN GARDE

Contre-indications: Hypersensibilité ▪ Crises aiguës d'asthme ▪ Intolérance connue à l'alcool (certains élixirs en contiennent) ▪ Application sur de grandes surfaces cutanées écorchées ou suintantes (usage topique).

Précautions et mises en garde: **GÉR.**: Les personnes âgées sont davantage prédisposées à des réactions indésirables et aux effets anticholinergiques du médicament (délire, confusion aiguë, étourdissements, xérostomie, vision trouble, rétention urinaire, constipation et tachycardie); il est conseillé de réduire la dose ou d'administrer un antihistaminique sans propriétés anticholinergiques ▪ Maladie hépatique grave ▪ Glaucome à angle fermé ▪ Ulcère gastroduodénal avec sténose, obstruction du pylore ou du duodénum ▪ Troubles convulsifs ▪ Hyperplasie de la prostate ▪ Obstruction du col de la vessie ▪ Asthme bronchique ▪ Hyperthyroïdie ▪ Maladie cardiovasculaire ou hypertension ▪ **OBST.**: L'innocuité du médicament n'a pas été établie ▪ Allaitement ▪ **PÉD.**: Risque d'excitation paradoxale chez les jeunes enfants ▪ Ne pas appliquer la diphenhydramine topique sur des ampoules, sur la chair à vif ou sur une lésion suintante. Ne pas utiliser en cas de varicelle, de rougeole ou sur de grandes surfaces de la peau.

RÉACTIONS INDÉSIRABLES ET EFFETS SECONDAIRES

SNC: somnolence, étourdissements, céphalées, excitation paradoxale (accrue chez les enfants).

ORLO: vision trouble, acouphènes.

Resp.: épaississement des sécrétions bronchiques.

CV: hypotension, palpitations.

GI: anorexie, sécheresse de la bouche (xérostomie), constipation, diarrhée.

GU: dysurie, mictions fréquentes, rétention urinaire.

Tég.: photosensibilité.

Locaux: douleurs au point d'injection IM.

INTERACTIONS

Médicament-médicament: Effets dépressifs additifs sur le SNC lors de l'usage concomitant de **médicaments ayant un effet dépresseur du SNC**, tels que les **antihistaminiques**, les **opioïdes**, les **hypnosédatifs**, et d'**alcool** ▪ Propriétés anticholinergiques additives lors de l'administration concomitante de **médicaments ayant des propriétés anticholinergiques**, tels que les **antidépresseurs tricycliques**, la **quinidine** ou le **disopyramide** ▪ Les **IMAO** intensifient et prolongent les effets anticholinergiques des antihistaminiques.

Médicament-produits naturels: La consommation concomitante de **kava**, de **valériane** et de **camomille** peut augmenter l'effet dépresseur du SNC de la diphenhydramine.

VOIES D'ADMINISTRATION ET POSOLOGIE

- **PO (adultes et enfants > 12 ans)**: *Antihistaminique, antiémétique et antivertigineux* – de 25 à 50 mg, toutes les 4 à 6 heures. *Hypnosédatif* – de 25 à 50 mg, de 20 à 30 minutes avant le coucher.
- **PO (enfants de 6 à 12 ans)**: De 12,5 mg à 25 mg, toutes les 4 à 6 heures; au maximum: 100 mg par jour.
- **PO (enfants de 2 à 5 ans)**: 6,25 mg, toutes les 4 à 6 heures; au maximum: 4 doses par jour.
- **PO (enfants < 2 ans)**: 3,13 mg, toutes les 4 à 6 heures; au maximum: 4 doses par jour.
- **IM, IV (adultes)**: De 10 à 50 mg, toutes les 2 à 3 heures, selon les besoins (on peut administrer jusqu'à 100 mg par dose; ne pas dépasser 400 mg par jour).
- **IM, IV (enfants)**: 5 mg/kg/jour ou 150 mg/m^2/jour, en 4 doses fractionnées, à administrer selon les besoins (ne pas dépasser 300 mg par jour).
- **Usage topique (adultes et enfants > 2 ans)**: Appliquer la diphenhydramine à 2 % en crème, 3 ou 4 fois par jour.

PRÉSENTATION (version générique disponible)

Capsules: 25 mg^{VL}, 50 mg^{VL} ▪ **Comprimés**: 25 mg^{VL}, 50 mg^{VL} ▪ **Comprimés à croquer**: 12,5 mg^{VL} ▪ **Élixir**: 12,5 mg/5 mL^{VL} ▪ **Sirop**: 6,25 mg/5 mL^{VL} ▪ **Solution pour injection**: 10 mg/mL^{Pr}, 50 mg/mL^{Pr} ▪ **Crème**: 2 %^{VL}

■ **En association avec**: analgésiques, décongestionnants et expectorants dans des préparations en vente libre contre les douleurs, l'insomnie, la toux et le rhume.

SOINS INFIRMIERS

D

ÉVALUATION DE LA SITUATION

- La diphenhydramine est un médicament à usages multiples. Déterminer la raison pour laquelle le médecin l'a prescrite et observer les symptômes qui s'appliquent au cas particulier du patient.

GÉR.: Les personnes âgées sont plus à risque de sédation et de confusion, car elles sont plus sensibles aux effets secondaires anticholinergiques. Rester à l'affût de ces effets secondaires et protéger le patient contre les chutes. Mettre en place des mesures visant à diminuer ce risque.

Prophylaxie et traitement de l'anaphylaxie: Rester à l'affût de l'urticaire et assurer la perméabilité des voies respiratoires.

Rhinite allergique: Déterminer le degré de congestion nasale; suivre de près la rhinorrhée et les éternuements.

Parkinsonisme et réactions extrapyramidales: Évaluer le type de dyskinésie avant et après l'administration du médicament.

Insomnie: Observer les habitudes de sommeil du patient.

Mal des transports: Suivre de près les nausées, les vomissements et les douleurs abdominales; ausculter les bruits intestinaux.

Soulagement de la toux: Déterminer la fréquence et la nature de la toux. Ausculter le murmure vésiculaire et noter la quantité et le type d'expectorations. Sauf contre-indication, conseiller au patient de consommer de 1 500 à 2 000 mL de liquides par jour afin de diminuer la viscosité des sécrétions bronchiques.

Prurit: Déterminer la gravité des démangeaisons, du rash et de l'inflammation.

Tests de laboratoire: La diphenhydramine peut diminuer la réponse cutanée aux tests d'allergie cutanés. Arrêter le traitement 4 jours avant ces tests.

DIAGNOSTICS INFIRMIERS POSSIBLES

- Habitudes de sommeil perturbées (Indications).
- Risque de déficit des volumes liquidiens (Indications).
- Risque d'accident (Effets secondaires).

INTERVENTIONS INFIRMIÈRES

- NE PAS CONFONDRE BENADRYL (DIPHENHYDRAMINE) AVEC BENYLIN (DEXTROMETHORPHAN).

Traitement de l'insomnie: administrer le médicament 20 minutes avant le coucher et planifier les soins infirmiers en conséquence afin d'interrompre le moins possible le sommeil du patient.

Prophylaxie du mal des transports: Administrer la diphenhydramine au moins 30 minutes et, de préférence, 1 ou 2 heures avant que le patient ne se trouve dans une circonstance où le mal des transports peut survenir.

PO: Administrer le médicament avec des aliments ou du lait afin de réduire l'irritation gastro-intestinale. On peut vider la capsule et prendre son contenu avec de l'eau ou des aliments.

IM: Administrer dans un muscle bien développé. Éviter les injections SC.

IV directe: On peut administrer la diphenhydramine sans la diluer. On peut aussi effectuer une dilution dans une solution de NaCl 0,9 % ou NaCl 0,4 5%, de D5%E ou D10%E, de D5%/NaCl 0,9 % ou de D5%/NaCl 0,45 % ou de D5%/NaCl 0,25 %, dans une solution de Ringer, dans une solution de lactate de Ringer et dans une solution de Ringer avec dextrose. Consulter les directives de chaque fabricant avant de reconstituer la préparation.

Vitesse d'administration: Ne pas dépasser 25 mg/min.

Associations compatibles dans la même seringue: atropine ■ butorphanol ■ chlorpromazine ■ cimétidine ■ dimenhydrinate ■ dropéridol ■ fentanyl ■ fluphénazine ■ glycopyrrolate ■ hydromorphone ■ hydroxyzine ■ mépéridine ■ métoclopramide ■ midazolam ■ morphine ■ nalbuphine ■ pentazocine ■ perphénazine ■ proclorpérazine ■ promazine ■ prométhazine ■ ranitidine ■ scopolamine ■ sufentanil.

Associations incompatibles dans la même seringue: halopéridol ■ pentobarbital ■ phénobarbital ■ phénytoïne ■ thiopental.

Compatibilité (tubulure en Y): acyclovir ■ aldesleukine ■ amifostine ■ aztréonam ■ ciprofloxacine ■ cisplatine ■ cladribine ■ cyclophosphamide ■ cytarabine ■ doxorubicine ■ filgrastim ■ fluconazole ■ fludarabine ■ gallium, nitrate de ■ granisétron ■ héparine ■ hydrocortisone ■ idarubicine ■ melphalan ■ mépéridine ■ méropénème ■ méthotrexate ■ ondansétron ■ paclitaxel ■ pipéracilline/tazobactam ■ potassium, chlorure de ■ propofol ■ sargramostim ■ sufentanil ■ tacrolimus ■ téniposide ■ thiotépa ■ vinorelbine ■ vitamines du complexe B avec C.

Incompatibilité (tubulure en Y): allopurinol ■ céfépime ■ cefmétazole ■ foscarnet.

ENSEIGNEMENT AU PATIENT ET À SES PROCHES

- Conseiller au patient de respecter rigoureusement la posologie recommandée et de ne pas dépasser la dose prescrite. Lui recommander de ne pas prendre de médicament en vente libre contenant de la diphenhydramine avec un autre produit contenant de la diphenhydramine, incluant la préparation topique.

GÉR.: Conseiller au patient âgé de ne pas prendre de produits de vente libre contenant de la diphenhydramine puisque les personnes âgées sont plus sensibles aux effets secondaires anticholinergiques.

- Prévenir le patient que la diphenhydramine peut provoquer de la somnolence. Lui conseiller de ne pas conduire et d'éviter les activités qui exigent sa vigilance jusqu'à ce qu'on ait la certitude que le médicament n'entraîne pas cet effet chez lui.

PÉD.: Prévenir les parents et les soignants que le médicament peut entraîner chez l'enfant une excitation paradoxale. Leur conseiller de bien calculer la dose à administrer; le surdosage, en particulier chez les nourrissons et les enfants, peut entraîner des hallucinations, des convulsions et la mort.

- Informer le patient que la diphenhydramine peut entraîner la sécheresse buccale. Lui conseiller de pratiquer une bonne hygiène buccale, de se rincer la bouche fréquemment avec de l'eau et de consommer de la gomme à mâcher ou des bonbons sans sucre pour diminuer cet effet. Lui conseiller de prévenir un professionnel de la santé si la sécheresse de la bouche persiste pendant plus de 2 semaines.
- Recommander au patient d'utiliser un écran solaire et de porter des vêtements protecteurs afin de prévenir les réactions de photosensibilité.
- Mettre en garde le patient contre la consommation d'alcool ou d'autres dépresseurs du SNC en même temps que la diphenhydramine.
- Recommander au patient qui prend de la diphenhydramine sous forme de préparation en vente libre de prévenir un professionnel de la santé si les symptômes s'aggravent ou persistent pendant plus de 7 jours.

Usage topique:

- Recommander au patient de nettoyer la peau affectée avant l'application, d'éviter d'appliquer la préparation sur une peau écorchée ou sur des ampoules, et d'arrêter le traitement et de communiquer avec un professionnel de la santé en cas d'irritation.
- Mettre en garde le patient contre l'utilisation de ce médicament sur des lésions dues à la varicelle ou à la rougeole ou sur des territoires cutanés étendus.

VÉRIFICATION DE L'EFFICACITÉ THÉRAPEUTIQUE

L'efficacité du traitement peut être démontrée par: la prévention ou la diminution de l'urticaire, en cas d'anaphylaxie ou d'autres réactions allergiques ▪ la sédation lorsque le médicament est administré comme hypnosédatif ▪ la prévention ou la diminution des nausées et des vomissements entraînés par le mal des transports ▪ la réduction des nausées et vomissements postopératoires ou des nausées causées par une néoplasie ou un traitement antinéoplasique ▪ le soulagement des démangeaisons (usage topique) ▪ la diminution de la fréquence et de l'intensité de la toux, sans suppression des réflexes tussigènes ▪ la diminution de la dyskinésie chez les patients souffrant de parkinsonisme ou manifestant des réactions extrapyramidales. ✳

DIPHÉNOXYLATE AVEC ATROPINE

Lomotil

CLASSIFICATION:

Antidiarrhéique

Grossesse – catégorie C

INDICATIONS

Traitement d'appoint de la diarrhée.

MÉCANISME D'ACTION

Inhibition d'une motilité gastro-intestinale excessive ▪ Structure similaire à celle des opioïdes, mais la préparation est dépourvue de propriétés analgésiques ▪ L'atropine est ajoutée pour décourager l'abus. ***Effets thérapeutiques:*** Ralentissement de la motilité gastro-intestinale, d'où diminution de la diarrhée.

PHARMACOCINÉTIQUE

Absorption: > 60 % (PO).

Distribution: Le diphénoxylate passe dans le lait maternel.

Métabolisme et excrétion: *Diphénoxylate* – métabolisme majoritairement hépatique; une fraction du médicament est transformée en un composé antidiarrhéique actif (la difénoxine). Excrétion urinaire minimale.

Demi-vie: *Diphénoxylate* – 2,5 heures.

Profil temps-action (effet antidiarrhéique)

	DÉBUT D'ACTION	PIC	DURÉE
Diphénoxylate – PO	45 – 60 min	2 h	3 – 4 h

CONTRE-INDICATIONS, PRÉCAUTIONS ET MISES EN GARDE

Contre-indications: Hypersensibilité ■ Maladie hépatique grave ■ Diarrhée infectieuse (attribuable à *E. coli*, *Salmonella* ou *Shigella*) ■ Diarrhée associée à la colite pseudomembraneuse ■ **PÉD.**: Enfants de moins de 2 ans.

Précautions et mises en garde: Patients déshydratés ■ Glaucome à angle fermé ■ Dépendance physique aux opioïdes ■ Maladies inflammatoires de l'intestin ■ **GÉR.**: Plus grande sensibilité aux effets du médicament ■ Hyperplasie de la prostate ■ **OBST., ALLAITEMENT**: L'innocuité du médicament n'a pas été établie ■ **PÉD.**: Prudence, surtout chez les patients atteints du syndrome de Down.

RÉACTIONS INDÉSIRABLES ET EFFETS SECONDAIRES

SNC: étourdissements, confusion, somnolence, céphalées, insomnie, nervosité.
ORLO: vision trouble, xérophtalmie.
CV: tachycardie.
GI: constipation, sécheresse de la bouche (xérostomie), épigastralgie, iléus, nausées, vomissements.
GU: rétention urinaire.
Tég.: rougeurs de la peau.

INTERACTIONS

Médicament-médicament: Effets dépressifs additifs sur le SNC lors de l'usage concomitant d'autres **dépresseurs du SNC** incluant l'**alcool**, les **antihistaminiques**, les **opioïdes**, et les **hypnosédatifs** ■ Propriétés anticholinergiques additives lors de l'administration concomitante d'autres **médicaments dotés de propriétés anticholinergiques** dont les **antidépresseurs tricycliques** ou le **disopyramide** ■ Les **IMAO** peuvent déclencher une crise hypertensive.

Médicament-produits naturels: Augmentation des effets anticholinergiques lors de la consommation concomitante de **datura**, de **stramoine** et de **scopolia**.

VOIES D'ADMINISTRATION ET POSOLOGIE

Les doses sont établies compte tenu de la teneur en diphénoxylate – un comprimé contient 2,5 mg de diphénoxylate et 0,025 mg d'atropine.

- **PO (adultes)**: Initialement, 5 mg, 3 ou 4 fois par jour; la dose d'entretien doit être déterminée dans chaque cas particulier (ne pas dépasser 20 mg par jour).
- **PO (enfants)**: Schémas posologique présentés à titre indicatif seulement. Adapter selon l'état nutritionnel et le degré de déshydratation de l'enfant: *de 2 à 5 ans (de 15 à 20 kg)*: 2,5 mg 2 fois jour; *de 6 à 8 ans (de 20 à 27 kg)*: 2,5 mg 3 fois par jour; *de 9 à 12 ans (de 27 à 36 kg)*: 2,5 mg 4 fois par jour.

PRÉSENTATION

Comprimés: 2,5 mg de diphénoxylate/0,025 mg d'atropine[N].

SOINS INFIRMIERS

ÉVALUATION DE LA SITUATION

- Observer la fréquence et la consistance des selles et ausculter les bruits intestinaux avant l'administration du médicament et pendant toute la durée du traitement.
- Effectuer le bilan hydroélectrolytique à intervalles réguliers et observer la turgescence de la peau à la recherche de signes de déshydratation.

Tests de laboratoire:
- On devrait effectuer des tests de la fonction hépatique à intervalles réguliers pendant toute la durée du traitement prolongé.
- Le diphénoxylate avec atropine peut entraîner une élévation des concentrations sériques d'amylase.

DIAGNOSTICS INFIRMIERS POSSIBLES

- Diarrhée (Indications).
- Constipation (Effets secondaires).
- Connaissances insuffisantes sur le traitement médicamenteux (Enseignement au patient et à ses proches).

INTERVENTIONS INFIRMIÈRES

- NE PAS CONFONDRE LOMOTIL AVEC LAMICTAL (LAMOTRIGINE) OU AVEC LAMISIL (TERBINAFINE).
- Le risque de dépendance augmente avec la dose et la durée d'utilisation. L'atropine est ajoutée à la préparation pour diminuer le risque d'abus.
- Les comprimés de diphénoxylate avec atropine peuvent être administrés avec des aliments si l'irritation gastro-intestinale devient gênante. On peut écraser les comprimés et les administrer avec la boisson choisie par le patient. Utiliser un récipient gradué pour mesurer la quantité de solution à administrer.

ENSEIGNEMENT AU PATIENT ET À SES PROCHES

- Conseiller au patient de respecter rigoureusement la posologie recommandée et de ne pas prendre une quantité plus grande de médicament que celle qui lui a été prescrite en raison du risque d'accoutumance, ainsi que du risque de surdosage chez les enfants. Expliquez aussi au patient que s'il n'a pas pu prendre son médicament au moment habituel, il doit le prendre aussitôt que possible à moins qu'il ne soit presque l'heure prévue pour la dose suivante; le prévenir qu'il ne doit jamais remplacer une dose manquée par une double dose.

- Prévenir le patient que ce médicament peut parfois provoquer de la somnolence. Lui conseiller de ne pas conduire et d'éviter les activités qui exigent sa vigilance jusqu'à ce qu'on ait la certitude que le médicament n'entraîne pas cet effet chez lui.
- Expliquer au patient que pour soulager la sécheresse de la bouche, il devrait se rincer fréquemment la bouche, consommer des bonbons ou de la gomme à mâcher sans sucre et pratiquer une bonne hygiène buccale.
- Recommander au patient d'éviter de boire de l'alcool ou de prendre d'autres dépresseurs du SNC en même temps que ce médicament.
- Conseiller au patient d'informer le professionnel de la santé de son traitement par ce médicament, avant de se soumettre à une intervention chirurgicale ou à un autre traitement.
- Conseiller au patient de prévenir un professionnel de la santé si la diarrhée persiste ou si de la fièvre, des douleurs abdominales ou des palpitations se manifestent.

VÉRIFICATION DE L'EFFICACITÉ THÉRAPEUTIQUE

L'efficacité du traitement peut être démontrée par: la diminution de la diarrhée; on doit poursuivre le traitement pendant 24 à 36 heures avant qu'on puisse décider que le médicament n'est pas efficace pour traiter la diarrhée aiguë. ✳

DIPYRIDAMOLE

Apo-Dipyridamole, Dipyridamole, Persantine

DIPYRIDAMOLE/ASPIRINE

Aggrenox

CLASSIFICATION:

Antiplaquettaire, agent diagnostique (vasodilatateur coronarien)

Grossesse – catégorie B

INDICATIONS

PO: Prévention des complications thromboemboliques postopératoires associées au remplacement prothétique des valves cardiaques ■ **IV:** Agent diagnostique qui remplace l'épreuve d'effort durant la scintigraphie myocardique.

Dipyridamole/aspirine: Prévention des accidents vasculaires cérébraux (AVC) chez les patients qui ont déjà subi un AVC ou une ischémie cérébrale transitoire (ICT).

D

MÉCANISME D'ACTION

PO: Diminution de l'agrégation plaquettaire par inhibition de l'enzyme phosphodiestérase ■ **IV:** Vasodilatation coronarienne par inhibition du captage de l'adénosine. ***Effets thérapeutiques:*** **PO:** Inhibition de l'agrégation plaquettaire et des épisodes ultérieurs de thromboembolie ■ **IV:** Dilatation des artères coronaires normales lors de la scintigraphie myocardique, réduisant ainsi le débit du sang dans les vaisseaux rétrécis et entraînant une distribution anormale du radioisotope.

PHARMACOCINÉTIQUE

Absorption: De 30 à 60 % (PO).

Distribution: Le médicament se répartit dans tout l'organisme. Il traverse la barrière placentaire et passe dans le lait maternel.

Métabolisme et excrétion: Métabolisme hépatique; excrétion biliaire.

Demi-vie: 10 heures.

Profil temps-action
(activité antiplaquettaire [PO]; vasodilatation coronarienne [IV])

	DÉBUT D'ACTION	PIC	DURÉE
PO	inconnu	inconnu	inconnue
IV	inconnu	6,5 min†	30 min

† À partir du début de la perfusion.

CONTRE-INDICATIONS, PRÉCAUTIONS ET MISES EN GARDE

Contre-indications: Hypersensibilité ■ États de choc et collapsus (ne pas administrer le dipyridamole par voie IV).

Précautions et mises en garde: Hypotension ■ **GÉR.:** Risque accru d'hypotension orthostatique ■ Anomalies plaquettaires ■ **OBST.:** Bien que l'innocuité du médicament n'ait pas été établie, il existe des précédents d'usage sans effets nocifs durant la grossesse ■ **ALLAITEMENT:** L'innocuité du médicament n'a pas été établie ■ **PÉD.:** Enfants < 12 ans (l'innocuité du médicament n'a pas été établie).

D

RÉACTIONS INDÉSIRABLES ET EFFETS SECONDAIRES

SNC: étourdissements, céphalées, syncope; *voie IV seulement* – ischémies cérébrales transitoires, faiblesse.
Resp.: *voie IV seulement* – bronchospasme.
CV: *voie IV seulement* – INFARCTUS DU MYOCARDE, hypotension, arythmies, bouffées vasomotrices.
GI: nausées, diarrhée, gêne gastro-intestinale, vomissements.
Tég.: rash.

INTERACTIONS

Médicament-médicament: Effets additifs sur l'agrégation plaquettaire lors de l'administration concomitante d'**aspirine**, de **clopidogrel** ou de **ticlopidine** ■ Risque accru de saignements lors de l'administration concomitante d'**anticoagulants**, de **thrombolytiques**, d'**anti-inflammatoires non stéroïdiens**, d'**acide valproïque** ou de **sulfinpyrazone** ■ Risque accru d'hypotension lors de la consommation concomitante d'**alcool** ■ Les **xanthines**, comme l'**aminophylline** et la **théophylline**, peuvent contrecarrer les effets du dipyridamole durant l'épreuve de scintigraphie myocardique.
Médicament-aliments: Les **dérivés de la xanthine**, comme la **caféine** que l'on retrouve dans le **café**, le **thé**, le **chocolat** et le **cola**, peuvent contrecarrer les effets du dipyridamole durant l'épreuve de scintigraphie myocardique.

VOIES D'ADMINISTRATION ET POSOLOGIE

- **PO (adultes)**: De 75 à 100 mg, 4 fois par jour. *En association avec l'aspirine* – 200 mg, 2 fois par jour.
- **IV (adultes)**: 0,142 mg/kg/min, à injecter en 4 minutes. Ne pas dépasser 60 mg.

PRÉSENTATION (version générique disponible)

Comprimés: 25 mg^Pr, 50 mg^Pr, 75 mg^Pr ■ **Capsules à libération prolongée**: En association avec aspirine (Aggrenox^Pr) (voir l'annexe U) ■ **Solution pour injection**: 5 mg/mL^Pr.

SOINS INFIRMIERS

ÉVALUATION DE LA SITUATION

PO: Mesurer la pression artérielle et le pouls avant le traitement et à intervalles réguliers pendant la période d'adaptation posologique.
GÉR.: Suivre de près les personnes âgées pour déceler l'hypotension orthostatique.
IV: PRENDRE LES SIGNES VITAUX DURANT LA PERFUSION ET PENDANT 10 À 15 MINUTES APRÈS L'AVOIR ARRÊTÉE. OBTENIR UN TRACÉ ÉCG DANS AU MOINS UNE DÉRIVATION. EN CAS DE DOULEUR THORACIQUE INTENSE OU DE BRONCHOSPASME, ADMINISTRER DE 50 À 250 mg D'AMINOPHYLLINE PAR VOIE IV À UN DÉBIT DE 50 À 100 mg EN 30 À 60 SECONDES. SI L'HYPOTENSION EST GRAVE, INSTALLER LE PATIENT EN DÉCUBITUS DORSAL, LA TÊTE PENCHÉE VERS L'ARRIÈRE. SI LA DOULEUR THORACIQUE N'EST PAS SOULAGÉE PAR UNE DOSE D'AMINOPHYLLINE DE 250 mg, ADMINISTRER DE LA NITROGLYCÉRINE PAR VOIE SUBLINGUALE. SI LA DOULEUR THORACIQUE PERSISTE MALGRÉ TOUT, AMORCER LE TRAITEMENT QUI S'IMPOSE EN CAS D'INFARCTUS DU MYOCARDE.
Tests de laboratoire: Noter le temps de saignement à intervalles réguliers pendant toute la durée du traitement.

DIAGNOSTICS INFIRMIERS POSSIBLES

- Débit cardiaque diminué (Indications).
- Connaissances insuffisantes sur le traitement médicamenteux (Enseignement au patient et à ses proches).

INTERVENTIONS INFIRMIÈRES

PO: Administrer le dipyridamole avec un grand verre d'eau, au moins 1 heure avant les repas ou 2 heures après, pour accélérer l'absorption. En cas d'irritation gastro-intestinale, on peut administrer le médicament avec des aliments ou immédiatement après les repas. On peut écraser les comprimés et les mélanger avec des aliments si le patient éprouve des difficultés de déglutition. Le pharmacien peut également délivrer le dipyridamole sous forme de suspension. Les granules de dipyridamole qui se trouvent à l'intérieur des capsules d'Aggrenox ne doivent pas être écrasés ni mâchés.
Perfusion: Diluer le médicament à une concentration de 1:2 au moins, dans une solution de D5%E, pour obtenir un volume total de 20 à 50 mL. Le dipyridamole non dilué peut provoquer l'irritation de la veine. Consulter les directives de chaque fabricant avant de reconstituer la préparation.
Vitesse d'administration: Administrer la perfusion en 4 minutes.

ENSEIGNEMENT AU PATIENT ET À SES PROCHES

PO:
- Conseiller au patient de respecter rigoureusement la posologie recommandée et de prendre le médica-

ment en espaçant uniformément les doses. S'il n'a pu prendre le médicament au moment habituel, il doit le prendre dès que possible, à moins que la dose suivante ne soit prévue dans moins de 4 heures. Le prévenir qu'il ne doit jamais remplacer une dose manquée par une double dose. Puisque le patient peut ne pas se rendre compte des bienfaits du médicament, l'inciter à continuer de prendre le dipyridamole en respectant rigoureusement les recommandations du médecin.

- Conseiller au patient de changer lentement de position afin de réduire le risque d'hypotension orthostatique.
- Mettre en garde le patient contre la consommation d'alcool qui peut potentialiser les effets hypotenseurs du médicament. Lui conseiller aussi de ne pas fumer, car la nicotine entraîne une vasoconstriction.
- Conseiller au patient de consulter un professionnel de la santé avant de prendre des médicaments en vente libre en même temps que le dipyridamole. Le prévenir qu'il ne doit prendre de l'aspirine que si le médecin le recommande et qu'il doit respecter ses consignes concernant la posologie. Lui conseiller également de se renseigner sur les traitements de rechange qui peuvent soulager les douleurs ou la fièvre.
- Recommander au patient de signaler au médecin tout saignement ou toute ecchymose inhabituels. L'usage concomitant d'un autre antiplaquettaire ou de warfarine peut augmenter le risque de saignements, mais ce médicament est habituellement utilisé pour des indications spécifiques.
- Conseiller au patient d'informer tous les professionnels de la santé de son traitement médicamenteux et, le cas échéant, de les prévenir qu'il prend un autre antiplaquettaire ou de la warfarine.

IV: Recommander au patient de signaler immédiatement à un professionnel de la santé la dyspnée ou les douleurs thoraciques.

- Conseiller au patient d'éviter de consommer du café, du thé, du chocolat, du cola ou tout autre aliment ou boisson contenant de la caféine dans les 24 heures qui précèdent une scintigraphie myocardique avec du dipyridamole.

VÉRIFICATION DE L'EFFICACITÉ THÉRAPEUTIQUE

L'efficacité du traitement peut être démontrée par: la prévention des complications thromboemboliques postopératoires associées au port d'une valve artificielle prothétique ■ la vasodilatation coronarienne lors des procédés d'imagerie diagnostique par scintigraphie myocardique ■ la prévention des AVC chez les patients qui ont déjà subi un AVC ou une ICT. ✳

DISOPYRAMIDE

Rythmodan, Rythmodan-LA

CLASSIFICATION:

Antiarythmique (classe IA)

Grossesse – catégorie C

INDICATIONS

Prévention et traitement des tachycardies ventriculaires soutenues. Traitement des arythmies ventriculaires symptomatiques confirmées lorsque les symptômes sont suffisamment graves pour nécessiter un traitement. **Usages non approuvés**: Prophylaxie et traitement des tachyarythmies supraventriculaires.

MÉCANISME D'ACTION

Diminution de l'excitabilité du myocarde et de la vitesse de conduction ■ Médicament doté de propriétés anticholinergiques ■ Faible effet sur la fréquence cardiaque, mais effet inotrope négatif direct. ***Effets thérapeutiques***: Suppression des arythmies ventriculaires.

PHARMACOCINÉTIQUE

Absorption: > 60 % (PO).

Distribution: Le médicament se répartit dans tout l'organisme et passe dans le lait maternel.

Métabolisme et excrétion: Métabolisme hépatique; 10 % excrété à l'état inchangé dans les fèces, et 50 %, à l'état inchangé par les reins.

Demi-vie: De 8 à 18 heures (prolongée en cas d'insuffisance rénale ou hépatique).

Profil temps-action (effets antiarythmiques)

	DÉBUT D'ACTION	PIC	DURÉE
PO	0,5 – 3,5 h	2,5 h	1,5 – 8,5 h
PO – LA†	0,5 – 3,5 h	4,9 h	12 h

† LA: libération prolongée ou retard.

CONTRE-INDICATIONS, PRÉCAUTIONS ET MISES EN GARDE

Contre-indications: Hypersensibilité ■ Choc cardiogénique ■ Bloc cardiaque du 2e et du 3e degré ■ Troubles graves de la conduction intraventriculaire ■ Syndrome de dysfonctionnement sinusal (en l'absence d'un stimulateur cardiaque) ■ Insuffisance rénale ■ Insuffisance cardiaque non compensée ■ Glaucome.

Précautions et mises en garde: Insuffisance cardiaque ou dysfonctionnement ventriculaire gauche (il est recommandé de réduire la dose) ■ Insuffisance hépatique ■

Hyperplasie de la prostate ■ Myasthénie grave ■ **OBST., ALLAITEMENT, PÉD.**: L'innocuité du médicament n'a pas été établie ■ **GÉR.**: Risque d'insuffisance cardiaque.

RÉACTIONS INDÉSIRABLES ET EFFETS SECONDAIRES

D

SNC: étourdissements, fatigue, céphalées.
ORLO: vision trouble, xérophtalmie, sécheresse de la gorge.
CV: INSUFFISANCE CARDIAQUE, arythmies, bloc AV, dyspnée, œdème, hypotension.
GI: constipation, sécheresse de la bouche (xérostomie), douleurs abdominales, flatulence, nausées.
GU: retard de la miction, rétention urinaire.
End.: hypoglycémie.
Divers: altération de la régulation thermique.

INTERACTIONS

Médicament-médicament: Le disopyramide peut potentialiser l'effet anticoagulant de la **warfarine** ■ La **rifampine**, le **phénobarbital** et la **phénytoïne** peuvent diminuer les concentrations sanguines et l'efficacité du disopyramide ■ La **cimétidine** ou l'**érythromycine** peuvent diminuer le métabolisme du disopyramide et en augmenter les concentrations sanguines ■ Risque d'effets cardiaques toxiques additifs lors de l'administration concomitante d'autres **antiarythmiques** (conduction prolongée et débit cardiaque réduit), et particulièrement du **vérapamil** (ne pas administrer le disopyramide 48 heures avant ou 24 heures après ces médicaments) ■ Risque d'effets secondaires anticholinergiques additifs lors de l'administration concomitante d'autres **médicaments dotés de propriétés anticholinergiques**, incluant les **antihistaminiques** et les **antidépresseurs tricycliques** ■ Risque accru d'arythmies lors de l'administration concomitante de **pimozide**.
Médicament-produits naturels: Effets anticholinergiques accrus lors de la consommation concomitante de **datura**, de **stramoine** et de **scopolia**.

VOIES D'ADMINISTRATION ET POSOLOGIE

- **PO (adultes > 50 kg)**: Initialement, une dose de 300 mg en capsules à libération immédiate, suivie d'une dose de 100 mg, toutes les 6 heures (aussi en capsules à libération immédiate), ou de 250 mg, toutes les 12 heures (sous forme de préparation à libération prolongée). Ne pas dépasser 800 mg par jour.
- **PO (adultes < 50 kg ou patients atteints de dysfonctionnement ventriculaire gauche)**: Initialement, une dose de 200 mg en capsules à libération immédiate, suivie d'une dose de 100 mg, toutes les 6 à 8 heures (aussi sous forme de capsules à libération immédiate).

INSUFFISANCE RÉNALE

- **PO (ADULTES)**: *CL_{CR} DE 30 À 40 mL/MIN* – DE 100 À 150 mg, TOUTES LES 8 HEURES; *CL_{CR} DE 15 À 30 mL/MIN* – DE 100 À 150 mg, TOUTES LES 12 HEURES; *CL_{CR} < 15 mL/MIN* – DE 100 À 150 mg, TOUTES LES 24 HEURES, SOUS FORME DE PRÉPARATION À ACTION IMMÉDIATE.

PRÉSENTATION (version générique disponible)

Capsules: 100 mg^Pr, 150 mg^Pr ■ **Comprimés à libération prolongée**: 250 mg^Pr.

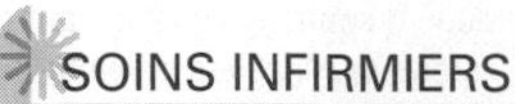

SOINS INFIRMIERS

ÉVALUATION DE LA SITUATION

- Mesurer la pression artérielle et le pouls et examiner l'ÉCG avant le traitement et à intervalles réguliers pendant toute sa durée. Mesurer le pouls avant d'administrer le médicament; ne pas administrer la dose et prévenir le médecin ou un autre professionnel de la santé si le pouls est inférieur à 60 battements par minute ou supérieur à 120 battements par minute ou si le rythme change considérablement.
- Effectuer le bilan quotidien des ingesta et des excreta et peser le patient tous les jours; observer le patient tous les jours pour déceler l'œdème et la rétention urinaire.
- RESTER À L'AFFÛT DES SIGNES D'INSUFFISANCE CARDIAQUE (ŒDÈME PÉRIPHÉRIQUE, RÂLES OU CRÉPITATIONS, DYSPNÉE, GAIN PONDÉRAL, TURGESCENCE DES JUGULAIRES). AVERTIR LE MÉDECIN OU UN AUTRE PROFESSIONNEL DE LA SANTÉ SI CES SIGNES APPARAISSENT.

Tests de laboratoire:

- Examiner à intervalles réguliers, tout au long du traitement, les résultats des tests des fonctions rénale et hépatique et les concentrations sériques de potassium.
- Le disopyramide peut entraîner l'élévation des concentrations sériques d'urée, de cholestérol et de triglycérides.
- Le médicament peut abaisser la glycémie.

DIAGNOSTICS INFIRMIERS POSSIBLES

- Débit cardiaque diminué (Indications).
- Atteinte à l'intégrité de la muqueuse buccale (Effets secondaires).
- Connaissances insuffisantes sur le traitement médicamenteux (Enseignement au patient et à ses proches).

INTERVENTIONS INFIRMIÈRES

- Lorsqu'on substitue le disopyramide au sulfate de quinidine ou au procaïnamide, administrer la dose d'entretien habituelle de disopyramide de 6 à 12 heures après la dernière dose de sulfate de quinidine ou de 3 à 6 heures après la dernière dose de procaïnamide.
- La préparation à libération prolongée (ou retard) est indiquée en traitement d'entretien seulement. Lorsqu'on substitue la préparation à libération prolongée à celle à libération immédiate, administrer la première dose de la préparation à libération prolongée 6 heures après la dernière dose de préparation à libération immédiate.

PO:

- Administrer sans égard aux repas. LES COMPRIMÉS À LIBÉRATION PROLONGÉE DOIVENT ÊTRE AVALÉS TELS QUELS, SANS ÊTRE COUPÉS, ÉCRASÉS OU MÂCHÉS.
- Le pharmacien peut préparer une suspension avec des capsules de 100 mg et du sirop au parfum de cerise.

ENSEIGNEMENT AU PATIENT ET À SES PROCHES

- Expliquer au patient qu'il doit prendre le médicament 24 heures sur 24, en respectant rigoureusement la posologie recommandée. Le prévenir qu'il ne doit pas arrêter de prendre le médicament sans consulter au préalable un professionnel de la santé. Lui expliquer que s'il n'a pu prendre le médicament au moment habituel, il doit le prendre dès que possible, à moins qu'il ne reste que 4 heures avant l'heure prévue pour la dose suivante. Le prévenir aussi qu'il ne doit jamais remplacer une dose manquée par une double dose.
- Prévenir le patient que le disopyramide peut provoquer des étourdissements. Lui conseiller de ne pas conduire et d'éviter les activités qui exigent sa vigilance jusqu'à ce qu'on ait la certitude que le médicament n'entraîne pas cet effet chez lui.
- Recommander au patient de changer lentement de position pour réduire le risque d'hypotension orthostatique.
- Conseiller au patient de pratiquer une bonne hygiène buccale, de se rincer la bouche fréquemment avec de l'eau et de consommer de la gomme à mâcher ou des bonbons sans sucre pour diminuer la sécheresse de la bouche.
- Mettre en garde le patient contre les écarts de température étant donné que ce médicament peut entraîner une altération de la régulation thermique. Lui conseiller d'utiliser un écran solaire et de porter des vêtements protecteurs afin de prévenir les réactions de photosensibilité.
- Recommander au patient de consulter un professionnel de la santé avant de prendre des médicaments en vente libre et d'éviter de consommer de l'alcool en même temps que ce médicament.
- Si la constipation devient gênante, inciter le patient à augmenter sa consommation de liquides et d'aliments riches en fibres et à faire plus d'exercice pour réduire cet effet secondaire.
- Recommander au patient de communiquer avec un professionnel de la santé si la sécheresse de la bouche, les mictions difficiles, la constipation ou la vision trouble persistent.

VÉRIFICATION DE L'EFFICACITÉ THÉRAPEUTIQUE

L'efficacité du traitement peut être démontrée par: la réduction des extrasystoles ventriculaires et des tachycardies ventriculaires ▪ la prévention d'autres arythmies. ✳

D

DIURÉTIQUES DE L'ANSE

bumétanide

Burinex

furosémide

Apo-Furosemide, Lasix, Lasix Special, Novo-Semide

CLASSIFICATION:

Diurétiques (de l'anse), antihypertenseurs

Grossesse – catégorie C (catégorie D en cas d'usage en présence d'hypertension gravidique)

INDICATIONS

Traitement de: l'œdème dû à l'insuffisance cardiaque ▪ la maladie hépatique ou rénale ▪ Traitement de l'hypertension (sauf le bumétanide). **Usages non approuvés:** *Furosémide* – traitement de l'hypercalcémie induite par le cancer.

MÉCANISME D'ACTION

Inhibition de la réabsorption du sodium et des chlorures au niveau de l'anse de Henle, ainsi que des tubes proximal et distal ▪ Augmentation de l'excrétion rénale de l'eau, du sodium, des chlorures, du magnésium, de l'hydrogène et du calcium ▪ Effets dilatateurs possibles sur les vaisseaux sanguins rénaux et périphériques ▪ Efficacité inaltérée même en présence d'une insuffisance rénale. ***Effets thérapeutiques:*** Diurèse et élimination des liquides en excès (œdème, épanchement pleural) ■ Abaissement de la pression artérielle.

PHARMACOCINÉTIQUE

Absorption: *Bumétanide* – > 80 % (PO); *furosémide* – de 60 à 75 % (PO) (moindre en présence d'insuffisance cardiaque décompensée ou d'insuffisance rénale); le médicament est également absorbé depuis les points d'injection IM.

Distribution: *Bumétanide* – inconnue; le *furosémide* traverse la barrière placentaire et passe dans le lait maternel.

Liaison aux protéines: de 91 à 97 %.

Métabolisme et excrétion: *Bumétanide* – métabolisme partiellement hépatique; 50 % éliminé à l'état inchangé par les reins et 20 % excrété dans les fèces. *Furosémide* – métabolisme partiellement hépatique (de 30 à 40 %), une partie est métabolisée par une voie non hépatique et une autre est excrétée à l'état inchangé par les reins.

Demi-vie: *Bumétanide* – de 60 à 90 minutes (de 6 à 15 heures chez les nouveau-nés); *furosémide* – de 30 à 60 minutes (prolongée en présence d'insuffisance rénale et chez les nouveau-nés; considérablement prolongée en présence d'insuffisance hépatique).

Profil temps-action (effet diurétique)

	DÉBUT D'ACTION	PIC	DURÉE
Bumétanide - PO	30 - 60 min	1 - 2 h	3 - 6 h
Furosémide - PO	30 - 60 min	1 - 2 h	6 - 8 h
Furosémide - IM	10 - 30 min	Inconnu	4 - 8 h
Furosémide - IV	5 min	30 min	2 h

CONTRE-INDICATIONS, PRÉCAUTIONS ET MISES EN GARDE

Contre-indications: Hypersensibilité ■ Risque de sensibilité croisée avec les thiazides et les sulfamides ■ Déséquilibre électrolytique préexistant non corrigé, coma hépatique ou anurie ■ Intolérance à l'alcool (certaines préparations liquides de furosémide peuvent contenir de l'alcool et leur administration devrait être évitée chez les patients présentant une telle intolérance).

Précautions et mises en garde: Maladie hépatique grave accompagnée de cirrhose ou d'ascite (risque de déclenchement d'un coma hépatique; il peut s'avérer nécessaire d'administrer en même temps des diurétiques épargneurs de potassium) ■ Déplétion électrolytique ■ **GÉR.**: Acuité auditive difficile à évaluer; risque accru d'hypotension et de déséquilibre électrolytique aux doses habituelles ■ Diabète ■ Azotémie accrue ■ Grossesse, allaitement ■ **PÉD.**: < 18 ans (l'innocuité de ces agents n'a pas été établie; le furosémide a cependant déjà été utilisé chez les enfants; par contre, il peut déclencher la formation de lithiases rénales ou intensifier le risque de persistance du canal artériel chez les prématurés; le bumétanide déplace fortement la bilirubine et devrait être utilisé avec précaution chez les nouveau-nés gravement malades ou souffrant d'ictère, en raison du risque de kernictère).

RÉACTIONS INDÉSIRABLES ET EFFETS SECONDAIRES

SNC: étourdissements, encéphalopathie, céphalées, insomnie, agitation.

ORLO: perte auditive, acouphènes.

CV: hypotension.

GI: constipation, diarrhée, sécheresse de la bouche (xérostomie), dyspepsie, nausées, vomissements.

GU: mictions fréquentes.

Tég.: photosensibilité, rash.

End.: hyperglycémie.

HÉ: déshydratation, hypochlorémie, hypokaliémie, hypomagnésémie, hyponatrémie, hypovolémie, alcalose métabolique.

Hémat.: dyscrasie sanguine (furosémide seulement).

Métab.: hyperglycémie, hyperuricémie.

Loc.: arthralgie, crampes musculaires, myalgie.

Divers: élévation des concentrations d'urée.

INTERACTIONS

Médicament-médicament: Effets hypotenseurs additifs lors de l'administration concomitante d'**antihypertenseurs** ou de **dérivés nitrés** ou d'une consommation excessive d'**alcool** ■ Effets hypokaliémiants additifs lors de l'administration concomitante d'autres **diurétiques**, de **pipéracilline**, d'**amphotéricine B**, de **laxatifs stimulants** et de **corticostéroïdes** ■ L'hypokaliémie peut augmenter la toxicité **digitalique** ■ Les diurétiques de l'anse diminuent l'excrétion du **lithium**, d'où risque d'intoxication ■ Risque accru d'ototoxicité lors de l'administration concomitante d'**aminosides** ■ Les diurétiques de l'anse peuvent accentuer l'efficacité de la **warfarine**, des **agents thrombolytiques** ou des **anticoagulants** ■ L'**indométhacine** peut atténuer l'effet des diurétiques de l'anse ■ Diminution de l'absorption lors de l'administration en concomitance de **sucralfate**.

VOIES D'ADMINISTRATION ET POSOLOGIE

Bumétanide

- **PO (adultes)**: 1 seule dose de 0,5 à 2 mg par jour. On peut administrer jusqu'à 2 doses additionnelles au cours de la journée, toutes les 4 à 5 heures (jusqu'à concurrence de 10 mg par jour). On peut également administrer les doses 1 jour sur 2 ou pendant des périodes de 3 ou 4 jours, suivies de périodes de repos de 1 ou 2 jours.

Furosémide

- **PO (adultes)**: *Diurétique* – initialement, de 20 à 80 mg par jour; on peut augmenter la dose par paliers de 20 à 40 mg, toutes les 6 à 8 heures, au besoin. On peut aussi adopter une posologie intermittente, avec administration du diurétique pendant 2 à 4 jours consécutifs (des doses jusqu'à 2,5 g par jour ont été utilisées en présence d'insuffisance rénale chronique et d'insuffisance cardiaque réfractaire). *Antihypertenseur* – de 40 à 80 mg par jour, en 2 doses fractionnées.
- **PO (enfants)**: La dose quotidienne totale (en prises fractionnées, toutes les 6 à 12 heures) ne devrait pas dépasser 2 mg/kg. Chez les nouveau-nés, on recommande d'administrer les doses à des intervalles plus espacés.
- **IM, IV (adultes)**: *Diurétique* – de 20 à 40 mg; on peut augmenter la dose par paliers de 20 mg, à administrer toutes les 2 heures jusqu'à l'obtention de l'effet désiré. *Œdème pulmonaire aigu* – initialement, 40 mg, à administrer lentement, et 80 mg, 1 heure plus tard, au besoin. On peut aussi administrer la dose en perfusion continue, à un débit de 0,1 à 0,4 mg/kg/h (on a déjà administré en présence d'insuffisance rénale chronique et d'insuffisance cardiaque réfractaire des doses allant jusqu'à 2,5 g par jour).
- **IM, IV (enfants)**: *Diurétique* – de 1 à 2 mg/kg/dose, toutes les 6 à 12 heures. On peut aussi administrer la dose en perfusion continue, à un débit de 0,05 mg/kg/h, en apportant les modifications qui s'imposent selon l'effet.

PRÉSENTATION

- **Bumétanide** (version générique disponible)
  Comprimés: 1 mg[Pr], 5 mg[Pr].
- **Furosémide** (version générique disponible)
  Comprimés: 20 mg[Pr], 40 mg[Pr], 80 mg[Pr], 500 mg[Pr] ■ **Solution orale**: 10 mg/mL[Pr] ■ **Solution pour injection**: 10 mg/mL[Pr].

SOINS INFIRMIERS

ÉVALUATION DE LA SITUATION

- Suivre de près l'hydratation pendant toute la durée du traitement. Peser le patient tous les jours, effectuer le bilan quotidien des ingesta et des excreta, déterminer l'emplacement et l'étendue de l'œdème, ausculter le murmure vésiculaire et inspecter l'état de la peau et des muqueuses. PRÉVENIR LE MÉDECIN OU UN AUTRE PROFESSIONNEL DE LA SANTÉ EN CAS DE SOIF INCOERCIBLE, DE SÉCHERESSE DE LA BOUCHE (XÉROSTOMIE), DE LÉTHARGIE, DE FAIBLESSE, D'HYPOTENSION OU D'OLIGURIE.
- Mesurer la pression artérielle et le pouls avant et pendant l'administration du médicament. Suivre la fréquence du renouvellement des ordonnances pour déterminer l'observance du traitement chez les patients qui reçoivent ce médicament pour le traitement de l'hypertension.

GÉR.: Le traitement par des diurétiques peut exposer les personnes âgées à un risque accru de chutes. Évaluer ce risque et prendre les mesures préventives qui s'imposent.

- Observer le patient qui reçoit des dérivés digitaliques à la recherche des signes et des symptômes suivants: anorexie, nausées, vomissements, crampes musculaires, paresthésie et confusion. Les patients prenant ces médicaments sont exposés à un risque accru de toxicité digitalique en raison de l'effet de déplétion potassique du diurétique. On peut administrer en concomitance des suppléments de potassium ou des diurétiques épargneurs de potassium pour prévenir l'hypokaliémie.
- Déterminer la présence d'acouphènes et le degré de la perte de l'acuité auditive. L'audiométrie est recommandée chez les patients recevant un traitement IV prolongé à des doses élevées. La perte auditive survient le plus souvent après l'administration IV d'une dose élevée ou après une injection IV trop rapide chez les patients dont la fonction rénale est diminuée ou chez ceux qui prennent en concomitance d'autres médicaments ototoxiques.
- Interroger le patient au sujet de ses antécédents d'allergie aux sulfamides.

Tests de laboratoire:

- Noter les concentrations d'électrolytes, les résultats des tests des fonctions rénale et hépatique, la glycémie et les concentrations d'acide urique, avant le traitement et à intervalles réguliers pendant toute sa durée. Les diurétiques de l'anse peuvent abaisser les concentrations sériques de potassium, de calcium et de magnésium et élever la glycémie, l'urémie et les concentrations de créatinine et d'acide urique.
- Le *bumétanide* peut élever les concentrations urinaires de phosphate.

DIAGNOSTICS INFIRMIERS POSSIBLES

- Excès de volume liquidien (Indications).
- Déficit de volume liquidien (Effets secondaires).

- Connaissances insuffisantes sur le traitement médicamenteux (Enseignement au patient et à ses proches).
- Non-observance du traitement médicamenteux (Enseignement au patient et à ses proches).

D

INTERVENTIONS INFIRMIÈRES

- Administrer le médicament le matin pour ne pas interrompre le cycle du sommeil.
- Lors de l'administration parentérale, on devrait choisir la voie IV plutôt que la voie IM.

PO:

- Administrer les doses par voie orale avec des aliments ou du lait afin de réduire l'irritation gastrique. On peut écraser les comprimés de *furosémide* pour en faciliter la prise par les patients qui éprouvent des difficultés de déglutition.
- Ne pas administrer une solution ou des comprimés de *furosémide* qui ont changé de couleur.

Furosémide

- Lorsque le furosémide est administré pour traiter l'hypercalcémie, il est important de procéder à un rééquilibrage électrolytique (sodium, potassium et magnésium) et de maintenir l'équilibre entre les échanges hydriques tout au long du traitement afin d'optimiser l'élimination rénale du calcium. Il sera important de corriger l'hypovolémie avec une solution de NaCl 0,9 % (pouvant varier de 3 à 6 L en 24 heures) et de vérifier les électrolytes toutes les 6 à 12 heures.

IV directe: Administrer le médicament non dilué.

Vitesse d'administration: Administrer lentement en 1 à 2 minutes.

Perfusion intermittente: Diluer les doses élevées de médicament dans une solution de D5%E, D10%E, D20%E, D5%/NaCl 0,9 %, de D5%/solution de lactate de Ringer, de NaCl 0,9 %, de lactate de sodium à 1/6 M ou dans une solution de lactate de Ringer. Utiliser la solution reconstituée en l'espace de 24 heures. Consulter les directives de chaque fabricant avant de reconstituer la préparation.

Vitesse d'administration: Pour prévenir l'ototoxicité chez l'adulte, administrer la solution par une tubulure en Y ou par un robinet à 3 voies à un débit inférieur à 4 mg/min. Utiliser une pompe de perfusion pour s'assurer que le patient reçoit la dose exacte.

Associations compatibles dans la même seringue: bléomycine ■ cisplatine ■ cyclophosphamide ■ fluorouracile ■ héparine ■ leucovorine calcique ■ méthotrexate ■ mitomycine.

Associations incompatibles dans la même seringue: doxapram ■ doxorubicine ■ dropéridol ■ métoclopramide ■ milrinone ■ vinblastine ■ vincristine.

Compatibilité (tubulure en Y): allopurinol sodique ■ amifostine ■ amikacine ■ amphotéricine B, cholestéryl sulfate d' ■ aztréonam ■ bléomycine ■ céfépime ■ cefmétazole ■ cisplatine ■ cladribine ■ cyclophosphamide ■ cytarabine ■ doxorubicine liposomale ■ fentanyl ■ fludarabine ■ fluorouracile ■ foscarnet ■ gallium, nitrate de ■ granisétron ■ héparine ■ hydrocortisone sodique, succinate d' ■ hydromorphone ■ indométhacine ■ kanamycine ■ leucovorine calcique ■ lorazépam ■ melphalan ■ méropénem ■ méthotrexate ■ mitomycine ■ nitroglycérine ■ paclitaxel ■ pipéracilline/tazobactam ■ potassium, chlorure de ■ propofol ■ ranitidine ■ rémifentanil ■ sargramostim ■ tacrolimus ■ téniposide ■ thiotépa ■ tobramycine ■ tolazoline ■ vitamines du complexe B avec C.

Incompatibilité (tubulure en Y): ciprofloxacine ■ diltiazem ■ dropéridol ■ esmolol ■ filgrastim ■ fluconazole ■ gentamicine ■ hydralazine ■ idarubicine ■ métoclopramide ■ midazolam ■ milrinone ■ morphine ■ nétilmicine ■ ondansétron ■ quinidine, gluconate de ■ thiopental ■ vécuronium ■ vinblastine ■ vincristine ■ vinorelbine.

ENSEIGNEMENT AU PATIENT ET À SES PROCHES

- Conseiller au patient de respecter rigoureusement la posologie recommandée. S'il n'a pas pu prendre le médicament au moment habituel, il doit le prendre dès que possible sans jamais remplacer une dose manquée par une double dose.
- Conseiller au patient de changer lentement de position pour réduire le risque d'hypotension orthostatique. Le prévenir que la consommation d'alcool, l'effort par temps chaud ou la station debout pendant de longues périodes peuvent aggraver l'hypotension orthostatique durant ce traitement.
- Conseiller au patient de demander à un professionnel de la santé s'il doit suivre un régime alimentaire riche en potassium (voir l'annexe J).
- Conseiller au patient de consulter un professionnel de la santé avant de prendre un médicament en vente libre en même temps qu'un diurétique.
- Recommander au patient qui doit suivre un traitement ou subir une intervention chirurgicale d'avertir le professionnel de la santé qu'il suit ce traitement médicamenteux.
- Recommander au patient d'utiliser un écran solaire et de porter des vêtements protecteurs afin de prévenir les réactions de photosensibilité.

Gér.: Prévenir les personnes âgées ou leurs soignants qu'il y a risque accru de chutes. Proposer des mesures de prévention.

- Recommander au patient de signaler immédiatement à un professionnel de la santé les symptômes suivants: faiblesse musculaire, crampes, nausées, étourdissements, engourdissement ou picotements au niveau des membres.
- Prévenir le patient diabétique qu'il doit suivre de près sa glycémie, les diurétiques de l'anse pouvant élever les concentrations de glucose sanguin.
- Insister sur l'importance des examens de suivi réguliers.

Hypertension:

- Conseiller au patient qui suit un traitement antihypertenseur de continuer à prendre le médicament même s'il se sent mieux. Lui expliquer que les diurétiques de l'anse stabilisent la pression artérielle, mais ne guérissent pas l'hypertension.
- Inciter le patient à appliquer d'autres mesures de réduction de l'hypertension: perdre du poids, faire régulièrement de l'exercice, réduire sa consommation de sel, diminuer le stress, boire avec modération et cesser de fumer.

VÉRIFICATION DE L'EFFICACITÉ THÉRAPEUTIQUE

L'efficacité du traitement peut être démontrée par: la diminution de l'œdème ■ la diminution du volume de l'abdomen ■ l'augmentation des excreta urinaires ■ la baisse de la pression artérielle ■ la diminution des concentrations sériques de calcium lorsque le diurétique de l'anse est utilisé pour traiter l'hypercalcémie. ✳

DIURÉTIQUES ÉPARGNEURS DE POTASSIUM

amiloride

Apo-Amiloride, Midamor

spironolactone

Aldactone, Novo-Spiroton

triamtérène/hydrochlorothiazide

Apo-Triazide, Novo-Triamzide, Nu-Triazide

Le triamtérène seul n'est plus commercialisé au Canada.

CLASSIFICATION:

Diurétiques (épargneurs de potassium)

Grossesse – amiloride: catégorie B (catégorie D, en cas d'usage en présence d'hypertension gravidique); spironolactone, triamtérène: catégorie C (catégorie D, en cas d'usage en présence d'hypertension gravidique)

INDICATIONS

Rééquilibrage des concentrations de potassium par suite des pertes induites par les autres diurétiques ■ Souvent en association avec d'autres agents (thiazidiques) pour traiter l'œdème ou l'hypertension ■ Traitement de l'hyperaldostéronisme (spironolactone seulement). **Usages non approuvés:** *Spironolactone* – traitement de l'insuffisance cardiaque (à de faibles doses).

MÉCANISME D'ACTION

Les diurétiques épargneurs de potassium favorisent l'excrétion du bicarbonate de sodium et du calcium tout en conservant les ions potassium et hydrogène. ***Effets thérapeutiques:*** Effet diurétique et antihypertenseur faible par rapport à celui des autres diurétiques ■ Conservation du potassium.

PHARMACOCINÉTIQUE

Absorption: *Amiloride* – de 15 à 25 % (PO); *spironolactone* – > 90 % (PO); *triamtérène* – de 30 à 70 % (PO).

Distribution: *Amiloride* et *triamtérène* – tout l'organisme; la *spironolactone* traverse la barrière placentaire et passe dans le lait maternel.

Liaison aux protéines: *Spironolactone, canrénone* – > 90 %.

Métabolisme et excrétion: *Amiloride* – 50 % éliminé à l'état inchangé dans l'urine et 40 % (non absorbé) dans les selles; *spironolactone* – transformée par le foie en son composé diurétique actif (canrénone); *triamtérène* – métabolisme partiellement hépatique; une petite fraction du médicament inchangé est excrétée.

Demi-vie: *Amiloride* – de 6 à 9 heures; *spironolactone* – de 13 à 24 heures (canrénone); *triamtérène* – de 100 à 150 minutes.

Profil temps-action (effet diurétique)

	Début d'action	Pic	Durée
Amiloride	2 h†	6 - 10 h†	24 h†
Spironolactone	24 - 48 h	2 - 3 jours‡	2 - 3 jours‡
Triamtérène	2 - 4 h†	1 - plusieurs jours	7 - 9 h†

† Une seule dose.

‡ Plusieurs doses.

D

CONTRE-INDICATIONS, PRÉCAUTIONS ET MISES EN GARDE

Contre-indications: Hypersensibilité ■ Hyperkaliémie ■ Anurie ■ Insuffisance rénale aiguë ■ Dysfonctionnement rénal grave ■ Dysfonctionnement hépatique grave (triamtérène) ■ Allaitement (triamtérène) ■ Néphropathie grave ou évolutive.

Précautions et mises en garde: Dysfonctionnement hépatique ■ **GÉR.**: Il est recommandé de réduire la dose chez les personnes âgées, débilitées ou diabétiques à cause de la diminution de la fonction rénale et du risque accru d'hyperkaliémie ■ Insuffisance rénale (concentrations d'urée > 11 mmol/L ou Cl_{Cr} < 30 mL/min) ■ Antécédents de goutte ou de lithiases rénales (triamtérène seulement) ■ **OBST., ALLAITEMENT, PÉD.**: L'innocuité de ces médicaments n'a pas été établie.

RÉACTIONS INDÉSIRABLES ET EFFETS SECONDAIRES

SNC: étourdissements, *spironolactone seulement* – ataxie, céphalées.

CV: arythmies.

GI: *amiloride* – constipation, irritation gastro-intestinale (plus fréquente lors de l'administration de spironolactone).

GU: impuissance, *triamtérène* – coloration bleuâtre de l'urine, lithiases rénales.

Tég.: *triamtérène* – photosensibilité.

End.: *spironolactone* – gynécomastie.

HÉ: hyperkaliémie, hyponatrémie.

Hémat.: *spironolactone* et *triamtérène* – dyscrasie sanguine.

Loc.: crampes musculaires.

Divers: réactions allergiques.

INTERACTIONS

Médicament-médicament: Effets hypotenseurs additifs lors de l'administration concomitante d'**antihypertenseurs** ou de **dérivés nitrés** ou d'une consommation excessive d'**alcool** ■ L'administration concomitante d'**inhibiteurs de l'ECA**, d'**indométhacine**, de **suppléments de potassium** ou de **cyclosporine** peut provoquer l'hyperkaliémie ■ Les diurétiques épargneurs de potassium diminuent l'excrétion de **lithium** ■ Les **anti-inflammatoires non stéroïdiens**, administrés en concomitance, peuvent diminuer la réponse antihypertensive au médicament ■ La spironolactone peut augmenter les effets de la **digoxine** ■ Le triamtérène diminue les effets de l'**acide folique** (il faudrait lui préférer la leucovorine) ■ Le triamtérène peut augmenter le risque de toxicité par l'**amantadine**.

VOIES D'ADMINISTRATION ET POSOLOGIE

Amiloride

- **PO (adultes)**: De 5 à 10 mg par jour (jusqu'à concurrence de 20 mg).

Spironolactone

- **PO (adultes)**: De 25 à 400 mg par jour, en une seule dose ou en 2 à 4 doses fractionnées.. *Insuffisance cardiaque (usage non approuvé)*: de 12,5 à 25 mg par jour.
- **PO (enfants)**: De 1 à 3 mg/kg par jour (de 30 à 90 mg/m^2/jour), en une seule dose ou en 2 à 4 doses fractionnées.

PRÉSENTATION

- **Amiloride**
  Comprimés: 5 mg[Pr] ■ **En association avec**: hydrochlorothiazide (Moduret[Pr]).
- **Spironolactone (version générique disponible)**
  Comprimés: 25 mg[Pr], 100 mg[Pr] ■ **En association avec**: hydrochlorothiazide (Aldactazide[Pr], Novo-Spirozine[Pr]).
- **Triamtérène**
  En association avec: hydrochlorothiazide (Apo-Triazide[Pr], Novo-Triamzide[Pr], Pro-Triazide[Pr]).

SOINS INFIRMIERS

ÉVALUATION DE LA SITUATION

- Effectuer le bilan quotidien des ingesta et des excreta et peser le patient tous les jours.
- Si le médicament est administré en traitement d'appoint de l'hypertension, mesurer la pression artérielle avant de l'administrer.
- Rester à l'affût des signes et des symptômes d'hypokaliémie (faiblesse, fatigue, apparition d'ondes U sur le tracé ÉCG, arythmies, polyurie, polydipsie). Observer le patient à intervalles fréquents pour déceler l'apparition des symptômes d'hyperkaliémie (fatigue, faiblesse musculaire, paresthésie, confusion, dyspnée, arythmies). Les patients souffrant de diabète ou de maladie rénale et les personnes âgées sont davantage prédisposés à ces symptômes.
- On recommande d'effectuer des ÉCG à intervalles réguliers chez les patients recevant un traitement prolongé.

Tests de laboratoire:

- Noter, avant le traitement et à intervalles réguliers pendant toute sa durée, les concentrations sériques de potassium. Ne pas administrer le médicament et informer le médecin ou un autre professionnel de la santé si l'hyperkaliémie s'installe.

- Noter, avant le traitement et à intervalles réguliers pendant toute sa durée, les concentrations d'urée, de créatinine sérique et d'électrolytes. Les diurétiques épargneurs de potassium peuvent élever les concentrations sériques de magnésium, d'acide urique, d'urée, de créatinine et de potassium et accroître l'activité de la rénine plasmatique et l'excrétion urinaire de calcium. Ils peuvent également diminuer les concentrations de sodium.
- Interrompre l'administration des diurétiques épargneurs de potassium 3 jours avant d'effectuer une épreuve d'hyperglycémie provoquée, en raison du risque d'hyperkaliémie grave.
- La *spironolactone* peut entraîner une fausse élévation des concentrations plasmatiques de cortisol. On devrait en interrompre l'administration de 4 à 7 jours avant ce dosage.
- Chez les patients prenant le *triamtérène*, noter également la numération plaquettaire, la numération globulaire et la formule leucocytaire à intervalles réguliers pendant toute la durée du traitement.

DIAGNOSTICS INFIRMIERS POSSIBLES

- Excès de volume liquidien (Indications).
- Connaissances insuffisantes sur le traitement médicamenteux (Enseignement au patient et à ses proches).

INTERVENTIONS INFIRMIÈRES

- Administrer ces médicaments le matin pour ne pas interrompre le cycle du sommeil.
- Administrer ces médicaments avec des aliments ou du lait afin de réduire l'irritation gastrique et d'augmenter la biodisponibilité.

ENSEIGNEMENT AU PATIENT ET À SES PROCHES

- Expliquer au patient qu'il doit continuer à prendre le médicament même s'il se sent mieux. Lui recommander de le prendre tous les jours à la même heure. S'il n'a pas pu prendre le médicament au moment habituel, il doit le prendre dès que possible à moins qu'il ne soit presque l'heure prévue pour la dose suivante. Le prévenir qu'il ne doit jamais remplacer une dose manquée par une double dose.
- Conseiller au patient d'éviter les substituts de sel et les aliments riches en potassium ou en sodium, sauf si un professionnel de la santé les a prescrits.
- Prévenir le patient que les diurétiques épargneurs de potassium peuvent parfois provoquer des étourdissements. Lui conseiller de ne pas conduire et d'éviter les activités qui exigent sa vigilance jusqu'à ce qu'on ait la certitude que son médicament n'entraîne pas cet effet chez lui.
- Conseiller au patient de consulter un professionnel de la santé avant de prendre des médicaments en vente libre, tels que des décongestionnants, des antitussifs, des préparations contre le rhume ou des coupe-faim, en même temps qu'un diurétique épargneur de potassium, en raison du risque d'élévation de la pression artérielle.
- Recommander au patient prenant le *triamtérène* d'utiliser un écran solaire et de porter des vêtements protecteurs pour prévenir les réactions de photosensibilité.
- Recommander au patient qui doit suivre un traitement ou subir une intervention chirurgicale de prévenir le professionnel de la santé qu'il suit un traitement avec ce type de médicaments.
- Signaler au patient que le triamtérène peut rendre l'urine bleuâtre.
- Recommander au patient de signaler à un professionnel de la santé les symptômes suivants: crampes ou faiblesse musculaires, fatigue, nausées intenses, vomissements ou diarrhée.
- Insister sur l'importance des examens de suivi qui permettent de déterminer les bienfaits du traitement.

Hypertension:

- Inciter le patient à appliquer d'autres mesures de réduction de l'hypertension: perdre du poids, réduire sa consommation de sel, diminuer le stress, boire de l'alcool avec modération, faire régulièrement de l'exercice et cesser de fumer. Le prévenir que les diurétiques épargneurs de potassium stabilisent la pression artérielle, mais ne guérissent pas l'hypertension.
- Montrer au patient et à ses proches comment mesurer la pression artérielle et leur recommander de prendre cette mesure toutes les semaines.

VÉRIFICATION DE L'EFFICACITÉ THÉRAPEUTIQUE

L'efficacité du traitement peut être démontrée par: l'augmentation de la diurèse et la diminution de l'œdème, avec maintien des concentrations de potassium sérique dans les limites acceptables ▪ la baisse de la pression artérielle ▪ la prévention de l'hypokaliémie chez les patients recevant des diurétiques ▪ une amélioration de l'état du patient qui souffre d'hyperaldostéronisme. ✳

D

DIURÉTIQUES THIAZIDIQUES

chlorthalidone

Apo-Chlorthalidone, Novo-Thalidone

hydrochlorothiazide

Apo-Hydro, Novo-Hydrazide, PMS-Hydrochlorothiazide

***CLASSIFICATION*:**

Antihypertenseurs, diurétiques (thiazidiques)

Grossesse – catégorie B (catégorie D, en cas d'usage en présence d'hypertension gravidique)

INDICATIONS

Traitement de l'hypertension légère à modérée ■ Traitement de l'œdème dû à : l'insuffisance cardiaque ■ un dysfonctionnement rénal ■ la cirrhose ■ une corticothérapie ■ une œstrogénothérapie.

MÉCANISME D'ACTION

Excrétion accrue du sodium et de l'eau par inhibition de la réabsorption du sodium au niveau du tubule distal ■ Effet favorable sur l'excrétion des chlorures, du potassium, du magnésium et du bicarbonate ■ Dilatation artériolaire possible. ***Effets thérapeutiques*:** Abaissement de la pression artérielle chez les patients hypertendus et diurèse par suite de la diminution de l'œdème.

PHARMACOCINÉTIQUE

Absorption: Rapide; *chlorthalidone* – de 30 à 60 % (PO); *hydrochlorothiazide* – de 60 à 80 % (PO).

Distribution: Les diurétiques thiazidiques se répartissent dans l'espace extracellulaire. Ils traversent la barrière placentaire et passent dans le lait maternel.

Métabolisme et excrétion: Excrétion majoritairement rénale à l'état inchangé.

Demi-vie: *Chlorthalidone* – de 35 à 50 heures; *hydrochlorothiazide* – de 6 à 15 heures.

Profil temps-action (effet diurétique)

	DÉBUT D'ACTION	PIC	DURÉE
Chlorthalidone	2 h	2 h	48 – 72 h
Hydrochlorothiazide†	2 h	3 – 6 h	6 – 12 h

† L'effet antihypertenseur apparaît de 3 à 4 jours après l'administration du médicament et atteint son maximum après 7 à 14 jours.

CONTRE-INDICATIONS, PRÉCAUTIONS ET MISES EN GARDE

Contre-indications: Hypersensibilité ■ Risque de réactions de sensibilité croisée avec d'autres diurétiques thiazidiques ou avec les sulfamides ■ Sensibilité connue aux ingrédients de la préparation ou aux composants du contenant (à noter: certaines préparations d'hydrochlorothiazide qu'on trouve sur le marché contiennent des sulfites) ■ Anurie ■ Coma ou précoma hépatique.

Précautions et mises en garde: Insuffisance rénale ou insuffisance hépatique grave ■ **OBST.**: Risque d'ictère ou de thrombopénie chez le nouveau-né ■ Allaitement.

RÉACTIONS INDÉSIRABLES ET EFFETS SECONDAIRES

SNC: étourdissements, somnolence, léthargie, faiblesse.

CV: hypotension.

GI: anorexie, crampes, hépatite, nausées, vomissements.

Tég.: photosensibilité, rash.

End.: hyperglycémie.

HÉ: hypokaliémie, déshydratation, hypercalcémie, alcalose hypochlorémique, hypomagnésémie, hyponatrémie, hypophosphatémie, hypovolémie.

Hémat.: dyscrasie sanguine.

Métab.: hyperuricémie, hyperlipidémie.

Loc.: crampes musculaires.

Divers: pancréatite.

INTERACTIONS

Médicament-médicament: Effets hypotenseurs additifs lors de l'administration concomitante d'autres **antihypertenseurs** ou de **dérivés nitrés** ou d'une consommation excessive d'**alcool** ■ Effets hypokaliémiants additifs lors de l'administration concomitante de **corticostéroïdes**, d'**amphotéricine B**, de **pipéracilline** ou de **ticarcilline** ■ Les diurétiques thiazidiques diminuent l'excrétion de **lithium** ■ La **cholestyramine** ou le **colestipol**, administrés en concomitance, diminuent l'absorption des diurétiques thiazidiques ■ L'hypokaliémie augmente le risque de toxicité **digitalique** ■ Les **anti-inflammatoires non stéroïdiens**, administrés en concomitance, peuvent diminuer l'efficacité des diurétiques thiazidiques ■ L'**allopurinol** peut augmenter le risque de réactions d'hypersensibilité.

Médicament-produits naturels: La **réglisse** et les **plantes laxatives stimulantes** (**aloès**, **cascara sagrada**, **séné**) peuvent augmenter le risque d'hypokaliémie ■ L'usage concomitant de **ginkgo biloba** peut diminuer l'efficacité antihypertensive des diurétiques thiazidiques.

VOIES D'ADMINISTRATION ET POSOLOGIE

Lorsqu'on utilise ces agents comme diurétiques chez les adultes, on peut les administrer 1 jour sur 2, ou 2 ou 3 jours par semaine.

Chlorthalidone

- **PO (adultes)**: De 25 à 100 mg, 1 fois par jour.

Hydrochlorothiazide

- **PO (adultes)**: De 12,5 à 100 mg par jour, en une seule dose ou en 2 doses fractionnées (jusqu'à concurrence de 200 mg par jour; ne pas dépasser 50 mg par jour pour traiter l'hypertension).
- **PO (enfants > 6 mois)**: De 1 à 2 mg/kg (de 30 à 60 mg/m^2 par jour), en une seule dose ou en 2 doses fractionnées.
- **PO (enfants < 6 mois)**: Jusqu'à concurrence de 3 mg/kg par jour.

PRÉSENTATION

- **Chlorthalidone** (version générique disponible)
  Comprimés: 50 mg^{Pr}, 100 mg^{Pr} ■ **En association avec**: aténolol.
- **Hydrochlorothiazide** (version générique disponible)
  Comprimés: 12,5 mg^{Pr}, 25 mg^{Pr}, 50 mg^{Pr}, 100 mg^{Pr} ■ **En association avec**: plusieurs médicaments dont amiloride, spironolactone, triamtérène, valsartan.

SOINS INFIRMIERS

ÉVALUATION DE LA SITUATION

- Mesurer la pression artérielle, effectuer le bilan quotidien des ingesta et des excreta et peser le patient tous les jours. Examiner quotidiennement les pieds, les jambes et la région sacrée pour déceler la formation d'un œdème.
- Observer le patient, particulièrement s'il prend des dérivés digitaliques, pour déceler les symptômes suivants: anorexie, nausées, vomissements, crampes musculaires, paresthésie et confusion. Prévenir le médecin ou un autre professionnel de la santé si ces signes de déséquilibre électrolytique se manifestent. Les patients prenant des dérivés digitaliques sont davantage prédisposés à une intoxication digitalique en raison de l'effet hypokaliémiant du diurétique.
- Interroger le patient à propos de ses antécédents d'allergie aux sulfamides.

Hypertension:

- Mesurer la pression artérielle avant le traitement et à intervalles réguliers pendant toute sa durée.
- Suivre la fréquence du renouvellement des ordonnances pour déterminer l'observance du traitement.

Tests de laboratoire:

- Noter les concentrations d'électrolytes (particulièrement de potassium), la glycémie, l'urémie et les concentrations sériques de créatinine et d'acide urique avant le traitement et à intervalles réguliers pendant toute sa durée.
- Les diurétiques thiazidiques peuvent augmenter les concentrations de glucose sérique et urinaire chez les diabétiques.
- Ces agents peuvent accroître les concentrations sériques de bilirubine, de calcium, de créatinine et d'acide urique et diminuer les concentrations sériques de magnésium, de potassium et de sodium ainsi que les concentrations urinaires de calcium.
- Les diurétiques thiazidiques peuvent diminuer les concentrations sériques d'iode protidique (PBI).
- Ces agents peuvent élever les concentrations sériques de cholestérol, de lipoprotéines de basse densité et de triglycérides.

D

DIAGNOSTICS INFIRMIERS POSSIBLES

- Excès de volume liquidien (Indications).
- Déficit de volume liquidien (Effets secondaires).
- Connaissances insuffisantes sur le traitement médicamenteux (Enseignement au patient et à ses proches).
- Non-observance du traitement médicamenteux (Enseignement au patient et à ses proches).

INTERVENTIONS INFIRMIÈRES

- Administrer le médicament le matin pour ne pas interrompre le cycle du sommeil.
- On peut choisir des schémas posologiques intermittents pour traiter l'œdème.
- Administrer le médicament avec des aliments ou du lait afin de réduire l'irritation gastrique. Si le patient éprouve des difficultés de déglutition, on peut écraser les comprimés et les mélanger à des liquides.

ENSEIGNEMENT AU PATIENT ET À SES PROCHES

- Conseiller au patient de prendre le médicament au même moment tous les jours. S'il n'a pas pu le prendre au moment habituel, il doit le prendre aussitôt que possible, mais non pas juste avant l'heure prévue pour la dose suivante. Le prévenir qu'il ne doit jamais remplacer une dose manquée par une dose double.
- Recommander au patient de se peser 2 fois par semaine et de signaler à un professionnel de la santé toute modification importante du poids.
- Recommander au patient de changer lentement de position pour prévenir le risque d'hypotension orthostatique. Lui expliquer que l'alcool peut intensifier l'effet hypotenseur du médicament.
- Recommander au patient d'utiliser un écran solaire et de porter des vêtements protecteurs pour prévenir les réactions de photosensibilité.

- Conseiller au patient de consulter un professionnel de la santé au sujet de ses besoins en potassium alimentaire (voir l'annexe J).
- Recommander au patient qui doit suivre un traitement ou subir une intervention chirurgicale de prévenir le professionnel de la santé qu'il suit un traitement par ce type de médicaments.
- Recommander au patient de signaler à un professionnel de la santé les symptômes suivants: faiblesse musculaire, crampes, nausées, vomissements, diarrhée ou étourdissements.
- Insister sur l'importance des examens réguliers de suivi.

Hypertension:

- Conseiller au patient qui suit un traitement antihypertenseur de continuer à prendre le médicament même s'il se sent mieux. Le prévenir que les diurétiques thiazidiques stabilisent la pression artérielle, mais ne guérissent pas l'hypertension.
- Inciter le patient à appliquer d'autres mesures de réduction de l'hypertension (perdre du poids, réduire sa consommation de sel, faire régulièrement de l'exercice, cesser de fumer, boire avec modération et diminuer le stress).
- Montrer au patient et à ses proches comment mesurer la pression artérielle et leur recommander de prendre cette mesure toutes les semaines.
- Conseiller au patient de consulter un professionnel de la santé avant de prendre des médicaments en vente libre, particulièrement des antitussifs ou des préparations contre le rhume, en même temps qu'un diurétique thiazidique.

VÉRIFICATION DE L'EFFICACITÉ THÉRAPEUTIQUE

L'efficacité du traitement peut être démontrée par: la baisse de la pression artérielle ■ l'augmentation du débit urinaire ■ la diminution de l'œdème.

DIVALPROEX SODIQUE,

voir Valproates

ALERTE CLINIQUE

DOBUTAMINE

Dobutrex

CLASSIFICATION:

Inotrope et cardiotonique, sympathomimétique

Grossesse – catégorie B

INDICATIONS

Traitement de courte durée (< 48 heures) de l'insuffisance cardiaque attribuable à une contractilité réduite, entraînée par une maladie cardiaque organique ou une intervention chirurgicale.

MÉCANISME D'ACTION

Stimulation des récepteurs bêta$_1$-adrénergiques (du myocarde) avec des effets relativement minimes sur la fréquence cardiaque ou sur les vaisseaux périphériques. ***Effets thérapeutiques:*** Élévation du débit cardiaque sans augmentation notable de la fréquence cardiaque.

PHARMACOCINÉTIQUE

Absorption: Biodisponibilité à 100 % (IV).

Distribution: Inconnue.

Métabolisme et excrétion: Métabolisme hépatique et autres tissus.

Demi-vie: 2 minutes.

Profil temps-action (effet inotrope)

	DÉBUT D'ACTION	PIC	DURÉE
IV	1 – 2 min	10 min	brève (quelques min)

CONTRE-INDICATIONS, PRÉCAUTIONS ET MISES EN GARDE

Contre-indications: Hypersensibilité à la dobutamine ou aux bisulfites ■ Sténose sous-aortique hypertrophique idiopathique.

Précautions et mises en garde: Antécédents d'hypertension (risque accru d'une réponse vasopressive exacerbée) ■ Infarctus du myocarde ■ Fibrillation auriculaire (un prétraitement par des dérivés digitaliques est conseillé) ■ Antécédents d'activité ectopique ventriculaire (risque d'exacerbation) ■ Hypovolémie (à corriger avant l'administration de cet agent) ■ **OBST., ALLAITEMENT:** L'innocuité du médicament n'a pas été établie ■ **PÉD.:** Bien que le risque de tachycardie soit accru, il existe des précédents d'usage pédiatrique.

RÉACTIONS INDÉSIRABLES ET EFFETS SECONDAIRES

SNC: céphalées.

Resp.: essoufflements.

CV: hypertension, augmentation de la fréquence cardiaque, contractions ventriculaires prématurées, angine de poitrine, arythmies, hypotension, palpitations.

GI: nausées, vomissements.

Locaux: phlébite.

Divers: réactions d'hypersensibilité, incluant le rash, la fièvre, les bronchospasmes ou l'éosinophilie, douleurs thoraciques non angineuses.

INTERACTIONS

Médicament-médicament: Le **nitroprusside** peut exercer un effet synergique sur l'élévation du débit cardiaque ■ Les **bêtabloquants**, administrés en concomitance, peuvent contrecarrer l'effet de la dobutamine ■ Risque accru d'arythmies ou d'hypertension lors de l'administration concomitante de certains **anesthésiques** (**halothane**), d'**IMAO**, d'**agents ocytociques** ou d'**antidépresseurs tricycliques**.

VOIES D'ADMINISTRATION ET POSOLOGIE

Voir le tableau des vitesses de perfusion qui se trouve à l'annexe C.

- **IV (adultes et enfants)**: Amorcer la perfusion à un débit lent (de 0,5 à 1 μg/kg/min) et l'ajuster à des intervalles de quelques minutes d'après la réponse du patient (écart posologique de 2 à 10 μg/kg/min, jusqu'à concurrence de 40 μg/kg/min).

PRÉSENTATION

Solution pour injection: 12,5 mg/mL, en fioles de 20 mL[Pr].

SOINS INFIRMIERS

ÉVALUATION DE LA SITUATION

- Mesurer constamment la pression artérielle et la fréquence cardiaque, suivre de près l'ÉCG, mesurer la pression capillaire pulmonaire bloquée, le débit cardiaque, la pression veineuse centrale et le débit urinaire durant l'administration de la dobutamine. Signaler au médecin toute modification importante des signes vitaux ou les arythmies. Lui demander de préciser les paramètres du pouls ou de la pression artérielle et les modifications de l'ÉCG dont il faut se servir pour adapter la dose ou pour arrêter le traitement.
- Palper les pouls périphériques et examiner l'aspect des membres à intervalles réguliers tout au long de l'administration de la dobutamine. Prévenir le médecin si la qualité du pouls se détériore ou si les membres deviennent froids ou tachetés.

Tests de laboratoire:

- Mesurer les concentrations de potassium au cours du traitement; la dobutamine peut entraîner l'hypokaliémie.
- Mesurer les concentrations d'électrolytes, d'urée et de créatinine ainsi que le temps de prothrombine toutes les semaines au cours d'un traitement prolongé.

Toxicité et surdosage: En cas de surdosage, réduire la dose ou interrompre le traitement. Aucun autre traitement n'est nécessaire étant donné que les effets de la dobutamine sont de courte durée.

DIAGNOSTICS INFIRMIERS POSSIBLES

- Débit cardiaque diminué (Indications).
- Irrigation tissulaire inefficace (Indications).

INTERVENTIONS INFIRMIÈRES

Alerte clinique: Les médicaments intraveineux vasoactifs peuvent être dangereux. Avant l'administration, il est recommandé de demander à un autre professionnel de la santé de vérifier l'ordonnance d'origine, le calcul des doses à administrer et le réglage de la pompe volumétrique. Ne pas confondre la dobutamine avec la dopamine. Si possible, la conserver séparément.

- Avant d'amorcer le traitement par la dobutamine, corriger l'hypovolémie par des solutions d'expansion volémique.
- Administrer la dobutamine dans une grosse veine et observer le point d'injection à intervalles fréquents. L'extravasation peut provoquer des douleurs et une inflammation.

IV: Diluer 250 mg (20 mL d'une fiole prédiluée) dans au moins 50 mL d'une solution de D5%E, de NaCl 0,9 %, de lactate de sodium, de NaCl 0,45 %, de D5%/NaCl 0,9 % ou 0,45 %, de D5%/solution de lactate de Ringer ou de lactate de Ringer. Les concentrations standard se situent entre 250 et 1 000 μg/mL. Les concentrations ne devraient pas dépasser 5 mg de dobutamine par mL. Même si la solution devient légèrement rosée, sa puissance n'est en rien altérée. La solution est stable pendant 48 heures à la température ambiante. Consulter les directives de chaque fabricant avant de reconstituer la préparation.

Perfusion continue: Administrer par une pompe à perfusion. La vitesse d'administration doit être adaptée d'après la réponse du patient (fréquence cardiaque, présence d'une activité ectopique, pression artérielle, débit urinaire, pression veineuse centrale, pression capillaire pulmonaire bloquée, débit cardiaque); voir l'annexe C.

Compatibilité (tubulure en Y): amifostine ■ amiodarone ■ amrinone ■ atracurium ■ aztréonam ■ brétylium ■ calcium, chlorure de ■ calcium, gluconate de ■ cisatracurium ■ ciprofloxacine ■ cladribine ■ diazépam ■ diltiazem ■ dopamine ■ doxorubicine liposomique ■ énalaprilate ■ famotidine ■ fentanyl ■ fluconazole ■ granisétron ■ halopéridol ■ hydromorphone ■ insuline ■ labétalol ■ lidocaïne ■ lorazépam ■ magnésium, sulfate de ■ mépéridine ■ milrinone ■ morphine ■

nitroglycérine ■ nitroprusside ■ noradrénaline ■ pancuronium ■ potassium, chlorure de ■ propofol ■ protamine ■ ranitidine ■ rémifentanil ■ streptokinase ■ tacrolimus ■ théophylline ■ thiotépa ■ tolazoline ■ vécuronium ■ vérapamil ■ zidovudine.

Incompatibilité (tubulure en Y): acyclovir ■ altéplase ■ aminophylline ■ céfamandole ■ céfazoline ■ céfépime ■ cefmétazole ■ éthacrynique, acide ■ foscarnet ■ hydrocortisone sodique, succinate d' ■ indométhacine ■ pénicilline ■ phytonadione ■ pipéracilline/tazobactam ■ warfarine.

D

ENSEIGNEMENT AU PATIENT ET À SES PROCHES

- Expliquer au patient la raison pour laquelle on doit lui administrer ce médicament et le surveiller étroitement.
- Recommander au patient de prévenir immédiatement un professionnel de la santé en cas de douleurs thoraciques, de dyspnée ou d'engourdissements, de picotements ou d'une sensation de brûlure au niveau des membres.
- Recommander au patient de prévenir immédiatement un professionnel de la santé en cas de douleur ou de gêne au point de ponction.

Soins à domicile:

- Recommander aux proches de signaler rapidement à un professionnel de la santé les signes suivants d'aggravation de l'insuffisance cardiaque: essoufflements, orthopnée, diminution de la tolérance à l'effort, ainsi que les douleurs abdominales, les nausées ou les vomissements.

VÉRIFICATION DE L'EFFICACITÉ THÉRAPEUTIQUE

L'efficacité du traitement peut être démontrée par: l'élévation du débit cardiaque ■ l'amélioration des paramètres hémodynamiques ■ l'augmentation du débit urinaire. ✳

ALERTE CLINIQUE

DOCÉTAXEL

Taxotere

CLASSIFICATION:

Antinéoplasique (taxoïde)

Grossesse – catégorie D

INDICATIONS

Traitement du cancer du sein avancé localisé ou métastatique, du cancer du poumon à petites cellules avancé localisé ou métastatique, du cancer ovarien métastatique après l'échec d'une chimiothérapie de première intention, du cancer de la prostate métastatique androgène indépendant ou réfractaire à l'hormonothérapie (en association avec la prednisone) et du carcinome spinocellulaire de la tête et du cou récurrent ou métastatique après l'échec d'une chimiothérapie.

MÉCANISME D'ACTION

Altération du fonctionnement normal des microtubules cellulaires intervenant pendant l'interphase et la mitose. ***Effets thérapeutiques:*** Destruction des cellules à réplication rapide, particulièrement des cellules malignes.

PHARMACOCINÉTIQUE

Absorption: Biodisponibilité à 100 % (IV).
Distribution: Inconnue.
Métabolisme et excrétion: Fort métabolisme hépatique; les métabolites sont éliminés dans les fèces.
Demi-vie: 11,1 heures.

Profil temps-action (effet sur la numération globulaire)

	Début d'action	Pic	Durée
IV	rapide	5 – 9 jours	15 jours

CONTRE-INDICATIONS, PRÉCAUTIONS ET MISES EN GARDE

Contre-indications: Hypersensibilité ■ Hypersensibilité au polysorbate 80 ■ Intolérance connue à l'alcool ■ Nombre de polynucléaires neutrophiles < $1,5 \times 10^9$/L ■ Insuffisance hépatique grave.

Précautions et mises en garde: **Obst.**: Grossesse ou allaitement, patientes en âge de procréer ■ **Péd.**: L'innocuité et l'efficacité du médicament n'ont pas été établies chez les enfants ■ **Gér.**: Augmentation de la fréquence des effets indésirables chez les personnes âgées.

RÉACTIONS INDÉSIRABLES ET EFFETS SECONDAIRES

SNC: fatigue, faiblesse.
Resp.: bronchospasme.
CV: ASCITE, TAMPONNADE CARDIAQUE, ÉPANCHEMENT PÉRICARDIQUE, ŒDÈME PULMONAIRE, œdème périphérique.
GI: diarrhée, nausées, stomatite, vomissements.
Tég.: alopécie, rash, dermatite, desquamation, œdème, érythème, affections unguéales.
Hémat.: anémie, thrombopénie, leucopénie.
Locaux: réactions au point d'injection.

Loc.: myalgie, arthralgie.
ORLO: larmoiement.
SN: déficits neurosensoriels, neuropathie périphérique.
Divers: réactions d'hypersensibilité, incluant l'ANAPHYLAXIE.

INTERACTIONS

Médicament-médicament: Risque d'aggravation de l'aplasie médullaire lors de l'administration concomitante d'autres **agents antinéoplasiques** ou d'une **radiothérapie** ■ La **cyclosporine**, le **kétoconazole**, l'**érythromycine** ou la **troléandomycine** peuvent modifier de façon marquée les effets du docétaxel.

VOIES D'ADMINISTRATION ET POSOLOGIE

IV (adultes): 100 mg/m^2, toutes les 3 semaines en monothérapie; 75 mg/m^2, toutes les 3 semaines en association.

PRÉSENTATION

Concentré pour injection: 20 mg de docétaxel/0,5 mL de polysorbate 80 avec une fiole de diluant incluse dans l'emballage (éthanol à 13 %)^{Pr}, 80 mg de docétaxel/0,5 mL de polysorbate 80 avec une fiole de diluant incluse dans l'emballage (éthanol à 13 %)^{Pr}.

SOINS INFIRMIERS

ÉVALUATION DE LA SITUATION

- Noter les signes vitaux avant et après l'administration du docétaxel.
- Examiner le point de perfusion pour en vérifier la perméabilité. Le docétaxel n'est pas un agent vésicant. En cas d'extravasation, interrompre immédiatement l'administration du docétaxel et aspirer le plus de volume possible à l'aide de l'aiguille IV déjà en place. Appliquer des compresses d'eau froide sur le point pendant 24 heures.
- SUIVRE CONSTAMMENT LES RÉACTIONS D'HYPERSENSIBILITÉ PENDANT TOUTE LA DURÉE DE LA PERFUSION. ELLES SE PRODUISENT LE PLUS SOUVENT APRÈS L'ADMINISTRATION DE LA PREMIÈRE ET DE LA DEUXIÈME DOSE DE DOCÉTAXEL ET SE MANIFESTENT PAR DES BRONCHOSPASMES, L'HYPOTENSION OU L'ÉRYTHÈME. ON PEUT TRAITER LES RÉACTIONS LÉGÈRES À MODÉRÉES SELON LE SYMPTÔME ET RALENTIR OU INTERROMPRE LA PERFUSION JUSQU'À CE QUE LA RÉACTION DISPARAISSE. LES RÉACTIONS GRAVES DICTENT L'ABANDON DE L'ADMINISTRATION DU DOCÉTAXEL ET L'AMORCE D'UN TRAITEMENT SYMPTOMATIQUE. NE PAS ADMINISTRER DE NOUVEAU LE DOCÉTAXEL À DES PATIENTS AYANT DES ANTÉCÉDENTS DE RÉACTIONS GRAVES. UN ŒDÈME GRAVE PEUT ÉGALEMENT SURVENIR. PESER LE PATIENT AVANT CHAQUE TRAITEMENT. L'ACCUMULATION DE LIQUIDES PEUT ENTRAÎNER UN ŒDÈME, UNE ASCITE OU DES ÉPANCHEMENTS PLEURAUX OU PÉRICARDIQUES. ON RECOMMANDE D'ADMINISTRER EN PRÉTRAITEMENT DES CORTICOSTÉROÏDES (TELLE LA DEXAMÉTHASONE À 8 mg, PAR VOIE ORALE, 2 FOIS PAR JOUR, PENDANT 5 JOURS, À PARTIR DE LA VEILLE DU JOUR OÙ L'ON ADMINISTRE LA PREMIÈRE DOSE DE DOCÉTAXEL) AFIN DE RÉDUIRE L'ŒDÈME ET LES RÉACTIONS D'HYPERSENSIBILITÉ. POUR TRAITER L'ŒDÈME, ON PEUT ÉGALEMENT ADMINISTRER DU FUROSÉMIDE PAR VOIE ORALE.
- Déceler les signes d'aplasie médullaire et la présence d'hémorragie (saignement des gencives, formation d'ecchymoses, pétéchies, présence de sang occulte dans les selles, l'urine et les vomissures) et, si le nombre de plaquettes est bas, éviter les injections IM et la prise de la température rectale. Appliquer une pression sur les points de ponction veineuse pendant 10 minutes. Suivre de près les signes d'infection en présence d'une neutropénie. Une anémie peut survenir. Rester à l'affût d'une fatigue accrue, de la dyspnée et de l'hypotension orthostatique.
- Déceler la présence d'un rash qui peut se manifester sur les pieds ou sur les mains, mais également sur les bras, le visage ou le thorax, habituellement accompagné de prurit. Le rash survient habituellement dans la semaine qui suit la perfusion et disparaît avant la perfusion suivante.
- Observer le patient pour déceler la présence d'un déficit neurosensoriel (paresthésie, dysesthésie, douleurs, brûlures). Le docétaxel peut également entraîner de la faiblesse. On peut administrer de la pyridoxine pour réduire ces symptômes. En cas de symptômes graves, on doit diminuer la dose ou arrêter le traitement.
- Rester à l'affût de signes d'arthralgie et de myalgie qui peuvent habituellement être soulagés par des analgésiques non opioïdes. Toutefois, ces symptômes peuvent devenir suffisamment graves pour dicter un traitement par des opioïdes.

Tests de laboratoire:

- Noter la numération globulaire et la formule leucocytaire avant chaque traitement. Le docétaxel entraîne fréquemment la neutropénie (nombre de polynucléaires neutrophiles $< 2 \times 10^9$/L), auquel cas il peut s'avérer nécessaire d'adapter la dose. Si le nombre de polynucléaires neutrophiles est inférieur à $1,5 \times 10^9$/L, on devrait interrompre l'administration du médicament. La neutropénie est réversible et non cumulative. Le nadir se produit en l'espace de 8 jours et dure 7 jours. Le docétaxel peut également entraîner la thrombopénie et l'anémie.

- Examiner les résultats des tests de la fonction hépatique (concentrations d'AST, d'ALT, de phosphatase alcaline, de bilirubine) avant chaque cycle. Si les concentrations sont élevées, la dose doit être diminuée, ou le traitement, suspendu.

DIAGNOSTICS INFIRMIERS POSSIBLES

- Risque d'infection (Réactions indésirables).
- Risque d'accident (Réactions indésirables).
- Connaissances insuffisantes sur le traitement médicamenteux (Enseignement au patient et à ses proches).

INTERVENTIONS INFIRMIÈRES

Alerte clinique: Des décès sont survenus lors de certaines chimiothérapies. Avant d'administrer l'agent, clarifier tous les points ambigus. Vérifier la limite des doses unitaires et quotidiennes ainsi que la dose à administrer pendant le traitement. Demander à un deuxième professionnel de la santé de vérifier une fois de plus l'ordonnance d'origine, les calculs et le réglage de la pompe à perfusion. Ne pas confondre Taxotère (docétaxel) et Taxol (paclitaxel).

- Les solutions devraient être préparées sous une hotte à flux laminaire. Porter des gants, une blouse et un masque pendant la manipulation de ce médicament. Jeter le matériel destiné à l'administration IV dans les contenants réservés à cet usage (voir l'annexe H).

Perfusion continue: Avant de faire la dilution, garder les fioles à la température ambiante pendant 5 minutes. Retirer tout le contenu de la fiole de diluant et le transvider dans la fiole de docétaxel. Mélanger la solution en faisant tourner délicatement la fiole pendant 45 secondes, sans la secouer. La solution devrait être transparente, mais de la mousse peut se former sur le dessus. Dans ce cas, laisser reposer la solution pendant quelques minutes, le temps que la mousse disparaisse. Ne pas poursuivre la préparation tant que la mousse est présente. Pour préparer la solution destinée à la perfusion, aspirer la quantité nécessaire de la solution à 10 mg/mL dans la seringue et l'injecter dans 250 mL d'une solution de NaCl 0,9% ou de D5%E pour obtenir une concentration de 0,3 à 0,74 mg/mL. Éviter d'utiliser des articles en PVC pour préparer la solution. Utiliser des sacs et des dispositifs de perfusion à revêtement de polyéthylène. Faire tourner le contenant de perfusion pour bien mélanger la solution. Ne pas administrer une solution trouble ou qui contient un précipité. Il n'est pas nécessaire d'utiliser un filtre intégré pour administrer la solution. Les solutions diluées sont stables pendant 8 heures au réfrigérateur ou à la température ambiante. Consulter les directives de chaque fabricant avant de reconstituer et de diluer la préparation.

Vitesse d'administration: Administrer la solution destinée à la perfusion en 1 heure.

Incompatibilité en addition au soluté: Aucune donnée disponible. Ne pas mélanger la solution à d'autres médicaments ou à d'autres solutions.

ENSEIGNEMENT AU PATIENT ET À SES PROCHES

- Demander au patient de prévenir un professionnel de la santé si les symptômes suivants se manifestent: fièvre > 38 °C, frissons, maux de gorge, signes d'infection, saignement des gencives, formation d'ecchymoses, pétéchies ou présence de sang dans les selles, l'urine et les vomissures. Lui recommander d'éviter les foules et les personnes contagieuses. Lui conseiller d'utiliser une brosse à dents à poils doux et un rasoir électrique.
- Recommander au patient d'éviter de consommer des boissons alcoolisées et de ne pas prendre de médicaments contenant de l'aspirine ou des AINS.
- Le docétaxel entraîne souvent la fatigue. Recommander au patient de prendre des périodes de repos, à intervalles fréquents, et de ralentir ses activités.
- Conseiller au patient de signaler à un professionnel de la santé les symptômes suivants: douleurs abdominales, jaunissement de la peau, faiblesse, paresthésie, démarche anormale, œdème des pieds ou douleurs articulaires ou musculaires.
- Recommander au patient d'examiner ses muqueuses buccales pour déceler l'érythème et les aphtes. En cas d'aphtes, lui conseiller de remplacer la brosse à dents par une brosse-éponge et de se rincer la bouche avec de l'eau après avoir bu ou mangé.
- Prévenir le patient qu'il risque de perdre ses cheveux; habituellement, ils commencent à tomber après 1 ou 2 doses, mais ils repoussent après l'arrêt du traitement. Explorer avec lui les stratégies lui permettant de s'adapter à ce changement.
- Expliquer au patient qu'il ne doit pas se faire vacciner sans recommandation expresse d'un professionnel de la santé.
- Insister sur l'utilité des tests de laboratoire réguliers permettant de déceler les effets secondaires du médicament.

VÉRIFICATION DE L'EFFICACITÉ THÉRAPEUTIQUE

L'efficacité du traitement peut être démontrée par: la diminution de la taille de la tumeur ou le ralentissement de la propagation du cancer.

DOCOSANOL

Abreva

CLASSIFICATION:

Antiviral (voie topique)

Grossesse – catégorie B

INDICATIONS

Traitement de l'infection par le virus de l'herpès simplex orofacial récurrent (boutons de fièvre, feux sauvages).

MÉCANISME D'ACTION

Prévention de la pénétration des cellules par le virus de l'herpès simplex, en empêchant la fusion des particules virales avec la membrane cellulaire. ***Effets thérapeutiques:*** Accélération de la cicatrisation ■ Durée écourtée des symptômes (douleur, brûlures, démangeaisons, picotements).

PHARMACOCINÉTIQUE

Absorption: Inconnue.

Distribution: Inconnue.

Métabolisme et excrétion: Inconnus.

Demi-vie: Inconnue.

Profil temps-action

	Début d'action	Pic	Durée
Voie topique	inconnu	inconnu	inconnue

CONTRE-INDICATIONS, PRÉCAUTIONS ET MISES EN GARDE

Conte-indications: Hypersensibilité au docosanol ou à l'un des ingrédients de la préparation (alcool benzylique, huile minérale, propylène glycol, stéarate ou distéarate de saccharose).

Précautions et mises en garde: Péd.: Enfants < 12 ans (l'innocuité de l'agent n'a pas été établie) ■ **Obst.:** N'utiliser qu'en cas de besoin incontestable.

RÉACTIONS INDÉSIRABLES ET EFFETS SECONDAIRES

Toutes les réactions locales se sont manifestées au siège de l'application.

Locaux: acné, démangeaisons, rash.

INTERACTIONS

Médicament-médicament: Aucune interaction notable.

VOIES D'ADMINISTRATION ET POSOLOGIE

Voie topique (adultes et enfants ≥ 12 ans): Appliquer une petite quantité, 5 fois par jour, sur les vésicules des lèvres ou du visage, jusqu'à leur guérison (ne pas utiliser pendant plus de 10 jours).

PRÉSENTATION

Crème: crème à 10 %, en tubes de 2 g^{VL}.

SOINS INFIRMIERS

ÉVALUATION DE LA SITUATION

- Suivre de près les lésions cutanées avant le traitement et à intervalles fréquents pendant toute sa durée.

DIAGNOSTICS INFIRMIERS POSSIBLES

- Atteinte à l'intégrité de la peau (Indications).
- Risque élevé d'infection (Indications).
- Connaissances insuffisantes sur l'évolution de la maladie et sur le traitement médicamenteux (Enseignement au patient et à ses proches).

INTERVENTIONS INFIRMIÈRES

Voie topique: Appliquer la crème sur les lésions, 5 fois par jour, dès les premiers signes de formation de vésicules ou de boutons.

ENSEIGNEMENT AU PATIENT ET À SES PROCHES

- Montrer au patient la technique correcte d'application du docosanol. Lui expliquer qu'il doit appliquer la crème sur les lèvres et le visage, en évitant le contact avec les yeux ou la région périorbitale. Insister sur le fait qu'il est important de se laver les mains après l'application ou après avoir touché les lésions, afin d'éviter la contamination d'autres parties du corps ou la transmission du virus à d'autres personnes.
- Recommander au patient de commencer l'application du docosanol dès que les premiers signes de

formation d'un bouton ou d'une vésicule se manifestent, même pendant la phase prodromique (sensation de brûlure, démangeaisons, picotements ou engourdissement).

- Expliquer au patient que le docosanol écourte l'épisode infectieux, mais ne guérit pas la maladie virale. La réactivation du virus peut être déclenchée par l'exposition aux rayons ultraviolets, au soleil ou au vent, le stress, la fatigue ou le froid. Les autres facteurs déclenchants sont notamment la fièvre, une blessure, les règles, les interventions dentaires et les maladies infectieuses (rhume, grippe).
- Recommander au patient de prévenir un professionnel de la santé si les lésions ne guérissent pas au bout de 14 jours ou s'il manifeste de la fièvre, un rash ou des ganglions lymphatiques tuméfiés.

VÉRIFICATION DE L'EFFICACITÉ THÉRAPEUTIQUE

L'efficacité du traitement peut être démontrée par: une diminution de la durée des symptômes d'un épisode infectieux dû au virus de l'herpès simplex (douleurs, brûlures, démangeaisons, picotements). ✳

DOCUSATE

docusate calcique

Calax, Novo-Docusate calcium, Ratio-Docusate calcium

docusate sodique

Apo-Docusate sodium, Colace, Novo-Docusate sodium, Ratio-Docusate sodium, Selax, Soflax

CLASSIFICATION:

Laxatif (émollient)

Grossesse – catégorie C

INDICATIONS

PO: Prévention de la constipation (chez les patients devant éviter des efforts reliés à la défécation, comme ceux ayant subi un infarctus du myocarde ou une chirurgie au rectum) ■ **IR**: Lavement pour ramollir un fécalome.

MÉCANISME D'ACTION

Effet favorable sur l'incorporation de l'eau dans les selles, entraînant le ramollissement de la masse fécale ■ Effet favorable sur la sécrétion d'électrolytes et d'eau dans le côlon. ***Effets thérapeutiques:*** Ramollissement des selles et leur évacuation.

PHARMACOCINÉTIQUE

Absorption: De petites quantités peuvent être absorbées depuis l'intestin grêle (PO). L'absorption depuis le rectum est inconnue.

Distribution: Inconnue.

Métabolisme et excrétion: Les quantités absorbées par voie orale sont éliminées dans la bile.

Demi-vie: Inconnue.

Profil temps-action (ramollissement des selles)

	DÉBUT D'ACTION	PIC	DURÉE
PO	24 – 48 h (jusqu'à 3 à 5 jours)	Inconnu	inconnue
IR	2 – 15 min	Inconnu	inconnue

CONTRE-INDICATIONS, PRÉCAUTIONS ET MISES EN GARDE

Contre-indications: Hypersensibilité ■ Douleurs abdominales, nausées ou vomissements, particulièrement si ces symptômes s'accompagnent de fièvre ou d'autres signes d'abdomen aigu.

Précautions et mises en garde: Administration excessive ou prolongée (risque de dépendance) ■ Usage déconseillé si l'on souhaite obtenir des résultats rapides ■ **OBST., ALLAITEMENT**: Précédents d'administration.

RÉACTIONS INDÉSIRABLES ET EFFETS SECONDAIRES

ORLO: irritation de la gorge.

GI: crampes légères.

Tég.: rash.

INTERACTIONS

Médicament-médicament: Ne pas administrer en même temps que de l'**huile minérale** (risque d'absorption de l'huile minérale).

VOIES D'ADMINISTRATION ET POSOLOGIE

Docusate calcique

- **PO (adultes)**: De 240 à 480 mg, 1 fois par jour.

Docusate sodique

- **PO (adultes et enfants > 12 ans)**: De 100 à 200 mg, 1 fois par jour.
- **PO (enfants de 6 à 12 ans)**: De 40 à 120 mg, 1 fois par jour.
- **PO (enfants de 3 à 6 ans)**: De 20 à 60 mg, 1 fois par jour.
- **PO (enfants < 3 ans)**: De 10 à 40 mg, 1 fois par jour.
- **IR (adultes)**: De 50 à 100 mg, dans 90 ou 100 mL de liquide de lavement.

PRÉSENTATION
(version générique disponible)

- **Docusate calcique**
  Capsules: 240 mg^{VL}.
- **Docusate sodique**
  Capsules: 100 mg^{VL}, 200 mg^{VL} ■ **Gouttes**: 10 mg/mL^{VL} ■ **Sirop**: 20 mg/5 mL^{VL} ■ **En association avec**: sennosides (Senokot-S^{VL}).

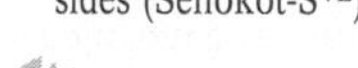

SOINS INFIRMIERS

ÉVALUATION DE LA SITUATION

- Déterminer le degré de distension abdominale, ausculter les bruits intestinaux, noter les habitudes normales d'élimination.
- Noter la couleur, la consistance et la quantité des selles produites.

DIAGNOSTICS INFIRMIERS POSSIBLES

- Constipation (Indications).
- Connaissances insuffisantes sur le traitement médicamenteux (Enseignement au patient et à ses proches).

INTERVENTIONS INFIRMIÈRES

- Ce médicament ne stimule pas le péristaltisme intestinal.
- Administrer le médicament avec un grand verre d'eau ou de jus. L'administration à jeun produit des résultats plus rapides.
- On peut diluer la solution orale dans du lait ou du jus de fruits pour en rendre le goût moins amer.
- Ne pas administrer le docusate dans les 2 heures qui suivent la prise d'huile minérale, en raison du risque d'absorption accrue.

ENSEIGNEMENT AU PATIENT ET À SES PROCHES

- Prévenir le patient que les laxatifs ne sont destinés qu'à un traitement de courte durée. Lui expliquer que le traitement prolongé peut entraîner un déséquilibre électrolytique et la dépendance.
- Recommander au patient de prendre d'autres mesures qui favorisent la défécation: augmenter la consommation de fibres alimentaires, boire plus de liquides (de 6 à 8 grands verres par jour) et faire de l'exercice. Lui expliquer que chaque personne a ses propres habitudes d'élimination et qu'il est tout aussi normal de déféquer 3 fois par jour que 3 fois par semaine.
- Recommander au patient souffrant de maladie cardiaque d'éviter les efforts de défécation (manœuvre de Valsalva).
- Prévenir le patient que les laxatifs sont déconseillés si la constipation s'accompagne de douleurs abdominales, de nausées, de vomissements ou de fièvre.
- Prévenir le patient qu'il ne doit pas prendre le docusate dans les 2 heures qui suivent la prise d'huile minérale.

VÉRIFICATION DE L'EFFICACITÉ THÉRAPEUTIQUE

L'efficacité du traitement peut être démontrée par: l'émission de selles molles et bien moulées, habituellement dans les 24 à 48 heures. Les résultats peuvent ne pas être manifestes avant 3 à 5 jours. Lors de l'administration des préparations rectales, les résultats se manifestent en l'espace de 2 à 15 minutes.

DOFÉTILIDE

Disponible par l'intermédiaire du Programme d'accès spécial de Santé Canada.

Tikosyn

CLASSIFICATION:
Antiarythmique (classe III)

Grossesse – catégorie C

INDICATIONS

Maintien d'un rythme sinusal normal (laps de temps prolongé jusqu'à la survenue d'un nouvel épisode de fibrillation ou de flutter auriculaires [FA/FAl]) chez des patients ayant subi un épisode de FA/FAl d'une durée de plus de 1 semaine, soumis à une cardioversion (rétablissement d'un rythme sinusal normal après un épisode de fibrillation ou de flutter auriculaires).

MÉCANISME D'ACTION

Blocage des canaux ioniques du cœur, responsables du transport du potassium ■ Prolongation de la durée du potentiel d'action monophasique ■ Prolongation de la période réfractaire. ***Effets thérapeutiques:*** Prévention de la récurrence des fibrillations ou flutters auriculaires ■ Rétablissement d'un rythme sinusal normal après un épisode de FA/FA1.

PHARMACOCINÉTIQUE

Absorption: > 90 % (PO).
Distribution: Inconnue.
Métabolisme et excrétion: Excrétion majoritairement rénale (80 %) sous forme inchangée; 20 % est excrété sous forme de métabolites inactifs. L'élimination rénale

implique la filtration glomérulaire et la sécrétion tubulaire (transport de cations). On note un certain degré de métabolisme hépatique par le système enzymatique du cytochrome P450 (isoenzyme CYP 3A4).

Demi-vie: 10 heures.

Profil temps-action

	DÉBUT D'ACTION	PIC	DURÉE
PO	quelques heures	2 - 3†	12 - 14 h

† Les concentrations à l'état d'équilibre sont atteintes après 2 ou 3 jours.

D

CONTRE-INDICATIONS, PRÉCAUTIONS ET MISES EN GARDE

Contre-indications: Hypersensibilité ■ Syndrome du QT long congénital ou acquis ■ Intervalle QT ou QT_c initial > 440 ms (500 ms chez les patients présentant des anomalies de conduction ventriculaire ■ Cl_{Cr} < 20 mL/min ■ Usage concomitant de vérapamil ou d'agents qui inhibent le système rénal de transport de cations, dont la cimétidine, le kétoconazole, le triméthoprime, le mégestrol ou la prochlorpérazine ■ Usage concomitant d'hydrochlorothiazide.

Précautions et mises en garde: Troubles électrolytiques sous-jacents (risque accru d'arythmies graves; corriger ces anomalies avant l'administration) ■ Cl_{Cr} de 20 à 60 mL/min (il est recommandé de diminuer la dose) ■ Insuffisance hépatique grave ■ **OBST.**: Grossesse (n'administrer que si les bienfaits pour la patiente dépassent les risques possibles auxquels est exposé le fœtus), allaitement ■ **PÉD.**: Enfants < 18 ans (l'innocuité de l'agent n'a pas été établie).

RÉACTIONS INDÉSIRABLES ET EFFETS SECONDAIRES

SNC: étourdissements, céphalées.

CV: ARYTHMIES VENTRICULAIRES, douleurs thoraciques, allongement de l'intervalle QT.

INTERACTIONS

Médicament-médicament: L'**hydrochlorothiazide** élève les concentrations de dofétilide, peut allonger l'intervalle QT et accroître le risque d'arythmies; l'usage concomitant est contre-indiqué ■ LES **INHIBITEURS DU TRANSPORT RÉNAL DE CATIONS**, NOTAMMENT LA **CIMÉTIDINE**, LE **TRIMÉTHOPRIME** ET LA **KÉTOCONAZOLE**, ADMINISTRÉS EN CONCOMITANCE, ÉLÈVENT LES CONCENTRATIONS SANGUINES ET LE RISQUE D'ARYTHMIES GRAVES; L'USAGE CONCOMITANT EST CONTRE-INDIQUÉ ■ L'**amiloride**, la **metformine**, le **mégestrol**, la **prochlorpérazine** et le **triamtérène** peuvent avoir des effets similaires ■ Les **phénothiazines**, les **antidépresseurs tricycliques**, certains **macrolides** (dont l'**érythromycine** et la **télithromycine**) et les **fluoroquinolones** peuvent allonger l'intervalle QT et accroître le risque d'arythmies; l'usage concomitant est contre-indiqué ■ Les concentrations sanguines et le risque d'arythmies sont également élevés par le **vérapamil**; l'usage concomitant est contre-indiqué (on recommande une période sans médicament de 2 jours) ■ Les **inhibiteurs du système enzymatique du cytochrome P450** (isoenzyme CYP3A4), notamment les **antibiotiques de type macrolide**, les **antifongique de type azole**, les **antirétroviraux de type inhibiteurs de la protéase**, les **antidépresseurs de type ISRS**, l'**amiodarone**, les **cannabinoïdes**, le **diltiazem**, la **quinine** et le **zafirlukast** peuvent également élever les concentrations sanguines et le risque d'arythmies; l'usage concomitant doit s'accompagner de prudence ■ L'usage concomitant d'autres **antiarythmiques de classe I ou III** est à proscrire à cause du risque accru d'arythmies ■ Les **phénothiazines** et les **antidépresseurs tricycliques** allongent également l'intervalle QT; il est déconseillé de les administrer en même temps que le dofétilide ■ L'hypokaliémie ou l'hypomagnésémie induites par les **diurétiques hypokaliémiants** élèvent le risque d'arythmies; corriger ces anomalies avant d'administrer l'agent ■ L'usage concomitant de **digoxine** peut également élever le risque d'arythmies.

Médicament-aliments: Le **jus de pamplemousse** peut élever les concentrations du médicament; éviter l'usage concomitant.

VOIES D'ADMINISTRATION ET POSOLOGIE

La posologie doit être adaptée compte tenu de la fonction rénale et de la mesure de l'intervalle QT.

- **PO (adultes)**: *Dose initiale* – 500 µg, 2 fois par jour; *dose d'entretien* – 250 µg, 2 fois par jour (ne pas dépasser 500 µg, 2 fois par jour).

INSUFFISANCE RÉNALE

- **PO (ADULTES)**: *CL_{CR} DE 40 À 60 mL/MIN: DOSE INITIALE* – 250 µg, 2 FOIS PAR JOUR; *DOSE D'ENTRETIEN* – 125 µg 2 FOIS PAR JOUR; *CL_{CR} DE 20 À 40 mL/MIN: DOSE INITIALE* – 125 µg, 2 FOIS PAR JOUR; *DOSE D'ENTRETIEN* – 125 µg, 1 FOIS PAR JOUR.

PRÉSENTATION

Capsules: 125 µg Pr, 250 µg Pr, 500 µg Pr.

SOINS INFIRMIERS

ÉVALUATION DE LA SITUATION

- SUIVRE DE PRÈS L'ÉCG, ET MESURER LE POULS ET LA PRESSION ARTÉRIELLE CONTINUELLEMENT EN DÉbut de traitement et pendant au moins 3 jours, puis à intervalles réguliers pendant toute la durée du traitement. Mesurer l'intervalle QT_C avant le début du traitement et tous les 3 mois tout au long du traitement. S'il dépasse les 440 ms (500 ms chez les patients présentant des anomalies de conduction ventriculaire), interrompre l'administration du dofétilide et suivre de près le patient jusqu'au moment où l'intervalle QT_C revient aux valeurs initiales.

- Suivre de près la pharmacothérapie (médicaments d'ordonnance et en vente libre et produits naturels ou à base de plantes médicinales) en prêtant une attention particulière aux agents qui interagissent avec le dofétilide (voir « Interactions »).

Tests de laboratoire: La clairance de la créatinine doit être calculée chez tous les patients avant l'administration de l'agent et tous les 3 mois pendant toute la durée du traitement.

DIAGNOSTICS INFIRMIERS POSSIBLES

- Débit cardiaque diminué (Indications).

INTERVENTIONS INFIRMIÈRES

- Le traitement par le dofétilide doit être commencé ou repris dans un milieu où l'on peut assurer une surveillance ÉCG constante et où l'on dispose d'un personnel ayant de l'expérience dans la prise en charge des arythmies ventriculaires graves. En raison du risque d'arythmies ventriculaires menaçantes pour la vie, le dofétilide est habituellement administré aux patients présentant des fibrillations ou un flutter auriculaires très symptomatiques.
- Les patients atteints de fibrillations auriculaires doivent recevoir une anticoagulothérapie conformément aux protocoles habituels, avant la cardioversion électrique ou pharmacologique.
- S'assurer que le patient dispose d'une provision suffisante de dofétilide à sa sortie de l'hôpital pour prévenir l'interruption du traitement.
- Les patients ne devraient pas quitter le centre hospitalier dans les 12 heures qui suivent la cardioversion visant le rétablissement d'un rythme sinusal normal.

PO: Administrer à la même heure tous les jours, sans égard aux repas.

ENSEIGNEMENT AU PATIENT ET À SES PROCHES

- Inciter le patient à prendre le médicament en suivant rigoureusement les recommandations du médecin, même s'il se sent mieux. Le prévenir qu'il ne doit jamais remplacer une dose manquée par une double dose, mais de prendre plutôt la dose suivante à l'heure prévue.
- Recommander au patient de lire le feuillet d'instructions avant de commencer le traitement et de le relire chaque fois que le traitement est recommencé. Insister sur le fait qu'il est important d'observer rigoureusement le traitement et les interactions médicamenteuses possibles tout comme de se soumettre à des suivis à intervalles réguliers pour réduire le risque d'arythmies graves.
- Montrer au patient et à ses proches comment mesurer le pouls. Leur recommander de signaler tout changement dans la fréquence du pouls et dans le rythme des battements à un professionnel de la santé.
- Prévenir le patient que le dofétilide peut provoquer des étourdissements. Lui conseiller de ne pas conduire et de ne pas s'engager dans des activités qui exigent sa vigilance jusqu'à ce qu'on ait la certitude que le médicament n'exerce pas cet effet chez lui.
- Conseiller au patient qui doit se soumettre à un autre traitement ou à une intervention chirurgicale de prévenir le professionnel de la santé qu'il prend du dofétilide.
- Expliquer au patient qu'il ne doit prendre aucun médicament en vente libre pendant son traitement par le dofétilide sans avoir consulté au préalable un professionnel de la santé.
- Recommander au patient de prévenir le médecin s'il s'est évanoui, s'il s'est senti étourdi ou si ses battements cardiaques se sont accélérés. S'il ne peut rejoindre le médecin, lui conseiller de se rendre au service des urgences le plus près de chez lui, d'emporter les capsules de dofétilide qui lui restent et de les montrer à un médecin ou à une infirmière. Il doit également prévenir immédiatement un professionnel de la santé en cas de déséquilibre électrolytique (diarrhée profuse et prolongée, transpiration, vomissements, perte d'appétit ou soif).
- Insister sur la nécessité des examens de suivi permettant de déterminer l'efficacité du traitement.

VÉRIFICATION DE L'EFFICACITÉ THÉRAPEUTIQUE

L'efficacité du traitement peut être démontrée par: la prévention de la récurrence des fibrillations ou du flutter auriculaires ■ la conversion de la fibrillation ou flutter auriculaires en rythme sinusal. ■ Si le rythme sinusal ne se rétablit pas en 24 heures après le début du traitement, il faut envisager une cardioversion électrique. ✳

D

DOLASÉTRON

Anzemet

CLASSIFICATION:

Antiémétique (antagoniste de la sérotonine [5-HT_3])

Grossesse – catégorie B

INDICATIONS

Prévention des nausées et des vomissements associés à une chimiothérapie émétisante, y compris le traitement par le cisplatine à fortes doses. **Usages non approuvés**: Prévention et traitement des nausées et des vomissements postopératoires.

MÉCANISME D'ACTION

Blocage des effets de la sérotonine au niveau des récepteurs 5-HT_3, situés sur les terminaisons du nerf vague et dans la zone gâchette chémoréceptrice du SNC. ***Effets thérapeutiques:*** Diminution de la fréquence et de la gravité des nausées et des vomissements associés à une intervention chirurgicale ou à une chimiothérapie émétisante.

PHARMACOCINÉTIQUE

Absorption: Bonne (PO).

Distribution: Inconnue.

Métabolisme et excrétion: Métabolisme rapide; transformation en hydrodolasétron, le métabolite actif. 61 % de l'hydrodolasétron est excrété par les reins.

Demi-vie: *Hydrodolasétron* – 8,1 heures (plus courte chez les enfants).

Profil temps-action (effet antiémétique)

	Début d'action	Pic	Durée
PO	inconnu	1 – 2 h	jusqu'à 24 h
IV	inconnu	15 – 30 min	jusqu'à 24 h

CONTRE-INDICATIONS, PRÉCAUTIONS ET MISES EN GARDE

Contre-indications: Hypersensibilité.

Précautions et mises en garde: Patients présentant des facteurs de risque qui peuvent allonger les intervalles de la conduction cardiaque, surtout l'intervalle QT_c (hypokaliémie, hypomagnésémie, traitement concomitant par un diurétique ou un antiarythmique de classe I et III, syndrome de Romano-Ward, doses élevées cumulatives d'anthracycline, bloc AV du 2ᵉ ou du 3ᵉ degré) ■ **Obst., allaitement**: L'innocuité du médicament n'a pas été établie ■ Insuffisance rénale grave ■ Insuffisance hépatique grave.

RÉACTIONS INDÉSIRABLES ET EFFETS SECONDAIRES

SNC: céphalées (fréquence accrue chez les patients cancéreux), étourdissements, fatigue, syncope.

CV: bradycardie, modifications du tracé de l'ÉCG (dont allongement de l'intervalle QT_c), hypertension, hypotension, tachycardie.

GI: diarrhée, dyspepsie.

GU: oligurie.

Tég.: prurit.

Divers: frissons, fièvre, douleurs.

INTERACTIONS

Médicament-médicament: L'administration concomitante de **diurétiques** ou d'**antiarythmiques** ou de **doses élevées cumulatives d'anthracycline** peut accroître le risque d'anomalies de conduction ■ Les concentrations sanguines et les effets du dolansétron sont augmentés par l'administration concomitante de **cimétidine** et d'**aténolol** ■ Les concentrations sanguines et les effets du dolansétron sont diminués par l'administration concomitante de **rifampicine**.

VOIES D'ADMINISTRATION ET POSOLOGIE

Prévention des nausées et des vomissements induits par la chimiothérapie

- **PO (adultes)**: 1 dose de 100 mg, administrée dans l'heure qui précède la chimiothérapie.
- **IV (adultes)**: 1 dose de 1,8 mg/kg, administrée 30 minutes avant la chimiothérapie (la dose habituelle est de 100 mg).

Prévention des nausées et des vomissements postopératoires (usage non approuvé)

- **PO (adultes)**: 1 dose de 100 mg, administrée 1 ou 2 heures avant la chirurgie.
- **IV (adultes)**: 1 dose de 12,5 mg, administrée 15 minutes avant la fin de l'anesthésie (prévention) ou lors de l'apparition de nausées ou de vomissements (traitement).

PRÉSENTATION

Comprimés: 50 mg^Pr, 100 mg^Pr ■ **Solution pour injection**: 20 mg/mL, en fioles de 5 mL^Pr.

SOINS INFIRMIERS

ÉVALUATION DE LA SITUATION

- Suivre de près les nausées, les vomissements et la distension abdominale; ausculter les bruits intestinaux avant et après l'administration du dolasétron.

- Noter les signes vitaux après l'administration du médicament. Après l'administration par voie IV, il y a risque d'hypotension grave, de bradycardie et de syncope.

DIAGNOSTICS INFIRMIERS POSSIBLES

- Alimentation déficiente (Indications).
- Connaissances insuffisantes sur le traitement médicamenteux (Enseignement au patient et à ses proches).

INTERVENTIONS INFIRMIÈRES

PO: Administrer dans l'heure qui précède la chimiothérapie ou dans les 2 heures qui précèdent l'intervention chirurgicale.

- La solution injectable de dolansétron peut être mélangée dans du jus de pomme ou du jus de pomme-raisin. Cette solution est stable pendant 2 heures à la température de la pièce.

IV: Administrer le médicament 30 minutes avant la chimiothérapie, 15 minutes avant la fin de l'anesthésie ou si les nausées et les vomissements se manifestent peu de temps après l'intervention chirurgicale.

IV directe: Le médicament peut être administré non dilué.

Vitesse d'administration: Administrer en 30 secondes au minimum.

Perfusion intermittente: Diluer dans 50 mL d'une des solutions suivantes: NaCl 0,9 %, D5%E, D5%E/NaCl 0,45 %, D5%E/lactate de Ringer, lactate de Ringer ou mannitol à 10 %. La solution est transparente et incolore. Elle est stable pendant 24 heures à la température ambiante ou pendant 48 heures si elle est réfrigérée après la dilution. Consulter les directives du fabricant avant de diluer le médicament.

Vitesse d'administration: Administrer chaque dose sous forme de perfusion IV en 15 minutes au maximum.

Incompatibilité (tubulure en Y): Le fabricant recommande de ne pas mélanger le dolansétron avec d'autres médicaments. Rincer la tubulure de perfusion avant et après l'administration du médicament.

ENSEIGNEMENT AU PATIENT ET À SES PROCHES

Recommander au patient de prévenir un professionnel de la santé si des nausées ou des vomissements surviennent.

VÉRIFICATION DE L'EFFICACITÉ THÉRAPEUTIQUE

L'efficacité du traitement peut être démontrée par: la prévention des nausées et des vomissements associés à une chimiothérapie émétisante ■ la prévention et le soulagement des nausées et des vomissements postopératoires. ✳

DOMPÉRIDONE

Apo-Domperidone, Dom-Domperidone, Gen-Domperidone, Motilidone, Novo-Domperidone, Nu-Domperidone, PHL-Domperidone, PMS-Domperidone, Ratio-Domperidone

Anciennement: Motilium

CLASSIFICATION:

Modificateur de la motilité des voies digestives supérieures

Grossesse – catégorie C

INDICATIONS

Traitement symptomatique des troubles de la motilité des voies digestives supérieures, associés à une gastrite chronique ou subaiguë et à la gastroparésie du diabète. On peut également prescrire la dompéridone dans la prévention des troubles digestifs et de l'hypotension orthostatique, associés aux agonistes dopaminergiques antiparkinsoniens et à la lévodopa. **Usages non approuvés**: Hypotension orthostatique ■ Traitement des nausées et des vomissements.

MÉCANISME D'ACTION

Blocage des récepteurs périphériques de la dopamine ■ Stimulation de la motilité des voies digestives hautes et accélération de la vidange gastrique. ***Effets thérapeutiques:*** Diminution des nausées et des vomissements ■ Diminution des symptômes de gastroparésie.

PHARMACOCINÉTIQUE

Absorption: Biodisponibilité de 13 à 17 % (PO).

Distribution: La dompéridone ne traverse pas facilement la barrière hématoencéphalique et ne devrait donc pas entraîner d'effets sur le SNC.

Liaison aux protéines: De 91,7 à 93 %.

Métabolisme et excrétion: Le médicament est métabolisé par hydroxylation et N-désalkylation oxydative. Les isoenzymes CYP3A4, 1A2 et 2E1 semblent intervenir dans ces métabolismes. 31 % de la dose est excrété dans les urines et on retrouve une fraction de 66 % dans les fèces pendant une période de 4 jours.

Demi-vie: De 12,6 à 16 heures.

Profil temps-action (concentrations plasmatiques)

	Début d'action	Pic	Durée
PO	inconnu	30 – 110 min	inconnue

D

CONTRE-INDICATIONS, PRÉCAUTIONS ET MISES EN GARDE

Contre-indications: Hypersensibilité ■ Occasions où la stimulation des voies digestives peut être dangereuse (p. ex., hémorragie digestive, obstruction mécanique ou perforation) ■ Tumeur hypophysaire à sécrétion de prolactine (prolactinome).

Précautions et mises en garde: Cancer du sein (ancien ou évolutif) ■ **OBST., ALLAITEMENT:** L'innocuité de l'agent n'a pas été établie ■ **PÉD.:** Incidence plus élevée des effets indésirables ■ Insuffisance hépatique ■ Allongement possible de l'intervalle QT_c.

RÉACTIONS INDÉSIRABLES ET EFFETS SECONDAIRES

SNC: maux de tête et migraines, sécheresse de la bouche (xérostomie).

ORLO: conjonctivite, stomatite.

End.: bouffées de chaleur, galactorrhée, gynécomastie, hyperprolactinémie, mastalgie, troubles menstruels.

Locaux: rash, prurit, urticaire.

INTERACTIONS

Médicament-médicament: L'administration concomitante d'**agents anticholinergiques** peut contrecarrer les effets bénéfiques de la dompéridone ■ Les **médicaments qui inhibent le CYP3A4** peuvent accroître les concentrations plasmatiques de dompéridone (p. ex., **antibiotiques macrolides**, **antifongiques azolés**, **inhibiteurs de la protéase du VIH**) ■ Les **médicaments qui induisent le CYP3A4** peuvent diminuer les concentrations plasmatiques de dompéridone (p. ex., **phénytoine**, **phénobarbital**) ■ La dompéridone peut entraver l'absorption des **préparations à libération prolongée ou entérosolubles** ■ Les **médicaments qui élèvent le pH gastrique** (p. ex., les **anti-H_2**, les **inhibiteurs de la pompe à protons**, les **antiacides**) peuvent diminuer l'absorption de la dompéridone.

VOIES D'ADMINISTRATION ET POSOLOGIE

- **PO (adultes):** *Troubles de la motilité des voies digestives supérieures* – initialement, 10 mg, 3 ou 4 fois par jour. Dans les cas graves ou résistants, on peut augmenter la dose jusqu'à 20 mg, 3 ou 4 fois par jour, si nécessaire. Des doses plus élevées peuvent se révéler nécessaires pour maîtriser les symptômes en cours d'adaptation de la posologie de l'agent antiparkinsonien.

PRÉSENTATION

Comprimés: 10 mg[Pr].

SOINS INFIRMIERS

ÉVALUATION DE LA SITUATION

Suivre de près les nausées et les vomissements; ausculter les bruits intestinaux et observer la distension abdominale avant et après l'administration de la dompéridone.

Tests de laboratoire:

- Examiner les résultats des tests de la fonction hépatique, car la dompéridone peut rarement élever les concentrations d'AST et d'ALT.
- La dompéridone peut également élever les concentrations de cholestérol dans de rares cas.
- La dompéridone peut accroître les concentrations sériques de prolactine, mais n'influe pas sur les concentrations d'aldostérone circulante.

DIAGNOSTICS INFIRMIERS POSSIBLES

- Alimentation déficiente (Indications).
- Risque d'accident (Effets secondaires).
- Connaissances insuffisantes sur le traitement médicamenteux (Enseignement au patient et à ses proches).

INTERVENTIONS INFIRMIÈRES

- Administrer les doses de 15 à 30 minutes avant les repas et au coucher.

ENSEIGNEMENT AU PATIENT ET À SES PROCHES

- Conseiller au patient de respecter rigoureusement la posologie recommandée. S'il n'a pas pu prendre le médicament au moment habituel, il doit le prendre aussitôt que possible, à moins que ce ne soit presque l'heure prévue pour la dose suivante.
- Conseiller au patient de pratiquer une bonne hygiène buccale, de se rincer la bouche avec de l'eau, de mâcher de la gomme ou de sucer des bonbons sans sucre pour diminuer la sécheresse de la bouche. Lui recommander de prévenir un professionnel de la santé si la sécheresse de la bouche persiste (on pourrait lui prescrire des substituts de salive). Lui recommander de consulter le dentiste si la sécheresse de la bouche gêne le port des prothèses dentaires.

VÉRIFICATION DE L'EFFICACITÉ THÉRAPEUTIQUE

L'efficacité du traitement peut être démontrée par: la prévention ou le soulagement des nausées et des vomissements ■ la diminution des symptômes de gastroparésie

■ la diminution des symptômes d'hypotension orthostatique et l'élévation de la pression artérielle en position debout.

DONÉPÉZIL

Aricept, Aricept RDT

CLASSIFICATION:
Cholinergique (inhibiteur de la cholinestérase)

Grossesse – catégorie C

INDICATIONS

Traitement symptomatique de la démence de type Alzheimer d'intensité légère ou modérée.

MÉCANISME D'ACTION

Amélioration de l'activité cholinergique par inhibition de l'acétylcholinestérase. ***Effets thérapeutiques:*** Diminution ou stabilisation des symptômes associés à la maladie d'Alzheimer ■ L'agent ne modifie pas l'évolution de la maladie.

PHARMACOCINÉTIQUE

Absorption: Bonne (PO).
Distribution: Inconnue.
Liaison aux protéines: 96 %.
Métabolisme et excrétion: Métabolisme partiellement hépatique (cytochromes CYP 2D6 et CYP 3A4); excrétion partiellement rénale (dont 17 % à l'état inchangé). Deux métabolites sont actifs sur le plan pharmacologique.
Demi-vie: 70 heures.

Profil temps-action (diminution des symptômes)

	DÉBUT D'ACTION	PIC	DURÉE
PO	inconnu	plusieurs semaines	6 semaines†

† Après arrêt du traitement, le patient retrouve son état cognitif initial.

CONTRE-INDICATIONS, PRÉCAUTIONS ET MISES EN GARDE

Contre-indications: Hypersensibilité au donépézil ou aux dérivés de pipéridine.
Précautions et mises en garde: Présence d'une maladie cardiaque sous-jacente, particulièrement le syndrome de dysfonctionnement sinusal ou des anomalies de conduction supraventriculaire ■ Antécédents d'ulcère ou traitement concomitant avec des AINS ■ Antécédents de convulsions ■ Antécédents d'asthme ou de bronchopneumopathie obstructive ■ **OBST., ALLAITEMENT, PÉD.:** L'innocuité du médicament n'a pas été établie (usage non approuvé).

RÉACTIONS INDÉSIRABLES ET EFFETS SECONDAIRES

SNC: céphalées, rêves bizarres, dépression, étourdissements, somnolence, fatigue, insomnie, syncope.
CV: fibrillation auriculaire, hypertension, hypotension, vasodilatation, bradycardie.
GI: diarrhée, nausées, anorexie, vomissements.
GU: mictions fréquentes.
Tég.: ecchymoses.
Métab.: bouffées de chaleur, perte de poids.
Loc.: arthrite, crampes musculaires.

INTERACTIONS

Médicament-médicament: Le donépézil accentue la relaxation musculaire induite par la **succinylcholine** ■ Le donépézil peut entraver les effets des **agents anticholinergiques** ■ Le médicament augmente les effets cholinergiques du **béthanéchol** ■ Risque accru d'hémorragie gastro-intestinale lors de l'administration concomitante d'**anti-inflammatoires non stéroïdiens** ■ La **quinidine** et le **kétoconazole** diminuent le métabolisme du donépézil ■ La **rifampine**, la **carbamazépine**, la **dexaméthasone**, le **phénobarbital** et la **phénytoïne** stimulent les enzymes qui métabolisent le donépézil et peuvent diminuer ses effets.
Médicament-produits naturels: La **stramoine** et le **scopolia** peuvent diminuer l'effet cholinergique du donépézil.

VOIES D'ADMINISTRATION ET POSOLOGIE

- **PO (adultes):** 5 mg, 1 fois par jour; après 4 à 6 semaines, on peut augmenter la dose jusqu'à 10 mg, 1 fois par jour. La dose ne devrait pas dépasser 5 mg/jour chez les femmes frêles.

PRÉSENTATION

Comprimés: 5 mg[Pr], 10 mg[Pr] ■ **Comprimés à dissolution rapide:** 5 mg[Pr], 10 mg[Pr].

SOINS INFIRMIERS

ÉVALUATION DE LA SITUATION

- Évaluer les fonctions cognitives (mémoire, attention, raisonnement, langage, capacité à accomplir des tâches simples) à intervalles réguliers pendant toute la durée du traitement.

- Mesurer la fréquence cardiaque à intervalles réguliers pendant toute la durée du traitement. Le donépézil peut induire une bradycardie.

DIAGNOSTICS INFIRMIERS POSSIBLES

- Opérations de la pensée perturbées (Indications).
- Risque d'accident (Indications).
- Connaissances insuffisantes sur le traitement médicamenteux (Enseignement au patient et à ses proches).

INTERVENTIONS INFIRMIÈRES

Administrer le donépézil sans égard aux repas. Les comprimés à dissolution orale doivent se dissoudre sur la langue; le patient doit boire ensuite un verre d'eau.

ENSEIGNEMENT AU PATIENT ET À SES PROCHES

- Insister sur le fait qu'il est important de prendre le donépézil tous les jours, en suivant rigoureusement la posologie recommandée. Si le patient n'a pas pu prendre le médicament au moment habituel, il devrait sauter cette dose et reprendre l'horaire habituel le lendemain. Le prévenir qu'il ne doit pas prendre une dose plus élevée que celle prescrite; des doses plus élevées n'augmentent pas les effets bénéfiques, mais peuvent entraîner un plus grand nombre d'effets secondaires.
- Prévenir le patient et ses proches que le donépézil peut provoquer des étourdissements.
- Recommander au patient et à ses proches de prévenir un professionnel de la santé en cas de nausées, de vomissements, de diarrhée ou de changement de la couleur des selles, ou encore si de nouveaux symptômes se manifestent ou si les symptômes déjà présents s'aggravent.
- Recommander au patient et à ses proches d'informer tous les professionnels de la santé de ce traitement médicamenteux avant de commencer un autre traitement ou de se soumettre à une intervention chirurgicale.
- Insister sur l'importance des examens de suivi réguliers pour déterminer les effets du traitement.

VÉRIFICATION DE L'EFFICACITÉ THÉRAPEUTIQUE

L'efficacité du traitement peut être démontrée par: l'amélioration ou la stabilisation des fonctions cognitives (mémoire, attention, raisonnement, langage, capacité à accomplir des tâches simples) chez les patients souffrant de la maladie d'Alzheimer. ✱

ALERTE CLINIQUE

DOPAMINE

Intropin

CLASSIFICATION:

Inotrope et cardiotonique, vasopresseur, sympathomimétique

Grossesse – catégorie C

INDICATIONS

Adjuvant aux mesures standard visant à améliorer: la pression artérielle ■ le débit cardiaque ■ le débit urinaire pour traiter le choc non corrigé par le rétablissement du volume sanguin.

MÉCANISME D'ACTION

Les faibles doses (de 0,5 à 2 µg/kg/min) stimulent les récepteurs dopaminergiques entraînant la dilatation des vaisseaux rénaux ■ Les doses plus élevées (de 2 à 10 µg/kg/min) stimulent les récepteurs dopaminergiques et bêta-adrénergiques entraînant la stimulation du cœur et la dilatation des vaisseaux rénaux ■ Les doses supérieures à 10 µg/kg/min stimulent les récepteurs alpha-adrénergiques et peuvent induire la constriction des vaisseaux rénaux. ***Effets thérapeutiques:*** Élévation du débit cardiaque et de la pression artérielle et amélioration du débit sanguin rénal.

PHARMACOCINÉTIQUE

Absorption: Biodisponibilité à 100 % (IV).
Distribution: Le médicament se répartit dans tout l'organisme; il ne traverse cependant pas la barrière hémato-encéphalique.
Métabolisme et excrétion: Métabolisme hépatique, rénal et plasmatique.
Demi-vie: 2 minutes.

Profil temps-action (effets hémodynamiques)

	DÉBUT D'ACTION	PIC	DURÉE
IV	1 – 2 min	jusqu'à 10 min	< 10 min

CONTRE-INDICATIONS, PRÉCAUTIONS ET MISES EN GARDE

Contre-indications: Phéochromocytome.
Précautions et mises en garde: Tachyarythmies ■ Hypersensibilité aux bisulfites (certains produits en renferment) ■ Hypovolémie ■ Infarctus du myocarde ■ Maladies vasculaires occlusives ■ **GÉR.**: Les personnes âgées peuvent être plus sensibles aux effets secondaires ■ **OBST., PÉD.**: Grossesse, allaitement et enfants (l'innocuité du médicament n'a pas été établie).

RÉACTIONS INDÉSIRABLES ET EFFETS SECONDAIRES

SNC: céphalées.
ORLO: mydriase (doses élevées).
Resp.: dyspnée.
CV: arythmies, hypotension, angine, modifications de l'ÉCG, palpitations, vasoconstriction.
GI: nausées, vomissements.
Tég.: pilo-érection.
Locaux: irritation au point d'injection IV.

INTERACTIONS

Médicament-médicament: L'usage concomitant d'**IMAO**, d'**alcaloïdes de l'ergot** (**ergotamine**), de **guanéthidine**, de **guanadrel** ou de certains **antidépresseurs** entraîne une hypertension grave ■ La **phénytoïne par voie IV**, administrée en concomitance, peut provoquer l'hypotension et la bradycardie ■ Les **anesthésiques généraux**, administrés en concomitance, peuvent entraîner des arythmies ■ Les **bêtabloquants** peuvent contrecarrer les effets cardiaques de la dopamine.

VOIES D'ADMINISTRATION ET POSOLOGIE

Consulter le tableau des vitesses de perfusion se trouvant à l'annexe C.

- **IV (adultes)**: Initialement, de 2 à 5 µg/kg/min; augmenter la dose par paliers de 5 à 10 µg/kg/min, jusqu'à une dose totale de 20 à 50 µg/kg/min. Si des doses plus élevées sont nécessaires, il est recommandé de vérifier fréquemment le débit urinaire. Adapter la posologie selon la réponse hémodynamique et rénale.

PRÉSENTATION (version générique disponible)

Solution pour injection (qui doit être diluée): en ampoules ou en fioles unidose de 5mL: 40 mg/mL^Pr ■ **Solution pour injection prémélangée**: 0,8 mg/mL^Pr, 1,6 mg/mL^Pr, 3,2 mg/mL^Pr dans 250 et 500 mL de solution D5%E^Pr.

SOINS INFIRMIERS

ÉVALUATION DE LA SITUATION

- Mesurer la pression artérielle, la fréquence cardiaque, le pouls, la pression capillaire pulmonaire bloquée, le débit cardiaque, la pression veineuse centrale (PVC) et le débit urinaire, et suivre le tracé de l'ÉCG, de façon continue pendant toute la durée de l'administration. Signaler au médecin tout changement important au niveau des signes vitaux ou l'apparition d'arythmies. Lui demander de préciser les paramètres du pouls et de la pression artérielle ainsi que les modifications de l'ÉCG dont il faut tenir compte afin de décider s'il faut adapter la posologie ou arrêter le traitement.
- Mesurer le débit urinaire à intervalles fréquents tout au long de l'administration. Prévenir rapidement le médecin si le débit urinaire diminue.
- Palper le pouls périphérique et examiner les membres à intervalles réguliers tout au long de l'administration. Avertir le médecin si la qualité du pouls se détériore ou si les membres deviennent froids ou tachetés.
- En présence d'hypotension, accélérer la vitesse d'administration. Si l'hypotension persiste, on peut administrer des vasoconstricteurs plus puissants (noradrénaline).

TOXICITÉ ET SURDOSAGE: En présence d'une hypertension excessive, ralentir la vitesse de perfusion ou interrompre le traitement jusqu'à ce que la pression artérielle diminue. Bien que des mesures supplémentaires ne soient habituellement pas nécessaires en raison de la courte durée d'action de la dopamine, on peut administrer de la phentolamine si l'hypertension persiste.

DIAGNOSTICS INFIRMIERS POSSIBLES

- Débit cardiaque diminué (Indications).
- Irrigation tissulaire inefficace (Indications).

INTERVENTIONS INFIRMIÈRES

ALERTE CLINIQUE: LES MÉDICAMENTS INTRAVEINEUX VASOACTIFS PEUVENT ÊTRE DANGEREUX. AVANT L'ADMINISTRATION, IL EST RECOMMANDÉ DE DEMANDER À UN AUTRE PROFESSIONNEL DE LA SANTÉ DE VÉRIFIER L'ORDONNANCE D'ORIGINE, LE CALCUL DES DOSES À ADMINISTRER ET LE RÉGLAGE DE LA POMPE VOLUMÉTRIQUE. NE PAS CONFONDRE LA DOBUTAMINE AVEC LA DOPAMINE. SI POSSIBLE, LA CONSERVER SÉPARÉMENT.

- Avant d'amorcer le traitement par la dopamine, corriger l'hypovolémie par des succédanés qui augmentent la masse plasmatique.
- ADMINISTRER LA PRÉPARATION DANS UNE GROSSE VEINE ET EXAMINER SOUVENT LE POINT D'INJECTION. L'EXTRAVASATION PEUT ENTRAÎNER UNE IRRITATION GRAVE, LA NÉCROSE ET LA DESQUAMATION DES TISSUS. EN CAS D'EXTRAVASATION, INFILTRER LA RÉGION ATTEINTE AVEC 10 À 15 mL DE SOLUTION DE NACL 0,9 % CONTENANT DE 5 À 10 mg DE PHENTOLAMINE. RÉDUIRE PROPORTIONNELLEMENT LA POSOLOGIE CHEZ LES ENFANTS. L'INFILTRATION DANS LES 12 HEURES QUI SUIVENT L'EXTRAVASATION ENTRAÎNE DES MODIFICATIONS HYPERÉMIQUES IMMÉDIATES.

Perfusion continue: Diluer de 200 à 400 mg de dopamine dans 250 à 500 mL d'une des solutions stériles IV suivantes: NaCl 0,9 %, D5%E, dextrose dans une solution de lactate de Ringer, D5%E/NaCl 0,45 % ou 0,9 %, ou solution de lactate de Ringer pour perfusion IV. Les concentrations habituellement utilisées sont de 800 µg/mL ou de 0,8 mg/mL (200 mg/250 mL) lorsque la masse plasmatique est suffisante, et de 1,6 mg/mL (400 mg/250 mL) ou de 3,2 mg/mL (800 mg/250 mL) lorsque le patient est soumis à une restriction liquidienne ou lorsqu'il est souhaitable de ralentir la vitesse d'administration. Diluer juste avant l'administration. La solution qui vire au jaune ou au brun est décomposée. Jeter toute solution qui est trouble, qui change de couleur ou qui contient un précipité. La solution est stable pendant 24 heures. Consulter les directives du fabricant avant de diluer le médicament.

Vitesse d'administration: Utiliser une pompe de perfusion afin de s'assurer que l'on injecte la dose exacte. La vitesse d'administration doit être adaptée selon la réponse au traitement (pression artérielle, fréquence cardiaque, débit urinaire, irrigation périphérique, présence d'activité ectopique, débit cardiaque); voir le tableau des vitesses de perfusion (annexe C). Diminuer la vitesse graduellement avant d'arrêter le traitement pour prévenir une chute marquée de la pression artérielle.

Compatibilité (tubulure en Y): adrénaline ▪ aldesleukine ▪ amifostine ▪ amiodarone ▪ amrinone ▪ atracurium ▪ aztréonam ▪ cefmétazole ▪ ciprofloxacine ▪ cladribine ▪ diltiazem ▪ dobutamine ▪ énalaprilate ▪ esmolol ▪ famotidine ▪ fentanyl ▪ fluconazole ▪ foscarnet ▪ granisétron ▪ halopéridol ▪ héparine ▪ hydrocortisone sodique, succinate de ▪ hydromorphone ▪ labétalol ▪ lidocaïne ▪ lorazépam ▪ mépéridine ▪ méthylprednisolone ▪ métronidazole ▪ midazolam ▪ milrinone ▪ morphine ▪ nitroglycérine ▪ nitroprusside ▪ noradrénaline ▪ ondansétron ▪ pancuronium ▪ pipéracilline/tazobactam ▪ potassium, chlorure de ▪ propofol ▪ ranitidine ▪ sargramostim ▪ streptokinase ▪ tacrolimus ▪ théophylline ▪ thiotépa ▪ tolazoline ▪ vécuronium ▪ vérapamil ▪ vitamines du complexe B avec C ▪ warfarine ▪ zidovudine.

Incompatibilité (tubulure en Y): acyclovir ▪ altéplase ▪ céfépime ▪ indométhacine ▪ insuline ▪ thiopental.

ENSEIGNEMENT AU PATIENT ET À SES PROCHES

- Expliquer au patient la raison pour laquelle on doit lui administrer ce médicament et assurer une surveillance étroite.
- Recommander au patient de prévenir immédiatement un professionnel de la santé en cas de douleurs thoraciques, de dyspnée ou d'engourdissements, de picotements ou d'une sensation de brûlure au niveau des membres.
- Recommander au patient de prévenir immédiatement un professionnel de la santé en cas de douleur ou de gêne au point d'injection.

VÉRIFICATION DE L'EFFICACITÉ THÉRAPEUTIQUE

L'efficacité du traitement peut être démontrée par: l'élévation de la pression artérielle ▪ l'amélioration de la circulation périphérique ▪ l'augmentation du débit urinaire. ✳

DOXAZOSINE

Apo-Doxazosin, Cardura, Gen-Doxazosin, Novo-Doxazosin

CLASSIFICATION:

Antihypertenseur (antagoniste alpha$_1$-adrénergique à action périphérique), traitement symptomatique de l'hyperplasie bénigne de la prostate

Grossesse – catégorie C

INDICATIONS

Traitement de l'hypertension en association avec d'autres agents ▪ Traitement des symptômes de l'hyperplasie bénigne de la prostate (HBP).

MÉCANISME D'ACTION

Dilatation des artères et des veines par blocage des récepteurs alpha$_1$-adrénergiques postsynaptiques ▪ Diminution de la résistance urétrale par blocage des récepteurs alpha$_1$-adrénergiques prostatiques. ***Effets thérapeutiques:*** Abaissement de la pression artérielle ▪ Soulagement des symptômes d'obstruction urétrale et d'HBP.

PHARMACOCINÉTIQUE

Absorption: Bonne (PO).

Distribution: Une certaine quantité de l'agent semble passer dans le lait maternel, mais la distribution du reste du médicament est inconnue.

Liaison aux protéines: De 98 à 99 %.

Métabolisme et excrétion: Fort métabolisme hépatique.

Demi-vie: 22 heures.

Profil temps-action (effet antihypertenseur)

	DÉBUT D'ACTION	PIC	DURÉE
PO	1 - 2 h	2 - 6 h	24 h

CONTRE-INDICATIONS, PRÉCAUTIONS ET MISES EN GARDE

Contre-indications: Hypersensibilité.

Précautions et mises en garde: Dysfonctionnement hépatique ■ **GÉR.**: Risque accru d'hypotension orthostatique ■ **OBST., ALLAITEMENT, PÉD.**: L'innocuité du médicament n'a pas été établie.

RÉACTIONS INDÉSIRABLES ET EFFETS SECONDAIRES

SNC: étourdissements, céphalées, dépression, somnolence, fatigue, nervosité, faiblesse.

ORLO: vision anormale, vision trouble, conjonctivite, épistaxis.

Resp.: dyspnée.

CV: hypotension orthostatique induite par la ou les premières doses, arythmies, douleurs thoraciques, œdème, palpitations.

GI: gêne abdominale, constipation, diarrhée, sécheresse de la bouche (xérostomie), flatulence, nausées, vomissements.

GU: diminution de la libido, dysfonctionnement sexuel.

Tég.: rougeurs du visage, rash, urticaire.

Loc.: arthralgie, arthrite, goutte, myalgie.

INTERACTIONS

Médicament-médicament: Effets hypotenseurs additifs lors de la consommation d'une grande quantité d'**alcool** ou lors de l'administration concomitante de **sildénafil**, de **tadalafil**, de **vardénafil**, d'autres **antihypertenseurs** ou de **dérivés nitrés** ■ Le médicament peut réduire l'effet antihypertenseur de la **clonidine**.

VOIES D'ADMINISTRATION ET POSOLOGIE

- **PO (adultes)**: *Hypertension* – 1 mg, 1 fois par jour; on peut augmenter graduellement cette dose, à intervalles de 2 semaines, jusqu'à concurrence de 2 à 16 mg par jour; l'incidence de l'hypotension orthostatique augmente de façon marquée à des doses > 4 mg par jour. *Hyperplasie bénigne de la prostate* – 1 mg, 1 fois par jour; on peut augmenter graduellement cette dose jusqu'à concurrence de 8 mg par jour.

PRÉSENTATION

Comprimés: 1 mg^{Pr}, 2 mg^{Pr}, 4 mg^{Pr}.

SOINS INFIRMIERS

ÉVALUATION DE LA SITUATION

- Mesurer la pression artérielle de 2 à 6 heures après les premières doses, pendant la période d'adaptation de la posologie et à intervalles réguliers pendant toute la durée du traitement. Informer le médecin de tout changement important.
- Suivre de près l'état du patient pour déceler l'hypotension orthostatique induite par la ou les premières doses et la syncope. L'incidence de ces effets peut être reliée à la dose administrée. Observer le patient attentivement pendant ce laps de temps et prendre toutes les précautions nécessaires pour prévenir les accidents.
- Effectuer le bilan quotidien des ingesta et des excreta et peser le patient tous les jours. L'observer quotidiennement, particulièrement au début du traitement, pour déceler la formation d'un œdème. Signaler au médecin tout gain de poids ou la présence d'un œdème.

Hyperplasie bénigne de la prostate: Avant le traitement et à intervalles réguliers pendant toute sa durée, suivre de près le patient pour déceler l'apparition des symptômes d'hyperplasie bénigne de la prostate: retard de la miction, miction incomplète, interruption du jet urinaire, modification de la puissance du jet et de la quantité d'urine éliminée, fuite postmictionnelle, effort pour amorcer la miction, dysurie, miction impérieuse.

DIAGNOSTICS INFIRMIERS POSSIBLES

- Élimination urinaire altérée (Indications).
- Risque d'accident (Effets secondaires).
- Connaissances insuffisantes sur le traitement médicamenteux (Enseignement au patient et à ses proches).

INTERVENTIONS INFIRMIÈRES

- Administrer la dose quotidienne au coucher.

Hypertension: La doxazosine doit être administrée en concomitance avec d'autres antihypertenseurs.

ENSEIGNEMENT AU PATIENT ET À SES PROCHES

- Expliquer au patient qu'il doit prendre la doxazosine tous les jours, à la même heure, même s'il se sent mieux. S'il n'a pu prendre le médicament au moment habituel, il doit le prendre aussitôt que possible, à moins que ce ne soit presque l'heure prévue pour la dose suivante. Le prévenir qu'il ne doit jamais remplacer une dose manquée par une double dose.
- Prévenir le patient que la doxazosine peut provoquer de la somnolence ou des étourdissements. Lui conseiller de ne pas conduire et d'éviter les activités qui exigent sa vigilance jusqu'à ce qu'on ait la certitude que le médicament n'entraîne pas ces effets chez lui.

D

- Recommander au patient de changer lentement de position pour diminuer le risque d'hypotension orthostatique.
- Conseiller au patient de consulter un professionnel de la santé avant de prendre un médicament en vente libre contre la toux, le rhume ou les allergies.
- Insister sur l'importance des examens de suivi permettant d'évaluer les bienfaits du traitement.

Hypertension:

- Montrer au patient et à ses proches comment mesurer la pression artérielle. Leur demander de prendre la pression artérielle au moins 1 fois par semaine et leur recommander de signaler au médecin tout changement important.
- Inciter le patient à suivre d'autres mesures de réduction de l'hypertension: perdre du poids, réduire sa consommation de sel, arrêter de fumer, consommer de l'alcool avec modération, faire régulièrement de l'exercice et diminuer le stress.

VÉRIFICATION DE L'EFFICACITÉ THÉRAPEUTIQUE

L'efficacité du traitement peut être démontrée par: la baisse de la pression artérielle sans manifestation d'effets secondaires ■ la diminution des symptômes urinaires associés à l'hyperplasie bénigne de la prostate.

DOXÉPINE

Apo-Doxépine, Novo-Doxépine, Sinequan, Zonalon

CLASSIFICATION:

Anxiolytique et hypnosédatif, antidépresseur (tricyclique), agent dermatologique (antiprurigineux)

Grossesse – catégorie C

INDICATIONS

PO: Traitement des diverses formes de dépression endogène (en association avec une psychothérapie) ■ Traitement de l'anxiété ■ **Usage topique**: Soulagement de courte durée du prurit associé à: une dermatite eczémateuse ■ une névrodermite circonscrite. **Usages non approuvés – PO**: Traitement des syndromes de douleurs chroniques ■ Traitement du prurit.

MÉCANISME D'ACTION

Prévention du recaptage de la noradrénaline et de la sérotonine par les neurones présynaptiques; l'accumulation de ces neurotransmetteurs potentialise leur activité ■ La doxépine est également dotée d'effets anticholinergiques importants ■ **Usage topique**: Effet antiprurigineux attribuable aux propriétés antihistaminiques du médicament. ***Effets thérapeutiques* – PO**: Soulagement de la dépression ■ Diminution de l'anxiété ■ **Usage topique**: Diminution du prurit.

PHARMACOCINÉTIQUE

Absorption: Bonne (PO). Fort métabolisme hépatique de premier passage. On note une certaine absorption systémique (préparation topique).

Distribution: Le médicament se répartit dans tout l'organisme. Il traverse probablement la barrière placentaire et passe dans le lait maternel.

Métabolisme et excrétion: Métabolisme hépatique. Une certaine portion est transformée en un composé antidépresseur actif. Plusieurs cycles entérohépatiques, sécrétion dans les sucs gastriques.

Demi-vie: De 8 à 25 heures.

Profil temps-action (effet antidépresseur)

	DÉBUT D'ACTION	PIC	DURÉE
PO	2 – 3 semaines	jusqu'à 6 semaines	plusieurs jours – semaines

CONTRE-INDICATIONS, PRÉCAUTIONS ET MISES EN GARDE

Contre-indications: Hypersensibilité ■ Intolérance aux bisulfites (certaines préparations de doxépine en contiennent) ■ Glaucome à angle fermé non traité ■ Début de la convalescence après un infarctus du myocarde ■ Insuffisance cardiaque aiguë ■ Pédiatrie ■ Rétention urinaire ■ Antécédents de dyscrasie sanguine ■ Maladie hépatique grave ■ Prise d'IMAO (attendre 14 jours entre l'arrêt de la prise de l'IMAO et le début du traitement par la doxépine et vice versa).

Précautions et mises en garde: GÉR.: Risque accru de chutes à cause de l'effet sédatif et anticholinergique de la doxépine. Il est recommandé de réduire la dose initiale ■ Une surveillance des idées suicidaires est indiquée chez tous les patients recevant ce médicament ■ Troubles bipolaires (l'administration d'un antidépresseur durant la phase dépressive d'un trouble bipolaire peut déclencher un épisode hypomaniaque ou maniaque) ■ Maladie cardiovasculaire préexistante (risque accru de réactions indésirables) ■ Hyperplasie bénigne de la prostate (prédisposition plus grande à la rétention urinaire) ■ Convulsions ■ Risque d'arythmies cardiaques transitoires chez des patients prenant en concomitance un médicament thyroïdien ou souffrant d'hyperthyroïdie ■ **OBST.**: On n'a pas mené d'études adéquates chez la femme enceinte. N'administrer la doxépine au cours de la grossesse que si les bienfaits éventuels l'emportent sur les risques possibles pour le fœtus ■ **ALLAITEMENT**: On n'a pas mené d'études adéquates chez la femme qui allaite. N'administrer la doxépine que si les bienfaits éventuels l'emportent sur les risques possibles pour le nourrisson.

RÉACTIONS INDÉSIRABLES ET EFFETS SECONDAIRES

SNC: fatigue, sédation, agitation, confusion, hallucinations.
ORLO: vision trouble, pression intraoculaire accrue.
CV: hypotension, arythmies, anomalies de l'ÉCG.
GI: constipation, sécheresse de la bouche (xérostomie), hépatite, gain d'appétit, nausées, iléus paralytique.
GU: rétention urinaire.
Tég.: photosensibilité, rash.
Hémat.: dyscrasie sanguine.
Divers: réactions d'hypersensibilité.

INTERACTIONS

On note les mêmes interactions en cas d'usage topique que d'administration par voie orale.
Médicament-médicament: La doxépine est métabolisée dans le foie par l'**isoenzyme 2D6 du cytochrome P450** et ses effets peuvent être modifiés par les **médicaments qui sont également métabolisés par cette enzyme**, incluant d'autres **antidépresseurs**, les **phénothiazines**, la **carbamazépine**, les **antiarythmiques de type 1C** (**propafénone**, **flécaïnide**); lors de l'administration concomitante de ces agents et de la doxépine, une réduction de la dose de l'un des médicaments ou des deux à la fois peut s'avérer nécessaire ■ L'usage concomitant d'autres **médicaments qui inhibent l'activité de cette enzyme**, incluant la **cimétidine**, la **quinidine**, l'**amiodarone** et le **ritonavir**, peut accroître les effets de la doxépine ■ La doxépine peut provoquer l'hypotension, la tachycardie et des réactions qui peuvent mettre la vie du patient en danger, si elle est administrée en même temps qu'un **IMAO** (éviter l'administration conjointe, attendre 14 jours entre l'arrêt du traitement par l'IMAO et le début du traitement par la doxépine et vice versa) ■ Il faudrait éviter l'usage concomitant d'**antidépresseurs du type ISRS**, en raison du risque de toxicité accrue (le traitement par la **fluoxétine** devrait être interrompu 5 semaines avant de commencer l'administration de la doxépine) ■ La doxépine peut inhiber la réponse thérapeutique à la **guanéthidine** ■ La **clonidine**, administrée en concomitance, peut provoquer une crise hypertensive; il faut donc éviter d'associer ces deux agents ■ L'administration concomitante de doxépine et de **lévodopa** peut retarder ou diminuer l'absorption de la lévodopa ou provoquer l'hypertension ■ Les concentrations sanguines du médicament et ses effets peuvent être diminués par les **rifamycines** ■ Effet dépresseur additif sur le SNC, lors de l'usage concomitant d'autres **dépresseurs du SNC**, incluant l'**alcool**, les **antihistaminiques**, la **clonidine**, les **opioïdes** et les **hypnosédatifs** ■ Les **barbituriques** peuvent modifier les concentrations sanguines de la doxépine et ses effets ■ Les effets secondaires **adrénergiques** et **anticholinergiques** peuvent être additifs lors de l'administration concomitante d'autres **agents dotés de ces mêmes propriétés** ■ Les **phénothiazines** et les **contraceptifs oraux** augmentent les concentrations de doxépine et peuvent entraîner une toxicité ■ Le **tabac** peut accélérer le métabolisme du médicament et en diminuer les effets.
Médicament-produits naturels: La consommation concomitante de **kava**, de **valériane** ou de **camomille** peut augmenter l'effet dépresseur sur le SNC ■ Risque d'augmentation des effets anticholinergiques lors de la consommation concomitante de **datura** et de **scopolia**.

VOIES D'ADMINISTRATION ET POSOLOGIE

- **PO (adultes)**: *Antidépresseur ou anxiolytique* – 25 mg, 3 fois par jour; on peut augmenter la dose, au besoin, jusqu'à concurrence de 150 mg par jour, chez les patients en consultation externe, ou de 300 mg par jour, chez les patients hospitalisés; chez certains patients, une posologie de 25 à 50 mg par jour peut s'avérer suffisante. Une fois que l'état du patient est stabilisé, on peut lui administrer la dose entière au coucher.
- **PO (personnes âgées)**: *Antidépresseur* – initialement, de 25 à 50 mg; on peut augmenter la dose, selon les besoins.
- **Usage topique (adultes)**: Appliquer 3 ou 4 fois par jour (espacer les applications de 3 à 4 heures) pendant une période pouvant aller jusqu'à 8 jours.

PRÉSENTATION
(version générique disponible)

Capsules: 10 mg^{Pr}, 25 mg^{Pr}, 50 mg^{Pr}, 75 mg^{Pr}, 100 mg^{Pr} ■ **Crème topique**: 5 %^{Pr}.

SOINS INFIRMIERS

ÉVALUATION DE LA SITUATION

- Mesurer la pression artérielle et le pouls avant l'administration du médicament et pendant toute la durée du traitement. Les patients recevant des doses élevées ou ayant des antécédents de maladie cardiovasculaire devraient se soumettre à un ÉCG avant le traitement et à intervalles réguliers pendant toute sa durée.

GÉR.: Évaluer le risque de chute chez les personnes âgées prenant ce médicament et mettre en place des mesures de prévention. Rester à l'affût des effets secondaires anticholinergiques.

Dépression: Évaluer fréquemment l'état mental du patient. Au début du traitement, des symptômes comme la confusion, l'agitation et des hallucinations peuvent se manifester et peuvent dicter une réduction de la dose. Suivre les sautes d'humeur. Rester à l'affût des tendances suicidaires, particulièrement au début du traitement. Limiter la quantité de médicament dont le patient peut disposer.

Anxiété: Évaluer la gravité de l'anxiété et ses manifestations avant le traitement et pendant toute sa durée.

Douleur: Évaluer l'intensité, le type et le siège de la douleur avant le traitement et à intervalles réguliers pendant toute sa durée.

Usage topique: Évaluer l'étendue du territoire prurigineux avant le traitement et à intervalles réguliers pendant toute sa durée.

Tests de laboratoire: Noter la numération globulaire et la formule leucocytaire, l'état de la fonction hépatique et la glycémie à intervalles réguliers pendant toute la durée du traitement. Le médicament peut entraîner une élévation des concentrations sériques de bilirubine et de phosphatase alcaline ainsi qu'une aplasie médullaire. La glycémie peut s'élever ou s'abaisser.

DIAGNOSTICS INFIRMIERS POSSIBLES

- Stratégies d'adaptation inefficaces (Indications).
- Risque d'accident (Effets secondaires).
- Connaissances insuffisantes sur le traitement médicamenteux (Enseignement au patient et à ses proches).

INTERVENTIONS INFIRMIÈRES

- NE PAS CONFONDRE LA DOXÉPINE AVEC LA DOXYCYCLINE.
- On peut administrer le médicament en une seule dose, au coucher, pour diminuer la sédation diurne. Les majorations de dose doivent également s'effectuer au coucher en raison du risque de sédation. L'adaptation posologique est un processus lent qui peut prendre de plusieurs semaines à plusieurs mois.

PO: Administrer le médicament au moment des repas ou immédiatement après pour diminuer l'irritation gastrique. Si le patient éprouve des difficultés de déglutition, on peut ouvrir les capsules et mélanger leur contenu à des aliments ou à des liquides.

Usage topique: Appliquer une mince couche de crème de doxépine seulement sur les surfaces affectées et frotter délicatement pour la faire pénétrer. Il ne faut l'appliquer que sur la peau atteinte; cette crème n'est pas destinée à l'usage ophtalmique ni à l'administration par voie orale ou à l'usage intravaginal.

ENSEIGNEMENT AU PATIENT ET À SES PROCHES

- Informer le patient que des effets secondaires systémiques peuvent se manifester lors de l'administration par voie orale ou de l'usage topique.
- Prévenir le patient que la doxépine peut parfois provoquer de la somnolence et rendre la vision trouble. Lui conseiller de ne pas conduire et d'éviter les activités qui exigent sa vigilance jusqu'à ce qu'on ait la certitude que le médicament n'entraîne pas ces effets chez lui.
- Prévenir le patient que l'hypotension orthostatique, la sédation et la confusion sont des effets courants de la doxépine au cours de l'étape initiale du traitement, particulièrement chez les personnes âgées. Protéger le patient des chutes et lui recommander de changer lentement de position.
- Recommander au patient de ne pas boire d'alcool et de ne pas prendre d'autres dépresseurs du SNC pendant toute la durée du traitement et pendant les 3 à 7 jours qui suivent l'arrêt de la médication.
- Conseiller au patient de prévenir un professionnel de la santé en cas de rétention urinaire, de sécheresse de la bouche ou de constipation persistante. Lui expliquer que les bonbons ou la gomme à mâcher sans sucre peuvent diminuer la sécheresse de la bouche et qu'une consommation accrue de liquides et d'aliments riches en fibres peut prévenir la constipation. Si ces symptômes persistent, une réduction de la dose ou l'abandon du traitement pourraient s'avérer nécessaires. Conseiller également au patient de consulter un professionnel de la santé si la sécheresse de la bouche persiste pendant plus de 2 semaines.
- Recommander au patient qui doit suivre un autre traitement ou subir une intervention chirurgicale d'informer le professionnel de la santé qu'il suit un traitement par ce médicament.

PO:

- Expliquer au patient qu'il doit respecter rigoureusement la posologie recommandée. S'il n'a pu prendre le médicament au moment habituel, il doit le prendre aussitôt que possible à moins que ce ne soit presque l'heure prévue pour la dose suivante. Si le patient prend le médicament 1 fois par jour, au coucher, lui conseiller de ne pas prendre la dose manquée le matin en raison des effets secondaires. Prévenir le patient que les effets du médicament pourraient ne pas être notables pendant au moins 2 semaines.

L'abandon brusque du traitement peut provoquer des nausées, des vomissements, la diarrhée, des céphalées, des troubles du sommeil s'accompagnant de rêves saisissants et l'irritabilité.

- Recommander au patient d'utiliser un écran solaire et des vêtements protecteurs afin de prévenir les réactions de photosensibilité.
- Inciter le patient à surveiller son alimentation, car le médicament peut lui donner plus d'appétit, ce qui risque d'entraîner un gain de poids indésirable.
- Prévenir le patient que le traitement de la dépression est habituellement de longue durée. Insister sur l'importance d'un suivi régulier permettant de déterminer les bienfaits du traitement et de déceler les effets secondaires.

Usage topique:

- Expliquer au patient qu'il doit appliquer le médicament selon la posologie recommandée; il ne doit pas utiliser une plus grande quantité de crème que celle prescrite, ni l'appliquer sur une plus grande surface que celle atteinte, ni l'utiliser à une plus grande fréquence que celle recommandée, ni prolonger le traitement au-delà de 8 jours.
- Prévenir le patient que la préparation topique peut entraîner des brûlures, des picotements, de l'œdème, des démangeaisons accrues ou une aggravation de l'eczéma. Si ces symptômes deviennent incommodants, les signaler à un professionnel de la santé.
- Prévenir le patient qu'il ne doit pas utiliser de pansements occlusifs en raison du risque d'une plus grande absorption systémique.
- Conseiller au patient de prévenir un professionnel de la santé en cas de somnolence excessive lors de l'application topique. On peut diminuer, dans ce cas, la fréquence des applications ou la quantité de crème appliquée ou encore réduire la surface traitée. Cet effet secondaire peut dicter l'abandon du traitement.

VÉRIFICATION DE L'EFFICACITÉ THÉRAPEUTIQUE

L'efficacité du traitement peut être démontrée par: un sentiment de mieux-être ■ un regain d'intérêt pour l'entourage ■ un gain d'appétit ■ un regain d'énergie ■ l'amélioration du sommeil ■ la diminution de l'anxiété ■ la diminution de la douleur chronique; les pleins effets thérapeutiques pourraient ne se manifester que de 2 à 6 semaines après le début du traitement par voie orale ■ la réduction du prurit associé à l'eczéma.

DOXERCALCIFÉROL,

voir Vitamine D (composés de)

ALERTE CLINIQUE

DOXORUBICINE

doxorubicine
Adriamycin
doxorubicine, liposomes péguylés
Caelyx
doxorubicine liposomale
Myocet

CLASSIFICATION:
Antinéoplasique (anthracycline)

Grossesse – catégorie D

INDICATIONS

Chlorhydrate de doxorubicine: En monothérapie ou en association avec d'autres modalités thérapeutiques en présence de diverses affections néoplasiques incluant: le cancer du sein ■ le cancer de l'ovaire ■ le cancer de la vessie ■ le cancer pulmonaire ■ le cancer de l'estomac ■ l'épithélioma de la tête et du cou ■ les neuroblastomes ■ les lymphomes malins et les leucémies ■ le sarcome des tissus mous ■ l'ostéosarcome ■ le cancer des testicules ■ le cancer de la thyroïde ■ **Liposomes péguylés de doxorubicine (Caelyx):** Traitement du sarcome de Kaposi associé au sida chez les patients ayant un taux de CD4 < 200/mm^3 et des lésions cutanéomuqueuses ou viscérales étendues, lorsque la maladie a évolué malgré d'autres traitements ou lorsque le patient ne peut tolérer les traitements classiques par des associations d'antinéoplasiques ■ Traitement du cancer métastatique de l'ovaire chez les patientes souffrant d'une maladie qui ne répond pas aux chimiothérapies à base de paclitaxel ou de platine. ■ En monothérapie, traitement du cancer du sein métastatique lorsque les risques cardiaques sont élevés ■ **Doxorubicine liposomale (Myocet):** Traitement de première intention du cancer du sein métastatique chez la femme.

MÉCANISME D'ACTION

Formation d'un complexe avec l'ADN, ce qui inhibe la synthèse de l'ADN et de l'ARN; l'effet spécifique s'exerce au cours de la phase S du cycle cellulaire ■ Propriétés immunosuppressives ■ Encapsulation dans un liposome qui augmente le captage par la tumeur, prolonge les effets de la doxorubicine et peut diminuer quelque peu ses effets toxiques. ***Effets thérapeutiques:*** Destruction des cellules à croissance rapide, particulièrement des cellules malignes.

PHARMACOCINÉTIQUE

Absorption: Biodisponibilité à 100 % (IV).

D

Distribution: La doxorubicine se répartit dans tout l'organisme, mais ne traverse pas la barrière hémato-encéphalique; elle se fixe en grande partie aux tissus. *Liposomes* – on trouve des concentrations plus élevées de médicament au niveau des lésions induites par le sarcome de Kaposi qu'au niveau de la peau normale.
Métabolisme et excrétion: Fort métabolisme hépatique et transformation en un composé actif. Excrétion majoritairement biliaire, dont 50 % sous forme inchangée. Moins de 5 % est éliminé sous forme inchangée dans l'urine.
Demi-vie: De 20 à 48 heures; *liposomes* – de 50 à 55 heures.

Profil temps-action (effet sur la numération globulaire)

	DÉBUT D'ACTION	PIC	DURÉE
IV	10 jours	14 jours	21 – 24 jours

CONTRE-INDICATIONS, PRÉCAUTIONS ET MISES EN GARDE

Contre-indications: Hypersensibilité ■ Patients ayant des antécédents de maladie cardiaque ou ayant déjà reçu les doses cumulatives totales d'anthracycline ■ Aplasie médullaire marquée et persistante ■ Insuffisance hépatique grave.
Précautions et mises en garde: Aplasie médullaire ■ Insuffisance hépatique (on recommande de réduire la dose si les concentrations sériques de bilirubine > 21 µmol/mL) ■ **OBST., ALLAITEMENT**: Patientes en âge de procréer, grossesse ou allaitement ■ **PÉD.**: Risque accru d'effets indésirables ■ **GÉR.**: Risque accru de cardiotoxicité ■ Antécédents de radiothérapie du médiastin ou administration concomitante de cyclophosphamide (risque accru de cardiotoxicité).

RÉACTIONS INDÉSIRABLES ET EFFETS SECONDAIRES

Chlorhydrate de doxorubicine
CV: CARDIOMYOPATHIE, modifications de l'ÉCG, arythmies.
GI: diarrhée, œsophagite, nausées, stomatite, vomissements, modification des concentrations de transaminases.
GU: urine de couleur rouge.
Tég.: alopécie, photosensibilité.
End.: stérilité, ralentissement de la croissance prépubertaire avec suppression temporaire de la fonction des gonades (enfants seulement).
Hémat.: anémie, leucopénie, thrombopénie, leucémies secondaires.
Locaux: phlébite au point d'injection IV, nécrose tissulaire.
Métab.: hyperuricémie.
Divers: réactions d'hypersensibilité.
Resp.: pneumopathie de rebond.

Liposomes péguylés de doxorubicine
SNC: faiblesse.
CV: CARDIOMYOPATHIE.
GI: nausées, diarrhée, concentrations accrues de phosphatase alcaline, candidose, stomatite, vomissements.
Tég.: alopécie, dysesthésie érythémateuse palmoplantaire, rash.
Hémat.: anémie, leucopénie, thrombopénie.
Locaux: réactions au point d'injection IV.
Divers: réactions aiguës associées à la perfusion, fièvre.

INTERACTIONS

Médicament-médicament: Aggravation de l'aplasie médullaire lors de l'administration concomitante d'autres **agents antinéoplasiques** ou d'une **radiothérapie** ■ Les enfants qui ont reçu en même temps la doxorubicine et la **dactinomycine** sont exposés à un risque accru de pneumopathie de rebond à tout moment à la suite d'une radiothérapie locale ■ La doxorubicine peut aggraver les réactions cutanées dans les régions qui ont déjà été exposées à une **radiothérapie** ■ Si le **paclitaxel** est administré en premier, la clairance de la doxorubicine est réduite, et l'incidence et la gravité de la neutropénie et de la stomatite sont accrues (ces effets sont moindres, si la doxorubicine est administrée en premier) ■ La toxicité hématologique est plus prononcée et dure plus longtemps lors de l'administration concomitante de **cyclosporine**; le risque de coma et de convulsions est également accru ■ L'administration concomitante de **progestatifs** augmente l'incidence et la gravité de la neutropénie et de la thrombopénie ■ Le **phénobarbital** peut augmenter la clairance de la doxorubicine et en diminuer les effets ■ La doxorubicine peut ralentir le métabolisme de la **phénytoïne** et en augmenter les effets ■ La **streptozocine** peut prolonger la demi-vie de la doxorubicine (il est recommandé de réduire la dose de doxorubicine) ■ Risque accru de cystite hémorragique lors de l'administration concomitante de **cyclophosphamide**, ou d'hépatite lors de l'administration concomitante de **mercaptopurine** ■ La **radiothérapie** ou le **cyclophosphamide** peuvent augmenter le risque de cardiotoxicité ■ La doxorubicine peut diminuer la réponse immunitaire et augmenter le risque de réactions indésirables dues aux **vaccins à virus vivants**.

VOIES D'ADMINISTRATION ET POSOLOGIE

On a déjà utilisé d'autres schémas posologiques.

Chlorhydrate de doxorubicine (Adriamycin PFS, Adriamycin RDF)

- **IV (adultes)**: De 60 à 75 mg/m² par jour, tous les 21 jours; 30 mg/m² par jour, pendant 3 jours, toutes les 4 semaines, ou 20 mg/m² par semaine. La dose cumulative totale ne devrait pas dépasser 550 mg/m² sans surveillance de la fonction cardiaque, ou 400 mg/m², chez les patients ayant déjà reçu une radiothérapie thoracique ou une autre chimiothérapie cardiotoxique.
- **IV (enfants)**: De 40 à 75 mg/m² par jour, tous les 21 jours.
- ***INSUFFISANCE HÉPATIQUE***

  IV (ADULTES): *BILIRUBINE DE 21 À 52 µmol/mL* – ADMINISTRER 50 % DE LA DOSE HABITUELLE. *BILIRUBINE DE 52 À 86 MOL/mL* – ADMINISTRER 25 % DE LA DOSE HABITUELLE.

Liposomes péguylés de doxorubicine (Caelyx)

- **IV (adultes)**: *Sarcome de Kaposi associé au sida* – 20 mg/m², toutes les 2 ou 3 semaines; *cancer métastatique de l'ovaire ou du sein* – 50 mg/m², toutes les 4 semaines.

Doxorubicine liposomale (Myocet)

- **IV (adultes)**: *Cancer du sein métastatique* – de 60 à 75 mg/m² en association avec le cyclophosphamide, toutes les 3 semaines.

PRÉSENTATION (version générique disponible)

- **Chlorhydrate de doxorubicine**

  Poudre pour injection: fioles de 10 mg, de 50 mg^Pr^ et de 150 mg^Pr^ ■ **Solution pour injection à 2 mg/mL**: fioles de 10 mg, de 50 mg et de 200 mg^Pr^.
- **Liposomes péguylés de doxorubicine (Caelyx)**

  Dispersion de liposomes pour injection à 2 mg/mL: fioles de 20 mg et de 50 mg de doxorubicine^Pr^.
- **Doxorubicine liposomale (Myocet)**

  Poudre pour injection: fioles de 50 mg^Pr^ avec un flacon de liposomes pour perfusion et un flacon de solution tampon.

SOINS INFIRMIERS

ÉVALUATION DE LA SITUATION

- Mesurer la pression artérielle, le pouls et la fréquence respiratoire, et prendre la température à intervalles fréquents pendant toute la durée de l'administration. Signaler au médecin tout changement important.
- Rester à l'affût des signes d'aplasie médullaire. Observer le patient de près afin de déceler les saignements: saignements des gencives, formation d'ecchymoses, pétéchies, présence de sang occulte dans les selles, l'urine et les vomissures. Éviter les injections IM et la prise de la température rectale si la numération plaquettaire est basse. Appliquer une pression sur les points de ponction veineuse pendant 10 minutes. Évaluer les signes d'infection en présence de neutropénie. Il y a risque d'anémie. Suivre de près le patient pour déceler une fatigue accrue, la dyspnée et l'hypotension orthostatique.
- Effectuer le bilan quotidien des ingesta et des excreta et signaler tout écart important. Inciter le patient à boire de 2 000 à 3 000 mL de liquides par jour si son état le permet. Le médecin peut également recommander l'administration d'allopurinol et l'alcalinisation de l'urine pour diminuer les concentrations sériques d'acide urique et pour prévenir la formation de calculs d'urate.
- Des nausées et des vomissements graves et prolongés peuvent survenir dans l'heure qui suit le traitement et persister pendant 24 heures. Il faudrait administrer des agents antiémétiques par voie parentérale de 30 à 45 minutes avant le traitement et à intervalles réguliers pendant les 24 heures qui suivent, selon les indications. Noter la quantité des vomissures et, si elle dépasse les paramètres habituels, en informer le médecin ou un autre professionnel de la santé afin qu'on puisse prévenir la déshydratation.
- SUIVRE DE PRÈS LE PATIENT POUR DÉCELER LES SIGNES DE CARDIOTOXICITÉ QUI PEUVENT SE MANIFESTER RAPIDEMENT ET ÊTRE PASSAGERS (ABAISSEMENT DES SEGMENTS S-T, APLATISSEMENT DES ONDES T, TACHYCARDIE SINUSALE, EXTRASYSTOLES) OU TARDIVEMENT (HABITUELLEMENT DE 1 À 6 MOIS APRÈS LE DÉBUT DU TRAITEMENT). LA CARDIOTOXICITÉ EST CARACTÉRISÉE PAR UNE INSUFFISANCE CARDIAQUE RÉFRACTAIRE (ŒDÈME PÉRIPHÉRIQUE, DYSPNÉE, RÂLES ET CRÉPITATIONS, GAIN PONDÉRAL). LE MÉDECIN PEUT RECOMMANDER UNE RADIOGRAPHIE PULMONAIRE, UNE ÉCHOCARDIOGRAPHIE, UNE ÉCG ET UNE ANGIOGRAPHIE ISOTOPIQUE, AVANT LE TRAITEMENT ET À INTERVALLES RÉGULIERS PENDANT TOUTE SA DURÉE. LA CARDIOTOXICITÉ EST PLUS FRÉQUENTE CHEZ LES ENFANTS ÂGÉS DE MOINS DE 2 ANS ET CHEZ LES PERSONNES ÂGÉES. ON PEUT ADMINISTRER DU DEXRAZOXANE POUR PRÉVENIR LA CARDIOTOXICITÉ CHEZ LES PATIENTS QUI ONT REÇU DES DOSES CUMULATIVES > 300 mg/m² (VOIR LA MONOGRAPHIE DU DEXRAZOXANE).
- Observer fréquemment le point d'injection IV pour déceler les rougeurs, l'irritation ou l'inflammation. La doxorubicine est un agent vésicant, mais elle

peut s'infiltrer sans causer de douleurs même si le sang reflue par aspiration dans l'aiguille de perfusion. Des lésions tissulaires graves peuvent survenir s'il y a extravasation. En cas d'extravasation, arrêter immédiatement la perfusion et la reprendre dans une autre veine pour administrer le restant de la dose. On ne recommande pas d'infiltrer localement un antidote. Conseiller au patient d'appliquer des compresses de glace (contenants réfrigérants), et de surélever et de garder au repos le membre affecté pendant 24 à 48 heures afin de réduire l'œdème; il peut ensuite reprendre ses activités habituelles selon sa tolérance. Si l'œdème, les rougeurs ou les douleurs persistent pendant plus de 48 heures, consulter immédiatement un médecin, car il pourrait s'avérer nécessaire de débrider la plaie.

- Examiner fréquemment les muqueuses buccales pour déceler la présence de stomatite. Il est recommandé d'espacer les traitements ou de réduire la dose si les lésions sont douloureuses ou si elles gênent le patient lorsqu'il mange.

Liposomes péguylés de doxorubicine:

- Rester à l'affût des réactions aiguës suivantes associées à la perfusion: rougeurs du visage, essoufflement, œdème du visage, céphalées, frissons, douleurs thoraciques, douleurs lombaires, oppression au niveau du thorax ou de la gorge, fièvre, tachycardie, prurit, rash, cyanose, syncope, bronchospasme, asthme ou apnée. Ces réactions peuvent être accompagnées d'hypotension. Elles disparaissent habituellement après un jour et ne sont habituellement manifestes que lors de l'administration de la première dose. Une vitesse de perfusion plus lente peut diminuer ces réactions qui semblent être attribuables aux liposomes.
- OBSERVER DE PRÈS LE PATIENT POUR DÉTECTER LES SIGNES OU LES SYMPTÔMES D'ANAPHYLAXIE: RASH, PRURIT, ŒDÈME LARYNGÉ OU RESPIRATION SIFFLANTE. ARRÊTER L'ADMINISTRATION DE DOXORUBICINE ET INFORMER LE MÉDECIN OU UN AUTRE PROFESSIONNEL DE LA SANTÉ IMMÉDIATEMENT SI UNE TELLE RÉACTION SE PRODUIT. GARDER DE L'ADRÉNALINE, UN ANTIHISTAMINIQUE ET LE MATÉRIEL DE RÉANIMATION À PORTÉE DE LA MAIN POUR PARER AUX RÉACTIONS D'ANAPHYLAXIE.
- Suivre de près la toxicité cutanée lors de l'administration prolongée; la dysesthésie érythémateuse palmoplantaire survient habituellement après 6 semaines de traitement et se manifeste par l'œdème, des douleurs et l'érythème au niveau des mains et des pieds. Elle peut évoluer vers la desquamation, mais régresse habituellement au bout de 2 semaines. Dans les cas graves, il peut s'avérer nécessaire de modifier les doses ultérieures de cet agent.

Tests de laboratoire:

- Noter la numération globulaire et la formule leucocytaire avant le traitement et à intervalles réguliers pendant toute sa durée. Le nadir des leucocytes se produit dans les 10 à 14 jours qui suivent l'administration. Les valeurs se rétablissent habituellement après 21 jours. La thrombopénie et l'anémie peuvent également se manifester. Il est recommandé de prolonger les écarts posologiques ou de réduire la dose si le nombre absolu de neutrophiles est $< 1 \times 10^9$/L ou si celui de plaquettes est $< 50 \times 10^9$/L.
- Noter les résultats des tests des fonctions rénale (concentrations d'urée et de créatinine) et hépatique (concentrations d'AST, d'ALT, de LDH et de bilirubine sérique), avant le traitement et à intervalles réguliers pendant toute sa durée. Il faut réduire la dose si les concentrations de bilirubine sont > 21 µmol/L ou si celles de créatinine sérique sont > 265 µmol/L.
- La doxorubicine peut entraîner une élévation des concentrations sériques et urinaires d'acide urique.

DIAGNOSTICS INFIRMIERS POSSIBLES

- Risque d'infection (Réactions indésirables).
- Débit cardiaque diminué (Réactions indésirables).
- Connaissances insuffisantes sur le traitement médicamenteux (Enseignement au patient et à ses proches).

INTERVENTIONS INFIRMIÈRES

ALERTE CLINIQUE: DES DÉCÈS SONT SURVENUS LORS DE CERTAINES CHIMIOTHÉRAPIES. AVANT D'ADMINISTRER L'AGENT, CLARIFIER TOUS LES POINTS AMBIGUS. VÉRIFIER LA LIMITE DES DOSES UNITAIRES ET QUOTIDIENNES AINSI QUE LA DOSE À ADMINISTRER PENDANT LE TRAITEMENT. DEMANDER À UN DEUXIÈME PROFESSIONNEL DE LA SANTÉ DE VÉRIFIER UNE FOIS DE PLUS L'ORDONNANCE D'ORIGINE, LES CALCULS ET LE RÉGLAGE DE LA POMPE À PERFUSION.

- IL EST IMPORTANT DE NE PAS CONFONDRE LE CHLORHYDRATE DE DOXORUBICINE (ADRIAMYCIN PFS) ET LES LIPOSOMES DE DOXORUBICINE (CAELYX, MYOCET) AVEC LA DAUNORUBICINE (CERUBIDINE) OU AVEC L'IDARUBICINE (IDAMYCINE). POUR ÉVITER TOUTE CONFUSION, LE MÉDECIN DEVRAIT INDIQUER SUR L'ORDONNANCE LA DÉNOMINATION COMMUNE ET LE NOM COMMERCIAL DU MÉDICAMENT.
- Préparer les solutions sous une hotte à flux laminaire. Porter des vêtements protecteurs ainsi que des gants et un masque pendant la manipulation du médicament. Mettre au rebut le matériel dans les contenants réservés à cet usage (voir l'annexe H).

- On peut utiliser des aiguilles en aluminium pour administrer la doxorubicine, mais il ne faut pas les laisser au contact de la solution qu'on conserve, car un contact prolongé entre la solution et l'aluminium entraîne un changement de couleur et la formation d'un précipité foncé. La solution est de couleur rouge.

Chlorhydrate de doxorubicine

- **IV directe**: Reconstituer 10 mg dans 5 mL, 50 mg dans 25 mL ou 150 mg dans 75 mL de solution de NaCl 0,9 % (non bactériostatique) pour injection pour obtenir une concentration finale de 2 mg/mL. Secouer délicatement la fiole pour en dissoudre entièrement le contenu. Ne pas ajouter à une autre solution destinée à la voie IV. La solution reconstituée est stable pendant 24 heures à la température ambiante et pendant 48 heures au réfrigérateur. Garder à l'abri des rayons du soleil. Consulter les directives du fabricant avant de diluer la préparation.
- ***Vitesse d'administration:*** Administrer chaque dose en au moins 3 à 5 minutes par une tubulure en Y par laquelle s'écoule librement une solution de NaCl 0,9 % ou de D5%E. Une administration trop rapide entraîne souvent des rougeurs au visage ou un érythème le long de la veine servant à la perfusion.
- **Associations compatibles dans la même seringue**: bléomycine ■ cisplatine ■ cyclophosphamide ■ dropéridol ■ leucovorine ■ méthotrexate ■ métoclopramide ■ mitomycine ■ vincristine.
- **Associations incompatibles dans la même seringue**: furosémide ■ héparine.
- **Compatibilité (tubulure en Y)**: amifostine ■ aztréonam ■ bléomycine ■ chlorpromazine ■ cimétidine ■ cisplatine ■ cladribine ■ cyclophosphamide ■ dexaméthasone ■ diphénhydramine ■ dropéridol ■ famotidine ■ filgrastim ■ fludarabine ■ fluorouracile ■ granisétron ■ hydromorphone ■ leucovorine calcique ■ lorazépam ■ melphalan ■ méthotrexate ■ méthylprednisolone ■ métoclopramide ■ mitomycine ■ morphine ■ ondansétron ■ paclitaxel ■ prochlorpérazine, édisylate de ■ prochlorpérazine ■ propofol ■ ranitidine ■ sargramostim ■ sodium, bicarbonate de ■ téniposide ■ thiotépa ■ vinblastine ■ vincristine ■ vinorelbine.
- **Incompatibilité (tubulure en Y)**: allopurinol ■ amphotéricine B, cholestérylsulfate d' ■ céfépime ■ gallium, nitrate de ■ ganciclovir ■ pipéracilline/tazobactam.

Liposomes péguylés de doxorubicine (Caelyx)

- **Perfusion intermittente**: Diluer la dose de liposomes péguylés de doxorubicine jusqu'à concurrence de 90 mg dans 250 mL d'une solution de D5%E. Ne pas utiliser d'autres diluants et surtout pas de diluants contenant un agent bactériostatique. La solution n'est pas transparente; c'est une dispersion liposomique translucide de couleur rouge. Ne pas utiliser de filtre intégré pour la perfusion. Réfrigérer les solutions diluées et les administrer dans les 24 heures qui suivent la dilution. Consulter les directives du fabricant avant de diluer la préparation.
- ***Vitesse d'administration:*** La vitesse initiale de perfusion devrait être de 1 mg/min pour réduire le risque de réactions à la perfusion. Si aucune réaction ne se manifeste, augmenter la vitesse de perfusion pour que l'administration du médicament soit terminée en 1 heure (cancer du sein ou de l'ovaire) ou en 30 minutes (sarcome de Kaposi). Ne pas administrer sous forme de bolus ni sous forme de solution non diluée. Une perfusion rapide peut entraîner un plus grand nombre de réactions liées à la perfusion.
- **Incompatibilité en addition au soluté**: Ne pas mélanger cet agent à d'autres solutions ou médicaments.

ENSEIGNEMENT AU PATIENT ET À SES PROCHES

- Recommander au patient de prévenir rapidement un professionnel de la santé si les signes suivants se manifestent: fièvre, maux de gorge, infection, saignements des gencives, ecchymoses, pétéchies, présence de sang dans l'urine, les selles et les vomissures, fatigue accrue, dyspnée ou hypotension orthostatique. Expliquer au patient qu'il doit éviter les foules et les personnes contagieuses. Lui conseiller d'utiliser une brosse à dents à poils doux et un rasoir électrique et de prendre garde aux chutes. Le prévenir qu'il ne doit pas consommer de boissons alcoolisées ni prendre des préparations contenant de l'aspirine ou des AINS en même temps que la doxorubicine en raison du risque d'hémorragie gastrique.
- Recommander au patient de signaler immédiatement les douleurs au point d'injection.
- Recommander au patient d'examiner ses muqueuses buccales à la recherche d'érythème et d'aphtes. En présence d'aphtes, lui conseiller de remplacer la brosse à dents par une brosse-éponge, de se rincer la bouche avec de l'eau après avoir bu ou mangé et de consulter un professionnel de la santé si les douleurs l'empêchent de s'alimenter. Pour soulager ces douleurs, il peut s'avérer nécessaire d'administrer des opioïdes. La stomatite risque surtout d'apparaître dans les 5 à 10 jours suivant l'administration d'une dose de doxorubicine; elle dure habituellement de 3 à 7 jours.
- Prévenir la patiente que ce médicament peut exercer des effets tératogènes; lui conseiller de continuer à prendre des mesures de contraception pendant

toute la durée du traitement et pendant au moins 4 mois après l'avoir arrêté. L'informer que ce médicament peut provoquer une suppression irréversible de la fonction des gonades.

- Recommander au patient de prévenir immédiatement un professionnel de la santé en cas d'extrasystoles, d'essoufflement, d'enflure des membres inférieurs ou d'irritation cutanée (œdème, douleurs ou rougeurs au niveau des pieds ou des mains).
- Expliquer au patient qu'il risque de perdre ses cheveux. Explorer avec lui les stratégies lui permettant de s'adapter à ce changement. Les cheveux recommencent à pousser de 2 à 3 mois environ après l'arrêt du traitement.
- Expliquer au patient qu'il ne doit pas se faire vacciner sans recommandation expresse d'un professionnel de la santé.
- Prévenir le patient que la doxorubicine peut rendre l'urine rouge pendant 1 ou 2 journées.
- Recommander au patient de prévenir un professionnel de la santé en cas d'irritation cutanée au niveau des régions qui ont déjà été traitées par radiothérapie.
- Recommander aux proches et aux soignants de prendre des précautions (porter des gants de latex) lorsqu'ils manipulent des liquides corporels pendant au moins 5 jours après le traitement.
- Inciter le patient à se soumettre à des tests de laboratoire à intervalles réguliers afin qu'on puisse déceler les effets secondaires du médicament.

VÉRIFICATION DE L'EFFICACITÉ THÉRAPEUTIQUE

L'efficacité du traitement peut être démontrée par: la régression des tumeurs ou l'arrêt de la propagation du cancer dans le cas de tumeurs solides ▪ l'amélioration de l'hématopoïèse chez les patients atteints de leucémie ▪ l'arrêt de l'évolution du sarcome de Kaposi chez les patients infectés par le VIH. ✳

DOXYCYCLINE,

voir Tétracyclines

DROPÉRIDOL

Dropéridol

CLASSIFICATION:

Antiémétique (butyrophénone)/anxiolytique et hypnosédatif/antipsychotique

Grossesse – catégorie C

INDICATIONS

Tranquillisant et adjuvant à l'anesthésie générale et locale ▪ Adjuvant à la neuroleptanalgésie en association avec le fentanyl ▪ Traitement du syndrome de Ménière (crise aiguë) ▪ **Usages non approuvés:** Diminution des nausées et des vomissements qui surviennent après une intervention chirurgicale ▪ Traitement des migraines (crise aiguë).

MÉCANISME D'ACTION

Action similaire à celle de l'halopéridol; modification des effets de la dopamine dans le SNC. ***Effets thérapeutiques:*** Apaisement du patient ▪ Diminution des nausées et des vomissements.

PHARMACOCINÉTIQUE

Absorption: Bonne (IM).

Distribution: Le médicament semble traverser la barrière hémato-encéphalique et placentaire.

Métabolisme et excrétion: Métabolisme majoritairement hépatique. 22 % est éliminé dans les fèces.

Demi-vie: 2,2 heures.

Profil temps-action

	DÉBUT D'ACTION	PIC	DURÉE†
IM, IV	3 – 10 min	30 min	2 – 4 h

† Durée de l'effet tranquillisant; la modification de l'état de la conscience peut se prolonger pendant 12 heures.

CONTRE-INDICATIONS, PRÉCAUTIONS ET MISES EN GARDE

Contre-indications: Hypersensibilité ▪ Intolérance connue ▪ **PÉD.:** Enfants âgés de moins de 2 ans (l'innocuité du médicament n'a pas été établie) ▪ Administration concomitante de médicaments allongeant l'intervalle QT ou risque d'allongement de l'intervalle QT (insuffisance cardiaque, bradycardie, prise de diurétiques, hypertrophie cardiaque, hypokaliémie, hypomagnésémie) ▪ QT_c allongé (> 440 ms chez les hommes et > 450 ms chez les femmes).

Précautions et mises en garde: Glaucome à angle fermé ▪ Dépression du SNC ▪ Maladie hépatique grave ▪ Maladie cardiaque grave ▪ **GÉR.:** Personnes âgées, patients débilités ou gravement malades (des doses plus faibles devraient être utilisées) ▪ Insuffisance respiratoire ▪ Tumeurs du SNC ▪ Occlusion intestinale ▪ Maladie de Parkinson ▪ Convulsions (le dropéridol peut abaisser le seuil de convulsions) ▪ Maladie rénale grave ▪ **OBST.:** Grossesse, allaitement (bien que l'innocuité du médicament n'ait pas été établie, il y a des précédents d'administration durant une césarienne, sans qu'une dépression respiratoire chez le nouveau-né se soit manifestée). ▪ Risque d'arythmies (administrer en milieu hospitalier) ▪ Association avec d'autres dépresseurs du SNC, tels que les benzodiazépines, les opioïdes et les anesthésiques volatils (l'utilisation concomitante peut provoquer une sédation excessive et augmente le risque d'arythmie; réduire la dose) ▪ Risque d'hypotension (particulièrement chez les patients hypovolémiques et chez ceux recevant des vasodilatateurs).

RÉACTIONS INDÉSIRABLES ET EFFETS SECONDAIRES

SNC: CONVULSIONS, SYNDROME MALIN DES NEUROLEPTIQUES, réactions extrapyramidales, anomalies de l'ÉEG, anxiété, confusion, étourdissements, sédation excessive, hallucinations, hyperactivité, dépression, cauchemars, agitation, dyskinésie tardive.
ORLO: vision trouble, xérophtalmie.
Resp.: DÉPRESSION RESPIRATOIRE, APNÉE, bronchospasme, laryngospasme.
CV: ARYTHMIES (incluant des torsades de pointe), hypotension, tachycardie, allongement de l'intervalle QT.
GI: constipation, sécheresse de la bouche (xérostomie).
Divers: frissons, transpiration au niveau du visage, tremblements.

INTERACTIONS

Médicament-médicament: Hypotension additive lors de l'administration concomitante d'**antihypertenseurs** ou de **dérivés nitrés** ▪ Dépression additive du SNC lors de l'usage concomitant d'autres **dépresseurs du SNC**, incluant l'**alcool**, les **antihistaminiques**, les **antidépresseurs**, les **opioïdes** et d'autres **sédatifs** ▪ Utilisation concomitante de **médicaments pouvant allonger l'intervalle QT** (risque accru d'arythmies mortelles) ▪ L'**adrénaline** peut paradoxalement abaisser la pression artérielle chez les patients recevant du dropéridol.
Médicament-produits naturels: La consommation concomitante de **kava**, de **valériane**, de **scutellaire**, de **camomille** ou de **houblon** peut aggraver la dépression respiratoire.

VOIES D'ADMINISTRATION ET POSOLOGIE

Les doses doivent être diminuées chez les patients âgés, affaiblis ou recevant des dépresseurs du SNC.

Emploi comme prémédication ou sans anesthésie générale durant les examens diagnostiques

- **IV, IM (adultes)**: De 2,5 à 10 mg, par voie IM, de 30 à 60 minutes avant l'intervention. On peut administrer des doses supplémentaires de 1,25 à 2,5 mg, par voie IV, selon les besoins.
- **IM, IV (enfants de 2 à 12 ans)**: De 0,1 à 0,15 mg/kg (emploi comme prémédication seulement).

Traitement d'appoint avant l'induction d'une anesthésie générale

- **IV (adultes)**: 0,25 mg/kg ou moins. On peut administrer des doses supplémentaires de 1,25 à 2,5 mg, par voie IV, selon les besoins.
- **IM, IV (enfants de 2 à 12 ans)**: De 0,1 à 0,15 mg/kg.

Traitement d'appoint lors d'une anesthésie locale

- **IM, IV (adultes)**: De 2,5 à 5 mg.

Traitement du syndrome de Ménière (crise aiguë)

- **IM (adultes)**: 5 mg en une seule dose.

Antiémétique

- **IV (adultes)**: De 0,5 à 1,25 mg, toutes les 4 heures, selon les besoins *(usage non approuvé)*.

Traitement des migraines (crise aiguë)

- **IM (adultes)**: 2,5 mg en une seule dose *(usage non approuvé)*.

PRÉSENTATION (version générique disponible)

Solution pour injection: 2,5 mg/mL[Pr], fioles de 2 mL.

SOINS INFIRMIERS

ÉVALUATION DE LA SITUATION

- Mesurer la pression artérielle et la fréquence cardiaque à intervalles fréquents pendant toute la durée du traitement. Prévenir immédiatement le médecin en cas de changement important. Pour traiter l'hypotension, on peut administrer des liquides par voie parentérale si l'hypovolémie est le facteur causal. Des vasopresseurs (noradrénaline, phényléphrine) peuvent s'avérer nécessaires. Ne pas administrer de l'adrénaline étant donné que le dropéridol renverse ses effets vasopresseurs et peut entraîner une hypotension paradoxale.
- Avant d'administrer le dropéridol, effectuer chez tous les patients un ÉCG dans 12 dérivations pour déterminer si l'intervalle QT est allongé. Dans ce cas, ne pas administrer le dropéridol. Surveiller l'ÉCG avant, pendant le traitement et pendant les 2 à 3 heures suivant l'administration du médicament pour détecter la présence d'arythmies.
- Déterminer le niveau de la sédation après l'administration du médicament.
- Tout au long du traitement, rester à l'affût des symptômes extrapyramidaux suivants: dystonie, crise oculogyre, extension du cou, fléchissement des bras, tremblements, agitation, hyperactivité, anxiété. En informer le médecin ou un autre professionnel de la santé, le cas échéant. On peut administrer un

agent antiparkinsonien anticholinergique pour traiter ces symptômes.

Nausées et vomissements: Noter les nausées et les vomissements ainsi que l'état d'hydratation; ausculter les bruits intestinaux et observer les douleurs abdominales avant et après l'administration du dropéridol.

DIAGNOSTICS INFIRMIERS POSSIBLES

- Risque d'accident (Effets secondaires).
- Connaissances insuffisantes sur le traitement médicamenteux (Enseignement au patient et à ses proches).

INTERVENTIONS INFIRMIÈRES

IV directe: Administrer le médicament non dilué.

Vitesse d'administration: Administrer chaque dose lentement en au moins 1 minute.

Perfusion intermittente: On peut ajouter le médicament à 250 mL de solution de D5%E, de NaCl 0,9% ou de lactate de Ringer.

Vitesse d'administration: Administrer par perfusion IV lente. Adapter la dose selon la réponse du patient.

Associations compatibles dans la même seringue: atropine ▪ bléomycine ▪ butorphanol ▪ chlorpromazine ▪ cimétidine ▪ cisplatine ▪ cyclophosphamide ▪ dimenhydrinate ▪ doxorubicine ▪ fentanyl ▪ glycopyrrolate ▪ hydroxyzine ▪ mépéridine ▪ métoclopramide ▪ midazolam ▪ mitomycine ▪ morphine ▪ nalbuphine ▪ pentazocine ▪ perphénazine ▪ prochlorpérazine ▪ promazine ▪ prométhazine ▪ scopolamine ▪ vinblastine ▪ vincristine.

Associations incompatibles dans la même seringue: fluorouracile ▪ furosémide ▪ héparine ▪ leucovorine calcique ▪ méthotrexate ▪ pentobarbital.

Compatibilité (tubulure en Y): amifostine ▪ aztréonam ▪ bléomycine ▪ buprénorphine ▪ cisatracurium ▪ cisplatine ▪ cyclophosphamide ▪ cytarabine ▪ doxorubicine ▪ doxorubicine liposomale ▪ filgrastim ▪ fluconazole ▪ fludarabine ▪ granisétron ▪ hydrocortisone sodique, succinate d' ▪ idarubicine ▪ melphalan ▪ mépéridine ▪ métoclopramide ▪ mitomycine ▪ ondansétron ▪ paclitaxel ▪ potassium, chlorure de ▪ propofol ▪ sargramostim ▪ téniposide ▪ thiotépa ▪ vinblastine ▪ vincristine ▪ vinorelbine ▪ vitamines du complexe B avec C.

Incompatibilité (tubulure en Y): allopurinol sodique ▪ amphotéricine B, complexe de cholestérylsulfate d' ▪ céfépime ▪ cefmétazole ▪ fluorouracile ▪ foscarnet ▪ furosémide ▪ leucovorine calcique ▪ nafcilline ▪ pipéracilline/ tazobactam.

Incompatibilité en addition au soluté: barbituriques.

ENSEIGNEMENT AU PATIENT ET À SES PROCHES

- Conseiller au patient de changer lentement de position pour réduire le risque d'hypotension orthostatique.
- Prévenir le patient que le dropéridol entraîne de la somnolence. Lui conseiller de demander de l'aide lorsqu'il se déplace.

VÉRIFICATION DE L'EFFICACITÉ THÉRAPEUTIQUE

L'efficacité du traitement peut être démontrée par: l'apaisement généralisé et la réduction de l'activité motrice ▪ la diminution des vertiges (maladie de Ménière) ▪ la diminution des nausées et des vomissements ▪ la diminution des douleurs (migraines).

DROSPIRÉNONE,

voir Contraceptifs hormonaux

DROTRÉCOGINE ALFA

Xigris

CLASSIFICATION:

Enzyme antithrombotique, profibrinolytique et anti-inflammatoire (protéine C activée recombinante)

Grossesse – catégorie C

INDICATIONS

Réduction de la mortalité chez les patients adultes atteints de septicémie grave, qui sont exposés à un risque élevé de décès (état septique grave avec atteinte d'organes cibles).

MÉCANISME D'ACTION

Activité antithrombotique, profibrinolytique et anti-inflammatoire diminuant la réponse inflammatoire systémique secondaire à la septicémie. ***Effets thérapeutiques:*** Diminution de la mortalité due à un état septique grave.

PHARMACOCINÉTIQUE

Absorption: Biodisponibilité à 100 % (IV).

Distribution: Inconnue.

Métabolisme et excrétion: Inconnus.

Demi-vie: Inconnue.

Profil temps-action

	DÉBUT D'ACTION	PIC	DURÉE
IV	inconnu	fin de la perfusion	inconnue

CONTRE-INDICATIONS, PRÉCAUTIONS ET MISES EN GARDE

Contre-indications: Hypersensibilité ▪ Risque élevé de saignements: hémorragie interne active ▪ accident vasculaire cérébral hémorragique (au cours des 3 mois précédents) ▪ chirurgie intracrânienne ou rachidienne récente ou traumatisme crânien grave ayant nécessité l'hospitalisation (au cours des 2 mois précédents) ▪ traumatisme associé à un risque accru d'hémorragie menaçant le pronostic vital ▪ présence d'un cathéter épidural ▪ tumeur ou lésion intracrânienne massive ou signe d'engagement cérébral ▪ Patients moribonds ▪ Patients infectés par le VIH, dont le nombre de CD4 $\leq 50/mm^3$ ▪ Patients souffrant d'une insuffisance rénale chronique nécessitant une dialyse ▪ Patients ayant subi une greffe pulmonaire, hépatique, pancréatique, intestinale ou de moelle osseuse.

Précautions et mises en garde: Administration concomitante d'héparine (≥ 15 unités/kg/h) ▪ Traitement thrombolytique (dans les 3 derniers jours) ▪ Administration d'un inhibiteur de la glycoprotéine IIb/IIIa ou d'un anticoagulant oral (dans les 7 derniers jours) ▪ Administration d'AAS (> 650 mg/jour) ou d'un autre antiagrégant plaquettaire (dans les 7 derniers jours) ▪ Numération plaquettaire < 30 000 × 10^6/L ▪ Temps de prothrombine – RNI > 3,0 ▪ Hémorragie gastro-intestinale (dans les 6 dernières semaines) ▪ Accident vasculaire cérébral ischémique (dans les 3 derniers mois) ▪ Malformation artérioveineuse ou anévrisme intracrânien ▪ Diathèse hémorragique connue ▪ Maladie hépatique chronique grave ▪ Risque de tout autre saignement grave ▪ Intervention chirurgicale (interrompre l'administration 2 heures avant, la reprendre 12 heures après, si l'hémostase est accomplie) ▪ **OBST.**: Grossesse (n'utiliser qu'en cas de besoin incontestable), allaitement ▪ **PÉD.**: L'innocuité de l'agent n'a pas été établie.

RÉACTIONS INDÉSIRABLES ET EFFETS SECONDAIRES

Hémat.: SAIGNEMENTS.

INTERACTIONS

Médicament-médicament: Risque accru de saignements graves lors de l'usage concomitant d'**antiplaquettaires**, d'**anticoagulants**, de **thrombolytiques** ou d'autres **agents qui peuvent affecter la coagulation**.

Médicament-produits naturels: Risque accru de saignements lors de l'usage concomitant d'**arnica**, de **camomille**, de **clou de girofle**, de **dong quai**, de **grande camomille**, d'**ail**, de **gingembre**, de **ginkgo**, de **ginseng panax** et **autres**.

VOIES D'ADMINISTRATION ET POSOLOGIE

IV (adultes): 24 µg/kg/h pendant 96 heures.

PRÉSENTATION

Poudre pour perfusion intraveineuse (à reconstituer): fioles de 5 mg^Pr^ et de 20 mg^Pr^.

SOINS INFIRMIERS

ÉVALUATION DE LA SITUATION

- DÉCELER TOUT AU LONG DU TRAITEMENT LES SIGNES DE SAIGNEMENTS ET D'HÉMORRAGIE (SAIGNEMENT DES GENCIVES OU DU NEZ, ECCHYMOSES, SELLES NOIRES GOUDRONNEUSES, HÉMATURIE, CHUTE DE L'HÉMATOCRITE; RÉSULTATS POSITIFS AU TEST AU GAÏAC POUR LA RECHERCHE DE SANG OCCULTE DANS LES SELLES, L'URINE OU LES PRODUITS D'ASPIRATION NASOGASTRIQUE). EN CAS D'HÉMORRAGIE GRAVE, ARRÊTER IMMÉDIATEMENT LA PERFUSION DE DROTRÉCOGINE. RECHERCHER LES AUTRES AGENTS QUI PEUVENT AFFECTER LA COAGULATION. UNE FOIS L'HÉMOSTASE ACCOMPLIE, ON POURRAIT ENVISAGER LA REPRISE DES PERFUSIONS PAR LA DROTRÉCOGINE.
- Déceler les signes d'infection (altération des signes vitaux, aspect de la plaie, des expectorations, de l'urine et des selles; augmentation du nombre de globules blancs) au début du traitement et pendant toute sa durée.

Tests de laboratoire: La prolongation du temps de céphaline activée (TCA) et du temps de Quick chez les patients atteints de septicémie grave peut être attribuable à la coagulopathie sous-jacente. La drotrécogine peut aussi modifier le temps de céphaline activée, mais a un effet minime sur le temps de Quick. Chez les patients sous drotrécogine, recourir au temps de Quick pour suivre l'état de la coagulation.

DIAGNOSTICS INFIRMIERS POSSIBLES

- Irrigation tissulaire inefficace (Indications).

INTERVENTIONS INFIRMIÈRES

- Arrêter la perfusion de drotrécogine 2 heures avant une chirurgie ou une intervention qui comporte un risque de saignements. Une fois qu'on a accompli l'hémostase, on peut reprendre la perfusion 12 heures après l'intervention.

Perfusion intermittente: Calculer la dose et le nombre de fioles à 5 mg ou à 20 mg nécessaires (les fioles contiennent plus de poudre pour en faciliter l'administration). Reconstituer le contenu de la fiole de 5 mg avec 2,5 mL et celui de la fiole de 20 mg avec 10 mL d'eau stérile pour préparations injectables pour atteindre une concentration de 2 mg/mL. Verser l'eau stérile lentement dans la fiole; éviter de l'inverser ou de la secouer. Pour dissoudre complètement la poudre, agiter doucement la fiole en faisant un mouvement de rotation. La solution reconstituée peut être diluée davantage avec du NaCl 0,9 % pour obtenir une concentration de 100 à 200 µg/mL, si on utilise une pompe à perfusion, ou une concentration de 100 à 1 000 µg/ mL, si on utilise un pousse-seringue. Retirer de la fiole la quantité de solution reconstituée nécessaire et l'ajouter au sac de perfusion contenant du NaCl 0,9 %; diriger la solution vers les parois du sac pour ne pas l'agiter. Inverser délicatement le sac pour bien mélanger. La solution reconstituée doit être utilisée dans les 3 heures et la perfusion doit être terminée dans les 14 heures qui suivent la préparation de la solution IV. Ne pas administrer une solution qui a changé de couleur ou qui contient des particules. Si la perfusion doit être interrompue, la reprendre à la vitesse d'administration initiale pour la mener à bien. Consulter les directives de chaque fabricant avant de reconstituer la préparation.

Vitesse d'administration: Administrer à une vitesse de 24 µg/kg/h pendant 96 heures. Il n'est pas recommandé d'ajuster la posologie ni d'administrer l'agent en bolus.

Incompatibilité (tubulure en Y): Administrer par une tubulure séparée ou par une lumière séparée d'un cathéter veineux central à plusieurs lumières.

Compatibilité en addition au soluté: N'administrer qu'avec du NaCl 0,9 %, du LR, du dextrose ou du dextrose mélangé à un soluté.

ENSEIGNEMENT AU PATIENT ET À SES PROCHES

- Expliquer au patient le but du traitement.

VÉRIFICATION DE L'EFFICACITÉ THÉRAPEUTIQUE

L'efficacité du traitement peut être démontrée par: la réduction de la mortalité chez les patients atteints de septicémie grave.

DUTASTÉRIDE

Avodart

CLASSIFICATION:

Inhibiteur des hormones androgènes
(inhibiteur de la 5 alpha-réductase de type I et II)

Grossesse – catégorie X

INDICATIONS

Traitement de l'hyperplasie bénigne de la prostate symptomatique.

MÉCANISME D'ACTION

Inhibition de l'enzyme 5 alpha-réductase de type I et II, responsable de la transformation de la testostérone en son puissant métabolite, la 5 alpha-dihydrotestostérone dans la prostate, le foie et la peau; la 5 alpha-dihydrotestostérone est en partie responsable de l'hyperplasie de la prostate. ***Effets thérapeutiques:*** Réduction de la taille de la prostate et, par le fait même, des symptômes urinaires.

PHARMACOCINÉTIQUE

Absorption: Rapide (PO); la biodisponibilité est d'environ 60 % (de 40 à 94 %).

Distribution: Volume de distribution considérable (de 300 à 500 L).

Liaison aux protéines: 99,5 %.

Métabolisme et excrétion: Métabolisme majoritairement hépatique par l'intermédiaire du CYP 450 3A4. Le dutastéride et ses métabolites sont excrétés majoritairement dans les fèces.

Demi-vie: Environ 3 à 5 semaines (demi-vie à l'équilibre).

Profil temps-action

(baisse des concentrations de dihydrotestostérone†)

	DÉBUT D'ACTION	PIC	DURÉE
PO	inconnu	1 – 2 semaines	inconnue

† Les effets cliniques, évalués par les symptômes urinaires, peuvent ne se manifester qu'après 3 à 12 mois de traitement.

CONTRE-INDICATIONS, PRÉCAUTIONS ET MISES EN GARDE

Contre-indications: Hypersensibilité au dutastéride ou à un autre inhibiteur de l'enzyme 5 alpha-réductase ■ Femmes ■ Grossesse ■ Enfants.

Précautions et mises en garde: Insuffisance hépatique ■ Uropathie obstructive ■ Don de sang ou de produits sanguins (il faut attendre au moins 6 mois après la prise de la dernière dose avant de pouvoir donner du sang, afin d'éviter l'exposition involontaire à ce médicament d'une femme enceinte devant recevoir une transfusion) ■ Prise concomitante de médicaments inhibant le cytochrome P450 3A4.

RÉACTIONS INDÉSIRABLES ET EFFETS SECONDAIRES

GU: baisse de la libido, impuissance, diminution du volume d'éjaculat, troubles de l'éjaculation, troubles de l'érection.
End.: gynécomastie.

INTERACTIONS

Médicament-médicament: Aucune interaction cliniquement significative n'a été signalée, mais le dutastéride étant métabolisé dans le foie, les concentrations plasmatiques peuvent s'élever lors de la prise concomitante de **médicaments qui inhibent le cytochrome P450 3A4**, notamment les suivants: **ritonavir**, **kétoconazole**, **itraconazole**, **vérapamil**, **diltiazem**, **cimétidine** et **ciprofloxacine**.

VOIES D'ADMINISTRATION ET POSOLOGIE

PO (adultes): 0,5 mg, 1 fois par jour.

PRÉSENTATION

Capsules: 0,5 mg[Pr].

SOINS INFIRMIERS

ÉVALUATION DE LA SITUATION

- Observer le patient avant le traitement et à intervalles réguliers pendant toute sa durée pour déceler les symptômes suivants d'hyperplasie de la prostate: retard de la miction, sensation d'évacuation incomplète de la vessie, jet mictionnel discontinu, modification de la force du jet mictionnel et de la quantité d'urine évacuée, fuite postmictionnelle, effort pour amorcer le jet, dysurie, miction impérieuse.
- Effectuer un toucher rectal avant le traitement et à intervalles réguliers pendant toute sa durée.

Tests de laboratoire: On peut établir les concentrations de l'antigène prostatique spécifique (APS) permettant de dépister le cancer de la prostate, avant le traitement et à intervalles réguliers pendant toute sa durée. Le médicament diminue les concentrations sériques de cet antigène. L'interprétation du résultat des tests d'APS doit être faite par un médecin. L'APS devrait diminuer d'environ 20 % durant le 1er mois et se stabiliser à environ 50 % de la valeur de base au courant des 6 premiers mois de traitement. Les valeurs devraient être mesurées au 3e et au 6e mois de traitement ainsi que pendant toute sa durée.

DIAGNOSTICS INFIRMIERS POSSIBLES

- Élimination urinaire altérée (Indications).
- Connaissances insuffisantes sur le traitement médicamenteux (Enseignement au patient et à ses proches).

INTERVENTIONS INFIRMIÈRES

- Administrer le médicament 1 fois par jour, sans égard aux repas. NE PAS CROQUER, BRISER OU MÂCHER LA CAPSULE.

ENSEIGNEMENT AU PATIENT ET À SES PROCHES

- Recommander au patient de prendre le dutastéride comme il lui a été prescrit, même si les symptômes s'améliorent ou demeurent inchangés. Il faut parfois administrer le médicament pendant 6 à 12 mois avant qu'on puisse évaluer la réponse au traitement.
- Expliquer au patient que s'il n'a pu prendre le médicament au moment habituel, il doit le prendre aussitôt que possible, sauf s'il est presque l'heure prévue pour la dose suivante. Le prévenir qu'il ne faut jamais remplacer une dose manquée par une double dose.
- Informer le patient qu'il peut être dangereux de partager ce médicament avec une autre personne.
- Informer le patient que la quantité d'éjaculat peut être moindre pendant le traitement, mais que ce phénomène n'altère pas la fonction sexuelle.
- EXPLIQUER AU PATIENT QUE LE DUTASTÉRIDE PEUT ÊTRE NOCIF POUR LE FŒTUS DE SEXE MASCULIN. LES FEMMES ENCEINTES OU CELLES QUI POURRAIENT LE DEVENIR DEVRAIENT ÉVITER DE S'EXPOSER AU SPERME D'UN PARTENAIRE TRAITÉ PAR LE DUTASTÉRIDE ET À TOUT CONTACT AVEC LA POUDRE DE DUTASTÉRIDE, EN RAISON DES RISQUES D'ABSORPTION. IL EST RECOMMANDÉ DE BIEN SE LAVER LES MAINS AVEC DE L'EAU ET DU SAVON S'IL Y A CONTACT AVEC LA CAPSULE OU LA POUDRE QU'ELLE CONTIENT.
- Informer le patient qu'il ne doit pas faire de don de sang ou de produits sanguins (il faut attendre au moins 6 mois après la prise de la dernière dose avant de pouvoir donner du sang afin d'éviter l'exposition involontaire à ce médicament d'une femme enceinte devant recevoir une transfusion).
- Insister sur l'importance des examens de suivi permettant d'évaluer l'efficacité du traitement.

VÉRIFICATION DE L'EFFICACITÉ THÉRAPEUTIQUE

L'efficacité du traitement peut être démontrée par: la diminution des symptômes urinaires associés à l'hyperplasie bénigne de la prostate.

ÉCONAZOLE,
voir Antifongiques topiques

ÉFAVIRENZ

Sustiva

CLASSIFICATION:

Antirétroviral (inhibiteur non nucléosidique de la transcriptase inverse [INNTI])

Grossesse – catégorie C

INDICATIONS

Traitement des infections par le virus d'immunodéficience humaine (VIH) en association avec d'autres antirétroviraux. **Usages non approuvés:** En association avec d'autres antirétroviraux, en prophylaxie après une exposition accidentelle au VIH.

MÉCANISME D'ACTION

Inhibition de la transcriptase inverse du VIH entraînant une interruption de la synthèse de l'ADN. ***Effets thérapeutiques:*** Ralentissement de l'évolution de la maladie causée par le VIH et diminution du nombre de ses complications ■ Augmentation du nombre de cellules CD4 et diminution de la charge virale.

PHARMACOCINÉTIQUE

Absorption: 50 % après un repas riche en matières grasses.

Distribution: L'agent pénètre dans le liquide céphalorachidien.

Liaison aux protéines: De 99,5 à 99,75 %.

Métabolisme et excrétion: Métabolisme majoritairement hépatique.

Demi-vie: *Après l'administration d'une seule dose* – de 52 à 76 heures; *après l'administration de plusieurs doses* – de 40 à 55 heures.

Profil temps-action

	DÉBUT D'ACTION	PIC	DURÉE
PO	rapide	3 - 5 h	24 h

CONTRE-INDICATIONS, PRÉCAUTIONS ET MISES EN GARDE

Contre-indications: Hypersensibilité ■ Administration concomitante de cisapride, de voriconazole, de midazolam, de triazolam et de dérivés de l'ergot.

Précautions et mises en garde: Nombreuses interactions médicamenteuses ■ Antécédents de maladie mentale ou de toxicomanie (augmentation du risque de symptômes psychiatriques) ■ Antécédents d'insuffisance hépatique (incluant l'infection par le virus de l'hépatite B ou C ou l'administration concomitante d'agents hépatotoxiques) ■ **PÉD.:** Incidence accrue de rash ■ **OBST.:** Grossesse ou allaitement (n'administrer aux femmes enceintes qu'en dernier recours; les patientes infectées par le VIH ne devraient pas allaiter).

RÉACTIONS INDÉSIRABLES ET EFFETS SECONDAIRES

SNC: rêves bizarres, dépression, étourdissements, somnolence, fatigue, céphalées, capacité de concentration altérée, insomnie, nervosité, symptômes psychiatriques.

GI: nausées, douleurs abdominales, anorexie, diarrhée, dyspepsie, flatulences.

GU: hématurie, calculs rénaux.

Tég.: RASH, sécrétion accrue de sueur, prurit.

SN: hypoesthésie.

Métab.: hypertriglycéridémie, modification de la distribution du tissu adipeux.

Divers: syndrome de reconstitution immunitaire.

INTERACTIONS

Médicament-médicament: L'éfavirenz induit (stimule) l'activité enzymatique du cytochrome P450 3A4; il faut donc s'attendre à ce qu'il modifie à la baisse les effets des autres **médicaments métabolisés par ce cytochrome**, incluant la **clarithromycine**, l'**atorvastatine**, la **simvastatine**, la **sertraline**, la **rifabutine** et la **méthadone** (un ajustement à la hausse de la dose peut être nécessaire); l'éfavirenz est lui aussi métabolisé par ce cytochrome ■ Risque accru de dépression du SNC lors de la prise concomitante d'autres **dépresseurs du SNC**, dont l'**alcool**, les **antidépresseurs**, les **antihistaminiques** et les **opioïdes** ■ LE MÉDICAMENT ENTRAÎNE L'ÉLÉVATION DES CONCENTRATIONS SANGUINES DE **CISAPRIDE**, DE **MIDAZOLAM**, DE **TRIAZOLAM** OU D'**ALCALOÏDES DE L'ERGOT** LORS D'UNE ADMINISTRATION CONCOMITANTE, CE QUI PEUT PROVOQUER DES RÉACTIONS INDÉSIRABLES POUVANT ÊTRE GRAVES, DONT DES ARYTHMIES, UNE DÉPRESSION DU SNC OU UNE DÉPRESSION RESPIRATOIRE ■ La **rifampine** réduit les concentrations sanguines d'éfavirenz. Un ajustement à la hausse de la dose d'éfavirenz peut être nécessaire ■ L'éfavirenz peut entraver l'efficacité des **contraceptifs oraux** (le risque d'interaction entre l'éfavirenz et les contraceptifs oraux n'étant pas entièrement établi, il faudrait utiliser une méthode fiable de contraception de type barrière en plus du contraceptif oral) ■ L'éfavirenz abaisse les concentrations sanguines de **voriconazole**

(il ne faut pas les administrer en association) ■ L'éfavirenz peut diminuer les concentrations plasmatiques de **kétoconazole** et d'**itraconazole** ■ À la suite de l'utilisation concomitante d'éfavirenz et de **carbamazépine**, les concentrations sanguines des deux médicaments diminuent (il ne faut pas les utiliser en association) ■ À la suite de l'utilisation concomitante d'éfavirenz et de **phénytoïne** ou de **phénobarbital**, les concentrations sanguines des deux médicaments diminuent (noter à intervalles réguliers les concentrations plasmatiques de l'anticonvulsivant) ■ Le médicament abaisse les concentrations sanguines d'**atazanavir**, d'**amprénavir**, d'**indinavir**, de **lopinavir/ritonavir** (il est recommandé d'augmenter la dose de ces médicaments) ■ À la suite de l'usage concomitant de **ritonavir**, les concentrations sanguines des deux agents s'élèvent et le risque de réactions indésirables, particulièrement d'hépatotoxicité, s'accroît ■ L'éfavirenz abaisse les concentrations sanguines de **saquinavir** (il ne faut pas utiliser en association le saquinavir comme seul inhibiteur des protéases) ■ L'éfavirenz peut entraver l'effet de la **warfarine** (suivre de près le RNI).

Médicament-aliments: La prise du médicament après un **repas riche en matières grasses** accroît l'absorption de l'éfavirenz de 50 %.

Médicament-produits naturels: L'usage concomitant de **millepertuis** peut entraîner la diminution des concentrations sanguines et de l'efficacité de l'éfavirenz, associée à l'émergence d'une résistance virale.

VOIES D'ADMINISTRATION ET POSOLOGIE

- **PO (adultes et enfants ≥ 40 kg):** 600 mg, 1 fois par jour.
- **PO (enfants de 32,5 à < 40 kg):** 400 mg, 1 fois par jour.
- **PO (enfants de 25 à < 32,5 kg):** 350 mg, 1 fois par jour.
- **PO (enfants de 20 à < 25 kg):** 300 mg, 1 fois par jour.
- **PO (enfants de 15 à < 20 kg):** 250 mg, 1 fois par jour.
- **PO (enfants de 13 à < 15 kg):** 200 mg, 1 fois par jour.

PRÉSENTATION

Capsules: 50 mg[Pr], 100 mg[Pr], 200 mg[Pr] ■ **Comprimés:** 600 mg[Pr].

SOINS INFIRMIERS

ÉVALUATION DE LA SITUATION

- Suivre de près le patient pour déceler tout changement dans la gravité des symptômes de l'infection par le VIH et tout symptôme d'infection opportuniste pendant toute la durée du traitement.
- Déceler le rash, particulièrement au cours du premier mois de traitement. Cet effet se manifeste habituellement au cours des deux premières semaines et disparaît malgré la poursuite du traitement dans l'espace de 1 mois. Le rash peut prendre la forme d'une lésion maculopapulaire s'accompagnant d'érythème et de prurit, mais peut aussi se présenter sous la forme d'une dermatite exfoliatrice ou du syndrome de Stevens-Johnson. Il survient plus fréquemment chez les enfants et peut être plus grave. Si le rash est grave ou s'accompagne d'ampoules, de desquamation ou de fièvre, ou s'il touche les muqueuses, il faut arrêter immédiatement le traitement. Lorsque le traitement par l'éfavirenz a été interrompu en raison du rash, on peut le reprendre si l'on administre en concomitance un antihistaminique ou un corticostéroïde.
- Observer étroitement le patient pour déceler les symptômes psychiatriques ou ceux touchant le SNC: étourdissements, capacité de concentration altérée, somnolence, rêves bizarres, insomnie. Les symptômes apparaissent habituellement 1 ou 2 jours après le début du traitement et disparaissent de 2 à 4 semaines plus tard. L'administration du médicament au coucher peut réduire les symptômes. L'usage concomitant d'alcool ou d'agents psychoactifs peut entraîner des effets additifs sur le SNC.
- Si une patiente enceinte est exposée à des antirétroviraux, l'inscrire dans le registre des femmes exposées aux antirétroviraux pendant leur grossesse, en composant le 1-800-258-4263.

Tests de laboratoire:

- Noter la charge virale et le nombre de cellules CD4 à intervalles réguliers pendant toute la durée du traitement.
- Noter les résultats des tests de la fonction hépatique chez les patients ayant des antécédents d'hépatite B ou C. Le médicament peut entraîner une élévation des concentrations d'AST, d'ALT et de GGT. En cas d'anomalies modérées à graves, relevées par les tests de la fonction hépatique, on devrait interrompre le traitement par l'éfavirenz jusqu'à ce que les concentrations reviennent à la normale. Si ces anomalies se manifestent de nouveau à la reprise du traitement, il faut l'arrêter.
- Le médicament peut entraîner une élévation des taux sériques de cholestérol total et de triglycérides.
- L'éfavirenz peut entraîner des résultats faussement positifs aux tests de dépistage des dérivés du cannabis dans les urines.

DIAGNOSTICS INFIRMIERS POSSIBLES

- Risque d'infection (Indications).
- Connaissances insuffisantes sur le traitement médicamenteux (Enseignement au patient et à ses proches).
- Non-observance du traitement médicamenteux (Enseignement au patient et à ses proches).

INTERVENTIONS INFIRMIÈRES

- On peut administrer le médicament avec ou sans aliments. Il ne faut cependant pas le prendre en même temps qu'un repas riche en matières grasses, en raison du risque accru d'effets indésirables.

ENSEIGNEMENT AU PATIENT ET À SES PROCHES

- Expliquer au patient qu'il doit respecter rigoureusement la posologie recommandée et qu'il doit toujours prendre ce médicament avec d'autres antirétroviraux. Le prévenir qu'il ne doit prendre que la quantité qui lui a été prescrite et qu'il ne doit pas arrêter le traitement sans avoir consulté au préalable un professionnel de la santé. S'il n'a pas pu prendre le médicament au moment habituel, il doit le prendre aussitôt que possible, sans jamais remplacer une dose manquée par une double dose.
- Recommander au patient de ne jamais donner l'éfavirenz à d'autres personnes.
- Prévenir le patient que l'éfavirenz peut parfois provoquer des étourdissements et de la somnolence ou altérer ses capacités de concentration. Lui conseiller de ne pas conduire et d'éviter les activités qui exigent sa vigilance jusqu'à ce qu'on ait la certitude que le médicament n'entraîne pas ces effets chez lui.
- Conseiller au patient de consulter un professionnel de la santé avant de prendre d'autres médicaments sur ordonnance ou en vente libre ou des produits naturels.
- Prévenir le patient que l'éfavirenz ne guérit pas le sida et n'empêche pas l'apparition d'infections associées ou opportunistes. Lui expliquer que ce médicament ne réduit pas le risque de transmission du VIH à d'autres personnes par les rapports sexuels ou par la contamination du sang. Inciter le patient à utiliser un condom et à éviter le partage d'aiguilles ou les dons de sang afin de prévenir la propagation du VIH. Informer le patient que les effets à long terme de l'éfavirenz sont encore inconnus.
- Recommander à la patiente qui prend des contraceptifs oraux d'utiliser une autre méthode de contraception non hormonale et de prévenir le professionnel de la santé si elle devient enceinte pendant le traitement par l'éfavirenz.
- Conseiller au patient d'informer un professionnel de la santé si un rash se manifeste.
- Prévenir le patient qu'il y a risque de redistribution ou d'accumulation de graisses corporelles à la suite de ce traitement antirétroviral, dont les causes et les conséquences à long terme sur la santé sont actuellement inconnues.
- Insister sur le fait qu'il est important de se soumettre à intervalles réguliers à des examens de suivi et à des analyses de sang permettant de déceler les effets secondaires et les bienfaits du traitement.

VÉRIFICATION DE L'EFFICACITÉ THÉRAPEUTIQUE

L'efficacité du traitement peut être démontrée par: le ralentissement de l'évolution de l'infection par le VIH et la diminution du nombre d'infections opportunistes chez les patients infectés ■ la diminution de la charge virale et l'augmentation du nombre de cellules CD4. ✳

ÉLÉTRIPTAN,

voir Agonistes de la sérotonine 5-HT_1

EMTRICITABINE

Emtriva

CLASSIFICATION:

Antirétroviral (inhibiteur nucléosidique de la transcriptase inverse)

Grossesse – catégorie B

INDICATIONS

Infection par le VIH (en association avec d'autres antirétroviraux). **Usages non approuvés:** En association avec d'autres antirétroviraux, prophylaxie après une exposition accidentelle au VIH.

MÉCANISME D'ACTION

Phosphorylation intracellulaire et inhibition de la transcriptase inverse du VIH, ce qui détruit la chaîne d'ADN virale. ***Effets thérapeutiques:*** Ralentissement de l'évolution de l'infection par le VIH et moindre risque d'apparition de ses complications ■ Augmentation du nombre de cellules CD4 et diminution de la charge virale.

PHARMACOCINÉTIQUE

Absorption: Rapide et massive. Biodisponibilité à 93 %.

Distribution: Inconnue.

Métabolisme et excrétion: Faible métabolisme; 86 % est excrété par les reins, et 14 %, dans les fèces.

Demi-vie: 10 heures.

Profil temps-action†

	DÉBUT D'ACTION	PIC	DURÉE
PO	rapide	1 - 2 h	24 h

† Lorsque la fonction rénale est normale.

CONTRE-INDICATIONS, PRÉCAUTIONS ET MISES EN GARDE

Contre-indications: Hypersensibilité ■ **PÉD.**: Enfants < 18 ans (l'innocuité de l'agent n'a pas été établie).

Précautions et mises en garde: Obésité, femmes, prise prolongée d'inhibiteurs nucléosidiques (il peut s'agir de facteurs de risque d'acidose lactique ou d'hépatomégalie) ■ **GÉR.**: Risque accru d'effets secondaires ■ Infection par le virus de l'hépatite B (risque d'exacerbation après l'arrêt du traitement) ■ Insuffisance rénale ■ **OBST.**: N'administrer qu'en cas de besoin incontestable ■ **ALLAITEMENT**: L'allaitement est déconseillé aux femmes infectées par le VIH.

RÉACTIONS INDÉSIRABLES ET EFFETS SECONDAIRES

SNC: étourdissements, céphalées, insomnie, faiblesse, dépression, cauchemars.

GI: douleurs abdominales, diarrhée, nausées, HÉPATOMÉGALIE GRAVE AVEC STÉATOSE, dyspepsie, vomissements.

Tég.: rash, modification de la couleur de la peau.

HÉ: ACIDOSE LACTIQUE.

Loc.: arthralgie, myalgie.

SN: neuropathie, paresthésie.

Resp.: toux, rhinite.

Divers: modification de la distribution du tissu adipeux, syndrome de reconstitution immunitaire.

INTERACTIONS

Médicament-médicament: Profil de résistance du VIH similaire à celui de la **lamivudine** (éviter l'usage concomitant).

VOIES D'ADMINISTRATION ET POSOLOGIE

- **PO (adultes ≥ 18 ans)**: 200 mg, 1 fois par jour.

Insuffisance rénale

- **PO (ADULTES ≥ 18 ANS)**: *CL_{CR} DE 30 À 49 mL/MIN* – 200 mg, TOUTES LES 48 HEURES; *CL_{CR} DE 15 À 29 mL/MIN* – 200 mg, TOUTES LES 72 HEURES; *CL_{CR} < 15 mL/MIN* – 200 mg, TOUTES LES 96 HEURES.

PRÉSENTATION

Capsules: 200 mg[Pr] ■ **En association avec**: ténofovir (Truvada[Pr]) (voir l'annexe U).

SOINS INFIRMIERS

ÉVALUATION DE LA SITUATION

- Rester à l'affût de tout changement qui intervient dans la gravité des symptômes de l'infection par le VIH et des symptômes d'infections opportunistes, pendant toute la durée du traitement.
- L'AGENT PEUT PROVOQUER UNE ACIDOSE LACTIQUE ET UNE HÉPATOMÉGALIE GRAVE AVEC STÉATOSE. CES COMPLICATIONS SONT PLUS PROBABLES CHEZ LES PATIENTS DE SEXE FÉMININ, CHEZ LES PERSONNES OBÈSES ET CHEZ CELLES QUI PRENNENT DES ANALOGUES NUCLÉOSIDIQUES PENDANT UN TEMPS PROLONGÉ. SUIVRE DE PRÈS LES SIGNES DE CES COMPLICATIONS (TAUX ACCRUS DE LACTATE SÉRIQUE, CONCENTRATIONS ÉLEVÉES D'ENZYMES HÉPATIQUES, HYPERTROPHIE DU FOIE DÉCELÉE À LA PALPATION). ARRÊTER LE TRAITEMENT DÈS L'APPARITION DE SIGNES CLINIQUES OU DE RÉSULTATS DE TESTS DE LABORATOIRE QUI ÉVOQUENT UN TEL PROBLÈME.
- Avant le traitement, soumettre le patient au test de dépistage de l'infection chronique par le virus de l'hépatite B (VHB). L'emtricitabine n'est pas indiquée dans le traitement de l'infection par le VHB. On a noté des cas d'exacerbation de l'infection par le VHB après l'arrêt du traitement par l'emtricitabine.
- Si une patiente enceinte est exposée à des antirétroviraux, l'inscrire dans le registre des femmes exposées aux antirétroviraux pendant leur grossesse, en composant le 1-800-258-4263.

Tests de laboratoire:

- Mesurer la charge virale et le nombre de cellules CD4 à intervalles réguliers pendant toute la durée du traitement.
- L'agent peut élever les taux d'AST, d'ALT, de bilirubine, de créatine kinase, d'amylase sérique, de lipase sérique et de triglycérides. Il peut élever ou abaisser la glycémie. Il peut diminuer le nombre de neutrophiles.

DIAGNOSTICS INFIRMIERS POSSIBLES

- Risque d'infection (Indications).
- Non-observance du traitement médicamenteux (Enseignement au patient et à ses proches).

INTERVENTIONS INFIRMIÈRES

PO: On peut administrer l'agent avec ou sans aliments.

ENSEIGNEMENT AU PATIENT ET À SES PROCHES

- Insister sur le fait qu'il faut prendre l'emtricitabine en respectant rigoureusement les recommandations du médecin et toujours en association avec d'autres antirétroviraux. Expliquer au patient qu'il ne doit pas prendre plus que la quantité prescrite ni arrêter le traitement sans consulter un professionnel de la santé au préalable. Le prévenir qu'il doit prendre toute dose oubliée dès qu'il s'en souvient à moins que ce ne soit presque l'heure prévue pour la dose suivante; lui expliquer qu'il ne faut jamais remplacer une dose manquée par une double dose.
- Prévenir le patient qu'il ne doit pas donner l'emtricitabine à d'autres personnes.
- Prévenir le patient que l'agent ne guérit pas l'infection par le VIH ni ne prévient les infections associées ou opportunistes. Il ne réduit pas le risque de transmission du VIH à d'autres personnes par les rapports sexuels ou par la contamination du sang. Inciter le patient à utiliser un condom et à éviter le partage d'aiguilles ou les dons de sang pour prévenir la propagation du VIH. Prévenir le patient que les effets de long cours de l'emtricitabine sont pour le moment inconnus.
- RECOMMANDER AU PATIENT DE PRÉVENIR UN PROFESSIONNEL DE LA SANTÉ IMMÉDIATEMENT SI DES SIGNES D'ACIDOSE LACTIQUE (FATIGUE OU FAIBLESSE, DOULEURS MUSCULAIRES INHABITUELLES, DIFFICULTÉS RESPIRATOIRES, DOULEURS D'ESTOMAC AVEC DES NAUSÉES ET DES VOMISSEMENTS, SENSATION DE FROID, SURTOUT AU NIVEAU DES EXTRÉMITÉS, ÉTOURDISSEMENTS OU BATTEMENTS CARDIAQUES RAPIDES ET IRRÉGULIERS) OU D'HÉPATOTOXICITÉ (JAUNISSEMENT DE LA PEAU OU DU BLANC DES YEUX, URINE DE COULEUR FONCÉE, SELLES DE COULEUR PÂLE, PERTE D'APPÉTIT PENDANT PLUSIEURS JOURS DE SUITE, NAUSÉES OU DOULEURS ABDOMINALES) SE MANIFESTENT. Ces symptômes peuvent se présenter plus fréquemment chez les sujets de sexe féminin, les personnes obèses ou celles qui prennent des médicaments comme l'emtricitabine pendant un laps de temps prolongé.
- Prévenir le patient qu'il y a risque de redistribution des tissus adipeux (obésité centrale, accumulation de graisses dans la région dorsocervicale ou bosse de bison, atrophie des tissus périphériques ou de ceux du visage, hypertrophie des tissus mammaires, apparence cushinoïde) et de changement de la couleur de la peau (hyperpigmentation de la paume des mains et de la plante des pieds).
- Insister sur l'importance des examens réguliers de suivi et des numérations globulaires permettant d'évaluer les progrès du traitement et de surveiller les effets secondaires.
- Recommander à la patiente d'informer un professionnel de la santé si elle pense être enceinte, si elle souhaite le devenir ou si elle allaite.

VÉRIFICATION DE L'EFFICACITÉ THÉRAPEUTIQUE

L'efficacité du traitement peut être démontrée par: le ralentissement de l'évolution de l'infection par le VIH et la diminution du risque d'infections opportunistes chez les patients infectés ■ la diminution de la charge virale et l'augmentation du nombre de CD4.

ÉNALAPRIL,

voir Inhibiteurs de l'enzyme de conversion de l'angiotensine (IECA)

ÉNALAPRILATE,

voir Inhibiteurs de l'enzyme de conversion de l'angiotensine (IECA)

ENFUVIRTIDE

Fuzeon

CLASSIFICATION:

Antirétroviral (inhibiteur de la fusion du VIH-1)

Grossesse – catégorie B

INDICATIONS

Traitement des infections par le VIH en association avec d'autres antirétroviraux chez les patients qui présentent des signes de réplication virale malgré un traitement antirétroviral en cours.

MÉCANISME D'ACTION

L'enfuvirtide empêche la pénétration du VIH-1 dans les cellules, en inhibant la fusion de l'enveloppe virale et de la membrane cellulaire. Il prévient les changements de conformation nécessaires à cette fusion en se fixant sur la première heptade répétée (HR1) de la sous-unité gp41 de l'enveloppe virale.

PHARMACOCINÉTIQUE

Absorption: L'absorption est proportionnelle à la dose. L'administration SC d'une dose de 90 mg procure une biodisponibilité absolue de 84,3 % ± 15,5 %.

Distribution: Volume de distribution de 5,5 ± 1,1 litres après une dose.

Liaison aux protéines: 92 %.

Métabolisme et excrétion: L'enfuvirtide étant un peptide, il est décomposé en ses acides aminés constitutifs. Ces derniers devraient ensuite se retrouver dans le capital des acides aminés de l'organisme. Aucune étude ne semble avoir déterminé la ou les voies d'élimination de l'enfuvirtide.

Demi-vie: 3,8 ± 0,6 heures.

Profil temps-action (diminution de la charge virale)

	DÉBUT D'ACTION	PIC	DURÉE
SC	inconnu	2 semaines	inconnue

CONTRE-INDICATIONS, PRÉCAUTIONS ET MISES EN GARDE

Contre-indications: Hypersensibilité à l'enfuvirtide ou à ses composants.

Précautions et mises en garde: Pneumonie bactérienne active ou état prédisposant à une pneumonie ■ Allaitement ■ **PÉD.**: Enfants < 6 ans (l'innocuité et la pharmacocinétique de l'agent n'ont pas été établies) ■ **GÉR.**: Personnes âgées > 65 ans (études insuffisantes à ce jour) ■ **OBST.**: Aucune étude contrôlée adéquate n'a été réalisée; administrer seulement si les avantages potentiels pour la mère justifient les risques potentiels pour le fœtus.

RÉACTIONS INDÉSIRABLES ET EFFETS SECONDAIRES

Lors des essais cliniques, l'enfuvirtide a toujours été évalué en association avec d'autres agents antirétroviraux. Par conséquent, on peut supposer que les effets indésirables observés ne sont pas exclusivement ceux de l'enfuvirtide.

SNC: vertiges, neuropathie périphérique, fatigue, hypoesthésie, troubles de l'attention, tremblements, anxiété, irritabilité, cauchemars.

ORLO: congestion nasale, sinusite, vertige, conjonctivite, otite, grippe.

Resp.: PNEUMONIE BACTÉRIENNE.

GI: nausées, diarrhée, reflux gastro-œsophagien, pancréatite, élévation des transaminases hépatiques.

Tég.: érythème, acné, eczéma séborrhéique, peau sèche, papillome cutané.

Hémat.: lymphadénopathie.

Métab.: perte d'appétit, perte de poids, anorexie, diabète, hypertriglycéridémie.

Loc.: myalgie.

Locaux: réactions au point d'injection.

Divers: RÉACTIONS D'HYPERSENSIBILITÉ, herpès simplex.

INTERACTIONS

Médicament-médicament: L'enfuvirtide n'est pas un inhibiteur du CYP450. Jusqu'à présent, on ne trouve dans les publications aucune mention d'interactions cliniquement significatives.

VOIES D'ADMINISTRATION ET POSOLOGIE

- **SC (adultes)**: 90 mg (1 mL), 2 fois par jour.
- **SC (enfants > 6 ans)**: 2,0 mg/kg, 2 fois par jour, jusqu'à concurrence de 90 mg, 2 fois par jour.

PRÉSENTATION

Poudre lyophilisée pour solution injectable: 108 mg[Pr] par fiole.

SOINS INFIRMIERS

ÉVALUATION DE LA SITUATION

- Observer le patient pendant toute la durée du traitement pour déceler l'aggravation des symptômes de l'infection par le VIH-1 ou les symptômes d'infections opportunistes.
- Rester à l'affût de réactions aux points d'injection (douleur, malaise, induration, érythème, nodules et kystes, prurit, ecchymoses). Ces effets sont fréquents, ils peuvent nécessiter l'administration d'analgésiques et limiter la capacité du patient de mener ses activités habituelles.
- Rester à l'affût des signes et des symptômes de pneumonie (toux avec fièvre, tachypnée, dyspnée) pendant toute la durée du traitement. Prévenir un professionnel de la santé immédiatement si de tels signes ou symptômes se manifestent. Les patients à plus haut risque de pneumonie sont notamment ceux ayant un compte initial de CD4 bas, ceux ayant une charge virale élevée, ceux qui utilisent des drogues IV, les fumeurs et les personnes ayant des antécédents de maladie pulmonaire.
- Rester à l'affût des réactions d'hypersensibilité (< 1 %), telles que les éruptions cutanées, la fièvre,

les nausées et les vomissements, les frissons, la raideur, l'hypotension et l'élévation des transaminases hépatiques. Le traitement à l'enfuvirtide doit être arrêté définitivement si des signes et des symptômes généraux qui évoquent une réaction d'hypersensibilité surviennent.

- Si une patiente enceinte est exposée à des antirétroviraux, l'inscrire dans le registre des femmes exposées aux antirétroviraux pendant leur grossesse, en composant le 1-800-258-4263.

Tests de laboratoire:

- Suivre de près la charge virale et le nombre de cellules CD4, avant le traitement et à intervalles réguliers pendant toute sa durée.
- Le médicament peut provoquer une éosinophilie et une élévation des taux sériques d'amylase, de lipase, de triglycérides, d'AST, d'ALT, de GGT et de CK.

TOXICITÉ ET SURDOSAGE: Il n'existe aucun antidote particulier de l'enfuvirtide. Le traitement d'un surdosage devrait comprendre des mesures générales de maintien des fonctions vitales.

DIAGNOSTICS INFIRMIERS POSSIBLES

- Risque d'infection (Indications, Réactions indésirables).
- Connaissances insuffisantes sur le traitement médicamenteux (Enseignement au patient et à ses proches).

INTERVENTIONS INFIRMIÈRES

- Le médicament doit être administré 2 fois par jour, par voie sous-cutanée. L'enfuvirtide doit être reconstitué avec 1,1 mL d'eau stérile pour injection. Une fois l'eau ajoutée, tapoter doucement la fiole pendant 10 secondes, puis la déposer jusqu'à dissolution complète de la poudre, ce qui peut prendre jusqu'à 45 minutes. Avant de prélever la solution à administrer, inspecter visuellement la fiole pour s'assurer que le contenu est entièrement dissous et que la solution est limpide, incolore et dépourvue de bulles ou de particules. Si des particules sont visibles, ne pas utiliser la fiole et la jeter ou la retourner à la pharmacie. Le médicament ne contient aucun agent de conservation. Une fois la préparation reconstituée, on devrait l'injecter immédiatement. Si c'est impossible, le produit reconstitué doit être gardé au réfrigérateur dans sa fiole jusqu'à son administration, et utilisé dans les 24 heures. La solution reconstituée réfrigérée doit être portée à la température ambiante avant d'être injectée et il faut inspecter de nouveau la fiole visuellement pour s'assurer que le contenu est entièrement dissous et que la solution est limpide, incolore et dénuée de bulles ou de particules.
- Le médicament s'administre par voie sous-cutanée dans le haut du bras, le devant de la cuisse ou dans l'abdomen. L'injection doit être administrée dans un point d'injection différent du précédent et exempt de réaction visible due à une dose antérieure. Ne pas injecter dans un grain de beauté, une verrue, une cicatrice, une ecchymose ou le nombril.

Associations compatibles dans la même seringue: Ne pas mélanger avec d'autres médicaments.

E

ENSEIGNEMENT AU PATIENT ET À SES PROCHES

- Conseiller au patient de s'injecter le médicament tous les jours à la même heure. S'il n'a pas pu se l'injecter au moment habituel, il doit le faire dès que possible, à moins que ce ne soit presque l'heure prévue pour la dose suivante. Lui conseiller de ne jamais remplacer une dose manquée par une double dose.
- Expliquer au patient et à ses soignants naturels la technique de préparation de l'injection ainsi que les règles d'asepsie à suivre lors de l'administration de l'enfuvirtide.
- L'enfuvirtide doit toujours être utilisé en concomitance avec d'autres antirétroviraux.
- Demander aux soignants naturels de communiquer immédiatement avec un professionnel de la santé s'ils se piquent accidentellement en administrant une injection au patient.
- Expliquer au patient les signes et les symptômes des réactions au point d'injection. Lui recommander de prévenir un professionnel de la santé s'il manifeste ces réactions.
- Prévenir le patient qu'il est possible de développer une réaction d'hypersensibilité à l'enfuvirtide. On doit lui conseiller d'interrompre le traitement et de consulter immédiatement un médecin si des signes ou des symptômes d'hypersensibilité apparaissent (éruptions cutanées, fièvre, nausées et vomissements, frissons, raideur, hypotension).
- Informer le patient qu'une fréquence plus élevée des pneumonies bactériennes a été observée chez les sujets sous traitement par l'enfuvirtide. Il doit consulter un médecin si des signes ou des symptômes évocateurs d'une pneumonie (toux accompagnée de fièvre, respiration rapide, essoufflement) apparaissent.
- Informer la patiente qu'on ignore si l'enfuvirtide passe dans le lait maternel. Étant donné le risque de transmission du VIH-1 et les effets indésirables possibles de l'enfuvirtide chez le nourrisson, l'allaitement est déconseillé aux mères qui reçoivent ce médicament.

- Expliquer au patient que l'enfuvirtide ne guérit pas l'infection par le VIH-1 et qu'il ne réduit pas le risque de transmission du VIH-1 à d'autres personnes par les rapports sexuels ou par la contamination du sang. Inciter le patient à utiliser un condom durant les rapports sexuels, à ne pas se servir des mêmes aiguilles qu'une autre personne et à ne pas donner du sang, afin de prévenir la transmission du virus du sida à autrui.
- Recommander au patient de signaler rapidement à un professionnel de la santé les signes d'infection aux points d'injection: écoulements, augmentation de la sensation de chaleur, de la rougeur, de l'enflure ou de la douleur.
- Insister sur le fait qu'il est important de se soumettre à intervalles réguliers à des examens de suivi et à des analyses de sang permettant de déceler les effets secondaires et les bienfaits du traitement.
- Recommander au patient d'éviter de prendre des médicaments en vente libre ou sur ordonnance sans consulter au préalable un professionnel de la santé.
- Informer le patient qu'aucune étude n'a été menée sur la capacité de conduire ou de faire fonctionner des machines pendant un traitement à l'enfuvirtide. Rien ne permet de croire que l'enfuvirtide pourrait nuire à cette capacité, mais ses effets indésirables doivent être pris en considération.

VÉRIFICATION DE L'EFFICACITÉ THÉRAPEUTIQUE

L'efficacité du traitement peut être démontrée par: la diminution de la charge virale et l'augmentation du nombre de cellules CD4 chez les patients infectés par le VIH-1 ▪ le ralentissement de l'évolution de l'infection par le VIH et la diminution du nombre d'infections opportunistes chez les patients infectés.

ÉNOXAPARINE,

voir Héparines de faible poids moléculaire/héparinoïdes

ENTACAPONE

Comtan

CLASSIFICATION:

Antiparkinsonien (inhibiteur de la catéchol-O-méthyltransférase)

Grossesse – catégorie C

INDICATIONS

Traitement adjuvant aux lévodopa/carbidopa ou carbidopa/bensérazide chez les patients atteints de la maladie de Parkinson idiopathique présentant des signes et des symptômes d'épuisement de l'effet thérapeutique de la médication en fin de dose.

MÉCANISME D'ACTION

Inhibition sélective et réversible de l'enzyme catéchol-O-méthyltransférase (COMT) ▪ Prévention de la décomposition de la lévodopa, grâce à l'inhibition de cette enzyme, ce qui accroît nettement la disponibilité du médicament dans le SNC. ***Effets thérapeutiques:*** Prolongation de la durée de la réponse à la lévodopa ▪ Diminution des signes et des symptômes de la maladie de Parkinson.

PHARMACOCINÉTIQUE

Absorption: Rapide (35 %) (PO).

Distribution: Inconnue.

Liaison aux protéines: 98 %.

Métabolisme et excrétion: Fort métabolisme et excrétion dans la bile; de très faibles quantités sont éliminées sous forme inchangée.

Demi-vie: *Phase initiale* – de 0,4 à 0,7 heure; *seconde phase* – 2,4 heures.

Profil temps-action (inhibition de la COMT)

	Début d'action	Pic	Durée
PO	inconnu	inconnu	jusqu'à 8 h

CONTRE-INDICATIONS, PRÉCAUTIONS ET MISES EN GARDE

Contre-indications: Hypersensibilité ▪ Traitement concomitant par un IMAO (cesser l'emploi de tout inhibiteur non sélectif de la MAO au moins 2 semaines avant d'entreprendre un traitement par l'entacapone) ▪ Antécédents de syndrome malin des neuroleptiques ou de rhabdomyolyse atraumatique ▪ Insuffisance hépatique ▪ Phéochromocytome (augmentation du risque de crise hypertensive).

Précautions et mises en garde: Traitement simultané par des médicaments métabolisés par la COMT ▪ **Obst., allaitement, péd.:** L'innocuité du médicament n'a pas été établie ▪ Coloration anormale des urines: l'emploi de l'entacapone peut entraîner une intensification inoffensive de la couleur des urines, qui peuvent devenir brun-orangé.

RÉACTIONS INDÉSIRABLES ET EFFETS SECONDAIRES

SNC: SYNDROME MALIN DES NEUROLEPTIQUES, étourdissements, hallucinations, syncope.
Resp.: infiltrats pulmonaires, épanchement pleural, épaississement pleural.
CV: hypotension.
GI: douleurs abdominales, diarrhée, nausées (pendant le traitement initial), fibrose rétropéritonéale.
GU: urine de couleur brun-orangé.
Loc.: RHABDOMYOLYSE.
SN: dyskinésie.

INTERACTIONS

Médicament-médicament: L'administration concomitante d'un **inhibiteur non sélectif de la MAO** n'est pas recommandée; les deux agents inhibent les voies métaboliques des catécholamines ■ L'usage concomitant de **médicaments métabolisés par la COMT**, tels que l'**isoprotérénol**, l'**adrénaline**, la **noradrénaline**, la **dopamine**, la **dobutamine** et le **méthyldopa** peut accroître le risque de tachycardie, d'arythmies et d'élévation de la pression artérielle ■ Le **probénécide**, la **cholestyramine**, l'**érythromycine**, la **rifampine**, l'**ampicilline** et le **chloramphénicol** peuvent entraver l'élimination biliaire de l'entacapone; l'administration concomitante de ces agents doit s'accompagner de prudence.

VOIES D'ADMINISTRATION ET POSOLOGIE

- **PO (adultes)**: 200 mg par dose de lévodopa/carbidopa ou de lévodopa/bensérazide, jusqu'à 8 fois par jour au maximum (1 600 mg/jour).

PRÉSENTATION

Comprimés: 200 mg[Pr].

SOINS INFIRMIERS

ÉVALUATION DE LA SITUATION

- Observer le patient, avant le traitement et pendant toute sa durée, à la recherche des symptômes parkinsoniens et extrapyramidaux suivants: agitation ou besoin de bouger sans cesse, rigidité, tremblements, mouvements d'émiettement, faciès figé, démarche traînante, spasmes musculaires, mouvements de torsion, difficultés d'élocution ou de déglutition, perte de l'équilibre. La dyskinésie peut s'aggraver si le traitement est poursuivi.
- Suivre de près l'apparition de la diarrhée. Cet effet se manifeste habituellement dans les 4 à 12 semaines qui suivent le début du traitement, mais peut survenir dès la première semaine ou même plusieurs mois après le début du traitement.
- OBSERVER LE PATIENT À LA RECHERCHE DES SIGNES SUIVANTS S'APPARENTANT AU SYNDROME MALIN DES NEUROLEPTIQUES: HYPERTHERMIE, RIGIDITÉ MUSCULAIRE, ALTÉRATION DE L'ÉTAT DE CONSCIENCE, ÉLÉVATION DES CONCENTRATIONS DE CPK. ON A ASSOCIÉ CES SYMPTÔMES À UNE DIMINUTION RAPIDE DE LA DOSE OU À L'ARRÊT DU TRAITEMENT PAR D'AUTRES MÉDICAMENTS DOPAMINERGIQUES. LE TRAITEMENT DOIT ÊTRE ARRÊTÉ GRADUELLEMENT.

E

DIAGNOSTICS INFIRMIERS POSSIBLES

- Mobilité physique réduite (Indications).
- Risque d'accident (Indications).
- Connaissances insuffisantes sur le traitement médicamenteux (Enseignement au patient et à ses proches).

INTERVENTIONS INFIRMIÈRES

- Il faut toujours administrer l'entacapone en même temps que la lévodopa/carbidopa ou la lévodopa/bensérazide. Le médicament n'exerce aucun effet antiparkinsonien par lui-même.

ENSEIGNEMENT AU PATIENT ET À SES PROCHES

- Conseiller au patient de respecter rigoureusement la posologie recommandée. S'il n'a pu prendre le médicament au moment habituel, il doit le prendre dès que possible, mais pas plus tard que 2 heures avant l'heure prévue pour la dose suivante. Avant d'arrêter le traitement par l'entacapone, on doit diminuer graduellement la dose pour éviter les réactions de sevrage.
- Prévenir le patient que l'entacapone peut provoquer des étourdissements et des hallucinations. Lui conseiller de ne pas conduire et d'éviter les activités qui exigent sa vigilance jusqu'à ce qu'on ait la certitude que le médicament n'entraîne pas ces effets chez lui.
- Prévenir le patient que l'entacapone peut entraîner des nausées, particulièrement au début du traitement, et que son urine peut devenir brun-orangé.
- Conseiller au patient de changer lentement de position afin de réduire le risque d'hypotension orthostatique.
- Recommander à la patiente de prévenir un professionnel de la santé si elle pense être enceinte ou si elle souhaite le devenir.
- Insister sur l'importance des examens de suivi réguliers.

VÉRIFICATION DE L'EFFICACITÉ THÉRAPEUTIQUE

L'efficacité du traitement peut être démontrée par: la diminution des signes et des symptômes de la maladie de Parkinson. ✳

E

ENTÉCAVIR

Baraclude

CLASSIFICATION:

Antiviral (analogue nucléosidique)

Grossesse – catégorie C

INDICATIONS

Infection chronique par le virus de l'hépatite B (VHB) chez l'adulte en présence d'une réplication virale active et de hausses persistantes des aminotransférases sériques (ALT ou AST) ou de maladie évolutive démontrée à l'histologie.

MÉCANISME D'ACTION

À la suite d'une phosphorylation intracellulaire, transformation en une forme active qui agit à l'instar d'un analogue de la guanosine, entravant la synthèse de l'ADN. ***Effets thérapeutiques:*** Diminution des lésions hépatiques provoquées par l'infection chronique par le VHB.

PHARMACOCINÉTIQUE

Absorption: Bonne (PO).
Distribution: Tous les tissus.
Métabolisme et excrétion: Excrétion urinaire sous forme inchangée, de l'ordre de 62 à 73 %.
Demi-vie: Plasmatique: de 128 à 149 heures; intracellulaire: 15 heures.

Profil temps-action

	DÉBUT D'ACTION	PIC	DURÉE
PO	rapide	0,5 - 1,5 h	24 h

CONTRE-INDICATIONS, PRÉCAUTIONS ET MISES EN GARDE

Contre-indications: Hypersensibilité ■ Allaitement.
Précautions et mises en garde: Insuffisance rénale (il est recommandé de diminuer la dose si la Cl_{Cr} est < 50 mL/min) ■ Receveurs d'une greffe de foie (il est recommandé de suivre de près la fonction rénale) ■ Co-infection par le VIH et le VHB (on ne peut exclure le risque de l'émergence d'un VIH résistant lorsqu'on envisage un traitement par entécavir chez un patient co-infecté par le VIH et le VHB, qui n'est pas sous traitement antirétroviral hautement actif (HAART)) ■ **GÉR.**: Personnes âgées (risque de détérioration de la fonction rénale liée au vieillissement) ■ **PÉD.**: Enfants < 16 ans (l'innocuité de l'agent n'a pas été établie) ■ **OBST.**: Grossesse (n'administrer qu'en cas de besoin incontestable en évaluant soigneusement les bienfaits par rapport aux risques).

RÉACTIONS INDÉSIRABLES ET EFFETS SECONDAIRES

SNC: étourdissements, fatigue, céphalées.
GI: dyspepsie, douleurs abdominales, nausées, HÉPATOMÉGALIE ACCOMPAGNÉE DE STÉATOSE.
HÉ: ACIDOSE LACTIQUE.

INTERACTIONS

Médicament-médicament: L'usage concomitant de médicaments qui peuvent détériorer la fonction rénale peut élever les concentrations sanguines d'entécavir et le risque de toxicité.

VOIES D'ADMINISTRATION ET POSOLOGIE

- **PO (adultes et enfants > 16 ans)**: 0,5 mg, 1 fois par jour; *antécédents de résistance à la lamivudine:* 1 mg, 1 fois par jour.

INSUFFISANCE RÉNALE

- **PO (ADULTES ET ENFANTS > 16 ANS)**: *CL_{CR} DE 30 À < 50 mL/MIN:* 0,25 mg, 1 FOIS PAR JOUR; *ANTÉCÉDENTS DE RÉSISTANCE À LA LAMIVUDINE:* 0,5 mg, 1 FOIS PAR JOUR. *CL_{CR} DE 10 À < 30 mL/MIN:* 0,15 mg, 1 FOIS PAR JOUR; *ANTÉCÉDENTS DE RÉSISTANCE À LA LAMIVUDINE:* 0,3 mg, 1 FOIS PAR JOUR. *CL_{CR} < 10 mL/MIN:* 0,05 mg, 1 FOIS PAR JOUR; *ANTÉCÉDENTS DE RÉSISTANCE À LA LAMIVUDINE:* 0,1 mg, 1 FOIS PAR JOUR.

PRÉSENTATION

Comprimés: 0,5 mg[Pr] ■ **Solution par voie orale (parfumée à l'orange)**: 0,05 mg/mL[Pr].

SOINS INFIRMIERS

ÉVALUATION DE LA SITUATION

- Rester à l'affût de l'hépatite (jaunisse, fatigue, anorexie, prurit) tout au long du traitement et pendant plusieurs mois après qu'il a pris fin. IL Y A RISQUE D'EXACERBATION APRÈS LA FIN DU TRAITEMENT.
- Si une patiente enceinte est exposée à l'entécavir, l'inscrire dans le registre des femmes exposées aux

antirétroviraux pendant leur grossesse, en composant le 1-800-258-4263.

Tests de laboratoire: Suivre de près la fonction hépatique tout au long du traitement et pendant plusieurs mois après qu'il a pris fin. L'agent peut élever les taux d'AST, d'ALT, de bilirubine, d'amylase, de lipase, de créatinine et de glucose sérique. Il peut diminuer le taux d'albumine sérique.

DIAGNOSTICS INFIRMIERS POSSIBLES

- Risque d'infection (Indications).
- Non-observance du traitement médicamenteux (Enseignement au patient et à ses proches).

INTERVENTIONS INFIRMIÈRES

PO: Administrer à jeun, au moins 2 heures avant ou après un repas. La solution orale est prête à être employée et il ne faut pas la diluer ni la mélanger avec de l'eau ou un autre liquide. Tenir la cuillère à la verticale et la remplir lentement jusqu'à la gradation qui correspond à la dose prescrite. Rincer la cuillère avec de l'eau après l'administration de chaque dose. Conserver le médicament dans son emballage à la température ambiante. Après ouverture du flacon, on peut utiliser la solution jusqu'à la date de péremption indiquée.

ENSEIGNEMENT AU PATIENT ET À SES PROCHES

- Inciter le patient à lire les renseignements destinés au patient à chaque renouvellement d'ordonnance et de prendre l'entécavir en respectant rigoureusement les recommandations du médecin. Prendre toute dose manquée le plus rapidement possible, à moins que ce ne soit presque l'heure prévue pour la dose suivante. Le prévenir qu'il ne doit jamais rester à court de médicament et lui conseiller de s'en procurer dès que ses provisions diminuent. Lui recommander de ne jamais doubler les doses. Insister sur la nécessité d'observer le traitement pendant toute sa durée, de ne pas prendre une quantité supérieure à celle qui lui a été prescrite et de ne pas arrêter le traitement sans avoir consulté un professionnel de la santé au préalable. Informer le patient qu'il y a risque d'exacerbation de l'hépatite après l'arrêt du traitement. Lui recommander de ne pas donner ce médicament à d'autres personnes.
- Informer le patient que l'entécavir ne guérit pas l'infection par le VHB, mais qu'il peut diminuer la charge virale et la capacité du virus de proliférer et d'infecter de nouvelles cellules hépatiques; l'agent peut aussi améliorer l'état du foie. L'entécavir ne réduit pas le risque de transmettre le VHB à d'autres personnes par les rapports sexuels ou par la contamination du sang. Inciter le patient à utiliser un condom et à éviter le partage d'aiguilles ou les dons de sang pour prévenir la propagation du VHB.
- Recommander au patient de prévenir un professionnel de la santé immédiatement si des signes d'acidose lactique (fatigue ou faiblesse, douleurs musculaires inhabituelles, difficultés respiratoires, douleurs d'estomac avec des nausées et des vomissements, sensation de froid, surtout au niveau des extrémités, étourdissements ou battements cardiaques rapides et irréguliers) ou d'hépatotoxicité (jaunissement de la peau ou du blanc des yeux, urine de couleur foncée, selles de couleur pâle, perte d'appétit pendant plusieurs jours de suite, nausées ou douleurs abdominales basses) se manifestent.
- L'entécavir peut provoquer des étourdissements. Conseiller au patient de ne pas conduire et de ne pas s'engager dans d'autres activités qui exigent sa vigilance jusqu'à ce qu'on ait la certitude que le médicament n'entraîne pas cet effet chez lui.
- Recommander au patient de consulter un professionnel de la santé avant de prendre d'autres médicaments d'ordonnance ou en vente libre ou des produits naturels en même temps que ce médicament.
- Recommander à la patiente d'informer un professionnel de la santé si elle pense être enceinte, si elle souhaite le devenir ou si elle allaite.
- Insister sur l'importance des examens réguliers de suivi et des numérations globulaires permettant d'évaluer les progrès du traitement et de surveiller les effets secondaires.

VÉRIFICATION DE L'EFFICACITÉ THÉRAPEUTIQUE

L'efficacité du traitement peut être démontrée par: la diminution des lésions hépatiques dues à l'infection chronique par le virus de l'hépatite B.

ÉPINÉPHRINE,

voir Adrénaline

ALERTE CLINIQUE

ÉPIRUBICINE

Pharmorubicin

CLASSIFICATION:

Antinéoplasique (anthracycline)

Grossesse – catégorie D

INDICATIONS

Monothérapie ou traitement d'association avec d'autres antinéoplasiques pour obtenir la régression de divers types de tumeurs, tels le lymphome et le cancer des poumons, du sein, des ovaires et de l'estomac.

MÉCANISME D'ACTION

Inhibition de la synthèse de l'ADN et de l'ARN par formation d'un complexe avec l'ADN. ***Effets thérapeutiques:*** Destruction des cellules à prolifération rapide, particulièrement les cellules malignes.

E

PHARMACOCINÉTIQUE

Absorption: Biodisponibilité à 100 % (IV).

Distribution: L'agent se répartit rapidement dans tout l'organisme; il se concentre dans les érythrocytes.

Métabolisme et excrétion: Métabolisme rapide et important dans le foie et d'autres tissus.

Demi-vie: 35 heures.

Profil temps-action (effet sur le nombre de globules blancs)

	DÉBUT D'ACTION	PIC	DURÉE
IV	inconnu	10 - 14 jours	21 jours

CONTRE-INDICATIONS, PRÉCAUTIONS ET MISES EN GARDE

Contre-indications: Hypersensibilité à l'épirubicine, à d'autres anthracyclines ou à des composés connexes ■ Myélosuppresion grave ■ Antécédents d'affections cardiaques graves (insuffisance cardiaque grave, infarctus du myocarde, arythmies graves) ■ Insuffisance hépatique grave ■ Administration antérieure de doxorubicine, de daunorubicine, de mitoxantrone ou de mitomycine C jusqu'à l'atteinte de la dose cumulative maximale.

Précautions et mises en garde: Insuffisance rénale grave (créatinine sérique > 442 µmol/L) - envisager l'administration de doses moins élevées ■ Insuffisance hépatique (on recommande de réduire la dose lorsque les concentrations de bilirubine sont > 21 µmol/L ou que l'AST dépasse de 2 à 4 fois la limite supérieure de la normale) ■ **GÉR.**: Femmes ≥ 70 ans (risque accru de toxicité) ■ Administration concomitante de cimétidine ■ **OBST.**: Patientes en âge de procréer ■ **PÉD.**: Enfants (l'innocuité de l'agent n'a pas été établie; risque accru de cardiotoxicité aiguë et d'insuffisance cardiaque chronique) ■ Grossesse ou allaitement.

RÉACTIONS INDÉSIRABLES ET EFFETS SECONDAIRES

SNC: léthargie.

CV: CARDIOTOXICITÉ (reliée à la dose).

GI: nausées, vomissements, anorexie, diarrhée, mucosite.

Tég.: alopécie, bouffées vasomotrices, démangeaisons, photosensibilité, réaction secondaire à la radiothérapie, rash, hyperpigmentation de la peau et des ongles.

End.: suppression de la fonction des gonades.

Hémat.: LEUCOPÉNIE, anémie, thrombopénie, leucémie, syndrome myélodysplasique.

Locaux: réactions au point d'injection, phlébite au point d'injection IV, nécrose tissulaire.

Métab.: bouffées de chaleur, hyperuricémie.

Divers: ANAPHYLAXIE, INFECTION.

INTERACTIONS

Médicament-médicament: La **cimétidine** entraîne l'élévation des concentrations sanguines et accroît le risque de toxicité grave; il faut éviter l'administration concomitante ■ Toxicité hématologique et gastro-intestinale additives lors de l'administration concomitante d'autres **antinéoplasiques** ou d'une **radiothérapie** ■ L'épirubicine peut diminuer la réponse des anticorps aux **vaccins à virus vivants** et augmenter le risque de réactions indésirables.

VOIES D'ADMINISTRATION ET POSOLOGIE

IV (adultes): On a déjà utilisé d'autres schémas posologiques.

- *Cancer du sein: monothérapie* - de 75 à 90 mg/m² tous les 21 jours, ou de 12,5 à 25 mg/m², toutes les semaines; *traitement d'association* - de 50 à 60 mg/m², toutes les 3 ou 4 semaines.
- *Cancer bronchopulmonaire à petites cellules: monothérapie* - de 90 à 120 mg/m², toutes les 3 semaines; *traitement d'association* - de 50 à 90 mg/m².
- *Cancer bronchopulmonaire non à petites cellules: monothérapie* - de 120 à 150 mg/m², toutes les 3 à 4 semaines; *traitement d'association* - de 90 à 120 mg/m², toutes les 3 à 4 semaines.
- *Lymphome non hodgkinien: monothérapie* - de 75 à 90 mg/m², tous les 21 jours; *traitement d'association* - de 60 à 75 mg/m².
- *Maladie de Hodgkin: traitement d'association* - 35 mg/m², toutes les 2 semaines, ou 70 mg/m², toutes les 3 à 4 semaines.
- *Cancer ovarien: monothérapie* - de 50 à 90 mg/m², toutes les 3 ou 4 semaines; *traitement d'association* - de 50 à 90 mg/m², toutes les 3 à 4 semaines.
- *Cancer de l'estomac: monothérapie* - de 75 à 100 mg/m²; *traitement d'association* - 80 mg/m².

INSUFFISANCE HÉPATIQUE

- **IV (ADULTES)**: *BILIRUBINE DE 21 À 51 µMOL/L OU AST DE 2 À 4 FOIS LA LIMITE SUPÉRIEURE DE LA*

NORMALE – ADMINISTRER 50 % DE LA DOSE DE DÉPART RECOMMANDÉE; *BILIRUBINE > 51 μMOL/L OU AST > 4 FOIS LA LIMITE SUPÉRIEURE DE LA NORMALE* – ADMINISTRER 25 % DE LA DOSE DE DÉPART RECOMMANDÉE.

PRÉSENTATION

Solution pour injection: fioles à dose unique de 10 mg/5 mL[Pr], fioles à dose unique de 50 mg/25 mL[Pr], fioles à dose unique de 200 mg/100 mL[Pr].

SOINS INFIRMIERS

ÉVALUATION DE LA SITUATION

- RESTER À L'AFFÛT DES SIGNES D'APLASIE MÉDULLAIRE. SUIVRE DE PRÈS LES SAIGNEMENTS: SAIGNEMENT DES GENCIVES, FORMATION D'ECCHYMOSES, PÉTÉCHIES, PRÉSENCE DE SANG OCCULTE DANS LES SELLES, L'URINE ET LES VOMISSEMENTS. ÉVITER LES INJECTIONS IM ET LA PRISE DE LA TEMPÉRATURE RECTALE. APPLIQUER UNE PRESSION SUR LES POINTS DE PONCTION VEINEUSE PENDANT 10 MINUTES. DÉCELER LES SIGNES D'INFECTION EN PRÉSENCE DE NEUTROPÉNIE. L'ANÉMIE PEUT SURVENIR. SUIVRE DE PRÈS LA FATIGUE ACCRUE, LA DYSPNÉE ET L'HYPOTENSION ORTHOSTATIQUE.
- Des nausées et des vomissements graves peuvent survenir. Administrer un antiémétique par voie parentérale de 30 à 45 minutes avant le traitement et à intervalles réguliers pendant les 24 heures qui suivent, selon les indications. Mesurer la quantité de vomissures et avertir le médecin ou un autre professionnel de la santé si cette quantité est supérieure à celle indiquée dans les directives visant à prévenir la déshydratation.
- IL FAUT EXAMINER AVANT LE DÉBUT DU TRAITEMENT L'ÉTAT DE LA FONCTION CARDIAQUE PAR ÉCG ET PAR ANGIOGRAPHIE ISOTOPIQUE À ENTRÉES MULTIPLES OU PAR ÉCHOCARDIOGRAPHIE. ÉVALUER À PLUSIEURS REPRISES AU COURS DU TRAITEMENT LA FRACTION D'ÉJECTION DU VENTRICULE GAUCHE. RESTER À L'AFFÛT DES SIGNES DE TOXICITÉ CARDIAQUE QUI PEUVENT SURVENIR TÔT (MODIFICATIONS DES ONDES ST-T, TACHYCARDIE SINUSALE ET EXTRASYSTOLES) OU TARDIVEMENT (PARFOIS PLUSIEURS MOIS ET MÊME PLUSIEURS ANNÉES APRÈS L'ARRÊT DU TRAITEMENT). LA TOXICITÉ CARDIAQUE TARDIVE SE CARACTÉRISE PAR LA CARDIOMYOPATHIE, LA TACHYCARDIE, L'ŒDÈME PÉRIPHÉRIQUE, LA DYSPNÉE, LES RÂLES ET LES CRÉPITATIONS, LE GAIN PONDÉRAL, L'HÉPATOMÉGALIE, L'ASCITE ET L'ÉPANCHEMENT PLEURAL. LA TOXICITÉ DÉPEND HABITUELLEMENT DE LA DOSE CUMULATIVE ADMINISTRÉE.
- Observer fréquemment le point d'injection pour déceler la rougeur, l'irritation ou l'inflammation. Une sensation de brûlure ou de piqûre lors de la perfusion peut être un signe d'infiltration. Dans ce cas, il faut arrêter la perfusion et la reprendre dans une autre veine. L'épirubicine est un agent vésicant, mais elle peut s'infiltrer sans douleur même lorsqu'il y a reflux du sang lors de l'aspiration par l'aiguille de perfusion. L'extravasation de l'épirubicine peut entraîner de graves lésions tissulaires. En cas d'extravasation, arrêter immédiatement la perfusion, puis administrer le reste de la dose dans une autre veine.
- Examiner fréquemment la muqueuse buccale pour déceler les signes suivants de stomatite: douleur, brûlure, érythème, aphtes, saignements, infection. Espacer les administrations et/ou réduire la dose si les lésions sont douloureuses ou si elles empêchent le patient de s'alimenter.

Tests de laboratoire:

- NOTER LA NUMÉRATION GLOBULAIRE ET LA FORMULE LEUCOCYTAIRE AVANT CHAQUE TRAITEMENT ET À INTERVALLES RÉGULIERS PENDANT TOUTE SA DURÉE. L'ÉPIRUBICINE NE DOIT PAS ÊTRE ADMINISTRÉE LORSQUE LE TAUX INITIAL DES POLYNUCLÉAIRES NEUTROPHILES EST $< 1,5 \times 10^9$/L. LE NADIR DES GLOBULES BLANCS SE PRODUIT DANS LES 10 À 14 JOURS QUI SUIVENT L'ADMINISTRATION. LES VALEURS SE RÉTABLISSENT HABITUELLEMENT DANS LES 21 JOURS SUIVANT LE DÉBUT DU TRAITEMENT. UNE THROMBOPÉNIE ET UNE ANÉMIE GRAVES PEUVENT AUSSI SURVENIR.
- Suivre de près la fonction rénale (urée et créatinine) et la fonction hépatique (AST, ALT, LDH et bilirubine sérique), avant le traitement et à intervalles réguliers pendant toute sa durée. Il faut réduire la dose lorsque la bilirubine est > 21 μmol/L, que l'AST est de 2 à 4 fois la limite supérieure de la normale ou que la créatinine sérique est > 442 μmol/L.

DIAGNOSTICS INFIRMIERS POSSIBLES

- Risque d'infection (Réactions indésirables).
- Débit cardiaque diminué (Réactions indésirables).
- Connaissances insuffisantes sur le traitement médicamenteux (Enseignement au patient et à ses proches).

INTERVENTIONS INFIRMIÈRES

ALERTE CLINIQUE: DES DÉCÈS SONT SURVENUS LORS DE CERTAINES CHIMIOTHÉRAPIES. AVANT D'ADMINISTRER L'AGENT, CLARIFIER TOUS LES POINTS AMBIGUS. VÉRIFIER

LA LIMITE DES DOSES UNITAIRES ET QUOTIDIENNES AINSI QUE LA DOSE À ADMINISTRER PENDANT LE TRAITEMENT. DEMANDER À UN AUTRE PROFESSIONNEL DE LA SANTÉ DE VÉRIFIER UNE FOIS DE PLUS L'ORDONNANCE D'ORIGINE, LES CALCULS ET LE RÉGLAGE DE LA POMPE À PERFUSION. L'ÉPIRUBICINE DOIT ÊTRE ADMINISTRÉE SOUS LA SUPERVISION D'UN MÉDECIN AYANT DE L'EXPÉRIENCE DANS L'UTILISATION DES ANTINÉOPLASIQUES.

- Les solutions doivent être préparées sous une hotte à flux laminaire. Il faut porter des gants, une blouse et un masque pendant qu'on manipule ce médicament. Jeter le matériel dans les contenants réservés à cet usage (voir l'annexe H).
- Avant d'amorcer le traitement par l'épirubicine, on peut administrer en prophylaxie un traitement anti-infectieux à base de triméthoprime/sulfaméthoxazole ou d'une fluoroquinolone et un traitement antiémétique.
- Ne pas administrer par voies SC ou IM.

Perfusion intermittente: Administrer la solution non diluée. Elle est de couleur rouge clair. Utiliser l'épirubicine dans les 24 heures suivant la perforation du bouchon en caoutchouc. Jeter toute solution inutilisée.

Vitesse d'administration: Administrer chaque dose de 100 à 120 mg en 15 à 20 minutes dans une tubulure en Y par laquelle s'écoule une solution de NaCl 0,9 % ou de D5%E. Des doses plus faibles peuvent être administrées en un minimum de 3 minutes. Ne pas administrer par bolus direct. Des rougeurs du visage et un érythème le long de la veine surviennent fréquemment si l'administration est trop rapide. Il y a risque de sclérose veineuse si l'épirubicine est administrée dans une petite veine ou à plusieurs reprises dans la même veine. Ne pas administrer dans les veines qui longent une articulation ou les extrémités des membres lorsque le retour veineux ou le drainage lymphatique est compromis.

Incompatibilité dans la même seringue: Ne pas mélanger à d'autres médicaments ou à des solutions alcalines ■ fluorouracile ■ héparine.

ENSEIGNEMENT AU PATIENT ET À SES PROCHES

- Recommander au patient de signaler rapidement à un professionnel de la santé les symptômes suivants: fièvre, maux de gorge, signes d'infection, saignement des gencives, ecchymoses, pétéchies, présence de sang dans les selles, les urines ou les vomissures, fatigue accrue, dyspnée ou hypotension orthostatique. Conseiller au patient d'éviter les foules et les personnes contagieuses. Lui recommander d'utiliser une brosse à dents à poils doux et un rasoir électrique et de prendre garde aux chutes. Le prévenir qu'il ne faut pas consommer de boissons alcoolisées ni prendre des AINS ou des médicaments à base d'aspirine, étant donné que ces agents peuvent déclencher une hémorragie gastro-intestinale.
- Recommander au patient de signaler immédiatement toute douleur au point d'injection.
- Recommander au patient d'examiner sa muqueuse buccale à la recherche d'érythème et d'aphtes. En présence d'aphtes, lui conseiller de remplacer la brosse à dents par une brosse-éponge, de se rincer la bouche avec de l'eau après avoir bu ou mangé et de consulter un professionnel de la santé si la douleur l'empêche de s'alimenter. En cas de douleur, un analgésique opioïde pourrait s'avérer utile. Lui expliquer que sa muqueuse buccale guérira habituellement dans les 3 semaines suivant le début du traitement.
- Prévenir la patiente que ce médicament peut avoir des effets tératogènes. Lui conseiller de prendre des mesures de contraception pendant toute la durée du traitement et pendant au moins 4 mois après l'avoir arrêté. L'informer avant le début du traitement que l'épirubicine peut provoquer une suppression irréversible de la fonction des gonades.
- Conseiller au patient de ne pas prendre de cimétidine pendant le traitement et de consulter un professionnel de la santé avant de prendre un médicament en vente libre.
- Recommander au patient de signaler immédiatement à un professionnel de la santé les vomissements, la déshydratation, la fièvre, les signes d'infection, les symptômes d'insuffisance cardiaque ou les douleurs au point d'injection. Il faut informer le patient du risque de lésions cardiaques irréversibles et de leucémie induite par le traitement.
- Expliquer au patient qu'il risque de perdre ses cheveux. Explorer avec lui les stratégies lui permettant de s'adapter à ce changement. Les cheveux recommencent à pousser 2 ou 3 mois après l'arrêt du traitement.
- Expliquer au patient qu'il ne doit pas se faire vacciner sans recommandation expresse d'un professionnel de la santé.
- Prévenir le patient que ce médicament peut rendre l'urine rouge pendant 1 ou 2 journées.
- Recommander au patient de prévenir un professionnel de la santé en cas d'irritation cutanée dans une région ayant été antérieurement traitée par radiothérapie. Le médicament peut entraîner une hyperpigmentation de la peau et des ongles. Conseiller au patient d'utiliser un écran solaire et de porter

des vêtements protecteurs pour prévenir les réactions de photosensibilité.
- Insister sur l'importance des tests de laboratoire effectués à intervalles réguliers permettant de suivre de près les effets secondaires du médicament.

VÉRIFICATION DE L'EFFICACITÉ THÉRAPEUTIQUE

L'efficacité du traitement peut être démontrée par: la diminution de la taille des tumeurs et la réduction de la propagation des métastases chez les patients présentant une tumeur solide ■ l'amélioration des paramètres hématologiques chez les patients présentant un lymphome ■ la diminution du risque de récidive chez les patients présentant une atteinte des ganglions axillaires par suite de la résection d'une tumeur due à un cancer primaire du sein. ✳

ÉPOÉTINE ALFA

Eprex

CLASSIFICATION:

Traitement de l'anémie, hormone régulatrice d'érythropoïèse

Grossesse – catégorie C

INDICATIONS

Traitement de l'anémie associée à l'insuffisance rénale chronique ■ Traitement de l'anémie secondaire à l'administration de zidovudine (AZT) chez les patients infectés par le VIH ■ Traitement de l'anémie induite par la chimiothérapie chez les patients présentant des tumeurs non myéloïdes ■ Traitement de patients devant subir une intervention chirurgicale majeure programmée afin de faciliter le prélèvement de sang autologue et de réduire l'exposition au sang allogénique.

MÉCANISME D'ACTION

Stimulation de l'érythropoïèse (production d'érythrocytes). ***Effets thérapeutiques:*** Maintien du nombre d'érythrocytes et même augmentation de ce nombre, réduisant ainsi le besoin de transfusion.

PHARMACOCINÉTIQUE

Absorption: Lente (SC). Biodisponibilité de 21 à 31 %.

Distribution: Inconnue.

Métabolisme et excrétion: Inconnus.

Demi-vie: De 4 à 13 heures.

Profil temps-action
(augmentation du nombre d'érythrocytes)

	DÉBUT D'ACTION†	PIC	DURÉE
IV, SC	2 – 6 semaines	en 2 mois	2 semaines‡

† Augmentation du nombre de réticulocytes.
‡ Après l'arrêt du traitement.

CONTRE-INDICATIONS, PRÉCAUTIONS ET MISES EN GARDE

Contre-indications: Survenue d'une érythroblastopénie à la suite d'un traitement par une hormone régulatrice de l'érythropoïèse ■ Hypersensibilité à l'albumine, aux produits dérivés de cellules de mammifères ou à l'un des ingrédients de la préparation ■ Hypertension non maîtrisée ■ Impossibilité de recevoir un traitement antithrombotique, pour quelque raison que ce soit ■ Prématurés et nouveau-nés (préparation contenant de l'alcool benzylique) ■ Patients souffrant d'une maladie coronarienne, artérielle périphérique, carotidienne ou vasculaire cérébrale grave, y compris un infarctus du myocarde ou un accident vasculaire cérébral récents, qui doivent subir une intervention chirurgicale non urgente et qui ne participent pas à un programme d'autotransfusion ■ Taux d'hémoglobine > 120 g/L.

Précautions et mises en garde: Antécédents de convulsions ■ Pendant l'hémodialyse, les patients ont parfois besoin d'une héparinisation accrue pour empêcher la formation de caillots dans le rein artificiel ■ L'innocuité et l'efficacité n'ont pas été établies chez les patients ayant une hémopathie sous-jacente ■ Antécédents de porphyrie ■ Antécédents de goutte ■ **OBST., ALLAITEMENT**: L'innocuité de l'agent n'a pas été établie chez la femme enceinte ou qui allaite ■ Taux d'érythropoïétine > 200 mU/mL.

RÉACTIONS INDÉSIRABLES ET EFFETS SECONDAIRES

SNC: CONVULSIONS, céphalées.

CV: hypertension, épisodes de thrombose (risque accru chez les patients en hémodialyse ou si le taux d'hémoglobine > 120 g/L).

Tég.: rash passager.

End.: rétablissement de la fécondité, retour des règles.

Hémat.: ÉRYTHROBLASTOPÉNIE.

INTERACTIONS

Médicament-médicament: L'administration d'époétine peut augmenter les besoins en **héparine** pour prévenir la coagulation du sang au cours de l'hémodialyse.

E

VOIES D'ADMINISTRATION ET POSOLOGIE

Anémie due à l'insuffisance rénale chronique

- **SC, IV (adultes)**: Initialement, de 50 à 100 unités/kg, 3 fois par semaine; on peut ensuite adapter la dose selon l'hématocrite et la concentration d'hémoglobine.
- **SC, IV (enfants)**: Initialement, 50 unités/kg, 3 fois par semaine; on peut ensuite adapter la dose selon l'hématocrite et la concentration d'hémoglobine.

Anémie consécutive au traitement à la zidovudine

- **IV, SC (adultes)**: Initialement, 100 unités/kg, 3 fois par semaine, pendant 8 semaines; si la réponse est insuffisante, on peut augmenter la dose, à raison de 50 à 100 unités/kg, 3 fois par semaine, toutes les 4 à 8 semaines, jusqu'à concurrence de 300 unités/kg, 3 fois par semaine.

Anémie induite par la chimiothérapie

- **SC (adultes)**: Initialement, 150 unités/kg, 3 fois par semaine, ou 40 000 unités, 1 fois par semaine; après 4 semaines, on peut augmenter la dose jusqu'à concurrence de 300 unités/kg, 3 fois par semaine, ou de 60 000 unités, 1 fois par semaine.

Intervention chirurgicale

- **SC, IV (adultes)**: *Pour réduire l'exposition au sang allogénique* – 600 unités/kg, par voie SC, 1 fois par semaine, soit les 21e, 14e et 7e jours avant l'intervention chirurgicale ainsi que le jour où elle a lieu, *ou* si la période avant l'intervention est < 3 semaines, 300 unités/kg/jour, par voie SC, pendant les 10 jours qui précèdent l'intervention chirurgicale, le jour de l'intervention et pendant les 4 jours qui suivent. *En association avec l'autotransfusion* – 600 unités/kg, par voie IV, 2 fois par semaine pendant les 3 semaines qui précèdent l'intervention.

PRÉSENTATION

Fioles à usages multiples (contenant de l'albumine humaine): 20 000 unités/mL[Pr] ▪ **Seringues préremplies à usage unique**: 1 000 UI/0,5 mL[Pr], 2 000 UI/0,5 mL[Pr], 3 000 UI/0,3 mL[Pr], 4 000 UI/0,4 mL[Pr], 5 000 UI/0,5 mL[Pr], 6 000 UI/0,6 mL[Pr], 8 000 UI/0,8 mL[Pr], 10 000 UI/mL[Pr], 20 000 UI/0,5 mL[Pr] et 40 000 UI/mL[Pr].

SOINS INFIRMIERS

ÉVALUATION DE LA SITUATION

- Mesurer la pression artérielle avant l'administration initiale et tout au long du traitement. Prévenir le médecin ou un professionnel de la santé en cas d'hypertension grave ou si la pression artérielle commence à s'élever. Un traitement antihypertenseur supplémentaire peut s'avérer nécessaire pendant le traitement initial.
- Suivre la réponse du patient au traitement pour déceler les symptômes suivants d'anémie: fatigue, dyspnée, pâleur.
- Déterminer l'état du shunt artérioveineux (frémissements et bruits) et celui du rein artificiel au cours de l'hémodialyse. On pourrait augmenter la dose d'héparine afin de prévenir la coagulation du sang. Les patients souffrant d'une maladie vasculaire sous-jacente devraient être suivis de près afin de déceler les signes d'insuffisance circulatoire.

Tests de laboratoire:

- L'époétine peut entraîner une augmentation du nombre de globules blancs et de plaquettes. Le médicament peut aussi écourter le temps de saignement.
- Noter les concentrations sériques de ferritine, de transferrine et de fer afin de déterminer la nécessité d'amorcer un traitement concomitant au fer. Le taux de saturation de la transferrine devrait être d'au moins 20 % et la concentration de ferritine devrait être d'au moins 100 ng/mL.

Anémie due à l'insuffisance rénale chronique

- Noter l'hématocrite avant l'administration, 2 fois par semaine au cours du traitement initial, pendant 2 à 6 semaines après l'adaptation de la dose et à intervalles réguliers après qu'on a atteint la valeur cible (de 30 à 36 %) et qu'on a déterminé la dose d'entretien. Il faudrait également noter d'autres paramètres hématopoïétiques (numération globulaire, formule leucocytaire et numération plaquettaire) avant le début du traitement et à intervalles réguliers pendant toute sa durée. Si l'hématocrite augmente de plus de 6 points de pourcentage en l'espace de 2 semaines, le risque de réaction hypertensive et de convulsions peut être accru. Il faudrait diminuer la dose et mesurer l'hématocrite 2 fois par semaine, pendant 2 à 6 semaines. Une adaptation posologique peut s'avérer nécessaire. Si l'hématocrite s'élève et approche les 36 %, on doit diminuer la dose pour le maintenir dans les valeurs cibles. Si l'hématocrite continue de s'élever et dépasse 36 %, on devrait interrompre l'administration jusqu'à ce qu'il diminue; on peut ensuite recommencer à administrer l'époétine à une dose plus faible. Si l'hématocrite ne s'élève pas de 5 à 6 points de pourcentage après 8 semaines et si les réserves en fer sont adéquates, on peut augmenter graduellement la dose à intervalles de 4 à 6 semaines jusqu'à l'obtention de la réponse souhaitée.
- Suivre de près les résultats des tests de la fonction rénale et la concentration des électrolytes, car, en

raison d'un sentiment de mieux-être, le patient pourrait ne pas observer les autres traitements de l'insuffisance rénale, d'où risque d'élévation des concentrations d'urée, de créatinine, d'acide urique, de phosphore et de potassium.

Anémie consécutive au traitement par la zidovudine: Avant d'amorcer le traitement, établir la concentration sérique d'érythropoïétine juste avant la transfusion. Les patients traités par la zidovudine, qui présentent des concentrations sériques endogènes d'érythropoïétine supérieures à 500 mU/mL, pourraient ne pas répondre au traitement. Mesurer l'hématocrite toutes les semaines pendant l'adaptation posologique. Si le traitement ne réduit pas les besoins en transfusion ou n'augmente pas de façon efficace l'hématocrite après 8 semaines, on peut augmenter la dose par paliers de 50 à 100 unités/kg, 3 fois par semaine. Évaluer la réponse et adapter la dose par paliers de 50 à 100 unités/kg, toutes les 4 à 8 semaines par la suite. Si on n'obtient pas de réponse satisfaisante avec une dose de 300 unités/kg, 3 fois par semaine, il est peu probable qu'une dose plus élevée entraîne une réponse. Lorsque la réponse souhaitée est atteinte, la dose d'entretien est adaptée selon les variations de la dose de zidovudine et les infections intercurrentes. Si l'hématocrite dépasse 40 %, interrompre la médication jusqu'à ce qu'il chute jusqu'à 36 %, puis la reprendre en diminuant la dose de 25 %.

Anémie induite par la chimiothérapie: Évaluer l'hématocrite et la concentration d'hémoglobine toutes les semaines jusqu'à ce que ces valeurs se stabilisent. Les patients présentant des concentrations sériques initiales plus faibles d'érythropoïétine peuvent répondre plus rapidement au traitement; l'époétine n'est pas recommandée si les concentrations d'érythropoïétine sont supérieures à 200 mU/mL. Si la réponse n'est pas adéquate après 8 semaines, on peut augmenter la dose jusqu'à 300 unités/kg, 3 fois par semaine, ou 60 000 unités, 1 fois par semaine. Si on n'obtient pas de réponse satisfaisante à cette dose, il est peu probable qu'une dose plus élevée entraîne une réponse. Si la concentration d'hémoglobine augmente de plus de 10 g/L au cours d'une période de 2 semaines ou si elle dépasse 120 g/L, on doit diminuer la dose d'environ 25 %. Si elle dépasse 130 g/L, on doit interrompre l'administration des doses jusqu'à l'obtention d'une hémoglobinémie de 120 g/L, puis reprendre le traitement à une dose inférieure de 25 % à la dose précédente.

Intervention chirurgicale: S'assurer avant le traitement que l'hématocrite est > 100 g/L et ≤ 130 g/L.

DIAGNOSTICS INFIRMIERS POSSIBLES

- Intolérance à l'activité (Indications).
- Connaissances insuffisantes sur le traitement médicamenteux (Enseignement au patient et à ses proches).
- Non-observance du traitement médicamenteux (Enseignement au patient et à ses proches).

INTERVENTIONS INFIRMIÈRES

- En cas d'anémie symptomatique grave, les transfusions continuent d'être nécessaires. Il faut administrer en concomitance un supplément de fer pendant toute la durée du traitement.
- PRENDRE LES PRÉCAUTIONS NÉCESSAIRES POUR PRÉVENIR LES CONVULSIONS CHEZ LE PATIENT DONT L'HÉMATOCRITE AUGMENTE DE PLUS DE 4 POINTS DE POURCENTAGE EN MOINS DE 2 SEMAINES OU DONT L'ÉTAT NEUROLOGIQUE SE MODIFIE. LE RISQUE DE CONVULSIONS EST PLUS ÉLEVÉ AU COURS DES 90 PREMIERS JOURS DE TRAITEMENT.
- Ne pas agiter la fiole pour ne pas inactiver le médicament. Conserver au réfrigérateur les fioles multidoses; le médicament est stable pendant 30 jours après qu'on a retiré la première dose.

SC: On utilise souvent cette voie d'administration chez les patients non dialysés.

IV directe: Administrer la solution non diluée.

Vitesse d'administration: On peut administrer le médicament par injection directe en 1 à 5 minutes, ou par bolus IV injecté dans la tubulure ou dans la veine à la fin d'une séance de dialyse.

ENSEIGNEMENT AU PATIENT ET À SES PROCHES

- Expliquer au patient l'utilité d'un traitement concomitant au fer (la production d'une quantité accrue d'érythrocytes ne peut se faire sans un apport de fer).
- Expliquer à la patiente qui est en âge de procréer que les règles et la fécondité peuvent se rétablir. Lui recommander de consulter un professionnel de la santé pour choisir une méthode de contraception appropriée.
- EXPLIQUER AU PATIENT EXPOSÉ AU RISQUE DE CONVULSIONS COMMENT PRÉVENIR LES BLESSURES. LUI CONSEILLER DE NE PAS CONDUIRE ET D'ÉVITER LES ACTIVITÉS QUI EXIGENT SA VIGILANCE.

Anémie due à l'insuffisance rénale chronique: Insister sur le fait qu'il est important d'observer les restrictions diététiques et de respecter rigoureusement le traitement médicamenteux recommandé et les rendez-vous fixés pour la dialyse. Expliquer au patient que les aliments riches en fer et pauvres en potassium sont notamment le foie, la viande de porc, de veau et de bœuf, les feuilles de moutarde et de navet, les pois, les œufs, le brocoli, le chou frisé, les mûres, les fraises, le jus de pomme, la pastèque, les flocons d'avoine et le pain enrichi. L'époétine donne une sensation de mieux-être, mais ne guérit pas la maladie rénale sous-jacente.

Soins à domicile: Expliquer au patient sous dialyse à domicile, jugé apte à s'administrer l'époétine efficacement et sans danger, la posologie, la technique d'administration et la méthode de mise au rebut du matériel. Lui remettre les renseignements destinés au patient sous dialyse à domicile en même temps que le médicament.

E

VÉRIFICATION DE L'EFFICACITÉ THÉRAPEUTIQUE

L'efficacité du traitement peut être démontrée par: l'augmentation de l'hématocrite jusqu'à 30 à 36 %, des concentrations d'hémoglobine et l'amélioration ultérieure des symptômes d'anémie chez les patients souffrant d'insuffisance rénale chronique ■ l'augmentation de l'hématocrite en cas d'anémie consécutive au traitement à la zidovudine ■ l'augmentation de l'hématocrite et des concentrations d'hémoglobine en cas d'anémie induite par la chimiothérapie ■ la réduction du besoin de recourir à des transfusions après une intervention chirurgicale. ✳

ÉPROSARTAN,
voir Antagonistes des récepteurs de l'angiotensine II

ALERTE CLINIQUE

EPTIFIBATIDE

Integrilin

CLASSIFICATION:

Antiplaquettaire (inhibiteur des récepteurs des glycoprotéines IIb/IIIa)

Grossesse – catégorie B

INDICATIONS

Traitement des patients souffrant d'un syndrome coronarien aigu (angine instable; infarctus du myocarde sans élévation du segment ST) incluant ceux dont l'état peut être maîtrisé par la pharmacothérapie et ceux qui devront subir une intervention coronarienne percutanée (ICP) ■ Traitement des patients qui subissent une intervention coronarienne percutanée, comportant l'installation d'une endoprothèse coronarienne ■ Traitement habituellement administré en concomitance avec l'aspirine et l'héparine.

MÉCANISME D'ACTION

Diminution de l'agrégation plaquettaire par l'inhibition réversible de la liaison du fibrinogène aux sites de liaison des glycoprotéines IIb/IIIa situés à la surface des plaquettes. ***Effets thérapeutiques:*** Inhibition de l'agrégation plaquettaire entraînant un moindre risque de nouvel IM, de décès ou d'ischémie rebelle au traitement et, par conséquent, la diminution du nombre d'interventions cardiaques d'urgence.

PHARMACOCINÉTIQUE

Absorption: 100 % (IV).

Distribution: Inconnue.

Métabolisme et excrétion: Élimination rénale à 50 %.

Demi-vie: 2,5 heures.

Profil temps-action (effet antiplaquettaire)

	DÉBUT D'ACTION	PIC	DURÉE
IV	immédiat	après le bolus	brève†

† L'inhibition est réversible après l'arrêt de la perfusion.

CONTRE-INDICATIONS, PRÉCAUTIONS ET MISES EN GARDE

Contre-indications: Hypersensibilité ■ Antécédents de diathèse hémorragique ou signes de saignement anormal au cours des 30 jours précédents ■ Hypertension grave non maîtrisée (pression systolique > 200 mm Hg ou diastolique > 110 mm Hg) ■ Intervention chirurgicale majeure dans les 6 semaines précédentes ■ Antécédents d'AVC dans les 30 jours précédents ou antécédents d'AVC hémorragiques quels qu'ils soient ■ Administration prévue ou concomitante d'un autre inhibiteur des récepteurs des glycoprotéines IIb/IIIa ■ Dialyse rénale ■ Maladie hépatique cliniquement importante.

Précautions et mises en garde: Nombre de plaquettes < 100 × 10^9/L ■ **GÉR.**: Risque accru de saignements ■ Insuffisance rénale (réduire la dose initiale et la vitesse de perfusion si la Cl_{Cr} est < 50 mL/min ou, faute de ce renseignement, si la créatinine sérique ≥ 177 µmol/L) ■ Patients < 70 kg (risque accru de petites hémorragies ou d'hémorragies importantes) ■ Intervention coronarienne percutanée (risque d'un plus grand nombre de complications hémorragiques [petites hémorragies ou hémorragies importantes], particulièrement à l'endroit où est établi l'abord fémoral servant à la mise en place de l'introducteur artériel fémoral) ■ **OBST., PÉD.**: Grossesse, allaitement, enfants (l'innocuité de l'agent n'a pas été établie; ne l'utiliser chez la femme enceinte qu'en cas d'absolue nécessité).

RÉACTIONS INDÉSIRABLES ET EFFETS SECONDAIRES

Chez les patients ayant reçu l'héparine, l'aspirine et l'eptifibatide en concomitance.

CV: hypotension.

Hémat.: thrombopénie, SAIGNEMENTS (incluant les saignements gastro-intestinaux et intracrâniens, l'hématurie et les hématomes).

INTERACTIONS

Médicament-médicament: Risque accru de saignements lors de l'administration concomitante d'autres **médicaments qui affectent l'hémostase** (**héparine** et **composés de type héparinique**, **warfarine**, **AINS**, **agents thrombolytiques**, **abciximab**, **tirofiban**, **lépirudine**, **dipyridamole**, **ticlodipine**, **clopidogrel**, **valproates**).

Médicament-produits naturels: Risque accru de saignements lors de la prise concomitante d'**ail**, d'**arnica**, de **camomille**, de **clou de girofle**, de **dong quai**, de **grande camomille**, de **gingembre**, de **ginkgo**, de **ginseng** et d'**autres produits**.

VOIES D'ADMINISTRATION ET POSOLOGIE

Syndrome coronarien aigu (angine instable ou IM sans élévation du segment ST)

- **IV (adultes ≤ 121 kg)**: 180 µg/kg sous forme de bolus, suivi d'une perfusion de 2 µg/kg/min jusqu'à la sortie de l'hôpital ou jusqu'au moment du pontage aortocoronarien (pendant 72 heures au maximum). Chez les patients subissant une intervention coronarienne percutanée, la perfusion d'eptifibatide doit être poursuivie et maintenue pendant une période de 18 à 24 heures après l'intervention, la durée de traitement pouvant aller jusqu'à 96 heures.
- **IV (adultes > 121 kg)**: Au maximum 22,6 mg sous forme de bolus, suivi d'une perfusion de 15 mg/h, ce qui représente la vitesse de perfusion maximale.
- **INSUFFISANCE RÉNALE:** *(CL_{CR} < 50 mL/MIN OU, FAUTE DE CE RENSEIGNEMENT, UNE CRÉATININÉMIE SUPÉRIEURE À 177 µmol/L)*

  IV (ADULTES ≤ 121 kg): 180 µg/kg SOUS FORME DE BOLUS, SUIVI D'UNE PERFUSION DE 1 µg/kg/MIN JUSQU'À LA SORTIE DE L'HÔPITAL OU JUSQU'AU MOMENT DU PONTAGE AORTOCORONARIEN (PENDANT 72 HEURES AU MAXIMUM).

  IV (ADULTES > 121 kg): AU MAXIMUM 22,6 mg SOUS FORME DE BOLUS, SUIVI D'UNE PERFUSION DE 7,5 mg/H, CE QUI REPRÉSENTE LA VITESSE DE PERFUSION MAXIMALE.

Intervention coronarienne percutanée

- **IV (adultes ≤ 121 kg)**: 180 µg/kg sous forme de bolus, suivi d'une perfusion de 2 µg/kg/min, et d'un second bolus de 180 µg/kg, administré 10 minutes après le premier. La perfusion doit se poursuivre jusqu'à la sortie de l'hôpital ou pendant une période maximale de 18 à 24 heures, selon la première éventualité. Une perfusion d'au moins 12 heures est recommandée.
- **IV (adultes > 121 kg)**: Au maximum 22,6 mg sous forme de bolus, suivi d'une perfusion de 15 mg/h, ce qui représente la vitesse de perfusion maximale.
- **INSUFFISANCE RÉNALE:** *(CL_{CR} < 50 mL/MIN OU, FAUTE DE CE RENSEIGNEMENT, UNE CRÉATININÉMIE SUPÉRIEURE À 177 µmol/L)*

  IV (ADULTES ≤ 121 kg): 180 µg/kg SOUS FORME DE BOLUS, SUIVI D'UNE PERFUSION DE 1 µg/kg/MIN, ET D'UN SECOND BOLUS DE 180 µg/kg, ADMINISTRÉ 10 MINUTES APRÈS LE PREMIER. LA PERFUSION DOIT SE POURSUIVRE JUSQU'À LA SORTIE DE L'HÔPITAL OU PENDANT UNE PÉRIODE MAXIMALE DE 18 À 24 HEURES, SELON LA PREMIÈRE ÉVENTUALITÉ. UNE PERFUSION D'AU MOINS 12 HEURES EST RECOMMANDÉE.

  IV (ADULTES > 121 kg): AU MAXIMUM 22,6 mg SOUS FORME DE BOLUS, SUIVI D'UNE PERFUSION DE 7,5 mg/H, CE QUI REPRÉSENTE LA VITESSE DE PERFUSION MAXIMALE.

PRÉSENTATION

Solution pour injection: fioles de 10 mL à 2 mg/mL[Pr], fioles de 100 mL à 0,75 mg/mL[Pr].

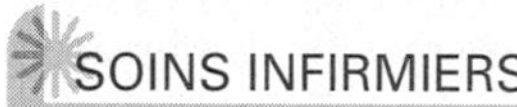

SOINS INFIRMIERS

ÉVALUATION DE LA SITUATION

- RESTER À L'AFFÛT DES SAIGNEMENTS. ILS SE PRODUISENT LE PLUS SOUVENT AU NIVEAU DES POINTS DONNANT ACCÈS AUX ARTÈRES EN VUE DU CATHÉTÉRISME CARDIAQUE OU AU NIVEAU DES TRACTUS GASTRO-INTESTINAL OU URINAIRE. IL FAUT LIMITER DANS LA MESURE DU POSSIBLE LES PONCTIONS ARTÉRIELLES ET VEINEUSES, LES INJECTIONS IM, L'INTRODUCTION DE CATHÉTERS URINAIRES, L'INTUBATION NASOTRACHÉALE ET NASOGASTRIQUE. ÉVITER LES POINTS D'INJECTION IV QUI NE PEUVENT ÊTRE COMPRIMÉS. SI LES SAIGNEMENTS NE PEUVENT ÊTRE ARRÊTÉS PAR PRESSION, IL FAUT CESSER IMMÉDIATEMENT L'ADMINISTRATION DE L'EPTIFIBATIDE ET DE L'HÉPARINE.

Tests de laboratoire:

- Avant d'amorcer le traitement par l'eptifibatide, relever la concentration d'hémoglobine ou l'hématocrite, le nombre de plaquettes, la concentration sérique de créatinine, le temps de prothrombine et le temps de céphaline activée. Mesurer aussi le temps de coagulation activée chez les patients devant subir une intervention coronarienne percutanée.
- Maintenir le temps de céphaline activée entre 50 et 70 secondes sauf si le patient doit subir une intervention coronarienne percutanée. Maintenir le temps de coagulation activée entre 200 et 300 secondes pendant cette intervention.
- Ne pas retirer la gaine artérielle sauf si le temps de céphaline activée est inférieur à 45 secondes ou que le temps de coagulation activée est inférieur à 150 secondes.
- Si le nombre de plaquettes descend sous la barre des 100 et si ce nombre est confirmé, il faut cesser l'administration de l'eptifibatide et de l'héparine, surveiller l'état du patient et démarrer le traitement de rigueur.

DIAGNOSTICS INFIRMIERS POSSIBLES

- Irrigation tissulaire inefficace (Indications).
- Connaissances insuffisantes sur le traitement médicamenteux (Enseignement au patient et à ses proches).

INTERVENTIONS INFIRMIÈRES

ALERTE CLINIQUE: DES SURDOSES ACCIDENTELLES D'UN INHIBITEUR DES RÉCEPTEURS DES GLYCOPROTÉINES IIb/IIIa ONT CAUSÉ DES COMPLICATIONS OU DES DÉCÈS PAR HÉMORRAGIE INTERNE OU PAR SAIGNEMENTS INTRACRÂNIENS. AVANT L'ADMINISTRATION, CLARIFIER TOUTE AMBIGUÏTÉ SUR LES ORDONNANCES ET FAIRE VÉRIFIER L'ORDONNANCE D'ORIGINE, LES CALCULS DES DOSES ET LA PROGRAMMATION DE LA POMPE À PERFUSION PAR UN AUTRE PROFESSIONNEL DE LA SANTÉ.

- La plupart des patients reçoivent de l'héparine et de l'aspirine en concomitance avec l'eptifibatide.
- Après l'intervention coronarienne percutanée, on peut retirer la gaine de l'artère fémorale durant le traitement par l'eptifibatide seulement lorsqu'on a cessé l'administration de l'héparine et que ses effets sont presque entièrement renversés.
- Ne pas administrer les solutions qui ont changé de couleur ou qui renferment des particules. Jeter toute portion inutilisée.

IV directe: ALERTE CLINIQUE: Prélever dans une seringue la dose destinée au bolus d'une fiole de 10 mL. Administrer la solution non diluée.

Vitesse d'administration: Administrer par intraveineuse directe en 1 ou 2 minutes.

Perfusion intermittente: Administrer la solution non diluée, prélevée directement de la fiole de 100 mL, à l'aide d'une pompe à perfusion. Percer le centre du bouchon en caoutchouc de la fiole de 100 mL à l'aide d'un dispositif d'injection intraveineuse à évent.

Vitesse d'administration: La vitesse d'administration est établie d'après le poids du patient. Voir la section «Voies d'administration et posologie».

Compatibilité (tubulure en Y): altéplase ▪ atropine ▪ D5%/NaCl 0,9% ▪ dobutamine ▪ héparine ▪ lidocaïne ▪ mépéridine ▪ métoprolol ▪ midazolam ▪ morphine ▪ NaCl 0,9% ▪ nitroglycérine ▪ potassium, chlorure de (jusqu'à 60 mmol/L) ▪ vérapamil.

Incompatibilité (tubulure en Y): furosémide.

ENSEIGNEMENT AU PATIENT ET À SES PROCHES

- Expliquer au patient le but du traitement par l'eptifibatide.
- RECOMMANDER AU PATIENT DE PRÉVENIR IMMÉDIATEMENT UN PROFESSIONNEL DE LA SANTÉ EN CAS DE SAIGNEMENTS.

VÉRIFICATION DE L'EFFICACITÉ THÉRAPEUTIQUE

L'efficacité du traitement peut être démontrée par: l'inhibition de l'agrégation plaquettaire, résultant en une réduction du risque d'un nouvel IM, de décès ou d'ischémie rebelle au traitement et, par conséquent, du nombre d'interventions cardiaques d'urgence.

ERGOCALCIFÉROL (VITAMINE D_2),

voir Vitamine D (composés de)

ERGONOVINE

Ergonovine

CLASSIFICATION:

Agent utilisé pendant la grossesse et l'allaitement, (ocytocique)

Grossesse – catégorie inconnue

INDICATIONS

Prévention ou traitement de l'hémorragie qui survient après l'accouchement ou après un avortement dû à l'atonie utérine. **Usages non approuvés:** Diagnostic des spasmes coronariens chez les patients souffrant d'angor de Prinzmetal sans occlusion coronarienne importante.

MÉCANISME D'ACTION

Stimulation directe des muscles lisses utérins et vasculaires. L'ergonovine produit également une vasoconstriction des artères coronaires. ***Effets thérapeutiques:*** Contractions utérines.

PHARMACOCINÉTIQUE

Absorption: Bonne (IM).
Distribution: Inconnue.
Métabolisme et excrétion: Inconnus. Métabolisme probablement hépatique.
Demi-vie: Inconnue.

Profil temps-action (contractions utérines)

	DÉBUT D'ACTION	PIC	DURÉE
IM	2 - 5 min	inconnu	3 h ou plus
IV	immédiat	inconnu	45 min

CONTRE-INDICATIONS, PRÉCAUTIONS ET MISES EN GARDE

Contre-indications: Antécédents de réaction allergique ou idiosyncrasie aux préparations d'ergot ■ Déclenchement ou intensification du travail de l'accouchement ■ Toxémie ■ Hypertension ■ Patientes exposées au risque d'un avortement spontané ■ **OBST.:** Prééclampsie ou éclampsie.
Précautions et mises en garde: Maladie hépatique ou rénale grave ■ Septicémie ■ **OBST.:** Troisième stade du travail ■ Usage prolongé (à éviter) ■ Patients sous anesthésie générale ■ Antécédents de maladie coronarienne ■ Hypertension (prédisposition accrue aux effets hypertenseurs).

RÉACTIONS INDÉSIRABLES ET EFFETS SECONDAIRES

SNC: étourdissements, céphalées.
ORLO: acouphènes.
Resp.: dyspnée.
CV: arythmies, douleurs thoraciques, hypertension, palpitations.
GI: <u>nausées</u>, <u>vomissements</u>.
Tég.: transpiration.
Divers: réactions allergiques.

INTERACTIONS

Médicament-médicament: Risque de vasoconstriction excessive lors de l'administration concomitante d'autres **vasopresseurs**, comme la **dopamine** ou la **nicotine** ■ Augmentation du risque de réactions indésirables lors de l'usage concomitant de **bromocriptine**.

VOIES D'ADMINISTRATION ET POSOLOGIE

Effet ocytocique

- **IM, IV (adultes):** 200 µg (0,2 mg), toutes les 2 à 4 heures, jusqu'à concurrence de 5 doses.

Agent d'induction de spasmes coronariens

- **IV (adultes):** 50 µg (0,05 mg), toutes les 5 minutes, jusqu'à l'apparition d'une douleur thoracique ou jusqu'à l'administration d'une dose totale de 400 µg (0,4 mg) (usage non approuvé).

E

PRÉSENTATION

Solution pour injection: 0,25 mg/mL[Pr].

SOINS INFIRMIERS

ÉVALUATION DE LA SITUATION

- Mesurer la pression artérielle, le pouls et la fréquence respiratoire toutes les 15 à 30 minutes jusqu'à ce que la patiente soit installée dans l'unité des soins postpartum et, par la suite, toutes les 1 ou 2 heures. Signaler au médecin les symptômes suivants: hypertension, douleurs thoraciques, arythmies, céphalées ou modification de l'état neurologique.
- Évaluer la quantité et le type de pertes vaginales. Signaler immédiatement au médecin les symptômes suivants d'hémorragie: saignements accrus, hypotension, pâleur, tachycardie.
- Palper le fond de l'utérus; en noter la position et la fermeté. Prévenir le médecin ou un professionnel de la santé si l'utérus ne se contracte pas en réponse à l'ergonovine. Rester à l'affût de l'apparition de crampes fortes; dans ce cas, la dose peut être réduite.
- Suivre de près les signes suivants d'ergotisme: sensation de froid, engourdissement des doigts et des orteils, nausées, vomissements, diarrhée, céphalées, douleurs musculaires, faiblesse.
- Si la patiente ne répond pas au traitement par l'ergonovine, vérifier les concentrations sériques de calcium. La correction de l'hypocalcémie peut favoriser la réponse à ce médicament.

Tests de laboratoire: L'ergonovine peut entraîner une diminution des concentrations sériques de prolactine, inhibant ainsi la production de lait maternel.

TOXICITÉ ET SURDOSAGE: La toxicité se manifeste d'abord par l'ergotisme et peut entraîner des convulsions et la gangrène. Il faut traiter les convulsions par un anticonvulsivant. Un vasodilatateur et de l'héparine peuvent être nécessaires pour améliorer la circulation au niveau des extrémités.

DIAGNOSTICS INFIRMIERS POSSIBLES

- Irrigation tissulaire inefficace (Indications).
- Risque d'accident (Effets secondaires).
- Connaissances insuffisantes sur le traitement médicamenteux (Enseignement au patient et à ses proches).

E

INTERVENTIONS INFIRMIÈRES

Ne pas administrer une solution qui a changé de couleur ou qui contient un précipité.

IM: Il est conseillé de privilégier la voie IM. Des contractions utérines fermes sont déclenchées en l'espace de quelques minutes. Pour obtenir le plein effet thérapeutique du médicament, on peut répéter l'administration toutes les 2 à 4 heures.

IV directe: La voie IV est réservée aux cas graves d'hémorragie utérine. Diluer l'agent dans 5 mL de solution de NaCl 0,9 %.

***Vitesse d'administration**:* Administrer la solution en au moins 1 minute par injection IV lente dans une tubulure en Y par laquelle s'écoule une solution de D5%E ou de NaCl 0,9 %. Consulter les directives du fabricant avant de reconstituer la préparation.

ENSEIGNEMENT AU PATIENT ET À SES PROCHES

- Expliquer à la patiente les symptômes de toxicité. L'inciter à signaler immédiatement l'apparition de ces symptômes.
- Prévenir la patiente que les crampes utérines prouvent que le traitement est efficace.
- Expliquer à la patiente qu'elle doit compter le nombre de serviettes hygiéniques qu'elle utilise pour déterminer l'intensité des saignements. Lui conseiller de signaler immédiatement à un professionnel de la santé l'intensification des saignements ou le passage de caillots.
- Conseiller à la patiente de signaler toute difficulté concernant l'allaitement.
- Conseiller à la patiente de ne pas fumer pendant le traitement à l'ergonovine, car la nicotine est également un vasoconstricteur.

VÉRIFICATION DE L'EFFICACITÉ THÉRAPEUTIQUE

***L'efficacité du traitement peut être démontrée par**:* des contractions et des crampes utérines permettant de prévenir ou d'arrêter l'hémorragie utérine après l'accouchement ou l'avortement ■ la vasoconstriction des artères coronaires lorsque le médicament est utilisé comme agent diagnostique. ✳

ERGOTAMINE

tartrate d'ergotamine/caféine

Cafergot

dihydroergotamine

DHE, Migranal

***CLASSIFICATION**:*

Agent utilisé dans le traitement des céphalées vasculaires (dérivé de l'ergot), antimigraineux

Grossesse - catégorie X

INDICATIONS

Crises aiguës de migraine, avec ou sans aura ■ **Dihydroergotamine IV**: Traitement des céphalées vasculaires apparentées, incluant les céphalées vasculaires de Horton.

MÉCANISME D'ACTION

Aux doses thérapeutiques, vasoconstriction des vaisseaux dilatés, par la stimulation des récepteurs alpha-adrénergiques et sérotoninergiques (5-HT) ■ Aux doses plus élevées, possibilité de blocage des récepteurs alpha-adrénergiques et de vasodilatation. ***Effets thérapeutiques**:* Constriction des ramifications dilatées de la carotide avec résolution des céphalées vasculaires.

PHARMACOCINÉTIQUE

Absorption: *Ergotamine* – faible (PO), mais la caféine administrée en concomitance permet d'en augmenter l'absorption. Très faible par voie sublinguale. *Dihydroergotamine* – rapide (IM ou SC). 32 % est absorbé par la muqueuse nasale.

Distribution: L'ergotamine traverse la barrière hémato-encéphalique et passe dans le lait maternel.

Liaison aux protéines: *Ergotamine* – de 93 à 98 %; *dihydroergotamine* – 90 %.

Métabolisme et excrétion: Une fraction très élevée des deux médicaments (90 %) est métabolisée par le foie (isoenzymes 3A4 du cytochrome P450). Certains métabolites sont actifs.

Demi-vie: *Ergotamine* – 2 phases: première phase, 2,7 heures; seconde phase, 21 heures. *Dihydroergotamine* – 2 phases: première phase, de 2,3 minutes à 1,45 heure; seconde phase, de 10 à 32 heures.

Profil temps-action (soulagement des céphalées)

	DÉBUT D'ACTION	PIC	DURÉE
Ergotamine PO	1 - 2 h (variable)	1 - 5 h	inconnue
Dihydroergotamine Voie intranasale	en 30 min	inconnu	inconnue
Dihydroergotamine IM, SC	15 - 30 min	15 min - 2 h	8 h
Dihydroergotamine IV	< 5 min	15 min - 2 h	8 h

CONTRE-INDICATIONS, PRÉCAUTIONS ET MISES EN GARDE

Contre-indications: Hypersensibilité à l'ergotamine, à la dihydroergotamine et aux alcaloïdes de l'ergot ■ Hypersensibilité à la caféine (association ergotamine/caféine) ■ Infections graves/septicémie ■ État de choc ■ Chirurgie vasculaire ■ Maladie vasculaire périphérique ■ Maladie vasculaire cérébrale ■ Artérite temporale ■ Maladie cardiovasculaire ■ Hypertension non maîtrisée ■ Arythmies cardiaques ■ Maladie rénale ou hépatique grave ■ Malnutrition ■ Grossesse ■ Allaitement ■ Ulcère gastroduodénal ■ Prurit grave ■ Utilisation dans les 24 heures précédant ou suivant la prise d'un agoniste 5-HT_1 d'un médicament contenant de l'ergotamine ou d'un dérivé de l'ergot ■ Administration concomitante d'inhibiteurs puissants des isoenzymes 3A4 du cytochrome P450 (p. ex., ritonavir, nelfinavir, indinavir, érythromycine, clarithromycine, kétoconazole, itraconazole) ■ Administration concomitante d'un vasoconstricteur périphérique ou central ■ Migraine hémiplégique, basilaire ou ophtalmoplégique.
Précautions et mises en garde: Maladie associée à une atteinte vasculaire périphérique, telle que le diabète ■ **PÉD.:** Enfants < 16 ans (l'innocuité de la dihydroergotamine n'a pas été établie), enfants < 6 ans (l'innocuité de l'ergotamine n'a pas été établie) ■ Intolérance connue à l'alcool (injection de dihydroergotamine seulement) ■ Complications fibreuses (fibrose pleurale, rétropéritonéale, valvulaire cardiaque).

RÉACTIONS INDÉSIRABLES ET EFFETS SECONDAIRES

SNC: étourdissements.
ORLO: rhinite (voie intranasale).
CV: INFARCTUS DU MYOCARDE, angine de poitrine, spasmes artériels, claudication intermittente, bradycardie sinusale, tachycardie sinusale.
GI: douleurs abdominales, nausées, vomissements, altération du goût (voie intranasale), diarrhée, polydipsie.
Loc.: rigidité des membres, douleurs musculaires, raideur du cou, raideur des épaules.
SN: faiblesse dans les jambes, sensation d'engourdissement ou de picotement au niveau des doigts et des orteils.
Divers: fatigue.

INTERACTIONS

Médicament-médicament: L'UTILISATION CONCOMITANTE D'INHIBITEURS PUISSANTS DES ISOENZYMES 3A4 DU CYTOCHROME P450, INCLUANT LES **INHIBITEURS DE LA PROTÉASE** (**RITONAVIR, NELFINAVIR** ET **INDINAVIR**), LES **MACROLIDES** (**ÉRYTHROMYCINE, CLARITHROMYCINE**) ET LES **ANTIFONGIQUES DE TYPE AZOLÉ** (**KÉTOCONAZOLE, ITRACONAZOLE**) PEUT ENTRAÎNER UN VASOSPASME OU UNE ISCHÉMIE CÉRÉBRALE OU PÉRIPHÉRIQUE ET EST CONTRE-INDIQUÉE ■ L'usage concomitant de **bêtabloquants**, de **contraceptifs oraux**, de **vasoconstricteurs** ou de **nicotine** (tabagisme abusif) peut accroître le risque de vasoconstriction périphérique ■ Lors de l'administration concomitante d'un traitement prophylactique au **méthysergide** (autre alcaloïde de l'ergot), la dose d'ergotamine devrait être réduite de 50 % ■ La dihydroergotamine inhibe les effets antiangineux des **dérivés nitrés** ■ L'administration concomitante de **vasoconstricteurs** peut entraîner des effets additifs (éviter cette association) ■ Les **agonistes 5-HT_1** (**almotriptan, élétriptan, naratriptan, rizatriptan, sumatriptan** et **zolmitriptan**), administrés en même temps, peuvent prolonger la vasoconstriction (prévoir un intervalle de 24 heures entre la prise des deux médicaments).

VOIES D'ADMINISTRATION ET POSOLOGIE

Ergotamine/caféine

- **PO, IR (adultes et enfants > 12 ans):** Initialement, 2 mg, puis 1 mg toutes les 30 minutes jusqu'à ce que la crise disparaisse ou jusqu'à concurrence d'une dose totale de 6 mg en 24 heures. Ne pas dépasser 10 mg en une semaine.
- **PO, IR (enfants 6 à 12 ans):** Initialement, 1 mg, puis 1 mg, toutes les 30 minutes jusqu'à ce que la crise disparaisse ou jusqu'à concurrence d'une dose totale de 3 mg en 24 heures. Ne pas dépasser 5 mg en une semaine.

Dihydroergotamine

- **IM, SC (adultes):** 1 mg; on peut répéter l'administration de 30 à 60 minutes plus tard jusqu'à concurrence de 3 mg (ne pas dépasser 3 mg/jour ou par crise et 6 mg/semaine).
- **IV (adultes):** 1 mg; on peut répéter l'administration 1 heure plus tard (ne pas dépasser 2 mg par crise migraineuse et 6 mg/semaine). *Céphalées vasculaires de Horton* – 0,5 mg.
- **Voie intranasale (adultes):** 1 vaporisation (0,5 mg) dans chaque narine, à répéter après 15 minutes s'il n'y a pas d'amélioration (dose totale de 2 mg). On ne doit pas recourir à plus de 4 vaporisations lors d'une même crise; de 6 à 8 heures au moins doivent s'écouler avant le traitement d'une autre crise

migraineuse par la DHE en vaporisateur nasal ou par tout autre agent renfermant de la DHE ou de l'ergotamine. Ne pas dépasser 8 vaporisations en 24 heures ou 24 vaporisations par semaine.

PRÉSENTATION

- **Ergotamine**

  Comprimés en association avec la caféine: 1 mg d'ergotamine[Pr] et 100 mg de caféine[Pr] ■ **Suppositoires en association avec la caféine**: 2 mg d'ergotamine[Pr] et 100 mg de caféine[Pr] ■ **En association avec**: barbituriques[Pr] et alcaloïde de la belladone[Pr].
- **Dihydroergotamine**

  Solution pour injection: 1 mg/mL[Pr] ■ **Vaporisateur nasal**: flacons de 1 mL renfermant 4 mg/mL[Pr] (avec pulvérisateur nasal).

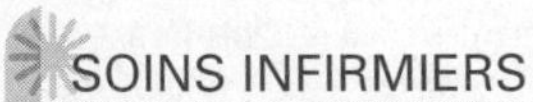

SOINS INFIRMIERS

ÉVALUATION DE LA SITUATION

- Déterminer la fréquence, le siège, la durée et les caractéristiques (douleurs, nausées, vomissements, troubles visuels) des céphalées chroniques. Au cours d'une crise aiguë, noter le type, le siège et l'intensité de la douleur, avant l'administration du médicament et 60 minutes plus tard.
- Mesurer la pression artérielle et le pouls périphérique à intervalles réguliers tout au long du traitement. Prévenir un professionnel de la santé si une hypertension notable se manifeste.
- Observer le patient à la recherche des signes suivants d'ergotisme: sensation de froid et engourdissement des orteils et des doigts, nausées, vomissements, céphalées, douleurs musculaires, faiblesse.
- Suivre de près les nausées et les vomissements. L'ergotamine stimule la zone gâchette chémoréceptrice. Chez les adultes, on peut administrer 10 mg de métoclopramide par voie IV de 3 à 5 minutes avant l'administration de la dihydroergotamine par voie IV. Chez les enfants, on peut administrer par voie orale le métoclopramide ou une phénothiazine antiémétique en prophylaxie, 1 heure avant l'administration de dihydroergotamine par voie IV. L'administration par voie orale peut réduire le risque d'effets secondaires extrapyramidaux ou autres, associés à la voie IV.

Toxicité et surdosage: La toxicité se manifeste par la gangrène et les symptômes suivants d'ergotisme grave: douleurs thoraciques, douleurs abdominales, paresthésie persistante des membres. Le médecin peut prescrire des vasodilatateurs, du dextran ou de l'héparine pour améliorer l'état de la circulation.

DIAGNOSTICS INFIRMIERS POSSIBLES

- Douleur aiguë (Indications).
- Risque d'accident (Effets secondaires).
- Connaissances insuffisantes sur le traitement médicamenteux (Enseignement au patient et à ses proches).

INTERVENTIONS INFIRMIÈRES

- Administrer le médicament aussitôt que le patient signale des symptômes prodromiques ou une céphalée.

IV directe: On peut administrer la dihydroergotamine sans la diluer au préalable. On peut aussi effectuer une dilution dans 50 mL d'une solution de NaCl 0,9% ou de D5%E. Consulter les directives de chaque fabricant avant de reconstituer la préparation.

Vitesse d'administration: *Sans dilution:* administrer en 1 minute. *Avec dilution:* administrer en 15 à 30 minutes.

ENSEIGNEMENT AU PATIENT ET À SES PROCHES

- Conseiller au patient de prendre l'ergotamine aux premiers signes d'une céphalée imminente et de ne pas dépasser la dose maximale prescrite par le médecin.
- Inciter le patient à se reposer dans une pièce sombre et tranquille après avoir pris l'ergotamine.
- Expliquer au patient les symptômes de toxicité. Lui conseiller de signaler ces symptômes le plus rapidement possible à un professionnel de la santé.
- Conseiller au patient de ne pas fumer et d'éviter de s'exposer au froid, car la vasoconstriction induite par le médicament peut altérer davantage la circulation périphérique.
- Prévenir le patient que l'ergotamine peut parfois provoquer des étourdissements. Lui conseiller de ne pas conduire et d'éviter les activités qui exigent sa vigilance jusqu'à ce qu'on ait la certitude que le médicament n'entraîne pas cet effet chez lui.
- Recommander au patient d'éviter de boire de l'alcool, car l'alcool peut déclencher des céphalées vasculaires.
- Conseiller à la patiente d'informer un professionnel de la santé si elle pense être enceinte ou si elle souhaite le devenir. L'usage de l'ergotamine pendant la grossesse est déconseillé.

IM, SC: Conseiller au patient de s'injecter la préparation aux premiers signes de céphalée et de répéter les injections toutes les 30 à 60 minutes, jusqu'à concurrence de 3 doses. Lui expliquer qu'une fois qu'on a établi la dose minimale efficace, il devrait adapter les doses en conséquence lors des crises suivantes.

Voie intranasale:

- Montrer au patient comment utiliser le vaporisateur nasal: amorcer le vaporisateur 4 fois avant d'administrer la dose. Administrer une vaporisation dans chaque narine, suivie, au besoin, 15 minutes plus tard, d'une nouvelle vaporisation dans chaque narine, soit 4 doses au total. Il ne faut pas pencher la tête ni renifler après la vaporisation. Prévenir le patient qu'il ne doit pas dépasser la dose prescrite. Une fois le vaporisateur ouvert, on doit le jeter dans les 8 heures qui suivent. Ne pas réfrigérer. Le dispositif peut être employé pour administrer les 4 doses prévues; il doit ensuite être jeté.
- Expliquer au patient qu'il ne doit pas prendre ces médicaments en l'absence de symptômes ou lorsque la céphalée ne correspond pas à une migraine typique.
- Recommander au patient de prévenir un professionnel de la santé si l'un des symptômes suivants se manifeste: sensation d'engourdissement ou de picotements au niveau des doigts ou des orteils; douleurs ou oppression thoracique; douleurs ou crampes musculaires dans les bras et les jambes; faiblesse dans les jambes; accélération ou ralentissement passager de la fréquence cardiaque; œdème ou démangeaisons.

VÉRIFICATION DE L'EFFICACITÉ THÉRAPEUTIQUE

L'efficacité du traitement peut être démontrée par: le soulagement de la douleur provoquée par les céphalées vasculaires.

ERTAPÉNEM

Invanz

CLASSIFICATION:

Antibiotique (carbapénem)

Grossesse – catégorie B

INDICATIONS

Traitement des infections suivantes de modérées à graves: infections intra-abdominales compliquées ▪ infections de la peau et des tissus mous compliquées ▪ pneumonie extrahospitalière ▪ infections urinaires compliquées (dont la pyélonéphrite) ▪ infections pelviennes aiguës, dont l'endomyométrite du post-partum ▪ Avortements septiques ▪ Infections gynécologiques postopératoires.

MÉCANISME D'ACTION

Effets thérapeutiques: Effet bactéricide contre les bactéries sensibles. **Spectre d'action:** L'agent agit sur les microorganismes aérobies à Gram positif suivants: *Staphylococcus aureus* (souches sensibles à la méthicilline seulement), *Staphylococcus epidermidis, Streptococcus agalactiæ, S. pneumoniæ* (souches sensibles à la pénicilline seulement) et *S. pyogenes* ▪ L'agent agit également sur les microorganismes aérobies à Gram négatif suivants: *Escherichia coli, Hæmophilus influenzæ* (souches non productrices de bêta-lactamase), *Klebsiella pneumoniæ, Moraxella catarrhalis* et *Providencia rettgeri* ▪ Le spectre englobe aussi les microorganismes anaérobies suivants: *Bacteroides fragilis, B. distasonis, B. ovatus, B. thetaiotamicron, B. uniformis, B. vulgatis Clostridium clostrioforme, Eubacterium lentum, Peptostreptococcus, Porphyromonas asaccharolytica* et *Prevotella bivia*.

PHARMACOCINÉTIQUE

Absorption: 90 % (IM); 100 % (IV).

Distribution: L'ertapénem passe dans le lait maternel.

Métabolisme et excrétion: Excrétion majoritairement rénale.

Demi-vie: 4 heures (prolongée en cas d'insuffisance rénale).

Profil temps-action

	DÉBUT D'ACTION	PIC	DURÉE
IM	rapide	2 h	24 h
IV	rapide	fin de la perfusion	24 h

CONTRE-INDICATIONS, PRÉCAUTIONS ET MISES EN GARDE

Contre-indications: Hypersensibilité ▪ Risque de sensibilité croisée avec les pénicillines, les céphalosporines et les autres carbapénems ▪ Hypersensibilité à la lidocaïne qui pourrait être utilisée à titre de diluant en vue de l'administration IM.

Précautions et mises en garde: Antécédents de plusieurs réactions d'hypersensibilité ▪ Troubles convulsifs ▪ **GÉR.:** Sensibilité accrue et diminution de la fonction rénale liée à l'âge ▪ **OBST., PÉD.:** Grossesse et allaitement ou nourrissons < 3 mois (l'innocuité de l'agent n'a pas été établie; n'utiliser pendant l'allaitement que si les bienfaits pour la mère dépassent les risques auxquels est exposé le fœtus; n'administrer pendant la grossesse qu'en cas de besoin incontestable).

E

RÉACTIONS INDÉSIRABLES ET EFFETS SECONDAIRES

SNC: CONVULSIONS, céphalées.

GI: COLITE PSEUDOMEMBRANEUSE, diarrhée, nausées, vomissements.

GU: vaginite.

Locaux: phlébite au point d'injection IV, douleur au point d'injection IM.

Divers: réactions d'hypersensibilité comprenant l'ANAPHYLAXIE.

INTERACTIONS

Médicament-médicament: Le **probénécide** diminue l'excrétion et élève les concentrations sanguines.

VOIES D'ADMINISTRATION ET POSOLOGIE

- **IV, IM (adultes, enfants ≥ 13 ans)**: 1 g, 1 fois par jour.
- **IV, IM (enfants 3 mois à 12 ans)**: 15 mg/kg (dose maximale: 500 mg) toutes les 12 heures.

INSUFFISANCE RÉNALE

- **IM, IV (ADULTES, ENFANTS ≥ 3 MOIS)**: *CL_{CR} < 30 mL/MIN/1,73M²* – 500 mg, 1 FOIS PAR JOUR.

PRÉSENTATION

Poudre pour perfusion IV (à reconstituer): 1 g/fiole[Pr].

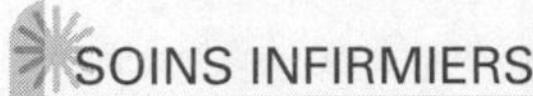

ÉVALUATION DE LA SITUATION

- Rechercher les signes d'infection (altération des signes vitaux, aspect de la plaie, des expectorations, de l'urine et des selles, accroissement du nombre de globules blancs) en début de traitement et pendant toute sa durée.
- Recueillir les antécédents du patient avant de commencer le traitement, afin de déterminer s'il a déjà pris une pénicilline, une céphalosporine ou un carbapénem et s'il a déjà manifesté une réaction à ces antibiotiques. Même les personnes n'ayant jamais manifesté de sensibilité à la pénicilline peuvent présenter une réaction allergique.
- Prélever des échantillons pour les cultures et les antibiogrammes avant le début du traitement. On peut administrer la première dose avant que les résultats soient connus.
- OBSERVER LE PATIENT POUR DÉCELER LES SIGNES ET LES SYMPTÔMES D'ANAPHYLAXIE (RASH, PRURIT, ŒDÈME LARYNGÉ, RESPIRATION SIFFLANTE). INTERROMPRE L'ADMINISTRATION DU MÉDICAMENT ET PRÉVENIR IMMÉDIATEMENT LE MÉDECIN SI DE TELS SIGNES OU SYMPTÔMES SE MANIFESTENT. GARDER À PORTÉE DE LA MAIN DE L'ADRÉNALINE, UN ANTIHISTAMINIQUE ET LE MATÉRIEL DE RÉANIMATION POUR PARER À UNE ÉVENTUELLE RÉACTION ANAPHYLACTIQUE.

Tests de laboratoire:

- Le médicament peut élever les taux d'AST, d'ALT et de phosphatase alcaline sérique.
- Il peut accroître le nombre de plaquettes et d'éosinophiles.

DIAGNOSTICS INFIRMIERS POSSIBLES

- Risque d'infection (Indications, Effets secondaires).

INTERVENTIONS INFIRMIÈRES

IM: Reconstituer le contenu de la fiole de 1 g avec 3,2 mL de lidocaïne à 1 %, sans adrénaline. Bien agiter pour former une solution. Retirer immédiatement le contenu et injecter en profondeur dans une masse musculaire volumineuse. Utiliser la solution reconstituée en l'espace de 1 heure.

Perfusion intermittente: Reconstituer le contenu de la fiole de 1 g avec 10 mL d'eau stérile ou bactériostatique pour injection ou avec du NaCl 0,9 % et bien agiter. Rediluer la solution ainsi obtenue dans 50 mL de NaCl 0,9 %. Administrer dans les 6 heures qui suivent la reconstitution.

Vitesse d'administration: Administrer en 30 minutes. Ne pas administrer par IV directe. Consulter les directives du fabricant avant de reconstituer la préparation.

Incompatibilité (tubulure en Y): Ne pas perfuser avec d'autres médicaments.

ENSEIGNEMENT AU PATIENT ET À SES PROCHES

- Conseiller au patient de signaler les signes de surinfection (excroissance noire et pileuse sur la langue, démangeaisons ou écoulements vaginaux, selles molles ou nauséabondes) et d'allergie. Lui recommander de consulter un professionnel de la santé avant de prendre un antidiarrhéique.
- RECOMMANDER AU PATIENT DE PRÉVENIR UN PROFESSIONNEL DE LA SANTÉ EN CAS DE FIÈVRE OU DE DIARRHÉE, PARTICULIÈREMENT SI SES SELLES CONTIENNENT DU SANG, DU PUS OU DU MUCUS. CONSEILLER AU PATIENT DE NE PAS TRAITER LA DIARRHÉE SANS AVOIR CONSULTÉ UN PROFESSIONNEL DE LA SANTÉ AU PRÉALABLE. LA DIARRHÉE PEUT SE MANIFESTER PLUSIEURS SEMAINES APRÈS L'ARRÊT DE L'ANTIBIOTHÉRAPIE.

VÉRIFICATION DE L'EFFICACITÉ THÉRAPEUTIQUE

L'efficacité du traitement peut être démontrée par: la résolution des signes et des symptômes d'infection. Le laps de temps jusqu'à une résolution complète dépend du microorganisme infectant et du siège de l'infection. ✳

ÉRYTHROMYCINES

érythromycine base
Apo-Erythro E-C, Eryc, Erythro, Novo-Rythro Encap, PCE

érythromycine, estolate d'
Novo-Rythro estolate

érythromycine, éthylsuccinate d'
Apo-Erythro-ES, EES, Erythro-ES, Novo-Rythro éthylsuccinate

érythromycine, lactobionate d'
Erythrocin

érythromycine, stéarate d'
Apo-Erythro-S, Erythrocin, Erythrocine Liquide, Érythromycine, Erytro-500, Novo-Rythro stéarate, Nu-Erythromycin-S

érythromycine (usage ophtalmique)†
AK-Mycin, Diomycin, Ilotycin, PMS-Érythromycine

érythromycine (usage topique)
Sans-Acne, Staticin, Erypak

CLASSIFICATION:
Antibiotiques (macrolides)

Grossesse – catégorie B

† Pour l'usage ophtalmique, voir l'annexe N.

INDICATIONS

Traitement des infections suivantes provoquées par les microorganismes sensibles:
IV, PO: infections des voies respiratoires supérieures et inférieures ▪ otite moyenne aiguë ▪ infections de la peau et des tissus mous ▪ coqueluche ▪ diphtérie ▪ érythrasma ▪ chancre mou ▪ conjonctivite ▪ listériose ▪ actinomycose ▪ lymphogranulome vénérien ▪ entérite due à *Campylobacter* ▪ maladie de Lyme ▪ urétrite non gonococcique ▪ syphilis ▪ maladie du légionnaire ▪ rhumatisme articulaire aigu ▪ Usage indiqué dans les cas suivants lorsque la pénicilline est l'agent le plus approprié, mais ne peut être administrée en raison de réactions d'hypersensibilité antérieures: infections à streptocoques ▪ syphilis ou gonorrhée ▪ **Usage topique**: traitement de l'acné ▪ infections superficielles de la peau ▪ **Usage ophtalmique**: infections superficielles de la conjonctive ou de la cornée ▪ prévention de l'ophtalmie du nouveau-né due à *N. gonorrhϾ* ou à *C. trachomatis.*

MÉCANISME D'ACTION

Inhibition de la synthèse des protéines au niveau de la sous-unité 50S du ribosome bactérien. ***Effets thérapeutiques:*** Action bactériostatique contre les bactéries sensibles. **Spectre d'action**: Action contre de nombreux coques à Gram positif incluant: les streptocoques ▪ les staphylocoques ▪ Action contre les bacilles à Gram positif incluant: *Clostridium* ▪ *Corynebacterium* ▪ Action contre plusieurs microorganismes pathogènes à Gram négatif, notamment: *Neisseria* ▪ *Hæmophilus influenzæ* ▪ *Legionella pneumophila* ▪ *Mycoplasma* et *Chlamydia* (habituellement sensibles à l'érythromycine).

PHARMACOCINÉTIQUE

Absorption: Bonne depuis le duodénum mais l'absorption varie selon le sel utilisé. L'absorption des comprimés entérosolubles est retardée. Minime, à la suite de l'administration par voie topique et ophtalmique.
Distribution: Tout l'organisme. L'érythromycine pénètre en quantité infime dans le liquide céphalorachidien, traverse la barrière placentaire et passe dans le lait maternel.
Liaison aux protéines: De 70 à 80 %; 96 % dans le cas de l'estolate.
Métabolisme et excrétion: Métabolisme partiellement hépatique; excrétion dans la bile, principalement à l'état inchangé. De petites quantités sont excrétées à l'état inchangé dans l'urine.
Demi-vie: Nouveau-nés: 2,1 heures; adultes: de 1,4 à 2 heures.

Profil temps-action (concentrations sanguines)

	DÉBUT D'ACTION	PIC	DURÉE
PO	1 h	1 – 4 h	6 – 12 h
IV	rapide	fin de la perfusion	6 – 12 h

CONTRE-INDICATIONS, PRÉCAUTIONS ET MISES EN GARDE

Contre-indications: Hypersensibilité ▪ Insuffisance hépatique (sel d'estolate) ▪ Usage concomitant de cisapride, d'astémizole, de terfénadine, de clozapine, d'alcaloïdes de l'ergot, de pimozide ▪ **OBST.**: Grossesse (sel d'estolate)

■ PÉD.: Nouveau-nés (les produits renfermant de l'alcool benzylique sont contre-indiqués).

Précautions et mises en garde: GÉR.: Risque accru d'ototoxicité lors d'administration de > 4 g IV par jour ■ Maladie hépatique ■ **OBST.:** Pour traiter les infections à *Chlamydia* ou la syphilis, administrer les produits qui ne renferment pas de sels d'estolate ■ Intolérance connue à l'alcool (la plupart des agents topiques) ■ Sensibilité à la tartrazine (certains produits renferment de la tartrazine – colorant jaune FDC n° 5).

E

RÉACTIONS INDÉSIRABLES ET EFFETS SECONDAIRES

SNC: convulsions (rare).
ORLO: ototoxicité.
CV: ALLONGEMENT DE L'INTERVALLE QT (pouvant résulter en torsades de pointe), ARYTHMIES VENTRICULAIRES.
GI: nausées, vomissements, douleurs abdominales, crampes, diarrhée, hépatite induite par les médicaments, sténose pylorique hypertrophique infantile, pancréatite induite par les médicaments (rare).
Tég.: rash.
Locaux: phlébite au point d'injection IV.
Divers: réactions allergiques, surinfection.

INTERACTIONS

Médicament-médicament: L'ADMINISTRATION CONCOMITANTE DE **PIMOZIDE** OU DE **CISAPRIDE** ACCROÎT LE RISQUE D'ARYTHMIES (L'USAGE CONCOMITANT EST CONTRE-INDIQUÉ); DES EFFETS SIMILAIRES PEUVENT ÊTRE OBSERVÉS AVEC LE **DILTIAZEM**, LE **VÉRAPAMIL**, LE **KÉTOCONAZOLE**, L'**ITRACONAZOLE** ET LES **INHIBITEURS DE LA PROTÉASE**; ÉVITER L'USAGE CONCOMITANT ■ L'administration concomitante de **rifabutine** ou de **rifampine** peut réduire les effets de l'érythromycine et accroître le risque de réactions gastro-intestinales ■ L'érythromycine augmente les concentrations d'**alfentanil**, d'**alprazolam**, de **buspirone**, de **clozapine**, de **bromocriptine**, de **diazépam,** de **théophylline**, de **carbamazépine**, de **cyclosporine**, de **disopyramide**, d'**alcaloïdes de l'ergot**, de **félodipine**, de **warfarine**, de **méthylprednisolone**, de **midazolam,** de **quinidine**, de **rifabutine**, de **sildénafil**, de **tacrolimus**, de **triazolam** ou de **vinblastine** et accroît la toxicité associée à ces médicaments ■ L'usage concomitant d'**inhibiteurs de la HMG-CoA réductase** accroît le risque de myopathie grave et de rhabdomyolyse ■ Risque d'élévation des concentrations sériques de **digoxine** chez un faible pourcentage de patients ■ La **théophylline** peut réduire les concentrations sériques d'érythromycine ■ La **clindamycine** peut inhiber les effets bénéfiques de l'érythromycine ■ L'application concomitante d'**agents irritants**, **abrasifs** ou **exfoliants** peut aggraver l'irritation.

VOIES D'ADMINISTRATION ET POSOLOGIE

250 mg d'érythromycine base ou d'estolate ou de stéarate d'érythromycine équivalent à 400 mg d'éthylsuccinate d'érythromycine. L'érythromycine par voie orale est commercialisée sous forme de base, d'estolate, d'éthylsuccinate, ou de stéarate et par voie parentérale, sous forme de lactobionate. L'érythromycine base est également utilisée dans des préparations pour usage topique ou ophtalmique. Les posologies qui suivent sont indiquées en termes d'érythromycine base.

PO (adultes), sauf mention contraire:

- *Acné* – 250 mg, toutes les 6 heures, *ou* 333 mg, toutes les 8 heures, *ou* 500 mg, toutes les 12 heures. Après 4 semaines, on peut entreprendre un traitement d'entretien de 333 à 500 mg, 1 fois par jour.
- *Angine streptococcique* – 500 mg, toutes les 12 heures; **(enfants):** de 5 à 7,5 mg/kg, toutes les 6 heures, *ou* de 10 à 15 mg/kg, toutes les 12 heures, pendant au moins 10 jours.
- *Antibactérien* – 250 mg, toutes les 6 heures, *ou* 333 mg, toutes les 8 heures, *ou* 500 mg, toutes les 12 heures; **(enfants):** de 7,5 à 25 mg/kg, toutes les 6 heures, *ou* de 15 à 25 mg/kg, toutes les 12 heures (au maximum, 4 g/jour).
- *Chancre mou* – 500 mg, toutes les 6 heures, pendant 7 jours.
- *Conjonctivite due à* Chlamydia – **(nouveau-né):** 12,5 mg/kg, toutes les 6 heures, pendant au moins 10 à 14 jours.
- *Coqueluche* – 500 mg, toutes les 6 heures, pendant 14 jours; **(enfants):** de 10 à 12,5 mg/kg, toutes les 6 heures (au maximum, 2 g/jour), pendant 10 jours.
- *Diphtérie* – 500 mg, toutes les 6 heures, pendant 7 jours; **(enfants):** de 10 à 12,5 mg/kg, toutes les 6 heures (au maximum, 2 g/jour), pendant 14 jours.
- *Entérite due à* Campylobacter – 250 mg, toutes les 6 heures, pendant 5 jours; **(enfants):** 10 mg/kg, toutes les 6 heures, pendant 5 jours.
- *Gastroparésie diabétique* – 250 mg, 3 fois par jour, 30 minutes avant les repas.
- *Lymphogranulome vénérien* – 500 mg, toutes les 6 heures, pendant 21 jours.
- *Maladie de Lyme* – 250 mg, toutes les 6 heures, pendant 10 à 21 jours; **(enfants):** 7,5 mg/kg, toutes les 6 heures, pendant 10 à 21 jours.
- *Maladie du légionnaire* – 500 mg à 1 g, toutes les 6 heures.
- *Pararickettsioses endocervicales ou cervicales* – 500 mg, toutes les 6 heures, pendant 7 jours; 250 mg, toutes les 6 heures, pendant 14 jours;

(enfants < 45 kg): 10 mg/kg, toutes les 6 heures, pendant 10 à 14 jours.

- *Pneumonie à Chlamydia* – **(nouveau-né):** 12,5 mg/kg, toutes les 6 heures, pendant 14 jours.
- *Prophylaxie contre les streptocoques* – 250 mg, toutes les 12 heures.
- *Salpingite aiguë due à* N. gonorrhϾæ – 250 mg, toutes les 6 heures, pendant 7 jours.
- *Urétrite non gonococcique,* U. urealyticum – 500 mg, toutes les 6 heures, pendant 7 jours, ou 250 mg, toutes les 6 heures, pendant 14 jours.

IV (adultes): De 250 à 500 mg, toutes les 6 heures. On peut utiliser jusqu'à 4 g/jour pour traiter les infections graves.

IV (enfants): De 15 à 20 mg/kg/jour, en 4 doses fractionnées.

Usage topique (adultes et enfants > 12 ans): 2 fois par jour.

Usage ophtalmique: *Infections oculaires externes* – 1 ou plusieurs fois par jour selon la gravité de l'infection. *Prévention de la conjonctivite du nouveau-né* – environ 0,5 à 1 cm d'onguent dans chaque sac conjonctival.

PRÉSENTATION (version générique disponible)

- **Érythromycine base**

  Comprimés: 250 mg[Pr], 500 mg[Pr] ■ **Comprimés à enrobage entérique:** 250 mg[Pr], 333 mg[Pr] ■ **Capsules entériques:** 250 mg[Pr], 333 mg[Pr].
- **Estolate d'érythromycine**

  Capsules: 250 mg [Pr] **Suspension orale:** 125 mg/5 mL[Pr], 250 mg/5 ml [Pr].
- **Éthylsuccinate d'érythromycine**

  Comprimés: 600 mg[Pr] ■ **Suspension orale:** 200 mg/5 mL[Pr], 400 mg/5 mL[Pr] ■ **En association avec:** sulfisoxazole (Pediazole)[Pr].
- **Lactobionate d'érythromycine**

  Poudre pour injection: 500 mg[Pr], 1 g[Pr].
- **Stéarate d'érythromycine**

  Comprimés pelliculés: 250 mg[Pr], 500 mg[Pr].
- **Préparations topiques**

  Lotion topique: 1,5 %[Pr], 2 %[Pr] ■ **En association avec:** peroxyde de benzoyl (Benzamycin)[Pr], alcool éthylique et Parsol MCX et Parsol 1789(Erysol)[Pr], trétinoïne (Stievamycin)[Pr].
- **Préparations ophtalmiques**

  Onguent ophtalmique: 0,5 %[Pr].

SOINS INFIRMIERS

ÉVALUATION DE LA SITUATION

- Observer le patient, au début du traitement et pendant toute sa durée, à la recherche des signes suivants d'infection: altération des signes vitaux; aspect de la plaie, des crachats, de l'urine et des selles; accroissement du nombre de globules blancs.
- Prélever des échantillons pour les cultures et les antibiogrammes avant le début du traitement. La première dose peut être administrée avant même que les résultats soient connus.

Tests de laboratoire:

- On devrait effectuer à intervalles réguliers des tests de la fonction hépatique chez les patients recevant des doses élevées dans le cadre d'un traitement prolongé.
- L'érythromycine peut entraîner l'élévation des concentrations sériques de bilirubine, d'AST, d'ALT et de phosphatase alcaline.
- Le médicament peut entraîner des concentrations urinaires de catécholamines faussement élevées.

DIAGNOSTICS INFIRMIERS POSSIBLES

- Risque d'infection (Indications, Effets secondaires).
- Connaissances insuffisantes sur le traitement médicamenteux (Enseignement au patient et à ses proches).
- Non-observance du traitement médicamenteux (Enseignement au patient et à ses proches).

INTERVENTIONS INFIRMIÈRES

- NE PAS CONFONDRE L'ÉRYTHROMYCINE AVEC L'AZITHROMYCINE.

PO:

- Administrer le médicament à intervalles réguliers. *Les comprimés pelliculés d'érythromycine (base et stéarate)* sont mieux absorbés s'ils sont pris à jeun, au moins 1 heure avant ou 2 heures après les repas. En cas d'irritation gastrique, on peut administrer le médicament avec des aliments. *Les comprimés d'érythromycine à enrobage entérique (base et estolate)* peuvent être pris sans égard aux repas. *L'éthylsuccinate d'érythromycine* est mieux absorbé s'il est pris avec des aliments. Il faut prendre chaque dose avec un grand verre d'eau.
- Utiliser un contenant gradué pour mesurer les préparations liquides. Bien agiter la solution avant de l'administrer.
- Les comprimés à croquer doivent être mâchés ou écrasés et ne doivent pas être avalés tels quels.

E

- IL NE FAUT PAS OUVRIR, ÉCRASER OU MÂCHER LES CAPSULES OU LES COMPRIMÉS À ACTION RETARD; DEMANDER AU PATIENT DE LES AVALER TELS QUELS. On peut ouvrir *les capsules d'érythromycine base à libération retard* et en saupoudrer le contenu sur de la compote de pomme, de la gelée ou de la crème glacée, immédiatement avant que le patient ne les consomme. Il faut s'assurer que le patient a pris tout le contenu de la capsule.

E

IV: Ajouter 10 mL d'eau stérile pour injection sans agent de conservation aux fioles de 250 mg ou de 500 mg, et 20 mL, aux fioles de 1 g. La solution reconstituée reste stable pendant 7 jours si elle est réfrigérée. Consulter les directives de chaque fabricant avant de reconstituer la préparation.

Perfusion intermittente: Diluer de nouveau dans 100 à 250 mL de solution de NaCl 0,9 % ou de solution de D5%E.

Vitesse d'administration: Administrer lentement pendant 20 à 60 minutes pour prévenir la phlébite. Suivre de près toute douleur le long de la veine; si elle se manifeste, ralentir la vitesse d'administration et appliquer de la glace. Prévenir le médecin ou un autre professionnel de la santé si la douleur ne peut être soulagée.

Perfusion continue: L'érythromycine peut également être administrée en perfusion dans les 4 heures qui suivent la dilution, à raison de 1 g par litre de solution de NaCl 0,9 %, de D5%E ou de lactate de Ringer.

Lactobionate d'érythromycine

Association incompatible dans la même seringue: héparine.

Compatibilité (tubulure en Y): acyclovir ■ amiodarone ■ cyclophosphamide ■ diltiazem ■ énalaprilate ■ esmolol ■ famotidine ■ foscarnet ■ héparine ■ hydromorphone ■ idarubicine ■ labétalol ■ lorazépam ■ magnésium, sulfate de ■ mépéridine ■ midazolam ■ morphine ■ multivitamines ■ perphénazine ■ tacrolimus ■ théophylline ■ vitamines du complexe B avec C ■ zidovudine.

Incompatibilité (tubulure en Y): cefmétazole ■ fluconazole.

Compatibilité en addition au soluté: cimétidine ■ hydrocortisone sodique, succinate d' ■ pentobarbital ■ potassium, chlorure de ■ prednisolone ■ ranitidine ■ sodium, bicarbonate de.

Incompatibilité en addition au soluté: héparine ■ métoclopramide ■ vitamines du complexe B avec C.

Préparation topique: Nettoyer la région atteinte avant d'appliquer l'onguent. Enfiler des gants pour l'appliquer.

ENSEIGNEMENT AU PATIENT ET À SES PROCHES

- Expliquer au patient qu'il doit prendre le médicament à intervalles réguliers, et qu'il doit utiliser toute la quantité qui lui a été prescrite même s'il se sent mieux. S'il n'a pas pu prendre le médicament au moment habituel, il doit le prendre dès que possible et espacer uniformément les doses suivantes prévues pour la journée. Le prévenir qu'il peut être dangereux de donner ce médicament à d'autres personnes.
- Prévenir le patient que l'érythromycine peut provoquer des nausées, des vomissements, de la diarrhée ou des crampes d'estomac; lui conseiller de prévenir un professionnel de la santé si ces effets persistent ou si les symptômes suivants se manifestent: douleurs abdominales intenses, jaunissement de la peau ou des yeux, urine foncée, selles de couleur pâle ou fatigue inhabituelle. Mettre en garde les parents contre le risque de sténose pylorique hypertrophique chez l'enfant. Leur conseiller de prévenir un professionnel de la santé si des vomissements et de l'irritabilité surviennent.
- Conseiller au patient de signaler à un professionnel de la santé les signes suivants de surinfection: excroissance pileuse noire sur la langue, démangeaisons ou pertes vaginales, selles molles ou nauséabondes.
- Inciter le patient à prévenir un professionnel de la santé si les symptômes ne s'améliorent pas.

VÉRIFICATION DE L'EFFICACITÉ THÉRAPEUTIQUE

L'efficacité du traitement peut être démontrée par: la disparition des signes et des symptômes d'infection; le temps de résolution dépend du microorganisme infectant et du siège de l'infection ■ la cicatrisation des lésions acnéiques.

ESCITALOPRAM

Cipralex

CLASSIFICATION:

Antidépresseur (inhibiteur sélectif du recaptage de la sérotonine [ISRS])

Grossesse – catégorie C (risque durant le 3e trimestre; voir «Précautions et mises en garde»)

INDICATIONS

Traitement de la dépression, souvent en association avec une psychothérapie ■ Anxiété généralisée.

MÉCANISME D'ACTION

Inhibition sélective du recaptage de la sérotonine dans le SNC. ***Effets thérapeutiques*:** Effet antidépresseur.

PHARMACOCINÉTIQUE

Absorption: 80 % (PO).
Distribution: L'agent passe dans le lait maternel.
Métabolisme et excrétion: Métabolisme majoritairement hépatique (principalement par les isoenzymes CYP3A4 et CYP2C19); 7 % est excrété à l'état inchangé par les reins.
Demi-vie: Prolongée chez les personnes âgées et les insuffisants hépatiques.

Profil temps-action (effet antidépresseur)

	DÉBUT D'ACTION	PIC	DURÉE
PO	en 1 – 4 semaines	inconnu	inconnue

CONTRE-INDICATIONS, PRÉCAUTIONS ET MISES EN GARDE

Contre-indications: Hypersensibilité ■ Traitement concomitant avec un IMAO (attendre 14 jours entre l'arrêt de la prise de l'IMAO et le début de la prise de ce médicament et vice versa) ■ Traitement concomitant par le pimozide ■ Usage concomitant de citalopram.
Précautions et mises en garde: Antécédents de manie (risque d'activation de la manie ou de l'hypomanie) ■ Antécédents de troubles convulsifs ■ La surveillance des idées suicidaires est indiquée chez tous les patients recevant ce médicament ■ Risque d'effets indésirables de type agitation grave et de blessures infligées à soi et aux autres ■ Ne pas mettre fin au traitement brusquement, en raison du risque de symptômes de sevrage ■ Période suivant immédiatement un infarctus du myocarde ■ Risque d'anomalies hémorragiques particulièrement chez les patients exposés à ce risque (p. ex., personnes âgées, patients ayant des antécédents d'hémorragie ou prenant des médicaments modifiant la coagulation) ■ Insuffisance cardiaque congestive aiguë ■ Diabète ■ Patients suicidaires ■ Insuffisance hépatique (il est recommandé de réduire la dose et d'utiliser le médicament avec prudence) ■ Insuffisance rénale (utiliser avec prudence chez les patients dont la Cl_{Cr} est < 30 mL/min) ■ **GÉR.:** Il est recommandé de réduire les doses ■ **PÉD.:** Risque accru de tentatives de suicide ou d'aggravation de l'idéation suicidaire, particulièrement en début de traitement ou pendant la période d'adaptation posologique chez les enfants ou les adolescents ■ Risque d'effets indésirables de type agitation grave et de blessures infligées à soi et aux autres (usage pédiatrique non approuvé) ■ **OBST.:** On n'a pas mené d'études adéquates chez la femme enceinte. N'administrer au cours de la grossesse que si les bienfaits éventuels pour la mère l'emportent sur les risques possibles pour le fœtus. Risque de complications après l'accouchement chez les nouveau-nés lorsque la mère a pris ce médicament durant le 3e trimestre de la grossesse ■ **ALLAITEMENT:** L'escitalopram passe dans le lait maternel et peut provoquer la léthargie chez le nouveau-né, qui, de ce fait, peut refuser de téter; peser les bienfaits par rapport aux risques.

E

RÉACTIONS INDÉSIRABLES ET EFFETS SECONDAIRES

SNC: <u>insomnie</u>, <u>étourdissements</u>, somnolence, fatigue.
GI: <u>diarrhée</u>, <u>nausées</u>, douleurs abdominales, constipation, sécheresse de la bouche (xérostomie), indigestion.
GU: anorgasmie, diminution de la libido, retard de l'éjaculation, impuissance.
Tég.: sécrétion accrue de sueur.
End.: syndrome de sécrétion inappropriée de l'hormone antidiurétique (SIADH).
HÉ: hyponatrémie.
Métab.: gain d'appétit.

INTERACTIONS

Médicament-médicament: RISQUE DE RÉACTIONS GRAVES POUVANT ÊTRE MORTELLES LORS DE L'USAGE CONCOMITANT D'**IMAO**; PRÉVOIR AU MOINS 14 JOURS SANS MÉDICATION ENTRE L'ADMINISTRATION DE L'ESCITALOPRAM ET CELLE DES IMAO ■ La prudence est de mise lors de l'administration concomitante d'autres médicaments ou substances à action centrale (notamment l'**alcool**, les **antihistaminiques**, les **analgésiques opioïdes** et les **hypnosédatifs**; la prise concomitante d'alcool est déconseillée) ■ L'usage concomitant de **sumatriptan** ou d'autres antimigraineux de la classe des **agonistes des récepteurs 5-HT_1** peut entraîner de la faiblesse, une hyperréflexie et des problèmes de coordination ■ Les effets sérotoninergiques peuvent être intensifiés par le **lithium** (l'usage concomitant doit être attentivement surveillé) ■ La **carbamazépine** peut diminuer les concentrations sanguines de l'agent ■ L'escitalopram peut élever les concentrations sanguines de **métoprolol** ■ L'usage concomitant d'**antidépresseurs tricycliques** doit s'accompagner de prudence en raison des modifications de la pharmacocinétique ■ L'administration concomitante de plusieurs doses d'un **inhibiteur puissant de l'isoenzyme CYP3A4** (par exemple, **fluconazole**, **kétoconazole**, **itraconazole**, **cimétidine** ou **érythromycine**) ou d'un **inhibiteur puissant de l'isoenzyme CYP2C19** (par exemple, **oméprazole**) peut augmenter les concentrations plasmatiques d'escitalopram.

Médicament-produits naturels: Risque accru de survenue d'un syndrome sérotoninergique lors de la prise concomitante de **millepertuis** et d'**adémétionine** (**SAMe**).

VOIES D'ADMINISTRATION ET POSOLOGIE

- **PO (adultes):** 10 mg, 1 fois par jour; on peut porter cette dose à 20 mg, 1 fois par jour, après 1 semaine.
- **PO (personnes âgées):** 5mg, 1 fois par jour; on peut porter cette dose à 10 mg, 1 fois par jour, après 1 semaine, si le patient la tolère bien.

INSUFFISANCE HÉPATIQUE

- **PO (ADULTES):** 5 mg, 1 FOIS PAR JOUR; ON PEUT PORTER CETTE DOSE À 10 mg, 1 FOIS PAR JOUR, APRÈS 1 SEMAINE, SI LE PATIENT LA TOLÈRE BIEN.

PRÉSENTATION

Comprimés: 10 mg^{Pr}, 20 mg^{Pr}.

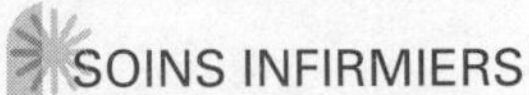

SOINS INFIRMIERS

ÉVALUATION DE LA SITUATION

- Suivre de près les sautes d'humeur et le niveau d'anxiété tout au long du traitement.
- Rester à l'affût des tendances suicidaires, particulièrement en début de traitement. Restreindre la quantité de médicament dont peut disposer le patient. Le risque peut être accru chez les enfants et les adolescents. Après le début du traitement, les enfants et les adolescents devraient être vus par un professionnel de la santé au moins 1 fois par semaine, pendant 4 semaines, toutes les 2 semaines, pendant les 4 semaines suivantes, et selon la décision du professionnel de la santé, par la suite.

DIAGNOSTICS INFIRMIERS POSSIBLES

- Stratégies d'adaptation inefficaces (Indications).
- Risque d'accident (Effets secondaires).
- Connaissances insuffisantes sur le traitement médicamenteux (Enseignement au patient et à ses proches).

INTERVENTIONS INFIRMIÈRES

- Ne pas administrer l'escitalopram et le citalopram en concomitance.
- Administrer en une seule dose, le matin ou le soir, sans égard aux repas.

ENSEIGNEMENT AU PATIENT ET À SES PROCHES

- Recommander au patient de prendre l'escitalopram en suivant rigoureusement la posologie recommandée. Lui conseiller de prendre toute dose manquée le jour même, dès que possible, d'en informer un professionnel de la santé et de reprendre l'horaire habituel le lendemain. Prévenir le patient qu'il ne doit jamais remplacer une dose manquée par une double dose ni arrêter le traitement abruptement; le sevrage doit se faire graduellement.
- Prévenir le patient que l'escitalopram peut provoquer des étourdissements. Lui conseiller de ne pas conduire et de ne pas s'engager dans d'autres activités qui exigent sa vigilance jusqu'à ce qu'on ait la certitude que le médicament ne provoque pas cet effet chez lui.
- Recommander au patient de ne pas prendre d'alcool et d'autres dépresseurs du SNC pendant le traitement et de consulter un professionnel de la santé avant de prendre d'autres médicaments d'ordonnance ou en vente libre ou des produits à base de plantes médicinales.
- Recommander à la patiente de prévenir un professionnel de la santé si elle pense être enceinte, si elle souhaite le devenir ou si elle allaite.
- PRÉVENIR LE PATIENT QU'IL NE FAUT PAS PRENDRE L'ESCITALOPRAM DANS LES 14 JOURS QUI SUIVENT L'ARRÊT DE LA PRISE D'UN IMAO ET QU'IL FAUT ATTENDRE AU MOINS 14 JOURS APRÈS L'ARRÊT DU TRAITEMENT PAR L'ESCITALOPRAM AVANT DE COMMENCER UN TRAITEMENT PAR UN IMAO.

VÉRIFICATION DE L'EFFICACITÉ THÉRAPEUTIQUE

L'efficacité du traitement peut être démontrée par: un sentiment de mieux-être ▪ un intérêt renouvelé pour l'entourage; il faut parfois compter de 1 à 4 semaines avant que les effets antidépresseurs se manifestent; le plein effet antidépresseur se produit après 4 à 6 semaines ▪ la diminution de l'anxiété.

ALERTE CLINIQUE

ESMOLOL

Brevibloc

CLASSIFICATION:

Antiarythmique (classe II) (bêtabloquant)

Grossesse – catégorie C

INDICATIONS

Traitement des tachycardies et de l'hypertension se manifestant pendant la période périopératoire chez les patients susceptibles de présenter un déséquilibre de l'oxygène au niveau du myocarde et qui, selon l'avis du médecin, présentent des risques de développer un état d'ischémie myocardique d'origine hémodynamique ■ Maîtrise rapide de la fréquence ventriculaire chez les patients présentant une fibrillation ou un flutter auriculaires, dans les cas où le choix d'un agent à courte durée d'action est souhaitable.

MÉCANISME D'ACTION

Blocage de la stimulation des récepteurs bêta$_1$-adrénergiques (du myocarde), habituellement sans affecter les récepteurs bêta$_2$ (pulmonaires, vasculaires ou utérins). ***Effets thérapeutiques:*** Ralentissement de la fréquence cardiaque ■ Diminution de la conduction auriculoventriculaire.

PHARMACOCINÉTIQUE

Absorption: Complète (IV).
Distribution: Tout l'organisme.
Métabolisme et excrétion: Le médicament est métabolisé par les enzymes des érythrocytes et du foie.
Demi-vie: 9 minutes.

Profil temps-action (effet antiarythmique)

	DÉBUT D'ACTION	PIC	DURÉE
IV	quelques minutes	inconnu	1 – 20 min

CONTRE-INDICATIONS, PRÉCAUTIONS ET MISES EN GARDE

Contre-indications: Insuffisance cardiaque décompensée ■ Choc cardiogénique ■ Bradycardie ou bloc cardiaque (bloc AV du 2e et du 3e degré) ■ Insuffisance ventriculaire droite due à une hypertension pulmonaire ■ Hypotension.
Précautions et mises en garde: GÉR.: Il est recommandé de diminuer la dose chez les personnes âgées (sensibilité accrue aux effets des bêtabloquants) ■ Maladies pulmonaires bronchospastiques ■ Diabète (l'esmolol peut masquer les symptômes d'hypoglycémie) ■ Antécédents de réactions allergiques graves (l'intensité des réactions peut être accrue) ■ **OBST., ALLAITEMENT, PÉD.:** L'innocuité du médicament n'a pas été établie chez les femmes enceintes ou qui allaitent ni chez les enfants.

RÉACTIONS INDÉSIRABLES ET EFFETS SECONDAIRES

SNC: fatigue, agitation, confusion, étourdissements, somnolence, faiblesse.
CV: hypotension, ischémie périphérique.
GI: nausées, vomissements.
Tég.: transpiration.
Locaux: réactions au point d'injection.

INTERACTIONS

Médicament-médicament: Risque de dépression additive du myocarde lors de l'administration concomitante d'une **anesthésie générale**, de **diltiazem** ou de **vérapamil** ■ Risque de bradycardie additive lors de l'administration concomitante de **dérivés digitaliques** ■ Risque d'hypotension additive lors de l'administration concomitante d'autres **antihypertenseurs** et de **dérivés nitrés** et lors de l'ingestion de quantités excessives d'**alcool** ■ La prise concomitante d'**amphétamines**, de **cocaïne**, d'**éphédrine**, d'**adrénaline**, de **noradrénaline**, de **phényléphrine** ou de **pseudoéphédrine** peut entraîner une stimulation alpha-adrénergique excessive (hypertension et bradycardie excessives) ■ L'administration concomitante d'une **hormonothérapie substitutive thyroïdienne** peut diminuer l'efficacité de l'esmolol ■ Risque de perte de l'efficacité de l'**insuline** ou des **hypoglycémiants oraux** (une adaptation posologique peut s'avérer nécessaire) ■ L'esmolol peut réduire l'efficacité de la **théophylline** ■ L'esmolol peut diminuer les effets bénéfiques sur les récepteurs bêtacardiaques de la **dopamine** ou de la **dobutamine** ■ La prudence est de mise lorsque l'esmolol est administré dans les 14 jours suivant un traitement par un **IMAO** (risque d'hypertension).

VOIES D'ADMINISTRATION ET POSOLOGIE

- **IV (adultes):** *Antiarythmique* – initialement, une dose d'attaque de 500 µg/kg, pendant 1 minute, suivie d'une perfusion de 50 µg/kg/min, pendant 4 minutes; en l'absence de réponse dans les 5 minutes qui suivent, administrer une deuxième dose d'attaque de 500 µg/kg, pendant 1 minute, et accélérer la vitesse de perfusion pour la faire passer à 100 µg/kg/min, pendant 4 minutes. En l'absence de réponse, administrer de nouveau la dose d'attaque de 500 µg/kg, pendant 1 minute, et accélérer la vitesse de perfusion par paliers de 50 µg/kg/min (ne pas dépasser 200 µg/kg/min). Lorsque l'objectif thérapeutique est atteint, éliminer les doses d'attaque et diminuer la dose par paliers de 25 µg/kg/min. *Tachycardie et hypertension peropératoires et postopératoires*: 1 500 µg/kg en bolus (en 30 secondes), puis perfusion de 150 µg/kg/min (le débit peut être accéléré jusqu'à 300 µg/kg/min en fonction des besoins).

PRÉSENTATION

Solution pour injection (prédiluée, destinée à la dose d'attaque): fioles de 10 mL à 10 mg/mL[Pr] ■ **Solution pour injection (à diluer avant l'administration):** fioles de 10 mL à 250 mg/mL[Pr].

SOINS INFIRMIERS

E

ÉVALUATION DE LA SITUATION

- Mesurer souvent la pression artérielle et la fréquence cardiaque et suivre de près l'ÉCG pendant la période d'adaptation posologique et à intervalles fréquents pendant toute la durée du traitement. Le risque d'hypotension est plus élevé dans les 30 premières minutes qui suivent le début de la perfusion d'esmolol.
- Effectuer le bilan quotidien des ingesta et des excreta et peser le patient tous les jours. Observer régulièrement le patient à la recherche des signes et des symptômes suivants d'insuffisance cardiaque: dyspnée, râles ou crépitations, gain pondéral, œdème périphérique, turgescence des jugulaires.
- Examiner fréquemment le point d'injection tout au long du traitement. Les concentrations supérieures à 10 mg/mL peuvent provoquer des rougeurs, de l'enflure, un changement de couleur de la peau et une sensation de brûlure au point d'injection. Ne pas utiliser d'aiguilles à papillon pour administrer ce médicament. En cas d'irritation veineuse, interrompre la perfusion et la poursuivre à un autre point d'injection.

Toxicité et surdosage:

- Observer le patient à la recherche des signes suivants de surdosage: bradycardie, étourdissements graves ou évanouissements, somnolence importante, dyspnée, bleuissement des ongles ou des paumes, convulsions. Prévenir immédiatement le médecin si ces signes surviennent.
- En cas de surdosage, administrer du glucagon par voie IV et amorcer le traitement des symptômes. Étant donné la courte durée d'action de l'esmolol, l'arrêt du traitement peut réduire la toxicité aiguë.

DIAGNOSTICS INFIRMIERS POSSIBLES

- Débit cardiaque diminué (Effets secondaires).
- Connaissances insuffisantes sur le traitement médicamenteux (Enseignement au patient et à ses proches).

INTERVENTIONS INFIRMIÈRES

Alerte clinique: L'ADMINISTRATION DES MÉDICAMENTS VASOACTIFS ADMINISTRÉS PAR VOIE IV COMPORTE UN RISQUE PAR ELLE-MÊME. L'ESMOLOL EST DISPONIBLE EN DEUX CONCENTRATIONS; DES DÉCÈS ONT ÉTÉ SIGNALÉS À LA SUITE DE L'ADMINISTRATION EN DOSE D'ATTAQUE DU CONTENU DE LA FIOLE DESTINÉE À LA PERFUSION, QUI RENFERME 2 500 mg DANS 10 mL D'ESMOLOL ET QUI DOIT ÊTRE DILUÉ EN VUE DE L'ADMINISTRATION. AVANT L'ADMINISTRATION, FAIRE VÉRIFIER L'ORDONNANCE D'ORIGINE, LE CALCUL DE LA DOSE ET LE RÉGLAGE DES POMPES À PERFUSION PAR UN DEUXIÈME PROFESSIONNEL DE LA SANTÉ.

- Pour substituer à l'esmolol un autre agent antiarythmique, administrer la première dose de cet agent et diminuer la dose d'esmolol de 50 %, 30 minutes plus tard. Si la réponse appropriée peut être maintenue pendant 1 heure après la deuxième dose de l'agent antiarythmique, arrêter l'administration de l'esmolol.

IV directe: La solution de 10 mg/mL peut être administrée non diluée.

Perfusion intermittente: Pour préparer la solution, prélever 20 mL d'un flacon de 500 mL de D5%E, de D5%/solution de lactate de Ringer, de D5%/NaCl 0,45 % ou 0,9 %, de NaCl 0,45 %, de NaCl 0,9 % ou de solution de lactate de Ringer. Ajouter 5 g d'esmolol au flacon de 500 mL pour obtenir une concentration de 10 mg/mL. La solution est transparente, d'incolore à jaune clair, et elle est stable pendant 24 heures à la température ambiante. Consulter les directives du fabricant avant de reconstituer la préparation.

Vitesse d'administration: La dose d'attaque d'esmolol doit être administrée pendant 1 minute, suivie d'une dose d'entretien par perfusion IV, pendant 4 minutes. Si la réponse n'est pas suffisante, répéter l'administration toutes les 5 minutes en augmentant la dose d'entretien. Pour adapter la dose, il faut se baser sur la fréquence cardiaque souhaitable ou sur l'abaissement de la pression artérielle qu'il faut éviter. La dose d'entretien ne devrait pas dépasser les 200 µg/kg/min et ne devrait pas être administrée pendant plus de 48 heures. Il ne faut pas arrêter brusquement les perfusions d'esmolol; éliminer les doses d'attaque et diminuer la dose par paliers de 25 µg/kg/min (voir l'annexe C).

Compatibilité (tubulure en Y): amikacine ■ aminophylline ■ amiodarone ■ ampicilline ■ atracurium ■ butorphanol ■ calcium, chlorure de ■ céfazoline ■ cefmétazole ■ céfopérazone ■ ceftazidime ■ ceftizoxime ■ chloramphénicol ■ cimétidine ■ clindamycine ■ diltiazem ■ dopamine ■ énalaprilate ■ érythromycine, lactobionate d' ■ famotidine ■ fentanyl ■ gentamicine ■ héparine ■ hydrocortisone sodique, succinate d' ■ insuline ■

labétalol ■ magnésium, sulfate de ■ méthyldopa ■ métronidazole ■ midazolam ■ morphine ■ nafcilline ■ nitroprusside ■ noradrénaline ■ pancuronium ■ pénicilline G potassique ■ phénytoïne ■ pipéracilline ■ polymyxine B ■ potassium, chlorure de ■ potassium, phosphate de ■ propofol ■ ranitidine ■ sodium, acétate de ■ streptomycine ■ tacrolimus ■ tobramycine ■ triméthoprim/sulfaméthoxazole ■ vancomycine ■ vécuronium.

Incompatibilité (tubulure en Y): furosémide ■ warfarine.

ENSEIGNEMENT AU PATIENT ET À SES PROCHES

- Prévenir le patient que l'esmolol peut parfois provoquer de la somnolence. Lui conseiller de demander de l'aide lors de ses déplacements.
- Recommander au patient de changer lentement de position pour réduire le risque d'hypotension orthostatique.
- Recommander au patient diabétique de surveiller de près sa glycémie, particulièrement en présence des symptômes suivants: faiblesse, malaise, irritabilité ou fatigue. Le prévenir que d'autres signes d'hypoglycémie, comme les étourdissements ou la transpiration, restent cependant présents.

VÉRIFICATION DE L'EFFICACITÉ THÉRAPEUTIQUE

L'efficacité du traitement peut être démontrée par: la maîtrise des arythmies, sans survenue d'effets secondaires nocifs. ✳

ESOMÉPRAZOLE

Nexium

CLASSIFICATION:

Antiulcéreux (inhibiteur de la pompe à protons)

Grossesse – catégorie B

INDICATIONS

Diminution de la sécrétion d'acide gastrique, en présence d'affections comme l'ulcère duodénal et gastrique ■ Œsophagite par érosion associée au reflux gastro-œsophagien ■ Reflux gastro-œsophagien symptomatique (brûlures d'estomac, régurgitations) ■ Ulcères gastriques associés aux AINS ■ **En association avec l'amoxicilline et la clarithromycine**: Éradication de *H. pylori* chez les patients ayant des antécédents d'ulcère duodénal ■ Ulcère duodénal associé à *H. pylori*.

MÉCANISME D'ACTION

L'esoméprazole est l'isomère S de l'oméprazole. Il est un inhibiteur spécifique de l'enzyme gastrique H^+, K^+-ATPase (pompe à protons), responsable des sécrétions acides des cellules pariétales de l'estomac, ce qui prévient l'entrée des ions hydrogène dans la lumière du tube gastrique. ***Effets thérapeutiques:*** Diminution de l'accumulation d'acide dans la lumière gastrique et réduction du reflux gastro-œsophagien ■ Cicatrisation des ulcères duodénaux et de ceux provoqués par l'œsophagite ■ Diminution des sécrétions acides caractérisant les états d'hypersécrétion.

E

PHARMACOCINÉTIQUE

Absorption: Biodisponibilité à 89 % à l'état d'équilibre (après plusieurs doses uniquotidiennes répétées).

Distribution: Volume de distribution à l'état d'équilibre de 0,22 L/kg de poids corporel.

Liaison aux protéines: 97 %.

Métabolisme et excrétion: Métabolisme hépatique par l'entremise du cytochrome P450 (2C19 et 3A4). Excrétion à 80 % sous forme de métabolites dans l'urine et à 20 % dans les fèces.

Demi-vie: De 1 à 1,5 heure.

Profil temps-action (suppression des sécrétions acides)

	DÉBUT D'ACTION	PIC	DURÉE
PO	inconnu	1,6 h	24 h

CONTRE-INDICATIONS, PRÉCAUTIONS ET MISES EN GARDE

Contre-indications: Hypersensibilité à l'esoméprazole, aux benzimidazoles substitués ou à l'un des autres ingrédients du médicament.

Précautions et mises en garde: Insuffisance hépatique grave (la dose quotidienne ne devait pas dépasser 20 mg) ■ **OBST.**: Utiliser seulement si les bienfaits dépassent les risques ■ **PÉD., ALLAITEMENT**: L'innocuité du médicament n'a pas été établie.

RÉACTIONS INDÉSIRABLES ET EFFETS SECONDAIRES

SNC: céphalées, étourdissements.

GI: flatulences, diarrhée, douleurs abdominales, nausées, vomissements, sécheresse de la bouche (xérostomie).

INTERACTIONS

Médicament-médicament: L'administration concomitante d'esoméprazole et de **diazépam** peut entraîner une diminution de la clairance de ce dernier et en augmenter les effets ■ L'esoméprazole est métabolisé par le cytochrome P450, principalement par les isoenzymes 2C19 et 3A4; aucune interaction cliniquement significative entre l'esoméprazole et les différents médicaments métabolisés par ces isoenzymes n'a été signalée ■ L'esoméprazole réduit l'absorption de l'**itraconazole**, du **kétoconazole,** du **fer** et de l'**indinavir**, car elle ne peut se faire qu'en milieu acide.

VOIES D'ADMINISTRATION ET POSOLOGIE

- **PO (adultes)**: *Œsophagite par reflux* – 40 mg, 1 fois par jour. La durée du traitement est de 4 à 8 semaines. Un second traitement de 4 semaines est recommandé si l'œsophagite n'est pas guérie ou si le patient ressent encore des symptômes. *Traitement d'entretien après guérison de l'œsophagite érosive* – 20 mg, 1 fois par jour. La durée maximale des études a été de 6 mois. *Reflux gastroœsophagien symptomatique (brûlures d'estomac ou régurgitations acides)* – 20 mg, 1 fois par jour. Le traitement recommandé est de 2 à 4 semaines. *Guérison des ulcères gastriques associés au traitement par des AINS* – 20 mg, 1 fois par jour, pendant 4 à 8 semaines. *Réduction du risque d'ulcères gastriques associés au traitement par des AINS* – 20 mg, 1 fois par jour. La durée maximale des études a été de 6 mois. *Ulcère duodénal évolutif associé à* H. pylori *ou éradication de* H. pylori *chez des patients ayant des antécédents d'ulcère duodénal* – triple thérapie: esoméprazole à 20 mg, clarithromycine à 500 mg et amoxicilline à 1 000 mg, à prendre 2 fois par jour pendant 7 jours.

PRÉSENTATION

Comprimés: 20 mg[Pr], 40 mg[Pr] ■ **En association avec**: amoxicilline et clarithromycine (Nexium 1-2-3 A[Pr]).

SOINS INFIRMIERS

ÉVALUATION DE LA SITUATION

Observer le patient à intervalles réguliers afin d'évaluer la douleur épigastrique ou abdominale et de déceler la présence de sang visible ou occulte dans les selles, les vomissements ou le liquide d'aspiration gastrique.

Tests de laboratoire:

- L'esoméprazole peut entraîner l'élévation des concentrations sériques d'ALT.
- Il peut aussi élever les concentrations sériques de gastrine au cours du traitement. Les concentrations reviennent à la normale dans les 4 semaines suivant l'arrêt du traitement par l'esoméprazole.
- L'agent peut modifier la concentration d'hémoglobine, le nombre de globules blanc, le nombre de plaquettes, le taux de sodium et de potassium sérique ainsi que le taux de thyroxine.

DIAGNOSTICS INFIRMIERS POSSIBLES

- Douleur aiguë (Indications).
- Connaissances insuffisantes sur le traitement médicamenteux (Enseignement au patient et à ses proches).

INTERVENTIONS INFIRMIÈRES

- Administrer le médicament sans égard aux repas. LE PATIENT DEVRAIT AVALER LES COMPRIMÉS TELS QUELS, SANS LES ÉCRASER, LES CROQUER OU LES MÂCHER. On peut aussi disperser les comprimés dans un demi-verre d'eau non gazéifiée. Aucun autre liquide ne convient, car l'enrobage gastrorésistant pourrait se dissoudre. Mélanger jusqu'à la désagrégation du comprimé et faire boire au patient immédiatement ou dans les 30 minutes qui suivent le mélange contenant les granules d'esoméprazole. Rincer le verre avec de l'eau et lui faire boire le restant de la solution.
- On peut aussi administrer les comprimés dispersés par sonde nasogastrique (calibre 8 – 20 Fr) à l'aide d'une seringue jetable de 25 à 60 mL. Le type de seringue utilisé doit permettre un raccord hermétique avec la sonde nasogastrique. Chaque comprimé doit être dispersé dans 50 mL d'eau, et ce mélange doit passer par le tube pour atteindre l'estomac. Après avoir administré la suspension, on devrait rincer le tube nasogastrique avec 25 à 50 mL d'eau pour nettoyer la seringue et le tube. Pour les sondes nasogastriques de gros calibre (c.-à-d. 14 Fr ou plus), on devrait réduire le volume à 25 mL.
- On peut administrer un antiacide en concomitance.

ENSEIGNEMENT AU PATIENT ET À SES PROCHES

- Conseiller au patient de respecter rigoureusement la posologie recommandée pendant toute la durée du traitement, même s'il se sent mieux. S'il n'a pu prendre le médicament au moment habituel, il doit le prendre aussitôt que possible, sauf s'il est presque l'heure prévue pour la dose suivante. Lui expliquer qu'il ne faut jamais remplacer une dose manquée par une double dose.
- Conseiller au patient de garder l'esoméprazole dans un endroit sec, à température ambiante contrôlée (de 15 °C à 30 °C), car les comprimés sont sensibles à l'humidité.

- Prévenir le patient que l'esoméprazole peut parfois provoquer des étourdissements. Lui conseiller de ne pas conduire et d'éviter des activités qui exigent sa vigilance jusqu'à ce qu'on ait la certitude que le médicament n'entraîne pas cet effet chez lui.
- Recommander au patient de ne pas prendre de médicaments renfermant de l'aspirine ni d'AINS, sauf recommandation contraire du médecin, et de ne pas consommer d'alcool ni d'aliments pouvant aggraver l'irritation gastrique.
- Recommander au patient de signaler rapidement à un professionnel de la santé la présence de selles noires et goudronneuses, de diarrhée, de douleurs abdominales ou de céphalées persistantes.

VÉRIFICATION DE L'EFFICACITÉ THÉRAPEUTIQUE

L'efficacité du traitement peut être démontrée par: le soulagement de la douleur abdominale ou la prévention de l'irritation ou des saignements gastriques; on peut constater la guérison de l'ulcère gastroduodénal par radiographie ou endoscopie ■ la diminution des symptômes de reflux gastro-œsophagien (une résolution des symptômes se produit généralement après 5 à 8 jours de traitement). Il faudrait poursuivre le traitement pendant 4 à 8 semaines après le premier épisode.

ESTROPIPATE

Ogen

CLASSIFICATION:

Hormone (œstrogène)

Grossesse – catégorie X

INDICATIONS

PO: Élément de l'hormonothérapie de substitution dans le traitement des symptômes vasomoteurs modérés à graves de la ménopause ■ Diverses carences œstrogéniques entraînées par: l'hypogonadisme (femmes), l'ovariectomie et l'insuffisance ovarienne primaire ■ Traitement d'appoint de l'ostéoporose postménopausique ■ Vaginite atrophique et atrophie vulvaire ■ On recommande l'usage concomitant de progestatifs au cours du traitement cyclique afin de réduire le risque de cancer de l'endomètre chez les patientes dont l'utérus est intact.

MÉCANISME D'ACTION

Les œstrogènes favorisent la croissance et le développement des organes sexuels et maintiennent les caractères sexuels secondaires chez la femme ■ Les effets métaboliques comprennent la réduction des concentrations sanguines de cholestérol, la synthèse des protéines et la rétention hydrosodée. ***Effets thérapeutiques:*** Rétablissement de l'équilibre hormonal en présence de divers états de carence.

PHARMACOCINÉTIQUE

Absorption: Bonne (PO).

Distribution: L'estropipate se répartit dans tout l'organisme. Il traverse la barrière placentaire et passe dans le lait maternel.

Métabolisme et excrétion: Majoritairement hépatique. L'estropipate subit plusieurs cycles entérohépatiques et son absorption depuis le tractus gastro-intestinal peut être accrue.

Demi-vie: Inconnue.

Profil temps-action (effets œstrogéniques)

	DÉBUT D'ACTION	PIC	DURÉE
PO	inconnu	inconnu	24 h

CONTRE-INDICATIONS, PRÉCAUTIONS ET MISES EN GARDE

Contre-indications: Maladie thromboembolique ■ Hypersensibilité ■ Antécédents personnels de cancer œstrogénodépendant ■ Hyperplasie de l'endomètre ■ Présence de migraine classique ■ Problèmes oculaires liés à une atteinte vasculaire ophtalmique ■ Maladies hépatiques évolutives ■ Antécédents d'accidents vasculaires cérébraux ■ Saignements vaginaux non diagnostiqués ■ **OBST.**: Risque d'effets nocifs sur le fœtus ■ Allaitement.

Précautions et mises en garde: Maladie cardiovasculaire sous-jacente ■ Maladies rénales graves ■ Ce type d'œstrogénothérapie comporte un risque accru de cancer de l'endomètre.

RÉACTIONS INDÉSIRABLES ET EFFETS SECONDAIRES

SNC: céphalées, étourdissements, léthargie, dépression.

ORLO: intolérance aux lentilles cornéennes, aggravation de la myopie ou de l'astigmatisme.

CV: INFARCTUS DU MYOCARDE, THROMBOEMBOLIE, œdème, hypertension.

GI: nausées, variations pondérales, anorexie, gain d'appétit, jaunisse, vomissements.

GU: *femmes* – aménorrhée, hémorragies utérines consécutives à l'œstrogénothérapie, dysménorrhée, érosions cervicales, perte de la libido, candidose vaginale; *hommes* – impuissance, atrophie testiculaire.

Tég.: acné, peau grasse, pigmentation, urticaire.

End.: gynécomastie (hommes), hyperglycémie.
HÉ: hypercalcémie, rétention hydrosodée.
Loc.: crampes dans les jambes.
Divers: sensibilité mammaire.

INTERACTIONS

Médicament-médicament: L'estropipate peut diminuer l'efficacité de la **warfarine**, des **hypoglycémiants oraux**, de l'**insuline** et des **antihypertenseurs** ■ Les **barbituriques**, la **carbamazépine** ou la **rifampine** peuvent diminuer l'efficacité de l'estropipate ■ L'**usage du tabac** (**cigarettes**) augmente le risque de réactions cardiovasculaires indésirables.

VOIES D'ADMINISTRATION ET POSOLOGIE

Symptômes vasomoteurs de la ménopause, vaginite atrophique, ostéoporose

- **PO (adultes)**: *Sous forme d'estropipate* – de 0,75 à 3 mg par jour ou en traitement cyclique.

PRÉSENTATION
(version générique disponible)

Comprimés: Doses exprimées en sulfate sodique d'estrone (équivalant en estropipate) 0,625 mg (0,75 mg)[Pr], 1,25 mg (1,5 mg)[Pr], 2,5 mg (3 mg)[Pr].

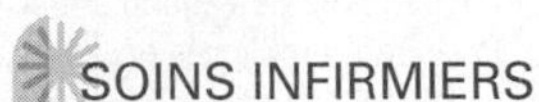

SOINS INFIRMIERS

ÉVALUATION DE LA SITUATION

- Mesurer la pression artérielle avant l'œstrogénothérapie et à intervalles réguliers pendant toute sa durée.
- Effectuer le bilan quotidien des ingesta et des excreta et peser la patiente toutes les semaines. Signaler au médecin toute variation pondérale importante ou un gain de poids constant.

Ménopause: Évaluer la fréquence et la gravité des symptômes vasomoteurs.

Tests de laboratoire:

- L'estropipate peut entraîner une élévation des taux de cholestérol HDL, de phospholipides et de triglycérides et une baisse des taux sériques de cholestérol LDL et de cholestérol total.
- L'estropipate peut entraîner l'élévation des concentrations sériques de glucose, de sodium, de cortisol, de prolactine, de prothrombine et des facteurs VII, VIII, IX et X. Il peut diminuer les concentrations sériques de folate, de pyridoxine, d'antithrombine III et les concentrations urinaires du prégnandiol.
- Suivre de près les résultats des tests de la fonction hépatique avant l'administration de l'estropipate et à intervalles réguliers tout au long du traitement.
- L'estropipate peut modifier les résultats des tests de la fonction thyroïdienne, entraîner des résultats faussement élevés à l'épreuve de l'agrégation plaquettaire induite par la noradrénaline et des résultats faussement bas au test à la métyrapone.

DIAGNOSTICS INFIRMIERS POSSIBLES

- Dysfonctionnement sexuel (Indications).
- Connaissances insuffisantes sur le traitement médicamenteux (Enseignement au patient et à ses proches).

INTERVENTIONS INFIRMIÈRES

- Pour réduire les nausées, administrer l'estropipate pendant le repas ou immédiatement après.

ENSEIGNEMENT AU PATIENT ET À SES PROCHES

- Conseiller à la patiente de respecter rigoureusement la posologie recommandée. Si elle n'a pas pu prendre le médicament au moment habituel, elle doit le prendre aussitôt que possible à moins que ce ne soit presque l'heure prévue pour la dose suivante. Il ne faut jamais remplacer une dose manquée par une double dose.
- Expliquer à la patiente le schéma posologique: traitement pendant 21 jours, sans traitement pendant 7 jours. L'inciter à prendre ces hormones tous les jours à la même heure.
- Si les nausées deviennent gênantes, recommander à la patiente de manger des aliments solides, qui peuvent souvent procurer un soulagement.
- Recommander à la patiente de prévenir un professionnel de la santé si les signes et les symptômes suivants se manifestent: rétention hydrique (œdème des chevilles et des pieds, gain de poids); TROUBLES THROMBOEMBOLIQUES (DOULEURS, ŒDÈME ET SENSIBILITÉ AU NIVEAU DES MEMBRES, CÉPHALÉES, DOULEURS THORACIQUES, VISION TROUBLE); dépression; dysfonctionnement hépatique (jaunissement de la peau ou des yeux, prurit, urine foncée, selles de couleur pâle); saignements vaginaux anormaux.
- Recommander à la patiente d'arrêter le traitement et de prévenir un professionnel de la santé si elle pense être enceinte.
- Prévenir la patiente que l'usage du tabac pendant l'œstrogénothérapie l'expose à des risques accrus d'effets secondaires graves, particulièrement si elle est âgée de plus de 35 ans.

- Inciter la patiente à utiliser un écran solaire et à porter des vêtements protecteurs afin de prévenir l'hyperpigmentation.
- Recommander à la patiente qui doit suivre un traitement ou subir une intervention chirurgicale d'avertir le professionnel de la santé qu'elle suit un traitement avec ces hormones.
- Expliquer à la patiente qui reçoit des œstrogènes pour le traitement de l'ostéoporose que l'exercice peut freiner et même renverser la perte de substance osseuse. Lui conseiller de consulter un professionnel de la santé au sujet de toute restriction éventuelle avant de s'engager dans un programme d'exercices.
- Insister sur l'importance des examens réguliers de suivi, tous les 6 à 12 mois, comprenant la mesure de la pression artérielle, l'examen des seins, de l'abdomen, des organes pelviens et le prélèvement de frottis vaginaux pour le test de Papanicolaou, et d'une mammographie, effectuée tous les 12 mois ou selon les recommandations du professionnel de la santé. Celui-ci devrait évaluer la possibilité d'interrompre le traitement tous les 3 à 6 mois. Si la patiente suit un traitement prolongé (non cyclique) ou si elle ne prend pas en même temps des progestatifs, on peut lui recommander une biopsie de l'endomètre si l'utérus est intact.

VÉRIFICATION DE L'EFFICACITÉ THÉRAPEUTIQUE

L'efficacité du traitement peut être démontrée par: la résolution des symptômes vasomoteurs de la ménopause ■ la diminution des démangeaisons, de l'inflammation ou de la sécheresse du vagin et de la vulve, provoquées par la ménopause ■ la normalisation des concentrations d'œstrogènes en cas d'ovariectomie ou d'hypogonadisme chez la femme ■ la prévention de l'ostéoporose. ✳

ÉTANERCEPT

Enbrel

CLASSIFICATION:

Agent antirhumatismal modificateur de la maladie [AARMM] (agent anti-TNF)

Grossesse – catégorie B

INDICATIONS

Traitement des poussées évolutives des formes modérées ou graves de la polyarthrite rhumatoïde chez les adultes (réduction des signes et des symptômes, induction d'une réponse clinique marquée, inhibition de la détérioration structurale et amélioration de la capacité physique). On peut l'administrer en association avec le méthotrexate ou en monothérapie ■ Atténuation des signes et des symptômes des poussées évolutives des formes modérées ou graves d'arthrite chronique juvénile polyarticulaire chez les patients âgés de 4 à 17 ans qui n'ont pas réagi de façon satisfaisante à au moins un traitement par un AARMM ■ Réduction des signes et des symptômes associés à la détérioration structurale provoquée par les poussées évolutives du rhumatisme psoriasique, inhibition de l'évolution de ces lésions et amélioration de la fonction physique chez les patients adultes. On peut l'administrer en association avec le méthotrexate chez les adultes qui n'ont pas répondu adéquatement au méthotrexate seul ■ Réduction des signes et des symptômes des poussées évolutives de la spondylarthrite ankylosante ■ Traitement des adultes atteints d'une forme chronique, modérée ou grave, de psoriasis en plaques dans le cadre d'un traitement général ou du traitement de la photothérapie.

MÉCANISME D'ACTION

Liaison au facteur de nécrose tumorale (TNF) entraînant son inactivation. Le TNF est l'un des médiateurs de la réponse inflammatoire. ***Effets thérapeutiques:*** Diminution de l'inflammation et ralentissement de l'évolution de la polyarthrite rhumatoïde, de la spondylarthrite ankylosante et du psoriasis.

PHARMACOCINÉTIQUE

Absorption: 60 % (SC).
Distribution: Inconnue.
Métabolisme et excrétion: Inconnus.
Demi-vie: 115 heures (intervalle de 98 à 300 heures).

Profil temps-action (diminution des symptômes)

	DÉBUT D'ACTION	PIC	DURÉE
SC	2 - 4 semaines	inconnu	inconnue

CONTRE-INDICATIONS, PRÉCAUTIONS ET MISES EN GARDE

Contre-indications: Hypersensibilité ■ Septicémie ■ Patients à risque de souffrir d'un état septique (p. ex., patients infectés par le VIH ou immunodéprimés) ■ ALLAITEMENT: Déterminer s'il convient de mettre fin à l'allaitement ou au traitement ■ Granulomatose de Wegener (sous traitement avec des agents immunodépresseurs) ■ Utilisation concomitante de cyclophosphamide ou d'anakinra.
Précautions et mises en garde: Trouble démyélinisant, préexistant ou d'apparition récente, touchant le système

nerveux central (sclérose en plaques, myélite, névrite optique) ■ Antécédents d'anomalies hématologiques notables ■ Patients souffrant d'une maladie chronique qui prédispose aux infections (p. ex., diabète avancé ou non équilibré) ■ Antécédents de tuberculose ou d'hépatite B (risque accru de réactivation de la maladie) ■ Allergie au latex (le capuchon de l'aiguille servant à l'administration du diluant renferme du latex) ■ Risque de réactions allergiques et d'anaphylaxie ■ Insuffisance cardiaque congestive ■ Formation d'autoanticorps (risque d'apparition du syndrome pseudolupique) ■ **GÉR.**: Risque plus élevé d'infections ■ **PÉD.**: Enfants exposés au virus de la varicelle (interrompre temporairement le traitement; envisager l'administration d'immunoglobulines de varicelle-zona). Ce médicament n'a pas été étudié chez les enfants < 4 ans ■ **OBST.**: Chez les femmes enceintes, n'administrer ce médicament qu'en cas d'absolue nécessité.

RÉACTIONS INDÉSIRABLES ET EFFETS SECONDAIRES

SNC: céphalées, étourdissements, faiblesse.
ORLO: rhinite, pharyngite, sinusite.
Resp.: infections des voies respiratoires supérieures, toux, maladie respiratoire.
GI: douleurs abdominales, dyspepsie.
Tég.: rash.
Hémat.: pancytopénie.
Locaux: réactions au point d'injection.
Divers: INFECTIONS, augmentation du risque de cancers, réaction d'hypersensibilité (rare).

INTERACTIONS

Médicament-médicament: L'étanercept peut réduire la production d'anticorps déclenchée par l'administration d'un **vaccin à virus vivants** et accroître le risque de réactions indésirables (ne pas administrer en concomitance) ■ L'utilisation concomitante d'étanercept, de **cyclophosphamide** et d'**anakinra** augmente le risque d'effets secondaires. Cette association n'est pas recommandée.

VOIES D'ADMINISTRATION ET POSOLOGIE

Polyarthrite rhumatoïde, rhumatisme psoriasique ou spondylarthrite ankylosante

- **SC (adultes)**: 50 mg, 1 fois par semaine.

Psoriasis en plaques

- **SC (adultes)**: 50 mg, 2 fois par semaine, pendant 3 mois. Par la suite, administrer la dose d'entretien de 50 mg par semaine. Une dose d'entretien de 50 mg, 2 fois par semaine, s'est également révélée efficace.

Arthrite chronique juvénile

- **SC (enfants de 4 à 17 ans)**: *Enfants ≥ 63 kg*: 0,8 mg/kg/semaine (maximum de 50 mg par semaine) en une seule dose; *enfants de 31 à 62 kg*: 0,8 mg/kg/semaine en 2 injections sous-cutanées soit le même jour, soit à des intervalles de 3 ou 4 jours; *enfants < 31 kg*: 0,8 mg/kg/semaine en une seule dose.

PRÉSENTATION

Poudre pour injection: fioles de 25 mg[Pr] ■ **Solution pour injection**: seringues jetables: 50 mg/mL[Pr], auto-injecteur: 50 mg/mL[Pr].

SOINS INFIRMIERS

ÉVALUATION DE LA SITUATION

- Déterminer l'amplitude des mouvements articulaires et la gravité de l'œdème des articulations ainsi que l'intensité de la douleur au niveau des articulations atteintes, avant le traitement et à intervalles réguliers pendant toute sa durée.
- Rester à l'affût des réactions suivantes au point d'injection: érythème, douleur, démangeaisons, œdème. Les réactions sont habituellement légères à modérées et persistent pendant 3 à 5 jours après l'injection.
- SURVEILLER LES PATIENTS QUI DÉVELOPPENT UNE NOUVELLE INFECTION PENDANT LEUR TRAITEMENT AVEC L'ÉTANERCEPT. CESSER LE TRAITEMENT PAR L'ÉTANERCEPT SI LE PATIENT CONTRACTE UNE INFECTION GRAVE OU S'IL DÉVELOPPE UN ÉTAT SEPTIQUE. NE PAS COMMENCER UN TRAITEMENT PAR L'ÉTANERCEPT CHEZ LES PATIENTS QUI PRÉSENTENT UNE INFECTION ACTIVE.

DIAGNOSTICS INFIRMIERS POSSIBLES

- Mobilité physique réduite (Indications).
- Douleur aiguë (Indications).
- Connaissances insuffisantes sur le traitement médicamenteux (Enseignement au patient et à ses proches).

INTERVENTIONS INFIRMIÈRES

- Le capuchon de l'aiguille destinée à l'administration du diluant renferme du latex. Il ne devrait donc pas être manipulé par des personnes allergiques à cette substance.

SC:

- Le contenu des flacons à usage multiple doit être reconstitué avec 1 mL de l'eau bactériostatique pour injection fournie par le fabricant. Injecter lentement le diluant dans la fiole pour prévenir la formation d'une mousse. Le produit moussera un peu. Tourner doucement la fiole pour dissoudre cette mousse, sans brasser ni agiter vigoureusement pour que le produit ne mousse pas trop. La dissolution prend habituellement moins de 10 minutes. La reconstitution de la solution avec l'eau bactériostatique pour préparations injectables fournie permet d'obtenir une solution à usages multiples, contenant un agent de conservation et utilisable pendant 14 jours. Dans le cas des enfants recevant une dose inférieure à 25 mg, on inscrira la date de la reconstitution dans l'espace marqué « Date de reconstitution/Mixing Date : » sur l'autocollant fourni et on apposera celui-ci sur le flacon immédiatement après la reconstitution de la solution. La solution doit être transparente et incolore; ne pas administrer la solution si elle a changé de couleur, si elle est trouble ou si elle renferme des particules. Ne prélever dans la seringue que la dose à administrer. Un peu de mousse peut rester dans la fiole. Ne pas filtrer la solution reconstituée pendant la préparation ou l'administration. La solution reconstituée peut être conservée dans le flacon d'origine pendant 14 jours au maximum à une température comprise entre 2 °C et 8 °C. Elle ne doit toutefois pas être laissée à la température ambiante pendant plus de 12 heures en tout durant cette période, ce qui comprend le temps de préparation et d'administration des injections. Consulter les directives du fabricant avant de reconstituer la préparation.

- La solution d'étanercept contenue dans les seringues préremplies ou dans les auto-injecteurs doit être conservée à une température de 2 °C à 8 °C. Avant son administration, la solution devrait être laissée à la température de la pièce (sans retirer le protecteur dc l'aiguille) pendant 15 à 30 minutes afin de diminuer les douleurs pendant l'injection.
- L'étanercept peut être injecté dans l'abdomen, la cuisse ou la portion supérieure du bras. Assurer la rotation des points d'injection. Ne pas administrer à moins de 2,5 cm d'un ancien point d'injection ou dans une région sensible, rouge, dure ou contusionnée.

Incompatibilité dans la même seringue: Ne pas mélanger à d'autres solutions ni diluer avec d'autres diluants.

ENSEIGNEMENT AU PATIENT ET À SES PROCHES

- Enseigner au patient la technique d'autoadministration et lui montrer comment conserver et mettre au rebut le matériel. La première injection doit être administrée sous la supervision d'un professionnel de la santé. Fournir au patient un contenant non perforable pour la mise au rebut du matériel usagé.
- Recommander au patient de ne pas recevoir de vaccin à virus vivants durant le traitement. Les enfants doivent recevoir leurs vaccins avant de commencer le traitement par l'étanercept. Les patients qui ont été exposés à la varicelle devraient interrompre passagèrement le traitement et on devrait envisager dans leur cas l'administration d'immunoglobulines de varicelle-zona.
- Expliquer au patient qu'il peut prendre simultanément le méthotrexate, un analgésique, un AINS, des corticostéroïdes et des salicylates.
- RECOMMANDER AU PATIENT DE SIGNALER À UN PROFESSIONNEL DE LA SANTÉ TOUTE INFECTION DES VOIES RESPIRATOIRES HAUTES OU AUTRE. L'ARRÊT DU TRAITEMENT POURRAIT S'IMPOSER EN CAS D'INFECTIONS GRAVES.

VÉRIFICATION DE L'EFFICACITÉ THÉRAPEUTIQUE

L'efficacité du traitement peut être démontrée par: la diminution des symptômes de polyarthrite rhumatoïde, d'arthrite chronique juvénile polyarticulaire, de rhumatisme psoriasique, de spondylarthrite ankylosante ou de psoriasis en plaques. Les symptômes peuvent cependant récidiver dans le mois qui suit l'arrêt du traitement. ✳

ÉTHAMBUTOL

Etibi

CLASSIFICATION:

Antituberculeux

Grossesse – catégorie B

INDICATIONS

Traitement, en association avec au moins un autre médicament, de la tuberculose en poussée évolutive ou d'autres infections mycobactériennes.

MÉCANISME D'ACTION

Inhibition de la croissance des mycobactéries. ***Effets thérapeutiques:*** Effet bactériostatique contre les mycobactéries sensibles.

PHARMACOCINÉTIQUE

Absorption: 80 % (PO).

Distribution: Dans la plupart des tissus et liquides physiologiques. L'éthambutol ne traverse qu'en très petites quantités la barrière hématoencéphalique. Il traverse la barrière placentaire et passe dans le lait maternel.
Métabolisme et excrétion: Métabolisme hépatique (50 %); excrétion rénale à l'état inchangé (50 %).
Demi-vie: De 3 à 4 heures (prolongée en cas d'insuffisance rénale ou hépatique).

E

Profil temps-action

	DÉBUT D'ACTION	PIC	DURÉE
PO	rapide	2-4 h	24 h

CONTRE-INDICATIONS, PRÉCAUTIONS ET MISES EN GARDE

Contre-indications: Hypersensibilité ■ Névrite optique.
Précautions et mises en garde: Insuffisance rénale ou hépatique graves (réduire la dose) ■ **PÉD.:** L'innocuité du médicament n'a pas été établie chez les enfants < 13 ans ■ **OBST.:** Bien que l'innocuité de l'éthambutol n'ait pas été établie, l'agent a déjà été administré en association avec l'isoniazide pour traiter la tuberculose chez les femmes enceintes sans provoquer d'effets nocifs chez le fœtus ■ Allaitement.

RÉACTIONS INDÉSIRABLES ET EFFETS SECONDAIRES

SNC: confusion, étourdissements, hallucinations, céphalées, malaise.
ORLO: <u>névrite optique</u>.
GI: douleurs abdominales, anorexie, HÉPATITE, nausées, vomissements.
Métab.: hyperuricémie.
Loc.: douleurs articulaires.
SN: névrite périphérique.
Divers: réactions anaphylactoïdes, fièvre.

INTERACTIONS

Médicament-médicament: Risques de neurotoxicité additive lors de l'administration concomitante d'autres **agents dotés de propriétés neurotoxiques**.

VOIES D'ADMINISTRATION ET POSOLOGIE

- **PO (adultes et enfants > 13 ans):** 15 mg/kg/jour, 1 fois par jour, si le patient n'a jamais pris d'agent antituberculeux. Si le patient a déjà été traité par un agent antituberculeux: 25 mg/kg/jour, 1 fois par jour, jusqu'à ce que les cultures et frottis bactériens soient négatifs, puis administrer 15 mg/kg/jour. On peut aussi administrer l'éthambutol à raison de 50 mg/kg (jusqu'à 2,5 g), 2 fois par semaine, *ou* de 25 à 30 mg/kg (jusqu'à 2,5 g), 3 fois par semaine.

PRÉSENTATION

Comprimés: 100 mg[Pr], 400 mg[Pr].

SOINS INFIRMIERS

ÉVALUATION DE LA SITUATION

- Prélever des échantillons pour les cultures de mycobactéries et les épreuves de sensibilité avant de commencer le traitement et à intervalles réguliers par la suite, afin de déceler l'émergence d'une résistance éventuelle.
- À intervalles réguliers, pendant toute la durée du traitement, ausculter le murmure vésiculaire et noter les caractéristiques des expectorations et la quantité expulsée.
- Examiner la vue du patient à intervalles fréquents tout au long du traitement. Conseiller au patient de prévenir immédiatement un professionnel de la santé si les signes suivants se manifestent: vision trouble, rétrécissement des champs visuels ou changement de la perception des couleurs. Si l'altération de la vision n'est pas diagnostiquée suffisamment tôt, elle risque d'être irréversible.

Tests de laboratoire: Examiner les résultats des tests des fonctions rénale et hépatique, la numération globulaire et les concentrations d'acide urique à intervalles réguliers tout au long du traitement. L'éthambutol entraîne fréquemment l'élévation des concentrations d'acide urique, ce qui peut déclencher une crise de goutte.

DIAGNOSTICS INFIRMIERS POSSIBLES

- Risque d'infection (Indications).
- Trouble de la perception sensorielle (Effets secondaires).
- Connaissances insuffisantes sur le traitement médicamenteux (Enseignement au patient et à ses proches).

INTERVENTIONS INFIRMIÈRES

- L'éthambutol est administré en une seule dose quotidienne et il doit être pris tous les jours à la même heure. Selon certains schémas posologiques, il faut administrer le médicament 2 ou 3 fois par semaine. L'éthambutol est habituellement administré en concomitance avec d'autres antituberculeux pour prévenir l'émergence d'une résistance bactérienne.
- Administrer l'éthambutol avec des aliments ou du lait afin de réduire les risques d'irritation gastrique.

ENSEIGNEMENT AU PATIENT ET À SES PROCHES

- Conseiller au patient de respecter rigoureusement la posologie recommandée. S'il n'a pas pu prendre le médicament au moment habituel, il doit le prendre aussitôt que possible à moins que ce ne soit presque l'heure prévue pour la dose suivante. Le prévenir qu'il ne doit jamais remplacer une dose manquée par une double dose. Le traitement peut durer plusieurs mois et même plusieurs années. Conseiller également au patient de ne pas arrêter le traitement avant d'avoir consulté un professionnel de la santé même si les symptômes semblent s'être résorbés.
- Recommander à la patiente de prévenir un professionnel de la santé si elle pense être enceinte.
- Conseiller au patient de prévenir un professionnel de la santé s'il ne note aucune amélioration en l'espace de 2 à 3 semaines, tout comme en cas de gain de poids imprévu ou de diminution de la diurèse.
- Insister sur l'importance des examens réguliers de suivi permettant d'évaluer les bienfaits du traitement et des examens de la vue, si des signes de névrite optique se manifestent.

VÉRIFICATION DE L'EFFICACITÉ THÉRAPEUTIQUE

L'efficacité du traitement peut être démontrée par: la résolution des symptômes cliniques de la tuberculose ■ la diminution du nombre de bactéries dans les échantillons de crachats ■ l'amélioration des signes révélés par la radiographie pulmonaire. Le traitement antituberculeux doit habituellement être poursuivi pendant au moins 1 ou 2 ans. ✳

ÉTHINYLŒSTRADIOL,

voir Contraceptifs hormonaux

ÉTHINYLŒSTRADIOL/ NORELGESTROMINE,

voir Contraceptifs hormonaux

ÉTHYNODIOL,

voir Contraceptifs hormonaux

ÉTIDRONATE

Co-étidronate, Didronel, Gen-Étidronate

CLASSIFICATION:

Régulateur du métabolisme osseux (bisphosphonate)

Grossesse – catégorie C

INDICATIONS

Traitement de la maladie osseuse de Paget ■ Traitement concomitant (diurèse saline) de l'hypercalcémie associée aux cancers ■ *En association avec du calcium (Didrocal):* Traitement de l'ostéoporose postménopausique établie, prévention de l'ostéoporose postménopausique chez les femmes à risque, prévention de l'ostéoporose provoquée par les corticostéroïdes. **Usages non approuvés:** Traitement et prophylaxie de la calcification hétérotopique associée à la présence d'une prothèse totale de la hanche ou à une lésion de la moelle épinière.

MÉCANISME D'ACTION

Inhibition de la croissance des cristaux d'hydroxyapatite de calcium par liaison au phosphate de calcium. ***Effets thérapeutiques:*** Diminution de la résorption osseuse et ralentissement du renouvellement de la substance osseuse.

PHARMACOCINÉTIQUE

Absorption: Faible (de 1 à 6 %, PO).
Distribution: La moitié de la dose absorbée se lie aux cristaux d'hydroxyapatite dans les régions où l'ostéogenèse est accrue.
Métabolisme et excrétion: Le médicament non absorbé est éliminé dans les fèces; 50 % de la dose absorbée est excrété à l'état inchangé par les reins.
Demi-vie: De 5 à 7 heures.

Profil temps-action (effets thérapeutiques)

	DÉBUT D'ACTION	PIC	DURÉE
PO (maladie osseuse de Paget)	1 mois†	inconnu	1 an
PO (ossification hétérotopique)	inconnu	inconnu	plusieurs mois
IV‡ (hypercalcémie)	24 h	3 jours	11 jours

† Mesuré par la diminution de l'hydroxyproline urinaire.
‡ Mesurés par la diminution de l'excrétion du calcium urinaire.

CONTRE-INDICATIONS, PRÉCAUTIONS ET MISES EN GARDE

Contre-indications: Hypersensibilité ■ Insuffisance rénale grave (créatinine sérique > 442 μmol/L) ■ Hypercalcémie due à l'hyperparathyroïdie ■ Ostéomalacie.

Précautions et mises en garde: Fracture des os longs ■ Insuffisance cardiaque ■ Hypocalcémie ■ Hypovitaminose D ■ Insuffisance rénale modérée (il est recommandé de diminuer la dose si la créatinine sérique se situe entre 221 et 433 μmol/L) ■ **OBST., ALLAITEMENT, PÉD.**: L'innocuité du médicament n'a pas été établie.

RÉACTIONS INDÉSIRABLES ET EFFETS SECONDAIRES

E

GI: diarrhée, nausées; *IV* – perte du goût, goût métallique.
GU: néphrotoxicité.
Tég.: rash.
Loc.: douleurs osseuses, sensibilité osseuse, microfractures.

INTERACTIONS

Médicament-médicament: Les **antiacides**, les **suppléments minéraux** ou les **tampons** (comme ceux qui entrent dans la composition de la didanosine) contenant du **calcium**, de l'**aluminium**, du **fer** ou du **magnésium** peuvent diminuer l'absorption de l'étidronate ■ Risque d'effets hypocalcémiques additifs lors de l'administration concomitante de **calcitonine**.
Médicament-aliments: Les aliments riches en **calcium**, en **aluminium**, en **fer** ou en **magnésium** peuvent diminuer l'absorption de l'étidronate.

VOIES D'ADMINISTRATION ET POSOLOGIE

Maladie osseuse de Paget

- **PO (adultes)**: De 5 à 10 mg/kg/jour, en une seule dose, pendant une période n'excédant pas 6 mois *ou* de 11 à 20 mg/kg/jour, pendant une période n'excédant pas 3 mois.

Hypercalcémie

- **PO (adultes)**: 20 mg/kg/jour, pendant 30 à 90 jours.
- **IV (adultes)**: 7,5 mg/kg/jour, pendant 3 jours.

Ostéoporose

- **PO (adultes)**: *En association avec le calcium (Didrocal):* 14 comprimés blancs de 400 mg d'étidronate disodique à prendre 1 fois/jour, pendant 14 jours, et 76 comprimés bleus de carbonate de calcium à prendre 1 fois/jour, pendant les 76 jours qui suivent. Traitement cyclique de 90 jours.

PRÉSENTATION

Comprimés: 200 mg^{Pr} ■ L'étidronate est également présent dans le produit Didrocal^{Pr} (traitement de 90 jours; les 14 premiers jours, il faut administrer des comprimés d'étidronate à 400 mg et les 76 jours qui suivent, des comprimés de carbonate de calcium).

SOINS INFIRMIERS

ÉVALUATION DE LA SITUATION

- Observer le patient, avant le traitement et pendant toute sa durée, à la recherche des symptômes suivants: douleurs osseuses, faiblesse ou perte de la capacité fonctionnelle. Les douleurs osseuses peuvent persister ou s'intensifier chez les patients souffrant de la maladie de Paget; elles disparaissent habituellement plusieurs jours ou plusieurs mois après l'arrêt du traitement. Consulter un professionnel de la santé à propos de l'administration d'un analgésique pour soulager la douleur.

Ossification hétérotopique: Suivre de près le patient à la recherche de signes d'inflammation et de douleur à l'emplacement de l'ossification et examiner la perte de capacité fonctionnelle si cette ossification se produit près d'une articulation.

Hypercalcémie:

- Suivre de près les symptômes suivants d'hypercalcémie: nausées, vomissements, anorexie, faiblesse, constipation, soif et arythmies cardiaques.
- Observer attentivement le patient pour déceler les signes et les symptômes suivants d'hypocalcémie: paresthésie, soubresauts musculaires, laryngospasme, coliques, arythmies cardiaques et signes de Chvostek ou de Trousseau. Afin de protéger contre les blessures les patients qui manifestent des symptômes, relever et rembourrer les ridelles du lit; garder le lit en position basse. Le risque d'hypocalcémie est le plus élevé après 3 jours de traitement continu par voie IV.

Tests de laboratoire:

- L'étidronate entrave le captage par les os du technétium^{99} utilisé lors des épreuves diagnostiques d'imagerie.
- *Maladie de Paget:* La diminution de l'excrétion urinaire d'hydroxyproline et des concentrations sériques de phosphatase alcaline constitue souvent le premier signe clinique d'un traitement efficace. Ces valeurs doivent être notées tous les 3 mois. On recommence le traitement lorsque les concentrations reviennent à 75 % des valeurs d'avant le traitement. Les concentrations de phosphate sérique doivent également être mesurées avant le traitement et 4 semaines après son début. On peut réduire la dose si les concentrations de phosphate sérique sont élevées sans diminution correspondante de l'excrétion urinaire d'hydroxyproline ou des concentrations sériques de phosphatase alcaline.

- *Hypercalcémie:* Noter les concentrations sériques de calcium et d'albumine afin de déterminer l'efficacité du traitement.
- Mesurer les concentrations sériques d'urée et de créatinine avant le traitement et à intervalles réguliers pendant toute sa durée. Des augmentations stables ou réversibles des concentrations d'urée et de créatinine peuvent se produire chez les patients présentant une hypercalcémie.

DIAGNOSTICS INFIRMIERS POSSIBLES

- Douleur aiguë (Indications, Effets secondaires).
- Risque d'accident (Indications).
- Connaissances insuffisantes sur le traitement médicamenteux (Enseignement au patient et à ses proches).

INTERVENTIONS INFIRMIÈRES

- NE PAS CONFONDRE L'ÉTIDRONATE AVEC L'ÉTOMIDATE.
- Administrer à jeun, car les aliments diminuent l'absorption du médicament.

Hypercalcémie: L'étidronate est utilisé comme traitement d'appoint après le rétablissement du débit urinaire par l'hydratation par voie IV et l'administration de diurétiques de l'anse.

- On peut commencer l'administration des doses orales le lendemain de la dernière dose IV.

Perfusion intermittente: Diluer la dose dans au moins 250 mL de NaCl 0,9 % ou de D5%E. La solution est stable pendant 24 heures, si elle est diluée dans du D5%E, et pendant 48 heures, si elle est diluée dans du NaCl 0,9 %.

Vitesse d'administration: Administrer les doses de 7,5 mg/kg en perfusion pendant au moins 2 heures.

ENSEIGNEMENT AU PATIENT ET À SES PROCHES

- Conseiller au patient de respecter rigoureusement la posologie recommandée. S'il n'a pu prendre le médicament au moment habituel, il doit le prendre aussitôt que possible à moins que ce ne soit presque l'heure prévue pour la dose suivante. Le prévenir qu'il ne doit jamais remplacer une dose manquée par une double dose. Lui expliquer qu'il ne faut pas prendre le médicament dans les 2 heures qui suivent ou précèdent les repas (particulièrement s'il consomme des aliments riches en calcium) ou la prise de vitamines ou d'antiacides, car l'absorption du médicament sera altérée.
- Recommander au patient de prévenir un professionnel de la santé en cas de diarrhée. Pour la maîtriser, celui-ci peut recommander de fractionner la dose quotidienne.
- Inciter le patient à suivre les recommandations diététiques et à consommer des aliments contenant des quantités appropriées de calcium et de vitamine D (voir l'annexe J).
- Recommander au patient de signaler à un professionnel de la santé l'apparition ou l'aggravation des douleurs durant le traitement.
- Expliquer au patient qui reçoit une dose par voie IV que le goût métallique n'est pas un effet inhabituel et qu'il disparaît généralement dans les quelques heures qui suivent.
- Recommander au patient de signaler immédiatement à un professionnel de la santé les signes suivants qui indiquent la réapparition de l'hypercalcémie: douleurs osseuses, anorexie, nausées, vomissements, soif, léthargie.
- Insister sur l'importance d'un suivi médical régulier pendant le traitement permettant de déterminer si l'état du patient s'améliore et, même après l'arrêt du traitement, pour déceler les premiers signes de rechute.

VÉRIFICATION DE L'EFFICACITÉ THÉRAPEUTIQUE

L'efficacité du traitement peut être démontrée par: la diminution des concentrations de calcium sérique ■ la diminution des douleurs et des fractures osseuses en cas de maladie osseuse de Paget ■ la prévention ou la diminution des signes d'ossification hétérotopique; les concentrations sériques normales de calcium sont habituellement atteintes dans les 2 à 8 jours en cas d'hypercalcémie associée à des métastases osseuses; on peut répéter le traitement 1 semaine plus tard ■ la prévention de l'ostéoporose ou le ralentissement de son évolution chez les femmes ménopausées ■ la prévention de l'ostéoporose induite par les corticostéroïdes. ✳

ÉTODOLAC

Apo-Etodolac, Gen-Etodolac, Taro-Etodolac

CLASSIFICATION:

Analgésique non opioïde, anti-inflammatoire non stéroïdien

Grossesse – catégories D (1er et 3e trimestres) et B (2e trimestre)

INDICATIONS

Traitement de l'arthrose ■ Traitement de la polyarthrite rhumatoïde ■ Soulagement des douleurs légères à modérées.

MÉCANISME D'ACTION

Inhibition de la synthèse des prostaglandines ■ Effet uricosurique. ***Effets thérapeutiques:*** Suppression de l'inflammation ■ Diminution de l'intensité de la douleur.

PHARMACOCINÉTIQUE

Absorption: Bonne (PO).
Distribution: Tout l'organisme.
Liaison aux protéines: > 99 %.
Métabolisme et excrétion: Métabolisme majoritairement hépatique; moins de 1 % est excrété à l'état inchangé dans l'urine.
Demi-vie: De 6 à 7 heures (dose unique); 7,3 heures (administration prolongée).

Profil temps-action (effets thérapeutiques)

	Début d'action	Pic	Durée
PO (analgésique)	0,5 h	1 – 2 h	4 – 12 h
PO (anti-inflammatoire)	plusieurs jours – semaines	inconnu	6 – 12 h

CONTRE-INDICATIONS, PRÉCAUTIONS ET MISES EN GARDE

Contre-indications: Hypersensibilité ■ Hémorragie digestive évolutive ou présence d'un ulcère gastroduodénal ■ Risque de réactions de sensibilité croisée avec d'autres agents anti-inflammatoires non stéroïdiens incluant l'aspirine ■ Antécédents d'ulcération récurrente ■ Maladie inflammatoire des voies gastro-intestinales ■ Syndrome complet ou partiel des polypes nasaux (usage déconseillé) ■ Altération ou forte dégradation de la fonction rénale (Cl_{Cr} < 30 mL/min) ■ Insuffisance hépatique ou autre maladie hépatique évolutive.
Précautions et mises en garde: Maladie cardiovasculaire ou facteurs de risque de maladies cardiovasculaires (risque accru de complications coronariennes, d'infarctus du myocarde ou d'accidents vasculaires cérébraux surtout lors d'un usage prolongé) ■ **OBST.:** Utilisation déconseillée pendant la deuxième partie de la grossesse ■ **ALLAITEMENT, PÉD.:** L'innocuité du médicament n'a pas été établie ■ **GÉR.:** Ces patients peuvent être davantage prédisposés aux réactions indésirables.

RÉACTIONS INDÉSIRABLES ET EFFETS SECONDAIRES

SNC: dépression, étourdissements, somnolence, insomnie, malaise, nervosité, syncope, faiblesse.
ORLO: vision trouble, photophobie, acouphènes.
Resp.: asthme.
CV: INSUFFISANCE CARDIAQUE, œdème, hypertension, palpitations.
GI: HÉMORRAGIE DIGESTIVE, dyspepsie, douleurs abdominales, constipation, diarrhée, hépatite médicamenteuse, sécheresse de la bouche (xérostomie), flatulence, gastrite, nausées, stomatite, soif, vomissements.
GU: dysurie, insuffisance rénale, mictions fréquentes.
Tég.: ecchymoses, bouffées vasomotrices, hyperpigmentation, prurit, rash, transpiration, DERMATITE EXFOLIATIVE, SYNDROME DE STEVENS-JOHNSON, ÉPIDERMOLYSE NÉCROSANTE SUBAIGUË.
Hémat.: anémie, allongement du temps de saignement, thrombopénie.
Divers: réactions allergiques incluant l'ANAPHYLAXIE, l'ŒDÈME ANGIONEUROTIQUE, frissons, fièvre.

INTERACTIONS

Médicament-médicament: L'**aspirine** peut réduire l'efficacité de l'étodolac ■ Intensification des effets indésirables sur l'appareil gastro-intestinal lors de l'administration concomitante d'**aspirine**, d'autres **agents anti-inflammatoires non stéroïdiens**, de **suppléments de potassium**, de **corticostéroïdes**, d'**agents antiplaquettaires** ou de la consommation d'**alcool** ■ L'utilisation prolongée d'étodolac avec de l'**acétaminophène** peut augmenter le risque de réactions rénales indésirables ■ L'étodolac peut réduire l'efficacité des **diurétiques** ou des **antihypertenseurs** ■ L'étodolac peut élever les concentrations sériques de **lithium** et augmenter le risque de toxicité ■ L'étodolac augmente le risque de toxicité reliée à un traitement par le **méthotrexate** ■ L'étodolac augmente le risque d'hémorragie lors de l'administration concomitante de **céfamandole**, de **céfotétane**, de **céfopérazone**, d'**acide valproïque**, de **plicamycine**, d'**agents thrombolytiques**, d'**agents antiplaquettaires** ou d'**anticoagulants** ■ Risque accru de réactions hématologiques indésirables lors de l'administration concomitante d'**agents antinéoplasiques** ou d'une **radiothérapie** ■ L'étodolac peut accroître le risque de néphrotoxicité associé à un traitement par la **cyclosporine**.
Médicament-produits naturels: On peut observer une augmentation du risque de saignement en cas de prise concomitante d'**arnica**, de **camomille**, de **girofle**, d'**ail**, de **dong quai**, de **grande camomille**, de **gingembre**, de **ginkgo biloba** et de **ginseng**.

VOIES D'ADMINISTRATION ET POSOLOGIE

- **PO (adultes):** *Analgésie* – de 200 à 400 mg, toutes les 6 à 8 heures, selon les besoins; durée maximale d'utilisation pour cette indication: 7 jours (ne pas dépasser 1 000 mg par jour). *Arthrose, polyarthrite* *rhumatoïde* – de 200 à 300 mg, 2 fois par jour ou une dose unique de 400 à 600 mg, le soir.

PRÉSENTATION

Capsules: 200 mgPr, 300 mgPr.

SOINS INFIRMIERS

ÉVALUATION DE LA SITUATION

- LES PATIENTS SOUFFRANT D'ASTHME, D'ALLERGIE INDUITE PAR L'ASPIRINE ET DE POLYPES NASAUX SONT DAVANTAGE PRÉDISPOSÉS AUX RÉACTIONS D'HYPERSENSIBILITÉ. SUIVRE DE PRÈS LA RHINITE, L'ASTHME ET L'URTICAIRE.

Arthrose et polyarthrite rhumatoïde: Suivre de près la douleur et la mobilité des articulations avant l'administration de l'étodolac et de 1 à 2 heures plus tard.

Douleur: Déterminer le siège, la durée et l'intensité de la douleur avant l'administration de l'étodolac et 60 minutes plus tard.

Tests de laboratoire:

- L'étodolac peut diminuer les concentrations d'hémoglobine, l'hématocrite et le nombre de globules blancs et de plaquettes.
- Après le début du traitement par l'étodolac, noter les résultats des tests de la fonction hépatique pendant les 8 premières semaines, et à intervalles réguliers tout au long du traitement. L'étodolac peut entraîner une élévation des concentrations sériques de phosphatase alcaline, de LDH, d'AST et d'ALT.
- Noter les concentrations d'urée, de créatinine sérique et d'électrolytes à intervalles réguliers tout au long du traitement. L'étodolac peut élever les concentrations d'urée, de créatinine sérique et d'électrolytes et diminuer les concentrations d'électrolytes urinaires.
- L'étodolac peut diminuer les concentrations sériques d'acide urique et en élever les concentrations urinaires.

DIAGNOSTICS INFIRMIERS POSSIBLES

- Douleur aiguë (Indications).
- Mobilité physique réduite (Indications).
- Connaissances insuffisantes sur le traitement médicamenteux (Enseignement au patient et à ses proches).

INTERVENTIONS INFIRMIÈRES

- L'administration de doses plus élevées que celles recommandées n'entraîne pas une efficacité accrue, mais peut accroître le nombre d'effets secondaires.
- Pour obtenir un effet initial rapide, administrer l'agent 30 minutes avant ou 2 heures après les repas. On peut administrer l'étodolac avec des aliments, du lait ou des antiacides renfermant de l'aluminium ou du magnésium pour diminuer l'irritation gastrique.
- Utiliser la dose minimale efficace pendant le moins de temps possible.

ENSEIGNEMENT AU PATIENT ET À SES PROCHES

- Conseiller au patient de prendre l'étodolac avec un grand verre d'eau; l'informer qu'il ne doit pas se coucher pendant les 15 à 30 minutes qui suivent.
- Conseiller au patient de respecter rigoureusement la posologie recommandée. S'il n'a pas pu prendre le médicament au moment habituel, il doit le prendre aussitôt que possible, à moins que ce ne soit presque l'heure prévue pour la dose suivante. Lui expliquer qu'il ne faut jamais remplacer une dose manquée par une double dose.
- Prévenir le patient que l'étodolac peut parfois provoquer des étourdissements ou de la somnolence. Lui conseiller de ne pas conduire et d'éviter les activités qui exigent sa vigilance jusqu'à ce qu'on ait la certitude que le médicament n'entraîne pas ces effets chez lui.
- RECOMMANDER AU PATIENT D'ÉVITER DE BOIRE DE L'ALCOOL ET DE CONSULTER UN PROFESSIONNEL DE LA SANTÉ AVANT DE PRENDRE UNE PRÉPARATION À BASE D'ASPIRINE OU D'ACÉTAMINOPHÈNE, UN ANTI-INFLAMMATOIRE NON STÉROÏDIEN OU UN AUTRE MÉDICAMENT EN VENTE LIBRE EN MÊME TEMPS QUE L'ÉTODOLAC.
- Recommander au patient qui doit suivre un traitement ou subir une intervention chirurgicale d'avertir le professionnel de la santé qu'il suit un traitement avec ce médicament.
- RECOMMANDER AU PATIENT DE COMMUNIQUER AVEC UN PROFESSIONNEL DE LA SANTÉ EN CAS DE RASH, DE DÉMANGEAISONS, DE TROUBLES VISUELS, D'ACOUPHÈNES, DE GAIN DE POIDS, D'ŒDÈME, DE SELLES NOIRES, DE CÉPHALÉES PERSISTANTES OU DE SYNDROME PSEUDOGRIPPAL (FRISSONS, FIÈVRE, DOULEURS MUSCULAIRES, DOULEURS).

VÉRIFICATION DE L'EFFICACITÉ THÉRAPEUTIQUE

L'efficacité du traitement peut être démontrée par: la diminution de l'intensité de la douleur ■ l'amélioration de la mobilité des articulations. Les patients qui ne répondent pas à un anti-inflammatoire non stéroïdien peuvent répondre à un autre. Il peut s'écouler 2 semaines avant d'obtenir le plein effet anti-inflammatoire.

ÉTONOGESTREL,
voir Contraceptifs hormonaux

ALERTE CLINIQUE

ÉTOPOSIDE

Vepesid

CLASSIFICATION:

Antinéoplasique (dérivé de la podophyllotoxine)

Grossesse – catégorie D

INDICATIONS

En monothérapie ou en association avec d'autres types de traitement (autres antinéoplasiques, radiothérapie, intervention chirurgicale) en présence de: ■ cancer des testicules ■ cancer pulmonaire à petites cellules ■ lymphome malin (histiocytaire). **Usages non approuvés:** Certaines leucémies.

MÉCANISME D'ACTION

Inhibition de l'ADN avant la mitose (effet spécifique sur une phase du cycle cellulaire). ***Effets thérapeutiques:*** Destruction des cellules à réplication rapide, particulièrement des cellules malignes.

PHARMACOCINÉTIQUE

Absorption: Variable (PO).

Distribution: L'agent se répartit rapidement dans l'organisme et ne semble pas pénétrer en grande quantité dans le liquide céphalorachidien; il semble cependant traverser la barrière placentaire et passe dans le lait maternel.

Liaisons aux protéines: 97 %.

Métabolisme et excrétion: Métabolisme partiellement hépatique; 45 % est excrété par les reins et 44% dans les selles.

Demi-vie: 7 heures (intervalle de 3 à 12 heures).

Profil temps-action (effets sur la numération globulaire)

	DÉBUT D'ACTION	PIC	DURÉE
PO	7 – 14 jours	9 – 16 jours	20 jours
IV	7 – 14 jours	9 – 16 jours	20 jours

CONTRE-INDICATIONS, PRÉCAUTIONS ET MISES EN GARDE

Contre-indications: Hypersensibilité ■ Leucopénie grave, thrombopénie, insuffisance rénale ou hépatique grave.

Précautions et mises en garde: Patientes en âge de procréer ■ Infection active ■ Aplasie médullaire ■ Insuffisance rénale ou hépatique (une modification de la posologie pourrait s'avérer nécessaire) ■ Autres maladies chroniques débilitantes ■ **PÉD.:** Nouveau-nés (la solution contient du polysorbate 80) ■ Grossesse ■ Allaitement ■ Intolérance connue à l'alcool benzylique, à l'alcool éthylique ou au polyéthylène glycol (étoposide par voie IV seulement).

RÉACTIONS INDÉSIRABLES ET EFFETS SECONDAIRES

SNC: somnolence, fatigue, céphalées, vertiges.

Resp.: ŒDÈME PULMONAIRE, bronchospasme.

CV: INSUFFISANCE CARDIAQUE, INFARCTUS DU MYOCARDE, hypotension (IV).

GI: nausées, vomissements, stomatite.

Tég.: alopécie.

End.: stérilité.

Hémat.: leucopénie, thrombopénie, leucémie.

Locaux: phlébite au point d'injection.

Loc.: crampes musculaires.

SN: neuropathie périphérique.

Divers: réactions allergiques incluant l'ANAPHYLAXIE, fièvre.

INTERACTIONS

Médicament-médicament: Risque d'aggravation de l'aplasie médullaire lors de l'administration concomitante d'autres **antinéoplasiques** ou d'une **radiothérapie** ■ L'étoposide peut altérer la réponse immunitaire normale aux **vaccins à virus vivants** et augmenter le risque de réactions indésirables.

VOIES D'ADMINISTRATION ET POSOLOGIE

Pour les posologies n'apparaissant pas ci-dessous, consulter les références les plus récentes en chimiothérapie.

- **IV (adultes):** De 50 à 100 mg/m² par jour, pendant 5 jours.
- **PO (adultes):** De 100 à 200 mg/m² (arrondir à 50 mg près) par jour, pendant 5 jours.

PRÉSENTATION

Capsules: 50 mg[Pr] ■ **Solution pour injection:** 20 mg/mL[Pr].

SOINS INFIRMIERS

ÉVALUATION DE LA SITUATION

- Mesurer la pression artérielle avant l'administration du médicament et toutes les 15 minutes tout au long de la perfusion. En cas d'hypotension, arrêter la perfusion et prévenir le médecin. Après avoir stabilisé la pression artérielle à l'aide de solutions IV et d'autres mesures de soutien, on peut reprendre la perfusion à un débit plus lent.

- OBSERVER LE PATIENT À LA RECHERCHE DES RÉACTIONS SUIVANTES D'HYPERSENSIBILITÉ : FIÈVRE, FRISSONS, PRURIT, URTICAIRE, BRONCHOSPASME, TACHYCARDIE, HYPOTENSION. SI CES SYMPTÔMES SE MANIFESTENT, ARRÊTER LA PERFUSION ET PRÉVENIR LE MÉDECIN. GARDER À PORTÉE DE LA MAIN DE L'ADRÉNALINE, UN ANTIHISTAMINIQUE, DES CORTICOSTÉROÏDES, DES SOLUTIONS DE REMPLISSAGE VASCULAIRE ET LE MATÉRIEL DE RÉANIMATION POUR PARER À UNE ÉVENTUELLE RÉACTION ANAPHYLACTIQUE.
- Rechercher les signes d'infection suivants : fièvre, frissons, toux, raucité de la voix, douleurs lombaires basses ou aux flancs, maux de gorge, mictions douloureuses ou difficiles. Si ces symptômes se manifestent, en informer le médecin.
- Suivre de près les saignements : saignement des gencives, formation d'ecchymoses, pétéchies, présence de sang dans les selles, l'urine et les vomissements. Éviter les injections IM et la prise de la température rectale. Appliquer une pression sur les points de ponction veineuse pendant 10 minutes.
- Effectuer le bilan quotidien des ingesta et des excreta, noter l'appétit du patient et la quantité d'aliments qu'il peut consommer. L'étoposide provoque des nausées et des vomissements chez 30 % des patients. L'administration prophylactique d'un antiémétique peut en réduire la fréquence et la durée.
- Adapter le régime alimentaire en fonction des aliments que le patient peut tolérer pour essayer de maintenir l'équilibre hydroélectrolytique et l'état nutritionnel.

Tests de laboratoire :

- Noter la numération globulaire et la formule leucocytaire avant l'administration de l'agent et à intervalles réguliers pendant toute la durée du traitement. Le nadir de la leucopénie se produit dans les 7 à 14 jours qui suivent l'administration de l'étoposide. Prévenir le médecin si le nombre de globules blancs est inférieur à 1×10^9/L. Le nadir de la thrombopénie se produit dans les 9 à 16 jours qui suivent l'administration. Prévenir le médecin si le nombre de plaquettes est inférieur à 75×10^9/L. Le nombre de globules blancs et de plaquettes revient à la normale dans les 20 jours.
- Étudier les résultats des tests de la fonction hépatique (concentrations d'AST, d'ALT, de LDH et de bilirubine) et des tests de la fonction rénale (urée, créatinine), avant le traitement et à intervalles réguliers pendant toute sa durée afin de déceler la toxicité hépatique et rénale.
- L'étoposide peut entraîner l'élévation des concentrations d'acide urique. Suivre de près ces concentrations à intervalles réguliers pendant toute la durée du traitement.

DIAGNOSTICS INFIRMIERS POSSIBLES

E

- Risque d'accident (Effets secondaires).
- Risque d'infection (Effets secondaires).
- Connaissances insuffisantes sur le traitement médicamenteux (Enseignement au patient et à ses proches).

INTERVENTIONS INFIRMIÈRES

ALERTE CLINIQUE : DES DÉCÈS SONT SURVENUS LORS DE CERTAINES CHIMIOTHÉRAPIES. AVANT D'ADMINISTRER L'AGENT, CLARIFIER TOUS LES POINTS AMBIGUS. VÉRIFIER LA LIMITE DES DOSES UNITAIRES ET QUOTIDIENNES AINSI QUE LA DOSE À ADMINISTRER PENDANT LE TRAITEMENT. DEMANDER À UN AUTRE PROFESSIONNEL DE LA SANTÉ DE VÉRIFIER UNE FOIS DE PLUS L'ORDONNANCE D'ORIGINE, LES CALCULS ET LE RÉGLAGE DE LA POMPE À PERFUSION.

- NE PAS CONFONDRE VEPESID (ÉTOPOSIDE) AVEC VERSED (MIDAZOLAM).
- Éviter tout contact avec la peau. Utiliser une tubulure de type Luer-Lock afin de prévenir les fuites accidentelles. En cas d'éclaboussure, laver immédiatement la peau avec de l'eau et du savon.
- La solution doit être préparée sous une hotte à flux laminaire. Porter des gants, un vêtement protecteur et un masque pendant la manipulation du médicament. Mettre au rebut le matériel dans les contenants réservés à cet usage (voir l'annexe H).

PO : Les capsules doivent être conservées à la température ambiante.

Perfusion intermittente : Diluer le contenu de la fiole de 5 mL avec 250 à 500 mL de solution de D5%E ou de NaCl 0,9 %, afin d'obtenir une concentration maximale de 200 à 400 µg/mL. La solution à 200 µg/mL est stable pendant 96 heures, et celle à 400 µg/mL, pendant 24 heures. Il n'est pas recommandé de préparer des concentrations supérieures à 400 µg/mL, car des cristaux peuvent se former. Jeter la solution qui contient des cristaux. Consulter les directives du fabricant avant de diluer la préparation.

Vitesse d'administration : Perfuser lentement pendant 30 à 60 minutes. Une hypotension passagère peut se manifester si la vitesse de perfusion est inférieure à 30 minutes.

Compatibilité (tubulure en Y): allopurinol ■ amifostine ■ aztréonam ■ cladribine ■ fludarabine ■ granisétron ■ melphalan ■ ondansétron ■ paclitaxel ■ pipéracilline/tazobactam ■ sagramostim ■ sodium, bicarbonate de ■ téniposide ■ thiotépa ■ vinorelbine.
Incompatibilité (tubulure en Y): céfépime ■ filgrastim ■ gallium, nitrate de ■ idarubicine.
Compatibilité en addition au soluté: carboplatine ■ cisplatine ■ cytarabine ■ floxuridine ■ fluorouracile ■ ifosfamide ■ ondansétron.

E

ENSEIGNEMENT AU PATIENT ET À SES PROCHES

- Conseiller au patient de respecter rigoureusement la posologie recommandée même si des nausées ou des vomissements surviennent. Si des vomissements surviennent peu de temps après l'administration de la dose, consulter le médecin. Si le patient n'a pas pu prendre le médicament au moment habituel, il ne doit pas prendre cette dose.
- Recommander au patient de signaler à un professionnel de la santé la fièvre, les frissons, les maux de gorge, les signes d'infection, le saignement des gencives, la formation d'ecchymoses, les pétéchies ou la présence de sang dans l'urine, les selles ou les vomissements. Le prévenir qu'il doit éviter les foules et les personnes contagieuses. Lui conseiller de ne pas consommer de boissons alcoolisées et de ne pas prendre de médicaments contenant de l'aspirine ou des AINS.
- RECOMMANDER AU PATIENT DE SIGNALER À UN PROFESSIONNEL DE LA SANTÉ LES BATTEMENTS RAPIDES DU CŒUR, LES DIFFICULTÉS RESPIRATOIRES, LES DOULEURS ABDOMINALES, LE JAUNISSEMENT DE LA PEAU, LA FAIBLESSE, LES PARESTHÉSIES OU LES TROUBLES DE LA DÉMARCHE.
- Recommander au patient d'observer ses muqueuses buccales à la recherche d'érythème et d'aphtes. En cas d'aphtes, lui conseiller de remplacer la brosse à dents par une brosse-éponge et de se rincer la bouche avec de l'eau après avoir bu ou mangé. On pourrait lui prescrire de la lidocaïne visqueuse en gargarisme si les douleurs l'empêchent de s'alimenter. La douleur associée à la stomatite peut dicter un traitement par des analgésiques opioïdes.
- Prévenir le patient qu'il risque de perdre ses cheveux. Explorer avec lui les stratégies lui permettant de s'adapter à ce changement.
- Recommander à la patiente d'utiliser une méthode contraceptive.
- Expliquer au patient qu'il ne doit pas se faire vacciner sans recommandation expresse d'un professionnel de la santé.
- Insister sur l'importance des tests de laboratoire à intervalles réguliers permettant de suivre les effets secondaires du médicament.

VÉRIFICATION DE L'EFFICACITÉ THÉRAPEUTIQUE

L'efficacité du traitement peut être démontrée par: la diminution de la taille des tumeurs solides ou le ralentissement de la propagation des métastases ■ l'amélioration de l'hématopoïèse chez les patients souffrant de leucémie. ✳

EXTRAIT THYROÏDIEN LYOPHILISÉ,

voir Thyroïdiennes, préparations

ÉZÉTIMIBE

Ezetrol

CLASSIFICATION:

Hypolipidémiant (inhibiteur de l'absorption du cholestérol)

Grossesse – catégorie C

INDICATIONS

Traitement d'appoint de l'hypercholestérolémie primaire, de l'hypercholestérolémie familiale homozygote et de la sitostérolémie homozygote (phytostérolémie), en association avec la diétothérapie et parfois avec d'autres agents (p. ex., inhibiteurs de l'HMG-CoA réductase [statines]) lorsque la diétothérapie et les autres mesures non pharmacologiques seules ne donnent pas les résultats escomptés.

MÉCANISME D'ACTION

Inhibition de l'absorption du cholestérol et des stérols végétaux apparentés au niveau de l'intestin grêle, ce qui réduit l'apport de cholestérol intestinal vers le foie. L'ézétimibe n'augmente pas l'excrétion des acides biliaires, contrairement aux chélateurs des acides biliaires, et n'inhibe pas la synthèse du cholestérol dans le foie, comme le font les statines. ***Effets thérapeutiques:*** Abaissement des réserves de cholestérol dans le foie et hausse de la clairance du cholestérol sanguin.

PHARMACOCINÉTIQUE

Absorption: Rapidement absorbé et fortement métabolisé par conjugaison en glucuronide phénolique (ézétimibe glucuronide). Le degré d'absorption et la biodisponibilité absolue sont variables.

Distribution: Inconnue.

Liaison aux protéines: 99,7 % pour l'ézétimibe et de 88 à 92 % pour son métabolite actif (ézétimibe glucuronide).

Métabolisme et excrétion: L'ézétimibe est principalement métabolisé dans l'intestin grêle et le foie par glucuronoconjugaison et fait ensuite l'objet d'une excrétion biliaire et rénale. Une très légère réaction oxydative a été observée. L'ézétimibe et son métabolite actif sont éliminés lentement du plasma, après une recirculation entérohépatique importante. Le médicament et son métabolite sont principalement excrétés dans les fèces, et le reste dans l'urine.

Demi-vie: 22 heures.

Profil temps-action (effet hypocholestérolémiant)

	DÉBUT D'ACTION	PIC	DURÉE
PO	< 1 semaine	2 - 4 semaines	inconnue

CONTRE-INDICATIONS, PRÉCAUTIONS ET MISES EN GARDE

Contre-indications: Hypersensibilité ■ Maladie hépatique évolutive ou élévation persistante et inexpliquée des transaminases sériques chez les patients qui reçoivent l'ézétimibe en association avec un inhibiteur de l'HMG-CoA réductase ■ **OBST., ALLAITEMENT**: L'ézétimibe est contre-indiqué chez la femme enceinte ou qui allaite lorsqu'il est associé à un inhibiteur de l'HMG-CoA réductase.

Précautions et mises en garde: Insuffisance hépatique modérée ou grave ■ **OBST., ALLAITEMENT**: L'innocuité du médicament, utilisé en monothérapie, n'a pas été établie chez la femme enceinte ou qui allaite ■ **PÉD.**: L'innocuité et l'efficacité du médicament n'ont pas été établies chez les enfants < 10 ans.

RÉACTIONS INDÉSIRABLES ET EFFETS SECONDAIRES

SNC: céphalées, étourdissements, fatigue.

ORLO: infection des voies respiratoires supérieures, ŒDÈME ANGIONEUROTIQUE, pharyngite, sinusite.

Resp.: toux.

CV: douleurs thoraciques, PALPITATIONS (UN CAS ACCOMPAGNÉ DE DOULEURS DANS LE BRAS).

GI: diarrhée, douleurs abdominales (UN CAS GRAVE ACCOMPAGNÉ DE PANNICULITE), élévation des enzymes hépatiques (surtout si l'agent est associé à un inhibiteur de l'HMG-CoA réductase).

Tég.: éruptions cutanées.

Loc.: arthralgie, douleurs dorsales, DOULEURS DANS LE BRAS (UN CAS ACCOMPAGNÉ DE PALPITATIONS), myalgie.

Divers: infection virale.

INTERACTIONS

Médicament-médicament: L'ézétimibe n'exerce aucun effet inducteur ou inhibiteur sur les isoenzymes CYP 1A2, 2D6, 2C8, 2C9 et 3A4 du cytochrome P450 ■ Les **chélateurs des acides biliaires** (**cholestyramine**), administrés en même temps, peuvent réduire la biodisponibilité de l'ézétimibe. Il est donc recommandé de prendre l'ézétimibe au moins 2 heures avant ou au moins 4 heures après les chélateurs des acides biliaires ■ On ne recommande pas d'administrer l'ézétimibe avec des **fibrates** (l'efficacité et l'innocuité n'ont pas été établies) ■ La **cyclosporine** augmente l'effet et la toxicité de l'ézétimibe.

VOIES D'ADMINISTRATION ET POSOLOGIE

- **PO (enfants ≥ 10 ans et adultes)**: 10 mg, 1 fois par jour, en monothérapie ou en association avec une statine, sans égard au moment la journée.

INSUFFISANCE HÉPATIQUE

- **PO (ADULTES)**: AUCUNE MODIFICATION DE LA POSOLOGIE N'EST NÉCESSAIRE EN PRÉSENCE D'UNE INSUFFISANCE HÉPATIQUE LÉGÈRE. L'ÉZÉTIMIBE N'EST PAS RECOMMANDÉ CHEZ LES PATIENTS SOUFFRANT D'INSUFFISANCE HÉPATIQUE MODÉRÉE OU GRAVE.

PRÉSENTATION

Comprimés: 10 mg[Pr].

SOINS INFIRMIERS

ÉVALUATION DE LA SITUATION

- Recueillir les données sur les habitudes alimentaires du patient, notamment sur sa consommation de matières grasses.

Tests de laboratoire:

- Noter les concentrations sériques de cholestérol et de triglycérides avant l'administration initiale, puis à intervalles réguliers, pendant toute la durée du traitement.
- Si l'ézétimibe est administré en association avec un inhibiteur de l'HMG-CoA réductase, vérifier les résultats des tests de la fonction hépatique, incluant les concentrations d'AST et d'ALT, avant l'administration initiale, de 6 à 12 semaines après le début du traitement ou après la majoration de la dose, et tous les 6 mois par la suite. Si les concentrations d'AST et d'ALT sont 3 fois supérieures à la normale,

il faut arrêter le traitement par les inhibiteurs de l'HMG-CoA réductase. Ces agents peuvent également élever les concentrations de phosphatase alcaline et de bilirubine.

- SI L'ÉZÉTIMIBE EST ADMINISTRÉ EN ASSOCIATION AVEC UN INHIBITEUR DE L'HMG-COA RÉDUCTASE, VÉRIFIER LES CONCENTRATIONS DE CPK EN CAS DE SENSIBILITÉ MUSCULAIRE. SI LES CONCENTRATIONS DE CPK SONT FORTEMENT ÉLEVÉES (PLUS DE 10 FOIS LA LSN) OU SI UNE MYOPATHIE SE MANIFESTE, IL FAUT ARRÊTER LE TRAITEMENT PAR L'INHIBITEUR DE L'HMG-COA RÉDUCTASE.

E

DIAGNOSTICS INFIRMIERS POSSIBLES

- Connaissances insuffisantes sur le traitement médicamenteux (Enseignement au patient et à ses proches).
- Non-observance du traitement médicamenteux (Enseignement au patient et à ses proches).

INTERVENTIONS INFIRMIÈRES

- Administrer l'ézétimibe avec ou sans aliments, sans égard au moment de la journée, mais de préférence à la même heure chaque jour.

ENSEIGNEMENT AU PATIENT ET À SES PROCHES

- Conseiller au patient de respecter rigoureusement la posologie recommandée, de ne pas sauter de dose et de ne pas remplacer une dose manquée par une double dose. Le médicament aide à réduire les taux sériques élevés de cholestérol, mais ne guérit pas l'hypercholestérolémie.
- Expliquer au patient que le traitement médicamenteux ne peut être efficace que s'il observe en même temps un régime pauvre en matières grasses, en cholestérol et en glucides, s'il boit de l'alcool avec modération, s'il fait de l'exercice, s'il perd du poids (le cas échéant) et s'il cesse de fumer.
- Si l'ézétimibe est pris en association avec un inhibiteur de l'HMG-CoA réductase, recommander au patient de prévenir un professionnel de la santé en cas de douleurs, de sensibilité ou de faiblesse musculaires inexpliquées, particulièrement si ces symptômes s'accompagnent de fièvre ou de malaise.
- Recommander à la patiente de prévenir immédiatement un professionnel de la santé si elle souhaite devenir enceinte ou si elle pense l'être.
- Recommander au patient d'éviter de consommer des médicaments en vente libre ou des produits naturels sans avoir consulté un professionnel de la santé.
- Recommander au patient qui doit suivre un traitement ou subir une intervention chirurgicale de prévenir le professionnel de la santé qu'il suit un traitement par ce type de médicament.
- Insister sur l'importance des examens de suivi permettant de déterminer l'efficacité du traitement et de déceler les effets secondaires.

VÉRIFICATION DE L'EFFICACITÉ THÉRAPEUTIQUE

L'efficacité du traitement peut être démontrée par: la baisse des concentrations sériques de cholestérol total, de cholestérol-LDL et d'apolipoprotéines B ■ l'élévation des concentrations de cholestérol-HDL ■ la diminution des concentrations de triglycérides. ✳

FACTEUR CITROVORUM,
voir Leucovorine calcique

FAMCICLOVIR

Apo-Famciclovir, Famvir, PMS-Famciclovir, Sandoz Famciclovir

CLASSIFICATION:
Antiviral

Grossesse – catégorie B

INDICATIONS

Traitement des infections aiguës provoquées par l'herpès zoster (zona) ■ Traitement et suppression des infections génitales herpétiques récurrentes chez les patients immunocompétents ■ Traitement des infections mucocutanées récurrentes provoquées par le virus herpès simplex chez les patients infectés par le VIH.

MÉCANISME D'ACTION

Inhibition de la synthèse de l'ADN viral seulement dans les cellules infectées par l'herpès. ***Effets thérapeutiques:*** Diminution de la durée des infections par l'herpès zoster et de la période d'excrétion virale ■ Prévention de la formation de lésions et accélération de la cicatrisation en présence d'infections récurrentes provoquées par l'herpès simplex.

PHARMACOCINÉTIQUE

Absorption: Le famciclovir est un promédicament; après son absorption, il est rapidement transformé dans la paroi intestinale en penciclovir, qui est le composé actif.
Distribution: Inconnue.
Métabolisme et excrétion: Excrétion majoritairement rénale.
Demi-vie: *Penciclovir* – de 2,1 à 3 heures (prolongée en cas d'insuffisance rénale).

Profil temps-action (penciclovir)

	DÉBUT D'ACTION	PIC	DURÉE
PO	rapide	0,9 h	8 - 12 h

CONTRE-INDICATIONS, PRÉCAUTIONS ET MISES EN GARDE

Contre-indications: Hypersensibilité.
Précautions et mises en garde: Insuffisance rénale (il est conseillé d'espacer les prises ou de réduire la dose si la Cl_{Cr} est < 60 mL/min – traitement du zona, ou si la Cl_{Cr} est < 40 mL/min – les autres indications) ■ **GÉR.**: Tenir compte du déclin de la fonction rénale associé au vieillissement ■ **OBST., ALLAITEMENT**: L'innocuité du médicament n'a pas été établie ■ **PÉD.**: L'innocuité du médicament n'a pas été établie chez les enfants < 18 ans ■ Les comprimés de famciclovir contiennent du lactose. Les personnes atteintes d'un trouble génétique rare d'intolérance au galactose, d'un grave déficit en lactase ou d'un syndrome de malabsorption du glucose/galactose ne doivent pas prendre ces comprimés.

F

RÉACTIONS INDÉSIRABLES ET EFFETS SECONDAIRES

SNC: céphalées, étourdissements, fatigue.
GI: diarrhée, nausées, vomissements.

INTERACTIONS

Médicament-médicament: Le **probénécide** élève les concentrations sanguines de penciclovir.

VOIES D'ADMINISTRATION ET POSOLOGIE

Zona

- **PO (adultes)**: 500 mg, toutes les 8 heures, pendant 7 jours. Le traitement doit être amorcé dans les 72 heures suivant le début de l'éruption.
- ***INSUFFISANCE RÉNALE***

  PO (ADULTES): *Cl_{CR} DE 40 À 59 mL/MIN* – 500 mg, TOUTES LES 12 HEURES; *Cl_{CR} DE 20 À 39 mL/MIN* – 500 mg, TOUTES LES 24 HEURES; *Cl_{CR} < 20 mL/MIN* – 250 mg, TOUTES LES 48 HEURES.

Récidives de l'herpès génital chez les patients immunocompétents

- **PO (adultes)**: 125 mg, toutes les 12 heures, pendant 5 jours. On recommande d'amorcer le traitement durant la phase prodromique ou le plus tôt possible après l'apparition des lésions.
- ***INSUFFISANCE RÉNALE***

  PO (ADULTES): *Cl_{CR} DE 20 À 39 mL/MIN* – 125 mg, TOUTES LES 24 HEURES; *Cl_{CR} < 20 mL/MIN* – 125 mg, TOUTES LES 48 HEURES.

Suppression des récidives de l'herpès génital chez les patients immunocompétents

- **PO (adultes)**: 250 mg, toutes les 12 heures, pendant une période allant jusqu'à 1 an.
- ***INSUFFISANCE RÉNALE***

  PO (ADULTES): *Cl_{CR} DE 20 À 39 mL/MIN* – 125 mg, TOUTES LES 12 HEURES; *Cl_{CR} < 20 mL/MIN* – 125 mg, TOUTES LES 24 HEURES.

Infections mucocutanées récurrentes dues au virus herpès simplex chez les patients infectés par le VIH

- **PO (adultes):** 500 mg, toutes les 12 heures, pendant 7 jours.
- ***INSUFFISANCE RÉNALE***
  PO (ADULTES): *CL_{CR} DE 20 À 39 mL/MIN* – 500 mg, TOUTES LES 24 HEURES; *CL_{CR} < 20 mL/MIN* – 250 mg, TOUTES LES 24 HEURES.

PRÉSENTATION

Comprimés: 125 mg[Pr], 250 mg[Pr], 500 mg[Pr].

F

SOINS INFIRMIERS

ÉVALUATION DE LA SITUATION

- Examiner les lésions avant le début du traitement et quotidiennement pendant toute sa durée.
- Rester à l'affût des signes d'algies postzostériennes pendant et après le traitement.

DIAGNOSTICS INFIRMIERS POSSIBLES

- Risque d'atteinte à l'intégrité de la peau (Indications).
- Risque d'infection (Indications, Enseignement au patient et à ses proches).
- Connaissances insuffisantes sur le traitement médicamenteux (Enseignement au patient et à ses proches).

INTERVENTIONS INFIRMIÈRES

- Il faut commencer le traitement au famciclovir dès que le diagnostic de zona est posé, au moins dans les 72 heures qui suivent le diagnostic, mais de préférence dans les 48 heures.
- On peut prendre le famciclovir sans égard aux repas.

ENSEIGNEMENT AU PATIENT ET À SES PROCHES

- Inciter le patient à suivre rigoureusement la posologie recommandée pendant toute la durée du traitement. S'il n'a pu prendre le médicament au moment habituel, il doit le prendre le plus rapidement possible à moins que ce ne soit presque l'heure prévue pour la dose suivante.
- Prévenir le patient que le famciclovir n'empêche pas la transmission de l'infection à d'autres personnes. Lui recommander de ne pas côtoyer des personnes immunosupprimées ou celles qui n'ont jamais eu la varicelle ou qui n'ont pas reçu de vaccin contre la varicelle jusqu'à ce que toutes les lésions de zona aient formé une croûte.
- Inciter le patient à utiliser des préservatifs pendant les rapports sexuels et à éviter les contacts sexuels pendant que des lésions sont présentes.
- Prévenir les patientes qui souffrent d'herpès génital qu'elles devraient se soumettre tous les ans à un test de Papanicolaou étant donné qu'elles sont davantage prédisposées au cancer du col de l'utérus.

VÉRIFICATION DE L'EFFICACITÉ THÉRAPEUTIQUE

L'efficacité du traitement peut être démontrée par: une formation plus rapide de croûtes et la disparition plus rapide des vésicules, des ulcérations et des croûtes chez les patients atteints d'herpès zoster aigu (zona) ■ la formation de croûtes et la cicatrisation des lésions en cas d'herpès génital et d'infections récurrentes provoquées par le virus herpès simplex mucocutané chez les patients infectés par le VIH ■ la prévention des infections génitales herpétiques récurrentes chez les patients immunocompétents. ✳

FAMOTIDINE,

voir Antagonistes des récepteurs H_2 de l'histamine

FÉLODIPINE

Plendil, Renedil, Sandoz-Félodipine

CLASSIFICATION:

Antihypertenseur (bloqueur des canaux calciques)

Grossesse – catégorie C

INDICATIONS

Traitement de l'hypertension. **Usages non approuvés:** Traitement de l'angine de poitrine et de l'angine vasospastique (angor de Prinzmetal) ■ Traitement de la maladie de Raynaud.

MÉCANISME D'ACTION

Inhibition du transport du calcium dans les cellules myocardiques et musculaires lisses vasculaires, entraînant l'inhibition du couplage excitation-contraction et de la contraction qui s'ensuit. ***Effets thérapeutiques:*** Vasodilatation périphérique entraînant une chute de la pression artérielle ■ Dilatation des coronaires se traduisant par la diminution de la fréquence et de la gravité des crises d'angine.

PHARMACOCINÉTIQUE

Absorption: Bonne (PO); premier passage hépatique important (biodisponibilité d'environ 15 %).

Distribution: Inconnue.

Liaison aux protéines: > 99 %.

Métabolisme et excrétion: Métabolisme hépatique important. Excrétion rénale majoritairement sous forme de métabolites; une faible fraction sous forme inchangée.

Demi-vie: De 11 à 16 heures.

Profil temps-action (effet antihypertenseur)

	DÉBUT D'ACTION	PIC	DURÉE
PO	1 h	2 – 4 h	jusqu'à 24 h

CONTRE-INDICATIONS, PRÉCAUTIONS ET MISES EN GARDE

Contre-indications: Hypersensibilité (risque de sensibilité croisée) ■ **OBST., ALLAITEMENT**: Le médicament est contre-indiqué chez les femmes enceintes, en âge de procréer ou qui allaitent.

Précautions et mises en garde: Pression artérielle systolique < 90 mm Hg ■ Insuffisance hépatique grave (il est recommandé de réduire la dose) ■ **GÉR.**: Il est recommandé de réduire la dose; risque accru d'hypotension ■ Insuffisance hépatique grave (réduire la dose) ■ Antécédents d'arythmies ventriculaires graves ou d'insuffisance cardiaque ■ **PÉD.**: L'innocuité du médicament n'a pas été établie ■ Sténose aortique.

RÉACTIONS INDÉSIRABLES ET EFFETS SECONDAIRES

SNC: céphalées, anxiété, confusion, étourdissements, somnolence, nervosité, troubles psychiatriques, faiblesse.

ORLO: vision trouble, problèmes d'équilibre, épistaxis.

Resp.: toux, dyspnée.

CV: ARYTHMIES, INSUFFISANCE CARDIAQUE, œdème périphérique, tachycardie, douleurs thoraciques, hypotension, palpitations, syncope, bradycardie.

GI: résultats anormaux aux tests de la fonction hépatique, anorexie, constipation, diarrhée, sécheresse de la bouche (xérostomie), dysgueusie, dyspepsie, nausées, vomissements.

GU: dysurie, nycturie, polyurie, troubles sexuels, mictions fréquentes.

Tég.: dermatite, érythème polymorphe, bouffées vasomotrices, diaphorèse accrue, photosensibilité, prurit, urticaire, rash.

End.: gynécomastie, hyperglycémie.

Hémat.: anémie, leucopénie, thrombopénie.

Mét.: gain pondéral.

Loc.: raideur des articulations, crampes musculaires.

SN: paresthésie, tremblements.

Divers: SYNDROME DE STEVENS-JOHNSON, hyperplasie gingivale.

INTERACTIONS

Médicament-médicament: Risque d'hypotension additive lors de l'administration concomitante de **fentanyl**, d'autres **antihypertenseurs**, de **dérivés nitrés** et de **quinidine** ou lors de la consommation de fortes quantités d'**alcool** ■ La prise concomitante d'**AINS** peut réduire les effets antihypertenseurs de la félodipine ■ L'administration concomitante de **bêtabloquants**, de **digoxine**, de **disopyramide** ou de **phénytoïne** peut entraîner de la bradycardie, des troubles de conduction ou l'insuffisance cardiaque ■ La **cimétidine**, l'**érythromycine**, l'**itraconazole** et le **kétoconazole** peuvent ralentir le métabolisme de la félodipine et accroître le risque de toxicité (une diminution de la dose peut être nécessaire).

Médicament-aliments: Le **jus de pamplemousse** élève les concentrations sanguines de félodipine (éviter la consommation concomitante).

VOIES D'ADMINISTRATION ET POSOLOGIE

- **PO (adultes)**: 5 mg, 1 fois par jour; on peut augmenter la dose, toutes les 2 semaines (écart posologique: de 2,5 à 10 mg, 1 fois par jour; dose maximale: 10 mg, 1 fois par jour).
- **PO (personnes âgées ou insuffisants hépatiques)**: 2,5 mg, 1 fois par jour (dose maximale: 10 mg, 1 fois par jour).

PRÉSENTATION

Comprimés à libération prolongée: 2,5 mg[Pr], 5 mg[Pr], 10 mg[Pr].

SOINS INFIRMIERS

ÉVALUATION DE LA SITUATION

- Mesurer la pression artérielle et le pouls avant le traitement, pendant la période d'adaptation posologique et à intervalles réguliers, pendant toute la durée du traitement. SUIVRE L'ÉCG À INTERVALLES RÉGULIERS AU COURS D'UN TRAITEMENT PROLONGÉ.
- EFFECTUER LE BILAN QUOTIDIEN DES INGESTA ET DES EXCRETA ET PESER LE PATIENT TOUS LES JOURS. RESTER À L'AFFÛT DES SIGNES D'INSUFFISANCE CARDIAQUE (ŒDÈME PÉRIPHÉRIQUE, RÂLES OU CRÉPITATIONS, DYSPNÉE, GAIN DE POIDS, TURGESCENCE DES JUGULAIRES).

Angine: Déterminer le siège, la durée et l'intensité de la douleur angineuse ainsi que les facteurs qui la déclenchent.

Hypertension: Vérifier la fréquence des renouvellements d'ordonnance afin d'évaluer l'observance du traitement.

Tests de laboratoire:

- Les concentrations totales de calcium sérique ne sont pas affectées par les bloqueurs des canaux calciques.
- Suivre les concentrations sériques de potassium à intervalles réguliers. L'hypokaliémie accroît le risque d'arythmies et devrait être corrigée.
- Noter les résultats des tests des fonctions rénale et hépatique à intervalles réguliers lors du traitement de longue durée. La félodipine peut entraîner une élévation des concentrations d'enzymes hépatiques après plusieurs jours de traitement, mais elles retournent à la normale après l'arrêt du traitement.

F

DIAGNOSTICS INFIRMIERS POSSIBLES

- Irrigation tissulaire inefficace (Indications).
- Douleur aiguë (Indications).
- Connaissances insuffisantes sur le traitement médicamenteux (Enseignement au patient et à ses proches).
- Non-observance du traitement médicamenteux (Enseignement au patient et à ses proches).

INTERVENTIONS INFIRMIÈRES

- La félodipine peut être administrée sans égard aux repas. En cas de troubles gastro-intestinaux, on peut l'administrer avec des aliments.
- Il NE FAUT PAS OUVRIR, ÉCRASER, BRISER NI MÂCHER LES COMPRIMÉS À LIBÉRATION PROLONGÉE. Il est normal que des comprimés vides se retrouvent dans les selles.

ENSEIGNEMENT AU PATIENT ET À SES PROCHES

- Expliquer au patient qu'il doit respecter rigoureusement la posologie recommandée, même s'il se sent mieux. S'il n'a pu prendre le médicament au moment habituel, il doit le prendre aussitôt que possible à moins que ce ne soit presque l'heure prévue pour la dose suivante. Le prévenir qu'il ne doit jamais remplacer une dose manquée par une double dose. Le traitement peut être interrompu graduellement.
- Enseigner au patient comment prendre son pouls. Lui conseiller de communiquer avec un professionnel de la santé si la fréquence cardiaque est < 50 bpm.
- Recommander au patient de changer lentement de position pour réduire le risque d'hypotension orthostatique.
- Prévenir le patient que la félodipine peut provoquer des étourdissements.
- Expliquer au patient qu'il est important de pratiquer une bonne hygiène dentaire et de consulter fréquemment le dentiste pour faire nettoyer ses dents afin de prévenir la sensibilité et le saignement des gencives ou une hyperplasie gingivale (hypertrophie des gencives).
- Expliquer au patient qu'il doit éviter de consommer de l'alcool ou des médicaments en vente libre, particulièrement des médicaments contre le rhume, sans avoir consulté au préalable un professionnel de la santé.
- Recommander au patient de signaler à un professionnel de la santé les symptômes suivants: battements cardiaques irréguliers, dyspnée, œdème des mains et des pieds, étourdissements prononcés, nausées, constipation, hypotension ou céphalées graves ou persistantes.
- Conseiller au patient de porter des vêtements de protection et d'utiliser un écran solaire pour prévenir les réactions de photosensibilité.
- Conseiller au patient d'informer tous les professionnels de la santé qu'il suit un traitement par ce médicament avant de se soumettre à une intervention chirurgicale ou à un traitement.

Angine:

- Recommander au patient qui suit un traitement parallèle par un dérivé nitré ou par un bêtabloquant de continuer à prendre les deux médicaments selon la posologie recommandée, et d'utiliser de la nitroglycérine sublinguale, selon les besoins, en cas de crises d'angine.
- Conseiller au patient de prévenir un professionnel de la santé si les douleurs thoraciques ne diminuent pas ou si elles s'aggravent après le traitement et si elles s'accompagnent de diaphorèse ou d'essoufflements ou encore si des céphalées graves et persistantes se manifestent.
- Inciter le patient à discuter avec un professionnel de la santé des restrictions à respecter sur le plan de l'effort avant de s'engager dans un programme d'exercices.

Hypertension:

- Encourager le patient à suivre rigoureusement les autres mesures thérapeutiques permettant de maîtriser l'hypertension: perdre du poids, suivre un régime hyposodé, cesser de fumer, consommer de l'alcool avec modération, faire régulièrement de l'exercice, gérer le stress. Le prévenir que ce médicament stabilise la pression artérielle, mais ne guérit pas l'hypertension.

- Enseigner au patient et à ses proches la façon de prendre la pression artérielle. Leur recommander de la mesurer toutes les semaines et de signaler à un professionnel de la santé tout changement important.

VÉRIFICATION DE L'EFFICACITÉ THÉRAPEUTIQUE

L'efficacité du traitement peut être démontrée par: une baisse de la pression artérielle ▪ une diminution de la fréquence et de la gravité des crises d'angine ▪ un moindre recours à des dérivés nitrés ▪ une meilleure tolérance à l'effort et un sentiment de mieux-être.

FÉNOFIBRATE

Apo-Fénofibrate, Apo-Féno-Micro, Apo-Féno-Super, Féno-Micro, Gen-Fénofibrate Micro, Lipidil EZ, Lipidil Micro, Lipidil Supra, Novo-Fénofibrate micronisé, PMS-Fénofibrate Micro

CLASSIFICATION:
Hypolipidémiant (dérivé de l'acide fénofibrique)

Grossesse – catégorie C

INDICATIONS

Traitement complémentaire de la diétothérapie ou d'autres mesures thérapeutiques en cas d'hyperlipidémie chez les patients qui ne répondent pas à un traitement non médicamenteux.

MÉCANISME D'ACTION

Activation d'un récepteur nucléaire spécifique, appelé récepteur-alpha activé de la prolifération des peroxysomes (PPAR), qui entraîne une baisse de la sécrétion des triglycérides, une diminution de la concentration de cholestérol LDL et une élévation correspondante de la concentration de cholestérol HDL. ***Effets thérapeutiques:*** Abaissement des concentrations de triglycérides ▪ Abaissement des concentrations de cholestérol LDL ▪ Augmentation des concentrations de cholestérol HDL.

PHARMACOCINÉTIQUE

Absorption: Bonne (de l'ordre de 60 %) (PO); l'absorption est accrue lorsque le médicament est pris avec des aliments.

Distribution: Inconnue.

Liaison aux protéines: 99 %.

Métabolisme et excrétion: Le médicament est rapidement transformé en acide fénofibrique, le métabolite actif, qui est ensuite métabolisé par le foie. L'acide fénofibrique et ses métabolites sont surtout excrétés dans les urines (60 %).

Demi-vie: De 20 à 24 heures.

Profil temps-action
(abaissement des concentrations de triglycérides)

	DÉBUT D'ACTION	PIC	DURÉE
PO	inconnu	2 semaines	inconnue

CONTRE-INDICATIONS, PRÉCAUTIONS ET MISES EN GARDE

Contre-indications: Hypersensibilité au fénofibrate, à tout autre ingrédient du médicament ou à tout autre médicament appartenant à la classe des fibrates ▪ Insuffisance hépatique (incluant la cirrhose biliaire primitive) ▪ Maladie préexistante de la vésicule biliaire ▪ Insuffisance rénale grave (Cl_{Cr} < 20 mL/min) ▪ Hyperlipoprotéinémies de type 1 ▪ Antécédents connus de réaction photoallergique ou phototoxique au cours d'un traitement par des fibrates ou le kétoprofène ▪ **OBST., ALLAITEMENT:** Éviter l'administration pendant la grossesse ou l'allaitement.

Précautions et mises en garde: **PÉD.:** L'innocuité du médicament n'a pas été établie chez les enfants.

RÉACTIONS INDÉSIRABLES ET EFFETS SECONDAIRES

SNC: fatigue, faiblesse, céphalées.
CV: arythmies.
GI: lithiase biliaire, pancréatite.
Tég.: rash, urticaire.
Loc.: myalgie, rhabdomyolyse.
Divers: réactions d'hypersensibilité.

INTERACTIONS

Médicament-médicament: Le fénofibrate intensifie les effets de la **warfarine** ▪ L'administration concomitante d'**inhibiteurs de la HMG-CoA réductase (statines)** peut accroître le risque de rhabdomyolyse (l'usage concomitant n'est pas recommandé) ▪ Les **résines hypocholestérolémiantes** peuvent ralentir l'absorption du fénofibrate (il faut prendre le fénofibrate, 1 heure avant ou de 4 à 6 heures après ces médicaments) ▪ L'administration concomitante de **cyclosporine** peut accroître les effets toxiques du fénofibrate.

VOIES D'ADMINISTRATION ET POSOLOGIE

- **PO (adultes):** *Capsules micronisées* – 200 mg, 1 fois par jour, ou 3 capsules de 67 mg réparties en 2 ou

3 prises par jour (dose maximale: 267 mg par jour). *Insuffisance rénale* – dose initiale: 67 mg, 1 fois par jour, qu'on peut majorer graduellement, selon les besoins. *Capsules micro-enrobées* – de 160 mg à 200 mg, 1 fois par jour. Si la Cl_{Cr} se situe entre 20 et 100 mL/minute, commencer le traitement à 100 mg, 1 fois par jour, et augmenter la dose graduellement selon la tolérance du patient et l'effet du médicament. *Comprimés nanocristalisés* – 145 mg, 1 fois par jour. Chez les personnes âgées et les insuffisants rénaux, il est recommandé de débuter à 48 mg, 1 fois par jour et d'ajuster la posologie selon la réponse du patient et sa tolérance au traitement. *Capsules régulières* – 100 mg, 3 fois par jour.

F

PRÉSENTATION

Capsules micronisées: 67 mg^Pr, 200 mg^Pr ■ **Comprimés micro-enrobés**: 100 mg^Pr, 160 mg^Pr ■ **Comprimés nanocristalisés**: 48 mg^Pr, 145 mg^Pr ■ **Capsules régulières**: 100 mg^Pr.

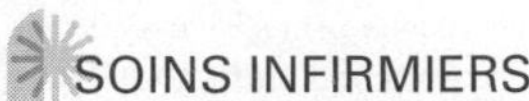

SOINS INFIRMIERS

ÉVALUATION DE LA SITUATION

- Recueillir les données sur les habitudes alimentaires du patient, notamment sur sa consommation de matières grasses. Il faut tout essayer pour normaliser les concentrations sériques de triglycérides du patient obèse par la diétothérapie et l'exercice et lui faire perdre du poids avant d'amorcer le traitement par le fénofibrate.
- Suivre de près le patient pour déceler la présence de lithiases biliaires. En cas de symptômes, il faut effectuer des tests de la fonction de la vésicule biliaire. Si une lithiase biliaire est présente, il faut cesser le traitement par le fénofibrate.

Tests de laboratoire:

- Noter les concentrations sériques de lipides avant le début du traitement afin de déterminer si les élévations sont constantes, puis à intervalles réguliers pendant toute sa durée.
- Surveiller les concentrations sériques d'AST et d'ALT à intervalles réguliers pendant toute la durée du traitement. Le médicament peut entraîner l'élévation de ces concentrations. Il faut arrêter le traitement si les concentrations s'élèvent au-delà de 3 fois la limite de la normale.
- Si le patient manifeste des douleurs musculaires pendant le traitement, il faut vérifier les concentrations de créatine-phosphokinase. Si ces concentrations sont très élevées ou si une myopathie s'installe, il faut cesser le traitement.
- Le fénofibrate peut entraîner une baisse légère à modérée des concentrations d'hémoglobine, de l'hématocrite et du nombre de globules blancs. Il faut mesurer ces paramètres à intervalles réguliers au cours des 12 premiers mois de traitement. Ils se stabilisent habituellement lors d'un traitement de longue durée.
- Chez les patients qui prennent en même temps des anticoagulants oraux, mesurer à intervalles fréquents le temps de prothrombine jusqu'à ce que ces valeurs se stabilisent.

DIAGNOSTICS INFIRMIERS POSSIBLES

- Connaissances insuffisantes sur la diétothérapie et le traitement médicamenteux (Enseignement au patient et à ses proches).
- Non-observance du traitement médicamenteux et de la diétothérapie (Enseignement au patient et à ses proches).

INTERVENTIONS INFIRMIÈRES

- Il faut prescrire une diétothérapie visant l'abaissement des taux de triglycérides avant d'amorcer le traitement et la maintenir pendant toute la durée du traitement hypolipidémiant.
- On peut augmenter la dose après avoir mesuré à plusieurs reprises les taux sériques de triglycérides à intervalles de 4 à 8 semaines.
- Les différentes préparations ne sont pas interchangeables.
- Administrer le médicament avec des aliments (comprimés ordinaires, préparation micronisé et micro-enrobé) ou sans égard aux repas (préparation nanocristalisée).

ENSEIGNEMENT AU PATIENT ET À SES PROCHES

- Conseiller au patient de respecter rigoureusement la posologie recommandée, de ne pas sauter de dose ni de remplacer une dose manquée par une double dose. Le prévenir que le médicament permet de normaliser les concentrations sériques élevées de triglycérides, mais il ne guérit pas l'hyperlipidémie.
- Expliquer au patient que le traitement ne peut être efficace que s'il suit en même temps une diétothérapie pauvre en matières grasses, en cholestérol, en glucides et en alcool, s'il fait de l'exercice et s'il cesse de fumer.
- Conseiller au patient d'informer un professionnel de la santé en cas de douleurs, de sensibilité ou de faiblesses musculaires inexpliquées, particulière-

ment si ces symptômes s'accompagnent de fièvre ou de malaises.

- Recommander à la patiente d'informer rapidement un professionnel de la santé si elle pense être enceinte ou si elle souhaite le devenir.
- Recommander au patient d'informer tous les professionnels de la santé qu'il suit un traitement par ce médicament avant de se soumettre à une intervention chirurgicale ou à un autre traitement.
- Insister sur l'importance d'un suivi médical permettant de déterminer l'efficacité du médicament et ses effets secondaires.

VÉRIFICATION DE L'EFFICACITÉ THÉRAPEUTIQUE

L'efficacité du traitement peut être démontrée par: la diminution des concentrations sériques de triglycérides ■ la diminution des concentrations sériques de cholestérol LDL ■ l'augmentation des concentrations sériques de cholestérol HDL.

ALERTE CLINIQUE

FENTANYL (VOIE PARENTÉRALE)

Fentanyl

CLASSIFICATION:

Analgésique opioïde (agoniste), anesthésique et adjuvant anesthésique

Grossesse – catégories C et D (en cas d'administration prolongée ou de doses élevées près du terme)

INDICATIONS

Analgésique de courte durée d'action au cours des étapes de prémédication, d'induction et de maintien de l'anesthésie, et, au besoin, pendant la période postopératoire immédiate (en salle de réveil) ■ Supplément analgésique opioïde destiné à l'anesthésie générale ou régionale ■ Prémédication anesthésique administrée en association avec un neuroleptique, tel le dropéridol injectable, pour l'induction de l'anesthésie, et comme agent d'appoint dans le maintien de l'anesthésie générale et régionale ■ Agent anesthésique associé à l'oxygène chez certains patients à risque élevé, dans les cas notamment d'interventions à cœur ouvert ou d'interventions neurologiques ou orthopédiques compliquées ■ **Voie épidurale**: Traitement postopératoire de la douleur consécutive aux interventions de chirurgie générale et aux césariennes.

MÉCANISME D'ACTION

Liaison aux récepteurs opioïdes du SNC modifiant la perception de la douleur et la réaction à celle-ci ■ Dépression du SNC. ***Effets thérapeutiques:*** Adjuvant à l'anesthésie ■ Soulagement de la douleur.

PHARMACOCINÉTIQUE

Absorption: Bonne (IM).

Distribution: Inconnue.

Métabolisme et excrétion: Métabolisme majoritairement hépatique. De 8 à 10 % est excrété à l'état inchangé par les reins.

Demi-vie: De 2 à 4 heures (prolongée après une circulation extracorporelle et chez les personnes âgées).

Profil temps-action (analgésie†)

	DÉBUT D'ACTION	PIC	DURÉE
IM	7 - 15 min	20 - 30 min	1 - 2 h
IV	1 - 2 min	3 - 5 min	0,5 - 1 h

† La dépression respiratoire peut durer plus longtemps que l'analgésie.

CONTRE-INDICATIONS, PRÉCAUTIONS ET MISES EN GARDE

Contre-indications: Hypersensibilité; risque de sensibilité croisée ■ Intolérance connue au médicament.

Précautions et mises en garde: Personnes âgées, patients débilités ou très malades ■ Diabète ■ Maladies pulmonaires ou hépatiques graves ■ Tumeurs du SNC ■ Pression intracrânienne accrue ■ Traumatisme crânien ■ Insuffisance surrénalienne ■ Douleurs abdominales non diagnostiquées ■ Hypothyroïdie ■ Alcoolisme ■ Maladie cardiaque (arythmies) ■ Grossesse, allaitement ■ **PÉD.**: Nouveau-nés et enfants < 3 mois (risque accru de dépression respiratoire); nouveau-nés (éviter les préparations injectables contenant des agents de conservation, car elles peuvent causer un « syndrome d'halètement » pouvant mener à une issue fatale); enfants < 2 ans (l'innocuité du médicament n'a pas été établie) ■ Risque de pharmacodépendance et d'abus.

RÉACTIONS INDÉSIRABLES ET EFFETS SECONDAIRES

SNC: confusion, excitation paradoxale ou délire, dépression postopératoire, somnolence postopératoire.

ORLO: vision double ou trouble.

Resp.: APNÉE, LARYNGOSPASME, bronchospasme allergique, DÉPRESSION RESPIRATOIRE.

CV: arythmies, bradycardie, dépression circulatoire, hypotension.

GI: spasmes biliaires, nausées et vomissements, constipation.

Tég.: démangeaisons au niveau du visage.
Loc.: rigidité des muscles squelettiques et thoraciques.

INTERACTIONS

Médicament-médicament: L'ADMINISTRATION DU FENTANYL CHEZ LES PATIENTS AYANT REÇU DES **IMAO** OU DE LA **PROCARBAZINE** DANS LES 14 JOURS PRÉCÉDENTS EST À ÉVITER (RISQUE DE RÉACTIONS IMPRÉVISIBLES QUI PEUVENT ÊTRE MORTELLES) ■ Dépression additive du SNC et du système respiratoire lors de l'usage concomitant d'**alcool**, d'**antihistaminiques**, de **phénothiazines**, de **barbituriques**, d'**antidépresseurs**, d'**hypnosédatifs** et d'autres **opioïdes** ■ L'administration d'**analgésiques opioïdes agonistes/antagonistes** (**nalbuphine**, **butorphanol**, **pentazocine**) peut diminuer l'analgésie et/ou déclencher des symptômes de sevrage chez les patients présentant une dépendance physique aux analgésiques opioïdes ■ Risque accru d'hypotension lors de l'administration simultanée de **benzodiazépines**.

F

VOIES D'ADMINISTRATION ET POSOLOGIE

Usage préopératoire

- **IM (adultes)**: De 0,7 à 1,4 µg/kg, de 30 à 60 minutes avant la chirurgie.

Adjuvant à l'anesthésie générale

- **IV (adultes)**: *Faible dose pour chirurgie mineure* – 2 µg/kg. *Dose moyenne pour chirurgie majeure* – de 2 à 20 µg/kg. *Dose élevée pour chirurgie majeure* – de 20 à 50 µg/kg.

Adjuvant à l'anesthésie régionale

- **IM, IV (adultes)**: De 0,7 à 1,4 µg/kg.

Anesthésie générale

- **IV (adultes et enfants > 12 ans)**: De 50 à 100 µg/kg (jusqu'à 150 µg/kg), en même temps que de l'oxygène et un myorelaxant.
- **IV (enfants de 2 à 12 ans)**: De 2 à 3 µg/kg.

Douleurs postopératoires

- **Voie épidurale (adultes)**: 1,5 µg/kg en bolus et/ou en perfusion continue de 1 µg/kg/h.

Sédation/analgésie

- **IV (adultes et enfants > 12 ans)**: De 0,5 à 1 µg/kg/dose; on peut répéter l'administration de cette dose toutes les 30 à 60 minutes, au besoin.
- **IV (enfants de 1 à 12 ans)**: *Bolus:* de 2 à 3 µg/kg/dose; on peut répéter l'administration de cette dose toutes les 30 à 60 minutes, au besoin. *Perfusion continue*: de 1 à 5 µg/kg/h après l'administration du bolus.
- **IV (nouveau-nés)**: *Bolus:* de 0,5 à 3 µg/kg/dose; on peut répéter l'administration de cette dose toutes les 30 à 60 minutes, au besoin. *Perfusion continue*: de 0,5 à 2 µg/kg/h après l'administration du bolus.

PRÉSENTATION

Solution pour injection: 0,05 mg/mL[N], en ampoules ou en flacons de 2 mL, de 5 mL, de 10 mL, de 20 mL.

SOINS INFIRMIERS

ÉVALUATION DE LA SITUATION

- ÉVALUER LE NIVEAU DE CONSCIENCE ET MESURER LA FRÉQUENCE RESPIRATOIRE ET LA PRESSION ARTÉRIELLE À INTERVALLES FRÉQUENTS TOUT AU LONG DU TRAITEMENT. PRÉVENIR IMMÉDIATEMENT LE MÉDECIN EN CAS DE MODIFICATION IMPORTANTE. LES EFFETS DÉPRESSEURS DU FENTANYL SUR LA RESPIRATION PEUVENT DURER PLUS LONGTEMPS QUE LES EFFETS ANALGÉSIQUES. DIMINUER LES DOSES ULTÉRIEURES DES AUTRES OPIOÏDES DE $^1/_4$ À $^1/_3$ DE LA DOSE HABITUELLE RECOMMANDÉE. SUIVRE DE PRÈS L'ÉTAT DU PATIENT.

GÉR.: Évaluer fréquemment les patients âgés, car ils sont plus sensibles aux effets des analgésiques opioïdes que les adultes plus jeunes et peuvent subir des effets indésirables et des complications respiratoires plus souvent.

PÉD.: Évaluer les enfants fréquemment, car ils sont plus sensibles aux effets des analgésiques opioïdes et peuvent subir des complications respiratoires, et manifester de l'excitabilité et de l'agitation plus souvent.

IM, IV: Lorsqu'on administre le fentanyl en tant qu'analgésique, déterminer le type, le siège et l'intensité de la douleur avant l'administration IM et 30 minutes après ou de 3 à 5 minutes après l'administration IV.

Tests de laboratoire: Le fentanyl peut entraîner l'élévation des concentrations sériques d'amylase et de lipase.

TOXICITÉ ET SURDOSAGE: Les symptômes de surdosage sont notamment la dépression respiratoire, l'hypotension, les arythmies, la bradycardie et les asystoles. On peut administrer de l'atropine pour traiter la bradycardie. Si la dépression respiratoire persiste après l'intervention chirurgicale, une ventilation artificielle prolongée pourrait s'imposer. S'il faut administrer un antagoniste des opioïdes pour renverser la dépression respiratoire ou le coma, l'antidote est la naloxone (Narcan). Diluer le contenu d'une ampoule de 0,4 mg de naloxone dans 10 mL de solution de NaCl 0,9 % et administrer 0,5 mL (0,02 mg) par IV directe, toutes les 2 minutes. Chez les enfants et les patients dont le poids est < 40 kg, diluer 0,1 mg de naloxone dans 10 mL de solution de NaCl 0,9 % pour obtenir une concentration de 10 μg/mL et administrer 0,5 μg/kg, toutes les 2 minutes. Afin de prévenir les symptômes de sevrage, les convulsions et les douleurs intenses, il faut adapter la posologie. L'administration de naloxone dans ces circonstances a entraîné, particulièrement chez les patients cardiaques, de l'hypertension et une tachycardie ayant parfois provoqué une insuffisance du ventricule gauche et de l'œdème pulmonaire.

DIAGNOSTICS INFIRMIERS POSSIBLES

- Douleur aiguë (Indications).
- Mode de respiration inefficace (Réactions indésirables).
- Risque d'accident (Effets secondaires).

INTERVENTIONS INFIRMIÈRES

- NE PAS CONFONDRE L'ALFENTANIL, LE FENTANYL ET LE SUFENTANIL.

ALERTE CLINIQUE: DES SURDOSES ACCIDENTELLES D'ANALGÉSIQUES OPIOÏDES ONT CAUSÉ DES DÉCÈS. ÉVALUER L'UTILISATION ANTÉRIEURE D'ANALGÉSIQUES OPIOÏDES PAR LE PATIENT ET SES BESOINS ACTUELS. AVANT L'ADMINISTRATION, CLARIFIER TOUTE ORDONNANCE AMBIGUË ET FAIRE VÉRIFIER L'ORDONNANCE D'ORIGINE ET LES CALCULS DES DOSES PAR UN AUTRE PROFESSIONNEL DE LA SANTÉ.

PÉD.: LES ERREURS DANS L'ADMINISTRATION DES ANALGÉSIQUES OPIOÏDES SONT FRÉQUENTES AU SEIN DE LA POPULATION PÉDIATRIQUE; ELLES COMPRENNENT DES ERREURS D'INTERPRÉTATION ET DE CALCUL DES DOSES AINSI QUE L'USAGE D'INSTRUMENTS DE MESURE INAPPROPRIÉS.

- UTILISER SEULEMENT DES PRÉPARATIONS SANS AGENTS DE CONSERVATION CHEZ LES NOUVEAU-NÉS ET POUR L'ADMINISTRATION ÉPIDURALE ET INTRATHÉCALE CHEZ TOUS LES PATIENTS.
- On peut administrer des benzodiazépines, avant d'administrer le fentanyl ou après, pour réduire la dose d'induction et la durée de la perte de conscience, et pour produire l'amnésie. Cette association peut également augmenter le risque d'hypotension.

ALERTE CLINIQUE: AU COURS DE L'ADMINISTRATION DU FENTANYL, GARDER À PORTÉE DE LA MAIN UN ANTAGONISTE DES OPIOÏDES, DE L'OXYGÈNE ET LES APPAREILS DE RÉANIMATION. LES DÉRIVÉS DU FENTANYL NE DOIVENT ÊTRE ADMINISTRÉS QUE PAR VOIE IV, DANS UN MILIEU OÙ L'ANESTHÉSIE EST SURVEILLÉE DE PRÈS (SALLE D'OPÉRATION, SERVICE DES URGENCES, UNITÉ DE SOINS INTENSIFS) ET OÙ ON DISPOSE D'APPAREILS DE MAINTIEN DES FONCTIONS VITALES. LEUR ADMINISTRATION EST RÉSERVÉE AU PERSONNEL DÛMENT FORMÉ EN RÉANIMATION ET EN PRISE EN CHARGE DES URGENCES DES TROUBLES RESPIRATOIRES.

IV directe: Administrer la solution non diluée.

Vitesse d'administration: Administrer lentement pendant 1 à 3 minutes. L'administration IV lente permet de réduire l'incidence ou la gravité de la rigidité musculaire, de la bradycardie ou de l'hypotension. Pour réduire la rigidité musculaire, on peut administrer en même temps des bloqueurs neuromusculaires.

Perfusion intermittente: On peut diluer le fentanyl dans une solution de D5%E ou de NaCl 0,9 %.

Associations compatibles dans la même seringue: atracurium ▪ atropine ▪ butorphanol ▪ chlorpromazine ▪ cimétidine ▪ dimenhydrinate ▪ diphenhydramine ▪ dropéridol ▪ héparine ▪ hydromorphone ▪ hydroxyzine ▪ mépéridine ▪ métoclopramide ▪ midazolam ▪ morphine ▪ pentazocine ▪ perphénazine ▪ prochlorpérazine, édisylate de ▪ promazine ▪ prométhazine ▪ ranitidine ▪ scopolamine.

Association incompatible dans la même seringue: pentobarbital.

Compatibilité (tubulure en Y): atracurium ▪ diltiazem ▪ dobutamine ▪ dopamine ▪ énalaprilate ▪ esmolol ▪ étomidate ▪ furosémide ▪ héparine ▪ hydrocortisone sodique, succinate d' ▪ hydromorphone ▪ labétolol ▪ lorazépam ▪ midazolam ▪ milrinone ▪ morphine ▪ nafcilline ▪ nitroglycérine ▪ noradrénaline ▪ pancuronium ▪ potassium, chlorure de ▪ propofol ▪ ranitidine ▪ sargramostim ▪ thiopental ▪ vécuronium ▪ vitamines du complexe B avec C.

Compatibilité en addition au soluté: bupivacaïne.

Incompatibilité en addition au soluté: méthohexital ▪ pentobarbital ▪ thiopental.

ENSEIGNEMENT AU PATIENT ET À SES PROCHES

- Expliquer au patient avant l'intervention chirurgicale l'utilité des anesthésiques et les effets qu'ils entraînent.
- Expliquer au patient la façon d'utiliser l'échelle d'évaluation de la douleur.
- Conseiller au patient de changer lentement de position pour réduire le risque d'hypotension orthostatique.

GÉR.: Les personnes âgées sont plus à risque d'hypotension orthostatique et donc de chutes. Expliquer au patient qu'il doit prendre des précautions jusqu'à ce que l'effet du médicament soit complètement résorbé.

- Prévenir le patient que le fentanyl provoque des étourdissements et de la somnolence. Lui conseiller de demander de l'aide lors de ses déplacements, de ne pas conduire et d'éviter les activités qui exigent sa vigilance pendant les 24 heures qui suivent l'administration du fentanyl lors d'une chirurgie d'un jour.

- Prévenir le patient qu'il ne doit pas consommer d'alcool ni prendre des dépresseurs du SNC dans les 24 heures qui suivent l'administration du fentanyl lors d'une chirurgie d'un jour.

VÉRIFICATION DE L'EFFICACITÉ THÉRAPEUTIQUE

L'efficacité du traitement peut être démontrée par: l'apaisement généralisé ■ la réduction de l'activité motrice ■ l'analgésie prononcée.

F

ALERTE CLINIQUE

FENTANYL (VOIE TRANSDERMIQUE)

Duragesic, RAN-fentanyl Système Transdermique, Ratio-Fentanyl

CLASSIFICATION:
Analgésique opioïde (agoniste)

Grossesse – catégories C et D (en cas d'administration prolongée ou de doses élevées près du terme)

INDICATIONS

Traitement des douleurs chroniques **persistantes** d'intensité modérée à forte qui ne sont pas bien maîtrisées par d'autres agents, comme les opioïdes d'association ou à action brève, et seulement chez les patients qui nécessitent une analgésie continue aux opioïdes à toute heure pendant une période prolongée et qui reçoivent déjà un traitement aux opioïdes à une dose quotidienne totale d'au moins l'équivalent morphine de la dose initiale minimum de fentanyl transdermique ■ LE FENTANYL TRANSDERMIQUE N'EST PAS RECOMMANDÉ POUR SOULAGER LA DOULEUR LÉGÈRE, INTERMITTENTE, POSTOPÉRATOIRE OU DE COURTE DURÉE. IL NE FAUT PAS L'UTILISER CHEZ DES PATIENTS NE PRÉSENTANT PAS DE TOLÉRANCE ACQUISE AUX OPIOÏDES.

MÉCANISME D'ACTION

Liaison aux récepteurs opioïdes du SNC modifiant ainsi la perception de la douleur et la réaction à celle-ci. ***Effets thérapeutiques:*** Diminution de l'intensité de la douleur chronique.

PHARMACOCINÉTIQUE

Absorption: 92 % de la dose par la surface de la peau recouverte du timbre transdermique, favorisant la formation d'un dépôt dans les couches épidermiques. La libération du fentanyl depuis le timbre transdermique dans la circulation générale augmente graduellement pour atteindre un débit constant, ce qui assure une libération continue pendant 72 heures.

Distribution: Le fentanyl traverse la barrière placentaire et passe dans le lait maternel.

Métabolisme et excrétion: Fort métabolisme hépatique. De 10 à 25 % est excrété à l'état inchangé par les reins.

Demi-vie: 17 heures après le retrait d'un seul timbre, mais elle passe à 21 heures après le retrait de plusieurs timbres successifs (en raison de la libération continue à partir des dépôts de médicament formés dans les couches cutanées).

Profil temps-action (diminution de la douleur)

	DÉBUT D'ACTION	PIC	DURÉE
Timbre transdermique	6 h†	12 – 24 h	72 h‡

† Atteinte des concentrations sanguines associées à l'effet analgésique; la réponse maximale et l'adaptation posologique peuvent prendre jusqu'à 6 jours.

‡ Laps de temps pendant lequel le timbre est en place.

CONTRE-INDICATIONS, PRÉCAUTIONS ET MISES EN GARDE

Contre-indications: Hypersensibilité au fentanyl ou aux adhésifs du timbre ■ Douleur aiguë ou postopératoire, y compris en cas d'intervention chirurgicale en clinique externe ou en chirurgie d'un jour ■ Douleur légère, intermittente ou de courte durée qui peut être soulagée par d'autres moyens ■ Patients ne présentant pas de tolérance acquise aux opioïdes (quelle que soit la dose, y compris celle de 12 µg/h) ■ Asthme bronchique aigu ou grave ■ Dépression respiratoire marquée, en particulier dans les milieux non surveillés qui manquent de matériel de réanimation ■ Iléus paralytique confirmé ou soupçonné ■ Augmentation de la pression intracrânienne.

Précautions et mises en garde: **GÉR.**: Il est conseillé de réduire la dose chez les personnes âgées > 60 ans et les patients cachectiques ou débilités en raison d'une modification du processus d'élimination du médicament) ■ Diabète ■ Maladies pulmonaires ou hépatiques graves ■ Tumeurs du SNC ■ Traumatisme crânien ■ Insuffisance surrénalienne ■ Douleurs abdominales non diagnostiquées ■ Hypothyroïdie ■ Intolérance à l'alcool (de petites quantités d'alcool traversent la peau) ■ Alcoolisme ■ Maladies cardiaques, particulièrement les bradyarythmies ■ Fièvre (libération accrue du fentanyl depuis le timbre transdermique) ■ Période d'adaptation posologique (l'administration d'autres analgésiques peut s'avérer nécessaire) ■ **OBST., PÉD.**: Grossesse, allaitement et enfants < 18 ans (l'innocuité du médicament n'a pas été établie) ■ Risque de pharmacodépendance et d'abus.

RÉACTIONS INDÉSIRABLES ET EFFETS SECONDAIRES

SNC: confusion, sédation, faiblesse, étourdissements, agitation.
Resp.: APNÉE, bronchoconstriction, laryngospasme, DÉPRESSION RESPIRATOIRE.
CV: bradycardie.
GI: anorexie, constipation, sécheresse de la bouche (xérostomie), nausées, vomissements.
Tég.: transpiration, érythème.
Locaux: réaction à l'endroit d'application du timbre.
Loc.: rigidité des muscles squelettiques et thoraciques.
Divers: dépendance physique, dépendance psychologique.

INTERACTIONS

Médicament-médicament: L'ADMINISTRATION DU FENTANYL CHEZ LES PATIENTS AYANT REÇU DES **IMAO** OU DE LA **PROCARBAZINE** DANS LES 14 JOURS PRÉCÉDENTS EST À ÉVITER (RISQUE DE RÉACTIONS IMPRÉVISIBLES QUI PEUVENT ÊTRE MORTELLES) ■ Dépression additive du SNC et du système respiratoire lors de l'usage concomitant d'**alcool**, d'**antihistaminiques**, de **phénothiazines**, de **barbituriques**, d'**antidépresseurs**, d'**hypnosédatifs** et d'autres **opioïdes** ■ L'administration d'**analgésiques opioïdes agonistes/antagonistes** (**nalbuphine**, **butorphanol**, **pentazocine**) peut diminuer l'analgésie et/ou déclencher des symptômes de sevrage chez les patients présentant une dépendance physique aux analgésiques opioïdes ■ L'administration concomitante d'**agents inducteurs du CYP 3A4** peut réduire l'efficacité du fentanyl ■ L'utilisation concomitante de **ritonavir**, ou d'autres **inhibiteurs puissants du CYP 3A4**, tels que **kétoconazole**, **itraconazole**, **clarithromycine**, **nelfinavir**, **néfazodone**, **diltiazem** et **érythromycine**, peut entraîner une augmentation du taux sérique de fentanyl et causer ainsi une dépression respiratoire grave.
Médicament-produits naturels: Effets dépresseurs additifs sur le SNC lors de l'usage concomitant de **kava**, de **valériane** et de **camomille**.

VOIES D'ADMINISTRATION ET POSOLOGIE

- **Timbre transdermique (adultes)**:
  Au moment où on passe au timbre, la dose initiale ne doit pas dépasser l'équivalent de la dose totale d'opioïdes que le patient recevait auparavant. Pour calculer la dose de fentanyl par voie transdermique à administrer aux patients qui reçoivent déjà des opioïdes, évaluer la dose de ces analgésiques qu'il a fallu leur administrer au cours des 24 dernières heures. En utilisant le tableau des analgésiques équivalents de l'annexe A, convertir cette dose en quantité équivalente de morphine orale par 24 heures. Pour la conversion en fentanyl transdermique, consulter le tableau de conversion du fentanyl de l'annexe A. L'administration de doses supplémentaires d'autres opioïdes ayant une courte durée d'action peut s'avérer nécessaire pour traiter les épisodes douloureux pendant la période d'adaptation de la posologie. Le timbre agit pendant 72 heures chez la plupart des patients. Chez certains patients, il faut changer le timbre toutes les 48 heures.
- **Timbre transdermique (adultes > 60 ans, patients débilités ou cachectiques)**: En fonction de l'évaluation clinique, il peut s'avérer approprié de commencer le traitement à une dose inférieure à celle indiquée dans les tableaux de conversion.

PRÉSENTATION

Timbre transdermique: 12 µg/h[N], 25 µg/h[N], 50 µg/h[N], 75 µg/h[N], 100 µg/h[N].

SOINS INFIRMIERS

ÉVALUATION DE LA SITUATION

- Noter le type, le siège et l'intensité de la douleur avant et 24 heures après l'application du timbre et, par la suite, à intervalles réguliers, tout au long du traitement. Il faut suivre de près la douleur ainsi que les adaptations posologiques pendant le traitement initial pour déterminer si le patient a ou non besoin de recevoir des doses supplémentaires d'analgésique lors d'un épisode douloureux.
- ÉVALUER LE NIVEAU DE CONSCIENCE ET MESURER LA FRÉQUENCE RESPIRATOIRE, LE POULS ET LA PRESSION ARTÉRIELLE AVANT L'APPLICATION DU TIMBRE ET À INTERVALLES RÉGULIERS, TOUT AU LONG DU TRAITEMENT. SI LA FRÉQUENCE RESPIRATOIRE EST < 10/MIN, ÉVALUER LE DEGRÉ DE SÉDATION. UNE STIMULATION PHYSIQUE PEUT SUFFIRE À PRÉVENIR L'HYPOVENTILATION. IL PEUT ÊTRE NÉCESSAIRE DE RÉDUIRE LA DOSE DE 25 À 50 %. LA SOMNOLENCE INITIALE S'ATTÉNUERA AVEC L'USAGE CONTINU.

GÉR.: Évaluer fréquemment les patients âgés, car ils sont plus sensibles aux effets des analgésiques opioïdes que les adultes plus jeunes et peuvent subir des effets indésirables et des complications respiratoires plus souvent.

F

- L'usage prolongé peut entraîner la dépendance physique et psychologique ainsi qu'une tolérance à l'effet du médicament, mais cela ne doit pas empêcher le patient de recevoir une quantité suffisante d'analgésique. La psychodépendance est rare chez la plupart des patients qui reçoivent des opioïdes pour soulager les douleurs intenses.
- Lors d'un traitement prolongé, il peut s'avérer nécessaire d'administrer des doses de plus en plus élevées pour soulager la douleur. Après avoir augmenté la dose, l'atteinte d'un équilibre peut prendre jusqu'à 6 jours; il faut habituellement appliquer l'un après l'autre 2 timbres successifs à dose plus élevée avant que l'on puisse augmenter de nouveau la dose.
- Déterminer les habitudes d'élimination fécale à intervalles réguliers. Pour réduire les effets constipants du médicament, augmenter l'apport de liquides et d'aliments riches en fibres et administrer des laxatifs. Sauf indication contraire, il faut administrer systématiquement un laxatif stimulant si le traitement par l'opioïde dure plus de 2 ou 3 jours.

Tests de laboratoire: Le fentanyl peut entraîner l'élévation des concentrations sériques d'amylase et de lipase.

TOXICITÉ ET SURDOSAGE: S'il est nécessaire d'utiliser un antagoniste des opioïdes pour renverser la dépression respiratoire ou le coma, l'antidote est la naloxone (Narcan). Diluer le contenu d'une ampoule de 0,4 mg de naloxone dans 10 mL de solution de NaCl 0,9% et administrer 0,5 mL (0,02 mg) par IV directe, toutes les 2 minutes. Chez les patients dont le poids est < 40 kg, diluer 0,1 mg de naloxone dans 10 mL de solution de NaCl 0,9% pour obtenir une concentration de 10 µg/mL et administrer 0,5 µg/kg, toutes les 2 minutes. Afin de prévenir les symptômes de sevrage, les convulsions et les douleurs intenses, il faut adapter la dose. Suivre le patient de près; il peut être nécessaire de répéter l'administration de la dose ou d'administrer la naloxone par perfusion en raison de l'effet du fentanyl, qui peut se maintenir malgré le retrait du timbre. Adapter la dose pour prévenir les symptômes de sevrage, les crises convulsives et la douleur intense.

DIAGNOSTICS INFIRMIERS POSSIBLES

- Douleur aiguë (Indications).
- Risque d'accident (Effets secondaires).
- Connaissances insuffisantes sur le traitement médicamenteux (Enseignement au patient et à ses proches).

INTERVENTIONS INFIRMIÈRES

ALERTE CLINIQUE: DES SURDOSES ACCIDENTELLES D'ANALGÉSIQUES OPIOÏDES ONT CAUSÉ DES DÉCÈS. ÉVALUER L'UTILISATION ANTÉRIEURE D'ANALGÉSIQUES OPIOÏDES PAR LE PATIENT ET SES BESOINS ACTUELS. AVANT L'UTILISATION, CLARIFIER TOUTE ORDONNANCE AMBIGUË ET FAIRE VÉRIFIER L'ORDONNANCE D'ORIGINE ET LES CALCULS DES DOSES PAR UN AUTRE PROFESSIONNEL DE LA SANTÉ.

- Administrer des doses supplémentaires d'opioïdes à action brève pour soulager la douleur en attendant que les effets analgésiques du timbre transdermique se manifestent. Le patient peut avoir besoin de recevoir des doses supplémentaires d'opioïde pour soulager un épisode douloureux. Si une dose supérieure à 100 µg/h s'avère nécessaire, appliquer plusieurs timbres.
- Pour adapter la posologie, il faut se fier à la perception de la douleur dont fait état le patient jusqu'à ce que l'effet analgésique survienne (baisse de 50 % de l'intensité de la douleur selon l'évaluation du patient sur une échelle analogique numérique ou visuelle ou selon le degré de satisfaction du patient à l'égard du soulagement de la douleur). On détermine la dose de fentanyl transdermique en calculant les besoins en analgésiques des 24 dernières heures et en transformant cette valeur en dose équivalente de morphine (voir l'annexe A). Le ratio de conversion de la morphine en fentanyl transdermique doit être calculé prudemment; 50 % des patients peuvent avoir besoin d'une dose plus élevée après l'application initiale. L'augmentation de la dose après 3 jours est basée sur les doses quotidiennes supplémentaires d'analgésiques qui ont dû être administrées.
- Les analgésiques non opioïdes administrés simultanément peuvent exercer des effets analgésiques additifs, ce qui permet parfois de diminuer les doses de l'opioïde.
- Pour substituer un autre opioïde à cet agent, retirer le timbre de fentanyl transdermique et amorcer le traitement avec le nouvel analgésique au cours des 12 heures qui suivent.
- Après un traitement prolongé, interrompre l'administration graduellement pour prévenir les symptômes de sevrage.

Timbre transdermique: Appliquer le timbre sur un territoire cutané plan (torse, dos, flancs ou partie supérieure du bras) qui n'est pas irrité et qui n'a pas été exposé à une radiothérapie. S'il faut préparer le territoire cutané, nettoyer la peau avec de l'eau et couper les poils (ne pas raser). Laisser sécher complètement la peau avant l'application. Appliquer le timbre immédiatement après l'avoir retiré de l'emballage, sans en modifier la forme (sans le couper). Retirer la doublure qui protège la couche adhésive et peser fermement avec la paume de la main pendant 30 secondes, surtout sur les bordures, pour assurer une bonne adhérence. Pour changer de timbre, le décoller et le replier de sorte que les bords adhésifs collent ensemble, puis le jeter immédiatement dans les toilettes et tirer la chasse d'eau. Appliquer ensuite un nouveau timbre sur un territoire cutané différent. Jeter tous les timbres inutilisés dans les toilettes après les avoir retirés de leur emballage; tirer la chasse d'eau.

ENSEIGNEMENT AU PATIENT ET À SES PROCHES

- Expliquer au patient ce qu'on entend par administration sur demande et à quel moment il doit réclamer l'analgésique.
- Montrer au patient comment appliquer le timbre transdermique et comment le mettre au rebut. DES DÉCÈS SONT SURVENUS CHEZ DES ENFANTS AYANT EU ACCÈS À DES TIMBRES USAGÉS JETÉS DE MANIÈRE INADÉQUATE. Informer le patient qu'il peut porter le timbre pendant qu'il prend son bain ou sa douche ou pendant qu'il se baigne.
- Prévenir le patient que le fentanyl transdermique peut provoquer des étourdissements et de la somnolence. Lui recommander de demander de l'aide lorsqu'il se déplace et lorsqu'il veut fumer. Lui conseiller de ne pas conduire et d'éviter les activités qui exigent sa vigilance jusqu'à ce qu'on ait la certitude que le médicament n'entraîne pas ces effets chez lui.
- Conseiller au patient de changer lentement de position pour réduire les étourdissements.
- Recommander au patient de ne pas prendre de l'alcool ou d'autres dépresseurs du SNC en même temps qu'il porte le timbre transdermique.
- Prévenir le patient que la fièvre, les couvertures chauffantes, les coussins chauffants, les saunas, les bains tourbillons et les lits d'eau chauffés augmentent la dose de fentanyl qui est libérée du timbre.
- Prévenir le patient qu'une bonne hygiène buccale, l'usage fréquent d'un rince-bouche et la gomme ou les bonbons sans sucre peuvent réduire la sécheresse de la bouche.
- Insister sur l'importance de la prévention de la constipation associée à la prise d'analgésiques opioïdes.

VÉRIFICATION DE L'EFFICACITÉ THÉRAPEUTIQUE

L'efficacité du traitement peut être démontrée par: la diminution de l'intensité de la douleur sans modification importante de l'état de conscience, de l'état respiratoire ou de la pression artérielle. ✳

FER, SUPPLÉMENTS DE

fer dextran
Dexiron, Infufer

fer saccharose
Venofer

fumarate ferreux
Euro-Fer, Neo-Fer, Novo-Fumar, Palafer, Palafer CF, Scheinpharm-Fer

gluconate ferreux
Apo-Ferrous Gluconate, Novo-Ferrogluc

sulfate ferreux
Apo-Ferrous Sulfate, Fer-In-Sol, Ferodan, Ferofate, Fero-Grad, Novo-Ferrosulfa, Pediafer, PMS-Ferrous Sulfate, Slow-FE

CLASSIFICATION:
Minéraux et électrolytes (antianémiques)

Grossesse – catégorie C (fer dextran, suppléments administrés par voie orale)

INDICATIONS

PO: Prévention et traitement de l'anémie ferriprive ▪ **IM, IV**: *fer dextran* – Traitement et prévention de l'anémie ferriprive chez les patients qui ne peuvent tolérer les suppléments administrés par voie orale ▪ **IV**: *fer saccharose* – Traitement des anémies associées à la dialyse.

MÉCANISME D'ACTION

Substance minérale essentielle que l'on trouve dans l'hémoglobine, la myoglobine et un certain nombre d'enzymes ▪ Le fer administré par voie parentérale pénètre dans la circulation sanguine et les organes du système réticulo-endothélial (foie, rate, moelle osseuse), où le fer est séparé du complexe qu'il forme avec le dextran et intègre les réserves de fer. ***Effets thérapeutiques:*** Prévention et traitement des carences en fer.

PHARMACOCINÉTIQUE

Absorption: De 5 à 10 % du fer alimentaire est absorbé. Dans les états de carence, l'absorption peut augmenter jusqu'à 30 %. Elle peut s'élever à 60 % lorsque le fer est administré dans un but thérapeutique. Les agents sont absorbés par transport actif et passif. Bonne absorption (IM).

Distribution: Le fer demeure dans l'organisme pendant plusieurs mois. Il traverse la barrière placentaire et pénètre dans le lait maternel.

Liaison aux protéines: ≥ 90 %.
Métabolisme et excrétion: La plus grande partie de la substance est réabsorbée. Les petites pertes quotidiennes sont attribuables à la desquamation cutanée et à l'élimination par la sueur, l'urine et la bile.
Demi-vie: *Fer dextran* – 6 heures.

Profil temps-action (effets sur l'érythropoïèse)

	DÉBUT D'ACTION	PIC	DURÉE
PO	4 jours	7 – 10 jours	2 – 4 mois
IM, IV	4 jours	1 – 2 semaines	plusieurs semaines ou mois

F

CONTRE-INDICATIONS, PRÉCAUTIONS ET MISES EN GARDE

Contre-indications: Hypersensibilité ■ Hémochromatose ■ Hémosidérose ■ Anémies hémolytiques et autres anémies non attribuables à une carence en fer ■ Administration concomitante du fer par voie orale et par voie parentérale ■ Pyélonéphrite aiguë, affections hépatiques aiguës, début de la grossesse.
Précautions et mises en garde: PO: Ulcère gastroduodénal ■ Colite ulcéreuse ou entérite régionale (l'état du patient peut s'aggraver) ■ Hypersensibilité ou intolérance à l'alcool ou à la tartrazine (éviter les préparations qui contiennent ces substances) ■ Utilisation abusive sans discernement (risque de surcharge en fer) ■ **IM, IV:** Maladies auto-immunes et arthrite (plus grande prédisposition aux réactions allergiques) ■ **GÉR.:** Utiliser des doses initiales plus faibles chez les personnes âgées ■ **ALLAITEMENT, PÉD.:** L'innocuité des préparations injectables n'a pas été établie ■ **IM, IV:** Insuffisance hépatique grave.
EXTRÊME PRUDENCE: GÉR.: UTILISER DES DOSES INITIALES PLUS FAIBLES CHEZ LES PERSONNES ÂGÉES ■ **ALLAITEMENT, PÉD.:** L'INNOCUITÉ DES PRÉPARATIONS INJECTABLES N'A PAS ÉTÉ ÉTABLIE.

RÉACTIONS INDÉSIRABLES ET EFFETS SECONDAIRES

SNC: *IM, IV* – CONVULSIONS, étourdissements, céphalées, syncope.
CV: *IM, IV* – hypotension, tachycardie.
GI: nausées; *PO* – constipation, selles foncées, diarrhée, douleurs épigastriques, hémorragie digestive; *IM, IV* – altération du goût, vomissements.
Tég.: *IM, IV* – bouffées vasomotrices, urticaire.
Locaux: douleur au point d'injection IM (fer dextran), phlébite au point d'injection IV, coloration sombre de la peau au point d'injection IM (fer dextran).
Loc.: arthralgie, myalgie.
Divers: coloration sombre des dents (préparations liquides), *IM, IV* – réactions allergiques incluant l'ANAPHYLAXIE, la fièvre et la lymphadénopathie.

INTERACTIONS

Médicament-médicament: Les **tétracyclines** et les **antiacides** inhibent l'absorption du fer en formant des composés insolubles ■ Le fer, administré en concomitance, peut diminuer l'absorption des **tétracyclines**, des **fluoroquinolones** ou de la **pénicillamine** ■ Le fer diminue l'absorption et les effets de la **lévodopa** et de la **méthyldopa** ■ Le fer peut réduire l'absorption de la **lévothyroxine** (administration concomitante à proscrire) ■ La **cimétidine**, administrée en concomitance, peut réduire l'absorption du fer ■ Des doses d'**acide ascorbique** ≥ 200 mg peuvent accroître l'absorption du fer de ≥ 30 % ■ L'administration concomitante de **chloramphénicol** ou de **vitamine E** peut modifier la réponse hématologique au traitement par le fer.
Médicament-aliments: L'absorption du fer est réduite de 30 à 50 %, s'il est pris en même temps que des **aliments**.

VOIES D'ADMINISTRATION ET POSOLOGIE

Fer dextran

La dose totale est calculée d'après la gravité de la carence et la quantité de sang perdu. Administrer une dose d'essai de 0,5 mL (25 mg) avant d'entreprendre le traitement. Attendre au moins 1 heure avant d'administrer le reste de la dose. Si aucune réaction indésirable n'est observée, le fer dextran peut être administré selon la posologie suivante jusqu'à ce que la dose totale nécessaire soit atteinte:

- **IM, IV (nourrissons < 5 kg):** Ne pas dépasser 25 mg par jour.
- **IM, IV (enfants < 10 kg et > 5 kg):** Ne pas dépasser 50 mg par jour.
- **IM, IV (adultes, enfants > 10 kg):** Ne pas dépasser 100 mg par jour.
- **IM, IV (adultes, enfants > 15 kg):** *Anémie ferriprive:* Dose totale (mL) = 0,004 42 (concentration souhaitable d'hémoglobine en g/L – concentration d'hémoglobine observée en g/L) × poids corporel maigre + (0,26 × poids corporel maigre).
- **IM, IV (enfants de 5 à 15 kg):** *Anémie ferriprive:* Dose totale (mL) = 0,004 42 (concentration souhaitable d'hémoglobine en g/L – concentration d'hémoglobine observée en g/L) × poids + (0,26 × poids).
- **IM, IV (adultes, enfants > 15 kg):** *Remplacement du fer perdu à la suite de saignements:* Fer de remplacement (en mg) = pertes sanguines (en mL) × hématocrite.

Fer saccharose

- **IV (adultes):** 100 mg, durant la séance de dialyse, jusqu'à un maximum de 3 fois par semaine.

Fumarate ferreux, gluconate ferreux, sulfate ferreux
Les doses par voie orale sont exprimées en mg de fer élémentaire. Voici un aperçu des doses équivalentes selon la teneur en fer élémentaire de chacun des sels: fumarate ferreux: 197 mg; gluconate ferreux: 560 mg; sulfate ferreux: 324 mg.

- **PO (adolescents et adultes)**: *Pour prévenir la carence* – de 8 à 13 mg/jour de fer élémentaire. *En cas de carence en fer* – de 50 à 100 mg de fer élémentaire, 3 fois par jour.
- **PO (enfants)**: *Pour prévenir la carence* – de 6 à 8 mg/jour de fer élémentaire. *En cas de carence* – de 3 à 6 mg/kg de fer élémentaire par jour, en 3 doses fractionnées.
- **PO (nourrissons < 4 mois)**: *Pour prévenir la carence* – 0,3 mg/jour de fer élémentaire. *En cas de carence* – de 3 à 6 mg/kg de fer élémentaire par jour, en 3 doses fractionnées.
- **PO (2e trimestre de grossesse)**: *Pour prévenir la carence* – une quantité supplémentaire de 5 mg/jour de fer élémentaire.
- **PO (3e trimestre de grossesse)**: *Pour prévenir la carence* – une quantité supplémentaire de 10 mg/jour de fer élémentaire.

PRÉSENTATION

- **Fer dextran (mg de fer élémentaire)**
  Solution pour injection: 50 mg/mL^{Pr}, en flacons de 1 mL et de 2 mL.
- **Fer saccharose (mg de fer élémentaire)**
  Solution pour injection: 20 mg/mL^{Pr}, en flacons de 5 mL.
- **Fumarate ferreux (fer élémentaire à 33 %)**
  Capsules: 300 mg^{VL} ■ **Suspension**: 300 mg/5 mL^{VL}.
- **Gluconate ferreux (fer élémentaire à 11,6 %)**
  Comprimés: 300 mg^{VL}, 324 mg^{VL}, 325 mg^{VL} ■ **Sirop**: (fer élémentaire) 7 mg/mL^{VL}.
- **Sulfate ferreux (fer élémentaire de 20 à 30 %)**
  Comprimés, capsules: 60 mg^{VL}, 300 mg^{VL}, 325 mg^{VL} ■ **Comprimés à libération prolongée**: 160 mg^{VL} ■ **Solutions orales**: 75 mg/mL^{VL}, 150 mg/5 mL^{VL} ■ **Gouttes**: (fer élémentaire) 6 mg/mL^{VL}, 15 mg/mL^{VL}, 25 mg/mL^{VL}.
- **En association avec**: acide ascorbique, antiacides, multivitamines et minéraux^{VL}.

SOINS INFIRMIERS

ÉVALUATION DE LA SITUATION

- Examiner l'état nutritionnel du patient et ses habitudes alimentaires afin de déterminer les causes possibles de l'anémie et le type d'enseignement qu'il faudra lui prodiguer.
- Suivre de près la fonction intestinale pour déceler la constipation ou la diarrhée. Prévenir le médecin ou un autre professionnel de la santé si ces symptômes surviennent et suivre la démarche des soins infirmiers qui s'impose.

Fer dextran et fer saccharose:

- Mesurer la pression artérielle et la fréquence cardiaque à intervalles fréquents à la suite de l'administration par voie IV, jusqu'à ce que les valeurs se stabilisent. Une perfusion rapide peut provoquer l'hypotension et des bouffées vasomotrices.
- SUIVRE DE PRÈS LES SIGNES ET LES SYMPTÔMES SUIVANTS D'ANAPHYLAXIE: RASH, PRURIT, ŒDÈME LARYNGÉ, RESPIRATION SIFFLANTE. SIGNALER IMMÉDIATEMENT CES SYMPTÔMES AU MÉDECIN. GARDER À PORTÉE DE LA MAIN DE L'ADRÉNALINE ET LE MATÉRIEL DE RÉANIMATION POUR PARER À UNE ÉVENTUELLE RÉACTION ANAPHYLACTIQUE.

Tests de laboratoire:

- Noter les concentrations d'hémoglobine et la numération réticulocytaire ainsi que l'hématocrite avant l'administration du médicament, toutes les 3 semaines, pendant les 2 premiers mois de traitement et à intervalles réguliers par la suite. On peut aussi évaluer l'efficacité du traitement par la mesure des concentrations sériques de ferritine et de fer.
- La présence de sang occulte dans les selles peut être masquée par la présence du fer qui rend les selles de couleur foncée. La méthode au gaïac peut parfois donner des résultats faussement positifs. Par contre, les résultats de la méthode à la benzidine ne seront pas affectés par l'administration de préparations de fer.

Fer dextran:

- Noter l'hématocrite, la numération réticulocytaire, les concentrations d'hémoglobine, de transferrine, de ferritine et de fer plasmatique ainsi que la capacité de fixation du fer, à intervalles réguliers tout au long du traitement. Les concentrations sériques de ferritine atteignent un pic dans les 7 à 9 jours et se rétablissent en 3 semaines. Les mesures des concentrations sériques de fer peuvent ne pas être entièrement fiables pendant 1 ou 2 semaines après le traitement par de fortes doses; par conséquent, on doit utiliser la concentration d'hémoglobine et l'hématocrite pour évaluer la réponse initiale. La concentration normale d'hémoglobine est 148 g/L, dans le cas des patients pesant plus de 15 kg, et de 120 g/L, dans le cas des patients pesant 15 kg ou moins.

- Le fer dextran peut rendre de couleur brunâtre le sang prélevé dans les 4 heures suivant l'administration. Il peut aussi entraîner une fausse élévation des concentrations sériques de bilirubine et une fausse diminution des valeurs sériques de calcium.
- Le temps de céphaline peut être prolongé lorsqu'on mélange l'échantillon de sang avec une solution anticoagulante de citrate de dextrose; utiliser plutôt une solution de citrate de sodium.

***Toxicité et surdosage*:**

- Les premiers symptômes du surdosage sont les maux d'estomac, la fièvre, les nausées, les vomissements (qui peuvent contenir du sang) et la diarrhée. Les symptômes tardifs sont le bleuissement des lèvres, des ongles et des paumes, la somnolence, la faiblesse, la tachycardie, les convulsions, l'acidose métabolique, les lésions hépatiques et le collapsus cardiovasculaire. Avant que les symptômes tardifs ne se manifestent, le patient peut paraître rétabli. Par conséquent, après la disparition des symptômes, il faut prolonger l'hospitalisation de 24 heures afin de pouvoir suivre de près toute manifestation tardive d'un état de choc ou d'une hémorragie digestive. Les complications tardives du surdosage comprennent l'occlusion intestinale, la sténose du pylore et l'ulcération de la muqueuse gastrique.
- Pour traiter le surdosage, il faut provoquer des vomissements avec du sirop d'ipéca. Si le patient est comateux ou en convulsion, il faut effectuer un lavage gastrique avec du bicarbonate de sodium. L'antidote à utiliser en cas de surdosage est la déféroxamine. Il est également conseillé d'administrer des traitements de soutien supplémentaires visant à maintenir l'équilibre hydroélectrolytique et à corriger l'acidose métabolique.

DIAGNOSTICS INFIRMIERS POSSIBLES

- Intolérance à l'activité (Indications).
- Connaissances insuffisantes sur le traitement médicamenteux et la diétothérapie (Enseignement au patient et à ses proches).

INTERVENTIONS INFIRMIÈRES

L'administration de fer par voie orale devrait être interrompue avant le début du traitement par voie parentérale.

PO:

- Pour que les préparations orales soient absorbées le plus efficacement possible, on doit les administrer 1 heure avant les repas ou 2 heures après. En cas d'irritation gastrique, administrer la préparation lors des repas. Les comprimés et les capsules doivent être pris avec un grand verre d'eau ou de jus. IL NE FAUT PAS OUVRIR, ÉCRASER NI MÂCHER LES CAPSULES À LIBÉRATION PROLONGÉE ET LES COMPRIMÉS ENTÉROSOLUBLES.
- Les préparations liquides peuvent tacher les dents. Diluer l'agent dans un grand verre (240 mL) d'eau ou de jus de fruits, dans le cas des adultes, ou dans un demi-verre (120 mL), dans le cas des enfants. Demander au patient de boire la préparation avec une paille ou de verser les gouttes au fond de la gorge. Le liquide ou le sirop Fer-In-Sol peut être dilué dans de l'eau ou dans du jus de fruits.
- Il ne faut pas prendre des antiacides, du café ou du thé ni consommer de produits laitiers, d'œufs ou de pain complet en même temps qu'on prend des sels ferreux ni dans l'heure qui suit. L'absorption du fer est réduite de 33 % si on administre du fer et du calcium avec des aliments. Si le patient doit prendre des suppléments de calcium, lui faire prendre du carbonate de calcium, puisqu'il ne diminue pas l'absorption des sels ferreux, si ces suppléments sont administrés entre les repas.

Fer dextran

- L'ampoule de 2 mL peut servir à l'administration IM ou IV.
- Avant d'administrer la dose initiale par voie IM ou IV, on devrait administrer une dose d'essai de 25 mg par la même voie, afin de vérifier la réaction du patient. La dose d'essai par voie IV devrait être administrée en 5 minutes, alors que celle par voie IM devrait être administrée au même point d'injection et selon la même technique que la dose thérapeutique. Le reste de la dose peut être administré 1 heure après, si aucune réaction indésirable ne s'est manifestée.
- **IM**: Injecter en profondeur, selon la technique du tracé en Z, dans le quadrant supérieur externe du muscle fessier, jamais dans le bras ou une autre partie exposée. Utiliser une aiguille de 5 à 7 cm de longueur, de calibre 19 ou 20. Ne pas utiliser la même aiguille pour aspirer l'agent de la fiole et pour l'injecter, afin de réduire le risque de tacher les tissus sous-cutanés. Ce genre de tache est habituellement permanente.
- **IV**: À la suite de l'administration par voie IV, le patient devrait demeurer allongé pendant au moins 30 minutes pour prévenir l'hypotension orthostatique.
- **IV directe**: Administrer la préparation non diluée.
- ***Vitesse d'administration*:** Administrer lentement, à raison de 50 mg (1 mL) en au moins 1 minute.
- **Perfusion intermittente**: On peut diluer l'agent dans 100 à 1 000 mL de solution de NaCl 0,9 % ou D5%E; le NaCl 0,9 % est le diluant privilégié, car

la dilution dans le D5%E augmente le risque de douleur et de phlébite.

- ***Vitesse d'administration:*** Administrer en 1 à 8 heures, après l'administration de la dose d'essai de 25 mg en 5 minutes. À la fin de la perfusion, rincer la tubulure avec 10 mL de solution de NaCl 0,9 %.
- Consulter les directives de chaque fabricant avant de reconstituer la préparation.
- **Incompatibilité (tubulure en Y):** Interrompre l'administration des autres solutions IV pendant la perfusion de la préparation de fer.
- **Incompatibilité en addition au soluté:** Les fabricants recommandent de ne pas mélanger le fer dextran avec d'autres solutions; cependant, on l'a déjà ajouté à des solutions de nutrition parentérale totale.

Fer saccharose

- **IV directe:** Administrer la préparation non diluée.
- ***Vitesse d'administration:*** Administrer lentement, à raison de 1 mL (20 mg de fer) par minute (c.-à-d. 5 minutes par flacon), sans excéder le contenu d'un flacon (100 mg de fer) par injection.
- **Perfusion intermittente:** Diluer 100 mg (5 mL) dans un maximum de 100 mL de NaCl 0,9% seulement. Les doses supérieures à 100 mg et jusqu'à 500 mg devraient être diluées dans 250 mL de NaCl 0,9%.
- ***Vitesse d'administration:*** Perfuser la dose de 100 mg en au moins 15 minutes. Les doses > 100 mg doivent être perfusées en 2 heures.
- Consulter les directives de chaque fabricant avant de reconstituer la préparation.
- **Incompatibilité (tubulure en Y):** Interrompre l'administration des autres solutions IV pendant la perfusion de la préparation de fer.
- **Incompatibilité en addition au soluté:** Les fabricants recommandent de ne pas mélanger le fer saccharose avec d'autres solutions.

ENSEIGNEMENT AU PATIENT ET À SES PROCHES

- Conseiller au patient de respecter rigoureusement la posologie recommandée. S'il n'a pas pu prendre le médicament au moment habituel, il doit le prendre aussitôt que possible dans les 12 heures qui suivent. Sinon, il devrait reprendre le schéma posologique prescrit; le prévenir qu'il ne faut jamais remplacer une dose manquée par une double dose.
- Prévenir le patient que ses selles peuvent devenir vert foncé ou noires, mais que ce changement est inoffensif.
- Recommander au patient de suivre un régime alimentaire riche en fer (voir l'annexe J).
- Informer les parents du risque de surcharge en fer auquel est exposé l'enfant. Le médicament doit être gardé dans son contenant d'origine, muni d'un bouchon de sécurité, hors de la portée des enfants. Ne jamais comparer les vitamines à des bonbons. Si l'on soupçonne un surdosage, il faut communiquer sans tarder avec un professionnel de la santé, étant donné que ce type de surdosage peut être mortel. Conseiller aux parents de garder à la maison du sirop d'ipéca et de communiquer avec le pédiatre, les services d'urgence ou un centre antipoison afin de recevoir des directives d'utilisation avant d'administrer l'agent.

Fer dextran: Une réaction retard peut survenir 1 ou 2 jours après l'administration et durer 3 ou 4 jours, dans le cas d'une administration par voie IV, et de 3 à 7 jours, dans le cas d'une administration par voie IM. Recommander au patient de communiquer avec un médecin en cas de fièvre, de frissons, de malaise, de douleurs musculaires ou articulaires, de nausées, de vomissements, d'étourdissements ou de douleurs lombaires.

VÉRIFICATION DE L'EFFICACITÉ THÉRAPEUTIQUE

L'efficacité du traitement peut être démontrée par: l'élévation des concentrations d'hémoglobine qui peuvent atteindre les valeurs normales après 1 à 2 mois de traitement; de 3 à 6 mois peuvent s'écouler avant que les réserves de fer de l'organisme reviennent à la normale ■ l'élévation des concentrations plasmatiques d'hémoglobine et de fer ainsi que de l'hématocrite par le fer dextran; le diagnostic d'anémie ferriprive devrait être reconfirmé si les concentrations d'hémoglobine n'augmentent pas de 10 g/L en l'espace de 2 semaines ■ amélioration de l'anémie chez les patients atteints d'une insuffisance rénale chronique.

FEXOFÉNADINE

Allegra

CLASSIFICATION:

Antihistaminique (antagoniste des récepteurs H_1 de l'histamine)

Grossesse – catégorie C

INDICATIONS

Soulagement des symptômes de rhinite allergique saisonnière ou apériodique ■ Soulagement des symptômes de l'urticaire idiopathique chronique.

MÉCANISME D'ACTION

Inhibition des effets de l'histamine au niveau des récepteurs périphériques H_1, incluant le prurit et l'urticaire ■ Effet asséchant au niveau de la muqueuse nasale. ***Effets thérapeutiques:*** Diminution des éternuements, de la rhinorrhée et des démangeaisons au niveau des yeux, du nez et de la gorge, associés aux allergies saisonnières ■ Diminution de l'urticaire.

PHARMACOCINÉTIQUE

F

Absorption: Rapide (PO).
Distribution: Inconnue.
Métabolisme et excrétion: 80 % est excrété dans l'urine et 11 % dans les fèces.
Demi-vie: 14,4 heures (accrue chez les insuffisants rénaux).
Profil temps-action (effet antihistaminique)

	DÉBUT D'ACTION	PIC	DURÉE
PO	en l'espace de 1 h	2 - 3 h	12 - 24 h

CONTRE-INDICATIONS, PRÉCAUTIONS ET MISES EN GARDE

Contre-indications: Hypersensibilité.
Précautions et mises en garde: Insuffisance rénale (on recommande d'accroître l'intervalle posologique) ■ **OBST., ALLAITEMENT**: L'innocuité du médicament n'a pas été établie ■ **PÉD.**: L'innocuité du médicament n'a pas été établie chez les enfants < 12 ans.

RÉACTIONS INDÉSIRABLES ET EFFETS SECONDAIRES

SNC: somnolence, fatigue.
GI: dyspepsie.
End.: dysménorrhée.

INTERACTIONS

Médicament-médicament: La prise simultanée d'**antiacides à base de magnésium et d'aluminium** peut diminuer l'absorption de la fexofénadine et, par conséquent, son efficacité.
Médicament-aliments: La consommation de **jus d'orange**, de **pomme** ou de **pamplemousse** peut diminuer l'absorption de la fexofénadine et, par conséquent, son efficacité.

VOIES D'ADMINISTRATION ET POSOLOGIE

Rhinite allergique saisonnière

- **PO (adultes et enfants ≥ 12 ans)**: *Comprimés 12 heures:* 60 mg, 2 fois par jour. *Comprimés 24 heures:* 120 mg, 1 fois par jour.

Rhinite allergique apériodique

- **PO (adultes et enfants ≥ 12 ans)**: *Comprimés 12 heures:* 60 mg, 2 fois par jour.

Urticaire idiopathique chronique

- **PO (adultes et enfants ≥ 12 ans)**: *Comprimés 12 heures:* 60 mg, 2 fois par jour.

INSUFFISANCE RÉNALE

- **PO (ADULTES)**: DÉBUTER AVEC 60 mg, 1 FOIS PAR JOUR.

PRÉSENTATION

Comprimés 12 heures: 60 mg[VL] ■ **Comprimés 24 heures**: 120 mg[VL] ■ **En association avec**: pseudoéphédrine (Allegra-D[VL]).

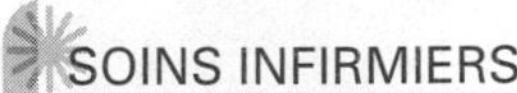

SOINS INFIRMIERS

ÉVALUATION DE LA SITUATION

- Suivre de près les symptômes d'allergie (rhinite, conjonctivite et urticaire), avant l'administration du médicament et à intervalles réguliers pendant toute la durée du traitement.
- Ausculter le murmure vésiculaire et noter les caractéristiques des sécrétions bronchiques. Maintenir l'apport de liquides entre 1 500 et 2 000 mL par jour pour diminuer la viscosité des sécrétions.

Tests de laboratoire: Le médicament peut entraîner des résultats faussement négatifs aux tests d'allergie cutanés; arrêter le traitement 3 jours avant ces tests.

DIAGNOSTICS INFIRMIERS POSSIBLES

- Dégagement inefficace des voies respiratoires (Indications).
- Risque d'accident (Réactions indésirables).
- Connaissances insuffisantes sur le traitement médicamenteux (Enseignement au patient et à ses proches).

INTERVENTIONS INFIRMIÈRES

- Administrer le médicament avec des aliments ou du lait afin de réduire l'irritation gastrique.

ENSEIGNEMENT AU PATIENT ET À SES PROCHES

- Conseiller au patient de respecter rigoureusement la posologie recommandée. S'il n'a pu prendre le médicament au moment habituel, il doit le prendre dès que possible à moins que ce ne soit presque l'heure prévue pour la dose suivante.
- Prévenir le patient que la fexofénadine peut provoquer de la somnolence, bien que le risque soit

moindre qu'avec les autres antihistaminiques. Lui conseiller de ne pas conduire et d'éviter les activités qui exigent sa vigilance jusqu'à ce qu'on ait la certitude que le médicament n'entraîne pas cet effet chez lui.
- Recommander au patient de prévenir un professionnel de la santé si les symptômes persistent.

VÉRIFICATION DE L'EFFICACITÉ THÉRAPEUTIQUE

L'efficacité du traitement peut être démontrée par: la diminution des symptômes allergiques.

FILGRASTIM

G-CSF, Neupogen

CLASSIFICATION:

Facteur stimulant de colonies de granulocytes (agent hématopoïétique)

Grossesse – catégorie C

INDICATIONS

Prévention de la neutropénie fébrile et des infections associées chez les patients qui ont reçu des agents antinéoplasiques myélodépresseurs pour traiter des affections malignes non myéloïdes ■ Diminution de la durée de la neutropénie et de la fièvre chez les patients atteints de leucémie myéloïde aiguë qui reçoivent une chimiothérapie d'induction ou de consolidation ■ Diminution de la durée et des séquelles de la neutropénie chez les patients présentant une affection maligne non myéloïde, qui reçoivent une chimiothérapie myélo-ablative suivie d'une greffe de moelle osseuse ■ Mobilisation des cellules souches hématopoïétique du sang périphérique afin qu'on puisse les récupérer par leucophérèse ■ Traitement de la neutropénie chronique grave ■ Neutropénie associée à une infection par le VIH.

MÉCANISME D'ACTION

Le filgrastim est une glycoprotéine qui se lie aux polynucléaires neutrophiles immatures et qui en stimule la division et la différenciation. Il active également les polynucléaires neutrophiles matures. ***Effets thérapeutiques:*** Réduction de l'incidence des infections chez les patients souffrant de neutropénie induite par la chimiothérapie ou d'une autre étiologie ■ Amélioration de la récolte de cellules souches pour la greffe de moelle osseuse.

PHARMACOCINÉTIQUE

Absorption: Bonne (SC).

Distribution: Inconnue.

Métabolisme et excrétion: Inconnus.

Demi-vie: 3,5 heures.

Profil temps-action (effet sur la formule leucocytaire)

	DÉBUT D'ACTION	PIC	DURÉE
IV, SC	inconnu	inconnu	4 jours†

† Rétablissement du nombre initial de polynucléaires neutrophiles.

CONTRE-INDICATIONS, PRÉCAUTIONS ET MISES EN GARDE

Contre-indications: Hypersensibilité au filgrastim ou aux produits dérivés de *Escherichia coli*.

Précautions et mises en garde: Leucémie myéloïde chronique ou myélodysplasie ■ Maladie cardiaque préexistante ■ **OBST., ALLAITEMENT, PÉD.:** L'innocuité du médicament n'a pas été établie.

RÉACTIONS INDÉSIRABLES ET EFFETS SECONDAIRES

Hémat.: leucocytose excessive.

Locaux: douleur, rougeur au point d'injection SC.

Loc.: douleurs osseuses médullaires.

INTERACTIONS

Médicament-médicament: L'administration simultanée d'**agents antinéoplasiques** peut entraîner des effets délétères sur les polynucléaires neutrophiles à prolifération rapide. Ne pas administrer le filgrastim 24 heures avant et 24 heures après la chimiothérapie ■ Le **lithium** peut potentialiser la production des polynucléaires neutrophiles; la prudence est de mise lors d'un usage concomitant.

VOIES D'ADMINISTRATION ET POSOLOGIE

Après une chimiothérapie myélodépressive

- **IV, SC (adultes):** 5 µg/kg/jour, en une seule injection quotidienne, pendant un maximum de 2 semaines. On peut augmenter la dose de 5 µg/kg par cycle de chimiothérapie selon le nombre absolu de polynucléaires neutrophiles.
- **SC (enfants):** 5 µg/kg/jour, en une seule injection quotidienne, pendant un maximum de 2 semaines. On peut augmenter la dose de 5 µg/kg par cycle de chimiothérapie selon le nombre absolu de polynucléaires neutrophiles.

Après la greffe de moelle osseuse

- **IV, SC (adultes):** 10 µg/kg/jour en perfusion IV d'une durée de 4 à 24 heures ou en perfusion SC continue pendant 24 heures; amorcer le traitement au moins 24 heures après la chimiothérapie et la greffe de moelle osseuse. Adapter les doses ultérieures selon le nombre absolu de polynucléaires neutrophiles.

Prélèvement de cellules souches du sang périphérique suivi d'un traitement

- **SC, IV (adultes)**: 10 µg/kg/jour en bolus SC ou en perfusion SC continue pendant au moins 4 jours avant la première leucophérèse; poursuivre jusqu'à la dernière leucophérèse; 5 µg/kg/jour en perfusion SC ou IV à débuter au moins 24 heures après la chimiothérapie et l'injection de cellules souches. Adapter les doses ultérieures selon le nombre absolu de polynucléaires neutrophiles.

F

Neutropénie chronique grave

- **SC (adultes)**: *Neutropénie congénitale* – 12 µg/kg/jour en une dose unique ou en doses fractionnées; *neutropénie idiopathique ou cyclique* – 5 µg/kg/jour en une dose unique ou en doses fractionnées (adapter la posologie pour maintenir le nombre absolu de polynucléaires neutrophiles entre 1,5 × 10^9/L et 10 × 10^9/L).

Infection par le VIH

- **SC (adultes)**: 1 µg/kg/jour, ou 300 µg, 3 fois par semaine en bolus, jusqu'à l'obtention et au maintien d'un nombre absolu de polynucléaires neutrophiles normal. Puis, établir la posologie minimale efficace pour maintenir un nombre normal.

PRÉSENTATION

Solution pour injection: fioles de 1 mL et de 1,6 mL à 300 µg/mL[Pr].

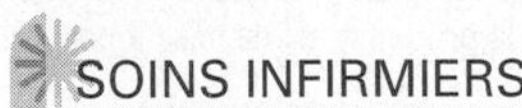

SOINS INFIRMIERS

ÉVALUATION DE LA SITUATION

- Mesurer la fréquence cardiaque, la pression artérielle et la fonction respiratoire avant l'administration du médicament et à intervalles réguliers tout au long du traitement.
- Suivre de près les douleurs osseuses tout au long du traitement. La douleur est habituellement de légère à modérée et peut être soulagée par des analgésiques non opioïdes. Parfois, il faut cependant administrer des opioïdes, particulièrement aux patients qui reçoivent de fortes doses de filgrastim par voie IV.

Tests de laboratoire:

- *Chimiothérapie:* examiner la numération globulaire, la formule leucocytaire, incluant l'analyse permettant de déceler la présence de cellules blastiques, ainsi que la numération plaquettaire, avant la chimiothérapie et 2 fois par semaine pendant toute la durée du traitement, afin de prévenir la leucocytose. Noter le nombre absolu des polynucléaires neutrophiles. Une élévation passagère survient 1 ou 2 jours après le début du traitement. Toutefois, il ne faut pas interrompre le traitement avant que le nombre absolu de polynucléaires neutrophiles après l'atteinte du nadir soit supérieur à 10 × 10^9/L.
- *Greffe de moelle osseuse:* la dose quotidienne est adaptée selon le nombre de polynucléaires neutrophiles. Lorsque le nombre absolu de polynucléaires neutrophiles est > 1,0 × 10^9/L pendant 3 jours consécutifs, la dose doit être réduite de 5 µg/kg/jour. S'il reste > 1,0 × 10^9/L pendant au moins 3 jours consécutifs de plus, on doit cesser le traitement par le filgrastim. Si ce nombre descend en dessous de 1,0 × 10^9/L, il faut reprendre le traitement à 5 µg/kg/jour.
- *Neutropénie chronique grave:* examiner la numération globulaire, la formule leucocytaire et la numération plaquettaire 2 fois par semaine, pendant les 4 premières semaines de traitement, et pendant 2 semaines après chaque adaptation posologique.
- Le filgrastim peut entraîner la diminution du nombre de plaquettes et une élévation transitoire des concentrations d'acide urique, de LDH et de phosphatase alcaline.

DIAGNOSTICS INFIRMIERS POSSIBLES

- Risque d'infection (Indications).
- Douleur aiguë (Effets secondaires).
- Connaissances insuffisantes sur le traitement médicamenteux (Enseignement au patient et à ses proches).

INTERVENTIONS INFIRMIÈRES

- Administrer le filgrastim au moins 24 heures après la chimiothérapie cytotoxique et au moins 24 heures après l'injection de moelle osseuse; ne pas administrer cet agent 24 heures avant la chimiothérapie.
- Garder la solution au réfrigérateur, mais non pas au congélateur. Ne pas secouer le contenant. La solution peut être réchauffée à la température ambiante jusqu'à 24 heures avant l'injection. Jeter toute solution qui est restée à la température ambiante pendant plus de 24 heures. La solution est présentée en fioles uniservice.

SC:

- S'il faut administrer une dose supérieure à 1 mL, on peut l'injecter en 2 points différents.
- Le filgrastim peut aussi être administré en perfusion SC continue pendant 24 heures après la greffe de moelle osseuse.

Perfusion continue: Diluer dans une solution de D5%E pour obtenir une concentration de plus de 15 µg de filgrastim/mL. Si la concentration finale se situe entre 5 et 15 µg/mL, il faut ajouter à la solution de D5%E, avant d'y injecter le filgrastim, de l'albumine humaine à une concentration de 2 mg/mL, afin de prévenir l'adsorption du médicament par les matières plastiques du dispositif d'administration du produit.

Vitesse d'administration:

- *Après la chimiothérapie,* la dose est administrée par perfusion d'une durée de 15 à 30 minutes ou en perfusion continue.
- *Après la greffe de moelle osseuse,* on doit administrer la dose sous forme de perfusion en 4 à 24 heures.

Compatibilité (tubulure en Y): acyclovir ■ allopurinol ■ amikacine ■ aminophylline ■ ampicilline ■ ampicilline/sulbactam ■ aztréonam ■ bléomycine ■ bumétanide ■ buprénorphine ■ butorphanol ■ calcium, gluconate de ■ carboplatine ■ carmustine ■ céfazoline ■ céfotétane ■ ceftazidime ■ chlorpromazine ■ cimétidine ■ cisplatine ■ cyclophosphamide ■ cytarabine ■ dacarbazine ■ daunorubicine ■ dexaméthasone ■ diphenhydramine ■ doxorubicine ■ doxycycline ■ dropéridol ■ énalaprilate ■ famotidine ■ floxuridine ■ fluconazole ■ fludarabine ■ gallium, nitrate de ■ ganciclovir ■ halopéridol ■ hydrocortisone ■ hydromorphone ■ idarubicine ■ ifosfamide ■ leucovorine calcique ■ lorazépam ■ méchloréthamine ■ melphalan ■ mépéridine ■ mesna ■ méthotrexate ■ métoclopramide ■ miconazole ■ minocycline ■ mitoxantrone ■ morphine ■ nalbuphine ■ nétilmicine ■ ondansétron ■ plicamycine ■ potassium, chlorure de ■ prométhazine ■ ranitidine ■ sodium, bicarbonate de ■ streptozocine ■ ticarcilline ■ ticarcilline/clavulanate ■ tobramycine ■ triméthoprime/sulfaméthoxazole ■ vancomycine ■ vinblastine ■ vincristine ■ vinorelbine ■ zidovudine.

Incompatibilité (tubulure en Y): amphotéricine B ■ céfépime ■ céfonicide ■ céfopérazone ■ céfotaxime ■ céfoxitine ■ ceftizoxime ■ ceftriaxone ■ céfuroxime ■ clindamycine ■ dactinomycine ■ étoposide ■ fluorouracile ■ furosémide ■ héparine ■ mannitol ■ méthylprednisolone sodique, succinate de ■ métronidazole ■ mezlocilline ■ mitomycine ■ pipéracilline ■ prochlorpérazine ■ thiotépa.

ENSEIGNEMENT AU PATIENT ET À SES PROCHES

Soins à domicile: Montrer au patient comment s'autoadministrer les injections et comment mettre au rebut le matériel à domicile. Prévenir le patient qu'il ne faut jamais réutiliser une aiguille, une fiole ou une seringue. Remettre au patient un contenant imperforable pour qu'il puisse jeter l'aiguille et la seringue.

VÉRIFICATION DE L'EFFICACITÉ THÉRAPEUTIQUE

L'efficacité du traitement peut être démontrée par: la réduction de l'incidence des infections chez les patients qui reçoivent des antinéoplasiques myélodépresseurs ■ la diminution de la durée et des séquelles de la neutropénie après une greffe de moelle osseuse ■ la diminution de l'incidence et de la durée des séquelles de la neutropénie chez les patients atteints de neutropénie chronique grave ■ un prélèvement plus efficace des cellules souches nécessaires à la greffe de moelle osseuse. ✳

F

FINASTÉRIDE

Propecia, Proscar

CLASSIFICATION:

Inhibiteur des hormones androgènes (inhibiteur de la 5 alpha-réductase de type II), stimulant de la repousse des cheveux

Grossesse – catégorie X

INDICATIONS

Traitement de l'hyperplasie bénigne de la prostate ■ Traitement de l'alopécie androgénétique (calvitie hippocratique) chez les hommes seulement.

MÉCANISME D'ACTION

Inhibition de l'enzyme 5-alpha-réductase, responsable de la transformation de la testostérone en son puissant métabolite, la 5-alpha-dihydrotestostérone, dans la prostate, le foie et la peau; la 5-alpha-testostérone est en partie responsable de l'hyperplasie de la prostate et de la perte de cheveux. ***Effets thérapeutiques:*** Réduction de la taille de la prostate et, par le fait même, des symptômes urinaires ■ Diminution de la perte de cheveux; stimulation de la repousse des cheveux.

PHARMACOCINÉTIQUE

Absorption: Bonne (63 %, PO).

Distribution: Le finastéride pénètre dans les tissus prostatiques et traverse la barrière hématoencéphalique. Le reste de la distribution est inconnu.

Liaison aux protéines: 90 %.

Métabolisme et excrétion: Le médicament est métabolisé en grande partie; 39 % est excrété sous forme de métabolites par les reins; 57 % dans les fèces.
Demi-vie: 6 heures (écart de 6 à 15 heures; légèrement prolongée chez les patients > 70 ans).

Profil temps-action
(baisse des concentrations de la dihydrotestostérone†)

	DÉBUT D'ACTION	PIC	DURÉE
PO	rapide	8 h	2 semaines

† Les effets cliniques, évalués par les symptômes au niveau des voies urinaires et la repousse des cheveux, peuvent ne se manifester qu'après plusieurs mois de traitement et se maintenir pendant 4 mois après que celui-ci a été arrêté.

F

CONTRE-INDICATIONS, PRÉCAUTIONS ET MISES EN GARDE

Contre-indications: Hypersensibilité ■ Femmes ■ Grossesse ■ Enfants.
Précautions et mises en garde: Insuffisance hépatique ou uropathie obstructive.

RÉACTIONS INDÉSIRABLES ET EFFETS SECONDAIRES

GU: baisse de la libido, diminution du volume d'éjaculat, impuissance.

INTERACTIONS

Médicament-médicament: Les **agents anticholinergiques**, les **bronchodilatateurs adrénergiques** et la **théophylline** peuvent atténuer les effets bénéfiques du finastéride.

VOIES D'ADMINISTRATION ET POSOLOGIE

- **PO (adultes):** *Hyperplasie bénigne de la prostate* – 5 mg, 1 fois par jour; *alopécie androgénétique* – 1 mg par jour.

PRÉSENTATION

Comprimés: 1 mg[Pr], 5 mg[Pr].

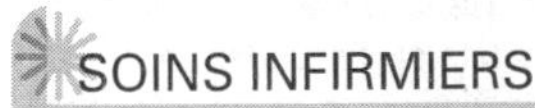

ÉVALUATION DE LA SITUATION

- Observer le patient avant le traitement et à intervalles réguliers pendant toute sa durée pour déceler les symptômes suivants d'hyperplasie de la prostate: retard de la miction, sensation d'évacuation incomplète de la vessie, jet mictionnel discontinu, modification de la force du jet mictionnel et de la quantité d'urine évacuée, fuite postmictionnelle, effort pour amorcer le jet, dysurie, miction impérieuse.
- En cas d'hyperplasie bénigne de la prostate, effectuer un toucher rectal avant le traitement et à intervalles réguliers pendant toute sa durée.

Tests de laboratoire: On peut établir les concentrations de l'antigène prostatique spécifique (APS) permettant de dépister le cancer de la prostate, avant le traitement et à intervalles réguliers pendant toute sa durée. Le médicament peut diminuer les concentrations sériques de cet antigène.

DIAGNOSTICS INFIRMIERS POSSIBLES

- Élimination urinaire altérée (Indications).
- Connaissances insuffisantes sur le traitement médicamenteux (Enseignement au patient et à ses proches).

INTERVENTIONS INFIRMIÈRES

- Administrer le médicament 1 fois par jour sans égard aux repas.

ENSEIGNEMENT AU PATIENT ET À SES PROCHES

- Recommander au patient de prendre le finastéride en suivant rigoureusement les recommandations du médecin même si les symptômes s'améliorent ou demeurent inchangés. Il faut parfois administrer le traitement pendant 6 à 12 mois avant qu'on puisse évaluer la réponse du patient.
- Informer le patient que la quantité d'éjaculat peut être moindre pendant le traitement, mais que ce phénomène n'altère pas la fonction sexuelle.
- EXPLIQUER AU PATIENT QUE LE FINASTÉRIDE PEUT ÊTRE NOCIF POUR LE FŒTUS DE SEXE MASCULIN. LES FEMMES ENCEINTES OU CELLES QUI POURRAIENT LE DEVENIR DEVRAIENT ÉVITER DE S'EXPOSER AU SPERME D'UN PARTENAIRE TRAITÉ PAR LE FINASTÉRIDE ET À TOUT CONTACT AVEC LA POUDRE DE FINASTÉRIDE EN RAISON DES RISQUES D'ABSORPTION.
- Insister sur l'importance des examens de suivi permettant d'évaluer l'efficacité du traitement.

VÉRIFICATION DE L'EFFICACITÉ THÉRAPEUTIQUE

L'efficacité du traitement peut être démontrée par: la diminution des symptômes urinaires associés à l'hyperplasie bénigne de la prostate ■ la repousse des cheveux en cas d'alopécie androgénétique. Il faut habituellement compter au moins 3 mois avant de pouvoir constater la repousse des cheveux. Il est recommandé de poursuivre le traitement pour en maintenir les effets. L'abandon du traitement entraîne le renversement des effets dans les 12 mois qui suivent.

FLÉCAÏNIDE

Apo-Flecainide, Tambocor

CLASSIFICATION:

Antiarythmique (classe IC)

Grossesse – catégorie C

INDICATIONS

Traitement des arythmies ventriculaires mettant la vie du patient en danger, incluant la tachycardie ventriculaire soutenue ■ Prévention des tachyarythmies supraventriculaires dont: les tachycardies supraventriculaires paroxystiques ■ la fibrillation auriculaire paroxystique ■ le flutter auriculaire.

MÉCANISME D'ACTION

Ralentissement de la conduction du tissu cardiaque par la modification du transport des ions à travers la membrane cellulaire. ***Effets thérapeutiques:*** Suppression des arythmies.

PHARMACOCINÉTIQUE

Absorption: Bonne (PO).
Distribution: Tout l'organisme.
Métabolisme et excrétion: Métabolisme majoritairement hépatique. Excrétion rénale à l'état inchangé (30 %).
Demi-vie: De 11 à 14 heures.

Profil temps-action (effet antiarythmique)

	DÉBUT D'ACTION	PIC	DURÉE
PO	plusieurs jours	plusieurs jours – semaines	12 h

CONTRE-INDICATIONS, PRÉCAUTIONS ET MISES EN GARDE

Contre-indications: Hypersensibilité ■ Choc cardiogénique ■ Dysfonctionnement du nœud sinusal ou bloc AV du 2e ou du 3e degré préexistants (en l'absence d'un stimulateur cardiaque) ■ Bloc de branche bifasciculaire ou trifasciculaire (en l'absence d'un stimulateur cardiaque).

Précautions et mises en garde: Insuffisance cardiaque (réduire la dose, au besoin) ■ Insuffisance rénale (réduire la dose si la Cl_{Cr} est < 35 mL/min) ■ **OBST., ALLAITEMENT, PÉD.**: L'innocuité du médicament n'a pas été établie.

RÉACTIONS INDÉSIRABLES ET EFFETS SECONDAIRES

SNC: étourdissements, anxiété, fatigue, céphalée, dépression.
ORLO: vision trouble, altération de l'acuité visuelle.
CV: ARYTHMIES, DOULEURS THORACIQUES, INSUFFISANCE CARDIAQUE.
GI: anorexie, constipation, nausées, douleurs d'estomac, vomissements.
Tég.: rash.
SN: tremblements.

INTERACTIONS

Médicament-médicament: Risque accru d'arythmies lors de l'administration concomitante d'autres **antiarythmiques** incluant les **bloqueurs des canaux calciques** ■ Le **disopyramide**, les **bêtabloquants** ou le **vérapamil**, administrés en concomitance, peuvent avoir des effets dépresseurs additifs sur le myocarde; il faut faire preuve de prudence lors de l'administration concomitante de ces agents ■ L'**amiodarone** double les concentrations sériques de flécaïnide (réduire la dose de flécaïnide de 50 %) ■ Le flécaïnide élève légèrement les concentrations sériques de **digoxine** (entre 15 et 25 %) ■ Lors d'un traitement concomitant aux **bêtabloquants**, il y a risque d'élévation des concentrations des deux médicaments ■ Les **agents alcalinisants** favorisent la réabsorption du flécaïnide, en élèvent les concentrations sanguines et peuvent engendrer une toxicité ■ Les **agents acidifiants** augmentent l'élimination rénale et peuvent réduire l'efficacité du flécaïnide (si le pH urinaire est < 5).

Médicament-aliments: Les **aliments qui alcalinisent l'urine** (pH > 7) élèvent aussi les concentrations sanguines de flécaïnide (**régime végétarien strict**) ■ Les **aliments ou boissons qui acidifient l'urine** (pH < 5) augmentent l'élimination rénale et peuvent réduire l'efficacité du flécaïnide (**jus de fruits acides**).

VOIES D'ADMINISTRATION ET POSOLOGIE

Tachycardie ventriculaire

- **PO (adultes)**: Initialement, 100 mg, toutes les 12 heures; augmenter la dose de 50 mg, 2 fois par jour tous les 4 jours, jusqu'à l'obtention d'une réponse ou jusqu'à l'atteinte de la dose quotidienne maximale totale de 400 mg. Chez certains patients, il faut fractionner la dose pour l'administrer toutes les 8 heures.

Tachyarythmies supraventriculaires paroxystiques/ fibrillation ou flutter auriculaire paroxystique

- **PO (adultes)**: Initialement, 50 mg, toutes les 12 heures, dose qu'on augmente par paliers de 50 mg, 2 fois par jour tous les 4 jours, jusqu'à l'obtention d'une réponse ou jusqu'à l'atteinte de la dose quotidienne maximale totale de 300 mg. Chez certains patients, il faut administrer la dose toutes les 8 heures.

INSUFFISANCE RÉNALE

- **PO (ADULTES):** *CL_{CR} < 35 mL/MIN* – INITIALEMENT, DE 50 À 100 mg, 1 FOIS PAR JOUR, OU 50 mg, TOUTES LES 12 HEURES ; L'ADAPTATION POSOLOGIQUE ULTÉRIEURE DOIT SE FAIRE SELON LES CONCENTRATIONS SANGUINES ÉVALUÉES À INTERVALLES FRÉQUENTS.

PRÉSENTATION

Comprimés: 50 mg[Pr], 100 mg[Pr].

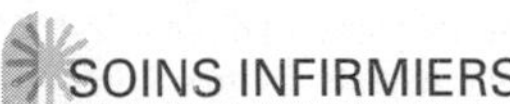

SOINS INFIRMIERS

F

ÉVALUATION DE LA SITUATION

- SUIVRE DE PRÈS L'ÉCG OU LE TRACÉ HOLTER AVANT LE TRAITEMENT ET À INTERVALLES RÉGULIERS PENDANT TOUTE SA DURÉE. LE FLÉCAÏNIDE PEUT ENTRAÎNER L'ÉLARGISSEMENT DES COMPLEXES QRS ET L'ALLONGEMENT DES INTERVALLES PR ET QT.
- Mesurer la pression artérielle et le pouls à intervalles réguliers pendant toute la durée du traitement.
- EFFECTUER LE BILAN QUOTIDIEN DES INGESTA ET DES EXCRETA ET PESER LE PATIENT TOUS LES JOURS. OBSERVER LE PATIENT À LA RECHERCHE DES SIGNES ET DES SYMPTÔMES SUIVANTS D'INSUFFISANCE CARDIAQUE : ŒDÈME PÉRIPHÉRIQUE, RÂLES ET CRÉPITATIONS, DYSPNÉE, GAIN DE POIDS, TURGESCENCE DES JUGULAIRES.

Tests de laboratoire:

- Interpréter les résultats des tests des fonctions hépatique, pulmonaire et rénale et noter la numération globulaire à intervalles réguliers chez le patient recevant un traitement prolongé. Il faut cesser le traitement par le flécaïnide en présence d'aplasie médullaire.
- Le flécaïnide peut entraîner l'élévation des concentrations sériques de phosphatase alcaline lors d'un traitement prolongé.

TOXICITÉ ET SURDOSAGE: Les concentrations sanguines thérapeutiques se situent entre 0,2 et 1 µg/mL. Il faut mesurer fréquemment les creux des concentrations plasmatiques pendant la période d'adaptation posologique chez les patients souffrant d'une maladie rénale ou hépatique grave ou chez ceux souffrant d'insuffisance cardiaque et d'insuffisance rénale modérée.

DIAGNOSTICS INFIRMIERS POSSIBLES

- Débit cardiaque diminué (Réactions indésirables).
- Connaissances insuffisantes sur le traitement médicamenteux (Enseignement au patient et à ses proches).

INTERVENTIONS INFIRMIÈRES

- Avant d'amorcer le traitement par le flécaïnide, il faut interrompre tout traitement antiarythmique antérieur (sauf l'administration de lidocaïne) pendant une période entre 2 et 4 demi-vies.
- Amorcer le traitement en milieu hospitalier afin de déceler toute aggravation des arythmies.
- Il faut espacer les modifications posologiques d'au moins 4 jours étant donné la longue demi-vie du flécaïnide.

PO: Si l'irritation gastrique devient gênante, administrer le flécaïnide aux repas.

ENSEIGNEMENT AU PATIENT ET À SES PROCHES

- Expliquer au patient qu'il doit respecter rigoureusement la posologie recommandée et prendre le médicament à intervalles réguliers, 24 heures sur 24, même s'il se sent mieux. S'il n'a pas pu prendre le médicament au moment habituel, il doit le prendre aussitôt que possible dans les 6 heures suivantes ; sinon, lui recommander de sauter cette dose. Une réduction graduelle de la dose peut s'avérer nécessaire.
- Prévenir le patient que le flécaïnide peut provoquer des étourdissements ou des troubles visuels. Lui conseiller de ne pas conduire et d'éviter les activités qui exigent sa vigilance jusqu'à ce qu'on ait la certitude que le médicament n'entraîne pas ces effets chez lui.
- Recommander au patient qui doit suivre un traitement ou subir une intervention chirurgicale d'avertir le professionnel de la santé qu'il suit un traitement par ce médicament.
- Recommander au patient de prévenir un professionnel de la santé en cas de douleurs thoraciques, d'essoufflements ou de diaphorèse.
- Conseiller au patient de porter sur lui en tout temps une pièce d'identité où sont inscrits son problème de santé et son traitement.
- Insister sur l'importance des examens de suivi permettant d'évaluer l'efficacité du traitement.

VÉRIFICATION DE L'EFFICACITÉ THÉRAPEUTIQUE

L'efficacité du traitement peut être démontrée par: la diminution de la fréquence des arythmies ventriculaires mettant la vie du patient en danger ■ la diminution des tachyarythmies supraventriculaires.

FLUCONAZOLE

Apo-Fluconazole, Diflucan, Novo-Fluconazole, PMS-Fluconazole

CLASSIFICATION:

Antifongique (par voie générale)

Grossesse – catégorie C

INDICATIONS

PO, IV: Traitement des infections fongiques dues à des microorganismes sensibles dont les suivantes: candidose oropharyngée ou œsophagienne ■ candidose profonde grave (incluant les candidoses urinaires, péritonéales et pulmonaires) ■ méningite cryptococcique ■ Prévention de la candidose chez les patients ayant subi une greffe de moelle osseuse ■ Prévention des récurrences de la méningite cryptococcique chez les patients atteints de sida ■ **PO**: Traitement de la candidose vaginale (par une seule dose de médicament. **Usages non approuvés**: Prévention de la candidose vaginale récurrente.

MÉCANISME D'ACTION

Inhibition de la synthèse des stérols fongiques, un élément essentiel de la paroi cellulaire. ***Effets thérapeutiques:*** Action fongistatique contre les microorganismes sensibles ■ Action fongicide possible lors de l'administration de concentrations élevées. **Spectre d'action**: *Cryptococcus neoformans* ■ espèces *Candida.*

PHARMACOCINÉTIQUE

Absorption: Bonne (PO).
Distribution: Tout l'organisme; l'agent pénètre bien dans le liquide céphalorachidien, les yeux et le péritoine.
Métabolisme et excrétion: Excrétion rénale à l'état inchangé (> 80 %); métabolisme hépatique (< 10 %).
Demi-vie: 30 heures (prolongée en cas d'insuffisance rénale).

Profil temps-action (concentrations sanguines)

	DÉBUT D'ACTION	PIC	DURÉE
PO	inconnu	1 - 2 h	24 h
IV	rapide	fin de la perfusion	24 h

CONTRE-INDICATIONS, PRÉCAUTIONS ET MISES EN GARDE

Contre-indications: Hypersensibilité au fluconazole ■ Administration concomitante de cisapride, de pimozide ou de terfénadine.
Précautions et mises en garde: Insuffisance rénale (réduire la dose si la Cl_{Cr} est < 50 mL/min) ■ Maladie hépatique sous-jacente ■ Patients prédisposés à des troubles du rythme cardiaque (risque d'allongement de l'intervalle QT_c) ■ Hypersensibilité à d'autres antifongiques de type azole ■ **GÉR.**: Risque accru de réactions indésirables (érythème, vomissements, diarrhée, convulsions). Pour établir la dose, il faut tenir compte de la diminution de la fonction rénale chez les patients âgés ■ **OBST.**: L'innocuité du fluconazole n'a pas été établie chez la femme enceinte ■ **ALLAITEMENT**: L'innocuité du fluconazole n'a pas été établie ■ **PÉD.**: L'innocuité du fluconazole n'a pas été établie chez les nouveau-nés.

RÉACTIONS INDÉSIRABLES ET EFFETS SECONDAIRES

L'incidence des réactions indésirables est plus élevée chez les patients infectés par le VIH.
SNC: céphalées, étourdissements, convulsions, paresthésie, tremblements, vertiges, insomnie, somnolence.
CV: allongement de l'intervalle QT, torsades de pointes.
GI: HÉPATOTOXICITÉ, gêne abdominale, diarrhée, nausées, vomissements, sécheresse de la bouche (xérostomie).
HÉ: hypokaliémie.
Tég.: éruptions cutanées, prurit, érythrodermies, incluant le SYNDROME DE STEVENS-JOHNSON.
Hémat.: leucopénie (neutropénie et agranulocytose), thrombopénie, anémie.
Métab.: hypertriglycéridémie.
Loc.: myalgies.
Divers: réactions allergiques, incluant l'ANAPHYLAXIE.

INTERACTIONS

Médicament-médicament: Le fluconazole, administré à des doses > 200 mg/jour, peut inhiber le cytochrome P450 3A4 et, par conséquent, élever les concentrations plasmatiques (efficacité et/ou toxicité accrues) des **médicaments métabolisés par cette enzyme** ■ Le **cisapride** et le **pimozide** élèvent les concentrations sanguines de fluconazole et le risque de réactions indésirables cardiovasculaires graves (l'usage concomitant est contre-indiqué) ■ Le fluconazole intensifie les effets de la **warfarine** ■ La **rifampine** et l'**isoniazide** diminuent les concentrations sanguines de fluconazole ■ Le fluconazole intensifie les effets hypoglycémiants du **tolbutamide**, du **glyburide** ou du **glipizide** ■ Le médicament élève les concentrations sanguines de **cyclosporine**, de **rifabutine**, de **tacrolimus**, de **théophylline**, de **zidovudine**, d'**alfentanil** et de **phénytoïne** et accroît le risque de toxicité associé à ces agents ■ Le médicament élève les concentrations sanguines des **benzodiazépines**, du **zolpidem**, de la **buspirone**, des **antidépresseurs tricycliques** et du **losartan** et accroît leur effet thérapeutique ■ Le fluconazole peut contrecarrer les effets de l'**amphotéricine B** ■ Le médicament ne doit pas être administré avec d'autres **médicaments allongeant l'intervalle** QT_c en raison du risque de torsades de pointes.

VOIES D'ADMINISTRATION ET POSOLOGIE

Le premier jour du traitement, l'administration d'une dose d'attaque équivalant à 2 fois la dose quotidienne habituelle permet d'atteindre une concentration plasmatique près de l'état d'équilibre dès le 2e jour. Chez les patients souffrant d'une infection aiguë, on recommande d'administrer, le 1er jour, une dose d'attaque équivalant à 2 fois la dose quotidienne; cependant, cette dose ne doit pas être supérieure à 400 mg chez l'adulte, et à 12 mg/kg, chez l'enfant.

Candidose oropharyngée

- **PO, IV (adultes)**: 100 mg, 1 fois par jour, pendant au moins 2 semaines afin de réduire les risques de rechute.
- **PO, IV (enfants)**: 3 mg/kg, 1 fois par jour, pendant au moins 2 semaines afin de réduire les risques de rechute.

F

Candidose œsophagienne

- **PO, IV (adultes)**: De 100 à 200 mg, 1 fois par jour, pendant au moins 3 semaines, dont 2 semaines au moins après la disparition des symptômes.
- **PO, IV (enfants)**: De 3 à 6 mg/kg, 1 fois par jour, pendant au moins 3 semaines, dont 2 semaines au moins après la disparition des symptômes.

Candidoses profondes

- **PO, IV (adultes)**: De 200 à 400 mg/jour, 1 fois par jour, pendant au moins 4 semaines, dont 2 semaines au moins après la disparition des symptômes.
- **PO, IV (enfants)**: De 6 à 12 mg/kg/jour, 1 fois par jour, pendant au moins 4 semaines, dont 2 semaines au moins après la disparition des symptômes (données provenant d'un essai non comparatif, sans insu, mené chez un petit nombre de patients).

Méningite cryptococcique

- **PO, IV (adultes)**: *Traitement* – de 200 à 400 mg, 1 fois par jour, jusqu'à l'obtention d'une réponse clinique favorable, mais pendant au moins 10 semaines. *Prophylaxie* – 200 mg, 1 fois par jour.
- **PO, IV (enfants)**: *Traitement* – de 6 à 12 mg/kg, 1 fois par jour. On recommande de prolonger le traitement initial de 10 à 12 semaines après obtention d'un résultat négatif à la culture du liquide céphalorachidien. *Prophylaxie* – 6 mg/kg, 1 fois par jour.

Prévention de la candidose après une greffe de moelle osseuse

- **PO, IV (adultes)**: 400 mg, 1 fois par jour; amorcer le traitement plusieurs jours avant l'intervention si l'on prévoit l'apparition d'une neutropénie grave et le poursuivre pendant les 7 jours qui suivent l'atteinte d'un nombre absolu des polynucléaires neutrophiles $> 1 \times 10^9$/L.

INSUFFISANCE RÉNALE

- **PO, IV (ADULTES)**: *CL_{CR} DE 21 À 50 mL/MIN* – 50 % DE LA DOSE HABITUELLE. *CL_{CR} DE 11 À 20 mL/MIN* – 25 % DE LA DOSE HABITUELLE. *HÉMODIALYSE PÉRIODIQUE:* 100 % DE LA DOSE HABITUELLE APRÈS CHAQUE SÉANCE.

Candidose vaginale

- **PO (adultes)**: une seule dose de 150 mg (aucune adaptation posologique n'est nécessaire en cas d'insuffisance rénale).

PRÉSENTATION

Comprimés: 50 mgPr, 100 mgPr ■ **Capsules**: 150 mgPr ■ **Suspension orale**: 50 mg/5 mLPr, en flacons de 35 mL ■ **Solution pour injection**: 2 mg/mLPr, en flacons de 100 mL.

SOINS INFIRMIERS

ÉVALUATION DE LA SITUATION

- Inspecter la région infectée et analyser les cultures fongiques de liquide céphalorachidien avant le traitement et à intervalles réguliers pendant toute sa durée.
- Il faut prélever des échantillons pour les mises en culture avant d'amorcer le traitement. La première dose peut être administrée avant que les résultats soient connus.

Tests de laboratoire:

- Noter les concentrations d'urée et de créatinine sérique avant le traitement et à intervalles réguliers pendant toute sa durée, car il faut adapter la posologie chez les patients qui souffrent d'insuffisance rénale.
- NOTER LES RÉSULTATS DES TESTS DE LA FONCTION HÉPATIQUE AVANT L'ADMINISTRATION DU FLUCONAZOLE ET À INTERVALLES RÉGULIERS TOUT AU LONG DU TRAITEMENT. LE FLUCONAZOLE PEUT ENTRAÎNER L'ÉLÉVATION DES CONCENTRATIONS D'AST, D'ALT, DE PHOSPHATASE ALCALINE SÉRIQUE ET DE BILIRUBINE.

DIAGNOSTICS INFIRMIERS POSSIBLES

- Risque d'infection (Indications).
- Connaissances insuffisantes sur le traitement médicamenteux (Enseignement au patient et à ses proches).

INTERVENTIONS INFIRMIÈRES

- NE PAS CONFONDRE DIFLUCAN (FLUCONAZOLE) AVEC DIPRIVAN (PROPOFOL).

PO: Bien agiter la suspension orale avant de l'administrer.

Perfusion intermittente:

- Ne pas administrer une solution qui est trouble ou qui contient un précipité. Si la bague de métal a été brisée, la solution n'est plus stérile. Le flacon est uniservice. Jeter toute portion inutilisée.
- En raison du risque d'embolie gazeuse, ne pas administrer par une tubulure qui fait partie d'un raccordement en série.

Vitesse d'administration: Perfuser à une vitesse maximale de 200 mg/h. Chez les enfants recevant une dose > 6 mg/kg, perfuser en 2 heures.

Compatibilité (tubulure en Y): acyclovir ■ aldesleukine ■ allopurinol ■ amifostine ■ amikacine ■ aminophylline ■ ampicilline/sulbactam ■ aztréonam ■ benztropine ■ céfalozine ■ céfépime ■ céfotétane ■ céfoxitine ■ chlorpromazine ■ cimétidine ■ dexaméthasone sodique, phosphate de ■ diltiazem ■ diphenhydramine ■ dobutamine ■ dopamine ■ dropéridol ■ famotidine ■ filgrastim ■ fludarabine ■ foscarnet ■ gallium, nitrate de ■ ganciclovir ■ gentamicine ■ granisétron ■ héparine ■ hydrocortisone ■ immunoglobuline ■ leucovorine ■ lorazépam ■ melphalan ■ mépéridine ■ méropénem ■ métoclopramide ■ métronidazole ■ midazolam ■ morphine ■ nafcilline ■ nitroglycérine ■ ondansétron ■ oxacilline ■ paclitaxel ■ pancuronium ■ pénicilline G potassique ■ phénytoïne ■ pipéracilline/tazobactam ■ prochlorpérazine ■ prométhazine ■ propofol ■ ranitidine ■ sargramostim ■ tacrolimus ■ téniposide ■ théophylline ■ thiotépa ■ ticarcilline/clavulanate ■ tobramycine ■ vancomycine ■ vécuronium ■ vinorelbine ■ zidovudine.

Incompatibilité (tubulure en Y): amphotéricine B ■ ampicilline ■ calcium, gluconate de ■ céfotaxime ■ ceftazidime ■ ceftriaxone ■ céfuroxime ■ chloramphénicol ■ clindamycine ■ diazépam ■ digoxine ■ érythromycine, lactobionate d' ■ furosémide ■ halopéridol ■ hydroxyzine ■ imipénem/cilastatine ■ pentamidine ■ pipéracilline ■ ticarcilline ■ triméthoprime/sulfaméthoxazole.

Incompatibilité en addition au soluté: Le fabricant ne recommande aucun mélange.

ENSEIGNEMENT AU PATIENT ET À SES PROCHES

- Expliquer au patient qu'il doit respecter rigoureusement la posologie recommandée et continuer à prendre le médicament même s'il se sent mieux. Lui conseiller de prendre le médicament au même moment, tous les jours. S'il n'a pas pu le prendre au moment habituel, il doit le prendre aussitôt que possible à moins que ce ne soit presque l'heure prévue pour la dose suivante, sans jamais remplacer une dose manquée par une double dose.
- Demander au patient de prévenir un professionnel de la santé si les douleurs abdominales, la fièvre ou la diarrhée s'aggravent ou si les signes et les symptômes suivants de dysfonction hépatique se manifestent: fatigue inhabituelle, anorexie, nausées, vomissements, jaunisse, urine foncée ou selles de couleur pâle, ou encore s'il ne note aucune amélioration après quelques jours de traitement.

VÉRIFICATION DE L'EFFICACITÉ THÉRAPEUTIQUE

L'efficacité du traitement peut être démontrée par: la résolution des signes et des symptômes d'infection fongique, confirmée par les résultats des tests de laboratoire; pour prévenir les rechutes, il faut parfois suivre le traitement pendant plusieurs semaines ou plusieurs mois après la résolution des symptômes ■ la prévention de la candidose chez les patients ayant subi une greffe de moelle osseuse ■ la diminution de l'irritation vaginale et de la gêne vaginale chez les patientes atteintes de candidose vaginale. Il faut reconfirmer le diagnostic par des frottis ou des cultures avant d'amorcer une deuxième cure afin d'écarter la présence de tout autre agent pathogène associé à la vulvovaginite. Les infections vaginales récurrentes peuvent être un signe de maladie généralisée.

F

FLUDROCORTISONE

Florinef

CLASSIFICATION:

Corticostéroïde (minéralocorticoïde), traitement de la maladie d'Addison

Grossesse – catégorie C

INDICATIONS

Traitement de la déperdition sodique et de l'hypotension dues à une insuffisance corticosurrénalienne (en association avec l'hydrocortisone ou la cortisone) ■ Traitement de la déperdition sodique entraînée par le syndrome génitosurrénal congénital (hyperplasie congénitale des surrénales). **Usages non approuvés:** Traitement de l'hypotension orthostatique idiopathique (en association avec un apport accru de sodium) ■ Traitement de l'acidose tubulaire rénale de type IV.

MÉCANISME D'ACTION

Réabsorption du sodium, excrétion de l'hydrogène et du potassium et rétention de l'eau par les effets sur les tubules rénaux distaux. ***Effets thérapeutiques:*** Maintien de l'équilibre sodique et stabilisation de la pression artérielle chez les patients souffrant d'insuffisance corticosurrénalienne.

PHARMACOCINÉTIQUE

Absorption: Bonne (PO).

Distribution: Le médicament semble se répartir dans tout l'organisme; il passe probablement dans le lait maternel.

Liaison aux protéines: Forte.

Métabolisme et excrétion: Métabolisme hépatique.

Demi-vie: 3,5 heures.

F

Profil temps-action (activité minéralocorticoïde)

	DÉBUT D'ACTION	PIC	DURÉE
PO	inconnu	inconnu	1 - 2 jours

CONTRE-INDICATIONS, PRÉCAUTIONS ET MISES EN GARDE

Contre-indications: Hypersensibilité ■ Infections fongiques systémiques.

Précautions et mises en garde: Insuffisance cardiaque ■ Maladie d'Addison (la réponse peut être exagérée) ■ La fludrocortisone peut masquer certaines signes d'infections et de nouvelles infections ■ Patients souffrant de la tuberculose ou manifestant une réactivité à la tuberculine ■ La fludrocortisone peut entraîner l'élévation de la pression artérielle, une rétention hydrosodée et une augmentation de l'excrétion de potassium ■ Éviter de vacciner les patients qui prennent de la fludrocortisone à cause du risque possible de complications neurologiques et du manque de production d'anticorps ■ **OBST., ALLAITEMENT, PÉD.:** L'innocuité du médicament n'a pas été établie.

RÉACTIONS INDÉSIRABLES ET EFFETS SECONDAIRES

SNC: étourdissements, céphalées.

CV: INSUFFISANCE CARDIAQUE, arythmies, œdème, hypertension.

GI: anorexie, nausées.

End.: suppression de la fonction des surrénales, gain pondéral.

HÉ: hypokaliémie, alcalose hypokaliémique.

Loc.: arthralgie, faiblesse musculaire, contracture des tendons.

SN: paralysie ascendante.

Divers: réactions d'hypersensibilité.

INTERACTIONS

Médicament-médicament: Les **diurétiques thiazidiques ou de l'anse**, la **pipéracilline** ou l'**amphotéricine B**, administrés en concomitance, peuvent induire une hypokaliémie exagérée ■ L'hypokaliémie peut augmenter le risque de toxicité de la **digoxine** ■ Risque de blocage neuromusculaire prolongé après l'administration de **bloquants neuromusculaires du type non dépolarisant** ■ Le **phénobarbital** ou la **rifampine** peuvent accélérer le métabolisme et réduire l'efficacité de la fludrocortisone.

Médicament-aliments: L'ingestion de grandes quantités de **sel** ou d'**aliments contenant du sodium** peut provoquer une rétention sodique excessive et une déperdition potassique.

VOIES D'ADMINISTRATION ET POSOLOGIE

- **PO (adultes):** *Insuffisance corticosurrénale* – 100 µg par jour (entre 100 µg, 3 fois par semaine, et 200 µg par jour). En cas d'hypertension transitoire induite par le traitement, on doit diminuer la dose à 50 µg par jour. Il est préférable d'administrer en même temps de 10 à 37,5 mg de cortisone ou de 10 à 20 mg d'hydrocortisone par jour en prises fractionnées. *Syndrome génitosurrénal* – de 100 à 200 µg par jour. *Hypotension orthostatique idiopathique* – de 50 à 200 µg par jour (usage non approuvé).

PRÉSENTATION

Comprimés: 100 µg (0,1 mg)^{Pr}.

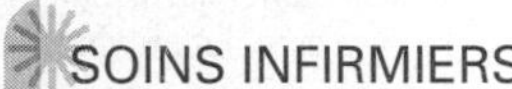

SOINS INFIRMIERS

ÉVALUATION DE LA SITUATION

- Mesurer la pression artérielle à intervalles réguliers tout au long du traitement. Prévenir un professionnel de la santé en cas de modification importante. L'hypotension peut indiquer que la dose administrée est insuffisante.
- Suivre de près les signes de rétention hydrique: peser le patient tous les jours, déceler l'œdème et ausculter les poumons à la recherche de râles ou de crépitations.
- Surveiller de près les patients atteints de la maladie d'Addison et arrêter le traitement en cas de gain de poids important ou d'une élévation marquée de la pression artérielle, d'œdème ou d'hypertrophie cardiaque. Les patients atteints de cette maladie sont plus sensibles aux effets de la fludrocortisone et pourraient manifester une réponse exagérée.

Tests de laboratoire: Mesurer les concentrations sériques d'électrolytes à intervalles réguliers tout au long du traitement. La fludrocortisone peut entraîner la diminution des concentrations sériques de potassium.

DIAGNOSTICS INFIRMIERS POSSIBLES

- Déficit de volume liquidien (Indications).
- Excès de volume liquidien (Effets secondaires).
- Connaissances insuffisantes sur le traitement médicamenteux (Enseignement au patient et à ses proches).

INTERVENTIONS INFIRMIÈRES

- Les comprimés sont sécables; on peut les diviser facilement s'il faut adapter la dose.

ENSEIGNEMENT AU PATIENT ET À SES PROCHES

- Conseiller au patient de respecter rigoureusement la posologie recommandée. S'il n'a pas pu prendre le médicament au moment habituel, il doit le prendre aussitôt que possible à moins que ce ne soit presque l'heure prévue pour la dose suivante. Lui expliquer qu'il lui faudrait peut-être suivre ce traitement toute sa vie durant; un sevrage brusque peut provoquer une crise addisonienne. Conseiller au patient de toujours garder une provision suffisante de médicament.
- Recommander au patient d'observer les modifications de régime alimentaire prescrites par le professionnel de la santé. Lui expliquer qu'il doit consommer des aliments riches en potassium (voir l'annexe J). La quantité de sodium alimentaire qu'il est autorisé à consommer dépend de la physiopathologie en cause.
- Recommander au patient de prévenir un professionnel de la santé en cas de gain de poids ou d'œdème, de faiblesse musculaire, de crampes, de nausées, d'anorexie ou d'étourdissements.
- Conseiller au patient de porter sur lui en tout temps une pièce d'identité où sont inscrits son problème de santé et son traitement.

VÉRIFICATION DE L'EFFICACITÉ THÉRAPEUTIQUE

L'efficacité du traitement peut être démontrée par: la normalisation de l'équilibre hydroélectrolytique sans hypokaliémie ni hypertension.

FLUMAZÉNIL

Anexate, Flumazenil

CLASSIFICATION:

Antidote (antagoniste des benzodiazépines)

Grossesse – catégorie C

INDICATIONS

Inversion totale ou partielle des effets des benzodiazépines utilisées comme anesthésiques généraux ou suppression de la sédation induite par les benzodiazépines lors d'interventions diagnostiques ou thérapeutiques ■ Traitement du surdosage intentionnel ou accidentel par les benzodiazépines.

MÉCANISME D'ACTION

Le flumazénil est un dérivé des benzodiazépines qui contrecarre les effets dépresseurs de celles-ci sur le SNC. Il n'exerce aucun effet sur la dépression du SNC induite par d'autres substances dont les opioïdes, l'alcool, les barbituriques ou les anesthésiques généraux. ***Effets thérapeutiques:*** Inversion des effets des benzodiazépines.

PHARMACOCINÉTIQUE

Absorption: Totale (IV).

Distribution: Inconnue.

Liaison aux protéines: 50 %, principalement à l'albumine.

Métabolisme et excrétion: Métabolisme majoritairement hépatique.

Demi-vie: Enfants – de 20 à 75 minutes; adultes – de 41 à 79 minutes.

Profil temps-action
(inversion des effets des benzodiazépines)

	DÉBUT D'ACTION	PIC	DURÉE
IV	1 – 2 min	6 – 10 min	1 – 2 h†

† Selon la dose ou la concentration de la benzodiazépine et la dose de flumazénil.

CONTRE-INDICATIONS, PRÉCAUTIONS ET MISES EN GARDE

Contre-indications: Hypersensibilité au flumazénil ou aux benzodiazépines ■ Patients sous benzodiazépines en raison d'une maladie qui met leur vie en danger, y compris les patients atteint de l'état de mal épileptique ou présentant une pression intracrânienne accrue ■ Patients épileptiques traités depuis longtemps par des benzodiazépines (l'arrêt brusque de l'effet protecteur des benzodiazépines peut induire des convulsions chez ces patients) ■ Surdosage massif par un antidépresseur cyclique.

Précautions et mises en garde: Surdosage par plusieurs dépresseurs du SNC (les effets des autres agents pourraient se manifester lorsque ceux des benzodiazépines disparaissent) ■ Antécédents de convulsions (les convulsions se manifesteront plus vraisemblablement chez les patients présentant des symptômes de sevrage aux hypnosédatifs, chez ceux qui ont reçu récemment des doses répétées de benzodiazépines ou chez ceux qui ont des antécédents de crises d'épilepsie) ▪ Traumatisme crânien (risque de pression intracrânienne accrue et de convulsions) ▪ **Grossesse, allaitement**: L'innocuité du médicament n'a pas été établie ▪ **Péd.**: L'innocuité du médicament n'a pas été établie chez les enfants < 18 ans ▪ Infarctus myocardique aigu ou arythmies cardiaques (risque d'augmentation du tonus sympathique, ce qui peut accroître l'instabilité électrique du cœur) ▪ Insuffisance hépatique.

F

RÉACTIONS INDÉSIRABLES ET EFFETS SECONDAIRES

SNC: CONVULSIONS, étourdissements, agitation, confusion, somnolence, labilité émotionnelle, fatigue, céphalées, troubles du sommeil.

ORLO: altération de l'ouïe, altération de la vue, vision trouble.

CV: arythmies, douleurs thoraciques, hypertension.

GI: nausées, vomissements, hoquets.

Tég.: bouffées vasomotrices, transpiration.

Locaux: douleurs ou réactions au point d'injection, phlébite.

SN: paresthésie.

Divers: rigidité, frissons.

INTERACTIONS

Médicament-médicament: Aucune interaction notable.

VOIES D'ADMINISTRATION ET POSOLOGIE

Inversion de la sédation ou de l'anesthésie générale

- **IV (adultes)**: 0,2 mg, à administrer en 15 secondes. On peut administrer des doses additionnelles de 0,1 mg à intervalles de 1 minute jusqu'à l'obtention des résultats souhaités. La dose totale maximale est de 1 mg.

Surdosage connu ou soupçonné par des benzodiazépines

- **IV (adultes)**: 0,3 mg, à administrer en 30 secondes. Cette dose initiale est suivie d'une série d'injections de 0,3 mg, à intervalles de 60 secondes. La dose maximale recommandée est de 2,0 mg. En cas de somnolence, une perfusion IV à une vitesse de 0,1 à 0,4 mg/h peut se révéler utile. La vitesse de la perfusion doit être adaptée à chaque cas selon le niveau de vigilance qu'on souhaite obtenir.

PRÉSENTATION

Solution pour injection: 0,1 mg/mL, en fioles de 5 mL[Pr].

SOINS INFIRMIERS

ÉVALUATION DE LA SITUATION

Évaluer le niveau de conscience et la fonction respiratoire avant le traitement et pendant toute sa durée. Observer le patient pendant 3 à 4 heures après l'administration pour déceler le retour de la sédation. Risque d'hypoventilation.

Surdosage par des benzodiazépines: Tenter d'établir l'heure de l'ingestion de même que la quantité et le type de benzodiazépine absorbée, car on pourra ainsi estimer la durée de la dépression du SNC.

DIAGNOSTICS INFIRMIERS POSSIBLES

- Risque d'accident (Indications).
- Risque d'intoxication (Indications).

INTERVENTIONS INFIRMIÈRES

- Avant d'administrer le flumazénil, s'assurer que les voies respiratoires du patient sont dégagées.
- Examiner fréquemment le point d'injection IV afin de déceler toute rougeur ou irritation. Administrer dans une tubulure en Y par laquelle s'écoule une solution IV et choisir une grosse veine pour réduire la douleur au point d'injection.
- Il faut ramener lentement le patient à un état de conscience afin de diminuer les effets indésirables dont la confusion, l'agitation, la labilité émotionnelle et les distorsions perceptuelles.
- PRENDRE LES PRÉCAUTIONS NÉCESSAIRES POUR PRÉVENIR LES CONVULSIONS. LES CONVULSIONS RISQUENT DE SE MANIFESTER PLUS VRAISEMBLABLEMENT CHEZ LES PATIENTS PRÉSENTANT DES SYMPTÔMES DE SEVRAGE ASSOCIÉS À UN HYPNOSÉDATIF, CHEZ CEUX AYANT REÇU RÉCEMMENT DES DOSES RÉPÉTÉES DE BENZODIAZÉPINES OU CHEZ CEUX AYANT DES ANTÉCÉDENTS DE CRISES ÉPILEPTIQUES. ON PEUT TRAITER LES CONVULSIONS PAR DES BENZODIAZÉPINES, DES BARBITURIQUES OU LA PHÉNYTOÏNE. IL PEUT ÊTRE NÉCESSAIRE D'ADMINISTRER DES DOSES DE BENZODIAZÉPINES PLUS ÉLEVÉES QUE LA NORMALE.

Surdosage soupçonné par les benzodiazépines: Si l'administration de flumazénil n'entraîne pas d'amélioration des symptômes, il faut rechercher d'autres causes de la diminution du niveau de conscience (alcool, barbituriques, opioïdes).

IV directe: Le flumazénil peut être administré non dilué ou dilué dans une seringue, dans une solution de D5%E, une solution de NaCl 0,9 % ou une solution de lactate de Ringer. Jeter toute solution diluée après 24 heures.

Vitesse d'administration: Administrer chaque dose en 15 à 30 secondes dans une grosse veine par une tubulure en Y par laquelle s'écoule une solution IV.

ENSEIGNEMENT AU PATIENT ET À SES PROCHES

- Expliquer au patient que le flumazénil n'inverse pas systématiquement l'effet amnésique des benzodiazépines. Fournir au patient et à ses proches des directives écrites sur les soins à administrer après l'intervention. Informer les proches que le patient peut donner l'impression qu'il a regagné toute sa conscience au moment de sa sortie de l'hôpital, mais que les effets sédatifs des benzodiazépines peuvent se manifester de nouveau. Prévenir le patient qu'il ne doit pas conduire ni s'engager dans d'autres activités qui exigent sa vigilance pendant au moins 24 heures après sa sortie de l'hôpital.
- Recommander au patient de ne pas boire d'alcool et de ne pas prendre des médicaments en vente libre pendant au moins 18 à 24 heures après sa sortie de l'hôpital.
- Conseiller au patient de ne reprendre ses activités habituelles qu'au moment où tous les effets résiduels de la benzodiazépine ont disparu.

VÉRIFICATION DE L'EFFICACITÉ THÉRAPEUTIQUE

L'efficacité du traitement peut être démontrée par: l'amélioration du niveau de conscience ■ la diminution de la dépression respiratoire induite par les benzodiazépines. ✳

FLUNISOLIDE,

voir Corticostéroïdes (voie intranasale)

FLUOCINOLONE,

voir Corticostéroïdes (topiques)

FLUOCINONIDE,

voir Corticostéroïdes (topiques)

FLUOROQUINOLONES

ciprofloxacine

Cipro, Cipro IV, Cipro XL, Gen-Ciprofloxacin, Novo-Ciprofloxacin, PMS-Ciprofloxacin, Ratio-Ciprofloxacin

lévofloxacine

Levaquin, Novo-Levofloxacin

moxifloxacine

Avelox

norfloxacine

Apo-Norflox, Noroxin, Novo-Norfloxacin, Riva-Norfloxacin

ofloxacine

Apo-Oflox, Floxin

CLASSIFICATION:

Antibiotiques

Grossesse – catégorie C (X pour l'administration pendant le 1er trimestre)

Pour l'usage ophtalmique, voir l'annexe N.

INDICATIONS

PO, IV: Traitement des infections urinaires et gynécologiques (à l'exception de la moxifloxacine ■ de la gonorrhée (à l'exception de la lévofloxacine et de la moxifloxacine) ■ de la prostatite (ciprofloxacine, ofloxacine) ■ des infections des voies respiratoires, y compris la sinusite (à l'exception de la norfloxacine) ■ des infections de la peau et de ses annexes (ciprofloxacine, lévofloxacine, ofloxacine) ■ des infections des os et des articulations (ciprofloxacine) ■ de la diarrhée infectieuse (ciprofloxacine) ■ des infections intra-abdominales (ciprofloxacine avec métronidazole, moxifloxacine) ■ Traitement de la neutropénie fébrile (ciprofloxacine).

MÉCANISME D'ACTION

Inhibition de la synthèse de l'ADN bactérien par l'inhibition de l'ADN-gyrase. ***Effets thérapeutiques:*** Destruction des bactéries sensibles. **Spectre d'action:** Spectre d'activité élargi, qui englobe de nombreux microorganismes à Gram positif dont les staphylocoques incluant les souches de *Staphylococcus epidermidis* ■ *Streptococcus pneumoniæ* ■ Action marquée contre les microorganismes à Gram négatif suivants: *Escherichia coli* ■ espèces *Klebsiella* ■ *Enterobacter* ■ *Salmonella* ■ *Shigella* ■ *Proteus vulgaris* ■ *Providencia stuartii* ■ *Providencia rettgeri* ■ *Morganella* *morganii* ■ *Pseudomonas æruginosa* ■ *Serratia* ■ espèces *Hæmophilus* ■ *Acinetobacter* ■ *Neisseria gonorrhϾ* et *Neisseria meningitidis* ■ *Moraxella catarrhalis* ■ *Yersinia* ■ *Vibrio* ■ *Brucella* ■ *Campylobacter* ■ espèces *Æromonas* ■ *Bacteroides fragilis* (moxifloxacine) ■ *Clostridium welchii* ■ *Gardnerella vaginalis* ■ *Peptococcus niger* ■ espèces *Peptostreptococcus* ■ Le spectre englobe aussi: *Chlamydia pneumoniæ* et *Chlamydia trachomatis* ■ *Legionella pneumoniæ* ■ *Mycobacterium tuberculosis* ■ *Mycoplasma pneumoniæ* ■ *Urea urealyticum.*

F

PHARMACOCINÉTIQUE

Absorption: Bonne (PO) (*ciprofloxacine* – 70 %; *moxifloxacine* – 90 %; *lévofloxacine* – 99 %; *norfloxacine* – entre 30 et 40 %; *ofloxacine* – 89 %).

Distribution: Tout l'organisme. On trouve de fortes concentrations dans les tissus et les urines. Tous ces agents semblent traverser la barrière placentaire. La *ciprofloxacine* et l'*ofloxacine* passe dans le lait maternel.

Métabolisme et excrétion: *Ciprofloxacine* – métabolisme hépatique à 15 %, de 40 à 50 % est excrété sous forme inchangée par les reins; *lévofloxacine* – 87 % est excrété sous forme inchangée dans les urines, de petites quantités sont métabolisées; *moxifloxacine* – métabolisme majoritairement hépatique, 20 % est excrété sous forme inchangée dans les urines, et 25 %, dans les fèces; *norfloxacine* – métabolisme hépatique à 10 %, 30 % est excrété sous forme inchangée par les reins, et 30 % sous forme inchangée dans les fèces; *ofloxacine* – de 70 à 80 % est excrété sous forme inchangée par les reins.

Demi-vie: *Ciprofloxacine* – 4 heures; *lévofloxacine* – de 6 à 8 heures; *moxifloxacine* – 12 heures; *norfloxacine* – 6,5 heures; *ofloxacine* – de 5 à 7 heures (toutes ces demi-vies sont accrues en présence d'insuffisance rénale).

Profil temps-action (concentrations sanguines)

	DÉBUT D'ACTION	PIC	DURÉE
Ciprofloxacine – PO	rapide	1 – 2 h	12 h
Ciprofloxacine – PO-LP	rapide	1 – 4 h	24 h
Ciprofloxacine – IV	rapide	fin de la perfusion	12 h
Lévofloxacine – PO	rapide	1 – 2 h	24 h
Lévofloxacine – IV	rapide	fin de la perfusion	24 h
Moxifloxacine – PO	en 1 h	1 – 3 h	24 h
Moxifloxacine – IV	rapide	fin de la perfusion	24 h
Ofloxacine – PO	rapide	1 – 2 h	12 h

CONTRE-INDICATIONS, PRÉCAUTIONS ET MISES EN GARDE

Contre-indications: Hypersensibilité. Risque de sensibilité croisée entre les agents ■ *Lévofloxacine* – antécédents de tendinites ou de rupture du tendon associée à l'administration d'un antibiotique de la famille des quinolones.

Précautions et mises en garde: Maladies sous-jacentes du SNC ■ Insuffisance rénale (si la Cl_{Cr} est ≤ 50 mL/min, réduire la dose de ciprofloxacine, de lévofloxacine, d'ofloxacine et de norfloxacine ■ *Moxifloxacine* – Administration concomitante d'amiodarone, de bépridil, de cisapride, de disopyramide, d'érythromycine, de pentamidine, de phénothiazines, de pimozide, de procaïnamide, de quinidine, de sotalol ou d'antidépresseurs tricycliques; allongement connu de l'intervalle QT ou administration concomitante d'agents allongeant cet intervalle ■ **GÉR.**: Risque accru de réactions indésirables chez les personnes âgées et les patients sous dialyse ■ **OBST., ALLAITEMENT, PÉD.**: L'innocuité de ces agents n'a pas été établie.

RÉACTIONS INDÉSIRABLES ET EFFETS SECONDAIRES

SNC: CONVULSIONS, étourdissements, somnolence, céphalées, insomnie, psychose aiguë, agitation, confusion, hallucinations, pression intracrânienne accrue, sensation de tête légère, tremblements.

CV: *Moxifloxacine* – ARYTHMIES, allongement des intervalles QT, vasodilatation.

GI: COLITE PSEUDOMEMBRANEUSE, douleurs abdominales, diarrhée, nausées, altération du goût.

GU: cystite interstitielle, vaginite.

Tég.: photosensibilité, rash.

End.: hyperglycémie, hypoglycémie.

Locaux: phlébite au point d'injection IV.

Loc.: tendinite, rupture de tendon.

Divers: réactions d'hypersensibilité y compris l'ANAPHYLAXIE et le SYNDROME DE STEVENS-JOHNSON, lymphadénopathie, neuropathie périphérique (lévofloxacine, ofloxacine, norfloxacine).

INTERACTIONS

Médicament-médicament: RISQUE ACCRU DE RÉACTIONS CARDIOVASCULAIRES GRAVES LORS DE L'ADMINISTRATION CONCOMITANTE DE MOXIFLOXACINE ET D'**AMIODARONE**, DE **BÉPRIDIL**, DE **CISAPRIDE**, DE **DISOPYRAMIDE**, D'**ÉRYTHROMYCINE**, DE **PENTAMIDINE**, DE **PHÉNOTHIAZINES**, DE **PIMOZIDE**, DE **PROCAÏNAMIDE**, DE **QUINIDINE**, DE **SOTALOL** ET D'**ANTIDÉPRESSEURS TRICYCLIQUES** ■ Ces agents élèvent les concentrations sériques de **théophylline**, ce qui peut entraîner une toxicité ■ Les

antiacides, les **sels de fer**, le **sous-salicylate de bismuth**, le **sucralfate** et les **sels de zinc**, administrés en même temps, diminuent l'absorption des fluoroquinolones ■ Ces agents peuvent intensifier les effets de la **warfarine** ■ On peut observer une diminution du taux sérique de **phénytoïne** et de son efficacité lors d'une utilisation concomitante ■ L'usage concomitant de **glyburide** et des autres **hypoglycémiants oraux** peut provoquer une hypoglycémie ■ Les **agents antinéoplasiques** peuvent abaisser les concentrations sériques des fluoroquinolones ■ La **cimétidine** peut entraver l'élimination des fluoroquinolones ■ Les effets bénéfiques de la ciprofloxacine peuvent être inhibés par la **nitrofurantoïne** ■ Le **probénécide** réduit l'élimination rénale des fluoroquinolones ■ Les fluoroquinolones peuvent accroître le risque de néphrotoxicité associé à la **cyclosporine** ■ L'administration concomitante de ciprofloxacine et de **foscarnet** peut élever le risque de convulsions ■ Une **corticothérapie** concomitante peut élever le risque de rupture de tendons.

Médicament-aliments: L'**alimentation par voie entérale** peut modifier l'absorption de ces agents (en raison des cations métalliques) ■ La ciprofloxacine ne doit pas être prise avec du **lait** ou du **yogourt**, mais elle peut être prise avec d'autres sources de calcium alimentaire ■ Les **aliments** et les **produits laitiers** réduisent l'absorption de la norfloxacine (la prendre 1 heure avant ou 2 heures après).

Médicament-produits naturels: Le **fenouil** peut diminuer l'absorption de la ciprofloxacine.

VOIES D'ADMINISTRATION ET POSOLOGIE

Ciprofloxacine

- **PO (adultes)**: *La plupart des infections* – de 500 à 750 mg, toutes les 12 heures. *Infections des voies urinaires* – de 250 à 500 mg, toutes les 12 heures, ou 500 mg (comprimés à libération prolongée), 1 fois par jour. *Infections des voies urinaires compliquées ou pyélonéphrite:* 1 000 mg (comprimés à libération prolongée), 1 fois par jour. *Gonorrhée* – une seule dose de 500 mg.
- **IV (adultes)**: *La plupart des infections* – 400 mg, toutes les 8 à 12 heures. *Infections des voies urinaires* – 200 mg, toutes les 12 heures.
- ***INSUFFISANCE RÉNALE***

  PO (ADULTES): *CL_{CR} DE 31 À 60 mL/MIN* –1 000 mg/JOUR AU MAXIMUM; *$CL_{CR} \leq 30$ mL/MIN* – 500 mg/JOUR AU MAXIMUM.

  IV (ADULTES): *CL_{CR} DE 31 À 60 mL/MIN* – 800 mg/JOUR, AU MAXIMUM; *$CL_{CR} \leq 30$ mL/MIN* – 400 mg/JOUR AU MAXIMUM.

Lévofloxacine

- **PO, IV (adultes)**: De 250 à 750 mg, toutes les 24 heures; *infections compliquées de la peau et annexes cutanées:* 1 000 mg par jour, en 2 doses fractionnées.
- ***INSUFFISANCE RÉNALE***

  PO, IV (ADULTES): *SINUSITE AIGUË, EXACERBATION BACTÉRIENNE AIGUË DE LA BRONCHITE CHRONIQUE, PNEUMONIE EXTRAHOSPITALIÈRE, INFECTIONS DE LA PEAU ET DES ANNEXES CUTANÉES NON COMPLIQUÉES, PROSTATITE BACTÉRIENNE CHRONIQUE – CL_{CR} DE 20 À 49 mL/MIN* – INITIALEMENT, 500 mg, PUIS 250 mg, TOUTES LES 24 HEURES; *CL_{CR} DE 10 À 19 mL/MIN* – INITIALEMENT, 500 mg, PUIS 250 mg, TOUTES LES 48 HEURES. *INFECTIONS DES VOIES URINAIRES COMPLIQUÉES – CL_{CR} DE 10 À 19 mL/MIN* – 250 mg, TOUTES LES 48 HEURES. *INFECTIONS DE LA PEAU ET DES ANNEXES CUTANÉES COMPLIQUÉES, PNEUMONIE NOSOCOMIALE, PNEUMONIE EXTRAHOSPITALIÈRE, EXACERBATION AIGUË DE LA BRONCHITE CHRONIQUE D'ORIGINE BACTÉRIENNE – CL_{CR} DE 20 À 49 mL/MIN* – INITIALEMENT, 750 mg, PUIS 750 mg, TOUTES LES 48 HEURES; *CL_{CR} DE 10 À 19 mL/MIN* – INITIALEMENT, 750 mg, PUIS 500 mg, TOUTES LES 48 HEURES.

Moxifloxacine

- **PO (adultes)**: *Pneumonie extrahospitalière légère à modérée* – 400 mg, 1 fois par jour, pendant 10 jours. *Sinusite bactérienne aiguë* – 400 mg, 1 fois par jour, pendant 7 à 10 jours. *Exacerbation bactérienne aiguë de la bronchite chronique* – 400 mg, 1 fois par jour, pendant 5 jours.
- **IV-PO (adultes)**: *Pneumonie extrahospitalière chez le patient hospitalisé* – 400 mg, 1 fois par jour, pendant 7 à 14 jours. *Infections intraabdominales compliquées* – 400 mg, 1 fois par jour, pendant 5 à 14 jours.

Norfloxacine

- **PO (adultes)**: *Infections des voies urinaires* – 400 mg, toutes les 12 heures. *Gonorrhée* – une seule dose de 800 mg.
- ***INSUFFISANCE RÉNALE***

  PO (ADULTES): *CL_{CR} DE 6,6 À 30 mL/MIN* – 400 mg, 1 FOIS PAR JOUR.

Ofloxacine

- **PO (adultes)**: *La plupart des infections* – 400 mg, toutes les 12 heures. *Prostatite, cervicite ou urétrite* – 300 mg, toutes les 12 heures. *Infections des voies urinaires* – 200 mg, toutes les 12 heures. *Gonorrhée* – une seule dose de 400 mg.

F

- *INSUFFISANCE RÉNALE*
 PO (ADULTES): *CL_{CR} DE 20 À 50 mL/MIN* – DOSE HABITUELLE, TOUTES LES 24 HEURES; *CL_{CR} < 20 mL/MIN* – LA MOITIÉ DE LA DOSE HABITUELLE, TOUTES LES 24 HEURES.

PRÉSENTATION

- **Ciprofloxacine**
 Comprimés: 250 mg^Pr^, 500 mg^Pr^, 750 mg^Pr^ ■ **Comprimés à libération prolongée**: 500 mg^Pr^, 1 000 mg^Pr^ ■ **Suspension orale**: 500 mg/5 mL, en flacons de 100 mL^Pr^ ■ **Solution pour injection**: 200 mg/20 mL^Pr^, 400 mg/40mL^Pr^ ■ **Solution prémélangée pour injection en mini-sac**: 200 mg/100 mL^Pr^, 400 mg/200 mL^Pr^.
- **Lévofloxacine**
 Comprimés: 250 mg^Pr^, 500 mg^Pr^ ■ **Solution pour injection**: 500 mg/20 mL^Pr^ ■ **Solution prémélangée pour injection en mini-sac**: 250 mg/50 mL^Pr^, 500 mg/100 mL^Pr^.
- **Moxifloxacine**
 Comprimés: 400 mg^Pr^ ■ **Solution prémélangée pour injection en mini-sac**: 400 mg/250 mL^Pr^.
- **Norfloxacine**
 Comprimés: 400 mg^Pr^.
- **Ofloxacine**
 Comprimés: 200 mg^Pr^, 300 mg^Pr^, 400 mg^Pr^.

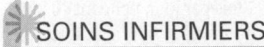

SOINS INFIRMIERS

ÉVALUATION DE LA SITUATION

- Au début du traitement et pendant toute sa durée, suivre de près l'évolution de l'infection: altération des signes vitaux, aspect de la plaie, des crachats, de l'urine et des selles; accroissement du nombre de globules blancs; résultats anormaux aux analyses d'urine; mictions fréquentes et impérieuses; urine trouble ou nauséabonde.
- Prélever des échantillons pour les cultures et les antibiogrammes avant le début du traitement. La première dose peut être administrée avant que les résultats soient connus. Pour prévenir l'émergence de bactéries résistantes, ces molécules devraient être utilisées seulement en présence d'une infection prouvée ou fortement suspectée et causée par un microorganisme sensible.
- OBSERVER LE PATIENT À LA RECHERCHE DES SIGNES ET SYMPTÔMES SUIVANTS D'ANAPHYLAXIE: RASH, PRURIT, ŒDÈME LARYNGÉ, RESPIRATION SIFFLANTE. S'ILS SE MANIFESTENT, CESSER LE TRAITEMENT ET COMMUNIQUER IMMÉDIATEMENT AVEC LE MÉDECIN OU UN AUTRE PROFESSIONNEL DE LA SANTÉ. GARDER À PORTÉE DE LA MAIN DE L'ADRÉNALINE, UN ANTIHISTAMINIQUE ET LE MATÉRIEL DE RÉANIMATION POUR TRAITER LES RÉACTIONS ANAPHYLACTIQUES.

***Tests de laboratoire*:**

- Les fluoroquinolones peuvent entraîner une élévation des concentrations sériques d'AST, d'ALT, de LDH, de bilirubine et de phosphatase alcaline.
- Les fluoroquinolones peuvent aussi abaisser le nombre de globules blancs et élever ou abaisser la glycémie, la glycosurie, l'hématurie, la protéinurie et l'albuminurie.
- La ciprofloxacine et la norfloxacine peuvent induire la cristallurie et une élévation des concentrations sériques d'urée et de créatinine.
- La moxifloxacine peut induire de l'hyperglycémie et de l'hyperlipidémie et modifier le temps de prothrombine. Elle peut aussi élever le nombre de globules blancs et les concentrations sériques de calcium, de chlorure, d'albumine et de globuline et réduire les concentrations de glucose et d'hémoglobine et le nombre d'érythrocytes, de polynucléaires neutrophiles, d'éosinophiles et de basophiles.

DIAGNOSTICS INFIRMIERS POSSIBLES

- Risque d'infection (Indication).
- Connaissances insuffisantes sur le traitement médicamenteux (Enseignement au patient et à ses proches).

INTERVENTIONS INFIRMIÈRES

- NE PAS CONFONDRE LA NORFLOXACINE AVEC NORFLEX (ORPHÉNADRINE).

PO:

- Le patient doit prendre la *norfloxacine* et l'*ofloxacine* à jeun, soit 1 heure avant ou 2 heures après les repas, avec un grand verre d'eau. La *moxifloxacine* peut être administrée sans égard aux repas. Il ne faut pas prendre des antiacides renfermant du magnésium ou de l'aluminium ou des préparations contenant du fer ou du zinc dans les 4 heures précédant ou dans les 2 heures (8 heures dans le cas de la moxifloxacine) suivant l'administration des fluoroquinolones.
- En cas d'irritation gastrique, on peut administrer la ciprofloxacine avec des aliments. Les aliments ralentissent et peuvent diminuer légèrement l'absorption de cet agent.
- Le lait et le yogourt réduisent l'absorption de la ciprofloxacine. Éviter d'en consommer en même temps.

Ciprofloxacine (suspension orale): Avant de faire boire la suspension au patient, bien agiter le flacon pendant environ 15 secondes. Administrer la quantité de suspension prescrite. Il ne faut pas croquer les microcapsules.

- Les comprimés de ciprofloxacine à libération prolongée doivent être avalés tels quels. Ils ne doivent pas être croqués, mâchés ou écrasés.

Ciprofloxacine

- **Perfusion intermittente**: Diluer dans une solution de NaCl 0,9 % ou de D5%E pour obtenir une concentration de 1 à 2 mg/mL. La solution est stable pendant 24 heures à la température ambiante ou pendant 72 heures au réfrigérateur. Consulter les directives de chaque fabricant avant de reconstituer la préparation. La ciprofloxacine est aussi présentée dans des sacs souples, prêts à l'emploi, sous forme de solution prémélangée. Dans ce cas, aucune autre dilution n'est nécessaire.
- ***Vitesse d'administration***: Afin de réduire l'irritation veineuse, administrer la préparation dans une grosse veine en 60 minutes.
- **Incompatibilité (tubulure en Y)**: Interrompre l'administration d'autres solutions pendant qu'on administre la ciprofloxacine.

Lévofloxacine

- **Perfusion intermittente**: Pour obtenir une concentration de 5 mg/mL, diluer dans une solution de NaCl 0,9 %, de D5%E, de D5%/NaCl 0,9 %, de D5%/NaCl 0,45 %, de D5%/lactate de Ringer, de D5%/Plasma-Lyte 56 ou de lactate de sodium. La lévofloxacine est aussi présentée dans des flacons ou des sacs souples, prêts à l'emploi, sous forme de solution prémélangée avec du D5%E. Dans ce cas, aucune autre dilution n'est nécessaire. Jeter toute portion inutilisée. La solution diluée est stable pendant 24 heures à la température ambiante et pendant 72 heures au réfrigérateur. Consulter les directives de chaque fabricant avant de reconstituer la préparation.
- ***Vitesse d'administration***: Administrer la dose de 250 mg et de 500 mg par perfusion pendant au moins 60 minutes. Administrer la dose de 750 mg par perfusion pendant au moins 90 minutes. Ne pas administrer en bolus rapide.
- **Compatibilité en addition au soluté**: chlorure de potassium.

Moxifloxacine.

- **Perfusion intermittente**: Les sacs contenant la solution prémélangée ne nécessitent pas de dilution supplémentaire. Consulter les directives de chaque fabricant avant de reconstituer la préparation.
- ***Vitesse d'administration***: Administrer par perfusion pendant au moins 60 minutes. Ne pas administrer en bolus rapide.
- **Compatibilité avec les solutions**: NaCl 0,9 %, D5%E, D10%E, lactate de Ringer.
- **Incompatibilité (tubulure en Y)**: Interrompre l'administration d'autres solutions pendant qu'on administre la moxifloxacine.

ENSEIGNEMENT AU PATIENT ET À SES PROCHES

- Expliquer au patient qu'il doit prendre le médicament à intervalles réguliers et finir toute la quantité qui lui a été prescrite en respectant rigoureusement la posologie recommandée, même s'il se sent mieux. S'il n'a pu prendre le médicament au moment habituel, il doit le prendre dès que possible à moins que ce ne soit presque l'heure prévue pour la dose suivante. Lui recommander de ne pas remplacer une dose manquée par une double dose. Insister sur le fait qu'il peut être dangereux de donner ce médicament à une autre personne. Prévenir le patient que les fluoroquinolones devraient être utilisées seulement pour traiter des infections bactériennes; elles sont inefficaces pour traiter des infections virales telles que le rhume et la grippe.
- Prévenir le patient qu'il doit informer immédiatement un professionnel de la santé s'il prend de la théophylline.
- Inciter le patient à boire au moins 1 500 à 2 000 mL de liquides par jour afin de prévenir la cristallurie.
- Prévenir le patient que les antiacides ou les préparations à base de fer et de zinc réduisent l'absorption des fluoroquinolones; il doit donc éviter de prendre la *norfloxacine* ou l'*ofloxacine* dans les 2 heures qui suivent; la *moxifloxacine* dans les 4 heures; la *ciprofloxacine* dans les 6 heures. À l'inverse, ne pas administrer ces préparations après l'administration des fluoroquinolones ou dans les 2 heures qui suivent (8 heures, dans le cas de la *moxifloxacine*).
- Prévenir le patient que les fluoroquinolones peuvent provoquer de la somnolence ou des étourdissements. Lui conseiller de ne pas conduire et d'éviter les activités qui exigent sa vigilance jusqu'à ce qu'on ait la certitude que le médicament n'entraîne pas ces effets chez lui.
- Recommander au patient d'informer un professionnel de la santé en présence de tout problème pouvant évoquer l'allongement de l'intervalle QT (antécédents personnels ou antécédents familiaux d'allongement de l'intervalle QT, états proarythmiques, tels que l'hypokaliémie, une bradycardie importante ou un infarctus du myocarde récent. Les patients ayant de tels antécédents ne devraient pas recevoir de fluoroquinolones.

- Recommander au patient d'utiliser un écran solaire et de porter des vêtements protecteurs, pendant le traitement et pendant 5 jours après l'avoir arrêté, pour prévenir les réactions de phototoxicité.
- Recommander au patient de se rincer fréquemment la bouche, de pratiquer une bonne hygiène buccale, de mâcher de la gomme ou de sucer des bonbons sans sucre pour diminuer la sécheresse de la bouche.
- Expliquer au patient atteint de gonorrhée que ses partenaires doivent aussi être traités.
- Conseiller au patient de consulter un professionnel de la santé avant de prendre tout autre médicament vendu sur ordonnance ou en vente libre.
- Recommander au patient de signaler les signes suivants de surinfection: excroissance pileuse sur la langue, démangeaisons ou pertes vaginales, selles molles ou nauséabondes.
- RECOMMANDER AU PATIENT DE COMMUNIQUER AVEC UN PROFESSIONNEL DE LA SANTÉ EN CAS DE FIÈVRE OU DE DIARRHÉE, PARTICULIÈREMENT SI SES SELLES CONTIENNENT DU SANG, DU PUS OU DU MUCUS. CONSEILLER AU PATIENT DE NE PAS TRAITER LA DIARRHÉE AVANT D'AVOIR CONSULTÉ UN PROFESSIONNEL DE LA SANTÉ.
- CONSEILLER AU PATIENT DE SIGNALER IMMÉDIATEMENT À UN PROFESSIONNEL DE LA SANTÉ LA PRÉSENCE DE RASH, DE DOULEURS OU D'INFLAMMATION AU NIVEAU DES TENDONS. DANS CE CAS, IL FAUT INTERROMPRE LE TRAITEMENT.

VÉRIFICATION DE L'EFFICACITÉ THÉRAPEUTIQUE

L'efficacité du traitement peut être démontrée par: la disparition des signes et symptômes d'infection; le temps de résolution dépend du microorganisme infectant et du siège de l'infection ■ la disparition des signes et des symptômes d'infection des voies urinaires ■ des résultats négatifs aux analyses des urines. ✳

ALERTE CLINIQUE

FLUOROURACILE

5-FU, Efudex, Fluoroplex, Fluorouracile

CLASSIFICATION:

Antinéoplasique (antimétabolite)

Grossesse – catégorie D

INDICATIONS

IV: En monothérapie ou en association avec d'autres modalités thérapeutiques (intervention chirurgicale, radiothérapie, administration d'autres antinéoplasiques) dans le traitement palliatif du cancer du côlon ■ du sein ■ du rectum ■ de l'estomac ■ du pancréas ■ de la prostate ■ de l'ovaire ■ de la tête et du cou ■ de la vessie ■ En monothérapie ou en association dans le traitement adjuvant du cancer du côlon, du rectum et du sein ■ **Usage topique**: *Crème 5 %* – traitement topique des kératoses prénéoplasiques et des épithéliomes basocellulaires superficiels ■ *Crème 1 %* – traitement topique des kératoses actiniques multiples.

MÉCANISME D'ACTION

Inhibition de la synthèse de l'ADN en prévenant la production de thymidine (effet spécifique sur la phase S du cycle cellulaire) et de l'ARN par l'incorporation du fluorouracil dans l'ARN. ***Effets thérapeutiques:*** Destruction des cellules à réplication rapide, particulièrement des cellules malignes.

PHARMACOCINÉTIQUE

Absorption: Faible (de 5 à 10 % par voie topique).
Distribution: Le fluorouracile se répartit dans tout l'organisme y compris dans le liquide céphalorachidien; il se concentre dans les tumeurs où il s'accumule.
Métabolisme et excrétion: Transformation en un métabolite actif. Métabolisme hépatique; de petites quantités sont excrétées sous forme inchangée dans l'urine.
Demi-vie: 20 minutes.

Profil temps-action
(effets sur la numération globulaire [voie IV]; effets dermatologiques [voie topique])

	DÉBUT D'ACTION	PIC	DURÉE
IV	7 -14 jours	9 - 21 (nadir)	30 jours
Voie topique	2 - 3 jours	2 - 6 semaines	1 - 2 mois

CONTRE-INDICATIONS, PRÉCAUTIONS ET MISES EN GARDE

Contre-indications: Hypersensibilité ■ Malnutrition ■ Aplasie médullaire ■ Infections potentiellement graves ■ Patients affaiblis ou dénutris.
Précautions et mises en garde: Infections ■ Autres maladies chroniques débilitantes ■ Obésité, œdème ou ascite (calculer la dose selon le poids idéal) ■ Insuffisance hépatique ■ **OBST.**: Grossesse et allaitement.

RÉACTIONS INDÉSIRABLES ET EFFETS SECONDAIRES

Plus vraisemblables lors de l'administration par voie générale que lors de l'usage topique.
CV: ISCHÉMIE MYOCARDIQUE, douleurs rétrosternales, changements asymptomatiques à l'ÉCG, arythmies.

SNC: dysfonction cérébelleuse aiguë.

GI: anorexie, diarrhée, nausées, stomatite, œsophagopharyngite, vomissements.

Tég.: alopécie, rash maculopapulaire, réactions inflammatoires locales (usage topique seulement), mélanose des ongles, perte des ongles, dysesthésie érythémateuse palmoplantaire, phototoxicité.

End.: stérilité.

Hémat.: anémie, leucopénie, thrombopénie.

Locaux: thrombophlébite.

ORLO: larmoiements excessifs.

Divers: fièvre.

INTERACTIONS

Médicament-médicament: L'administration concomitante d'**irinotécan** peut entraîner une toxicité importante (déshydratation, neutropénie, septicémie) ■ Effets additifs sur l'aplasie médullaire lors de l'administration concomitante d'autres **dépresseurs de la moelle osseuse**, incluant d'autres **antinéoplasiques** et la **radiothérapie** ■ Le fluorouracile peut diminuer la réponse des anticorps aux **vaccins à virus vivants** et augmenter le risque de réactions indésirables ■ La **leucovorine calcique** peut intensifier les effets thérapeutiques et la toxicité du fluorouracile; l'association de ces agents peut être utile.

VOIES D'ADMINISTRATION ET POSOLOGIE

Les doses peuvent varier grandement selon la tumeur, l'état du patient et les protocoles utilisés.

- **IV (adultes)**: *Dose initiale* – 12 mg/kg/jour (500 mg/m^2), pendant 5 jours; répéter tous les 28 jours. La dose quotidienne ne doit pas excéder 800 mg. *Dose d'entretien* – répéter la dose initiale en commençant 28 jours après le début du traitement antérieur ou administrer une dose d'entretien de 10 à 15 mg/kg par semaine. ***Patients dont l'état général est précaire:*** *Dose initiale* – de 6 à 10 mg/kg/jour (de 250 à 400 mg/m^2/jour), pendant 5 jours; répéter tous les 28 jours.
- **Voie intra-artérielle (adultes)**: De 5 à 7 mg/kg/jour en perfusion continue pendant 24 heures.

Kératoses prénéoplasique et carcinome basocellulaire superficiel

- **Préparation topique (adultes)**: Appliquer la crème à 5 %, 2 fois par jour, pendant 2 à 4 semaines. La guérison complète n'apparaît parfois que 1 ou 2 mois après l'arrêt du traitement.

Kératoses actiniques (solaires)

- **Préparation topique (adultes)**: Appliquer la crème à 1 %, 2 fois par jour, pendant 2 à 6 semaines.

PRÉSENTATION

Solution pour injection: 50 mg/mL, en fioles de 10 ou 100 mL[Pr] ■ **Crème**: 5 %, en tubes de 40 g[Pr]; 1 %, en tubes de 30 g[Pr].

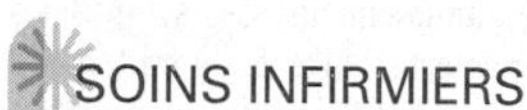

ÉVALUATION DE LA SITUATION

- Prendre les signes vitaux avant le traitement et à intervalles fréquents pendant toute sa durée.
- Examiner les muqueuses, noter le nombre et la consistance des selles et la fréquence des vomissements. Rester à l'affût des signes d'infection suivants: fièvres, frissons, maux de gorge, toux, raucité de la voix, douleurs dans le bas du dos ou aux flancs, mictions difficiles ou douloureuses. Suivre de près les saignements: saignement des gencives, formation d'ecchymoses, pétéchies, présence de sang occulte dans les selles, l'urine et les vomissements. Éviter les injections IM et la prise de la température rectale. Appliquer une pression sur les points de ponction veineuse pendant 10 minutes. Prévenir le médecin si les symptômes suivants de toxicité se manifestent: stomatite ou œsophagopharyngite, vomissements impossibles à réprimer, diarrhée, saignements gastro-intestinaux, ischémie myocardique, nombre de globules blancs inférieur à 3,5 × 10^9/L, nombre de plaquettes inférieur à 100 × 10^9/L, hémorragie de quelque nature que ce soit. Le traitement peut être suspendu dans ce cas. On peut le reprendre à une plus faible dose, une fois que les effets secondaires ont disparu.
- Examiner fréquemment les points d'injection IV pour déceler l'inflammation et l'infiltration. Demander au patient de prévenir l'infirmière en cas de douleur ou d'irritation au point d'injection. Le médicament peut provoquer la thrombophlébite. En cas d'extravasation, arrêter la perfusion et recommencer dans une autre veine afin d'éviter la lésion des tissus sous-cutanés. En prévenir immédiatement le médecin. Le traitement classique comprend l'application de compresses de glace.
- Examiner la peau pendant toute la durée du traitement pour déceler la présence d'une dysesthésie érythémateuse palmoplantaire, se manifestant par des picotements aux mains et aux pieds, suivis de douleurs, d'érythème et d'œdème.
- Effectuer le bilan quotidien des ingesta et des excreta, évaluer l'appétit du patient et noter son apport alimentaire. Les effets gastriques surviennent habituellement le 4e jour de traitement. En adaptant le

F

régime selon les aliments que le patient peut tolérer, on peut maintenir l'équilibre hydroélectrolytique et l'état nutritionnel.

- Observer le patient à la recherche des symptômes suivants de dysfonctionnement cérébelleux: faiblesse, ataxie et étourdissements. Ces symptômes peuvent persister même après l'arrêt du traitement.

Usage topique: Examiner la peau atteinte avant le traitement et pendant toute sa durée.

Tests de laboratoire:

- Le fluorouracile peut diminuer les concentrations plasmatiques d'albumine.
- Examiner les résultats des tests des fonctions hépatique (AST, ALT, LDH et bilirubine sérique), rénale et hématologique (hématocrite, hémoglobine, nombre de globules blancs et de plaquettes) avant le traitement et à intervalles réguliers pendant toute sa durée. Une numération globulaire devrait être effectuée tous les jours au cours du traitement par voie IV. Prévenir le médecin immédiatement si le nombre de globules blancs est inférieur à $3,5 \times 10^9$/L, ou celui de plaquettes, à 100×10^9/L. Il s'agit de critères qui peuvent dicter l'arrêt du traitement. Le nadir de la leucopénie survient habituellement dans les 9 à 21 jours qui suivent l'administration. Les valeurs se rétablissent vers le 30e jour. Le fluorouracile peut également provoquer une thrombopénie.
- Le fluorouracile peut accroître l'excrétion urinaire d'acide 5-hydroxy-indol-acétique (5-HIAA).

DIAGNOSTICS INFIRMIERS POSSIBLES

- Risque d'infection (Effets secondaires).
- Alimentation déficiente (Effets secondaires).
- Connaissances insuffisantes sur le traitement médicamenteux (Enseignement au patient et à ses proches).

INTERVENTIONS INFIRMIÈRES

ALERTE CLINIQUE: DES DÉCÈS SONT SURVENUS LORS DE CERTAINES CHIMIOTHÉRAPIES. AVANT D'ADMINISTRER L'AGENT, CLARIFIER TOUS LES POINTS AMBIGUS. VÉRIFIER LA LIMITE DES DOSES UNITAIRES ET QUOTIDIENNES AINSI QUE LA DOSE À ADMINISTRER PENDANT LE TRAITEMENT. DEMANDER À UN AUTRE PROFESSIONNEL DE LA SANTÉ DE VÉRIFIER UNE FOIS DE PLUS L'ORDONNANCE D'ORIGINE, LES CALCULS ET LE RÉGLAGE DE LA POMPE À PERFUSION. LE CHIFFRE 5 (5-FLUOROURACILE) FAIT PARTIE DU NOM DE L'AGENT ET NE FAIT NULLEMENT RÉFÉRENCE À LA TENEUR DU MÉDICAMENT.

- Préparer les solutions IV sous une hotte à flux laminaire. Porter des vêtements protecteurs incluant des gants et un masque pendant la manipulation du fluorouracile. Mettre au rebut le matériel dans les contenants réservés à cet usage (voir l'annexe H). Consulter les directives de chaque fabricant avant de reconstituer la préparation.

IV directe: Le fluorouracile peut être administré non dilué.

Vitesse d'administration: L'administration en bolus rapide (en 1 à 2 minutes) donne les résultats les plus efficaces, mais la toxicité peut se manifester plus rapidement.

Perfusion intermittente:

- Le fluorouracile peut être dilué dans une solution de D5%E ou de NaCl 0,9%.
- Afin de maintenir la stabilité du médicament, utiliser une tubulure et des sacs en plastique pour perfusion IV. La solution est stable pendant 24 heures à la température ambiante; ne pas réfrigérer. La solution est d'incolore à jaune pâle. Jeter toute solution trouble ou qui a changé de couleur de façon notable. Si des cristaux se forment dans la solution, la chauffer jusqu'à 55 °C, la secouer vigoureusement et la laisser refroidir jusqu'à la température du corps.

Vitesse d'administration: Si on administre la préparation en 2 à 8 heures, on retarde considérablement l'apparition d'effets toxiques.

Compatibilité dans la même seringue: bléomycine ■ cisplatine ■ cyclophosphamide ■ furosémide ■ héparine ■ leucovorine ■ méthotrexate ■ métoclopramide ■ mitomycine ■ vinblastine ■ vincristine.

Incompatibilité dans la même seringue: dropéridol ■ épirubicine.

Compatibilité (tubulure en Y): allopurinol ■ amifostine ■ aztréonam ■ bléomycine ■ céfépime ■ cisplatine ■ cyclophosphamide ■ doxorubicine ■ fludarabine ■ furosémide ■ granisétron ■ héparine ■ hydrocortisone ■ leucovorine ■ mannitol ■ melphalan ■ méthotrexate ■ métoclopramide ■ mitomycine ■ paclitaxel ■ pipéracilline/tazobactam ■ potassium, chlorure de ■ propofol ■ sargramostim ■ téniposide ■ thiotépa ■ vinblastine ■ vincristine ■ vitamines du complexe B avec C.

Incompatibilité (tubulure en Y): dropéridol ■ filgrastim ■ gallium, nitrate de ■ vinorelbine.

Compatibilité en addition au soluté: bléomycine ■ cyclophosphamide ■ D5%E avec une solution de lactate de Ringer ■ étoposide ■ floxuridine ■ ifosfamide ■ méthotrexate ■ mitoxantrone ■ prednisolone ■ vincristine.

Incompatibilité en addition au soluté: carboplatine ■ cisplatine ■ cytarabine ■ diazépam ■ doxorubicine ■ leucovorine ■ métoclopramide ■ morphine.

Préparation topique: Consulter le médecin avant d'utiliser les préparations topiques afin de déterminer les soins qu'il recommande pour préparer la peau. Les pansements occlusifs trop ajustés sont déconseillés en raison du risque d'irritation des tissus environnants sains. On devrait habituellement opter pour un pansement léger de gaze pour des raisons esthétiques seulement. Porter des gants lors de l'application du médicament. Ne pas utiliser d'applicateur métallique.

ENSEIGNEMENT AU PATIENT ET À SES PROCHES

- Recommander au patient de signaler à un professionnel de la santé les symptômes suivants: fièvre, frissons, maux de gorge, signes d'infection, jaunissement de la peau ou des yeux, douleurs abdominales ou lombaires, enflure des pieds ou des jambes, saignements des gencives, formation d'ecchymoses, pétéchies, présence de sang dans les urines, les selles ou les vomissures. Inciter le patient à éviter les foules et les personnes contagieuses. Lui recommander d'utiliser une brosse à dents à poils doux et un rasoir électrique, de ne pas boire d'alcool et de ne pas prendre de produits à base d'aspirine ou des AINS.
- Conseiller au patient de se rincer la bouche avec de l'eau après avoir bu ou mangé et de ne pas utiliser de la soie dentaire afin de réduire les risques de stomatite. Lui recommander d'utiliser de la lidocaïne visqueuse si les douleurs à la bouche l'empêchent de manger. La douleur associée à la stomatite peut dicter un traitement par un opioïde.
- Prévenir le patient qu'il risque de perdre ses cheveux. Explorer avec lui les stratégies lui permettant de s'adapter à ce changement.
- Expliquer à la patiente qu'elle devrait prendre des mesures contraceptives pendant toute la durée du traitement.
- Recommander au patient d'utiliser un écran solaire et de porter des vêtements protecteurs pour prévenir les réactions de phototoxicité.
- Recommander au patient de ne pas se faire vacciner sans en avoir discuté préalablement avec un professionnel de la santé.
- Insister sur l'importance des tests de laboratoire à intervalles réguliers permettant d'évaluer les bienfaits du traitement et de déceler les effets secondaires.

Préparation topique: Expliquer au patient la méthode d'application de la crème, en insistant sur le fait qu'il doit éviter tout contact avec les yeux et qu'il doit user de prudence lorsqu'il applique le médicament près de la bouche et du nez. Si le patient ne porte pas de gants lors de l'application du médicament, l'avertir qu'il est important de se laver soigneusement les mains après le traitement. Lui expliquer que l'érythème, la desquamation, les phlyctènes avec prurit et une sensation de brûlure sont des effets prévisibles du traitement. Il faut arrêter le traitement en cas d'apparition d'érosions, d'ulcérations et de nécrose des tissus, qui peuvent se produire dans les 2 à 6 semaines qui suivent le début des applications (de 10 à 12 semaines dans le cas d'un carcinome basocellulaire). La peau guérit dans les 4 à 8 semaines suivantes.

VÉRIFICATION DE L'EFFICACITÉ THÉRAPEUTIQUE

L'efficacité du traitement peut être démontrée par: la diminution de la taille et de la propagation de la tumeur ■ la disparition des kératoses ou du carcinome basocellulaire superficiel. ✳

F

FLUORURE, SUPPLÉMENTS DE

préparations orales

Fluor-A-Day, Fluridrops, Fluoritabs, Fluorosol, Fluotic

préparations topiques liquides

Fluorinse, Oral-B solution anti-caries, Oro NaF Daily Rinse+Fluoride

CLASSIFICATION:

Oligo-élément, soins dentaires, traitement de l'otospongiose

Grossesse – catégorie inconnue

INDICATIONS

Prévention de la carie dentaire chez les enfants, lorsque les concentrations en fluorure de l'eau potable sont insuffisantes ■ Traitement de l'otospongiose (Fluotic).

MÉCANISME D'ACTION

Le fluorure s'incorpore aux os et aux dents et il stabilise la matrice cristalline. Il favorise la reminéralisation et peut ralentir la formation de la plaque dentaire. Le fluorure présent sur l'émail dentaire favorise la résistance aux substances acides et prévient la carie. ***Effets thérapeutiques:*** Réduction du nombre de caries chez les enfants.

PHARMACOCINÉTIQUE

Absorption: Bonne (PO).

Distribution: L'agent est emmagasiné dans les os et dans les dents pendant leur croissance. Il traverse facilement la barrière placentaire et passe en petites quantités dans le lait maternel.

Métabolisme et excrétion: 50 % excrété par voie rénale à l'état inchangé. De petites quantités sont excrétées dans les fèces et la sueur.

Demi-vie: Inconnue.

Profil temps-action

	DÉBUT D'ACTION	PIC	DURÉE
PO	inconnu	30 – 60 min	inconnue

CONTRE-INDICATIONS, PRÉCAUTIONS ET MISES EN GARDE

F

Contre-indications: Hypersensibilité ■ Intolérance à la tartrazine et à d'autres additifs; ne pas en administrer les produits qui en contiennent aux patients ayant de tels antécédents ■ Insuffisance rénale grave ■ Ulcère gastroduodénal en poussée évolutive ■ Enfants < 18 ans (Fluotic) ■ Grossesse.

Précautions et mises en garde: Circonstances où la teneur en fluorure de l'eau est inconnue ■ Régime hyposodé ■ Présence de plus de 0,7 mg/L de fluorure dans l'eau potable.

RÉACTIONS INDÉSIRABLES ET EFFETS SECONDAIRES

SNC: céphalées, faiblesse.

GI: gêne gastro-intestinale.

Tég.: eczéma, dermatite atopique, urticaire.

Divers: taches sur les dents (toxicité).

INTERACTIONS

Médicament-médicament: Les **suppléments calciques**, administrés simultanément, entravent l'absorption des préparations à base de fluorure de calcium et du fluorure ■ L'**hydroxyde d'aluminium** diminue l'absorption du fluorure.

Médicament-aliments: Les **produits laitiers**, pris en même temps, entravent l'absorption du fluorure et des préparations à base de fluorure de calcium.

VOIES D'ADMINISTRATION ET POSOLOGIE

2,2 mg de fluorure de sodium = 1 mg de fluor élémentaire

Selon l'Association dentaire canadienne, on ne doit pas administrer de fluorure lorsque l'eau potable renferme plus de 0,3 mg/L de fluorure.

Préparations orales – concentration de fluorure dans l'eau potable < 0,3 mg/L

- **(Enfants < 3 ans)**: usage déconseillé.
- **(Enfants de 3 à 5 ans)**: 0,25 ou 0,5 mg (fluor élémentaire) par jour, selon le dentifrice utilisé.
- **(Enfants de 6 à 13 ans)**: 1 mg (fluor élémentaire) par jour.

Traitement de l'otospongiose

- **PO (adultes)**: 20 mg (fluorure de sodium), 3 fois par jour (Fluotic).

PRÉSENTATION (selon la teneur en fluorure de sodium)

Comprimés à croquer: 0,55 mg^{VL}, 1,1 mg^{VL}, 2,21 mg^{VL} ■ **Comprimés**: 2,21 mg^{VL}, 20 mg^{Pr} (Fluotic) ■ **Pastilles**: 2,21 mg^{VL} ■ **Gouttes**: 5,56 mg/mL^{VL}, 7,04 mg/mL^{VL} ■ **Liquide oral**: 6,9 mg/mL^{VL}, 7,04 mg/mL ^{VL} ■ **Rince-bouche**: 0,023 %^{VL}, 0,05 %^{VL} et 0,2 %^{VL} ■ **En association avec**: multivitamines^{VL}, cétylpyridinium^{VL}.

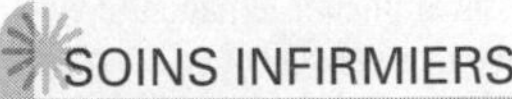

SOINS INFIRMIERS

ÉVALUATION DE LA SITUATION

- Examiner les dents à intervalles réguliers pour déceler l'apparition de taches. En informer le dentiste, le cas échéant.

DIAGNOSTICS INFIRMIERS POSSIBLES

- Connaissances insuffisantes sur le traitement médicamenteux (Enseignement au patient et à ses proches).

INTERVENTIONS INFIRMIÈRES

- On peut administrer les gouttes sans les diluer ou on peut les mélanger à des aliments ou à des liquides.
- Il ne faut pas administrer le fluorure de sodium dans les 2 heures qui suivent la consommation de lait ou de produits laitiers puisque ces aliments peuvent en réduire l'absorption.

ENSEIGNEMENT AU PATIENT ET À SES PROCHES

- Expliquer au patient qu'il doit prendre les suppléments de fluorure selon les directives accompagnant chaque préparation.
- Prévenir le patient que les rince-bouche sont plus efficaces s'il les utilise immédiatement après s'être brossé les dents ou après avoir passé la soie dentaire, juste avant d'aller se coucher. Lui expliquer qu'il doit cracher l'excédent de salive; il ne faut pas avaler le produit. Lui conseiller de ne pas boire, ni manger ni se rincer la bouche pendant les 30 minutes qui suivent le traitement.
- Encourager le patient à subir à intervalles réguliers des examens dentaires permettant d'évaluer l'état de ses dents.

VÉRIFICATION DE L'EFFICACITÉ THÉRAPEUTIQUE

L'efficacité du traitement peut être démontrée par: la prévention de la carie dentaire. ✻

FLUOXÉTINE

Alti-Fluoxétine, FXT, Gen-Fluoxétine, PMS-Fluoxétine, Prozac, Rhoxal-Fluoxétine

CLASSIFICATION:

Antidépresseur (inhibiteur sélectif du recaptage de la sérotonine [ISRS])

Grossesse – catégorie D (risque durant le 3e trimestre; voir «Précautions et mises en garde»)

INDICATIONS

Soulagement symptomatique de la dépression (y compris la dépression chez les personnes âgées), souvent en association avec la psychothérapie ■ Trouble obsessionnel-compulsif (TOC) ■ Boulimie. **Usages non approuvés:** Anorexie ■ Trouble déficitaire de l'attention et hyperactivité (TDAH) ■ Neuropathie diabétique ■ Fibromyalgie ■ Obésité ■ Trouble panique ■ Syndrome prémenstruel ■ Phénomène de Raynaud.

MÉCANISME D'ACTION

Inhibition du recaptage de la sérotonine dans le SNC. ***Effets thérapeutiques:*** Effet antidépresseur ■ Diminution des comportements associés au TOC et à la boulimie.

PHARMACOCINÉTIQUE

Absorption: Bonne (PO).

Distribution: L'agent traverse la barrière hématoencéphalique.

Liaison aux protéines: 94,5 %.

Métabolisme et excrétion: Fort métabolisme hépatique. Une fraction est transformée en norfluoxétine, un métabolite actif. Ce métabolite subit également un fort métabolisme hépatique. Une fraction de la fluoxétine et de son métabolite (12 % et 7 %) est excrétée par les reins sous forme inchangée.

Demi-vie: De 1 à 3 jours (norfluoxétine: de 5 à 7 jours).

Profil temps-action (effet antidépresseur)

	DÉBUT D'ACTION	PIC	DURÉE
PO	1 – 4 semaines	inconnu	2 semaines

CONTRE-INDICATIONS, PRÉCAUTIONS ET MISES EN GARDE

Contre-indications: Hypersensibilité ■ Administration concomitante d'IMAO (attendre au moins 14 jours entre l'arrêt du traitement par de l'IMAO et le début du traitement par la fluoxétine, ou au moins 5 semaines entre l'arrêt du traitement par la fluoxétine et le début du traitement par l'IMAO).

Précautions et mises en garde: Insuffisance hépatique ou rénale grave (l'adaptation de la posologie peut s'avérer nécessaire) ■ Antécédents de convulsions ■ Il est conseillé de suivre de près les idées suicidaires chez tous les patients recevant ce médicament ■ Patients débilités (risque accru de convulsions) ■ Diabète ■ Maladie chronique ou polypharmacothérapie (réduire les doses ou prolonger l'intervalle entre les doses, au besoin) ■ Diabète ■ Antécédents de manie ■ Risque d'anomalies hémorragiques, particulièrement chez les patients à risque d'hémorragie (p. ex., personnes âgées, antécédents d'hémorragie, patients prenant des médicaments modifiant la coagulation) ■ Antécédents de troubles épileptiques ■ Risque d'effets indésirables de type agitation grave et de blessures infligées à soi-même ou aux autres (adultes et enfants) ■ **OBST.:** Il n'existe pas d'études adéquates chez la femme enceinte. N'administrer ce médicament au cours de la grossesse que si les bienfaits éventuels pour la patiente l'emportent sur les risques possibles auxquels on expose le fœtus. Il y a des risques de complication après accouchement chez les nouveau-nés lorsque la mère a pris ce médicament durant le 3e trimestre ■ **ALLAITEMENT:** Les femmes sous fluoxétine ne doivent pas allaiter, sauf si le médecin traitant juge que l'allaitement est nécessaire, auquel cas le nourrisson doit être surveillé étroitement ■ **PÉD.:** L'innocuité et l'efficacité de la fluoxétine n'ont pas été établies ■ **GÉR.:** La fluoxétine n'a été évaluée qu'à une dose de 20 mg/jour chez les personnes âgées déprimées. Une posologie réduite ou des prises moins fréquentes peuvent être efficaces et doivent être envisagées en cas de maladie concomitante ou de prise de plusieurs médicaments. Cette population est exposée à un risque accru de stimulation excessive du SNC, de troubles du sommeil et d'agitation ■ Éviter de mettre fin abruptement au traitement en raison du risque de symptômes de sevrage.

RÉACTIONS INDÉSIRABLES ET EFFETS SECONDAIRES

SNC: CONVULSIONS, anxiété, somnolence, céphalées, insomnie, nervosité, rêves bizarres, étourdissements, fatigue, hypomanie, manie, faiblesse.

ORLO: congestion nasale, troubles visuels.

Resp.: toux.

CV: douleurs thoraciques, palpitations.
GI: diarrhée, douleurs abdominales, altération du goût, anorexie, constipation, sécheresse de la bouche (xérostomie), dyspepsie, nausées, vomissements, perte de poids.
GU: dysfonctionnement sexuel, mictions fréquentes.
Tég.: sécrétion excessive de sueur, prurit, érythème noueux, rougeurs du visage, rash.
End.: dysménorrhée.
Loc.: arthralgie, douleurs lombaires, myalgie.
SN: tremblements.
Divers: réactions allergiques, fièvre, syndrome pseudogrippal, bouffées de chaleur, réactions d'hypersensibilité.

INTERACTIONS

Médicament-médicament: INTERROMPRE L'ADMINISTRATION DES **IMAO** 14 JOURS AVANT LE DÉBUT DU TRAITEMENT PAR LA FLUOXÉTINE; L'ADMINISTRATION CONCOMITANTE PEUT ENTRAÎNER DE LA CONFUSION, DE L'AGITATION, DES CONVULSIONS, DE L'HYPERTENSION ET DE L'HYPERPYREXIE (SYNDROME SÉROTONINERGIQUE). ARRÊTER L'ADMINISTRATION DE LA FLUOXÉTINE AU MOINS 5 SEMAINES AVANT D'AMORCER LE TRAITEMENT PAR LES IMAO ■ La fluoxétine inhibe l'activité du cytochrome P450 2D6 dans le foie et intensifie les effets des **médicaments métabolisés par cette enzyme** ■ La fluoxétine ralentit le métabolisme de l'**alprazolam** et en intensifie les effets (réduire la dose d'alprazolam de moitié) ■ Les **médicaments qui inhibent l'activité du cytochrome P450** (incluant le **ritonavir**, le **saquinavir** et l'**efavirenz**) peuvent augmenter le risque d'apparition du syndrome sérotoninergique ■ Diminuer la dose de fluoxétine de 70 % en cas de prise concomitante de **ritonavir**; en cas de traitement par la fluoxétine, commencer par une dose de 10 mg par jour ■ Risque d'élévation des concentrations d'**antidépresseurs tricycliques** (incluant l'**imipramine** et la **désipramine**), administrés en concomitance; diminuer la dose de ces médicaments et suivre leurs concentrations plasmatiques ■ Risque d'augmentation ou de diminution des taux de **lithium** après la prise concomitante de fluoxétine. Des effets toxiques dus au lithium ont été signalés. On doit donc surveiller les taux de lithium quand ces deux agents sont pris en concomitance ■ Risque d'effets secondaires (sensations de faiblesse, d'hyperréflexie et d'incoordination) lors de la prise concomitante d'**agonistes des récepteurs 5HT$_1$ (triptans)** ■ Effets additifs sur la dépression du SNC lors de l'usage concomitant d'**alcool**, d'**antihistaminiques**, d'autres **antidépresseurs**, d'**opioïdes** ou d'**hypnosédatifs** ■ Risque accru d'effets secondaires et de réactions indésirables lors de l'administration concomitante d'autres **antidépresseurs**, de **tryptophane** ou de **phénothiazines** ■ La fluoxétine peut accroître l'efficacité ou le risque de toxicité de la **carbamazépine**, de la **clozapine**, de la **digoxine**, de l'**halopéridol**, de la **phénytoïne**, du **lithium** et de la **warfarine** ■ La fluoxétine peut réduire les effets de la **buspirone** ■ La **cyproheptadine** peut réduire ou annuler les effets de la fluoxétine ■ La fluoxétine peut accroître la sensibilité aux **agents adrénergiques** et le risque de syndrome sérotoninergique ■ Cet agent peut modifier l'activité d'autres **médicaments qui se lient fortement aux protéines plasmatiques**.
Médicament-produits naturels: La consommation concomitante de **millepertuis** ou de **SAMe** peut augmenter le risque de syndrome sérotoninergique.

VOIES D'ADMINISTRATION ET POSOLOGIE

- **PO (adultes)**: *Dépression* – posologie initiale: 20 mg par jour, le matin. Après plusieurs semaines, on peut majorer la dose de 20 mg par jour à intervalles hebdomadaires. Les doses de plus de 20 mg par jour doivent être administrées en 2 prises fractionnées, à prendre le matin et le midi. *TOC* – de 20 à 60 mg par jour. *Boulimie* – 60 mg par jour (il peut être nécessaire de majorer la dose en l'espace de plusieurs jours). On doit mesurer les taux d'électrolytes avant de commencer le traitement. Pour toutes ces indications, la dose quotidienne ne doit pas dépasser 80 mg.
- **PO (personnes âgées)**: Au départ, 10 mg par jour, le matin; on peut augmenter cette dose (ne pas dépasser 60 mg par jour).

PRÉSENTATION

Capsules: 10 mg^{Pr}, 20 mg^{Pr}, 40 mg^{Pr} ■ **Solution orale**: 20 mg/5 mL^{Pr}.

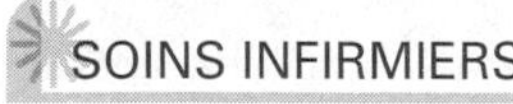

SOINS INFIRMIERS

ÉVALUATION DE LA SITUATION

- Suivre de près les sautes d'humeur. Signaler au médecin ou à un autre professionnel de la santé l'aggravation de l'anxiété, de l'agitation ou de l'insomnie.
- Observer les tendances suicidaires, particulièrement durant le traitement initial. Réduire la quantité de médicament dont le patient peut disposer.
- Suivre de près l'appétit du patient et son alimentation. Peser le patient toutes les semaines. Prévenir le médecin ou un autre professionnel de la santé en cas de perte constante de poids. Adapter le régime alimentaire selon les aliments que le patient peut

tolérer pour favoriser le maintien de l'état nutritionnel.

- Observer le patient à la recherche des signes suivants de réactions d'hypersensibilité: urticaire, fièvre, arthralgie, œdème, syndrome du canal carpien, rash, lymphadénopathie et détresse respiratoire. Prévenir le médecin ou un autre professionnel de la santé si ces symptômes se manifestent; ils disparaissent habituellement lors de l'arrêt du traitement par la fluoxétine, mais l'administration d'antihistaminiques ou de corticostéroïdes peut s'avérer nécessaire.

Trouble obsessionnel-compulsif: Observer la fréquence des comportements obsessionnels compulsifs. Noter à quel point de telles pensées ou comportements empêchent le patient de poursuivre ses activités quotidiennes.

Boulimie: Évaluer la fréquence de la consommation excessive d'aliments et des vomissements pendant toute la durée du traitement.

Tests de laboratoire:

- Noter les résultats de la numération globulaire et leucocytaire à intervalles réguliers, tout au long du traitement. Prévenir le médecin en cas de leucopénie, d'anémie, de thrombopénie ou d'allongement du temps de saignement.
- Une protéinurie et une légère élévation des concentrations d'AST peuvent survenir au cours des réactions d'hypersensibilité.
- La fluoxétine peut élever les concentrations sériques de phosphatase alcaline, d'ALT, d'urée, et de créatine phosphokinase, ou entraîner l'hypo-uricémie, l'hypocalcémie, l'hypoglycémie ou l'hyperglycémie et l'hyponatrémie.

DIAGNOSTICS INFIRMIERS POSSIBLES

- Stratégies d'adaptation inefficaces (Indications).
- Risque d'accident (Effets secondaires).
- Connaissances insuffisantes sur le traitement médicamenteux (Enseignement au patient et à ses proches).

INTERVENTIONS INFIRMIÈRES

- Administrer une seule dose, le matin. Chez certains patients, il peut s'avérer nécessaire d'administrer une quantité plus élevée de fluoxétine en doses fractionnées.
- La fluoxétine peut être administrée avec des aliments pour réduire l'irritation gastro-intestinale.

ENSEIGNEMENT AU PATIENT ET À SES PROCHES

- Conseiller au patient de respecter rigoureusement la posologie recommandée. S'il n'a pas pu prendre le médicament au moment habituel, lui conseiller de ne pas prendre cette dose et de revenir au schéma habituel. Lui recommander de ne jamais remplacer une dose manquée par une double dose. Le prévenir qu'il ne doit pas arrêter le traitement sans avoir consulté un professionnel de la santé; l'abandon du traitement peut entraîner de l'anxiété, de l'insomnie et de la nervosité.
- Prévenir le patient que la fluoxétine peut altérer sa capacité de jugement et peut provoquer de la somnolence, des étourdissements et une vision trouble. Lui recommander de ne pas conduire et d'éviter les activités qui exigent sa vigilance jusqu'à ce qu'on ait la certitude que le médicament n'entraîne pas ces effets chez lui.
- Conseiller au patient d'éviter la consommation d'alcool ou la prise d'autres dépresseurs du SNC pendant le traitement et de consulter un professionnel de la santé avant de prendre d'autres médicaments en même temps que la fluoxétine.
- Recommander au patient de changer lentement de position afin de prévenir les étourdissements.
- Expliquer au patient qu'il peut soulager la sécheresse de la bouche en se rinçant souvent la bouche, en pratiquant une bonne hygiène buccale et en consommant des bonbons ou de la gomme à mâcher sans sucre. Si la sécheresse de la bouche persiste pendant plus de 2 semaines, lui recommander de consulter un professionnel de la santé qui pourra lui prescrire des substituts de salive.
- Conseiller à la patiente de prévenir un professionnel de la santé si elle pense être enceinte ou si elle souhaite le devenir.
- Recommander au patient d'utiliser un écran solaire et des vêtements protecteurs afin de prévenir les réactions de photosensibilité.
- Prévenir le patient que la fluoxétine peut réduire la libido.
- Conseiller au patient de prévenir un professionnel de la santé en cas de réactions d'hypersensibilité ou si les céphalées, les nausées, l'anorexie, l'anxiété ou l'insomnie persistent.
- Insister sur l'importance des examens de suivi permettant de déterminer les bienfaits du traitement. Encourager le patient à s'engager dans une psychothérapie.

VÉRIFICATION DE L'EFFICACITÉ THÉRAPEUTIQUE

L'efficacité du traitement peut être démontrée par: une sensation de mieux-être ▪ un regain d'intérêt pour l'entourage; les effets antidépresseurs peuvent ne pas se manifester avant 1 à 4 semaines ▪ la diminution de la

F

fréquence des comportements obsessionnels-compulsifs ■ la diminution de la consommation excessive d'aliments et des vomissements chez les patients atteints de boulimie.

FLUPHÉNAZINE

décanoate de fluphénazine
Modecate, PMS-Fluphénazine Décanoate, Rho-Fluphénazine Décanoate

hydrochlorure de fluphénazine
Apo-Fluphenazine

CLASSIFICATION:
Antipsychotique (phénothiazine)

Grossesse – catégorie C

INDICATIONS

Traitement des manifestations schizophréniques et des troubles psychotiques qui ne sont pas associés à la déficience mentale.

MÉCANISME D'ACTION

Modification des effets de la dopamine dans le SNC ■ Action anticholinergique et blocage alpha-adrénergique. ***Effets thérapeutiques:*** Diminution des signes et des symptômes de psychose.

PHARMACOCINÉTIQUE

Absorption: Bonne (PO, IM). Les sels de décanoate ont un début d'action retardé et des effets prolongés en raison d'une libération retardée de la base d'huile et, par la suite, des tissus adipeux.

Distribution: L'agent se répartit dans tout l'organisme. Il traverse la barrière hématoencéphalique et placentaire et passe dans le lait maternel.

Liaison aux protéines: ≥ 90 %.

Métabolisme et excrétion: Métabolisme majoritairement hépatique, qui comprend plusieurs cycles entérohépatiques.

Demi-vie: *Chlorhydrate de fluphénazine* – de 4,7 à 15,3 heures; *décanoate de fluphénazine* – de 6,8 à 9,6 jours.

Profil temps-action (effets antipsychotiques)

	Début d'action	Pic	Durée
Chlorhydrate PO	1 h	inconnu	6 – 8 h
Décanoate IM	24 – 72 h	inconnu	≥ 4 semaines

CONTRE-INDICATIONS, PRÉCAUTIONS ET MISES EN GARDE

Contre-indications: Hypersensibilité ■ Risque de réactions de sensibilité croisée avec d'autres phénothiazines ■ Glaucome à angle fermé ■ Aplasie médullaire ■ Maladies hépatique ou cardiovasculaire graves ■ Hypersensibilité à l'huile de sésame (sels de décanoate) ■ Intolérance à l'alcool ou à la tartrazine (éviter l'usage des produits qui contiennent ces substances chez les patients qui ne les tolèrent pas) ■ Utilisation concomitante de pimozide.

Précautions et mises en garde: **GÉR.:** Il pourrait s'avérer nécessaire de réduire la dose initiale chez les personnes âgées ou débilitées ■ Diabète ■ Maladies respiratoires ■ Hyperplasie de la prostate ■ Tumeurs du SNC ■ Épilepsie ■ Occlusion intestinale ■ **OBST., ALLAITEMENT:** L'innocuité des fluphénazines n'a pas été établie.

RÉACTIONS INDÉSIRABLES ET EFFETS SECONDAIRES

SNC: réactions extrapyramidales, sédation, dyskinésie tardive.

ORLO: vision trouble, xérophtalmie, opacité du cristallin.

CV: hypotension, tachycardie.

GI: anorexie, constipation, hépatite induite par les médicaments, sécheresse de la bouche (xérostomie), occlusion intestinale.

GU: rétention urinaire.

Tég.: photosensibilité, modification de la pigmentation, rash.

End.: galactorrhée.

Hémat.: AGRANULOCYTOSE, leucopénie.

Divers: réactions allergiques, hyperthermie.

INTERACTIONS

Médicament-médicament: L'usage concomitant de **pimozide** devrait être évité en raison d'effets secondaires cardiaques additifs (allongement de l'intervalle QT) ■ Effets hypotenseurs additifs lors de l'administration concomitante d'**antihypertenseurs** ■ Effets additifs sur la dépression du SNC lors de l'usage concomitant d'autres **dépresseurs du SNC** dont l'**alcool**, les **antidépresseurs**, les **antihistaminiques**, les **IMAO**, les **opioïdes**, les **hypnosédatifs** ou les **anesthésiques généraux** ■ Le **phénobarbital** peut accélérer le métabolisme des fluphénazines et en réduire l'efficacité ■ L'administration concomitante de **lithium** peut provoquer l'une des réactions suivantes: diminution de l'absorption des fluphénazines, augmentation de l'excrétion du lithium, risque accru de réactions extrapyramidales ou dissimulation des premiers signes de toxicité par le lithium ■ L'usage concomitant de **mépéridine** peut produire une sédation excessive et de l'hypotension ■ Les **antiacides à base d'aluminium** ou les **antidiarrhéiques adsorbants** (**kaolin**) peuvent diminuer l'absorption des fluphénazines prises par voie orale ■ Risque accru d'agranulocytose lors de l'administration simultanée d'**agents antithyroïdiens** ■ Les fluphénazines peuvent réduire les effets antiparkinsoniens de la **lévodopa** et de la **bromocriptine** ■ Les fluphénazines diminuent l'effet vasopresseur de l'**adrénaline** et de la **noradrénaline** ■ Les **bêtabloquants** peuvent inhiber le métabolisme de l'un des médicaments ou des deux à la fois entraînant une intensification de la réponse ■ Risque accru d'effets anticholinergiques lors de l'administration concomitante d'autres **agents dotés de propriétés anticholinergiques**, dont les **antihistaminiques**, les **antidépresseurs tricycliques**, le **disopyramide** ou la **quinidine** ■ Risque de diminution des effets pharmacologiques des **amphétamines**.

VOIES D'ADMINISTRATION ET POSOLOGIE

Décanoate de fluphénazine

- **IM, SC (adultes)**: Initialement, de 2,5 à 12,5 mg (une dose initiale de 12,5 mg est généralement bien tolérée). Administrer une 2e dose de 12,5 mg ou de 25 mg après 4 à 10 jours. On peut majorer lentement la dose selon les besoins (ne pas dépasser 100 mg par dose). Une dose de 25 mg ou moins, toutes les 2 ou 3 semaines, suffit généralement à maîtriser les symptômes.

Chlorhydrate de fluphénazine

- **PO (adultes)**: *Dose initiale* – de 2,5 à 10 mg par jour en prises fractionnées, toutes les 6 à 8 heures. *Dose d'entretien* – de 1 à 5 mg par jour.
- **PO (personnes âgées ou débilitées)**: Initialement, de 1 à 2,5 mg par jour.

PRÉSENTATION
(version générique disponible)

Décanoate de fluphénazine (solution pour injection): 100 mg/mL^Pr ■ **Chlorhydrate de fluphénazine (comprimés)**: 1 mg^Pr, 2 mg^Pr, 5 mg^Pr ■ **Chlorhydrate de fluphénazine (élixir parfum d'orange)**: 2,5 mg/5 mL^Pr.

SOINS INFIRMIERS

ÉVALUATION DE LA SITUATION

- Évaluer l'état de conscience du patient (orientation, humeur, comportement) avant le traitement et à intervalles réguliers pendant toute sa durée.
- Mesurer la pression artérielle (en position assise, debout et en position couchée), le pouls et la fréquence respiratoire, effectuer un ÉCG avant l'administration initiale et à intervalles fréquents pendant la période d'adaptation de la posologie. Les fluphénazines peuvent entraîner des modifications des ondes Q et T sur l'ÉCG.
- Observer attentivement le patient lorsqu'on lui administre le médicament pour s'assurer qu'il l'a bien avalé.
- Noter la consommation de liquides et l'état de la fonction intestinale. Un apport accru de liquides et un régime alimentaire riche en fibres peuvent réduire les effets constipants de ces médicaments.
- Suivre le patient tous les 2 mois, tout au long du traitement, et pendant 8 à 12 semaines après l'avoir mené à terme pour déceler les signes d'akathisie (agitation, incapacité de rester en place) et les symptômes extrapyramidaux (*parkinsoniens* – difficulté d'élocution ou de déglutition, perte d'équilibre, mouvements d'émiettement, faciès figé, démarche traînante, rigidité, tremblements; *dystonique* – spasmes musculaires, tortillements, soubresauts, incapacité de bouger les yeux, faiblesses des bras et des jambes). Dans certains cas, il faudra réduire la dose ou abandonner le traitement. On peut administrer du trihexyphénidyle ou de la diphenhydramine pour maîtriser ces symptômes.
- Rester à l'affût des symptômes de dyskinésie tardive (mouvements rythmiques incontrôlables du visage, de la bouche, de la langue ou de la mâchoire et mouvements involontaires des membres, claquement des lèvres ou moue, gonflement des joues; mastication incontrôlable, mouvements rapides de la langue). Signaler immédiatement ces symptômes qui pourraient être irréversibles.
- Observer le patient à la recherche des signes suivants du syndrome malin des neuroleptiques: fièvre, détresse respiratoire, tachycardie, convulsions, diaphorèse, hypertension ou hypotension, pâleur, fatigue, rigidité musculaire marquée, perte de la maîtrise de la vessie. Signaler immédiatement ces symptômes.

Tests de laboratoire:

- IL FAUT ÉVALUER LA NUMÉRATION GLOBULAIRE ET LA FORMULE LEUCOCYTAIRE ET EFFECTUER DES EXAMENS OCULAIRES À INTERVALLES RÉGULIERS PENDANT TOUTE LA DURÉE DU TRAITEMENT. LES FLUPHÉNAZINES PEUVENT ENTRAÎNER UNE BAISSE DE L'HÉMATOCRITE, DES CONCENTRATIONS D'HÉMOGLOBINE ET DU NOMBRE DE GLOBULES BLANCS, DE GRANULOCYTES ET DE PLAQUETTES. ELLES PEUVENT ÉLEVER LA BILIRUBINE ET LES CONCENTRATIONS D'ALT, D'AST ET DE PHOSPHATASE ALCALINE. L'AGRANULOCYTOSE PEUT SE MANIFESTER DE 4 À 10 SEMAINES APRÈS LE DÉBUT DU TRAITEMENT; LE

RÉTABLISSEMENT SE PRODUIT DE 1 À 2 SEMAINES APRÈS L'AVOIR ARRÊTÉ. IL Y A RISQUE DE RÉCURRENCE SI L'ON REPREND LE TRAITEMENT. DES ANOMALIES DE LA FONCTION HÉPATIQUE PEUVENT DICTER L'ABANDON DU TRAITEMENT.

- Les fluphénazines peuvent entraîner des résultats faussement positifs ou faussement négatifs aux tests de grossesse et des résultats faussement positifs aux épreuves de dosage de la bilirubine urinaire.

DIAGNOSTICS INFIRMIERS POSSIBLES

F

- Opérations de la pensée perturbées (Indications).
- Connaissances insuffisantes sur le traitement médicamenteux (Enseignement au patient et à ses proches).
- Non-observance du traitement médicamenteux (Enseignement au patient et à ses proches).

INTERVENTIONS INFIRMIÈRES

- Même si la solution vire au jaune pâle ou devient ambrée, sa puissance n'est en rien altérée.
- Éviter les éclaboussures sur les mains, afin de réduire les risques de dermatite de contact. En cas d'éclaboussures, bien se laver les mains.
- Pour ne pas rendre les préparations injectables troubles, il faut les extraire de la fiole en utilisant une seringue sèche et une aiguille sèche de calibre 21.

PO: Diluer le concentré juste avant de l'administrer dans 120 à 240 mL d'eau, de lait, de boisson gazéifiée, de soupe ou de jus de tomates ou de fruits. Ne pas mélanger à des boissons renfermant de la caféine (cola, café), des tanins (thé) ou des pectines (jus de pomme).

SC: Le décanoate est dissous dans l'huile de sésame, ce qui en assure une longue durée d'action. Il peut être administré par voie SC ou IM.

IM:

- La dose IM correspond habituellement à $^1/_3$ ou à $^1/_2$ de la dose PO.
- Injecter profondément dans le muscle fessier à l'aide d'une seringue sèche et d'une aiguille de calibre 21. Demander au patient de rester couché pendant 30 minutes pour prévenir l'hypotension.

ENSEIGNEMENT AU PATIENT ET À SES PROCHES

- Expliquer au patient qu'il doit respecter rigoureusement la posologie recommandée; le prévenir qu'il ne doit jamais sauter de dose ni remplacer une dose manquée par une double dose. S'il n'a pas pu prendre le médicament au moment prévu, il devrait le prendre dans l'heure qui suit ou sauter cette dose et reprendre le schéma habituel (si le médecin lui a prescrit plus de 1 dose par jour). S'il ne doit prendre que 1 dose par jour, la prendre dès que possible sauf s'il est presque l'heure prévue pour la dose suivante. Le sevrage brusque peut provoquer une gastrite, des nausées, des vomissements, des étourdissements, des céphalées, de la tachycardie et de l'insomnie.
- Informer le patient qu'il risque de manifester des symptômes extrapyramidaux ou une dyskinésie tardive. Lui recommander de signaler immédiatement ces symptômes à un professionnel de la santé.
- Recommander au patient de changer lentement de position afin de réduire le risque d'hypotension orthostatique.
- Prévenir le patient que les fluphénazines peuvent provoquer de la somnolence. Lui conseiller de ne pas conduire et d'éviter les activités qui exigent sa vigilance jusqu'à ce qu'on ait la certitude que le médicament n'entraîne pas cet effet chez lui.
- Mettre en garde le patient contre la consommation d'alcool ou d'autres dépresseurs du SNC en même temps que ce médicament.
- Recommander au patient d'utiliser un écran solaire et de porter des vêtements protecteurs lorsqu'il s'expose au soleil, car, sous l'effet du soleil, les surfaces exposées peuvent devenir bleu-gris; cette réaction peut disparaître après l'arrêt du traitement. Recommander également au patient d'éviter les températures extrêmes, car les fluphénazines altèrent la thermorégulation.
- Conseiller au patient de se rincer fréquemment la bouche avec de l'eau, de pratiquer une bonne hygiène buccale et de consommer de la gomme ou des bonbons sans sucre pour soulager la sécheresse de la bouche. Lui recommander de consulter un professionnel de la santé si la sécheresse de la bouche persiste pendant plus de 2 semaines.
- Informer le patient que les fluphénazines peuvent modifier la couleur de l'urine qui peut devenir de rose à rouge-brun.
- Informer le patient qu'il doit prévenir sans délai un professionnel de la santé en cas de maux de gorge, de fièvre, de saignements ou d'ecchymoses inhabituels, de rash, de faiblesse, de tremblements, de troubles de la vue, d'urine de couleur foncée ou de selles couleur de glaise.
- Recommander au patient qui doit suivre un traitement ou subir une intervention chirurgicale de prévenir le professionnel de la santé qu'il suit un traitement par ce médicament.
- Insister sur l'importance des examens réguliers de suivi, incluant les examens de la vue lors d'un trai-

tement prolongé, et inciter le patient à suivre une psychothérapie.

VÉRIFICATION DE L'EFFICACITÉ THÉRAPEUTIQUE

L'efficacité du traitement peut être démontrée par: la diminution de l'agitation et un moindre recours à des comportements paranoïdes ou au repli sur soi.

FLURAZÉPAM

Apo-Flurazépam, Bio-Flurazépam, Dalmane, Flurazépam, Novo-Flupam, PMS-Flurazépam, Somnol, Som Pam

CLASSIFICATION:

Anxiolytique et hypnosédatif (benzodiazépine)

Grossesse – catégorie X

INDICATIONS

Traitement de courte durée de l'insomnie (< 4 semaines).

MÉCANISME D'ACTION

Dépression du SNC, probablement attribuable à la potentialisation de l'acide gamma-aminobutyrique (GABA), un neurotransmetteur inhibiteur. ***Effets thérapeutiques:*** Amélioration du sommeil.

PHARMACOCINÉTIQUE

Absorption: Bonne (PO).

Distribution: L'agent se répartit dans tout l'organisme et traverse la barrière hématoencéphalique. Il traverse probablement la barrière placentaire et passe dans le lait maternel. Lors d'une administration prolongée, le médicament s'accumule dans les tissus.

Liaison aux protéines: 97 % (l'un des métabolites actifs).

Métabolisme et excrétion: Métabolisme hépatique. Certains métabolites ont un effet hypnotique.

Demi-vie: 2,3 heures (la demi-vie des métabolites actifs peut durer de 30 à 200 heures).

Profil temps-action (effet hypnotique)

	DÉBUT D'ACTION	PIC	DURÉE
PO	15 – 45 min	0,5 – 1 h	7 – 8 h

CONTRE-INDICATIONS, PRÉCAUTIONS ET MISES EN GARDE

Contre-indications: Hypersensibilité connue au médicament ou à d'autres benzodiazépines (allergie croisée) ■ Glaucome à angle fermé ■ Myasthénie grave ■ **OBST., ALLAITEMENT:** L'innocuité du médicament n'a pas été établie (absence de données pertinentes chez l'humain).

Précautions et mises en garde: Altération de la fonction hépatique ■ Insuffisance respiratoire grave ou apnée du sommeil ■ Insuffisance rénale grave ■ Comportement suicidaire ou antécédents de toxicomanie ou de pharmacodépendance ■ **GÉR.:** Il est recommandé de réduire la dose chez les personnes âgées ou débilitées ■ Coma ou dépression préexistante du SNC ■ **PÉD.:** L'innocuité du médicament n'a pas été établie chez les enfants < 15 ans.

F

RÉACTIONS INDÉSIRABLES ET EFFETS SECONDAIRES

SNC: confusion, somnolence diurne, difficultés de concentration, étourdissements, céphalées, léthargie, dépression mentale, excitation paradoxale.

ORLO: vision trouble.

GI: constipation, diarrhée, nausées, vomissements.

Tég.: rash.

SN: ataxie.

Divers: dépendance physique, dépendance psychologique, tolérance aux effets du médicament.

INTERACTIONS

Médicament-médicament: Risque de dépression additive du SNC, lors de l'usage concomitant d'**alcool**, d'**antidépresseurs**, d'**antihistaminiques** et d'**opiacés** ■ La **cimétidine**, les **contraceptifs oraux**, le **disulfirame**, la **fluoxétine**, l'**isoniazide**, le **kétoconazole**, le **métoprolol**, le **propoxyphène**, le **propranolol** ou l'**acide valproïque** peuvent ralentir le métabolisme du flurazépam et en accroître les effets ■ Le flurazépam peut diminuer l'efficacité de la **lévodopa** ■ La **rifampine** ou les **barbituriques** peuvent accélérer le métabolisme du flurazépam et en diminuer l'efficacité ■ La **théophylline** peut diminuer les effets sédatifs du flurazépam.

Médicament-produits naturels: Le **kava**, le **houblon**, la **scutellaire**, la **valériane** et la **camomille** peuvent accentuer la dépression du SNC.

VOIES D'ADMINISTRATION ET POSOLOGIE

- **PO (adultes):** De 15 à 30 mg, au coucher.
- **PO (personnes âgées ou débilitées):** Initialement, 15 mg au coucher; on peut majorer la dose si besoin est.

PRÉSENTATION (version générique disponible)

Capsules: 15 mg$^{T\backslash C}$, 30 mg$^{T\backslash C}$ ■ **Comprimés:** 15 mg$^{T\backslash C}$, 30 mg$^{T\backslash C}$.

SOINS INFIRMIERS

ÉVALUATION DE LA SITUATION

- Noter les habitudes de sommeil du patient avant le traitement et à intervalles réguliers pendant toute sa durée.

GÉR.: Évaluer le risque de chutes et mettre en place les mesures préventives.

- Le traitement prolongé peut entraîner une dépendance psychologique ou physique. Réduire la quantité de médicament dont le patient peut disposer, particulièrement si ce dernier est dépressif ou suicidaire ou s'il a des antécédents de toxicomanie.

DIAGNOSTICS INFIRMIERS POSSIBLES

- Habitudes de sommeil perturbées (Indications).
- Risque d'accident (Effets secondaires).
- Connaissances insuffisantes sur le traitement médicamenteux (Enseignement au patient et à ses proches).

INTERVENTIONS INFIRMIÈRES

- Surveiller le patient lors de ses déplacements ou de son transport après l'administration du médicament. Retirer les cigarettes. Relever les ridelles du lit et laisser la sonnette d'alarme à portée de sa main en tout temps.
- Si le patient éprouve des difficultés de déglutition, on peut ouvrir les capsules et les mélanger à des aliments ou à des liquides.

ENSEIGNEMENT AU PATIENT ET À SES PROCHES

- Conseiller au patient de respecter rigoureusement la posologie recommandée. Lui expliquer aussi qu'il est important de préparer un cadre propice au sommeil: la pièce doit être sombre et calme; la nicotine et le café sont à proscrire.
- Prévenir le patient que le flurazépam peut provoquer de la somnolence diurne. Lui conseiller de ne pas conduire et d'éviter les activités qui exigent sa vigilance jusqu'à ce qu'on ait la certitude que le médicament n'entraîne pas cet effet chez lui.

GÉR.: Enseigner au patient et à ses proches les mesures préventives visant à réduire le risque de chutes.

- Prévenir le patient qu'il ne doit pas consommer d'alcool ni prendre des dépresseurs du SNC en même temps que le flurazépam.
- Conseiller à la patiente d'informer immédiatement un professionnel de la santé si elle pense être enceinte ou si elle souhaite le devenir.

VÉRIFICATION DE L'EFFICACITÉ THÉRAPEUTIQUE

L'efficacité du traitement peut être démontrée par: l'amélioration du sommeil. Les pleins effets hypnotiques du médicament se manifestent 2 ou 3 nuits après le début du traitement et peuvent durer 1 ou 2 nuits après qu'il a été arrêté.

FLURBIPROFÈNE

Ansaid, Apo-Flurbiprofen, Froben, Froben SR, Novo-Flurbiprofen, Nu-Flurbiprofen, Ratio-Flurbiprofen

CLASSIFICATION:

Anti-inflammatoire non stéroïdien, analgésique non opioïde

Grossesse – catégories D (1er et 3e trimestres) et B (2e trimestre)

Pour l'usage ophtalmique, voir l'annexe N.

INDICATIONS

PO: Traitement des maladies inflammatoires dont: la polyarthrite rhumatoïde ■ l'arthrose ■ la spondylite ankylosante ■ Usage à titre d'analgésique non opioïde (pour le soulagement de la douleur légère à modérée accompagnée d'inflammation comme la bursite, la tendinite, les traumas des tissus mous) ■ Traitement de la dysménorrhée.

MÉCANISME D'ACTION

Inhibition de la synthèse des prostaglandines, ce qui réduit l'inflammation et la douleur. ***Effets thérapeutiques:*** Suppression de l'inflammation et de la douleur.

PHARMACOCINÉTIQUE

Absorption: Bonne (PO).

Distribution: Inconnue.

Liaison aux protéines: 99 %.

Métabolisme et excrétion: Métabolisme majoritairement hépatique. De 20 à 25 % est excrété à l'état inchangé par les reins.

Demi-vie: De 3 à 6 heures.

Profil temps-action (effet anti-inflammatoire)

	DÉBUT D'ACTION	PIC	DURÉE
PO	quelques jours – 1 semaine	1 – 2 semaines	inconnue

CONTRE-INDICATIONS, PRÉCAUTIONS ET MISES EN GARDE

Contre-indications: Hypersensibilité ■ Risque de réactions de sensibilité croisée avec d'autres agents anti-inflammatoires non stéroïdiens incluant l'aspirine ■ Syndrome complet ou partiel des polypes nasaux ■ Ulcère ou hémorragie digestive en poussée évolutive ■ Contexte périopératoire en cas de pontage aortocoronarien ■ Enfants.

Précautions et mises en garde: Maladie cardiovasculaire ou facteurs de risque de maladie cardiovasculaire (risque accru de complications coronariennes, d'infarctus du myocarde ou d'accidents vasculaires cérébraux surtout lors d'un usage prolongé) ■ Antécédents d'ulcère ■ Diabète ■ Troubles hémorragiques ■ **OBST., ALLAITEMENT:** Usage déconseillé ■ **GÉR.:** Patients âgés (réduire la dose; ces patients peuvent être davantage prédisposés aux réactions indésirables).

RÉACTIONS INDÉSIRABLES ET EFFETS SECONDAIRES

SNC: étourdissements, somnolence, céphalées, insomnie, dépression mentale, troubles psychiques.

ORLO: vision trouble, opacité de la cornée, acouphènes.

CV: modification de la pression artérielle, œdème, palpitations.

GI: HÉMORRAGIE DIGESTIVE, douleurs abdominales, brûlures d'estomac, nausées, sensation de plénitude gastrique, constipation, diarrhée, hépatite médicamenteuse, stomatite.

GU: incontinence.

Tég.: sudation accrue, rash, DERMATITE EXFOLIATIVE, SYNDROME DE STEVENS-JOHNSON, ÉPIDERMOLYSE NÉCROSANTE SUBAIGUË.

Hémat.: dyscrasie sanguine, allongement du temps de saignement.

Loc.: myalgie.

Divers: réactions allergiques comprenant l'ANAPHYLAXIE, frissons, fièvre.

INTERACTIONS

Médicament-médicament: L'**aspirine** peut réduire l'efficacité du flurbiprofène ■ L'**aspirine**, les autres **agents anti-inflammatoires non stéroïdiens**, les **suppléments de potassium** et les **corticostéroïdes**, tout comme l'**alcool**, intensifient les effets secondaires gastro-intestinaux ■ L'administration prolongée de flurbiprofène en même temps que l'**acétaminophène** peut augmenter le risque de réactions rénales indésirables ■ Le flurbiprofène peut réduire l'efficacité des **diurétiques** ou des **antihypertenseurs** ■ Le flurbiprofène peut intensifier l'effet hypoglycémiant de l'**insuline** ou des **hypoglycémiants oraux** ■ Le flurbiprofène augmente le risque de toxicité par le **méthotrexate** ■ Le **probénécide** augmente le risque de toxicité par le flurbiprofène ■ Risque accru d'hémorragie lors de l'administration concomitante de **céfamandole**, de **céfotétane**, de **céfopérazone**, d'**agents antiplaquettaires**, de **plicamycine**, d'**héparine**, d'**agents thrombolytiques**, d'**acide valproïque** ou de **warfarine** ■ Risque accru de réactions hématologiques indésirables lors de l'administration concomitante d'**agents antinéoplasiques** ou d'une **radiothérapie** ■ Risque accru de toxicité rénale lors de l'administration concomitante d'autres **agents néphrotoxiques** ■ L'administration concomitante d'**anti-inflammatoires non stéroïdiens** par voie orale et topique devrait être réduite au minimum.

Médicament-produits naturels: Risque accru de saignement lors de la prise concomitante d'**arnica**, de **camomille**, d'**ail**, de **dong quai**, de **grande camomille**, de **gingembre**, de **ginkgo biloba** et de **ginseng**.

VOIES D'ADMINISTRATION ET POSOLOGIE

- **PO (adultes):** *Anti-inflammatoire* – de 100 à 300 mg par jour, en 2 à 4 doses fractionnées (ne pas dépasser 300 mg par jour ou 100 mg par dose). *Traitement de la dysménorrhée* – 50 mg, 4 fois par jour. *Douleur légère à modérée* – 50 mg, toutes les 4 à 6 heures, selon les besoins.

PRÉSENTATION (version générique disponible)

Comprimés: 50 mg[Pr], 100 mg[Pr] ■ **Capsules à libération retard:** 200 mg[Pr].

SOINS INFIRMIERS

ÉVALUATION DE LA SITUATION

- LES PATIENTS SOUFFRANT D'ASTHME, D'ALLERGIE INDUITE PAR L'ASPIRINE ET DE POLYPES NASAUX SONT DAVANTAGE PRÉDISPOSÉS À DES RÉACTIONS D'HYPERSENSIBILITÉ. SUIVRE DE PRÈS LA RHINITE, L'ASTHME ET L'URTICAIRE.

Arthrite: Suivre de près la douleur et déterminer la mobilité des articulations, avant l'administration du flurbiprofène et à intervalles réguliers pendant toute la durée du traitement.

Tests de laboratoire:

- Le flurbiprofène peut allonger le temps de saignement; cet effet peut durer pendant moins de 24 heures.
- Le flurbiprofène peut entraîner une baisse des concentrations d'hémoglobine, de l'hématocrite, du nombre de leucocytes et de plaquettes.

- Noter les résultats des tests de la fonction hépatique à intervalles réguliers pendant toute la durée du traitement. Le médicament peut entraîner une élévation des concentrations sériques de phosphatase alcaline, de LDH, d'AST et d'ALT.
- Mesurer les concentrations d'urée, de créatinine sérique et d'électrolytes à intervalles réguliers pendant toute la durée du traitement. Le médicament peut élever les concentrations d'urée, de créatinine sérique et d'électrolytes et diminuer les concentrations d'électrolytes urinaires.

F

DIAGNOSTICS INFIRMIERS POSSIBLES

- Douleur aiguë (Indications).
- Mobilité physique réduite (Indications).
- Connaissances insuffisantes sur le traitement médicamenteux (Enseignement au patient et à ses proches).

INTERVENTIONS INFIRMIÈRES

- L'administration de doses plus élevées que celles recommandées n'accentue pas l'efficacité du médicament, mais pourrait augmenter le risque d'effets secondaires.
- Pour obtenir un effet initial rapide, administrer le flurbiprofène 30 minutes avant ou 2 heures après les repas. ADMINISTRER L'AGENT APRÈS LES REPAS OU AVEC DES ALIMENTS OU ENCORE AVEC UN ANTIACIDE RENFERMANT DE L'ALUMINIUM OU DU MAGNÉSIUM POUR RÉDUIRE L'IRRITATION GASTRIQUE. IL NE FAUT PAS ÉCRASER NI MÂCHER LES CAPSULES À LIBÉRATION PROLONGÉE.

ENSEIGNEMENT AU PATIENT ET À SES PROCHES

Arthrite:

- Conseiller au patient de prendre le flurbiprofène avec un grand verre d'eau et d'éviter de se coucher pendant les 15 à 30 minutes qui suivent.
- Conseiller au patient de respecter rigoureusement la posologie recommandée. S'il n'a pu prendre le médicament au moment habituel, il doit le faire dès que possible à moins que ce ne soit presque l'heure prévue pour la dose suivante. Le prévenir qu'il ne doit jamais remplacer une dose manquée par une double dose.
- Prévenir le patient que le flurbiprofène peut parfois provoquer de la somnolence ou des étourdissements. Lui conseiller de ne pas conduire et d'éviter les activités qui exigent sa vigilance jusqu'à ce qu'on ait la certitude que le médicament n'entraîne pas ces effets chez lui.
- Recommander au patient d'éviter de boire de l'alcool et de consulter un professionnel de la santé avant de prendre une préparation à base d'aspirine ou d'acétaminophène, un autre AINS ou un autre médicament en vente libre en même temps que le flurbiprofène.
- Recommander au patient qui doit suivre un traitement ou subir une intervention chirurgicale de prévenir le professionnel de la santé qu'il suit un traitement médicamenteux.
- RECOMMANDER AU PATIENT DE COMMUNIQUER AVEC UN PROFESSIONNEL DE LA SANTÉ EN CAS DE RASH, DE DÉMANGEAISONS, DE TROUBLES VISUELS, D'ACOUPHÈNES, DE GAIN DE POIDS, D'ŒDÈME, DE SELLES NOIRES, DE CÉPHALÉES PERSISTANTES OU DE SYMPTÔMES PSEUDOGRIPPAUX, TELS QUE FRISSONS, FIÈVRE, DOULEURS MUSCULAIRES OU AUTRES DOULEURS.

VÉRIFICATION DE L'EFFICACITÉ THÉRAPEUTIQUE

L'efficacité du traitement peut être démontrée par: la diminution de l'intensité de la douleur ■ l'amélioration de la mobilité des articulations; les patients qui ne répondent pas à un anti-inflammatoire non stéroïdien peuvent répondre à un autre.

FLUTAMIDE

Apo-Flutamide, Euflex, Flutamide, Novo-Flutamide, PMS-Flutamide

CLASSIFICATION:

Antinéoplasique (hormone de synthèse)

Grossesse – catégorie D

INDICATIONS

Traitement du cancer de la prostate métastasé (stade D2) en association avec des analogues de l'hormone de libération de la gonadotrophine (LH-RH) ou avec l'orchidectomie. Aussi en association avec un analogue de la LH-RH, avant et pendant une radiothérapie externe traditionnelle, chez les patients atteints d'un volumineux cancer localisé de la prostate au stade B2 ou au stade C.

MÉCANISME D'ACTION

Inhibition des effets des hormones androgènes (testostérone) au niveau cellulaire. ***Effets thérapeutiques:*** Ralentissement de la croissance des tumeurs malignes de la prostate sensibles aux hormones androgènes.

PHARMACOCINÉTIQUE

Absorption: Bonne (PO).

Distribution: Inconnue.

Métabolisme et excrétion: Métabolisme majoritairement hépatique; 23 % est transformé en un autre composé antiandrogène (l'a-hydroxyflutamide).

Demi-vie: *Flutamide* – inconnue; *a-hydroxyflutamide* – de 6 à 8 heures.

Profil temps-action

	DÉBUT D'ACTION	PIC	DURÉE
PO	inconnu	inconnu	inconnue

CONTRE-INDICATIONS, PRÉCAUTIONS ET MISES EN GARDE

Contre-indications: Hypersensibilité ■ Insuffisance hépatique grave ■ Femmes.

Précautions et mises en garde: Maladie cardiovasculaire grave.

RÉACTIONS INDÉSIRABLES ET EFFETS SECONDAIRES

Les effets secondaires sont principalement provoqués par l'analogue de la LH-RH lorsque le flutamide est utilisé en association.

SNC: anxiété, confusion, somnolence, dépression, nervosité.

CV: œdème, hypertension.

GI: HÉPATOTOXICITÉ, diarrhée, nausées, vomissements.

GU: impuissance, perte de la libido.

Tég.: photosensibilité, rash.

End.: gynécomastie, galactorrhée.

Divers: rougeurs du visage.

INTERACTIONS

Médicament-médicament: Le flutamide et les **analogues de la LH-RH** agissent en synergie ■ Le flutamide peut augmenter les concentrations plasmatiques de la **théophylline**.

VOIES D'ADMINISTRATION ET POSOLOGIE

- **PO (adultes)**: 1 dose de 250 mg, toutes les 8 heures, administrée en concomitance avec un analogue de la LH-RH. Commencer l'administration en même temps que celle de l'analogue de la LH-RH ou 24 heures plus tôt.

PRÉSENTATION

Comprimés: 250 mg^{Pr}.

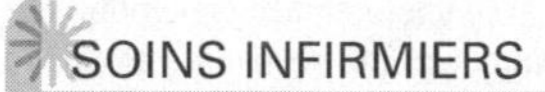

SOINS INFIRMIERS

ÉVALUATION DE LA SITUATION

- Suivre de près la diarrhée, les nausées et les vomissements. Modifier le régime en fonction des aliments que le patient peut tolérer. Prévenir le médecin si ces symptômes s'aggravent.

Tests de laboratoire:

- Le flutamide peut entraîner l'élévation des concentrations d'AST, d'ALT, de bilirubine et de créatinine sérique. Mesurer les concentrations d'ALT avant le traitement, mensuellement pendant les 4 premiers mois de traitement et à intervalles réguliers par la suite. Si les concentrations d'ALT ou d'AST s'élèvent à plus du double de la limite supérieure de la normale, il faut arrêter immédiatement l'administration du flutamide. Il faut aussi effectuer un test de la fonction hépatique dès l'apparition des nausées, des vomissements, des douleurs abdominales, de la fatigue, de l'anorexie, de l'ictère ou du prurit ou dès que l'urine devient foncée.
- Le flutamide peut entraîner une élévation des concentrations d'œstradiol et de testostérone.

DIAGNOSTICS INFIRMIERS POSSIBLES

- Dysfonctionnement sexuel (Effets secondaires).
- Connaissances insuffisantes sur le traitement médicamenteux (Enseignement au patient et à ses proches).

INTERVENTIONS INFIRMIÈRES

Administrer en association avec un analogue de la LH-RH.

ENSEIGNEMENT AU PATIENT ET À SES PROCHES

- Expliquer au patient qu'il doit prendre le flutamide en association avec un analogue de la LH-RH, si tel est le cas. Lui conseiller de respecter rigoureusement la posologie recommandée. S'il n'a pu prendre le médicament au moment habituel, il doit le faire dès que possible à moins que ce ne soit presque l'heure prévue pour la dose suivante. Il ne faut jamais remplacer une dose manquée par une double dose.
- Mettre en garde le patient contre la manifestation des effets secondaires suivants qui peuvent être entraînés par l'analogue de la LH-RH: rougeurs du visage, diminution de la libido, impuissance et gynécomastie. Les principaux effets secondaires du flutamide seul sont la diarrhée et la gynécomastie, mais il faut l'administrer en association avec d'autres

médicaments ou avec une orchidectomie pour que son effet thérapeutique puisse se manifester.

- Recommander au patient d'informer immédiatement un professionnel de la santé si l'un des effets suivants se manifeste: urine foncée, démangeaisons, perte de l'appétit, nausées, vomissements, douleur au côté droit ou jaunissement des yeux ou de la peau. L'hépatotoxicité disparaît habituellement à l'arrêt du traitement par le flutamide, mais elle peut être évolutive et d'issue fatale. Elle dicte donc une attention médicale immédiate.

F

VÉRIFICATION DE L'EFFICACITÉ THÉRAPEUTIQUE

L'efficacité du traitement peut être démontrée par: le ralentissement de la propagation du cancer de la prostate.

FLUTICASONE,

voir Corticostéroïdes (inhalation), Corticostéroïdes (topiques) et Corticostéroïdes (voie intranasale)

FLUVASTATINE,

voir Inhibiteurs de l'HMG-CoA réductase

FLUVOXAMINE

Apo-Fluvoxamine, Dom-Fluvoxamine, Luvox, Novo-Fluvoxamine, Nu-Fluvoxamine

CLASSIFICATION:

Antidépresseur (inhibiteur sélectif du recaptage de la sérotonine [ISRS]), antiobsessionnel

Grossesse – catégorie C (risque durant le 3e trimestre; voir «Précautions et mises en garde»)

INDICATIONS

Dépression ▪ Trouble obsessionnel-compulsif.

MÉCANISME D'ACTION

Inhibition du recaptage de la sérotonine dans le SNC. ***Effets thérapeutiques:*** Effet antidépresseur ▪ Diminution des comportements obsessionnels-compulsifs.

PHARMACOCINÉTIQUE

Absorption: 53 % (PO).

Distribution: La fluvoxamine passe dans le lait maternel et pénètre dans le SNC. Le reste de sa distribution demeure inconnu.

Métabolisme et excrétion: Élimination majoritairement rénale.

Demi-vie: De 13,6 à 15,6 heures.

Profil temps-action
(effet sur l'amélioration des comportements obsessionnels-compulsifs)

	DÉBUT D'ACTION	PIC	DURÉE
PO	dans les 2 à 3 semaines	plusieurs mois	inconnue

CONTRE-INDICATIONS, PRÉCAUTIONS ET MISES EN GARDE

Contre-indications: Hypersensibilité à la fluvoxamine ou à un autre ISRS ▪ Administration concomitante d'un IMAO ▪ Administration concomitante de terfénadine, d'astémizole ou de cisapride ▪ Administration concomitante de tizanidine.

Précautions et mises en garde: Antécédents de troubles épileptiques ▪ Diabète ▪ Il est conseillé de suivre de près les idées suicidaires chez tous les patients recevant ce médicament ▪ Risque d'effets indésirables de type agitation grave et de blessures infligées à soi-même ou aux autres (adultes et enfants) ▪ Risque d'anomalies hémorragiques, particulièrement chez les patients à risque d'hémorragie (p. ex., personnes âgées, antécédents d'hémorragie, patients prenant des médicaments modifiant la coagulation) ▪ Insuffisance rénale ou hépatique (commencer le traitement par une dose faible et suivre de près l'état du patient) ▪ **GÉR.:** Administrer une dose initiale moins élevée et la majorer plus lentement ▪ **OBST.:** Il n'existe pas d'études adéquates chez la femme enceinte. N'administrer cet agent au cours de la grossesse que si les bienfaits éventuels pour la patiente l'emportent sur les risques possibles auxquels on expose le fœtus. Il y a des risques de complication après accouchement chez les nouveau-nés lorsque la mère a pris ce médicament durant le 3e trimestre ▪ **ALLAITEMENT:** Possibilité de réactions indésirables graves chez les nouveau-nés, il faut décider soit de cesser l'allaitement, soit de cesser la prise du médicament, compte tenu de l'importance du médicament pour la mère ▪ **PÉD.:** L'innocuité et l'efficacité de cet agent n'ont pas été établies ▪ Éviter de mettre fin abruptement au traitement en raison du risque de symptômes de sevrage ▪ Risque d'intensification des effets de l'alcool.

RÉACTIONS INDÉSIRABLES ET EFFETS SECONDAIRES

SNC: étourdissements, somnolence, céphalées, insomnie, nervosité, faiblesse, agitation, anxiété, apathie,

labilité émotionnelle, réactions maniaques, dépression mentale, réactions psychotiques, syncope.
ORLO: sinusite.
Resp.: toux, dyspnée.
CV: œdème, hypertension, palpitations, hypotension orthostatique, tachycardie, vasodilatation.
GI: constipation, diarrhée, sécheresse de la bouche (xérostomie), dyspepsie, nausées, anorexie, dysphagie, élévation des concentrations d'enzymes hépatiques, flatulence, vomissements.
GU: baisse de la libido, dysfonctionnement sexuel.
Tég.: sécrétion excessive de sueur.
Métab.: gain pondéral, perte pondérale.
Loc.: hypertonie, myoclonie, mouvements brefs et saccadés.
SN: hypokinésie, hyperkinésie, tremblements.
Divers: réactions allergiques, frissons, symptômes pseudogrippaux, maux de dents, caries, bâillements.

INTERACTIONS

Médicament-médicament: L'ADMINISTRATION CONCOMITANTE D'**IMAO** PEUT ENTRAÎNER DES RÉACTIONS GRAVES POUVANT ÊTRE D'ISSUE FATALE (SYNDROME SÉROTONINERGIQUE) ■ L'administration concomitante de **tizanidine** en augmente les effets secondaires (hypotension, sédation) et est contre-indiquée ■ L'administration concomitante de **terfénadine**, d'**astémizole** ou de **cisapride** augmente les concentrations plasmatiques des médicaments et est contre-indiquée ■ L'usage de la **cigarette** (**nicotine**) peut réduire l'efficacité de la fluvoxamine ■ L'administration concomitante d'**antidépresseurs tricycliques** peut élever les concentrations plasmatiques de fluvoxamine ■ La fluvoxamine peut ralentir le métabolisme et accentuer les effets de certains **bêtabloquants** (**propranolol**), de certaines **benzodiazépines** (ne pas administrer simultanément du **diazépam**), de la **carbamazépine**, de la **méthadone**, du **lithium**, de la **théophylline** (administrer $^1/_3$ de la dose habituelle), du **tolbutamide**, de la **warfarine** et du **L-tryptophane** ■ La fluvoxamine élève les concentrations sanguines de la **clozapine** et le risque de toxicité associé à cet agent (une adaptation de la dose peut s'avérer nécessaire).

VOIES D'ADMINISTRATION ET POSOLOGIE

- **PO (adultes)**: *Dose initiale* – 50 mg par jour, au coucher; majorer par paliers de 50 mg, tous les 4 à 7 jours jusqu'à l'obtention de l'effet souhaité. Si la dose quotidienne est de plus de 150 mg, administrer en 2 doses également fractionnées ou administrer une dose plus importante au coucher (ne pas dépasser 300 mg par jour). *Dose d'entretien* – adapter la posologie à intervalles réguliers afin d'administrer la plus faible dose pouvant maîtriser les symptômes.

PRÉSENTATION

Comprimés: 50 mg^Pr^, 100 mg^Pr^.

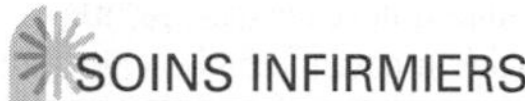

SOINS INFIRMIERS

ÉVALUATION DE LA SITUATION

- Suivre de près les changements d'humeur. Évaluer la fréquence des comportements obsessionnels-compulsifs. Observer à quel point ces pensées et ces comportements empêchent le patient de mener à bien ses activités quotidiennes. Signaler au médecin l'aggravation de l'anxiété, de la nervosité ou de l'insomnie.
- Observer les tendances suicidaires, particulièrement durant le traitement initial. Réduire la quantité de médicament dont le patient peut disposer.
- Suivre de près l'appétit du patient et son alimentation. Noter son poids toutes les semaines. Signaler toute perte importante de poids. Adapter le régime selon les aliments que le patient peut tolérer pour favoriser le maintien de l'état nutritionnel.

TOXICITÉ ET SURDOSAGE: Les symptômes les plus courants de toxicité incluent la somnolence, les vomissements, la diarrhée et les étourdissements. Les symptômes suivants peuvent aussi se manifester: coma, tachycardie, bradycardie, hypotension, anomalies de l'ÉCG, résultats anormaux aux tests de la fonction hépatique et convulsions. Administrer un traitement symptomatique de soutien.

DIAGNOSTICS INFIRMIERS POSSIBLES

- Stratégies d'adaptation inefficaces (Indications).
- Risque d'accident (Effets secondaires).
- Connaissances insuffisantes sur le traitement médicamenteux (Enseignement au patient et à ses proches).

INTERVENTIONS INFIRMIÈRES

- Initialement, administrer une seule dose, au coucher. Augmenter la posologie tous les 4 à 7 jours, au besoin, selon la tolérance du patient.
- La fluvoxamine peut être administrée sans égard aux repas.

ENSEIGNEMENT AU PATIENT ET À SES PROCHES

- Conseiller au patient de respecter rigoureusement la posologie recommandée. Lui recommander de ne

F

pas sauter de dose et de ne pas remplacer une dose manquée par une double dose. Comme de 2 à 3 semaines peuvent s'écouler avant de pouvoir observer une amélioration des symptômes, expliquer au patient qu'il devrait continuer de prendre le médicament tel qu'il lui a été prescrit.

- Prévenir le patient que la fluvoxamine peut provoquer de la somnolence et des étourdissements. Lui recommander de ne pas conduire et d'éviter les activités qui exigent sa vigilance jusqu'à ce qu'on ait la certitude que le médicament n'entraîne pas ces effets chez lui.
- Conseiller au patient d'éviter la consommation d'alcool ou la prise d'autres dépresseurs du SNC pendant le traitement et de consulter un professionnel de la santé avant de prendre d'autres médicaments en même temps que la fluvoxamine.
- Conseiller à la patiente de prévenir un professionnel de la santé si elle allaite, si elle pense être enceinte ou si elle souhaite le devenir.
- Recommander au patient d'informer un professionnel de la santé en cas de rash ou d'urticaire ou si les céphalées, les nausées, l'anorexie, l'anxiété ou l'insomnie persistent.
- Insister sur l'importance des examens de suivi permettant de déterminer les bienfaits du traitement.

VÉRIFICATION DE L'EFFICACITÉ THÉRAPEUTIQUE

L'efficacité du traitement peut être démontrée par: un sentiment de mieux-être ■ un moindre recours à des comportements obsessionnels-compulsifs. ✳

FOLATE,

voir Acide folique

FONDAPARINUX SODIQUE

Arixtra

CLASSIFICATION:

Anticoagulant (antithrombotique synthétique)

Grossesse – catégorie B

INDICATIONS

Prophylaxie des troubles thromboemboliques veineux consécutifs à une chirurgie orthopédique des membres inférieurs, par exemple, en cas de fracture de la hanche, de chirurgie du genou ou d'arthroplastie de la hanche ■ Traitement de la thrombose veineuse profonde aiguë et de l'embolie pulmonaire aiguë.

MÉCANISME D'ACTION

Le fondaparinux sodique est un inhibiteur synthétique spécifique du facteur X activé (Xa). Il agit en potentialisant l'effet de l'antithrombine III (ATIII) qui inhibe de façon sélective le facteur Xa. La neutralisation du facteur Xa interrompt la séquence des réactions en cascade qui se déclenchent pendant la coagulation sanguine, inhibant ainsi la formation de thrombine et prévenant la formation du thrombus. ***Effets thérapeutiques:*** Prévention de la formation de thrombus.

PHARMACOCINÉTIQUE

Absorption: Rapide et complète (SC); biodisponibilité à 100 %.

Distribution: Dans le sang. Liaison sélective à l'ATIII (au moins 94 %), mais sans liaison notable aux autres protéines plasmatiques.

Métabolisme et excrétion: Peu ou pas de métabolisme. Excrétion majoritairement urinaire sous forme inchangée.

Demi-vie: De 17 à 21 heures.

Profil temps-action (effet anticoagulant)

	DÉBUT D'ACTION	PIC	DURÉE
SC	rapide	2 - 3 h	jusqu'à 24 h

CONTRE-INDICATIONS, PRÉCAUTIONS ET MISES EN GARDE

Contre-indications: Hypersensibilité connue au fondaparinux ■ Thrombopénie qui s'accompagne d'un résultat positif du test d'agrégation plaquettaire *in vitro* en présence du fondaparinux ■ Saignement évolutif significatif sur le plan clinique ■ Endocardite bactérienne aiguë ■ Insuffisance rénale grave (Cl_{Cr} < 30 mL/min) ■ Faible poids corporel (< 50 kg).

Précautions et mises en garde: Administration réservée à la voie SC ■ Insuffisance hépatique grave ■ Insuffisance rénale modérée (Cl_{Cr} de 30 à 50 mL/min) ■ Anesthésie rachidienne ou péridurale (risque accru d'hématomes rachidiens ou périduraux, particulièrement en cas de traitement concomitant par des agents influant sur l'hémostase, tels les AINS ou les antiagrégants plaquettaires, ou par d'autres agents affectant la coagulation, de ponctions épidurales ou rachidiennes répétées ou traumatiques, ou de l'installation d'un cathéter péridural à demeure) ■ **GÉR.:** Risque d'hémorragie et d'effets indésirables graves qui s'élève avec l'âge; de plus, l'excrétion rénale pourrait être diminuée

■ **OBST., ALLAITEMENT, PÉD.**: L'innocuité du médicament n'a pas été établie.

EXTRÊME PRUDENCE: CHEZ LES PATIENTS PRÉSENTANT UN RISQUE ACCRU D'HÉMORRAGIE: TROUBLES CONGÉNITAUX OU ACQUIS DE L'HÉMOSTASE ■ MALADIE, ULCÈRE OU SAIGNEMENTS GASTRO-INTESTINAUX ■ HÉMORRAGIE CÉRÉBRALE RÉCENTE ■ INTERVENTION CHIRURGICALE RÉCENTE AU CERVEAU, À LA COLONNE VERTÉBRALE OU AUX YEUX.

RÉACTIONS INDÉSIRABLES ET EFFETS SECONDAIRES

SNC: étourdissements, céphalées, insomnie, confusion, HÉMATOME INTRARACHIDIEN.
CV: œdème, hypotension.
GI: constipation, nausées, vomissements, diarrhée, dyspepsie, élévation réversible des enzymes hépatiques.
GU: infection des voies urinaires, rétention urinaire.
HÉ: hypokaliémie.
Tég.: éruptions cutanées, purpura, prurit, hématome.
Hémat.: HÉMORRAGIE, anémie, thrombopénie.
Locaux: érythème au point d'injection, irritation locale, douleurs, augmentation des exsudations de la plaie.
Divers: fièvre.

INTERACTIONS

Médicament-médicament: Les **anticoagulants oraux** (**warfarine** ou **acénocoumarol**) ou les **médicaments qui inhibent la fonction plaquettaire**, dont l'**aspirine**, les **AINS**, le **dipyridamole**, le **clopidogrel**, la **ticlopidine**, l'**abciximab**, l'**eptifibatide**, le **tirofiban** et le **dextran**, administrés en concomitance, peuvent augmenter le risque d'hémorragie. Dans les essais cliniques menés sur le fondaparinux, la prise concomitante d'**anticoagulants oraux** (**warfarine**), d'**inhibiteurs des plaquettes** (**aspirine**), d'**AINS** (**piroxicam**) et de **digoxine** n'a pas modifié les paramètres pharmacocinétiques et pharmacodynamiques du fondaparinux ou des autres médicaments étudiés ■ Avant de commencer le traitement par le fondaparinux, il faut cesser l'administration des **agents susceptibles d'accroître le risque d'hémorragie**. Au cas où un tel traitement concomitant serait indispensable, il convient de surveiller étroitement l'état du patient.

VOIES D'ADMINISTRATION ET POSOLOGIE

Prophylaxie en cas de chirurgie orthopédique

- **SC (adultes)**: 2,5 mg, 1 fois par jour, après l'intervention chirurgicale. Une fois l'hémostase établie, ATTENDRE AU MOINS 6 HEURES APRÈS LA FIN DE L'INTERVENTION CHIRURGICALE pour administrer la dose initiale. Généralement, la durée de traitement est de 7 ± 2 jours, mais il devrait se poursuivre aussi longtemps que le risque de thromboembolie veineuse persiste (pendant 24 jours au maximum).

Traitement de la thrombose veineuse profonde aiguë et de l'embolie pulmonaire aiguë

- **SC (adultes)**: 5 mg (< 50 kg), 7,5 mg (de 50 à 100 kg) ou 10 mg (> 100 kg), 1 fois par jour. L'administration concomitante d'un anticoagulant oral doit être commencée le plus tôt possible. L'administration du fondaparinux doit se poursuivre pendant au moins 5 jours et jusqu'à ce que l'effet d'une anticoagulothérapie par voie orale soit établi (RNI de 2,0 à 3,0).

F

PRÉSENTATION

Solution pour injection: seringues préremplies: 2,5 mg/0,5 mL[Pr], 5 mg/0,4 mL[Pr], 7,5 mg/0,6 mL[Pr], 10 mg/0,8 mL[Pr].

SOINS INFIRMIERS

ÉVALUATION DE LA SITUATION

- RESTER À L'AFFÛT DES SIGNES SUIVANTS D'HÉMORRAGIE: SAIGNEMENT DES GENCIVES ET DU NEZ, FORMATION INHABITUELLE D'ECCHYMOSES, SELLES NOIRES GOUDRONNEUSES, HÉMATURIE, CHUTE DE L'HÉMOGLOBINE OU DE LA PRESSION ARTÉRIELLE, PRÉSENCE DE SANG OCCULTE DANS LES SELLES, SAIGNEMENT AU SIÈGE D'UNE CHIRURGIE. PRÉVENIR LE MÉDECIN SI CES SYMPTÔMES SE MANIFESTENT.
- Suivre de près les réactions d'hypersensibilité: frissons, fièvre, urticaire, enflure des lèvres, difficultés respiratoires, etc. Signaler ces réactions au médecin.
- Rester à l'affût des signes et des symptômes d'atteinte neurologique (paralysie) chez les patients porteurs d'un cathéter péridural.

SC: Observer étroitement la formation d'hématomes et d'ecchymoses ou l'apparition d'une inflammation au point d'injection.

Tests de laboratoire:

- NOTER LA NUMÉRATION GLOBULAIRE ET PLAQUETTAIRE. EXAMINER LES SELLES À INTERVALLES RÉGULIERS PENDANT TOUTE LA DURÉE DU TRAITEMENT POUR DÉCELER LA PRÉSENCE DE SANG OCCULTE. EN CAS DE THROMBOPÉNIE, SUIVRE DE PRÈS L'ÉTAT DU PATIENT. SI LA NUMÉRATION PLAQUETTAIRE CHUTE SOUS LE SEUIL DES 50×10^9/L, ON DEVRAIT CESSER D'ADMINISTRER LE FONDAPARINUX. SI LES VALEURS DE L'HÉMATOCRITE OU LES CONCENTRATIONS D'HÉMOGLOBINE CHUTENT SOUDAINEMENT, RECHERCHER LES FOYERS HÉMORRAGIQUES POSSIBLES.

- Épreuves de coagulation: Il n'est pas nécessaire de suivre le temps de céphaline activée (TCA), le temps de coagulation activée, le temps de Quick (TQ) et les rapports normalisés internationaux (RNI) plasmatiques, car le fondaparinux ne modifie pas ces paramètres.
- Cet agent peut provoquer l'élévation des concentrations d'AST et d'ALT ou une hypokaliémie.

Toxicité et surdosage: Un saignement mineur nécessite rarement un traitement spécifique, et il suffit en général de réduire la posologie ou de retarder l'administration des doses suivantes. En cas de surdosage entraînant des complications hémorragiques, on doit cesser le traitement et rechercher la cause primaire de l'hémorragie, puis amorcer le traitement approprié.

F

DIAGNOSTICS INFIRMIERS POSSIBLES

- Irrigation tissulaire inefficace (Indications).
- Risque d'accident (Effets secondaires).
- Connaissances insuffisantes sur le traitement médicamenteux (Enseignement au patient et à ses proches).

INTERVENTIONS INFIRMIÈRES

- **SC:** Administrer profondément dans le tissu SC uniquement. Alterner les points d'injection entre les sections antérolatérales gauche et droite et postérolatérales gauche et droite de la paroi abdominale. Faire entrer l'aiguille sur toute sa longueur à un angle de 90° dans un pli cutané retenu entre le pouce et l'index; garder le pli cutané pendant toute la durée de l'injection. Ne pas aspirer ni masser. Assurer la rotation des points d'injection chaque jour. NE PAS ADMINISTRER PAR VOIE IM en raison du risque de formation d'hématomes. La solution devrait être transparente; ne pas injecter de solution contenant des particules ou des dépôts.
- En cas de formation excessive d'ecchymoses, il peut s'avérer utile de masser le point d'injection avec un cube de glace avant d'administrer le médicament.
- Pour éviter la perte de médicament, ne pas tenter d'évacuer la petite bulle d'air contenue dans la seringue avant d'injecter la dose.

ENSEIGNEMENT AU PATIENT ET À SES PROCHES

- CONSEILLER AU PATIENT DE SIGNALER IMMÉDIATEMENT À UN PROFESSIONNEL DE LA SANTÉ LES SAIGNEMENTS OU LES ECCHYMOSES INHABITUELS, LES ÉTOURDISSEMENTS, LES DÉMANGEAISONS, LE RASH, LA FIÈVRE, L'ŒDÈME OU LES DIFFICULTÉS RESPIRATOIRES.
- Prévenir le patient que, si la chirurgie est prévue à l'avance, il doit avertir le médecin qu'il prend déjà des médicaments antiplaquettaires ou qui influent sur la coagulation du sang (par exemple, warfarine, acénocoumarol, aspirine, clopidogrel, ticlopidine, dipyridamole) pour que celui-ci puisse évaluer la pertinence de cette médication.
- Prévenir le patient que s'il consulte un autre médecin ou un dentiste pendant le traitement par le fondaparinux, il doit l'informer qu'il est sous traitement par Arixtra.
- Conseiller au patient de ne pas prendre d'aspirine, d'anti-inflammatoires non stéroïdiens ou d'autres médicaments pouvant modifier la coagulation du sang, pendant le traitement au fondaparinux, sans consulter un professionnel de la santé au préalable.
- Conseiller au patient de ne pas cesser le traitement avant la date prévue par le médecin, en raison du risque de formation d'un caillot sanguin dans une veine de la jambe ou dans le poumon. Le médecin évaluera la durée de traitement chez chaque patient.
- Informer le patient qu'il devrait jeter la seringue usagée dans un endroit sûr, inaccessible aux enfants ou aux animaux domestiques.
- Conservation: Conserver les seringues de fondaparinux à une température se situant entre 15 °C et 30 °C. Ne pas réfrigérer ni congeler le médicament. Garder hors de la portée et de la vue des enfants.

VÉRIFICATION DE L'EFFICACITÉ THÉRAPEUTIQUE

L'efficacité du traitement peut être démontrée par: la prévention des troubles thromboemboliques veineux.

FORMOTÉROL

Foradil, Oxeze

CLASSIFICATION:

Bronchodilatateur (agoniste bêta-adrénergique)

Grossesse – catégorie C

INDICATIONS

Traitement et prévention des symptômes des maladies pulmonaires obstructives réversibles, dont l'asthme, chez des patients ≥ 6 ans qui: ont besoin d'un traitement d'entretien biquotidien et à long terme de l'asthme ■ ont parfois besoin de recourir à un bronchodilatateur ■ présentent une bronchoconstriction aiguë (Oxeze seulement) ■ souffrent d'asthme nocturne ■ présentent une bronchoconstriction provoquée par l'effort (Oxeze seulement) ■ Traitement prolongé de la bronchopneumopathie chronique obstructive (BPCO) chez l'adulte, y compris la bronchite chronique et l'emphysème.

MÉCANISME D'ACTION

Accumulation de l'adénosine monophosphate cyclique (AMPc) au niveau des récepteurs bêta-adrénergiques, ce qui entraîne la relaxation des muscles lisses des voies respiratoires ■ Spécificité relative pour les récepteurs bêta$_2$-pulmonaires. ***Effets thérapeutiques:*** Bronchodilatation.

PHARMACOCINÉTIQUE

Absorption: Rapide (inhalation). De 21 à 37 % de la dose administrée se dépose dans les poumons.
Distribution: Inconnue.
Métabolisme et excrétion: Métabolisme majoritairement hépatique. De 6 à 10 % est excrété dans l'urine sous forme inchangée.
Demi-vie: De 8 à 14 heures.

Profil temps-action (bronchodilatation)

	DÉBUT D'ACTION	PIC	DURÉE
Inhalation	1 – 3 min	15 min	12 h

CONTRE-INDICATIONS, PRÉCAUTIONS ET MISES EN GARDE

Contre-indications: Hypersensibilité au formotérol ou au lactose inhalé ■ Tachyarythmies.
Précautions et mises en garde: Maladie cardiovasculaire (cardiopathies ischémiques, hypertension, arythmies cardiaques et insuffisance cardiaque grave) ■ Diabète ■ Hyperthyroïdie ■ Phéochromocytome ■ Usage excessif (risque de tolérance et de bronchospasme paradoxal) ■ **OBST.**: L'innocuité du formotérol n'a pas été établie. Risque d'inhibition des contractions au cours du travail; n'administrer que si les bienfaits possibles pour la mère dépassent les risques auxquels est exposé le fœtus ■ **ALLAITEMENT:** L'innocuité du formotérol n'a pas été établie; n'administrer que si les bienfaits possibles pour la mère dépassent les risques auxquels est exposé le nouveau-né ■ **PÉD.:** Enfants âgés < 6 ans (utilisation au besoin: enfants âgés < 12 ans).

RÉACTIONS INDÉSIRABLES ET EFFETS SECONDAIRES

SNC: étourdissements, fatigue, céphalées, insomnie, malaise, nervosité.
Resp.: BRONCHOSPASME PARADOXAL.
CV: angine, arythmies, hypertension, hypotension, palpitations, tachycardie.
GI: sécheresse de la bouche (xérostomie), nausées.
HÉ: hypokaliémie.
Métab.: hyperglycémie, acidose métabolique.
Loc.: crampes musculaires.
SN: tremblements.
Divers: réactions allergiques incluant l'ANAPHYLAXIE.

INTERACTIONS

Médicament-médicament: L'USAGE CONCOMITANT D'**IMAO**, D'**ANTIDÉPRESSEURS TRICYCLIQUES** OU D'AUTRES **AGENTS QUI PEUVENT ALLONGER L'INTERVALLE QT$_C$** PEUT ENTRAÎNER DES ARYTHMIES GRAVES; UNE EXTRÊME PRUDENCE EST DE MISE ■ Risque accru d'hypokaliémie lors de l'usage concomitant de **théophylline**, de **corticostéroïdes** et de **diurétiques hypokaliémiants** ■ Les **bêtabloquants** peuvent diminuer les effets thérapeutiques du formotérol ■ L'usage concomitant d'**agents adrénergiques** peut accroître les effets adrénergiques du formotérol.

F

VOIES D'ADMINISTRATION ET POSOLOGIE

Traitement d'entretien de l'asthme

- **Inhalation (adultes):** *Foradil:* 1 gélule (12 µg), toutes les 12 heures, à utiliser avec l'inhalateur Aerolizer. La dose quotidienne maximale est de 48 µg. *Oxeze:* de 6 à 12 µg, toutes les 12 heures. La dose quotidienne maximale est de 48 µg.
- **Inhalation (enfants ≥ 6 ans):** *Foradil:* 1 gélule (12 µg), toutes les 12 heures, à utiliser avec l'inhalateur Aerolizer. La dose quotidienne maximale est de 48 µg. *Oxeze:* de 6 à 12 µg, toutes les 12 heures. La dose quotidienne maximale est de 24 µg.

Traitement au besoin (bronchoconstriction aiguë)

- **Inhalation (adultes et adolescents ≥ 12 ans):** *Oxeze:* de 6 à 12 µg, au besoin. La dose quotidienne maximale est de 72 µg.

Prévention du bronchospasme induit par l'effort

- **Inhalation (adultes et enfants ≥ 6 ans):** *Oxeze:* de 6 à 12 µg, au moins 15 minutes avant l'effort.

Traitement prolongé de la BPCO

- **Inhalation (adultes):** *Foradil et Oxeze:* de 12 à 24 µg, toutes les 12 heures.

PRÉSENTATION

Turbuhaler (Oxeze): 6 µg/dose[Pr], 12 µg/dose[Pr] ■ **En association avec:** budésonide (Symbicort) ■ **Gélules pour Aerolizer (Foradil):** 12 µg[Pr].

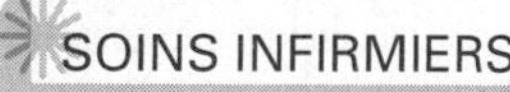

SOINS INFIRMIERS

ÉVALUATION DE LA SITUATION

- Ausculter les bruits respiratoires, mesurer le pouls et la pression artérielle, avant l'administration du médicament et lorsque les concentrations atteignent un pic. Noter la quantité, la couleur et les caractéristiques des expectorations. Rester à l'affût des réactions indésirables chez les patients qui prennent des doses élevées.

- Noter les résultats des tests de la fonction respiratoire, avant de commencer le traitement et à intervalles réguliers pendant toute sa durée, pour évaluer l'efficacité du médicament.
- SUIVRE DE PRÈS L'APPARITION D'UN BRONCHOSPASME PARADOXAL (RESPIRATION SIFFLANTE). S'IL SURVIENT, ARRÊTER L'ADMINISTRATION DU MÉDICAMENT ET PRÉVENIR IMMÉDIATEMENT LE MÉDECIN OU UN AUTRE PROFESSIONNEL DE LA SANTÉ.
- Suivre l'ÉCG à intervalles réguliers tout au long du traitement. L'agent peut allonger l'intervalle QTc.
- RESTER À L'AFFÛT DES SIGNES D'ANAPHYLAXIE (DYSPNÉE, RASH, ŒDÈME LARYNGÉ) PENDANT TOUTE LA DURÉE DU TRAITEMENT.

Tests de laboratoire: Risque d'élévation des concentrations sériques de glucose et de diminution des concentrations sériques de potassium.

DIAGNOSTICS INFIRMIERS POSSIBLES

- Dégagement inefficace des voies respiratoires (Indications).

INTERVENTIONS INFIRMIÈRES

Aerolizer - Foradil: Retirer le capuchon. Pour ouvrir l'inhalateur, tenir le socle fermement et faire pivoter l'embout buccal dans le sens de la flèche. Sortir la gélule de la plaquette alvéolée. Il est important de ne sortir la gélule qu'au moment où elle est prête à utiliser. Placer la gélule dans le compartiment à gélule situé dans le socle de l'inhalateur. Refermer l'embout buccal. En maintenant l'inhalateur en position verticale, appuyer fermement sur les 2 boutons-poussoirs bleus **une seule fois** pour percer la gélule. Relâcher les boutons-poussoirs. Bien que la gélule soit maintenant percée, la poudre ne sera pas libérée tant qu'elle ne sera pas inhalée. (**Remarque:** Il est possible à cette étape que la gélule se fragmente et que de petits fragments de gélatine entrent en contact avec la bouche et la gorge. Cette gélatine est comestible et n'est donc pas nocive. En prenant les mesures suivantes, on peut réduire au minimum le risque de fragmentation de la gélule: percer la gélule une seule fois; conserver les gélules à la température ambiante, dans un endroit sec; conserver les gélules dans la plaquette alvéolée jusqu'à ce qu'elles soient prêtes à l'utilisation.) Expirer à fond. Placer l'embout buccal dans la bouche et incliner légèrement la tête vers l'arrière. Serrer les lèvres autour de l'embout buccal et inspirer de façon régulière aussi profondément que possible. Au moment de l'inspiration, le médicament sera inhalé dans les poumons. Un ronronnement devrait se faire entendre au moment de l'inspiration parce que l'inhalation fait tourner la gélule dans l'inhalateur. Si le ronronnement n'est pas entendu, il se peut que la gélule soit coincée dans le compartiment à gélule. Si tel est le cas, ouvrir l'inhalateur délicatement et dégager la gélule avec les doigts. La gélule ne peut être dégagée en appuyant à répétition sur les boutons-poussoirs. Si on entend un ronronnement, retirer l'inhalateur de la bouche **en retenant la respiration** aussi longtemps que possible sans en être incommodé, puis expirer. Après utilisation, ouvrir l'inhalateur et s'assurer que la gélule est vide. S'il reste de la poudre, refermer l'inhalateur et répéter l'inhalation. Retirer la gélule vide. Fermer l'embout buccal. Remettre le capuchon.

Turbuhaler - Oxeze: Dévisser et enlever le couvercle. **Tourner:** Tenir l'inhalateur à la verticale, molette vers le bas. Pour charger une dose, tourner la molette turquoise le plus loin possible dans une direction, puis la ramener à la position initiale. **Déclic:** Le «déclic» que l'on entend signifie que l'inhalateur est prêt à l'utilisation. **Expirer.** Ne **jamais** expirer dans l'embout buccal. **Inhaler:** Placer l'embout buccal entre les dents et refermer les lèvres. Inspirer **vivement et profondément** par la bouche. Ne pas mordiller l'embout buccal ni le serrer avec les dents. (**Remarque:** Ne pas utiliser l'inhalateur Turbuhaler s'il est endommagé ou si l'embout buccal s'est détaché.) **Avant d'expirer, retirer l'inhalateur de la bouche.** Si plus de 1 dose a été prescrite, répéter les étapes ci-dessus. Revisser le couvercle. Si l'inhalateur Oxeze Turbuhaler tombe par terre ou s'il est agité ou si l'expiration se fait accidentellement dans le dispositif après son chargement, la dose sera perdue. Il faut alors en charger une deuxième et l'inhaler. (**Remarque:** Ne jamais expirer dans l'embout buccal. Toujours revisser le couvercle après l'emploi. Étant donné que la quantité de poudre libérée est très petite, il se peut qu'on ne sente pas le goût du médicament après l'inhalation. Toutefois, si les instructions ont été rigoureusement suivies, la dose a été inhalée.) **Nettoyage:** Nettoyer la partie extérieure de l'embout buccal chaque semaine à l'aide d'un papier-mouchoir sec. Ne jamais utiliser d'eau ni un autre liquide pour le nettoyer. Si du liquide entre dans l'inhalateur, cela peut nuire à son fonctionnement.

ENSEIGNEMENT AU PATIENT ET À SES PROCHES

- Encourager le patient à prendre le formotérol en respectant rigoureusement les recommandations du médecin et à ne pas interrompre le traitement, même s'il se sent mieux, sans en avoir parlé au préalable à un professionnel de la santé. S'il suit un traitement qui prévoit la prise des doses à une heure précise, lui recommander de prendre toute dose omise dès que possible. Préciser qu'il ne doit jamais remplacer une dose manquée par une double dose. Lui conseiller d'utiliser un bronchodilatateur à action rapide si les symptômes se manifestent avant l'heure prévue pour la dose suivante (Foradil) ou d'utiliser le formotérol au besoin, si le médecin le recommande (Oxeze).

- Faire la démonstration du mode d'emploi de l'inhalateur Aerolizer ou de Turbuhaler, selon le cas.

Aerolizer:

- Expliquer au patient qu'il doit toujours utiliser le nouvel inhalateur qui lui est remis à chaque renouvellement d'ordonnance. Lui recommander de décoller l'étiquette « à utiliser avant le » que le pharmacien a collé sur la boîte et de la coller sur le capuchon de l'inhalateur Aerolizer. Si la date de péremption n'a pas été précisée, il faut compter 4 mois à partir de la date de l'achat, et écrire cette date sur l'étiquette. Insister sur le fait qu'après la date de péremption, il faut utiliser un nouvel inhalateur et une nouvelle plaquette alvéolaire.
- Informer le patient que, dans de rares cas, les gélules peuvent se casser en petits morceaux qui devraient être retenus par le filtre de l'inhalateur. Cependant, il arrive rarement que de petits fragments de médicament pénètrent dans la bouche ou dans la gorge après inhalation. La fragmentation des gélules risque moins de se produire si les conditions de conservation sont respectées rigoureusement, si les capsules sont retirées de la plaquette alvéolaire juste avant l'utilisation et si les gélules ne sont percées qu'une seule fois.
- Recommander au patient de garder à portée de la main un bronchodilatateur à action rapide qu'il peut utiliser en tout temps pour soulager les symptômes des crises aiguës d'asthme (Foradil).
- Recommander au patient de prévenir un professionnel de la santé sans tarder si l'essoufflement n'est pas soulagé par le médicament ou s'il manifeste des nausées, des vomissements, des tremblements, des céphalées, des battements de cœur rapides ou irréguliers ou des troubles du sommeil.
- Conseiller au patient de prévenir un professionnel de la santé s'il ne répond pas à la dose habituelle de formotérol. Dans ce cas, il faut réévaluer son état et la posologie du médicament, et envisager l'administration de corticostéroïdes. Le besoin de recourir plus souvent à l'inhalation pour traiter les symptômes est un indice de maîtrise insuffisante de l'asthme et du besoin d'en réévaluer le traitement.
- Recommander au patient de consulter un professionnel de la santé avant de prendre des médicaments en vente libre, des produits naturels ou d'autres types d'agents utilisés en médecine douce. Lui conseiller de ne pas fumer et d'éviter les autres irritants des voies respiratoires.
- Recommander à la patiente de prévenir un professionnel de la santé si elle pense être enceinte, si elle souhaite le devenir ou si elle allaite.

VÉRIFICATION DE L'EFFICACITÉ THÉRAPEUTIQUE

L'efficacité du traitement peut être démontrée par: la prévention des bronchospasmes ▪ le traitement des bronchoconstrictions aiguës (Oxeze) ▪ le soulagement des symptômes de la BPCO. ✳

F

FOSAMPRÉNAVIR

Telzir

CLASSIFICATION:

Antirétroviral (inhibiteur de la protéase)

Grossesse – catégorie C

INDICATIONS

En association avec d'autres antirétroviraux pour traiter l'infection par le VIH. **Usages non approuvés**: En association avec d'autres antirétroviraux, prophylaxie après une exposition accidentelle au VIH.

MÉCANISME D'ACTION

Inhibition de l'activité de la protéase du VIH et prévention du clivage des polyprotéines virales. ***Effets thérapeutiques:*** Augmentation du nombre de cellules CD4 et réduction de la charge virale, ce qui ralentit l'évolution de l'infection par le VIH et en diminue les séquelles.

PHARMACOCINÉTIQUE

Absorption: Le fosamprénavir est un promédicament. À la suite de l'administration par voie orale, il est rapidement transformé en amprénavir par la paroi intestinale.

Distribution: La pénétration dans les érythrocytes dépend de la concentration.

Métabolisme et excrétion: Métabolisme majoritairement hépatique (par le système enzymatique du CYP3A4). L'excrétion rénale est minime.

Demi-vie: 7,7 heures.

Profil temps-action

	DÉBUT D'ACTION	PIC	DURÉE
PO	rapide	1,5 - 4 h	12 - 24 h

CONTRE-INDICATIONS, PRÉCAUTIONS ET MISES EN GARDE

Contre-indications: Hypersensibilité au médicament ■ Insuffisance hépatique grave ■ Usage concomitant de flécaïnide, de propafénone, de rifampine, de dérivés de l'ergot (dihydroergotamine, ergonovine, ergotamine), de pimozide, de cisapride, de midazolam, de diazépam, de flurazépam ou de triazolam.

Précautions et mises en garde: Nombreuses interactions médicamenteuses ■ Hypersensibilité aux sulfamides (risque de réaction croisée) ■ Hémophilie (risque accru de saignements) ■ Diabète (risque d'aggravation de l'hyperglycémie) ■ **GÉR.**: Tenir compte de la diminution de la masse corporelle et de l'insuffisance hépatique et cardiaque, liées au vieillissement, ainsi que des maladies concomitantes et des autres traitements médicamenteux ■ Insuffisance hépatique de légère à modérée ■ Prise concomitante de médicaments métabolisés par le système enzymatique CYP3A4 ou qui l'influencent (la surveillance des concentrations sériques et la modification des doses ou des intervalles posologiques peuvent être de mise) ■ **OBST., PÉD.**: Grossesse, allaitement, enfants < 18 ans (l'innocuité du médicament n'a pas été établie; l'allaitement est déconseillé aux patientes infectées par le VIH).

EXTRÊME PRUDENCE: ADMINISTRATION CONCOMITANTE D'AMIODARONE, DE LIDOCAÏNE PAR VOIE PARENTÉRALE, D'ANTIDÉPRESSEURS TRICYCLIQUES OU DE QUINIDINE (RISQUE D'INTERACTIONS MÉDICAMENTEUSES POUVANT METTRE LA VIE DU PATIENT EN DANGER).

RÉACTIONS INDÉSIRABLES ET EFFETS SECONDAIRES

En association avec d'autres antirétroviraux.

SNC: céphalées, fatigue, troubles thymiques.

GI: diarrhée, nausées, vomissements, douleurs abdominales, élévation des concentrations d'enzymes hépatiques.

Tég.: rash.

End.: intolérance au glucose, hyperglycémie.

Hémat.: neutropénie.

Métab.: modification de la distribution du tissu adipeux, élévation des taux de triglycérides.

Divers: réactions allergiques, comprenant le SYNDROME DE STEVENS-JOHNSON, syndrome de reconstitution immunitaire.

INTERACTIONS

Médicament-médicament: L'amprénavir, la fraction active de la molécule de fosamprénavir, est métabolisé par le CYP3A4; il inhibe également ce système enzymatique. L'effet de tout autre **médicament qui est métabolisé ou influencé par ce système** peut être modifié par l'usage concomitant ■ L'**amprénavir** et le fosamprénavir ne doivent pas être utilisés en concomitance, car une telle administration n'apporte aucun bienfait, alors qu'elle augmente le risque de toxicité ■ L'USAGE CONCOMITANT DE **FLECAÏNIDE**, DE **PROPAFÉNONE**, DE **RIFAMPINE**, DE **DÉRIVÉS DE L'ERGOT** (**DIHYDROERGOTAMINE**, **ERGOTAMINE**, **ERGONOVINE**), DE **PIMOZIDE**, DE **CISAPRIDE**, DE **DIAZÉPAM**, DE **FLURAZÉPAM**, DE **MIDAZOLAM** OU DE **TRIAZOLAM** PEUT ENTRAÎNER DES RÉACTIONS INDÉSIRABLES GRAVES POUVANT ÊTRE MORTELLES, NOTAMMENT ARYTHMIES, SÉDATION EXCESSIVE, MYOPATHIE OU PERTE DE LA RÉPONSE VIROLOGIQUE, ET IL EST CONTRE-INDIQUÉ ■ Les concentrations sanguines du médicament sont abaissées par l'**éfavirenz** (en cas d'usage concomitant, l'ajout de ritonavir pourrait s'avérer nécessaire), le **lopinavir/ritonavir**, le **saquinavir**, la **carbamazépine**, le **phénobarbital**, la **phénytoïne**, la **dexaméthasone** et les **antagonistes des récepteurs H_2 de l'histamine**; rester à l'affût de la diminution de l'effet antirétroviral ■ Les concentrations sont élevées par l'**abacavir** et l'**indinavir** ■ L'administration concomitante de **delavirdine** entraîne l'élévation des concentrations du médicament et la diminution des concentrations de delavirdine (la prise concomitante n'est pas recommandée) ■ L'agent peut abaisser le taux de **méthadone** ■ Élévation des concentrations et risque accru de toxicité lors de l'usage concomitant d'**amiodarone**, de **lidocaïne**, de **quinidine** (suivre de près les concentrations sanguines), de **kétoconazole** et d'**itraconazole** (la dose d'itraconazole ou de kétoconazole ne doit pas dépasser 200 mg/jour, lorsque le fosamprénavir est administré avec le ritonavir ou 400 mg/jour, lorsqu'il est utilisé sans ce dernier), de **rifabutine** (rester à l'affût de la neutropénie, diminuer la dose de rifabutine de 50 % lors de l'usage concomitant de fosamprénavir ou de 75 % lors de l'usage concomitant de fosamprénavir avec le ritonavir), de **lovastatine** ou de **simvastatine** (la prise concomitante n'est pas recommandée), d'**atorvastatine** (la dose ne doit pas dépasser 20 mg/jour ou envisager l'administration d'un autre inhibiteur de l'HMG-CoA réductase), de **cyclosporine** ou de **tacrolimus** (suivre les concentrations sanguines de l'immunosuppresseur), de **bloqueurs des canaux calciques** (une surveillance clinique est recommandée), de certaines **benzodiazépines** (**alprazolam**, **clorazépate**); (la réduction de la dose de benzodiazépine peut s'avérer nécessaire), de

sildénafil, de **tadalafil** et de **vardénafil** (la prudence est de mise; rester à l'affût des effets toxiques; abaisser la dose de sildénafil à 25 mg, toutes les 48 heures; dans le cas du tadalafil, la dose unique ne doit pas dépasser 10 mg en 72 heures; dans le cas du vardénafil, la dose ne doit pas dépasser 2,5 mg, toutes les 24 heures, sans administration conjointe de ritonavir, ou 2,5 mg, toutes les 72 heures, avec administration conjointe de ritonavir) et d'**antidépresseurs tricycliques** (il est recommandé de suivre de près les concentrations sanguines) ▪ L'agent peut modifier les effets de la **warfarine** (surveiller le RNI) ou des **contraceptifs hormonaux** (utiliser une autre méthode de contraception) ▪ Les **antiacides** et la **didanosine** (en raison du tampon qu'elle contient) peuvent réduire l'absorption du médicament (espacer les administrations de 1 heure).

Médicament-produits naturels: L'usage concomitant de **millepertuis** est contre-indiqué; risque de diminution des concentrations sanguines et de la réponse virologique.

VOIES D'ADMINISTRATION ET POSOLOGIE

- **PO (adultes)**: 1 400 mg, 1 fois par jour avec du ritonavir à 200 mg, 1 fois par jour, ou 700 mg, 2 fois par jour avec du ritonavir à 100 mg, 2 fois par jour. Si l'on ajoute l'éfavirenz au régime uniquotidien contenant le fosamprénavir et le ritonavir, il faudrait ajouter 100 mg de ritonavir de plus (au total, 300 mg).

PRÉSENTATION

Comprimés: 700 mg[Pr] ▪ **Suspension buvable**: 50 mg/mL[Pr].

SOINS INFIRMIERS

ÉVALUATION DE LA SITUATION

- Évaluer le patient tout au long du traitement pour déceler tout changement au niveau de l'aggravation des symptômes de l'infection par le VIH ainsi que l'apparition des symptômes d'infections opportunistes.
- Rester à l'affût des allergies aux sulfamides. Il y a risque de sensibilité croisée.
- RECHERCHER LES RÉACTIONS CUTANÉES TOUT AU LONG DU TRAITEMENT. Ces réactions peuvent être graves et même mortelles. Arrêter le traitement en cas de réactions graves ou de rash modéré s'accompagnant de symptômes généraux.
- Si une patiente enceinte est exposée à des antirétroviraux, l'inscrire dans le registre des femmes exposées aux antirétroviraux pendant leur grossesse, en composant le 1-800-258-4263.

***Tests de laboratoire*:**

- Suivre la charge virale et le nombre de cellules CD4 à intervalles réguliers tout au long du traitement.
- L'agent peut élever la glycémie et les taux de triglycérides.
- Il peut élever les taux d'AST et d'ALT.
- Il peut provoquer une neutropénie.

DIAGNOSTICS INFIRMIERS POSSIBLES

- Risque d'infection (Indications).
- Non-observance du traitement médicamenteux (Enseignement au patient et à ses proches).

INTERVENTIONS INFIRMIÈRES

PO: On peut administrer l'agent avec ou sans aliments.

- La suspension doit être prise sans aliments et à jeun. Elle doit être conservée entre 2 °C et 30 °C. Ne pas la congeler. Il faut la mettre au rebut 28 jours après l'ouverture du flacon.

ENSEIGNEMENT AU PATIENT ET À SES PROCHES

- Insister sur le fait qu'il est important de prendre le fosamprénavir en suivant rigoureusement les recommandations du médecin. Recommander au patient de lire les renseignements destinés au patient avant de commencer le traitement et à chaque renouvellement d'ordonnance. Le fosamprénavir doit toujours être pris en association avec d'autres antirétroviraux. Prévenir le patient qu'il ne doit prendre que la quantité de médicament qui lui a été prescrite et qu'il ne doit pas arrêter de prendre ce médicament avant d'avoir consulté un professionnel de la santé au préalable. Lui expliquer qu'il doit prendre toute dose manquée aussitôt que possible et revenir ensuite à son horaire habituel. L'informer qu'il ne faut jamais remplacer une dose manquée par une double dose.
- Prévenir le patient qu'il ne doit pas donner le fosamprénavir à d'autres personnes.
- Informer le patient que l'agent ne guérit pas le sida ni ne prévient les infections associées ou opportunistes. Il ne réduit pas le risque de transmission du VIH à d'autres personnes par les rapports sexuels ou par la contamination du sang. Inciter le patient à utiliser un condom et à éviter le partage d'aiguilles ou les dons de sang pour prévenir la propagation du VIH. Prévenir le patient que les effets de long cours du fosamprénavir sont pour le moment inconnus.

- Insister sur le fait qu'il est important d'informer tous les professionnels de la santé de tous les médicaments pris couramment et qu'il ne faut pas prendre de médicaments d'ordonnance ou en vente libre ni de produits naturels sans avoir consulté un professionnel de la santé au préalable en raison du risque d'interactions médicamenteuses graves.
- Prévenir le patient qu'il peut se produire une redistribution ou une accumulation de graisses corporelles en association avec le traitement antirétroviral, dont les causes et les conséquences à long terme sur la santé sont actuellement inconnues.
- Prévenir la patiente que l'agent peut diminuer l'efficacité des contraceptifs hormonaux; lui conseiller d'utiliser une méthode de contraception non hormonale tout au long du traitement.
- Conseiller au patient de consulter un professionnel de la santé si des nausées, des vomissements, la diarrhée ou un rash surviennent.
- Insister sur l'importance des numérations globulaires et des examens de suivi réguliers permettant de déterminer les progrès du traitement et de surveiller les effets secondaires.

VÉRIFICATION DE L'EFFICACITÉ THÉRAPEUTIQUE

L'efficacité du traitement peut être démontrée par: le ralentissement de l'évolution de l'infection par le VIH et la diminution du nombre d'infections opportunistes chez les patients infectés ■ la diminution de la charge virale et l'augmentation du nombre de CD4. ✳

FOSCARNET

Ce médicament n'est pas commercialisé au Canada. Disponible par l'intermédiaire du Programme d'accès spécial de Santé Canada.

CLASSIFICATION:
Antiviral

Grossesse – catégorie C

INDICATIONS

Usages non approuvés: Traitement de la rétinite provoquée par le cytomégalovirus (CMV) chez les patients infectés par le VIH ■ Traitement de l'herpès mucocutané résistant à l'acyclovir, chez les patients immunodéprimés.

MÉCANISME D'ACTION

Prévention de la réplication virale par inhibition de l'ADN-polymérase virale et de la transcriptase inverse.

Effets thérapeutiques: Action virostatique contre les virus sensibles incluant le CMV.

PHARMACOCINÉTIQUE

Absorption: Biodisponibilité à 100 % (IV).

Distribution: Le médicament pénètre en quantités variables dans le liquide céphalorachidien. Il peut se concentrer dans les os et en être libéré lentement.

Métabolisme et excrétion: De 80 à 90 % est excrété à l'état inchangé dans l'urine.

Demi-vie: De 3 à 6 heures (chez les patients ayant une fonction rénale normale). Une demi-vie plus longue, de l'ordre de 90 heures, peut traduire la libération du médicament des os.

Profil temps-action

	DÉBUT D'ACTION	PIC	DURÉE
IV	rapide	fin de la perfusion	8 - 24 h

CONTRE-INDICATIONS, PRÉCAUTIONS ET MISES EN GARDE

Contre-indications: Hypersensibilité.

Précautions et mises en garde: Insuffisance rénale (réduire la dose si la Cl_{Cr} se situe entre 1,4 et 1,6 mL/min/kg) ■ Administration concomitante de médicaments néphrotoxiques ■ Antécédents de convulsions ■ **OBST., ALLAITEMENT, PÉD.:** L'innocuité de l'agent n'a pas été établie.

RÉACTIONS INDÉSIRABLES ET EFFETS SECONDAIRES

SNC: CONVULSIONS, céphalées, anxiété, confusion, étourdissements, fatigue, malaises, dépression, faiblesse.

ORLO: conjonctivite, douleurs oculaires, anomalies de la vision.

Resp.: toux, dyspnée.

CV: douleurs thoraciques, anomalies de l'ÉCG, œdème, palpitations.

GI: diarrhée, nausées, vomissements, douleurs abdominales, altération du goût, anorexie, constipation, dyspepsie.

GU: insuffisance rénale, albuminurie, dysurie, nycturie, polyurie, rétention urinaire.

Tég.: sécrétion accrue de sueur, prurit, rash, ulcérations cutanées.

HÉ: hypocalcémie, hypokaliémie, hypomagnésémie, hyperphosphatémie, hypophosphatémie.

Hémat.: anémie, granulopénie, leucopénie, thrombopénie.

Locaux: douleur ou inflammation au point d'injection.

Loc.: arthralgie, myalgie, douleurs lombaires, contractions musculaires involontaires.

SN: ataxie, hypoesthésie, neuropathie, paresthésie, tremblements.

Divers: fièvre, frissons, syndrome pseudogrippal, lymphome, sarcome.

INTERACTIONS

Médicament-médicament: L'administration concomitante de **pentamidine** par voie parentérale peut provoquer une hypocalcémie grave mettant la vie du patient en danger ■ Risque accru de néphrotoxicité lors de l'administration simultanée d'autres **agents néphrotoxiques (amphotéricine B, aminosides)**.

VOIES D'ADMINISTRATION ET POSOLOGIE

- **IV (adultes)**: *Rétinite provoquée par le CMV* – initialement, 60 mg/kg, toutes les 8 heures, ou 90 mg/kg, toutes les 12 heures, pendant 2 à 3 semaines, puis de 90 à 120 mg/kg par jour en une seule dose. En cas d'insuffisance rénale de quelque gravité que ce soit, réduire la dose; *herpès* – 40 mg/kg, toutes les 8 à 12 heures, pendant 2 à 3 semaines ou jusqu'à la guérison. En cas d'insuffisance rénale de quelque gravité que ce soit, réduire la dose.

PRÉSENTATION

Ce médicament n'est pas commercialisé au Canada.
Solution pour injection: 24 mg/mL (fiole de 250 mL).

SOINS INFIRMIERS

ÉVALUATION DE LA SITUATION

Rétinite à CMV:

- Avant de commencer le traitement par le foscarnet, il faut établir le diagnostic de rétinite à CMV par ophtalmoscopie. On doit également effectuer un examen ophtalmoscopique au terme du traitement d'induction et toutes les 4 semaines pendant le traitement d'entretien.
- On peut faire des cultures de CMV (à partir des prélèvements d'urine, de sang et de sécrétions de la gorge) avant de commencer l'administration du médicament. Toutefois, des résultats négatifs après la mise en culture des CMV n'écartent pas la possibilité qu'une rétinite à CMV soit présente.

Herpès: Évaluer les lésions avant le traitement et tous les jours pendant toute sa durée.

Tests de laboratoire:

- Noter les concentrations sériques de créatinine avant le début du traitement, 2 ou 3 fois par semaine pendant le traitement d'induction et au moins toutes les semaines au cours du traitement d'entretien. Noter la clairance de la créatinine en l'espace de 24 heures, avant le traitement et à intervalles réguliers pendant toute sa durée. Si la clairance de la créatinine chute en dessous de 0,4 mL/min/kg, il faut arrêter l'administration du foscarnet.
- Mesurer les concentrations sériques de calcium, de magnésium, de potassium et de phosphore avant le début du traitement, 2 ou 3 fois par semaine au cours du traitement d'induction et au moins toutes les 1 ou 2 semaines au cours du traitement d'entretien. Le foscarnet peut réduire ces concentrations.
- Le foscarnet peut entraîner l'anémie, la granulopénie, la leucopénie et la thrombopénie. Il peut aussi élever les concentrations d'AST et d'ALT et entraîner un rapport albumine-globuline anormal.

DIAGNOSTICS INFIRMIERS POSSIBLES

- Risque d'infection (Indications).
- Connaissances insuffisantes sur le traitement médicamenteux (Enseignement au patient et à ses proches).

INTERVENTIONS INFIRMIÈRES

- Avant d'amorcer la première perfusion, il faut noter la diurèse et hydrater adéquatement le patient en lui administrant de 750 à 1 000 mL de NaCl 0,9 % ou de D5%E, puis, lors de l'administration de chaque dose, on doit aussi lui administrer de 750 à 1 000 mL de ces solutés, en même temps que de 90 à 120 mg/kg de foscarnet, ou 500 mL en même temps que de 40 à 60 mg/kg de foscarnet pour prévenir la toxicité rénale.

Perfusion intermittente:

- On peut administrer le médicament par une tubulure centrale dans une solution standard de 24 mg/mL non diluée. Si l'on administre la solution par une tubulure périphérique, *il faut la diluer* jusqu'à une concentration de 12 mg/mL dans une solution de D5%E ou de NaCl 0,9 %, afin de prévenir l'irritation veineuse. Ne pas administrer la solution si elle a changé de couleur ou si elle contient des particules. Utiliser la solution dans les 24 heures qui suivent la dilution. Consulter les directives du fabricant avant de reconstituer la préparation.
- On calcule la dose selon le poids du patient. Afin de prévenir le surdosage, on peut jeter la solution en excès avant d'administrer le médicament.
- Les patients dont la rétinite à CMV évolue pendant le traitement d'entretien peuvent être soumis à un nouveau traitement d'induction, suivi d'un traitement d'entretien.

Vitesse d'administration:

- Administrer la préparation à un débit maximal de 1 mg/kg/min. Il faut perfuser les doses de 40 ou de 60 mg/kg en au moins 1 heure, celles de 90 mg/kg, en 1,5 à 2 heures, et la dose d'entretien de 90 à 120 mg/kg, en 2 heures.
- Utiliser une pompe à perfusion pour assurer le débit exact.

Compatibilité (tubulure en Y): aldesleukine ▪ amikacine ▪ aminophylline ▪ ampicilline ▪ aztréonam ▪ benzquinamide ▪ céfazoline ▪ céfopérazone ▪ céfoxitine ▪ ceftazidime ▪ ceftizoxime ▪ ceftriaxone ▪ céfuroxine ▪ chloramphénicol ▪ cimétidine ▪ clindamycine ▪ dexaméthasone ▪ dopamine ▪ érythromycine, lactobionate d' ▪ fluconazole ▪ flucytosine ▪ furosémide ▪ gentamicine ▪ héparine ▪ hydrocortisone ▪ hydromorphone ▪ imipénem/cilastatine ▪ métoclopramide ▪ métronidazole ▪ miconazole ▪ morphine ▪ nafcilline ▪ oxacilline ▪ pénicilline G potassique ▪ phénytoïne ▪ pipéracilline ▪ ranitidine ▪ ticarcilline/clavulanate ▪ tobramycine.

Incompatibilité (tubulure en Y): Le fabricant ne recommande pas l'administration du foscarnet dans la même tubulure de perfusion IV par laquelle passent d'autres médicaments ou solutions sauf une solution de D5%E ou de NaCl 0,9 % ▪ acyclovir ▪ amphotéricine B ▪ diazépam ▪ digoxine ▪ diphenhydramine ▪ dobutamine ▪ dropéridol ▪ ganciclovir ▪ halopéridol ▪ leucovorine ▪ midazolam ▪ pentamidine ▪ prochlorpérazine ▪ prométhazine ▪ trimétrexate.

ENSEIGNEMENT AU PATIENT ET À SES PROCHES

- Expliquer au patient que le foscarnet ne guérit pas la rétinite à CMV. La rétinite peut évoluer chez les patients qui présentent un déficit immunitaire pendant et après le traitement. Conseiller au patient de se soumettre à des examens ophtalmiques à intervalles réguliers.
- Recommander au patient de signaler sans tarder à un professionnel de la santé les picotements autour de la bouche, l'engourdissement des membres ou la paresthésie, symptômes qui peuvent se manifester pendant la perfusion ou après celle-ci. Si ces signes de déséquilibre électrolytique surviennent pendant l'administration du médicament, il faut arrêter la perfusion et obtenir immédiatement du laboratoire des échantillons permettant de déterminer les concentrations sériques d'électrolytes.
- Insister sur l'importance des examens de suivi fréquents permettant de suivre la fonction rénale et les concentrations d'électrolytes.

VÉRIFICATION DE L'EFFICACITÉ THÉRAPEUTIQUE

L'efficacité du traitement peut être démontrée par: la résolution des symptômes de la rétinite à CMV chez les patients atteints du sida ▪ la formation d'une croûte sur les lésions et la cicatrisation des lésions en cas d'infections herpétiques. ✳

FOSINOPRIL,

voir Inhibiteurs de l'enzyme de conversion de l'angiotensine (IECA)

FOSPHÉNYTOÏNE,

voir Phénytoïne

FRAGMENTS D'ANTICORPS SPÉCIFIQUES DE LA DIGOXINE [Fab (OVINS)]

Digibind

CLASSIFICATION:

Antidote (digoxine, digitoxine)

Grossesse – catégorie C

INDICATIONS

Traitement du surdosage massif (mettant la vie du patient en danger) par la digoxine ou la digitoxine.

MÉCANISME D'ACTION

Fragments Fab d'anticorps d'origine ovine qui se fixent à la digoxine ou à la digitoxine du sang et favorisent leur élimination. ***Effets thérapeutiques:*** Liaison à la digoxine ou à la digitoxine, ce qui en favorise l'élimination, prévenant ainsi les effets toxiques du surdosage.

PHARMACOCINÉTIQUE

Absorption: L'administration est réservée à la voie IV; dans ce cas, la biodisponibilité est à 100 %.

Distribution: Tous les espaces extracellulaires.

Métabolisme et excrétion: Excrétion rénale sous forme de complexe lié (fragment Fab d'anticorps spécifique de la digoxine plus digoxine ou digitoxine).

Demi-vie: De 14 à 20 heures.

Profil temps-action
(renversement des arythmies et de l'hyperkaliémie; le renversement de l'effet inotrope peut prendre plusieurs heures)

	DÉBUT D'ACTION	PIC	DURÉE
IV	30 min (variable)	inconnu	plusieurs jours

CONTRE-INDICATIONS, PRÉCAUTIONS ET MISES EN GARDE

Contre-indications: Aucune contre-indication connue.

Précautions et mises en garde: Hypersensibilité connue aux protéines ou aux produits d'origine ovine (mouton) ■ Risque de réactions anaphylactiques ou d'hypersensibilité ■ Allergie à la papaïne, à la chymopapaïne ou à d'autres extraits de papaye (risque plus élevé de réactions allergiques) ■ Patients ayant déjà reçu un traitement avec des fragments d'anticorps spécifiques de la digoxine (risque plus élevé de réactions allergiques) ■ Insuffisance rénale ■ Le suivi de la kaliémie s'impose ■ **OBST., ALLAITEMENT, PÉD.**: L'innocuité du médicament n'a pas été établie.

RÉACTIONS INDÉSIRABLES ET EFFETS SECONDAIRES

CV: fibrillation auriculaire rebond, insuffisance cardiaque rebond.

HÉ: HYPOKALIÉMIE.

Divers: RÉACTIONS D'HYPERSENSIBILITÉ, ANAPHYLAXIE, fièvre.

INTERACTIONS

Médicament-médicament: L'agent inhibe la réponse à la **digoxine** ou à la **digitoxine**.

VOIES D'ADMINISTRATION ET POSOLOGIE

38 mg de fragments d'anticorps (Fab) spécifiques de la digoxine se lient à 0,5 mg de digitoxine ou de digoxine. Chaque fiole contient 38 mg de fragments d'anticorps (Fab) spécifiques de la digoxine. Une fois qu'on a déterminé la dose (en mg) nécessaire chez l'adulte, on doit la transformer en nombre de fioles à administrer en arrondissant à la fiole suivante près.

Cas d'ingestion aiguë d'une quantité déterminée

- **IV (adultes et enfants)**: *Ingestion de digoxine en comprimés ou en solution orale ou administration de digoxine par voie IM* – dose de fragments d'anticorps (Fab) spécifiques de la digoxine à administrer (en mg) = dose de digoxine ingérée (mg) × 0,8 ÷ 0,5 × 38. *Administration de digoxine par voie IV ou ingestion de digitoxine en comprimés* – dose de fragments d'anticorps (Fab) spécifiques de la digoxine à administrer (en mg) = dose de digoxine ou digitoxine ingérée (mg) ÷ 0,5 × 38.

Concentrations sériques connues de digoxine ou de digitoxine (CSD) à l'équilibre

- **IV (adultes et enfants)**: *Intoxication par la digoxine* – dose de fragments d'anticorps (Fab) spécifiques de la digoxine à administrer (en mg) = CSD (nmol/L) × 0,781 × poids corporel (kg) ÷ 100 × 38. *Intoxication par la digitoxine* – dose de fragments d'anticorps (Fab) spécifiques de la digoxine à administrer (en mg) = CSD (nmol/L) × 0,765 × poids corporel (kg) ÷ 1 000 × 38.

Chez les enfants et les adultes, il faudrait administrer les doses approximatives suivantes d'anticorps (Fab) spécifiques de la digoxine, en fonction des concentrations sériques de digoxine à l'équilibre.

Dose approximative de fragments d'anticorps (Fab) spécifiques de la digoxine en mg ou en nombre de fioles (f) d'après la concentration sérique de digoxine à l'état d'équilibre

POIDS CORPOREL (kg)	CONCENTRATIONS SÉRIQUES DE DIGOXINE À L'ÉQUILIBRE (EN nmol/L)						
	1	2	4	8	12	16	20
1	0,3 mg	0,6 mg	1,2 mg	2,5 mg	4 mg	5 mg	6 mg
3	1 mg	2 mg	4 mg	8 mg	11 mg	15 mg	18 mg
5	1,5 mg	3 mg	6 mg	12 mg	18 mg	24 mg	30 mg
10	3 mg	6 mg	12 mg	24 mg	36 mg	48 mg	60 mg
20	6 mg	12 mg	24 mg	48 mg	72 mg	95 mg	119 mg
40	0,5 f	1 f	2 f	3 f	4 f	5 f	7 f
60	0,5 f	1 f	2 f	4 f	6 f	8 f	10 f
70	1 f	2 f	3 f	5 f	7 f	9 f	11 f
80	1 f	2 f	3 f	5 f	8 f	10 f	13 f
100	1 f	2 f	4 f	7 f	10 f	13 f	16 f

Tableau tiré de la monographie du produit (CPS 2007).

Cas d'ingestion aiguë d'une quantité indéterminée

- **IV (adultes)**: 760 mg (20 fioles).
- **IV (enfants)**: Commencer par 380 mg (10 fioles). Après que le médecin a observé la réaction du patient, il peut décider de poursuivre le traitement avec 10 fioles de plus, au besoin.

Cas d'intoxication pendant un traitement prolongé (patients en état de détresse aiguë ou chez qui on ignore la CSD)

- **IV (adultes)**: 228 mg (6 fioles).
- **IV (enfants ≤ 20 kg))**: 38 mg (1 fiole), habituellement.

PRÉSENTATION

38 mg de fragments d'anticorps (Fab) spécifiques de la digoxine/fiole[Pr].

F

SOINS INFIRMIERS

ÉVALUATION DE LA SITUATION

- Examiner l'ÉCG, mesurer le pouls, la pression artérielle et la température avant le traitement et pendant toute sa durée. Chez les patients souffrant de fibrillation auriculaire, la réponse ventriculaire peut être rapide en raison de la diminution des concentrations de digoxine ou de digitoxine.
- Suivre de près les signes suivants qui indiquent l'aggravation de l'insuffisance cardiaque: œdème périphérique, dyspnée, râles et crépitations, gain pondéral.

F

Tests de laboratoire:

- Noter les concentrations sériques de digoxine ou de digitoxine avant d'administrer la préparation.
- NOTER À INTERVALLES FRÉQUENTS DURANT TOUTE LA DURÉE DU TRAITEMENT LES CONCENTRATIONS SÉRIQUES DE POTASSIUM. AVANT LE TRAITEMENT, L'HYPERKALIÉMIE ACCOMPAGNE HABITUELLEMENT L'ÉTAT TOXIQUE. LES CONCENTRATIONS PEUVENT DIMINUER RAPIDEMENT; TRAITER L'HYPOKALIÉMIE SANS TARDER.
- Les concentrations sériques de digoxine ou de digitoxine non liée chutent rapidement après l'administration de la préparation. Les concentrations sériques totales s'élèvent brusquement après l'administration, mais comme elles sont liées aux molécules des fragments (Fab), elles sont inactives. Elles diminueront jusqu'à des valeurs infimes en l'espace de plusieurs jours. Les données sur les concentrations sériques de digoxine ou de digitoxine ne sont pas valables pendant les 5 à 7 jours qui suivent l'administration de l'agent.

DIAGNOSTICS INFIRMIERS POSSIBLES

- Connaissances insuffisantes sur le traitement médicamenteux (Enseignement au patient et à ses proches).

INTERVENTIONS INFIRMIÈRES

- Durant l'administration de cet agent, garder à portée de la main le matériel et les médicaments nécessaires à la réanimation cardiorespiratoire.
- Attendre plusieurs jours avant de redigitaliser le patient pour que les fragments (Fab) puissent être complètement éliminés de l'organisme.

Dose-test:

- En cas de risque élevé d'allergie aux fragments d'anticorps spécifiques de la digoxine (patients avec des antécédents d'allergie ou qui ont déjà été traités par des fragments d'anticorps spécifiques de la digoxine) ou aux protéines d'origine ovine, effectuer un test cutané allergologique avant d'administrer l'antidote. Préparer la solution destinée au test cutané en diluant 0,1 mL de la solution reconstituée (9,5 mg/mL) dans 9,9 mL de solution de NaCl 0,9 % pour obtenir une solution de 95 µg/mL (10 mL). Le test peut être administré par injection intradermique ou par scarification. Pour l'administration intradermique, injecter 0,1 mL (9,5 µg) d'antidote. Pour le test par scarification, déposer une goutte de solution sur la peau et faire une incision de 6 mm à travers la goutte à l'aide d'une aiguille stérile. Quelle que soit la méthode utilisée, vérifier 20 minutes plus tard si une papule entourée d'érythème s'est formée. Si le test cutané est positif, n'administrer le médicament qu'en cas d'absolue nécessité. Traiter préalablement le patient avec des corticostéroïdes et de la diphénhydramine. Le médecin devra être prêt à traiter une réaction anaphylactique.

Perfusion intermittente:

- Reconstituer la dose de 38 mg destinée à l'administration par voie IV dans 4 mL d'eau stérile et mélanger délicatement. La concentration de la solution sera de 9,5 mg/mL. On peut effectuer une nouvelle dilution avec une solution de NaCl 0,9 % destinée à la perfusion IV. La solution reconstituée doit être utilisée immédiatement, mais elle est stable pendant 4 heures au réfrigérateur. Consulter les directives du fabricant avant de reconstituer la préparation.
- Chez les nourrissons et les jeunes enfants, suivre de près la surcharge hydrique. Pour administrer de petites doses, on peut diluer le contenu de la fiole de 38 mg/4mL, une fois reconstituée, dans 34 mL de solution de NaCl 0,9 % pour obtenir une concentration de 1 mg/mL (38 mg/38 mL). Consulter les directives du fabricant avant de reconstituer la préparation. Administrer la préparation à l'aide d'une seringue à tuberculine.
- ***Vitesse d'administration:*** Administrer la solution reconstituée par perfusion IV à travers un filtre membranaire ayant une porosité de 0,22 µm, pendant 15 à 30 minutes. Si l'arrêt cardiaque est imminent, on peut administrer la préparation par injection IV directe rapide. Ne pas utiliser cette méthode chez d'autres patients en raison du risque accru de réactions indésirables.

Incompatibilité: Aucune donnée disponible à ce sujet. Ne pas mélanger l'antidote à d'autres médicaments ou solutions.

ENSEIGNEMENT AU PATIENT ET À SES PROCHES

- Expliquer au patient la méthode de traitement et le but de l'intervention.

- Prévenir le patient que s'il présente des signes d'une réaction allergique retardée (érythème, prurit, urticaire) après son départ de l'hôpital, il doit en informer un professionnel de la santé.

VÉRIFICATION DE L'EFFICACITÉ THÉRAPEUTIQUE

L'efficacité du traitement peut être démontrée par: la résolution des signes et des symptômes d'intoxication par la digoxine ou la digitoxine ■ la diminution des concentrations de digoxine ou de digitoxine sans effets secondaires importants. ✳

FUROSÉMIDE,

voir Diurétiques (de l'anse)

GABAPENTINE

Apo-Gabapentin, Dom-Gabapentin, Neurontin, PMS-Gabapentin.

CLASSIFICATION:

Anticonvulsivant

Grossesse – catégorie C

INDICATIONS

Chez l'adulte dont l'état n'est pas stabilisé par le traitement classique, traitement d'appoint de l'épilepsie. **Usages non approuvés:** Traitement de la douleur chronique.

G

MÉCANISME D'ACTION

Mécanisme d'action inconnu. Le médicament pourrait modifier le passage des acides aminés au travers des membranes neuronales. ***Effets thérapeutiques:*** Diminution de la fréquence des crises épileptiques.

PHARMACOCINÉTIQUE

Absorption: Bonne (PO) grâce à un système de transport actif. À des doses plus élevées, le système est saturé et l'absorption du médicament diminue (la biodisponibilité de la gabapentine se situe entre 60 %, pour une dose de 300 mg, et 35 %, pour une dose de 1 600 mg).
Distribution: Le médicament traverse la barrière hématoencéphalique.
Métabolisme et excrétion: Presque tout le médicament est éliminé à l'état inchangé par les reins.
Demi-vie: De 5 à 7 heures (fonction rénale normale); jusqu'à 132 heures en présence d'anurie.

Profil temps-action

	DÉBUT D'ACTION	PIC	DURÉE
PO	rapide	2 – 4 h	inconnue

CONTRE-INDICATIONS, PRÉCAUTIONS ET MISES EN GARDE

Contre-indications: Hypersensibilité.
Précautions et mises en garde: Insuffisance rénale (diminuer la dose ou prolonger l'écart posologique, ou les deux, si la $Cl_{Cr} \leq 60$ mL/min) ■ **GÉR.:** Tenir compte de la diminution de la fonction rénale chez la personne âgée ■ **OBST., ALLAITEMENT, PÉD. (< 12 ANS):** L'innocuité du médicament n'a pas été établie.

RÉACTIONS INDÉSIRABLES ET EFFETS SECONDAIRES

SNC: confusion, somnolence, anxiété, étourdissements, hostilité, malaises, vertiges, faiblesse.
ORLO: vision anormale, nystagmus.
CV: hypertension.
GI: anorexie, flatulence, gingivite.
Loc.: arthralgie.
SN: ataxie, réflexes modifiés, hyperkinésie, paresthésie.
Divers: œdème facial.

INTERACTIONS

Médicament-médicament: Les **antiacides** peuvent diminuer l'absorption de la gabapentine • Risque accru de dépression du SNC lors de l'administration concomitante d'autres **dépresseurs du SNC**.

VOIES D'ADMINISTRATION ET POSOLOGIE

- **PO (adultes et enfants > 12 ans):** L'écart posologique habituel se situe entre 900 et 1 800 mg par jour, administrés en 3 doses fractionnées (les doses ne devraient pas être espacées de plus de 12 heures). On peut amorcer le traitement à 300 mg, 3 fois par jour, ou augmenter la dose de la façon suivante: 1 dose de 300 mg, le premier jour, 2 doses de 300 mg, le deuxième jour, 3 doses de 300 mg, le troisième jour. On peut poursuivre cette adaptation posologique rapide jusqu'à l'obtention de l'effet souhaité.

INSUFFISANCE RÉNALE

- **PO (ADULTES ET ENFANTS > 12 ANS):** *CL_{CR} DE 30 À 60 mL/MIN* – 300 mg, 2 FOIS PAR JOUR; *CL_{CR} DE 15 À 30 mL/MIN* – 300 mg, 1 FOIS PAR JOUR; *CL_{CR} < 15 mL/MIN* – 300 mg, TOUS LES 2 JOURS; LES ADAPTATIONS POSOLOGIQUES PEUVENT ÊTRE POURSUIVIES SELON LA RÉPONSE DU PATIENT AU TRAITEMENT.

PRÉSENTATION

Capsules: 100 mg[Pr], 300 mg[Pr], 400 mg[Pr] ■ **Comprimés:** 600 mg[Pr], 800 mg[Pr].

SOINS INFIRMIERS

ÉVALUATION DE LA SITUATION

Convulsions: Déterminer le siège, la durée et les caractéristiques des convulsions.
Douleur chronique: Évaluer le siège, les caractéristiques et l'intensité de la douleur à intervalles réguliers pendant toute la durée du traitement.

Tests de laboratoire:

- La gabapentine peut entraîner des résultats faussement positifs lors du dosage des protéines urinaires par l'épreuve sur bâtonnet réactif *N-Multistix SG* d'*Ames*; il faudrait opter pour les épreuves de précipitation par l'acide sulfosalicylique.
- Le médicament peut provoquer la leucopénie.

DIAGNOSTICS INFIRMIERS POSSIBLES

- Risque d'accident (Effets secondaires).
- Connaissances insuffisantes sur le traitement médicamenteux (Enseignement au patient et à ses proches).

INTERVENTIONS INFIRMIÈRES

- On peut administrer le médicament sans égard aux repas.
- Avant d'arrêter le traitement, il faudrait réduire graduellement la dose de gabapentine pendant une semaine. Éviter le sevrage brusque, car il peut accroître la fréquence des crises d'épilepsie.

ENSEIGNEMENT AU PATIENT ET À SES PROCHES

- Inciter le patient à respecter rigoureusement la posologie recommandée. S'il doit prendre le médicament 3 fois par jour, il ne devrait pas espacer les doses de plus de 12 heures. S'il n'a pas pu prendre le médicament au moment habituel, il doit le faire dès que possible. S'il reste moins de 2 heures avant la dose suivante, il doit prendre cette dose immédiatement et attendre de 1 à 2 heures avant de prendre la suivante, puis il doit revenir à l'horaire habituel. Prévenir le patient qu'il ne doit pas remplacer une dose manquée par une double dose ni arrêter brusquement la prise de ce médicament, car il risque d'accroître la fréquence des crises d'épilepsie.
- Prévenir le patient qu'il ne doit pas prendre la gabapentine dans les 2 heures qui précèdent ou qui suivent la prise d'un antiacide.
- Prévenir le patient que la gabapentine peut provoquer de la somnolence et des étourdissements. Lui conseiller de ne pas conduire et d'éviter les activités qui exigent sa vigilance jusqu'à ce qu'on ait la certitude que le médicament n'entraîne pas ces effets chez lui. Lui expliquer qu'il ne pourra reprendre la conduite automobile que si le médecin l'y autorise, une fois que les crises ont été maîtrisées.
- Recommander à la patiente d'informer un professionnel de la santé si elle pense être enceinte ou souhaite le devenir, si elle a l'intention d'allaiter ou si elle allaite.
- Recommander au patient qui doit suivre un traitement ou subir une intervention chirurgicale d'avertir le professionnel de la santé qu'il suit un traitement par ce médicament.
- Conseiller au patient de porter sur lui en tout temps une pièce d'identité où sont inscrits sa maladie et son traitement médicamenteux.

VÉRIFICATION DE L'EFFICACITÉ THÉRAPEUTIQUE

L'efficacité du traitement peut être démontrée par: la diminution ou la suppression des crises épileptiques ▪ la baisse d'intensité de la douleur chronique.

GALANTAMINE

Reminyl, Reminyl ER

CLASSIFICATION:

Traitement de la maladie d'Alzheimer (inhibiteur de la cholinestérase)

Grossesse – catégorie B

G

INDICATIONS

Traitement symptomatique de la démence de type Alzheimer d'intensité légère ou modérée.

MÉCANISME D'ACTION

Amélioration de l'activité cholinergique par inhibition de l'acétylcholinestérase. ***Effets thérapeutiques:*** Diminution passagère de certains épisodes de démence associés à la maladie d'Alzheimer ▪ L'agent ne modifie pas l'évolution de la maladie.

PHARMACOCINÉTIQUE

Absorption: Bonne (PO). Biodisponibilité à 88,5 %.
Distribution: Inconnue.
Liaison aux protéines: 18 %.
Métabolisme et excrétion: Métabolisme hépatique (par les CYP2D6, CYP3A4 et la glycuroconjugaison) et excrétion à l'état inchangé dans l'urine (32 %).
Demi-vie: De 8,5 à 9,7 heures.

Profil temps-action (diminution des symptômes)

	Début d'action	Pic	Durée
PO	inconnu	plusieurs semaines	6 semaines†

† Après l'arrêt du traitement, les valeurs initiales se rétablissent.

CONTRE-INDICATIONS, PRÉCAUTIONS ET MISES EN GARDE

Contre-indications: Hypersensibilité à la galantamine, à d'autres dérivés alcaloïdes tertiaires ou à tout autre ingrédient du médicament.
Précautions et mises en garde: Présence d'une maladie cardiaque sous-jacente, particulièrement syndrome de dysfonctionnement sinusal ou anomalies de conduction supraventriculaire (les cholinomimétiques peuvent exercer des effets vagotoniques sur la fréquence cardiaque, p. ex., bradycardie et bloc cardiaque) ▪ Utilisation

concomitante d'un médicament pouvant diminuer la fréquence cardiaque (risque accru de bradycardie) ■ Antécédents de syncope ■ Antécédents d'ulcère, de saignements digestifs ou traitement concomitant par des anti-inflammatoires non stéroïdiens ■ Antécédents de convulsions ■ Antécédents d'asthme grave ou de bronchopneumopathie obstructive ■ **OBST., ALLAITEMENT, PÉD.**: L'innocuité du médicament n'a pas été établie ■ Insuffisance hépatique grave ■ Insuffisance rénale grave (Cl_{Cr} < 9 mL/min) ■ **GÉR.**: Personnes âgées ≥ 85 ans (peu de données sur ce groupe d'âge) ■ Risque accru de mortalité par atteinte cardiovasculaire.

G

RÉACTIONS INDÉSIRABLES ET EFFETS SECONDAIRES

Hémat.: anémie.
SNC: céphalées, dépression, étourdissements, somnolence, fatigue, insomnie, tremblements, CRISES CONVULSIVES.
CV: bradycardie, syncope, douleurs thoraciques.
GI: diarrhée, nausées, anorexie, vomissements, douleurs abdominales, dyspepsie, flatulence.
GU: infection des voies urinaires, incontinence.
Métab.: perte de poids.
SN: tremblements.

INTERACTIONS

Médicament-médicament: La galantamine accentue la relaxation musculaire induite par des **curarisants** comme la **succinylcholine**, administrés pendant une anesthésie ■ La galantamine peut entraver les effets des **agents anticholinergiques** ■ Le médicament augmente les effets cholinergiques du **béthanéchol**, des autres **agonistes cholinergiques** et des autres **inhibiteurs de la cholinestérase** ■ Risque accru d'hémorragie gastro-intestinale lors de l'administration concomitante d'**anti-inflammatoires non stéroïdiens** ■ Le **kétoconazole** (inhibiteur du CYP3A4 et du CYP2D6), la **paroxétine** (inhibiteur du CYP2D6), l'**amitriptyline**, la **fluvoxamine** et la **quinidine** diminuent le métabolisme de la galantamine et peuvent en augmenter les effets.

VOIES D'ADMINISTRATION ET POSOLOGIE

- **PO (adultes)**: *Comprimés de Reminyl* – 4 mg, 2 fois par jour. Après un minimum de 4 semaines, augmenter la dose pour la passer à 8 mg, 2 fois par jour. Si cette dose d'entretien initiale est bien tolérée après un minimum de 4 semaines de plus, on peut envisager une majoration supplémentaire de la posologie pour aller jusqu'à 12 mg, 2 fois par jour. *Capsules à libération prolongée de Reminyl ER* – 8 mg, 1 fois par jour. Après un minimum de 4 semaines, augmenter la dose pour la passer à 16 mg, 1 fois par jour. Si cette dose d'entretien initiale est bien tolérée après un minimum de 4 semaines de plus, on peut envisager une majoration supplémentaire de la posologie pour aller jusqu'à 24 mg, 1 fois par jour.

INSUFFISANCE HÉPATIQUE MODÉRÉE

- COMMENCER LE TRAITEMENT À UNE DOSE DE 4 mg DE REMINYL, 1 FOIS PAR JOUR, PENDANT AU MOINS 1 SEMAINE OU 8 mg DE REMINYL ER, TOUS LES 2 JOURS, PENDANT AU MOINS UNE SEMAINE. ENSUITE, MAJORER LA POSOLOGIE POUR LA PASSER À 4 mg DE REMINYL, 2 FOIS PAR JOUR, OU 8 mg DE REMINYL ER, 1 FOIS PAR JOUR, PENDANT AU MOINS 4 SEMAINES. NE PAS DÉPASSER 16 mg/JOUR.

INSUFFISANCE RÉNALE

- *CL_{CR} DE 9 À 60 mL/MIN* – LA PRUDENCE EST DE MISE LORS DE LA MAJORATION DE LA POSOLOGIE CHEZ CETTE POPULATION. DE PLUS, LA DOSE D'ENTRETIEN NE DEVRAIT GÉNÉRALEMENT PAS DÉPASSER 16 mg PAR JOUR.

PRÉSENTATION

Comprimés: 4 mg^{Pr}, 8 mg^{Pr}, 12 mg^{Pr} ■ **Capsules à libération prolongée**: 8 mg^{Pr}, 16 mg^{Pr}, 24 mg^{Pr}.

SOINS INFIRMIERS

ÉVALUATION DE LA SITUATION

- Évaluer le fonctionnement cognitif (mémoire, attention, raisonnement, langage, capacité à accomplir des tâches simples) à intervalles réguliers pendant toute la durée du traitement.
- Mesurer la fréquence cardiaque à intervalles réguliers pendant toute la durée du traitement. La galantamine peut induire une bradycardie.

DIAGNOSTICS INFIRMIERS POSSIBLES

- Opérations de la pensée perturbées (Indications).
- Risque d'accident (Indications).
- Connaissances insuffisantes sur le traitement médicamenteux (Enseignement au patient et à ses proches).

INTERVENTIONS INFIRMIÈRES

- Le patient devrait maintenir la même dose pendant un minimum de 4 semaines avant de l'augmenter.

PO: Administrer la galantamine de préférence avec les repas du matin et du soir (Reminyl) et avec le repas du matin (Reminyl ER). Il pourrait être nécessaire d'administrer des antiémétiques pour maintenir l'équilibre électrolytique.

ENSEIGNEMENT AU PATIENT ET À SES PROCHES

- Insister sur le fait qu'il est important de prendre la galantamine tous les jours en suivant rigoureusement la posologie recommandée. Si le patient n'a pas pu prendre le médicament au moment habituel, il doit le prendre aussitôt que possible, à moins que ce ne soit presque l'heure prévue pour la dose suivante. Le prévenir qu'il ne doit jamais remplacer une dose manquée par une double dose. Lui expliquer qu'il peut être dangereux de donner ce médicament à une autre personne. Le prévenir qu'il ne doit pas prendre une dose plus élevée que celle prescrite; des doses plus élevées n'augmentent pas les effets bénéfiques, mais peuvent entraîner un plus grand nombre d'effets secondaires.
- Prévenir le patient et ses proches que, chaque fois qu'on interrompt le traitement durant plusieurs jours, il faut le reprendre à la dose quotidienne la plus faible qui soit, puis majorer la posologie jusqu'à l'atteinte de la dose d'entretien en cours.
- Prévenir le patient et ses proches que la galantamine peut provoquer des étourdissements.
- Recommander au patient et à ses proches de prévenir un professionnel de la santé en cas de nausées et de vomissements persistants pendant plus de 7 jours, de diarrhée ou de changement de la couleur des selles, ou encore si de nouveaux symptômes se manifestent ou si les symptômes déjà présents s'aggravent.
- Recommander au patient et à ses proches d'informer tous les professionnels qu'il suit un traitement par ce médicament avant de se soumettre à une intervention chirurgicale ou à un autre traitement.
- Insister sur l'importance des examens de suivi réguliers pour déterminer les effets du traitement.

VÉRIFICATION DE L'EFFICACITÉ THÉRAPEUTIQUE

L'efficacité du traitement peut être démontrée par: l'amélioration du fonctionnement cognitif (mémoire, attention, raisonnement, langage, capacité à accomplir des tâches simples) chez les patients souffrant de la maladie d'Alzheimer. ✳

GANCICLOVIR

Cytovene, Vitrasert

CLASSIFICATION:

Antiviral

Grossesse – catégorie C

INDICATIONS

IV: Traitement de la rétinite à cytomégalovirus (CMV) chez les patients immunodéprimés, y compris ceux présentant une immunosuppression iatrogène à la suite d'une chimiothérapie antinéoplasique ou d'une transplantation d'organe, ou ceux présentant une infection par le VIH (le ganciclovir peut être utilisé en association avec le foscarnet) ■ Prévention de l'infection à CMV chez les patients ayant reçu une greffe, qui sont exposés au risque de contracter ce type de rétinite ■ **PO**: Traitement d'entretien de la rétinite à CMV stabilisée à la suite d'un premier traitement IV chez les patients présentant un déficit immunitaire (y compris ceux qui sont atteints du sida) ■ Prévention de la rétinite à CMV chez les receveurs de greffe d'organe plein, exposés au risque de contracter une infection à CMV.

MÉCANISME D'ACTION

Sous l'action du cytomégalovirus, le ganciclovir est transformé en sa forme active (phosphate de ganciclovir) à l'intérieur de la cellule hôte où il inhibe l'ADN-polymérase virale. ***Effets thérapeutiques:*** Effet antiviral dirigé surtout contre les cellules infectées par le cytomégalovirus.

PHARMACOCINÉTIQUE

Absorption: De 5 à 9 % (PO). Biodisponibilité à 100 % (IV). L'effet de l'implant intravitréen est local.

Distribution: Tout l'organisme; l'agent pénètre dans le liquide céphalorachidien.

Métabolisme et excrétion: 90 % du médicament est excrété à l'état inchangé par les reins.

Demi-vie: 2,9 heures (prolongée en cas d'insuffisance rénale).

Profil temps-action

	Début d'action	Pic	Durée
PO	rapide	1,8 - 3 h	3 - 8 h
IV	rapide	fin de la perfusion	12 - 24 h
Implant intravitréen	rapide	inconnu	5 - 8 mois

CONTRE-INDICATIONS, PRÉCAUTIONS ET MISES EN GARDE

Contre-indications: Hypersensibilité au ganciclovir, au valganciclovir ou à l'acyclovir ■ Ne pas administrer aux patients qui présentent un nombre absolu de neutrophiles (NAN) inférieur à $0,5 \times 10^9$/L, un nombre de plaquettes inférieur à 25×10^9/L ou un taux d'hémoglobine inférieur à 80 g/L.

Précautions et mises en garde: Insuffisance rénale (réduire la dose si la Cl_{Cr} est < 70 mL/min) ■ Personnes âgées (il est recommandé de réduire la dose) ■ Risque de toxicité hématologique ■ Risque de néoplasie ■ **OBST., ALLAITEMENT, PÉD.**: L'innocuité du médicament n'a pas été établie ■ Stérilité temporaire ou permanente probable chez l'homme. Risque de stérilité chez la femme.

RÉACTIONS INDÉSIRABLES ET EFFETS SECONDAIRES

SNC: CONVULSIONS, rêves bizarres, coma, confusion, étourdissements, somnolence, céphalées, malaise, nervosité.
ORLO: décollement de la rétine; *voie intravitréenne seulement* – baisse de l'acuité visuelle, hémorragie vitrée, hyphéma, pointes de pression intraoculaire, opacités du cristallin, anomalies maculaires, modifications des nerfs optiques, uvéite.
Resp.: dyspnée.
CV: arythmies, œdème, hypertension, hypotension.
GI: HÉMORRAGIE GASTRIQUE, douleurs abdominales, élévation des concentrations d'enzymes hépatiques, nausées, vomissements.
GU: suppression de la fonction des gonades, hématurie, toxicité rénale.
Tég.: alopécie, photosensibilité, prurit, rash, urticaire.
End.: hypoglycémie.
Hémat.: neutropénie, thrombopénie, anémie, éosinophilie, leucopénie.
Locaux: douleur ou phlébite au point d'injection IV.
SN: ataxie, tremblements.
Divers: fièvre.

INTERACTIONS

Médicament-médicament: Les **agents antinéoplasiques**, la **radiothérapie** ou la **zidovudine**, administrés simultanément, peuvent augmenter le risque d'aplasie médullaire ■ Le **probénécide** peut augmenter la toxicité du ganciclovir ■ L'administration concomitante d'**imipénem/cilastatine** peut augmenter le risque de convulsions ■ L'administration concomitante d'autres **agents néphrotoxiques**, de **cyclosporine** ou d'**amphotéricine B** augmente le risque de néphrotoxicité ■ Le ganciclovir élève les concentrations sériques de **didanosine** et peut ainsi en augmenter la toxicité.

VOIES D'ADMINISTRATION ET POSOLOGIE

- **IV (adultes)**: *Traitement d'induction* – 5 mg/kg, toutes les 12 heures, pendant 14 à 21 jours. *Traitement d'entretien* – 5 mg/kg, 1 fois par jour, 7 jours par semaine, ou 6 mg/kg, 1 fois par jour, 5 jours par semaine. Si la maladie évolue, on peut administrer cette dose à intervalles de 12 heures. *Prévention chez les receveurs de greffe* – 5 mg/kg, toutes les 12 heures, pendant 7 à 14 jours, puis 5 mg/kg par jour, 7 jours par semaine, ou 6 mg/kg, 5 jours par semaine.
- **PO (adultes)**: *Traitement d'entretien* – après un traitement d'au moins 3 semaines par la solution IV, on peut administrer le médicament par voie orale à raison de 1 000 mg, 3 fois par jour (avec des aliments), ou de 500 mg, toutes les 3 heures, lorsque le patient est éveillé. *Prévention de la rétinite à CMV chez les receveurs de greffe* – 1 000 mg, 3 fois par jour.
- ***INSUFFISANCE RÉNALE:*** CHEZ LES INSUFFISANTS RÉNAUX (CL_{CR} < 70 mL/MIN), ON RECOMMANDE DE RÉDUIRE LA POSOLOGIE. (VOIR LA MONOGRAPHIE DU FABRICANT.)
- **Implant intravitréen (adultes)**: Implant de 4,5 mg.

PRÉSENTATION

Capsules: 250 mg[Pr], 500 mg[Pr] ■ **Poudre pour injection**: 500 mg/fiole[Pr] ■ **Implant intravitréen**: 4,5 mg[Pr].

SOINS INFIRMIERS

ÉVALUATION DE LA SITUATION

- Avant d'administrer le ganciclovir, il faut confirmer le diagnostic de rétinite à cytomégalovirus par ophtalmoscopie.
- Avant de commencer le traitement, prélever des échantillons d'urine, de sang ou de sécrétions de la gorge pour une mise en culture permettant de déceler la présence du cytomégalovirus. Il n'est pas justifié d'écarter le diagnostic de rétinite à cytomégalovirus, même lorsque les résultats sont négatifs. Si les symptômes ne disparaissent pas après plusieurs semaines, il est possible qu'il se soit développé une résistance au ganciclovir. On devrait effectuer des examens ophtalmiques toutes les semaines, pendant la phase d'induction, et toutes les 2 semaines, pendant la phase d'entretien, ou plus fréquemment si la région maculaire ou le nerf optique sont menacés. La rétinite à CMV peut continuer d'évoluer pendant ou après le traitement par le ganciclovir.
- Rester à l'affût des signes suivants d'infection: fièvre, frissons, toux, enrouement, douleurs lombaires ou aux flancs, mictions difficiles ou douloureuses. Prévenir le médecin si ces symptômes se manifestent.
- Surveiller les saignements: saignement des gencives, ecchymoses, pétéchies, présence de sang occulte dans les selles, l'urine ou les vomissements. Éviter les injections par voie IM et la prise de température rectale. Appliquer une pression sur les points de ponction veineuse pendant 10 minutes.

Tests de laboratoire:

- Noter le nombre de neutrophiles et de plaquettes au moins tous les 2 jours, si le ganciclovir est administré 2 fois par jour, et 1 fois par semaine, par la suite. Bien que la granulopénie se manifeste habituellement au cours des 2 premières semaines de traitement, elle peut survenir à tout moment. Ne pas administrer le ganciclovir si le nombre de neutrophiles est < $0,5 \times 10^9$/L et si celui des plaquettes est < 25×10^9/L. Ces valeurs commencent à se rétablir de 3 à 7 jours après l'arrêt du traitement.
- Noter les concentrations d'urée et de créatinine sérique au moins toutes les 2 semaines pendant toute la durée du traitement.
- Suivre les résultats des tests de la fonction hépatique (AST, ALT, bilirubine sérique, phosphatase alcaline) à intervalles réguliers pendant toute la durée du traitement. Le ganciclovir peut en élever les concentrations.
- Le médicament peut entraîner une baisse de la glycémie.

DIAGNOSTICS INFIRMIERS POSSIBLES

- Risque d'infection (Indications, Enseignement au patient et à ses proches).
- Connaissances insuffisantes sur le traitement médicamenteux (Enseignement au patient et à ses proches).

INTERVENTIONS INFIRMIÈRES

- NE PAS CONFONDRE CYTOVENE (GANCICLOVIR) AVEC CYTOSAR (CYTARABINE).
- Préparer la solution sous une hotte à flux laminaire. Porter des vêtements de protection, des gants et un masque lors de la préparation du médicament. Après l'administration, jeter le matériel de perfusion IV dans les contenants réservés à cette fin (voir l'annexe H).
- Ne pas administrer le médicament par voie SC ou IM, en raison des risques d'irritation cutanée grave.

PO: Administrer les capsules avec des aliments.

IV:

- Surveiller le point de perfusion afin de déceler l'apparition d'une phlébite. Pour la prévenir, assurer la rotation des points de perfusion.
- Assurer une hydratation adéquate pendant toute la durée du traitement.

Perfusion intermittente:

- Reconstituer 500 mg de ganciclovir dans 10 mL d'eau stérile pour injection pour obtenir une concentration de 50 mg/mL. Ne pas diluer dans de l'eau bactériostatique contenant des parabènes étant donné qu'un précipité peut se former. Bien agiter le récipient pour dissoudre complètement le médicament. Si la solution change de couleur ou si des particules sont présentes, jeter la fiole. La solution reconstituée est stable pendant 12 heures à la température ambiante; ne pas la réfrigérer.
- Diluer la solution reconstituée dans une des solutions suivantes: D5%E, NaCl 0,9%, solution de Ringer ou solution de lactate de Ringer, jusqu'à une concentration maximale de 10 mg/mL. La solution doit être utilisée dans les 24 heures qui suivent la dilution. Elle peut être réfrigérée, mais non congelée. Consulter les directives du fabricant avant de reconstituer la préparation.

Vitesse d'administration: Administrer lentement, en 1 heure, par une pompe à perfusion munie d'un filtre intégré. Une administration rapide peut augmenter la toxicité.

Compatibilité (tubulure en Y): cisplatine ■ cyclophosphamide ■ énalaprilate ■ filgrastim ■ fluconazole ■ melphalan ■ méthotrexate ■ paclitaxel ■ tacrolimus ■ téniposide ■ thiotépa.

Incompatibilité (tubulure en Y): aldesleukine ■ amifostine ■ aztréonam ■ cytarabine ■ doxorubicine ■ fludarabine ■ foscarnet ■ ondansétron ■ pipéracilline/tazobactam ■ sargramostim ■ vinorelbine.

G

ENSEIGNEMENT AU PATIENT ET À SES PROCHES

- Conseiller au patient de prendre le ganciclovir par voie orale avec des aliments et de respecter rigoureusement la posologie recommandée.
- Expliquer au patient que le ganciclovir ne guérit pas la rétinite à cytomégalovirus. La rétinite peut continuer à évoluer pendant et après le traitement chez les patients présentant un déficit immunitaire. Insister sur l'importance d'un suivi ophtalmique régulier. La durée du traitement préventif est basée sur la durée et la gravité de l'immunosuppression.
- CONSEILLER AU PATIENT DE PRÉVENIR UN PROFESSIONNEL DE LA SANTÉ EN CAS DE FIÈVRE, DE FRISSONS, DE MAUX DE GORGE, D'AUTRES SIGNES D'INFECTION, DE SAIGNEMENT DES GENCIVES, D'ECCHYMOSES, DE PÉTÉCHIES OU DE PRÉSENCE DE SANG DANS L'URINE, LES SELLES OU LES VOMISSEMENTS. PRÉVENIR LE PATIENT QU'IL DOIT ÉVITER LES FOULES ET LES PERSONNES CONTAGIEUSES. LUI CONSEILLER D'UTILISER UNE BROSSE À DENTS À POILS DOUX ET UN RASOIR ÉLECTRIQUE. LE PRÉVENIR ÉGALEMENT QU'IL NE DOIT PAS PRENDRE DE BOISSONS ALCOOLISÉES NI DE PRÉPARATIONS CONTENANT DE L'ASPIRINE OU DES AINS.
- Prévenir la patiente que le ganciclovir peut avoir des effets tératogènes; lui recommander d'utiliser

une méthode contraceptive non hormonale au cours du traitement et au moins 90 jours après.
- Inciter le patient à utiliser un écran solaire et à porter des vêtements protecteurs pour prévenir les réactions de photosensibilité.
- Expliquer au patient qu'il est important de se soumettre à des analyses sanguines fréquentes permettant de suivre de près les numérations globulaires.

VÉRIFICATION DE L'EFFICACITÉ THÉRAPEUTIQUE

L'efficacité du traitement peut être démontrée par: la résolution des symptômes de rétinite à cytomégalovirus chez les patients présentant un déficit immunitaire ▪ la prévention de la rétinite à cytomégalovirus chez les patients greffés, exposés au risque de contracter cette infection. ✳

G

GÉFITINIB

Iressa

CLASSIFICATION:

Antinéoplasique (inhibiteur de l'activation des kinases)

Grossesse – catégorie D

INDICATIONS

Patients atteints du cancer du poumon non à petites cellules, tirant profit de leur traitement courant par le géfitinib et qui sont porteurs d'une tumeur EGFR positive ou de statut inconnu pour ce qui est de l'EGFR.

MÉCANISME D'ACTION

Inhibition de l'activation des kinases contenues dans les récepteurs transmembranaires, dont celui du facteur de croissance épidermique (EGFR-TK). ***Effets thérapeutiques:*** Destruction des cellules à réplication rapide, particulièrement des cellules cancéreuses.

PHARMACOCINÉTIQUE

Absorption: Biodisponibilité à 60 % (PO).

Distribution: Tous les tissus.

Métabolisme et excrétion: Métabolisme majoritairement hépatique (par le système enzymatique du CYP 3A4); l'agent est éliminé dans les fèces; < 4 % est excrété dans l'urine.

Demi-vie: 48 heures.

Profil temps-action

	DÉBUT D'ACTION	PIC	DURÉE
PO	inconnu	inconnu	inconnue

CONTRE-INDICATIONS, PRÉCAUTIONS ET MISES EN GARDE

Contre-indications: Hypersensibilité ▪ Tumeur EGFR négative.

Précautions et mises en garde: Fibrose pulmonaire idiopathique (risque accru de toxicité pulmonaire) ▪ Usage concomitant d'inhibiteurs puissants du système enzymatique du CYP 3A4 (risque accru de toxicité) ▪ Patients à risque de présenter un intervalle QT allongé ▪ **OBST.:** Grossesse et allaitement ▪ **PÉD.:** L'innocuité et l'efficacité de l'agent n'ont pas été établies.

RÉACTIONS INDÉSIRABLES ET EFFETS SECONDAIRES

CNS: faiblesse.

ORLO: croissance aberrante des cils, conjonctivite, érosion de la cornée/ulcérations, douleurs oculaires, diminution de la vision.

CV: œdème périphérique.

Resp.: TOXICITÉ PULMONAIRE, dyspnée.

GI: diarrhée, nausées, vomissements, anorexie, hépatotoxicité, aphtes.

Hémat.: saignements.

Tég.: acné, sécheresse de la peau, rash, prurit.

Métab.: perte de poids.

Divers: réactions allergiques, comprenant l'ŒDÈME ANGIONEUROTIQUE.

INTERACTIONS

Médicament-médicament: Les **inducteurs puissants du système enzymatique du CYP 3A4**, notamment la **rifampine** et la **phénytoïne**, diminuent les concentrations sanguines et les effets du géfitinib ▪ Les **inhibiteurs puissants du système enzymatique du CYP 3A4**, notamment le **kétoconazole** et l'**itraconazole**, élèvent les concentrations sanguines et les effets du géfitinib (la prudence est de mise) ▪ L'absorption et l'efficacité peuvent être réduites par les **médicaments qui élèvent le pH gastrique**, notamment la **cimétidine** et la **ranitidine** ▪ Le risque de saignements et le RNI peuvent être accrus lors de l'usage concomitant de **warfarine** ▪ L'usage concomitant de **vinorelbine** peut accroître le risque de neutropénie ou aggraver cette dernière.

VOIES D'ADMINISTRATION ET POSOLOGIE

- **PO (adultes):** 250 mg, 1 fois par jour.

PRÉSENTATION

Comprimés: 250 mg[Pr].

SOINS INFIRMIERS

ÉVALUATION DE LA SITUATION

- RESTER À L'AFFÛT DES SIGNES DE TOXICITÉ PULMONAIRE (DYSPNÉE, TOUX, FIÈVRE). SI UNE MALADIE PULMONAIRE INTERSTITIELLE EST CONFIRMÉE, ARRÊTER L'ADMINISTRATION DU GÉFITINIB ET AMORCER LE TRAITEMENT APPROPRIÉ.
- Rester à l'affût des symptômes oculaires, comme la douleur, tout au long du traitement. L'interruption du traitement et le retrait des cils aberrants peuvent être nécessaires. Une fois que les symptômes et les modifications oculaires se sont résorbés, le traitement peut être repris.
- ***Tests de laboratoire:*** Suivre les résultats des tests de la fonction hépatique à intervalles réguliers. L'agent peut élever les concentrations de transaminases, de bilirubine et de phosphatase alcaline. Arrêter l'administration du géfitinib si ces élévations sont importantes.
- Suivre de près les modifications du RNI chez les patients prenant de la warfarine, car il peut s'élever.

DIAGNOSTICS INFIRMIERS POSSIBLES

- Diarrhée (Réactions indésirables).
- Atteinte à l'intégrité de la peau (Effets secondaires).
- Dégagement inefficace des voies respiratoires (Réactions indésirables).

INTERVENTIONS INFIRMIÈRES

PO: Administrer 1 comprimé par jour, sans égard aux repas.

- On peut interrompre brièvement le traitement (14 jours) chez les patients souffrant d'une diarrhée forte, s'accompagnant de déshydratation ou chez les patients présentant des réactions cutanées indésirables. Reprendre le traitement à la dose de 250 mg.

ENSEIGNEMENT AU PATIENT ET À SES PROCHES

- Recommander au patient de prendre le géfitinib en suivant rigoureusement les recommandations du médecin.
- Conseiller au patient de prévenir rapidement un professionnel de la santé, en cas de diarrhée, de nausées ou de vomissements persistants ou d'anorexie, en cas d'essoufflements ou de toux ou de leur aggravation et en cas d'irritation oculaire ou de tout autre nouveau symptôme.
- Recommander à la patiente de prévenir un professionnel de la santé si elle pense être enceinte, si elle souhaite le devenir ou si elle allaite.

VÉRIFICATION DE L'EFFICACITÉ THÉRAPEUTIQUE

L'efficacité du traitement peut être démontrée par: la diminution de la taille et de la propagation des tumeurs en cas de cancer pulmonaire non à petites cellules.

ALERTE CLINIQUE

GEMCITABINE

Gemzar

CLASSIFICATION:

Antinéoplasique (antimétabolite, analogue des nucléosides)

Grossesse – catégorie D

INDICATIONS

Traitement du cancer du pancréas localisé de stade avancé ou métastatique ■ En monothérapie ou en association avec le cisplatine – traitement du cancer du poumon non à petites cellules, localisé, de stade avancé ou métastatique ■ En association avec le cisplatine – traitement du cancer transitionnel de la vessie localisé de stade avancé ou métastatique.

MÉCANISME D'ACTION

Inhibition de la synthèse de l'ADN (effet spécifique sur une phase du cycle cellulaire). ***Effets thérapeutiques:*** Destruction des cellules à réplication rapide, particulièrement des cellules malignes.

PHARMACOCINÉTIQUE

Absorption: Biodisponibilité à 100 % (IV).
Distribution: Inconnue.
Métabolisme et excrétion: La gemcitabine est transformée dans les cellules en métabolites actifs, soit en nucléosides diphosphates et triphosphates. Ces métabolites sont principalement excrétés par les reins.
Demi-vie: De 32 à 94 minutes.

Profil temps-action (effets sur la numération globulaire)

	DÉBUT D'ACTION	PIC	DURÉE
IV	inconnu	inconnu	inconnue

CONTRE-INDICATIONS, PRÉCAUTIONS ET MISES EN GARDE

Contre-indications: Hypersensibilité.
Précautions et mises en garde: Maladie cardiovasculaire ■ Insuffisance rénale ou hépatique (risque accru de toxicité) ■ Autres maladies chroniques débilitantes ■ **PÉD.**: L'innocuité et l'efficacité de la gencitabine n'ont

pas été établies ■ OBST.: Grossesse ou allaitement, patientes en âge de procréer.

RÉACTIONS INDÉSIRABLES ET EFFETS SECONDAIRES

Resp.: TOXICITÉ PULMONAIRE, dyspnée, bronchospasmes.

CV: ARYTHMIES, ACCIDENT VASCULAIRE CÉRÉBRAL, INFARCTUS DU MYOCARDE, œdème, hypertension.

GI: HÉPATOTOXICITÉ, diarrhée, nausées, stomatite, élévations passagères des concentrations des transaminases hépatiques, vomissements.

G

GU: SYNDROME HÉMOLYTIQUE ET URÉMIQUE, hématurie, protéinurie.

Tég.: alopécie, rash.

Hémat.: anémie, leucopénie, thrombopénie.

Locaux: réactions au point d'injection.

SN: paresthésie.

Divers: symptômes pseudogrippaux, fièvre, réactions anaphylactoïdes, effet radiosensibilisant.

INTERACTIONS

Médicament-médicament: Aplasie médullaire additive lors de l'administration concomitante d'autres **antinéoplasiques** ou d'une **radiothérapie** ■ La gemcitabine peut diminuer la réponse des anticorps aux **vaccins à virus vivants** et augmenter le risque de réactions indésirables.

VOIES D'ADMINISTRATION ET POSOLOGIE

On peut utiliser d'autres schémas posologiques.

Cancer du pancréas

- **IV (adultes)**: 1 000 mg/m², 1 fois par semaine, pendant 7 semaines consécutives, suivies d'une période sans médication de 1 semaine. On peut ensuite administrer le médicament 1 fois par semaine, pendant 3 semaines consécutives, suivies d'une période sans médication de 1 semaine (cycle de 4 semaines).

Cancer du poumon non à petites cellules (monothérapie)

- **IV (adultes)**: 1 000 mg/m², 1 fois par semaine, pendant 3 semaines consécutives, suivies d'une période sans médication de 1 semaine. Par la suite, on répète le cycle de 4 semaines.

Cancer du poumon non à petites cellules (en association avec le cisplatine)

- **IV (adultes)**: 1 000 mg/m², les 1er, 8e et 15e jours de chaque cycle de 28 jours (administrer également le cisplatine le 1er jour) *ou* 1 250 mg/m², les 1er et 8e jours de chaque cycle de 21 jours (administrer également le cisplatine le 1er jour).

Cancer transitionnel de la vessie

- **IV (adultes)**: 1 000 mg/m², les 1er, 8e et 15e jours de chaque cycle de 28 jours (administrer également le cisplatine le 1er jour).

PRÉSENTATION

Poudre pour injection: fioles de 200 mg^Pr^, fioles de 1 g^Pr^.

SOINS INFIRMIERS

ÉVALUATION DE LA SITUATION

- Prendre les signes vitaux avant l'administration et à intervalles réguliers pendant toute la durée du traitement.
- Observer le point d'injection pendant l'administration. Même si la gemcitabine n'est pas considérée comme un agent vésicant, des réactions locales peuvent survenir.
- Rester à l'affût d'une aplasie médullaire. Suivre de près les saignements (saignement des gencives, formation d'ecchymoses, pétéchies, présence de sang occulte dans les selles, l'urine et les vomissements). Éviter les injections IM et la prise de la température rectale si la numération plaquettaire est basse. Appliquer une pression sur les points de ponction veineuse pendant 10 minutes. Rester à l'affût des signes d'infection en présence d'une neutropénie. Une anémie peut survenir. Suivre de près la fatigue accrue, la dyspnée et l'hypotension orthostatique.
- Effectuer le bilan quotidien des ingesta et des excreta, suivre de près l'appétit du patient et son apport nutritionnel. Des nausées et des vomissements de légers à modérés surviennent fréquemment. On peut administrer des antiémétiques à titre prophylactique.

Tests de laboratoire:

- Noter la numération globulaire, la formule leucocytaire et la numération plaquettaire avant l'administration initiale et avant l'administration de chaque dose. Les lignes directrices concernant la dose sont fondées sur la numération globulaire. Si le nombre absolu de granulocytes est $> 1 \times 10^9$/L et le nombre de plaquettes $> 100 \times 10^9$/L, on peut administrer la dose complète. Si le nombre absolu de granulocytes se situe entre $0{,}5 \times 10^9$/L et 1×10^9/L et le nombre de plaquettes entre 50×10^9/L et 100×10^9/L, on peut administrer 75 % de la dose. Arrêter le traitement si le nombre absolu de granulocytes est inférieur à $0{,}5 \times 10^9$/L ou celui des plaquettes est inférieur à 50×10^9/L.
- Noter les résultats des tests des fonctions rénale et hépatique avant le traitement et à intervalles réguliers

pendant toute sa durée. La gemcitabine peut entraîner des élévations passagères des concentrations sériques d'AST, d'ALT, de phosphatase alcaline et de bilirubine.

- La gemcitabine peut également élever les concentrations d'urée et de créatinine sérique et entraîner une protéinurie et une hématurie.

DIAGNOSTICS INFIRMIERS POSSIBLES

- Risque d'infection (Réactions indésirables).
- Connaissances insuffisantes sur le traitement médicamenteux (Enseignement au patient et à ses proches).

INTERVENTIONS INFIRMIÈRES

ALERTE CLINIQUE: DES DÉCÈS SONT SURVENUS LORS DE CERTAINES CHIMIOTHÉRAPIES. AVANT D'ADMINISTRER L'AGENT, CLARIFIER TOUS LES POINTS AMBIGUS. VÉRIFIER LA LIMITE DES DOSES UNITAIRES ET QUOTIDIENNES AINSI QUE LA DOSE À ADMINISTRER PENDANT LE TRAITEMENT. DEMANDER À UN DEUXIÈME PROFESSIONNEL DE LA SANTÉ DE VÉRIFIER UNE FOIS DE PLUS L'ORDONNANCE D'ORIGINE, LES CALCULS DES DOSES ET LE RÉGLAGE DE LA POMPE À PERFUSION.

- Préparer les solutions sous une hotte à flux laminaire. Porter des vêtements protecteurs, des gants et un masque pendant la manipulation du médicament. Jeter le matériel destiné à l'administration IV dans les contenants réservés à cet usage (voir l'annexe H).

Perfusion intermittente: Reconstituer le contenu d'une fiole de 200 mg avec 5 mL de solution de NaCl 0,9 % sans agent de conservation ou celui d'une fiole de 1 g avec 25 mL de solution de NaCl 0,9 %, pour obtenir une concentration de 38 mg/mL. La reconstitution de la solution à une concentration supérieure à 40 mg/mL peut entraîner une dissolution incomplète et doit être évitée. La solution peut être diluée davantage dans une solution de NaCl 0,9 %, pour obtenir des concentrations allant jusqu'à 0,1 mg/mL. La solution est d'incolore ou jaune paille clair. Ne pas administrer la solution si elle a changé de couleur ou si elle renferme des particules. La solution reconstituée est stable pendant 24 heures à la température ambiante. Jeter les portions inutilisées. Ne pas réfrigérer la solution, car il y a risque de formation de cristaux.
Vitesse d'administration: Administrer en 30 minutes. Les perfusions d'une durée supérieure à 60 minutes sont associées à un plus grand risque de toxicité.
Incompatibilité en addition au soluté: Données non disponibles. Ne pas mélanger à d'autres solutions ou médicaments.

ENSEIGNEMENT AU PATIENT ET À SES PROCHES

- Recommander au patient de prévenir un professionnel de la santé si les symptômes suivants se manifestent: fièvre, frissons, maux de gorge, signes d'infection, saignement des gencives, formation d'ecchymoses, pétéchies, présence de sang dans l'urine, les selles ou les vomissements. Prévenir le patient qu'il doit éviter les foules et les personnes contagieuses. Lui conseiller d'utiliser une brosse à dents à poils doux et un rasoir électrique. Le prévenir qu'il ne doit pas prendre de boissons alcoolisées ni de préparations contenant de l'aspirine ou des AINS.
- Recommander au patient d'examiner ses muqueuses buccales pour déceler l'érythème et les aphtes. En cas d'aphtes, lui conseiller de remplacer la brosse à dents par une brosse-éponge et de se rincer la bouche avec de l'eau après avoir bu ou mangé. La douleur provoquée par la stomatite peut nécessiter l'usage d'analgésiques opioïdes.
- Recommander au patient de prévenir un professionnel de la santé en cas de symptômes pseudogrippaux (fièvre, anorexie, céphalées, toux, frissons, myalgie), d'enflure des pieds ou des jambes ou d'essoufflements.
- Expliquer au patient qu'il risque de perdre ses cheveux. Explorer avec lui les stratégies lui permettant de s'adapter à ce changement.
- Expliquer à la patiente que ce médicament peut avoir des effets tératogènes; elle doit donc prendre des mesures contraceptives tout au long du traitement.
- Expliquer au patient qu'il ne doit pas se faire vacciner sans recommandation expresse d'un professionnel de la santé.
- Insister sur l'importance des tests de laboratoire effectués à intervalles réguliers pour déceler les effets secondaires.

VÉRIFICATION DE L'EFFICACITÉ THÉRAPEUTIQUE

L'efficacité du traitement peut être démontrée par: l'amélioration des symptômes chez les patients atteints d'un cancer du pancréas ■ la diminution de la taille et de l'étendue des lésions cancéreuses pulmonaires ou vésicales.

GEMFIBROZIL

Apo-Gemfibrozil, Gen-Gemfibrozil, Lopid, Novo-Gemfibrozil, PMS-Gemfibrozil

CLASSIFICATION:
Hypolipidémiant (dérivé de l'acide fénofibrique)

Grossesse – catégorie C

INDICATIONS

Hypertriglycéridémie (concentration sérique de triglycérides élevée), comme adjuvant à la diétothérapie et à l'exercice physique ■ Hypercholestérolémie (hyperlipidémie de type IIa et IIb), afin de régulariser le taux de lipides (diminution des concentrations de triglycérides et de cholestérol LDL, élévation des concentrations de cholestérol HDL). Le traitement de l'hyperlipidémie devrait toujours inclure la diétothérapie, la poursuite d'un programme d'exercices et la perte de poids.

MÉCANISME D'ACTION

Inhibition de la lipolyse périphérique ■ Diminution de la production hépatique de triglycérides ■ Diminution de la production de protéines qui transportent les triglycérides ■ Élévation des concentrations de cholestérol HDL. ***Effets thérapeutiques:*** Diminution des concentrations de triglycérides plasmatiques et élévation des concentrations de cholestérol HDL.

PHARMACOCINÉTIQUE

Absorption: Bonne (PO).
Distribution: Inconnue.
Métabolisme et excrétion: Métabolisme partiellement hépatique. Excrétion rénale à 70 % (surtout à l'état inchangé) et fécale à 6 %.
Demi-vie: De 1,3 à 1,5 heure.

Profil temps-action
(effet sur la diminution des concentrations de triglycérides liés aux VLDL)

	DÉBUT D'ACTION	PIC	DURÉE
PO	2 - 5 jours	4 semaines	plusieurs mois

CONTRE-INDICATIONS, PRÉCAUTIONS ET MISES EN GARDE

Contre-indications: Hypersensibilité ■ Cirrhose biliaire primitive ■ Maladie de la vésicule biliaire ■ Maladie hépatique ou rénale ■ **OBST., ALLAITEMENT, PÉD.:** L'innocuité du médicament n'a pas été établie pendant la grossesse ou l'allaitement ni chez les enfants ■ Traitement d'une hyperlipoprotéinémie de type I.

RÉACTIONS INDÉSIRABLES ET EFFETS SECONDAIRES

SNC: étourdissements, céphalées.
ORLO: vision trouble.
GI: douleurs abdominales, diarrhée, douleurs épigastriques, flatulence, formation de calculs biliaires, brûlures d'estomac, nausées, vomissements.
Tég.: alopécie, rash, urticaire.
Hémat.: anémie, leucopénie.
Loc.: myosite.

INTERACTIONS

Médicament-médicament: Le gemfibrozil peut intensifier l'effet de la **warfarine** ■ L'administration concomitante d'**inhibiteurs de l'HMG-CoA réductase** peut accroître le risque de rhabdomyolyse (éviter l'usage concomitant) ■ Les **chélateurs de l'acide biliaire** peuvent diminuer la biodisponibilité du gemfibrozil (espacer l'administration des deux médicaments d'au moins 2 heures) ■ Le gemfibrozil peut augmenter l'effet du **répaglinide** et accroître ainsi le risque d'hypoglycémie grave (éviter l'usage concomitant).

VOIES D'ADMINISTRATION ET POSOLOGIE

- **PO (adultes):** 600 mg, 2 fois par jour, 30 minutes avant le déjeuner et le souper. La dose maximale est de 1 500 mg par jour.

PRÉSENTATION

Comprimés: 600 mg[Pr] ■ **Capsules:** 300 mg[Pr].

SOINS INFIRMIERS

ÉVALUATION DE LA SITUATION

- Recueillir des données sur les habitudes alimentaires du patient, notamment sur sa consommation de matières grasses et d'alcool.

Tests de laboratoire:

- Noter les concentrations sériques de cholestérol et de triglycérides, ainsi que les concentrations de LDL et de VLDL, avant le traitement et à intervalles réguliers pendant toute sa durée. Il faut arrêter le traitement en cas d'élévation paradoxale des concentrations lipidiques.
- Suivre de près les résultats des tests de la fonction hépatique avant le traitement et à intervalles réguliers pendant toute sa durée. Le gemfibrozil peut entraîner l'élévation des concentrations de bilirubine sérique, de phosphatase alcaline, de créatine kinase (CK), de LDH, d'AST et d'ALT. En cas d'élévation marquée de ces valeurs, le traitement devrait être arrêté.
- Noter la numération globulaire et évaluer le bilan électrolytique tous les 3 à 6 mois et, ensuite, 1 fois par année, pendant toute la durée du traitement. Le gemfibrozil peut diminuer légèrement les concentrations d'hémoglobine, l'hématocrite et le nombre de globules blancs; il peut entraîner la diminution des concentrations sériques de potassium.
- Le gemfibrozil peut élever légèrement la glycémie.

DIAGNOSTICS INFIRMIERS POSSIBLES

- Connaissances insuffisantes sur le traitement médicamenteux (Enseignement au patient et à ses proches).

- Non-observance du traitement médicamenteux (Enseignement au patient et à ses proches).

INTERVENTIONS INFIRMIÈRES

- Administrer le gemfibrozil 30 minutes avant le déjeuner et le souper.

ENSEIGNEMENT AU PATIENT ET À SES PROCHES

- Inciter le patient à suivre rigoureusement la posologie recommandée. S'il n'a pas pu prendre le médicament au moment habituel, il doit le prendre aussitôt que possible à moins que ce ne soit presque l'heure prévue pour la dose suivante. Le prévenir qu'il ne doit jamais remplacer une dose manquée par une double dose.
- Expliquer au patient qu'il doit réduire sa consommation de matières grasses, de cholestérol, de glucides et d'alcool, faire régulièrement de l'exercice et cesser de fumer.
- Conseiller au patient de prévenir rapidement un professionnel de la santé si l'un des signes ou des symptômes suivants se manifeste : douleurs abdominales graves accompagnées de nausées et de vomissements, fièvre, frissons, mal de gorge, rash, diarrhée, crampes musculaires, gêne abdominale ou flatulence persistante.

VÉRIFICATION DE L'EFFICACITÉ THÉRAPEUTIQUE

L'efficacité du traitement peut être démontrée par : la baisse des concentrations sériques de triglycérides et de cholestérol et l'amélioration du ratio cholestérol HDL : cholestérol total. On doit habituellement arrêter le traitement si aucune réponse clinique ne se manifeste en l'espace de 3 mois. ✳

GENTAMICINE,
voir Aminosides

GLICLAZIDE,
voir Hypoglycémiants (oraux)

GLIMÉPIRIDE,
voir Hypoglycémiants (oraux)

GLUCAGON

Glucagon

CLASSIFICATION :

Hormone pancréatique (agent hyperglycémiant)

Grossesse – catégorie B

INDICATIONS

Traitement de courte durée de l'hypoglycémie grave, lorsqu'il est impossible d'administrer du glucose ■ Agent diagnostique d'appoint destiné aux examens radiologiques de l'appareil gastro-intestinal. **Usages non approuvés :** Antidote des agents suivants : bêtabloquants ■ bloqueurs des canaux calciques.

MÉCANISME D'ACTION

Stimulation de la production hépatique de glucose à partir des réserves de glycogène (glycogénolyse) ■ Relaxation des muscles du tractus gastro-intestinal (estomac, duodénum, intestin grêle et côlon), d'où une inhibition passagère de la motilité ■ Effets inotropes et chronotropes positifs. ***Effets thérapeutiques :*** Élévation de la glycémie ■ Relaxation des muscles gastro-intestinaux, ce qui facilite les examens radiologiques.

PHARMACOCINÉTIQUE

Absorption : Bonne (IM et SC).

Distribution : Inconnue.

Métabolisme et excrétion : Métabolisme hépatique, plasmatique et rénal important.

Demi-vie : De 8 à 18 minutes.

Profil temps-action (effets thérapeutiques)

	DÉBUT D'ACTION	PIC	DURÉE
IM (effet hyperglycémiant)	en l'espace de 10 min	30 min	60 - 90 min
IV (effet hyperglycémiant)	en l'espace de 10 min	5 min	60 - 90 min
SC (effet hyperglycémiant)	en l'espace de 10 min	30 - 45 min	60 - 90 min
IV (effet sur les muscles gastro-intestinaux)	45 s (dose de 0,25 à 2 mg)	inconnu	9 - 17 min (dose de 0,25 à 0,5 mg); 22 - 25 min (dose de 2 mg)
IM (effet sur les muscles gastro-intestinaux)	8 - 10 min (dose de 1 mg); 4 - 7 min (dose de 2 mg)	inconnu	9 - 27 min (dose de 1 mg); 21 - 32 min (dose de 2 mg)

G

CONTRE-INDICATIONS, PRÉCAUTIONS ET MISES EN GARDE

Contre-indications: Hypersensibilité au glucagon, à la glycérine ou aux autres excipients ■ Phéochromocytome.

Précautions et mises en garde: Antécédents évoquant un insulinome ou un phéochromocytome ■ Jeûne prolongé, inanition, insuffisance surrénalienne ou hypoglycémie chronique (seulement de faibles concentrations de glucose peuvent être libérées) ■ Lorsque le médicament est destiné à l'inhibition de la motilité gastrique, la prudence est de mise chez les personnes âgées ou chez celles souffrant de maladie cardiaque ou de diabète ■ **OBST., ALLAITEMENT**: L'innocuité du médicament n'a pas été établie.

G

RÉACTIONS INDÉSIRABLES ET EFFETS SECONDAIRES

CV: élévation passagère de la fréquence cardiaque et de la pression artérielle.

GI: nausées, vomissements.

HÉ: hypokaliémie.

Divers: réactions d'hypersensibilité, incluant l'ANAPHYLAXIE.

INTERACTIONS

Médicament-médicament: Les doses élevées de glucagon peuvent intensifier l'effet de la **warfarine** ■ Le glucagon peut contrecarrer la réponse à l'**insuline** ou aux **hypoglycémiants oraux** ■ L'**adrénaline** peut intensifier et prolonger l'effet hyperglycémiant du glucagon ■ Chez les patients sous traitement concomitant par des **bêtabloquants**, il y a risque d'une plus grande élévation de la fréquence cardiaque et de la pression artérielle.

VOIES D'ADMINISTRATION ET POSOLOGIE

Hypoglycémie

- **IV, IM, SC (adultes et enfants ≥ 20 kg)**: 1 mg; au besoin, on peut répéter l'administration de cette dose 15 minutes plus tard.
- **IV, IM, SC (enfants < 20 kg ou âgés de < 6 à 8 ans)**: 0,5 mg ou de 20 à 30 µg/kg; au besoin, on peut répéter l'administration de cette dose 15 minutes plus tard.

Examen radiologique de l'appareil gastro-intestinal

- **IM, IV (adultes)**: De 0,25 à 2 mg, selon la région à explorer et la durée de l'examen (0,5 mg par voie IV ou 2 mg par voie IM pour la relaxation de l'estomac, 2 mg par voie IM, 10 minutes avant l'examen de l'intestin grêle).

PRÉSENTATION

Poudre pour injection: fioles de 1 mg^Pr (sous forme de trousse d'urgence en cas de crise hypoglycémique et de trousse diagnostique).

SOINS INFIRMIERS

ÉVALUATION DE LA SITUATION

- Avant l'administration initiale et à intervalles réguliers tout au long du traitement, rechercher les signes et les symptômes suivants d'hypoglycémie: transpiration, faim, faiblesse, céphalées, étourdissements, tremblements, irritabilité, tachycardie, anxiété.
- Suivre de près l'état neurologique du patient tout au long du traitement. Prendre les mesures nécessaires pour le protéger contre les accidents provoqués par les convulsions, les chutes ou l'aspiration. Lors du traitement du choc insulinique, on doit administrer de 0,5 à 1 mg si le patient est comateux depuis 1 heure; le patient se réveille habituellement en l'espace de 10 à 25 minutes. En l'absence de réponse, administrer de nouveau cette dose. Aussitôt que possible après le réveil, et particulièrement chez les enfants, administrer des glucides supplémentaires pour reconstituer la réserve de glycogène hépatique et pour prévenir une hypoglycémie secondaire.
- Déterminer l'état nutritionnel du patient. Chez les patients dont la réserve de glycogène est réduite (comme dans les cas d'inanition, d'hypoglycémie chronique et d'insuffisance surrénalienne), il faut administrer du glucose plutôt que du glucagon.
- Suivre de près l'apparition des nausées et des vomissements après l'administration du médicament. Protéger le patient dont l'état de conscience est altéré contre les risques d'aspiration en l'installant en décubitus latéral; garder à portée de la main un dispositif d'aspiration. En cas de vomissements, prévenir le médecin qui devrait prescrire du glucose par voie parentérale pour éviter les épisodes récurrents d'hypoglycémie.

Tests de laboratoire:

- Doser la glycémie tout au long de l'épisode, durant le traitement et pendant 3 ou 4 heures après que le patient a repris connaissance. Pour obtenir rapidement des résultats, on utilise la méthode par prélèvement de sang capillaire du bout du doigt. Le médecin peut prescrire des tests de laboratoire pour valider ces résultats. Il faut cependant traiter le patient sans attendre les résultats de ces tests, étant donné le danger de lésions neurologiques et même de mort.

- Des doses élevées de glucagon peuvent entraîner une diminution de la concentration sérique de potassium.

DIAGNOSTICS INFIRMIERS POSSIBLES

- Risque d'accident (Indications).
- Connaissances insuffisantes sur le traitement médicamenteux (Enseignement au patient et à ses proches).
- Non-observance du traitement médicamenteux (Enseignement au patient et à ses proches).

INTERVENTIONS INFIRMIÈRES

- On peut administrer le glucagon par voies SC, IM ou IV. Reconstituer la solution avec le diluant fourni par le fabricant. Examiner la solution avant de l'administrer; n'utiliser que les solutions transparentes et aqueuses. Le médicament non dilué devrait être gardé à la température ambiante. La solution diluée devrait être utilisée immédiatement après sa reconstitution.
- Administrer des suppléments de glucides par voie IV ou par voie orale pour favoriser l'élévation de la glycémie.

IV: Reconstituer la solution avec le diluant fourni par le fabricant. Utiliser la solution reconstituée immédiatement. La concentration finale ne doit pas dépasser 1 mg/mL. Jeter toute portion inutilisée. Consulter les directives de chaque fabricant avant de reconstituer la préparation

IV directe: Administrer la solution à un débit inférieur à 1 mg/min. On peut l'administrer par une tubulure IV par laquelle passe une solution de D5%E. On peut également administrer la solution en même temps qu'un bolus IV de dextrose.

Incompatibilité en addition au soluté: NaCl 0,9 %, chlorure de calcium, chlorure de potassium.

ENSEIGNEMENT AU PATIENT ET À SES PROCHES

Expliquer au patient et à ses proches les signes et les symptômes d'hypoglycémie. Recommander au patient de prendre du glucose par voie orale dès que ces symptômes apparaissent. L'administration du glucagon doit être réservée au patient qui éprouve des difficultés de déglutition en raison de l'altération de l'état de conscience.

Soins à domicile:

- Expliquer aux proches du patient la méthode de préparation de la solution, de l'aspiration dans la seringue et d'administration de l'injection. Les inciter à prévenir immédiatement un professionnel de la santé qu'on a administré du glucagon pour recevoir des consignes quant au traitement ultérieur, à l'ajustement de la dose d'insuline ou aux modifications diététiques.
- Prévenir les proches que le patient devrait recevoir du glucose par voie orale dès que son état de conscience le permet.
- Expliquer aux proches qu'il faut installer le patient sur le côté jusqu'à ce qu'il reprenne entièrement conscience. Les prévenir que le glucagon peut provoquer des nausées et des vomissements. Il y a risque d'aspiration si le patient vomit lorsqu'il est installé en décubitus dorsal.
- Conseiller au patient de vérifier tous les mois la date de péremption inscrite sur l'emballage et de remplacer immédiatement le médicament périmé.
- Expliquer au patient l'utilisation de sa médication hypoglycémiante ainsi que la diétothérapie et le programme d'exercices à suivre.
- Conseiller au patient souffrant de diabète d'avoir toujours à portée de la main du sucre (un sachet de sucre ou un bonbon) et de porter en tout temps un bracelet d'identité où sont inscrits son problème de santé et son traitement médicamenteux.

VÉRIFICATION DE L'EFFICACITÉ THÉRAPEUTIQUE

L'efficacité du traitement peut être démontrée par: l'élévation de la glycémie jusqu'aux concentrations normales et l'amélioration de l'état de conscience ▪ la relaxation des muscles lisses de l'estomac, du duodénum, de l'intestin grêle et du gros intestin chez les patients qui doivent se soumettre à un examen radiologique du tractus gastro-intestinal.

GLYBURIDE,

voir Hypoglycémiants (oraux)

GLYCOPYRROLATE

Glycopyrrolate, Robinul

CLASSIFICATION:

Anticholinergique (antispasmodique)

Grossesse - catégorie B

INDICATIONS

Traitement de nombreuses affections gastro-intestinales susceptibles de répondre à un traitement anticholinergique ▪ Agent préanesthésique antimuscarinique: inhibition de la salivation et des sécrétions excessives des voies respiratoires avant une intervention chirurgicale ■ Au cours du renversement du blocage neuromusculaire induit par les bloqueurs neuromusculaires non dépolarisants, le glycopyrrolate protège des effets muscariniques périphériques (tels que la bradycardie et les sécrétions excessives) des agents cholinergiques comme la néostigmine et la pyridostigmine. **Usages non approuvés - SC**: Diminution des sécrétions respiratoires chez les patients en phase terminale.

MÉCANISME D'ACTION

Inhibition de l'effet de l'acétylcholine au niveau des sites des récepteurs postganglionnaires et sur les muscles lisses qui répondent à l'acétylcholine, mais qui ne reçoivent pas d'innervation cholinergique ■ Diminution de la sécrétion de sueur, de la salivation et des sécrétions des voies respiratoires (faibles doses) ■ Accélération de la fréquence cardiaque (doses moyennes) ■ Diminution de la motilité du tractus gastro-intestinal et des voies génito-urinaires (doses élevées). ***Effets thérapeutiques:*** Diminution des sécrétions du tractus gastro-intestinal et des voies respiratoires.

PHARMACOCINÉTIQUE

Absorption: Incomplète (PO); bonne (IM).

Distribution: Le mode de distribution n'est pas totalement élucidé. Le médicament traverse faiblement la barrière hématoencéphalique et l'œil. Il traverse la barrière placentaire.

Métabolisme et excrétion: Élimination majoritairement fécale, à l'état inchangé, par excrétion biliaire.

Demi-vie: 1,7 heure (entre 0,6 et 4,6 heures).

Profil temps-action (effets anticholinergiques)

	DÉBUT D'ACTION	PIC	DURÉE
IM	15 - 30 min	30 - 45 min	4 - 6 h
IV	1 min	inconnu	2 - 7 h†

† L'effet antisécrétoire dure 7 heures au maximum; l'effet antivagal dure de 2 à 3 heures.

CONTRE-INDICATIONS, PRÉCAUTIONS ET MISES EN GARDE

Contre-indications: Hypersensibilité ■ Glaucome à angle fermé ■ Hémorragie aiguë ■ Sténose pylorique ■ Sténose avec rétention gastrique importante ■ Obstruction duodénale ■ Achalasie œsophagienne ■ Cardiospasme ■ Hyperplasie de la prostate ■ Iléus paralytique ■ Atonie intestinale ■ Affection pulmonaire chronique (patients âgés ou débilités) ■ Rectocolite hémorragique grave ■ Mégacôlon toxique ■ Myasthénie grave ■ **PÉD.**: À cause de sa teneur en alcool benzylique, le glycopyrrolate en fioles multidoses ne devrait pas être utilisé chez les nouveau-nés.

Précautions et mises en garde: **GÉR.**: Les personnes âgées ont une prédisposition accrue à des réactions indésirables ■ **PÉD.**: Les jeunes enfants ont une prédisposition accrue à des réactions indésirables ■ Infections intra-abdominales ■ **PÉD.**: Les enfants atteints de maladies telles que le syndrome de Down ne devraient pas recevoir d'anticholinergiques; si cette administration est nécessaire, la dose habituelle devrait être réduite de moitié ■ Maladies rénale, hépatique ou pulmonaire chroniques ■ Hernie hiatale accompagnée d'un reflux gastroœsophagien ■ Affection du système nerveux autonome ■ Hyperthyroïdie ■ Cardiopathie ischémique ■ Insuffisance cardiaque congestive ■ Arythmies cardiaques ■ Hypertension ■ **OBST., ALLAITEMENT**: L'innocuité du médicament n'a pas été établie.

RÉACTIONS INDÉSIRABLES ET EFFETS SECONDAIRES

SNC: confusion, somnolence.

ORLO: vision trouble, cycloplégie, xérophtalmie, mydriase.

CV: tachycardie, hypotension orthostatique, palpitations.

GI: sécheresse de la bouche (xérostomie), constipation.

GU: retard de la miction avec effort pour uriner, rétention urinaire.

INTERACTIONS

Médicament-médicament: Effets anticholinergiques additifs lors de l'administration d'autres **préparations anticholinergiques** comprenant les **antihistaminiques**, les **phénothiazines**, les **antidépresseurs tricycliques**, la **quinidine** et le **disopyramide** ■ Le glycopyrrolate peut modifier l'absorption d'autres **médicaments administrés par voie orale** en ralentissant la motilité du tractus gastro-intestinal ■ Les **antiacides** ou les **antidiarrhéiques adsorbants** diminuent l'absorption des anticholinergiques ■ Le glycopyrrolate peut aggraver le risque de lésions de la muqueuse gastro-intestinale chez les patients qui prennent des comprimés de **chlorure de potassium** par voie orale ■ Risque accru de réactions cardiovasculaires indésirables en cas d'anesthésie par le **cyclopropane** ■ L'usage concomitant peut diminuer l'absorption du **kétoconazole** (administrer le glycopyrrolate 2 heures après le kétoconazole).

VOIES D'ADMINISTRATION ET POSOLOGIE

Médication préanesthésique pour diminuer les sécrétions au cours d'une intervention chirurgicale

- **IM (adultes)**: 0,005 mg/kg, de 30 à 60 minutes avant l'intervention.

- **IM (enfants)**: De 0,005 à 0,01 mg/kg, de 30 à 60 minutes avant l'intervention.

Médication peropératoire
- **IV (adultes)**: 0,1 mg, toutes les 2 à 3 minutes.
- **IV (enfants)**: 0,005 mg/kg, toutes les 2 à 3 minutes (ne pas dépasser 0,1 mg par dose).

Renversement du blocage neuromusculaire
- **IV (adultes et enfants)**: 0,2 mg par mg de néostigmine ou par 5 mg de pyridostigmine, administrées simultanément.

Gastroentérologie
- **IM (adultes)**: De 0,1 à 0,2 mg, toutes les 4 heures, 3 ou 4 fois par jour.

PRÉSENTATION

Solution pour injection: 200 µg (0,2 mg)/mL[Pr].

SOINS INFIRMIERS

ÉVALUATION DE LA SITUATION

- Mesurer la fréquence cardiaque, la pression artérielle et la fréquence respiratoire avant l'administration par voie parentérale et à intervalles réguliers pendant toute la durée du traitement.

PÉD.: Demeurer à l'affût de l'hyperexcitabilité, un effet paradoxal qui peut survenir chez les enfants.

- Effectuer le bilan quotidien des ingesta et des excreta chez les personnes âgées ou chez les patients ayant subi une intervention chirurgicale, car le glycopyrrolate peut provoquer une rétention urinaire. Inciter le patient à uriner avant de lui administrer le médicament.
- Observer régulièrement les signes de distension abdominale et ausculter les bruits intestinaux. Si la constipation devient gênante, augmenter la consommation de liquides et servir au patient des aliments riches en fibres pour soulager les effets constipants du glycopyrrolate.
- Le patient qui suit un traitement prolongé doit faire mesurer régulièrement sa pression intraoculaire.

Tests de laboratoire:
- Le glycopyrrolate contrecarre les effets de la pentagastrine et de l'histamine, qui sont administrées lors des tests d'évaluation des sécrétions d'acide gastrique. Ne pas administrer le médicament 24 heures avant ces tests.
- Le médicament peut entraîner la diminution des concentrations d'acide urique chez les patients souffrant de goutte ou d'hyperuricémie.

Toxicité et surdosage: En cas de surdosage, l'antidote est la néostigmine.

DIAGNOSTICS INFIRMIERS POSSIBLES

- Atteinte à l'intégrité de la muqueuse buccale (Effets secondaires).
- Constipation (Effets secondaires).
- Connaissances insuffisantes sur le traitement médicamenteux (Enseignement au patient et à ses proches).

INTERVENTIONS INFIRMIÈRES

- Ne pas administrer la solution si elle est trouble ou si elle a changé de couleur.

IM: On peut administrer la solution sans la diluer ou on peut la mélanger à une solution de D5%E ou de NaCl 0,9 %. Consulter les directives du fabricant avant de diluer la préparation.

IV directe: On peut administrer la solution sans la diluer par une tubulure en Y.

Vitesse d'administration: Administrer la solution à un débit maximal de 0,2 mg/min.

Associations compatibles dans la même seringue: chlorpromazine ■ cimétidine ■ codéine ■ diphenhydramine ■ dropéridol ■ dropéridol/fentanyl ■ hydromorphone ■ hydroxyzine ■ lévorphanol ■ lidocaïne ■ mépéridine ■ midazolam ■ morphine ■ nalbuphine ■ néostigmine ■ prochlorpérazine ■ promazine ■ prométhazine ■ propiomazine ■ pyridostigmine ■ ranitidine ■ triflupromazine.

Associations incompatibles dans la même seringue: chloramphénicol ■ dexaméthasone ■ diazépam ■ dimenhydrinate ■ méthohexital ■ pentazocine ■ pentobarbital ■ sécobarbital ■ sodium, bicarbonate de ■ thiopental.

Compatibilité en addition au soluté: solution de D5%E et de NaCl 0,45 % ■ solution de D5%E ■ solution de NaCl à 0,9 % ■ solution de Ringer. Administrer immédiatement après l'admixtion.

Incompatibilité en addition au soluté: méthylprednisolone sodique, succinate de.

ENSEIGNEMENT AU PATIENT ET À SES PROCHES

- Expliquer au patient qu'il doit respecter rigoureusement la posologie recommandée et qu'il ne doit jamais augmenter la dose. S'il n'a pu prendre le médicament au moment habituel, il doit le prendre dès que possible à moins que ce ne soit presque l'heure prévue pour la dose suivante.
- Prévenir le patient que le glycopyrrolate peut provoquer de la somnolence et une vision trouble. Lui recommander de ne pas conduire et d'éviter les

autres activités qui exigent sa vigilance jusqu'à ce qu'on ait la certitude que le médicament n'entraîne pas ces effets chez lui.

- Expliquer au patient que pour soulager la sécheresse de la bouche, il devrait se rincer fréquemment la bouche, consommer des bonbons ou de la gomme à mâcher sans sucre et pratiquer une bonne hygiène buccale. Si la sécheresse de la bouche persiste pendant plus de 2 semaines, lui conseiller de consulter un professionnel de la santé au sujet de la possibilité d'utiliser des substituts de salive.
- Recommander au patient recevant le glycopyrrolate de changer lentement de position pour réduire le risque d'hypotension orthostatique induite par le médicament.
- Recommander au patient d'éviter les températures extrêmes, car le glycopyrrolate diminue les sécrétions de sueur et peut augmenter le risque d'un coup de chaleur.
- Conseiller au patient de signaler immédiatement à un professionnel de la santé les douleurs oculaires ou une sensibilité accrue à la lumière. Insister sur l'importance des examens ophtalmiques réguliers pendant toute la durée du traitement.
- Conseiller au patient de consulter un professionnel de la santé avant de prendre un médicament en vente libre en même temps que le glycopyrrolate.

VÉRIFICATION DE L'EFFICACITÉ THÉRAPEUTIQUE

L'efficacité du traitement peut être démontrée par: l'inhibition de la salivation avant une intervention chirurgicale ■ le renversement des effets des médicaments cholinergiques ■ la diminution de la motilité gastro-intestinale. ✳

GOSÉRÉLINE

Zoladex, Zoladex LA

CLASSIFICATION:

Antinéoplasique (hormone de synthèse), analogue de l'hormone de libération de la gonadotrophine

Grossesse – catégories X

INDICATIONS

Traitement palliatif du cancer de la prostate hormonodépendant de stade avancé (stade M_1 de la classification *Tumor-Node-Metastasis* [TNM] ou stade D_2 de la classification de l'*American Urologic Association* [AUA]) ■ En association avec un antiandrogène non stéroïdien et la radiothérapie, traitement du cancer localisé de la prostate de stade avancé lorsque la tumeur est volumineuse (stades T2b-T2c-T3-T4) ■ Adjuvant à la radiothérapie dans le traitement du cancer de la prostate avancé (stades T3 et T4) ■ Traitement de remplacement de la chimiothérapie adjuvante standard chez les femmes non ménopausées atteintes d'un cancer du sein hormonodépendant de stade précoce chez lesquelles une chimiothérapie n'est pas possible ■ Traitement palliatif du cancer du sein hormonodépendant avancé, chez les femmes périménopausées et préménopausées ■ Traitement hormonal de l'endométriose (soulagement de la douleur et résorption des lésions) ■ Amincissement de l'endomètre avant ablation en cas de ménométrorragie.

MÉCANISME D'ACTION

Forme synthétique de l'hormone de libération de la gonadotrophine (GnRH ou LH-RH). Inhibition de la production de gonadotrophine par l'hypophyse. Initialement, les concentrations d'hormone lutéinisante (LH), d'hormone folliculostimulante (FSH), d'œstradiol et de testostérone augmentent. L'administration continue entraîne une réduction de la production hormonale, particulièrement de testostérone et d'œstradiol.
Effets thérapeutiques: Ralentissement de la propagation du cancer de la prostate ou du sein ■ Régression de l'endométriose et diminution de la douleur ■ Amincissement de l'endomètre.

PHARMACOCINÉTIQUE

Absorption: Bonne (SC).
Distribution: Inconnue.
Métabolisme et excrétion: Métabolisme hépatique à moins de 10 %, le reste étant excrété par les reins (soit plus de 90 %, dont une fraction de 20 % seulement sous forme inchangée).
Demi-vie: 4,2 heures (hommes) ou 2,3 heures (femmes).

Profil temps-action
(diminution des concentrations sériques de testostérone ou d'œstradiol)

	DÉBUT D'ACTION	PIC	DURÉE
SC	inconnu	3 - 4 semaines	pendant le traitement

CONTRE-INDICATIONS, PRÉCAUTIONS ET MISES EN GARDE

Contre-indications: Hypersensibilité ■ Saignements vaginaux d'étiologie indéterminée ■ Grossesse ou allaitement.
Précautions et mises en garde: **PÉD.:** Enfants < 18 ans (l'innocuité du médicament n'a pas été établie) ■ Métastases vertébrales.

RÉACTIONS INDÉSIRABLES ET EFFETS SECONDAIRES

SNC: céphalées, anxiété, dépression, étourdissements, fatigue, insomnie, faiblesse.

Resp.: dyspnée.

CV: ACCIDENT VASCULAIRE CÉRÉBRAL, INFARCTUS DU MYOCARDE, EMBOLIE PULMONAIRE, INSUFFISANCE CARDIAQUE CONGESTIVE, vasodilatation, douleurs thoraciques, hypertension, palpitations, thrombophlébite, fibrillation auriculaire.

GI: anorexie, constipation, diarrhée, nausées, ulcère, vomissements.

GU: insuffisance rénale, obstruction des voies urinaires.

Tég.: transpiration, rash, sécheresse vaginale.

End.: diminution de la libido, impuissance, engorgement mammaire, sensibilité mammaire, gynécomastie, stérilité, kyste ovarien, syndrome d'hyperstimulation ovarienne.

HÉ: œdème périphérique.

Hémat.: anémie.

Métab.: goutte, hyperglycémie, hyperlipidémie.

Loc.: douleurs osseuses accrues, arthralgie, diminution de la densité osseuse.

Divers: bouffées de chaleur, frissons, fièvre, gain de poids.

INTERACTIONS

Médicament-médicament: Aucune interaction notable.

VOIES D'ADMINISTRATION ET POSOLOGIE

- **SC (adultes)**: 3,6 mg, toutes les 4 semaines ou, pour Zoladex LA, 10,8 mg, toutes les 12 semaines. *Amincissement de l'endomètre* – 2 injections de 3,6 mg, à 4 semaines d'intervalle; pratiquer l'intervention 2 semaines après la deuxième injection.

PRÉSENTATION

Implant: 3,6 mg[Pr], 10,8 mg[Pr] (forme LA).

SOINS INFIRMIERS

ÉVALUATION DE LA SITUATION

Cancer:

- Chez le patient ayant des métastases au niveau de la colonne vertébrale, suivre de près l'intensification des douleurs lombaires et la diminution des fonctions sensorimotrices.
- Pendant le traitement initial, effectuer le bilan des ingesta et des excreta et rester à l'affût d'une distension de la vessie chez les patients présentant un risque d'obstruction des voies urinaires.

Endométriose: Surveiller les signes et les symptômes d'endométriose avant le traitement et à intervalles réguliers pendant toute sa durée. L'aménorrhée survient habituellement dans les 8 semaines suivant l'administration initiale et les règles recommencent environ 8 semaines après la fin du traitement.

Tests de laboratoire:

- Au début, les concentrations d'hormone lutéinisante (LH) et d'hormone folliculostimulante (FSH) augmentent, puis elles diminuent, ce qui entraîne des concentrations de testostérone équivalentes à celles qu'on trouve chez les castrats, environ 3 semaines après l'élévation initiale de ces concentrations.
- Noter les concentrations sériques de phosphatase acide et d'antigènes prostatiques spécifiques à intervalles réguliers pendant toute la durée du traitement (cancer de la prostate). Le médicament peut entraîner des élévations passagères des concentrations sériques de phosphatase acide, qui reviennent habituellement aux valeurs initiales dans les 4 semaines suivant le début du traitement et qui peuvent diminuer au-dessous des valeurs initiales ou revenir à celles-ci si elles étaient élevées avant le traitement.
- Le médicament peut entraîner une hypercalcémie chez les patients souffrant de cancer du sein ou de la prostate, associé à des métastases osseuses.
- Le médicament peut provoquer une élévation des concentrations sériques de cholestérol HDL, de cholestérol LDL et de triglycérides.

DIAGNOSTICS INFIRMIERS POSSIBLES

- Dysfonctionnement sexuel (Effets secondaires).
- Connaissances insuffisantes sur le traitement médicamenteux (Enseignement au patient et à ses proches).

INTERVENTIONS INFIRMIÈRES

- On insère un implant dans le tissu sous-cutané de la paroi abdominale au-dessous du nombril, tous les mois ou tous les 3 mois (forme LA). On peut administrer un anesthésique local avant l'injection.
- Si, pour une raison quelconque, on doit retirer l'implant, on peut le localiser par ultrasons.

ENSEIGNEMENT AU PATIENT ET À SES PROCHES

- Prévenir le patient que les douleurs osseuses peuvent s'intensifier au début du traitement. Elles disparaîtront avec le temps. Conseiller au patient de consulter un professionnel de la santé concernant l'utilisation d'analgésiques pour soulager la douleur.

G

- Conseiller à la patiente de prévenir un professionnel de la santé si elle continue d'avoir un cycle menstruel régulier.
- Prévenir la patiente que le médicament peut provoquer des bouffées de chaleur. Lui conseiller de prévenir un professionnel de la santé si elles deviennent gênantes.
- Recommander au patient de prévenir rapidement un professionnel de la santé s'il éprouve des difficultés de miction.
- Insister sur le fait qu'il est important de respecter le schéma thérapeutique prévoyant l'administration du médicament tous les mois ou tous les 3 mois.

G

VÉRIFICATION DE L'EFFICACITÉ THÉRAPEUTIQUE

L'efficacité du traitement peut être démontrée par: l'arrêt de la propagation du cancer de la prostate ▪ la réduction des symptômes de cancer du sein avancé chez les femmes périménopausées ou préménopausées ▪ la diminution de la propagation du cancer du sein ▪ la diminution des signes et des symptômes d'endométriose (habituellement, dans les 4 semaines qui suivent l'installation de l'implant) ▪ l'amincissement de l'endomètre avant ablation en raison d'une ménométrorragie. ✳

GRANISÉTRON

Kytril

CLASSIFICATION:

Antiémétique (antagoniste des récepteurs de la sérotonine [5-HT_3])

Grossesse – catégorie B

INDICATIONS

Prévention des nausées et des vomissements associés à la chimiothérapie ou consécutifs à une radiothérapie ▪ Prévention et traitement des nausées et des vomissements postopératoires chez l'adulte < 65 ans.

MÉCANISME D'ACTION

Inhibition des effets de la sérotonine au niveau des récepteurs (antagoniste spécifique) situés sur les terminaisons du nerf vague et dans la zone gâchette chémoréceptrice. ***Effets thérapeutiques:*** Diminution de la fréquence et de la gravité des nausées et des vomissements provoqués par la chimiothérapie, la radiothérapie ou la chirurgie.

PHARMACOCINÉTIQUE

Absorption: 50 % (PO).

Distribution: Inconnue (on sait cependant que le médicament se répartit dans les érythrocytes).

Métabolisme et excrétion: Métabolisme majoritairement hépatique. 12 % est excrété à l'état inchangé dans l'urine.

Demi-vie: *Patients cancéreux* – de 8 à 9 heures (écart de 0,9 à 31,1 heures); *volontaires en santé* – 4,9 heures (de 0,9 à 15,2 heures); *patients âgés* – 7,7 heures (de 2,6 à 17,7 heures).

Profil temps-action

	DÉBUT D'ACTION	PIC	DURÉE
PO	rapide	60 min	24 h
IV	rapide	30 min	jusqu'à 24 h

CONTRE-INDICATIONS, PRÉCAUTIONS ET MISES EN GARDE

Contre-indications: Hypersensibilité.

Précautions et mises en garde: **OBST.:** Grossesse ou allaitement (l'innocuité du médicament n'a pas été établie) ▪ **PÉD.:** Enfants < 18 ans (l'innocuité du médicament n'a pas été établie) ▪ Éviter l'utilisation de produits contenant de l'alcool benzylique chez les nouveau-nés.

RÉACTIONS INDÉSIRABLES ET EFFETS SECONDAIRES

SNC: céphalées, agitation, anxiété, stimulation du SNC, somnolence, faiblesse.

CV: hypertension.

GI: constipation, diarrhée, concentrations élevées des enzymes hépatiques, altération du goût.

Divers: réactions anaphylactoïdes, fièvre.

INTERACTIONS

Médicament-médicament: L'usage concomitant d'**agents provoquant des réactions extrapyramidales** peut augmenter le risque de telles réactions au granisétron.

VOIES D'ADMINISTRATION ET POSOLOGIE

Prévention des nausées et des vomissements induits par la chimiothérapie

- **PO (adultes):** 1 dose de 1 mg, administrée au moins 60 minutes avant la chimiothérapie, suivie de 1 dose de 1 mg, administrée 12 heures plus tard, les jours où le patient est soumis à ce traitement. On peut également administrer une seule dose de 2 mg, 1 heure avant la chimiothérapie.

- **IV (adultes)**: 10 μg/kg, dans les 30 minutes qui précèdent la chimiothérapie, le jour ou les jours où ce traitement est administré.

Prévention des nausées et des vomissements induits par la radiothérapie

- **PO (adultes)**: 1 dose de 1 mg, administrée au moins 60 minutes avant la radiothérapie, suivie de 1 dose de 1 mg, administrée 12 heures plus tard, les jours où le patient est soumis à ce traitement. On peut également administrer une seule dose de 2 mg, 1 heure avant la radiothérapie.

Prévention et traitement des nausées et des vomissements postopératoires

- **IV (adultes < 65 ans)**: *Prévention* – 1 mg avant l'induction ou avant la fin de l'anesthésie. *Traitement* – 1 mg.

PRÉSENTATION

Comprimés: 1 mg[Pr] ▪ **Solution pour injection**: 1 mg/mL[Pr].

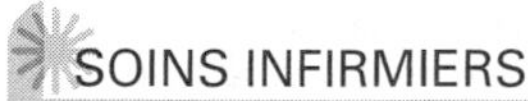

SOINS INFIRMIERS

ÉVALUATION DE LA SITUATION

- Suivre de près les nausées, les vomissements et la distension abdominale et ausculter les bruits intestinaux, avant et après l'administration du granisétron.
- Pendant toute la durée du traitement, surveiller l'apparition des effets extrapyramidaux suivants: mouvements involontaires, grimaces, rigidité, démarche traînante, tremblements des mains. Ces symptômes se manifestent rarement et ils sont habituellement associés à l'usage concomitant d'autres médicaments qui produisent ces effets.

Tests de laboratoire: Le granisétron peut entraîner l'élévation des concentrations d'AST et d'ALT.

DIAGNOSTICS INFIRMIERS POSSIBLES

- Alimentation déficiente (Indications).
- Connaissances insuffisantes sur le traitement médicamenteux (Enseignement au patient et à ses proches).

INTERVENTIONS INFIRMIÈRES

- Le granisétron est administré seulement les jours où le patient reçoit la chimiothérapie ou la radiothérapie. Il s'est avéré inutile de l'administrer les autres jours.

PO: Administrer la première dose dans l'heure qui précède la chimiothérapie ou la radiothérapie, et la deuxième, 12 heures plus tard.

IV directe: La solution peut être administrée non diluée ou diluée dans 20 à 50 mL d'une solution de NaCl 0,9 % ou de D5%E. La solution devrait être préparée au moment de l'administration, mais elle reste stable pendant 24 heures à la température ambiante.

Vitesse d'administration: Administrer le granisétron non dilué pendant 30 secondes, ou dilué pendant 5 minutes.

Compatibilité (tubulure en Y): acyclovir ▪ allopurinol ▪ amifostine ▪ amikacine ▪ aminophylline ▪ amphotéricine B, cholestéryle d' ▪ ampicilline ▪ ampicilline/sulbactam ▪ aztréonam ▪ bléomycine ▪ bumétanide ▪ buprénorphine ▪ butorphanol ▪ calcium, gluconate de ▪ carboplatine ▪ carmustine ▪ céfazoline ▪ céfépime ▪ céfonicide ▪ céfopérazone ▪ céfotaxime ▪ céfotétane ▪ céfoxitine ▪ ceftazidime ▪ ceftizoxime ▪ ceftriaxone ▪ céfuroxime ▪ chlorpromazine ▪ cimétidine ▪ ciprofloxacine ▪ cisplatine ▪ cladribine ▪ clindamycine ▪ cyclophosphamide ▪ cytarabine ▪ dacarbazine ▪ dactinomycine ▪ daunorubicine ▪ dexaméthasone ▪ diphenhydramine ▪ dobutamine ▪ dopamine ▪ doxorubicine ▪ doxorubicine liposomale ▪ doxycycline ▪ dropéridol ▪ énalaprilate ▪ étoposide ▪ famotidine ▪ filgrastim ▪ fluconazole ▪ fluorouracile ▪ floxuridine ▪ fludarabine ▪ furosémide ▪ gallium, nitrate de ▪ ganciclovir ▪ gentamicine ▪ halopéridol ▪ héparine ▪ hydrocortisone ▪ hydromorphone ▪ idarubicine ▪ ifosfamide ▪ imipénem/cilastatine ▪ leucovorine ▪ lorazépam ▪ magnésium, sulfate de ▪ méchloréthamine ▪ melphalan ▪ mépéridine ▪ mesna ▪ méthotrexate ▪ méthylprednisolone ▪ métoclopramide ▪ métronidazole ▪ mezlocilline ▪ miconazole ▪ minocycline ▪ mitomycine ▪ mitoxantrone ▪ morphine ▪ nalbuphine ▪ nétilmicine ▪ ofloxacine ▪ paclitaxel ▪ pipéracilline ▪ pipéracilline/tazobactam ▪ plicamycine ▪ potassium, chlorure de ▪ prochlorpérazine ▪ prométhazine ▪ propofol ▪ ranitidine ▪ rémifentanil ▪ sargramostim ▪ sodium, bicarbonate de ▪ streptozocine ▪ téniposide ▪ thiotépa ▪ ticarcilline ▪ ticarcilline/clavulanate ▪ tobramycine ▪ triméthoprime/sulfaméthoxazole ▪ vancomycine ▪ vinblastine ▪ vincristine ▪ vinorelbine ▪ zidovudine.

Incompatibilité (tubulure en Y): amphotéricine B.

Incompatibilité en addition au soluté: Le granisétron ne devrait pas être mélangé à d'autres médicaments.

ENSEIGNEMENT AU PATIENT ET À SES PROCHES

Recommander au patient de prévenir immédiatement un professionnel de la santé s'il note des mouvements involontaires des yeux, du visage ou des membres.

G

VÉRIFICATION DE L'EFFICACITÉ THÉRAPEUTIQUE

L'efficacité du traitement peut être démontrée par: la prévention des nausées et des vomissements associés à une chimiothérapie ou à une radiothérapie qui provoque de telles réactions ■ la prévention ou le traitement des nausées et des vomissements postopératoires.

GUAIFÉNÉSINE

Balminil Expectorant, Benylin-E, Guaifenesine, Robitussin

CLASSIFICATION:

Expectorant

Grossesse – catégorie C

G

INDICATIONS

Soulagement symptomatique des maladies respiratoires associées à une toux productive avec présence de mucus dans les voies respiratoires. On peut aussi l'administrer dans le traitement de la toux sèche, improductive, pour faciliter l'expectoration des sécrétions épaisses et visqueuses.

MÉCANISME D'ACTION

Diminution de la viscosité des sécrétions tenaces par l'augmentation de la quantité de liquides présents dans les voies respiratoires. ***Effets thérapeutiques:*** Diminution de la viscosité des mucosités, ce qui en facilite l'élimination par expectoration.

PHARMACOCINÉTIQUE

Absorption: Bonne (PO).
Distribution: Inconnue.
Métabolisme et excrétion: Excrétion rénale sous forme de métabolites.
Demi-vie: Inconnue.

Profil temps-action (effet expectorant)

	Début d'action	Pic	Durée
PO	30 min	inconnu	4 – 6 h
PO – LP†	inconnu	inconnu	12 h

† LP = libération prolongée.

CONTRE-INDICATIONS, PRÉCAUTIONS ET MISES EN GARDE

Contre-indications: Hypersensibilité ■ Les patients ayant une hypersensibilité ou une intolérance à l'alcool, à l'aspartame, à la saccharine, au sucre ou à la tartrazine doivent éviter les associations médicamenteuses contenant ces substances.

Précautions et mises en garde: Toux qui persiste depuis plus de 1 semaine ou qui s'accompagne de fièvre, d'hémoptysie, d'une éruption cutanée, de maux de tête persistants ou d'un mal de gorge intense (il est conseillé de consulter un professionnel de la santé au préalable) ■ Grossesse ■ Patients recevant du disulfirame (les préparations liquides peuvent contenir de l'alcool) ■ Patients diabétiques (certaines préparations peuvent contenir du sucre).

RÉACTIONS INDÉSIRABLES ET EFFETS SECONDAIRES

SNC: étourdissements, céphalées.
GI: nausées, diarrhée, douleurs d'estomac, vomissements.
Tég.: rash, urticaire.

INTERACTIONS

Médicament-médicament: Aucune interaction notable.

VOIES D'ADMINISTRATION ET POSOLOGIE

- **PO (adultes et enfants ≥ 12 ans):** De 200 à 400 mg, toutes les 4 à 6 heures (ne pas dépasser 2 400 mg par jour).
- **PO (enfants de 6 à 11 ans):** De 100 à 200 mg, toutes les 4 à 6 heures (ne pas dépasser 1 200 mg par jour).
- **PO (enfants de 2 à 5 ans):** De 50 à 100 mg, toutes les 4 à 6 heures (ne pas dépasser 600 mg par jour).

PRÉSENTATION (version générique disponible)

Sirop: 100 mg/5 mL[VL], 200 mg/5 mL[VL] ■ **Solution orale:** 100 mg/5 mL[VL] ■ **En association avec:** analgésiques/antipyrétiques, antihistaminiques, décongestionnants et antitussifs[Pr, VL]. Voir l'annexe U.

SOINS INFIRMIERS

ÉVALUATION DE LA SITUATION

- Noter la fréquence et la nature de la toux, ausculter le murmure vésiculaire et noter les caractéristiques des sécrétions bronchiques à intervalles réguliers tout au long du traitement. Sauf en cas de contre-indications, maintenir un apport liquidien de 1 500 à 2 000 mL par jour afin de diminuer la viscosité des sécrétions.

DIAGNOSTICS INFIRMIERS POSSIBLES

- Dégagement inefficace des voies respiratoires (Indications).

- Connaissances insuffisantes sur le traitement médicamenteux (Enseignement au patient et à ses proches).

INTERVENTIONS INFIRMIÈRES

- Servir un grand verre d'eau au patient après chaque dose de guaifénésine, afin de diminuer la viscosité des sécrétions.

ENSEIGNEMENT AU PATIENT ET À SES PROCHES

- Expliquer au patient les méthodes lui permettant de tousser efficacement: s'asseoir en gardant le dos bien droit et prendre plusieurs respirations profondes avant de tousser.
- Prévenir le patient que la guaifénésine peut parfois provoquer des étourdissements. Lui conseiller de ne pas conduire et d'éviter les activités qui exigent sa vigilance jusqu'à ce qu'on ait la certitude que le médicament n'entraîne pas cet effet chez lui.
- Expliquer au patient les mesures à prendre pour calmer une toux chronique non productive: parler peu, cesser de fumer, humidifier l'air de la pièce, mâcher de la gomme ou sucer des bonbons durs sans sucre.
- Recommander au patient de prévenir un professionnel de la santé si la toux persiste au-delà de 1 semaine ou si elle s'accompagne de fièvre, de rash, de céphalées persistantes ou de maux de gorge.

VÉRIFICATION DE L'EFFICACITÉ THÉRAPEUTIQUE

L'efficacité du traitement peut être démontrée par: une expectoration plus facile des mucosités associées aux infections des voies respiratoires supérieures. ✳

HALCINONIDE,
voir Corticostéroïdes (topiques)

HALOBÉTASOL,
voir Corticostéroïdes (topiques)

HALOPÉRIDOL
Apo-Haloperidol, Haldol, Haloperidol LA, Novo-Peridol, Peridol, PMS Haloperidol LA

CLASSIFICATION:
Antipsychotique (butyrophénone)

Grossesse – catégorie C

H

INDICATIONS
Traitement des psychoses aiguës et chroniques, de l'agitation aiguë, du délire et des crises de manie ■ Maîtrise des symptômes de la maladie de Gilles de la Tourette ■ Traitement du comportement agité et agressif chez les patients présentant un syndrome cérébral chronique ou une arriération mentale. **Usages non approuvés**: Traitement des nausées et des vomissements induits par une intervention chirurgicale ou la chimiothérapie ■ Traitement du hoquet incoercible.

MÉCANISME D'ACTION
Modification des effets de la dopamine dans le SNC ■ Effets anticholinergiques et alpha-adrénolytiques. ***Effets thérapeutiques:*** Diminution des signes et des symptômes de psychoses ■ Amélioration du comportement chez les enfants souffrant du syndrome de Gilles de la Tourette ou d'autres troubles comportementaux.

PHARMACOCINÉTIQUE
Absorption: Bonne (PO et IM). Le sel de décanoate est absorbé lentement et a une longue durée d'action.
Distribution: On trouve des concentrations élevées dans le foie. L'halopéridol traverse la barrière placentaire et passe dans le lait maternel.
Liaison aux protéines: 90 %.
Métabolisme et excrétion: Métabolisme hépatique.
Demi-vie: De 21 à 24 heures.

Profil temps-action (activité antipsychotique)

	DÉBUT D'ACTION	PIC	DURÉE
PO	2 h	2 - 6 h	8 - 12 h
IM	20 - 30 min	30 - 45 min	4 - 8 h†
IM (décanoate)	3 - 9 jours	inconnu	1 mois

† Les effets peuvent persister pendant plusieurs jours.

CONTRE-INDICATIONS, PRÉCAUTIONS ET MISES EN GARDE
Contre-indications: Hypersensibilité ■ Glaucome à angle fermé ■ Aplasie médullaire ■ Dépression du SNC ■ État comateux ■ État dépressif grave ■ Antécédents de maladies spasmodiques ■ **GÉR.**: Patients séniles présentant des antécédents de symptômes pseudoparkinsoniens ■ Lésions des noyaux basaux ou maladie de Parkinson, sauf lorsqu'il s'agit de dyskinésies résultant d'un traitement par la lévodopa ■ Trouble hépatique ou cardiovasculaire grave ■ Intolérance ou hypersensibilité à la tartrazine, à l'huile de sésame ou à l'alcool benzylique (éviter, dans ce cas, l'administration des produits qui contiennent ces substances) ■ **PÉD.**: L'innocuité du médicament n'a pas été établie chez les enfants < 3 ans ■ **OBST., ALLAITEMENT**: Utiliser seulement si les bienfaits pour la mère dépassent les risques pour le fœtus.
Précautions et mises en garde: **GÉR.**: Réduire la dose chez les personnes âgées ou débilitées ■ Cardiopathie ■ Diabète ■ Insuffisance respiratoire ■ Hyperplasie de la prostate ■ Tumeurs du SNC ■ Occlusion intestinale ■ Convulsions.

RÉACTIONS INDÉSIRABLES ET EFFETS SECONDAIRES
SNC: CONVULSIONS, réactions extrapyramidales, confusion, somnolence, agitation, dyskinésie tardive.
ORLO: vision trouble, xérophtalmie.
Resp.: dépression respiratoire.
CV: hypotension, tachycardie.
GI: constipation, sécheresse de la bouche (xérostomie), anorexie, hépatite, iléus.
GU: rétention urinaire.
Tég.: diaphorèse, photosensibilité, rash.
End.: galactorrhée.
Hémat.: anémie, leucopénie.
Métab.: hyperpyrexie.
Divers: SYNDROME MALIN DES NEUROLEPTIQUES, réactions d'hypersensibilité.

INTERACTIONS
Médicament-médicament: Effets hypotenseurs additifs lors de l'administration concomitante d'**antihypertenseurs** ou de **dérivés nitrés** ou de l'ingestion rapide de grandes quantités d'**alcool** ■ Effets anticholinergiques additifs lors de l'administration concomitante de **médicaments dotés de propriétés anticholinergiques**, dont les **antihistaminiques**, les **antidépresseurs**, l'**atropine**, les **phénothiazines**, la **quinidine** et le **disopyramide** ■ Effets dépresseurs additifs sur le SNC, lors de l'usage concomitant d'autres **dépresseurs du SNC**,

dont l'**alcool**, les **antihistaminiques**, les **analgésiques opioïdes** et les **hypnosédatifs** ■ Risque d'hypotension grave et de tachycardie lors de l'administration concomitante d'**adrénaline** ■ L'halopéridol peut diminuer les effets thérapeutiques de la **lévodopa** et du **pergolide** ■ Risque d'apparition du syndrome encéphalopathique aigu, en cas d'administration concomitante de **lithium** ■ Risque de manifestations de démence lors de l'administration concomitante de **méthyldopa**.

Médicament-produits naturels: Effets dépresseurs additifs sur le SNC lors de l'usage concomitant de **kava**, de **valériane** et de **camomille**.

VOIES D'ADMINISTRATION ET POSOLOGIE

Halopéridol

- **PO (adultes)**: De 0,5 à 5 mg, 2 ou 3 fois par jour (chez certains patients, on doit parfois administrer des doses quotidiennes pouvant atteindre 100 mg par jour).
- **PO (personnes âgées ou patients débilités)**: De 0,5 à 2 mg, 2 fois par jour, au départ; la dose peut être augmentée graduellement selon les besoins.
- **PO (enfants de 3 à 12 ans, de 15 à 40 kg)**: De 0,25 à 0,5 mg/jour, en 2 ou 3 doses fractionnées, puis augmenter la posologie de 0,25 à 0,5 mg par jour, à intervalles de 5 à 7 jours, jusqu'à un maximum de 0,15 mg/kg/jour.
- **IM (adultes)**: De 2 à 5 mg, toutes les 4 à 6 heures (ne pas dépasser 100 mg par jour).
- **IV (adultes)**: De 1 à 2 mg, toutes les 2 à 4 heures.

Décanoate d'halopéridol

- **IM (adultes)**: De 10 à 15 fois la dose quotidienne précédente administrée par voie orale, sans dépasser 100 mg initialement, tous les mois (ne pas dépasser 300 mg par mois).

PRÉSENTATION (version générique disponible)

Comprimés: 0,5 mg^{Pr}, 1 mg^{Pr}, 2 mg^{Pr}, 5 mg^{Pr}, 10 mg^{Pr}, 20 mg^{Pr} ■ **Concentré oral**: 2 mg/mL^{Pr} ■ **Halopéridol (solution pour injection)**: 5 mg/mL^{Pr} ■ **Décanoate d'halopéridol (solution pour injection)**: 50 mg/mL^{Pr}, 100 mg/mL^{Pr}.

SOINS INFIRMIERS

ÉVALUATION DE LA SITUATION

- Déterminer l'état de conscience du patient (orientation spatiotemporelle, humeur, comportement), avant le traitement et à intervalles réguliers pendant toute sa durée.
- Mesurer la pression artérielle (en position assise, debout et couchée) et le pouls, avant l'administration du médicament et à intervalles fréquents pendant la période d'adaptation de la posologie. Le médicament peut modifier l'intervalle QT sur l'ÉCG.
- Observer attentivement le patient au moment de l'administration du médicament pour s'assurer qu'il l'a bien avalé.
- Effectuer le bilan quotidien des ingesta et des excreta et peser le patient tous les jours. Particulièrement chez les personnes âgées, observer les signes et les symptômes suivants de déshydratation: diminution de la soif, léthargie, hémoconcentration.
- Déterminer la quantité de liquides consommée et l'état de la fonction intestinale. L'augmentation de la consommation de fibres alimentaires et de liquides permet de réduire les effets constipants de l'halopéridol.
- Rester à l'affût des symptômes d'akathisie (agitation ou désir de bouger continuellement), qui peuvent apparaître dans les 6 heures suivant la première dose et qui peuvent être difficiles à distinguer de ceux de l'agitation psychotique; pour les distinguer les uns des autres, on peut administrer de la benztropine. Observer attentivement le patient pour déceler l'apparition de symptômes extrapyramidaux (*symptômes parkinsoniens:* difficulté d'élocution ou de déglutition, perte de l'équilibre, mouvements d'émiettement, faciès figé, démarche traînante, rigidité, tremblements; *symptômes dystoniques:* spasmes musculaires, torsions, secousses musculaires, incapacité de bouger les yeux, faiblesse des bras ou des jambes).
- Suivre de près l'apparition de symptômes de dyskinésie tardive (mouvements rythmiques et incontrôlés de la bouche, du visage et des membres; émission de bruits secs avec les lèvres, moue; gonflement des joues; mastication incontrôlée; mouvements rapides de la langue). Signaler immédiatement au médecin ces symptômes, qui peuvent être irréversibles.
- RESTER À L'AFFÛT DES SYMPTÔMES SUIVANTS DU SYNDROME MALIN DES NEUROLEPTIQUES: FIÈVRE, DÉTRESSE RESPIRATOIRE, TACHYCARDIE, CONVULSIONS, DIAPHORÈSE, HYPERTENSION OU HYPOTENSION, PÂLEUR, FATIGUE, RIGIDITÉ MUSCULAIRE MARQUÉE, PERTE DE LA MAÎTRISE DE LA VESSIE. INFORMER IMMÉDIATEMENT LE MÉDECIN DE CES SYMPTÔMES. LE MÉDICAMENT PEUT ÉGALEMENT INDUIRE UNE LEUCOCYTOSE, DES RÉSULTATS ÉLEVÉS AUX TESTS DE LA FONCTION HÉPATIQUE OU DES CONCENTRATIONS ÉLEVÉES DE CRÉATINE-KINASE.

H

Tests de laboratoire: Noter à intervalles réguliers tout au long du traitement la numération globulaire, la formule leucocytaire et les résultats des tests de la fonction hépatique.

DIAGNOSTICS INFIRMIERS POSSIBLES

- Opérations de la pensée perturbées (Indications).
- Connaissances insuffisantes sur le traitement médicamenteux (Enseignement au patient et à ses proches).

INTERVENTIONS INFIRMIÈRES

- Éviter le contact de la peau avec la solution orale, en raison du risque de dermatite.

PO:

- Administrer le médicament avec des aliments ou un grand verre d'eau ou de lait afin de réduire l'irritation gastrique.
- Utiliser un récipient gradué pour administrer la dose exacte. Ne pas diluer le concentré dans du café ou du thé; un précipité pourrait se former. On peut administrer le médicament sans le diluer, mais on peut le diluer au besoin dans au moins 60 mL de liquide.

IM: Injecter lentement dans un muscle bien développé, selon la technique du tracé en Z, en utilisant une aiguille de 5 cm, de calibre 21. Ne pas administrer plus de 3 mL par point d'injection. La solution peut virer au jaune pâle sans que sa puissance soit modifiée. Conseiller au patient de rester couché pendant au moins 30 minutes après l'injection afin de réduire les effets hypotenseurs de l'halopéridol.

IV directe: Le médicament peut être administré non dilué pour maîtriser rapidement la psychose aiguë ou le délire.

Vitesse d'administration: Administrer la préparation à une vitesse de 5 mg/min au minimum.

Perfusion intermittente: La solution peut être diluée dans 50 mL de D5%E.

Vitesse d'administration: Administrer la préparation en 30 minutes.

- Consulter les directives de chaque fabricant avant de reconstituer la préparation.

Associations compatibles dans la même seringue: hydromorphone ■ sufentanil.

Associations incompatibles dans la même seringue: héparine ■ kétorolac.

Compatibilité (tubulure en Y): amifostine ■ aztréonam ■ cimétidine ■ cisatracurium ■ cladribine ■ dobutamine ■ dopamine ■ doxorubicine liposomale ■ famotidine ■ filgrastim ■ fludarabine ■ granisétron ■ lidocaïne ■ lorazépam ■ melphalan ■ midazolam ■ nitroglycérine ■ noradrénaline ■ ondansétron ■ paclitaxel ■ phényléphrine ■ propofol ■ rémifentanil ■ sufentanil ■ tacrolimus ■ téniposide ■ théophylline ■ thiotépa ■ vinorelbine.

Incompatibilité (tubulure en Y): amphotéricine B, cholestéryle d' ■ céfépime ■ cefmétazole ■ fluconazole ■ foscarnet ■ gallium, nitrate de ■ héparine ■ pipéracilline/tazobactam ■ sargramostim.

ENSEIGNEMENT AU PATIENT ET À SES PROCHES

- Conseiller au patient de respecter rigoureusement la posologie recommandée. S'il n'a pu prendre le médicament au moment habituel, il doit le prendre dès que possible, en espaçant à des intervalles égaux les autres prises de la journée. Parfois, plusieurs semaines peuvent s'écouler avant de pouvoir noter les effets souhaités. Prévenir le patient qu'il ne doit jamais augmenter la dose ni arrêter le traitement sans avoir consulté un professionnel de la santé au préalable. Le sevrage brusque peut provoquer des étourdissements, des nausées, des vomissements, de l'irritation gastrique, des tremblements ou des mouvements involontaires de la bouche, de la langue ou de la mâchoire.
- Prévenir le patient que l'halopéridol peut provoquer des symptômes extrapyramidaux et la dyskinésie tardive. Lui recommander de signaler immédiatement ces symptômes à un professionnel de la santé.
- Recommander au patient de changer lentement de position afin de réduire le risque d'hypotension orthostatique.
- Prévenir le patient que l'halopéridol peut provoquer de la somnolence. Lui conseiller de ne pas conduire et d'éviter les activités qui exigent sa vigilance jusqu'à ce qu'on ait la certitude que le médicament n'entraîne pas cet effet chez lui.
- Mettre en garde le patient contre la consommation d'alcool ou d'autres dépresseurs du SNC en même temps que l'halopéridol.
- Inciter le patient à utiliser un écran solaire et à porter des vêtements protecteurs lors des expositions au soleil pour prévenir les réactions de photosensibilité. Lui recommander également d'éviter les températures extrêmes, car l'halopéridol altère la thermorégulation.
- Conseiller au patient de se rincer fréquemment la bouche, de pratiquer une bonne hygiène buccale et de consommer de la gomme ou des bonbons sans sucre pour soulager la sécheresse de la bouche.
- Recommander au patient qui doit suivre un traitement ou subir une intervention chirurgicale de prévenir le professionnel de la santé qu'il suit un traitement médicamenteux.

- Conseiller au patient de signaler rapidement à un professionnel de la santé la faiblesse, les tremblements, les troubles visuels, l'urine foncée ou les selles couleur de glaise, les maux de gorge ou la fièvre.
- Insister sur l'importance des examens réguliers de suivi.

VÉRIFICATION DE L'EFFICACITÉ THÉRAPEUTIQUE

L'efficacité du traitement peut être démontrée par: la diminution des hallucinations, de l'insomnie, de l'agitation, de l'hostilité et du délire ▪ la diminution des tics gestuels et vocaux, qui accompagnent le syndrome de Gilles de la Tourette ▪ l'amélioration du comportement chez les enfants présentant des troubles graves du comportement. En l'absence d'un effet thérapeutique après 2 à 4 semaines de traitement, on peut augmenter la dose.

ALERTE CLINIQUE

HÉPARINE

Hepalean, Hepalean-Lok, Héparine Léo, Solution de rinçage héparinée

CLASSIFICATION:
Anticoagulant, antithrombotique

Grossesse – catégorie C

INDICATIONS

Prophylaxie et traitement des divers troubles thromboemboliques incluant: la thromboembolie veineuse ▪ l'embolie pulmonaire ▪ la fibrillation auriculaire accompagnée d'embolie ▪ la coagulation intravasculaire disséminée (aiguë ou chronique) ▪ la thromboembolie artérielle périphérique ▪ Maintien de la perméabilité des cathéters IV en utilisant de très faibles doses: entre 10 et 100 unités (solution de rinçage à l'héparine) ▪ Circulation extracorporelle et transfusions sanguines.

MÉCANISME D'ACTION

Potentialisation des effets inhibiteurs de l'antithrombine sur le facteur Xa et la thrombine ▪ À de faibles doses, prévention de la transformation de la prothrombine en thrombine, grâce aux effets sur le facteur Xa ▪ À des doses plus élevées, neutralisation de la thrombine, ce qui prévient la transformation du fibrinogène en fibrine. ***Effets thérapeutiques:*** Prévention de la formation de thrombus ▪ Prévention de la croissance des thrombus existants (pleine dosc).

PHARMACOCINÉTIQUE

Absorption: Bonne (SC).

Distribution: L'héparine ne traverse pas la barrière placentaire, ni ne passe dans le lait maternel.

Liaison aux protéines: Très élevée (liaison aux lipoprotéines de basse densité, aux globulines et au fibrinogène).

Métabolisme et excrétion: L'héparine semble être éliminée de l'organisme par le système réticuloendothélial (ganglions lymphatiques, rate).

Demi-vie: De 1 à 2 heures (plus la dose est élevée, plus la demi-vie se prolonge). La demi-vie est modifiée par l'obésité, la fonction rénale et la fonction hépatique, ou par la présence d'une tumeur maligne, d'une embolie pulmonaire ou d'une infection.

Profil temps-action (effet anticoagulant)

	DÉBUT D'ACTION	PIC	DURÉE
SC	20 – 60 min	2 h	8 – 12 h
IV	immédiat	5 – 10 min	2 – 6 h

CONTRE-INDICATIONS, PRÉCAUTIONS ET MISES EN GARDE

Contre-indications: Hypersensibilité ▪ Hémorragie non maîtrisée ▪ Thrombopénie grave ▪ Plaies ouvertes (pleine dose) ▪ **PÉD.:** Nourrissons prématurés (l'usage de la préparation contenant de l'alcool benzylique est déconseillé dans leur cas).

Précautions et mises en garde: Maladie rénale ou hépatique grave ▪ Rétinopathie (patients hypertendus ou diabétiques) ▪ Hypertension non traitée ▪ Ulcère ▪ Lésions de la moelle épinière ou du cerveau ▪ Antécédents de troubles de la coagulation congénitaux ou acquis ▪ Tumeur maligne ▪ **GÉR.:** Femmes âgées de plus de 60 ans (risque accru d'hémorragie) ▪ **OBST.:** Dernier trimestre et au tout début du post-partum (on peut utiliser le médicament pendant la grossesse, mais il faut faire preuve de prudence pendant la période mentionnée).

EXTRÊME PRUDENCE: HYPERTENSION GRAVE NON MAÎTRISÉE ▪ ENDOCARDITE BACTÉRIENNE, TROUBLES DE LA COAGULATION ▪ MALADIE, ULCÈRE OU SAIGNEMENTS GASTRO-INTESTINAUX ▪ ACCIDENT VASCULAIRE HÉMORRAGIQUE ▪ INTERVENTION CHIRURGICALE RÉCENTE AU SNC OU AUX YEUX ▪ SAIGNEMENTS OU ULCÈRE GASTRO-INTESTINAL EN POUSSÉE ÉVOLUTIVE ▪ ANTÉCÉDENTS DE THROMBOPÉNIE LIÉE À L'HÉPARINE.

RÉACTIONS INDÉSIRABLES ET EFFETS SECONDAIRES

GI: hépatite induite par le médicament.

Tég.: alopécie (usage prolongé), rash, urticaire.

Hémat.: HÉMORRAGIE, anémie, thrombopénie.
Locaux: douleurs au point d'injection.
Loc.: ostéoporose (usage prolongé).
Divers: fièvre, hypersensibilité.

INTERACTIONS

L'héparine est souvent administrée en concomitance ou en séquence avec d'autres agents modifiant la coagulation. Le risque d'interactions pouvant être graves est maximal en cas de traitement anticoagulant administré à pleines doses.

Médicament-médicament: L'administration concomitante de **médicaments qui affectent la fonction plaquettaire**, dont l'**aspirine**, les **anti-inflammatoires non stéroïdiens**, le **clopidogrel**, le **dipyridamole**, certaines **pénicillines**, la **ticlopidine**, l'**abciximab**, l'**eptifibatide**, le **tirofiban** et le **dextran**, peut augmenter le risque d'hémorragie ■ L'administration concomitante de **médicaments qui entraînent une hypoprothrombinémie**, dont la **quinidine**, le **céfamandole**, le **cefmétazole**, la **céfopérazone**, le **céfotétane**, la **plicamycine** et l'**acide valproïque**, peut augmenter le risque d'hémorragie ■ L'administration concomitante d'**agents thrombolytiques** augmente le risque d'hémorragie ■ Les héparines modifient le temps de prothrombine nécessaire pour évaluer la réponse à la **warfarine** ■ Les **dérivés digitaliques**, les **tétracyclines**, la **nicotine** et les **antihistaminiques** peuvent diminuer l'effet anticoagulant de l'héparine ■ L'administration de la **streptokinase** peut entraîner une résistance relative à l'héparine.

Médicament-produits naturels: Le risque de saignements est accru en cas de consommation concomitante d'**ail**, d'**anis**, d'**arnica**, de **camomille**, de **dong quai**, de **girofle**, de **gingembre**, de **ginkgo** et de **ginseng**.

VOIES D'ADMINISTRATION ET POSOLOGIE

Idéalement, la dose d'héparine doit être ajustée de telle sorte que le TCA atteigne un intervalle thérapeutique cible, basé sur le dosage d'une héparine «étalon-or». En traitement, on vise un TCA allant de 1,5 à 2,5 fois le temps du témoin.

Anticoagulation thérapeutique

- **IV (adultes)**: *Bolus intermittent* – comme il nécessite l'administration de doses totales importantes, vraisemblablement responsables de l'incidence élevée d'hémorragie, le bolus intermittent n'est pas recommandé. Administrer 10 000 unités, suivies de 5 000 à 10 000 unités, toutes les 4 à 6 heures.
- *Perfusion continue* – 5 000 unités, suivies de 30 000 à 40 000 unités, par 24 heures (approximativement de 15 à 18 unités/kg/h) *ou* bolus de 80 unités/kg, suivies de 18 unités/kg/h.
- **IV (enfants)**: *Perfusion continue* – bolus initial de 75 à 100 unités/kg, puis 28 unités/kg/h chez les nourrissons, 20 unités/kg/h chez les enfants > 1 an, et 18 unités/kg/h chez les enfants plus âgés.
- **SC (adultes)**: 5 000 unités par voie IV, suivies d'une dose initiale par voie SC de 10 000 à 20 000 unités, puis de 8 000 à 10 000 unités, toutes les 8 heures, ou de 15 000 à 20 000 unités, toutes les 12 heures.

Prophylaxie des épisodes de thromboembolie

- **SC (adultes)**: 5 000 unités, toutes les 8 à 12 heures (on peut commencer l'administration 2 heures avant l'intervention chirurgicale).

Intervention chirurgicale cardiovasculaire

- **IV (adultes)**: 150 unités/kg, au minimum (300 unités/kg si l'intervention dure moins de 60 minutes ou 400 unités/kg si elle dure plus de 60 minutes).

Solution de rinçage à l'héparine

- **IV (adultes et enfants)**: De 10 à 100 unités/mL pour remplir le dispositif d'injection intermittente jusqu'à l'embout de l'aiguille; remplacer après chaque usage.

PRÉSENTATION (version générique disponible)

- **Héparine sodique**

  Solution pour injection: 10 unités/mL^{Pr}, 100 unités/mL^{Pr}, 1 000 unités/mL^{Pr}, 10 000 unités/mL^{Pr}, 25 000 unités/mL^{Pr} ■ **Solution prémélangée pour injection**: 1 000 unités/500 mL NaCl 0,9%^{Pr}, 2 000 unités/1 000 mL NaCl 0,9%^{Pr}, 20 000 unités/500 mL D5%^{Pr}, 25 000 unités/250 mL D5%^{Pr}, 25 000 unités/500 mL D5%^{Pr}.

SOINS INFIRMIERS

ÉVALUATION DE LA SITUATION

- RECHERCHER LES SIGNES SUIVANTS D'HÉMORRAGIE: SAIGNEMENT DES GENCIVES ET DU NEZ, FORMATION INHABITUELLE D'ECCHYMOSES, SELLES NOIRES GOUDRONNEUSES, HÉMATURIE, CHUTE DE L'HÉMATOCRITE OU DE LA PRESSION ARTÉRIELLE, PRÉSENCE DE SANG OCCULTE DANS LES SELLES. PRÉVENIR LE MÉDECIN SI CES SYMPTÔMES SE MANIFESTENT.
- Rechercher les signes qui révèlent que la thrombose s'aggrave ou qu'elle touche d'autres territoires. Les symptômes dépendent du territoire touché.
- Suivre de près les réactions d'hypersensibilité: frissons, fièvre, urticaire. Signaler ces réactions au médecin.

SC: Observer étroitement la formation d'hématomes et d'ecchymoses ou l'apparition d'une inflammation au point d'injection.

Tests de laboratoire:

- Noter le temps de céphaline activée (TCA) et l'hématocrite, avant l'administration de l'héparine et à intervalles réguliers tout au long du traitement. Lors d'une *perfusion intermittente*, il faut noter le temps de céphaline activée (TCA), 30 minutes avant chaque dose, durant le traitement initial et à intervalles réguliers, par la suite. Lors d'une *perfusion continue*, on doit surveiller le temps de céphaline activée (TCA), toutes les 4 heures, au début du traitement. Lors d'un traitement par voie *SC*, on peut prélever les échantillons de sang nécessaires à la détermination du temps de céphaline activée (TCA), de 4 à 6 heures après l'injection.
- Noter le nombre de plaquettes tous les 2 ou 3 jours, pendant toute la durée du traitement. L'héparine peut provoquer une thrombopénie légère qui survient le 4e jour du traitement, mais qui se résorbe même si l'on poursuit l'administration. La thrombopénie qui dicte l'arrêt de l'administration de l'héparine peut survenir le 8e jour de traitement. Les patients ayant déjà reçu un traitement à l'héparine sont exposés à un risque plus élevé de thrombopénie grave pendant plusieurs mois après le traitement initial.
- L'héparine peut allonger le temps de prothrombine (PT), entraîner des concentrations sériques élevées de thyroxine et de résine T_3 et des résultats faussement négatifs au test de captage du fibrinogène marqué à l'iode^{125}.
- L'héparine peut entraîner la diminution des concentrations sériques de triglycérides et de cholestérol et l'élévation des concentrations plasmatiques d'acides gras libres.
- L'héparine peut également provoquer une hyperkaliémie et l'élévation des concentrations d'AST et d'ALT.

Toxicité et surdosage: Le sulfate de protamine est l'antidote de l'héparine. Toutefois, en raison de la courte demi-vie de l'héparine, on peut souvent traiter le surdosage en arrêtant l'administration du médicament.

DIAGNOSTICS INFIRMIERS POSSIBLES

- Irrigation tissulaire inefficace (Indications).
- Risque d'accident (Effets secondaires).
- Connaissances insuffisantes sur le traitement médicamenteux (Enseignement au patient et à ses proches).

INTERVENTIONS INFIRMIÈRES

Alerte clinique: L'ADMINISTRATION ACCIDENTELLE DE 2 HÉPARINES (HÉPARINE NON FRACTIONNÉE ET HÉPARINE DE FAIBLE POIDS MOLÉCULAIRE) A ENTRAINÉ DE GRAVES EFFETS SECONDAIRES ALLANT JUSQU'À LA MORT. VÉRIFIER LA MÉDICATION COURANTE ET RÉCENTE DU PATIENT (URGENCE, BLOC OPÉRATOIRE) AVANT D'ADMINISTRER DE L'HÉPARINE NON FRACTIONNÉE OU DE L'HÉPARINE DE FAIBLE POIDS MOLÉCULAIRE. DES ERREURS SONT AUSSI ATTRIBUABLES À DE MAUVAIS CALCULS DE LA DOSE OU À LA MAUVAISE PROGRAMMATION DE LA POMPE À PERFUSION. TOUJOURS FAIRE CONFIRMER LES ORDONNANCES, LE CALCUL DES DOSES ET LES PROGRAMMATIONS DE LA POMPE PAR UN AUTRE PROFESSIONNEL DE LA SANTÉ. NE PAS CONFONDRE LES FIOLES D'HÉPARINE AVEC LES FIOLES D'INSULINE.

- Signaler à tous les membres de l'équipe de soins que le patient suit un traitement anticoagulant. Appliquer une pression sur les points d'injection et de ponction veineuse pour prévenir le saignement ou la formation d'un hématome. Éviter d'administrer par voie IM d'autres médicaments en raison du risque de formation d'hématomes.
- Avant d'administrer l'héparine, vérifier la dose exacte à injecter en présence d'un autre professionnel de la santé.
- Chez les patients qui suivent un traitement anticoagulant prolongé, commencer l'administration de l'anticoagulant par voie orale, 4 ou 5 jours avant d'arrêter le traitement à l'héparine.
- La solution est incolore à jaune pâle.

SC: Administrer profondément dans le tissu souscutané. Alterner les points d'injection entre la paroi abdominale gauche et droite, au-dessus de la crête iliaque. Introduire l'aiguille, sur toute sa longueur, à un angle de 45° ou de 90°, dans un pli cutané retenu entre le pouce et l'index; garder le pli cutané pendant toute la durée de l'injection. Nc pas aspirer ni masser. Assurer la rotation des points d'injection à intervalles fréquents. Ne pas administrer par voie IM en raison du risque de formation d'hématomes. La solution devrait être transparente; ne pas injecter de solution contenant des particules.

IV directe: Habituellement, il faut administrer une dose d'attaque avant le début de la perfusion continue.

Vitesse d'administration: On peut administrer la préparation sans la diluer, en au moins 1 minute.

Perfusion intermittente/continue: Diluer l'héparine dans la quantité prescrite de solution de NaCl 0,9%, de D5%E ou de solution de Ringer pour injection, et administrer par perfusion intermittente ou continue. S'assurer que l'héparine est bien mélangée dans la solution en renversant le contenant au moins 6 fois au début, puis en mélangeant la solution à intervalles réguliers pendant la perfusion. On peut aussi utiliser les sacs contenant une solution prémélangée. Consulter les directives de chaque fabricant avant de reconstituer la préparation.

Vitesse d'administration: La perfusion peut être administrée pendant 4 à 24 heures. Utiliser une pompe à perfusion pour s'assurer qu'on a administré la dose exacte. Voir le tableau des vitesses de perfusion à l'annexe C.

Solution de rinçage à l'héparine: Afin d'éviter la formation de caillots dans les dispositifs de perfusion intermittente (solution de rinçage à l'héparine), injecter de 10 à 100 unités d'héparine diluée dans 0,5 à 1 mL de solution après chaque injection de médicament ou toutes les 8 à 12 heures. Pour prévenir le risque d'incompatibilité avec le médicament à administrer, rincer le dispositif avec de l'eau stérile ou avec une solution de NaCl 0,9% pour injection, avant et après l'administration du médicament en question.

H

Associations compatibles dans la même seringue: adrénaline ▪ aminophylline ▪ amphotéricine B ▪ ampicilline ▪ atropine ▪ bléomycine ▪ céfamandole ▪ céfazoline ▪ céfopérazone ▪ céfotaxime ▪ céfoxitine ▪ chloramphénicol ▪ cimétidine ▪ cisplatine ▪ clindamycine ▪ cyclophosphamide ▪ diazoxide ▪ digoxine ▪ dimenhydrinate ▪ fentanyl ▪ fluorouracile ▪ furosémide ▪ leucovorine ▪ lidocaïne ▪ méthotrexate ▪ métoclopramide ▪ mezlocilline ▪ mitomycine ▪ nafcilline ▪ naloxone ▪ néostigmine ▪ pancuronium ▪ pénicilline G ▪ phénobarbital ▪ pipéracilline ▪ succinylcholine ▪ triméthoprime/sulfaméthoxazole ▪ vérapamil ▪ vincristine.

Associations incompatibles dans la même seringue: amikacine ▪ amiodarone ▪ chlorpromazine ▪ diazépam ▪ doxorubicine ▪ dropéridol ▪ dropéridol avec fentanyl ▪ érythromycine, lactobionate d' ▪ gentamicine ▪ halopéridol ▪ kanamycine ▪ mépéridine ▪ méthicilline ▪ méthotriméprazine ▪ nétilmicine ▪ pentazocine ▪ prométhazine ▪ streptomycine ▪ tobramycine ▪ triflupromazine ▪ vancomycine ▪ warfarine.

Compatibilité (tubulure en Y): acyclovir ▪ adrénaline ▪ aldesleukine ▪ allopurinol ▪ amifostine ▪ aminophylline ▪ ampicilline ▪ ampicilline/sulbactam ▪ atracurium ▪ atropine ▪ aztréonam ▪ bétaméthasone ▪ bléomycine ▪ calcium, gluconate de ▪ céfazoline ▪ céfotétane ▪ ceftazidime ▪ ceftriaxone ▪ céphapirine ▪ chlordiazépoxide ▪ chlorpromazine ▪ cimétidine ▪ cisplatine ▪ cladribine ▪ clindamycine ▪ cyanocobalamine ▪ cyclophosphamide ▪ cytarabine ▪ dexaméthasone ▪ digoxine ▪ diphenhydramine ▪ dopamine ▪ doxorubicine liposomale ▪ édrophonium ▪ énalaprilate ▪ érythromycine, lactobionate d' ▪ esmolol ▪ éthacrynate ▪ famotidine ▪ fentanyl ▪ fluconazole ▪ fludarabine ▪ fluorouracile ▪ foscarnet ▪ furosémide ▪ gallium, nitrate de ▪ hydralazine ▪ hydrocortisone ▪ hydromorphone ▪ insuline ▪ isoprotérénol ▪ kanamycine ▪ leucovorine ▪ lidocaïne ▪ lorazépam ▪ magnésium, sulfate de ▪ melphalan ▪ mépéridine ▪ méropénem ▪ méthicilline ▪ méthotrexate ▪ méthoxamine ▪ méthyldopate ▪ méthylergonovine ▪ métoclopramide ▪ métronidazole ▪ midazolam ▪ milrinone ▪ minocycline ▪ mitomycine ▪ morphine ▪ nafcilline ▪ néostigmine ▪ nitroglycérine ▪ nitroprusside ▪ noradrénaline ▪ œstrogènes conjugués ▪ ondansétron ▪ oxacilline ▪ oxytocine ▪ paclitaxel ▪ pancuronium ▪ pénicilline G potassique ▪ pentazocine ▪ pipéracilline ▪ pipéracilline/tazobactam ▪ potassium, chlorure de ▪ prednisolone ▪ procaïnamide ▪ prochlorpérazine ▪ propofol ▪ propranolol ▪ pyridostigmine ▪ ranitidine ▪ rémifentanil ▪ sargramostim ▪ scopolamine ▪ sodium, bicarbonate de ▪ streptokinase ▪ succinylcholine ▪ tacrolimus ▪ téniposide ▪ théophylline ▪ thiotépa ▪ ticarcilline ▪ ticarcilline/clavulanate ▪ triméthobenzamide ▪ triméthophane, camsylate de ▪ vécuronium ▪ vinblastine ▪ vincristine ▪ vinorelbine ▪ warfarine ▪ zidovudine.

Incompatibilité (tubulure en Y): alteplase ▪ amiodarone ▪ amphotéricine B, cholestéryle d' ▪ ciprofloxacine ▪ diazépam ▪ doxycycline ▪ ergotamine, tartrate de ▪ filgrastim ▪ gentamicine ▪ halopéridol ▪ idarubicine ▪ méthotriméprazine ▪ phénytoïne ▪ tobramycine ▪ triflupromazine ▪ vancomycine.

Compatibilité en addition au soluté: On recommande de ne pas mélanger l'héparine avec d'autres médicaments lors d'un traitement anticoagulant, même lorsqu'il s'agit de médicaments compatibles, car on pourrait être obligé de modifier la vitesse d'administration de l'héparine, ce qui risquerait de modifier la vitesse d'administration des autres médicaments mélangés dans la même solution. Cependant, en cas d'admixtion, les médicaments suivants sont compatibles: aminophylline ▪ amphotéricine ▪ calcium, gluconate de ▪ céfépime ▪ céphapirine ▪ chloramphénicol ▪ clindamycine ▪ colistiméthate ▪ dopamine ▪ érythromycine, gluceptate d' ▪ fluconazole ▪ flumazénil ▪ furosémide ▪ lidocaïne ▪ magnésium, sulfate de ▪ méropénem ▪ méthyldopa ▪ méthylprednisolone ▪ nafcilline ▪ octréotide ▪ potassium, chlorure de ▪ prednisolone ▪ promazine ▪ ranitidine ▪ sodium, bicarbonate de ▪ vérapamil ▪ vitamines du complexe B ▪ vitamines du complexe B avec C. Également, solutions destinées à la nutrition parentérale totale ou émulsions de lipides.

Incompatibilité en addition au soluté: alteplase ▪ amikacine ▪ ciprofloxacine ▪ cytarabine ▪ daunorubicine ▪ érythromycine, lactobionate d' ▪ gentamicine ▪ hyaluronidase ■ kanamycine ■ mépéridine ■ méthadone ■ morphine ■ polymyxine B ■ streptomycine.

ENSEIGNEMENT AU PATIENT ET À SES PROCHES

- CONSEILLER AU PATIENT DE SIGNALER IMMÉDIATEMENT À UN PROFESSIONNEL DE LA SANTÉ LES SAIGNEMENTS OU LES ECCHYMOSES INHABITUELS.
- Conseiller au patient de ne pas prendre de médicaments contenant de l'aspirine ou des AINS pendant le traitement à l'héparine.
- Recommander au patient d'éviter les injections IM et les activités pendant lesquelles il risque de se blesser. Lui recommander également d'utiliser au cours du traitement à l'héparine une brosse à dents à poils doux et un rasoir électrique.
- Recommander au patient qui doit suivre un traitement ou subir une intervention chirurgicale de prévenir le professionnel de la santé qu'il suit un traitement à l'héparine.
- Conseiller au patient de porter constamment sur lui une pièce d'identité où il est mentionné qu'il suit un traitement anticoagulant.

VÉRIFICATION DE L'EFFICACITÉ THÉRAPEUTIQUE

L'efficacité du traitement peut être démontrée par: l'allongement du temps de céphaline activée (TCA) de 1,5 à 2,5 fois par rapport au temps témoin, en l'absence de signes d'hémorragie ■ la prévention de la thrombose veineuse profonde et de l'embolie pulmonaire ■ la perméabilité des cathéters IV.

ALERTE CLINIQUE

HÉPARINES DE FAIBLE POIDS MOLÉCULAIRE/ HÉPARINOÏDES

daltéparine
Fragmin

danaparoïde (héparinoïde)
Orgaran

énoxaparine
Lovenox, Lovenox HP

nadroparine calcique
Fraxiparine, Fraxiparine Forte

tinzaparine
Innohep

CLASSIFICATION:
Anticoagulants, antithrombotiques

Grossesse – catégorie B

INDICATIONS

Prophylaxie de divers troubles thromboemboliques incluant la thrombose veineuse profonde et l'embolie pulmonaire, à la suite d'interventions chirurgicales qui augmentent habituellement le risque de telles complications (prothèse de la hanche et du genou, intervention à l'abdomen) ■ **Énoxaparine, nadroparine et daltéparine seulement**: Prévention des complications ischémiques (avec l'aspirine) dans les cas suivants: angine instable ■ IM sans onde Q ■ **Énoxaparine, daltéparine, nadroparine calcique, tinzaparine**: Traitement de la thrombose veineuse profonde ■ **Énoxaparine, tinzaparine**: Traitement de l'embolie pulmonaire ■ **Daltéparine, nadroparine calcique, tinzaparine**: Prévention de la coagulation lors de l'hémodialyse ■ **Danaparoïde seulement**: Patients souffrant ou ayant des antécédents de thrombopénie aiguë provoquée par l'héparine.

MÉCANISME D'ACTION

Potentialisation des effets inhibiteurs de l'antithrombine sur le facteur Xa et la thrombine ■ Le danaparoïde est un héparinoïde. ***Effets thérapeutiques:*** Prévention de la formation de thrombus.

PHARMACOCINÉTIQUE

Absorption: Tous les agents sont détruits par des enzymes présentes dans le tractus gastro-intestinal, d'où la nécessité de les administrer par voie parentérale. Bonne (SC: daltéparine 87 %, énoxaparine 92 %, danaparoïde 100 %, nadroparine 89 %, tinzaparine 90 %).

Distribution: Inconnue.

Métabolisme et excrétion: *Daltéparine* – inconnus; *danaparoïde et tinzaparine* – principalement excrétés par les reins; *énoxaparine et nadroparine* – faible métabolisme hépatique; élimination par voie rénale.

Demi-vie: *Daltéparine* – de 2,1 à 2,3 heures (prolongée en cas d'insuffisance rénale); *danaparoïde* – 24 heures; *énoxaparine* – de 3 à 6 heures; *tinzaparine* – inconnue; *nadroparine* – 3,5 heures (prolongée en cas d'insuffisance rénale).

H

Profil temps-action (effet anticoagulant)

	DÉBUT D'ACTION	PIC	DURÉE
Daltéparine SC	rapide	4 h	jusqu'à 24 h
Danaparoïde SC	inconnu	2 – 5 h	12 h
Énoxaparine SC	inconnu	inconnu	12 h
Nadroparine SC	inconnu	4 h	18 h
Tinzaparine SC	rapide	4 – 6 h	24 h

CONTRE-INDICATIONS, PRÉCAUTIONS ET MISES EN GARDE

Contre-indications: Hypersensibilité aux agents spécifiques ou aux produits du porc, une hypersensibilité croisée peut survenir entre les différents agents ■ Hémorragie non maîtrisée ■ Intolérance ou hypersensibilité aux sulfites (éviter l'usage de la tinzaparine) et à l'alcool benzylique (ne pas administrer la daltéparine, la tinzaparine, le danaparoïde ou l'énoxaparine présentés en fiole à doses multiples; vérifier les monographies de chacun des produits avant l'administration) ■ Hypertension grave non traitée ■ Antécédents de thrombopénie liée à l'héparine ou à une héparine de faible poids moléculaire ■ **Danaparoïde**: Endocardite bactérienne ■ Antécédents de thrombopénie au danaparoïde ■ Rétinopathie hémorragique ou diabétique ■ Intervention chirurgicale au cerveau, à la moelle épinière, aux yeux ou aux oreilles.

Précautions et mises en garde: Maladies rénale ou hépatique graves (adapter la dose d'énoxaparine si la Cl_{Cr} est < 30 mL/min) ■ Poids < 45 kg (adapter la dose d'énoxaparine) ■ Rétinopathie (patients hypertendus ou diabétiques) ■ Ulcère récent ■ Anesthésie rachidienne ou péridurale (risque accru d'hématomes rachidiens ou périduraux, particulièrement en cas de traitement concomitant par des AINS, de ponctions péridurales répétées ou traumatiques ou de l'installation d'une sonde péridurale à demeure) ■ Antécédents de troubles de la coagulation congénitaux ou acquis ■ **GÉR.**: L'élimination de l'énoxaparine est plus lente chez les personnes âgées ■ Tumeur maligne ■ **OBST., ALLAITEMENT, PÉD.**: L'innocuité du médicament n'a pas été établie.

EXTRÊME PRUDENCE: ANESTHÉSIE RACHIDIENNE OU PÉRIDURALE (RISQUE ÉLEVÉ D'HÉMATOMES INTRARACHIDIENS, PARTICULIÈREMENT LORS DE L'USAGE DE CATHÉTERS PÉRIDURAUX POSTOPÉRATOIRES OU LORS DE L'ADMINISTRATION CONCOMITANTE DE MÉDICAMENTS INFLUANT SUR L'HÉMOSTASE, COMME LES ANTI-INFLAMMATOIRES NON STÉROÏDIENS (AINS), LES INHIBITEURS PLAQUETTAIRES OU D'AUTRES MÉDICAMENTS QUI INFLUENT SUR LA COAGULATION. LE RISQUE SEMBLE ÉGALEMENT AUGMENTÉ DANS LES CAS D'INTERVENTIONS PÉRIDURALES OU RACHIDIENNES TRAUMATIQUES OU RÉPÉTÉES ■ HYPERTENSION GRAVE NON MAÎTRISÉE ■ ENDOCARDITE BACTÉRIENNE, TROUBLES DE LA COAGULATION ■ MALADIE, ULCÈRE OU SAIGNEMENTS GASTROINTESTINAUX ■ ACCIDENT VASCULAIRE HÉMORRAGIQUE ■ INTERVENTION CHIRURGICALE RÉCENTE AU SNC OU AUX YEUX ■ SAIGNEMENTS OU ULCÈRE GASTROINTESTINAL EN POUSSÉE ÉVOLUTIVE.

RÉACTIONS INDÉSIRABLES ET EFFETS SECONDAIRES

SNC: étourdissements, céphalées, insomnie.

CV: œdème.

GI: constipation, nausées, élévations réversibles des enzymes hépatiques, vomissements.

GU: rétention urinaire.

Tég.: ecchymoses, prurit, rash, urticaire.

Hémat.: HÉMORRAGIE, anémie, thrombopénie.

Locaux: érythème au point d'injection, hématome, irritation, douleurs.

Divers: fièvre.

INTERACTIONS

Médicament-médicament: En cas d'administration concomitante de **warfarine** ou de **médicaments qui affectent la fonction plaquettaire**, dont l'**aspirine**, les **AINS**, le **dipyridamole**, certaines **pénicillines**, le **clopidogrel**, la **ticlopidine**, l'**abciximab**, l'**eptifibatide**, le **tirofiban** et le **dextran**, le risque d'hémorragie est accru.

Médicament-produits naturels: Le risque de saignements est accru en cas de consommation concomitante d'**ail**, d'**arnica**, de **camomille**, de **dong quai**, de **girofle**, de **gingembre**, de **ginkgo**, de **ginseng** et de certains **autres produits**.

VOIES D'ADMINISTRATION ET POSOLOGIE

Daltéparine

- **SC (adultes)**: *Prophylaxie de la thrombose veineuse profonde chez les patients médicaux choisis*: 5 000 UI anti-Xa, 1 fois par jour. *Prophylaxie de la thrombose veineuse profonde avant une chirurgie majeure* – 2 500 UI anti-Xa, de 1 à 2 heures avant l'intervention, puis chaque matin, pendant au moins 5 à 7 jours. *Prophylaxie de la thrombose veineuse profonde avant une chirurgie orthopédique de la hanche* – 5 000 UI anti-Xa, la veille de l'opération, puis tous les soirs, pendant au moins 5 à 7 jours, ou 2 500 UI anti-Xa, de 1 à 2 heures avant la chirurgie, et 1 fois de plus, de 8 à 12 heures plus tard, puis 5 000 UI anti-Xa, chaque matin, pendant au moins 5 à 7 jours. *Traitement de la thrombose veineuse profonde* – 200 UI anti-Xa/kg/jour. La dose unique quotidienne ne doit pas dépasser

18 000 UI. *Traitement de la thrombose veineuse profonde chez les patients à haut risque d'hémorragie* – 100 UI antiXa/kg en 12 heures par perfusion continue. *Prévention de la coagulation durant l'hémodialyse ou l'hémoperfusion* – de 30 à 40 UI anti-Xa/kg en bolus IV au début de la dialyse, puis de 10 à 15 UI anti-Xa/kg/h en perfusion IV. *Traitement de l'angor instable ou de l'IM sans onde Q, en concomitance avec l'AAS (de 100 à 325 mg par jour)* – 120 UI anti-Xa/kg, 2 fois par jour (sans dépasser 10 000 UI par dose), pendant un maximum de 6 jours.

Danaparoïde

- **SC (adultes):** *Prophylaxie de la thrombose veineuse profonde après une chirurgie orthopédique, thoracique ou abdominale majeure* – 750 UI d'anti-Xa, toutes les 12 heures, pendant une période pouvant atteindre 14 jours.
- **SC (adultes): patients présentant une thrombopénie induite par l'héparine:** *Prophylaxie de la thrombose veineuse profonde – présence de thrombopénie induite par l'héparine:* (patients pesant ≤ 90 kg) 750 UI, 2 ou 3 fois par jour, pendant 7 à 10 jours. Pour atteindre rapidement des concentrations prophylactiques, on peut administrer un bolus IV initial de 1 250 UI; (patients pensant > 90 kg) 1 250 UI, 2 ou 3 fois par jour, pendant 7 à 10 jours. Pour atteindre rapidement des concentrations prophylactiques, on peut administrer un bolus IV initial de 1 250 UI; *antécédents de thrombopénie induite par l'héparine (> 3 mois):* (patient pesant ≤ 90 kg) 750 UI, 2 ou 3 fois par jour, pendant 7 à 10 jours; (patients pesant > 90 kg) 1 250 UI, 2 ou 3 fois par jour, pendant 7 à 10 jours.
- **IV (adultes): Patients présentant une thrombopénie induite par l'héparine:** *Traitement de la thrombose veineuse profonde ou de l'embolie pulmonaire – Patients ≤ 55 kg:* 1 250 à 1 500 UI en bolus IV, puis 400 UI/h pour 4 heures, 300 UI/h pour 4 heures, puis 150 à 200 UI/h par la suite. Ajuster la vitesse de perfusion afin de maintenir les niveaux plasmatiques d'activité d'anti-Xa entre 0,5 et 0,8 unité/mL. *Patients > 55 kg et ≤ 90 kg:* 2 250 à 2 500 UI en bolus IV, puis 400 UI/h pour 4 heures, 300 UI/h pour 4 heures, puis 150 à 200 UI/h par la suite. Ajuster la vitesse de perfusion afin de maintenir les niveaux plasmatiques d'activité d'anti-Xa entre 0,5 et 0,8 unité/mL. *Patients > 90 kg:* 3 750 UI en bolus IV, puis 400 UI/h pour 4 heures, 300 UI/h pour 4 heures, puis 150 à 200 UI/h par la suite. Ajuster la vitesse de perfusion afin de maintenir les niveaux plasmatiques d'activité d'anti-Xa entre 0,5 et 0,8 unité/mL.

Énoxaparine

- **SC (adultes):** *Prophylaxie de la thrombose veineuse profonde chez les patients médicaux choisis* – 40 mg, 1 fois par jour, pendant 6 à 11 jours. *Prophylaxie de la thrombose veineuse profonde lors d'une chirurgie orthopédique* – 30 mg, toutes les 12 heures, pendant 7 à 14 jours, en commençant de 12 à 24 heures après l'intervention. *Prophylaxie de la thrombose veineuse profonde avant une chirurgie colorectale, abdominale, gynécologique ou urologique* – 40 mg, 2 heures avant la chirurgie, puis quotidiennement pendant 7 à 10 jours. *Traitement de la thrombose veineuse profonde* – 1,5 mg/kg, 1 fois par jour, ou 1 mg/kg, toutes les 12 heures. *Traitement de l'angor instable ou de l'IM sans onde Q, en concomitance avec l'AAS (de 100 à 325 mg/jour)* – 1 mg/kg, toutes les 12 heures (sans dépasser 100 mg par dose), pendant 2 à 8 jours.

Nadroparine calcique

- **SC (adultes):** *Prophylaxie de la thrombose veineuse profonde avant une chirurgie majeure* – 2 850 UI anti-Xa, de 2 à 4 heures avant l'intervention, puis quotidiennement, pendant au moins 7 jours. *Prophylaxie de la thrombose veineuse profonde avant une chirurgie orthopédique* – 38 UI anti-Xa/kg, 12 heures avant l'intervention, et 12 heures après, ensuite, quotidiennement pendant 3 jours, puis, 57 UI anti-Xa/kg quotidiennement, pendant au moins 7 jours. *Traitement de la thrombose veineuse profonde* – 171 UI anti-Xa/kg, 1 fois par jour, pendant 10 jours. La dose quotidienne unique ne doit pas dépasser 17 000 UI. *Traitement de la thrombose veineuse profonde chez les patients à haut risque d'hémorragie* – 86 UI anti-Xa/kg, 2 fois par jour pendant 10 jours. *Prévention de la coagulation lors de l'hémodialyse et de l'hémoperfusion* – 65 UI anti-Xa/kg dans la tubulure intra-artérielle. *Traitement de l'angor instable ou de l'IM sans onde Q en concomitance avec l'AAS (de 100 à 325 mg/jour)* – 86 UI anti-Xa/kg en bolus IV initialement, puis 86 UI anti-Xa/kg, toutes les 12 heures. La durée habituelle du traitement est de 6 jours.

Tinzaparine

- **SC (adultes):** *Prophylaxie de la thrombose veineuse profonde avant une chirurgie majeure* – 3 500 UI anti-Xa, 2 heures avant l'intervention, puis 3 500 UI anti-Xa, quotidiennement, pendant 7 à 10 jours. *Prophylaxie de la thrombose veineuse profonde avant une chirurgie orthopédique de la hanche* – 50 UI anti-Xa/kg, 2 heures avant l'intervention, puis 50 UI anti-Xa/kg, quotidiennement, pendant 7 à 10 jours, ou 75 UI anti-Xa/kg, 1 fois par jour après l'intervention, puis, pendant 7 à 10 jours.

Prophylaxie de la thrombose veineuse profonde avant une chirurgie du genou – 75 UI anti-Xa/kg, 1 fois par jour après l'intervention, puis, pendant 7 à 10 jours. *Traitement de la thrombose veineuse profonde* – 175 UI anti-Xa/kg, 1 fois par jour, pendant 7 jours. *Prévention de la coagulation lors de l'hémodialyse et de l'hémoperfusion* – 4 500 UI anti-Xa dans la tubulure artérielle au début d'une séance de 4 heures ou moins.

PRÉSENTATION

- **Daltéparine**
  Solution pour injection: ampoules: 10 000 UI anti-Xa/mL[Pr], flacons: 25 000 UI anti-Xa/mL[Pr], seringues préremplies: 2 500 UI anti-Xa/0,2 mL[Pr], 5 000 UI anti-Xa/0,2 mL[Pr], 7 500 UI anti-Xa/0,3 mL[Pr], 10 000 UI anti-Xa/0,4 mL[Pr], 12 500 UI anti-Xa/0,5 mL[Pr], 15 000 UI anti-Xa/0,6 mL[Pr], 18 000 UI anti-Xa/0,72 mL[Pr].
- **Danaparoïde**
  Solution pour injection: 750 UI anti-Xa/0,6 mL[Pr], en ampoules.
- **Énoxaparine**
  Solution pour injection: 30 mg/0,3 mL (dans des seringues préremplies)[Pr], 40 mg/0,4 mL (dans des seringues préremplies)[Pr], 60 mg/0,6 mL (dans des seringues préremplies)[Pr], 80 mg/0,8 mL (dans des seringues préremplies)[Pr], 100 mg/1 mL (dans des seringues préremplies)[Pr], 120 mg/0,8 mL (dans des seringues préremplies HP)[Pr], 150 mg/1 mL (dans des seringues préremplies HP)[Pr], 300 mg/3 mL (flacons multidoses)[Pr].
- **Nadroparine calcique**
  Fraxiparine - Solution pour injection: ampoules: 9 500 UI anti-Xa/mL[Pr], seringues préremplies: 2 850 UI anti-Xa/0,3 mL[Pr], 3 800 UI anti-Xa/0,4 mL[Pr], 5 700 UI anti-Xa/0,6 mL[Pr], 7 600 UI anti-Xa/0,8 mL[Pr], 9 500 UI anti-Xa/1 mL[Pr].
  Fraxiparine Forte - Solution pour injection: ampoules: 19 000 UI anti-Xa/mL[Pr], seringues préremplies: 11 400 UI anti-Xa/0,6 mL[Pr], 15 200 UI anti-Xa/0,8 mL[Pr], 19 000 UI anti-Xa/1 mL[Pr].
- **Tinzaparine**
  Solution pour injection: Fioles: 10 000 UI anti-Xa/mL[Pr], 20 000 UI anti-Xa/mL[Pr]; seringues: 10 000 UI anti-Xa/1 mL[Pr], 20 000 UI anti-Xa/1 mL[Pr].

SOINS INFIRMIERS

ÉVALUATION DE LA SITUATION

- RECHERCHER LES SIGNES SUIVANTS D'HÉMORRAGIE: SAIGNEMENT DES GENCIVES ET DU NEZ, FORMATION INHABITUELLE D'ECCHYMOSES, SELLES NOIRES GOUDRONNEUSES, HÉMATURIE, CHUTE DE L'HÉMATOCRITE OU DE LA PRESSION ARTÉRIELLE, PRÉSENCE DE SANG OCCULTE DANS LES SELLES, SAIGNEMENT AU SIÈGE D'UNE CHIRURGIE. PRÉVENIR LE MÉDECIN SI CES SYMPTÔMES SE MANIFESTENT.
- Rechercher les signes qui révèlent que la thrombose s'aggrave ou qu'elle touche d'autres territoires. Les symptômes dépendent du territoire touché. Suivre l'état neurologique à intervalles fréquents et rester à l'affût des signes d'atteinte neurologique. Un traitement urgent pourrait être nécessaire.
- Suivre de près les réactions d'hypersensibilité: frissons, fièvre, urticaire. Signaler ces réactions au médecin.
- Rester à l'affût des signes et des symptômes d'atteinte neurologique chez les patients porteurs d'un cathéter péridural.

SC: Observer étroitement la formation d'hématomes et d'ecchymoses ou l'apparition d'une inflammation au point d'injection.

Tests de laboratoire:

- Noter la numération globulaire et le nombre de plaquettes. Examiner les selles à intervalles réguliers pendant toute la durée du traitement pour déceler la présence de sang occulte. En cas de thrombopénie, suivre de près l'état du patient. Si les valeurs de l'hématocrite chutent soudainement, rechercher les foyers hémorragiques possibles. Il n'est pas nécessaire de suivre en particulier le temps de céphaline activée (TCA).
- Ces agents peuvent provoquer l'élévation des concentrations d'AST et d'ALT.

TOXICITÉ ET SURDOSAGE: *Énoxaparine* – en cas de surdosage, administrer 1 mg de sulfate de protamine (injection IV lente) par mg d'énoxaparine. *Daltéparine* – en cas de surdosage, administrer 1 mg de sulfate de protamine (injection IV lente) par 100 UI d'anti-facteur Xa. Si le TCA, mesuré de 2 à 4 heures après l'administration du sulfate de protamine, demeure prolongé, on peut administrer une deuxième perfusion de protamine à 0,5 mg par 100 UI d'anti-facteur Xa de daltéparine. Le sulfate de protamine n'est qu'un antidote partiel du *danaparoïde*. En cas de surdosage, cesser l'administration du danaparoïde. En cas d'hémorragie, administrer du sang ou des produits sanguins, selon les besoins.

DIAGNOSTICS INFIRMIERS POSSIBLES

- Irrigation tissulaire inefficace (Indications).
- Risque d'accident (Effets secondaires).
- Connaissances insuffisantes sur le traitement médicamenteux (Enseignement au patient et à ses proches).

INTERVENTIONS INFIRMIÈRES

ALERTE CLINIQUE: L'ADMINISTRATION ACCIDENTELLE DE 2 HÉPARINES (HÉPARINE NON FRACTIONNÉE ET HÉPARINE DE FAIBLE POIDS MOLÉCULAIRE) A ENTRAINÉ DE GRAVES EFFETS SECONDAIRES ALLANT JUSQU'À LA MORT. VÉRIFIER LA MÉDICATION COURANTE ET RÉCENTE DU PATIENT (URGENCE, BLOC OPÉRATOIRE) AVANT D'ADMINISTRER DE L'HÉPARINE NON FRACTIONNÉE OU DE L'HÉPARINE DE FAIBLE POIDS MOLÉCULAIRE.

- Ces agents et l'héparine non fractionnée ou les autres préparations d'héparine de faible poids moléculaire ne sont pas interchangeables (unité pour unité).

SC:

- Administrer profondément dans le tissu SC. Alterner les points d'injection entre les sections antérolatérales gauche et droite et postérolatérales gauche et droite de la paroi abdominale, le haut de la cuisse ou les fesses. Faire entrer l'aiguille sur toute sa longueur à un angle de 45° ou de 90° dans un pli cutané retenu entre le pouce et l'index; garder le pli cutané pendant toute la durée de l'injection. Ne pas aspirer ni masser. Assurer la rotation des points d'injection à intervalles fréquents. Ne pas administrer par voie IM en raison du risque de formation d'hématomes. La solution devrait être transparente; ne pas injecter de solution contenant des particules.
- En cas de formation excessive d'ecchymoses, il peut s'avérer utile de masser le point d'injection avec un cube de glace avant d'administrer le médicament.

Danaparoïde

IV directe: Pour le bolus de charge seulement: administrer sans dilution ou diluer dans 50 à 100 mL de NaCl 0,9 % ou de D5%E. Consulter les directives de chaque fabricant avant de reconstituer la préparation.

Vitesse d'administration: Administrer sans dilution en 5 minutes ou en 15 à 30 minutes si dilué.

Perfusion intermittente/continue: Pour la dose d'entretien: diluer 2 250 UI dans 250 mL de NaCl 0,9 % ou de D5%E pour obtenir une concentration finale de 9 UI/mL. Consulter les directives de chaque fabricant avant de reconstituer la préparation.

Vitesse d'administration: Utiliser une pompe à perfusion pour s'assurer qu'on administre la dose exacte: 400 UI/h (44 mL/h) pour 4 heures, 300 UI/h (33 mL/h) pour 4 heures, puis 150 à 200 UI/h (17-22 mL/h). Ajuster la vitesse de perfusion afin de maintenir les niveaux plasmatiques d'activité anti-Xa entre 0,5 et 0,8 unité/mL.

Énoxaparine

- Pour éviter la perte de médicament, ne pas évacuer les bulles d'air de la seringue avant d'injecter la dose.
- Pour assurer une absorption adéquate, le fabricant recommande d'injecter l'énoxaparine dans les sections antérolatérales gauche et droite et postérolatérales gauche et droite de la paroi abdominale seulement.
- Pour réduire le risque d'hémorragie après l'exploration instrumentale en cas d'angine instable, on doit respecter étroitement les intervalles recommandés entre les doses. Laisser la gaine vasculaire en place pendant 6 à 8 heures après l'administration de la dose d'énoxaparine. Administrer la dose suivante d'énoxaparine plus de 6 à 8 heures après le retrait de la gaine. Observer attentivement le patient pour déceler l'hémorragie ou la formation d'un hématome.

Tinzaparine

- La tinzaparine devrait être administrée tous les jours pendant un minimum de 6 jours, et ce jusqu'à ce que l'anticoagulothérapie à la warfarine donne les résultats escomptés (RNI de 2,0 pendant 2 jours consécutifs). Démarrer l'administration de warfarine dans les 24 à 72 heures qui suivent le début du traitement à la tinzaparine.
- La solution pour injection est claire et incolore ou légèrement jaune; ne pas administrer une solution qui a changé de couleur ou qui contient des particules.
- Les fioles multidoses contiennent de l'alcool benzylique; administrer avec prudence chez les femmes enceintes.

ENSEIGNEMENT AU PATIENT ET À SES PROCHES

- Conseiller au patient de signaler immédiatement à un professionnel de la santé les saignements ou les ecchymoses inhabituels, les étourdissements, les démangeaisons, le rash, la fièvre, l'œdème ou les difficultés respiratoires.
- Conseiller au patient de ne pas prendre d'aspirine (acide acétylsalicylique), de naproxène ou d'ibuprofène pendant le traitement à l'héparine sans consulter un professionnel de la santé au préalable.

VÉRIFICATION DE L'EFFICACITÉ THÉRAPEUTIQUE

L'efficacité du traitement peut être démontrée par: la prévention de la thrombose veineuse profonde et de l'embolie pulmonaire ■ l'amélioration des signes et des symptômes de thrombose veineuse profonde ■ la prévention des complications ischémiques (en association avec l'aspirine) chez les patients souffrant d'angine instable ou ayant subi un IM sans onde Q.

HORMONES DE CROISSANCE

somatotrophine (recombinante)

Humatrope, Nutropin, Nutropin AQ, Saizen, Serostim

somatrem (recombinant)

Protropin

CLASSIFICATION:

Hormones hypophysaires (hormones de croissance)

Grossesse – catégorie C

H

INDICATIONS

Retard de la croissance chez l'enfant, associé à une insuffisance rénale chronique (Nutropin, Saizen) ■ Retard de la croissance chez l'enfant, dû à une carence en somatotrophine ou en hormone de croissance (Humatrope, Nutropin, Protropin, Saizen) ■ Nanisme associé au syndrome de Turner (Humatrope, Nutropin, Saizen) ■ Carence en hormone de croissance chez l'adulte (Humatrope, Nutropin, Saizen) ■ Syndrome de dépérissement ou cachexie associés au sida (Serostim).

MÉCANISME D'ACTION

Stimulation de la croissance (du squelette et des cellules) ■ Nombreux effets métaboliques, dont: une synthèse accrue des protéines ■ un métabolisme accru des glucides ■ la mobilisation des lipides ■ la rétention du sodium, du phosphore et du potassium ■ La séquence d'acides aminés de la somatotrophine est identique à celle de l'hormone de croissance humaine; cependant, le somatrem possède un acide aminé de plus. Les deux agents sont synthétisés par la technologie de recombinaison de l'ADN. ***Effets thérapeutiques:*** Stimulation de la croissance du squelette chez les enfants qui présentent une carence en somatotrophine ■ Traitement de substitution de la somatotrophine chez les adultes carencés ■ Traitement du syndrome de dépérissement chez les patients atteints du sida.

PHARMACOCINÉTIQUE

Absorption: Bonne (SC et IM).

Distribution: Répartition dans les organes fortement irrigués (foie, reins).

Métabolisme et excrétion: Le médicament se décompose dans les cellules rénales en acides aminés qu'on retrouve dans la circulation sanguine; métabolisme partiellement hépatique.

Demi-vie: *SC* – 3,8 heures; *IM* – 4,9 heures.

Profil temps-action (effets sur la croissance)

	Début d'action	Pic	Durée
IM, SC	en l'espace de 3 mois	inconnu	12 – 48 h

CONTRE-INDICATIONS, PRÉCAUTIONS ET MISES EN GARDE

Contre-indications: Soudure des cartilages épiphysaires ■ Néoplasies évolutives ■ Hypersensibilité au m-crésol ou à la glycérine (Humatrope) ou à l'alcool benzylique (Nutropin, Protropin, Saizen), contenus dans l'eau bactériostatique pour injection USP servant à la reconstitution de la préparation ■ Maladie aiguë très grave à la suite de complications chirurgicales ou traumatismes accidentels multiples ■ Insuffisance respiratoire aiguë ■ Patients atteints du syndrome de Prader-Labhart-Willi, très obèses ou atteints d'insuffisance respiratoire ■ Rétinopathie diabétique proliférative ou préproliférative (Saizen).

Précautions et mises en garde: Carence en hormone de croissance secondaire à une lésion intracrânienne ■ Carence coexistante en ACTH (corticotrophine) ■ Diabète (risque d'insulinorésistance) ■ Dysfonctionnement thyroïdien ■ **Obst., allaitement**: L'innocuité de ces agents n'a pas été établie.

RÉACTIONS INDÉSIRABLES ET EFFETS SECONDAIRES

CV: œdème des mains et des pieds.

Endo.: hyperglycémie, hypothyroïdie, insulinorésistance.

Locaux: douleurs au point d'injection.

Loc.: *Serostim seulement* – syndrome du tunnel carpien, douleurs musculosquelettiques.

INTERACTIONS

Médicament-médicament: L'administration de doses élevées (équivalent à 10 à 15 mg/m²/jour) de **corticostéroïdes** peut diminuer la réponse à la somatotrophine.

VOIES D'ADMINISTRATION ET POSOLOGIE

Humatrope

- **SC (adultes)**: 0,006 mg/kg/jour (0,18 UI/kg/jour) en une injection SC quotidienne; la dose peut être augmentée jusqu'à 0,0125 mg/kg/jour (0,375 UI/kg/jour).
- **SC (enfants)**: *Syndrome de Turner* – la posologie hebdomadaire maximale est de 0,375 mg/kg (1,125 UI/kg), fractionnée en doses égales à administrer tous les 1 ou 2 jours (3 fois/semaine).
- **IM, SC (enfants)**: 0,18 mg/kg (0,54 UI/kg) par semaine, en doses fractionnées, tous les jours, 1 jour sur 2 (3 fois/semaine) ou 6 fois par semaine (jusqu'à

un maximum de 0,3 mg/kg ou 0,9 UI/kg par semaine).

Nutropin/Nutropin AQ

- **SC, IM (enfants):** La dose maximale est de 0,3 mg/kg/semaine (0,9 UI/kg/semaine). La dose quotidienne se calcule selon la formule suivante: dose/injection (mg) = poids du patient (kg) × 0,043 (maximum) mg/kg. *Insuffisance rénale chronique* – la dose maximale est de 0,35 mg/kg/semaine (1,05 UI/kg/semaine). La dose quotidienne se calcule selon la formule suivante: dose/injection (mg) = poids du patient (kg) × 0,05 (maximum) mg/kg.
- **SC (enfants):** *Syndrome de Turner* – la posologie recommandée est de 0,375 mg/kg/semaine au maximum, répartie en 3 à 7 doses égales par semaine.
- **SC (adultes):** 0,042 mg/kg/semaine au maximum, par injection sous-cutanée quotidienne; la dose peut être augmentée jusqu'à 0,175 mg/kg/semaine chez les sujets < 35 ans ou jusqu'à 0,0875 mg/kg/semaine chez les sujets ≥ 35 ans.

Protropin

- **IM, SC:** La dose maximale est de 0,3 mg/kg/semaine (environ 0,9 UI/kg/semaine). La dose quotidienne se calcule selon la formule suivante: dose/injection (mg) = poids du patient (kg) × 0,043 (maximum) mg/kg.

Saizen

- **SC, IM (enfants):** 0,2 mg/kg/semaine, jusqu'à un maximum de 0,27 mg/kg/semaine. Cette dose hebdomadaire peut être fractionnée en 3 injections IM ou en 3, 6 ou 7 injections SC. *Insuffisance rénale chronique* – 0,35 mg/kg/semaine.

Serostim

- **SC (adultes):** *> 55 kg* – 6 mg, 1 fois par jour; *de 45 à 55 kg* – 5 mg, 1 fois par jour; *de 35 à 45 kg* – 4 mg, 1 fois par jour; *< 35 kg* – 0,1 mg/kg, 1 fois par jour.

PRÉSENTATION

- **Somatrem (Protropin)**
  Poudre pour injection: 10 mg (30 UI)/fiole[Pr].
- **Humatrope**
  Poudre pour injection: 5 mg (15 UI)/fiole[Pr], 6 mg (18 UI)/cartouche[Pr], 12 mg (36 UI)/cartouche[Pr], 24 mg (72 UI)/cartouche[Pr].
- **Nutropin**
  Poudre pour injection: 5 mg (15 UI)/fiole[Pr], 10 mg (30 UI)/fiole[Pr].
- **Nutropin AQ**
  Solution pour injection: 5 mg (15 UI)/mL, en fioles de 2 mL[Pr].
- **Saizen**
  Poudre pour injection: 1,33 mg/fiole[Pr], 3,33 mg/fiole[Pr], 5 mg/fiole[Pr], 8,8 mg/fiole[Pr].
- **Serostim**
  Poudre pour injection: 4 mg/fiole[Pr], 5 mg/fiole[Pr], 6 mg/fiole[Pr], 8,88 mg/fiole[Pr].

SOINS INFIRMIERS

ÉVALUATION DE LA SITUATION

Retard de la croissance: Déterminer l'âge osseux tous les ans et mesurer le taux de croissance, la taille et le poids du patient tous les 3 à 6 mois, tout au long du traitement.

H

Syndrome du dépérissement ou de la cachexie associés au sida: Réévaluer le traitement chez les patients qui continuent de perdre du poids au cours des 2 premières semaines de traitement.

Tests de laboratoire:

- Noter avant le traitement et pendant toute sa durée, les résultats des tests de la fonction thyroïdienne. Le médicament peut diminuer les concentrations de T_4, le captage de l'iode radioactif et la capacité de liaison à la thyroxine. En cas d'hypothyroïdie, pour rendre la somatotrophine efficace, il faut administrer en association une hormonothérapie thyroïdienne substitutive. Le traitement par la somatotrophine peut accroître les concentrations sériques de phosphore inorganique, de phosphatase alcaline et de parathormone.
- Noter la glycémie à intervalles réguliers pendant toute la durée du traitement. Chez les patients diabétiques, il pourrait s'avérer nécessaire d'administrer une dose plus élevée d'insuline.
- Suivre de près la formation d'anticorps neutralisants, si l'enfant ne grandit pas de plus de 2,5 cm en 6 mois.

DIAGNOSTICS INFIRMIERS POSSIBLES

- Image corporelle perturbée (Indications).
- Connaissances insuffisantes sur le traitement médicamenteux (Enseignement au patient et à ses proches).

INTERVENTIONS INFIRMIÈRES

- Assurer la rotation des points d'injection.

Somatrem: Reconstituer le contenu d'une fiole de 10 mg avec 1 à 10 mL d'eau bactériostatique pour injection. Ajouter l'eau en la faisant couler sur les parois de la fiole de verre. Ne pas secouer la fiole; agiter la fiole dans un mouvement de rotation lent jusqu'à la dissolution complète de la poudre. La solution est transparente; ne pas utiliser les solutions troubles. Jeter la fiole après en avoir retiré la dose.

Humatrope: Reconstituer chaque fiole de 5 mg avec 1,5 à 5 mL du diluant fourni. La solution demeure stable au réfrigérateur pendant une période allant jusqu'à 21 jours.

Nutropin/Nutropin AQ: Reconstituer chaque fiole de Nutropin de 5 mg avec 1 à 5 mL d'eau bactériostatique pour injection et chaque fiole de 10 mg avec 1 à 10 mL d'eau bactériostatique pour injection. Nutropin AQ est présenté en solution prête à être utilisée; aucune reconstitution n'est donc nécessaire. Les solutions reconstituées sont stables pendant 14 jours au réfrigérateur.

H

Saizen: Reconstituer chaque fiole de 1,33 mg avec jusqu'à 1 mL de solution de NaCl pour injection USP, chaque fiole de 3,33 mg, avec jusqu'à 5 mL de solution de NaCl pour injection USP ou de solution de NaCL bactériostatique pour injection USP, et chaque fiole de 5 mg et de 8,8 mg, avec 1 à 3 mL d'eau pour injection ou d'eau bactériostatique pour injection. Les solutions reconstituées avec un diluant ne contenant pas d'agents bactériostatiques doivent être utilisées immédiatement, et celles diluées avec un diluant contenant un agent bactériostatique (alcool benzylique) sont stables pendant 14 jours au réfrigérateur.

Serostim: Reconstituer chaque fiole avec 1 mL d'eau stérile pour injection. Utiliser dans les 24 heures suivant la reconstitution de la préparation.

- Consulter les directives de chaque fabricant avant de reconstituer la préparation.

ENSEIGNEMENT AU PATIENT ET À SES PROCHES

- Montrer au patient et aux parents comment reconstituer le médicament, comment choisir le point d'injection, comment administrer l'injection IM ou SC et comment mettre au rebut les aiguilles et les seringues. Lui expliquer le schéma posologique. Conseiller aux parents de signaler à un professionnel de la santé les douleurs persistantes ou l'œdème au point d'injection.
- Expliquer les raisons qui sous-tendent l'interdiction d'utiliser cette hormone pour accroître la performance athlétique. L'administration de cet agent chez des personnes ne souffrant pas de carence en hormone de croissance ou dont les cartilages épiphysaires sont soudés peut entraîner l'acromégalie (épaississement des traits du visage, hypertrophie des mains, des pieds et des viscères, élévation de la glycémie et hypertension).
- Insister sur l'importance d'un suivi régulier par un endocrinologue qui pourra s'assurer que le taux de croissance est adéquat, vérifier les résultats des tests de laboratoire et déterminer l'âge osseux par examen radiologique.
- Expliquer aux parents et à l'enfant que cet agent est synthétique; il n'y a par conséquent aucun risque de transmission du syndrome de Creutzfeldt-Jacob, comme auparavant, lorsque la somatotrophine était extraite de cadavres humains.

VÉRIFICATION DE L'EFFICACITÉ THÉRAPEUTIQUE

L'efficacité du traitement peut être démontrée par: l'atteinte d'une taille adulte chez l'enfant souffrant d'un arrêt de croissance secondaire à une carence en hormone de croissance hypophysaire; le traitement ne peut être administré qu'avant la soudure des cartilages épiphysaires (jusqu'à l'âge de 14 à 15 ans, chez les filles, et de 15 à 16 ans, chez les garçons) ▪ la substitution de la somatotrophine chez les adultes présentant une carence ▪ un gain de poids chez les patients atteints du sida. ✳

HUILE MINÉRALE

Fleet à l'huile minérale, Lansoÿl, Lansoÿl sans sucre, Nujol

CLASSIFICATION:

Laxatif (lubrifiant)

Grossesse – catégorie C

INDICATIONS

Lubrifiant intestinal indiqué dans le traitement de la constipation occasionnelle et passagère ▪ Diminution de l'effort d'évacuation après une chirurgie ou dans d'autres circonstances particulières.

MÉCANISME D'ACTION

Lubrification des selles et de l'intestin par un enduit qui favorise le passage de la masse fécale ▪ Amélioration de la rétention hydrique dans les selles. ***Effets thérapeutiques:*** Ramollissement de la masse fécale et élimination ultérieure.

PHARMACOCINÉTIQUE

Absorption: Minime (PO ou IR).

Distribution: Faible en raison de la faible absorption systémique.

Métabolisme et excrétion: Inconnus. L'effet est principalement local; l'huile minérale non absorbée est évacuée en même temps que la masse fécale.

Demi-vie: Inconnue.

Profil temps-action (effet laxatif)

	DÉBUT D'ACTION	PIC	DURÉE
PO	6 – 8 h	inconnu	inconnue
IR	2 – 15 min	inconnu	inconnue

CONTRE-INDICATIONS, PRÉCAUTIONS ET MISES EN GARDE

Contre-indications: Hypersensibilité ▪ Appendicite ▪ Diverticulite ▪ Occlusion intestinale ▪ Colite ulcéreuse, saignement rectal ▪ Colostomie ou iléostomie ▪ Dysphagie ▪ **PÉD.**: Enfants < 6 ans (PO) et enfants < 2 ans (IR).

Précautions et mises en garde: Fièvre ▪ Nausées ▪ Vomissements ▪ Douleurs abdominales ▪ **PÉD., GÉR.**: Risque accru de pneumonie graisseuse lors de l'utilisation chez les enfants, les personnes âgées ou les patients débilités ▪ **OBST.**: La prise prolongée diminue l'absorption des vitamines liposolubles.

RÉACTIONS INDÉSIRABLES ET EFFETS SECONDAIRES

Resp.: pneumonie graisseuse.

GI: fuite d'huile minérale par le rectum, irritation anale.

INTERACTIONS

Médicament-médicament: L'administration concomitante de **docusate** (**sodique** ou **calcique**) peut augmenter l'absorption systémique de l'huile minérale qui se distribue alors dans la muqueuse intestinale, les ganglions lymphatiques mésentériques, le foie et la rate ▪ L'huile minérale diminue l'absorption des **vitamines liposolubles (A, D, E, K)**.

Médicament-aliments: L'huile minérale diminue l'absorption des **vitamines liposolubles (A, D, E, K)**.

VOIES D'ADMINISTRATION ET POSOLOGIE

Gelée orale

- **PO (adultes et enfants > 12 ans)**: De 15 à 60 mL (préparation sans sucre – de 15 à 45 mL), 1 fois par jour dans la journée (ne pas prendre au coucher).
- **PO (enfants de 6 à 12 ans)**: De 5 à 20 mL (préparation sans sucre – de 5 à 15 mL), 1 fois par jour dans la journée (ne pas prendre au coucher).

Liquide oral

- **PO (adultes)**: De 15 à 45 mL, 1 fois par jour dans la journée (ne pas prendre au coucher).
- **PO (enfants > 6 ans)**: De 10 à 15 mL, 1 fois par jour dans la journée (ne pas prendre au coucher).

Lavement rectal

- **IR (adultes et enfants > 12 ans)**: 120 mL, en une seule dose.
- **IR (enfants de 2 à 12 ans)**: 60 mL, en une seule dose.

PRÉSENTATION

Gelée orale: 78 % d'huile minérale[VL] (Lansoÿl avec ou sans sucre) ▪ **Liquide oral**: 100 % d'huile minérale lourde[VL] ▪ **Lavement rectal**: 100 % d'huile minérale[VL], en flacons de 130 mL munis d'une canule rectale.

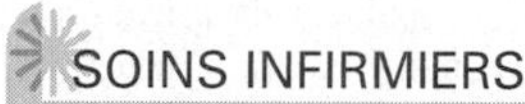

SOINS INFIRMIERS

ÉVALUATION DE LA SITUATION

- Suivre de près la distension abdominale, ausculter les bruits intestinaux et noter les habitudes d'élimination intestinale.
- Noter la couleur, la consistance et la quantité des selles.

DIAGNOSTICS INFIRMIERS POSSIBLES

- Constipation (Indications).
- Connaissances insuffisantes sur le traitement médicamenteux (Enseignement au patient et à ses proches).

INTERVENTIONS INFIRMIÈRES

- Ce médicament ne stimule pas le péristaltisme intestinal.
- Administrer l'huile minérale avec prudence aux enfants ou aux patients alités pour prévenir la pneumonie graisseuse par aspiration. Ne pas administrer l'huile minérale aux patients qui se trouvent en position couchée.

PO:

- Habituellement, le médicament devrait être administré dans la journée; ne pas administrer au coucher pour prévenir la pneumonie graisseuse par aspiration. Ne pas l'administrer dans les 2 heures qui suivent ou qui précèdent les repas, car l'huile minérale peut altérer l'absorption des éléments nutritifs et des vitamines.
- Espacer de 2 heures l'administration d'un laxatif émollient, car l'absorption de l'huile minérale peut être accrue.

ENSEIGNEMENT AU PATIENT ET À SES PROCHES

- Prévenir le patient que les laxatifs devraient être utilisés pendant de courtes périodes seulement. Le traitement prolongé peut altérer l'absorption des nutriments et des vitamines A, D, E et K.

- Conseiller au patient de ne pas prendre ce médicament dans les 2 heures qui suivent ou qui précèdent les repas ou la prise d'un autre médicament.
- Inciter le patient à prendre d'autres mesures qui favorisent l'élimination intestinale: augmenter la consommation d'aliments riches en fibres, augmenter la consommation de liquides et faire de l'exercice. Lui expliquer que les habitudes d'élimination intestinale varient d'une personne à l'autre et qu'il est tout aussi normal de déféquer 3 fois par jour que 3 fois par semaine.
- Conseiller au patient souffrant de maladie cardiaque d'éviter les efforts reliés à la défécation (manœuvre de Valsalva).
- Prévenir le patient que des doses élevées d'huile minérale peuvent entraîner des fuites d'huile par le rectum; lui conseiller de protéger ses vêtements. On peut prévenir ces fuites en réduisant la dose ou en la fractionnant.
- Recommander au patient de ne pas prendre de laxatif en présence de douleurs abdominales, de nausées, de vomissements ou de fièvre.

VÉRIFICATION DE L'EFFICACITÉ THÉRAPEUTIQUE

L'efficacité du traitement peut être démontrée par: l'évacuation de selles molles et bien moulées, habituellement dans les 6 à 8 heures. En général, on peut obtenir des résultats dans les 2 à 15 minutes qui suivent l'administration IR.

HYDRALAZINE

Apo-Hydralazine, Apresoline, Novo-Hylazin

CLASSIFICATION:

Antihypertenseur (vasodilatateur)

Grossesse – catégorie C

INDICATIONS

PO: Traitement de deuxième intention de l'hypertension, y compris des urgences hypertensives ■ Traitement de l'hypertension pendant la grossesse ■ Traitement de rechange de l'insuffisance cardiaque de classe II ou III de la NYHA, en association avec du dinitrate d'isosorbide chez les patients qui ne tolèrent pas les inhibiteurs de l'ECA ■ **IV**: Traitement de l'hypertension grave.

MÉCANISME D'ACTION

Vasodilatation directe des artérioles périphériques. ***Effets thérapeutiques:*** Abaissement de la pression artérielle chez les patients hypertendus et diminution de la postcharge chez les patients souffrant d'insuffisance cardiaque.

PHARMACOCINÉTIQUE

Absorption: Bonne et rapide (PO).

Distribution: L'hydralazine se répartit dans tout l'organisme. Elle traverse la barrière placentaire et passe dans le lait maternel à de très faibles concentrations.

Métabolisme et excrétion: Métabolisme dans la muqueuse gastro-intestinale et le foie. Excrétion majoritairement rénale sous forme de métabolites inactifs, 10% de la dose administrée par voie orale se retrouve dans les fèces.

Demi-vie: De 2 à 8 heures.

Profil temps-action (effet antihypertenseur)

	DÉBUT D'ACTION	PIC	DURÉE
PO	45 min	2 h	2 - 4 h
IM	10 - 30 min	1 h	3 - 8 h
IV	5 - 20 min	15 - 30 min	2 - 6 h

CONTRE-INDICATIONS, PRÉCAUTIONS ET MISES EN GARDE

Contre-indications: Hypersensibilité ■ Lupus érythémateux disséminé ■ Tachycardie et insuffisance cardiaque graves avec débit cardiaque élevé ■ Insuffisance myocardique due à une obstruction myocardique ■ Anévrisme disséquant aigu de l'aorte ■ Cœur pulmonaire ■ Cardite rhumatismale touchant la valvule mitrale.

Précautions et mises en garde: Névrite périphérique pouvant être liée à un effet antipyridoxine ■ Maladie cardiovasculaire ■ Maladies rénale et hépatiques graves.

RÉACTIONS INDÉSIRABLES ET EFFETS SECONDAIRES

SNC: étourdissements, somnolence, céphalées.

CV: tachycardie, angine, arythmies, œdème, hypotension orthostatique.

GI: diarrhée, nausées, vomissements.

Tég.: rash.

HÉ: rétention sodique.

Loc.: arthralgie, arthrite.

SN: neuropathie périphérique.

Divers: syndrome lupique induit par le médicament.

INTERACTIONS

Médicament-médicament: Effets hypotenseurs additifs, lors de l'administration concomitante d'autres **antihypertenseurs** ou de **dérivés nitrés** et de l'ingestion rapide de grandes quantités d'**alcool** ■ Les **IMAO**

peuvent intensifier l'état hypotensif ■ L'hydralazine peut réduire les effets vasopresseurs de l'**adrénaline** ■ L'administration concomitante d'**AINS** peut diminuer la réponse antihypertensive ■ Les **bêtabloquants** diminuent la tachycardie induite par l'hydralazine (on peut administrer un traitement d'association pour cette raison) ■ Le **métoprolol** et le **propranolol** élèvent les concentrations d'hydralazine ■ L'hydralazine élève les concentrations sanguines de **métoprolol** et de **propranolol**.

VOIES D'ADMINISTRATION ET POSOLOGIE

- **PO (adultes)**: *Hypertension* – 10 mg, 4 fois par jour, au départ. Après 2 à 4 jours, on peut augmenter la dose jusqu'à 25 mg, 4 fois par jour, pour le reste de la première semaine. Ensuite, on peut augmenter la dose par paliers de 25 mg par jour, à intervalles de 1 semaine, jusqu'à 50 mg, 4 fois par jour (jusqu'à 200 mg par jour). Une fois la dose d'entretien établie, on peut administrer le médicament 2 fois par jour. *Insuffisance cardiaque congestive (en association avec le dinitrate d'isosorbide)* – de 50 à 100 mg, toutes les 8 heures, au départ. Dose d'entretien: de 200 à 600 mg par jour, administrés en doses fractionnées toutes les 4 à 12 heures.
- **PO (enfants)**: *Hypertension* – 0,75 mg/kg/jour, en 4 doses fractionnées (au maximum: 25 mg/dose). On peut augmenter la dose graduellement jusqu'à 7 mg/kg/jour au maximum, en l'espace de 3 à 4 semaines. Dose maximale: 200 mg/jour.
- **IV (adultes)**: *Hypertension* – de 10 à 20 mg, dose qu'on peut répéter selon les besoins, à intervalles de 20 à 30 minutes. *Urgence hypertensive durant la grossesse* – de 5 à 10 mg, toutes les 20 à 30 minutes, au besoin.
- **IM, IV (enfants)**: *Hypertension* – de 1,7 à 3,5 mg/kg/jour, en 4 à 6 doses fractionnées (au maximum: 20 mg/dose).

PRÉSENTATION
(version générique disponible)

Comprimés: 10 mg[Pr], 25 mg[Pr], 50 mg[Pr] ■ **Solution pour injection**: 20 mg/mL[Pr].

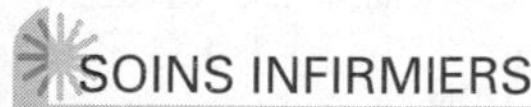

SOINS INFIRMIERS

ÉVALUATION DE LA SITUATION

- Mesurer souvent la pression artérielle et le pouls pendant la période d'adaptation de la posologie et à intervalles réguliers pendant toute la durée du traitement. Prévenir le médecin ou un autre professionnel de la santé si des changements importants surviennent.
- Surveiller la fréquence du renouvellement des ordonnances pour déterminer l'observance du traitement.

Tests de laboratoire:

- Noter la numération globulaire, les concentrations d'électrolytes, la présence des cellules LE et les titres d'anticorps antinucléaires avant l'administration initiale et à intervalles réguliers tout au long du traitement prolongé.
- L'hydralazine peut entraîner des résultats faussement positifs au test de Coombs direct.

DIAGNOSTICS INFIRMIERS POSSIBLES

- Irrigation tissulaire inefficace (Indications).
- Connaissances insuffisantes sur le traitement médicamenteux (Enseignement au patient et à ses proches).
- Non-observance du traitement médicamenteux (Enseignement au patient et à ses proches).

INTERVENTIONS INFIRMIÈRES

- NE PAS CONFONDRE L'HYDRALAZINE AVEC L'HYDROXYZINE.
- Le médicament ne doit être administré par voie IV ou IM que si le patient est incapable de prendre la forme orale.
- On peut administrer l'hydralazine en association avec des diurétiques ou des bêtabloquants pour pouvoir en réduire la dose et, par conséquent, les effets secondaires.

PO:

- Il faut toujours administrer l'hydralazine avec des aliments pour en favoriser l'absorption.
- Dans le cas des patients ayant des difficultés de déglutition, le pharmacien peut préparer une solution orale à partir de la solution d'hydralazine pour injection.

IV directe:

- Injecter la solution non diluée. Après avoir aspiré la solution dans la seringue, l'utiliser dès que possible. L'hydralazine change de couleur au contact d'un filtre métallique.
- Consulter les directives de chaque fabricant avant de reconstituer la préparation.

Vitesse d'administration: Administrer à un débit de 10 mg pendant au moins 1 minute. **PÉD.**: Administrer à un débit de 0,2 mg/kg/min chez les enfants. Après l'injection, mesurer la pression artérielle et le pouls à intervalles fréquents.

Compatibilité (tubulure en Y): héparine ▪ hydrocortisone sodique, succinate d' ▪ potassium, chlorure de ▪ vérapamil ▪ vitamines du complexe B avec C.

Incompatibilité (tubulure en Y): aminophylline ▪ ampicilline ▪ furosémide.

Compatibilité en addition au soluté: mélange de dextrose et de soluté salin ▪ mélange de dextrose et de solution de Ringer ▪ D5% dans une solution de lactate de Ringer ▪ D5%E ou D10%E ▪ D10% dans une solution de lactate de Ringer ▪ solution de NaCl 0,45% et 0,9% ▪ solution de Ringer ou solution de lactate de Ringer.

ENSEIGNEMENT AU PATIENT ET À SES PROCHES

H

- Expliquer au patient qu'il doit continuer à prendre le médicament même s'il se sent mieux. Lui conseiller de prendre le médicament au même moment, tous les jours. La dernière dose de la journée devrait être prise au coucher. Si le patient n'a pas pu prendre le médicament au moment habituel, il doit le prendre aussitôt que possible mais ne jamais remplacer une dose manquée par une double dose. S'il n'a pas pu prendre plus de 2 doses consécutives, il doit en prévenir un professionnel de la santé. Le sevrage brusque peut entraîner une élévation soudaine de la pression artérielle. Prévenir le patient que l'hydralazine stabilise la pression artérielle mais ne guérit pas l'hypertension.
- Inciter le patient à suivre d'autres mesures de réduction de l'hypertension: perdre du poids, réduire sa consommation de sel, cesser de fumer, boire de l'alcool avec modération, faire régulièrement de l'exercice et diminuer le stress.
- Montrer au patient et à ses proches comment mesurer la pression artérielle. Leur demander de prendre la pression artérielle 1 fois par semaine et leur recommander de signaler à un professionnel de la santé tous les changements importants.
- Conseiller au patient de se peser 2 fois par semaine et d'examiner ses pieds et ses chevilles afin de déceler la rétention hydrique.
- Prévenir le patient que l'hydralazine peut provoquer de la somnolence. Lui conseiller de ne pas conduire et d'éviter les activités qui exigent sa vigilance jusqu'à ce qu'on ait la certitude que le médicament n'entraîne pas cet effet chez lui.
- Recommander au patient de changer lentement de position pour prévenir le risque d'hypotension orthostatique.
- Conseiller au patient de consulter un professionnel de la santé avant de prendre un médicament contre la toux, le rhume ou les allergies en même temps que l'hydralazine.
- Recommander au patient qui doit suivre un traitement ou subir une intervention chirurgicale de prévenir le professionnel de la santé qu'il suit un traitement par cet agent.
- Recommander au patient de signaler immédiatement à un professionnel de la santé les symptômes suivants: fatigue généralisée, fièvre, douleurs musculaires ou articulaires, douleurs thoraciques, rash, maux de gorge ou engourdissements, picotements, douleurs ou faiblesse au niveau des mains et des pieds. La vitamine B_6 (pyridoxine) peut soulager la névrite périphérique.
- Insister sur l'importance des examens de suivi permettant d'évaluer les bienfaits du médicament.

VÉRIFICATION DE L'EFFICACITÉ THÉRAPEUTIQUE

L'efficacité du traitement peut être démontrée par: la baisse de la pression artérielle sans manifestation d'effets secondaires ▪ la diminution de la post-charge chez les patients souffrant d'insuffisance cardiaque.

HYDROCHLOROTHIAZIDE,

voir Diurétiques (thiazidiques)

ALERTE CLINIQUE

HYDROCODONE

Hycodan

CLASSIFICATION:

Antitussif, analgésique opioïde

Grossesse – catégories C et D (en cas d'usage prolongé ou de dose élevée administrée près du terme)

INDICATIONS

Antitussif (monothérapie mais, généralement, en traitement d'association avec des décongestionnants, des antihistaminiques ou des expectorants). **Usages non approuvés:** Traitement de la douleur modérée ou grave.

MÉCANISME D'ACTION

Suppression du réflexe de la toux par une action centrale directe ▪ Liaison aux récepteurs opioïdes du SNC. Modification de la perception de la douleur et de la réaction aux stimuli douloureux tout en entraînant une dépression généralisée du SNC. ***Effets thérapeutiques:***

Diminution de l'intensité des douleurs modérées ■ Suppression du réflexe de la toux.

PHARMACOCINÉTIQUE

Absorption: Bonne (PO).
Distribution: Inconnue.
Métabolisme et excrétion: Métabolisme majoritairement hépatique.
Demi-vie: 3,8 heures.

Profil temps-action (effet analgésique)

	DÉBUT D'ACTION	PIC	DURÉE
PO	10 - 30 min	30 - 60 min	4 - 6 h

CONTRE-INDICATIONS, PRÉCAUTIONS ET MISES EN GARDE

Contre-indications: Hypersensibilité à l'hydrocodone ou à l'un des ingrédients de la préparation ■ Présence de lésions intracrâniennes associées à une pression intracrânienne accrue, traumatisme crânien ■ Dépression respiratoire ■ Patients recevant des **IMAO** ■ Les patients ayant une hypersensibilité ou une intolérance à l'alcool, à l'aspartame, à la saccharine, au sucre ou à la tartrazine doivent éviter les associations de médicaments contenant ces substances.

Précautions et mises en garde: Maladies rénale, hépatique ou pulmonaire graves ■ Hypothyroïdie ■ Insuffisance surrénalienne ■ Alcoolisme ■ Personnes âgées ou patients débilités (réduire la dose initiale; prédisposition accrue à la dépression du SNC et à la constipation) ■ Douleurs abdominales non diagnostiquées ■ Grossesse ■ Allaitement ■ Hyperplasie de la prostate ■ Risque de pharmacodépendance et d'abus.

RÉACTIONS INDÉSIRABLES ET EFFETS SECONDAIRES

SNC: confusion, sédation, dysphorie, euphorie, sensation de flottement, hallucinations, céphalées, rêves bizarres.
ORLO: vision trouble, diplopie, myosis.
Resp.: DÉPRESSION RESPIRATOIRE.
CV: hypotension, bradycardie.
GI: constipation, nausées, vomissements.
GU: rétention urinaire.
Tég.: transpiration.
Divers: dépendance physique, dépendance psychologique, tolérance aux effets du médicament.

INTERACTIONS

Médicament-médicament: L'HYDROCODONE NE DOIT PAS ÊTRE ADMINISTRÉE CHEZ LES PATIENTS RECEVANT DES **IMAO** OU DE LA **PROCARBAZINE**, CAR ELLE PEUT PROVOQUER DES RÉACTIONS GRAVES ET IMPRÉVISIBLES ■ Dépression additive du SNC et du système respiratoire lors de l'usage concomitant d'**alcool**, d'**antihistaminiques**, de **phénothiazines**, de **barbituriques**, d'**antidépresseurs**, d'**hypnosédatifs** et d'autres **opioïdes** ■ L'administration d'**analgésiques opioïdes agonistes/antagonistes** (**nalbuphine**, **butorphanol**, **pentazocine**) peut diminuer l'analgésie et/ou déclencher des symptômes de sevrage chez les patients présentant une dépendance physique aux analgésiques opioïdes.

Médicament-produits naturels: Effets dépresseurs additifs sur le SNC lors de l'usage concomitant de **kava**, de **valériane**, de **scutellaire**, de **camomille** et de **houblon**.

VOIES D'ADMINISTRATION ET POSOLOGIE

Hydrocodone

- **PO (adultes):** *Antitussif* – 5 mg, toutes les 4 heures, selon les besoins (dose unique maximale: 15 mg; dose quotidienne maximale: 30 mg).
- **PO (enfants > 12 ans):** 5 mg, toutes les 4 heures, selon les besoins (dose unique maximale: 10 mg; dose quotidienne maximale: 30 mg).
- **PO (enfants de 2 à ≤ 12 ans):** 2,5 mg, toutes les 4 heures, selon les besoins (dose unique maximale: 5 mg; dose quotidienne maximale: 15 mg).
- **PO (enfants < 2 ans):** 1,25 mg, toutes les 4 heures selon les besoins (dose unique maximale: 1,25 mg; dose quotidienne maximale: 7,5 mg).

PRÉSENTATION

Comprimés: 5 mg^{N} ■ **Sirop:** 1 mg/mL^{N} ■ **En association avec:** antihistaminiques, caféine, guaïfénésine ou décongestionnants^{N}. Voir l'annexe U.

SOINS INFIRMIERS

ÉVALUATION DE LA SITUATION

- ÉVALUER LE NIVEAU DE CONSCIENCE ET MESURER LA PRESSION ARTÉRIELLE, LE POULS ET LA FRÉQUENCE RESPIRATOIRE AVANT L'ADMINISTRATION DU MÉDICAMENT ET À INTERVALLES RÉGULIERS PAR LA SUITE. SI LA FRÉQUENCE RESPIRATOIRE EST < 10/MIN, ÉVALUER LE DEGRÉ DE SÉDATION. UNE STIMULATION PHYSIQUE PEUT SUFFIRE POUR PRÉVENIR UNE HYPOVENTILATION IMPORTANTE. IL PEUT S'AVÉRER NÉCESSAIRE DE RÉDUIRE LA DOSE DE 25 À 50 %. LA SOMNOLENCE INITIALE DISPARAÎT MALGRÉ LA POURSUITE DU TRAITEMENT.

GÉR.: Évaluer les patients âgés à intervalles fréquents, car ils sont plus sensibles aux effets des analgésiques opioïdes que les adultes plus jeunes et peuvent subir

H

plus souvent des effets indésirables et des complications respiratoires.

PÉD.: Évaluer les enfants à intervalles plus fréquents, car ils sont plus sensibles aux effets des analgésiques opioïdes et peuvent manifester plus souvent des complications respiratoires, ou se montrer excités ou agités.

- Examiner la fonction intestinale du patient à intervalles réguliers. La consommation accrue de liquides et d'aliments riches en fibres et la prise de laxatifs peuvent réduire les effets constipants du médicament. Sauf contre-indication, les laxatifs stimulants devraient être administrés de façon systématique si le traitement par un analgésique opioïde dure plus de 2 ou 3 jours.

Douleur:

- Déterminer le type de douleur, son siège et son intensité, avant l'administration du médicament et 60 minutes (pic) après. Lorsqu'on décide de majorer la dose d'un analgésique opioïde, on devrait l'augmenter de 25 à 50 % jusqu'à ce qu'on note une réduction de 50 % de la douleur, selon l'évaluation qu'en fait le patient d'après une échelle numérique ou visuelle ou jusqu'à ce qu'il signale un soulagement suffisant de la douleur. On peut administrer sans danger une nouvelle dose au moment du pic, si la dose précédente s'est avérée inefficace et si les effets secondaires ont été minimes.
- On devrait utiliser le tableau des équivalences de l'annexe A lorsqu'on décide de changer de mode d'administration ou de type d'opioïde.
- L'usage prolongé peut entraîner une dépendance physique et psychologique ainsi qu'une tolérance aux effets du médicament, mais cela ne doit pas empêcher le patient de recevoir une quantité suffisante d'analgésiques. La psychodépendance est rare chez la plupart des patients qui reçoivent de l'hydrocodone pour des raisons médicales. Si des doses de plus en plus élevées sont nécessaires pour soulager la douleur, on peut envisager de substituer au médicament un analgésique opioïde plus puissant.

Toux: Évaluer la toux et le murmure vésiculaire pendant le traitement antitussif.

Tests de laboratoire: L'hydrocodone peut élever les concentrations plasmatiques d'amylase et de lipase.

TOXICITÉ ET SURDOSAGE: S'il est nécessaire d'administrer un opioïde antagoniste pour renverser la dépression respiratoire ou le coma, l'antidote est la naloxone (Narcan). Diluer l'ampoule de naloxone à 0,4 mg dans 10 mL de solution de NaCl 0,9 % et administrer 0,5 mL (0,02 mg) par bolus IV direct, toutes les 2 minutes. Dans le cas des enfants et des patients pesant < 40 kg, diluer 0,1 mg de naloxone dans 10 mL de solution de NaCl 0,9 % pour obtenir une concentration de 10 µg/mL et administrer 0,5 µg/kg, toutes les 2 minutes. Adapter graduellement la dose pour prévenir les symptômes de sevrage, les convulsions et la douleur intense.

DIAGNOSTICS INFIRMIERS POSSIBLES

- Douleur aiguë (Indications).
- Trouble de la perception visuelle et auditive (Effets secondaires).
- Risque d'accident (Effets secondaires).

INTERVENTIONS INFIRMIÈRES

ALERTE CLINIQUE: DES SURDOSES ACCIDENTELLES D'ANALGÉSIQUES OPIOÏDES ONT CAUSÉ DES DÉCÈS. AVANT L'ADMINISTRATION, CLARIFIER TOUTES LES ORDONNANCES AMBIGUËS ET FAIRE VÉRIFIER L'ORDONNANCE D'ORIGINE ET LE CALCUL DES DOSES PAR UN AUTRE PROFESSIONNEL DE LA SANTÉ.

- NE PAS CONFONDRE L'HYDROCODONE AVEC L'HYDROCORTISONE.
- Pour augmenter l'effet analgésique de l'hydrocodone, avant de l'administrer, expliquer au patient la valeur thérapeutique de ce médicament.
- Les doses administrées selon un horaire fixe peuvent être plus efficaces que celles administrées sur demande. L'analgésique s'avère plus efficace s'il est administré avant que la douleur ne devienne intense.
- L'association avec des analgésiques non opioïdes peut avoir des effets analgésiques additifs et permettre d'administrer des doses plus faibles d'hydrocodone. La présence d'autres ingrédients non opioïdes, surtout à des doses maximales, limite la nécessité de majorer les doses d'hydrocodone.
- Après un traitement prolongé, interrompre l'administration graduellement pour prévenir les symptômes de sevrage.
- On peut administrer le médicament avec des aliments ou du lait pour réduire l'irritation gastrique.

ENSEIGNEMENT AU PATIENT ET À SES PROCHES

- Conseiller au patient de respecter rigoureusement la posologie recommandée et de ne pas prendre une dose supérieure à celle recommandée.
- Expliquer au patient ce qu'on entend par administration sur demande et à quel moment il doit réclamer l'analgésique.
- Prévenir le patient que l'hydrocodone peut provoquer des étourdissements et de la somnolence. Lui recommander de demander de l'aide lorsqu'il se déplace et lorsqu'il veut fumer. Lui conseiller de ne pas conduire et d'éviter les activités qui exigent sa vigilance jusqu'à ce qu'on ait la certitude que le médicament n'entraîne pas ces effets chez lui.

- Recommander au patient de changer lentement de position pour diminuer le risque d'hypotension orthostatique.
- Inciter le patient à ne pas boire d'alcool et à ne pas prendre d'autres dépresseurs du SNC en même temps que l'hydrocodone.
- Conseiller au patient de se tourner dans le lit, de tousser et de faire des exercices de respiration profonde toutes les 2 heures pour prévenir l'atélectasie.
- Recommander au patient de se rincer fréquemment la bouche, de pratiquer une bonne hygiène buccale et de consommer de la gomme ou des bonbons sans sucre pour soulager la sécheresse de la bouche.
- Insister sur l'importance de la prévention de la constipation associée à la prise d'analgésiques opioïdes.

PÉD.: MONTRER AUX PARENTS OU AUX SOIGNANTS COMMENT MESURER AVEC PRÉCISION LE MÉDICAMENT SOUS FORME LIQUIDE ET LEUR RECOMMANDER D'UTILISER SEULEMENT LA MESURE FOURNIE AVEC LE MÉDICAMENT.

VÉRIFICATION DE L'EFFICACITÉ THÉRAPEUTIQUE

L'efficacité du traitement peut être démontrée par: la diminution de l'intensité de la douleur sans modification importante de l'état de conscience ou de l'état respiratoire ■ la suppression de la toux improductive.

HYDROCORTISONE,

voir Corticostéroïdes (topiques) et Corticostéroïdes (voie générale)

ALERTE CLINIQUE

HYDROMORPHONE

Dilaudid, Dilaudid-HP, Dilaudid-HP-Plus, Dilaudid-XP, Hydromorph Contin, Hydromorphone, PMS-Hydromorphone

CLASSIFICATION:

Analgésique opioïde (agoniste)

Grossesse – catégories C et D (en cas d'usage prolongé ou de dose élevée administrée près du terme)

INDICATIONS

Douleur modérée à grave (en monothérapie ou en association avec des analgésiques non opioïdes) ■ **Préparation à libération contrôlée**: Soulagement de la douleur intense exigeant l'emploi prolongé d'une préparation opioïde administrée par voie orale. **Usages non approuvés**: Traitement de la toux (doses plus faibles).

MÉCANISME D'ACTION

Liaison aux récepteurs opioïdes du SNC ■ Modification de la perception de la douleur et de la réaction aux stimuli douloureux tout en entraînant une dépression généralisée du SNC ■ Suppression du réflexe de la toux par une action centrale directe. ***Effets thérapeutiques:*** Diminution de l'intensité de la douleur modérée ou grave ■ Suppression de la toux.

PHARMACOCINÉTIQUE

Absorption: Bonne (PO, IR, SC et IM). Les doses orale et parentérale ne sont pas équivalentes. Les capsules à libération contrôlée procurent une analgésie équivalente à celle entraînée par les comprimés à libération traditionnelle, administrés toutes les 4 heures.

Distribution: Tout l'organisme. L'hydromorphone traverse la barrière placentaire et passe dans le lait maternel.

Métabolisme et excrétion: Métabolisme majoritairement hépatique.

Demi-vie: De 2 à 4 heures.

Profil temps-action (effet analgésique)

	DÉBUT D'ACTION	PIC	DURÉE
PO	30 min	90 – 120 min	4 – 5 h
PO (capsule à libération contrôlée)	60 min et +	4 – 5 h	12 h
SC	15 min	30 – 90 min	4 – 5 h
IM	15 min	30 – 60 min	4 – 5 h
IV	10 – 15 min	15 – 30 min	2 – 3 h
IR	15 – 30 min	30 – 90 min	4 – 5 h

CONTRE-INDICATIONS, PRÉCAUTIONS ET MISES EN GARDE

Contre-indications: Hypersensibilité ■ Hypersensibilité aux bisulfites (ne pas administrer dans ce cas les préparations qui contiennent ces additifs) ■ Traumatisme crânien ■ Pression intracrânienne accrue ■ Crises d'asthme ou autres troubles obstructifs des voies respiratoires ou dépression respiratoire ■ Alcoolisme aigu ■ Delirium tremens ■ Dépression grave du SNC ■ Troubles convulsifs ■ Abdomen aigu soupçonné ■ Prise concomitante d'IMAO, ainsi que durant les 14 jours suivant l'arrêt de ce traitement ■ **ALLAITEMENT**: Administration prolongée à proscrire.

Précautions et mises en garde: **OBST.**: Grossesse ■ Maladies rénale, hépatique ou pulmonaire graves ■ Hypothyroïdie ■ Insuffisance surrénalienne ■ Personnes âgées ou patients débilités (réduire la dose initiale) ■ Hyperplasie de la prostate ■ **PÉD.**: Nouveau-nés et enfants < 3 mois (risque accru de dépression respiratoire); nouveau-nés: éviter les préparations injectables contenant des agents de conservation et les solutions buvables contenant du benzoate de sodium, car elles

H

peuvent causer un syndrome de halètement pouvant mener à une issue fatale ■ Risque de pharmacodépendance et d'abus.

RÉACTIONS INDÉSIRABLES ET EFFETS SECONDAIRES

SNC: confusion, sédation, étourdissements, dysphorie, euphorie, sensation de flottement, hallucinations, céphalées, rêves bizarres.
ORLO: vision trouble, diplopie, myosis.
Resp.: DÉPRESSION RESPIRATOIRE.
CV: hypotension, bradycardie.
GI: constipation, nausées, vomissements.
GU: rétention urinaire.
Tég.: rougeurs du visage, transpiration.
Divers: dépendance physique, dépendance psychologique, tolérance aux effets du médicament.

H

INTERACTIONS

Médicament-médicament: L'HYDROMORPHONE EST CONTRE-INDIQUÉE CHEZ LES PATIENTS RECEVANT DES **IMAO** OU DE LA **PROCARBAZINE**, CAR ELLE PEUT PROVOQUER DES RÉACTIONS GRAVES ET IMPRÉVISIBLES ■ Dépression additive du SNC et du système respiratoire lors de l'usage concomitant d'**alcool**, d'**antihistaminiques**, de **phénothiazines**, de **barbituriques**, d'**antidépresseurs**, d'**hypnosédatifs** et d'autres **opioïdes** ■ L'administration d'**analgésiques opioïdes agonistes/antagonistes** (**nalbuphine**, **butorphanol**, **pentazocine**) peut diminuer l'analgésie et/ou déclencher des symptômes de sevrage chez les patients présentant une dépendance physique aux analgésiques opioïdes.
Médicament-produits naturels: Effets dépresseurs additifs sur le SNC lors de l'usage concomitant de **kava**, de **valériane**, de **scutellaire**, de **camomille** et de **houblon**.

VOIES D'ADMINISTRATION ET POSOLOGIE

Les doses dépendent de l'intensité de la douleur et de la tolérance du patient. Les doses peuvent être augmentées selon sa réponse et sa tolérance.

Analgésique

- **PO (adultes)**: Initialement, de 2 à 4 mg, toutes les 4 à 6 heures. Pour obtenir une analgésie continue plus stable, on peut passer à la préparation à libération contrôlée, à la même posologie quotidienne totale d'hydromorphone, divisée en 2 doses égales, administrées à 12 heures d'intervalle.
- **PO (enfants)**: Initialement, de 0,03 à 0,08 mg/kg, toutes les 4 à 6 heures.
- **IV, IM, SC (adultes)**: Initialement, de 1 à 2 mg, toutes les 4 à 6 heures, selon les besoins; on peut augmenter cette dose.
- **IV, IM, SC (enfants)**: Initialement, 0,015 mg/kg, toutes les 4 à 6 heures.
- **IV (adultes)**: *Perfusion continue* – de 0,2 à 30 mg/h, selon l'usage de l'analgésique opioïde antérieur. On peut administrer un bolus initial correspondant à 2 fois la dose en mg/h, puis des bolus « secondaires » correspondant à 50 à 100 % de la dose en mg/h.
- **IR (adultes)**: Initialement, 3 mg, toutes les 6 à 8 heures, selon les besoins.

PRÉSENTATION (version générique disponible)

Comprimés: 1 mg^N, 2 mg^N, 4 mg^N, 8 mg^N ■ **Capsules à libération contrôlée** (Hydromorph Contin): 3 mg^N, 6 mg^N, 12 mg^N, 18 mg^N, 24 mg^N, 30 mg^N ■ **Solution orale**: 1 mg/mL^N ■ **Solution pour injection**: 2 mg/mL^N, en ampoules de 1 mL; 10 mg/mL^N (Dilaudid-HP), en flacons de 1 mL, 5 mL et 50 mL; 20 mg/mL^N (Dilaudid-HP-Plus), en flacons de 50 mL; 50 mg/mL^N (Dilaudid-XP), en flacons de 50 mL ■ **Poudre stérile pour injection**: 250 mg^N ■ **Suppositoires**: 3 mg^N.

SOINS INFIRMIERS

ÉVALUATION DE LA SITUATION

- ÉVALUER LE NIVEAU DE CONSCIENCE ET MESURER LA PRESSION ARTÉRIELLE, LE POULS ET LA FRÉQUENCE RESPIRATOIRE AVANT L'ADMINISTRATION DU MÉDICAMENT ET À INTERVALLES RÉGULIERS PENDANT TOUTE LA DURÉE DU TRAITEMENT. SI LA FRÉQUENCE RESPIRATOIRE EST < 10/MIN, ÉVALUER LE DEGRÉ DE SÉDATION. IL PEUT S'AVÉRER NÉCESSAIRE DE RÉDUIRE LA DOSE DE 25 À 50 %. LA SOMNOLENCE INITIALE DISPARAÎT MALGRÉ LA POURSUITE DU TRAITEMENT.

GÉR.: Évaluer les patients âgés à intervalles fréquents, car ils sont plus sensibles aux effets des analgésiques opioïdes que les adultes plus jeunes et peuvent subir plus souvent des effets indésirables et des complications respiratoires.

PÉD.: Évaluer les enfants à intervalles plus fréquents, car ils sont plus sensibles aux effets des analgésiques opioïdes et peuvent manifester plus souvent des complications respiratoires, ou se montrer excités et agités.

- Examiner la fonction intestinale du patient à intervalles réguliers. La consommation accrue de liquides et d'aliments riches en fibres et la prise de laxatifs peuvent réduire les effets constipants du médicament. Sauf contre-indication, les laxatifs stimulants devraient être administrés de façon systématique si le traitement par un analgésique opioïde dure plus de 2 ou 3 jours.

Douleur:

- Déterminer le type de douleur, son siège et son intensité, avant l'administration du médicament, 1 heure après l'administration IM et 5 minutes (pic) après l'administration IV. Lorsqu'on décide de majorer la dose d'analgésique opioïde, on devrait l'augmenter de 25 à 50 % jusqu'à ce qu'on note une réduction de 50 % de la douleur, selon l'évaluation qu'en fait le patient d'après une échelle numérique ou visuelle ou jusqu'à ce qu'il signale un soulagement suffisant de la douleur. On peut administrer sans danger une nouvelle dose au moment du pic, si la dose précédente s'est avérée inefficace et si les effets secondaires ont été minimes.
- En cas de perfusion continue, on devrait administrer des doses additionnelles en bolus toutes les 15 à 30 minutes, selon les besoins, si des douleurs surgissent en cours de traitement. La dose du bolus correspond habituellement à la quantité de médicament administrée en 1 heure de perfusion continue.
- Lors la prise de capsules à libération contrôlée, on devrait administrer des doses additionnelles d'opioïdes à courte durée d'action, que l'on appelle entre-doses, toutes les 1 à 4 heures, selon les besoins, si des douleurs surgissent en cours de traitement. L'entre-dose correspond habituellement à entre 10 et 15 % de la dose quotidienne totale.
- On devrait utiliser le tableau des équivalences de l'annexe A lorsqu'on décide de changer de mode d'administration ou de type d'opioïde.
- L'usage prolongé peut entraîner une dépendance physique et psychologique ainsi qu'une tolérance aux effets du médicament, mais cela ne doit pas empêcher le patient de recevoir une quantité suffisante d'analgésiques. La psychodépendance est rare chez la plupart des patients qui reçoivent de l'hydromorphone pour des raisons médicales. Lors d'un traitement prolongé, il faut parfois administrer des doses de plus en plus élevées pour soulager la douleur.

Toux: Évaluer la toux et le murmure vésiculaire pendant le traitement antitussif.

Tests de laboratoire: L'hydromorphone peut élever les concentrations plasmatiques d'amylase et de lipase.

TOXICITÉ ET SURDOSAGE: S'il est nécessaire d'administrer un antagoniste opioïde pour renverser la dépression respiratoire ou le coma, l'antidote est la naloxone (Narcan). Diluer l'ampoule de naloxone à 0,4 mg dans 10 mL de solution de NaCl 0,9 % et administrer 0,5 mL (0,02 mg) par bolus IV direct, toutes les 2 minutes. Dans le cas des enfants et des patients pesant < 40 kg, diluer 0,1 mg de naloxone dans 10 mL de solution de NaCl 0,9 % pour obtenir une concentration de 10 µg/mL et administrer 0,5 µg/kg, toutes les 2 minutes. Adapter la dose pour éviter les symptômes de sevrage, les convulsions et la douleur intense.

DIAGNOSTICS INFIRMIERS POSSIBLES

- Douleur aiguë (Indications).
- Altération de la perception visuelle et auditive (Effets secondaires).
- Risque d'accident (Effets secondaires).

INTERVENTIONS INFIRMIÈRES

ALERTE CLINIQUE: DES SURDOSES ACCIDENTELLES D'ANALGÉSIQUES OPIOÏDES ONT CAUSÉ DES DÉCÈS. ÉVALUER L'UTILISATION ANTÉRIEURE D'ANALGÉSIQUES OPIOÏDES PAR LE PATIENT ET SES BESOINS ACTUELS. AVANT L'ADMINISTRATION, CLARIFIER TOUTES LES ORDONNANCES AMBIGUËS ET FAIRE VÉRIFIER L'ORDONNANCE D'ORIGINE, LE CALCUL DES DOSES ET LE RÉGLAGE DE LA POMPE À PERFUSION PAR UN AUTRE PROFESSIONNEL DE LA SANTÉ.

- NE PAS CONFONDRE L'HYDROMORPHONE AVEC LA MÉPÉRIDINE OU LA MORPHINE; DES ERREURS ONT DÉJÀ MENÉ À UNE ISSUE FATALE. NE PAS CONFONDRE LES CONCENTRATIONS ÉLEVÉES (HP, HP-PLUS ET XP) AVEC LES CONCENTRATIONS NORMALES.

PÉD.: LES ERREURS DANS L'ADMINISTRATION DES ANALGÉSIQUES OPIOÏDES SONT FRÉQUENTES DANS LA POPULATION PÉDIATRIQUE; ELLES COMPRENNENT DES ERREURS D'INTERPRÉTATION ET DE CALCULS DES DOSES AINSI QUE L'USAGE D'INSTRUMENTS DE MESURE INAPPROPRIÉS.

- UTILISER SEULEMENT DES PRÉPARATIONS SANS AGENT DE CONSERVATION CHEZ LES NOUVEAU-NÉS AINSI QUE POUR L'ADMINISTRATION ÉPIDURALE ET INTRATHÉCALE CHEZ TOUS LES PATIENTS.
- Pour augmenter l'effet analgésique de l'hydromorphone, avant de l'administrer, expliquer au patient la valeur thérapeutique de ce médicament.
- Les doses administrées selon un horaire fixe peuvent être plus efficaces que celles administrées sur demande. L'analgésique s'avère plus efficace s'il est administré avant que la douleur ne devienne intense.
- L'association avec des analgésiques non opioïdes peut avoir des effets analgésiques additifs et permettre d'administrer des doses plus faibles d'hydromorphone.
- Après un traitement prolongé, interrompre l'administration graduellement pour prévenir les symptômes de sevrage.

PO: On peut administrer le médicament avec des aliments ou du lait pour réduire l'irritation gastrique.

Préparation à action prolongée: Les capsules d'hydromorphone à libération contrôlée doivent être avalées telles quelles et ne doivent être ni mâchées ni écrasées. La prise de capsules brisées, mâchées ou écrasées pourrait entraîner la libération et l'absorption rapides d'une dose d'hydromorphone qui risque d'être mortelle.

IV directe: Diluer le médicament dans au moins 5 mL d'eau stérile ou de NaCl 0,9 %. Inspecter la solution pour déceler la présence de particules. Même si le médicament prend une couleur légèrement jaunâtre, son efficacité n'est pas altérée. Garder l'hydromorphone à la température ambiante. Consulter les directives de chaque fabricant avant de reconstituer la préparation.

H

Vitesse d'administration: Administrer lentement, à un débit inférieur à 2 mg en 3 à 5 minutes.

ALERTE CLINIQUE: UNE ADMINISTRATION TROP RAPIDE PEUT PROVOQUER UNE DÉPRESSION RESPIRATOIRE ACCRUE, DE L'HYPOTENSION ET UN COLLAPSUS CIRCULATOIRE.

Associations compatibles dans la même seringue: atropine ▪ bupivacaïne ▪ ceftazidime ▪ chlorpromazine ▪ cimétidine ▪ diphenhydramine ▪ fentanyl ▪ glycopyrrolate ▪ hydroxyzine ▪ lorazépam ▪ midazolam ▪ pentobarbital ▪ prométhazine ▪ ranitidine ▪ scopolamine ▪ téniposide ▪ thiéthylpérazine ▪ triméthobenzamide.

Associations incompatibles dans la même seringue: ampicilline ▪ diazépam ▪ phénobarbital ▪ phénytoïne.

Compatibilité (tubulure en Y): acyclovir ▪ amifostine ▪ amikacine ▪ aztréonam ▪ céfamandole ▪ céfazoline ▪ céfépime ▪ céfopérazone ▪ céfotaxime ▪ céfoxitine ▪ ceftazidime ▪ ceftizoxime ▪ céfuroxime ▪ céphalothine ▪ céphapirine ▪ chloramphénicol ▪ cisatracurium ▪ cisplatine ▪ clindamycine ▪ cyclophosphamide ▪ cytarabine ▪ doxorubicine ▪ doxorubicine liposomale ▪ doxycycline ▪ érythromycine, lactobionate d' ▪ filgrastim ▪ fludarabine ▪ foscarnet ▪ gentamicine ▪ granisétron ▪ kanamycine ▪ magnésium, sulfate de ▪ melphalan ▪ méthotrexate ▪ métronidazole ▪ mezlocilline ▪ nafcilline ▪ ondansétron ▪ oxacilline ▪ paclitaxel ▪ pénicilline G potassique ▪ pipéracilline ▪ pipéracilline/tazobactam ▪ rémifentanil ▪ thiotépa ▪ ticarcilline ▪ tobramycine ▪ triméthoprime/sulfaméthoxazole ▪ vancomycine ▪ vinorelbine.

Incompatibilité (tubulure en Y): amphotéricine B liposomale ▪ diazépam ▪ gallium, nitrate de ▪ minocycline ▪ phénobarbital ▪ phénytoïne ▪ sargramostim.

Compatibilité en addition au soluté: ondansétron.

Incompatibilité en addition au soluté: sodium, bicarbonate de ▪ thiopental.

Solutions compatibles: ▪ D5%E ▪ D5%/NaCl 0,45 % ▪ D5%/NaCl 0,9 % ▪ D5%/solution de lactate de Ringer ▪ D5%/solution de Ringer ▪ NaCl 0,45 % ou 0,9 % ▪ solution de Ringer et solution de lactate de Ringer.

ENSEIGNEMENT AU PATIENT ET À SES PROCHES

- Expliquer au patient ce qu'on entend par administration sur demande et à quel moment il doit réclamer l'analgésique.

ALERTE CLINIQUE: PRÉVENIR LES PROCHES QU'IL NE FAUT PAS ADMINISTRER DE DOSES D'ACP À UN PATIENT QUI DORT, EN RAISON DES RISQUES DE SÉDATION, DE SURDOSAGE ET DE DÉPRESSION RESPIRATOIRE.

- Prévenir le patient que l'hydromorphone peut provoquer des étourdissements et de la somnolence. Lui recommander de demander de l'aide lorsqu'il se déplace et lorsqu'il veut fumer. Lui conseiller de ne pas conduire et d'éviter les activités qui exigent sa vigilance jusqu'à ce qu'on ait la certitude que le médicament n'entraîne pas ces effets chez lui.
- Recommander au patient de changer lentement de position pour diminuer le risque d'hypotension orthostatique.
- Inciter le patient à ne pas boire d'alcool et à ne pas prendre d'autres dépresseurs du SNC en même temps que l'hydromorphone.
- Conseiller au patient de se tourner dans le lit, de tousser et de faire des exercices de respiration profonde toutes les 2 heures pour prévenir l'atélectasie.

Soins à domicile: **ALERTE CLINIQUE**: EXPLIQUER AU PATIENT ET À SES PROCHES COMMENT ET QUAND ADMINISTRER L'HYDROMORPHONE ET COMMENT ENTRETENIR LE MATÉRIEL DE PERFUSION. **PÉD.**: MONTRER AUX PARENTS OU AUX SOIGNANTS COMMENT MESURER AVEC PRÉCISION LE MÉDICAMENT SOUS FORME LIQUIDE ET LEUR RECOMMANDER D'UTILISER SEULEMENT LA MESURE FOURNIE AVEC LE MÉDICAMENT.

- Insister sur l'importance de la prévention de la constipation associée à la prise d'analgésiques opioïdes.

VÉRIFICATION DE L'EFFICACITÉ THÉRAPEUTIQUE

L'efficacité du traitement peut être démontrée par: la diminution de l'intensité de la douleur sans modification importante de l'état de conscience ou de l'état respiratoire ▪ la suppression de la toux. ✳

HYDROXOCOBALAMINE,

voir Vitamine B_{12} (préparations)

HYDROXYCHLOROQUINE

Apo-Hydroxyquine, Gen-Hydroxychloroquine, Plaquenil

CLASSIFICATION:

Antipaludéen, anti-inflammatoire (agent antirhumatismal modificateur de la maladie [AARMM])

Grossesse – catégorie C

INDICATIONS

Traitement suppressif (chimioprophylaxie) de la malaria et traitement des crises aiguës ■ Traitement de la polyarthrite rhumatoïde grave et du lupus érythémateux disséminé.

MÉCANISME D'ACTION

Inhibition de la synthèse protéique des microorganismes sensibles, par inhibition de la polymérase de l'ADN et de l'ARN. ***Effets thérapeutiques:*** Destruction des plasmodies qui provoquent la malaria ■ Propriétés anti-inflammatoires.

PHARMACOCINÉTIQUE

Absorption: Variable (de 31 à 100 % PO).

Distribution: Tout l'organisme et en fortes concentrations dans les tissus (particulièrement dans le foie). L'hydroxychloroquine passe probablement dans le lait maternel.

Métabolisme et excrétion: Métabolisme partiellement hépatique avec transformation en métabolites actifs. Excrétion partiellement rénale à l'état inchangé.

Demi-vie: De 72 à 120 heures.

Profil temps-action

	DÉBUT D'ACTION	PIC	DURÉE
PO	rapide†	1 – 2 h	plusieurs jours – semaines

† L'effet antiarthritique peut ne pas se manifester avant 6 semaines.

CONTRE-INDICATIONS, PRÉCAUTIONS ET MISES EN GARDE

Contre-indications: Hypersensibilité aux amino-4-quinoléines ■ Rétinopathie préexistante ■ Antécédents de lésions oculaires induites par l'hydroxychloroquine ou la chloroquine ■ **PÉD.**: Enfants < 6 ans (les comprimés de 200 mg ne sont pas adaptés à un poids corporel < 35 kg).

Précautions et mises en garde: Administration concomitante de médicaments hépatotoxiques ou néphrotoxique ■ Insuffisance hépatique ou rénale ■ Antécédents de maladie hépatique ou d'alcoolisme ■ Taux insuffisants de G-6-PD ■ Changement de l'acuité visuelle, du champ visuel ou des zones maculaires de la rétine (arrêter le traitement immédiatement) ■ Psoriasis ou porphyrie ■ Troubles gastro-intestinaux, neurologiques ou hématologiques ■ Aplasie médullaire ■ Obésité (déterminer la dose en fonction du poids corporel idéal) ■ **OBST., ALLAITEMENT**: Éviter l'usage sauf en cas de traitement ou de prévention de la malaria ou de traitement d'un abcès amibien ■ **PÉD.**: L'usage prolongé augmente la sensibilité aux effets secondaires. L'innocuité et l'efficacité n'ont pas été établies en cas de polyarthrite rhumatoïde ou de lupus érythémateux disséminé.

RÉACTIONS INDÉSIRABLES ET EFFETS SECONDAIRES

SNC: CONVULSIONS, agressivité, anxiété, apathie, confusion, fatigue, céphalées, irritabilité, modifications de la personnalité, psychoses.

ORLO: kératite, ototoxicité, rétinopathie, acouphènes, troubles visuels.

CV: modifications de l'ÉCG, hypotension.

GI: crampes abdominales, anorexie, diarrhée, gêne épigastrique, nausées, vomissements, insuffisance hépatique.

Tég.: prurit, changements de pigmentation de la peau et des muqueuses, décoloration des cheveux et alopécie, photosensibilité, syndrome de Stevens-Johnson, dermatoses.

Hémat.: AGRANULOCYTOSE, ANÉMIE APLASIQUE, leucopénie, thrombopénie.

SN: neuromyopathie, névrite périphérique.

INTERACTIONS

Médicament-médicament: L'administration concomitante d'**agents hépatotoxiques** peut accroître le risque d'hépatotoxicité ■ Risque accru de toxicité hématologique, lors de l'administration concomitante de **pénicillamine** ■ L'administration concomitante d'**agents ayant des propriétés toxiques pour la peau** peut accroître le risque de dermatoses ■ L'hydroxychloroquine, administrée en même temps que des **vaccins antirabiques obtenus sur des cellules diploïdes humaines**, peut réduire les titres des anticorps de la rage ■ L'administration concomitante d'**acidifiants urinaires** peut accroître l'excrétion rénale de l'hydroxychloroquine ■ L'hydroxychloroquine peut élever les concentrations sériques de **digoxine** ■ L'hydroxychloroquine pouvant accentuer les effets d'un traitement hypoglycémiant, il peut-être nécessaire de diminuer les doses d'**insuline** ou de **médicaments antidiabétiques**.

H

VOIES D'ADMINISTRATION ET POSOLOGIE

LES DOSES POUR ADULTES SONT INDIQUÉES EN TERMES DE SULFATE D'HYDROXYCHLOROQUINE. LES DOSES POUR ENFANTS SONT INDIQUÉES EN TERMES D'HYDROXYCHLOROQUINE BASE. UN COMPRIMÉ DE 200 mg DE SULFATE D'HYDROXYCHLOROQUINE ÉQUIVAUT À 155 mg D'HYDROXYCHLOROQUINE BASE.

Malaria

- **PO (adultes)**: *Suppression* – 400 mg, 1 fois par semaine; commencer le traitement 2 semaines avant l'arrivée dans la zone endémique; s'il n'est pas commencé avant l'exposition, administrer 1 dose de charge de 800 mg, en 2 prises espacées de 6 heures. Le patient devrait continuer le traitement pendant 8 semaines après avoir quitté cette région. *Traitement* – 800 mg, puis 400 mg, de 6 à 8 heures plus tard. Administrer ensuite 1 dose quotidienne de 400 mg pendant 2 jours, pour un total de 2 g d'hydroxychloroquine. Une dose unique de 800 mg s'est également révélée efficace.
- **PO (nourrissons et enfants)**: *Suppression* – 5 mg de base/kg, 1 fois par semaine; commencer le traitement 2 semaines avant l'arrivée dans la zone endémique; s'il n'est pas commencé avant l'exposition, administrer 1 dose de charge de 10 mg de base/kg, en 2 prises espacées de 6 heures. Le patient devrait continuer le traitement pendant 8 semaines après avoir quitté cette région. Ne pas dépasser la dose recommandée chez l'adulte, quel que soit le poids corporel de l'enfant. *Traitement* – 10 mg de base/kg (ne pas dépasser 620 mg de base); ensuite, 5 mg de base/kg (ne pas dépasser 310 mg de base), 6 heures après la première dose; ensuite, 5 mg de base/kg, 18 heures après la deuxième dose, et 5 mg de base/kg, 24 heures après la troisième dose. La dose totale est de 25 mg de base/kg, administrés en 3 jours.

Polyarthrite rhumatoïde

- **PO (adultes)**: Initialement, de 400 à 600 mg par jour, puis de 200 à 400 mg par jour, en traitement d'entretien.

Lupus érythémateux disséminé

- **PO (adultes)**: 400 mg, 1 ou 2 fois par jour, puis de 200 à 400 mg par jour, en traitement d'entretien.

PRÉSENTATION

Comprimés: 200 mg (155 mg d'hydroxychloroquine base)Pr.

SOINS INFIRMIERS

ÉVALUATION DE LA SITUATION

- Examiner le réflexe tendineux à intervalles réguliers afin de déceler le degré de faiblesse musculaire. Arrêter le traitement si cette réaction se manifeste.
- Chez les patients qui suivent un traitement prolongé à des doses élevées, il faudrait effectuer des examens ophtalmiques avant l'administration initiale et tous les 3 à 6 mois pendant toute la durée du traitement afin de déceler les lésions de la rétine.

Malaria ou lupus érythémateux: Observer quotidiennement le patient pendant toute la durée du traitement pour déterminer si les signes et les symptômes de la maladie se sont améliorés.

Polyarthrite rhumatoïde: Noter mensuellement l'intensité de la douleur articulaire, l'enflure des articulations et l'amplitude des mouvements.

Tests de laboratoire: NOTER LES NUMÉRATIONS GLOBULAIRE ET PLAQUETTAIRE À INTERVALLES RÉGULIERS PENDANT TOUTE LA DURÉE DU TRAITEMENT. L'HYDROXYCHLOROQUINE PEUT DIMINUER LE NOMBRE DE GLOBULES ROUGES ET BLANCS ET LE NOMBRE DE PLAQUETTES. SI L'ON NOTE UNE DIMINUTION MARQUÉE QUI N'EST PAS LIÉE AU PROCESSUS PATHOLOGIQUE, ON DEVRAIT INTERROMPRE LE TRAITEMENT PAR L'HYDROXYCHLOROQUINE.

DIAGNOSTICS INFIRMIERS POSSIBLES

- Risque d'infection (Indications).
- Douleur chronique (Indications).
- Connaissances insuffisantes sur le traitement médicamenteux (Enseignement au patient et à ses proches).

INTERVENTIONS INFIRMIÈRES

- Administrer le médicament avec du lait ou des aliments pour réduire le risque de douleurs gastrointestinales.
- Dans le cas des patients ayant des difficultés de déglutition, on peut écraser les comprimés et les mélanger à une cuillerée à thé de confiture ou de gelée.

Prophylaxie de la malaria: Il faudrait commencer le traitement à l'hydroxychloroquine, 2 semaines avant l'exposition probable aux plasmodies et le poursuivre pendant 8 semaines après avoir quitté la région endémique.

ENSEIGNEMENT AU PATIENT ET À SES PROCHES

- Expliquer au patient qu'il doit respecter rigoureusement la posologie recommandée et continuer à prendre l'hydroxychloroquine même s'il se sent mieux. S'il n'a pas pu prendre le médicament au moment habituel, il doit le prendre aussitôt que possible, sauf si c'est presque l'heure prévue pour la dose suivante. L'avertir qu'il ne doit jamais remplacer une dose manquée par une double dose.

- Recommander au patient d'éviter de boire de l'alcool pendant qu'il prend de l'hydroxychloroquine.
- RECOMMANDER AU PATIENT DE GARDER L'HYDROXYCHLOROQUINE HORS DE LA PORTÉE DES ENFANTS; DES DÉCÈS SONT SURVENUS PAR SUITE DE L'INGESTION DE 3 OU DE 4 COMPRIMÉS.
- Expliquer au patient qui suit un traitement prolongé à fortes doses qu'il doit se soumettre à des examens ophtalmiques à intervalles réguliers. L'informer que le risque de lésions oculaires peut être réduit s'il porte des verres fumés lorsque la lumière est vive. Lui conseiller de porter des vêtements protecteurs et d'utiliser un écran solaire pour réduire le risque de dermatose.
- Recommander au patient de signaler immédiatement à un professionnel de la santé les maux de gorge, la fièvre, les saignements ou les ecchymoses inhabituels, la vision trouble, les modifications de la vue, les acouphènes, les troubles auditifs ou la faiblesse musculaire.

Prophylaxie de la malaria:

- Passer en revue les moyens de réduire l'exposition aux moustiques: utiliser un insectifuge, porter des chemises à manches longues et des pantalons, s'abriter derrière une moustiquaire.
- Recommander au patient de consulter un professionnel de la santé s'il fait de la fièvre pendant le voyage ou pendant les 2 mois qui suivent le moment où il a quitté la région endémique.

Polyarthrite rhumatoïde: Conseiller au patient de signaler à un professionnel de la santé l'absence de toute amélioration dans les quelques jours suivant le début du traitement. La pleine efficacité du traitement de la polyarthrite rhumatoïde peut ne pas être manifeste avant 6 mois.

VÉRIFICATION DE L'EFFICACITÉ THÉRAPEUTIQUE

L'efficacité du traitement peut être démontrée par: la prévention ou la résolution de la malaria ▪ la diminution des signes et des symptômes de polyarthrite rhumatoïde ▪ la diminution des symptômes de lupus érythémateux. ✳

HYDROXYURÉE

Apo-Hydroxyurea, Gen-Hydroxyurea, Hydrea

CLASSIFICATION:

Antinéoplasique (antimétabolite)

Grossesse – catégorie D

INDICATIONS

Traitement de l'épithélioma spinocellulaire épidermoïde primaire de la tête et du cou (à l'exclusion des lèvres) en association avec la radiothérapie ▪ Traitement de la leucémie myéloïde chronique et réfractaire ▪ Traitement des mélanomes. **Usages non approuvés**: Traitement du cancer des ovaires ▪ Réduction des crises douloureuses associées à la drépanocytose et du besoin de recourir à des transfusions chez les patients adultes ayant des antécédents de crises récurrentes, d'intensité modérée à grave (au moins 3 crises au cours de l'année précédente).

MÉCANISME D'ACTION

Inhibition de la synthèse de l'ADN (effet spécifique sur la phase S du cycle cellulaire). ***Effets thérapeutiques:*** Destruction des cellules à réplication rapide, particulièrement des cellules malignes ▪ Diminution de la fréquence des crises douloureuses et du besoin de recourir à des transfusions en cas de drépanocytose.

PHARMACOCINÉTIQUE

Absorption: Bonne (PO).

Distribution: L'hydroxyurée traverse la barrière hématoencéphalique et se concentre dans les globules rouges et blancs.

Métabolisme et excrétion: 50 % du médicament est excrété à l'état inchangé par les reins; 50 % est métabolisé par le foie.

Demi-vie: De 3 à 4 heures.

Profil temps-action (effets sur la numération globulaire)

	DÉBUT D'ACTION	PIC	DURÉE
PO	7 jours	10 jours	7-15 jours après l'arrêt du traitement

CONTRE-INDICATIONS, PRÉCAUTIONS ET MISES EN GARDE

Contre-indications: Hypersensibilité à l'hydroxyurée ou à tout autre ingrédient du produit ▪ Aplasie médullaire.

Précautions et mises en garde: Patients en âge de procréer ▪ Grossesse ou allaitement ▪ Insuffisance rénale (on recommande un suivi étroit des paramètres hématologiques; il peut s'avérer nécessaire de réduire la dose) ▪ Insuffisance hépatique (on recommande un suivi étroit des paramètres hématologiques) ▪ Maladies infectieuses évolutives ▪ Autres maladies chroniques débilitantes ▪ Patients obèses ou œdémateux (la dose devrait être déterminée en fonction du poids idéal) ▪ Radiothérapie (effet radiosensibilisant) ▪ **GÉR.**: Risque accru d'effets indésirables; il peut s'avérer nécessaire de diminuer la dose ▪ Infection par le VIH traitée par des antirétroviraux ▪ **PÉD.**: L'innocuité et l'efficacité du médicalement n'ont pas été établies.

RÉACTIONS INDÉSIRABLES ET EFFETS SECONDAIRES

CV: vasculite.
SNC: somnolence (doses élevées).
GI: anorexie, diarrhée, nausées, vomissements, constipation, hépatite, stomatite.
GU: dysurie, stérilité, dysfonctionnement des tubules rénaux.
Tég.: alopécie, érythème, prurit, rash.
Hémat.: leucopénie, anémie, thrombopénie.
Métab.: hyperuricémie.
Divers: frissons, fièvre, malaise.

INTERACTIONS

Médicament-médicament: Effets additifs sur la réserve médullaire lors de l'administration simultanée d'**agents dépresseurs de la moelle osseuse** ou d'une **radiothérapie** ▪ Le médicament peut réduire la réponse des anticorps aux **vaccins à virus vivants** et augmenter le risque de réactions indésirables ▪ Le traitement d'association d'hydroxyurée et de certains **antirétroviraux**, en particulier la **didanosine** plus **stadivuline**, a été associé à des cas de pancréatite, d'hépatite et de neuropathies périphériques graves.

VOIES D'ADMINISTRATION ET POSOLOGIE

Cancer au niveau de la tête et du cou, mélanome malin

- **PO (adultes)**: 80 mg/kg en une seule dose par jour, tous les 3 jours. Le traitement devrait être amorcé 7 jours avant la radiothérapie et poursuivi par la suite.

Leucémie myéloïde chronique réfractaire

- **PO (adultes)**: De 20 à 30 mg/kg par jour, en 1 dose par jour.

Drépanocytose

- **PO (adultes et enfants)**: 15 mg/kg/jour, 1 fois par jour, dose qu'on peut augmenter de 5 mg/kg/jour, toutes les 12 semaines, jusqu'à concurrence de 35 mg/kg/jour *(usage non approuvé)*.

PRÉSENTATION
(version générique disponible)

Capsules: 500 mg[Pr].

SOINS INFIRMIERS

ÉVALUATION DE LA SITUATION

- Rechercher les signes et les symptômes suivants d'infection: fièvre, maux de gorge, toux, enrouement, douleurs lombaires ou aux flancs, mictions difficiles ou douloureuses. Si ces symptômes se manifestent, en informer immédiatement le médecin.
- Il y a risque d'anémie. Suivre de près la fatigue, la dyspnée et l'hypotension orthostatique.
- Suivre de près les saignements: saignement des gencives, formation d'ecchymoses, pétéchies, présence de sang occulte dans les selles, dans l'urine et dans les vomissures. Éviter les injections IM et la prise de la température rectale; appliquer une pression sur les points de ponction veineuse pendant au moins 10 minutes.
- Effectuer le bilan quotidien des ingesta et des excreta, noter l'appétit du patient et sa consommation de nourriture. Maintenir une alimentation adéquate en modifiant le régime en fonction des aliments que le patient peut tolérer.

Tests de laboratoire:

- Noter la numération globulaire et la formule leucocytaire avant l'administration initiale et à intervalles réguliers pendant toute la durée du traitement. La leucopénie apparaît dans les 10 jours qui suivent le début du traitement. Le nombre de globules blancs se rétablit habituellement dans les 30 jours. Prévenir le médecin si le nombre de globules blancs est inférieur à $2,5 \times 10^9$/L ou si une chute soudaine survient. Le médicament peut élever passagèrement le volume globulaire moyen.
- Chez les patients souffrant de *drépanocytose*, noter la numération globulaire et la formule leucocytaire toutes les 2 semaines. Le traitement devrait être interrompu si le nombre de polynucléaires neutrophiles est $< 2 \times 10^9$/L, si celui des plaquettes est $< 80 \times 10^9$/L, si l'hémoglobine est < 45 g/L ou si le nombre de réticulocytes est $< 80 \times 10^9$/L et lorsque l'hémoglobine est < 90 g/L. Chez la plupart des patients, il est nécessaire d'interrompre le traitement à intervalles réguliers jusqu'à ce que les numérations globulaires reviennent à des concentrations acceptables.
- Noter les résultats des tests de la fonction rénale (concentrations sériques d'urée, de créatinine et d'acide urique) et hépatique (concentrations d'AST,

d'ALT, de bilirubine et de LDH), avant le traitement et à intervalles réguliers pendant toute sa durée. L'hydroxyurée peut entraîner l'élévation des concentrations sériques d'urée, de créatinine et d'acide urique.

DIAGNOSTICS INFIRMIERS POSSIBLES

- Risque d'accident (Effets secondaires).
- Risque d'infection (Effets secondaires).
- Connaissances insuffisantes sur le traitement médicamenteux (Enseignement au patient et à ses proches).

INTERVENTIONS INFIRMIÈRES

- Chez le patient éprouvant des difficultés de déglutition, on peut ouvrir les capsules, en vider le contenu dans un verre d'eau et l'administrer immédiatement. Une certaine quantité de poudre inerte peut flotter à la surface de l'eau. Si de la poudre se disperse accidentellement, l'essuyer immédiatement à l'aide d'un chiffon humide jetable.

ENSEIGNEMENT AU PATIENT ET À SES PROCHES

- Conseiller au patient de respecter rigoureusement la posologie recommandée, même si les nausées, les vomissements et la diarrhée persistent et de consulter un professionnel de la santé si les vomissements se produisent peu de temps après la prise de la dose. Si le patient n'a pas pu prendre le médicament au moment habituel, il doit le prendre aussitôt que possible à moins que ce ne soit presque l'heure prévue pour la dose suivante. L'avertir qu'il ne doit jamais remplacer une dose manquée par une double dose. Lui conseiller de consulter un professionnel de la santé s'il a sauté plus de 1 dose.
- Recommander au patient de signaler à un professionnel de la santé la fièvre, les frissons, les maux de gorge, les signes d'infection, la perte d'appétit, les nausées, les vomissements, la diarrhée, les saignements des gencives, la formation d'ecchymoses, les pétéchies ou la présence de sang dans les urines, les selles ou les vomissures. Inciter le patient à éviter les foules et les personnes contagieuses. Lui recommander d'utiliser une brosse à dent à poils doux et un rasoir électrique. Mettre en garde le patient contre la consommation de boissons alcoolisées ou de produits contenant de l'aspirine ou des AINS.
- Informer le patient qu'un traitement prolongé par l'hydroxyurée peut accroître le risque de cancer.
- Recommander au patient d'examiner sa muqueuse buccale pour déceler l'érythème et l'aphte. En cas d'aphte, lui conseiller de remplacer la brosse à dents par une brosse-éponge, de se rincer la bouche avec de l'eau après avoir bu ou mangé et de consulter un professionnel de la santé si les douleurs l'empêchent de s'alimenter. La douleur associée à la stomatite peut dicter un traitement par des analgésiques opioïdes.
- Expliquer au patient qui reçoit des doses élevées que l'hydroxyurée peut entraîner la somnolence. Lui conseiller de ne pas conduire et d'éviter les activités qui exigent sa vigilance jusqu'à ce qu'on ait la certitude que ce médicament n'entraîne pas cet effet chez lui.
- Conseiller au patient de consulter un professionnel de la santé avant de prendre tout autre médicament en vente libre ou sur ordonnance en même temps que l'hydroxyurée.
- Expliquer à la patiente qu'elle doit prendre des mesures contraceptives tout au long du traitement même si l'aménorrhée survient. Cependant, la prévenir que l'hydroxyurée peut la rendre stérile. Expliquer aussi au patient qu'il ne doit pas procréer pendant le traitement à l'hydroxyurée.
- Expliquer au patient qu'il ne doit pas se faire vacciner sans recommandation expresse d'un professionnel de la santé.
- Insister sur l'importance des examens médicaux de suivi et des tests de laboratoire permettant de déterminer l'efficacité du médicament et d'en déceler les effets secondaires.

Leucémie: Inciter le patient à boire de 2 000 à 3 000 mL de liquides par jour si son état le permet. Le médecin peut lui prescrire de l'allopurinol et l'alcalinisation de l'urine pour prévenir la formation de calculs d'urate.

VÉRIFICATION DE L'EFFICACITÉ THÉRAPEUTIQUE

L'efficacité du traitement peut être démontrée par: la diminution de la taille des tumeurs et le ralentissement de la propagation du cancer ▪ l'amélioration des valeurs hématologiques en cas de leucémie (le traitement doit être interrompu si le nombre de globules blancs est inférieur à $2,5 \times 10^9$/L ou celui de plaquettes à 100×10^9/L; on peut le reprendre lorsque ces valeurs se rapprochent des limites normales, habituellement dans les 3 jours qui suivent) ▪ la réduction des crises douloureuses en cas de drépanocytose. ✳

HYDROXYZINE

Apo-Hydroxyzine, Atarax, Novo-Hydroxyzin, Nu-Hydroxyzine, PMS-Hydroxyzine, Riva-Hydroxyzin

CLASSIFICATION:

Antihistaminique, anxiolytique et hypnosédatif (antihistaminique)

Grossesse – catégorie C

INDICATIONS

PO: Traitement de l'anxiété ■ Sédation préopératoire ■ Traitement antiémétique (contre-indiqué en cas de grossesse) ■ Traitement du prurit ■ Traitement de l'alcoolisme aigu ou chronique ■ **IM**: Patient hystérique ou extrêmement perturbé ■ Traitement de l'alcoolisme chronique ou aigu ■ Médication adjuvante préopératoire et postopératoire pour calmer l'anxiété, pour permettre une réduction substantielle de la dose d'analgésiques opioïdes et pour maîtriser les vomissements.

MÉCANISME D'ACTION

Dépression du SNC au niveau sous-cortical ■ Propriétés anticholinergiques, antihistaminiques et antiémétiques. ***Effets thérapeutiques:*** Sédation ■ Apaisement de l'anxiété ■ Soulagement des nausées et des vomissements ■ Soulagement des symptômes allergiques associés à la libération d'histamine, incluant le prurit.

PHARMACOCINÉTIQUE

Absorption: Bonne (PO et IM).

Distribution: Inconnue.

Métabolisme et excrétion: Métabolisme entièrement hépatique; élimination fécale par excrétion biliaire.

Demi-vie: 3 heures.

Profil temps-action

(effets sédatifs, antiémétiques, antiprurigineux)

	DÉBUT D'ACTION	PIC	DURÉE
PO	15 – 30 min	2 – 4 h	4 – 6 h
IM	15 – 30 min	2 – 4 h	4 – 6 h

CONTRE-INDICATIONS, PRÉCAUTIONS ET MISES EN GARDE

Contre-indications: Hypersensibilité ■ Grossesse.

Précautions et mises en garde: Dysfonction hépatique grave ■ Antécédents de troubles épileptiques ■ **GÉR.**: Les personnes âgées sont plus sensibles aux effets secondaires anticholinergiques. Il est indiqué de réduire la dose ■ **PÉD.**: La solution pour injection peut contenir de l'alcool benzylique qui est contre-indiqué chez les nouveau-nés (< 1 mois). L'utilisation durant le travail de l'accouchement ne comporte cependant aucun danger ■ **ALLAITEMENT**: L'innocuité du médicament n'a pas été établie.

RÉACTIONS INDÉSIRABLES ET EFFETS SECONDAIRES

SNC: somnolence, agitation, ataxie, étourdissements, céphalées, faiblesse.

Resp.: respiration sifflante.

GI: sécheresse de la bouche (xérostomie), goût amer, constipation, nausées.

GU: rétention urinaire.

Tég.: bouffées vasomotrices.

Locaux: douleurs au point d'injection IM, abcès au point d'injection IM.

Divers: oppression thoracique.

INTERACTIONS

Médicament-médicament: Effets dépresseurs additifs sur le SNC, lors de l'usage concomitant d'autres **dépresseurs du SNC**, incluant l'**alcool**, les **antidépresseurs**, les **antihistaminiques**, les **analgésiques opioïdes** et les **hypnosédatifs** ■ Effets anticholinergiques additifs, lors de l'administration concomitante de **médicaments ayant des propriétés anticholinergiques**, incluant les **antihistaminiques**, les **antidépresseurs**, l'**atropine**, l'**halopéridol**, les **phénothiazines**, la **quinidine** et le **disopyramide** ■ L'agent peut contrecarrer l'effet vasopresseur de l'**adrénaline**.

Médicament-produits naturels: L'utilisation concomitante avec le **kava**, la **valériane** et la **camomille** peut augmenter l'effet dépresseur sur le SNC ■ Risque d'intensification des effets secondaires anticholinergiques lors de la consommation concomitante de **trompette des anges**, de **datura** et de **scopolia**.

VOIES D'ADMINISTRATION ET POSOLOGIE

- **PO (adultes)**: De 25 à 100 mg, 3 ou 4 fois par jour.
- **PO (enfants > 6 ans)**: De 50 à 100 mg par jour, en doses fractionnées.
- **PO (enfants < 6 ans)**: De 30 à 50 mg par jour, en doses fractionnées.
- **IM (adultes)**: *Urgence psychiatrique ou crise émotive et alcoolisme* – de 50 à 100 mg, toutes les 4 à 6 heures, au besoin. *Antiémétique, adjuvant aux analgésiques opioïdes* – de 25 à 100 mg.
- **IM (enfants)**: *Antiémétique, adjuvant aux analgésiques opioïdes* – de 0,5 à 1 mg/kg, toutes les 4 à 6 heures.

PRÉSENTATION
(version générique disponible)

Capsules: 10 mg^{Pr}, 25 mg^{Pr}, 50 mg^{Pr} ▪ **Sirop**: 10 mg/5 mL^{Pr} ▪ **Solution pour injection**: 50 mg/mL^{Pr}.

SOINS INFIRMIERS

ÉVALUATION DE LA SITUATION

- Déterminer si le patient est en état de sédation profonde et prendre les mesures de sécurité qui s'imposent: remonter les ridelles du lit, garder le lit en position basse, placer la sonnette d'appel à portée de la main, suivre de près les déplacements et les changements de position.

GÉR.: Les personnes âgées sont plus sensibles aux effets secondaires anticholinergiques de l'hydroxyzine ainsi qu'à ses effets au niveau du SNC: délire, confusion aiguë, étourdissements, xérostomie, vision trouble, rétention urinaire, constipation et tachycardie. Noter la somnolence, l'agitation, la sédation excessive et les autres effets secondaires systémiques. Évaluer les risques de chutes et mettre en place les mesures de prévention qui s'imposent.

Anxiété: Noter l'état de conscience, l'humeur et le comportement du patient.

Nausées et vomissements: Noter l'intensité des nausées ainsi que la fréquence et la quantité des vomissements.

Prurit: Déterminer la gravité du prurit et les caractéristiques de la peau affectée.

Tests de laboratoire: Le médicament peut entraîner des résultats faussement négatifs aux tests d'allergie cutanés. Interrompre l'administration de l'hydroxyzine au moins 72 heures avant ces tests.

DIAGNOSTICS INFIRMIERS POSSIBLES

- Anxiété (Indications).
- Atteinte à l'intégrité de la peau (Indications).
- Risque d'accident (Effets secondaires).

INTERVENTIONS INFIRMIÈRES

- NE PAS CONFONDRE L'HYDROXYZINE AVEC L'HYDRALAZINE OU ATARAX (HYDROXYZINE) AVEC ATIVAN (LORAZÉPAM).

PO: Chez les patients éprouvant des difficultés de déglutition, on peut percer les capsules d'hydroxyzine et en administrer le contenu dans un aliment ou un jus.

IM: Administrer l'injection par voie IM profondément dans un muscle bien développé, de préférence selon la technique du tracé en Z. L'injection est extrêmement douloureuse. Ne pas administrer dans le muscle deltoïde. Si le médicament doit être administré à un enfant, utiliser de préférence la partie médiane externe de la cuisse. Les injections sous-cutanées ou intra-artérielles peuvent provoquer des lésions tissulaires importantes, la nécrose des tissus et la formation d'une escarre. Les injections par voie IV peuvent provoquer l'hémolyse. Assurer la rotation fréquente des points d'injection.

Associations compatibles dans la même seringue: atropine ▪ benzquinamide ▪ buprénorphine ▪ butorphanol ▪ chlorpromazine ▪ cimétidine ▪ codéine ▪ diphenhydramine ▪ doxapram ▪ dropéridol ▪ fentanyl ▪ fluphénazine ▪ glycopyrrolate ▪ hydromorphone ▪ lidocaïne ▪ mépéridine ▪ méthotriméprazine ▪ métoclopramide ▪ midazolam ▪ morphine ▪ nalbuphine ▪ oxymorphone ▪ pentazocine ▪ perphénazine ▪ procaïne ▪ prochlorpérazine ▪ promazine ▪ prométhazine ▪ scopolamine ▪ sufentanil ▪ thiothixène.

Associations incompatibles dans la même seringue: chloramphénicol ▪ dimenhydrinate ▪ halopéridol ▪ héparine ▪ kétorolac ▪ pénicilline G potassique ▪ pentobarbital ▪ phénobarbital ▪ phénytoïne ▪ ranitidine ▪ vitamines du complexe B avec C.

ENSEIGNEMENT AU PATIENT ET À SES PROCHES

- Conseiller au patient de respecter rigoureusement la posologie recommandée. S'il n'a pu prendre le médicament au moment habituel, il doit le prendre dès que possible, à moins que ce ne soit presque l'heure prévue pour la dose suivante. L'avertir qu'il ne doit jamais remplacer une dose manquée par une double dose.
- Prévenir le patient que l'hydroxyzine peut provoquer de la somnolence ou des étourdissements. Lui conseiller de ne pas conduire et d'éviter les activités qui exigent sa vigilance jusqu'à ce qu'on ait la certitude que le médicament n'entraîne pas ces effets chez lui.

GÉR.: Prévenir le patient ou les soignants que les personnes âgées sont exposées à un plus grand risque de chutes et d'effets secondaires au niveau du SNC.

- Conseiller au patient de ne pas consommer d'alcool ou d'autres dépresseurs du SNC en même temps que cet agent.
- Conseiller au patient de pratiquer une bonne hygiène buccale, de se rincer la bouche fréquemment avec de l'eau et de consommer de la gomme à mâcher ou des bonbons sans sucre pour diminuer la sécheresse de la bouche. Si la sécheresse de la bouche persiste pendant plus de 2 semaines, l'inciter à consulter un professionnel de la santé qui pourra lui recommander des substituts de salive.

VÉRIFICATION DE L'EFFICACITÉ THÉRAPEUTIQUE

L'efficacité du traitement peut être démontrée par: l'apaisement de l'anxiété ■ le soulagement des nausées et des vomissements ■ le soulagement du prurit ■ la sédation lorsque le médicament est administré comme hypnosédatif. ✳

HYOSCINE,

voir Scopolamine

H

IBUPROFÈNE

Advil, Apo-Ibuprofen, Ibuprofen, Motrin IB, Novo-Profen

CLASSIFICATION:

Antipyrétique, analgésique non opioïde, anti-inflammatoire non stéroïdien

Grossesse – catégories D (1er et 3e trimestres) et B (2e trimestre)

INDICATIONS

Adultes: Soulagement de la douleur associée aux céphalées, aux maux de dents, à la dysménorrhée ainsi qu'aux douleurs musculaires, articulaires et osseuses, telles que foulures, entorses et lombalgies ■ Traitement des troubles inflammatoires incluant: la polyarthrite rhumatoïde ■ l'arthrose ■ Abaissement de la fièvre et des malaises causés par le rhume ordinaire.

Enfants: Soulagement passager de la fièvre, des céphalées, des douleurs articulaires, musculaires et osseuses bénignes ■ Soulagement des courbatures et de la fièvre causées par le rhume ordinaire, la grippe, le mal de gorge, le mal d'oreille ou la vaccination.

MÉCANISME D'ACTION

Inhibition de la synthèse des prostaglandines. ***Effets thérapeutiques:*** Suppression de la douleur et de l'inflammation ■ Abaissement de la fièvre.

PHARMACOCINÉTIQUE

Absorption: Bonne (PO).

Distribution: L'agent passe en quantités minimes dans le lait maternel.

Liaison aux protéines: 99 %.

Métabolisme et excrétion: Métabolisme majoritairement hépatique. De petites quantités (de l'ordre de 1 %) sont excrétées à l'état inchangé par les reins.

Demi-vie: Enfants: de 1 à 2 heures; adultes: de 2 à 4 heures.

Profil temps-action (effets thérapeutiques)

	DÉBUT D'ACTION	PIC	DURÉE
PO (antipyrétique)	30 min - 2,5 h	2 - 4 h	6 - 8 h
PO (analgésique)	30 min	1 - 2 h	4 - 6 h
PO (anti-inflammatoire)	7 jours	1 - 2 semaines	inconnue

CONTRE-INDICATIONS, PRÉCAUTIONS ET MISES EN GARDE

Contre-indications: Hypersensibilité ■ Antécédents de polypes nasaux, de bronchospasme ou d'œdème de Quincke induits par l'aspirine, l'ibuprofène ou les autres AINS ■ Risque de réactions de sensibilité croisée avec d'autres anti-inflammatoires non stéroïdiens, incluant l'aspirine ■ Hémorragie digestive ou ulcère gastroduodénal en poussées évolutives ■ Lupus érythémateux disséminé.

Précautions et mises en garde: Maladies cardiovasculaires, rénales ou hépatiques graves ■ Déshydratation, usage concomitant de médicaments néphrotoxiques (risque accru de néphrotoxicité) ■ Alcoolisme chronique ■ Antécédents d'ulcère gastroduodénal ■ Phénylcétonurie (les comprimés à croquer contiennent de l'aspartame et ne devraient pas être administrés aux patients souffrant de cette maladie) ■ **GÉR.**: Risque accru d'effets indésirables liés à une diminution de la fonction rénale et hépatique, aux maladies concomitantes et aux médicaments ■ **OBST.**: Précédents d'hypertension pulmonaire persistante chez le nouveau-né ■ **PÉD.**: L'innocuité chez les enfants de moins de 6 mois n'a pas été établie ■ **ALLAITEMENT**: Utiliser avec précautions. Cependant, il existe des précédents d'utilisation sans danger.

I

RÉACTIONS INDÉSIRABLES ET EFFETS SECONDAIRES

SNC: céphalées, étourdissements, somnolence, troubles psychiques.

ORLO: amblyopie, vision trouble, acouphènes.

CV: arythmies, œdème.

GI: HÉMORRAGIE DIGESTIVE, HÉPATITE, constipation, dyspepsie, nausées, vomissements, malaises abdominaux.

GU: cystite, hématurie, insuffisance rénale.

Tég.: rash, DERMATITE EXFOLIATIVE, SYNDROME DE STEVENS-JOHNSON, ÉPIDERMOLYSE NÉCROSANTE SUBAIGUË.

Hémat.: dyscrasie sanguine, allongement du temps de saignement.

Divers: réactions allergiques incluant l'ANAPHYLAXIE.

INTERACTIONS

Médicament-médicament: Risque de diminution de l'effet cardioprotecteur de l'**aspirine** ■ L'administration concomitante d'**aspirine** peut réduire l'efficacité de l'ibuprofène ■ Effets secondaires gastro-intestinaux additifs lors de l'usage concomitant d'**aspirine**, d'autres **AINS**, de **corticostéroïdes** ou d'**alcool** ■ L'usage prolongé d'ibuprofène avec de l'**acétaminophène** peut accroître le risque de réactions rénales indésirables ■ L'ibuprofène peut diminuer l'efficacité des **diurétiques** ou des **antihypertenseurs** ■ L'agent peut intensifier les effets hypoglycémiants de l'**insuline** ou des **hypoglycémiants oraux** ■ L'ibuprofène peut entraîner une légère élévation des concentrations sériques de **digoxine** ■ L'ibuprofène peut entraîner l'élévation des concentrations sériques de **lithium** et augmenter le risque de toxicité ■ Le médicament accroît le risque de toxicité par le **méthotrexate** ■ Le **probénécide** accroît le risque de toxicité par l'ibuprofène ■ Risque accru de saignements lors de l'administration concomitante de **céfamandole**, de **céfotétane**, de **céfopérazone**, d'**acide valproïque**, de **plicamycine**, d'**agents thrombolytiques**, de **warfarine** et d'**agents agissant sur la fonction plaquettaire**, incluant le **clopidogrel**, la **ticlopidine**, l'**abciximab**, l'**eptifibatide** ou le **tirofiban** ■ Risque accru de réactions hématologiques indésirables lors de l'administration concomitante d'**antinéoplasiques** ou d'une **radiothérapie** ■ L'administration concomitante de **cyclosporine** accroît le risque de néphrotoxicité.

Médicament-produits naturels: Risque accru de saignements en cas de consommation concomitante d'**arnica**, de **camomille**, d'**ail**, de **gingembre**, de **ginkgo**, de **ginseng** et de certains autres produits.

VOIES D'ADMINISTRATION ET POSOLOGIE

Analgésie

- **PO (adultes):** *Anti-inflammatoire: polyarthrite rhumatoïde et arthrose* – la posologie initiale est de 1 200 mg par jour, divisée en 3 ou 4 doses. Selon l'effet thérapeutique obtenu, la dose peut être ajustée à la baisse ou à la hausse, sans dépasser 2 400 mg par jour. *Analgésique/antidysménorrhéique/antipyrétique* – de 200 à 400 mg, toutes les 4 à 6 heures (ne pas dépasser 1 200 mg par jour, sauf recommandation médicale).
- **PO (enfants de 6 mois à 12 ans):** *Antalgique* – 10 mg/kg/jour, en doses fractionnées (ne pas dépasser 40 mg/kg/jour). *Antipyrétique* – 5 mg/kg, lorsque la température est inférieure à 39,2 °C, ou 10 mg/kg, lorsque la température est supérieure à 39,2 °C (ne pas dépasser 40 mg/kg/jour); on peut répéter l'administration de cette dose toutes les 6 à 8 heures, sans dépasser 4 doses par jour.

Médicaments en vente libre réservés à l'usage pédiatrique

- **PO (enfants de 11 ans, de 32 à 43,9 kg):** 300 mg, toutes les 6 à 8 heures.
- **PO (enfants de 9 ou de 10 ans, de 27 à 31,9 kg):** 250 mg, toutes les 6 à 8 heures.
- **PO (enfants de 6 à 8 ans, de 22 à 26,9 kg):** 200 mg, toutes les 6 à 8 heures.
- **PO (enfants de 4 ou de 5 ans, de 16 à 21,9 kg):** 150 mg, toutes les 6 à 8 heures.
- **PO (enfants de 2 ou de 3 ans, de 11 à 15,9 kg):** 100 mg, toutes les 6 à 8 heures.
- **PO (enfants < 2 ans):** Consulter le médecin.

PRÉSENTATION (version générique disponible)

Comprimés/caplets: 100 mg^{VL}, 200 mg^{VL}, 300 mg^{VL}, 400 mg^{VL}, 600 mg^{Pr} ■ **Capsules (liquigel):** 200 mg^{VL}, 300 mg^{VL} ■ **Comprimés/caplets à croquer (parfum d'orange):** 50 mg^{VL}, 100 mg^{VL} ■ **Liquide (parfum de fruits, de raisin):** 100 mg/5 mL^{VL} ■ **Suspension orale (parfum de fruits, de gomme, de raisin):** 100 mg/5 mL^{VL}, 100 mg/2,5 mL^{VL} ■ **Gouttes pédiatriques (parfum de fruits, de raisin):** 40 mg/mL^{VL} ■ **En association avec:** décongestionnants^{VL}.

SOINS INFIRMIERS

ÉVALUATION DE LA SITUATION

- LES PATIENTS SOUFFRANT D'ASTHME, D'ALLERGIE INDUITE PAR L'ASPIRINE ET DE POLYPES SONT DAVANTAGE PRÉDISPOSÉS À DES RÉACTIONS D'HYPERSENSIBILITÉ. OBSERVER LE PATIENT À LA RECHERCHE DE SIGNES DE RHINITE, D'ASTHME ET D'URTICAIRE.

GÉR.: Risque élevé de mauvais résultats ou de décès par saignements digestifs. La diminution de la fonction rénale liée à l'âge augmente le risque de toxicité rénale et hépatique. Observer le patient à la recherche de signes de saignements digestifs (selles noires, hypotension, vertiges), de diminution de la fonction rénale (élévation de l'urée et de la créatinine sérique, diminution de l'excrétion d'urine) et de diminution de la fonction hépatique (élévation des enzymes hépatiques, teint ictérique).

Douleur: Noter le type de douleur, son siège et son intensité, avant l'administration du médicament et de 1 à 2 heures après.

Arthrite: Évaluer la douleur et l'amplitude du mouvement des articulations avant l'administration et de 1 à 2 heures après.

Fièvre: Prendre la température et noter les signes connexes suivants: diaphorèse, tachycardie, malaise.

Tests de laboratoire:

- Obtenir les concentrations sériques d'urée et de créatinine ainsi que la numération globulaire et les résultats des tests de la fonction hépatique à intervalles réguliers, tout au long d'un traitement prolongé.
- L'ibuprofène peut entraîner l'élévation des concentrations sériques de potassium, d'urée, de créatinine, de phosphatase alcaline, de LDH, d'AST et d'ALT. Le médicament peut diminuer la clairance de la créatinine et abaisser la glycémie, les concentrations d'hémoglobine et l'hématocrite ainsi que le nombre de globules blancs et de plaquettes.

- L'ibuprofène peut allonger le temps de saignement, phénomène qui peut durer jusqu'à 2 jours après l'arrêt du traitement.

DIAGNOSTICS INFIRMIERS POSSIBLES

- Douleur aiguë (Indications).
- Mobilité physique réduite (Indications).
- Connaissances insuffisantes sur le traitement médicamenteux (Enseignement au patient et à ses proches).

INTERVENTIONS INFIRMIÈRES

- L'administration de doses supérieures à celles qui sont recommandées n'accroît pas l'efficacité du médicament mais augmente le risque de réactions indésirables.

GÉR.: Utiliser la dose minimale efficace pendant la plus courte période de temps possible.

- Si on administre l'ibuprofène et un analgésique opioïde en concomitance, on peut intensifier les effets analgésiques de ce dernier, ce qui permet de réduire la dose de l'analgésique opioïde.

PO: Pour obtenir un effet initial rapide, administrer le médicament 30 minutes avant les repas ou 2 heures après. On peut administrer le médicament avec des aliments, du lait ou un antiacide pour réduire l'irritation gastrique. On peut écraser les comprimés et les mélanger à des liquides ou à des aliments.

Dysménorrhée: Administrer le médicament dès que possible après le début des règles. L'administration prophylactique ne s'est pas avérée efficace.

ENSEIGNEMENT AU PATIENT ET À SES PROCHES

- Conseiller au patient de prendre l'ibuprofène avec un grand verre d'eau et de ne pas se coucher pendant les 15 à 30 minutes qui suivent.
- Conseiller au patient de respecter rigoureusement la posologie recommandée. S'il n'a pu prendre le médicament au moment habituel, il doit le prendre dès que possible, à moins que ce ne soit presque l'heure prévue pour la dose suivante. L'avertir qu'il ne doit jamais remplacer une dose manquée par une double dose.

PÉD.: Enseigner aux parents la façon adéquate de calculer et de mesurer les doses. Insister sur le fait qu'il est important d'utiliser les mesures recommandées par le pharmacien.

- Prévenir le patient que l'ibuprofène peut provoquer de la somnolence ou des étourdissements. Lui conseiller de ne pas conduire et d'éviter les activités qui exigent sa vigilance jusqu'à ce qu'on ait la certitude que le médicament n'entraîne pas ces effets chez lui.
- Conseiller au patient d'éviter de consommer de l'alcool et de consulter un professionnel de la santé avant de prendre de l'aspirine, de l'acétaminophène ou tout autre médicament en vente libre en même temps que l'ibuprofène.
- Recommander au patient qui doit suivre un autre traitement ou subir une intervention chirurgicale d'avertir le professionnel de la santé qu'il suit un traitement par ce médicament.
- Inciter le patient à utiliser des écrans solaires et à porter des vêtements protecteurs pour prévenir les réactions de photosensibilité.
- Recommander au patient de ne pas prendre des préparations d'ibuprofène en vente libre pendant plus de 10 jours pour soulager la douleur, ou pendant plus de 3 jours pour traiter la fièvre, et de consulter un professionnel de la santé si les symptômes persistent ou s'aggravent.

PÉD.: Recommander aux parents ou aux soignants de bien vérifier les étiquettes des produits en vente libre pour s'assurer qu'ils ne donnent pas à l'enfant plus d'un produit contenant de l'ibuprofène en concomitance.

PÉD: Expliquer aux parents ou aux soignants qu'il ne faut pas administrer d'ibuprofène aux enfants présentant des risques de déshydratation (à cause de vomissements répétés, de diarrhée ou d'un faible apport liquidien). La déshydratation peut augmenter le risque de toxicité rénale.

- AVERTIR LE PATIENT QUE LA CONSOMMATION DE 3 VERRES D'ALCOOL OU PLUS PAR JOUR PEUT ACCROÎTRE LE RISQUE D'HÉMORRAGIE DIGESTIVE ASSOCIÉE À L'IBUPROFÈNE.
- Recommander au patient de communiquer avec un professionnel de la santé en cas de rash, de démangeaisons, de troubles visuels, d'acouphènes, de gain de poids, d'œdème, de selles noires, de céphalées persistantes ou de syndrome pseudogrippal (frissons, fièvre, douleurs musculaires).

VÉRIFICATION DE L'EFFICACITÉ THÉRAPEUTIQUE

L'efficacité du traitement peut être démontrée par: la diminution de l'intensité de la douleur ■ la mobilité accrue des articulations; le soulagement partiel des douleurs arthritiques est habituellement notable dans les 7 jours, mais le plein effet du médicament peut ne se manifester qu'après 1 ou 2 semaines de traitement ininterrompu; les patients qui ne répondent pas à un AINS peuvent répondre à un autre ■ l'abaissement de la fièvre.

IBUTILIDE

Corvert

CLASSIFICATION:

Antiarythmique (classe III)

Grossesse – catégorie C

INDICATIONS

Rétablissement rapide d'un rythme sinusal normal à la suite d'une fibrillation ou d'un flutter auriculaires d'apparition récente, incluant le traitement de la fibrillation ou du flutter auriculaires survenant dans la semaine suivant un pontage aortocoronarien ou une chirurgie valvulaire. L'ibutilide devrait être considéré comme une solution de rechange à la cardioversion électrique.

I

MÉCANISME D'ACTION

Activation du courant de sodium qui pénètre lentement dans les tissus cardiaques, d'où un retard de la repolarisation et une prolongation de la durée du potentiel d'action et de la période réfractaire efficace ▪ Léger ralentissement du rythme sinusal et de la conduction AV. ***Effets thérapeutiques:*** Rétablissement d'un rythme sinusal normal.

PHARMACOCINÉTIQUE

Absorption: 100 % (IV).

Distribution: Inconnue.

Métabolisme et excrétion: Métabolisme majoritairement hépatique (un métabolite est actif). Excrétion rénale (sous forme de métabolites).

Demi-vie: 6 heures (de 2 à 12 heures).

Profil temps-action (effet antiarythmique)

	DÉBUT D'ACTION	PIC	DURÉE
IV	en 30 – 90 min	inconnu	jusqu'à 24 h

CONTRE-INDICATIONS, PRÉCAUTIONS ET MISES EN GARDE

Contre-indications: Hypersensibilité.

Précautions et mises en garde: Insuffisance cardiaque ou dysfonctionnement ventriculaire gauche (risque accru d'arythmies plus graves pendant la perfusion) ▪ **OBST., ALLAITEMENT, PÉD. (< 18 ANS)**: L'innocuité du médicament n'a pas été établie.

RÉACTIONS INDÉSIRABLES ET EFFETS SECONDAIRES

SNC: céphalées.

CV: <u>arythmies</u>.

GI: nausées.

INTERACTIONS

Médicament-médicament: L'**amiodarone**, le **disopyramide**, le **procaïnamide**, la **quinidine** et le **sotalol** ne devraient pas être administrés en même temps que l'ibutilide ou dans les 4 heures suivant ou précédant le traitement par cet agent, en raison des effets additifs sur la période réfractaire efficace ▪ Les effets proarythmiques de l'ibutilide peuvent être intensifiés par les **phénothiazines**, les **antidépresseurs tricycliques**, les **tétracycliques** et certains **antihistaminiques**; leur usage concomitant devrait être évité.

VOIES D'ADMINISTRATION ET POSOLOGIE

Fibrillation ou flutter auriculaire

- **IV (adultes ≥ 60 kg)**: 1 mg en perfusion; on peut répéter l'administration de cette dose 10 minutes après la première perfusion, si nécessaire.
- **IV (adultes < 60 kg)**: 0,01 mg/kg en perfusion; on peut répéter l'administration de cette dose 10 minutes après la première perfusion, si nécessaire.

Fibrillation ou flutter auriculaire après une chirurgie cardiaque

- **IV (adultes ≥ 60 kg)**: 0,5 mg en perfusion; on peut répéter l'administration de cette dose 10 minutes après la première perfusion, si nécessaire.
- **IV (adultes < 60 kg)**: 0,005 mg/kg en perfusion; on peut répéter l'administration de cette dose 10 minutes après la première perfusion, si nécessaire.

PRÉSENTATION

Solution pour injection: 0,1 mg/mL, en fioles de 10 mL[Pr].

SOINS INFIRMIERS

ÉVALUATION DE LA SITUATION

- Suivre l'ÉCG tout au long de la perfusion et pendant les 4 heures qui suivent ou jusqu'à ce que les intervalles QT se normalisent. Interrompre le traitement si les arythmies prennent fin, tout comme en cas de tachycardie ventriculaire soutenue ou d'allongement des intervalles QT ou QTc. L'ibutilide peut avoir des effets proarythmiques. Ces arythmies peuvent être graves et mettre la vie du patient en danger. On devrait s'assurer que des médecins ayant de l'expérience dans le traitement des arythmies ventriculaires et dans l'usage de médicaments et d'appareils spécialisés (défibrillateurs classiques ou à synchronisation automatique) se trouvent sur place tout au long du traitement et de la période pendant laquelle il faut garder le patient sous étroite observation.

DIAGNOSTICS INFIRMIERS POSSIBLES

- Débit cardiaque diminué (Indications).
- Connaissances insuffisantes sur le traitement médicamenteux (Enseignement au patient et à ses proches).

INTERVENTIONS INFIRMIÈRES

- Le traitement antiarythmique par voie orale peut être amorcé 4 heures après la perfusion par l'ibutilide.

Perfusion intermittente: Le médicament peut être administré non dilué ou dilué dans 50 mL de solution de NaCl 0,9 % ou de D5%E, jusqu'à l'atteinte d'une concentration d'environ 0,017 mg/mL. La solution, diluée ou non diluée, devrait être utilisée immédiatement après le mélange. Consulter les directives du fabricant avant de diluer le médicament.
Vitesse d'administration: Administrer en 10 minutes.
Incompatibilité en addition au soluté: Renseignements non disponibles; ne pas mélanger avec d'autres solutions ou médicaments.

ENSEIGNEMENT AU PATIENT ET À SES PROCHES

- Informer le patient des raisons pour lesquelles on lui administre l'ibutilide.

VÉRIFICATION DE L'EFFICACITÉ THÉRAPEUTIQUE

L'efficacité du traitement peut être démontrée par: le rétablissement d'un rythme sinusal normal à la suite d'une tachycardie ou d'une fibrillation auriculaires récentes. ✳

ALERTE CLINIQUE

IDARUBICINE

Idamycin

CLASSIFICATION:

Antinéoplasique (anthracycline)

Grossesse - catégorie D

INDICATIONS

Traitement de première ligne de la leucémie aiguë non lymphoblastique (LANL) ou des cas réfractaires de cette maladie ■ Traitement de deuxième ligne de la leucémie aiguë lymphoblastique (LAL), chez les adultes et les enfants. **Usages non approuvés:** Traitement de la leucémie myélogène aiguë dans le cadre d'une chimiothérapie d'association.

MÉCANISME D'ACTION

Inhibition de la synthèse de l'acide nucléique. ***Effets thérapeutiques:*** Destruction des cellules à réplication rapide, particulièrement des cellules malignes.

PHARMACOCINÉTIQUE

Absorption: Biodisponibilité à 100 % (IV).
Distribution: Répartition rapide et forte liaison aux tissus. Le recaptage cellulaire est très élevé.
Métabolisme et excrétion: Métabolisme hépatique important (le médicament subit également un métabolisme extrahépatique). Un des métabolites est actif (idarubicinol). Excrétion majoritairement biliaire et urinaire sous forme d'idarubicinol.
Demi-vie: 22 heures (de 11 à 25 heures).

Profil temps-action (effets sur la numération globulaire)

	DÉBUT D'ACTION	PIC	DURÉE
IV	inconnu	10 - 14 jours	21 jours

CONTRE-INDICATIONS, PRÉCAUTIONS ET MISES EN GARDE

Contre-indications: Antécédents d'hypersensibilité à l'idarubicine ou aux anthracénédiones ■ Aplasie médullaire ■ Insuffisance rénale grave ■ Insuffisance hépatique grave ■ Cardiopathie grave ■ Infarctus du myocarde récent ■ Prise antérieure des doses cumulatives maximales d'anthracycline.
Précautions et mises en garde: **OBST.:** Patientes en âge de procréer, grossesse, allaitement ■ **PÉD.:** L'innocuité du médicament n'a pas été établie ■ Infections actives ■ Personnes âgées ■ Autres maladies chroniques débilitantes ■ Insuffisance hépatique (une réduction de la dose peut s'avérer nécessaire; éviter l'administration si les concentrations de bilirubine sont > 85 µmol/L) ■ Insuffisance rénale ■ Cardiopathie préexistante ■ Traitement antérieur par des anthracyclines.

RÉACTIONS INDÉSIRABLES ET EFFETS SECONDAIRES

SNC: céphalées, modifications de l'état mental.
Resp.: toxicité pulmonaire, réactions pulmonaires allergiques.
CV: ARYTHMIES, CARDIOTOXICITÉ, INSUFFISANCE CARDIAQUE.
GI: crampes abdominales, diarrhée, inflammation des muqueuses, nausées, vomissements, colite.
Tég.: alopécie, photosensibilité, rash, vésication.
End.: suppression de la fonction des gonades.
Hémat.: HÉMORRAGIE, anémie, leucopénie, thrombopénie, leucémie secondaire.
Locaux: phlébite au point d'injection IV.

Métab.: hyperuricémie.
SN: neuropathie périphérique.
Divers: ANAPHYLAXIE, fièvre.

INTERACTIONS

Médicament-médicament: Les autres **antinéoplasiques** ou la **radiothérapie** peuvent aggraver l'aplasie médullaire ■ L'idarubicine peut diminuer la réponse aux **vaccins à virus vivants** et augmenter le risque de réactions indésirables.

VOIES D'ADMINISTRATION ET POSOLOGIE

- **IV (adultes)**: *Leucémie aiguë non lymphoblastique* – 12 mg/m²/jour, pendant 3 jours, en association avec la cytarabine, ou 8 mg/m²/jour, pendant 5 jours, si l'agent est administré seul.
- **IV (adultes)**: *Leucémie aiguë lymphoblastique* – 12 mg/m²/jour, pendant 3 jours, si l'agent est administré seul.
- **IV (enfants)**: *Leucémie aiguë lymphoblastique* – 10 mg/m²/jour, pendant 3 jours, si l'agent est administré seul.

On peut également utiliser d'autres schémas thérapeutiques.

PRÉSENTATION

Poudre pour injection: fioles de 5 mg^Pr^ et de 10 mg^Pr^.

SOINS INFIRMIERS

ÉVALUATION DE LA SITUATION

- Mesurer la pression artérielle, le pouls, la fréquence respiratoire et la température à intervalles réguliers pendant toute la durée de l'administration. Prévenir le médecin en cas de changement notable.
- Déceler l'aplasie médullaire. Suivre de près les signes et les symptômes de saignement: saignement des gencives, formation d'ecchymoses, pétéchies, présence de sang occulte dans les selles, l'urine et les vomissements. Éviter les injections IM et la prise de la température rectale. Appliquer une pression sur les points de ponction veineuse pendant 10 minutes. Évaluer les signes d'infection en présence d'une neutropénie. Une anémie peut survenir. Rester à l'affût d'une fatigue accrue, de la dyspnée et de l'hypotension orthostatique.
- Effectuer le bilan quotidien des ingesta et des excreta et prévenir le médecin de tout écart notable. Inciter le patient à boire de 2 à 3 L de liquides par jour, si son état le permet. On peut également lui prescrire de l'allopurinol et l'alcalinisation de l'urine pour diminuer les concentrations sériques d'acide urique et pour prévenir la formation de calculs d'urate.
- Des nausées ou des vomissements intenses et persistants peuvent se manifester 1 heure après le traitement et durer jusqu'à 24 heures. Administrer des antiémétiques par voie parentérale de 30 à 45 minutes avant le traitement et à intervalles réguliers pendant les 24 heures suivantes, selon les indications. Afin de prévenir la déshydratation, noter la quantité de vomissures et prévenir le médecin si elle est supérieure à celle qui est contenue dans les directives de l'établissement.
- Suivre de près les signes suivants de toxicité myocardique: arythmies qui mettent la vie du patient en danger, cardiomyopathie et insuffisance cardiaque (œdème périphérique, dyspnée, râles et crépitations, gain pondéral). Avant le traitement, et à intervalles réguliers pendant toute sa durée, on devrait suivre de près les radiographies pulmonaires, les ÉCG et les échocardiographies, et déterminer la fraction d'éjection par angiographie isotopique.
- Observer fréquemment le point d'injection IV pour déceler la rougeur, l'irritation ou l'inflammation. L'infiltration du médicament n'est pas nécessairement douloureuse. En cas d'extravasation, arrêter immédiatement la perfusion et la reprendre dans une autre veine afin de prévenir la lésion des tissus sous-cutanés. Le traitement de l'extravasation inclut la mise au repos et l'élévation du membre ainsi que l'application de compresses de glace (appliquer pendant 30 minutes, immédiatement, et pendant 30 minutes par la suite, 4 fois par jour, pendant 3 jours). En présence de douleur, d'érythème ou de vésication durant plus de 48 heures, une chirurgie plastique immédiate devrait être envisagée.

Tests de laboratoire:

- Noter la numération globulaire, la formule leucocytaire et le nombre de plaquettes avant le traitement et à intervalles réguliers pendant toute sa durée. Le nadir de la leucopénie et de la thrombopénie survient après 10 à 14 jours, et se rétablit 21 jours après le traitement.
- Vérifier les résultats des tests de la fonction hépatique et rénale avant le traitement et pendant toute sa durée. L'idarubicine peut entraîner l'hyperuricémie. Elle peut également entraîner des élévations passagères des concentrations d'AST, d'ALT, de LDH, de phosphatase alcaline sérique et de bilirubine.

DIAGNOSTICS INFIRMIERS POSSIBLES

- Risque d'infection (Réactions indésirables).

- Alimentation déficiente (Réactions indésirables).
- Connaissances insuffisantes sur le traitement médicamenteux (Enseignement au patient et à ses proches).

INTERVENTIONS INFIRMIÈRES

ALERTE CLINIQUE: DES DÉCÈS SONT SURVENUS LORS DE CERTAINES CHIMIOTHÉRAPIES. AVANT D'ADMINISTRER L'AGENT, CLARIFIER TOUS LES POINTS AMBIGUS. VÉRIFIER LA LIMITE DES DOSES UNITAIRES ET QUOTIDIENNES AINSI QUE LA DOSE À ADMINISTRER PENDANT LE TRAITEMENT. DEMANDER À UN DEUXIÈME PROFESSIONNEL DE LA SANTÉ DE VÉRIFIER UNE FOIS DE PLUS L'ORDONNANCE D'ORIGINE, LES CALCULS ET LE RÉGLAGE DE LA POMPE À PERFUSION.

- NE PAS CONFONDRE ADRIAMYCIN (DOXORUBICINE) AVEC IDAMYCIN (IDARUBICINE).
- Préparer les solutions IV sous une hotte à flux laminaire (hotte biologique de classe II). Porter des gants, des vêtements de protection et un masque pendant la manipulation de ce médicament. Mettre au rebut le matériel dans les contenants réservés à cet usage (voir l'annexe H).
- Consulter la monographie de la cytarabine pour obtenir des renseignements sur l'administration concomitante de cytarabine et d'idarubicine.

IV directe:

- Reconstituer le contenu des fioles de 5 et de 10 mg avec 5 et 10 mL, respectivement, d'eau stérile pour injection (non bactériostatique), pour obtenir une concentration de 1 mg/mL. Le contenu des fioles est sous pression négative; introduire l'aiguille avec prudence. Consulter les directives du fabricant avant de reconstituer la préparation.
- La solution reconstituée est stable pendant 24 heures à la température ambiante et pendant 48 heures au réfrigérateur entre 2 et 8 °C. Jeter toute portion inutilisée. Protéger la solution de la lumière.

Vitesse d'administration: Administrer chacune des doses lentement, en 5 à 10 minutes, dans une tubulure en Y par laquelle s'écoule une solution de NaCl 0,9 %. La tubulure peut être raccordée à une aiguille à ailettes et la solution doit être injectée de préférence dans une grosse veine.

Incompatibilité dans la même seringue: héparine.

Compatibilité (tubulure en Y): amikacine ▪ aztréonam ▪ cimétidine ▪ cyclophosphamide ▪ cytarabine ▪ diphenhydramine ▪ dropéridol ▪ érythromycine, lactobionate d' ▪ filgrastim ▪ imipénem/cilastatine ▪ magnésium, sulfate de ▪ mannitol ▪ melphalan ▪ métoclopramide ▪ potassium, chlorure de ▪ ranitidine ▪ sargramostim ▪ vinorelbine.

Incompatibilité (tubulure en Y): acyclovir ▪ ampicilline/sulbactam ▪ céfazoline ▪ céfépime ▪ ceftazidime ▪ clindamycine ▪ dexaméthasone ▪ étoposide ▪ furosémide ▪ gentamicine ▪ héparine ▪ hydrocortisone, succinate sodique d' ▪ lorazépam ▪ mépéridine ▪ méthotrexate ▪ mezlocilline ▪ pipéracilline/tazobactam ▪ sodium, bicarbonate de ▪ téniposide ▪ vancomycine ▪ vincristine.

ENSEIGNEMENT AU PATIENT ET À SES PROCHES

- Recommander au patient de signaler rapidement à un professionnel de la santé la fièvre, les maux de gorge, les signes d'infection, le saignement des gencives, la formation d'ecchymoses, les pétéchies, la présence de sang dans les selles, l'urine et les vomissements ainsi que la fatigue accrue, la dyspnée ou l'hypotension orthostatique. Prévenir le patient qu'il doit éviter les foules et les personnes contagieuses. Lui conseiller d'utiliser une brosse à dents à poils doux et un rasoir électrique, et de prendre garde aux chutes. Le prévenir également qu'il ne doit pas prendre de boissons alcoolisées ni de préparations contenant de l'aspirine ou des AINS, en raison des risques d'hémorragie digestive.
- Recommander au patient de signaler immédiatement toute douleur au point d'injection.
- Recommander au patient d'examiner ses muqueuses buccales à la recherche d'érythème et d'aphtes. En présence d'aphtes, lui conseiller de remplacer la brosse à dents par une brosse-éponge, de se rincer la bouche avec de l'eau après avoir bu ou mangé et de consulter un professionnel de la santé si les douleurs l'empêchent de s'alimenter. Il ne faut pas entreprendre un nouveau cycle par l'idarubicine avant la disparition de l'inflammation de la muqueuse; les doses suivantes devraient être réduites de 25 %. La douleur associée à la stomatite peut dicter un traitement par des analgésiques opioïdes.
- Expliquer à la patiente que ce médicament peut avoir des effets tératogènes. Lui conseiller de continuer à prendre des mesures de contraception pendant toute la durée du traitement et pendant au moins 4 mois après l'avoir arrêté.
- Recommander au patient de prévenir immédiatement un professionnel de la santé en cas d'extrasystoles, d'essoufflements ou d'œdème des membres inférieurs.
- Inciter le patient à utiliser des écrans solaires et à porter des vêtements protecteurs pour prévenir les réactions de photosensibilité.

- Expliquer au patient qu'il risque de perdre ses cheveux. Explorer avec lui les stratégies lui permettant de s'adapter à ce changement.
- Expliquer au patient qu'il ne doit pas se faire vacciner sans recommandation expresse d'un professionnel de la santé.
- Informer le patient que son urine peut prendre une couleur rougeâtre pendant 1 à 2 jours après l'administration du médicament.
- Inciter le patient à se soumettre à des tests de laboratoire à intervalles réguliers permettant de déceler les effets secondaires du médicament.

VÉRIFICATION DE L'EFFICACITÉ THÉRAPEUTIQUE

L'efficacité du traitement peut être démontrée par: l'amélioration de l'hématopoïèse en présence de leucémie. ✳

I

IFOSFAMIDE

Ifex

CLASSIFICATION:

Antinéoplasique (alkylant)

Grossesse – catégorie D

INDICATIONS

Sarcome des tissus mous en monothérapie (en première ou en deuxième intention) ■ Cancer du pancréas en monothérapie (en deuxième intention) ■ Cancer du col de l'utérus en monothérapie ou en association avec le cisplatine et la bléomycine, en cas de maladie avancée ou récurrente. **Usages non approuvés:** Traitement du cancer des cellules germinales des testicules en association avec d'autres agents.

MÉCANISME D'ACTION

Après sa transformation en composés actifs, l'ifosfamide entrave la réplication de l'ADN et la transcription de l'ARN en inhibant, en fin de compte, la synthèse des protéines (effet non spécifique sur le cycle cellulaire). ***Effets thérapeutiques:*** Destruction des cellules à réplication rapide et, particulièrement, des cellules malignes.

PHARMACOCINÉTIQUE

Absorption: Biodisponibilité à 100 % (IV). L'agent reste inactif jusqu'à sa transformation en métabolites.

Distribution: L'agent passe dans le lait maternel.

Métabolisme et excrétion: Métabolisme hépatique et transformation en composés antinéoplasiques actifs.

Demi-vie: 1 800 mg/m^2: de 4 à 7 heures; de 3 800 à 5 000 mg/m^2: de 11 à 15 heures.

Profil temps-action (effet sur les numérations globulaires)

	DÉBUT D'ACTION	PIC	DURÉE
IV	inconnu	7 - 10 jours	14 - 21 jours

CONTRE-INDICATIONS, PRÉCAUTIONS ET MISES EN GARDE

Contre-indications: Hypersensibilité ■ Infections actives ■ Leucopénie grave ■ Thrombopénie ■ Affection rénale ou hépatique grave ■ Obstruction du débit urinaire ■ Cystite ■ Artériosclérose cérébrale avancée.

Précautions et mises en garde: **OBST.:** Grossesse, allaitement, patientes en âge de procréer ■ Aplasie médullaire ■ Personnes âgées ■ Autres maladies chroniques débilitantes ■ Enfants ■ Chirurgie (retard de la cicatrisation).

RÉACTIONS INDÉSIRABLES ET EFFETS SECONDAIRES

SNC: toxicité du SNC (somnolence, confusion, hallucinations, coma), dysfonctionnement des nerfs crâniens, désorientation, étourdissements.

CV: cardiotoxicité.

GI: nausées, vomissements, anorexie, constipation, diarrhée, hépatotoxicité.

GU: cystite hémorragique, dysurie, suppression de la fonction des gonades, toxicité rénale.

Métab.: acidose.

Tég.: alopécie.

Hémat.: anémie, leucopénie, thrombopénie.

Locaux: phlébite.

Divers: réactions allergiques.

INTERACTIONS

Médicament-médicament: Les autres **antinéoplasiques** ou la **radiothérapie** peuvent aggraver l'aplasie médullaire ■ L'**allopurinol** et le **phénobarbital** peuvent accroître la toxicité de l'ifosfamide ■ Le médicament peut réduire la réponse aux **vaccins à virus vivants** et augmenter le risque de réactions indésirables. ■ L'ifosfamide peut intensifier l'effet de la **warfarine**.

VOIES D'ADMINISTRATION ET POSOLOGIE

- **IV (adultes):** De 50 à 60 mg/kg/jour (ou de 2 000 à 2 400 mg/m^2/jour), pendant 5 jours consécutifs, en association avec le mesna. On peut répéter l'administration de cette dose après un arrêt de la médication d'au moins 3 à 4 semaines.

On peut également utiliser d'autres schémas thérapeutiques.

PRÉSENTATION (version générique disponible)

Poudre pour injection: fioles de 1 g^{Pr} et de 3 g^{Pr}.

SOINS INFIRMIERS

ÉVALUATION DE LA SITUATION

- Mesurer la pression artérielle, le pouls, la fréquence respiratoire et la température à intervalles réguliers tout au long de l'administration. Informer le médecin de tout changement marqué.
- Mesurer la diurèse à intervalles réguliers pendant toute la durée du traitement. Prévenir le médecin en cas d'hématurie. Encourager l'adulte à boire au moins 3 000 mL de liquides par jour et l'enfant, entre 1 000 et 2 000 mL de liquides par jour, si son état le permet, pour réduire le risque de cystite hémorragique. Pour prévenir la cystite hémorragique, on administre simultanément le mesna.
- Suivre de près l'état neurologique du patient. On devrait interrompre le traitement par l'ifosfamide en cas de symptômes graves touchant le SNC (agitation, confusion, hallucinations, fatigue inhabituelle). Les symptômes diminuent habituellement dans les 3 jours suivant l'arrêt du traitement, mais peuvent persister plus longtemps. De rares cas de décès ont été signalés.
- Noter les nausées, les vomissements et l'appétit du patient. Peser le patient toutes les semaines. L'administration d'antiémétiques avant le traitement permet de réduire les effets gastro-intestinaux. Adapter le régime alimentaire selon les aliments que le patient peut tolérer.
- Rester à l'affût des signes d'aplasie médullaire. Suivre de près les saignements: saignement des gencives, formation d'ecchymoses, pétéchies, présence de sang occulte dans les selles, l'urine et les vomissements. Éviter les injections IM et la prise de la température rectale. Appliquer une pression sur les points de ponction veineuse pendant 10 minutes. Évaluer les signes d'infection en présence d'une neutropénie. Une anémie peut survenir. Rester à l'affût de la fatigue accrue, de la dyspnée et de l'hypotension orthostatique.

Tests de laboratoire:

- Noter la numération globulaire, la formule leucocytaire et le nombre de plaquettes avant l'administration et à intervalles réguliers pendant toute la durée du traitement. Ne pas administrer l'agent si le nombre de globules blancs est inférieur à 2×10^9/L ou celui des plaquettes, à 50×10^9/L. Le nadir de la leucopénie et de la thrombopénie survient dans les 7 à 10 jours et se rétablit habituellement dans les 14 à 21 jours.
- Noter les résultats de l'analyse des urines avant d'administrer chacune des doses. Ne pas administrer le médicament si l'analyse des urines révèle que le nombre de globules rouges est supérieur à 10 par champ à fort grossissement.
- L'ifosfamide peut entraîner l'élévation des concentrations d'enzymes hépatiques et de bilirubine sérique.
- Suivre de près les concentrations d'AST, d'ALT, de phosphatase alcaline sérique, de bilirubine et de LDH, avant le traitement et à intervalles réguliers pendant toute sa durée.
- Noter les concentrations d'urée, de créatinine sérique, de phosphate et de potassium à intervalles réguliers pendant toute la durée du traitement.

I

DIAGNOSTICS INFIRMIERS POSSIBLES

- Risque d'infection (Effets secondaires).
- Image corporelle perturbée (Effets secondaires).
- Connaissances insuffisantes sur le traitement médicamenteux (Enseignement au patient et à ses proches).

INTERVENTIONS INFIRMIÈRES

Préparer les solutions IV sous une hotte à flux laminaire (hotte biologique de classe II). Porter des gants, des vêtements de protection et un masque pendant la manipulation de ce médicament. Mettre au rebut le matériel dans les contenants réservés à cet usage (voir l'annexe H).

IV: Diluer le contenu des fioles de 1 g dans 20 mL d'eau stérile pour injection et celui des fioles de 3 g dans 60 mL d'eau stérile pour injection. Utiliser la solution reconstituée ainsi que ses dilutions dans les 24 heures qui suivent leur préparation ou dans les 72 heures, si elles sont conservées au réfrigérateur dans des fioles de verre ou des sacs Viaflex®. Consulter les directives du fabricant avant de reconstituer la préparation.

Perfusion intermittente: On peut effectuer une nouvelle dilution pour obtenir une concentration de 0,6 à 20 mg/mL dans une solution de D5%E, de NaCl 0,9 % ou de lactate de Ringer.

Vitesse d'administration: La perfusion doit durer au moins 30 minutes.

Compatibilité dans la même seringue: mesna.

Perfusion continue: Le médicament a aussi été administré en perfusion continue d'une durée de 72 heures.
Compatibilité (tubulure en Y): allopurinol sodique ■ amphotéricine B, cholestéryle de ■ aztréonam ■ doxorubicine liposomale ■ filgrastim ■ fludarabine ■ gallium, nitrate de ■ melphalan ■ ondansétron ■ paclitaxel ■ pipéracilline/tazobactam ■ sargramostim ■ sodium, bicarbonate de ■ téniposide ■ vinorelbine.
Incompatibilité (tubulure en Y): céfépime ■ méthotrexate.
Compatibilité en addition au soluté: carboplatine ■ cisplatine ■ étoposide ■ fluorouracile ■ mesna.

ENSEIGNEMENT AU PATIENT ET À SES PROCHES

- Inciter le patient à boire beaucoup de liquides pendant toute la durée du traitement et à uriner fréquemment afin de réduire l'irritation de la vessie due aux métabolites excrétés par les reins. Lui recommander de signaler immédiatement à un professionnel de la santé la présence d'hématurie.
- Recommander au patient de signaler rapidement à un professionnel de la santé la fièvre, les frissons, la toux, l'enrouement, les maux de gorge, les signes d'infection, les douleurs lombaires ou aux flancs, les mictions difficiles ou douloureuses, le saignement des gencives, la formation d'ecchymoses, les pétéchies, la présence de sang dans les selles, l'urine ou les vomissements et la confusion.
- Prévenir le patient qu'il doit éviter les foules et les personnes contagieuses. Lui conseiller d'utiliser une brosse à dents à poils doux et un rasoir électrique, et de prendre garde aux chutes. Le prévenir qu'il ne doit pas prendre de boissons alcoolisées ni de préparations contenant de l'aspirine ou des AINS, en raison du risque d'hémorragie digestive.
- Conseiller à la patiente de prendre des mesures contraceptives pendant le traitement.
- Expliquer au patient qu'il risque de perdre ses cheveux. Explorer avec lui les stratégies lui permettant de s'adapter à ce changement.
- Expliquer au patient qu'il ne doit pas se faire vacciner sans recommandation expresse d'un professionnel de la santé. Le médicament peut réduire la réponse aux vaccins à virus vivants et augmenter le risque de réactions indésirables.

VÉRIFICATION DE L'EFFICACITÉ THÉRAPEUTIQUE

L'efficacité du traitement peut être démontrée par: la diminution de la taille de la tumeur ou le ralentissement de la propagation du cancer. ✳

ALERTE CLINIQUE

IMATINIB

Gleevec

CLASSIFICATION:
Antinéoplasique (inhibiteur de l'activation des kinases)

Grossesse – catégorie D

INDICATIONS

Leucémie myéloïde chronique (LMC) en crise blastique, en phase accélérée ou en phase chronique, après échec du traitement par l'interféron alpha chez les patients porteurs du chromosome Philadelphie ■ Tumeurs stromales gastro-intestinales métastatiques et non résécables ■ Adultes atteints de leucémie myéloïde chronique, porteurs du chromosome Philadelphie.

MÉCANISME D'ACTION

Inhibition des kinases qui pourraient être produites par les lignées cellulaires malignes. ***Effets thérapeutiques:*** Inhibition de la production de lignées cellulaires malignes avec diminution de la prolifération des cellules atteintes de leucémie, en cas de LMC, ou des cellules cancéreuses, en cas de tumeur stromale gastro-intestinale.

PHARMACOCINÉTIQUE

Absorption: Bonne (98 % PO).
Distribution: Inconnue.
Liaison aux protéines: 95 %.
Métabolisme et excrétion: Métabolisme majoritairement hépatique, principalement par le système enzymatique du CYP3A4; transformation en imatinib n-déméthylé, qui est aussi actif que l'imatinib. Excrétion majoritairement fécale sous forme de métabolite; 5 % est excrété sous forme inchangée dans l'urine.
Demi-vie: *Imatinib* – 18 heures; *imatinib n-déméthylé* – 40 heures.

Profil temps-action

	Début d'action	Pic	Durée
PO	inconnu	2 – 4 h	24 h

CONTRE-INDICATIONS, PRÉCAUTIONS ET MISES EN GARDE

Contre-indications: Hypersensibilité.
Précautions et mises en garde: Insuffisance hépatique (il est recommandé de suspendre le traitement si la bilirubine est > 3 fois la limite supérieure de la normale ou les transaminases hépatiques sont > 5 fois la limite supérieure de la normale) ■ **GÉR.:** Risque accru

d'œdème ■ **Péd.**: L'innocuité de l'agent n'a pas été établie ■ **Obst.**: Grossesse ou allaitement.

RÉACTIONS INDÉSIRABLES ET EFFETS SECONDAIRES

SNC: fatigue, céphalées, faiblesse.

Resp.: toux, dyspnée, épistaxis, nasopharyngite, pneumonie.

GI: HÉPATOTOXICITÉ, douleurs abdominales, anorexie, constipation, diarrhée, dyspepsie, nausées, vomissements.

Tég.: ÉRYTHÈME POLYMORPHE, SYNDROME DE STEVENS-JOHNSON, pétéchies, prurit, rash.

HÉ: œdème (comprenant l'épanchement pleural, l'épanchement péricardique, l'anasarque, l'œdème superficiel et la rétention hydrique), hypokaliémie.

Hémat.: SAIGNEMENTS, NEUTROPÉNIE, THROMBOPÉNIE.

Métab.: gain de poids.

Loc.: arthralgie, crampes musculaires, douleurs musculosquelettiques, myalgie.

Divers: fièvre, sueurs nocturnes.

INTERACTIONS

Médicament-médicament: Les concentrations sanguines et les effets sont accrus lors de l'usage concomitant d'**inhibiteurs du CYP3A4** comme le **kétoconazole** ■ Les concentrations sanguines et les effets peuvent être diminués par la **phénytoïne**, la **rifampicine** et les autres inducteurs du CYP3A4 ■ L'agent élève les concentrations sanguines de la **simvastatine** ■ L'utilisation concomitante de **warfarine** peut augmenter le RNI et le risque de saignements ■ L'imatinib inhibe les systèmes enzymatiques suivants: **CYP2C9**, **CYP2D6**, **CYP3A4/5** et peut donc modifier les effets des autres **médicaments métabolisés par ces systèmes**.

Médicament-produits naturels: Le **jus de pamplemousse** peut augmenter les concentrations et la toxicité de l'imatinib. Le **millepertuis** peut diminuer l'efficacité de l'imatinib.

VOIES D'ADMINISTRATION ET POSOLOGIE

Leucémie myéloïde chronique

- **PO (adultes)**: *Phase chronique* – 400 mg, 1 fois par jour, qu'on peut porter à 600 mg, 1 fois par jour; *phase accélérée ou crise blastique* – 600 mg, 1 fois par jour; on peut porter la dose à 800 mg par jour, administrée à raison de 400 mg, 2 fois par jour, compte tenu des circonstances, de la tolérabilité et de la réponse.
- **PO (enfants ≥ 3 ans)**: 260 mg/m²/jour; on peut porter la posologie à 340 mg/m²/jour en 1 seule dose ou en 2 doses fractionnées *(usage non approuvé)*.

Tumeurs stromales gastro-intestinales

- **PO (adultes)**: 400 mg/jour ou 600 mg/jour, en 1 seule dose. La dose peut être augmentée jusqu'à 800 mg/jour chez les patients tolérant bien le traitement, mais dont la réponse est insuffisante.

Insuffisance hépatique

EN CAS D'ÉLÉVATION DE LA BILIRUBINE À PLUS DE 3 FOIS LA LIMITE SUPÉRIEURE DE LA NORMALE OU DES TRANSAMINASES À PLUS DE 5 FOIS LA LIMITE SUPÉRIEURE DE LA NORMALE, IL FAUT INTERROMPRE LE TRAITEMENT JUSQU'À CE QUE LA BILIRUBINE DIMINUE À MOINS DE 1,5 FOIS LA LIMITE SUPÉRIEURE DE LA NORMALE ET LES TRANSAMINASES, À MOINS DE 2,5 FOIS LA LIMITE SUPÉRIEURE DE LA NORMALE. ON PEUT ENSUITE REPRENDRE LE TRAITEMENT AUX POSOLOGIES SUIVANTES:

- **PO (ADULTES)**: 300 mg, 1 FOIS PAR JOUR, QU'ON PEUT PORTER À 400 mg, 1 FOIS PAR JOUR.
- **PO (ENFANTS)**: 200 mg/m²/JOUR; ON PEUT PORTER LA POSOLOGIE À 260 mg/m²/JOUR EN 1 SEULE DOSE OU EN 2 DOSES FRACTIONNÉES *(USAGE NON APPROUVÉ)*.

PRÉSENTATION

Comprimés: 100 mg^Pr^, 400 mg^Pr^.

SOINS INFIRMIERS

ÉVALUATION DE LA SITUATION

- Suivre de près la rétention hydrique. Peser le patient à intervalles réguliers et rester à l'affût des épanchements pleuraux et péricardiques, de l'œdème pulmonaire, de l'ascite (dyspnée, œdème périorbital, œdème des pieds et des chevilles, gain de poids). Évaluer tout gain de poids inattendu. L'œdème est habituellement traité avec des diurétiques. LA RÉTENTION HYDRIQUE GÉNÉRALISÉE EST HABITUELLEMENT LIÉE À LA DOSE; ELLE EST PLUS COURANTE EN PHASE ACCÉLÉRÉE OU EN CRISE BLASTIQUE ET PLUS FRÉQUENTE CHEZ LES PERSONNES ÂGÉES. LE TRAITEMENT CONSISTE HABITUELLEMENT EN L'ADMINISTRATION DE DIURÉTIQUES, LA PRISE DE MESURES DE SOUTIEN ET L'ABANDON DU TRAITEMENT PAR L'IMATINIB.
- Suivre de près les signes vitaux; l'agent peut provoquer la fièvre.
- ***Tests de laboratoire:*** SUIVRE DE PRÈS LES RÉSULTATS DES TESTS DE LA FONCTION HÉPATIQUE AVANT LE TRAITEMENT, TOUS LES MOIS PENDANT TOUTE SA DURÉE OU CHAQUE FOIS QUE L'ÉTAT CLINIQUE DU PATIENT L'EXIGE. L'AGENT PEUT ÉLEVER LES CONCENTRATIONS DE TRANSAMINASES ET DE BILIRUBINE,

I

ÉLÉVATIONS QUI PEUVENT PERSISTER HABITUELLEMENT PENDANT 1 SEMAINE ET QUI PEUVENT DICTER LA RÉDUCTION DE LA DOSE OU L'INTERRUPTION DU TRAITEMENT. SI LA BILIRUBINE S'ÉLÈVE À PLUS DE 3 FOIS LA LIMITE SUPÉRIEURE DE LA NORMALE OU LES TRANSAMINASES À PLUS DE 5 FOIS LA LIMITE SUPÉRIEURE DE LA NORMALE, NE PAS ADMINISTRER JUSQU'À CE QUE LES CONCENTRATIONS DE BILIRUBINE REVIENNENT À MOINS DE 1,5 FOIS LA LIMITE SUPÉRIEURE DE LA NORMALE ET CELLES DE TRANSAMINASES À MOINS DE 2,5 FOIS LA LIMITE SUPÉRIEURE DE LA NORMALE. LE TRAITEMENT PEUT ÊTRE POURSUIVI À UNE POSOLOGIE PLUS BASSE (LES PATIENTS QUI PRENNENT 400 mg/JOUR DOIVENT RECEVOIR 300 mg/JOUR ET CEUX PRENANT 600 mg/JOUR DOIVENT RECEVOIR 400 mg/JOUR).

- SUIVRE LA NUMÉRATION GLOBULAIRE TOUTES LES SEMAINES, PENDANT LE PREMIER MOIS, TOUTES LES DEUX SEMAINES, PENDANT LE DEUXIÈME MOIS, ET À INTERVALLES RÉGULIERS TOUT AU LONG DU TRAITEMENT. L'AGENT PEUT PROVOQUER UNE NEUTROPÉNIE ET UNE THROMBOPÉNIE, QUI DURENT HABITUELLEMENT DE 2 À 3 SEMAINES ET DE 3 À 4 SEMAINES, RESPECTIVEMENT, AINSI QUE L'ANÉMIE. IL FAUT HABITUELLEMENT RÉDUIRE LES DOSES, MAIS PARFOIS L'ARRÊT DU TRAITEMENT PEUT S'IMPOSER (VOIR INTERVENTIONS INFIRMIÈRES).
- L'agent peut provoquer de l'hypokaliémie.

DIAGNOSTICS INFIRMIERS POSSIBLES

- Risque d'accident (Réactions indésirables).

INTERVENTIONS INFIRMIÈRES

ALERTE CLINIQUE: DES DÉCÈS SONT SURVENUS LORS DE CERTAINES CHIMIOTHÉRAPIES. AVANT D'ADMINISTRER L'AGENT, CLARIFIER TOUS LES POINTS AMBIGUS. VÉRIFIER UNE FOIS DE PLUS LA LIMITE DES DOSES UNITAIRES ET QUOTIDIENNES AINSI QUE CELLES À ADMINISTRER PENDANT LE TRAITEMENT. DEMANDER À UN DEUXIÈME PROFESSIONNEL DE LA SANTÉ DE VÉRIFIER L'ORDONNANCE D'ORIGINE ET LES CALCULS DES DOSES. LE MÉDICAMENT NE DOIT ÊTRE ADMINISTRÉ QUE SOUS LA SURVEILLANCE D'UN MÉDECIN EXPÉRIMENTÉ DANS LE TRAITEMENT DES PATIENTS ATTEINTS DE LEUCÉMIE MYÉLOÏDE CHRONIQUE.

- Les patients sous anticoagulothérapie peuvent recevoir de l'héparine standard ou à faible poids moléculaire au lieu de la warfarine, en raison du risque d'augmentation du RNI.
- Le traitement doit être poursuivi tant que le patient en tire profit.

PO: Administrer avec des aliments et un grand verre d'eau pour réduire l'irritation gastro-intestinale.

- On peut disperser les comprimés dans de l'eau ou dans du jus de pomme (50 mL pour les comprimés à 100 mg et 100 mL pour ceux à 400 mg), et bien les mélanger avec une cuillère, si le patient ne peut avaler des comprimés. Administrer aussitôt.
- Chez les patients en traitement de la *LMC en phase chronique* ou *d'une tumeur stromale gastro-intestinale* dont le NAN chute $< 1,0 \times 10^9$/L ou le nombre des plaquettes $< 50 \times 10^9$/L, arrêter l'administration de l'imatinib jusqu'à ce que le NAN remonte $\geq 1,5 \times 10^9$/L et la numération plaquettaire soit $\geq 75 \times 10^9$/L. Reprendre alors le traitement par l'imatinib à une dose de 400 mg/jour ou de 600 mg/jour (soit la dose administrée avant la survenue de l'effet indésirable). En cas de récurrence d'une diminution du NAN ou du nombre des plaquettes, reprendre de nouveau le traitement à une dose réduite (300 mg/jour ou 400 mg/jour), lorsque les valeurs se rétablissent.
- Chez les patients en traitement de la *phase accélérée* ou *de la crise blastique* dont le NAN chute $< 0,5 \times 10^9$/L ou le nombre des plaquettes $< 10 \times 10^9$/L, on doit déterminer, par une biopsie ou une aspiration de moelle, si la cytopénie est liée à la leucémie. Si tel n'est pas le cas, réduire la dose à 400 mg/jour. Si la cytopénie persiste pendant 2 semaines, réduire la dose à 300 mg/jour. Si la cytopénie persiste pendant 4 semaines et si elle n'est toujours pas liée à la leucémie, arrêter l'administration de l'imatinib jusqu'à ce que le NAN soit $\geq 1 \times 10^9$/L et la numération plaquettaire $\geq 20 \times 10^9$/L. Reprendre ensuite le traitement par l'imatinib à 300 mg/jour.

ENSEIGNEMENT AU PATIENT ET À SES PROCHES

- Expliquer au patient le but du traitement par l'imatinib.

VÉRIFICATION DE L'EFFICACITÉ THÉRAPEUTIQUE

L'efficacité du traitement peut être déterminée par: la diminution de la production de cellules leucémiques chez les patients atteints de LMC et de cellules cancéreuses et chez ceux présentant une tumeur stromale gastro-intestinale.

IMIPÉNEM/CILASTATINE

Primaxin

CLASSIFICATION:

Antibiotique (carbapénem)

Grossesse – catégorie C

INDICATIONS

Traitement des infections suivantes: infections des voies respiratoires inférieures ■ infections des voies urinaires ■ infections intra-abdominales ■ infections gynécologiques ■ infections de la peau et des tissus mous ■ infections des os et des articulations ■ bactériémie ■ endocardite due à *S. aureus* ■ septicémie ■ infections polymicrobiennes.

MÉCANISME D'ACTION

Liaison à la paroi de la cellule bactérienne, entraînant la destruction de la bactérie ■ L'association avec la cilastatine empêche l'inactivation rénale de l'imipénem, ce qui entraîne des concentrations urinaires élevées ■ Le médicament résiste à l'action de nombreuses enzymes qui décomposent la plupart des autres pénicillines et pénicillinases. ***Effets thérapeutiques:*** Effet bactéricide contre les bactéries sensibles. **Spectre d'action**: Le spectre d'action est large ■ Le médicament est actif contre la plupart des coques aérobies à Gram positif dont: *Streptococcus pneumoniæ* ■ les streptocoques bêta-hémolytiques du groupe A ■ les entérocoques ■ *Staphylococcus aureus* ■ Le médicament est aussi actif contre de nombreux microorganismes à Gram négatif dont: *Escherichia coli* ■ *Klebsiella* ■ *Acinetobacter* ■ *Proteus* ■ *Serratia* ■ *Pseudomonas æruginosa* ■ Le médicament est également actif contre: *Salmonella* ■ *Shigella* ■ *Neisseria gonorrhϾ* ■ de nombreux autres microorganismes anaérobies.

PHARMACOCINÉTIQUE

Absorption: Biodisponibilité à 100 % (IV).

Distribution: Répartition dans tout l'organisme. L'agent traverse la barrière placentaire et passe dans le lait maternel.

Métabolisme et excrétion: *Imipénem et cilastatine* – 70 % excrété à l'état inchangé par les reins.

Demi-vie: *Imipénem et cilastatine* – 1 heure (prolongée en cas d'insuffisance rénale).

Profil temps-action

	DÉBUT D'ACTION	PIC	DURÉE
IV	rapide	fin de la perfusion	6 - 8 h

CONTRE-INDICATIONS, PRÉCAUTIONS ET MISES EN GARDE

Contre-indications: Hypersensibilité.

Précautions et mises en garde: Risque de réactions de sensibilité croisée avec les pénicillines et les céphalosporines ■ Antécédents de réactions d'hypersensibilité multiples ■ Troubles convulsifs ■ Personnes âgées ■ Insuffisance rénale (réduire la dose si la Cl_{Cr} est ≤ 70 mL/min/1,73 m^2) ■ **OBST., ALLAITEMENT, PÉD. (< 3 MOIS)**: L'innocuité du médicament n'a pas été établie.

RÉACTIONS INDÉSIRABLES ET EFFETS SECONDAIRES

SNC: CONVULSIONS, étourdissements, somnolence.

CV: hypotension.

GI: COLITE PSEUDOMEMBRANEUSE, diarrhée, nausées, vomissements.

Tég.: rash, prurit, transpiration, urticaire.

Hémat.: éosinophilie.

Locaux: phlébite au point d'injection IV.

Divers: réactions allergiques incluant l'ANAPHYLAXIE, fièvre et surinfection.

INTERACTIONS

Médicament-médicament: Le mélange avec des **aminosides** peut entraîner l'inactivation de cette association médicamenteuse ■ Le **probénécide** diminue l'excrétion rénale et augmente les concentrations sanguines d'imipénem/cilastatine ■ L'administration concomitante de **ganciclovir** ou de **cyclosporine** accroît le risque de convulsions (éviter l'administration concomitante de ganciclovir).

VOIES D'ADMINISTRATION ET POSOLOGIE

- **IV (adultes)**: *Infections légères* – 250 mg, toutes les 6 heures. *Infections modérées* – 500 mg, toutes les 8 heures. *Infections graves* – de 500 mg, toutes les 6 heures, à 1 g, toutes les 6 à 8 heures.
- ***INSUFFISANCE RÉNALE***

  IV (ADULTES):

  POSOLOGIE QUOTIDIENNE DANS LE CAS DES INFECTIONS DUES AUX BACTÉRIES SENSIBLES: Cl_{CR} DE 31 À 70 mL/MIN – 500 mg, TOUTES LES 8 HEURES (NE PAS DÉPASSER 1,5 g PAR JOUR); *Cl_{CR} DE 21 À 30 mL/MIN* – 500 mg, TOUTES LES 12 HEURES (NE PAS DÉPASSER 1 g PAR JOUR); *Cl_{CR} DE 6 À 20 mL/MIN* – 250 mg OU 3,5 mg/kg (LA PLUS PETITE DOSE DES DEUX), TOUTES LES 12 HEURES (NE PAS DÉPASSER 0,5 g PAR JOUR). NE PAS ADMINISTRER AUX PATIENTS DONT LA CLAIRANCE DE LA CRÉATININE EST < 5 mL/MIN SAUF S'ILS SONT HÉMODIALYSÉS DANS LES 48 HEURES (CONSULTER LES DIRECTIVES DU FABRICANT).

  POSOLOGIE QUOTIDIENNE DANS LE CAS DES INFECTIONS DUES À DES BACTÉRIES MOINS SENSIBLES: Cl_{CR} DE 31 À 70 mL/MIN – 500 mg, TOUTES LES 6 HEURES (NE PAS DÉPASSER 2 g PAR JOUR); *Cl_{CR} DE 21 À 30 mL/MIN* – 500 mg, TOUTES LES 8 HEURES (NE PAS DÉPASSER 1,5 g PAR JOUR); *Cl_{CR} DE 6 À 20 mL/MIN* – 500 mg OU 3,5 mg/kg (LA PLUS PETITE DOSE DES DEUX), TOUTES LES 12 HEURES (NE

PAS DÉPASSER 1 g PAR JOUR). NE PAS ADMINISTRER AUX PATIENTS DONT LA CLAIRANCE DE LA CRÉATININE EST < 5 mL/MIN SAUF S'ILS SONT HÉMODIALYSÉS DANS LES 48 HEURES (CONSULTER LES DIRECTIVES DU FABRICANT).

- **IV (nourrissons ≥ 3 mois [infections ne touchant pas le SNC]):** De 15 à 25 mg/kg, toutes les 6 heures (ne pas dépasser 2 g par jour).

PRÉSENTATION

Poudre pour injection IV: imipénem à 250 mg/cilastatine à 250 mg^Pr^, imipénem à 500 mg/cilastatine à 500 mg^Pr^. L'association est aussi présentée en flacons ADD-Vantage.

SOINS INFIRMIERS

ÉVALUATION DE LA SITUATION

- Au début du traitement et pendant toute sa durée, suivre de près les signes suivants d'infection: altération des signes vitaux; aspect de la plaie, des expectorations, de l'urine et des selles; accroissement du nombre de globules blancs.
- Recueillir les antécédents du patient avant d'amorcer le traitement afin de déterminer ses réactions antérieures à une pénicilline. Même les personnes n'ayant jamais manifesté une sensibilité aux pénicillines peuvent présenter une réaction allergique.
- Prélever des échantillons pour les cultures et les antibiogrammes avant le début du traitement. La première dose peut être administrée avant que les résultats soient connus.
- SUIVRE DE PRÈS LES SIGNES ET LES SYMPTÔMES SUIVANTS D'ANAPHYLAXIE: RASH, PRURIT, ŒDÈME LARYNGÉ, RESPIRATION SIFFLANTE. SI CES SYMPTÔMES SE MANIFESTENT, ARRÊTER LE TRAITEMENT ET PRÉVENIR IMMÉDIATEMENT LE MÉDECIN. GARDER À PORTÉE DE LA MAIN DE L'ADRÉNALINE, UN ANTIHISTAMINIQUE ET LE MATÉRIEL DE RÉANIMATION POUR PARER À UNE ÉVENTUELLE RÉACTION ANAPHYLACTIQUE.

Tests de laboratoire:

- Le médicament peut entraîner l'élévation passagère des concentrations d'urée, d'AST, d'ALT, de LDH, de phosphatase alcaline sérique, de bilirubine et de créatinine.
- L'imipénem/cilastatine peut diminuer les concentrations d'hémoglobine et l'hématocrite.
- Le médicament peut entraîner des résultats positifs au test de Coombs.

DIAGNOSTICS INFIRMIERS POSSIBLES

- Risque d'infection (Indications, Effets secondaires).
- Connaissances insuffisantes sur le traitement médicamenteux (Enseignement au patient et à ses proches).

INTERVENTIONS INFIRMIÈRES

Perfusion intermittente:

- Reconstituer le contenu des flacons destinés à la perfusion avec 100 mL de diluant compatible. Commencer par reconstituer le contenu d'une fiole de 250 ou de 500 mg avec 10 mL de diluant compatible (NaCl 0,9 % ou D5%E) et bien agiter. Transvaser la solution obtenue dans un récipient contenant les 90 mL de diluant restant. Répéter l'opération en rinçant la fiole dont le contenu vient d'être reconstitué avec 10 mL de diluant et bien agiter afin de s'assurer que tout le médicament a été utilisé. Transvaser tout le contenu de la fiole dans le contenant pour perfusion.
- Agiter jusqu'à ce que la solution devienne transparente.
- Les *diluants compatibles* sont les suivants: solutions de NaCl 0,9 %, de D5%E ou de D10%E, de D5%/bicarbonate de sodium 0,02 %, de D5%/NaCl 0,9 %, de D5%/NaCl 0,45 %, de D5%/NaCl 0,225 %, de D5%/chlorure de potassium 0,15 % et solutions de mannitol à 5 % ou à 10 %. La solution peut être de transparente à jaunâtre. Ne pas administrer la solution si elle est trouble. La solution est stable pendant 4 heures à la température ambiante et pendant 24 heures au réfrigérateur. Consulter les directives du fabricant avant de reconstituer la préparation.

Vitesse d'administration:

- Administrer la dose de 250 mg ou de 500 mg en 20 à 30 minutes et la dose de 1 g en 40 à 60 minutes. Ne pas administrer par IV directe.
- La perfusion rapide peut entraîner des nausées, des vomissements, une fatigue ou une faiblesse inhabituelles, des étourdissements ou une sécrétion accrue de sueur. Si ces symptômes se manifestent, ralentir la vitesse de perfusion. Il peut s'avérer nécessaire d'arrêter l'administration.

Compatibilité (tubulure en Y): acyclovir ▪ aztréonam ▪ cisatracurium ▪ céfépime ▪ diltiazem ▪ famotidine ▪ filgrastim ▪ fludarabine ▪ foscarnet ▪ idarubicine ▪ insuline ▪ melphalan ▪ méthotrexate ▪ ondansétron ▪ rémifentanil ▪ tacrolimus ▪ téniposide ▪ vinorelbine ▪ zidovudine.

Incompatibilité (tubulure en Y): amphotéricine B, cholestéryl d' ■ fluconazole ■ gallium, nitrate de ■ mépéridine ■ sargramostim ■ sodium, bicarbonate de.
Incompatibilité en addition au soluté: Les aminosides administrés en concomitance peuvent inactiver le médicament. En cas d'administration concomitante, choisir des points d'injection différents, si possible, et attendre 1 heure entre les deux injections. Si un deuxième point d'injection n'est pas accessible, rincer la tubulure entre l'administration des deux médicaments.

ENSEIGNEMENT AU PATIENT ET À SES PROCHES

- Conseiller au patient de signaler l'allergie et les signes suivants de surinfection: excroissance pileuse noire sur la langue, démangeaisons ou pertes vaginales, selles molles ou nauséabondes.
- RECOMMANDER AU PATIENT DE COMMUNIQUER AVEC UN PROFESSIONNEL DE LA SANTÉ EN CAS DE FIÈVRE OU DE DIARRHÉE, PARTICULIÈREMENT SI LES SELLES RENFERMENT DU SANG, DU PUS OU DU MUCUS. CONSEILLER AU PATIENT DE NE PAS TRAITER LA DIARRHÉE SANS CONSULTER AU PRÉALABLE UN PROFESSIONNEL DE LA SANTÉ. CES SYMPTÔMES PEUVENT SURVENIR MÊME PLUSIEURS SEMAINES APRÈS L'ARRÊT DU TRAITEMENT.

VÉRIFICATION DE L'EFFICACITÉ THÉRAPEUTIQUE

L'efficacité du traitement peut être démontrée par: la disparition des signes et des symptômes d'infection. Le temps de résolution dépend du microorganisme infectant et du siège de l'infection. ✳

IMIPRAMINE

Apo-Imipramine, Novo-Pramine, Tofranil

CLASSIFICATION:

Antidépresseur (tricyclique)

Grossesse – catégorie C (risque durant le 3e trimestre; voir «Précautions et mises en garde»)

INDICATIONS

Soulagement des symptômes de dépression (en association avec la psychothérapie). **Usages non approuvés:** Traitement d'appoint de la douleur chronique et de l'incontinence (chez les adultes) ■ Traitement de l'énurésie chez les enfants de plus de 5 ans ■ Prophylaxie des céphalées de Horton et des migraines.

MÉCANISME D'ACTION

Potentialisation des effets de la sérotonine et de la noradrénaline ■ Propriétés anticholinergiques importantes. ***Effets thérapeutiques:*** Effet antidépresseur qui se manifeste graduellement en l'espace de plusieurs semaines.

PHARMACOCINÉTIQUE

Absorption: Bonne (PO).
Distribution: Tout l'organisme. L'imipramine traverse probablement la barrière placentaire et passe dans le lait maternel.
Liaison aux protéines: De 89 à 95 %.
Métabolisme et excrétion: Fort métabolisme hépatique. Une certaine fraction est transformée en métabolites actifs. Le médicament subit plusieurs cycles entérohépatiques et il est sécrété dans les sucs gastriques.
Demi-vie: De 8 à 16 heures.

Profil temps-action (effet antidépresseur)

	DÉBUT D'ACTION	PIC	DURÉE
PO	plusieurs heures	2 – 6 semaines	plusieurs semaines

CONTRE-INDICATIONS, PRÉCAUTIONS ET MISES EN GARDE

Contre-indications: Hypersensibilité au médicament ou à ses excipients ■ Glaucome ■ Administration en association avec un IMAO (attendre 14 jours entre l'arrêt de la prise de l'IMAO et le début du traitement par l'imipramine et vice versa) ■ Phase qui suit immédiatement un infarctus du myocarde ■ Insuffisance cardiaque aiguë ■ Affections hépatiques ou rénales ■ Antécédents de dyscrasie sanguine.
Précautions et mises en garde: La surveillance des idées suicidaires est recommandée chez tous les patients prenant ce médicament ■ **OBST.:** Il n'existe pas d'études adéquates menées chez la femme enceinte. N'utiliser ce médicament pendant la grossesse que si les bienfaits éventuels l'emportent sur les risques possibles. Il y a des risques de complication après l'accouchement chez les nouveau-nés lorsque la mère a pris ce médicament durant le 3e trimestre ■ **ALLAITEMENT:** L'imipramine passe dans le lait maternel; en interrompre graduellement l'administration chez la mère qui allaite ou sevrer le nourrisson ■ **PÉD.:** L'innocuité et l'efficacité de l'imipramine n'ont pas été établies. Il y a risque de changements comportementaux et émotifs, incluant l'automutilation ■ **GÉR.:** Plus grande prédisposition aux réactions indésirables ■ Maladie cardiovasculaire préexistante ■ Risque d'arythmie cardiaque transitoire chez des patients prenant en concomitance un médicament thyroïdien ou souffrant d'hyperthyroïdie ■ Patients porteurs d'une tumeur adrénomédullaire (p. ex., phéochromocytome,

neuroblastome): risque de crise hypertensive ■ Risque d'iléus paralytique, en particulier chez les patients âgés ou hospitalisés ■ Ne pas mettre fin brusquement au traitement en raison du risque de symptômes de sevrage ■ Hommes souffrant d'hyperplasie de la prostate (risque de rétention urinaire) ■ Convulsions ou antécédents de crises convulsives ■ Risque de réactions de sensibilité croisée avec d'autres antidépresseurs.

RÉACTIONS INDÉSIRABLES ET EFFETS SECONDAIRES

SNC: somnolence, fatigue, agitation, confusion, hallucinations, insomnie.
ORLO: vision trouble, xérophtalmie.
CV: ARYTHMIES, hypotension, modifications de l'ÉCG.
GI: constipation, sécheresse de la bouche (xérostomie), nausées, iléus paralytique.
GU: rétention urinaire.
Tég.: photosensibilité.
End.: gynécomastie.
Hémat.: dyscrasie sanguine.

INTERACTIONS

Médicament-médicament: L'IMIPRAMINE PEUT PROVOQUER L'HYPOTENSION, LA TACHYCARDIE ET DES RÉACTIONS POUVANT ÊTRE D'ISSUE FATALE LORS DE L'ADMINISTRATION CONCOMITANTE D'**IMAO** (ÉVITER L'ADMINISTRATION CONJOINTE; INTERROMPRE LE TRAITEMENT 2 SEMAINES AVANT D'ADMINISTRER L'IMIPRAMINE) ■ L'ADMINISTRATION CONCOMITANTE D'**ANTIDÉPRESSEURS DU TYPE ISRS** PEUT AUGMENTER LA TOXICITÉ ET DEVRAIT ÊTRE ÉVITÉE (INTERROMPRE LE TRAITEMENT PAR LA **FLUOXÉTINE**, 5 SEMAINES AVANT D'ADMINISTRER L'IMIPRAMINE) ■ L'IMIPRAMINE PEUT PROVOQUER UNE CRISE HYPERTENSIVE LORSQU'ELLE EST ADMINISTRÉE EN MÊME TEMPS QUE LA **CLONIDINE** (ÉVITER L'ADMINISTRATION CONJOINTE) ■ L'imipramine est métabolisée dans le foie par le cytochrome **P450 2D6** et son action pourrait être modifiée par les **agents qui sont aussi métabolisés par cette enzyme**, incluant les autres **antidépresseurs**, les **phénothiazines**, la **carbamazépine**, les **antiarythmiques de type 1C** (**propafénone**, **flécaïnide**); en cas d'administration concomitante, il peut s'avérer nécessaire de réduire la dose de l'un ou de l'autre des médicaments ou des deux à la fois ■ Les autres médicaments qui inhibent l'activité de l'enzyme, incluant la **cimétidine**, la **quinidine**, l'**amiodarone** et le **ritonavir**, administrés en concomitance, peuvent intensifier les effets de l'imipramine ■ L'imipramine peut annuler la réponse au traitement par la **guanéthidine**, la **réserpine** et l'**alphaméthyldopa** ■ L'imipramine peut retarder ou réduire l'absorption de la **lévodopa** ou entraîner l'hypertension en cas d'administration concomitante ■ La **rifamycine** peut réduire les concentrations sanguines et les effets de l'imipramine ■ Effets dépresseurs additifs sur le SNC lors de l'usage concomitant d'autres **dépresseurs du SNC**, dont l'**alcool**, les **antihistaminiques**, la **clonidine**, les **analgésiques opioïdes** et les **hypnosédatifs** ■ Les **barbituriques** peuvent modifier les concentrations sanguines et les effets de l'imipramine ■ Les effets secondaires **adrénergiques** et **anticholinergiques** peuvent être additifs lors de l'administration d'autres agents dotés de ces propriétés ■ Les **phénothiazines** ou les **contraceptifs oraux** élèvent les concentrations d'imipramine et peuvent provoquer une toxicité ■ L'administration concomitante d'**agents antiarythmiques** du type **quinidine** augmente les risques cardiovasculaires ■ L'imipramine peut potentialiser les effets cardiovasculaires de la **noradrénaline** ou de l'**adrénaline**, des **amphétamines**, de même que des gouttes nasales et des anesthésiques locaux qui contiennent des **sympathomimétiques** (comme l'**isoprénaline**, l'**éphédrine**, la **phényléphrine**) ■ La **cimétidine** ou le **méthylphénidate**, administrés en concomitance, inhibent le métabolisme de plusieurs antidépresseurs tricycliques, dont l'imipramine, ce qui entraîne une augmentation des concentrations plasmatiques de cette dernière ■ L'**amitriptyline** et la **lévothyroxine**, administrées en concomitance, peuvent augmenter les effets secondaires cardiovasculaires de l'imipramine ■ La **nicotine** peut accélérer le métabolisme du médicament et en diminuer l'efficacité.

VOIES D'ADMINISTRATION ET POSOLOGIE

- **PO (adultes)**: Initialement, 25 mg, 3 fois par jour; augmenter la dose graduellement jusqu'à 150 mg par jour (ne pas dépasser 200 mg par jour). Lorsque la dose d'entretien a été déterminée, la dose quotidienne totale peut être administrée au coucher, pourvu qu'elle soit bien tolérée.
- **PO (personnes âgées)**: Initialement, de 30 à 40 mg au coucher, en doses fractionnées, puis augmenter la dose graduellement jusqu'à un maximum de 100 mg par jour.

PRÉSENTATION

Comprimés: 10 mg[Pr], 25 mg[Pr], 50 mg[Pr], 75 mg[Pr].

SOINS INFIRMIERS

ÉVALUATION DE LA SITUATION

- Mesurer la pression artérielle et le pouls avant l'administration du médicament et pendant toute la durée du traitement initial.

- ÉVALUER L'ÉCG À INTERVALLES RÉGULIERS CHEZ LES PERSONNES ÂGÉES OU LES PATIENTS SOUFFRANT D'UNE MALADIE CARDIAQUE ET AVANT LA MAJORATION DE LA DOSE, CHEZ LES ENFANTS SOUFFRANT D'ÉNURÉSIE. L'IMIPRAMINE PEUT ALLONGER LES INTERVALLES PR ET QT, ET APLATIR LES ONDES T.

Dépression: Évaluer fréquemment l'état de conscience du patient. Lors du traitement initial, la confusion, l'agitation et des hallucinations qui peuvent se manifester dictent parfois une réduction de la dose. Noter les changements d'humeur. Rester à l'affût des tendances suicidaires, particulièrement en début de traitement. Diminuer la quantité de médicament dont le patient peut disposer.

Énurésie: Évaluer la fréquence de l'énurésie tout au long du traitement.

Douleur: Déterminer le siège, la durée et l'intensité de la douleur à intervalles réguliers tout au long du traitement.

***Tests de laboratoire*:**

- Vérifier la formule leucocytaire ainsi que les résultats des tests de la fonction hépatique et rénale, avant d'amorcer un traitement de longue durée ou à fortes doses et à intervalles réguliers par la suite.
- Mesurer les concentrations sériques chez les patients qui ne répondent pas à la dose thérapeutique habituelle. Les concentrations plasmatiques thérapeutiques se situent entre 535 et 1 070 nmol/L.
- L'imipramine peut modifier la glycémie.

***TOXICITÉ ET SURDOSAGE*:**

- Les symptômes d'un surdosage aigu comprennent la difficulté de se concentrer, la confusion, l'agitation, les convulsions, la somnolence, la mydriase, les arythmies, la fièvre, les hallucinations, les vomissements et la dyspnée.
- On traite le surdosage par un lavage gastrique et l'administration de charbon activé et d'un purgatif. Maintenir les fonctions cardiaque et respiratoire (suivre de près l'ÉCG pendant au moins 5 jours) et prendre la température du patient. On peut administrer de la digoxine pour traiter l'insuffisance cardiaque, ainsi que des antiarythmiques et des anticonvulsivants.

DIAGNOSTICS INFIRMIERS POSSIBLES

- Stratégies d'adaptation inefficaces (Indications).
- Élimination urinaire altérée (Indications).
- Connaissances insuffisantes sur le traitement médicamenteux (Enseignement au patient et à ses proches).

INTERVENTIONS INFIRMIÈRES

- NE PAS CONFONDRE L'IMIPRAMINE AVEC LA DÉSIPRAMINE.
- Si les doses doivent être augmentées, la première dose majorée devrait être administrée à l'heure du coucher en raison des effets sédatifs de l'imipramine. La majoration des doses est un processus lent qui peut prendre de quelques semaines à quelques mois. On peut administrer la dose totale au coucher pour réduire la sédation diurne.
- Administrer le médicament avec des aliments ou immédiatement après pour diminuer l'irritation gastro-intestinale.

ENSEIGNEMENT AU PATIENT ET À SES PROCHES

- Conseiller au patient de respecter rigoureusement la posologie recommandée. S'il n'a pu prendre le médicament au moment habituel, il doit le prendre dès que possible, à moins que ce ne soit presque l'heure prévue pour la dose suivante. Si le patient doit prendre une seule dose à l'heure du coucher, lui recommander de ne pas prendre le médicament le matin en raison des effets secondaires. Prévenir le patient que les effets du médicament peuvent ne pas se manifester avant 2 semaines au moins. Le sevrage brusque peut provoquer des nausées, des vomissements, la diarrhée, des céphalées, de l'insomnie associée à des rêves saisissants et de l'irritabilité.
- Prévenir le patient que l'imipramine peut provoquer des étourdissements et rendre la vision trouble. Lui conseiller de ne pas conduire et d'éviter les activités qui exigent sa vigilance jusqu'à ce qu'on ait la certitude que le médicament n'entraîne pas ces effets chez lui.
- Conseiller au patient de prévenir un professionnel de la santé si sa vision change. L'informer que, pendant un traitement prolongé, on pourrait lui prescrire des tests à intervalles réguliers pour déceler le glaucome.
- Recommander au patient de changer lentement de position afin de réduire le risque d'hypotension orthostatique.
- Recommander au patient d'éviter de boire de l'alcool et de ne pas prendre d'autres dépresseurs du SNC pendant toute la durée du traitement et pendant les 3 à 7 jours qui suivent l'arrêt de la médication.
- Conseiller au patient de prévenir un professionnel de la santé en cas de rétention urinaire, de sécheresse de la bouche ou de constipation persistante. Lui expliquer que les bonbons ou la gomme à mâcher sans sucre peuvent diminuer la sécheresse de la bouche et qu'une consommation accrue de liquides et d'aliments riches en fibres peut prévenir la constipation. Si les symptômes persistent, il peut

s'avérer nécessaire de réduire la dose ou d'interrompre le traitement. Conseiller au patient de consulter un professionnel de la santé si la sécheresse de la bouche persiste pendant plus de 2 semaines.

- Recommander au patient d'utiliser des écrans solaires et de porter des vêtements protecteurs afin de prévenir les réactions de photosensibilité.
- Inciter le patient à surveiller son alimentation, car l'imipramine peut lui donner plus d'appétit, ce qui risque d'entraîner un gain pondéral indésirable. Informer le patient qu'il faudrait peut-être augmenter l'apport de riboflavine dans son alimentation; lui conseiller de consulter un professionnel de la santé à ce sujet.
- Recommander au patient qui doit suivre un autre traitement ou subir une intervention chirurgicale d'avertir le professionnel de la santé qu'il suit un traitement par ce médicament.
- Prévenir le patient que le traitement de la dépression est habituellement prolongé. Insister sur l'importance d'un suivi régulier permettant de déterminer les bienfaits du médicament.

ENFANTS:

- Informer les parents que les effets secondaires qui peuvent se manifester le plus souvent sont la nervosité, l'insomnie, la fatigue inhabituelle et les nausées et vomissements légers. Leur recommander de prévenir un professionnel de la santé si ces symptômes s'aggravent.
- Recommander aux parents de garder le médicament hors de la portée des enfants, pour réduire le risque de surdosage accidentel.

VÉRIFICATION DE L'EFFICACITÉ THÉRAPEUTIQUE

L'efficacité du traitement peut être démontrée par: un sentiment de mieux-être ■ un regain d'intérêt pour l'entourage ■ un gain d'appétit ■ un regain d'énergie ■ l'amélioration du sommeil chez les patients traités pour la dépression; le plein effet thérapeutique de l'imipramine pourrait ne pas être notable avant 2 à 6 semaines de traitement ■ la disparition de l'énurésie chez les enfants de plus de 5 ans ■ la diminution des douleurs neurogènes chroniques. ✳

IMMUNOGLOBULINE Rh_0(D)

WinRho SDF

CLASSIFICATION:

Agent d'immunisation passive (immunoglobulines)

Grossesse – catégorie C

INDICATIONS

IM, IV: Prévention de l'iso-immunisation par l'antigène Rh chez les femmes $Rh_0(D)^-$, qui ont été exposées à du sang $Rh_0(D)^+$ dans les cas suivants: accouchement d'un nouveau-né $Rh_0(D)^+$ ■ avortement ou fausse couche d'un fœtus $Rh_0(D)^+$ ■ amniocentèse, prélèvement de villosités choriales, hémorragie transplacentaire, rupture de grossesse tubaire ou traumatisme intra-abdominal pendant la grossesse, sauf si le type sanguin du fœtus ou du père est certainement $Rh_0(D)^-$ ■ transfusion accidentelle de sang $Rh_0(D)^+$ à un patient $Rh_0(D)^-$ (fillette ou femme adulte en âge de procréer) ■ **IV:** Traitement du purpura thrombopénique auto-immun (PTI).

MÉCANISME D'ACTION

Prévention de la production d'anticorps anti-Rh_0(D) chez les patients $Rh_0(D)^-$, qui ont été exposés à du sang $Rh_0(D)^+$ ■ Augmentation du nombre de plaquettes chez les patients souffrant de PTI. ***Effets thérapeutiques:*** Prévention de la réponse des anticorps et de la maladie hémolytique du nouveau-né (érythroblastose fœtale) lors des futures grossesses, chez une femme ayant déjà porté un fœtus $Rh_0(D)^+$ ■ Prévention de la sensibilisation du sang Rh_0(D) par suite d'une transfusion accidentelle ■ Diminution des saignements chez les patients souffrant de PTI.

PHARMACOCINÉTIQUE

Absorption: Bonne (IM).

Distribution: Inconnue.

Métabolisme et excrétion: Inconnus.

Demi-vie: *IM* – 30 jours; *IV* – 24 jours.

Profil temps-action

	DÉBUT D'ACTION	PIC	DURÉE
IM	rapide	5 – 10 jours	inconnue
IV†	inconnu	2 h	inconnue

† Lors du traitement du PTI, le nombre de plaquettes commence à augmenter après 1 ou 2 jours, atteint un pic après 5 à 7 jours et se maintient pendant 30 jours.

CONTRE-INDICATIONS, PRÉCAUTIONS ET MISES EN GARDE

Contre-indications: ***Prévention de l'iso-immunisation par l'antigène Rh*** – Patients $Rh_0(D)^+$ ou Du^+, y compris les nouveau-nés ■ Femmes $Rh_0(D)^-$ dont l'immunisation contre le facteur Rh est démontrée par les tests de dépistage manuel standard des anticorps Rh ■ Personnes ayant déjà présenté des réactions anaphylactiques ou d'autres réactions systémiques importantes aux immunoglobulines ■ **PTI** – Patients $Rh_0(D)^-$ ■ Patients splénectomisés ■ Patients allergiques aux dérivés plasmatiques.

Précautions et mises en garde: Patients ayant une carence en IgA (risque de développer des anticorps IgA et des réactions anaphylactiques) ■ Patients souffrant de PTI, en présence d'une anémie préexistante (réduire la dose, si l'hémoglobine < 100 g/L; EXTRÊME PRUDENCE, SI L'HÉMOGLOBINE < 80 g/L).

RÉACTIONS INDÉSIRABLES ET EFFETS SECONDAIRES

Hémat.: anémie, hémolyse intravasculaire (si l'agent est administré en cas de PTI).
Locaux: douleurs au point d'injection IM.
Divers: fièvre.

INTERACTIONS

Médicament-médicament: Les immunoglobulines peuvent diminuer la réponse des anticorps à certains **vaccins à virus vivants** (**rougeole**, **rubéole, oreillons**).

VOIES D'ADMINISTRATION ET POSOLOGIE

- **Après l'accouchement**
  IM, IV (adultes): 600 UI (120 µg), dans les 72 heures qui suivent l'accouchement.
- **Avant l'accouchement**
  IV, IM (adultes): 1 500 UI (300 µg) d'immunoglobuline Rh_0(D), à la 28e semaine de gestation.
- **Menace d'avortement imminent**
  IM, IV (adultes): 1 500 UI (300 µg), le plus rapidement possible.
- **Après un avortement, une amniocentèse ou une autre intervention; gestation > 34 semaines**
  IM, IV (adultes): 600 UI (120 µg), dans les 72 heures qui suivent l'intervention.
- **Après une amniocentèse ou un prélèvement des villosités choriales; gestation < 34 semaines**
  IM, IV (adultes): 1 500 UI (300 µg), dans les 72 heures qui suivent l'intervention; répéter toutes les 12 semaines pendant toute la durée de la grossesse.
- **Transfusion accidentelle de sang incompatible**
  IM (adultes): 60 UI (12 µg) par mL de sang entier *ou* 120 UI (24 µg) par mL de globules rouges. Administrer 6 000 UI (1 200 µg) toutes les 12 heures, jusqu'à la dose totale calculée.
  IV (adultes): 45 UI (9 µg) par mL de sang entier *ou* 90 UI (18 µg) par mL de globules rouges. Administrer 3 000 UI (600 µg) toutes les 8 heures, jusqu'à la dose totale calculée.
- **Purpura thrombopénique auto-immun (PTI)**
  IV (adultes et enfants): Initialement, de 25 à 50 µg (de 125 à 250 UI)/kg (si l'hémoglobine < 100 g/L, réduire la dose jusqu'à 25 à 40 µg [de 125 à 200 UI]/kg); la fréquence d'administration et les doses suivantes sont déterminées par la réponse clinique (écart posologique: de 25 à 60 µg [de 125 à 300 UI]/kg). Chaque dose peut être administrée en 1 seule fois ou en 2 fois, à des jours différents.

PRÉSENTATION

Produit lyophilisé pour injection: 600 UI (120 µg)/fiole^Pr^; 1 500 UI (300 µg)/fiole^Pr^; 5 000 UI (1 000 µg)/fiole^Pr^.

SOINS INFIRMIERS

ÉVALUATION DE LA SITUATION

IV: Chez les patients recevant l'immunoglobuline Rh_0(D) par voie IV, prendre les signes vitaux à intervalles réguliers, pendant toute la durée du traitement.
PTI: SUIVRE DE PRÈS LES SIGNES ET LES SYMPTÔMES D'HÉMOLYSE INTRAVASCULAIRE (DOULEURS LOMBAIRES, GRANDS FRISSONS, HÉMOGLOBINURIE), D'ANÉMIE ET D'INSUFFISANCE RÉNALE. SI DES TRANSFUSIONS S'AVÈRENT NÉCESSAIRES, UTILISER UN CONCENTRÉ DE GLOBULES ROUGES (CULOT SANGUIN) $RH_0(D)^-$ POUR PRÉVENIR L'EXACERBATION DE L'HÉMOLYSE INTRAVASCULAIRE.

Tests de laboratoire:

- *Grossesse*: Effectuer un test de compatibilité croisée avec le sang de la mère et le sang cordonal du nouveau-né et un typage du sang afin de déterminer le besoin de recourir au traitement. Le sang de la mère doit être $Rh_0(D)^-$ et Du^- et celui du nourrisson, $Rh_0(D)^+$. S'il subsiste un doute quant au type sanguin du nourrisson ou si le père est Rh_0 $(D)^+$, on devrait administrer le médicament.
- Dans le cas où la mère est traitée par l'immunoglobuline Rh_0 (D) avant l'accouchement, on peut noter chez le nouveau-né un résultat faiblement positif au test de Coombs direct, effectué sur des prélèvements de son sang ou de sang cordonal.

PTI: Pour déterminer l'efficacité du traitement, noter le nombre de plaquettes, de globules rouges et de réticulocytes ainsi que la concentration d'hémoglobine.

DIAGNOSTICS INFIRMIERS POSSIBLES

- Connaissances insuffisantes sur le traitement médicamenteux (Enseignement au patient et à ses proches).

INTERVENTIONS INFIRMIÈRES

- Ne pas administrer ces agents à un nourrisson, à une personne $Rh_0(D)^+$ ou à un sujet de type $Rh_0(D)^-$ mais qui a déjà été sensibilisé à l'antigène Rh_0(D). Toutefois, il n'y a pas plus de risque que si l'on administre le traitement à une femme qui n'a pas été sensibilisée. Par conséquent, lorsqu'il subsiste un doute, administrer l'immunoglobuline Rh_0(D).

IM:

- Reconstituer les fioles de 600, de 1 500 et de 5 000 UI avec 1,25, 1,25 et 8,5 mL, respectivement, du diluant stérile fourni. Injecter le diluant en le laissant couler sur la paroi interne de la fiole et mouiller les granules en faisant tourner délicatement la fiole jusqu'à leur dissolution. Ne pas secouer le contenant. Consulter les directives du fabricant avant de reconstituer la préparation.
- Administrer dans le muscle deltoïde. La dose devrait être administrée dans les 3 heures (jusqu'à un maximum de 72 heures) qui suivent l'accouchement, la fausse couche, l'avortement ou la transfusion.
- Ne pas administrer l'*immunoglobuline $Rh_0(D)$* ou l'*immunoglobuline $Rh_0(D)$ en microdose* par voie intraveineuse.

IV directe: Reconstituer les fioles de 600, de 1 500 et de 5 000 UI avec 2,5, 2,5 et 8,5 mL, respectivement, du diluant stérile fourni. Injecter le diluant en le laissant couler sur la paroi interne de la fiole et mouiller les granules en faisant tourner délicatement la fiole jusqu'à leur dissolution. Ne pas secouer le contenant. Consulter les directives du fabricant avant de reconstituer la préparation.

Vitesse d'administration: Administrer en 3 à 5 minutes.

ENSEIGNEMENT AU PATIENT ET À SES PROCHES

Grossesse: Expliquer à la patiente que le but du traitement est de protéger les enfants $Rh_0(D)^+$ qu'elle aura à l'avenir.

PTI: Expliquer au patient le but du traitement.

VÉRIFICATION DE L'EFFICACITÉ THÉRAPEUTIQUE

L'efficacité du traitement peut être démontrée par: la prévention de l'érythroblastose du nouveau-né chez les nourrissons futurs dont le sang sera de type Rh_0^+ ■ la prévention de la sensibilisation au Rh_0^+ après une transfusion accidentelle ■ la diminution de la fréquence des épisodes de saignement chez les patients souffrant de PTI. ✳

INDAPAMIDE

Apo-Indapamide, Dom-Indapamide, Gen-Indapamide, Indapamide, Lozide, Novo-Indapamide, Nu-Indapamide, PMS-Indapamide, Riva-Indapamide, Tria-Indapamide

CLASSIFICATION:
Antihypertenseur, diurétique (thiazidique et dérivé ayant une structure proche)

Grossesse – catégorie B (catégorie D, en cas d'utilisation en présence d'hypertension gravidique)

INDICATIONS

Traitement de l'hypertension légère à modérée (en monothérapie ou en association avec d'autres médicaments) ■ **Usages non approuvés:** Œdème attribuable à l'insuffisance cardiaque ou à d'autres causes.

MÉCANISME D'ACTION

Augmentation de l'excrétion du sodium et de l'eau par l'inhibition de la réabsorption du sodium dans les tubules distaux ■ Effet favorable sur l'excrétion du chlorure, du potassium, du magnésium et du bicarbonate ■ Dilatation artériolaire possible. ***Effets thérapeutiques:*** Abaissement de la pression artérielle chez les hypertendus et diurèse se traduisant par une diminution de l'œdème.

PHARMACOCINÉTIQUE

Absorption: Bonne (PO).

Distribution: Répartition dans tout l'organisme.

Métabolisme et excrétion: Métabolisme majoritairement hépatique. Excrétion rénale (7 % sous forme inchangée).

Demi-vie: De 14 à 18 heures.

Profil temps-action (effet antihypertenseur)

	DÉBUT D'ACTION	PIC	DURÉE
PO (une seule dose)	inconnu	24 h	inconnue
PO (plusieurs doses)	1 – 2 semaines	8 – 12 semaines	jusqu'à 8 semaines

CONTRE-INDICATIONS, PRÉCAUTIONS ET MISES EN GARDE

Contre-indications: Hypersensibilité ■ Anurie ■ Oligurie grave évolutive ■ Coma hépatique.

Précautions et mises en garde: Insuffisance rénale ou insuffisance hépatique graves ■ **GÉR.:** Sensibilité accrue aux effets du médicament ■ **OBST., ALLAITEMENT, PÉD.:** L'innocuité du médicament n'a pas été établie ■ Risque de réactions de sensibilité croisée avec d'autres sulfamides.

RÉACTIONS INDÉSIRABLES ET EFFETS SECONDAIRES

SNC: étourdissements, somnolence, léthargie.

CV: arythmies, hypotension.

GI: anorexie, crampes, nausées, vomissements.
Tég.: photosensibilité, rash.
End.: hyperglycémie.
HÉ: hypokaliémie, déshydratation, alcalose hypochlorémique, hyponatrémie, hypovolémie.
Métab.: hyperuricémie.
Loc.: crampes musculaires.

INTERACTIONS

Médicament-médicament: Effets additifs sur l'hypotension, lors de l'administration concomitante d'autres **antihypertenseurs** ou de **dérivés nitrés** et lors de l'ingestion d'**alcool** ■ Effets additifs sur l'hypokaliémie, lors de l'administration concomitante de **corticostéroïdes**, d'**amphotéricine B**, de **pipéracilline** ou de **ticarcilline** ■ L'indapamide diminue l'excrétion du **lithium** pouvant provoquer, de ce fait, une toxicité ■ L'hypokaliémie entraînée par l'agent peut accroître le risque de toxicité **digitalique**.
Médicament-produits naturels: La **réglisse** et les **plantes laxatives stimulantes** (**aloès, cascara sagrada, séné**), consommées en concomitance, peuvent augmenter le risque d'hypokaliémie.

VOIES D'ADMINISTRATION ET POSOLOGIE

- **PO (adultes)**: *Hypertension* – de 1,25 à 2,5 mg par jour, en 1 seule prise quotidienne, le matin.

PRÉSENTATION (version générique disponible)

Comprimés: 1,25 mg^{Pr}, 2,5 mg^{Pr}.

SOINS INFIRMIERS

ÉVALUATION DE LA SITUATION

- Prendre quotidiennement la pression artérielle, effectuer le bilan des ingesta et des excreta, peser le patient et examiner ses pieds, ses jambes et la région sacrée pour déceler l'œdème.
- Observer le patient, particulièrement s'il prend des dérivés digitaliques, pour déceler les signes et les symptômes suivants: anorexie, nausées, vomissements, crampes musculaires, paresthésie et confusion. Prévenir le médecin si ces signes de déséquilibre électrolytique se manifestent. Le risque de toxicité digitalique est plus élevé chez ces patients à cause de l'effet de déplétion potassique du diurétique.
- Déterminer si le patient est allergique aux sulfamides.

Tests de laboratoire: Noter la glycémie et les concentrations sériques d'électrolytes (particulièrement de potassium), d'urée, de créatinine et d'acide urique à intervalles réguliers pendant toute la durée du traitement. L'indapamide peut diminuer les concentrations de potassium, de sodium et de chlorure, et élever la glycémie. Chez les diabétiques, il peut s'avérer nécessaire d'accroître les doses d'hypoglycémiants oraux ou d'insuline. Le médicament entraîne une élévation moyenne de 59 μmol/L des concentrations d'acide urique; il risque de déclencher une crise de goutte.

DIAGNOSTICS INFIRMIERS POSSIBLES

- Excès de volume liquidien (Indications).
- Risque de déficit de volume liquidien (Effets secondaires).
- Connaissances insuffisantes sur le traitement médicamenteux (Enseignement au patient et à ses proches).

INTERVENTIONS INFIRMIÈRES

- Administrer le médicament le matin pour prévenir l'interruption du cycle du sommeil.
- Administrer l'indapamide avec des aliments ou du lait pour réduire l'irritation gastro-intestinale.

ENSEIGNEMENT AU PATIENT ET À SES PROCHES

- Expliquer au patient qu'il doit prendre le médicament à la même heure tous les jours. S'il n'a pas pu prendre le médicament au moment habituel, il doit le prendre aussitôt que possible, à moins que ce ne soit presque l'heure prévue pour la dose suivante. L'avertir qu'il ne doit jamais remplacer une dose manquée par une double dose. Expliquer également au patient qui reçoit l'indapamide pour le traitement de l'hypertension qu'il doit continuer de prendre le médicament même s'il se sent mieux. L'indapamide stabilise la pression artérielle mais ne guérit pas l'hypertension.
- Conseiller au patient de changer lentement de position pour réduire le risque d'hypotension orthostatique. Lui expliquer que l'alcool peut aggraver l'hypotension orthostatique.
- Recommander au patient d'utiliser des écrans solaires (mais d'éviter ceux qui renferment du PABA ou acide p-aminobenzoïque) et de porter des vêtements protecteurs lorsqu'il s'expose au soleil pour prévenir les réactions de photosensibilité.
- Conseiller au patient de suivre un régime alimentaire riche en potassium (voir l'annexe J).
- Recommander au patient de signaler à un professionnel de la santé les symptômes suivants: faiblesse musculaire, crampes, nausées ou étourdissements.

- Conseiller au patient de consulter un professionnel de la santé avant de prendre un médicament en vente libre pendant le traitement à l'indapamide.
- Insister sur l'importance des examens de suivi réguliers.

Hypertension:

- Montrer au patient et à ses proches comment prendre la pression artérielle et leur recommander de la mesurer au moins 1 fois par semaine et de signaler à un professionnel de la santé tout écart important.
- Inciter le patient à appliquer d'autres mesures de réduction de l'hypertension: perdre du poids, réduire sa consommation de sel, faire régulièrement de l'exercice, cesser de fumer, consommer l'alcool avec modération et diminuer le stress.

VÉRIFICATION DE L'EFFICACITÉ THÉRAPEUTIQUE

L'efficacité du traitement peut être démontrée par: la stabilisation de la pression artérielle ■ la diminution de l'œdème dû à l'insuffisance cardiaque.

I

INDINAVIR

Crixivan

CLASSIFICATION:

Antirétroviral (inhibiteur de la protéase)

Grossesse – catégorie C

INDICATIONS

Traitement de l'infection par le VIH, en association avec d'autres antirétroviraux. **Usages non approuvés:** En association avec d'autres antirétroviraux, prophylaxie après exposition accidentelle au VIH.

MÉCANISME D'ACTION

Inhibition dc l'action de la protéase du VIH et prévention du clivage des polyprotéines virales. ***Effets thérapeutiques:*** Ralentissement de l'évolution de l'infection par le VIH et de ses complications.

PHARMACOCINÉTIQUE

Absorption: Rapide (PO). L'absorption est réduite de 78 % lorsque l'indinavir est pris en même temps qu'un repas standard riche en calories, en matières grasses et en protéines.

Distribution: Inconnue.

Métabolisme et excrétion: Fort métabolisme hépatique; moins de 20 % est excrété à l'état inchangé dans l'urine.

Demi-vie: 1,8 heure.

Profil temps-action

	Début d'action	Pic	Durée
PO	rapide	1 h	8 h

CONTRE-INDICATIONS, PRÉCAUTIONS ET MISES EN GARDE

Contre-indications: Hypersensibilité ■ Traitement concomitant par le cisapride, le pimozide, l'amiodarone, les alcaloïdes de l'ergot (dihydroergotamine, ergonovine, ergotamine, méthylergonovine), le midazolam ou le triazolam.

Précautions et mises en garde: Nombreuses interactions médicamenteuses ■ Insuffisance hépatique (réduire la dose) ■ Hémophilie (risque accru d'hémorragie) ■ Diabète (risque d'aggravation de l'hyperglycémie) ■ **Obst., Péd.:** Grossesse, allaitement ou enfants (l'innocuité du médicament n'a pas été établie; l'allaitement est déconseillé chez les patientes infectées par le VIH) ■ Déshydratation.

RÉACTIONS INDÉSIRABLES ET EFFETS SECONDAIRES

SNC: étourdissements, somnolence, fatigue, céphalées, insomnie, faiblesse.

GI: douleurs abdominales, régurgitation acide, dysgueusie, hyperbilirubinémie asymptomatique, diarrhée, nausées, vomissements.

GU: lithiase rénale.

End.: hyperglycémie.

HÉ: ACIDOCÉTOSE.

Hémat: anémie hémolytique, thrombopénie.

Loc.: douleurs lombaires, douleurs au flanc.

Divers: hyperlipidémie, modification de la distribution du tissu adipeux, syndrome de reconstitution immunitaire.

INTERACTIONS

Médicament-médicament: L'USAGE CONCOMITANT DE **CISAPRIDE**, DE **PIMOZIDE**, D'**AMIODARONE**, D'**ERGONOVINE**, DE **MÉTHYLERGONOVINE**, DE **DIHYDROERGOTAMINE**, D'**ERGOTAMINE**, DE **MIDAZOLAM**, OU DE **TRIAZOLAM** EST CONTRE-INDIQUÉ, ÉTANT DONNÉ LE RISQUE ACCRU DE RÉACTIONS INDÉSIRABLES GRAVES OU MENAÇANTES POUR LA VIE, INCLUANT LES ARYTHMIES, LA SÉDATION EXCESSIVE ET LA VASOCONSTRICTION ■ La **rifampine** réduit les concentrations sanguines de l'indinavir; on doit éviter de les administrer en concomitance ■ La **carbamazépine**, le **phénobarbital** et la **phénytoïne** peuvent réduire les concentrations sanguines d'indinavir et diminuer son efficacité ■ L'indinavir augmente le risque de myopathie associé à l'**atorvastatine**, à la **lovastatine** ou à la **simvastatine** ■ L'indinavir élève les concentrations sanguines de la **rifabutine** (réduire de moitié la dose de rifabutine) et des **contraceptifs oraux** ■ La **rifabutine**, la **névirapine** et l'**éfavirenz** réduisent les concentrations d'indinavir; si un traitement concomitant par la rifabutine ou l'éfavirenz est nécessaire, augmenter la posologie d'indinavir jusqu'à concurrence de 1 000 mg, toutes les 8 heures ■ Le **kétoconazole**, l'**itraconazole** et la **délavirdine** élèvent les concentrations sanguines d'indinavir (réduire la dose d'indinavir jusqu'à 600 mg, toutes les 8 heures) ■ L'indinavir modifie l'absorption de la **didanosine** (prendre à au moins 1 heure d'intervalle) ■ L'administration concomitante d'**atazanavir** peut accroître le risque d'hyperbilirubinémie, et il faut l'éviter ■ L'indinavir peut élever les concentrations sanguines du **sildénafil**, du **tadalafil** et du **vardénafil**, et en intensifier les effets (suivre de près l'état du patient et utiliser des doses beaucoup plus faibles).

Médicament-produits naturels: L'usage concomitant de **millepertuis** entraîne une diminution marquée des concentrations sanguines et de l'efficacité de l'indinavir, associée à l'émergence d'une résistance virale.

Médicament-aliments: Les **aliments à forte teneur en matières grasses ou en protéines** et le **jus de pamplemousse** réduisent de façon marquée l'absorption du médicament.

VOIES D'ADMINISTRATION ET POSOLOGIE

- **PO (adultes)**: 800 mg, toutes les 8 heures.
- **PO (enfants de 3 à 18 ans)**: 500 mg/m², toutes les 8 heures; ne pas dépasser la dose recommandée chez l'adulte.

Surface corporelle (m²)	Dose (mg) à administrer toutes les 8 heures
0,5	300
0,75	400
1	500
1,25	600
1,5	800

Insuffisance hépatique légère ou modérée attribuable à une cirrhose

- **PO (adultes)**: 600 mg, toutes les 8 heures.

PRÉSENTATION

Capsules: 200 mg[Pr], 400 mg[Pr].

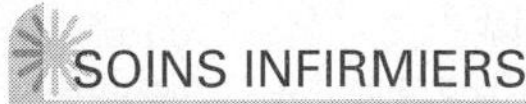

SOINS INFIRMIERS

ÉVALUATION DE LA SITUATION

- Tout au long du traitement, rester à l'affût de toute modification sur le plan de la gravité des symptômes de l'infection par le VIH et de l'apparition d'infections opportunistes.
- Si une patiente enceinte est exposée à des antirétroviraux, l'inscrire dans le registre des femmes exposées aux antirétroviraux pendant leur grossesse, en composant le 1 800 258 4263.

Tests de laboratoire:

- Noter la charge virale et le nombre de CD4 à intervalles réguliers tout au long du traitement.
- Le médicament peut provoquer l'hyperglycémie.
- Le médicament peut entraîner l'élévation des concentrations sériques d'AST, d'ALT, de bilirubine totale et d'amylase.

DIAGNOSTICS INFIRMIERS POSSIBLES

- Risque d'infection (Indications).
- Connaissances insuffisantes sur le traitement médicamenteux (Enseignement au patient et à ses proches).
- Non-observance du traitement médicamenteux (Enseignement au patient et à ses proches).

INTERVENTIONS INFIRMIÈRES

- NE PAS CONFONDRE DENAVIR (PENCICLOVIR) ET L'INDINAVIR.
- Administrer le médicament avec de l'eau, 1 heure avant ou 2 heures après les repas. On peut le prendre avec d'autres liquides (lait écrémé, jus, café, thé) ou avec un repas léger (biscottes et confiture, café au lait écrémé et sucre, flocons de maïs avec du lait écrémé et sucre). Recommander au patient d'éviter de prendre un repas riche en matières grasses ou en protéines dans les 2 heures précédant ou suivant la prise de l'indinavir.
- Les patients qui suivent un traitement concomitant par la didanosine devraient espacer la prise des deux médicaments d'au moins 1 heure.

ENSEIGNEMENT AU PATIENT ET À SES PROCHES

- Insister sur le fait qu'il est important de suivre rigoureusement la posologie recommandée et de prendre le médicament à des intervalles égaux tout au long de la journée. Recommander au patient de ne pas dépasser la dose prescrite et de ne pas cesser de prendre le médicament sans avoir consulté au préalable un professionnel de la santé. S'il n'a pas pu prendre le médicament au moment habituel, il doit le prendre aussitôt que possible. L'avertir qu'il ne doit jamais remplacer une dose manquée par une double dose.
- Informer le patient qu'il ne doit pas partager l'indinavir avec d'autres personnes.

- Recommander au patient de garder l'indinavir dans son flacon d'origine, contenant un agent dessiccateur; l'indinavir est sensible à l'humidité.
- Prévenir le patient que l'indinavir peut favoriser la formation de calculs rénaux. Lui conseiller de boire au moins 1,5 L d'eau par jour. Si des calculs se sont formés, il peut s'avérer nécessaire d'interrompre le traitement pendant 1 à 3 jours.
- INFORMER LE PATIENT QUE L'INDINAVIR PEUT INDUIRE L'HYPERGLYCÉMIE. LUI CONSEILLER DE PRÉVENIR UN PROFESSIONNEL DE LA SANTÉ SI LES SYMPTÔMES SUIVANTS SE MANIFESTENT: SOIF OU FAIM ACCRUE, PERTE DE POIDS INEXPLIQUÉE, MICTIONS PLUS FRÉQUENTES, FATIGUE ET SÉCHERESSE OU DÉMANGEAISONS DE LA PEAU.
- Conseiller au patient de consulter un professionnel de la santé avant de prendre d'autres médicaments (sur ordonnance ou en vente libre et produits naturels), en même temps que l'indinavir.
- Expliquer au patient qui suit un traitement concomitant par la didanosine que les deux médicaments doivent être pris à jeun, à 1 heure d'intervalle.
- Expliquer au patient que le médicament ne guérit pas le sida et qu'il ne réduit pas le risque de transmission du VIH à d'autres personnes par les rapports sexuels ou par la contamination du sang. L'inciter à utiliser un condom, à ne pas se servir des mêmes aiguilles qu'une autre personne et à ne pas donner du sang afin de prévenir la transmission du virus du sida à autrui.
- Prévenir le patient que l'indinavir peut provoquer de la somnolence ou des étourdissements. Lui conseiller de ne pas conduire et d'éviter les activités qui exigent sa vigilance jusqu'à ce qu'on ait la certitude que le médicament n'entraîne pas ces effets chez lui.
- Prévenir le patient qu'il peut se produire une redistribution ou une accumulation de graisses corporelles en association avec le traitement antirétroviral, dont les causes et les conséquences à long terme sur la santé sont actuellement inconnues.
- Insister sur le fait qu'il est important de se soumettre à intervalles réguliers à des examens de suivi et à des analyses de sang permettant de déceler les effets secondaires et les bienfaits du traitement.

VÉRIFICATION DE L'EFFICACITÉ THÉRAPEUTIQUE

L'efficacité du traitement peut être démontrée par: le ralentissement de l'évolution de l'infection par le VIH et la diminution du risque d'infections opportunistes ■ l'augmentation du nombre de CD4 et la diminution de la charge virale. ✳

INDOMÉTHACINE

Apo-Indomethacin, Indomethacine, Indocid, Novo-Méthacin, Nu-Indo, Pro-Indo, Ratio-Indo, Rhodacine, Sab-Indomethacine, Indocid P.D.A.

CLASSIFICATION:

Analgésique non opioïde, anti-inflammatoire non stéroïdien

Grossesse – catégories D (1er et 3e trimestres) et B (2e trimestre)

INDICATIONS

PO, IR: Traitement des maladies inflammatoires incluant: la polyarthrite rhumatoïde ■ la goutte ■ l'arthrose ■ la spondylarthrite ankylosante ■ Traitement généralement réservé aux patients qui ne répondent pas aux agents traditionnels ■ **IV:** Fermeture du canal artériel chez les prématurés lorsque le traitement habituel est inefficace.

MÉCANISME D'ACTION

Inhibition de la synthèse des prostaglandines. ***Effets thérapeutiques:*** *PO, IR* – Suppression de la douleur et de l'inflammation ■ *IV* – Fermeture du canal artériel.

PHARMACOCINÉTIQUE

Absorption: Bonne (PO et IR).

Distribution: L'agent traverse la barrière hématoencéphalique et placentaire, et passe dans le lait maternel.

Liaison aux protéines: 99 %.

Métabolisme et excrétion: Métabolisme majoritairement hépatique.

Demi-vie: Nouveau-nés < 2 semaines: 20 heures; nouveau-nés > 2 semaines: 11 heures; adultes: de 2,6 à 11 heures.

Profil temps-action (effets thérapeutiques)

	DÉBUT D'ACTION	PIC	DURÉE
PO (analgésique)	30 min	0,5 – 2 h	4 – 6 h
PO (anti-inflammatoire)	jusqu'à 7 jours	1 – 2 semaines	inconnue
IV (fermeture du canal artériel)	jusqu'à 48 h	inconnu	inconnue

CONTRE-INDICATIONS, PRÉCAUTIONS ET MISES EN GARDE

Contre-indications: Hypersensibilité ■ Risque de réactions de sensibilité croisée avec d'autres anti-inflammatoires non stéroïdiens dont l'aspirine ■ Hémorragie digestive active ■ Ulcère gastro-intestinal évolutif ■ Gastrite ■ Entérite régionale ■ Diverticulite ■ Rectocolite hémorragique ■ Antécédents de lésions gastro-intestinales récidivantes.

IR: Antécédents de rectite ou de saignements rectaux récents.

IV: Infection non traitée ■ Saignements ■ Thrombopénie ■ Coagulopathie ■ Entérocolite nécrosante ■ Altération importante de la fonction rénale ■ Ictère ■ Maladies hépatiques ■ Cardiopathies congénitales.

Précautions et mises en garde: Maladies cardiovasculaires ■ **GÉR.**: Risque accru de réactions indésirables chez les personnes âgées ■ Grossesse ■ Allaitement.

RÉACTIONS INDÉSIRABLES ET EFFETS SECONDAIRES

SNC: étourdissements, somnolence, céphalées, troubles psychiques.

ORLO: vision trouble, acouphènes.

CV: arythmies, œdème.

GI: *PO* – HÉPATITE MÉDICAMENTEUSE, SAIGNEMENTS GASTRO-INTESTINAUX, constipation, dyspepsie, nausées, vomissements, malaise; *IR* – irritation rectale, ténesme.

GU: cystite, hématurie, insuffisance rénale.

Tég.: rash.

HÉ: *PO* – hyperkaliémie; *IV* – hyponatrémie dilutionnelle, hypoglycémie.

Hémat.: dyscrasie sanguine, allongement du temps de saignement.

Locaux: phlébite au point d'injection IV.

Divers: réactions allergiques incluant l'ANAPHYLAXIE.

INTERACTIONS

Médicament-médicament: L'usage concomitant d'**aspirine** peut réduire l'efficacité de l'indométhacine ■ L'usage concomitant d'**aspirine**, d'autres **AINS**, de **corticostéroïdes** ou d'**alcool** accroît le risque d'irritation gastro-intestinale ■ L'administration prolongée d'indométhacine avec de l'**acétaminophène** peut accroître le risque de réactions rénales indésirables ■ L'effet thérapeutique des **diurétiques** et des **antihypertenseurs** peut être diminué ■ L'indométhacine peut accroître l'hypoglycémie provoquée par l'**insuline** ou les **hypoglycémiants oraux** ■ Le médicament peut entraîner une augmentation du risque de toxicité par le **lithium** ou la **zidovudine** (l'usage concomitant de zidovudine devrait être évité) ■ L'indométhacine accroît le risque de toxicité par le **méthotrexate** ■ Le **probénécide** accroît le risque de toxicité par l'indométhacine ■ L'administration concomitante de **céfamandole**, de **céfotétane**, de **céfopérazone**, d'**acide valproïque**, de **plicamycine**, d'**agents thrombolytiques**, de **warfarine** et d'**agents modifiant la fonction plaquettaire**, incluant le **clopidogrel**, la **ticlopidine**, l'**abciximab**, l'**eptifibatide** ou le **tirofiban**, peut augmenter le risque de saignements ■ L'administration concomitante d'**antinéoplasiques** ou d'une **radiothérapie** accroît le risque de réactions hématologiques indésirables ■ L'administration concomitante de **cyclosporine** augmente le risque de néphrotoxicité ■ L'usage concomitant de **diurétiques épargneurs de potassium** peut provoquer l'hyperkaliémie ■ *IV* – L'indométhacine peut accroître les concentrations de **dérivés digitaliques**, d'**aminosides**, de **lithium** et de **méthotrexate** chez les nourrissons.

Médicament-produits naturels: Risque accru de saignements en cas de consommation concomitante d'**ail**, d'**anis**, d'**arnica**, de **camomille**, de **dong quai**, de **girofle**, de **gingembre**, de **ginkgo** et de **ginseng**.

VOIES D'ADMINISTRATION ET POSOLOGIE

Anti-inflammatoire

- **PO (adultes)**: *Antiarthritique* – 25 mg, 2 ou 3 fois par jour (ne pas dépasser 200 mg). On peut administrer une seule dose de 100 mg, au coucher. *Antigoutte* – 50 mg, 3 fois par jour, pour soulager la douleur; ensuite, réduire la dose graduellement.
- **IR (adultes)**: De 100 à 200 mg/jour; les doses quotidiennes supérieures à 100 mg doivent être fractionnées en 2 prises.
- **PO (enfants)**: *Antiarthritique* – de 2 à 4 mg/kg, en doses fractionnées (maximum de 4 mg/kg/jour ou 200 mg).

Fermeture du canal artériel

- **IV (nouveau-nés)**: La posologie varie selon l'âge du nouveau-né au moment où le traitement est commencé. Initialement, 0,2 mg/kg dans tous les cas, puis 1 ou 2 doses à intervalles de 12 à 24 heures selon l'âge du nouveau-né lors de l'administration de la première dose: 0,1 mg/kg, si le nouveau-né est âgé de moins de 48 heures; 0,2 mg/kg, s'il est âgé de 2 à 7 jours; 0,25 mg/kg, s'il est âgé de plus de 7 jours.

PRÉSENTATION (version générique disponible)

Capsules: 25 mg[Pr], 50 mg[Pr] ■ **Suppositoires**: 50 mg[Pr], 100 mg[Pr] ■ **Poudre pour injection**: fioles de 1 mg[Pr].

SOINS INFIRMIERS

ÉVALUATION DE LA SITUATION

- LES PATIENTS SOUFFRANT D'ASTHME, D'ALLERGIE INDUITE PAR L'ASPIRINE ET DE POLYPES NASAUX SONT DAVANTAGE PRÉDISPOSÉS À DES RÉACTIONS D'HYPERSENSIBILITÉ. SUIVRE DE PRÈS LA RHINITE, L'ASTHME ET L'URTICAIRE.

Arthrite: Déterminer le degré de mobilité des articulations ainsi que le type de douleur, son siège et son intensité, avant l'administration et de 1 à 2 heures après.

Persistance du canal artériel:

- Ausculter les bruits du cœur, mesurer la fréquence cardiaque et la pression artérielle, effectuer un échocardiogramme et examiner la fonction respiratoire à intervalles réguliers pendant toute la durée du traitement.
- Effectuer le bilan des ingesta et des excreta. Il faut habituellement restreindre l'apport de liquides pendant toute la durée du traitement.

Tests de laboratoire:

- Chez les patients recevant un traitement prolongé, noter à intervalles réguliers les concentrations sériques d'urée, de créatinine et de potassium, la numération globulaire et les résultats des tests de la fonction hépatique.
- L'indométhacine peut entraîner l'élévation des concentrations sériques de potassium, de créatinine, d'urée, d'ALT et d'AST, et modifier la glycémie. Cet agent peut réduire les concentrations d'hémoglobine et l'hématocrite ainsi que le nombre de globules blancs et de plaquettes, et la clairance de la créatinine. Le temps de saignement peut également être allongé pendant plusieurs jours après l'arrêt du traitement.
- Le médicament peut élever la glycosurie et la protéinurie.

DIAGNOSTICS INFIRMIERS POSSIBLES

- Douleur aiguë (Indications).
- Mobilité physique réduite (Indications).
- Connaissances insuffisantes sur le traitement médicamenteux (Enseignement au patient et à ses proches).

INTERVENTIONS INFIRMIÈRES

- En cas de traitement prolongé, on devrait administrer la plus faible dose qui permet de maîtriser les symptômes.

PO: Administrer après les repas ou avec des aliments ou un antiacide pour réduire l'irritation gastrique.

IV directe: Reconstituer avec 2 mL de solution de NaCl 0,9 % ou d'eau stérile pour injection sans agent de conservation pour obtenir une concentration de 0,5 mg/mL. Reconstituer immédiatement avant l'administration et jeter toute portion inutilisée. Ne pas diluer de nouveau; ne pas mélanger à d'autres médicaments. Ne pas administrer dans le cordon ombilical ni dans les vaisseaux situés près de l'artère mésentérique supérieure, puisque cela pourrait causer une vasoconstriction et compromettre ainsi l'apport sanguin aux intestins. Ne pas administrer par voie intrathécale. Consulter les directives de chaque fabricant avant de reconstituer la préparation.

Vitesse d'administration: Administrer en 20 à 30 minutes. Éviter l'extravasation afin de prévenir l'irritation des tissus.

Compatibilité (tubulure en Y): furosémide ■ insuline ■ nitroprussiate ■ potassium, chlorure de ■ sodium, bicarbonate de.

Incompatibilité (tubulure en Y): calcium, gluconate de ■ cimétidine ■ dobutamine ■ dopamine ■ gentamicine ■ tobramycine ■ tolazoline.

IR: Inciter le patient à retenir le suppositoire pendant 1 heure après l'administration.

ENSEIGNEMENT AU PATIENT ET À SES PROCHES

- Conseiller au patient de prendre le médicament avec un grand verre d'eau et d'éviter de se coucher pendant les 15 à 30 minutes qui suivent l'administration.
- Conseiller au patient de respecter rigoureusement la posologie recommandée. S'il n'a pu prendre le médicament au moment habituel, il doit le prendre dès que possible, à moins que ce ne soit presque l'heure prévue pour la dose suivante. Le prévenir qu'il ne doit jamais remplacer une dose manquée par une double dose.
- Prévenir le patient que l'indométhacine peut provoquer de la somnolence ou des étourdissements. Lui conseiller de ne pas conduire et d'éviter les activités qui exigent sa vigilance jusqu'à ce qu'on ait la certitude que le médicament n'entraîne pas ces effets chez lui.
- Conseiller au patient d'éviter de boire de l'alcool et de consulter un professionnel de la santé avant de prendre de l'aspirine, d'autres AINS, de l'acétaminophène ou tout autre médicament en vente libre en même temps que l'indométhacine.
- Inciter le patient à utiliser des écrans solaires et à porter des vêtements protecteurs pour prévenir les réactions de photosensibilité.
- Recommander au patient qui doit suivre un autre traitement ou subir une intervention chirurgicale d'avertir le professionnel de la santé qu'il suit un traitement par ce médicament.
- CONSEILLER AU PATIENT DE SIGNALER À UN PROFESSIONNEL DE LA SANTÉ LES SYMPTÔMES SUIVANTS: RASH, DÉMANGEAISONS, FRISSONS, FIÈVRE, DOULEURS MUSCULAIRES, TROUBLES VISUELS, GAIN DE POIDS, ŒDÈME, DOULEURS ABDOMINALES, SELLES NOIRES OU CÉPHALÉES PERSISTANTES.

Persistance du canal artériel: Expliquer aux parents la raison d'être du traitement et la nécessité d'exercer une surveillance étroite.

VÉRIFICATION DE L'EFFICACITÉ THÉRAPEUTIQUE

L'efficacité du traitement peut être démontrée par: la diminution de l'intensité de la douleur modérée ▪ l'amélioration de la mobilité des articulations; le soulagement partiel des douleurs arthritiques survient habituellement dans les 2 semaines suivant le début du traitement, mais le plein effet thérapeutique n'est parfois notable qu'après 1 mois de traitement ininterrompu; les patients qui ne répondent pas à un AINS peuvent répondre à un autre ▪ la fermeture du canal artériel. ✳

INFLIXIMAB

Remicade

CLASSIFICATION:

Agent antirhumatismal modificateur de la maladie [AARMM]; anti-inflammatoire gastro-intestinal (anticorps monoclonal)

Grossesse – catégorie C

INDICATIONS

Traitement, en association avec le méthotrexate, des poussées évolutives des formes modérées ou graves de la polyarthrite rhumatoïde ▪ Traitement de la spondylarthrite ankylosante chez les patients dont la réponse au traitement standard n'est pas satisfaisante ou qui le tolèrent mal ▪ Traitement des formes modérées à graves de la maladie de Crohn, chez les adultes dont la réponse au traitement standard n'est pas satisfaisante ▪ Traitement de la maladie de Crohn avec fistulisation, chez les adultes réfractaires à un traitement standard complet et approprié ▪ Traitement de la colite ulcéreuse des formes modérée à grave, chez les patients dont la réponse au traitement standard n'est pas satisfaisante ▪ Traitement de l'arthrite, chez les patients atteints de rhumatisme psoriasique ▪ Traitement des adultes atteints des formes modérée à grave du psoriasis en plaques chronique.

MÉCANISME D'ACTION

Neutralisation et prévention de l'activité du facteur de nécrose tumorale alpha (TNF alpha), d'où une action anti-inflammatoire et antiproliférative. ***Effets thérapeutiques:*** Diminution des signes et des symptômes, ainsi que de la vitesse de destruction des articulations et amélioration de la capacité fonctionnelle chez les patients souffrant de polyarthrite rhumatoïde, de spondylarthrite ankylosante et de rhumatisme psoriasique ▪ Diminution des signes et des symptômes de la maladie de Crohn, incluant les fistules entérocutanées exsudatives ▪ Diminution des symptômes, induction de la rémission clinique et moindre besoin de recourir à des corticostéroïdes, voire possibilité d'en arrêter la prise chez les patients souffrant de colite ulcéreuse.

PHARMACOCINÉTIQUE

Absorption: Complète (IV).

Distribution: Principalement dans les compartiments vasculaires.

Métabolisme et excrétion: Inconnus.

Demi-vie: 9,5 jours.

Profil temps-action (symptômes de la maladie de Crohn)

	DÉBUT D'ACTION	PIC	DURÉE
IV	1 – 2 semaines	inconnu	12 – 48 semaines†

† Après la perfusion.

CONTRE-INDICATIONS, PRÉCAUTIONS ET MISES EN GARDE

Contre-indications: Hypersensibilité à l'infliximab, aux protéines murines ou aux autres composantes de la préparation ▪ Patients souffrant d'infections graves comme la septicémie, la formation d'abcès, la tuberculose et les infections opportunistes ▪ Patients atteints d'une insuffisance cardiaque congestive modérée ou grave ▪ Utilisation concomitante d'anakinra ▪ **ALLAITEMENT**: Les femmes prenant l'infliximab ne doivent pas allaiter pendant le traitement et pendant au moins 6 mois après l'avoir fini.

Précautions et mises en garde: Patients traités de nouveau après une période sans traitement de 2 ans (risque accru de réactions indésirables) ▪ Tuberculose (y compris la forme latente) ▪ Insuffisance cardiaque légère (cesser le traitement en cas d'apparition ou d'aggravation des symptômes d'insuffisance cardiaque) ▪ Antécédents d'hépatite B ou maladie active ▪ Trouble démyélinisant préexistant ou d'apparition récente touchant le SNC (sclérose en plaques, myélite, névrite optique) ▪ Risque de réactions allergiques et d'anaphylaxie ▪ Formation d'auto-anticorps (risque d'apparition du syndrome pseudolupique) ▪ Personnes âgées ▪ **OBST.**: L'administration durant la grossesse est déconseillée. Utiliser un moyen contraceptif efficace pendant le traitement par l'infliximab ainsi que pendant au moins 6 mois par la suite ▪ **PÉD.**: L'innocuité du médicament n'a pas été établie ■ **GÉR.**: Risque plus élevé d'infections et d'effets secondaires.

RÉACTIONS INDÉSIRABLES ET EFFETS SECONDAIRES

SNC: fatigue, céphalées, anxiété, dépression, étourdissements, insomnie.

ORLO: conjonctivite.

Resp.: infection des voies respiratoires supérieures, bronchite, toux, dyspnée, laryngite, pharyngite, réactions allergiques touchant les voies respiratoires, rhinite, sinusite.

CV: douleurs thoraciques, hypertension, hypotension, épanchement péricardique, tachycardie, insuffisance cardiaque congestive.

GI: douleurs abdominales, nausées, vomissements, constipation, diarrhée, dyspepsie, flatulence, hépatotoxicité, occlusion intestinale, douleurs buccales, maux de dents, stomatite ulcérative.

GU: dysurie, mictions fréquentes, infection des voies urinaires.

Tég.: acné, alopécie, sécheresse de la peau, ecchymoses, eczéma, érythème, formation d'hématomes, sécrétion accrue de sueur, bouffées vasomotrices, prurit, urticaire, rash.

Loc.: arthralgie, arthrite, douleurs lombaires, contractions involontaires des muscles, myalgie.

SN: paresthésie.

Divers: INFECTIONS (incluant la réactivation d'une tuberculose, une pneumonie ou une infection fongique envahissante), fièvre, réactions lors de la perfusion IV, frissons, syndrome pseudogrippal, herpès, zona, réactions d'hypersensibilité, risque accru de lymphome, syndrome lupoïde, muguet, douleurs, œdème périphérique, vasculite.

INTERACTIONS

Médicament-médicament: L'usage concomitant d'**étanercept** ou d'**anakinra** augmente le risque d'infections graves. Cette association n'est pas recommandée ■ Il est déconseillé d'administrer en concomitance un **vaccin à virus vivants.**

VOIES D'ADMINISTRATION ET POSOLOGIE

Polyarthrite rhumatoïde

- **IV (adultes)**: 3 mg/kg, en perfusion, suivie de doses supplémentaires de 3 mg/kg, 2 et 6 semaines plus tard, et toutes les 8 semaines par la suite. En cas de réponse insatisfaisante, il est possible de porter la dose à 10 mg/kg au maximum ou d'administrer une perfusion toutes les 4 semaines (en association avec le méthotrexate).

Spondylarthrite ankylosante

- **IV (adultes)**: 5 mg/kg, en perfusion, suivie de doses supplémentaires de 5 mg/kg, 2 et 6 semaines plus tard, et toutes les 6 à 8 semaines par la suite.

Maladie de Crohn modérée ou grave

- **IV (adultes)**: *Traitement d'induction* – 5 mg/kg, en perfusion, suivis de doses supplémentaires de 5 mg/kg, 2 et 6 semaines plus tard. *Traitement d'entretien* – 5 mg/kg, en perfusion, toutes les 8 semaines. Dans le cas des patients dont la réponse demeure insatisfaisante, on peut envisager de porter la dose à 10 mg/kg au maximum.

Maladie de Crohn avec fistulisation

- **IV (adultes)**: *Traitement d'induction* – 5 mg/kg, en perfusion, suivis de doses supplémentaires de 5 mg/kg, 2 et 6 semaines plus tard. *Traitement d'entretien* – 5 mg/kg, en perfusion, toutes les 8 semaines. Les patients qui n'auront pas réagi favorablement au traitement par l'infliximab après 14 semaines sont peu susceptibles d'y répondre même si on continue de leur administrer ce médicament. Dans leur cas, il faudrait envisager de mettre fin à ce traitement.

Colite ulcéreuse

- **IV (adultes)**: *Traitement d'induction* – 5 mg/kg, en perfusion, suivis de doses supplémentaires de 5 mg/kg, 2 et 6 semaines plus tard. *Traitement d'entretien* – 5 mg/kg, en perfusion, toutes les 8 semaines pendant une période maximale de 30 semaines. Chez certains patients, on peut envisager de porter la dose à 10 mg/kg au maximum, pour maintenir la réponse clinique et la rémission.

Rhumatisme psoriasique

- **IV (adultes)**: 5 mg/kg, en perfusion, suivis de doses supplémentaires de 5 mg/kg, 2 et 6 semaines plus tard, et toutes les 8 semaines par la suite. Si aucune réponse ne s'est manifestée après 24 semaines, il ne faut pas administrer d'autres perfusions d'infliximab.

Psoriasis en plaques chronique

- **IV (adultes)**: 5 mg/kg, en perfusion, suivis de doses supplémentaires de 5 mg/kg, 2 et 6 semaines plus tard, et toutes les 8 semaines par la suite. Si aucune réponse ne s'est manifestée après 14 semaines, il ne faut pas administrer d'autres perfusions d'infliximab.

PRÉSENTATION

Poudre pour injection: fiole de 100 mg^{Pr}.

SOINS INFIRMIERS

ÉVALUATION DE LA SITUATION

- Rester à l'affût des signes et des symptômes de la maladie de Crohn, avant, pendant et après le traitement.
- Déceler les réactions induites par la perfusion (fièvre, frissons, urticaire, prurit), pendant la perfusion et pendant les 2 heures qui suivent. Les symptômes disparaissent habituellement à l'arrêt de la perfusion. Les réactions sont plus courantes après la première ou la deuxième perfusion. La fréquence des réactions peut être réduite par l'administration d'agents immunosuppresseurs.
- Faire un test à la tuberculine pour détecter une tuberculose latente avant le début du traitement par l'infliximab. On peut commencer un traitement contre la tuberculose latente avant celui par l'infliximab.
- Rester à l'affût des réactions d'hypersensibilité (urticaire, dyspnée, hypotension) tout au long de la perfusion. Arrêter l'administration de l'infliximab en cas de réaction grave. Il faut garder des médicaments (antihistaminiques, acétaminophène, corticostéroïdes, adrénaline) et le matériel de réanimation à la portée de la main pour parer à toute réaction grave.

Polyarthrite rhumatoïde: Évaluer la douleur et l'amplitude des mouvements articulaires avant le traitement et à intervalles réguliers pendant toute sa durée.

Maladie de Crohn et colite ulcéreuse: Évaluer les signes et les symptômes avant le traitement, à intervalles réguliers pendant toute sa durée et après qu'il a pris fin.

Tests de laboratoire:

- L'infliximab peut entraîner l'élévation des concentrations d'anticorps antinucléaires. La fréquence de cette réaction peut être réduite par l'administration d'un traitement immunosuppresseur initial.
- Noter les résultats des tests de la fonction hépatique avant le début du traitement et à intervalles réguliers pendant toute sa durée. Il y a risque d'une augmentation faible ou modérée de l'AST et de l'ALT sans évolution vers une insuffisance hépatique. En cas de jaunisse ou d'élévation de l'ALT de 5 fois la limite supérieure de la normale ou plus, arrêter le traitement par l'infliximab.
- Vérifier le nombre de globules blancs et la formule leucocytaire à intervalles réguliers pendant toute la durée du traitement. Il y a risque de leucopénie, de neutropénie, de thrombopénie et de pancytopénie. Arrêter le traitement par l'infliximab si des symptômes de dyscrasie sanguine (p.ex., fièvre persistante) se manifestent.

DIAGNOSTICS INFIRMIERS POSSIBLES

- Diarrhée (Indications).
- Risque d'infection (Réactions indésirables).
- Connaissances insuffisantes sur le traitement médicamenteux (Enseignement au patient et à ses proches).

INTERVENTIONS INFIRMIÈRES

Perfusion intermittente: Calculer le nombre total de fioles nécessaires. Reconstituer le contenu de chaque fiole avec 10 mL d'eau stérile pour injection en se servant d'une seringue munie d'une aiguille de calibre 21 ou plus petit. Diriger le jet vers les côtés de la fiole. Si le contenu de la fiole n'est pas sous vide, ne pas l'utiliser. Pour diluer la poudre, tourner délicatement la fiole, sans l'agiter. La solution peut mousser lors de la reconstitution; laisser reposer pendant 5 minutes. La solution est opalescente, d'incolore à jaune pâle; on peut cependant noter la présence de quelques particules translucides étant donné que l'infliximab est une protéine. Ne pas utiliser la solution si elle a changé de couleur ou si des particules opaques ou des particules autres que celles qui sont translucides se sont formées. Prélever le volume de la dose totale d'infliximab et l'ajouter lentement dans un sac pour perfusion contenant 250 mL de solution de NaCl 0,9 %. La concentration maximale recommandée est de 4 mg/mL. Mélanger délicatement. La perfusion devrait être amorcée dans les 3 heures suivant la préparation. La solution est incompatible avec le matériel en chlorure de polyvinyle. Préparer dans un flacon en verre ou dans un sac de polypropylène ou de polyoléfine. Ne pas réutiliser la solution ni garder les portions inutilisées.

Vitesse d'administration: Administrer en au moins 2 heures au moyen d'un appareil de perfusion, par une tubulure de perfusion en polyéthylène dotée d'un filtre stérile intégré, non pyrogène, à faible fixation protéinique, dont les pores ne dépassent pas 1,2 µm.

Incompatibilité (tubulure en Y): Ne pas administrer par la même tubulure que d'autres agents.

ENSEIGNEMENT AU PATIENT ET À SES PROCHES

- Informer le patient que des réactions indésirables (myalgie, rash, fièvre, polyarthralgie, prurit) peuvent survenir de 3 à 12 jours après un traitement par l'infliximab, administré plus de 2 ans après un traitement antérieur. Habituellement, ces symptômes diminuent ou disparaissent dans les 1 à 3 jours.

I

Recommander au patient de prévenir un professionnel de la santé si ces symptômes se manifestent.

- Prévenir le patient que l'infliximab peut provoquer des étourdissements. Lui conseiller de ne pas conduire et d'éviter les activités qui exigent sa vigilance jusqu'à ce qu'on ait la certitude que le médicament n'entraîne pas cet effet chez lui.

VÉRIFICATION DE L'EFFICACITÉ THÉRAPEUTIQUE

L'efficacité du traitement peut être démontrée par: la diminution des signes et des symptômes, ainsi que de la vitesse de destruction des articulations et l'amélioration de la capacité fonctionnelle, chez les patients souffrant de polyarthrite rhumatoïde, de spondylarthrite ankylosante et de rhumatisme psoriasique ■ la diminution des signes et des symptômes de la maladie de Crohn et du nombre de fistules entérocutanées exsudatives ■ la diminution des symptômes, l'induction de la rémission clinique et un moindre besoin de recourir à des corticostéroïdes, voire la possibilité d'en arrêter la prise chez les patients souffrant de colite ulcéreuse.

INHIBITEURS DE LA MONOAMINE-OXYDASE (IMAO)

phénelzine
Nardil

tranylcypromine
Parnate

CLASSIFICATION:
Antidépresseurs

Grossesse – catégorie C

INDICATIONS

Traitement de la dépression névrotique, non endogène ou atypique, chez les patients qui ne peuvent tolérer d'autres modes de traitement (antidépresseurs tricycliques, ISRS ou électrochocs) ou qui n'ont pas répondu à ces traitements ■ Traitement de certaines dépressions réactionnelles lorsque les électrochocs ne sont pas indiqués (tranylcypromine).

MÉCANISME D'ACTION

Inhibition de la monoamine-oxydase, ce qui entraîne une accumulation de divers neurotransmetteurs (dopamine, adrénaline, noradrénaline et sérotonine). ***Effets thérapeutiques:*** Amélioration de l'humeur chez les patients dépressifs.

PHARMACOCINÉTIQUE

Absorption: Bonne (PO).

Distribution: Les deux agents traversent la barrière placentaire et passent probablement dans le lait maternel.

Métabolisme et excrétion: Métabolisme hépatique.

Demi-vie: Inconnue.

Profil temps-action (effet antidépresseur)

	DÉBUT D'ACTION	PIC	DURÉE
Phénelzine	1 - 4 semaines	2 - 6 semaines	2 semaines
Tranylcypromine	2 jours - 3 semaines	2 - 3 semaines	3 - 5 jours

CONTRE-INDICATIONS, PRÉCAUTIONS ET MISES EN GARDE

Contre-indications: Hypersensibilité ■ Maladie hépatique et antécédents de troubles hépatiques ■ Dyscrasie sanguine (tranylcypromine) ■ Maladie rénale grave ■ Maladie vasculaire cérébrale ■ Maladie cardiovasculaire ■ Phéochromocytome ■ Insuffisance cardiaque ■ Antécédents de céphalées ■ Traitement concomitant par d'autres IMAO ■ Traitement concomitant par les dérivés de la dibenzazépine, comme l'amitriptyline, la nortriptyline, la protriptyline, la désipramine, l'imipramine, la doxépine, la perphénazine, la carbamazépine, la cyclobenzaprine, l'amoxapine, la maprotiline ou la trimipramine ■ Traitement concomitant par des ISRS (fluoxétine, fluvoxamine, paroxétine, sertraline) ■ Usage concomitant d'antidépresseurs, tels que le bupropion, la trazodone ou la venlafaxine ■ Usage concomitant de sympathomimétiques (adrénaline, amphétamines, cocaïne, éphédrine, dopamine, méthylphénidate, noradrénaline) ■ Usage concomitant de buspirone, de cocaïne, de dextrométhorphane, de dépresseurs du SNC (alcool, certains narcotiques), de guanéthidine, de lévodopa, de L-tryptophane, de L-tyrosine, de mépéridine, de méthyldopa, de phénylalanine, de réserpine ■ Traitement concomitant par des produits grand public contre le rhume, le rhume des foins ou des produits amaigrissants contenant un vasoconstricteur, tels que la phénylpropanolamine ou la phényléphrine ■ Interventions chirurgicales non urgentes exigeant une anesthésie générale ■ Traitement concomitant par des anesthésiques locaux contenant les vasoconstricteurs sympathomimétiques ■ Consommation concomitante d'aliments riches en tyramine ou d'aliments riches en protéines ayant subi une modification par maturation, fermentation, marinade, fumaison ou contamination bactérienne (fromages vieillis, harengs marinés, bière, vin, foie, extraits de levure, saucissons secs, etc.) ■ Consommation excessive de caféine (café, thé, cola, chocolat, etc.).

Précautions et mises en garde: Risque de crise hypertensive (une surveillance étroite de la pression artérielle est indiquée) ■ La surveillance des idées suicidaires est indiquée chez tous les patients recevant ce médicament ■ Antécédents de manie ou d'hypomanie ■ Antécédents de pharmacodépendance ■ Maladie cardiovasculaire symptomatique ■ Hyperthyroïdie ■ Troubles convulsifs ■ Éviter de mettre fin abruptement au traitement, en raison du risque de symptômes de sevrage ■ **GÉR.**: Risque accru de réactions indésirables ■ **PÉD.**: Risque accru de pensées et de comportements suicidaires chez les enfants et les adolescents. L'innocuité de ces médicaments n'a pas été étudiée ■ **OBST., ALLAITEMENT**: L'innocuité de ces agents n'a pas été établie.

EXTRÊME PRUDENCE: INTERVENTION CHIRURGICALE (DANS LA MESURE DU POSSIBLE, LE TRAITEMENT DEVRAIT ÊTRE INTERROMPU PLUSIEURS SEMAINES AVANT L'INTERVENTION CHIRURGICALE EN RAISON DU RISQUE ACCRU DE RÉACTIONS IMPRÉVISIBLES).

RÉACTIONS INDÉSIRABLES ET EFFETS SECONDAIRES

SNC: CONVULSIONS, étourdissements, céphalées, insomnie, agitation, faiblesse, confusion, somnolence.
ORLO: vision trouble, glaucome, nystagmus.
CV: CRISE HYPERTENSIVE, arythmies, hypotension orthostatique, œdème.
GI: diarrhée, douleurs abdominales, anorexie, constipation, sécheresse de la bouche (xérostomie), nausées, vomissements.
GU: dysurie, incontinence urinaire, rétention urinaire.
Tég.: rash.
End.: hypoglycémie.
SN: arthralgie.

INTERACTIONS (VOIR CONTRE-INDICATIONS)

Médicament-médicament: DES RÉACTIONS INDÉSIRABLES GRAVES, POUVANT ÊTRE D'ISSUE FATALE, PEUVENT SURVENIR EN CAS D'ADMINISTRATION CONCOMITANTE D'AUTRES **ANTIDÉPRESSEURS**, DE **CARBAMAZÉPINE**, DE **CYCLOBENZAPRINE**, DE **MAPROTILINE**, DE **PROCARBAZINE** OU DE **SÉLÉGILINE**. RETARDER LES TRAITEMENTS D'AU MOINS 2 SEMAINES AVANT LE PASSAGE À UN AUTRE MÉDICAMENT OU VICE-VERSA (5 SEMAINES APRÈS LA FIN DU TRAITEMENT PAR LA **FLUOXÉTINE**) ■ L'**ADRÉNALINE**, LES **AMPHÉTAMINES**, LA **MÉTHYLDOPA**, LA **LÉVODOPA**, LA **DOPAMINE**, LA **NORADRÉNALINE**, LA **GUANÉTHIDINE**, LA **RÉSERPINE** OU LES **VASOCONSTRICTEURS**, ADMINISTRÉS AVEC UN IMAO, PEUVENT ENTRAÎNER UNE CRISE HYPERTENSIVE ■ LES **OPIOÏDES**, ADMINISTRÉS EN CONCOMITANCE, PEUVENT INDUIRE L'HYPERTENSION OU L'HYPOTENSION, LE COMA, DES CONVULSIONS ET MÊME LA MORT (ÉVITER L'USAGE DE LA **MÉPÉRIDINE** DANS LES 14 À 21 JOURS SUIVANT OU PRÉCÉDANT LE TRAITEMENT PAR UN IMAO – RÉDUIRE LA DOSE INITIALE DES AUTRES AGENTS À 25 % DE LA DOSE HABITUELLE) ■ L'usage concomitant de **dextrométhorphane** peut induire l'hypertension, l'excitation et l'hyperpyrexie; des effets similaires peuvent survenir lors de l'administration concomitante de **tryptophane** (éviter toute association avec du tryptophane ou commencer le traitement à de très faibles doses) ■ Risque d'hypertension en cas d'administration concomitante de **buspirone**; attendre 10 jours entre les deux traitements ■ Risque de stimulation excessive du SNC et d'hypertension en cas d'administration concomitante de **méthylphénidate** ■ Risque d'hypotension additive lors d'un traitement concomitant par des **antihypertenseurs** ou d'une **anesthésie rachidienne** ■ Risque d'hypoglycémie additive en cas d'usage concomitant d'**insulines** ou d'**hypoglycémiants oraux**.

Médicament-aliments: Risque de crise hypertensive en cas de consommation d'aliments riches en **tyramine** (voir l'annexe J) ■ La consommation d'aliments ou de boissons riches en **caféine** augmente le risque d'hypertension et d'arythmies.

VOIES D'ADMINISTRATION ET POSOLOGIE

Phénelzine

- **PO (adultes)**: 15 mg, 3 fois par jour; augmenter la dose jusqu'à 60 à 90 mg par jour, en prises fractionnées, puis la réduire graduellement jusqu'à la plus petite dose efficace (15 mg par jour ou tous les 2 jours).

Tranylcypromine

- **PO (adultes)**: 10 mg, 2 fois par jour (matin et après-midi); si la réponse est insuffisante après 2 à 3 semaines, on peut augmenter la dose jusqu'à 20 mg, le matin, et 10 mg, l'après-midi. Lorsqu'on administre la tranylcypromine en même temps que des électrochocs, on utilise habituellement 10 mg, 2 fois par jour, pendant le traitement par les électrochocs, puis on diminue la posologie pour la faire passer à 10 mg, 1 fois par jour, en traitement d'entretien.

PRÉSENTATION

- **Phénelzine**
  Comprimés: 15 mg[Pr].
- **Tranylcypromine**
  Comprimés: 10 mg[Pr].

I

SOINS INFIRMIERS

ÉVALUATION DE LA SITUATION

- Suivre l'état mental, les changements d'humeur et le degré d'anxiété à intervalles fréquents. Rester à l'affût des idées suicidaires, particulièrement au début du traitement. Limiter la quantité de médicament dont le patient peut disposer.
- MESURER LA PRESSION ARTÉRIELLE ET LE POULS AVANT LE TRAITEMENT ET À INTERVALLES RÉGULIERS PENDANT TOUTE SA DURÉE. INFORMER LE MÉDECIN DE TOUT CHANGEMENT MARQUÉ.
- Effectuer le bilan quotidien des ingesta et des excreta, et peser le patient tous les jours. Suivre de près l'œdème périphérique et la rétention urinaire.

I

Tests de laboratoire:

- Noter les résultats des tests de la fonction hépatique à intervalles réguliers chez les patients qui reçoivent un traitement de longue durée ou à doses élevées.
- Suivre de près la glycémie chez les patients diabétiques; il y a risque d'hypoglycémie.

TOXICITÉ ET SURDOSAGE:

- LA CONSOMMATION CONCOMITANTE D'ALIMENTS RICHES EN TYRAMINE ET DE NOMBREUX MÉDICAMENTS PEUT ENTRAÎNER UNE CRISE HYPERTENSIVE METTANT LA VIE DU PATIENT EN DANGER. LES SIGNES ET LES SYMPTÔMES D'UNE CRISE HYPERTENSIVE SONT LES SUIVANTS: DOULEURS THORACIQUES, TACHYCARDIE, CÉPHALÉES INTENSES, NAUSÉES ET VOMISSEMENTS, PHOTOSENSIBILITÉ ET DILATATION DES PUPILLES. LE TRAITEMENT DE CETTE CRISE COMPREND, ENTRE AUTRES, L'ADMINISTRATION DE PHENTOLAMINE PAR VOIE IV.
- Les symptômes du surdosage sont les suivants: anxiété, irritabilité, tachycardie, hypertension ou hypotension, détresse respiratoire, étourdissements, somnolence, hallucinations, confusion, convulsions, fièvre et diaphorèse. Pour contrer ces symptômes, il faut effectuer un lavage gastrique et assurer un traitement de soutien.

DIAGNOSTICS INFIRMIERS POSSIBLES

- Stratégies d'adaptation inefficaces (Indications).
- Connaissances insuffisantes sur le traitement médicamenteux (Enseignement au patient et à ses proches).
- Non-observance du traitement médicamenteux (Enseignement au patient et à ses proches).

INTERVENTIONS INFIRMIÈRES

- Ne pas administrer ces médicaments le soir, étant donné que la stimulation psychomotrice peut entraîner de l'insomnie ou d'autres troubles du sommeil.

PO: En cas de difficultés de déglutition, on peut écraser les comprimés et les mélanger avec des aliments ou des liquides.

ENSEIGNEMENT AU PATIENT ET À SES PROCHES

- Conseiller au patient de respecter rigoureusement la posologie recommandée. S'il n'a pu prendre le médicament au moment habituel, il doit le prendre dans les 2 heures, sinon il doit sauter cette dose et reprendre son schéma posologique habituel. Le traitement ne devrait pas être interrompu brusquement, en raison du risque de symptômes de sevrage: nausées, vomissements, malaises, cauchemars, agitation, psychose, convulsions.
- METTRE LE PATIENT EN GARDE CONTRE LA CONSOMMATION D'ALCOOL, DE DÉPRESSEURS DU SNC, DE MÉDICAMENTS EN VENTE LIBRE OU D'ALIMENTS OU BOISSONS QUI RENFERMENT DE LA TYRAMINE (VOIR L'ANNEXE J), TOUT AU LONG DU TRAITEMENT ET PENDANT AU MOINS 2 SEMAINES APRÈS L'AVOIR ARRÊTÉ, EN RAISON DU RISQUE DE CRISE HYPERTENSIVE. LUI CONSEILLER DE COMMUNIQUER IMMÉDIATEMENT AVEC UN PROFESSIONNEL DE LA SANTÉ SI DES SYMPTÔMES DE CRISE HYPERTENSIVE SE MANIFESTENT.
- Prévenir le patient que les IMAO peuvent provoquer de la somnolence ou des étourdissements. Lui conseiller de ne pas conduire et d'éviter les activités qui exigent sa vigilance jusqu'à ce qu'on ait la certitude que ces médicaments n'entraînent pas ces effets chez lui.
- Recommander au patient de changer lentement de position afin de réduire le risque d'hypotension orthostatique. Les personnes âgées sont prédisposées à cet effet secondaire.
- Recommander au patient de consulter un professionnel de la santé en cas de sécheresse de la bouche, de rétention urinaire ou de constipation. Lui conseiller de se rincer fréquemment la bouche, de pratiquer une bonne hygiène buccale et de consommer de la gomme ou des bonbons sans sucre pour soulager la sécheresse de la bouche. L'augmentation de la consommation de liquides et de fibres ainsi que l'exercice peuvent prévenir la constipation.
- Recommander au patient de consulter un professionnel de la santé en cas de céphalées graves, de palpitations, d'une sensation d'oppression au niveau du thorax ou de la gorge, de transpiration, d'étour-

dissements, de raideurs à la nuque, de nausées ou de vomissements.

- Recommander au patient qui doit suivre un autre traitement ou subir une intervention chirurgicale d'avertir le professionnel de la santé qu'il suit un traitement avec un de ces médicaments. Dans la mesure du possible, le traitement devrait être interrompu au moins 2 semaines avant l'intervention chirurgicale.
- Conseiller au patient de porter en tout temps un bracelet d'identité où sont inscrits son problème de santé et son traitement médicamenteux.
- Insister sur le fait qu'il est important d'entreprendre une psychothérapie, si celle-ci est recommandée par un professionnel de la santé, et de se soumettre à des examens de suivi permettant d'évaluer l'efficacité du traitement. Des tests ophtalmologiques devraient également être effectués à intervalles réguliers lors d'un traitement de longue durée.

VÉRIFICATION DE L'EFFICACITÉ THÉRAPEUTIQUE

L'efficacité du traitement peut être démontrée par: l'amélioration de l'humeur chez les patients dépressifs ■ la baisse de l'anxiété ■ un gain d'appétit ■ un regain d'énergie ■ l'amélioration du sommeil ■ Les effets thérapeutiques du médicament peuvent ne pas se manifester avant 1 à 4 semaines.

INHIBITEURS DE L'ANHYDRASE CARBONIQUE

acétazolamide

Apo-Acetazolamide, Diamox

méthazolamide

Apo-Methazolamide, Neptazane

CLASSIFICATION:

Anticonvulsivants, diurétiques, agents utilisés dans le traitement du glaucome (inhibiteurs de l'anhydrase carbonique)

Grossesse – catégorie C

Les renseignements sur les inhibiteurs de l'anhydrase carbonique pour usage ophtalmique se trouvent à l'annexe N.

INDICATIONS

Diminution de la pression intraoculaire lors du traitement du glaucome chronique (angle ouvert) et du glaucome secondaire, ainsi que traitement préopératoire du glaucome aigu à angle fermé, afin d'abaisser la pression intraoculaire avant l'intervention chirurgicale ■ **Acétazolamide -** Traitement d'appoint des convulsions réfractaires ■ Œdème dû à une insuffisance cardiaque ou à des médicaments. **Usages non approuvés: Acétazolamide -** prévention de la formation de calculs rénaux composés d'acide urique ou de cystine ■ traitement du mal d'altitude (forme aiguë).

MÉCANISME D'ACTION

Diminution de la sécrétion de l'humeur aqueuse par l'inhibition de l'anhydrase carbonique dans le processus ciliaire de l'œil ■ Inhibition de l'anhydrase carbonique rénale entraînant une excrétion urinaire spontanément résolutive du sodium, du potassium, du bicarbonate et de l'eau ■ Diminution possible de la décharge anormale des neurones par inhibition de l'anhydrase carbonique du SNC et de la diurèse qui en résulte ■ Diurèse alcaline qui prévient également la précipitation de l'acide urique ou de la cystine contenus dans les voies urinaires. ***Effets thérapeutiques:*** Abaissement de la pression intraoculaire ■ Maîtrise de certains types de convulsions ■ Prévention et traitement du mal d'altitude (forme aiguë) ■ Prévention de la formation de calculs rénaux composés d'acide urique et de cystine.

PHARMACOCINÉTIQUE

Absorption: Bonne (PO). Biodisponibilité à 100 % (IV).
Distribution: Les inhibiteurs de l'anhydase carbonique traversent la barrière placentaire. L'acétazolamide passe dans le lait maternel.
Liaison aux protéines: *Acétazolamide* – de 90 à 95 %. *Méthazolamide* – environ 55 %.
Métabolisme et excrétion: *Acétazolamide* – excrétion à l'état inchangé dans l'urine de 70 à 100 %. *Méthazolamide* –Métabolisme partiellement hépatique. De 15 à 30 % est excrété à l'état inchangé dans l'urine.
Demi-vie: *Acétazolamide* – de 2,4 à 5,8 heures. *Méthazolamide* – 14 heures.

Profil temps-action (diminution de la pression intraoculaire)

	DÉBUT D'ACTION	PIC	DURÉE
Acétazolamide PO	1 h	2 - 4 h	8 - 12 h
Acétazolamide IV	2 min	15 min	4 - 5 h
Méthazolamide PO	2 - 4 h	6 - 8 h	10 - 18 h

CONTRE-INDICATIONS, PRÉCAUTIONS ET MISES EN GARDE

Contre-indications: Risque d'hypersensibilité ou de sensibilité croisée avec les sulfamides ■ Il est déconseillé d'administrer en même temps les inhibiteurs de l'anhydrase carbonique par voie orale et ceux qui sont destinés à un usage ophtalmique (brinzolamide et dorzolamide) ▪ Faibles concentrations sériques de sodium ou de potassium ▪ Insuffisance rénale ou hépatique graves ▪ Insuffisance surrénalienne ▪ Cirrhose (risque accru d'encéphalopathie hépatique) ▪ Acidose hyperchlorémique ▪ *Acétazolamide* – patients souffrant de glaucome chronique non congestif à angle fermé (administration prolongée).

Précautions et mises en garde: Maladie respiratoire chronique ou acidose respiratoire (risque de déclencher ou d'aggraver l'acidose) ▪ Anomalies électrolytiques ▪ Diabète (risque d'élévation du taux de glucose sanguin ou urinaire) ▪ **OBST.:** Grossesse (éviter l'utilisation pendant le premier trimestre) ou allaitement ▪ **PÉD.:** L'innocuité du médicament n'a pas été établie.

RÉACTIONS INDÉSIRABLES ET EFFETS SECONDAIRES

SNC: dépression, fatigue, faiblesse, somnolence.
ORLO: myopie passagère, acouphènes.
GI: anorexie, goût métallique, nausées, vomissements.
GU: cristallurie, calculs rénaux.
Tég.: rash, photosensibilité.
End.: hyperglycémie.
HÉ: acidose hyperchlorémique, hypokaliémie.
Hémat.: ANÉMIE APLASIQUE, ANÉMIE HÉMOLYTIQUE, LEUCOPÉNIE, THROMBOPÉNIE.
Métab.: perte de poids, hyperuricémie.
SN: paresthésie.
Divers: réactions allergiques incluant l'ANAPHYLAXIE et le SYNDROME DE STEVENS-JOHNSON.

INTERACTIONS

Médicament-médicament: Ces médicaments augmentent l'excrétion rénale des **barbituriques**, de l'**aspirine** et du **lithium**, ce qui peut en diminuer l'efficacité ▪ Les inhibiteurs de l'anhydrase carbonique diminuent l'excrétion des **amphétamines**, de la **quinidine**, du **procaïnamide** et, parfois, des **antidépresseurs tricycliques**, d'où un risque d'intoxication par ces agents ▪ L'utilisation concomitante de **topiramate** peut augmenter le risque de lithiase rénale ▪ L'hypokaliémie causée par les inhibiteurs de l'anhydrase carbonique peut augmenter le risque d'intoxication par la **digoxine** ▪ Risque d'élévation des concentrations de **cyclosporine** lors de l'administration concomitante d'acétazolamide.

VOIES D'ADMINISTRATION ET POSOLOGIE

Acétazolamide

- **PO (adultes):** *Glaucome* – de 250 à 1 000 mg par jour, en 1 seule dose ou en 2 à 4 doses fractionnées (jusqu'à 250 mg, toutes les 4 heures). *Épilepsie* – de 8 à 30 mg/kg/jour, en 1 seule dose ou en 2 à 4 doses fractionnées (maximum: 1 000 mg par jour). *Insuffisance cardiaque, œdème induit par les médicaments* – la posologie recommandée est de 250 à 375 mg, 1 fois par jour, le matin; l'effet diurétique est plus efficace lorsqu'on administre le médicament un jour sur deux. *Mal d'altitude* – de 500 à 1 000 mg/jour, que l'on prendra en 2 ou 3 doses fractionnées, 48 heures avant l'ascension et tout au long de celle-ci par la suite, si besoin est.
- **PO (enfants):** *Glaucome* – de 8 à 30 mg/kg/jour, en 3 doses fractionnées. Ne pas dépasser 1 g/jour. *Épilepsie* – de 8 à 30 mg/kg/jour, en 1 seule dose ou en 2 à 4 doses fractionnées (maximum: 1 000 mg par jour).
- **IV (adultes):** *Glaucome aigu* – de 250 à 500 mg; on peut répéter l'administration de 2 à 4 heures plus tard.
- **IV (enfants):** *Glaucome aigu* – de 20 à 40 mg/kg/jour, en 4 doses fractionnées. Ne pas dépasser 1 g/jour.

Méthazolamide

- **PO (adultes):** De 50 à 100 mg, 2 ou 3 fois par jour.

PRÉSENTATION

- **Acétazolamide**
  Comprimés: 250 mg^{Pr} ▪ **Poudre pour injection:** 500 mg (produit non commercialisé au Canada, disponible par l'intermédiaire du Programme d'accès spécial de Santé Canada).
- **Méthazolamide**
  Comprimés: 50 mg^{Pr}.

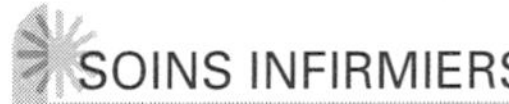

SOINS INFIRMIERS

ÉVALUATION DE LA SITUATION

- Rester à l'affût des signes suivants d'hypokaliémie: faiblesse musculaire, malaise, fatigue, modifications de l'ÉCG, vomissements.
- Vérifier si le patient n'est pas allergique aux sulfamides.

Pression intraoculaire: Suivre de près la gêne oculaire ou la diminution de l'acuité visuelle.

Convulsions: Observer étroitement l'état neurologique des patients qui reçoivent l'acétazolamide pour maîtriser les convulsions. Prendre les précautions de rigueur dans ce cas.

Mal d'altitude: Suivre de près le patient pour s'assurer que la gravité des symptômes suivants a diminué: céphalées, nausées, vomissements, fatigue, étourdissements, somnolence, essoufflement. Prévenir immédiatement le médecin ou un autre professionnel de la santé si les symptômes neurologiques ou la dyspnée s'aggravent, ou si des râles ou des crépitations surviennent.

Tests de laboratoire:

- Examiner les concentrations d'électrolytes sériques et la numération globulaire et plaquettaire avant l'administration du médicament et à intervalles réguliers lors d'un traitement prolongé. Le médicament peut diminuer les concentrations de potassium et de bicarbonate ainsi que le nombre de leucocytes et d'érythrocytes, et élever les concentrations sériques de chlorure.
- Le médicament peut élever la glycémie et la glycosurie; noter soigneusement la glycémie et la glycosurie des patients diabétiques.
- Le médicament peut entraîner des résultats faussement positifs lors du dosage des protéines urinaires et des 17-hydroxycorticostéroïdes.
- Le médicament peut entraîner une élévation des concentrations sanguines d'ammoniaque, de bilirubine et d'acide urique, ainsi que des concentrations urinaires de calcium et d'urobilinogène urinaire. Il peut diminuer les concentrations urinaires de citrate.

DIAGNOSTICS INFIRMIERS POSSIBLES

- Trouble de la perception visuelle (Indications).
- Connaissances insuffisantes sur le traitement médicamenteux (Enseignement au patient et à ses proches).

INTERVENTIONS INFIRMIÈRES

- Encourager le patient à consommer de 2 à 3 L de liquides par jour, sauf contre-indication, pour prévenir la cristallurie et la formation de calculs rénaux.
- On devrait administrer un supplément de potassium sans chlorure en même temps que les inhibiteurs de l'anhydrase carbonique.

PO: Administrer le médicament avec des aliments pour réduire l'irritation gastro-intestinale. Dans le cas des patients qui éprouvent des difficultés de déglutition, on peut broyer les comprimés et les mélanger à un sirop de fruits pour en atténuer le goût amer.

ENSEIGNEMENT AU PATIENT ET À SES PROCHES

- Expliquer au patient qu'il doit respecter rigoureusement la posologie recommandée. S'il n'a pu prendre le médicament au moment habituel, il doit le prendre aussitôt que possible, sauf si c'est presque l'heure prévue pour la dose suivante. Le prévenir qu'il ne faut pas remplacer une dose manquée par une double dose. Chez les patients qui suivent un traitement anticonvulsif, on devrait éventuellement réduire graduellement la posologie avant d'arrêter l'administration du médicament.
- INFORMER LE PATIENT QU'IL DOIT PRÉVENIR UN PROFESSIONNEL DE LA SANTÉ EN CAS D'ENGOURDISSEMENT OU DE PICOTEMENTS AU NIVEAU DES MEMBRES, DE FAIBLESSE, DE RASH, DE MAL DE GORGE, DE SAIGNEMENTS INHABITUELS, DE FORMATION D'ECCHYMOSES AU MOINDRE TRAUMATISME OU DE FIÈVRE. EN PRÉSENCE DE RÉACTIONS HÉMATOPOÏÉTIQUES, DE FIÈVRE, DE RASH OU DE TROUBLES RÉNAUX, ON DEVRAIT CESSER LE TRAITEMENT PAR L'INHIBITEUR DE L'ANHYDRASE CARBONIQUE.
- Prévenir le patient que ce type de médicament peut parfois provoquer de la somnolence. Lui conseiller de ne pas conduire et d'éviter les activités qui exigent sa vigilance jusqu'à ce qu'on ait la certitude que l'agent qu'il prend n'entraîne pas cet effet chez lui.
- Inciter le patient à utiliser des écrans solaires et à porter des vêtements protecteurs pour prévenir les réactions de photosensibilité.

Pression intraoculaire: Inciter le patient à passer des examens ophtalmologiques à intervalles réguliers, car la perte de la vue peut être graduelle et indolore.

VÉRIFICATION DE L'EFFICACITÉ THÉRAPEUTIQUE

L'efficacité du traitement peut être démontrée par: la diminution de la pression intraoculaire, lorsqu'on administre le médicament pour traiter le glaucome (si le traitement échoue ou si le patient ne peut tolérer un inhibiteur de l'anhydrase carbonique, un autre pourrait être plus efficace et mieux toléré) ■ la diminution de la fréquence des convulsions ■ la prévention de l'apparition du mal d'altitude ■ la prévention de la formation de calculs de cystine ou d'acide urique dans les voies urinaires. ✳

INHIBITEURS DE L'ENZYME DE CONVERSION DE L'ANGIOTENSINE (IECA)

bénazépril

Apo-Benazepril, Lotensin

captopril

Apo-Capto, Capoten, Gen-Captopril, Novo-Captopril, PMS-Captopril

I

cilazapril
Inhibace, Novo-Cilazapril, PMS-Cilazapril

énalapril, énalaprilate
Vasotec, Vasotec IV

fosinopril
Apo-Fosinopril, Gen-Fosinopril, Monopril, Novo-Fosinopril

lisinopril
Apo-Lisinopril, Prinivil, Zestril

périndopril
Coversyl

quinapril
Accupril

ramipril
Apo-Ramipril, Altace

trandolapril
Mavik

CLASSIFICATION:
Antihypertenseurs (inhibiteurs de l'ECA)

Grossesse – catégories C (1er trimestre) et D (2e et 3e trimestres)

INDICATIONS

Hypertension – en monothérapie ou en association avec d'autres agents ■ **Captopril, cilazapril, énalapril, fosinopril, lisinopril, périndopril, quinapril:** Traitement de l'insuffisance cardiaque ■ **Captopril, lisinopril, ramipril, trandolapril:** Réduction du risque de décès ou d'apparition d'une insuffisance cardiaque par suite d'un infarctus du myocarde ■ **Captopril, énalapril, ramipril, trandolapril:** Ralentissement de l'évolution du dysfonctionnement du ventricule gauche vers une insuffisance cardiaque patente ■ **Captopril:** Ralentissement de l'évolution de la néphropathie diabétique ■ **Périndopril, ramipril:** Prévention des événements cardiaques.

MÉCANISME D'ACTION

Inhibition de la transformation de l'angiotensine I en angiotensine II, un vasoconstricteur. Les IECA inhibent la dégradation de la bradykinine, un vasodilatateur, et d'autres prostaglandines vasodilatatrices. Ils élèvent les concentrations plasmatiques de rénine et abaissent celles d'aldostérone. Ces effets entraînent une vasodilatation générale. ***Effets thérapeutiques:*** Abaissement de la pression artérielle chez les patients hypertendus ■ Diminution de la post-charge chez les patients atteints d'insuffisance cardiaque ■ Ralentissement de l'évolution vers une insuffisance cardiaque patente (seulement certains agents) ■ Prolongation de la survie après un infarctus du myocarde (seulement certains agents) ■ Ralentissement de l'évolution de la néphropathie diabétique (captopril seulement) ■ Diminution des événements cardiovasculaires d'issue fatale et non fatale chez les patients à risque (périndopril et ramipril seulement).

PHARMACOCINÉTIQUE

Absorption: *Bénazépril* – 37 % (PO). *Captopril* – 75 % (PO); de 30 à 55 %, lorsque le médicament est pris avec des aliments. *Cilazapril* – 75 % (PO). *Énalapril* – 60 % (PO). *Énalaprilate* – biodisponibilité à 100 % (IV). *Fosinopril* – 36 % (PO). *Lisinopril* – 25 % (PO; très variable). *Périndopril* – 75 % (PO); transformation rapide en périndoprilate, le métabolite actif, dont la biodisponibilité est à 35 %. *Quinapril* – 60 % (PO) (les aliments riches en matières grasses en diminuent l'absorption). *Ramipril* – de 50 à 60 % (PO). *Trandolapril* – transformation en trandolaprilate (forme active); la biodisponibilité du trandolapril est de 10 % et celle du trandolaprilate, de 70 %.

Distribution: Tous les IECA traversent la barrière placentaire. *Bénazépril, bénazéprilate, captopril, énalapril, énalaprilate et fosinoprilate* – de faibles quantités passent dans le lait maternel. *Lisinopril* – quantités infimes dans le SNC. *Quinapril* – ce médicament passe dans le lait maternel. *Ramipril* – ce médicament ne passe probablement pas dans le lait maternel. *Trandolapril* – ce médicament passe probablement dans le lait maternel.

Liaison aux protéines: *Bénazépril* – 96,7 % (*bénazéprilate* – 95,3 %), *fosinopril* – de 89 à 99,8 %, *quinapril* – 97 %.

Métabolisme et excrétion: *Bénazépril* – métabolisme hépatique, avec transformation en bénazéprilate, le métabolite actif; excrétion rénale à 20 % et excrétion non rénale de 10 à 11 % (élimination biliaire). *Captopril* – métabolisme hépatique à 50 %, avec transformation en composés inactifs; excrétion rénale à 95 % (50 % sous forme inchangée). *Cilazapril* – métabolisme hépatique et sanguin, avec transformation en cilazaprilate, le métabolite actif; excrétion rénale à plus de 90 %, sous forme de cilazaprilate principalement. *Énalapril, énalaprilate* – métabolisme hépatique, avec transformation en énalaprilate, le métabolite actif; excrétion rénale à 61 % (18 % sous forme d'énalapril et 43 % sous forme d'énalaprilate); 33 % est éliminé dans les fèces (6 % sous forme d'énalapril et 27 % sous forme d'énalaprilate). *Fosinopril* – métabolisme par le foie et la muqueuse gastro-intestinale, avec transformation en fosinoprilate, le métabolite actif; excrétion rénale à 50 % et fécale à 50 %. *Lisinopril* – excrétion rénale à 100 %. *Périndopril* – métabolisme hépatique, avec transformation en périndoprilate, le métabolite actif; le périndoprilate et ses métabolites sont principalement excrétés par les reins. *Quinapril* – métabolisme hépatique, avec transformation en quinaprilate, le métabolite actif; excrétion rénale à 61 % et fécale à 33 %. *Ramipril* – métabolisme hépatique, avec transformation en ramiprilate, le métabolite actif; excrétion rénale à 60 % et fécale à 40 %. *Trandolapril* – métabolisme hépatique, avec transformation en trandolaprilate, le métabolite actif; excrétion rénale à 33 % et fécale à 66 %, principalement sous forme de trandolaprilate.

Demi-vie: *Bénazéprilate* – de 10 à 11 heures. *Captopril* – < 3 heures (prolongée en cas d'insuffisance rénale). *Cilazaprilate* – de 30 à 50 heures. *Énalaprilate* – 11 heures (prolongée en cas d'insuffisance rénale). *Fosinoprilate* – 12 heures. *Lisinopril* – 12 heures (prolongée en cas d'insuffisance rénale). *Périndoprilate* – 10 heures, avec une demi-vie d'élimination terminale prolongée de 30 à 120 heures, qui témoigne de la lente dissociation des sites de liaison tissulaire et du plasma. *Quinaprilate* – 2 heures. *Ramiprilate* – de 13 à 17 heures (prolongée en cas d'insuffisance rénale). *Trandolaprilate* – de 16 à 24 heures.

Profil temps-action
(effet sur la pression artérielle – une seule dose)†

	Début d'action	Pic	Durée
Bénazépril	en 1 h	2 - 4 h	24 h
Captopril	15 - 60 min	60 - 90 min	6 - 12 h
Cilazapril	1 h	3 - 7 h	> 24 h
Énalapril PO	1 h	4 - 6 h	12 - 24 h
Énalapril IV	15 min	1 - 4 h	6 h
Fosinopril	en 1 h	2 - 6 h	24 h
Lisinopril	1 h	6 h	24 h
Périndopril	1 h	3 - 7 h	24 h
Quinapril	en 1 h	2 - 4 h	jusqu'à 24 h
Ramipril	1 - 2 h	4 - 6 h	24 h
Trandolapril	1 - 4 h	6 - 8 h	24 h

† Plusieurs semaines peuvent s'écouler avant que les pleins effets du médicament deviennent manifestes.

CONTRE-INDICATIONS, PRÉCAUTIONS ET MISES EN GARDE

Contre-indications: Hypersensibilité (risque de réactions de sensibilité croisée avec les autres IECA) ■ **OBST.:** Risque accru de malformations congénitales majeures lors de l'utilisation au cours du premier trimestre; morbidité et mortalité fœtales importantes lors de l'utilisation au cours des 2e et 3e trimestres ■ Œdème angioneurotique lié à l'utilisation antérieure de n'importe quel IECA.

Précautions et mises en garde: Insuffisance rénale, insuffisance hépatique, hypovolémie, hyponatrémie ou traitement diurétique concomitant (réduction de la dose initiale recommandée pour la plupart des agents) ■ **GÉR.:** Il est recommandé de diminuer la dose chez les personnes âgées ou débilitées ■ Patients hypertendus de race noire (la monothérapie est moins efficace, un traitement additionnel pourrait être de mise) ■ Sténose aortique, cardiomyopathie hypertrophique ■ Maladie vasculaire cérébrale ou ischémie cardiaque ■ Anesthésie ou intervention chirurgicale (risque d'exacerbation de l'hypotension) ■ **ALLAITEMENT, PÉD.:** L'innocuité de la plupart des agents n'a pas été établie chez les femmes qui allaitent et chez les enfants.

EXTRÊME PRUDENCE: ANTÉCÉDENTS FAMILIAUX D'ŒDÈME ANGIONEUROTIQUE.

I

RÉACTIONS INDÉSIRABLES ET EFFETS SECONDAIRES

SNC: étourdissements, fatigue, céphalées, insomnie, faiblesse.

Resp.: toux.

CV: hypotension, angine de poitrine, tachycardie.

GI: altération du goût, anorexie, diarrhée, hépatotoxicité (rare), nausées.

GU: protéinurie, impuissance, insuffisance rénale.

Tég.: rash.

HÉ: hyperkaliémie.

Hémat.: AGRANULOCYTOSE, NEUTROPÉNIE (CAPTOPRIL SEULEMENT).

Divers: ŒDÈME ANGIONEUROTIQUE, fièvre.

INTERACTIONS

Médicament-médicament: Effets hypotenseurs excessifs lors de l'administration concomitante de **diurétiques** ■ L'administration concomitante d'autres **antihypertenseurs**, de **dérivés nitrés**, de **phénothiazines** ou l'ingestion de grandes quantités d'**alcool** peuvent entraîner un effet hypotenseur additif, effet pouvant aussi survenir lors d'une **intervention chirurgicale** ou d'une **anesthésie générale** ■ L'administration simultanée de **suppléments potassiques**, de **diurétiques épargneurs de potassium**, d'**indométhacine**, de **succédanés de sel** ou de **cyclosporine** peut entraîner de l'hyperkaliémie ■ Les **anti-inflammatoires non stéroïdiens** peuvent atténuer l'effet antihypertenseur des IECA ■ Les **antiacides** peuvent réduire l'absorption des IECA ■ Les IECA peuvent élever les concentrations sériques de **digoxine** et de **lithium** ainsi que le risque de toxicité par ces médicaments ■ Le **probénécide** diminue l'excrétion du captopril et en élève les concentrations ■ L'administration simultanée d'**allopurinol** peut accroître le risque de réactions d'hypersensibilité ■ La **capsaïcine** peut accroître l'incidence de la toux ■ La **rifampine** peut réduire l'efficacité de l'énalapril ■ Le quinapril peut réduire l'absorption de la **tétracycline** (en raison de la présence de magnésium dans les comprimés).

Médicament-aliments: Les **aliments** diminuent la transformation du périndopril en périndoprilate. Ils diminuent également l'absorption du captopril et du cilazapril.

VOIES D'ADMINISTRATION ET POSOLOGIE

Bénazépril

- **PO (adultes)**: 10 mg par jour, en 1 seule prise ou en 2 prises fractionnées, posologie qu'on peut augmenter graduellement à des intervalles de 2 semaines; dose d'entretien habituelle: 20 mg par jour, en 1 seule prise ou en 2 prises fractionnées. La dose quotidienne maximale est de 40 mg. Commencer le traitement par 5 mg par jour chez les patients prenant un diurétique.
- ***INSUFFISANCE RÉNALE***
  PO (ADULTES): Cl_{CR} < *30 mL/MIN* – AMORCER LE TRAITEMENT PAR UNE DOSE DE 5 mg PAR JOUR.

Captopril

- **PO (adultes)**: *Hypertension* – 25 mg par jour, en 2 ou en 3 prises; on peut augmenter cette dose à des intervalles de 1 ou 2 semaines, jusqu'à concurrence de 150 mg, 3 fois par jour (dose habituelle: 50 mg, 3 fois par jour; amorcer le traitement par une dose de 6,25 à 12,5 mg, 2 ou 3 fois par jour, chez les patients prenant un diurétique). *Insuffisance cardiaque* – de 6,25 à 12,5 mg, 3 fois par jour (chez les patients normotendus ou hypotendus, qui ont été soumis à un traitement énergique par des diurétiques et qui peuvent présenter une hyponatrémie et/ou une hypovolémie). Chez la plupart des patients la dose initiale est de 25 mg, 3 fois par jour. On peut augmenter cette dose jusqu'à concurrence de 50 à 100 mg, 3 fois par jour (posologie habituelle de 12,5 à 450 mg par jour). *Après un infarctus du myocarde* – dose d'essai de 6,25 mg, suivie d'une dose de 12,5 mg, 3 fois par jour; on peut augmenter cette dose jusqu'à concurrence de 50 mg, 3 fois par jour. *Néphropathie diabétique* – 25 mg, 3 fois par jour.
- ***INSUFFISANCE RÉNALE***
  PO (ADULTES): AMORCER LE TRAITEMENT PAR UNE DOSE DE 6,25 À 12,5 mg, 2 OU 3 FOIS PAR JOUR.

Cilazapril

- **PO (adultes)**: *Hypertension* – initialement, 2,5 mg, 1 fois par jour; on peut porter la dose à 5 mg par jour, si nécessaire, après un intervalle d'au moins 2 semaines (dose quotidienne maximale: 10 mg). Chez les patients prenant un diurétique, amorcer le traitement à une dose de 0,5 mg, 1 fois par jour. *Insuffisance cardiaque* – 0,5 mg, 1 fois par jour (commencer le traitement sous étroite surveillance médicale); la dose peut être portée à 1 mg, 1 fois par jour, en l'espace de 5 jours (posologie habituelle de 1 à 2,5 mg, 1 fois par jour selon la réponse au traitement et la tolérance du patient).
- ***INSUFFISANCE RÉNALE***
  PO (ADULTES): Cl_{CR} > *40 mL/MIN* – 1 mg, 1 FOIS PAR JOUR (DOSE QUOTIDIENNE MAXIMALE: 5 mg); Cl_{CR} *DE 10 À 40 mL/MIN* – 0,5 mg, 1 FOIS PAR JOUR (DOSE QUOTIDIENNE MAXIMALE: 2,5 mg); Cl_{CR} < *10 mL/MIN* – DE 0,25 À 0,5 mg, 1 OU 2 FOIS PAR SEMAINE, SELON LA RÉPONSE AU TRAITEMENT.

Énalapril, énalaprilate

- **PO (adultes)**: *Hypertension* – 5 mg, 1 fois par jour; on peut augmenter cette dose, selon la réponse clinique (posologie habituelle: de 10 à 40 mg par jour, en 1 seule prise ou en 2 prises fractionnées; amorcer le traitement à une dose de 2,5 mg, 1 fois par jour, chez les patients prenant un diurétique). *Insuffisance cardiaque* – 2,5 mg, 1 fois par jour; on peut augmenter la dose selon la réponse clinique (posologie habituelle: de 5 à 20 mg par jour, en 1 seule prise ou en 2 prises fractionnées). La dose quotidienne maximale est de 40 mg. *Dysfonctionnement asymptomatique du ventricule gauche* – 2,5 mg, 1 fois par jour; on peut augmenter la dose selon la réponse clinique (posologie habituelle: de 5 à 20 mg par jour, en 1 seule prise ou en 2 prises fractionnées). La dose quotidienne maximale est de 40 mg.
- **PO (personnes âgées)**: 2,5 mg, 1 fois par jour initialement; augmenter la dose selon la réponse clinique et la tolérance du patient.
- **PO (enfants < 16 ans)**: 0,08 mg/kg (maximum de 5 mg), 1 fois par jour; augmenter la dose selon la réponse clinique et la tolérance du patient. La dose maximale quotidienne est de 0,58 mg/kg (ou 40 mg).
- **IV (adultes)**: 1,25 mg (0,625 mg chez les patients prenant un diurétique), toutes les 6 heures. La dose quotidienne maximale est de 20 mg.
- ***INSUFFISANCE RÉNALE***
  PO (ADULTES): $Cl_{CR} \leq$ *30 mL/MIN* – AMORCER LE TRAITEMENT PAR UNE DOSE DE 2,5 mg, 1 FOIS PAR JOUR.
  IV (ADULTES): $Cl_{CR} \leq$ *30 mL/MIN* – AMORCER LE TRAITEMENT PAR UNE DOSE DE 0,625 mg, TOUTES LES 6 HEURES; AJUSTER SELON LA RÉPONSE CLINIQUE.

Fosinopril

- **PO (adultes)**: *Hypertension* – 10 mg, 1 fois par jour; on peut augmenter cette dose, selon les besoins (posologie: de 20 à 40 mg, 1 fois par jour). *Insuffisance cardiaque* – 10 mg, 1 fois par jour (5 mg, chez les patients qui ont subi une diurèse vigoureuse); on peut augmenter cette dose graduellement, pendant plusieurs semaines, pour atteindre 40 mg, 1 fois par jour (posologie habituelle: de 20 à 40 mg par jour).

Lisinopril

- **PO (adultes)**: *Hypertension* – 10 mg, 1 fois par jour; on peut augmenter cette dose jusqu'à concurrence de 20 à 40 mg par jour (amorcer le traitement par une dose de 5 mg par jour, chez les patients prenant un diurétique). La dose quotidienne maximale est de 80 mg. *Insuffisance cardiaque* – 2,5 mg, 1 fois par jour; on peut augmenter la dose selon la réponse clinique et la tolérance du patient (posologie habituelle: de 5 à 20 mg, 1 fois par jour). *Prolongation de la survie après un infarctus du myocarde* – 5 mg, 1 fois par jour, pendant 2 jours, puis 10 mg, 1 fois par jour.
- ***INSUFFISANCE RÉNALE***

  PO (ADULTES): *CL_{CR} DE 10 À 30 mL/MIN* – INITIALEMENT, DE 2,5 À 5 mg, 1 FOIS PAR JOUR; *CL_{CR} < 10 mL/MIN* – INITIALEMENT, 2,5 mg, 1 FOIS PAR JOUR; ON PEUT AUGMENTER CETTE DOSE, SELON LA RÉPONSE CLINIQUE, JUSQU'À CONCURRENCE DE 40 mg PAR JOUR.

Périndopril

- **PO (adultes)**: *Hypertension* – 4 mg, 1 fois par jour; on peut augmenter la dose jusqu'à concurrence de 8 mg par jour, en 1 seule prise ou en 2 prises fractionnées (amorcer le traitement par 2 mg, 1 fois par jour, chez les patients prenant un diurétique). *Insuffisance cardiaque* – 2 mg, 1 fois par jour; on peut porter la dose à 4 mg, 1 fois par jour, après 2 à 4 semaines. La dose quotidienne habituelle est de 4 mg. *Prévention des événements cardiaques* – 4 mg, 1 fois par jour, pendant 2 semaines (chez les personnes âgées de > 75 ans, débuter à une dose de 2 mg, 1 fois par jour pendant la première semaine, puis porter à 4 mg, 1 fois par jour pendant la deuxième semaine); on peut ensuite augmenter la dose selon la tolérance du patient, jusqu'à une dose d'entretien de 8 mg, 1 fois par jour.
- **PO (personnes âgées)**: 2 mg, 1 fois par jour; on peut augmenter la dose jusqu'à concurrence de 4 mg par jour, en 1 seule prise ou en 2 prises fractionnées.
- ***INSUFFISANCE RÉNALE***

  PO (ADULTES): *CL_{CR} DE 30 À 60 mL/MIN* – INITIALEMENT, 2 mg, 1 FOIS PAR JOUR; *CL_{CR} DE 15 À 30 mL/MIN* – 2 mg, TOUS LES 2 JOURS; *CL_{CR} < 15 mL/MIN* – 2 mg, LE JOUR DE LA DIALYSE.

Quinapril

- **PO (adultes)**: *Hypertension* – initialement, de 10 à 20 mg, 1 fois par jour; on peut augmenter cette dose, à intervalles d'au moins 2 semaines, jusqu'à concurrence de 40 mg par jour, en 1 seule prise ou en 2 prises fractionnées. Amorcer le traitement par une dose de 5 mg par jour, chez les patients prenant un diurétique. *Insuffisance cardiaque* – initialement, 5 mg, 1 fois par jour; on peut augmenter cette dose selon la réponse clinique et la tolérance du patient jusqu'à concurrence de 40 mg par jour, en 2 prises fractionnées.
- ***INSUFFISANCE RÉNALE***

  PO (ADULTES): *CL_{CR} > 60 mL/MIN* – AMORCER LE TRAITEMENT PAR UNE DOSE DE 10 mg, 1 FOIS PAR JOUR; *CL_{CR} DE 30 À 60 mL/MIN* – AMORCER LE TRAITEMENT PAR UNE DOSE DE 5 mg, 1 FOIS PAR JOUR; *CL_{CR} DE 10 À 30 mL/MIN* – AMORCER LE TRAITEMENT PAR UNE DOSE DE 2,5 mg, 1 FOIS PAR JOUR; *CL_{CR} < 10 mL/MIN* – L'INNOCUITÉ DU MÉDICAMENT, DANS CE CAS, N'A PAS ÉTÉ ÉTABLIE.

Ramipril

- **PO (adultes)**: *Hypertension* – 2,5 mg, 1 fois par jour; on peut augmenter graduellement cette dose à intervalles d'au moins 2 semaines pour atteindre 20 mg par jour, en 1 seule prise ou en 2 prises fractionnées (amorcer le traitement par une dose de 1,25 mg par jour chez les patients prenant un diurétique). *Insuffisance cardiaque après un infarctus du myocarde* – initialement, de 1,25 à 2,5 mg, 2 fois par jour; on peut augmenter cette dose selon la tolérance du patient jusqu'à concurrence de 5 mg, 2 fois par jour. *Prévention des événements cardiaques* – 2,5 mg, 1 fois par jour; on peut augmenter graduellement la dose pour atteindre la dose d'entretien habituelle de 10 mg par jour.
- ***INSUFFISANCE RÉNALE***

  PO (ADULTES): *HYPERTENSION* – *CL_{CR} DE 10 À 40 mL/MIN* – AMORCER LE TRAITEMENT À UNE DOSE DE 1,25 mg, 1 FOIS PAR JOUR; ON PEUT AUGMENTER GRADUELLEMENT LA DOSE JUSQU'À CONCURRENCE DE 5 mg PAR JOUR. *CL_{CR} < 10 mL/MIN* – AMORCER LE TRAITEMENT À UNE DOSE DE 1,25 mg, 1 FOIS PAR JOUR; ON PEUT AUGMENTER GRADUELLEMENT LA DOSE JUSQU'À CONCURRENCE DE 2,5 mg PAR JOUR.

INSUFFISANCE CARDIAQUE APRÈS UN INFARCTUS DU MYOCARDE – CL_{CR} DE 20 À 50 mL/MIN – AMORCER LE TRAITEMENT À UNE DOSE DE 1,25 mg, 1 FOIS PAR JOUR; ON PEUT AUGMENTER LA DOSE AVEC PRUDENCE JUSQU'À 1,25 mg, 2 FOIS PAR JOUR.

Trandolapril

- **PO (adultes)**: *Hypertension* – 1 mg, 1 fois par jour; on peut augmenter cette dose, toutes les semaines, pour atteindre 4 mg, 1 fois par jour; une administration biquotidienne peut être de mise chez certains patients (amorcer le traitement par une dose de 0,5 mg par jour, chez les patients prenant un diurétique). *Insuffisance cardiaque ou dysfonctionnement du ventricule gauche après un infarctus du myocarde* – initialement, 1 mg, 1 fois par jour; augmenter graduellement cette dose pour atteindre, si possible, 4 mg, 1 fois par jour.
- ***INSUFFISANCE RÉNALE***
  PO (ADULTES): *CL_{CR} < 30 mL/MIN* – AMORCER LE TRAITEMENT À UNE DOSE DE 0,5 mg, 1 FOIS PAR JOUR; ON PEUT AUGMENTER GRADUELLEMENT CETTE DOSE, SANS DÉPASSER 1 mg PAR JOUR. *CL_{CR} < 30 mL/MIN* – NE PAS DÉPASSER 0,5 mg PAR JOUR.
- ***INSUFFISANCE HÉPATIQUE***
  PO (ADULTES): AMORCER LE TRAITEMENT À UNE DOSE DE 0,5 mg, 1 FOIS PAR JOUR; ON PEUT AUGMENTER GRADUELLEMENT CETTE DOSE.

PRÉSENTATION

- **Bénazépril** (version générique disponible)
  Comprimés: 5 mg^{Pr}, 10 mg^{Pr}, 20 mg^{Pr}.
- **Captopril** (version générique disponible)
  Comprimés: 12,5 mg^{Pr}, 25 mg^{Pr}, 50 mg^{Pr}, 100 mg^{Pr}.
- **Cilazapril** (version générique disponible)
  Comprimés: 1 mg^{Pr}, 2,5 mg^{Pr}, 5 mg^{Pr} ■ **En association avec**: hydrochlorothiazide (Inhibace $plus^{Pr}$).
- **Énalapril** (version générique disponible)
  Comprimés: 2,5 mg^{Pr}, 5 mg^{Pr}, 10 mg^{Pr}, 20 mg^{Pr} ■ **En association avec**: hydrochlorothiazide ($Vaseretic^{Pr}$).
- **Énalaprilate**
  Solution pour injection: 1,25 mg/mL^{Pr}.
- **Fosinopril** (version générique disponible)
  Comprimés: 10 mg^{Pr}, 20 mg^{Pr}.
- **Lisinopril** (version générique disponible)
  Comprimés: 2,5 mg^{Pr}, 5 mg^{Pr}, 10 mg^{Pr}, 20 mg^{Pr} ■ **En association avec**: hydrochlorothiazide ($Prinzide^{Pr}$, $Zestoretic^{Pr}$).
- **Périndopril**
  Comprimés: 2 mg^{Pr}, 4 mg^{Pr}, 8 mg^{Pr} ■ **En association avec**: indapamide ($Coversyl^{Pr}$ Plus).
- **Quinapril**
  Comprimés: 5 mg^{Pr}, 10 mg^{Pr}, 20 mg^{Pr}, 40 mg^{Pr} ■ **En association avec**: hydrochlorothiazide ($Accuretic^{Pr}$).
- **Ramipril** (version générique disponible)
  Capsules: 1,25 mg^{Pr}, 2,5 mg^{Pr}, 5 mg^{Pr}, 10 mg^{Pr}, 15 mg^{Pr} ■ **En association avec**: hydrochlorothiazide ($Altace^{Pr}$ HCT).
- **Trandolapril**
  Capsules: 0,5 mg^{Pr}, 1 mg^{Pr}, 2 mg^{Pr}, 4 mg^{Pr} ■ **En association avec**: vérapamil ($Tarka^{Pr}$).

SOINS INFIRMIERS

ÉVALUATION DE LA SITUATION

Hypertension:

- Mesurer la pression artérielle et le pouls à intervalles fréquents pendant la période initiale d'ajustement de la posologie et à intervalles réguliers, pendant toute la durée du traitement. Avertir le médecin ou un autre professionnel de la santé s'il y a des changements importants.
- Vérifier la fréquence du renouvellement des ordonnances afin d'établir l'observance du traitement.

Insuffisance cardiaque: Peser régulièrement le patient et suivre de près les signes suivants pour déterminer si la surcharge liquidienne a été contrée: œdème périphérique, râles et crépitations, dyspnée, gain pondéral, turgescence des jugulaires.

Tests de laboratoire:

- Noter à intervalles réguliers les concentrations d'urée, de créatinine et d'électrolytes. Ces médicaments peuvent entraîner l'élévation des concentrations sériques de potassium, l'élévation passagère des concentrations sériques d'urée et de créatinine, et la diminution des concentrations de sodium. L'élévation des concentrations sériques d'urée ou de créatinine peut dicter une réduction de la dose ou l'arrêt du traitement.
- Vérifier l'hémogramme à intervalles réguliers tout au long du traitement. Ces médicaments peuvent entraîner, dans de rares cas, une légère baisse des concentrations d'hémoglobine et de l'hématocrite.
- Ces médicaments peuvent entraîner une élévation des concentrations d'AST, d'ALT, de phosphatase alcaline, de bilirubine sérique, d'acide urique et de glucose.
- Effectuer le dosage des protéines avant le traitement et à intervalles réguliers pendant une période allant jusqu'à un an chez les patients atteints d'insuffisance rénale ou chez ceux recevant > 150 mg/

jour de captopril. Si la protéinurie est trop élevée ou s'aggrave, réévaluer l'utilité du traitement par un IECA.

- Ces médicaments peuvent positiver les titres des ANA (anticorps antinucléaires).
- *Captopril*: le médicament peut entraîner des résultats faussement positifs lors du dosage des cétones dans l'urine.
- VÉRIFIER LA NUMÉRATION ET LA FORMULE LEUCOCYTAIRE, AVANT L'ADMINISTRATION INITIALE, TOUS LES MOIS PENDANT LES 3 À 6 PREMIERS MOIS DE TRAITEMENT, ET À INTERVALLES RÉGULIERS PAR LA SUITE, PENDANT UN AN, CHEZ LES PATIENTS EXPOSÉS AU RISQUE DE NEUTROPÉNIE (PATIENTS ATTEINTS D'INSUFFISANCE RÉNALE OU DE COLLAGÉNOSE AVEC MANIFESTATIONS VASCULAIRES OU CEUX RECEVANT DE FORTES DOSES), AINSI QU'AUX PREMIERS SIGNES D'INFECTION. ARRÊTER LE TRAITEMENT SI LE NOMBRE DE POLYNUCLÉAIRES NEUTROPHILES EST < $1{,}0 \times 10^9$/L.

DIAGNOSTICS INFIRMIERS POSSIBLES

- Débit cardiaque diminué (Indications).
- Connaissances insuffisantes sur le traitement médicamenteux (Enseignement au patient et à ses proches).
- Non-observance du traitement médicamenteux (Enseignement au patient et à ses proches).

INTERVENTIONS INFIRMIÈRES

PO: Une chute brusque de la pression artérielle en l'espace de 1 à 3 heures après l'administration de la première dose peut dicter l'expansion volémique avec un soluté salin normal, mais, en général, cela ne justifie pas l'arrêt du traitement. L'interruption du traitement par les diurétiques, 1 semaine avant le début du traitement par les IECA, peut diminuer le risque d'hypotension. Suivre de près la pression artérielle pendant au moins 1 heure après qu'elle a été stabilisée. Reprendre le traitement par les diurétiques si la pression artérielle n'est pas maîtrisée.

Captopril

PO: Administrer le médicament 1 heure avant ou 2 heures après les repas. On peut réduire les comprimés en poudre si le patient éprouve des difficultés de déglutition. Les comprimés peuvent avoir une odeur de soufre.

- On peut préparer une solution orale en réduisant en poudre un comprimé à 25 mg et en le dissolvant dans 25 à 100 mL d'eau. Bien mélanger pendant au moins 5 minutes et administrer dans les 30 minutes.

Énalaprilate

IV directe: On peut administrer l'énalaprilate sous forme non diluée.

***Vitesse d'administration*:** Administrer en au moins 5 minutes.

Perfusion intermittente: Diluer dans 50 mL de D5%E, de NaCl 0,9 %, de D5%/NaCl 0,9 % ou de D5%E avec une solution de lactate de Ringer. La solution diluée est stable pendant 24 heures. Consulter les directives du fabricant avant de reconstituer la préparation.

***Vitesse d'administration*:** Administrer la perfusion lentement.

Compatibilité (tubulure en Y): allopurinol ▪ amifostine ▪ amikacine ▪ aminophylline ▪ ampicilline ▪ ampicilline/sulbactam ▪ aztréonam ▪ butorphanol ▪ calcium, gluconate de ▪ céfazoline ▪ céfopérazone ▪ ceftazidime ▪ ceftizoxime ▪ chloramphénicol ▪ cimétidine ▪ cladribine ▪ clindamycine ▪ dextran 40 ▪ dobutamine ▪ dopamine ▪ érythromycine, lactobionate d' ▪ esmolol ▪ famotidine ▪ fentanyl ▪ filgrastim ▪ ganciclovir ▪ gentamycine ▪ granisétron ▪ héparine ▪ hétastarch ▪ hydrocortisone sodique, succinate d' ▪ labétalol ▪ lidocaïne ▪ magnésium, sulfate de ▪ melphalan ▪ méropénem ▪ méthylprednisolone sodique, succinate de ▪ métronidazole ▪ morphine ▪ nafcilline ▪ nicardipine ▪ nitroprusside ▪ pénicilline G potassique ▪ phénobarbital ▪ pipéracilline ▪ pipéracilline/tazobactam ▪ potassium, chlorure de ▪ potassium, phosphate de ▪ propofol ▪ ranitidine ▪ sodium, acétate de ▪ téniposide ▪ thiotépa ▪ tobramycine ▪ triméthoprime/sulfaméthoxazole ▪ vancomycine ▪ vinorelbine.

Incompatibilité (tubulure en Y): amphotéricine B ▪ céfépime ▪ phénytoïne.

Compatibilité en addition au soluté: dobutamine ▪ dopamine ▪ héparine ▪ méropénem ▪ nitroglycérine ▪ nitroprusside ▪ potassium, chlorure de.

Ramipril

PO: On peut ouvrir les capsules et en saupoudrer le contenu sur de la compote de pommes, l'ajouter à du jus de pomme, ou le dissoudre dans 125 mL d'eau, dans le cas des patients qui éprouvent des difficultés de déglutition, sans que l'efficacité du médicament en soit diminuée. Les mélanges ainsi préparés peuvent être conservés jusqu'à 24 heures à la température ambiante ou jusqu'à 48 heures au réfrigérateur.

ENSEIGNEMENT AU PATIENT ET À SES PROCHES

- Conseiller au patient de respecter rigoureusement la posologie recommandée, de prendre le médicament à la même heure tous les jours, et de continuer le traitement même s'il se sent bien. S'il n'a pas pu prendre le médicament au moment habituel, il doit le prendre aussitôt que possible à moins qu'il ne soit presque l'heure de prendre la dose suivante. L'avertir qu'il ne doit pas remplacer une dose manquée par une double dose. Prévenir le patient qu'il ne doit arrêter le traitement par un IECA que sur recommandation d'un professionnel de la santé.

- Recommander au patient d'éviter de consommer des succédanés de sel ou des aliments à forte teneur en potassium ou en sodium, sauf si le professionnel de la santé le recommande (voir l'annexe J).
- Conseiller au patient de changer de position lentement afin de réduire le risque d'hypotension, particulièrement après l'administration de la dose initiale. Lui expliquer que les efforts physiques par temps chaud peuvent augmenter les effets hypotenseurs des IECA.
- Conseiller au patient de consulter un professionnel de la santé avant de prendre des médicaments en vente libre, particulièrement des médicaments contre le rhume.
- Prévenir le patient que le médicament peut parfois provoquer des étourdissements.
- Recommander au patient qui doit suivre un nouveau traitement ou subir une intervention chirurgicale, d'informer le professionnel de la santé qu'il suit un traitement par des IECA.
- Expliquer au patient que le médicament peut entraîner une altération du goût qui disparaît en 8 à 12 semaines, même si le traitement est poursuivi.
- RECOMMANDER AU PATIENT DE SIGNALER À UN PROFESSIONNEL DE LA SANTÉ LES SYMPTÔMES SUIVANTS: RASH, APHTES, MAUX DE GORGE, FIÈVRE, ŒDÈME DES MAINS OU DES PIEDS, POULS IRRÉGULIER, DOULEURS THORACIQUES, TOUX SÈCHE, RAUCITÉ DE LA VOIX, ŒDÈME DU VISAGE, DES YEUX, DES LÈVRES OU DE LA LANGUE, DIFFICULTÉS DE DÉGLUTITION, DIFFICULTÉS RESPIRATOIRES, altération persistante du goût ou rash persistant. Une toux sèche peut se manifester et ne disparaître qu'après l'arrêt du traitement. Lui conseiller de consulter un professionnel de la santé si la toux devient gênante et de le prévenir en cas de nausées, de vomissements ou de diarrhée qui persistent.
- Insister sur l'importance des examens de suivi permettant d'évaluer l'efficacité du traitement.

Hypertension:

- Inciter le patient à appliquer d'autres mesures de réduction de l'hypertension: perdre du poids, cesser de fumer, boire avec modération, faire de l'exercice régulièrement et diminuer le stress. Lui expliquer que le médicament stabilise la pression artérielle, mais ne guérit pas l'hypertension.
- Montrer au patient et à ses proches comment mesurer la pression artérielle. Leur demander de mesurer la pression artérielle au moins 1 fois par semaine et de signaler tout changement important à un professionnel de la santé.

VÉRIFICATION DE L'EFFICACITÉ THÉRAPEUTIQUE

L'efficacité du traitement peut être démontrée par: la baisse de la pression artérielle sans manifestation d'effets indésirables ■ la diminution des signes et des symptômes d'insuffisance cardiaque ■ la réduction du risque de décès ou d'apparition d'une insuffisance cardiaque après un infarctus du myocarde ■ le ralentissement de l'évolution de la néphropathie diabétique ■ la prévention d'événements cardiovasculaires chez les patients à risque. ✳

INHIBITEURS DE L'HMG-CoA RÉDUCTASE

atorvastatine
Lipitor

fluvastatine
Lescol, Lescol XL

lovastatine
Apo-Lovastatin, Gen-Lovastatin, Mevacor, Novo-Lovastatin, PMS-Lovastatin, Ratio-Lovastatin

pravastatine
Apo-Pravastatin, Gen-Pravastatin, Lin-Pravastatin, Novo-Pravastatin, PMS-Pravastatin, Pravachol, Ratio-Pravastatin

rosuvastatin
Crestor

simvastatine
Apo-Simvastatin, Gen-Simvastatin, Novo-Simvastatin, PMS-Simvastatin, Ratio-Simvastatin, Zocor

CLASSIFICATION:
Hypolipidémiants

Grossesse – catégorie X

INDICATIONS

Traitement d'appoint de l'hypercholestérolémie primaire et des dyslipidémies mixtes, en association avec la diétothérapie ■ Traitement de la dysbêtalipoprotéinémie, caractérisée par des taux élevés de triglycérides, mais des taux normaux de LDL, et de l'hypertriglycéridémie familiale (atorvastatine) ■ Réduction du risque d'infarctus du myocarde et d'AVC chez l'adulte hypertendu souffrant de diabète de type 2, sans aucun signe clinique de maladie coronarienne, mais présentant d'autres facteurs de risque, tels que l'âge ≥ 55 ans, la rétinopathie, l'albuminurie ou le tabagisme (atorvastatine) ■ Réduction du risque d'infarctus du myocarde chez l'adulte hypertendu sans aucun signe clinique de maladie coronarienne, mais présentant au moins 3 des facteurs de risque coronarien parmi les suivants: âge ≥ 55 ans, sexe masculin, tabagisme, diabète de type 2, hypertrophie ventriculaire gauche, certaines anomalies de l'ÉCG, microalbuminurie ou protéinurie, rapport cholestérol total/cholestérol-HDL ≥ 6 et antécédents familiaux de maladie coronarienne prématurée (atorvastatine) ■ Réduction du risque de décès toutes causes confondues ou par atteinte coronarienne, d'infarctus du myocarde et d'AVC ischémique chez les patients présentant un risque élevé d'événements coronariens en raison d'une maladie coronarienne ou d'une autre maladie artérielle occlusive et chez les patients diabétiques âgés > 40 ans (simvastatine) ■ Retard dans la survenue d'un premier événement cardiaque majeur chez les patients atteints de maladie coronarienne, ayant subi une intervention coronarienne percutanée (fluvastatine) ■ Réduction du risque de décès par atteinte coronarienne, d'infarctus du myocarde, d'AVC et d'ischémie cérébrale transitoire, réduction du besoin de recourir à une intervention de revascularisation du myocarde et réduction du nombre total de jours d'hospitalisation chez les patients atteints d'une maladie coronarienne et présentant un taux de cholestérol normal à modérément élevé (pravastatine) ■ Ralentissement de l'évolution de l'athérosclérose coronarienne et carotidienne (lovastatine).

MÉCANISME D'ACTION

Inhibition de l'enzyme 3-hydroxy-3-méthylglutaryl-coenzyme A (HMG-CoA) réductase qui catalyse une étape précoce de la synthèse du cholestérol. ***Effets thérapeutiques:*** Abaissement des concentrations de cholestérol total et de cholestérol-LDL. Légère élévation des concentrations de cholestérol HDL et abaissement des concentrations de cholestérol VLDL et de triglycérides ■ Ralentissement de l'évolution de l'athérosclérose coronarienne et carotidienne, d'où une réduction de l'incidence des infarctus du myocarde, des AVC et des accidents ischémiques transitoires.

PHARMACOCINÉTIQUE

Absorption: *Atorvastatine* – rapide, biodisponibilité à 14 % (PO) (30 % pour l'activité hypolipidémiante). *Fluvastatine* – 98 %, biodisponiblité à 24 % (PO). *Lovastatine* – faible et variable absolue, biodisponibilité à < 5 % (PO). *Pravastatine* – faible et variable, biodisponibilité à 17 % (PO); *Rosuvastatine* – biodisponibilité à 20 % (PO). *Simvastatine* – 85 %, biodisponibilité absolue à < 5 % (PO).

Distribution: *Atorvastatine* – passe probablement dans le lait maternel. *Fluvastatine* – passe dans le lait maternel. *Lovastatine* – traverse la barrière hémato-encéphalique et placentaire. *Pravastatine* – pénètre dans les hépatocytes, site de son action; passe en petites quantités dans le lait maternel.

Liaison aux protéines: *Atorvastatine* – ≥ 98 %. *Fluvastatine* – 98 %. *Rosuvastatine* – 90 %.

Métabolisme et excrétion: Métabolisme majoritairement hépatique, dans la plupart des cas, lors d'un premier passage, pour tous les agents (l'*atorvastatine*, la *lovastatine* et la *simvastatine* sont métabolisées par le CYP3A4). Excrétion dans la bile et dans les fèces. Excrétion rénale en petites quantités (*atorvastatine* – < 2 %; *fluvastatine* – 5 %, *pravastatine* – 20 %; *lovastatine* – 10 %; *rosuvastatine* – 10 %; *simvastatine* – 13 %). L'*atorvastatine* a 2 métabolites hypolipidémiants.

Demi-vie: *Atorvastatine* – 14 heures (activité hypolipidémiante due à l'atorvastatine et à ses métabolites – de 20 à 30 heures). *Fluvastatine* – 1,2 heure. *Lovastatine* – 3 heures. *Pravastatine* – de 1,3 à 2,7 heures. *Rosuvastatine* – 19 heures. *Simvastatine* – inconnue.

Profil temps-action (effet hypocholestérolémiant)

	Début d'action	Pic	Durée
Atorvastatine	inconnu	inconnu	20 - 30 h
Fluvastatine	1 - 2 semaines	4 - 6 semaines	inconnue
Lovastatine	2 semaines	4 - 6 semaines	6 semaines†
Pravastatine	inconnu	inconnu	inconnue
Rosuvastatine	inconnu	2 - 4 semaines	inconnue
Simvastatine	1 semaine	4 semaines	inconnue

† Après l'arrêt du traitement.

CONTRE-INDICATIONS, PRÉCAUTIONS ET MISES EN GARDE

Contre-indications: Hypersensibilité ■ Risque de réactions de sensibilité croisée entre les agents ■ Maladie hépatique en poussée évolutive ou élévations persistantes inexpliquées du taux sérique de transaminases dépassant 3 fois la limite supérieure de la normale ■ **OBST.**: L'administration chez la femme enceinte expose le fœtus à un risque important qui dépasse les bienfaits ■ **ALLAITEMENT**: L'innocuité de ces agents n'a pas été établie et on ignore dans quelle mesure ils se retrouvent dans le lait maternel ■ Patients asiatiques (rosuvastatine, dose de 40 mg) ■ Facteurs prédisposant à la myopathie ou à la rhabdomyolyse: antécédents personnels ou familiaux de troubles musculaires héréditaires, antécédents de toxicité musculaire consécutive à la prise d'un autre inhibiteur de l'HMG-CoA réductase, insuffisance hépatique grave, insuffisance rénale grave (Cl_{Cr} < 30 mL/min), hypothyroïdie, alcoolisme, circonstances pouvant provoquer une augmentation du taux plasmatique du médicament (rosuvastatine, dose de 40 mg).

Précautions et mises en garde: Antécédents de maladie hépatique ■ Alcoolisme ■ Insuffisance rénale (on recommande de réduire la dose si la Cl_{Cr} < 30 mL/min) ■ Infection aiguë grave ■ Intervention chirurgicale majeure ■ Traumatisme ■ Myopathie ■ Antécédents personnels ou familiaux de troubles musculaires héréditaires ■ Antécédents de toxicité musculaire consécutive à la prise d'un autre inhibiteur de l'HMG-CoA réductase ■ Hypothyroïdie ■ Exercice physique excessif ■ **GÉR.**: Il est recommandé de réduire la dose chez les personnes âgées > 70 ans (plus à risque de souffrir de myopathie) ■ Femmes en âge de procréer ■ **PÉD.**: L'innocuité du médicament n'a pas été établie chez les enfants < 10 ans (atorvastatine), < 16 ans (pravastatine), < 18 ans (fluvastatine, lovastatine, rosuvastatine, simvastatine).

RÉACTIONS INDÉSIRABLES ET EFFETS SECONDAIRES

SNC: étourdissements, céphalées, insomnie, faiblesse.
ORLO: rhinite; *lovastatine* – vision trouble.
Resp.: bronchite.
GI: crampes abdominales, constipation, diarrhée, flatulence, brûlures d'estomac, dysgueusie, hépatite induite par le médicament, dyspepsie, élévation des enzymes hépatiques, nausées, pancréatite.
GU: impuissance.
Tég.: rash, prurit.
Loc.: RHABDOMYOLYSE, arthralgie, arthrite, myalgie, myosite.
Divers: réactions d'hypersensibilité.

INTERACTIONS

Médicament-médicament: Les **chélateurs des acides biliaires** peuvent réduire la biodisponibilité des inhibiteurs de l'HMG-CoA réductase ■ Les **dérivés de l'acide fibrique** (**bezafibrate**, **fénofibrate** et **gemfibrozil**) et la **niacine** peuvent augmenter le risque de myopathie avec ou sans rhabdomyolyse ■ Risque accru de myopathie avec ou sans rhabdomyolyse lors de l'administration concomitante d'inhibiteurs et substrats du CYP3A4, tels l'**amiodarone**, la **clarithromycine**, la **cyclosporine**, le **diltiazem**, l'**érythromycine**, les **inhibiteurs de la protéase**, l'**itraconazole**, le **kétoconazole** et la **télithromycine** (atorvastatine, lovastatine et simvastatine) ■ Le **lopinavir** et le **ritonavir** augmentent les concentrations sanguines de la rosuvastatine ■ Risque accru de myopathie avec ou sans rhabdomyolyse lors de l'administration concomitante de **niacine** et de lovastatine ■ La **rifampicine** peut diminuer les taux plasmatiques des inhibiteurs de l'HMG-CoA réductase ■ L'atorvastatine et la simvastatine peuvent élever légèrement les concentrations sériques de **digoxine** ■ L'atorvastatine peut accroître les concentrations des **contraceptifs oraux** ■ Le **fluconazole** augmente les concentrations sanguines de la fluvastatine ■ Les inhibiteurs de l'HMG-CoA réductase peuvent intensifier les effets de la **warfarine**.

Médicament-produits naturels: Le **millepertuis** peut diminuer les concentrations sanguines et l'efficacité de la lovastatine et de la simvastatine.

Médicament-aliments: Les **aliments** augmentent les concentrations sanguines de la lovastatine ■ Le **jus de pamplemousse** augmente les concentrations sanguines et le risque de myopathie avec ou sans rhabdomyolyse, entraîné par l'atorvastatine, la lovastatine et la simvastatine.

VOIES D'ADMINISTRATION ET POSOLOGIE

Atorvastatine

- **PO (adultes)**: De 10 à 20 mg, 1 fois par jour, au départ (commencer par 40 mg, 1 fois par jour, si le cholestérol-LDL doit être diminué de > 45 %); on peut augmenter la dose toutes les 2 à 4 semaines, jusqu'à un maximum de 80 mg par jour. Écart posologique habituel: de 10 à 80 mg par jour.
- **PO (enfants de 10 à 17 ans)**: 10 mg, 1 fois par jour, au départ; on peut augmenter la dose après 4 semaines, jusqu'à un maximum de 20 mg par jour.

Fluvastatine

- **PO (adultes)**: De 20 à 40 mg, 1 fois par jour, au coucher; on peut augmenter la dose toutes les 4 semaines, jusqu'à un maximum de 80 mg par jour. Écart posologique: de 20 à 80 mg par jour. La dose de 80 mg par jour doit être fractionnée en 2 doses de 40 mg (préparation régulière) ou administrée en 1 seule fois (préparation à action prolongée).

Lovastatine

- **PO (adultes)**: 20 mg, 1 fois par jour, au repas du soir. Augmenter la posologie à intervalles de 4 semaines, jusqu'à un maximum de 80 mg par jour, en une seule dose ou en doses fractionnées.

Pravastatine

- **PO (adultes)**: De 20 à 40 mg, 1 fois par jour, au coucher. Écart posologique habituel: de 10 à 80 mg par jour.

- *INSUFFISANCE HÉPATIQUE OU RÉNALE*
  PO (ADULTES): CL_{CR} < 30 mL/MIN – LA DOSE INITIALE NE DEVRAIT PAS DÉPASSER 10 mg, 1 FOIS PAR JOUR.

Rosuvastatine

- **PO (adultes)**: 10 mg, 1 fois par jour, le matin ou le soir. Augmenter la posologie, si nécessaire, après 2 à 4 semaines, pour la passer à 20 mg, 1 fois par jour. Dans les cas d'hypercholestérolémie grave, une dose de départ de 20 mg peut être envisagée. Ne pas dépasser 40 mg, 1 fois par jour.
- *INSUFFISANCE HÉPATIQUE*
  PO (ADULTES): AUCUNE MODIFICATION DE LA POSOLOGIE N'EST NÉCESSAIRE EN PRÉSENCE D'INSUFFISANCE HÉPATIQUE LÉGÈRE OU MODÉRÉE. NE PAS DÉPASSER 20 mg, 1 FOIS PAR JOUR, EN PRÉSENCE D'INSUFFISANCE HÉPATIQUE GRAVE.
- *INSUFFISANCE RÉNALE*
  PO (ADULTES): AUCUNE MODIFICATION N'EST NÉCESSAIRE EN PRÉSENCE D'INSUFFISANCE RÉNALE LÉGÈRE OU MODÉRÉE. SI L'INSUFFISANCE RÉNALE EST GRAVE (CL_{CR} < 30 mL/MIN), NE PAS DÉPASSER 10 mg, 1 FOIS PAR JOUR.

Simvastatine

- **PO (adultes)**: De 10 à 20 mg, 1 fois par jour, le soir (commencer par 40 mg, 1 fois par jour si le cholestérol-LDL doit être diminué de > 45%).

PRÉSENTATION

- **Atorvastatine**
  Comprimés: 10 mg^{Pr}, 20 mg^{Pr}, 40 mg^{Pr}, 80 mg^{Pr} ■ **En association avec**: amlodipine (Caduet).
- **Fluvastatine**
  Capsules: 20 mg^{Pr}, 40 mg^{Pr} ■ **Comprimés à libération prolongée**: 80 mg^{Pr}.
- **Lovastatine** (versions génériques disponibles)
  Comprimés: 20 mg^{Pr}, 40 mg^{Pr} ■ **En association avec**: niacine (Advicor).
- **Pravastatine** (versions génériques disponibles)
  Comprimés: 10 mg^{Pr}, 20 mg^{Pr}, 40 mg^{Pr} ■ **En association avec**: acide acétylsalicylique (PravASA).
- **Rosuvastatine**
  Comprimés: 5 mg^{Pr}, 10 mg^{Pr}, 20 mg^{Pr}, 40 mg^{Pr}.
- **Simvastatine** (versions génériques disponibles)
  Comprimés: 5 mg^{Pr}, 10 mg^{Pr}, 20 mg^{Pr}, 40 mg^{Pr}, 80 mg^{Pr}.

SOINS INFIRMIERS

ÉVALUATION DE LA SITUATION

- Recueillir les données sur les habitudes alimentaires du patient, notamment sur sa consommation de matières grasses.

Tests de laboratoire:

- Noter les concentrations sériques de cholestérol et de triglycérides avant l'administration initiale, après 4 à 6 semaines, puis, à intervalles réguliers, pendant toute la durée du traitement.
- Vérifier les résultats des tests de la fonction hépatique, incluant les concentrations d'AST, avant l'administration initiale, de 6 à 12 semaines après le début du traitement ou après la majoration de la dose, puis tous les 6 mois. Si les concentrations d'AST sont 3 fois supérieures à la normale, il faut arrêter le traitement par les inhibiteurs de l'HMG-CoA réductase. Ces agents peuvent également élever les concentrations de phosphatase alcaline et de bilirubine.
- VÉRIFIER LES CONCENTRATIONS DE CPK EN CAS DE SENSIBILITÉ MUSCULAIRE. SI LES CONCENTRATIONS DE CPK SONT FORTEMENT ÉLEVÉES OU SI UNE MYOPATHIE SE MANIFESTE, IL FAUT ARRÊTER LE TRAITEMENT PAR LES INHIBITEURS DE L'HMG-COA RÉDUCTASE.

DIAGNOSTICS INFIRMIERS POSSIBLES

- Connaissances insuffisantes sur le traitement médicamenteux (Enseignement au patient et à ses proches).
- Non-observance du traitement médicamenteux (Enseignement au patient et à ses proches).

INTERVENTIONS INFIRMIÈRES

- NE PAS CONFONDRE PRAVACHOL (PRAVASTATINE) AVEC PRÉVACID (LANSOPRAZOLE).

PO:

- Administrer la *lovastatine* avec des aliments. L'administration à jeun réduit l'absorption d'environ 30 %. Il faut administrer la dose uniquotidienne initiale au repas du soir.
- Administrer la *fluvastatine*, la *pravastatine* et la *simvastatine* 1 fois par jour, dans la soirée. On peut administrer ces médicaments sans égard aux repas.
- L'*atorvastatine* et la *rosuvastatine* peuvent être administrées à n'importe quel moment de la journée, sans égard aux repas.
- Si les inhibiteurs de l'HMG-CoA réductase sont administrés en association avec des chélateurs des acides biliaires (cholestyramine, colestipol), les administrer 1 heure avant ou au moins de 4 à 6 heures après ces agents.

ENSEIGNEMENT AU PATIENT ET À SES PROCHES

- Conseiller au patient de respecter rigoureusement la posologie recommandée, de ne pas sauter de dose et de ne pas remplacer une dose manquée par une double dose. Le médicament aide à réduire les taux sériques élevés de cholestérol, mais ne guérit pas l'hypercholestérolémie.

- Expliquer au patient que le traitement médicamenteux ne peut être efficace que s'il observe en même temps un régime pauvre en matières grasses, en cholestérol et en glucides, s'il évite de boire de l'alcool, s'il fait de l'exercice et s'il cesse de fumer.
- RECOMMANDER AU PATIENT DE PRÉVENIR UN PROFESSIONNEL DE LA SANTÉ EN CAS DE DOULEURS, DE SENSIBILITÉ OU DE FAIBLESSE MUSCULAIRES INEXPLIQUÉES, PARTICULIÈREMENT SI CES SYMPTÔMES S'ACCOMPAGNENT DE FIÈVRE OU DE MALAISE.
- Inciter le patient à utiliser des écrans solaires et à porter des vêtements protecteurs pour prévenir les réactions de photosensibilité (effet rare).
- Recommander à la patiente de prévenir immédiatement un professionnel de la santé si elle pense être enceinte ou désire le devenir.
- Recommander au patient qui doit suivre un traitement ou subir une intervention chirurgicale de prévenir le professionnel de la santé qu'il suit un traitement par ce type de médicament.
- Insister sur l'importance des examens de suivi permettant de déterminer l'efficacité du traitement et de déceler les effets secondaires.

VÉRIFICATION DE L'EFFICACITÉ THÉRAPEUTIQUE

L'efficacité du traitement peut être démontrée par: la baisse des concentrations sériques de cholestérol-LDL, de cholestérol-VLDL et de cholestérol total ▪ l'élévation des concentrations de cholestérol-HDL ▪ la diminution des concentrations de triglycérides ▪ la réduction du risque de décès, d'infarctus du myocarde, d'AVC et d'ischémie cérébrale transitoire ▪ la réduction du besoin de recourir à une revascularisation coronarienne ▪ le ralentissement de l'évolution de l'athérosclérose coronarienne et carotidienne. ✳

ALERTE CLINIQUE

INSULINE (ACTION INTERMÉDIAIRE)

insuline NPH (suspension d'insuline isophane)

Humulin N, Novolin ge NPH

CLASSIFICATION:

Antidiabétique, hormone pancréatique

Grossesse – catégorie B

INDICATIONS

Traitement du diabète (de type 1 ou de type 2).

MÉCANISME D'ACTION

Abaissement de la glycémie par augmentation de la captation cellulaire du glucose au niveau des cellules musculaires et adipeuses, et par inhibition de la sortie du glucose du foie ▪ Inhibition de la lipolyse et de la protéolyse ▪ Stimulation de la synthèse des protéines. ***Effets thérapeutiques:*** Équilibrage de la glycémie chez les patients diabétiques.

PHARMACOCINÉTIQUE

Absorption: Bonne (SC). La vitesse d'absorption dépend du point d'injection, du volume injecté et d'autres facteurs.
Distribution: Tout l'organisme.
Métabolisme et excrétion: Métabolisme hépatique, splénique, rénal et musculaire.
Demi-vie: De 5 à 6 minutes (prolongée chez les diabétiques; la demi-vie biologique est plus longue).

Profil temps-action (effet hypoglycémiant)

	DÉBUT D'ACTION	PIC	DURÉE
Insuline NPH SC	1 – 2 h	4 – 12 h	jusqu'à 24 h

CONTRE-INDICATIONS, PRÉCAUTIONS ET MISES EN GARDE

Contre-indications: Allergie ou hypersensibilité à un type particulier d'insuline, d'agent de conservation ou d'additif ▪ Hypoglycémie ▪ L'insuline NPH ne doit pas être administrée par voie IV ni utilisée dans le traitement du coma.
Précautions et mises en garde: Stress ou infection (les besoins en insuline peuvent varier) ▪ **OBST.:** Les besoins en insuline peuvent varier selon le trimestre de la grossesse ▪ **ALLAITEMENT:** Les femmes qui allaitent peuvent avoir besoin d'adapter leur dose d'insuline ▪ Insuffisance hépatique (les besoins en insuline peuvent diminuer en raison d'une déficience de la gluconéogenèse et de l'atténuation du métabolisme insulinique) ▪ Insuffisance rénale (les besoins en insuline peuvent diminuer).

RÉACTIONS INDÉSIRABLES ET EFFETS SECONDAIRES

Tég.: urticaire.
End.: HYPOGLYCÉMIE, hyperglycémie rebond (effet de Somogyi).
Locaux: lipodystrophie (lipoatrophie, lipohypertrophie), démangeaisons, rougeurs, œdème.
Divers: réactions allergiques, incluant l'ANAPHYLAXIE.

INTERACTIONS

Médicament-médicament: Les **bêtabloquants** peuvent masquer certains signes et symptômes d'hypoglycémie et en retarder la disparition ■ Les **diurétiques thiazidiques**, les **corticostéroïdes**, les **sympathomimétiques**, les **hormones thyroïdiennes**, les **œstrogènes**, les **antipsychotiques atypiques** et les **inhibiteurs de la protéase (antirétroviraux)** peuvent accroître les besoins en insuline ■ Les **stéroïdes anabolisants (testostérone)**, l'**alcool**, les **IMAO**, les **hypoglycémiants oraux**, l'**octréotide**, les **inhibiteurs de l'enzyme de conversion de l'angiotensine (IECA)** et les **salicylates** peuvent réduire les besoins en insuline.
Médicament-produits naturels: La **glucosamine** peut entraver l'équilibrage de la glycémie.

VOIES D'ADMINISTRATION ET POSOLOGIE

La dose dépend de la glycémie, de la réponse au traitement et de nombreux autres facteurs.

- **SC (adultes et enfants):** De 0,5 à 1 U/kg/jour.

PRÉSENTATION

Au Canada, toutes les insulines sont présentées à une concentration de 100 unités/mL.
Insuline NPH: fioles de 10 mL^{Phc}, cartouches de 3 mL^{Phc}.

SOINS INFIRMIERS

ÉVALUATION DE LA SITUATION

- SUIVRE À INTERVALLES RÉGULIERS, PENDANT TOUTE LA DURÉE DU TRAITEMENT, LES SIGNES ET LES SYMPTÔMES D'HYPOGLYCÉMIE (ANXIÉTÉ, FRISSONS, SUEURS FROIDES, CONFUSION, PEAU PÂLE ET FROIDE, DIFFICULTÉS DE CONCENTRATION, SOMNOLENCE, FAIM EXCESSIVE, CÉPHALÉES, IRRITABILITÉ, NAUSÉES, NERVOSITÉ, POULS RAPIDE, TREMBLEMENTS, FATIGUE OU FAIBLESSE INHABITUELLES) et d'hyperglycémie (confusion, somnolence, rougeur et sécheresse de la peau, haleine fruitée, mictions fréquentes, perte d'appétit, fatigue, soif inhabituelle).
- Peser le patient à intervalles réguliers. Les modifications de poids peuvent dicter l'adaptation de la posologie d'insuline.

Tests de laboratoire:

- L'insuline peut abaisser les concentrations sériques de phosphates inorganiques, de magnésium et de potassium.
- Suivre la glycémie et la cétonémie toutes les 6 heures pendant toute la durée du traitement (plus fréquemment en présence d'acidocétose ou de stress). L'efficacité du traitement peut également être déterminée par la mesure de l'hémoglobine glyquée.

TOXICITÉ ET SURDOSAGE: LE SURDOSAGE SE MANIFESTE PAR DES SYMPTÔMES D'HYPOGLYCÉMIE. ON PEUT TRAITER L'HYPOGLYCÉMIE LÉGÈRE EN ADMINISTRANT DU GLUCOSE PAR VOIE ORALE. L'HYPOGLYCÉMIE GRAVE EST UNE URGENCE, CAR ELLE PEUT METTRE EN DANGER LA VIE DU PATIENT. LE TRAITEMENT CONSISTE À ADMINISTRER DU GLUCOSE PAR VOIE IV, DU GLUCAGON OU DE L'ADRÉNALINE.

DIAGNOSTICS INFIRMIERS POSSIBLES

- Connaissances insuffisantes sur le traitement médicamenteux (Enseignement au patient et à ses proches).
- Non-observance du traitement médicamenteux (Enseignement au patient et à ses proches).

I

INTERVENTIONS INFIRMIÈRES

ALERTE CLINIQUE: LES ERREURS LIÉES À L'INSULINOTHÉRAPIE ONT ENTRAÎNÉ DES ACCIDENTS ET MÊME DES DÉCÈS. SE RENSEIGNER AUPRÈS DU MÉDECIN TRAITANT AU SUJET DE TOUTES LES ORDONNANCES QUI SEMBLENT AMBIGUËS.

- IL EXISTE DIFFÉRENTS TYPES D'INSULINES. VÉRIFIER LE TYPE, LA DOSE ET LA DATE DE PÉREMPTION DE L'INSULINE AVEC UN AUTRE PROFESSIONNEL DE LA SANTÉ. NE PAS SUBSTITUER UN TYPE D'INSULINE À UN AUTRE SANS RECOMMANDATION EXPRESSE DU MÉDECIN OU D'UN AUTRE PROFESSIONNEL DE LA SANTÉ.
- N'utiliser *que* les seringues à insuline pour prélever la dose. Les unités inscrites sur la seringue doivent correspondre aux unités d'insuline par mL. On peut se procurer des seringues spécialement destinées au prélèvement des doses inférieures à 50 unités. Avant de prélever la dose, faire tourner la fiole dans la paume des mains pour bien disperser la solution; ne pas agiter.
- Lorsqu'on doit mélanger les insulines, prélever d'abord l'insuline régulière, l'insuline aspart ou l'insuline lispro pour éviter la contamination de la fiole contenant ce type d'insuline. Les mélanges d'insulines ne doivent pas être utilisés pour l'administration par voie IV ou par pompe SC.
- Conserver l'insuline au frais; il n'est pas nécessaire de garder la fiole entamée au réfrigérateur. Celle-ci se conservera pendant 28 jours à une température ne dépassant pas les 30 °C, à l'abri de la chaleur et de la lumière directe. Il est recommandé de jeter les fioles 28 jours après les avoir ouvertes pour prévenir la prolifération des microorganismes. Ne pas

utiliser l'insuline si elle a changé de couleur ou si elle est anormalement visqueuse.

- L'insuline NPH ne doit pas être utilisée pour traiter l'acidocétose.

SC:

- Faire la rotation des points d'injection.
- Administrer dans l'abdomen, la cuisse ou le haut du bras. Pincer la peau, introduire l'aiguille, injecter l'insuline et retirer l'aiguille. Maintenir une légère pression sur le point d'injection sans masser.
- Administrer l'insuline NPH de 30 à 60 minutes avant un repas.

ENSEIGNEMENT AU PATIENT ET À SES PROCHES

- Montrer au patient comment s'autoadministrer l'insuline et préciser le type d'insuline qu'il doit utiliser, le matériel dont il doit se servir (seringue, cartouche, tampons d'alcool), le mode de conservation de l'agent et la méthode de mise au rebut des seringues. Insister sur le fait qu'il est important de ne pas changer de marque d'insuline ou de seringue, qu'il faut choisir soigneusement les points d'injection et en assurer la rotation et qu'il est vital d'observer le schéma posologique prescrit.
- Faire la démonstration du mode de mélange des insulines: prélever d'abord l'insuline régulière, l'insuline aspart ou l'insuline lispro, tourner la fiole d'insuline à action intermédiaire dans la paume des mains sans l'agiter (en raison du risque de fausser les doses); prélever ensuite l'insuline à action intermédiaire.
- Expliquer au patient que ce médicament équilibre la glycémie, mais ne guérit pas le diabète. Le traitement est de longue durée.
- Faire la démonstration du dosage de la glycémie et de la cétonémie. Ces dosages doivent être exécutés attentivement pendant des périodes de stress ou pendant une maladie. Il faut prévenir un professionnel de la santé si des modifications importantes surviennent.
- Insister sur le fait qu'il est important de suivre les consignes des professionnels de la santé concernant l'alimentation et les exercices.
- Conseiller au patient de consulter un professionnel de la santé avant de prendre en concomitance d'autres médicaments d'ordonnance ou en vente libre, des produits naturels ou de l'alcool.
- Recommander au patient qui doit suivre un autre traitement ou subir une intervention chirurgicale d'avertir le professionnel de la santé qu'il suit un traitement à l'insuline.
- Recommander au patient de communiquer avec un professionnel de la santé s'il souffre de nausées, de vomissements ou de fièvre, s'il est incapable de suivre le régime alimentaire habituel ou si la glycémie n'est pas équilibrée.
- EXPLIQUER AU PATIENT QUELS SONT LES SIGNES ET LES SYMPTÔMES D'HYPOGLYCÉMIE ET D'HYPERGLYCÉMIE, ET LES MESURES À PRENDRE S'ILS SE MANIFESTENT.
- Demander à la patiente de prévenir le professionnel de la santé si elle pense être enceinte ou désire le devenir.
- Inciter le patient souffrant de diabète à toujours garder sur lui du sucre (bonbons, sachets de sucre) et une pièce d'identité où sont inscrits sa maladie et son traitement médicamenteux.
- Insister sur l'importance des examens de suivi réguliers.

VÉRIFICATION DE L'EFFICACITÉ THÉRAPEUTIQUE

L'efficacité du traitement peut être démontrée par: l'équilibrage de la glycémie sans apparition d'épisodes d'hypoglycémie ou d'hyperglycémie. ✳

ALERTE CLINIQUE

INSULINE (ACTION RAPIDE)

insuline régulière

Humulin R, Novolin ge Toronto

CLASSIFICATION:

Antidiabétique, hormone pancréatique

Grossesse – catégorie B

INDICATIONS

Traitement du diabète (de type 1 ou de type 2) ■ Traitement d'urgence du coma ou du précoma diabétiques ■ Administration durant une intervention chirurgicale chez les diabétiques.

MÉCANISME D'ACTION

Abaissement de la glycémie par augmentation de la captation cellulaire du glucose au niveau des cellules musculaires et adipeuses, et par inhibition de la sortie du glucose du foie ■ Inhibition de la lipolyse et de la protéolyse ■ Stimulation de la synthèse des protéines. ***Effets thérapeutiques:*** Équilibrage de la glycémie chez les patients diabétiques.

PHARMACOCINÉTIQUE

Absorption: Rapide (SC).
Distribution: Tout l'organisme.
Métabolisme et excrétion: Métabolisme hépatique, splénique, rénal et musculaire.
Demi-vie: De 5 à 6 minutes (prolongée chez les diabétiques; la demi-vie biologique est plus longue).

Profil temps-action (effet hypoglycémiant)

	DÉBUT D'ACTION	PIC	DURÉE
Insuline régulière IV	10 - 30 min	15 - 30 min	30 - 60 min
Insuline régulière SC	30 - 60 min	2 - 4 h	5 - 7 h

CONTRE-INDICATIONS, PRÉCAUTIONS ET MISES EN GARDE

Contre-indications: Allergie ou hypersensibilité à un type particulier d'insuline, d'agent de conservation ou d'additif ■ Hypoglycémie.

Précautions et mises en garde: Stress ou infection (les besoins en insuline peuvent varier) ■ **OBST.**: Les besoins en insuline peuvent varier selon le trimestre de la grossesse ■ **ALLAITEMENT**: Les femmes qui allaitent peuvent avoir besoin d'adapter leur dose d'insuline ■ Insuffisance hépatique (les besoins en insuline peuvent diminuer en raison d'une déficience de la gluconéogenèse et de l'atténuation du métabolisme insulinique) ■ Insuffisance rénale (les besoins en insuline peuvent diminuer).

RÉACTIONS INDÉSIRABLES ET EFFETS SECONDAIRES

Tég.: urticaire.
End.: HYPOGLYCÉMIE, hyperglycémie rebond (effet de Somogyi).
Locaux: lipodystrophie (lipoatrophie, lipohypertrophie), démangeaisons, rougeurs, œdème.
Divers: réactions allergiques, incluant l'ANAPHYLAXIE.

INTERACTIONS

Médicament-médicament: Les **bêtabloquants** peuvent masquer certains signes et symptômes d'hypoglycémie et en retarder la disparition ■ Les **diurétiques thiazidiques**, les **corticostéroïdes**, les **sympathomimétiques**, les **hormones thyroïdiennes**, les **œstrogènes**, les **antipsychotiques atypiques** et les **inhibiteurs de la protéase (antirétroviraux)** peuvent accroître les besoins en insuline ■ Les **stéroïdes anabolisants (testostérone)**, l'**alcool**, les **IMAO**, les **hypoglycémiants oraux**, l'**octréotide**, les **inhibiteurs de l'enzyme de conversion de l'angiotensine (IECA)** et les **salicylates** peuvent réduire les besoins en insuline.

Médicament-produits naturels: La **glucosamine** peut entraver l'équilibrage de la glycémie.

VOIES D'ADMINISTRATION ET POSOLOGIE

La dose dépend de la glycémie, de la réponse au traitement et de nombreux autres facteurs.

Acidocétose
- **IV (adultes)**: 0,1 U/kg/heure en perfusion continue.
- **IV (enfants)**: Dose individualisée selon le poids du patient.

Traitement d'entretien
- **SC (adultes et enfants)**: De 0,5 à 1 U/kg/jour.

PRÉSENTATION

Au Canada, toutes les insulines sont présentées à une concentration de 100 unités/mL.
Insuline régulière: fioles de 10 mL[Phc], cartouches de 3 mL[Phc].

I

SOINS INFIRMIERS

ÉVALUATION DE LA SITUATION

- SUIVRE À INTERVALLES RÉGULIERS, PENDANT TOUTE LA DURÉE DU TRAITEMENT, LES SIGNES ET LES SYMPTÔMES D'HYPOGLYCÉMIE (ANXIÉTÉ, FRISSONS, SUEURS FROIDES, CONFUSION, PEAU PÂLE ET FROIDE, DIFFICULTÉS DE CONCENTRATION, SOMNOLENCE, FAIM EXCESSIVE, CÉPHALÉES, IRRITABILITÉ, NAUSÉES, NERVOSITÉ, POULS RAPIDE, TREMBLEMENTS, FATIGUE OU FAIBLESSE INHABITUELLES) et d'hyperglycémie (confusion, somnolence, rougeur et sécheresse de la peau, haleine fruitée, mictions fréquentes, perte d'appétit, fatigue, soif inhabituelle).
- Peser le patient à intervalles réguliers. Les modifications de poids peuvent dicter l'adaptation de la posologie d'insuline.

Tests de laboratoire:
- L'insuline peut abaisser les concentrations sériques de phosphates inorganiques, de magnésium et de potassium.
- Suivre la glycémie et la cétonémie toutes les 6 heures pendant toute la durée du traitement (plus fréquemment en présence d'acidocétose ou de stress). L'efficacité du traitement peut également être déterminée par la mesure de l'hémoglobine glyquée.

TOXICITÉ ET SURDOSAGE: LE SURDOSAGE SE MANIFESTE PAR DES SYMPTÔMES D'HYPOGLYCÉMIE. ON PEUT TRAITER L'HYPOGLYCÉMIE LÉGÈRE EN ADMINISTRANT DU GLUCOSE PAR VOIE ORALE. L'HYPOGLYCÉMIE GRAVE EST UNE URGENCE, CAR ELLE PEUT METTRE EN DANGER LA VIE DU

PATIENT. LE TRAITEMENT CONSISTE À ADMINISTRER DU GLUCOSE PAR VOIE IV, DU GLUCAGON OU DE L'ADRÉNALINE.

DIAGNOSTICS INFIRMIERS POSSIBLES

- Connaissances insuffisantes sur le traitement médicamenteux (Enseignement au patient et à ses proches).
- Non-observance du traitement médicamenteux (Enseignement au patient et à ses proches).

INTERVENTIONS INFIRMIÈRES

ALERTE CLINIQUE: LES ERREURS LIÉES À L'INSULINOTHÉRAPIE ONT ENTRAÎNÉ DES ACCIDENTS ET MÊME DES DÉCÈS. SE RENSEIGNER AUPRÈS DU MÉDECIN TRAITANT AU SUJET DE TOUTES LES ORDONNANCES QUI SEMBLENT AMBIGUËS.

- IL EXISTE DIFFÉRENTS TYPES D'INSULINES. VÉRIFIER LE TYPE, LA DOSE ET LA DATE DE PÉREMPTION DE L'INSULINE AVEC UN AUTRE PROFESSIONNEL DE LA SANTÉ. NE PAS SUBSTITUER UN TYPE D'INSULINE À UN AUTRE SANS RECOMMANDATION EXPRESSE DU MÉDECIN OU D'UN AUTRE PROFESSIONNEL DE LA SANTÉ.
- N'utiliser *que* les seringues à insuline pour prélever la dose. Les unités inscrites sur la seringue doivent correspondre aux unités d'insuline par mL. On peut se procurer des seringues spécialement destinées au prélèvement des doses inférieures à 50 unités. Avant de prélever la dose, faire tourner la fiole dans la paume des mains pour bien disperser la solution; ne pas agiter.
- Lorsqu'on doit mélanger les insulines, prélever d'abord l'insuline régulière pour éviter la contamination de la fiole contenant ce type d'insuline. Les mélanges d'insulines ne doivent pas être utilisés pour l'administration par voie IV ou par pompe SC.
- Conserver l'insuline au frais; il n'est pas nécessaire de garder la fiole entamée au réfrigérateur. Celle-ci se conservera pendant 28 jours à une température ne dépassant pas les 30 °C, à l'abri de la chaleur et de la lumière directe. Il est recommandé de jeter les fioles 28 jours après les avoir ouvertes pour prévenir la prolifération des microorganismes. Ne pas administrer l'insuline si elle a changé de couleur ou si elle est anormalement visqueuse.

SC:

- Faire la rotation des points d'injection.
- Administrer dans l'abdomen, la cuisse ou le haut du bras. Pincer la peau, introduire l'aiguille, injecter l'insuline et retirer l'aiguille. Maintenir une légère pression sur le point d'injection, sans masser.
- Administrer l'insuline régulière de 15 à 30 minutes avant un repas.

IV: L'insuline régulière peut être administrée par voie IV.

IV directe: On peut administrer l'insuline non diluée par voie IV, directement dans une veine ou dans une tubulure en Y.

Perfusion continue: On peut diluer l'insuline pour perfusion dans les solutions IV courantes; toutefois, avant d'atteindre le système veineux, l'insuline pourrait perdre sa puissance d'au moins 20 à 80 % à cause du contact avec le contenant ou la tubulure de verre ou de plastique.

Vitesse d'administration: La vitesse de perfusion doit être prescrite par le médecin; l'administration doit se faire à l'aide d'une pompe IV afin de s'assurer que le patient reçoit la dose exacte.

Compatibilité (tubulure en Y): ampicilline ▪ ampicilline/sulbactam ▪ aztréonam ▪ céfazoline ▪ céfotétane ▪ dobutamine ▪ famotidine ▪ gentamicine ▪ héparine ▪ imipénem/cilastatine ▪ indométhacine ▪ magnésium, sulfate de ▪ mépéridine ▪ morphine ▪ oxytocine ▪ pentobarbital ▪ potassium, chlorure de ▪ ritodrine ▪ sodium, bicarbonate de ▪ tacrolimus ▪ terbutaline ▪ ticarcilline ▪ ticarcilline/clavulanate ▪ tobramycine ▪ vancomycine ▪ vitamines du complexe B avec C.

Compatibilité en addition au soluté: L'insuline peut être ajoutée à une solution d'APT (alimentation parentérale totale).

ENSEIGNEMENT AU PATIENT ET À SES PROCHES

- Montrer au patient comment s'autoadministrer l'insuline et préciser le type d'insuline qu'il doit utiliser, le matériel dont il doit se servir (seringue, cartouche, tampons d'alcool), le mode de conservation de l'agent et la méthode de mise au rebut des seringues. Insister sur le fait qu'il est important de ne pas changer de marque d'insuline ou de seringue, qu'il faut choisir soigneusement les points d'injection et en assurer la rotation, et qu'il est vital d'observer le schéma posologique prescrit.
- Faire la démonstration du mode de mélange des insulines: prélever d'abord l'insuline régulière, et tourner la fiole d'insuline à action intermédiaire dans la paume des mains sans l'agiter (en raison du risque de fausser les doses); prélever ensuite l'insuline à action intermédiaire.
- Expliquer au patient que ce médicament équilibre la glycémie, mais ne guérit pas le diabète. Le traitement est de longue durée.
- Faire la démonstration du dosage de la glycémie et de la cétonémie. Ces dosages doivent être exécutés attentivement pendant des périodes de stress ou pendant une maladie. Il faut prévenir un profes-

sionnel de la santé si des modifications importantes surviennent.

- Insister sur le fait qu'il est important de suivre les consignes des professionnels de la santé concernant l'alimentation et les exercices.
- Conseiller au patient de consulter un professionnel de la santé avant de prendre en concomitance d'autres médicaments d'ordonnance ou en vente libre, des produits naturels ou de l'alcool.
- Recommander au patient qui doit suivre un autre traitement ou subir une intervention chirurgicale d'avertir le professionnel de la santé qu'il suit un traitement à l'insuline.
- Recommander au patient de communiquer avec un professionnel de la santé s'il souffre de nausées, de vomissements ou de fièvre, s'il est incapable de suivre le régime alimentaire habituel ou si la glycémie n'est pas équilibrée.
- EXPLIQUER AU PATIENT QUELS SONT LES SIGNES ET LES SYMPTÔMES D'HYPOGLYCÉMIE ET D'HYPERGLYCÉMIE, ET LES MESURES À PRENDRE S'ILS SE MANIFESTENT.
- Demander à la patiente de prévenir le professionnel de la santé si elle pense être enceinte ou désire le devenir.
- Inciter le patient souffrant de diabète à toujours garder sur lui du sucre (bonbons, sachets de sucre) et une pièce d'identité où sont inscrits sa maladie et son traitement médicamenteux.
- Insister sur l'importance des examens de suivi réguliers.

VÉRIFICATION DE L'EFFICACITÉ THÉRAPEUTIQUE

L'efficacité du traitement peut être démontrée par: l'équilibrage de la glycémie sans apparition d'épisodes d'hypoglycémie ou d'hyperglycémie. ✳

ALERTE CLINIQUE

INSULINES (ACTION PROLONGÉE)

insuline détémir

Levemir

insuline glargine

Lantus

CLASSIFICATION:

Antidiabétiques, hormones pancréatiques

Grossesse – catégorie C

INDICATIONS

Traitement des patients atteints de diabète de type 1 ou de type 2 ayant besoin d'insuline (basale) à action prolongée pour maintenir une homéostasie glucidique normale. Il est recommandé d'utiliser ce type d'insuline en association avec une insuline prandiale à action rapide ou à action très rapide.

MÉCANISME D'ACTION

Abaissement de la glycémie par augmentation de la captation cellulaire du glucose au niveau des cellules musculaires et adipeuses, et par inhibition de la sortie du glucose du foie ■ Inhibition de la lipolyse et de la protéolyse ■ Stimulation de la synthèse des protéines. ***Effets thérapeutiques:*** Équilibrage de la glycémie chez les patients diabétiques.

PHARMACOCINÉTIQUE

Absorption: Bonne, mais retardée et prolongée (SC). La vitesse d'absorption dépend du type d'insuline, du point d'injection, du volume injecté et d'autres facteurs.

Distribution: Tout l'organisme.

Métabolisme et excrétion: Métabolisme hépatique, splénique, rénal et musculaire.

Demi-vie: *Insuline détémir* – de 5 à 7 heures. *Insuline glargine* – inconnue.

Profil temps-action (effet hypoglycémiant)

	DÉBUT D'ACTION	PIC	DURÉE
Insuline détémir SC	3 – 4 h	6 – 8 h	24 h
Insuline glargine SC	1 – 2 h	aucun (action constante)	jusqu'à 24 h

CONTRE-INDICATIONS, PRÉCAUTIONS ET MISES EN GARDE

Contre-indications: Allergie ou hypersensibilité à un type particulier d'insuline, d'agent de conservation ou d'additif ■ Hypoglycémie ■ Les insulines détémir et glargine ne doivent pas être administrées par voie IV ni utilisées dans le traitement du coma.

Précautions et mises en garde: Stress ou infection (les besoins en insuline peuvent varier) ■ **OBST., ALLAITEMENT:** L'innocuité de ces insulines n'a pas été établie chez la femme enceinte ou qui allaite ■ **PÉD.:** L'innocuité de ces insulines n'a pas été établie chez les enfants < 7 ans (glargine) ni chez les enfants < 18 ans (détémir) ■ Insuffisance hépatique (les besoins en insuline peuvent diminuer en raison d'une déficience de la gluconéogenèse et de l'atténuation du métabolisme insulinique) ■ Insuffisance rénale (les besoins en insuline peuvent diminuer) ■ **GÉR.:** Adapter les doses avec prudence chez les personnes âgées afin de prévenir l'hypoglycémie ■ Changement de type ou de marque d'insuline (un suivi étroit de la glycémie s'impose).

RÉACTIONS INDÉSIRABLES ET EFFETS SECONDAIRES

Tég.: urticaire.
End.: HYPOGLYCÉMIE, hyperglycémie rebond (effet de Somogyi).
Locaux: lipodystrophie (lipoatrophie, lipohypertrophie), démangeaisons, rougeurs, œdème.
Hémat.: production d'anticorps anti-insuline.
Divers: réactions allergiques, incluant l'ANAPHYLAXIE.

INTERACTIONS

Médicament-médicament: Les **bêtabloquants** peuvent masquer certains signes et symptômes d'hypoglycémie et en retarder la disparition ■ Les **diurétiques thiazidiques**, les **corticostéroïdes**, les **sympathomimétiques**, les **hormones thyroïdiennes**, les **œstrogènes**, les **antipsychotiques atypiques** et les **inhibiteurs de la protéase (antirétroviraux)** peuvent accroître les besoins en insuline ■ Les **stéroïdes anabolisants (testostérone)**, l'**alcool**, les **IMAO**, les **hypoglycémiants oraux**, l'**octréotide**, les **inhibiteurs de l'enzyme de conversion de l'angiotensine (IECA)** et les **salicylates** peuvent réduire les besoins en insuline.
Médicament-produits naturels: La **glucosamine** peut entraver l'équilibrage de la glycémie.

VOIES D'ADMINISTRATION ET POSOLOGIE

La dose dépend de la glycémie, de la réponse au traitement et de nombreux autres facteurs.

Insuline détémir

- L'insuline détémir doit être administrée 1 ou 2 fois par jour, en fonction des besoins du patient. La posologie doit être individualisée et déterminée, selon les conseils du médecin, en fonction des besoins du patient.
- Chez les patients qui ont besoin de 2 injections par jour pour optimiser l'équilibrage glycémique, la dose du soir peut être administrée au souper ou au coucher.
- **SC (diabète de type 1)**: Administrer 1 fois par jour, au souper ou au coucher.
- **SC (diabète de type 2)**: Dose initiale de 0,1 à 0,2 UI/kg, 1 fois par jour, au souper ou au coucher, puis adapter selon la réponse au traitement.
- **Substitution par l'insuline détémir d'une insuline à action intermédiaire (NPH)**: Il peut s'avérer nécessaire d'adapter la dose et le moment de l'administration en vue d'atteindre la cible de glycémie; il se peut qu'il soit nécessaire d'adapter aussi le traitement antidiabétique concomitant (doses et moment de l'administration des insulines à courte durée d'action, administrées en concomitance, ou doses des agents antidiabétiques oraux).

Insuline glargine

- **SC (diabète de type 1)**: Administrer 1 fois par jour, au coucher.
- **SC (diabète de type 2) (patients n'ayant jamais reçu d'insuline et traités par des hypoglycémiants oraux)**: Dose initiale: 10 UI, 1 fois par jour, au coucher, puis adapter la posologie selon la réponse au traitement. La dose totale quotidienne se situe entre 2 et 90 UI.
- **Substitution par l'insuline glargine d'une insuline à action intermédiaire (NPH)**: Si le patient reçoit 1 dose d'insuline à action intermédiaire par jour, on recommande de la remplacer par l'insuline glargine à la même dose (UI), administrée 1 fois par jour, au coucher. Lors des études pendant lesquelles on est passé de l'insuline humaine NPH, administrée 2 fois par jour, à Lantus, administré 1 fois par jour, la dose initiale (UI) a dû être généralement réduite d'environ 20 % (par rapport au nombre d'UI quotidiennes totales d'insuline humaine NPH), durant la première semaine de traitement, puis adaptée en fonction de la réponse du patient.

PRÉSENTATION

Au Canada, toutes les insulines sont présentées à une concentration de 100 unités/mL. L'insuline détémir et l'insuline glargine sont des solutions aqueuses claires et incolores; elles ne contiennent pas de particules visibles. Leur action est prolongée, mais il ne s'agit pas d'une suspension.
Insuline détémir: cartouches de 3 mL[Phc] ■ **Insuline glargine**: fioles de 10 mL[Phc], cartouches de 3 mL[Phc].

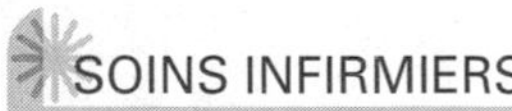

SOINS INFIRMIERS

ÉVALUATION DE LA SITUATION

- SUIVRE À INTERVALLES RÉGULIERS PENDANT TOUTE LA DURÉE DU TRAITEMENT, LES SIGNES ET LES SYMPTÔMES D'HYPOGLYCÉMIE (ANXIÉTÉ, FRISSONS, SUEURS FROIDES, CONFUSION, PEAU PÂLE ET FROIDE, DIFFICULTÉS DE CONCENTRATION, SOMNOLENCE, FAIM EXCESSIVE, CÉPHALÉES, IRRITABILITÉ, NAUSÉES, NERVOSITÉ, POULS RAPIDE, TREMBLEMENTS, FATIGUE OU FAIBLESSE INHABITUELLES) et d'hyperglycémie (confusion, somnolence, rougeur et sécheresse de la peau, haleine fruitée, mictions fréquentes, perte d'appétit, fatigue, soif inhabituelle).

- Peser le patient à intervalles réguliers. Les modifications de poids peuvent dicter l'adaptation de la posologie d'insuline.

Tests de laboratoire:

- L'insuline peut abaisser les concentrations sériques de phosphates inorganiques, de magnésium et de potassium.
- Suivre la glycémie et la cétonémie toutes les 6 heures pendant toute la durée du traitement (plus fréquemment en présence d'acidocétose ou de stress). L'efficacité du traitement peut également être déterminée par la mesure de l'hémoglobine glyquée.

TOXICITÉ ET SURDOSAGE: LE SURDOSAGE SE MANIFESTE PAR DES SYMPTÔMES D'HYPOGLYCÉMIE. ON PEUT TRAITER L'HYPOGLYCÉMIE LÉGÈRE EN ADMINISTRANT DU GLUCOSE PAR VOIE ORALE. L'HYPOGLYCÉMIE GRAVE EST UNE URGENCE, CAR ELLE PEUT METTRE EN DANGER LA VIE DU PATIENT. LE TRAITEMENT CONSISTE À ADMINISTRER DU GLUCOSE PAR VOIE IV, DU GLUCAGON OU DE L'ADRÉNALINE. LA RÉCUPÉRATION APRÈS UN ÉPISODE D'HYPOGLYCÉMIE PEUT ÊTRE RETARDÉE EN RAISON DE L'EFFET PROLONGÉ DE CES INSULINES.

DIAGNOSTICS INFIRMIERS POSSIBLES

- Connaissances insuffisantes sur le traitement médicamenteux (Enseignement au patient et à ses proches).
- Non-observance du traitement médicamenteux (Enseignement au patient et à ses proches).

INTERVENTIONS INFIRMIÈRES

- **ALERTE CLINIQUE**: LES ERREURS LIÉES À L'INSULINOTHÉRAPIE ONT ENTRAÎNÉ DES ACCIDENTS ET MÊME DES DÉCÈS. SE RENSEIGNER AUPRÈS DU MÉDECIN TRAITANT AU SUJET DE TOUTES LES ORDONNANCES QUI SEMBLENT AMBIGUËS.
- IL EXISTE DIFFÉRENTS TYPES D'INSULINES. VÉRIFIER LE TYPE, LA DOSE ET LA DATE DE PÉREMPTION DE L'INSULINE AVEC UN AUTRE PROFESSIONNEL DE LA SANTÉ. NE PAS SUBSTITUER UN TYPE D'INSULINE À UN AUTRE SANS RECOMMANDATION EXPRESSE DU MÉDECIN OU D'UN AUTRE PROFESSIONNEL DE LA SANTÉ.
- N'utiliser *que* les seringues à insuline pour prélever la dose. Les unités inscrites sur la seringue doivent correspondre aux unités d'insuline par mL. Avant de prélever la dose, faire tourner la fiole dans la paume des mains pour bien disperser la solution; ne pas agiter.
- **ALERTE CLINIQUE**: NE PAS MÉLANGER AVEC D'AUTRES INSULINES OU SOLUTIONS; NE PAS UTILISER DE SERINGUES CONTENANT TOUT AUTRE PRODUIT MÉDICAMENTEUX OU RÉSIDU. SI UNE INSULINE À ACTION RAPIDE OU TRÈS RAPIDE DOIT ÊTRE ADMINISTRÉE SIMULTANÉMENT, UTILISER DES SERINGUES DISTINCTES ET DES POINTS D'INJECTION DIFFÉRENTS. LA SOLUTION DOIT ÊTRE CLAIRE ET INCOLORE.
- Conserver l'insuline au frais; il n'est pas nécessaire de garder la fiole entamée au réfrigérateur. Celle-ci se conservera pendant 28 jours à une température ne dépassant pas les 30 °C, à l'abri de la chaleur et de la lumière directe. Il est recommandé de jeter les fioles 28 jours après les avoir ouvertes pour prévenir la prolifération des microorganismes. Ne pas utiliser l'insuline si elle a changé de couleur ou si elle est anormalement visqueuse.
- Il peut s'avérer nécessaire d'adapter les doses d'insuline à courte durée d'action (régulière, aspart ou lispro) lorsqu'on amorce le traitement par l'insuline détémir ou l'insuline glargine.

SC: Faire la rotation des points d'injection.

- Administrer dans l'abdomen, la cuisse ou le haut du bras. Pincer la peau, introduire l'aiguille, injecter l'insuline et retirer l'aiguille. Maintenir une légère pression sur le point d'injection sans masser.
- Lorsque l'insuline détémir est prescrite 1 fois par jour, l'administrer au souper ou au coucher.
- Administrer l'insuline glargine 1 fois par jour, au coucher.

ENSEIGNEMENT AU PATIENT ET À SES PROCHES

- Montrer au patient comment s'autoadministrer l'insuline et préciser le type d'insuline qu'il doit utiliser, le matériel dont il doit se servir (seringue, cartouche, tampons d'alcool), le mode de conservation de l'agent et la méthode de mise au rebut des seringues. Insister sur le fait qu'il est important de ne pas changer de marque d'insuline ou de seringue, qu'il faut choisir soigneusement les points d'injection et en assurer la rotation, et qu'il est vital d'observer le schéma posologique prescrit.
- Informer le patient que l'insuline détémir et l'insuline glargine NE DOIVENT PAS ÊTRE MÉLANGÉES avec d'autres types d'insulines.
- Expliquer au patient que ce médicament équilibre la glycémie, mais ne guérit pas le diabète. Le traitement est de longue durée.
- Faire la démonstration du dosage de la glycémie et de la cétonémie. Ces dosages doivent être exécutés attentivement pendant les périodes de stress ou pendant une maladie. Il faut prévenir un professionnel de la santé si des modifications importantes surviennent.

I

- Insister sur le fait qu'il est important de suivre les consignes des professionnels de la santé concernant l'alimentation et les exercices.
- Conseiller au patient de consulter un professionnel de la santé avant de prendre en concomitance d'autres médicaments d'ordonnance ou en vente libre, des produits naturels ou de l'alcool.
- Recommander au patient qui doit suivre un autre traitement ou subir une intervention chirurgicale d'avertir le professionnel de la santé qu'il suit un traitement à l'insuline.
- Recommander au patient de communiquer avec un professionnel de la santé s'il souffre de nausées, de vomissements ou de fièvre, s'il est incapable de suivre le régime alimentaire habituel ou si la glycémie n'est pas équilibrée.
- EXPLIQUER AU PATIENT QUELS SONT LES SIGNES ET LES SYMPTÔMES D'HYPOGLYCÉMIE ET D'HYPERGLYCÉMIE, ET LES MESURES À PRENDRE S'ILS SE MANIFESTENT.
- Demander à la patiente de prévenir le professionnel de la santé si elle pense être enceinte ou désire le devenir.
- Inciter le patient souffrant de diabète à toujours garder sur lui du sucre (bonbons, sachets de sucre) et une pièce d'identité où sont inscrits sa maladie et son traitement médicamenteux.
- Insister sur l'importance des examens de suivi réguliers.

VÉRIFICATION DE L'EFFICACITÉ THÉRAPEUTIQUE

L'efficacité du traitement peut être démontrée par: l'équilibrage de la glycémie sans apparition d'épisodes d'hypoglycémie ou d'hyperglycémie.

ALERTE CLINIQUE

INSULINES (ACTION TRÈS RAPIDE)

insuline aspart
NovoRapid

insuline lispro
Humalog

CLASSIFICATION:
Antidiabétiques, hormones pancréatiques

Grossesse – catégorie B

INDICATIONS

Traitement du diabète (de type 1 ou de type 2).

MÉCANISME D'ACTION

Abaissement de la glycémie par augmentation de la captation cellulaire du glucose au niveau des cellules musculaires et adipeuses, et par inhibition de la sortie du glucose du foie ■ Inhibition de la lipolyse et de la protéolyse ■ Stimulation de la synthèse des protéines. ***Effets thérapeutiques:*** Équilibrage de la glycémie chez les patients diabétiques.

PHARMACOCINÉTIQUE

Absorption: Rapide (SC).
Distribution: Tout l'organisme.
Métabolisme et excrétion: Métabolisme hépatique, splénique, rénal et musculaire.
Demi-vie: De 5 à 6 minutes (prolongée chez les diabétiques; la demi-vie biologique est plus longue).

Profil temps-action (effet hypoglycémiant)

	DÉBUT D'ACTION	PIC	DURÉE
Insuline aspart SC	10 - 15 min	1 - 3 h	3 - 5 h
Insuline lispro SC	15 - 30 min	0,75 - 2,5 h	3,5 - 4,75 h

CONTRE-INDICATIONS, PRÉCAUTIONS ET MISES EN GARDE

Contre-indications: Allergie ou hypersensibilité à un type particulier d'insuline, d'agent de conservation ou d'additif ■ Hypoglycémie.

Précautions et mises en garde: Stress ou infection (les besoins en insuline peuvent varier) ■ **OBST.:** Les besoins en insuline peuvent varier selon le trimestre de la grossesse ■ **ALLAITEMENT:** Les femmes qui allaitent peuvent avoir besoin d'adapter leur dose d'insuline ■ Insuffisance hépatique (les besoins en insuline peuvent diminuer en raison d'une déficience de la gluconéogenèse et de l'atténuation du métabolisme insulinique) ■ Insuffisance rénale (les besoins en insuline peuvent diminuer).

RÉACTIONS INDÉSIRABLES ET EFFETS SECONDAIRES

Tég.: urticaire.
End.: HYPOGLYCÉMIE, hyperglycémie rebond (effet de Somogyi).
Locaux: lipodystrophie (lipoatrophie, lipohypertrophie), démangeaisons, rougeurs, œdème.
Divers: réactions allergiques, incluant l'ANAPHYLAXIE.

INTERACTIONS

Médicament-médicament: Les **bêtabloquants** peuvent masquer certains signes et symptômes d'hypoglycémie, et en retarder la disparition ■ Les **diurétiques thiazidiques**, les **corticostéroïdes**, les **sympathomimétiques**, les **hormones thyroïdiennes**, les **œstrogènes**, les **antipsychotiques atypiques** et les **inhibiteurs de la protéase (antirétroviraux)** peuvent accroître les besoins en insuline ■ Les **stéroïdes anabolisants (testostérone)**, l'**alcool**, les **IMAO**, les **hypoglycémiants oraux**, l'**octréotide**, les **inhibiteurs de l'enzyme de conversion de l'angiotensine (IECA)** et les **salicylates** peuvent réduire les besoins en insuline.

Médicament-produits naturels: La **glucosamine** peut entraver l'équilibrage de la glycémie.

VOIES D'ADMINISTRATION ET POSOLOGIE

La dose dépend de la glycémie, de la réponse au traitement et de nombreux autres facteurs.

- **SC (adultes et enfants)**: De 0,5 à 1 U/kg/jour.

PRÉSENTATION

Au Canada, toutes les insulines sont présentées à une concentration de 100 unités/mL.

Insuline aspart: fioles de 10 mL^{Phc}, cartouches de 3 mL^{Phc} ■ **Insuline lispro**: fioles de 10 mL^{Phc}, cartouches de 3 mL^{Phc}, stylos-injecteurs de 3 mL^{Phc}.

SOINS INFIRMIERS

ÉVALUATION DE LA SITUATION

- SUIVRE À INTERVALLES RÉGULIERS, PENDANT TOUTE LA DURÉE DU TRAITEMENT, LES SIGNES ET LES SYMPTÔMES D'HYPOGLYCÉMIE (ANXIÉTÉ, FRISSONS, SUEURS FROIDES, CONFUSION, PEAU PÂLE ET FROIDE, DIFFICULTÉS DE CONCENTRATION, SOMNOLENCE, FAIM EXCESSIVE, CÉPHALÉES, IRRITABILITÉ, NAUSÉES, NERVOSITÉ, POULS RAPIDE, TREMBLEMENTS, FATIGUE OU FAIBLESSE INHABITUELLES) et d'hyperglycémie (confusion, somnolence, rougeur et sécheresse de la peau, haleine fruitée, mictions fréquentes, perte d'appétit, fatigue, soif inhabituelle).
- Peser le patient à intervalles réguliers. Les modifications de poids peuvent dicter l'adaptation de la posologie d'insuline.

Tests de laboratoire:

- L'insuline peut abaisser les concentrations sériques de phosphates inorganiques, de magnésium et de potassium.
- Suivre la glycémie et la cétonémie toutes les 6 heures pendant toute la durée du traitement (plus fréquemment en présence d'acidocétose ou de stress). L'efficacité du traitement peut également être déterminée par la mesure de l'hémoglobine glyquée.

TOXICITÉ ET SURDOSAGE: LE SURDOSAGE SE MANIFESTE PAR DES SYMPTÔMES D'HYPOGLYCÉMIE. ON PEUT TRAITER L'HYPOGLYCÉMIE LÉGÈRE EN ADMINISTRANT DU GLUCOSE PAR VOIE ORALE. L'HYPOGLYCÉMIE GRAVE EST UNE URGENCE, CAR ELLE PEUT METTRE EN DANGER LA VIE DU PATIENT. LE TRAITEMENT CONSISTE À ADMINISTRER DU GLUCOSE PAR VOIE IV, DU GLUCAGON OU DE L'ADRÉNALINE.

DIAGNOSTICS INFIRMIERS POSSIBLES

- Connaissances insuffisantes sur le traitement médicamenteux (Enseignement au patient et à ses proches).
- Non-observance du traitement médicamenteux (Enseignement au patient et à ses proches).

INTERVENTIONS INFIRMIÈRES

- **ALERTE CLINIQUE**: LES ERREURS LIÉES À L'INSULINOTHÉRAPIE ONT ENTRAÎNÉ DES ACCIDENTS ET MÊME DES DÉCÈS. SE RENSEIGNER AUPRÈS DU MÉDECIN TRAITANT AU SUJET DE TOUTES LES ORDONNANCES QUI SEMBLENT AMBIGUËS.
- IL EXISTE DIFFÉRENTS TYPES D'INSULINES. VÉRIFIER LE TYPE, LA DOSE ET LA DATE DE PÉREMPTION DE L'INSULINE AVEC UN AUTRE PROFESSIONNEL DE LA SANTÉ. NE PAS SUBSTITUER UN TYPE D'INSULINE À UN AUTRE SANS RECOMMANDATION EXPRESSE DU MÉDECIN OU D'UN AUTRE PROFESSIONNEL DE LA SANTÉ.
- N'utiliser *que* les seringues à insuline pour prélever la dose. Les unités inscrites sur la seringue doivent correspondre aux unités d'insuline par mL. N'utiliser *que* les seringues à insuline de 100 unités pour prélever la dose d'*insuline lispro*. Avant de prélever la dose, faire tourner la fiole dans la paume des mains pour bien disperser la solution; ne pas agiter.
- Lorsqu'on doit mélanger les insulines, prélever d'abord l'insuline aspart ou l'insuline lispro pour éviter la contamination de la fiole contenant ce type d'insuline. Les mélanges d'insulines ne doivent pas être utilisés pour l'administration par pompe SC.
- Conserver l'insuline au frais; il n'est pas nécessaire de garder la fiole entamée au réfrigérateur. Celle-ci se conservera pendant 28 jours à une température ne dépassant pas les 30 °C, à l'abri de la chaleur et de la lumière directe. Il est recommandé de jeter les fioles 28 jours après les avoir ouvertes pour prévenir la prolifération des microorganismes. Ne pas utiliser l'insuline si elle a changé de couleur ou si elle est anormalement visqueuse.
- Étant donné la courte durée d'action de l'insuline aspart et de l'insuline lispro, il peut s'avérer nécessaire d'administrer un traitement d'appoint par une insuline à action intermédiaire ou prolongée pour équilibrer la glycémie.

I

SC:
- Faire la rotation des points d'injection.
- Administrer dans l'abdomen, la cuisse ou le haut du bras. Pincer la peau, introduire l'aiguille, injecter l'insuline et retirer l'aiguille. Maintenir une légère pression sur le point d'injection sans masser.
- Administrer l'insuline aspart ou l'insuline lispro dans les 15 minutes précédant un repas.

ENSEIGNEMENT AU PATIENT ET À SES PROCHES

- Montrer au patient comment s'autoadministrer l'insuline et préciser le type d'insuline qu'il doit utiliser, le matériel dont il doit se servir (seringue, cartouche, tampons d'alcool), le mode de conservation de l'agent et la méthode de mise au rebut des seringues. Insister sur le fait qu'il est important de ne pas changer de marque d'insuline ou de seringue, qu'il faut choisir soigneusement les points d'injection et en assurer la rotation, et qu'il est vital d'observer le schéma posologique prescrit.
- Faire la démonstration du mode de mélange des insulines: prélever d'abord l'insuline aspart ou l'insuline lispro, tourner la fiole d'insuline à action intermédiaire dans la paume des mains sans l'agiter (en raison du risque de fausser les doses); prélever ensuite l'insuline à action intermédiaire.
- Expliquer au patient que ce médicament équilibre la glycémie, mais ne guérit pas le diabète. Le traitement est de longue durée.
- Faire la démonstration du dosage de la glycémie et de la cétonémie. Ces dosages doivent être exécutés attentivement pendant les périodes de stress ou pendant une maladie. Il faut prévenir un professionnel de la santé si des modifications importantes surviennent.
- Insister sur le fait qu'il est important de suivre les consignes des professionnels de la santé concernant l'alimentation et les exercices.
- Conseiller au patient de consulter un professionnel de la santé avant de prendre en concomitance d'autres médicaments d'ordonnance ou en vente libre, des produits naturels ou de l'alcool.
- Recommander au patient qui doit suivre un autre traitement ou subir une intervention chirurgicale d'avertir le professionnel de la santé qu'il suit un traitement à l'insuline.
- Recommander au patient de communiquer avec un professionnel de la santé s'il souffre de nausées, de vomissements ou de fièvre, s'il est incapable de suivre le régime alimentaire habituel ou si la glycémie n'est pas équilibrée.
- EXPLIQUER AU PATIENT QUELS SONT LES SIGNES ET LES SYMPTÔMES D'HYPOGLYCÉMIE ET D'HYPERGLYCÉMIE, ET LES MESURES À PRENDRE S'ILS SE MANIFESTENT.
- Demander à la patiente de prévenir le professionnel de la santé si elle pense être enceinte ou désire le devenir.
- Inciter le patient souffrant de diabète à toujours garder sur lui du sucre (bonbons, sachets de sucre) et une pièce d'identité où sont inscrits sa maladie et son traitement médicamenteux.
- Insister sur l'importance des examens de suivi réguliers.

VÉRIFICATION DE L'EFFICACITÉ THÉRAPEUTIQUE

L'efficacité du traitement peut être démontrée par: l'équilibrage de la glycémie sans apparition d'épisodes d'hypoglycémie ou d'hyperglycémie. ✳

ALERTE CLINIQUE

INSULINES (MÉLANGES)

insuline lispro protamine
Humalog Mix25, Humalog Mix50

insuline NPH avec insuline régulière
Humulin 30/70, Novolin ge 10/90, Novolin ge 20/80, Novolin ge 30/70, Novolin ge 40/60, Novolin ge 50/50

CLASSIFICATION:
Antidiabétiques, hormones pancréatiques

Grossesse – catégorie B

INDICATIONS

Traitement du diabète (de type 1 ou de type 2).

MÉCANISME D'ACTION

Abaissement de la glycémie par augmentation de la captation cellulaire du glucose au niveau des cellules musculaires et adipeuses, et par inhibition de la sortie du glucose du foie ▪ Inhibition de la lipolyse et de la protéolyse ▪ Stimulation de la synthèse des protéines. ***Effets thérapeutiques:*** Équilibrage de la glycémie chez les patients diabétiques.

PHARMACOCINÉTIQUE

Absorption: Bonne (SC). La vitesse d'absorption dépend du point d'injection, du volume injecté et d'autres facteurs.
Distribution: Tout l'organisme.

Métabolisme et excrétion: Métabolisme hépatique, splénique, rénal et musculaire.
Demi-vie: Variable selon le type d'insuline (prolongée chez les diabétiques; la demi-vie biologique est plus longue).
Profil temps-action: (effet hypoglycémiant)

	DÉBUT D'ACTION	PIC	DURÉE
Insuline lispro protamine SC	15 - 30 min	2,8 h	jusqu'à 24 h
Insuline NPH/régulière SC	30 min	4 - 8 h	jusqu'à 24 h

CONTRE-INDICATIONS, PRÉCAUTIONS ET MISES EN GARDE

Contre-indications: Allergie ou hypersensibilité à un type particulier d'insuline, d'agent de conservation ou d'additif ▪ Hypoglycémie ▪ Les mélanges d'insulines ne doivent pas être administrés par voie IV ni utilisés dans le traitement du coma.
Précautions et mises en garde: Stress ou infection (les besoins en insuline peuvent varier) ▪ **OBST.**: Les besoins en insuline peuvent varier selon le trimestre de la grossesse ▪ **ALLAITEMENT**: Les femmes qui allaitent peuvent avoir besoin d'adapter leur dose d'insuline ▪ **PÉD.**: L'innocuité et l'efficacité de l'insuline lispro protamine chez les enfants n'ont pas été établies ▪ Insuffisance hépatique (les besoins en insuline peuvent diminuer en raison d'une déficience de la gluconéogenèse et de l'atténuation du métabolisme insulinique) ▪ Insuffisance rénale (les besoins en insuline peuvent diminuer).

RÉACTIONS INDÉSIRABLES ET EFFETS SECONDAIRES

Tég.: urticaire.
End.: HYPOGLYCÉMIE, hyperglycémie rebond (effet de Somogyi).
Locaux: lipodystrophie (lipoatrophie, lipohypertrophie), démangeaisons, rougeurs, œdème.
Divers: réactions allergiques, incluant l'ANAPHYLAXIE.

INTERACTIONS

Médicament-médicament: Les **bêtabloquants** peuvent masquer certains signes et symptômes d'hypoglycémie, et en retarder la disparition ▪ Les **diurétiques thiazidiques**, les **corticostéroïdes**, les **sympathomimétiques**, les **hormones thyroïdiennes**, les **œstrogènes**, les **antipsychotiques atypiques** et les **inhibiteurs de la protéase (antirétroviraux)** peuvent accroître les besoins en insuline ▪ Les **stéroïdes anabolisants (testostérone)**, l'**alcool**, les **IMAO**, les **hypoglycémiants oraux**, l'**octréotide**, les **inhibiteurs de l'enzyme de conversion de l'angiotensine (IECA)** et les **salicylates** peuvent réduire les besoins en insuline.
Médicament-produits naturels: La **glucosamine** peut entraver l'équilibrage de la glycémie.

VOIES D'ADMINISTRATION ET POSOLOGIE

La dose dépend de la glycémie, de la réponse au traitement et de nombreux autres facteurs.
- **SC (adultes et enfants)**: De 0,5 à 1 U/kg/jour.

PRÉSENTATION

Au Canada, toutes les insulines sont présentées à une concentration de 100 unités/mL
Insuline lispro protamine: cartouches de 3 mL^{Phc}, stylos-injecteurs de 3 mL^{Phc} ▪ **Insuline NPH et insuline régulière**: fioles de 10 mL^{Phc}, cartouches de 3 mL^{Phc}, 30/70: seringues jetables de 3 mL^{Phc}.

SOINS INFIRMIERS

ÉVALUATION DE LA SITUATION

- SUIVRE À INTERVALLES RÉGULIERS, PENDANT TOUTE LA DURÉE DU TRAITEMENT, LES SIGNES ET LES SYMPTÔMES D'HYPOGLYCÉMIE (ANXIÉTÉ, FRISSONS, SUEURS FROIDES, CONFUSION, PEAU PÂLE ET FROIDE, DIFFICULTÉS DE CONCENTRATION, SOMNOLENCE, FAIM EXCESSIVE, CÉPHALÉES, IRRITABILITÉ, NAUSÉES, NERVOSITÉ, POULS RAPIDE, TREMBLEMENTS, FATIGUE OU FAIBLESSE INHABITUELLES) et d'hyperglycémie (confusion, somnolence, rougeur et sécheresse de la peau, haleine fruitée, mictions fréquentes, perte d'appétit, fatigue, soif inhabituelle).
- Peser le patient à intervalles réguliers. Les modifications de poids peuvent dicter l'adaptation de la posologie d'insuline.

Tests de laboratoire:
- L'insuline peut abaisser les concentrations sériques de phosphates inorganiques, de magnésium et de potassium.
- Suivre la glycémie et la cétonémie toutes les 6 heures pendant toute la durée du traitement (plus fréquemment en présence d'acidocétose ou de stress). L'efficacité du traitement peut également être déterminée par la mesure de l'hémoglobine glyquée.

TOXICITÉ ET SURDOSAGE: LE SURDOSAGE SE MANIFESTE PAR DES SYMPTÔMES D'HYPOGLYCÉMIE. ON PEUT TRAITER L'HYPOGLYCÉMIE LÉGÈRE EN ADMINISTRANT DU GLUCOSE PAR VOIE ORALE. L'HYPOGLYCÉMIE GRAVE EST UNE URGENCE, CAR ELLE PEUT METTRE EN DANGER LA VIE DU PATIENT. LE TRAITEMENT CONSISTE À ADMINISTRER DU GLUCOSE PAR VOIE IV, DU GLUCAGON OU DE L'ADRÉNALINE.

DIAGNOSTICS INFIRMIERS POSSIBLES

- Connaissances insuffisantes sur le traitement médicamenteux (Enseignement au patient et à ses proches).
- Non-observance du traitement médicamenteux (Enseignement au patient et à ses proches).

INTERVENTIONS INFIRMIÈRES

ALERTE CLINIQUE: LES ERREURS LIÉES À L'INSULINOTHÉRAPIE ONT ENTRAÎNÉ DES ACCIDENTS ET MÊME DES DÉCÈS. SE RENSEIGNER AUPRÈS DU MÉDECIN TRAITANT AU SUJET DE TOUTES LES ORDONNANCES QUI SEMBLENT AMBIGUËS.

- IL EXISTE DIFFÉRENTS TYPES D'INSULINES. VÉRIFIER LE TYPE, LA DOSE ET LA DATE DE PÉREMPTION DE L'INSULINE AVEC UN AUTRE PROFESSIONNEL DE LA SANTÉ. NE PAS SUBSTITUER UN TYPE D'INSULINE À UN AUTRE SANS RECOMMANDATION EXPRESSE DU MÉDECIN OU D'UN AUTRE PROFESSIONNEL DE LA SANTÉ.
- N'utiliser *que* les seringues à insuline pour prélever la dose. Les unités inscrites sur la seringue doivent correspondre aux unités d'insuline par mL. On peut se procurer des seringues spécialement destinées au prélèvement des doses inférieures à 50 unités. N'utiliser *que* les seringues à insuline de 100 unités pour prélever la dose d'*insuline lispro protamine*. Avant de prélever la dose, faire tourner la fiole dans la paume des mains pour bien disperser la solution; ne pas agiter.
- Conserver l'insuline au frais; il n'est pas nécessaire de garder la fiole entamée au réfrigérateur. Celle-ci se conservera pendant 28 jours à une température ne dépassant pas les 30 °C, à l'abri de la chaleur et de la lumière directe. Il est recommandé de jeter les fioles 28 jours après les avoir ouvertes pour prévenir la prolifération des microorganismes. Ne pas utiliser l'insuline si elle a changé de couleur ou si elle est anormalement visqueuse.

SC:

- Faire la rotation des points d'injection.
- Administrer dans l'abdomen, la cuisse ou le haut du bras. Pincer la peau, introduire l'aiguille, injecter l'insuline et retirer l'aiguille. Maintenir une légère pression sur le point d'injection, sans masser.
- Administrer l'insuline lispro protamine dans les 15 minutes précédant un repas.
- Administrer le mélange d'insuline NPH/insuline régulière de 15 à 30 minutes avant un repas.

ENSEIGNEMENT AU PATIENT ET À SES PROCHES

- Montrer au patient comment s'autoadministrer l'insuline et préciser le type d'insuline qu'il doit utiliser, le matériel dont il doit se servir (seringue, cartouche, tampons d'alcool), le mode de conservation de l'agent et la méthode de mise au rebut des seringues. Insister sur le fait qu'il est important de ne pas changer de marque d'insuline ou de seringue, qu'il faut choisir soigneusement les points d'injection et en assurer la rotation, et qu'il est vital d'observer le schéma posologique prescrit.
- Expliquer au patient que ce médicament équilibre la glycémie, mais ne guérit pas le diabète. Le traitement est de longue durée.
- Faire la démonstration du dosage de la glycémie et de la cétonémie. Ces dosages doivent être exécutés attentivement pendant les périodes de stress ou pendant une maladie. Il faut prévenir un professionnel de la santé si des modifications importantes surviennent.
- Insister sur le fait qu'il est important de suivre les consignes des professionnels de la santé concernant l'alimentation et les exercices.
- Conseiller au patient de consulter un professionnel de la santé avant de prendre en concomitance d'autres médicaments d'ordonnance ou en vente libre, des produits naturels ou de l'alcool.
- Recommander au patient qui doit suivre un autre traitement ou subir une intervention chirurgicale d'avertir le professionnel de la santé qu'il suit un traitement à l'insuline.
- Recommander au patient de communiquer avec un professionnel de la santé s'il souffre de nausées, de vomissements ou de fièvre, s'il est incapable de suivre le régime alimentaire habituel ou si la glycémie n'est pas équilibrée.
- EXPLIQUER AU PATIENT QUELS SONT LES SIGNES ET LES SYMPTÔMES D'HYPOGLYCÉMIE ET D'HYPERGLYCÉMIE, ET LES MESURES À PRENDRE S'ILS SE MANIFESTENT.
- Demander à la patiente de prévenir le professionnel de la santé si elle pense être enceinte ou désire le devenir.
- Inciter le patient souffrant de diabète à toujours garder sur lui du sucre (bonbons, sachets de sucre) et une pièce d'identité où sont inscrits sa maladie et son traitement médicamenteux.
- Insister sur l'importance des examens de suivi réguliers.

VÉRIFICATION DE L'EFFICACITÉ THÉRAPEUTIQUE

L'efficacité du traitement peut être démontrée par: l'équilibrage de la glycémie sans apparition d'épisodes d'hypoglycémie ou d'hyperglycémie.

INTERFÉRON ALPHA

peginterféron alpha-2a
Pegasys
interféron alpha-2b (recombinant)
Intron A
peginterféron alpha-2b
Unitron PEG
interféron alphacon-1
Infergen

CLASSIFICATION:
Modulateur des réactions biologiques (interféron)

Grossesse – catégorie C

INDICATIONS

Peginterféron alpha-2a: Traitement de l'hépatite C chronique (traitement d'association avec la ribavirine possible) ■ Traitement de l'hépatite B chronique de formes AgHBe-positive et AgHBe-négative, chez les patients présentant une inflammation du foie et des signes de réplication virale. **Interféron alpha-2b**: Traitement de la leucémie myéloïde chronique, de la thrombocytose associée à la leucémie myéloïde chronique, du myélome multiple, du lymphome non hodgkinien, de l'épithélioma basocellulaire, de la leucémie à tricholeucocytes (cellules chevelues), du mélanome malin, du sarcome de Kaposi lié au sida, du condylome acuminé (intralésionnel), de l'hépatite B chronique active et de l'hépatite C chronique. **Peginterféron alpha-2b**: Traitement de l'hépatite C chronique en association avec la ribavirine ou en monothérapie en cas d'intolérance ou de contre-indication à la ribavirine. **Interféron alphacon-1**: Traitement de l'hépatite C chronique.

MÉCANISME D'ACTION

Les interférons sont des protéines capables de modifier la réponse immunitaire, et qui ont des effets antiprolifératifs sur les cellules tumorales. L'interféron alpha-2b et l'interféron alphacon-1 sont obtenus par les techniques de l'ADN recombinant; le peginterféron est un dérivé pégylé de l'interféron alpha, qui a une durée d'action prolongée. ■ Les interférons ont aussi des effets antiviraux. ***Effets thérapeutiques:*** Effets antinéoplasiques, antiviraux et antiprolifératifs ■ Chez les patients atteints d'hépatite, ralentissement de l'évolution des lésions hépatiques.

PHARMACOCINÉTIQUE

Absorption: L'agent administré par voie orale n'est pas absorbé. Bonne absorption (> 80% IM et SC). Absorption systémique minimale à la suite de l'administration intralésionnelle.

Distribution: Inconnue.

Métabolisme et excrétion: Élimination hépatique, rénale et biliaire (mineure). *Peginterféron alpha-2a* – moins de 10 % est éliminé par les reins; le reste est métabolisé. *Peginterféron alpha-2b* – 30 % est excrété par les reins.

Demi-vie: *Interféron alpha-2b* – de 2 à 3 heures. *Peginterféron alpha-2a* – 80 heures. *Peginterféron alpha-2b* – 40 heures. *Interféron aphacon-1* – inconnue.

Profil temps-action

	DÉBUT D'ACTION	PIC	DURÉE
Interféron alpha-2b, IM, SC	1 – 3 mois	inconnu	3 – 5 jours (RC)
Interféron alpha-2b, IM, SC	inconnu	3 – 5 jours	3 – 5 jours (NP)
Interféron alpha-2b, IM, SC	2 semaines	inconnu	inconnue (FH)
Interféron alpha-2b	inconnu	4 – 8 semaines	inconnue (IL)
Peginterféron alpha-2b, SC	inconnu	6 mois ou plus	inconnue

NP: effet sur la numération plaquettaire; RC: réponse clinique; IL: régression des lésions; FH: effet sur la fonction hépatique, chez les patients atteints d'hépatite.

CONTRE-INDICATIONS, PRÉCAUTIONS ET MISES EN GARDE

Contre-indications: Hypersensibilité aux interférons alpha ou à tout autre ingrédient du produit ■ Insuffisance rénale grave (les patients dont la Cl_{Cr} < 50 mL/min ne doivent pas être traités à l'aide de l'intron-A associé à la ribavirine) ■ Hépatite auto-immune ou toute autre maladie auto-immune (Unitron PEG) ■ Affection mentale grave ou antécédents de trouble mental grave, anomalie thyroïdienne réfractaire, épilepsie, insuffisance rénale (Cl_{Cr} < 50 mL/min) ou hépatopathie décompensée (Unitron PEG) ■ Hépatopathie décompensée ou hépatite auto-immune (Infergen).

Précautions et mises en garde: Maladies cardiovasculaire, pulmonaire, rénale ou hépatique graves ■ Infections actives ■ Antécédents de troubles endocriniens ■ Antécédents psychiatriques ou maladie sous-jacente touchant le SNC ■ Réserve médullaire réduite ou aplasie médullaire ■ Présence de varicelle, de zona ou d'herpès labial (risque de réactivation ou de dissémination de la maladie) ■ Radiothérapie antérieure ou concomitante ■ Maladies auto-immunes (risque accru d'exacerbation) ■ **GÉR.**: Risque accru de réactions indésirables ■ **OBST.**: Femmes en âge de procréer, grossesse, allaitement ■ **PÉD.**: Enfants < 18 ans (l'innocuité de ces agents n'a pas été établie) ▪ Sarcome de Kaposi lié au sida dans la phase viscérale rapide (Intron-A).

Extrême prudence: ANTÉCÉDENTS DE DÉPRESSION OU DE TENTATIVE DE SUICIDE.

RÉACTIONS INDÉSIRABLES ET EFFETS SECONDAIRES

SNC: TROUBLES NEUROPSYCHIATRIQUES, étourdissements, confusion, dépression s'accompagnant d'idéation suicidaire, insomnie, nervosité, difficultés de concentration, perturbation de la pensée.

ORLO: vision trouble.

CV: ÉPISODES ISCHÉMIQUES, arythmies, douleurs thoraciques.

GI: COLITE, PANCRÉATITE, anorexie, perte d'appétit, diarrhée, sécheresse de la bouche (xérostomie), nausées, stomatite, altération du goût, vomissements, perte de poids, hépatite médicamenteuse (plus fréquente en présence de sarcome de Kaposi).

GU: suppression de la fonction des gonades.

Tég.: prurit, rash, alopécie, sécheresse de la peau, transpiration.

End.: troubles thyroïdiens (plus fréquents en présence de sarcome de Kaposi).

Hémat.: LEUCOPÉNIE, THROMBOPÉNIE, anémie, anémie hémolytique (lors d'administration conjointe de ribavirine).

Loc.: crampes dans les jambes, douleurs musculosquelettiques.

SN: neuropathie périphérique.

Divers: MALADIES AUTO-IMMUNES, MALADIES INFECTIEUSES, réactions allergiques comprenant l'ANAPHYLAXIE, frissons, fièvre, syndrome pseudogrippal.

INTERACTIONS

Médicament-médicament: Myélosuppression additive lors de l'administration concomitante d'autres **antinéoplasiques** ou d'une **radiothérapie** ▪ Risque accru de dépression du SNC lors de l'usage concomitant de **dépresseurs du SNC**, comprenant l'**alcool**, les **antihistaminiques**, les **hypnosédatifs** et les **opioïdes** ▪ Risque de ralentissement du métabolisme, d'élévation des concentrations sanguines et d'intensification des effets toxiques de la **théophylline** et de la **méthadone** ▪ Risque accru de réactions indésirables à la **zidovudine** ▪ La **ribavirine** élève le risque d'anémie hémolytique, particulièrement si la Cl_{Cr} < 50 mL/min (éviter l'usage concomitant dans la mesure du possible).

Médicament-produits naturels: Éviter l'usage concomitant d'**échinacée** et de **mélatonine.**

VOIES D'ADMINISTRATION ET POSOLOGIE

Interféron alpha-2b (Intron-A)

- **IV (adultes):** *Mélanome malin* – 20 millions d'unités/m^2/jour, pendant 5 jours consécutifs par semaine, pendant les 4 semaines initiales; par la suite, administrer une dose d'entretien par voie SC.
- **IM, SC (adultes):** *Leucémie à tricholeucocytes (cellules chevelues)* – 2 millions d'unités/m^2 par voie SC, 3 fois par semaine. *Leucémie myéloïde chronique* – de 4 à 5 millions d'unités/m^2 par voie SC, 1 fois par jour, jusqu'à la maîtrise de la leucocytose. Une fois la leucocytose maîtrisée, on peut administrer de 4 à 5 millions d'unités/m^2, 3 fois par semaine. Des doses allant de 0,5 à 10 millions d'unités/m^2 peuvent être nécessaires. *Thrombocytose associée à la leucémie myéloïde chronique* – de 4 à 5 millions d'unités/m^2 par voie SC, 1 fois par jour, jusqu'au rétablissement du nombre de plaquettes. Une fois le nombre de plaquettes rétabli, on peut administrer de 4 à 5 millions d'unités/m^2, 3 fois par semaine. Des doses allant de 0,5 à 10 millions d'unités/m^2 peuvent être nécessaires. *Lymphome non hodgkinien (traitement adjuvant à la chimiothérapie)* – 5 millions d'unités par voie SC, 3 fois par semaine, pendant 18 mois. *Mélanome malin* – 10 millions d'unités/m^2/jour, 3 fois par semaine, pendant 48 semaines, après administration de l'agent à la posologie initiale par voie IV. *Myélome multiple* – 3 millions d'unités/m^2 par voie SC, 3 fois par semaine, chez les patients qui se trouvent à la phase stationnaire qui suit la chimiothérapie. *Sarcome de Kaposi* – 30 millions d'unités/m^2, 3 fois par semaine. *Hépatite B chronique active* – 5 millions d'unités/jour ou 10 millions d'unités, 3 fois par semaine, pendant 16 semaines. *Hépatite C chronique* – 3 millions d'unités, 3 fois par semaine. La dose peut être augmentée jusqu'à 10 millions d'unités, 3 fois par semaine, si le patient ne répond pas au traitement. Le traitement peut se poursuivre jusqu'à 18 mois.
- **SC (enfants > 3 ans):** *Traitement de l'hépatite B ou C* – 3 millions d'unités/m^2, 3 fois par semaine, pendant la première semaine; porter ensuite la dose à 6 millions d'unités/m^2, 3 fois par semaine (ne pas dépasser 10 millions d'unités/dose) pendant 16 à 24 semaines (*usage non approuvé chez les enfants*).
- **IL (adultes):** *Condylome acuminé* – 1 million unités/lésion, 3 fois par semaine, pendant 3 semaines; ne traiter que 5 lésions par cycle. *Épithéliome basocellulaire* – pour des lésions inférieures à 2 cm^2, injecter 1,5 million d'unités dans la lésion, 3 fois par semaine, pendant 3 semaines. Pour des lésions de taille supérieure à 2 cm^2, injecter 0,5 million

d'unités/cm² de la surface initiale de la lésion jusqu'à un maximum de 5 millions d'unités dans la lésion, 3 fois par semaine, pendant 3 semaines.

Peginterféron alpha-2a (Pegasys)

- **SC (adultes)**: 180 µg, 1 fois par semaine, pendant 48 semaines.

Interféron alphacon-1 (Infergen)

- **SC (adultes)**: 9 µg, 3 fois par semaine, pendant 24 semaines. Les patients qui ont toléré un traitement initial et qui n'ont pas répondu par la suite ou qui ont rechuté à l'arrêt du traitement peuvent être traités à nouveau avec 15 µg, 3 fois par semaine, pendant 48 semaines.

Peginterféron alpha-2b (Unitron PEG)

- **SC (adultes)**: 1 µg/kg, 1 fois par semaine, pendant 48 semaines.

PRÉSENTATION

- **Peginterféron alpha-2a (Pegasys)**
  Solution pour injection: 180 µg/mL[Pr] en ampoules uniservice ▪ **Seringues préremplies**: 180 µg/0,5 mL[Pr]. **En association avec**: ribavirine (Pegasys RBV[Pr]).
- **Interféron alpha-2b (Intron-A)**
  Poudre pour injection: fioles de 10 millions d'unités[Pr] et de 18 millions d'unités[Pr] ▪ **Solution pour injection**: fioles de 18 millions d'unités (6 millions d'unités/mL)[Pr], fioles de 10 millions d'unités (10 millions d'unités/mL)[Pr] ou fioles de 25 millions d'unités (10 millions d'unités/mL)[Pr] ▪ **Solution pour injection par stylo multidoses (cartouche en verre)**: 15 millions d'unités par 1,2 mL[Pr], 30 millions d'unités par 1,2 mL[Pr], 60 millions d'unités par 1,2 mL[Pr].
- **Interféron alphacon-1 (Infergen)**
  Solution pour injection: fioles: 9 µg/0,3 mL[Pr] et 15 µg/0,5 mL[Pr].
- **Peginterféron alpha-2b (Unitron PEG)**
  Poudre lyophilisée pour injection: 50 µg/0,5 mL[Pr], 80 µg/0,5 mL[Pr], 120 µg/0,5 mL[Pr], 150 µg/0,5 mL[Pr]. **En association avec**: ribavirine (Pegentron[Pr]).

SOINS INFIRMIERS

ÉVALUATION DE LA SITUATION

- RECHERCHER LES SIGNES DE TROUBLES NEUROPSYCHIATRIQUES (IRRITABILITÉ, ANXIÉTÉ, DÉPRESSION, IDÉATION SUICIDAIRE, COMPORTEMENT AGRESSIF). IL PEUT S'AVÉRER NÉCESSAIRE D'ARRÊTER LE TRAITEMENT PAR L'INTERFÉRON ALPHA-2A.
- SUIVRE DE PRÈS LES SIGNES D'INFECTION (ALTÉRATION DES SIGNES VITAUX, ACCROISSEMENT DU NOMBRE DE LEUCOCYTES) TOUT AU LONG DU TRAITEMENT. ARRÊTER LE TRAITEMENT PAR L'INTERFÉRON ALPHA-2A EN CAS D'INFECTION GRAVE ET COMMENCER UNE ANTIBIOTHÉRAPIE.
- RESTER À L'AFFÛT DES MALADIES CARDIOVASCULAIRES (MESURER LE POULS ET LA PRESSION ARTÉRIELLE, ÉVALUER LES DOULEURS THORACIQUES). IL Y A RISQUE D'INFARCTUS DU MYOCARDE.
- Rechercher les signes de colite (douleurs abdominales, diarrhée sanguinolente, fièvre) et de pancréatite (nausées, vomissements, douleurs abdominales) tout au long du traitement. Arrêter le traitement si ces signes se manifestent; ils peuvent mener à une issue fatale. La colite disparaît habituellement en 1 à 3 semaines après l'arrêt du traitement.
- Rester à l'affût du syndrome pseudogrippal (fièvre, frissons, myalgie, céphalées). Les symptômes surviennent souvent brusquement dans les 3 à 6 heures qui suivent le début du traitement. Ils ont tendance à diminuer même si le traitement est poursuivi. Pour diminuer ces symptômes, on peut administrer de l'acétaminophène.
- Rester à l'affût d'une dépression médullaire. Rechercher les saignements (saignement des gencives, formation d'ecchymoses, pétéchies, sang dans les selles, l'urine et les vomissures) et éviter les injections IM et la prise de la température rectale, si le nombre de plaquettes est bas. Appliquer une pression sur les points de ponction veineuse pendant 10 minutes. En cas de neutropénie, rester à l'affût des signes d'infection. Il y a risque d'anémie. Suivre de près la fatigue accrue, la dyspnée et l'hypotension orthostatique.
- L'agent peut provoquer des nausées et des vomissements. On peut administrer des antiémétiques en prophylaxie. Suivre de près les ingesta et les excreta, le poids quotidien et l'appétit. Modifier l'alimentation selon la tolérance en cas d'anorexie. Encourager le patient à prendre au moins 2 litres de liquides par jour, si son état le permet.

Peginterféron alpha: Évaluer l'état des poumons (murmure vésiculaire, respirations) à intervalles réguliers tout au long du traitement.

- Effectuer un examen ophtalmologique avant le début du traitement. Suivre les patients atteints de diabète ou de rétinopathie hypertensive à intervalles réguliers pendant toute la durée du traitement. Arrêter le traitement en cas d'apparition d'une nouvelle maladie de l'œil ou de l'aggravation de celle existante.

Sarcome de Kaposi: Suivre de près le nombre, la taille et le caractère des lésions, avant le traitement et pendant toute sa durée.

Tests de laboratoire:

- **Atteinte systémique**: SUIVRE LA NUMÉRATION GLOBULAIRE ET LA FORMULE LEUCOCYTAIRE AVANT LE TRAITEMENT ET À INTERVALLES RÉGULIERS PENDANT TOUTE SA DURÉE. IL Y A RISQUE DE LEUCOPÉNIE, DE NEUTROPÉNIE, DE THROMBOPÉNIE, DE DIMINUTION DES CONCENTRATIONS D'HÉMOGLOBINE, DE CHUTE DE L'HÉMATOCRITE ET D'ANÉMIE HÉMOLYTIQUE. Les nadirs de la leucopénie et de la thrombopénie se produisent dans les 3 à 5 jours suivant le traitement, et les valeurs se rétablissent dans les 3 à 5 jours qui suivent l'arrêt du traitement par l'*interféron alpha-2b*. Si la numération granulocytaire est < 0,75 × 10^9/L ou la numération plaquettaire est < 50 × 10^9/L, réduire la dose d'interféron alpha-2b de 50 %. Si la numération granulocytaire est < 0,5 × 10^9/L ou la numération plaquettaire est < 30 × 10^9/L, interrompre l'administration de l'*interféron alpha-2b* jusqu'à ce que le nombre de plaquettes ou de granulocytes se normalise ou revienne aux valeurs initiales; reprendre ensuite le traitement à 100 % de la dose.
- Le nombre de plaquettes doit être ≥ 90 × 10^9/L et le NAN ≥1,5 × 10^9/L avant qu'on puisse amorcer un traitement par le peginterféron. Habituellement, cet agent entraîne une chute des concentrations d'hémoglobine, de l'hématocrite, du nombre de leucocytes, du NAN, ainsi que du nombre de lymphocytes et de plaquettes au cours des 2 premières semaines de traitement.
- Suivre les résultats des tests de la fonction hépatique (AST, ALT, LDH, bilirubine, phosphatase alcaline), du dosage des triglycérides et des tests de la fonction rénale (urée, créatinine, acide urique, analyse des urines) avant le traitement et à intervalles réguliers pendant toute sa durée. La créatinine sérique devrait être < 1,5 fois la limite supérieure de la normale, avant de commencer à administrer le peginterféron.
- **Hépatite**: Suivre de près les concentrations de TSH si une insuffisance thyroïdienne est décelée.
- **Leucémie à tricholeucocytes (cellules chevelues)**: Mesurer le nombre de cellules chevelues périphériques et médullaires avant le traitement et pendant toute sa durée.

DIAGNOSTICS INFIRMIERS POSSIBLES

- Risque d'accident (Effets secondaires).
- Risque d'infection (Effets secondaires).

INTERVENTIONS INFIRMIÈRES

- Préparer les solutions sous une hotte à flux laminaire. Porter des gants, une blouse et un masque pendant les manipulations. Jeter le matériel dans des contenants réservés à cet usage (voir l'annexe H).

Interféron alpha-2b (Intron-A)

- **IM, SC**: Préférer la voie sous-cutanée chez les patients dont le nombre de plaquettes est < 50 × 10^9/L.
- Reconstituer le contenu des fioles de 10 millions d'unités ainsi que celui des fioles de 18 millions d'unités avec 1 mL du diluant fourni par le fabricant (eau bactériostatique pour injection). Agiter légèrement. La solution peut être d'incolore à jaune pâle. Réfrigérer après la reconstitution. La solution est stable pendant 1 mois si elle est réfrigérée. Consulter les recommandations du fabricant avant de reconstituer la préparation.
- **IL**: Reconstituer le contenu de la fiole de 10 millions d'unités avec 1 mL d'eau bactériostatique pour injection. Administrer à l'aide d'une seringue à tuberculine de petit calibre (de 0,3 ou de 0,5 mm). Injecter chaque dose de 0,1 mL dans le centre de la base de la verrue par une technique intradermique. On peut traiter jusqu'à 5 lésions à la fois.

Peginterféron alpha-2a (Pegasys)

- Le contenu des fioles et des seringues préremplies n'est pas interchangeable. S'il faut changer de contenant, recalculer la dose. La solution doit être d'incolore à jaune pâle. Ne pas administrer de solution qui est trouble ou qui contient un précipité.
- Réchauffer la solution en la roulant délicatement entre la paume des mains; ne pas agiter la fiole.
- Suivre les consignes du *Guide des médicaments* pour l'utilisation des seringues préremplies.
- Administrer dans la cuisse ou l'abdomen.

Interféron alphacon-1 (Infergen)

- Conserver au réfrigérateur, à une température de 2 à 8 °C. Ne pas congeler. Éviter de secouer énergiquement. Ne pas utiliser au-delà de la date de péremption. On peut laisser Infergen se réchauffer à la température ambiante juste avant l'injection.

Peginterféron alpha-2b (Unitron PEG)

- Reconstituer le contenu de la fiole avec 0,7 mL d'eau stérile pour injection fournie par le fabricant. Prélever 0,5 mL de la solution obtenue. Administrer immédiatement; la solution est stable pendant 24 heures si elle est réfrigérée. Inspecter la solution avant de l'administrer. Elle doit être transparente et incolore. Ne pas administrer de solution qui a changé de couleur ou qui contient un précipité; en prévenir le pharmacien. Réfrigérer la solution et la garder à l'abri de la lumière. Ne pas la congeler. Laisser la solution se réchauffer à la température ambiante. Jeter toute portion inutilisée. Consulter les recommandations du fabricant avant de reconstituer la préparation.

- **SC**: Administrer dans l'abdomen ou le côté extérieur du bras ou de la cuisse. Observer le point d'injection 2 heures après l'administration, pour déceler la rougeur, la tuméfaction ou la sensibilité au toucher.

ENSEIGNEMENT AU PATIENT ET À SES PROCHES

- Conseiller au patient de suivre rigoureusement la posologie recommandée par le médecin. S'il a oublié une dose, l'omettre et reprendre l'horaire habituel. Lui recommander de prévenir un professionnel de la santé s'il a omis plus de 1 dose.

Soins à domicile: Enseigner au patient et à ses proches la bonne technique de préparation et d'administration de l'injection ainsi que la manipulation appropriée du matériel et sa mise au rebut. Leur conseiller de lire les consignes d'utilisation avant l'administration et lors de chaque renouvellement d'ordonnance pour voir si des changements ont été apportés. Expliquer au patient qu'il ne doit pas remplacer une marque par une autre avant d'avoir consulté un professionnel de la santé; il y a risque de modification involontaire de la dose.

- Expliquer au patient qu'une réaction pseudogrippale peut survenir de 3 à 6 heures après l'administration. Lui conseiller de prendre de l'acétaminophène avant l'injection et toutes les 3 ou 4 heures par la suite, selon les besoins, pour enrayer les symptômes.
- Réexpliquer au patient les effets secondaires. L'administration de l'interféron peut être passagèrement interrompue ou la dose diminuée de 50 % en cas d'effet secondaire grave.
- RECOMMANDER AU PATIENT DE PRÉVENIR IMMÉDIATEMENT UN PROFESSIONNEL DE LA SANTÉ EN CAS DE FIÈVRE, DE FRISSONS, DE TOUX, D'ENROUEMENT, DE MAUX DE GORGE, DE SIGNES D'INFECTION, DE DOULEURS AU DOS OU AUX FLANCS, DE MICTIONS DOULOUREUSES OU DIFFICILES, DE SAIGNEMENT DES GENCIVES, DE FORMATION D'ECCHYMOSES, DE PÉTÉCHIES, DE PRÉSENCE DE SANG DANS LES SELLES, L'URINE OU LES VOMISSURES, DE FATIGUE ACCRUE, DE DYSPNÉE OU D'HYPOTENSION ORTHOSTATIQUE. CONSEILLER AU PATIENT D'ÉVITER LES FOULES ET LES PERSONNES AYANT CONTRACTÉ UNE INFECTION. LUI RECOMMANDER D'UTILISER UNE BROSSE À DENTS À POILS DOUX ET UN RASOIR ÉLECTRIQUE, ET DE PRENDRE GARDE AUX CHUTES. L'inciter à ne pas consommer des boissons alcoolisées ni à prendre des médicaments contenant de l'aspirine ou des AINS, en raison du risque de saignements gastriques.
- Informer le patient du risque de dépression et lui conseiller de prévenir un professionnel de la santé s'il se sent déprimé.
- Expliquer au patient qu'il risque de perdre ses cheveux. Explorer avec lui les stratégies lui permettant de s'adapter à ce changement.
- Expliquer à la patiente que l'interféron peut entraver la fécondité, mais qu'elle doit prendre des mesures contraceptives tout au long du traitement pour prévenir les effets nocifs du médicament chez le fœtus.
- Conseiller au patient de ne pas se faire vacciner sans avoir consulté au préalable un professionnel de la santé.
- Insister sur la nécessité de se soumettre à intervalles réguliers à des analyses de laboratoire permettant de suivre les effets secondaires.

Peginterféron: Prévenir le patient que le peginterféron alpha-2a ne diminue pas le risque de transmission du virus de l'hépatite C à d'autres personnes ni ne prévient la cirrhose, l'insuffisance hépatique ou le cancer du foie.

VÉRIFICATION DE L'EFFICACITÉ THÉRAPEUTIQUE

L'efficacité du traitement peut être démontrée par: la normalisation des paramètres hématologiques (hémoglobine, granulocytes neutrophiles, plaquettes, monocytes et cellules chevelues médullaires et périphériques) en présence de leucémie à tricholeucocytes. La réponse pourrait ne pas se manifester avant 1 à 3 mois, lors du traitement par l'*interféron alpha-2a* ou avant 6 mois, lors du traitement par l'*interféron alpha-2b* ▪ la diminution de la taille et du nombre de lésions en présence de sarcome de Kaposi. Le traitement doit parfois être poursuivi pendant 6 mois, avant qu'une pleine réponse se manifeste. On arrête le traitement lorsqu'on ne constate plus d'amélioration clinique et que les paramètres sont restés stables pendant 3 mois ▪ l'amélioration des paramètres hématologiques chez les patients atteints de leucémie myélogène chronique ▪ la prolongation de la durée de la rémission et de la survie chez les patients atteints de mélanome malin ▪ la disparition des verrues génitales ou la diminution de leur nombre. La réponse en cas de condylome acuminé se manifeste habituellement en l'espace de 4 à 8 semaines. Parfois on doit prolonger un cycle de traitement jusqu'à 16 semaines; un deuxième cycle pourrait être entrepris si les verrues génitales persistent et si les valeurs de laboratoire restent dans les limites acceptables ▪ la diminution des symptômes et l'amélioration des résultats de tests de la fonction hépatique chez les patients atteints d'hépatite B ▪ le ralentissement de l'évolution des lésions hépatiques chez les patients atteints d'hépatite C chronique. ✱

INTERFÉRON BÊTA

interféron bêta-1a
Avonex, Avonex PS, Rebif

interféron bêta-1b
Betaseron

CLASSIFICATION:
Immunomodulateur

Grossesse – catégorie C

INDICATIONS

Avonex et Avonex PS: Traitement des patients présentant des formes rémittentes ou évolutives secondaires de la sclérose en plaques et de ceux ayant subi un épisode de démyélinisation unique dont l'IRM a mis en évidence des lésions caractéristiques de la sclérose en plaques ■ **Rebif:** Traitement des formes rémittentes ou progressives secondaires de la sclérose en plaques. **Usages non approuvés: Interféron bêta-1a:** Traitement du condylome acuminé ne répondant pas aux traitements classiques ■ **Interféron bêta-1b:** Traitement de la sclérose en plaques rémittente ou des formes évolutives secondaires chez les patients ambulatoires.

MÉCANISME D'ACTION

Propriétés antivirales et immunorégulatrices dues aux interactions avec des récepteurs spécifiques de la surface des cellules ■ Agent produit par les techniques de recombinaison de l'ADN. ***Effets thérapeutiques:*** Réduction de l'incidence des récidives (dysfonctionnement neurologique) et ralentissement des déficiences physiques chez les patients atteints de sclérose en plaques.

PHARMACOCINÉTIQUE

Absorption: *Interféron bêta-1b* (50 % SC).

Distribution: Inconnue.

Métabolisme et excrétion: Inconnus.

Demi-vie: *Interféron bêta-1a* – 8,6 heures (SC), 10 heures (IM) – *Interféron bêta-1b* – de 8 minutes à 4,3 heures (IV).

Profil temps-action

	DÉBUT D'ACTION	PIC	DURÉE
Interféron bêta-1a IM†	dans les 12 h	48 h	4 jours
Interféron bêta-1b SC‡	rapide	1 – 8 h	inconnue

† Modification de la réponse biologique.

‡ Concentrations sériques.

CONTRE-INDICATIONS, PRÉCAUTIONS ET MISES EN GARDE

Contre-indications: Hypersensibilité à l'interféron bêta naturel ou recombinant, à l'albumine humaine, au latex ou à un ingrédient de la préparation ■ Grossesse.

Précautions et mises en garde: Antécédents de tentatives de suicide ou de dépression ■ Antécédents de convulsions ■ Maladie cardiovasculaire ■ Patientes en âge de procréer ■ Allaitement ■ **PÉD.:** Enfants < 18 ans (l'innocuité du médicament n'a pas été établie) ■ Insuffisance rénale grave ■ Insuffisance hépatique ou administration concomitante d'un médicament hépatotoxique ■ Aplasie médullaire ■ **GÉR.:** Personnes > 65 ans (peu de données disponibles).

RÉACTIONS INDÉSIRABLES ET EFFETS SECONDAIRES

SNC: CONVULSIONS, céphalées, faiblesse, anxiété, confusion, dépersonnalisation, somnolence, labilité affective, évanouissements, dépression, troubles du sommeil, IDÉES SUICIDAIRES.

ORLO: conjonctivite, laryngite, otite.

Resp.: dyspnée, infection des voies respiratoires supérieures.

CV: douleurs thoraciques, œdème, hypertension, palpitations, troubles vasculaires périphériques, tachycardie, vasodilatation.

GI: constipation, diarrhée, dyspepsie, nausées, vomissements, douleurs abdominales, hépatite auto-immune, anorexie, élévation des enzymes hépatiques, DYSFONCTIONNEMENT HÉPATIQUE, troubles gastro-intestinaux.

GU: cystite, kyste ovarien, douleurs pelviennes.

Tég.: transpiration, alopécie, photosensibilité, phototoxicité.

End.: troubles menstruels, douleurs mammaires, hypoglycémie, ménorragie, fausse couche.

Hémat.: neutropénie, anémie, éosinophilie, pancytopénie, thrombopénie.

Locaux: réactions au point d'injection (plus fréquentes lors de l'administration d'interféron bêta-1b), nécrose au point d'injection.

Métab.: perte pondérale, dysfonction thyroïdienne.

Loc.: myalgie, arthralgie, spasmes musculaires.

Divers: réactions allergiques dont l'ANAPHYLAXIE, frissons, fièvre, symptômes pseudogrippaux, douleur, troubles auto-immuns.

INTERACTIONS

Médicament-médicament: Risque d'aggravation de l'aplasie médullaire lors de l'administration concomitante d'autres **dépresseurs de la moelle osseuse**, incluant les **antinéoplasiques** ■ L'utilisation concomitante de

médicaments hépatotoxiques peut augmenter le risque d'hépatotoxicité (élévation des enzymes hépatiques).

Médicament-produits naturels: Éviter la consommation concomitante de produits naturels **immunomodulateurs**, comme l'**astragale**, l'**échinacée** et la **mélatonine**.

VOIES D'ADMINISTRATION ET POSOLOGIE

Interféron bêta-1a

- **Avonex et Avonex PS: IM (adultes)**: 30 µg, 1 fois par semaine. Les patients atteints de sclérose en plaques évolutive secondaire, qui présentent des poussées répétitives, peuvent tirer profit d'une augmentation de la dose allant jusqu'à 60 µg, 1 fois par semaine.
- **Rebif**: *Sclérose en plaques* – **SC (adultes)**: 44 µg (12 MUI), 3 fois par semaine. La dose peut être diminuée à 22 µg (6 MUI), 3 fois par semaine, si le patient ne peut tolérer la dose plus élevée. Pour réduire les manifestations indésirables, on peut administrer 20 % de la dose pendant les 2 premières semaines, 50 % de la dose pendant les 3e et 4e semaines, et 100 % de la dose à partir de la 5e semaine. *Condylome acuminé* – **voie intralésionnelle ou périlésionnelle (adultes)**: 3,67 µg (1 MUI) par lésion, 3 fois par semaine, pendant 3 semaines. Les seringues préremplies ne doivent pas être utilisées à cette fin (*usage non approuvé*).

Interféron bêta-1b (Betaseron)

- **SC (adultes)**: 0,25 mg (8 MUI), 1 jour sur 2. Pour réduire les manifestations indésirables, on peut administrer 50 % de la dose pendant les 2 premières semaines de traitement, puis 100 % de la dose à partir de la 3e semaine.

PRÉSENTATION

- **Interféron bêta-1a**

  Avonex: poudre pour injection: 33 µg (6,6 MUI)/fiole[Pr], 66 µg (13,2 MUI)/fiole[Pr] ■ **Avonex PS (seringue préremplie)**: 30 µg (6,0 MUI)/ 0,5 mL[Pr] ■ **Rebif: poudre pour injection**: 11 µg (3 MUI)/flacon[Pr] ■ **seringues préremplies**: 8,8 µg (2,4 MUI)[Pr], 22 µg (6 MUI)/0,5mL[Pr], 44 µg (12 MUI)/0,5 mL[Pr].
- **Interféron bêta-1b (Betaseron)**

  Poudre pour injection: 0,3 mg (9,6 MUI)/fiole[Pr].

SOINS INFIRMIERS

ÉVALUATION DE LA SITUATION

- Évaluer la fréquence des exacerbations des symptômes de la sclérose en plaques à intervalles réguliers tout au long du traitement.
- Rester à l'affût de la dépression tout au long du traitement. En cas de dépression, prévenir immédiatement le médecin ou un autre professionnel de la santé.

Tests de laboratoire: Suivre les concentrations d'hémoglobine, la formule leucocytaire et le nombre de plaquettes, et effectuer d'autres analyses sanguines, incluant les tests de la fonction hépatique, avant l'administration du médicament et à intervalles réguliers tout au long du traitement. Il peut s'avérer nécessaire d'arrêter temporairement le traitement, si le nombre de polynucléaires neutrophiles est inférieur à $0,75 \times 10^9$/L, si les concentrations d'AST ou d'ALT dépassent 10 fois la limite supérieure de la normale ou si les concentrations sériques de bilirubine dépassent 5 fois la limite supérieure de la normale. Dès que le nombre absolu de polynucléaires neutrophiles dépasse $0,75 \times 10^9$/L ou que les concentrations d'enzymes hépatiques reviennent à la normale, le traitement peut être repris à 50 % de la dose initiale.

I

DIAGNOSTICS INFIRMIERS POSSIBLES

Connaissances insuffisantes sur le traitement médicamenteux (Enseignement au patient et à ses proches).

INTERVENTIONS INFIRMIÈRES

- NE PAS CONFONDRE LES AGENTS. L'INTERFÉRON BÊTA-1A ET L'INTERFÉRON BÊTA-1B NE SONT PAS INTERCHANGEABLES.

Interféron bêta-1a: *Avonex:* Reconstituer avec 1,1 mL du diluant fourni et faire rouler délicatement le flacon entre les mains pour dissoudre la poudre. Garder la solution reconstituée au réfrigérateur; injecter dans les 6 heures suivant la reconstitution. *Avonex PS*: La solution fournie en seringues préremplies est prête pour l'administration. *Rebif:* Reconstituer la poudre lyophilisée avec le diluant fourni et administrer immédiatement. La solution fournie en seringues préremplies est prête pour l'administration. Administrer au même moment de la journée (matin ou soir), les mêmes jours de la semaine (lundi, mercredi et vendredi) à au moins 48 heures d'intervalle. Faire la rotation des points d'injection pour diminuer le risque de réaction. Jeter toute portion inutilisée. Conserver au réfrigérateur. Les seringues préremplies peuvent être conservées à la température de la pièce (jusqu'à 25 °C) pendant un maximum de 30 jours.

Interféron bêta-1b *(Betaseron)*:

- Pour reconstituer, injecter 1,2 mL du diluant fourni dans la fiole d'interféron bêta-1b, pour obtenir une concentration de 0,25 mg (8 millions d'UI)/mL. Faire rouler délicatement la fiole entre les mains pour dissoudre complètement la poudre; ne pas agiter. Ne pas utiliser les solutions qui ont changé de couleur ou qui contiennent des particules. Garder la solution reconstituée au réfrigérateur et injecter dans les 3 heures suivant la reconstitution.

- Après avoir reconstitué la solution, prélever 1 mL dans une seringue munie d'une aiguille de calibre 27 et injecter par voie SC dans l'abdomen, la fesse ou la cuisse. Mettre au rebut toute portion inutilisée; les fioles sont réservées à un usage unique.

ENSEIGNEMENT AU PATIENT ET À SES PROCHES

Soins à domicile: Montrer au patient la technique d'injection et la méthode d'entretien et de mise au rebut du matériel. Recommander au patient de ne pas réutiliser les aiguilles ou les seringues et lui fournir un contenant imperforable pour la mise au rebut.

- Conseiller au patient de suivre rigoureusement la posologie recommandée; l'enjoindre de ne pas changer de dose ni d'intervalle entre les injections sans consulter d'abord un professionnel de la santé. Les patients devraient recevoir de l'information par écrit sur le médicament lors de la remise de chaque produit.
- Informer le patient que des symptômes pseudogrippaux (fièvre, frissons, myalgie, transpiration, malaise) peuvent survenir en cours de traitement. Lui conseiller de prendre de l'acétaminophène pour soulager la fièvre et la myalgie.
- Inciter le patient à utiliser des écrans solaires et à porter des vêtements protecteurs pour prévenir les réactions de photosensibilité.
- Inciter la patiente à prévenir un professionnel de la santé si elle pense être enceinte ou désire le devenir. Ce médicament peut provoquer une fausse couche.

VÉRIFICATION DE L'EFFICACITÉ THÉRAPEUTIQUE

L'efficacité du traitement peut être démontrée par: la diminution de la fréquence des récidives (dysfonctionnement neurologique) chez les patients atteints de sclérose en plaques rémittente et évolutive secondaire. ✳

IODE, IODURES

iodure de potassium
ThyroSafe

iodure de potassium, solution saturée
Ce médicament n'est pas commercialisé au Canada.

iodure de sodium
Micro I

iode, solution forte d'
Solution de Lugol

CLASSIFICATION:
Antithyroïdiens

Grossesse – catégories D et inconnue (iodure de sodium)

INDICATIONS

Traitement d'appoint en association avec d'autres antithyroïdiens pour préparer le patient à la thyroïdectomie ▪ Traitement des crises thyréotoxiques ▪ Radioprotection, à la suite de l'absorption accidentelle (urgence nucléaire) ou de l'administration d'iode radioactif ▪ Traitement supplétif en cas de nutrition parentérale de longue durée. **Usages non approuvés:** Traitement substitutif.

MÉCANISME D'ACTION

Inhibition rapide de la libération et de la synthèse d'hormones thyroïdiennes ▪ Diminution de la vascularité de la glande thyroïde ▪ Diminution du captage thyroïdien de l'iode radioactif à la suite de l'absorption accidentelle (urgence nucléaire) ou de l'administration d'isotopes radioactifs de l'iode ▪ L'iode est une composante essentielle de l'hormone thyroïdienne. ***Effets thérapeutiques:*** Maîtrise de l'hyperthyroïdie ▪ Diminution de l'hémorragie durant une intervention chirurgicale à la thyroïde ▪ Traitement supplétif ou substitutif ▪ Diminution de l'incidence du cancer thyroïdien à la suite d'une absorption accidentelle d'iode radioactif.

PHARMACOCINÉTIQUE

Absorption: L'agent est transformé dans le tractus gastro-intestinal et pénètre dans la circulation sous forme d'iode; il est également absorbé par la peau et les poumons; il peut aussi se former par recyclage des iodothyronines.

Distribution: L'iode se concentre dans la glande thyroïde et dans les muscles; on le retrouve également dans la peau, les os, les tissus mammaires et les cheveux. Il traverse la barrière placentaire et passe dans le lait maternel.

Métabolisme et excrétion: L'iode est capté par la glande thyroïde, puis il est éliminé par les reins, le foie, la peau, les poumons et les intestins.

Demi-vie: Inconnue.

Profil temps-action (effet sur la glande thyroïde)

	DÉBUT D'ACTION	PIC	DURÉE
PO	24 h	10 - 15 jours	variable
IV	rapide	inconnu	inconnue

CONTRE-INDICATIONS, PRÉCAUTIONS ET MISES EN GARDE

Contre-indications: Hypersensibilité.

Précautions et mises en garde: Tuberculose ■ Bronchite ■ Hyperkaliémie ■ Insuffisance rénale ■ **OBST., ALLAITEMENT, PÉD.**: Bien que l'iode soit nécessaire pendant la grossesse, des quantités excessives peuvent entraîner des anomalies de la fonction thyroïdienne ou le goitre chez le nouveau-né; un usage excessif pendant l'allaitement peut causer un rash ou la suppression de la fonction thyroïdienne chez le nourrisson.

RÉACTIONS INDÉSIRABLES ET EFFETS SECONDAIRES

GI: diarrhée, irritation gastro-intestinale.
Tég.: éruptions acnéiformes.
End.: hypothyroïdie, hyperthyroïdie, hyperplasie de la thyroïde.
HÉ: hyperkaliémie (iodure de potassium seulement).
Divers: hypersensibilité, iodisme.

INTERACTIONS

Médicament-médicament: Le **lithium**, administré en concomitance, peut provoquer une hypothyroïdie additive ■ Intensification de l'effet antithyroïdien du **méthimazole** et du **propylthiouracile** ■ Risque d'hyperkaliémie additive lors de l'usage concomitant de l'iodure de potassium et de **diurétiques épargneurs de potassium**, d'**inhibiteurs de l'enzyme de conversion de l'angiotensine**, de **bloqueurs des récepteurs de l'angiotensine** ou de **suppléments de potassium**.

VOIES D'ADMINISTRATION ET POSOLOGIE

Iodure de potassium, solution saturée = 1 g d'iodure de potassium/mL; iodure de potassium (comprimés): 65 mg/comprimé; solution de Lugol (*solution forte d'iode*) = iode à 50 mg/mL plus iodure de potassium à 100 mg/mL; iodure de sodium = 118 µg d'iodure de sodium (100 µg d'iodure)/mL.

Préparation à la thyroïdectomie

- **(É.-U.): PO (adultes et enfants)**: *Solution forte d'iode* – de 3 à 5 gouttes (de 0,1 à 0,3 mL), 3 fois par jour, pendant les 10 jours précédant l'intervention. *Solution saturée d'iodure de potassium* – de 1 à 5 gouttes (de 50 à 250 mg), 3 fois par jour, pendant les 10 à 14 jours précédant l'intervention.

Crise thyréotoxique

- **(É.-U.): PO (adultes et enfants)**: *Solution forte d'iode* – 1 mL dans de l'eau, 3 fois par jour. *Solution saturée d'iodure de potassium* – 5 gouttes (250 mg), 3 fois par jour.

Radioprotection (en situation d'urgence nucléaire, seulement sur recommandations des autorités de santé publique)

- **PO (adultes incluant les femmes enceintes et les enfants > 12 ans)**: 130 mg d'iodure de potassium.
- **PO (enfants 3 à 12 ans)**: 65 mg d'iodure de potassium.
- **PO (enfants de 1 mois à 3 ans)**: 32 mg d'iodure de potassium.
- **PO (enfants < 1 mois)**: 16 mg d'iodure de potassium.

Supplément nutritionnel

- **IV (adultes)**: De 1 à 2 µg d'iode élémentaire/kg/jour, ajoutés à la nutrition parentérale.
- **IV (enfants)**: De 2 à 3 µg d'iode élémentaire/kg/jour, ajoutés à la nutrition parentérale.

PRÉSENTATION

- **Iodure de potassium** (version générique disponible)
  Solution saturée: 1 g d'iodure de potassium/mL (on ne trouve pas la solution dans le commerce, mais elle peut être fabriquée par un pharmacien) ■ **Comprimés**: 65 mg[VL].
- **Iodure de sodium**
  Solution pour injection: 100 µg d'iodure (118 mg d'iodure de sodium)/mL, en flacons de 10 mL[Pr] ■ **Solution pour injection en association avec**: chrome, cuivre, manganèse, sélénium et zinc.
- **Solution forte d'iode** (version générique disponible)
  Solution orale: iode à 50 mg/mL avec iodure de potassium à 100 mg/mL (iode à 5 % avec iodure de potassium à 10 %), plusieurs formats de flacon disponibles[VL].

SOINS INFIRMIERS

ÉVALUATION DE LA SITUATION

- Suivre de près les signes et les symptômes suivants d'iodisme: goût métallique, stomatite, lésions de la peau, symptômes de rhume, troubles gastro-intestinaux graves. Prévenir le médecin dès l'apparition de ces symptômes.
- Suivre de près les symptômes suivants d'hyperthyroïdie: tachycardie, palpitations, nervosité, insomnie, diaphorèse, intolérance à la chaleur, tremblements, perte de poids.
- Suivre de près les réactions d'hypersensibilité: rash, prurit, œdème laryngé, respiration sifflante. Arrêter

d'administrer le médicament et prévenir le médecin dès l'apparition des symptômes.

Tests de laboratoire:

- Examiner les résultats des tests de la fonction thyroïdienne avant le traitement et à intervalles réguliers pendant toute sa durée. L'agent peut modifier les résultats de la scintigraphie thyroïdienne et peut diminuer la fixation par la thyroïde de l'iode^{131}, de l'iode^{123} et du pertechnétate sodique ^{99m}Tc lors des tests de captage thyroïdien.
- Noter les concentrations sériques de potassium à intervalles réguliers pendant toute la durée du traitement.

DIAGNOSTICS INFIRMIERS POSSIBLES

Connaissances insuffisantes sur le traitement médicamenteux (Enseignement au patient et à ses proches).

I

INTERVENTIONS INFIRMIÈRES

PO:

- Mélanger la solution à un grand verre de jus de fruits, d'eau, de bouillon ou de lait. Administrer le médicament après les repas afin de réduire l'irritation gastro-intestinale.
- La solution est normalement transparente et incolore. Si on la laisse reposer, elle peut prendre une teinte foncée sans que son effet soit altéré. Mettre au rebut les solutions de couleur jaune brunâtre.
- Des cristaux peuvent se former, particulièrement si la solution est gardée au réfrigérateur, mais ils se dissolvent lorsqu'on l'agite et qu'on la laisse à la température ambiante.

IV: L'administration parentérale ne devrait être utilisée que lorsque l'administration orale est impossible.

Perfusion continue: L'iodure de sodium est ajouté aux solutions de nutrition parentérale totale.

Compatibilité en addition au soluté: électrolytes ▪ métaux à l'état de traces ▪ solutions d'acides aminés ▪ solutions de dextrose.

ENSEIGNEMENT AU PATIENT ET À SES PROCHES

- Conseiller au patient de respecter rigoureusement la posologie recommandée. S'il n'a pu prendre le médicament au moment habituel, il doit le prendre dès que possible, à moins que ce ne soit presque l'heure prévue pour la dose suivante. L'avertir qu'il ne doit jamais remplacer une dose manquée par une double dose.
- Recommander à la patiente d'informer le professionnel de la santé, avant de commencer le traitement, si elle pense être enceinte ou désire le devenir.
- Recommander au patient de demander à un professionnel de la santé s'il doit éviter les aliments riches en iode (fruits de mer, sel iodé, chou, chou frisé, navets) ou en potassium (voir l'annexe J).
- Conseiller au patient de consulter un professionnel de la santé avant de prendre un médicament contre le rhume, car certaines de ces préparations peuvent contenir de l'iode comme expectorant.

Hyperthyroïdie: Conseiller au patient de suivre rigoureusement la posologie recommandée. Une dose manquée peut déclencher l'hyperthyroïdie.

Supplément nutritionnel: Expliquer au patient les besoins en iode de l'organisme et inventorier avec lui les aliments riches en iode.

VÉRIFICATION DE L'EFFICACITÉ THÉRAPEUTIQUE

L'efficacité du traitement peut être démontrée par: la résolution des symptômes de crise thyroïdienne ▪ la diminution de la taille et de la vascularité de la glande thyroïde avant une thyroïdectomie; l'administration d'iodures pour traiter l'hyperthyroïdie est habituellement limitée à 2 semaines ▪ la protection de la glande thyroïde contre les effets de l'iode radioactif ▪ la prévention et le traitement de la carence en iode.

IPRATROPIUM (INHALATION)

Apo-Ipravent, Atrovent, Atrovent HFA, Gen-Ipratropium, Novo-Ipramide, Ratio-Ipratropium

CLASSIFICATION:

Bronchodilatateur (anticholinergique), anti-allergique topique (anticholinergique topique)

Grossesse – catégorie B

INDICATIONS

Inhalation: Bronchodilatation, dans le traitement d'entretien du bronchospasme associé à la bronchopneumopathie chronique obstructive (BPCO), comprenant la bronchite chronique et l'emphysème ▪ **Voie intranasale:** Traitement de la rhinorrhée, associée à la rhinite allergique et non allergique apériodique (solution à 0,03 %) ou au rhume de cerveau (solution à 0,06 %).

MÉCANISME D'ACTION

Inhalation: Inhibition des récepteurs cholinergiques du muscle lisse des bronches entraînant la baisse des concentrations de guanosine monophosphate cyclique (GMPc). La diminution des concentrations de GMPc entraîne une bronchodilatation locale ■ **Voie intranasale**: L'application locale inhibe les sécrétions des glandes qui tapissent la muqueuse nasale. ***Effets thérapeutiques:*** **Inhalation**: Bronchodilatation sans effets anticholinergiques systémiques ■ **Voie intranasale**: Diminution de la rhinorrhée.

PHARMACOCINÉTIQUE

Absorption: Absorption systémique minime (2 % pour la solution en inhalation; 20 % pour l'aérosol en inhalation; < 20 % par voie intranasale).
Distribution: L'ipratropium ne semble pas traverser la barrière hémato-encéphalique.
Métabolisme et excrétion: Les faibles quantités absorbées sont métabolisées par le foie.
Demi-vie: 2 heures.

Profil temps-action (bronchodilatation)

	Début d'action	Pic	Durée
Inhalation	5 - 15 min	1 - 2 h	3 - 4 h (jusqu'à 8 h)
Voie intranasale	15 min	1 - 4 h	6 - 12 h

CONTRE-INDICATIONS, PRÉCAUTIONS ET MISES EN GARDE

Contre-indications: Hypersensibilité à l'ipratropium, à l'atropine ou aux autres composants du produit ■ Hypersensibilité à la lécithine de soya ou aux produits alimentaires de la même catégorie, tels que la fève de soya et les arachides (inhalateur doseur).
Précautions et mises en garde: Usage déconseillé en présence de bronchospasme aigu ■ Obstruction du col de la vessie, hyperplasie de la prostate, glaucome ou rétention urinaire ■ **Gér.**: sensibilité accrue aux effets du médicament (anticholinergique) ■ **Obst., allaitement, Péd.**: L'innocuité du médicament n'a pas été établie chez les femmes enceintes ou qui allaitent et chez les enfants < 12 ans (aérosol en inhalation et par voie intranasale) ou < 5 ans (solution en inhalation).

RÉACTIONS INDÉSIRABLES ET EFFETS SECONDAIRES

SNC: étourdissements, céphalées, nervosité.
ORLO: vision trouble, maux de gorge. *Voie intranasale seulement* - épistaxis, sécheresse ou irritation nasales.
Resp.: bronchospasme, toux.
CV: hypotension, palpitations.
GI: irritation gastrique, nausées.
Tég.: rash.
Divers: réactions allergiques.

INTERACTIONS

Médicament-médicament: L'utilisation concomitante d'autres **bronchodilatateurs par inhalation** dont l'une des composantes propulsives est un **fluorocarbure** pourrait intensifier les effets toxiques du fluorocarbure ■ Effets anticholinergiques additifs lors de l'administration concomitante d'autres **médicaments dotés de propriétés anticholinergiques** (**antihistaminiques, phénothiazines, disopyramide**).

VOIES D'ADMINISTRATION ET POSOLOGIE

Inhalation (adultes): *Inhalateur doseur* - 2 inhalations, 3 ou 4 fois par jour. Ne pas dépasser 12 inhalations en 24 heures ni faire inhaler à des intervalles inférieurs à 4 heures. Pendant le traitement initial, on peut aller jusqu'à 4 inhalations en une séance. *Nébuliseur* - de 250 à 500 µg, toutes les 4 à 6 heures, selon les besoins. Pour le traitement d'entretien de la BPCO, la dose recommandée est de 500 µg, 3 ou 4 fois par jour.
Inhalation (enfants de 5 à 12 ans): *Nébuliseur* - de 125 à 250 µg, toutes les 4 à 6 heures, selon les besoins.
Voie intranasale (adultes et enfants ≥ 12 ans): *Rhinite non allergique apériodique ou allergique* - 2 vaporisations de la solution à 0,03 % dans chaque narine, 2 ou 3 fois par jour (21 µg par vaporisation). *Rhume de cerveau* - 2 vaporisations de la solution à 0,06 % dans chaque narine, 3 ou 4 fois par jour (42 µg par vaporisation), pendant 4 jours.

I

PRÉSENTATION (version générique disponible)

Inhalation doseur: 20 µg/vaporisation, en vaporisateurs de 140 et de 200 doses[Pr] ■ **Solution pour inhalation**: 125 µg/mL[Pr] en flacons unidose; 250 µg/mL[Pr] en flacons unidose ou multidoses ■ **Vaporisateur nasal**: solution à 0,03 % - 21 µg/vaporisation, en flacons de 30 mL (345 vaporisations par flacon)[Pr], solution à 0,06 % - 42 µg/vaporisation, en flacons de 15 mL (165 vaporisations par flacon)[Pr].

SOINS INFIRMIERS

ÉVALUATION DE LA SITUATION

- Déterminer si le patient est allergique à l'atropine, puisque les sujets souffrant de ce type d'allergie peuvent également être sensibles à l'ipratropium.

Inhalation: Suivre de près la fonction respiratoire: ausculter le murmure vésiculaire, mesurer la fréquence respiratoire et le pouls, évaluer la gravité de la dyspnée, avant l'administration et au pic de l'effet de la médication. Consulter le médecin ou un autre professionnel de la santé au sujet des solutions de rechange en présence d'un bronchospasme grave, puisque le début d'action de l'ipratropium est trop lent en cas de détresse aiguë. En cas de bronchospasme paradoxal (respiration sifflante), arrêter d'administrer et prévenir immédiatement le médecin ou un autre professionnel de la santé.

Vaporisateur nasal: Déceler la présence de rhinorrhée.

DIAGNOSTICS INFIRMIERS POSSIBLES

- Dégagement inefficace des voies respiratoires (Indications).
- Intolérance à l'activité (Indications).
- Connaissances insuffisantes sur le traitement médicamenteux (Enseignement au patient et à ses proches).

INTERVENTIONS INFIRMIÈRES

Inhalation:

- Le mode d'administration des médicaments par inhalation est indiqué à l'annexe G.
- Lorsque l'ipratropium est administré en même temps que d'autres médicaments à inhaler, administrer le bronchodilatateur adrénergique en premier, l'ipratropium en deuxième, et les corticostéroïdes en troisième. Espacer l'inhalation des différents médicaments de 5 minutes.
- La solution pour *nébulisation* peut être diluée dans une solution de NaCl 0,9 % sans agent de conservation. La solution diluée peut être gardée 24 heures à la température ambiante ou 48 heures au réfrigérateur. On peut la mélanger avec du salbutamol, du cromoglycate ou du métaprotérénol (tous sans agent de conservation) si on l'utilise dans l'heure qui suit.

ENSEIGNEMENT AU PATIENT ET À SES PROCHES

- Montrer au patient comment utiliser l'inhalateur doseur, le nébuliseur ou le vaporisateur nasal. L'inciter à suivre rigoureusement la posologie recommandée. S'il n'a pu prendre le médicament au moment habituel, il doit le prendre dès que possible à moins que ce ne soit presque l'heure prévue pour la dose suivante. Recommander au patient d'espacer les autres doses de façon uniforme pendant le reste de la journée et de ne pas remplacer une dose manquée par une double dose.
- Recommander au patient de se rincer la bouche avec de l'eau après chaque inhalation, de pratiquer une bonne hygiène orale et de consommer de la gomme ou des bonbons sans sucre pour diminuer la sécheresse de la bouche. Lui conseiller de prévenir un professionnel de la santé en cas de stomatite ou de sécheresse de la bouche persistant pendant plus de 2 semaines.

Inhalation:

- Prévenir le patient qu'il ne doit pas prendre plus de 12 doses en 24 heures. Lui conseiller de communiquer avec un professionnel de la santé s'il n'y a pas d'amélioration des symptômes dans les 30 minutes suivant l'administration ou si son état s'aggrave.
- Expliquer au patient qu'il doit se soumettre à des tests de la fonction pulmonaire avant le début du traitement et à intervalles réguliers pendant toute sa durée afin de déterminer l'efficacité de l'ipratropium.
- Prévenir le patient que la vaporisation de l'ipratropium dans les yeux peut entraîner une vision trouble ou l'irritation oculaire.
- Conseiller au patient de communiquer avec un professionnel de la santé si les symptômes suivants se manifestent: toux, nervosité, céphalées, étourdissements, nausées ou douleurs gastriques.

Vaporisateur nasal:

- Montrer au patient comment utiliser le vaporisateur nasal. Lui demander de se moucher d'abord délicatement. Lui expliquer qu'il ne doit pas inspirer pendant qu'il vaporise, pour que le médicament reste dans les voies nasales. Avant l'usage initial, activer 7 fois la pompe. En cas d'usage régulier, il n'est plus nécessaire de la réamorcer. Si la pompe n'est pas réutilisée pendant 24 heures, il faut l'activer 2 fois avant de vaporiser l'agent dans les narines. Si elle n'est pas utilisée pendant plus de 7 jours, il faut l'amorcer de nouveau en l'activant 7 fois.
- Conseiller au patient de communiquer avec un professionnel de la santé s'il n'y a pas d'amélioration des symptômes dans les 1 à 2 semaines ou si son état s'aggrave.

VÉRIFICATION DE L'EFFICACITÉ THÉRAPEUTIQUE

L'efficacité du traitement peut être démontrée par: la diminution de la dyspnée ■ le soulagement de la rhinorrhée associée à la rhinite allergique et non allergique apériodique ou au rhume de cerveau.

IRBESARTAN,

voir Antagonistes des récepteurs de l'angiotensine II

ALERTE CLINIQUE

IRINOTÉCAN

Camptosar

CLASSIFICATION:

Antinéoplasique (inhibiteur enzymatique)

Grossesse – catégorie D

INDICATIONS

En association avec d'autres agents pour le traitement de première intention du cancer métastatique du côlon ou du rectum. ■ Traitement du cancer métastatique du rectum ou du côlon n'ayant pas répondu à un traitement antérieur incluant le 5-fluorouracile ou ayant récidivé après un tel traitement.

MÉCANISME D'ACTION

Modification de la synthèse de l'ADN par l'inhibition de l'enzyme topoisomérase. ***Effets thérapeutiques:*** Destruction des cellules à réplication rapide, particulièrement des cellules malignes.

PHARMACOCINÉTIQUE

Absorption: Biodisponibilité à 100 % (IV).

Distribution: Inconnue.

Liaison aux protéines: *Irinotécan* – de 30 à 68 %. *SN-38 (métabolite actif)* – 95 %.

Métabolisme et excrétion: Transformation par le foie en SN-38, un métabolite actif, qui est également métabolisé par le foie. Excrétion rénale de petites quantités d'irinotécan et de son métabolite.

Demi-vie: *Irinotécan* – 6 heures. *SN-38 (métabolite actif)* – 10 heures.

Profil temps-action (effets hématologiques)

	Début d'action	Pic	Durée
IV	inconnu	21 – 29 jours	27 – 34 jours

CONTRE-INDICATIONS, PRÉCAUTIONS ET MISES EN GARDE

Contre-indications: Hypersensibilité ■ Administration concomitante d'antifongiques azolés (kétoconazole, fluconazole, itraconazole) ■ Intolérance héréditaire au fructose (l'agent contient du sorbitol).

Précautions et mises en garde: Antécédents de radiothérapie pelvienne ou abdominale ■ Radiothérapie ■ Infections ■ Aplasie médullaire ■ Maladie chronique concomitante ou affaiblissement généralisé ■ Concentrations sériques de bilirubine de 17,1 à 34,2 µmol/L (il est recommandé de réduire la dose initiale) ■ **Gér.:** Personnes âgées (sensibilité accrue aux réactions indésirables; amorcer le traitement à des doses plus faibles) ■ Antécédents de diarrhée importante ou d'aplasie médullaire grave chez les patients sous irinotécan (reprendre le traitement à une dose plus faible après le rétablissement) ■ **Obst.:** Patientes en âge de procréer ■ Grossesse ou allaitement ■ **Péd.:** L'innocuité du médicament n'a pas été établie.

RÉACTIONS INDÉSIRABLES ET EFFETS SECONDAIRES

SNC: étourdissements, céphalées, insomnie, faiblesse.

ORLO: rhinite, larmoiement.

Resp.: toux, dyspnée.

CV: œdème, vasodilatation.

GI: DIARRHÉE, ÉLÉVATION DES ENZYMES HÉPATIQUES, douleurs ou crampes abdominales, anorexie, constipation, dyspepsie, flatulence, nausées, stomatite, vomissements, distension abdominale, ulcération du côlon.

Tég.: alopécie, rash, transpiration.

HÉ: déshydratation.

Hémat.: anémie, leucopénie, thrombopénie.

Locaux: réactions au point d'injection.

Métab.: perte pondérale.

Loc.: douleurs lombaires.

Divers: ANAPHYLAXIE, bouffées de chaleur, frissons, fièvre.

I

INTERACTIONS

Médicament-médicament: L'administration concomitante d'**antifongiques azolés** (**fluconazole, kétoconazole, itraconazole**) est contre-indiquée (toxicité accrue) ■ L'association avec le **flourouracile** peut entraîner des toxicités importantes (déshydratation, neutropénie, septicémie) ■ Les autres **antinéoplasiques** ou une **radiothérapie** peuvent aggraver l'aplasie médullaire ■ Les **laxatifs** doivent être utilisés avec prudence (risque d'exacerbation de la diarrhée) ■ Les **diurétiques** peuvent accroître le risque de déshydratation en cas de diarrhée (l'administration de ce type de médicament peut être interrompue pendant le traitement selon l'état du patient) ■ La **dexaméthasone**, utilisée comme antiémétique, peut accroître le risque d'hyperglycémie et de lymphopénie ■ La **prochlorpérazine**, administrée le même jour que l'irinotécan, peut accroître le risque d'akathisie. ■ Certains antibiotiques (**fluoroquinolones**, **macrolides**) et certains antihypertenseurs (**vérapamil**, **diltiazem** et **nifédipine**) peuvent augmenter la toxicité de l'irinotécan. ■ Certains médicaments peuvent diminuer l'efficacité de l'irinotécan (**phénytoine**, **corticostéroïdes**, **phénobarbital**, **carbamazépine**).

Médicament-produits naturels: Le **millepertuis** peut diminuer l'efficacité de l'irinotécan.

Médicament-aliments: Le **jus de pamplemousse** peut augmenter le risque de toxicité.

VOIES D'ADMINISTRATION ET POSOLOGIE

On a également utilisé des schémas thérapeutiques autres que les suivants.

Monothérapie

- **IV (adultes):** *Schéma hebdomadaire* – 125 mg/m^2, 1 fois par semaine, pendant 4 semaines; observer ensuite une période sans médication de 2 semaines. On peut répéter ce cycle en utilisant des doses allant de 50 à 150 mg/m^2, selon la tolérance du patient et le degré de toxicité. *Schéma d'administration séquentielle* – 350 mg/m^2, 1 fois toutes les 3 semaines.
- **IV (personnes > 70 ans):** Amorcer le traitement à une dose de 300 mg/m^2, à administrer toutes les 3 semaines.

INSUFFISANCE HÉPATIQUE

UNE RÉDUCTION DE LA DOSE EST RECOMMANDÉE SI LES CONCENTRATIONS SÉRIQUES DE BILIRUBINE SONT DE 17,1 À 34,2 µmol/L.

Association avec le flourouracile et la leucovorine

- **IV (adultes):** *Schéma hebdomadaire* (bolus) – 125 mg/m^2, 1 fois par semaine, pendant 4 semaines; observer ensuite une période sans médication de 2 semaines. On peut répéter ce cycle en utilisant des doses adaptées selon la tolérance du patient et le degré de toxicité. *Schéma d'administration séquentielle* (perfusion) – 180 mg/m^2, 1 fois toutes les 2 semaines, pour 3 doses (aux 1er, 15e et 29e jours); observer ensuite une période sans médication de 1 semaine. On peut répéter ce cycle en utilisant des doses adaptées selon la tolérance du patient et le degré de toxicité.

PRÉSENTATION

Solution pour injection: 20 mg/mL, en flacons de 2 mL^{Pr}, 5 mL^{Pr} et 25 mL^{Pr}.

SOINS INFIRMIERS

ÉVALUATION DE LA SITUATION

- Suivre de près les signes vitaux à intervalles réguliers tout au long de l'administration du médicament.
- Surveiller l'apparition d'une aplasie médullaire. Suivre de près les saignements (saignement des gencives, formation d'ecchymoses, pétéchies, présence de sang occulte dans les selles, l'urine et les vomissements). Éviter les injections IM et la prise de la température rectale si le nombre de plaquettes est bas. Appliquer une pression sur les points de ponction veineuse pendant 10 minutes. Évaluer les signes d'infection en présence d'une neutropénie. Une anémie peut survenir. Suivre de près la fatigue accrue, la dyspnée et l'hypotension orthostatique.
- Observer étroitement le patient pour déceler la diarrhée. Deux types de diarrhée peuvent survenir. Le premier survient dans les 24 heures suivant l'administration du médicament, et peut être précédé de crampes et de transpiration. On peut administrer dans ce cas de 0,25 à 1 mg d'atropine, par voie IV ou SC, pour soulager les symptômes. UNE DIARRHÉE POUVANT METTRE LA VIE DU PATIENT EN DANGER PEUT SURVENIR PLUS DE 24 HEURES APRÈS L'ADMINISTRATION D'UNE DOSE ET ÊTRE ACCOMPAGNÉE D'UNE FORTE DÉSHYDRATATION ET D'UN DÉSÉQUILIBRE ÉLECTROLYTIQUE. POUR TRAITER CE DERNIER TYPE DE DIARRHÉE, IL FAUT ADMINISTRER RAPIDEMENT DU LOPÉRAMIDE À 4 mg, INITIALEMENT, PUIS À 2 mg, TOUTES LES 2 HEURES, JUSQU'À CE QUE LA DIARRHÉE S'ARRÊTE PENDANT AU MOINS 12 HEURES (OU 4 mg, TOUTES LES 4 HEURES, PENDANT LES HEURES DE SOMMEIL). ON DOIT AMORCER UN TRAITEMENT HYDROÉLECTROLYTIQUE DE SUBSTITUTION POUR PRÉVENIR LES COMPLICATIONS. RETARDER L'ADMINISTRATION DES DOSES D'IRINOTÉCAN CHEZ LES PATIENTS MANIFESTANT UNE DIARRHÉE ACTIVE JUSQU'À 24 HEURES APRÈS SA RÉSOLUTION. LES DOSES SUIVANTES D'IRINOTÉCAN DOIVENT ÊTRE DIMINUÉES EN CAS DE DIARRHÉE DE GRADE 2, 3 OU 4.
- Les nausées et les vomissements sont courants. Il faut administrer en prétraitement de la dexaméthasone à 10 mg, associée à des agents comme l'ondansétron ou le granisétron, au moins 30 minutes avant l'administration de l'irinotécan. On peut administrer la prochlorpérazine les jours suivants, mais cet agent peut augmenter le risque d'akathisie s'il est administré le même jour que l'irinotécan.
- Observer fréquemment le point d'injection IV pour déceler l'inflammation. Éviter l'extravasation. En cas d'extravasation, arrêter immédiatement la perfusion et la reprendre dans une autre veine afin de prévenir la lésion du tissu sous-cutané. On recommande de rincer le point d'injection avec de l'eau stérile et d'appliquer des compresses de glace sur la peau.

Tests de laboratoire:

- Avant l'administration de chaque dose, noter la numération globulaire, la formule leucocytaire et le nombre de plaquettes. Cesser temporairement le traitement par l'irinotécan si le nombre absolu de polynucléaires neutrophiles est $< 0,5 \times 10^9$/L ou en cas de fièvre neutropénique. On peut envisager l'administration d'un facteur de croissance des colonies en cas de baisse importante sur le plan clinique du nombre de globules blancs ($< 2 \times 10^9$/L), de polynucléaires neutrophiles ($< 1 \times 10^9$/L) ou de la concentration d'hémoglobine (< 90 g/L).

- L'IRINOTÉCAN PEUT ÉLEVER LES CONCENTRATIONS DE PHOSPHATASE ALCALINE SÉRIQUE ET D'AST.

DIAGNOSTICS INFIRMIERS POSSIBLES

- Risque d'infection (Réactions indésirables).
- Connaissances insuffisantes sur le traitement médicamenteux (Enseignement au patient et à ses proches).

INTERVENTIONS INFIRMIÈRES

Préparer les solutions sous une hotte à flux laminaire. Porter des gants, des vêtements de protection et un masque pendant la manipulation de ce médicament. Mettre au rebut le matériel dans les contenants réservés à cet usage (voir l'annexe H).

Perfusion intermittente: Diluer le contenu des fioles dans une solution de D5%E ou de NaCl 0,9 % pour obtenir une concentration de 0,12 à 2,8 mg/mL. On utilise habituellement comme diluant 500 mL de D5%E. La solution est jaune pâle. Ne pas administrer la solution si elle est trouble ou si elle contient des particules. La solution pour perfusion est stable pendant 24 heures à la température ambiante et pendant 48 heures au réfrigérateur si elle est diluée dans du D5%E (risque de précipitation si la solution diluée dans du NaCl 0,9 % est réfrigérée). Étant donné le risque de contamination microbienne pendant le processus de dilution, on devrait utiliser les solutions dans les 24 heures suivant leur dilution, si elles ont été gardées au réfrigérateur, ou dans les 6 heures, si elles ont été laissées à la température ambiante. Ne pas réfrigérer les solutions diluées avec du NaCl 0,9 %.

Vitesse d'administration: Administrer la dose en 90 minutes.

Incompatibilité en addition au soluté: Données non disponibles. Ne pas mélanger avec d'autres solutions ou d'autres médicaments.

ENSEIGNEMENT AU PATIENT ET À SES PROCHES

- RECOMMANDER AU PATIENT DE SIGNALER IMMÉDIATEMENT À UN PROFESSIONNEL DE LA SANTÉ LA DIARRHÉE, PARTICULIÈREMENT SI ELLE SURVIENT PLUS DE 24 HEURES APRÈS L'ADMINISTRATION DE LA DOSE. ELLE PEUT S'ACCOMPAGNER D'UNE FORTE DÉSHYDRATATION ET D'UN DÉSÉQUILIBRE ÉLECTROLYTIQUE. PUISQU'ELLE PEUT METTRE LA VIE DU PATIENT EN DANGER, ELLE DEVRAIT ÊTRE TRAITÉE SANS TARDER.
- Recommander au patient de signaler rapidement à un professionnel de la santé la fièvre, les frissons, les maux de gorge, les signes d'infection, le saignement des gencives, la formation d'ecchymoses, les pétéchies ou la présence de sang dans les selles, l'urine et les vomissements. Expliquer au patient qu'il doit éviter les foules et les personnes contagieuses. Lui conseiller d'utiliser une brosse à dents à poils doux et un rasoir électrique. Le prévenir qu'il ne doit pas prendre de boissons alcoolisées ni de préparations contenant de l'aspirine ou des AINS.
- Recommander au patient de signaler immédiatement à l'infirmière toute douleur au point d'injection.
- Recommander au patient de communiquer avec un professionnel de la santé en cas de vomissements, d'évanouissements ou d'étourdissements.
- Expliquer au patient qu'il risque de perdre ses cheveux. Explorer avec lui les stratégies lui permettant de s'adapter à ce changement.
- Expliquer à la patiente que ce médicament peut avoir des effets tératogènes. Lui conseiller de prendre des mesures de contraception pendant toute la durée du traitement.
- Expliquer au patient qu'il ne doit pas se faire vacciner sans la recommandation d'un professionnel de la santé.
- Inciter le patient à se soumettre à des intervalles réguliers à des tests de laboratoire permettant de déceler les effets secondaires du médicament.

VÉRIFICATION DE L'EFFICACITÉ THÉRAPEUTIQUE

L'efficacité du traitement peut être démontrée par: la diminution de la taille de la tumeur et le ralentissement de la propagation du cancer.

ISONIAZIDE

Dom-Isoniazid, Isotamine, PMS-Isoniazid

CLASSIFICATION:

Antituberculeux (antimycobactérien)

Grossesse – catégorie C

INDICATIONS

En association avec d'autres médicaments: traitement de premier recours de la tuberculose pulmonaire et extrapulmonaire en évolution ■ En monothérapie: prophylaxie de la tuberculose chez les patients exposés à la forme active de la maladie.

MÉCANISME D'ACTION

Inhibition de la synthèse de la paroi des cellules mycobactériennes et modification du métabolisme. ***Effets thérapeutiques:*** Effet bactériostatique ou bactéricide contre les mycobactéries sensibles.

PHARMACOCINÉTIQUE

Absorption: Bonne (PO).

Distribution: Répartition dans tout l'organisme. L'isoniazide traverse facilement la barrière hématoencéphalique. Il traverse la barrière placentaire et passe dans le lait maternel aux mêmes concentrations que dans le plasma.

Métabolisme et excrétion: 50 % métabolisé par le foie à une vitesse qui varie considérablement d'une personne à une autre. Le reste est excrété à l'état inchangé par les reins.

Demi-vie: De 1 à 4 heures.

Profil temps-action

	Début d'action	Pic	Durée
PO	Rapide	1 - 2 h	jusqu'à 24 h

CONTRE-INDICATIONS, PRÉCAUTIONS ET MISES EN GARDE

Contre-indications: Hypersensibilité ■ Maladie hépatique aiguë ■ Antécédents d'hépatite induite par l'isoniazide.

Précautions et mises en garde: Antécédents de lésions hépatiques ou d'alcoolisme ■ Femmes de race noire ou d'origine hispanique, postpartum ou patients > 50 ans (risque accru d'hépatite induite par le médicament) ■ Insuffisance rénale grave (il peut s'avérer nécessaire de réduire la dose) ■ Malnutrition, diabète ou alcoolisme chronique (risque accru de neuropathie) ■ **OBST., ALLAITEMENT:** Bien que l'innocuité du médicament n'ait pas été établie, l'agent a été administré en association avec l'éthambutol pour traiter la tuberculose chez les femmes enceintes, sans provoquer d'effets nocifs chez le fœtus.

RÉACTIONS INDÉSIRABLES ET EFFETS SECONDAIRES

SNC: psychose, convulsions.

ORLO: troubles de la vue.

GI: HÉPATITE MÉDICAMENTEUSE, nausées, vomissements.

Tég.: rash.

End.: gynécomastie.

Hémat.: dyscrasie.

SN: neuropathie périphérique.

Divers: fièvre.

INTERACTIONS

Médicament-médicament: Toxicité additive sur le SNC lors de l'administration concomitante d'autres **antituberculeux** ■ L'isoniazide peut entraver l'efficacité du **vaccin BCG** ■ L'isoniazide inhibe le métabolisme de la **phénytoïne** ■ Les **antiacides contenant de l'aluminium** peuvent réduire l'absorption de l'isoniazide ■ L'administration concomitante de **disulfirame** peut entraîner des réactions psychotiques et des troubles de la coordination ■ L'administration concomitante de **pyridoxine** peut prévenir la neuropathie ■ Risque accru d'hépatotoxicité lors de l'administration concomitante d'autres **agents hépatotoxiques**, incluant l'**alcool** et la **rifampine** ■ L'isoniazide peut réduire les concentrations sanguines et l'efficacité du **kétoconazole** ■ L'administration concomitante de **carbamazépine** augmente les concentrations sanguines de cette dernière et le risque d'hépatotoxicité.

Médicament-aliments: L'ingestion d'aliments ayant une forte teneur en **tyramine** peut entraîner des réactions graves (voir l'annexe J).

VOIES D'ADMINISTRATION ET POSOLOGIE

Traitement de la tuberculose

- **PO (adultes):** *En association avec d'autres traitements* – de 5 à 10 mg/kg, 1 fois par jour, jusqu'à concurrence de 300 mg, pendant un minimum de 6 mois, *ou* 15 mg/kg (jusqu'à 900 mg par dose), 2 ou 3 fois par semaine.
- **PO (enfants):** *En association avec d'autres traitements* – de 10 à 20 mg/kg, 1 fois par jour, jusqu'à concurrence de 300 mg, pendant un minimum de 6 mois, *ou* de 20 à 40 mg/kg (jusqu'à 900 mg par dose), 2 fois par semaine.

Prophylaxie de la tuberculose

- **PO (adultes):** 300 mg, 1 fois par jour, pendant 6 à 12 mois. Chez les patients qui risquent de ne pas observer le traitement: 1 dose de 15 mg/kg (jusqu'à concurrence de 900 mg par dose), 2 fois par semaine peut remplacer le traitement quotidien.
- **PO (enfants):** De 10 à 15 mg/kg, 1 fois par jour, jusqu'à concurrence de 300 mg, pendant 6 à 12 mois.

PRÉSENTATION (version générique disponible)

Comprimés: 50 mg^{Pr}, 100 mg^{Pr}, 300 mg^{Pr} ■ **Sirop:** 50 mg/5 mL^{Pr} ■ **En association avec:** rifampine et pyrazinamide (Rifater)^{Pr}.

SOINS INFIRMIERS

ÉVALUATION DE LA SITUATION

Prélever des échantillons pour les cultures de mycobactéries et les épreuves de sensibilité avant de commencer le traitement et à intervalles réguliers par la suite afin de déceler une résistance éventuelle.

Tests de laboratoire: EXAMINER LES RÉSULTATS DES TESTS DE LA FONCTION HÉPATIQUE, AVANT LE TRAITEMENT ET TOUS LES MOIS PAR LA SUITE. L'ÉLÉVATION DES CONCENTRATIONS D'AST, D'ALT ET DE BILIRUBINE SÉRIQUE PEUT RÉVÉLER UNE HÉPATITE MÉDICAMENTEUSE. LES FEMMES DE RACE NOIRE OU D'ORIGINE HISPANIQUE, LES FEMMES EN POSTPARTUM ET LES PATIENTS > 50 ANS SONT EXPOSÉS À UN RISQUE PLUS ÉLEVÉ. LE RISQUE EST MOINS ÉLEVÉ CHEZ LES ENFANTS; LES TESTS DE LA FONCTION HÉPATIQUE DOIVENT DONC HABITUELLEMENT ÊTRE EFFECTUÉS MOINS FRÉQUEMMENT DANS LEUR CAS.

TOXICITÉ ET SURDOSAGE: En cas de surdosage en isoniazide, amorcer le traitement à la pyridoxine (vitamine B_6).

DIAGNOSTICS INFIRMIERS POSSIBLES

- Risque d'infection (Indications).
- Connaissances insuffisantes sur le traitement médicamenteux (Enseignement au patient et à ses proches).
- Non-observance du traitement médicamenteux (Enseignement au patient et à ses proches).

INTERVENTIONS INFIRMIÈRES

PO: En cas d'irritation gastrique, l'isoniazide peut être administré avec des aliments ou des antiacides; cependant, les antiacides contenant de l'aluminium ne devraient pas être pris dans l'heure qui suit ou qui précède.

ENSEIGNEMENT AU PATIENT ET À SES PROCHES

- Conseiller au patient de respecter rigoureusement la posologie recommandée. S'il n'a pu prendre le médicament au moment habituel, il doit le prendre dès que possible, à moins que ce ne soit presque l'heure prévue pour la dose suivante. L'avertir qu'il ne doit jamais remplacer une dose manquée par une double dose. Insister sur le fait qu'il est important de poursuivre le traitement, même après la disparition des symptômes. Le traitement peut durer de 6 mois à 2 ans.
- CONSEILLER AU PATIENT DE PRÉVENIR RAPIDEMENT UN PROFESSIONNEL DE LA SANTÉ SI DES SIGNES OU DES SYMPTÔMES D'HÉPATITE (JAUNISSEMENT DES YEUX ET DE LA PEAU, NAUSÉES, VOMISSEMENTS, ANOREXIE, URINE DE COULEUR FONCÉE, FATIGUE INHABITUELLE OU FAIBLESSE) OU DE NÉVRITE PÉRIPHÉRIQUE (ENGOURDISSEMENTS, PICOTEMENTS, PARESTHÉSIE) SE MANIFESTENT. ON PEUT ADMINISTRER EN MÊME TEMPS DE LA PYRIDOXINE POUR PRÉVENIR L'APPARITION DE LA NEUROPATHIE. RECOMMANDER AU PATIENT DE SIGNALER IMMÉDIATEMENT À UN PROFESSIONNEL DE LA SANTÉ LA MODIFICATION DE L'ACUITÉ VISUELLE, LES DOULEURS AUX YEUX OU LES TROUBLES DE LA VUE.
- METTRE EN GARDE LE PATIENT CONTRE LA CONSOMMATION CONCOMITANTE D'ALCOOL QUI PEUT ACCROÎTRE LE RISQUE D'HÉPATOTOXICITÉ. Lui conseiller d'éviter la consommation de fromage suisse ou de Cheshire, de poisson (thon, bonite ou sardines) et de tout aliment pouvant contenir de la tyramine (voir l'annexe J), puisque ces aliments peuvent entraîner des démangeaisons ou des rougeurs de la peau, une sensation de chaleur, des battements de cœur rapides ou forts, des sueurs, des frissons, une sensation de peau moite et froide, des céphalées ou une sensation de tête légère.
- Insister sur l'importance des examens réguliers de suivi et des examens de la vue permettant d'évaluer les bienfaits du traitement et de suivre les effets secondaires.

VÉRIFICATION DE L'EFFICACITÉ THÉRAPEUTIQUE

L'efficacité du traitement peut être démontrée par: la résolution des signes et des symptômes de tuberculose ▪ des résultats négatifs à l'analyse des échantillons d'expectorations ▪ la prophylaxie de la tuberculose chez les personnes ayant été exposées à la forme active de la maladie.

ISOPROPYLE, MYRISTATE D', ET CYCLOMÉTHICONE

Resultz

CLASSIFICATION:

Agent dermatologique (pédiculicide)

Grossesse – catégorie C (cyclométhicone), catégorie inconnue (myristate d'isopropyle)

INDICATIONS

Traitement de la pédiculose (*Pediculus humanus capitis* ou pou de tête).

I

MÉCANISME D'ACTION

Dissolution de la cire qui recouvre l'exosquelette du pou de tête, entraînant la déshydratation, puis la mort du parasite. ***Effets thérapeutiques:*** Destruction des parasites.

PHARMACOCINÉTIQUE

Absorption: Inconnue.
Distribution: Inconnue.
Métabolisme et excrétion: Inconnus.
Demi-vie: Inconnue.

Profil temps-action (action pédiculicide)

	DÉBUT D'ACTION	PIC	DURÉE
Usage topique	inconnu	inconnu	inconnue

CONTRE-INDICATIONS, PRÉCAUTIONS ET MISES EN GARDE

Contre-indications: Hypersensibilité au myristate d'isopropyle ou au cyclométhicone ■ Irritation ou infection de la peau présente ou en voie de se développer ■ Infestation des sourcils ou des cils.
Précautions et mises en garde: **OBST., ALLAITEMENT**: Absence de données ■ **PÉD.**: Enfants < 4 ans.

RÉACTIONS INDÉSIRABLES ET EFFETS SECONDAIRES

Tég.: prurit, rash, irritation, rougeurs.

INTERACTIONS

Médicament-médicament: Inconnues.

VOIES D'ADMINISTRATION ET POSOLOGIE

- **Usage topique (adultes et enfants ≥ 4 ans)**: *Premier jour* – appliquer le produit sur les cheveux secs et masser pour le faire pénétrer dans toute la chevelure, en insistant au niveau des tempes et de la nuque, jusqu'à ce que le cuir chevelu soit complètement imprégné. Laisser agir pendant 10 minutes, puis rincer les cheveux à l'eau tiède et les laver, au besoin. *Septième jour* – répéter l'application. *Quantité nécessaire de produit*: cheveux courts – de 30 à 60 mL par application (au total, de 60 à 120 mL) ■ cheveux aux épaules – de 60 à 90 mL par application (au total, de 120 à 180 mL) ■ cheveux longs – de 90 à 120 mL par application (au total, de 180 à 240 mL).

PRÉSENTATION

Produit de rinçage: teneur à 50 %, en flacons de 120 et de 240 mL[VL].

SOINS INFIRMIERS

ÉVALUATION DE LA SITUATION

- Examiner le cuir chevelu du patient et des membres de sa famille à la recherche de poux et d'œufs (lentes), avant l'application du myristate d'isopropyle, tous les jours entre les traitements et pendant au moins 2 semaines après le dernier traitement.

DIAGNOSTICS INFIRMIERS POSSIBLES

- Connaissances insuffisantes sur le traitement médicamenteux (Enseignement au patient et à ses proches).

INTERVENTIONS INFIRMIÈRES

- La préparation est réservée à l'application topique.

ENSEIGNEMENT AU PATIENT ET À SES PROCHES

- Recommander au patient de prévenir un professionnel de la santé en cas d'irritation ou d'infection cutanées, ou d'une infestation dans les sourcils ou les cils.
- Recommander au patient d'éviter tout contact avec les yeux. Lui conseiller de bien les fermer et ne pas les ouvrir tant que le produit n'a pas été bien éliminé par rinçage. Il peut se protéger les yeux avec une débarbouillette ou une serviette, ou d'une autre manière. Le cas échéant, lui conseiller de se rincer abondamment les yeux à l'eau et de prévenir un professionnel de la santé si l'irritation oculaire persiste.
- Expliquer au patient que les autres personnes habitant sous le même toit devraient également passer un examen de dépistage des poux. Si un membre de la famille est infesté, traiter cette personne dès que possible.
- Expliquer au patient les méthodes permettant de prévenir la réinfestation: laver à la machine, à l'eau très chaude, tous les vêtements, casquettes, écharpes, serviettes, vêtements d'extérieur et linge de maison, et les faire sécher dans une sécheuse à haute température pendant au moins 20 minutes; faire nettoyer à sec les vêtements qu'on ne peut laver; faire tremper les brosses et les peignes dans de l'eau chaude (au moins 54 °C) savonneuse pendant 5 à 10 minutes, puis les rincer; ne pas utiliser le même peigne ou la même brosse qu'une autre personne; faire un shampooing aux perruques et postiches; passer l'aspirateur sur les tapis et les meubles rembourrés; laver les jouets dans de l'eau chaude savonneuse; conserver les articles ne pouvant être lavés dans un sac en plastique hermétiquement

fermé pendant 2 semaines. Les matelas qui ont servi à une personne infestée ne doivent pas être utilisés pendant 48 heures.

- Informer le patient qu'il doit protéger les vêtements et les meubles avec une serviette parce que le produit peut tacher les tissus.
- Le prévenir que le produit rend glissantes les surfaces dures, comme le plancher et la baignoire.
- Recommander aux parents d'informer l'infirmière de l'école ou la garderie que l'enfant a des poux, pour que l'infestation puisse être enrayée.
- Recommander au patient d'appliquer le produit sur les cheveux secs et de masser pour le faire bien pénétrer jusqu'à ce que le cuir chevelu, surtout les côtés et la nuque (à l'arrière de la tête, sous les cheveux), soit complètement imprégné. Cette opération peut prendre plusieurs minutes. Comme les poux peuvent se déplacer rapidement sur la tige du cheveu, il est important d'appliquer le produit aussi bien sur le cuir chevelu que sur toute la longueur du cheveu, de la racine jusqu'à l'extrémité. Laisser agir pendant 10 minutes, puis rincer abondamment les cheveux à l'eau chaude et les laver, au besoin. Peigner les cheveux avec un peigne fin afin de retirer les poux morts et les lentes (cette étape n'est pas obligatoire, mais peut être utile pour des raisons esthétiques).
- Recommander au patient de répéter l'application du produit, 6 jours après la première application, car certains œufs n'ont peut-être pas été tués par le premier traitement. Ces œufs peuvent éclore et doivent être éliminés lors d'un second traitement.
- Si l'infestation revient ou persiste après la seconde application, recommander au patient de consulter un médecin.

VÉRIFICATION DE L'EFFICACITÉ THÉRAPEUTIQUE

L'efficacité du traitement peut être démontrée par: la disparition des poux et des lentes. ✳

ISOSORBIDE

isosorbide, dinitrate d'

Apo-ISDN, Isordil

isosorbide, mononitrate d'

Apo-ISMN, Imdur

CLASSIFICATION:

Antiangineux (dérivés nitrés et nitrates)

Grossesse – catégorie C

INDICATIONS

Traitement aigu des crises d'angine (forme sublinguale seulement) ■ Prophylaxie prolongée de l'angine de poitrine (dinitrate et mononitrate).

MÉCANISME D'ACTION

Vasodilatation (la vasodilatation veineuse est plus importante que la vasodilatation artérielle) ■ Diminution de la pression et du volume (précharge) télédiastoliques du ventricule gauche. Effet net: réduction de la consommation d'oxygène par le myocarde ■ Augmentation du débit coronarien par la dilatation des coronaires et amélioration de l'irrigation des territoires ischémiés par la circulation collatérale. ***Effets thérapeutiques:*** Soulagement des crises d'angine et élévation du débit cardiaque.

PHARMACOCINÉTIQUE

Absorption: Bonne (PO et voie sublinguale).

Distribution: Inconnue.

Métabolisme et excrétion: Métabolisme majoritairement hépatique.

Demi-vie: *Dinitrate d'isosorbide* – 50 minutes. *Mononitrate d'isosorbide* – 5 heures.

Profil temps-action (effets cardiovasculaires)

	Début d'action	Pic	Durée
Dinitrate, voie sublinguale	2 - 5 min	inconnu	1 - 3 h
Dinitrate, PO	20 - 40 min	inconnu	4 - 6 h
Mononitrate, PO - LP†	inconnu	inconnu	10 - 12 h

† Libération prolongée.

CONTRE-INDICATIONS, PRÉCAUTIONS ET MISES EN GARDE

Contre-indications: Hypersensibilité ■ Anémie grave ■ Usage concomitant de sildénafil, de tadalafil ou de vardénafil ■ Collapsus cardiovasculaire associé à une hypotension marqué ■ Hypotension orthostatique ■ Insuffisance myocardique due à une obstruction ■ Pression intracrânienne accrue ■ Traumatisme crânien ou hémorragie cérébrale.

Précautions et mises en garde: Hypotension ou patients prédisposés (p. ex., hypovolémiques) ■ Maladie hépatique ou rénale grave ■ **Obst.**: Grossesse (risque d'altération de la circulation utéroplacentaire) ■ **Allaitement, Péd.**: L'innocuité du médicament n'a pas été établie ■ **Gér.**: Les personnes âgées sont exposées à un plus grand risque d'hypotension (commencer le traitement à une dose plus faible).

RÉACTIONS INDÉSIRABLES ET EFFETS SECONDAIRES

SNC: étourdissements, céphalées, appréhension, faiblesse.

CV: hypotension, tachycardie, bradycardie paradoxale, syncope.

GI: douleurs abdominales, nausées, vomissements.

Divers: tolérance croisée, bouffées vasomotrices, tolérance à l'effet du médicament.

INTERACTIONS

Médicament-médicament: L'usage concomitant de **sildénafil,** de **tadalafil** ou de **vardénafil** peut entraîner une hypotension marquée, qui risque d'être d'issue fatale (l'usage concomitant est contre-indiqué) ■ Effets additifs sur l'hypotension, lors de l'administration concomitante d'**antihypertenseurs** (particulièrement les **bloqueurs des canaux calciques**), de **bêtabloquants** et de **phénothiazines** ■ L'**alcool** peut accroître la sensibilité aux effets hypotenseurs des dérivés nitrés ■ Les **alcaloïdes de l'ergot** (p. ex., **dihydroergotamine, ergotamine)** inhibent les effets des dérivés nitrés.

VOIES D'ADMINISTRATION ET POSOLOGIE

Dinitrate d'isosorbide

- **Comprimés sublinguaux (adultes)**: *Crise aiguë d'angine de poitrine* – laisser dissoudre 1 ou 2 comprimés de 5 mg sous la langue. Des doses additionnelles peuvent être administrées à intervalles de 5 minutes, au besoin. Consulter d'urgence un médecin s'il n'y a pas de soulagement après l'administration de 3 doses. *Prophylaxie des crises d'angine de poitrine* – de 5 à 10 mg, par voie sublinguale, toutes les 2 à 4 heures. Il est possible d'administrer de 5 à 10 mg par voie sublinguale de 10 à 15 minutes avant des situations susceptibles de déclencher une crise d'angine.
- **PO (adultes)**: *Prophylaxie à long terme de l'angine de poitrine* – de 10 à 30 mg, 3 fois par jour, selon la réponse du patient.

Mononitrate d'isosorbide

- **PO (adultes)**: De 30 à 60 mg, 1 fois par jour; on peut augmenter la dose jusqu'à 120 à 240 mg, 1 fois par jour (ne pas dépasser 240 mg par jour).

PRÉSENTATION (version générique disponible)

- **Dinitrate d'isosorbide**
  Comprimés sublinguaux: 5 mg[Pr] ■ **Comprimés**: 10 mg[Pr], 30 mg[Pr].
- **Mononitrate d'isosorbide**
  Comprimés à libération prolongée: 60 mg[Pr].

SOINS INFIRMIERS

ÉVALUATION DE LA SITUATION

- Déterminer le siège, la durée et l'intensité de la douleur angineuse de même que les facteurs qui la déclenchent.
- Mesurer la pression artérielle et le pouls à intervalles réguliers pendant la période d'adaptation posologique.

Tests de laboratoire:

- Le médicament peut entraîner des résultats faussement bas lors du dosage du cholestérol sérique.
- Des doses excessives peuvent accroître les concentrations de méthémoglobine.
- Le médicament peut élever les concentrations urinaires d'acide vanylmandélique.

DIAGNOSTICS INFIRMIERS POSSIBLES

- Irrigation tissulaire inefficace (Indications).
- Intolérance à l'activité (Indications).
- Connaissances insuffisantes sur le traitement médicamenteux (Enseignement au patient et à ses proches).

INTERVENTIONS INFIRMIÈRES

Dinitrate d'isosorbide

PO: Administrer le médicament 1 heure avant les repas ou 2 heures après, avec un grand verre d'eau, pour accélérer l'absorption.

Voie sublinguale: Les comprimés sublinguaux doivent être gardés sous la langue jusqu'à leur dissolution.

- Il ne faut pas manger, boire ni fumer jusqu'à ce que le comprimé soit dissous. Administrer un nouveau comprimé si le comprimé sublingual a été avalé par inadvertance.

Mononitrate d'isosorbide

- NE PAS CONFONDRE IMDUR AVEC IMURAN (AZATHIOPRINE), INDERAL (PROPRANOLOL) OU K-DUR (CHLORURE DE POTASSIUM).

PO: Les comprimés à libération prolongée doivent être avalés tels quels ou divisés en deux. Ils ne doivent pas être écrasés, brisés ni croqués. Les selles peuvent parfois sembler contenir un comprimé entier; en fait, il s'agit seulement de la matrice qui est restée intacte après la libération du médicament.

ENSEIGNEMENT AU PATIENT ET À SES PROCHES

- Inciter le patient à respecter rigoureusement la posologie recommandée même s'il se sent mieux. S'il n'a pas pu prendre le médicament au moment habituel, il doit le prendre dès que possible, sauf si la dose suivante doit être prise dans les 2 heures (6 heures dans le cas des préparations à libération prolongée). Prévenir le patient qu'il ne doit jamais remplacer une dose manquée par une double dose, ni interrompre brusquement le traitement.

- Expliquer au patient que seuls les comprimés sublinguaux conviennent au traitement des crises d'angine. Les autres comprimés n'agissent pas assez rapidement.
- Recommander au patient de changer lentement de position afin de réduire le risque d'hypotension orthostatique.
- Prévenir le patient que l'isosorbide peut provoquer des étourdissements. Lui conseiller de ne pas conduire et d'éviter les activités qui exigent sa vigilance jusqu'à ce qu'on ait la certitude que le médicament n'entraîne pas cet effet chez lui.
- Mettre le patient en garde contre la consommation d'alcool en même temps que ce médicament. Lui conseiller de consulter un professionnel de la santé avant de prendre un médicament en vente libre ou un produit naturel pendant son traitement au dinitrate ou au mononitrate d'isosorbide.
- Prévenir le patient que les céphalées sont un effet secondaire courant, qui devrait diminuer en intensité à mesure que le traitement se poursuit. On pourrait lui prescrire de l'acétaminophène pour le traitement de ces céphalées. Lui recommander de voir un professionnel de la santé si les céphalées sont graves ou persistantes. Le prévenir qu'il ne doit pas modifier la dose pour éviter les céphalées.
- Conseiller au patient de prévenir un professionnel de la santé en cas de sécheresse de la bouche ou de vision trouble.
- Prévenir le patient qu'il peut retrouver dans ses selles une partie des comprimés à libération prolongée, mais qu'il s'agit de la partie inactive du comprimé.

VÉRIFICATION DE L'EFFICACITÉ THÉRAPEUTIQUE

L'efficacité du traitement peut être démontrée par: la diminution de la fréquence et de l'intensité des crises d'angine ■ l'augmentation de la tolérance à l'effort.

ITRACONAZOLE

Sporanox

CLASSIFICATION:

Antifongique par voie générale (de type azole)

Grossesse – catégorie C

INDICATIONS

Capsules par voie orale: Traitement de: l'histoplasmose pulmonaire chronique ■ la blastomycose ■ l'aspergillose pulmonaire envahissante et non envahissante ■ l'onychomycose ■ la sporotrichose cutanée et lymphatique ■ la paracoccidioïdomycose ■ la chromomycose ■ les dermatomycoses dues à *Tinea corporis*, *cruris* et *pedis*, et à *Pityriasis versicolor* quand le traitement par voie orale est justifié ■ les candidoses buccales et bucco-œsophagiennes ■ **Solution orale:** Traitement des candidoses buccales ou œsophagiennes chez les patients adultes séropositifs pour le VIH ou immunodéprimés (sauf les patients neutropéniques).

MÉCANISME D'ACTION

Inhibition de la synthèse des stérols fongiques, un élément essentiel de la paroi cellulaire. ***Effets thérapeutiques:*** Effets fongistatiques contre les microorganismes sensibles. **Spectre d'action:** *Histoplasma capsulatum*, *Blastomyces dermatitidis*, *Cryptococcus neoformans*, *Aspergillus fumigatus*, *Candida*, *Tinea unguium* et les espèces *Trichophyton*.

PHARMACOCINÉTIQUE

Absorption: Les aliments améliorent l'absorption après l'administration PO des capsules, mais diminuent l'absorption de la solution. Comme les capsules et les solutions ne sont pas bioéquivalentes, on ne peut pas les substituer les unes aux autres.

Distribution: Les concentrations tissulaires sont plus élevées que les concentrations plasmatiques. Le médicament ne pénètre pas dans le liquide céphalorachidien, mais passe dans le lait maternel.

Liaison aux protéines: *Itraconazole* – 99,8 %. *Hydroxyitraconazole* – 99,5 %.

Métabolisme et excrétion: Métabolisme majoritairement hépatique; excrétion fécale. L'hydroxyitraconazole, le principal métabolite, a un effet antifongique.

Demi-vie: 21 heures.

Profil temps-action (concentrations sanguines)

	DÉBUT D'ACTION	PIC	DURÉE
PO	rapide	4 h	12 – 24 h

CONTRE-INDICATIONS, PRÉCAUTIONS ET MISES EN GARDE

Contre-indications: Hypersensibilité ■ Risque de réactions de sensibilité croisée avec d'autres antifongiques de type azole (miconazole, kétoconazole) ■ L'administration concomitante d'itraconazole et de certains médicaments métabolisés par l'isoenzyme 3A4 du cytochrome P450 (CYP3A4) peut entraîner une augmentation des concentrations plasmatiques de ces médicaments menant à des manifestations indésirables pouvant mettre la vie du patient en danger (quinidine, dofétilide, cisapride, pimozide, midazolam oral, triazolam) ■ Administration concomitante d'inhibiteurs de la HMG-CoA réductase métabolisés par le CYP3A4, tels que la simvastatine ou la lovastatine ■ Administration concomitante des alcaloïdes de l'ergot, tels que la dihydroergotamine, l'ergométrine (ergonovine) et l'ergotamine ■ Administration concomitante d'élétriptan ■ Traitement de l'onychomycose ou de la dermatomycose chez un patient présentant des signes de dysfonction ventriculaire, telle l'insuffisance cardiaque ou ayant ces antécédents ■ Traitement de l'onychomycose ou de la dermatomycose (*Tinea corporis*, *Tinea cruris*, *Tinea pedis* et *Pityriasis versicolor*) chez la femme enceinte ou envisageant une grossesse.

I

Précautions et mises en garde: Insuffisance hépatique (une réduction de la dose peut être nécessaire) ■ Risque de toxicité hépatique importante même chez les patients ne souffrant pas d'insuffisance cardiaque. Un suivi de la fonction hépatique est indiqué ■ Insuffisance rénale grave (Cl_{Cr} < 30 mL/min) ■ Patient sidéen ou neutropénique (risque de diminution des concentrations plasmatiques) ■ Achlorhydrie ou hypochlorhydrie (diminution de l'absorption) ■ Allaitement ■ Femmes en âge de procréer (la patiente doit adopter une méthode contraceptive pendant le traitement et pendant les 2 mois qui suivent) ■ **OBST., PÉD.**: L'innocuité du médicament n'a pas été établie.

RÉACTIONS INDÉSIRABLES ET EFFETS SECONDAIRES

SNC: étourdissements, somnolence, fatigue, céphalées, malaise.

ORLO: acouphènes.

CV: insuffisance cardiaque, œdème, hypertension.

GI: HÉPATOTOXICITÉ, nausées, douleurs abdominales, anorexie, diarrhée, flatulence, vomissements.

GU: albuminurie, baisse de la libido, impuissance.

Tég.: NÉCROLYSE ÉPIDERMIQUE TOXIQUE, photosensibilité, prurit, rash.

End.: insuffisance surrénalienne.

HÉ: hypokaliémie.

Loc.: rhabdomyolyse.

Divers: réactions allergiques incluant l'ANAPHYLAXIE, fièvre.

INTERACTIONS

Médicament-médicament: L'itraconazole est un puissant inhibiteur du système d'enzymes hépatiques **P4503A** et peut donc augmenter les concentrations sanguines ainsi que les effets des **médicaments qui sont métabolisés par ce système** ■ RISQUE ACCRU D'ARYTHMIES CARDIAQUES D'ISSUE FATALE LORS DE L'ADMINISTRATION CONCOMITANTE DE **QUINIDINE**, DE **DOFÉTILIDE**, DE **CISAPRIDE** OU DE **PIMOZIDE** (l'utilisation concomitante est contre-indiquée et peut entraîner un allongement de l'intervalle QT_c, des torsades de pointes, des arythmies ventriculaires ou la mort) ■ L'itraconazole peut accroître le risque de sédation excessive associé au **midazolam** ou au **triazolam** (l'utilisation concomitante est contre-indiquée) ■ Risque accru de myopathie en cas d'administration concomitante de **simvastatine**, d'**atorvastatine** ou de **lovastatine** (usage concomitant contre-indiqué) ■ L'utilisation concomitante des alcaloïdes de l'ergot (**dihydroergotamine**, **ergonovine**, **ergotamine**) est contre-indiquée, en raison du risque accru de vasoconstriction pouvant entraîner une ischémie grave ■ L'itraconazole peut également accroître les concentrations sanguines de **fentanyl**, de **warfarine**, de **ritonavir**, d'**indinavir**, de **saquinavir**, d'**alcaloïdes de la pervenche**, de **busulfan**, de **diazépam**, de **félodipine**, de **nicardipine**, de **nifédipine**, de **nimodipine**, de **cyclosporine**, de **vardénafil**, de **tacrolimus**, de **sildénafil**, de **méthylprednisolone**, de **digoxine**, de **phénytoïne**, d'**hypoglycémiants oraux** et de **quinidine**, et accroître le risque d'intoxication par ces agents ■ Les **antiacides**, le **sucralfate** (prendre ces agents 2 heures après l'itraconazole), les **bloqueurs des récepteurs H_2 de l'histamine**, les **inhibiteurs de la pompe à protons** (tels que le **lansoprazole**, le **rabéprazole**, l'**oméprazole**, l'**esoméprazole**, le **pantoprazole**) ou d'autres **agents qui augmentent le pH gastrique**, incluant le tampon que renferme la **didanosine**, peuvent réduire l'absorption de l'itraconazole ■ La **phénytoïne**, le **phénobarbital**, l'**isoniazide**, la **rifampine**, la **rifabutine** et la **carbamazépine** accélèrent le métabolisme et réduisent les concentrations sanguines de l'itraconazole (il peut s'avérer nécessaire d'augmenter la dose) ■ En cas d'hypokaliémie, le risque de toxicité associé aux **glucosides cardiotoniques** est accru ■ La **clarithromycine**, l'**erythromycine**, le **ritonavir** et l'**indinavir** peuvent accroître les concentrations sanguines d'itraconazole.

Médicament-aliments: Les **aliments** augmentent l'absorption des capsules d'itraconazole mais diminuent celle de la solution.

VOIES D'ADMINISTRATION ET POSOLOGIE

Capsules

Aspergillose pulmonaire

- **PO (adultes)**: 200 mg, 1 fois par jour, pendant 3 à 4 mois.

Aspergillose pulmonaire envahissante

- **PO (adultes)**: 200 mg, 2 fois par jour, pendant 3 à 4 mois.

Blastomycose et histoplasmose pulmonaire chronique

- **PO (adultes)**: 200 mg, 1 fois par jour; on peut augmenter la dose par paliers de 100 mg par jour, jusqu'à 200 mg, 2 fois par jour, pendant au moins 3 mois.

Sporotrichose

- **PO (adultes)**: 100 mg, 1 fois par jour, pendant 3 mois.

Paracoccidioïdomycose

- **PO (adultes)**: 100 mg, 1 fois par jour, pendant 6 mois.

Chromomycose due à **Fonsecæa pedrosoi**

- **PO (adultes)**: 200 mg, 1 fois par jour, pendant 6 mois.

Chromomycose due à **Cladosporium carrionii**

- **PO (adultes)**: 100 mg, 1 fois par jour, pendant 3 mois.

Dermatomycose

- ***Tinea corporis* ou *cruris*: PO (adultes)**: 100 mg, 1 fois par jour, pendant 14 jours, ou 200 mg, 1 fois par jour, pendant 7 jours.
- ***Tinea pedis*: PO (adultes)**: 100 mg, 1 fois par jour, pendant 28 jours, ou 200 mg, 2 fois par jour, pendant 7 jours.
- ***Pityriasis versicolor***: 200 mg, 1 fois par jour, pendant 7 jours.

Onychomycose

- **PO (adultes)**: 200 mg, 2 fois par jour, pendant 1 semaine, puis une période de 3 semaines sans traitement. *Infection des ongles des doigts* – 2 cycles de 1 semaine. *Infection des ongles des orteils avec ou sans atteinte des ongles des doigts* – 3 cycles de 1 semaine.

Candidoses buccale et bucco-œsophagienne

- **PO (adultes)**: 100 mg, 1 fois par jour, pendant 2 semaines. Dans le cas des patients neutropéniques ou sidéens: 200 mg, 1 fois par jour, pendant 2 semaines. En présence d'une candidose bucco-œsophagienne, le traitement doit durer 4 semaines.

Solution orale

Candidose

- **PO (adultes)**: *Candidose oropharyngée* – 200 mg (20 mL) par jour, en 1 dose ou en doses fractionnées, pendant 1 à 2 semaines. *Candidose œsophagienne* – 100 mg (10 mL), 1 fois par jour, pendant au moins 3 semaines; poursuivre le traitement pendant 2 semaines après la disparition des symptômes. On peut augmenter la dose à 200 mg/jour selon la réponse au traitement.

PRÉSENTATION

Capsules: 100 mg[Pr] ■ **Solution orale**: 10 mg/mL[Pr].

SOINS INFIRMIERS

ÉVALUATION DE LA SITUATION

- Avant le traitement et à intervalles réguliers pendant toute sa durée, rester à l'affût des signes et des symptômes d'infection: altération des signes vitaux, murmure vésiculaire, accroissement du nombre de globules blancs, aspect des expectorations, des muqueuses de la bouche et du pharynx, et des lits unguéaux.
- Prélever des échantillons destinés à la mise en culture avant d'amorcer le traitement. On peut cependant démarrer le traitement sans attendre les résultats.

Tests de laboratoire:

- Noter les résultats des tests de la fonction hépatique, avant le traitement et à intervalles réguliers pendant toute sa durée, particulièrement en présence d'anomalies préexistantes de la fonction hépatique. Interrompre le traitement par l'itraconazole si les valeurs anormales persistent ou s'aggravent.
- Noter les concentrations sériques de potassium. L'itraconazole peut provoquer une hypokaliémie.

DIAGNOSTICS INFIRMIERS POSSIBLES

- Risque d'infection (Indications).
- Connaissances insuffisantes sur le traitement médicamenteux (Enseignement au patient et à ses proches).
- Non-observance du traitement médicamenteux (Enseignement au patient et à ses proches).

INTERVENTIONS INFIRMIÈRES

Les capsules et la solution orale ne sont pas interchangeables. Seule la solution orale est efficace en cas de candidose oropharyngée.

Capsules:

- Administrer avec un repas complet pour réduire le risque de nausées et de vomissements, et pour accroître l'absorption.
- Ne pas administrer l'itraconazole avec des antiacides ou d'autres médicaments qui augmentent le pH gastrique, car ces agents peuvent en diminuer l'absorption.

Solution orale: Administrer sans aliments dans la mesure du possible. Demander au patient de se rincer vigoureusement la bouche avec 10 mL de solution à la fois, pendant plusieurs secondes, puis d'avaler. Il ne doit pas se rincer la bouche à l'eau immédiatement après.

I

ENSEIGNEMENT AU PATIENT ET À SES PROCHES

- Conseiller au patient de respecter rigoureusement la posologie recommandée, même s'il se sent mieux. Les doses devraient être prises à la même heure chaque jour.
- Prévenir le patient que l'itraconazole peut parfois provoquer de la somnolence. Lui conseiller de ne pas conduire et d'éviter les activités qui exigent sa vigilance jusqu'à ce qu'on ait la certitude que le médicament n'entraîne pas cet effet chez lui.
- Recommander au patient de cesser la prise d'itraconazole et de consulter un professionnel de la santé en présence des signes ou des symptômes suivants de dysfonctionnement hépatique (fatigue inhabituelle, anorexie, nausées, vomissements, jaunisse, urine foncée ou selles pâles) ou d'insuffisance cardiaque (dyspnée, œdème périphérique, gain de poids).
- Conseiller au patient de consulter un professionnel de la santé avant de prendre tout autre médicament en vente libre ou sur ordonnance, ou des produits naturels, en même temps que l'itraconazole.
- Recommander au patient d'utiliser des écrans solaires et des vêtements protecteurs afin de prévenir les réactions de photosensibilité.

VÉRIFICATION DE L'EFFICACITÉ THÉRAPEUTIQUE

L'efficacité du traitement peut être démontrée par: la résolution des signes cliniques et l'amélioration des résultats des tests indiquant une infection fongique. La durée minimale du traitement en présence d'une infection fongique systémique est de 3 mois. Un traitement d'une durée inadéquate peut mener à la récurrence de l'infection.

KÉTOCONAZOLE

Apo-Ketoconazole, Nizoral, Novo-Ketoconazole, Nu-Ketocon

CLASSIFICATION:
Antifongique (par voie générale)

Grossesse – catégorie C

Pour l'usage topique, voir Antifongiques topiques.

INDICATIONS

Traitement des infections fongiques suivantes: candidose (disséminée, oro-œsophagienne et mucocutanée chronique) ■ Mycoses des cheveux ou du cuir chevelu ■ pityriasis versicolor ■ chromomycose ■ coccidioïdomycose ■ paracoccidioïdomycose ■ histoplasmose ■ blastomycose sud-américaine ■ dermatophytoses graves, réfractaires aux autres formes de traitement. **Usages non approuvés:** Traitement du cancer de la prostate à un stade avancé ■ Traitement du syndrome de Cushing.

MÉCANISME D'ACTION

Inhibition de la synthèse des stérols fongiques, un élément essentiel de la paroi cellulaire ■ Inhibition de la synthèse des corticostéroïdes. ***Effets thérapeutiques:*** Effet fongicide ou fongistatique contre les microorganismes sensibles, selon le microorganisme infectant et le foyer de l'infection. **Spectre d'action:** Le médicament agit contre de nombreux champignons pathogènes dont: *Blastomyces* ■ *Candida* ■ *Coccidioides* ■ *Cryptococcus* ■ *Histoplasma* ■ un grand nombre de dermatophytes.

PHARMACOCINÉTIQUE

Absorption: L'absorption par le tractus gastro-intestinal dépend du pH; un pH accru diminue l'absorption.

Distribution: Tout l'organisme. Pénétration dans le SNC imprévisible et minime. Le kétoconazole traverse la barrière placentaire et passe dans le lait maternel.

Liaison aux protéines: 99 %.

Métabolisme et excrétion: Métabolisme hépatique partiel. Excrétion dans les fèces par voie biliaire.

Demi-vie: 8 heures.

Profil temps-action (concentrations sanguines)

	DÉBUT D'ACTION	PIC	DURÉE
PO	rapide	1 - 4 h	24 h

CONTRE-INDICATIONS, PRÉCAUTIONS ET MISES EN GARDE

Contre-indications: Hypersensibilité ■ Risque de réactions de sensibilité croisée avec d'autres antifongiques de type azole (miconazole, itraconazole) ■ Troubles hépatiques ■ Femmes en âge de procréer qui n'utilisent pas de méthode de contraception efficace.

Précautions et mises en garde: Risque d'inhibition de la synthèse du cortisol et de la testostérone, en particulier lors de l'administration de fortes doses. On recommande de ne pas administrer plus de 400 mg par jour ■ Risque d'hépatotoxicité, en particulier chez les patients à risque ■ Achlorhydrie ou hypochlorhydrie ■ Alcoolisme ■ Grossesse ■ Allaitement ■ Enfants < 2 ans.

RÉACTIONS INDÉSIRABLES ET EFFETS SECONDAIRES

SNC: étourdissements, somnolence.

ORLO: photophobie.

GI: HÉPATITE MÉDICAMENTEUSE, nausées, vomissements, douleurs abdominales, constipation, diarrhée, flatulence.

GU: azoospermie, baisse de la libido chez l'homme, dérèglement du cycle menstruel, oligospermie.

Tég.: rash.

End.: gynécomastie.

INTERACTIONS

Médicament-médicament: Le kétoconazole inhibe le système enzymatique hépatique P4503A4, ce qui entraîne une diminution du métabolisme et un risque d'intensification des effets ou de la toxicité des **bloqueurs des canaux calciques**, de la **cyclosporine**, du **tacrolimus**, du **sirolimus**, des **corticostéroïdes** (une réduction de la dose peut être nécessaire), des **sulfonylurés**, des **hypoglycémiants oraux**, de la **buspirone**, de la **clarithromycine** de l'**érythromycine**, du **cyclophosphamide**, de la **dompéridone**, du **tamoxifène**, des **antidépresseurs tricycliques**, de la **trazodone**, de la **carbamazépine**, de la **loratadine**, du **zolpidem**, de la **vincristine**, de la **vinblastine**, de l'**ifosfamide**, de l'**alprazolam**, du **midazolam**, du **triazolam**, de l'**alfentanil**, du **fentanyl**, de la **méthadone**, du **donépézil**, du **sufentanil**, de l'**atorvastatine**, de la **cérivastatine**, de la **lovastatine**, de la **simvastatine**, de l'**amprénavir**, de l'**indinavir** (une baisse de la dose de l'indinavir est recommandée), du **nelfinavir**, du **ritonavir**, du **saquinavir**, du **cisapride** (usage concomitant contre-indiqué), de la **quinidine**, du **sildénafil** et du **vardénafil** ■ Baisse de l'absorption lors de l'administration concomitante de médicaments élevant le pH gastrique, dont les **antiacides** et le **sulcralfate** (attendre 2 heures avant d'administrer le kétoconazole), les **antagonistes des récepteurs H_2 de**

K

l'histamine, la **didanosine** (en raison du tampon) et les inhibiteurs de la pompe à protons (**lansoprazole**, **oméprazole**, **rabéprazole**) ■ Le kétoconazole peut diminuer l'efficacité des **contraceptifs oraux** (il est recommandé d'utiliser une autre méthode contraceptive) ■ Hépatotoxicité additive lors de l'usage concomitant d'**agents hépatotoxiques**, incluant l'**alcool** ■ La prise concomitante d'**alcool** peut entraîner une réaction s'apparentant à celle qui est induite par le disulfirame ■ La **rifampine** ou l'**isoniazide** peuvent réduire les concentrations et l'efficacité de l'agent ■ Le kétoconazole peut augmenter l'efficacité ou le risque de toxicité lié à la **warfarine** (risque accru de saignements) ou à la **phénytoïne**, lors d'un traitement concomitant ■ Le kétoconazole peut diminuer l'absorption et l'efficacité de la **théophylline**.

VOIES D'ADMINISTRATION ET POSOLOGIE

K

- **PO (adultes)**: 200 mg, 1 fois par jour; la durée du traitement varie selon l'infection (ne pas dépasser 400 mg/jour).
- **PO (enfants > 2 ans)**: De 3,3 à 6,6 mg/kg/jour, 1 fois par jour.

PRÉSENTATION

Comprimés: 200 mg[Pr].

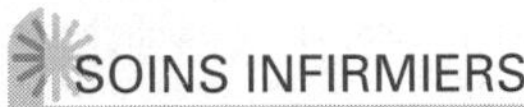

SOINS INFIRMIERS

ÉVALUATION DE LA SITUATION

- Suivre de près le patient à la recherche des symptômes d'infection, avant le traitement et à intervalles réguliers pendant toute sa durée.
- Prélever des échantillons pour la mise en culture avant d'amorcer le traitement. On peut commencer le traitement avant même que les résultats soient connus.

Tests de laboratoire:

- IL FAUT EFFECTUER DES TESTS DE LA FONCTION HÉPATIQUE AVANT D'AMORCER LE TRAITEMENT, TOUS LES MOIS, PENDANT LES 3 OU 4 PREMIERS MOIS, ET À INTERVALLES RÉGULIERS PAR LA SUITE JUSQU'À LA FIN DU TRAITEMENT. LE KÉTOCONAZOLE PEUT ÉLEVER LES CONCENTRATIONS D'AST, D'ALT, DE PHOSPHATASE ALCALINE SÉRIQUE ET DE BILIRUBINE. IL FAUT CESSER L'ADMINISTRATION DU KÉTOCONAZOLE AU MOINDRE SIGNE D'ANOMALIE.
- Le kétoconazole peut entraîner une baisse des concentrations sériques de testostérone.

DIAGNOSTICS INFIRMIERS POSSIBLES

- Risque d'infection (Indications).
- Connaissances insuffisantes sur le traitement médicamenteux (Enseignement au patient et à ses proches).
- Non-observance du traitement médicamenteux (Enseignement au patient et à ses proches).

INTERVENTIONS INFIRMIÈRES

- NE PAS CONFONDRE NIZORAL (KÉTOCONAZOLE) AVEC NEORAL (CYCLOSPORINE).
- Administrer l'agent avec des repas ou des collations pour réduire les nausées et les vomissements.
- Ne pas administrer d'antagonistes des récepteurs H_2 de l'histamine, de sucralfate ou d'antiacides dans les 2 heures précédant ou suivant l'administration du kétoconazole.
- Chez les patients atteints d'achlorhydrie, dissoudre chaque comprimé dans 4 mL de solution aqueuse de HCl à 0,2 N. Demander au patient de boire la suspension avec une paille de plastique ou de verre de façon à éviter tout contact avec les dents. Lui faire ensuite prendre un verre d'eau et lui demander de bien se rincer la bouche, puis d'avaler.

ENSEIGNEMENT AU PATIENT ET À SES PROCHES

- Recommander au patient de respecter rigoureusement la posologie recommandée et de poursuivre le traitement même s'il se sent mieux. Le prévenir qu'il doit prendre le médicament à la même heure, chaque jour. S'il n'a pas pu prendre le médicament au moment habituel, il doit le prendre aussitôt que possible. S'il est presque l'heure de la dose suivante, il doit prendre le médicament aussitôt et retarder la prise de la dose suivante de 10 à 12 heures.
- Prévenir le patient que le kétoconazole peut provoquer des étourdissements et de la somnolence. Lui conseiller de ne pas conduire et d'éviter les activités qui exigent sa vigilance jusqu'à ce qu'on ait la certitude que le médicament n'entraîne pas ces effets chez lui.
- Recommander au patient de ne pas prendre d'antiacides en vente libre dans les 2 heures avant ou suivant la prise du kétoconazole.
- Recommander au patient de porter des lunettes de soleil et d'éviter toute exposition prolongée à la lumière vive afin de prévenir les réactions de photophobie.
- Conseiller au patient d'éviter de boire de l'alcool en même temps qu'il prend ce médicament, en raison du risque de réactions s'apparentant à celles qui sont entraînées par le disulfirame (bouffées vasomotrices,

rash, œdème périphérique, nausées, céphalées) et du risque accru d'hépatotoxicité.

- CONSEILLER AU PATIENT DE SIGNALER À UN PROFESSIONNEL DE LA SANTÉ LES DOULEURS ABDOMINALES, LA FIÈVRE OU UNE DIARRHÉE IMPORTANTE AINSI QUE LA PRÉSENCE DE SIGNES ET DE SYMPTÔMES DE DYSFONCTIONNEMENT HÉPATIQUE (FATIGUE INHABITUELLE, ANOREXIE, NAUSÉES, VOMISSEMENTS, JAUNISSE, URINE FONCÉE OU SELLES DE COULEUR PÂLE).

VÉRIFICATION DE L'EFFICACITÉ THÉRAPEUTIQUE

L'efficacité du traitement peut être démontrée par: la résolution des signes cliniques et la normalisation des résultats des examens de laboratoire liés à l'infection fongique. (La durée minimale de traitement de la candidose est de 1 à 2 semaines et des autres infections fongiques généralisées, de 6 mois. La candidose mucocutanée chronique dicte habituellement un traitement d'entretien.) ✳

KÉTOPROFÈNE

Apo-Keto, Apo-Keto-E, Apo-Keto SR, Nu-Ketoprofen, Nu-Ketoprofen-E, Orudis, Orudis E, Orudis SR, PMS-Ketoprofen, Rhodis

CLASSIFICATION:

Anti-inflammatoire non stéroïdien, analgésique non opioïde

Grossesse – catégories D (1er et 3e trimestres) et B (2e trimestre)

INDICATIONS

Maladies inflammatoires dont: la polyarthrite rhumatoïde ▪ la spondylarthrite ankylosante ▪ l'arthrose ▪ Douleur légère à modérée, incluant celle qui accompagne la dysménorrhée et la fièvre.

MÉCANISME D'ACTION

Inhibition de la synthèse des prostaglandines. ***Effets thérapeutiques:*** Suppression de l'inflammation et de la douleur ▪ Abaissement de la fièvre.

PHARMACOCINÉTIQUE

Absorption: Bonne (PO).

Distribution: Inconnue.

Liaison aux protéines: 99 %.

Métabolisme et excrétion: Métabolisme hépatique à 60 %. Une certaine fraction est excrétée par les reins.

Demi-vie: De 2 à 4 heures.

Profil temps-action (effets thérapeutiques)

	DÉBUT D'ACTION	PIC	DURÉE
PO (analgésique)	dans les 60 min	1 h	4 - 6 h
PO (anti-inflammatoire)	de quelques jours à 1 semaine	inconnu	jusqu'à 24 h (libération prolongée)

CONTRE-INDICATIONS, PRÉCAUTIONS ET MISES EN GARDE

Contre-indications: Hypersensibilité ▪ Risque de réactions de sensibilité croisée avec d'autres AINS incluant l'aspirine ▪ Syndrome complet ou partiel de polypes nasaux, ou patients chez lesquels l'asthme, l'anaphylaxie, l'urticaire, la rhinite ou toute autre manifestation allergique a été déclenchée par l'aspirine ou d'autres AINS ▪ Hémorragie digestive ▪ Ulcère gastroduodénal évolutif, antécédents d'ulcère gastroduodénal récurrent ou d'affection inflammatoire évolutive des voies digestives ▪ Atteinte hépatique notable ou évolutive ▪ Dysfonctionnement rénal grave ou évolutif ▪ Douleur périopératoire après installation d'un tuteur coronarien.

Précautions et mises en garde: Maladie cardiovasculaire, hépatique ou rénale grave ▪ Antécédents d'ulcère ▪ Insuffisance rénale ▪ **GÉR.:** Personnes âgées, de petite taille ou insuffisants rénaux (la préparation à libération prolongée est déconseillée) ▪ Alcoolisme chronique ▪ Intolérance à la tartrazine (ne pas administrer les agents qui renferment cette substance aux patients ayant de tels antécédents) ▪ **OBST., ALLAITEMENT, PÉD.:** L'innocuité du médicament n'a pas été établie; en éviter l'administration au cours de la deuxième moitié de la grossesse.

RÉACTIONS INDÉSIRABLES ET EFFETS SECONDAIRES

SNC: somnolence, céphalées, étourdissements.

ORLO: vision trouble, acouphènes.

CV: œdème.

GI: HÉPATITE MÉDICAMENTEUSE, HÉMORRAGIE DIGESTIVE, constipation, diarrhée, dyspepsie, nausées, vomissements, anorexie, gêne, flatulence.

GU: cystite, hématurie, insuffisance rénale.

Tég: photosensibilité, rash, DERMATITE EXFOLIATIVE, SYNDROME DE STEVENS-JOHNSON, ÉPIDERMOLYSE NÉCROSANTE SUBAIGUË.

End.: gynécomastie.

Hémat.: dyscrasie sanguine, prolongation du temps de saignement.

K

SN: myalgie.

Divers: réactions allergiques incluant l'ANAPHYLAXIE et la fièvre.

INTERACTIONS

Médicament-médicament: L'**aspirine** modifie la distribution, le métabolisme et l'excrétion du kétoprofène (une administration concomitante n'est pas recommandée) ■ L'administration concomitante d'**autres agents anti-inflammatoires non stéroïdiens** et de **corticostéroïdes**, ou l'ingestion d'**alcool** intensifient les effets secondaires gastro-intestinaux ■ L'administration prolongée de kétoprofène et d'**acétaminophène** en concomitance peut augmenter le risque de réactions rénales indésirables ■ Le kétoprofène peut réduire l'efficacité des **diurétiques** ou des **antihypertenseurs** ■ Le kétoprofène peut intensifier l'effet hypoglycémiant de l'**insuline** ou des **hypoglycémiants oraux à base de sulfonylurée** ■ Le kétoprofène peut élever les concentrations sériques de **lithium** et le risque de toxicité associé ■ Le kétoprofène augmente le risque de toxicité associé au **méthotrexate** ■ Le **probénécide** augmente le risque de toxicité associé au kétoprofène (l'administration concomitante n'est pas recommandée) ■ Risque accru d'hémorragie lors de l'administration concomitante de **céfamandole**, de **céfotétane**, de **céfopérazone**, d'**acide valproïque**, de **plicamycine**, d'**agents thrombolytiques**, de **clopidogrel**, de **ticlopidine**, d'**eptifibatide**, de **tirofiban** ou d'**anticoagulants** ■ Risque accru de réactions hématologiques indésirables lors de l'administration concomitante d'**agents antinéoplasiques** ou d'une **radiothérapie** ■ Risque accru de toxicité rénale lors de l'administration concomitante de **cyclosporine**.

Médicament-produits naturels: Risque accru de saignements en cas de consommation concomitante d'**ail**, d'**anis**, d'**arnica**, de **camomille**, de **dong quai**, de **girofle**, de **gingembre**, de **ginkgo** et de **ginseng**.

VOIES D'ADMINISTRATION ET POSOLOGIE

- **PO, IR (adultes)**: *Anti-inflammatoire* – de 150 à 300 mg par jour, en 3 ou 4 doses fractionnées, *ou* de 150 à 300 mg, en 1 ou 2 doses fractionnées, pour la présentation à libération prolongée. *Analgésique* – de 150 à 200 mg par jour, en 1 à 4 doses fractionnées, selon la présentation utilisée. *Sujets âgés et insuffisants rénaux* – réduire la posologie initiale de un tiers ou de moitié.

PRÉSENTATION (version générique disponible)

Comprimés à enrobage entérique: 50 mg^{Pr}, 100 mg^{Pr}, 200 mg^{Pr} ■ **Capsules**: 50 mg^{Pr} ■ **Capsules à libération prolongée**: 150 mg^{Pr}, 200 mg^{Pr} ■ **Suppositoires**: 50 mg^{Pr}, 100 mg^{Pr}.

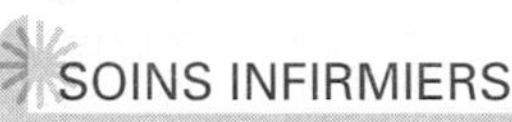

SOINS INFIRMIERS

ÉVALUATION DE LA SITUATION

- LES PATIENTS SOUFFRANT D'ASTHME, D'ALLERGIE INDUITE PAR L'ASPIRINE OU DE POLYPES NASAUX SONT DAVANTAGE PRÉDISPOSÉS AUX RÉACTIONS D'HYPERSENSIBILITÉ. SUIVRE DE PRÈS LA RHINITE, LA RESPIRATION SIFFLANTE ET L'URTICAIRE.

Arthrite: Évaluer l'intensité de la douleur et l'amplitude des mouvements articulaires, avant l'administration du kétoprofène et une heure après.

Douleur: Suivre de près la douleur (type, siège et intensité) avant l'administration du kétoprofène et 1 heure après.

Tests de laboratoire:

- Chez les patients recevant un traitement prolongé, noter à intervalles réguliers les concentrations sériques d'urée et de créatinine, ainsi que la numération globulaire et les résultats des tests de la fonction hépatique.
- L'agent peut élever les concentrations sériques de potassium, d'urée, de créatinine, de phosphatase alcaline, ainsi que celles de LDH, d'AST et d'ALT, et réduire la glycémie, les concentrations d'hémoglobine et l'hématocrite, ainsi que le nombre de leucocytes et de plaquettes, et la clairance de la créatinine.
- Le kétoprofène peut allonger le temps de saignement de 3 ou de 4 minutes.
- Le kétoprofène peut modifier le dosage de l'albuminurie, de la bilirubine, du 17-cétostéroïde et du 17-hydrocorticostéroïde urinaire.

DIAGNOSTICS INFIRMIERS POSSIBLES

- Douleur aiguë (Indications).
- Mobilité physique réduite (Indications).
- Connaissances insuffisantes sur le traitement médicamenteux (Enseignement au patient et à ses proches).

INTERVENTIONS INFIRMIÈRES

- L'administration de doses plus élevées que celles qui sont recommandées n'améliore pas l'efficacité du médicament, mais pourrait augmenter le risque d'effets secondaires.
- L'administration concomitante d'analgésiques opioïdes peut intensifier les effets analgésiques, ce qui permet d'abaisser les doses d'opioïdes.

- L'effet analgésique est plus efficace si l'agent est administré avant que la douleur devienne intense.

PO:

- Pour obtenir un effet initial rapide, administrer 30 minutes avant ou 2 heures après les repas. On peut administrer les capsules avec des aliments, du lait ou un antiacide renfermant de l'hydroxyde d'aluminium et de magnésium pour réduire l'irritation gastrique.
- LES CAPSULES À LIBÉRATION PROLONGÉE DOIVENT ÊTRE AVALÉES TELLES QUELLES; IL NE FAUT PAS LES OUVRIR NI LES MÂCHER.

Dysménorrhée: Administrer l'agent dès que possible après le début des règles. On n'a pas prouvé l'efficacité d'un traitement prophylactique.

ENSEIGNEMENT AU PATIENT ET À SES PROCHES

- Conseiller au patient de prendre le kétoprofène avec un grand verre d'eau et d'éviter de se coucher pendant les 15 à 30 minutes qui suivent.
- Conseiller au patient de respecter rigoureusement la posologie recommandée. S'il n'a pu prendre le médicament au moment habituel, il doit le faire dès que possible à moins que ce ne soit presque l'heure prévue pour la dose suivante. Le prévenir qu'il ne faut jamais remplacer une dose manquée par une double dose.
- Prévenir le patient que le kétoprofène peut parfois provoquer de la somnolence ou des étourdissements. Lui conseiller de ne pas conduire et d'éviter les activités qui exigent sa vigilance jusqu'à ce qu'on ait la certitude que le médicament n'entraîne pas ces effets chez lui.
- Recommander au patient d'éviter de boire de l'alcool et de consulter un professionnel de la santé avant de prendre une préparation à base d'aspirine ou d'acétaminophène, ou un autre médicament en vente libre en même temps que le kétoprofène.
- Recommander au patient qui doit suivre un autre traitement ou subir une intervention chirurgicale d'avertir le professionnel de la santé qu'il suit un traitement avec ce médicament.
- Recommander au patient d'utiliser des écrans solaires et de porter des vêtements protecteurs pour prévenir les réactions de photosensibilité.
- PRÉVENIR LE PATIENT QUE S'IL PREND 3 VERRES D'ALCOOL OU PLUS PAR JOUR PENDANT CE TRAITEMENT, IL PEUT ACCROÎTRE LE RISQUE D'HÉMORRAGIE DIGESTIVE.
- Recommander au patient de communiquer avec un professionnel de la santé en cas de rash, de démangeaisons, de troubles visuels, d'acouphènes, de gain de poids, d'œdème, de selles noires, de céphalées persistantes ou de symptômes pseudogrippaux (frissons, fièvre, douleurs musculaires, douleurs).

VÉRIFICATION DE L'EFFICACITÉ THÉRAPEUTIQUE

L'efficacité du traitement peut être démontrée par: l'amélioration de la mobilité des articulations ▪ la diminution de l'intensité de la douleur; la douleur arthritique peut commencer à diminuer quelques jours ou 1 semaine après le début du traitement; l'efficacité maximale peut ne pas être notable avant 1 à 2 semaines. Les patients qui ne répondent pas à un anti-inflammatoire non stéroïdien peuvent répondre à un autre. ✳

KÉTOROLAC

Apo-Ketorolac, Novo-Ketorolac, Ratio-Ketorolac, Toradol, Toradol IM

CLASSIFICATION:

Anti-inflammatoire non stéroïdien, analgésique non opioïde

Grossesse – catégories D (1er et 3e trimestres) et B (2e trimestre)

Pour l'usage ophtalmique, voir l'annexe N.

INDICATIONS

PO: Traitement de courte durée (jusqu'à 5 jours tout au plus, après une intervention chirurgicale, ou jusqu'à 7 jours en cas de douleurs musculosquelettiques) de la douleur aiguë, modérée à modérément intense, y compris la douleur postopératoire, la douleur musculosquelettique aiguë due à un traumatisme et les crampes utérines du postpartum ▪ **IM**: Traitement de courte durée (ne dépassant pas 2 jours) de la douleur aiguë, modérée ou intense, y compris celle qui suit les interventions chirurgicales abdominales, orthopédiques et gynécologiques majeures. La durée totale du traitement combiné par voies IM et orale ne doit pas dépasser 5 jours.

MÉCANISME D'ACTION

Inhibition de la synthèse des prostaglandines entraînant une analgésie par médiation périphérique ▪ Propriétés anti-inflammatoires et antipyrétiques. ***Effets thérapeutiques:* PO, IM**: Diminution de la douleur.

PHARMACOCINÉTIQUE

Absorption: Rapide et totale (PO, IM).

Distribution: De faibles concentrations de kétorolac passent dans le lait maternel.

Métabolisme et excrétion: Métabolisme à 50 % hépatique. Le kétorolac et ses métabolites sont principalement excrétés par les reins (92 %); 6 % sont excrétés dans les fèces.

Demi-vie: 4,5 heures (de 3,8 à 6,3 heures; prolongée chez les personnes âgées et les insuffisants rénaux).

Profil temps-action (effets analgésiques)

	DÉBUT D'ACTION	PIC	DURÉE
PO	inconnu	2-3 h	4-6 h ou plus
IM	10 min	1-2 h	6 h ou plus

CONTRE-INDICATIONS, PRÉCAUTIONS ET MISES EN GARDE

Contre-indications: Hypersensibilité ■ Risque de réactions de sensibilité croisée avec d'autres AINS ■ Syndrome complet ou partiel de polypes nasaux, ou patients chez lesquels l'asthme, l'anaphylaxie, l'urticaire, la rhinite ou toute autre manifestation allergique a été déclenchée par l'aspirine ou d'autres AINS ■ Ulcère gastroduodénal évolutif, antécédents d'ulcère récurrent ou maladie inflammatoire active des voies digestives ■ Atteinte hépatique importante ou évolutive ■ Dysfonctionnement rénal grave ou évolutif ■ Traitement concomitant avec d'autres AINS ■ Usage préopératoire ou périopératoire ■ Usage postopératoire en présence de troubles de la coagulation ■ **OBST.**: Travail de l'accouchement ■ Administration épidurale et intrathécale de la solution IM ■ Usage concomitant de probénécide et d'oxpentifylline.

Précautions et mises en garde: Antécédents d'hémorragie digestive ■ Insuffisance rénale (réduire la dose, au besoin) ■ Maladie cardiovasculaire ou facteurs de risque de maladie cardiovasculaire (risque accru de complications thrombotiques, d'infarctus du myocarde, d'AVC, surtout lors d'un usage prolongé) ■ Intolérance connue à l'alcool (injection seulement) ■ **OBST., ALLAITEMENT, PÉD.**: Usage déconseillé au cours de la deuxième moitié de la grossesse. L'innocuité n'a pas été établie chez les enfants < 16 ans. ■ **GÉR.**: Les personnes âgées sont davantage prédisposées à des saignements gastro-intestinaux.

RÉACTIONS INDÉSIRABLES ET EFFETS SECONDAIRES

SNC: somnolence, altération des opérations de la pensée, étourdissements, euphorie, céphalées.

Resp.: asthme, dyspnée.

CV: œdème, pâleur, vasodilatation.

GI: HÉMORRAGIE DIGESTIVE, altération du goût, diarrhée, sécheresse de la bouche (xérostomie), dyspepsie, douleurs gastro-intestinales, nausées.

GU: oligurie, néphrotoxicité, mictions fréquentes.

Tég: prurit, purpura, transpiration, urticaire, DERMATITE EXFOLIATIVE, SYNDROME DE STEVENS-JOHNSON, ÉPIDERMOLYSE NÉCROSANTE SUBAIGUË.

Hémat.: allongement du temps de saignement.

Locaux: douleur au point d'injection.

SN: paresthésie.

Divers: réactions allergiques incluant l'ANAPHYLAXIE.

INTERACTIONS

Médicament-médicament: Le kétorolac peut diminuer l'efficacité de l'**aspirine** administrée en prévention cardiovasculaire ■ L'**aspirine**, prise en concomitance, peut réduire l'efficacité du kétorolac ■ L'administration concomitante d'**aspirine**, d'autres **AINS**, de **suppléments de potassium** et de **glucocorticoïdes** ou l'ingestion d'**alcool** intensifient les effets secondaires gastro-intestinaux ■ L'administration prolongée de kétorolac en même temps que la prise d'**acétaminophène** peut augmenter le risque de réactions rénales indésirables ■ Le kétorolac peut réduire l'efficacité des **diurétiques** ou des **antihypertenseurs** ■ Le kétorolac peut élever les concentrations sériques de **lithium** et le risque de toxicité associé ■ Le kétorolac augmente le risque de toxicité associé au **méthotrexate** ■ Risque accru d'hémorragie lors de l'administration concomitante de **céfamandole**, de **céfotétane**, de **céfopérazone**, d'**acide valproïque**, de **clopidogrel**, de **ticlodipine**, de **tirofiban**, d'**eptifibatide**, de **plicamycine**, d'**agents thrombolytiques** ou d'**anticoagulants** ■ Risque accru de réactions hématologiques indésirables lors de l'administration concomitante d'**agents antinéoplasiques** ou d'une **radiothérapie** ■ Risque accru de toxicité rénale lors de l'administration concomitante de **cyclosporine** ■ Le **probénécide** élève les concentrations sanguines de kétorolac et le risque d'effets indésirables (administration concomitante déconseillée).

Médicament-produits naturels: Risque accru de saignements en cas de consommation concomitante d'**ail**, d'**anis**, d'**arnica**, de **camomille**, de **dong quai**, de **girofle**, de **gingembre**, de **ginkgo** et de **ginseng**.

VOIES D'ADMINISTRATION ET POSOLOGIE

La durée totale du traitement combiné par voies IM et orale ne doit pas dépasser 5 jours.

- **PO (adultes)**: 10 mg, toutes les 4 à 6 heures, selon les besoins (ne pas dépasser 40 mg/jour). La durée maximale du traitement est de 5 jours, en cas de douleurs postopératoires, et de 7 jours, en cas de douleurs musculosquelettiques.

- **IM (adultes < 65 ans)**: De 10 à 30 mg, toutes les 4 à 6 heures, selon les besoins (ne pas dépasser 120 mg/jour) ; ne pas administrer le médicament pendant plus de 2 jours.
- **IM (adultes > 65 ans, < 50 kg ou insuffisants rénaux)**: 10 mg, toutes les 4 à 6 heures, selon les besoins (ne pas dépasser 60 mg/jour) ; ne pas administrer le traitement pendant plus de 2 jours.

PRÉSENTATION

Comprimés: 10 mg^Pr ■ **Solution pour injection IM**: 10 mg/mL^Pr et 30 mg/mL^Pr, en fioles de 1 mL.

SOINS INFIRMIERS

ÉVALUATION DE LA SITUATION

- LES PATIENTS SOUFFRANT D'ASTHME, D'ALLERGIE INDUITE PAR L'ASPIRINE OU DE POLYPES NASAUX SONT DAVANTAGE PRÉDISPOSÉS AUX RÉACTIONS D'HYPERSENSIBILITÉ. SUIVRE DE PRÈS LA RHINITE, L'ASTHME ET L'URTICAIRE.

Douleur: Évaluer la douleur (type, siège et intensité) avant l'administration du kétorolac, et de 1 à 2 heures après.

Tests de laboratoire:

- Chez les patients recevant un traitement prolongé, effectuer à intervalles réguliers des tests de la fonction hépatique, particulièrement pour déterminer les valeurs d'ALT et d'AST. Il y a risque d'élévation de ces concentrations.
- Risque de prolongation du temps de saignement pouvant persister jusqu'à 24 à 48 heures après l'arrêt du traitement.
- Risque d'élévation des concentrations d'urée, de créatinine sérique et de potassium.

DIAGNOSTICS INFIRMIERS POSSIBLES

- Douleur aiguë (Indications).
- Connaissances insuffisantes sur le traitement médicamenteux (Enseignement au patient et à ses proches).

INTERVENTIONS INFIRMIÈRES

- L'administration de doses plus élevées que celles qui sont recommandées n'améliore pas l'efficacité du médicament, mais pourrait augmenter le risque d'effets secondaires. LA DURÉE DU TRAITEMENT PAR LE KÉTOROLAC, TOUTES VOIES D'ADMINISTRATION CONFONDUES, NE DOIT PAS DÉPASSER DE 5 À 7 JOURS.
- L'administration concomitante d'analgésiques opioïdes peut intensifier les effets analgésiques, ce qui permet de diminuer les doses d'opioïdes.

ENSEIGNEMENT AU PATIENT ET À SES PROCHES

- Expliquer au patient comment et à quel moment il est approprié de demander un analgésique.
- Conseiller au patient de respecter rigoureusement la posologie recommandée. S'il n'a pu prendre le médicament au moment habituel, il doit le faire dès que possible à moins que ce ne soit presque l'heure prévue pour la dose suivante. Le prévenir qu'il ne doit jamais remplacer une dose manquée par une double dose.
- Prévenir le patient que le kétorolac peut parfois provoquer de la somnolence ou des étourdissements. Lui conseiller de ne pas conduire et d'éviter les activités qui exigent sa vigilance jusqu'à ce qu'on ait la certitude que le médicament n'entraîne pas ces effets chez lui.
- Recommander au patient d'éviter de boire de l'alcool et de consulter un professionnel de la santé avant de prendre une préparation à base d'aspirine ou d'acétaminophène, un AINS ou un autre médicament en vente libre en même temps que le kétorolac.
- Recommander au patient qui doit suivre un autre traitement ou subir une intervention chirurgicale d'avertir le professionnel de la santé qu'il suit un traitement par ce médicament.
- Recommander au patient de communiquer avec un professionnel de la santé en cas de rash, de démangeaisons, de troubles visuels, d'acouphènes, de gain de poids, d'œdème, de selles noires, de céphalées persistantes ou de symptômes pseudogrippaux (frissons, fièvre, douleurs musculaires, douleurs).

VÉRIFICATION DE L'EFFICACITÉ THÉRAPEUTIQUE

L'efficacité du traitement peut être démontrée par: la diminution de l'intensité de la douleur. Les patients qui ne répondent pas à un AINS peuvent répondre à un autre.

K

ALERTE CLINIQUE

LABÉTALOL

Apo-Labétalol, Labétalol, Trandate

CLASSIFICATION:

Antihypertenseur (bêtabloquant)

Grossesse – catégorie C

INDICATIONS

Traitement de l'hypertension en monothérapie ou en association ▪ Traitement d'urgence de l'hypertension grave (voie intraveineuse).

MÉCANISME D'ACTION

Blocage de la stimulation des récepteurs bêta$_1$-adrénergiques (myocardiques) et bêta$_2$-adrénergiques (pulmonaires, vasculaires ou utérins) ▪ Inhibition de l'effet du blocage alpha-adrénergique qui peut aggraver l'hypotension orthostatique. ***Effets thérapeutiques:*** Abaissement de la pression artérielle.

L

PHARMACOCINÉTIQUE

Absorption: Bonne (PO), mais métabolisme hépatique de premier passage important, se traduisant par une biodisponibilité à 25 %.

Distribution: Une petite fraction de médicament pénètre dans le SNC. Le labétalol traverse la barrière placentaire et passe dans le lait maternel.

Métabolisme et excrétion: Métabolisme hépatique important. Excrétion rénale à 50 % et fécale à 50 % (sous forme de métabolites).

Demi-vie: De 3 à 8 heures.

Profil temps-action (effets cardiovasculaires)

	DÉBUT D'ACTION	PIC	DURÉE
PO	1 - 2 h	2 - 4 h	8 - 12 h
IV	1 - 5 min	5 min	16 - 18 h

CONTRE-INDICATIONS, PRÉCAUTIONS ET MISES EN GARDE

Contre-indications: Hypersensibilité ▪ Insuffisance cardiaque non compensée ▪ Œdème pulmonaire ▪ Choc cardiogénique ou autres états d'hypotension ▪ Bradycardie sinusale ou bloc cardiaque de 2e ou de 3e degré ▪ Maladie pulmonaire (y compris l'asthme) ▪ Allaitement.

Précautions et mises en garde: Insuffisance rénale ▪ Insuffisance hépatique ▪ **GÉR.**: Il est recommandé de réduire la dose initiale chez les personnes âgées ou débilitées, puisqu'elles sont plus sensibles aux bêtabloquants ▪ Diabète (le médicament peut masquer les symptômes d'hypoglycémie) ▪ Thyrotoxicose (le médicament peut en masquer les symptômes) ▪ Antécédents de réactions allergiques graves (les réactions peuvent être plus intenses) ▪ **OBST., PÉD.**: L'innocuité du médicament n'a pas été établie chez les femmes enceintes et les enfants; risque de bradycardie, d'hypotension, d'hypoglycémie ou de dépression respiratoire chez le fœtus ou le nouveau-né.

RÉACTIONS INDÉSIRABLES ET EFFETS SECONDAIRES

SNC: fatigue, faiblesse, anxiété, dépression, étourdissements, somnolence, insomnie, perte de mémoire, modification des opérations de la pensée, nervosité, cauchemars.

ORLO: vision trouble, xérophtalmie, enchifrènement.

Resp.: bronchospasme, respiration sifflante.

CV: ARYTHMIE, BRADYCARDIE, INSUFFISANCE CARDIAQUE, ŒDÈME PULMONAIRE, hypotension orthostatique, vasoconstriction périphérique.

GI: constipation, diarrhée, nausées.

GU: impuissance, baisse de la libido.

Tég.: démangeaisons, rash.

End.: hyperglycémie, hypoglycémie.

Loc.: arthralgie, douleurs lombaires, crampes musculaires.

SN: paresthésie.

Divers: lupus érythémateux induit par le médicament.

INTERACTIONS

Médicament-médicament: Les **anesthésiques généraux par voie IV**, le **diltiazem** et le **vérapamil** peuvent exercer des effets additifs sur la dépression du myocarde ▪ Risque accru de bradycardie lors de l'administration concomitante de **dérivés digitaliques** ▪ Risque d'effets hypotenseurs additifs lors de la prise concomitante d'**antihypertenseurs** ou de **dérivés nitrés** ainsi que de l'ingestion rapide de grandes quantités d'**alcool** ▪ Le labétalol peut réduire l'efficacité de la **théophylline** et des **bronchodilatateurs bêta-adrénergiques** ▪ Le médicament peut diminuer les effets cardiovasculaires bénéfiques sur les récepteurs bêta$_1$ de la **dopamine** et de la **dobutamine** ▪ Il faut administrer le médicament avec prudence dans les 14 jours qui suivent un traitement par un **IMAO** (risque d'hypertension) ▪ Les effets du labétalol peuvent être intensifiés par le **propanolol** ou la **cimétidine** ▪ Les **AINS** peuvent réduire l'effet antihypertenseur du labétalol.

VOIES D'ADMINISTRATION ET POSOLOGIE

- **PO (adultes)**: Initialement, 100 mg, 2 fois par jour, en monothérapie ou avec un diurétique; majorer la dose, selon la réponse au traitement ou la tolérance

du patient, toutes les semaines ou 2 fois par semaine (écart posologique habituel: de 400 à 800 mg par jour, en 2 doses fractionnées; des doses allant jusqu'à 1,2 g par jour ont déjà été administrées).
- **IV (adultes)**: Initialement, 20 mg (0,25 mg/kg); on peut administrer des doses additionnelles allant de 20 à 80 mg, toutes les 10 minutes, selon la réponse au traitement ou la tolérance du patient (ne pas dépasser 300 mg au total), ou perfusion IV de 0,5 à 2 mg/min, à adapter selon la réponse au traitement et la tolérance du patient (écart posologique habituel: de 50 à 200 mg au total).

PRÉSENTATION

Comprimés: 100 mg[Pr], 200 mg[Pr] ▪ **Solution pour injection**: 5 mg/mL[Pr].

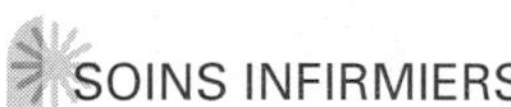

SOINS INFIRMIERS

ÉVALUATION DE LA SITUATION

- Mesurer la pression artérielle et le pouls à intervalles fréquents pendant toute la période d'adaptation posologique, et à intervalles réguliers pendant toute la durée du traitement. Rester à l'affût de la survenue d'un épisode d'hypotension orthostatique pendant qu'on aide le patient à se lever.
- Vérifier la fréquence des renouvellements des ordonnances pour évaluer l'observance du traitement.
- Les patients recevant le *labétalol par voie IV* doivent rester en position couchée pendant l'administration du médicament et pendant les 3 heures qui suivent. Mesurer les signes vitaux toutes les 5 à 15 minutes pendant l'administration du médicament et pendant plusieurs heures par la suite.
- EFFECTUER LE BILAN QUOTIDIEN DES INGESTA ET DES EXCRETA; PESER LE PATIENT TOUS LES JOURS. RESTER À L'AFFÛT DES SIGNES ET DES SYMPTÔMES SUIVANTS DE SURCHARGE HYDRIQUE: ŒDÈME PÉRIPHÉRIQUE, DYSPNÉE, RÂLES OU CRÉPITATIONS, FATIGUE, GAIN PONDÉRAL, TURGESCENCE DES JUGULAIRES.

Tests de laboratoire:
- Le labétalol peut élever les concentrations d'urée, de lipoprotéines sériques, de potassium, de triglycérides et d'acide urique.
- Le labétalol peut accroître les titres des anticorps antinucléaires.
- Le labétalol peut élever la glycémie.
- Le labétalol peut élever les concentrations sériques de phosphatase alcaline, de LDH, d'AST et d'ALT. Arrêter le traitement en présence de jaunisse ou de résultats de laboratoire indiquant un dysfonctionnement hépatique.

TOXICITÉ ET SURDOSAGE:
- Suivre de près les patients recevant des bêtabloquants afin de déceler les signes suivants de surdosage: bradycardie, étourdissements graves ou évanouissements, somnolence prononcée, dyspnée, bleuissement des ongles ou des paumes des mains, convulsions. En informer immédiatement le médecin ou un autre professionnel de la santé.
- On a utilisé du glucagon pour traiter la bradycardie et l'hypotension.

DIAGNOSTICS INFIRMIERS POSSIBLES

- Débit cardiaque diminué (Indications).
- Connaissances insuffisantes sur le traitement médicamenteux (Enseignement au patient et à ses proches).
- Non-observance du traitement médicamenteux (Enseignement au patient et à ses proches).

L

INTERVENTIONS INFIRMIÈRES

ALERTE CLINIQUE: LES MÉDICAMENTS VASOACTIFS ADMINISTRÉS PAR VOIE IV COMPORTENT UN DANGER PAR EUX-MÊMES. AVANT L'ADMINISTRATION, FAIRE VÉRIFIER L'ORDONNANCE D'ORIGINE, LE CALCUL DE LA DOSE ET LE RÉGLAGE DES POMPES À PERFUSION PAR UN DEUXIÈME PROFESSIONNEL DE LA SANTÉ.
- L'arrêt d'un traitement concomitant par la clonidine doit se faire graduellement, en arrêtant d'abord le traitement par le bêtabloquant. On peut ensuite, quelques jours plus tard, cesser le traitement par la clonidine.

PO:
- Mesurer le pouls à l'apex du cœur avant d'administrer le médicament. S'il est inférieur à 50 battements par minute ou si des arythmies surviennent, ne pas administrer le médicament et en informer le médecin ou un autre professionnel de la santé.
- Administrer le labétalol au moment des repas ou tout de suite après pour en favoriser l'absorption.

IV directe: Administrer le médicament sans le diluer.

Vitesse d'administration: Administrer lentement en 2 minutes.

Perfusion continue: Ajouter 200 mg à 160 mL de diluant (1 mg/1 mL de solution) ou 200 mg à 250 mL de diluant (2 mg/3 mL de solution). Les diluants compatibles sont les suivants: D5%E, NaCl 0,9 %, D5%/NaCl 0,25 %, D5%/NaCl 0,9 %, D5%/solution de Ringer, D5%/solution de lactate de Ringer, solution de Ringer et solution de lactate de Ringer. Consulter les directives du fabricant avant de reconstituer la préparation.

Vitesse d'administration: Administrer à un débit de 0,5 à 2 mg/min et adapter la dose pour obtenir la réponse voulue. Administrer à l'aide d'une pompe à perfusion afin de s'assurer que le patient reçoit la dose exacte.
Compatibilité (tubulure en Y): amikacine ■ aminophylline ■ amiodarone ■ ampicilline ■ butorphanol ■ calcium, gluconate de ■ céfazoline ■ ceftazidime ■ ceftizoxime ■ chloramphénicol ■ cimétidine ■ clindamycine ■ énalaprilate ■ érythromycine, lactobionate d' ■ esmolol ■ famotidine ■ fentanyl ■ gentamicine ■ lidocaïne ■ magnésium, sulfate de ■ mépéridine ■ métronidazole ■ midazolam ■ morphine ■ nitroglycérine ■ nitroprusside ■ oxacilline ■ pénicilline G potassique ■ pipéracilline ■ potassium, chlorure de ■ potassium, phosphate de ■ ranitidine ■ sodium, acétate de ■ tobramycine ■ triméthroprime/sulfaméthoxazole ■ vancomycine.
Incompatibilité (tubulure en Y): amphotéricine B, cholestéryle d' ■ céfopérazone ■ nafcilline ■ warfarine.
Incompatibilité en addition au soluté: bicarbonate de sodium.

L

ENSEIGNEMENT AU PATIENT ET À SES PROCHES

- Prévenir le patient qu'il doit prendre le labétalol au même moment de la journée en suivant rigoureusement la posologie recommandée et qu'il ne doit pas arrêter le traitement même s'il se sent bien. L'avertir qu'il ne doit jamais sauter de dose ni remplacer une dose manquée par une double dose. S'il n'a pu prendre le médicament au moment habituel, il doit le prendre aussitôt que possible, mais au moins 8 heures avant l'heure prévue pour la dose suivante. UN SEVRAGE BRUSQUE PEUT PROVOQUER DES ARYTHMIES MORTELLES, L'HYPERTENSION OU L'ISCHÉMIE DU MYOCARDE.
- Conseiller au patient d'avoir une réserve suffisante de médicament pour les fins de semaine, les congés et les vacances. Lui conseiller également de conserver une ordonnance dans son portefeuille pour parer à toute urgence.
- Montrer au patient et à ses proches comment prendre le pouls et la pression artérielle. Leur demander de mesurer le pouls tous les jours et la pression artérielle 2 fois par semaine. Recommander au patient de ne pas prendre la dose et de communiquer avec un professionnel de la santé si le pouls est de moins de 50 battements/minute ou si la pression artérielle change notablement.
- Prévenir le patient que le labétalol peut parfois provoquer des étourdissements. Lui conseiller de ne pas conduire et d'éviter les activités qui exigent sa vigilance jusqu'à ce qu'on ait la certitude que le médicament n'entraîne pas cet effet chez lui. Conseiller au patient recevant le labétalol par voie IV de demander de l'aide s'il désire se lever ou se déplacer.
- Conseiller au patient de changer lentement de position pour réduire le risque d'hypotension orthostatique, particulièrement pendant la phase initiale du traitement ou lors des majorations de la dose. Expliquer au patient qui prend du labétalol par voie orale qu'il doit être extrêmement vigilant s'il consomme de l'alcool, s'il doit rester debout pendant de longues périodes de temps, s'il fait des efforts ou s'il est exposé à des températures élevées, car le risque d'hypotension orthostatique est dans ces cas plus grand.
- Prévenir le patient que le médicament peut le rendre plus sensible au froid.
- Conseiller le patient de consulter un professionnel de la santé avant de prendre des médicaments en vente libre, particulièrement des préparations contre le rhume, ou des produits naturels en même temps que le labétalol.
- Recommander au patient diabétique de mesurer sa glycémie, particulièrement lorsqu'il se sent faible, irritable ou fatigué, ou lorsqu'il ressent un malaise. Le labétalol peut masquer la tachycardie et les tremblements, en tant que signes d'hypoglycémie, bien que des étourdissements et la transpiration puissent toujours se manifester.
- RECOMMANDER AU PATIENT DE SIGNALER À UN PROFESSIONNEL DE LA SANTÉ LES SYMPTÔMES SUIVANTS: RALENTISSEMENT DU POULS, DIFFICULTÉS RESPIRATOIRES, RESPIRATION SIFFLANTE, MAINS ET PIEDS FROIDS, ÉTOURDISSEMENTS, SENSATION DE TÊTE LÉGÈRE, CONFUSION, DÉPRESSION, RASH, FIÈVRE, MAUX DE GORGE, SAIGNEMENTS INHABITUELS OU FORMATION D'ECCHYMOSES.
- Recommander au patient qui doit suivre un autre traitement ou subir une intervention chirurgicale d'avertir le professionnel de la santé qu'il prend du labétalol.
- Conseiller au patient de porter sur lui en tout temps un bracelet d'identité où sont inscrits son problème de santé et son traitement médicamenteux.

Hypertension: Inciter le patient à appliquer d'autres mesures de réduction de l'hypertension: perdre du poids, réduire sa consommation de sel, diminuer le stress, faire régulièrement de l'exercice, boire de l'alcool avec modération et cesser de fumer. Le prévenir que le labétalol stabilise la pression artérielle, mais ne guérit pas l'hypertension.

VÉRIFICATION DE L'EFFICACITÉ THÉRAPEUTIQUE

L'efficacité du traitement peut être démontrée par: la baisse de la pression artérielle.

LACTULOSE

Apo-Lactulose, Euro-Lac, Gen-Lac, PMS-Lactulose, Ratio-Lactulose

CLASSIFICATION:

Laxatif (osmotique), traitement de l'encéphalopathie portocave, acidifiant du côlon

Grossesse – catégorie B

INDICATIONS

Traitement de la constipation chronique chez les adultes et les personnes âgées ■ Prévention et traitement de l'encéphalopathie hépatique portocave.

MÉCANISME D'ACTION

Augmentation du contenu hydrique des selles et leur ramollissement ■ Abaissement du pH à l'intérieur du côlon, entraînant la transformation de l'ammoniaque en ammonium qui est moins absorbé et, par le fait même, la diminution des concentrations sanguines d'ammoniaque. ***Effets thérapeutiques:*** Soulagement de la constipation ■ Diminution des concentrations sanguines d'ammoniaque, accompagnée d'une amélioration de l'état mental des patients atteints d'encéphalopathie hépatique.

PHARMACOCINÉTIQUE

Absorption: Minime (PO).
Distribution: Inconnue.
Métabolisme et excrétion: Le lactulose absorbé est excrété sous forme inchangée dans l'urine. Le lactulose qui n'est pas absorbé est métabolisé par les bactéries du côlon et transformé en acides lactique, acétique et formique.
Demi-vie: Inconnue.

Profil temps-action (soulagement de la constipation)

	Début d'action	Pic	Durée
PO	24 – 48 h	inconnu	inconnue

CONTRE-INDICATIONS, PRÉCAUTIONS ET MISES EN GARDE

Contre-indications: Patients suivant un régime pauvre en galactose.

Précautions et mises en garde: Douleurs abdominales, nausées, fièvre ou vomissements ■ Diabète ■ Usage excessif ou prolongé (risque de dépendance) ■ **OBST., ALLAITEMENT, PÉD.:** L'innocuité du médicament n'a pas été établie chez les femmes enceintes ou qui allaitent, ni chez les enfants ≤ 16 ans.

RÉACTIONS INDÉSIRABLES ET EFFETS SECONDAIRES

GI: éructations, crampes, ballonnement, flatulence, diarrhée.
End.: hyperglycémie (patients diabétiques).

INTERACTIONS

Médicament-médicament: Il ne faut pas administrer le lactulose en concomitance avec d'autres **laxatifs** lors du traitement de l'encéphalopathie hépatique (en raison de l'incapacité d'établir la dose optimale de lactulose) ■ Les **antibiotiques** peuvent réduire l'efficacité du traitement de l'encéphalopathie hépatique.

VOIES D'ADMINISTRATION ET POSOLOGIE

Constipation

- **PO (adultes):** De 15 à 30 mL par jour et jusqu'à 60 mL par jour, en 1 ou 2 doses fractionnées.
- **PO (enfants):** De 1 à 3 mL/kg par jour, en doses fractionnées (ne pas dépasser la dose maximale recommandée chez l'adulte) (usage non approuvé).

Encéphalopathie hépatique portocave

- **PO (adultes):** 30 mL, de 2 à 4 fois par jour; adapter la dose en vue de l'émission de 2 ou de 3 selles par jour.
- **PO (nourrissons):** De 2,5 à 10 mL par jour, en doses fractionnées (usage non approuvé).
- **PO (enfants et adolescents):** De 40 à 90 mL par jour, en doses fractionnées; adapter la dose en vue de l'émission de 2 ou de 3 selles par jour (usage non approuvé).
- **IR (adultes):** 300 mL (200 g), dilués et administrés sous forme de lavement à garder pendant 30 à 60 minutes, toutes les 4 à 6 heures.

PRÉSENTATION (version générique disponible)

Sirop: 667 mg de lactulose/mL[VL].

SOINS INFIRMIERS

ÉVALUATION DE LA SITUATION

- Suivre de près la distension abdominale, ausculter les bruits intestinaux, noter les habitudes normales d'élimination intestinale.

- Noter la couleur, la consistance et la quantité des selles évacuées.

Encéphalopathie hépatique portocave: Évaluer l'état mental du patient (orientation, degré de conscience) avant le début du traitement et à intervalles réguliers pendant toute sa durée.

Tests de laboratoire:

- Le lactulose abaisse les concentrations sanguines d'ammoniaque de 25 à 50 %.
- Le médicament peut élever la glycémie chez les patients diabétiques.
- Lors de l'usage prolongé, noter à intervalles réguliers les concentrations sériques d'électrolytes. Le médicament peut induire la diarrhée, d'où risque d'hypokaliémie et d'hypernatrémie.

DIAGNOSTICS INFIRMIERS POSSIBLES

- Constipation (Indications).
- Connaissances insuffisantes sur le traitement médicamenteux (Enseignement au patient et à ses proches).

L

INTERVENTIONS INFIRMIÈRES

- Lors du traitement de l'encéphalopathie hépatique, il faut adapter la dose jusqu'à ce que le patient produise 2 ou 3 selles molles par jour. Au cours du traitement initial, on peut administrer de 30 à 45 mL, toutes les heures, pour induire rapidement la défécation.
- La coloration foncée de la solution n'est pas un signe d'altération de sa puissance.

PO: Mélanger le lactulose avec du jus de fruits, de l'eau, du lait ou des boissons gazéifiées aux agrumes pour en améliorer le goût. Administrer avec un grand verre (240 mL) d'eau ou de jus. Pour un effet plus rapide, administrer à jeun.

Voie rectale: Administrer le lavement à l'aide d'une sonde rectale à ballonnet. Mélanger 300 mL de lactulose à 700 mL d'eau ou de solution de NaCl 0,9%. Demander au patient de retenir le lavement pendant 30 à 60 minutes. Si l'évacuation se produit avant ce laps de temps, on peut répéter l'administration.

ENSEIGNEMENT AU PATIENT ET À SES PROCHES

- Encourager le patient à recourir à d'autres moyens de régulation de la fonction intestinale, par exemple consommer plus de fibres alimentaires et de liquides, et faire plus d'exercice. Lui expliquer que la fréquence de l'élimination intestinale varie d'une personne à l'autre et qu'il est tout aussi normal d'avoir 3 selles par jour que 3 selles par semaine.
- Prévenir le patient que ce médicament peut entraîner des éructations, de la flatulence ou des crampes abdominales. Lui recommander de prévenir un professionnel de la santé si ces effets deviennent gênants ou si la diarrhée survient.

VÉRIFICATION DE L'EFFICACITÉ THÉRAPEUTIQUE

L'efficacité du traitement peut être démontrée par: l'émission de selles molles et bien moulées, en général, dans les 24 à 48 heures ▪ la disparition de la confusion, de l'apathie et de l'irritation, et l'amélioration de l'état mental chez les patients atteints d'encéphalopathie hépatique portocave. On peut noter une amélioration dans les 2 heures suivant le lavement ou dans les 24 à 48 heures suivant l'administration par voie orale. ✳

LAMIVUDINE

3TC, Heptovir

CLASSIFICATION:

Antirétroviral (inhibiteur nucléosidique de la transcriptase inverse)

Grossesse – catégorie C

INDICATIONS

Traitement des infections par le VIH en association avec d'autres agents antirétroviraux ▪ Traitement des patients atteints d'hépatite B chronique et qui présentent des signes de réplication du virus de l'hépatite B (VHB). **Usages non approuvés:** En association avec d'autres antirétroviraux, prophylaxie après exposition accidentelle au VIH.

MÉCANISME D'ACTION

Après sa transformation intracellulaire en sa forme active (lamivudine-5-triphosphate), la lamivudine inhibe la synthèse de l'ADN viral en bloquant la transcriptase inverse. ***Effets thérapeutiques:*** Ralentissement de l'évolution de l'infection par le VIH et diminution de l'incidence de ses complications ▪ Augmentation du nombre de cellules CD4 et diminution de la charge virale ▪ Prévention des lésions hépatiques dues aux infections chroniques de l'hépatite B; diminution de la charge virale.

PHARMACOCINÉTIQUE

Absorption: Bonne (PO – 86 % chez les adultes, 66 % chez les nourrissons et les enfants).

Distribution: Espace extravasculaire. Une certaine fraction pénètre dans le liquide céphalorachidien; le reste de la distribution demeure inconnu.
Métabolisme et excrétion: Excrétion majoritairement urinaire sous forme inchangée; moins de 5 %, métabolisé par le foie.
Demi-vie: *Adultes* – 3,7 heures. *Enfants* – 2 heures.

Profil temps-action

	DÉBUT D'ACTION	PIC	DURÉE
PO	inconnu	1 h†	12 h

† À jeun; 3,2 h si la lamivudine est prise avec des aliments. Les aliments ne modifient pas la quantité totale de médicament absorbée.

CONTRE-INDICATIONS, PRÉCAUTIONS ET MISES EN GARDE

Contre-indications: Hypersensibilité.
Précautions et mises en garde: Hypertension ■ Insuffisance rénale (allonger l'intervalle entre les doses/réduire la dose si la Cl_{Cr} < 50 mL/min) ■ Hémophilie (risque accru d'hémorragie) ■ Diabète (risque d'aggravation de l'hyperglycémie) ■ Femmes, exposition prolongée, obésité, antécédents de maladie hépatique (risque accru d'acidose lactique et d'hépatomégalie grave accompagnée de stéatose) ■ Infection concomitante par le virus de l'hépatite B (risque de récurrence de l'hépatite après arrêt du traitement par la lamivudine) ■ Personnes âgées (une réduction de la dose peut être nécessaire) ■ **OBST., PÉD.**: Grossesse et enfants < 3 mois (l'innocuité de la lamivudine n'a pas été établie) ■ **ALLAITEMENT**: Déconseillé chez les patientes infectées par le VIH.
EXTRÊME PRUDENCE: PÉD.: Enfants ayant des antécédents de pancréatite (n'utiliser ce médicament que s'il n'y a pas d'autre solution).

RÉACTIONS INDÉSIRABLES ET EFFETS SECONDAIRES

Réactions signalées lors de l'administration simultanée de zidovudine.
SNC: CONVULSIONS, fatigue, céphalées, insomnie, malaise, dépression, étourdissements.
Resp.: toux.
GI: HÉPATOMÉGALIE AVEC STÉATOSE, PANCRÉATITE (risque accru chez les enfants), anorexie, diarrhée, nausées, vomissements, gêne abdominale, résultats anormaux aux tests de la fonction hépatique, dyspepsie.
Tég.: alopécie, érythème polymorphe, rash, urticaire.
End.: hyperglycémie.
HÉ: acidose lactique.
Hémat.: anémie, neutropénie.
Loc.: douleurs musculosquelettiques, arthralgie, faiblesse musculaire, myalgie, rhabdomyolyse.
SN: neuropathie.
Divers: réactions d'hypersensibilité, incluant l'ANAPHYLAXIE et le SYNDROME DE STEVENS-JOHNSON, modification de la distribution du tissu adipeux, syndrome de reconstitution immunitaire.

INTERACTIONS

Médicament-médicament: Le **triméthoprime/sulfaméthoxazole** augmente les concentrations sanguines de lamivudine (une adaptation de la posologie peut s'avérer nécessaire en cas d'insuffisance rénale) ■ Risque accru de pancréatite, si la lamivudine est administrée en même temps que des **agents qui induisent une pancréatite** ■ La lamivudine peut augmenter le risque de neuropathie périphérique lors de l'administration concomitante d'autres **médicaments qui induisent une neuropathie** ■ Profil de résistance du VIH similaire à celui à l'**emtricitabine** (éviter l'usage concomitant).

VOIES D'ADMINISTRATION ET POSOLOGIE

Infection par le VIH

- **PO (adultes et enfants > 12 ans et > 50 kg)**: 150 mg, 2 fois par jour, ou 300 mg, 1 fois par jour, en association avec d'autres agents antirétroviraux.
- **PO (adultes < 50 kg)**: 2 mg/kg, 2 fois par jour.
- **PO (enfants de 3 mois à 12 ans)**: 4 mg/kg, 2 fois par jour (jusqu'à 150 mg, 2 fois par jour), en association avec d'autres agents antirétroviraux.
- ***INSUFFISANCE RÉNALE***
  PO (ADULTES ET ENFANTS > 12 ANS): *Cl_{CR} DE 30 À 50 mL/MIN* – 150 mg, 1 FOIS PAR JOUR. *Cl_{CR} DE 15 À 29 mL/MIN* – PREMIÈRE DOSE DE 150 mg, PUIS 100 mg, 1 FOIS PAR JOUR. *Cl_{CR} DE 5 À 14 mL/MIN* – PREMIÈRE DOSE DE 150 mg, PUIS 50 mg, 1 FOIS PAR JOUR. *Cl_{CR} < 5 mL/MIN* – PREMIÈRE DOSE DE 50 mg, PUIS 25 mg, 1 FOIS PAR JOUR.

Hépatite B chronique

- **PO (adultes)**: 100 mg, 1 fois par jour.
- ***INSUFFISANCE RÉNALE***
  PO (ADULTES): *Cl_{CR} DE 30 À 49 mL/MIN* – PREMIÈRE DOSE DE 100 mg, PUIS 50 mg, 1 FOIS PAR JOUR. *Cl_{CR} DE 15 À 29 mL/MIN* – PREMIÈRE DOSE DE 100 mg, PUIS 25 mg, 1 FOIS PAR JOUR. *Cl_{CR} DE 5 À 14 mL/MIN* – PREMIÈRE DOSE DE 35 mg, PUIS 15 mg, 1 FOIS PAR JOUR. *Cl_{CR} < 5 mL/MIN* – PREMIÈRE DOSE DE 35 mg, PUIS 10 mg, 1 FOIS PAR JOUR.

PRÉSENTATION

Comprimés: 100 mg[Pr], 150 mg[Pr], 300 mg[Pr] ■ **Solution orale (parfum de fraise et banane)**: 5 mg/mL[Pr], 10 mg/mL[Pr] ■ **En association avec**: abacavir (Kivexa[Pr]), zidovudine (Combivir[Pr]), abacavir et zidovudine (Trizivir[Pr]). Voir l'annexe U.

L

SOINS INFIRMIERS

ÉVALUATION DE LA SITUATION

VIH:

- Examiner le patient, avant le traitement et pendant toute sa durée, pour déceler toute aggravation des symptômes de l'infection par le VIH ou l'apparition de symptômes d'infections opportunistes.
- Rester à l'affût des signes et des symptômes suivants de neuropathie périphérique: engourdissements, sensation de brûlure, fourmillements ou douleurs au niveau des pieds ou des mains. Il peut s'avérer difficile de distinguer cette neuropathie de celle accompagnant une infection grave par le VIH. Elle peut dicter l'arrêt du traitement.
- À INTERVALLES RÉGULIERS, TOUT AU LONG DU TRAITEMENT, OBSERVER LE PATIENT, PARTICULIÈREMENT S'IL S'AGIT D'UN ENFANT, À LA RECHERCHE DES SIGNES SUIVANTS DE PANCRÉATITE: NAUSÉES, VOMISSEMENTS ET DOULEURS ABDOMINALES. IL PEUT S'AVÉRER NÉCESSAIRE D'ARRÊTER LE TRAITEMENT.
- Si une patiente enceinte est exposée à des antirétroviraux, l'inscrire dans le registre des femmes exposées aux antirétroviraux pendant leur grossesse, en composant le 1 800 258 4263.

Hépatite B chronique: Pendant toute la durée du traitement, rester à l'affût des signes suivants d'hépatite: jaunisse, fatigue, anorexie et prurit.

Tests de laboratoire:

- Suivre de près la charge virale et le nombre de cellules CD4, avant le traitement et à intervalles réguliers pendant toute sa durée.
- NOTER À INTERVALLES RÉGULIERS PENDANT TOUTE LA DURÉE DU TRAITEMENT LES CONCENTRATIONS SÉRIQUES D'AMYLASE, DE LIPASE ET DE TRIGLYCÉRIDES. DES CONCENTRATIONS ÉLEVÉES PEUVENT RÉVÉLER LA PRÉSENCE DE PANCRÉATITE ET DICTENT L'ARRÊT DU TRAITEMENT.
- SUIVRE DE PRÈS LA FONCTION HÉPATIQUE. LA LAMIVUDINE PEUT ENTRAÎNER UNE ÉLÉVATION DES CONCENTRATIONS D'AST, D'ALT, DE CPK, DE BILIRUBINE ET DE PHOSPHATASE ALCALINE, MAIS ELLES REVIENNENT HABITUELLEMENT À LA NORMALE APRÈS INTERRUPTION DU TRAITEMENT. L'ACIDOSE LACTIQUE PEUT SURVENIR EN PRÉSENCE D'UNE TOXICITÉ HÉPATIQUE ENTRAÎNANT UNE STÉATOSE HÉPATIQUE, QUI PEUT ÊTRE D'ISSUE FATALE, PARTICULIÈREMENT CHEZ LES FEMMES.
- Dans de rares cas, la lamivudine peut induire une neutropénie et l'anémie.

DIAGNOSTICS INFIRMIERS POSSIBLES

- Risque d'infection (Indications).
- Connaissances insuffisantes sur le traitement médicamenteux (Enseignement au patient et à ses proches).

INTERVENTIONS INFIRMIÈRES

- NE PAS CONFONDRE LA LAMIVUDINE AVEC LA LAMOTRIGINE (LAMICTAL).
- NE PAS CONFONDRE LES COMPRIMÉS ET LES SOLUTIONS BUVABLES DE 3TC ET D'HEPTOVIR. CES PRÉPARATIONS CONTIENNENT TOUTES DE LA LAMIVUDINE, MAIS À DES DOSES OU À DES CONCENTRATIONS DIFFÉRENTES, QUI SONT ADAPTÉES AU TRAITEMENT DE L'HÉPATITE B OU DE L'INFECTION PAR LE VIH. La dose de lamivudine utilisée en traitement de l'hépatite B ne convient pas aux patients qui sont infectés à la fois par l'hépatite B et le VIH. Si l'on doit administrer de la lamivudine à ces patients, il faut recourir à la dose plus forte, indiquée dans le traitement d'association anti-VIH.
- La lamivudine peut être administrée avec ou sans aliments.

ENSEIGNEMENT AU PATIENT ET À SES PROCHES

- Demander au patient de prendre la lamivudine, exactement comme elle lui a été prescrite, toutes les 12 heures. Insister sur le fait qu'il est important d'observer rigoureusement le traitement, de ne pas prendre plus de médicament que la quantité exacte qui lui a été prescrite, et de consulter un professionnel de la santé avant d'arrêter la prise de la lamivudine. Expliquer au patient que s'il n'a pu prendre le médicament au moment habituel, il doit le prendre aussitôt que possible, à moins que ce ne soit presque l'heure prévue pour la dose suivante. Le prévenir qu'il ne doit jamais remplacer une dose manquée par une double dose. Insister sur le fait qu'il ne faut pas donner ce médicament à d'autres personnes.
- Expliquer au patient que la lamivudine ne guérit pas l'infection par le VIH ni ne prévient les infections opportunistes ou toute autre infection connexe. Elle ne réduit pas le risque de transmission du VIH par les rapports sexuels ou par la contamination du sang. Conseiller au patient d'utiliser un condom lors des rapports sexuels, de ne pas partager ses seringues et de ne pas faire de dons de sang afin de prévenir la transmission du virus à d'autres personnes. Prévenir le patient que les effets au long cours de la lamivudine demeurent inconnus.
- Recommander au patient de signaler immédiatement à un professionnel de la santé tout signe de neuropathie périphérique ou de pancréatite.
- Prévenir le patient diabétique que les solutions buvables de lamivudine contiennent du sucre.

- Recommander au patient de prévenir un professionnel de la santé immédiatement, si des signes d'acidose lactique (fatigue ou faiblesse, douleurs musculaires inhabituelles, difficultés respiratoires, douleurs à l'estomac avec des nausées et des vomissements, sensation de froid, surtout au niveau des extrémités, étourdissements ou battements cardiaques rapides et irréguliers) ou d'hépatotoxicité (jaunissement de la peau ou du blanc des yeux, urine de couleur foncée, selles de couleur pâle, perte d'appétit pendant plusieurs jours de suite, nausées ou douleurs abdominales) se manifestent. Ces symptômes peuvent se présenter plus fréquemment chez les sujets de sexe féminin, les personnes obèses ou celles qui prennent des médicaments comme la lamivudine pendant un laps de temps prolongé.
- Informer le patient que le traitement antirétroviral peut entraîner une redistribution ou une accumulation des graisses corporelles, dont les causes et les conséquences à long terme sur la santé sont actuellement inconnues.
- Conseiller au patient de consulter un professionnel de la santé avant de prendre d'autres médicaments (sur ordonnance ou en vente libre) ou des produits naturels en même temps que la lamivudine.
- Insister sur l'importance des examens réguliers de suivi et des tests sanguins permettant de déceler l'évolution de la maladie et les effets secondaires de la lamivudine.

VÉRIFICATION DE L'EFFICACITÉ THÉRAPEUTIQUE

L'efficacité du traitement peut être démontrée par: le ralentissement de l'évolution de l'infection par le VIH et l'apparition plus tardive de ses complications ■ la diminution de la charge virale et l'accroissement du nombre de cellules CD4 chez les patients atteints d'une infection par le VIH ■ l'amélioration de l'activité nécro-inflammatoire hépatique ■ l'augmentation de la séroconversion de l'AgHBe ■ la diminution de la charge virale du VHB ou le retour à la normale des taux d'aminotransférases sériques, ou les deux. ✳

LAMOTRIGINE

Apo-Lamotrigine, Ge-Lamotrigine, Lamictal, Novo-Lamotrigine, PMS-Lamotrigine

CLASSIFICATION:
Anticonvulsivant

Grossesse – catégorie C

INDICATIONS

Traitement d'appoint chez les patients adultes atteints d'épilepsie dont l'état n'est pas maîtrisé de façon satisfaisante par les traitements traditionnels ■ Monothérapie chez les adultes, après retrait des antiépileptiques administrés en concomitance ■ Traitement d'appoint chez les enfants et les adultes présentant des crises épileptiques associées au syndrome de Lennox-Gastaut.

MÉCANISME D'ACTION

Stabilisation de la membrane neuronale par inhibition du transport du sodium. ***Effets thérapeutiques:*** Diminution de la fréquence des crises.

PHARMACOCINÉTIQUE

Absorption: 98 % (PO).

Distribution: La lamotrigine passe dans le lait maternel. Elle se lie fortement aux tissus renfermant de la mélanine (yeux, peau pigmentée).

Métabolisme et excrétion: Métabolisme majoritairement hépatique (métabolites inactifs). Excrétion majoritairement rénale (10 % excrété sous forme inchangée).

Demi-vie: 25 heures (lors d'une monothérapie prolongée par la lamotrigine), 14 heures (avec inducteur enzymatique), 59 heures (avec acide valproïque) et 28 heures (avec inducteur enzymatique et acide valproïque).

Profil temps-action

	Début d'action	Pic	Durée
PO	inconnu	1,4 – 4,8 h	inconnue

CONTRE-INDICATIONS, PRÉCAUTIONS ET MISES EN GARDE

Contre-indications: Hypersensibilité.

Précautions et mises en garde: Maladie rénale (réduire la dose d'entretien, au besoin) ■ Maladie cardiaque ■ Maladie hépatique ■ Grossesse ■ Allaitement ■ **Péd.:** Enfants < 16 ans (l'innocuité de la monothérapie n'a pas été établie); utilisation possible chez les enfants de 2 à 16 ans atteints du syndrome de Lennox-Gastaut.

RÉACTIONS INDÉSIRABLES ET EFFETS SECONDAIRES

SNC: <u>ataxie</u>, <u>étourdissements</u>, <u>céphalées</u>, modification du comportement, dépression, somnolence, insomnie, tremblements.

ORLO: vision trouble, vision double, rhinite.

GI: <u>nausées</u>, <u>vomissements</u>.

GU: vaginite.

Tég.: <u>photosensibilité</u>, <u>rash</u>.

Loc.: arthralgie.

Divers: réactions allergiques incluant le syndrome de Stevens-Johnson.

INTERACTIONS

Médicament-médicament: La **carbamazépine** peut réduire les concentrations de lamotrigine (avec élévation des concentrations d'un métabolite actif de la carbamazépine) ■ Le **phénobarbital**, la **phénytoïne** ou la **primidone**, administrés en concomitance, abaissent les concentrations de lamotrigine ■ Par suite de l'administration concomitante d'**acide valproïque**, les concentrations de lamotrigine doublent et celles d'acide valproïque sont diminuées (il faut réduire d'au moins de moitié la dose de lamotrigine).

VOIES D'ADMINISTRATION ET POSOLOGIE

En association avec d'autres antiépileptiques

- **PO (adultes > 12 ans)**: *Patients prenant de la carbamazépine, du phénobarbital, de la phénytoïne ou de la primidone* – 50 mg par jour, en une seule dose, pendant les 2 premières semaines, puis 50 mg, 2 fois par jour, pendant les 2 semaines suivantes; majorer ensuite la posologie de 100 mg toutes les semaines ou deux, jusqu'à l'atteinte d'une dose d'entretien de 150 à 250 mg, 2 fois par jour (ne pas dépasser 500 mg par jour). *Patients prenant de la carbamazépine, du phénobarbital, de la phénytoïne ou de la primidone avec de l'acide valproïque* – 25 mg par jour, pendant les 2 premières semaines, puis 25 mg, 2 fois par jour, pendant les 2 semaines suivantes; majorer ensuite la dose de 25 à 50 mg, toutes les semaines ou deux, jusqu'à l'atteinte d'une dose d'entretien de 50 à 100 mg, 2 fois par jour (ne pas dépasser 200 mg par jour).
- **PO (enfants de 2 à 12 ans)**: *Patients prenant de la carbamazépine, du phénobarbital, de la phénytoïne ou de la primidone* – 0,3 mg/kg, 2 fois par jour (arrondir à la baisse aux 5 mg les plus près) pendant les 2 premières semaines, puis 0,6 mg/kg (arrondir à la baisse aux 5 mg les plus près), 2 fois par jour, pendant les 2 semaines suivantes; majorer ensuite la dose de 1,2 mg/kg, toutes les semaines ou deux, jusqu'à l'atteinte d'une dose d'entretien de 2,5 à 7,5 mg/kg, 2 fois par jour (ne pas dépasser 400 mg par jour, en 2 doses fractionnées). *Patients prenant de la carbamazépine, du phénobarbital, de la phénytoïne ou de la primidone avec de l'acide valproïque* – 0,15 mg/kg/jour, 1 fois par jour (arrondir à la baisse aux 5 mg les plus près), pendant les 2 premières semaines; si la dose initiale calculée se situe entre 2,5 et 5 mg/jour, cette dose devrait être de 5 mg, 1 jour sur 2, pendant 2 semaines. Administrer ensuite 0,3 mg/kg, 1 fois par jour (arrondir à la baisse aux 5 mg les plus près), pendant les 2 semaines suivantes, puis majorer la dose de 0,3 mg/kg (arrondir à la baisse aux 5 mg les plus près), toutes les semaines ou deux, jusqu'à l'atteinte d'une dose d'entretien de 1 à 5 mg/kg/jour (ne pas dépasser 200 mg/jour, en 1 ou 2 doses fractionnées).

Passage à la monothérapie

- **PO (adultes et enfants ≥ 16 ans)**: 50 mg/jour pendant 2 semaines, ensuite 50 mg, 2 fois par jour, pendant 2 semaines; majorer ensuite de 100 mg/jour, toutes les 1 ou 2 semaines, jusqu'à l'atteinte d'une dose d'entretien de 300 à 500 mg/jour, en 2 doses fractionnées; lorsque la dose cible est atteinte, diminuer la dose des autres antiépileptiques de 20 % de la dose initiale toutes les semaines, pendant 5 semaines.

PRÉSENTATION

Comprimés: 25 mg^Pr, 100 mg^Pr, 150 mg^Pr ■ **Comprimés à croquer dispersables**: 2 mg^Pr, 5 mg^Pr.

SOINS INFIRMIERS

ÉVALUATION DE LA SITUATION

- Déterminer la fréquence, le siège, la durée et les caractéristiques des convulsions.
- EXAMINER LE PATIENT À INTERVALLES FRÉQUENTS, PENDANT TOUTE LA DURÉE DU TRAITEMENT, POUR DÉCELER LA PRÉSENCE D'UN RASH. IL FAUT ARRÊTER LE TRAITEMENT PAR LA LAMOTRIGINE AUX PREMIERS SIGNES DE RASH; CETTE RÉACTION PEUT METTRE LA VIE DU PATENT EN DANGER. IL Y A ÉGALEMENT RISQUE D'APPARITION DU SYNDROME DE STEVENS-JOHNSON OU D'UNE ÉRYTHRODERMIE BULLEUSE AVEC ÉPIDERMOLYSE. LE RASH SURVIENT HABITUELLEMENT DANS LES 2 À 8 PREMIÈRES SEMAINES DE TRAITEMENT ET, PLUS FRÉQUEMMENT, CHEZ LES PATIENTS PRENANT PLUSIEURS ANTIÉPILEPTIQUES, PARTICULIÈREMENT DE L'ACIDE VALPROÏQUE. SON INCIDENCE EST BEAUCOUP PLUS ÉLEVÉE CHEZ LES PATIENTS < 16 ANS.

Tests de laboratoire: On devrait noter les concentrations de lamotrigine à intervalles réguliers pendant toute la durée du traitement, particulièrement chez les patients prenant d'autres anticonvulsivants. L'intervalle thérapeutique des concentrations plasmatiques n'a pas été établi.

DIAGNOSTICS INFIRMIERS POSSIBLES

- Risque d'atteinte à l'intégrité de la peau (Indications).
- Risque d'accident (Effets secondaires).

- Connaissances insuffisantes sur le traitement médicamenteux (Enseignement au patient et à ses proches).

INTERVENTIONS INFIRMIÈRES

- NE PAS CONFONDRE LA LAMOTRIGINE (LAMICTAL) AVEC LA TERBINAFINE (LAMISIL).
- NE PAS CONFONDRE LA LAMOTRIGINE AVEC LA LAMIVUDINE.
- La lamotrigine peut être administrée sans égards aux repas.
- Il faut arrêter graduellement le traitement par la lamotrigine, pendant une période d'au moins 2 semaines, sauf si, pour des raisons de sécurité, le sevrage doit se faire plus rapidement. L'arrêt brusque du traitement peut accroître la fréquence des convulsions.

Comprimés à croquer dispersables: Ces comprimés peuvent être avalés tels quels, croqués ou dispersés dans de l'eau ou du jus de fruits. Si le patient les croque, il doit ensuite boire de l'eau ou du jus pour les avaler plus facilement.

ENSEIGNEMENT AU PATIENT ET À SES PROCHES

- Expliquer au patient qu'il doit prendre la lamotrigine en suivant rigoureusement la posologie recommandée. S'il n'a pu prendre le médicament au moment habituel, il doit le prendre aussitôt que possible, sauf s'il est presque l'heure prévue pour la dose suivante. Le prévenir qu'il ne doit jamais remplacer une dose manquée par une double dose ni arrêter brusquement la prise de la lamotrigine. Le sevrage doit être graduel, sinon, les convulsions risquent d'augmenter en fréquence.
- Recommander au patient d'informer immédiatement un professionnel de la santé si un rash se manifeste ou si les convulsions deviennent plus fréquentes.
- Prévenir le patient que la lamotrigine peut provoquer des étourdissements, de la somnolence et une vision trouble. Lui conseiller de ne pas conduire et d'éviter les activités qui exigent sa vigilance jusqu'à ce qu'on ait la certitude que le médicament n'entraîne pas ces effets chez lui. Le patient ne doit pas conduire jusqu'à ce que le médecin lui en donne l'autorisation, une fois les convulsions maîtrisées.
- Inciter le patient à utiliser des écrans solaires et à porter des vêtements protecteurs pour prévenir les réactions de photosensibilité.
- Recommander à la patiente d'informer un professionnel de la santé si elle pense être enceinte ou désire le devenir ou, encore, si elle allaite.
- Recommander au patient qui doit suivre un autre traitement ou subir une intervention chirurgicale d'avertir le professionnel de la santé qu'il suit un traitement avec ce médicament.
- Conseiller au patient de porter sur lui en tout temps un bracelet d'identité où sont inscrits son problème de santé et son traitement médicamenteux.

VÉRIFICATION DE L'EFFICACITÉ THÉRAPEUTIQUE

L'efficacité du traitement peut être démontrée par: la suppression des convulsions ou la réduction de leur fréquence.

LANSOPRAZOLE

Prevacid, Prevacid FasTab

LANSOPRAZOLE/ CLARITHROMYCINE/ AMOXICILLINE

Hp-PAC

CLASSIFICATION:

Antiulcéreux (inhibiteur de la pompe à protons)

Grossesse – catégorie B

INDICATIONS

Traitement des affections nécessitant une réduction de la sécrétion d'acide gastrique dont: l'ulcère duodénal ■ l'ulcère gastrique ■ l'œsophagite par reflux gastro-œsophagien incluant le syndrome de Barrett et les cas réfractaires à une cure appropriée par des antagonistes des récepteurs H_2 de l'histamine ■ le reflux gastro-œsophagien (RGO) ■ les brûlures d'estomac et autres symptômes associés au reflux gastro-œsophagien ■ Traitement de l'hypersécrétion pathologique, dont le syndrome de Zollinger-Ellison ■ Cicatrisation de l'ulcère gastrique secondaire à la prise d'AINS; traitement de l'ulcère gastrique secondaire à la prise d'AINS chez les patients qui continuent à prendre ces médicaments ■ Réduction du risque d'ulcère gastrique secondaire à la prise d'AINS chez les patients qui ont des antécédents d'ulcères gastriques et qui doivent continuer à prendre un AINS ■ **En association avec l'amoxicilline et la clarithromycine:** Éradication de *H. pylori* chez les patients ayant des antécédents d'ulcère duodénal ■ Ulcère duodénal associé à *H. pylori*.

MÉCANISME D'ACTION

Inhibition spécifique de l'enzyme gastrique H^+, K^+-ATPase (pompe à protons), responsable de la sécrétion

L

acide par les cellules pariétales de l'estomac, ce qui prévient l'entrée des ions hydrogène dans la lumière du tube gastrique. ***Effets thérapeutiques:*** Réduction de l'accumulation d'acide dans la lumière gastrique, ce qui diminue le reflux d'acide ▪ Guérison de l'ulcère gastroduodénal et de ceux qui sont provoqués par l'œsophagite.

PHARMACOCINÉTIQUE

Absorption: 80 % (PO).
Distribution: Inconnue.
Liaison aux protéines: 97 %.
Métabolisme et excrétion: Métabolisme majoritairement hépatique, avec transformation en composés inactifs. À l'intérieur des cellules, transformation en au moins 2 autres composés antisécrétoires.
Demi-vie: Moins de 2 heures (plus longue chez les personnes âgées et les insuffisants hépatiques).

Profil temps-action (suppression des sécrétions acides)

	DÉBUT D'ACTION	PIC	DURÉE
PO	rapide	inconnu	plus de 24 h

L

CONTRE-INDICATIONS, PRÉCAUTIONS ET MISES EN GARDE

Contre-indications: Hypersensibilité.
Précautions et mises en garde: GÉR.: La dose d'entretien chez les personnes âgées ne doit pas dépasser 30 mg/jour, sauf si l'on désire réduire davantage la quantité d'acide ▪ Insuffisance hépatique grave (ne pas dépasser 30 mg/jour chez ces patients) ▪ **OBST., ALLAITEMENT, PÉD.:** L'innocuité du médicament n'a pas été établie chez les femmes enceintes ou chez celles qui allaitent, ni chez les enfants < 1 an.

RÉACTIONS INDÉSIRABLES ET EFFETS SECONDAIRES

SNC: étourdissements, céphalées.
GI: diarrhée, douleurs abdominales, nausées.
Tég.: rash.

INTERACTIONS

Médicament-médicament: Le **sulcrafate** réduit l'absorption du lansoprazole (il faut prendre le lansoprazole 30 minutes avant le sulcrafate) ▪ Le lansoprazole peut réduire l'absorption des médicaments nécessitant un pH acide, tels que le **kétoconazole**, l'**itraconazole,** les **esters d'ampicilline**, les **sels ferreux** et la **digoxine** ▪ Risque accru de saignements lors d'usage concomitant de **warfarine** (suivre le RNI et le temps de prothrombine).

VOIES D'ADMINISTRATION ET POSOLOGIE

- **PO (adultes):** *Œsophagite (incluant le syndrome de Barrett)* – 30 mg par jour, pendant 4 à 8 semaines; puis, au besoin, 15 mg/jour en traitement d'entretien. *Guérison des ulcères gastriques associés au traitement par des AINS* – de 15 à 30 mg, 1 fois par jour, pendant 8 semaines. *Réduction du risque d'ulcères gastriques associés au traitement par les AINS* – 15 mg, 1 fois par jour, pendant 12 semaines. *RGO (adultes)* – 15 mg/jour, pendant un maximum de 8 semaines. *RGO; œsophagite érosive et non érosive (enfants)* – chez l'enfant de 1 à 11 ans, la posologie par voie orale recommandée est de 15 mg (chez l'enfant pesant ≤ 30 kg), et de 30 mg (chez l'enfant pesant > 30 kg), 1 fois par jour, pendant un maximum de 12 semaines; chez l'adolescent de 12 à 17 ans, on peut utiliser la posologie recommandée chez l'adulte. *Ulcère duodénal* et *ulcère gastrique* – 15 mg/jour, pendant 2 à 4 semaines et 4 à 8 semaines, respectivement. *Ulcère duodénal associé à* H. pylori – 30 mg, 2 fois par jour, en association avec la clarithromycine et l'amoxicilline, pendant 7, 10 ou 14 jours, ou 30 mg, 3 fois par jour, en association avec l'amoxicilline, pendant 14 jours. *Hypersécrétions pathologiques* – 60 mg, 1 fois par jour; on peut augmenter la dose jusqu'à concurrence de 90 mg, 2 fois par jour. Si la posologie quotidienne est supérieure à 120 mg, l'administrer en doses fractionnées.

PRÉSENTATION

Capsules à libération prolongée et comprimés à dissolution rapide: 15 mg[Pr], 30 mg[Pr] ▪ **En association avec:** amoxicilline et clarithromycine, dans une trousse favorisant l'observance du traitement (Hp-PAC)[Pr].

SOINS INFIRMIERS

ÉVALUATION DE LA SITUATION

- Observer le patient à intervalles réguliers afin de déceler toute douleur épigastrique ou abdominale, et suivre de près la présence de sang visible ou occulte dans les selles, les vomissements ou le liquide d'aspiration gastrique.

Tests de laboratoire:

- Le lansoprazole peut modifier les résultats des tests de la fonction hépatique indiquant des taux accrus d'AST, d'ALT, de phosphatase alcaline, de LDH et de bilirubine.
- Le médicament peut élever les concentrations de créatinine sérique et élever ou abaisser les concentrations d'électrolytes.
- Le lansoprazole peut modifier le nombre d'érythrocytes, de leucocytes et de plaquettes.
- Il peut aussi élever les concentrations de gastrine, donner un rapport anormal albumine-globuline,

induire l'hyperlipidémie et élever ou abaisser les taux de cholestérol.

- Effectuer le suivi du RNI et du temps de prothrombine chez les patients prenant de la warfarine.

DIAGNOSTICS INFIRMIERS POSSIBLES

- Douleur aiguë (Indications).
- Connaissances insuffisantes sur le traitement médicamenteux (Enseignement au patient et à ses proches).

INTERVENTIONS INFIRMIÈRES

- Administrer le médicament avant les repas. LES CAPSULES À LIBÉRATION PROLONGÉE ET LES COMPRIMÉS À DISSOLUTION RAPIDE NE DOIVENT PAS ÊTRE ÉCRASÉS, MÂCHÉS OU CROQUÉS.

PO (capsules): Dans le cas des patients ayant des difficultés de déglutition, on peut ouvrir les capsules et saupoudrer avec les granules qu'elles contiennent 1 cuillerée à table de compote de pommes, de pouding, de fromage cottage ou de yogourt; faire avaler immédiatement ce mélange au patient. Il ne faut pas écraser ni croquer le contenu des capsules.

PO (comprimés): On recommande de placer le comprimé sur la langue et de le laisser se désintégrer avec ou sans eau jusqu'à ce que les granules puissent être avalés. Le comprimé se désintègre habituellement en moins de 1 minute. Chez les adultes ou les enfants incapables d'avaler le comprimé, on peut l'administrer au moyen d'une seringue destinée à l'administration par voie orale: placer un comprimé de 15 mg dans une seringue destinée à l'administration par voie orale et aspirer environ 4 mL d'eau, ou un comprimé de 30 mg et aspirer environ 10 mL d'eau. Agiter doucement pour obtenir une dispersion rapide. Une fois le comprimé dispersé, administrer le contenu de la seringue dans la bouche du patient dans les 15 minutes. Après l'administration, aspirer environ 2 mL (5 mL pour le comprimé de 30 mg) d'eau de plus, agiter doucement, puis administrer le contenu de la seringue dans la bouche du patient.

Sonde nasogastrique (capsule): Chez le patient nécessitant une sonde nasogastrique, ouvrir la capsule de lansoprazole à libération prolongée, ajouter les granules intacts à 40 mL de jus de pomme ou d'eau, et administrer le mélange dans l'estomac par la sonde. Rincer ensuite la sonde avec du jus de pomme ou de l'eau. Dans le cas de l'administration de lansoprazole par une jéjunostomie, on l'a déjà mélangé à une solution contenant 2,5 mL de bicarbonate de sodium à 4,2% et 2,5 mL d'eau.

Sonde nasogastrique (comprimé): Chez le patient nécessitant une sonde nasogastrique, introduire un comprimé de 15 mg dans une seringue, et aspirer 4 mL d'eau, ou un comprimé de 30 mg, et aspirer 10 mL d'eau. Agiter doucement pour obtenir une dispersion rapide. Une fois le comprimé dispersé, administrer le contenu de la seringue dans la sonde nasogastrique du patient dans les 15 minutes. Après l'administration, aspirer environ 5 mL d'eau de plus, agiter doucement, puis rincer avec cette solution la sonde nasogastrique.

- On peut administrer un antiacide simultanément.

ENSEIGNEMENT AU PATIENT ET À SES PROCHES

- Conseiller au patient de respecter rigoureusement la posologie recommandée pendant toute la durée du traitement, même s'il se sent mieux.
- Recommander au patient de ne pas prendre de médicaments renfermant de l'aspirine ni d'AINS, sauf recommandation contraire du médecin, et de ne pas consommer d'alcool ni d'aliments pouvant aggraver l'irritation gastrique.
- Prévenir le patient que le lansoprazole peut provoquer de la somnolence. Lui conseiller de ne pas conduire et d'éviter les activités qui exigent sa vigilance jusqu'à ce qu'on ait la certitude que le médicament n'entraîne pas cet effet chez lui.
- Recommander au patient de signaler immédiatement à un professionnel de la santé la présence de selles noires et goudronneuses, de diarrhée ou de douleurs abdominales.

VÉRIFICATION DE L'EFFICACITÉ THÉRAPEUTIQUE

L'efficacité du traitement peut être démontrée par: le soulagement de la douleur abdominale ou la prévention de l'irritation ou des saignements gastriques; on peut constater la guérison de l'ulcère gastroduodénal par radiographie ou endoscopie; on doit maintenir le traitement pendant la durée prescrite; le traitement de l'hypersécrétion pathologique peut être de longue durée ■ la guérison de l'œsophagite; le traitement peut durer jusqu'à 8 semaines, mais on peut le prolonger jusqu'à 12 mois (traitement d'entretien).

LÉFLUNOMIDE

Apo-Léflunomide, Arava, Novo-Léflunomide, PMS-Léflunomide

CLASSIFICATION:

Agent antirhumatismal modificateur de la maladie (AARMM) (immunomodulateur)

Grossesse – catégorie X

INDICATIONS

Traitement de la polyarthrite rhumatoïde évolutive chez l'adulte.

MÉCANISME D'ACTION

Inhibition d'une enzyme nécessaire à la synthèse de la pyrimidine; effets antiprolifératif et anti-inflammatoire. ***Effets thérapeutiques:*** Diminution de la douleur et de l'inflammation, ralentissement de l'évolution de la polyarthrite rhumatoïde et amélioration de la capacité fonctionnelle.

PHARMACOCINÉTIQUE

Absorption: 80 % (PO); le léflunomide est rapidement transformé en métabolite M1, lequel est responsable de l'effet pharmacologique.

Distribution: Le léflunomide traverse la barrière placentaire.

Liaison aux protéines: 99 %.

Métabolisme et excrétion: Métabolisme majoritairement hépatique. Les métabolites sont excrétés dans l'urine (43 %) et les fèces (48 %). Recyclage biliaire.

L

Demi-vie: De 14 à 18 jours.

Profil temps-action (effet antirhumatismal)

	DÉBUT D'ACTION	PIC	DURÉE
PO	1 mois	3-6 mois	plusieurs semaines - mois†

† En raison de la persistance du métabolite actif.

CONTRE-INDICATIONS, PRÉCAUTIONS ET MISES EN GARDE

Contre-indications: Hypersensibilité ■ Femmes enceintes ou en âge de procréer qui n'utilisent pas de méthode contraceptive fiable avant le traitement, pendant celui-ci et pendant les 2 années qui suivent (ou tant que le taux plasmatique du métabolite actif n'est pas inférieur à 0,02 mg/L) ■ Dysfonctionnement hépatique important, incluant un résultat positif au test de dépistage de l'hépatite B ou C ■ Insuffisance rénale modérée à grave, syndrome néphrotique ou hypoprotéinémie grave ■ Immunodéficience (p. ex., sida) ■ Infection grave ■ Aplasie médullaire grave ou anémie, leucopénie, neutropénie ou thrombopénie importantes ■ Enfants < 18 ans ■ Allaitement ■ Vaccination par des virus vivants ■ Hommes désirant procréer.

Précautions et mises en garde: Une étroite surveillance médicale est de mise ■ Tuberculose.

RÉACTIONS INDÉSIRABLES ET EFFETS SECONDAIRES

SNC: céphalées, étourdissements, faiblesse.

Resp.: bronchite, toux accrue, pharyngite, pneumonie, infection respiratoire, rhinite, sinusite.

CV: douleurs thoraciques, hypertension.

GI: diarrhée, nausées, douleurs abdominales, taux anormaux d'enzymes hépatiques et hépatotoxicité (rare), anorexie, dyspepsie, gastroentérite, aphtes buccaux, vomissements.

GU: infection des voies urinaires.

Tég.: alopécie, rash, peau sèche, eczéma, prurit.

HÉ: hypokaliémie.

Métab.: perte pondérale.

Loc.: arthralgie, douleurs dorsales, troubles articulaires, crampes dans les jambes, synovite, ténosynovite.

SN: paresthésie.

Locaux: réactions allergiques, syndrome grippal, infection incluant la SEPTICÉMIE, douleurs.

INTERACTIONS

Médicament-médicament: La **cholestyramine** et le **charbon activé** peuvent entraîner une baisse marquée et rapide des concentrations sanguines du métabolite actif ■ L'administration concomitante de **médicaments hépatotoxiques, hématotoxiques** ou **immunosuppresseurs,** comme le **méthotrexate,** augmente le risque d'hépatotoxicité ■ La prise concomitante d'**alcool** augmente les risques d'hépatotoxicité ■ L'administration concomitante de **rifampine** élève les concentrations sanguines de métabolite actif ■ Risque accru de saignements lors de l'administration concomitante de **warfarine** ■ Il est déconseillé d'administrer le léflunomide en même temps que d'autres **AARMM,** car l'innocuité de cette association n'a pas été étudiée ■ L'utilisation de **vaccins à virus vivants** n'est pas recommandée. Il faut attendre au moins 6 mois après l'interruption du traitement par le léflunomide avant d'administrer un vaccin à virus vivants.

VOIES D'ADMINISTRATION ET POSOLOGIE

- **PO (adultes)**: *Dose d'attaque* - 100 mg, 1 fois par jour, pendant 3 jours. *Dose d'entretien* - 20 mg, 1 fois par jour (en cas d'intolérance, on peut diminuer la dose jusqu'à 10 mg).

PRÉSENTATION

Comprimés: 10 mg^{Pr}, 20 mg^{Pr}, 100 mg^{Pr}.

SOINS INFIRMIERS

ÉVALUATION DE LA SITUATION

- Déterminer l'amplitude des mouvements articulaires et la gravité de l'œdème des articulations ainsi que l'intensité de la douleur au niveau des articulations atteintes, avant le traitement et à intervalles réguliers pendant toute sa durée.

Tests de laboratoire:

- Évaluer la fonction hépatique tout au long du traitement. Il faut déterminer les concentrations d'ALT avant le traitement, puis, tous les mois, pendant la phase initiale de traitement, jusqu'à ce que l'état du patient se stabilise. Par la suite, les tests de la fonction hépatique pourront être faits toutes les 6 à 8 semaines. Le léflunomide peut élever les concentrations d'ALT et d'AST, mais ce phénomène est réversible si l'on diminue la dose ou si l'on arrête le traitement. Si les concentrations d'ALT sont plus du double des valeurs initiales, abaisser la dose jusqu'à 10 mg/jour et poursuivre le traitement. Suivre de près les concentrations après la réduction de la dose; plusieurs semaines peuvent s'écouler avant que les concentrations plasmatiques s'abaissent en raison de la longue demi-vie du médicament. Si la hausse des concentrations est > 2 fois plus élevée, mais ≤ 3 fois plus élevée que les valeurs initiales, malgré une réduction de la dose, il faut effectuer une biopsie hépatique si l'on décide de poursuivre le traitement. Si les concentrations d'ALT sont > 3 fois plus élevées que les valeurs initiales, malgré la réduction de la dose, il faut arrêter le traitement par le léflunomide et administrer de la cholestyramine (voir Toxicité et surdosage). Suivre de près le patient et lui administrer de nouveau de la cholestyramine, selon les besoins.
- Noter la numération globulaire et plaquettaire tous les mois, pendant les 6 mois qui suivent le début du traitement, et toutes les 6 à 8 semaines par la suite. Si le léflunomide est administré en même temps que d'autres médicaments immunosuppresseurs, assurer un suivi mensuel. En cas de dépression de la moelle osseuse, arrêter l'administration de léflunomide et procéder à l'élimination du médicament (voir la marche à suivre à la rubrique Interventions infirmières).
- Dans de rares cas, le léflunomide peut élever les concentrations de phosphatase alcaline et de bilirubine.

Toxicité et surdosage: En cas de surdosage ou de toxicité marquée, administrer 8 g de cholestyramine, 3 fois par jour, pendant 24 heures, ou 50 mg de charbon activé par voie orale ou par sonde nasogastrique, toutes les 6 heures, pendant 24 heures, afin d'accélérer l'élimination de l'agent.

DIAGNOSTICS INFIRMIERS POSSIBLES

- Mobilité physique réduite (Indications).
- Douleur aiguë (Indications).
- Connaissances insuffisantes sur le traitement médicamenteux (Enseignement au patient et à ses proches).

INTERVENTIONS INFIRMIÈRES

Amorcer le traitement par une dose d'attaque de 100 mg par jour, pendant 3 jours, suivie d'une dose de 20 mg par jour. Réduire la dose jusqu'à 10 mg par jour si le médicament n'est pas bien toléré.

Marche à suivre pour éliminer le médicament: On doit suivre cette méthode lorsqu'on veut abaisser les concentrations plasmatiques jusqu'à un niveau non décelable, soit à moins de 0,02 mg/L après l'arrêt du traitement par le léflunomide. Administrer 8 g de cholestyramine, 3 fois par jour, pendant 11 jours. (Il n'est pas nécessaire de le faire pendant 11 jours consécutifs, à moins qu'on ne souhaite une baisse rapide des concentrations.) S'assurer que les concentrations sont inférieures à 0,02 mg/L, à l'aide de deux épreuves distinctes, effectuées à au moins 14 jours d'intervalle. Si les concentrations plasmatiques sont supérieures à 0,02 mg/L, envisager la poursuite du traitement par la cholestyramine. Si l'on ne suit pas la méthode d'élimination du médicament, 2 ans peuvent s'écouler avant que les concentrations ne soient plus décelables.

ENSEIGNEMENT AU PATIENT ET À SES PROCHES

- Recommander au patient de prendre le léflunomide en suivant rigoureusement la posologie recommandée.
- Prévenir le patient que le léflunomide peut parfois provoquer des étourdissements. Lui conseiller de ne pas conduire et d'éviter les activités qui exigent sa vigilance jusqu'à ce qu'on ait la certitude que le médicament n'entraîne pas cet effet chez lui.
- Prévenir la patiente en âge de procréer que le léflunomide entraîne des effets tératogènes. Les femmes qui désirent devenir enceintes doivent se soumettre à l'intervention d'élimination du médicament (voir la rubrique Interventions infirmières). Il faut aussi s'assurer que les concentrations plasmatiques du métabolite M1 sont inférieures à 0,02 mg/L. Les hommes qui désirent procréer doivent aussi prendre 8 g de cholestyramine, 3 fois par jour, pendant 11 jours, afin de réduire tout risque possible.
- Conseiller au patient de consulter un professionnel de la santé avant de prendre en concomitance tout autre médicament. Le patient peut continuer de prendre de l'aspirine, un AINS ou de faibles doses de corticostéroïdes pendant ce traitement, mais il devra peut-être abandonner tout autre traitement de la polyarthrite rhumatoïde.

- Expliquer au patient qu'il risque de perdre ses cheveux. Explorer avec lui les stratégies lui permettant de s'adapter à ce changement.
- Recommander au patient de ne pas se faire vacciner par un produit à virus vivants, durant et après le traitement, sans avoir consulté un professionnel de la santé au préalable.

VÉRIFICATION DE L'EFFICACITÉ THÉRAPEUTIQUE

L'efficacité du traitement peut être démontrée par: la diminution des signes et des symptômes de polyarthrite rhumatoïde, et le ralentissement de l'évolution de la maladie (érosion et pincement de l'interligne articulaire), observé par radiographie. ✳

LÉPIRUDINE (ADNr)

Refludan

CLASSIFICATION:

Anticoagulant (inhibiteur de la thrombine)

Grossesse – catégorie B

INDICATIONS

Traitement de la maladie thromboembolique et prévention de ses complications chez les patients atteints de thrombopénie induite par l'héparine ▪ Anticoagulation en présence d'un syndrome coronarien aigu, notamment angine instable et infarctus du myocarde sans élévation du segment ST (en association avec de l'aspirine).

MÉCANISME D'ACTION

Effet anticoagulant par inhibition des effets de la thrombine ▪ Médicament obtenu par la technologie de l'ADN recombinant. ***Effet thérapeutique:*** Anticoagulation avec prévention des complications thromboemboliques.

PHARMACOCINÉTIQUE

Absorption: Biodisponibilité à 100 % (IV).

Distribution: Surtout dans les liquides extracellulaires.

Métabolisme et excrétion: Métabolisme par la libération des acides aminés résultant de la décomposition du médicament; 48 % est excrété dans l'urine, dont 35 % à l'état inchangé.

Demi-vie: 1,3 heure.

Profil temps-action (effet anticoagulant)

	DÉBUT D'ACTION	PIC	DURÉE
IV	en 30 – 90 min	inconnu	jusqu'à 24 h

CONTRE-INDICATIONS, PRÉCAUTIONS ET MISES EN GARDE

Contre-indications: Hypersensibilité ▪ Syndrome coronarien aigu: anomalie hémostatique généralisée (p. ex., hémophilie, maladie de Christmas, purpura thrombopénique idiopathique), saignement actif provenant d'une lésion locale, notamment un ulcère aigu ou un carcinome ulcératif, et chirurgie ou trauma crânien, spinal, oculaire ou auriculaire, ou choc.

Précautions et mises en garde: Administration concomitante d'un thrombolytique (déconseillée en raison d'un risque accru de saignements pouvant menacer le pronostic vital) ▪ Ponction récente d'un gros vaisseau ou biopsie récente d'organe ▪ Anomalie de vaisseau ou d'organe ▪ Antécédents récents d'AVC ou d'intervention chirurgicale intracérébrale ▪ Hypertension grave non maîtrisée ▪ Endocardite bactérienne ▪ Diathèse hémorragique ▪ Chirurgie majeure récente ▪ Ulcère gastroduodénal actif récent ▪ Signes manifestes de saignement ▪ Saignement majeur récent ▪ Insuffisance hépatique grave ▪ Insuffisance rénale grave (il faut éviter ou arrêter la perfusion si la Cl_{Cr} < 15 mL/min) ▪ Insuffisance rénale modérée (si la Cl_{Cr} est de 15 à 50 mL/min, il est recommandé de réduire la dose administrée en bolus et en perfusion d'entretien) ▪ Poids corporel inférieur à 50 kg (risque de saignement plus élevé) ▪ **GÉR.:** Le dysfonctionnement rénal est fréquent chez les patients > 65 ans (une attention spéciale doit être portée au choix de la dose et à la surveillance de la fonction rénale) ▪ **OBST., PÉD.:** Grossesse, allaitement ou enfants (l'innocuité du médicament n'a pas été établie).

RÉACTIONS INDÉSIRABLES ET EFFETS SECONDAIRES

SNC: fièvre.

Hémat.: SAIGNEMENTS.

Divers: réactions allergiques comprenant l'ANAPHYLAXIE.

INTERACTIONS

Médicament-médicament: Risque accru de saignements lors de l'administration concomitante d'**agents thrombolytiques**, de **warfarine**, d'**AINS**, d'**acide valproïque**, d'**inhibiteurs de l'agrégation plaquettaire**, notamment l'**aspirine**, le **dipyridamole**, le **clopidogrel**, la **ticlopidine**, l'**abciximab**, le **tirofiban** et l'**eptifibatide**.

VOIES D'ADMINISTRATION ET POSOLOGIE

Syndrome coronarien aigu

- **IV (adultes)**: 0,4 mg/kg (ne pas dépasser 40 mg) sous forme de bolus pendant 15 à 20 s, suivi d'une perfusion de 0,15 mg/ kg/h (ne pas dépasser 15 mg/h) initialement; les adaptations ultérieures de la posologie devraient être effectuées d'après les résultats des tests de laboratoire (TCA), mais on ne doit jamais dépasser une vitesse d'administration de 0,21 mg/ kg/h, sans chercher à dépister d'éventuelles anomalies de la coagulation.
- ***INSUFFISANCE RÉNALE***

  CRÉATININÉMIE > 177 µmol/L – LE TRAITEMENT EST DÉCONSEILLÉ; *CRÉATININÉMIE DE 133 À 177 µmol/L* – 0,2 mg/kg, SOUS FORME DE BOLUS PENDANT 15 À 20 S, ENSUITE 0,075 mg/kg/H. SI, AU COURS DU TRAITEMENT, LA CRÉATININÉMIE DU PATIENT SE SITUE ENTRE 133 ET 221 µmol/L, ON DOIT DIMINUER LA VITESSE DE PERFUSION DE 50 % ET ÉVALUER LA CRÉATININÉMIE DE 6 À 8 HEURES PLUS TARD.

Thrombopénie induite par l'héparine

- **IV (adultes)**: 0,4 mg/kg (ne pas dépasser 44 mg) sous forme de bolus pendant 15 à 20 s, suivi d'une perfusion de 0,15 mg/ kg/h (ne pas dépasser 16,5 mg/h) initialement; les adaptations ultérieures de la posologie devraient être effectuées d'après les résultats des tests de laboratoire (TCA), mais on ne doit jamais dépasser une vitesse d'administration de 0,21 mg/ kg/h, sans chercher à dépister d'éventuelles anomalies de la coagulation.
- ***INSUFFISANCE RÉNALE***

  IV (ADULTES): 0,2 mg/kg SOUS FORME DE BOLUS PENDANT 15 À 20 S, ENSUITE, SI LA *CL_{CR} 45-60 mL/MIN* – 0,075 mg/kg/H; SI LA *CL_{CR} 30–44 mL/MIN* – 0,045 mg/kg/H; SI LA *CL_{CR} 15–29 ML/MIN* – 0,0225 mg/kg/H; *SI LA CL_{CR} < 15 mL/MIN*, – ÉVITER OU ARRÊTER LA PERFUSION. ON PEUT ENVISAGER D'INJECTER UN BOLUS ADDITIONNEL DE 0,1 mg/kg DE POIDS CORPOREL TOUS LES 2 JOURS, SELON LES RÉSULTATS DES TCA.

PRÉSENTATION

Poudre pour injection: 50 mg/fiole[Pr].

SOINS INFIRMIERS

ÉVALUATION DE LA SITUATION

- RECHERCHER LES SIGNES DE SAIGNEMENT ET D'HÉMORRAGIE (SAIGNEMENT DES GENCIVES OU DU NEZ, FORMATION INHABITUELLE D'ECCHYMOSES, SELLES NOIRES ET GOUDRONNEUSES, HÉMATURIE, CHUTE DE L'HÉMATOCRITE, DE L'HÉMOGLOBINE OU DE LA PRESSION ARTÉRIELLE, RÉSULTATS POSITIFS AU TEST AU GAÏAC DES MATIÈRES FÉCALES). PRÉVENIR LE MÉDECIN, LE CAS ÉCHÉANT.
- Suivre de près le patient pour déceler les réactions d'hypersensibilité (frissons, fièvre, urticaire). Informer le médecin de ces signes.

Tests de laboratoire:

- La posologie doit être adaptée selon le ratio TCA (TCA du patient à un moment donné sur une valeur de référence du TCA, qui est habituellement la moyenne de l'intervalle normal). L'intervalle cible du ratio TCA durant le traitement devrait se situer entre 1,5 et 2,5.
- Déterminer le TCA initial avant le traitement; ne pas commencer l'administration chez les patients dont le ratio est > 2,5.
- Le premier TCA doit être calculé 4 heures après le début du traitement et au moins 1 fois par jour par la suite, tout au long du traitement. Une surveillance plus fréquente est nécessaire chez les patients atteints d'insuffisance hépatique ou rénale grave.
- Si le ratio TCA n'est pas dans la zone cible, le confirmer avant de modifier la dose, à moins que les circonstances cliniques ne dictent des mesures immédiates. Si le ratio confirmé dépasse l'intervalle cible, arrêter la perfusion pendant 2 heures. La recommencer à 50 % de la dose précédente sans administration préalable d'un bolus et déterminer le TCA, 4 heures plus tard.
- Si le ratio confirmé se situe sous l'intervalle cible, accélérer la vitesse de la perfusion par paliers de 20 % et déterminer le ratio 4 heures plus tard.
- ***TOXICITÉ ET SURDOSAGE:*** SI DES SAIGNEMENTS MENAÇANTS POUR LA VIE SURVIENNENT ET QU'ON SOUPÇONNE QUE LES CONCENTRATIONS PLASMATIQUES DE LÉPIRUDINE SONT ÉLEVÉES, ARRÊTER LA PERFUSION, MESURER LE TCA ET LES AUTRES TEMPS DE COAGULATION, MESURER L'HÉMOGLOBINE ET PRÉPARER LE PATIENT À UNE TRANSFUSION DE SANG. ON NE CONNAÎT PAS D'ANTIDOTE SPÉCIFIQUE.

DIAGNOSTICS INFIRMIERS POSSIBLES

- Irrigation tissulaire inefficace (Indications).
- Risque d'accident (Effets secondaires).

INTERVENTIONS INFIRMIÈRES

- Informer tout le personnel chargé des soins du patient que ce dernier est sous anticoagulothérapie. Appliquer une pression sur tous les points de ponction veineuse et d'injection pour prévenir les saignements et la formation d'hématomes. Éviter les injections

L

par voie IM à cause du risque de formation d'hématomes.

- Chez les patients qui doivent recevoir des dérivés de warfarine en vue d'une anticoagulothérapie par voie orale, diminuer graduellement la dose de lépirudine pour atteindre un ratio TCA tout juste supérieur à 1,5 avant de commencer l'anticoagulothérapie par voie orale.

IV directe: Reconstituer le contenu de chaque fiole avec 1 mL d'eau stérile pour injection ou de NaCl 0,9 %. Agiter délicatement. On doit obtenir une solution transparente et incolore en l'espace de quelques secondes à 3 minutes. Ne pas utiliser de solution trouble ou qui contient des particules. Prélever le contenu de la fiole avec une seringue de 10 mL et le diluer avec de l'eau stérile pour injection, du NaCl 0,9% ou du D5%E pour obtenir un volume total de 10 mL et une concentration finale de 5 mg/mL. Consulter les directives du fabricant avant de reconstituer la préparation.

Vitesse d'administration: Administrer lentement en 15 à 20 secondes.

Perfusion continue: Reconstituer le contenu de 2 fioles avec 1 mg par fiole d'eau stérile pour injection ou de NaCl 0,9 %. Injecter le contenu dans un sac pour perfusion renfermant 500 mL ou 250 mL de NaCl 0,9 % ou de D5%E, pour obtenir une concentration de 0,2 mg/mL ou de 0,4 mg/mL, respectivement. La solution est stable pendant 24 heures à la température ambiante. Jeter toute portion inutilisée. Consulter les directives du fabricant avant de reconstituer la préparation.

Vitesse d'administration: Perfuser à une vitesse de 0,15 mg/kg/h. Utiliser une pompe à perfusion pour assurer l'administration d'une dose exacte.

Incompatibilité en addition au soluté: Ne pas mélanger à d'autres médicaments.

ENSEIGNEMENT AU PATIENT ET À SES PROCHES

- Conseiller au patient de signaler immédiatement à un professionnel de la santé tout symptôme associé à un saignement inhabituel ou la formation d'hématomes.
- Recommander au patient d'éviter les injections IM ainsi que les activités pouvant entraîner des blessures et d'utiliser une brosse à dents à poils doux et un rasoir électrique tout au long du traitement.

VÉRIFICATION DE L'EFFICACITÉ THÉRAPEUTIQUE

L'efficacité du traitement peut être démontrée par: un ratio TCA se situant entre 1,5 et 2,5, sans signes d'hémorragie ■ la prise en charge efficace et la prévention de la maladie thromboembolique et de ses complications. ✳

LÉTROZOLE

Femara

CLASSIFICATION:

Antinéoplasique (agent hormonal – inhibiteur de l'aromatase)

Grossesse – catégorie D

INDICATIONS

Traitement de première intention du cancer du sein d'un stade avancé chez les femmes ménopausées ■ Traitement du cancer du sein avancé ou métastatique chez les femmes ménopausées lorsque la maladie évolue à la suite d'un traitement anti-œstrogénique ■ Traitement adjuvant du cancer du sein au stade précoce avec récepteurs hormonaux positifs chez les femmes ménopausées ■ Traitement adjuvant prolongé du cancer du sein au stade précoce avec récepteurs hormonaux positifs chez les femmes ménopausées ayant déjà reçu un traitement adjuvant standard par le tamoxifène pendant 5 ans environ.

MÉCANISME D'ACTION

Inhibition de l'enzyme aromatase, qui est partiellement responsable de la transformation des précurseurs des œstrogènes. ***Effets thérapeutiques:*** Abaissement des concentrations d'œstrogènes circulants, ce qui pourrait arrêter l'évolution des tumeurs du sein sensibles aux œstrogènes et diminuer ainsi le risque de récidive ou d'évolution de la maladie.

PHARMACOCINÉTIQUE

Absorption: Rapide et totale.

Distribution: Inconnue.

Métabolisme et excrétion: Métabolisme majoritairement hépatique.

Demi-vie: 2 jours.

Profil temps-action

(abaissement des concentrations sériques d'œstradiol)

	DÉBUT D'ACTION	PIC	DURÉE
PO	inconnu	2 – 3 jours	inconnue

CONTRE-INDICATIONS, PRÉCAUTIONS ET MISES EN GARDE

Contre-indications: Hypersensibilité ■ État endocrinien préménopausique. **OBST.**: Grossesse et allaitement.

Précautions et mises en garde: Insuffisance hépatique grave ■ **PÉD.**: L'innocuité du médicament n'a pas été établie.

RÉACTIONS INDÉSIRABLES ET EFFETS SECONDAIRES

SNC: anxiété, dépression, étourdissements, somnolence, fatigue, céphalées, vertige, faiblesse.
Resp.: toux, dyspnée, épanchement pleural.
CV: douleurs thoraciques, œdème, hypertension, complications vasculaires cérébrales, complications thromboemboliques.
GI: nausées, douleurs abdominales, anorexie, constipation, diarrhée, dyspepsie, vomissements.
Tég.: alopécie, rougeurs du visage, sécrétion accrue de sueur, prurit, rash.
HÉ: hypercalcémie.
Mét.: hypercholestérolémie, gain pondéral.
Loc.: douleurs musculosquelettiques, arthralgie, fractures, ostéoporose.

INTERACTIONS

Médicament-médicament: Aucune interaction notable.

VOIES D'ADMINISTRATION ET POSOLOGIE

Traitement du cancer du sein avancé ou métastatique

- **PO (adultes)**: 2,5 mg, 1 fois par jour.

Traitement adjuvant ou adjuvant prolongé du cancer du sein précoce

- **PO (adultes)**: 2,5 mg, 1 fois par jour, pendant 5 ans.

PRÉSENTATION

Comprimés: 2,5 mg[Pr].

SOINS INFIRMIERS

ÉVALUATION DE LA SITUATION

- Suivre la patiente à intervalles réguliers, pendant toute la durée du traitement, pour évaluer l'intensité de la douleur et déceler les autres effets secondaires.

Tests de laboratoire: Le médicament peut entraîner une élévation des concentrations de cholestérol et de transaminases.

DIAGNOSTICS INFIRMIERS POSSIBLES

- Douleur aiguë (Effets secondaires).
- Connaissances insuffisantes sur le traitement médicamenteux (Enseignement au patient et à ses proches).

INTERVENTIONS INFIRMIÈRES

- Le médicament peut être pris sans égard aux repas.

ENSEIGNEMENT AU PATIENT ET À SES PROCHES

- Recommander à la patiente de prendre le médicament exactement comme il lui a été prescrit.
- Expliquer à la patiente quelles sont les réactions indésirables possibles et lui conseiller de communiquer avec un professionnel de la santé si ces réactions lui posent des problèmes.

VÉRIFICATION DE L'EFFICACITÉ THÉRAPEUTIQUE

L'efficacité du traitement peut être démontrée par: le ralentissement de l'évolution de la maladie chez les femmes atteintes d'un cancer du sein d'un stade avancé ■ la diminution du risque de récidive ou d'évolution de la maladie.

LEUCOVORINE CALCIQUE

Synonymes: acide folinique, facteur citrovorum

Lederle Leucovorin, Leucovorin

CLASSIFICATION:

Antidote (du méthotrexate)/vitamine (dérivé de l'acide folique)

Grossesse – catégorie C

L

INDICATIONS

Diminution de la toxicité du méthotrexate et des toxicités secondaires à l'élimination difficile de cet agent ■ Traitement de l'anémie mégaloblastique due à une carence en folate, comme dans le cas de la sprue, d'une carence alimentaire ou d'anémies mégaloblastiques pendant la grossesse et l'enfance ■ Prétraitement, suivi de l'administration de 5-FU dans le traitement du cancer colorectal.

MÉCANISME D'ACTION

Forme réduite de l'acide folique servant de cofacteur à la synthèse de l'ADN et de l'ARN. ***Effets thérapeutiques:*** Inversion des effets toxiques des antagonistes de l'acide folique ■ Renversement des effets de la carence en acide folique ■ Augmentation de la cytotoxicité des fluoropyrimidines (5-FU).

PHARMACOCINÉTIQUE

Absorption: 38 % (PO). La biodisponibilité diminue à mesure que les doses augmentent. L'absorption atteint un point de saturation aux doses de plus de 25 mg.
Distribution: Tout l'organisme, avec concentration dans le SNC et le foie.
Métabolisme et excrétion: Une importante fraction est transformée en dérivés tétrahydrofoliques dont le 5-méthyltétrahydrofolate, forme sous laquelle le médicament est mis en réserve dans l'organisme en quantités importantes.

Demi-vie: *5-méthyltétrahydrofolate* – 3,5 heures.

Profil temps-action

	DÉBUT D'ACTION	PIC	DURÉE
PO	20 - 30 min	1,7 h	3 - 6 h
IM	10 - 20 min	0,7 h	3 - 6 h
IV	< 5 min	inconnu	3 - 6 h

CONTRE-INDICATIONS, PRÉCAUTIONS ET MISES EN GARDE

Contre-indications: Hypersensibilité ■ Anémie non diagnostiquée (la leucovorine calcique peut masquer l'évolution de l'anémie pernicieuse) ■ **PÉD.**: Nourrissons (ne pas leur administrer les préparations renfermant de l'alcool benzylique).

Précautions et mises en garde: **OBST.**: Grossesse et allaitement (bien que l'innocuité du médicament n'ait pas été établie, il existe des antécédents d'utilisation sans danger dans le traitement de l'anémie mégaloblastique pendant la grossesse) ■ ADMINISTRATION CONCOMITANTE DE FORTES DOSES DE MÉTHOTREXATE: IL FAUT SYNCHRONISER PARFAITEMENT LES DOSES ET CONNAÎTRE LES CONCENTRATIONS DE MÉTHOTREXATE ■ Ascite ■ Insuffisance rénale ■ Déshydratation ■ Épanchement pleural ■ pH urinaire < 7.

RÉACTIONS INDÉSIRABLES ET EFFETS SECONDAIRES

Hémat.: thrombocytose (méthotrexate par voie intra-artérielle seulement).

Divers: réactions allergiques (rash, urticaire, respiration sifflante), pyrexie.

INTERACTIONS

Médicament-médicament: La leucovorine calcique peut réduire l'effet anticonvulsivant des **barbituriques**, de la **phénytoïne** ou de la **primidone** ■ L'administration concomitante de **triméthoprime/sulfaméthoxazole** peut réduire l'effet antibiotique et entraîner des résultats médiocres dans le traitement de la pneumonie à *Pneumocystis carinii* chez les patients infectés par le VIH ■ La leucovorine calcique peut intensifier les effets thérapeutiques et la toxicité du **fluorouracile**; l'association de ces agents peut être utile.

VOIES D'ADMINISTRATION ET POSOLOGIE

Élimination du méthotrexate ou surdosage accidentel

La leucovorine doit être administrée aussitôt que possible, dans les 24 heures suivant l'administration du méthotrexate.

- **PO, IM, IV (adultes et enfants)**: *Élimination normale du méthotrexate* – 10 mg/m², toutes les 6 heures (par voie IV ou IM), jusqu'à ce que la concentration de méthotrexate soit inférieure à 5×10^{-8} M. Si la créatine sérique est de 50 % supérieure aux valeurs initiales après 24 heures ou si les concentrations de méthotrexate sont supérieures à 5×10^{-6} M après 24 heures, ou supérieures à 9×10^{-7} M après 48 heures, majorer la dose de leucovorine jusqu'à concurrence de 100 mg/m², à administrer par voie IV toutes les 3 heures, jusqu'à l'atteinte de concentrations de méthotrexate inférieures à 5×10^{-8} M.

Cancer colorectal avancé

- **IV (adultes)**: 200 mg/m², suivis de 370 mg/m² de 5-fluorouracile, pendant 5 jours consécutifs, toutes les 4 semaines.

Anémie mégaloblastique

- **PO, IM, IV (adultes et enfants)**: Jusqu'à 1 mg par jour. Une dose supérieure à 1 mg/jour ne s'avère pas plus efficace.

PRÉSENTATION (version générique disponible)

Comprimés: 5 mg[Pr] ■ **Solution pour injection**: fioles de 50 mg[Pr], de 300 mg[Pr] et de 500 mg[Pr] ■ **Solution pour injection**: 10 mg/mL, en fioles de 50 mg[Pr] et de 500 mg[Pr].

SOINS INFIRMIERS

ÉVALUATION DE LA SITUATION

- Suivre de près l'apparition des nausées et des vomissements attribuables au traitement par le méthotrexate ou au surdosage par un inhibiteur de l'acide folique (pyriméthamine et triméthoprime). Il pourrait s'avérer nécessaire d'administrer la leucovorine par voie parentérale pour s'assurer que le patient reçoit la dose appropriée.
- Suivre de près l'apparition d'une réaction allergique: rash, urticaire, respiration sifflante. Prévenir le médecin si ces symptômes se manifestent.

Anémie mégaloblastique: Déterminer le degré de faiblesse et de fatigue.

Tests de laboratoire:

- *Élimination du méthotrexate ou surdosage accidentel* – Noter les concentrations sériques de méthotrexate afin de déterminer la dose à administrer et l'efficacité du traitement. Les concentrations de leucovorine calcique devraient être égales ou supérieures à celles du méthotrexate. Le traitement doit se poursuivre jusqu'à ce que les concentrations sériques de méthotrexate soient inférieures à 5×10^{-8} M.

- Noter la clairance de la créatinine et la concentration sérique de créatinine avant l'administration du médicament et toutes les 24 heures, tout au long du traitement, afin de déceler les effets toxiques du méthotrexate. Une élévation de plus de 50 %, après 24 heures, par rapport à la concentration antérieure au traitement, est associée à une toxicité rénale grave.
- Obtenir le pH de l'urine, toutes les 6 heures, pendant toute la durée du traitement. Le pH doit demeurer > 7 pour qu'on puisse diminuer les effets néphrotoxiques des doses élevées de méthotrexate. Le médecin peut prescrire du bicarbonate de sodium ou de l'acétazolamide pour alcaliniser l'urine.
- *Anémie mégaloblastique* – Noter les concentrations plasmatiques d'acide folique, l'hémoglobine, l'hématocrite et le nombre de réticulocytes avant le traitement et à intervalles réguliers pendant toute sa durée.

DIAGNOSTICS INFIRMIERS POSSIBLES

- Risque d'accident (Indications).
- Alimentation déficiente (Indications).
- Connaissances insuffisantes sur le traitement médicamenteux (Enseignement au patient et à ses proches).

INTERVENTIONS INFIRMIÈRES

- NE PAS CONFONDRE L'ACIDE FOLINIQUE (LEUCOVORINE CALCIQUE) AVEC L'ACIDE FOLIQUE. NE PAS CONFONDRE L'ACIDE FOLINIQUE AVEC LEUKERAN (CHLORAMBUCIL) OU PROLEUKIN (ALDESLEUKINE).
- S'assurer que la leucovorine calcique se trouve à portée de la main avant l'administration de fortes doses de méthotrexate. ADMINISTRER LA LEUCOVORINE DANS LES 24 HEURES SUIVANT L'ADMINISTRATION DU MÉTHOTREXATE.
- Administrer l'agent dès que possible après la prise de doses toxiques de l'inhibiteur de l'acide folique (pyriméthamine et triméthoprime), puisque l'efficacité du médicament commence à s'atténuer 1 heure après le surdosage.

IM: Administrer dans le deltoïde plutôt que dans le muscle fessier.

IV directe: Administrer par voie parentérale chez les patients présentant une toxicité gastro-intestinale, accompagnée de nausées et de vomissements, ou lorsque la dose est supérieure à 25 mg.

Vitesse d'administration: Ne pas administrer à un débit supérieur à 160 mg/min (16 mL de solution à 10 mg/mL/min).

Perfusion intermittente: La leucovorine peut être diluée dans 100 à 500 mL de solution de D%5E, de D%10E, de NaCl 0,9 %, de solution de Ringer ou de solution de lactate de Ringer. La solution est stable pendant 24 heures. Consulter les recommandations du fabricant avant de diluer la préparation.

Compatibilité (tubulure en Y): amifostine ■ aztréonam ■ bléomycine ■ céfépime ■ cisplatine ■ cyclophosphamide ■ doxorubicine ■ filgrastim ■ fluconazole ■ fluorouracile ■ furosémide ■ héparine ■ méthotrexate ■ métoclopramide ■ mitomycine ■ pipéracilline/tazobactame ■ tacrolimus ■ téniposide ■ thiotépa ■ vinblastine ■ vincristine.

Incompatibilité (tubulure en Y): dropéridol ■ foscarnet ■ sodium, bicarbonate de.

ENSEIGNEMENT AU PATIENT ET À SES PROCHES

- Expliquer au patient le but du traitement. Insister sur le fait qu'il est primordial de respecter rigoureusement la posologie recommandée. Conseiller au patient de prévenir un professionnel de la santé s'il n'a pu prendre une dose.

Élimination du méthotrexate ou surdosage accidentel: Recommander au patient de boire au moins 3 000 mL de liquides par jour pendant le traitement, si son état le permet.

Carence en acide folique: Encourager le patient à consommer des aliments riches en acide folique (protéines d'origine animale, son, haricots secs et légumes à feuilles vertes).

VÉRIFICATION DE L'EFFICACITÉ THÉRAPEUTIQUE

L'efficacité du traitement peut être démontrée par: la résorption de la toxicité médullaire et gastro-intestinale en cas de surdosage par un inhibiteur de l'acide folique ■ une sensation de mieux-être et l'élévation de la production de normoblastes chez les patients souffrant d'anémie mégaloblastique.

LEUPROLIDE

Eligard, Lupron, Lupron Depot

CLASSIFICATION:

Antinéoplasique (hormone de synthèse), analogue de l'hormone de libération de la gonadotrophine

Grossesse – catégorie X

INDICATIONS

Solution pour injection ou préparation retard (Lupron ou Lupron depot): Traitement palliatif du cancer avancé de la prostate sensible aux hormones sexuelles (le leuprolide peut être administré en association avec le flutamide ou le bicalutamide) ■ Traitement de la puberté précoce d'origine centrale ■ Traitement de l'endométriose. **Préparation retard (Eligard)**: Traitement palliatif du cancer avancé de la prostate.

MÉCANISME D'ACTION

Analogue synthétique de l'hormone de libération de la gonadotrophine (LH-RH) ■ Initialement, élévation transitoire des concentrations de stéroïdes gonadiques (testostérone chez l'homme et œstradiol chez la femme); toutefois, ces concentrations diminuent lors de l'administration continue du médicament ■ Réduction des concentrations de gonadotrophine, de testostérone et d'œstradiol. ***Effets thérapeutiques:*** Diminution des concentrations de testostérone et, par conséquent, ralentissement de la propagation du cancer de la prostate ■ Diminution de la douleur et des lésions associées à l'endométriose ■ Ralentissement de la croissance des fibromes ■ Retard de la puberté.

PHARMACOCINÉTIQUE

L

Absorption: Rapide et presque complète (SC). Absorption plus lente de la préparation retard (IM ou SC).
Distribution: Inconnue.
Métabolisme et excrétion: Inconnus.
Demi-vie: 3 heures.

Profil temps-action
(diminution des concentrations hormonales [testostérone, œstradiol])

	DÉBUT D'ACTION†	PIC‡	DURÉE§
SC	durant la 1re semaine	2 - 4 semaines	4 - 12 semaines
IM	durant la 1re semaine	2 - 4 semaines	4 - 12 semaines
IM - retard	durant la 1re semaine	2 - 4 semaines	4 - 12 semaines

† Élévation passagère des concentrations de testostérone et d'œstradiol.
‡ Baisse maximale des concentrations de testostérone et d'œstradiol.
§ Rétablissement de la fonction normale des glandes pituitaires et des gonades; en présence d'aménorrhée, le retour des règles survient normalement dans les 60 à 90 jours après la fin du traitement.

CONTRE-INDICATIONS, PRÉCAUTIONS ET MISES EN GARDE

Contre-indications: Intolérance ou hypersensibilité aux analogues synthétiques de la LH-RH ■ Grossesse ou allaitement ■ Saignement vaginal anormal dont la cause n'a pas été diagnostiquée.
Précautions et mises en garde: Hypersensibilité à l'alcool benzylique (induration et érythème au point d'injection SC) ■ Uropathie obstructive ■ Métastases vertébrales.

RÉACTIONS INDÉSIRABLES ET EFFETS SECONDAIRES

SNC: étourdissements, céphalées, syncope; *préparation retard* – somnolence, troubles de la personnalité; *SC* – anxiété, vision trouble, léthargie, troubles de la mémoire, sautes d'humeur.
ORLO: vision trouble; *SC* – troubles de l'ouïe.
Resp.: hémoptysie; *préparation retard* – épistaxis, nodules dans la gorge; *SC* – toux, frottement pleural, fibrose pulmonaire; infiltrat pulmonaire.
CV: INFARCTUS DU MYOCARDE, EMBOLIE PULMONAIRE, angine, arythmies; *préparation retard* – vasodilatation; *SC* – accidents ischémiques transitoires, AVC.
GI: anorexie, diarrhée, dysphagie, nausées, vomissements; *préparation retard* – gingivite; *SC* – HÉMORRAGIE GASTRO-INTESTINALE, dysfonctionnement hépatique, ulcère gastroduodénal, polypes rectaux, altération du goût.
GU: diminution de la taille des testicules, dysurie, incontinence, douleurs aux testicules; *préparation retard* – troubles cervicaux; *SC* – spasme de la vessie, œdème pénien, douleurs prostatiques, obstruction urinaire.
Tég.: *préparation retard* – pousse des poils, rash; *SC* – peau sèche, alopécie, pigmentation, cancer de la peau, lésions cutanées.
End.: œdème mammaire, sensibilité mammaire, diabète.
HÉ: hypercalcémie, œdème des membres inférieurs.
Locaux: brûlures, démangeaisons, œdème au point d'injection.
Métab.: *préparation retard* – hyperuricémie.
Loc.: fibromyalgie, intensification transitoire de la douleur osseuse (cancer de la prostate seulement); *SC* – spondylarthrite ankylosante, douleurs articulaires, fibrose pelvienne, douleur à l'os temporal.
SN: *SC* – neuropathie périphérique.
Divers: rougeurs du visage, frissons, baisse de la libido, fièvre; *préparation retard* – odeurs corporelles, épistaxis.

INTERACTIONS

Médicament-médicament: Effets antinéoplasiques additifs lors de l'administration concomitante d'**agents antiandrogènes (bicalutamide, flutamide)**.

VOIES D'ADMINISTRATION ET POSOLOGIE

Cancer de la prostate

- **SC (adultes)**: 1 mg par jour (Lupron); 7,5 mg, 1 fois par mois, ou 22,5 mg, tous les 3 mois, ou 30 mg, tous les 4 mois, ou 45 mg, tous les 6 mois, sous forme d'injection retard (Eligard).
- **IM (adultes)**: 7,5 mg, 1 fois par mois, ou 22,5 mg, tous les 3 mois, ou 30 mg, tous les 4 mois, sous forme d'injection retard (Lupron Depot).

Endométriose

- **IM (adultes)**: 3,75 mg, 1 fois par mois, ou 11,25 mg, tous les 3 mois, sous forme d'injection retard (Lupron Depot).

Puberté précoce d'origine centrale

Dans le cas de l'administration par voie IM, on peut majorer la dose de 3,75 mg, toutes les 4 semaines, selon les besoins; d'autres adaptations posologiques peuvent s'avérer nécessaires.

- **SC (enfants)**: 50 µg/kg/jour; on peut augmenter la dose de 10 µg/kg/jour, selon les besoins. Dose maximale: 100 µg/kg par jour (Lupron).
- **IM (enfants > 37,5 kg)**: 15 mg, toutes les 4 semaines (Lupron Depot).
- **IM (enfants de 25 à 37,5 kg)**: 11,25 mg, toutes les 4 semaines (Lupron Depot).
- **IM (enfants < 25 kg)**: 7,5 mg, toutes les 4 semaines (Lupron Depot).

PRÉSENTATION

Solution pour injection (Lupron): 5 mg/mL, en fioles de 2,8 mL^Pr ■ **Suspension à effet prolongé pendant 1 mois**: seringues préremplies, à double compartiment, de 3,75 mg^Pr et de 7,5 mg^Pr ■ **Matrice polymérique pour injection SC à effet prolongé pendant 1 mois**: 2 seringues préremplies de 7,5 mg^Pr, à mélanger avant l'administration ■ **Suspension à effet prolongé pendant 3 mois**: seringues préremplies, à double compartiment, de 11,25 mg^Pr et de 22,5 mg^Pr ■ **Matrice polymérique pour injection SC à effet prolongé pendant 3 mois**: 2 seringues préremplies de 22,5 mg^Pr, à mélanger avant l'administration ■ **Suspension à effet prolongé pendant 4 mois**: seringues préremplies, à double compartiment, de 30 mg^Pr ■ **Matrice polymérique pour injection SC à effet prolongé pendant 4 mois**: 2 seringues préremplies de 30 mg^Pr, à mélanger avant l'administration ■ **Matrice polymérique pour injection SC à effet prolongé pendant 6 mois**: 2 seringues préremplies de 45 mg^Pr, à mélanger avant l'administration.

SOINS INFIRMIERS

ÉVALUATION DE LA SITUATION

Cancer de la prostate:

- Rester à l'affût de l'intensification de la douleur osseuse, particulièrement au cours des quelques premières semaines de traitement. Chez le patient présentant des métastases aux vertèbres, suivre de près l'intensification des douleurs lombaires et la diminution de la fonction sensorimotrice.
- Effectuer le bilan des ingesta et des excreta. Chez le patient présentant une obstruction urinaire, suivre de près, également, la distension de la vessie au cours du traitement initial.

Endométriose: Suivre de près la douleur endométriale avant le début du traitement et à intervalles réguliers pendant toute sa durée.

Puberté précoce d'origine centrale:

- Avant le traitement, ce diagnostic doit être confirmé par l'apparition des caractéristiques sexuelles secondaires chez les filles de moins de 8 ans et les garçons de moins de 9 ans; il faut effectuer un examen physique et endocrinien complet, incluant la mesure de la taille et du poids, et une radiographie des mains et des poignets, établir les concentrations totales des stéroïdes sexuels (œstradiol ou testostérone), les concentrations d'hormone corticosurrénale et de gonadotrophine chorionique humaine de type bêta, et effectuer un test de stimulation de la gonadolibérine et une tomodensitométrie de la tête. Il faut vérifier ces paramètres après 1 mois ou 2 et tous les 6 à 12 mois pendant toute la durée du traitement.
- Suivre de près l'apparition des signes de puberté précoce (règles, développement des seins, croissance des testicules) à intervalles réguliers pendant toute la durée du traitement. Il faut majorer la dose jusqu'à l'arrêt de l'évolution de la maladie selon des preuves cliniques ou des résultats des tests de laboratoire. Il faut songer à arrêter le traitement avant l'âge de 11 ans chez les filles et de 12 ans chez les garçons.

Tests de laboratoire:

- Le leuprolide entraîne, au départ, l'élévation des concentrations d'hormone lutéinisante (LH) et folliculostimulante (FSH), suivie d'une baisse de ces concentrations. Chez les hommes, ce phénomène entraîne l'atteinte de concentrations de testostérone équivalentes à celle qu'on trouve à la suite d'une castration, de 2 à 4 semaines après l'élévation initiale des concentrations.
- Suivre de près les concentrations de testostérone, de phosphatase acide prostatique et d'APS pour évaluer la réponse au traitement. On peut noter une élévation passagère de ces concentrations au cours du premier mois de traitement du cancer de la prostate.
- Le leuprolide peut entraîner l'élévation des concentrations d'urée, de calcium sérique, d'acide urique, de LDH, de phosphatase alcaline et d'AST, et peut induire l'hypoprotéinémie, l'hyperglycémie, l'hyperlipidémie et l'hyperphosphatémie. Il peut aussi élever le nombre de globules blancs et prolonger le temps de prothrombine et de céphaline. Il peut également réduire le nombre de plaquettes et abaisser les concentrations sériques de potassium.

DIAGNOSTICS INFIRMIERS POSSIBLES

- Dysfonctionnement sexuel (Effets secondaires).

L

- Connaissances insuffisantes sur le traitement médicamenteux (Enseignement au patient et à ses proches).

INTERVENTIONS INFIRMIÈRES

- Utiliser la seringue fournie par le fabricant. Assurer la rotation des points d'injection.
- Le leuprolide retard est réservé à l'administration IM (Lupron Depot) ou SC (Eligard).
- *Préparation retard Lupron Depot*: Visser le piston blanc sur le disque de caoutchouc à l'extrémité de la seringue, jusqu'à ce que le disque commence à tourner. Retirer et jeter la languette antimanipulation qui se trouve à la base de l'aiguille. Bien serrer le mécanisme de verrouillage Luer, en tournant l'aiguille dans le sens des aiguilles d'une montre, jusqu'à ce qu'elle ne bouge plus. Éviter de trop serrer. La seringue étant en position verticale, faire passer le solvant dans le compartiment se trouvant près de l'aiguille en poussant lentement le piston jusqu'à ce que le premier disque se trouve au niveau de la ligne bleue, au milieu du corps de la seringue. Agiter doucement la seringue pour bien mélanger les particules et pour obtenir une suspension homogène. La suspension aura une consistance laiteuse. Si les microsphères (particules) adhèrent au disque, frapper la seringue du doigt. Enlever ensuite la gaine de l'aiguille et pousser le piston pour expulser l'air de la seringue. Administrer enfin l'injection IM selon la méthode habituelle. Comme la suspension se dépose très rapidement après la reconstitution, il est fortement recommandé d'administrer la préparation dès qu'elle a été reconstituée. Agiter la seringue de nouveau si les particules se déposent. Conserver à la température ambiante; bien que la solution soit stable pendant 24 heures après la reconstitution, il faut la jeter si elle n'est pas administrée immédiatement étant donné qu'elle ne renferme aucun agent de conservation.
- *Préparation retard Eligard*: Laisser le produit atteindre la température de la pièce. Sortir les seringues de leur pochette, enlever les embouts et fixer les seringues l'une à l'autre. Faire passer la préparation d'une seringue dans l'autre et vice versa, jusqu'à ce que la solution devienne homogène (ou qu'une suspension se forme, dans le cas de la dose de 45 mg). Détacher les seringues et fixer l'aiguille stérile à la seringue mâle pour administrer l'agent par voie SC dans un endroit où le tissu sous-cutané est suffisant, mou ou lâche. Une fois le mélange fait, le produit doit être administré dans les 30 minutes.

ENSEIGNEMENT AU PATIENT ET À SES PROCHES

Prévenir le patient que le médicament peut entraîner des rougeurs du visage. Lui recommander de communiquer avec un professionnel de la santé si celles-ci deviennent gênantes.

Cancer de la prostate:

- Montrer au patient et à ses proches comment administrer les injections. Lire avec eux les renseignements destinés aux patients, imprimés sur le dépliant fourni avec la trousse d'administration du leuprolide.
- Conseiller au patient de respecter rigoureusement la posologie recommandée. S'il n'a pas pu s'administrer le médicament au moment habituel, il doit le faire dès que possible, sauf s'il se rend compte de l'oubli le lendemain seulement (préparation SC, administrée 1 fois par jour).
- Prévenir le patient que les douleurs osseuses peuvent s'intensifier au début du traitement, mais qu'elles disparaîtront après quelque temps. Lui conseiller de demander à un professionnel de la santé s'il peut recourir à un analgésique pour soulager la douleur.
- Recommander au patient de prévenir immédiatement un professionnel de la santé en cas de difficultés de miction, de faiblesse ou d'engourdissements.

Endométriose: Conseiller à la patiente d'utiliser pendant le traitement une autre méthode contraceptive que les contraceptifs oraux. La prévenir que l'aménorrhée est prévisible, mais qu'on ne peut la considérer comme une garantie de contraception.

Puberté précoce d'origine centrale:

- Montrer au patient et à ses parents comment administrer les injections SC. Insister sur le fait qu'il est important d'administrer le médicament au même moment chaque jour. Assurer la rotation des points d'injection à intervalles réguliers.
- Expliquer au patient et à ses parents que si l'injection n'est pas administrée quotidiennement, le processus pubertaire risque d'être réactivé (préparation SC, administrée 1 fois par jour).
- Prévenir la patiente et ses parents qu'au cours des 2 premiers mois de traitement, elle peut noter un léger flux menstruel ou des saignotements. Si ce phénomène se poursuit pendant plus de 2 mois, il faut en informer un professionnel de la santé.
- Recommander au patient et à ses parents de prévenir un professionnel de la santé immédiatement en cas d'irritation au point d'injection ou de signes ou de symptômes inhabituels.

VÉRIFICATION DE L'EFFICACITÉ THÉRAPEUTIQUE

L'efficacité du traitement peut être démontrée par: le ralentissement de la propagation du cancer de la prostate ■ la diminution des lésions et de la douleur associées à l'endométriose ■ la résolution des signes de puberté précoce d'origine centrale.

LÉVÉTIRACÉTAM

Apo-Levetiracetam, Co-Levetiracetam, Keppra

CLASSIFICATION:

Anticonvulsivant (pyrrolidine)

Grossesse – catégorie C

INDICATIONS

Traitement d'appoint chez les patients épileptiques dont les crises ne sont pas convenablement maîtrisées par les traitements classiques.

MÉCANISME D'ACTION

Le mécanisme d'action exact du lévétiracétam n'a pas encore été complètement élucidé, mais il semble qu'il diffère de celui des antiépileptiques d'usage courant. Des études *in vitro* ont révélé que le médicament n'entraîne pas de déplacement significatif des ligands des sites récepteurs, comme les benzodiazépines, le GABA, la glycine ou le NMDA. De plus, il ne module pas les canaux sodiques qui dépendent du voltage ni les canaux calciques de type T, et n'induit pas la modulation classique du système GABAergique. ***Effets thérapeutiques:*** Diminution de l'activité convulsivante.

PHARMACOCINÉTIQUE

Absorption: 100 % (PO).

Distribution: Le volume de distribution s'approche du volume d'eau intracellulaire et extracellulaire. L'agent et ses métabolites traversent la barrière placentaire et le médicament passe dans le lait maternel.

Liaison aux protéines: < 10 %.

Métabolisme et excrétion: Métabolisme faible. L'hydrolyse enzymatique du groupe carboxamide constitue la principale voie métabolique du médicament (24 % de la dose). Cette biotransformation n'est pas modifiée par l'action du cytochrome P450 hépatique. Excrétion majoritairement rénale (66 % sous forme inchangée). Les métabolites n'exercent pas d'activité pharmacodynamique connue et sont excrétés par les reins.

Demi-vie: De 6 à 8 heures; plus longue chez les insuffisants rénaux et les personnes âgées, principalement en raison d'une clairance rénale réduite.

Profil temps-action

	DÉBUT D'ACTION	PIC	DURÉE
PO	inconnu	1,3 h†	inconnue

† Le pic plasmatique peut passer à 1,5 h en cas de prise concomitante de nourriture.

CONTRE-INDICATIONS, PRÉCAUTIONS ET MISES EN GARDE

Contre-indications: Hypersensibilité au lévétiracétam ou à toute substance inactive entrant dans la composition des comprimés.

Précautions et mises en garde: Anomalies hématologiques ■ Insuffisance rénale ■ **OBST., ALLAITEMENT, PÉD. (< 18 ANS):** L'innocuité et l'efficacité du médicament n'ont pas été établies ■ **GÉR.:** En raison du risque d'altération de la fonction rénale chez les personnes âgées, il peut s'avérer nécessaire de diminuer la dose.

RÉACTIONS INDÉSIRABLES ET EFFETS SECONDAIRES

SNC: amnésie, asthénie (fatigue), étourdissements, somnolence, symptômes comportementaux ou psychiatriques non psychotiques (agitation, réactions antisociales, anxiété, apathie, dépersonnalisation, dépression, labilité émotionnelle, euphorie, hostilité, nervosité, névrose, troubles de la personnalité et tentatives de suicide) et psychotiques (hallucinations, réactions paranoïdes, psychose et dépression psychotique), troubles de la coordination (ataxie, démarche anormale, incoordination), troubles de la pensée, vertiges.

ORLO: infection des voies respiratoires supérieures (pharyngite, rhinite, sinusite), rhume banal.

GI: problèmes dentaires.

Hémat.: ecchymoses, TROUBLES SANGUINS ET LYMPHATIQUES (LEUCOPÉNIE, NEUTROPÉNIE, PANCYTOPÉNIE ET THROMBOPÉNIE).

INTERACTIONS

Médicament-médicament: Aucune interaction pharmacocinétique cliniquement significative.

VOIES D'ADMINISTRATION ET POSOLOGIE

- **PO (adultes):** Initialement, 500 mg, 2 fois par jour; on peut augmenter la dose par paliers de 1 000 mg par jour, toutes les 2 semaines, selon la réponse clinique du patient et sa tolérance. Ne pas dépasser une dose de 3 000 mg par jour, soit 1 500 mg, 2 fois par jour.

INSUFFISANCE HÉPATIQUE

- **PO (ADULTES):** AUCUNE MODIFICATION N'EST NÉCESSAIRE EN PRÉSENCE D'UNE INSUFFISANCE HÉPATIQUE

DE LÉGÈRE À MODÉRÉE. EN PRÉSENCE D'INSUFFISANCE HÉPATIQUE GRAVE, LA CLAIRANCE DE LA CRÉATININE PEUT DONNER LIEU À UNE SOUS-ESTIMATION DE L'INSUFFISANCE RÉNALE. PAR CONSÉQUENT, ON RECOMMANDE UNE RÉDUCTION DE 50 % DE LA DOSE D'ENTRETIEN QUOTIDIENNE, LORSQUE LA CL_{CR} EST < 70 mL/MIN.

INSUFFISANCE RÉNALE

- **PO (ADULTES)**: *CL_{CR} ≥ 80 mL/MIN* – COMME CI-DESSUS; *CL_{CR} DE 50 À 79 mL/MIN* – DE 500 À 1 000 mg, 2 FOIS PAR JOUR; *CL_{CR} DE 30 À 49 mL/MIN* – DE 250 À 750 mg, 2 FOIS PAR JOUR; *CL_{CR} < 30 mL/MIN* – DE 250 À 500 mg, 2 FOIS PAR JOUR. *INSUFFISANCE TERMINALE, PATIENTS DIALYSÉS* – DE 500 À 1 000 mg PAR JOUR; ON RECOMMANDE UNE DOSE SUPPLÉMENTAIRE DE 250 À 500 mg APRÈS LA DIALYSE.

PRÉSENTATION

Comprimés: 250 mg[Pr], 500 mg[Pr], 750 mg[Pr].

SOINS INFIRMIERS

ÉVALUATION DE LA SITUATION

- Évaluer le siège, la durée, la fréquence et les caractéristiques des crises convulsives. On peut surveiller à intervalles réguliers l'ÉEG pendant toute la durée du traitement.
- SUIVRE DE PRÈS LES SIGNES D'ANOMALIES HÉMATOLOGIQUES: MAUX DE GORGE, FIÈVRE, LÉTHARGIE, FAIBLESSE, MALAISES, SYMPTÔMES PSEUDOGRIPPAUX, SAIGNEMENTS OU ECCHYMOSES INHABITUELS, SAIGNEMENT DU NEZ OU PÉTÉCHIES.
- Suivre de près les effets secondaires sur le SNC, tels l'amnésie, l'asthénie (fatigue), les étourdissements, la somnolence, les symptômes comportementaux ou psychiatriques non psychotiques (agitation, réactions antisociales, anxiété, apathie, dépersonnalisation, dépression, labilité émotionnelle, euphorie, hostilité, nervosité, névrose, troubles de la personnalité et tentatives de suicide) et psychotiques (hallucinations, réactions paranoïdes, psychose et dépression psychotique), les troubles de la coordination (ataxie, démarche anormale, incoordination), les troubles de la pensée, les vertiges. Ces effets sont plus importants durant les 4 premières semaines de traitement.

DIAGNOSTICS INFIRMIERS POSSIBLES

- Risque d'accident (Indications, Effets secondaires).
- Connaissances insuffisantes sur le traitement médicamenteux (Enseignement au patient et à ses proches).
- Non-observance du traitement médicamenteux (Enseignement au patient et à ses proches).

INTERVENTIONS INFIRMIÈRES

- NE PAS CONFONDRE KEPPRA AVEC KALETRA (LOPINAVIR/RITONAVIR).
- Prendre les mesures qui s'imposent en cas de crise convulsive.
- Administrer le lévétiracétam avec ou sans aliments.
- Au moment du sevrage, il est recommandé de réduire la dose graduellement.

ENSEIGNEMENT AU PATIENT ET À SES PROCHES

- Conseiller au patient de respecter rigoureusement la posologie recommandée, de ne pas sauter de dose et de ne pas remplacer une dose manquée par une double dose.
- Prévenir le patient qui suit un traitement prolongé qu'il ne doit pas arrêter de prendre le médicament sans avoir consulté un professionnel de la santé au préalable. L'arrêt brusque du traitement peut déclencher des convulsions ou l'état de mal épileptique.
- Prévenir le patient que le lévétiracétam peut provoquer de la somnolence, de la fatigue et des troubles de la coordination. Ces effets semblent survenir surtout au cours des 4 premières semaines de traitement, mais disparaissaient habituellement même si on le poursuit. Conseiller au patient de ne pas conduire et d'éviter les activités qui exigent sa vigilance jusqu'à ce qu'on ait la certitude que le médicament n'entraîne pas ces effets chez lui. Recommander au patient de ne reprendre la conduite automobile que si le médecin l'autorise à le faire, après s'être assuré que les crises ont été maîtrisées.
- Conseiller au patient de ne pas boire d'alcool et de ne pas prendre d'autres dépresseurs du SNC en même temps que ce médicament.
- Conseiller au patient de porter sur lui en tout temps une pièce d'identité où sont inscrits son trouble de santé et son traitement médicamenteux.
- Conseiller au patient d'informer rapidement un professionnel de la santé de l'apparition des symptômes suivants: maux de gorge, fièvre, léthargie, faiblesse, malaises, symptômes pseudogrippaux, saignements ou ecchymoses inhabituels, saignement du nez ou pétéchies.
- Recommander au patient qui doit suivre un traitement ou subir une intervention chirurgicale de prévenir le professionnel de la santé qu'il suit un traitement par ce médicament.
- Recommander à la patiente qui prend un contraceptif oral de prêter attention à tout saignement ou saignotement vaginal anormal et, le cas échéant, de les signaler à un professionnel de la santé. Demander à la patiente de prévenir un professionnel de la

santé si elle pense être enceinte ou désire le devenir ou, encore, si elle allaite.

- Insister sur l'importance des examens médicaux réguliers permettant d'évaluer l'efficacité du traitement et les effets secondaires.

VÉRIFICATION DE L'EFFICACITÉ THÉRAPEUTIQUE

L'efficacité du traitement peut être démontrée par: la diminution ou l'arrêt des crises convulsives.

LÉVODOPA

Ce médicament n'est pas commercialisé au Canada.

BENSÉRAZIDE/LÉVODOPA

Prolopa

CARBIDOPA/LÉVODOPA

Apo-Levocarb, Apo-Levocarb CR, Dom-Levocarbidopa, Novo-Levocarbidopa, Nu-Levocarb, Sinemet, Sinemet CR

CLASSIFICATION:

Antiparkinsoniens (agonistes de la dopamine)

Grossesse – catégories inconnue (bensérazide/lévodopa) et C (carbidopa/lévodopa)

INDICATIONS

Traitement de la maladie de Parkinson (déconseillé en cas de parkinsonisme d'origine médicamenteuse).

MÉCANISME D'ACTION

La lévodopa est transformée en dopamine dans le SNC où elle sert de neurotransmetteur ■ La carbidopa et le bensérazide, des inhibiteurs de la décarboxylase, empêchent le métabolisme périphérique de la lévodopa. ***Effets thérapeutiques:*** Soulagement des tremblements et de la rigidité qui caractérisent le syndrome parkinsonien.

PHARMACOCINÉTIQUE

Absorption: Bonne (PO).

Distribution: Tout l'organisme. *Lévodopa* – elle pénètre dans le SNC en faible concentration. *Carbidopa* – elle ne traverse pas la barrière hématoencéphalique, mais traverse la barrière placentaire. Les deux agents passent dans le lait maternel.

Métabolisme et excrétion: *Lévodopa* – métabolisée principalement par le tractus gastro-intestinal et le foie. *Carbidopa* – 30 % est excrété à l'état inchangé par les reins.

Demi-vie: *Lévodopa* – 1 heure. *Carbidopa* – de 1 à 2 heures.

Profil temps-action (effets antiparkinsoniens)

	DÉBUT D'ACTION	PIC	DURÉE
Carbidopa	inconnu	inconnu	5 – 24 h
Lévodopa	10 – 15 minutes	inconnu	5 – 24 h ou plus
Carbidopa/lévodopa à action prolongée	inconnu	2 h	12 h

CONTRE-INDICATIONS, PRÉCAUTIONS ET MISES EN GARDE

Contre-indications: Hypersensibilité ■ Glaucome à angle fermé ■ Traitement concomitant par un IMAO (prévoir 14 jours entre l'arrêt de l'administration de l'IMAO et le début de l'administration du médicament) ■ Patients chez qui les amines sympathomimétiques sont contre-indiquées ■ Mélanome malin ■ Lésions cutanées non diagnostiquées ■ **OBST.:** Grossesse ou femmes en âge de procréer qui n'emploient pas de méthode contraceptive adéquate (l'innocuité du médicament n'a pas été établie) ■ **ALLAITEMENT** ■ **PÉD.:** Enfants et jeunes adultes < 25 ans (bensérazide/lévodopa); enfants < 18 ans (carbidopa/lévodopa) ■ Patients en décompensation endocrinienne, rénale, hépatique, cardiovasculaire, hématologique ou pulmonaire (y compris l'asthme bronchique).

Précautions et mises en garde: Antécédents d'ulcère gastroduodénal ■ Antécédents de convulsions ■ Glaucome à angle ouvert ■ Maladies mentales avec une composante psychiatrique ■ Risque d'une réaction de type syndrome malin des neuroleptiques (caractérisé par l'élévation de la température, la rigidité musculaire, des changements de l'état de conscience et une instabilité autonome), en cas de diminution rapide de la dose ■ Risque de narcolepsie (celle-ci ne survient pas nécessairement en début de traitement; les patients devraient également être informés qu'un endormissement soudain peut survenir sans signes avant-coureurs).

RÉACTIONS INDÉSIRABLES ET EFFETS SECONDAIRES

SNC: <u>mouvements involontaires</u>, anxiété, étourdissements, hallucinations, perte de mémoire, problèmes psychiatriques.

ORLO: vision trouble, mydriase.

GI: <u>nausées</u>, <u>vomissements</u>, anorexie, sécheresse de la bouche (xérostomie), hépatotoxicité.

Tég.: mélanome.

Hémat.: anémie hémolytique, leucopénie.

Divers: urine ou sueur de couleur plus foncée.

INTERACTIONS

Médicament-médicament: L'administration simultanée d'**IMAO** peut déclencher une crise hypertensive ■ Risque accru d'arythmies lors de l'usage concomitant d'**anesthésiques à base d'hydrocarbures destinés à l'inhalation** (particulièrement l'**halothane**; si cela est possible, arrêter le traitement de 6 à 8 heures avant l'anesthésie) ■ Les **phénothiazines**, l'**halopéridol**, les **opioïdes**, la **papavérine**, la **phénytoïne** et la **réserpine** peuvent contrecarrer l'effet de la lévodopa ■ Les doses élevées de **pyroxidine** peuvent renverser les effets de la lévodopa ■ L'administration concomitante de **méthyldopa** peut entraver l'efficacité de la lévodopa et accroître le risque d'effets secondaires sur le SNC ■ L'administration concomitante de **sympathomimétiques** (p. ex., l'**adrénaline**, la **noradrénaline** ou l'**isoprotérénol**, qui stimulent le système nerveux sympathique) devrait être évitée, car la lévodopa risque de potentialiser les effets de ces médicaments ■ Les **suppléments de fer** diminuent l'absorption de la lévodopa ■ Le **métoclopramide** augmente l'absorption de la lévodopa et peut également avoir des effets délétères sur le traitement par cet agent, en raison de ses propriétés antagonistes sur les récepteurs dopaminergiques ■ L'**isoniazide** peut réduire les effets thérapeutiques de la lévodopa ■ L'administration simultanée d'**antihypertenseurs** peut entraîner des effets hypotenseurs additifs ■ L'usage simultané d'**anticholinergiques** peut réduire l'absorption de la lévodopa ■ Risque accru de réactions indésirables lors de l'usage concomitant de **sélégine** ou de **cocaïne**.

Médicament-produits naturels: Le **kava** peut diminuer l'efficacité de la lévodopa.

Médicament-aliments: Les aliments riches en **pyridoxine** peuvent renverser l'effet de la lévodopa.

VOIES D'ADMINISTRATION ET POSOLOGIE

Lévodopa

Ce médicament n'est pas commercialisé au Canada.

Carbidopa/lévodopa

Les comprimés renferment 10/100, 25/100 ou 25/250 mg de carbidopa et de lévodopa, respectivement.

- **PO (adultes)**: 25 mg de carbidopa/100 mg de lévodopa, 3 fois par jour; on peut augmenter cette dose tous les 3 jours, jusqu'à l'obtention de l'effet souhaité. La dose maximale de lévodopa est de 1 500 mg/jour. La dose quotidienne devrait être fractionnée en 4 à 6 doses.

Carbidopa/lévodopa à libération prolongée

Les comprimés à libération prolongée renferment 25/100 ou 50/200 mg de carbidopa et de lévodopa, respectivement.

- **PO (adultes)**: Initialement, 25 mg de carbidopa/100 mg de lévodopa, 2 fois par jour (à un intervalle d'au moins 6 heures). Dose quotidienne initiale maximale: 600 mg de lévodopa. *Substitution à un traitement standard par la carbidopa/lévodopa* – amorcer le traitement par une dose de lévodopa d'au moins 10 % supérieure/jour (il peut s'avérer nécessaire d'administrer jusqu'à 30 % de plus), à des intervalles de 4 à 8 heures, lorsque le patient est éveillé. Espacer de 3 jours les adaptations posologiques; des doses plus élevées et des intervalles posologiques plus courts peuvent être nécessaires chez certains patients.

Bensérazide/lévodopa

Les capsules renferment 12,5/50, 25/100 ou 50/200 mg de bensérazide et de lévodopa, respectivement.

- **PO (adultes)**: 25 mg de bensérazide/100 mg de lévodopa, 1 ou 2 fois par jour. Majorer cette dose à raison de 1 capsule de cette teneur tous les 3 ou 4 jours, au besoin. La posologie optimale est de 4 à 8 capsules de 25 mg de bensérazide/100 mg lévodopa, en 4 à 6 doses.

PRÉSENTATION

- **Lévodopa**

  Ce médicament n'est pas commercialisé au Canada.
- **Carbidopa/lévodopa**

  Comprimés: 10 mg de carbidopa/100 mg de lévodopa[Pr], 25 mg de carbidopa/100 mg de lévodopa[Pr], 25 mg de carbidopa/250 mg de lévodopa[Pr] ■ **Comprimés à action prolongée**: 25 mg de carbidopa/100 mg de lévodopa[Pr], 50 mg de carbidopa/200 mg de lévodopa[Pr].
- **Bensérazide/lévodopa**

  Capsules: 12,5 mg de bensérazide/50 mg de lévodopa[Pr], 25 mg de bensérazide/100 mg de lévodopa[Pr], 50 mg de bensérazide/200 mg de lévodopa[Pr].

SOINS INFIRMIERS

ÉVALUATION DE LA SITUATION

- Observer le patient pendant toute la durée du traitement à la recherche des symptômes parkinsoniens suivants: akinésie, rigidité, tremblements, mouvements d'émiettement, démarche traînante, faciès figé, mouvements de torsion, bouche ouverte laissant échapper la salive (sialorrhée). En raison des fluctuations de réponse (effet « on-off »), certains symptômes peuvent survenir ou s'améliorer brusquement.

- Mesurer la pression artérielle et le pouls à intervalles fréquents pendant la période d'adaptation posologique.

Tests de laboratoire:

- Le médicament peut entraîner des résultats faussement positifs au test de Coombs ainsi que des concentrations faussement élevées d'acide urique sérique et urinaire, de gonadotrophine sérique, de noradrénaline urinaire et de protéines urinaires.
- Le médicament peut entraîner des résultats faussement positifs au dosage de l'acétonurie par la méthode du bâtonnet.
- Les patients suivant un traitement prolongé doivent se soumettre à intervalles réguliers à des tests de la fonction hépatique et rénale, et à des analyses visant à déterminer la numération globulaire. Le médicament peut élever les concentrations d'urée, d'AST, d'ALT, de bilirubine, de phosphatase alcaline, de LDH et d'iode lié aux protéines.

TOXICITÉ ET SURDOSAGE: Suivre de près les signes suivants de toxicité: soubresauts musculaires involontaires, grimaces, clignements spasmodiques des yeux, protrusion exagérée de la langue, modification du comportement. Prévenir immédiatement le médecin ou un autre professionnel de la santé si ces symptômes se manifestent.

DIAGNOSTICS INFIRMIERS POSSIBLES

- Mobilité physique réduite (Indications).
- Risque d'accident (Indications).
- Connaissances insuffisantes sur le traitement médicamenteux (Enseignement au patient et à ses proches).

INTERVENTIONS INFIRMIÈRES

- NE PAS CONFONDRE LA LÉVODOPA AVEC LE MÉTHYLDOPA.
- Pour les préparations associant la carbidopa et la lévodopa, les chiffres suivant le nom du médicament représentent le nombre de milligrammes de chacun de ces médicaments.
- Demander au médecin ou à un autre professionnel de la santé s'il faut continuer d'administrer le médicament au patient qui doit rester à jeun ou qui doit subir une intervention chirurgicale.
- Administrer le médicament peu de temps avant les repas pour réduire l'irritation gastrique. Si l'on administre le médicament pendant ou après les repas, on risque de retarder les effets de la lévodopa. Cependant, une telle administration peut être nécessaire pour réduire l'irritation gastrique. Si le patient éprouve des difficultés de déglutition, demander conseil au pharmacien.
- ON PEUT ADMINISTRER LA MOITIÉ OU LA TOTALITÉ DU COMPRIMÉ À ACTION PROLONGÉE, MAIS IL NE FAUT PAS ÉCRASER NI CROQUER CE GENRE DE COMPRIMÉ.

ENSEIGNEMENT AU PATIENT ET À SES PROCHES

- Conseiller au patient de respecter rigoureusement la posologie recommandée. S'il n'a pu prendre le médicament au moment habituel, il doit le prendre aussitôt que possible, mais au moins 2 heures avant l'heure prévue pour la dose suivante. Le prévenir qu'il ne doit pas remplacer une dose manquée par une double dose.
- Expliquer au patient qu'il peut réduire l'irritation gastrique s'il prend le médicament peu avant les repas, mais que les aliments riches en protéines peuvent diminuer les effets de la lévodopa. Conseiller au patient de répartir les aliments contenant des protéines entre tous les repas pour assurer un apport protéique adéquat et pour conserver l'efficacité du médicament. Lui recommander de ne pas modifier de façon exagérée son alimentation pendant le traitement sans consulter un professionnel de la santé au préalable.
- Prévenir le patient que le médicament peut provoquer de la somnolence et des étourdissements. Lui conseiller de ne pas conduire et d'éviter les activités qui exigent sa vigilance jusqu'à ce qu'on ait la certitude que le médicament n'entraîne pas ces effets chez lui.
- Conseiller au patient de changer lentement de position afin de réduire le risque d'hypotension orthostatique. Lui recommander de prévenir un professionnel de la santé si elle survient.
- Conseiller au patient de se rincer fréquemment la bouche, de pratiquer une bonne hygiène buccale et de consommer de la gomme à mâcher ou des bonbons sans sucre pour diminuer la sécheresse de la bouche.
- Conseiller au patient de surveiller toute modification des lésions cutanées. Le cas échéant, en informer immédiatement un professionnel de la santé, car la lévodopa peut activer un mélanome malin.
- Conseiller au patient de consulter un professionnel de la santé avant de prendre un médicament en vente libre, particulièrement des préparations contre le rhume. De fortes quantités de vitamine B_6 (pyridoxine) peuvent diminuer les effets de la lévodopa.
- Prévenir le patient que son urine ou sa sueur peuvent prendre une couleur foncée, mais que cet effet n'est pas nuisible.
- Recommander au patient de signaler à un professionnel de la santé les symptômes suivants: palpitations, rétention urinaire, mouvements involontaires,

modifications du comportement, nausées et vomissements graves, ou nouvelles lésions cutanées. Il peut être nécessaire de réduire la dose.

VÉRIFICATION DE L'EFFICACITÉ THÉRAPEUTIQUE

L'efficacité du traitement peut être démontrée par: la disparition des signes et des symptômes parkinsoniens. Les effets thérapeutiques deviennent habituellement manifestes après 2 ou 3 semaines de traitement, mais parfois ils ne sont notables qu'après 6 mois. Chez les patients qui prennent ce médicament pendant plusieurs années, l'effet peut diminuer. L'efficacité du traitement peut parfois être rétablie après un arrêt temporaire de la médication. ✳

LÉVOFLOXACINE,
voir Fluoroquinolones

LÉVONORGESTREL,
voir Contraceptifs hormonaux

LÉVOTHYROXINE,
voir Thyroïdiennes, préparations

ALERTE CLINIQUE

LIDOCAÏNE (VOIE PARENTÉRALE)
Xylocaine, Xylocard

LIDOCAÏNE (ANESTHÉSIQUE LOCAL)
Xylocaine

LIDOCAÏNE (ANESTHÉSIE DES MUQUEUSES)
Lidodan, Xylocaine visqueuse

LIDOCAÏNE (TOPIQUE)
Solarcaine, Xylocaine, Zilactin-L

CLASSIFICATION:

Anesthésique et adjuvant anesthésique (local, topique, anesthésie des muqueuses), antiarythmique (classe IB)

Grossesse – catégorie B

INDICATIONS

IV: Arythmies ventriculaires ▪ **Anesthésie locale**: Infiltration/anesthésie topique ou anesthésie des muqueuses.

MÉCANISME D'ACTION

IV: Suppression de l'automaticité et de la dépolarisation spontanée des ventricules pendant la diastole, en modifiant le flux des ions sodium à travers les membranes cellulaires. Peu d'effets, sinon aucun, sur la fréquence cardiaque ▪ **Anesthésie locale**: Anesthésie locale par l'inhibition du passage des ions sodium à travers les membranes neuronales, empêchant ainsi le déclenchement et la transmission des influx nerveux normaux. ***Effets thérapeutiques:*** Maîtrise des arythmies ventriculaires ▪ Anesthésie locale.

PHARMACOCINÉTIQUE

Absorption: Une certaine quantité est absorbée par suite de l'application locale.

Distribution: Répartition dans tout l'organisme, avec concentration dans les tissus adipeux. La lidocaïne traverse la barrière hématoencéphalique et placentaire.

Métabolisme et excrétion: Métabolisme majoritairement hépatique.

Demi-vie: Biphasique – phase initiale: de 7 à 30 minutes; phase terminale: de 90 à 120 minutes.

Profil temps-action (IV = effets antiarythmiques; application locale = effets anesthésiques)

	Début d'action	Pic	Durée
IV	immédiat	immédiat	10 – 20 min (jusqu'à plusieurs heures après une perfusion continue)
Topique	rapide	inconnu	1 – 3 h

CONTRE-INDICATIONS, PRÉCAUTIONS ET MISES EN GARDE

Ces contre-indications, précautions et mises en garde s'appliquent surtout à l'usage par voie générale.

Contre-indications: Hypersensibilité; risque d'hypersensibilité croisée ▪ Traitement des arythmies chez les enfants (l'innocuité de cet agent n'a pas été établie) ▪ Syndrome d'Adams-Stokes ou blocs sinoauriculaire, auriculoventriculaire ou intraventriculaire de degré avancé.

Précautions et mises en garde: Maladie hépatique, insuffisance cardiaque, poids inférieur à 50 kg, personnes âgées (réduire le bolus ou la dose d'entretien) ▪ Dépression respiratoire, choc ou bloc cardiaque ▪ **OBST., ALLAITEMENT**: L'innocuité de la lidocaïne n'a pas été établie.

RÉACTIONS INDÉSIRABLES ET EFFETS SECONDAIRES

Ces réactions et effets sont surtout associés à l'administration par voie systémique.

SNC: CONVULSIONS, confusion, somnolence, étourdissements, nervosité, tremblements.

ORLO: *application sur les muqueuses* – baisse ou abolition du réflexe de déglutition.

CV: ARRÊT CARDIAQUE, arythmies, bradycardie, hypotension.

GI: nausées, vomissements.

Locaux: picotements, brûlures, eczéma de contact, érythème.

Divers: réactions allergiques, incluant l'ANAPHYLAXIE.

INTERACTIONS

Ces interactions s'appliquent surtout à l'administration par voie systémique.

Médicament-médicament: Dépression et toxicité cardiaque additives lors de l'administration concomitante de **phénytoïne**, de **quinidine**, de **procaïnamide** ou de **propranolol** ■ La **cimétidine** et les **bêtabloquants** peuvent ralentir le métabolisme de la lidocaïne et accroître le risque de toxicité.

VOIES D'ADMINISTRATION ET POSOLOGIE

Les vitesses de perfusion sont indiquées à l'annexe C.

Antiarythmique

- **IV (adultes)**: Bolus de 50 à 100 mg; on peut répéter cette dose après 10 minutes, puis administrer en perfusion, à un débit de 1 à 2 mg/min (de 15 à 30 µg/kg/min; jusqu'à 300 mg, en 1 heure).

Application locale

- **Infiltration (adultes et enfants)**: Infiltrer la région touchée selon les besoins (plus la fréquence et la quantité de médicament augmentent, plus le risque d'absorption systémique et de réactions indésirables s'élève).
- **Préparation topique (adultes)**: Appliquer selon les besoins (ne pas appliquer plus de 20 g/jour de pommade).
- **Application sur les muqueuses (adultes)**: *Anesthésie des muqueuses buccales* – on peut appliquer de 5 à 10 mL de lidocaïne visqueuse à 2 % (6 doses par jour, au maximum) pour soulager la douleur buccale ou pharyngienne. *Anesthésie de l'urètre chez la femme* – de 5 à 10 mL de gelée à 2 %. *Anesthésie de l'urètre chez l'homme* – de 5 à 10 mL de gelée à 2 %, avant l'introduction de la sonde, ou 30 à 40 mL de gelée à 2 %, avant la cystoscopie ou toute autre intervention similaire. On peut utiliser les solutions topiques pour anesthésier les muqueuses du larynx, de la trachée ou de l'œsophage.

PRÉSENTATION (version générique disponible)

Injection IV directe: 20 mg/mL (2 %)Pr ■ **Solution prémélangée pour perfusion IV**: 2 mg/mL (0,2 %)Pr, 4 mg/ mL (0,4 %)Pr ■ **Injection pour infiltration locale/anesthésie par blocage nerveux**: 0,5 %Pr, 1 %Pr, 1,5 %Pr, 2 %Pr ■ **En association avec**: adrénaline pour des infiltrations localesPr ■ **Gelée**: 2 %Pr ■ **Liquide**: 5 %Pr ■ **Pommade**: 5 %VL ■ **Solution**: 4 %Pr ■ **Solution visqueuse**: 2 %VL ■ **En association avec**: prilocaïne.

SOINS INFIRMIERS

ÉVALUATION DE LA SITUATION

Antiarythmique: SUIVRE CONTINUELLEMENT L'ÉCG, MESURER LA PRESSION ARTÉRIELLE ET LA FONCTION RESPIRATOIRE À INTERVALLES RÉGULIERS PENDANT TOUTE LA DURÉE DE L'ADMINISTRATION.

Anesthésique: Déterminer le degré d'engourdissement de la région touchée.

Tests de laboratoire:

- Noter les concentrations sériques d'électrolytes à intervalles réguliers pendant le traitement de longue durée.

TOXICITÉ ET SURDOSAGE:

- Noter les concentrations sériques de lidocaïne, à intervalles réguliers pendant toute la durée d'un traitement prolongé ou à de fortes doses. Les concentrations sériques thérapeutiques de lidocaïne se situent entre 5 et 25 µmol/L (entre 1,5 et 6 µg/mL).
- Les signes et les symptômes de toxicité incluent la confusion, l'excitation, la vision trouble ou double, les nausées, les vomissements, les acouphènes, les tremblements, les soubresauts musculaires, les convulsions, les difficultés respiratoires, les étourdissements graves ou les évanouissements, et une fréquence cardiaque d'une lenteur inhabituelle.
- Si des symptômes de surdosage se manifestent, interrompre la perfusion et observer étroitement le patient.

DIAGNOSTICS INFIRMIERS POSSIBLES

- Débit cardiaque diminué (Indications).
- Douleur aiguë (Indications).
- Connaissances insuffisantes sur le traitement médicamenteux (Enseignement au patient et à ses proches).

INTERVENTIONS INFIRMIÈRES

ALERTE CLINIQUE: LA LIDOCAÏNE EST ABSORBÉE RAPIDEMENT À TRAVERS LA MUQUEUSE. UNE POSOLOGIE EXCESSIVE DE GELÉE OU UN TROP GRAND NOMBRE DE

L

VAPORISATIONS PEUVENT PROVOQUER DES RÉACTIONS TOXIQUES GÉNÉRALES AIGUËS PROVENANT SURTOUT DES SYSTÈMES NERVEUX CENTRAL ET CARDIOVASCULAIRE. UTILISER LA PLUS FAIBLE POSOLOGIE CAPABLE DE PRODUIRE UNE ANESTHÉSIE EFFICACE.

Vaporisateur pour la gorge: S'assurer que le réflexe de déglutition est intact avant de permettre au patient de boire ou de manger.

IV: Seules les solutions à 2 % sont administrées par voie IV directe.

IV directe: Administrer une dose d'attaque non diluée de 1 mg/kg, à un débit de 25 à 50 mg, en 1 minute. On peut administrer 10 minutes plus tard une deuxième dose. Administrer ensuite par perfusion. Ne pas administrer par injection IV les préparations de lidocaïne renfermant des agents de conservation ou d'autres médicaments, comme l'adrénaline.

Perfusion continue: Utiliser la solution prémélangée pour perfusion IV. Si elle n'est pas disponible, préparer la perfusion en ajoutant 1 g de lidocaïne à 250, à 500 ou à 1 000 mL de solution de D5%E. La solution est stable pendant 24 heures. Les autres solutions compatibles sont les suivantes: D5%/solution de lactate de Ringer, D5%/NaCl 0,45 %, D5%/NaCl 0,9 %, NaCl 0,45 %, NaCl 0,9 % et solution de lactate de Ringer. Consulter les directives de chaque fabricant avant de reconstituer la préparation.

Vitesse d'administration: Administrer à l'aide d'une pompe à perfusion afin d'injecter la dose exacte, à un débit de 1 ou 2 mg/min (consulter le tableau des vitesses de perfusion de l'annexe C).

Compatibilité (tubulure en Y): alteplase ▪ amiodarone ▪ amrinone ▪ céfazoline ▪ ciprofloxacine ▪ diltiazem ▪ dobutamine ▪ dopamine ▪ énalaprilat ▪ étomidate ▪ famotidine ▪ halopéridol ▪ labétalol ▪ mépéridine ▪ morphine ▪ nitroglycérine ▪ nitroprusside ▪ potassium, chlorure de ▪ propofol ▪ streptokinase ▪ théophylline ▪ vitamines du complexe B avec C.

Incompatibilité (tubulure en Y): thiopental.

Infiltration: La lidocaïne peut être administrée en même temps que l'adrénaline pour réduire l'absorption par voie générale et pour prolonger l'anesthésie.

ENSEIGNEMENT AU PATIENT ET À SES PROCHES

Prévenir le patient que la lidocaïne peut provoquer de la somnolence et des étourdissements. Lui recommander de demander de l'aide lorsqu'il se déplace.

VÉRIFICATION DE L'EFFICACITÉ THÉRAPEUTIQUE

L'efficacité du traitement peut être démontrée par: la réduction des arythmies ventriculaires ▪ l'anesthésie locale. ✳

LIDOCAÏNE/PRILOCAÏNE

EMLA

CLASSIFICATION:

Anesthésique et adjuvant anesthésique (anesthésique local)

Grossesse – catégorie B

INDICATIONS

Anesthésie locale en vue d'interventions mineures douloureuses dont: l'introduction d'un cathéter ou d'une aiguille ▪ une ponction artérielle, veineuse ou lombaire ▪ des injections intramusculaires ▪ une incision de la peau ▪ un traitement au laser ▪ la circoncision ▪ Application sur la muqueuse génitale en vue d'une intervention mineure ou de l'anesthésie par infiltration.

MÉCANISME D'ACTION

Anesthésie locale produite par inhibition du transport des ions à travers la membrane neuronale, ce qui prévient le déclenchement et la transmission des influx nerveux normaux. L'association des deux anesthésiques est appliquée sous forme de crème sous un pansement occlusif. Le médicament actif est libéré dans le derme et l'épiderme où il s'accumule dans les régions où se situent les récepteurs dermiques de la douleur et les terminaisons nerveuses. ***Effets thérapeutiques:*** L'effet anesthésique est localisé dans la région où le médicament est appliqué.

PHARMACOCINÉTIQUE

Absorption: De petites quantités sont absorbées par voie générale pendant tout le temps où le timbre EMLA est en place, soit 4 heures.

Distribution: Les petites quantités absorbées se répartissent dans tout l'organisme et traversent les barrières placentaire et hématoencéphalique.

Métabolisme et excrétion: *Lidocaïne* – métabolisme majoritairement hépatique. *Prilocaïne* – métabolisme hépatique et rénal.

Demi-vie: *Lidocaïne* – phase initiale: de 7 à 30 minutes; phase terminale: de 90 à 120 minutes. *Prilocaïne* de 10 à 50 minutes.

Profil temps-action (anesthésie locale)

	DÉBUT D'ACTION	PIC	DURÉE†
Topique	15 min	3 h	1 - 2 h

† Après le retrait du pansement occlusif.

CONTRE-INDICATIONS, PRÉCAUTIONS ET MISES EN GARDE

Contre-indications: Hypersensibilité à la lidocaïne, à la prilocaïne ou à tout autre anesthésique local de type amide ▪ Hypersensibilité à tout autre ingrédient de la préparation ▪ Application dans l'oreille moyenne ▪ Méthémoglobinémie congénitale ou idiopathique ▪ **PÉD.**: Nourrissons de moins de 6 mois ▪ Enfants âgés de 6 à 12 mois qui reçoivent des agents produisant de la méthémoglobine.

Précautions et mises en garde: Usage répété ou sur de grandes surfaces (risque accru d'absorption par voie générale) ▪ **GÉR.**: Risque d'absorption cutanée plus grande et d'effets indésirables accrus chez les personnes âgées et les patients très malades ou débilités ▪ Maladie hépatique grave ▪ Tout état associé à la méthémoglobinémie (incluant une carence en G-6-PD) ▪ **PÉD.**: Enfants de moins de 20 kg (la surface traitée et la durée du traitement doivent être limitées) ▪ **OBST.**: Moins de 37 semaines de gestation (la surface traitée et la durée du traitement doivent être limitées) ▪ Allaitement ▪ Circonstances cliniques où la crème peut pénétrer ou passer dans l'oreille moyenne.

RÉACTIONS INDÉSIRABLES ET EFFETS SECONDAIRES

Locaux: pâleur, rougeur, altération de la sensibilité thermique, œdème, démangeaisons, rash.

Divers: réactions allergiques, incluant l'ANAPHYLAXIE.

INTERACTIONS

Médicament-médicament: L'administration concomitante d'**antiarythmiques de classe I** (comme la **mexilétine)** peut entraîner des effets cardiovasculaires indésirables ▪ L'usage concomitant d'autres **anesthésiques locaux** peut entraîner une toxicité additive ▪ Risque accru de méthémoglobinémie chez les enfants, lors de l'administration concomitante de **sulfamides** (éviter l'usage concomitant chez les enfants < 12 mois).

VOIES D'ADMINISTRATION ET POSOLOGIE

- **Topique (adultes et enfants)**: *Interventions dermiques mineures dont la ponction veineuse et la mise en place d'une canule IV* – appliquer 2,5 g (la moitié du tube de 5 g) sur une surface de peau de 20 à 25 cm^2, couvrir d'un pansement occlusif, ou appliquer un disque anesthésique pendant au moins 1 heure. *Interventions dermiques majeures dont la greffe de peau mince* – appliquer 2 g/10 cm^2 de peau, couvrir d'un pansement occlusif pendant au moins 2 heures. *Peau des organes génitaux chez l'homme* – anesthésique d'appoint avant l'anesthésie locale par infiltration; appliquer une couche épaisse sur la peau, laisser agir pendant 5 à 10 minutes; l'anesthésie locale par infiltration doit être effectuée immédiatement après le retrait de la crème. *Muqueuses génitales chez la femme* – appliquer une couche épaisse, laisser agir pendant 5 à 10 minutes.
- **Topique (enfants de 6 à 12 mois et > 5 kg)**: Appliquer au moins 1 heure avant le début de l'intervention. La dose ne doit pas dépasser 2 g; ne pas appliquer sur une surface de plus de 16 cm^2 pendant plus de 4 heures.

PRÉSENTATION

Crème: lidocaïne à 2,5 % et prilocaïne à 2,5 %, en tubes de 5 et de 30 g^{VL} ▪ **Disque anesthésique**: lidocaïne à 2,5 % et prilocaïne à 2,5 %, sous forme de timbre adhésif (1 g/10 cm^2)^{VL}.

SOINS INFIRMIERS

ÉVALUATION DE LA SITUATION

- Bien observer la surface de la peau pour déceler la présence d'une éventuelle lésion. Appliquer seulement sur une peau intacte.
- Évaluer l'effet anesthésique sur la surface d'application après le retrait du timbre et avant l'intervention.

DIAGNOSTICS INFIRMIERS POSSIBLES

- Douleur aiguë (Indications).
- Connaissances insuffisantes sur le traitement médicamenteux (Enseignement au patient et à ses proches).

INTERVENTIONS INFIRMIÈRES

- En prévision d'une intervention dermique mineure (ponction veineuse, installation d'une canule IV, ponction artérielle ou lombaire), appliquer en une couche épaisse 2,5 g de crème (la moitié du tube de 5 g) pour une surface de 20 à 25 cm^2 sur la région où sera effectuée l'intervention. Retirer la pièce centrale prédécoupée du pansement occlusif (fourni avec le tube de 5 g) et le papier protecteur. Recouvrir avec le pansement la couche épaisse de crème de lidocaïne/prilocaïne. Ne pas étaler ni ne faire pénétrer la crème. Lisser doucement les bords du pansement, et s'assurer qu'il est bien fixé pour éviter les fuites. Retirer le cadre en papier et noter l'heure d'application sur le pansement. Appliquer la crème de lidocaïne/prilocaïne au moins 1 heure avant le début d'une intervention mineure (ponction veineuse, installation d'une canule IV). L'anesthésie peut être plus marquée si l'application dure de 90 à 120 minutes. Après avoir retiré le pansement occlusif, essuyer la crème. Nettoyer toute la surface avec une solution antiseptique et préparer le patient à l'intervention.

- En prévision d'interventions dermiques majeures (prélèvement d'un greffon de peau), suivre les mêmes étapes en utilisant de plus grandes quantités de crème de lidocaïne/prilocaïne et le pansement occlusif de la taille appropriée. Il faut appliquer la crème au moins 2 heures avant toute intervention dermique majeure.
- Pour appliquer le disque anesthésique, plier le coin de la languette en aluminium vers l'arrière. En tenant ensuite le coin de la couche beige, séparer les 2 couches. Ne pas toucher au disque blanc et rond qui contient la crème de lidocaïne/prilocaïne. Placer sur la surface à anesthésier et presser fermement les bords pour assurer une bonne adhérence à la peau; ne pas presser le centre du disque. Marquer l'heure de l'application avec un stylo à bille sur la bordure du disque. Appliquer au moins 1 heure avant l'intervention. Après avoir retiré le disque, essuyer la crème. Nettoyer toute la surface avec une solution antiseptique et préparer le patient à l'intervention.

L

ENSEIGNEMENT AU PATIENT ET À SES PROCHES

- Expliquer au patient et aux parents l'objectif du traitement. Informer le patient que la crème de lidocaïne/prilocaïne peut éliminer toute sensation au niveau de la surface où elle est appliquée. Lui expliquer que pour prévenir tout traumatisme de la région, il doit éviter de gratter ou de frotter la surface, ou de l'exposer à des températures extrêmes (froides ou chaudes) jusqu'au retour de la sensibilité.

Soins à domicile: Montrer au patient ou à un proche comment appliquer le produit. Lui fournir un croquis pour circonscrire la surface d'application.

VÉRIFICATION DE L'EFFICACITÉ THÉRAPEUTIQUE

L'efficacité du traitement peut être démontrée par: l'anesthésie de la surface où le produit est appliqué. ✳

LINDANE

Hexit, PMS-Lindane

CLASSIFICATION:

Pédiculicide, scabicide

Grossesse – catégorie B

INDICATIONS

Traitement de deuxième recours de l'infestation par des arthropodes parasites (gale, poux de tête, de corps et du pubis) chez les patients qui ne répondent pas aux agents moins toxiques ou qui ne les tolèrent pas.

MÉCANISME D'ACTION

Le lindane entraîne la destruction des arthropodes parasites. ***Effets thérapeutiques***: Traitement curatif de l'infestation par les arthropodes parasites.

PHARMACOCINÉTIQUE

Absorption: Par suite de l'application de la préparation topique, une absorption systémique importante (de 9 à 13 %) se produit lentement.

Distribution: Le lindane est emmagasiné dans les tissus adipeux.

Métabolisme et excrétion: Métabolisme hépatique.

Demi-vie: 18 heures (nourrissons et enfants).

Profil temps-action (effet antiparasitaire)

	Début d'action	Pic	Durée
Topique	rapide	rapide	190 min

CONTRE-INDICATIONS, PRÉCAUTIONS ET MISES EN GARDE

Contre-indications: Hypersensibilité ■ Rash, abrasion ou inflammation de la peau (l'absorption est accrue) ■ **Péd.**: Enfants de 2 ans ou moins (risque accru de toxicité du SNC).

Précautions et mises en garde: **Obst.**: Ne pas dépasser la dose recommandée; ne pas administrer plus de 2 cures ■ **Péd.**: Risque accru d'absorption systémique et d'effets secondaires sur le SNC ■ Enfants de 6 ans et moins ■ Antécédents de convulsions ■ Allaitement.

RÉACTIONS INDÉSIRABLES ET EFFETS SECONDAIRES

Toutes les réactions indésirables, sauf les réactions dermiques, sont un signe d'absorption systémique et de toxicité.

SNC: CONVULSIONS, céphalées.

CV: tachycardie.

GI: nausées, vomissements.

Tég.: dermatite de contact (applications répétées), irritation locale.

INTERACTIONS

Médicament-médicament: L'usage concomitant de **préparations topiques pour la peau, le cuir chevelu ou les cheveux** peut accroître le risque d'absorption systémique. ■ L'usage concomitant de **médicaments pouvant abaisser le seuil convulsif** entraîne un risque accru de convulsions.

VOIES D'ADMINISTRATION ET POSOLOGIE

Gale

- **Préparation topique (adultes et enfants):** Appliquer la lotion à 1 % sur toutes les surfaces cutanées du cou aux orteils, laisser agir pendant 8 heures et enlever en lavant à fond; il peut s'avérer nécessaire de devoir répéter le traitement, une nouvelle fois, 1 semaine plus tard.

Poux de tête ou du pubis

- **Préparation topique (adultes et enfants):** De 15 à 30 mL (jusqu'à 60 mL) de shampooing; laisser agir pendant 4 minutes et rincer; il peut s'avérer nécessaire de devoir répéter le traitement, une nouvelle fois, 1 semaine plus tard.

PRÉSENTATION (version générique disponible)

Lotion: 1 %[VL] ■ **Shampooing:** 1 %[VL].

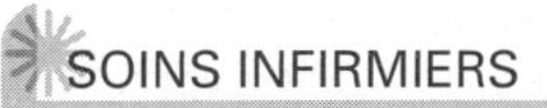

SOINS INFIRMIERS

ÉVALUATION DE LA SITUATION

- Examiner la peau et les cheveux à la recherche de signes d'infestation, avant et après le traitement.
- Examiner les membres de la famille et les personnes ayant eu des contacts étroits avec le patient pour déterminer s'ils sont infestés. Lorsque le lindane est utilisé dans le traitement de la pédiculose du pubis ou de la gale, il faut administrer simultanément un traitement prophylactique aux partenaires sexuels.

DIAGNOSTICS INFIRMIERS POSSIBLES

- Atteinte à l'intégrité de la peau (Indications).
- Connaissances insuffisantes sur le traitement médicamenteux (Enseignement au patient et à ses proches).

INTERVENTIONS INFIRMIÈRES

Préparation topique:

- Lorsqu'on doit administrer le lindane à autrui, on doit porter des gants afin de prévenir l'absorption systémique.
- Ne pas appliquer sur des plaies (égratignures, coupures, lésions de la peau ou du cuir chevelu) afin de réduire l'absorption systémique. Éviter tout contact avec les yeux; en cas de contact accidentel, bien rincer l'œil avec de l'eau et prévenir le médecin ou un autre professionnel de la santé.
- Prendre les mesures d'isolement de mise.

Lotion: Demander au patient de prendre un bain et de bien se laver avec de l'eau et du savon. Il doit bien s'essuyer et attendre un peu avant d'appliquer le lindane. Il doit, ensuite, appliquer une quantité suffisante de lotion pour couvrir toute la surface corporelle d'une mince couche de lindane à partir du cou jusqu'aux orteils (60 mL chez l'adulte). Le patient doit garder le médicament sur la peau pendant 8 à 12 heures, et ensuite l'enlever à l'eau. En cas de rash, de sensation de brûlure ou de démangeaisons, il faut laver la peau pour enlever le médicament et prévenir le médecin ou un autre professionnel de la santé.

Shampooing: Verser une quantité suffisante de shampooing pour en imbiber les cheveux et le cuir chevelu (30 mL, cheveux courts; 45 mL, cheveux mi-longs; 60 mL, cheveux longs). Bien faire pénétrer, puis laisser agir pendant 4 minutes. Ensuite, utiliser assez d'eau pour bien faire mousser; rincer abondamment et laisser sécher. Si on applique le shampooing dans la douche ou le bain, ne pas laisser couler le lindane le long du corps ou dans l'eau dans laquelle le patient est assis. Une fois que les cheveux sont secs, utiliser un peigne fin pour enlever les lentes et leurs enveloppes. On peut aussi appliquer du shampooing sur les peignes et les brosses afin de prévenir la propagation de l'infestation.

L

ENSEIGNEMENT AU PATIENT ET À SES PROCHES

- Montrer au patient comment appliquer l'agent. Le prévenir qu'il ne doit répéter le traitement que sur recommandation d'un professionnel de la santé. Lui expliquer les mesures d'hygiène qu'il doit prendre pour prévenir et enrayer l'infestation. Le mettre en garde contre les risques de contamination. Lui expliquer aussi les raisons pour lesquelles il faut examiner toutes les personnes qui vivent sous le même toit et traiter simultanément le partenaire sexuel.
- Conseiller au patient de laver tous les vêtements qu'il a portés récemment de même que sa literie et ses serviettes dans de l'eau très chaude ou de les faire nettoyer afin d'empêcher la réinfestation ou la propagation.
- Expliquer au patient qu'il ne doit pas appliquer d'autres crèmes ou huiles pendant le traitement puisqu'elles augmentent l'absorption systémique du lindane et peuvent entraîner une intoxication.
- Prévenir le patient que les démangeaisons peuvent persister après le traitement. Il doit consulter un professionnel de la santé au sujet de l'utilisation d'hydrocortisone topique ou d'antihistaminiques.

- Conseiller au patient d'appliquer de la vaseline sur ses cils, 3 fois par jour pendant 1 semaine.
- PRÉVENIR LE PATIENT QU'ON NE PEUT REPÉTER LE TRAITEMENT AVANT 7 JOURS ; ON NE DOIT TRAITER DE NOUVEAU QUE SI L'ON TROUVE DES POUX VIVANTS.

Shampooing: Prévenir le patient qu'il ne faut utiliser le shampooing qu'en présence d'infestation et que cette préparation n'est pas destinée à un usage régulier. Insister sur le fait qu'il faut éviter tout contact avec les yeux.

PÉD.: CONSEILLER AUX PARENTS DE SURVEILLER ÉTROITEMENT LEUR ENFANT À LA RECHERCHE DE SIGNES DE TOXICITÉ DU SNC (CONVULSIONS, ÉTOURDISSEMENTS, MALADRESSE, PALPITATIONS, CRAMPES MUSCULAIRES, NERVOSITÉ, AGITATION, IRRITABILITÉ, NAUSÉES, VOMISSEMENTS) PENDANT LE TRAITEMENT ET IMMÉDIATEMENT APRÈS.

PÉD.: Couvrir les mains des jeunes enfants pour éviter une ingestion accidentelle par succion du pouce.

VÉRIFICATION DE L'EFFICACITÉ THÉRAPEUTIQUE

L'efficacité du traitement peut être démontrée par: la résolution des signes d'infestation (gale ou poux).

LINÉZOLIDE

Zyvoxam

CLASSIFICATION:

Antibiotique (oxazolidinone)

Grossesse – catégorie C

INDICATIONS

Traitement des infections suivantes: infections dues à *Enterococcus fæcium* résistant à la vancomycine ■ pneumonie nosocomiale due à *Staphylococcus aureus* (souches sensibles et résistantes à la méthicilline) ou *Streptococcus pneumoniæ* (souches sensibles à la pénicilline seulement) ■ infections compliquées de la peau et des tissus mous dues à *Staphylococcus aureus* (souches sensibles et résistantes à la méthicilline) et à *Streptococcus pyogenes* ou *Streptococcus agalactiæ* (comprenant les infections du pied chez le diabétique) ■ infections non compliquées de la peau et des tissus mous dues à *Staphylococcus aureus* (souches sensibles à la méthicilline seulement) et à *Streptococcus pyogenes* ■ pneumonie extrahospitalière due à *Streptococcus pneumoniæ* (souches sensibles à la pénicilline seulement) ou à *Staphylococcus aureus* (souches sensibles et résistantes à la méthicilline).

MÉCANISME D'ACTION

Inhibition de la synthèse de la protéine bactérienne au niveau du ribosome 23S de la sous-unité 50S. ***Effets thérapeutiques:*** Effet bactéricide contre les streptocoques et bactériostatique contre les entérocoques et les staphylocoques.

PHARMACOCINÉTIQUE

Absorption: Rapide et totale (100 %).

Distribution: Tous les tissus bien irrigués.

Métabolisme et excrétion: Métabolisme majoritairement hépatique à 65 % ; excrétion urinaire à l'état inchangé à 30 %.

Demi-vie: 6,4 heures.

Profil temps-action

	DÉBUT D'ACTION	PIC	DURÉE
PO	rapide	1 –2 h	12 h
IV	rapide	fin de la perfusion	12 h

CONTRE-INDICATIONS, PRÉCAUTIONS ET MISES EN GARDE

Contre-indications: Hypersensibilité.

Précautions et mises en garde: Thrombopénie, usage concomitant d'agents antiplaquettaires ou diathèse hémorragique (vérifier plus fréquemment la numération plaquettaire) ■ Consommation de grandes quantités d'aliments ou de boissons riches en tyramine (risque accru de réponse vasopressive ; voir l'annexe J) ■ **OBST.**: Grossesse et allaitement (l'innocuité de l'agent n'a pas été établie).

RÉACTIONS INDÉSIRABLES ET EFFETS SECONDAIRES

CV: céphalées, insomnie.

GI: COLITE PSEUDOMEMBRANEUSE, diarrhée, élévation des résultats aux tests de la fonction hépatique, nausées, altération du goût, vomissements.

HÉ: ACIDOSE LACTIQUE.

Hémat.: anémie, neutropénie, thrombopénie, pancytopénie.

SN: neuropathie optique, neuropathie périphérique.

INTERACTIONS

Médicament-médicament: Le linézolide a les propriétés d'un inhibiteur réversible non sélectif de la monoamine oxydase ; la réponse aux **sympathicomimétiques à action indirecte**, aux **vasopresseurs**, aux **agents sérotoninergiques** (comme les **ISRS** et la majorité des **antidépresseurs** ou la **sibutramine**) ou aux **agents dopaminergiques** peut être accrue ■ Les doses initiales d'**adrénergiques**, comme la **dopamine** ou l'**adrénaline**, doivent être plus faibles et adaptées soigneusement.

Médicament-aliments: En raison des propriétés d'inhibiteur de la monoamine oxydase de cet agent, il faut éviter de consommer de grandes quantités d'aliments ou de boissons contenant de la **tyramine** (risque accru de réponse vasopressive; voir l'annexe J).

VOIES D'ADMINISTRATION ET POSOLOGIE

Infections à Enterococcus fæcium résistant à la vancomycine

- **PO, IV (adultes et enfants ≥ 12 ans)**: 600 mg, toutes les 12 heures, pendant 14 à 28 jours.
- **PO, IV (enfants ≤ 11 ans)**: 10 mg/kg, toutes les 8 heures, pendant 14 à 28 jours. (Durant la première semaine de vie, les nouveau-nés peuvent recevoir initialement 10 mg/kg, toutes les 12 heures.)

Pneumonie, infections compliquées de la peau et des tissus mous

- **PO, IV (adultes et enfants ≥ 12 ans)**: 600 mg, toutes les 12 heures, pendant 10 à 14 jours.
- **PO, IV (enfants ≤ 11 ans)**: 10 mg/kg, toutes les 8 heures, pendant 10 à 14 jours. (Durant la première semaine de vie, les nouveau-nés peuvent recevoir initialement 10 mg/kg, toutes les 12 heures.)

Infections non compliquées de la peau et des tissus mous

- **PO (adultes et enfants ≥ 12 ans)**: 400 mg, toutes les 12 heures, pendant 10 à 14 jours.
- **PO, IV (enfants de 5 à 11 ans)**: 10 mg/kg, toutes les 12 heures, pendant 10 à 14 jours.
- **PO, IV (enfants < 5 ans)**: 10 mg/kg, toutes les 8 heures, pendant 10 à 14 jours. (Durant la première semaine de vie, les nouveau-nés peuvent recevoir initialement 10 mg/kg, toutes les 12 heures.)

PRÉSENTATION

Comprimés: 600 mg[Pr] ■ **Solution pour injection**: 600 mg/sac de 300 mL[Pr].

SOINS INFIRMIERS

ÉVALUATION DE LA SITUATION

- Suivre de près le patient pour déceler les signes d'infection (altération des signes vitaux, aspect de la plaie, des crachats, de l'urine et des selles, nombre de leucocytes) au début du traitement et pendant toute sa durée.
- Prélever des échantillons pour les cultures et les antibiogrammes avant le début du traitement. Les premières doses peuvent être administrées avant que les résultats soient connus.
- Le médicament peut provoquer une acidose lactique. Prévenir le médecin en cas de nausées et de vomissements récurrents, d'une acidose inexpliquée ou de taux faibles de bicarbonate.
- Suivre de près la vision chez les patients qui prennent du linézolide pendant plus de 28 jours ou qui signalent des symptômes visuels (modifications de l'acuité visuelle ou de la perception des couleurs, vision brouillée ou anomalies du champ visuel) sans égard à la durée du traitement. L'apparition de symptômes d'atteinte de la fonction visuelle dicte une évaluation ophtalmologique immédiate. En cas de neuropathie optique, il faut reconsidérer le bien-fondé du traitement.
- Le médicament peut causer une colite pseudomembraneuse: Suivre de près la fonction intestinale (bruits intestinaux, fréquence et consistance des selles, présence de sang dans les selles) tout au long du traitement.

Tests de laboratoire:

- Risque de dépression médullaire, d'anémie, de leucopénie et de pancytopénie. Suivre de près la numération globulaire et plaquettaire, toutes les semaines, particulièrement chez les patients exposés à un risque élevé de saignements, qui présentent une dépression médullaire préexistante, qui prennent en même temps d'autres médicaments qui peuvent provoquer une dépression médullaire ou qui doivent suivre le traitement pendant > 2 semaines. Arrêter l'antibiothérapie si une dépression médullaire survient ou si elle s'aggrave.
- L'agent peut élever les taux d'AST, d'ALT, de LDH, de phosphatase alcaline et d'urée.

L

DIAGNOSTICS INFIRMIERS POSSIBLES

Risque d'infection (Indications).

INTERVENTIONS INFIRMIÈRES

- Aucune adaptation posologique n'est nécessaire lorsqu'on passe de l'administration IV à celle par voie orale.

PO: On peut administrer le médicament avec ou sans aliments.

Perfusion intermittente: La solution pour injection doit être administrée à partir d'un sac à usage unique, prêt à servir. Ne pas perfuser une solution contenant des particules.

Vitesse d'administration: Administrer en 30 à 120 minutes. Ne pas raccorder à d'autres tubulures IV. Rincer la tubulure avant et après la perfusion.

Compatibilité (tubulure en Y): acyclovir ■ alfentanil ■ amikacine ■ aminophylline ■ ampicilline ■ ampicilline/sulbactam ■ aztréonam ■ buprénorphine ■ butorphanol ■ calcium, gluconate de ■ carboplatine ■ céfazoline ■ céfoxitine ■ ceftazidime ■ céfuroxime ■ cimétidine ■ ciprofloxacine ■ cisatracurium ■ cisplatine ■ clindamycine

■ cyclophosphamide ■ cyclosporine ■ cytarabine ■ D5/NaCl 0,45 % ■ D5/NaCl 0,9 % ■ D5%E ■ dexmédétomidine ■ digoxine ■ diphenhydramine ■ dobutamine ■ dopamine ■ doxorubicine ■ doxycycline ■ dropéridol ■ énalaprilate ■ esmolol ■ étoposide, phosphate de ■ famotidine ■ fénoldopam ■ fentanyl ■ fluconazole ■ fluorouracile ■ furosémide ■ ganciclovir ■ gemcitabine ■ gentamicine ■ granisétron ■ halopéridol ■ héparine ■ hydrocortisone ■ hydromorphone ■ ifosfamide ■ imipénem/cilastatine ■ labétalol ■ lactate de Ringer pour injection ■ leucovorine ■ lévofloxacine ■ lidocaïne ■ lorazépam ■ magnésium, sulfate de ■ mannitol ■ mépéridine ■ méropénem ■ mesna ■ méthotrexate ■ méthylprednisolone ■ métoclopramide ■ métronidazole ■ midazolam ■ minocycline ■ mitoxantrone ■ nalbuphine ■ NaCl 0,9 % ■ naloxone ■ nitroglycérine ■ ofloxacine ■ ondansétron, ■ orphine ■ paclitaxel ■ pentobarbital ■ phénobarbital ■ piperacilline ■ piperacilline/tazobactam ■ potassium, chlorure de ■ prochlorpérazine ■ prométhazine ■ propranolol ■ ranitidine ■ rémifentanil ■ Ringer, solution pour injection ■ sodium, bicarbonate de ■ sufentanil ■ théophylline ■ ticarcilline ■ tobramycine ■ vancomycine ■ vécuronium ■ vérapamil ■ vincristine ■ zidovudine.
Incompatibilité (tubulure en Y): amphotéricine B ■ ceftriaxone ■ chlorpromazine ■ diazépam ■ érythromycine ■ pentamidine ■ phénytoïne ■ triméthoprime/sulfaméthoxazole.

ENSEIGNEMENT AU PATIENT ET À SES PROCHES

- Conseiller au patient qui reçoit le linézolide par voie orale de respecter rigoureusement les recommandations du médecin et de prendre toute la quantité qui lui a été prescrite, même s'il se sent mieux. S'il n'a pas pu prendre le médicament au moment habituel, le prendre dès que possible à moins que ce ne soit presque l'heure prévue pour la dose suivante. Insister sur le fait qu'il ne faut pas remplacer une dose manquée par une double dose.
- Conseiller au patient d'éviter de consommer des quantités importantes d'aliments et de boissons contenant de la tyramine (voir l'annexe J). Le prévenir qu'il y a risque de réaction hypertensive.
- Recommander au patient de prévenir un professionnel de la santé s'il a des antécédents d'hypertension et de lui demander conseil avant de prendre un autre médicament d'ordonnance ou en vente libre ou des produits naturels, particulièrement, s'il s'agit de médicaments contre le rhume, de décongestionnants ou d'antidépresseurs.
- Conseiller au patient de prévenir un professionnel de la santé si des changements de la vision se produisent pendant le traitement par le linézolide.
- Conseiller au patient de prévenir un professionnel de la santé en cas d'engourdissements, de picotements ou de sensation de brûlure au niveau des extrémités.
- Conseiller au patient de prévenir un professionnel de la santé s'il ne note aucune amélioration en l'espace de quelques jours.

VÉRIFICATION DE L'EFFICACITÉ THÉRAPEUTIQUE

L'efficacité du traitement peut être démontrée par: la résolution des signes et des symptômes d'infection; le temps de résolution dépend du microorganisme infectant et du siège de l'infection.

LIOTHYRONINE,
voir Thyroïdiennes, préparations

LISINOPRIL,
voir Inhibiteurs de l'enzyme de conversion de l'angiotensine (IECA)

LITHIUM

Apo-Lithium Carbonate, Carbolith, Duralith, Lithane, PMS-Lithium

CLASSIFICATION:
Antimaniaque

Grossesse – catégorie D

INDICATIONS

Traitement de divers troubles psychiatriques, particulièrement des troubles bipolaires (traitement des épisodes hypomaniaques et maniaques aigus, et prévention de leur récurrence). **Usages non approuvés**: Traitement adjuvant chez des patients souffrant de dépression ne répondant que partiellement aux antidépresseurs ■ Prophylaxie des céphalées vasculaires de Horton chroniques.

MÉCANISME D'ACTION

Modification du transport de cations dans les nerfs et dans les muscles ■ Influence possible sur le recaptage des neurotransmetteurs. ***Effets thérapeutiques:*** Effets antimaniaques et antidépresseurs.

PHARMACOCINÉTIQUE

Absorption: Complète (PO).

Distribution: L'agent se répartit dans de nombreux tissus et liquides; les concentrations dans le liquide céphalorachidien correspondent à 50 % des concentrations plasmatiques. Il traverse la barrière placentaire et passe dans le lait maternel.

Métabolisme et excrétion: Excrétion à l'état pratiquement inchangé par les reins.

Demi-vie: De 20 à 27 heures.

Profil temps-action (effets antimaniaques)

	DÉBUT D'ACTION	PIC	DURÉE
PO, PO-LP†	5 - 7 jours	10 - 21 jours	plusieurs jours

† LP = libération prolongée.

CONTRE-INDICATIONS, PRÉCAUTIONS ET MISES EN GARDE

Contre-indications: Hypersensibilité ■ Maladies cardiaque ou rénale graves ■ Patients déshydratés ou débilités ■ Administration réservée aux cas où le traitement et les concentrations sanguines peuvent être suivis de près ■ Hypersensibilité ou intolérance à l'alcool ou à la tartrazine (ne pas administrer dans ce cas les produits qui renferment ces substances).

Précautions et mises en garde: **GÉR.**: Réduire la dose initiale chez les personnes âgées ou débilitées ■ Maladie cardiaque, rénale ou thyroïdienne de quelque gravité que ce soit ■ Diabète ■ **PÉD.**: L'innocuité du lithium n'a pas été établie ■ **OBST.**: Utiliser avec prudence. Le lithium a été associé à des risques de malformation chez le nouveau-né. N'utiliser le lithium que si aucun autre traitement n'est possible. **ALLAITEMENT**: Le lithium passe dans le lait maternel à des concentrations allant de 30 à 100 % des concentrations sériques maternelles. Utiliser avec prudence. Il peut être justifié de mesurer les concentrations sériques chez le nourrisson.

RÉACTIONS INDÉSIRABLES ET EFFETS SECONDAIRES

SNC: CONVULSIONS, fatigue, céphalées, perte de mémoire, ataxie, confusion, étourdissements, somnolence, retard psychomoteur, agitation, stupeur.

ORLO: aphasie, vision trouble, dysarthrie, acouphènes.

CV: ARYTHMIES, modification de l'ÉCG, œdème, hypotension.

GI: douleurs abdominales, anorexie, ballonnement, diarrhée, nausées, sécheresse de la bouche (xérostomie), goût métallique.

GU: polyurie, glycosurie, diabète insipide, toxicité rénale.

Tég.: éruptions acnéiformes, folliculite, alopécie, perte des sensations, prurit.

End.: hypothyroïdie, goitre, hyperglycémie, hyperthyroïdie.

HÉ: hyponatrémie.

Hémat.: leucocytose.

Mét.: gain de poids.

Loc.: faiblesse musculaire, hyperirritabilité, rigidité.

SN: tremblements.

INTERACTIONS

Médicament-médicament: Le lithium peut prolonger l'effet des **bloqueurs neuromusculaires** ■ Risque de toxicité neurologique lors de l'administration concomitante d'**halopéridol** ■ Les **diurétiques**, la **méthyldopa**, le **probénécide**, la **fluoxétine** et les **AINS**, administrés en concomitance, peuvent accroître le risque de toxicité ■ Risque d'élévation des concentrations sanguines lors de l'usage concomitant d'**inhibiteurs de l'enzyme de conversion de l'angiotensine** ou d'**antagonistes des récepteurs de l'angiotensine II** ■ Le lithium peut réduire les effets de la **chlorpromazine** ■ La **chlorpromazine** peut masquer les premiers signes de toxicité du lithium ■ Risque d'effets hypothyroïdiens additifs lors de l'administration concomitante d'**iodure de potassium** ou d'**agents antithyroïdiens** ■ L'**aminophylline**, les **phénothiazines** et les **médicaments renfermant des quantités importantes de sodium** peuvent accroître l'élimination rénale et réduire l'efficacité du lithium.

Médicament-produits naturels: Les produits contenant de la caféine (**café, cola, guarana, maté, thé**) peuvent abaisser les concentrations sériques de lithium et en diminuer ainsi l'efficacité.

Médicament-aliments: Une modification importante de la consommation de **sodium** peut modifier l'élimination rénale du lithium. L'augmentation de l'apport de sodium accroîtra l'élimination rénale.

L

VOIES D'ADMINISTRATION ET POSOLOGIE

La dose précise se fonde sur les concentrations sériques de lithium; 300 mg de carbonate de lithium contiennent 8 mmol de lithium.

- **PO (adultes)**: *Comprimés, capsules* – initialement, de 300 à 600 mg, 3 fois par jour; la dose d'entretien habituelle est de 300 mg, 3 ou 4 fois par jour. *Comprimés à libération prolongée* – le premier jour: de 600 à 900 mg, en 2 doses fractionnées. À partir du deuxième jour: de 1 200 mg à 1 800 mg par jour, en 2 doses fractionnées; la posologie moyenne recommandée est de 900 mg par jour, en 1 seule dose, administrée au coucher. Normalement, cette dose peut se situer entre 600 et 1 200 mg par jour.

PRÉSENTATION (version générique disponible)

Capsules: 150 mg^Pr^, 300 mg^Pr^, 600 mg^Pr^ ■ **Comprimés à libération prolongée:** 300 mg^Pr^ ■ **Sirop:** 300 mg (8 mmol de lithium)/5 mL^Pr^.

SOINS INFIRMIERS

ÉVALUATION DE LA SITUATION

- Observer l'humeur, l'idéation et le comportement du patient à intervalles réguliers. Prendre les précautions nécessaires si le patient a des idées suicidaires.
- Effectuer le bilan des ingesta et des excreta. Signaler tout écart important dans les valeurs totales. Sauf contre-indication, inciter le patient à boire au moins de 2 000 à 3 000 mL de liquides par jour. Peser le patient au moins tous les 3 mois.

Tests de laboratoire: Noter à intervalles réguliers, pendant toute la durée du traitement, les résultats des tests de la fonction rénale et thyroïdienne, le nombre de globules blancs et la formule leucocytaire, les concentrations sériques d'électrolytes et la glycémie.

Toxicité et surdosage:

- Noter les concentrations sériques de lithium, 2 fois par semaine au début du traitement, et tous les 2 à 3 mois pendant un traitement prolongé. Les échantillons de sang doivent être prélevés le matin, juste avant d'administrer la dose, et au moins 10 à 12 heures après la dernière dose. Les concentrations thérapeutiques se situent entre 0,5 et 1,5 mmol/L.
- Rester à l'affût des signes et des symptômes suivants de toxicité du lithium: vomissements, diarrhée, troubles de l'élocution, perte de coordination, somnolence, faiblesse musculaire ou soubresauts musculaires. Si ces symptômes se manifestent, prévenir le médecin avant d'administrer la dose suivante.

DIAGNOSTICS INFIRMIERS POSSIBLES

- Opérations de la pensée perturbées (Indications).
- Risque de violence envers soi ou les autres (Indications).
- Non-observance du traitement médicamenteux (Enseignement au patient et à ses proches).

INTERVENTIONS INFIRMIÈRES

- Administrer le lithium avec des aliments ou du lait afin de diminuer l'irritation gastro-intestinale. Les capsules à libération prolongée doivent être avalées telles quelles sans être scindées, écrasées ou croquées. Les comprimés à libération prolongée peuvent être avalés tels quels ou scindés en deux. Ils ne doivent pas être écrasés ou croqués.

ENSEIGNEMENT AU PATIENT ET À SES PROCHES

- Conseiller au patient de respecter rigoureusement la posologie recommandée même s'il se sent mieux. S'il n'a pu prendre le médicament au moment habituel, il doit le prendre dès que possible à moins que la dose suivante ne soit prévue dans les 2 heures (dans les 6 heures, s'il s'agit d'une préparation à libération prolongée).
- Prévenir le patient que le lithium peut provoquer de la somnolence ou des étourdissements. Lui conseiller de ne pas conduire et d'éviter les activités qui exigent sa vigilance jusqu'à ce qu'on ait la certitude que ce médicament n'entraîne pas ces effets chez lui.
- Puisque les faibles concentrations de sodium peuvent prédisposer le patient à la toxicité, lui conseiller de boire de 2 000 à 3 000 mL de liquides par jour et d'opter constamment pour un régime alimentaire à teneur modérée en sodium. Lui conseiller également d'éviter la consommation excessive de café, de thé ou de boissons à base de cola en raison de leur effet diurétique et de ne pas s'engager dans des activités qui entraînent des pertes excessives de sodium (efforts excessifs, exercice par temps chaud, sauna). Lui conseiller de communiquer avec un professionnel de la santé en cas de fièvre, de vomissements et de diarrhée, puisqu'ils entraînent aussi une déplétion sodique.
- Prévenir le patient qu'il peut prendre du poids. Lui expliquer les principes d'un régime alimentaire hypocalorique.
- Conseiller au patient de consulter un professionnel de la santé avant de prendre un médicament en vente libre pendant qu'il suit le traitement au lithium.
- Conseiller à la patiente de prendre des mesures contraceptives et de prévenir un professionnel de la santé si elle pense être enceinte ou désire le devenir ou, encore, si elle allaite.
- Expliquer au patient les effets secondaires du lithium et les symptômes de toxicité. Insister sur le fait qu'il est important d'arrêter immédiatement le traitement en cas de signes de toxicité et de les signaler à un professionnel de la santé.
- EXPLIQUER AU PATIENT SOUFFRANT DE MALADIE CARDIAQUE OU À CELUI QUI EST ÂGÉ DE PLUS DE 40 ANS QU'IL DOIT SE SOUMETTRE À UN ÉCG AVANT LE TRAITEMENT ET À INTERVALLES RÉGULIERS PENDANT TOUTE SA DURÉE. LUI CONSEILLER DE PRÉVENIR UN PROFESSIONNEL DE LA SANTÉ EN CAS

D'ÉVANOUISSEMENTS, DE POULS IRRÉGULIER OU DE DIFFICULTÉS RESPIRATOIRES.

- Insister sur l'importance des tests de laboratoire permettant de déceler la toxicité du lithium.

VÉRIFICATION DE L'EFFICACITÉ THÉRAPEUTIQUE

L'efficacité du traitement peut être démontrée par: la résolution des symptômes maniaques (hyperactivité, élocution précipitée, manque de jugement, diminution du besoin de sommeil) ■ la diminution de l'incidence des sautes d'humeur en cas de trouble bipolaire ■ l'amélioration de l'affect en cas de trouble unipolaire. L'amélioration de l'état du patient n'est parfois notable qu'après 1 à 3 semaines. ✳

LOPÉRAMIDE

Apo-Loperamide, Diarr-Eze, Imodium, Novo-Loperamide, PMS-Loperamide

CLASSIFICATION:

Antidiarrhéique

Grossesse – catégorie B

INDICATIONS

Traitement d'appoint de la diarrhée aiguë ■ Traitement de la diarrhée chronique associée aux maladies intestinales inflammatoires ■ Diminution du volume des évacuations après iléostomie.

MÉCANISME D'ACTION

Inhibition du péristaltisme et prolongation du transit intestinal par effet direct sur les nerfs de la paroi de l'intestin ■ Réduction du volume fécal, augmentation de la viscosité et de la masse fécales avec diminution parallèle des pertes de liquides et d'électrolytes. ***Effets thérapeutiques:*** Soulagement de la diarrhée.

PHARMACOCINÉTIQUE

Absorption: 40 % (PO).

Distribution: Inconnue. L'agent ne traverse pas la barrière hématoencéphalique.

Liaison aux protéines: 97 %.

Métabolisme et excrétion: Le lopéramide est métabolisé en partie par le foie et subit plusieurs cycles entérohépatiques. Excrétion fécale à 30 %; excrétion urinaire en quantités infimes.

Demi-vie: 10,8 heures.

Profil temps-action (soulagement de la diarrhée)

	DÉBUT D'ACTION	PIC	DURÉE
PO	1 h	2,5 – 5 h	10 h

CONTRE-INDICATIONS, PRÉCAUTIONS ET MISES EN GARDE

Contre-indications: Hypersensibilité ■ Patients chez lesquels la constipation doit être évitée ■ Douleurs abdominales d'étiologie inconnue, particulièrement lorsqu'elles s'accompagnent de fièvre ■ Administration déconseillée dans les cas où il faut éviter d'inhiber le péristaltisme (p. ex., colite pseudomembraneuse) ■ Intolérance à l'alcool (préparation liquide seulement) ■ **PÉD.:** L'innocuité de l'agent n'a pas été établie chez les enfants < 2 ans.

Précautions et mises en garde: Dysfonctionnement hépatique ■ **GÉR.:** Sensibilité accrue aux effets secondaires ■ **OBST.:** Grossesse, allaitement.

RÉACTIONS INDÉSIRABLES ET EFFETS SECONDAIRES

SNC: somnolence, étourdissements.

GI: constipation, douleurs abdominales, ballonnements et gêne abdominaux, sécheresse de la bouche (xérostomie), nausées, vomissements.

Divers: réactions allergiques.

INTERACTIONS

Médicament-médicament: Effets dépressifs additifs sur le SNC lors de l'usage concomitant de **dépresseurs du SNC**, y compris l'**alcool**, les **antihistaminiques**, les **opioïdes** et les **hypnosédatifs** ■ Effets anticholinergiques additifs lors de l'administration concomitante de **médicaments dotés de propriétés anticholinergiques**, y compris les **antidépresseurs** et les **antihistaminiques**.

Médicament-produits naturels: Le **kava**, la **valériane**, la **scutellaire**, la **camomille** et le **houblon** peuvent accentuer la dépression du SNC.

VOIES D'ADMINISTRATION ET POSOLOGIE

- **PO (adultes et enfants > 12 ans):** 4 mg au départ, puis 2 mg après chaque émission de selles liquides. La dose d'entretien habituelle est de 4 à 8 mg par jour (ne pas dépasser 16 mg par jour).
- **PO (enfants de 8 à 12 ans, poids > 30 kg):** Posologie initiale recommandée le premier jour: 2 mg, 3 fois (ne pas dépasser 6 mg/24 h; la préparation en vente libre ne doit pas être administrée pendant plus de 2 jours).
- **PO (enfants de 5 à 8 ans, poids de 20 à 30 kg):** Posologie initiale recommandée le premier jour: 2 mg, 2 fois

(ne pas dépasser 4 mg/24 h; la préparation en vente libre ne doit pas être administrée pendant plus de 2 jours).

- **PO (enfants de 2 à 5 ans, poids de 10 à 20 kg):** Posologie initiale recommandée le premier jour: 1 mg, 3 fois (ne pas dépasser 3 mg/24 h; la préparation en vente libre ne doit pas être administrée pendant plus de 2 jours).

Chez les **enfants**, après le premier jour de traitement, il est recommandé d'administrer le lopéramide à raison de 1 mg/10 kg de poids corporel, seulement après une selle molle et sans dépasser la dose quotidienne maximale.

PRÉSENTATION (version générique disponible)

Comprimés: 2 mg^VL ■ **Comprimés Vit-dissous:** 2 mg^VL ■ **Liquide:** 1 mg/5 mL^VL ■ **En association avec:** siméthicone (Imodium Avancé^VL).

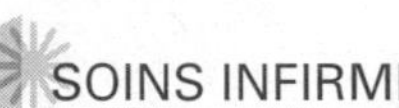

SOINS INFIRMIERS

ÉVALUATION DE LA SITUATION

- Observer la fréquence et la consistance des selles, et ausculter les bruits intestinaux avant le traitement et pendant toute sa durée.
- Noter le bilan hydroélectrolytique et observer la peau à la recherche de signes de déshydratation.

DIAGNOSTICS INFIRMIERS POSSIBLES

- Diarrhée (Indications).
- Risque d'accident (Effets secondaires).
- Connaissances insuffisantes sur le traitement médicamenteux (Enseignement au patient et à ses proches).

INTERVENTIONS INFIRMIÈRES

- Administrer l'agent avec des liquides clairs afin de prévenir la déshydratation qui pourrait accompagner la diarrhée.

ENSEIGNEMENT AU PATIENT ET À SES PROCHES

- Conseiller au patient de respecter rigoureusement la posologie recommandée. Le prévenir qu'il ne doit pas prendre les doses manquées ni doubler la dose. En cas de diarrhée aiguë, on pourrait lui recommander de prendre le médicament après chaque émission de selles liquides. Conseiller au patient de ne pas dépasser le nombre maximal de doses recommandées.
- Prévenir le patient que le lopéramide peut provoquer de la somnolence. Lui conseiller de ne pas conduire et d'éviter les activités qui exigent sa vigilance jusqu'à ce qu'on ait la certitude que le médicament n'entraîne pas cet effet chez lui.
- Conseiller au patient de se rincer fréquemment la bouche, de pratiquer une bonne hygiène buccale et de consommer de la gomme à mâcher ou des bonbons sans sucre pour soulager la sécheresse de la bouche.
- Prévenir le patient qu'il doit éviter de boire de l'alcool et de prendre d'autres dépresseurs du SNC pendant le traitement au lopéramide.
- Conseiller au patient de prévenir un professionnel de la santé si la diarrhée persiste ou si elle s'accompagne de fièvre, de douleurs abdominales ou de ballonnements.

VÉRIFICATION DE L'EFFICACITÉ THÉRAPEUTIQUE

L'efficacité du traitement peut être démontrée par: la diminution de la diarrhée ■ en cas de diarrhée aiguë, il faut arrêter le traitement en l'absence de toute amélioration après 48 heures ■ en cas de diarrhée chronique, en l'absence de toute amélioration après au moins 10 jours de traitement à la dose maximale, le lopéramide n'est vraisemblablement pas efficace.

LOPINAVIR/RITONAVIR

Kaletra

CLASSIFICATION:

Antirétroviral (inhibiteur de la protéase, inhibiteur métabolique [ritonavir])

Grossesse – catégorie C

INDICATIONS

Infection par le VIH (en association avec d'autres antirétroviraux). **Usages non approuvés:** En association avec d'autres antirétroviraux, prophylaxie après une exposition accidentelle au VIH.

MÉCANISME D'ACTION

Lopinavir – inhibition de la protéase du VIH et prévention du clivage des polyprotéines virales. *Ritonavir* – bien que le ritonavir ait des effets antirétroviraux par lui-même (inhibition de l'action de la protéase du VIH), on l'associe au lopinavir pour qu'il inhibe le métabolisme de ce dernier en élevant ainsi ses concentrations plasmatiques. ***Effets thérapeutiques:*** Augmentation du nombre de CD4 et diminution de la charge virale, ce qui ralentit l'évolution de l'infection par le VIH et en diminue les complications.

PHARMACOCINÉTIQUE

Absorption: Bonne (PO), accrue par les aliments.
Distribution: *Ritonavir* – l'agent pénètre faiblement dans le SNC.
Liaison aux protéines: *Lopinavir* – de 98 à 99 %.
Métabolisme et excrétion: *Lopinavir* – métabolisme hépatique total par le cytochrome P4503A; le ritonavir est un puissant inhibiteur de cette enzyme. *Ritonavir* – fort métabolisme hépatique (par les enzymes CYP3A et CYP2D6); un des métabolites est doté d'une activité antirétrovirale; 3,5 % est excrété à l'état inchangé dans l'urine.
Demi-vie: *Lopinavir* – de 5 à 6 heures; *ritonavir* – de 3 à 5 heures.

Profil temps-action

	Début d'action	Pic	Durée
Lopinavir PO	rapide	4h	12 h
Ritonavir PO	rapide	4h†	12 h

† Avec des aliments.

CONTRE-INDICATIONS, PRÉCAUTIONS ET MISES EN GARDE

Contre-indications: Hypersensibilité ▪ Usage concomitant de cisapride, de dihydroergotamine, d'ergotamine, d'ergonovine, de méthylergonovine, de midazolam, de pimozide, de rifampine, de simvastatine, de lovastatine et de triazolam, dont le métabolisme dépend fortement des enzymes CYP3A et dont les concentrations sanguines accrues peuvent entraîner des complications graves, voire mortelles ▪ Usage concomitant de millepertuis (*Hypericum perforatum*) ▪ Hypersensibilité ou intolérance à l'huile de ricin (présente dans les capsules et la solution).
Précautions et mises en garde: Nombreuses interactions médicamenteuses ▪ Intolérance connue à l'alcool (la solution destinée à la voie orale en contient) ▪ Hémophilie (risque accru d'hémorragie) ▪ Diabète (risque d'aggravation de l'hyperglycémie) ▪ Dysfonctionnement hépatique, antécédents d'hépatite (en raison du contenu en ritonavir) ▪ Antécédents de pancréatite (plus grand risque de récurrence pendant le traitement avec ce médicament) ▪ **Obst.**: Grossesse ou allaitement (l'innocuité de l'agent n'a pas été établie; l'allaitement est déconseillé aux patientes infectées par le VIH) ▪ **Péd.**: Enfants < 6 mois (l'innocuité de cette association n'a pas été établie).
Extrême prudence: L'usage concomitant de sildénafil, de vardénafil ou de tadalafil doit s'accompagner d'une extrême prudence en raison des risques d'hypotension, de syncope, de changements de la vision et d'érection prolongée.

RÉACTIONS INDÉSIRABLES ET EFFETS SECONDAIRES

SNC: céphalées, insomnie, faiblesse.
GI: diarrhée (plus fréquente chez les enfants), douleurs abdominales, nausées, pancréatite, altération du goût (chez les enfants), vomissements (plus fréquents chez les enfants), élévation des concentrations de transaminases hépatiques.
Tég.: rash.
Métab.: hyperglycémie, hyperlipidémie, hypertriglycéridémie.
Divers: modification de la distribution du tissu adipeux, syndrome de reconstitution immunitaire.

INTERACTIONS

Médicament-médicament: Le lopinavir/ritonavir est métabolisé par le CYP3A; il inhibe également ce système enzymatique. L'effet de tout autre médicament qui est métabolisé ou influencé par ce système peut être modifié lors d'un usage concomitant ▪ L'USAGE CONCOMITANT DE **CISAPRIDE**, DE **DIHYDROERGOTAMINE**, D'**ERGOTAMINE**, D'**ERGONOVINE**, DE **MÉTHYLERGONOVINE**, DE **MIDAZOLAM**, DE **PIMOZIDE**, DE **RIFAMPINE**, DE **SIMVASTATINE**, DE **LOVASTATINE** ET DE **TRIAZOLAM** EST CONTRE-INDIQUÉ EN RAISON DU RISQUE D'INTERACTIONS MÉDICAMENTEUSES QUI PEUVENT ÊTRE GRAVES, VOIRE MORTELLES ▪ L'usage concomitant de **rifampine** diminue l'efficacité du traitement antirétroviral et il est donc contre-indiqué ▪ L'usage concomitant de **sildénafil**, de **vardénafil** ou de **tadalafil** doit s'accompagner d'une extrême prudence en raison du risque d'hypotension, de syncope, de changements de la vision et d'érection prolongée (suivre de près l'état du patient et réduire la dose de sildénafil à 25 mg, toutes les 48 heures, et celle de tadalafil à 10 mg, toutes les 72 heures; éviter l'usage du vardénafil) ▪ L'usage concomitant d'**atorvastatine** augmente le risque de rhabdomyolyse (administrer la plus faible dose possible d'atorvastatine et suivre de près l'état du patient) ▪ L'usage concomitant d'**éfavirenz** ou de **névirapine** diminue les concentrations de l'association lopinavir/ritonavir et son efficacité (augmenter les doses et éviter l'administration uniquotidienne) ▪ La **délavirdine** élève les concentrations de lopinavir ▪ L'association lopinavir/ritonavir élève les concentrations d'**indinavir**, de **saquinavir** et de **ténofovir** ▪ L'association lopinavir/ritonavir peut abaisser les concentrations d'**abacavir** et de **zidovudine** ▪ L'usage concomitant d'**amprénavir** ou de **nelfinavir** entraîne l'élévation des concentrations d'amprénavir ou de nelfinavir et la diminution des concentrations de lopinavir (augmenter les doses de lopinavir/ritonavir et éviter l'administration uniquotidienne) ▪ L'association lopinavir/ritonavir élève les concentrations d'**amiodarone**, de **lidocaïne** et de **quinidine** (utiliser avec prudence; il est recommandé de mesurer les concentrations sanguines) ▪ L'association lopinavir/ritonavir pourrait élever les concentrations de **flécaïnide** et de **propafénone** (utiliser avec prudence) ▪ L'usage concomitant d'anticonvulsivants, dont la **carbamazépine**, le **phénobarbital** ou la **phénytoïne** peut diminuer l'efficacité du lopinavir (utiliser avec prudence et éviter l'administration uniquotidienne) ▪ L'association lopinavir/ritonavir élève les concentrations de **trazodone**, de **digoxine** et de **bloqueurs des canaux calciques dihydropyridiniques** (**amlodipine**, **félodipine**, **nifédipine**) (la surveillance clinique est de mise) ▪ L'association lopinavir/ritonavir peut modifier les concentrations de **warfarine** et réduire l'efficacité de cette dernière (surveiller le RNI) ▪ Elle élève les concentrations de **clarithromycine** (il est recommandé de réduire la dose chez les patients dont la Cl_{Cr} ≤ 60 mL/min) ▪ L'association lopinavir/ritonavir élève les concentrations d'**itraconazole** et de **kétoconazole** (les doses élevées d'antifongiques sont déconseillées) ▪ L'association lopinavir/ritonavir pourrait abaisser les concentrations de **voriconazole** ▪ Elle élève les concentrations de **rifabutine** (il est recommandé de réduire la dose) ▪ Elle abaisse les concentrations sanguines d'**atovaquone** (une majoration des doses peut être de mise) ▪ La **dexaméthasone** abaisse les concentrations sanguines de lopinavir et peut en réduire l'efficacité ▪ La solution administrée par voie orale contient de l'alcool et peut provoquer une intolérance si le patient prend du **disulfirame** ou du **métronidazole** ▪ L'association lopinavir/ritonavir peut accroître les concentrations et le risque de toxicité des immunosuppresseurs, comme la **cyclosporine** ou le **tacrolimus** (il est recommandé de suivre de près les concentrations sanguines) ▪ Elle peut diminuer les concentrations et les effets de la **méthadone** (augmenter, au besoin, la dose de **méthadone**) ▪ Elle peut abaisser les concentrations et l'efficacité contraceptive de certains **contraceptifs oraux contenant des œstrogènes**, notamment de l'**éthinylœstradiol** (il est recommandé d'utiliser une autre méthode ou de prendre des mesures contraceptives additionnelles) ▪ L'association lopinavir/ritonavir peut élever les concentrations de **fluticasone** en inhalation (éviter l'usage concomitant).

Médicament-produits naturels: L'usage concomitant de **millepertuis** entraîne une diminution marquée des concentrations sanguines et de l'efficacité du lopinavir/ritonavir, associée à l'émergence d'une résistance virale.

VOIES D'ADMINISTRATION ET POSOLOGIE

- **PO (adultes et enfants > 40 kg):** *Patients n'ayant jamais reçu d'antirétroviraux* – 400/100 mg (3 capsules ou 2 comprimés, ou 5 mL de solution orale), 2 fois par jour *OU* une seule dose quotidienne de 800/200 mg (6 capsules ou 4 comprimés, ou 10 mL de solution orale). *Patients ayant déjà reçu des antirétroviraux* – 400/100 mg (3 capsules ou 2 comprimés, ou 5 mL de solution orale), 2 fois par jour. La dose uniquotidienne n'est autorisée que chez l'adulte. L'administration uniquotidienne n'est pas recommandée chez les patients qui ont déjà reçu des antirétroviraux.
- **PO (enfants pesant de 15 à 40 kg):** 10 mg/kg de l'équivalent du contenu en lopinavir, 2 fois par jour.
- **PO (enfants pesant de 7 à < 15 kg):** 12 mg/kg de l'équivalent du contenu en lopinavir, 2 fois par jour.

Prise concomitante d'éfavirenz, de névirapine, de fosamprénavir, d'amprénavir ou de nelfinavir

- **PO (adultes et enfants pesant > 40 kg):** *Patients n'ayant jamais reçu d'antirétroviraux* – 400/100 mg (2 comprimés), 2 fois par jour. *Patients ayant déjà reçu des antirétroviraux* – 600/150 mg (3 comprimés), 2 fois par jour *OU* 533/133 mg (4 capsules ou 6,5 mL de solution orale), 2 fois par jour.
- **PO (enfants pesant de 15 à 40 kg):** 11 mg/kg de l'équivalent du contenu en lopinavir, 2 fois par jour.
- **PO (enfants pesant de 7 à < 15 kg):** 13 mg/kg de l'équivalent du contenu en lopinavir, 2 fois par jour.

PRÉSENTATION

Capsules: 133,3 mg de lopinavir/33 mg de ritonavir[Pr].

Comprimés enrobés: 200 mg de lopinavir/50 mg de ritonavir[Pr].

Solution orale (parfum de barbe à papa ou de vanille): 80 mg lopinavir/20 mg ritonavir par mL (contient 42,4 % d'alcool), en flacons de 160 mL[Pr].

SOINS INFIRMIERS

ÉVALUATION DE LA SITUATION

- Rester à l'affût de tout changement qui intervient dans la gravité des symptômes de l'infection par le VIH et de l'apparition de symptômes d'infections opportunistes pendant toute la durée du traitement.
- Rechercher les signes de pancréatite (nausées, vomissements, douleurs abdominales, élévations des taux sériques de lipase ou d'amylase) à intervalles réguliers pendant toute la durée du traitement. L'arrêt du traitement pourrait s'imposer.

- Si une patiente enceinte est exposée à des antirétroviraux, l'inscrire dans le registre des femmes exposées aux antirétroviraux pendant leur grossesse, en composant le 1 800 258 4263.

Tests de laboratoire:

- Suivre la charge virale et le nombre de cellules CD4 à intervalles réguliers tout au long du traitement.
- Mesurer les taux de triglycérides et de cholestérol avant le début du traitement et à intervalles réguliers pendant toute sa durée.
- Il y a risque d'hyperglycémie.
- Il y a risque d'élévation des concentrations sériques d'AST, d'ALT, de GGT et de bilirubine totale.

DIAGNOSTICS INFIRMIERS POSSIBLES

- Risque d'infection (Indications).
- Non-observance du traitement médicamenteux (Enseignement au patient et à ses proches).

INTERVENTIONS INFIRMIÈRES

- NE PAS CONFONDRE KALETRA (LOPINAVIR/RITONAVIR) AVEC KEPPRA (LÉVÉTIRACÉTAM).
- Les patients qui prennent en même temps de la didanosine doivent prendre celle-ci 1 heure avant ou 2 heures après avoir pris le lopinavir/ritonavir.

PO: Administrer les capsules et la solution orale avec des aliments pour améliorer l'absorption. Les comprimés peuvent être pris avec ou sans nourriture.

- La solution orale est de jaune pâle à orangé.
- Les capsules et la solution orale sont stables jusqu'à leur date de péremption si elles sont gardées au réfrigérateur ou pendant 42 jours si elles sont gardées à la température ambiante. Les comprimés ne doivent pas être réfrigérés.

ENSEIGNEMENT AU PATIENT ET À SES PROCHES

- Insister sur le fait qu'il faut prendre le lopinavir/ritonavir en respectant rigoureusement les recommandations du médecin et en espaçant également les heures des prises au cours de la journée. Expliquer au patient qu'il ne doit pas prendre plus que la quantité prescrite ni arrêter le traitement par cette association médicamenteuse ou par tout autre antirétroviral sans consulter un professionnel de la santé au préalable. Le prévenir qu'il doit prendre toute dose oubliée dès qu'il s'en souvient, sans jamais remplacer une dose manquée par une double dose.
- Prévenir le patient qu'il ne doit pas donner le lopinavir/ritonavir à d'autres personnes.
- Conseiller au patient de consulter un professionnel de la santé avant de prendre d'autres médicaments d'ordonnance ou en vente libre, ou des produits naturels, et particulièrement du millepertuis.
- Prévenir le patient que le lopinavir/ritonavir ne guérit pas l'infection par le VIH ni ne prévient les infections associées ou opportunistes. Il ne réduit pas le risque de transmission du VIH à d'autres personnes par les rapports sexuels ou le sang. Inciter le patient à utiliser un condom et à éviter le partage d'aiguilles ou les dons de sang pour prévenir la propagation du VIH. Prévenir le patient que les effets au long cours du lopinavir/ritonavir sont pour le moment inconnus.
- Informer le patient que le lopinavir/ritonavir peut provoquer de l'hyperglycémie. Lui conseiller de prévenir un professionnel de la santé en cas de faim ou de soif accrue, d'une perte de poids inexpliquée ou d'une fréquence accrue des mictions.
- Conseiller à la patiente qui prend des contraceptifs oraux d'utiliser une méthode non hormonale de contraception pendant le traitement par le lopinavir/ritonavir.
- Mettre en garde le patient prenant du sildénafil, du tadalafil ou du vardénafil contre le risque accru d'effets secondaires de ces agents (hypotension, changements de la vision, érection prolongée). Lui recommander de prévenir rapidement un professionnel de la santé si ces effets se manifestent.
- Prévenir le patient qu'il y a risque de redistribution des tissus adipeux (obésité centrale, accumulation de graisses dans la région dorsocervicale ou bosse de bison, atrophie des tissus périphériques, hypertrophie des tissus mammaires, apparence cushinoïde). La cause de cet effet et ses répercussions à long terme ne sont pas connues.
- Recommander à la patiente d'informer un professionnel de la santé si elle pense être enceinte ou désire le devenir ou, encore, si elle allaite.
- Insister sur l'importance des examens réguliers de suivi et des numérations globulaires permettant d'évaluer les progrès du traitement et de surveiller les effets secondaires.

VÉRIFICATION DE L'EFFICACITÉ THÉRAPEUTIQUE

L'efficacité du traitement peut être démontrée par: le ralentissement de l'évolution de l'infection par le VIH et la diminution du risque d'infections opportunistes ▪ la diminution de la charge virale et l'augmentation du nombre de CD4.

LORATADINE

Allertin, Apo-Loratadine, Claritin

CLASSIFICATION:

Antihistaminique (inhibiteur des récepteurs H_1 de l'histamine)

Grossesse – catégorie B

INDICATIONS

Soulagement des symptômes de rhinite allergique saisonnière et apériodique, tels que les éternuements, l'écoulement nasal, l'irritation oculaire et le prurit nasal et oculaire ▪ Soulagement des symptômes et des signes de l'urticaire idiopathique chronique et d'autres dermatopathies allergiques.

MÉCANISME D'ACTION

Blocage au niveau des récepteurs H_1 des effets périphériques de l'histamine libérée lors des réactions allergiques. ***Effets thérapeutiques:*** Diminution des symptômes de réactions allergiques (éternuements, rhinorrhée, larmoiements, rougeurs oculaires, prurit).

PHARMACOCINÉTIQUE

Absorption: 80 % (PO).

Distribution: Inconnue.

Liaison aux protéines: *Loratadine* – 97 %. *Descarboéthoxyloratadine* – de 73 à 77 %.

Métabolisme et excrétion: Fort métabolisme hépatique et transformation notable en un métabolite actif, la descarboéthoxyloratidine.

Demi-vie: *Loratadine* – de 7,8 à 11 heures. *Descarboéthoxyloratadine* – 20 heures.

Profil temps-action (effets antihistaminiques)

	Début d'action	Pic	Durée
PO	1 - 3 h	8 - 12 h	> 24 h

CONTRE-INDICATIONS, PRÉCAUTIONS ET MISES EN GARDE

Contre-indications: Hypersensibilité.

Précautions et mises en garde: Insuffisance hépatique grave (il est recommandé de réduire la dose initiale à 5 mg, 1 fois par jour, ou 10 mg, 1 jour sur 2) ▪ **OBST.**: Ce médicament est déconseillé chez les femmes enceintes, sauf avis médical contraire ▪ **ALLAITEMENT**: Ce médicament est déconseillé pendant l'allaitement, sauf avis médical contraire ▪ **PÉD.**: L'innocuité du médicament n'a pas été établie chez les enfants < 2 ans.

RÉACTIONS INDÉSIRABLES ET EFFETS SECONDAIRES

SNC: confusion, somnolence (rare), excitation paradoxale.

ORLO: vision trouble.

GI: sécheresse de la bouche (xérostomie), gêne gastro-intestinale.

Tég.: photosensibilité, rash.

Métab.: gain de poids.

INTERACTIONS

Médicament-médicament: Les interactions suivantes sont susceptibles de se produire, mais plus rarement que dans le cas des antihistaminiques plus sédatifs: effets additifs sur la dépression du SNC lors de l'usage concomitant d'**alcool**, d'**antidépresseurs**, d'**opioïdes** et d'**hypnosédatifs** ▪ Les **IMAO** pourraient augmenter et prolonger l'effet sédatif des antihistaminiques ▪ Les médicaments qui diminuent le métabolisme hépatique (le **kétoconazole**, l'**érythromycine** ou la **cimétidine**), pris en concomitance, peuvent augmenter la concentration plasmatique de loratadine sans toutefois entraîner de changement clinique notable.

Médicament-produits naturels: La consommation concomitante de **kava**, de **valériane** et de **camomille** peut augmenter l'effet dépresseur du SNC de la loratadine.

Médicament-aliments: L'absorption de la loratadine est accrue par la consommation d'aliments.

VOIES D'ADMINISTRATION ET POSOLOGIE

- **PO (comprimés) (adultes et enfants ≥ 12 ans)**: 10 mg, 1 fois par jour.
- **PO (sirop) (adultes et enfants ≥ 10 ans, poids > 30 kg)**: 10 mg, 1 fois par jour.
- **PO (sirop) (enfants de 2 à 9 ans, poids ≤ 30 kg)**: 5 mg, 1 fois par jour.
- ***INSUFFISANCE HÉPATIQUE GRAVE***

  PO (ADULTES): 5 mg, 1 FOIS PAR JOUR, OU 10 mg, 1 JOUR SUR 2.

PRÉSENTATION

Comprimés à dissolution rapide: 10 mg^VL ▪ **Comprimés**: 10 mg^VL ▪ **Sirop**: 1 mg/mL^VL ▪ **En association avec**: pseudoéphédrine (Claritin Extra, Chlor-Tripolon ND SRT, Liberator)^VL.

SOINS INFIRMIERS

ÉVALUATION DE LA SITUATION

- Avant le traitement et à intervalles réguliers pendant toute sa durée, rester à l'affût des symptômes suivants d'allergie: rhinite, conjonctivite, urticaire.

- Ausculter le murmure vésiculaire et déterminer les caractéristiques des sécrétions bronchiques. Maintenir la consommation de liquides entre 1 500 et 2 000 mL par jour pour diminuer la viscosité des sécrétions.

Tests de laboratoire: La loratadine peut entraîner des résultats faussement négatifs aux tests d'allergie cutanée.

DIAGNOSTICS INFIRMIERS POSSIBLES

- Dégagement inefficace des voies respiratoires (Indications).
- Risque d'accident (Effets secondaires).
- Connaissances insuffisantes sur le traitement médicamenteux (Enseignement au patient et à ses proches).

INTERVENTIONS INFIRMIÈRES

PO: Administrer la loratadine 1 fois par jour, à jeun.

- *Comprimés à dissolution rapide*: Placer le comprimé sur la langue. Il se dissout rapidement et peut être pris avec ou sans liquide. Administrer à jeun.

ENSEIGNEMENT AU PATIENT ET À SES PROCHES

- Conseiller au patient de prendre la loratadine 1 heure avant les repas ou 2 heures après.
- Prévenir le patient que la loratadine peut provoquer de la somnolence ou des étourdissements. Lui conseiller de ne pas conduire et d'éviter les activités exigeant sa vigilance jusqu'à ce qu'on ait la certitude que le médicament n'entraîne pas ces effets chez lui.
- Conseiller au patient d'utiliser un écran solaire et de porter des vêtements protecteurs pour prévenir les réactions de photosensibilité.
- Recommander au patient d'éviter de boire de l'alcool ou de prendre d'autres dépresseurs du SNC en même temps que ce médicament.
- Expliquer au patient que pour soulager la sécheresse de la bouche, il doit se rincer fréquemment la bouche, consommer des bonbons ou de la gomme à mâcher sans sucre et pratiquer une bonne hygiène buccale. Recommander au patient de consulter un professionnel de la santé si la sécheresse de la bouche persiste pendant plus de 2 semaines.
- Conseiller au patient de communiquer immédiatement avec un professionnel de la santé en cas d'étourdissements, d'évanouissement, d'arythmies et de palpitations, ou si les symptômes persistent.

VÉRIFICATION DE L'EFFICACITÉ THÉRAPEUTIQUE

L'efficacité du traitement peut être démontrée par: la diminution des symptômes d'allergie.

LORAZÉPAM

Apo-Lorazépam, Ativan, Dom-Lorazépam, Lorazépam, Novo-Lorazem, Nu-Loraz, PMS-Lorazépam

CLASSIFICATION:

Anxiolytique et hypnosédatif (benzodiazépine), anticonvulsivant

Grossesse – catégorie D

INDICATIONS

Traitement d'appoint de l'anxiété ■ Diminution de l'anxiété préopératoire ■ Traitement de l'état de mal épileptique (IV). **Usages non approuvés – IV**: Antiémétique avant la chimiothérapie.

MÉCANISME D'ACTION

Dépression du SNC, probablement par potentialisation de l'activité de l'acide gamma-aminobutyrique (GABA), un neurotransmetteur inhibiteur. ***Effets thérapeutiques:*** Sédation ■ Soulagement de l'anxiété ■ Diminution des convulsions.

L

PHARMACOCINÉTIQUE

Absorption: Bonne (PO); rapide et totale (IM). Voie sublinguale – plus rapide que PO et similaire à la voie IM.

Distribution: Tout l'organisme. Le lorazépam traverse la barrière hématoencéphalique et placentaire, et passe dans le lait maternel.

Liaison aux protéines: 87 %.

Métabolisme et excrétion: Métabolisme hépatique important. Excrétion rénale principalement sous forme de métabolites.

Demi-vie: De 10 à 20 heures.

Profil temps-action (sédation)

	DÉBUT D'ACTION	PIC†	DURÉE
PO	30 - 60 min	60 - 90 min	6 - 8 h
SL	15 - 30 min	60 - 90 min	6 - 8 h
IM	15 - 30 min	1 - 2 h	6 - 8 h
IV	15 - 30 min	15 - 20 min	6 - 8 h

† Effet amnésique.

CONTRE-INDICATIONS, PRÉCAUTIONS ET MISES EN GARDE

Contre-indications: Hypersensibilité ■ Risque de sensibilité croisée avec d'autres benzodiazépines ■ Coma ou dépression préexistante du SNC ■ Glaucome à angle fermé aigu ■ Myasthénie grave.

Précautions et mises en garde: Insuffisance hépatique, rénale ou pulmonaire grave ■ Antécédents de tentatives de suicide ou de toxicomanie ■ **GÉR.**: Il est recommandé de réduire la dose chez les personnes âgées ou débilitées ■ **PÉD.**: L'innocuité du produit injectable n'a pas été établie chez les enfants < 18 ans ■ **OBST., ALLAITEMENT:** L'innocuité du lorazépam n'a pas été établie chez la femme enceinte ou qui allaite (le médicament traverse la barrière placentaire et passe dans le lait maternel).

RÉACTIONS INDÉSIRABLES ET EFFETS SECONDAIRES

SNC: étourdissements, somnolence, léthargie, sensation de tête légère, céphalées, dépression, excitation paradoxale.
ORLO: vision trouble.
Resp.: dépression respiratoire.
CV: *IV rapide seulement* – APNÉE, ARRÊT CARDIAQUE, bradycardie, hypotension.
GI: constipation, diarrhée, nausées, vomissements.
Tég.: rash.
Divers: dépendance physique, dépendance psychologique, tolérance aux effets du médicament.

INTERACTIONS

Médicament-médicament: Dépression additive du SNC lors de l'usage concomitant d'autres **dépresseurs du SNC**, y compris l'**alcool**, les **antihistaminiques**, les **antidépresseurs**, les **opioïdes** et d'autres **hypnosédatifs**, incluant d'autres benzodiazépines ■ Le lorazépam peut diminuer l'efficacité de la **lévodopa** ■ L'**usage du tabac** peut accélérer le métabolisme et réduire l'efficacité du lorazépam ■ Le **probénécide** peut ralentir le métabolisme du lorazépam et en intensifier les effets.
Médicament-produits naturels: Le **kava**, la **valériane** et la **camomille** peuvent accentuer la dépression du SNC.

VOIES D'ADMINISTRATION ET POSOLOGIE

- **PO (adultes):** *Anxiété* – initialement, 2 mg par jour, en doses fractionnées. L'écart posologique habituel est de 2 à 3 mg par jour. La dose quotidienne maximale est de 6 mg.
- **PO (personnes âgées ou débilitées):** *Anxiété* – initialement, la dose ne doit pas dépasser 0,5 mg par jour.
- **SL (adultes):** *Sédation préopératoire* – 0,05 mg/kg (ne pas dépasser 4 mg), de 1 à 2 heures avant l'intervention.
- **IM (adultes):** *Sédation préopératoire* – 0,05 mg/kg (ne pas dépasser 4 mg), de 2 à 3 heures avant l'intervention.
- **IV (adultes):** *Sédation préopératoire* – 0,044 mg/kg (ne pas dépasser 2 mg), de 15 à 20 minutes avant l'intervention. *Anticonvulsivant* – 0,05 mg/kg, jusqu'à 4 mg; on peut administrer de nouveau cette dose de 10 à 15 minutes plus tard (ne pas dépasser 8 mg/12 h).

PRÉSENTATION (version générique disponible)

Comprimés ordinaires et comprimés sublinguaux: 0,5 mg[T\C], 1 mg[T\C], 2 mg[T\C] ■ **Solution pour injection:** 4 mg/mL[T\C].

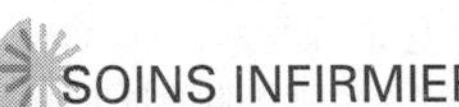

SOINS INFIRMIERS

ÉVALUATION DE LA SITUATION

Anxiété:

- Déterminer le degré d'anxiété et ses manifestations avant le traitement et à intervalles réguliers pendant toute sa durée.
- Le traitement prolongé à des doses élevées peut entraîner une dépendance psychologique ou physique. Réduire la quantité de médicament dont le patient peut disposer.

État de mal épileptique: Évaluer le siège, la durée, les caractéristiques et la fréquence des convulsions. **GÉR.**: Les personnes âgées ou débilitées sont plus sensibles aux effets sur le SNC; prendre les mesures qui s'imposent pour prévenir les chutes.
PÉD.: Chez les nouveau-nés, le métabolisme du lorazépam peut être entravé; rester à l'affût d'une dépression prolongée du SNC.
Tests de laboratoire: Les patients qui reçoivent des doses élevées doivent se soumettre à intervalles réguliers aux tests de la fonction hépatique, rénale et hématologique.

DIAGNOSTICS INFIRMIERS POSSIBLES

- Anxiété (Indications).
- Risque d'accident (Indications, Effets secondaires).
- Connaissances insuffisantes sur le traitement médicamenteux (Enseignement au patient et à ses proches).

INTERVENTIONS INFIRMIÈRES

- NE PAS CONFONDRE ATIVAN (LORAZÉPAM) AVEC ATARAX (HYDROXYZINE).
- Après administration par voie parentérale, demander au patient de garder le lit et l'observer étroitement pendant au moins 8 heures.

PO: On peut également administrer le comprimé par voie sublinguale (usage non approuvé) si l'on désire un effet plus rapide.
IM: Afin d'obtenir un effet optimal, administrer les injections IM profondément dans le tissu musculaire, au moins 2 heures avant l'intervention chirurgicale.

IV directe: Diluer immédiatement avant l'administration dans une quantité égale d'eau stérile, de D5%E ou de NaCl 0,9 % pour injection. Ne pas utiliser la solution si elle est colorée ou si elle renferme un précipité. Consulter les directives de chaque fabricant avant de reconstituer la préparation.

Vitesse d'administration: ADMINISTRER LA SOLUTION PAR IV DIRECTE DANS UNE TUBULURE EN Y, À UN DÉBIT DE 2 mg PAR MINUTE. L'INJECTION RAPIDE PEUT ENTRAÎNER L'APNÉE, L'HYPOTENSION, LA BRADYCARDIE OU L'ARRÊT CARDIAQUE.

Compatibilité (tubulure en Y): acyclovir ▪ adrénaline ▪ albumine ▪ allopurinol ▪ amifostine ▪ amikacine ▪ amphotéricine B, cholestéryl d' ▪ atracurium ▪ bumétanide ▪ céfépime ▪ cefmétazole ▪ céfotaxime ▪ ciprofloxacine ▪ cisatracurium ▪ cisplatine ▪ cladribine ▪ clonidine ▪ cyclophosphamide ▪ cytarabine ▪ dexaméthasone, phosphate sodique de ▪ diltiazem ▪ dobutamine ▪ dopamine ▪ doxorubicine ▪ doxorubicine liposomique ▪ érythromycine, lactobionate d' ▪ étomidate ▪ famotidine ▪ fentanyl ▪ filgrastim ▪ fluconazole ▪ fludarabine ▪ furosémide ▪ gentamicine ▪ granisétron ▪ halopéridol ▪ héparine ▪ hydrocortisone, succinate sodique d' ▪ hydromorphone ▪ labétalol ▪ melphalan ▪ méthotrexate ▪ métronidazole ▪ midazolam ▪ milrinone ▪ morphine ▪ nitroglycérine ▪ noradrénaline ▪ paclitaxel ▪ pancuronium ▪ pipéracilline ▪ pipéracilline/tazobactam ▪ potassium, chlorure de ▪ propofol ▪ ranitidine ▪ rémifentanil ▪ tacrolimus ▪ téniposide ▪ thiotépa ▪ triméthoprime/sulfaméthoxazole ▪ vancomycine ▪ vécuronium ▪ vinorelbine ▪ zidovudine.

Incompatibilité (tubulure en Y): aldesleukine ▪ floxacilline ▪ gallium, nitrate de ▪ idarubicine ▪ imipénem/cilastatine ▪ oméprazole ▪ ondansétron ▪ sargramostim ▪ sufentanil.

ENSEIGNEMENT AU PATIENT ET À SES PROCHES

- Expliquer au patient qu'il doit respecter rigoureusement la posologie recommandée. L'avertir qu'il ne doit jamais sauter de dose, ni remplacer une dose manquée par une double dose. Si le médicament s'avère moins efficace après quelques semaines, il faut en prévenir un professionnel de la santé, sans augmenter les doses. Le sevrage brusque peut provoquer des tremblements, des nausées, des vomissements ou des crampes abdominales et musculaires.
- Prévenir le patient que le lorazépam peut parfois provoquer de la somnolence ou des étourdissements. Lui conseiller de ne pas conduire et d'éviter les activités qui exigent sa vigilance jusqu'à ce qu'on ait la certitude que le médicament n'entraîne pas ces effets chez lui.

GÉR.: Prévenir le patient âgé qu'il y un risque accru d'effets sur le SNC et de chutes.

- Prévenir le patient qu'il ne doit pas consommer d'alcool ni prendre d'autres dépresseurs du SNC en même temps que ce médicament.
- Recommander à la patiente de prévenir immédiatement un professionnel de la santé si elle pense être enceinte ou désire le devenir ou, encore, si elle allaite.
- Insister sur l'importance des examens de suivi permettant d'évaluer l'efficacité du médicament.

VÉRIFICATION DE L'EFFICACITÉ THÉRAPEUTIQUE

L'efficacité du traitement peut être démontrée par: un sentiment de mieux-être ▪ la diminution de la sensation subjective d'anxiété sans sédation excessive ▪ la diminution de l'anxiété préopératoire ▪ l'amnésie postopératoire ▪ la disparition des convulsions en cas d'état de mal épileptique.

LOSARTAN,

voir Antagonistes des récepteurs de l'angiotensine II

LOVASTATINE,

voir Inhibiteurs de l'HMG-CoA réductase

LOXAPINE

Apo-Loxapine, Dom-Loxapine, Loxapac, Nu-Loxapine, PMS-Loxapine

CLASSIFICATION:

Antipsychotique

Grossesse – catégorie C

INDICATIONS

Traitement des manifestations de la schizophrénie.

MÉCANISME D'ACTION

Blocage possible de la dopamine aux sites des récepteurs postsynaptiques dans le SNC. ***Effets thérapeutiques:*** Diminution du comportement schizophrénique.

PHARMACOCINÉTIQUE

Absorption: Rapide et complète (PO et IM).

Distribution: Inconnue.
Métabolisme et excrétion: Métabolisme majoritairement hépatique. Une certaine fraction est transformée en composés antipsychotiques actifs.
Demi-vie: 19 heures.

Profil temps-action (effet antipsychotique)

	DÉBUT D'ACTION	PIC	DURÉE
PO	30 min	1,5 - 3 h	12 h
IM	30 min	inconnu	inconnue

CONTRE-INDICATIONS, PRÉCAUTIONS ET MISES EN GARDE

Contre-indications: Hypersensibilité ou intolérance à la loxapine ou à l'amoxapine ■ Coma ■ Dépression du SNC ■ Insuffisance circulatoire.
Précautions et mises en garde: Glaucome ■ Hommes âgés ou souffrant d'hyperplasie de la prostate (prédisposition accrue à la rétention urinaire) ■ **GÉR.**: Prédisposition accrue aux réactions indésirables ■ Occlusion intestinale ■ Antécédents de convulsions ■ Alcoolisme ■ Maladie cardiovasculaire ■ Insuffisance hépatique ■ **PÉD.**: L'innocuité du médicament n'a pas été établie chez les enfants < 16 ans ■ **OBST., ALLAITEMENT**: L'innocuité n'a pas été établie.

RÉACTIONS INDÉSIRABLES ET EFFETS SECONDAIRES

SNC: somnolence, syndromes extrapyramidaux, incluant le SYNDROME MALIN DES NEUROLEPTIQUES, dyskinésie tardive, insomnie, étourdissements, léthargie, sensation de tête légère, syncope, céphalées, ataxie, faiblesse, confusion.
ORLO: congestion nasale, vision trouble, opacité du cristallin.
CV: tachycardie, hypotension.
GI: constipation, sécheresse de la bouche (xérostomie), hépatite, nausées, vomissements, iléus.
GU: rétention urinaire.
Tég.: rash, dermatite, photosensibilité faciale, œdème, séborrhée, modification de la pigmentation.
End.: galactorrhée.
Hémat.: AGRANULOCYTOSE.
Divers: réactions allergiques.

INTERACTIONS

Médicament-médicament: La loxapine peut diminuer les effets des **antiparkinsoniens** ■ La loxapine peut diminuer les concentrations sériques de **carbamazépine** ■ La loxapine inhibe les effets alpha-adrénergiques de l'**adrénaline** (risque d'hypotension et de tachycardie) ■ Dépression additive du SNC lors de l'usage concomitant d'autres **dépresseurs du SNC**, y compris l'**alcool**, les **antihistaminiques**, les **analgésiques opioïdes** et les **hypnosédatifs** ■ L'administration concomitante d'**antiacides** ou d'**antidiarrhéiques adsorbants** peut réduire l'absorption de la loxapine ■ Les **antidépresseurs** ou les **IMAO**, administrés en concomitance, peuvent prolonger la dépression du SNC et intensifier les effets anticholinergiques ■ Il faut utiliser la loxapine avec précaution lorsqu'elle est administrée en concomitance avec d'autres médicaments qui allongent l'intervalle QTc (**amantadine, amiodarone, ampicilline, antidépresseurs tricycliques, chlorpromazine, citalopram, clarithromycine, cotrimoxazole, disopyramide, dompéridone, érythromycine, indapamide, lithium, moxifloxacine, procaïnamide, quétiapine, quinidine, thioridazine**) à cause du risque d'allongement additionnel de l'intervalle QTc et d'arythmies mortelles, telles les torsades de pointes.

VOIES D'ADMINISTRATION ET POSOLOGIE

- **PO (adultes)**: 10 mg, 2 fois par jour; on peut augmenter graduellement la dose au cours des 7 à 10 premiers jours de traitement, selon la réponse au traitement ou la tolérance du patient. La dose d'entretien habituelle est de 60 à 100 mg par jour, en 2 ou 4 doses fractionnées. Chez les patients très malades, on doit parfois administrer une dose initiale allant jusqu'à 50 mg et des doses d'entretien allant jusqu'à 250 mg par jour.
- **IM (adultes)**: De 12,5 à 50 mg, toutes les 4 à 6 heures ou plus, selon la réponse au traitement ou la tolérance du patient.

PRÉSENTATION

Comprimés: 2,5 mg[Pr], 5 mg[Pr], 10 mg[Pr], 25 mg[Pr], 50 mg[Pr] ■ **Solution injectable**: 50 mg/mL[Pr] ■ **Liquide oral**: 25 mg/mL[Pr].

SOINS INFIRMIERS

ÉVALUATION DE LA SITUATION

- Déterminer, avant le traitement et à intervalles réguliers pendant toute sa durée, l'état de conscience du patient (délire, hallucinations, comportement).
- Mesurer le pouls et la pression artérielle (en position assise, couchée et debout) avant l'administration initiale et à intervalles fréquents pendant la période d'adaptation de la posologie.
- Observer attentivement le patient pendant qu'il prend le médicament pour s'assurer qu'il l'a bien avalé.

- Surveiller l'apparition des symptômes extrapyramidaux suivants: akathisie – agitation; dystonie – spasmes musculaires et mouvements de contorsion; pseudoparkinsonisme – faciès figé, rigidité, tremblements, bouche ouverte laissant s'échapper la salive (sialorrhée), démarche traînante et dysphagie. Signaler immédiatement à un professionnel de la santé l'apparition de ces symptômes, car une réduction de la dose ou l'arrêt du traitement pourraient s'imposer. Le médecin pourrait également prescrire un agent antiparkinsonien (trihexiphénidyle, benztropine) pour maîtriser ces symptômes.
- Suivre de près l'apparition de la dyskinésie tardive qui se traduit par des mouvements rythmiques de la bouche, du visage et des membres. Avertir immédiatement un professionnel de la santé si ces symptômes se manifestent, car de tels effets secondaires peuvent être irréversibles.
- Noter la fréquence et la consistance des selles. La consommation accrue de fibres alimentaires et de liquides peut aider à réduire la constipation.
- La loxapine abaisse le seuil de convulsion. Prendre les précautions de mise dans le cas des patients ayant des antécédents de troubles convulsifs.
- SURVEILLER L'APPARITION DU SYNDROME MALIN DES NEUROLEPTIQUES SE MANIFESTANT PAR LES SYMPTÔMES SUIVANTS: FIÈVRE, DÉTRESSE RESPIRATOIRE, TACHYCARDIE, CONVULSIONS, DIAPHORÈSE, HYPERTENSION OU HYPOTENSION, PÂLEUR, FATIGUE. SIGNALER IMMÉDIATEMENT À UN PROFESSIONNEL DE LA SANTÉ L'APPARITION DE CES SYMPTÔMES.

Tests de laboratoire:

- Noter la numération globulaire et la formule leucocytaire avant le traitement et à intervalles réguliers pendant toute sa durée.
- Examiner les résultats des tests de la fonction hépatique avant le traitement et à intervalles réguliers pendant toute sa durée.

TOXICITÉ ET SURDOSAGE: Les effets antiémétiques de la loxapine peuvent inhiber l'effet du sirop d'ipéca. En cas de surdosage, effectuer un lavage gastrique, administrer un barbiturique pour maîtriser les convulsions et prodiguer les soins de soutien qui s'imposent en présence de fluctuations de la température corporelle. En cas d'hypotension, administrer des liquides par voie IV, de la noradrénaline ou de la phényléphrine. Ne pas administrer d'adrénaline, car elle pourrait aggraver l'hypotension.

DIAGNOSTICS INFIRMIERS POSSIBLES

- Opérations de la pensée perturbées (Indications).
- Risque d'accident (Réactions indésirables).
- Connaissances insuffisantes sur le traitement médicamenteux (Enseignement au patient et à ses proches).

INTERVENTIONS INFIRMIÈRES

PO:

- Administrer les comprimés avec des aliments ou du lait pour réduire l'irritation gastrique.
- Diluer la solution orale dans du jus d'orange ou de pamplemousse, immédiatement avant l'administration. Mesurer la dose à l'aide du compte-gouttes fourni.

IM:

- Ne pas administrer la préparation par voie SC. Injecter lentement et en profondeur dans un muscle bien développé. Une légère coloration ambrée n'altère en rien la puissance de la solution. Ne pas administrer la solution si elle a fortement changé de couleur ou si elle renferme un précipité.
- Maintenir le patient en position couchée pendant au moins 30 minutes après l'administration par voie parentérale afin de réduire les effets hypotenseurs de la loxapine.

ENSEIGNEMENT AU PATIENT ET À SES PROCHES

- Conseiller au patient de respecter rigoureusement la posologie recommandée. S'il n'a pas pu prendre le médicament au moment habituel, il doit le prendre dès que possible, jusqu'à 1 heure avant l'heure prévue pour la dose suivante. Chez les patients suivant un traitement prolongé avec des fortes doses, un arrêt graduel de la médication pourrait s'avérer nécessaire afin d'éviter l'apparition des symptômes suivants de sevrage: dyskinésie, tremblements, étourdissements, nausées et vomissements.
- Montrer au patient recevant la solution orale comment mesurer la dose avec le compte-gouttes fourni.
- Mettre en garde le patient contre le risque d'apparition de symptômes extrapyramidaux ou d'une dyskinésie tardive. L'inciter à avertir immédiatement un professionnel de la santé si ces symptômes se manifestent.
- Recommander au patient de changer lentement de position afin de réduire le risque d'hypotension orthostatique.
- Prévenir le patient que la loxapine peut provoquer de la somnolence. Lui conseiller de ne pas conduire et d'éviter les activités qui exigent sa vigilance jusqu'à ce qu'on ait la certitude que le médicament n'entraîne pas cet effet chez lui.
- Recommander au patient d'utiliser des crèmes solaires et de porter des vêtements protecteurs afin de prévenir les réactions de photosensibilité.

- Mettre en garde le patient contre la consommation concomitante d'alcool, d'autres dépresseurs du SNC ou de médicaments en vente libre, sans avoir consulté au préalable un professionnel de la santé.
- Conseiller au patient de se rincer fréquemment la bouche, de pratiquer une bonne hygiène buccale et de consommer de la gomme à mâcher ou des bonbons sans sucre pour soulager la sécheresse de la bouche. Lui recommander de consulter un professionnel de la santé si la sécheresse de la bouche persiste pendant plus de 2 semaines.
- Conseiller à la patiente de prendre des mesures contraceptives et de prévenir un professionnel de la santé si elle pense être enceinte ou désire le devenir ou, encore, si elle allaite.
- Recommander au patient qui doit suivre un autre traitement ou subir une intervention chirurgicale de prévenir le professionnel de la santé qu'il suit un traitement avec ce médicament.
- Conseiller au patient d'informer rapidement un professionnel de la santé de l'apparition des symptômes suivants: maux de gorge, fièvre, saignements ou ecchymoses inhabituels, rash, faiblesse, tremblements, troubles visuels, urine de couleur foncée ou selles couleur de glaise.
- Insister sur l'importance des examens réguliers de suivi, des examens de la vue, des tests diagnostiques et d'une psychothérapie.

VÉRIFICATION DE L'EFFICACITÉ THÉRAPEUTIQUE

L'efficacité du traitement peut être démontrée par: la diminution des manifestations de la schizophrénie et de l'idéation psychotique. ✳

MAGALDRATE,
voir Magnésium et d'aluminium, sels de

MAGNÉSIUM, SELS DE (VOIE ORALE)

carbonate de magnésium
Gaviscon

chlorure de magnésium (magnésium à 12 %; 4,9 mmol de magnésium/g)
Slow-Mag

citrate de magnésium (magnésium à 16,2 %; 2,2 mmol de magnésium/g)
Citromag

glucoheptonate de magnésium (magnésium à 5,1 %)
Ratio-Magnésium

hydroxyde de magnésium (magnésium à 41,7 %; 17,15 mmol de magnésium/g)
Phillips Lait de magnésie

oxyde de magnésium (magnésium à 60,3 %; 24,8 mmol de magnésium/g)
Pico-Salax

CLASSIFICATION:
Minéraux et électrolytes, laxatifs (salins), antiulcéreux (antiacides)

Grossesse – catégorie inconnue

INDICATIONS

Traitement et prévention de l'hypomagnésémie ■ Autres indications: laxatif ■ évacuation intestinale en vue d'une intervention chirurgicale ou d'un examen radiologique ■ Le lait de magnésie et le carbonate de magnésium sont utilisés comme antiacides.

MÉCANISME D'ACTION

Rôle essentiel à l'action de nombreuses enzymes ■ Rôle important dans la neurotransmission et dans l'excitabilité musculaire ■ Augmentation de la pression osmotique au niveau du tractus gastro-intestinal par attraction de l'eau dans la lumière, ce qui entraîne des mouvements péristaltiques. ***Effets thérapeutiques:*** Substitution en cas d'états de carence ■ Évacuation des matières du côlon.

PHARMACOCINÉTIQUE

Absorption: Jusqu'à 30 % (PO).
Distribution: Tout l'organisme. L'agent traverse la barrière placentaire et passe dans le lait maternel.
Métabolisme et excrétion: Excrétion majoritairement rénale.
Demi-vie: Inconnue.

Profil temps-action (effet laxatif)

	DÉBUT D'ACTION	PIC	DURÉE
PO	3-6 h	inconnu	inconnue

CONTRE-INDICATIONS, PRÉCAUTIONS ET MISES EN GARDE

Contre-indications: Insuffisance rénale ■ Hypersensibilité à l'un des ingrédients ■ Occlusion intestinale connue ou soupçonnée ■ Diarrhée chronique ■ Hypermagnésémie ■ Hypocalcémie ■ Anurie ■ Bloc cardiaque ■ **OBST.:** Période active du travail de l'accouchement ou dans les 2 heures suivant ou précédant l'accouchement (à moins d'usage en cas d'accouchement prématuré).
Précautions et mises en garde: Régime hyposodé (certaines préparations contiennent beaucoup de sodium).

RÉACTIONS INDÉSIRABLES ET EFFETS SECONDAIRES

GI: diarrhée.
Tég.: rougeurs du visage, transpiration.

INTERACTIONS

Médicament-médicament: Potentialisation des effets des **bloqueurs neuromusculaires** ■ Risque de diminution de l'absorption des **fluoroquinolones**, de la **nitrofurantoïne** et des **tétracyclines** lors d'un usage concomitant.

VOIES D'ADMINISTRATION ET POSOLOGIE

Prévention des carences (besoins quotidiens en mg de magnésium)

- **PO (adultes et enfants ≥ 10 ans):** *Adolescents et hommes adultes* – de 130 à 250 mg par jour; *adolescentes et femmes adultes* – de 135 à 210 mg par jour; *femmes enceintes* – de 195 à 245 mg par jour; *femmes qui allaitent* – de 245 à 265 mg par jour.
- **PO (enfants de 7 à 10 ans):** De 100 à 135 mg par jour.
- **PO (enfants de 4 à 6 ans):** 65 mg par jour.
- **PO (enfants nouveau-nés et jusqu'à 3 ans):** De 20 à 50 mg par jour.

Traitement des carences (en mg de magnésium)

- **PO (adultes):** De 100 à 600 mg par jour, en 3 ou 4 doses fractionnées (voir la monographie de chacun des produits).

M

- **PO (enfants de 6 à 11 ans):** De 3 à 6 mg/kg/jour, en 3 ou 4 doses fractionnées (au maximum, 400 mg/jour).

Laxatif

- **PO (adultes):** *Citrate de magnésium* – de 75 à 300 mL. *Hydroxyde de magnésium (lait de magnésie)* – de 30 à 60 mL, en une seule dose ou en doses fractionnées. *Oxyde de magnésium (Pico-Salax)* – 1 sachet avant 8 h, la veille de l'examen ou de l'intervention chirurgicale, et 1 sachet, entre 14 h et 16 h, la veille de l'examen ou de l'intervention chirurgicale.
- **PO (enfants de 7 à 14 ans):** *Citrate de magnésium* – de 60 à 200 mL. *Hydroxyde de magnésium (lait de magnésie)* – de 7 à 30 mL, en une seule dose ou en doses fractionnées.
- **PO (enfants de 1 à 6 ans):** *Oxyde de magnésium (Pico-Salax)* – ¼ sachet, avant 8 h la veille de l'examen ou de l'intervention chirurgicale, et ¼ sachet, entre 14 h et 16 h, la veille de l'examen ou de l'intervention chirurgicale.
- **PO (enfants de 6 à 12 ans):** *Oxyde de magnésium (Pico-Salax)* – ½ sachet, avant 8 h, la veille de l'examen ou l'intervention chirurgicale, et ½ sachet, entre 14 h et 16 h, la veille de l'examen ou de l'intervention chirurgicale.

M

Antiacide

- **PO (adultes):** *Hydroxyde de magnésium (lait de magnésie)* – de 2 à 4 comprimés ou de 5 à 20 mL de suspension avec un peu d'eau (jusqu'à 4 fois par jour). *Carbonate de magnésium (Gaviscon)* – croquer de 2 à 4 comprimés dès l'apparition des symptômes (au maximum, 16 comprimés en 24 heures).
- **PO (enfants de 7 à 14 ans):** *Hydroxyde de magnésium (lait de magnésie)* – 1 comprimé (jusqu'à 4 fois par jour).

PRÉSENTATION

- **Carbonate de magnésium**
  Comprimés: 40 mg de magnésium^{VL}.
- **Chlorure de magnésium**
  Comprimés à libération prolongée: 535 mg (64 mg de magnésium)^{VL}.
- **Citrate de magnésium (version générique disponible)**
  Solution orale: flacons de 300 mL (contenant 15 g de citrate de magnésium)^{VL}.
- **Hydroxyde de magnésium (version générique disponible)**
  Liquide: 400 mg/5 mL^{VL} ■ **Comprimés à croquer:** 311 mg^{VL}.
- **Oxyde de magnésium (version générique disponible)**
  Sachets: 3,5 g d'oxyde de magnésium^{VL}.

SOINS INFIRMIERS

ÉVALUATION DE LA SITUATION

Laxatif:

- Suivre de près la distension abdominale, ausculter les bruits intestinaux et observer les habitudes normales d'élimination.
- Déterminer la couleur, la consistance et la quantité des selles produites.

Antiacide: Suivre de près les brûlures d'estomac et l'indigestion; déterminer le siège, la durée et les caractéristiques de la douleur gastrique ainsi que les facteurs qui la déclenchent.

DIAGNOSTICS INFIRMIERS POSSIBLES

- Constipation (Indications).
- Connaissances insuffisantes sur le traitement médicamenteux (Enseignement au patient et à ses proches).

INTERVENTIONS INFIRMIÈRES

- Le comprimé doit être bien mâché avant d'être avalé afin de l'empêcher d'atteindre l'intestin grêle sous forme non dissoute. Demander ensuite au patient de boire un demi-verre d'eau.
- *Citrate de magnésium:* Réfrigérer les solutions afin qu'elles gardent leur puissance et un goût agréable. On peut administrer le médicament avec des glaçons. Ne pas laisser le contenant de citrate de magnésium ouvert, car la solution deviendra moins effervescente avec le temps, ce qui n'en affectera pas la puissance, mais en altérera le goût.
- *Hydroxyde de magnésium:* Bien agiter la solution avant de l'administrer.

Antiacide:

- Administrer le médicament de 1 à 3 heures après les repas et au coucher.
- Les préparations sous forme de poudre ou de liquide sont considérées comme plus efficaces que les comprimés.

Laxatif: Pour obtenir un effet plus rapide, administrer à jeun. Afin de prévenir la déshydratation et d'accélérer les effets du médicament, demander au patient de prendre les doses de laxatif avec un verre de liquide. Ne pas administrer le médicament au coucher ou en fin de journée.

ENSEIGNEMENT AU PATIENT ET À SES PROCHES

- Demander au patient de ne pas prendre le médicament dans les 2 heures qui précèdent ou qui suivent la prise d'un autre médicament, particulièrement de fluoroquinolones, de nitrofurantoïne et de tétracyclines.

Antiacide: Inciter le patient à consulter un professionnel de la santé s'il doit prendre des antiacides pendant plus de 2 semaines ou si les symptômes récidivent. Lui recommander de consulter également un professionnel de la santé si la douleur n'est pas soulagée ou si les symptômes suivants d'hémorragie digestive se manifestent: selles noires et goudronneuses et vomissures ayant l'aspect du marc de café.

Laxatif:

- Prévenir le patient que les laxatifs devraient être pris pendant de courtes périodes seulement. Le traitement prolongé peut entraîner un déséquilibre électrolytique et l'accoutumance.
- Recommander au patient de prendre d'autres mesures qui favorisent l'élimination fécale: consommer des aliments riches en fibres, augmenter la consommation de liquides, faire de l'exercice. Expliquer au patient que chaque personne a ses propres habitudes d'élimination et qu'il est tout aussi normal de déféquer 3 fois par jour que 3 fois par semaine.
- Recommander au patient de prévenir un professionnel de la santé si la constipation n'est pas soulagée et si des saignements rectaux ou des symptômes de déséquilibre électrolytique (crampes ou douleurs musculaires, faiblesse, étourdissements, etc.) se manifestent.

VÉRIFICATION DE L'EFFICACITÉ THÉRAPEUTIQUE

L'efficacité du traitement peut être démontrée par: le soulagement de la douleur et de l'irritation gastriques ■ l'évacuation de selles molles et bien formées, habituellement dans les 3 à 6 heures qui suivent l'administration de la préparation ■ la prévention des carences en magnésium et le soulagement de leurs symptômes.

MAGNÉSIUM ET D'ALUMINIUM, SELS DE

hydroxyde d'aluminium
Alugel, Alu-Tab, Amphojel, Basaljel

hydroxyde de magnésium et hydroxyde d'aluminium
Alumag, Diovol, Diovol Ex, Gelusil, Gelusil Extra-Puissant, Maalox, Maalox TC, Mylanta Double concentration simple, Neutralca-S

magaldrate
Riopan, Riopan Extra Fort

CLASSIFICATION:
Antiulcéreux (antiacides)

Grossesse – catégorie inconnue

INDICATIONS

Traitement d'appoint de la douleur provoquée par l'ulcère gastroduodénal et effet positif sur la guérison des ulcères duodénaux et gastriques ■ Traitement de divers troubles gastriques incluant: l'hyperacidité ■ l'indigestion ■ le reflux gastro-œsophagien ■ les brûlures d'estomac ■ L'hydroxyde d'aluminium est également administré dans le traitement de l'hyperphosphatémie associée à l'insuffisance rénale.

MÉCANISME D'ACTION

Après dissolution dans l'estomac, neutralisation de l'acide gastrique ■ Inactivation de la pepsine, si le pH ≥ 4 ■ L'hydroxyde d'aluminium se lie aux phosphates dans le tractus gastro-intestinal pour former un composé non absorbable. ***Effets thérapeutiques:*** Neutralisation de l'acide gastrique avec guérison ultérieure des ulcères et diminution de la douleur qu'ils provoquent ■ L'hydroxyde d'aluminium abaisse les concentrations sériques de phosphate.

PHARMACOCINÉTIQUE

Absorption: Nulle lors d'un usage régulier; de 15 à 30 % de magnésium et une plus faible quantité d'aluminium peuvent être absorbés lors d'un usage prolongé.
Distribution: Les petites quantités de magnésium et d'aluminium absorbées se répartissent dans tout l'organisme, traversent la barrière placentaire et passent dans le lait maternel. L'aluminium s'accumule dans le SNC.
Métabolisme et excrétion: Excrétion rénale.
Demi-vie: Inconnue.

Profil temps-action (effet sur le pH gastrique)

	DÉBUT D'ACTION	PIC	DURÉE
PO (aluminium)	légèrement retardé	30 min	30 min – 1 h (à jeun); 3 h (après un repas)
PO (magnésium)	immédiat	30 min	30 min – 1 h (à jeun); 3 h (après un repas)

CONTRE-INDICATIONS, PRÉCAUTIONS ET MISES EN GARDE

Contre-indications: Alcalose ■ Hypermagnésémie ■ Douleurs abdominales graves de cause inconnue, particulièrement si elles s'accompagnent de fièvre ■ Anurie

M

(le magnésium est contre-indiqué dans ce cas) ■ Intolérance à la tartrazine ou au sucre (ne pas administrer dans ce cas les produits qui contiennent ces additifs).

Précautions et mises en garde: Insuffisance rénale de quelque gravité que ce soit (les antiacides contenant du magnésium sont déconseillés dans ce cas) ■ Déshydratation ■ Hémorragie digestive haute.

RÉACTIONS INDÉSIRABLES ET EFFETS SECONDAIRES

GI: *sels d'aluminium* – constipation; *sels de magnésium* – diarrhée.

HÉ: *sels d'aluminium* – hypophosphatémie; *sels de magnésium* – hypermagnésémie.

INTERACTIONS

Médicament-médicament: Les sels de magnésium et d'aluminium modifient l'absorption de nombreux **médicaments administrés par voie orale** ■ Ces agents détruisent l'enrobage des **médicaments à libération entérique**, entraînant leur libération prématurée dans l'estomac, d'où un faible risque d'absorption ou d'effets secondaires ■ Risque de réduction de l'absorption des **tétracyclines**, des **phénothiazines**, du **kétoconazole**, de l'**itraconazole**, des **sels de fer**, des **fluoroquinolones** et de l'**isoniazide**, administrés en concomitance (prendre les antiacides 2 heures avant ou 2 heures après) ■ Si le pH de l'urine est augmenté à cause de l'administration de doses élevées, les concentrations plasmatiques de **salicylates** peuvent diminuer, tandis que les concentrations plasmatiques de **quinidine**, de **flécaïnide** et d'**amphétamine** peuvent s'élever ■ Risque de diminution de la liaison du **sucralfate** à la muqueuse gastrique ulcérée.

VOIES D'ADMINISTRATION ET POSOLOGIE

Les doses varient selon les concentrations des ingrédients de l'agent choisi. En général, on administre de 5 à 30 mL ou de 1 à 4 comprimés, de 20 à 60 minutes et 3 heures après les repas et au coucher. Pendant la toute première phase de guérison de l'ulcère gastroduodénal, il peut s'avérer nécessaire d'administrer le médicament plus fréquemment.

Ulcère gastroduodénal

- **PO (adultes)**: *Ulcères gastroduodénaux non compliqués* – administrer l'agent 1 heure et 3 heures après les repas et au coucher. On peut administrer des doses additionnelles en cas de récurrence des symptômes; continuer le traitement pendant 4 à 6 semaines dans le cas des ulcères duodénaux et jusqu'à la guérison dans le cas des ulcères gastriques.

Reflux gastro-œsophagien

- **PO (adultes)**: *Traitement de courte durée* – antiacide en suspension, toutes les 30 à 60 minutes. *Traitement d'entretien* – administrer l'agent 1 heure et 3 heures après les repas et au coucher; on peut administrer des doses additionnelles en cas de récurrence des symptômes.

Hémorragie digestive et ulcère dû au stress

- **PO (adultes)**: Administrer l'agent toutes les heures ou selon les besoins, pour maintenir le pH de l'aspirat nasogastrique à un niveau supérieur à 3,5.

Prévention de l'aspiration gastro-intestinale induite par l'anesthésie

- **PO (adultes)**: Administrer l'antiacide en suspension, 30 minutes avant l'anesthésie générale.

Hyperphosphatémie (hydroxyde d'aluminium seulement)

- **PO (adultes)**: La dose doit être adaptée proportionnellement aux résultats du contrôle des concentrations de phosphates, sous la supervision d'un néphrologue.

PRÉSENTATION (version générique disponible)

- **Hydroxyde d'aluminium**
  Comprimés: 600 mg[VL] ■ **Capsules**: 500 mg[VL] ■ **Suspension**: 320 mg/5 mL[VL] ■ **Liquide**: 300 mg/5 mL[VL].
- **Magaldrate**
  Comprimés: 480 mg[VL] ■ **Comprimés à croquer**: 480 mg[VL] ■ **Suspension**: 480 mg/5 mL[VL] ■ **En association avec**: siméthicone[VL].
- **Hydroxyde de magnésium et hydroxyde d'aluminium**
  Comprimés réguliers: hydroxyde d'aluminium à 200 mg et hydroxyde de magnésium à 200 mg[VL] ■ **Comprimés extraforts et suspension**: plusieurs concentrations contenant diverses teneurs des 2 ingrédients[VL] ■ **En association avec**: siméthicone[VL].

SOINS INFIRMIERS

ÉVALUATION DE LA SITUATION

Antiacide: Suivre de près les brûlures d'estomac et l'indigestion; déterminer le siège, la durée et les caractéristiques de la douleur gastrique ainsi que les facteurs qui la déclenchent.

Tests de laboratoire:

- Noter les concentrations sériques de phosphate, de calcium et de potassium à intervalles réguliers pendant un traitement prolongé. L'agent peut élever les concentrations sériques de calcium et réduire celles de phosphate.
- Ces agents peuvent entraîner une hypergastrinémie et élever le pH du sang et des urines.

- Ces agents contrecarrent les effets de la pentagastrine et de l'histamine lors des tests de sécrétion d'acide gastrique. Éviter de les administrer dans les 24 heures précédant un tel test.

DIAGNOSTICS INFIRMIERS POSSIBLES

- Douleur aiguë (Indications).
- Connaissances insuffisantes sur le traitement médicamenteux (Enseignement au patient et à ses proches).

INTERVENTIONS INFIRMIÈRES

Le magnésium et l'aluminium sont combinés sous forme d'antiacide pour équilibrer les effets constipants de l'aluminium et les effets laxatifs du magnésium.

- Le comprimé doit être bien mâché avant d'être avalé afin de l'empêcher d'atteindre l'intestin grêle sous forme non dissoute. Demander ensuite au patient de boire un demi-verre d'eau.
- Bien agiter les suspensions avant de les administrer.
- Pour obtenir un effet antiacide, administrer l'agent, 1 et 3 heures après les repas et au coucher.

ENSEIGNEMENT AU PATIENT ET À SES PROCHES

- Inciter le patient à consulter un professionnel de la santé s'il doit prendre des antiacides pendant plus de 2 semaines ou si les symptômes récidivent. Lui recommander de consulter également un professionnel de la santé si la douleur n'est pas soulagée ou si les symptômes suivants d'hémorragie digestive se manifestent: selles noires et goudronneuses et vomissures ayant l'aspect du marc de café.
- Prévenir le patient qu'il ne faut pas prendre cette préparation dans les 2 heures qui précèdent ou qui suivent la prise d'autres médicaments.
- Certains antiacides peuvent contenir de grandes quantités de sodium. Conseiller au patient qui doit suivre un régime alimentaire hyposodé de vérifier la teneur en sodium de la préparation lors d'un traitement prolongé à des doses élevées.

PÉD.: Les produits associant le magnésium et l'aluminium peuvent causer de sérieux effets indésirables chez les enfants, particulièrement dans le cas de ceux dont la fonction rénale est diminuée ou qui souffrent de déshydratation. Prévenir les parents et les soignants que l'administration d'antiacides en vente libre chez l'enfant est déconseillée en l'absence d'une évaluation médicale.

VÉRIFICATION DE L'EFFICACITÉ THÉRAPEUTIQUE

L'efficacité du traitement peut être démontrée par: le soulagement de la douleur et de l'irritation gastriques ■ la diminution des concentrations sériques de phosphate.

ALERTE CLINIQUE

MAGNÉSIUM, SULFATE DE

(magnésium à 9,9 %; 4 mmol de magnésium/g)

CLASSIFICATION:

Anticonvulsivant, minéraux et électrolytes (suppléments de magnésium)

Grossesse – catégorie D

INDICATIONS

Traitement et prévention de l'hypomagnésémie ■ Traitement anticonvulsivant en cas d'éclampsie ou de prééclampsie graves ■ Traitement de l'hypertension, de l'encéphalopathie et des convulsions associées à la néphrite aiguë de l'enfant. **Usages non approuvés**: Accouchement prématuré ■ Traitement des torsades de pointes ■ Traitement adjuvant comme bronchodilatateur en cas d'asthme aigu de modéré à grave.

MÉCANISME D'ACTION

Rôle essentiel à l'action de nombreuses enzymes ■ Rôle important dans la neurotransmission et l'excitabilité musculaire. ***Effets thérapeutiques***: Substitution en cas d'états de carence ■ Résolution de l'éclampsie.

PHARMACOCINÉTIQUE

Absorption: Complète (IV). Bonne (IM).

Distribution: L'agent se répartit dans tout l'organisme, traverse la barrière placentaire et passe dans le lait maternel.

Métabolisme et excrétion: Excrétion majoritairement rénale.

Demi-vie: Inconnue.

Profil temps-action (effet anticonvulsivant)

	DÉBUT D'ACTION	PIC	DURÉE
IM	60 min	inconnu	3 – 4 h
IV	immédiat	inconnu	30 min

CONTRE-INDICATIONS, PRÉCAUTIONS ET MISES EN GARDE

Contre-indications: Hypermagnésémie ■ Hypocalcémie ■ Anurie ■ Bloc cardiaque ■ **OBST.**: Période active du travail de l'accouchement ou dans les 2 heures suivant ou précédant l'accouchement (à moins d'usage en cas d'accouchement prématuré).

Précautions et mises en garde: Insuffisance rénale de quelque degré que ce soit ■ Patients recevant des dérivés digitaliques.

RÉACTIONS INDÉSIRABLES ET EFFETS SECONDAIRES

SNC: somnolence.
Resp.: diminution de la fréquence respiratoire.
CV: arythmies, bradycardie, hypotension.
GI: diarrhée.
Tég.: rougeurs du visage, transpiration.
Métab.: hypothermie.

INTERACTIONS

Médicament-médicament: Le sulfate de magnésium potentialise les effets des **bloqueurs neuromusculaires** et des **bloqueurs des canaux calciques**.

VOIES D'ADMINISTRATION ET POSOLOGIE

Traitement des carences (dose exprimée en mg de magnésium)

- **IM (adultes)**: *Carence grave* – de 8 à 12 g/jour en doses fractionnées; *carence légère* – 1 g, toutes les 6 heures, pour un total de 4 doses.
- **IV (adultes)**: *Carence grave* – de 5 à 8 g à perfuser à une vitesse de 0,5 à 1 g/h. Au maximum, 16 g/24 h *ou* 5 g dans 1 litre de D5%E ou de NaCl 0,9 % pour injection, qu'on administre lentement en 3 heures.

M

Éclampsie et prééclampsie

- **IM, IV (adultes)**: Initialement, 4 ou 5 g dans 100 à 250 mL de D5%E ou de NaCl 0,9 %, à administrer à une vitesse de 150 mg/min (environ 20 à 30 minutes), puis une perfusion continue de 1 à 4 g/h jusqu'à entre 12 et 24 heures postpartum. Ajuster la perfusion pour obtenir des concentrations plasmatiques de magnésium de 1,7 à 3,1 mmol/L *ou* 4 ou 5 g, par perfusion IV (dans 250 mL de D5%E ou de NaCl 0,9 % pour injection), en même temps que l'injection IM de 5 g dans une fesse, puis 4 ou 5 g par voie IM, toutes les 4 heures (ne pas dépasser de 30 à 40 g par jour ou 30 g en 24 heures en présence d'anurie). D'autres régimes posologiques ont été utilisés.

Nutrition parentérale

- **IV (adultes)**: De 5 à 20 mmol par jour.
- **IV (nourrissons)**: De 0,125 à 0,3 mmol par jour.

Crises convulsives

- **IM, IV (enfants)**: De 20 à 100 mg (de 0,1 à 0,5 mL de la solution à 20 %) par kilogramme de poids corporel; répéter toutes les 4 à 6 heures au besoin.

PRÉSENTATION (version générique disponible)

Solution pour injection: solution à 20 %^{Pr} (ampoules de 10 mL) et à 50 %^{Pr} (ampoules de 2 mL, de 10 mL et de 50 mL).

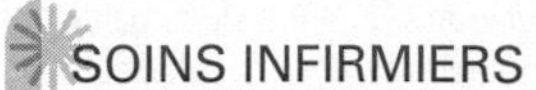

SOINS INFIRMIERS

ÉVALUATION DE LA SITUATION

Hypomagnésémie ou traitement anticonvulsivant:

- Mesurer le pouls, la pression artérielle et la fréquence respiratoire et suivre de près l'ÉCG à intervalles fréquents tout au long de l'administration du sulfate de magnésium par voie parentérale. La fréquence respiratoire devrait être d'au moins 16 respirations à la minute avant de pouvoir administrer la dose.
- Noter l'état neurologique du patient avant le traitement et pendant toute sa durée. Prendre toutes les précautions nécessaires en cas de crise. Le réflexe rotulien devrait être déterminé avant l'administration de la dose par voie parentérale de sulfate de magnésium. En l'absence de réponse, ne pas administrer de nouvelles doses jusqu'à l'obtention d'une réponse positive.
- Si la mère a reçu du sulfate de magnésium, suivre de près l'état du nouveau-né afin de déceler l'hypotension, l'hyporéflexie et la dépression respiratoire.
- Mesurer les ingesta et les excreta. La diurèse devrait être maintenue à au moins 100 mL/4 h.

Tests de laboratoire: Évaluer les concentrations sériques de magnésium et la fonction rénale à intervalles réguliers tout au long de l'administration du sulfate de magnésium par voie parentérale.

DIAGNOSTICS INFIRMIERS POSSIBLES

- Risque d'accident (Indications, Effets secondaires).
- Connaissances insuffisantes sur le traitement médicamenteux (Enseignement au patient et à ses proches).

INTERVENTIONS INFIRMIÈRES

ALERTE CLINIQUE: DES SURDOSAGES ACCIDENTELS ONT ENTRAÎNÉ DE SÉRIEUX EFFETS SECONDAIRES ET DES DÉCÈS. TOUJOURS DEMANDER À UN AUTRE PROFESSIONNEL DE LA SANTÉ DE REVÉRIFIER L'ORDONNANCE D'ORIGINE, LE CALCUL DE LA DOSE ET LE RÉGLAGE DE LA POMPE. NE PAS CONFONDRE LES DOSES EN MILLIGRAMMES (mg) AVEC CELLES EN GRAMMES (g) ET EN MILLIMOLES (mmol).

IM:

- Administrer l'injection profondément dans le muscle fessier. Administrer les injections suivantes en alternant les points de ponction.
- Chez l'adulte, administrer les concentrations à 20 % ou à 50 %, et chez l'enfant < 14 ans, la concentration à 20 %.

IV directe: Diluer de 1 à 2 g de la solution à 50 % dans 10 mL de D5%E ou de NaCl 0,9 %.
Vitesse d'administration: Injecter en 1 à 2 minutes (en cas d'arrêt cardiaque).
Perfusion continue: Diluer dans une solution compatible, à une concentration maximale de 200 mg/mL.
Vitesse d'administration: Utiliser une pompe à perfusion pour régler le débit avec précision. La vitesse d'administration ne devrait pas dépasser 150 mg/min.
Compatibilité (tubulure en Y): acyclovir ■ aldesleukine ■ amifostine ■ amikacine ■ ampicilline ■ aztréonam ■ céfamandole ■ céfazoline ■ céfopérazone ■ céfotaxime ■ céfoxitine ■ céphalothine ■ céphapirine ■ chloramphénicol ■ clindamycine ■ dobutamine ■ doxycycline ■ énalaprilate ■ érythromycine, lactobionate d' ■ esmolol ■ famotidine ■ fludarabine ■ gallium, nitrate de ■ gentamicine ■ granisétron ■ héparine ■ hydrocortisone sodique, succinate d' ■ hydromorphone ■ idarubicine ■ insuline ■ kanamycine ■ labétalol ■ mépéridine ■ métronidazole ■ minocycline ■ morphine ■ nafcilline ■ ondansétron ■ oxacilline ■ paclitaxel ■ pénicilline G potassique ■ pipéracilline ■ pipéracilline/tazobactam ■ potassium, chlorure de ■ sargramostim ■ thiotépa ■ ticarcilline ■ tobramycine ■ triméthoprime/sulfaméthoxazole ■ vancomycine ■ vitamines du complexe B avec C.
Incompatibilité (tubulure en Y): céfépime.

ENSEIGNEMENT AU PATIENT ET À SES PROCHES

- Expliquer au patient et à ses proches le but du traitement.

VÉRIFICATION DE L'EFFICACITÉ THÉRAPEUTIQUE

L'efficacité du traitement peut être démontrée par: le rétablissement des concentrations sériques normales de magnésium ■ la suppression des convulsions associées aux toxémies de la grossesse.

MANNITOL

Mannitol, Osmitrol, Resectisol

CLASSIFICATION:
Diurétique (osmotique)

Grossesse – catégorie C

INDICATIONS

IV: Traitement d'appoint des troubles suivants: insuffisance rénale oligurique aiguë ■ œdème cérébral ■ pression intracrânienne ou intraoculaire ■ certains surdosages toxiques. **Usages non approuvés:** Irrigation génito-urinaire (lors d'interventions transurétrales – solution à 2,5 % à 5 % seulement).

MÉCANISME D'ACTION

Augmentation de la pression osmotique du filtrat glomérulaire inhibant ainsi la réabsorption de l'eau et des électrolytes ■ Induction de l'excrétion: de l'eau ■ du sodium ■ du potassium ■ des chlorures ■ du calcium ■ du phosphore ■ du magnésium ■ de l'urée ■ de l'acide urique. ***Effets thérapeutiques:*** Mobilisation de l'excès de liquides en cas d'insuffisance rénale oligurique ou d'œdème ■ Réduction de la pression intraoculaire ou intracrânienne ■ Augmentation de l'excrétion urinaire de certaines substances toxiques ■ Diminution de l'hémolyse en cas d'usage à titre de solution d'irrigation après une prostactectomie transurétrale.

PHARMACOCINÉTIQUE

Absorption: Biodisponibilité à 100 % (IV). Le mannitol peut être absorbé dans une certaine mesure lorsqu'il est utilisé à titre de solution d'irrigation.
Distribution: Le mannitol s'accumule seulement dans les espaces extracellulaires. Il ne traverse habituellement pas la barrière hématoencéphalique ni oculaire.
Métabolisme et excrétion: Métabolisme hépatique; excrétion rénale minime.
Demi-vie: 100 minutes.

Profil temps-action (effet diurétique)

	Début d'action	Pic	Durée
IV	30 - 60 min	1 h	6 - 8 h

CONTRE-INDICATIONS, PRÉCAUTIONS ET MISES EN GARDE

Contre-indications: Hypersensibilité ■ Insuffisance cardiaque grave ■ Œdème pulmonaire ■ Insuffisance rénale avancée ou signes cliniques d'atteinte rénale progressive irréversible ■ Anurie ■ Déshydratation grave ■ Hémorragie intracrânienne active.
Précautions et mises en garde: OBST., ALLAITEMENT: L'innocuité du médicament n'a pas été établie.

RÉACTIONS INDÉSIRABLES ET EFFETS SECONDAIRES

SNC: confusion, céphalées.
ORLO: vision trouble, rhinite.
CV: expansion volémique passagère, douleurs thoraciques, insuffisance cardiaque, œdème pulmonaire, tachycardie.
GI: nausées, soif, vomissements.

GU: insuffisance rénale, rétention urinaire.
HÉ: déshydratation, hyperkaliémie, hypernatrémie, hypokaliémie, hyponatrémie.
Locaux: phlébite au point d'injection IV.

INTERACTIONS

Médicament-médicament: L'hypokaliémie augmente le risque de toxicité attribuable aux **dérivés digitaliques**.

VOIES D'ADMINISTRATION ET POSOLOGIE

Le mannitol est destiné à l'administration IV seulement. L'écart thérapeutique se situe entre 50 et 200 g par 24 heures. La dose totale, la concentration et la vitesse d'administration varient selon l'état clinique du patient et la gravité de l'affection traitée. On peut d'abord administrer une dose d'essai de 0,2 g/kg, en 3 à 5 minutes; elle devrait produire une excrétion urinaire excédant 40 mL à l'heure au cours des 2 ou 3 heures suivantes.

- **IV (adultes)**: *Œdème, insuffisance rénale oligurique* – de 50 à 100 g pendant une période allant de 90 minutes à plusieurs heures, afin de maintenir un débit urinaire > 100 mL/h. *Réduction de la pression intracrânienne/intraoculaire* – de 1,5 à 2 g/kg ont été utilisés sous forme de solution de 15 à 25 % en 30 à 60 minutes.

M

PRÉSENTATION
(version générique disponible)

Solution pour injection IV: solution à 10 %[Pr], à 20 %[Pr] et à 25 %[Pr] ■ **Solution pour l'irrigation de l'appareil génito-urinaire**: solution à 5 %[Pr] ■ **En association avec**: sorbitol pour irrigation de l'appareil génito-urinaire[Pr].

SOINS INFIRMIERS

ÉVALUATION DE LA SITUATION

- Mesurer les signes vitaux, le débit urinaire, la pression veineuse centrale et la pression des artères pulmonaires avant l'administration et toutes les heures pendant toute la durée du traitement. Suivre de près les signes et les symptômes de déshydratation (diminution de la turgescence de la peau, sécheresse de la peau et des muqueuses, fièvre, soif) ou de surcharge liquidienne (pression veineuse centrale accrue, dyspnée, râles et crépitations, œdème).
- Suivre de près l'anorexie, la faiblesse musculaire, l'engourdissement, les picotements, la paresthésie, la confusion et la soif excessive. Prévenir immédiatement le médecin si ces symptômes de déséquilibre électrolytique se manifestent.

Pression intracrânienne accrue: Noter l'état neurologique et la pression intracrânienne du patient si le mannitol est administré pour réduire l'œdème cérébral.
Pression intraoculaire accrue: Suivre de près les douleurs oculaires accrues ou persistantes ou la diminution de l'acuité visuelle.
Tests de laboratoire: Noter à intervalles réguliers, tout au long du traitement, les résultats des tests de l'exploration fonctionnelle rénale et les concentrations sériques d'électrolytes.

DIAGNOSTICS INFIRMIERS POSSIBLES

- Excès de volume liquidien (Indications).
- Risque de déficit des volumes liquidiens (Effets secondaires).

INTERVENTIONS INFIRMIÈRES

- Observer le point de perfusion à intervalles fréquents pour déceler l'infiltration. L'extravasation peut provoquer l'irritation et la nécrose tissulaires.
- La perte excessive d'eau et d'électrolytes peut entraîner des déséquilibres importants. La natrémie et la kaliémie doivent être surveillées étroitement durant l'administration du mannitol.
- Consulter le médecin au sujet de l'installation d'une sonde de Foley à demeure (sauf si le mannitol est administré pour réduire la pression intraoculaire).

IV: Administrer la solution non diluée par perfusion IV. Si la solution contient des cristaux, réchauffer le flacon dans de l'eau chaude et l'agiter vigoureusement. Ne pas administrer la solution si les cristaux ne se sont pas dissous. Laisser tiédir la solution pour qu'elle puisse atteindre la température du corps. Utiliser un filtre pour la perfusion des solutions à 20 % et à 25 %.
Dose d'essai: Administrer en 3 à 5 minutes pour produire un débit urinaire de 40 mL à l'heure. Si le débit de l'urine n'augmente pas au cours des 2 ou 3 heures suivantes, administrer une deuxième dose d'essai. Si le débit urinaire n'est pas d'au moins 40 mL à l'heure, pendant 2 ou 3 heures après l'administration de la deuxième dose d'essai, il faudrait réévaluer l'état du patient.
Oligurie: La vitesse d'administration devrait être ajustée de façon à obtenir un débit urinaire de 100 mL à l'heure.
Pression intracrânienne accrue: Chez l'adulte, perfuser la dose en 30 à 60 minutes.
Pression intraoculaire accrue: Administrer la dose en 30 à 60 minutes. Si le mannitol est utilisé avant une intervention chirurgicale, l'administrer de 60 à 90 minutes avant l'intervention.
Compatibilité (tubulure en Y): aztréonam ■ fludarabine ■ fluorouracile ■ gallium, nitrate de ■ idarubicine ■ mel-

phalan ▪ ondansétron ▪ paclitaxel ▪ pipéracilline/tazobactam ▪ téniposide ▪ thiotépa ▪ vinorelbine.
Incompatibilité (tubulure en Y): céfépime ▪ filgrastim.

ENSEIGNEMENT AU PATIENT ET À SES PROCHES

▪ Expliquer au patient le but du traitement.

VÉRIFICATION DE L'EFFICACITÉ THÉRAPEUTIQUE

L'efficacité du traitement peut être démontrée par: l'obtention d'un débit urinaire d'au moins 40 mL à l'heure ou l'augmentation du débit urinaire selon les paramètres établis par le médecin ▪ la réduction de la pression intracrânienne ▪ la réduction de la pression intraoculaire ▪ l'excrétion de certaines substances toxiques.

MÉBENDAZOLE

Vermox

CLASSIFICATION:
Anthelminthique
Grossesse – catégorie C

INDICATIONS

Traitement des infections helminthiques simples ou mixtes dues aux: trichocéphales (trichocéphalose) ▪ oxyures (oxyurose) ▪ ascaris (ascaridiase) ▪ ankylostomes (ankylostomiase) ▪ vers solitaires (téniase).

MÉCANISME D'ACTION

Inhibition du captage du glucose et d'autres éléments nutritifs par les helminthes sensibles. ***Effets thérapeutiques:*** Destruction des parasites, des œufs et des kystes hydatiques (action vermicide et ovocide).

PHARMACOCINÉTIQUE

Absorption: De 2 à 10 % (PO).
Distribution: Inconnue.
Métabolisme et excrétion: Élimination fécale à plus de 95 %. Métabolisme majoritairement hépatique du médicament absorbé; de petites quantités sont excrétées à l'état inchangé par les reins.
Demi-vie: De 2,5 à 9 heures (prolongée en cas d'insuffisance hépatique).

Profil temps-action

	DÉBUT D'ACTION	PIC	DURÉE
PO	inconnu	2 - 5 h	inconnue

CONTRE-INDICATIONS, PRÉCAUTIONS ET MISES EN GARDE

Contre-indications: Hypersensibilité.
Précautions et mises en garde: Dysfonctionnement hépatique ▪ Maladie de Crohn ▪ Colite ulcéreuse ▪ **OBST.**: On peut utiliser le médicament seulement si les avantages pour la mère l'emportent sur les risques pour le fœtus ▪ Allaitement ▪ **PÉD.**: Enfants < 2 ans (l'innocuité du médicament n'a pas été établie).

RÉACTIONS INDÉSIRABLES ET EFFETS SECONDAIRES

On observe la plupart des effets secondaires et réactions indésirables lors d'un traitement à doses élevées seulement.
SNC: CONVULSIONS (rares), étourdissements, céphalées.
ORLO: acouphènes.
GI: douleurs abdominales, diarrhée, augmentation des concentrations d'enzymes hépatiques (traitement prolongé à doses élevées), nausées, vomissements.
Tég.: rash, urticaire.
Hémat.: agranulocytose, myélodépression réversible (leucopénie, thrombopénie).
SN: engourdissements.
Divers: fièvre.

INTERACTIONS

Médicament-médicament: La **carbamazépine** et la **phénytoïne** peuvent accélérer le métabolisme et réduire l'efficacité du traitement chez les patients qui reçoivent des doses élevées.
Médicament-aliments: L'absorption du médicament peut être augmentée par les **aliments riches en matières grasses**.

VOIES D'ADMINISTRATION ET POSOLOGIE

Oxyurose

▪ **PO (adultes et enfants > 2 ans)**: 100 mg, en une seule dose; répéter après 2 ou 4 semaines.

Trichocéphalose, ascaridiase, ankylostomiase, strongyloïdose, téniase ou infections mixtes

▪ **PO (adultes et enfants > 2 ans)**: 100 mg, 2 fois par jour, pendant 3 jours. En l'absence de guérison 3 semaines après le traitement, amorcer une 2e cure.

PRÉSENTATION

Comprimés à croquer: 100 mg[Pr].

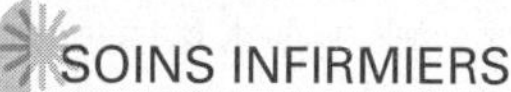

SOINS INFIRMIERS

ÉVALUATION DE LA SITUATION

Oxyurose: Examiner la région périanale afin de déceler la présence de vers adultes. Effectuer un prélèvement de la région périanale à l'aide d'un adhésif, avant le traitement et une semaine après qu'il a été mené à terme, afin de déceler la présence d'œufs. Répéter le test de dépistage avec l'adhésif tous les matins avant la défécation ou le bain, pendant au moins 3 jours. Les patients ne sont pas considérés comme guéris à moins que le test périanal donne des résultats négatifs pendant 7 jours.

Ascaridiase: Examiner les selles avant le traitement et de 1 à 3 semaines après qu'il a été mené à terme.

Tests de laboratoire:

- Le mébendazole peut entraîner l'élévation passagère des concentrations sériques d'urée, d'ALT, d'AST et de phosphatase alcaline. On devrait suivre de près les résultats des tests de la fonction hépatiques à intervalles réguliers lors d'un traitement prolongé.
- Déterminer la numération globulaire avant le traitement, 2 ou 3 fois par semaine du 10e au 25e jour et toutes les semaines par la suite, chez les patients qui reçoivent des doses élevées ou un traitement prolongé. Le mébendazole peut provoquer une leucopénie et une thrombopénie réversibles.
- Le mébendazole peut entraîner la réduction des concentrations sériques d'hémoglobine.

M

DIAGNOSTICS INFIRMIERS POSSIBLES

- Risque d'infection (Indications).
- Connaissances insuffisantes sur le traitement médicamenteux (Enseignement au patient et à ses proches).

INTERVENTIONS INFIRMIÈRES

- Aucun régime alimentaire spécial, jeûne, laxatif ou lavement n'est nécessaire avant l'administration du mébendazole.

PO: Le comprimé de mébendazole peut être croqué, avalé tel quel ou écrasé et mélangé avec des aliments. Les patients recevant des doses élevées devraient prendre les comprimés avec des aliments riches en matières grasses pour accroître l'absorption du médicament.

Oxyurose: Toutes les personnes vivant sous le même toit devraient être traitées simultanément; le traitement doit être répété après 2 ou 3 semaines.

Ankylostomiase et trichocéphalose: En cas d'anémie, le patient devrait prendre tous les jours un supplément de fer pendant qu'il prend du mébendazole ainsi que pendant les 6 mois qui suivent la fin de ce traitement.

ENSEIGNEMENT AU PATIENT ET À SES PROCHES

- Conseiller au patient de respecter rigoureusement la posologie recommandée pendant toute la durée du traitement et de continuer à prendre le mébendazole même s'il se sent mieux. S'il n'a pas pu prendre le médicament au moment habituel, il doit le prendre aussitôt que possible. S'il doit le prendre 2 fois par jour, il doit espacer les prises de 4 à 5 heures ou doubler la dose suivante. Une deuxième cure peut s'avérer nécessaire.
- Expliquer au patient les mesures d'hygiène qu'il doit prendre pour diminuer les risques de réinfection: se laver les mains avec du savon avant de manger et après être allé aux toilettes; désinfecter les toilettes tous les jours; ne pas se toucher la bouche avec les mains; laver tous les fruits et légumes; ne pas marcher pieds nus.
- Prévenir le patient que le mébendazole peut provoquer des étourdissements. Lui conseiller de ne pas conduire et d'éviter les activités qui exigent sa vigilance jusqu'à ce qu'on ait la certitude que le médicament n'entraîne pas cet effet chez lui.
- Conseiller au patient de consulter un professionnel de la santé si aucune amélioration ne survient après quelques jours.
- Insister sur l'importance des examens de suivi permettant d'évaluer l'efficacité du traitement, particulièrement si le médicament est pris à doses élevées.

Oxyurose: Recommander au patient de laver (sans secouer) toute la literie, les sous-vêtements, les serviettes et les vêtements de nuit après le traitement afin d'éviter le risque de réinfection.

VÉRIFICATION DE L'EFFICACITÉ THÉRAPEUTIQUE

L'efficacité du traitement peut être démontrée par: la disparition des signes et symptômes d'infection ou des résultats négatifs aux analyses des échantillons de selles et des prélèvements périanaux. Le délai de guérison complète dépend du type de parasite. ✳

MÉCHLORÉTHAMINE

Mustargen

CLASSIFICATION:

Antinéoplasique (alkylant)

Grossesse – catégorie D

INDICATIONS

IV: Traitement palliatif de la maladie de Hodgkin (stades III et IV), des lymphomes non hodgkiniens, de la leucémie myéloïde chronique, de la leucémie lymphoïde chronique, de la polyglobulie essentielle, du mycosis fongoïde et de l'épithélioma bronchopulmonaire ■ **Voie intrapleurale, intrapéritonéale ou intrapéricardique**: Traitement palliatif des métastases d'épithéliomas qui entraînent un épanchement.

MÉCANISME D'ACTION

Inhibition de la synthèse de l'ADN et de l'ARN par formation de liaisons transversales (effet non spécifique sur une phase du cycle cellulaire). ***Effets thérapeutiques:*** Destruction des cellules à croissance rapide, particulièrement des cellules malignes.

PHARMACOCINÉTIQUE

Absorption: L'administration est réservée à la voie IV et intracavitaire. Par suite de l'instillation intracavitaire, une certaine quantité de méchloréthamine est absorbée.

Distribution: Inconnue.

Métabolisme et excrétion: La méchloréthamine se décompose rapidement dans les tissus et les liquides organiques.

Demi-vie: Inconnue.

Profil temps-action (effets sur la numération globulaire)

	DÉBUT D'ACTION	PIC	DURÉE
Globules blancs	24 h	7 - 14 jours	10 - 21 jours
Plaquettes	inconnu	9 - 16 jours	20 jours

CONTRE-INDICATIONS, PRÉCAUTIONS ET MISES EN GARDE

Contre-indications: Hypersensibilité ■ Présence d'une maladie infectieuse.

Précautions et mises en garde: Aplasie médullaire ■ Antécédents de radiothérapie ou de chimiothérapie (réduire la dose) ■ Obésité ou œdème important (la dose devrait être calculée à partir du poids sec idéal) ■ Personnes âgées ou patients présentant des maladies chroniques débilitantes ■ **OBST.**: Patientes en âge de procréer, grossesse, allaitement.

RÉACTIONS INDÉSIRABLES ET EFFETS SECONDAIRES

SNC: CONVULSIONS, étourdissements, céphalées, vertiges, faiblesse.

GI: nausées, vomissements, anorexie, diarrhée.

GU: stérilité.

Tég.: rash, alopécie.

Hémat.: LEUCOPÉNIE, THROMBOPÉNIE, anémie.

Locaux: nécrose tissulaire, phlébite au point d'injection IV.

Métab.: hyperuricémie.

Divers: réactivation du zona.

INTERACTIONS

Médicament-médicament: Aplasie médullaire additive lors de l'administration concomitante d'autres **agents antinéoplasiques** ou d'une **radiothérapie** ■ La méchloréthamine peut diminuer la réponse des anticorps aux **vaccins à virus vivants** et augmenter le risque de réactions indésirables.

VOIES D'ADMINISTRATION ET POSOLOGIE

- **IV (adultes)**: 0,4 mg/kg de poids corporel sec idéal, en une seule dose ou en doses fractionnées de 0,1 à 0,2 mg/kg/jour. Les doses administrées lors des cycles suivants sont déterminées en fonction de la numération globulaire.
- **Voie intracavitaire (adultes)**: Le choix de la posologie et de la technique utilisées se fonde sur la voie d'administration endocavitaire. La dose habituelle est de 0,4 mg/kg, bien qu'on ait déjà administré une dose de 0,2 mg/kg par voie intrapéricardique.

PRÉSENTATION

Poudre pour injection: flacons de 10 mg[Pr].

SOINS INFIRMIERS

M

ÉVALUATION DE LA SITUATION

- Mesurer fréquemment la pression artérielle, le pouls et la fréquence respiratoire pendant toute la durée du traitement. Prévenir le médecin en cas de changement marqué.
- Examiner fréquemment le point d'injection pour déceler la rougeur, l'irritation ou l'inflammation. L'extravasation dans les tissus sous-cutanés entraîne une inflammation douloureuse. On note habituellement une induration du point d'injection avec risque de formation d'une escarre. En cas d'extravasation, arrêter la perfusion et la recommencer ailleurs pour éviter la lésion des tissus sous-cutanés. Infiltrer rapidement dans la région affectée une solution de thiosulfate sodique isotonique à 4 % (prélever 1,6 mL de thiosulfate sodique à 25 % et le diluer dans 8,4 mL d'eau stérile pour injection); appliquer ensuite des compresses de glace pendant 6 à 12 heures, selon les recommandations du médecin.
- Effectuer le bilan des ingesta et des excreta. Noter l'appétit et l'apport nutritionnel du patient. Les nausées et les vomissements peuvent survenir de 1 à 3 heures après le traitement; les vomissements peuvent persister pendant 8 heures, et les nausées, pendant 24 heures. Administrer des antiémétiques par voie parentérale de 30 à 45 minutes avant le

traitement et à intervalles réguliers au cours des 24 heures qui suivent, selon les recommandations du médecin. Modifier le régime alimentaire selon les aliments que le patient peut tolérer afin de maintenir l'équilibre hydroélectrolytique et l'apport nutritionnel.

- RESTER À L'AFFÛT D'UNE APLASIE MÉDULLAIRE. SUIVRE DE PRÈS LES SAIGNEMENTS: SAIGNEMENT DES GENCIVES, ECCHYMOSES, PÉTÉCHIES, PRÉSENCE DE SANG OCCULTE DANS LES SELLES, L'URINE ET LES VOMISSEMENTS. ÉVITER LES INJECTIONS IM ET LA PRISE DE LA TEMPÉRATURE RECTALE SI LA NUMÉRATION PLAQUETTAIRE EST BASSE. APPLIQUER UNE PRESSION SUR LES POINTS DE PONCTION VEINEUSE PENDANT 10 MINUTES. SURVEILLER LES SIGNES D'INFECTION EN CAS DE NEUTROPÉNIE. Une anémie peut survenir. Suivre de près une fatigue accrue, la dyspnée et l'hypotension orthostatique.
- Rester à l'affût des symptômes suivants de goutte: concentrations accrues d'acide urique, douleurs articulaires et œdème. Inciter le patient à boire au moins 2 litres de liquide par jour si son état le permet. On peut lui administrer de l'allopurinol pour diminuer les concentrations d'acide urique. Le médecin peut recommander l'alcalinisation de l'urine pour accroître l'excrétion d'acide urique.

Voie intracavitaire: Une douleur survient souvent après l'injection intracavitaire et peut persister pendant 2 ou 3 jours. Évaluer fréquemment la douleur et la traiter à l'aide d'analgésiques, selon les besoins.

Tests de laboratoire:

- NOTER LA NUMÉRATION GLOBULAIRE ET LA FORMULE LEUCOCYTAIRE AVANT LE TRAITEMENT ET À INTERVALLES RÉGULIERS PENDANT TOUTE SA DURÉE. LE NADIR DE LA LEUCOPÉNIE SURVIENT DANS LES 7 À 14 JOURS. PRÉVENIR LE MÉDECIN SI LE NOMBRE DE LEUCOCYTES EST $< 1{,}0 \times 10^9$/L. LE NADIR DE LA THROMBOPÉNIE SURVIENT DANS LES 9 À 16 JOURS. PRÉVENIR LE MÉDECIN SI LE NOMBRE DE PLAQUETTES EST $< 75 \times 10^9$/L. LE NOMBRE DE LEUCOCYTES ET DE PLAQUETTES REVIENT À LA NORMALE DANS LES 20 JOURS QUI SUIVENT.
- Noter les résultats des tests de la fonction hépatique (AST, ALT, LDH et bilirubine) et ceux de la fonction rénale (urée et créatinine), avant le début du traitement et à intervalles réguliers pendant toute sa durée, afin de déceler les signes d'hépatotoxicité et de néphrotoxicité.
- Noter les concentrations d'acide urique avant le traitement et à intervalles réguliers pendant toute sa durée. La méchloréthamine peut entraîner l'élévation des concentrations sériques et urinaires d'acide urique.

DIAGNOSTICS INFIRMIERS POSSIBLES

- Risque d'infection (Réactions indésirables).
- Alimentation déficiente (Réactions indésirables).
- Connaissances insuffisantes sur le traitement médicamenteux (Enseignement au patient et à ses proches).

INTERVENTIONS INFIRMIÈRES

- Préparer la solution sous une hotte à flux laminaire. Porter des gants, une blouse et un masque pendant la manipulation de ce médicament. Tout le matériel qui a été en contact avec ce médicament doit être décontaminé avant d'être mis au rebut. Faire tremper les gants, les tubulures IV, les seringues, etc., dans une solution de thiosulfate de sodium à 5 % et de bicarbonate de sodium à 5 % pendant 45 minutes. Mélanger les portions du médicament inutilisées à des quantités égales de cette solution.
- Mettre au rebut tout le matériel contaminé dans les contenants réservés à cet usage. Ce médicament est **très toxique** et autant la poudre que la solution doivent être manipulées avec soin. Éviter l'inhalation de la poussière ou des vapeurs, ainsi que le contact avec la peau ou les muqueuses, et particulièrement avec les yeux. Si le médicament touche la peau, rincer la région atteinte avec beaucoup d'eau pendant 15 minutes et, ensuite, avec une solution de thiosulfate de sodium à 2 %. Si le médicament touche l'œil, rincer avec une solution de NaCl 0,9 % et prévenir immédiatement le médecin. Relire et respecter les règlements particuliers concernant la manipulation de ce produit avant de l'utiliser (voir l'annexe H).

IV directe: Jeter la fiole si l'on observe, avant de reconstituer le médicament, que des gouttelettes d'eau se sont formées. Reconstituer à raison de 10 mg dans 10 mL de solution de NaCl 0,9 % ou d'eau stérile pour injection. Ne pas retirer l'aiguille du bouchon de la fiole avant d'agiter la solution. Laisser la solution se dissoudre complètement. La solution reconstituée se décompose en l'espace de 15 minutes. Administrer immédiatement. Ne pas utiliser une solution qui a changé de couleur ou qui contient un précipité.

Vitesse d'administration: Prélever la quantité désirée de médicament et l'administrer en 3 à 5 minutes par une tubulure en Y par laquelle s'écoule une solution de NaCl 0,9 %.

Compatibilité (tubulure en Y): amifostine ▪ aztréonam ▪ filgrastim ▪ fludarabine ▪ granisétron ▪ melphalan ▪ ondansétron ▪ sargramostim ▪ téniposide ▪ vinorelbine.

Incompatibilité (tubulure en Y): céfépime.

Voie intracavitaire: On peut diluer de nouveau la solution dans 50 à 100 mL de solution de NaCl 0,9 %.

Demander conseil au médecin au sujet de l'administration d'analgésiques et des changements de position nécessaires afin de s'assurer que la méchloréthamine se répartit dans toute la surface cavitaire. Le liquide restant dans la cavité peut être retiré après 24 à 36 heures.

ENSEIGNEMENT AU PATIENT ET À SES PROCHES

- RECOMMANDER AU PATIENT DE SIGNALER IMMÉDIATEMENT À UN PROFESSIONNEL DE LA SANTÉ LES SYMPTÔMES SUIVANTS: FIÈVRE, FRISSONS, TOUX, ENROUEMENT, MAUX DE GORGE, SIGNES D'INFECTION, DOULEURS LOMBAIRES OU AUX FLANCS, MICTIONS DOULOUREUSES OU DIFFICILES, SAIGNEMENT DES GENCIVES, FORMATION D'ECCHYMOSES, PÉTÉCHIES, PRÉSENCE DE SANG DANS L'URINE, LES SELLES OU LES VOMISSEMENTS, FATIGUE ACCRUE, DYSPNÉE OU HYPOTENSION ORTHOSTATIQUE. INCITER LE PATIENT À ÉVITER LES FOULES ET LES PERSONNES CONTAGIEUSES. LUI CONSEILLER D'UTILISER UNE BROSSE À DENTS À POILS DOUX ET UN RASOIR ÉLECTRIQUE ET DE PRENDRE GARDE AUX CHUTES. LUI RECOMMANDER DE NE PAS PRENDRE D'ALCOOL NI DE PRÉPARATIONS À BASE D'ACIDE ACÉTYLSALICYLIQUE OU D'AINS EN RAISON DU RISQUE DE SAIGNEMENTS GASTRIQUES.
- Expliquer à la patiente que ce médicament peut provoquer une suppression irréversible de la fonction des gonades; toutefois, lui recommander de continuer à prendre des mesures contraceptives pendant le traitement et pendant au moins 4 mois après l'avoir arrêté, car la méchloréthamine peut avoir des effets tératogènes.
- Prévenir le patient qu'il risque de perdre ses cheveux. Explorer avec lui les stratégies lui permettant de s'adapter à ce changement.
- Prévenir le patient qu'il ne doit pas se faire vacciner sans recommandation expresse d'un professionnel de la santé.
- Conseiller au patient de prévenir un professionnel de la santé si un rash survient. Le rash peut indiquer une réaction idiosyncrasique ou la réactivation du zona.
- Insister sur l'importance des tests de laboratoire à intervalles réguliers permettant de déceler les effets secondaires.

VÉRIFICATION DE L'EFFICACITÉ THÉRAPEUTIQUE

L'efficacité du traitement peut être démontrée par: la diminution de la taille de la tumeur et le ralentissement de la propagation des cellules malignes ▪ l'amélioration de l'état hématologique, en cas de leucémie.

MÉCLIZINE

Bonamine

CLASSIFICATION:

Antiémétique, antihistaminique

Grossesse – catégorie B

INDICATIONS

Prévention et traitement symptomatique de la nausée, des vomissements et des vertiges associés: au mal des transports ▪ au mal des rayons ▪ au syndrome de Ménière ▪ à la labyrinthite et à d'autres troubles de l'appareil vestibulaire.

MÉCANISME D'ACTION

Agent doté de propriétés anticholinergiques centrales et de propriétés antihistaminiques; effets dépresseurs sur le SNC ▪ Diminution de l'excitabilité du labyrinthe de l'oreille moyenne et de la conduction de ses voies vestibulaires cérébelleuses. ***Effets thérapeutiques:*** Diminution des symptômes du mal des transports ▪ Diminution des vertiges dus à une maladie vestibulaire.

M

PHARMACOCINÉTIQUE

Absorption: Bonne (PO).

Distribution: Inconnue.

Métabolisme et excrétion: Inconnus.

Demi-vie: 6 heures.

Profil temps-action (effets antihistaminiques)

	DÉBUT D'ACTION	PIC	DURÉE
PO	1 h	inconnu	8 - 24 h

CONTRE-INDICATIONS, PRÉCAUTIONS ET MISES EN GARDE

Contre-indications: Hypersensibilité.

Précautions et mises en garde: Hyperplasie bénigne de la prostate ▪ Glaucome à angle fermé ▪ Personnes âgées ou patients très jeunes (sensibilité accrue; risque accru de réactions indésirables) ▪ **OBST.**: On devrait évaluer les avantages potentiels par rapport aux risques du traitement ▪ Enfants < 12 ans ou allaitement (l'innocuité du médicament n'a pas été établie).

RÉACTIONS INDÉSIRABLES ET EFFETS SECONDAIRES

SNC: somnolence, fatigue.

ORLO: vision trouble.

GI: sécheresse de la bouche (xérostomie).

INTERACTIONS

Médicament-médicament: Dépression additive du SNC, lors de l'usage concomitant d'autres **dépresseurs du SNC**, incluant l'**alcool**, les **antihistaminiques**, les **opioïdes** et les **hypnosédatifs** ■ Effets anticholinergiques additifs lors de l'administration concomitante d'autres **agents dotés de propriétés anticholinergiques**, incluant certains **antihistaminiques**, les **antidépresseurs**, l'**atropine**, l'**halopéridol**, les **phénothiazines**, la **quinidine** et le **disopyramide**.

VOIES D'ADMINISTRATION ET POSOLOGIE

- **PO (adultes):** *Mal des transports* – de 25 à 50 mg, 1 heure avant le voyage; on peut répéter l'administration toutes les 24 heures. *Labyrinthite et autres troubles de l'appareil vestibulaire* – de 25 à 100 mg par jour, en doses fractionnées, selon la réponse clinique. *Mal des rayons* – 50 mg, de 2 à 12 heures avant le traitement par irradiation.
- **PO (enfants > 12 ans):** L'enfant doit recevoir environ la moitié de la dose adulte.

PRÉSENTATION

M

Comprimés à croquer: 25 mg[VL].

SOINS INFIRMIERS

ÉVALUATION DE LA SITUATION

- Observer le patient pour déterminer le degré de sédation entraîné par le médicament.

Mal des transports: Noter les nausées et les vomissements avant l'administration du médicament et 60 minutes après.

Vertiges: Déterminer l'intensité des vertiges à intervalles réguliers chez les patients recevant la méclizine pour le traitement de la labyrinthite.

Tests de laboratoire: Le médicament peut entraîner des résultats faussement négatifs aux tests d'allergie cutanés. Arrêter l'administration de la méclizine 72 heures avant le test.

DIAGNOSTICS INFIRMIERS POSSIBLES

- Risque d'accident (Effets secondaires).
- Connaissances insuffisantes sur le traitement médicamenteux (Enseignement au patient et à ses proches).

INTERVENTIONS INFIRMIÈRES

- Administrer le médicament par voie orale avec des aliments, de l'eau ou du lait afin de réduire l'irritation gastro-intestinale. Les comprimés à croquer peuvent être mâchés ou avalés tels quels.

ENSEIGNEMENT AU PATIENT ET À SES PROCHES

- Conseiller au patient de respecter rigoureusement la posologie recommandée. S'il n'a pu prendre le médicament au moment habituel, il doit le prendre dès que possible, à moins que ce ne soit presque l'heure prévue pour la dose suivante. L'avertir qu'il ne doit jamais remplacer une dose manquée par une double dose.
- Prévenir le patient que la méclizine peut provoquer de la somnolence. Lui conseiller de ne pas conduire et d'éviter les activités exigeant sa vigilance jusqu'à ce qu'on ait la certitude que le médicament n'entraîne pas cet effet chez lui.
- Pour soulager la sécheresse de la bouche, conseiller au patient de se rincer fréquemment la bouche, de pratiquer une bonne hygiène orale et de consommer de la gomme à mâcher ou des bonbons sans sucre.
- Mettre en garde le patient contre la consommation d'alcool ou d'autres dépresseurs du SNC en même temps que la méclizine.

Mal des transports: Prévenir le patient qu'il doit prendre la méclizine au moins 1 heure avant le voyage, en prophylaxie du mal des transports.

VÉRIFICATION DE L'EFFICACITÉ THÉRAPEUTIQUE

L'efficacité du traitement peut être démontrée par: la prévention et le traitement des symptômes du mal des transports ■ la prévention et le traitement des vertiges entraînés par une maladie vestibulaire.

MÉDROXYPROGESTÉRONE

Alti-MPA, Apo-Medroxy, Depo-Provera, Dom-Medroxyprogesterone, Gen-Medroxy, Novo-Medrone, PMS-Medroxyprogesterone, Provera

CLASSIFICATION:

Antinéoplasique (hormone de synthèse), progestatif et contraceptif hormonal

Grossesse – catégorie D

Pour l'usage contraceptif, voir Contraceptifs hormonaux.

INDICATIONS

PO: Hormonothérapie de substitution visant à contrebalancer l'effet des œstrogènes sur l'endomètre ■ Traitement des troubles menstruels ■ Traitement adjuvant ou palliatif du cancer récidivant ou métastatique de l'endomètre ■ Traitement adjuvant ou palliatif du cancer du sein hormonodépendant, récidivant et métastatique chez la femme postménopausée ■ **IM**: Prévention de la grossesse ■ Traitement de l'endométriose ■ Traitement adjuvant ou palliatif des cancers récurrents ou métastatiques de l'endomètre ou du rein ■ Traitement adjuvant ou palliatif du cancer du sein hormonodépendant chez la femme postménopausée.

MÉCANISME D'ACTION

Forme synthétique de progestérone; ses effets comprennent la modification des sécrétions de l'endomètre, l'élévation de la température corporelle basale, des modifications histologiques de l'épithélium vaginal, la relaxation des muscles lisses utérins, la croissance des tissus alvéolaires mammaires, l'inhibition hypophysaire et le saignement de retrait en présence d'œstrogènes. ***Effets thérapeutiques:*** Diminution de l'hyperplasie de l'endomètre chez les femmes ménopausées qui reçoivent un traitement concomitant par des œstrogènes (l'association avec les œstrogènes diminue les symptômes vasomoteurs et prévient l'ostéoporose) ■ Rétablissement de l'équilibre hormonal et suppression des saignements utérins ■ Traitement du cancer de l'endomètre ou du rein ■ Prévention de la grossesse.

PHARMACOCINÉTIQUE

Absorption: De 0,6 à 10 % (PO).
Distribution: L'agent passe dans le lait maternel.
Métabolisme et excrétion: Métabolisme hépatique.
Demi-vie: *1re phase* – 52 minutes; *2e phase* – 230 minutes; *biologique* – 14,5 heures.

Profil temps-action (effets thérapeutiques)

	DÉBUT D'ACTION	PIC	DURÉE
PO	inconnu	inconnu	inconnue
IM†	plusieurs semaines ou mois	plusieurs mois	inconnue‡

† Effets antinéoplasiques.
‡ L'effet contraceptif dure 3 mois.

CONTRE-INDICATIONS, PRÉCAUTIONS ET MISES EN GARDE

Contre-indications: Hypersensibilité ■ Hypersensibilité aux parabènes (suspension IM seulement) ■ Grossesse ■ Rétention fœtale ■ Maladie thromboembolique, maladie vasculaire cérébrale ou antécédents de ces maladies ■ Maladie hépatique grave ■ Cancer du sein ou des organes génitaux ■ Saignements vaginaux ou urinaires non diagnostiqués ■ Pathologie du sein non diagnostiquée ■ Administration par voie IV de la suspension pour injection destinée à la voie IM.
Précautions et mises en garde: Antécédents de maladie hépatique ■ Maladie rénale ■ Maladie cardiovasculaire ■ Troubles convulsifs ■ Dépression ■ **ALLAITEMENT**: En cas d'usage comme contraceptif, la mère devrait attendre 6 semaines après l'accouchement avant de pouvoir allaiter ■ Porphyrie.

RÉACTIONS INDÉSIRABLES ET EFFETS SECONDAIRES

SNC: dépression.
ORLO: thrombose de la rétine.
CV: EMBOLIE PULMONAIRE, thromboembolie, thrombophlébite.
GI: hépatite, hémorragie des gencives.
GU: érosions cervicales.
Tég.: chloasma, mélasme, rash.
End.: aménorrhée, saignements en cours de traitement, sensibilité mammaire, modifications du flux menstruel, galactorrhée, hyperglycémie, saignotements.
HÉ: œdème.
Divers: réactions allergiques, incluant l'ANAPHYLAXIE et l'ŒDÈME ANGIONEUROTIQUE, gain de poids, perte de poids.

INTERACTIONS

Médicament-médicament: La médroxyprogestérone peut diminuer l'efficacité de la **bromocriptine** administrée en concomitance pour traiter la galactorrhée et l'aménorrhée ■ La **carbamazépine**, le **phénobarbital**, la **phénytoïne**, la **rifampine** ou la **rifabutine** peuvent réduire l'efficacité contraceptive du médicament ■ L'**aminoglutéthimide** peut réduire l'absorption du médicament pris par voie orale.

VOIES D'ADMINISTRATION ET POSOLOGIE

Femmes ménopausées recevant une œstrogénothérapie concomitante

- **PO (adultes)**: De 5 à 10 mg par jour, pendant 12 à 14 jours par mois, ou de 2,5 à 5 mg, tous les jours.

Aménorrhée secondaire

- **PO (adultes)**: De 5 à 10 mg par jour, pendant 12 à 14 jours par mois; amorcer le traitement après avoir écarté la présence d'une grossesse.

Saignements utérins anormaux

- **PO (adultes)**: De 5 à 10 mg par jour, pendant 10 à 14 jours; amorcer le traitement entre le 12e et le 16e jour présumé ou calculé du cycle menstruel. Ce schéma posologique peut être répété au cours de 2 cycles consécutifs ou plus et doit se poursuivre pendant 2 cycles supplémentaires après l'arrêt des saignements.

Cancer du rein ou de l'endomètre

- **PO (adultes)**: *Cancer de l'endomètre* – de 200 à 400 mg par jour.

- **IM (adultes)**: *Cancer du rein et de l'endomètre* – de 400 à 1 000 mg par semaine; on peut répéter l'administration toutes les semaines; si une amélioration est notée, il faudrait essayer de diminuer la dose en la faisant passer à 400 mg par mois.

Cancer mammaire
- **PO (adultes)**: 400 mg par jour, en doses fractionnées.
- **IM (adultes)**: 500 mg par jour, pendant 28 jours; par la suite, en dose d'entretien, 500 mg, 2 fois par semaine, tant que la patiente répond au traitement.

Contraception
- **IM (adultes)**: 150 mg tous les 3 mois; on administre cette dose au cours des 5 premiers jours qui suivent le début d'une menstruation normale, ou au cours des 5 premiers jours postpartum, si la mère n'allaite pas.

Endométriose
- **IM (adultes)**: 50 mg, toutes les semaines, ou 100 mg, toutes les 2 semaines, pendant au moins 6 mois.

PRÉSENTATION

Comprimés: 2,5 mg[Pr], 5 mg[Pr], 10 mg[Pr], 100 mg[Pr] ■ **Suspension pour injection retard**: 50 mg/mL[Pr], 150 mg/mL[Pr] ■ **En association avec:** œstrogènes conjugués (Premplus) – 0,625 d'œstrogènes conjugués et 2,5 ou 5 mg de médroxyprogestérone[Pr].

M

SOINS INFIRMIERS

ÉVALUATION DE LA SITUATION

- Mesurer la pression artérielle à intervalles réguliers tout au long du traitement.
- Déterminer la durée habituelle du cycle menstruel de la patiente. Commencer l'administration du médicament n'importe quel jour du cycle chez les patientes souffrant d'aménorrhée, et entre le 12e et le 16e jour du cycle, chez les patientes présentant des saignements anormaux.
- Effectuer le bilan des ingesta et des excreta et peser la patiente toutes les semaines. Signaler au médecin toute modification importante ou un gain pondéral constant.

Tests de laboratoire:
- Noter les résultats des tests de la fonction hépatique avant le début du traitement et à intervalles réguliers pendant toute sa durée.
- La médroxyprogestérone peut entraîner l'élévation des concentrations de phosphatase alcaline. Elle peut diminuer les concentrations de prégnandiol éliminé dans l'urine.
- La médroxyprogestérone peut entraîner l'élévation des concentrations sériques de LDL et la diminution des concentrations sériques de HDL.
- Le médicament peut modifier les résultats des tests de la fonction thyroïdienne.

DIAGNOSTICS INFIRMIERS POSSIBLES

- Dysfonctionnement sexuel (Indications).
- Irrigation tissulaire inefficace (Effets secondaires).
- Connaissances insuffisantes sur le traitement médicamenteux (Enseignement au patient et à ses proches).

INTERVENTIONS INFIRMIÈRES

- Seule la présentation en fioles à 150 mg/mL devrait être utilisée dans un but contraceptif.
- La préparation injectable peut entraîner une perte de densité minérale osseuse, surtout chez la femme de moins de 21 ans. Cette préparation ne devrait être utilisée pendant plus de 2 ans que dans le cas de la femme chez laquelle aucune autre méthode de contraception n'est envisageable. Si l'usage à long terme est inévitable, la patiente devrait prendre des suppléments de calcium et de vitamine D et se soumettre à un suivi régulier de la densité minérale osseuse.

IM:
- Bien agiter la fiole avant de préparer la dose IM. Administrer profondément dans le muscle.
- Si l'injection de routine n'est pas administrée dans les 13 semaines qui suivent une injection préalable, il faut effectuer un test de grossesse avant d'administrer la dose suivante pour s'assurer que la patiente n'est pas enceinte.
- Chez les patientes souffrant de cancer, il faut parfois administrer initialement la dose IM toutes les semaines. Une fois l'état de la patiente stabilisé, la dose IM pourrait n'être nécessaire que 1 fois par mois.

ENSEIGNEMENT AU PATIENT ET À SES PROCHES

- Expliquer à la patiente le schéma posologique. Lui recommander de prendre le médicament à la même heure tous les jours. Si elle n'a pas pu prendre le médicament au moment habituel, elle doit le prendre dès que possible à moins que ce ne soit presque l'heure prévue pour la dose suivante. L'avertir qu'il ne faut jamais remplacer une dose manquée par une double dose.
- Prévenir la patiente qui reçoit la médroxyprogestérone pour le traitement de l'aménorrhée qu'un saignement de retrait peut se manifester dans les 3 à 7 jours qui suivent l'arrêt du traitement.

- EXPLIQUER À LA PATIENTE LES DONNÉES CONTENUES DANS LE DÉPLIANT DE CONDITIONNEMENT. INSISTER SUR LE FAIT QU'IL EST IMPORTANT DE PRÉVENIR UN PROFESSIONNEL DE LA SANTÉ SI LES EFFETS SECONDAIRES SUIVANTS SE MANIFESTENT : MODIFICATIONS DE LA VISION, FAIBLESSE SOUDAINE, MANQUE DE COORDINATION, DIFFICULTÉS D'ÉLOCUTION, CÉPHALÉES, DOULEURS AU NIVEAU DE LA JAMBE OU DU MOLLET, ESSOUFFLEMENTS, DOULEURS THORACIQUES, MODIFICATION DES SAIGNEMENTS VAGINAUX, JAUNISSEMENT DE LA PEAU, ŒDÈME DES MEMBRES, DÉPRESSION OU RASH. Les patientes qui reçoivent la médroxyprogestérone comme traitement anticancéreux pourraient ne pas avoir lu le dépliant.
- Conseiller à la patiente de toujours disposer d'une provision de médroxyprogestérone suffisante pour 1 mois.
- Montrer à la patiente la méthode d'autoexamen des seins. Lui conseiller d'effectuer cet examen tous les mois. Une sensibilité mammaire accrue peut survenir.
- Prévenir la patiente que des saignements des gencives peuvent survenir lors du traitement par la médroxyprogestérone. Lui recommander de pratiquer une bonne hygiène buccale et de se faire examiner et traiter les dents à intervalles réguliers.
- Recommander à la patiente de prévenir le professionnel de la santé si elle n'a pas eu ses règles au moment habituel ou si elle pense être enceinte. La prévenir qu'il ne faudrait pas qu'une grossesse survienne dans les 3 mois qui suivent l'arrêt du traitement afin de réduire les risques d'effets nocifs chez le fœtus.
- Prévenir la patiente que la médroxyprogestérone peut entraîner l'apparition du mélasme (taches brunes sur le visage) lors des expositions au soleil. Lui recommander de ne pas s'exposer au soleil, d'utiliser un écran solaire et de porter des vêtements protecteurs.
- Insister sur l'importance d'un suivi médical régulier comprenant la prise de la pression artérielle, l'examen des seins, de l'abdomen et du pelvis et le test de Papanicolaou, tous les 6 à 12 mois.

IM: Recommander à la patiente de consommer régulièrement des produits alimentaires riches en vitamine D et en calcium pour prévenir la perte minérale osseuse.

VÉRIFICATION DE L'EFFICACITÉ THÉRAPEUTIQUE

L'efficacité du traitement peut être démontrée par: la régularisation du cycle menstruel ■ la diminution de l'hyperplasie de l'endomètre chez les femmes ménopausées qui reçoivent une œstrogénothérapie concomitante ■ la maîtrise de la propagation des métastases, en cas de cancer de l'endomètre ou du rein. ✱

MÉGESTROL

Apo-Megestrol, Lin-Megestrol, Megace, Megace OS, Nu-Megestrol

CLASSIFICATION:

Antinéoplasique (hormone de synthèse), progestatif, antianorexique, anticachectique

Grossesse – catégories D (comprimés) et X (suspension)

INDICATIONS

Traitement palliatif ou adjuvant du cancer de l'endomètre et du sein inopérable et récurrent et traitement palliatif du cancer avancé de la prostate ■ Traitement de l'anorexie, de la perte de poids et de la cachexie associées au cancer métastatique ■ **Suspension orale**: Traitement de l'anorexie, de la perte de poids et de la cachexie associées au sida.

MÉCANISME D'ACTION

L'effet antinéoplasique peut être le résultat de l'inhibition de la fonction hypophysaire. ***Effets thérapeutiques:*** Diminution de la taille de la tumeur ■ Gain d'appétit et de poids chez les patients atteints de sida ou de cancer métastatique.

M

PHARMACOCINÉTIQUE

Absorption: Bonne (PO). Il existe cependant une grande variabilité interindividuelle dans la vitesse et l'importance de l'absorption.

Distribution: Inconnue.

Liaison aux protéines: ≥ 90 %.

Métabolisme et excrétion: Métabolisme hépatique (100 %).

Demi-vie: 38 heures (de 13 à 104 heures).

Profil temps-action (effet antinéoplasique)

	DÉBUT D'ACTION	PIC	DURÉE
PO	plusieurs semaines – mois	2 mois	inconnue

CONTRE-INDICATIONS, PRÉCAUTIONS ET MISES EN GARDE

Contre-indications: Hypersensibilité ■ **OBST.**: Épreuves diagnostiques de la grossesse (le mégestrol n'est pas destiné à cet usage).

Précautions et mises en garde: **OBST.**: Grossesse, rétention fœtale ou allaitement ■ Hémorragie vaginale non diagnostiquée ■ Maladie hépatique grave ■ Intolérance à l'alcool (éviter l'administration de la suspension chez les patients présentant ce type d'intolérance) ■ Diabète ■ Dépression ■ Maladie rénale ■ Antécédents de thrombophlébite ■ Maladie cardiovasculaire ■ Troubles convulsifs ■ **Péd.**: L'innocuité et l'efficacité du médicament n'ont pas été établies chez les enfants.

RÉACTIONS INDÉSIRABLES ET EFFETS SECONDAIRES

CV: THROMBOEMBOLIE, œdème.
GI: irritation gastrique, nausées, vomissements.
Tég.: alopécie.
End.: inhibition asymptomatique des glandes surrénales (traitement chronique).
Hémat.: thrombophlébite.
GU: hémorragies intermenstruelles.
Métab.: gain pondéral, intolérance au glucose.
Loc.: syndrome du tunnel carpien.

INTERACTIONS

Médicament-médicament: Aucune interaction notable.

VOIES D'ADMINISTRATION ET POSOLOGIE

- **PO (adultes)**: *Cancer du sein* – 160 mg/jour ou 125 mg/m^2/jour, en une seule dose ou en doses fractionnées. *Cancer de l'endomètre* – de 80 à 320 mg/jour ou 62,5 à 250 mg/m^2/jour en doses fractionnées. *Cancer de la prostate* – 120 mg/jour ou 93,8 mg/m^2/jour en une seule prise, en association avec 1 comprimé de 0,1 mg de diéthylstilbestrol. *Anorexie, cachexie ou perte de poids associées au cancer* – de 400 à 800 mg, 1 fois par jour. *Anorexie, cachexie ou perte de poids associées au sida* – de 400 à 800 mg, 1 fois par jour sous forme de suspension orale.

PRÉSENTATION (version générique disponible)

Comprimés: 40 mg^{Pr}, 160 mg^{Pr} ■ **Suspension orale (parfum de citron-lime)**: 40 mg/mL^{Pr}.

SOINS INFIRMIERS

ÉVALUATION DE LA SITUATION

- SUIVRE DE PRÈS L'ÉTAT DU PATIENT POUR DÉCELER L'ŒDÈME, LA DOULEUR OU UNE SENSIBILITÉ AU NIVEAU DES JAMBES. PRÉVENIR LE MÉDECIN SI CES SIGNES DE THROMBOPHLÉBITE DES VEINES PROFONDES SE MANIFESTENT.

Anorexie: Suivre de près le poids, l'appétit et l'apport nutritionnel des patients atteints de sida ou de cancer métastatique.

DIAGNOSTICS INFIRMIERS POSSIBLES

- Connaissances insuffisantes sur le traitement médicamenteux (Enseignement au patient et à ses proches).

INTERVENTIONS INFIRMIÈRES

- En raison de la dose élevée qu'il faut administrer, la suspension est la forme posologique la plus pratique chez les patients atteints du sida.
- Administrer le médicament avec les repas si l'irritation gastrique devient gênante.

ENSEIGNEMENT AU PATIENT ET À SES PROCHES

- Conseiller au patient de respecter rigoureusement la posologie recommandée. Le prévenir qu'il ne doit pas sauter de dose ni remplacer une dose manquée par une double dose. S'il n'a pas pu prendre le médicament au moment habituel, il doit le prendre dès que possible à moins que ce ne soit presque l'heure prévue pour la dose suivante. Diminuer graduellement les doses avant d'arrêter définitivement l'administration du mégestrol.
- Recommander à la patiente de signaler au médecin tout saignement vaginal inhabituel. CONSEILLER AUX PATIENTS DES DEUX SEXES DE SIGNALER TOUT SIGNE DE THROMBOPHLÉBITE DES VEINES PROFONDES.
- Prévenir la patiente que le mégestrol peut avoir des effets tératogènes. Lui conseiller de prendre des moyens de contraception pendant toute la durée du traitement et pendant au moins 4 mois après l'avoir arrêté.
- Prévenir le patient qu'il risque de perdre ses cheveux. Explorer avec lui les stratégies lui permettant de s'adapter à ce changement.

VÉRIFICATION DE L'EFFICACITÉ THÉRAPEUTIQUE

L'efficacité du traitement peut être démontrée par: le ralentissement ou l'arrêt de la propagation de la tumeur de l'endomètre ou du sein; les effets thérapeutiques se manifestent habituellement dans les 2 mois qui suivent le début du traitement ■ l'amélioration de l'appétit et un gain de poids chez les patients atteints de sida ou de cancer métastatique.

MÉLOXICAM

Apo-Meloxicam, Co-Meloxicam, Gen-Meloxicam, Mobicox, Novo-Meloxicam, PMS-Meloxicam, Ratio-Meloxicam

CLASSIFICATION:

Anti-inflammatoire non stéroïdien, analgésique non opioïde

Grossesse – catégories D (1er et 3e trimestres) et B (2e trimestre)

INDICATIONS

Traitement symptomatique de la polyarthrite rhumatoïde et de la douleur arthrosique (arthrose, maladie articulaire dégénérative) chez l'adulte.

MÉCANISME D'ACTION

Inhibition de la synthèse des prostaglandines, probablement par inhibition de l'enzyme cyclo-oxygénase ▪ Propriétés analgésiques, anti-inflammatoires et antipyrétiques. ***Effets thérapeutiques:*** Diminution de la douleur et de l'inflammation.

PHARMACOCINÉTIQUE

Absorption: L'absorption du médicament se fait pendant un laps de temps prolongé. Biodisponibilité à 89 % (PO).

Distribution: Inconnue.

Liaison aux protéines: 99,4 %.

Métabolisme et excrétion: Métabolisme hépatique important par le biais du P450. Élimination urinaire et fécale, principalement sous forme de métabolites.

Demi-vie: 20,1 heures.

Profil temps-action (concentrations sanguines)

	DÉBUT D'ACTION	PIC	DURÉE
PO	inconnu	5 – 6 h	24 h

CONTRE-INDICATIONS, PRÉCAUTIONS ET MISES EN GARDE

Contre-indications: Hypersensibilité ▪ Antécédents de crises aiguës d'asthme ou de symptômes d'asthme, d'urticaire, de polypes nasaux, d'anaphylaxie, de rhinite, d'œdème de Quincke ou de toute autre manifestation allergique à la suite de la prise d'aspirine ou d'autres AINS ▪ Ulcère gastroduodénal en évolution ▪ Usage concomitant d'autres AINS ▪ Insuffisance hépatique grave ▪ Insuffisance rénale grave sans dialyse ▪ **PÉD.**: Enfants et adolescents < 18 ans (l'innocuité et l'efficacité de l'agent n'ont pas été établies) ▪ **OBST.**: 3e trimestre de la grossesse (le médicament peut entraîner l'obturation prématurée du canal artériel) ▪ Allaitement.

Précautions et mises en garde: Maladie cardiovasculaire ou facteurs de risque de maladies cardiovasculaires (risque accru de complications coronariennes, d'infarctus du myocarde ou d'accidents vasculaires cérébraux surtout lors d'un usage prolongé) ▪ Traitement concomitant par des corticostéroïdes oraux ou des anticoagulants, traitement prolongé par des AINS, usage du tabac, alcoolisme, patients âgés ou en mauvaise santé (risque accru d'hémorragie digestive) ▪ Néphropathie, insuffisance cardiaque ou dysfonctionnement hépatique préexistants, traitement concomitant par un diurétique ou un IECA ▪ **GÉR.**: Risque accru d'insuffisance rénale ▪ Déshydratation grave (corriger les déficits avant d'administrer le médicament) ▪ Insuffisance cardiaque ou hypertension (risque accru de rétention liquidienne et d'œdème) ▪ Insuffisance rénale, diabète, usage concomitant de bêtabloquants, d'IECA ou de certains diurétiques (risque d'hyperkaliémie) ▪ Asthme préexistant.

EXTRÊME PRUDENCE: ANTÉCÉDENTS D'ULCÈRE OU D'HÉMORRAGIE DIGESTIVE.

RÉACTIONS INDÉSIRABLES ET EFFETS SECONDAIRES

SNC: étourdissements, céphalées, insomnie.

Resp.: asthme, BRONCHOSPASME, dyspnée, infections des voies respiratoires supérieures, pharyngite, toux.

CV: ANGINE DE POITRINE, ARYTHMIES, INFARCTUS DU MYOCARDE, INSUFFISANCE CARDIAQUE, œdème, PALPITATIONS, TACHYCARDIE.

GI: constipation, diarrhée, douleurs abdominales, dyspepsie, élévation de l'AST, de l'ALT et de la GGT, flatulence, HÉMORRAGIE DIGESTIVE, HÉPATITE MÉDICAMENTEUSE, ICTÈRE (rare), INSUFFISANCE HÉPATIQUE (rare), nausées, ULCÈRE GASTRIQUE OU DUODÉNAL, vomissements.

GU: hématurie, infection urinaire, INSUFFISANCE RÉNALE AIGUË.

Tég.: éruptions cutanées, prurit, DERMATITE EXFOLIATIVE, SYNDROME DE STEVENS-JOHNSON, ÉPIDERMOLYSE NÉCROSANTE SUBAIGUË.

Hémat.: ANÉMIE, AGRANULOCYTOSE (rare), anomalies de la numération globulaire, THROMBOPÉNIE.

Loc.: arthralgie, lombalgie.

Divers: réaction allergique, RÉACTIONS ANAPHYLACTOÏDES OU ANAPHYLACTIQUES, Y COMPRIS LE CHOC (rare), symptômes pseudogrippaux.

INTERACTIONS

Médicament-médicament: Le méloxicam est éliminé en grande partie par les isoenzymes CYP 2C9 (voie principale) et 3A4 (voie mineure) du cytochrome P450. Il faut donc user de prudence lors de l'administration concomitante de **médicaments qui inhibent ces isoenzymes ou sont métabolisés par elles** ▪ Le méloxicam peut réduire l'efficacité des **IECA**, du **furosémide** et des **diurétiques thiazidiques** ▪ L'administration concomitante d'**aspirine** peut augmenter davantage le risque d'ulcères gastro-intestinaux ou d'autres complications que si le méloxicam est administré seul ▪ Risque accru de saignements lors de l'administration concomitante d'**anticoagulants**, tels que la **warfarine** ▪ Risque accru de cytopénie lors de l'administration concomitante d'un **médicament qui pourrait être myélotoxique**,

M

en particulier le **méthotrexate** ■ Risque accru d'effets indésirables gastro-intestinaux, tels que les ulcères et l'hémorragie, lors de l'administration concomitante de **glucocorticoïdes**, surtout chez les personnes âgées ■ Le méloxicam peut élever les concentrations sériques de **lithium** ■ La **cholestyramine** augmente la clairance et diminue la demi-vie du méloxicam.

VOIES D'ADMINISTRATION ET POSOLOGIE

- **PO (adultes)**: De 7,5 à 15 mg, 1 fois par jour, quel que soit le moment de la journée.

Insuffisance rénale grave (patient dialysé)

- **PO (adultes)**: La dose ne devrait pas dépasser 7,5 mg, 1 fois par jour.

PRÉSENTATION

Comprimés: 7,5 mg[Pr], 15 mg[Pr].

SOINS INFIRMIERS

ÉVALUATION DE LA SITUATION

M

- Les patients souffrant d'asthme, d'allergie induite par l'aspirine et de polypes nasaux sont davantage prédisposés à des réactions d'hypersensibilité. Observer le patient à la recherche de signes de rhinite, d'asthme et d'urticaire.
- Suivre de près l'amplitude des mouvements, le degré d'enflure et la douleur au niveau des articulations touchées, avant l'administration du médicament et de 1 à 2 heures par la suite.
- Déterminer si le patient est allergique à l'aspirine ou aux AINS. Les patients allergiques ne devraient pas recevoir de méloxicam.

Tests de laboratoire:

- Obtenir les concentrations sériques d'urée et de créatinine ainsi que la numération globulaire et les résultats des tests de la fonction hépatique à intervalles réguliers tout au long d'un traitement prolongé. Le méloxicam peut provoquer une anémie, une thrombopénie et une leucopénie, et entraîner des résultats anormaux aux tests des fonctions hépatique et rénale.
- Le temps de saignement peut être prolongé.

DIAGNOSTICS INFIRMIERS POSSIBLES

- Mobilité physique réduite (Indications).
- Douleur aiguë (Indications).
- Connaissances insuffisantes sur le traitement médicamenteux (Enseignement au patient et à ses proches).

INTERVENTIONS INFIRMIÈRES

- L'administration de doses supérieures à celles recommandées n'accroît pas l'efficacité du médicament, mais augmente le risque de réactions indésirables. Utiliser la dose minimale efficace pendant la plus courte durée de traitement possible.
- Administrer le méloxicam avec ou sans aliments, quel que soit le moment de la journée.

ENSEIGNEMENT AU PATIENT ET À SES PROCHES

- Conseiller au patient de prendre le méloxicam avec un grand verre d'eau et de ne pas se coucher pendant les 15 à 30 minutes qui suivent.
- Conseiller au patient de respecter rigoureusement la posologie recommandée, de ne pas sauter de dose et de ne pas remplacer une dose manquée par une double dose.
- Le méloxicam aide à soulager l'enflure des articulations, la rougeur et la douleur associées à l'arthrite, mais il ne guérit pas cette maladie.
- Expliquer au patient que, dans le cas de certaines formes d'arthrite, les pleins effets thérapeutiques du méloxicam pourraient ne pas se faire sentir avant 2 semaines.
- Conseiller au patient de ne pas prendre d'aspirine, de composés à base d'aspirine, d'AINS ni d'autres médicaments utilisés pour soulager les symptômes d'arthrite pendant qu'il prend le méloxicam, sauf si son médecin le lui a recommandé.
- Conseiller au patient d'éviter l'alcool pendant qu'il prend ce médicament étant donné que le méloxicam pourrait augmenter le risque de troubles gastriques.
- Recommander au patient de prévenir un professionnel de la santé sans tarder en cas de gain de poids inexpliqué, de signes ou de symptômes de toxicité gastro-intestinale (douleurs abdominales, selles noirâtres), de rash cutané ou d'œdème. Lui conseiller de cesser de prendre le méloxicam et de prévenir le médecin si les signes et les symptômes suivants d'hépatotoxicité se manifestent: nausées, fatigue, léthargie, prurit, jaunisse, sensibilité au niveau du quadrant supérieur droit de l'abdomen, symptômes pseudogrippaux.
- Conseiller au patient de consulter un professionnel de la santé si des signes et des symptômes d'anémie surviennent (faiblesse, fatigue, maux de tête, vertiges, etc.).
- Prévenir le patient que certains AINS peuvent provoquer de la somnolence ou de la fatigue chez certaines personnes. Lui conseiller de ne pas conduire

et d'éviter les activités exigeant sa vigilance jusqu'à ce qu'on ait la certitude que ce médicament n'entraîne pas ces effets chez lui.

- Certaines personnes peuvent être plus sensibles à la lumière du soleil lorsqu'elles prennent ce médicament. Conseiller au patient d'utiliser un écran solaire et de porter des vêtements protecteurs pour prévenir les réactions de photosensibilité.
- Conseiller à la patiente de prévenir le médecin sans délai si elle pense être enceinte ou si elle souhaite le devenir.
- Insister sur l'importance des examens médicaux et des examens diagnostiques de suivi.

VÉRIFICATION DE L'EFFICACITÉ THÉRAPEUTIQUE

L'efficacité du traitement peut être démontrée par: la réduction de la douleur articulaire chez les patients souffrant d'arthrose ▪ la réduction de la douleur, de la sensibilité et de l'enflure des articulations chez les patients souffrant de polyarthrite rhumatoïde ▪ les patients qui ne répondent pas à un AINS peuvent répondre à un autre. ✳

MELPHALAN

Alkeran

CLASSIFICATION:

Antinéoplasique (alkylant)

Grossesse - catégorie D

INDICATIONS

En monothérapie ou en association avec d'autres modalités thérapeutiques en présence de: myélome multiple ▪ cancer des ovaires non résécable ▪ mélanome malin - perfusion hyperthermique d'un membre isolé, à titre de traitement adjuvant à une intervention chirurgicale. **Usages non approuvés:** Cancer du sein ▪ Leucémie myélogène chronique ▪ Sarcome ostéogénique.

MÉCANISME D'ACTION

Inhibition de la synthèse de l'ADN et de l'ARN par alkylation (effet non spécifique sur une phase du cycle cellulaire). ***Effets thérapeutiques:*** Destruction des cellules à croissance rapide, particulièrement les cellules malignes ▪ Propriétés immunosuppressives.

PHARMACOCINÉTIQUE

Absorption: Incomplète et variable (PO).

Distribution: Répartition rapide dans l'eau corporelle totale.

Liaison aux protéines: ≤ 30 %.

Métabolisme et excrétion: Métabolisme rapide pendant que le melphalan est dans le sang. Excrétion rénale faible (10 % sous forme inchangée).

Demi-vie: 1,5 heure.

Profil temps-action (effets sur la numération globulaire)

	DÉBUT D'ACTION	PIC	DURÉE
PO	5 jours	2 - 3 semaines	5 - 6 semaines

CONTRE-INDICATIONS, PRÉCAUTIONS ET MISES EN GARDE

Contre-indications: Hypersensibilité au melphalan ou au chlorambucil ▪ Résistance au melphalan ▪ Radiothérapie récente ou concomitante ▪ Aplasie médullaire.

Précautions et mises en garde: Patientes en âge de procréer ▪ Infections en évolution ▪ Personnes âgées ou patients souffrant de maladies chroniques débilitantes ▪ Dysfonctionnement rénal (réduire la dose si l'urée est ≥ 10,7 mmol/L) ▪ Grossesse ou allaitement ▪ Enfants (l'innocuité du médicament n'a pas été établie).

M

RÉACTIONS INDÉSIRABLES ET EFFETS SECONDAIRES

Resp.: dysplasie bronchopulmonaire, fibrose pulmonaire.

GI: MALADIE VÉNO-OCCLUSIVE HÉPATIQUE, diarrhée, hépatite, nausées, stomatite, vomissements.

GU: stérilité, insuffisance rénale.

Tég.: alopécie, prurit, rash.

End.: cycle menstruel irrégulier.

Hémat.: leucopénie, thrombopénie, anémie.

Métab.: hyperuricémie.

Divers: réactions allergiques, incluant l'ANAPHYLAXIE (plus fréquente lors de l'administration IV).

INTERACTIONS

Médicament-médicament: Aplasie médullaire additive lors de l'administration concomitante d'autres **agents antinéoplasiques** ou d'une **radiothérapie** ▪ Le melphalan peut diminuer la réponse des anticorps aux **vaccins à virus vivants** et augmenter le risque de réactions indésirables ▪ La **carmustine**, administrée en concomitance, peut accroître le risque de toxicité pulmonaire ▪ L'usage concomitant de **cyclosporine** par voie IV peut accroître le risque d'insuffisance rénale ▪ L'**acide nalidixique**, administré en concomitance, peut accroître le risque d'entérocolite.

VOIES D'ADMINISTRATION ET POSOLOGIE

Myélome multiple

- **PO (adultes)**: Initialement, 6 mg, 1 fois par jour, pendant 2 ou 3 semaines; arrêter le traitement pendant environ 4 semaines, puis le reprendre à raison de 2 mg, 1 fois par jour, lorsque le nombre de leucocytes et de plaquettes augmente (au besoin, on adapte la dose selon les résultats des numérations globulaires) ou initialement, 0,15 mg/kg/jour, pendant 7 jours; arrêter ensuite le traitement pendant au moins 14 jours (jusqu'à 5 ou 6 semaines), puis le reprendre à raison de 0,05 mg/kg/jour ou moins (dose d'entretien). D'autres schémas posologiques ont aussi été utilisés.
- **IV (adultes)**: 16 mg/m^2, toutes les 2 semaines (4 doses), puis toutes les 4 semaines.

Mélanome malin

- **Intra-artérielle (adultes)**: Perfusion hyperthermique d'un membre isolé en traitement d'appoint lors d'une intervention chirurgicale: 1 mg/kg (membre supérieur) ou 1,5 mg/kg (membre inférieur). La dose maximale est de 80 mg pour un membre supérieur et de 120 mg pour un membre inférieur. Aussitôt qu'on obtient l'hyperthermie du membre, on injecte le melphalan en 3 doses égales, à intervalles de 5 minutes, dans la tubulure artérielle du dispositif de perfusion.

Cancer des ovaires

- **PO (adultes)**: 0,2 mg/kg/jour pendant 5 jours, toutes les 4 ou 5 semaines.

PRÉSENTATION

Comprimés: 2 mg^{Pr} ▪ **Poudre pour injection**: 50 mg^{Pr}.

SOINS INFIRMIERS

ÉVALUATION DE LA SITUATION

- Suivre de près les signes d'infection: fièvre, frissons, maux de gorge, toux, enrouement, douleurs lombaires ou aux flancs, mictions difficiles ou douloureuses. Prévenir le médecin si ces symptômes se manifestent.
- Suivre de près les saignements: saignement des gencives, ecchymoses, pétéchies, présence de sang occulte dans les selles, l'urine et les vomissements. Éviter les injections par voie IM et la prise de la température par voie rectale. Appliquer une pression sur les points de ponction veineuse pendant 10 minutes.
- Le melphalan peut provoquer des nausées et des vomissements. Effectuer le bilan des ingesta et des excreta. Observer l'appétit du patient et noter son apport nutritionnel. On peut administrer un antiémétique en prophylaxie. Modifier le régime alimentaire selon les aliments que le patient peut tolérer.
- Surveiller les symptômes suivants de goutte: concentrations accrues d'acide urique, douleurs articulaires et œdème. Inciter le patient à boire au moins 2 litres de liquides par jour si son état le permet. On peut administrer de l'allopurinol pour réduire les concentrations d'acide urique.
- L'anémie peut survenir. Suivre de près la fatigue accrue et la dyspnée.
- DÉTERMINER SI LE PATIENT EST ALLERGIQUE AU CHLORAMBUCIL. DES RÉACTIONS DE SENSIBILITÉ CROISÉE PEUVENT SE MANIFESTER.

Tests de laboratoire:

- Noter la numération globulaire et la formule leucocytaire, toutes les semaines, pendant toute la durée du traitement. Le nadir de la leucopénie survient dans les 2 à 3 semaines. Prévenir le médecin si le nombre de leucocytes est $< 3 \times 10^9$/L. Le nadir de la thrombopénie survient dans les 2 à 3 semaines. Prévenir le médecin si le nombre de plaquettes est $< 100 \times 10^9$/L. Le nombre de leucocytes et de plaquettes revient à la normale dans les 5 à 6 semaines qui suivent.
- Noter les résultats des tests de la fonction hépatique (AST, ALT, LDH et bilirubine) et ceux de la fonction rénale (urée et créatinine) avant le début du traitement et à intervalles réguliers pendant toute sa durée, afin de déceler les signes d'hépatotoxicité et de néphrotoxicité.
- Le melphalan peut entraîner l'élévation des concentrations d'acide urique. Mesurer les concentrations d'acide urique à intervalles réguliers tout au long du traitement.
- Le melphalan peut entraîner l'élévation des concentrations d'acide 5-hydroxy-indol-acétique (5-HIAA) par suite de la désintégration de la tumeur.

DIAGNOSTICS INFIRMIERS POSSIBLES

- Risque d'accident (Effets secondaires).
- Risque d'infection (Effets secondaires).
- Connaissances insuffisantes sur le traitement médicamenteux (Enseignement au patient et à ses proches).

INTERVENTIONS INFIRMIÈRES

- Préparer la solution sous une hotte à flux laminaire. Porter un masque, des gants et un vêtement protecteur pendant la manipulation de ce médicament. Mettre au rebut le matériel IV dans les contenants réservés à cette fin (voir l'annexe H).
- Si la solution entre en contact avec la peau ou les muqueuses, les laver immédiatement à l'eau savonneuse.

PO: Le médecin peut prescrire le melphalan en doses fractionnées ou en une seule dose quotidienne.

Perfusion intermittente: Reconstituer le médicament avec 10 mL du diluant fourni par le fabricant afin d'obtenir une concentration de 5 mg/mL et bien agiter jusqu'à dissolution complète. Consulter les directives du fabricant avant de reconstituer la préparation. Diluer immédiatement la dose dans une solution de NaCl 0,9% afin d'obtenir une concentration ≤ 0,45 mg/mL. Administrer la perfusion dans les 50 minutes suivant la reconstitution de la préparation. Ne pas réfrigérer.

Vitesse d'administration: Administrer la solution en au moins 15 minutes.

Compatibilité (tubulure en Y): acyclovir ■ amikacine ■ aminophylline ■ ampicilline ■ aztréonam ■ bléomycine ■ bumétanide ■ buprénorphine ■ butorphanol ■ calcium, gluconate de ■ carboplatine ■ carmustine ■ céfazoline ■ céfopérazone ■ céfotaxime ■ céfotétane ■ ceftazidime ■ ceftizoxime ■ ceftriaxone ■ céfuroxime ■ cimétidine ■ cisplatine ■ clindamycine ■ cyclophosphamide ■ cytarabine ■ dacarbazine ■ dactinomycine ■ daunorubicine ■ dexaméthasone ■ diphenhydramine ■ doxorubicine ■ doxycycline ■ dropéridol ■ énalaprilate ■ étoposide ■ famotidine ■ floxuridine ■ fluconazole ■ fludarabine ■ fluorouracile ■ furosémide ■ gallium, nitrate de ■ ganciclovir ■ gentamicine ■ halopéridol ■ héparine ■ hydrocortisone ■ hydromorphone ■ idarubicine ■ ifosfamide ■ imipénem/cilastatine ■ lorazépam ■ mannitol ■ méchloréthamine ■ mépéridine ■ mesna ■ méthotrexate ■ métoclopramide ■ métronidazole ■ miconazole ■ minocycline ■ mitomycine ■ mitoxantrone ■ morphine ■ nalbuphine ■ nétilmicine ■ ondansétron ■ pentostatine ■ pipéracilline ■ plicamycine ■ potassium, chlorure de ■ prochlorpérazine, édisylate de ■ prométhazine ■ ranitidine ■ sodium, bicarbonate de ■ streptozocine ■ téniposide ■ thiotépa ■ ticarcilline ■ ticarcilline/clavulanate ■ tobramycine ■ triméthoprime/sulfaméthoxazole ■ vancomycine ■ vinblastine ■ vincristine ■ vinorelbine ■ zidovudine.

Incompatibilité (tubulure en Y): amphotéricine B ■ chlorpromazine.

ENSEIGNEMENT AU PATIENT ET À SES PROCHES

- Conseiller au patient de respecter rigoureusement la posologie recommandée même si des nausées ou des vomissements surviennent. L'inciter à demander conseil à un professionnel de la santé si les vomissements surviennent peu de temps après la prise du médicament. Si le patient n'a pu prendre le médicament au moment habituel, il ne doit pas le prendre du tout.
- Recommander au patient de signaler au médecin les symptômes suivants: fièvre, frissons, dyspnée, toux persistante, maux de gorge, signes d'infection, saignement des gencives, formation d'ecchymoses, pétéchies, présence de sang dans l'urine, les selles ou les vomissements. Inciter le patient à éviter les foules et les personnes contagieuses. Lui recommander d'utiliser une brosse à dents à poils doux et un rasoir électrique et de ne pas prendre d'alcool ni de préparations à base d'aspirine ou d'AINS.
- Conseiller au patient de signaler à un professionnel de la santé le rash, les démangeaisons, les douleurs articulaires ou l'œdème.
- Recommander au patient d'examiner ses muqueuses buccales pour déceler l'érythème et les aphtes. En cas d'aphtes, lui conseiller de remplacer la brosse à dents par une brosse-éponge et de se rincer la bouche avec de l'eau après avoir bu ou mangé. Lui conseiller de consulter le médecin si la douleur l'empêche de s'alimenter. La douleur associée à la stomatite peut dicter l'administration d'analgésiques opioïdes.
- Recommander à la patiente de continuer à prendre des mesures contraceptives tout au long du traitement, car bien que le melphalan puisse réduire la fécondité, il peut avoir des effets tératogènes.
- Prévenir le patient qu'il ne doit pas se faire vacciner sans recommandation expresse d'un professionnel de la santé.
- Insister sur l'importance des tests de laboratoire à intervalles réguliers permettant de déceler les effets secondaires du médicament.

VÉRIFICATION DE L'EFFICACITÉ THÉRAPEUTIQUE

L'efficacité du traitement peut être démontrée par: la diminution de la taille de la tumeur et le ralentissement de la propagation des cellules malignes.

MÉMANTINE

Ebixa

CLASSIFICATION:

Antagoniste du récepteur N-méthyl-D-aspartate (NMDA)

Grossesse – catégorie B (l'innocuité réelle n'a pas été établie)

INDICATIONS

Traitement symptomatique de la démence modérée à grave, associée à la maladie d'Alzheimer. La mémantine

M

peut être administrée en monothérapie ou comme adjuvant aux inhibiteurs de la cholinestérase.

MÉCANISME D'ACTION

Antagonisme non compétitif pour la fixation au récepteur NMDA avec une affinité faible à modérée (canaux ouverts); la mémantine se fixe préférentiellement aux canaux cationiques dépendant du récepteur NMDA. Elle bloque les effets des taux toniques anormalement élevés de glutamate, qui pourraient entraîner une dysfonction neuronale. La mémantine n'affecte pas directement les récepteurs de l'acétylcholine ni la transmission cholinergique, lesquels sont responsables des effets indésirables cholinomimétiques (p. ex., hyperacidité gastrique, nausées et vomissements) associés aux inhibiteurs de l'acétylcholinestérase. La mémantine exerce des effets antagonistes sur le récepteur 5-HT_3 avec une puissance semblable à celle qu'elle exerce sur le récepteur NMDA. ***Effets thérapeutiques:*** Pour le moment, on ne dispose pas de données cliniques qui montrent que la mémantine prévient ou ralentit la neurodégénérescence, ni qu'elle modifie le cours du processus de démence sous-jacent chez les patients atteints de la maladie d'Alzheimer. Stabilisation ou diminution des symptômes associés à la maladie d'Alzheimer.

M

PHARMACOCINÉTIQUE

Absorption: Biodisponibilité à 100 % (PO). Cinétique linéaire à l'intérieur de l'intervalle posologique.

Distribution: La mémantine traverse rapidement la barrière hématoencéphalique.

Liaison aux protéines plasmatiques: 45 %.

Métabolisme et excrétion: Métabolisme faible. Biotransformation en 3 métabolites qui ont peu d'effets antagonistes au niveau du récepteur NMDA. Le cytochrome P450 ne joue pas de rôle important dans le métabolisme de la mémantine. Excrétion majoritairement rénale (de 75 à 90 % sous forme inchangée). L'excrétion rénale se fait en partie par sécrétion tubulaire. Une réabsorption tubulaire intervient également dans ce processus. Le taux d'élimination rénale de la mémantine en présence d'urines alcalines peut être réduit d'un facteur de 7 à 9, ce qui entraîne des concentrations élevées de médicament dans le plasma.

Demi-vie: De 60 à 80 heures.

Profil temps-action (amélioration clinique)

	Début d'action	Pic	Durée
PO	14 jours	inconnu	inconnue

CONTRE-INDICATIONS, PRÉCAUTIONS ET MISES EN GARDE

Contre-indications: Hypersensibilité.

Précautions et mises en garde: Antécédents de troubles convulsifs ■ Troubles génito-urinaires qui augmentent le pH des urines (diminution de l'élimination urinaire de la mémantine). L'alcalinisation des urines peut être due à un changement draconien de l'alimentation, comme le passage d'un régime carnivore à un régime végétarien, ou à des médicaments (p. ex., inhibiteurs de l'anhydrase carbonique, bicarbonate de sodium ou ingestion massive d'antiacides). Elle peut aussi être due à une acidose tubulaire rénale ou à une infection grave des voies urinaires par des bactéries du genre *Proteus* ■ Troubles cardiovasculaires (p. ex., hypertension artérielle non maîtrisée, infarctus du myocarde récent, insuffisance cardiaque non compensée [classe III ou IV selon la NYHA]) ■ Troubles ophtalmiques (concentrations plus élevées dans le liquide lacrymal que dans le plasma). Risque d'aggravation d'une affection de la cornée (on devrait surveiller l'état des yeux du patient à intervalles réguliers) ■ Insuffisance rénale modérée à grave (la dose doit être diminuée en cas d'insuffisance rénale modérée) ■ Patients ≥ 85 ans ■ Maladies concomitantes graves (l'innocuité de la mémantine n'a pas été établie) ■ **Obst.**: Grossesse et allaitement (l'innocuité du médicament n'a pas été établie) ■ **Péd.**: Enfants (l'innocuité et l'efficacité de la mémantine n'ont pas été établies).

RÉACTIONS INDÉSIRABLES ET EFFETS SECONDAIRES

SNC: agitation, anorexie, anxiété, asthénie, automutilation, céphalées, confusion, CONVULSIONS, dépression, étourdissements, fatigue, hallucinations, insomnie, somnolence, syncope, tremblements, troubles de la personnalité.

ORLO: infection des voies respiratoires supérieures.

Resp.: bronchite, dyspnée, toux.

CV: ANGINE DE POITRINE, BRADYCARDIE, douleurs thoraciques, hypertension, INSUFFISANCE CARDIAQUE, THROMBOPHLÉBITE.

GI: constipation, diarrhée, douleurs abdominales, incontinence fécale, nausées, vomissements.

GU: infection urinaire, incontinence urinaire, pollakiurie, troubles prostatiques.

HÉ: déshydratation, œdème périphérique.

Tég.: éruptions cutanées.

Hémat.: anémie.

Métab.: gain pondéral.

Loc.: arthralgies, dorsalgies.

Divers: chutes, démarche anormale, douleurs, fièvre, symptômes pseudogrippaux.

INTERACTIONS

Médicament-médicament: Des études *in vitro* réalisées avec plusieurs substrats des enzymes du CYP450 (CYP 1A2, 2A6, 2C9, 2D6, 2E1 et 3A4) ont révélé une inhibition minime de ces enzymes par la mémantine. On ne s'attend donc à aucune interaction pharmacocinétique avec les **médicaments métabolisés par ces enzymes** ▪ La clairance de la mémantine est réduite d'environ 80 % en présence d'urines alcalines à un pH de 8. L'alcalinisation des urines peut entraîner une accumulation du médicament et aussi une fréquence accrue de ses effets indésirables. Les **inhibiteurs de l'anhydrase carbonique** (p. ex., l'**acétazolamide**) et le **bicarbonate de sodium** peuvent modifier le pH urinaire ▪ La mémantine peut potentialiser les effets de la **lévodopa**, des **agonistes dopaminergiques** et des **anticholinergiques** ▪ Les **médicaments éliminés par le même système rénal de transport des cations que la mémantine**, comme la **ranitidine**, la **quinidine**, le **triamtérène** et l'**hydrochlorothiazide**, administrés en concomitance, pourraient modifier les taux plasmatiques de chacun de ces agents ▪ Les **composés dont la structure chimique s'apparente à celle des antagonistes des récepteurs NMDA** (p. ex., l'**amantadine**, la **kétamine**, le **dextrométhorphane**) pourraient augmenter les effets indésirables (principalement liés au SNC).

VOIES D'ADMINISTRATION ET POSOLOGIE

- **PO (adultes):** 5 mg, 1 fois par jour, pendant 1 semaine. On augmente la posologie de 5 mg/jour après une semaine (5 mg, 2 fois par jour) selon la réponse et la tolérance du patient, puis de 5 mg/jour de plus toutes les semaines, jusqu'à l'atteinte de la dose d'entretien de 10 mg, 2 fois par jour.
- ***INSUFFISANCE RÉNALE***

  Cl_{CR} *> 60 mL/MIN* – AUCUNE MODIFICATION DE LA DOSE; Cl_{CR} *DE 40 À 60 mL/MIN* – DIMINUER LA DOSE POUR LA PORTER À 10 mg PAR JOUR; Cl_{CR} *< 40 mL/MIN* – USAGE DÉCONSEILLÉ.

PRÉSENTATION

Comprimés: 10 mg[Pr].

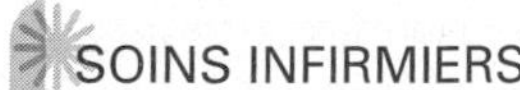

SOINS INFIRMIERS

ÉVALUATION DE LA SITUATION

- Évaluer le fonctionnement cognitif (mémoire, attention, raisonnement, langage, capacité à accomplir des tâches simples) à intervalles réguliers, pendant toute la durée du traitement.

Tests de laboratoire: Mesurer les concentrations d'hémoglobine à intervalles réguliers. La mémantine peut provoquer de l'anémie.

DIAGNOSTICS INFIRMIERS POSSIBLES

- Opérations de la pensée perturbées (Indications).
- Risque d'accident (Réactions indésirables).
- Connaissances insuffisantes sur le traitement médicamenteux (Enseignement au patient et à ses proches).

INTERVENTIONS INFIRMIÈRES

- Ne pas majorer les doses plus souvent que toutes les semaines.
- Administrer la mémantine avec ou sans aliments.
- Il ne faut pas mâcher les comprimés, mais on peut les fractionner.

ENSEIGNEMENT AU PATIENT ET À SES PROCHES

- Expliquer au patient et à ses proches qu'ils doivent respecter rigoureusement la posologie recommandée. Si le patient n'a pu prendre le médicament au moment habituel, il doit le prendre aussitôt que possible, à moins que ce ne soit presque le moment prévu pour la dose suivante. Le prévenir qu'il ne doit jamais remplacer une dose manquée par une double dose; des doses plus élevées n'augmentent pas les effets bénéfiques, mais peuvent entraîner un plus grand nombre d'effets secondaires. Conseiller également au patient de ne pas arrêter le traitement avant d'avoir consulté un professionnel de la santé.
- Prévenir le patient et ses proches que la mémantine peut provoquer des étourdissements et de la somnolence. Conseiller au patient de ne pas conduire et d'éviter les activités qui exigent sa vigilance jusqu'à ce qu'on ait la certitude que le médicament n'entraîne pas ces effets chez lui.
- Recommander au patient et à ses proches de prévenir un professionnel de la santé en cas de crises convulsives, d'élévation de la pression artérielle ou de problèmes cardiaques (p. ex., angine de poitrine, bradycardie, symptômes d'insuffisance cardiaque).
- Recommander au patient et à ses proches de prévenir tous les professionnels de la santé avant tout autre traitement ou avant une intervention chirurgicale que le patient suit ce traitement médicamenteux.
- Recommander au patient et à ses proches de ne pas modifier abruptement l'alimentation du patient (p. ex., passage d'une alimentation normale à une alimentation végétarienne stricte). Les effets du médicament pourraient être accrus.
- Recommander au patient et à ses proches de communiquer avec un professionnel de la santé en cas

d'infection des voies urinaires. Les effets de la mémantine pourraient être accrus.

- Insister sur l'importance des examens de suivi réguliers pouvant déterminer les effets du traitement.
- Recommander au patient et à ses proches de faire surveiller l'état des yeux du patient à intervalles réguliers.

VÉRIFICATION DE L'EFFICACITÉ THÉRAPEUTIQUE

L'efficacité du traitement peut être démontrée par: l'amélioration du fonctionnement cognitif (mémoire, attention, raisonnement, langage, capacité à accomplir des tâches simples) chez les patients souffrant de la maladie d'Alzheimer. ✳

ALERTE CLINIQUE

MÉPÉRIDINE

Synonyme: péthidine

Demerol

CLASSIFICATION:

Analgésique opioïde (agoniste)

Grossesse – catégories C et D (en cas d'usage prolongé ou de doses élevées administrées près du terme)

INDICATIONS

Soulagement de la douleur modérée à grave, en monothérapie ou en association avec des analgésiques non opioïdes ■ Adjuvant à l'anesthésie ■ Analgésie au cours du travail de l'accouchement ■ Sédation préopératoire. **Usages non approuvés:** Frissons.

MÉCANISME D'ACTION

Liaison aux récepteurs opioïdes du SNC ■ Modification de la perception de la douleur et de la réaction aux stimuli douloureux, s'accompagnant d'une dépression généralisée du SNC. ***Effets thérapeutiques:*** Diminution de l'intensité de la douleur.

PHARMACOCINÉTIQUE

Absorption: 50 % (PO); bonne (IM). Les doses par voies orale et parentérale ne sont pas équivalentes.

Distribution: Tout l'organisme. La mépéridine traverse la barrière placentaire et passe dans le lait maternel.

Liaison aux protéines: Élevée.

Métabolisme et excrétion: Métabolisme majoritairement hépatique. Une certaine fraction est transformée en norméperidine, qui peut s'accumuler et provoquer des convulsions; 5 % est excrété à l'état inchangé par les reins.

Demi-vie: *Nouveau-nés:* de 12 à 39 heures; *enfants:* de 2 à 3 heures; *adultes:* de 3 à 5 heures (prolongée en cas de dysfonctionnement hépatique ou rénal); *norméperidine:* de 15 à 20 heures.

Profil temps-action (effet analgésique)

	Début d'action	Pic	Durée
PO	15 min	60 min	2-5 h
IM	10-15 min	30-50 min	2-5 h
SC	10-15 min	40-60 min	2-5 h
IV	immédiat	5-7 min	2-5 h

CONTRE-INDICATIONS, PRÉCAUTIONS ET MISES EN GARDE

Contre-indications: Hypersensibilité ■ Hypersensibilité aux bisulfites (certains produits injectables renferment ces additifs) ■ Traitement par les IMAO au cours des 14 à 21 jours précédents.

Précautions et mises en garde: Traumatisme crânien ■ Pression intracrânienne accrue ■ Maladies rénale, hépatique ou pulmonaire graves ■ Troubles convulsifs (risque d'aggravation des convulsions préexistantes) ■ Hypothyroïdie ■ Insuffisance surrénalienne ■ Alcoolisme ■ **GÉR.:** Personnes âgées ou patients débilités (il est conseillé de réduire la dose initiale) ■ Douleurs abdominales non diagnostiquées ■ Hyperplasie de la prostate ■ **OBST.:** Travail de l'accouchement (risque de dépression respiratoire chez le nouveau-né); grossesse et allaitement (administration prolongée à proscrire) ■ Patients souffrant d'insuffisance rénale ou présentant des brûlures sur une grande surface corporelle ■ Doses élevées (> 600 mg/jour) ou traitement prolongé (> 2 jours): risque accru de stimulation du SNC et de convulsions dues à l'accumulation de norméperidine ■ **PÉD.:** Risque accru de convulsions dues à l'accumulation de norméperidine chez les enfants; nouveau-nés et enfants < 3 mois (risque accru de dépression respiratoire); nouveau-nés (éviter les préparations injectables contenant des agents de conservation, car elles peuvent provoquer un syndrome de halètement pouvant être mortel) ■ Risque de pharmacodépendance et d'abus.

RÉACTIONS INDÉSIRABLES ET EFFETS SECONDAIRES

SNC: CONVULSIONS, confusion, sédation, dysphorie, euphorie, sensation de flottement, hallucinations, céphalées, rêves bizarres.

ORLO: vision trouble, diplopie, myosis.

Resp.: DÉPRESSION RESPIRATOIRE.

CV: hypotension, bradycardie.

GI: constipation, nausées, vomissements.

GU: rétention urinaire.

Tég.: bouffées vasomotrices, transpiration.

Divers: dépendance physique, dépendance psychologique, tolérance aux effets du médicament.

INTERACTIONS

Médicament-médicament: LA MÉPÉRIDINE NE DOIT PAS ÊTRE ADMINISTRÉE CHEZ LES PATIENTS RECEVANT DES **IMAO** OU LA **PROCARBAZINE** (RISQUE DE RÉACTIONS MORTELLES; LA MÉPÉRIDINE EST CONTRE-INDIQUÉE DANS LES 14 À 21 JOURS SUIVANT UN TRAITEMENT PAR UN IMAO) ■ Dépression additive du SNC et du système respiratoire lors de l'usage concomitant d'**alcool**, d'**antihistaminiques**, de **phénothiazines**, de **barbituriques**, d'**antidépresseurs**, d'**hypnosédatifs** et d'autres **opioïdes** ■ L'administration d'**analgésiques opioïdes agonistes/antagonistes** (**nalbuphine**, **butorphanol**, **pentazocine**) peut diminuer l'analgésie et/ou déclencher des symptômes de sevrage chez les patients présentant une dépendance physique aux analgésiques opioïdes ■ Les **antirétroviraux inhibiteurs de la protéase** peuvent intensifier les effets et les réactions indésirables de cet agent (usage concomitant à éviter) ■ La **phénytoïne** accélère le métabolisme de la mépéridine et peut en diminuer les effets ■ La **chlorpromazine** et la **thioridazine** peuvent accroître le risque de réactions indésirables (usage concomitant à éviter).

Médicament-produits naturels: Effets dépresseurs additifs sur le SNC lors de l'usage concomitant de **kava**, de **valériane** et de **camomille**. L'usage concomitant de **millepertuis** n'est pas recommandé, en raison du risque accru d'effets indésirables graves.

VOIES D'ADMINISTRATION ET POSOLOGIE

- **PO, IM, SC, IV (adultes)**: *Analgésie* – de 50 à 150 mg, toutes les 3 à 4 heures, au besoin. *Analgésie au cours du travail de l'accouchement* – de 50 à 100 mg par voie IM ou SC lorsque les contractions deviennent régulières; on peut répéter l'administration toutes les 1 à 3 heures. *Sédation préopératoire* – de 50 à 100 mg par voie IM ou SC, de 30 à 90 minutes avant l'anesthésie.
- **PO, IM, SC (enfants)**: *Analgésie* – de 1,1 à 1,8 mg/kg/dose, toutes les 3 à 4 heures, au besoin (ne pas dépasser 100 mg par dose). *Sédation préopératoire* – de 1 à 2 mg/kg/dose par voie IM ou SC, de 30 à 90 minutes avant l'anesthésie (ne pas dépasser la dose recommandée chez l'adulte).
- **PO, IM, IV, SC (personnes âgées)**: Réduire la posologie.

PRÉSENTATION
(version générique disponible)

Comprimés: 50 mg[N] ■ **Solutions pour injection**: 50 mg/mL[N], 75 mg/mL[N], 100 mg/mL[N].

SOINS INFIRMIERS

ÉVALUATION DE LA SITUATION

- Déterminer le type de douleur, son siège et son intensité, avant l'administration du médicament, 1 heure après l'administration PO, SC et IM, et 5 minutes (pic) après l'administration IV. Lorsqu'on majore la dose d'un opioïde, on devrait l'augmenter de 25 à 50 % jusqu'à ce qu'on note une réduction de 50 % de la douleur, selon l'évaluation qu'en fait le patient sur une échelle numérique ou visuelle ou jusqu'à ce qu'il signale un soulagement adéquat de la douleur. On peut administrer sans danger une autre dose au moment du pic, si la dose précédente s'est avérée inefficace et si les effets secondaires sont minimes.
- Utiliser un tableau de doses équianalgésiques (voir l'annexe A) lorsqu'on change de voie d'administration ou qu'on substitue à cet agent un autre opioïde.
- ÉVALUER L'ÉTAT DE CONSCIENCE DU PATIENT ET MESURER SA PRESSION ARTÉRIELLE, SON POULS ET SA FRÉQUENCE RESPIRATOIRE AVANT ET À INTERVALLES RÉGULIERS TOUT AU LONG DE L'ADMINISTRATION DE CE MÉDICAMENT. SI LA FRÉQUENCE RESPIRATOIRE EST < 10/MIN, ÉVALUER LE DEGRÉ DE SÉDATION. IL PEUT S'AVÉRER NÉCESSAIRE DE RÉDUIRE LA DOSE DE 25 À 50 %. LA SOMNOLENCE INITIALE DIMINUE LORS D'UN TRAITEMENT PROLONGÉ.

GÉR.: Évaluer les personnes âgées à intervalles fréquents, car elles sont plus sensibles aux effets des analgésiques opioïdes que les adultes plus jeunes et peuvent manifester plus souvent des réactions indésirables ou subir des complications respiratoires.

PÉD.: Évaluer les enfants à intervalles fréquents, car ils sont plus sensibles aux effets des analgésiques opioïdes et peuvent subir plus souvent des complications respiratoires ou se montrer excités ou irritables.

- Examiner la fonction intestinale du patient à intervalles réguliers. La consommation accrue de liquides et d'aliments riches en fibres et la prise de laxatifs peuvent réduire, voire prévenir, les effets constipants du médicament. Sauf contre-indication, des laxatifs stimulants devraient être administrés de façon systématique si le traitement par un opioïde dure plus de 2 ou 3 jours.

M

- L'usage prolongé peut entraîner la dépendance physique et psychologique ainsi qu'une tolérance aux effets du médicament, mais cela ne doit pas empêcher le patient de recevoir une quantité suffisante d'analgésiques. La dépendance psychologique est rare chez la plupart des patients qui reçoivent la mépéridine pour traiter la douleur. Lors d'un traitement prolongé, il faut parfois administrer des doses de plus en plus élevées pour soulager la douleur.
- CHEZ LES PATIENTS QUI SUIVENT UN TRAITEMENT PROLONGÉ OU À DOSES ÉLEVÉES, RESTER À L'AFFÛT DES SIGNES DE STIMULATION DU SNC (AGITATION, IRRITABILITÉ, CONVULSIONS), ATTRIBUABLES À L'ACCUMULATION DU MÉTABOLITE NORMÉPÉRIDINE. LE RISQUE DE TOXICITÉ AUGMENTE EN CAS D'ADMINISTRATION DE DOSES SUPÉRIEURES À 600 mg/24 H, D'ADMINISTRATION PROLONGÉE (> 2 JOURS) ET D'INSUFFISANCE RÉNALE.

GÉR.: La mépéridine, comme les autres opioïdes, peut entraîner le délire chez les personnes âgées; elles sont également exposées à un risque plus élevé de toxicité associée à la normépéridine. Évaluer ces patients à intervalles fréquents.

Tests de laboratoire: La mépéridine peut élever les concentrations plasmatiques d'amylase et de lipase.

M

TOXICITÉ ET SURDOSAGE: S'il est nécessaire d'administrer un antagoniste opioïde pour renverser la dépression respiratoire ou le coma, l'antidote est la naloxone (Narcan). Diluer le contenu de l'ampoule de naloxone à 0,4 mg dans 10 mL de solution de NaCl 0,9 % et administrer 0,5 mL (0,02 mg) par bolus IV direct, toutes les 2 minutes. Dans le cas des enfants et des patients pesant moins de 40 kg, diluer 0,1 mg de naloxone dans 10 mL de solution de NaCl 0,9 % pour obtenir une concentration de 10 µg/mL et administrer 0,5 µg/kg, toutes les 2 minutes. Ajuster graduellement la dose pour prévenir les symptômes de sevrage, les convulsions et la douleur intense. CHEZ LES PATIENTS QUI REÇOIVENT UN TRAITEMENT PROLONGÉ PAR LA MÉPÉRIDINE, LA NALOXONE PEUT PROVOQUER DES CONVULSIONS EN ÉLIMINANT LES EFFETS DÉPRESSEURS SUR LE SNC DE LA MÉPÉRIDINE, CE QUI REND PRÉDOMINANTS LES EFFETS CONVULSIFS DE LA NORMÉPÉRIDINE. SUIVRE LE PATIENT DE PRÈS.

DIAGNOSTICS INFIRMIERS POSSIBLES

- Douleur aiguë (Indications).
- Trouble de la perception visuelle et auditive (Effets secondaires).
- Risque d'accident (Effets secondaires).

INTERVENTIONS INFIRMIÈRES

ALERTE CLINIQUE: DES SURDOSES ACCIDENTELLES D'ANALGÉSIQUES OPIOÏDES ONT CAUSÉ DES DÉCÈS. ÉVALUER L'UTILISATION ANTÉRIEURE D'ANALGÉSIQUES OPIOÏDES PAR LE PATIENT ET SES BESOINS ACTUELS. AVANT L'ADMINISTRATION, CLARIFIER TOUS LES POINTS AMBIGUS SUR LES ORDONNANCES ET FAIRE VÉRIFIER L'ORDONNANCE D'ORIGINE ET LE CALCUL DES DOSES PAR UN AUTRE PROFESSIONNEL DE LA SANTÉ.

- NE PAS CONFONDRE LA MÉPÉRIDINE AVEC LA MORPHINE OU L'HYDROMORPHONE; DES ERREURS ONT MENÉ À UNE ISSUE FATALE.

PÉD.: LES ERREURS DANS L'ADMINISTRATION DES ANALGÉSIQUES OPIOÏDES SONT FRÉQUENTES CHEZ LES ENFANTS. ELLES COMPRENNENT DES ERREURS D'INTERPRÉTATION ET DE CALCUL DES DOSES AINSI QUE L'USAGE D'INSTRUMENTS DE MESURE INAPPROPRIÉS.

- UTILISER SEULEMENT DES PRÉPARATIONS SANS AGENT DE CONSERVATION CHEZ LES NOUVEAU-NÉS, AINSI QU'EN CAS D'ADMINISTRATION ÉPIDURALE ET INTRATHÉCALE CHEZ TOUS LES PATIENTS.
- Pour augmenter l'effet analgésique de la mépéridine, avant de l'administrer, expliquer au patient la valeur thérapeutique de ce médicament.
- Les doses administrées selon un horaire fixe peuvent être plus efficaces que celles administrées sur demande. L'analgésique s'avère plus efficace s'il est administré avant que la douleur ne devienne intense.
- Les analgésiques non opioïdes, administrés en concomitance, peuvent exercer des effets analgésiques additifs, ce qui permet parfois d'administrer des doses plus faibles d'opioïdes.
- La dose administrée par voie orale est de 50 % moins efficace que la dose parentérale. Lors du passage au traitement par voie orale, il peut s'avérer nécessaire d'augmenter la dose (voir l'annexe A).
- Après un traitement prolongé, interrompre l'administration graduellement pour prévenir les symptômes de sevrage.

PO: On peut administrer le médicament avec des aliments ou du lait pour réduire l'irritation gastrique.

SC: L'administration répétée de doses SC peut provoquer une irritation locale.

IV directe: Diluer le médicament jusqu'à une concentration de 10 mg/mL avec de l'eau stérile ou avec une solution de NaCl 0,9 % pour injection.

Vitesse d'administration: ADMINISTRER LENTEMENT EN AU MOINS 5 MINUTES. UNE ADMINISTRATION TROP RAPIDE PEUT AGGRAVER LA DÉPRESSION RESPIRATOIRE ET PROVOQUER DE L'HYPOTENSION ET UN COLLAPSUS CIRCULATOIRE.

Associations compatibles dans la même seringue: atropine ■ chlorpromazine ■ dimenhydrinate ■ diphenhydramine ■ dropéridol ■ glycopyrrolate ■ hydroxyzine ■ métoclopramide ■ midazolam ■ perphénazine ■ prochlorpérazine ■ promazine ■ prométhazine ■ scopolamine.

Associations incompatibles dans la même seringue: héparine ■ pentobarbital.

Compatibilité (tubulure en Y): amifostine ■ amikacine ■ ampicilline ■ aténolol ■ céfazoline ■ céfotaxime ■ céfoxitine ■ ceftazidime ■ ceftriaxone ■ céfuroxime ■ chloramphénicol ■ cisatracurium ■ clindamycine ■ dexaméthasone ■ diltiazem ■ diphenhydramine ■ dobutamine ■ dopamine ■ doxycycline ■ dropéridol ■ érythromycine, lactobionate d' ■ famotidine ■ filgrastim ■ fluconazole ■ fludarabine ■ gallium, nitrate de ■ gentamicine ■ héparine ■ hydrocortisone sodique, succinate d' ■ insuline ■ labétolol ■ lidocaïne ■ magnésium ■ paclitaxel ■ pénicilline G potassique ■ pipéracilline ■ pipéracilline/tazobactam ■ potassium, chlorure de ■ propranolol ■ ranitidine ■ rémifentanil ■ téniposide ■ thiotépa ■ ticarcilline ■ ticarcilline/clavulanate ■ tobramycine ■ triméthoprime/sulfaméthoxazole ■ vancomycine ■ vérapamil ■ vinorelbine.

Incompatibilité (tubulure en Y): amphotéricine B, cholestéryle d' ■ céfépime ■ doxorubicine liposomale ■ idarubicine ■ imipénem/cilastatine ■ minocycline.

ENSEIGNEMENT AU PATIENT ET À SES PROCHES

- Expliquer au patient ce qu'on entend par administration sur demande et à quel moment il doit réclamer l'analgésique. **ALERTE CLINIQUE**: PRÉVENIR LES PROCHES QU'IL NE FAUT PAS ADMINISTRER DE DOSES D'ACP À UN PATIENT QUI DORT, EN RAISON DES RISQUES DE SÉDATION, DE SURDOSAGE ET DE DÉPRESSION RESPIRATOIRE.
- Conseiller au patient de respecter rigoureusement la posologie recommandée. Si la dose devient moins efficace après quelques semaines, lui demander de ne pas l'augmenter sans avoir consulté d'abord un professionnel de la santé.
- Prévenir le patient que la mépéridine peut provoquer des étourdissements et de la somnolence. Lui recommander de demander de l'aide lorsqu'il se déplace et lorsqu'il veut fumer. Lui conseiller de ne pas conduire et d'éviter les activités qui exigent sa vigilance jusqu'à ce qu'on ait la certitude que le médicament n'entraîne pas ces effets chez lui.
- Recommander au patient de changer lentement de position pour diminuer le risque d'hypotension orthostatique.
- Inciter le patient à ne pas boire d'alcool et à ne pas prendre d'autres dépresseurs du SNC en même temps que la mépéridine.
- Informer le patient qui reçoit un traitement ambulatoire qu'il peut réduire les nausées et les vomissements en demeurant couché.
- Conseiller au patient de se tourner dans le lit, de tousser et de faire des exercices de respiration profonde toutes les 2 heures pour prévenir l'atélectasie.
- Insister sur le fait qu'il est important de prévenir la constipation associée à la prise des analgésiques opioïdes.

VÉRIFICATION DE L'EFFICACITÉ THÉRAPEUTIQUE

L'efficacité du traitement peut être démontrée par: la diminution de l'intensité de la douleur sans modification importante de l'état de conscience ou de la fonction respiratoire. ✳

MÉROPÉNEM

Merrem

CLASSIFICATION:

Antibiotique (carbapénem)

Grossesse – catégorie B

M

INDICATIONS

Traitement des infections suivantes: infections intra-abdominales ■ méningite bactérienne ■ infections de la peau et des tissus mous ■ pneumonie nosocomiale ■ septicémie bactérienne due à *E.coli*. **Usages non approuvés**: Neutropénie fébrile.

MÉCANISME D'ACTION

Liaison à la paroi de la cellule bactérienne, entraînant la destruction de la bactérie. Le méropénem résiste à l'action de nombreuses enzymes qui décomposent la plupart des autres pénicillines et les antibiotiques apparentés. ***Effets thérapeutiques***: Effet bactéricide contre les bactéries sensibles. **Spectre d'action**: Le méropénem agit contre les microorganismes à Gram positif suivants: *Staphylococcus aureus*, *Streptococcus pneumoniæ*, groupe des streptocoques viridans, *Enterococcus fæcalis* ■ Son spectre englobe également les microorganismes à Gram négatif suivants: *Escherichia coli*, *Hæmophilus influenzæ*, *Klebsiella pneumoniæ*, *Neisseria meningitidis*, *Pseudomonas æruginosa*, *Proteus mirabilis* ■ L'agent agit également sur les microorganismes anaérobies suivants: *Bacteroides fragilis*, groupe des bactéroïdes fragiles, espèces *Peptostreptococcus*.

PHARMACOCINÉTIQUE

Absorption: Biodisponibilité à 100 % (IV).

Distribution: Tous les liquides et tissus; l'agent pénètre dans le liquide céphalorachidien lorsque les méninges sont enflammées.

Métabolisme et excrétion: Excrétion rénale (de 65 à 83 % sous forme inchangée).

Demi-vie: Nourrissons de 3 mois à 2 ans: 1,4 h; enfants > 2 ans et adultes: 1 h (prolongée en cas d'insuffisance rénale).

Profil temps-action

	DÉBUT D'ACTION	PIC	DURÉE
IV	Rapide	fin de la perfusion	8 h

CONTRE-INDICATIONS, PRÉCAUTIONS ET MISES EN GARDE

Contre-indications: Hypersensibilité au méropénem, à l'imipénem ou à l'ertapénem ▪ Hypersensibilité marquée aux autres bêtalactamines (pénicillines ou céphalosporines; il y a risque de sensibilité croisée).

Précautions et mises en garde: Insuffisance rénale (risque accru de thrombopénie et de convulsions; il est recommandé de réduire la dose si la Cl_{Cr} <50 mL/min) ▪ Antécédents de convulsions, de lésions au cerveau ou de méningite ▪ **OBST., ALLAITEMENT, PÉD.:** Enfants < 3 mois – l'"innocuité de l'agent n'a pas été établie.

M

RÉACTIONS INDÉSIRABLES ET EFFETS SECONDAIRES

SNC: CONVULSIONS, étourdissements, céphalées.

Resp.: APNÉE.

GI: COLITE PSEUDOMEMBRANEUSE, constipation, diarrhée, glossite (plus fréquente chez les enfants), nausées, muguet (plus fréquent chez les enfants), vomissements.

Tég.: moniliase (enfants seulement), prurit, rash.

Locaux: inflammation au point d'injection, phlébite.

Divers: réactions allergiques comprenant l'ANAPHYLAXIE.

INTERACTIONS

Médicament-médicament: Le **probénécide** diminue l'excrétion rénale et accroît les concentrations sanguines (il n'est pas recommandé d'administrer en même temps ces deux médicaments).

VOIES D'ADMINISTRATION ET POSOLOGIE

- **IV (adultes):** De 0,5 à 1 g, toutes les 8 heures. *Méningite* – 2 g, toutes les 8 heures.
- **IV (enfants de ≥ 3 mois à 12 ans):** *Infections intra-abdominales* – 20 mg/kg, toutes les 8 heures; *méningite* – 40 mg/kg, toutes les 8 heures (maximum 2 g, toutes les 8 heures).

INSUFFISANCE RÉNALE

- **IV (ADULTES):** *CL_{CR} DE 26 À 50 mL/MIN* – 1 g, TOUTES LES 12 HEURES; *CL_{CR} DE 10 À 25 mL/MIN* – 500 mg, TOUTES LES 12 HEURES; *CL_{CR} < 10 mL/MIN* – 500 mg, TOUTES LES 24 HEURES.

PRÉSENTATION

Poudre pour injection: 500 mg^{Pr}, 1 g^{Pr}.

SOINS INFIRMIERS

ÉVALUATION DE LA SITUATION

- Rester à l'affût des signes d'infection (altération des signes vitaux, aspect de la plaie, des crachats, de l'urine et des selles, accroissement du nombre de globules blancs) au début du traitement et pendant toute sa durée.
- Recueillir les antécédents du patient avant d'amorcer le traitement afin de déterminer ses réactions antérieures à une pénicilline. Même les personnes n'ayant jamais manifesté de sensibilité à la pénicilline peuvent présenter une réaction allergique.
- Prélever des échantillons pour les cultures et les antibiogrammes avant le début du traitement. La première dose peut être administrée avant que les résultats soient connus.
- RESTER À L'AFFÛT DES SIGNES ET DES SYMPTÔMES SUIVANTS D'ANAPHYLAXIE (RASH, PRURIT, ŒDÈME LARYNGÉ, RESPIRATION SIFFLANTE). SI CES RÉACTIONS SE MANIFESTENT, ARRÊTER L'ADMINISTRATION DU MÉDICAMENT ET PRÉVENIR LE MÉDECIN IMMÉDIATEMENT. GARDER À PORTÉE DE LA MAIN DE L'ADRÉNALINE, UN ANTIHISTAMINIQUE ET LE MATÉRIEL DE RÉANIMATION POUR PARER À TOUTE ÉVENTUELLE RÉACTION ANAPHYLACTIQUE.
- Examiner les points de ponction à intervalles réguliers pendant l'administration pour déceler la phlébite, la douleur et la tuméfaction.

Tests de laboratoire:

- Suivre de près les paramètres hématologiques et les fonctions rénale et hépatique à intervalles réguliers pendant toute la durée du traitement.
- L'urée, l'AST, l'ALT, la LDH, la créatinine, la bilirubine et la phosphatase alcaline peuvent s'élever passagèrement.
- La concentration d'hémoglobine et l'hématocrite peuvent chuter.

- L'antibiotique peut positiver le test de Coombs direct et indirect.

DIAGNOSTICS INFIRMIERS POSSIBLES

- Risque d'infection (Indications, Effets secondaires).
- Connaissances insuffisantes sur le traitement médicamenteux (Enseignement au patient et à ses proches).

INTERVENTIONS INFIRMIÈRES

IV: Reconstituer avec 25 à 50 mL de NaCl 0,9 %, de D5E, de D10E, de D5/NaCl 0,9 %, de D5/NaCl 0,25 %, d'eau stérile pour injection, de bicarbonate de sodium à 5%, de D5/LR ou de lactate de Ringer pour injection. Échelle des concentrations de 1 à 40 mg/mL.

IV directe: Reconstituer le contenu de la fiole avec de l'eau stérile pour injection (10 et 20 mL pour une fiole de 500 mg et de 1 g, respectivement) pour obtenir une concentration finale de 50 mg/mL.

Vitesse d'administration: On peut administrer le médicament sous forme de bolus pendant 5 minutes.

Perfusion intermittente: Reconstituer le contenu de la fiole avec de l'eau stérile pour injection (10 et 20 mL pour une fiole de 500 mg et de 1 g, respectivement) pour obtenir une concentration finale de 50 mg/mL.

Vitesse d'administration: Administrer en 15 à 30 minutes. Consulter les directives du fabricant avant de reconstituer la préparation.

Compatibilité (tubulure en Y): aminophylline ■ atropine ■ cimétidine ■ dexaméthasone ■ digoxine ■ diphenhydramine ■ docétaxel ■ énalaprilate ■ fluconazole ■ furosémide ■ gentamicine ■ héparine ■ insuline régulière ■ métoclopramide ■ morphine ■ noradrénaline ■ phénobarbital ■ vancomycine.

Incompatibilité (tubulure en Y): amphotéricine B ■ diazépam ■ métronidazole.

Incompatibilité en addition au soluté: Information inconnue. Ne pas mélanger avec d'autres antibiotiques.

ENSEIGNEMENT AU PATIENT ET À SES PROCHES

- Conseiller au patient de signaler les signes de surinfection (excroissance noire et pileuse sur la langue, démangeaisons et écoulements vaginaux, selles molles ou nauséabondes) et d'allergie.
- Le méropénem peut provoquer des étourdissements. Conseiller au patient de ne pas conduire et de ne pas s'engager dans d'autres activités qui exigent sa vigilance jusqu'à ce qu'on ait la certitude que le médicament n'entraîne pas cet effet chez lui.
- CONSEILLER AU PATIENT DE PRÉVENIR UN PROFESSIONNEL DE LA SANTÉ EN CAS DE FIÈVRE OU DE DIARRHÉE, PARTICULIÈREMENT SI SES SELLES CONTIENNENT DU SANG, DU PUS OU DU MUCUS. LUI RECOMMANDER DE NE PAS TRAITER LA DIARRHÉE SANS CONSULTER AU PRÉALABLE UN PROFESSIONNEL DE LA SANTÉ. CE SYMPTÔME PEUT SURVENIR PLUSIEURS SEMAINES APRÈS L'ARRÊT DU TRAITEMENT.

VÉRIFICATION DE L'EFFICACITÉ THÉRAPEUTIQUE

L'efficacité du traitement peut être démontrée par: la résolution des signes et des symptômes d'infection. Le temps nécessaire à une résolution complète dépend du microorganisme infectant et du siège de l'infection. ✳

MÉSALAMINE

Synonyme: acide 5-aminosalicylique

Asacol, Mesasal, Novo-5-asa, Pentasa, Salofalk

CLASSIFICATION:

Anti-inflammatoire local non stéroïdien (entérocolique)

Grossesse – catégorie B

M

INDICATIONS

Pentasa oral, Salofalk oral: Traitement des maladies inflammatoires de l'intestin, incluant: la colite ulcéreuse ■ la rectite ■ la rectosigmoïdite ■ la maladie de Crohn ■ ***Pentasa suspension rectale:*** Traitement de la colite ulcéreuse distale ■ ***Pentasa suppositoire rectal:*** Traitement de la rectite ulcéreuse ■ ***Salofalk suspension rectal:*** Traitement de la colite ulcéreuse distale ■ ***Salofalk suppositoire rectal:*** Traitement de la colite ulcéreuse distale et de la rectite ulcéreuse ■ ***Asacol, Mesasal:*** Traitement de la colite ulcéreuse.

MÉCANISME D'ACTION

Action anti-inflammatoire locale au niveau du côlon, probablement due à l'inhibition de la synthèse des prostaglandines. ***Effets thérapeutiques:*** Réduction des symptômes des maladies inflammatoires de l'intestin.

PHARMACOCINÉTIQUE

Absorption: 28 % (PO); de 10 à 30 % (IR) absorbé à partir du côlon, selon la durée de la rétention.

Distribution: Inconnue.

Métabolisme et excrétion: Métabolisme présent, mais inconnu. Excrétion dans les fèces à l'état inchangé.

Demi-vie: *PO* – 12 heures (de 2 à 15 heures); *IR* – de 0,5 à 1,5 heure.

Profil temps-action (amélioration sur le plan clinique)

	DÉBUT D'ACTION	PIC	DURÉE
PO	inconnu	inconnu	6 - 8 h
IR	3 - 21 jours	inconnu	24 h

CONTRE-INDICATIONS, PRÉCAUTIONS ET MISES EN GARDE

Contre-indications: Réactions d'hypersensibilité aux salicylates et à la mésalamine ▪ Occlusion des voies urinaires ou intestinales ▪ Ulcère gastrique ou duodénal ▪ **PÉD.**: Enfants < 2 ans.

Précautions et mises en garde: Réactions d'hypersensibilité aux sulfamides ou à la sulfasalazine ▪ Risque de réactions de sensibilité croisée avec le furosémide, les sulfonylurées (hypoglycémiants) ou les inhibiteurs de l'anhydrase carbonique ▪ Insuffisance hépatique ou rénale grave ▪ Carence en G-6-PD ▪ Hypersensibilité aux bisulfites (lavement à la mésalamine seulement) ▪ Porphyrie ▪ **OBST., ALLAITEMENT**: L'innocuité du médicament n'a pas été établie.

RÉACTIONS INDÉSIRABLES ET EFFETS SECONDAIRES

M

SNC: céphalées, étourdissements, malaise, faiblesse.

ORLO: pharyngite, rhinite.

CV: péricardite.

GI: diarrhée, éructations (PO), flatulence, nausées, vomissements.

GU: néphrite interstitielle, pancréatite, insuffisance rénale.

Tég.: alopécie, rash.

Locaux: irritation anale (lavement, suppositoires).

Loc.: douleurs lombaires.

Divers: ANAPHYLAXIE, syndrome d'intolérance aiguë, fièvre.

INTERACTIONS

Médicament-médicament: La mésalamine peut diminuer le métabolisme et augmenter la toxicité de l'**azathioprine** et de la **mercaptopurine** ▪ L'effet hypoglycémiant des **sulfonylurées** peut être augmenté lors de l'usage concomitant de mésalamine ▪ Risque possible d'insuffisance rénale lors d'utilisation concomitante d'autres **agents néphrotoxiques** comme les **AINS** et l'**azathioprine** ▪ Lors de l'utilisation concomitante de **warfarine**, le RNI du patient peut s'élever.

VOIES D'ADMINISTRATION ET POSOLOGIE

- **PO (adultes)**: La dose quotidienne est de 2 à 4 g (Pentasa), de 1,5 à 3 g (Mesasal), de 3 g ou de 4 g (Salofalk) ou de 0,8 à 4,8 g (Asacol), en 3 ou 4 prises fractionnées.
- **IR (adultes)**: *Suppositoires* – la dose quotidienne est de 500 mg, 2 ou 3 fois par jour, ou 1 g, au coucher. *Lavement* – phase aiguë: 4 g au coucher, à retenir pendant 8 heures. *Lavement* – prévention des récidives: 2 g au coucher, à retenir pendant 8 heures, ou 4 g, tous les 2 ou 3 jours.

PRÉSENTATION

Comprimés entérosolubles: 400 mg^{Pr}, 500 mg^{Pr}, 800 mg^{Pr} ▪ **Comprimés à libération retard**: 250 mg^{Pr}, 500 mg^{Pr} ▪ **Lavements**: 1 g/100 mL^{Pr}, 4 g/100 mL^{Pr} ▪ **Suppositoires**: 500 mg^{Pr}, 1 000 mg^{Pr} ▪ **Suspensions rectales**: 2 g/60 g^{Pr}, 4 g/60 g^{Pr}.

SOINS INFIRMIERS

ÉVALUATION DE LA SITUATION

- DÉTERMINER SI LE PATIENT EST ALLERGIQUE AUX SULFAMIDES OU AUX SALICYLATES. LE PATIENT ALLERGIQUE À LA SULFASALAZINE PEUT PRENDRE DE LA MÉSALAMINE OU DE L'OLSALAZINE SANS PROBLÈMES, MAIS LE TRAITEMENT DOIT ÊTRE INTERROMPU EN CAS DE RASH OU DE FIÈVRE.
- Effectuer le bilan des ingesta et des excreta. L'apport de liquides devrait être suffisant pour maintenir un débit urinaire d'au moins 1 200 à 1 500 mL par jour afin de prévenir la cristallurie et la formation de calculs.

Maladie inflammatoire de l'intestin: Évaluer les douleurs abdominales et la fréquence, la quantité et la consistance des selles au début du traitement et pendant toute sa durée.

***Tests de laboratoire*:**

- Noter les résultats de l'examen des urines, l'urée et les concentrations de créatinine sérique avant le traitement et à intervalles réguliers par la suite. La mésalamine peut provoquer une toxicité rénale.
- La mésalamine peut élever les concentrations d'AST et d'ALT. Elle peut également entraîner une élévation des concentrations sériques de phosphatase alcaline, de GGTP, de LDH, d'amylase et de lipase.

DIAGNOSTICS INFIRMIERS POSSIBLES

- Douleur aiguë (Indications).
- Diarrhée (Indications).
- Connaissances insuffisantes sur le traitement médicamenteux (Enseignement au patient et à ses proches).

INTERVENTIONS INFIRMIÈRES

- NE PAS CONFONDRE ASACOL (MÉSALAMINE) AVEC OS-CAL (CARBONATE DE CALCIUM).

PO: Administrer le médicament avant les repas et à l'heure du coucher, avec un grand verre d'eau. Les comprimés doivent être avalés tels quels sans être brisés; garder intact l'enrobage externe. On peut parfois retrouver des comprimés intacts ou partiellement intacts dans les selles. Si ce phénomène est fréquent, recommander au patient d'en informer un professionnel de la santé.

IR:

- Le patient devrait aller à la selle avant l'administration de la préparation rectale.
- Éviter de manipuler à l'excès les *suppositoires*. Retirer le papier d'aluminium et introduire délicatement la pointe du suppositoire dans le rectum sans exercer de pression excessive. Le suppositoire devrait être retenu pendant au moins 1 à 3 heures pour que le patient puisse en tirer un maximum de bienfaits.
- Administrer le lavement 1 fois par jour, au coucher. La solution devrait être retenue pendant environ 8 heures. Avant d'administrer la *suspension rectale*, bien agiter le flacon et retirer le capuchon protecteur. Installer le patient en position couchée sur le côté gauche, et lui demander de garder sa jambe gauche allongée et sa jambe droite fléchie pour se soutenir ou de ramener ses genoux vers sa poitrine. Introduire délicatement la pointe de l'applicateur dans le rectum, en la pointant vers le nombril. Comprimer uniformément le flacon pour administrer la plus grande partie de la préparation.

ENSEIGNEMENT AU PATIENT ET À SES PROCHES

- Enseigner au patient la bonne méthode d'administration. Lui conseiller de respecter rigoureusement la posologie recommandée, même s'il se sent mieux. S'il n'a pu prendre le médicament au moment habituel, il doit le prendre dès que possible, à moins que ce ne soit presque l'heure prévue pour la dose suivante.
- Prévenir le patient que la mésalamine peut provoquer des étourdissements. Lui conseiller de ne pas conduire et d'éviter les activités qui exigent sa vigilance jusqu'à ce qu'on ait la certitude que le médicament n'entraîne pas cet effet chez lui.
- Recommander au patient d'informer un professionnel de la santé si les symptômes suivants se manifestent: rash, maux de gorge, fièvre, aphtes, saignements inhabituels ou formation d'ecchymoses, respiration sifflante ou urticaire.
- Conseiller au patient de consulter un professionnel de la santé si les symptômes ne s'améliorent pas après 1 ou 2 mois de traitement.
- Recommander au patient de consulter un professionnel de la santé si les symptômes s'aggravent ou ne s'améliorent pas. Si des symptômes d'intolérance aiguë se manifestent (crampes, douleurs abdominales aiguës, diarrhée sanguinolente, fièvre, céphalées, rash), lui conseiller d'interrompre le traitement et d'en informer immédiatement un professionnel de la santé.
- Informer le patient qu'il devrait peut-être se soumettre à intervalles réguliers à une rectoscopie et à une sigmoïdoscopie pour qu'on puisse déterminer sa réponse au traitement.

IR:

- Demander au patient d'utiliser la *suspension rectale* au coucher et de la retenir toute la nuit pour obtenir de meilleurs résultats.
- Recommander au patient de ne pas changer de marque de mésalamine sans avoir consulté un professionnel de la santé au préalable.

M

VÉRIFICATION DE L'EFFICACITÉ THÉRAPEUTIQUE

L'efficacité du traitement peut être démontrée par: la diminution de la diarrhée et des douleurs abdominales ■ le rétablissement d'un mode d'élimination intestinale normale chez les patients souffrant d'une maladie inflammatoire de l'intestin; les effets du médicament peuvent se manifester dans les 3 à 21 jours suivant le début du traitement; le traitement dure habituellement de 3 à 6 semaines ■ le maintien de la rémission chez les patients souffrant d'une maladie inflammatoire de l'intestin.

MESNA

Uromitexan

CLASSIFICATION:

Antidote (prévention de la toxicité associée aux oxazaphosphorines), uroprotecteur

Grossesse – catégorie B

INDICATIONS

Diminution et prévention de la cystite hémorragique induite par des oxazaphosphorines (voir Cyclophosphamide et Ifosfamide).

MÉCANISME D'ACTION

Liaison aux métabolites toxiques de l'ifosfamide et du cyclophosphamide dans les reins. ***Effets thérapeutiques:*** Prévention de la cystite hémorragique induite par l'ifosfamide ou le cyclophosphamide.

PHARMACOCINÉTIQUE

Absorption: Variable (PO – de 45 à 79 %). Biodisponibilité à 100 % (IV). L'administration par voie orale à la suite d'une dose IV peut augmenter l'exposition systémique au mesna.

Distribution: Inconnue.

Métabolisme et excrétion: Métabolisme rapide, avec transformation en disulfite de mesna, puis nouvelle transformation en mesna dans les reins, où l'agent peut se lier aux métabolites toxiques de l'ifosfamide ou du cyclophosphamide. Excrétion rénale (de 18 à 26 % sous forme de mesna libre).

Demi-vie: *Mesna* – 0,36 heure (IV); de 1,2 à 8,3 heures (IV suivi de PO); *disulfide de mesna* – 1,17 heure.

Profil temps-action (effet détoxifiant)

	Début d'action	Pic	Durée
IV, PO	rapide	inconnu	4 h

M

CONTRE-INDICATIONS, PRÉCAUTIONS ET MISES EN GARDE

Contre-indications: Hypersensibilité au mesna ou à d'autres dérivés du caoutchouc.

Précautions et mises en garde: Obst., Allaitement: L'innocuité du médicament n'a pas été établie.

RÉACTIONS INDÉSIRABLES ET EFFETS SECONDAIRES

SNC: étourdissements, somnolence, céphalées.

GI: anorexie, diarrhée, nausées, goût désagréable, vomissements.

Tég.: bouffées vasomotrices.

Loc.: réactions au point d'injection.

Divers: symptômes pseudogrippaux.

INTERACTIONS

Médicament-médicament: Aucune interaction notable.

VOIES D'ADMINISTRATION ET POSOLOGIE

- **IV (adultes):** Administrer une dose de mesna équivalente à 20 % de la dose d'oxazaphosphorine au même moment que cet agent ainsi que 4 et 8 heures plus tard.
- **PO (adultes):** Administrer une dose de mesna équivalente à 40 % de la dose d'oxazaphosphorine au même moment que cet agent ainsi que 4 et 8 heures plus tard (ou une dose IV de mesna équivalente à 20 % de la dose d'oxazaphosphorine au même moment que cet agent, puis une dose PO de mesna équivalente à 40 % de la dose d'oxazaphosphorine, 4 et 8 heures plus tard).

PRÉSENTATION

Solution pour injection: 100 mg/mL, en ampoules de 4 mL[Pr] et de 10 mL[Pr].

SOINS INFIRMIERS

ÉVALUATION DE LA SITUATION

- Chez le patient recevant de l'ifosfamide ou du cyclophosphamide, déceler l'apparition d'une cystite hémorragique.

Tests de laboratoire: Le mesna peut entraîner des résultats faussement positifs au dosage de la cétonurie.

DIAGNOSTICS INFIRMIERS POSSIBLES

- Connaissances insuffisantes sur le traitement médicamenteux (Enseignement au patient et à ses proches).

INTERVENTIONS INFIRMIÈRES

- Administrer le premier bolus au même moment que l'ifosfamide ou le cyclophosphamide, la deuxième dose, 4 heures plus tard, et la troisième dose, 8 heures plus tard. Maintenir le même schéma posologique lors de l'administration de chaque dose d'ifosfamide ou de cyclophosphamide.

PO: Des deuxième et troisième doses ont déjà été administrées par voie orale. La solution orale a été préparée avec 20 ou 50 mg de mesna par mL, en diluant la préparation parentérale avec un sirop (solution stable pendant 7 jours à la température ambiante). On l'a également diluée dans des boissons gazeuses ou dans du jus de pomme ou d'orange, pour obtenir des concentrations de 2, de 10 ou de 50 mg/mL (la solution est stable pendant 24 heures au réfrigérateur). Si la dose de mesna administrée par voie orale est vomie dans les 2 heures suivant son administration, répéter l'administration de cette dose ou utiliser la voie IV.

IV directe: Diluer le contenu des ampoules de 4 et de 10 mL, d'une teneur de 100 mg/mL, dans 16 ou 40 mL, respectivement, de solution D5%E, de NaCl 0,9 %, de D5%/NaCl 0,45 % ou de solution de lactate de Ringer, jusqu'à l'obtention d'une concentration finale de 20 mg/mL. Garder la solution au réfrigérateur. Utiliser la préparation dans les 24 heures qui suivent. Jeter toute portion inutilisée.

IV intermittente: Administrer la solution diluée dans 50 à 100 mL de diluant en 15 à 30 minutes. La solution peut aussi être administrée en perfusion continue.
Association compatible dans la même seringue: ifosfamide.
Compatibilité (tubulure en Y): amifostine ▪ aztréonam ▪ céfépime ▪ filgrastim ▪ fludarabine ▪ gallium, nitrate de ▪ granisétron ▪ melphalan ▪ méthotrexate ▪ ondansétron ▪ paclitaxel ▪ pipéracilline/tazobactam ▪ sargramostim ▪ téniposide ▪ thiotépa ▪ vinorelbine.
Compatibilité en addition au soluté: cyclophosphamide ▪ ifosfamide.
Incompatibilité en addition au soluté: carboplatine ▪ cisplatine.

ENSEIGNEMENT AU PATIENT ET À SES PROCHES

- Prévenir le patient que le goût désagréable est un effet prévisible se manifestant pendant l'administration du médicament.
- Conseiller au patient de prévenir un professionnel de la santé si les nausées, les vomissements ou la diarrhée persistent ou si cette dernière est grave.

VÉRIFICATION DE L'EFFICACITÉ THÉRAPEUTIQUE

L'efficacité du traitement peut être démontrée par: la prévention de la cystite hémorragique associée au traitement par l'ifosfamide ou le cyclosphosphamide. ✳

MESTRANOL,
voir Contraceptifs hormonaux

MÉTAPROTÉRÉNOL,
voir Orciprénaline

METFORMINE

Apo-Metformin, Glucophage, Glumetza, Novo-Metformin, Nu-Metformin, PMS-Metformin, Ratio-Metformin, Rhoxal-Metformine

CLASSIFICATION:
Antidiabétique (biguanide)

Grossesse – catégorie B

INDICATIONS

Maîtrise de l'hyperglycémie en présence de diabète de type 2 sensible à la metformine, stable, léger et non susceptible d'entraîner une cétose lorsqu'on ne peut pas équilibrer la glycémie par la diétothérapie, l'exercice et la perte de poids. Ce médicament peut être associé à des sulfamides hypoglycémiants oraux.

MÉCANISME D'ACTION

Diminution de la production de glucose par le foie ▪ Diminution de l'absorption du glucose par les intestins ▪ Augmentation de la sensibilité à l'insuline. ***Effets thérapeutiques:*** Équilibrage de la glycémie.

PHARMACOCINÉTIQUE

Absorption: De 50 à 60 % (PO).
Distribution: La metformine passe dans le lait maternel à des taux équivalents à ceux qu'on retrouve dans le plasma.
Métabolisme et excrétion: Élimination rénale surtout sous forme inchangée.
Demi-vie: De 9 à 17 heures.

Profil temps-action (équilibrage de la glycémie)

	DÉBUT D'ACTION	PIC	DURÉE
PO	plusieurs jours	2 – 4 semaines	12 h (24 h pour les comprimés à action prolongée)

CONTRE-INDICATIONS, PRÉCAUTIONS ET MISES EN GARDE

Contre-indications: Hypersensibilité ▪ Diabète de type 1 ▪ Acidose métabolique aiguë ou chronique et antécédents d'acidocétose de quelque cause que ce soit ▪ Antécédents d'acidose lactique ▪ Insuffisance rénale ▪ Néphropathie ou dysfonctionnement rénal sous-jacent (créatinine sérique > 136 µmol/L chez l'homme ou > 124 µmol/L chez la femme, ou encore une clairance de la créatinine < 60 mL/min) ▪ Études radiographiques concomitantes nécessitant l'administration IV d'une substance de contraste iodée (interrompre temporairement l'administration de la metformine) ▪ Insuffisance hépatique ▪ Insuffisance cardiaque dictant une pharmacothérapie ▪ Alcoolisme ▪ Déshydratation ▪ Collapsus cardiovasculaire et états pathologiques compliqués d'hypoxémie ▪ Stress dû à une infection, à une blessure ou à une intervention chirurgicale ▪ Phase de récupération postopératoire ▪ **OBST.**: L'innocuité du médicament n'a pas été établie chez la femme enceinte.
Précautions et mises en garde: **GÉR.**: Il peut s'avérer nécessaire de réduire la dose chez les personnes âgées ou débilitées ▪ Insuffisance hypophysaire ou hyperthyroïdie ▪ **ALLAITEMENT**: Le médicament passe dans le lait maternel; employer la metformine avec prudence chez la femme qui allaite ▪ **PÉD.**: L'innocuité et l'efficacité du médicament n'ont pas été établies chez l'enfant.

M

RÉACTIONS INDÉSIRABLES ET EFFETS SECONDAIRES

GI: ballonnement, diarrhée, nausées, vomissements, goût métallique désagréable.
End.: hypoglycémie.
HÉ: ACIDOSE LACTIQUE.
Divers: réduction des concentrations de vitamine B_{12}.

INTERACTIONS

Médicament-médicament: L'administration d'une **substance de contraste à base d'iode** ou une consommation abusive de grandes quantités d'**alcool** en une seule fois ou de façon prolongée peuvent élever le risque d'acidose lactique ■ L'**amiloride**, la **digoxine**, la **morphine**, le **procaïnamide**, la **quinidine**, la **ranitidine**, le **triamtérène**, le **triméthoprime**, les **bloqueurs des canaux calciques** et la **vancomycine** peuvent entrer en compétition avec la metformine au cours du processus d'élimination. Dans ce cas, on peut noter une modification des réponses au traitement ■ La **cimétidine** et le **furosémide** peuvent augmenter les effets de la metformine ■ La **nifédipine** augmente l'absorption de la metformine et peut en intensifier les effets.
Médicament-produits naturels: La **glucosamine**, consommée en concomitance, peut entraver l'équilibrage de la glycémie ■ Le **chrome** et la **coenzyme Q-10** peuvent entraîner des effets hypoglycémiants additifs.

VOIES D'ADMINISTRATION ET POSOLOGIE

- **PO (adultes)**: *Comprimé à libération immédiate* – 500 mg, 3 ou 4 fois par jour, ou 850 mg, 2 ou 3 fois par jour, jusqu'à concurrence de 2 550 mg par jour, en doses fractionnées. *Comprimé à libération prolongée* – dose initiale de 1 000 mg, 1 fois par jour avec le repas du soir. La dose peut ensuite être augmentée par paliers de 500 mg, à intervalles de 7 jours, selon la réponse au traitement et la tolérance du patient. Dose quotidienne maximale: 2 000 mg.

PRÉSENTATION

Comprimés à libération immédiate: 500 mg^{Pr}, 850 mg^{Pr} ■ **Comprimés à libération prolongée**: 500 mg^{Pr} ■ **En association avec**: rosiglitazone (Avandamet^{Pr}).

SOINS INFIRMIERS

ÉVALUATION DE LA SITUATION

- En cas d'administration concomitante de sulfamides hypoglycémiants, rester à l'affût des signes et des symptômes suivants d'hypoglycémie: douleurs abdominales, transpiration, faim, faiblesse, étourdissements, céphalées, tremblements, tachycardie, anxiété.
- SUIVRE DE PRÈS L'APPARITION D'UNE CÉTOACIDOSE OU D'UNE ACIDOSE LACTIQUE CHEZ LES PATIENTS DONT LA GLYCÉMIE EST BIEN ÉQUILIBRÉE PAR LA METFORMINE, MAIS QUI CONTRACTENT UNE NOUVELLE MALADIE OU QUI PRÉSENTENT DES RÉSULTATS ANORMAUX AUX TESTS DE LABORATOIRE. MESURER LES ÉLECTROLYTES SÉRIQUES, LA CÉTONÉMIE ET LA GLYCÉMIE ET, SI CELA EST INDIQUÉ, LE pH SANGUIN, LES CONCENTRATIONS DE LACTATE, DE PYRUVATE ET DE METFORMINE. EN PRÉSENCE DE N'IMPORTE QUELLE FORME D'ACIDOSE, ARRÊTER IMMÉDIATEMENT L'ADMINISTRATION DE METFORMINE ET TRAITER L'ACIDOSE.

Tests de laboratoire:

- Suivre, à intervalles réguliers, pendant toute la durée du traitement, la glycémie et la concentration d'hémoglobine glyquée afin d'évaluer l'efficacité du médicament. La metformine peut entraîner des résultats faussement positifs au dosage de la cétonurie.
- Le patient devrait surveiller systématiquement sa glycémie et la faire mesurer tous les 3 mois par un professionnel de la santé, afin de déterminer l'efficacité du traitement.
- Vérifier les résultats des tests de la fonction rénale avant le traitement et au moins 1 fois par année pendant toute sa durée. Arrêter le traitement par la metformine si une insuffisance rénale se manifeste.
- Suivre de près les concentrations sériques de vitamine B_{12} annuellement ou tous les 2 ans, lors d'un traitement de longue durée. La metformine peut entraver l'absorption de cette vitamine.

DIAGNOSTICS INFIRMIERS POSSIBLES

- Alimentation excessive (Indications).
- Connaissances insuffisantes sur le traitement médicamenteux (Enseignement au patient et à ses proches).
- Non-observance du traitement médicamenteux (Enseignement au patient et à ses proches).

INTERVENTIONS INFIRMIÈRES

- Il peut s'avérer nécessaire d'administrer de l'insuline aux patients dont la glycémie a été stabilisée, mais qui font de la fièvre, qui sont exposés au stress, à un traumatisme ou à une infection ou qui doivent subir une intervention chirurgicale. Interrompre l'administration de la metformine et attendre la fin de l'épisode aigu avant de reprendre le traitement.
- On devrait interrompre temporairement l'administration de la metformine chez les patients qui doivent subir une intervention chirurgicale et, de ce fait,

diminuer leur consommation d'aliments et de liquides. Reprendre l'administration du médicament lorsque le patient a de nouveau le droit de prendre des aliments et des liquides par la bouche et lorsque sa fonction rénale s'est rétablie.

- Interrompre le traitement par la metformine avant les analyses nécessitant l'injection IV d'une substance de contraste à base d'iode et attendre 48 heures avant de le reprendre.
- Administrer la metformine avec des aliments pour réduire les effets gastro-intestinaux. LES COMPRIMÉS À LIBÉRATION PROLONGÉE DOIVENT ÊTRE AVALÉS TELS QUELS ; IL NE FAUT PAS LES COUPER, LES ÉCRASER OU LES MÂCHER.

ENSEIGNEMENT AU PATIENT ET À SES PROCHES

- Conseiller au patient de prendre le médicament tous les jours à la même heure, en suivant rigoureusement la posologie recommandée. S'il n'a pas pu prendre le médicament au moment habituel, il doit le prendre dès que possible à moins que ce ne soit presque l'heure prévue pour la dose suivante. Le prévenir qu'il ne doit pas remplacer une dose manquée par une double dose.
- Expliquer au patient que la metformine permet de stabiliser la glycémie, mais ne peut guérir le diabète. Le traitement à l'aide de cet agent est habituellement de longue durée.
- Inciter le patient à suivre la diétothérapie, la pharmacothérapie et le programme d'exercices prescrits afin de prévenir les épisodes d'hypoglycémie ou d'hyperglycémie.
- Expliquer au patient les signes d'hypoglycémie et d'hyperglycémie. Si des symptômes d'hypoglycémie se manifestent, lui recommander de prendre un verre de jus d'orange ou un verre d'eau auquel il ajoute 2 ou 3 cuillerées à thé de sucre, de miel ou de sirop de maïs et de prévenir un professionnel de la santé.
- Montrer au patient comment mesurer sa glycémie et sa cétonurie. Lui recommander de surveiller étroitement les résultats de ces tests en période de stress ou de maladie et de prévenir immédiatement un professionnel de la santé si des modifications importantes surviennent.
- EXPLIQUER AU PATIENT QU'EN PRÉSENCE D'UNE INFECTION GRAVE, DE DÉSHYDRATATION OU DE DIARRHÉE INTENSE OU PERSISTANTE, OU EN CAS D'EXAMENS MÉDICAUX OU D'UNE INTERVENTION CHIRURGICALE, LE RISQUE D'ACIDOSE LACTIQUE PEUT DICTER L'ARRÊT DU TRAITEMENT PAR LA METFORMINE. LUI RECOMMANDER DE SIGNALER IMMÉDIATEMENT À UN PROFESSIONNEL DE LA SANTÉ LES SYMPTÔMES SUIVANTS D'ACIDOSE LACTIQUE : FRISSONS, DIARRHÉE, ÉTOURDISSEMENTS, HYPOTENSION, DOULEURS MUSCULAIRES, SOMNOLENCE, POULS FAIBLE OU FRÉQUENCE CARDIAQUE RALENTIE, DYSPNÉE OU FAIBLESSE.
- Conseiller au patient de consulter un professionnel de la santé avant de prendre d'autres médicaments d'ordonnance ou en vente libre, des produits naturels ou de l'alcool en même temps que la metformine.
- Expliquer à la patiente que l'insuline est le médicament de choix pour équilibrer la glycémie au cours de la grossesse. Lui conseiller de ne pas prendre de contraceptifs oraux, mais d'utiliser une autre méthode de contraception et d'informer rapidement un professionnel de la santé si elle pense être enceinte ou si elle souhaite le devenir.
- Prévenir le patient que la metformine peut lui donner un goût désagréable ou métallique, symptôme qui disparaît habituellement de façon spontanée.
- Recommander au patient qui doit suivre un autre traitement ou subir une intervention chirurgicale d'avertir le professionnel de la santé qu'il suit un traitement par ce médicament.
- Conseiller au patient de toujours avoir sur lui du sucre (sachets de sucre ou bonbons) et une pièce d'identité où sont inscrits son problème de santé et son traitement médicamenteux.
- Recommander au patient de signaler à un professionnel de la santé les symptômes suivants : diarrhée, nausées, vomissements, douleurs d'estomac ou sensation de plénitude gastrique.
- Insister sur l'importance des examens de suivi et des contrôles réguliers de la glycémie, de l'hémoglobine glyquée, de la fonction rénale et des paramètres hématologiques.

VÉRIFICATION DE L'EFFICACITÉ THÉRAPEUTIQUE

L'efficacité du traitement peut être démontrée par : l'équilibrage de la glycémie sans épisodes d'hypoglycémie ou d'hyperglycémie. L'équilibre peut être atteint en quelques jours, mais le plein effet du traitement peut ne pas se manifester avant 2 semaines. ✳

M

ALERTE CLINIQUE

MÉTHADONE

Metadol, Méthadone

CLASSIFICATION :

Analgésique opioïde (agoniste)

Grossesse – catégories B et D (en cas d'usage prolongé ou de doses élevées administrées près du terme)

INDICATIONS

Soulagement des douleurs intenses en soins palliatifs et de la douleur chronique ■ Désintoxication et traitement d'entretien chez les patients présentant une dépendance aux opioïdes.

MÉCANISME D'ACTION

Liaison aux récepteurs des opioïdes du SNC ■ Modification de la perception de la douleur et de la réaction aux stimuli douloureux avec dépression généralisée du SNC. ***Effets thérapeutiques:*** Diminution de l'intensité de la douleur ■ Suppression des symptômes de sevrage lors des cures de désintoxication ou d'entretien en cas de dépendance à l'héroïne ou aux autres opioïdes.

PHARMACOCINÉTIQUE

Absorption: Bonne (PO).

Distribution: Tout l'organisme. La méthadone traverse la barrière placentaire et passe dans le lait maternel.

Liaison aux protéines: Élevée.

Métabolisme et excrétion: Métabolisme hépatique; certains métabolites sont actifs et peuvent s'accumuler en cas d'administration prolongée.

Demi-vie: De 15 à 25 heures (prolongée lors d'une utilisation à long terme).

Profil temps-action (effet analgésique)

	DÉBUT D'ACTION	PIC	DURÉE
PO	30 - 60 min	90 - 120 min	6 - 12 h; 24 - 48 h lors d'une utilisation prolongée

CONTRE-INDICATIONS, PRÉCAUTIONS ET MISES EN GARDE

Contre-indications: Hypersensibilité ■ Diarrhée due à un empoisonnement, jusqu'à l'élimination de la toxine du tractus gastro-intestinal ■ Dépression respiratoire aiguë, crise d'asthme aiguë et obstruction des voies respiratoires supérieures ■ Personnes n'ayant jamais consommé d'opioïdes auparavant.

Précautions et mises en garde: Hypertrophie ventriculaire, usage concomitant de diurétiques, hypokaliémie, hypomagnésémie, antécédents de troubles de conduction cardiaque, usage concomitant de médicament affectant la conduction ou autre facteur de risque d'arythmies ■ Traitement concomitant par un IMAO ■ Traumatisme crânien ■ Pression intracrânienne accrue ■ Maladies rénale, hépatique ou pulmonaire graves ■ Hypothyroïdie ■ Insuffisance surrénalienne ■ Alcoolisme ■ **GÉR.:** Personnes âgées ou patients débilités (il est conseillé de réduire la dose) ■ Douleurs abdominales non diagnostiquées ■ Hyperplasie de la prostate ou rétrécissement de l'urètre ■ **OBST.:** On considère souvent qu'il est plus sûr et plus raisonnable de prescrire de la méthadone durant la grossesse que de risquer que la mère continue de consommer des drogues illicites ■ **ALLAITEMENT:** On retrouve des quantités variables de méthadone dans le lait maternel; en règle générale, on considère son emploi compatible avec l'allaitement ■ **PÉD.:** L'efficacité et l'innocuité de la méthadone chez les enfants < 18 ans n'ont pas été établies ■ Risque de pharmacodépendance et d'abus.

RÉACTIONS INDÉSIRABLES ET EFFETS SECONDAIRES

SNC: confusion, sédation, étourdissements, dysphorie, euphorie, sensation de flottement, hallucinations, céphalées, rêves bizarres.

ORLO: vision trouble, diplopie, myosis.

Resp.: DÉPRESSION RESPIRATOIRE.

CV: hypotension, bradycardie, allongement de l'intervalle QT.

GI: constipation, nausées, vomissements.

GU: rétention urinaire.

Tég.: transpiration, rougeurs du visage.

Divers: dépendance physique, dépendance psychologique, tolérance aux effets du médicament.

INTERACTIONS

Médicament-médicament: ADMINISTRER LA MÉTHADONE AVEC UNE EXTRÊME PRUDENCE CHEZ LES PATIENTS PRENANT DES **IMAO** (la dose initiale doit être réduite à 25 % de la dose habituelle) ■ Une extrême prudence est de mise lors de l'usage concomitant d'autres **médicaments pouvant allonger l'intervalle QT**, notamment les **antiarythmiques de classes I et III**, les **neuroleptiques** et **antidépresseurs tricycliques**, les **macrolides**, la **pentamidine** et les **fluoroquinolones** ■ L'usage concomitant de **médicaments qui augmentent le risque d'hypokaliémie ou d'hypomagnésémie** (comme les **laxatifs**, les **diurétiques**, les **minéralocorticoïdes**) augmente le risque d'arythmies ■ Dépression additive du SNC et du système respiratoire lors de l'usage concomitant d'**alcool**, d'**antihistaminiques**, de **phénothiazines**, de **barbituriques**, d'**antidépresseurs**, d'**hypnosédatifs** et d'autres **opioïdes** ■ L'administration d'**analgésiques opioïdes agonistes/antagonistes** (**nalbuphine**, **butorphanol**, **pentazocine**) peut diminuer l'analgésie et/ou déclencher des symptômes de sevrage chez les patients présentant une dépendance physique aux analgésiques opioïdes ■ La méthadone étant métabolisée par le CYP 3A4, les **inhibiteurs du cytochrome 3A4** (par exemple le **fluconazole**, le **voriconazole** et l'**érythromicine**) peuvent élever les concentrations de méthadone (une réduction de la dose peut être nécessaire) ■ La **phénytoïne**, le **phénobarbital**, la

carbamazépine, l'**amprénavir**, le **fosamprénavir**, la **délavirdine**, la **névirapine**, le **nelfinavir**, l'**éfavirenz**, le **ritonavir**, le **lopinavir/ritonavir** et la **rifampine** peuvent accélérer le métabolisme de la méthadone, réduire son effet analgésique et déclencher un syndrome de sevrage ■ La **fluvoxamine** peut accroître la dépression du SNC et déclencher un syndrome de sevrage ■ La méthadone peut accroître les concentrations sanguines de **désipramine** et de **zidovudine** et en intensifier les effets ■ La méthadone peut diminuer les concentrations sanguines de **didanosine** et de **stavudine**.

Médicament-produits naturels: L'usage concomitant de **millepertuis** n'est pas recommandé en raison du risque de diminution des concentrations de méthadone et de la survenue de réactions de sevrage ■ Effets dépresseurs additifs sur le SNC lors de l'usage concomitant de **kava**, de **valériane** et de **camomille**.

VOIES D'ADMINISTRATION ET POSOLOGIE

Des doses élevées peuvent être nécessaires pour obtenir un effet analgésique lors d'un traitement prolongé; on peut réduire l'intervalle entre les prises ou augmenter la posologie si les douleurs réapparaissent.

- **PO (adultes)**: *Analgésie* – initialement de 2,5 à 10 mg, toutes les 4 à 8 heures, pendant les 3 à 5 premiers jours; espacer ensuite les prises pour les ramener à un intervalle de 8 à 12 heures, selon les besoins du patient. La posologie doit être individualisée et certains patients peuvent avoir besoin de doses qui se situent en dehors de cet intervalle. On recommande de porter une attention particulière à la posologie de la méthadone lorsque celle-ci est substituée à un autre opioïde dans le traitement de douleurs intenses. En effet, la puissance analgésique relative de la méthadone est beaucoup plus élevée qu'on le croyait auparavant et l'adaptation posologique nécessaire lorsqu'on change de médicament peut varier grandement selon la dose de l'autre opioïde que le patient recevait antérieurement. *Désintoxication* – de 15 à 40 mg, 1 fois par jour ou la quantité nécessaire pour prévenir le syndrome de sevrage. La posologie peut être réduite tous les 1 ou 2 jours; la dose d'entretien est établie en fonction de la réponse de chaque patient. La désintoxication à la méthadone implique l'administration de doses décroissantes de l'agent pendant une période n'excédant pas 180 jours. *Traitement d'entretien* – la posologie initiale doit être ajustée individuellement, selon la tolérance aux opioïdes du patient, tout en visant la prévention du syndrome de sevrage. On peut administrer jusqu'à 120 mg par jour.

PRÉSENTATION

Comprimés: 1 mg^{N}, 5 mg^{N}, 10 mg^{N}, 25 mg^{N} ■ **Solution orale**: 1 mg/mL^{N}, 10 mg/mL^{N}.

SOINS INFIRMIERS

ÉVALUATION DE LA SITUATION

- Pour prescrire de la méthadone au Québec, le médecin doit avoir une autorisation du Collège des médecins de la province. L'autorisation émise pour le traitement de la douleur est différente de celle émise pour la désintoxication. La distribution de la méthadone par les pharmaciens pour la désintoxication est, elle aussi, réglementée et étroitement encadrée.

Douleur: Déterminer le type de douleur, son siège et son intensité, avant l'administration du médicament et de 1 à 2 heures (pic) après. Lorsqu'on majore la dose d'un opioïde, on devrait l'augmenter de 25 à 50 % jusqu'à ce qu'on note une réduction de 50 % de la douleur, selon l'évaluation qu'en fait le patient sur une échelle numérique ou visuelle, ou jusqu'à ce qu'il signale un soulagement adéquat de la douleur. On peut administrer sans danger une autre dose au moment du pic, si la dose précédente s'est avérée inefficace et si les effets secondaires ont été minimes. En raison des effets cumulatifs de la méthadone, il faut parfois effectuer des adaptations posologiques à intervalles réguliers.

- Les doses de méthadone administrées aux patients suivant une cure d'entretien ne préviennent que le syndrome de sevrage et ne procurent *aucune analgésie*. Il faut administrer des doses additionnelles d'opioïdes pour traiter la douleur.
- Consulter un tableau d'équivalences (voir l'annexe A) lorsqu'on doit changer de mode d'administration ou substituer à cet agent un autre opioïde.
- ÉVALUER L'ÉTAT DE CONSCIENCE DU PATIENT ET MESURER SA PRESSION ARTÉRIELLE, SON POULS ET SA FRÉQUENCE RESPIRATOIRE AVANT ET À INTERVALLES RÉGULIERS PENDANT L'ADMINISTRATION DE CET AGENT. SI LA FRÉQUENCE RESPIRATOIRE EST < 10/MIN, ÉVALUER LE DEGRÉ DE SÉDATION. IL PEUT S'AVÉRER NÉCESSAIRE DE RÉDUIRE LA DOSE DE 25 À 50 %. LA SOMNOLENCE INITIALE DISPARAÎT AU FIL DU TRAITEMENT.
- Examiner la fonction intestinale du patient à intervalles réguliers. La consommation accrue de liquides et d'aliments riches en fibres et la prise de laxatifs peuvent réduire les effets constipants du médicament. Sauf contre-indication, les laxatifs stimulants devraient être administrés de façon systématique si

M

le traitement par un opioïde dure plus de 2 ou de 3 jours.

- L'usage prolongé peut entraîner la dépendance physique et psychologique ainsi qu'une tolérance aux effets du médicament, mais cela ne doit pas empêcher le patient de recevoir une quantité suffisante d'analgésiques. La dépendance psychologique est rare chez la plupart des patients qui reçoivent de la méthadone pour des raisons médicales. Des doses de plus en plus élevées peuvent s'avérer nécessaires pour soulager la douleur en cas de traitement prolongé.

Dépendance aux opioïdes: Rester à l'affût des signes de sevrage aux opioïdes (irritabilité, écoulement nasal et oculaire, crampes abdominales, courbatures, diaphorèse, perte d'appétit, frissons, mydriase, trouble du sommeil, fatigue, bâillements).

Tests de laboratoire: La méthadone peut élever les concentrations plasmatiques d'amylase et de lipase.

TOXICITÉ ET SURDOSAGE: S'il est nécessaire d'administrer un antagoniste opioïde pour renverser la dépression respiratoire ou le coma, l'antidote est la naloxone (Narcan). Diluer le contenu de l'ampoule de naloxone à 0,4 mg dans 10 mL de solution de NaCl 0,9 % et administrer 0,5 mL (0,02 mg) par bolus IV direct, toutes les 2 minutes. Dans le cas des enfants et des patients pesant moins de 40 kg, diluer 0,1 mg de naloxone dans 10 mL de solution de NaCl 0,9 % pour obtenir une concentration de 10 µg/mL et administrer 0,5 µg/kg, toutes les 2 minutes. Adapter la dose pour prévenir les symptômes de sevrage, les convulsions et la douleur intense.

M

DIAGNOSTICS INFIRMIERS POSSIBLES

- Douleur aiguë (Indications).
- Trouble de la perception visuelle et auditive (Effets secondaires).
- Risque d'accident (Effets secondaires).

INTERVENTIONS INFIRMIÈRES

ALERTE CLINIQUE: DES SURDOSES ACCIDENTELLES D'ANALGÉSIQUES OPIOÏDES ONT CAUSÉ DES DÉCÈS. AVANT L'ADMINISTRATION, CLARIFIER TOUS LES POINTS AMBIGUS SUR LES ORDONNANCES ET FAIRE VÉRIFIER L'ORDONNANCE D'ORIGINE ET LE CALCUL DES DOSES PAR UN AUTRE PROFESSIONNEL DE LA SANTÉ.

- Pour augmenter l'effet analgésique de la méthadone, expliquer au patient la valeur thérapeutique de ce médicament avant de l'administrer.
- Les doses administrées selon un horaire fixe peuvent être plus efficaces que celles administrées sur demande. Le médicament s'avère plus efficace s'il est administré avant que la douleur ne devienne intense. Dans le cas des patients souffrant de douleurs intenses chroniques, on recommande d'administrer les doses selon un horaire fixe.
- Les analgésiques non opioïdes, administrés simultanément, peuvent exercer des effets analgésiques additifs, ce qui permet parfois de diminuer les doses d'opioïde.
- Après un traitement prolongé, interrompre l'administration graduellement pour prévenir les symptômes de sevrage.
- Le médicament peut être administré avec des aliments ou du lait pour réduire l'irritation gastrique.
- Avant l'administration, diluer chaque dose de 10 mg/mL de concentré oral avec au moins 30 mL d'eau ou d'un autre liquide.

ENSEIGNEMENT AU PATIENT ET À SES PROCHES

- Expliquer au patient ce qu'on entend par administration sur demande et à quel moment il doit réclamer l'analgésique.
- Recommander au patient de respecter rigoureusement la posologie de la méthadone. Si la dose prescrite devient moins efficace après quelques semaines, il ne faut pas l'augmenter sans avoir consulté un professionnel de la santé au préalable.
- Prévenir le patient que la méthadone peut provoquer des étourdissements et de la somnolence. Lui recommander de demander de l'aide lorsqu'il se déplace et lorsqu'il veut fumer. Lui conseiller de ne pas conduire et d'éviter les activités qui exigent sa vigilance jusqu'à ce qu'on ait la certitude que le médicament n'entraîne pas ces effets chez lui.
- Recommander au patient de changer lentement de position pour diminuer le risque d'hypotension orthostatique.
- Recommander au patient d'éviter de boire de l'alcool et de ne pas prendre d'autres dépresseurs du SNC en même temps que la méthadone.
- Recommander au patient de se tourner dans le lit, de tousser et de faire des exercices de respiration profonde toutes les 2 heures pour prévenir l'atélectasie.
- Insister sur le fait qu'il est important de prévenir la constipation associée à la prise d'analgésiques opioïdes.

VÉRIFICATION DE L'EFFICACITÉ THÉRAPEUTIQUE

L'efficacité du traitement peut être démontrée par: la diminution de l'intensité de la douleur sans modification importante de l'état de la conscience ou de l'état de la respiration ■ la prévention de l'apparition de symptômes de sevrage lors des cures de désintoxication des toxicomanes qui abusent de l'héroïne et d'autres analgésiques opioïdes.

MÉTHAZOLAMIDE,
voir Inhibiteurs de l'anhydrase carbonique

MÉTHIMAZOLE

Tapazole

CLASSIFICATION:
Antithyroïdien

Grossesse – catégorie D

INDICATIONS

Traitement médicamenteux de l'hyperthyroïdie ▪ Traitement d'appoint visant à maîtriser l'hyperthyroïdie en préparation à une thyroïdectomie partielle ou à un traitement par de l'iode radioactif lorsque la thyroïdectomie est contre-indiquée ou déconseillée.

MÉCANISME D'ACTION

Inhibition de la synthèse des hormones thyroïdiennes. ***Effets thérapeutiques:*** Diminution des signes et des symptômes d'hyperthyroïdie.

PHARMACOCINÉTIQUE

Absorption: Rapide (PO). Biodisponibilité à 93 %.
Distribution: Le médicament traverse la barrière placentaire et passe dans le lait maternel à des concentrations élevées.
Métabolisme et excrétion: Métabolisme majoritairement hépatique; environ 10 % est éliminé à l'état inchangé dans l'urine.
Demi-vie: De 4 à 6 heures.

Profil temps-action (effet sur l'état de la thyroïde)

	DÉBUT D'ACTION	PIC	DURÉE
PO	1 semaine	4 - 10 semaines	plusieurs semaines

CONTRE-INDICATIONS, PRÉCAUTIONS ET MISES EN GARDE

Contre-indications: Hypersensibilité.
Précautions et mises en garde: Aplasie médullaire ▪ Patients > 40 ans (risque accru d'agranulocytose) ▪ **OBST.:** Grossesse (la prudence est de mise; des troubles thyroïdiens peuvent se manifester chez le fœtus) ▪ Allaitement.

RÉACTIONS INDÉSIRABLES ET EFFETS SECONDAIRES

SNC: somnolence, céphalées, vertiges.
GI: diarrhée, hépatite, perte du goût, nausées, parotidite, vomissements.
Tég.: rash, changement de couleur de la peau, urticaire.
Hémat.: AGRANULOCYTOSE, anémie, leucopénie, thrombopénie.
Loc.: arthralgie.
Divers: fièvre, lymphadénopathie.

INTERACTIONS

Médicament-médicament: Aplasie médullaire additive lors de l'administration simultanée d'**agents antinéoplasiques** ou d'une **radiothérapie** ▪ L'**iodure de potassium** ou l'**amiodarone**, administrés simultanément, peuvent intensifier l'effet antithyroïdien du méthimazole ▪ Risque accru d'agranulocytose lors de l'administration simultanée de **phénothiazines** ▪ Le méthimazole peut modifier la réponse du patient à la **warfarine** et à la **digoxine**.

M

VOIES D'ADMINISTRATION ET POSOLOGIE

Le traitement peut durer de 6 mois à plusieurs années; habituellement, la durée moyenne est de 1 an.

- **PO (adultes):** La dose quotidienne peut être prise en 1 fois ou répartie en 2 ou 3 doses égales, prises à intervalles réguliers. *Traitement initial: Hyperthyroïdie bénigne* – 15 mg par jour; *hyperthyroïdie de gravité moyenne* – de 30 à 40 mg par jour; *hyperthyroïdie grave* – 60 mg par jour. *Traitement d'entretien:* de 5 à 15 mg par jour.
- **PO (enfants):** *Traitement initial* – 0,4 mg/kg/jour (au maximum: 30 mg/jour), en 1 fois ou en 2 ou 3 doses égales, prises à intervalles réguliers. *Traitement d'entretien* – environ la moitié de la dose d'attaque.

PRÉSENTATION

Comprimés: 5 mg[Pr].

SOINS INFIRMIERS

ÉVALUATION DE LA SITUATION

- Suivre de près la réponse du patient pour déceler les symptômes suivants d'hyperthyroïdie ou de thyrotoxicose: tachycardie, palpitations, nervosité,

insomnie, fièvre, diaphorèse, intolérance à la chaleur, tremblements, perte de poids, diarrhée.
- Suivre de près l'apparition de l'hypothyroïdie: intolérance au froid, constipation, peau sèche, céphalées, apragmatisme, fatigue ou faiblesse. Une adaptation de la posologie peut s'avérer nécessaire.
- Suivre de près l'apparition du rash ou d'une tuméfaction des ganglions lymphatiques du cou. Si ces symptômes se manifestent, il peut s'avérer nécessaire d'interrompre le traitement.

Tests de laboratoire:
- Vérifier les résultats des tests de la fonction thyroïdienne avant le traitement, puis tous les mois au cours du traitement initial et, par la suite, tous les 2 à 3 mois pendant toute la durée du traitement.
- EXAMINER LE NOMBRE DE GLOBULES BLANCS ET LA FORMULE LEUCOCYTAIRE À INTERVALLES RÉGULIERS PENDANT TOUTE LA DURÉE DU TRAITEMENT. L'AGRANULOCYTOSE PEUT SURVENIR RAPIDEMENT. ELLE SE MANIFESTE HABITUELLEMENT AU COURS DES 3 PREMIERS MOIS DE TRAITEMENT ET ELLE EST PLUS FRÉQUENTE CHEZ LES PATIENTS > 40 ANS ET CHEZ CEUX RECEVANT UNE DOSE SUPÉRIEURE À 40 mg PAR JOUR. EN CAS D'AGRANULOCYTOSE, IL FAUT ARRÊTER LE TRAITEMENT.
- Le méthimazole peut entraîner l'élévation des concentrations d'AST, d'ALT, de LDH, de phosphatase alcaline et de bilirubine sérique ainsi que l'allongement du temps de prothrombine.

DIAGNOSTICS INFIRMIERS POSSIBLES

- Connaissances insuffisantes sur le traitement médicamenteux (Enseignement au patient et à ses proches).
- Non-observance du traitement médicamenteux (Enseignement au patient et à ses proches).

INTERVENTIONS INFIRMIÈRES

- Administrer le méthimazole au même moment tous les jours par rapport à l'heure des repas. Les aliments peuvent augmenter ou diminuer l'absorption du médicament.

ENSEIGNEMENT AU PATIENT ET À SES PROCHES

- Conseiller au patient de suivre rigoureusement la posologie recommandée et de prendre le méthimazole à intervalles réguliers. S'il n'a pas pu prendre le médicament au moment habituel, il doit le prendre dès que possible; s'il est presque l'heure prévue pour la dose suivante, il devrait prendre les 2 doses ensemble. Conseiller au patient de consulter un professionnel de la santé s'il a sauté plus de 1 dose ou s'il veut arrêter le traitement.
- Conseiller au patient de se peser 2 ou 3 fois par semaine et de prévenir un professionnel de la santé si des changements importants surviennent.
- Prévenir le patient que le méthimazole peut provoquer de la somnolence. Lui conseiller de ne pas conduire et d'éviter les activités qui exigent sa vigilance jusqu'à ce qu'on ait la certitude que le médicament n'entraîne pas cet effet chez lui.
- Recommander au patient de consulter un professionnel de la santé au sujet des sources alimentaires d'iode: sel iodé, algues, crustacés.
- Recommander au patient de signaler rapidement à un professionnel de la santé les maux de gorge, la fièvre, les frissons, les céphalées, les malaises, la faiblesse, le jaunissement des yeux ou de la peau, les saignements ou les ecchymoses inhabituels, le rash ou les symptômes d'hyperthyroïdie ou d'hypothyroïdie.
- Conseiller au patient de consulter un professionnel de la santé avant de prendre un médicament en vente libre ou un produit naturel en même temps que cet agent.
- Recommander au patient de porter sur lui en tout temps une pièce d'identité où est inscrit son traitement médicamenteux.
- Recommander au patient qui doit suivre un autre traitement ou subir une intervention chirurgicale d'avertir le professionnel de la santé qu'il suit un traitement par ce médicament.
- Insister sur l'importance des examens réguliers de suivi permettant d'évaluer l'évolution de la maladie et de vérifier les effets secondaires du traitement.

VÉRIFICATION DE L'EFFICACITÉ THÉRAPEUTIQUE

L'efficacité du traitement peut être démontrée par: la diminution de la gravité des symptômes d'hyperthyroïdie (diminution de la fréquence du pouls et gain de poids) ■ le rétablissement des résultats des tests de la fonction thyroïdienne.

MÉTHOCARBAMOL

Methocarbamol, Methoxacet, Methoxisal, Robaxacet, Robaxin, Robaxisal

CLASSIFICATION:

Relaxant musculosquelettique (à action centrale)

Grossesse – catégorie C

INDICATIONS

Adjuvant pharmaceutique au repos et à la physiothérapie en vue de soulager les spasmes musculaires associés à des maladies musculosquelettiques aiguës douloureuses.

MÉCANISME D'ACTION

Relaxation des muscles squelettiques, probablement par dépression du SNC. ***Effets thérapeutiques:*** Relaxation des muscles squelettiques.

PHARMACOCINÉTIQUE

Absorption: Bonne (PO).

Distribution: Répartition dans tout l'organisme. L'agent traverse la barrière placentaire et passe dans le lait maternel en faibles quantités.

Métabolisme et excrétion: Métabolisme hépatique.

Demi-vie: De 1 à 2 heures.

Profil temps-action (relaxation des muscles squelettiques)

	Début d'action	Pic	Durée
PO	30 min	2 h	inconnue
IM	rapide	inconnu	inconnue
IV	immédiat	fin de la perfusion	inconnue

CONTRE-INDICATIONS, PRÉCAUTIONS ET MISES EN GARDE

Contre-indications: Hypersensibilité ■ Hypersensibilité au propylène glycol (préparations parentérales) ■ Insuffisance rénale connue ou soupçonnée (préparation parentérales).

Précautions et mises en garde: **Obst., allaitement, péd.**: L'innocuité du médicament n'a pas été établie ■ Convulsions (préparations parentérales) ■ **Gér.**: Piètre tolérance aux effets anticholinergiques.

RÉACTIONS INDÉSIRABLES ET EFFETS SECONDAIRES

SNC: CONVULSIONS (voies IV, IM seulement), étourdissements, somnolence, sensation de tête légère.

ORLO: vision trouble, congestion nasale.

CV: *IV* – bradycardie, hypotension.

GI: anorexie, dyspepsie, nausées.

GU: urine brune, noire ou verte.

Tég.: rougeurs du visage (voie IV seulement), prurit, rash, urticaire.

Locaux: douleur au point d'injection IM, phlébite au point d'injection IV.

Divers: réactions allergiques incluant l'ANAPHYLAXIE (voies IM et IV seulement), fièvre.

INTERACTIONS

Médicament-médicament: Dépression additive du SNC lors de l'usage concomitant d'autres **dépresseurs du SNC** incluant l'**alcool**, les **antihistaminiques**, les **analgésiques opioïdes** et les **hypnosédatifs**.

Médicament-produits naturels: Le **kava**, la **valériane**, la **scutellaire**, la **camomille** et le **houblon**, consommés en concomitance, peuvent accentuer la dépression du SNC.

VOIES D'ADMINISTRATION ET POSOLOGIE

- **PO (adultes)**: 1,5 g, 4 fois par jour pendant 48 à 72 heures en présence de spasmes aigus du muscle strié. Dans les cas graves, la dose peut être portée jusqu'à 8 g par jour. On peut ensuite réduire la dose jusqu'à 4 ou 4,5 g par jour, en 4 à 6 prises.
- **IM, IV (adultes)**: 1 g, à répéter toutes les 8 heures, au besoin; ne pas dépasser 3 g par jour pendant 3 jours consécutifs.

PRÉSENTATION

Comprimés: 500 mg^{Pr}, 750 mg^{Pr} ■ **En association avec**: aspirine (Robaxisal)^{VL}, acétaminophène (Robaxacet)^{VL}, aspirine, caféine et codéine (Robaxisal)^{N} et acétaminophène, caféine et codéine (Robaxacet-8)^{N} ■ **Solution pour injection**: 100 mg/mL, en ampoules de 10 mL^{Pr}.

M

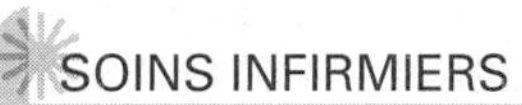

SOINS INFIRMIERS

ÉVALUATION DE LA SITUATION

- Noter l'intensité de la douleur, la rigidité des muscles et l'amplitude des mouvements avant le début du traitement et à intervalles réguliers pendant toute sa durée.
- Mesurer le pouls et la pression artérielle toutes les 15 minutes tout au long de l'administration par voie parentérale.

Gér.: Rester à l'affût des effets anticholinergiques (somnolence et fatigue).

- APRÈS L'ADMINISTRATION PAR VOIE PARENTÉRALE, RESTER À L'AFFÛT DES RÉACTIONS ALLERGIQUES SUIVANTES: RASH, ASTHME, URTICAIRE, RESPIRATION SIFFLANTE, HYPOTENSION. GARDER À LA PORTÉE DE LA MAIN DE L'ADRÉNALINE ET DE L'OXYGÈNE POUR CONTRER UNE TELLE RÉACTION.
- Examiner le point d'injection IV. L'injection est hypertonique et peut provoquer une thrombophlébite. Éviter l'extravasation.

Tests de laboratoire: Le méthocarbamol peut entraîner des concentrations urinaires d'acide 5-hydroxy-indolacétique et d'acide vanillylmandélique faussement élevées.

DIAGNOSTICS INFIRMIERS POSSIBLES

- Douleur aiguë (Indications).
- Mobilité physique réduite (Indications).
- Risque d'accident (Effets secondaires).

INTERVENTIONS INFIRMIÈRES

- Prendre des mesures de sécurité, selon les besoins. Suivre de près les déplacements et le transport des patients.

PO: On peut administrer le méthocarbamol avec des aliments pour réduire l'irritation gastrique. Les comprimés de méthocarbamol peuvent être écrasés et mélangés à des aliments ou à des liquides pour en faciliter la déglutition. Pour administrer le médicament par une sonde nasogastrique, écraser le comprimé et le mettre en suspension dans de l'eau ou dans une solution saline.
IM: Dose maximale: 500 mg dans chaque muscle fessier. Ne pas administrer par voie sous-cutanée.
IV directe: Injecter la solution non diluée. La vitesse d'administration maximale est de 300 mg/min.
Perfusion intermittente: Diluer 1 g dans un volume allant jusqu'à 250 mL de D5%E ou de NaCl 0,9 %. Perfuser en l'espace de 3 à 4 heures.

- Les patients doivent demeurer en position couchée pendant au moins 15 minutes après l'administration IV pour réduire l'intensité des effets secondaires.
- Consulter les directives de chaque fabriquant avant de reconstituer la préparation.

M

ENSEIGNEMENT AU PATIENT ET À SES PROCHES

- Conseiller au patient de respecter rigoureusement la posologie recommandée. Lui expliquer que s'il n'a pu prendre le médicament au moment habituel, il doit le faire dans l'heure qui suit, sinon il doit reprendre son horaire habituel. Le prévenir qu'il ne doit jamais remplacer une dose manquée par une double dose.
- Inciter le patient à appliquer les autres mesures prescrites pour contrer les spasmes musculaires: repos, physiothérapie, application de chaleur.
- Prévenir le patient que le méthocarbamol peut provoquer des étourdissements, de la somnolence et une vision trouble. Lui conseiller de ne pas conduire et d'éviter les activités qui exigent sa vigilance jusqu'à ce qu'on ait la certitude que le médicament n'entraîne pas ces effets chez lui.
- Recommander au patient de changer lentement de position pour réduire le risque d'hypotension orthostatique.
- Conseiller au patient d'éviter de boire de l'alcool et de ne pas prendre d'autres dépresseurs du SNC en même temps que ce médicament.
- Prévenir le patient que ses urines peuvent devenir noires, brunes ou vertes, particulièrement si on les laisse décanter.
- Recommander au patient de signaler à un professionnel de la santé le rash, les démangeaisons, la fièvre ou la congestion nasale.
- Insister sur l'importance des examens de suivi réguliers permettant d'évaluer les bienfaits du traitement.

VÉRIFICATION DE L'EFFICACITÉ THÉRAPEUTIQUE

L'efficacité du traitement peut être démontrée par: la réduction des spasmes musculaires et de la douleur musculosquelettique ▪ l'augmentation de l'amplitude des mouvements.

ALERTE CLINIQUE

MÉTHOTREXATE

Apo-Méthotrexate, Ratio-Méthotrexate

CLASSIFICATION:

Antinéoplasique, antirhumatismal (ARMM), immunosuppresseur (antimétabolite)

Grossesse – catégorie X

INDICATIONS

Monothérapie ou traitement d'association avec d'autres modalités thérapeutiques (autres antinéoplasiques, chirurgie ou radiothérapie) en présence des affections suivantes: choriocarcinome et autres maladies trophoblastiques similaires ▪ leucémie ▪ lymphome non hodgkinien ▪ cancer du sein ▪ cancer de la tête ▪ cancer du cou ▪ cancer de l'estomac ▪ métastases d'origine inconnue ▪ cancer de la vessie ▪ lymphome de Burkitt ▪ mycose fongoïde ▪ lymphome de stade avancé chez l'enfant ▪ Antirhumatismal modificateur de la maladie (ARMM): Traitement du psoriasis ou du rhumatisme psoriasique et de la polyarthrite rhumatoïde invalidants et graves qui ne répondent pas au traitement habituel ▪ Arthrite séronégative invalidante grave. **Usages non approuvés:** Grossesse ectopique.

MÉCANISME D'ACTION

Altération du métabolisme de l'acide folique, entraînant l'inhibition de la synthèse de l'ADN et de la reproduction cellulaire (action spécifique sur la phase S du cycle cellulaire) ▪ Activité immunosuppressive. ***Effets thérapeutiques:*** Destruction des cellules à réplication rapide, particulièrement des cellules malignes et effet immunosuppresseur.

PHARMACOCINÉTIQUE

Absorption: Bonne à faible dose (PO). Saturation de l'absorption lors de l'administration de doses de plus de 30 mg/m^2 (PO).

Distribution: Le méthotrexate traverse les membranes cellulaires par transport actif et se répartit dans tout l'organisme. Il n'atteint pas de concentrations thérapeutiques dans le liquide céphalorachidien. Il traverse la barrière placentaire et passe dans le lait maternel où on le retrouve à faible concentration.

Métabolisme et excrétion: Excrétion rénale (sous forme inchangée).

Demi-vie: *Faible dose* – de 3 à 10 heures; *dose élevée* – de 8 à 15 heures (prolongée en cas d'insuffisance rénale).

Profil temps-action (effet sur la numération globulaire)

	Début d'action	Pic	Durée
PO, IM, IV	4 - 7 jours	7 - 14 jours	21 jours

CONTRE-INDICATIONS, PRÉCAUTIONS ET MISES EN GARDE

Contre-indications: Hypersensibilité ▪ Grossesse ou allaitement ▪ Alcoolisme, maladie hépatique alcoolique, maladie hépatique chronique, syndrome d'immunodéficience ou dyscrasie préexistante (pour le traitement du psoriasis ou de la polyarthrite rhumatoïde) ▪ Ne pas utiliser de produit contenant de l'alcool benzylique chez les nouveau-nés.

Précautions et mises en garde: Insuffisance rénale (une diminution de dose peut s'avérer nécessaire) ▪ Insuffisance hépatique (risque important d'hépatotoxicité) ▪ Patientes en âge de procréer ▪ Infections actives ▪ Aplasie médullaire ▪ Patients âgés ou souffrant d'autres maladies chroniques débilitantes ▪ Présence d'un 3e espace (p. ex., épanchement pleural, ascite) ▪ Administration concomitante d'AINS ▪ Radiothérapie concomitante ▪ Ulcère gastroduodénal ▪ Colite ulcéreuse ▪ **Péd.**: L'innocuité de cet agent pour d'autres utilisations que le cancer n'a pas été établie.

RÉACTIONS INDÉSIRABLES ET EFFETS SECONDAIRES

SNC: arachnoïdite (voie intrathécale seulement), étourdissements, somnolence, céphalées, malaise.

ORLO: vision trouble, dysarthrie, cécité transitoire.

Resp.: FIBROSE PULMONAIRE, pneumonite interstitielle.

GI: anorexie, hépatotoxicité, nausées, stomatite, vomissements, douleurs abdominales.

GU: stérilité, néphropathie.

Tég.: alopécie, érosion douloureuse des plaques (lors du traitement du psoriasis), photosensibilité, prurit, rash, ulcération de la peau, urticaire.

Hémat.: ANÉMIE APLASIQUE, anémie, leucopénie, thrombopénie.

Métab.: hyperuricémie.

Loc.: ostéonécrose, fractures de stress.

Divers: frissons, fièvre, nécrose des tissus mous.

INTERACTIONS

Médicament-médicament: Les médicaments suivants peuvent accroître la toxicité du méthotrexate: **salicylates** à doses élevées, **anti-inflammatoires non stéroïdiens**, **phénytoïne**, **tétracyclines**, **probénécide**, **triméthoprime/sulfaméthoxazole**, **oméprazole**, **pantoprazole**, **pénicillines** et **pyriméthamine** ▪ Hépatotoxicité additive lors de l'administration simultanée d'autres **médicaments hépatotoxiques**, incluant l'**azathioprine**, la **sulfasalazine** et les **rétinoïdes** ▪ Néphrotoxicité additive lors de l'administration d'autres **médicaments néphrotoxiques** ▪ Aplasie médullaire additive lors de l'administration concomitante d'autres **antinéoplasiques** ou d'une **radiothérapie** ▪ La **radiothérapie** augmente le risque de nécrose des tissus mous et d'ostéonécrose ▪ Le méthotrexate peut diminuer la réponse des anticorps aux **vaccins à virus vivants** et augmenter le risque de réactions indésirables ▪ Risque accru de réactions neurologiques lors de l'administration concomitante d'**acyclovir** (voie intrathécale seulement) ▪ L'**asparaginase** peut diminuer les effets du méthotrexate ▪ L'administration concomitante de **léflunomide** augmente le risque de pancytopénie ▪ L'administration concomitante de **mercaptopurine** ou de **théophylline** peut élever la concentration plasmatique de ces agents.

Médicament-produits naturels: La consommation concomitante d'**échinacée** et de **mélatonine** peut entraver l'immunosuppression ▪ La **caféine** et le **guarana** peuvent diminuer l'efficacité du méthotrexate.

VOIES D'ADMINISTRATION ET POSOLOGIE

Néoplasmes trophoblastiques

- **PO, IM (adultes)**: De 15 à 30 mg par jour, pendant 5 jours; ce régime, en alternance avec des périodes sans traitement de 1 semaine ou plus, peut être répété de 3 à 5 fois.

Cancer du sein

- **IV (adultes)**: 40 mg/m^2 les 1er et 8e jours (en association avec d'autres agents; de nombreux régimes sont utilisés).
- **IV (adultes > 60 ans)**: réduire la dose à 30 mg/m^2.

Cancer de la tête et du cou

- **IV (adultes)**: De 40 à 200 mg/m^2 (en association avec d'autres agents; de nombreux autres régimes sont utilisés).

M

Cancer de l'estomac

- **IV (adultes)**: 1,5 g/m^2, le premier jour en association avec le 5-FU, la leucovorine et la doxorubicine, tous les 29 jours; répéter pendant 6 cycles de traitement.

Cancer de la vessie

- **PO, IM (adultes)**: 30 mg/m^2 les 1er et 8e jours (en association avec d'autres agents; de nombreux régimes sont utilisés).
- **PO, IM (adultes > 70 ans)**: Administrer 80 % de toutes les doses.

Leucémie lymphoïde aiguë

- **PO (adultes)**: *Traitement d'induction* – 3,3 mg/m^2 par jour, habituellement en même temps que la prednisone, seul ou en association avec d'autres agents.
- **PO, IM (adultes)**: *Traitement d'entretien* – 30 mg/m^2 par semaine, en 2 doses fractionnées, en association avec d'autres agents.
- **IV (adultes)**: *Traitement d'entretien* – 2,5 mg/kg, toutes les 2 semaines.

POUR L'ADMINISTRATION PAR VOIE INTRATHÉCALE, UTILISER TOUJOURS LA PRÉPARATION SANS AGENTS DE CONSERVATION.

M

- **Voie intrathécale (adultes)**: 12 mg/m^2 ou une dose maximale de 15 mg.
- **Voie intrathécale (enfants ≥ 3 ans)**: 12 mg.
- **Voie intrathécale (enfants de 2 ans)**: 10 mg.
- **Voie intrathécale (enfants de 1 an)**: 8 mg.
- **Voie intrathécale (enfants < 1 an)**: 6 mg.

Lymphome de Burkitt

- **PO (adultes)**: De 10 à 25 mg/jour, pendant 4 à 8 jours, puis une période de repos de 7 à 10 jours. Administration possible en association avec d'autres agents. *Lymphosarcome de stade III* – en association avec d'autres agents: de 0,625 à 2,5 mg/kg/jour.

Psoriasis

Le traitement peut être précédé par l'administration d'une dose d'essai de 5 à 10 mg.

- **IM ou IV (adultes)**: De 10 à 25 mg, 1 fois par semaine jusqu'à obtention de l'effet désiré.
- **PO (adultes)**: 2,5 mg, toutes les 12 heures, à raison de 3 doses par semaine (la dose peut être augmentée selon la réponse). Ne pas dépasser 30 mg par semaine.

Polyarthrite rhumatoïde

Le traitement peut être précédé par l'administration d'une dose d'essai de 5 à 10 mg.

- **PO (adultes)**: 7,5 mg, 1 fois par semaine (2,5 mg, toutes les 12 heures, jusqu'à concurrence de 3 doses ou une dose unique; la dose peut être augmentée selon la réponse). Ne pas dépasser 20 mg par semaine; lorsqu'on a obtenu une réponse, il faut réduire la dose.

Mycose fongoïde

- **PO (adultes)**: De 2,5 à 10 mg par jour, pendant plusieurs semaines ou mois.
- **IM (adultes)**: 50 mg, 1 fois par semaine, ou 25 mg, 2 fois par semaine.

Grossesse ectopique

- **IM (adultes)**: 50 mg/m^2 pour 1 dose *(usage non approuvé)*.

PRÉSENTATION (version générique disponible)

Comprimés: 2,5 mg^{Pr}, 10 mg^{Pr} ■ **Solution pour injection sans agents de conservation**: 10 mg/mL^{Pr}, 25 mg/mL^{Pr} (disponible en différents formats) ■ **Solution pour injection avec agents de conservation**: 25 mg/mL^{Pr} (disponible en différents formats).

SOINS INFIRMIERS

ÉVALUATION DE LA SITUATION

- Mesurer la pression artérielle, le pouls et la fréquence respiratoire à intervalles réguliers pendant toute la durée de l'administration. Informer le médecin de tout changement notable.
- Suivre de près les douleurs abdominales, la diarrhée ou la stomatite. Prévenir le médecin si ces symptômes surviennent, car ils peuvent dicter l'arrêt du traitement.
- Déceler l'apparition d'une aplasie médullaire. Suivre de près les saignements: saignement des gencives, ecchymose, pétéchies, présence de sang dans les selles, l'urine et les vomissements. Éviter les injections par voie IM et la prise de la température par voie rectale, si la numération thrombocytaire est basse. Appliquer une pression sur les points de ponction veineuse pendant au moins 10 minutes. Surveiller les signes d'infection en cas de neutropénie. L'anémie peut survenir. Suivre de près la fatigue accrue, la dyspnée et l'hypotension orthostatique.
- Effectuer le bilan quotidien des ingesta et des excreta et peser le patient tous les jours. Prévenir le médecin en cas de changements importants dans les valeurs totales.
- RESTER À L'AFFÛT DES SYMPTÔMES DE TOXICITÉ PULMONAIRE QUI PEUVENT SE MANIFESTER À UN STADE PRÉCOCE PAR UNE TOUX SÈCHE ET NON PRODUCTIVE.
- Observer l'apparition des symptômes suivants de goutte: élévation des concentrations d'acide urique,

douleurs articulaires et œdème. Inciter le patient à boire au moins 2 litres de liquides par jour si son état le permet. On peut administrer de l'allopurinol ou alcaliniser l'urine afin de diminuer les concentrations d'acide urique.

- Noter l'état nutritionnel du patient. Administrer un antiémétique avant le traitement et à intervalles réguliers pendant toute sa durée et adapter l'alimentation selon les aliments qu'il peut tolérer, pour maintenir l'équilibre hydroélectrolytique et l'apport nutritionnel.

Voie intrathécale: Suivre de près la rigidité de la nuque, les céphalées, la fièvre, la confusion, la somnolence, les étourdissements, la faiblesse ou les convulsions.

Polyarthrite rhumatoïde: Noter l'intensité de la douleur et l'amplitude des mouvements avant le début du traitement et à intervalles réguliers pendant toute sa durée.

Psoriasis: Évaluer les lésions cutanées avant le traitement et à intervalles réguliers pendant toute sa durée.

Tests de laboratoire:

- Noter la numération globulaire et la formule leucocytaire avant le traitement et à intervalles fréquents pendant toute sa durée. Le nadir de la leucopénie et de la thrombopénie survient en l'espace de 7 à 14 jours. Le nombre de leucocytes et de thrombocytes revient habituellement à la normale 7 jours après les nadirs. Prévenir le médecin en cas de chute soudaine des valeurs.
- Noter les résultats des tests des fonctions rénale (concentrations d'urée et de créatinine) et hépatique (concentrations d'AST, d'ALT, de bilirubine et de LDH), avant le début du traitement et à intervalles réguliers pendant toute sa durée. Suivre de près le pH de l'urine avant d'administrer des doses élevées de méthotrexate et toutes les 6 heures pendant la récupération par la leucovorine. Maintenir le pH de l'urine au-dessus de 7 pour prévenir les lésions rénales.
- Le méthotrexate peut entraîner l'élévation des concentrations sériques d'acide urique, particulièrement au cours du traitement initial de la leucémie et du lymphome.

Toxicité et surdosage:

- Lors d'un traitement à doses élevées, le patient doit recevoir un traitement de récupération par la leucovorine dans les 24 à 48 heures afin de prévenir une toxicité d'issue fatale. Suivre de près les concentrations sériques de méthotrexate toutes les 12 à 24 heures au cours du traitement par des doses élevées, jusqu'à ce que ces concentrations descendent en dessous de 0,05 µmol/L. Cette surveillance est essentielle pour établir la dose appropriée de leucovorine et la durée du traitement de récupération. L'alcalinisation des urines peut également être nécessaire.
- En cas de surdosage massif, il peut s'avérer nécessaire d'hydrater le patient et d'alcaliniser son urine afin de prévenir des lésions des tubules rénaux. Surveiller l'état hydroélectrolytique du patient. On peut recourir à une hémodialyse à l'aide d'un dialyseur à flux élevé pour favoriser l'élimination du médicament, jusqu'à ce que les concentrations soient < 0,05 µmol/L.

DIAGNOSTICS INFIRMIERS POSSIBLES

- Risque d'infection (Réactions indésirables).
- Alimentation déficiente (Réactions indésirables).
- Connaissances insuffisantes sur le traitement médicamenteux (Enseignement au patient et à ses proches).

INTERVENTIONS INFIRMIÈRES

Alerte clinique: Des décès sont survenus lors de certaines chimiothérapies. Avant d'administrer l'agent, clarifier tous les points ambigus. Vérifier la limite des doses unitaires et quotidiennes ainsi que la dose à administrer pendant le traitement. Demander à un autre professionnel de la santé de vérifier une fois de plus l'ordonnance d'origine, le calcul des doses et le réglage de la pompe à perfusion. Le méthotrexate est administré à plus petites doses, à intervalles moins fréquents et souvent 1 fois par semaine lorsqu'il est utilisé dans des indications non oncologiques. Ne pas confondre les doses oncologiques avec les doses non oncologiques de méthotrexate.

- Préparer les solutions pour injection sous une hotte à flux laminaire. Porter des gants, un vêtement protecteur et un masque pendant la manipulation du méthotrexate. Mettre au rebut le matériel dans les contenants réservés à cette fin (voir l'annexe H).

IV directe: Ne pas utiliser les préparations qui ont changé de couleur ou qui contiennent un précipité. Jeter toute portion inutilisée. Consulter les directives du fabricant avant de diluer la préparation.

Vitesse d'administration: Administrer à un débit de moins de 10 mg/min dans une tubulure en Y ou dans le robinet à trois voies d'une tubulure IV par laquelle s'écoule une solution compatible.

Perfusion intermittente ou continue: On peut diluer la préparation dans une solution de D5%E, de D5%/NaCl 0,9 % ou de NaCl 0,9 % et l'administrer sous forme de perfusion intermittente ou continue.

Vitesse d'administration: Administrer le méthotrexate à un débit de 4 à 20 mg à l'heure.

Compatibilité (tubulure en Y): amifostine ▪ amphotéricine B, cholestéryle d' ▪ asparaginase ▪ bléomycine ▪

M

céfépime ■ ceftriaxone ■ cimétidine ■ cisplatine ■ cyclophosphamide ■ cytarabine ■ daunorubicine ■ diphenhydramine ■ doxorubicine ■ doxorubicine liposomale ■ étoposide ■ famotidine ■ filgrastim ■ fludarabine ■ fluorouracile ■ furosémide ■ gallium, nitrate de ■ ganciclovir ■ granisétron ■ héparine ■ hydromorphone ■ imipénem/cilastatine ■ leucovorine ■ lorazépam ■ melphalan ■ mesna ■ méthylprednisolone, succinate sodique de ■ sargramostim ■ téniposide ■ thiotépa ■ vancomycine ■ vinblastine ■ vincristine ■ vinorelbine.

Incompatibilité (tubulure en Y): chlorpromazine ■ idarubicine ■ ifosfamide ■ midazolam ■ nalbuphine ■ prométhazine.

Compatibilité en addition au soluté: cyclophosphamide ■ cytarabine ■ fluorouracile ■ sodium, bicarbonate de.

Voie intrathécale: Diluer le méthotrexate sans agents de conservation avec une solution de NaCl 0,9 % sans agents de conservation, une solution B de Elliot ou avec le liquide céphalorachidien du patient jusqu'à l'obtention d'une concentration de 1 mg/mL. On peut administrer le méthotrexate par ponction lombaire ou par un réservoir d'Ommaya. Utiliser immédiatement la préparation afin de prévenir toute contamination bactérienne.

M

ENSEIGNEMENT AU PATIENT ET À SES PROCHES

- Conseiller au patient de suivre rigoureusement la posologie recommandée. S'il n'a pas pu prendre le médicament au moment habituel, il ne doit pas le prendre du tout. Lui recommander de prévenir un professionnel de la santé si les vomissements surviennent peu de temps après la prise du médicament.
- Recommander au patient de signaler rapidement à un professionnel de la santé la fièvre, les frissons, la toux, l'enrouement, les maux de gorge, les signes d'infection, les douleurs lombaires ou aux flancs, les mictions difficiles ou douloureuses, le saignement des gencives, la formation d'ecchymoses, les pétéchies, la présence de sang dans les selles, l'urine ou les vomissements, la fatigue accrue, la dyspnée ou l'hypotension orthostatique. Prévenir le patient qu'il doit éviter les foules et les personnes contagieuses. Lui conseiller d'utiliser une brosse à dents à poils doux et un rasoir électrique et de prendre garde aux chutes. Le prévenir qu'il ne doit pas prendre de boissons alcoolisées ni de préparations contenant de l'aspirine ou des AINS, en raison des risques d'hémorragie digestive.
- Recommander au patient d'examiner sa muqueuse buccale à la recherche d'érythème et d'aphtes. En présence d'aphtes, lui recommander de remplacer la brosse à dents par une brosse-éponge et de se rincer la bouche avec de l'eau après avoir bu ou mangé. Il peut utiliser un médicament topique si la douleur buccale l'empêche de s'alimenter. La douleur associée à la stomatite peut dicter le traitement par un analgésique opioïde.
- Conseiller au patient de consulter un professionnel de la santé avant de prendre des médicaments en vente libre ou des produits naturels.
- Prévenir le patient que le méthotrexate peut avoir des effets tératogènes. Lui conseiller de prendre des mesures de contraception pendant toute la durée du traitement et pendant au moins 3 mois (hommes) ou un cycle ovulatoire (femmes) après l'avoir arrêté.
- Expliquer au patient qu'il risque de perdre ses cheveux; explorer avec lui les stratégies lui permettant de s'adapter à ce changement.
- Prévenir le patient qu'il ne doit pas se faire vacciner sans recommandation expresse d'un professionnel de la santé.
- Recommander au patient d'utiliser un écran solaire et de porter des vêtements protecteurs afin de prévenir les réactions de photosensibilité.
- Insister sur l'importance des tests de laboratoire à intervalles réguliers permettant de suivre de près les effets secondaires du médicament.

VÉRIFICATION DE L'EFFICACITÉ THÉRAPEUTIQUE

L'efficacité du traitement peut être démontrée par: l'amélioration des paramètres hématopoïétiques en cas de leucémie ■ la diminution des symptômes d'atteinte méningée en présence de leucémie ■ la diminution de la taille des lymphomes non hodgkiniens et d'autres tumeurs solides et de la propagation des métastases ■ la cicatrisation des lésions cutanées en cas de psoriasis grave ■ la diminution des douleurs articulaires et de l'œdème et l'amélioration de la mobilité chez les patients souffrant de polyarthrite rhumatoïde ■ la régression des lésions en cas de mycose fongoïde. ✳

MÉTHOTRIMÉPRAZINE

Apo-Methoprazine, Novo-Meprazine, Nozinan, PMS-Méthotriméprazine, Riva-Meprazine

CLASSIFICATION:

Antipsychotique (phénothiazine), antiémétique

Grossesse – catégorie C

INDICATIONS

Traitement des troubles psychotiques ■ Traitement des troubles accompagnés d'angoisse, d'anxiété et de tension. **Usages non approuvés**: Traitement de la douleur ■ Potentialisation de l'anesthésie ■ Sédation et analgésie préopératoires et postopératoires ■ Traitement de l'insomnie ■ Prévention des nausées et des vomissements d'origine centrale.

MÉCANISME D'ACTION

Modification des effets de la dopamine dans le SNC ■ Suppression des influx sensoriels entraînant l'élévation du seuil de la douleur ■ Induction de l'amnésie ■ Blocage des récepteurs alpha-adrénergiques, d'où risque d'hypotension orthostatique. ***Effets thérapeutiques:*** Réduction de l'intensité de la douleur ■ Potentialisation de l'anesthésie ■ Sédation ■ Diminution des signes et des symptômes de psychose ■ Soulagement de l'anxiété et de l'angoisse ■ Soulagement des nausées et des vomissements.

PHARMACOCINÉTIQUE

Absorption: Bonne (PO et IM).
Distribution: La méthotriméprazine pénètre dans le liquide céphalorachidien et traverse la barrière placentaire. Elle passe en quantités minimes dans le lait maternel.
Métabolisme et excrétion: Métabolisme majoritairement hépatique. Certains métabolites sont actifs. 1 % est excrété à l'état inchangé par les reins.
Demi-vie: De 15 à 30 heures.

Profil temps-action (effet analgésique)

	DÉBUT D'ACTION	PIC	DURÉE
IM	inconnu	20 – 40 min	4 h

CONTRE-INDICATIONS, PRÉCAUTIONS ET MISES EN GARDE

Contre-indications: Hypersensibilité aux phénothiazines ou aux sulfites ■ États de coma ou de dépression du SNC dus à l'alcool, aux hypnotiques, aux analgésiques et aux opioïdes ■ Maladies rénale, cardiaque ou hépatique graves ■ Dyscrasie sanguine.
Précautions et mises en garde: Antécédents de convulsions ■ Antécédents de surdose de dépresseurs du SNC ■ **OBST.**: Risque de travail prématuré, utiliser avec prudence principalement pendant le 1er trimestre. Utiliser seulement si les avantages pour la patiente dépassent les risques pour le fœtus ■ **ALLAITEMENT**: L'innocuité du médicament n'a pas été établie ■ Administration prolongée (> 30 jours) ■ **GÉR.**: Il est recommandé de réduire la dose initiale chez les personnes âgées ou débilitées ■ Glaucome ■ Hyperplasie bénigne de la prostate ■ Hypotension.

RÉACTIONS INDÉSIRABLES ET EFFETS SECONDAIRES

SNC: somnolence, sédation excessive, amnésie, désorientation, euphorie, céphalées, faiblesse, troubles de l'élocution, réactions extrapyramidales incluant le SYNDROME MALIN DES NEUROLEPTIQUES, dyskinésie tardive, CONVULSIONS.

ORLO: congestion nasale.

CV: hypotension orthostatique, tachycardie, bradycardie, palpitations.

GI: gêne abdominale, sécheresse de la bouche (xérostomie), nausées, vomissements.

GU: difficultés de miction.

Locaux: douleur au point d'injection.

Métab.: gain pondéral.

Divers: frissons.

INTERACTIONS

Médicament-médicament: Dépression additive du SNC lors de l'usage concomitant d'autres **dépresseurs du SNC** incluant l'**alcool**, les **antihistaminiques**, les **antidépresseurs**, les **analgésiques opioïdes** et les **hypnosédatifs** (réduire les doses de barbituriques ou d'opioïdes d'au moins la moitié lors d'une administration concomitante) ■ Effets anticholinergiques additifs lors de l'administration concomitante d'**antihistaminiques**, d'**antidépresseurs**, de **phénothiazines**, de **quinidine**, de **disopyramide**, d'**atropine** ou de **scopolamine** (réduire les doses d'atropine ou de scopolamine, administrées en concomitance) ■ La méthotriméprazine renverse les effets vasopresseurs de l'**adrénaline** (éviter l'usage concomitant; s'il faut administrer un vasopresseur, opter pour la phényléphrine, la méthoxamine ou la noradrénaline) ■ Hypotension additive lors de l'ingestion d'**alcool** ou de l'administration concomitante de **dérivés nitrés**, d'**IMAO** ou d'**antihypertenseurs** ■ Risque d'allongement de l'intervalle QT. Utiliser avec précaution lors de l'administration concomitante de **médicaments pouvant allonger l'intervalle QT**.

M

VOIES D'ADMINISTRATION ET POSOLOGIE

Psychoses, douleurs intenses

- **IM (adultes)**: De 75 à 100 mg, en 3 ou 4 injections.
- **PO (adultes)**: Initialement, de 50 à 75 mg par jour, en 2 ou 3 prises fractionnées; augmenter jusqu'à l'obtention de l'effet désiré (on peut administrer 1 g et plus par jour).

Prémédication, douleurs postopératoires
- **IM (adultes)**: De 10 à 25 mg, toutes les 8 heures. La dernière dose de la prémédication, administrée 1 heure avant l'intervention chirurgicale, peut être de 25 à 50 mg.
- **PO (adultes)**: De 20 à 40 mg, toutes les 8 heures.

Potentialisation de l'anesthésie
- **IV (adultes)**: De 10 à 25 mg en perfusion pendant l'intervention chirurgicale ou pendant le travail.

Insomnie
- **PO (adultes)**: De 10 à 25 mg le soir, au coucher.

Angoisse, anxiété, douleurs modérées
- **PO (adultes)**: Initialement, de 6 à 25 mg par jour, en 3 prises fractionnées lors des repas; augmenter par paliers pour atteindre la dose efficace.
- **PO (enfants)**: Initialement, 0,25 mg/kg par jour, en 2 ou 3 prises fractionnées; cette dose peut être augmentée graduellement jusqu'à l'atteinte de la dose efficace. Ne pas dépasser 40 mg par jour chez l'enfant < 12 ans.
- **IM (enfants)**: De 0,0625 à 0,125 mg/kg par jour en 1 ou plusieurs injections.
- **IV (enfants)**: 0,0625 mg/kg en perfusion lente pendant l'intervention chirurgicale.

M

PRÉSENTATION

Comprimés: 2 mg^Pr^, 5 mg^Pr^, 25 mg^Pr^, 50 mg^Pr^ ■ **Solution injectable**: 25 mg/mL^Pr^ ■ **Liquide oral**: 5 mg/mL^Pr^ ■ **Gouttes orales**: 40 mg/mL^Pr^.

SOINS INFIRMIERS

ÉVALUATION DE LA SITUATION

- Déterminer le type de douleur, son siège et son intensité, avant l'administration du médicament et 30 minutes plus tard.
- Déterminer, avant le traitement et à intervalles réguliers pendant toute sa durée, l'état de conscience du patient (délire, hallucinations, comportement).
- Mesurer le pouls et la pression artérielle (en position assise, couchée et debout) avant l'administration initiale et à intervalles fréquents pendant la période d'adaptation de la posologie.
- Observer attentivement le patient pendant qu'il prend le médicament pour s'assurer qu'il l'a bien avalé.
- Surveiller l'apparition des symptômes extrapyramidaux suivants: akathisie – agitation; dystonie – spasmes musculaires et mouvements de contorsion; pseudoparkinsonisme – faciès figé, rigidité, tremblements, bouche ouverte laissant s'échapper la salive (sialorrhée), démarche traînante et dysphagie. Signaler immédiatement à un professionnel de la santé l'apparition de ces symptômes, car une réduction de la dose ou l'arrêt du traitement pourraient s'imposer. Le médecin pourrait également prescrire un agent antiparkinsonien (trihexiphénidyle, benztropine) pour maîtriser ces symptômes.
- Suivre de près l'apparition de la dyskinésie tardive qui se traduit par des mouvements rythmiques de la bouche, du visage et des membres. Avertir immédiatement un professionnel de la santé si ces symptômes se manifestent, car de tels effets secondaires peuvent être irréversibles.
- Noter la fréquence et la consistance des selles. La consommation accrue de fibres alimentaires et de liquides peut aider à réduire la constipation.
- La méthotriméprazine abaisse le seuil de convulsion. Prendre les précautions de mise dans le cas des patients ayant des antécédents de troubles convulsifs.
- SURVEILLER L'APPARITION DU SYNDROME MALIN DES NEUROLEPTIQUES SE MANIFESTANT PAR LES SYMPTÔMES SUIVANTS: FIÈVRE, DÉTRESSE RESPIRATOIRE, TACHYCARDIE, CONVULSIONS, DIAPHORÈSE, HYPERTENSION OU HYPOTENSION, PÂLEUR, FATIGUE. SIGNALER IMMÉDIATEMENT À UN PROFESSIONNEL DE LA SANTÉ L'APPARITION DE CES SYMPTÔMES.

Tests de laboratoire:
- Noter la numération globulaire et la formule leucocytaire avant le traitement et à intervalles réguliers pendant toute sa durée.
- Examiner les résultats des tests de la fonction hépatique avant le traitement et à intervalles réguliers pendant toute sa durée lors d'un traitement prolongé (> 30 jours).

DIAGNOSTICS INFIRMIERS POSSIBLES

- Douleur aiguë (Indications).
- Risque d'accident (Réactions indésirables).
- Connaissances insuffisantes sur le traitement médicamenteux (Enseignement au patient et à ses proches).

INTERVENTIONS INFIRMIÈRES

- Pour prévenir la dermatite de contact, éviter les éclaboussures de la solution injectable sur les mains.
- L'administration des phénothiazines devrait être arrêtée 48 heures avant la myélographie par le métrizamide et reprise seulement 24 heures plus tard, car ces agents abaissent le seuil de convulsion.

IM: Ne pas injecter la solution par voie SC. Injecter lentement et profondément dans un muscle bien développé. Assurer la rotation des points d'injection.

IV: Diluer la dose dans 250 mL (enfants) ou 500 mL (adultes) d'une solution de D5%E. Consulter les directives de chaque fabricant avant d'administrer la préparation.

Vitesse d'administration: Administrer lentement à un débit de 20 à 40 gouttes par minute.

Associations compatibles dans la même seringue: atropine ▪ scopolamine.

ENSEIGNEMENT AU PATIENT ET À SES PROCHES

- Expliquer au patient ce qu'on entend par administration sur demande et à quel moment il doit réclamer l'analgésique.
- Conseiller au patient de changer lentement de position et de rester couché pendant 6 à 12 heures après l'administration de la méthotriméprazine injectable afin de diminuer le risque d'hypotension orthostatique.
- Prévenir le patient que la méthotriméprazine peut provoquer de la somnolence. Lui recommander de demander de l'aide lorsqu'il se déplace, de ne pas conduire et d'éviter les activités qui exigent sa vigilance jusqu'à ce qu'on ait la certitude que le médicament n'entraîne pas cet effet chez lui.
- Recommander au patient d'éviter de boire de l'alcool et de ne pas prendre de dépresseurs du SNC en concomitance avec la méthotriméprazine.

PO: Conseiller au patient de respecter rigoureusement la posologie recommandée. S'il n'a pas pu prendre le médicament au moment habituel, il doit le prendre dès que possible, jusqu'à 1 heure avant l'heure prévue pour la dose suivante. Chez les patients suivant un traitement prolongé avec de fortes doses, un arrêt graduel de la médication pourrait s'avérer nécessaire afin de prévenir l'apparition des symptômes suivants de sevrage: dyskinésie, tremblements, étourdissements, nausées et vomissements.

- Mettre en garde le patient contre le risque d'apparition de symptômes extrapyramidaux ou d'une dyskinésie tardive. L'inciter à avertir immédiatement un professionnel de la santé si ces symptômes se manifestent.
- Conseiller à la patiente de prendre des mesures contraceptives et de prévenir un professionnel de la santé si elle pense être enceinte.
- Insister sur l'importance des examens réguliers de suivi, des examens de la vue, des tests diagnostiques et d'une psychothérapie.
- Recommander au patient qui doit suivre un autre traitement ou subir une intervention chirurgicale de prévenir le professionnel de la santé qu'il suit un traitement par ce médicament.
- Expliquer au patient qu'il peut soulager la sécheresse de la bouche en se rinçant souvent la bouche, en pratiquant une bonne hygiène buccale et en consommant des bonbons ou de la gomme à mâcher sans sucre.
- Conseiller au patient de prévenir rapidement un professionnel de la santé en cas de maux de gorge, de fièvre, de saignements ou d'ecchymoses inhabituels, de rash, de faiblesse, de tremblements, d'urine de couleur foncée ou de selles couleur de glaise.

VÉRIFICATION DE L'EFFICACITÉ THÉRAPEUTIQUE

L'efficacité du traitement peut être démontrée par: la diminution de l'intensité de la douleur ▪ la sédation ▪ la potentialisation de l'anesthésie ▪ un moindre recours à un comportement excitable ou paranoïaque et au repli sur soi ▪ le soulagement de l'anxiété et de l'angoisse ▪ le soulagement des nausées et des vomissements.

MÉTHYLDOPA

Aldomet, Apo-Methyldopa, Novo-Medopa, Nu-Medopa

CLASSIFICATION:

Antihypertenseur (agoniste alpha-adrénergique à action centrale)

Grossesse – catégorie B

M

INDICATIONS

Traitement de l'hypertension de divers degrés (en monothérapie ou en association avec d'autres agents) ▪ Traitement de l'hypertension gravidique.

MÉCANISME D'ACTION

Stimulation des récepteurs alpha-adrénergiques centraux entraînant la diminution du débit sympathique vers le cœur, les reins et les vaisseaux sanguins. L'effet global est une diminution de la pression artérielle et de la résistance périphérique et une légère baisse de la fréquence cardiaque, sans modification du débit cardiaque. ***Effets thérapeutiques:*** Abaissement de la pression artérielle.

PHARMACOCINÉTIQUE

Absorption: 50 % (PO).

Distribution: L'agent traverse la barrière hémato-encéphalique et placentaire et passe en faibles quantités dans le lait maternel.

Métabolisme et excrétion: Métabolisme hépatique (50 %). Excrétion rénale (70 %) et fécale (30 %).
Demi-vie: 1,7 heure.

Profil temps-action (effet antihypertenseur)

	DÉBUT D'ACTION	PIC	DURÉE
PO	3-6 h	6-9 h	24-48 h

CONTRE-INDICATIONS, PRÉCAUTIONS ET MISES EN GARDE

Contre-indications: Hypersensibilité ■ Maladie hépatique active ■ Antécédents de troubles hépatiques ou anémie hémolytique induits par un traitement antérieur par la méthyldopa ■ Traitement concomitant par un IMAO.

Précautions et mises en garde: Antécédents de maladie hépatique ■ Insuffisance rénale ■ **GÉR.**: Il est recommandé de diminuer la dose chez les personnes âgées ou débilitées (risque accru de réactions indésirables).

RÉACTIONS INDÉSIRABLES ET EFFETS SECONDAIRES

M

SNC: sédation, perte de l'acuité mentale, dépression.
ORLO: congestion nasale.
CV: MYOCARDITE, bradycardie, œdème, hypotension orthostatique.
GI: HÉPATITE MÉDICAMENTEUSE, diarrhée, sécheresse de la bouche (xérostomie).
GU: impuissance.
Hémat.: éosinophilie, anémie hémolytique.
Divers: fièvre.

INTERACTIONS

Médicament-médicament: Hypotension additive lors de l'administration concomitante d'autres **antihypertenseurs** et de **dérivés nitrés**, lors de l'**anesthésie** ou lors de l'ingestion de grandes quantités d'**alcool** ■ Les **amphétamines**, les **barbituriques**, les **antidépresseurs tricycliques**, les **anti-inflammatoires non stéroïdiens** et les **phénothiazines**, administrés en concomitance, peuvent réduire l'effet antihypertenseur de la méthyldopa ■ Effets accrus et risque de psychose en cas d'administration concomitante d'**halopéridol** ■ Une stimulation excessive du système sympathique peut survenir lors de l'administration concomitante d'**IMAO** ou d'**agents sympathomimétiques** ■ Risque de potentialisation des effets du **tolbutamide** ■ La méthyldopa peut aggraver la toxicité reliée au **lithium** ■ Hypotension additive et effets toxiques sur le SNC lors de l'administration concomitante de **lévodopa** ■ Risque de dépression additive du SNC en cas d'administration concomitante d'**antihistaminiques**, d'**hypnosédatifs**, de certains **antidépresseurs** et d'**opioïdes**, ainsi qu'en cas d'ingestion d'**alcool** ■ L'usage concomitant de **bêtabloquants non sélectifs** peut, dans de rares cas, entraîner une hypertension paradoxale ■ L'administration concomitante de **fer** diminue l'absorption de la méthyldopa (administrer cette dernière 2 heures avant ou 6 heures après le fer).

VOIES D'ADMINISTRATION ET POSOLOGIE

- **PO (adultes)**: 250 mg, 2 ou 3 fois par jour (ne pas dépasser 500 mg par jour en cas d'administration concomitante d'antihypertenseurs autres que des diurétiques thiazidiques); la dose peut être augmentée ou diminuée tous les 2 jours, selon la réponse au traitement et la tolérance du patient; la posologie d'entretien habituelle est de 500 mg à 2 g par jour, administrée en 2 à 4 doses fractionnées (ne pas dépasser 3 g par jour).
- **PO (personnes âgées ou débilitées)**: 125 mg, 2 fois par jour; la dose peut être augmentée par paliers de 125 mg tous les 2 ou 3 jours, selon la réponse au traitement et la tolérance du patient (ne pas dépasser 1 g par jour).
- **PO (enfants)**: 10 mg/kg par jour, en 2 à 4 prises; la dose peut être augmentée ou diminuée tous les 2 jours (choisir comme posologie maximale 65 mg/kg/jour ou 3 g par jour, selon celle qui est la plus basse).

INSUFFISANCE RÉNALE

- **PO (ADULTES)**: CL_{CR} > *50 mL/MIN* – ADMINISTRER LES DOSES À INTERVALLE DE 8 HEURES; CL_{CR} *DE 10 À 50 mL/MIN* – ADMINISTRER LES DOSES À INTERVALLE DE 8 À 12 HEURES; CL_{CR} < *10 mL/MIN* – ADMINISTRER LES DOSES À INTERVALLE DE 12 À 24 HEURES.

PRÉSENTATION (version générique disponible)

Comprimés: 125 mg[Pr], 250 mg[Pr], 500 mg[Pr].

SOINS INFIRMIERS

ÉVALUATION DE LA SITUATION

- Mesurer la pression artérielle et le pouls à intervalles fréquents au cours de la période initiale d'adaptation de la posologie et à intervalles réguliers pendant toute la durée du traitement. Signaler tout changement important.
- Surveiller la fréquence du renouvellement des ordonnances pour déterminer l'observance du traitement.
- Effectuer le bilan quotidien des ingesta et des excreta, peser le patient tous les jours; suivre quotidiennement la formation d'œdème, particulièrement au début du traitement. Prévenir un professionnel de la santé en cas de gain de poids ou d'œdème, car la

rétention du sodium et de l'eau peut être traitée par des diurétiques.

- Suivre de près la dépression ou d'autres modifications de l'état de conscience. Prévenir immédiatement un professionnel de la santé si ces symptômes se manifestent.
- MESURER LA TEMPÉRATURE DU PATIENT TOUT AU LONG DU TRAITEMENT. LA FIÈVRE PEUT SURVENIR PEU APRÈS L'AMORCE DU TRAITEMENT ET PEUT S'ACCOMPAGNER D'UNE ÉOSINOPHILIE ET DE MODIFICATIONS DE LA FONCTION HÉPATIQUE. SUIVRE LES RÉSULTATS DES TESTS DE LA FONCTION HÉPATIQUE EN CAS DE FIÈVRE INEXPLIQUÉE.

Tests de laboratoire:

- Vérifier les résultats des tests des fonctions rénale et hépatique et noter la numération globulaire avant le début du traitement et à intervalles réguliers pendant toute sa durée.
- Vérifier les résultats du test de Coombs direct avant le traitement, après 6 et 12 mois de traitement et à intervalles réguliers par la suite. La méthyldopa peut positiver le test de Coombs, mais il s'agit rarement d'un signe d'anémie hémolytique.
- La méthyldopa peut entraîner l'élévation des concentrations sériques d'urée, de créatinine, de potassium, de sodium, de prolactine, d'acide urique, d'AST, d'ALT, de phosphatase alcaline et de bilirubine.
- La méthyldopa peut prolonger le temps de prothrombine.

DIAGNOSTICS INFIRMIERS POSSIBLES

- Risque d'accident (Effets secondaires).
- Connaissances insuffisantes sur le traitement médicamenteux (Enseignement au patient et à ses proches).
- Non-observance du traitement médicamenteux (Enseignement au patient et à ses proches).

INTERVENTIONS INFIRMIÈRES

- NE PAS CONFONDRE LA MÉTHYLDOPA AVEC LA LÉVODOPA.
- La rétention hydrique et l'expansion du volume vasculaire peuvent entraîner une tolérance aux effets du médicament, qui surviendra dans les 2 à 3 mois qui suivent le début du traitement. On peut ajouter des diurétiques au traitement à ce moment-là afin de continuer à maîtriser l'hypertension.
- Majorer la dose de médicament dans la soirée afin de diminuer la somnolence diurne.

ENSEIGNEMENT AU PATIENT ET À SES PROCHES

- Expliquer au patient qu'il doit continuer à prendre le médicament même s'il se sent bien. Lui recommander de prendre le médicament tous les jours à la même heure; la dernière dose de la journée devrait être prise au coucher. S'il n'a pu prendre le médicament au moment habituel, il doit le prendre aussitôt que possible à moins que ce ne soit presque l'heure prévue pour la dose suivante. Le prévenir qu'il ne faut jamais remplacer une dose manquée par une double dose.
- Inciter le patient à appliquer d'autres mesures d'abaissement de l'hypertension: perdre du poids, réduire sa consommation de sel, faire régulièrement de l'exercice, cesser de fumer, boire de l'alcool avec modération et diminuer le stress. Lui expliquer que la méthyldopa stabilise la pression artérielle mais ne guérit pas l'hypertension.
- Enseigner au patient et à ses proches la méthode de prise de la pression artérielle. Leur demander de mesurer la pression artérielle au moins 1 fois par semaine et de prévenir un professionnel de la santé si des changements importants surviennent.
- Prévenir le patient que son urine peut devenir foncée ou virer au rouge-noir lorsqu'on la laisse décanter.
- Prévenir le patient que la méthyldopa peut provoquer de la somnolence. Lui conseiller de ne pas conduire et d'éviter les activités qui exigent sa vigilance jusqu'à ce qu'on ait la certitude que le médicament n'entraîne pas cet effet chez lui. La somnolence disparaît habituellement après 7 à 10 jours de traitement continu.
- Conseiller au patient de changer lentement de position afin de réduire le risque d'hypotension orthostatique.
- Conseiller au patient de pratiquer une bonne hygiène buccale, de se rincer la bouche fréquemment avec de l'eau et de consommer de la gomme à mâcher ou des bonbons sans sucre pour diminuer la sécheresse de la bouche. Si la sécheresse de la bouche persiste pendant plus de 2 semaines, l'inciter à consulter un professionnel de la santé.
- Recommander au patient d'éviter de boire de l'alcool et de ne pas prendre d'autres dépresseurs du SNC en même temps que la méthyldopa.
- Conseiller au patient de consulter un professionnel de la santé avant de prendre un médicament contre la toux, le rhume ou les allergies.
- Recommander au patient qui doit suivre un autre traitement ou subir une intervention chirurgicale de prévenir le professionnel de la santé qu'il suit un traitement par ce médicament.
- Recommander au patient de signaler à un professionnel de la santé les symptômes suivants: fièvre, douleurs musculaires ou syndrome pseudogrippal.

VÉRIFICATION DE L'EFFICACITÉ THÉRAPEUTIQUE

L'efficacité du traitement peut être démontrée par: la baisse de la pression artérielle sans apparition d'effets indésirables.

MÉTHYLPHÉNIDATE

Concerta, Apo-Méthylphénidate, Biphentin, Novo-Méthylphénidate, PMS-Méthylphénidate, Ratio-Méthylphénidate, Ritalin, Ritalin-SR

CLASSIFICATION:
Stimulant du SNC

Grossesse – catégorie C

INDICATIONS

Traitement d'appoint du trouble déficitaire de l'attention avec hyperactivité ■ Traitement symptomatique de la narcolepsie. **Usages non approuvés:** Traitement de certaines formes de dépression lorsqu'on ne peut utiliser des antidépresseurs classiques.

MÉCANISME D'ACTION

Stimulation du SNC et de l'appareil respiratoire, avec faible activité sympathomimétique. ***Effets thérapeutiques:*** Prolongation de la durée de la concentration en cas de trouble déficitaire de l'attention avec hyperactivité ■ Augmentation de l'activité motrice et de la vigilance et diminution de la fatigue chez les patients narcoleptiques.

PHARMACOCINÉTIQUE

Absorption: Bonne (PO), bien que l'absorption des comprimés à libération prolongée (SR) soit retardée. *Concerta, Biphentin:* libération biphasique permettant d'obtenir un premier pic de la concentration, environ 1 heure après l'administration, puis une augmentation graduelle pendant les 5 à 9 heures suivantes.

Distribution: Inconnue.

Métabolisme et excrétion: Métabolisme hépatique à 80 %.

Demi-vie: De 2 à 4 heures.

Profil temps-action (stimulation du SNC)

	DÉBUT D'ACTION	PIC	DURÉE
PO	inconnu	1 - 3 h	4 - 6 h
PO - LP †	inconnu	4 - 7 h	3 - 12 h

† LP = libération prolongée.

CONTRE-INDICATIONS, PRÉCAUTIONS ET MISES EN GARDE

Contre-indications: Hypersensibilité ■ États d'hyperexcitation ■ Hyperthyroïdie ■ Personnalités psychotiques, patients ayant manifesté des tendances suicidaires ou homicides ■ Glaucome ■ Tics moteurs ■ Tachyarythmies ■ Angine de poitrine grave ■ Usage concomitant ou récent (< 14 jours) d'IMAO.

Précautions et mises en garde: Antécédents de maladie cardiovasculaire ■ Hypertension ■ Diabète ■ **GÉR.:** L'innocuité du médicament chez les personnes âgées ou débilitées n'a pas été établie ■ Usage continu (risque de dépendance psychologique ou physique) ■ Troubles convulsifs (le médicament peut abaisser le seuil convulsif) ■ **OBST., ALLAITEMENT:** L'innocuité du médicament n'a pas été établie ■ **PÉD.:** Risque de suppression de la croissance en cas d'une utilisation prolongée ■ *Concerta* devrait être utilisé avec prudence chez les patients présentant un rétrécissement ou une occlusion des voies digestives (risque accru d'occlusion).

RÉACTIONS INDÉSIRABLES ET EFFETS SECONDAIRES

SNC: hyperactivité, insomnie, agitation, tremblements, étourdissements, céphalées, irritabilité.

ORLO: vision trouble.

CV: hypertension, palpitations, tachycardie, hypotension.

GI: anorexie, constipation, crampes, diarrhée, sécheresse de la bouche (xérostomie), goût métallique, nausées, vomissements.

Tég.: rash.

SN: akathisie, dyskinésie.

Divers: fièvre, réactions d'hypersensibilité, dépendance physique, dépendance psychologique, arrêt du gain pondéral (enfants), tolérance aux effets du médicament.

INTERACTIONS

Médicament-médicament: Effets sympathomimétiques additifs lors de l'administration concomitante d'autres **agents sympathomimétiques**, incluant les **vasoconstricteurs** et les **décongestionnants** ■ L'usage concomitant d'**IMAO** ou de **vasopresseurs** peut déclencher une crise hypertensive (l'utilisation concomitante ou dans les 14 jours précédents est une contre-indication) ■ Risque d'inhibition du métabolisme de la **warfarine**, des **anticonvulsivants**, des **antidépresseurs tricycliques** et des **inhibiteurs sélectifs du recaptage de la sérotonine** et d'intensification de leurs effets ■ Le **pimozide**, administré en concomitance, peut masquer la cause des tics (éviter l'usage concomitant) ■ L'utilisation concomitante de la **clonidine** peut entraîner des modifications importantes sur l'ÉCG (diminuer la dose de méthylphénidate de 40 %).

Médicament-aliments: La consommation excessive d'aliments ou de boissons contenant de la **caféine** (**café**, **boissons à base de cola**, **thé**) peut entraîner une stimulation additive du SNC.

Médicament-produits naturels: Les produits contenant de la **caféine** (**café**, **cola**, **guarana**, **maté**, **thé**) peuvent intensifier les effets stimulants ■ Le **millepertuis** peut augmenter les effets indésirables graves (l'usage concomitant est déconseillé).

VOIES D'ADMINISTRATION ET POSOLOGIE

- **PO (adultes):** De 5 à 20 mg, 2 ou 3 fois par jour. Une fois la dose d'entretien établie, on peut passer à la préparation à libération prolongée, à raison de 20 mg, de 1 à 3 fois par jour, à intervalles de 8 heures.
  Biphentin: 10 mg ou 0,25 mg/kg, 1 fois par jour. La dose peut être majorée par paliers de 10 mg par semaine jusqu'à une dose de 1 mg/kg (maximum: 80 mg).
- **PO (enfants > 6 ans):** 5 mg, avant le petit-déjeuner et le dîner; augmenter par paliers de 5 à 10 mg à des intervalles hebdomadaires (ne pas dépasser 60 mg par jour). Une fois la dose d'entretien établie, on peut passer à la préparation à libération prolongée, à raison de 20 mg, de 1 à 3 fois par jour, à intervalles de 8 heures.
  Concerta: *Patients n'ayant jamais pris de méthylphénidate* – 18 mg, 1 fois par jour. La dose peut être majorée jusqu'à un maximum de 54 mg, 1 fois par jour. *Patients recevant déjà du méthylphénidate* – 18 mg, 1 fois par jour, si le patient prenait 5 mg, 2 ou 3 fois par jour, ou 20 mg par jour de la préparation libération prolongée; 36 mg, 1 fois par jour, si le patient prenait 10 mg, 2 ou 3 fois par jour, ou 40 mg par jour de la préparation à libération prolongée; 54 mg, 1 fois par jour, si le patient prenait 15 mg, 2 ou 3 fois par jour, ou 60 mg par jour de la préparation à libération prolongée.
  Biphentin: *Patients n'ayant jamais pris de méthylphénidate* – 10 mg, 1 fois par jour, jusqu'à 0,3 mg/kg, 1 fois par jour. La dose peut être majorée par paliers de 10 mg par semaine jusqu'à une dose maximum de 1 mg/kg/jour (maximum: 60 mg). *Patients recevant déjà du méthylphénidate* – la dose quotidienne de méthylphénidate à libération immédiate peut être donnée en dose uniquotidienne, le matin.

PRÉSENTATION
(version générique disponible)

Comprimés: 5 mg^{C}, 10 mg^{C}, 20 mg^{C} ■ **Comprimés à libération prolongée (Ritalin SR):** 20 mg^{C} ■ **Comprimés 12 heures (Concerta):** 18 mg^{C}, 27 mg^{C}, 36 mg^{C}, 54 mg^{C} ■ **Capsules à libération prolongée (Biphentin):** 10 mg^{C}, 15 mg^{C}, 20 mg^{C}, 30 mg^{C}, 40 mg^{C}, 50 mg^{C}, 60 mg^{C}.

SOINS INFIRMIERS

ÉVALUATION DE LA SITUATION

- Mesurer la pression artérielle, le pouls et la fréquence respiratoire avant l'administration et à intervalles réguliers pendant toute la durée du traitement.

PÉD.: Suivre de près la croissance en mesurant la taille et le poids de l'enfant qui suit un traitement prolongé.

- Le méthylphénidate peut provoquer un faux sentiment d'euphorie et de bien-être. Prévoir des repos fréquents et suivre de près l'apparition d'une dépression rebond, une fois les effets du médicament dissipés.
- L'usage du méthylphénidate comporte des risques élevés de dépendance et d'abus. La tolérance survient rapidement; ne pas augmenter la dose.

Trouble déficitaire de l'attention avec hyperactivité: PÉD.: Noter la durée de l'attention, la maîtrise des impulsions et les interactions de l'enfant avec autrui. On peut interrompre le traitement pendant un certain temps afin de déterminer si les symptômes sont suffisamment graves pour en justifier la poursuite.

Narcolepsie: Observer la fréquence des épisodes de narcolepsie et les consigner dans les dossiers.

Tests de laboratoire: Mesurer la numération globulaire et plaquettaire ainsi que la formule leucocytaire à intervalles réguliers chez les patients qui reçoivent un traitement prolongé.

DIAGNOSTICS INFIRMIERS POSSIBLES

- Opérations de la pensée perturbées (Effets secondaires).
- Connaissances insuffisantes sur le traitement médicamenteux (Enseignement au patient et à ses proches).

INTERVENTIONS INFIRMIÈRES

- Administrer le médicament avec ou après un repas. LES COMPRIMÉS À LIBÉRATION PROLONGÉE (RITALIN SR, CONCERTA) DEVRAIENT ÊTRE AVALÉS TELS QUELS SANS LES BRISER, ÉCRASER OU CROQUER. ON PEUT OUVRIR LES CAPSULES À LIBÉRATION PROLONGÉE (BIPHENTIN) ET EN SAUPOUDRER LE CONTENU SUR DES ALIMENTS, MAIS IL NE FAUT PAS LES ÉCRASER NI LES CROQUER. On doit s'assurer que le patient prend toute la quantité de nourriture sur laquelle on a saupoudré le contenu de la capsule, immédiatement après l'avoir préparée. Ne pas préparer à l'avance.

M

ENSEIGNEMENT AU PATIENT ET À SES PROCHES

- Conseiller au patient de suivre rigoureusement la posologie recommandée. S'il n'a pas pu prendre le médicament au moment habituel, il devrait prendre les autres doses de la journée en les espaçant également, sans jamais doubler les doses. Afin de réduire les risques d'insomnie, la dernière dose de la journée devrait être prise avant 18 heures. Insister sur le fait qu'il ne faut pas modifier la posologie sans consulter un professionnel de la santé. Le sevrage brusque après un traitement à doses élevées peut provoquer une fatigue extrême ou la dépression mentale.
- Recommander au patient de se peser 2 ou 3 fois par semaine et de signaler à un professionnel de la santé toute perte de poids.
- Prévenir le patient que le méthylphénidate peut provoquer des étourdissements ou une vision trouble. Lui conseiller de ne pas conduire et d'éviter les activités qui exigent sa vigilance jusqu'à ce qu'on ait la certitude que le médicament n'entraîne pas ces effets chez lui.
- Prévenir le patient ou les parents que les comprimés de Concerta ne se dissolvent pas complètement une fois que tout le médicament a été libéré. Une partie du comprimé peut donc se retrouver dans les selles, ce qui est normal.
- Conseiller au patient d'éviter de consommer des boissons à base de caféine en même temps que ce médicament.
- Recommander au patient de signaler à un professionnel de la santé la nervosité, l'insomnie, les palpitations, les vomissements, le rash ou la fièvre.
- Informer le patient que le médecin peut prescrire des arrêts temporaires de la médication lui permettant d'évaluer les bienfaits du traitement et de diminuer la dépendance.
- Insister sur l'importance des examens réguliers de suivi permettant d'évaluer les bienfaits du traitement.

Trouble déficitaire de l'attention avec hyperactivité: PÉD.: Conseiller aux parents d'informer l'infirmière de l'école du traitement que suit leur enfant.

VÉRIFICATION DE L'EFFICACITÉ THÉRAPEUTIQUE

L'efficacité du traitement peut être démontrée par: la diminution de la fréquence des symptômes narcoleptiques ■ la prolongation de la durée de l'attention et l'amélioration des interactions sociales en présence du trouble déficitaire de l'attention avec hyperactivité. ✳

MÉTHYLPREDNISOLONE,

voir Corticostéroïdes (topiques) et Corticostéroïdes (voie générale)

MÉTOCLOPRAMIDE

Apo-Metoclop, Metoclopramide Omega, Nu-Metoclopramide, PMS-Métoclopramide

CLASSIFICATION:

Antiémétique, modificateur de la motilité des voies digestives

Grossesse – catégorie B

INDICATIONS

Prévention des vomissements induits par la chimiothérapie ■ Adjuvant facilitant l'intubation de l'intestin grêle lors des procédés radiographiques ■ Prévention des nausées et des vomissements postopératoires ■ Traitement d'appoint du ralentissement de la vidange gastrique associé à une gastrite subaiguë ou chronique ou à des séquelles consécutives à une intervention chirurgicale. **Usages non approuvés:** Traitement du hoquet ■ Adjuvant au traitement des migraines accompagnées de nausées ou de vomissements ■ Traitement de la gastroparésie diabétique ■ Traitement du reflux œsophagien.

MÉCANISME D'ACTION

Blocage des récepteurs dopaminergiques dans la zone gâchette chémoréceptrice du SNC ■ Stimulation de la motilité des voies digestives hautes et accélération de la vidange gastrique. ***Effets thérapeutiques:*** Diminution des nausées et des vomissements ■ Diminution des symptômes de gastroparésie ■ Facilitation du passage de la sonde nasogastrique dans l'intestin grêle.

PHARMACOCINÉTIQUE

Absorption: Bonne (PO, IR, IM).

Distribution: Tous les tissus et liquides de l'organisme. Le métoclopramide traverse la barrière hémato-encéphalique et placentaire et on le retrouve dans le lait maternel à des concentrations plus élevées que dans le plasma.

Métabolisme et excrétion: Métabolisme partiellement hépatique. Élimination rénale (25 % sous forme inchangée).

Demi-vie: De 2,5 à 5 heures.

Profil temps-action (effet sur le péristaltisme)

	DÉBUT D'ACTION	PIC	DURÉE
PO	30 - 60 min	inconnu	1 - 2 h
IM	10 - 15 min	inconnu	1 - 2 h
IV	1 - 3 min	immédiat	1 - 2 h

CONTRE-INDICATIONS, PRÉCAUTIONS ET MISES EN GARDE

Contre-indications: Hypersensibilité ■ Risque d'occlusion, de perforation ou d'hémorragie gastro-intestinale ■ Phéochromocytome.

Précautions et mises en garde: Antécédents de dépression ■ Cancer du sein (l'élévation des concentrations de prolactine par le métoclopramide pourrait stimuler les cellules cancéreuses) ■ Diabète (risque de modification de la réponse à l'insuline) ■ **OBST., ALLAITEMENT**: L'innocuité du médicament n'a pas été établie ■ **PÉD.**: Fréquence accrue de réactions extrapyramidales. Nouveau-nés (certains sirops peuvent contenir du benzoate, un métabolite de l'alcool benzylique qui risque de provoquer le syndrome mortel de halètement; la diminution de la clairance chez le nouveau-né peut élever les concentrations plasmatiques et le risque de méthémoglobinémie) ■ **GÉR.**: Fréquence accrue de réactions extrapyramidales et de sédation ■ Antécédents de convulsions ■ Patients recevant d'autres médicaments qui peuvent entraîner des réactions extrapyramidales ■ Patients recevant d'autres dépresseurs du SNC ■ Maladie de Parkinson.

RÉACTIONS INDÉSIRABLES ET EFFETS SECONDAIRES

SNC: SYNDROME MALIN DES NEUROLEPTIQUES, somnolence, réactions extrapyramidales, agitation, anxiété, dépression, irritabilité, dyskinésie tardive.

CV: arythmies (tachycardie supraventriculaire, bradycardie), hypertension, hypotension.

GI: constipation, diarrhée, sécheresse de la bouche (xérostomie), nausées.

End.: gynécomastie.

Hémat.: méthémoglobinémie, neutropénie, leucopénie, agranulocytose.

INTERACTIONS

Médicament-médicament: Effets additifs sur la dépression du SNC lors de l'usage concomitant d'autres **dépresseurs du SNC**, incluant l'**alcool**, les **antidépresseurs**, les **antihistaminiques**, les **opioïdes** ou les **hypnosédatifs** ■ Le métoclopramide peut accroître l'absorption de la **cyclosporine** et le risque de toxicité ■ Le métoclopramide peut affecter l'absorption gastro-intestinale d'autres **médicaments administrés par voie orale** en raison de son effet sur la motilité gastro-intestinale ■ Le métoclopramide peut exacerber l'hypotension au cours d'une **anesthésie générale** ■ Risque accru de réactions extrapyramidales lors de l'administration concomitante d'agents comme l'**halopéridol** ou les **phénothiazines** ■ Les **opioïdes** et les **anticholinergiques** peuvent contrecarrer les effets gastro-intestinaux du métoclopramide ■ Le métoclopramide doit être administré avec prudence lors de la prise concomitante d'**IMAO** (libération des catécholamines) ■ Le métoclopramide peut augmenter le blocage neuromusculaire attribuable à la **succinylcholine** ■ Le métoclopramide peut réduire l'efficacité de la **lévodopa** ■ Le métoclopramide peut augmenter les concentrations plasmatiques de **tacrolimus**.

VOIES D'ADMINISTRATION ET POSOLOGIE

Prévention des vomissements dus à la chimiothérapie

- **IV (adultes)**: De 1 à 2 mg/kg; administrer une deuxième dose, 2 heures plus tard, et une troisième dose, 4 heures plus tard, s'il y a lieu.
- **IV (enfants)**: De 0,5 à 1,5 mg/kg/dose (ne pas dépasser 2 mg/kg/dose ou 10 mg/kg/jour) avant la chimiothérapie, puis 3 doses, toutes les 2 à 3 heures et au besoin par la suite. On recommande l'administration concomitante de diphenhydramine pour réduire ou pour contrer les réactions dystoniques.

Facilitation de l'intubation de l'intestin grêle

- **IV (adultes)**: 10 mg.
- **IV, PO, IM (enfants)**: De 2,5 à 5 mg dans le cas des enfants de 6 à 14 ans, et 0,1 mg/kg dans celui des enfants < 6 ans.

Prévention des nausées et vomissements postopératoires

- **IM (adultes)**: De 10 à 20 mg vers la fin de l'intervention. On peut répéter l'administration toutes les 4 à 6 heures.
- **IM, IV (enfants)**: De 0,1 à 0,2 mg/kg/dose vers la fin de l'intervention. On peut répéter l'administration après 6 à 8 heures, si nécessaire *(usage non approuvé)*.

Accélération de la vidange gastrique

- **PO (adultes)**: De 5 à 10 mg, 3 ou 4 fois par jour, avant les repas et au coucher.
- **IM, IV (adultes)**: 10 mg, 2 ou 3 fois par jour, selon les besoins.
- **PO (enfants)**: Enfants de 5 à 14 ans – administrer de 2,5 à 5 mg, 3 fois par jour, avant les repas; enfants < 5 ans – administrer de 0,3 à 0,5 mg/kg/jour avec les repas, en 3 doses fractionnées. Ne pas dépasser 0,5 mg/kg/jour.

Reflux gastro-œsophagien

- **PO (adultes):** De 10 à 15 mg, jusqu'à 4 fois par jour, avant les repas et au coucher *(usage non approuvé)*.
- **PO (nouveau-nés et enfants):** De 0,4 à 0,8 mg/kg/jour, en 4 doses fractionnées *(usage non approuvé)*.

Gastroparésie diabétique

- **PO, IV (adultes):** De 5 à 10 mg avant les repas et au coucher pendant 2 à 8 semaines. Envisager l'administration parentérale dans les cas graves. Reprendre le traitement si les symptômes se manifestent de nouveau *(usage non approuvé)*.

Traitement du hoquet

- **PO, IM (adultes):** De 10 à 20 mg, 4 fois par jour par voie orale. La première dose de 10 mg peut être donnée par voie IM *(usage non approuvé)*.

PRÉSENTATION (version générique disponible)

Comprimés: 5 mg[Pr], 10 mg[Pr] ■ **Sirop:** 250 mg/250 mL[Pr], 500 mg/500 mL[Pr] ■ **Solution pour injection:** 10 mg/2 mL[Pr], 50 mg/10 mL[Pr], 150 mg/30 mL[Pr].

M

SOINS INFIRMIERS

ÉVALUATION DE LA SITUATION

- Suivre de près les nausées et les vomissements; ausculter les bruits intestinaux et observer la distension abdominale avant et après l'administration du métoclopramide.
- Rester à l'affût des symptômes extrapyramidaux, à intervalles réguliers, tout au long du traitement (*symptômes parkinsoniens:* difficultés d'élocution ou de déglutition, perte de l'équilibre, mouvements d'émiettement, faciès figé, démarche traînante, rigidité, tremblements; *symptômes dystoniques:* spasmes musculaires, torsions, secousses musculaires, incapacité de bouger les yeux, faiblesse des bras ou des jambes). Ces symptômes peuvent apparaître plusieurs semaines ou même plusieurs mois après le début du traitement et sont réversibles une fois qu'on l'a arrêté. Les réactions dystoniques peuvent survenir dans les minutes suivant la perfusion IV et cesser dans les 24 heures suivant l'abandon du métoclopramide. On peut les traiter avec 50 mg de diphenhydramine par voie IM ou les prévenir avec 1 mg/kg de diphenhydramine par voie IV, administré 15 minutes avant la perfusion du métoclopramide par voie IV.
- Suivre de près l'apparition de la dyskinésie tardive qui se traduit par les symptômes suivants: mouvements rythmiques incontrôlés des mâchoires, de la bouche, du visage et des membres; émission de bruits secs avec les lèvres, moue; gonflement des joues; mastication incontrôlée; mouvements rapides de la langue. Ces symptômes se manifestent habituellement après au moins 1 an de traitement continu. Prévenir immédiatement le médecin si ces symptômes se manifestent, car de tels effets secondaires peuvent être irréversibles. Suivre de près l'apparition du syndrome malin des neuroleptiques qui se traduit par les symptômes suivants: hyperthermie, rigidité musculaire, altération de l'état de conscience, pouls ou pression artérielle irréguliers, tachycardie et diaphorèse.
- Observer le patient à intervalles réguliers, tout au long du traitement, pour déceler les signes de dépression.

Tests de laboratoire:

- Le métoclopramide peut modifier les résultats des tests de la fonction hépatique.
- Le métoclopramide peut accroître les concentrations sériques de prolactine et d'aldostérone.

DIAGNOSTICS INFIRMIERS POSSIBLES

- Alimentation déficiente (Indications).
- Risque d'accident (Effets secondaires).
- Connaissances insuffisantes sur le traitement médicamenteux (Enseignement au patient et à ses proches).

INTERVENTIONS INFIRMIÈRES

PO: Administrer les doses 30 minutes avant les repas et au coucher.

IM: Pour prévenir les nausées et les vomissements postopératoires, injecter le médicament par voie IM lorsque l'intervention chirurgicale touche à sa fin.

IR: Les suppositoires peuvent être confectionnés par le pharmacien. Administrer un suppositoire de 30 à 60 minutes avant chaque repas et au coucher.

IV directe: Administrer la dose par voie IV, 30 minutes avant l'administration de l'agent chimiothérapeutique. ***Vitesse d'administration:*** Administrer les doses lentement pendant 1 ou 2 minutes. L'administration rapide peut provoquer de l'agitation et une sensation d'anxiété, passagères mais intenses, suivies de somnolence.

Perfusion intermittente: On peut diluer la solution destinée à la perfusion IV dans 50 mL de solution de D5%E, de NaCl 0,9 %, de D5%/NaCl 0,45 %, de solution de Ringer ou de solution de lactate de Ringer. La solution diluée est stable pendant 48 heures si elle est protégée de la lumière et pendant 24 heures si elle est gardée sous un éclairage normal. Consulter les directives du fabricant avant de diluer la préparation.

Vitesse d'administration: Perfuser lentement pendant au moins 15 minutes.

Associations compatibles dans la même seringue: bléomycine ▪ butorphanol ▪ cyclophosphamide ▪ cytarabine ▪ dexaméthasone ▪ doxorubicine ▪ fluorouracile ▪ héparine ▪ hydrocortisone ▪ leucovorine ▪ mépéridine ▪ méthotriméprazine ▪ méthylprednisolone, succinate sodique de ▪ mitomycine ▪ morphine ▪ ranitidine ▪ vinblastine ▪ vincristine.

Compatibilité (tubulure en Y): acyclovir ▪ aldesleukine ▪ amifostine ▪ aztréonam ▪ bléomycine ▪ ciprofloxacine ▪ cisplatine ▪ cyclophosphamide ▪ cytarabine ▪ diltiazem ▪ doxorubicine ▪ dropéridol ▪ famotidine ▪ filgrastim ▪ fluconazole ▪ fludarabine ▪ fluorouracile ▪ foscarnet ▪ gallium, nitrate de ▪ héparine ▪ idarubicine ▪ leucovorine ▪ melphalan ▪ mépéridine ▪ méthotrexate ▪ mitomycine ▪ morphine ▪ ondansétron ▪ paclitaxel ▪ pipéracilline/tazobactam ▪ sargramostim ▪ sufentanil ▪ tacrolimus ▪ téniposide ▪ thiotépa ▪ vinblastine ▪ vincristine ▪ vinorelbine ▪ zidovudine.

Incompatibilité (tubulure en Y): céfépime ▪ furosémide.

ENSEIGNEMENT AU PATIENT ET À SES PROCHES

- Conseiller au patient de suivre rigoureusement la posologie recommandée. S'il n'a pas pu prendre le médicament au moment habituel, il doit le prendre aussitôt que possible à moins que ce ne soit presque l'heure prévue pour la dose suivante. **PÉD.**: Lors de l'utilisation de la solution orale chez l'enfant, on a signalé des surdosages non intentionnels. Montrer aux parents comment lire correctement l'étiquette et administrer le médicament.
- Prévenir le patient que le métoclopramide peut provoquer de la somnolence. Lui conseiller de ne pas conduire et d'éviter les activités qui exigent sa vigilance jusqu'à ce qu'on ait la certitude que le médicament n'entraîne pas cet effet chez lui.
- Conseiller au patient d'éviter de boire de l'alcool et de ne pas prendre d'autres dépresseurs du SNC durant le traitement par le métoclopramide.
- Recommander au patient de signaler immédiatement à un professionnel de la santé les mouvements involontaires des yeux, du visage ou des membres.

VÉRIFICATION DE L'EFFICACITÉ THÉRAPEUTIQUE

L'efficacité du traitement peut être démontrée par: la prévention ou le soulagement des nausées et des vomissements ▪ la diminution des symptômes de gastroparésie ▪ la facilitation de l'intubation de l'intestin grêle ▪ la diminution des symptômes de reflux œsophagien.

MÉTOLAZONE

Zaroxolyn

CLASSIFICATION:

Antihypertenseur, diurétique (thiazidique et dérivé ayant une structure proche)

Grossesse – catégorie B (catégorie D, en cas d'hypertension gravidique)

INDICATIONS

Hypertension légère à modérée ▪ Œdème attribuable à l'insuffisance cardiaque ou au syndrome néphrotique.

MÉCANISME D'ACTION

Excrétion accrue du sodium et de l'eau par l'inhibition de la réabsorption sodique au niveau des tubules distaux ▪ Excrétion accrue des chlorures, du potassium et du magnésium ▪ Dilatation artériolaire possible. ***Effets thérapeutiques:*** Abaissement de la pression artérielle chez les patients hypertendus ▪ Diurèse suivie de la diminution de l'œdème. L'effet peut se poursuivre en cas d'insuffisance rénale.

PHARMACOCINÉTIQUE

Absorption: Variable.

Distribution: Inconnue.

Métabolisme et excrétion: Excrétion rénale (sous forme inchangée).

Demi-vie: 8 heures.

Profil temps-action (effet diurétique†)

	DÉBUT D'ACTION	PIC	DURÉE
PO	1 h	2 h	12 – 24 h

† Le plein effet antihypertenseur peut ne se manifester qu'après plusieurs jours ou plusieurs semaines.

CONTRE-INDICATIONS, PRÉCAUTIONS ET MISES EN GARDE

Contre-indications: Hypersensibilité ▪ Risque de réactions de sensibilité croisée avec d'autres sulfamides ▪ Anurie ▪ Coma ou précoma hépatique.

Précautions et mises en garde: Insuffisance hépatique grave ▪ **GÉR.**: Sensibilité accrue aux effets du médicament ▪ **OBST., ALLAITEMENT, PÉD.**: L'innocuité du médicament n'a pas été établie; les enfants peuvent être plus sensibles aux effets diurétiques et hypokaliémiants.

RÉACTIONS INDÉSIRABLES ET EFFETS SECONDAIRES

SNC: somnolence, léthargie.

M

CV: douleurs thoraciques, hypotension, palpitations.
GI: anorexie, ballonnements, crampes, hépatite, nausées, vomissements.
Tég.: photosensibilité, rash.
End.: hyperglycémie.
HÉ: hypokaliémie, déshydratation, hypercalcémie, alcalose hypochlorémique, hypomagnésémie, hyponatrémie, hypophosphatémie, hypovolémie.
Hémat.: dyscrasie.
Métab.: hyperuricémie.
Loc.: crampes musculaires.
Divers: frissons, pancréatite.

INTERACTIONS

Médicament-médicament: Effet hypotenseur additif lors de l'administration concomitante d'autres **antihypertenseurs** ou de **dérivés nitrés** et lors de l'ingestion de grandes quantités d'**alcool** ▪ Effet hypokaliémiant additif, lors de l'administration concomitante de **corticostéroïdes**, d'**amphotéricine B**, de **pipéracilline** ou de **ticarcilline** ▪ La métolazone entraîne l'hypokaliémie, ce qui peut augmenter le risque de toxicité **digitalique** ▪ La métolazone diminue l'excrétion du **lithium** et peut provoquer une toxicité ▪ Le métolazone peut diminuer l'efficacité de la **méthénamine**.
Médicament-produits naturels: Les **plantes laxatives stimulantes** (**aloès**, **cascara sagrada**, **séné**) peuvent augmenter le risque d'hypokaliémie.
Médicament-aliments: Les **aliments** peuvent augmenter l'absorption de cet agent.

VOIES D'ADMINISTRATION ET POSOLOGIE

- **PO (adultes)**: *Doses d'attaque: Œdème dû à l'insuffisance cardiaque* – de 5 à 10 mg, 1 fois par jour. *Œdème dû à des maladies rénales* – de 5 à 20 mg, 1 fois par jour. *Hypertension essentielle, de légère à modérée* – de 2,5 à 5 mg, 1 fois par jour. *Doses d'entretien:* à adapter selon chaque cas particulier. Lorsqu'on a ramené la dose quotidienne à 2,5 mg, on peut la diminuer une fois de plus, en n'administrant le médicament que 1 jour sur 2.

PRÉSENTATION

Comprimés: 2,5 mg[Pr].

SOINS INFIRMIERS

ÉVALUATION DE LA SITUATION

- Mesurer la pression artérielle, effectuer le bilan quotidien des ingesta et des excreta et peser le patient tous les jours. Examiner quotidiennement les pieds, les jambes et la région sacrée pour déceler la formation d'œdème.
- Suivre de près, particulièrement chez le patient qui prend des dérivés digitaliques, les symptômes suivants: anorexie, nausées, vomissements, crampes musculaires, paresthésie et confusion. Informer le médecin ou un autre professionnel de la santé si ces signes de déséquilibre électrolytique se manifestent. Les patients digitalisés sont davantage prédisposés à la toxicité digitalique en raison de l'effet de déplétion potassique du diurétique.
- Interroger le patient à propos de ses antécédents d'allergie aux sulfamides.

Hypertension:

- Mesurer la pression artérielle avant le traitement et à intervalles réguliers pendant toute sa durée.
- Noter la fréquence des renouvellements des ordonnances afin de déterminer l'observance du traitement.

Tests de laboratoire:

- Noter les concentrations d'électrolytes (particulièrement celles de potassium), la glycémie, l'urée, les concentrations de créatinine sérique et d'acide urique avant le traitement et à intervalles réguliers pendant toute sa durée.
- La métolazone peut entraîner l'élévation des concentrations de glucose sérique et urinaire chez les patients diabétiques.
- L'agent peut entraîner l'élévation des concentrations sériques de bilirubine, de calcium, de créatinine et d'acide urique et la diminution des concentrations sériques de magnésium, de potassium et de sodium ainsi que des concentrations urinaires de calcium.
- La métolazone peut entraîner la diminution des concentrations sériques d'iode lié aux protéines.
- L'agent peut entraîner l'élévation des concentrations sériques de cholestérol, de lipoprotéines de basse densité et de triglycérides.

DIAGNOSTICS INFIRMIERS POSSIBLES

- Excès de volume liquidien (Indications).
- Risque de déficit des volumes liquidiens (Effets secondaires).
- Connaissances insuffisantes sur le traitement médicamenteux (Enseignement au patient et à ses proches).

INTERVENTIONS INFIRMIÈRES

- Administrer le médicament le matin afin d'éviter l'interruption du cycle du sommeil.
- On peut utiliser un schéma posologique intermittent afin d'assurer un traitement continu de l'œdème.

PO: On peut administrer la métolazone avec des aliments ou du lait afin de réduire l'irritation gastrique.

ENSEIGNEMENT AU PATIENT ET À SES PROCHES

- Conseiller au patient de prendre ce médicament au même moment tous les jours. S'il n'a pas pu le prendre au moment habituel, il doit le prendre aussitôt que possible, à moins que ce ne soit presque l'heure prévue pour la dose suivante. L'avertir qu'il ne doit jamais remplacer une dose manquée par une double dose.
- Recommander au patient de se peser 2 fois par semaine et de signaler à un professionnel de la santé toute modification importante du poids.
- Recommander au patient de changer lentement de position pour prévenir le risque d'hypotension orthostatique. Lui expliquer que l'alcool peut intensifier l'effet antihypertenseur du médicament.
- Inciter le patient à utiliser un écran solaire et à porter des vêtements protecteurs pour prévenir les réactions de photosensibilité.
- Recommander au patient de discuter de ses besoins en potassium alimentaire avec un professionnel de la santé (voir l'annexe J).
- Recommander au patient qui doit suivre un autre traitement ou subir une intervention chirurgicale d'avertir le professionnel de la santé qu'il suit un traitement avec ce médicament.
- Inciter le patient à signaler à un professionnel de la santé les symptômes suivants: faiblesse musculaire, crampes, nausées, vomissements, diarrhée ou étourdissements.
- Insister sur l'importance des examens réguliers de suivi.

Hypertension:

- Expliquer au patient qu'il doit continuer de prendre le médicament même s'il se sent mieux. La métolazone stabilise la pression artérielle mais ne guérit pas l'hypertension.
- Inciter le patient à appliquer d'autres mesures de réduction de l'hypertension: perdre du poids, réduire sa consommation de sel, faire régulièrement de l'exercice, cesser de fumer, boire de l'alcool avec modération et diminuer le stress.
- Montrer au patient et à ses proches comment prendre la pression artérielle et les inciter à la mesurer 1 fois par semaine.
- Conseiller au patient de consulter un professionnel de la santé avant de prendre un médicament en vente libre, particulièrement des préparations contre la toux ou le rhume, en même temps que la métolazone.

VÉRIFICATION DE L'EFFICACITÉ THÉRAPEUTIQUE

L'efficacité du traitement peut être démontrée par: la baisse de la pression artérielle ▪ l'augmentation du débit urinaire ▪ la diminution de l'œdème.

ALERTE CLINIQUE

MÉTOPROLOL

Apo-Metoprolol, Betaloc, Betaloc Durules, Gen-Metoprolol, Lopresor, Lopresor SR, Novo-Metoprol, PMS-Metoprolol-L

CLASSIFICATION:

Antiangineux, antiarythmique (classe II), antihypertenseur (bêtabloquant cardiosélectif)

Grossesse – catégories C (1er trimestre) et D (2e et 3e trimestres)

INDICATIONS

Traitement de l'hypertension légère à modérée ▪ Traitement prolongé de l'angine de poitrine ▪ Prévention de l'infarctus du myocarde (IM) et diminution de la mortalité chez les patients ayant subi un IM récent. **Usages non approuvés**: Tachycardie, arythmies ventriculaires ▪ Prophylaxie des migraines ▪ Tremblements ▪ Traitement du comportement agressif ▪ Traitement de l'akathisie médicamenteuse induite par les neuroleptiques ▪ Anxiété.

MÉCANISME D'ACTION

Blocage de la stimulation des récepteurs bêta$_1$-adrénergiques (myocardiques) avec moins d'effets sur les récepteurs bêta$_2$-adrénergiques (pulmonaires, vasculaires ou utérins). ***Effets thérapeutiques:*** Abaissement de la pression artérielle et diminution de la fréquence cardiaque ▪ Diminution de la fréquence des crises d'angine de poitrine ▪ Diminution des infarctus récurrents et des décès par atteinte cardiovasculaire chez les patients ayant subi un infarctus du myocarde.

PHARMACOCINÉTIQUE

Absorption: Bonne (PO).

Distribution: L'agent traverse la barrière hématoencéphalique et placentaire et passe en faibles quantités dans le lait maternel.

Métabolisme et excrétion: Métabolisme majoritairement hépatique. Excrétion rénale (95 % sous forme de métabolites et 5 % sous forme inchangée).

Demi-vie: De 3 à 7 heures.

Profil temps-action (effets cardiovasculaires)

	Début d'action	Pic	Durée
PO†	< 1 h	inconnu	6 - 12 h
PO - LP‡	inconnu	6 - 12 h	24 h
IV	immédiat	20 min	5 - 8 h

† Au cours d'un traitement prolongé, les effets maximaux sur la pression artérielle peuvent ne pas se manifester pendant la première semaine. Les effets antihypertenseurs peuvent persister jusqu'à 4 semaines après l'arrêt du traitement.

‡ LP = libération prolongée.

CONTRE-INDICATIONS, PRÉCAUTIONS ET MISES EN GARDE

Contre-indications: Hypersensibilité connue au métoprolol ou à d'autres bêtabloquants ■ Insuffisance cardiaque non compensée ■ Œdème pulmonaire ■ Choc cardiogénique ■ Bradycardie ou bloc cardiaque (bloc AV du 2e et 3e degré) ■ Insuffisance ventriculaire droite secondaire à une hypertension pulmonaire ■ Syndrome de dysfonctionnement sinusal ■ Artériopathies périphériques graves ■ Anesthésie au moyen d'agents dépresseurs du myocarde ■ Phéochromocytome non traité ■ Asthme ou maladies respiratoires obstructives (administration par voie IV).

M

Précautions et mises en garde: Insuffisance cardiaque compensée ■ Insuffisance rénale ■ Insuffisance hépatique ■ **Gér.**: Il est recommandé de réduire la dose initiale chez les personnes âgées ou débilitées (sensibilité accrue aux bêtabloquants) ■ Maladie pulmonaire bronchospastique (incluant l'asthme); l'effet sélectif sur les récepteurs bêta$_1$-adrénergiques peut disparaître à des doses élevées ■ Diabète (le médicament peut masquer les signes et les symptômes d'hypoglycémie) ■ Thyrotoxicose (le médicament peut en masquer les symptômes) ■ Antécédents de réactions allergiques graves (l'intensité des réactions peut être accrue) ■ **Obst., allaitement**: L'innocuité du médicament n'a pas été établie; le métoprolol ne devrait pas être administré aux femmes enceintes ou qui allaitent ■ **Péd.**: L'innocuité et l'efficacité de l'agent n'ont pas été établies.

RÉACTIONS INDÉSIRABLES ET EFFETS SECONDAIRES

SNC: fatigue, faiblesse, anxiété, dépression, étourdissements, somnolence, insomnie, pertes de mémoire, modification de l'état de conscience, nervosité, cauchemars.

ORLO: vision trouble, rhinorrhée.

Resp.: bronchospasme, respiration sifflante.

CV: BRADYCARDIE, INSUFFISANCE CARDIAQUE, ŒDÈME PULMONAIRE, hypotension, vasoconstriction périphérique.

GI: constipation, diarrhée, hépatite, sécheresse de la bouche (xérostomie), flatulence, douleurs gastriques, brûlures d'estomac, anomalies des résultats des tests de la fonction hépatique, nausées, vomissements.

GU: impuissance, perte de la libido, mictions fréquentes.

Tég.: rash.

End.: hyperglycémie, hypoglycémie.

Loc.: arthralgie, douleurs lombaires, douleurs articulaires.

Divers: syndrome lupique d'origine médicamenteuse.

INTERACTIONS

Médicament-médicament: L'**anesthésie générale**, le **diltiazem** et le **vérapamil** peuvent avoir un effet additif sur la dépression du myocarde ■ Risque de bradycardie additive lors de l'administration concomitante de **dérivés digitaliques** ■ Risque d'hypotension additive lors de l'administration concomitante d'**antihypertenseurs** ou de **dérivés nitrés** ainsi que lors de l'ingestion de grandes quantités d'**alcool** ■ L'usage concomitant d'**amphétamines**, de **cocaïne**, d'**éphédrine**, d'**adrénaline**, de **noradrénaline**, de **phényléphrine** ou de **pseudoéphédrine** peut entraîner une réponse hypertensive excessive et une bradycardie ■ Le métoprolol peut modifier l'efficacité des **insulines** ou des **hypoglycémiants oraux** (des adaptations posologiques peuvent s'avérer nécessaires) ■ Le métoprolol peut réduire les effets bénéfiques de la **dopamine** ou de la **dobutamine** sur les récepteurs bêta$_1$ cardiaques ■ Le métoprolol peut provoquer l'hypertension s'il est administré dans les 14 jours qui suivent un traitement par un **IMAO** ■ Les **inhibiteurs puissants du CYP2D6** (**fluoxétine**, **paroxétine**, **bupropion**, **thioridazine**, **quinidine**, **propafénone**, **ritonavir**, **diphenhydramine**, **hydroxychloroquine**, **quinine**, **terbinafine**, **cimétidine**, **ranitidine**) peuvent augmenter les concentrations plasmatiques du métoprolol.

VOIES D'ADMINISTRATION ET POSOLOGIE

- **PO (adultes)**: *Antihypertenseur/antiangineux* – 100 mg par jour, en 2 prises; la dose peut être majorée tous les 7 jours, selon la réponse au traitement et la tolérance du patient, jusqu'à concurrence de 400 mg par jour. Les produits à libération prolongée sont administrés 1 fois par jour et sont habituellement utilisés durant le traitement d'entretien après établissement de la dose. *Infarctus du myocarde, traitement précoce* – de 25 à 50 mg (15 minutes après la dernière dose par voie IV), toutes les 6 heures, pendant 48 heures, puis 100 mg, 2 fois par jour. *Infarctus du myocarde, traitement tardif* – 100 mg, 2 fois par jour dès que l'état clinique du patient le permettra (en général, de 3 à 10 jours après la phase aiguë).

- **IV (adultes)**: *Infarctus du myocarde* – 5 mg, toutes les 2 minutes, 3 fois, puis passer au traitement par voie orale.

PRÉSENTATION

Comprimés (version générique disponible): 25 mgPr, 50 mgPr, 100 mgPr ▪ **Comprimés à libération prolongée**: 100 mgPr, 200 mgPr ▪ **Solution pour injection**: 1 mg/mLPr.

SOINS INFIRMIERS

ÉVALUATION DE LA SITUATION

- Suivre la pression artérielle, l'ÉCG et le pouls à intervalles fréquents pendant la période d'adaptation posologique et à intervalles réguliers pendant toute la durée du traitement.
- PRENDRE LES SIGNES VITAUX ET SUIVRE L'ÉCG TOUTES LES 5 À 15 MINUTES PENDANT L'ADMINISTRATION PAR VOIE PARENTÉRALE ET PENDANT PLUSIEURS HEURES PAR LA SUITE. SI LA FRÉQUENCE CARDIAQUE EST < 40 BPM, PARTICULIÈREMENT SI LE DÉBIT CARDIAQUE EST ÉGALEMENT RÉDUIT, ADMINISTRER DE L'ATROPINE À 0,25 mg OU À 0,5 mg PAR VOIE IV.
- EFFECTUER LE BILAN QUOTIDIEN DES INGESTA ET DES EXCRETA ET PESER LE PATIENT TOUS LES JOURS. SUIVRE À INTERVALLES RÉGULIERS LES SIGNES ET LES SYMPTÔMES SUIVANTS D'INSUFFISANCE CARDIAQUE: DYSPNÉE, RÂLES ET CRÉPITATIONS, GAIN PONDÉRAL, ŒDÈME PÉRIPHÉRIQUE, TURGESCENCE DES JUGULAIRES.

Angine: Évaluer la fréquence et les caractéristiques des crises d'angine à intervalles réguliers tout au long du traitement.

Tests de laboratoire:

- Le métoprolol peut entraîner l'élévation de l'urée ainsi que des concentrations sériques de lipoprotéines, de potassium, de triglycérides et d'acide urique.
- Le métoprolol peut entraîner l'élévation de la glycémie.
- Le métoprolol peut entraîner l'élévation des concentrations sériques de phosphatase alcaline, de LDH, d'AST et d'ALT.

DIAGNOSTICS INFIRMIERS POSSIBLES

- Débit cardiaque diminué (Effets secondaires).
- Connaissances insuffisantes sur le traitement médicamenteux (Enseignement au patient et à ses proches).
- Non-observance du traitement médicamenteux (Enseignement au patient et à ses proches).

INTERVENTIONS INFIRMIÈRES

ALERTE CLINIQUE: L'ADMINISTRATION DES MÉDICAMENTS VASOACTIFS PAR VOIE IV COMPORTE UN RISQUE PAR ELLE-MÊME. AVANT L'ADMINISTRATION, FAIRE VALIDER L'ORDONNANCE D'ORIGINE ET LE CALCUL DE LA DOSE PAR UN DEUXIÈME PROFESSIONNEL DE LA SANTÉ.

- NE PAS CONFONDRE LE MÉTOPROLOL AVEC LE MISOPROSTOL.

PO:

- Prendre le pouls apical avant d'administrer le médicament. Si la fréquence cardiaque est < 50 bpm ou en cas d'arythmie, consulter le médecin ou un autre professionnel de la santé avant d'administrer le médicament.
- Administrer le médicament avec des aliments ou tout de suite après les repas.
- LES COMPRIMÉS À LIBÉRATION PROLONGÉE DEVRAIENT ÊTRE AVALÉS TELS QUELS; NE PAS LES ÉCRASER, LES BRISER OU LES MÂCHER.

IV directe: On peut injecter 3 doses de 5 mg rapidement, à intervalles de 2 minutes. Le traitement par voie orale devrait commencer 15 minutes après la dernière dose par voie IV.

Compatibilité (tubulure en Y): altéplase ▪ mépéridine ▪ morphine.

Incompatibilité (tubulure en Y): cholestéryl d'amphotéricine B.

M

ENSEIGNEMENT AU PATIENT ET À SES PROCHES

- Conseiller au patient de suivre rigoureusement la posologie recommandée et de prendre le médicament à la même heure, tous les jours, même s'il se sent bien. Lui expliquer qu'il ne doit pas sauter de dose ni remplacer une dose manquée par une double dose. S'il n'a pas pu prendre le médicament au moment habituel, il doit le prendre aussitôt que possible, mais au moins 8 heures avant l'heure prévue pour la dose suivante. Le sevrage brusque peut déclencher l'hypertension, l'ischémie du myocarde ou des arythmies mettant la vie en danger.
- Enseigner au patient et à ses proches comment prendre le pouls et la pression artérielle. Leur demander de mesurer le pouls tous les jours et la pression artérielle 2 fois par semaine et de signaler tout changement important à un professionnel de la santé.
- Prévenir le patient que le métoprolol peut provoquer des étourdissements. Lui conseiller de ne pas conduire et d'éviter les activités qui exigent sa vigilance jusqu'à ce qu'on ait la certitude que le médicament n'entraîne pas cet effet chez lui.
- Recommander au patient de changer lentement de position afin de réduire le risque d'hypotension orthostatique.

- Prévenir le patient que le médicament peut le rendre plus sensible au froid.
- Conseiller au patient de consulter un professionnel de la santé avant de prendre des médicaments en vente libre, particulièrement des médicaments contre le rhume, ou un produit naturel en même temps que le métoprolol. Les patients qui suivent un traitement antihypertenseur devraient également éviter de boire des quantités excessives de café, de thé et de boissons à base de cola.
- Recommander au patient diabétique de mesurer soigneusement sa glycémie, particulièrement lorsqu'il se sent fatigué, faible ou irritable. Le médicament bloque tous les signes d'hypoglycémie, sauf la transpiration.
- Recommander au patient de signaler à un professionnel de la santé les symptômes suivants: ralentissement du pouls, troubles respiratoires, respiration sifflante, mains et pieds froids, étourdissements, sensation de tête légère, confusion, état dépressif, rash, fièvre, maux de gorge, saignements ou ecchymoses inhabituels.
- Recommander au patient qui doit suivre un autre traitement ou subir une intervention chirurgicale d'avertir le professionnel de la santé qu'il suit un traitement par ce médicament.
- Conseiller au patient de toujours porter sur lui une pièce d'identité où sont inscrits sa maladie et son traitement médicamenteux.

Hypertension: Inciter le patient à appliquer d'autres mesures d'abaissement de l'hypertension: perdre du poids, réduire sa consommation de sel, diminuer le stress, faire régulièrement de l'exercice, boire de l'alcool avec modération et cesser de fumer. Expliquer au patient que le métoprolol stabilise la pression artérielle, mais ne guérit pas l'hypertension.

VÉRIFICATION DE L'EFFICACITÉ THÉRAPEUTIQUE

L'efficacité du traitement peut être démontrée par: la baisse de la pression artérielle ▪ la réduction de la fréquence des crises d'angine ▪ l'amélioration de la tolérance à l'effort ▪ la prévention de l'infarctus du myocarde.

MÉTRONIDAZOLE

Apo-Metronidazole, Flagyl, Florazole ER, MetroCreme, MetroGel, MetroLotion, Nidagel, Noritate

CLASSIFICATION:

Anti-infectieux, antiprotozoaire

Grossesse – catégorie B (administration contre-indiquée pendant le 1er trimestre)

INDICATIONS

PO, IV: Traitement des infections suivantes provoquées par des microorganismes anaérobies: infections intra-abdominales ▪ infections gynécologiques ▪ infections périodontiques ▪ infections des voies respiratoires inférieures ▪ infections du SNC ▪ Traitement de la colite pseudomembraneuse induite par les antibiotiques ▪ **PO**: Infections à *Trichomonas* chez l'homme et chez la femme ▪ Amibiase hépatique ou intestinale ▪ Giardiase ▪ Traitement de l'ulcère gastroduodénal dû à *Helicobacter pylori*, en association avec l'oméprazole et la clarithromycine ▪ **Préparation topique**: Traitement des papules, des pustules et de l'érythème inflammatoire de la rosacée ▪ **Préparation vaginale**: Traitement de la vaginose bactérienne. **Usages non approuvés – PO, IV**: Infections de la peau et de ses annexes ▪ Infections des os et des articulations ▪ Septicémie ▪ Endocardite ▪ **IV**: Prophylaxie périopératoire lors des interventions colorectales.

MÉCANISME D'ACTION

Inhibition de la synthèse de l'ADN et des protéines des microorganismes sensibles. ***Effets thérapeutiques:*** Action bactéricide, trichomonacide ou amœbicide. **Spectre d'action**: Action notable surtout contre les bactéries anaérobies incluant: *Bacteroïdes* ▪ *Clostridium* ▪ *Fusobacterium* ▪ *Peptococcus* ▪ *Peptostreptococcus* ▪ Le métronidazole est également actif contre: ▪ *Trichomonas vaginalis* ▪ *Entamœba histolytica* ▪ *Giardia lamblia* ▪ *Helicobacter pylori* ▪ *Clostridium difficile*.

PHARMACOCINÉTIQUE

Absorption: 80 % (PO); minime (voies topique ou vaginale).

Distribution: Dans la plupart des liquides et tissus de l'organisme incluant le liquide céphalorachidien. Le métronidazole traverse la barrière placentaire et passe rapidement dans la circulation fœtale. Il passe également dans le lait maternel à des concentrations équivalentes à celles qu'on trouve dans le plasma.

Métabolisme et excrétion: Métabolisme hépatique partiel (de 30 à 60 %). Excrétion urinaire partielle à l'état inchangé (20 %) et élimination fécale de 6 à 15 %.

Demi-vie: *Nouveau-nés:* de 25 à 75 heures; *enfants et adultes:* de 6 à 12 heures.

Profil temps-action
(PO, IV = délai d'action ; topique = amélioration des signes de rosacée)

	DÉBUT D'ACTION	PIC	DURÉE
PO	rapide	1 – 2 h	8 h
PO libération prolongée	rapide	inconnu	jusqu'à 24 h
IV	rapide	fin de la perfusion	6 – 8 h
Préparation topique	3 semaines	9 semaines	12 h (durée d'action de chaque application)
Préparation vaginale	inconnu	6 – 12 h	12 h

CONTRE-INDICATIONS, PRÉCAUTIONS ET MISES EN GARDE

Contre-indications: Hypersensibilité ■ Hypersensibilité aux parabènes (préparation topique seulement) ■ Antécédents de convulsions ou de troubles neurologiques ■ Antécédents de dyscrasie sanguine ■ Hypothyroïdie ■ Hyposurrénalisme ■ **OBST.**: 1er trimestre de la grossesse.

Précautions et mises en garde: Insuffisance hépatique grave (il est recommandé de réduire la dose) ■ **OBST.**: Grossesse (bien que l'innocuité du médicament n'ait pas été établie, on l'a utilisé pour traiter la trichomonase au cours des 2e et 3e trimestres de la grossesse, mais il ne s'agissait pas d'un traitement à dose unique) ■ **ALLAITEMENT**: Au besoin, administrer un traitement à dose unique et interrompre l'allaitement pendant les 24 heures qui suivent ■ **PÉD.**: L'innocuité de la préparation IV n'a pas été établie ; l'expérience clinique avec les préparations orales est limitée, il est donc particulièrement important de surveiller de près les enfants soumis à ce traitement ■ Patients qui reçoivent des corticostéroïdes ou qui ont une prédisposition à l'œdème (la solution injectable contient 28 mmol de sodium/g de métronidazole).

RÉACTIONS INDÉSIRABLES ET EFFETS SECONDAIRES

SNC: CONVULSIONS, étourdissements, céphalées, ataxie transitoire, confusion.

ORLO: larmoiement (préparation topique seulement).

GI: douleurs abdominales, anorexie, nausées, diarrhée, sécheresse de la bouche (xérostomie), excroissance pileuse sur la langue, glossite, goût désagréable, vomissements.

Tég.: rash, urticaire ; *voie topique seulement* – brûlures, légère sécheresse, irritation cutanée, rougeurs passagères.

Hémat.: éosinophilie transitoire, leucopénie.

Locaux: phlébite au point d'injection IV.

SN: neuropathie périphérique.

Divers: surinfection, réactions de type disulfirame lors de la consommation d'alcool, coloration foncée de l'urine.

INTERACTIONS

Médicament-médicament: La **cimétidine** peut ralentir le métabolisme du métronidazole ■ Le **phénobarbital** et la **rifampine** accélèrent le métabolisme du métronidazole et peuvent en réduire l'efficacité ■ Le métronidazole augmente les effets de la **warfarine** ■ Une réaction semblable à celle au disulfirame peut survenir lors de l'ingestion simultanée d'**alcool** ■ Le métronidazole peut provoquer une psychose aiguë et de la confusion lors de l'administration simultanée de **disulfirame** ■ Risque accru de leucopénie lors de l'administration simultanée d'**azathioprine** ■ Le métronidazole augmente les concentrations et le risque de toxicité du **lithium**, de la **cyclosporine**, de la **phénytoïne**, du **busulfan** et du **fluorouracile** ■ Le métronidazole augmente la toxicité du **propylèneglycol**, contenu par exemple dans la solution buvable d'amprénavir.

VOIES D'ADMINISTRATION ET POSOLOGIE

- **PO (adultes)**: *Infections dues à des microorganismes anaérobies* – 500 mg, toutes les 8 heures (ou 7,5 mg/kg, toutes les 6 à 8 heures, ne pas dépasser 4 g par jour). *Trichomonase* – de 250 à 500 mg, toutes les 12 heures, pendant 7 à 10 jours ou une seule dose de 2 g après un repas. *Amibiase* – de 500 à 750 mg, toutes les 8 heures, pendant 5 à 10 jours. *Giardiase* – 2 g par jour, pendant 3 jours (au coucher avec de la nourriture) ou 250 mg, 2 ou 3 fois par jour pendant 5 à 7 jours. *Traitement de la colite pseudomembraneuse à* C. difficile – de 250 à 500 mg, 3 ou 4 fois par jour, pendant 7 à 14 jours. *Infection due à* H. pylori – 250 mg, 4 fois par jour, ou 500 mg, 2 fois par jour, pendant 1 ou 2 semaines (en association avec d'autres agents). *Vaginoses bactériennes* – 500 mg, 2 fois par jour, pendant 7 jours ou 750 mg (comprimé à libération prolongée), 1 fois par jour, pendant 7 jours ou une seule dose de 2 g après un repas.
- **PO (enfants)**: *Infections dues à des microorganismes anaérobies* – de 15 à 30 mg/kg/jour en 3 ou 4 prises fractionnées (ne pas dépasser 4 g par jour). *Trichomonase* – de 15 à 20 mg/kg/jour, en 3 prises fractionnées toutes les 8 heures, pendant 7 jours (maximum 250 mg, 3 fois par jour) ou 40 mg/kg (maximum 2 g) en une seule dose. *Amibiase* – de 35 à 50 mg/kg/jour, en 3 prises fractionnées toutes les 8 heures, pendant 5 à 10 jours (ne pas dépasser 750 mg par dose). *Giardiase* – de 25 à 35 mg/kg/jour en 2 prises fractionnées, pendant 5 à 7 jours.

- **IV (adultes)**: *Infections dues à des microorganismes anaérobies* - 500 mg, toutes les 8 heures ou 7,5 mg/kg, toutes les 6 à 8 heures (ne pas dépasser 4 g par jour). *Amibiase* - de 500 à 750 mg, toutes les 8 heures, pendant 5 à 10 jours. *Traitement de la colite pseudomembraneuse à* C. difficile - 500 mg, toutes les 8 heures, pendant 7 à 14 jours.
- **IV (enfants)**: *Infections dues à des microorganismes anaérobies* - 30 mg/kg/jour en doses fractionnées, toutes les 6 ou 8 heures (ne pas dépasser 4 g par jour).
- **PO, IV (nouveau-nés de 0 à 4 semaines)**: *Poids* < *1 200* g - 7,5 mg/kg, toutes les 48 heures. *Âge postnatal* ≤ *7 jours et poids de 1 200 à 2 000* g - 7,5 mg/kg, toutes les 24 heures. *Âge postnatal* ≤ *7 jours et poids* > *2 000* g - 15 mg/kg/jour, divisé en 2 doses, administrées toutes les 12 heures. *Âge postnatal* > *7 jours et poids de 1 200 à 2 000* g - 15 mg/kg/jour, divisé en 2 doses, administrées toutes les 12 heures. *Âge postnatal* > *7 jours et poids* > *2 000* g - 30 mg/kg/jour, divisé en 2 doses, administrées toutes 12 heures.
- **Préparation topique (adultes)**: *Rosacée* - appliquer une mince couche sur la région atteinte, 2 fois par jour.
- **Préparation vaginale (adultes)**: *Trichomonase* - le contenu d'un applicateur (crème à 10 %), 1 ou 2 fois par jour, pendant 10 à 20 jours. *Vaginose bactérienne* - le contenu d'un applicateur (gel à 0,75 %), 2 fois par jour, pendant 5 jours.

M

PRÉSENTATION (version générique disponible)

Comprimés: 250 mg[Pr] ■ **Comprimés à libération prolongée** (Florazole ER): 750 mg[Pr] ■ **Capsules**: 500 mg[Pr] ■ **Solution prémélangée pour injection**: (prête à l'emploi) 500 mg/100 mL[Pr] ■ **Gel topique**: 0,75 %[Pr], en tube de 60 g ■ **Crème topique**: 0,75 %[Pr], en tube de 60 g, et 1 %[Pr], en tube de 30 et 45 g ■ **Gel vaginal**: 0,75 %, en tube de 70 g[Pr] ■ **Crème vaginale**: 10 %, en tube de 60 g[Pr] ■ **Lotion**: 0,75 %, en bouteille de 120 mL[Pr] ■ **En association avec**: nystatine (Flagystatin) ■ Parsol MCX et Parsol 1789 (Rosasol) (voir l'annexe U).

SOINS INFIRMIERS

ÉVALUATION DE LA SITUATION

- Au début du traitement et pendant toute sa durée, surveiller les signes suivants d'infection: altération des signes vitaux, aspect de la plaie, des crachats, de l'urine et des selles; accroissement du nombre de globules blancs.
- Prélever des échantillons pour les cultures et les antibiogrammes avant de commencer le traitement. On peut administrer la première dose avant de recevoir les résultats.
- Suivre l'état neurologique du patient pendant et après les perfusions IV. Signaler au médecin les engourdissements, la paresthésie, la faiblesse, l'ataxie ou les convulsions.
- Effectuer le bilan quotidien des ingesta et des excreta et peser le patient tous les jours, particulièrement s'il doit suivre un régime hyposodé. Une dose de 500 mg de métronidazole injectable contient 14 mmol de sodium.

Giardiase: Faire analyser 3 échantillons de selles, prélevés à plusieurs jours d'intervalle, en commençant 3 ou 4 semaines après le début du traitement.

Tests de laboratoire: Le métronidazole peut modifier les concentrations sériques d'AST, d'ALT et de LDH.

DIAGNOSTICS INFIRMIERS POSSIBLES

- Risque d'infection (Indications).
- Diarrhée (Indications).
- Connaissances insuffisantes sur le traitement médicamenteux (Enseignement au patient et à ses proches).

INTERVENTIONS INFIRMIÈRES

PO: Administrer le métronidazole avec des aliments ou du lait pour réduire l'irritation gastrique. On peut écraser les comprimés ordinaires si le patient éprouve des difficultés de déglutition. Ne pas écraser, briser ou mâcher les comprimés à libération prolongée.

Perfusion intermittente: Les préparations prêtes à utiliser sont diluées d'avance (5 mg/mL). Les minisacs de plastique préremplis ne devraient pas être utilisés pour des raccords en série, en raison du risque d'aéro-embolie. Des cristaux peuvent se former lors de la réfrigération, mais se dissolvent à la température ambiante. Consulter les directives de chaque fabricant avant d'utiliser la préparation.

Vitesse d'administration: Administrer les doses en perfusion lente. Chaque dose doit être perfusée en 30 à 60 minutes.

Compatibilité (tubulure en Y): acyclovir ■ allopurinol ■ amifostine ■ céfépime ■ cisatracurium ■ clarithromycine ■ cyclophosphamide ■ diltiazem ■ docétaxel ■ dopamine ■ doxorubicine liposomale ■ énalaprilat ■ esmolol ■ étoposide ■ fluconazole ■ forcarnet ■ gatifloxacine ■ gemcitabine ■ granisétron ■ héparine ■ hydromorphone ■ labétalol ■ linezolid ■ lorazépam ■ magnésium, sulfate de ■ melphalan ■ mépéridine ■ méthylprednisolone ■ midazolam ■ morphine ■ perphénazine ■ pipéracilline/tazobactam ■ rémifentanil ■ tacrolimus ■ téniposide ■ théophylline ■ thiotépa ■ vinorelbine.

Incompatibilité (tubulure en Y): Le fabricant recommande d'arrêter l'administration IV du soluté principal pendant la perfusion du métronidazole ■ amphotéricine B cholestéryle, sulfate d' ■ filgastrim.

Incompatibilité en addition au soluté: Ne pas mélanger avec d'autres médicaments.

Préparation topique: Nettoyer la région atteinte avant d'appliquer la préparation. Appliquer une mince couche de la préparation topique, 2 fois par jour, le matin et le soir, et faire pénétrer en massant. Éviter tout contact avec les yeux.

ENSEIGNEMENT AU PATIENT ET À SES PROCHES

- Conseiller au patient de suivre rigoureusement la posologie recommandée, même s'il se sent mieux et d'espacer les prises à intervalles égaux. Le prévenir qu'il ne faut pas sauter de dose ni remplacer une dose manquée par une double dose. S'il n'a pas pu prendre le médicament au moment habituel, il doit le prendre dès que possible à moins que ce ne soit presque l'heure prévue pour la dose suivante.
- Prévenir le patient qui reçoit le médicament pour le traitement de la trichomonase que le partenaire sexuel peut le réinfecter même s'il est asymptomatique, raison pour laquelle il faut le traiter simultanément. Le patient devrait également pratiquer l'abstinence ou utiliser un préservatif afin de prévenir la réinfection.
- Recommander au patient d'éviter de consommer des boissons alcoolisées, des médicaments contenant de l'alcool ou des préparations contenant de l'alcool pendant le traitement par le métronidazole (même s'il ne s'agit que du gel vaginal) et pendant au moins 24 heures après l'avoir arrêté. Le métronidazole peut provoquer une réaction semblable à celle au disulfirame, se manifestant par des rougeurs du visage, des nausées, des vomissements, des céphalées ou des crampes abdominales.
- Prévenir le patient que le métronidazole peut provoquer des étourdissements ou une sensation de tête légère. Lui conseiller de ne pas conduire et d'éviter les activités qui exigent sa vigilance jusqu'à ce qu'on ait la certitude que le médicament n'entraîne pas ces effets chez lui.
- Informer le patient que le médicament peut entraîner un goût métallique désagréable.
- Conseiller au patient de consulter un professionnel de la santé avant de prendre un médicament en vente libre ou un produit naturel en même temps que le métronidazole.
- Conseiller au patient de se rincer fréquemment la bouche, de pratiquer une bonne hygiène buccale et de consommer de la gomme à mâcher ou des bonbons sans sucre pour réduire la sécheresse de la bouche. Lui recommander de prévenir un professionnel de la santé si la sécheresse de la bouche persiste pendant plus de 2 semaines.
- Recommander à la patiente de prévenir un professionnel de la santé avant de commencer le traitement par le métronidazole si elle pense être enceinte.
- Prévenir le patient que le métronidazole peut rendre l'urine foncée.
- Conseiller au patient de consulter un professionnel de la santé en l'absence d'une amélioration dans les quelques jours qui suivent le début du traitement ou si les signes et les symptômes suivants de surinfection se manifestent: excroissance noire et pileuse sur la langue, démangeaisons ou pertes vaginales, selles molles ou nauséabondes.

Préparation vaginale: Montrer à la patiente comment appliquer le gel vaginal. Lui conseiller d'éviter les rapports sexuels lors du traitement par le gel vaginal.

Préparation topique: Montrer au patient comment appliquer le gel topique. On peut utiliser des produits cosmétiques après l'application du gel.

VÉRIFICATION DE L'EFFICACITÉ THÉRAPEUTIQUE

L'efficacité du traitement peut être démontrée par: la disparition des signes et des symptômes d'infection; le temps de résolution dépend du microorganisme infectant et du siège de l'infection ■ une amélioration notable de la rosacée dans les 3 semaines suivant l'application du gel topique; on peut poursuivre l'application pendant 9 semaines. ✳

MEXILÉTINE

Novo-Mexiletine

CLASSIFICATION:

Antiarythmique (classe IB)

Grossesse – catégorie C

INDICATIONS

Prophylaxie et traitement des arythmies ventriculaires graves incluant la tachycardie ventriculaire. **Usages non approuvés:** Traitement de la douleur neuropathique chronique.

M

MÉCANISME D'ACTION

Diminution de la durée du potentiel d'action et de la période réfractaire effective dans les tissus cardiaques de conduction par modification du transport du sodium à travers la membrane des cellules du myocarde ■ Le médicament a peu ou pas d'effet sur la fréquence cardiaque. ***Effets thérapeutiques:*** Maîtrise des arythmies ventriculaires.

PHARMACOCINÉTIQUE

Absorption: Bonne (PO).

Distribution: L'agent passe dans le lait maternel à des concentrations semblables à celles qu'on trouve dans le plasma.

Métabolisme et excrétion: Métabolisme majoritairement hépatique. Excrétion rénale (10 % sous forme inchangée).

Demi-vie: De 10 à 14 heures.

Profil temps-action (effets antiarythmiques†)

	Début d'action	Pic	Durée
PO	30 min - 2 h	2 - 3 h	8 - 12 h

† Si une dose d'attaque a été administrée.

M

CONTRE-INDICATIONS, PRÉCAUTIONS ET MISES EN GARDE

Contre-indications: Hypersensibilité ■ Choc cardiogénique ■ Bloc cardiaque du 2e ou du 3e degré (en l'absence d'un stimulateur cardiaque) ■ Période de 3 mois suivant un infarctus ■ Fraction d'éjection du ventricule gauche < 35 %.

Précautions et mises en garde: Anomalies de conduction du nœud SA ou de conduction intraventriculaire ■ Hypotension ■ Insuffisance cardiaque ■ Insuffisance hépatique grave (il est conseillé de réduire la dose) ■ **OBST., PÉD.**: L'innocuité du médicament n'a pas été établie ■ Allaitement.

RÉACTIONS INDÉSIRABLES ET EFFETS SECONDAIRES

SNC: étourdissements, nervosité, confusion, fatigue, céphalées, trouble du sommeil.

ORLO: vision trouble, acouphènes.

Resp.: dyspnée.

CV: ARYTHMIES, douleurs thoraciques, œdème, palpitations.

GI: NÉCROSE HÉPATIQUE, brûlures gastriques, nausées, vomissements.

Tég.: rash.

Hémat.: dyscrasie.

SN: tremblements, troubles de coordination, paresthésie.

INTERACTIONS

Médicament-médicament: Les **opioïdes**, l'**atropine** et les **antiacides** peuvent ralentir l'absorption de la mexilétine ■ Le **métoclopramide** peut accélérer l'absorption de la mexilétine ■ La **phénytoïne**, la **rifampine** et le **phénobarbital** ainsi que le **tabac** (**nicotine**) peuvent accélérer le métabolisme et diminuer l'efficacité de la mexilétine ■ La mexilétine peut accroître les concentrations sanguines de **théophylline** et le risque de toxicité ■ Risque d'effets cardiaques additifs lors de l'administration simultanée d'autres **antiarythmiques** ■ Les **médicaments qui modifient de façon notable le pH de l'urine** peuvent modifier les concentrations sanguines de mexilétine (l'alcalinisation de l'urine augmente la réabsorption de la mexilétine et, par le fait même, les concentrations sanguines; l'acidification de l'urine augmente l'excrétion de la mexilétine et en diminue les concentrations sanguines).

Médicament-aliments: Les **aliments qui modifient de façon notable le pH de l'urine** peuvent modifier les concentrations sanguines de mexilétine. L'alcalinisation de l'urine augmente la réabsorption de la mexilétine et, par le fait même, les concentrations sanguines; l'acidification de l'urine augmente l'excrétion du médicament et peut en diminuer l'efficacité (voir l'annexe J).

VOIES D'ADMINISTRATION ET POSOLOGIE

- **PO (adultes - arythmies ventriculaires)**: Initialement, 200 mg toutes les 8 heures, jusqu'à un maximum de 1 200 mg en 3 ou 4 doses fractionnées. On peut modifier la dose à raison de 50 à 100 mg, tous les 2 ou 3 jours. La dose efficace se situe habituellement entre 600 et 900 mg par jour. Chez certains patients, il peut s'avérer nécessaire d'administrer le médicament toutes les 6 heures. Chez les patients nécessitant une réduction rapide des arythmies ventriculaires, on peut administrer une dose d'attaque de 400 mg, suivie 8 heures plus tard de 200 mg, toutes les 8 heures.
- **PO (adultes - douleurs neuropathiques)**: *Usages non approuvés* - initialement, 200 mg, 1 fois par jour. Porter la dose à 200 mg, 2 fois par jour, puis à 200 mg, 3 fois par jour à intervalles de 2 jours. Ne pas dépasser 1 200 mg par jour.

PRÉSENTATION

Capsules: 100 mg^Pr, 200 mg^Pr.

ÉVALUATION DE LA SITUATION

- MESURER LE POULS ET LA PRESSION ARTÉRIELLE ET SUIVRE DE PRÈS L'ÉCG À INTERVALLES RÉGULIERS

TOUT AU LONG DU TRAITEMENT. UNE SURVEILLANCE CONSTANTE À L'AIDE D'UN APPAREIL HOLTER ET DE RADIOGRAPHIES PULMONAIRES PEUT S'AVÉRER NÉCESSAIRES POUR DÉTERMINER L'EFFICACITÉ DU MÉDICAMENT. CES DONNÉES PEUVENT ÉGALEMENT SERVIR DE GUIDE POUR L'ADAPTATION DE LA POSOLOGIE.

Douleur: Évaluer le type, le siège et l'intensité de la douleur avant le traitement et à intervalles réguliers pendant toute sa durée.

Tests de laboratoire:

- La mexilétine peut parfois positiver le dosage des anticorps antinucléaires.
- LA MEXILÉTINE PEUT ENTRAÎNER UNE ÉLÉVATION PASSAGÈRE DES CONCENTRATIONS D'AST ET D'ALT.
- La mexilétine peut provoquer la thrombopénie quelques jours après le début du traitement. La numération globulaire revient habituellement aux valeurs normales dans le mois qui suit l'arrêt du traitement.

TOXICITÉ ET SURDOSAGE: On peut déterminer les concentrations sériques de mexilétine au cours de la période d'adaptation de la posologie. Les effets secondaires sont plus fréquents si on administre le médicament à des concentrations > 11 µmol/L.

DIAGNOSTICS INFIRMIERS POSSIBLES

- Débit cardiaque diminué (Indications).
- Connaissances insuffisantes sur le traitement médicamenteux (Enseignement au patient et à ses proches).

INTERVENTIONS INFIRMIÈRES

- Lorsqu'on substitue la mexilétine à un autre antiarythmique, on doit administrer la première dose de mexilétine de 6 à 12 heures après la dernière dose de quinidine, de 3 à 6 heures après la dernière dose de procaïnamide ou de 6 à 12 heures après la dernière dose de disopyramide. Lorsqu'on substitue la mexilétine à la lidocaïne par voie parentérale, on doit réduire la dose de lidocaïne ou en arrêter l'administration 1 ou 2 heures après l'administration de la mexilétine ou administrer des doses initiales plus faibles de mexilétine.
- Chez les patients souffrant d'arythmies qui peuvent mettre la vie en danger, la substitution par la mexilétine du traitement par un autre agent antiarythmique doit se faire en milieu hospitalier.

PO: Administrer la mexilétine avec des aliments ou des antiacides pour réduire l'irritation gastrique.

ENSEIGNEMENT AU PATIENT ET À SES PROCHES

- Conseiller au patient de suivre rigoureusement la posologie recommandée et de prendre le médicament à des intervalles égaux, même s'il se sent mieux. S'il n'a pas pu prendre le médicament au moment habituel, il doit le prendre dans les 4 heures qui suivent ou ne pas prendre cette dose. Lui recommander de ne pas sauter de dose ni de remplacer une dose manquée par une double dose.
- MONTRER AU PATIENT COMMENT MESURER LE POULS. LUI CONSEILLER DE COMMUNIQUER AVEC UN PROFESSIONNEL DE LA SANTÉ SI SON POULS EST INFÉRIEUR À 50 BPM OU S'IL DEVIENT IRRÉGULIER.
- Prévenir le patient que la mexilétine peut provoquer des étourdissements et une sensation de tête légère. Lui conseiller de ne pas conduire et d'éviter les activités qui exigent sa vigilance jusqu'à ce qu'on ait la certitude que le médicament n'entraîne pas ces effets chez lui.
- Inciter le patient à éviter toute modification de l'alimentation qui peut entraîner une acidification ou une alcalinisation notables de l'urine (les aliments en question sont indiqués à l'annexe J).
- Recommander au patient qui doit suivre un autre traitement ou subir une intervention chirurgicale d'avertir le professionnel de la santé qu'il souffre d'arythmies et qu'il suit un traitement par ce médicament.
- Conseiller au patient de signaler à un professionnel de la santé les symptômes suivants: fatigue généralisée, jaunissement de la peau ou des yeux, fièvre, maux de gorge, tout comme des effets secondaires persistants.
- Conseiller au patient de porter sur lui en tout temps une pièce d'identité où sont inscrits son problème de santé et son traitement.

VÉRIFICATION DE L'EFFICACITÉ THÉRAPEUTIQUE

L'efficacité du traitement peut être démontrée par: la diminution de la fréquence des arythmies ventriculaires graves ou leur suppression ■ la diminution de l'intensité de la douleur neuropathique grave.

MICONAZOLE,

voir Antifongiques topiques et Antifongiques vaginaux

ALERTE CLINIQUE

MIDAZOLAM

Apo-Midazolam, Midazolam, Versed

CLASSIFICATION:

Anxiolytique et hypnosédatif (benzodiazépine)

Grossesse – catégorie D

M

INDICATIONS

IM: Prémédication avant une intervention chirurgicale ou diagnostique ▪ **IV**: Sédation, soulagement de l'anxiété et amnésie lors d'interventions thérapeutiques, diagnostiques ou radiographiques (sédation consciente) ▪ Adjuvant à l'induction de l'anesthésie et élément d'une anesthésie équilibrée ▪ Sous forme de perfusion continue, sédation des patients soumis à une ventilation mécanique, sous anesthésie ou dans le cadre de soins d'urgence ▪ **Péd. (IM ou IV)**: Sédation, soulagement de l'anxiété ou amnésie lors d'interventions diagnostiques ou thérapeutiques, comme prémédication avant une anesthésie ou comme composante de l'anesthésie pendant les interventions chirurgicales ou pendant les soins de réanimation.

MÉCANISME D'ACTION

Dépression généralisée du SNC par un effet s'exerçant à de nombreux niveaux de ce système ▪ Effets probablement attribuables à la médiation par l'acide gamma-aminobutyrique (GABA), un neurotransmetteur inhibiteur. ***Effets thérapeutiques:*** Sédation de courte durée ▪ Amnésie postopératoire.

M

PHARMACOCINÉTIQUE

Absorption: > 90 % (IM); 100 % (IV).

Distribution: L'agent traverse la barrière hémato-encéphalique et placentaire.

Liaison aux protéines: 97 %.

Métabolisme et excrétion: Métabolisme hépatique, avec transformation en hydroxymidazolam, un métabolite actif, et en 2 autres métabolites inactifs (métabolisés par le cytochrome P450 3A4); excrétion rénale sous forme de métabolites.

Demi-vie: De 1 à 12 heures (prolongée en cas d'insuffisance rénale ou hépatique, d'insuffisance cardiaque ou d'obésité et chez les personnes âgées).

Profil temps-action (sédation)

	Début d'action	Pic	Durée
IM	15 min	30 - 60 min	2 - 6 h
IV	1,5 - 5 min	rapide	2 - 6 h

CONTRE-INDICATIONS, PRÉCAUTIONS ET MISES EN GARDE

Contre-indications: Hypersensibilité (risque de réactions de sensibilité croisée avec d'autres benzodiazépines) ▪ Insuffisance pulmonaire aiguë ▪ Bronchopneumopathie chronique obstructive ▪ Glaucome à angle fermé.

Précautions et mises en garde: Choc (sauf dans les unités de soins intensifs) ▪ Coma ou dépression préexistante du SNC (sauf dans les unités de soins intensifs) ▪ **Péd.**: Ne pas administrer les produits renfermant de l'alcool benzylique aux nouveau-nés et aux enfants prématurés; calculer la dose en fonction du poids corporel idéal chez les enfants obèses ▪ **Obst., allaitement**: L'innocuité du médicament n'a pas été établie chez la femme enceinte ou qui allaite ▪ Insuffisance cardiaque ▪ Insuffisance rénale ▪ Insuffisance hépatique grave ▪ **Gér.**: Il est recommandé de réduire la dose chez les personnes âgées ou débilitées ▪ Myasthénie (risque augmenté de décompensation respiratoire).

RÉACTIONS INDÉSIRABLES ET EFFETS SECONDAIRES

SNC: agitation, somnolence, sédation excessive, céphalées.

ORLO: vision trouble.

Resp.: APNÉE, LARYNGOSPASME, DÉPRESSION RESPIRATOIRE, bronchospasme, toux.

CV: ARRÊT CARDIAQUE, arythmies.

GI: hoquet, nausées, vomissements.

Tég.: rash.

Locaux: phlébite au point d'injection IV, douleur au point d'injection IM.

INTERACTIONS

Médicament-médicament: Dépression additive du SNC lors de l'usage concomitant d'**alcool**, d'**antihistaminiques**, d'**analgésiques opioïdes** et d'**hypnosédatifs** (diminuer la dose de midazolam de 30 à 50 % en cas d'administration concomitante) ▪ Risque accru d'hypotension lors de l'administration simultanée d'**antihypertenseurs** ou de **dérivés nitrés**, ou lors de l'ingestion de grandes quantités d'**alcool** ▪ Le midazolam est métabolisé par le cytochrome P450 3A4; on peut s'attendre à ce que les **médicaments qui induisent ce système ou qui l'inhibent** modifient les effets du midazolam ▪ La **carbamazépine**, la **phénytoïne**, la **rifampine**, la **rifabutine** et le **phénobarbital** réduisent les concentrations de midazolam ▪ Les agents suivants ralentissent le métabolisme du midazolam et peuvent intensifier ses effets: **érythromycine**, **clarithromycine**, **cimétidine**, **ranitidine**, **diltiazem**, **vérapamil**, **fluconazole**, **itraconazole** et **kétoconazole**.

Médicament-aliments: Le **jus de pamplemousse** ralentit le métabolisme du midazolam et peut en intensifier les effets.

VOIES D'ADMINISTRATION ET POSOLOGIE

Il faut adapter la dose à chaque cas particulier et la diminuer chez les personnes âgées et chez les patients ayant déjà reçu un sédatif.

Sédation préopératoire, soulagement de l'anxiété et amnésie

- **IM (adultes autrement en bonne santé < 55 ans):** De 0,07 à 0,08 mg/kg, de 30 à 60 minutes avant l'intervention (la dose habituelle est de 5 mg).
- **IM (adultes ≥ 55 ans, débilités ou souffrant d'une maladie chronique):** De 0,02 à 0,03 mg/kg, de 30 à 60 minutes avant l'intervention (la dose habituelle se situe entre 1 et 3 mg).
- **IM (enfants):** De 0,1 à 0,15 mg/kg, jusqu'à 0,5 mg/kg; ne pas dépasser 10 mg par dose.

Sédation consciente lors d'interventions de courte durée

- **IV (adultes et enfants autrement en bonne santé > 12 ans et < 55 ans):** Dose initiale de 2 à 2,5 mg. On peut majorer cette dose selon la réponse du patient. Il est rarement nécessaire d'administrer des doses supérieures à 5 mg (maximum 0,1 mg/kg). Réduire la dose de 30 %, si des opioïdes ou d'autres dépresseurs du SNC sont administrés. Des doses d'entretien équivalant à 25 % de la dose initiale peuvent être administrées selon les besoins.
- **IV (personnes ≥ 55 ans, débilitées ou souffrant d'une maladie chronique):** Dose initiale de 1 à 1,5 mg. On peut augmenter cette dose selon la réponse du patient. Il est rarement nécessaire d'administrer des doses supérieures à 3,5 mg (dose maximale 0,07 mg/kg). Réduire la dose de 30 %, si des opioïdes ou d'autres dépresseurs du SNC sont administrés. Des doses d'entretien équivalant à 25 % de la dose initiale peuvent être administrées selon les besoins.

Sédation consciente lors d'interventions de courte durée ou avant l'anesthésie

- **IV (enfants de 6 mois à 5 ans):** De 0,05 à 0,1 mg/kg (la dose totale ne doit pas dépasser 0,6 mg/kg).
- **IV (enfants de 6 à 12 ans):** Dose initiale de 0,025 à 0,050 mg/kg (la dose totale ne doit pas dépasser 0,4 mg/kg).

Induction de l'anesthésie (adjuvant)

Au besoin, on peut administrer une dose additionnelle équivalant à 25 % de la dose initiale.

- **IV (adultes autrement en bonne santé < 55 ans):** Dose initiale de 0,3 à 0,35 mg/kg (la dose totale ne doit pas dépasser 0,6 mg/kg). Si le patient a déjà reçu un opioïde ou un dépresseur du SNC, la dose initiale est de 0,15 à 0,35 mg/kg.
- **IV (personnes ≥ 55 ans):** Dose initiale de 0,3 mg/kg. Si le patient a déjà reçu un opioïde ou un dépresseur du SNC, la dose initiale est de 0,2 mg/kg.
- **IV (adultes débilités ou souffrant de maladies chroniques):** Dose initiale de 0,15 à 0,25 mg/kg. Si le patient a déjà reçu un opioïde ou un dépresseur du SNC, la dose initiale est de 0,15 à 0,2 mg/kg.

Sédation lors de soins d'urgence

- **IV (adultes ne recevant aucun autre opioïde ni dépresseur du SNC):** Dose initiale de 0,015 à 0,03 mg/kg, s'il faut administrer une dose d'attaque; on peut augmenter ou réduire cette dose par paliers équivalant à 25 à 50 % de la dose initiale, à intervalles de 30 minutes, jusqu'à l'obtention de l'effet souhaité; on peut ensuite administrer le médicament par perfusion à un débit de 0,01 à 0,03 mg/kg/h (dose maximale: de 0,07 à 0,15 mg/kg/h).
- **IV (adultes ayant reçu une prémédication ou recevant des opioïdes ou des dépresseurs du SNC):** Dose initiale de 0,015 à 0,03 mg/kg, s'il faut administrer une dose d'attaque; on peut augmenter ou réduire cette dose par paliers équivalant à 25 à 50 % de la dose initiale, à intervalles de 30 minutes, jusqu'à l'obtention de l'effet souhaité; on peut ensuite administrer le médicament par perfusion à un débit de 0,01 à 0,03 mg/kg/h (dose maximale: de 0,07 mg/kg/h).
- **IV (enfants):** *Patients intubés seulement* – dose d'attaque de 0,05 à 0,2 mg/kg; administrer ensuite par perfusion à un débit de 0,001 à 0,002 mg/kg/min (de 1 à 2 g/kg/min).
- **IV (nouveau-nés prématurés et nés à terme):** *Patients intubés seulement* – de 0,000 5 à 0,001 mg/kg/min (de 0,5 à 1 µg/kg/min). Il ne faut pas administrer de dose d'attaque chez le nouveau-né (à terme ou prématuré).

PRÉSENTATION

Solution pour injection: 1 mg/mL^{Pr}, 5 mg/mL^{Pr}.

SOINS INFIRMIERS

ÉVALUATION DE LA SITUATION

- Noter le degré de sédation et l'état de conscience du patient tout au long de l'administration du médicament et pendant les 2 à 6 heures qui suivent.
- Mesurer la pression artérielle, le pouls et la fréquence respiratoire tout au long de l'administration IV. Garder à portée de la main de l'oxygène et le matériel de réanimation pour parer à toute urgence.

Toxicité et surdosage:

- En cas de surdosage, mesurer continuellement le pouls, la fréquence respiratoire et la pression artérielle. Maintenir la perméabilité des voies aériennes et assister la ventilation, selon les besoins. En cas

d'hypotension, administrer des liquides par voie IV, repositionner le patient et lui administrer des vasopresseurs.
- Les effets du midazolam peuvent être renversés par le flumazénil (Anexate).

DIAGNOSTICS INFIRMIERS POSSIBLES

- Mode de respiration inefficace (Réactions indésirables).
- Risque d'accident (Effets secondaires).
- Connaissances insuffisantes sur le traitement médicamenteux (Enseignement au patient et à ses proches).

INTERVENTIONS INFIRMIÈRES

- NE PAS CONFONDRE VERSED (MIDAZOLAM) AVEC VEPESID (ÉTOPOSIDE).

ALERTE CLINIQUE: NE PAS ACCEPTER D'ORDONNANCE OÙ LA DOSE DE MIDAZOLAM EST PRESCRITE EN VOLUME; EXIGER QUE LES ORDONNANCES SOIENT RÉDIGÉES EN mg. AVANT L'ADMINISTRATION, FAIRE VALIDER L'ORDONNANCE D'ORIGINE ET LE CALCUL DE LA DOSE PAR UN DEUXIÈME PROFESSIONNEL DE LA SANTÉ.

IM: Injecter profondément dans une grande masse musculaire.

M

IV directe:

- Administrer la préparation sans la diluer ou la diluer dans une solution de D5%E ou de NaCl 0,9 % et l'administrer dans une tubulure en Y.
- Lorsqu'on administre le midazolam en même temps que des analgésiques opioïdes, la dose devrait être réduite de 30 à 50 %.

Vitesse d'administration: Administrer chacune des doses lentement, en 2 à 5 minutes. Observer attentivement le point d'injection IV afin de prévenir l'extravasation. Adapter la dose selon la réponse du patient. Une injection rapide, particulièrement chez les nouveau-nés, a provoqué une hypotension grave.

Perfusion continue: Diluer 5 mg/mL dans une solution de NaCl 0,9 % ou de D5%E, jusqu'à l'obtention d'une concentration de 0,5 mg/mL. Consulter les directives du fabricant avant de diluer la préparation.

Vitesse d'administration: Le midazolam ne doit être administré que par une personne ayant la formation requise en anesthésie. Le débit de perfusion chez l'adulte est habituellement de 0,02 à 0,1 mg/kg/h, chez l'enfant, de 0,001 à 0,002 mg/kg/min, et chez le nouveau-né, de 0,000 5 à 0,001 mg/kg/min. Adapter la dose pour obtenir le niveau de sédation souhaité. Évaluer la sédation à intervalles réguliers et ajuster le débit à la hausse ou à la baisse, de 25 à 50 %, selon les besoins.

Associations compatibles dans la même seringue: atropine ■ benzquinamide ■ buprénorphine ■ butorphanol ■ cimétidine ■ fentanyl ■ glycopyrrolate ■ hydromorphone ■ mépéridine ■ métoclopramide ■ morphine ■ nalbuphine ■ scopolamine ■ sufentanil ■ thiéthylpérazine ■ triméthobenzamide.

Associations incompatibles dans la même seringue: prochlorpérazine ■ ranitidine.

Compatibilité (tubulure en Y): amikacine ■ amiodarone ■ atracurium ■ bumétanide ■ calcium, gluconate de ■ céfazoline ■ céfotaxime ■ cimétidine ■ ciprofloxacine ■ clindamycine ■ digoxine ■ dopamine ■ érythromycine, lactobionate d' ■ esmolol ■ étomidate ■ famotidine ■ fentanyl ■ fluconazole ■ gentamicine ■ halopéridol ■ héparine ■ insuline ■ labétolol ■ méthylprednisolone ■ métronidazole ■ morphine ■ nitroglycérine ■ nitroprusside ■ noradrénaline ■ pancuronium ■ pipéracilline ■ potassium, chlorure de ■ ranitidine ■ sufentanil ■ théophylline ■ tobramycine ■ vancomycine ■ vécuronium.

Incompatibilité (tubulure en Y): albumine ■ ampicilline ■ ceftazidime ■ céfuroxime ■ clonidine ■ dexaméthasone ■ floxacilline ■ foscarnet ■ furosémide ■ hydrocortisone ■ imipénem/cilastatine ■ méthotrexate ■ nafcilline ■ oméprazole ■ sodium, bicarbonate de ■ triméthoprime/sulfaméthoxazole.

ENSEIGNEMENT AU PATIENT ET À SES PROCHES

- Expliquer au patient que ce médicament entraînera une perte de mémoire et de ce fait ses souvenirs de l'intervention seront estompés.
- Prévenir le patient que le midazolam peut provoquer de la somnolence ou des étourdissements. Lui conseiller de demander de l'aide lors de ses déplacements, de ne pas conduire et d'éviter les activités qui exigent sa vigilance pendant les 24 heures qui suivent l'administration de ce médicament.
- Recommander à la patiente qui pense être enceinte d'en informer le professionnel de la santé, avant que ce médicament ne lui soit administré.
- Recommander au patient d'éviter de boire de l'alcool et de ne pas prendre d'autres dépresseurs du SNC dans les 24 heures qui suivent l'administration du midazolam.

VÉRIFICATION DE L'EFFICACITÉ THÉRAPEUTIQUE

L'efficacité du traitement peut être démontrée par: la sédation au cours des interventions chirurgicales, diagnostiques et endoscopiques et l'amnésie par la suite ■ la sédation et l'amnésie chez les patients soumis à une ventilation mécanique lors de soins d'urgence.

MIDODRINE

Apo-Midodrine, Amatine

CLASSIFICATION:

Vasopresseur

Grossesse - catégorie C

INDICATIONS

Soulagement des symptômes d'hypotension orthostatique chronique, dus à une insuffisance d'origine autonome chez les patients atteints des syndromes de Bradbury-Eggleston ou de Shy-Drager, de diabète et de la maladie de Parkinson.

MÉCANISME D'ACTION

La midodrine est un bioprécurseur; son effet thérapeutique est dû et directement relié à sa transformation après absorption en desglymidodrine ■ La desglymidodrine est un stimulant des récepteurs alpha$_1$-adrénergiques ayant peu d'effet sur les récepteurs bêta-adrénergiques. L'élévation de la pression artérielle est due presque entièrement à une élévation de la résistance périphérique. ***Effets thérapeutiques:*** Hausse des pressions systolique et diastolique, en orthostatisme, en position assise ou en décubitus, chez les patients atteints d'hypotension orthostatique.

PHARMACOCINÉTIQUE

Absorption: Rapide et presque complète (PO). Biodisponibilité à 93 % (sous forme de desglymidodrine, le métabolite actif).

Distribution: Peu étudiée. La midodrine traverse difficilement la barrière hématoencéphalique.

Liaison aux protéines: Faible.

Métabolisme et excrétion: Métabolisme hépatique partiel; également métabolisme dans plusieurs tissus. Élimination majoritairement rénale (midodrine et desglymidodrine).

Demi-vie: Desglymidodrine: environ 3 heures.

Profil temps-action

	DÉBUT D'ACTION	PIC	DURÉE
PO	45 - 90 min	1 h	2 - 6 h

CONTRE-INDICATIONS, PRÉCAUTIONS ET MISES EN GARDE

Contre-indications: Hypersensibilité ■ Hypertension persistante et excessive préexistante en décubitus ■ Cardiopathie organique grave ■ Maladie rénale aiguë ■ Rétention urinaire ■ Phéochromocytome ■ Thyrotoxicose.

Précautions et mises en garde: Hypertension en décubitus: la réaction la plus grave associée à la midodrine est une élévation marquée de la pression artérielle en décubitus qui, si elle est soutenue, peut provoquer un accident vasculaire cérébral, un infarctus du myocarde, une insuffisance cardiaque globale, une insuffisance rénale ou des problèmes similaires qui, seuls ou en association, peuvent mener à une issue fatale. Les symptômes d'hypertension en décubitus sont observés plus fréquemment au début du traitement et au cours du processus d'adaptation de la posologie ■ Bradycardie: La prudence est de mise si la midodrine est administrée en même temps que des glucosides cardiaques (digoxine), des agents psychopharmacologiques, des bêtabloquants ou d'autres agents qui, directement ou indirectement, ralentissent la fréquence cardiaque ■ Tachycardie ■ Diabète ■ Insuffisance rénale ■ Insuffisance hépatique ■ Occlusion des voies urinaires, vessie neurogène ou troubles semblables ■ **PÉD.:** L'innocuité et l'efficacité du médicament n'ont pas été établies ■ **OBST., ALLAITEMENT:** L'innocuité du médicament n'a pas été établie.

M

RÉACTIONS INDÉSIRABLES ET EFFETS SECONDAIRES

SNC: étourdissements, céphalées.

CV: HYPERTENSION EN DÉCUBITUS et en position assise.

GI: nausées.

GU: troubles urinaires, dysurie, mictions impérieuses, rétention urinaire, mictions fréquentes.

Tég.: prurit, éruptions cutanées.

Divers: réactions pilomotrices, frissons, paresthésie, douleurs.

INTERACTIONS

Médicament-médicament: Les **glucosides cardiaques** (**digoxine**), administrés en concomitance, peuvent aggraver ou déclencher la bradycardie, un bloc AV ou des arythmies ■ **Agents sympathomimétiques:** Les **médicaments qui stimulent les récepteurs alpha-adrénergiques** (p. ex., **phényléphrine**, **pseudoéphédrine**, **éphédrine** ou **dihydroergotamine**) peuvent aggraver ou potentialiser les effets vasopresseurs de la midodrine ■ **Agents sympatholytiques:** Les **antagonistes des récepteurs alpha-adrénergiques** (p. ex., **phentolamine**, **prazosine**, **doxazosine** et **labétalol**) peuvent inhiber l'effet vasopresseur de la midodrine ■ **Corticostéroïdes:** Les patients prenant des corticostéroïdes ayant des propriétés minéralocorticoïdes (**fludrocortisone**) peuvent éprouver à la suite d'un traitement à la midodrine un effet vasopresseur excessif, surtout en décubitus ■ Il existe un risque d'interaction avec les **médicaments subissant une**

élimination par sécrétion tubulaire active par le système de sécrétion des bases, comme la **metformine**, la **cimétidine**, la **ranitidine**, le **procaïnamide**, le **triamtérène**, la **flécaïnide** et la **quinidine**, étant donné que la desglymidodrine est éliminée par cette voie.

Médicament-aliments: L'ingestion de grandes quantités de **sel** ou d'**aliments contenant du sodium** peut provoquer une rétention sodique excessive et accroître les effets hypertenseurs de la midodrine.

VOIES D'ADMINISTRATION ET POSOLOGIE

- **PO (adultes):** *Dose d'attaque habituelle:* 2,5 mg, 3 fois par jour. Augmenter la posologie selon les besoins de chaque patient. La plupart des cas sont maîtrisés avec 30 mg ou moins par jour, administrés en 3 ou 4 prises fractionnées. On peut administrer la midodrine jusqu'à 6 fois par jour. *Dose maximale recommandée:* 30 mg par jour. Chez certains patients, la première dose matinale doit être plus élevée que les doses ultérieures. Dans certains cas, la midodrine a été administrée 3 fois par jour, selon le schéma posologique suivant: le matin (1 ou 2 heures avant le lever), au milieu de l'avant-midi et au milieu de l'après-midi.

M

INSUFFISANCE RÉNALE OU HÉPATIQUE

- **PO (ADULTES):** UTILISER AVEC PRUDENCE. CHEZ CES PATIENTS, LA DOSE D'ATTAQUE NE DOIT PAS DÉPASSER 2,5 mg.

PRÉSENTATION

Comprimés: 2,5 mg^{Pr}, 5 mg^{Pr}.

SOINS INFIRMIERS

ÉVALUATION DE LA SITUATION

- Le traitement par la midodrine devrait être amorcé sous surveillance médicale étroite, dans un milieu thérapeutique contrôlé, comme un hôpital, une clinique ou un cabinet médical. La pression artérielle (en décubitus et en position assise) devrait être prise toutes les heures, au cours des 3 heures suivant la première et la deuxième dose d'un schéma posologique basé sur 3 prises quotidiennes. On adoptera la même démarche chaque fois qu'on doit augmenter la posologie.
- Mesurer la pression artérielle à intervalles réguliers tout au long du traitement. Prévenir un professionnel de la santé en cas de modification importante.

Tests de laboratoire: On n'a pas noté de changements cliniquement significatifs dans les résultats des épreuves de laboratoire.

DIAGNOSTICS INFIRMIERS POSSIBLES

- Manque de connaissances sur le traitement médicamenteux (Enseignement au patient et à ses proches).

INTERVENTIONS INFIRMIÈRES

- Les comprimés de 2,5 mg et de 5 mg sont sécables; on peut les diviser facilement s'il faut ajuster la dose.
- Chez les patients prenant la midodrine 3 fois par jour, l'horaire habituel des prises est le suivant: de 1 à 2 heures avant le lever, au milieu de l'avant-midi et au milieu de l'après-midi.
- Pour diminuer les risques d'hypertension en décubitus, on peut recommander au patient de ne pas prendre le médicament après le repas du soir ou dans les 4 heures qui précèdent l'heure du coucher.
- On peut prendre le médicament sans égard aux repas.

ENSEIGNEMENT AU PATIENT ET À SES PROCHES

- Durant la période de surveillance médicale étroite, on devrait enseigner au patient ou à un proche vivant avec lui la façon correcte de mesurer la pression artérielle. On doit leur expliquer qu'il faut la prendre en position couchée et assise tous les jours, pendant au moins 1 mois après le début du traitement par la midodrine, et 2 fois par semaine par la suite.
- Expliquer au patient qu'il doit interrompre la prise de la midodrine et prévenir aussitôt le médecin si sa pression artérielle, en n'importe quelle position, s'élève au-dessus de 180/100 mm Hg.
- Conseiller au patient de respecter rigoureusement la posologie recommandée. S'il n'a pas pu prendre le médicament au moment habituel, il doit le prendre aussitôt que possible à moins que ce ne soit presque l'heure prévue pour la dose suivante. Conseiller au patient de toujours garder une provision suffisante de médicament.
- Recommander au patient d'observer les modifications de régime alimentaire prescrites par le professionnel de la santé.
- Recommander au patient de prévenir un professionnel de la santé si les symptômes suivants d'hypertension en décubitus se manifestent: palpitations, bourdonnements d'oreilles (acouphènes), céphalées, vision brouillée, etc.
- Prévenir le patient qui manifeste une bradycardie qu'il doit signaler tout signe ou symptôme évoquant la bradycardie (ralentissement du pouls, aggravation des étourdissements, syncope, palpitations) et ne plus prendre la midodrine avant d'avoir consulté son médecin.

- Prévenir le patient qu'il doit signaler promptement tout signe de rétention urinaire possible (p. ex., retard de la miction ou changement de fréquence).
- Recommander au patient de ne pas prendre de médicaments en vente libre refermant des agents sympathomimétiques vasoconstricteurs (p. ex., phényléphrine, pseudoéphédrine, éphédrine ou dihydroergotamine) en concomitance avec la midodrine. Lui conseiller de toujours consulter le pharmacien avant de prendre un médicament en vente libre.
- Conseiller au patient de porter sur lui en tout temps une pièce d'identité où sont inscrits son problème de santé et son traitement.

VÉRIFICATION DE L'EFFICACITÉ THÉRAPEUTIQUE

L'efficacité du traitement peut être démontrée par: la diminution des symptômes d'hypotension orthostatique.

MIGLUSTAT

Zavesca

CLASSIFICATION:

Inhibiteur de la glucosylcéramide synthase, analogue synthétique de la D-glucose

Grossesse – catégorie X

INDICATIONS

Maladie de Gaucher de type 1, de légère à modérée, lorsque le traitement par remplacement enzymatique (TRE) ne fait pas partie des options thérapeutiques.

MÉCANISME D'ACTION

Inhibition compétitive et réversible de la glucosylcéramide synthase, l'enzyme qui intervient la première dans une série de réactions assurant la synthèse des glycosphingolipides. En présence de maladie de Gaucher, les glucosylcéramides (un type de glycosphingolipide) s'accumulent dans les tissus. ***Effets thérapeutiques:*** Diminution de la synthèse et de l'accumulation des glycosphingolipides à base de glucosylcéramide et, par conséquent, diminution des lésions tissulaires provoquées par le glucosylcéramide.

PHARMACOCINÉTIQUE

Absorption: Bonne (PO).

Distribution: Tissus extravasculaires.

Métabolisme et excrétion: Aucun métabolisme. Excrétion majoritairement rénale (sous forme inchangée).

Demi-vie: De 6 à 7 heures.

Profil temps-action

	DÉBUT D'ACTION	PIC	DURÉE
PO	inconnu	2 - 2,5 h	8 h

CONTRE-INDICATIONS, PRÉCAUTIONS ET MISES EN GARDE

Contre-indications: Hypersensibilité ■ Grossesse ■ Insuffisance rénale grave (Cl_{Cr} < 30 mL/min).

Précautions et mises en garde: Insuffisance rénale de légère à modérée (il est recommandé de modifier la posologie si la Cl_{Cr} est < 70 mL/min) ■ **GÉR.:** Commencer le traitement à une faible dose chez les personnes âgées, en raison de la diminution de la masse corporelle, des fonctions cardiaque, hépatique et rénale, ainsi que de la présence possible d'autres maladies chroniques et de traitements médicamenteux concomitants ■ **PÉD.:** L'innocuité de l'agent n'a pas été établie chez les enfants < 18 ans ■ Allaitement.

RÉACTIONS INDÉSIRABLES ET EFFETS SECONDAIRES

SNC: céphalées.

GI: douleurs abdominales, diarrhée, flatulence, nausées, anorexie, dyspepsie.

GU: diminution de la fécondité chez l'homme.

Hémat.: thrombopénie.

Métab.: perte de poids.

SN: paresthésie, neuropathie périphérique, tremblements.

INTERACTIONS

Médicament-médicament: Aucune interaction cliniquement significative n'a été signalée.

VOIES D'ADMINISTRATION ET POSOLOGIE

- **PO (adultes):** 100 mg, 3 fois par jour, à intervalles également espacés.

INSUFFISANCE RÉNALE

- **PO (ADULTES):** *CL_{CR} 50–70 mL/MIN* – 100 mg, 2 FOIS PAR JOUR; *CL_{CR} 30–50 mL/MIN* – 100 mg, 1 FOIS PAR JOUR.

PRÉSENTATION

Capsules: 100 mg[Pr].

SOINS INFIRMIERS

ÉVALUATION DE LA SITUATION

- Il faut effectuer des évaluations neurologiques au départ et tous les 6 mois par la suite, pendant toute la durée du traitement. Si des symptômes de neuropathie périphériques se manifestent (engourdissements, picotements), il faudrait envisager l'abandon du traitement.

- Rester à l'affût des tremblements. Ils peuvent commencer pendant le premier mois de traitement et pourraient disparaître en l'espace de 1 à 3 mois; il pourrait cependant s'avérer nécessaire d'abandonner le traitement.
- Suivre de près la diarrhée et la perte de poids. Conseiller au patient souffrant de diarrhée d'éviter les aliments riches en hydrates de carbone.

Tests de laboratoire: L'agent peut entraîner une thrombopénie.

DIAGNOSTICS INFIRMIERS POSSIBLES

- Connaissances insuffisantes sur l'évolution de la maladie et sur le traitement médicamenteux (Enseignement au patient et à ses proches).

INTERVENTIONS INFIRMIÈRES

PO: Administrer le médicament 3 fois par jour, à des intervalles également espacés. Les capsules doivent être avalées telles quelles avec de l'eau. On peut administrer l'agent avec ou sans aliments.

M

ENSEIGNEMENT AU PATIENT ET À SES PROCHES

- Conseiller au patient de prendre le miglustat à la même heure chaque jour, en respectant rigoureusement les recommandations du médecin. S'il n'a pas pu prendre le médicament au moment habituel, lui recommander de sauter cette dose et de prendre la suivante à l'heure habituelle. Le prévenir qu'il est dangereux de donner ce médicament à d'autres personnes.
- Recommander à la patiente d'informer immédiatement un professionnel de la santé si elle est enceinte, si elle souhaite le devenir ou si elle allaite. Conseiller au patient des deux sexes d'avoir recours à une méthode de contraception fiable tout au long du traitement et pendant les 3 mois qui suivent.
- Recommander au patient de consulter un professionnel de la santé avant de prendre des médicaments d'ordonnance ou en vente libre ou des produits à base de plantes médicinales en même temps que le miglustat.
- Recommander au patient de prévenir un professionnel de la santé en cas d'engourdissements, de douleurs ou de brûlures au niveau des mains ou des pieds, ou si des tremblements apparaissent ou s'aggravent.

VÉRIFICATION DE L'EFFICACITÉ THÉRAPEUTIQUE

L'efficacité du traitement peut être démontrée par: la diminution du volume de la rate et du foie chez les patients qui souffrent de la maladie de Gaucher. ✳

ALERTE CLINIQUE

MILRINONE

Apo-Milrinone injectable, Primacor

CLASSIFICATION:

Inotrope et cardiotonique, vasodilatateur

Grossesse – catégorie C

INDICATIONS

Traitement de courte durée de l'insuffisance cardiaque globale grave (y compris les états de faible débit après une chirurgie) qui ne répond pas au traitement habituel par des dérivés digitaliques, des diurétiques et des vasodilatateurs.

MÉCANISME D'ACTION

Augmentation de la contractilité du myocarde ■ Diminution de la précharge et de la postcharge par un effet direct de dilatation du muscle lisse vasculaire. ***Effets thérapeutiques:*** Augmentation du débit cardiaque (effet inotrope).

PHARMACOCINÉTIQUE

Absorption: Biodisponibilité à 100 % (IV).

Distribution: Inconnue.

Métabolisme et excrétion: Excrétion rénale (de 80 à 90 % sous forme inchangée).

Demi-vie: 2,3 heures (prolongée en cas d'insuffisance cardiaque).

Profil temps-action (effets hémodynamiques)

	DÉBUT D'ACTION	PIC	DURÉE
IV	5 – 15 min	inconnu	3 – 6 h

CONTRE-INDICATIONS, PRÉCAUTIONS ET MISES EN GARDE

Contre-indications: Hypersensibilité.

Précautions et mises en garde: Cardiopathie valvulaire pulmonaire ou aortique grave ■ Rétrécissement aortique sous-valvulaire hypertrophique (risque accru d'obstruction de la voie d'éjection) ■ Antécédents d'arythmies, d'anomalies électrolytiques, de concentrations anormales de digoxine ou de cathétérisme vasculaire (risque accru d'arythmies ventriculaires) ■ Insuffisance rénale (il est recommandé de réduire la vitesse de perfusion si la Cl_{Cr} est < 50 mL/min) ■ **OBST., ALLAITEMENT, PÉD.**: L'innocuité du médicament n'a pas été établie.

RÉACTIONS INDÉSIRABLES ET EFFETS SECONDAIRES

SNC: céphalées, tremblements.
CV: ARYTHMIES VENTRICULAIRES, angine de poitrine, douleurs thoraciques, hypotension, arythmies supraventriculaires.
Tég.: rash.
GI: résultats anormaux aux tests de la fonction hépatique.
HÉ: hypokaliémie.
Hémat.: thrombopénie.

INTERACTIONS

Médicament-médicament: Aucune interaction notable.

VOIES D'ADMINISTRATION ET POSOLOGIE

- **IV (adultes)**: *Dose d'attaque* de 50 µg/kg, suivie d'une *perfusion* de 0,50 µg/kg/min (le débit peut aller de 0,375 à 0,75 µg/kg/min).

PRÉSENTATION

Solution pour injection: 1 mg/mL[Pr], en fioles de 10 mL et de 20 mL.

SOINS INFIRMIERS

ÉVALUATION DE LA SITUATION

- Mesurer la fréquence cardiaque et la pression artérielle tout au long de l'administration. On devrait ralentir ou arrêter l'administration de la milrinone si la pression artérielle chute excessivement.
- Effectuer le bilan quotidien des ingesta et des excreta et peser le patient tous les jours. Observer le patient pour déterminer si les signes et les symptômes suivants d'insuffisance cardiaque ont disparu: œdème périphérique, dyspnée, râles et crépitations, gain pondéral; vérifier si les paramètres hémodynamiques suivants se sont améliorés: élévation du débit et de l'index cardiaques, diminution de la pression capillaire pulmonaire. Corriger les effets d'un traitement antérieur intensif par des diurétiques pour favoriser une pression de remplissage adéquate.
- SUIVRE L'ÉCG TOUT AU LONG DE LA PERFUSION. LES ARYTHMIES SONT COURANTES ET PEUVENT METTRE LA VIE DU PATIENT EN DANGER. LE RISQUE D'ARYTHMIES VENTRICULAIRES EST ACCRU CHEZ LES PATIENTS AYANT DES ANTÉCÉDENTS D'ARYTHMIES, D'ANOMALIES ÉLECTROLYTIQUES, DE CONCENTRATIONS ANORMALES DE DIGOXINE OU DE CATHÉTÉRISME VASCULAIRE.

***Tests de laboratoire*:**
- Examiner à intervalles fréquents tout au long de l'administration les concentrations d'électrolytes et les résultats des tests de la fonction rénale. Pour réduire le risque d'arythmies, corriger l'hypokaliémie avant d'administrer la milrinone.
- Noter la numération plaquettaire tout au long du traitement.

***TOXICITÉ ET SURDOSAGE*: ALERTE CLINIQUE**: LE SURDOSAGE SE MANIFESTE PAR DE L'HYPOTENSION. ON DEVRAIT, DANS CE CAS, RÉDUIRE LA DOSE OU ARRÊTER LE TRAITEMENT. IL POURRAIT S'AVÉRER NÉCESSAIRE DE RECOURIR À DES MESURES DE SOUTIEN.

DIAGNOSTICS INFIRMIERS POSSIBLES

- Débit cardiaque diminué (Indications).
- Connaissances insuffisantes sur le traitement médicamenteux (Enseignement au patient et à ses proches).

INTERVENTIONS INFIRMIÈRES

ALERTE CLINIQUE: LORS DE L'ADMINISTRATION DE LA MILRINONE, ON A SIGNALÉ DES ERREURS AYANT PARFOIS MENÉ À UNE ISSUE FATALE. AVANT L'ADMINISTRATION, IL EST RECOMMANDÉ DE DEMANDER À UN AUTRE PROFESSIONNEL DE LA SANTÉ DE VÉRIFIER L'ORDONNANCE D'ORIGINE, LE CALCUL DES DOSES ET LE RÉGLAGE DE LA POMPE VOLUMÉTRIQUE.

IV directe: On peut administrer la dose d'attaque sans la diluer au préalable.

***Vitesse d'administration*:** Administrer la dose d'attaque en 10 minutes.

Perfusion continue: On peut diluer le contenu de la fiole de 20 mg avec 180 mL de diluant pour obtenir une concentration de 100 µg/mL, avec 113 mL de diluant pour obtenir une concentration de 150 µg/mL, ou avec 80 mL de diluant pour obtenir une concentration de 200 µg/mL. Les diluants compatibles sont les solutions de NaCl 0,9 % et 0,45 % et de D5%E. Ne pas utiliser une solution qui a changé de couleur ou qui contient des particules. Consulter les directives du fabricant avant de diluer la préparation.

***Vitesse d'administration*:** Adapter le débit de la perfusion selon la réponse clinique et hémodynamique du patient.

Associations compatibles dans la même seringue: adrénaline ■ atropine ■ calcium, chlorure de ■ digoxine ■ lidocaïne ■ morphine ■ propranolol ■ sodium, bicarbonate de ■ vérapamil.

M

Association incompatible dans la même seringue: furosémide.
Compatibilité (tubulure en Y): digoxine ■ propranolol ■ quinidine, gluconate de.
Incompatibilité (tubulure en Y): furosémide ■ procaïnamide.

ENSEIGNEMENT AU PATIENT ET À SES PROCHES

Expliquer au patient et à ses proches la raison pour laquelle on doit lui administrer ce médicament. La milrinone ne guérit pas l'insuffisance cardiaque, mais peut en maîtriser les symptômes pendant un certain temps.

VÉRIFICATION DE L'EFFICACITÉ THÉRAPEUTIQUE

L'efficacité du traitement peut être démontrée par: la résolution des signes et des symptômes d'insuffisance cardiaque ■ l'amélioration des paramètres hémodynamiques.

MINOCYCLINE,

voir Tétracyclines

MINOXIDIL (VOIE GÉNÉRALE)

Loniten

CLASSIFICATION:
Antihypertenseur (vasodilatateur)

Grossesse – catégorie C

INDICATIONS

Traitement de l'hypertension symptomatique grave ou de l'hypertension associée à la lésion des organes cibles, qui n'a pas pu être maîtrisée par des traitements d'association plus classiques.

MÉCANISME D'ACTION

Relaxation directe du muscle lisse vasculaire, probablement par inhibition de la phosphodiestérase, ce qui entraîne une vasodilatation qui est plus prononcée au niveau des artérioles qu'au niveau des veines. ***Effets thérapeutiques:*** Abaissement de la pression artérielle.

PHARMACOCINÉTIQUE

Absorption: Bonne (PO).
Distribution: Tout l'organisme. L'agent passe dans le lait maternel.
Métabolisme et excrétion: Métabolisme hépatique à 90 %.
Demi-vie: 4,2 heures.

Profil temps-action (effet antihypertenseur)

	DÉBUT D'ACTION	PIC	DURÉE
PO	30 min	2 - 3 h	2 - 5 jours

CONTRE-INDICATIONS, PRÉCAUTIONS ET MISES EN GARDE

Contre-indications: Hypersensibilité ■ Phéochromocytome ■ Hypertension pulmonaire associée à une sténose mitrale.
Précautions et mises en garde: Infarctus du myocarde récent ■ Insuffisance rénale grave (on peut administrer le médicament en présence d'une insuffisance rénale modérée) ■ **OBST., ALLAITEMENT**: L'innocuité du médicament n'a pas été établie ■ Rétention hydrosodée, insuffisance cardiaque ■ **GÉR.**: Les personnes âgées peuvent être plus sensibles aux effets indésirables étant donné la diminution de leurs fonctions hépatique, cardiaque et rénale, reliées au processus du vieillissement.

RÉACTIONS INDÉSIRABLES ET EFFETS SECONDAIRES

SNC: céphalées.
Resp.: ŒDÈME PULMONAIRE.
CV: INSUFFISANCE CARDIAQUE, modifications de l'ÉCG (modification des ondes T), tachycardie, angine de poitrine, épanchement péricardique.
GI: nausées.
Tég.: hypertrichose, modification de la pigmentation, rash.
End.: gynécomastie, irrégularités du cycle menstruel.
HÉ: rétention hydrosodée.
Divers: claudication intermittente.

INTERACTIONS

Médicament-médicament: Hypotension additive lors de l'administration concomitante d'autres **antihypertenseurs** ou de **dérivés nitrés** ou lors de l'ingestion d'**alcool** ■ Les **anti-inflammatoires non stéroïdiens** peuvent diminuer l'efficacité antihypertensive du minoxidil.

VOIES D'ADMINISTRATION ET POSOLOGIE

- **PO (adultes et enfants > 12 ans)**: 5 mg/jour, en 2 doses fractionnées; on peut augmenter la dose à des intervalles de 3 jours ou plus. La dose habituelle se situe entre 10 et 40 mg/jour; la posologie maximale est de 100 mg/jour.

- **PO (enfants < 12 ans):** 0,2 mg/kg/jour, en 2 doses fractionnées; on peut augmenter graduellement la dose à des intervalles de 3 jours ou plus. La dose habituelle est de 0,25 à 1 mg/kg/jour; la dose quotidienne ne doit pas dépasser 50 mg.

PRÉSENTATION

Comprimés: 2,5 mg^{Pr}, 10 mg^{Pr}.

SOINS INFIRMIERS

ÉVALUATION DE LA SITUATION

- Mesurer fréquemment le pouls et la pression artérielle pendant la période initiale d'adaptation de la posologie et à intervalles réguliers pendant toute la durée du traitement. Prévenir le médecin de tout changement important.
- Surveiller la fréquence du renouvellement des ordonnances pour déterminer l'observance du traitement.
- Effectuer le bilan quotidien des ingesta et des excreta, peser le patient tous les jours et suivre de près l'œdème, surtout au début du traitement. Prévenir le médecin en cas de gain de poids ou d'œdème, car la rétention hydrosodée peut être traitée par des diurétiques.

Tests de laboratoire:

- Examiner les résultats des tests des fonctions rénale et hépatique, la numération globulaire et les concentrations d'électrolytes, avant le début du traitement et à intervalles réguliers pendant toute sa durée.
- Le minoxidil peut entraîner l'élévation des concentrations d'urée, de créatinine, de phosphatase alcaline et de sodium, et intensifier l'activité de la rénine plasmatique. Il peut également entraîner la diminution du nombre de globules rouges, de l'hémoglobine et de l'hématocrite. Les valeurs hématologiques et rénales se rétablissent habituellement au fil du traitement.

DIAGNOSTICS INFIRMIERS POSSIBLES

- Irrigation tissulaire inefficace (Indications).
- Connaissances insuffisantes sur le traitement médicamenteux (Enseignement au patient et à ses proches).

INTERVENTIONS INFIRMIÈRES

- On peut administrer le minoxidil sans égard aux repas.
- Il peut être nécessaire d'interrompre graduellement le traitement afin de prévenir l'hypertension rebond.
- Sauf chez les patients hémodialysés, le minoxidil doit être administré avec un diurétique.
- À moins qu'une maîtrise rapide des symptômes ne soit nécessaire, adapter la posologie tous les 3 jours afin que le médicament puisse exercer ses pleins effets.

ENSEIGNEMENT AU PATIENT ET À SES PROCHES

- Expliquer au patient la raison pour laquelle il doit poursuivre la prise de ce médicament même s'il se sent mieux. Lui conseiller de prendre le médicament à la même heure tous les jours. S'il n'a pas pu le prendre au moment habituel, il doit le prendre dès que possible dans les quelques heures qui suivent l'heure prévue, autrement il devrait sauter cette dose et reprendre l'horaire habituel. Il ne faut jamais remplacer une dose manquée par une double dose. Prévenir le patient qu'il ne doit pas arrêter de prendre le minoxidil ni aucun autre antihypertenseur sans consulter un professionnel de la santé au préalable. Le minoxidil stabilise la pression artérielle mais ne guérit pas l'hypertension.
- Inciter le patient à appliquer d'autres mesures de réduction de l'hypertension: perdre du poids, réduire sa consommation de sel, cesser de fumer, boire avec modération, faire régulièrement de l'exercice et diminuer le stress.
- Montrer au patient et à ses proches comment prendre la pression artérielle et le pouls. Leur recommander de mesurer la pression artérielle au moins 1 fois par semaine et de signaler à un professionnel de la santé tout changement important. Leur conseiller de prévenir également un professionnel de la santé si la fréquence du pouls au repos monte de plus de 20 bpm au-dessus des valeurs initiales.
- Recommander au patient de se peser tous les jours et de signaler à un professionnel de la santé tout gain rapide de poids de plus de 2,5 kg ou tout signe de rétention hydrique.
- Recommander au patient de changer lentement de position pour réduire le risque d'hypotension orthostatique.
- Conseiller au patient de consulter un professionnel de la santé avant de prendre des médicaments contre la toux, le rhume ou les allergies.
- Expliquer au patient que les crèmes dépilatoires peuvent ralentir la croissance pileuse accrue. Ce phénomène est passager et disparaît dans les 1 à 6 mois qui suivent l'arrêt du traitement par le minoxidil.
- Conseiller au patient de signaler à un professionnel de la santé les symptômes suivants: enflure inhabituelle du visage, des membres ou de l'abdomen,

M

troubles respiratoires, particulièrement en position couchée, apparition ou aggravation d'une angine, indigestion grave, étourdissements ou évanouissement.

VÉRIFICATION DE L'EFFICACITÉ THÉRAPEUTIQUE

L'efficacité du traitement peut être démontrée par: la baisse de la pression artérielle sans apparition d'effets secondaires graves. ✳

MIRTAZAPINE

Apo-Mirtazapine, Dom-Mirtazapine, Novo-Mirtazapine, Novo-Mirtazapine OD, Remeron, Remeron RD, Riva-Mirtazapine

CLASSIFICATION:
Antidépresseur (tétracyclique)

Grossesse – catégorie C (risque durant le 3e trimestre; voir «Précautions et mises en garde»)

M

INDICATIONS

Traitement de la dépression.

MÉCANISME D'ACTION

Potentialisation des effets de la noradrénaline et de la sérotonine. ***Effets thérapeutiques:*** Effet antidépresseur, qui peut prendre plusieurs semaines avant de se manifester.

PHARMACOCINÉTIQUE

Absorption: Bonne (PO). Biodisponibilité à 50 % (PO).

Distribution: Inconnue.

Liaison aux protéines: 85 %.

Métabolisme et excrétion: Métabolisme majoritairement hépatique (par les enzymes P450 2D6, 1A2 et 3A); les métabolites sont excrétés dans l'urine (75 %) et les fèces (15 %).

Demi-vie: De 20 à 40 heures.

Profil temps-action (effet antidépresseur)

	DÉBUT D'ACTION	PIC	DURÉE
PO	1 – 2 semaines	6 semaines ou plus	inconnue

CONTRE-INDICATIONS, PRÉCAUTIONS ET MISES EN GARDE

Contre-indications: Hypersensibilité.

Précautions et mises en garde: Risque chez les adultes et les enfants d'effets indésirables de type agitation grave parallèlement à des blessures infligées à soi-même ou aux autres ■ Éviter de mettre fin abruptement au traitement en raison du risque de symptômes de sevrage ■ Risque d'agranulocytose: en cas de maux de gorge, de fièvre, de stomatite ou d'autres signes d'infection ainsi que d'une faible numération des globules blancs, il faut interrompre le traitement par la mirtazapine et observer le patient étroitement ■ Antécédents de convulsions ■ Une surveillance des idées suicidaires est indiquée chez tous les patients recevant ce médicament ■ Antécédents de manie ou d'hypomanie ■ Antécédents de maladie systémique concomitante ■ Antécédents de maladies cardiovasculaires ou de cardiopathies pouvant être aggravées par l'hypotension (antécédents d'infarctus du myocarde, d'angine ou d'accident ischémique cérébral) et par des états prédisposant les patients à l'hypotension (déshydratation, hypovolémie et traitement par des antihypertenseurs) ■ **GÉR.:** Les personnes âgées pourraient être plus sensibles aux effets indésirables ■ Insuffisance rénale ou hépatique (une réduction de la dose peut s'avérer nécessaire) ■ **OBST.:** Il n'existe pas d'études adéquates menées chez la femme enceinte. N'administrer au cours de la grossesse que si les bienfaits éventuels pour la femme enceinte l'emportent sur les risques possibles pour le fœtus. Risque de complication chez le nouveau-né lorsque la mère a pris ce médicament durant le 3e trimestre ■ **ALLAITEMENT:** L'innocuité du médicament n'a pas été établie ■ **PÉD.:** L'innocuité et l'efficacité de l'agent n'ont pas été établies ■ Traitement concomitant par un IMAO (attendre 14 jours entre l'arrêt de la prise de l'IMAO et le début du traitement par la mirtazapine ou vice versa) ■ Risque de gain d'appétit et de gain pondéral.

RÉACTIONS INDÉSIRABLES ET EFFETS SECONDAIRES

SNC: somnolence, rêves anormaux, modes de pensée anormaux, agitation, anxiété, apathie, confusion, étourdissements, malaise, faiblesse.

ORLO: sinusite.

Resp.: dyspnée, toux accrue.

CV: œdème, hypotension, vasodilatation.

GI: constipation, sécheresse de la bouche (xérostomie), gain d'appétit, douleurs abdominales, anorexie, élévation des concentrations d'enzymes hépatiques, nausées, vomissements.

GU: mictions fréquentes.

Tég.: prurit, rash.

HÉ: soif accrue.

Hémat.: AGRANULOCYTOSE.

Métab.: gain pondéral, hypercholestérolémie, hypertriglycéridémie.
Loc.: arthralgie, douleurs lombaires, myalgie.
SN: hyperkinésie, hypoesthésie, secousses musculaires.
Divers: syndrome pseudogrippal.

INTERACTIONS

Médicament-médicament: LA MIRTAZAPINE PEUT ENTRAÎNER L'HYPERTENSION, DES CONVULSIONS ET LA MORT EN CAS D'ADMINISTRATION CONCOMITANTE D'**IMAO**; NE PAS ADMINISTRER LA MIRTAZAPINE DANS LES 14 JOURS SUIVANT OU PRÉCÉDANT LE TRAITEMENT PAR UN IMAO ■ Effets additifs sur la dépression du SNC lors de l'usage concomitant d'autres **dépresseurs du SNC** dont l'**alcool** et les **benzodiazépines** ■ Les **agents modifiant le métabolisme hépatique (métabolisés par l'entremise des cytochromes P450 2D6, 1A2, 3A4)** peuvent diminuer l'efficacité de la mirtazapine.
Médicament-produits naturels: La consommation concomitante de **kava**, de **valériane**, de **véronique**, de **camomille** ou de **houblon** peut entraîner un effet additif sur la dépression du SNC ■ La consommation concomitante de **millepertuis** ou de **SAMe** augmente le risque d'effets secondaires sérotoninergiques, incluant le syndrome sérotoninergique.

VOIES D'ADMINISTRATION ET POSOLOGIE

- **PO (adultes)**: Dose initiale de 15 mg par jour, 1 fois par jour au coucher; on peut augmenter cette dose toutes les 1 ou 2 semaines, jusqu'à concurrence de 45 mg par jour.

PRÉSENTATION

Comprimés: 15 mg[Pr], 30 mg[Pr], 45 mg[Pr] ■ **Comprimés à dissolution rapide**: 15 mg[Pr], 30 mg[Pr], 45 mg[Pr].

SOINS INFIRMIERS

ÉVALUATION DE LA SITUATION

- Évaluer l'état mental du patient à intervalles fréquents. Rester à l'affût des idées suicidaires, particulièrement au début du traitement. Limiter la quantité de médicament dont le patient peut disposer.
- Mesurer la pression artérielle et le pouls à intervalles réguliers pendant la période initiale de traitement. Prévenir le médecin de tout changement important.
- Surveiller l'apparition de convulsions chez les patients ayant des antécédents de convulsions ou d'alcoolisme. Prendre les précautions qui s'imposent.

Tests de laboratoire: NOTER LA NUMÉRATION GLOBULAIRE ET LES RÉSULTATS DES TESTS DE LA FONCTION HÉPATIQUE AVANT LE TRAITEMENT ET À INTERVALLES RÉGULIERS PENDANT TOUTE SA DURÉE.

DIAGNOSTICS INFIRMIERS POSSIBLES

- Stratégies d'adaptation inefficaces (Indications).
- Anxiété (Indications).
- Connaissances insuffisantes sur le traitement médicamenteux (Enseignement au patient et à ses proches).

INTERVENTIONS INFIRMIÈRES

- La mirtazapine peut être administrée en une seule dose au coucher afin de diminuer la somnolence ou les étourdissements excessifs.
- Le médicament peut être pris sans égard aux aliments.

Comprimés à dissolution rapide: Ne pas essayer de sortir le comprimé en le poussant au travers du papier aluminium. Bien se sécher les mains. Replier la pellicule protectrice et retirer le comprimé. Le placer immédiatement sur la langue; il se dissoudra en quelques secondes. L'avaler avec la salive. Il n'est pas nécessaire de le prendre avec des liquides.

ENSEIGNEMENT AU PATIENT ET À SES PROCHES

- Conseiller au patient de respecter rigoureusement la posologie recommandée. S'il n'a pu prendre le médicament au moment habituel, il doit le prendre dès que possible, à moins que ce ne soit presque l'heure prévue pour la dose suivante. Sinon, lui recommander de sauter cette dose et de reprendre le schéma posologique habituel. Si le médicament n'est pris qu'une seule fois par jour, au coucher, le patient ne doit pas prendre la dose manquée le matin suivant; lui recommander de consulter plutôt un professionnel de la santé. Il ne faut pas arrêter le traitement brusquement, mais plutôt réduire graduellement la dose.
- Prévenir le patient que la mirtazapine peut provoquer de la somnolence ou des étourdissements. Lui conseiller de ne pas conduire et d'éviter les activités qui exigent sa vigilance jusqu'à ce qu'on ait la certitude que le médicament n'entraîne pas ces effets chez lui.
- Recommander au patient de changer lentement de position afin de réduire le risque d'hypotension orthostatique.
- Recommander au patient d'éviter de boire de l'alcool et de ne pas prendre d'autres dépresseurs du SNC pendant le traitement et pendant au moins 3 à 7 jours après l'avoir arrêté.
- Conseiller au patient d'informer un professionnel de la santé en cas de sécheresse de la bouche, de

rétention urinaire ou de constipation. Lui conseiller de se rincer fréquemment la bouche, de pratiquer une bonne hygiène buccale et de consommer de la gomme ou des bonbons sans sucre pour soulager la sécheresse de la bouche. L'augmentation de l'apport de liquides et de fibres ainsi que l'exercice peuvent prévenir la constipation.

- Recommander au patient de surveiller son apport nutritionnel. Un plus grand appétit peut mener à un gain de poids non souhaité.
- Conseiller au patient de consulter un professionnel de la santé avant de prendre un médicament en ventre libre contre le rhume en même temps que la mirtazapine.
- Recommander au patient qui doit suivre un autre traitement ou subir une intervention chirurgicale d'avertir le professionnel de la santé qu'il suit un traitement par ce médicament.
- Le traitement de la dépression peut être de longue durée. Insister sur l'importance des examens de suivi permettant de vérifier l'efficacité du médicament et d'en déceler les effets secondaires.

M

VÉRIFICATION DE L'EFFICACITÉ THÉRAPEUTIQUE

L'efficacité du traitement peut être démontrée par: la résolution des symptômes de dépression ■ un sentiment de mieux-être ■ un regain d'intérêt pour les activités habituelles ■ un gain d'appétit ■ une plus grande énergie ■ une amélioration du sommeil. Les effets thérapeutiques peuvent apparaître en l'espace de 1 semaine, bien qu'il faille habituellement attendre plusieurs semaines avant qu'on note une amélioration. ✳

MISOPROSTOL

Apo-Misoprostol, Cytotec, Novo-Misoprostol, PMS-Misoprostol

CLASSIFICATION:

Antiulcéreux, cytoprotecteur

Grossesse – catégorie X

INDICATIONS

Prévention et traitement des ulcères gastro-intestinaux induits par les AINS chez les patients à haut risque (antécédents d'ulcère gastro-intestinal, administration de fortes doses d'AINS, utilisation concomitante de corticostéroïdes ou d'anticoagulants et âge > 60 ans). **Usages non approuvés:** Traitement des ulcères duodénaux ■ En association avec la mifépristone pour mettre fin médicalement à une grossesse intra-utérine.

MÉCANISME D'ACTION

Action qui ressemble à celle des analogues des prostaglandines: diminution des sécrétions d'acide gastrique (effet antisécrétoire) et augmentation de la production de mucus et de la sécrétion de bicarbonate dans le duodénum (effet cytoprotecteur). ***Effets thérapeutiques:*** Prévention et traitement de l'ulcération gastrique provoquée par les AINS.

PHARMACOCINÉTIQUE

Absorption: Bonne (PO). Le misoprostol est rapidement transformé en sa forme active (acide de misoprostol).

Distribution: Inconnue.

Liaison aux protéines: 85 %.

Métabolisme et excrétion: Métabolisme partiel; excrétion rénale.

Demi-vie: De 20 à 40 minutes.

Profil temps-action (effets sur la sécrétion d'acide gastrique)

	Début d'action	Pic	Durée
PO	30 min	inconnu	3-6 h

CONTRE-INDICATIONS, PRÉCAUTIONS ET MISES EN GARDE

Contre-indications: Hypersensibilité aux prostaglandines, aux analogues de la prostaglandine ou à tout autre excipient de la préparation ■ **Obst.:** En raison de ses propriétés abortives, le misoprostol ne doit pas être administré aux femmes enceintes pour réduire le risque d'ulcères induits par les AINS.

Précautions et mises en garde: Patientes en âge de procréer ■ **Péd.:** L'innocuité du médicament n'a pas été établie chez les patients < 18 ans ■ **Allaitement:** Compte tenu du risque important de diarrhée chez le nouveau-né, il ne faut administrer le misoprostol que si ses bienfaits pour la mère dépassent indiscutablement les risques auxquels on expose l'enfant.

RÉACTIONS INDÉSIRABLES ET EFFETS SECONDAIRES

SNC: céphalées.

GI: douleurs abdominales, diarrhée, constipation, dyspepsie, flatulence, nausées, vomissements.

GU: fausses couches, troubles menstruels.

INTERACTIONS

Médicament-médicament: Risque accru de diarrhée lors de l'administration concomitante d'**antiacides contenant du magnésium**.

VOIES D'ADMINISTRATION ET POSOLOGIE

- **PO (adultes)**: *Prévention et traitement des ulcères gastriques induits par les AINS* – de 400 à 800 µg par jour, en 4 doses fractionnées. En cas d'intolérance, on peut réduire la posologie, pour la passer à 100 µg, 4 fois par jour. *Induction de l'avortement, en association avec la mifépristone* – administrer de 400 à 600 µg par voie intravaginale en 1 ou 2 doses fractionnées égales après une dose unique de 600 mg de mifépristone par voie orale. Chez les femmes enceintes de moins de 63 jours, on peut aussi administrer 200 mg de mifépristone par voie orale, puis, de 36 à 48 heures plus tard, 800 µg de misoprostol par voie intravaginale.

PRÉSENTATION

Comprimés: 100 µg[Pr], 200 µg[Pr] ■ **En association avec**: diclofénac à 50 mg ou à 75 mg (Arthrotec)[Pr] avec 200 µg de misoprostol.

SOINS INFIRMIERS

ÉVALUATION DE LA SITUATION

- Observer le patient à intervalles réguliers pour déceler les douleurs abdominales ou épigastriques et la présence de sang occulte ou franc dans les selles, les vomissements ou les sécrétions gastriques.
- Faire passer un test de grossesse aux patientes en âge de procréer. On amorce habituellement le traitement le deuxième ou le troisième jour du cycle menstruel si le test de grossesse est négatif.

DIAGNOSTICS INFIRMIERS POSSIBLES

- Douleur aiguë (Indications).
- Connaissances insuffisantes sur le traitement médicamenteux (Enseignement au patient et à ses proches).

INTERVENTIONS INFIRMIÈRES

- Le traitement par le misoprostol devrait être amorcé au début du traitement par les AINS.
- Administrer le médicament aux repas et au coucher pour réduire la gravité de la diarrhée.
- Les antiacides peuvent être administrés avant ou après le misoprostol pour soulager la douleur. Éviter les antiacides qui contiennent du magnésium, en raison du risque accru de diarrhée associé au misoprostol.

ENSEIGNEMENT AU PATIENT ET À SES PROCHES

- Conseiller au patient de suivre rigoureusement la posologie recommandée pendant toute la durée du traitement, même s'il se sent mieux. S'il n'a pu prendre le médicament au moment habituel, il doit le prendre dès que possible, à moins que ce ne soit presque l'heure prévue pour la dose suivante. L'avertir qu'il ne doit jamais remplacer une dose manquée par une double dose. Lui expliquer qu'il peut être dangereux de donner ce médicament à une autre personne.
- Prévenir la patiente que le misoprostol provoque des fausses couches. Il faut informer de cet effet verbalement et par écrit toute femme en âge de procréer et lui recommander de prendre des mesures de contraception pendant toute la durée du traitement. Si on soupçonne une grossesse, il faut arrêter de prendre le misoprostol et prévenir immédiatement un professionnel de la santé.
- Informer le patient du risque de diarrhée. Lui conseiller de prévenir un professionnel de la santé si la diarrhée persiste pendant plus de 1 semaine. Lui conseiller également de communiquer avec un professionnel de la santé si les selles deviennent noires et goudronneuses ou si des douleurs abdominales graves surviennent.
- Conseiller au patient d'éviter de boire de l'alcool et de ne pas consommer des aliments qui peuvent aggraver l'irritation gastrique.

M

VÉRIFICATION DE L'EFFICACITÉ THÉRAPEUTIQUE

L'efficacité du traitement peut être démontrée par: la prévention des ulcères gastriques chez les patients recevant un traitement prolongé par des AINS.

MITOMYCINE

Mitomycin

CLASSIFICATION:

Antinéoplasique (antibiotique antitumoral)

Grossesse – D

INDICATIONS

Traitement palliatif de l'adénocarcinome de l'estomac et du côlon ■ Traitement topique, en monothérapie, du carcinome superficiel de type transitionnel de la vessie. **Usages non approuvés**: Traitement palliatif des cancers suivants: cancer du sein ■ tumeurs de la tête et du cou ■ cancer épidermoïde avancé des voies biliaires, des poumons et du col.

MÉCANISME D'ACTION

Principalement, inhibition de la synthèse de l'ADN par la formation de liaisons transversales; également, inhibition de la synthèse des protéines et de l'ARN (toutes les phases du cycle cellulaire). ***Effets thérapeutiques:*** Destruction des cellules à réplication rapide, particulièrement des cellules malignes.

PHARMACOCINÉTIQUE

Absorption: Biodisponibilité à 100 % (IV).

Distribution: Tout l'organisme avec concentration dans les tissus tumoraux; sans pénétration dans le liquide céphalorachidien.

Métabolisme et excrétion: Métabolisme principalement hépatique; excrétion rénale et fécale (< 10 % à l'état inchangé dans les urines et la bile).

Demi-vie: 50 minutes.

Profil temps-action (effet sur la numération globulaire)

	DÉBUT D'ACTION	PIC	DURÉE
IV	3 - 8 semaines	4 - 8 semaines	jusqu'à 3 mois

M

CONTRE-INDICATIONS, PRÉCAUTIONS ET MISES EN GARDE

Contre-indications: Hypersensibilité ou réaction idiosyncrasique ▪ Thrombopénie, leucopénie ou troubles de coagulation.

Précautions et mises en garde: OBST.: Patientes en âge de procréer, grossesse ou allaitement ▪ Infections actives ▪ Aplasie médullaire ▪ Personnes âgées ou patients souffrant d'autres maladies chroniques débilitantes ▪ Dysfonctionnement hépatique ▪ Antécédents de troubles pulmonaires ▪ Insuffisance rénale.

RÉACTIONS INDÉSIRABLES ET EFFETS SECONDAIRES

Resp.: TOXICITÉ PULMONAIRE.

CV: œdème.

GI: nausées, vomissements, anorexie, stomatite.

GU: stérilité, insuffisance rénale, irritation locale (intravésical), hématurie (intravésical).

Tég.: alopécie, desquamation, rash.

Hémat.: leucopénie, thrombopénie, anémie.

Locaux: phlébite au point d'injection IV, vésication.

Divers: SYNDROME HÉMOLYTIQUE ET URÉMIQUE, fièvre, malaise prolongé.

INTERACTIONS

Médicament-médicament: Aplasie médullaire additive lors de l'administration concomitante d'autres **antinéoplasiques** ou d'une **radiothérapie** ▪ La mitomycine peut diminuer la réponse des anticorps aux **vaccins à virus vivants** et augmenter le risque de réactions indésirables ▪ L'administration concomitante ou séquentielle d'**alcaloïdes de la pervenche** peut entraîner une toxicité respiratoire.

VOIES D'ADMINISTRATION ET POSOLOGIE

- **IV (adultes):** 20 mg/m^2 en une seule dose ou 2 traitements à raison de 2 mg/m^2/jour, pendant 5 jours, espacés par une période sans traitement de 2 jours (dose totale de 20 mg/m^2, administrée pendant 10 jours). Le traitement peut être répété toutes les 6 à 8 semaines.
- **Voie intravésicale (adultes):** De 20 à 40 mg, 1 fois par semaine pendant 8 semaines, sous forme d'une solution à une concentration de 1 mg/mL. La solution doit demeurer 2 heures dans la vessie. Le patient peut changer de position toutes les 15 minutes pour maximiser l'exposition vésicale.

PRÉSENTATION

Poudre stérile pour injection: fioles de 5 mg[Pr] et de 20 mg[Pr].

SOINS INFIRMIERS

ÉVALUATION DE LA SITUATION

- Mesurer les signes vitaux à intervalles réguliers tout au long de l'administration.
- Surveiller l'apparition d'une aplasie médullaire. Suivre de près les saignements: saignement des gencives, formation d'ecchymoses, pétéchies, présence de sang occulte dans les selles, dans l'urine et dans les vomissements. Éviter les injections IM et la prise de la température rectale si la numération plaquettaire est basse. Appliquer une pression sur les points de ponction veineuse pendant 10 minutes. En cas de neutropénie, rester à l'affût des signes d'infection. Il y a risque d'anémie. Suivre de près la fatigue accrue, la dyspnée et l'hypotension orthostatique.
- Effectuer le bilan des ingesta et des excreta; noter l'appétit du patient et son apport nutritionnel. Les nausées et les vomissements se manifestent habituellement 1 ou 2 heures après l'administration du médicament. Les vomissements peuvent s'arrêter dans les 3 à 4 heures; les nausées peuvent persister pendant 2 ou 3 jours. Le médecin peut recommander l'administration prophylactique d'un antiémétique. Afin de favoriser le maintien de l'équilibre hydroélectrolytique et l'état nutritionnel, adapter le régime

alimentaire du patient en fonction des aliments qu'il peut tolérer.

- EXAMINER L'ÉTAT DE LA FONCTION RESPIRATOIRE ET NOTER LES RÉSULTATS DES RADIOGRAPHIES PULMONAIRES AVANT LE TRAITEMENT ET À INTERVALLES RÉGULIERS PENDANT TOUTE SA DURÉE. LA TOUX, LE BRONCHOSPASME, L'HÉMOPTYSIE OU LA DYSPNÉE SURVIENNENT HABITUELLEMENT APRÈS L'ADMINISTRATION DE PLUSIEURS DOSES ET PEUVENT INDIQUER LA PRÉSENCE D'UNE TOXICITÉ PULMONAIRE, QUI POURRAIT METTRE LA VIE DU PATIENT EN DANGER.
- CHEZ LE PATIENT QUI REÇOIT UN TRAITEMENT PROLONGÉ, RESTER À L'AFFÛT D'UN SYNDROME HÉMOLYTIQUE ET URÉMIQUE QUI PEUT ÊTRE D'ISSUE FATALE. LES SYMPTÔMES COMPRENNENT L'ANÉMIE HÉMOLYTIQUE MICROANGIOPATHIQUE, LA THROMBOPÉNIE, L'INSUFFISANCE RÉNALE ET L'HYPERTENSION.

Tests de laboratoire:

- Noter la numération globulaire, la formule leucocytaire, la numération plaquettaire et la présence de globules rouges fragmentés sur des frottis de sang périphérique, avant le traitement, à intervalles réguliers pendant toute sa durée et pendant plusieurs mois par la suite.
- Les nadirs de la leucopénie et de la thrombopénie surviennent dans les 4 à 8 semaines qui suivent le début du traitement. Prévenir le médecin si le nombre de leucocytes est < 4,0 × 10^9/L, si le nombre de plaquettes est < 150 × 10^9/L ou s'il diminue graduellement. Le nombre de leucocytes et de plaquettes se rétablit dans les 10 semaines qui suivent l'arrêt du traitement. L'aplasie médullaire est cumulative et peut être irréversible. Ne pas administrer un nouveau traitement jusqu'à ce que le nombre de leucocytes soit > 3 × 10^9/L et celui des plaquettes > 75 × 10^9/L.
- Noter les résultats des tests des fonctions hépatique (AST, ALT, LDH, bilirubine) et rénale (urée, créatinine) avant le traitement et à intervalles réguliers pendant toute sa durée pour déceler les signes d'hépatotoxicité et de néphrotoxicité. Prévenir le médecin si les concentrations de créatinine sont supérieures à 150 µmol/L.

DIAGNOSTICS INFIRMIERS POSSIBLES

- Risque d'accident (Effets secondaires).
- Risque d'infection (Effets secondaires).
- Image corporelle perturbée (Effets secondaires).

INTERVENTIONS INFIRMIÈRES

- Préparer la solution sous une hotte à flux laminaire. Porter des gants, un vêtement protecteur et un masque pendant la manipulation de ce médicament. Mettre au rebut le matériel ayant servi à la préparation dans les contenants réservés à cette fin (voir l'annexe H).
- Vérifier la perméabilité de la voie IV. L'extravasation peut provoquer une nécrose tissulaire grave. Si le patient se plaint de douleurs au point d'injection IV, arrêter immédiatement l'administration et reprendre la perfusion à un autre point. Prévenir immédiatement le médecin en cas d'extravasation.

IV directe: Reconstituer le contenu de la fiole à 5 mg avec 10 mL et celle de la fiole à 20 mg, avec 40 mL d'eau stérile pour injection. Bien agiter la fiole; on doit laisser la préparation reposer à la température ambiante pendant un certain temps afin que l'agent se dissolve complètement; la solution a une couleur bleu-gris à mauve. La solution reconstituée est stable pendant 24 heures à la température ambiante et pendant 3 jours au réfrigérateur. Consulter les directives du fabricant avant de reconstituer la préparation.

Vitesse d'administration: On peut administrer le médicament par injection directe en 5 à 10 minutes dans une tubulure IV par où s'écoule une solution de NaCl 0,9 % ou de D5%E.

Compatibilité (tubulure en Y): amifostine ■ bléomycine ■ cisplatine ■ cyclophosphamide ■ doxorubicine ■ dropéridol ■ fluorouracile ■ furosémide ■ héparine ■ leucovorine ■ melphalan ■ méthotrexate ■ métoclopramide ■ ondansétron ■ téniposide ■ thiotépa ■ vinblastine ■ vincristine.

Incompatibilité (tubulure en Y): aztréonam ■ céfépime ■ filgrastim ■ pipéracilline/tazobactam ■ sargramostim ■ vinorelbine.

ENSEIGNEMENT AU PATIENT ET À SES PROCHES

- Conseiller au patient de signaler rapidement à un professionnel de la santé les symptômes suivants: fièvre, frissons, toux, enrouement, maux de gorge, signes d'infection, douleurs lombaires ou aux flancs, mictions douloureuses ou difficiles, saignement des gencives, formation d'ecchymoses, pétéchies ou présence de sang dans les urines, les selles ou les vomissements, fatigue accrue, dyspnée ou hypotension orthostatique. Conseiller au patient d'éviter les foules et les personnes contagieuses. Lui recommander d'utiliser une brosse à dents à poils doux et un rasoir électrique. Mettre en garde le patient contre les chutes. Lui recommander de ne pas consommer de boissons alcoolisées ni de prendre des médicaments contenant de l'aspirine ou des anti-inflammatoires non stéroïdiens, en raison du risque de saignements gastriques.

- Conseiller au patient de signaler à un professionnel de la santé les symptômes suivants: diminution du débit urinaire, œdème des membres inférieurs, essoufflement, ulcération de la peau ou nausées persistantes.
- Recommander au patient d'examiner sa muqueuse buccale à la recherche d'érythèmes et d'aphtes. En présence d'aphtes, lui recommander d'utiliser une brosse-éponge et de se rincer la bouche avec de l'eau après avoir bu et mangé. Il peut utiliser des agents topiques si la douleur l'empêche de s'alimenter. La douleur associée à la stomatite peut dicter l'utilisation d'analgésiques opioïdes.
- Expliquer au patient qu'il risque de perdre ses cheveux. Explorer avec lui les stratégies lui permettant de s'adapter à ce changement.
- Prévenir la patiente que même si la mitomycine peut la rendre stérile, elle doit continuer à prendre des mesures de contraception puisque ce médicament peut avoir des effets tératogènes.
- Prévenir le patient qu'il ne doit pas se faire vacciner sans recommandation expresse d'un professionnel de la santé.
- Insister sur le fait qu'il est nécessaire d'effectuer des tests de laboratoire à intervalles réguliers pour pouvoir déceler les effets secondaires du médicament.

M

VÉRIFICATION DE L'EFFICACITÉ THÉRAPEUTIQUE

L'efficacité du traitement peut être démontrée par: la diminution de la taille des tumeurs malignes et le ralentissement de la propagation des métastases. ✳

MITOXANTRONE

Mitoxantrone

CLASSIFICATION:

Antinéoplasique (antibiotique antitumoral)

Grossesse – catégorie D

INDICATIONS

Traitement de la leucémie aiguë non lymphocytaire (LANL) de l'adulte en association avec d'autres antinéoplasiques ■ Traitement des cancers suivants: cancer du sein ■ hépatome ■ leucémie récurrente de l'adulte ■ lymphome. **Usages non approuvés**: Chimiothérapie initiale chez les patients souffrant de douleurs associées à un cancer avancé de la prostate, rebelle à l'hormonothérapie, en association avec des corticostéroïdes.

MÉCANISME D'ACTION

Inhibition de la synthèse de l'ADN (effet indépendant du cycle cellulaire). ***Effets thérapeutiques:*** Destruction des cellules à réplication rapide, particulièrement des cellules malignes ■ Diminution de la douleur chez les patients souffrant de cancer avancé de la prostate.

PHARMACOCINÉTIQUE

Absorption: Biodisponibilité à 100 % (IV).

Distribution: Tout l'organisme. Pénétration en quantités limitées dans le liquide céphalorachidien.

Métabolisme et excrétion: Élimination principalement par clairance hépatobiliaire; excrétion rénale (< 10 % sous forme inchangée).

Demi-vie: 5,8 jours.

Profil temps-action (effet sur la numération globulaire)

	DÉBUT D'ACTION	PIC	DURÉE
IV	inconnu	10 jours	21 jours

CONTRE-INDICATIONS, PRÉCAUTIONS ET MISES EN GARDE

Contre-indications: Hypersensibilité aux anthracyclines ■ Administration intrathécale ■ Aplasie médullaire ■ Insuffisance hépatique grave ■ Insuffisance cardiaque.

Précautions et mises en garde: Antécédents de maladie cardiaque ■ **OBST.**: Patientes en âge de procréer, grossesse ou allaitement ■ Infections actives ■ Aplasie médullaire ■ Antécédents de radiothérapie du médiastin ■ Patients âgés ou présentant d'autres maladies chroniques débilitantes ■ **PÉD.**: L'innocuité du médicament n'a pas été établie ■ Dysfonctionnement hépatobiliaire ou numération globulaire réduite (réduire la dose) ■ Sclérose en plaques (risque accru de toxicité cardiaque) ■ Asthme ou allergie (risque accru de réactions allergiques).

RÉACTIONS INDÉSIRABLES ET EFFETS SECONDAIRES

SNC: CONVULSIONS, céphalées.

ORLO: sclérotiques de couleur bleu-vert, conjonctivite.

Resp.: toux, dyspnée.

CV: CARDIOTOXICITÉ, arythmies, modifications de l'ÉCG, œdème.

GI: douleurs abdominales, diarrhée, toxicité hépatique, nausées, stomatite, vomissements, constipation, anorexie.

GU: urine de couleur bleu-vert, suppression de la fonction des gonades, insuffisance rénale.

Tég.: alopécie, rash, coloration bleu de la peau en cas d'extravasation.

Hémat.: anémie, leucopénie, thrombopénie, leucémie secondaire.

Métab.: hyperuricémie.

Divers: fièvre, réactions d'hypersensibilité, incluant l'ANAPHYLAXIE.

INTERACTIONS

Médicament-médicament: Aplasie médullaire additive lors de l'administration concomitante d'autres **antinéoplasiques** ou d'une **radiothérapie** ▪ Risque accru de cardiomyopathie en cas de traitement préalable par une **anthracycline** (**daunorubicine**, **doxorubicine**, **idarubicine**) ou de **radiothérapie du médiastin** ▪ La mitoxantrone peut diminuer la réponse des anticorps aux **vaccins à virus vivants** et augmenter le risque de réactions indésirables.

VOIES D'ADMINISTRATION ET POSOLOGIE

Leucémie aiguë récurrente

- **IV (adultes)**: 12 mg/m^2/jour, pendant 5 jours consécutifs (dose totale: 60 mg/m^2).

Leucémie aiguë non lymphocytaire

- **IV (adultes)**: *Traitement d'association* – dose d'induction: de 10 à 12 mg/m^2/jour, pendant 3 jours (en association avec la cytosine arabinoside à 100 mg/m^2/jour en perfusion continue, pendant 7 jours). Si un deuxième traitement s'avère nécessaire, on peut utiliser la même association et la même posologie quotidienne; par contre, la durée de traitement par la mitoxantrone est de 2 jours et celle par la cytosine arabinoside est de 5 jours.

Cancer du sein, hépatome, lymphome (en monothérapie)

- **IV (adultes)**: 14 mg/m^2, en une seule dose, pouvant être répétée tous les 21 jours. On peut administrer une dose initiale de 12 mg/m^2 chez les patients dont la réserve médullaire est diminuée.

Traitement d'association pour le cancer du sein et le lymphome

- **IV (adultes)**: La posologie initiale devrait être réduite de 2 à 4 mg/m^2 par rapport à la posologie habituelle administrée en monothérapie. La posologie qu'il faudra établir par la suite dépend du degré et de la durée de la suppression médullaire.

PRÉSENTATION

Solution pour injection: 2 mg/mL, en fioles de 20 mg^{Pr} et de 25 mg^{Pr}.

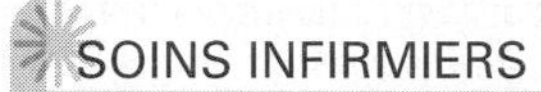

SOINS INFIRMIERS

ÉVALUATION DE LA SITUATION

- Suivre de près l'apparition des réactions d'hypersensibilité suivantes: rash, urticaire, bronchospasme, tachycardie, hypotension. Si ces symptômes se manifestent, arrêter la perfusion et prévenir le médecin. Garder à portée de la main de l'adrénaline, un antihistaminique et le matériel de réanimation pour contrer toute réaction anaphylactique éventuelle.
- Rester à l'affût de l'apparition d'une aplasie médullaire. Suivre de près les saignements: saignement des gencives, formation d'ecchymoses, pétéchies, présence de sang occulte dans les selles, dans l'urine et dans les vomissements. Éviter les injections IM et la prise de la température rectale si la numération plaquettaire est basse. Appliquer une pression sur les points de ponction veineuse pendant 10 minutes. En cas de neutropénie, rester à l'affût des signes d'infection. Il y a risque d'anémie. Suivre de près la fatigue accrue, la dyspnée et l'hypotension orthostatique.
- Effectuer le bilan des ingesta et des excreta, noter l'appétit du patient et son apport nutritionnel. Suivre de près les nausées et les vomissements. Demander au médecin si l'on peut administrer un antiémétique en prophylaxie. Modifier le régime alimentaire du patient en fonction des éléments qu'il peut tolérer afin de favoriser le maintien de l'équilibre hydroélectrolytique et l'état nutritionnel.
- EXAMINER LES RADIOGRAPHIES PULMONAIRES, L'ÉCG, L'ÉCHOCARDIOGRAPHIE ET LES RÉSULTATS DE L'ANGIOGRAPHIE ISOTOPIQUE POUR DÉTERMINER LA FRACTION D'ÉJECTION AVANT LE TRAITEMENT ET À INTERVALLES RÉGULIERS PENDANT TOUTE SA DURÉE. LES PATIENTS SOUFFRANT DE SCLÉROSE EN PLAQUES, DONT LA FRACTION D'ÉJECTION DU VENTRICULE GAUCHE EST < 50 %, NE DEVRAIENT PAS RECEVOIR DE MITOXANTRONE. LA MITOXANTRONE PEUT PROVOQUER UNE CARDIOTOXICITÉ, PARTICULIÈREMENT CHEZ LES PATIENTS AYANT REÇU DE LA DAUNORUBICINE OU DE LA DOXORUBICINE. SUIVRE DE PRÈS LES RÂLES ET LES CRÉPITATIONS, LA DYSPNÉE, L'ŒDÈME, LA TURGESCENCE DES JUGULAIRES, LES MODIFICATIONS DE L'ÉCG, LES ARYTHMIES ET LES DOULEURS THORACIQUES. EN PRÉSENCE DE SIGNE OU DE SYMPTÔME D'INSUFFISANCE CARDIAQUE OU AVANT CHAQUE DOSE DE MITOXANTRONE CHEZ LES PATIENTS SOUFFRANT DE SCLÉROSE EN PLAQUES, SUIVRE DE PRÈS LA FRACTION D'ÉJECTION DU VENTRICULE GAUCHE PAR ÉCHOCARDIOGRAPHIE OU PAR ANGIOGRAPHIE ISOTOPIQUE. L'INSUFFISANCE CARDIAQUE

PEUT S'INSTALLER DURANT LE TRAITEMENT OU DANS LES MOIS OU LES ANNÉES QUI SUIVENT L'ARRÊT DU TRAITEMENT, ET ELLE PEUT ÊTRE D'ISSUE FATALE. LE RISQUE D'INSUFFISANCE CARDIAQUE EST ACCRU CHEZ LES PATIENTS AYANT REÇU UNE DOSE CUMULATIVE > 140 mg/m^2.

- Rester à l'affût des symptômes suivants de goutte: concentrations accrues d'acide urique, douleurs articulaires et œdème. Inciter le patient à boire au moins 2 litres de liquide par jour si son état le permet. On peut administrer de l'allopurinol pour diminuer les concentrations sériques d'acide urique.

Tests de laboratoire:

- Noter la numération globulaire et la formule leucocytaire avant le traitement et à intervalles réguliers pendant toute sa durée. Le nadir de la leucopénie survient habituellement dans les 10 jours suivant le début du traitement et les valeurs se rétablissent généralement dans les 21 jours.
- Examiner les résultats des tests des fonctions hépatique (concentrations d'AST, d'ALT, de LDH et de bilirubine) et rénale (urée et créatinine sérique) avant le traitement et à intervalles réguliers pendant toute sa durée, pour déceler l'hépatotoxicité et la néphrotoxicité.
- La mitoxantrone peut entraîner l'élévation des concentrations d'acide urique. Suivre de près ces concentrations à intervalles réguliers pendant toute la durée du traitement.

DIAGNOSTICS INFIRMIERS POSSIBLES

- Risque d'accident (Effets secondaires).
- Risque d'infection (Effets secondaires).
- Image corporelle perturbée (Effets secondaires).

INTERVENTIONS INFIRMIÈRES

- Préparer les solutions sous une hotte à flux laminaire. Porter des gants, un vêtement protecteur et un masque pendant la manipulation de ce médicament. Mettre au rebut le matériel dans les contenants réservés à cette fin (voir l'annexe H).
- Éviter tout contact avec la peau. Utiliser une tubulure Luer-Lock pour prévenir les fuites accidentelles. En cas de contact avec la peau, la laver immédiatement à l'eau et au savon.
- Nettoyer les éclaboussures avec une solution aqueuse d'hypochlorite de calcium. Mélanger la solution en ajoutant 5,5 parties (par poids) d'hypochlorite de calcium à 13 parties d'eau.

IV: Examiner les points d'injection IV. En cas d'extravasation, interrompre l'administration et la reprendre à un autre point d'injection. La mitoxantrone n'est pas vésicante.

IV directe: Diluer la solution dans au moins 50 mL de solution de NaCl 0,9 % ou de D5%E. Jeter toute portion inutilisée selon les directives de l'établissement.

Vitesse d'administration: Administrer lentement en au moins 3 minutes, dans une tubulure IV par où s'écoule une solution de NaCl 0,9 % ou de D5%E.

Perfusion intermittente: On peut diluer davantage la préparation dans une solution de D5%E, de NaCl 0,9 % ou de D5%/NaCl 0,9 %. Utiliser la solution immédiatement.

Compatibilité (tubulure en Y): amifostine ▪ filgrastim ▪ fludarabine ▪ melphalan ▪ ondansétron ▪ sargramostim ▪ téniposide ▪ thiotépa ▪ vinorelbine.

Incompatibilité (tubulure en Y): amphotéricine B, cholestéryle d' ▪ aztréonam ▪ céfépime ▪ doxorubicine liposomale ▪ paclitaxel ▪ pipéracilline/tazobactam.

Compatibilité en addition au soluté: cyclophosphamide ▪ cytarabine ▪ fluorouracile ▪ hydrocortisone sodique, succinate d' ▪ potassium, chlorure de.

Incompatibilité en addition au soluté: héparine.

ENSEIGNEMENT AU PATIENT ET À SES PROCHES

- Conseiller au patient de signaler rapidement à un professionnel de la santé les symptômes suivants: fièvre, frissons, toux, enrouement, maux de gorge, signes d'infection, douleurs lombaires ou aux flancs, mictions douloureuses ou difficiles, saignement des gencives, formation d'ecchymoses, pétéchies ou présence de sang dans les urines, les selles ou les vomissements, fatigue accrue, dyspnée ou hypotension orthostatique. Conseiller au patient d'éviter les foules et les personnes contagieuses. Lui recommander d'utiliser une brosse à dents à poils doux et un rasoir électrique. Mettre en garde le patient contre les chutes. Lui recommander de ne pas consommer de boissons alcoolisées ni de prendre des médicaments contenant de l'aspirine ou des AINS, en raison du risque de saignements gastriques.
- Conseiller au patient de signaler à un professionnel de la santé les douleurs abdominales, le jaunissement de la peau, la toux, la diarrhée ou un débit urinaire réduit.
- Prévenir le patient que son urine et les sclérotiques peuvent virer au bleu-vert.
- Recommander au patient d'examiner sa muqueuse buccale à la recherche d'érythème et d'aphtes. En présence d'aphtes, lui conseiller de remplacer la brosse à dents par une brosse-éponge et de se rincer la bouche avec de l'eau après avoir bu et mangé. Il peut utiliser des agents topiques si la douleur l'empêche de s'alimenter. La douleur associée à la

stomatite peut être traitée par des analgésiques opioïdes.

- Expliquer au patient qu'il risque de perdre ses cheveux. Explorer avec lui les stratégies lui permettant de s'adapter à ce changement.
- Expliquer à la patiente que même si la mitoxantrone peut la rendre stérile, elle doit continuer à prendre des mesures de contraception pendant toute la durée du traitement en raison des risques d'effets tératogènes de ce médicament.
- Recommander au patient de ne pas se faire vacciner sans recommandation expresse d'un professionnel de la santé.
- Insister sur le fait qu'il est nécessaire d'effectuer des tests de laboratoire à intervalles réguliers permettant de suivre de près les effets secondaires du médicament.

VÉRIFICATION DE L'EFFICACITÉ THÉRAPEUTIQUE

L'efficacité du traitement peut être démontrée par: la diminution de la production et de la propagation de cellules leucémiques ▪ la diminution de la douleur chez les patients souffrant du cancer de la prostate.

MOFÉTILMYCOPHÉNOLATE

CellCept

MYCOPHÉNOLATE SODIQUE

Myfortic

CLASSIFICATION:
Immunosuppresseur

Grossesse – catégorie C

INDICATIONS

Mofétilmycophénolate: Prévention de la réaction de rejet chez les adultes ayant subi une greffe rénale, hépatique ou cardiaque allogène (en association avec la cyclosporine et des corticostéroïdes) ▪ Prévention de la réaction de rejet chez les enfants de 2 à 18 ans ayant subi une greffe rénale allogène (en association avec la cyclosporine et des corticostéroïdes) ▪ ***Mycophénolate sodique:*** Prévention de la réaction de rejet chez les patients ayant subi une greffe rénale allogène (en association avec la cyclosporine et des corticostéroïdes).

MÉCANISME D'ACTION

Inhibition de l'inosine-monophosphate-déshydrogénase, enzyme qui participe à la synthèse des purines. Cette inhibition bloque la prolifération des lymphocytes T et B. ***Effets thérapeutiques:*** Prévention des réactions de rejet de greffes.

PHARMACOCINÉTIQUE

Absorption: Bonne (PO). L'absorption du mycophénolate sodique est retardée par rapport à celle du mofétilmycophénolate.
Distribution: Inconnue.
Liaison aux protéines: *Acide mycophénolique* – 97 %.
Métabolisme et excrétion: Le mofétilmycophénolate est métabolisé par hydrolyse (100 %), ce qui entraîne la formation de l'acide mycophénolique, son métabolite actif. Le mycophénolate sodique se transforme en acide mycophénolique dans le tractus gastro-intestinal. L'acide mycophénolique subit un fort métabolisme et une certaine recirculation entérohépatique. Faible excrétion rénale (< 1 % d'acide mycophénolique sous forme inchangée).
Demi-vie: *Acide mycophénolique* – 17,9 heures.

Profil temps-action
(concentrations sanguines d'acide mycophénolique)

	DÉBUT D'ACTION	PIC	DURÉE
mofétilmycophénolate - PO	rapide	0,8 – 1,3 h	inconnue
mycophénolate sodique - PO	rapide	1,5 – 2,75 h	inconnue

CONTRE-INDICATIONS, PRÉCAUTIONS ET MISES EN GARDE

Contre-indications: Hypersensibilité.
Précautions et mises en garde: Affection grave du tractus gastro-intestinal en évolution (incluant des antécédents d'ulcère ou d'hémorragie digestive) ▪ Insuffisance rénale chronique grave (ne pas dépasser 1 g, 2 fois par jour de mofétilmycophénolate, si la clairance de la créatinine est < 25 mL/min/1,73 m^2 chez les greffés rénaux) ▪ Retard de fonctionnement de la greffe à la suite d'une transplantation (risque élevé de toxicité) ▪ **PÉD.:** L'innocuité et l'efficacité du mofétilmycophénolate n'ont pas été établies chez les enfants recevant une greffe cardiaque ou hépatique; les données sur le mycophénolate sodique sont limitées ▪ **OBST.:** Grossesse, patientes en âge de procréer ou allaitement ▪ Déficit héréditaire en hypoxanthine-guanine-phosphoribosyl-transférase ▪ Phénylcétonurie (la solution orale contient de l'aspartame) ▪ **GÉR.:** Risque accru d'effets indésirables associés à l'immunosuppression.

RÉACTIONS INDÉSIRABLES ET EFFETS SECONDAIRES

GI: HÉMORRAGIE DIGESTIVE, diarrhée, vomissements.
Hémat.: leucopénie.
Divers: septicémie, infections, risque accru de cancer.

INTERACTIONS

Médicament-médicament: L'usage concomitant de l'**azathioprine** est déconseillé (effets inconnus) ■ L'**acyclovir** et le **ganciclovir** sont en compétition avec l'acide mycophénolique pour l'excrétion rénale et, chez les insuffisants rénaux, peuvent accroître leur toxicité réciproque ■ Les antiacides à base de **magnésium** et d'**aluminium** réduisent l'absorption de l'acide mycophénolique (éviter l'administration concomitante) ■ La **cholestyramine** et le **colestipol** réduisent l'absorption de l'acide mycophénolique (éviter l'administration concomitante) ■ Les **salicylates** peuvent accroître la toxicité du mofétilmycophénolate ■ Ces agents peuvent entraver l'effet des **contraceptifs oraux** (il faut choisir une autre méthode de contraception efficace) ■ Le mofétilmycophénolate peut diminuer la réponse des anticorps aux **vaccins à virus vivants** et augmenter le risque de réactions indésirables. Par contre, le vaccin contre l'influenza peut être utile.

Médicament-aliments: Si le médicament est administré avec des **aliments**, les pics des concentrations sanguines d'acide mycophénolique sont fortement réduits.

M

VOIES D'ADMINISTRATION ET POSOLOGIE

Administration en association avec la cyclosporine et des corticostéroïdes.

Mofétilmycophénolate (Cellcept)

Greffe rénale

- **PO, IV (adultes):** 1 g, 2 fois par jour; on peut commencer l'administration IV dans les 24 heures suivant la greffe, puis passer au traitement par voie orale le plus tôt possible (on déconseille de poursuivre l'administration IV au-delà de 14 jours).
- ***INSUFFISANCE RÉNALE EN CAS DE GREFFE RÉNALE***
  PO, IV (ADULTES): CL_{CR} < 25 *mL/MIN* – LA DOSE QUOTIDIENNE NE DEVRAIT PAS DÉPASSER 2 g.

Greffe cardiaque

- **PO, IV (adultes):** 1,5 g, 2 fois par jour; on peut commencer l'administration IV dans les 24 heures suivant la greffe, puis passer au traitement par voie orale le plus tôt possible (on déconseille de poursuivre l'administration IV au-delà de 14 jours).

Greffe hépatique

- **PO, IV (adultes):** 1 g, 2 fois par jour par voie IV; on peut commencer l'administration IV dans les 24 heures suivant la greffe, puis passer au traitement par voie orale le plus tôt possible à raison de 1,5 g, 2 fois par jour (on déconseille de poursuivre l'administration IV au-delà de 14 jours).

Greffe rénale

- **PO (enfant de 2 à 18 ans):** 600 mg/m^2 de la suspension orale, 2 fois par jour (dose maximale: 2 g/jour). Surface corporelle de 1,25 à 1,5 m^2: 750 mg sous forme de gélules, 2 fois par jour. Surface corporelle > 1,5 m^2: 1 g sous forme de gélules ou de comprimés, 2 fois par jour.

Mycophénolate sodique (Myfortic)

Greffe rénale

- **PO (adultes):** 720 mg, 2 fois par jour.

PRÉSENTATION

- **Mofétilmycophénolate**
  Capsules: 250 mg[Pr] ■ **Comprimés:** 500 mg[Pr] ■ **Poudre pour injection:** 500 mg/fioles de 20 mL[Pr] ■ **Poudre pour suspension orale:** flacons de 225 mL[Pr].
- **Mycophénolate sodique**
  Comprimés: 180 mg[Pr] et 360 mg[Pr].

SOINS INFIRMIERS

ÉVALUATION DE LA SITUATION

- Évaluer les symptômes de rejet d'organe tout au long du traitement.

Tests de laboratoire:

- Noter la numération globulaire et la formule leucocytaire, toutes les semaines pendant le premier mois, 2 fois par mois pendant le deuxième et le troisième mois du traitement, puis tous les mois, pour le reste de la première année. La neutropénie se manifeste le plus souvent dans les 31 à 180 jours suivant la greffe. Si le NAN est < $1,3 \times 10^9$/L, la dose doit être réduite ou le traitement interrompu.
- Surveiller les résultats des tests des fonctions hépatique et rénale et l'équilibre hydroélectrolytique à intervalles réguliers tout au long du traitement. Le mycophénolate peut entraîner une élévation des concentrations sériques de phosphatase alcaline, d'AST, d'ALT, de LDH et de créatinine. Il peut également provoquer une hypercalcémie, une hypocalcémie, une hyperuricémie, une hyperlipidémie, une hypoglycémie et une hypoprotéinémie.

DIAGNOSTICS INFIRMIERS POSSIBLES

- Risque d'infection (Réactions indésirables).
- Connaissances insuffisantes sur le traitement médicamenteux (Enseignement au patient et à ses proches).

INTERVENTIONS INFIRMIÈRES

- La dose initiale de mofétilmycophénolate devrait être administrée dans les 72 heures suivant la greffe.
- Les femmes en âge de procréer devraient obtenir un résultat négatif à un test sérique ou urinaire de gros-

sesse dans la semaine suivant le début du traitement.

PO:

- Administrer à jeun, 1 heure avant le repas ou 2 heures après. LES CAPSULES DEVRAIENT ÊTRE AVALÉES TELLES QUELLES; NE PAS LES OUVRIR, LES ÉCRASER OU LES MÂCHER. LE MOFÉTILMYCOPHÉNOLATE PEUT ÊTRE TÉRATOGÈNE; LE CONTENU DES CAPSULES NE DOIT PAS ÊTRE INHALÉ NI ENTRER EN CONTACT AVEC LA PEAU OU LES MUQUEUSES. Le pharmacien peut préparer une solution si le patient ne peut avaler les comprimés ou les capsules.
- Ne pas administrer le mofétilmycophénolate en même temps que des antiacides renfermant du magnésium ou de l'aluminium.

IV: La voie IV est réservée aux patients incapables de prendre le médicament par voie orale. On devrait passer à la forme orale du médicament aussitôt que le patient peut tolérer les capsules ou les comprimés.

Perfusion intermittente: Reconstituer le contenu de chaque fiole avec 14 mL de solution de D5%E. Agiter délicatement pour dissoudre la poudre. La solution est jaune pâle; la jeter si elle a changé de couleur ou si elle contient des particules. Diluer de nouveau le contenu de 2 fioles (dose de 1 g) avec 140 mL de solution de D5%E ou de 3 fioles (dose de 1,5 g) avec 210 mL de solution de D5%E, pour obtenir une concentration de 6 mg/mL. La solution reste stable pendant 4 heures. Consulter les directives du fabricant avant de reconstituer et de diluer la préparation.

Vitesse d'administration: Administrer la solution en 2 heures, sous forme de perfusion IV lente.

Incompatibilité (tubulure en Y): Ne pas faire d'admixtion, ne pas administrer le mofétilmycophénolate dans la même tubulure que d'autres médicaments.

ENSEIGNEMENT AU PATIENT ET À SES PROCHES

- Conseiller au patient de prendre le médicament à la même heure chaque jour. Lui recommander de ne pas sauter de dose ni de remplacer une dose manquée par une double dose, ni d'arrêter le traitement sans avoir consulté un professionnel de la santé au préalable.
- Insister sur le fait qu'il est important de suivre le traitement pour le reste de sa vie afin de prévenir le rejet de la greffe. Passer en revue les symptômes de rejet de la greffe et conseiller au patient d'informer immédiatement un professionnel de la santé en cas d'apparition de signes de rejet ou d'infection.
- Informer la patiente qu'il est important d'utiliser simultanément deux formes fiables de contraception, sauf si l'abstinence est la méthode choisie et ce, avant et pendant le traitement ainsi que 6 semaines après qu'il a pris fin.
- Conseiller au patient d'éviter tout contact avec des personnes contagieuses.
- Informer le patient du risque accru d'apparition de lymphomes et d'autres tumeurs malignes. Inciter le patient à utiliser un écran solaire et à porter des vêtements protecteurs pour réduire le risque de cancer de la peau.
- Recommander au patient de consulter un professionnel de la santé avant de prendre d'autres médicaments en même temps que le mofétilmycophénolate.
- Insister sur l'importance des tests de laboratoire de routine, permettant d'assurer le suivi.

VÉRIFICATION DE L'EFFICACITÉ THÉRAPEUTIQUE

L'efficacité du traitement peut être démontrée par: la prévention des réactions de rejet des organes greffés.

MOMÉTASONE,

voir Corticostéroïdes (topiques) et Corticostéroïdes (voie intranasale)

MONTÉLUKAST

Singulair

CLASSIFICATION:

Bronchodilatateur (antagoniste des récepteurs des leucotriènes)

Grossesse – catégorie B

INDICATIONS

Prévention et traitement au long cours de l'asthme ■ Soulagement des symptômes de la rhinite allergique saisonnière (patients ≥ 15 ans).

MÉCANISME D'ACTION

Inhibition des effets des leucotriènes, médiateurs des réactions suivantes: œdème des voies aériennes ■ constriction des muscles lisses ■ modification de l'activité cellulaire ■ Diminution du processus inflammatoire, faisant partie des manifestations de l'asthme et de la rhinite allergique. ***Effets thérapeutiques:*** Diminution de la fréquence et de la gravité des crises d'asthme aiguës ■ Diminution de la gravité de la rhinite allergique.

M

PHARMACOCINÉTIQUE

Absorption: De 63 à 73 % (PO).
Distribution: Inconnue.
Liaison aux protéines: 99 %.
Métabolisme et excrétion: Métabolisme principalement hépatique (par les enzymes P450 3A4 et 2C9). Excrétion principalement fécale et biliaire.
Demi-vie: De 2,7 à 5,5 heures.

Profil temps-action (diminution des symptômes de l'asthme)

	DÉBUT D'ACTION	PIC†	DURÉE
PO	en l'espace de 24 h	2 - 4 h	24 h
PO (comprimé à croquer)	en l'espace de 24 h	2 - 2,5 h	24 h

† Concentrations sanguines.

CONTRE-INDICATIONS, PRÉCAUTIONS ET MISES EN GARDE

Contre-indications: Hypersensibilité.
Précautions et mises en garde: Crises d'asthme aiguës ▪ Phénylcétonurie (les comprimés à croquer contiennent de l'aspartame) ▪ Insuffisance hépatique (il peut s'avérer nécessaire de réduire la dose) ▪ Réduction de la dose des corticostéroïdes administrés par voie orale (risque accru de troubles éosinophiliques) ▪ **OBST., ALLAITEMENT:** L'innocuité de l'agent n'a pas été établie chez la femme enceinte ou qui allaite ▪ **PÉD.:** L'efficacité de l'agent n'a pas été établie chez les enfants < 2 ans.

M

RÉACTIONS INDÉSIRABLES ET EFFETS SECONDAIRES

SNC: fatigue, céphalées, faiblesse.
ORLO: congestion nasale, otite (enfants), sinusite (enfants).
Resp.: toux.
GI: douleurs abdominales, diarrhée (enfants), dyspepsie, nausées (enfants), élévation des concentrations d'enzymes hépatiques.
Tég.: rash.
Divers: troubles éosinophiliques (incluant le SYNDROME DE CHURG ET STRAUSS), fièvre.

INTERACTIONS

Médicament-médicament: Aucune interaction notable.

VOIES D'ADMINISTRATION ET POSOLOGIE

- **PO (adultes et enfants ≥ 15 ans):** 10 mg, 1 fois par jour, en soirée.
- **PO (enfants de 6 à 14 ans):** 5 mg, 1 fois par jour (comprimés à croquer), en soirée.
- **PO (enfants de 2 à 5 ans):** 4 mg, 1 fois par jour (comprimés à croquer ou sachets de granulés), en soirée.

PRÉSENTATION

Comprimés: 10 mg^{Pr} ▪ **Comprimés à croquer (parfum de cerise):** 4 mg^{Pr}, 5 mg^{Pr} ▪ **Sachets de granulés:** 4 mg^{Pr}.

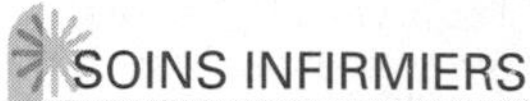

SOINS INFIRMIERS

ÉVALUATION DE LA SITUATION

- Évaluer le murmure vésiculaire et la fonction respiratoire avant le traitement et à intervalles réguliers pendant toute sa durée.
- Évaluer les symptômes d'allergie (rhinite, conjonctivite, urticaire) avant le traitement et à intervalles réguliers pendant toute sa durée.

Tests de laboratoire: Le montélukast peut entraîner une élévation des concentrations d'AST et d'ALT.

DIAGNOSTICS INFIRMIERS POSSIBLES

- Dégagement inefficace des voies respiratoires (Indications).
- Connaissances insuffisantes sur le traitement médicamenteux (Enseignement au patient et à ses proches).

INTERVENTIONS INFIRMIÈRES

- Sous la supervision d'un professionnel de la santé, on peut réduire les doses de corticostéroïdes administrées par inhalation graduellement; ne pas interrompre le traitement brusquement.
- Administrer le médicament 1 fois par jour, en soirée.
- Les sachets de granulés doivent être ouverts juste avant l'administration du médicament. Les granulés peuvent être avalés directement ou mélangés à des aliments mous, froids ou gardés à la température ambiante. Le contenu du sachet doit être pris en entier dans les 15 minutes suivant son ouverture. Ne pas conserver le mélange granulés/aliments en vue d'un usage ultérieur. Les granulés ne doivent pas être dissous dans un liquide. Par contre, l'enfant peut prendre des liquides après avoir avalé les granulés.

ENSEIGNEMENT AU PATIENT ET À SES PROCHES

- Recommander au patient de prendre ce médicament 1 fois par jour, en soirée, même s'il ne présente pas de symptômes d'asthme. L'avertir qu'il ne doit jamais remplacer une dose manquée par une double dose, ni cesser le traitement sans consulter un professionnel de la santé.
- Enseigner au patient le mode d'administration des granulés.

- Conseiller au patient de ne pas interrompre ni réduire la dose des autres médicaments contre l'asthme sans consulter un professionnel de la santé au préalable.
- Informer le patient que le montélukast n'est pas destiné au traitement des crises d'asthme aiguës, mais qu'on peut continuer de le prendre lors d'une exacerbation aiguë. Le patient devrait toujours avoir sur lui un médicament à action rapide pour contrer le bronchospasme. Lui recommander d'informer un professionnel de la santé s'il a besoin de prendre plus que le nombre maximal de doses de bronchodilatateur à action rapide recommandé pour une période de 24 heures.

VÉRIFICATION DE L'EFFICACITÉ THÉRAPEUTIQUE

L'efficacité du traitement peut être démontrée par: la prévention et la réduction des symptômes d'asthme ■ la réduction de la gravité de la rhinite allergique.

ALERTE CLINIQUE

MORPHINE

Kadian, M-Eslon, Morphine HP, Morphitec, M.O.S., M.O.S.-Sulfate, M.O.S.-S.R., MS Contin, MS IR, Ratio-Morphine, Statex

CLASSIFICATION:

Analgésique opioïde (agoniste)

Grossesse – catégories C et D (en cas d'usage prolongé ou d'administration de doses élevées près du terme)

INDICATIONS

Traitement de la douleur modérée à intense ■ Traitement de la douleur associée à l'infarctus du myocarde ■ **Préparation à libération contrôlée**: Soulagement de la douleur modérée à intense exigeant l'administration prolongée d'une préparation opioïde par voie orale. **Usages non approuvés**: Traitement de l'œdème pulmonaire.

MÉCANISME D'ACTION

Liaison aux récepteurs opioïdes du SNC. Modification de la perception de la douleur et de la réaction aux stimuli douloureux, s'accompagnant d'une dépression généralisée du SNC. ***Effets thérapeutiques:*** Diminution de l'intensité de la douleur.

PHARMACOCINÉTIQUE

Absorption: Variable (environ 30 à 40 % PO); plus prévisible par voie IR, SC ou IM. Les doses par voies orale et parentérale ne sont pas équivalentes.

Distribution: Tout l'organisme. La morphine traverse la barrière placentaire et passe dans le lait maternel en petites quantités.

Métabolisme et excrétion: Métabolisme majoritairement hépatique. Les métabolites sont éliminés par les reins.

Demi-vie: *Prématurés:* de 10 à 20 heures; *nouveau-nés:* 7,6 heures; *enfants de 1 à 3 mois:* de 5 à 10 heures; *enfants de 6 mois à 2,5 ans:* 2,9 heures; *enfants de 3 à 6 ans:* 1 à 2 heures; *adultes:* de 2 à 4 heures.

Profil temps-action (analgésie)

	DÉBUT D'ACTION	PIC	DURÉE
PO	30 – 60 min	60 – 120 min	4 – 5 h
PO (forme longue action)	60 min et +	inconnu	12 – 24 h selon la forme utilisée
IM	10 – 30 min	30 – 60 min	4 – 5 h
SC	10 – 20 min	50 – 90 min	4 – 5 h
IR	20 – 60 min	inconnu	4 – 5 h
IV	Rapide	20 min	4 – 5 h
Épidurale	15 – 60 min	inconnu	jusqu'à 24 h
Intrathécale	rapide (quelques min)	inconnu	jusqu'à 24 h

M

CONTRE-INDICATIONS, PRÉCAUTIONS ET MISES EN GARDE

Contre-indications: Hypersensibilité ■ Hypersensibilité à la tartrazine, aux bisulfites ou à l'alcool (certains produits renferment ces additifs et leur administration devrait être évitée chez les patients présentant ce type d'hypersensibilité) ■ Dépression respiratoire aiguë ■ Asthme aigu ■ Obstruction des voies respiratoires supérieures ■ Cœur pulmonaire ■ Arythmies cardiaques ■ Alcoolisme aigu ■ Delirium tremens ■ Dépression grave du SNC ■ Troubles convulsifs ■ Augmentation de la pression intracrânienne ou céphalorachidienne ■ Traumatisme crânien ■ Tumeur cérébrale ■ Abdomen aigu soupçonné ■ Diarrhée due à un empoisonnement ■ Traitement concomitant par les IMAO ou prise au cours des 14 jours précédents.

Précautions et mises en garde: Maladies rénale, hépatique ou pulmonaire graves ■ Hypothyroïdie ■ Insuffisance surrénalienne ■ Antécédents d'alcoolisme ou de toxicomanie ■ **GÉR.**: Personnes âgées ou patients débilités (réduire la dose initiale) ■ Douleurs abdominales non diagnostiquées ■ Hyperplasie de la prostate ou rétrécissement urétral ■ Troubles des voies biliaires ■ Patients qui subissent des interventions qui réduisent rapidement la douleur (cordotomie, radiothérapie); on devrait interrompre le traitement par des agents à action prolongée 24 heures au préalable et administrer des agents à action brève ■ **OBST.**: Grossesse ou allaitement (éviter l'usage prolongé; précédents d'usage au cours du travail de l'accouchement, mais risque de dépression respiratoire chez le nouveau-né) ■ **PÉD.**: Nouveau-nés et enfants < 3 mois (risque accru de dépression respiratoire); nouveau-nés (éviter les préparations injectables contenant des agents de conservation et les solutions buvables contenant du benzoate de sodium, car elles peuvent causer un syndrome de halètement pouvant être mortel) ■ Risque de pharmacodépendance et d'abus.

RÉACTIONS INDÉSIRABLES ET EFFETS SECONDAIRES

SNC: confusion, sédation, étourdissements, dysphorie, euphorie, sensation de flottement, hallucinations, céphalées, rêves bizarres.

ORLO: vision trouble, diplopie, myosis.

Resp.: DÉPRESSION RESPIRATOIRE.

CV: hypotension, bradycardie.

GI: constipation, nausées, vomissements.

GU: rétention urinaire.

Tég.: rougeurs de la peau, démangeaisons, transpiration.

Divers: dépendance physique, dépendance psychologique, tolérance aux effets du médicament.

INTERACTIONS

Médicament-médicament: LA MORPHINE NE DOIT PAS ÊTRE ADMINISTRÉE CHEZ LES PATIENTS RECEVANT DES **IMAO** OU LA **PROCARBAZINE,** CAR ELLE PEUT PROVOQUER DES RÉACTIONS GRAVES ET IMPRÉVISIBLES ■ LA MORPHINE EST CONTRE-INDIQUÉE DANS LES 14 JOURS SUIVANT UN TRAITEMENT PAR UN IMAO ■ Effet dépresseur additif sur le SNC lors de l'usage concomitant d'**alcool**, d'**antihistaminiques**, de **phénothiazines**, de **barbituriques**, d'**antidépresseurs** et d'**hypnosédatifs** ■ L'administration d'**analgésiques opioïdes agonistes/antagonistes** (**nalbuphine**, **butorphanol**, **pentazocine**) peut diminuer l'analgésie et/ou déclencher des symptômes de sevrage chez les patients présentant une dépendance physique aux analgésiques opioïdes.

Médicament-produits naturels: Effets dépresseurs additifs sur le SNC lors de l'usage concomitant de **kava**, de **valériane**, de **scutellaire**, de **camomille** et de **houblon**.

VOIES D'ADMINISTRATION ET POSOLOGIE

Des doses plus élevées peuvent être nécessaires lors d'un traitement prolongé.

- **PO, IR (adultes ≥ 50 kg)**: *Dose de départ habituelle pour soulager la douleur modérée ou intense chez les patients n'ayant jamais pris d'opioïdes* – de 10 à 30 mg, toutes les 4 heures. Une fois la dose quotidienne déterminée, il est possible de passer à une préparation à action prolongée, en fractionnant la dose pour qu'elle soit administrée toutes les 12 heures (M-Eslon, MS Contin,) ou toutes les 24 heures (Kadian).
- **PO, IR (enfants et adultes < 50 kg)**: *Dose de départ habituelle pour soulager la douleur modérée ou intense chez les patients n'ayant jamais pris d'opioïdes* – de 0,15 à 0,3 mg/kg, toutes les 4 heures.
- **IM, IV, SC (adultes ≥ 50 kg)**: *Dose de départ habituelle pour soulager la douleur modérée ou intense chez les patients n'ayant jamais pris d'opioïdes* – de 5 à 15 mg, toutes les 3 ou 4 heures.
- **IM, IV, SC (enfants et adultes < 50 kg)**: *Dose de départ habituelle pour soulager la douleur modérée ou intense chez les patients n'ayant jamais pris d'opioïdes* – de 0,05 à 0,2 mg/kg, toutes les 3 ou 4 heures; au maximum: 15 mg/dose.
- **IM, IV, SC (nouveau-nés)**: De 0,05 à 0,1 mg/kg, toutes les 4 à 8 heures. Utiliser une préparation sans agent de conservation.
- **IV, SC (adultes)**: *Perfusion continue* – de 0,8 à 10 mg/h, dose qui peut être précédée d'un bolus (les débits de perfusion peuvent varier grandement selon la tolérance du patient).
- **IV, SC (enfants)**: *Perfusion continue, douleur postopératoire* – de 0,01 à 0,04 mg/kg/h.
- **IV (nouveau-nés)**: *Perfusion continue* – de 0,01 à 0,03 mg/kg/h. Utiliser une préparation sans agent de conservation.
- **Voie épidurale (adultes)**: *Injection intermittente* – 5 mg/jour (initialement). Si un soulagement n'est pas obtenu après 60 minutes, administrer des doses supplémentaires de 1 à 2 mg (dose maximum: 10 mg/jour). Utiliser une préparation sans agent de conservation. *Perfusion continue* – de 2 à 4 mg/jour, dose qu'on peut augmenter de 1 à 2 mg/jour.
- **Voie épidurale (enfants)**: De 0,03 à 0,05 mg/kg (dose maximum: 0,1 mg/kg ou 5 mg/24 h). Utiliser une préparation sans agent de conservation.
- **Voie intrathécale (adultes)**: De 0,2 mg à 1 mg/jour, en une seule dose. Utiliser une préparation sans agent de conservation.

PRÉSENTATION (version générique disponible)

La morphine est présentée sous de multiples formes de comprimés, de comprimés et de capsules à action prolongée, de solutions, de solutions concentrées, de suppositoires et de préparations injectables à différentes concentrations[N].

SOINS INFIRMIERS

ÉVALUATION DE LA SITUATION

- Déterminer le type de douleur, son siège et son intensité, avant l'administration du médicament, 1 heure après l'administration PO, SC et IM, et 20 minutes (pic) après l'administration IV. Lorsqu'on majore la dose d'un opioïde, on devrait l'augmenter de 25 à 50 % jusqu'à ce qu'on note une réduction de 50 % de la douleur, selon l'évaluation qu'en fait le patient sur une échelle numérique ou visuelle ou jusqu'à ce qu'il signale un soulagement adéquat de la douleur. Pendant qu'on adapte la dose de morphine à action brève, on peut administrer sans danger une deuxième dose au moment du pic, si la dose précédente s'est avérée inefficace et si les effets secondaires sont minimes.
- Les patients sous perfusion continue devraient recevoir des doses additionnelles en bolus toutes les 15 à 30 minutes, selon les besoins, pour soulager la douleur survenant en cours de traitement. Le bolus correspond habituellement à la quantité de médicament administrée par heure en perfusion continue.
- Les patients qui prennent de la morphine à action prolongée peuvent avoir besoin de doses additionnelles d'un opioïde à action brève pour soulager la douleur survenant en cours de traitement. Ces doses devraient être équivalentes à 10 à 15 % de la dose quotidienne et données toutes les 1 à 4 heures, selon les besoins.
- Utiliser un tableau d'équivalences (voir l'annexe A) lorsqu'on doit changer de mode d'administration ou de type d'opioïde.

ALERTE CLINIQUE: ÉVALUER L'ÉTAT DE CONSCIENCE, MESURER LA PRESSION ARTÉRIELLE, LE POULS ET LA FRÉQUENCE RESPIRATOIRE AVANT ET À INTERVALLES RÉGULIERS DURANT L'ADMINISTRATION. SI LA FRÉQUENCE RESPIRATOIRE EST < 10/MIN, ÉVALUER LE DEGRÉ DE SÉDATION. UNE STIMULATION PHYSIQUE PEUT ÊTRE SUFFISANTE POUR PRÉVENIR UNE HYPOVENTILATION IMPORTANTE. IL PEUT S'AVÉRER NÉCESSAIRE DE RÉDUIRE LA DOSE DE 25 À 50 %. LA SOMNOLENCE INITIALE DISPARAÎT AU FIL DU TRAITEMENT.

GÉR.: Évaluer les personnes âgées à intervalles fréquents, car elles sont plus sensibles aux effets des analgésiques opioïdes que les adultes plus jeunes et peuvent manifester plus souvent des réactions indésirables ou subir des complications respiratoires.

PÉD.: Évaluer les enfants à intervalles fréquents, car ils sont plus sensibles aux effets des analgésiques opioïdes et peuvent subir plus souvent des complications respiratoires ou se montrer excités ou irritables.

- L'usage prolongé peut entraîner la dépendance physique et psychologique ainsi qu'une tolérance aux effets du médicament, mais cela ne doit pas empêcher le patient de recevoir une quantité suffisante d'analgésiques. La dépendance psychologique est rare chez la plupart des patients qui reçoivent de la morphine pour des raisons médicales. Lors d'un traitement prolongé, il faut parfois administrer des doses de plus en plus élevées pour soulager la douleur.
- Examiner la fonction intestinale du patient à intervalles réguliers. La consommation accrue de liquides et d'aliments riches en fibres et la prise de laxatifs peuvent réduire les effets constipants du médicament. Sauf contre-indication, des laxatifs stimulants devraient être administrés de façon systématique si le traitement par un produit opioïde dure plus de 2 ou 3 jours.

Tests de laboratoire: La morphine peut élever les concentrations plasmatiques d'amylase et de lipase.

TOXICITÉ ET SURDOSAGE: S'il est nécessaire d'administrer un antagoniste opioïde pour renverser la dépression respiratoire ou le coma, l'antidote est la naloxone (Narcan). Diluer l'ampoule de naloxone à 0,4 mg dans 10 mL de solution de NaCl 0,9 % et administrer 0,5 mL (0,02 mg) par bolus IV direct, toutes les 2 minutes. Dans le cas des enfants et des patients pesant moins de 40 kg, diluer 0,1 mg de naloxone dans 10 mL de solution de NaCl 0,9 % pour obtenir une concentration de 10 µg/mL et administrer 0,5 µg/kg, toutes les 2 minutes. Adapter la dose pour prévenir les symptômes de sevrage, les convulsions et la douleur intense.

DIAGNOSTICS INFIRMIERS POSSIBLES

- Douleur aiguë (Indications).
- Trouble de la perception visuelle et auditive (Effets secondaires).
- Risque d'accident (Effets secondaires).
- Connaissances insuffisantes sur le traitement médicamenteux (Enseignement au patient et à ses proches).

INTERVENTIONS INFIRMIÈRES

ALERTE CLINIQUE: NE PAS CONFONDRE LA MORPHINE AVEC L'HYDROMORPHONE OU LA MÉPÉRIDINE; DES ERREURS ONT MENÉ À UNE ISSUE FATALE. NE PAS CONFONDRE LES CONCENTRATIONS ÉLEVÉES (HP) AVEC LES CONCENTRATIONS ORDINAIRES.

- DES SURDOSES ACCIDENTELLES D'ANALGÉSIQUES OPIOÏDES ONT CAUSÉ DES DÉCÈS. ÉVALUER L'UTILISATION ANTÉRIEURE D'ANALGÉSIQUES OPIOÏDES PAR LE PATIENT ET SES BESOINS ACTUELS. AVANT L'ADMINISTRATION, CLARIFIER TOUS LES POINTS AMBIGUS SUR LES ORDONNANCES ET FAIRE VÉRIFIER L'ORDONNANCE D'ORIGINE, LES CALCULS DES DOSES ET LE

RÉGLAGE DE LA POMPE À PERFUSION PAR UN AUTRE PROFESSIONNEL DE LA SANTÉ.

PÉD.: LES ERREURS DANS L'ADMINISTRATION DES ANALGÉSIQUES OPIOÏDES SONT FRÉQUENTES CHEZ LES ENFANTS; ELLES COMPRENNENT DES ERREURS D'INTERPRÉTATION ET DE CALCULS DES DOSES AINSI QUE L'USAGE D'INSTRUMENTS DE MESURE INAPPROPRIÉS.

- UTILISER SEULEMENT DES PRÉPARATIONS SANS AGENT DE CONSERVATION CHEZ LES NOUVEAU-NÉS ET LORS DE L'ADMINISTRATION ÉPIDURALE ET INTRATHÉCALE CHEZ TOUS LES PATIENTS.
- Pour augmenter l'effet analgésique de la morphine, avant de l'administrer, expliquer au patient la valeur thérapeutique de ce médicament.
- Les doses administrées selon un horaire fixe peuvent être plus efficaces que celles administrées sur demande. L'analgésique s'avère plus efficace s'il est administré avant que la douleur ne devienne intense.
- L'association avec des analgésiques non opioïdes peut avoir des effets analgésiques additifs et permettre d'administrer des doses plus faibles.
- Si l'on substitue les comprimés à libération prolongée à d'autres opioïdes ou à d'autres formes de morphine, administrer par voie orale une dose quotidienne totale de morphine équivalente à la dose quotidienne précédente (voir l'annexe A), fractionnée pour qu'elle soit administrée toutes les 12 heures (M-Eslon, MS Contin,) ou toutes les 24 heures (Kadian).
- Après un traitement prolongé, interrompre l'administration graduellement pour prévenir les symptômes de sevrage.

PO:

- On peut administrer le médicament avec des aliments ou du lait pour réduire l'irritation gastrique.
- Administrer la solution à l'aide d'un dispositif bien calibré. Pour améliorer le goût de la solution, on peut la diluer dans un verre de jus de fruits juste avant de l'administrer.
- LES COMPRIMÉS À LIBÉRATION PROLONGÉE DOIVENT ÊTRE AVALÉS TELS QUELS. IL NE FAUT PAS LES ÉCRASER, LES MÂCHER OU LES BRISER (EN RAISON DU RISQUE DE LIBÉRATION RAPIDE ET D'ABSORPTION D'UNE DOSE POUVANT S'AVÉRER TOXIQUE).
- On peut ouvrir les capsules de *Kadian* et de *M-Eslon* et saupoudrer leur contenu sur de la compote de pomme immédiatement avant l'administration. LES GRANULES NE DOIVENT PAS ÊTRE MÂCHÉS, ÉCRASÉS OU DISSOUS.

IV: La solution est incolore ou jaune clair (selon la concentration). Ne pas administrer une solution qui a changé de couleur.

IV directe: Diluer le médicament dans au moins 5 mL d'eau stérile ou de solution de NaCl 0,9% pour injection.

***VITESSE D'ADMINISTRATION*: ALERTE CLINIQUE**: ADMINISTRER DE 2,5 À 15 mg EN 4 À 5 MINUTES. UNE ADMINISTRATION TROP RAPIDE PEUT AGGRAVER LA DÉPRESSION RESPIRATOIRE ET INDUIRE L'HYPOTENSION ET UN COLLAPSUS CIRCULATOIRE.

Perfusion continue: On peut ajouter le médicament à une solution de D5%E, de D10%E, de NaCl 0,9 % ou 0,45 %, ou encore à une solution de Ringer ou de lactate de Ringer, de dextrose dans une solution saline ou de dextrose dans une solution de Ringer ou de lactate de Ringer à une concentration de 0,1 à 1 mg/mL ou plus. Consulter les directives de chaque fabricant avant de reconstituer la préparation.

***Vitesse d'administration*:**

- Administrer à l'aide d'une pompe à perfusion permettant de régler le débit. La dose doit être adaptée pour assurer le soulagement de la douleur sans sédation, dépression respiratoire ou hypotension excessives.
- On peut administrer la préparation par une pompe d'analgésie contrôlée par le patient (ACP) qu'il peut faire fonctionner lorsqu'il en ressent le besoin.

Associations compatibles dans la même seringue: adrénaline ■ atropine ■ bupivacaïne ■ cimétidine ■ dimenhydrinate ■ diphenhydramine ■ dropéridol ■ glycopyrrolate ■ hydroxyzine ■ kétamine ■ métoclopramide ■ midazolam ■ milrinone ■ perphénazine ■ promazine ■ ranitidine ■ scopolamine.

Compatibilité (tubulure en Y): allopurinol ■ amifostine ■ amikacine ■ aminophylline ■ amiodarone ■ ampicilline ■ aténolol ■ atracurium ■ calcium, chlorure de ■ céfazoline ■ céfotaxime ■ céfoxitine ■ ceftazidime ■ ceftriaxone ■ céfuroxime ■ chloramphénicol ■ cisplatine ■ cladribine ■ clindamycine ■ cyclophosphamide ■ cytarabine ■ dexaméthasone sodique, phosphate de ■ digoxine ■ diltiazem ■ dobutamine ■ dopamine ■ doxorubicine ■ doxycycline ■ énalaprilat ■ érythromycine, lactobionate d' ■ esmolol ■ étomidate ■ famotidine ■ filgrastim ■ fluconazole ■ fludarabine ■ foscarnet ■ gentamicine ■ granisétron ■ héparine ■ hydrocortisone sodique, succinate d' ■ insuline ■ kanamycine ■ labétolol ■ lidocaïne ■ lorazépam ■ magnésium, sulfate de ■ melphalan ■ méropénème ■ méthotrexate ■ méthyldopa ■ méthylprednisolone ■ métoclopramide ■ métoprolol ■ métronidazole ■ midazolam ■ milrinone ■ nitroprusside ■ noradrénaline ■ ondansétron ■ oxacilline ■ oxytocine ■ paclitaxel ■ pancuronium ■ pénicilline G potassique ■ pipéracilline ■ pipéracilline/tazobactam ■ potassium, chlorure de ■ propofol ■ propranolol ■ ranitidine ■ sodium, bicarbonate de ■

téniposide ■ thiotépa ■ ticarcilline ■ ticarcilline/clavulanate ■ tobramycine ■ triméthoprime/sulfaméthoxazole ■ vancomycine ■ vécuronium ■ vinorelbine ■ vitamines du complexe B avec C ■ warfarine ■ zidovudine.

Incompatibilité (tubulure en Y): céfépime ■ gallium, nitrate de ■ minocycline.

ENSEIGNEMENT AU PATIENT ET À SES PROCHES

- Expliquer au patient ce qu'on entend par administration sur demande et à quel moment il doit réclamer l'analgésique. **ALERTE CLINIQUE**: PRÉVENIR LES PROCHES QU'IL NE FAUT PAS ADMINISTRER DE DOSES D'ACP À UN PATIENT QUI DORT, EN RAISON DES RISQUES DE SÉDATION, DE SURDOSAGE ET DE DÉPRESSION RESPIRATOIRE.
- Prévenir le patient que la morphine peut provoquer des étourdissements et de la somnolence. Lui recommander de demander de l'aide lorsqu'il se déplace et lorsqu'il veut fumer. Lui conseiller de ne pas conduire et d'éviter les activités qui exigent sa vigilance jusqu'à ce qu'on ait la certitude que le médicament n'entraîne pas ces effets chez lui.
- Recommander au patient de changer lentement de position pour diminuer le risque d'hypotension orthostatique.
- Inciter le patient à ne pas boire d'alcool et à ne pas prendre d'autres dépresseurs du SNC en même temps que la morphine.
- Conseiller au patient de se tourner dans le lit, de tousser et de faire des exercices de respiration profonde toutes les 2 heures pour prévenir l'atélectasie.
- **Soins à domicile**: **ALERTE CLINIQUE**: EXPLIQUER AU PATIENT ET À SES PROCHES COMMENT ET QUAND ADMINISTRER LA MORPHINE ET COMMENT ENTRETENIR LE MATÉRIEL DE PERFUSION ■ **PÉD.**: ENSEIGNER AUX PARENTS OU AUX SOIGNANTS COMMENT MESURER AVEC PRÉCISION LE MÉDICAMENT EN LIQUIDE ET LEUR RECOMMANDER D'UTILISER SEULEMENT LA MESURE FOURNIE.
- Insister sur le fait qu'il est primordial de prévenir la constipation aussi longtemps que le patient prend de la morphine.

VÉRIFICATION DE L'EFFICACITÉ THÉRAPEUTIQUE

L'efficacité du traitement peut être démontrée par: la diminution de l'intensité de la douleur sans modification importante de l'état de conscience ou de la fonction respiratoire. ✳

MOXIFLOXACINE,
voir Fluoroquinolones

MUPIROCINE

Bactroban, Taro-Mupirocin

CLASSIFICATION:
Antibiotique (topique)

Grossesse - catégorie B

INDICATIONS

Voie topique: Traitement des affections suivantes: impétigo ■ lésions cutanées traumatiques (jusqu'à 10 cm de longueur ou surface de 100 cm^2), dues à une infection par *Staphylococcus aureus* et *Streptococcus pyogenes*. **Usages non approuvés - voie nasale**: Éradication du *Staphylococcus aureus* résistant à la méthicilline (SARM) qui colonise les voies nasales de certains patients.

MÉCANISME D'ACTION

Inhibition de la synthèse des protéines bactériennes. ***Effets thérapeutiques:*** Inhibition de la croissance et de la reproduction bactériennes. **Spectre d'action**: Activité notable surtout contre les microorganismes à Gram positif, incluant *S. aureus* ■ les streptocoques bêtahémolytiques ■ Résolution de l'impétigo ■ Éradication de l'état de porteur de *S. aureus*.

PHARMACOCINÉTIQUE

Absorption: L'absorption systémique est minime.

Distribution: Le médicament demeure dans la couche cornée (couche la plus éloignée de l'épiderme) pendant de longues périodes (72 heures).

Métabolisme et excrétion: Métabolisme au niveau de la peau; l'agent est éliminé par desquamation.

Demi-vie: Inconnue.

Profil temps-action (effet antibiotique)

	DÉBUT D'ACTION	PIC	DURÉE
Préparation topique†	inconnu	3 - 5 jours	72 h

† Cicatrisation des lésions.

CONTRE-INDICATIONS, PRÉCAUTIONS ET MISES EN GARDE

Contre-indications: Hypersensibilité à la mupirocine ou au polyéthylèneglycol.

M

Précautions et mises en garde: OBST., ALLAITEMENT: L'innocuité du médicament n'a pas été établie ■ Insuffisance rénale modérée ou grave.

RÉACTIONS INDÉSIRABLES ET EFFETS SECONDAIRES

SNC: céphalées (voie nasale).

Resp.: pharyngite, rhinite (voie nasale).

GI: nausées (voie nasale).

Tég.: sensation de brûlure, démangeaisons, douleurs, picotements.

INTERACTIONS

Médicament-médicament: La mupirocine administrée par voie nasale ne devrait pas être utilisée en même temps que d'autres **produits destinés à l'administration intranasale**.

VOIES D'ADMINISTRATION ET POSOLOGIE

- **Voie topique (adultes et enfants):** Appliquer 3 fois par jour.
- **Voie nasale (adultes et enfants):** *Usage non approuvé* – appliquer 0,5 g, 2 fois par jour dans chaque narine pendant 5 jours (jusqu'à 7 à 14 jours).

PRÉSENTATION

Onguent: à 2 %, en tubes de 15 g^{VL} et de 30 g^{VL} ■ **Crème:** à 2 %, en tubes de 15 g^{VL} et de 30 g^{VL}.

SOINS INFIRMIERS

ÉVALUATION DE LA SITUATION

- Examiner les lésions avant le traitement et tous les jours pendant toute sa durée.

DIAGNOSTICS INFIRMIERS POSSIBLES

- Risque d'atteinte à l'intégrité de la peau (Indications).
- Risque d'infection (Indications, Enseignement au patient et à ses proches).
- Connaissances insuffisantes sur le traitement médicamenteux (Enseignement au patient et à ses proches).

INTERVENTIONS INFIRMIÈRES

Préparation topique: Nettoyer la région à l'eau et au savon et bien assécher. Appliquer une petite quantité d'onguent de mupirocine sur la région affectée, 3 fois par jour. Bien faire pénétrer en massant délicatement. On peut couvrir la région traitée avec un pansement de gaze.

Préparation nasale: Appliquer une petite quantité d'onguent de mupirocine (environ 0,5 g) dans chaque narine, 2 fois par jour (matin et soir). Après l'application, presser légèrement les ailes du nez et relâcher. Répéter cette opération pendant 1 minute.

ENSEIGNEMENT AU PATIENT ET À SES PROCHES

- Montrer au patient comment appliquer l'onguent de mupirocine. Lui conseiller de suivre rigoureusement la posologie recommandée pendant toute la durée du traitement. S'il n'a pu appliquer le médicament au moment habituel, il doit le faire dès que possible, à moins que ce ne soit presque l'heure prévue pour l'application suivante.
- Enseigner au patient et à ses proches les mesures d'hygiène à suivre pour prévenir la propagation de l'impétigo.
- Conseiller aux parents de prévenir l'infirmière de l'école que l'enfant souffre d'impétigo afin qu'elle puisse prendre des mesures de dépistage et de prévention de la contamination.
- Recommander au patient de consulter le médecin si les symptômes ne se sont pas améliorés dans les 3 à 5 jours qui suivent le début du traitement.

VÉRIFICATION DE L'EFFICACITÉ THÉRAPEUTIQUE

L'efficacité du traitement peut être démontrée par: la cicatrisation des lésions cutanées; en l'absence d'une réponse clinique en l'espace de 3 à 5 jours, il faut réévaluer l'état du patient ■ l'éradication de l'état de porteur de souches de *S. aureus* résistant à la méthicilline chez les patients et les travailleurs de la santé, lors des éclosions en milieu hospitalier.

MYCOPHÉNOLATE SODIQUE,

voir Mofétilmycophénolate

NABUMÉTONE

Apo-Nabumetone, Gen-Nabumetone, Novo-Nabumetone, Relafen, Sandoz Nabumetone

CLASSIFICATION:

Anti-inflammatoire non stéroïdien

Grossesse – catégories D (1er et 3e trimestres) et B (2e trimestre)

INDICATIONS

Traitement symptomatique des états aigus de polyarthrite rhumatoïde et d'arthrose.

MÉCANISME D'ACTION

Inhibition de la synthèse des prostaglandines. ***Effets thérapeutiques:*** Suppression de l'inflammation et de la douleur.

PHARMACOCINÉTIQUE

Absorption: 80 % (PO – pour le nabumétone qui est un promédicament); transformation rapide de 35 % en acide 6-méthoxy-2-naphthylacétique (6-MNA), qui est le médicament actif.

Distribution: Inconnue.

Liaison aux protéines: > 99 %.

Métabolisme et excrétion: Métabolisme hépatique (le 6-MNA est transformé en composés inactifs).

Demi-vie: 24 heures (prolongée en cas d'insuffisance rénale grave).

Profil temps-action (analgésie et effets anti-inflammatoires)

	DÉBUT D'ACTION	PIC	DURÉE
PO	1 – 2 jours	quelques jours à 2 semaines	12 – 24 h

CONTRE-INDICATIONS, PRÉCAUTIONS ET MISES EN GARDE

Contre-indications: Hypersensibilité ■ Risque de réactions de sensibilité croisée avec d'autres AINS incluant l'aspirine ■ Contexte périopératoire en cas de pontage aortocoronarien ■ **OBST., ALLAITEMENT, PÉD.:** L'innocuité de l'agent n'a pas été établie.

Précautions et mises en garde: Maladies cardiovasculaire, hépatique ou rénale graves ■ Antécédents d'ulcère ■ Ulcère ou hémorragie digestive évolutive.

RÉACTIONS INDÉSIRABLES ET EFFETS SECONDAIRES

SNC: agitation, anxiété, confusion, dépression, étourdissements, somnolence, fatigue, céphalées, insomnie, malaise, faiblesse.

ORLO: vision anormale, acouphènes.

Resp.: dyspnée, pneumopathie d'hypersensibilité.

CV: œdème, rétention liquidienne, vasculite.

GI: HÉMORRAGIE DIGESTIVE, douleurs abdominales, diarrhée, résultats anormaux aux tests de la fonction hépatique, anorexie, constipation, sécheresse de la bouche (xérostomie), dyspepsie, flatulence, gastrite, gastroentérite, gain d'appétit, nausées, stomatite, vomissements.

GU: albuminurie, azotémie, néphrite interstitielle.

Tég.: sécrétion accrue de sueur, photosensibilité, prurit, rash, DERMATITE EXFOLIATIVE, SYNDROME DE STEVENS-JOHNSON, ÉPIDERMOLYSE NÉCROSANTE SUBAIGUË.

Hémat.: allongement du temps de saignement.

Métab.: gain de poids.

SN: paresthésie, tremblements.

Divers: réactions allergiques comprenant l'ANAPHYLAXIE et l'ŒDÈME ANGIONEUROTIQUE.

INTERACTIONS

Médicament-médicament: L'**aspirine**, les autres **AINS**, les **suppléments de potassium** et les **corticostéroïdes**, tout comme l'**alcool**, intensifient les effets secondaires gastro-intestinaux ■ L'administration prolongée de nabumétone avec de l'**acétaminophène** peut augmenter le risque de réactions rénales indésirables ■ La nabumétone peut réduire l'efficacité des **diurétiques** ou des **antihypertenseurs** ■ La nabumétone peut intensifier l'effet hypoglycémiant de l'**insuline** ou des **hypoglycémiants oraux** ■ La nabumétone élève le risque de toxicité associé au **méthotrexate** ■ Risque accru d'hémorragie lors de l'administration de **céfamandole**, de **céfotétane**, de **céfopérazone**, d'**acide valproïque**, de **plicamycine**, d'**anticoagulants**, de **ticlopidine**, de **clopidogrel**, d'**eptifibatide**, de **tirofiban** ou d'**agents thrombolytiques** ■ Risque accru de réactions hématologiques indésirables lors de l'administration d'**agents antinéoplasiques** ou d'une **radiothérapie** ■ Risque accru de toxicité rénale lors de l'administration de **cyclosporine**.

VOIES D'ADMINISTRATION ET POSOLOGIE

- **PO (adultes):** 1 000 mg par jour, en une seule dose; on peut majorer la posologie jusqu'à concurrence de 2 000 mg par jour, en une seule dose ou en 2 doses fractionnées.

PRÉSENTATION

Comprimés: 500 mgPr, 750 mgPr.

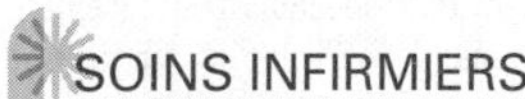

SOINS INFIRMIERS

ÉVALUATION DE LA SITUATION

- LES PATIENTS SOUFFRANT D'ASTHME, D'ALLERGIE INDUITE PAR L'ASPIRINE OU DE POLYPES NASAUX

N

SONT DAVANTAGE PRÉDISPOSÉS AUX RÉACTIONS D'HYPERSENSIBILITÉ. SUIVRE DE PRÈS LA RHINITE, L'ASTHME ET L'URTICAIRE.

- Suivre de près la douleur et déterminer la mobilité des articulations, avant l'administration de la nabumétone et à intervalles réguliers pendant toute la durée du traitement.

Tests de laboratoire:

- Mesurer les concentrations d'urée et de créatinine sérique ainsi que la numération globulaire; chez les patients recevant un traitement prolongé par la nabumétone, noter les résultats des tests de la fonction hépatique à intervalles réguliers pendant toute la durée du traitement.
- Le médicament peut entraîner une élévation des concentrations sériques de potassium, d'urée, de créatinine, de phosphatase alcaline, de LDH, d'AST et d'ALT. La nabumétone peut entraîner une baisse de la glycémie, des concentrations d'hémoglobine, de l'hématocrite, du nombre de leucocytes et de plaquettes, et réduire la clairance de la créatinine.
- La nabumétone peut allonger le temps de saignement.

DIAGNOSTICS INFIRMIERS POSSIBLES

N

- Douleur aiguë (Indications).
- Mobilité physique réduite (Indications).
- Connaissances insuffisantes sur le traitement médicamenteux (Enseignement au patient et à ses proches).

INTERVENTIONS INFIRMIÈRES

- L'administration de doses plus élevées que celles recommandées n'accroît pas l'efficacité du médicament, mais pourrait augmenter le risque d'effets secondaires. **GÉR.**: Administrer la dose minimale efficace pendant la plus courte durée de traitement possible.
- Administrer la nabumétone avec des aliments ou avec un antiacide pour réduire l'irritation gastrique et pour augmenter l'absorption du médicament.

ENSEIGNEMENT AU PATIENT ET À SES PROCHES

- Conseiller au patient de prendre la nabumétone avec un grand verre d'eau et d'éviter de se coucher pendant les 15 à 30 minutes qui suivent.
- Conseiller au patient de respecter rigoureusement la posologie recommandée. S'il n'a pu prendre le médicament au moment habituel, il doit le faire dès que possible à moins que ce ne soit presque l'heure prévue pour la dose suivante. Le prévenir qu'il ne doit jamais remplacer une dose manquée par une double dose.
- Prévenir le patient que la nabumétone peut parfois provoquer de la somnolence, des étourdissements ou des troubles de la vue. Lui conseiller de ne pas conduire et d'éviter les activités qui exigent sa vigilance jusqu'à ce qu'on ait la certitude que le médicament n'entraîne pas ces effets chez lui.
- Recommander au patient d'utiliser un écran solaire et de porter des vêtements protecteurs pour prévenir les réactions de photosensibilité.
- Recommander au patient d'éviter de boire de l'alcool et de consulter un professionnel de la santé avant de prendre une préparation à base d'aspirine ou d'acétaminophène ou un autre médicament en vente libre en même temps que la nabumétone.
- Recommander au patient qui doit suivre un traitement ou subir une intervention chirurgicale de prévenir le professionnel de la santé qu'il suit un traitement par ce médicament.
- Recommander au patient de communiquer avec un professionnel de la santé en cas de rash, de démangeaisons, de troubles visuels, d'acouphènes, de gain de poids, d'œdème, de selles noires, de céphalées persistantes ou de symptômes pseudogrippaux, tels que frissons, fièvre, douleurs musculaires ou autres douleurs.

VÉRIFICATION DE L'EFFICACITÉ THÉRAPEUTIQUE

L'efficacité du traitement peut être démontrée par: la diminution de l'intensité de la douleur et l'amélioration de la mobilité des articulations. Un soulagement partiel des douleurs arthritiques survient habituellement dans la semaine qui suit le début du traitement, mais les pleins effets du médicament peuvent ne se manifester qu'après 2 semaines ou plus d'un traitement continu. Les patients qui ne répondent pas à un anti-inflammatoire non stéroïdien peuvent répondre à un autre. ✳

NADOLOL

Apo-Nadolol, Corgard, Novo-Nadolol

CLASSIFICATION:

Antiangineux, antihypertenseur (bêtabloquant)

Grossesse – catégories C (1er trimestre) et D (2e et 3e trimestres)

INDICATIONS

Prophylaxie de l'angine de poitrine ■ Traitement de l'hypertension légère à modérée, administré seul ou en association avec d'autres médicaments.

MÉCANISME D'ACTION

Blocage de la stimulation des récepteurs adrénergiques bêta$_1$ (du myocarde) et des récepteurs bêta$_2$ (pulmonaires, vasculaires ou utérins). ***Effets thérapeutiques:*** Ralentissement de la fréquence cardiaque et abaissement de la pression artérielle.

PHARMACOCINÉTIQUE

Absorption: 37 % (PO).
Distribution: L'agent pénètre dans le SNC en quantités infimes, traverse la barrière placentaire et passe dans le lait maternel.
Métabolisme et excrétion: Excrétion rénale sous forme inchangée (20 %) et fécale sous forme inchangée (70 %).
Demi-vie: De 20 à 24 heures (prolongée en cas d'insuffisance rénale).

Profil temps-action (effet antihypertenseur)

	Début d'action	Pic	Durée
PO†	jusqu'à 5 jours	6 – 9 jours	24 h

† Lors d'une administration prolongée.

CONTRE-INDICATIONS, PRÉCAUTIONS ET MISES EN GARDE

Contre-indications: Insuffisance cardiaque ■ Choc cardiogénique ■ Bradycardie ou bloc cardiaque (bloc AV du 2e et 3e degré) ■ Rhinite allergique ■ Bronchospasmes (y compris l'asthme bronchique) ou bronchopneumopathie obstructive chronique grave ■ Insuffisance ventriculaire droite secondaire à l'hypertension pulmonaire ■ Anesthésie au moyen de substances qui induisent une insuffisance du myocarde.
Précautions et mises en garde: Insuffisance rénale ■ **Gér.**: Il est recommandé de réduire la dose initiale chez les personnes âgées ou débilitées ■ Diabète (le nadolol peut masquer les symptômes d'hypoglycémie) ■ Thyrotoxicose (le médicament peut en masquer les symptômes) ■ Antécédents de réactions allergiques graves (l'intensité des réactions peut être accrue) ■ **Obst., Allaitement, Péd.**: L'innocuité du médicament n'a pas été établie chez la femme enceinte ou qui allaite ni chez l'enfant; il traverse la barrière placentaire et peut entraîner la bradycardie, l'hypotension, l'hypoglycémie et la dépression respiratoire chez le fœtus ou le nouveau-né.

RÉACTIONS INDÉSIRABLES ET EFFETS SECONDAIRES

SNC: fatigue, faiblesse, anxiété, dépression, étourdissements, somnolence, insomnie, perte de mémoire, modifications des opérations de la pensée, cauchemars.
ORLO: vision trouble, xérophtalmie, congestion nasale.
Resp.: bronchospasme, respiration sifflante.
CV: ARYTHMIES, BRADYCARDIE, INSUFFISANCE CARDIAQUE, ŒDÈME PULMONAIRE, hypotension orthostatique, vasoconstriction périphérique.
GI: constipation, diarrhée, nausées.
GU: impuissance, baisse de la libido.
Tég.: démangeaisons, rash.
End.: hyperglycémie, hypoglycémie.
Loc.: arthralgie, douleurs lombaires, crampes musculaires.
SN: paresthésie.
Divers: syndrome lupique d'origine médicamenteuse.

INTERACTIONS

Médicament-médicament: Risque de dépression additive du myocarde lors de l'administration concomitante d'une **anesthésie générale**, de **phénytoïne** par voie IV, de **diltiazem** ou de **vérapamil** ■ Risque de bradycardie additive lors de l'administration concomitante de **dérivés digitaliques** ■ Risque d'hypotension additive lors de l'administration concomitante d'autres **antihypertenseurs** et de **dérivés nitrés**, ainsi que lors de l'ingestion de grandes quantités d'**alcool** ■ La prise concomitante d'**amphétamines**, de **cocaïne**, d'**éphédrine**, d'**adrénaline**, de **noradrénaline**, de **phényléphrine** ou de **pseudoéphédrine** peut entraîner une stimulation alpha-adrénergique à laquelle rien ne s'oppose (hypertension et bradycardie excessives) ■ L'administration concomitante de **clonidine** accentue l'hypotension et la bradycardie ■ L'administration concomitante de **préparations thyroïdiennes** peut diminuer l'efficacité du nadolol ■ Risque de modification de l'efficacité de l'**insuline** ou des **hypoglycémiants oraux** (une adaptation posologique peut s'avérer nécessaire) ■ Le nadolol peut augmenter les concentrations sériques de **théophylline** ■ Le nadolol peut diminuer les effets bénéfiques sur les récepteurs bêtacardiaques de la **dopamine** ou de la **dobutamine** ■ La prudence est de mise lorsque le nadolol est administré dans les 14 jours suivant un traitement par un **IMAO** (risque d'hypertension) ■ L'administration concomitante d'un **AINS** peut diminuer l'effet antihypertenseur du nadolol.

VOIES D'ADMINISTRATION ET POSOLOGIE

- **PO (adultes)**: *Antiangineux* – initialement, 40 mg, 1 fois par jour; on peut majorer la dose par paliers de 40 à 80 mg par jour, tous les 3 à 7 jours, selon la réponse au traitement et la tolérance du patient (jusqu'à concurrence de 240 mg par jour). *Antihypertenseur* – initialement, 40 mg, 1 fois par jour; on peut majorer la dose par paliers de 40 à 80 mg par jour, tous les 7 jours, selon la réponse au traitement et la tolérance du patient (jusqu'à concurrence de 320 mg par jour).

N

■ *INSUFFISANCE RÉNALE*
PO (ADULTES): CL_{CR} DE 10 À 50 mL/MIN – ADMINISTRER 50 % DE LA DOSE HABITUELLE; CL_{CR} < 10 mL/MIN – ADMINISTRER 25 % DE LA DOSE HABITUELLE.

PRÉSENTATION (version générique disponible)

Comprimés: 40 mg[Pr], 80 mg[Pr], 160 mg[Pr].

SOINS INFIRMIERS

ÉVALUATION DE LA SITUATION

- MESURER LA PRESSION ARTÉRIELLE ET LE POULS À INTERVALLES FRÉQUENTS PENDANT LA PÉRIODE D'ADAPTATION POSOLOGIQUE ET À INTERVALLES RÉGULIERS PENDANT TOUTE LA DURÉE DU TRAITEMENT. SUIVRE DE PRÈS LES SIGNES D'HYPOTENSION ORTHOSTATIQUE LORSQU'ON AIDE LE PATIENT À SE LEVER.
- EFFECTUER LE BILAN QUOTIDIEN DES INGESTA ET DES EXCRETA ET PESER LE PATIENT TOUS LES JOURS. OBSERVER RÉGULIÈREMENT LE PATIENT À LA RECHERCHE DES SIGNES ET DES SYMPTÔMES SUIVANTS DE SURCHARGE LIQUIDIENNE: ŒDÈME PÉRIPHÉRIQUE, DYSPNÉE, RÂLES OU CRÉPITATIONS, FATIGUE, GAIN PONDÉRAL, TURGESCENCE DES JUGULAIRES.

Hypertension: Suivre la fréquence de renouvellement des ordonnances pour déterminer l'observance du traitement.

Angine: Déterminer la fréquence et les caractéristiques des crises d'angine à intervalles réguliers pendant toute la durée du traitement.

Tests de laboratoire:

- Le nadolol peut élever les concentrations d'urée, de lipoprotéines sériques, de potassium, de triglycérides et d'acide urique.
- Le nadolol peut entraîner une élévation des titres des anticorps antinucléaires.
- Il peut provoquer une élévation de la glycémie.

TOXICITÉ ET SURDOSAGE: Suivre de près les patients recevant des bêtabloquants afin de déceler les signes suivants de surdosage: bradycardie, étourdissements graves ou évanouissements, somnolence prononcée, dyspnée, ongles ou paumes des mains bleutés, convulsions. Communiquer immédiatement avec le médecin ou un autre professionnel de la santé si ces signes se manifestent.

DIAGNOSTICS INFIRMIERS POSSIBLES

- Débit cardiaque diminué (Effets secondaires).
- Connaissances insuffisantes sur le traitement médicamenteux (Enseignement au patient et à ses proches).
- Non-observance du traitement médicamenteux (Enseignement au patient et à ses proches).

INTERVENTIONS INFIRMIÈRES

- Il faut arrêter le traitement concomitant par la clonidine graduellement, en cessant d'abord le traitement par le bêtabloquant et, plusieurs jours plus tard, celui par la clonidine.
- Mesurer le pouls à l'apex du cœur avant d'administrer le médicament. S'il est inférieur à 50 battements par minute ou s'il y a arythmie, ne pas administrer le nadolol et en avertir le médecin ou un autre professionnel de la santé.
- Administrer le médicament à jeun ou avec des aliments.
- On peut écraser le comprimé de nadolol et le mélanger à des aliments.

ENSEIGNEMENT AU PATIENT ET À SES PROCHES

- Prévenir le patient qu'il doit prendre le nadolol quotidiennement, au même moment de la journée, en suivant rigoureusement les recommandations du médecin. Lui expliquer qu'il doit continuer à prendre le médicament même s'il se sent bien. L'avertir qu'il ne doit jamais sauter de dose ni remplacer une dose manquée par une double dose. S'il n'a pu prendre le médicament au moment habituel, il doit le prendre aussitôt que possible, mais au moins 8 heures avant l'heure prévue pour la dose suivante. UN SEVRAGE BRUSQUE PEUT PROVOQUER DES ARYTHMIES METTANT LA VIE EN DANGER, L'HYPERTENSION OU L'ISCHÉMIE DU MYOCARDE.
- Conseiller au patient de toujours avoir une réserve suffisante de médicament à sa disposition. Lui conseiller également de conserver une ordonnance dans son portefeuille pour parer à toute urgence.
- ENSEIGNER AU PATIENT ET À SES PROCHES LA MÉTHODE DE PRISE DU POULS ET DE LA PRESSION ARTÉRIELLE. LEUR DEMANDER DE MESURER LE POULS TOUS LES JOURS ET LA PRESSION ARTÉRIELLE AU MOINS 2 FOIS PAR SEMAINE. SI LE POULS EST INFÉRIEUR À 50 BATTEMENTS PAR MINUTE OU SI LA PRESSION ARTÉRIELLE VARIE DE FAÇON MARQUÉE, LUI CONSEILLER D'EN INFORMER UN PROFESSIONNEL DE LA SANTÉ.
- Prévenir le patient que le nadolol peut parfois provoquer des étourdissements. Lui conseiller de ne pas conduire et d'éviter les activités qui exigent sa vigilance jusqu'à ce qu'on ait la certitude que le médicament n'entraîne pas cet effet chez lui.
- Conseiller au patient de changer lentement de position pour réduire le risque d'hypotension orthostatique, particulièrement au début du traitement ou lors de la majoration de la dose.
- Prévenir le patient que le médicament peut le rendre plus sensible au froid.

- Conseiller au patient de consulter un professionnel de la santé avant de prendre des médicaments en vente libre, particulièrement des préparations contre le rhume, en même temps que le nadolol.
- Recommander au patient diabétique de mesurer sa glycémie, particulièrement lorsqu'il se sent fatigué, faible ou irritable ou lorsqu'il ressent un malaise. Le nadolol peut masquer certains signes d'hypoglycémie, mais non pas la transpiration et les étourdissements.
- Recommander au patient de signaler au médecin les symptômes suivants: ralentissement du pouls, difficultés respiratoires, respiration sifflante, mains et pieds froids, étourdissements, confusion, dépression, rash, fièvre, maux de gorge, saignements inhabituels ou ecchymoses.
- Recommander au patient qui doit suivre un autre traitement ou subir une intervention chirurgicale d'avertir le professionnel de la santé qu'il prend du nadolol.
- Conseiller au patient de porter sur lui en tout temps une pièce d'identité où sont inscrits son problème de santé et sa médication.

Hypertension: Inciter le patient à appliquer d'autres mesures de réduction de l'hypertension: perdre du poids, réduire sa consommation de sel, diminuer le stress, faire régulièrement de l'exercice, boire avec modération et cesser de fumer. Le nadolol stabilise la pression artérielle, mais ne guérit pas l'hypertension.
Angine: Prévenir le patient qu'il ne doit pas faire d'efforts excessifs même si ses douleurs de poitrine diminuent.

VÉRIFICATION DE L'EFFICACITÉ THÉRAPEUTIQUE

L'efficacité du traitement peut être démontrée par: la baisse de la pression artérielle ■ la diminution de la fréquence des crises d'angine ■ la tolérance accrue à l'effort. Les effets du médicament peuvent ne se manifester que 5 jours après le début du traitement.

NADROPARINE CALCIQUE,

voir Héparines de faible poids moléculaire/héparinoïdes

NAFARÉLINE

Synarel

CLASSIFICATION:

Analogue de l'hormone de libération de la gonadotrophine (GnRH)

Grossesse – catégorie X

INDICATIONS

Hormonothérapie de l'endométriose ■ Soulagement de la douleur ■ Réduction de la dimension et du nombre de plaques d'endométriose.

MÉCANISME D'ACTION

Analogue synthétique de l'hormone de libération de la gonadotrophine (GnRH). L'agent accroît initialement la production hypophysaire d'hormone lutéinisante (LH) et d'hormone folliculostimulante (FSH), ce qui stimule la stéroïdogenèse ovarienne. L'administration prolongée entraîne une diminution de la production de gonadotrophine. Les lésions dues à l'endométriose sont sensibles aux hormones ovariennes. ***Effets thérapeutiques:*** Diminution des lésions dues à l'endométriose et de la douleur qu'elle provoque.

PHARMACOCINÉTIQUE

Absorption: Bonne (IN).
Distribution: Inconnue.
Métabolisme et excrétion: Excrétion fécale (de 20 à 40 %) et rénale (3 % sous forme inchangée).
Demi-vie: 3 heures.

Profil temps-action (baisse de la stéroïdogenèse ovarienne)

	Début d'action	Pic	Durée
Voie intranasale	en l'espace de 4 semaines	3 - 4 semaines	3 - 6 mois†

† Soulagement des symptômes d'endométriose après l'arrêt du traitement.

CONTRE-INDICATIONS, PRÉCAUTIONS ET MISES EN GARDE

Contre-indications: Hypersensibilité à la gonadolibérine, à ses analogues ou à un des excipients du produit ■ **Obst., allaitement**: L'innocuité du médicament n'a pas été établie ■ Hémorragies vaginales anormales non diagnostiquées ■ Femmes < 18 ans.
Précautions et mises en garde: Rhinite.

RÉACTIONS INDÉSIRABLES ET EFFETS SECONDAIRES

SNC: instabilité émotionnelle, céphalées, dépression, insomnie.
ORLO: irritation nasale.
CV: œdème.
GU: sécheresse vaginale.
Tég.: acné, hirsutisme, séborrhée.
End.: arrêt des règles, stérilité, diminution du volume des seins.
Loc.: diminution de la densité osseuse, myalgie.
Divers: baisse de la libido, bouffées vasomotrices, réactions d'hypersensibilité, gain pondéral.

INTERACTIONS

Médicament-médicament: L'administration concomitante d'un **décongestionnant nasal topique** peut réduire l'absorption de la nafaréline (administrer le décongestionnant au moins 2 heures après la nafaréline).

VOIES D'ADMINISTRATION ET POSOLOGIE

- **Voie intranasale (adultes):** *Endométriose* – 1 vaporisation (200 µg) dans une narine, le matin et 1 vaporisation dans l'autre narine, le soir (400 µg par jour). Le traitement doit débuter entre le 2e et le 4e jour du cycle menstruel. Dans le cas des patientes chez lesquelles 400 µg n'entraînent pas d'aménorrhée après 2 mois, on peut augmenter la dose de façon à administrer 1 vaporisation dans chaque narine, matin et soir (800 µg par jour). La durée recommandée du traitement est de 6 mois.

PRÉSENTATION

Vaporisateur nasal: 2 mg/mL, en flacons de 8 mL (200 µg par vaporisation)Pr.

SOINS INFIRMIERS

N

ÉVALUATION DE LA SITUATION

Endométriose: Suivre à intervalles réguliers, pendant toute la durée du traitement, la douleur provoquée par l'endométriose.

DIAGNOSTICS INFIRMIERS POSSIBLES

- Douleur aiguë (Indications).
- Dysfonctionnement sexuel (Indications, Effets secondaires).
- Connaissances insuffisantes sur le traitement médicamenteux (Enseignement au patient et à ses proches).

INTERVENTIONS INFIRMIÈRES

Endométriose: Amorcer le traitement entre le 2e et le 4e jour du cycle menstruel et le poursuivre pendant 6 mois.

ENSEIGNEMENT AU PATIENT ET À SES PROCHES

- Montrer à la patiente comment utiliser le vaporisateur nasal. Lui expliquer qu'elle doit renverser légèrement la tête vers l'arrière et attendre 30 secondes entre les vaporisations.
- Recommander à la patiente de consulter un professionnel de la santé si une rhinite survient au cours du traitement. Si elle doit recourir à un décongestionnant topique, lui conseiller de ne pas l'utiliser dans les 2 heures qui suivent la prise de nafaréline. Dans la mesure du possible, il faut éviter d'éternuer pendant la prise de la dose de nafaréline et immédiatement après.

Endométriose:

- Expliquer à la patiente qu'il faut vaporiser l'agent 1 fois dans une narine, le matin, et 1 fois dans l'autre narine, le soir, pour prendre une dose totale de 400 µg par jour. Si la dose est majorée jusqu'à 800 µg par jour, elle doit vaporiser l'agent 1 fois dans chaque narine (2 vaporisations), matin et soir. Si la dose qui lui est prescrite est de 400 µg par jour, un flacon devrait lui suffire pour 30 jours.
- Recommander à la patiente d'utiliser pendant ce traitement une autre méthode de contraception que des contraceptifs oraux. La prévenir que l'aménorrhée est un effet normal du traitement. Lui recommander de prévenir un professionnel de la santé si le cycle menstruel reste régulier ou si elle n'a pas pu prendre plusieurs doses successives.
- Prévenir la patiente que le médicament peut entraîner des bouffées vasomotrices. Lui conseiller de consulter un professionnel de la santé si celles-ci deviennent gênantes.

VÉRIFICATION DE L'EFFICACITÉ THÉRAPEUTIQUE

L'efficacité du traitement peut être démontrée par: la diminution des lésions et des douleurs provoquées par l'endométriose.

ALERTE CLINIQUE

NALBUPHINE

Nubain

CLASSIFICATION:

Analgésique opioïde (agoniste-antagoniste)

Grossesse – catégorie C

INDICATIONS

Soulagement de la douleur modérée à grave ■ Autres indications: analgésique pendant le travail de l'accouchement ■ analgésique avant une intervention chirurgicale ■ supplément à l'analgésie lors d'une intervention chirurgicale.

MÉCANISME D'ACTION

Liaison aux récepteurs des opioïdes du SNC ■ Modification de la perception de la douleur et de la réaction aux stimuli douloureux avec dépression généralisée du SNC ■ Propriétés antagonistes partielles qui peuvent entraîner des symptômes de sevrage aux opioïdes en cas de pharmacodépendance physique. ***Effets thérapeutiques:*** Diminution de l'intensité de la douleur.

PHARMACOCINÉTIQUE

Absorption: Bonne (IM et SC).

Distribution: La nalbuphine semble traverser la barrière placentaire et passer dans le lait maternel.

Métabolisme et excrétion: Métabolisme majoritairement hépatique; élimination majoritairement fécale par excrétion biliaire. De petites quantités de nalbuphine sont excrétées à l'état inchangé dans l'urine.

Demi-vie: 5 heures.

Profil temps-action (effet analgésique)

	DÉBUT D'ACTION	PIC	DURÉE
IM	< 15 min	60 min	3 - 6 h
SC	< 15 min	inconnu	3 - 6 h
IV	2 - 3 min	30 min	3 - 6 h

CONTRE-INDICATIONS, PRÉCAUTIONS ET MISES EN GARDE

Contre-indications: Hypersensibilité à la nalbuphine ou à tout autre ingrédient de la préparation.

Précautions et mises en garde: Traumatisme crânien ■ Pression intracrânienne accrue ■ Maladies rénale, hépatique ou pulmonaire graves ■ Hypothyroïdie ■ Insuffisance surrénalienne ■ Alcoolisme ■ Personnes âgées ou patients débilités (réduire la dose) ■ Douleurs abdominales non diagnostiquées ■ Hyperplasie de la prostate ■ Traitement récent par des opioïdes agonistes ■ Dépendance physique aux opioïdes, chez les patients qui n'ont pas été désintoxiqués (risque de déclenchement d'un syndrome de sevrage) ■ **PÉD.**: Enfants < 12 ans (l'efficacité et l'innocuité de la nalbuphine n'ont pas été établies) ■ **OBST.**: Le médicament a déjà été utilisé pendant le travail de l'accouchement, mais il peut entraîner une dépression respiratoire chez le nouveau-né ■ **ALLAITEMENT**: L'innocuité du médicament n'a pas été établie.

RÉACTIONS INDÉSIRABLES ET EFFETS SECONDAIRES

SNC: étourdissements, céphalées, sédation, confusion, dysphorie, euphorie, sensation de flottement, hallucinations, rêves bizarres.

ORLO: vision trouble, diplopie, myosis (doses élevées).

Resp.: DÉPRESSION RESPIRATOIRE.

CV: hypertension, hypotension orthostatique, palpitations.

GI: sécheresse de la bouche (xérostomie), nausées, vomissements, constipation, iléus.

GU: mictions impérieuses.

Tég.: sensation de peau moite et froide, transpiration.

Divers: dépendance physique, dépendance psychologique, tolérance aux effets du médicament.

INTERACTIONS

Médicament-médicament: LA NALBUPHINE DOIT ÊTRE ADMINISTRÉE AVEC UNE EXTRÊME PRUDENCE AUX PATIENTS RECEVANT DES **IMAO** (RISQUE DE RÉACTIONS GRAVES ET IMPRÉVISIBLES; DIMINUER LA DOSE DE NALBUPHINE DE 25 %) ■ Dépression additive du SNC et du système respiratoire lors de l'usage concomitant d'**alcool**, d'**antihistaminiques,** de **phénothiazines**, de **barbituriques**, **d'antidépresseurs**, d'**hypnosédatifs** et d'autres **opioïdes** ■ Le médicament peut déclencher des symptômes de sevrage chez les patients qui présentent une dépendance physique aux **opioïdes agonistes** ■ Éviter l'usage concomitant d'autres **analgésiques de type opioïde agoniste** (risque de diminution de l'effet analgésique).

Médicament-produits naturels: Effets dépresseurs additifs sur le SNC lors de l'usage concomitant de **kava**, de **valériane**, de **scutellaire**, de **camomille** et de **houblon**.

N

VOIES D'ADMINISTRATION ET POSOLOGIE

- **IM, SC, IV (adultes)**: La dose habituelle est de 10 mg, toutes les 3 à 6 heures (une seule dose ne doit pas dépasser 20 mg, et la dose quotidienne totale, 160 mg).

PRÉSENTATION

Solution pour injection: 10 mg/mL, en ampoules de 1 mL[N]; 20 mg/mL, en ampoules de 1 mL[N].

SOINS INFIRMIERS

ÉVALUATION DE LA SITUATION

- Noter le type, le siège et l'intensité de la douleur, avant l'administration du médicament et 1 heure après l'administration par voie IM ou 30 minutes (pic) après l'administration par voie IV. Lors de l'adaptation des doses d'opioïdes, on devrait majorer les doses de 25 à 50 % jusqu'à ce qu'on note une réduction de 50 % de la douleur, selon l'évaluation qu'en fait le patient sur une échelle numérique ou visuelle ou jusqu'à ce qu'il signale un soulagement adéquat. On peut administrer sans danger une deuxième dose au moment du pic, si la dose précédente s'est avérée inefficace et si les effets secondaires sont minimes. Chez les patients ayant besoin de doses supérieures à 20 mg, on peut substituer à la nalbuphine un opioïde agoniste. La nalbuphine n'est pas recommandée en traitement prolongé ou en traitement de première intention des douleurs aiguës ou de celles dues au cancer.

- On devrait utiliser un tableau d'équivalences (voir l'annexe A) lorsqu'on change de voie d'administration ou de type d'opioïde.
- ÉVALUER L'ÉTAT DE CONSCIENCE ET LA FONCTION RESPIRATOIRE DU PATIENT, MESURER SA PRESSION ARTÉRIELLE ET SON POULS AVANT L'ADMINISTRATION DU MÉDICAMENT ET À INTERVALLES RÉGULIERS PENDANT TOUTE LA DURÉE DU TRAITEMENT. SI LA FRÉQUENCE RESPIRATOIRE EST INFÉRIEURE À 10 RESPIRATIONS À LA MINUTE, ÉVALUER LE NIVEAU DE SÉDATION. Une stimulation physique peut être suffisante pour prévenir une hypoventilation importante. Il peut s'avérer nécessaire de diminuer la dose de 25 à 50 %. La nalbuphine entraîne une dépression respiratoire, mais qui ne s'accentue pas de façon notable lors de l'administration de doses plus élevées.
- Déterminer les antécédents de prise d'analgésiques opioïdes. En raison de ses propriétés antagonistes, le médicament peut induire chez les personnes présentant une dépendance physique aux opioïdes les symptômes suivants de sevrage: vomissements, agitation, crampes abdominales, pression artérielle accrue et fièvre.
- Bien que le risque de dépendance à la nalbuphine soit plus faible que dans le cas d'autres opioïdes, un traitement prolongé par cet agent peut entraîner une dépendance physique et psychologique ainsi qu'une tolérance aux effets du médicament, ce qui ne doit cependant pas empêcher le patient de recevoir une quantité suffisante d'analgésique. La dépendance psychologique est rare chez la plupart des patients qui reçoivent la nalbuphine pour soulager la douleur. Si une tolérance aux effets du médicament se développe, il faudrait envisager l'administration d'un autre opioïde agoniste pour soulager efficacement la douleur.

Tests de laboratoire: Le médicament peut entraîner l'élévation des concentrations sériques d'amylase et de lipase.

TOXICITÉ ET SURDOSAGE: En cas de surdosage par la nalbuphine, la dépression respiratoire ou le coma peuvent être renversés par la naloxone (Narcan), qui en est l'antidote. Diluer le contenu d'une ampoule à 0,4 mg de naloxone dans 10 mL de solution de NaCl 0,9 % et administrer 0,5 mL (0,02 mg) par bolus IV direct, toutes les 2 minutes. Chez les enfants et les patients pesant < 40 kg, diluer 0,1 mg de naloxone dans 10 mL de solution de NaCl 0,9 % pour obtenir une concentration de 10 µg/mL et administrer 0,5 µg/kg, toutes les 2 minutes. Adapter la dose pour prévenir les symptômes de sevrage, les convulsions et les douleurs intenses.

DIAGNOSTICS INFIRMIERS POSSIBLES

- Douleur aiguë (Indications).
- Risque d'accident (Effets secondaires).
- Trouble de la perception sensorielle (visuelle, auditive) (Effets secondaires).

INTERVENTIONS INFIRMIÈRES

ALERTE CLINIQUE: DES SURDOSES ACCIDENTELLES D'ANALGÉSIQUES OPIOÏDES ONT CAUSÉ DES DÉCÈS. AVANT L'ADMINISTRATION, CLARIFIER TOUS LES POINTS AMBIGUS SUR LES ORDONNANCES ET FAIRE VÉRIFIER L'ORDONNANCE D'ORIGINE ET LE CALCUL DES DOSES PAR UN AUTRE PROFESSIONNEL DE LA SANTÉ.

- Pour augmenter l'effet analgésique de la nalbuphine, expliquer au patient la valeur thérapeutique de ce médicament avant de l'administrer.
- Les doses administrées selon un horaire fixe peuvent être plus efficaces que celles administrées au besoin. L'analgésie s'avère plus efficace si le médicament est administré avant que la douleur ne devienne intense.
- Les analgésiques non opioïdes, administrés simultanément, peuvent exercer des effets analgésiques additifs, ce qui permet de diminuer les doses d'opioïde.

IM: Administrer les injections IM profondément dans un muscle bien développé. Assurer la rotation des points d'injection.

IV directe: On peut administrer le médicament par voie IV sans le diluer ou le diluer avec du D5%E ou du NaCl 0,9 % pour injection pour obtenir un volume total de 10 mL.

Vitesse d'administration: Injecter lentement une dose de 10 mg pendant 3 à 5 minutes.

Associations compatibles dans la même seringue: atropine ▪ cimétidine ▪ diphenhydramine ▪ dropéridol ▪ glycopyrrolate ▪ hydroxyzine ▪ lidocaïne ▪ midazolam ▪ prochlorpérazine ▪ ranitidine ▪ scopolamine.

Associations incompatibles dans la même seringue: diazépam ▪ kétorolac ▪ pentobarbital.

Compatibilité (tubulure en Y): amifostine ▪ filgrastim ▪ fludarabine ▪ melphalan ▪ paclitaxel ▪ téniposide ▪ thiotépa ▪ vinorelbine.

Incompatibilité (tubulure en Y): céfépime ▪ méthotrexate ▪ pipéracilline/tazobactam ▪ sodium, bicarbonate de.

ENSEIGNEMENT AU PATIENT ET À SES PROCHES

- Expliquer au patient ce qu'on entend par administration au besoin et à quel moment il doit demander un analgésique.
- Prévenir le patient que la nalbuphine peut provoquer de la somnolence ou des étourdissements. Lui recommander de demander de l'aide lorsqu'il se déplace et lui conseiller de ne pas conduire et d'éviter les activités qui exigent sa vigilance jusqu'à ce qu'on ait la certitude que le médicament n'entraîne pas ces effets chez lui.
- Recommander au patient de changer lentement de position pour diminuer le risque d'hypotension orthostatique.
- Conseiller au patient de pratiquer une bonne hygiène buccale, de se rincer la bouche fréquemment avec de l'eau et de consommer de la gomme ou des bonbons sans sucre pour diminuer la sécheresse de la bouche.
- Recommander au patient de se tourner dans le lit, de tousser et de faire des exercices de respiration profonde toutes les 2 heures pour prévenir l'atélectasie.
- Mettre en garde le patient contre l'usage concomitant d'alcool ou d'autres dépresseurs du SNC.

VÉRIFICATION DE L'EFFICACITÉ THÉRAPEUTIQUE

L'efficacité du traitement peut être démontrée par: la diminution de l'intensité de la douleur sans altération importante de l'état de conscience ou de la fonction respiratoire. ✳

NALOXONE

Narcan

CLASSIFICATION:

Antidote (antagoniste des opioïdes)

Grossesse – catégorie B

INDICATIONS

Renversement de la dépression du SNC et de la dépression respiratoire provoquées par les opioïdes ■ Agent utilisé pour le diagnostic d'une intoxication aiguë due à un surdosage soupçonné par les opioïdes.

MÉCANISME D'ACTION

Inhibition compétitive des effets des opioïdes, y compris la dépression du SNC et la dépression respiratoire, sans entraîner d'effets agonistes (semblables aux effets des opioïdes). ***Effets thérapeutiques:*** Renversement des signes associés au surdosage par les opioïdes.

PHARMACOCINÉTIQUE

Absorption: Bonne (IM ou SC).

Distribution: Répartition rapide dans les tissus. La naloxone traverse la barrière placentaire.

Métabolisme et excrétion: Métabolisme hépatique.

Demi-vie: De 60 à 90 minutes (jusqu'à 3 heures chez les nouveau-nés).

Profil temps-action (renversement des effets des opioïdes)

	DÉBUT D'ACTION	PIC	DURÉE
IV	1 – 2 min	inconnu	45 min
IM, SC	2 – 5 min	inconnu	> 45 min

CONTRE-INDICATIONS, PRÉCAUTIONS ET MISES EN GARDE

Contre-indications: Hypersensibilité.

Précautions et mises en garde: Maladie cardiovasculaire ■ Dépendance physique aux opioïdes (l'agent risque de déclencher des symptômes de sevrage graves) ■ **OBST.:** Risque de symptômes de sevrage chez la mère et le fœtus, si la mère présente une dépendance aux opioïdes ■ **ALLAITEMENT:** L'innocuité du médicament n'a pas été établie ■ **PÉD.:** Nouveau-nés de mères présentant une dépendance aux opioïdes.

RÉACTIONS INDÉSIRABLES ET EFFETS SECONDAIRES

CV: hypertension, hypotension, fibrillation ventriculaire, tachycardie ventriculaire.
GI: nausées, vomissements.

INTERACTIONS

Médicament-médicament: La naloxone peut déclencher des symptômes de sevrage chez les patients présentant une dépendance physique aux **opioïdes** ■ Des doses plus élevées peuvent s'avérer nécessaires pour renverser les effets du **butorphanol**, de la **nalbuphine**, de la **pentazocine** ou du **propoxyphène** ■ La naloxone peut contrecarrer les effets des **analgésiques opioïdes** administrés à la suite d'une intervention chirurgicale.

VOIES D'ADMINISTRATION ET POSOLOGIE

Dépression respiratoire postopératoire induite par un opioïde

- **IV (adultes):** De 0,1 à 0,2 mg, toutes les 2 ou 3 minutes, jusqu'à l'obtention de la réponse souhaitée. Il peut être nécessaire de répéter l'administration de

N

ces doses à des intervalles de 1 à 2 heures selon la quantité, le type d'opioïde et le laps de temps écoulé depuis la dernière administration de l'opioïde.

- **IV (enfants)**: De 0,005 mg à 0,01 mg; on peut répéter l'administration toutes les 2 ou 3 minutes, jusqu'à l'obtention de la réponse souhaitée. Il peut être nécessaire de répéter l'administration de ces doses à des intervalles de 1 à 2 heures selon la quantité, le type d'opioïde et le laps de temps écoulé depuis la dernière administration de l'opioïde.
- **IM, IV, SC (nouveau-nés)**: 0,01 mg/kg; on peut répéter l'administration toutes les 2 ou 3 minutes, jusqu'à l'obtention de la réponse souhaitée. Il peut être nécessaire de répéter l'administration de ces doses à des intervalles de 1 à 2 heures selon la quantité, le type d'opioïde et le laps de temps écoulé depuis la dernière administration de l'opioïde.

Surdosage connu ou soupçonné d'un opioïde

- **IV (adultes)**: De 0,4 à 2 mg, on peut répéter l'administration toutes les 2 ou 3 minutes, jusqu'à l'obtention de la réponse souhaitée. *Perfusion continue* – administrer au débit qui peut améliorer la fonction respiratoire sans renverser l'analgésie ou provoquer un effet de sevrage (environ 0,4 mg/h). Si la voie IV n'est pas accessible, il faudrait utiliser la voie IM ou SC. Le diagnostic d'une toxicité induite ou partiellement induite par un opioïde doit être remis en question si aucune réaction n'a été observée après l'administration de 10 mg de naloxone.
- **IV (enfants)**: *Dose d'attaque:* 0,01 mg/kg. Si la première dose n'a pas produit le niveau désiré d'amélioration clinique, on peut administrer une nouvelle dose de 0,1 mg/kg. On peut aussi administrer ces doses par voie IM ou SC.

N

PRÉSENTATION
(version générique disponible)

Solution pour injection: 0,4 mg/mL[Pr], ampoules de 1 mL et fioles de 10 mL; 1 mg/mL[Pr], fioles de 2 mL.

SOINS INFIRMIERS

ÉVALUATION DE LA SITUATION

- Noter la fréquence, le rythme et la profondeur des respirations. Suivre de près l'ÉCG et l'état de conscience, mesurer le pouls et la pression artérielle à intervalles fréquents, pendant les 3 ou 4 heures qui suivent le pic prévu des concentrations sanguines. Après un surdosage modéré par un opioïde dont la demi-vie est courte, une stimulation physique peut s'avérer suffisante pour prévenir une hypoventilation importante. LES EFFETS DE PLUSIEURS OPIOÏDES PEUVENT PERSISTER PLUS LONGTEMPS QUE CEUX DE LA NALOXONE. DANS CE CAS, IL PEUT S'AVÉRER NÉCESSAIRE DE RÉPÉTER L'ADMINISTRATION DE L'AGENT.
- Les patients qui ont reçu des opioïdes pendant plus de 1 semaine sont extrêmement sensibles aux effets de la naloxone. Il faut diluer le médicament et l'administrer avec prudence.
- Noter l'intensité de la douleur après l'administration de la naloxone, lorsque ce médicament est destiné au traitement de la dépression respiratoire postopératoire. La naloxone diminue la dépression respiratoire, mais elle renverse aussi l'analgésie.
- Surveiller les signes et les symptômes suivants d'une réaction de sevrage aux opioïdes: vomissements, agitation, crampes abdominales, élévation de la pression artérielle et fièvre. Les symptômes peuvent se manifester en quelques minutes ou dans les 2 heures qui suivent l'administration. La gravité des symptômes dépend de la dose de naloxone, de l'opioïde ayant entraîné le surdosage et de l'importance de la dépendance physique.
- L'absence d'une amélioration notable indique que les symptômes sont attribuables à l'évolution de la maladie ou à un autre dépresseur du SNC non opioïde ne réagissant pas à la naloxone.

TOXICITÉ ET SURDOSAGE: La naloxone est un antagoniste pur qui n'est pas doté de propriétés agonistes et qui entraîne une toxicité minimale.

DIAGNOSTICS INFIRMIERS POSSIBLES

- Mode de respiration inefficace (Indications).
- Stratégies d'adaptation inefficaces (Indications).
- Douleur aiguë (Interactions).

INTERVENTIONS INFIRMIÈRES

- Des doses plus élevées de naloxone peuvent s'avérer nécessaires pour contrecarrer les effets du butorphanol, de la nalbuphine, de la pentazocine et du propoxyphène.
- Garder à portée de la main le matériel de réanimation, de l'oxygène, des vasopresseurs et l'appareillage destiné à la ventilation assistée afin de pouvoir mener à bien le traitement à la naloxone, selon les besoins.

IV directe:

- En cas de surdosage soupçonné par les opioïdes, administrer la naloxone non diluée.
- Chez les patients présentant une dépression respiratoire induite par un opioïde, diluer 0,4 mg de

naloxone dans 10 mL d'eau stérile ou de solution de NaCl 0,9 % pour injection. Consulter les directives de chaque fabricant avant d'effectuer la dilution.

- Chez les enfants ou les personnes pesant < 40 kg, diluer 0,1 mg de naloxone dans 10 mL d'eau stérile ou de solution de NaCl 0,9 % pour injection pour obtenir une concentration de 10 µg/mL.

Vitesse d'administration:

- En cas de surdosage soupçonné par les opioïdes, administrer la naloxone à un débit de 0,1 à 0,4 mg, pendant 15 secondes.
- Chez les patients qui ont développé une *dépression respiratoire induite par un opioïde*, administrer la solution diluée de 0,4 mg/10 mL à un débit de 0,5 mL (0,02 mg) par IV directe, toutes les 2 minutes. Adapter la dose pour prévenir les symptômes de sevrage et les douleurs intenses. Des doses excessives administrées après une intervention chirurgicale peuvent entraîner les symptômes suivants: agitation, douleurs, hypotension, hypertension, œdème pulmonaire, tachycardie ou fibrillation ventriculaires et convulsions.
- Chez les enfants ou les personnes < 40 kg, administrer la solution à 10 µg/mL à un débit de 0,5 µg/kg, toutes les 1 ou 2 minutes. Adapter la dose afin de prévenir les symptômes de sevrage, les convulsions et les douleurs intenses.

Perfusion continue: Diluer le médicament dans une solution de D5%E ou de NaCl 0,9 % pour injection. La dilution de 2 mg de naloxone dans 500 mL donne une concentration de 4 µg/mL. La solution est stable pendant 24 heures. Jeter toute portion inutilisée. Consulter les directives de chaque fabricant avant d'effectuer la dilution.

- Adapter la dose selon la réponse du patient au traitement. Des doses additionnelles administrées par voie SC ou IM ou par perfusion continue peuvent assurer des effets de plus longue durée.
- Adapter les doses avec prudence chez les patients qui ont subi une intervention chirurgicale afin de ne pas contrecarrer l'analgésie postopératoire.

Incompatibilité en addition au soluté: Préparations renfermant du bisulfite ou des sulfites et solutions dont le pH est alcalin.

ENSEIGNEMENT AU PATIENT ET À SES PROCHES

- Lorsque la naloxone commence à agir, expliquer au patient le but et les effets de ce traitement.

VÉRIFICATION DE L'EFFICACITÉ THÉRAPEUTIQUE

L'efficacité du traitement peut être démontrée par: une respiration appropriée ■ un regain de la vigilance sans que des douleurs marquées ni des symptômes de sevrage se manifestent.

NANDROLONE, DÉCANOATE DE

Deca-Durabolin

CLASSIFICATION:

Hormone androgène et stéroïde anabolisant

Grossesse – catégorie X

INDICATIONS

Adjuvant thérapeutique de l'ostéoporose sénile et postménopausique ■ Nanisme pituitaire ■ Traitement des états dans lesquels il est souhaitable d'amorcer une puissante action régénératrice des tissus ou de ménager les protéines.

MÉCANISME D'ACTION

Action anabolique sur les protéines et action inhibitrice du catabolisme sur les tissus ■ Stimulation de la production d'érythropoïétine avec possibilité d'un effet stimulant direct sur la moelle osseuse. ***Effets thérapeutiques:*** Gain de poids ■ Augmentation du nombre de globules rouges et des concentrations d'hémoglobine.

PHARMACOCINÉTIQUE

Absorption: Bonne (IM).

Distribution: Inconnue.

Métabolisme et excrétion: Inconnus.

Demi-vie: Inconnue.

Profil temps-action

	DÉBUT D'ACTION	PIC	DURÉE
IM	inconnu	3 – 6 jours	inconnue

CONTRE-INDICATIONS, PRÉCAUTIONS ET MISES EN GARDE

Contre-indications: Hypersensibilité ■ Grossesse ■ Hypersensibilité à l'huile de sésame (ne pas administrer dans ce cas les produits qui contiennent cet additif) ■ Cancer du sein chez l'homme ■ Insuffisance hépatique grave ou affection hépatique accompagnée de trouble excrétoire de la bilirubine ■ Néphrose ou phase néphrotique de la néphrite ■ Cancer de la prostate.

Précautions et mises en garde: Insuffisance cardiaque ou hépatique ■ Cancer avancé du sein accompagné d'hypercalcémie ■ Coronaropathie ou antécédents d'infarctus du myocarde ■ Diabète ■ Hyperplasie bénigne de la prostate ■ Enfants ■ Personnes âgées ■ Allaitement.

RÉACTIONS INDÉSIRABLES ET EFFETS SECONDAIRES

SNC: insomnie.

CV: œdème.

GI: plénitude gastrique, diarrhée, dysfonctionnement hépatique.

GU: modification de la libido, impuissance, hyperplasie de la prostate.

Tég.: acné.

End.: <u>virilisation chez les femmes et les garçons prépubères.</u>

HÉ: hypercalcémie.

Loc.: crampes musculaires.

Divers: frissons.

INTERACTIONS

N

Médicament-médicament: Risque accru d'hépatotoxicité lors de l'administration d'autres **agents hépatotoxiques** ■ Risque accru d'hémorragie lors de l'utilisation concomitante de **warfarine**, d'**anti-inflammatoires non stéroïdiens** et de **salicylates**.

VOIES D'ADMINISTRATION ET POSOLOGIE

- **IM (adultes et enfants ≥ 14 ans):** De 50 à 100 mg, toutes les 3 à 4 semaines.
- **IM (enfants de 2 à 13 ans):** De 25 à 50 mg, toutes les 3 ou 4 semaines.

PRÉSENTATION

Solution pour injection: 100 mg/mL, en fioles de 2 mL[C].

SOINS INFIRMIERS

ÉVALUATION DE LA SITUATION

- Observer la réponse du patient à la recherche des symptômes suivants d'anémie: fatigue, dyspnée, pâleur.

Tests de laboratoire: Déterminer la numération globulaire à intervalles réguliers, pendant toute la durée du traitement.

DIAGNOSTICS INFIRMIERS POSSIBLES

- Intolérance à l'activité (Indications).
- Connaissances insuffisantes sur le traitement médicamenteux (Enseignement au patient et à ses proches).

INTERVENTIONS INFIRMIÈRES

Administrer l'injection en profondeur dans le muscle fessier.

ENSEIGNEMENT AU PATIENT ET À SES PROCHES

- Expliquer au patient le but du traitement.
- Recommander au patient de prévenir un professionnel de la santé en cas d'œdème ou de signes excessifs de virilisation.
- Insister sur l'importance des examens de suivi réguliers permettant de suivre l'évolution de l'état du patient et de déterminer s'il est utile de poursuivre le traitement.

VÉRIFICATION DE L'EFFICACITÉ THÉRAPEUTIQUE

L'efficacité du traitement peut être démontrée par: l'amélioration des états reliés à l'ostéoporose, au nanisme pituitaire ou aux états dans lesquels on doit amorcer une action régénératrice des tissus ou ménager les protéines. ✳

NAPROXÈNE

Apo-Naproxen, Apo-Naprox EC, Apo-Naproxen SR, Gen-Naproxen, Gen-Naproxen EC, Naprosyn, Naprosyn-E, Naprosyn-SR, Naproxen, Naxen, Novo-Naprox, Novo-Naprox EC, Novo-Naprox SR, Nu-Naprox, PMS-Naproxen, Ratio-Naproxen, Riva-Naproxen, Sab-Naproxen

NAPROXÈNE SODIQUE

Anaprox, Anaprox DS, Apo-Napro-Na, Apo-Napro-Na DS, Naprelan, Naproxen-NA, Naproxen-NA DF, Novo-Naprox Sodium, Novo-Naprox Sodium DS

CLASSIFICATION:

Analgésique non opioïde, anti-inflammatoire non stéroïdien

Grossesse – catégories D (1er et 3e trimestres) et B (2e trimestre)

INDICATIONS

Traitement de la douleur légère à modérée ■ Dysménorrhée ■ Douleur associée aux crampes du postpartum

■ Maladies inflammatoires incluant: la polyarthrite rhumatoïde ■ l'arthrose ■ la spondylarthrite ankylosante ■ la polyarthrite juvénile.

MÉCANISME D'ACTION

Inhibition de la synthèse des prostaglandines. ***Effets thérapeutiques:*** Soulagement de la douleur ■ Suppression de l'inflammation.

PHARMACOCINÉTIQUE

Absorption: Complète (PO). Le sel sodique (Anaprox) est absorbé plus rapidement.

Distribution: L'agent traverse la barrière placentaire et passe dans le lait maternel en petites quantités.

Liaison aux protéines: > 99 %.

Métabolisme et excrétion: Métabolisme majoritairement hépatique.

Demi-vie: *Enfants < 8 ans:* de 8 à 17 heures; *enfants de 8 à 14 ans:* de 8 à 10 heures; *adultes:* de 10 à 20 heures.

Profil temps-action (effets thérapeutiques)

	DÉBUT D'ACTION	PIC	DURÉE
PO (analgésique)	1 h	inconnu	8 - 12 h
PO (anti-inflammatoire)	14 jours	2 - 4 semaines	inconnue

CONTRE-INDICATIONS, PRÉCAUTIONS ET MISES EN GARDE

Contre-indications: Hypersensibilité ■ Syndrome complet ou partiel de polypes nasaux ou patients chez lesquels l'asthme, l'anaphylaxie, la rhinite, l'urticaire ou toute autre manifestation allergique sont déclenchés par l'aspirine ou d'autres AINS ■ Hémorragie digestive évolutive ■ Ulcère ■ Antécédents d'ulcère récidivant ■ Maladies inflammatoires de l'appareil digestif en phase évolutive ■ Insuffisance hépatique ou rénale grave ■ Maladie hépatique évolutive ■ Usage concomitant d'autres AINS ■ **PÉD.**: Enfants < 12 ans (suppositoires) et/ou enfants < 2 ans. Il y a risque de pseudoporphyrie (incidence de 12 % chez les enfants atteints de polyarthrite juvénile; si cet effet survient, il faut cesser le traitement).

Précautions et mises en garde: Maladie cardiovasculaire ou facteurs de risque de maladie cardiovasculaire (risque accru de complications thrombotiques, d'infarctus du myocarde, d'accident vasculaire cérébral, surtout lors d'un usage prolongé) ■ Antécédents d'ulcère ■ Abus ou consommation régulière d'alcool ■ **OBST., ALLAITEMENT**: L'innocuité du médicament n'a pas été établie; éviter l'usage durant la deuxième moitié de la grossesse ■ **GÉR.**: Ces patients peuvent être davantage prédisposés aux réactions indésirables.

RÉACTIONS INDÉSIRABLES ET EFFETS SECONDAIRES

SNC: étourdissements, somnolence, céphalées.

ORLO: acouphènes.

Resp.: dyspnée.

CV: œdème, palpitations, tachycardie.

GI: HÉPATITE MÉDICAMENTEUSE, HÉMORRAGIE DIGESTIVE, constipation, dyspepsie, nausées, anorexie, diarrhée, malaises, flatulence, vomissements.

GU: cystite, hématurie, insuffisance rénale.

Tég.: photosensibilité, rash, transpiration, pseudoporphyrie (incidence de 12 % chez les enfants atteints de polyarthrite juvénile).

Hémat.: dyscrasie sanguine, allongement du temps de saignement.

Divers: réactions allergiques incluant l'ANAPHYLAXIE et le SYNDROME DE STEVENS-JOHNSON.

INTERACTIONS

Médicament-médicament: L'**aspirine** entraîne la baisse des concentrations sanguines de naproxène et peut en réduire l'efficacité lors d'une administration concomitante ■ Risque accru de saignements lors de l'administration concomitante d'**anticoagulants**, d'**agents thrombolytiques**, d'**eptifibatide**, de **tirofiban**, de **céfamandole**, de **céfotétane**, de **céfopérazone**, d'**acide valproïque**, de **clopidogrel**, de **ticlopidine** et de **plicamycine** ■ Effets secondaires gastro-intestinaux additifs lors de l'usage concomitant d'**aspirine**, de **corticostéroïdes**, de **suppléments de potassium** et d'autres **anti-inflammatoires non stéroïdiens** ■ Le **probénécide** élève les concentrations sanguines de naproxène et peut en accroître la toxicité ■ Risque accru de photosensibilité lors de l'administration concomitante d'autres **agents photosensibilisants** ■ Le médicament accroît le risque de toxicité par le **méthotrexate**, les **antinéoplasiques** ou la **radiothérapie** ■ Le naproxène peut entraîner l'élévation des concentrations sériques de **lithium** et augmenter le risque de toxicité associé à cet agent lors d'une administration concomitante ■ L'administration concomitante d'**acétaminophène** pendant une période prolongée ou de **cyclosporine** peut accroître le risque de réactions rénales indésirables ■ Le naproxène peut diminuer l'efficacité des **inhibiteurs de l'enzyme de conversion de l'angiotensine**, des **antagonistes des récepteurs de l'angiotensine II** et du **furosémide** ■ L'agent peut intensifier les effets hypoglycémiants de l'**insuline** ou des **hypoglycémiants oraux**.

VOIES D'ADMINISTRATION ET POSOLOGIE

Remarque: 275 mg de naproxène sodique équivalent à 250 mg de naproxène.

Arthrose/polyarthrite rhumatoïde/spondylarthrite ankylosante

- **PO (adultes)**: *Naproxène* – de 500 à 1 500 mg par jour, en doses fractionnées (jusqu'à 1,5 g par jour). *Naproxène à libération prolongée* – 750 mg, 1 fois par jour.
- **IR (adultes)**: Un suppositoire de 500 mg peut remplacer l'une des doses orales chez l'adulte qui reçoit 1 000 mg/jour.

Analgésie/lésions musculosquelettiques

- **PO (adultes)**: *Naproxène* – de 750 mg à 1 000 mg par jour, en 2 ou 3 doses fractionnées. *Naproxène sodique* – dose initiale de 550 mg, suivie de 275 mg, toutes les 6 à 8 heures, au besoin (jusqu'à 1 375 g par jour), ou 550 mg, 2 fois par jour.

Dysménorrhée

- **PO (adultes)**: *Naproxène* – dose initiale de 500 mg, suivie de 250 mg, toutes les 6 à 8 heures, au besoin (jusqu'à 1,25 g par jour), ou 500 mg, 2 fois par jour. *Naproxène sodique* – dose initiale de 550 mg, suivie de 275 mg, toutes les 6 à 8 heures, au besoin (jusqu'à 1 375 g par jour), ou 550 mg, 2 fois par jour.

Polyarthrite juvénile

- **PO (enfants)**: 5 mg/kg, 2 fois par jour, à intervalles de 12 heures, sous forme de suspension.

N

PRÉSENTATION

- **Naproxène (version générique disponible)** **Comprimés**: 125 mg[Pr], 250 mg[Pr], 375 mg[Pr], 500 mg[Pr] ■ **Comprimés entérosolubles**: 250 mg[Pr], 375 mg[Pr], 500 mg[Pr] ■ **Comprimés à libération prolongée**: 750 mg[Pr] ■ **Suspension orale**: 125 mg/5 mL[Pr] ■ **Suppositoires**: 500 mg[Pr].
- **Naproxène sodique (version générique disponible)** **Comprimés**: 275 mg[Pr], 550 mg[Pr].

SOINS INFIRMIERS

ÉVALUATION DE LA SITUATION

- LES PATIENTS SOUFFRANT D'ASTHME, D'ALLERGIE INDUITE PAR L'ASPIRINE ET DE POLYPES NASAUX SONT DAVANTAGE PRÉDISPOSÉS À DES RÉACTIONS D'HYPERSENSIBILITÉ. SUIVRE DE PRÈS LA RHINITE, L'ASTHME ET L'URTICAIRE.

Douleur: Noter le type de douleur, son siège et son intensité, avant l'administration du médicament et de 1 à 2 heures plus tard.

Arthrite: Suivre de près la douleur et déterminer la mobilité des articulations avant l'administration et de 1 à 2 heures plus tard.

Tests de laboratoire:

- Examiner à intervalles réguliers, tout au long du traitement prolongé, les concentrations sériques d'urée et de créatinine ainsi que la numération globulaire et les résultats des tests de la fonction hépatique.
- Le naproxène peut entraîner l'élévation des concentrations sériques de potassium, d'urée, de créatinine, de phosphatase alcaline, de LDH, d'AST et d'ALT. Par contre, il peut réduire la glycémie, les concentrations d'hémoglobine et l'hématocrite, ainsi que le nombre de leucocytes et de plaquettes et la clairance de la créatinine.
- Le naproxène peut allonger le temps de saignement jusqu'à 4 jours après l'arrêt du traitement.
- Le naproxène peut modifier les résultats des tests urinaires de dépistage de l'acide 5-hydroxy-indoleacétique (5-HIAA) et des stéroïdes.

DIAGNOSTICS INFIRMIERS POSSIBLES

- Douleur aiguë (Indications).
- Mobilité physique réduite (Indications).
- Connaissances insuffisantes sur le traitement médicamenteux (Enseignement au patient et à ses proches).

INTERVENTIONS INFIRMIÈRES

- L'administration de doses plus élevées que celles recommandées n'accroît pas l'efficacité du médicament, mais peut augmenter le risque d'effets secondaires.
- L'administration concomitante d'analgésiques opioïdes peut intensifier les effets analgésiques du naproxène, ce qui permet parfois de réduire la dose d'opioïde.
- L'analgésique est plus efficace s'il est administré avant que la douleur ne devienne intense.

PO: Pour obtenir un effet initial rapide, administrer 30 minutes avant les repas ou 2 heures après. On peut administrer le naproxène avec des aliments, du lait ou des antiacides pour réduire l'irritation gastrique. Les aliments ralentissent, mais ne réduisent pas l'absorption de ce médicament. Ne pas mélanger la suspension avec un antiacide ou un autre liquide avant de l'administrer.

Dysménorrhée: Administrer le naproxène dès que possible après le début des règles. L'efficacité du traitement prophylactique n'a pas été prouvée.

ENSEIGNEMENT AU PATIENT ET À SES PROCHES

- Conseiller au patient de prendre le naproxène avec un grand verre d'eau et de ne pas se coucher pendant les 15 à 30 minutes qui suivent.

- Conseiller au patient de respecter rigoureusement la posologie recommandée. S'il n'a pu prendre le médicament au moment habituel, il doit le prendre dès que possible, à moins que ce ne soit presque l'heure prévue pour la dose suivante. L'avertir qu'il ne doit jamais remplacer une dose manquée par une double dose.
- Prévenir le patient que le naproxène peut provoquer de la somnolence ou des étourdissements. Lui conseiller de ne pas conduire et d'éviter les activités qui exigent sa vigilance jusqu'à ce qu'on ait la certitude que le médicament n'entraîne pas ces effets chez lui.
- CONSEILLER AU PATIENT D'ÉVITER DE PRENDRE DE L'ALCOOL, DE L'ASPIRINE, DE L'ACÉTAMINOPHÈNE OU TOUT AUTRE MÉDICAMENT EN VENTE LIBRE EN MÊME TEMPS QUE LE NAPROXÈNE, SANS CONSULTER AU PRÉALABLE UN PROFESSIONNEL DE LA SANTÉ. LA CONSOMMATION DE 3 VERRES D'ALCOOL OU PLUS PAR JOUR PENDANT LE TRAITEMENT AU NAPROXÈNE PEUT ACCROÎTRE LE RISQUE D'HÉMORRAGIE DIGESTIVE.
- Recommander au patient qui doit suivre un autre traitement ou subir une intervention chirurgicale de prévenir le professionnel de la santé qu'il suit un traitement avec ce médicament.
- Inciter le patient à utiliser un écran solaire et à porter des vêtements protecteurs pour prévenir les réactions de photosensibilité.
- Recommander au patient de consulter un professionnel de la santé en cas de rash, de démangeaisons, de troubles visuels, d'acouphènes, de gain de poids, d'œdème, de selles noires, de céphalées persistantes ou de syndrome pseudogrippal (frissons, fièvre, douleurs musculaires, douleur).

VÉRIFICATION DE L'EFFICACITÉ THÉRAPEUTIQUE

L'efficacité du traitement peut être démontrée par: le soulagement de la douleur ■ l'amélioration de la mobilité des articulations. Le soulagement partiel des douleurs arthritiques survient habituellement dans les 2 semaines qui suivent le début du traitement, mais le plein effet du médicament peut ne se manifester qu'après 2 à 4 semaines. Les patients qui ne répondent pas à un anti-inflammatoire non stéroïdien peuvent répondre à un autre. ✳

NARATRIPTAN,

voir Agonistes de la sérotonine 5-HT$_1$

NATÉGLINIDE

Starlix

CLASSIFICATION:

Antidiabétique (méglitinide)

Grossesse – catégorie C

INDICATIONS

En monothérapie, en complément aux mesures diététiques et à l'exercice, pour abaisser la glycémie chez les patients atteints de diabète de type 2 ■ En association avec la metformine, lorsque la diétothérapie et l'exercice en concomitance avec le natéglinide ou la metformine, employés seuls, ne permettent pas d'équilibrer adéquatement la glycémie.

MÉCANISME D'ACTION

Stimulation de la libération d'insuline depuis les cellules bêta du pancréas par la fermeture des canaux potassiques, ce qui entraîne l'ouverture des canaux calciques. Il s'ensuit une libération d'insuline. L'action du médicament dépend du bon fonctionnement des cellules des îlots pancréatiques. ***Effets thérapeutiques:*** Abaissement de la glycémie.

PHARMACOCINÉTIQUE

Absorption: 73 % (PO).
Distribution: Inconnue.
Liaison aux protéines: 98 %.
Métabolisme et excrétion: Métabolisme hépatique, principalement par le CYP2C9 (70 %) et par le CYP3A4 (30 %). Excrétion rénale (83 %; 16 % du médicament est excrété sous forme inchangée) et fécale (10 %).
Demi-vie: 1,5 heure.

Profil temps-action (effet sur la glycémie)

	DÉBUT D'ACTION	PIC	DURÉE
PO	15 min	1 – 2 h	4 h

CONTRE-INDICATIONS, PRÉCAUTIONS ET MISES EN GARDE

Contre-indications: Hypersensibilité ■ Acidocétose diabétique ■ Diabète de type 1.

Précautions et mises en garde: Insuffisance hépatique modérée ou grave (l'innocuité et l'efficacité du médicament n'ont pas été établies) ■ **OBST., ALLAITEMENT:** L'innocuité du médicament n'a pas été établie chez la femme enceinte ou qui allaite (il est recommandé d'administrer de l'insuline pour équilibrer le diabète pendant la grossesse et l'allaitement) ■ **PÉD.:** L'innocuité et

N

l'efficacité du médicament n'ont pas été établies chez les enfants.

RÉACTIONS INDÉSIRABLES ET EFFETS SECONDAIRES

SNC: étourdissements, fatigue.
End.: HYPOGLYCÉMIE (tremblements, sudation, étourdissements, asthénie).
GU: polyurie.
Tég.: éruptions cutanées, prurit, urticaire.
Divers: soif.

INTERACTIONS

Médicament-médicament: L'administration concomitante de **sulfinpyrazone** ou de tout autre **inhibiteur de l'isoenzyme CYP2C9** peut ralentir le métabolisme du natéglinide et augmenter le risque d'hypoglycémie ■ Les effets des antidiabétiques oraux peuvent être accrus par les **AINS**, les **salicylates** (tels que l'**aspirine**), les **IMAO** et les **bêtabloquants non sélectifs** ■ Les effets des antidiabétiques oraux peuvent être diminués par les **diurétiques thiazidiques**, les **corticostéroïdes**, les **préparations thyroïdiennes** et les **agents sympathomimétiques**.
Médicament-produits naturels: La **glucosamine** peut entraver l'équilibrage de la glycémie.

N

VOIES D'ADMINISTRATION ET POSOLOGIE

- **PO (adultes)**: *Posologie de départ et d'entretien* – 120 mg, 3 fois par jour avant les repas (généralement le déjeuner, le dîner et le souper). Si la réponse n'est pas satisfaisante, on peut porter la dose à 180 mg, 3 fois par jour avant les repas, ou ajouter de la metformine au traitement. *Posologie initiale* – chez les patients dont l'hémoglobine glyquée est près de l'objectif thérapeutique (HbA_{1c} < 0,075), 60 mg, 3 fois par jour avant les repas.

PRÉSENTATION

Comprimés: 60 mg^{Pr}, 120 mg^{Pr}, 180 mg^{Pr}.

SOINS INFIRMIERS

ÉVALUATION DE LA SITUATION

- OBSERVER LE PATIENT À LA RECHERCHE DES SIGNES ET DES SYMPTÔMES SUIVANTS D'HYPOGLYCÉMIE: TRANSPIRATION, FAIM, NAUSÉES, FAIBLESSE, ÉTOURDISSEMENTS, CÉPHALÉES, TREMBLEMENTS, PALPITATIONS, ANXIÉTÉ. L'hypoglycémie peut être difficile à déceler chez les personnes âgées et chez les patients recevant des bêtabloquants. L'hypoglycémie survient plus fréquemment lorsque l'apport énergétique est insuffisant, après une activité physique intense et prolongée ou lorsque le patient consomme de l'alcool ou prend plusieurs agents hypoglycémiants.

Tests de laboratoire: Pour évaluer l'efficacité du médicament, suivre, à intervalles réguliers pendant toute la durée du traitement, la glycémie à jeun et 1 à 2 heures après le repas ainsi que la concentration d'hémoglobine glyquée.

TOXICITÉ ET SURDOSAGE: Le surdosage se manifeste par des symptômes d'hypoglycémie. On peut traiter l'hypoglycémie légère en administrant du glucose par voie orale. L'hypoglycémie grave est une urgence, car elle peut mettre en danger la vie du patient. Le traitement consiste à administrer du glucose par voie IV, du glucagon ou de l'adrénaline.

DIAGNOSTICS INFIRMIERS POSSIBLES

- Alimentation excessive (Indications).
- Connaissances insuffisantes sur le traitement médicamenteux (Enseignement au patient et à ses proches).
- Non-observance du traitement médicamenteux (Enseignement au patient et à ses proches).

INTERVENTIONS INFIRMIÈRES

- Il peut s'avérer nécessaire d'administrer de l'insuline aux patients dont la glycémie a été stabilisée, mais qui font de la fièvre, qui sont exposés au stress, à un traumatisme ou à une infection ou qui doivent subir une intervention chirurgicale. Interrompre l'administration du natéglinide et attendre la fin de l'épisode aigu avant de reprendre le traitement.
- On devrait interrompre passagèrement l'administration du natéglinide chez les patients qui doivent subir une intervention chirurgicale.
- Le natéglinide n'est pas administré en doses fixes. La dose dépend des mesures de la glycémie prises à intervalles réguliers; la réponse au traitement prolongé dépend des concentrations d'hémoglobine glyquée. En l'absence d'une réponse satisfaisante, on peut ajouter au traitement de la metformine. Si le traitement d'association échoue également, il peut s'avérer nécessaire de cesser l'administration de l'hypoglycémiant oral et de le remplacer par l'insuline.
- Lorsque le natéglinide remplace un autre hypoglycémiant oral, il peut être administré le jour suivant l'arrêt de l'ancien traitement. Suivre de près la glycémie. L'interruption du traitement par un hypoglycémiant oral à action prolongée peut dicter une surveillance étroite de la glycémie pendant au moins 1 semaine.
- Administrer le natéglinide immédiatement avant le repas (soit 1 minute avant), mais son ingestion peut

se faire jusqu'à 30 minutes avant le repas. Les patients qui sautent un repas devraient aussi sauter une dose. On doit avaler les comprimés entiers, avec un verre d'eau.

ENSEIGNEMENT AU PATIENT ET À SES PROCHES

- Conseiller au patient de prendre le médicament avant chaque repas, en suivant rigoureusement les recommandations du professionnel de la santé.
- Si le patient oublie de prendre un comprimé, lui dire de sauter simplement la dose en question et de prendre le médicament avant le repas suivant, sans doubler la dose pour compenser.
- Expliquer au patient que le natéglinide permet de normaliser la glycémie, mais ne peut guérir le diabète. Le traitement à l'aide de cet agent est habituellement de longue durée.
- Inciter le patient à suivre la diétothérapie, la pharmacothérapie et le programme d'exercices prescrits afin de prévenir les épisodes d'hypoglycémie ou d'hyperglycémie.
- Expliquer au patient les signes d'hypoglycémie et d'hyperglycémie. Si des symptômes d'hypoglycémie se manifestent, lui recommander de prendre un verre de jus d'orange ou bien 2 ou 3 cuillerées à thé de sucre, de miel ou de sirop de maïs dans un verre d'eau, et de prévenir un professionnel de la santé.
- Montrer au patient comment mesurer sa glycémie. Lui recommander de surveiller étroitement les résultats de ces tests en période de stress ou de maladie et de prévenir immédiatement un professionnel de la santé si des modifications importantes surviennent.
- Conseiller au patient d'éviter de boire de l'alcool et de consulter un professionnel de la santé avant de prendre d'autres médicaments d'ordonnance ou en vente libre en même temps que le natéglinide.
- Expliquer à la patiente que l'insuline est le médicament de prédilection pour équilibrer la glycémie au cours de la grossesse. Lui conseiller d'informer rapidement un professionnel de la santé si elle pense être enceinte ou si elle souhaite le devenir.
- Recommander au patient qui doit suivre un autre traitement ou subir une intervention chirurgicale d'avertir le professionnel de la santé qu'il suit un traitement avec ce médicament.
- Conseiller au patient de toujours avoir sur lui du sucre (sachets de sucre ou bonbons) et une pièce d'identité où sont inscrits son problème de santé et son traitement médicamenteux.
- Insister sur l'importance des examens de suivi et des dosages réguliers de la glycémie et de l'hémoglobine glyquée.

VÉRIFICATION DE L'EFFICACITÉ THÉRAPEUTIQUE

L'efficacité du traitement peut être démontrée par: l'équilibrage de la glycémie sans épisodes d'hypoglycémie ou d'hyperglycémie. ✵

NÉDOCROMIL,

voir Stabilisateurs des mastocytes

ALERTE CLINIQUE

NELFINAVIR

Viracept

CLASSIFICATION:

Antirétroviral (inhibiteur de la protéase)

Grossesse – catégorie B (voir « Précautions et mises en garde »)

INDICATIONS

Traitement de l'infection par le VIH en association avec d'autres antirétroviraux.

MÉCANISME D'ACTION

Inhibition de l'action de la protéase du VIH et prévention du clivage des polyprotéines virales. ***Effets thérapeutiques:*** Augmentation du nombre de cellules CD4 et diminution de la charge virale ▪ Ralentissement de l'évolution de l'infection par le VIH et de l'apparition de ses complications.

PHARMACOCINÉTIQUE

Absorption: Rapide (PO). Les aliments augmentent considérablement l'absorption.

Distribution: Inconnue.

Liaison aux protéines: > 98 %.

Métabolisme et excrétion: Fort métabolisme hépatique (par le CYP P450 3A4); excrétion fécale sous forme de métabolites (78 %) et à l'état inchangé (22 %); de 1 à 2 % excrété à l'état inchangé dans l'urine.

Demi-vie: De 3,5 à 5 heures.

Profil temps-action

	Début d'action	Pic	Durée
PO	rapide	2-4 h	8 h

CONTRE-INDICATIONS, PRÉCAUTIONS ET MISES EN GARDE

Contre-indications: Hypersensibilité ▪ Traitement concomitant par le cisapride, le pimozide, l'amiodarone, la

N

quinidine, la lovastatine, la simvastatine, les alcaloïdes de l'ergot (dihydroergotamine, ergonovine, ergotamine, méthylergonovine), le midazolam ou le triazolam.

Précautions et mises en garde: Nombreuses interactions médicamenteuses ■ Hémophilie (risque accru d'hémorragie) ■ Diabète (risque d'aggravation de l'hyperglycémie) ■ Insuffisance hépatique ■ **ALLAITEMENT:** Les patientes infectées par le VIH ne devraient pas allaiter.

ALERTE CLINIQUE: Santé Canada a émis en septembre 2007 l'avis suivant concernant le nelfinavir: « Toutes les présentations de nelfinavir contiennent une faible quantité de méthanesulfonate d'éthyle, une impureté issue de la fabrication du médicament, qui pourrait être cancérigène chez l'humain. Les médecins doivent évaluer les risques et les bienfaits d'un traitement par le nelfinavir. De façon générale, Santé Canada recommande de remplacer le nelfinavir par une autre solution thérapeutique, si ce changement peut se faire en toute sécurité. Les femmes enceintes et les enfants pourraient être plus vulnérables aux effets néfastes du méthanesulfonate d'éthyle; leur traitement devrait donc être modifié le plus rapidement possible. »

RÉACTIONS INDÉSIRABLES ET EFFETS SECONDAIRES

SNC: CONVULSIONS, anxiété, dépression, étourdissements, somnolence, labilité émotionnelle, céphalées, hyperkinésie, insomnie, malaises, migraines, troubles du sommeil, idées suicidaires, faiblesse.

ORLO: iritis aiguë, pharyngite, rhinite, sinusite.

Resp.: dyspnée.

GI: diarrhée, anorexie, dyspepsie, valeurs élevées lors des tests de la fonction hépatique, douleurs épigastriques, flatulence, hémorragie gastrique, hépatite, nausées, aphtes buccaux, pancréatite, vomissements.

GU: lithiase rénale, dysfonctionnement sexuel.

Derm.: prurit, rash, transpiration, urticaire.

End.: hyperglycémie.

HÉ: déshydratation.

Hémat.: anémie, leucopénie, thrombopénie.

Métab.: hyperlipidémie, hyperuricémie, modification de la distribution du tissu adipeux.

Loc.: arthralgie, arthrite, douleurs lombaires, myalgie, myopathie.

SN: myasthénie, paresthésie.

Divers: réactions allergiques, fièvre, syndrome de reconstitution immunitaire.

INTERACTIONS

Médicament-médicament: Le nelfinavir est un inhibiteur et un substrat du CYP P450 3A4. L'USAGE CONCOMITANT DE **CISAPRIDE**, DE **PIMOZIDE**, D'**AMIODARONE**, DE **QUINIDINE**, D'**ERGONOVINE**, DE **MÉTHYLERGONOVINE**, DE **DIHYDROERGOTAMINE**, D'**ERGOTAMINE**, DE **LOVASTATINE**, DE **SIMVASTATINE**, DE **MIDAZOLAM** ET DE **TRIAZOLAM** EST CONTRE-INDIQUÉ, ÉTANT DONNÉ LE RISQUE ACCRU DE RÉACTIONS INDÉSIRABLES GRAVES OU MENAÇANTES POUR LA VIE, INCLUANT LES ARYTHMIES, LA RHABDOMYOLYSE, LA SÉDATION EXCESSIVE ET LA VASOCONSTRICTION ■ Le nelfinavir ralentit le métabolisme de la **rifabutine** et peut en accroître les effets (réduire de moitié la dose de rifabutine et administrer le nelfinavir à une dose de 1 250 mg toutes les 12 heures) ■ La **rifampine** abaisse les concentrations plasmatiques de nelfinavir (éviter l'usage concomitant) ■ Les stimulants puissants du CYP 3A, comme la **carbamazépine**, le **phénobarbital**, et la **phénytoïne**, peuvent abaisser les concentrations plasmatiques de nelfinavir et favoriser l'émergence d'une résistance virale ■ L'**oméprazole** peut abaisser les concentrations plasmatiques de nelfinavir ■ Le **kétoconazole**, la **délavirdine**, l'**éfavirenz**, l'**indinavir**, **le saquinavir** et le **ritonavir** peuvent élever les concentrations plasmatiques de nelfinavir et en augmenter les effets ■ La **névirapine** peut abaisser les concentrations plasmatiques de nelfinavir ■ Le nelfinavir abaisse les concentrations plasmatiques de **délavirdine** et de **zidovudine** ■ Le nelfinavir élève les concentrations plasmatiques d'**indinavir**, de **saquinavir**, de **tacrolimus**, de **sirolimus**, de **cyclosporine** et d'**azithromycine** ■ La **didanosine** devant être prise à jeun, le nelfinavir doit être administré avec un repas 1 heure après ou plus de 2 heures avant la didanosine ■ Le nelfinavir peut diminuer les concentrations sanguines des **contraceptifs oraux** et en diminuer ainsi l'efficacité (utiliser une autre méthode contraceptive) ■ Le nelfinavir peut diminuer les concentrations sanguines de **méthadone** (une augmentation de la dose de méthadone peut être nécessaire) ■ Le nelfinavir élève les concentrations plasmatiques d'**atorvastatine** et augmente le risque d'effets indésirables (utiliser la plus petite dose d'atorvastatine) ■ L'indinavir peut élever les concentrations sanguines de **sildénafil**, de **tadalafil** et de **vardénafil** et en intensifier les effets (suivre de près l'état du patient et utiliser des doses beaucoup plus faibles).

Médicament-aliments: Les **aliments** augmentent l'absorption du nelfinavir.

Médicament-produits naturels: L'usage concomitant de **millepertuis** diminue de façon marquée les concentrations sanguines et l'efficacité du nelfinavir, favorisant ainsi l'émergence d'une résistance virale.

VOIES D'ADMINISTRATION ET POSOLOGIE

- **PO (adultes et enfants > 13 ans):** 750 mg, 3 fois par jour, ou 1 250 mg, 2 fois par jour, en association avec d'autres antirétroviraux.

- **PO (enfants de 2 à 13 ans):** De 25 à 30 mg/kg/dose, 3 fois par jour (ne pas dépasser 750 mg, 3 fois par jour).

PRÉSENTATION

Comprimés: 250 mg^{Pr}, 625 mg^{Pr}.

SOINS INFIRMIERS

ÉVALUATION DE LA SITUATION

- Pendant toute la durée du traitement, rester à l'affût de toute modification qui intervient au niveau de la gravité des symptômes de l'infection par le VIH et de l'apparition d'infections opportunistes.
- Si une patiente enceinte est exposée à des antirétroviraux, l'inscrire dans le registre des femmes exposées aux antirétroviraux pendant leur grossesse, en composant le 1-800-258-4263.

Tests de laboratoire: Noter la charge virale et le nombre de cellules CD4 à intervalles réguliers tout au long du traitement. Le médicament peut provoquer l'hyperglycémie. Il peut entraîner l'élévation des concentrations sériques d'AST, d'ALT, de bilirubine totale, de phosphatase alcaline, de LDH et de créatine-kinase (CPK), et provoquer l'anémie, la leucopénie, la thrombopénie, l'hyperlipidémie et l'hyperuricémie.

DIAGNOSTICS INFIRMIERS POSSIBLES

- Risque d'infection (Indications).
- Connaissances insuffisantes sur le traitement médicamenteux (Enseignement au patient et à ses proches).
- Non-observance du traitement médicamenteux (Enseignement au patient et à ses proches).

INTERVENTIONS INFIRMIÈRES

- NE PAS CONFONDRE LE NELFINAVIR (VIRACEPT) AVEC LA NÉVIRAPINE (VIRAMUNE).
- Administrer le médicament avec des aliments (repas ou collation).
- Chez les patients qui ne peuvent avaler les comprimés, on peut les dissoudre, entiers ou préalablement écrasés, dans une petite quantité d'eau, ou encore les écraser et les mélanger à une petite quantité de nourriture. Une fois que les comprimés ont été mélangés à des aliments ou dissous dans l'eau, le patient doit prendre la préparation au complet pour s'assurer qu'il a absorbé toute la dose. Lui recommander d'avaler immédiatement le mélange dès qu'il a été préparé, de rincer le verre en ajoutant un peu d'eau et de la boire pour s'assurer qu'il a pris toute la dose. Les jus ou les aliments acides (p. ex., le jus d'orange, le jus de pomme ou la compote de pommes) ne devraient pas être mélangés à Viracept, car la préparation pourrait avoir un goût amer.

ENSEIGNEMENT AU PATIENT ET À SES PROCHES

- Expliquer au patient qu'il est important de suivre rigoureusement la posologie recommandée et de prendre le nelfinavir à des intervalles égaux tout au long de la journée. Lui recommander de ne pas dépasser la dose prescrite et de ne pas cesser de prendre le médicament sans avoir consulté au préalable un professionnel de la santé. S'il n'a pas pu prendre le médicament au moment habituel, il doit le prendre aussitôt que possible. L'avertir qu'il ne doit jamais remplacer une dose manquée par une double dose.
- Informer le patient qu'il ne doit pas partager le nelfinavir avec d'autres personnes.
- Conseiller au patient de consulter un professionnel de la santé avant de prendre d'autres médicaments (sur ordonnance ou en vente libre et des produits naturels), en même temps que le nelfinavir.
- Expliquer au patient que le nelfinavir ne guérit pas le sida, qu'il n'empêche pas l'apparition d'infections associées ou opportunistes et qu'il ne réduit pas le risque de transmission du VIH à autrui par les rapports sexuels ou par la contamination du sang. L'inciter à éviter les rapports sexuels ou à utiliser un condom, et à éviter le partage d'aiguilles ou les dons de sang afin de prévenir la propagation du VIH. Prévenir le patient que les effets à longue échéance du nelfinavir restent inconnus.
- Informer le patient que le nelfinavir peut causer l'hyperglycémie. Lui conseiller de prévenir un professionnel de la santé si les symptômes suivants se manifestent: soif ou faim accrue, perte de poids inexpliquée, mictions plus fréquentes, fatigue, sécheresse de la peau ou démangeaisons.
- Prévenir le patient qu'en cas de diarrhée il peut prendre un antidiarrhéique en vente libre tel que le lopéramide, lequel ralentit la motilité gastro-intestinale.
- Conseiller à la patiente qui prend des contraceptifs oraux d'utiliser un autre moyen de contraception (non hormonal) pendant toute la durée du traitement par le nelfinavir.
- Prévenir le patient qu'il peut se produire une redistribution ou une accumulation de graisses corporelles à la suite du traitement antirétroviral, dont les causes et les conséquences à long terme sur la santé sont actuellement inconnues.

- Insister sur le fait qu'il est important de se soumettre à intervalles réguliers à des examens de suivi et à des analyses de sang permettant de déceler les effets secondaires et les bienfaits du traitement.

VÉRIFICATION DE L'EFFICACITÉ THÉRAPEUTIQUE

L'efficacité du traitement peut être démontrée par: le ralentissement de l'évolution de l'infection par le VIH et la diminution du risque d'infections opportunistes ■ l'augmentation du nombre de cellules CD4 et la diminution de la charge virale. ✳

NÉOMYCINE,
voir Aminosides

NÉOSTIGMINE

Neostigmine Omega, PMS-Neostigmine, Prostigmin

CLASSIFICATION:
Cholinergique (inhibiteur de la cholinestérase), antimyasthénique

Grossesse – catégorie C

INDICATIONS

PO et voie parentérale: Augmentation de la force musculaire dans le cadre du traitement des symptômes de la myasthénie grave ■ **Voie parentérale**: Prévention et traitement de l'atonie intestinale postopératoire et de la rétention urinaire ■ Renversement des effets des bloqueurs neuromusculaires de type non dépolarisant.

MÉCANISME D'ACTION

Inhibition de la décomposition de l'acétylcholine entraînant son accumulation et la prolongation de son effet ■ Myosis, élévation du tonus des muscles intestinaux et locomoteurs, constriction bronchique et urétérale, bradycardie, salivation, larmoiement et transpiration accrus. ***Effets thérapeutiques:*** Amélioration de la fonction musculaire chez les patients souffrant de myasthénie grave; vidange de la vessie chez les patients souffrant de rétention urinaire ou renversement des effets des bloqueurs neuromusculaires de type non dépolarisant.

PHARMACOCINÉTIQUE

Absorption: Faible (PO), ce qui dicte le recours à des doses plus élevées que celles administrées par voie parentérale.

Distribution: Le médicament ne semble pas traverser la barrière placentaire ni passer dans le lait maternel.

Métabolisme et excrétion: Métabolisme par les cholinestérases plasmatiques et le foie.

Demi-vie: *PO et IV* – de 40 à 60 minutes; *IM* – de 50 à 90 minutes.

Profil temps-action
(effets cholinergiques; tonus musculaire accru)

	DÉBUT D'ACTION	PIC	DURÉE
PO	45 – 75 min	inconnu	2 – 4 h
IM	10 – 30 min	20 – 30 min	2 – 4 h
IV	10 – 30 min	20 – 30 min	2 – 4 h

CONTRE-INDICATIONS, PRÉCAUTIONS ET MISES EN GARDE

Contre-indications: Hypersensibilité ■ Obstruction mécanique du tractus gastro-intestinal ou des voies urinaires ■ Péritonite ■ Viabilité intestinale douteuse ■ Utilisation conjointe de bloqueurs neuromusculaires de type dépolarisant ■ À ne pas utiliser lors d'une anesthésie par le cyclopropane ou l'halothane, mais utilisation possible une fois que ces agents ont été éliminés ■ Asthme bronchique.

Précautions et mises en garde: Lors de l'utilisation de doses élevées, il est indiqué d'administrer simultanément de l'atropine ■ Antécédents d'asthme ■ Ulcère ■ Maladie cardiovasculaire ■ Épilepsie ■ Hyperthyroïdie ■ Risque d'hypotension et de bradycardie si la néostigmine est utilisée comme antagoniste des bloqueurs neuromusculaires de type non dépolarisant ■ **OBST.**: Risque d'irritation utérine par suite de l'administration par voie IV près du terme; risque de faiblesse musculaire chez le nouveau-né ■ Allaitement.

RÉACTIONS INDÉSIRABLES ET EFFETS SECONDAIRES

SNC: CONVULSIONS, étourdissements, faiblesse.
ORLO: larmoiement, myosis.
Resp.: bronchospasme, sécrétions excessives.
CV: bradycardie, hypotension.
GI: crampes abdominales, diarrhée, salivation excessive, nausées, vomissements.
Tég.: transpiration, rash.

INTERACTIONS

Médicament-médicament: Les **médicaments dotés de propriétés anticholinergiques**, dont les **antihistaminiques**, les **antidépresseurs**, l'**atropine**, l'**halopéridol**, les **phénothiazines**, la **quinidine** et le **disopyramide**, peuvent contrecarrer les effets de la néostigmine ■ La néostigmine prolonge l'effet des **relaxants musculaires**

de type dépolarisant (succinylcholine, décaméthonium) ■ Toxicité additive lors de l'administration simultanée d'autres **inhibiteurs de la cholinestérase**, dont l'**écothiopate**.

VOIES D'ADMINISTRATION ET POSOLOGIE

Myasthénie grave

- **PO (adultes)**: De 75 à 300 mg, répartis sur 24 heures, selon les besoins.
- **SC, IM (adultes)**: 1 mg, toutes les heures (lors de crises myasthéniques).

Prévention de l'atonie intestinale postopératoire

- **IM, SC (adultes)**: 250 µg, avant ou immédiatement après l'opération; répéter toutes les 4 à 6 heures par voie SC.

Traitement de l'atonie intestinale postopératoire

- **IM, IV lent, SC (adultes)**: 500 µg; on peut répéter l'administration de cette dose toutes les 4 à 5 heures, jusqu'au rétablissement de l'état du patient.

Prévention de la rétention urinaire

- **IM, SC (adultes)**: 250 µg, avant ou immédiatement après l'opération; répéter l'administration de cette dose toutes les 4 à 6 heures par voie SC.

Traitement de la rétention urinaire

- **IM, SC (adultes)**: 500 µg; si la miction ne peut se produire dans l'heure qui suit, procéder à un cathétérisme. Ensuite, poursuivre avec 500 µg, toutes les 3 heures, à 5 reprises au moins.

Antagonistes des bloqueurs neuromusculaires de type non dépolarisant

- **IV (adultes)**: Administrer lentement de 0,5 à 2 mg; administrer au préalable de 0,6 à 1,2 mg d'atropine par voie IV.

PRÉSENTATION (version générique disponible)

Comprimés: 15 mg^{Pr} ■ **Solution pour injection**: 1:400 (2,5 mg/mL), en fioles de 5 mL^{Pr}, 1:1 000 (1 mg/mL), en fioles de 10 mL^{Pr}, 1:2 000 (0,5 mg/mL), en ampoules de 1 mL et fioles de 10 mL^{Pr}.

SOINS INFIRMIERS

ÉVALUATION DE LA SITUATION

Mesurer le pouls, la fréquence respiratoire et la pression artérielle avant l'administration de la néostigmine. Prévenir le médecin en cas de changements marqués au niveau de la fréquence cardiaque.

Myasthénie grave:

- Examiner les réactions neuromusculaires, y compris la capacité vitale, le ptosis, la diplopie, la capacité de mastication, la capacité de déglutition, la préhension manuelle et la démarche, avant l'administration du médicament et au moment de son effet maximal. Conseiller au patient de tenir un journal où il notera quotidiennement son état et les effets du médicament.
- Surveiller les signes suivants de surdosage, de dosage insuffisant ou de résistance au traitement: faiblesse musculaire, dyspnée, dysphagie. En cas de surdosage, les symptômes se manifestent habituellement dans l'heure qui suit l'administration alors que, en cas de dosage insuffisant, ils apparaissent 3 heures après l'administration ou plus tard. Les symptômes de surdosage (crise cholinergique) peuvent aussi inclure l'intensification des sécrétions pulmonaires et de la salivation, la bradycardie, les nausées, les vomissements, les crampes, la diarrhée et la diaphorèse. On peut distinguer le surdosage d'un dosage insuffisant par un test au Tensilon (chlorure d'édrophonium).

Atonie intestinale postopératoire: Examiner l'abdomen: suivre de près la distension abdominale et ausculter les bruits intestinaux. On peut installer un cathéter rectal afin de faciliter l'expulsion des gaz.

Rétention urinaire: Suivre de près la distension vésicale. Effectuer le bilan des ingesta et des excreta. Si le patient ne peut uriner dans l'heure qui suit l'administration de néostigmine, envisager la possibilité d'installer un cathéter.

Antagoniste des bloqueurs neuromusculaires de type non dépolarisant: Suivre le renversement des effets des bloqueurs neuromusculaires à l'aide d'un stimulateur des nerfs périphériques. Le rétablissement musculaire s'effectue habituellement dans l'ordre suivant: diaphragme, muscles intercostaux, muscles des cordes vocales et de la gorge, muscles abdominaux, muscles des membres, muscles masticateurs et muscles releveurs de la paupière. Suivre de près la faiblesse musculaire résiduelle et la détresse respiratoire pendant toute la période de récupération. Garder les voies aériennes dégagées et maintenir la ventilation jusqu'au rétablissement de la respiration normale.

TOXICITÉ ET SURDOSAGE: En cas de surdosage, l'antidote est l'atropine.

DIAGNOSTICS INFIRMIERS POSSIBLES

- Mobilité physique réduite (Indications).
- Mode de respiration inefficace (Indications).
- Connaissances insuffisantes sur le traitement médicamenteux (Enseignement au patient et à ses proches).

N

INTERVENTIONS INFIRMIÈRES

- Les doses par voies orale et parentérale ne sont pas interchangeables.
- Lorsque l'agent est utilisé comme antagoniste des bloqueurs neuromusculaires de type non dépolarisant, on peut administrer de l'atropine avant la néostigmine ou en association avec celle-ci afin de prévenir ou de traiter la bradycardie.

PO: Administrer le médicament avec du lait ou des aliments pour en réduire les effets secondaires. Chez les patients éprouvant des difficultés de mastication, on peut administrer la néostigmine 30 minutes avant les repas.

IV directe: Administrer les doses sans les diluer. On peut injecter la néostigmine dans une tubulure en Y par où s'écoule une solution de D5%E, de NaCl 0,9 %, de Ringer ou de lactate de Ringer.

***Vitesse d'administration*:** Administrer à raison de 0,5 mg par minute.

Associations compatibles dans la même seringue: glycopyrrolate ■ héparine ■ pentobarbital ■ thiopental.

Compatibilité (tubulure en Y): héparine ■ hydrocortisone sodique, succinate d' ■ potassium, chlorure de ■ vitamines du complexe B avec C.

N

ENSEIGNEMENT AU PATIENT ET À SES PROCHES

- Conseiller au patient de respecter rigoureusement la posologie recommandée. Le prévenir qu'il ne doit ni sauter de dose ni remplacer une dose manquée par une double dose. Les patients présentant des antécédents de dysphagie devraient recourir en tout temps à un réveille-matin mécanique ou à piles afin de pouvoir prendre le médicament exactement à l'heure prévue. Les patients souffrant de dysphagie peuvent être incapables d'avaler le médicament si la dose n'est pas prise à l'heure prévue. Si la dose est prise en retard, une crise myasthénique peut se déclencher. La prise prématurée du médicament peut entraîner une crise cholinergique. Les patients souffrant de myasthénie grave doivent suivre ce traitement pendant toute leur vie.
- Conseiller au patient souffrant de myasthénie grave d'espacer ses activités afin d'éviter la fatigue.
- Conseiller au patient de toujours porter sur lui une pièce d'identité où sont inscrits son état de santé et son traitement médicamenteux.

VÉRIFICATION DE L'EFFICACITÉ THÉRAPEUTIQUE

***L'efficacité du traitement peut être démontrée par*:** le soulagement du ptosis et de la diplopie ■ l'amélioration de la mastication, de la déglutition, de la force des membres et de la respiration, sans apparition de symptômes cholinergiques en cas de myasthénie grave ■ le soulagement ou la prévention de l'atonie intestinale postopératoire ■ le soulagement de la rétention urinaire non obstructive ■ le renversement des effets des bloqueurs neuromusculaires du type non dépolarisant lors d'une anesthésie générale. ✳

NÉVIRAPINE

Viramune

***CLASSIFICATION*:**

Antirétroviral (inhibiteur non nucléosidique de la transcriptase inverse [INNTI])

Grossesse – catégorie C

INDICATIONS

Traitement des infections par le VIH en association avec d'autres agents antirétroviraux.

MÉCANISME D'ACTION

Liaison à la transcriptase inverse inhibant ainsi la synthèse de l'ADN viral. ***Effets thérapeutiques*:** Ralentissement de l'évolution de l'infection au VIH et de l'apparition de ses complications.

PHARMACOCINÉTIQUE

Absorption: > 90 % (PO).

Distribution: La névirapine traverse la barrière placentaire et passe dans le lait maternel; elle pénètre dans le liquide céphalorachidien à des concentrations qui équivalent à 45 % des concentrations plasmatiques.

Métabolisme et excrétion: Fort métabolisme hépatique; des quantités minimes sont excrétées à l'état inchangé dans l'urine.

Demi-vie: De 25 à 30 heures (lors de l'administration de plusieurs doses).

Profil temps-action

	DÉBUT D'ACTION	PIC	DURÉE
PO	rapide	4 h	12 h

CONTRE-INDICATIONS, PRÉCAUTIONS ET MISES EN GARDE

Contre-indications: Hypersensibilité ■ Utilisation concomitante de kétoconazole ■ Trouble hépatique grave ou taux d'AST ou d'ALT avant le traitement > 5 fois la limite supérieure de la normale ■ Patients qui ont dû interrompre le traitement en raison d'une éruption cutanée grave, d'une éruption cutanée accompagnée de symptômes constitutionnels, de réactions d'hypersensibilité ou d'hépatite clinique due à la névirapine ■ Patients dont les taux d'AST ou d'ALT dépassait de 5 fois la limite supérieure de la normale pendant le traitement par névirapine.

Précautions et mises en garde: Nombreuses interactions médicamenteuses ■ Insuffisance rénale ou hépatique ■ Femmes adultes dont la numération des lymphocytes CD4+ est supérieure à 250 cellules/mm^3, y compris les femmes enceintes recevant un traitement prolongé contre l'infection par le VIH (plus grand risque de manifestations hépatiques indésirables graves) ■ Hommes adultes dont la numération des lymphocytes CD4+ est supérieure à 400 cellules/mm^3 ■ **OBST., PÉD.**: Grossesse ou enfants (l'innocuité du médicament n'a pas été établie) ■ **ALLAITEMENT**: Les patientes infectées par le VIH ne devraient pas allaiter.

RÉACTIONS INDÉSIRABLES ET EFFETS SECONDAIRES

Effets observés au cours du traitement d'association.

SNC: céphalées.

GI: HÉPATOTOXICITÉ (y compris des cas graves et potentiellement mortels d'hépatotoxicité et d'hépatite fulminante d'issue fatale), concentrations accrues d'enzymes hépatiques, nausées, douleurs abdominales, diarrhée, hépatite, stomatite ulcéreuse.

Tég.: ÉRUPTIONS CUTANÉES (POUVANT ÉVOLUER VERS UNE ÉRYTHRODERMIE BULLEUSE AVEC ÉPIDERMOLYSE OU VERS LE SYNDROME DE STEVENS-JOHNSON).

Hémat.: granulopénie (risque accru chez les enfants).

Loc.: myalgie.

SN: paresthésie, neuropathie périphérique.

Divers: fièvre, réactions d'hypersensibilité (caractérisées par une éruption cutanée et accompagnée de symptômes généraux, tels que fièvre, arthralgie, myalgie et lymphadénopathie et d'un ou de plusieurs des symptômes suivants: hépatite, éosinophilie, granulopénie, dysfonction rénale ou autres lésions viscérales), modification de la distribution du tissu adipeux, syndrome de reconstitution immunitaire.

INTERACTIONS

Médicament-médicament: La névirapine induit les systèmes enzymatiques hépatiques **P450 3A4** et **2B6** et peut affecter le sort des **médicaments qui sont métabolisés par ce système enzymatique** ■ La névirapine diminue considérablement les concentrations de **kétoconazole** (une administration concomitante est contre-indiquée) ■ Chez les patients qui présentent une dépendance physique à la **méthadone**, la névirapine peut déclencher des symptômes de sevrage à la méthadone dans les 2 semaines qui suivent le début du traitement ■ L'agent peut diminuer les concentrations plasmatiques des **contraceptifs hormonaux** et en réduire ainsi l'efficacité (l'usage concomitant de contraceptifs hormonaux devrait être évité) ■ L'agent peut diminuer les concentrations plasmatiques et l'efficacité des médicaments suivants: **éfavirenz**, **indinavir**, **lopinavir**, **nelfinavir**, **saquinavir**, **amiodarone**, **disopyramide**, **lidocaïne**, **carbamazépine**, **clonazépam**, **ethosuximide**, **itraconazole**, **voriconazole**, **diltiazem**, **nifédipine**, **vérapamil**, **cyclophosphamide**, **ergotamine**, **cyclosporine**, **tacrolimus**, **sirolimus**, **cisapride**, **fentanyl** (faire un suivi étroit lors de l'usage concomitant) ■ La **rifampine** diminue les concentrations sanguines de névirapine ainsi que son efficacité (éviter l'usage concomitant) ■ La névirapine peut modifier les concentrations sanguines et augmenter l'efficacité de la **rifabutine** et le risque de toxicité qui en découle (l'administration concomitante doit se faire seulement sous une étroite surveillance) ■ Le **fluconazole** élève les concentrations sanguines de névirapine et en augmente le risque de toxicité (suivre de près l'apparition d'effets indésirables causés par la névirapine) ■ La névirapine diminue les concentrations et l'efficacité de la **clarithromycine** (utiliser un autre antibiotique) ■ La névirapine peut augmenter le risque de saignements provoqués par la **warfarine** (suivre le RNI) ■ L'utilisation de **prednisone** dans les 2 premières semaines de traitement augmente le risque d'éruptions cutanées ■ Risque accru d'éruptions cutanées, en cas de traitement concomitant par d'autres **médicaments qui provoquent souvent des éruptions cutanées**, comme le **trimétoprime/sulfaméthoxazole** et l'**abacavir**.

Médicament-produits naturels: L'usage concomitant de **millepertuis** diminue de façon marquée les concentrations sanguines et l'efficacité de la névirapine, et favorise l'émergence d'une résistance virale.

N

VOIES D'ADMINISTRATION ET POSOLOGIE

- **PO (adultes)**: 200 mg par jour, pendant les 2 premières semaines, puis 200 mg, 2 fois par jour (en association avec d'autres agents antirétroviraux). Il est très important de commencer le traitement à une dose de 200 mg, 1 fois par jour, pendant les 2 premières semaines, car ce schéma posologique permet de réduire la fréquence des éruptions cutanées graves. En cas d'apparition d'éruptions cutanées, ne pas administrer 2 fois par jour. Si le traitement est interrompu pendant plus de 7 jours, le recommencer par une dose quotidienne de 200 mg, 1 fois par jour, pendant 14 jours.

PRÉSENTATION

Comprimés: 200 mg^{Pr}.

SOINS INFIRMIERS

ÉVALUATION DE LA SITUATION

- Observer le patient pendant toute la durée du traitement pour déceler l'aggravation des symptômes de l'infection au VIH et l'apparition des symptômes d'une infection opportuniste.
- SUIVRE DE PRÈS LE PATIENT POUR DÉCELER LE RASH (DE LÉGER À MODÉRÉ : ÉRYTHÈME OU ÉRUPTION MACULOPAPULEUSE ; URTICAIRE, ÉRUPTIONS PRURIGINEUSES SURÉLEVÉES AVEC BORDURES – S'ACCOMPAGNANT DE SYMPTÔMES CONSTITUTIONNELS : FIÈVRE, VÉSICATION, LÉSIONS BUCCALES ÉROSIVES, CONJONCTIVITE, ŒDÈME DU VISAGE, MYALGIE, ARTHRALGIE), PARTICULIÈREMENT AU COURS DES 6 PREMIÈRES SEMAINES DE TRAITEMENT. SI LE RASH EST GRAVE (ÉRUPTIONS ÉRYTHÉMATEUSES OU MACULOPAPULEUSES ÉTENDUES AVEC ŒDÈME ANGIONEUROTIQUE OU DESQUAMATIONS HUMIDES) OU S'IL S'ACCOMPAGNE DE SYMPTÔMES GÉNÉRAUX (RÉACTION RESSEMBLANT À LA MALADIE SÉRIQUE, SYNDROME DE STEVENS-JOHNSON, ÉRYTHRODERMIE BULLEUSE AVEC ÉPIDERMOLYSE), IL FAUT ARRÊTER LE TRAITEMENT IMMÉDIATEMENT. LA PREDNISONE OU LES ANTIHISTAMINIQUES NE SONT PAS EFFICACES POUR PRÉVENIR OU POUR TRAITER CES PROBLÈMES CUTANÉS. ON PEUT POURSUIVRE LE TRAITEMENT À LA NÉVIRAPINE, SI LE RASH EST DE LÉGER À MODÉRÉ, ET S'IL NE S'ACCOMPAGNE PAS DE SYMPTÔMES CONSTITUTIONNELS OU D'ÉLÉVATION DES TAUX D'ALT OU D'AST, MAIS IL NE FAUT PAS REPRENDRE CE TRAITEMENT UNE FOIS QU'ON L'A ARRÊTÉ. SI LE RASH EST GRAVE OU S'IL S'ACCOMPAGNE DE SYMPTÔMES CONSTITUTIONNELS, DE DYSFONCTIONNEMENT ORGANIQUE OU D'UNE ÉLÉVATION DES TAUX D'ALT OU D'AST, IL FAUT ABANDONNER DÉFINITIVEMENT LE TRAITEMENT PAR LA NÉVIRAPINE.
- Si une patiente enceinte est exposée à des antirétroviraux, l'inscrire dans le registre des femmes exposées aux antirétroviraux pendant leur grossesse, en composant le 1-800-258-4263.

Tests de laboratoire :

- Noter la charge virale et le nombre de cellules CD4 à intervalles réguliers pendant toute la durée du traitement.
- ÉVALUER LA FONCTION HÉPATIQUE INITIALEMENT ET À INTERVALLES FRÉQUENTS AU COURS DES 18 PREMIÈRES SEMAINES DE TRAITEMENT POUR DÉCELER LES EFFETS TOXIQUES DE L'AGENT, PARTICULIÈREMENT FRÉQUENTS AU COURS DES 6 PREMIÈRES SEMAINES. LA TOXICITÉ PEUT ÊTRE ASYMPTOMATIQUE AVEC ÉLÉVATION DES TAUX D'ALT OU D'AST SANS SIGNES OU SYMPTÔMES CLINIQUES, OU ENCORE S'ACCOMPAGNER D'AU MOINS UN TYPE DE SYMPTÔME (RASH, SYMPTÔMES PSEUDOGRIPPAUX, FIÈVRE), AVEC ÉLÉVATION DES TAUX D'ENZYMES HÉPATIQUES. LA TOXICITÉ PEUT ÉVOLUER VERS L'INSUFFISANCE HÉPATIQUE ET LE DÉCÈS. SI DES SIGNES DE TOXICITÉ HÉPATIQUE SE MANIFESTENT, ABANDONNER DÉFINITIVEMENT LE TRAITEMENT PAR LA NÉVIRAPINE.

DIAGNOSTICS INFIRMIERS POSSIBLES

- Risque d'infection (Indications).
- Connaissances insuffisantes sur le traitement médicamenteux (Enseignement au patient et à ses proches).
- Non-observance du traitement médicamenteux (Enseignement au patient et à ses proches).

INTERVENTIONS INFIRMIÈRES

- NE PAS CONFONDRE LA NÉVIRAPINE (VIRAMUNE) AVEC LE NELFINAVIR (VIRACEPT).
- La névirapine peut être administrée sans égard aux repas.
- Si le traitement est interrompu pendant plus de 7 jours, l'amorcer de nouveau en administrant une dose de 200 mg, 1 fois par jour, pendant 14 jours, puis majorer la dose jusqu'à 200 mg, 2 fois par jour.

ENSEIGNEMENT AU PATIENT ET À SES PROCHES

- Expliquer au patient qu'il est important de prendre la névirapine en suivant rigoureusement les recommandations du médecin et en espaçant les prises également, tout au long de la journée. Le prévenir qu'il ne doit pas prendre une plus grande quantité de médicament que celle qui lui a été prescrite et qu'il ne doit pas arrêter le traitement sans consulter un professionnel de la santé au préalable. S'il n'a pu prendre le médicament à l'heure prévue, il devrait le prendre aussitôt que possible, sans jamais remplacer une dose manquée par une double dose.
- Informer le patient qu'il ne doit pas partager la névirapine avec d'autres personnes.
- Conseiller au patient de ne pas prendre d'autres médicaments (sur ordonnance ou en vente libre et des produits naturels) en même temps que la névirapine, sans consulter au préalable un professionnel de la santé.
- Prévenir le patient que la névirapine ne guérit pas le sida et n'empêche pas l'apparition d'infections associées ou opportunistes. Lui expliquer que ce médicament ne réduit pas le risque de transmission du VIH à autrui par les rapports sexuels ou par la contamination du sang. Inciter le patient à utiliser

un condom, et à éviter le partage d'aiguilles ou les dons de sang afin de prévenir la propagation du VIH. Informer le patient que les effets à long terme de la névirapine sont pour le moment inconnus.

- Prévenir la patiente qui prend des contraceptifs oraux qu'elle doit utiliser une méthode de contraception non hormonale au cours du traitement par la névirapine.
- RECOMMANDER AU PATIENT DE PRÉVENIR IMMÉDIATEMENT UN PROFESSIONNEL DE LA SANTÉ SI DES SIGNES ET DES SYMPTÔMES D'HÉPATITE (SYMPTÔMES PSEUDOGRIPPAUX, FATIGUE, NAUSÉES, MANQUE D'APPÉTIT, JAUNISSEMENT DE LA PEAU OU DU BLANC DES YEUX, URINES FONCÉES, SELLES PÂLES, DOULEUR OU SENSIBILITÉ AU TOUCHER DU CÔTÉ GAUCHE EN DESSOUS DES CÔTES) OU DES RÉACTIONS CUTANÉES S'ACCOMPAGNANT DE SYMPTÔMES (SYMPTÔMES PSEUDOGRIPPAUX, FIÈVRES, DOULEURS MUSCULAIRES, CONJONCTIVITE, VÉSICULES, APHTES BUCCAUX, ŒDÈME DU VISAGE, FATIGUE) SE MANIFESTENT, CAR IL FAUT ALORS ABANDONNER IMMÉDIATEMENT LE TRAITEMENT PAR LA NÉVIRAPINE.
- Insister sur le fait qu'il est important de se soumettre à intervalles réguliers à des examens de suivi et à des analyses sanguines permettant de déterminer l'évolution de l'infection et de déceler les effets secondaires du médicament.

VÉRIFICATION DE L'EFFICACITÉ THÉRAPEUTIQUE

L'efficacité du traitement peut être démontrée par: le ralentissement de l'évolution de l'infection par le VIH et la diminution du risque d'infections opportunistes ■ la réduction de la charge virale et l'augmentation du nombre de cellules CD4. ✳

NIACINAMIDE,
voir Niacine

NIACINE

Synonyme: acide nicotinique

Acti-Niacin, Formula #7, Niacine, Novo-Niacin, Niaspan, Vitamine B_3

NIACINAMIDE

Synonyme: nicotinamide

Niacinamide

CLASSIFICATION:
Hypolipidémiants, vitamines B3 hydrosolubles

Grossesse – catégorie C

INDICATIONS

Traitement et prévention de la carence en niacine (pellagre) ■ Traitement d'appoint de certaines hyperlipidémies (niacine seulement).

MÉCANISME D'ACTION

Coenzymes essentielles pour le métabolisme lipidique, la glycogénolyse et la respiration tissulaire ■ Diminution de la synthèse des lipoprotéines et des triglycérides lors de l'administration de fortes doses, par inhibition de la libération des acides gras libres des tissus adipeux et par diminution de la synthèse hépatique des lipoprotéines (niacine seulement) ■ Vasodilatation périphérique lors de l'administration de fortes doses (niacine seulement). ***Effets thérapeutiques:*** Diminution des concentrations sanguines de lipides (niacine seulement) ■ Supplément en cas de carence.

PHARMACOCINÉTIQUE

Absorption: Bonne (PO).

Distribution: L'agent se répartit dans tout l'organisme après transformation en niacinamide et passe dans le lait maternel.

Métabolisme et excrétion: La niacine, à doses physiologiques, subit un métabolisme hépatique; le niacinamide, produit du métabolisme de la niacine, subit à son tour un métabolisme hépatique. À doses thérapeutiques, seule une partie subit un métabolisme, le reste est excrété sous forme inchangée par les reins.

Demi-vie: 45 minutes.

Profil temps-action
(effet sur les concentrations sanguines de lipides)

	DÉBUT D'ACTION	PIC	DURÉE
PO (cholestérol)	plusieurs jours	inconnu	inconnue
PO (triglycérides)	plusieurs heures	inconnu	inconnue

CONTRE-INDICATIONS, PRÉCAUTIONS ET MISES EN GARDE

Contre-indications: Hypersensibilité à la niacine ou au niacinamide ■ Maladie hépatique évolutive ■ Ulcère gastroduodénal ■ Hyperuricémie avec antécédents de rhumatisme goutteux ■ Hyperglycémie non maîtrisée ■ Hypotension grave.

Précautions et mises en garde: Maladie hépatique ■ Antécédents d'ulcère gastroduodénal ■ Goutte ■ Diabète

■ **OBST., ALLAITEMENT**: L'innocuité des doses élevées pour traiter les dyslipidémies n'a pas été établie chez la femme enceinte ou qui allaite.

RÉACTIONS INDÉSIRABLES ET EFFETS SECONDAIRES

Ces réactions indésirables et effets secondaires ont été notés lors du traitement de l'hyperlipidémie.

SNC: céphalées.

ORLO: vision trouble, perte de la vision centrale, proptose, amblyopie toxique.

CV: hypotension orthostatique.

GI: HÉPATOTOXICITÉ (comprimés oraux à action prolongée seulement), irritation gastro-intestinale, ballonnement, diarrhée, sécheresse de la bouche (xérostomie), flatulence, brûlures d'estomac, faim douloureuse, nausées, ulcère gastroduodénal.

Tég.: rougeurs du visage et du cou, prurit, sensation de brûlure, peau sèche, hyperpigmentation, activité accrue des glandes sébacées, rash, sensation de picotement ou de fourmillement au niveau de la peau.

Métab.: glycosurie, hyperglycémie, hyperuricémie.

INTERACTIONS

Médicament-médicament: Risque accru de myopathie lors de l'administration concomitante d'**inhibiteurs de l'HMG-CoA réductase** ■ Hypotension additive lors de l'administration concomitante d'**agents vasoactifs** ou de **ganglioplégiques** (**guanéthidine**, **guanadrel**).

VOIES D'ADMINISTRATION ET POSOLOGIE

Niacine

- **PO (adultes)**: *Apports individuels recommandés* – de 6 à 18 mg par jour. *Hyperlipidémie – Comprimé à libération immédiate:* initialement, 50 mg, 3 fois par jour; doubler la dose tous les 5 jours pour atteindre de 1,5 à 2 g par jour, en 3 ou 4 doses fractionnées. La dose quotidienne maximale est de 4 g, si elle est bien tolérée. *Comprimé à libération prolongée:* initialement, 500 mg, 1 fois par jour, au coucher; augmenter par paliers de 500 mg, toutes les 4 semaines jusqu'à une dose quotidienne maximale de 2 000 mg.

***Niacine ou niacinamide* – traitement de la pellagre**:

- **PO (adultes)**: De 300 à 500 mg par jour, en doses fractionnées (la dose quotidienne maximale est de 500 mg).
- **PO (enfants)**: De 100 à 300 mg par jour, en doses fractionnées.

INSUFFISANCE RÉNALE

- **PO (ADULTES)**: *CL_{CR} DE 10À 50 mL/MIN* – ADMINISTRER 50 % DE LA DOSE QUOTIDIENNE TOTALE EN DOSES FRACTIONNÉES; CL_{CR} < 10 mL/MIN – ADMINISTRER 25 % DE LA DOSE QUOTIDIENNE TOTALE EN DOSES FRACTIONNÉES.

PRÉSENTATION

- **Niacine (version générique disponible)**
  Comprimés: 50 mg[VL], 100 mg[VL], 250 mg[VL], 500 mg[VL] ■ **Comprimés à libération retard**: 500 mg[VL] ■ **Capsules à libération retard**: 300 mg[VL], 400 mg[VL] ■ **Comprimés à libération prolongée**: 500 mg[Pr], 750 mg[Pr], 1 000 mg[Pr] ■ **Poudre orale**: 800 mg/1,25 mL[VL] ■ **En association avec**: autres vitamines ■ **En association avec**: lovastatine (Advicor).
- **Niacinamide (version générique disponible)**
  Comprimés: 100 mg[VL], 500 mg[VL] ■ **Poudre orale**: 750 mg/1,25 mL[VL] ■ **En association avec**: autres vitamines.

SOINS INFIRMIERS

ÉVALUATION DE LA SITUATION

Carences en vitamines: Suivre de près le patient, avant le début du traitement et à intervalles réguliers pendant toute sa durée, à la recherche des signes suivants de carence en niacine: *pellagre* – dermatite, stomatite, glossite, anémie, nausées et vomissements, confusion, perte de la mémoire et délire.

Hyperlipidémie: Recueillir les antécédents alimentaires du patient, particulièrement en ce qui a trait à sa consommation de matières grasses.

Tests de laboratoire:

- Noter à intervalles réguliers, pendant un traitement prolongé à de fortes doses, les concentrations sériques de glucose et d'acide urique et les résultats des tests de la fonction hépatique. Prévenir le médecin ou un autre professionnel de la santé en cas d'élévation des concentrations d'AST, d'ALT ou de LDH. Le médicament peut allonger le temps de prothrombine et entraîner la diminution des concentrations sériques d'albumine.
- L'administration de fortes doses peut entraîner l'élévation des concentrations sériques de glucose et d'acide urique.
- Lorsque la niacine est administrée en tant qu'hypolipidémiant, noter, avant le traitement et à intervalles réguliers pendant toute sa durée, les concentrations sériques de cholestérol et de triglycérides.

DIAGNOSTICS INFIRMIERS POSSIBLES

- Alimentation déficiente (Indications).

- Connaissances insuffisantes sur le traitement médicamenteux (Enseignement au patient et à ses proches).
- Non-observance du traitement médicamenteux (Enseignement au patient et à ses proches).

INTERVENTIONS INFIRMIÈRES

- Étant donné qu'il est rare que le patient présente une carence en vitamine B seulement, on administre habituellement plusieurs vitamines en association.
- Administrer l'agent avec des aliments ou du lait pour réduire l'irritation gastro-intestinale.
- LES COMPRIMÉS ET LES CAPSULES À LIBÉRATION PROLONGÉE DOIVENT ÊTRE AVALÉS TELS QUELS SANS ÊTRE ÉCRASÉS, BRISÉS OU MÂCHÉS. Utiliser un récipient gradué pour mesurer avec précision les doses de préparation liquide.

ENSEIGNEMENT AU PATIENT ET À SES PROCHES

- Prévenir le patient qu'une rougeur de la peau et une sensation de chaleur, particulièrement au niveau du visage, du cou et des oreilles, des démangeaisons ou des picotements et des céphalées peuvent se manifester dans les 2 à 4 heures suivant la prise de ce médicament. Ces effets sont habituellement passagers et disparaissent si le traitement est poursuivi. Si la rougeur est gênante ou persistante, lui conseiller de prendre de l'aspirine, 30 minutes avant chaque dose. Afin de réduire ces rougeurs, on peut aussi majorer la dose de médicament moins rapidement.
- Recommander au patient de changer lentement de position pour diminuer le risque d'hypotension orthostatique.
- EXPLIQUER AU PATIENT PRENANT DES COMPRIMÉS DE NIACINE À LIBÉRATION PROLONGÉE QU'IL DOIT SIGNALER À UN PROFESSIONNEL DE LA SANTÉ LES SIGNES SUIVANTS D'HÉPATOTOXICITÉ: COULEUR PLUS FONCÉE DE L'URINE, SELLES DE COULEUR GRIS PÂLE, PERTE D'APPÉTIT, FORTES DOULEURS D'ESTOMAC, JAUNISSEMENT DES YEUX OU DE LA PEAU.
- Insister sur l'importance des examens de suivi permettant d'évaluer l'efficacité du traitement.

Carences en vitamines:

- Inciter le patient à respecter rigoureusement les recommandations du professionnel de la santé relatives à l'alimentation. Lui expliquer que la meilleure source de vitamines est une alimentation bien équilibrée comprenant les aliments des 4 principaux groupes alimentaires.
- Informer le patient que les aliments riches en niacine sont les viandes, les œufs, le lait et les produits laitiers; la perte de vitamines est faible lors d'une cuisson ordinaire.
- Prévenir le patient qui s'autoadministre des suppléments vitaminiques qu'il ne doit pas dépasser les apports quotidiens recommandés (voir l'annexe K). L'efficacité de fortes doses dans le traitement de diverses maladies n'a pas été prouvée et leur administration peut entraîner des effets secondaires.

Hyperlipidémie: Expliquer au patient qu'outre la prise de ce médicament, il doit se conformer à certaines restrictions alimentaires (matières grasses, cholestérol, glucides, alcool), faire de l'exercice et arrêter de fumer.

VÉRIFICATION DE L'EFFICACITÉ THÉRAPEUTIQUE

L'efficacité du traitement peut être démontrée par: la prévention et le traitement de la carence en niacine ■ la baisse des concentrations sériques de cholestérol et de triglycérides et l'élévation des concentrations sériques de cholestérol HDL. ✳

NICOTINAMIDE,
voir Niacine

NICOTINE

gomme à mâcher
Nicorette, Nicorette Plus

inhalateur
Nicorette Inhaler

timbre transdermique
Habitrol, Nicoderm, Nicotrol, Prostep

vaporisateur nasal
Ce médicament n'est pas commercialisé au Canada.

CLASSIFICATION:
Aide antitabagique

Grossesse – catégories C (gomme) et D (inhalateur, timbre transdermique)

INDICATIONS

Traitement d'appoint pour protéger le patient des effets psychopharmacologiques associés aux symptômes de sevrage lors de l'abandon de la cigarette, ou de l'abstinence temporaire.

MÉCANISME D'ACTION

Source de nicotine pendant le sevrage graduel de la cigarette. ***Effets thérapeutiques:*** Diminution des effets

N

accompagnant le sevrage nicotinique (irritabilité, insomnie, somnolence, céphalées et gain d'appétit).

PHARMACOCINÉTIQUE

Absorption: *Gomme à mâcher* – L'agent est lentement absorbé depuis la muqueuse buccale pendant la mastication. *Inhalateur* – une fraction de 50 % de la dose de 4 mg est absorbée par voie systémique; l'absorption par les muqueuses buccales est lente. Une grande partie de la nicotine libérée par l'inhalateur se dépose dans la bouche. *Timbre transdermique* – 68 % de la nicotine libérée par le timbre est absorbé par la peau (Nicoderm).

Distribution: L'agent passe dans le lait maternel.

Métabolisme et excrétion: Métabolisme majoritairement hépatique. Une faible quantité est métabolisée par les reins et les poumons. Excrétion rénale (de 10 à 20 % sous forme inchangée).

Demi-vie: De 1 à 2 heures.

Profil temps-action

	DÉBUT D'ACTION	PIC	DURÉE
gomme (Nicorette)	rapide	15 - 30 min	inconnue
inhalateur (Nicotrol)	lent	15 min après la fin de l'inhalation	inconnue
timbre transdermique (Nicoderm)	rapide	2 - 4 h	inconnue
timbre transdermique (Habitrol)	rapide	6 - 12 h	inconnue
timbre transdermique (Prostep)	rapide	9 h	inconnue

CONTRE-INDICATIONS, PRÉCAUTIONS ET MISES EN GARDE

Contre-indications: Maladie cardiovasculaire grave ■ Accident vasculaire cérébral récent ■ Atteinte de l'articulation temporomandibulaire (gomme à mâcher seulement) ■ Affection cutanée pouvant gêner l'utilisation du timbre ■ Grossesse, allaitement ■ **PÉD.**: Enfants (< 18 ans) ■ Usage concomitant de tabac ■ Non fumeurs ou fumeurs occasionnels ■ Hypersensibilité au menthol (inhalateur seulement).

Précautions et mises en garde: Maladie cardiovasculaire y compris l'hypertension ■ Diabète ■ Phéochromocytome ■ Maladies vasculaires périphériques ■ Problèmes dentaires (gomme seulement) ■ Antécédents de troubles nasaux chroniques (inhalateur seulement) ■ Œsophagite, pharyngite ou stomatite (gomme et inhalateur) ■ Hyperthyroïdie ■ Ulcère gastroduodénal ■ Maladie hépatique ■ Patients < 50 kg ou qui fument < 10 cigarettes par jour (utiliser une dose initiale plus faible).

RÉACTIONS INDÉSIRABLES ET EFFETS SECONDAIRES

SNC: céphalées, insomnie, rêves inhabituels, étourdissements, somnolence, manque de concentration, nervosité, faiblesse.

ORLO: *gomme* – sinusite; *inhalateur* – pharyngite, irritation locale de la bouche ou de la gorge.

Resp.: *inhalateur* – bronchospasme, toux accrue.

CV: tachycardie, fibrillation auriculaire, douleurs thoraciques, hypertension.

GI: douleurs abdominales, altération du goût, constipation, diarrhée, sécheresse de la bouche (xérostomie), dyspepsie, nausées, vomissements; *gomme* – éructations, gain d'appétit, salivation accrue, lésions buccales, douleurs dans la bouche, hoquet.

Tég.: *timbre transdermique* – sensation de brûlure au point d'application, érythème, prurit, hypersensibilité cutanée, rash, transpiration.

End.: dysménorrhée.

Loc.: arthralgie, douleurs lombaires, myalgie; *gomme* – douleurs des muscles de la mâchoire.

SN: paresthésie.

Divers: allergie, douleurs.

INTERACTIONS

Médicament-médicament: Les **hydrocarbures** et les **constituants de la fumée de cigarette** accélèrent le métabolisme de plusieurs médicaments et en diminuent les effets. Ces effets sont graduellement renversés lors du sevrage nicotinique ■ Lors du sevrage nicotinique, les besoins en **insuline** peuvent être diminués ■ Les effets de l'**acétaminophène**, du **furosémide**, de la **caféine**, de l'**imipramine**, de l'**oxazépam**, de la **pentazocine**, du **propranolol**, d'autres **bêtabloquants**, des **antagonistes adrénergiques** (**prazosine**, **labétalol**) et de la **théophylline** peuvent être accentués lors du sevrage nicotinique en raison du ralentissement du métabolisme; une réduction de la dose pendant le sevrage peut s'avérer nécessaire ■ Il peut s'avérer nécessaire d'augmenter les doses d'**isoprotérénol** ou de **phényléphrine** en raison des concentrations plus faibles de catécholamines circulantes pendant le sevrage nicotinique ■ Le traitement concomitant par le **bupropion** peut entraîner une hypertension artérielle maligne.

VOIES D'ADMINISTRATION ET POSOLOGIE

- **Timbre transdermique (adultes)**: *Habitrol* – 21 mg par jour, pendant 3 à 4 semaines, 14 mg par jour, pendant 3 à 8 semaines, puis 7 mg par jour, pendant 3 à 4 semaines (durée totale du traitement: de 7 à 12 semaines); le timbre doit être porté pendant 24 heures. *Nicoderm* – 21 mg par jour, pendant 6 semaines, 14 mg par jour, pendant 2 semaines, puis 7 mg par jour, pendant 2 semaines (durée totale du traitement: de 8 à 12 semaines); le timbre doit être porté pendant 24 heures. *Nicotrol* – 15 mg, 16 heures par jour, pendant 6 semaines, puis 10 mg, 16 heures par jour, pendant 2 semaines, puis 5 mg, 16 heures par jour, pendant 2 semaines (durée totale du traitement: 10 semaines); le timbre doit être retiré au coucher. *Prostep* – 22 mg par jour, pendant 4 à 8 semaines, et 11 mg, pendant 2 à 4 semaines (durée totale du traitement: de 6 à 12 semaines); le timbre doit être porté pendant 24 heures.

- **Timbre transdermique (adultes < 45 kg, ceux qui fument < 10 cigarettes par jour ou ceux qui souffrent d'une maladie cardiovasculaire sous-jacente)**: *Habitrol* – 14 mg par jour, pendant 4 à 8 semaines, puis 7 mg par jour, pendant 2 à 4 semaines (durée totale du traitement: de 7 à 12 semaines); le timbre doit être porté pendant 24 heures. *Nicoderm* – 14 mg par jour, pendant 6 semaines, puis 7 mg par jour, pendant 2 à 4 semaines. *Prostep* – 11 mg par jour, pendant 6 à 8 semaines.
- **Gomme (adultes)**: De 2 à 4 mg, selon les besoins; la dose est déterminée par l'intensité du besoin de fumer et par la vitesse de mastication, ou selon un horaire fixe, toutes les 1 ou 2 heures. Besoins initiaux habituels: 10 morceaux par jour (ne pas dépasser 20 morceaux par jour).
- **Inhalateur (adultes)**: Les patients doivent être encouragés à utiliser au moins 6 cartouches par jour pendant les 3 à 6 premières semaines de traitement. Des doses supplémentaires peuvent être nécessaires, soit jusqu'à 12 cartouches par jour pendant une durée pouvant aller jusqu'à 12 semaines. Une réduction graduelle de la dose doit être entreprise après 12 semaines de traitement initial et se poursuivre pendant au maximum 12 semaines de plus. Il faut inhaler le contenu de chaque cartouche fréquemment, à intervalles réguliers, jusqu'à ce qu'elle soit vide (20 minutes environ)

PRÉSENTATION

Gomme à mâcher (Nicorette): 2 mg^{VL}, 4 mg^{VL} ■ **Système d'inhalation (Nicorette)**: Trousse de départ incluant: un embout buccal et 30 cartouches^{VL} ■ **Timbre transdermique (Habitrol)**: 7 mg/jour^{VL}, 14 mg/jour^{VL}, 21 mg/jour^{VL} ■ **Timbre transdermique (Nicotrol)**: 5 mg/16 h^{VL}, 10 mg/16 h^{VL}, 15 mg/16 h^{VL} ■ **Timbre transdermique (Nicoderm)**: 7 mg/jour^{VL}, 14 mg/jour^{VL}, 21 mg/jour^{VL} ■ **Timbre transdermique (Prostep)**: 11 mg/jour^{VL}, 22 mg/jour^{VL}.

SOINS INFIRMIERS

ÉVALUATION DE LA SITUATION

- Noter, avant le traitement, les antécédents suivants de tabagisme: nombre de cigarettes fumées par jour, moment où le besoin de fumer se manifeste, teneur en nicotine de la marque de cigarette préférée, quantité de fumée inhalée.
- Évaluer à intervalles réguliers, pendant toute la durée du traitement, les symptômes de sevrage: irritabilité, somnolence, fatigue, céphalées, besoin impérieux de nicotine.
- Évaluer à intervalles réguliers pendant toute la durée du traitement les progrès réalisés sur le plan du sevrage à la nicotine.

Gomme: Noter les antécédents d'atteinte à l'articulation temporomandibulaire ou de dysfonctionnement de cette articulation.

Toxicité et surdosage: Suivre de près les nausées, les vomissements, la diarrhée, la salivation accrue, les douleurs abdominales, les céphalées, les étourdissements, les troubles auditifs ou visuels, la faiblesse, la dyspnée, l'hypotension et le pouls irrégulier.

DIAGNOSTICS INFIRMIERS POSSIBLES

- Stratégies d'adaptation inefficaces (Indications).
- Connaissances insuffisantes sur le traitement médicamenteux (Enseignement au patient et à ses proches).

INTERVENTIONS INFIRMIÈRES

Gomme: Conserver les gommes à l'abri de la lumière; l'exposition à la lumière les fait brunir.

Timbre transdermique: Déterminer si le timbre doit être porté pendant 16 ou 24 heures. Le timbre *Nicotrol* devrait être collé au lever et retiré au coucher.

ENSEIGNEMENT AU PATIENT ET À SES PROCHES

- Expliquer au patient qu'il doit absolument cesser de fumer dès le début du traitement et pendant toute sa durée.
- Encourager le patient à participer à un programme de renoncement au tabac pendant qu'il utilise ce produit.
- Lire avec le patient le mode d'emploi qui se trouve dans l'emballage.
- Expliquer au patient comment jeter ce produit. Insister sur le fait qu'il est important de le garder hors de la portée des enfants.

N

- Insister sur le fait qu'il est important de consulter régulièrement un professionnel de la santé qui pourra suivre les progrès enregistrés par le patient.

Gomme:

- Expliquer au patient le but de ce traitement d'appoint. Lui conseiller de mâcher une gomme chaque fois qu'il éprouve un besoin impérieux de fumer ou selon un horaire fixe (pendant la journée, toutes les 1 à 2 heures) en respectant les recommandations du professionnel de la santé. Lui recommander de mâcher la gomme lentement. Il doit mastiquer 1 ou 2 fois, puis garder la gomme entre la gencive et la joue jusqu'à ce que la sensation de picotement disparaisse (après 1 minute environ). Lui recommander de répéter ces deux opérations pendant environ 30 minutes. Expliquer au patient que s'il mâche rapidement et vigoureusement la gomme, des effets secondaires similaires à ceux provoqués par la consommation d'un nombre excessif de cigarettes peuvent se manifester: céphalées, étourdissements, nausées, salivation accrue, brûlures d'estomac et hoquet.
- Informer le patient que la gomme a un léger goût de tabac et de poivre. Le prévenir qu'au début, de nombreux patients trouvent que ce goût est désagréable et légèrement irritant pour la bouche, mais ces inconvénients disparaissent après plusieurs jours de traitement.
- Recommander au patient d'avoir de la gomme sur lui en tout temps pendant toute la durée du traitement.
- Recommander au patient de ne pas manger d'aliments ni boire de boissons acides (café, jus, vin, boissons gazeuses), 15 minutes avant de prendre une gomme de nicotine et pendant qu'il la mâche, pour ne pas entraver l'absorption de la nicotine par la muqueuse buccale.
- Les patients portant des prothèses dentaires peuvent habituellement mâcher cette gomme. Conseiller au patient de consulter le dentiste si la gomme adhère aux ponts.
- Expliquer au patient qu'il peut arrêter le traitement lorsque 1 ou 2 gommes par jour suffisent à satisfaire ses besoins en nicotine. Lui expliquer aussi que pour réduire graduellement la dose, en l'espace de 2 à 3 mois, il peut diminuer la dose quotidienne par une gomme ou plus, tous les 4 à 7 jours, réduire le temps de mâchage de chaque gomme de 30 minutes à entre 10 et 15 minutes, pendant 4 à 7 jours et, ensuite, diminuer le nombre de gommes utilisées. Il peut aussi mâcher 1 ou plusieurs gommes sans sucre au lieu de gommes de nicotine, et augmenter ce nombre tous les 4 à 7 jours, ou encore remplacer 1 dose de 4 mg par 1 de 2 mg. Lui expliquer qu'il peut mettre en pratique n'importe laquelle de ces solutions ou toutes à la fois. La durée du traitement ne devrait pas dépasser 6 mois, en raison de la dépendance physique et psychologique qu'il peut entraîner. L'arrêt prématuré du traitement peut entraîner les symptômes de sevrage suivants: anxiété, irritabilité, gêne gastro-intestinale, céphalées, somnolence ou besoin impérieux de tabac.
- Prévenir le patient qu'il ne doit pas avaler la gomme.
- Expliquer au patient qu'il doit envelopper la gomme avant de la jeter pour éviter tout risque d'ingestion par un enfant ou par un animal. Lui conseiller de communiquer immédiatement avec le centre antipoison, le service d'urgence ou un professionnel de la santé si un enfant a avalé la gomme.
- Insister sur le fait qu'il faut arrêter le traitement par la gomme et prévenir un professionnel de la santé en cas de grossesse.

Timbre transdermique:

- Expliquer au patient le mode d'emploi du timbre. Appliquer le timbre à la même heure tous les jours. Garder le timbre dans son sachet scellé jusqu'au moment de l'utilisation. Appliquer sur la partie supérieure du bras ou sur le torse; la surface de la peau doit être propre et sèche, sans poils, résidus d'huile, cicatrices, coupures, brûlures ou irritation. Presser fortement le timbre avec la paume de la main, pendant 10 secondes, particulièrement sur les bordures, afin d'assurer une bonne adhérence. On peut porter le timbre pendant la douche, le bain ou la baignade. Appliquer un nouveau timbre si le premier se détache ou tombe. Se laver les mains à l'eau après avoir manipulé le timbre; le savon augmente l'absorption de la nicotine. Il ne faut pas essayer de diminuer la dose, en coupant le timbre. Ne pas coller le timbre toujours au même endroit, mais plutôt alterner les endroits où on l'applique. Pour mettre au rebut le timbre, le plier pour coller ensemble les deux côtés de la surface adhésive et le replacer dans le sachet protecteur ou dans du papier d'aluminium; le garder hors de la portée des enfants.
- Expliquer au patient que les rougeurs, les démangeaisons et la sensation de brûlure de la peau disparaissent habituellement dans l'heure qui suit la pose du timbre. Si des signes de réactions allergiques (urticaire, rash généralisé) ou des réactions cutanées locales persistantes (érythème grave, prurit, œdème) se manifestent, recommander au patient de les signaler à un professionnel de la santé et de ne pas appliquer un nouveau timbre.

N

- Prévenir le patient que la nicotine peut parfois provoquer de la somnolence ou des étourdissements. Lui conseiller de ne pas conduire et d'éviter les activités qui exigent sa vigilance jusqu'à ce qu'on ait la certitude que le médicament n'entraîne pas ces effets chez lui.

VÉRIFICATION DE L'EFFICACITÉ THÉRAPEUTIQUE

L'efficacité du traitement peut être démontrée par: l'abandon de la cigarette ■ la diminution des symptômes de sevrage nicotinique chez les patients participant à un programme surveillé de renoncement au tabac. Le traitement par la gomme et l'inhalateur de nicotine ne doit pas se prolonger au-delà de 6 mois; chez la plupart des patients le sevrage devrait être graduel, après 3 mois de traitement. Si le patient est incapable de cesser de fumer après 4 semaines de traitement, il ne devrait plus utiliser le timbre transdermique ou l'inhalateur, car il est peu probable qu'il puisse cesser l'usage du tabac pendant cette cure. La durée du traitement par le timbre transdermique ne devrait pas dépasser 20 semaines.

NICOTINIQUE (ACIDE),
voir Niacine

NIFÉDIPINE

Adalat XL, Apo-Nifed, Apo-Nifed PA, Gen-Nifedipine, Gen-Nifedipine PA, Nu-Nifed, Nu-Nifedipine PA, PMS-Nifedipine

CLASSIFICATION:

Antiangineux, antihypertenseur (bloqueur des canaux calciques)

Grossesse – catégorie C

INDICATIONS

Traitement de: l'hypertension (comprimés à libération prolongée seulement) ■ l'angine de poitrine.

MÉCANISME D'ACTION

Inhibition de la pénétration des ions calcium dans les cellules du myocarde et des muscles lisses vasculaires, ce qui entraîne l'inhibition du couplage excitation-contraction et de la contraction suivante. ***Effets thérapeutiques:*** Vasodilatation systémique entraînant une chute de la pression artérielle ■ Vasodilatation coronarienne se traduisant par une diminution de la fréquence et de la gravité des crises d'angine.

PHARMACOCINÉTIQUE

Absorption: Bonne (PO), mais métabolisme de premier passage important; biodisponibilité de 45 à 70 % pour la préparation ordinaire et à 80 % pour les préparations à libération prolongée (formes PA et XL).

Distribution: L'agent traverse la barrière placentaire.

Liaison aux protéines: De 90 à 96 %.

Métabolisme et excrétion: Métabolisme hépatique. Excrétion sous forme de métabolites inactifs par les reins (de 60 à 80 %) et dans les fèces (20 %).

Demi-vie: De 2 à 5 heures.

Profil temps-action (effet sur la pression artérielle)

	DÉBUT D'ACTION	PIC	DURÉE
PO	20 min	inconnu	6 – 8 h
PO – PA	30 min	4 h	12 h
PO – XL	inconnu	6 h	24 h

CONTRE-INDICATIONS, PRÉCAUTIONS ET MISES EN GARDE

Contre-indications: Hypersensibilité ■ Collapsus cardiovasculaire ■ Pression artérielle < 90 mm Hg ■ Infarctus du myocarde (préparation à libération immédiate) ■ Grossesse et allaitement.

Précautions et mises en garde: Insuffisance hépatique grave (il est recommandé de réduire la dose) ■ **GÉR.:** Il est recommandé de réduire la dose chez les personnes âgées ou débilitées; risque accru d'hypotension ■ Insuffisance vasculaire cérébrale ■ Insuffisance cardiaque ■ **PÉD.:** L'innocuité du médicament n'a pas été établie chez les enfants ■ Rétrécissement gastro-intestinal (Adalat XL).

RÉACTIONS INDÉSIRABLES ET EFFETS SECONDAIRES

SNC: céphalées, rêves bizarres, anxiété, confusion, étourdissements, somnolence, agitation, nervosité, troubles psychiatriques, faiblesse.

ORLO: vision trouble, perte d'équilibre, épistaxis, acouphènes.

Resp.: toux, dyspnée, essoufflement.

CV: ARYTHMIES, INSUFFISANCE CARDIAQUE, œdème périphérique, bradycardie, douleurs thoraciques, hypotension, palpitations, syncope, tachycardie.

GI: résultats anormaux aux tests de la fonction hépatique, anorexie, constipation, diarrhée, sécheresse de la bouche (xérostomie), dysgueusie, dyspepsie, nausées, vomissements.

GU: dysurie, nycturie, polyurie, dysfonctionnement sexuel, mictions fréquentes.

Tég.: bouffées vasomotrices, dermatite, érythème polymorphe, sécrétion accrue de sueur, photosensibilité, prurit/urticaire, rash.

End.: gynécomastie, hyperglycémie.

Hémat.: anémie, leucopénie, thrombopénie.

Métab.: gain pondéral.

Loc.: rigidité des articulations, crampes musculaires.

SN: paresthésie, tremblements.

Divers: SYNDROME DE STEVENS-JOHNSON, hyperplasie gingivale.

INTERACTIONS

Médicament-médicament: Risque d'hypotension additive lors de l'administration concomitante de **fentanyl**, d'autres **antihypertenseurs**, de **dérivés nitrés** et de **quinidine** ou lors de la consommation de grandes quantités d'**alcool** ■ Les effets antihypertenseurs peuvent être réduits lors de l'usage concomitant d'**anti-inflammatoires non stéroïdiens** ■ La nifédipine peut élever les concentrations de **digoxine** et augmenter le risque de toxicité ■ Risque accru de bradycardie, d'anomalies de conduction ou d'insuffisance cardiaque lors de l'administration concomitante de **bêtabloquants**, de **digoxine**, de **disopyramide** ou de **phénytoïne** ■ La **cimétidine** et le **propranolol** peuvent ralentir le métabolisme de la nifédipine et augmenter le risque de toxicité ■ La nifédipine peut ralentir le métabolisme de la **cyclosporine**, de la **prazosine** ou de la **carbamazépine** et augmenter le risque de toxicité ■ La nifédipine peut entraîner une baisse des concentrations de **quinidine** ■ Les **médicaments qui inhibent le CYP3A4 (kétoconazole, itraconazole, fluconazole, cimétidine, cyclosporine, érythromycine, clarithromycine, fluoxétine, amprénavir, indinavir, nelfinavir, ritonavir, saquinavir, terfénadine**) peuvent élever les concentrations sanguines de la nifédipine ■ Les **médicaments qui induisent ce cytochrome** (**phénobarbital**, **phénytoïne**, **rifampine**) peuvent diminuer les concentrations sanguines de nifédipine.

Médicament-aliments: Le **jus de pamplemousse** élève les concentrations sanguines de nifédipine.

VOIES D'ADMINISTRATION ET POSOLOGIE

- **PO (adultes)**: *Capsules à libération immédiate – angine:* de 10 à 20 mg, 3 fois par jour (ne pas dépasser 120 mg par jour). *Comprimés à libération prolongée (PA) – hypertension:* de 10 à 20 mg, 2 fois par jour (ne pas dépasser 80 mg par jour). *Comprimés à libération prolongée (XL) – angine:* de 30 à 60 mg, 1 fois par jour (ne pas dépasser 90 mg par jour). *Hypertension:* de 20 à 30 mg, 1 fois par jour (ne pas dépasser 90 mg par jour).

PRÉSENTATION (version générique disponible)

Capsules: 5 mg[Pr], 10 mg[Pr] ■ **Comprimés à libération prolongée (PA ou 2 fois par jour)**: 10 mg[Pr], 20 mg[Pr] ■ **Comprimés à libération prolongée (XL ou 1 fois par jour)**: 20 mg[Pr], 30 mg[Pr], 60 mg[Pr].

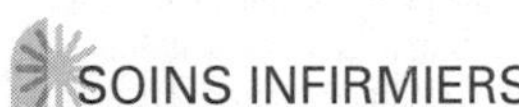

SOINS INFIRMIERS

ÉVALUATION DE LA SITUATION

- Mesurer la pression artérielle et le pouls avant l'administration initiale au cours de l'adaptation de la posologie et à intervalles réguliers pendant toute la durée du traitement. SUIVRE L'ÉCG À INTERVALLES RÉGULIERS PENDANT TOUTE LA DURÉE DU TRAITEMENT PROLONGÉ.
- Effectuer le bilan quotidien des ingesta et des excreta et peser le patient tous les jours. Rester à l'affût des signes d'insuffisance cardiaque (œdème périphérique, râles ou crépitations, dyspnée, gain pondéral, turgescence des jugulaires).

GÉR.: Évaluer le risque de chute et prendre les mesures permettant de les prévenir.

- Chez les patients recevant des dérivés digitaliques et la nifédipine en concomitance, noter régulièrement les concentrations sériques du dérivé digitalique et suivre de près les signes et les symptômes de toxicité digitalique.

Angine: Déterminer le siège, la durée et l'intensité de la douleur angineuse, ainsi que les facteurs qui la déclenchent.

Tests de laboratoire:

- Les concentrations totales de calcium sérique ne sont pas modifiées par les bloqueurs des canaux calciques.
- Noter à intervalles réguliers les concentrations sériques de potassium. L'hypokaliémie augmente le risque d'arythmies et devrait être traitée.
- Vérifier à intervalles réguliers les résultats des tests des fonctions hépatique et rénale chez les patients qui suivent un traitement prolongé. Après plusieurs jours de traitement, les concentrations d'enzymes hépatiques peuvent augmenter; elles reviennent à la normale après l'arrêt du traitement.

DIAGNOSTICS INFIRMIERS POSSIBLES

- Débit cardiaque diminué (Indications).
- Douleur aiguë (Indications).

- Connaissances insuffisantes sur le traitement médicamenteux (Enseignement au patient et à ses proches).

INTERVENTIONS INFIRMIÈRES

- NE PAS CONFONDRE LA NIFÉDIPINE AVEC LA NIMODIPINE.
- La nifédipine peut être administrée sans égard aux repas. On peut l'administrer avec des aliments si l'irritation gastrique devient gênante.
- IL NE FAUT PAS OUVRIR, ÉCRASER, BRISER OU MÂCHER LES PRÉPARATIONS À LIBÉRATION PROLONGÉE. Il ne faut pas s'inquiéter des capsules vides qui se retrouvent dans les selles.
- Ne pas servir au patient du jus de pamplemousse et la nifédipine en concomitance.

ENSEIGNEMENT AU PATIENT ET À SES PROCHES

- Conseiller au patient de suivre rigoureusement la posologie recommandée même s'il se sent bien. S'il n'a pu prendre le médicament au moment habituel, il doit le prendre aussitôt que possible, à moins que ce ne soit presque l'heure prévue pour la dose suivante. Le prévenir qu'il ne doit jamais remplacer une dose manquée par une double dose. Avant d'arrêter complètement le traitement à la nifédipine, il faudrait probablement en diminuer les doses graduellement.
- Recommander au patient de changer lentement de position pour réduire le risque d'hypotension orthostatique.
- Prévenir le patient que la nifédipine peut parfois provoquer des étourdissements.

GÉR.: Mettre en garde le patient et ses proches contre le risque de chute et leur enseigner les mesures préventives afin d'en réduire le risque à domicile.

- Expliquer au patient qu'il est important de pratiquer une bonne hygiène dentaire et de consulter fréquemment le dentiste pour se faire nettoyer les dents afin de prévenir la sensibilité, le saignement ou l'hyperplasie des gencives.
- Conseiller au patient de ne pas boire d'alcool et de consulter un professionnel de la santé avant de prendre des médicaments en vente libre, surtout des préparations contre le rhume, ou des produits naturels en même temps que la nifédipine.
- Recommander au patient de communiquer avec un professionnel de la santé si les symptômes suivants se manifestent: battements cardiaques irréguliers, dyspnée, enflure des mains et des pieds, étourdissements prononcés, nausées, constipation, hypotension ou céphalées graves ou persistantes.
- Recommander au patient d'utiliser un écran solaire et de porter des vêtements protecteurs afin de prévenir les réactions de photosensibilité.

Angine:

- Inciter le patient qui suit simultanément un traitement par un dérivé nitré ou par un bêtabloquant à continuer de prendre les 2 médicaments selon les recommandations du médecin et à prendre de la nitroglycérine sublinguale, selon les besoins, en cas de crise d'angine.
- Recommander au patient de prévenir un professionnel de la santé si les douleurs thoraciques ne sont pas soulagées par le traitement, si elles s'aggravent ou si elles s'accompagnent de diaphorèse, ou encore s'il souffre d'essoufflements ou de céphalées persistantes.
- Conseiller au patient de s'informer auprès d'un professionnel de la santé des restrictions à respecter sur le plan de l'effort avant de s'engager dans un programme d'exercices.

Hypertension:

- Encourager le patient à appliquer les autres mesures permettant de maîtriser l'hypertension: perdre du poids, suivre un régime hyposodé, cesser de fumer, consommer de l'alcool avec modération, faire régulièrement de l'exercice, gérer le stress. Le prévenir que ce médicament stabilise la pression artérielle, mais ne guérit pas l'hypertension.
- Montrer au patient et à ses proches comment prendre la pression artérielle. Leur recommander de la mesurer toutes les semaines et de signaler tout changement important à un professionnel de la santé.

VÉRIFICATION DE L'EFFICACITÉ THÉRAPEUTIQUE

L'efficacité du traitement peut être démontrée par: une baisse de la pression artérielle ■ une diminution de la fréquence et de la gravité des crises d'angine ■ un moindre recours à des dérivés nitrés ■ une meilleure tolérance à l'effort et un sentiment de mieux-être.

NILUTAMIDE

Anandron

CLASSIFICATION:

Antinéoplasique (hormone de synthèse), antiandrogène non stéroïdien

Grossesse – catégorie C

INDICATIONS

Traitement du cancer métastatique de la prostate de stade D_2 (en association avec la castration chirurgicale).

MÉCANISME D'ACTION

Inhibition des effets des hormones androgènes (testostérone) au niveau cellulaire. ***Effets thérapeutiques:*** Ralentissement de la propagation du cancer de la prostate.

PHARMACOCINÉTIQUE

Absorption: Rapide et entière (PO).

Distribution: Inconnue.

Métabolisme et excrétion: Métabolisme principalement hépatique; 1 métabolite possède une certaine activité antiandrogène. Très faible excrétion rénale (< 2 % sous forme inchangée).

Demi-vie: De 23 à 87 heures.

Profil temps-action (effet antiandrogène)

	DÉBUT D'ACTION	PIC	DURÉE
PO	rapide	inconnu	24 - 72 h

CONTRE-INDICATIONS, PRÉCAUTIONS ET MISES EN GARDE

N

Contre-indications: Hypersensibilité ▪ Insuffisance hépatique grave ▪ Insuffisance respiratoire grave ▪ Femmes et enfants (l'innocuité de l'agent n'a pas été établie).

Précautions et mises en garde: Antécédents de maladie hépatique ou d'alcoolisme ▪ Antécédents de problèmes respiratoires.

RÉACTIONS INDÉSIRABLES ET EFFETS SECONDAIRES

SNC: étourdissements.

ORLO: difficultés d'adaptation à l'obscurité, vision anormale.

Resp.: pneumonie interstitielle.

CV: hypertension.

GI: HÉPATOTOXICITÉ, constipation, hépatite, élévation des concentrations d'enzymes hépatiques, nausées.

Tég.: bouffées de chaleur, alopécie, transpiration, réaction de type disulfirame.

INTERACTIONS

Médicament-médicament: Le nilutamide peut accentuer les effets de la **warfarine**, de la **phénytoïne**, du **propranolol**, du **chlordiazépoxide**, de la **lidocaïne**, du **diazépam** et de la **théophylline** ▪ Le nilutamide peut entraîner une intolérance à l'**alcool**.

VOIES D'ADMINISTRATION ET POSOLOGIE

- **PO (adultes):** 300 mg, 1 fois par jour (avant le petit-déjeuner), pendant 30 jours, puis 150 mg, 1 fois par jour.

PRÉSENTATION

Comprimés: 50 mg[Pr].

SOINS INFIRMIERS

ÉVALUATION DE LA SITUATION

- Le patient devrait se soumettre à une radiographie thoracique avant le début du traitement. Suivre l'état du patient à la recherche des symptômes suivants de pneumonie interstitielle: dyspnée, aggravation d'une dyspnée préexistante. Si ces symptômes se manifestent, on devrait cesser l'administration de nilutamide jusqu'à ce que la cause en soit déterminée. La pneumonie interstitielle survient habituellement au cours des 3 premiers mois de traitement et elle est presque toujours réversible si le traitement est interrompu.

Tests de laboratoire:

- VÉRIFIER LES RÉSULTATS DES TESTS DE LA FONCTION HÉPATIQUE, AVANT LE TRAITEMENT ET TOUS LES 3 MOIS PENDANT TOUTE SA DURÉE. SI LES CONCENTRATIONS D'AST OU D'ALT SONT SUPÉRIEURES À 2 OU 3 FOIS LES VALEURS NORMALES, ON DEVRAIT INTERROMPRE LE TRAITEMENT.
- Le nilutamide peut entraîner l'hyperglycémie, une élévation des concentrations sériques de phosphatase alcaline, d'urée et de créatinine et la leucopénie.

DIAGNOSTICS INFIRMIERS POSSIBLES

- Risque d'accident (Effets secondaires).
- Connaissances insuffisantes sur le traitement médicamenteux (Enseignement au patient et à ses proches).

INTERVENTIONS INFIRMIÈRES

- Le médicament doit être pris avant le petit-déjeuner.

ENSEIGNEMENT AU PATIENT ET À SES PROCHES

- Conseiller au patient de suivre rigoureusement la posologie recommandée. S'il n'a pu prendre le nilutamide au moment habituel, il doit le prendre aussitôt que possible, à moins que ce ne soit presque l'heure prévue pour la dose suivante. Le prévenir qu'il ne doit pas remplacer une dose manquée par une double dose.

- Prévenir le patient qu'il risque de connaître des problèmes d'adaptation à l'obscurité, d'où la difficulté de conduire la nuit ou de traverser des tunnels. Lui conseiller de porter des lunettes teintées pour minimiser cet effet.
- RECOMMANDER AU PATIENT DE SIGNALER IMMÉDIATEMENT AU MÉDECIN LES SIGNES ET LES SYMPTÔMES SUIVANTS : URINE FONCÉE, FATIGUE, DOULEURS ABDOMINALES, COLORATION JAUNE DES YEUX OU DE LA PEAU OU SYMPTÔMES GASTRO-INTESTINAUX INEXPLIQUÉS. L'HÉPATOTOXICITÉ DISPARAÎT HABITUELLEMENT LORS DE L'ARRÊT DU TRAITEMENT PAR LE NILUTAMIDE. TOUTEFOIS, ELLE PEUT S'AGGRAVER GRADUELLEMENT ET ÊTRE D'ISSUE FATALE, DICTANT UNE ATTENTION MÉDICALE IMMÉDIATE.

VÉRIFICATION DE L'EFFICACITÉ THÉRAPEUTIQUE

L'efficacité du traitement peut être démontrée par: le ralentissement de la propagation du cancer de la prostate. ✳

NIMODIPINE

Nimotop

CLASSIFICATION:

Bloqueur des canaux calciques: traitement d'appoint de l'hémorragie sous-arachnoïdienne

Grossesse – catégorie C

INDICATIONS

Traitement d'appoint de l'hémorragie sous-arachnoïdienne.

MÉCANISME D'ACTION

Inhibition de la pénétration des ions calcium dans les cellules des muscles lisses vasculaires, ce qui entraîne l'inhibition du couplage excitation-contraction et de la contraction suivante ▪ Vasodilatateur périphérique puissant. ***Effets thérapeutiques:*** Prévention des spasmes vasculaires après une hémorragie sous-arachnoïdienne, ce qui entraîne moins de troubles neurologiques.

PHARMACOCINÉTIQUE

Absorption: Bonne (PO), mais biodisponibilité faible à la suite d'un métabolisme hépatique important.

Distribution: La nimodipine traverse la barrière hémato-encéphalique; pour le reste, la distribution est inconnue.

Liaison aux protéines: > 95 %.

Métabolisme et excrétion: Métabolisme majoritairement hépatique; faible excrétion rénale (≤ 10 % sous forme inchangée).

Demi-vie: De 1 à 2 heures.

Profil temps-action (vasodilatation)

	DÉBUT D'ACTION	PIC	DURÉE
PO	inconnu	1 h	4 h

CONTRE-INDICATIONS, PRÉCAUTIONS ET MISES EN GARDE

Contre-indications: Hypersensibilité.

Précautions et mises en garde: Syndrome de dysfonctionnement sinusal ▪ Bloc AV du 2ᵉ et du 3ᵉ degré (sauf si le patient est porteur d'un stimulateur cardiaque) ▪ Pression artérielle < 90 mm Hg ▪ Insuffisance hépatique grave (il est recommandé de réduire la dose) ▪ Personnes âgées (il est recommandé de réduire la dose; risque accru d'hypotension) ▪ Insuffisance rénale grave ▪ Œdème cérébral ou forte élévation de la pression intracrânienne ▪ Infarctus du myocarde ou angine de poitrine instable ▪ Antécédents d'arythmies ventriculaires graves ou d'insuffisance cardiaque ▪ **OBST., ALLAITEMENT, PÉD.:** L'innocuité du médicament n'a pas été établie.

N

RÉACTIONS INDÉSIRABLES ET EFFETS SECONDAIRES

SNC: rêves bizarres, anxiété, confusion, étourdissements, somnolence, céphalées, nervosité, troubles psychiatriques, faiblesse.

ORLO: vision trouble, perte d'équilibre, épistaxis, acouphènes.

Resp.: toux, dyspnée.

CV: ARYTHMIES, INSUFFISANCE CARDIAQUE, bradycardie, douleurs thoraciques, hypotension, palpitations, œdème périphérique, syncope, tachycardie.

GI: résultats anormaux aux tests de la fonction hépatique, anorexie, constipation, diarrhée, sécheresse de la bouche (xérostomie), dysgueusie, dyspepsie, nausées, vomissements.

GU: dysurie, nycturie, polyurie, dysfonctionnement sexuel, mictions fréquentes.

Tég.: dermatite, érythème polymorphe, bouffées vasomotrices, sécrétion accrue de sueur, photosensibilité, prurit et urticaire, rash.

End.: gynécomastie, hyperglycémie.

Hémat.: anémie, leucopénie, thrombopénie.

Métab.: gain pondéral.

Loc.: rigidité des articulations, crampes musculaires.

SN: paresthésie, tremblements.

Divers: SYNDROME DE STEVENS-JOHNSON, hyperplasie gingivale.

INTERACTIONS

Médicament-médicament: La nimodipine est métabolisée par le cytochrome P450 3A4. Les **médicaments métabolisés par le CYP450-3A4, ou inducteurs ou inhibiteurs de ce cytochrome** risquent d'interagir avec la nimodipine ■ Risque d'hypotension additive lors de l'administration concomitante de **fentanyl**, d'autres **antihypertenseurs**, de **dérivés nitrés** et de **quinidine** ou lors de la consommation de grandes quantités d'**alcool** ■ Risque accru de bradycardie, d'anomalies de conduction ou d'insuffisance cardiaque lors de l'administration concomitante de **bêtabloquants**, de **digoxine**, de **disopyramide** ou de **phénytoïne**.

Médicament-aliments: Le **jus de pamplemousse** augmente les concentrations plasmatiques et l'effet de la nimodipine.

VOIES D'ADMINISTRATION ET POSOLOGIE

- **PO (adultes)**: 60 mg, toutes les 4 heures, pendant 21 jours; le traitement devrait être amorcé dans les 96 heures qui suivent l'hémorragie sous-arachnoïdienne.
- ***INSUFFISANCE HÉPATIQUE***

  PO (ADULTES): 30 mg, TOUTES LES 4 HEURES, PENDANT 21 JOURS; LE TRAITEMENT DEVRAIT ÊTRE AMORCÉ DANS LES 96 HEURES QUI SUIVENT L'HÉMORRAGIE SOUS-ARACHNOÏDIENNE.

PRÉSENTATION

Capsules: 30 mg^{Pr}.

SOINS INFIRMIERS

ÉVALUATION DE LA SITUATION

- Évaluer l'état neurologique du patient (état de conscience, mouvements) avant le traitement et à intervalles réguliers pendant toute sa durée.
- Mesurer la pression artérielle et le pouls avant l'administration initiale et à intervalles réguliers pendant toute la durée du traitement.
- EFFECTUER LE BILAN QUOTIDIEN DES INGESTA ET DES EXCRETA ET PESER LE PATIENT TOUS LES JOURS. RESTER À L'AFFÛT DES SIGNES D'INSUFFISANCE CARDIAQUE (ŒDÈME PÉRIPHÉRIQUE, RÂLES OU CRÉPITATIONS, DYSPNÉE, GAIN PONDÉRAL, TURGESCENCE DES JUGULAIRES).

Tests de laboratoire:

- Les concentrations totales de calcium sérique ne sont pas modifiées par les bloqueurs des canaux calciques.
- Noter à intervalles réguliers les concentrations sériques de potassium. L'hypokaliémie augmente le risque d'arythmies et devrait être traitée.
- Examiner à intervalles réguliers les résultats des tests des fonctions hépatique et rénale. Après plusieurs jours de traitement, les concentrations d'enzymes hépatiques peuvent augmenter; elles reviennent à la normale après l'arrêt du traitement.
- La nimodipine peut parfois entraîner une diminution du nombre de plaquettes.

DIAGNOSTICS INFIRMIERS POSSIBLES

- Irrigation tissulaire inefficace (Indications).
- Connaissances insuffisantes sur le traitement médicamenteux (Enseignement au patient et à ses proches).

INTERVENTIONS INFIRMIÈRES

- NE PAS CONFONDRE LA NIMODIPINE AVEC LA NICARDIPINE OU LA NIFÉDIPINE.
- Amorcer le traitement dans les 96 heures qui suivent une hémorragie sous-arachnoïdienne et poursuivre l'administration toutes les 4 heures pendant 21 jours consécutifs.
- Si le patient ne peut avaler la capsule, on peut en perforer les deux extrémités à l'aide d'une aiguille stérile de calibre 18 et en aspirer le contenu dans une seringue. Verser ensuite dans de l'eau ou dans une sonde nasogastrique et rincer avec 30 mL de soluté physiologique.

ENSEIGNEMENT AU PATIENT ET À SES PROCHES

- Conseiller au patient de suivre rigoureusement la posologie recommandée même s'il se sent bien. S'il n'a pu prendre le médicament au moment habituel, il doit le prendre aussitôt que possible, à moins que ce ne soit presque l'heure prévue pour la dose suivante. Le prévenir qu'il ne doit jamais remplacer une dose manquée par une double dose. Recommander au patient de changer lentement de position pour réduire le risque d'hypotension orthostatique.
- Prévenir le patient que la nimodipine peut parfois provoquer de la somnolence ou des étourdissements. Lui conseiller de ne pas conduire et d'éviter les activités qui exigent sa vigilance jusqu'à ce qu'on ait la certitude que le médicament n'entraîne pas ces effets chez lui.
- Conseiller au patient de ne pas boire d'alcool et de consulter un professionnel de la santé avant de prendre des médicaments en vente libre, surtout des préparations contre le rhume, en même temps que la nimodipine.

N

- RECOMMANDER AU PATIENT DE COMMUNIQUER AVEC UN PROFESSIONNEL DE LA SANTÉ SI LES SYMPTÔMES SUIVANTS SE MANIFESTENT : BATTEMENTS CARDIAQUES IRRÉGULIERS, DYSPNÉE, ENFLURE DES MAINS ET DES PIEDS, ÉTOURDISSEMENTS PRONONCÉS, NAUSÉES, CONSTIPATION, HYPOTENSION OU CÉPHALÉES GRAVES OU PERSISTANTES.
- Recommander au patient d'utiliser un écran solaire et de porter des vêtements protecteurs afin de prévenir les réactions de photosensibilité.

VÉRIFICATION DE L'EFFICACITÉ THÉRAPEUTIQUE

L'efficacité du traitement peut être démontrée par : une amélioration des troubles neurologiques attribuables au vasospasme qui suit une hémorragie sous-arachnoïdienne. ✳

NITROFURANTOÏNE

Apo-Nitrofurantoin, Macrobid, Macrodantin, Novo-Furantoin

CLASSIFICATION :

Anti-infectieux (antibactérien des voies urinaires)

Grossesse – catégorie B

INDICATIONS

Traitement des infections urinaires aiguës non compliquées dues à des microorganismes sensibles. La nitrofurantoïne n'est pas efficace dans le traitement des infections bactériennes systémiques ■ **Usages non approuvés :** Traitement suppressif de longue durée des infections des voies urinaires.

MÉCANISME D'ACTION

Inhibition des enzymes bactériennes. ***Effets thérapeutiques :*** Action bactéricide ou bactériostatique contre les microorganismes sensibles. **Spectre d'action :** Cet agent agit contre de nombreux microorganismes à Gram négatif et contre certains microorganismes à Gram positif, notamment : *Citrobacter* ■ *Corynebacterium* ■ *Enterobacter* ■ *Escherichia coli* ■ *Klebsiella* ■ *Neisseria* ■ *Salmonella* ■ *Shigella* ■ *Staphylococcus aureus* ■ *Staphylococcus epidermitis* ■ *Enterococcus*.

PHARMACOCINÉTIQUE

Absorption : Rapide (PO) ; plus lente, mais plus complète lors de l'administration de la préparation contenant des macrocristaux (Macrodantin).

Distribution : L'agent traverse la barrière placentaire et passe dans le lait maternel.

Métabolisme et excrétion : Métabolisme partiellement hépatique. Excrétion rénale sous forme inchangée (de 30 à 50 %).

Demi-vie : 20 minutes (prolongée en cas d'insuffisance rénale).

Profil temps-action (concentrations urinaires)

	DÉBUT D'ACTION	PIC	DURÉE
PO	inconnu	30 min	6 - 12 h

CONTRE-INDICATIONS, PRÉCAUTIONS ET MISES EN GARDE

Contre-indications : Hypersensibilité ■ Oligurie, anurie ou insuffisance rénale avec une clairance de la créatinine < 60 mL/min ■ **OBST., PÉD. :** Nouveau-nés < 1 mois et grossesse près du terme (risque accru d'anémie hémolytique chez le nouveau-né).

Précautions et mises en garde : Anémie, diabète, déséquilibre électrolytique, carence en vitamine B et maladie débilitante (risque accru de neuropathie) ■ Carence en glucose-6-phosphate-déshydrogénase (G-6-PD) (risque d'anémie hémolytique) ■ **GÉR. :** Les personnes âgées sont exposées à un risque accru de réactions pulmonaires, hépatiques et rénales ■ **OBST. :** Grossesse et allaitement (antécédents d'utilisation sans danger pendant la grossesse même si l'innocuité du médicament n'a pas été établie ; l'allaitement peut entraîner l'hémolyse chez les nourrissons présentant une carence en G-6-PD).

RÉACTIONS INDÉSIRABLES ET EFFETS SECONDAIRES

SNC : étourdissements, somnolence, céphalées.
ORLO : nystagmus.
Resp. : pneumopathie inflammatoire.
CV : douleurs thoraciques.
GI : COLITE PSEUDOMEMBRANEUSE, anorexie, nausées, vomissements, douleurs abdominales, diarrhée, hépatite médicamenteuse.
GU : urine de couleur rouille ou brune.
Tég. : photosensibilité.
Hémat. : dyscrasie sanguine, anémie hémolytique.
SN : neuropathie périphérique, dont la névrite optique.
Divers : réactions d'hypersensibilité.

INTERACTIONS

Médicament-médicament : Les **médicaments uricosuriques**, tels que le **probénécide** et la **sulfinpyrazone**, peuvent inhiber la sécrétion rénale tubulaire de la nitrofurantoïne. L'augmentation des concentrations sériques qui en découle peut accroître la toxicité, et la baisse

N

des concentrations urinaires peut amoindrir l'efficacité du médicament ■ Les **antiacides** peuvent réduire l'absorption de la nitrofurantoïne ■ Risque accru de neurotoxicité lors de l'administration de **médicaments neurotoxiques** ■ Risque accru d'hépatotoxicité lors de l'administration de **médicaments hépatotoxiques** ■ Risque accru de pneumopathie inflammatoire lors de l'administration de **médicaments entraînant une toxicité pulmonaire** ■ Ne pas administrer avec des **médicaments pouvant causer une insuffisance rénale**.

VOIES D'ADMINISTRATION ET POSOLOGIE

- **PO (adultes et enfants > 12 ans)**: *Infection active* – de 50 à 100 mg, 4 fois par jour, *ou* 100 mg, toutes les 12 heures (sous forme de préparation à libération prolongée). *Traitement suppressif de longue durée (usage non approuvé)* – de 50 à 100 mg, en une seule dose, le soir.
- **PO (enfants > 1 mois)**: *Infection active* – de 5 à 7 mg/kg/jour, administré en 4 doses fractionnées. *Traitement suppressif de longue durée (usage non approuvé)* – 1 mg/kg/jour, en une seule dose ou en 2 doses fractionnées.

PRÉSENTATION
(version générique disponible)

Comprimés: 50 mg[Pr], 100 mg[Pr] ■ **Capsules**: 50 mg[Pr], 100 mg[Pr] ■ **Capsules à libération prolongée**: 100 mg[Pr].

SOINS INFIRMIERS

ÉVALUATION DE LA SITUATION

- Avant le traitement et à intervalles réguliers pendant toute sa durée, suivre de près les signes et les symptômes suivants d'infection urinaire: mictions fréquentes, besoin impérieux d'uriner, mictions qui s'accompagnent de douleurs ou de brûlures, fièvre, urine trouble ou nauséabonde.
- Prélever des échantillons pour la mise en cultures et les antibiogrammes avant l'administration du médicament et pendant toute la durée du traitement.
- Effectuer le bilan des ingesta et des excreta. Signaler tout écart important.
- L'administration de nitrofurantoïne peut entraîner des réactions pulmonaires d'hypersensibilité, chroniques, subaiguës ou aiguës. Les réactions pulmonaires chroniques se produisent généralement chez les patients ayant reçu un traitement de 6 mois ou plus. Malaise, dyspnée d'effort, toux et altération de la fonction pulmonaire sont des manifestations courantes qui peuvent se produire insidieusement. La présence de pneumonie ou de fibrose interstitielle diffuse, ou des deux, constatée à l'examen radiologique et histologique, est également une manifestation courante de la réaction pulmonaire chronique. La fièvre est rarement élevée. La gravité des réactions pulmonaires chroniques et le degré de la résolution semblent être rattachés à la durée du traitement après l'apparition des premiers signes cliniques. La fonction pulmonaire peut être altérée de façon permanente, même après l'arrêt du traitement à la nitrofurantoïne. Le risque est accru lorsque les réactions pulmonaires ne sont pas dépistées au stade précoce. Dans les réactions pulmonaires subaiguës, la fièvre et l'éosinophilie s'observent moins fréquemment que dans la forme aiguë. Le rétablissement après l'arrêt du traitement peut demander plusieurs mois. Si les symptômes ne sont pas associés à la prise du médicament et que l'administration de nitrofurantoïne n'est pas interrompue, ces symptômes sont susceptibles de s'aggraver. Les réactions aiguës fréquentes sont les suivantes: fièvre, frissons, toux, douleurs thoraciques, dyspnée, infiltrations pulmonaires avec consolidation ou épanchement pleural décelé par rayons X, et éosinophilie. Les réactions aiguës se produisent généralement durant la première semaine de traitement et sont réversibles lorsqu'il est interrompu.

Tests de laboratoire:

- Suivre de près la numération globulaire chez les patients soumis à un traitement de longue durée.
- La nitrofurantoïne peut entraîner l'élévation de la glycémie et des concentrations sériques de bilirubine, de phosphatase alcaline, d'urée et de créatinine.

DIAGNOSTICS INFIRMIERS POSSIBLES

- Risque d'infection (Indications).
- Connaissances insuffisantes sur le traitement médicamenteux (Enseignement au patient et à ses proches).

INTERVENTIONS INFIRMIÈRES

- Administrer la nitrofurantoïne avec des aliments ou du lait pour réduire l'irritation gastro-intestinale, pour retarder et intensifier l'absorption, pour augmenter les concentrations maximales et pour prolonger la durée des concentrations thérapeutiques dans l'urine.
- Ne pas écraser les comprimés; ne pas ouvrir les capsules à libération prolongée.

ENSEIGNEMENT AU PATIENT ET À SES PROCHES

- Prévenir le patient qu'il doit prendre le médicament à intervalles réguliers, exactement comme il lui a été prescrit. S'il n'a pas pu le prendre au moment habituel, il doit le faire dès que possible et prendre la dose suivante en l'espaçant de 2 à 4 heures. Lui recommander de ne pas sauter de dose ni de remplacer une dose manquée par une double dose.

- Prévenir le patient que la nitrofurantoïne peut parfois provoquer des étourdissements et de la somnolence. Lui conseiller de ne pas conduire et d'éviter les activités qui exigent sa vigilance jusqu'à ce qu'on ait la certitude que le médicament n'entraîne pas ces effets chez lui.
- Prévenir le patient que son urine peut virer au jaune rouille ou au brun, mais que ce changement de couleur n'a aucun effet sur le plan clinique.
- Conseiller au patient de prévenir un professionnel de la santé si les symptômes suivants se manifestent: fièvre, frissons, toux, douleurs thoraciques, dyspnée, rash, engourdissements ou picotements au niveau des doigts et des orteils ou gêne gastro-intestinale intolérable. Recommander au patient d'informer également un professionnel de la santé si les signes suivants de surinfection se manifestent: urine laiteuse et nauséabonde, irritation périnéale, dysurie.
- CONSEILLER AU PATIENT DE PRÉVENIR UN PROFESSIONNEL DE LA SANTÉ EN CAS DE FIÈVRE OU DE DIARRHÉE, PARTICULIÈREMENT SI SES SELLES CONTIENNENT DU SANG, DU PUS OU DU MUCUS. LE PRÉVENIR QU'IL NE DOIT RIEN PRENDRE POUR TRAITER LA DIARRHÉE AVANT D'AVOIR CONSULTÉ UN PROFESSIONNEL DE LA SANTÉ.
- Inciter le patient à prévenir un professionnel de la santé s'il ne note aucune amélioration quelques jours après le début du traitement.

VÉRIFICATION DE L'EFFICACITÉ THÉRAPEUTIQUE

L'efficacité du traitement peut être démontrée par: la disparition des signes et des symptômes d'infection; le traitement doit être maintenu pendant un minimum de 7 jours et pendant au moins 3 jours de plus après que l'urine est devenue stérile ■ la diminution de la fréquence des infections lors d'un traitement suppressif prolongé. ✳

NITROGLYCÉRINE

comprimés sublingaux
Nitrostat

pommade
Nitrol

pulvérisateur lingual
Gen-Nitro SL, Nitrolingual, Rho-Nitro

solution intraveineuse
Nitroject, Tridil

timbre transdermique
Minitran, Nitro-Dur, Transderm-Nitro, Trinipatch

CLASSIFICATION:
Antiangineux (dérivé nitré et nitrate), vasodilatateur coronarien

Grossesse – catégorie B

INDICATIONS

Vaporisateur lingual, comprimés sublinguaux: Traitement de courte durée et prophylaxie de l'angine de poitrine ■ **Pommade, timbre transdermique**: Traitement prophylactique prolongé de l'angine de poitrine ■ **IV**: Traitement d'appoint de l'infarctus aigu du myocarde ■ Traitement de l'angine de poitrine chez les patients qui ne répondent pas aux traitements classiques ■ Induction d'une hypotension contrôlée pendant une intervention chirurgicale ■ Agent hypotenseur lors d'une crise hypertensive. **Usages non approuvés**: Traitement de l'insuffisance cardiaque lorsque les traitement habituels sont inefficaces ou contre-indiqués.

N

MÉCANISME D'ACTION

Augmentation du débit coronarien par dilatation des artères coronaires et par amélioration de l'irrigation des territoires ischémiés par la circulation collatérale ■ Vasodilatation (la vasodilatation veineuse est plus importante que la vasodilatation artérielle) ■ Diminution de la pression et du volume télédiastoliques du ventricule gauche (précharge) ■ Réduction de la consommation d'oxygène par le myocarde. ***Effets thérapeutiques:*** Soulagement ou prévention des crises d'angine ■ Élévation du débit cardiaque ■ Diminution de la pression artérielle.

PHARMACOCINÉTIQUE

Absorption: Bonne (PO, transcutanée, transmuqueuse et sublinguale).

Distribution: Inconnue.

Métabolisme et excrétion: Métabolisme hépatique rapide et presque complet. On observe également un métabolisme par les enzymes du sang.

Demi-vie: De 1 à 4 minutes.

Profil temps-action (effets cardiovasculaires)

	DÉBUT D'ACTION	PIC	DURÉE
Vaporisation linguale	2 - 4 min	4 - 10 min	10 - 30 min
Comprimés sublinguaux	1 - 3 min	4 - 8 min	10 - 30 min
Pommade (transdermique)	20 - 60 min	30 - 120 min	4 - 8 h
Timbre transdermique	40 - 60 min	1 - 3 h	jusqu'à 24 h†
IV	immédiat	inconnu	plusieurs minutes

† L'effet se maintient tant et si longtemps que le timbre reste en place, pendant un laps de temps allant jusqu'à 24 heures. Après le retrait du timbre, la concentration sérique diminue et atteint des taux indétectables en moins de 2 heures.

CONTRE-INDICATIONS, PRÉCAUTIONS ET MISES EN GARDE

Contre-indications: Hypersensibilité ■ Anémie grave (possibilité de formation de méthémoglobine) ■ Hypotension ou hypovolémie non corrigées ■ Tamponnade cardiaque ■ Péricardite constrictive ■ Traumatisme crânien ou hémorragie cérébrale ■ Usage concomitant de sildénafil, de tadalafil et de vardénafil.

Précautions et mises en garde: Intolérance à l'alcool (doses IV importantes seulement) ■ Glaucome ■ Myocardiopathie hypertrophique ■ Insuffisance hépatique grave ■ Pression capillaire pulmonaire normale ou basse (IV) ■ Cardioversion (retirer le timbre transdermique au préalable) ■ **OBST.**: Risque d'altération de la circulation maternofœtale ■ **ALLAITEMENT, PÉD.**: L'innocuité du médicament n'a pas été établie.

RÉACTIONS INDÉSIRABLES ET EFFETS SECONDAIRES

SNC: étourdissements, céphalées, appréhension, agitation, faiblesse.

ORLO: vision trouble.

CV: hypotension, tachycardie, syncope.

GI: douleurs abdominales, nausées, vomissements.

Tég.: dermatite de contact (timbre transdermique ou pommade).

Hémat.: méthémoglobinémie (doses très élevées).

Divers: intoxication à l'alcool (doses IV importantes seulement), tolérance croisée, bouffées vasomotrices, tolérance aux effets du médicament.

INTERACTIONS

Médicament-médicament: L'UTILISATION CONCOMITANTE DE **DÉRIVÉS NITRÉS**, QUELS QU'ILS SOIENT, ET DE **SILDÉNAFIL**, DE **TADALAFIL** OU DE **VARDÉNAFIL** ACCROÎT LE RISQUE D'HYPOTENSION GRAVE QUI POURRAIT MENER À UNE ISSUE FATALE; L'ADMINISTRATION CONCOMITANTE EST DONC CONTRE-INDIQUÉE. IL FAUT PRÉVOIR AU MOINS 24 HEURES ENTRE LA PRISE DE SILDÉNAFIL OU DE VARDÉNAFIL ET LA PRISE D'UN DÉRIVÉ NITRÉ. POUR LE TADALAFIL, L'INTERVALLE DOIT ÊTRE D'AU MOINS 48 HEURES ■ Hypotension additive lors de l'administration concomitante d'**antihypertenseurs**, de **bêtabloquants**, de **bloqueurs des canaux calciques**, d'**halopéridol** et de **phénothiazines** ou lors de la consommation de grandes quantités d'**alcool** ■ L'action des dérivés nitrés est contrecarrée par les **alcaloïdes de l'ergot**, ce qui peut déclencher une crise d'angine ■ Les **agents dotés de propriétés anticholinergiques** (**antidépresseurs tricycliques**, **antihistaminiques**, **phénothiazines**) peuvent diminuer l'absorption de la nitroglycérine administrée par voie sublinguale ou transmuqueuse ou en vaporisateur.

VOIES D'ADMINISTRATION ET POSOLOGIE

- **Comprimés sublinguaux (adultes)**: De 0,3 à 0,6 mg; en cas de crise aiguë, on peut répéter l'administration de cette dose toutes les 5 minutes, pendant 15 minutes. On peut administrer un comprimé en prophylaxie, de 5 à 10 minutes avant que le patient entreprenne des activités pouvant déclencher une crise aiguë.
- **Vaporisateur lingual (adultes)**: 1 ou 2 vaporisations (ne pas inhaler); on peut répéter les vaporisations toutes les 5 minutes, pendant 15 minutes. On peut administrer 1 ou 2 vaporisations en prophylaxie, de 5 à 10 minutes avant que le patient entreprenne des activités pouvant déclencher une crise aiguë.
- **IV (adultes)**: 5 µg/min; augmenter par paliers de 5 µg/min, toutes les 3 à 5 minutes, jusqu'à concurrence de 20 µg/min, puis par paliers de 10 à 20 µg/min, toutes les 3 à 5 minutes (la dose doit être déterminée d'après les paramètres hémodynamiques).
- **Timbre transdermique, pommade (adultes)**: *Pommade* – de 1,25 à 10 cm (2,5 cm ≅ 15 mg), toutes les 4 à 8 heures (jusqu'à concurrence de 12,5 cm ou d'une application toutes les 4 heures). *Timbre transdermique* – de 0,2 à 0,6 mg/h jusqu'à concurrence de 0,8 mg/h. Le timbre devrait être porté pendant 12 à 14 heures par jour. Pour prévenir la tolérance aux effets du médicament, il faut observer un laps de temps sans utilisation de dérivés nitrés de 10 à 12 heures par jour.

PRÉSENTATION (version générique disponible)

Comprimés sublinguaux: 0,3 mg^{Phc}, 0,6 mg^{Phc} ■ **Vaporisateur lingual**: 0,4 mg/vaporisation, en flacons de 75 doses^{Phc} et de 200 doses^{Phc} ■ **Timbres transdermiques**: 0,2 mg/h^{Phc}, 0,3 mg/h^{Phc}, 0,4 mg/h^{Phc}, 0,6 mg/h^{Phc}, 0,8 mg/h^{Phc} ■ **Pommade**: 2 %^{Phc} ■ **Solution pour injection**: 1 mg/mL^{Pr}, 5 mg/mL^{Pr}, en flacons de 10 mL ■

Solution prémélangée pour injection: 25 mg/250 mL de D5%E^{Pr}, 50 mg/ 250 mL de D5%E^{Pr}, 100 mg/250 mL de D5%E^{Pr}.

SOINS INFIRMIERS

ÉVALUATION DE LA SITUATION

- Évaluer le siège, la durée et l'intensité de la douleur angineuse de même que les facteurs qui la déclenchent.
- Mesurer la pression artérielle et le pouls avant et après l'administration. Surveiller constamment l'ÉCG et la pression artérielle chez les patients recevant la nitroglycérine par voie IV. Il peut s'avérer nécessaire d'évaluer d'autres paramètres hémodynamiques.

Tests de laboratoire:

- La nitroglycérine peut entraîner l'élévation des concentrations urinaires de catécholamine et d'acide vanilmandélique.
- L'administration de doses très élevées peut entraîner l'élévation des concentrations de méthémoglobine.
- La nitroglycérine peut entraîner des concentrations sériques faussement élevées de cholestérol.

DIAGNOSTICS INFIRMIERS POSSIBLES

- Douleur aiguë (Indications).
- Irrigation tissulaire inefficace (Indications).
- Connaissances insuffisantes sur le traitement médicamenteux (Enseignement au patient et à ses proches).

INTERVENTIONS INFIRMIÈRES

Voie sublinguale: Les comprimés sublinguaux doivent être gardés sous la langue jusqu'à leur dissolution. Il ne faut pas manger, boire ou fumer jusqu'à ce que le comprimé se soit dissous.

IV: Diluer les doses et les administrer par perfusion. Les nécessaires de perfusion standard en chlorure de polyvinyle (CPV) peuvent adsorber jusqu'à 80 % de la nitroglycérine en solution. Utiliser exclusivement des flacons en verre ou des sacs de plastique et des tubulures spécialement destinées à l'administration de nitroglycérine.

Perfusion continue: Diluer dans une solution de D5%E ou de NaCl 0,9% à une concentration de 50 à 200 µg/mL, selon la tolérance du patient aux liquides (le tableau des vitesses de perfusion se trouve à l'annexe C). La solution est stable pendant 48 heures à la température ambiante. Elle n'est pas explosive ni avant ni après la dilution.

Vitesse d'administration: Utiliser une pompe à perfusion afin d'assurer l'administration de quantités précises de médicament. Adapter la vitesse de perfusion selon la réaction du patient.

Compatibilité (tubulure en Y): amiodarone ▪ atracurium ▪ diltiazem ▪ dobutamine ▪ dopamine ▪ esmolol ▪ famotidine ▪ halopéridol ▪ héparine ▪ insuline ▪ labétalol ▪ lidocaïne ▪ midazolam ▪ nitroprusside ▪ pancuronium ▪ ranitidine ▪ streptokinase ▪ tacrolimus ▪ théophylline ▪ vécuronium.

Compatibilité en addition au soluté: Le fabricant ne recommande pas de mélanger la nitroglycérine à d'autres médicaments.

Préparation topique:

- Il faut assurer la rotation des sièges d'application des timbres ou de la pommade afin de prévenir l'irritation cutanée. Retirer l'ancien timbre ou les restes de pommade avant une nouvelle application.
- On peut augmenter la dose jusqu'à la dose la plus élevée qui ne provoque pas d'hypotension symptomatique.
- Pour appliquer la pommade, se servir du papier applicateur qui se trouve dans l'emballage. Sortir du tube une quantité de pommade qui correspond à la graduation inscrite sur le papier applicateur. Étaler une couche mince et uniforme de pommade à l'aide du papier applicateur sur une peau glabre (poitrine, abdomen, cuisses; éviter les parties distales des membres) pour en recouvrir un territoire cutané de 5 × 7,5 cm. Ne pas toucher la pommade avec les mains. Il ne faut pas masser ni faire pénétrer la pommade pour ne pas en accélérer l'absorption et pour ne pas en entraver l'effet prolongé. Appliquer un pansement occlusif sur recommandation seulement.
- Les timbres transdermiques peuvent être appliqués sur n'importe quelle surface cutanée glabre (éviter les parties distales des membres ou les régions qui présentent des coupures ou des callosités). Appliquer une forte pression sur le timbre, particulièrement sur les bordures, afin d'assurer une bonne adhérence à la peau. Appliquer un nouveau timbre si le premier se détache ou tombe. Les timbres sont imperméables; il ne faut donc pas les enlever lors des douches ou des bains. Il ne faut pas essayer d'adapter la dose en coupant le timbre. Ne pas changer de marque puisque les doses contenues dans les différents timbres peuvent ne pas être équivalentes. Retirer le timbre avant la cardioversion ou la défibrillation afin de prévenir les brûlures. Les timbres peuvent être portés pendant 12 à 14 heures et être enlevés la nuit pendant 10 à 12 heures pour prévenir la tolérance à l'effet du médicament.

ENSEIGNEMENT AU PATIENT ET À SES PROCHES

- Conseiller au patient de respecter rigoureusement la posologie recommandée, même s'il se sent mieux. S'il n'a pu appliquer le timbre ou la pommade au moment habituel, il doit en faire l'application dès que possible et retirer le timbre ou la pommade au moment habituel prévu. Le prévenir qu'il ne faut jamais remplacer une dose manquée par une double dose. Lui recommander de ne pas interrompre brusquement le traitement, car un sevrage graduel pourrait s'imposer pour prévenir l'angine rebond.
- Recommander au patient de changer lentement de position pour réduire le risque d'hypotension orthostatique.
- Conseiller au patient d'éviter de boire de l'alcool pendant qu'il suit le traitement à la nitroglycérine. Lui recommander de consulter un professionnel de la santé avant de prendre un médicament en vente libre ou un produit naturel en même temps que la nitroglycérine.
- Prévenir le patient que les céphalées sont un effet secondaire courant qui devrait diminuer en intensité à mesure que le traitement se poursuit. On pourrait lui prescrire de l'acétaminophène pour soulager ces céphalées. Recommander au patient de prévenir un professionnel de la santé si les céphalées sont graves ou persistantes.
- Conseiller au patient de prévenir un professionnel de la santé en cas de sécheresse de la bouche ou de vision trouble.

Crises aiguës d'angine: Recommander au patient de s'asseoir et de prendre le médicament aux premiers signes de crise. Le soulagement survient habituellement dans les 5 minutes. Il peut prendre une deuxième dose, s'il n'obtient pas de soulagement dans les 5 minutes. Si la douleur persiste après l'administration de 3 comprimés ou vaporisations à intervalles de 5 minutes, en l'espace de 15 minutes, il faut contacter les services médicaux d'urgence pour que le patient soit conduit à l'urgence.

Voie sublinguale: Expliquer au patient qu'il doit conserver les comprimés dans leur flacon de verre d'origine ou dans un contenant métallique spécial et qu'il doit retirer le coton. Les comprimés perdent de leur puissance s'ils sont conservés dans des contenants en plastique ou en carton ou s'ils sont mélangés à d'autres comprimés ou capsules. L'exposition à l'air, à la chaleur et à l'humidité peut aussi diminuer la puissance du comprimé. Recommander au patient de ne pas ouvrir fréquemment le flacon, de ne pas manipuler les comprimés et de ne pas conserver le flacon près du corps (par exemple dans la poche de sa chemise) ni dans la boîte à gants de la voiture.

Vaporisateur lingual: Il ne faut pas agiter le vaporisateur. Recommander au patient de soulever la langue et de vaporiser la dose en dessous. La dose peut aussi être vaporisée sur la langue. Il ne faut pas inhaler le produit vaporisé. Voir la méthode d'administration à l'annexe G.

VÉRIFICATION DE L'EFFICACITÉ THÉRAPEUTIQUE

L'efficacité du traitement peut être démontrée par: la diminution de la fréquence et de l'intensité des crises d'angine ■ l'augmentation de la tolérance à l'effort; lors d'un traitement prolongé, on peut réduire la tolérance aux effets du médicament en administrant la nitroglycérine de façon intermittente, c'est-à-dire pendant 12 à 14 heures, et en arrêtant de l'administrer pendant les 10 à 12 heures suivantes ■ une hypotension contrôlée au cours d'une intervention chirurgicale ■ la maîtrise de la pression artérielle lors d'une crise hypertensive.

NITROPRUSSIDE

Synonyme: nitroprussiate de sodium

Nipride

CLASSIFICATION:

Antihypertenseur (vasodilatateur)

Grossesse – catégorie C

INDICATIONS

Traitement des crises hypertensives. **Usages non approuvés**: Induction d'une hypotension contrôlée pendant l'anesthésie ■ Amélioration de la fonction cardiaque dans les cas d'insuffisance cardiaque réfractaire et d'infarctus du myocarde (en monothérapie ou en association avec la dopamine).

MÉCANISME D'ACTION

Vasodilatation périphérique par une action directe sur les muscles lisses des veines et des artérioles. ***Effets thérapeutiques:*** Abaissement rapide de la pression artérielle ■ Diminution de la précharge et de la postcharge cardiaques.

PHARMACOCINÉTIQUE

Absorption: Biodisponibilité à 100 % (IV).

Distribution: Inconnue.

Métabolisme et excrétion: Lors du métabolisme, le nitroprusside est rapidement transformé en cyanure dans les érythrocytes et dans les tissus, puis en thiocyanate, dans le foie.

Demi-vie: 2 minutes.

Profil temps-action (effet hypotenseur)

	DÉBUT D'ACTION	PIC	DURÉE
IV	immédiat	rapide	1 - 10 min

CONTRE-INDICATIONS, PRÉCAUTIONS ET MISES EN GARDE

Contre-indications: Hypersensibilité ■ Hypertension compensatrice (shunt artérioveineux ou coarctation aortique) ■ Anémie non corrigée ■ Hypovolémie non corrigée ■ Diminution de l'irrigation cérébrale ■ Maladies hépatique et rénale graves ■ Atrophie optique de Leber ■ États morbides associés à une carence en vitamine B_{12}.

Précautions et mises en garde: Maladie rénale (risque accru d'accumulation de thiocyanate) ■ Maladie hépatique (risque accru d'accumulation de cyanure) ■ **GÉR.**: Sensibilité accrue ■ Hypothyroïdie ■ Hyponatrémie ■ Carence en vitamine B_{12} ■ **OBST.**: L'innocuité du médicament n'a pas été établie.

RÉACTIONS INDÉSIRABLES ET EFFETS SECONDAIRES

SNC: <u>étourdissements</u>, <u>céphalées</u>, agitation.

ORLO: vision trouble, acouphènes.

CV: dyspnée, hypotension, palpitations.

GI: <u>douleurs abdominales</u>, <u>nausées</u>, vomissements.

HÉ: acidose.

Locaux: phlébite au point d'injection IV.

Divers: INTOXICATION AU CYANURE, intoxication au thiocyanate.

INTERACTIONS

Médicament-médicament: Effets hypotenseurs accrus lors de l'administration concomitante de **ganglioplégiques**, d'**anesthésiques généraux** et d'autres **antihypertenseurs** ■ Les **œstrogènes** et les **agents sympathomimétiques** peuvent diminuer la réponse au nitroprusside.

VOIES D'ADMINISTRATION ET POSOLOGIE

- **IV (adultes et enfants)**: Initialement, de 0,3 µg/kg/min à 0,5 µg/kg/min; on peut augmenter la dose, selon les besoins, jusqu'à 10 µg/kg/min. Si cette vitesse de perfusion ne réussit pas à faire baisser la tension artérielle en moins de 10 minutes, cesser l'administration du produit. La dose habituelle est de 3 µg/kg/min.

PRÉSENTATION

Poudre pour injection: 50 mg/fiole[Pr].

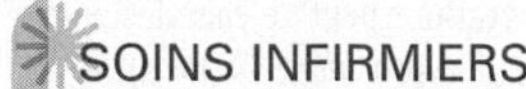

SOINS INFIRMIERS

ÉVALUATION DE LA SITUATION

- Mesurer la pression artérielle et le pouls et surveiller l'ÉCG fréquemment pendant toute la durée du traitement; une surveillance continue est préférable. Consulter le médecin au sujet des paramètres qu'il recommande. Observer les signes d'hypertension rebond après l'arrêt du traitement par le nitroprusside.
- Il est recommandé de suivre de près la pression capillaire pulmonaire chez les patients qui ont subi un infarctus du myocarde ou qui souffrent d'insuffisance cardiaque.

Tests de laboratoire:

- Le nitroprusside peut entraîner la diminution des concentrations de bicarbonate, de la pression partielle de gaz carbonique ($PaCO_2$) et du pH.
- Le nitroprusside peut entraîner l'élévation des concentrations de lactate.
- Le nitroprusside peut entraîner l'élévation des concentrations sériques de cyanure et de thiocyanate.
- Surveiller les concentrations sériques de méthémoglobine chez les patients recevant > 10 mg/kg, qui manifestent des signes d'un transport inadéquat de l'oxygène malgré un débit cardiaque et une $PaCO_2$ adéquats (le sang est de couleur marron chocolat et cette couleur ne change pas même lorsqu'il est exposé à l'air). Le traitement de la méthémoglobinémie consiste à administrer de 1 à 2 mg/kg de bleu de méthylène par voie IV en l'espace de plusieurs minutes.

TOXICITÉ ET SURDOSAGE:

- En cas d'hypotension grave, on peut inverser rapidement les effets du médicament, en l'espace de 1 à 10 minutes, en diminuant la vitesse de perfusion ou en l'arrêtant temporairement. On peut installer le patient en position de Trendelenburg afin de maximiser le retour veineux.
- NOTER TOUS LES JOURS LES CONCENTRATIONS PLASMATIQUES DE THIOCYANATE CHEZ LES PATIENTS RECEVANT DES PERFUSIONS PROLONGÉES À UNE VITESSE > 3 µg/kg/MIN, OU DE 1 µg/kg/MIN, CHEZ LES PATIENTS ANURIQUES. LES CONCENTRATIONS DE THIOCYANATE NE DOIVENT PAS DÉPASSER 1 mmol/L.
- Les signes et les symptômes d'intoxication au thiocyanate incluent les acouphènes, les psychoses toxiques, l'hyperréflexie, la confusion, la faiblesse, les convulsions et le coma.

- L'intoxication au cyanure peut se manifester par l'acidose lactique, l'hypoxémie, la tachycardie, l'altération de l'état de conscience, les convulsions et une haleine ayant une odeur caractéristique d'amandes.
- Le traitement de courte durée de l'intoxication au cyanure consiste en l'administration de 300 mg de *nitrite de sodium* (sous forme de solution à 3 %) IV pendant 5 minutes. Cet agent agit comme un tampon pour le cyanure en transformant 10 % de l'hémoglobine en méthémoglobine. Si l'administration de nitrite de sodium est retardée, on devrait écraser une ampoule de *nitrite d'amyle* et en faire inhaler le contenu pendant 15 à 30 secondes par minute en attendant de pouvoir commencer le traitement par le nitrite de sodium. Au terme de la perfusion de nitrite de sodium, administrer du *thiosulfate de sodium* à une dose 12,5 g (50 mL) IV en 10 minutes (disponible en solutions à 25 %). Cette solution transforme le cyanure en thiocyanate, qui peut par la suite être éliminé. Si cela s'avère nécessaire, le traitement entier peut être répété 30 minutes plus tard, à 50 % des doses initiales.

DIAGNOSTICS INFIRMIERS POSSIBLES

N

- Irrigation tissulaire inefficace (Indications).

INTERVENTIONS INFIRMIÈRES

- Si la perfusion d'une dose de 10 µg/kg/min pendant 10 minutes ne réduit pas suffisamment la pression artérielle, le fabricant recommande de cesser le traitement.
- On peut administrer le nitroprusside en association avec un agent inotrope (dopamine, dobutamine) lors du traitement de l'insuffisance ventriculaire gauche, si des doses appropriées de nitroprusside rétablissent le débit cardiaque, mais entraînent une hypotension excessive.

Perfusion continue:

- Reconstituer 50 mg avec 3 mL de solution de D5%E pour injection sans agents de conservation. Consulter les directives du fabricant avant de reconstituer la préparation. Diluer de nouveau dans 250 à 1 000 mL de solution de D5%E pour obtenir des concentrations de 200 à 500 µg/mL. Ne pas utiliser d'autres diluants pour la reconstitution ou la perfusion. Envelopper le flacon à perfusion dans du papier d'aluminium pour protéger son contenu de la lumière; il n'est cependant pas nécessaire d'en recouvrir les tubulures destinées à l'administration. Les sacs de plastique de couleur ambre n'assurent pas une protection suffisante contre la lumière; l'emballage doit être opaque. La solution fraîchement préparée a une légère teinte brunâtre; jeter la solution si elle devient brun foncé, orange, bleue, verte ou rouge foncé. Il faut utiliser la solution dans les 24 heures suivant sa préparation.
- Éviter l'extravasation.

Vitesse d'administration: Utiliser une pompe à perfusion afin d'assurer l'administration d'une quantité exacte de médicament (consulter le tableau des vitesses de perfusion de l'annexe C).

Compatibilité (tubulure en Y): atracurium ■ diltiazem ■ dobutamine ■ dopamine ■ énalaprilate ■ esmolol ■ famotidine ■ héparine ■ insuline ■ labétalol ■ lidocaïne ■ midazolam ■ morphine ■ nitroglycérine ■ pancuronium ■ tacrolimus ■ théophylline ■ vécuronium.

Incompatibilité en addition au soluté: Ne pas mélanger à d'autres médicaments.

ENSEIGNEMENT AU PATIENT ET À SES PROCHES

- Recommander au patient de signaler immédiatement l'apparition d'acouphènes, la dyspnée, les étourdissements, les céphalées ou la vision trouble.

VÉRIFICATION DE L'EFFICACITÉ THÉRAPEUTIQUE

L'efficacité du traitement peut être démontrée par: la baisse de la pression artérielle sans manifestation d'effets secondaires ■ l'amélioration des signes d'une insuffisance cardiaque réfractaire ou du choc cardiogénique.

NIZATIDINE,

voir Antagonistes des récepteurs H_2 de l'histamine

NORELGESTROMINE,

voir Contraceptifs hormonaux

NORÉTHINDRONE,

voir Contraceptifs hormonaux

NORFLOXACINE,

voir Fluoroquinolones

NORGESTIMATE,

voir Contraceptifs hormonaux

NORGESTREL,
voir Contraceptifs hormonaux

NORTRIPTYLINE

Apo-Nortriptyline, Aventyl, Dom-Nortriptiline, Gen-Nortriptyline, Norventyl, Novo-Nortriptyline, Nu-Nortriptyline, PMS-Nortriptyline

CLASSIFICATION:
Antidépresseur (tricyclique)

Grossesse – catégorie C

INDICATIONS

Soulagement des symptômes de dépression ■ Douleur neuropathique.

MÉCANISME D'ACTION

Potentialisation des effets de la sérotonine et de la noradrénaline au niveau du SNC ■ Propriétés anticholinergiques importantes. ***Effets thérapeutiques:*** Effet antidépresseur qui se manifeste graduellement en l'espace de plusieurs semaines.

PHARMACOCINÉTIQUE

Absorption: Bonne (PO).
Distribution: Tout l'organisme. La nortriptyline traverse probablement la barrière placentaire et se retrouve dans le lait maternel à faibles concentrations.
Liaison aux protéines: 92 %.
Métabolisme et excrétion: Métabolisme majoritairement hépatique, surtout lors d'un premier passage. Une certaine fraction est transformée en composés actifs. Le médicament subit plusieurs cycles entérohépatiques et il est sécrété dans les sucs gastriques.
Demi-vie: De 18 à 28 heures.

Profil temps-action (effet antidépresseur)

	DÉBUT D'ACTION	PIC	DURÉE
PO	2 – 3 semaines	6 semaines	inconnue

CONTRE-INDICATIONS, PRÉCAUTIONS ET MISES EN GARDE

Contre-indications: Hypersensibilité ■ Risque d'allergie croisée lors de l'administration d'autres antidépresseurs tricycliques ■ Administration en association avec un IMAO (prévoir 14 jours entre l'arrêt du traitement par l'IMAO et le début de l'administration de nortriptyline et vice versa) ■ Phase aiguë de rétablissement après un infarctus du myocarde ■ Insuffisance cardiaque congestive.

Précautions et mises en garde: Suivre de près les idées suicidaires chez tous les patients recevant ce médicament ■ Troubles bipolaires (l'emploi d'antidépresseurs durant la phase dépressive d'un trouble bipolaire peut déclencher un épisode hypomaniaque ou maniaque) ■ Risque de dyscrasie sanguine ■ Risque d'arythmies cardiaques transitoires chez les patients prenant en concomitance un médicament destiné au traitement des troubles thyroïdiens ou souffrant d'hyperthyroïdie ■ Éviter de mettre fin abruptement au traitement en raison du risque de symptômes de sevrage ■ **GÉR.:** Les personnes âgées sont davantage prédisposées aux réactions indésirables; il est recommandé de réduire la dose. Les hommes âgés souffrant d'hyperplasie de la prostate sont davantage prédisposés à la rétention urinaire ■ Maladie cardiovasculaire préexistante ■ Convulsions ou antécédents de convulsions ■ Asthme ■ Glaucome à angle fermé ■ **OBST.:** L'innocuité du médicament n'a pas été établie ■ **ALLAITEMENT:** Risque de sédation chez le nourrisson ■ **PÉD.:** Enfants < 6 ans.

RÉACTIONS INDÉSIRABLES ET EFFETS SECONDAIRES

SNC: somnolence, fatigue, léthargie, agitation, confusion, réactions extrapyramidales, hallucinations, céphalées, insomnie.
ORLO: vision trouble, sécheresse des yeux (xérophtalmie), sécheresse de la bouche (xérostomie).
CV: ARYTHMIES, hypotension, modifications de l'ÉCG.
GI: constipation, nausées, iléus paralytique, goût désagréable.
GU: rétention urinaire.
Tég.: photosensibilité.
End.: gynécomastie.
Hémat.: dyscrasie sanguine.
Métab.: gain pondéral.

INTERACTIONS

Médicament-médicament: LA NORTRIPTYLINE PEUT PROVOQUER L'HYPERTENSION, L'HYPERPYREXIE, DES CONVULSIONS ET LA MORT SI ELLE EST ADMINISTRÉE EN MÊME TEMPS QU'UN **IMAO** (ÉVITER L'ADMINISTRATION CONJOINTE; INTERROMPRE LE TRAITEMENT 2 SEMAINES AVANT D'ADMINISTRER LA NORTRIPTYLINE ET VICE VERSA) ■ Le médicament peut entraver la réponse thérapeutique à la plupart des **antihypertenseurs** ■ La nortriptyline peut provoquer une crise hypertensive si elle est administrée en même temps que la **clonidine** ■ Effets dépresseurs additifs sur le SNC lors de l'usage concomitant d'autres **dépresseurs du SNC**, dont l'**alcool**, les **antihistaminiques**, les **opioïdes** et les **hypnosédatifs** ■ Les

effets sympathomimétiques peuvent être additifs lors de l'administration d'**agents adrénergiques**, y compris les **vasoconstricteurs** et les **décongestionnants** ■ Effets anticholinergiques additifs lors de l'administration d'autres **agents dotés de ces propriétés**, y compris les **antihistaminiques**, les **antidépresseurs**, l'**atropine**, l'**halopéridol**, les **phénothiazines**, la **quinidine** et le **disopyramide** ■ La **cimétidine**, la **fluoxétine** et les **contraceptifs oraux** entraînent l'élévation des concentrations sanguines et augmentent le risque de toxicité ■ Les concentrations plasmatiques de la nortriptyline peuvent diminuer lors de l'administration concomitante d'**agents qui induisent le CYP1A2 et/ou le CYP2D6**, comme les **barbituriques**, la **carbamazépine**, la **phénytoïne** ou la **rifampine** ■ Les concentrations plasmatiques de nortriptyline peuvent augmenter lors de l'administration concomitante d'un **agent qui inhibe le CYP1A2 et/ou le CYP2D6**, comme l'**amiodarone**, le **célécoxib**, la **chloroquine**, la **cimétidine**, la **ciprofloxacine**, la **clarithromycine**, l'**érythromycine**, l'**éthynylœstradiol**, l'**isoniazide**, le **kétoconazole**, la **méthadone**, la **mexilétine**, le **propranolol**, la **quinidine** et les **ISRS** ■ Risque accru de neurotoxicité (p. ex., tremblements, ataxie, convulsions) lors de l'utilisation concomitante de **lithium** ■ L'administration concomitante de **lévothyroxine** peut augmenter les effets secondaires cardiovasculaires ■ Risque accru d'agranulocytose lors de l'administration concomitante d'**agents antithyroïdiens**.
Médicament-produits naturels: La consommation concomitante de **kava**, de **valériane** ou de **camomille** peut intensifier l'effet dépresseur sur le SNC de la nortriptyline ■ Le **datura** et le **scopolia** augmentent les effets secondaires cholinergiques.

VOIES D'ADMINISTRATION ET POSOLOGIE

Dépression

- **PO (adultes)**: Initialement, 25 mg, 1 ou 2 fois par jour; augmenter graduellement la dose jusqu'à concurrence de 200 mg par jour.
- **PO (personnes âgées)**: Initialement, de 10 à 25 mg, au coucher. On peut augmenter cette dose de 10 à 25 mg par jour à des intervalles de 1 semaine; la dose d'entretien habituelle est de 50 à 75 mg par jour.
- **PO (enfants de 6 à 12 ans)**: De 10 à 20 mg par jour en doses fractionnées.
- **PO (adolescents)**: De 30 à 50 mg par jour en doses fractionnées; dose maximale habituelle: 150 mg/jour.

Douleur neuropathique

- **PO (adultes)**: Initialement, de 10 à 25 mg, au coucher. On peut augmenter cette dose de 10 à 25 mg par jour à des intervalles de 1 semaine, jusqu'à ce que la douleur soit soulagée ou que surviennent des effets secondaires (ne pas dépasser 200 mg).

PRÉSENTATION

Capsules: 10 mg[Pr], 25 mg[Pr].

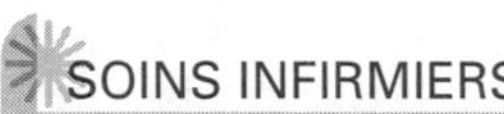

SOINS INFIRMIERS

ÉVALUATION DE LA SITUATION

- Évaluer l'état de conscience et l'affect du patient. Rester à l'affût des tendances suicidaires, particulièrement en début de traitement. Diminuer la quantité de médicament dont le patient peut disposer.
- Mesurer la pression artérielle et le pouls avant l'administration du médicament et pendant toute la durée du traitement initial. Prévenir le médecin en cas de baisse marquée de la pression artérielle ou d'une élévation brusque de la fréquence du pouls.
- ÉVALUER L'ÉCG À INTERVALLES RÉGULIERS CHEZ LES PERSONNES ÂGÉES OU CHEZ LES PATIENTS CARDIAQUES. LA NORTRIPTYLINE PEUT ALLONGER LES INTERVALLES PR ET QT ET APLATIR LES ONDES T.

Douleur: Déterminer le siège, le type et l'intensité de la douleur avant le traitement et à intervalles réguliers pendant toute sa durée.

Tests de laboratoire:

- Noter à intervalles réguliers la numération globulaire et la formule leucocytaire, la glycémie ainsi que les résultats des tests de la fonction hépatique. La nortriptyline peut élever les concentrations sériques de bilirubine et de phosphatase alcaline. Elle peut entraîner une aplasie médullaire. Elle peut élever ou diminuer la glycémie.
- On peut mesurer les concentrations sériques chez les patients qui ne répondent pas à la dose thérapeutique habituelle. Les concentrations plasmatiques thérapeutiques se situent entre 190 et 570 nmol/L.
- La nortriptyline peut modifier la glycémie.

TOXICITÉ ET SURDOSAGE:

- Les symptômes d'un surdosage aigu comprennent l'impossibilité de se concentrer, la confusion, l'agitation, les convulsions, la somnolence, la mydriase, les arythmies, la fièvre, les hallucinations, les vomissements et la dyspnée.
- Le traitement du surdosage inclut le lavage gastrique et l'administration de charbon activé et d'un purgatif. Maintenir la fonction cardiaque (suivre de près l'ÉCG pendant au moins 5 jours), la fonction respiratoire et la température du patient. On peut administrer de la digoxine pour traiter l'insuffisance cardiaque, ainsi que des antiarythmiques et des anticonvulsivants.

N

DIAGNOSTICS INFIRMIERS POSSIBLES

- Stratégies d'adaptation inefficaces (Indications).
- Risque d'accident (Effets secondaires).
- Connaissances insuffisantes sur le traitement médicamenteux (Enseignement au patient et à ses proches).

INTERVENTIONS INFIRMIÈRES

- NE PAS CONFONDRE LA NORTRYPTILINE AVEC LA DÉSIPRAMINE.
- Administrer la nortriptyline avec les repas pour diminuer l'irritation gastrique.
- On peut administrer la dose totale au coucher pour réduire la sédation diurne. Si la dose doit être majorée, cette majoration doit avoir lieu au coucher en raison des effets sédatifs du médicament.

ENSEIGNEMENT AU PATIENT ET À SES PROCHES

- Conseiller au patient de respecter rigoureusement la posologie recommandée. S'il n'a pu prendre le médicament au moment habituel, il doit le prendre dès que possible, à moins que ce ne soit presque l'heure prévue pour la dose suivante. Si le patient doit prendre une seule dose à l'heure du coucher, lui recommander de ne pas prendre la dose manquée le matin en raison des effets secondaires de ce médicament. Prévenir le patient que les effets du médicament peuvent ne pas se manifester avant 2 semaines au moins. L'arrêt brusque du traitement peut provoquer des nausées, des vomissements, la diarrhée, des céphalées, de l'insomnie associée à des rêves saisissants et de l'irritabilité.
- Prévenir le patient que la nortriptyline peut provoquer de la somnolence et rendre la vision trouble. Lui conseiller de ne pas conduire et d'éviter les activités qui exigent sa vigilance jusqu'à ce qu'on ait la certitude que le médicament n'entraîne pas ces effets chez lui.
- Conseiller au patient de prévenir un professionnel de la santé si sa vision change. L'informer que pendant un traitement prolongé on pourrait lui prescrire des examens ophtalmologiques à intervalles réguliers pour déceler le glaucome.
- Recommander au patient de changer lentement de position afin de réduire le risque d'hypotension orthostatique. (Cet effet secondaire est moins prononcé dans le cas de la nortriptyline que dans le cas des autres antidépresseurs tricycliques.)
- Recommander au patient d'éviter de boire de l'alcool et de ne pas prendre d'autres dépresseurs du SNC pendant toute la durée du traitement et pendant les 3 à 7 jours qui suivent l'arrêt de la médication.
- Conseiller au patient de prévenir un professionnel de la santé en cas de rétention urinaire, de sécheresse de la bouche ou de constipation persistante. Lui expliquer que les bonbons ou la gomme à mâcher sans sucre peuvent diminuer la sécheresse de la bouche et qu'une consommation accrue de liquides et d'aliments riches en fibres peut prévenir la constipation. Si les symptômes persistent, il peut s'avérer nécessaire de réduire la dose ou d'interrompre le traitement. Conseiller au patient de consulter un professionnel de la santé si la sécheresse de la bouche persiste pendant plus de 2 semaines.
- Recommander au patient d'utiliser un écran solaire et de porter des vêtements protecteurs afin de prévenir les réactions de photosensibilité.
- Inciter le patient à surveiller son alimentation, car la nortriptyline peut lui donner plus d'appétit, ce qui risque d'entraîner un gain pondéral indésirable.
- Prévenir la patiente que la nortriptyline peut exercer des effets tératogènes. Lui recommander de communiquer immédiatement avec un professionnel de la santé si elle pense être enceinte ou si elle souhaite le devenir.
- Recommander au patient qui doit suivre un autre traitement ou subir une intervention chirurgicale d'avertir le professionnel de la santé qu'il suit un traitement par ce médicament.
- Prévenir le patient que le traitement de la dépression est habituellement de longue durée. Insister sur l'importance d'un suivi régulier et des séances de psychothérapie, si elles lui sont prescrites.

VÉRIFICATION DE L'EFFICACITÉ THÉRAPEUTIQUE

L'efficacité du traitement peut être démontrée par: un sentiment accru de mieux-être ▪ un regain d'intérêt pour l'entourage ▪ un gain d'appétit ▪ un regain d'énergie ▪ l'amélioration du sommeil ▪ la diminution de l'intensité des douleurs neuropathiques. Le plein effet thérapeutique de la nortriptyline pourrait ne pas être notable avant 2 à 6 semaines de traitement.

NYSTATINE

Dom-Nystatin, Mycostatin, Nadostine, Nilstat, Nyaderm, PMS-Nystatin, Ratio-Nystatin

CLASSIFICATION:

Antifongique (par voie générale)

Grossesse – catégorie C

Pour les autres préparations de nystatine, voir Antifongiques topiques et Antifongiques vaginaux.

N

INDICATIONS

PO: Traitement préventif et curatif des candidoses de la cavité orale et de l'œsophage et de la moniliase intestinale ■ Prévention de la prolifération de *Candida* durant une antibiothérapie ou une corticothérapie.

MÉCANISME D'ACTION

Liaison à la membrane de la cellule fongique entraînant la fuite du contenu intracellulaire. ***Effets thérapeutiques:*** Effet fongicide ou fongistatique. **Spectre d'action**: Le médicament agit contre la plupart des espèces pathogènes de *Candida*, y compris *C. albicans*.

PHARMACOCINÉTIQUE

Absorption: Négligeable; l'effet est local.

Distribution: Inconnue.

Métabolisme et excrétion: Excrétion fécale à l'état inchangé.

Demi-vie: Inconnue.

Profil temps-action (effets antifongiques)

	Début d'action	Pic	Durée
PO	rapide	inconnu	2 h

N

CONTRE-INDICATIONS, PRÉCAUTIONS ET MISES EN GARDE

Contre-indications: Hypersensibilité ■ Hypersensibilité ou intolérance à l'alcool éthylique ou à l'alcool benzylique (éviter dans ce cas l'usage des préparations qui contiennent ces additifs).

Précautions et mises en garde: Porteurs de prothèses dentaires (il faut faire tremper les dentiers dans une suspension de nystatine).

RÉACTIONS INDÉSIRABLES ET EFFETS SECONDAIRES

GI: diarrhée, nausées, douleurs gastriques (doses élevées), vomissements.

Tég.: dermatite de contact, syndrome de Stevens-Johnson.

INTERACTIONS

Médicament-médicament: Aucune interaction notable.

VOIES D'ADMINISTRATION ET POSOLOGIE

- **PO (adultes et enfants)**: De 100 000 à 600 000 unités, 4 fois par jour, en suspension orale, ou 500 000 unités, 3 fois par jour, en comprimés oraux (au besoin, on peut doubler la dose chez l'adulte).
- **PO (nourrissons)**: 100 000 unités, 3 ou 4 fois par jour.

PRÉSENTATION

Suspension orale: 100 000 unités/mL, en flacons de 5 à 500 mL[Pr] ■ **Comprimés**: 500 000 unités[Pr].

SOINS INFIRMIERS

ÉVALUATION DE LA SITUATION

- Examiner les muqueuses atteintes avant le traitement et à intervalles fréquents par la suite. Une irritation accrue de la muqueuse peut dicter l'arrêt du traitement.

DIAGNOSTICS INFIRMIERS POSSIBLES

- Atteinte à l'intégrité de la peau (Indications).
- Risque d'infection (Indications).
- Connaissances insuffisantes sur le traitement médicamenteux (Enseignement au patient et à ses proches).

INTERVENTIONS INFIRMIÈRES

PO:

- Pour administrer la suspension, déposer la moitié de la dose de chaque côté de la bouche. Demander au patient de garder la suspension dans la bouche ou de la faire tourner dans la bouche pendant plusieurs minutes et de se gargariser avec elle, avant de l'avaler. Utiliser un récipient gradué pour mesurer les doses de suspension. Bien agiter la suspension avant de l'administrer.

Péd.: Chez les nourrissons et les nouveau-nés, bien badigeonner avec la suspension l'intérieur de la bouche.

- Pour traiter les candidoses buccales, on peut administrer les comprimés vaginaux de nystatine par voie orale.
- Afin de prévenir les rechutes à la suite du traitement par voie orale, il faut le poursuivre pendant les 48 heures qui suivent la disparition des symptômes et l'obtention de cultures négatives.
- Un traitement de 2 semaines est habituellement suffisant, mais il est parfois nécessaire de le prolonger.

ENSEIGNEMENT AU PATIENT ET À SES PROCHES

- Recommander au patient de respecter rigoureusement la posologie recommandée. S'il n'a pas pu utiliser le médicament au moment habituel, il doit le faire aussitôt que possible à moins que ce ne soit presque l'heure prévue pour la dose suivante. Le prévenir qu'il ne doit pas remplacer une dose manquée par une double dose. Il devrait poursuivre le traitement pendant au moins 2 jours après la disparition des symptômes.

PÉD.: Informer les parents et les soignants des nourrissons et des enfants de la posologie et du mode d'administration appropriés. Leur rappeler qu'ils doivent utiliser uniquement la mesure fournie avec le produit.

- Conseiller au patient de communiquer avec un professionnel de la santé si l'irritation des muqueuses s'aggrave ou si aucune réponse thérapeutique n'est notée.

VÉRIFICATION DE L'EFFICACITÉ THÉRAPEUTIQUE

L'efficacité du traitement peut être démontrée par: la diminution de la stomatite. ✳

OCTRÉOTIDE

Octreotide, Sandostatin, Sandostatin LAR

CLASSIFICATION:

Antidiarrhéique, hormone gastro-intestinale, octapeptide synthétique analogue de la somatostatine

Grossesse – catégorie B

INDICATIONS

Traitement de la diarrhée grave et des bouffées vasomotrices chez les patients présentant des tumeurs endocrines au niveau du tractus gastro-intestinal, incluant les tumeurs carcinoïdes métastatiques et les tumeurs contenant des peptides intestinaux vasoactifs (VIPomes) ▪ Soulagement des symptômes et réduction de la croissance de la tumeur chez les patients présentant un adénome de l'hypophyse volumineux associé à l'acromégalie ▪ Prévention des complications des chirurgies pancréatiques à haut risque ▪ Traitement d'urgence de la rupture des varices gastro-œsophagiennes chez les patients atteints de cirrhose. **Usages non approuvés:** Traitement de la diarrhée chez les patients atteints du sida ou chez ceux présentant des fistules.

MÉCANISME D'ACTION

O

Inhibition de la sécrétion de la sérotonine et des peptides gastroentérohépatiques ▪ Augmentation de l'absorption des liquides et des électrolytes depuis le tractus gastro-intestinal et prolongation du temps de transit ▪ Diminution des concentrations de métabolites sérotoninergiques ▪ Inhibition des sécrétions d'hormone de croissance, d'insuline et de glucagon. ***Effets thérapeutiques:*** Maîtrise des bouffées vasomotrices et de la diarrhée graves, associées aux tumeurs endocrines au niveau du tractus gastro-intestinal.

PHARMACOCINÉTIQUE

Absorption: Bonne (SC et IM de la préparation retard).

Distribution: Inconnue.

Liaison aux protéines: 65 %.

Métabolisme et excrétion: Excrétion rénale (32 % sous forme inchangée).

Demi-vie: 1,5 heure.

Profil temps-action (maîtrise des symptômes)

	DÉBUT D'ACTION	PIC	DURÉE
SC, IV	inconnu	inconnu	jusqu'à 12 h
IM (LAR)†	inconnu	2 semaines	jusqu'à 4 semaines

† Préparation retard.

CONTRE-INDICATIONS, PRÉCAUTIONS ET MISES EN GARDE

Contre-indications: Hypersensibilité.

Précautions et mises en garde: Maladie de la vésicule biliaire (risque accru de formation de calculs) ▪ Insuffisance rénale (une réduction de la dose pourrait s'avérer nécessaire) ▪ Hyperglycémie ou hypoglycémie (risque de modification de la glycémie) ▪ Malabsorption des matières grasses (risque d'aggravation) ▪ **OBST., ALLAITEMENT:** L'innocuité du médicament n'a pas été établie.

RÉACTIONS INDÉSIRABLES ET EFFETS SECONDAIRES

SNC: étourdissements, somnolence, fatigue, céphalées, faiblesse.

ORLO: troubles visuels.

CV: œdème, hypotension orthostatique, palpitations.

GI: douleurs abdominales, cholélithiase, diarrhée, malabsorption des matières grasses, nausées, vomissements.

Tég.: bouffées vasomotrices.

End.: hyperglycémie, hypoglycémie.

Locaux: douleur au point d'injection.

INTERACTIONS

Médicament-médicament: L'octréotide peut modifier les besoins en **insuline** et en **hypoglycémiants oraux** ▪ L'octréotide peut entraîner la diminution des concentrations sanguines de **cyclosporine**.

VOIES D'ADMINISTRATION ET POSOLOGIE

Dans la plupart des cas, il est recommandé d'administrer l'octréotide par voie SC. On a déjà administré un bolus par voie IV dans certaines situations d'urgence.

Tumeurs carcinoïdes

- **SC (adultes):** *Sandostatin* – 50 µg au départ, 1 ou 2 fois par jour, puis de 100 à 600 µg par jour, en 2 à 4 doses fractionnées pendant les 2 premières semaines de traitement (écart posologique: entre 50 et 1 500 µg par jour).
- **IM (adultes):** *Sandostatin LAR* – 20 mg, toutes les 4 semaines pendant 2 mois; on peut majorer cette dose, au besoin.

VIPomes

- **SC (adultes):** *Sandostatin* – 50 µg au départ, 1 ou 2 fois par jour, puis de 200 à 300 µg par jour, en 2 à 4 doses fractionnées pendant les 2 premières semaines de traitement (écart posologique: entre 150 et 750 µg par jour).
- **IM (adultes):** *Sandostatin LAR* – 20 mg, toutes les 4 semaines, pendant 2 mois; on peut majorer cette dose, au besoin.

Suppression de l'hormone de croissance (acromégalie)

- **SC (adultes)**: *Sandostatin* – de 50 à 100 µg, 2 ou 3 fois par jour (de 100 à 300 µg/jour).
- **IM (adultes)**: *Sandostatin LAR* – 20 mg, toutes les 4 semaines, pendant 3 mois; la posologie sera ensuite adaptée selon les concentrations d'hormone de croissance.

Prévention des complications des chirurgies pancréatiques

- **SC (adultes)**: *Sandostatin* – 100 µg, 3 fois par jour, pendant 7 jours (commencer 1 heure avant la laparoscopie).

Traitement d'urgence de la rupture des varices gastro-œsophagiennes chez les patients atteints de cirrhose

- **IV (adultes)**: *Sandostatin* – de 25 à 50 µg/h en perfusion continue pendant 48 heures; si le risque de récidive est élevé, continuer pendant 5 jours au maximum.

PRÉSENTATION

Solution pour injection: ampoules de 1 mL[Pr]: 50, 100 ou 500 µg/mL; fioles multidoses de 5 mL[Pr]: 200 µg/mL ■ **Solution pour injection retard**: fioles unidoses: 10 mg[Pr], 20 mg[Pr], 30 mg[Pr].

SOINS INFIRMIERS

ÉVALUATION DE LA SITUATION

- Observer la fréquence et la consistance des selles et ausculter les bruits intestinaux pendant toute la durée du traitement.
- Mesurer le pouls et la pression artérielle avant le traitement et à intervalles réguliers pendant toute sa durée.
- Effectuer le bilan hydroélectrolytique et observer la peau à la recherche de signes de déshydratation.
- Observer chez les patients diabétiques l'apparition des signes d'hypoglycémie. Il peut s'avérer nécessaire de diminuer les doses d'insuline et de sulfonylurée et d'administrer du diazoxide.
- Observer l'apparition des signes de maladie de la vésicule biliaire; évaluer la douleur et étudier les résultats des échographies de la vésicule biliaire et des voies biliaires avant l'administration initiale et à intervalles réguliers pendant un traitement prolongé.

Tests de laboratoire:

- Noter les concentrations urinaires d'acide 5-hydroxy-indole-acétique et les concentrations plasmatiques de sérotonine et de substance P chez les patients qui présentent des carcinoïdes, les concentrations plasmatiques des peptides intestinaux vasoactifs, chez les patients atteints d'un VIPome, les concentrations de T_4 libre et les concentrations sériques de glucose, avant le traitement et à intervalles réguliers pendant toute sa durée, chez tous les patients traités par l'octréotide.
- Noter, à intervalles réguliers, la quantité de graisses fécales contenues dans les selles de 72 heures et la concentration sérique de carotène pour déceler l'aggravation de la malabsorption des matières grasses induite par le médicament.
- L'octréotide peut entraîner une légère élévation des enzymes hépatiques.
- L'octréotide peut entraîner une diminution des concentrations sériques de thyroxine (T_4).

DIAGNOSTICS INFIRMIERS POSSIBLES

- Diarrhée (Indications).
- Connaissances insuffisantes sur le traitement médicamenteux (Enseignement au patient et à ses proches).

INTERVENTIONS INFIRMIÈRES

- Ne pas administrer la solution si elle a changé de couleur ou si elle renferme des particules. On devrait réfrigérer les ampoules, mais on peut aussi les conserver à la température ambiante pendant les quelques jours où elles seront utilisées. Jeter toute portion inutilisée.

SC:

- Administrer le plus petit volume nécessaire afin d'obtenir la dose efficace tout en prévenant la douleur au point d'injection. Assurer la rotation des points d'injection. Éviter d'administrer plusieurs injections au même endroit en un court laps de temps. Les points d'injection à privilégier sont la hanche, la cuisse ou l'abdomen.
- Laisser reposer le médicament à la température ambiante avant de l'injecter pour réduire les réactions locales au point d'injection.
- Administrer les injections entre les repas et au coucher pour éviter les effets indésirables gastro-intestinaux.

IM:

- Mélanger la solution IM en ajoutant le diluant inclus dans la trousse. Une fois la solution préparée, l'administrer immédiatement dans le muscle fessier. Éviter la région deltoïde en raison de la douleur due à l'injection.
- Afin de maintenir des concentrations thérapeutiques dans le plasma, les patients présentant des tumeurs carcinoïdes ou un VIPome devraient continuer de recevoir la dose SC pendant les 2 semaines qui suivent la substitution par la préparation IM à effet retard.

IV directe: En situations d'urgence, on a déjà administré des bolus intraveineux.

IV perfusion continue:

- Le contenu de l'ampoule ou du flacon doit être dilué dans une solution de NaCl 0,9 %. Le volume de dilution dépend du mode de perfusion et doit être ajusté pour maintenir une vitesse de 25 à 50 µg/h.
- Consulter les directives de chaque fabricant avant de reconstituer la préparation.

ENSEIGNEMENT AU PATIENT ET À SES PROCHES

- Prévenir le patient que l'octréotide peut provoquer des étourdissements, de la somnolence ou des troubles de la vue. Lui conseiller de ne pas conduire et d'éviter les activités qui exigent sa vigilance jusqu'à ce qu'on ait la certitude que le médicament n'entraîne pas ces effets chez lui.
- Recommander au patient de changer lentement de position afin de réduire le risque d'hypotension orthostatique.

Soins à domicile: Montrer au patient qui suit un traitement à domicile comment injecter l'octréotide et le conserver, et comment mettre au rebut le matériel utilisé.

- Conseiller au patient de respecter rigoureusement la posologie recommandée. S'il n'a pu prendre le médicament au moment habituel, il doit le prendre dès que possible et revenir ensuite à l'horaire régulier. Le prévenir qu'il ne faut jamais prendre une double dose.

O

VÉRIFICATION DE L'EFFICACITÉ THÉRAPEUTIQUE

L'efficacité du traitement peut être démontrée par: la diminution de la gravité de la diarrhée et le rééquilibrage électrolytique chez les patients qui présentent une tumeur carcinoïde ou un VIPome ▪ le soulagement des symptômes et l'inhibition de la croissance tumorale chez les patients présentant un adénome de l'hypophyse associé à l'acromégalie ▪ le traitement de la diarrhée chez les patients atteints du sida.

OCYTOCINE,
voir Oxytocine

ŒSTRADIOL

Estrace

œstradiol, anneau vaginal

Estring

œstradiol, cypionate d'

Ce médicament n'est pas commercialisé au Canada.

œstradiol, gel

Estrogel

œstradiol, comprimé vaginal

Vagifem

œstradiol, timbre transdermique

Climara, Estraderm, Estradot, Oesclim, Sandoz Estradiol dermVivelle

œstradiol/acétate de noréthindrone, timbre transdermique

Estalis, Estalis-Sequi, Estracomb

œstradiol, valérianate d'

Ce médicament n'est pas commercialisé au Canada.

CLASSIFICATION:

Hormones (œstrogènes)

Grossesse – catégorie X

INDICATIONS

PO, transdermique: Remplacement des œstrogènes (hormonothérapie de substitution) dans le traitement des symptômes vasomoteurs de la ménopause et de divers états de carence œstrogénique dont: l'hypogonadisme (femmes) ▪ l'ovariectomie ▪ l'insuffisance ovarienne primaire ▪ Traitement et prévention de l'ostéoporose postménopausique ▪ **Gel:** Soulagement des symptômes ménopausiques et postménopausiques ▪ Traitement de la vaginite atrophique ▪ **Voie intravaginale:** Traitement de la vaginite atrophique pouvant survenir à la ménopause ▪ On recommande l'usage concomitant de progestatifs au cours d'un traitement cyclique afin de réduire le risque de cancer de l'endomètre chez les patientes dont l'utérus est intact.

MÉCANISME D'ACTION

Les œstrogènes favorisent la croissance et le développement des organes sexuels et maintiennent les caractéristiques sexuelles secondaires chez la femme ▪ Les effets métaboliques comprennent la réduction des concentrations sanguines de cholestérol, la synthèse des protéines et la rétention hydrosodée. ***Effets thérapeutiques:*** Rétablissement de l'équilibre hormonal en présence de divers états de carence ▪ Traitement des tumeurs sensibles aux hormones.

PHARMACOCINÉTIQUE

Absorption: Bonne (PO); rapide (peau et muqueuses).
Distribution: Tout l'organisme. L'agent traverse la barrière placentaire et passe dans le lait maternel.

Métabolisme et excrétion: Métabolisme majoritairement hépatique et tissulaire. L'œstradiol subit plusieurs cycles entérohépatiques et son absorption depuis le tractus gastro-intestinal peut être accrue.

Demi-vie: Inconnue.

Profil temps-action (effets œstrogéniques)

	DÉBUT D'ACTION	PIC	DURÉE
PO	inconnu	inconnu	inconnue
TD†	inconnu	inconnu	3 – 4 jours (Estraderm) 7 jours (Climara)
Anneau vaginal	inconnu	inconnu	90 jours
Comprimé vaginal	inconnu	inconnu	3 – 4 jours
Anneau vaginal	inconnu	inconnu	90 jours

† Timbre transdermique.

CONTRE-INDICATIONS, PRÉCAUTIONS ET MISES EN GARDE

Contre-indications: Maladie thromboembolique ■ Saignements vaginaux non diagnostiqués ■ **OBST.**: Risque d'effets nocifs sur le fœtus ■ Allaitement ■ Hypersensibilité ■ Antécédents personnels de cancer œstrogénodépendant ■ Hyperplasie de l'endomètre ■ Migraine classique ■ Problèmes oculaires liés à une atteinte vasculaire ophtalmique ■ Maladies hépatiques évolutives ■ Antécédents d'accidents vasculaires cérébraux ■ Antécédents de porphyrie.

Précautions et mises en garde: Maladie cardiovasculaire sous-jacente ■ Maladies rénales graves ■ Ce type d'œstrogénothérapie comporte un risque accru de cancer de l'endomètre.

RÉACTIONS INDÉSIRABLES ET EFFETS SECONDAIRES

SNC: céphalées, étourdissements, léthargie.

ORLO: intolérance aux lentilles cornéennes, aggravation de la myopie ou de l'astigmatisme.

CV: INFARCTUS DU MYOCARDE, THROMBOEMBOLIE, œdème, hypertension.

GI: nausées, variations pondérales, anorexie, gain d'appétit, jaunisse, vomissements.

GU: *femmes* – aménorrhée, dysménorrhée, hémorragies utérines de l'œstrogénothérapie, érosions cervicales, perte de la libido, candidose vaginale; *hommes* – impuissance, atrophie testiculaire.

Tég.: peau grasse, acné, pigmentation, urticaire.

End.: gynécomastie (hommes), hyperglycémie.

HÉ: hypercalcémie, rétention hydrosodée.

Loc.: crampes dans les jambes.

Divers: sensibilité mammaire.

INTERACTIONS

Médicament-médicament: L'œstradiol peut modifier les besoins en **warfarine**, en **hypoglycémiants oraux** ou en **insuline** ■ Les **barbituriques** ou la **rifampine** peuvent diminuer l'efficacité de l'œstradiol ■ L'utilisation d'œstradiol par les fumeuses est associée à un risque accru d'effets secondaires cardiovasculaires.

VOIES D'ADMINISTRATION ET POSOLOGIE

Les œstrogènes doivent être utilisés à la dose minimale efficace pendant la plus courte période de temps possible, compte tenu des objectifs recherchés.

Symptômes de la ménopause, vaginite atrophique, hypogonadisme chez la femme, insuffisance ovarienne primaire, ostéoporose

- **PO (adultes)**: De 0,5 à 2 mg par jour ou traitement cyclique.
- **Voie transdermique (adultes)**: *Estraderm* – Timbre transdermique de 25, 50 ou 100 µg/24 h, à appliquer 2 fois par semaine. *Estradot* – Timbre transdermique de 25, 37,5, 50, 75 ou 100 µg/24 h, à appliquer 2 fois par semaine. *Climara* – Timbre transdermique de 25, 50, 75 ou 100 µg/24 h, à appliquer 1 fois par semaine. *Estalis* – Timbre transdermique de 140/50 ou 250/50 µg/24 h, à appliquer 2 fois par semaine. *Vivelle* – Timbre transdermique de 37,5 à 100 µg/24 h, à appliquer 2 fois par semaine. Des progestatifs peuvent être utilisés pendant 10 à 14 jours par mois.
- **Gel (adultes)**: *Estrogel* – 2,5 g par jour, en traitement cyclique.

Traitement de la vaginite atrophique

- **Voie intravaginale (adultes)**: *Estring* – 1 anneau (2 mg) à insérer dans le vagin tous les 90 jours. *Vagifem* – 25 µg, 1 fois par jour, pendant 14 jours (phase initiale), puis 25 µg, 2 fois par semaine (phase d'entretien).

PRÉSENTATION

Comprimés oraux: 0,5 mg[Pr], 1 mg[Pr], 2 mg[Pr] ■ **Comprimé vaginal**: 25 µg[Pr] ■ **Timbre transdermique**: libération de 25 µg/24 h[Pr], de 37,5 µg/24 h[Pr], de 50 µg/ 24 h[Pr], de 75 µg/24 h[Pr], de 100 µg/24 h[Pr] ■ **Anneau vaginal**: libération de 2 mg en 90 jours[Pr] ■ **Gel**: Flacon-doseur de 80 g[Pr] ■ **Diverses associations d'œstradiol** avec, entre autres, de l'acétate de noréthindrone et du benzilylhydrazone énanthate de testostérone: Estalis[Pr], Estalis-Sequi[Pr], Estracomb[Pr].

O

SOINS INFIRMIERS

ÉVALUATION DE LA SITUATION

- Mesurer la pression artérielle avant l'œstrogénothérapie et à intervalles réguliers pendant toute sa durée.
- Effectuer le bilan quotidien des ingesta et des excreta et peser la patiente toutes les semaines. Signaler toute variation pondérale importante ou un gain de poids constant.

Ménopause: Évaluer la fréquence et la gravité des symptômes vasomoteurs.

Tests de laboratoire:

- L'œstradiol peut entraîner l'élévation des taux de cholestérol HDL, de phospholipides et de triglycérides et la baisse des taux sériques de cholestérol LDL et de cholestérol total.
- L'œstradiol peut entraîner l'élévation des concentrations sériques de glucose, de sodium, de cortisol, de prolactine, de prothrombine et des facteurs VII, VIII, IX et X. Il peut diminuer les concentrations sériques de folate, de pyridoxine et d'antithrombine III, ainsi que les concentrations urinaires du prégnandiol.
- Suivre de près les résultats des tests de la fonction hépatique avant l'administration de l'œstradiol et à intervalles réguliers tout au long du traitement.
- L'œstradiol peut modifier les résultats du dosage des hormones thyroïdiennes, entraîner des résultats faussement élevés à l'épreuve de l'agrégation plaquettaire induite par la noradrénaline et des résultats faussement bas au test à la métyrapone.
- L'hormone peut induire une hypercalcémie chez les patientes présentant des lésions osseuses métastatiques.

O

DIAGNOSTICS INFIRMIERS POSSIBLES

- Dysfonctionnement sexuel (Indications).
- Connaissances insuffisantes sur le traitement médicamenteux (Enseignement au patient et à ses proches).

INTERVENTIONS INFIRMIÈRES

PO: Pour réduire les nausées, administrer l'œstradiol pendant le repas ou immédiatement après.

Voie intravaginale: Le fabricant fournit l'applicateur avec la crème. La dose est inscrite sur l'applicateur. Laver l'applicateur avec de l'eau chaude et un savon doux après chaque utilisation.

Timbre transdermique: Lorsqu'on substitue aux comprimés oraux le timbre transdermique, appliquer le timbre 1 semaine après la prise de la dernière dose par voie orale ou lorsque les symptômes réapparaissent.

ENSEIGNEMENT AU PATIENT ET À SES PROCHES

- Conseiller à la patiente de respecter rigoureusement la posologie recommandée. Si elle n'a pas pu prendre le médicament au moment habituel, elle doit le prendre aussitôt que possible à moins que ce ne soit presque l'heure prévue pour la dose suivante. Il ne faut jamais remplacer une dose manquée par une double dose.
- Si les nausées deviennent gênantes, recommander à la patiente de manger des aliments solides qui peuvent souvent procurer un soulagement.
- Expliquer à la patiente le schéma posologique et le calendrier du traitement d'entretien. La prévenir que l'interruption brusque du traitement peut provoquer un saignement de retrait.
- Recommander à la patiente de prévenir un professionnel de la santé si les signes et les symptômes suivants se manifestent: rétention hydrique (œdème des chevilles et des pieds, gain de poids); troubles thromboemboliques (douleurs, œdème et sensibilité au niveau des membres, céphalées, douleurs thoraciques, vision trouble); dépression; dysfonctionnement hépatique (jaunissement de la peau ou des yeux, prurit, urine foncée, selles de couleur pâle).
- Recommander à la patiente d'arrêter le traitement et de prévenir un professionnel de la santé si elle pense être enceinte.
- Recommander à la patiente qui doit suivre un traitement ou subir une intervention chirurgicale d'avertir le professionnel de la santé qu'elle suit ce type d'hormonothérapie.
- Prévenir la patiente que l'usage du tabac pendant l'œstrogénothérapie l'expose à des risques accrus d'effets secondaires graves, particulièrement si elle est âgée de plus de 35 ans.
- Inciter la patiente à utiliser un écran solaire et à porter des vêtements protecteurs afin de prévenir l'hyperpigmentation.
- Expliquer à la patiente qui reçoit l'œstradiol pour le traitement de l'ostéoporose que l'exercice peut freiner et même renverser la perte de substance osseuse. Lui conseiller de consulter un professionnel de la santé au sujet de toute restriction éventuelle avant de s'engager dans un programme d'exercices.
- Insister sur l'importance des examens réguliers de suivi, tous les 6 à 12 mois, comprenant la prise de la pression artérielle, l'examen des seins, de l'abdomen et des organes pelviens et le prélèvement de frottis vaginaux pour le test de Papanicolaou, et d'une mammographie, tous les 12 mois ou selon les recommandations du professionnel de la santé. Celui-ci devrait évaluer la possibilité d'interrompre

le traitement tous les 3 à 6 mois. Si la patiente suit un traitement prolongé (non cyclique) ou si elle ne prend pas en même temps des progestatifs, on peut lui recommander une biopsie de l'endomètre si l'utérus est intact.

Voie intravaginale:

- Montrer à la patiente la façon d'utiliser l'applicateur. Lui conseiller de rester allongée pendant au moins 30 minutes après l'application du médicament. Lui recommander d'utiliser une serviette hygiénique pour protéger ses vêtements, mais non pas un tampon. Si elle n'a pu appliquer la crème à l'heure habituelle, lui recommander de sauter cette dose et de reprendre le schéma posologique habituel.
- Recommander à la patiente d'utiliser l'applicateur fourni avec le comprimé vaginal. Lui conseiller de l'introduire le plus profondément possible dans le vagin, sans forcer.

Anneau vaginal: Recommander à la patiente de donner une forme ovale à l'anneau et de l'introduire dans le tiers supérieur du dôme vaginal. Un positionnement précis n'est pas essentiel. Lorsque l'anneau est en place, la patiente ne devrait pas le sentir. Si l'anneau la gêne, il n'est probablement pas installé assez profondément dans le vagin. Il suffit alors de le pousser doucement un peu plus loin. Il faut laisser l'anneau en place pendant 90 jours. Il ne devrait pas gêner les rapports sexuels. Expliquer à la patiente que si l'effort ou la défécation font descendre l'anneau, elle devrait le repousser plus profondément dans le vagin avec le doigt. S'il est éjecté, elle devrait le rincer à l'eau tiède et le réintroduire dans le vagin. Pour le retirer, elle devrait glisser un doigt dans l'anneau et le sortir.

Timbre transdermique: Expliquer à la patiente qu'elle doit d'abord se laver les mains et les sécher; appliquer ensuite le timbre sur la peau intacte dans une partie de l'abdomen dépourvue de poils (ne pas l'appliquer sur les seins ou à la taille). Exercer une pression sur le timbre pendant 10 secondes afin d'assurer une bonne adhérence à la peau (particulièrement autour des bordures). Éviter les régions où les vêtements peuvent frotter dessus. Changer d'emplacement lors de chaque nouvelle application afin de prévenir les risques d'irritation cutanée. Ne pas réutiliser le même emplacement avant 1 semaine. On peut recoller le timbre s'il s'est détaché.

Gel: Enfoncer fermement le poussoir une première fois en recueillant le gel dans la main. Appliquer le gel sur un bras. Enfoncer le poussoir une deuxième fois, et étendre cette fois-ci le gel sur l'autre bras. On recommande d'appliquer Estrogel sur les deux bras. On peut également l'appliquer sur l'abdomen ou sur la face interne des cuisses. Il n'est pas nécessaire de changer régulièrement l'endroit où le gel est appliqué (ne pas appliquer le gel sur les seins). Ne pas l'appliquer non plus sur le visage, ni sur une peau irritée ou abîmée. Laisser sécher le gel pendant 2 minutes environ avant de s'habiller.

VÉRIFICATION DE L'EFFICACITÉ THÉRAPEUTIQUE

L'efficacité du traitement peut être démontrée par: la résolution des symptômes vasomoteurs de la ménopause ▪ la diminution des démangeaisons, de l'inflammation ou de la sécheresse du vagin et de la vulve provoquées par la ménopause ▪ la normalisation des concentrations d'œstrogènes en cas d'ovariectomie ou d'hypogonadisme chez la femme ▪ la prévention de l'ostéoporose.

ŒSTROGÈNES CONJUGUÉS

C.E.S., Congest, Premarin

ŒSTROGÈNES CONJUGUÉS (SYNTHÉTIQUES, A)

Ces préparations ne sont pas commercialisées au Canada.

CLASSIFICATION:

Hormones (œstrogènes)

Grossesse – catégorie X

O

INDICATIONS

PO: Élément de l'hormonothérapie de substitution dans le traitement des symptômes vasomoteurs de la ménopause ▪ Traitement de diverses carences œstrogéniques dont: l'hypogonadisme (femmes) ▪ l'ovariectomie ▪ l'insuffisance ovarienne primaire ▪ Traitement d'appoint de l'ostéoporose postménopausique ▪ Vaginite atrophique et atrophie vulvaire ▪ Traitement d'appoint du cancer de la prostate ou du cancer du sein postménopausique évolutifs, inopérables ▪ **IM, IV:** Hémorragie utérine provoquée par un déséquilibre hormonal ▪ **Voie intravaginale:** Traitement de l'atrophie vaginale, de la dyspareunie et de la *kraurosis vulvæ* ▪ On recommande l'usage concomitant des progestatifs au cours du traitement cyclique afin de réduire le risque de cancer de l'endomètre chez les patientes dont l'utérus est intact.

MÉCANISME D'ACTION

Les œstrogènes favorisent la croissance et le développement des organes sexuels et maintiennent les caractéristiques sexuelles secondaires chez la femme ▪ Les effets métaboliques comprennent la réduction des concentrations sanguines de cholestérol, la synthèse des protéines et la rétention hydrosodée. ***Effets thérapeutiques:*** Rétablissement de l'équilibre hormonal en présence de divers états de carence et traitement des tumeurs sensibles aux hormones.

PHARMACOCINÉTIQUE

Absorption: Bonne (PO); rapide (peau et muqueuses).
Distribution: Tout l'organisme. Ces hormones traversent la barrière placentaire et passent dans le lait maternel.
Métabolisme et excrétion: Métabolisme majoritairement hépatique et tissulaire. Les œstrogènes conjugués subissent plusieurs cycles entérohépatiques et leur absorption depuis le tractus gastro-intestinal peut être accrue.
Demi-vie: Inconnue.

Profil temps-action (effets des œstrogènes)†

	Début d'action	Pic	Durée
PO	rapide	inconnu	24 h
IM	retardé	inconnu	6 – 12 h
IV	rapide	inconnu	6 – 12 h

† L'effet sur les tumeurs peut prendre de nombreuses semaines.

CONTRE-INDICATIONS, PRÉCAUTIONS ET MISES EN GARDE

0

Contre-indications: Maladie thromboembolique ■ Saignements vaginaux non diagnostiqués ■ **Obst.**: Risque d'effets nocifs sur le fœtus ■ Allaitement ■ Hypersensibilité ■ Hyperplasie de l'endomètre ■ Antécédents personnels de cancer œstrogénodépendant ■ Migraine classique ■ Problèmes oculaires liés à une atteinte vasculaire ophtalmique ■ Maladies hépatiques évolutives ■ Antécédents d'accidents vasculaires cérébraux.
Précautions et mises en garde: Utilisation à long terme (plus de 4 à 5 ans); risques accrus d'infarctus du myocarde, d'accident vasculaire cérébral, de cancer du sein invasif, d'embolie pulmonaire et de thrombose veineuse profonde chez les femmes ménopausées ■ Maladie cardiovasculaire sous-jacente ■ Maladies rénales graves ■ Ce type d'œstrogénothérapie comporte un risque accru de cancer de l'endomètre.

RÉACTIONS INDÉSIRABLES ET EFFETS SECONDAIRES (usage par voie générale)

SNC: céphalées, étourdissements, léthargie, dépression.
ORLO: intolérance aux lentilles cornéennes, aggravation de la myopie ou de l'astigmatisme.
CV: INFARCTUS DU MYOCARDE, THROMBOEMBOLIE, œdème, hypertension.
GI: nausées, variations pondérales, anorexie, gain d'appétit, jaunisse, vomissements.
GU: *femmes* – aménorrhée, hémorragies utérines consécutives à l'œstrogénothérapie, dysménorrhée, érosion cervicale, perte de la libido, candidose vaginale; *hommes* – impuissance, atrophie testiculaire.
Tég.: acné, peau grasse, pigmentation, urticaire.
End.: gynécomastie (hommes), hyperglycémie.
HÉ: hypercalcémie, rétention hydrosodée.
Loc.: crampes dans les jambes.
Divers: sensibilité mammaire.

INTERACTIONS

Médicament-médicament: Les œstrogènes conjugués peuvent modifier les besoins en **warfarine**, en **hypoglycémiants oraux** ou en **insuline** ■ Les **barbituriques** ou la **rifampicine** peuvent diminuer l'efficacité des œstrogènes conjugués ■ L'**usage du tabac** augmente le risque de réactions cardiovasculaires indésirables.
Médicament-produits naturels: Le **millepertuis** peut diminuer les taux ainsi que l'efficacité des œstrogènes conjugués.

VOIES D'ADMINISTRATION ET POSOLOGIE

Ovariectomie, insuffisance ovarienne primaire
- **PO (adultes)**: 1,25 mg par jour ou en traitement cyclique.

Ostéoporose
- **PO (adultes)**: 0,625 mg par jour.

Symptômes ménopausiques
- **PO (adultes)**: De 0,625 à 1,25 mg par jour ou en traitement cyclique.

Hypogonadisme
- **PO (adultes)**: De 0,3 à 0,625 mg par jour ou en traitement cyclique.

Cancer du sein inopérable chez les femmes ménopausées et les hommes
- **PO (adultes)**: 10 mg, 3 fois par jour.

Cancer inopérable de la prostate
- **PO (adultes)**: De 1,25 à 2,5 mg, 3 fois par jour.

Hémorragie utérine
- **IM et IV (adultes)**: 25 mg; on peut répéter l'administration de cette dose de 6 à 12 heures plus tard, au besoin.

Vaginite atrophique
- **Voie intravaginale (adultes)**: De 0,5 à 2 g de crème tous les jours pendant 3 semaines; observer une pause de 1 semaine, puis reprendre le traitement.
- **PO (adultes)**: De 0,3 à 1,25 mg par jour ou en traitement cyclique.

PRÉSENTATION (version générique disponible)

Comprimés: 0,3 mg[Pr], 0,625 mg[Pr], 0,9 mg[Pr], 1,25 mg[Pr], 2,5 mg[Pr] ■ **Poudre pour injection**: 25 mg/fiole[Pr] ■ **Crème vaginale**: 0,625 mg/g[Pr] ■ **En association avec**: médroxyprogestérone, dans un conditionnement favorisant l'observance du traitement (Premplus[Pr]).

SOINS INFIRMIERS

ÉVALUATION DE LA SITUATION

- Mesurer la pression artérielle avant le début de l'œstrogénothérapie et à intervalles réguliers pendant toute sa durée.
- Effectuer le bilan quotidien des ingesta et des excreta et peser la patiente toutes les semaines. Signaler au médecin toute variation pondérale importante ou un gain de poids constant.

Ménopause: Évaluer la fréquence et la gravité des symptômes vasomoteurs.

Tests de laboratoire:

- Les œstrogènes conjugués peuvent entraîner une élévation des taux de cholestérol HDL, de phospholipides et de triglycérides et une baisse des taux sériques de cholestérol LDL et de cholestérol total.
- Les œstrogènes conjugués peuvent entraîner l'élévation des concentrations sériques de glucose, de sodium, de cortisol, de prolactine, de prothrombine et des facteurs VII, VIII, IX et X. Ils peuvent diminuer les concentrations sériques de folate, de pyridoxine et d'antithrombine III, ainsi que les concentrations urinaires de prégnandiol.
- Suivre de près les résultats des tests de la fonction hépatique avant l'administration des œstrogènes conjugués et à intervalles réguliers tout au long du traitement.
- Les œstrogènes conjugués peuvent modifier les résultats du dosage des hormones thyroïdiennes, entraîner des résultats faussement élevés à l'épreuve de l'agrégation plaquettaire induite par la noradrénaline et des résultats faussement bas au test à la métyrapone.
- L'hormone peut induire une hypercalcémie chez les patients présentant des lésions osseuses métastatiques.

DIAGNOSTICS INFIRMIERS POSSIBLES

- Dysfonctionnement sexuel (Indications).
- Connaissances insuffisantes sur le traitement médicamenteux (Enseignement au patient et à ses proches).

INTERVENTIONS INFIRMIÈRES

- Les œstrogènes devraient être administrés à la dose minimale efficace et pendant la plus courte période de temps possible compte tenu des objectifs recherchés.

PO: Pour réduire les nausées, administrer ces hormones pendant le repas ou immédiatement après.

Voie intravaginale: Le fabricant fournit l'applicateur avec la crème. La dose est inscrite sur l'applicateur. Laver l'applicateur avec de l'eau chaude et un savon doux après chaque utilisation.

IM:

- Pour reconstituer la solution, retirer au moins 5 mL d'air de la fiole contenant la poudre sèche et introduire lentement le diluant stérile en le laissant couler le long de la paroi. Agiter délicatement la fiole pour diluer la poudre; ne pas agiter trop vigoureusement. La solution est stable pendant 60 jours au réfrigérateur. Ne pas utiliser la solution si elle contient un précipité ou si elle a une couleur foncée. Consulter les directives du fabricant avant de reconstituer la préparation.
- Préférer la voie IV en raison de la rapidité de la réponse.

IV directe: Reconstituer la solution de la même façon que pour la voie IM. Injecter dans l'embout distal d'une tubulure IV par laquelle s'écoule une solution de NaCl 0,9 %, une solution de D5%E ou une solution de lactate de Ringer. Consulter les directives du fabricant avant de reconstituer la préparation.

Vitesse d'administration: Pour prévenir les bouffées de chaleur, administrer lentement (ne pas dépasser un débit de 5 mg/min). Consulter les directives du fabricant avant de reconstituer la préparation.

Compatibilité (tubulure en Y): héparine ■ potassium, chlorure de ■ vitamines du complexe B avec C.

Incompatibilité en addition au soluté: acide ascorbique ou solutions acides.

O

ENSEIGNEMENT AU PATIENT ET À SES PROCHES

PO: Conseiller à la patiente de respecter rigoureusement la posologie recommandée. Si elle n'a pas pu prendre le médicament au moment habituel, elle doit le prendre aussitôt que possible à moins que ce ne soit presque l'heure prévue pour la dose suivante. Il ne faut jamais remplacer une dose manquée par une double dose.

- Expliquer à la patiente le schéma posologique et le calendrier du traitement d'entretien. La prévenir que l'interruption brusque du traitement peut provoquer un saignement de retrait. Les saignements devraient apparaître pendant la semaine où le traitement par les œstrogènes conjugués est interrompu.

- Si les nausées deviennent gênantes, recommander au patient de manger des aliments solides qui peuvent souvent procurer un soulagement.
- Recommander à la patiente de prévenir un professionnel de la santé si les signes et les symptômes suivants se manifestent: rétention hydrique (œdème des chevilles et des pieds, gain de poids); TROUBLES THROMBOEMBOLIQUES (DOULEURS, ŒDÈME ET SENSIBILITÉ AU NIVEAU DES MEMBRES, CÉPHALÉES, DOULEURS THORACIQUES, VISION TROUBLE); dépression; dysfonctionnement hépatique (jaunissement de la peau ou des yeux, prurit, urine foncée, selles de couleur pâle); saignements vaginaux anormaux.
- Recommander à la patiente d'arrêter le traitement et de prévenir un professionnel de la santé si elle pense être enceinte.
- Prévenir la patiente que l'usage du tabac pendant l'œstrogénothérapie l'expose à des risques accrus d'effets secondaires graves, particulièrement dans le cas des femmes > 35 ans.
- Inciter la patiente à utiliser un écran solaire et à porter des vêtements protecteurs afin de prévenir l'hyperpigmentation.
- Recommander à la patiente qui doit suivre un traitement ou subir une intervention chirurgicale d'avertir le professionnel de la santé qu'elle suit ce type d'hormonothérapie.
- Expliquer à la patiente qui reçoit des œstrogènes pour le traitement de l'ostéoporose que l'exercice peut freiner et même renverser la perte de substance osseuse. Lui conseiller de consulter un professionnel de la santé au sujet de toute restriction éventuelle avant de s'engager dans un programme d'exercices.
- Insister sur l'importance des examens réguliers de suivi, tous les 6 à 12 mois, comprenant la prise de la pression artérielle, l'examen des seins, de l'abdomen, des organes pelviens et le prélèvement de frottis vaginaux pour le test de Papanicolaou, et d'une mammographie, tous les 12 mois ou selon les recommandations du professionnel de la santé. Celui-ci devrait évaluer la possibilité d'interrompre le traitement tous les 3 à 6 mois. Si la patiente suit un traitement prolongé (non cyclique) ou si elle ne prend pas en même temps des progestatifs, on peut lui recommander une biopsie de l'endomètre si l'utérus est intact.
- Informer la patiente que les œstrogènes ne devraient pas être utilisés pour réduire le risque de maladies cardiovasculaires. Ils peuvent accroître le risque de maladies cardiovasculaires et de cancer du sein.

Voie intravaginale: Montrer à la patiente la façon d'utiliser l'applicateur. Lui conseiller de rester allongée pendant au moins 30 minutes après l'application du médicament. Lui recommander d'utiliser une serviette hygiénique pour protéger ses vêtements, mais non pas un tampon. Si elle n'a pu appliquer la crème à l'heure habituelle, lui recommander de sauter cette dose et de reprendre le schéma posologique habituel.

VÉRIFICATION DE L'EFFICACITÉ THÉRAPEUTIQUE

L'efficacité du traitement peut être démontrée par: la résolution des symptômes vasomoteurs de la ménopause ■ la diminution des démangeaisons, de l'inflammation ou de la sécheresse du vagin et de la vulve, provoquées par la ménopause ■ la normalisation des concentrations d'œstrogènes en cas d'ovariectomie ou d'hypogonadisme chez la femme ■ l'arrêt de la propagation des cancers évolutifs du sein ou de la prostate ■ la prévention de l'ostéoporose.

OFLOXACINE,
voir Fluoroquinolones

OLANZAPINE

Zyprexa, Zyprexa Zydis, Zyprexa Intramusculaire

CLASSIFICATION:

Antipsychotique (thiénobenzodiazépine)

Grossesse – catégorie C

INDICATIONS

Traitement de la schizophrénie et des troubles psychotiques apparentés en phase aiguë ou traitement d'entretien ■ Traitement de courte durée des épisodes maniaques ou mixtes du trouble bipolaire I ■ **IM seulement**: maîtrise rapide de l'agitation en présence de schizophrénie, de troubles psychotiques apparentés ou de manie liée au trouble bipolaire.

MÉCANISME D'ACTION

Antagoniste des effets de la dopamine et de la sérotonine de type 2 au niveau du SNC ■ Propriétés anticholinergiques, antihistaminiques et alpha$_1$-adrénolytiques. ***Effets thérapeutiques:*** Diminution du nombre d'épisodes de psychose.

PHARMACOCINÉTIQUE

Absorption: Bonne (PO), mais l'olanzapine est rapidement métabolisée au cours d'un premier passage hépatique, ce qui entraîne une biodisponibilité de 60 %.

Les comprimés oraux ordinaires et à dissolution rapide sont bioéquivalents. À la suite de l'administration IM, les concentrations sériques sont 5 fois plus élevées que dans le cas de la prise par voie orale.
Distribution: Tout l'organisme.
Liaison aux protéines: 93 %.
Métabolisme et excrétion: Métabolisme hépatique important (la plus grande partie du médicament est métabolisée par le P450 CYP 1A2); excrétion rénale (7 % sous forme inchangée).
Demi-vie: De 21 à 54 heures.
Profil temps-action (effet antipsychotique)

	Début d'action	Pic	Durée
PO	inconnu	6 h	inconnue
IM	rapide	15 - 45 min	2 - 4 h

CONTRE-INDICATIONS, PRÉCAUTIONS ET MISES EN GARDE

Contre-indications: Hypersensibilité ■ **Comprimés à dissolution rapide seulement:** Phénylcétonurie (les comprimés contiennent de l'aspartame).
Précautions et mises en garde: Insuffisance hépatique ■ **Gér.:** Il est recommandé de réduire la dose initiale chez les personnes âgées ou chez les patients débilités et les insuffisants rénaux ou hépatiques; l'utilisation chez les personnes âgées atteintes de psychoses reliées à la démence les expose à un risque accru de décès et de morbidité cardiovasculaire ■ Maladie cardiovasculaire ou vasculaire cérébrale ■ Antécédents de convulsions ■ Antécédents de tentatives de suicide ■ Diabète ou facteurs de risque de diabète (problèmes de maîtrise glycémique) ■ Hyperplasie de la prostate ■ Glaucome à angle fermé ■ Antécédents d'iléus paralytique ■ **Obst., allaitement, péd.:** L'innocuité du médicament n'a pas été établie chez les femmes enceintes et chez celles qui allaitent ni chez les enfants < 18 ans.

RÉACTIONS INDÉSIRABLES ET EFFETS SECONDAIRES

SNC: SYNDROME MALIN DES NEUROLEPTIQUES, CONVULSIONS, agitation, étourdissements, céphalées, sédation, faiblesse, dystonie, insomnie, changement d'humeur, troubles de la personnalité, trouble de la parole, dyskinésie tardive.
ORLO: amblyopie, rhinite, ptyalisme, pharyngite.
Resp.: toux, dyspnée.
CV: hypotension orthostatique (risque accru lors de l'administration par voie IM), tachycardie, douleurs thoraciques.
GI: constipation, sécheresse de la bouche (xérostomie), douleurs abdominales, gain d'appétit, nausées.
GU: diminution de la libido, incontinence urinaire.
Tég.: photosensibilité.
End.: diabète, goitre.
HÉ: soif accrue.
Métab.: gain pondéral, dyslipidémie, perte pondérale.
Loc.: hypertonie, douleurs articulaires.
SN: tremblements.
Divers: fièvre, syndrome pseudogrippal.

INTERACTIONS

Médicament-médicament: Les effets de l'olanzapine peuvent être diminués par l'administration concomitante de **carbamazépine**, d'**oméprazole** ou de **rifampicine** ■ Effets hypotenseurs additifs lors de l'administration concomitante d'**antihypertenseurs** ■ Effets additifs sur la dépression du SNC lors de l'usage concomitant d'**alcool** ou d'autres **dépresseurs du SNC** ■ L'olanzapine peut renverser les effets de la **lévodopa** ou ceux d'autres **agonistes de la dopamine**.

VOIES D'ADMINISTRATION ET POSOLOGIE

- **PO (adultes - la plupart des patients):** *Schizophrénie* - initialement, de 5 à 10 mg par jour; on peut augmenter la dose à intervalles d'au moins 1 semaine, par paliers de 5 mg par jour (ne pas dépasser 15 mg par jour). *Manie liée à un trouble bipolaire* - initialement, de 10 à 15 mg, 1 fois par jour. On peut ensuite augmenter la dose par paliers de 5 mg par jour (dose maximale: 20 mg par jour).
- **PO (adultes - personnes âgées ≥ 65 ans, patients débilités ou femmes non fumeuses):** Amorcer le traitement à 1 dose de 5 mg par jour.
- **IM (adultes):** *Agitation aiguë* - 1 dose de 5 à 10 mg, qu'on peut être répétée 2 heures plus tard si besoin est. Si une troisième dose est nécessaire, on doit l'administrer 4 heures après la deuxième dose. La dose quotidienne maximale est de 20 mg par jour.

PRÉSENTATION

Comprimés: 2,5 mg^Pr^, 5 mg^Pr^, 7,5 mg^Pr^, 10 mg^Pr^, 15 mg^Pr^ ■ **Comprimés à dissolution rapide (Zydis):** 5 mg^Pr^, 10 mg^Pr^, 15 mg^Pr^ ■ **Poudre pour injection intramusculaire:** 10 mg^Pr^.

SOINS INFIRMIERS

ÉVALUATION DE LA SITUATION

- Déterminer, avant le traitement et à intervalles réguliers pendant toute sa durée, l'état mental du patient (orientation, humeur, comportement).

- Mesurer la pression artérielle (en position assise, en station debout et en décubitus), le pouls et la fréquence respiratoire et observer l'ÉCG avant l'administration initiale et à intervalles fréquents pendant la période d'adaptation de la posologie.
- Observer étroitement le patient pendant qu'il prend le médicament pour s'assurer qu'il l'a bien avalé.
- Déterminer l'apport liquidien et l'état de la fonction intestinale. Une consommation accrue de liquides et de fibres alimentaires peut prévenir la constipation.
- Suivre de près le patient pour déceler l'akathisie (agitation ou désir de bouger continuellement) et les symptômes extrapyramidaux (*symptômes parkinsoniens:* difficulté d'élocution ou de déglutition, perte de l'équilibre, mouvements d'émiettement, faciès figé, démarche traînante, rigidité, tremblements, spasmes musculaires dystoniques, torsions, secousses musculaires, incapacité de bouger les yeux, faiblesse des bras ou des jambes), tous les 2 mois pendant toute la durée du traitement et de 8 à 12 semaines après qu'il a été mené à terme. Informer immédiatement le médecin de l'apparition de ces symptômes; il peut s'avérer nécessaire de réduire la dose ou d'abandonner le traitement. On peut administrer du trihexyphénidyle ou de la diphenhydramine pour maîtriser ces symptômes.
- Suivre de près l'apparition de la dyskinésie tardive qui se traduit par les symptômes suivants: mouvements rythmiques de la bouche, du visage et des membres, émission de bruits secs avec les lèvres, moue, gonflement des joues, mastication incontrôlée, mouvements rapides de la langue. Prévenir immédiatement le médecin si ces symptômes se manifestent, car de tels effets secondaires peuvent être irréversibles.
- SUIVRE DE PRÈS L'APPARITION DES SYMPTÔMES SUIVANTS DU SYNDROME MALIN DES NEUROLEPTIQUES: FIÈVRE, DÉPRESSION RESPIRATOIRE, TACHYCARDIE, CONVULSIONS, DIAPHORÈSE, HYPERTENSION OU HYPOTENSION, PÂLEUR, FATIGUE, FORTE RIGIDITÉ MUSCULAIRE, PERTE DE LA MAÎTRISE DE LA VESSIE. SIGNALER IMMÉDIATEMENT AU MÉDECIN L'APPARITION DE CES SYMPTÔMES.

Tests de laboratoire: Déterminer la numération globulaire, noter les résultats des tests de la fonction hépatique et effectuer des examens ophtalmologiques à intervalles réguliers tout au long du traitement. L'olanzapine peut entraîner une diminution du nombre de plaquettes et une élévation des concentrations de bilirubine, d'AST, d'ALT, de GGT, de créatine-kinase et de phosphatase alcaline.

DIAGNOSTICS INFIRMIERS POSSIBLES

- Opérations de la pensée perturbées (Indications).
- Connaissances insuffisantes sur le traitement médicamenteux (Enseignement au patient et à ses proches).
- Non-observance du traitement médicamenteux (Enseignement au patient et à ses proches).

INTERVENTIONS INFIRMIÈRES

- NE PAS CONFONDRE ZYPREXA (OLANZAPINE) AVEC CELEXA (CITALOPRAM)

PO: Le médicament peut être administré sans égard aux repas.

- Les comprimés à dissolution rapide doivent être manipulés avec prudence, avec les mains sèches. On doit détacher une alvéole de la plaquette en suivant le pointillé et retirer la pellicule protectrice en évitant de pousser le comprimé au travers de la pellicule. Soulever avec soin le comprimé en poussant le dessous de l'alvéole. En évitant de toucher le comprimé avec les mains, le placer directement dans la bouche du patient. Le comprimé commence à se dissoudre dans la bouche en quelques secondes avec ou sans prise de liquide.

IM: Reconstituer le contenu de la fiole avec 2,1 mL d'eau stérile pour injection afin d'obtenir une concentration de 5 mg/mL. La solution obtenue doit être claire et jaunâtre. Ne pas administrer de solution qui a changé de couleur ou qui contient des particules. Injecter lentement et profondément dans un muscle bien développé. Ne pas administrer par voie SC ou IV. La solution reconstituée doit être utilisée dans l'heure suivant sa reconstitution. Jeter toute portion inutilisée. Consulter les directives de chaque fabricant avant d'administrer la préparation.

ENSEIGNEMENT AU PATIENT ET À SES PROCHES

- Expliquer au patient qu'il doit respecter rigoureusement la posologie recommandée; l'avertir qu'il ne doit jamais sauter de dose, ni remplacer une dose manquée par une double dose. Un sevrage graduel peut s'avérer nécessaire.
- Mettre en garde le patient contre le risque de symptômes extrapyramidaux et de dyskinésie tardive. L'inciter à prévenir immédiatement un professionnel de la santé si ces symptômes se manifestent.
- Recommander au patient de changer lentement de position afin de réduire le risque d'hypotension orthostatique.
- Prévenir le patient que l'olanzapine peut provoquer de la somnolence. Lui conseiller de ne pas conduire et d'éviter les activités qui exigent sa vigilance jusqu'à ce qu'on ait la certitude que le médicament n'entraîne pas cet effet chez lui.

- Prévenir le patient qu'il doit éviter de boire de l'alcool et de prendre d'autres médicaments d'ordonnance ou en vente libre ou des produits naturels pendant le traitement à l'olanzapine.
- Recommander au patient d'utiliser un écran solaire et de porter des vêtements protecteurs lors des expositions au soleil. Lui recommander également d'éviter les températures extrêmes, les exercices vigoureux, les sorties par temps chaud, les douches ou les bains chauds, car ce médicament altère la thermorégulation.
- Conseiller au patient de se rincer fréquemment la bouche, de pratiquer une bonne hygiène buccale et de consommer de la gomme à mâcher ou des bonbons sans sucre pour soulager la sécheresse de la bouche. Lui recommander de consulter un professionnel de la santé si la sécheresse de la bouche persiste pendant plus de 2 semaines.
- Recommander au patient qui doit suivre un autre traitement ou subir une intervention chirurgicale d'avertir le professionnel de la santé qu'il suit un traitement par ce médicament.
- Conseiller au patient d'informer rapidement un professionnel de la santé de l'apparition des symptômes suivants: maux de gorge, fièvre, saignements ou ecchymoses inhabituels, rash, faiblesse, tremblements, troubles visuels, urine de couleur foncée ou selles grises.
- Recommander à la patiente de prévenir un professionnel de la santé si elle pense être enceinte ou souhaite le devenir, ou si elle allaite ou prévoit le faire.
- Insister sur l'importance des examens réguliers de suivi et de la participation active à une psychothérapie.

VÉRIFICATION DES RÉSULTATS

L'efficacité du traitement peut être démontrée par: la diminution de comportements tels que l'excitation, la paranoïa ou le repli sur soi. ✳

OLSALAZINE

Dipentum

CLASSIFICATION:

Anti-inflammatoire local non stéroïdien (entérocolique)

Grossesse – catégorie C

INDICATIONS

Traitement à long terme des patients dont la rectocolite hémorragique est en rémission ■ Traitement de la rectocolite hémorragique aiguë, d'intensité faible à modérée, avec ou sans l'utilisation concomitante de stéroïdes.

MÉCANISME D'ACTION

Action anti-inflammatoire locale au niveau du côlon, probablement due à l'inhibition de la synthèse des prostaglandines. ***Effets thérapeutiques:*** Réduction des symptômes de la maladie intestinale inflammatoire.

PHARMACOCINÉTIQUE

Absorption: Effet local dans le côlon; de 98 à 99 % est transformé en mésalamine (5-acide-aminosalicylique).

Distribution: Effet local au niveau du côlon.

Métabolisme et excrétion: 2 % est absorbé dans la circulation générale et est rapidement métabolisé; élimination majoritairement fécale sous forme de mésalamine.

Demi-vie: 0,9 heure.

Profil temps-action (concentrations plasmatiques)

	DÉBUT D'ACTION	PIC	DURÉE
PO	inconnu	1 h; 4 – 8 h	12 h

CONTRE-INDICATIONS, PRÉCAUTIONS ET MISES EN GARDE

Contre-indications: Réactions d'hypersensibilité aux salicylates ou à l'olsalazine.

Précautions et mises en garde: Risque d'exacerbation des symptômes de la colite (moins de 1 % des patients atteints de rectocolite hémorragique) ■ **OBST., ALLAITEMENT, PÉD.:** L'innocuité de l'agent n'a pas été établie ■ Insuffisance rénale (risque accru d'atteinte tubulaire rénale).

O

RÉACTIONS INDÉSIRABLES ET EFFETS SECONDAIRES

SNC: ataxie, confusion, étourdissement, somnolence, céphalées, dépression, psychoses, agitation.

GI: diarrhée, douleurs abdominales, anorexie, exacerbation de la colite, hépatite médicamenteuse, nausées, vomissements.

Tég.: démangeaisons, rash.

Hémat.: dyscrasie sanguine.

INTERACTIONS

Médicament-médicament: L'utilisation concomitante de **warfarine** peut entraîner une élévation du RNI.

VOIES D'ADMINISTRATION ET POSOLOGIE

- **PO (adultes):** Débuter par 250 mg, 2 fois par jour, dose qu'on peut augmenter par la suite selon la réponse du patient. La dose habituelle pour le traitement est de 500 mg, 4 fois par jour et, pour la prophylaxie, de 500 mg, 2 fois par jour.

PRÉSENTATION

Capsules: 250 mg.

SOINS INFIRMIERS

ÉVALUATION DE LA SITUATION

- Rester à l'affût des signes d'allergie aux sulfamides et aux salicylates. Les patients allergiques à la sulfasalazine peuvent prendre la mésalamine ou l'olsalazine sans danger, mais il faut abandonner le traitement en cas de rash ou de fièvre.
- Effectuer le bilan des ingesta et des excreta. Le patient doit boire suffisamment de liquides pour maintenir un débit urinaire d'au moins 1 200 à 1 500 mL par jour afin de prévenir la cristallurie et la formation de calculs.
- Évaluer les douleurs abdominales et la fréquence, la quantité et la consistance des selles au début du traitement et pendant toute sa durée.

Tests de laboratoire:

- Noter les résultats des analyses des urines, l'urée et les concentrations de créatinine sérique avant le traitement et pendant toute sa durée.
- L'olsalazine peut élever les taux d'AST et d'ALT.
- Suivre la numération globulaire avant le traitement et tous les 3 à 6 mois pendant le traitement prolongé. Abandonner le traitement à l'olsalazine en cas de dyscrasie sanguine.

O

DIAGNOSTICS INFIRMIERS POSSIBLES

- Douleur aiguë (Indications).
- Diarrhée (Indications).

INTERVENTIONS INFIRMIÈRES

PO: Administrer le médicament avec des aliments, à intervalles réguliers, en doses également fractionnées.

ENSEIGNEMENT AU PATIENT ET À SES PROCHES

- Recommander au patient de suivre rigoureusement les recommandations du médecin et de continuer à prendre l'olsalazine même s'il se sent mieux. S'il n'a pas pu prendre le médicament au moment habituel, lui conseiller de le prendre dès que possible à moins que ce ne soit presque l'heure prévue pour la dose suivante.
- Le médicament peut provoquer des étourdissements. Conseiller au patient de ne pas conduire et de ne pas s'engager dans d'autres activités qui exigent sa vigilance jusqu'à ce qu'on ait la certitude que le médicament n'entraîne pas cet effet chez lui.
- Recommander au patient de prévenir un professionnel de la santé en cas de rash, de maux de gorge, de fièvre, d'aphtes, de saignements inhabituels ou de formation inexpliquée d'ecchymoses, de respiration sifflante, de fièvre ou d'urticaire.
- Conseiller au patient de prévenir un professionnel de la santé si les symptômes ne s'améliorent pas après 1 ou 2 mois de traitement.
- Conseiller au patient d'arrêter le traitement si des symptômes d'intolérance aiguë se manifestent (crampes, douleurs abdominales aiguës, diarrhée, fièvre, maux de tête, rash), et d'en informer immédiatement un professionnel de la santé.
- Expliquer au patient qu'il devrait se soumettre à intervalles réguliers à des rectoscopies et à des sigmoïdoscopies afin qu'on puisse déterminer sa réponse au traitement.

VÉRIFICATION DE L'EFFICACITÉ THÉRAPEUTIQUE

L'efficacité du traitement peut être déterminée par: la diminution de la diarrhée et des douleurs abdominales ▪ le rétablissement d'un mode d'élimination intestinale normale; les effets du traitement peuvent se manifester en l'espace de 3 à 21 jours ▪ le maintien de la rémission chez les patients atteints de rectocolite hémorragique.

OMALIZUMAB

Xolair

CLASSIFICATION:

Anticorps monoclonal neutralisant les IgE (Anti-IgE)

Grossesse – catégorie B

INDICATIONS

Traitement de l'asthme persistant de modéré à grave chez les adultes et les adolescents (≥ 12 ans) qui ont obtenu un résultat positif à un test cutané ou à une épreuve de réactivité *in vitro* après avoir été exposés à un pneumoallergène apériodique, et dont les symptômes ne sont pas parfaitement maîtrisés au moyen d'une corticothérapie en inhalation.

MÉCANISME D'ACTION

L'omalizumab est un anticorps monoclonal recombinant obtenu par génie génétique, qui se lie à l'immunoglobuline E humaine (IgE) et empêche sa liaison avec le récepteur, réduisant ainsi la quantité d'IgE libres, propres à déclencher la cascade inflammatoire allergique. ***Effets thérapeutiques:*** Diminution de la fréquence des crises d'asthme et amélioration de la maîtrise des symptômes asthmatiques.

PHARMACOCINÉTIQUE

Absorption: Lente (62 % SC).
Distribution: L'agent traverse la barrière placentaire et passe dans le lait maternel.
Métabolisme et excrétion: Métabolisme par le système réticulo-endothélial et les cellules endothéliales du foie.
Demi-vie: 26 jours.

Profil temps-action (effets sur les taux d'IgE)

	DÉBUT D'ACTION	PIC	DURÉE
SC	1 - 2 h	inconnu	2 - 4 semaines

CONTRE-INDICATIONS, PRÉCAUTIONS ET MISES EN GARDE

Contre-indications: Hypersensibilité.
Précautions et mises en garde: Crises aiguës d'asthme ■ Infestations parasitaires ou autres troubles associés à l'IgE ■ **PÉD.**: L'innocuité et l'efficacité du médicament n'ont pas été établies chez les enfants < 12 ans ■ **OBST., ALLAITEMENT**: L'innocuité du médicament n'a pas été établie chez la femme enceinte ou qui allaite.

RÉACTIONS INDÉSIRABLES ET EFFETS SECONDAIRES

SNC: céphalées, étourdissements, fatigue.
Resp.: infections des voies respiratoires supérieures (p. ex., sinusite, pharyngite).
Loc.: douleur aux jambes, fractures.
Locaux: <u>réactions au point d'injection</u> (ecchymose, rougeur, sensation de chaleur, brûlures, picotements, démangeaisons, éruptions urticariennes, douleur, indurations, formation de masse et inflammation).
Divers: infections virales, douleurs, affections malignes, réactions allergiques locales ou générales (urticaire, dermatite, prurit), ANAPHYLAXIE (ŒDÈME DE LA GORGE OU DE LA LANGUE).

INTERACTIONS

Médicament-médicament: Aucune interaction médicamenteuse n'a été signalée.

VOIES D'ADMINISTRATION ET POSOLOGIE

- **SC (adultes et adolescents ≥ 12 ans)**: De 150 à 375 mg, toutes les 2 ou 4 semaines. La dose et la fréquence d'administration dépendent des concentrations sériques d'IgE totales, mesurées *avant* le début du traitement, ainsi que du poids corporel. Les doses supérieures à 150 mg devront être fractionnées afin de n'administrer qu'un maximum de 150 mg par point d'injection.

PRÉSENTATION

Poudre pour injection: 150 mg/fiole[Pr].

SOINS INFIRMIERS

ÉVALUATION DE LA SITUATION

- Ausculter le murmure vésiculaire et examiner la fonction respiratoire, avant le traitement et à intervalles réguliers pendant toute sa durée.
- Évaluer les symptômes d'allergies (rhinite, conjonctivite, urticaire), avant le traitement et à intervalles réguliers pendant toute sa durée.
- GARDER LE PATIENT SOUS OBSERVATION APRÈS LA PREMIÈRE INJECTION, AINSI QU'APRÈS LES INJECTIONS SUIVANTES. ÉVALUER LES SIGNES DE RÉACTIONS ALLERGIQUES: URTICAIRE, ŒDÈME DE LA LANGUE ET/OU DE LA GORGE. IL Y A RISQUE D'ANAPHYLAXIE. CONSERVER À PORTÉE DE LA MAIN LES MÉDICAMENTS SERVANT AU TRAITEMENT DES RÉACTIONS D'HYPERSENSIBILITÉ, Y COMPRIS L'ANAPHYLAXIE.
- Évaluer la présence de réaction au point d'injection: ecchymose, rougeur, sensation de chaleur, brûlures, picotements, démangeaisons, éruptions urticariennes, douleurs, indurations, formation de masse et inflammation. Ces réactions apparaissent habituellement dans l'heure qui suit l'injection, durent < 8 jours et leur fréquence diminue lors des injections ultérieures.

Tests de laboratoire: Avant de démarrer le traitement, mesurer les concentrations sériques d'IgE totales et le poids corporel afin de déterminer la dose appropriée. Les concentrations sériques d'IgE totales augmentent après l'administration de l'omalizumab en raison de la formation du complexe omalizumab: IgE. Elles peuvent demeurer élevées jusqu'à 1 an après l'arrêt du traitement par l'omalizumab. Par conséquent, leur dosage en cours de traitement ne peut pas servir de guide permettant de réévaluer le schéma posologique.

DIAGNOSTICS INFIRMIERS POSSIBLES

- Dégagement inefficace des voies respiratoires (Indications).
- Connaissances insuffisantes sur le traitement médicamenteux (Enseignement au patient et à ses proches).

INTERVENTIONS INFIRMIÈRES

Poudre stérile pour reconstitution: Pour reconstituer la préparation, injecter 1,4 mL d'eau stérile pour injection

USP avec une seringue de 3 mL munie d'une aiguille de calibre 18 dans la fiole d'omalizumab suivant une technique aseptique standard. Remuer la fiole doucement, en la faisant tourner, afin d'humidifier la poudre de façon uniforme pendant environ 1 minute. Ne pas secouer la fiole. Une fois la poudre humidifiée, remuer la fiole durant 5 à 10 secondes, à intervalles d'environ 5 minutes, afin de dissoudre toutes les particules résiduelles. Il est possible que le contenu de certaines fioles ne puisse se dissoudre complètement avant 20 minutes. À l'aide d'une nouvelle seringue munie d'une aiguille de calibre 18, prélever le volume correspondant à la dose désirée. La concentration de la solution est de 150 mg/1,2 mL par fiole (125 mg/mL). Remplacer l'aiguille de calibre 18 par une aiguille de calibre 25 en prévision de l'injection sous-cutanée. La solution reconstituée est plutôt visqueuse. L'injection peut donc durer de 5 à 10 secondes. Les doses > 150 mg doivent être injectées en plusieurs points. Ne pas utiliser de solutions ayant changé de couleur ou qui contiennent des particules étrangères ou des particules agglomérées.

- Les fioles sont à usage unique seulement et ne contiennent pas d'agent de conservation. Il est recommandé d'utiliser l'omalizumab immédiatement après la reconstitution (c'est-à-dire dans les 4 heures). Conserver les fioles contenant la solution reconstituée à l'abri des rayons du soleil.
- Conserver les fioles au réfrigérateur (de 2 °C à 8 °C). Ne pas congeler. Vérifier la date de péremption du produit.

O

ENSEIGNEMENT AU PATIENT ET À SES PROCHES

- Recommander au patient de respecter les rendez-vous pris avec le médecin ou l'infirmière qui lui injectera le produit, afin que les injections soient administrées à intervalles réguliers, même si les symptômes sont absents. L'avertir qu'il ne doit jamais cesser le traitement sans consulter un professionnel de la santé.
- Prévenir le patient qu'il ne doit pas interrompre la corticothérapie orale ou en inhalation lorsqu'il démarre le traitement par l'omalizumab. Toute diminution de la dose de corticostéroïdes doit se faire sous la surveillance directe d'un médecin et, au besoin, graduellement.
- Conseiller au patient de ne pas interrompre le traitement ni de réduire la dose des autres médicaments contre l'asthme sans consulter un professionnel de la santé au préalable. Il faut aussi lui préciser que son asthme ne s'atténuera pas immédiatement après le début du traitement par l'omalizumab.
- Informer le patient que l'omalizumab n'est pas destiné au traitement des crises aiguës d'asthme et qu'il ne doit pas être employé pour le traitement du bronchospasme aigu ni de l'état de mal asthmatique.
- Prévenir le patient que l'omalizumab peut provoquer des étourdissements ou de la fatigue. Lui conseiller de ne pas conduire et d'éviter les activités qui exigent sa vigilance jusqu'à ce qu'on ait la certitude que le médicament n'entraîne pas ces effets chez lui.

VÉRIFICATION DE L'EFFICACITÉ THÉRAPEUTIQUE

L'efficacité du traitement peut être démontrée par: la réduction de la fréquence des crises d'asthme et l'amélioration de la maîtrise des symptômes asthmatiques. ✳

OMÉPRAZOLE

Apo-Oméprazole, Losec, Losec MUPS

CLASSIFICATION:

Antiulcéreux (inhibiteur de la pompe à protons), traitement d'éradication de H. pylori

Grossesse – catégorie C

INDICATIONS

Traitement du reflux gastro-œsophagien (RGO) symptomatique et de l'œsophagite par RGO ■ Traitement de l'ulcère duodénal et gastrique (induit ou non par les AINS) ■ Traitement de l'hypersécrétion pathologique, dont le syndrome de Zollinger-Ellison ■ **En association avec l'amoxicilline et la clarithromycine ou le métronidazole et la clarithromycine**: Éradication de *H. pylori* chez les patients ayant des antécédents d'ulcère duodénal ■ Ulcère duodénal associé à *H. pylori*.

MÉCANISME D'ACTION

Inhibition spécifique de l'enzyme gastrique H^+, K^+-ATPase (pompe à protons), responsable des sécrétions acides des cellules pariétales de l'estomac, ce qui prévient l'entrée des ions hydrogène dans la lumière du tube gastrique. ***Effets thérapeutiques:*** Réduction de l'accumulation d'acide dans la lumière gastrique, ce qui diminue le reflux gastro-œsophagien ■ Guérison de l'ulcère gastroduodénal.

PHARMACOCINÉTIQUE

Absorption: Rapide (PO).

Distribution: Toutes les cellules pariétales gastriques.

Liaison aux protéines: 95 %.
Métabolisme et excrétion: Métabolisme majoritairement hépatique.
Demi-vie: De 0,5 à 1 heure (de plus longue durée en présence de maladie hépatique).

Profil temps-action (suppression des sécrétions acides)

	DÉBUT D'ACTION	PIC	DURÉE
PO	en 1 h	en 2 h	72 - 96 h

CONTRE-INDICATIONS, PRÉCAUTIONS ET MISES EN GARDE

Contre-indications: Hypersensibilité.
Précautions et mises en garde: Maladie hépatique (une réduction de la dose peut s'avérer nécessaire) ■ **OBST., ALLAITEMENT, PÉD.**: L'innocuité du médicament n'a pas été établie chez les femmes enceintes, chez celles qui allaitent et chez les enfants < 18 ans ■ **GÉR.**: La dose quotidienne ne doit pas dépasser 20 mg.

RÉACTIONS INDÉSIRABLES ET EFFETS SECONDAIRES

SNC: étourdissements, somnolence, fatigue, céphalées, faiblesse.
CV: douleurs thoraciques.
GI: douleurs abdominales, régurgitations acides, constipation, diarrhée, flatulence, nausées, vomissements.
Tég.: démangeaisons, rash.
Divers: réactions allergiques.

INTERACTIONS

Médicament-médicament: L'oméprazole est métabolisé par le cytochrome **CYP450** et peut entrer en compétition avec d'autres **agents métabolisés par ce système enzymatique** ■ L'oméprazole ralentit le métabolisme de la **phénytoïne**, du **diazépam**, du **flurazépam**, du **triazolam**, de la **cyclosporine**, du **disulfirame** et de la **warfarine** et peut en accentuer les effets ■ L'oméprazole peut modifier l'absorption des **médicaments nécessitant un pH acide**, tels que le **kétoconazole**, les **esters d'ampicilline**, la **cyanocobolamine** et les **sels ferreux** ■ L'oméprazole a été administré avec des **antiacides** sans qu'on signale d'interaction ■ Risque accru de saignements lors de l'usage concomitant de **warfarine** (suivre le RNI et le temps de prothrombine).

VOIES D'ADMINISTRATION ET POSOLOGIE

- **PO (adultes)**: *RGO* – 20 mg, 1 fois par jour pendant 4 semaines; dose d'entretien: 10 mg, 1 fois par jour. *Œsophagite par RGO* – 20 mg, 1 fois par jour, pendant 4 semaines. Si l'œsophagite par reflux n'est pas guérie après ce traitement initial, on recommande un traitement additionnel de 4 semaines. *Œsophagite par reflux réfractaire* – 40 mg, 1 fois par jour, pendant 8 semaines. *Traitement d'entretien de l'œsophagite par reflux* –10 mg, 1 fois par jour (selon des études d'une durée de 12 mois et en traitement d'entretien continu chez un nombre limité de patients, pendant un laps de temps allant jusqu'à 6 ans). S'il y a récidive, on peut augmenter la dose pour la passer à 20 mg ou à 40 mg, 1 fois par jour. *Traitement de l'ulcère duodénal et gastrique (induit ou non par les AINS)* – 20 mg, 1 fois par jour, pendant 4 semaines. On peut augmenter la dose jusqu'à 40 mg dans les cas réfractaires. La durée du traitement est de 2 semaines, en cas d'ulcère duodénal, et de 4 semaines, en cas d'ulcère gastrique et d'ulcère induit par les AINS (le traitement peut être prolongé d'autant, si besoin est). Les doses d'entretien sont généralement de 10 mg, 1 fois par jour, en cas d'ulcère duodénal, et de 20 mg, 1 fois par jour, en cas d'ulcère gastrique. *Ulcère gastroduodénal associé à* H. pylori – *triple thérapie par l'oméprazole, l'amoxicilline et la clarithromycine (ou Losec 1-2-3 A)*: 20 mg d'oméprazole, 1 000 mg d'amoxicilline et 500 mg de clarithromycine, 2 fois par jour, pour chacun des médicaments, pendant 7 jours; *triple thérapie par l'oméprazole, le métronidazole et la clarithromycine (ou Losec 1-2-3 M)*: 20 mg d'oméprazole, 500 mg de métronidazole et 250 mg de clarithromycine, 2 fois par jour, pour chacun des médicaments, pendant 7 jours. Pour assurer la guérison et la maîtrise des symptômes, il est recommandé de continuer l'administration de l'oméprazole à 20 mg par jour, pendant 3 semaines, en cas d'ulcère duodénal, et jusqu'à 12 semaines, en cas d'ulcère gastrique. *Syndrome de Zollinger-Ellison* – initialement, 60 mg, 1 fois par jour; on peut augmenter la dose jusqu'à concurrence de 120 mg, 3 fois par jour. Si la dose quotidienne est supérieure à 80 mg, administrer en doses fractionnées.

O

PRÉSENTATION

Comprimés à libération retard: 10 mg^{Pr}, 20 mg^{Pr} ■ **Gélules**: 10 mg^{Pr}, 20 mg^{Pr}, 40 mg^{Pr} ■ **Capsules**: 10 mg^{Pr} ■ **En association avec**: amoxicilline et clarithromycine (Losec 1-2-3 A^{Pr}); métronidazole et clarithromycine (Losec 1-2-3 M^{Pr}).

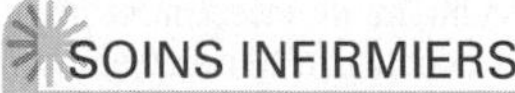

SOINS INFIRMIERS

ÉVALUATION DE LA SITUATION

Observer le patient à intervalles réguliers afin d'évaluer la douleur épigastrique ou abdominale et de déceler la présence de sang visible ou occulte dans les selles, les vomissements ou le liquide d'aspiration gastrique.

Tests de laboratoire:

- Noter, à intervalles réguliers pendant toute la durée du traitement, la numération globulaire et la formule leucocytaire.
- L'oméprazole peut entraîner l'élévation des concentrations sériques d'AST, d'ALT, de phosphatase alcaline et de bilirubine.
- Il peut aussi élever les concentrations sériques de gastrine pendant la 1re ou la 2e semaine de traitement. Les concentrations reviennent à la normale à l'arrêt du traitement par l'oméprazole.
- Effectuer un suivi du RNI et du temps de prothrombine chez les patients prenant de la warfarine.

DIAGNOSTICS INFIRMIERS POSSIBLES

- Douleur aiguë (Indications).
- Connaissances insuffisantes sur le traitement médicamenteux (Enseignement au patient et à ses proches).

INTERVENTIONS INFIRMIÈRES

- Administrer le médicament avant les repas, de préférence le matin. LE PATIENT DEVRAIT AVALER LES CAPSULES ET LES COMPRIMÉS TELS QUELS, SANS LES ÉCRASER, LES OUVRIR OU LES MÂCHER.
- On peut administrer un antiacide en concomitance.

O

ENSEIGNEMENT AU PATIENT ET À SES PROCHES

- Conseiller au patient de respecter rigoureusement la posologie recommandée pendant toute la durée du traitement, même s'il se sent mieux. S'il n'a pu prendre le médicament au moment habituel, il doit le prendre aussitôt que possible, sauf s'il est presque l'heure prévue pour la dose suivante. Le prévenir qu'il ne doit jamais remplacer une dose manquée par une double dose.
- Prévenir le patient que l'oméprazole peut parfois provoquer de la somnolence ou des étourdissements. Lui conseiller de ne pas conduire et d'éviter les activités qui exigent sa vigilance jusqu'à ce qu'on ait la certitude que le médicament n'entraîne pas ces effets chez lui.
- Recommander au patient de ne pas prendre de médicaments renfermant de l'aspirine ni d'AINS, sauf recommandation contraire du médecin, et de ne pas consommer d'alcool ni d'aliments pouvant aggraver l'irritation gastrique.
- Recommander au patient de signaler rapidement à un professionnel de la santé la présence de selles noires et goudronneuses, de diarrhée, de douleurs abdominales ou de céphalées persistantes.

VÉRIFICATION DE L'EFFICACITÉ THÉRAPEUTIQUE

L'efficacité du traitement peut être démontrée par: le soulagement de la douleur abdominale ou la prévention de l'irritation ou des saignements gastriques; on peut constater la guérison de l'ulcère gastroduodénal par radiographie ou endoscopie ■ la diminution des symptômes de reflux gastro-œsophagien. Il faudrait poursuivre le traitement pendant 4 à 8 semaines après le premier épisode. ✳

ONDANSÉTRON

Apo-Ondansétron, Novo-Ondansétron, PMS-Ondansétron, Ratio-Ondansétron, Sandoz Ondansétron, Zofran, Zofran ODT

CLASSIFICATION:

Antiémétique (antagoniste de la sérotonine [5-HT$_3$])

Grossesse – catégorie B

INDICATIONS

Prévention des nausées et des vomissements associés à une chimiothérapie ou à une radiothérapie ■ Prévention et traitement des nausées et des vomissements suivant une intervention chirurgicale.

MÉCANISME D'ACTION

Inhibition des effets de la sérotonine au niveau des sites récepteurs de la 5-HT (antagoniste spécifique), situés sur les terminaisons du nerf vague et dans la zone gâchette chémoréceptrice du SNC. ***Effets thérapeutiques:*** Diminution de la fréquence et de la gravité des nausées et des vomissements suivant une chimiothérapie ou une intervention chirurgicale.

PHARMACOCINÉTIQUE

Absorption: 50 % (PO). Biodisponibilité à 100 % (IV).

Distribution: Inconnue.

Métabolisme et excrétion: Métabolisme majoritairement hépatique. Excrétion rénale faible (5 % sous forme inchangée).

Demi-vie: De 3,5 à 5,5 heures.

Profil temps-action (effet antiémétique)

	DÉBUT D'ACTION	PIC	DURÉE
PO, IV	rapide	15 – 30 min	4 – 8 h

CONTRE-INDICATIONS, PRÉCAUTIONS ET MISES EN GARDE

Contre-indications: Hypersensibilité.

Précautions et mises en garde: Insuffisance hépatique modérée à grave (ne pas dépasser 8 mg par jour) ■ Chirurgie abdominale (le médicament peut masquer un iléus) ■ **OBST., PÉD.:** Grossesse, allaitement ou enfants < 3 ans (l'innocuité du médicament n'a pas été établie) ■ Allongement de l'intervalle QT ■ Phénylcétonurie (les comprimés à dissolution orale renferment de l'aspartame; administrer avec prudence aux patients atteints de ce trouble).

RÉACTIONS INDÉSIRABLES ET EFFETS SECONDAIRES

SNC: céphalées, étourdissements, somnolence, fatigue, faiblesse.

GI: constipation, diarrhée, douleurs abdominales, sécheresse de la bouche (xérostomie), concentrations accrues des enzymes hépatiques.

SN: réactions extrapyramidales.

INTERACTIONS

Médicament-médicament: L'efficacité de l'ondansétron peut être diminuée par les **agents qui augmentent l'activité des enzymes hépatiques** (p. ex., la **phénytoïne**, la **carbamazépine** et la **rifampicine**).

VOIES D'ADMINISTRATION ET POSOLOGIE

Le choix de la voie d'administration et de la dose devrait être établi selon les besoins du patient; la dose se situe généralement entre 8 et 32 mg par jour.

- **PO, IV (adultes et enfants > 12 ans):** *Prévention des nausées et des vomissements induits par la chimiothérapie* – 8 mg par perfusion IV, 30 minutes avant la chimiothérapie; on peut ou non administrer par la suite 1 mg/h, par perfusion continue pendant 24 heures au maximum, *ou* 32 mg en une seule dose (à diluer dans une solution compatible) par perfusion IV en au moins 15 minutes, 30 minutes avant la chimiothérapie (des doses plus faibles ont déjà été administrées). On administre après la chimiothérapie 8 mg par voie orale, toutes les 8 à 12 heures, pendant 5 jours au maximum. *Prévention des nausées et des vomissements induits par la radiothérapie* – 8 mg par voie orale, 1 ou 2 heures avant la radiothérapie; après la radiothérapie, on peut répéter l'administration toutes les 8 heures, pendant 5 jours au maximum, selon le type de rayons, l'endroit où ils sont administrés et leur intensité. *Prévention des nausées et des vomissements postopératoires* – une dose unique de 16 mg par voie orale, 1 heure avant le début de l'anesthésie, *ou* 4 mg en injection IV lente, au moment de l'induction de l'anesthésie. *Traitement des nausées et des vomissements postopératoires* – 4 mg en injection intraveineuse lente.
- **PO, IV (enfants de 4 à 12 ans):** *Prévention des nausées et des vomissements induits par la chimiothérapie* – de 3 à 5 mg/m^2, en perfusion IV, pendant les 15 minutes qui précèdent la chimiothérapie; après la chimiothérapie, on peut administrer 1 comprimé de 4 mg par voie orale, toutes les 8 heures, pendant 5 jours au maximum.

INSUFFISANCE HÉPATIQUE

- **PO, IV (ADULTES):** NE PAS DÉPASSER 8 mg PAR JOUR. CETTE DOSE TOTALE PEUT ÊTRE ADMINISTRÉE EN 1 FOIS PAR VOIE IV OU ORALE.

PRÉSENTATION (version générique disponible)

Comprimés à dissolution orale (renfermant de l'aspartame) ODT: 4 mg[Pr], 8 mg[Pr] ■ **Comprimés:** 4 mg[Pr], 8 mg[Pr] ■ **Solution orale (parfum de fraise):** 4 mg/5 mL[Pr] ■ **Solution pour injection:** 2 mg/mL, en ampoules de 2 mL[Pr] et de 4 mL[Pr] et en fioles de 20 mL[Pr].

SOINS INFIRMIERS

ÉVALUATION DE LA SITUATION

- Suivre de près les nausées, les vomissements et la distension abdominale et ausculter les bruits intestinaux avant et après l'administration de l'ondansétron.
- Suivre de près, à intervalles réguliers pendant toute la durée du traitement, les effets extrapyramidaux suivants: mouvements involontaires, grimaces, rigidité, démarche traînante, tremblements des mains.

Tests de laboratoire: L'ondansétron peut entraîner l'élévation passagère des concentrations sériques de bilirubine, d'AST et d'ALT.

DIAGNOSTICS INFIRMIERS POSSIBLES

- Alimentation déficiente (Indications).
- Diarrhée ou constipation (Effets secondaires).
- Connaissances insuffisantes sur le traitement médicamenteux (Enseignement au patient et à ses proches).

INTERVENTIONS INFIRMIÈRES

PO:

- Administrer la première dose avant le début des vomissements.

O

- Administrer le médicament sans le diluer.
- Manipuler la forme ODT à dissolution rapide avec les mains sèches. Peler le dessus de l'emballage et retirer le comprimé. Placez immédiatement le comprimé sur la langue du patient. Le médicament se dissout en quelques secondes et est ensuite avalé avec la salive. Il n'est pas nécessaire d'ingérer de liquide après avoir pris cette préparation.

IV directe: Administrer la solution non diluée immédiatement avant le début de l'anesthésie.

Vitesse d'administration: Administrer en 2 à 5 minutes.

Perfusion intermittente: Diluer la dose avec 50 mL de solution pour perfusion IV compatible – *ampoules:* D5%E, NaCl 0,9 %, mannitol 10 %, solution de Ringer pour injection, KCl 0,3 %/NaCl 0,9 %, KCl 0,3 %/ D5%E; *flacons:* D5%E, NaCl 0,9 %, D5%/NaCl 0,9 %, D5%/NaCl 0,45 % ou NaCl 3 % pour injection. La solution est transparente et incolore; après dilution, elle est stable pendant 24 heures à la température ambiante ou pendant 72 heures au réfrigérateur. Consulter les directives de chaque fabricant avant de faire la dilution.

Vitesse d'administration: Administrer chaque dose sous forme de perfusion IV pendant 15 minutes.

Compatibilité (tubulure en Y): aldesleukine ■ amifostine ■ amikacine ■ aztréonam ■ bléomycine ■ carboplatine ■ carmustine ■ céfazoline ■ cefmétazole ■ céfotaxime ■ céfoxitine ■ ceftazidime ■ ceftizoxime ■ céfuroxime ■ chlorpromazine ■ cimétidine ■ cisatracurium ■ cisplatine ■ cladribine ■ clindamycine ■ cyclophosphamide ■ cytarabine ■ dacarbazine ■ dactinomycine ■ daunorubicine ■ dexaméthasone sodique, phosphate de ■ diphenhydramine ■ dopamine ■ doxorubicine ■ doxorubicine liposomale ■ doxycycline ■ dropéridol ■ étoposide ■ famotidine ■ filgrastim ■ floxuridine ■ fluconazole ■ fludarabine ■ gallium, nitrate de ■ gentamicine ■ halopéridol ■ héparine ■ hydrocortisone sodique, succinate d' ■ hydrocortisone sodique, phosphate d' ■ hydromorphone ■ ifosfamide ■ imipénem/ cilastatine ■ magnésium, sulfate de ■ mannitol ■ méchloréthamine ■ melphalan ■ mépéridine ■ mesna ■ méthotrexate ■ métoclopramide ■ miconazole ■ mitomycine ■ mitoxantrone ■ morphine ■ paclitaxel ■ pentostatine ■ pipéracilline/tazobactam ■ potassium, chlorure de ■ prochlorpérazine, édisylate de ■ ranitidine ■ rémifentanil ■ sodium, acétate de ■ streptozocine ■ téniposide ■ thiotépa ■ ticarcilline ■ ticarcilline/ clavulanate ■ vancomycine ■ vinblastine ■ vincristine ■ vinorelbine ■ zidovudine.

Incompatibilité (tubulure en Y): acyclovir ■ allopurinol ■ aminophylline ■ amphotéricine B ■ amphotéricine B, cholestéryl d' ■ ampicilline ■ ampicilline/sulbactam ■ céfépime ■ céfopérazone ■ furosémide ■ ganciclovir ■ lorazépam ■ méthylprednisolone sodique, succinate de ■ mezlocilline ■ pipéracilline ■ sargramostim ■ sodium, bicarbonate de.

ENSEIGNEMENT AU PATIENT ET À SES PROCHES

- Conseiller au patient de respecter rigoureusement la posologie recommandée.
- Recommander au patient de prévenir immédiatement un professionnel de la santé s'il note des mouvements involontaires des yeux, du visage ou des membres.

VÉRIFICATION DE L'EFFICACITÉ THÉRAPEUTIQUE

L'efficacité du traitement peut être démontrée par: la prévention des nausées et des vomissements associés à une chimiothérapie initiale ou à des traitements répétés de chimiothérapie qui provoquent de telles réactions ■ la prévention et le traitement des nausées et des vomissements postopératoires ■ la prévention des nausées et des vomissements induits par la radiothérapie. ✳

OPRELVÉKINE

Ce médicament n'est pas commercialisé au Canada. Disponible par l'intermédiaire du Programme d'accès spécial de Santé Canada.

CLASSIFICATION:

Facteurs de croissance thrombopoïétique

Grossesse – catégorie C

INDICATIONS

Prévention de la thrombopénie grave et recours moindre aux transfusions de plaquettes par suite d'une chimiothérapie myélodépressive en présence de tumeurs non myéloïdes chez les patients qui sont exposés à un risque élevé de thrombopénie grave.

MÉCANISME D'ACTION

Stimulation de la production de mégacaryocytes et de plaquettes. ***Effets thérapeutiques:*** Augmentation de la numération plaquettaire.

PHARMACOCINÉTIQUE

Absorption: > 80 % (SC).

Distribution: Inconnue.

Métabolisme et excrétion: Métabolisme important; excrétion rénale (sous forme de métabolites).

Demi-vie: 6,9 heures.

Profil temps-action
(augmentation de la numération plaquettaire)

	Début d'action	Pic	Durée
SC	5 - 9 jours	inconnu	7 - 14 jours†

† Après l'arrêt du traitement, le nombre de plaquettes continue d'augmenter pendant 7 jours; il revient aux valeurs initiales après 14 jours.

CONTRE-INDICATIONS, PRÉCAUTIONS ET MISES EN GARDE

Contre-indications: Hypersensibilité.

Précautions et mises en garde: Toute maladie où une rétention hydrosodée poserait problème (insuffisance cardiaque, maladie rénale) ■ Épanchement péricardique ou ascite préexistants (risque d'exacerbation) ■ Antécédents d'arythmies auriculaires (particulièrement si le patient reçoit un traitement cardiaque ou a déjà suivi un traitement par la doxorubicine) ■ Œdème papillaire ou tumeurs du SNC ■ Grossesse ou enfants (l'innocuité du médicament n'a pas été établie) ■ Allaitement ■ Chimiothérapie myéloablative (usage non approuvé en raison du risque de toxicité) ■ Antécédents d'AVC ou d'ischémie cérébrale transitoire (ICT) ■ Insuffisance rénale (une diminution de dose peut être nécessaire si la Cl_{Cr} < 30 mL/min).

RÉACTIONS INDÉSIRABLES ET EFFETS SECONDAIRES

Ces effets sont survenus chez les patients qui avaient reçu une chimiothérapie myélodépressive récente.

SNC: étourdissements, céphalées, insomnie, nervosité, faiblesse.

ORLO: hémorragie conjonctivale, vision trouble, œdème papillaire, pharyngite, rhinite, névrite.

Resp.: toux, dyspnée, épanchement pleural.

CV: fibrillation auriculaire, œdème, palpitations, syncope, tachycardie, vasodilatation, arythmies ventriculaires, AVC.

GI: anorexie, constipation, diarrhée, dyspepsie, inflammation des muqueuses, nausées, candidose buccale, vomissements, douleurs abdominales.

Tég.: alopécie, ecchymoses, rash.

HÉ: rétention hydrosodée, anémie dilutionnelle.

Locaux: réactions au point d'injection.

Loc.: douleurs osseuses, myalgie.

Divers: frissons, fièvre, infection, douleurs, réactions allergiques incluant l'ANAPHYLAXIE.

INTERACTIONS

Médicament-médicament: Aucune interaction notable.

VOIES D'ADMINISTRATION ET POSOLOGIE

- **SC (adultes):** 50 µg/kg, 1 fois par jour, pendant 10 à 21 jours.

INSUFFISANCE RÉNALE

- **SC (ADULTES):** CL_{CR} < 30 mL/MIN – 25 µg/kg, 1 FOIS PAR JOUR, PENDANT 10 À 21 JOURS.

PRÉSENTATION

Ce médicament n'est pas commercialisé au Canada.

SOINS INFIRMIERS

ÉVALUATION DE LA SITUATION

- Observer le patient à la recherche de signes de rétention hydrosodée (dyspnée à l'effort, œdème périphérique) pendant toute la durée du traitement. La rétention hydrosodée est un effet secondaire courant, qui disparaît habituellement plusieurs jours après l'arrêt du traitement par l'oprelvékine.

Tests de laboratoire:

- Noter la numération plaquettaire avant le traitement et à intervalles réguliers pendant toute sa durée, particulièrement au moment où le nadir devrait être atteint. Le traitement est poursuivi jusqu'à ce que le nombre de plaquettes après le nadir soit > 50×10^9/L.
- On devrait noter la numération globulaire avant le traitement et à intervalles réguliers pendant toute sa durée. La concentration d'hémoglobine, l'hématocrite et le nombre de globules rouges peuvent diminuer en raison d'un volume plasmatique accru (anémie par hémodilution), habituellement, dans les 3 à 5 jours qui suivent le début du traitement. Cette diminution est généralement réversible dans la semaine qui suit l'arrêt du traitement.
- Vérifier les concentrations des électrolytes chez les patients recevant un traitement prolongé par des diurétiques. L'hypokaliémie peut être d'issue fatale.
- L'oprelvékine peut entraîner une élévation des concentrations de fibrinogène plasmatique.

DIAGNOSTICS INFIRMIERS POSSIBLES

- Excès de volume liquidien (Effets secondaires).
- Connaissances insuffisantes sur le traitement médicamenteux (Enseignement au patient et à ses proches).

INTERVENTIONS INFIRMIÈRES

- Le traitement devrait être amorcé dans les 6 à 24 heures suivant la fin de la chimiothérapie et être poursuivi pendant 10 à 21 jours, selon la numération plaquettaire.

- On devrait interrompre le traitement au moins 2 jours avant le cycle suivant de chimiothérapie.

ENSEIGNEMENT AU PATIENT ET À SES PROCHES

- Expliquer au patient la méthode appropriée de préparation et d'administration du médicament. Lui fournir un récipient imperforable destiné à la mise au rebut des aiguilles.
- Prévenir le patient que l'oprelvékine peut rendre passagèrement la vision trouble ou provoquer des étourdissements. Lui conseiller de ne pas conduire et d'éviter les activités qui exigent sa vigilance jusqu'à ce qu'on ait la certitude que le médicament n'entraîne pas ces effets chez lui.
- Conseiller à la patiente d'informer un professionnel de la santé si elle pense être enceinte ou si elle souhaite le devenir.
- Expliquer au patient les effets secondaires de ce médicament et lui conseiller de prévenir un professionnel de la santé si les douleurs thoraciques, l'essoufflement, la fatigue, la vision trouble ou le rythme cardiaque irrégulier persistent.

VÉRIFICATION DE L'EFFICACITÉ THÉRAPEUTIQUE

L'efficacité du traitement peut être démontrée par: une augmentation de la numération plaquettaire $\geq 50 \times 10^9$/L après l'atteinte du nadir. ✳

O

ORCIPRÉNALINE

Synonyme: métaprotérénol

Apo-Orciprenaline

CLASSIFICATION:

Bronchodilatateur (agoniste bêta-adrénergique)

Grossesse – catégorie C

INDICATIONS

Bronchodilatateur pour le traitement du bronchospasme qui accompagne les affections suivantes: asthme bronchique ■ bronchite chronique ■ emphysème pulmonaire.

MÉCANISME D'ACTION

Accumulation de l'adénosine monophosphate cyclique (AMPc) au niveau des récepteurs bêta-adrénergiques ■ Bronchodilatation ■ Sélectivité relative pour les récepteurs bêta$_2$-adrénergiques (pulmonaires); effet moindre sur les récepteurs bêta$_1$-adrénergiques (cardiaques). ***Effets thérapeutiques:*** Bronchodilatation.

PHARMACOCINÉTIQUE

Absorption: 40 % (PO).

Distribution: Inconnue.

Métabolisme et excrétion: Métabolisme hépatique important. Excrétion rénale sous forme de métabolites inactifs.

Demi-vie: Inconnue.

Profil temps-action (bronchodilatation)

	Début d'action	Pic	Durée
PO	30 min	2 - 4 h	4 h

CONTRE-INDICATIONS, PRÉCAUTIONS ET MISES EN GARDE

Contre-indications: Hypersensibilité ■ Tachyarythmies.

Précautions et mises en garde: Maladie cardiaque ■ Hypertension ■ Hyperthyroïdie ■ Diabète ■ Troubles convulsifs ■ **Gér.:** Il est recommandé de réduire la dose chez les personnes âgées (risque accru de réactions indésirables) ■ **Obst., allaitement:** L'innocuité du médicament n'a pas été établie chez la femme enceinte ou qui allaite.

RÉACTIONS INDÉSIRABLES ET EFFETS SECONDAIRES

SNC: nervosité, agitation, tremblements, céphalées, insomnie.

Resp.: BRONCHOSPASME PARADOXAL.

CV: angine, arythmies, hypertension, tachycardie.

GI: nausées, vomissements.

End.: hyperglycémie.

INTERACTIONS

Médicament-médicament: L'usage concomitant d'autres **agents adrénergiques (sympathomimétiques)** entraîne des effets secondaires adrénergiques additifs ■ L'usage concomitant d'**IMAO** peut mener à une crise hypertensive ■ Les **bêtabloquants** peuvent inhiber l'effet thérapeutique de l'agent.

VOIES D'ADMINISTRATION ET POSOLOGIE

- **PO (adultes):** 20 mg, 3 ou 4 fois par jour.
- **PO (enfants > 9 ans):** 20 mg, 3 ou 4 fois par jour.
- **PO (enfants de 6 à 9 ans):** 10 mg, 3 ou 4 fois par jour.
- **PO (enfants de 2 à 6 ans):** De 1,3 à 2,6 mg/kg/jour, en doses fractionnées, administrées toutes les 6 à 8 heures.
- **PO (enfants < 2 ans):** 0,4 mg/kg/dose, 3 ou 4 fois par jour ou toutes les 8 à 12 heures.

PRÉSENTATION (version générique disponible)

Sirop: 10 mg/5 mL[Pr].

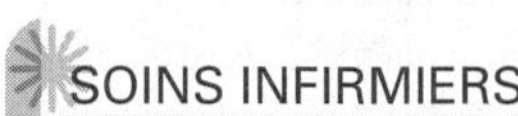

SOINS INFIRMIERS

ÉVALUATION DE LA SITUATION

Bronchodilatateur:

- Ausculter le murmure vésiculaire, mesurer la fréquence respiratoire, le pouls et la pression artérielle avant l'administration et au moment du pic de l'effet. Noter la quantité, la couleur et les caractéristiques des expectorations. Signaler tout résultat anormal.
- Noter les résultats des tests de la fonction pulmonaire avant d'amorcer le traitement et à intervalles réguliers pendant toute sa durée afin de déterminer si le médicament est efficace.
- Suivre de près les signes de bronchospasme paradoxal (respiration sifflante). Si ce trouble se manifeste, interrompre le traitement et en informer immédiatement le médecin ou un autre professionnel de la santé.

Tests de laboratoire: L'orciprénaline peut entraîner la diminution des concentrations sériques de potassium, qui est habituellement passagère et liée à la dose; ce phénomène se produit rarement aux doses recommandées et est plus marqué lors d'un usage fréquent de doses élevées.

TOXICITÉ ET SURDOSAGE:

- Les symptômes du surdosage sont notamment l'agitation persistante, les douleurs ou l'oppression thoracique, la baisse ou l'élévation de la pression artérielle, les étourdissements, l'hyperglycémie, l'hypokaliémie, les convulsions, les tachyarythmies, les tremblements persistants et les vomissements.
- Pour traiter ces symptômes, il faut arrêter l'administration des agonistes bêta-adrénergiques et entreprendre un traitement symptomatique de soutien. Il faut administrer avec prudence les bêtabloquants cardiosélectifs puisqu'ils peuvent induire un bronchospasme.

DIAGNOSTICS INFIRMIERS POSSIBLES

- Dégagement inefficace des voies respiratoires (Indications).
- Connaissances insuffisantes sur le traitement médicamenteux (Enseignement au patient et à ses proches).

INTERVENTIONS INFIRMIÈRES

- Administrer le médicament avec les repas afin de réduire l'irritation gastrique.

ENSEIGNEMENT AU PATIENT ET À SES PROCHES

- Conseiller au patient de respecter rigoureusement la posologie recommandée. S'il n'a pu prendre le médicament au moment habituel, il doit le prendre dès que possible et espacer les autres doses à intervalles réguliers. L'avertir qu'il ne doit jamais remplacer une dose manquée par une double dose. RECOMMANDER AU PATIENT DE NE PAS DÉPASSER LA DOSE RECOMMANDÉE; UN SURDOSAGE PEUT ENTRAÎNER DES RÉACTIONS INDÉSIRABLES, UN BRONCHOSPASME PARADOXAL OU LA PERTE D'EFFICACITÉ DU MÉDICAMENT.
- Conseiller au patient de consulter immédiatement un professionnel de la santé si l'essoufflement n'est pas soulagé par le médicament ou s'il s'accompagne de diaphorèse, d'étourdissements, de palpitations ou de douleurs thoraciques.
- Conseiller au patient de consulter un professionnel de la santé avant de prendre un médicament en vente libre, un produit naturel ou de l'alcool, en même temps que l'orciprénaline. Recommander également au patient de ne pas fumer et d'éviter l'exposition aux autres substances qui irritent l'appareil respiratoire. Inciter le patient à boire suffisamment de liquides (de 2 à 3 L par jour) afin de mieux liquéfier les sécrétions tenaces.

VÉRIFICATION DE L'EFFICACITÉ THÉRAPEUTIQUE

L'efficacité du traitement peut être démontrée par: la prévention ou le soulagement du bronchospasme ■ une plus grande facilité à respirer.

ORLISTAT

Xenical

CLASSIFICATION:

Agent antiobésité (inhibiteur des lipases gastro-intestinales)

Grossesse – catégorie B

INDICATIONS

Traitement de l'obésité (perte pondérale et maintien du poids) en association avec un régime légèrement hypocalorique, chez les patients dont l'indice de masse corporelle (IMC) est ≥ 30 kg/m^2 ou ≥ 27 kg/m^2, en présence de facteurs de risque additionnels (diabète, hypertension, hyperlipidémie) ■ Réduction du risque

O

d'un nouveau gain de poids après perte pondérale ■ Réduction du risque de diabète de type 2, chez les personnes obèses et intolérantes au glucose.

MÉCANISME D'ACTION

Diminution de l'absorption des graisses alimentaires par inhibition réversible des enzymes (lipases) qui sont nécessaires à la décomposition des graisses et à leur absorption ultérieure. ***Effets thérapeutiques:*** Perte pondérale et maintien du poids chez les patients obèses.

PHARMACOCINÉTIQUE

Absorption: Minime (PO).

Distribution: L'agent se lie très peu aux érythrocytes.

Liaison aux protéines: 99 % (*in vitro*).

Métabolisme et excrétion: Excrétion majoritairement fécale.

Demi-vie: De 1 à 2 heures.

Profil temps-action (effets sur les graisses fécales)

	DÉBUT D'ACTION	PIC	DURÉE
PO	24 – 48 h	inconnu	48 – 72 h†

† Après l'arrêt du traitement.

CONTRE-INDICATIONS, PRÉCAUTIONS ET MISES EN GARDE

O

Contre-indications: Hypersensibilité ■ Syndrome de malabsorption chronique ou cholestase.

Précautions et mises en garde: Grossesse ou allaitement ■ **PÉD.:** L'innocuité du médicament n'a pas été établie chez les enfants < 12 ans.

RÉACTIONS INDÉSIRABLES ET EFFETS SECONDAIRES

Lors de l'utilisation initiale du médicament; l'incidence diminue lors d'un traitement prolongé.

GI: défécation impérieuse, flatulence avec pertes de matières fécales, défécation accrue, évacuation huileuse, taches huileuses, incontinence fécale.

INTERACTIONS

Médicament-médicament: L'orlistat réduit l'absorption de certaines **vitamines liposolubles** et du **bêtacarotène**.

VOIES D'ADMINISTRATION ET POSOLOGIE

PO (adultes et enfants ≥ 12 ans): 120 mg, 3 fois par jour, avec chaque repas contenant des matières grasses.

PRÉSENTATION

Capsules: 120 mg[Pr].

SOINS INFIRMIERS

ÉVALUATION DE LA SITUATION

- Suivre la perte de poids du patient et adapter, selon les besoins, les doses des médicaments administrés en concomitance (antihypertenseurs, antidiabétiques, hypolipémiants).

DIAGNOSTICS INFIRMIERS POSSIBLES

- Image corporelle perturbée (Indications).
- Alimentation excessive (Indications).
- Connaissances insuffisantes sur le traitement médicamenteux (Enseignement au patient et à ses proches).

INTERVENTIONS INFIRMIÈRES

- NE PAS CONFONDRE XELODA (CAPÉCITABINE) ET XENICAL (ORLISTAT).
- Administrer une capsule, 3 fois par jour, avec les repas ou dans l'heure qui suit. Si le patient saute un repas ou si le repas ne renferme pas de matières grasses, il peut ne pas prendre la dose prévue d'orlistat.
- Le patient devrait prendre tous les jours des suppléments de multivitamines comprenant les vitamines D, E et K et du bêtacarotène, au moins 2 heures avant ou après la prise de la dose d'orlistat.
- Administrer 6 g de psyllium avec chaque dose d'orlistat ou 12 g au coucher pour réduire la fréquence et l'intensité des effets secondaires gastro-intestinaux.

ENSEIGNEMENT AU PATIENT ET À SES PROCHES

- Conseiller au patient de prendre l'orlistat au moment des repas, en suivant rigoureusement la posologie recommandée. Lui signaler qu'il peut omettre une dose d'orlistat s'il saute un repas ou si le repas ne contient pas de matières grasses. Le prévenir qu'il ne doit pas prendre de dose plus élevée que celle recommandée, car il n'en tirera aucun bienfait supplémentaire.
- Expliquer au patient qu'il doit suivre un régime hypocalorique. L'apport quotidien en matières grasses devrait être réparti entre les 3 repas principaux. Les repas ne devraient pas contenir plus de 30 % de matières grasses. La prise d'orlistat en même temps qu'un repas riche en matières grasses peut augmenter les effets secondaires gastro-intestinaux.
- Conseiller au patient de pratiquer des activités physiques régulières, approuvées par un professionnel de la santé, en même temps qu'il suit le traitement par l'orlistat et le régime hypocalorique.

- Informer le patient des effets secondaires courants d'orlistat (taches huileuses, flatuosités avec pertes de matières fécales, besoin impérieux de déféquer, selles huileuses ou graisseuses, écoulement huileux, nombre accru de défécations, incapacité de se retenir). L'huile présente dans les selles peut être transparente ou peut prendre une couleur orangée ou brunâtre. Les effets secondaires gastro-intestinaux se manifestent habituellement au cours des premières semaines de traitement et sont plus nombreux après un repas riche en matières grasses. Ces effets peuvent diminuer ou disparaître ou peuvent persister pendant 6 mois ou plus.
- Recommander au patient de consulter un professionnel de la santé avant de prendre un autre médicament sur ordonnance, en vente libre ou à base de plantes médicinales en même temps que l'orlistat.
- Conseiller à la patiente d'informer un professionnel de la santé si elle pense être enceinte ou si elle souhaite le devenir.

VÉRIFICATION DE L'EFFICACITÉ THÉRAPEUTIQUE

L'efficacité du traitement peut être démontrée par: une perte pondérale lente et constante si le traitement s'accompagne d'un régime hypocalorique. ✳

OSELTAMIVIR

Tamiflu

CLASSIFICATION:

Antiviral (inhibiteur sélectif de la neuraminidase)

Grossesse – catégorie C

INDICATIONS

Traitement de la grippe aiguë sans complications, due au virus de la grippe de type A et de type B chez les adultes et les enfants ≥ 1 an, qui présentent des symptômes depuis 2 jours au maximum ■ Prévention de la grippe chez les adultes et les enfants ≥ 1 an, après un contact étroit avec une personne infectée (cas primaire). L'oseltamivir ne remplace pas la vaccination antigrippale, qui reste la méthode de prévention privilégiée contre la grippe.

MÉCANISME D'ACTION

Inhibition de l'enzyme neuraminidase, ce qui modifie l'agrégation et la libération des particules virales. ***Effets thérapeutiques:*** Soulagement des symptômes grippaux et diminution de leur durée (lorsque l'agent est utilisé en traitement) ou diminution de l'incidence de la grippe fébrile (lorsque l'agent est utilisé en prévention).

PHARMACOCINÉTIQUE

Absorption: Rapide (PO). La biodisponibilité du métabolite actif est d'environ 75 %.

Distribution: Inconnue.

Liaison aux protéines: 42 % pour l'oseltamivir et environ 3 % pour son métabolite actif.

Métabolisme et excrétion: L'oseltamivir est un promédicament qui est transformé en métabolite actif par les estérases hépatiques. Le métabolite actif ne subit aucune autre biotransformation et est éliminé dans l'urine (> 99 %).

Demi-vie: De 1 à 3 heures (de 6 à 10 heures pour le métabolite actif).

Profil temps-action

	Début d'action	Pic	Durée
PO	24 h	inconnu	inconnue

CONTRE-INDICATIONS, PRÉCAUTIONS ET MISES EN GARDE

Contre-indications: Hypersensibilité ■ Enfants < 1 an.

Précautions et mises en garde: **Obst.:** L'innocuité de l'agent n'a pas été établie. Utiliser seulement si les bienfaits escomptés justifient les risques auxquels on expose le fœtus ■ **Allaitement:** On ignore si l'oseltamivir ou son métabolite actif passent dans le lait maternel; le médicament ne doit donc pas être administré aux mères qui allaitent des enfants < 1 an à cause des risques possibles pour le nourrisson allaité ■ Insuffisance rénale ou hépatique ■ Risque de réactions neuropsychiatriques surtout signalées chez les enfants (délire et automutilation) ■ Intolérance héréditaire au fructose (suspension buvable).

O

RÉACTIONS INDÉSIRABLES ET EFFETS SECONDAIRES

SNC: céphalées, étourdissements, fatigue, insomnie.

ORLO: conjonctivite, épistaxis, otite moyenne, troubles auriculaires, rhinorrhée, infections des voies respiratoires supérieures.

Resp.: asthme, bronchite, PNEUMONIE, toux.

CV: ANGINE INSTABLE.

GI: colite pseudomembraneuse, diarrhée, dyspepsie, douleur abdominale, ÉLÉVATION DES ENZYMES HÉPATIQUES, HÉPATOTOXICITÉ, nausées, vomissements.

Hémat.: ANÉMIE.

Loc.: courbatures.

Locaux: RÉACTIONS D'HYPERSENSIBILITÉ (DERMATITE, RASH, ECZÉMA, URTICAIRE, ÉRYTHÈME POLYMORPHE, SYNDROME DE STEVENS-JOHNSON) (rare).

Divers: ALLERGIE (RÉACTIONS ANAPHYLACTIQUES OU ANAPHYLACTOÏDES, ŒDÈME FACIAL) (rare).

INTERACTIONS

Médicament-médicament: Aucune interaction cliniquement significative.

VOIES D'ADMINISTRATION ET POSOLOGIE

Traitement de la grippe

- **PO (adultes et adolescents ≥ 13 ans)**: 75 mg, 2 fois par jour pendant 5 jours. Le traitement doit commencer au plus tard 2 jours après le début des symptômes de la grippe.
- **PO (enfants de 1 à 12 ans)**: *≤ 15 kg* – 30 mg; *de 15 à 23 kg* – 45 mg; *de 24 à 40 kg* – 60 mg; *> 40 kg* – 75 mg. Toutes ces doses doivent être administrées 2 fois par jour pendant 5 jours. Le traitement doit commencer au plus tard 2 jours après l'apparition des symptômes de la grippe.

Prévention de la grippe

Le traitement doit commencer au plus tard 2 jours après l'exposition au cas primaire (personne infectée) présentant déjà des symptômes et se poursuivre pendant au moins 10 jours. Les enfants et les personnes âgées peuvent excréter le virus pendant un maximum de 14 jours après le début de la maladie. Si le cas primaire est un enfant ou une personne âgée, le traitement préventif par l'oseltamivir devrait donc se poursuivre pendant 14 jours.

- **PO (adultes et adolescents ≥ 13 ans)**: 75 mg, 1 fois par jour.
- **PO (enfants de 1 à 12 ans)**: *≤ 15 kg* – 30 mg; *de 15 à 23 kg* – 45 mg; *de 24 à 40 kg* – 60 mg; *> 40 kg* – 75 mg. Toutes ces doses doivent être administrées 1 fois par jour.

INSUFFISANCE RÉNALE

- **PO (TRAITEMENT DE LA GRIPPE)**: *CL_{CR} DE 10 À 30 mL/MIN* – 75 mg, 1 FOIS PAR JOUR PENDANT 5 JOURS.
- **PO (PRÉVENTION DE LA GRIPPE)**: *CL_{CR} DE 10 À 30 mL/MIN* – 75 mg, TOUS LES 2 JOURS, OU 30 mg DE SUSPENSION, TOUS LES JOURS.

PRÉSENTATION

Gélules: 75 mg^{Pr} ■ **Poudre pour suspension buvable (saveur de fruits)**: 12 mg/mL^{Pr}.

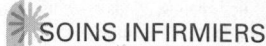

SOINS INFIRMIERS

ÉVALUATION DE LA SITUATION

- Rechercher les signes et les symptômes de grippe (fièvre, céphalées, myalgie, toux, maux de gorge) avant d'administrer le médicament. Déterminer la durée des symptômes. N'administrer ce médicament qu'aux patients qui présentent des symptômes depuis 2 jours ou moins. Un traitement de soutien additionnel pourrait être indiqué pour prendre en charge les symptômes.

DIAGNOSTICS INFIRMIERS POSSIBLES

- Risque d'infection (Indications).
- Connaissances insuffisantes sur le traitement médicamenteux (Enseignement au patient et à ses proches).

INTERVENTIONS INFIRMIÈRES

- Administrer le médicament avec ou sans aliments. Toutefois, la prise avec des aliments pourrait améliorer la tolérance chez certains patients.
- La suspension buvable doit être reconstituée avant l'emploi. Commencer par tapoter le flacon à plusieurs reprises pour disperser la poudre, puis mesurer 52 mL d'eau avec une éprouvette graduée et ajouter cette quantité au flacon. Bien agiter pendant 15 secondes. Enlever ensuite le couvercle de sécurité et introduire le bouchon de raccord dans le goulot du flacon, puis remettre le couvercle de sécurité. La concentration de la suspension reconstituée est de 12 mg/mL et le contenu net du flacon est de 75 mL. La suspension ainsi reconstituée se conserve pendant 10 jours au réfrigérateur.
- Bien agiter la suspension avant chaque usage.
- Une seringue pour administration orale portant des graduations de 30, 45 et 60 mg est fournie; pour mesurer la dose de 75 mg, additionner 30 et 45 mg.

ENSEIGNEMENT AU PATIENT ET À SES PROCHES

- Prévenir le patient qu'il doit respecter rigoureusement la posologie recommandée et qu'il doit prendre toute la quantité de médicament qui lui a été prescrite, même s'il se sent mieux. S'il n'a pu prendre le médicament au moment habituel, il doit le prendre dès que possible à moins que ce ne soit presque l'heure prévue pour la dose suivante. Le prévenir qu'il ne doit jamais remplacer une dose manquée par une double dose.
- Avertir le patient qu'il ne doit pas donner ce médicament à d'autres personnes même si celles-ci présentent les mêmes symptômes.

- Avertir le patient que l'oseltamivir ne remplace pas la vaccination contre la grippe. Il devrait recevoir chaque année le vaccin contre la grippe suivant les recommandations des autorités gouvernementales.
- Montrer au patient qui prend la suspension comment se servir de la seringue destinée à l'administration par voie orale.

VÉRIFICATION DE L'EFFICACITÉ THÉRAPEUTIQUE

L'efficacité du traitement peut être démontrée par: la prévention ou la diminution des signes et des symptômes de grippe (fièvre, céphalées, myalgie, toux, maux de gorge).

OXALIPLATINE

Eloxatin

CLASSIFICATION:
Antinéoplasique

Grossesse – catégorie D

INDICATIONS

En association avec le 5–fluorouracile (5-FU) et la leucovorine dans le traitement du cancer métastatique du côlon ou du rectum. **Usages non approuvés:** Traitement adjuvant du cancer du côlon ■ Traitement du cancer de l'ovaire qui a évolué malgré un traitement par d'autres agents.

MÉCANISME D'ACTION

Inhibition de la réplication et de la transcription de l'ADN par l'incorporation du platine dans les ponts intercaténaires normaux (effet indépendant du cycle cellulaire). ***Effets thérapeutiques:*** Destruction des cellules à réplication rapide, et particulièrement des cellules malignes.

PHARMACOCINÉTIQUE

Absorption: Biodisponibilité à 100 % (IV).
Distribution: Répartition dans tous les tissus.
Liaison aux protéines: > 90 % (platine).
Métabolisme et excrétion: Biotransformation non enzymatique rapide et massive; excrétion principalement rénale sous forme de platine.
Demi-vie: 391 heures.
Profil temps-action

	DÉBUT D'ACTION	PIC	DURÉE
IV	inconnu	inconnu	inconnue

CONTRE-INDICATIONS, PRÉCAUTIONS ET MISES EN GARDE

Contre-indications: Hypersensibilité ■ Hypersensibilité aux autres composés à base de platine ■ **OBST.:** Grossesse et allaitement ■ Insuffisance rénale grave (Cl_{Cr} < 30 mL/min).
Précautions et mises en garde: Insuffisance rénale modérée ■ **GÉR.:** Risque accru de réactions indésirables ■ **PÉD.:** L'innocuité de l'agent n'a pas été établie.

RÉACTIONS INDÉSIRABLES ET EFFETS SECONDAIRES

Les réactions indésirables signalées découlent de l'administration de l'association oxaliplatine, 5–FU et leucovorine.
SNC: fatigue.
CV: douleurs thoraciques, œdème, thromboembolie.
Resp.: FIBROSE PULMONAIRE, PNEUMOPATHIE INTERSTITIELLE, toux, dyspnée.
GI: diarrhée, nausées, vomissements, douleurs abdominales, anorexie, reflux gastro-œsophagien, stomatite, HÉPATOTOXICITÉ.
HÉ: déshydratation, hypokaliémie.
Tég.: rash.
Hémat.: LEUCOPÉNIE, NEUTROPÉNIE, THROMBOPÉNIE, anémie.
Locaux: réactions au point d'injection, nécrose cutanée.
Loc.: douleurs lombaires.
SN: neurotoxicité.
Divers: ANAPHYLAXIE/RÉACTIONS ANAPHYLACTOÏDES, fièvre.

INTERACTIONS

Médicament-médicament: L'usage concomitant d'**agents néphrotoxiques** peut accroître la toxicité du médicament ■ L'association oxaliplatine, 5–FU et leucovorine peut augmenter le RNI chez les patients sous **anticoagulants oraux**.

VOIES D'ADMINISTRATION ET POSOLOGIE

- **IV (adultes):** *Premier jour* – 85 mg/m^2 avec 200 mg/m^2 de leucovorine, administrée en même temps, pendant 2 à 6 heures, puis un bolus de 400 mg/m^2 de 5-FU, pendant 2 à 4 minutes, et ensuite 600 mg/m^2 de 5-FU, en perfusion pendant 22 heures. *Deuxième jour* – 200 mg/m^2 de leucovorine pendant 2 heures, puis un bolus de 400 mg/m^2 de 5-FU, pendant 2 à 4 minutes, et ensuite 600 mg/m^2 de 5-FU, en perfusion pendant 22 heures. Ce cycle est répété toutes les 2 semaines. En cas de neurotoxicité ou d'autres réactions indésirables graves, la diminution ou la modification de la posologie peut s'imposer.

PRÉSENTATION

Solution pour injection: 5 mg/mL, en fioles de 10 mL (50 mg)Pr, 5 mg/mL, en fioles de 20 mL (100 mg) Pr.

SOINS INFIRMIERS

ÉVALUATION DE LA SITUATION

- Rester à l'affût d'une neuropathie périphérique sensorielle. La *neuropathie aiguë* s'installe dans les quelques heures à 1 ou 2 jours après administration et disparaît dans les 14 jours; on note de fréquentes récurrences lors des administrations ultérieures (paresthésie passagère, dysesthésie ou hypoesthésie au niveau des mains, des pieds, de la région péribuccale ou de la gorge). Les symptômes peuvent être déclenchés ou exacerbés par l'exposition au froid ou le contact avec des objets froids. Les autres symptômes peuvent être notamment des spasmes des mâchoires, une sensation anormale au niveau de la langue, la dysarthrie, les douleurs oculaires et une sensation d'oppression thoracique. La *neuropathie persistante* (> 14 jours) se caractérise par la paresthésie, la dysesthésie et l'hypoesthésie, mais peut aussi s'accompagner de déficits de proprioception qui peuvent faire obstacle aux activités de la vie quotidienne (capacité de marcher, d'écrire, d'avaler). Une neuropathie persistante peut s'installer sans phase aiguë préalable et peut persister après l'abandon du traitement par l'oxaliplatine.
- RECHERCHER LES SIGNES DE FIBROSE PULMONAIRE (TOUX SÈCHE, DYSPNÉE, CRÉPITATIONS, INFILTRATS RADIOLOGIQUES). LA FIBROSE PULMONAIRE PEUT ÊTRE MORTELLE; ABANDONNER LE TRAITEMENT À L'OXALIPLATINE SI ELLE SURVIENT.
- Suivre de près les signes d'anaphylaxie (rash, urticaire, tuméfaction des lèvres ou de la langue, toux soudaine). Garder à portée de la main de l'adrénaline, des corticostéroïdes et des antihistaminiques.

Tests de laboratoire: Obtenir la numération et la formule leucocytaires, la concentration d'hémoglobine, le nombre de plaquettes et les résultats des analyses de sang (ALT, AST, bilirubine et créatinine) avant chaque cycle de chimiothérapie.

DIAGNOSTICS INFIRMIERS POSSIBLES

- Nausée (Réactions indésirables).

INTERVENTIONS INFIRMIÈRES

- L'extravasation risque de provoquer des douleurs et une inflammation locales qui peuvent être graves et entraîner la nécrose des tissus.
- Administrer des antiémétiques avec ou sans dexaméthasone en prémédication. Une hydratation préalable n'est pas nécessaire.

Perfusion intermittente: Protéger la solution concentrée de la lumière; ne pas la congeler. Diluer avec 250 à 500 mL de D5%E. NE PAS UTILISER DE NACL 0,9 % NI AUCUNE AUTRE SOLUTION CONTENANT DU CHLORURE COMME DILUANT. Consulter les directives du fabricant avant de diluer la solution. Ne pas utiliser d'aiguille en aluminium ni de récipients ayant des parties en aluminium; l'aluminium peut provoquer la décomposition des composés de platine. On peut garder la solution diluée pendant 24 heures au réfrigérateur ou pendant 6 heures à la température ambiante. La solution diluée n'est pas sensible à la lumière. Ne pas administrer de solutions qui ont changé de couleur ou qui contiennent des particules.

Vitesse d'administration: Administrer l'oxaliplatine en même temps que la leucovorine, dans des sacs séparés, par une tubulure en Y, pendant 120 minutes. Si on prolonge la perfusion pour la faire durer 6 heures, on pourrait diminuer les effets toxiques aigus. On ne doit pas changer la durée de la perfusion du flurouracil et de la leucovorine.

Incompatibilité (tubulure en Y): Solutions alcalines, solutions contenant du chlorure. Rincer les tubulures de perfusion avec du D5%E, avant d'administrer d'autres solutions ou médicaments.

ENSEIGNEMENT AU PATIENT ET À SES PROCHES

- Informer le patient et ses proches du risque de neuropathie périphérique, qui pourrait être aggravée par l'exposition au froid ou le contact avec des objets froids. Recommander au patient d'éviter de consommer des boissons froides, de mettre des glaçons dans les boissons ou d'utiliser des cryosacs, et de se couvrir la peau avant de s'exposer au froid ou de toucher des objets froids. Lui conseiller de se couvrir avec une couverture pendant la perfusion, de ne pas prendre de respirations profondes dans l'air froid, de porter des vêtements chauds, de se couvrir le nez et la bouche avec une écharpe ou de porter une cagoule pour réchauffer l'air qui pénètre dans les poumons, d'enfiler des gants avant de saisir des objets du réfrigérateur ou du congélateur, de ne consommer que des liquides tièdes ou à la température ambiante, de toujours boire à l'aide d'une paille, de ne pas sucer de la glace concassée en cas de nausées, de se souvenir que la plupart des objets métalliques (portières de voitures, boîtes postales) sont froids et de ne les toucher qu'avec une main gantée, et de ne pas trop climatiser la voiture ou les

O

pièces de la maison. Lui conseiller également, s'il a froid aux mains, de les laver à l'eau chaude. Lui demander d'informer le médecin ou l'infirmière avant la perfusion suivante de son état de santé depuis le dernier traitement.

- Recommander au patient de prévenir un professionnel de la santé sans tarder si des signes de numération globulaire basse (fièvre, infection) ou des vomissements prolongés, de la diarrhée persistante, des signes de déshydratation, une toux ou des difficultés respiratoires, la soif, la sécheresse de la bouche, des étourdissements, des problèmes de miction ou des signes de réactions allergiques se manifestent.

VÉRIFICATION DE L'EFFICACITÉ THÉRAPEUTIQUE

L'efficacité du traitement peut être démontrée par: la diminution de la taille de la tumeur et le ralentissement de la propagation des métastases.

OXAPROZINE

Apo-Oxaprozin, Daypro, Rhoxal-Oxaprozin

CLASSIFICATION:

Anti-inflammatoire non stéroïdien, analgésique non opioïde

Grossesse – catégories D (1er et 3e trimestres) et B (2e trimestre)

INDICATIONS

Traitement aigu ou prolongé de la polyarthrite rhumatoïde et de l'arthrose.

MÉCANISME D'ACTION

Inhibition de la synthèse des prostaglandines. ***Effets thérapeutiques:*** Suppression de la douleur et de l'inflammation.

PHARMACOCINÉTIQUE

Absorption: 80 % (PO); 35 % est transformé rapidement en un métabolite actif.

Distribution: Inconnue.

Liaison aux protéines: 99,9 %.

Métabolisme et excrétion: Le métabolite actif de l'oxaprozine est métabolisé par le foie et transformé en composés inactifs.

Demi-vie: De 42 à 50 heures.

Profil temps-action (effet antirhumatismal)

	DÉBUT D'ACTION	PIC	DURÉE
PO	dans les 7 jours	inconnu	inconnue

CONTRE-INDICATIONS, PRÉCAUTIONS ET MISES EN GARDE

Contre-indications: Hypersensibilité ■ Risque de réactions de sensibilité croisée avec d'autres AINS incluant l'aspirine ■ Antécédents d'asthme, d'urticaire ou de réactions de type allergique à l'aspirine ou aux autres AINS, incluant la triade de réactions provoquées par l'aspirine (asthme, polype nasal, réactions graves d'hypersensibilité) ■ Hémorragie digestive ou ulcère en phase évolutive ■ Contexte périopératoire en cas de pontage aortocoronarien ■ Antécédents d'ulcère récurrent ou maladie inflammatoire évolutive du système gastro-intestinal ■ Maladie hépatique grave ■ Insuffisance rénale (Cl_{Cr} < 30 mL/min).

Précautions et mises en garde: Maladie cardiovasculaire ou facteurs de risque de maladie cardiovasculaire (risque accru de complications thrombotiques, d'infarctus du myocarde et d'accident vasculaire cérébral, surtout lors d'un usage prolongé) ■ **OBST., ALLAITEMENT, PÉD.**: L'innocuité du médicament n'a pas été établie ■ **GÉR.**: Les personnes âgées sont plus à risque d'hémorragies digestives. Une adaptation de la dose peut s'avérer nécessaire en raison de la diminution de la fonction rénale reliée à l'âge.

RÉACTIONS INDÉSIRABLES ET EFFETS SECONDAIRES

SNC: agitation, anxiété, confusion, dépression, étourdissements, somnolence, fatigue, céphalées, insomnie, malaise, faiblesse.

ORLO: vision anormale, acouphènes.

Resp.: dyspnée, pneumopathie d'hypersensibilité.

CV: œdème, vasculite.

GI: HÉMORRAGIE DIGESTIVE, douleurs abdominales, diarrhée, dyspepsie, résultats anormaux aux tests de la fonction hépatique, anorexie, ictère cholestatique, constipation, sécheresse de la bouche (xérostomie), ulcère duodénal, flatulence, gastrite, gain d'appétit, nausées, stomatite, vomissements.

GU: albuminurie, azotémie, néphrite interstitielle.

Tég.: DERMATITE EXFOLIATIVE, SYNDROME DE STEVENS-JOHNSON, ÉPIDERMOLYSE NÉCROSANTE SUBAIGUË, sécrétion accrue de sueur, photosensibilité, prurit, rash.

Hémat.: allongement du temps de saignement.

Métab.: gain pondéral.

SN: paresthésie, tremblements.

Divers: réactions allergiques incluant l'ANAPHYLAXIE, ŒDÈME ANGIONEUROTIQUE.

INTERACTIONS

Médicament-médicament: L'administration concomitante d'**aspirine**, d'autres **AINS**, de **suppléments de potassium** ou de **corticostéroïdes**, ainsi que la prise d'**alcool**, intensifient les effets secondaires gastro-intestinaux et augmentent la toxicité ■ L'administration prolongée d'oxaprozine en même temps que de l'**acétaminophène** peut augmenter le risque de réactions rénales indésirables ■ L'oxaprozine peut réduire l'efficacité des **diurétiques** ou des **antihypertenseurs** ■ L'oxaprozine peut intensifier l'effet hypoglycémiant de l'**insuline** ou des **hypoglycémiants oraux** ■ L'oxaprozine augmente le risque de toxicité associé au **méthotrexate** ■ Risque accru d'hémorragie lors de l'administration concomitante de **céfamandole**, de **céfotétane**, de **céfopérazone**, de **plicamycine**, d'**agents thrombolytiques**, d'**anticoagulants**, de **ticlopidine**, de **clopidogrel**, d'**eptifibatide** ou de **tirofiban** ■ Risque accru de réactions hématologiques indésirables lors de l'administration simultanée d'**agents antinéoplasiques** ou d'une **radiothérapie**.

Médicament-produits naturels: Risque accru de saignements en cas de consommation concomitante d'**ail**, d'**arnica**, **de camomille**, de **girofle**, de **gingembre**, de **ginkgo** et de **ginseng**.

O

VOIES D'ADMINISTRATION ET POSOLOGIE

- **PO (adultes)**: *Polyarthrite rhumatoïde* – 1 200 mg, 1 fois par jour; on peut réduire ou augmenter la dose selon la réponse du patient. Ne pas dépasser 1 800 mg/jour ou 26 mg/kg/jour. La dose de 1 800 mg par jour devrait être réservée aux patients de > 50 kg, ayant une fonction rénale et hépatique normale, et dont la gravité de la maladie dicte l'administration d'une dose élevée. Chez les patients ayant un faible poids, souffrant d'une forme légère de la maladie ou présentant une insuffisance rénale, on peut amorcer le traitement par 1 dose de 600 mg par jour. Les doses quotidiennes > 1 200 mg devraient être administrées 2 fois par jour (1 200 mg, le matin, et 600 mg, le soir). *Arthrose* –1 200 mg, 1 fois par jour; on peut réduire la dose à 600 mg, 1 fois par jour, selon la réponse du patient.
- **PO (personnes âgées)**: Commencer le traitement à 1 dose de 600 mg, 1 fois par jour.

PRÉSENTATION
(version générique disponible)

Comprimés: 600 mg^{Pr}.

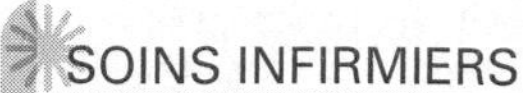

SOINS INFIRMIERS

ÉVALUATION DE LA SITUATION

- LES PATIENTS SOUFFRANT D'ASTHME, D'ALLERGIE INDUITE PAR L'ASPIRINE OU DE POLYPES NASAUX SONT DAVANTAGE PRÉDISPOSÉS AUX RÉACTIONS D'HYPERSENSIBILITÉ. SUIVRE DE PRÈS L'APPARITION DE SYMPTÔMES DE RHINITE, D'ASTHME OU D'URTICAIRE.
- Évaluer l'intensité de la douleur et l'amplitude des mouvements avant l'administration de l'oxaprozine et à intervalles réguliers pendant toute la durée du traitement.

Tests de laboratoire:

- L'oxaprozine peut allonger le temps de saignement, effet qui peut persister jusqu'à 2 semaines après l'arrêt du traitement.
- Chez les patients recevant un traitement prolongé, noter à intervalles réguliers les concentrations sériques d'urée et de créatinine, ainsi que la numération globulaire et les résultats des tests de la fonction hépatique. L'agent peut élever les concentrations sériques de potassium, d'urée, de créatinine, de phosphatase alcaline ainsi que celles de LDH, d'AST et d'ALT. À l'opposé, le médicament peut réduire la glycémie, les concentrations d'hémoglobine et l'hématocrite, ainsi que le nombre de leucocytes et de plaquettes et la Cl_{Cr}.

DIAGNOSTICS INFIRMIERS POSSIBLES

- Douleur aiguë (Indications).
- Connaissances insuffisantes sur le traitement médicamenteux (Enseignement au patient et à ses proches).

INTERVENTIONS INFIRMIÈRES

- L'administration de doses plus élevées que celles recommandées n'améliore pas l'efficacité du médicament, mais pourrait augmenter le risque d'effets secondaires.
- Administrer l'oxaprozine avec des aliments ou des antiacides pour réduire l'irritation gastrique.

ENSEIGNEMENT AU PATIENT ET À SES PROCHES

- Conseiller au patient de prendre l'oxaprozine avec un grand verre d'eau et d'éviter de se coucher pendant les 15 à 30 minutes qui suivent.
- Conseiller au patient de respecter rigoureusement la posologie recommandée. S'il n'a pu prendre le médicament au moment habituel, il doit le faire dès que possible à moins que ce ne soit presque l'heure

prévue pour la dose suivante. Le prévenir qu'il ne faut jamais remplacer une dose manquée par une double dose.

- Prévenir le patient que l'oxaprozine peut parfois provoquer de la somnolence ou des étourdissements. Lui conseiller de ne pas conduire et d'éviter les activités qui exigent sa vigilance jusqu'à ce qu'on ait la certitude que le médicament n'entraîne pas ces effets chez lui.
- Recommander au patient d'éviter de boire de l'alcool et de consulter un professionnel de la santé avant de prendre une préparation à base d'aspirine ou d'acétaminophène, un autre médicament en vente libre ou un produit naturel en même temps que l'oxaprozine.
- Recommander au patient qui doit suivre un autre traitement ou subir une intervention chirurgicale d'avertir le professionnel de la santé qu'il suit un traitement avec ce médicament. Le traitement par l'oxaprozine devrait être interrompu 2 semaines avant toute intervention chirurgicale.
- Recommander au patient d'utiliser un écran solaire et de porter des vêtements protecteurs pour prévenir les réactions de photosensibilité.
- Recommander au patient de communiquer avec un professionnel de la santé en cas de rash, de démangeaisons, de troubles visuels, d'acouphènes, de gain de poids, d'œdème, de selles noires, de céphalées persistantes ou de symptômes pseudogrippaux (frissons, fièvre, douleurs musculaires, douleurs).

VÉRIFICATION DE L'EFFICACITÉ THÉRAPEUTIQUE

L'efficacité du traitement peut être démontrée par: la diminution de l'intensité de la douleur et l'amélioration de la mobilité des articulations; l'efficacité maximale peut ne pas être notable avant 2 semaines ou plus de traitement continu. Les patients qui ne répondent pas à un anti-inflammatoire non stéroïdien peuvent répondre à un autre.

OXAZÉPAM

Apo-Oxazépam, Bio-Oxazépam, Novoxapam, Oxazepam, PMS-Oxazepam, Riva-Oxazépam, Serax

CLASSIFICATION:
Anxiolytique et hypnosédatif (benzodiazépine)

Grossesse – catégorie D

INDICATIONS

Traitement de l'anxiété ■ Traitement des symptômes du sevrage alcoolique.

MÉCANISME D'ACTION

Dépression du SNC, probablement par potentialisation de l'activité neuro-inhibitrice de l'acide gamma-aminobutyrique (GABA). ***Effets thérapeutiques:*** Soulagement de l'anxiété ■ Diminution des symptômes du sevrage alcoolique.

PHARMACOCINÉTIQUE

Absorption: Bonne (PO), mais plus lente que celle des autres benzodiazépines.

Distribution: L'agent se répartit dans tout l'organisme et traverse la barrière hématoencéphalique. Il traverse probablement la barrière placentaire et passe dans le lait maternel. Lors d'une administration prolongée, le médicament s'accumule dans les tissus.

Liaison aux protéines: De 86 à 99 %.

Métabolisme et excrétion: Métabolisme hépatique. Excrétion rénale (principalement sous forme de métabolites inactifs).

Demi-vie: De 5 à 15 heures.

Profil temps-action (sédation)

	DÉBUT D'ACTION	PIC	DURÉE
PO	45 - 90 min	inconnu	6 - 12 h

O

CONTRE-INDICATIONS, PRÉCAUTIONS ET MISES EN GARDE

Contre-indications: Hypersensibilité ■ Risque de réactions de sensibilité croisée avec d'autres benzodiazépines ■ Glaucome à angle fermé ■ Myasthénie grave.

Précautions et mises en garde: Dysfonctionnement hépatique ■ Dépression majeure ou psychose, lorsque l'anxiété n'est pas un facteur prédominant ■ Comportement suicidaire ou antécédents de tentatives de suicide, de toxicomanie ou de pharmacodépendance ■ **GÉR.:** Il est recommandé de réduire la dose initiale chez les personnes âgées ou débilitées ■ Coma ou dépression préexistante du SNC ■ Insuffisance pulmonaire grave ou apnée du sommeil ■ **OBST., ALLAITEMENT:** L'administration de cet agent chez la femme enceinte ou qui allaite n'est pas recommandée.

RÉACTIONS INDÉSIRABLES ET EFFETS SECONDAIRES

SNC: étourdissements, somnolence, confusion, sensation de tête légère, céphalées, troubles de mémoire, dépression mentale, excitation paradoxale, troubles de l'élocution.

ORLO: vision trouble.
Resp.: dépression respiratoire.
CV: tachycardie.
GI: constipation, diarrhée, hépatite médicamenteuse, nausées, vomissements.
GU: troubles urinaires.
Tég.: rash.
Hémat.: leucopénie.
Divers: dépendance physique, dépendance psychologique, tolérance aux effets du médicament.

INTERACTIONS

Médicament-médicament: Dépression additive du SNC lors de l'usage concomitant d'autres **dépresseurs du SNC**, y compris l'**alcool**, les **antihistaminiques**, les **antidépresseurs**, les **opioïdes** et les autres **hypnosédatifs** (incluant d'autres **benzodiazépines**) ■ La **phénytoïne**, administrée en concomitance, peut diminuer l'efficacité de l'oxazépam ■ La **théophylline** peut réduire les effets sédatifs de l'oxazépam.
Médicament-produits naturels: Le **kava**, le **houblon**, la **scutellaire**, la **valériane** et la **camomille** peuvent accentuer la dépression du SNC.

VOIES D'ADMINISTRATION ET POSOLOGIE

- **PO (adultes)**: *Anxiolytique* – de 10 à 30 mg, 3 ou 4 fois par jour. *Hypnosédatif/traitement des symptômes du sevrage alcoolique* – de 15 à 30 mg, 3 ou 4 fois par jour.
- **PO (personnes âgées ou débilitées)**: Initialement, de 5 à 10 mg, de 1 à 3 fois par jour; on peut majorer la dose, selon l'efficacité du traitement et la tolérance du patient.

O

PRÉSENTATION (version générique disponible)

Comprimés: 10 mg[T\C], 15 mg[T\C], 30 mg[T\C].

SOINS INFIRMIERS

ÉVALUATION DE LA SITUATION

- Noter le degré d'anxiété et de sédation (ataxie, étourdissements, troubles d'élocution), à intervalles réguliers pendant toute la durée du traitement.
- Noter les habitudes de sommeil du patient avant le traitement et à intervalles réguliers pendant toute sa durée.

GÉR.: Évaluer les effets au niveau du SNC et le risque de chutes et mettre en place les mesures préventives.

- Le traitement prolongé à des doses élevées peut entraîner une dépendance psychologique ou physique. Limiter la quantité de médicament dont le patient peut disposer.

Tests de laboratoire: Noter à intervalles réguliers les résultats des tests de la fonction hépatique et la numération globulaire chez les patients qui reçoivent un traitement prolongé.

DIAGNOSTICS INFIRMIERS POSSIBLES

- Anxiété (Indications).
- Risque d'accident (Effets secondaires).
- Connaissances insuffisantes sur le traitement médicamenteux (Enseignement au patient et à ses proches).

INTERVENTIONS INFIRMIÈRES

- Vers la fin du traitement, il faut interrompre graduellement l'administration de l'oxazépam. L'arrêt brusque de la médication peut entraîner les symptômes de sevrage suivants: insomnie, irritabilité, nervosité, tremblements.
- Administrer l'oxazépam avec des aliments si l'irritation gastrique devient gênante.

ENSEIGNEMENT AU PATIENT ET À SES PROCHES

- Conseiller au patient de respecter rigoureusement la posologie recommandée. S'il n'a pas pu prendre le médicament au moment habituel, il doit le prendre dans l'heure qui suit; sinon, il doit sauter cette dose et reprendre l'horaire habituel. Le prévenir qu'il ne doit pas doubler la dose ni l'augmenter. Lui conseiller de prévenir un professionnel de la santé si la dose est moins efficace après quelques semaines.
- Prévenir le patient que l'oxazépam peut entraîner de la somnolence ou des étourdissements. Lui conseiller de ne pas conduire et d'éviter les activités qui exigent sa vigilance jusqu'à ce qu'on ait la certitude que le médicament n'entraîne pas ces effets chez lui.

GÉR.: Expliquer au patient et à ses proches les mesures à prendre pour prévenir le risque de chutes.

- Recommander au patient d'éviter de boire de l'alcool. Lui conseiller de consulter un professionnel de la santé avant de prendre des préparations en vente libre contenant des antihistaminiques ou de l'alcool.
- Conseiller à la patiente d'informer un professionnel de la santé si elle pense être enceinte ou si elle souhaite le devenir.
- Recommander au patient qui doit suivre un autre traitement ou subir une intervention chirurgicale d'avertir le professionnel de la santé qu'il suit un traitement par ce médicament.
- Insister sur l'importance des examens de suivi permettant d'évaluer l'efficacité du médicament.

VÉRIFICATION DE L'EFFICACITÉ THÉRAPEUTIQUE

L'efficacité du traitement peut être démontrée par: la diminution de la sensation d'anxiété ■ une meilleure capacité d'adaptation ■ la prévention ou le soulagement de l'agitation aiguë, des tremblements et des hallucinations au cours du sevrage alcoolique.

OXCARBAZÉPINE

Apo-Oxcarbazepine, Trileptal

CLASSIFICATION:

Anticonvulsivant

Grossesse – catégorie C

INDICATIONS

Monothérapie ou traitement d'appoint des crises partielles chez les adultes atteints d'épilepsie ■ Traitement d'appoint des crises partielles chez les patients âgés de 6 à 16 ans. **Usages non approuvés:** Traitement de la névralgie essentielle du trijumeau.

MÉCANISME D'ACTION

Blocage des canaux sodiques dans les membranes neuronales, stabilisant ainsi les états d'hyperexcitabilité par inhibition des décharges neuronales à répétition et par ralentissement de la propagation des influx synaptiques. ***Effets thérapeutiques:*** Diminution de la fréquence des crises épileptiques.

PHARMACOCINÉTIQUE

Absorption: Bonne (PO). Transformation rapide en son métabolite pharmacologiquement actif, l'hydroxy-10 oxcarbazépine (MHD).

Distribution: L'agent passe dans le lait maternel en quantités importantes.

Métabolisme et excrétion: Le médicament est surtout transformé en MHD, lequel est principalement excrété par les reins.

Demi-vie: *Oxcarbazépine* – 2 heures; *MHD* – 9 heures.

Profil temps-action

	DÉBUT D'ACTION	PIC	DURÉE
PO	rapide	4 – 5 h†	12 h

† Les concentrations de MHD à l'état d'équilibre sont atteintes après 2 ou 3 jours de traitement à une posologie biquotidienne.

CONTRE-INDICATIONS, PRÉCAUTIONS ET MISES EN GARDE

Contre-indications: Hypersensibilité; risque de sensibilité croisée avec la carbamazépine.

Précautions et mises en garde: Insuffisance rénale (il est recommandé de réduire la dose si la Cl_{Cr} est < 30 mL/min) ■ **OBST., ALLAITEMENT:** Administrer ce médicament seulement si ses bienfaits escomptés justifient le risque possible auquel est exposé le fœtus ■ **PÉD.:** L'innocuité du médicament n'a pas été établie chez les enfants < 4 ans.

RÉACTIONS INDÉSIRABLES ET EFFETS SECONDAIRES

SNC: étourdissements et vertiges, somnolence et fatigue, céphalées, symptômes cognitifs.

ORLO: vision anormale, vision double, nystagmus.

GI: douleurs abdominales, dyspepsie, nausées, vomissements, soif.

Tég.: acné, rash, urticaire.

HÉ: hyponatrémie.

SN: ataxie, troubles de la démarche, tremblements.

Divers: réactions allergiques, HYPERSENSIBILITÉ MULTIORGANIQUE et réactions dermatologiques graves, dont le SYNDROME DE STEVENS-JOHNSON, lymphadénopathie.

INTERACTIONS

Médicament-médicament: L'oxcarbazépine peut inhiber l'isoenzyme **CYP 2C19** et pourrait donc modifier les effets d'autres **médicaments qui sont métabolisés par cette isoenzyme**. L'oxcarbazépine et le MHD exercent des effets sur l'isoenzyme **P450 3A4/5** et ils pourraient modifier les effets d'autres **médicaments qui sont métabolisés par cette isoenzyme**, ce qui pourrait entraîner une réduction des concentrations et de l'efficacité des **contraceptifs oraux**, de la **félodipine**, de la **nifédipine** et de la **nimodipine**. De plus, comme l'oxcarbazépine est elle-même métabolisée par les enzymes du **cytochrome P450**, les autres **médicaments qui modifient l'activité de ces enzymes** peuvent modifier la réponse au traitement par l'oxcarbazépine ■ Risque de dépression additive du SNC lors de l'usage concomitant d'autres **dépresseurs du SNC**, y compris l'**alcool**, les **antihistaminiques**, les **antidépresseurs**, les **hypnosédatifs** et les **opioïdes** ■ La **carbamazépine**, le **phénobarbital**, la **phénytoïne**, l'**acide valproïque** et le **vérapamil**, administrés en concomitance, abaissent les concentrations de l'oxcarbazépine ■ L'oxcarbazépine peut élever les concentrations sériques de **phénytoïne** et intensifier ses effets (il peut s'avérer nécessaire de réduire la dose de phénytoïne).

O

VOIES D'ADMINISTRATION ET POSOLOGIE

- **PO (adultes)**: *Traitement d'appoint* – 300 mg, 2 fois par jour; on peut majorer la dose par paliers allant jusqu'à 600 mg par jour, à des intervalles de 1 semaine, jusqu'à concurrence de 1 200 mg par jour (une dose de 2 400 mg par jour peut s'avérer nécessaire); *passage à la monothérapie* – 300 mg, 2 fois par jour; on peut majorer la dose par paliers de 600 mg par jour, à des intervalles de 1 semaine, tout en diminuant graduellement pendant 3 à 6 semaines les doses des autres médicaments antiépileptiques; la dose d'oxcarbazépine devrait être augmentée jusqu'à concurrence de 2 400 mg par jour, pendant 2 à 4 semaines; *début de la monothérapie* – 300 mg, 2 fois par jour; augmenter la dose de 300 mg par jour, à intervalles de 3 jours, jusqu'à concurrence de 1 200 mg par jour.
- **PO (enfants de 6 à 16 ans)**: *Traitement d'appoint* – de 4 à 5 mg/kg, 2 fois par jour (jusqu'à concurrence de 600 mg par jour); majorer la dose pendant une période de 2 semaines pour atteindre 900 mg par jour, chez les patients pesant entre 20 et 29 kg, 1 200 mg par jour, chez les patients pesant de 29,1 à 39 kg, et 1 800 mg par jour, chez les patients pesant plus de 39 kg (écart posologique: de 6 à 51 mg/kg par jour).

O

INSUFFISANCE RÉNALE

- **PO (ADULTES)**: *Cl_{CR} < 30 mL/MIN* – AMORCER LE TRAITEMENT À UNE DOSE DE 300 mg PAR JOUR ET L'AUGMENTER LENTEMENT JUSQU'À L'OBTENTION DE LA RÉPONSE SOUHAITÉE.

PRÉSENTATION

Comprimés: 150 mg[Pr], 300 mg[Pr], 600 mg[Pr] ■ **Suspension orale**: 300 mg/5 mL[Pr].

SOINS INFIRMIERS

ÉVALUATION DE LA SITUATION

Crises épileptiques:

- Déterminer la fréquence, le type, la durée et les caractéristiques des crises épileptiques.
- Examiner le patient à la recherche de changements au niveau du SNC, qui peuvent se manifester sous forme de symptômes cognitifs (ralentissement psychomoteur, problèmes de concentration, troubles d'élocution ou de langage), de somnolence, de fatigue ou d'anomalies de la coordination (ataxie, modification de la démarche).

Tests de laboratoire: Noter les résultats de l'ÉCG et les concentrations sériques d'électrolytes avant le traitement et à intervalles réguliers pendant toute sa durée. L'oxcarbazépine peut entraîner une hyponatrémie qui se manifeste habituellement au cours des 3 premiers mois de traitement. Dans ce cas, il peut s'avérer nécessaire de réduire la dose, de diminuer l'apport liquidien ou de cesser le traitement. Les concentrations de sodium reviennent à la normale dans les quelques jours qui suivent l'arrêt du traitement.

DIAGNOSTICS INFIRMIERS POSSIBLES

- Risque d'accident (Effets secondaires).
- Connaissances insuffisantes sur le traitement médicamenteux (Enseignement au patient et à ses proches).

INTERVENTIONS INFIRMIÈRES

- Prendre les précautions nécessaires en cas de crises épileptiques, selon les directives de l'établissement.
- Administrer l'oxcarbazépine 2 fois par jour sans égard aux repas.

ENSEIGNEMENT AU PATIENT ET À SES PROCHES

- Expliquer au patient qu'il doit prendre les doses d'oxcarbazépine à des intervalles égaux, en suivant rigoureusement la posologie recommandée. S'il n'a pas pu prendre le médicament au moment habituel, il doit le prendre aussitôt que possible, sauf s'il est presque l'heure prévue pour la dose suivante. Le prévenir qu'il ne doit jamais remplacer une dose manquée par une double dose. Lui expliquer qu'il doit prévenir un professionnel de la santé s'il n'a pas pu prendre plusieurs doses. Le sevrage doit être graduel, sinon la fréquence des crises épileptiques risque d'augmenter.
- Prévenir le patient que l'oxcarbazépine peut provoquer des étourdissements, de la somnolence ou des changements au niveau du SNC. Lui conseiller de ne pas conduire et d'éviter les activités qui exigent sa vigilance jusqu'à ce qu'on ait la certitude que le médicament n'entraîne pas ces effets chez lui. Le prévenir qu'il ne doit pas conduire jusqu'à ce que le médecin ne lui en donne l'autorisation, une fois les crises épileptiques maîtrisées.
- Prévenir le patient qu'il doit éviter de boire de l'alcool et de prendre d'autres dépresseurs du SNC pendant le traitement à l'oxcarbazépine.
- Recommander à la patiente d'utiliser une méthode contraceptive non hormonale pendant toute la durée du traitement et jusqu'au cycle menstruel suivant. Lui conseiller d'informer un professionnel de la santé

si elle pense être enceinte ou si elle souhaite le devenir.

- Recommander au patient qui doit suivre un autre traitement ou subir une intervention chirurgicale d'avertir le professionnel de la santé qu'il suit un traitement par ce médicament.
- Conseiller au patient de porter sur lui en tout temps un bracelet d'identité où sont inscrits son problème de santé et son traitement médicamenteux.

VÉRIFICATION DE L'EFFICACITÉ THÉRAPEUTIQUE

L'efficacité du traitement peut être démontrée par: la suppression des crises épileptiques ou la réduction de leur fréquence.

OXTRIPHYLLINE,

voir Bronchodilatateurs (xanthines)

OXYBUTYNINE

Apo-Oxybutynine, Ditropan, Ditropan XL, Dom-Oxybutynine, Gen-Oxybutynine, Oxytrol (transdermique), Novo-Oxybutynine, PMS-Oxybutynine, Riva-Oxybutynine, Uromax

CLASSIFICATION:
Anticholinergique (antispasmodique urinaire)

Grossesse – catégorie B

INDICATIONS

Traitement des symptômes urinaires suivants pouvant être associés à une vessie neurogène ou hyperactive: mictions fréquentes ■ mictions impérieuses ■ nycturie ■ incontinence ■ dysurie.

MÉCANISME D'ACTION

Inhibition de l'action de l'acétylcholine au niveau des récepteurs postganglionnaires ■ Effet spasmolytique direct sur les muscles lisses, y compris les muscles lisses de la vessie, sans affecter les muscles lisses vasculaires. ***Effets thérapeutiques:*** Augmentation de la capacité de la vessie ■ Retard du besoin d'uriner ■ Diminution des épisodes d'incontinence, du besoin impérieux d'uriner et de la fréquence des mictions et moindre risque de pertes accidentelles d'urine associées à une vessie hyperactive.

PHARMACOCINÉTIQUE

Absorption: Rapide (PO). Premier passage hépatique important; les comprimés à libération prolongée apportent un soulagement de plus longue durée. L'absorption transdermique se produit par diffusion à travers une peau intacte, sans métabolisme de premier passage hépatique.

Distribution: Importante.

Métabolisme et excrétion: Métabolisme hépatique et intestinal. Excrétion rénale très faible (moins de 0,1 % sous forme inchangée).

Demi-vie: *Oxybutynine:* 2 heures; *métabolites:* de 7 à 8 heures.

Profil temps-action (effet urinaire spasmolytique)

	Début d'action	Pic	Durée
PO	30 – 60 min	3 – 6 h	6 – 10 h (jusqu'à 24 h, comprimé à libération prolongée)
Transdermique	en 24 h	36 h	3 – 4 jours

CONTRE-INDICATIONS, PRÉCAUTIONS ET MISES EN GARDE

Contre-indications: Hypersensibilité ■ Glaucome à angle fermé non maîtrisé ■ Occlusion ou atonie intestinale ■ Mégacôlon toxique ■ Iléus paralytique ■ Myasthénie grave ■ Hémorragie aiguë accompagnée d'un état de choc ■ Uropathie obstructive ■ Rétention gastrique.

Précautions et mises en garde: Obst.: Grossesse et allaitement (inhibition possible de la lactation) ■ Maladie cardiovasculaire ■ Hyperplasie bénigne de la prostate ■ Hyperthyroïdie ■ Rectocolite hémorragique grave ■ Œsophagite de reflux ■ Prise de médicaments pouvant causer ou exacerber une œsophagite ■ **Gér.:** Personnes âgées (risque accru de réactions indésirables anticholinergiques) ■ **Péd.:** Enfants < 5 ans (l'innocuité du médicament n'a pas été établie) ■ Maladie hépatique ou rénale.

RÉACTIONS INDÉSIRABLES ET EFFETS SECONDAIRES

SNC: étourdissements, somnolence, hallucinations, insomnie, faiblesse.

ORLO: vision trouble, cycloplégie, pression intraoculaire accrue, mydriase, photophobie.

CV: palpitations, tachycardie.

GI: sensation de ballonnement, constipation, sécheresse de la bouche (xérostomie), nausées, vomissements.

GU: impuissance, retard de la miction (avec effort pour uriner), rétention urinaire.

Tég.: sécrétion réduite de sueur, urticaire, réaction au siège d'application (transdermique).

End.: suppression de la lactation.

Métab.: hyperthermie.

Divers: réactions allergiques, fièvre, bouffées vasomotrices.

INTERACTIONS

Médicament-médicament: Effets anticholinergiques additifs lors de l'administration concomitante d'autres **agents dotés de propriétés anticholinergiques**, tels que l'**amantadine**, les **antidépresseurs**, les **phénothiazines**, le **disopyramide** et l'**halopéridol** ▪ Dépression additive du SNC lors de l'usage concomitant d'autres **dépresseurs du SNC**, y compris l'**alcool**, les **antihistaminiques**, les **antidépresseurs**, les **opioïdes** et les **hypnosédatifs** ▪ L'oxybutynine peut élever les concentrations sériques de **nitrofurantoïne** et accroître le risque de toxicité par ce médicament ▪ L'oxybutynine peut diminuer l'efficacité de la **lévodopa** ▪ L'oxybutynine peut augmenter l'absorption de l'**aténolol** ▪ L'administration concomitante d'**halopéridol** peut entraîner une dyskinésie tardive, une aggravation de la schizophrénie et une diminution des concentrations d'halopéridol ▪ L'administration concomitante de **médicaments pouvant causer une œsophagite**, comme la **doxycycline** et les **bisphosphonates,** peut exacerber une œsophagite ▪ Augmentation des concentrations plasmatiques et du risque de toxicité lors de l'administration concomitante de **kétoconazole** ou d'autres **inhibiteurs du CYP P450 3A4**.

VOIES D'ADMINISTRATION ET POSOLOGIE

- **PO (adultes)**: 5 mg, 2 ou 3 fois par jour (ne pas dépasser 5 mg, 4 fois par jour) pour la préparation ordinaire, et de 5 à 10 mg, 1 fois par jour, pour la préparation à libération prolongée. La dose peut être augmentée toutes les semaines par paliers de 5 mg (maximum 30 mg/jour pour Ditropan XL et 20 mg/jour pour Uromax).
- **Timbre transdermique (adultes)**: 1 timbre de 3,9 mg/jour, tous les 3 à 4 jours (2 fois par semaine).
- **PO (enfants > 5 ans)**: 5 mg, 2 ou 3 fois par jour (ne pas dépasser 15 mg par jour) pour la préparation ordinaire.

O

PRÉSENTATION
(version générique disponible)

Comprimés: 2,5 mg[Pr], 5 mg[Pr] ▪ **Comprimés à libération prolongée**: 5 mg[Pr], 10 mg[Pr], 15 mg[Pr] ▪ **Sirop**: 5 mg/5 mL[Pr] ▪ **Système transdermique**: 36 mg (libération de 3,9 mg par jour)[Pr].

SOINS INFIRMIERS

ÉVALUATION DE LA SITUATION

- Noter le mode d'élimination urinaire, faire le bilan des ingesta et des excreta, examiner l'abdomen afin de déceler la distension de la vessie, avant le début du traitement et pendant toute sa durée. Pour évaluer les résidus postmictionnels, on peut procéder à des cathétérismes. La cystométrie, permettant de diagnostiquer le type de dysfonctionnement vésical, est habituellement effectuée avant que l'oxybutynine ne soit prescrite.

GÉR.: Chez les patients âgés, rester à l'affût d'effets anticholinergiques comme la somnolence et la faiblesse.

DIAGNOSTICS INFIRMIERS POSSIBLES

- Élimination urinaire altérée (Indications).
- Douleur aiguë (Indications).
- Connaissances insuffisantes sur le traitement médicamenteux (Enseignement au patient et à ses proches).

INTERVENTIONS INFIRMIÈRES

- NE PAS CONFONDRE DITROPAN (OXYBUTYNINE) AVEC LE DIAZÉPAM.

PO: L'oxybutynine peut être administrée à jeun ou avec des aliments ou du lait pour prévenir l'irritation gastrique.

Transdermique: Appliquer le timbre 2 fois par semaine, en conservant toujours les mêmes jours (dimanche/mercredi ou lundi/jeudi) sur la hanche, l'abdomen ou les fesses, sur une peau propre, sèche et exempte d'irritation. Le timbre doit être porté en tout temps.

ENSEIGNEMENT AU PATIENT ET À SES PROCHES

- Conseiller au patient de respecter rigoureusement la posologie recommandée. S'il n'a pas pu prendre le médicament au moment habituel, il doit le prendre dès que possible, à moins que ce ne soit presque l'heure prévue pour la dose suivante.
- Prévenir le patient que l'oxybutynine peut provoquer de la somnolence ou une vision trouble. Lui conseiller de ne pas conduire et d'éviter les activités qui exigent sa vigilance jusqu'à ce qu'on ait la certitude que le médicament n'entraîne pas ces effets chez lui.
- Prévenir le patient qu'il doit éviter de boire de l'alcool et de prendre d'autres dépresseurs du SNC pendant le traitement à l'oxybutynine.
- Conseiller au patient de se rincer fréquemment la bouche, de pratiquer une bonne hygiène buccale et de consommer de la gomme à mâcher ou des bonbons sans sucre pour soulager la sécheresse de la bouche. Lui recommander de consulter un professionnel de la santé si la sécheresse de la bouche persiste pendant plus de 2 semaines.
- Expliquer au patient que l'oxybutynine peut diminuer les sécrétions de sueur. Lui recommander

d'éviter les activités épuisantes par temps chaud en raison des risques d'hyperthermie.

- Recommander au patient de porter des lunettes fumées lorsqu'il est en plein soleil en raison du risque de sensibilité accrue à la lumière.
- Conseiller au patient de prévenir un professionnel de la santé en cas de rétention urinaire ou de constipation persistante. Lui expliquer qu'il peut prévenir la constipation en adoptant un régime alimentaire riche en fibres, en buvant plus de liquides et en faisant de l'exercice.
- Insister sur la nécessité d'un suivi médical constant. On peut effectuer à intervalles réguliers des cystométries pour évaluer l'efficacité du traitement et des examens ophtalmiques pour déceler tout signe de glaucome, particulièrement chez les patients > 40 ans.

Timbre transdermique: Enseigner au patient la technique d'application et de mise au rebut du timbre. Ouvrir le sachet en tirant le long des flèches. Appliquer immédiatement ½ timbre sur la peau en enlevant la moitié de la pellicule protectrice et le coller fermement sur la peau. Appliquer ensuite la seconde moitié en pliant le timbre en deux et en le déroulant sur la peau pendant qu'on enlève la pellicule protectrice. Appuyer fermement sur le timbre. Pour enlever: tirer lentement sur le timbre, le plier en deux en collant ensemble les côtés adhésifs et le jeter. Laver le siège de l'application avec de l'eau savonneuse ou nettoyer avec une petite quantité d'huile pour bébé.

VÉRIFICATION DE L'EFFICACITÉ THÉRAPEUTIQUE

L'efficacité du traitement peut être démontrée par: le soulagement du spasme de la vessie et des symptômes connexes (mictions fréquentes, mictions impérieuses, nycturie et incontinence) chez les patients présentant une vessie neurogène ou hyperactive.

ALERTE CLINIQUE

OXYCODONE

Oxycontin, Oxy-IR, Supeudol

CLASSIFICATION:

Analgésique opioïde (agoniste)

Grossesse – catégories B et D (usage prolongé ou doses élevées près du terme)

INDICATIONS

Soulagement de la douleur modérée à intense ■ **Préparation à libération contrôlée:** Soulagement de la douleur modérée à intense exigeant l'administration prolongée d'une préparation opioïde par voie orale.

MÉCANISME D'ACTION

Liaison aux récepteurs des opioïdes du SNC ■ Modification de la perception de la douleur et de la réaction aux stimuli douloureux, avec dépression généralisée du SNC. ***Effets thérapeutiques:*** Diminution de l'intensité de la douleur.

PHARMACOCINÉTIQUE

Absorption: Bonne (PO et IR).

Distribution: Le médicament se répartit dans tout l'organisme. Il traverse la barrière placentaire et passe dans le lait maternel.

Métabolisme et excrétion: Métabolisme hépatique.

Demi-vie: De 2 à 4 heures.

Profil temps-action (effets analgésiques)

	DÉBUT D'ACTION	PIC	DURÉE
PO	10 – 15 min	60 – 90 min	3 – 6 h
PO-LP†	60 min et +	3 h	12 h

† LP = libération prolongée.

CONTRE-INDICATIONS, PRÉCAUTIONS ET MISES EN GARDE

Contre-indications: Hypersensibilité ■ Crise d'asthme ou troubles obstructifs des voies aériennes et dépression respiratoire aiguë ■ Cœur pulmonaire ■ Alcoolisme aigu ■ Delirium tremens ■ Dépression grave du système nerveux central ■ Troubles convulsifs ■ Pression intracrânienne accrue ■ Traumatisme crânien ■ Abdomen aigu soupçonné ■ Prise concomitante d'IMAO (ou dans les 14 jours qui suivent ou qui précèdent un tel traitement).

Précautions et mises en garde: Maladies rénale, hépatique ou pulmonaire graves ■ Hypothyroïdie ■ Insuffisance surrénalienne ■ Personnes âgées ou patients débilités (il est recommandé de réduire la dose initiale) ■ Douleur abdominale non diagnostiquée ■ Hyperplasie de la prostate ■ **OBST.:** Grossesse et allaitement (administration prolongée à proscrire) ■ Risque de pharmacodépendance et d'abus.

RÉACTIONS INDÉSIRABLES ET EFFETS SECONDAIRES

SNC: confusion, sédation, étourdissements, dysphorie, euphorie, sensation de flottement, hallucinations, céphalées, rêves bizarres.

ORLO: vision trouble, diplopie, myosis.

Resp.: DÉPRESSION RESPIRATOIRE.

CV: hypotension orthostatique.

GI: constipation, sécheresse de la bouche (xérostomie), nausées, vomissements.

GU: rétention urinaire.

Tég.: bouffées vasomotrices, transpiration.

Divers: dépendance physique, dépendance psychologique, tolérance aux effets du médicament.

INTERACTIONS

Médicament-médicament: RISQUE DE RÉACTIONS IMPRÉVISIBLES CHEZ LES PATIENTS PRENANT DES **IMAO** – UNE GRANDE PRUDENCE EST DE MISE LORS D'UN TRAITEMENT CONCOMITANT (RÉDUIRE LA DOSE INITIALE D'OXYCODONE À 25 % DE LA DOSE HABITUELLE) ■ Dépression additive du SNC et du système respiratoire lors de l'usage concomitant d'**alcool**, d'**antihistaminiques**, de **phénothiazines**, de **barbituriques**, d'**antidépresseurs**, d'**hypnosédatifs** et d'autres **opioïdes** ■ L'administration d'**analgésiques opioïdes agonistes/antagonistes** (**nalbuphine**, **butorphanol**, **pentazocine**) peut diminuer l'analgésie et/ou déclencher des symptômes de sevrage chez les patients présentant une dépendance physique aux opioïdes.

Médicament-produits naturels: Effets dépresseurs additifs sur le SNC lors de la consommation concomitante de kava, de valériane, de scutellaire, de camomille et de houblon.

VOIES D'ADMINISTRATION ET POSOLOGIE

Les doses dépendent de l'intensité de la douleur et de la tolérance du patient. On peut les augmenter, selon la réponse et la tolérance du patient.

- **PO (adultes)**: Initialement, de 5 à 10 mg, toutes les 4 à 6 heures, selon les besoins. Une fois la dose quotidienne établie, il est possible de passer à une préparation à libération prolongée, en fractionnant la dose de manière à l'administrer toutes les 12 heures (OxyContin).
- **PO (enfants)**: Initialement, de 0,05 à 0,2 mg/kg/dose, toutes les 4 à 6 heures, selon les besoins.
- **IR (adultes)**: Initialement, de 10 à 20 mg, 3 ou 4 fois par jour, selon les besoins.

PRÉSENTATION

Comprimés: 5 mg[N], 10 mg[N], 20 mg[N] ■ **Comprimés à libération contrôlée**: 5 mg[N], 10 mg[N], 20 mg[N], 40 mg[N], 80 mg[N] ■ **Suppositoires**: 10 mg[N], 20 mg[N] ■ **En association avec**: acétaminophène ou aspirine (voir l'annexe U).

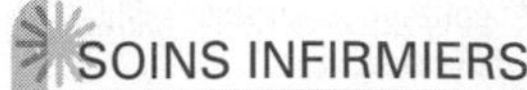

SOINS INFIRMIERS

ÉVALUATION DE LA SITUATION

- Déterminer le type de douleur, son siège et son intensité, avant l'administration du médicament et 1 heure après l'administration. Lorsqu'on majore la dose d'un opioïde, on devrait l'augmenter de 25 à 50 % jusqu'à ce qu'on note une réduction de 50 % de la douleur, selon l'évaluation qu'en fait le patient sur une échelle numérique ou visuelle, ou jusqu'à ce qu'il signale un soulagement adéquat de la douleur. On peut administrer sans danger une deuxième dose au moment du pic, si la dose précédente s'est avérée inefficace et si les effets secondaires sont minimes.
- Les patients prenant des comprimés à libération contrôlée devraient également recevoir des doses d'un opioïde à action brève, si des douleurs surviennent entre les prises. Ces doses devraient être équivalentes à 10 à 15 % de la dose quotidienne; on devrait les administrer toutes les 1 à 4 heures, selon les besoins.
- Utiliser un tableau d'équivalences (voir l'annexe A) au moment de changer de voie d'administration ou de marque d'opioïde.

ALERTE CLINIQUE: ÉVALUER L'ÉTAT DE CONSCIENCE, MESURER LA PRESSION ARTÉRIELLE, LE POULS ET LA FRÉQUENCE RESPIRATOIRE AVANT L'ADMINISTRATION DE CE MÉDICAMENT ET À INTERVALLES RÉGULIERS TOUT AU LONG DU TRAITEMENT. SI LA FRÉQUENCE RESPIRATOIRE EST < 10/MIN, ÉVALUER LE DEGRÉ DE SÉDATION. UNE STIMULATION PHYSIQUE PEUT SUFFIRE À PRÉVENIR UNE HYPOVENTILATION IMPORTANTE. IL PEUT S'AVÉRER NÉCESSAIRE DE RÉDUIRE LA DOSE DE 25 À 50 %. LA SOMNOLENCE INITIALE DISPARAÎT AU FIL DU TRAITEMENT.

GÉR.: Évaluer les patients âgés à intervalles fréquents, car ils sont plus sensibles aux effets des analgésiques opioïdes que les adultes plus jeunes; chez eux, les effets indésirables et les complications respiratoires peuvent être plus fréquents.

PÉD.: Évaluer les enfants à intervalles fréquents, car ils sont plus sensibles aux effets des analgésiques opioïdes; chez eux, les complications respiratoires, l'excitation et l'agitation peuvent être plus fréquentes.

- L'usage prolongé peut entraîner la dépendance physique et psychologique ainsi qu'une tolérance aux effets du médicament, mais cela ne doit pas empêcher le patient de recevoir une quantité suffisante d'analgésiques. La dépendance psychologique est rare chez la plupart des patients qui reçoivent l'oxycodone pour le traitement de la douleur. Lors d'un traitement prolongé, il faut parfois administrer des doses de plus en plus élevées pour soulager la douleur.

- Examiner le mode d'élimination intestinale du patient à intervalles réguliers. La consommation accrue de liquides et d'aliments riches en fibres et la prise de laxatifs peuvent réduire les effets constipants du médicament. Sauf contre-indication, des laxatifs stimulants devraient être administrés de façon systématique si le traitement par un opioïde dure plus de 2 ou 3 jours.

Tests de laboratoire: Le médicament peut entraîner l'élévation des concentrations plasmatiques d'amylase et de lipase.

Toxicité et surdosage: S'il est nécessaire d'administrer un antagoniste opioïde pour renverser la dépression respiratoire ou le coma, l'antidote est la naloxone (Narcan). Diluer le contenu de l'ampoule de naloxone à 0,4 mg dans 10 mL de solution de NaCl 0,9 % et administrer 0,5 mL (0,02 mg) par bolus IV direct, toutes les 2 minutes. Dans le cas des enfants et des patients < 40 kg, diluer 0,1 mg de naloxone dans 10 mL de solution de NaCl 0,9 % pour obtenir une concentration de 10 µg/mL et administrer 0,5 µg/kg, toutes les 2 minutes. Adapter la dose pour prévenir les symptômes de sevrage, les convulsions et la douleur intense.

DIAGNOSTICS INFIRMIERS POSSIBLES

- Douleur aiguë (Indications).
- Trouble de la perception visuelle et auditive (Effets secondaires).
- Risque d'accident (Effets secondaires).

INTERVENTIONS INFIRMIÈRES

Alerte clinique: DES SURDOSES ACCIDENTELLES D'ANALGÉSIQUES OPIOÏDES ONT CAUSÉ DES DÉCÈS. AVANT D'ADMINISTRER L'AGENT, CLARIFIER TOUS LES POINTS AMBIGUS ET FAIRE VÉRIFIER L'ORDONNANCE D'ORIGINE ET LE CALCUL DES DOSES PAR UN AUTRE PROFESSIONNEL DE LA SANTÉ.

- NE PAS CONFONDRE PERCOCET AVEC PERCODAN.
- NE PAS CONFONDRE L'OXYCODONE AVEC OXYCONTIN.
- **Péd.:** LES ERREURS DE MÉDICATION CONCERNANT LES ANALGÉSIQUE OPIOÏDES SONT FRÉQUENTES DANS LA POPULATION PÉDIATRIQUE ET COMPRENNENT DES ERREURS D'INTERPRÉTATION, DE CALCUL DES DOSES ET D'USAGE D'INSTRUMENTS DE MESURE INAPPROPRIÉS.
- Pour augmenter l'effet analgésique de l'oxycodone, avant de l'administrer, expliquer au patient la valeur thérapeutique de ce médicament.
- Les doses administrées selon un horaire fixe peuvent être plus efficaces que celles administrées sur demande. L'analgésique s'avère plus efficace s'il est administré avant que la douleur ne devienne intense.
- L'association avec des analgésiques non opioïdes peut avoir des effets analgésiques additifs et permettre d'administrer des doses plus faibles d'oxycodone.
- Après un traitement prolongé, interrompre l'administration graduellement pour prévenir les symptômes de sevrage.

PO:

- On peut administrer le médicament avec des aliments ou du lait pour réduire l'irritation gastrique.
- LES COMPRIMÉS À LIBÉRATION PROLONGÉE DOIVENT ÊTRE AVALÉS TELS QUELS, SANS ÊTRE MÂCHÉS OU ÉCRASÉS. LA PRISE DE COMPRIMÉS BRISÉS, MÂCHÉS OU ÉCRASÉS POURRAIT ENTRAÎNER LA LIBÉRATION ET L'ABSORPTION RAPIDES D'UNE DOSE D'OXYCODONE QUI POURRAIT ÊTRE MORTELLE.

Comprimés à libération contrôlée: Évaluer d'abord la dose d'opioïde à action brève nécessaire pour soulager la douleur pendant 24 heures, puis adapter cette dose à la présentation sous forme de comprimés à libération contrôlée.

ENSEIGNEMENT AU PATIENT ET À SES PROCHES

- Expliquer au patient ce qu'on entend par administration sur demande et à quel moment il doit réclamer l'analgésique.
- Prévenir le patient que l'oxycodone peut provoquer des étourdissements et de la somnolence. Lui recommander de demander de l'aide lorsqu'il se déplace et lorsqu'il veut fumer. Lui conseiller de ne pas conduire et d'éviter les activités qui exigent sa vigilance jusqu'à ce qu'on ait la certitude que le médicament n'entraîne pas ces effets chez lui.
- Prévenir les patients qui prennent des comprimés d'Oxycontin que l'enveloppe du médicament peut se retrouver dans les selles.
- Recommander au patient de changer lentement de position pour diminuer le risque d'hypotension orthostatique.
- Inciter le patient à ne pas boire d'alcool et à ne pas prendre d'autres dépresseurs du SNC en même temps que l'oxycodone.
- Conseiller au patient de se tourner dans le lit, de tousser et de faire des exercices de respiration profonde toutes les 2 heures pour prévenir l'atélectasie.
- Insister sur l'importance de la prévention de la constipation associée à la prise d'analgésiques opioïdes.

VÉRIFICATION DE L'EFFICACITÉ THÉRAPEUTIQUE

L'efficacité du traitement peut être démontrée par: la diminution de l'intensité de la douleur sans modification importante de l'état de conscience ou de la fonction respiratoire. ✳

OXYTOCINE

Synonyme: ocytocine

Oxytocine

CLASSIFICATION:

Agent utilisé pendant la grossesse et l'allaitement (ocytocique)

Grossesse – catégorie inconnue

INDICATIONS

Antepartum: déclenchement du travail lorsque la grossesse est arrivée à terme et qu'une raison médicale le justifie: incompatibilité du facteur Rhésus, diabète de la mère, prééclampsie bénigne, rupture prématurée des membranes ■ Stimulation des contractions de l'utérus dans certains cas d'inertie utérine ■ Facilitation d'un avortement incomplet ou inévitable ■ **Postpartum**: stimulation des contractions utérines pendant le 3e stade du travail et maîtrise de l'hémorragie de la délivrance après l'expulsion du placenta. **Usages non approuvés**: Surveillance fœtale (test de stress provoqué par des contractions, appelé parfois épreuve à l'ocytocine).

MÉCANISME D'ACTION

Stimulation du muscle lisse de l'utérus déclenchant des contractions utérines similaires à celles produites lors du travail spontané ■ Stimulation du muscle lisse de la glande mammaire favorisant la lactation ■ Effets vasopresseurs et antidiurétiques. ***Effets thérapeutiques:*** Déclenchement du travail (IV).

PHARMACOCINÉTIQUE

Absorption: 100 % (IV)

Distribution: Liquides extracellulaires. Une petite fraction pénètre dans la circulation fœtale.

Métabolisme et excrétion: Métabolisme rénal et hépatique.

Demi-vie: De 3 à 9 minutes.

Profil temps-action (contractions utérines)

	DÉBUT D'ACTION	PIC	DURÉE
IV	immédiat	inconnu	1 h
IM	3 - 5 min	inconnu	30 - 60 min

CONTRE-INDICATIONS, PRÉCAUTIONS ET MISES EN GARDE

Contre-indications: Hypersensibilité ■ Disproportion céphalopelvienne prononcée ■ Toxémie grave ■ Mauvaise présentation ou position du fœtus ou placenta prævia ■ Naissance prématurée ou rigidité du col ■ Prédisposition à la rupture de l'utérus ■ Césarienne antérieure ou autre intervention chirurgicale utérine ■ Travail avec hypertonie utérine ou emploi prolongé dans les cas d'inertie utérine ■ Facteurs prédisposant à l'embolie thromboplastique ou amniotique ■ Affections médicales ou obstétricales graves et tout état accompagné de souffrance fœtale ■ Accouchement anticipé par césarienne ■ Indisponibilité du médecin.

Précautions et mises en garde: 1re et 2e phases du travail.

RÉACTIONS INDÉSIRABLES ET EFFETS SECONDAIRES

Réactions indésirables chez la mère, survenues par suite de l'administration par voie IV seulement.

SNC: *mère* – COMA, CONVULSIONS; *fœtus* – HÉMORRAGIE INTRACRÂNIENNE.

Resp.: *fœtus* – ASPHYXIE, hypoxie.

CV: *mère* – hypotension; *fœtus* – arythmies.

HÉ: *mère* – hypochlorémie, hyponatrémie, intoxication hydrique.

Divers: *mère* – motilité accrue de l'utérus, contractions douloureuses, décollement placentaire, diminution du débit sanguin utérin, hypersensibilité.

INTERACTIONS

Médicament-médicament: Risque d'hypertension grave lorsque l'oxytocine est administrée après des **vasopresseurs** ■ L'administration concomitante d'une anesthésie au **cyclopropane** peut entraîner une hypotension excessive.

VOIES D'ADMINISTRATION ET POSOLOGIE

Déclenchement et stimulation du travail

- **IV (adultes)**: De 1 à 4 milliunités à la minute; augmenter par paliers de 1 ou 2 milliunités, jusqu'à ce que les contractions deviennent efficaces (habituellement, 5 ou 6 milliunités à la minute; maximum de 20 milliunités à la minute), puis diminuer la dose.

Hémorragie postpartum

- **IV (adultes)**: De 5 à 10 unités perfusées lentement.
- **IM (adultes)**: De 5 à 10 unités administrées après la délivrance (3e stade du travail).

Avortement incomplet ou inévitable

- **IV (adultes)**: 10 unités perfusées à une vitesse de 10 à 20 milliunités à la minute.

PRÉSENTATION (version générique disponible)

Solution pour injection: 10 unités/mL, en ampoules de 1 mLPr et de 5 mLPr.

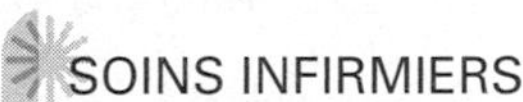

SOINS INFIRMIERS

ÉVALUATION DE LA SITUATION

- Il faut déterminer le degré de maturité du fœtus et sa présentation, ainsi que l'éventualité d'une disproportion céphalopelvienne avant d'administrer l'ocytocine dans le but de déclencher le travail.
- Déterminer à intervalles fréquents au cours de l'administration la nature, la fréquence et la durée des contractions, le tonus de l'utérus au repos et la fréquence cardiaque du fœtus. Si les contractions se produisent à moins de 2 minutes d'intervalle et si leur intensité est supérieure à entre 50 et 65 mm Hg, si elles durent de 60 à 90 secondes ou plus, ou si la fréquence cardiaque du fœtus se modifie considérablement, arrêter la perfusion, tourner la patiente sur le côté gauche afin de prévenir l'anoxie fœtale et appeler le médecin sans délai.
- Mesurer fréquemment la pression artérielle et le pouls de la mère et surveiller continuellement la fréquence cardiaque du fœtus pendant toute la durée de l'administration.
- L'ocytocine entraîne parfois une intoxication hydrique. Surveiller de près la patiente pour déceler les signes et les symptômes suivants d'intoxication: somnolence, apragmatisme, confusion, céphalées, anurie. Prévenir le médecin aussitôt que ces symptômes se manifestent.

Tests de laboratoire: Effectuer le bilan électrolytique de la patiente. La rétention hydrique peut entraîner l'hypochlorémie ou l'hyponatrémie.

DIAGNOSTICS INFIRMIERS POSSIBLES

- Connaissances insuffisantes sur le traitement médicamenteux (Enseignement au patient et à ses proches).

INTERVENTIONS INFIRMIÈRES

- Ne pas administrer l'ocytocine par plusieurs voies simultanément.

Perfusion continue:

- Renverser le sac afin de bien mélanger la solution. Garder la solution au réfrigérateur, mais non pas au congélateur.
- Utiliser une pompe à perfusion afin d'assurer l'administration de doses exactes. Le sac d'ocytocine doit être raccordé par une tubulure en Y à une tubulure IV par où s'écoule une solution de NaCl 0,9 %, qui pourrait être utilisée si des réactions indésirables surviennent.
- Garder à portée de la main du sulfate de magnésium pour assurer la relaxation du myomètre, si besoin est.

Déclenchement et stimulation du travail: Diluer 1 mL (10 unités) dans 1 L de solution pour perfusion compatible pour obtenir 10 milliunités/mL. Toute solution doit être utilisée dans les 24 heures suivant la préparation. Consulter les directives du fabricant avant de diluer la préparation.

Vitesse d'administration: *Déclenchement et stimulation du travail* – commencer la perfusion à une vitesse de 1 à 4 milliunités/min (de 0,1 à 0,4 mL/min ou de 2 à 8 gouttes/min). On peut l'augmenter de 1 à 2 milliunités/min (de 0,1 à 0,2 mL/min ou de 2 à 4 gouttes/min) au maximum, jusqu'à ce que les contractions deviennent régulières sans dépasser 20 milliunités/min (2 mL/min ou 40 gouttes/min).

Hémorragie postpartum: **IM**: Administrer de 5 à 10 unités.

IV: voir ci-dessus « Déclenchement et stimulation du travail ».

Compatibilité (tubulure en Y): héparine ▪ hydrocortisone sodique, succinate d' ▪ insuline ▪ mépéridine ▪ morphine ▪ potassium, chlorure de ▪ vitamines du complexe B avec C.

Compatibilité en addition au soluté: mélanges de dextrose et de solution de Ringer ou de lactate de Ringer ▪ mélanges de dextrose et de soluté salin ▪ solution de Ringer ou de lactate de Ringer pour injection ▪ D5%E ▪ D10%E ▪ NaCl 0,45 % ▪ NaCl 0,9 %.

ENSEIGNEMENT AU PATIENT ET À SES PROCHES

- Prévenir la patiente que les contractions qu'elle ressentira après le début de l'administration ressembleront aux crampes menstruelles.

VÉRIFICATION DE L'EFFICACITÉ THÉRAPEUTIQUE

L'efficacité du traitement peut être démontrée par: le déclenchement de contractions efficaces ▪ le raffermissement du tonus utérin.

O

ALERTE CLINIQUE

PACLITAXEL

Apo-Paclitaxel, Taxol

PACLITAXEL LIÉ À L'ALBUMINE

Abraxane

CLASSIFICATION:

Antinéoplasique (taxane)

Grossesse – catégorie D

INDICATIONS

Traitement de première intention du cancer avancé des ovaires, en association avec le cisplatine ■ Traitement de deuxième intention du cancer métastatique des ovaires n'ayant pas répondu au traitement classique ■ Traitement adjuvant du cancer du sein avec atteinte des ganglions, administré à la suite d'une chimiothérapie d'association classique ■ Traitement de deuxième intention du cancer métastatique du sein n'ayant pas répondu au traitement classique ■ Traitement de première intention du cancer du poumon non à petites cellules ■ Traitement de deuxième intention du sarcome de Kaposi au stade avancé chez les personnes atteintes du sida, après échec du traitement par une anthracycline liposomale ■ **Paclitaxel lié à l'albumine:** traitement du cancer du sein métastatique.

MÉCANISME D'ACTION

Inhibition de la fonction normale des microtubules, nécessaire à l'interphase et à la mitose. ***Effets thérapeutiques:*** Destruction des cellules à croissance rapide, particulièrement des cellules malignes.

PHARMACOCINÉTIQUE

Absorption: Biodisponibilité à 100 % (IV).

Distribution: Inconnue.

Métabolisme et excrétion: Métabolisme majoritairement hépatique. Excrétion rénale faible (moins de 4 % sous forme inchangée).

Demi-vie: *Paclitaxel:* de 5,3 à 17,4 heures; *paclitaxel lié à l'albumine:* 27 heures.

Profil temps-action (effet sur la numération leucocytaire)

	DÉBUT D'ACTION	PIC	DURÉE
IV	inconnu	11 jours	3 semaines

CONTRE-INDICATIONS, PRÉCAUTIONS ET MISES EN GARDE

Contre-indications: Hypersensibilité au paclitaxel ou à l'huile de ricin polyoxéthylique ■ Patients dont le nombre de neutrophiles est $\leq 1,5 \times 10^9$/L ■ Patients atteints du sida, souffrant du sarcome de Kaposi, et dont le nombre de neutrophiles est $\leq 1 \times 10^9$/L.

Précautions et mises en garde: Insuffisance hépatique grave ■ **GÉR.:** Risque accru de neuropathies et de problèmes cardiovasculaires ■ Intolérance connue à l'alcool ■ **OBST.:** Grossesse, allaitement *ou* femmes en âge de procréer ■ Infection active ■ Aplasie médullaire ■ Maladies chroniques débilitantes ■ **PÉD.:** L'innocuité du médicament n'a pas été établie.

RÉACTIONS INDÉSIRABLES ET EFFETS SECONDAIRES

SNC: malaise, faiblesse.

CV: anomalies de l'ÉCG, bradycardie, hypotension.

GI: diarrhée, nausées, vomissements, résultats anormaux aux tests de la fonction hépatique, stomatite.

Tég.: alopécie, rash maculopapulaire, prurit, réaction secondaire à la radiothérapie.

Hémat.: anémie, leucopénie, thrombopénie.

Loc.: arthralgie, myalgie.

SN: neuropathie périphérique.

Divers: réactions d'hypersensibilité, incluant l'ANAPHYLAXIE et le SYNDROME DE STEVENS-JOHNSON, NÉCROLYSE ÉPIDERMIQUE TOXIQUE.

INTERACTIONS

Médicament-médicament: LE **KÉTOCONAZOLE** PEUT INHIBER LE MÉTABOLISME DU PACLITAXEL ET ACCROÎTRE LE RISQUE D'UNE INTOXICATION GRAVE; L'ADMINISTRATION CONCOMITANTE DE CES DEUX AGENTS DEVRAIT S'ACCOMPAGNER DE PRUDENCE ■ La **cyclosporine**, la **doxorubicine**, la **félodipine**, le **diazépam** et le **midazolam** peuvent aussi diminuer le métabolisme et augmenter la toxicité du paclitaxel ■ Risque accru d'aplasie médullaire lors de l'administration d'autres **antinéoplasiques** ou d'une **radiothérapie** ■ Le **phénobarbital** et la **carbamazépine** peuvent diminuer les concentrations plasmatiques et l'efficacité du paclitaxel ■ La **radiothérapie** concomitante augmente le risque de pneumonie radique ■ L'aplasie médullaire s'aggrave lorsque le paclitaxel est administré après le **cisplatine** ■ Risque d'élévation des concentrations plasmatiques et de la toxicité de la **doxorubicine** lors d'une administration concomitante ■ Le paclitaxel peut réduire la réponse des anticorps aux **vaccins à virus vivants** et augmenter le risque de réactions indésirables.

VOIES D'ADMINISTRATION ET POSOLOGIE

Outre les suivants, de nombreux schémas thérapeutiques sont utilisés.

Paclitaxel (Taxol)

Cancer des ovaires

- **IV (adultes)**: *Patientes n'ayant jamais reçu de traitement* – 175 mg/m^2 en 3 heures, toutes les 3 semaines, puis le cisplatine à 75 mg/m^2; *patientes ayant déjà reçu un traitement* – 175 mg/m^2 en 3 heures, toutes les 3 semaines.

Cancer du sein

- **IV (adultes)**: *Traitement adjuvant du cancer du sein avec atteinte des ganglions* – 175 mg/m^2 en 3 heures, toutes les 3 semaines, pendant 4 cycles, administrés à la suite de la chimiothérapie d'association classique. *Progression des métastases ou rechute dans les 6 mois suivant le traitement adjuvant* – 175 mg/m^2 en 3 heures, toutes les 3 semaines.

Cancer du poumon non à petites cellules

- **IV (adultes)**: 175 mg/m^2 en 3 heures, toutes les 3 semaines, puis le cisplatine.

Paclitaxel lié à l'albumine (Abraxane)

- **IV (adultes)**: *Cancer du sein métastatique* – 260 mg/m^2, en 30 minutes, toutes les 3 semaines.

PRÉSENTATION

Concentré pour injection: fioles de 30 mg/5 mL^{Pr}, de 100 mg/16,7 mL^{Pr} et de 300 mg/50 mL^{Pr} ▪ **Poudre de nanoparticules liées à l'albumine pour injection (Abraxane)**: fioles de 100 mg^{Pr}.

SOINS INFIRMIERS

ÉVALUATION DE LA SITUATION

- Suivre à intervalles fréquents les signes vitaux, particulièrement durant la première heure de la perfusion.
- PACLITAXEL: SUIVRE DE PRÈS LES RÉACTIONS D'HYPERSENSIBILITÉ PENDANT LES 30 PREMIÈRES MINUTES DE L'ADMINISTRATION ET À INTERVALLES FRÉQUENTS PAR LA SUITE. CES RÉACTIONS SONT FRÉQUENTES (19 %) ET SURVIENNENT HABITUELLEMENT DURANT LES 10 PREMIÈRES MINUTES DE PERFUSION DU PACLITAXEL, APRÈS LA PREMIÈRE OU LA DEUXIÈME DOSE. ON RECOMMANDE D'ADMINISTRER À TOUS LES PATIENTS UN TRAITEMENT PRÉALABLE, QUI DEVRAIT INCLURE DE LA DEXAMÉTHASONE À 20 mg, PAR VOIE ORALE, 12 HEURES ET 6 HEURES AVANT L'ADMINISTRATION DU PACLITAXEL (10 mg CHEZ LES PATIENTS DONT L'INFECTION PAR LE VIH EST À UN STADE AVANCÉ), DE LA DIPHENHYDRAMINE À 50 mg, PAR VOIE IV, DE 30 À 60 MINUTES AVANT L'ADMINISTRATION DU PACLITAXEL ET DE LA CIMÉTIDINE À 300 mg OU DE LA RANITIDINE À 50 mg, PAR VOIE IV, DE 30 À 60 MINUTES AVANT L'ADMINISTRATION DU PACLITAXEL. LES MANIFESTATIONS LES PLUS COURANTES SONT LA DYSPNÉE, L'HYPOTENSION ET LES DOULEURS THORACIQUES. LE CAS ÉCHÉANT, ARRÊTER LA PERFUSION ET PRÉVENIR LE MÉDECIN. LE TRAITEMENT PEUT INCLURE L'ADMINISTRATION DE BRONCHODILATATEURS, D'ADRÉNALINE, D'ANTIHISTAMINIQUES ET DE CORTICOSTÉROÏDES. GARDER À PORTÉE DE LA MAIN CES AGENTS ET LE MATÉRIEL DE RÉANIMATION POUR PARER À UNE ÉVENTUELLE RÉACTION ANAPHYLACTIQUE. LES AUTRES MANIFESTATIONS D'UNE RÉACTION D'HYPERSENSIBILITÉ SONT LES BOUFFÉES VASOMOTRICES ET LE RASH.
- Aucune prémédication contre les réactions d'hypersensibilité n'est nécessaire lors de l'administration du paclitaxel lié à l'albumine.
- Suivre de près la fonction cardiovasculaire, particulièrement pendant la première heure de la perfusion. L'hypotension et la bradycardie surviennent couramment, mais elles ne dictent habituellement aucun traitement. On recommande de surveiller l'ÉCG tout au long du traitement seulement chez les patients présentant de graves anomalies de conduction sous-jacentes.
- Déceler l'apparition d'une aplasie médullaire. Suivre de près les saignements (saignement des gencives, formation d'ecchymoses, pétéchies, présence de sang occulte dans les selles, l'urine et les vomissements). Éviter les injections IM et la prise de la température par voie rectale si le nombre de plaquettes est bas. Appliquer une pression sur les points de ponction veineuse pendant 10 minutes. Évaluer les signes d'infection en présence d'une neutropénie. Une anémie peut survenir. Suivre de près les signes de fatigue accrue, de dyspnée et d'hypotension orthostatique. Au besoin, on peut administrer un facteur stimulant les colonies de granulocytes (G-CSF).
- Déceler l'apparition d'une neuropathie périphérique. En cas de symptômes graves, il faut réduire les doses ultérieures de 20 %.
- Effectuer le bilan des ingesta et des excreta, noter l'appétit du patient et son apport nutritionnel. Le paclitaxel entraîne des nausées et des vomissements chez 60 % des patients. Un antiémétique peut être administré en prophylaxie. La modification de l'alimentation en fonction des aliments que le patient peut tolérer permet de maintenir son équilibre hydroélectrolytique et son état nutritionnel.

- Noter la présence d'arthralgie et de myalgie, qui apparaissent habituellement dans les 2 ou 3 jours suivant le traitement et disparaissent dans les 5 jours. La douleur est habituellement soulagée par des analgésiques non opioïdes, mais elle peut être suffisamment intense pour justifier un traitement par des analgésiques opioïdes.

Tests de laboratoire:
- Suivre de près la numération globulaire et la formule leucocytaire avant le traitement et à intervalles réguliers pendant toute sa durée. Le nadir de la leucopénie se produit en l'espace de 11 jours et se rétablit dans les 4 à 10 jours suivants. Prévenir le médecin si le nombre de neutrophiles est $< 1,5 \times 10^9$/L (ou $< 1 \times 10^9$/L en présence du sarcome de Kaposi relié au sida) ou si le nombre de plaquettes est $< 100 \times 10^9$/L. Le traitement est habituellement interrompu jusqu'à ce que le nombre de neutrophiles soit $> 1,5 \times 10^9$/L (ou $> 1 \times 10^9$/L en présence du sarcome de Kaposi relié au sida) et celui de plaquettes $> 100 \times 10^9$/L.
- Noter les résultats des tests de la fonction hépatique (AST, ALT, LDH, bilirubine), avant le traitement et à intervalles réguliers pendant toute sa durée, pour déceler une toxicité hépatique.
- Le paclitaxel peut élever les concentrations sériques de triglycérides.

DIAGNOSTICS INFIRMIERS POSSIBLES

P

- Risque d'infection (Réactions indésirables).
- Risque d'accident (Réactions indésirables).
- Connaissances insuffisantes sur le traitement médicamenteux (Enseignement au patient et à ses proches).

INTERVENTIONS INFIRMIÈRES

- **ALERTE CLINIQUE:** DES DÉCÈS SONT SURVENUS LORS DE CERTAINES CHIMIOTHÉRAPIES. AVANT D'ADMINISTRER L'AGENT, CLARIFIER TOUS LES POINTS AMBIGUS. VÉRIFIER LA LIMITE DES DOSES UNITAIRES ET QUOTIDIENNES AINSI QUE LA DOSE À ADMINISTRER PENDANT LE TRAITEMENT. DEMANDER À UN AUTRE PROFESSIONNEL DE LA SANTÉ DE VÉRIFIER UNE FOIS DE PLUS L'ORDONNANCE D'ORIGINE, LE CALCUL DES DOSES ET LE RÉGLAGE DE LA POMPE À PERFUSION.
- NE PAS CONFONDRE TAXOL (PACLITAXEL) AVEC TAXOTÈRE (DOCÉTAXEL). NE PAS CONFONDRE LE PACLITAXEL AVEC PAXIL (PAROXÉTINE).
- Préparer la solution sous une hotte à flux laminaire. Porter un masque, un vêtement protecteur et des gants pendant la manipulation de ce médicament. Mettre au rebut le matériel dans des contenants réservés à cet usage (voir l'annexe H).

Paclitaxel lié à l'albumine (Abraxane)

Perfusion intermittente: Reconstituer la préparation en ajoutant 20 mL de NaCl 0,9 % au contenu de chaque fiole pendant au moins 1 minute pour obtenir une concentration de 5 mg/mL. Diriger le NaCl sur les parois pour éviter la formation de mousse. Laisser la fiole reposer pendant au moins 5 minutes pour assurer l'hydratation adéquate de la poudre. Agiter ou tourner délicatement la fiole pendant au moins 2 minutes pour permettre à la poudre de se dissoudre complètement. Éviter la formation de mousse. Si de la mousse ou des grumeaux se forment, laisser reposer pendant au moins 15 minutes jusqu'à ce qu'ils disparaissent. La solution doit être laiteuse et homogène, sans particules visibles. Si des particules ou des sédiments sont visibles, inverser doucement la fiole pour les remettre en suspension. Injecter la quantité nécessaire dans un sac de PVC vide. Ne pas utiliser de filtre pour l'administration. Ne pas utiliser de solution ayant changé de couleur ou présentant des particules. Les solutions reconstituées devraient être utilisées immédiatement, mais sont stables pendant 8 heures au réfrigérateur si on les protège de la lumière. Les solutions dans un sac de PVC sont stables pendant 8 heures à la température de la pièce. Jeter toute portion inutilisée. Consulter les directives du fabricant avant de reconstituer le produit.

Vitesse d'administration: Administrer pendant 30 minutes. Surveiller le point d'injection à la recherche d'une infiltration.

Paclitaxel

Perfusion continue: Diluer le paclitaxel avant de l'injecter. Diluer le contenu d'une fiole de 5 mL (30 mg) pour obtenir une concentration de 0,3 à 1,2 mg/mL avec les diluants suivants: NaCl 0,9%, D5%E, D5%/NaCl 0,9% ou D5%/solution de Ringer. La solution est normalement trouble; il faut vérifier avant de l'administrer qu'elle ne contient pas de particules et qu'elle n'a pas changé de couleur. Utiliser un filtre intégré dont les pores ne dépassent pas 0,22 µm. Les solutions sont stables pendant 27 heures à la lumière et à la température ambiante. Ne pas utiliser de contenants ou de tubulures en chlorure de polyvinyle (PVC). Consulter les directives de chaque fabricant avant de faire une dilution.

Vitesse d'administration: La dose administrée doit être perfusée en 3 heures.

Compatibilité (tubulure en Y): acyclovir ▪ amikacine ▪ aminophylline ▪ ampicilline/sulbactam ▪ bléomycine ▪ butorphanol ▪ calcium, chlorure de ▪ carboplatine ▪ céfépime ▪ céfotétane ▪ ceftazidime ▪ ceftriaxone ▪ cimétidine ▪ cisplatine ▪ cladribine ▪ cyclophosphamide ▪ cytarabine ▪ dacarbazine ▪ dexaméthasone ▪ diphenhydramine ▪ doxorubicine ▪ dropéridol ▪ étoposide ■ famotidine ■ floxuridine ■ fluconazole ■ fluorouracile ■ furosémide ■ ganciclovir ■ gentamicine ■ granisétron ■ halopéridol ■ héparine ■ hydrocortisone ■ hydromorphone ■ ifosfamide ■ lorazépam ■ magnésium, sulfate de ■ mannitol ■ mépéridine ■ mesna ■ méthotrexate ■ métoclopramide ■ morphine ■ nalbuphine ■ ondansétron ■ pentostatine ■ potassium, chlorure de ■ prochlorpérazine, édisylate de ■ propofol ■ ranitidine ■ sodium, bicarbonate de ■ thiotépa ■ vancomycine ■ vinblastine ■ vincristine ■ zidovudine.

Incompatibilité (tubulure en Y): amphotéricine B ■ amphotéricine B, cholestéryle d' ■ chlorpromazine ■ doxorubicine liposomale ■ méthylprednisolone sodique, succinate de ■ mitoxantrone.

ENSEIGNEMENT AU PATIENT ET À SES PROCHES

- Conseiller au patient de signaler rapidement à un professionnel de la santé les symptômes suivants: fièvre, frissons, toux, enrouement, maux de gorge, signes d'infection, douleurs lombaires ou aux flancs, mictions douloureuses ou difficiles, saignement des gencives, formation d'ecchymoses, pétéchies ou présence de sang dans les urines, les selles ou les vomissements, fatigue accrue, dyspnée ou hypotension orthostatique. L'inciter à éviter les foules et les personnes contagieuses. Lui recommander d'utiliser une brosse à dents à poils doux et un rasoir électrique. Mettre en garde le patient contre les chutes. Lui recommander de ne pas consommer de boissons alcoolisées ni de prendre de médicaments contenant de l'aspirine ou des anti-inflammatoires non stéroïdiens en raison du risque d'hémorragie gastrique.
- Recommander au patient de prévenir un professionnel de la santé en cas de douleurs abdominales, de jaunissement de la peau, de faiblesse, de paresthésie, de trouble de la démarche ou de douleurs musculaires ou articulaires.
- Recommander au patient d'examiner sa muqueuse buccale à la recherche d'érythème ou d'aphtes. En cas d'aphtes, lui conseiller de remplacer la brosse à dents par une brosse-éponge et de se rincer fréquemment la bouche avec de l'eau après avoir bu et mangé. La stomatite disparaît habituellement dans les 5 à 7 jours.
- Expliquer au patient qu'il risque de perdre ses cheveux. Les cheveux tombent habituellement entre le 14e et le 21e jour qui suivent l'administration, mais ils repoussent à la fin du traitement. Explorer avec lui les stratégies lui permettant de s'adapter à ces changements.
- Recommander à la patiente en âge de procréer d'adopter une méthode de contraception non hormonale. Recommander aux hommes de ne pas procréer pendant le traitement au paclitaxel.
- Expliquer au patient qu'il ne doit pas se faire vacciner sans recommandation expresse d'un professionnel de la santé.
- Insister sur l'importance des tests de laboratoire à intervalles réguliers permettant suivre de près les effets secondaires.

VÉRIFICATION DE L'EFFICACITÉ THÉRAPEUTIQUE

L'efficacité du traitement peut être démontrée par: la diminution de la taille de la tumeur et le ralentissement de la propagation des cellules malignes.

PALIFERMIN

Kepivance

CLASSIFICATION:

Agent cytoprotecteur (facteur de croissance des kératinocytes [ADNr])

Grossesse – catégorie C

INDICATIONS

Diminution de la fréquence et de la durée des mucosites buccales graves, induites par un traitement myéloablatif des hémopathies malignes chez les patients devant recevoir une greffe de cellules souches hématopoïétiques.

MÉCANISME D'ACTION

Stimulation de la prolifération des cellules épithéliales. ***Effets thérapeutiques:*** Diminution de l'incidence et de la durée des mucosites.

PHARMACOCINÉTIQUE

Absorption: Biodisponibilité à 100 % (IV).
Distribution: Compartiments extravasculaires.
Métabolisme et excrétion: Inconnus.
Demi-vie: 4,5 heures.

Profil temps-action (concentrations)

	DÉBUT D'ACTION	PIC	DURÉE
IV	inconnu	fin de la perfusion	inconnue

CONTRE-INDICATIONS, PRÉCAUTIONS ET MISES EN GARDE

Contre-indications: Hypersensibilité au palifermin ou à d'autres protéines dérivées de *E. coli*.

Précautions et mises en garde: PÉD., ALLAITEMENT: L'innocuité de l'agent n'a pas été établie ■ **OBST.:** N'utiliser ce médicament que si ses bienfaits chez la mère dépassent les risques auxquels est exposé le fœtus ■ Cancer non hématologique (l'innocuité de l'agent n'a pas été établie).

RÉACTIONS INDÉSIRABLES ET EFFETS SECONDAIRES

Tég.: toxicité cutanée, rash.

GI: toxicité buccale.

Métab.: élévation des taux d'amylase et de lipase.

Loc.: arthralgie.

SN: dysesthésie.

Divers: douleurs.

INTERACTIONS

Médicament-médicament: L'agent se lie à l'**héparine** et l'inactive (rincer les tubulures entre les utilisations) ■ L'administration dans les 24 heures qui précèdent ou qui suivent un **traitement myéloablatif (chimiothérapie/radiothérapie)** augmente la gravité et la durée de la mucosite.

VOIES D'ADMINISTRATION ET POSOLOGIE

- **IV (adultes):** 60 µg/kg/jour pendant 3 jours avant et 3 jours après un traitement myéloablatif. Administrer les doses pendant 3 jours consécutifs avant une chimiothérapie myéloablative (la troisième dose de 24 à 48 heures avant la chimiothérapie) et pendant 3 jours consécutifs après une chimiothérapie myéloablative (la quatrième dose, le même jour que la perfusion de cellules souches hématopoïétiques, et au moins 4 jours après l'administration de la dose la plus récente de palifermin) pour un total de 6 doses.

P

PRÉSENTATION

Poudre pour injection: 6,25 mg par fiole[Pr].

SOINS INFIRMIERS

ÉVALUATION DE LA SITUATION

- Évaluer la gravité de la mucosite buccale avant le traitement et à intervalles réguliers pendant toute sa durée.

Tests de laboratoire: L'agent peut élever les concentrations sériques de lipase et d'amylase; cette élévation est habituellement réversible.

- L'agent peut induire une protéinurie.

DIAGNOSTICS INFIRMIERS POSSIBLES

- Douleur aiguë (Indications).

INTERVENTIONS INFIRMIÈRES

- Ne pas administrer le palifermin durant les 24 heures qui précèdent ou qui suivent une chimiothérapie myéloablative ni pendant la perfusion de tels agents.

IV directe: Reconstituer la poudre de palifermin en injectant lentement 1,2 mL d'eau stérile pour injection par une méthode aseptique, pour obtenir une concentration de 5 mg/mL. Tourner lentement la fiole, sans la secouer ni l'agiter vigoureusement. La solution doit être transparente et incolore; ne pas administrer de solution qui a changé de couleur ou qui contient des particules. La dissolution prend habituellement moins de 5 minutes. Administrer immédiatement après la reconstitution ou réfrigérer et administrer dans les 24 heures. Consulter les directives du fabricant avant de reconstituer la préparation. Ne pas congeler. Laisser la solution se réchauffer à la température ambiante pendant 1 heure au plus. Garder à l'abri de la lumière. Jeter le palifermin après sa date de péremption ou s'il est resté à la température ambiante pendant plus de 1 heure.

Vitesse d'administration: Administrer sous forme de bolus. Ne pas utiliser de filtre.

Incompatibilité (tubulure en Y): héparine. Si l'on utilise une solution d'héparine pour maintenir la perméabilité d'une tubulure IV, la rincer avec du NaCl 0,9% avant et après l'administration de palifermin.

ENSEIGNEMENT AU PATIENT ET À SES PROCHES

- Informer le patient des données probantes sur la croissance des tumeurs issues des cultures cellulaires et des modèles animaux, causée par de fortes doses de palifermin.
- Recommander au patient de prévenir un professionnel de la santé en cas de rash, d'érythème, de prurit, de dysesthésie buccale et péribuccale, de modification de la coloration de la langue, d'épaississement de la langue ou d'altération du goût.

VÉRIFICATION DE L'EFFICACITÉ THÉRAPEUTIQUE

L'efficacité du traitement peut être démontrée par: la diminution de la fréquence et de la durée de la mucosite buccale chez les patients recevant un traitement myéloablatif nécessitant un soutien autologue par des cellules souches hématopoïétiques.

PAMIDRONATE

Aredia, PMS-Pamidronate, Ratio-Pamidronate

CLASSIFICATION:

Régulateur du métabolisme osseux (bisphosphonate), modificateur des électrolytes (hypocalcémique)

Grossesse – catégorie D

INDICATIONS

Traitement de l'hypercalcémie d'origine tumorale après une réhydratation appropriée ■ Traitement de l'ostéolyse associée au myélome multiple ou aux métastases osseuses lytiques ■ Traitement de la maladie de Paget symptomatique.

MÉCANISME D'ACTION

Inhibition de la résorption osseuse. ***Effets thérapeutiques:*** Diminution des taux sériques de calcium ■ Réduction de la destruction osseuse en présence d'un myélome multiple ou de métastases osseuses ■ Prévention des complications intervenant au niveau du squelette en présence de la maladie de Paget.

PHARMACOCINÉTIQUE

Absorption: Biodisponibilité à 100 % (IV).

Distribution: Répartition rapide dans les os. L'agent atteint des concentrations élevées dans les os, le foie, la rate, les dents et le cartilage trachéal. Environ 50 % de chaque dose est absorbé par les os, puis est lentement libéré.

Métabolisme et excrétion: Excrétion rénale (50 % sous forme inchangée).

Demi-vie: La demi-vie d'élimination à partir du plasma est biphasique, la première phase dure 1,6 heure, et la deuxième, 27,2 heures. La demi-vie d'élimination à partir des os est de 300 jours.

Profil temps-action (effet sur les taux sériques de calcium)

	DÉBUT D'ACTION	PIC	DURÉE
IV	24 h	7 jours	inconnue

CONTRE-INDICATIONS, PRÉCAUTIONS ET MISES EN GARDE

Contre-indications: Hypersensibilité au pamidronate, aux autres biphosphonates ou au mannitol.

Précautions et mises en garde: Maladie cardiovasculaire sous-jacente, particulièrement l'insuffisance cardiaque (amorcer avec prudence l'hydratation par un soluté) ■ Insuffisance rénale (on recommande de réduire la dose) ■ **OBST., ALLAITEMENT, PÉD.:** L'innocuité du médicament n'a pas été établie.

RÉACTIONS INDÉSIRABLES ET EFFETS SECONDAIRES

SNC: fatigue.

ORLO: conjonctivite, vision brouillée, douleur et inflammation oculaire, rhinite.

Resp.: râles.

CV: arythmies, hypertension, syncope, tachycardie.

GI: nausées, douleurs abdominales, anorexie, constipation, vomissements.

HÉ: hypocalcémie, hypokaliémie, hypomagnésémie, hypophosphatémie, surcharge liquidienne.

Hémat.: leucopénie, anémie.

Locaux: phlébite au point d'injection.

Métab.: hypothyroïdie.

Loc.: raideurs musculaires, douleurs osseuses.

Divers: fièvre, douleurs généralisées.

INTERACTIONS

Médicament-médicament: L'hypokaliémie et l'hypomagnésémie peuvent accroître le risque de toxicité **digitalique** ■ Le **calcium** et la **vitamine D** contrecarrent les effets bénéfiques du pamidronate.

VOIES D'ADMINISTRATION ET POSOLOGIE

Hypercalcémie d'origine tumorale

- **IV (adultes):** *Hypercalcémie modérée* – de 30 à 90 mg; on peut répéter l'administration de cette dose 7 jours plus tard.

Ostéolyse due au myélome multiple et aux métastases osseuses

- **IV (adultes):** 90 mg, toutes les 3 ou 4 semaines.

Maladie de Paget

- **IV (adultes):** De 180 à 210 mg par traitement; la dose peut être administrée à raison de 30 mg par semaine, pendant 6 semaines (180 mg au total), ou une dose initiale de 30 mg, suivie de 60 mg, toutes les 2 semaines, pour 3 doses (210 mg au total). Les effets secondaires de type pseudogrippaux ne surviennent qu'après administration de la première dose, c'est pourquoi il est nécessaire d'administrer une dose initiale de 30 mg.

PRÉSENTATION

Solution pour injection: 30 mg/fiole^{Pr}, 60 mg/fiole^{Pr}, 90 mg/fiole^{Pr}.

P

SOINS INFIRMIERS

ÉVALUATION DE LA SITUATION

- Noter les ingesta et les excreta et mesurer la pression artérielle à intervalles fréquents pendant toute la durée du traitement. Rester à l'affût des signes de surcharge liquidienne (œdème, râles et crépitations).
- Suivre de près les symptômes d'hypercalcémie (nausées, vomissements, anorexie, faiblesse, constipation, soif et arythmies).
- Rester à l'affût des signes d'hypocalcémie (paresthésie, contractions musculaires, laryngospasme et signe de Chvostek ou de Trousseau). Protéger les patients qui manifestent des symptômes en remontant et en rembourrant les ridelles du lit; garder le lit en position basse.
- Déceler les signes de phlébite au point d'injection IV (douleur, rougeur, œdème). Le cas échéant, on devrait traiter les symptômes.
- Évaluer la douleur osseuse. Il peut s'avérer nécessaire d'administrer un traitement par des analgésiques opioïdes ou non opioïdes.

Tests de laboratoire: Surveiller étroitement les concentrations d'électrolytes (incluant le calcium, le phosphate, le potassium et le magnésium), l'hémoglobine et les taux de créatinine. On devrait noter la numération globulaire et plaquettaire au cours des 2 premières semaines de traitement.

P

DIAGNOSTICS INFIRMIERS POSSIBLES

- Douleur aiguë (Indications, Effets secondaires).
- Risque d'accident (Indications).
- Connaissances insuffisantes sur le traitement médicamenteux (Enseignement au patient et à ses proches).

INTERVENTIONS INFIRMIÈRES

- On devrait amorcer une hydratation vigoureuse par soluté afin de maintenir un débit urinaire de 2 000 mL par 24 heures tout au long du traitement. Cette hydratation devrait être démarrée avec prudence chez les patients souffrant de maladie cardiovasculaire sous-jacente, particulièrement d'insuffisance cardiaque.
- En cas d'hypercalcémie grave, le traitement devrait être amorcé à une dose de 90 mg.

IV: Reconstituer la solution en ajoutant 10 mL d'eau stérile pour injection à chaque fiole, afin d'obtenir une concentration de 30 mg/10 mL, de 60 mg/10 mL ou de 90 mg/10 mL. Laisser le médicament se dissoudre avant de le retirer de la fiole. La solution est stable pendant 24 heures au réfrigérateur. Consulter les directives du fabricant avant de reconstituer la préparation.

Hypercalcémie: Diluer de nouveau dans une solution de NaCl 0,9 % ou de D5%E, selon la dose à administrer: 30 mg dans 125 mL, 60 mg dans 250 mL ou 90 mg dans 500 mL. La solution est stable pendant 24 heures à la température ambiante.

Vitesse d'administration: Administrer la perfusion en 2 à 4 heures selon la dose, sans dépasser 22,5 mg/h.

Myélome multiple: Diluer 90 mg dans 500 mL de solution de NaCl 0,9 % ou de D5%E.

Vitesse d'administration: Administrer la solution en 4 heures.

Métastases osseuses: Diluer 90 mg dans 250 mL de NaCl 0,9 % ou de D5%E.

Vitesse d'administration: Administrer la solution en 2 heures.

Maladie de Paget: Diluer chaque dose de 30 mg et de 60 mg dans 250 et 500 mL, respectivement, de solution de NaCl 0,9 % ou de D5%E.

Vitesse d'administration: Administrer la solution à un débit de 15 mg/h.

Incompatibilité en addition au soluté: Solutions renfermant du calcium, comme la solution de Ringer.

ENSEIGNEMENT AU PATIENT ET À SES PROCHES

- Recommander au patient de signaler rapidement à un professionnel de la santé les signes suivants de récurrence de l'hypercalcémie: douleurs osseuses, anorexie, nausées, vomissements, soif, léthargie.
- Recommander au patient de signaler à l'infirmière toute douleur au point de perfusion.
- Recommander au patient d'informer un professionnel de la santé si la douleur osseuse est intense ou persistante.
- Recommander au patient d'éviter toute chirurgie dentaire durant le traitement puisque le rétablissement pourrait être prolongé.
- Insister sur la nécessité des examens de suivi pendant le traitement, afin d'en évaluer les résultats, et même après l'arrêt du traitement, afin de pouvoir déceler une rechute.

VÉRIFICATION DE L'EFFICACITÉ THÉRAPEUTIQUE

L'efficacité du traitement peut être démontrée par: la diminution des taux sériques de calcium ■ la réduction de la douleur associée à l'ostéolyse.

PANCRÉLIPASE

Cotazym, Cotazym-65 B, Cotazym E.C.S., Pancrease, Pancrease MT, Ultrase, Ultrase MT, Viokase

CLASSIFICATION:

Enzymes pancréatiques

Grossesse – catégorie C

INDICATIONS

Traitement de l'insuffisance pancréatique observée dans les cas suivants: pancréatite chronique ▪ pancréatectomie ▪ fibrose kystique ▪ dérivation au niveau du tractus gastro-intestinal ▪ stéatorrhée ▪ obstruction du canal pancréatique ou biliaire par une tumeur ▪ autres syndromes de malabsorption.

MÉCANISME D'ACTION

Effet lipolytique, amylolytique et protéolytique. ***Effets thérapeutiques:*** Amélioration de la digestion des graisses, des glucides et des protéines dans le tractus gastro-intestinal.

PHARMACOCINÉTIQUE

Absorption: Inconnue.

Distribution: Inconnue.

Métabolisme et excrétion: Inconnus.

Demi-vie: Inconnue.

Profil temps-action (effets digestifs)

	DÉBUT D'ACTION	PIC	DURÉE
PO	rapide	inconnu	inconnue

CONTRE-INDICATIONS, PRÉCAUTIONS ET MISES EN GARDE

Contre-indications: Hypersensibilité aux protéines de porc ou aux additifs ▪ Pancréatite aiguë ou poussées aiguës d'une maladie pancréatique chronique.

Précautions et mises en garde: OBST.: Grossesse ou allaitement (l'innocuité du médicament n'a pas été établie).

RÉACTIONS INDÉSIRABLES ET EFFETS SECONDAIRES

ORLO: congestion nasale.

Resp.: dyspnée, essoufflement, respiration sifflante.

GI: douleurs abdominales (doses élevées seulement), diarrhée, nausées, crampes gastriques, irritation buccale, occlusion ou sténose intestinale, colopathie fibreuse.

GU: hématurie, hyperuricosurie.

Tég.: rash, urticaire.

Métab.: hyperuricémie.

Divers: réactions allergiques.

INTERACTIONS

Médicament-médicament: Les **antiacides** (comme le **carbonate de calcium** ou l'**hydroxyde de magnésium**), administrés simultanément, peuvent diminuer l'efficacité de la pancrélipase ▪ La pancrélipase peut diminuer l'absorption des **préparations à base de fer**, administrées simultanément.

Médicament-aliments: Les **aliments alcalins** détruisent l'enrobage des produits entérosolubles.

VOIES D'ADMINISTRATION ET POSOLOGIE

- **PO (adultes et enfants):** De 1 à 3 capsules ordinaires ou 1 ou 2 capsules contenant des microsphères entérosolubles ou 0,7 g de poudre, immédiatement avant ou pendant les repas et 1 capsule à chaque collation, selon les recommandations du médecin; on peut augmenter la dose selon les besoins. Une marge posologique est proposée, mais la réponse aux enzymes varie énormément d'un individu à l'autre.

PRÉSENTATION (version générique disponible)

Comprimés, capsules, capsules contenant des microsphères entérosolubles ▪ **Poudre**, en plusieurs teneurs différentes.

SOINS INFIRMIERS

ÉVALUATION DE LA SITUATION

- Évaluer l'état nutritionnel du patient (taille, poids, épaisseur des plis cutanés, circonférence des muscles du bras et résultats des tests de laboratoire), avant le traitement et à intervalles réguliers pendant toute sa durée.
- Examiner les selles pour déceler la stéatorrhée (augmentation anormale des graisses fécales). Les selles seront nauséabondes et mousseuses.
- Déterminer si le patient est allergique aux produits du porc; l'hypersensibilité à la pancrélipase est également possible.

Tests de laboratoire: La pancrélipase peut entraîner une élévation des concentrations sériques et urinaires d'acide urique.

DIAGNOSTICS INFIRMIERS POSSIBLES

- Alimentation déficiente (Indications).
- Connaissances insuffisantes sur le traitement médicamenteux (Enseignement au patient et à ses proches).

P

INTERVENTIONS INFIRMIÈRES

- Administrer la pancrélipase immédiatement avant ou pendant les repas et les collations.
- On peut ouvrir les capsules et en saupoudrer le contenu sur les aliments. Il ne faut pas mâcher les capsules à enrobage entérosoluble remplies de granules (en saupoudrer le contenu sur des aliments mous pouvant être avalés sans mastication, comme la compote de pommes ou les gelées).
- Les acides détruisent la pancrélipase. On peut administrer avec les préparations sans enrobage entérosoluble du bicarbonate de sodium ou des antiacides contenant de l'aluminium pour neutraliser le pH gastrique. Les granules à enrobage entérosoluble résistent au pH acide de l'estomac. Il ne faut pas les mâcher ni les mélanger à des aliments alcalins avant de les ingérer, sinon leur enrobage serait détruit.

ENSEIGNEMENT AU PATIENT ET À SES PROCHES

- Inciter le patient à observer rigoureusement les recommandations diététiques du professionnel de la santé (il s'agit généralement d'un régime hypercalorique, hyperprotéique, pauvre en matières grasses). La posologie devrait être adaptée selon la teneur en matières grasses des aliments. Habituellement, 300 mg de pancrélipase suffisent pour la digestion de 17 g de matières grasses d'origine alimentaire. Expliquer au patient que s'il ne peut prendre le médicament au moment habituel, il doit sauter cette dose.
- Recommander au patient de ne pas mâcher les comprimés; il doit les avaler rapidement avec beaucoup de liquide pour prévenir l'irritation de la bouche et de la gorge. Lui conseiller de s'asseoir lorsqu'il prend son médicament afin d'en faciliter la déglutition. Lui expliquer que s'il mange immédiatement après avoir pris le médicament, il peut mieux s'assurer qu'il l'a réellement dégluti et qu'il n'est pas resté collé à la bouche ou à l'œsophage pendant une période prolongée. Conseiller au patient d'éviter de renifler la poudre contenue dans les capsules en raison du risque d'une réaction de sensibilité au niveau du nez et de la gorge (congestion nasale ou détresse respiratoire).
- Conseiller au patient de prévenir un professionnel de la santé en cas de douleurs articulaires, d'œdème des jambes, de douleurs gastriques ou de rash.

VÉRIFICATION DE L'EFFICACITÉ THÉRAPEUTIQUE

L'efficacité du traitement peut être démontrée par: l'amélioration de l'état nutritionnel des patients souffrant d'insuffisance pancréatique ■ la normalisation des matières fécales chez les patients souffrant de stéatorrhée. ✳

ALERTE CLINIQUE

PANCURONIUM

Pancuronium

CLASSIFICATION:

Bloqueur neuromusculaire du type non dépolarisant

Grossesse – catégorie C

INDICATIONS

Paralysie des muscles squelettiques et facilitation de l'intubation après induction de l'anesthésie lors d'une intervention chirurgicale ■ Augmentation de la compliance pulmonaire lors de la ventilation artificielle.

MÉCANISME D'ACTION

Inhibition de la transmission neuromusculaire par blocage de l'effet de l'acétylcholine à la jonction neuromusculaire. Absence d'effets analgésiques ou anxiolytiques. ***Effets thérapeutiques:*** Paralysie des muscles squelettiques.

PHARMACOCINÉTIQUE

Absorption: Biodisponibilité à 100 % (IV).

Distribution: Distribution rapide dans le liquide extracellulaire. De petites quantités traversent la barrière placentaire.

Métabolisme et excrétion: Excrétion majoritairement rénale (sous forme inchangée); de petites quantités sont éliminées dans la bile.

Demi-vie: 2 heures.

Profil temps-action (blocage neuromusculaire)

	DÉBUT D'ACTION	PIC	DURÉE
IV	30 – 45 s	3 – 4,5 min	35 – 45 min

CONTRE-INDICATIONS, PRÉCAUTIONS ET MISES EN GARDE

Contre-indications: Hypersensibilité au pancuronium et aux bromures.

Précautions et mises en garde: Maladie cardiovasculaire sous-jacente (risque accru d'arythmies) ■ Déshydratation ou déséquilibre électrolytique (corriger le problème au préalable) ■ Cas où la libération d'histamine peut poser problème ■ Fractures ou spasmes musculaires ■ Personnes âgées ou insuffisants rénaux (élimination réduite) ■ Hyperthermie (accroissement de la durée ou de l'intensité de la paralysie) ■ Insuffisance hépatique importante (modification de la réponse) ■ Choc ■ Brûlures sur une grande surface corporelle (résistance accrue aux effets du pancuronium) ■ Faibles concentrations plasmatiques de pseudocholinestérase (parfois dues à l'anémie, à la déshydratation, aux insecticides ou aux inhibiteurs de la cholinestérase, à une maladie hépatique grave, à la grossesse ou à une prédisposition héréditaire) ■ **OBST., PÉD.**: L'innocuité du médicament n'a pas été établie; la plupart des agents ont été utilisés sans danger lors d'accouchements par césarienne; certains agents ont été utilisés sans danger chez des enfants.

EXTRÊME PRUDENCE: Maladies neuromusculaires, comme la myasthénie grave (on peut administrer une petite dose d'essai pour évaluer la réponse au médicament).

RÉACTIONS INDÉSIRABLES ET EFFETS SECONDAIRES

Resp.: bronchospasme.

CV: hypertension, tachycardie.

GI: salivation excessive.

Tég.: rash.

Divers: réactions allergiques, incluant l'ANAPHYLAXIE.

INTERACTIONS

Médicament-médicament: L'intensité et la durée de la paralysie peuvent être prolongées en cas de prétraitement par la **succinylcholine**, un **anesthésique général** (par inhalation), des **aminosides**, de la **vancomycine**, des **tétracyclines**, de la **clindamycine**, de la **lidocaïne** et d'autres **anesthésiques locaux**, du **lithium**, de la **quinidine**, du **procaïnamide**, des **bêtabloquants**, des **diurétiques hypokaliémiants et hypomagnésémiants** ■ Les **anesthésiques par inhalation**, incluant l'**enflurane**, l'**isoflurane**, l'**halothane**, le **desflurane** et le **sévoflurane**, peuvent intensifier les effets du pancuronium ■ Chez les patients recevant un traitement de longue durée par la **carbamazépine**, des **corticostéroïdes** ou la **phénytoïne**, il peut s'avérer nécessaire d'administrer l'agent à une vitesse accrue; par ailleurs, sa durée d'action peut être réduite.

VOIES D'ADMINISTRATION ET POSOLOGIE

- **IV (adultes et enfants > 1 mois)**: Initialement, de 40 à 100 µg/kg; administrer des doses supplémentaires de 10 µg/kg toutes les 25 à 60 minutes pour maintenir la paralysie. L'administration du pancuronium doit être supervisée par des cliniciens d'expérience.

PRÉSENTATION (version générique disponible)

Solution pour injection: 1 mg/mL, en fioles de 5 mL[Pr] et de 10 mL[Pr]; 2 mg/mL, en ampoules de 2 mL[Pr] et de 5 mL[Pr].

SOINS INFIRMIERS

ÉVALUATION DE LA SITUATION

- Suivre continuellement la fonction respiratoire pendant toute la durée du traitement par des bloqueurs neuromusculaires. Ces médicaments ne devraient être utilisés que pour faciliter l'intubation ou, encore, chez les patients déjà intubés.
- Évaluer la réponse neuromusculaire pendant l'intervention chirurgicale par la stimulation des nerfs périphériques. La paralysie des muscles est initialement sélective et elle se produit habituellement dans l'ordre suivant: muscles releveurs des paupières, muscles masticateurs, muscles des membres, muscles abdominaux, muscles de la glotte, muscles intercostaux et diaphragme. Le rétablissement de la fonction musculaire se produit habituellement dans l'ordre inverse.
- Mesurer la fréquence cardiaque et la pression artérielle, et examiner l'ÉCG à intervalles réguliers pendant toute la durée du traitement.
- Pendant la période de récupération, suivre de près les symptômes de faiblesse musculaire et de détresse respiratoire.
- Surveiller fréquemment le point de perfusion. Si des signes d'irritation tissulaire ou d'extravasation apparaissent, cesser l'administration et reprendre la perfusion dans une autre veine.

TOXICITÉ ET SURDOSAGE:

- En cas de surdosage, stimuler les nerfs périphériques pour déterminer le degré de blocage neuromusculaire. Maintenir la perméabilité des voies aériennes et la ventilation jusqu'au rétablissement de la respiration normale.
- On peut administrer des agents anticholinestérasiques (néostigmine, pyridostigmine) pour contrecarrer les effets des bloqueurs neuromusculaires, dès que le patient a commencé à se rétablir spontanément. L'atropine est habituellement administrée avant les agents anticholinestérasiques ou en même temps qu'eux pour contrecarrer les effets muscariniques.
- Il peut s'avérer nécessaire d'administrer un apport liquidien adéquat (cristalloïdes) et des vasopresseurs pour traiter l'hypotension grave ou le choc.

P

DIAGNOSTICS INFIRMIERS POSSIBLES

- Mode de respiration inefficace (Indications).
- Communication verbale altérée (Effets secondaires).
- Peur (Effets secondaires).

INTERVENTIONS INFIRMIÈRES

Alerte clinique: Les bloqueurs neuromusculaires peuvent avoir des effets dangereux. Des erreurs de médication, parfois mortelles, impliquant le pancuronium ont été signalées lors d'un soutien inadéquat de la ventilation. Ce médicament doit être bien identifié lorsqu'on le conserve au même endroit que d'autres médicaments dans une unité de soins.

- La dose doit être adaptée d'après la réponse du patient.
- Les bloqueurs neuromusculaires *ne* modifient *pas* l'état de conscience ni le seuil de la douleur. Il faut *toujours* assurer une anesthésie ou une analgésie adéquates lorsque ces agents sont utilisés en tant qu'adjuvants lors d'une intervention chirurgicale ou d'une autre intervention douloureuse. On doit administrer simultanément des benzodiazépines ou des analgésiques lors d'un traitement prolongé par des bloqueurs neuromusculaires pendant la ventilation artificielle, car le patient est éveillé et capable d'éprouver toutes les sensations.
- Si les yeux du patient restent ouverts tout au long de l'administration prolongée, on devrait protéger la cornée par des larmes artificielles.
- Garder le pancuronium au réfrigérateur. Afin de prévenir l'absorption du médicament par les matières plastiques, il ne devrait pas être conservé dans des seringues de plastique. On peut toutefois l'administrer par de telles seringues.
- La plupart des bloqueurs neuromusculaires sont incompatibles avec les barbituriques et le bicarbonate de sodium. Ne pas faire de mélanges.

IV directe: Administrer des doses supplémentaires toutes les 20 à 60 minutes, selon les besoins. La dose doit être adaptée d'après la réponse du patient.

Perfusion intermittente: On peut diluer le pancuronium dans une solution de NaCl 0,9%, de D5%E, de D5%/NaCl 0,9 % ou dans une solution de lactate de Ringer. La solution est stable pendant 48 heures. Consulter les directives du fabricant avant de diluer la préparation.

Vitesse d'administration: Adapter la vitesse d'administration d'après la réaction du patient.

Association compatible dans la même seringue: héparine.

Compatibilité (tubulure en Y): adrénaline ▪ aminophylline ▪ céfazoline ▪ céfuroxime ▪ cimétidine ▪ dobutamine ▪ dopamine ▪ esmolol ▪ étomidate ▪ fentanyl ▪ fluconazole ▪ gentamicine ▪ héparine ▪ hydrocortisone sodique, succinate d' ▪ isoprotérénol ▪ lorazépam ▪ midazolam ▪ morphine ▪ nitroglycérine ▪ nitroprusside ▪ ranitidine ▪ triméthoprime/sulfaméthoxazole ▪ vancomycine.

Incompatibilité (tubulure en Y): diazépam ▪ thiopental.

ENSEIGNEMENT AU PATIENT ET À SES PROCHES

- Étant donné que les bloqueurs neuromusculaires, administrés seuls, ne modifient pas l'état de conscience, expliquer toutes les interventions au patient qui reçoit un traitement par un tel agent sans anesthésie générale.
- Expliquer au patient que ses capacités de communication se rétabliront lorsque les effets du médicament s'épuiseront.

VÉRIFICATION DE L'EFFICACITÉ THÉRAPEUTIQUE

L'efficacité du traitement peut être démontrée par: la suppression adéquate des soubresauts musculaires, testée par la stimulation des nerfs périphériques et confirmée par une paralysie musculaire ▪ une compliance pulmonaire accrue lors de la ventilation artificielle.

PANTOPRAZOLE

Panto IV, Pantoloc

CLASSIFICATION:

Antiulcéreux (inhibiteur de la pompe à protons)

Grossesse – catégorie B

INDICATIONS

PO: Traitement des affections où une diminution de la sécrétion d'acide gastrique est nécessaire, telles que: ulcère duodénal et gastrique ▪ œsophagite par érosion associée au reflux gastro-œsophagien ▪ Réduction du risque d'ulcère gastrique secondaire à la prise d'AINS chez les patients qui ont des antécédents d'ulcère gastrique et qui doivent continuer à prendre un AINS ▪ *En association avec la clarithromycine et l'amoxicilline ou le métronidazole:* Éradication de *H. pylori* chez les patients ayant des antécédents d'ulcère duodénal ▪ Ulcère duodénal associé à *H. pylori* ▪ **IV**: Traitement de l'œsophagite associée au reflux gastro-œsophagien, lorsqu'il est nécessaire de diminuer rapidement l'acidité gastrique chez les patients hospitalisés qui ne peuvent prendre le médicament par voie orale ▪ Hypersécrétion pathologique associée au syndrome de Zollinger-Ellison, chez les patients hospitalisés qui ne peuvent pas prendre de médicaments par voie orale.

MÉCANISME D'ACTION

Inhibition spécifique de l'enzyme gastrique H^+, K^+-ATPase (pompe à protons), responsable des sécrétions acides des cellules pariétales de l'estomac, ce qui prévient l'entrée des ions hydrogène dans la lumière du tube gastrique. ***Effets thérapeutiques:*** Diminution de l'accumulation d'acide dans la lumière gastrique et réduction du reflux gastro-œsophagien ■ Cicatrisation des ulcères duodénaux et de ceux provoqués par l'œsophagite ■ Diminution des sécrétions acides caractérisant les états d'hypersécrétion.

PHARMACOCINÉTIQUE

Absorption: Les comprimés sont à délitement entérique; ils ne sont absorbés qu'après leur passage par l'estomac.

Distribution: Inconnue.

Liaison aux protéines: 98 %.

Métabolisme et excrétion: Métabolisme majoritairement hépatique, sous l'action du cytochrome P450. Excrétion urinaire (71 % sous forme de métabolites) et fécale (18 % sous forme de métabolites).

Demi-vie: 1 heure.

Profil temps-action (suppression des sécrétions acides)

	DÉBUT D'ACTION†	PIC	DURÉE‡
PO	2,5 h	inconnu	1 semaine

† Début d'action = 51 % d'inhibition enzymatique.

‡ Durée = retour à la normale après arrêt du traitement.

CONTRE-INDICATIONS, PRÉCAUTIONS ET MISES EN GARDE

Contre-indications: Hypersensibilité.

Précautions et mises en garde: Insuffisance hépatique grave ■ **OBST., ALLAITEMENT, PÉD.:** L'innocuité du médicament n'a pas été établie.

RÉACTIONS INDÉSIRABLES ET EFFETS SECONDAIRES

SNC: céphalées.

GI: douleurs abdominales, diarrhée, éructations, flatulence.

End.: hyperglycémie.

INTERACTIONS

Médicament-médicament: Risque de réduction de l'absorption des médicaments nécessitant un pH acide, tels que le **kétoconazole**, l'**itraconazole**, les **esters d'ampicilline**, les **sels ferreux** et la **digoxine** ■ Risque accru de saignement lors de l'usage concomitant de **warfarine** (suivre le RNI et le temps de prothrombine).

VOIES D'ADMINISTRATION ET POSOLOGIE

- **PO (adultes):** *Ulcère duodénal et gastrique* - 40 mg 1 fois par jour, le matin. La durée du traitement est habituellement de 2 semaines en cas d'ulcère duodénal et de 4 semaines en cas d'ulcère gastrique. Le traitement peut être prolongé d'autant, si besoin est. *Traitement de l'œsophagite associée au reflux gastro-œsophagien, reflux gastro-œsophagien* - 40 mg, 1 fois par jour, le matin, pendant 4 semaines; si besoin est, on peut prolonger le traitement de 4 semaines; *prévention des récidives* - 20 mg, 1 fois par jour le matin. *Réduction du risque d'ulcères gastriques associés au traitement par des AINS* - 20 mg, 1 fois par jour. *Ulcère duodénal associé à* H. pylori - *trithérapie:* pantoprazole à 40 mg, clarithromycine à 500 mg et métronidazole à 500 mg, à prendre 2 fois par jour, pendant 7 jours; **ou**: pantoprazole à 40 mg, clarithromycine à 500 mg et amoxicilline à 1 000 mg, à prendre 2 fois par jour, pendant 7 jours.
- **IV (adultes):** *Œsophagite par reflux* - 40 mg par jour, en perfusion IV pendant 15 minutes, ou par injection progressive pendant 2 à 5 minutes. *Hypersécrétion pathologique associée au syndrome de Zollinger-Ellison* - 80 mg, toutes les 12 heures, par perfusion IV pendant 15 minutes. On a également administré des doses de 120 mg, toutes les 12 heures, et de 80 mg, toutes les 8 heures, pour maintenir le débit d'acide en dessous de 10 mEq/h.

PRÉSENTATION

Comprimés à enrobage entérique: 20 mg[Pr], 40 mg[Pr] ■ **Poudre pour injection:** 40 mg/fiole[Pr].

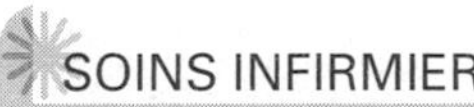

SOINS INFIRMIERS

ÉVALUATION DE LA SITUATION

- Suivre de près, à intervalles réguliers, la présence de douleurs épigastriques ou abdominales et de sang occulte ou apparent dans les selles, les vomissements ou les échantillons prélevés par aspiration gastrique.

Tests de laboratoire: Le médicament peut entraîner des résultats anormaux aux tests de la fonction hépatique, notamment une élévation des concentrations d'AST, d'ALT, de phosphatase alcaline et de bilirubine.

P

DIAGNOSTICS INFIRMIERS POSSIBLES

- Douleur aiguë (Indications).
- Connaissances insuffisantes sur le traitement médicamenteux (Enseignement au patient et à ses proches).

INTERVENTIONS INFIRMIÈRES

- Les patients recevant du pantoprazole IV devraient passer au pantoprazole par voie orale dès que leur situation le permet.

PO:

- On peut administrer le médicament le matin, avec ou sans aliments. IL NE FAUT PAS BRISER, ÉCRASER OU MÂCHER LES COMPRIMÉS.
- On peut administrer en même temps des antiacides.

IV: Reconstituer la fiole de 40 mg avec 10 mL de solution de NaCl 0,9%. On obtient ainsi une concentration de 4 mg/mL de pantoprazole, qu'on peut administrer par injection progressive pendant 2 à 5 minutes. La solution doit être utilisée dans les 24 heures qui suivent l'ouverture de la fiole. Consulter les directives du fabricant avant de reconstituer la préparation.

IV directe: Administrer la solution à 4 mg/mL sans dilution supplémentaire.

Vitesse d'administration: Administrer en 2 à 5 minutes.

Perfusion intermittente: Avant d'administrer, il faut diluer une fois de plus la solution de 4 mg/mL dans 90 mL de solution de NaCl 0,9 % ou de D5%E, pour obtenir une concentration de 0,4 mg/mL. La solution doit être utilisée dans les 24 heures qui suivent l'ouverture de la fiole. Consulter les directives du fabricant avant de reconstituer la préparation.

Vitesse d'administration: Administrer en 15 minutes à une vitesse < 3 mg/min.

ENSEIGNEMENT AU PATIENT ET À SES PROCHES

- Inciter le patient à respecter rigoureusement la posologie recommandée et à prendre toute la quantité de médicament qui lui a été prescrite même s'il se sent mieux.
- Mettre en garde le patient contre la consommation d'alcool, de produits renfermant de l'aspirine ou des anti-inflammatoires non stéroïdiens, sauf recommandation contraire du médecin, et d'aliments qui peuvent provoquer une irritation gastrique.
- Recommander au patient de signaler immédiatement à un professionnel de la santé la présence de selles noires et goudronneuses, de diarrhée ou de douleurs abdominales.

VÉRIFICATION DE L'EFFICACITÉ THÉRAPEUTIQUE

L'efficacité du traitement peut être démontrée par: la cicatrisation des ulcérations chez les patients souffrant d'œsophagite par érosion. Il faudrait poursuivre le traitement pendant un maximum de 8 semaines après le premier épisode.

PARICALCITOL,
voir Vitamine D (composés de)

PAROXÉTINE

Apo-Paroxétine, Dom-Paroxétine, Gen-Paroxétine, Paxil, Paxil Cr, Ratio-Paroxétine

CLASSIFICATION:

Antidépresseur (inhibiteur sélectif du recaptage de la sérotonine), antiobsessionnel, traitement de la panique et de la phobie sociale

Grossesse – catégorie C (risque durant le 3e trimestre; voir «Précautions et mises en garde»)

INDICATIONS

Comprimé ordinaire et à longue durée d'action: Dépression ■ trouble panique ■ phobie sociale ■ **Comprimé ordinaire**: Trouble obsessionnel-compulsif (souvent en association avec une psychothérapie) ■ anxiété généralisée ■ état de stress post-traumatique ■ **Comprimé à longue durée d'action**: Trouble dysphorique prémenstruel.

MÉCANISME D'ACTION

Inhibition du recaptage de la sérotonine par les neurones du SNC. Faible effet sur la noradrénaline et la dopamine. ***Effets thérapeutiques:*** Effet antidépresseur ■ Diminution de la fréquence des crises de panique, du comportement obsessionnel-compulsif ou des épisodes de phobie sociale ■ Amélioration de la symptomatologie présente chez les patients souffrant d'un état de stress post-traumatique ■ Amélioration de la dysphorie précédant la menstruation.

PHARMACOCINÉTIQUE

Absorption: Bonne (PO).

Distribution: Large distribution dans les liquides et les tissus de l'organisme, y compris le SNC. La paroxétine passe dans le lait maternel.

Liaison aux protéines: 95 %.

Métabolisme et excrétion: Métabolisme majoritairement hépatique (en partie par le CYP450 2D6); 2 % est excrété à l'état inchangé dans l'urine.

Demi-vie: 21 heures.

Profil temps-action (effet antidépresseur)

	DÉBUT D'ACTION	PIC	DURÉE
PO	1 - 4 semaines	inconnu	inconnue

CONTRE-INDICATIONS, PRÉCAUTIONS ET MISES EN GARDE

Contre-indications: Hypersensibilité ■ Traitement concomitant par un IMAO (prévoir 14 jours entre l'arrêt de l'administration de l'IMAO et le début de l'administration de la paroxétine, et vice versa; risque de réactions graves pouvant mener à une issue fatale) ■ Traitement concomitant par la thioridazine (prévoir 14 jours entre l'arrêt de l'administration de la thioridazine et le début de l'administration de la paroxétine, et vice versa; risque de réactions graves pouvant mener à une issue fatale) ■ Traitement concomitant par le pimozide.

Précautions et mises en garde: Risque d'effets indésirables de type agitation grave, parallèlement à des blessures infligées à soi-même ou aux autres ■ Éviter de mettre fin abruptement au traitement en raison du risque de symptômes de sevrage ■ Insuffisance hépatique ou rénale grave, personnes âgées ou patients débilités (amorcer le traitement à des doses plus faibles; la dose quotidienne ne devrait pas dépasser 40 mg) ■ Antécédents de troubles épileptiques ■ Électrochocs concomitants ■ Antécédents de manie ou d'hypomanie ■ La surveillance des idées suicidaires est indiquée chez tous les patients recevant ce médicament ■ Antécédents de maladie systémique concomitante, d'infarctus du myocarde récent ou de cardiopathie instable récente ■ Risque d'élévation des taux de cholestérol LDL (ces données doivent être prises en compte lorsqu'on traite des patients présentant des facteurs de risque cardiaque sous-jacents) ■ Risque de saignements (la prudence est de mise chez les patients prédisposés ou prenant simultanément des médicaments qui élèvent le risque de saignement) ■ Glaucome à angle fermé ■ **OBST.**: L'utilisation durant le 1er trimestre de la grossesse augmente le risque de malformation congénitale. Il importe d'évaluer les bienfaits escomptés par rapport au risque. Risque de complications chez le nouveau-né lorsque la mère a pris ce médicament durant le 3e trimestre ■ **ALLAITEMENT**: La paroxétine pénètre dans le lait maternel. Les femmes traitées par la paroxétine ne doivent pas allaiter, à moins que le médecin traitant juge l'allaitement nécessaire. En pareil cas, le nourrisson doit être surveillé de près ■ **PÉD.**: L'innocuité et l'efficacité de l'agent n'ont pas été établies.

RÉACTIONS INDÉSIRABLES ET EFFETS SECONDAIRES

SNC: anxiété, étourdissements, somnolence, céphalées, insomnie, faiblesse, agitation, amnésie, confusion, instabilité affective, sensation « droguée », manque de concentration, malaises, dépression, syncope.

ORLO: vision trouble, rhinite.

Resp.: toux, pharyngite, troubles respiratoires, bâillements.

CV: douleurs thoraciques, œdème, hypertension, palpitations, hypotension orthostatique, tachycardie, vasodilatation.

GI: constipation, diarrhée, sécheresse de la bouche (xérostomie), nausées, douleurs abdominales, perte d'appétit, dyspepsie, flatulence, gain d'appétit, altération du goût, vomissements.

GU: troubles éjaculatoires, diminution de la libido, troubles génitaux, troubles urinaires, mictions fréquentes.

Tég.: transpiration, photosensibilité, prurit, rash.

Métab.: gain de poids, perte de poids.

Loc.: douleurs lombaires, myalgie, myasthénie, myopathie.

SN: tremblements, myoclonie, paresthésie.

Divers: frissons, fièvre.

INTERACTIONS

Médicament-médicament: RISQUE DE RÉACTIONS GRAVES ET MÊME MORTELLES (HYPERTHERMIE, RIGIDITÉ, MYOCLONIE, INSTABILITÉ NEUROVÉGÉTATIVE, AVEC FLUCTUATION DES SIGNES VITAUX ET AGITATION EXTRÊME POUVANT MENER AU DÉLIRE ET AU COMA) LORS DE L'ADMINISTRATION CONCOMITANTE D'UN **IMAO**. IL FAUT CESSER L'ADMINISTRATION DES IMAO AU MOINS 14 JOURS AVANT D'AMORCER LE TRAITEMENT PAR LA PAROXÉTINE. DE MÊME, IL FAUT ARRÊTER L'ADMINISTRATION DE LA PAROXÉTINE AU MOINS 14 JOURS AVANT D'ENTREPRENDRE LE TRAITEMENT PAR UN IMAO ■ La paroxétine peut ralentir le métabolisme et augmenter les effets de certains **médicaments métabolisés par le foie**, notamment des autres **antidépresseurs**, des **phénothiazines** (la **thioridazine** est contre-indiquée), des **antiarythmiques du groupe IC**, du **pimozide** (usage contre-indiqué), de la **procyclidine** et de la **quinidine**. L'usage concomitant de ces médicaments et de la paroxétine devrait s'accompagner de prudence ■ La **cimétidine** élève les concentrations sanguines de paroxétine ■ Le **phénobarbital**, l'association **fosamprénavir/ritonavir** et la **phénytoïne** peuvent diminuer l'efficacité de la paroxétine ■ La consommation simultanée

P

d'**alcool** est déconseillée ■ Si elle est administrée en concomitance avec la **théophylline**, la paroxétine peut augmenter les concentrations plasmatiques de celle-ci ■ L'utilisation concomitante de **neuroleptiques** peut parfois donner lieu à des symptômes évoquant le syndrome malin des neuroleptiques ■ L'usage concomitant de **médicaments sérotoninergique** (p.ex., **tryptophane**, **linézolide**, **lithium**, **tramadol**) augmente le risque de syndrome sérotoninergique ■ Risque de faiblesse, d'hyperréflexie et d'incoordination lors de l'utilisation concomitante de **tryptans**, tel que le **sumatriptan** ■ Si elle est administrée en concomitance avec la **warfarine**, la paroxétine peut augmenter le risque de saignement sans que le RNI soit modifié.
Médicament-produits naturels: La consommation concomitante de **millepertuis** ou de **SAMe** augmente le risque d'effets secondaires sérotoninergiques, incluant le syndrome sérotoninergique.

VOIES D'ADMINISTRATION ET POSOLOGIE

Comprimé ordinaire

Dépression
- **PO (adultes)**: Initialement, 20 mg, 1 fois par jour le matin; on peut augmenter la dose de 10 mg par jour, à des intervalles hebdomadaires (écart posologique: de 20 à 50 mg par jour).

Trouble panique
- **PO (adultes)**: Initialement, 10 mg, 1 fois par jour; on peut augmenter la dose de 10 mg par jour, à des intervalles hebdomadaires (écart posologique: de 10 à 60 mg par jour).

Phobie sociale
- **PO (adultes)**: Initialement, 20 mg par jour; on peut augmenter la dose de 10 mg par jour, à des intervalles hebdomadaires (écart posologique: de 20 à 50 mg par jour).

Trouble obsessionnel-compulsif
- **PO (adultes)**: Initialement, 20 mg, 1 fois par jour; on peut augmenter la dose de 10 mg par jour, à des intervalles hebdomadaires (écart posologique: de 20 à 60 mg par jour).

Anxiété généralisée
- **PO (adultes)**: Initialement, 20 mg par jour; on peut augmenter la dose de 10 mg par jour, à des intervalles hebdomadaires (écart posologique: de 20 à 50 mg par jour).

Syndrome post-traumatique
- **PO (adultes)**: Initialement, 20 mg par jour; on peut augmenter la dose de 10 mg par jour, à des intervalles hebdomadaires (écart posologique: de 20 à 50 mg par jour).

Toutes les indications
- **PO (personnes âgées ou patients débilités)**: Initialement, 10 mg par jour; on peut augmenter la dose lentement (ne pas dépasser 40 mg par jour).

INSUFFISANCE HÉPATIQUE
- **PO (ADULTES)**: *INSUFFISANCE HÉPATIQUE GRAVE* – INITIALEMENT, 10 mg PAR JOUR; ON PEUT AUGMENTER LA DOSE LENTEMENT (NE PAS DÉPASSER 40 mg PAR JOUR).

INSUFFISANCE RÉNALE
- **PO (ADULTES)**: *INSUFFISANCE RÉNALE GRAVE* – INITIALEMENT, 10 mg PAR JOUR; ON PEUT AUGMENTER LA DOSE LENTEMENT (NE PAS DÉPASSER 40 mg PAR JOUR).

Comprimé à longue durée d'action

Dépression
- **PO (adultes)**: Initialement, 25 mg, 1 fois par jour le matin; on peut augmenter la dose de 12,5 mg par jour, à des intervalles hebdomadaires (écart posologique: de 25 à 62,5 mg par jour).

Trouble panique
- **PO (adultes)**: Initialement, 12,5 mg, 1 fois par jour; on peut augmenter la dose de 12,5 mg par jour, à des intervalles hebdomadaires (écart posologique: de 12,5 à 75 mg par jour).

Phobie sociale
- **PO (adultes)**: Initialement, 12,5 mg par jour; on peut augmenter la dose de 12,5 mg par jour, à des intervalles hebdomadaires (écart posologique: de 12,5 à 37,5 mg par jour).

Trouble dysphorique prémenstruel
- **PO (adultes)**: 12,5 mg, 1 fois par jour, pendant une période commençant 14 jours avant l'apparition prévue des règles et se terminant le premier jour de la menstruation (phase lutéale du cycle menstruel). La dose peut être portée à 25 mg, 1 fois par jour, si la patiente ne répond pas à la dose de départ. On peut envisager une administration quotidienne continue pendant tout le cycle menstruel, si l'efficacité de l'administration pendant la phase lutéale est sous-optimale. Il est recommandé d'effectuer les adaptations posologiques à intervalles d'au moins 1 semaine.

Toutes les indications
- **PO (personnes âgées ou patients débilités)**: Initialement, 12,5 mg par jour; on peut augmenter la dose lentement (ne pas dépasser 50 mg par jour).

INSUFFISANCE HÉPATIQUE
- **PO (ADULTES)**: *INSUFFISANCE HÉPATIQUE GRAVE* – INITIALEMENT, 12,5 mg PAR JOUR; ON PEUT AUG-

P

MENTER LA DOSE LENTEMENT (NE PAS DÉPASSER 50 mg PAR JOUR).

INSUFFISANCE RÉNALE

- **PO (ADULTES)**: *INSUFFISANCE RÉNALE GRAVE* – INITIALEMENT, 12,5 mg PAR JOUR; ON PEUT AUGMENTER LA DOSE LENTEMENT (NE PAS DÉPASSER 50 mg PAR JOUR).

PRÉSENTATION

Comprimés: 10 mg[Pr], 20 mg[Pr], 30 mg[Pr], 40 mg[Pr] ■ **Comprimés à libération prolongée**: 12,5 mg[Pr], 25 mg[Pr].

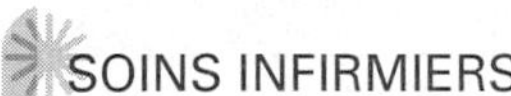

SOINS INFIRMIERS

ÉVALUATION DE LA SITUATION

- Suivre de près l'appétit du patient et son apport nutritionnel. Le peser toutes les semaines. Prévenir le médecin ou un autre professionnel de la santé en cas de perte constante de poids. Adapter le régime selon les aliments que le patient peut tolérer afin de maintenir son état nutritionnel.

Dépression:

- Suivre de près les changements d'humeur. Informer le médecin ou un autre professionnel de la santé si le patient devient plus anxieux ou nerveux ou si l'insomnie s'aggrave.
- Observer les tendances suicidaires, particulièrement durant le traitement initial. Réduire la quantité de médicament dont le patient peut disposer.

Trouble obsessionnel-compulsif: Noter la fréquence des comportements obsessionnels-compulsifs et le degré auquel ces pensées et ces comportements entravent le fonctionnement quotidien.

Crises de panique: Évaluer la fréquence et la gravité des crises de panique.

Phobie sociale: Évaluer la fréquence et la gravité des épisodes de phobie.

Syndrome post-traumatique: Évaluer les manifestations de l'état de stress post-traumatique à intervalles réguliers tout au long du traitement.

Trouble dysphorique prémenstruel: Évaluer les symptômes du trouble dysphorique prémenstruel avant et durant le traitement.

Tests de laboratoire: Noter la numération globulaire et la formule leucocytaire tout au long du traitement. Prévenir le médecin en cas de leucopénie ou d'anémie.

DIAGNOSTICS INFIRMIERS POSSIBLES

- Stratégies d'adaptation inefficaces (Indications).
- Risque d'accident (Effets secondaires).
- Connaissances insuffisantes sur le traitement médicamenteux (Enseignement au patient et à ses proches).

INTERVENTIONS INFIRMIÈRES

- NE PAS CONFONDRE LA PAROXÉTINE (PAXIL) AVEC LE PACLITAXEL (TAXOL).
- Réévaluer à intervalles réguliers la dose et le besoin de poursuivre le traitement.
- Administrer la paroxétine en une seule dose, le matin. On peut l'administrer avec des aliments pour réduire l'irritation gastrique.
- Les comprimés à longue durée d'action doivent être avalés entiers. Ne pas les écraser, les couper ou les mâcher.

ENSEIGNEMENT AU PATIENT ET À SES PROCHES

- Conseiller au patient de respecter rigoureusement la posologie recommandée. S'il n'a pu prendre le médicament au moment habituel, il doit le prendre dès que possible et revenir ensuite à son horaire habituel. Lui recommander de ne jamais remplacer une dose manquée par une double dose. Conseiller au patient de ne pas abandonner le traitement sans avoir consulté au préalable un professionnel de la santé. La dose quotidienne devra être diminuée graduellement. Un sevrage rapide peut entraîner des étourdissements, des modifications sensorielles, de l'agitation, de l'anxiété, des nausées et la diaphorèse.
- Prévenir le patient que la paroxétine peut provoquer de la somnolence ou des étourdissements. Lui conseiller de ne pas conduire et d'éviter les activités qui exigent sa vigilance jusqu'à ce qu'on ait la certitude que le médicament n'entraîne pas ces effets chez lui.
- Conseiller au patient d'éviter de consommer de l'alcool et de prendre d'autres dépresseurs du SNC en même temps que la paroxétine. Lui recommander de consulter un professionnel de la santé avant de prendre tout autre médicament ou produit naturel en même temps que la paroxétine.
- Expliquer au patient qu'il peut soulager la sécheresse de la bouche en se rinçant souvent la bouche, en pratiquant une bonne hygiène buccale et en consommant de la gomme ou des bonbons sans sucre. Si la sécheresse de la bouche persiste pendant plus de 2 semaines, lui conseiller de consulter un professionnel de la santé, qui pourra lui recommander des substituts de salive.
- Inciter le patient à utiliser un écran solaire et à porter des vêtements protecteurs pour prévenir les réactions de photosensibilité.

- Conseiller à la patiente de prévenir un professionnel de la santé si elle pense être enceinte, si elle souhaite le devenir ou si elle allaite.
- Recommander au patient de prévenir un professionnel de la santé si les céphalées, la faiblesse, les nausées, l'anorexie, l'anxiété ou l'insomnie persistent.
- Insister sur l'importance des examens de suivi permettant de déterminer les effets du traitement. Inciter le patient à suivre une psychothérapie.

VÉRIFICATION DE L'EFFICACITÉ THÉRAPEUTIQUE

L'efficacité du traitement peut être démontrée par: une sensation de mieux-être ■ un regain d'intérêt pour l'entourage; les effets antidépresseurs peuvent ne pas se manifester avant 1 à 4 semaines ■ une diminution des comportements obsessionnels-compulsifs ■ une diminution de la fréquence et de la gravité des crises de panique ■ une diminution de la fréquence et de la gravité des épisodes de phobie ■ l'amélioration des manifestations de l'état de stress post-traumatique ■ l'amélioration de la dysphorie due à la menstruation. ✻

PEGASPARGASE

Ce médicament n'est pas commercialisé au Canada. Disponible par l'intermédiaire du Programme d'accès spécial de Santé Canada.

CLASSIFICATION:
Antinéoplasique (enzyme)

Grossesse – catégorie C

P

INDICATIONS

Traitement de la leucémie lymphoblastique aiguë (LLA); on peut l'utiliser chez les patients présentant une hypersensibilité connue aux autres formes de L-asparaginase. La pegaspargase ne doit pas être employée seule dans le traitement anticancéreux d'induction ou d'entretien, à moins que le recours à un traitement d'association n'ait été jugé inopportun.

MÉCANISME D'ACTION

Composé formé par la liaison de la L-asparaginase au polyéthylèneglycol. Ce composé entraîne la déplétion de l'asparagine que les cellules leucémiques ne peuvent synthétiser. Les cellules normales étant capables de produire leur propre asparagine, elles sont moins sensibles à ses effets. La liaison au polyéthylèneglycol rend l'asparaginase moins antigénique et donc moins susceptible d'induire des réactions d'hypersensibilité. ***Effets thérapeutiques:*** Destruction des cellules leucémiques.

PHARMACOCINÉTIQUE

Absorption: Biodisponibilité à 100 % (IV).

Distribution: Inconnue.

Métabolisme et excrétion: Métabolisme par les protéases sériques et dans le système réticuloendothélial.

Demi-vie: 5,7 jours (raccourcie chez les patients ayant déjà présenté une hypersensibilité à la L-asparaginase naturelle).

Profil temps-action (déplétion de l'asparagine)

	DÉBUT D'ACTION	PIC	DURÉE
IV	rapide	inconnu	14 jours

CONTRE-INDICATIONS, PRÉCAUTIONS ET MISES EN GARDE

Contre-indications: Pancréatite ou antécédents de pancréatite à la suite d'un traitement par la L-asparaginase ■ Antécédent de réactions hémorragiques ou de thrombose grave à la suite d'un traitement par la L-asparaginase ■ Antécédent de réaction anaphylactique à la pegaspargase.

Précautions et mises en garde: Antécédent de réactions d'hypersensibilité à d'autres médicaments ■ **OBST.:** Patients en âge de procréer, grossesse ou allaitement (l'innocuité du médicament n'a pas été établie).

RÉACTIONS INDÉSIRABLES ET EFFETS SECONDAIRES

SNC: CONVULSIONS, céphalées, malaise.

GI: PANCRÉATITE, douleurs abdominales, anomalies des résultats des tests de la fonction hépatique, anorexie, diarrhée, œdème de la lèvre, nausées, vomissements.

CV: thrombose.

Tég.: jaunisse.

End.: hyperglycémie.

HÉ: œdème périphérique.

Hémat.: diminution du fibrinogène, coagulation intravasculaire disséminée, anémie hémolytique, taux accru de thromboplastine, leucopénie, pancytopénie, thrombopénie.

Locaux: hypersensibilité au point d'injection, douleur au point d'injection, thrombose.

Loc.: arthralgie, myalgie, douleurs dans les membres.

SN: paresthésie.

Divers: frissons, réactions d'hypersensibilité incluant l'ANAPHYLAXIE, sueurs nocturnes.

INTERACTIONS

Médicament-médicament: La pegaspargase peut modifier la réponse aux **anticoagulants** ou aux **agents antiplaquettaires** ■ La pegaspargase peut modifier la réponse à d'autres **médicaments métabolisés par le foie**.

VOIES D'ADMINISTRATION ET POSOLOGIE

- **IM, IV**: 2 500 UI/m^2, les 1er et 15e jours (habituellement en association avec d'autres agents), en traitement d'induction.

PRÉSENTATION

Ce médicament n'est pas commercialisé au Canada.

SOINS INFIRMIERS

ÉVALUATION DE LA SITUATION

- Déterminer si le patient a déjà manifesté des réactions d'hypersensibilité à la L-asparaginase naturelle. Rester à l'affût des réactions d'hypersensibilité (urticaire, diaphorèse, œdème facial, douleurs articulaires, hypotension, bronchospasme). Garder à portée de la main de l'adrénaline et le matériel de réanimation pour parer à toute urgence. Une réaction peut survenir jusqu'à 2 heures après l'administration.
- Déceler l'apparition d'une aplasie médullaire. Suivre de près la fièvre, les maux de gorge et les signes d'infection. Noter la numération plaquettaire tout au long du traitement. Suivre de près les saignements (saignement des gencives, formation d'ecchymoses, pétéchies, présence de sang occulte dans les selles, l'urine et les vomissements). Éviter les injections IM et la prise de la température rectale. Appliquer une pression sur les points de ponction veineuse pendant 10 minutes. Une anémie peut survenir. Suivre de près les signes de fatigue accrue, de dyspnée et d'hypotension orthostatique.
- RESTER À L'AFFÛT DES SIGNES DE PANCRÉATITE (NAUSÉES, VOMISSEMENTS, DOULEURS ABDOMINALES).
- Suivre de près les nausées, les vomissements et l'appétit. Peser le patient toutes les semaines. On peut administrer des antiémétiques prophylactiques avant d'administrer la pegaspargase.

***Tests de laboratoire*:**

- Noter la numération globulaire avant le traitement et à intervalles réguliers pendant toute sa durée. La pegaspargase peut modifier les résultats des tests de coagulation, réduire la concentration de fibrinogène et prolonger le temps de prothrombine et le temps de céphaline.
- Examiner à intervalles fréquents les concentrations sériques d'amylase pour déceler l'apparition d'une pancréatite.
- Suivre de près la glycémie; la pegaspargase peut entraîner l'hyperglycémie.
- La pegaspargase peut entraîner l'élévation des concentrations sériques d'urée et de créatinine.
- La toxicité hépatique peut se manifester par une concentration accrue d'AST, d'ALT ou de bilirubine. Les résultats des tests de la fonction hépatique reviennent habituellement à la normale après le traitement.
- La pegaspargase peut réduire les concentrations sériques de calcium.
- La pegaspargase peut entraîner l'élévation des concentrations sériques et urinaires d'acide urique et l'hyponatrémie.

DIAGNOSTICS INFIRMIERS POSSIBLES

- Risque d'infection (Réactions indésirables).
- Connaissances insuffisantes sur le traitement médicamenteux (Enseignement au patient et à ses proches).

INTERVENTIONS INFIRMIÈRES

- NE PAS CONFONDRE LA PEGASPARGASE AVEC L'ASPARAGINASE.
- La voie IM est la voie d'administration privilégiée en raison d'un moindre risque de réactions indésirables.
- Préparer les solutions sous une hotte à flux laminaire. Porter des gants, des vêtements protecteurs et un masque pendant la manipulation de ce médicament. Mettre au rebut le matériel dans les contenants réservés à cette fin (voir l'annexe H).

IM: Ne pas injecter plus de 2 mL à la fois. Si le volume d'injection est supérieur à 2 mL, administrer par plusieurs points.

Perfusion intermittente:

- Diluer chaque dose dans 100 mL de solution de NaCl 0,9 % ou de D5%E. Ne pas agiter la solution. Ne pas utiliser la solution si elle est trouble ou si elle contient un précipité.
- N'utiliser qu'une dose par fiole; ne pas introduire l'aiguille dans la fiole une deuxième fois. Jeter toute portion inutilisée.
- Garder la solution au réfrigérateur, mais ne pas la congeler. La congélation inactive la pegaspargase, sans en changer l'aspect.

***Vitesse d'administration*:** Administrer l'agent en 1 à 2 heures au moyen d'une tubulure en Y par laquelle s'écoule déjà une autre solution de NaCl 0,9 % ou de D5%E.

P

Incompatibilité en addition au soluté: On ne possède aucune donnée à cet égard. Ne pas mélanger à d'autres médicaments ou solutions, sauf celles indiquées ci-dessus.

ENSEIGNEMENT AU PATIENT ET À SES PROCHES

- Informer le patient du risque de réactions d'hypersensibilité, incluant l'anaphylaxie.
- Signaler au patient que l'usage concomitant d'autres médicaments peut augmenter le risque de saignement et la toxicité de la pegaspargase. Lui recommander de consulter un professionnel de la santé avant de prendre d'autres médicaments, même s'il s'agit de médicaments en vente libre.
- Conseiller au patient de signaler à un professionnel de la santé les symptômes suivants: douleurs abdominales, nausées et vomissements graves, jaunisse, fièvre, frissons, maux de gorge, saignement ou formation d'ecchymoses, soif ou mictions excessives, aphtes buccaux. Recommander au patient d'éviter les foules et les personnes contagieuses. Lui conseiller d'utiliser une brosse à dents à poils doux et un rasoir électrique et de prendre garde aux chutes. Recommander également au patient d'éviter de consommer des boissons alcoolisées et de ne pas prendre de médicaments contenant de l'aspirine ou des AINS en raison du risque d'hémorragie gastrique.
- Prévenir le patient qu'il ne doit recevoir aucun vaccin sans demander au préalable l'avis d'un professionnel de la santé. Informer les parents que le traitement peut modifier le schéma de vaccination de leur enfant.
- Expliquer au patient qu'il doit se soumettre à intervalles réguliers à des examens diagnostiques permettant de suivre l'apparition d'effets secondaires.

VÉRIFICATION DE L'EFFICACITÉ THÉRAPEUTIQUE

L'efficacité du traitement peut être démontrée par: l'amélioration de l'état hématologique des patients souffrant de leucémie. ✳

PEGFILGRASTIM

Neulasta

CLASSIFICATION:

Facteur de croissance hématopoïétique

Grossesse – catégorie C

INDICATIONS

Diminution de l'incidence des neutropénies fébriles chez les patients atteints de cancers non myéloïdes qui reçoivent un traitement par des antinéoplasiques myélosuppresseurs.

MÉCANISME D'ACTION

Le filgrastim est une glycoprotéine qui se lie aux granulocytes neutrophiles et en stimule la division et la différenciation. Il active également les granulocytes neutrophiles qui ont atteint la maturité. La liaison à une molécule de polyéthylène glycol prolonge ses effets. ***Effets thérapeutiques:*** Diminution de l'incidence des infections chez les patients neutropéniques à la suite d'une chimiothérapie.

PHARMACOCINÉTIQUE

Absorption: Bonne (SC).
Distribution: Inconnue.
Métabolisme et excrétion: Inconnus.
Demi-vie: De 25 à 49 heures.

Profil temps-action

	DÉBUT D'ACTION	PIC	DURÉE
SC	inconnu	inconnu	inconnue

CONTRE-INDICATIONS, PRÉCAUTIONS ET MISES EN GARDE

Contre-indications: Hypersensibilité au filgrastim, au pegfilgrastim ou aux protéines dérivées de *Escherichia coli.*
Précautions et mises en garde: Patients atteints de drépanocytose (risque accru de crise drépanocytaire) ▪ Usage concomitant de lithium ▪ Cancer à caractéristiques myéloïdes ▪ **OBST., ALLAITEMENT:** L'innocuité de l'agent n'a pas été établie ▪ **PÉD.:** L'innocuité de l'agent n'a pas été établie; ne pas utiliser la dose fixe de 6 mg chez les nourrissons, les enfants ou les adolescents frêles pesant < 45 kg ▪ Administration d'une chimiothérapie s'accompagnant d'une myélosupression différée (p. ex., nitroso-urée, mitomycine), d'un antimétabolique (p. ex., 5-FU) ou d'une radiothérapie, car l'innocuité de telles associations n'est pas établie.

RÉACTIONS INDÉSIRABLES ET EFFETS SECONDAIRES

Resp.: SYNDROME DE DÉTRESSE RESPIRATOIRE DE L'ADULTE.
Hémat.: CRISE DRÉPANOCYTAIRE, rupture de la rate, leucocytose.
Loc.: douleurs osseuses.
Divers: réactions allergiques comprenant L'ANAPHYLAXIE.

INTERACTIONS

Médicament-médicament: L'usage concomitant d'**antinéoplasiques** peut avoir des effets délétères sur les granulocytes neutrophiles à prolifération rapide; ne pas administrer l'agent pendant les 14 jours qui précèdent et les 24 heures qui suivent une chimiothérapie ▪ Le **lithium** peut potentialiser la libération de granulocytes neutrophiles; l'usage concomitant doit s'accompagner de prudence.

VOIES D'ADMINISTRATION ET POLOSOLGIE

- **SC (adultes)**: 6 mg par cycle de chimiothérapie.

PRÉSENTATION

Solution pour injection sous-cutanée: 6 mg/0,6 mL en seringues préremplies[Pr].

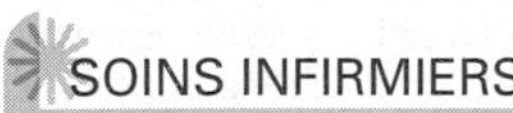

SOINS INFIRMIERS

ÉVALUATION DE LA SITUATION

- Évaluer la douleur osseuse tout au long du traitement. Elle est habituellement de légère à modérée et peut être soulagée par des analgésiques non opioïdes; cependant, il est parfois nécessaire d'administrer des analgésiques opioïdes.
- RESTER À L'AFFÛT DES SIGNES DE SYNDROME DE DÉTRESSE RESPIRATOIRE DE L'ADULTE (FIÈVRE, INFILTRATIONS PULMONAIRES, DÉTRESSE RESPIRATOIRE). SI UN TEL SYNDROME SURVIENT, LE TRAITER ET ABANDONNER LE TRAITEMENT AU PEGFILGRASTIM OU L'INTERROMPRE JUSQU'À LA DISPARITION DES SYMPTÔMES.

Tests de laboratoire:

- Obtenir la numération globulaire et plaquettaire avant la chimiothérapie. Suivre à intervalles réguliers l'hématocrite et la numération plaquettaire et leucocytaire.
- L'agent peut élever les concentrations de LDH, de phosphatase alcaline et d'acide urique.

DIAGNOSTICS INFIRMIERS POSSIBLES

- Risque d'infection (Indications).
- Douleur aiguë (Effets secondaires).

INTERVENTIONS INFIRMIÈRES

- Ne pas administrer le pegfilgrastim durant les 24 heures qui suivent et les 14 jours qui précèdent une chimiothérapie cytotoxique.
- Maintenir l'hydratation chez les patients atteints de drépanocytose qui reçoivent du pegfilgrastim; les suivre de près pour dépister une crise drépanocytaire.

SC: Administrer par voie sous-cutanée une fois par cycle de chimiothérapie. Ne pas administrer de solutions qui ont changé de couleur ou qui contiennent des particules. Ne pas agiter. Garder au réfrigérateur. On peut laisser la solution à la température ambiante pendant 72 heures, mais il faut la protéger de la lumière.

- L'agent est fourni dans des seringues préremplies. Après l'administration, pour prévenir les piqûres, utiliser le protecteur d'aiguille UltraSafe: placer les mains en arrière de l'aiguille, saisir la gaine d'une main et la faire glisser vers l'avant jusqu'à ce que l'aiguille soit complètement recouverte et que le verrouillage à déclic soit en position. Si on n'entend pas de déclic, le protecteur pourrait ne pas être complètement activé. Mettre au rebut la seringue préremplie recouverte du protecteur d'aiguille dans des contenants imperforables.

ENSEIGNEMENT AU PATIENT ET À SES PROCHES

- RECOMMANDER AU PATIENT DE PRÉVENIR IMMÉDIATEMENT UN PROFESSIONNEL DE LA SANTÉ EN CAS DE SIGNES DE RÉACTIONS ALLERGIQUES (ESSOUFFLEMENT, URTICAIRE, RASH, PRURIT, ŒDÈME LARYNGÉ) OU DE RUPTURE DE LA RATE (DOULEURS DANS LE QUADRANT SUPÉRIEUR GAUCHE DE L'ABDOMEN OU DANS L'ÉPAULE GAUCHE).
- Insister sur l'importance de l'observance du traitement et des numérations globulaires régulières.

Soins à domicile: Montrer au patient la méthode correcte de mise au rebut du matériel utilisé à domicile. Lui expliquer qu'il ne doit pas réutiliser les aiguilles, seringues ou restes de médicament. Lui remettre un contenant imperforable pour la mise au rebut des seringues préremplies.

VÉRIFICATION DE L'EFFICACITÉ THÉRAPEUTIQUE

L'efficacité du traitement peut être démontrée par: la diminution de l'incidence des neutropénies fébriles chez les patients qui reçoivent des antinéoplasiques myélosuppresseurs. ✳

PEGINTERFÉRON ALPHA-2A,

voir Interféron alpha

PEGINTERFÉRON ALPHA-2B,

voir Interféron alpha

P

PEMETREXED

Alimta

CLASSIFICATION:

Antinéoplasique (antimétabolite, antagoniste des folates)

Grossesse – catégorie D

INDICATIONS

Traitement de première intention du mésothéliome pleural malin (avec le cisplatine) lorsque la tumeur n'est pas résécable ou lorsque le patient n'est pas candidat à la chirurgie ■ Cancer du poumon non à petites cellules avancé ou métastatique, chez des patients déjà traités par une chimiothérapie.

MÉCANISME D'ACTION

Interruption des processus métaboliques folate-dépendants qui participent à la synthèse de la purine et de la thymidine. Transformation intracellulaire en polyglutamate, qui prolonge la durée d'action. ***Effets thérapeutiques:*** Ralentissement de la croissance et de la propagation des cellules cancéreuses.

PHARMACOCINÉTIQUE

Absorption: Biodisponibilité à 100 % (IV).

Distribution: Inconnue

Métabolisme et excrétion: Métabolisme minimal; excrétion rénale (de 70 à 90 % sous forme inchangée).

Demi-vie: 3,5 heures (fonction rénale normale).

Profil temps-action (effet hématologique)

	DÉBUT D'ACTION	PIC	DURÉE
IV	inconnu	8 jours	15 jours

CONTRE-INDICATIONS, PRÉCAUTIONS ET MISES EN GARDE

Contre-indications: Hypersensibilité ■ Cl_{Cr} < 45 mL/min.

Précautions et mises en garde: Usage concomitant d'AINS ■ Insuffisance rénale modérée (Cl_{Cr} de 45 à 80 mL/min) ■ Accumulation de liquide dans le troisième espace (ascite, épanchement pleural); envisager un drainage avant le traitement ■ Insuffisance hépatique (il est recommandé de modifier la posologie) ■ **PÉD.**: L'innocuité de l'agent n'a pas été établie ■ **OBST.**: Grossesse, allaitement.

RÉACTIONS INDÉSIRABLES ET EFFETS SECONDAIRES

Resp.: pharyngite.

CV: douleurs thoraciques.

GI: constipation, nausées, stomatite, vomissements, anorexie, diarrhée, œsophagite, douleurs buccales.

Tég.: desquamation, rash.

Hémat.: anémie, leucopénie, thrombopénie.

SN: neuropathie.

Divers: fièvre, infection, réaction d'hypersensibilité, incluant l'ANAPHYLAXIE.

INTERACTIONS

Médicament-médicament: Les **AINS** élèvent les concentrations sanguines et le risque de toxicité; chez les patients ayant une fonction rénale normale, on peut utiliser des AINS à courte durée d'action; chez les patients ayant une Cl_{Cr} de 45 à 80 mL/min, on doit administrer les AINS à courte durée d'action avec prudence et ne pas les administrer pendant les 2 jours qui précèdent et qui suivent le traitement ou le jour même du traitement; chez tous les patients, ne pas administrer les AINS à longue durée d'action pendant les 5 jours qui précèdent et les 2 jours qui suivent le traitement ou le jour même du traitement ■ Le **probénécide** élève les concentrations sanguines de pemetrexed ■ Les **agents néphrotoxiques**, administrés en concomitance, élèvent le risque de néphrotoxicité.

VOIES D'ADMINISTRATION ET POSOLOGIE

- **IV (adultes)**: *Mésothéliome* – 500 mg/m^2, le premier jour de chaque cycle de 21 jours (avec le cisplatine); en même temps, hydrater le patient et lui administrer en prétraitement de l'acide folique, de la vitamine B_{12} et de la dexaméthasone. Il est recommandé d'adapter la posologie pour prévenir les toxicités hématologiques et non hématologiques dont la neurotoxicité. *Cancer du poumon non à petites cellules* – 500 mg/m^2, le premier jour de chaque cycle de 21 jours (il est recommandé d'administrer en prétraitement des corticostéroïdes, de l'acide folique et de la vitamine B_{12}). Il est également recommandé d'adapter la posologie pour prévenir les toxicités hématologiques et non hématologiques dont la neurotoxicité.

PRÉSENTATION

Poudre lyophilisée pour perfusion: fioles de 500 mg^{Pr}.

SOINS INFIRMIERS

ÉVALUATION DE LA SITUATION

- Rechercher le rash tout au long du traitement. Le prétraitement par la dexaméthasone, la veille, le jour et le lendemain de l'administration réduit la fréquence et la gravité de la réaction.

Mésothéliome:

- Suivre de près les toxicités hématologiques et digestives (mucosite, diarrhée). En cas de toxicités non hématologiques de grade 3 ou 4 (à l'exception de la mucosite), administrer 75 % de la dose antérieure de pemetrexed et de cisplatine. En cas de mucosite de grade 3 ou 4, administrer 50 % de la dose antérieure de pemetrexed et 100 % de la dose antérieure de cisplatine.
- SUIVRE DE PRÈS LA DÉPRESSION MÉDULLAIRE. Rechercher les saignements (saignement des gencives, formation d'ecchymoses, pétéchies, présence de sang dans les selles, les urines et les vomissures); éviter les injections IM et la prise de la température par voie rectale, si le nombre de plaquettes est bas. Appliquer une pression sur les points de ponction IV pendant 10 minutes. En cas de neutropénie, rechercher les signes d'infection. L'anémie peut survenir; rester à l'affût d'une fatigue accrue, de la dyspnée et de l'hypotension orthostatique.
- Rester à l'affût de la neurotoxicité tout au long du traitement. En cas de neurotoxicité de grade 0 ou 1, conserver 100 % de la dose antérieure. En cas de neurotoxicité de grade 2, administrer 100 % de la dose antérieure de pemetrexed et 50 % de la dose antérieure de cisplatine. En cas de neurotoxicité de grade 3 ou 4, arrêter le traitement.

Tests de laboratoire: Obtenir les numérations globulaire et plaquettaire à leur nadir (8e jour), à leur rétablissement (15e jour) et avant d'administrer chaque dose; suivre à intervalles réguliers les résultats des analyses de sang pour évaluer les fonctions rénale et hépatique. L'agent peut induire l'anémie, la leucopénie, la neutropénie et la thrombopénie. Ne pas recommencer un nouveau cycle de traitement avant que le NAN n'atteigne $1,5 \times 10^9$/L au minimum, le nombre de plaquettes 100×10^9/L au minimum et la clairance de la créatinine 45 mL/min au minimum. Si le nadir du NAN est inférieur à $0,5 \times 10^9$/L et si celui des plaquettes est supérieur ou égal à 50×10^9/L, diminuer les doses de pemetrexed et de cisplatine à 75 % de la dose antérieure. Si le nadir des plaquettes est inférieur à 50×10^9/L, sans égard au nadir du NAN, diminuer les doses de pemetrexed et de cisplatine de 50 %.

DIAGNOSTICS INFIRMIERS POSSIBLES

- Risque d'accident (Réactions indésirables).

INTERVENTIONS INFIRMIÈRES

- Le pemetrexed doit être administré sous la surveillance d'un médecin ayant de l'expérience dans l'administration des agents chimiothérapeutiques.
- Préparer la solution sous une hotte à flux laminaire. Porter un masque, un vêtement protecteur et des gants pendant la manipulation de ce médicament. Mettre au rebut le matériel dans des contenants réservés à cet usage (voir l'annexe H).
- Pour réduire les risques d'intoxication, administrer au patient 0,4 mg (1 mg au maximum) d'acide folique par jour, pendant les 7 jours qui précèdent l'administration de la première dose de pemetrexed, poursuivre cette administration pendant tout le traitement et l'arrêter 21 jours après l'administration de la dernière dose de pemetrexed. Les patients doivent également recevoir une injection de vitamine B_{12} de 1 000 µg au cours de la semaine qui précède l'administration de la première dose de pemetrexed et tous les 3 cycles, par la suite jusqu'à 21 jours après la dernière dose de pemetrexed. Les doses suivantes de vitamine B_{12} peuvent être administrées le même jour que le pemetrexed.

Perfusion intermittente: Reconstituer le contenu de la fiole de 500 mg avec 20 mL de NaCl 0,9 % sans agents de conservation, pour obtenir une solution de 25 mg/mL. Tourner délicatement la fiole jusqu'à ce que la poudre soit complètement dissoute. La solution doit être transparente et d'incolore à jaune ou à vert-jaune. Ne pas administrer une solution qui a changé de couleur ou qui contient des particules. Diluer une fois de plus avec 100 mL de NaCl 0,9 % sans agents de conservation. La solution est stable à la température ambiante ou au réfrigérateur pendant 24 heures au maximum.

Vitesse d'administration: Administrer pendant 10 minutes.

Incompatibilité en addition au soluté: Solutions contenant du calcium, comme le lactate de Ringer et la solution de Ringer.

P

ENSEIGNEMENT AU PATIENT ET À SES PROCHES

- Insister sur le fait qu'il est important de prendre en prophylaxie de l'acide folique et de la vitamine B_{12} pour réduire les toxicités digestives et hématologiques induites par le traitement.
- Conseiller à la patiente d'éviter la grossesse pendant le traitement. Si une grossesse est planifiée ou soupçonnée, il faut en prévenir rapidement un professionnel de la santé.

VÉRIFICATION DE L'EFFICACITÉ THÉRAPEUTIQUE

L'efficacité du traitement peut être démontrée par: le ralentissement de la croissance des mésothéliomes et de l'évolution du cancer pulmonaire non à petites cellules ainsi que de la dissémination des cellules cancéreuses. 

PÉMOLINE

Disponible par l'intermédiaire du Programme d'accès spécial de Santé Canada.

CLASSIFICATION:
Stimulant du SNC

Grossesse – catégorie B

INDICATIONS

Traitement d'appoint du trouble déficitaire de l'attention avec hyperactivité (TDAH) chez les enfants > 6 ans (il ne s'agit pas d'un traitement de première intention). **Usages non approuvés:** Traitement de la fatigue ou de la dépression mentale ■ Traitement de la schizophrénie ■ Stimulant chez les patients âgés.

MÉCANISME D'ACTION

Stimulation du SNC, probablement par médiation dopaminergique ■ Augmentation de l'activité motrice et de la vigilance, diminution de la fatigue et de l'appétit et légère euphorie. ***Effets thérapeutiques:*** Prolongation de la durée de l'attention chez les enfants atteints du TDAH.

PHARMACOCINÉTIQUE

Absorption: Bonne (PO).
Distribution: Inconnue.
Métabolisme et excrétion: Métabolisme hépatique (50 %). Excrétion rénale (40 % sous forme inchangée).
Demi-vie: De 9 à 14 heures.

Profil temps-action
(effets sur le trouble déficitaire de l'attention avec hyperactivité)

	DÉBUT D'ACTION	PIC	DURÉE
PO	plusieurs jours – semaines	2 – 3 semaines	plusieurs jours

CONTRE-INDICATIONS, PRÉCAUTIONS ET MISES EN GARDE

Contre-indications: Hypersensibilité ■ Maladie hépatique.
Précautions et mises en garde: Insuffisance rénale ■ État affectif instable ou psychose ■ Antécédents de troubles convulsifs ■ Tics ■ **OBST., ALLAITEMENT:** L'innocuité du médicament n'a pas été établie.

RÉACTIONS INDÉSIRABLES ET EFFETS SECONDAIRES

SNC: CONVULSIONS, insomnie, étourdissements, mouvements dyskinétiques, céphalées, irritabilité, dépression, nervosité (doses élevées).
CV: tachycardie (doses élevées).
GI: INSUFFISANCE HÉPATIQUE, anorexie, hépatite médicamenteuse.
Tég.: rash, transpiration.
Métab.: perte de poids.
Divers: fièvre.

INTERACTIONS

Médicament-médicament: Risque de stimulation additive du SNC lors de l'usage concomitant d'autres **stimulants du SNC** ou d'**agents adrénergiques**, incluant les **décongestionnants** ■ L'usage concomitant d'**IMAO** peut entraîner des crises hypertensives, le coma, la dépression respiratoire ou la mort. (L'usage concomitant ou dans les 14 jours suivant l'arrêt de l'IMAO n'est pas recommandé.)

VOIES D'ADMINISTRATION ET POSOLOGIE

- **PO (enfants > 6 ans):** Initialement, 37,5 mg en une seule dose, le matin; on peut augmenter la dose de 18,75 mg à des intervalles de 1 semaine, jusqu'à obtention de la réponse optimale. (La dose d'entretien habituelle se situe entre 56,25 et 75 mg par jour; ne pas dépasser 112,5 mg par jour.)

PRÉSENTATION

Disponible par l'intermédiaire du Programme d'accès spécial de Santé Canada.
Capsule: 37,5 mg Pr, 75 mg Pr.

SOINS INFIRMIERS

ÉVALUATION DE LA SITUATION

- Noter la durée de l'attention, les tics moteurs ou verbaux, la maîtrise des impulsions et les interactions avec autrui chez les enfants souffrant d'un trouble déficitaire de l'attention avec hyperactivité. On peut interrompre l'administration du médicament à intervalles réguliers pour déterminer si les symptômes justifient la poursuite du traitement.
- Mesurer à intervalles réguliers la taille et le poids des enfants recevant un traitement prolongé pour évaluer leur croissance. Prévenir le médecin ou un autre professionnel de la santé en cas d'arrêt de la croissance.

Tests de laboratoire: ON DEVRAIT NOTER LES CONCENTRATIONS SÉRIQUES D'ALT AVANT LE TRAITEMENT, PUIS TOUTES LES 2 SEMAINES PENDANT TOUTE SA DURÉE. SI LE TRAITEMENT EST INTERROMPU PUIS REPRIS, ON DEVRAIT MENER DES TESTS DE LA FONCTION HÉPATIQUE AVANT DE REPRENDRE LA MÉDICATION ET TOUTES LES 2 SEMAINES PAR LA SUITE. LE TRAITEMENT PAR LA

PÉMOLINE DEVRAIT ÊTRE ARRÊTÉ SI LES CONCENTRATIONS D'ALT DEVIENNENT CLINIQUEMENT ÉLEVÉES OU CORRESPONDENT À PLUS DE 2 FOIS LA LIMITE SUPÉRIEURE DE LA NORMALE, OU SI DES SYMPTÔMES D'INSUFFISANCE HÉPATIQUE SE MANIFESTENT. LA PÉMOLINE PEUT ENTRAÎNER L'ÉLÉVATION DES CONCENTRATIONS DE LDH, DE PHOSPHATASE ALCALINE, D'AST ET D'ALT.

DIAGNOSTICS INFIRMIERS POSSIBLES

- Habitudes de sommeil perturbées (Effets secondaires).
- Connaissances insuffisantes sur le traitement médicamenteux (Enseignement au patient et à ses proches).

INTERVENTIONS INFIRMIÈRES

- Lorsque les symptômes du trouble déficitaire de l'attention avec hyperactivité sont maîtrisés, on peut envisager de réduire la dose ou d'interrompre le traitement durant l'été, les week-ends ou lorsque l'enfant est soumis à un moindre stress.

PO: Administrer la dose quotidienne le matin, avec ou après le repas, pour diminuer l'anorexie.

ENSEIGNEMENT AU PATIENT ET À SES PROCHES

- Recommander au patient de prendre le médicament le matin afin de prévenir les troubles du sommeil. S'il n'a pu prendre le médicament au moment habituel, il doit le prendre dès que possible; s'il ne peut le prendre que le jour suivant, il doit sauter cette dose et reprendre le programme thérapeutique prescrit. Lui expliquer qu'il ne doit jamais remplacer une dose manquée par une double dose. Lors d'un traitement à la pémoline, le risque de dépendance et d'abus est élevé. La tolérance aux effets du médicament se manifeste rapidement; ne pas augmenter la dose. Inciter le patient à consulter un professionnel de la santé avant de cesser le traitement. Chez le patient suivant un traitement prolongé, il faut réduire graduellement la dose afin de prévenir les symptômes de sevrage. Le sevrage brusque après un traitement à des doses élevées peut provoquer une fatigue extrême et la dépression.
- Prévenir le patient que la pémoline peut entraîner des étourdissements. Lui conseiller de ne pas conduire et d'éviter les activités qui exigent sa vigilance jusqu'à ce qu'on ait la certitude que le médicament n'entraîne pas cet effet chez lui.
- Conseiller au patient de ne pas consommer des quantités importantes de caféine.
- Informer le patient du risque d'insuffisance hépatique. Les parents devraient signer un consentement éclairé concernant ce risque avant le début du traitement. Recommander au patient ou aux parents de prévenir immédiatement un professionnel de la santé en présence des signes et des symptômes suivants: peau ou sclérotiques jaunes, anorexie, troubles gastro-intestinaux, selles pâles ou urine foncée, palpitations, transpiration, fièvre ou tremblements incontrôlés. Leur recommander de prévenir également un professionnel de la santé si la nervosité, l'agitation, l'insomnie ou les étourdissements s'aggravent.
- Informer le patient qu'on peut lui prescrire un arrêt temporaire de la médication permettant d'évaluer les bienfaits du traitement et de diminuer le risque de dépendance.
- Insister sur l'importance des examens réguliers de suivi permettant d'évaluer les bienfaits du traitement.

Trouble déficitaire de l'attention avec hyperactivité: Recommander aux parents d'informer l'infirmière de l'école que l'enfant suit un traitement par ce médicament.

VÉRIFICATION DE L'EFFICACITÉ THÉRAPEUTIQUE

L'efficacité du traitement peut être démontrée par: un effet calmant associé à une hyperactivité moindre et à une durée prolongée de l'attention chez les enfants souffrant d'un trouble déficitaire de l'attention avec hyperactivité. Des effets bénéfiques notables peuvent ne pas se manifester avant la troisième ou la quatrième semaine de traitement, car l'état clinique du patient s'améliore graduellement. ✳

P

PENCICLOVIR

Denavir

CLASSIFICATION:

Antiviral (topique)

Grossesse – catégorie B

INDICATION

Herpès labial récurrent (feux sauvages) chez l'adulte.

MÉCANISME D'ACTION

Inhibition de la synthèse de l'ADN viral et de sa réplication. ***Effets thérapeutiques:*** Diminution de la durée et de l'étendue de la lésion, ainsi que de la douleur.

PHARMACOCINÉTIQUE

Absorption: 0 % (topique).

Distribution: Inconnue.

Métabolisme et excrétion: Transformation intracellulaire en sa forme triphosphate active; excrétion rénale.
Demi-vie: De 2 à 2,5 heures.

Profil temps-action

	DÉBUT D'ACTION	PIC	DURÉE
Topique	inconnu	inconnu	inconnue

CONTRE-INDICATIONS, PRÉCAUTIONS ET MISES EN GARDE

Contre-indications: Hypersensibilité au penciclovir ou à un autre ingrédient de la préparation.
Précautions et mises en garde: OBST.: Grossesse ou allaitement ■ **PÉD.:** L'innocuité de l'agent n'a pas été établie ■ Patients immunocompromis (l'innocuité de l'agent n'a pas été établie).

RÉACTIONS INDÉSIRABLES ET EFFETS SECONDAIRES

Locaux: réactions au siège de l'application.

INTERACTIONS

Médicament-médicament: Aucune interaction notable.

VOIES D'ADMINISTRATION ET POSOLOGIE

- **PO (adultes):** Appliquer la crème dès l'apparition des premiers symptômes, et toutes les 2 heures par la suite, pendant 4 jours, durant les heures de veille.

P

PRÉSENTATION

Crème: 1 %, tubes de 2 g[Pr].

SOINS INFIRMIERS

ÉVALUATION DE LA SITUATION

- Évaluer les lésions avant le traitement et pendant toute sa durée.

DIAGNOSTICS INFIRMIERS POSSIBLES

- Risque d'atteinte à l'intégrité de la peau (Indications).
- Risque d'infection (Indications, Enseignement au patient et à ses proches).
- Connaissances insuffisantes sur le traitement médicamenteux (Enseignement au patient et à ses proches).

INTERVENTIONS INFIRMIÈRES

- NE PAS CONFONDRE DENAVIR (PENCICLOVIR) AVEC L'INDINAVIR.
- Commencer le traitement le plus rapidement possible, pendant la phase prodromique ou dès l'apparition des lésions.
- Appliquer sur les lèvres et le visage seulement; éviter l'application sur les muqueuses ou la région périoculaire.

ENSEIGNEMENT AU PATIENT ET À SES PROCHES

- Recommander au patient d'appliquer le médicament en respectant rigoureusement les recommandations du médecin pendant toute la durée de traitement prescrite. S'il n'a pas pu appliquer le médicament à l'heure prévue, l'appliquer dès que possible, puis continuer l'application toutes les 2 heures. Le prévenir qu'il ne doit pas utiliser le penciclovir plus souvent ou plus longtemps que le médecin ne l'a prescrit.
- Informer le patient que l'application d'autres crèmes, lotions ou onguents en vente libre peut retarder la guérison et favoriser la propagation des lésions.

VÉRIFICATION DE L'EFFICACITÉ THÉRAPEUTIQUE

L'efficacité du traitement peut être démontrée par: une cicatrisation plus rapide des lésions et la diminution de la douleur provoquée par le virus de l'herpès labial.

PÉNICILLAMINE

Cuprimine

CLASSIFICATION:
Agent antirhumatismal modificateur de la maladie [AARMM], antiurolithique, antidote (chélateur)

Grossesse – catégorie D

INDICATIONS

Traitement de la polyarthrite rhumatoïde grave et évolutive, rebelle au traitement classique ■ Traitement de la maladie de Wilson due à l'accumulation de dépôts de cuivre ■ Traitement de la cystinurie récurrente ■ Traitement du saturnisme chronique.

MÉCANISME D'ACTION

Effet antirhumatismal probablement attribuable à une fonction lymphocytaire accrue ■ Chélation des métaux lourds, incluant le cuivre, le mercure, le plomb et le fer et formation de complexes excrétés par les reins ■ Formation de complexes solubles avec la cystine, facilement excrétés par les reins. ***Effets thérapeutiques:*** Ralentissement de l'évolution de la polyarthrite rhumatoïde ▪ Diminution de l'accumulation de dépôts de cuivre chez les patients souffrant de la maladie de Wilson ▪ Réduction de la formation de calculs de cystine dans les reins.

PHARMACOCINÉTIQUE

Absorption: Bonne (PO).

Distribution: La pénicillamine traverse la barrière placentaire.

Métabolisme et excrétion: Une partie du médicament est excrétée dans l'urine sous forme de complexe pénicillamine-métaux lourds, une deuxième partie est excrétée dans l'urine sous forme de complexe pénicillamine-cystine et une troisième est métabolisée par le foie.

Demi-vie: De 1 à 7,5 heures (de 4 à 6 jours en cas d'usage prolongé).

Profil temps-action

	DÉBUT D'ACTION	PIC	DURÉE
PO (antirhumatismal)	2 - 3 mois	inconnu	1 - 3 mois
PO (maladie de Wilson)	1 - 3 mois	inconnu	inconnue

CONTRE-INDICATIONS, PRÉCAUTIONS ET MISES EN GARDE

Contre-indications: Patients recevant des sels d'or, des antipaludéens, des cytotoxiques, de l'oxyphenbutazone ou de la phénylbutazone ▪ Antécédents ou signes d'insuffisance rénale (risque accru d'effets nocifs sur les reins chez les patients souffrant de polyarthrite rhumatoïde) ▪ Antécédents d'anémie aplasique ou d'agranulocytose attribuables à la pénicillamine ▪ Patients atteints de saturnisme chronique chez lesquels un cliché radiologique révèle la présence, dans le tube digestif, de substances renfermant du plomb ▪ **OBST.**: Il n'est pas recommandé d'administrer la pénicillamine pendant la grossesse, sauf pour le traitement de la maladie de Wilson ou de certains cas de cystinurie ▪ Allaitement.

Précautions et mises en garde: Hypersensibilité ▪ Risque de réactions de sensibilité croisée avec la pénicilline (risque théorique) ▪ Risque de décès associé à certaines affections comme l'anémie aplasique, l'agranulocytose, la thrombopénie, le syndrome de Goodpasture et la myasthénie grave ▪ Protéinurie et hématurie ▪ Risque d'hépatotoxicité ▪ Risque de neurotoxicité ▪ Risque de pemphigus ▪ Risque de fièvre médicamenteuse accompagnée ou non d'une éruption cutanée maculaire ▪ Risque d'hypogueusie ▪ Traitement concomitant par des suppléments de fer ▪ Les patients souffrant de polyarthrite rhumatoïde, dont l'alimentation n'est pas parfaitement équilibrée, doivent prendre un supplément quotidien de pyridoxine ▪ Patients devant subir une intervention chirurgicale (le médicament peut retarder la cicatrisation de la plaie) ▪ **PÉD.**: Risque accru de toxicité hématologique; il est recommandé de réduire la dose ▪ **OBST.**: En présence de maladie de Wilson, limiter la dose quotidienne à < 1 g. Si un accouchement par césarienne est prévu, réduire la dose quotidienne jusqu'à 250 mg pendant les 6 dernières semaines de grossesse et jusqu'à la cicatrisation de l'incision.

RÉACTIONS INDÉSIRABLES ET EFFETS SECONDAIRES

ORLO: vision trouble, douleurs oculaires.

Resp.: toux, essoufflement, respiration sifflante.

GI: altération du goût, anorexie, ictère cholestatique, diarrhée, pancréatite médicamenteuse, dyspepsie, douleurs épigastriques, dysfonctionnement hépatique, nausées, aphtes buccaux, vomissements.

GU: protéinurie.

Tég.: pemphigus, ecchymoses, urticaire, démangeaisons, rash, formation de rides.

Hémat.: ANÉMIE APLASIQUE, anémie, éosinophilie, leucopénie, thrombopénie, thrombocytose.

Loc.: arthralgie, polyarthrite migratoire.

SN: syndrome myasthénique.

Divers: SYNDROME DE GOODPASTURE (GLOMÉRULONÉPHRITE ET HÉMORRAGIE INTRA-ALVÉOLAIRE), réactions allergiques, fièvre, lymphadénopathie, syndrome lupoïde.

INTERACTIONS

Médicament-médicament: Risque accru d'effets nocifs hématologiques lors de l'administration concomitante d'**antinéoplasiques**, d'**agents immunosuppresseurs** et de **sels d'or** (éviter l'administration concomitante) ▪ Les **suppléments de fer**, administrés en concomitance, diminuent l'absorption de la pénicillamine ▪ L'utilisation concomitante d'un **supplément de sels minéraux** peut inhiber la réponse à la pénicillamine ▪ La pénicillamine peut réduire les concentrations sériques de **digoxine**.

Médicament-aliments: La pénicillamine peut augmenter les besoins en **pyridoxine** (**vitamine B_6**).

VOIES D'ADMINISTRATION ET POSOLOGIE

Il est important de recommander aux patients de prendre la pénicillamine à jeun, au moins 1 heure avant les repas ou 2 heures après, et d'espacer d'au moins 1 heure la prise de tout autre médicament ou aliment ou la consommation de lait, pour assurer une meilleure absorption et pour réduire le risque d'une éventuelle inactivation par fixation à un métal.

P

Agent antirhumatismal

- **PO (adultes)**: de 125 à 250 mg par jour, en une seule dose; on peut augmenter lentement la dose jusqu'à concurrence de 1,5 g par jour.

Chélateur (maladie de Wilson)

- **PO (adultes)**: 250 mg, 4 fois par jour. La dose peut être augmentée selon le dosage urinaire du cuivre. Il est rarement nécessaire de dépasser 2 g/jour. Chez les malades qui ne peuvent pas tolérer la posologie initiale de 1 g/jour, il est préférable de commencer le traitement avec une dose de 250 mg/jour et de l'augmenter graduellement jusqu'à l'atteinte de la dose appropriée, permettant ainsi une meilleure maîtrise des effets du médicament et la diminution de l'incidence des effets secondaires.

Cystinurie

- **PO (adultes)**: 500 mg, 4 fois par jour (écart posologique: de 1 à 4 g/jour).
- **PO (enfants)**: 7,5 mg/kg, 4 fois par jour.

Saturnisme chronique

- **PO (adultes)**: de 900 à 1 500 mg/jour, en 3 doses fractionnées, pendant 1 ou 2 semaines, puis 750 mg/jour, en doses fractionnées.
- **PO (enfants)**: de 30 à 40 mg/kg/jour ou de 600 à 750 mg/m^2/jour, sans dépasser 750 mg/jour en une seule fois ou en 2 doses fractionnées.

PRÉSENTATION

Capsules: 250 mg[Pr].

SOINS INFIRMIERS

ÉVALUATION DE LA SITUATION

- Effectuer le bilan quotidien des ingesta et des excreta, peser le patient tous les jours et l'observer attentivement pendant toute la durée du traitement pour déceler l'œdème. Prévenir le médecin ou un autre professionnel de la santé en cas d'œdème ou de gain pondéral.
- Suivre de près les réactions allergiques (rash, fièvre). Interrompre le traitement et le reprendre à une dose plus faible (250 mg par jour), puis l'augmenter graduellement. On peut administrer de la prednisone à 20 mg par jour, pendant les premières semaines de traitement afin de réduire la gravité des réactions. On peut aussi administrer des antihistaminiques pour soulager le prurit.

Arthrite: Noter l'intensité de la douleur et l'ampleur des mouvements des articulations à intervalles réguliers tout au long du traitement.

Cystinurie: Noter tous les ans les résultats des examens radiologiques des reins pour déceler la formation de calculs.

Tests de laboratoire:

- Noter la numération globulaire et la formule leucocytaire, la numération plaquettaire et les résultats de l'analyse des urines (particulièrement pour déceler la protéinurie et l'hématurie) au moins toutes les 2 semaines durant les 6 premiers mois de traitement ou après la majoration de la dose, et, tous les mois, par la suite. La pénicillamine peut provoquer de la leucopénie, de l'anémie et de la thrombopénie. Interrompre le traitement si le nombre de globules blancs est $< 3,5 \times 10^9$/L, de polynucléaires neutrophiles $< 2 \times 10^9$/L, de monocytes $< 0,5 \times 10^9$/L, de plaquettes $< 100 \times 10^9$/L ou en cas d'hématurie.
- Examiner les résultats des tests de la fonction hépatique tous les 6 mois durant les 18 premiers mois de traitement.
- La pénicillamine peut entraîner un résultat positif au dosage des anticorps antinucléaires.
- La pénicillamine peut entraîner l'hypoglycémie.
- *Arthrite:* Noter les concentrations de protéines dans les urines de 24 heures à intervalles de 1 ou 2 semaines chez les patients présentant une protéinurie modérée.
- *Maladie de Wilson:* Noter les concentrations urinaires de cuivre avant le début du traitement et peu après, puis tous les 3 mois tout au long d'un traitement continu.
- *Cystinurie:* Mesurer les concentrations urinaires de cystine. L'excrétion de cystine dans l'urine devrait se maintenir à moins de 100 mg chez les patients ayant des antécédents de douleurs ou de calculs ou entre 100 et 200 mg chez les patients n'ayant pas d'antécédents de calculs.

DIAGNOSTICS INFIRMIERS POSSIBLES

- Douleur aiguë (Indications).
- Connaissances insuffisantes sur le traitement médicamenteux (Enseignement au patient et à ses proches).

INTERVENTIONS INFIRMIÈRES

- Administrer la pénicillamine à jeun, au moins 1 heure avant les repas ou 2 heures après. L'administration d'autres médicaments doit être espacée d'au moins 1 heure afin d'assurer l'absorption maximale de la pénicillamine.
- Ne pas administrer la pénicillamine en même temps que des préparations contenant du fer.

- La pénicillamine augmente les besoins quotidiens en pyridoxine. Il peut s'avérer nécessaire de prescrire des suppléments de pyridoxine (vitamine B_6) à raison de 25 mg par jour chez les patients dont l'état nutritionnel est altéré.

Arthrite:

- Une adaptation de la posologie peut s'avérer nécessaire tous les 2 ou 3 mois tout au long du traitement.
- Si aucune amélioration n'est observée après 3 ou 4 mois de traitement à des doses de 1 à 1,5 g par jour, il faut arrêter l'administration du médicament.

Maladie de Wilson: On peut administrer du sulfure de potassium (de 10 à 40 mg) avec des aliments afin de réduire l'absorption du cuivre.

ENSEIGNEMENT AU PATIENT ET À SES PROCHES

- Conseiller au patient de respecter rigoureusement la posologie recommandée. Dans le cas de prises uniquotidiennes, si le patient n'a pu prendre le médicament au moment habituel, il doit le prendre dès que possible au cours de la même journée; s'il doit prendre le médicament 2 fois par jour, il doit le prendre dès que possible à moins que ce ne soit presque l'heure prévue pour la dose suivante. En cas de prises plus fréquentes, il doit prendre le médicament dans l'heure suivante, sinon il doit sauter cette dose. Le prévenir qu'il ne faut jamais remplacer une dose manquée par une double dose.
- Prévenir le patient qu'il doit consulter un professionnel de la santé avant d'arrêter de prendre le médicament, car l'interruption du traitement peut entraîner des réactions de sensibilité lorsqu'il est repris. Le traitement doit être repris en commençant par la plus faible dose qu'on augmentera graduellement.
- Prévenir le patient que la pénicillamine peut altérer la sensibilité gustative. On peut traiter l'hypogueusie par l'administration de 5 à 10 mg de cuivre par jour. Lui recommander de mélanger de 5 à 10 gouttes de solution de sulfate de cuivre à 4 % à du jus de fruits et de prendre le mélange 2 fois par jour. Ce type de traitement est contre-indiqué chez les patients souffrant de la maladie de Wilson.
- Recommander au patient qui doit suivre un autre traitement ou subir une intervention chirurgicale d'avertir le professionnel de la santé qu'il suit un traitement avec ce médicament. La dose de pénicillamine doit rester faible jusqu'à la cicatrisation complète de la plaie.
- Recommander au patient de prévenir un professionnel de la santé en cas de rash, de saignements ou d'ecchymoses inhabituels, de maux de gorge, de dyspnée d'effort, de toux ou de respiration sifflante inexpliquées, de fièvre, de frissons ou d'autres effets inhabituels.
- Insister sur l'importance des examens réguliers de suivi permettant d'évaluer les bienfaits du traitement.

Maladie de Wilson: Recommander au patient de demander à un professionnel de la santé quelles sont les restrictions alimentaires qu'il devrait observer. Une alimentation à faible teneur en cuivre pourrait s'avérer nécessaire. Conseiller au patient d'éviter de consommer du chocolat, des noix, des fruits de mer, des champignons, du foie, de la mélasse, du brocoli et des céréales enrichies de cuivre. Si l'eau potable contient plus de 100 µg/L de cuivre, il devrait boire de l'eau distillée ou déminéralisée.

Cystinurie:

- Recommander au patient de consommer au moins 2 000 à 3 000 mL de liquides par jour, en prenant de plus grandes quantités le soir.
- Recommander au patient de demander à un professionnel de la santé quelles sont les restrictions alimentaires qu'il devrait observer. Une alimentation à faible teneur en méthionine peut s'avérer nécessaire pour réduire la production de cystine, mais, en raison de sa faible teneur en protéines, elle est contre-indiquée chez les enfants en période de croissance ou chez les femmes enceintes.

VÉRIFICATION DE L'EFFICACITÉ THÉRAPEUTIQUE

L'efficacité du traitement peut être démontrée par: la diminution de la douleur et l'augmentation de l'amplitude des mouvements chez les patients souffrant de polyarthrite rhumatoïde ■ la prévention et le traitement des symptômes de la maladie de Wilson ■ la prévention et le traitement des calculs rénaux chez les patients présentant des concentrations excessives de cystine dans l'urine.

P

PÉNICILLINES

pénicilline G potassique
Novo-Pen G, Pénicilline G potassique

pénicilline G sodique
Crystapen, Schein pénicilline G Na, Pénicilline G sodique

pénicilline V
Apo-Pen VK, Novo-Pen-VK, Nu-Pen-VK, Pen-Vee

pénicilline G procaïnique
Ce médicament n'est pas commercialisé au Canada.

pénicilline G benzathinique

Disponible par l'intermédiaire du Programme d'accès spécial de Santé Canada.

CLASSIFICATION:

Antibiotiques

Grossesse - catégorie B

INDICATIONS

Traitement d'une vaste gamme d'infections dues à des souches pathogènes sensibles, incluant: la pneumonie à pneumocoques ■ la pharyngite à streptocoques ■ la syphilis ■ la gonorrhée (souches sensibles à la pénicilline seulement) ■ les infections de la peau et des tissus mous ■ l'actinomycose ■ Prévention du rhumatisme articulaire aigu.

MÉCANISME D'ACTION

Liaison à la paroi de la cellule bactérienne entraînant sa destruction. ***Effets thérapeutiques:*** Effet bactéricide contre les bactéries sensibles. **Spectre d'action:** Activité contre: la plupart des agents pathogènes à Gram positif dont de nombreux streptocoques (*Streptococcus pneumoniæ*, streptocoques bêtahémolytiques du groupe A) et les staphylocoques (souches ne produisant pas de pénicillinase) ■ certains microorganismes à Gram négatif dont *Neisseria meningitidis* et *Neisseria gonorrhϾ (seules les souches sensibles à la pénicilline)* ■ les spirochètes et certaines bactéries anaérobies.

P

PHARMACOCINÉTIQUE

Absorption: Variable (PO). La *pénicilline V* résiste à la décomposition par le milieu acide du tractus gastrointestinal. *Pénicilline benzathine:* Absorption retardée et prolongée résultant en des taux sériques soutenus (IM).

Distribution: Répartition dans tout l'organisme, bien qu'en l'absence d'une inflammation des méninges, la pénicilline ne pénètre dans le système nerveux central qu'en quantités infimes. Elle traverse la barrière placentaire et passe dans le lait maternel.

Liaison aux protéines: 60 %.

Métabolisme et excrétion: Métabolisme hépatique faible. Excrétion majoritairement rénale.

Demi-vie: De 30 à 60 minutes.

Profil temps-action (concentrations sanguines)

	DÉBUT D'ACTION	PIC	DURÉE
Pénicilline PO	rapide	0,5 - 1 h	4 - 6 h
Pénicilline G - IM	rapide	0,25 - 0,5 h	4 - 6 h
Pénicilline G - IV	rapide	fin de la perfusion	4 - 6 h
Pénicilline G benzathinique - IM	retardé	12 - 24 h	3 semaines

CONTRE-INDICATIONS, PRÉCAUTIONS ET MISES EN GARDE

Contre-indications: Antécédents d'hypersensibilité aux pénicillines (risque de réactions de sensibilité croisée avec les céphalosporines) ■ Hypersensibilité à la tartrazine (éviter dans ce cas l'administration des pénicillines qui peuvent contenir cet additif) ■ Hypersensibilité à la benzathine (préparations contenant la pénicilline G benzathinique seulement) ■ Infections dues à des microorganismes produisant de la bêtalactamase ■ Application topique (hypersensibilisation).

Précautions et mises en garde: GÉR.: Tenir compte de la diminution de la masse musculaire, ainsi que de la diminution des fonctions rénale, hépatique et cardiaque, des maladies concomitantes et de la médication ■ Insuffisance rénale grave (il est recommandé de réduire la dose) ■ **OBST.:** Sans risque pour le fœtus ■ **ALLAITEMENT:** Bien que cet antibiotique soit généralement considéré comme sûr, de faibles quantités peuvent passer dans le lait maternel (risque d'altération de la flore intestinale, de diarrhée et de réactions d'hypersensibilité chez le nourrisson).

RÉACTIONS INDÉSIRABLES ET EFFETS SECONDAIRES

SNC: CONVULSIONS.

GI: diarrhée, douleurs épigastriques, nausées, vomissements, colite pseudomembraneuse.

GU: néphrite interstitielle.

Tég.: rash, urticaire.

Hémat.: éosinophilie, anémie hémolytique, leucopénie.

Locaux: douleur au point d'injection IM, phlébite au point d'injection IV.

Divers: réactions allergiques incluant l'ANAPHYLAXIE et la MALADIE SÉRIQUE, surinfection.

INTERACTIONS

Médicament-médicament: La pénicilline V peut diminuer l'efficacité des contraceptifs oraux ■ Le **probénécide** diminue l'excrétion rénale de la pénicilline et en augmente les concentrations sanguines (on peut utiliser un traitement d'association dans ce but) ■ La **néomycine** peut diminuer l'absorption de la pénicilline V ■ Lors d'une administration concomitante, l'élimination du **méthotrexate** est réduite et le risque de toxicité grave est accru.

VOIES D'ADMINISTRATION ET POSOLOGIE

Remarque: 1 mg de pénicilline G = 1 600 unités; la pénicilline G sodique renferme 2 mmol de sodium/million d'unités; la pénicilline G potassique renferme 1,7 mmol de potassium et 0,3 mmol de sodium/million d'unités.

Pénicilline G

- **IM, IV (adultes et enfants > 12 ans) :** De 1 million d'unités/jour par voie IM à 20 millions d'unités/jour par voie IV, en 4 à 6 doses fractionnées. Des doses plus fortes peuvent être nécessaires pour traiter les infections plus graves.
- **IM, IV (enfants de 1 mois à 12 ans) :** De 50 000 à 250 000 unités/kg/jour en 4 doses fractionnées. Des doses plus fortes (de 250 000 à 400 000 unités/kg/jour, en doses fractionnées, toutes les 4 à 6 heures) peuvent être nécessaires pour traiter les infections plus graves.
- **IM, IV (nourrissons de 1 semaine à 1 mois) :** De 50 000 à 200 000 unités/kg/jour, en doses fractionnées toutes les 6 heures (si le poids est > 2 kg), toutes les 8 heures (si le poids est ≥ 1,2 kg à ≤ 2 kg) ou toutes les 12 heures (si le poids est < 1,2 kg).
- **IM, IV (nourrissons < 1 semaine) :** De 50 000 à 100 000 unités/kg/jour, en doses fractionnées, toutes les 8 heures (si le poids est > 2 kg) ou toutes les 12 heures (si le poids est ≤ 2 kg).
- **Méningite due aux streptocoques du groupe B chez les nouveau-nés :** De 250 000 à 400 000 unités/kg/jour, en doses fractionnées, toutes les 6 à 8 heures.
- ***INSUFFISANCE RÉNALE :*** *CL_{CR} < 30 mL/MIN* – ADMINISTRER TOUTES LES 8 HEURES ; *CL_{CR} < 10 mL/MIN* – ADMINISTRER TOUTES LES 12 HEURES.

Pénicilline V

- **PO (adultes et enfants > 12 ans) :** *La plupart des infections* – 500 000 unités, toutes les 6 à 8 heures. Il est recommandé d'administrer la dose toutes les 6 heures dans le traitement de la pharyngite ou des infections pneumococciques des voies respiratoires. *Prévention du rhumatisme articulaire aigu* – 250 000 unités, toutes les 12 heures.
- **PO (enfants < 12 ans) :** De 25 000 à 90 000 unités/kg/jour en 3 à 6 doses fractionnées.

Pénicilline G benzathinique

- **IM :** *Syphilis primaire, syphilis secondaire, syphilis récente latente* – 2,4 millions d'unités, pour une seule dose. *Syphilis tardive latente, syphilis tertiaire* – 2,4 millions d'unités, 1 fois par semaine, pour 3 doses.

PRÉSENTATION (version générique disponible)

- **Pénicilline G potassique**
  Poudre pour injection : 1 million d'unités/fiole[Pr], 5 millions d'unités/fiole[Pr], 10 millions d'unités/fiole[Pr].
- **Pénicilline G sodique**
  Poudre pour injection : 1 million d'unités/fiole[Pr], 5 millions d'unités/fiole[Pr], 10 millions d'unités/fiole[Pr].
- **Pénicilline V**
  Comprimés : 500 000 unités (300 mg)[Pr] ▪ **Solution orale :** 200 000 unités (125 mg)/5 mL[Pr], 400 000 unités (250 mg)/5 mL[Pr], 500 000 unités (300 mg)/5 mL[Pr] ▪ **Suspension orale :** 300 000 unités (180 mg)/5 mL[Pr], 500 000 unités (300 mg)/5 mL[Pr].
- **Pénicilline G procaïnique**
  Ce médicament n'est pas commercialisé au Canada.
- **Pénicilline G benzathinique**
  Disponible par l'intermédiaire du Programme d'accès spécial de Santé Canada.
  Poudre pour injection : 1,2 million d'unités/fiole[Pr].

SOINS INFIRMIERS

ÉVALUATION DE LA SITUATION

- Au début du traitement et pendant toute sa durée, rester à l'affût des signes suivants d'infection : altération des signes vitaux, aspect de la plaie, des crachats, de l'urine et des selles, accroissement du nombre de leucocytes.
- Recueillir les antécédents du patient avant d'amorcer le traitement afin de déterminer ses réactions antérieures à une pénicilline ou à une céphalosporine. Même les personnes n'ayant jamais manifesté de sensibilité à la pénicilline peuvent présenter une réaction allergique.
- Prélever les échantillons pour les cultures et les antibiogrammes avant le début du traitement. La première dose peut être administrée avant que les résultats soient connus.
- RESTER À L'AFFÛT DES SIGNES ET DES SYMPTÔMES SUIVANTS D'ANAPHYLAXIE : RASH, PRURIT, ŒDÈME LARYNGÉ, RESPIRATION SIFFLANTE. SI CES RÉACTIONS SE MANIFESTENT, ARRÊTER L'ADMINISTRATION DU MÉDICAMENT ET PRÉVENIR IMMÉDIATEMENT LE MÉDECIN OU UN AUTRE PROFESSIONNEL DE LA SANTÉ. GARDER À PORTÉE DE LA MAIN DE L'ADRÉNALINE, UN ANTIHISTAMINIQUE ET LE MATÉRIEL DE RÉANIMATION POUR PARER À UNE ÉVENTUELLE RÉACTION ANAPHYLACTIQUE.

Tests de laboratoire :

- La pénicilline peut positiver le test de Coombs direct.
- Une hyperkaliémie peut survenir par suite de l'administration de doses élevées de pénicilline G potassique.

P

- Mesurer les concentrations sériques de sodium chez les patients souffrant d'hypertension ou d'insuffisance cardiaque. Une hypernatrémie peut survenir après l'administration de doses élevées de pénicilline G sodique.
- La pénicilline peut entraîner une élévation des concentrations sériques d'AST, d'ALT, de LDH et de phosphatase alcaline.
- La pénicilline peut entraîner une leucopénie ou une neutropénie, particulièrement en cas de traitement prolongé ou d'insuffisance hépatique.

DIAGNOSTICS INFIRMIERS POSSIBLES

- Risque d'infection (Indications, Effets secondaires).
- Connaissances insuffisantes sur le traitement médicamenteux (Enseignement au patient et à ses proches).
- Non-observance du traitement médicamenteux (Enseignement au patient et à ses proches).

INTERVENTIONS INFIRMIÈRES

PO:

- Administrer la pénicilline à intervalles réguliers. La pénicilline V peut être administrée sans égard aux repas.
- Utiliser un récipient gradué pour mesurer les préparations liquides.

IM, IV: Reconstituer la solution avec de l'eau stérile pour injection, de solution de D5%E ou de NaCl 0,9 %, en suivant les directives du fabricant.

P

IM:

- Bien mélanger la préparation avant de l'administrer. Injecter profondément dans un muscle bien développé à un débit lent et régulier afin de prévenir le blocage de l'aiguille. Bien masser le point d'injection. L'injection accidentelle dans un nerf ou à sa proximité peut entraîner une douleur et un dysfonctionnement graves.

Pénicilline G benzathinique: Cette préparation de pénicilline se présente sous forme de poudre à diluer. Une fois reconstituée, elle forme une suspension et non une solution. Diluer la poudre juste avant de l'administrer. Si la dilution ne précède pas immédiatement l'injection, un précipité qui bloquera l'aiguille peut se former. Consulter les directives du fabricant avant de reconstituer la préparation.

- On peut diluer la pénicilline G potassique ou sodique avec de la lidocaïne à 1 % ou à 2 % (sans adrénaline) afin de réduire la douleur provoquée par l'injection IM.
- Ne jamais administrer la pénicilline G benzathinique par voie IV, en raison du risque de réactions graves, telles qu'une embolie ou une réaction toxique.

IV:

- Changer de point d'injection toutes les 48 heures afin de prévenir la phlébite.
- Administrer lentement la pénicilline destinée aux injections IV et observer de près le patient pour déceler les signes d'hypersensibilité.

Perfusion intermittente: Diluer les doses de 3 millions d'unités ou moins dans au moins 50 mL et celles de plus de 3 millions d'unités dans 100 mL de solution de D5%E ou de NaCl 0,9%.

Vitesse d'administration: Perfuser en 1 à 2 heures, chez les adultes, et en 15 à 30 minutes, chez les enfants.

Pénicilline G potassique

Compatibilité (tubulure en Y): acyclovir ■ amiodarone ■ cyclophosphamide ■ diltiazem ■ énalaprilate ■ esmolol ■ fluconazole ■ foscarnet ■ héparine ■ hydromorphone ■ labétolol ■ magnésium, sulfate de ■ mépéridine ■ morphine ■ perphénazine ■ potassium, chlorure de ■ tacrolimus ■ vérapamil ■ vitamines du complexe B avec C.

Incompatibilité (tubulure en Y): Si des aminosides et des pénicillines doivent être administrés en même temps, choisir des points d'injection séparés et espacer les injections d'au moins 1 heure.

Incompatibilité en addition au soluté: La pénicilline est incompatible avec les aminosides; ne pas mélanger.

Pénicilline G sodique

Incompatibilité (tubulure en Y): Si des aminosides et des pénicillines doivent être administrés en même temps, choisir des points d'injection séparés et espacer les injections d'au moins 1 heure.

Incompatibilité en addition au soluté: La pénicilline est incompatible avec les aminosides; ne pas mélanger.

ENSEIGNEMENT AU PATIENT ET À SES PROCHES

- Recommander au patient de prendre toute la quantité de médicament qui lui a été prescrite, à intervalles réguliers, même s'il se sent mieux. Insister sur le fait qu'il peut être dangereux de donner ce médicament à une autre personne.
- Recommander au patient de signaler à un professionnel de la santé tout signe d'allergie et les signes suivants de surinfection: excroissance noire et pileuse sur la langue, démangeaisons et écoulements vaginaux, selles molles ou nauséabondes.
- CONSEILLER AU PATIENT DE CONSULTER UN PROFESSIONNEL DE LA SANTÉ EN CAS DE FIÈVRE OU DE DIARRHÉE, PARTICULIÈREMENT SI SES SELLES RENFERMENT DU SANG, DU PUS OU DU MUCUS. LUI RECOMMANDER DE NE PAS TRAITER LA DIARRHÉE SANS

AVOIR CONSULTÉ UN PROFESSIONNEL DE LA SANTÉ AU PRÉALABLE.

- Recommander au patient de prévenir un professionnel de la santé si les symptômes ne diminuent pas.
- Recommander à la patiente qui utilise des contraceptifs oraux de se servir jusqu'aux règles suivantes d'une méthode de contraception non hormonale additionnelle durant l'antibiothérapie par la pénicilline V.
- Conseiller au patient allergique à la pénicilline de toujours porter sur lui une pièce d'identité mentionnant cette information.

VÉRIFICATION DE L'EFFICACITÉ THÉRAPEUTIQUE

L'efficacité du traitement peut être démontrée par: la disparition des signes et des symptômes d'infection; le temps de la résolution dépend du microorganisme infectant et du siège de l'infection ▪ la prévention du rhumatisme articulaire aigu. ✳

PENTAMIDINE

Pentamidine

CLASSIFICATION:

Anti-infectieux (antiprotozoaire)

Grossesse – catégorie C

INDICATIONS

Injection: Traitement de la pneumonie attribuable à *Pneumocystis carinii* ▪ **Inhalation**: Prévention de la pneumonie à *Pneumocystis carinii* chez les sujets VIH positifs, exposés à un risque élevé, défini par l'un des critères suivants ou par les deux à la fois: antécédents d'un ou de plusieurs épisodes de pneumonie à *Pneumocystis carinii*; numération lymphocytaire des cellules CD_4 + périphériques (cellules T auxiliaires) inférieure ou égale à 200/µL, ou taux de CD_4 inférieur à 20 % du nombre total de lymphocytes. **Usages non approuvés – Inhalation**: Traitement de la pneumonie attribuable à *Pneumocystis carinii*.

MÉCANISME D'ACTION

Inhibition probable de la synthèse de l'ADN ou de l'ARN des protozoaires. ***Effets thérapeutiques:*** Destruction des protozoaires sensibles.

PHARMACOCINÉTIQUE

Absorption: Absorption systémique négligeable (par inhalation).

Distribution: Tout l'organisme. L'agent ne traverse pas la barrière hématoencéphalique. Il se concentre dans le foie, les reins, les poumons et la rate et reste emmagasiné pendant une période prolongée dans certains tissus.

Métabolisme et excrétion: Excrétion rénale sous forme inchangée et de métabolites.

Demi-vie: De 6,4 à 9,4 heures (prolongée en cas d'insuffisance rénale).

Profil temps-action

	DÉBUT D'ACTION	PIC	DURÉE
IV	inconnu	fin de la perfusion	24 h
Inhalation	inconnu	inconnu	inconnue

CONTRE-INDICATIONS, PRÉCAUTIONS ET MISES EN GARDE

Contre-indications: Antécédents d'hypersensibilité à la pentamidine ou à un de ses sels.

Précautions et mises en garde: Hypotension ▪ Hypertension ▪ Hypoglycémie ▪ Hyperglycémie ▪ Hypocalcémie ▪ Leucopénie ▪ Thrombopénie ▪ Anémie ▪ Insuffisance rénale (réduire la dose) ▪ Diabète ▪ Insuffisance hépatique ▪ Maladie cardiovasculaire ▪ Aplasie médullaire, traitement antinéoplasique ou radiothérapie préalables ▪ **OBST., ALLAITEMENT**: L'innocuité du médicament n'a pas été établie.

RÉACTIONS INDÉSIRABLES ET EFFETS SECONDAIRES

Sauf indication contraire, les effets secondaires et les réactions ci-dessous ont été observés par suite de l'administration du médicament par voie parentérale.

SNC: anxiété, céphalées, confusion, étourdissements, hallucinations.

ORLO: *inhalation* – sensation de brûlure dans la gorge.

Resp.: *inhalation* – bronchospasme, toux.

CV: ARYTHMIES, HYPOTENSION.

GI: PANCRÉATITE, douleurs abdominales, anorexie, hépatite médicamenteuse, nausées, goût métallique désagréable, vomissements.

GU: néphrotoxicité.

Tég.: pâleur, rash.

End.: HYPOGLYCÉMIE, hyperglycémie.

HÉ: hyperkaliémie, hypocalcémie.

Hémat.: anémie, leucopénie, thrombopénie.

Locaux: *IV* – phlébite, prurit, urticaire au point d'injection; *IM* – abcès stérile au point d'injection.

Divers: réactions allergiques incluant l'ANAPHYLAXIE et le SYNDROME DE STEVENS-JOHNSON, frissons, fièvre.

P

INTERACTIONS

Les interactions ci-dessous ont été observées lors de l'administration du médicament par voie parentérale.

Médicament-médicament: L'ADMINISTRATION CONCOMITANTE D'**ÉRYTHROMYCINE** PAR VOIE IV PEUT ACCROÎTRE LE RISQUE D'ARYTHMIES POUVANT METTRE LA VIE DU PATIENT EN DANGER ■ Toxicité rénale additive lors de l'usage concomitant d'autres **agents pouvant provoquer une toxicité rénale**, incluant les **aminosides**, l'**amphotéricine B** et la **vancomycine** ■ Aplasie médullaire additive lors de l'usage concomitant d'**antinéoplasiques** ou dans le cas d'une **radiothérapie** préalable ■ Risque accru de pancréatite lors de l'administration concomitante de **didanosine** ■ Risque accru de néphrotoxicité, d'hypocalcémie et d'hypomagnésémie lors de l'administration concomitante de **foscarnet**.

VOIES D'ADMINISTRATION ET POSOLOGIE

- **IV, IM (adultes et enfants):** De 3 à 4 mg/kg, 1 fois par jour, pendant 14 à 21 jours.
- **Inhalation (adultes):** 300 mg, toutes les 4 semaines, administrés par un nébuliseur Respirgard II.

PRÉSENTATION
(version générique disponible)

Poudre pour injection: 300 mg/fiole[Pr].

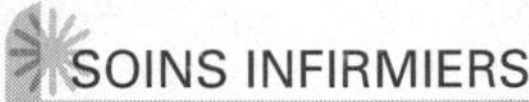

SOINS INFIRMIERS

ÉVALUATION DE LA SITUATION

- Au début du traitement et pendant toute sa durée, suivre de près les signes suivants d'infection: altération des signes vitaux, aspect des crachats, accroissement du nombre de globules blancs. Suivre de près la fonction respiratoire (fréquence et caractéristique des respirations, murmure vésiculaire, dyspnée, aspect des crachats).
- Prélever des échantillons pour l'analyse des cultures et des antibiogrammes avant le début du traitement. On peut administrer la première dose avant que les résultats de ces analyses soient connus.

IM, IV:

- MESURER LA PRESSION ARTÉRIELLE À INTERVALLES FRÉQUENTS PENDANT ET APRÈS L'ADMINISTRATION DE LA PENTAMIDINE PAR VOIE IM OU IV. LE PATIENT DOIT RESTER COUCHÉ DURANT L'ADMINISTRATION DU MÉDICAMENT. UNE HYPOTENSION SOUDAINE ET GRAVE PEUT SURVENIR APRÈS L'ADMINISTRATION D'UNE SEULE DOSE. GARDER À PORTÉE DE LA MAIN LE MATÉRIEL DE RÉANIMATION CARDIORESPIRATOIRE.
- SURVEILLER LES SIGNES D'HYPOGLYCÉMIE (ANXIÉTÉ, FRISSONS, DIAPHORÈSE, PEAU PÂLE ET FROIDE, CÉPHALÉES, FAIM ACCRUE, NAUSÉES, NERVOSITÉ, TREMBLEMENTS) et d'hyperglycémie (somnolence, peau sèche et rouge, haleine ayant une odeur fruitée, soif accrue, mictions accrues, perte d'appétit). Ces signes peuvent se manifester jusqu'à plusieurs mois après l'arrêt du traitement.
- MESURER LE POULS ET EXAMINER L'ÉCG AVANT LE TRAITEMENT ET À INTERVALLES RÉGULIERS PENDANT TOUTE SA DURÉE. ON A SIGNALÉ DES DÉCÈS ATTRIBUABLES À DES ARYTHMIES, À LA TACHYCARDIE ET À UNE TOXICITÉ CARDIAQUE.

Inhalation: Pour écarter la présence de la tuberculose, on devrait soumettre le patient à un test cutané à la tuberculine, prendre une radiographie pulmonaire et mettre en culture ses expectorations avant l'administration du médicament.

Tests de laboratoire:

- *IM, IV* – Mesurer la glycémie avant le traitement, tous les jours pendant toute sa durée et pendant plusieurs mois par la suite. On a déjà signalé des cas d'hypoglycémie grave et de diabète irréversible.
- Mesurer les concentrations sériques d'urée et de créatinine avant le traitement et quotidiennement pendant toute sa durée pour déceler l'apparition d'une toxicité rénale. La pentamidine peut entraîner une élévation des concentrations de ces substances.
- Examiner les numérations globulaire et plaquettaire avant le traitement et tous les 3 jours pendant toute sa durée. La pentamidine peut provoquer la leucopénie, l'anémie et la thrombopénie.
- La pentamidine peut entraîner une élévation des concentrations sériques de bilirubine, de phosphatase alcaline, d'AST et d'ALT. Il faut effectuer ces tests de la fonction hépatique avant le traitement et tous les 3 jours pendant toute sa durée.
- Suivre de près les concentrations sériques de calcium et de magnésium avant le traitement et tous les 3 jours pendant toute sa durée, car la pentamidine peut provoquer une hypocalcémie et une hypomagnésémie.
- La pentamidine peut entraîner une élévation des concentrations sériques de potassium.

DIAGNOSTICS INFIRMIERS POSSIBLES

- Risque d'infection (Indications, Effets secondaires).
- Connaissances insuffisantes sur le traitement médicamenteux (Enseignement au patient et à ses proches).

INTERVENTIONS INFIRMIÈRES

- La pentamidine doit être administrée selon un horaire fixe pendant toute la durée du traitement. S'il est impossible d'administrer la dose au moment habituel, on doit le faire dès que possible. S'il est presque l'heure prévue pour la dose suivante, on doit sauter cette dose et reprendre l'horaire habituel. Il ne faut jamais remplacer une dose manquée par une double dose.

IM: Diluer 300 mg de pentamidine avec 3 mL d'eau stérile pour injection, pour obtenir une concentration de 100 mg/mL. L'administration par voie IM devrait être réservée aux patients ayant une masse musculaire adéquate. Le médicament devrait alors être injecté profondément, selon la technique en Z. L'injection peut provoquer des abcès stériles.

Perfusion intermittente: Pour reconstituer la solution, ajouter 3 mL d'eau stérile pour injection à la fiole de 300 mg, pour obtenir une concentration de 100 mg/mL. Retirer la dose et diluer une fois de plus dans 50 à 500 mL de solution de D5%E ou de NaCl 0,9 %. La solution diluée dans du D5%E ou du NaCl 0,9 % de façon à obtenir une concentration finale d'environ 2 mg/mL est stable pendant 24 heures à la température ambiante. Jeter toute portion inutilisée.

Vitesse d'administration: Administrer la perfusion lentement, en 1 à 3 heures.

Compatibilité (tubulure en Y): diltiazem ▪ zidovudine.

Incompatibilité (tubulure en Y): céfazoline ▪ céfotaxime ▪ céfoxitine ▪ ceftazidime ▪ ceftriaxone ▪ fluconazole ▪ foscarnet.

Inhalation:

- Si le patient doit prendre un bronchodilatateur par inhalation, administrer le bronchodilatateur de 5 à 10 minutes avant la pentamidine.
- Administrer l'agent dans une pièce bien aérée.
- La pentamidine semble se répartir plus uniformément si le patient reste couché pendant l'administration.
- Diluer 300 mg dans 6 mL d'eau stérile pour injection. Vider la solution reconstituée dans un nébuliseur Respirgard II. Ne pas diluer avec une solution de NaCl 0,9 % ni mélanger à d'autres médicaments, car un précipité se formera dans la solution. Ne pas utiliser le nébuliseur Respirgard II pour administrer d'autres médicaments.
- Administrer la dose à inhaler à l'aide du nébuliseur jusqu'à ce que la chambre soit vide, soit pendant environ 30 à 45 minutes.

ENSEIGNEMENT AU PATIENT ET À SES PROCHES

Inciter le patient à prendre toute la quantité de pentamidine qui lui a été prescrite, même s'il se sent mieux.

IV:

- Conseiller au patient de signaler rapidement à un professionnel de la santé les symptômes suivants: fièvre, maux de gorge, signes d'infection, saignement des gencives, formation d'ecchymoses, pétéchies ou présence de sang dans les urines, les selles ou les vomissements. Conseiller au patient d'éviter les foules et les personnes contagieuses. Lui recommander d'utiliser une brosse à dents à poils doux et un rasoir électrique. Mettre en garde le patient contre les chutes. Éviter les injections IM et la prise de la température rectale. Recommander au patient de ne pas consommer de boissons alcoolisées ni de prendre des médicaments contenant de l'aspirine ou des anti-inflammatoires non stéroïdiens, en raison du risque d'hémorragie gastrique.
- Recommander au patient de changer lentement de position afin de réduire le risque d'hypotension orthostatique.

Inhalation:

- Expliquer au patient que le goût métallique désagréable est un effet secondaire prévisible de la pentamidine, mais qu'il ne s'agit pas d'un effet nuisible.
- Expliquer au patient qui continue de fumer que le risque de bronchospasme et de toux est accru pendant le traitement.

VÉRIFICATION DE L'EFFICACITÉ THÉRAPEUTIQUE

L'efficacité du traitement peut être démontrée par: la prévention ou la disparition des signes et des symptômes de pneumonie à *Pneumocystis carinii*, chez les patients VIH positifs. ✳

P

ALERTE CLINIQUE

PENTAZOCINE

Talwin

CLASSIFICATION:

Analgésique opioïde (agoniste-antagoniste)

Grossesse – catégories C et D (en usage prolongé ou à doses élevées près du terme)

INDICATIONS

Soulagement des douleurs chroniques ou aiguës, de modérées à intenses ▪ Analgésie durant le travail de l'accouchement ▪ Sédation avant une intervention chirurgicale ▪ Supplément lors d'une anesthésie équilibrée.

MÉCANISME D'ACTION

Liaison aux récepteurs des opioïdes du SNC ▪ Modification de la perception de la douleur et de la réaction aux stimuli douloureux avec dépression généralisée du SNC ■ Propriétés antagonistes partielles qui peuvent déclencher des symptômes de sevrage aux opioïdes en cas de dépendance physique. ***Effets thérapeutiques:*** Soulagement de la douleur modérée à intense.

PHARMACOCINÉTIQUE

Absorption: Bonne (PO).

Distribution: Le médicament se répartit largement dans l'organisme. Il traverse le placenta.

Métabolisme et excrétion: Métabolisme majoritairement hépatique. De petites quantités sont excrétées à l'état inchangé par les reins.

Demi-vie: De 2 à 5 heures.

Profil temps-action (effet analgésique)

	Début d'action	Pic	Durée
PO	15 - 30 min	60 - 90 min	3 h
IM et SC	15 - 20 min	30 - 60 min	2 - 3 h
IV	2 - 3 min	15 - 30 min	2 - 3 h

CONTRE-INDICATIONS, PRÉCAUTIONS ET MISES EN GARDE

Contre-indications: Hypersensibilité à la pentazocine ou à un de ses composés.

Précautions et mises en garde: Dépendance physique aux opioïdes (le médicament peut déclencher des symptômes de sevrage) ■ Traumatisme crânien ■ Troubles convulsifs ■ Antécédents de pharmacodépendance ■ Pression intracrânienne accrue ■ Maladies rénale, hépatique ou pulmonaire graves ■ Hypothyroïdie ■ Insuffisance surrénalienne ■ Alcoolisme ■ Personnes âgées, patients débilités ou patients souffrant d'insuffisance hépatique grave (il est recommandé de réduire la dose) ■ Troubles des voies biliaires ■ Douleurs abdominales non diagnostiquées ■ Hyperplasie de la prostate ■ Patients ayant reçu un traitement récent par des agonistes opioïdes ■ Allergie aux sulfites (les comprimés contiennent du métabisulfite) ■ **Obst.**: Bien que le médicament ait été administré durant le travail de l'accouchement, il peut entraîner une dépression respiratoire chez le nouveau-né ■ **Allaitement, Péd.**: L'innocuité du médicament n'a pas été établie ■ Risque de pharmacodépendance et d'abus.

RÉACTIONS INDÉSIRABLES ET EFFETS SECONDAIRES

SNC: étourdissements, euphorie, hallucinations, céphalées, sédation, confusion, dysphorie, sensation de flottement, rêves bizarres.

ORLO: vision trouble, diplopie, myosis (fortes doses).

Resp.: DÉPRESSION RESPIRATOIRE.

CV: hypertension, hypotension, palpitations.

GI: nausées, constipation, sécheresse de la bouche (xérostomie), iléus, vomissements.

GU: rétention urinaire.

Locaux: lésions tissulaires aux points d'injection souscutanée.

Tég.: peau moite et froide, transpiration.

Divers: dépendance physique, dépendance psychologique, tolérance aux effets du médicament.

INTERACTIONS

Médicament-médicament: RISQUE DE RÉACTIONS IMPRÉVISIBLES CHEZ LES PATIENTS RECEVANT EN CONCOMITANCE UN **IMAO** (RÉDUIRE LA DOSE INITIALE DE PENTAZOCINE JUSQU'À 25 % DE LA DOSE HABITUELLE) ■ Dépression additive du SNC et du système respiratoire lors de l'usage concomitant d'**alcool**, d'**antihistaminiques**, de **phénothiazines**, de **barbituriques**, d'**antidépresseurs**, d'**hypnosédatifs** et d'autres **opioïdes** ■ La pentazocine peut déclencher des symptômes de sevrage chez les patients présentant une dépendance physique aux **analgésiques opioïdes agonistes** ■ Le médicament peut diminuer les effets analgésiques d'autres **analgésiques opioïdes** administrés en concomitance.

Médicament-produits naturels: Effets dépresseurs additifs sur le SNC lors de la consommation concomitante de **kava**, de **valériane**, de **scutellaire**, de **camomille** et de **houblon**.

VOIES D'ADMINISTRATION ET POSOLOGIE

- **PO (adultes)**: De 50 à 100 mg, toutes les 3 à 4 heures. En raison du risque de sédation marquée chez les personnes âgées, maintenir une posologie réduite chez ce groupe de patients.
- **IV, IM, SC (adultes)**: Dose initiale de 30 mg. Par la suite, la posologie peut être adaptée selon la réaction du patient et l'intensité de la douleur, soit de 30 à 60 mg, toutes les 3 à 4 heures (une dose unique ne doit normalement pas excéder 1 mg/kg par voie IM ou SC, ou 0,5 mg/kg par voie IV. La dose quotidienne totale ne doit pas dépasser 360 mg). *Travail de l'accouchement* – 20 mg IV ou 30 mg IM lorsque les contractions deviennent régulières; on peut répéter cette dose 2 ou 3 fois, à intervalles de 2 à 3 heures.

PRÉSENTATION

Comprimés: 50 mg^{N} ■ **Solution pour injection**: 30 mg/mL^{N}.

SOINS INFIRMIERS

ÉVALUATION DE LA SITUATION

- Déterminer le type de douleur, son siège et son intensité, avant l'administration du médicament et 60 minutes (pic) après l'administration PO. Lorsqu'on majore la dose d'un opioïde, on devrait l'augmenter de 25 à 50 % jusqu'à ce qu'on note une réduction de 50 % de la douleur, selon l'évaluation qu'en fait le patient sur une échelle numérique ou visuelle analogue ou jusqu'à ce que le patient signale un soulagement adéquat de la douleur. On peut administrer sans danger une autre dose au moment du pic, si la dose précédente s'est avérée inefficace et que les effets secondaires sont minimes. Chez les patients ayant besoin de doses supérieures à 100 mg, on devrait remplacer la pentazocine par un agoniste opioïde. La pentazocine n'est pas recommandée en traitement prolongé ou de première intention en cas de douleur aiguë ou liée au cancer.
- On devrait utiliser un tableau d'équivalences (voir l'annexe A) au moment de changer de voie d'administration ou de type d'opioïde.
- ÉVALUER L'ÉTAT DE CONSCIENCE, MESURER LA PRESSION ARTÉRIELLE, LE POULS ET LA FRÉQUENCE RESPIRATOIRE AVANT ET À INTERVALLES RÉGULIERS PENDANT TOUTE LA DURÉE DE L'ADMINISTRATION. SI LA FRÉQUENCE RESPIRATOIRE EST < 10/MIN, ÉVALUER LE DEGRÉ DE SÉDATION. DES STIMULI PHYSIQUES PEUVENT PARFOIS SUFFIRE POUR PRÉVENIR UNE HYPOVENTILATION IMPORTANTE. IL PEUT S'AVÉRER NÉCESSAIRE DE RÉDUIRE LA DOSE DE 25 À 50 %. La pentazocine entraîne une dépression respiratoire, mais cet effet n'augmente pas de façon marquée si la dose est accrue.

GÉR.: Évaluer les patients âgés à intervalles fréquents, car ils sont plus sensibles aux effets des analgésiques opioïdes que les adultes plus jeunes; chez eux, les effets indésirables et les complications respiratoires peuvent être plus fréquents.

- Recueillir des données sur les antécédents de prise d'analgésiques. En raison de ses propriétés antagonistes, le médicament peut induire chez les patients dépendants aux opioïdes les symptômes de sevrage suivants: vomissements, agitation, crampes abdominales, pression artérielle accrue et fièvre.
- Bien que le risque de dépendance soit faible, l'administration prolongée de cet agent peut entraîner une dépendance physique et psychologique ainsi qu'une tolérance aux effets du médicament, mais cela ne doit pas empêcher le patient de recevoir une quantité suffisante d'analgésiques. La psychodépendance est rare chez la plupart des patients qui reçoivent de la pentazocine pour des raisons médicales. Si une tolérance aux effets du médicament se développe, il peut s'avérer nécessaire de remplacer la pentazocine par un analgésique opioïde agoniste pour soulager la douleur.

Tests de laboratoire: La pentazocine peut entraîner une élévation des concentrations sériques d'amylase et de lipase.

TOXICITÉ ET SURDOSAGE: S'il est nécessaire d'administrer un antagoniste opioïde pour renverser la dépression respiratoire ou le coma, l'antidote est la naloxone (Narcan). Diluer l'ampoule de naloxone à 0,4 mg dans 10 mL de solution de NaCl 0,9 % et administrer 0,5 mL (0,02 mg) par bolus IV direct, toutes les 2 minutes. Dans le cas des patients < 40 kg, diluer 0,1 mg de naloxone dans 10 mL de solution de NaCl 0,9 % pour obtenir une concentration de 10 µg/mL et administrer 0,5 µg/kg, toutes les 2 minutes. Adapter graduellement la dose pour prévenir les symptômes de sevrage, les convulsions et la douleur intense.

DIAGNOSTICS INFIRMIERS POSSIBLES

- Douleur aiguë (Indications).
- Risque d'accident (Effets secondaires).
- Trouble de la perception visuelle et auditive (Effets secondaires).

INTERVENTIONS INFIRMIÈRES

ALERTE CLINIQUE: DES SURDOSES ACCIDENTELLES D'ANALGÉSIQUES OPIOÏDES ONT CAUSÉ DES DÉCÈS. ÉVALUER L'UTILISATION ANTÉRIEURE D'ANALGÉSIQUES OPIOÏDES PAR LE PATIENT ET SES BESOINS COURANTS. AVANT L'ADMINISTRATION, CLARIFIER TOUTES LES AMBIGÜITÉS DE L'ORDONNANCE ET FAIRE VÉRIFIER L'ORDONNANCE D'ORIGINE ET LE CALCUL DES DOSES PAR UN AUTRE PROFESSIONNEL DE LA SANTÉ.

- Pour augmenter l'effet analgésique de la pentazocine, avant de l'administrer, expliquer au patient la valeur thérapeutique de ce médicament.
- Les doses administrées selon un horaire fixe peuvent être plus efficaces que celles administrées sur demande. L'analgésique s'avère plus efficace s'il est administré avant que la douleur ne devienne intense.
- L'association avec des analgésiques non opioïdes peut avoir des effets analgésiques additifs et permettre d'administrer des doses plus faibles de pentazocine.
- Après un traitement prolongé, interrompre l'administration graduellement pour prévenir les symptômes de sevrage.

IM, SC: Administrer l'injection IM profondément dans un muscle bien développé en assurant la rotation des points d'injection. L'administration SC répétée peut provoquer des lésions tissulaires.

IV directe: Diluer chaque 5 mg avec 1 mL d'eau stérile pour injection.

Vitesse d'administration: Administrer lentement, à une vitesse de 5 mg/min.

Associations compatibles dans la même seringue: atropine ■ chlorpromazine ■ cimétidine ■ dimenhydrinate ■ diphenhydramine ■ dropéridol ■ hydroxyzine ■ métocloparmide ■ perphénazine ■ prochlorpérazine ■ prométhazine ■ ranitidine ■ scopolamine.

Incompatibilité dans la même seringue: glycopyrrolate ■ héparine ■ pentobarbital.

Compatibilité (tubulure en Y): héparine ■ hydrocortisone ■ potassium, chlorure de ■ vitamines du complexe B avec C.

ENSEIGNEMENT AU PATIENT ET À SES PROCHES

- Expliquer au patient ce qu'on entend par administration sur demande et à quel moment il doit réclamer l'analgésique.
- Prévenir le patient que la pentazocine peut provoquer des étourdissements, de la somnolence ou des hallucinations, particulièrement chez les personnes âgées. Lui recommander de demander de l'aide lorsqu'il se déplace. Lui conseiller de ne pas conduire et d'éviter les activités qui exigent sa vigilance jusqu'à ce qu'on ait la certitude que le médicament n'entraîne pas ces effets chez lui. Mettre en place des stratégies de prévention des chutes et enseigner au patient et à sa famille les méthodes de prévention à cet égard.
- Recommander au patient de changer lentement de position pour diminuer le risque d'hypotension orthostatique.
- Inciter le patient à ne pas boire d'alcool et à ne pas prendre d'autres dépresseurs du SNC en même temps que la pentazocine.
- Conseiller au patient de se tourner dans le lit, de tousser et de faire des exercices de respiration profonde toutes les 2 heures pour prévenir l'atélectasie.
- Recommander au patient de se rincer fréquemment la bouche, de pratiquer une bonne hygiène buccale et de consommer de la gomme ou des bonbons sans sucre pour aider à soulager la sécheresse de la bouche.

VÉRIFICATION DE L'EFFICACITÉ THÉRAPEUTIQUE

L'efficacité du traitement peut être démontrée par: la diminution de l'intensité de la douleur sans modification importante de l'état de conscience ou de l'état respiratoire. ✳

PENTOBARBITAL

Nembutal

CLASSIFICATION:

Anticonvulsivant (barbiturique), anxiolytique et hypnosédatif

Grossesse – catégorie D

INDICATIONS

Induction d'un état de sédation ou d'hypnose ■ Sédation préopératoire ■ À doses anesthésiques, dans le traitement d'urgence de certains états convulsifs associés au tétanos, à l'état de mal épileptique et aux réactions toxiques à la strychnine ou aux anesthésiques locaux. **Usages non approuvés – IV**: Induction du coma chez certains patients souffrant d'ischémie cérébrale et traitement de la pression intracrânienne accrue (doses élevées).

MÉCANISME D'ACTION

Dépression du SNC probablement par potentialisation de l'acide gamma-aminobutyrique (GABA), qui est un neurotransmetteur inhibiteur ■ Dépression du SNC à tous les niveaux, incluant la dépression de la zone sensorielle du cortex, la diminution de l'activité motrice et la modification de la fonction cérébelleuse ■ Effet anticonvulsivant attribuable à la diminution de la transmission synaptique et à l'élévation du seuil de convulsions ■ Diminution possible du débit sanguin cérébral, de l'œdème cérébral et de la pression intracrânienne (voie IV seulement). ***Effets thérapeutiques:*** Sédation ou induction du sommeil.

PHARMACOCINÉTIQUE

Absorption: Bonne (IM).

Distribution: Tout l'organisme. Les concentrations les plus élevées se retrouvent dans le cerveau et le foie. L'agent traverse la barrière placentaire et passe dans le lait maternel.

Métabolisme et excrétion: Métabolisme hépatique. De petites quantités sont excrétées par les reins.

Demi-vie: De 35 à 50 heures.

Profil temps-action (sédation)

	DÉBUT D'ACTION	PIC	DURÉE†
IM	10 – 25 min	inconnu	1 – 4 h
IV	immédiat	1 min	15 min

† Effet hypnotique; les effets sédatifs durent plus longtemps.

CONTRE-INDICATIONS, PRÉCAUTIONS ET MISES EN GARDE

Contre-indications: Hypersensibilité aux barbituriques ■ Antécédents de dépendance aux hypnosédatifs (sauf en cas d'urgence) ■ Dépression respiratoire grave ■ Porphyrie latente ou manifeste ■ Risque de délire (ne pas administrer le médicament seul pour calmer la douleur) ■ **GÉR.**: Confusion nocturne et agitation ■ Patients suicidaires ou ayant des antécédents de toxicomanie.

Précautions et mises en garde: Coma ou dépression préexistante du SNC (à moins que le médicament ne soit administré pour induire le coma) ■ Dysfonction hépatique ■ Insuffisance rénale grave ■ Douleurs violentes réfractaires ■ Grossesse ou allaitement ■ **GÉR.**: Il est recommandé de réduire la dose initiale ■ Hypersensibilité ou intolérance à l'alcool ou au propylène glycol (éviter les préparations qui contiennent ces additifs chez ce type de patients).

RÉACTIONS INDÉSIRABLES ET EFFETS SECONDAIRES

SNC: somnolence, sensation d'euphorie, léthargie, délire, excitation, dépression, vertiges.

Resp.: dépression respiratoire; *IV* – LARYNGOSPASME, bronchospasme.

CV: *IV* – hypotension.

GI: constipation, diarrhée, nausées, vomissements.

Tég.: rash, urticaire.

Locaux: phlébite au point d'injection IV.

Loc.: arthralgie, myalgie, névralgie.

Divers: réactions d'hypersensibilité incluant l'ŒDÈME ANGIONEUROTIQUE et la MALADIE SÉRIQUE, dépendance physique, dépendance psychologique.

INTERACTIONS

Médicament-médicament: Effets dépressifs additifs sur le SNC lors de l'usage concomitant d'autres **dépresseurs du SNC** dont l'**alcool**, les **antihistaminiques**, les **analgésiques opioïdes** et d'autres **hypnosédatifs** ■ Le médicament peut activer les enzymes hépatiques qui métabolisent d'autres médicaments, diminuant ainsi leur efficacité. Il s'agit des médicaments suivants: **contraceptifs oraux**, **warfarine**, **chloramphénicol**, **cyclosporine**, **dacarbazine**, **corticostéroïdes**, **antidépresseurs tricycliques** et **quinidine** ■ Le pentobarbital peut accroître le risque d'intoxication hépatique par l'**acétaminophène** ■ Les **IMAO**, l'**acide valproïque** ou le **divalproex**, administrés en concomitance, peuvent ralentir le métabolisme du pentobarbital et intensifier ses effets sédatifs.

VOIES D'ADMINISTRATION ET POSOLOGIE

- **IM (adultes et enfants):** La posologie dépend de l'âge, du poids et de l'état du malade. Chez les adultes, elle va de 150 à 200 mg; chez les enfants, elle est fréquemment de 2 à 6 mg/kg sans dépasser 100 mg par dose.
- **IV (adultes et enfants):** Il n'existe pas de posologie courante ou soumise à une règle fixe. Il est recommandé de fractionner les doses. La première dose fractionnée peut être de 100 mg, chez les adultes, et de 50 mg, chez les enfants. Attendre 1 minute ou plus avant d'administrer une deuxième injection afin de pouvoir évaluer les résultats de la première. Si une quantité additionnelle est nécessaire, on poursuivra l'administration par petites doses fractionnées de 50 mg chez les adultes et de 25 mg chez les enfants, à des intervalles de 1 minute pour pouvoir évaluer les réactions du patient, jusqu'à ce que l'on puisse obtenir l'effet désiré. En cas d'états convulsifs, on administrera la posologie la plus basse possible pour ne pas aggraver la dépression qui peut survenir. La plupart des cas de convulsions peuvent être enrayés grâce à une faible dose d'attaque, suivie par l'administration à intervalles réguliers de doses fractionnées, jusqu'à concurrence de 200 à 500 mg, selon la réponse du patient (adulte normal).

PRÉSENTATION

Solution pour injection: 50 mg/mL, en ampoules de 2 mL[C].

P

SOINS INFIRMIERS

ÉVALUATION DE LA SITUATION

- Suivre de près la fonction respiratoire, mesurer le pouls et la pression artérielle à intervalles fréquents chez les patients recevant le pentobarbital par voie IV. Garder à portée de la main le matériel de réanimation et de respiration artificielle. La gravité de la dépression respiratoire est proportionnelle à la dose administrée.
- Suivre de près la douleur chez les patients ayant subi une intervention chirurgicale. Le pentobarbital peut augmenter la réaction aux stimuli douloureux.

Œdème cérébral: Suivre de près la pression intracrânienne et le degré de conscience du patient en cas de coma induit par le barbiturique.

Convulsions: Évaluer le siège, la durée et les caractéristiques des convulsions. Mettre en place des mesures de précaution.

DIAGNOSTICS INFIRMIERS POSSIBLES

- Risque d'accident (Effets secondaires).
- Connaissances insuffisantes sur le traitement médicamenteux (Enseignement au patient et à ses proches).

INTERVENTIONS INFIRMIÈRES

- Surveiller les déplacements du patient après l'administration du médicament et retirer les cigarettes. Remonter les ridelles du lit et laisser la sonnette d'appel à portée de la main en tout temps. Garder le lit en position basse.

IM: Ne pas administrer par voie SC. Administrer les injections IM profondément dans le muscle fessier pour diminuer l'irritation des tissus. Ne pas injecter plus de 5 mL dans un seul point étant donné le risque d'irritation tissulaire.

IV directe:

- On peut administrer les doses telles quelles ou les diluer dans de l'eau stérile, dans une solution de NaCl 0,45 % ou de NaCl 0,9 %, de D5%E ou de D10%E, de solution de Ringer ou de lactate de Ringer, dans une solution qui associe du dextrose et du soluté salin, du dextrose et de la solution de Ringer ou du dextrose et de la solution de lactate de Ringer. Ne pas administrer la solution si elle a changé de couleur ou si elle contient des particules.
- La solution est très alcaline; éviter l'extravasation, en raison des risques de lésion et de nécrose des tissus.

P

Vitesse d'administration: Administrer l'injection à un débit maximal de 50 mg/min. Ajuster lentement la dose jusqu'à l'obtention de la réaction désirée. L'administration rapide peut provoquer une dépression respiratoire, l'apnée, le laryngospasme, le bronchospasme ou l'hypertension.

Association compatible dans la même seringue: scopolamine.

Association incompatible dans la même seringue: glycopyrrolate.

Compatibilité (tubulure en Y): acyclovir ■ insuline régulière.

ENSEIGNEMENT AU PATIENT ET À SES PROCHES

- Prévenir le patient que le pentobarbital peut provoquer une somnolence diurne. Lui conseiller de ne pas conduire et d'éviter les activités qui exigent sa vigilance jusqu'à ce qu'on ait la certitude que le médicament n'entraîne pas cet effet chez lui.
- Conseiller au patient d'éviter de boire de l'alcool et de prendre des dépresseurs du SNC en concomitance avec ce médicament.
- Recommander à la patiente de prévenir immédiatement un professionnel de la santé si elle pense être enceinte.

VÉRIFICATION DE L'EFFICACITÉ THÉRAPEUTIQUE

L'efficacité du traitement peut être démontrée par: la prévention de l'anoxie cérébrale ■ la diminution ou la disparition des convulsions sans sédation excessive. ✳

PENTOXIFYLLINE

Apo-Pentoxifylline SR, Ratio-Pentoxifylline, Trental

CLASSIFICATION:

Agent vasoactif (diminution de la viscosité du sang)

Grossesse – catégorie C

INDICATIONS

Traitement symptomatique des patients atteints d'affections vasculaires périphériques oblitérantes chroniques. La pentoxifylline peut soulager les signes et les symptômes associés à l'altération du flux sanguin, tels que la claudication intermittente ou les ulcères trophiques.

MÉCANISME D'ACTION

Augmentation de la souplesse des globules rouges par l'élévation des concentrations d'adénosine monophosphate cyclique (AMPc) ■ Diminution de la viscosité du sang par inhibition de l'agrégation plaquettaire et par diminution du fibrinogène. ***Effets thérapeutiques***: Amélioration du flux sanguin périphérique.

PHARMACOCINÉTIQUE

Absorption: Bonne (PO), mais métabolisme de premier passage hépatique important (biodisponibilité absolue à 20 %).

Distribution: L'agent se lie à la membrane érythrocytaire, traverse la barrière placentaire et passe dans le lait maternel.

Métabolisme et excrétion: Métabolisme par les globules rouges et le foie. Excrétion rénale sous forme de métabolites.

Demi-vie: De 25 à 50 minutes.

Profil temps-action (amélioration du flux sanguin)

	DÉBUT D'ACTION	PIC	DURÉE
PO	2 - 4 semaines	8 semaines	8 h

CONTRE-INDICATIONS, PRÉCAUTIONS ET MISES EN GARDE

Contre-indications: Hypersensibilité ▪ Intolérance aux autres dérivés de xanthine (caféine, théobromine et théophylline) ▪ Infarctus aigu du myocarde ▪ Coronaropathie grave ▪ Hémorragie active ou patients à risque d'hémorragie ▪ Ulcères gastroduodénaux en poussée évolutive ou antécédents récents.

Précautions et mises en garde: Insuffisance hépatique (une réduction de la dose peut s'avérer nécessaire) ▪ Insuffisance rénale (une réduction de la dose peut être nécessaire) ▪ **GÉR.:** Il est recommandé d'adapter la dose chez les personnes âgées ou débilitées puisqu'elles présentent un risque accru de réactions indésirables ▪ **OBST., ALLAITEMENT, PÉD.:** L'innocuité du médicament n'a pas été établie chez les femmes enceintes ou qui allaitent ni chez les enfants < 18 ans.

RÉACTIONS INDÉSIRABLES ET EFFETS SECONDAIRES

SNC: agitation, étourdissements, somnolence, céphalées, insomnie, nervosité.

ORLO: vision trouble.

Resp.: dyspnée.

Hémat.: pancytopénie, purpura, thrombopénie, leucopénie, anémie, anémie aplasique.

CV: angine, arythmies, œdème, bouffées vasomotrices, hypotension.

GI: gêne abdominale, éructations, ballonnements, diarrhée, dyspepsie, flatulences, nausées, vomissements.

SN: tremblements.

INTERACTIONS

Médicament-médicament: Risque d'hypotension additive lors de l'administration concomitante d'**antihypertenseurs** et de **dérivés nitrés** ▪ La pentoxifylline peut accroître le risque de saignements en cas d'administration concomitante de **warfarine**, d'**héparine**, d'**énoxaparine**, de **daltéparine**, d'**aspirine**, d'**AINS**, de **clopidogrel**, de **ticlopidine**, d'**eptifibatide**, de **tirofiban** ou d'**agents thrombolytiques** ▪ La pentoxifylline peut accroître le risque de toxicité associée à la **théophylline** ▪ L'usage du **tabac** (**nicotine**) peut réduire les effets bénéfiques de la pentoxifylline.

Médicament-produits naturels: Risque accru de saignements lors de la consommation concomitante de **fenouil**, d'**arnica**, de **camomille**, de **trèfle**, de **dong quai**, de **fenugrec**, d'**ail**, de **gingembre**, de **ginkgo**, de **ginseng** et de **réglisse**.

VOIES D'ADMINISTRATION ET POSOLOGIE

- **PO (adultes):** La dose initiale recommandée est de 400 mg, 2 fois par jour. La dose d'entretien habituelle est de 400 mg, 2 ou 3 fois par jour. La dose quotidienne maximale est de 1 200 mg.

PRÉSENTATION

Comprimés à libération prolongée: 400 mg^Pr^.

SOINS INFIRMIERS

ÉVALUATION DE LA SITUATION

- Suivre de près la claudication intermittente avant le traitement et à intervalles réguliers pendant toute sa durée.
- Mesurer la pression artérielle à intervalles réguliers chez les patients recevant un traitement antihypertenseur concomitant.

DIAGNOSTICS INFIRMIERS POSSIBLES

- Douleur aiguë (Indications).
- Intolérance à l'activité (Indications).
- Connaissances insuffisantes sur le traitement médicamenteux (Enseignement au patient et à ses proches).

INTERVENTIONS INFIRMIÈRES

- Administrer la pentoxifylline avec des aliments afin de réduire l'irritation gastro-intestinale. DEMANDER AU PATIENT D'AVALER LES COMPRIMÉS TELS QUELS SANS LES ÉCRASER, LES BRISER NI LES MÂCHER.
- En cas d'effets sur l'appareil gastro-intestinal ou sur le SNC, administrer le médicament seulement 2 fois par jour. Cesser l'administration si les effets secondaires persistent.

ENSEIGNEMENT AU PATIENT ET À SES PROCHES

- Conseiller au patient de respecter rigoureusement la posologie recommandée. S'il n'a pu prendre le médicament au moment habituel, il doit le prendre dès que possible, à moins que ce ne soit presque l'heure prévue pour la dose suivante. Conseiller au patient de consulter un professionnel de la santé avant d'arrêter de prendre le médicament, car plusieurs semaines peuvent s'écouler avant que les effets de cet agent se manifestent.

P

- Prévenir le patient que la pentoxifylline peut entraîner des étourdissements et une vision trouble. Lui conseiller de ne pas conduire et d'éviter les activités qui exigent sa vigilance jusqu'à ce qu'on ait la certitude que le médicament n'entraîne pas ces effets chez lui.
- Recommander au patient d'éviter de fumer puisque la nicotine a un effet vasoconstricteur.
- Recommander au patient de prévenir un professionnel de la santé en cas de nausées, de vomissements, de gêne gastro-intestinale, de somnolence, d'étourdissements et de céphalées persistantes.

VÉRIFICATION DE L'EFFICACITÉ THÉRAPEUTIQUE

L'efficacité du traitement peut être démontrée par: le soulagement des crampes des muscles du mollet, des fesses, des cuisses et des pieds qui surviennent pendant l'effort ■ l'amélioration de l'endurance pendant la marche. Les effets thérapeutiques peuvent se manifester en l'espace de 2 à 4 semaines, mais le traitement devrait être poursuivi pendant au moins 8 semaines. ✳

PÉRINDOPRIL,

voir Inhibiteurs de l'enzyme de conversion de l'angiotensine (IECA)

P

PERMÉTHRINE

Kwellada-P, Nix

CLASSIFICATION:

Agent dermatologique (pédiculicide, ovicide et scabicide topique)

Grossesse – catégorie B

INDICATIONS

Après-shampooing à 1 %: Traitement des infestations causées par *Pediculus humanus var. capitis* (pou de tête) et ses lentes (œufs) ■ **Crème et lotion à 5 %:** Éradication de *Sarcoptes scabiei* (gale). **Usages non approuvés:** *Lotion à 1 %:* Prévention de l'infestation de poux en cas d'épidémie.

MÉCANISME D'ACTION

Retard de la repolarisation de la membrane des cellules nerveuses et paralysie du parasite par inhibition du transport sodique cellulaire normal. ***Effets thérapeutiques:*** Destruction des parasites.

PHARMACOCINÉTIQUE

Absorption: L'absorption systémique est minime (< 2 %). Le médicament reste dans les cheveux pendant 10 jours.

Distribution: Inconnue.

Métabolisme et excrétion: Le médicament est inactivé rapidement par les enzymes.

Demi-vie: Inconnue.

Profil temps-action (effet pédiculicide)

	DÉBUT D'ACTION	PIC	DURÉE
Topique	10 min	inconnu	14 jours

CONTRE-INDICATIONS, PRÉCAUTIONS ET MISES EN GARDE

Contre-indications: Hypersensibilité à la perméthrine ou à l'un de ses composants, à un pyréthroïde synthétique, à la pyréthrine (insecticides ou pesticides pour usage vétérinaire) ou au chrysanthème.

Précautions et mises en garde: Grossesse ou allaitement ■ **PÉD.:** Enfants < 2 ans (après-shampooing à 1 %) ■ Nourrissons < 2 mois (lotion et crème à 5 %).

RÉACTIONS INDÉSIRABLES ET EFFETS SECONDAIRES

Tég.: sensation de brûlure, démangeaisons, rash, rougeur, sensation de picotement, enflure.

SN: engourdissement, fourmillements.

INTERACTIONS

Médicament-médicament: Aucune interaction notable.

VOIES D'ADMINISTRATION ET POSOLOGIE

Poux (traitement)

- **Usage topique (adultes et enfants > 2 ans):** Appliquer en une seule fois l'après-shampooing à 1 % sur les cheveux et laisser agir pendant 10 minutes, puis rincer.

Gale

- **Usage topique (adultes et enfants):** Appliquer par massage la crème ou la lotion à 5 % sur toutes les surfaces cutanées touchées; laisser agir pendant 12 à 14 heures, puis laver la peau pour enlever l'agent.
- **Usage topique (nourrissons > 2 mois):** Appliquer par massage la crème ou la lotion à 5 %, de la tête à la plante des pieds en incluant le cuir chevelu, les tempes et le front; laisser agir pendant 12 à 14 heures,

puis laver la peau pour enlever l'agent. Ces enfants doivent être traités sous la supervision d'un médecin.

PRÉSENTATION

Lotion: teneur à 5 % en flacons de 50 mL[VL] et de 200 mL[VL] ■ **Crème**: teneur à 5 %, en tubes de 30 g[VL] et de 60 g[VL] ■ **Après-shampooing**: teneur à 1 %, en flacons de 50 mL[VL], de 59 mL[VL] et de 200 mL[VL].

SOINS INFIRMIERS

ÉVALUATION DE LA SITUATION

Poux: Examiner le cuir chevelu à la recherche de poux et d'œufs (lentes) avant l'application de la perméthrine et 1 semaine plus tard.

Gale: Examiner la peau pour déceler la gale, avant et après le traitement.

DIAGNOSTICS INFIRMIERS POSSIBLES

- Entretien inefficace du domicile (Indications).
- Déficit de soins personnels: se laver et effectuer ses soins d'hygiène (Indications).
- Connaissances insuffisantes sur le traitement médicamenteux (Enseignement au patient et à ses proches).

INTERVENTIONS INFIRMIÈRES

- Les préparations sont réservées à l'application topique.

ENSEIGNEMENT AU PATIENT ET À SES PROCHES

- Recommander au patient de prévenir un professionnel de la santé en cas de démangeaisons, d'engourdissement, de rougeur ou de rash du cuir chevelu.
- Recommander au patient d'éviter tout contact avec les yeux. Le cas échéant, lui conseiller de se rincer abondamment les yeux à l'eau et de prévenir un professionnel de la santé si l'irritation oculaire persiste.
- Expliquer au patient que les autres personnes habitant sous le même toit devraient également passer un examen de dépistage des poux.
- Expliquer au patient les méthodes permettant de prévenir la réinfestation: laver à la machine, à l'eau très chaude, tous les vêtements, incluant les vêtements d'extérieur et le linge de maison, et les faire sécher dans une sécheuse à air chaud pendant au moins 20 minutes; faire nettoyer à sec les vêtements qu'on ne peut laver; faire tremper les brosses et les peignes dans de l'eau chaude (54 °C) savonneuse pendant 5 à 10 minutes; ne pas utiliser le même peigne ou la même brosse qu'une autre personne; faire un shampooing aux perruques et postiches; passer l'aspirateur sur les tapis et les meubles rembourrés; laver les jouets dans de l'eau chaude savonneuse; conserver les articles ne pouvant être lavés dans un sac en plastique hermétiquement fermé pendant 2 semaines.
- Dans le cas de l'enfant, recommander aux parents d'informer l'infirmière de l'école ou la garderie de la présence de poux pour que l'infestation puisse être enrayée.

Poux:

- Recommander au patient de se laver les cheveux avec un shampooing ordinaire, de les rincer et de les sécher avec une serviette. Bien mélanger l'après-shampooing avant de l'appliquer. En imbiber le cuir chevelu et les cheveux. Le patient devrait utiliser autant de solution que nécessaire pour en recouvrir toute la chevelure et jeter la portion inutilisée. Laisser agir pendant 10 minutes, puis rincer abondamment les cheveux et sécher avec une serviette propre. Peigner les cheveux avec un peigne fin afin de retirer les poux morts et les lentes (cette étape n'est pas obligatoire, mais peut être utile pour des raisons cosmétiques). Les écoles exigent généralement que les enfants soient débarrassés des lentes avant de retourner en classe.
- Expliquer au patient que la perméthrine le protégera de la réinfestation pendant 2 semaines. Les effets de la perméthrine se poursuivent même si le patient recommence à utiliser un shampooing ordinaire.

Gale: Expliquer au patient qu'il doit faire pénétrer profondément la préparation dans la peau, de la tête à la plante des pieds. Chez les nourrissons, il faut traiter la lisière des cheveux, le cou, le cuir chevelu, les tempes et le front. Il faut laisser la préparation sur la peau pendant 12 à 14 heures et laver ensuite à l'eau les régions traitées. Une application suffit.

VÉRIFICATION DE L'EFFICACITÉ THÉRAPEUTIQUE

L'efficacité du traitement peut être démontrée par: la disparition des poux et des lentes 1 semaine après le traitement; une seconde application est indiquée si l'on décèle des poux à ce moment-là ■ l'éradication de la gale après une application.

PÉTHIDINE,

voir Mépéridine

P

PHÉNAZOPYRIDINE

Phenazo, Pyridium

CLASSIFICATION:

Analgésique non opioïde (urinaire)

Grossesse – catégorie B

INDICATIONS

Soulagement des symptômes urinaires suivants dus à une infection, à un traumatisme, à une chirurgie ou à une autre intervention urologique: douleur ■ pollakiurie ■ sensation de brûlure ■ mictions impérieuses ■ mictions fréquentes.

MÉCANISME D'ACTION

Action directe sur la muqueuse des voies urinaires pour produire un effet analgésique ou anesthésique local ■ Absence d'effets antimicrobiens. ***Effets thérapeutiques:*** Soulagement des symptômes urinaires.

PHARMACOCINÉTIQUE

Absorption: Bonne (PO).

Distribution: Inconnue. De petites fractions traversent la barrière placentaire.

Métabolisme et excrétion: Excrétion rénale rapide sous forme inchangée.

Demi-vie: Inconnue.

P

Profil temps-action (analgésie des voies urinaires)

	DÉBUT D'ACTION	PIC	DURÉE
PO	inconnu	5-6 h	6-8 h

CONTRE-INDICATIONS, PRÉCAUTIONS ET MISES EN GARDE

Contre-indications: Hypersensibilité ■ Insuffisance hépatique grave ■ Insuffisance rénale ■ Glomérulonéphrite ■ Urémie ■ Pyélonéphrite durant la grossesse.

Précautions et mises en garde: Hépatite ■ **OBST.**: Grossesse ou allaitement (l'innocuité du médicament n'a pas été établie) ■ Carence en G-6-PD.

RÉACTIONS INDÉSIRABLES ET EFFETS SECONDAIRES

SNC: céphalées, vertiges.

GI: hépatotoxicité, nausées.

GU: coloration de l'urine en rouge ou orange, insuffisance rénale.

Tég.: rash.

Hémat.: anémie hémolytique, méthémoglobinémie.

INTERACTIONS

Médicament-médicament: Aucune interaction notable.

VOIES D'ADMINISTRATION ET POSOLOGIE

- **PO (adultes)**: 200 mg, 3 fois par jour, pendant 2 jours.
- **PO (enfants de 6 à 12 ans)**: 4 mg/kg/dose, 3 fois par jour, pendant 2 jours.

PRÉSENTATION (version générique disponible)

Comprimés: 100 mg[Pr], 200 mg[Pr].

SOINS INFIRMIERS

ÉVALUATION DE LA SITUATION

- Suivre de près les mictions impérieuses ou fréquentes et la douleur à la miction avant le traitement et pendant toute sa durée.

Tests de laboratoire:

- Examiner à intervalles réguliers tout au long du traitement les résultats des tests de la fonction rénale.
- La phénazopyridine peut modifier les résultats des analyses urinaires basées sur la coloration: glucose, corps cétoniques, bilirubine, stéroïdes, protéines.

DIAGNOSTICS INFIRMIERS POSSIBLES

- Douleur aiguë (Indications).
- Élimination urinaire altérée (Indications).
- Connaissances insuffisantes sur le traitement médicamenteux (Enseignement au patient et à ses proches).

INTERVENTIONS INFIRMIÈRES

- Il faut arrêter l'administration de la phénazopyridine dès que la douleur ou la gêne ont été soulagées, habituellement 2 jours après le début du traitement de l'infection des voies urinaires, car elle peut masquer les signes et les symptômes d'un échec du traitement d'une infection urinaire. Le patient doit cependant poursuivre l'antibiothérapie prescrite pendant toute la durée recommandée.
- La coloration en jaune de la peau ou de la sclérotique (blanc de l'œil) peut indiquer une accumulation de phénazopyridine due à une insuffisance rénale, ce qui dicte l'interruption du traitement.
- Administrer la phénazopyridine avec des aliments ou après les repas pour réduire l'irritation gastrique. Il ne faut pas écraser ni croquer les comprimés.

ENSEIGNEMENT AU PATIENT ET À SES PROCHES

- Conseiller au patient de respecter rigoureusement la posologie recommandée. S'il n'a pu prendre le médicament au moment habituel, il doit le faire dès que possible à moins que ce ne soit presque l'heure prévue pour la dose suivante.
- Prévenir le patient que même si l'on arrête le traitement par la phénazopyridine, une fois la douleur ou la gêne soulagées, il doit continuer de prendre les antibiotiques que le médecin lui a prescrits, pendant toute la durée recommandée. Lui conseiller de ne pas prendre les comprimés de phénazopyridine inutilisés qu'il a conservés, sans avoir consulté au préalable un professionnel de la santé.
- Expliquer au patient que le médicament rendra l'urine de couleur rouge orangé et qu'il risque de tacher ses vêtements ou ses draps. Lui conseiller de porter des serviettes hygiéniques pour garder ses vêtements propres. La phénazopyridine peut aussi tacher les lentilles cornéennes souples.
- Recommander au patient de prévenir un professionnel de la santé en cas de rash, de modification de la couleur de la peau ou des yeux ou de fatigue inhabituelle.

VÉRIFICATION DE L'EFFICACITÉ THÉRAPEUTIQUE

L'efficacité du traitement peut être démontrée par: la diminution de la douleur et de la sensation de brûlure pendant les mictions.

PHÉNELZINE,

voir Inhibiteurs de la monoamine-oxydase (IMAO)

PHÉNOBARBITAL

Bellergal Spacetabs, Phenobarbital, PMS-Phenobarbital

CLASSIFICATION:

Anticonvulsivant, anxiolytique et hypnosédatif (barbiturique)

Grossesse – catégorie D

INDICATIONS

Anticonvulsivant en cas de crises tonicocloniques généralisées (grand mal) ou de crises complexes partielles ■ État de mal épileptique ■ Sédation préopératoire et autres circonstances où la sédation peut s'avérer nécessaire ■ Insomnie. **Usages non approuvés:** Prévention et traitement de l'hyperbilirubinémie.

MÉCANISME D'ACTION

Dépression du SNC à tous les niveaux ■ Dépression de la zone sensorielle du cortex, diminution de l'activité motrice et modification de la fonction cérébelleuse ■ Inhibition de la transmission dans le système nerveux et élévation du seuil de convulsion ■ Induction (accélération) de l'activité des enzymes hépatiques qui métabolisent les médicaments, la bilirubine et d'autres composés. ***Effets thérapeutiques:*** Effets anticonvulsivants ■ Sédation.

PHARMACOCINÉTIQUE

Absorption: > 60 % (PO).

Distribution: Inconnue.

Métabolisme et excrétion: Métabolisme majoritairement hépatique (75 %); excrétion rénale (25 % sous forme inchangée).

Demi-vie: De 2 à 6 jours.

Profil temps-action (sédation)†

	DÉBUT D'ACTION	PIC	DURÉE
PO	30 - 60 min	inconnu	10 - 12 h
IM, SC	10 - 30 min	inconnu	4 - 6 h
IV	5 min	15 min	4 - 6 h

† Le plein effet anticonvulsivant se manifeste après 2 à 3 semaines de traitement, sauf si une dose d'attaque a été administrée.

CONTRE-INDICATIONS, PRÉCAUTIONS ET MISES EN GARDE

Contre-indications: Hypersensibilité ■ Porphyrie ■ Dépression respiratoire grave ou insuffisance pulmonaire ■ Insuffisance hépatique ■ Insuffisance rénale ■ Apnée du sommeil ■ Patients suicidaires ■ Alcoolisme ■ Pharmacodépendance ■ Douleurs intenses non soulagées.

Précautions et mises en garde: GÉR.: Il est recommandé de réduire la dose ■ Usage à titre d'hypnotique réservé à un traitement de courte durée (l'administration prolongée peut entraîner une dépendance) ■ **OBST.:** L'administration prolongée provoque une pharmacodépendance chez le nourrisson; le médicament peut entraîner des troubles de la coagulation et des malformations chez le fœtus; l'administration de phénobarbital au terme de la grossesse peut provoquer la dépression respiratoire chez le nouveau-né ■ Coma ou dépression préexistante du SNC ■ Allaitement ■ Intolérance connue à l'alcool (élixir seulement).

RÉACTIONS INDÉSIRABLES ET EFFETS SECONDAIRES

SNC: sensation ébrieuse, delirium, dépression, somnolence, excitation, léthargie, vertiges.
Resp.: dépression respiratoire; *IV* – LARYNGOSPASME, bronchospasme.
CV: *IV* – hypotension.
GI: constipation, diarrhée, nausées, vomissements.
Tég.: photosensibilité, rash, urticaire.
Locaux: phlébite au point d'injection IV.
Loc.: arthralgie, myalgie, névralgie.
Divers: réactions d'hypersensibilité incluant l'ŒDÈME ANGIONEUROTIQUE et la MALADIE SÉRIQUE, dépendance physique, dépendance psychologique.

INTERACTIONS

Médicament-médicament: Effets dépressifs additifs sur le SNC lors de l'usage concomitant d'autres **dépresseurs du SNC** dont l'**alcool**, les **antihistaminiques**, les **analgésiques opioïdes** et d'autres **hypnosédatifs** ■ Le phénobarbital peut activer les enzymes hépatiques qui métabolisent d'autres médicaments, diminuant ainsi leur efficacité. Il s'agit des médicaments suivants: **contraceptifs oraux**, **warfarine**, **chloramphénicol**, **cyclosporine**, **dacarbazine**, **corticostéroïdes**, **antidépresseurs tricycliques** et **quinidine** ■ Le phénobarbital peut accroître le risque d'intoxication hépatique par l'**acétaminophène** ■ Les **IMAO**, l'**acide valproïque** ou le **divalproex**, administrés en concomitance, peuvent diminuer le métabolisme du phénobarbital et intensifier ses effets sédatifs ■ Le phénobarbital peut augmenter le risque de toxicité hématologique du **cyclophosphamide**.

P

VOIES D'ADMINISTRATION ET POSOLOGIE

- **PO (adultes)**: *Anticonvulsivant* – de 60 à 250 mg par jour, en une seule dose ou en 2 ou 3 doses fractionnées. *Sédatif* – de 30 à 120 mg par jour, en 2 ou 3 doses fractionnées. *Hypnotique* – de 100 à 320 mg, au coucher.
- **PO (enfants)**: *Anticonvulsivant* – de 1 à 6 mg/kg/jour, en une seule dose ou en doses fractionnées. *Sédatif* – 2 mg/kg, 3 fois par jour.
- **IM, IV (enfants)**: *Sédation préopératoire* – de 1 à 3 mg/kg, de 1 à 2 heures avant l'intervention chirurgicale.
- **IM, IV (adultes)**: *Sédatif* – de 30 à 120 mg par jour, en 2 ou 3 doses fractionnées. *Sédation préopératoire* – de 130 à 200 mg, de 1 à 2 heures avant l'intervention chirurgicale. *Hypnotique* – de 100 à 325 mg.
- **IV (adultes)**: *Anticonvulsivant* – au départ, de 100 à 320 mg, selon les besoins (dose totale de 600 mg/24 h). *État de mal épileptique* – de 10 à 20 mg/kg, répéter toutes les 20 minutes, au besoin, jusqu'à ce que la crise soit maîtrisée ou jusqu'à l'atteinte d'une dose totale de 1 à 2 g.
- **IV (enfants)**: *Anticonvulsivant* – de 1 à 6 mg/kg/jour. *État de mal épileptique* – de 10 à 20 mg/kg, répéter, au besoin, en administrant une dose de 5 à 10 mg/kg, toutes les 20 minutes jusqu'à ce que la crise soit maîtrisée ou jusqu'à l'atteinte d'une dose totale de 40 mg/kg.

PRÉSENTATION (version générique disponible)

Comprimés: 15 mg^C^, 30 mg^C^, 60 mg^C^, 100 mg^C^ ■ **Élixir**: 25 mg/5 mL^C^ ■ **Solution pour injection**: 30 mg/mL^C^, 120 mg/mL^C^ ■ **En association avec**: plusieurs autres médicaments.

SOINS INFIRMIERS

ÉVALUATION DE LA SITUATION

- SUIVRE DE PRÈS LA FONCTION RESPIRATOIRE, MESURER LE POULS ET LA PRESSION ARTÉRIELLE À INTERVALLES FRÉQUENTS CHEZ LES PATIENTS RECEVANT LE PHÉNOBARBITAL PAR VOIE IV. GARDER À PORTÉE DE LA MAIN LE MATÉRIEL DE RÉANIMATION ET DE RESPIRATION ARTIFICIELLE. LA GRAVITÉ DE LA DÉPRESSION RESPIRATOIRE EST PROPORTIONNELLE À LA DOSE.
- Le traitement prolongé peut entraîner une dépendance psychologique ou physique. Diminuer la quantité de médicament dont le patient peut disposer, particulièrement s'il est déprimé ou suicidaire ou s'il a des antécédents de toxicomanie.

GÉR.: Paradoxalement, la somnolence peut être précédée de phénomènes transitoires d'euphorie, d'exaltation, d'excitation et de confusion. Suivre de près ces effets secondaires.

Convulsions: Déterminer le siège, la durée et les caractéristiques des convulsions.

Sédation:

- Déterminer le niveau de conscience du patient et le degré d'anxiété qu'il manifeste lorsque le phénobarbital est administré comme sédatif avant une intervention chirurgicale.
- Suivre de près la douleur chez les patients ayant subi une intervention chirurgicale. Le phénobarbital peut augmenter la sensibilité aux stimuli douloureux.

Tests de laboratoire:

- Noter à intervalles réguliers les résultats des tests des fonctions hépatique et rénale ainsi que la numération globulaire chez les patients recevant un traitement prolongé.

- Mesurer les concentrations sériques de folate à intervalles réguliers pendant toute la durée du traitement puisque les besoins en folate des patients suivant un traitement anticonvulsivant de longue durée par le phénobarbital sont accrus.
- Le phénobarbital peut entraîner une baisse des concentrations sériques de bilirubine chez les nouveau-nés, chez les patients atteints d'hyperbilirubinémie congénitale non hémolytique et non conjuguée et chez les patients épileptiques.

Toxicité et surdosage: On peut mesurer à intervalles réguliers les concentrations sériques de phénobarbital lorsque le médicament est administré comme anticonvulsivant. Les concentrations sanguines thérapeutiques sont de 65 à 170 µmol/L. Les symptômes de toxicité incluent la confusion, la somnolence, la dyspnée, les troubles de l'élocution et la démarche chancelante.

DIAGNOSTICS INFIRMIERS POSSIBLES

- Risque d'accident (Indications, Effets secondaires).
- Connaissances insuffisantes sur le traitement médicamenteux (Enseignement au patient et à ses proches).

INTERVENTIONS INFIRMIÈRES

- NE PAS CONFONDRE LE PHÉNOBARBITAL AVEC LE PENTOBARBITAL.
- Surveiller les déplacements du patient après l'administration du médicament. Remonter les ridelles du lit et laisser la sonnette d'appel à porter de la main. Garder le lit en position basse. Prendre les précautions qui s'imposent en cas de crise convulsive.
- Lorsque l'on substitue un autre anticonvulsivant au phénobarbital, il faut réduire graduellement la dose de phénobarbital tout en augmentant la dose du nouveau médicament afin de maintenir les effets anticonvulsivants.

PO: Dans le cas des patients éprouvant des difficultés de déglutition, on peut écraser les comprimés et les mélanger à des aliments ou à des liquides (ne pas administrer à l'état sec). La solution orale peut être prise non diluée ou mélangée avec de l'eau, du lait ou du jus. Utiliser un récipient gradué pour mesurer les préparations liquides.

IM: Administrer les injections IM profondément dans le muscle fessier pour diminuer l'irritation des tissus. Ne pas injecter plus de 5 mL dans un seul point en raison du risque d'irritation tissulaire.

IV: Les concentrations maximales dans le cerveau ne sont parfois pas atteintes avant 15 à 30 minutes. Administrer la plus faible dose possible et attendre que son efficacité puisse se manifester avant d'administrer une seconde dose, afin de prévenir la dépression induite par l'accumulation de barbiturique.

IV directe:

- Diluer une fois de plus dans 10 mL d'eau stérile. Consulter les directives de chaque fabricant avant de reconstituer la préparation. Ne pas utiliser une solution qui ne devient pas tout à fait transparente dans les 5 minutes suivant la reconstitution ou qui contient un précipité. Jeter la poudre ou la solution exposée à l'air pendant plus de 30 minutes.
- La solution est très alcaline; éviter l'extravasation en raison des risques de lésion et de nécrose des tissus.

Vitesse d'administration: Administrer à un débit maximal de 60 mg/min. Adapter lentement la dose jusqu'à l'obtention de la réaction désirée. L'administration rapide peut provoquer une dépression respiratoire.

Compatibilité (tubulure en Y): énalaprilate ▪ méropenem ▪ propofol ▪ sufentanil.

Incompatibilité (tubulure en Y): hydromorphone.

ENSEIGNEMENT AU PATIENT ET À SES PROCHES

- Conseiller au patient de respecter rigoureusement la posologie recommandée. S'il n'a pu prendre le médicament au moment habituel, il doit le faire dès que possible à moins que ce ne soit presque l'heure prévue pour la dose suivante. Le prévenir qu'il ne doit jamais remplacer une dose manquée par une double dose.
- Prévenir le patient qui suit un traitement prolongé qu'il ne doit pas arrêter de prendre le médicament sans avoir consulté un professionnel de la santé au préalable. L'arrêt brusque du traitement peut déclencher des convulsions ou l'état de mal épileptique.
- Prévenir le patient que le phénobarbital peut provoquer la somnolence diurne. Lui conseiller de ne pas conduire et d'éviter les activités qui exigent sa vigilance jusqu'à ce qu'on ait la certitude que le médicament n'entraîne pas cet effet chez lui. Recommander au patient de ne reprendre la conduite automobile que si le médecin l'autorise à le faire après s'être assuré que les crises ont été maîtrisées.
- Conseiller au patient de ne pas boire d'alcool et de ne pas prendre d'autres dépresseurs du SNC en même temps que ce médicament.
- Recommander à la patiente qui prend un contraceptif oral d'utiliser une autre méthode contraceptive non hormonale pendant toute la durée du traitement et jusqu'aux règles suivantes. Lui conseiller de prévenir immédiatement un professionnel de la santé si elle pense être enceinte ou si elle souhaite le devenir.

- Recommander au patient de prévenir un professionnel de la santé en cas de fièvre, de maux de gorge, d'aphtes, de saignements ou d'ecchymoses inhabituels, de saignements du nez ou de pétéchies.

VÉRIFICATION DE L'EFFICACITÉ THÉRAPEUTIQUE

L'efficacité du traitement peut être démontrée par: la diminution ou l'arrêt des convulsions sans sédation excessive; le plein effet anticonvulsivant peut ne pas se manifester avant plusieurs semaines ■ la sédation préopératoire ■ l'amélioration du sommeil ■ la baisse des concentrations sériques de bilirubine.

PHENTOLAMINE

Phentolamine, Rogitine

CLASSIFICATION:

Antihypertenseur (antagoniste alpha-adrénergique à action périphérique)

Grossesse – catégorie C

INDICATIONS

IV: Prévention et maîtrise des épisodes d'hypertension chez les patients souffrant de phéochromocytome, lors de la phase préopératoire et durant l'ablation de la tumeur ■ Diagnostic de phéochromocytome (test à la phentolamine) ■ **Infiltration**: Prévention de la formation d'escarres et traitement de la nécrose tissulaire en cas d'extravasation, lors de l'administration de noradrénaline. **Usages non approuvés – IM, IV**: Traitement de l'hypertension associée à un excès d'activité adrénergique (sympathique), comme celle qui suit l'administration de phényléphrine, la consommation d'aliments contenant de la tyramine par les patients recevant un IMAO ou le sevrage de la clonidine.

MÉCANISME D'ACTION

Blocage incomplet et de courte durée des récepteurs alpha-adrénergiques situés principalement dans les muscles lisses et les glandes exocrines ■ Induction d'hypotension par relaxation directe des muscles vasculaires lisses et par blocage des récepteurs alpha. ***Effets thérapeutiques:*** Abaissement de la pression artérielle en cas d'hypertension attribuable à un excès d'activité adrénergique (sympathique) ■ **Infiltration**: Renversement de la vasoconstriction provoquée par la noradrénaline ou la dopamine.

PHARMACOCINÉTIQUE

Absorption: Bonne (IM).

Distribution: Inconnue.

Métabolisme et excrétion: Excrétion rénale (10 % sous forme inchangée).

Demi-vie: Inconnue.

Profil temps-action (blocage alpha-adrénergique)

	DÉBUT D'ACTION	PIC	DURÉE
IM	inconnu	20 min	30 – 45 min
IV	immédiat	2 min	15 – 30 min

CONTRE-INDICATIONS, PRÉCAUTIONS ET MISES EN GARDE

Contre-indications: Hypersensibilité ■ Hypersensibilité connue aux sulfites ■ Infarctus du myocarde ou antécédents d'infarctus, insuffisance coronarienne, angine ou autres signes évocateurs de maladie coronarienne ■ Hypotension.

Précautions et mises en garde: Ulcère gastroduodénal ■ **GÉR.**: Prédisposition accrue aux effets hypotenseurs; il est recommandé de réduire la dose ■ **OBST., ALLAITEMENT**: L'innocuité du médicament n'a pas été établie ■ Insuffisance rénale ■ Artériosclérose cérébrale.

RÉACTIONS INDÉSIRABLES ET EFFETS SECONDAIRES

Administration par voie parentérale.

SNC: SPASME VASCULAIRE CÉRÉBRAL, étourdissements, faiblesse.

ORLO: congestion nasale.

CV: HYPOTENSION, INFARCTUS DU MYOCARDE, angine, arythmies, tachycardie.

GI: douleurs abdominales, diarrhée, nausées, vomissements, aggravation de l'ulcère gastroduodénal.

Tég.: bouffées vasomotrices.

INTERACTIONS

Médicament-médicament: La phentolamine contrecarre les effets des **stimulants alpha-adrénergiques** ■ La phentolamine peut diminuer la réaction vasopressive à l'**éphédrine** et à la **phényléphrine** ■ L'administration concomitante d'**adrénaline** peut entraîner une hypotension grave ■ La **guanéthidine**, administrée en concomitance, peut provoquer une hypotension et une bradycardie exagérées ■ La phentolamine diminue la vasoconstriction périphérique entraînée par des doses élevées de **dopamine**.

VOIES D'ADMINISTRATION ET POSOLOGIE

Hypertension associée au phéochromocytome, avant et pendant l'intervention chirurgicale
- **IV (adultes)**: De 2 à 5 mg, de 1 à 2 heures avant l'intervention; répéter l'administration de cette dose selon les besoins.

Prévention et de la nécrose tissulaire provoquée par l'extravasation de noradrénaline
- **Infiltration (adultes)**: De 5 à 10 mg dans 10 mL de NaCl 0,9%.

Diagnostic du phéochromocytome
- **IV (adultes)**: 5 mg.
- **IV (enfants)**: 1 mg.
- **IM (adultes)**: 5 mg.
- **IM (enfants)**: 3 mg.

PRÉSENTATION

Solution pour injection: 5 mg/mL[Pr], 10 mg/mL[Pr].

SOINS INFIRMIERS

ÉVALUATION DE LA SITUATION

- MESURER LA PRESSION ARTÉRIELLE ET LE POULS ET EXAMINER LE TRACÉ DE L'ÉCG TOUTES LES 2 MINUTES PENDANT L'ADMINISTRATION IV. EN CAS DE CRISE HYPOTENSIVE, L'ADMINISTRATION D'ADRÉNALINE EST CONTRE-INDIQUÉE, CAR ELLE POURRAIT ENTRAÎNER UNE DIMINUTION PARADOXALE ADDITIVE DE LA PRESSION ARTÉRIELLE. CEPENDANT, ON PEUT UTILISER DE LA NORADRÉNALINE.

DIAGNOSTICS INFIRMIERS POSSIBLES

- Irrigation tissulaire inefficace (Indications).
- Risque d'accident (Indications).
- Connaissances insuffisantes sur le traitement médicamenteux (Enseignement au patient et à ses proches).

INTERVENTIONS INFIRMIÈRES

- Garder le patient en position couchée pendant toute la durée de l'administration par voie parentérale.
- Injecter à une vitesse de 5 mg/min.

Perfusion continue: Diluer de 5 à 10 mg de phentolamine dans 500 mL de NaCl 0,9 %.

Vitesse d'administration: Adapter la vitesse de perfusion à la réponse du patient.

- On peut également ajouter 10 mg de phentolamine par 1 000 mL de solution contenant de la noradrénaline pour prévenir la formation d'une escarre ou la nécrose tissulaire. Ce procédé ne modifie pas l'effet vasopresseur de la noradrénaline.

Compatibilité dans la même seringue: papavérine.

Compatibilité (tubulure en Y): amiodarone.

Compatibilité en addition au soluté: dobutamine ■ noradrénaline.

Infiltration: Diluer de 5 à 10 mg de phentolamine dans 10 mL de solution de NaCl 0,9 %. Infiltrer rapidement le territoire où l'extravasation a eu lieu. Afin que le traitement soit efficace, on doit administrer le médicament dans les 12 heures suivant l'extravasation.

ENSEIGNEMENT AU PATIENT ET À SES PROCHES

- Recommander au patient de changer lentement de position pour diminuer le risque d'hypotension orthostatique.
- Conseiller au patient d'informer un professionnel de la santé s'il ressent des douleurs thoraciques durant la perfusion IV.

VÉRIFICATION DE L'EFFICACITÉ THÉRAPEUTIQUE

L'efficacité du traitement peut être démontrée par: l'abaissement de la pression artérielle ■ la prévention de la nécrose tissulaire et de la formation d'escarres en cas d'extravasation lors de l'administration de noradrénaline, de dopamine ou de phényléphrine.

P

PHÉNYTOÏNE et FOSPHÉNYTOÏNE

phénytoïne

Dilantin, Novo-Phenytoin, Phenytoine, Taro-Phenytoin, Tremytoine

fosphénytoïne

Cerebyx

CLASSIFICATION:

Anticonvulsivants (hydantoïne), antiarythmiques (classe IB)

Grossesse – catégorie D

INDICATIONS

Phénytoïne: Traitement et prévention des crises tonicocloniques généralisées (grand mal) et des crises partielles complexes ■ **Fosphénytoïne**: Traitement de courte durée (moins de 5 jours) des convulsions lorsqu'il est impossible d'administrer la phénytoïne par voie orale ■ Traitement et prévention des convulsions pendant une neurochirurgie. **Usages non approuvés – Phénytoïne**:

Antiarythmique, particulièrement en cas d'arythmies associées à une toxicité digitalique ■ Soulagement de la douleur provoquée par la névralgie du trijumeau.

MÉCANISME D'ACTION

Inhibition de la propagation de la crise convulsive par modification du transport des ions sodium ■ Effets antiarythmiques découlant de l'amélioration de la conduction AV ■ Diminution possible de la transmission synaptique ■ La fosphénytoïne est rapidement transformée en phénytoïne, laquelle est à l'origine de ses effets pharmacologiques. ***Effets thérapeutiques:*** Diminution de l'activité convulsivante ■ Maîtrise des arythmies ventriculaires ■ Diminution de la douleur.

PHARMACOCINÉTIQUE

Absorption: *Phénytoïne* – Lente (PO). Disponibilité variant selon la préparation; les capsules contiennent de la phénytoïne sodique à libération prolongée. La libération des autres formes galéniques est rapide. *Fosphénytoïne* – Cet agent est rapidement transformé en phénytoïne par suite de l'administration par voie IV. Biodisponibilité à 100 % (IM).

Distribution: Ces médicaments se répartissent dans le liquide céphalorachidien et dans d'autres liquides et tissus de l'organisme, surtout dans les tissus adipeux. Ils traversent la barrière placentaire et passent dans le lait maternel; les concentrations sont similaires chez la mère et le fœtus.

P

Métabolisme et excrétion: *Phénytoïne* – Métabolisme majoritairement hépatique. Des quantités minimes sont excrétées dans l'urine.

Demi-vie: *Fosphénytoïne* – 15 minutes; *phénytoïne* – 22 heures (la demi-vie est plus longue lorsque les concentrations sanguines sont élevées).

Profil temps-action (effet anticonvulsivant)

	DÉBUT D'ACTION†	PIC	DURÉE
Fosphénytoïne IM	inconnu	30 min	jusqu'à 24 h
Fosphénytoïne IV	15 - 45 min	15 - 60 min	jusqu'à 24 h
Phénytoïne PO	2 - 24 h (1 semaine)	1,5 - 3 h	6 - 12 h
Phénytoïne PO-LP‡	2 - 24 h (1 semaine)	4 - 12 h	12 - 36 h
Phénytoïne IV	1 - 2 h (1 semaine)	rapide	12 - 24 h
Phénytoïne IM	inconnu (erratique)	erratique	12 - 24 h

† Laps de temps qui s'écoule jusqu'à ce que l'on note le début de l'action sans administration d'une dose d'attaque.

‡ LP = libération prolongée.

CONTRE-INDICATIONS, PRÉCAUTIONS ET MISES EN GARDE

Contre-indications: Hypersensibilité ■ Hypersensibilité au propylène glycol (injection de phénytoïne seulement) ■ Bradycardie sinusale, bloc sino-auriculaire (SA), bloc AV du deuxième ou du troisième degré ou syndrome d'Adams-Stokes.

Précautions et mises en garde: Maladie hépatique ou rénale (risque accru de réactions indésirables; il est recommandé de réduire la dose en cas d'insuffisance hépatique) ■ Personnes âgées ou patients souffrant de maladies cardiaque ou respiratoire graves (administration parentérale – risque accru de réactions indésirables graves, particulièrement lors de l'utilisation de phénytoïne par voie IV) ■ Obésité (la dose initiale de phénytoïne devrait être calculée selon le poids idéal + 1,33 fois le poids excédentaire) ■ **OBST., ALLAITEMENT:** L'innocuité de ces agents n'a pas été établie; l'administration prolongée peut déclencher le syndrome fœtal de l'hydantoïne; l'administration au terme de la grossesse peut provoquer l'hémorragie chez le nouveau-né. ■ Intolérance à l'alcool (la phénytoïne en solution pour injection et en suspension orale seulement).

RÉACTIONS INDÉSIRABLES ET EFFETS SECONDAIRES

La plupart des réactions et effets mentionnés se manifestent lors de l'administration prolongée de phénytoïne.

SNC: ataxie, agitation, œdème cérébral, coma, étourdissements, somnolence, dysarthrie, dyskinésie, syndrome extrapyramidal, céphalées, nervosité, faiblesse.

ORLO: diplopie, nystagmus, acouphènes.

CV: hypotension (risque accru lors de l'administration IV de phénytoïne), tachycardie, vasodilatation.

GI: hyperplasie gingivale, nausées, altération du goût, anorexie, constipation, hépatite médicamenteuse, sécheresse de la bouche (xérostomie), vomissements, perte de poids.

GU: urine de couleur rose, rouge et rouge-brun.

Tég.: hypertrichose, rash, dermatite exfoliative, prurit.

HÉ: hypocalcémie.

Hémat.: AGRANULOCYTOSE, ANÉMIE APLASIQUE, leucopénie, anémie mégaloblastique, thrombopénie.

Loc.: douleurs lombaires, ostéomalacie, douleurs pelviennes.

Divers: réactions allergiques, incluant le SYNDROME DE STEVENS-JOHNSON, fièvre, lymphadénopathie.

INTERACTIONS

Médicament-médicament: La **phénylbutazone**, le **disulfirame**, l'**amiodarone**, l'**isoniazide**, le **chloramphénicol**, le **vaccin antigrippal**, les **sulfamides**, la **fluoxétine**, les **benzodiazépines**, l'**oméprazole**, l'**itraconazole**, le **kétoconazole**, le **fluconazole**, le **miconazole**, les **œstrogènes**, l'**halothane**, le **méthylphénidate**, les **phénothiazines**, les **salicylates**, le **tolbutamide**, la **trazodone**, le **felba-**

mate, la **cimétidine** et l'ingestion rapide de grandes quantités d'**alcool** peuvent élever les concentrations sanguines de phénytoïne ■ Les **barbituriques** ou la **carbamazépine**, administrés en concomitance, ainsi que la consommation régulière d'**alcool**, peuvent diminuer les concentrations sanguines de phénytoïne ■ La phénytoïne peut modifier les effets de la **digoxine**, de la **warfarine**, du **felbamate**, des **corticostéroïdes**, de la **doxycycline**, de la **rifampine**, de la **quinidine**, de la **méthadone**, de la **cyclosporine** et des **œstrogènes** ■ Risque d'hypotension additive lors de l'administration concomitante par voie IV de phénytoïne et de **dopamine** ■ Dépression additive du SNC lors de l'administration d'autres **dépresseurs du SNC**, y compris l'**alcool**, les **antihistaminiques**, les **antidépresseurs**, les **opioïdes**, et les **hypnosédatifs** ■ Les **antiacides** peuvent diminuer l'absorption de la phénytoïne administrée par voie orale ■ La phénytoïne peut réduire l'efficacité de la **streptozocine** ou de la **théophylline** ■ Risque de dépression cardiaque additive lors de l'administration concomitante de **propranolol** ou de **lidocaïne** ■ Le **calcium** et le **sulcrafate**, administrés en concomitance, réduisent l'absorption de la phénytoïne.

Médicament-aliments: La phénytoïne peut diminuer l'absorption de l'**acide folique** ■ En cas d'**alimentation entérale** simultanée, l'absorption de la phénytoïne peut être réduite.

VOIES D'ADMINISTRATION ET POSOLOGIE

Fosphénytoïne

Toutes les doses sont exprimées en unités équivalentes de phénytoïne sodique (EP).

- **IV (adultes)**: *État de mal épileptique - dose d'attaque*: de 15 à 20 mg d'EP/kg.
- **IV, IM (adultes)**: *Dose d'attaque et dose d'entretien administrées dans les cas non urgents* - respectivement, de 10 à 20 mg d'EP/kg et de 4 à 6 mg d'EP/kg/jour.
- **IV, IM (adultes)**: *Remplacement de la phénytoïne orale par la fosphénytoïne par voie IM ou IV* - administrer la même dose quotidienne (la biodisponibilité des capsules de Dilantin est d'environ 90 %, et celle de la fosphénytoïne par voie IM ou IV, de 100 %).

Phénytoïne (anticonvulsivant)

L'administration IM ne devrait se faire qu'en dernier recours. La posologie devrait être augmentée de 50 % par rapport à la posologie quotidienne par voie orale établie antérieurement.

- **PO (adultes)**: *Dose d'attaque* - 100 mg, 3 fois/jour; *dose d'entretien* - de 300 à 400 mg/jour, 1 dose de 600 mg/jour peut être nécessaire dans certains cas. Lorsque les symptômes sont maîtrisés par 1 dose de 100 mg, 3 fois/jour, on peut administrer cette dose quotidienne en une seule fois.
- **PO (enfants)**: Au départ, 5 mg/kg/jour, jusqu'à un maximum de 300 mg/jour, en 2 ou 3 prises; *dose d'entretien* - de 4 à 8 mg/kg/jour (250 mg/m^2), en 2 ou 3 doses fractionnées (ne pas dépasser 300 mg/jour).
- **IV (adultes)**: *État de mal épileptique* - de 15 à 20 mg/kg, puis 100 mg, toutes les 6 à 8 heures. Le débit ne doit pas dépasser 50 mg/min.
- **IV (enfants)**: *État de mal épileptique* - de 15 à 20 mg/kg, à un débit de 1 à 3 mg/kg/min.

PRÉSENTATION

- **Fosphénytoïne**
  Solution pour injection: 75 mg/mL (équivalant à 50 mg de phénytoïne sodique), en flacons unidoses de 2 mL[Pr].
- **Phénytoïne (version générique disponible)**
  Comprimés à croquer: 50 mg[Pr] ■ **Suspension orale**: 30 mg/5 mL[Pr], 125 mg/5 mL[Pr] ■ **Capsules à libération prolongée**: 30 mg[Pr], 100 mg[Pr] ■ **Solution pour injection**: 50 mg/mL, en ampoules de 2 mL[Pr] et de 5 mL[Pr], en fioles de 2 mL[Pr] et de 5 mL[Pr].

SOINS INFIRMIERS

P

ÉVALUATION DE LA SITUATION

Convulsions: Évaluer le siège, la durée, la fréquence et les caractéristiques des crises convulsives. On devrait surveiller l'ÉEG à intervalles réguliers pendant toute la durée du traitement.

Arythmies: Surveiller continuellement l'ÉCG durant le traitement des arythmies.

Névralgie: Suivre de près la douleur (siège, durée, intensité, facteurs déclenchants), avant le traitement et à intervalles réguliers pendant toute sa durée.

Phénytoïne:

- Suivre de près l'hygiène buccale du patient. Un nettoyage vigoureux, commençant dans les 10 jours suivant le début du traitement par la phénytoïne, peut aider à maîtriser l'hyperplasie gingivale.
- SUIVRE DE PRÈS LES SIGNES DU SYNDROME D'HYPERSENSIBILITÉ À LA PHÉNYTOÏNE (FIÈVRE, RASH, LYMPHADÉNOPATHIE). LE RASH SURVIENT HABITUELLEMENT DANS LES 2 PREMIÈRES SEMAINES DE TRAITEMENT. LE SYNDROME D'HYPERSENSIBILITÉ SE MANIFESTE HABITUELLEMENT ENTRE LA 3e ET LA 8e SEMAINE, MAIS IL PEUT APPARAÎTRE JUSQU'À LA 12e SEMAINE APRÈS LE DÉBUT DU TRAITEMENT. CE

SYNDROME, DONT L'ISSUE PEUT ÊTRE FATALE, PEUT ENTRAÎNER UNE INSUFFISANCE RÉNALE, UNE RHABDOMYOLYSE OU UNE NÉCROSE HÉPATIQUE.

Fosphénytoïne:

- Surveiller continuellement la pression artérielle, l'ÉCG et la fonction respiratoire pendant l'administration de la fosphénytoïne et pendant toute la durée du pic plasmatique (de 10 à 20 minutes après la perfusion).
- OBSERVER ATTENTIVEMENT LE PATIENT POUR DÉCELER LE RASH. IL FAUT ARRÊTER LE TRAITEMENT PAR LA FOSPHÉNYTOÏNE AUX PREMIERS SIGNES DE RÉACTIONS CUTANÉES. LES RÉACTIONS INDÉSIRABLES GRAVES, TELLES QUE LA DERMATITE EXFOLIATRICE, PURPURIQUE OU BULLEUSE OU LE LUPUS ÉRYTHÉMATEUX, LE SYNDROME DE STEVENS-JOHNSON OU L'ÉRYTHRODERMIE BULLEUSE AVEC ÉPIDERMOLYSE SONT DES CONTRE-INDICATIONS ABSOLUES À L'UTILISATION ULTÉRIEURE DE LA PHÉNYTOÏNE OU DE LA FOSPHÉNYTOÏNE. SI DES ÉRUPTIONS CUTANÉES PLUS BÉNIGNES SURVIENNENT (D'APPARENCE ROUGEOLEUSE OU SCARLATINEUSE), ON PEUT REPRENDRE LE TRAITEMENT PAR LA FOSPHÉNYTOÏNE APRÈS LA DISPARITION DU RASH. SI LE RASH SE MANIFESTE DE NOUVEAU, IL FAUT ÉVITER TOUT TRAITEMENT ULTÉRIEUR PAR LA FOSPHÉNYTOÏNE OU LA PHÉNYTOÏNE.

Tests de laboratoire:

Phénytoïne:

- NOTER LA NUMÉRATION GLOBULAIRE ET PLAQUETTAIRE, LES CONCENTRATIONS SÉRIQUES DE CALCIUM ET D'ALBUMINE ET LES RÉSULTATS DES ANALYSES DES URINES ET DES TESTS DES FONCTIONS HÉPATIQUE ET THYROÏDIENNE AVANT L'ADMINISTRATION INITIALE, 1 FOIS PAR MOIS PENDANT LES PREMIERS MOIS, PUIS À INTERVALLES RÉGULIERS PENDANT TOUTE LA DURÉE DU TRAITEMENT.
- La phénytoïne peut entraîner l'élévation des concentrations sériques de phosphatase alcaline et de GGT ainsi que de la glycémie.
- Il faut mesurer à intervalles réguliers pendant le traitement prolongé les concentrations sériques de folate.

TOXICITÉ ET SURDOSAGE:

Phénytoïne:

- Noter à intervalles réguliers les concentrations sériques de phénytoïne. Les concentrations sanguines thérapeutiques se situent entre 40 et 80 µmol/L chez les patients présentant des concentrations sériques normales d'albumine et une fonction rénale normale. Chez les patients présentant une altération de la liaison protéique (nouveau-nés, insuffisants rénaux, patients atteints d'hypoalbuminémie ou ayant subi un traumatisme aigu), il faut suivre de près les concentrations sériques de phénytoïne libre, qui devraient se situer entre 4 et 8 µmol/L.
- Les signes et les symptômes toxiques graduels incluent le nystagmus, l'ataxie, la confusion, les nausées, les troubles de l'élocution et les étourdissements.

DIAGNOSTICS INFIRMIERS POSSIBLES

- Risque d'accident (Indications).
- Atteinte à l'intégrité de la muqueuse buccale (Effets secondaires).
- Connaissances insuffisantes sur le traitement médicamenteux (Enseignement au patient et à ses proches).

INTERVENTIONS INFIRMIÈRES

- NE PAS CONFONDRE LA FOSPHÉNYTOÏNE (CEREBYX) AVEC LE CÉLÉCOXIB (CELEBREX) OU LE CITALOPRAM (CELEXA).
- Prendre les mesures qui s'imposent en cas de crise convulsive.
- Lors de la substitution de la phénytoïne par un autre anticonvulsivant, il faut adapter la posologie graduellement, pendant plusieurs semaines.
- Lorsqu'on substitue à la fosphénytoïne la phénytoïne par voie orale, on peut administrer la même dose quotidienne totale en une seule fois. Contrairement à la phénytoïne par voie parentérale, la fosphénytoïne peut être administrée par voie IM.
- L'effet anticonvulsivant de la fosphénytoïne n'est pas immédiat. Il faut habituellement prendre des mesures additionnelles (incluant l'administration parentérale de benzodiazépines) pour le traitement immédiat de l'état de mal épileptique. Après l'administration d'une dose d'attaque de fosphénytoïne, il faut administrer un traitement anticonvulsivant d'entretien.

PO:

- Administrer le médicament avec les repas ou immédiatement après afin de réduire l'irritation gastro-intestinale. Bien mélanger les préparations liquides avant de les verser. Utiliser un récipient gradué pour administrer la dose exacte. Les comprimés à croquer doivent être écrasés ou bien mâchés avant d'être avalés. Afin de prévenir le contact direct du médicament alcalin avec les muqueuses, conseiller au patient d'avaler d'abord une gorgée de liquide, de prendre ensuite le médicament et de boire un grand verre d'eau ou de lait ou de manger quelque chose.
- Si le patient est alimenté par voie entérale, il faut prévoir un intervalle de 2 heures entre l'alimentation par voie entérale et l'administration de la phénytoïne. Si la phénytoïne est administrée par tube

nasogastrique, rincer le tube avec 60 à 120 mL d'eau avant et après l'administration.

- Les comprimés à croquer de phénytoïne et les capsules de phénytoïne sodique ne sont pas interchangeables puisqu'ils ne sont pas bioéquivalents.
- Les capsules de Dilantin peuvent être administrées 1 fois par jour. Les autres présentations de Dilantin pourraient entraîner des concentrations sériques toxiques si la dose totale est administrée 1 fois par jour.

Phénytoïne:

IV: la couleur légèrement jaune de la solution ne signifie pas que sa puissance est altérée. Si elle est réfrigérée, la solution peut former un précipité qui se dissoudra lorsqu'elle sera laissée à la température ambiante. Jeter toute solution qui n'est pas transparente.

- Afin de prévenir la précipitation et de réduire l'irritation veineuse locale, perfuser une solution de NaCl 0,9 % à la suite de l'administration de phénytoïne. Éviter l'extravasation; la phénytoïne a un effet caustique sur les tissus.

IV directe: Administrer à un débit ne dépassant pas 50 mg/min (25 mg/min, et même plus lentement, soit de 5 à 10 mg/min, chez les patients prédisposés à l'hypotension, chez ceux prenant des médicaments sympathomimétiques, chez les patients atteints de maladie cardiaque et chez les personnes âgées; de 1 à 3 mg/kg/min chez les enfants et de 0,5 mg/kg/min chez les nouveau-nés). L'administration rapide peut provoquer une hypotension grave, un collapsus cardiovasculaire ou une dépression du SNC.

Perfusion intermittente: Mélanger la phénytoïne à 50 mL de solution de NaCl 0,9 %, au maximum, pour obtenir une concentration de 1 à 10 mg/mL. Administrer le mélange immédiatement après l'avoir préparé. Utiliser une tubulure dotée d'un filtre intégré de 0,22 µm.

Vitesse d'administration: Terminer la perfusion en l'espace de 1 heure, à un débit inférieur à 50 mg/min. Suivre la fonction cardiaque et la pression artérielle tout au long de la perfusion.

Compatibilité (tubulure en Y): esmolol ▪ famotidine ▪ fluconazole ▪ foscarnet ▪ tacrolimus.

Incompatibilité (tubulure en Y): ciprofloxacine ▪ diltiazem ▪ énalaprilate ▪ hydromorphone ▪ potassium, chlorure de ▪ sufentanil ▪ vitamines du complexe B avec C.

Incompatibilité en addition au soluté: Ne pas mélanger avec d'autres solutions ou médicaments, particulièrement avec le dextrose, car un précipité se formera.

Fosphénytoïne:

IV directe: Diluer la fosphénytoïne dans une solution de D5%E ou de NaCl 0,9 % pour obtenir une concentration de 1,5 à 25 mg d'EP/mL. On peut conserver la solution reconstituée pendant 24 heures au réfrigérateur.

Vitesse d'administration: Administrer à un débit inférieur à 150 mg d'EP/min afin de réduire le risque d'hypotension.

Incompatibilité en addition au soluté: Les données ne sont pas disponibles. Ne pas mélanger avec d'autres solutions ou médicaments.

ENSEIGNEMENT AU PATIENT ET À SES PROCHES

- Prévenir le patient que le médicament peut provoquer la somnolence et des étourdissements. Lui conseiller de ne pas conduire et d'éviter les activités qui exigent sa vigilance jusqu'à ce qu'on ait la certitude que le médicament n'entraîne pas ces effets chez lui. Recommander au patient de ne reprendre la conduite automobile que si le médecin l'autorise à le faire après s'être assuré que les crises ont été maîtrisées.
- Conseiller au patient de porter sur lui en tout temps une pièce d'identité où sont inscrits son trouble de santé et son traitement médicamenteux.
- Inciter le patient à prévenir un professionnel de la santé si les symptômes suivants se manifestent: rash, nausées ou vomissements graves, somnolence, troubles d'élocution, démarche chancelante, enflure des ganglions, gencives sensibles ou qui saignent, jaunissement des yeux ou de la peau, douleurs articulaires, fièvre, maux de gorge, saignements ou ecchymoses inhabituels ou céphalées persistantes.
- Insister sur l'importance des examens médicaux réguliers permettant d'évaluer l'efficacité du traitement. Le patient devrait se soumettre à des examens physiques de routine, particulièrement à un examen de la peau et des ganglions lymphatiques et à un ÉEG.

Phénytoïne:

- Conseiller au patient de prendre le médicament tous les jours en respectant rigoureusement la posologie recommandée. S'il doit prendre le médicament 1 fois par jour, il devrait prendre toute dose manquée dès que possible, après quoi il devrait revenir à l'horaire habituel. S'il doit prendre plusieurs doses par jour, il doit prendre la dose manquée dès que possible dans les 4 heures précédant la dose suivante. Le prévenir qu'il ne faut jamais remplacer une dose manquée par une double dose. L'inciter à consulter un professionnel de la santé s'il n'a pu prendre la phénytoïne 2 jours de suite. Le sevrage brusque peut provoquer un état de mal épileptique.

- Recommander au patient d'éviter de boire de l'alcool ou de prendre des médicaments en vente libre en même temps que la phénytoïne, sans consulter au préalable un professionnel de la santé.
- Expliquer au patient l'importance d'une bonne hygiène buccale. L'inciter à se soumettre à des soins d'hygiène dentaire à intervalles réguliers afin de prévenir la sensibilité, les saignements et l'hyperplasie des gencives. L'amorce d'un programme d'hygiène buccale dans les 10 jours suivant le début du traitement par la phénytoïne peut réduire la gravité de l'hyperplasie gingivale et sa propagation. Les patients < 23 ans et ceux qui prennent des doses supérieures à 500 mg par jour sont particulièrement prédisposés à l'hyperplasie gingivale.
- Informer le patient que les diverses marques de phénytoïne ne sont pas nécessairement équivalentes. Lui recommander de vérifier auprès d'un professionnel de la santé s'il doit changer de marque ou de présentation.
- Informer le patient que la phénytoïne peut colorer l'urine en rose, rouge ou rouge-brun, mais que ce changement de couleur n'est pas important.
- Recommander au patient diabétique de mesurer soigneusement sa glycémie et de signaler à un professionnel de la santé tout changement important.
- Recommander au patient qui doit suivre un traitement ou subir une intervention chirurgicale d'avertir le professionnel de la santé qu'il suit un traitement par ce médicament.
- Prévenir le patient qu'il ne doit pas prendre la phénytoïne dans les 2 à 3 heures précédant ou suivant la prise d'antiacides ou d'antidiarrhéiques.
- Recommander à la patiente qui prend un contraceptif oral d'utiliser une autre méthode de contraception non hormonale pendant toute la durée du traitement et jusqu'aux règles suivantes. Lui conseiller de prévenir immédiatement un professionnel de la santé si elle pense être enceinte ou si elle souhaite le devenir.

VÉRIFICATION DE L'EFFICACITÉ THÉRAPEUTIQUE

L'efficacité du traitement peut être démontrée par: la diminution ou l'arrêt des crises sans sédation excessive ▪ la suppression des arythmies ▪ le soulagement de la douleur attribuable à la névralgie.

PHOSPHATE/BIPHOSPHATE

Fleet Lavement, Fleet Lavement pédiatrique, Fleet Phospho-Soda

CLASSIFICATION:
Laxatif (salin)

Grossesse – catégorie inconnue

INDICATIONS

Évacuation intestinale en vue d'une intervention chirurgicale ou d'un examen radiologique ▪ Traitement intermittent de la constipation chronique.

MÉCANISME D'ACTION

Effet osmotique dans la lumière du tractus gastro-intestinal ▪ Effets laxatifs entraînés par la rétention de l'eau et stimulation du péristaltisme ▪ Stimulation de la motilité gastro-intestinale et inhibition de l'absorption des liquides et des électrolytes par l'intestin grêle. ***Effets thérapeutiques:*** Soulagement de la constipation ▪ Évacuation des matières du côlon.

PHARMACOCINÉTIQUE

Absorption: Faible (PO ou IR).
Distribution: Inconnue.
Métabolisme et excrétion: Inconnus.
Demi-vie: Inconnue.

Profil temps-action (effet laxatif)

	DÉBUT D'ACTION	PIC	DURÉE
PO	0,5 – 3 h	inconnu	inconnue
IR	2 – 5 min	inconnu	inconnue

CONTRE-INDICATIONS, PRÉCAUTIONS ET MISES EN GARDE

Contre-indications: Appendicite (ou symptômes) ▪ Colite ulcéreuse ▪ Iléite ▪ Néphropathie ▪ Cardiopathie ▪ Hypertension ▪ Occlusion intestinale ▪ Saignement rectal ▪ Ascite (Fleet Phospho-Soda) ▪ Mégacôlon congénital (Fleet Phospho-Soda) ▪ Régime hyposodé (Fleet Phospho-Soda).

Précautions et mises en garde: Usage excessif ou prolongé (risque d'accoutumance) ▪ Déséquilibre électrolytique ou déshydratation grave ▪ **OBST., ALLAITEMENT:** Ce médicament n'est pas recommandé chez la femme enceinte ou qui allaite (risque de rétention sodique et d'œdème) ▪ Asthénie ▪ Douleurs abdominales, nausées ou vomissements, particulièrement s'ils s'accompagnent de fièvre ou d'autres signes d'abdomen aigu ▪ **PÉD.:** L'utilisation de ce produit n'est pas recommandé chez les enfants < 6 mois (Fleet Lavement pédiatrique), les enfants < 2 ans (Fleet Lavement) et les enfants < 6 ans (Fleet Phospho-Soda).

RÉACTIONS INDÉSIRABLES ET EFFETS SECONDAIRES

GI: crampes, nausées.
HÉ: hyperphosphatémie, hypocalcémie, hypokaliémie, rétention sodique.

INTERACTIONS

Médicament-médicament: Aucune interaction notable.

VOIES D'ADMINISTRATION ET POSOLOGIE

- **PO (adultes et enfants > 12 ans)**: *Laxatif* – 20 mL, 1 fois par jour de Fleet Phospho-Soda.
- **PO (enfants)**: De 10 à 11 ans – 10 mL, 1 fois par jour; de 6 à 9 ans – 5 mL, 1 fois par jour de Fleet Phospho-Soda.
- **PO (adultes)**: *Purgatif* – 45 mL de Fleet Phospho-Soda. Ne pas administrer plus de 45 mL en 24 heures.
- **IR (adultes)**: 120 mL de Fleet Lavement.
- **IR (enfants de 2 à 12 ans)**: 60 mL de Fleet Lavement.

PRÉSENTATION

Solution orale: 2,4 g de phosphate monobasique de sodium et 0,9 g de phosphate dibasique de sodium/5 mL, en flacons de 45 mL[VL] ■ **Lavement**: 16 g de phosphate monobasique de sodium et 6 g de phosphate dibasique de sodium/100 mL, en flacons de 65 et de 130 mL[VL].

SOINS INFIRMIERS

ÉVALUATION DE LA SITUATION

- Suivre de près la fièvre et la distension abdominale, ausculter les bruits intestinaux et observer les habitudes normales d'élimination.
- Déterminer la couleur, la consistance et la quantité des selles produites.

Tests de laboratoire: L'agent peut entraîner une élévation des concentrations sériques de sodium et de phosphore et une diminution des concentrations sériques de calcium et de potassium, ainsi que l'acidose. Les déséquilibres électrolytiques sont normalement transitoires, ne nécessitent pas de traitement et n'entraînent habituellement pas de réactions indésirables.

DIAGNOSTICS INFIRMIERS POSSIBLES

- Constipation (Indications).
- Connaissances insuffisantes sur le traitement médicamenteux (Enseignement au patient et à ses proches).

INTERVENTIONS INFIRMIÈRES

- Ne pas administrer le laxatif au coucher ou tard dans la journée.

PO: Pour obtenir un effet laxatif rapide, administrer la préparation à jeun. Mélanger la dose avec au moins la moitié d'un verre d'eau froide. Servir ensuite au patient un autre verre d'eau froide.
IR: Demander au patient de s'allonger sur le côté gauche et de plier légèrement les genoux. Introduire 5 cm de la pointe lubrifiée dans le rectum, en la dirigeant vers le nombril. Presser doucement le contenant jusqu'à ce qu'il soit vide. Arrêter en cas de résistance, puisqu'il y a risque de perforation si l'on force le contenu dans le rectum.

ENSEIGNEMENT AU PATIENT ET À SES PROCHES

- Prévenir le patient que les laxatifs ne devraient être pris que pendant un court laps de temps. Le traitement prolongé peut entraîner un déséquilibre électrolytique et l'accoutumance.
- Prévenir le patient qui suit un régime hyposodé que cet agent a une teneur élevée en sodium.
- Conseiller au patient de ne pas prendre la préparation par voie orale dans les 2 heures suivant ou précédant la prise d'autres médicaments.
- Recommander au patient de prendre d'autres mesures qui favorisent l'élimination intestinale: consommer des aliments riches en fibres, augmenter sa consommation de liquides, faire de l'exercice. Expliquer au patient que chaque personne a ses propres habitudes d'élimination et qu'il est aussi normal de déféquer 3 fois par jour que 3 fois par semaine.
- Recommander au patient de prévenir un professionnel de la santé si la constipation n'est pas soulagée et si des saignements rectaux ou des symptômes de déséquilibre électrolytique (crampes ou douleurs musculaires, faiblesse, étourdissements, etc.) se manifestent.

VÉRIFICATION DE L'EFFICACITÉ THÉRAPEUTIQUE

L'efficacité du traitement peut être démontrée par: l'évacuation de selles molles et bien moulées ■ l'évacuation des matières du côlon.

PHYTONADIONE

Synonyme: vitamine K
AquaMEPHYTON

CLASSIFICATION:
Vitamine K (liposoluble), antidote

Grossesse – catégorie C

P

INDICATIONS

Prévention et traitement de l'hypoprothrombinémie pouvant être attribuable à des doses excessives d'anticoagulants oraux, de salicylates, à certains antibiotiques, à une carence en vitamine K, à une alimentation parentérale prolongée et à des facteurs qui empêchent l'absorption ou la synthèse de la vitamine K ■ Prévention et traitement des hémorragies du nouveau-né.

MÉCANISME D'ACTION

Élément nécessaire à la synthèse hépatique des facteurs de coagulation II (prothrombine), VII, IX et X. ***Effets thérapeutiques:*** Prévention de l'hémorragie provoquée par l'hypoprothrombinémie.

PHARMACOCINÉTIQUE

Absorption: Bonne (PO, IM ou SC). La présence de sels biliaires et de lipases pancréatiques est nécessaire à l'absorption de l'agent pris par voie orale. Une certaine quantité de vitamine K est produite par les bactéries du tractus gastro-intestinal.

Distribution: La phytonadione traverse la barrière placentaire, mais ne passe pas dans le lait maternel.

Métabolisme et excrétion: Métabolisme hépatique rapide.

Demi-vie: Inconnue.

Profil temps-action

	DÉBUT D'ACTION	PIC†	DURÉE‡
PO	6 - 12 h	inconnu	24 - 48 h
IM, SC	1 - 2 h	3 - 6 h	12 - 24 h
IV	1 - 2 h	3 - 6 h	12 - 24 h

† Arrêt de l'hémorragie.
‡ Normalisation du temps de prothrombine.

CONTRE-INDICATIONS, PRÉCAUTIONS ET MISES EN GARDE

Contre-indications: Hypersensibilité.

Précautions et mises en garde: Insuffisance hépatique.

EXTRÊME PRUDENCE: Des réactions graves ainsi que des décès sont survenus pendant et tout de suite après une injection IV de phytonadione, bien qu'on ait pris soin de bien diluer la préparation et d'éviter une perfusion rapide. Il faut réserver la voie IV pour les cas où l'on estime qu'il est justifié d'exposer le patient à des risques graves.

RÉACTIONS INDÉSIRABLES ET EFFETS SECONDAIRES

GI: irritation gastrique, goût inhabituel.
Tég.: bouffées vasomotrices, rash, urticaire.
Hémat.: anémie hémolytique.
Locaux: érythème, douleur au point d'injection, œdème.
Divers: réactions allergiques, hyperbilirubinémie (doses élevées chez les nouveau-nés prématurés), ictère nucléaire (doses élevées chez les nouveau-nés prématurés).

INTERACTIONS

Médicament-médicament: La phytonadione inhibe les effets anticoagulants de la **warfarine** ■ La **quinidine**, la **quinine** ou les doses élevées de **salicylates** ou d'**antibiotiques** à large spectre, administrées en concomitance, peuvent augmenter les besoins en vitamine K ■ La **cholestyramine**, le **colestipol**, les **huiles minérales** et le **sucralfate** peuvent diminuer l'absorption de la vitamine K depuis le tractus gastro-intestinal.

VOIES D'ADMINISTRATION ET POSOLOGIE

L'administration de la phytonadione par voie IV devrait être réservée aux cas d'urgence ou lorsqu'il n'est pas possible d'utiliser les autres voies d'administration. La phytonadione existe seulement en solution injectable, mais on peut l'utiliser pour administration par voie orale.

Traitement de l'hypoprothrombinémie

- **PO, SC, IM (adultes):** De 2,5 à 10 mg, dose pouvant être répétée après 6 à 8 heures. Dans quelques rares cas, on a dû administrer des doses allant jusqu'à 25 à 50 mg.
- **PO, SC, IM (enfants):** De 2,5 à 10 mg, dose pouvant être répétée après 6 à 8 heures.
- **IM, SC (nourrissons):** De 1 à 2 mg, dose pouvant être répétée après 4 à 8 heures.

Prévention de l'hypoprothrombinémie pendant l'alimentation parentérale totale

- **IM (adultes):** De 5 à 10 mg, 1 fois par semaine.
- **IM (enfants):** De 2 à 5 mg, 1 fois par semaine.

Surdose d'anticoagulants oraux

- **PO, SC, IV (adultes):** De 1 à 10 mg, selon le RNI et la présence ou non d'hémorragie. La dose peut être répétée de 12 à 48 heures plus tard, selon la réponse à la dose initiale.
- **PO, SC, IV (enfants):** De 0,5 à 5 mg.

Prévention du syndrome hémorragique du nouveau-né

- **IM (nouveau-nés):** Une seule injection dans les 6 heures qui suivent la naissance. *Poids à la naissance > 1 500 g* – 1 mg; *poids à la naissance < 1 500 g* – 0,5 mg.
- **PO (nouveau-nés):** 2 mg, administrés lors de la première tétée, à l'âge de 2 à 4 semaines, puis à l'âge de 6 à 8 semaines, pour un total de 3 doses. On doit utiliser la voie orale lorsque les parents refusent l'injection IM.

Traitement du syndrome hémorragique du nouveau-né

- **IM, SC (nouveau-nés)**: 1 mg.

PRÉSENTATION

Solution pour injection: 2 mg/mL, en ampoules de 0,5 mL[Pr], 10 mg/mL, en ampoules de 1 mL[Pr].

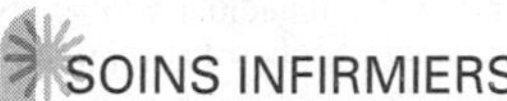

SOINS INFIRMIERS

ÉVALUATION DE LA SITUATION

- Suivre de près les saignements francs et occultes (présence de sang occulte dans les selles, l'urine et les vomissements). Mesurer le pouls et la pression artérielle à intervalles fréquents. Prévenir immédiatement le médecin si des symptômes d'hémorragie interne ou de choc hypovolémique se manifestent. Afin de prévenir tout risque de nouveau traumatisme, informer tout le personnel que le patient est prédisposé aux saignements. Exercer une pression sur tous les points de ponction veineuse pendant au moins 5 minutes; éviter toute injection IM superflue.

PÉD.: Rester à l'affut des réactions indésirables et des effets secondaires. Les enfants sont particulièrement sensibles aux effets de la vitamine K, ce qui peut augmenter le risque d'effets secondaires. Les nouveau-nés, particulièrement les prématurés, sont plus sensibles que les enfants plus âgés.

Tests de laboratoire: Noter le temps de prothrombine avant le traitement par la vitamine K et pendant toute sa durée, afin de déterminer la réponse du patient et le besoin de poursuivre le traitement.

DIAGNOSTICS INFIRMIERS POSSIBLES

- Alimentation déficiente (Indications).
- Atteinte à l'intégrité des tissus (Indications).
- Connaissances insuffisantes sur le traitement médicamenteux (Enseignement au patient et à ses proches).

INTERVENTIONS INFIRMIÈRES

- En raison du risque de réactions d'hypersensibilité grave, on ne recommande pas d'administrer de la vitamine K par voie IV.
- En raison du début d'action retardé de ce médicament, il peut également s'avérer nécessaire d'administrer du plasma ou du sang entier en cas d'hémorragie grave.
- La phytonadione est l'antidote de la warfarine et de la nicoumalone en cas de surdosage, mais elle ne contrecarre pas l'activité anticoagulante de l'héparine ou d'autres anticoagulants.

PO: Utiliser la solution injectable. Diluer dans environ 100 mL d'eau ou de jus et faire boire immédiatement.

IM: Ne pas administrer par voie IM en cas de surdosage par des anticoagulants oraux en raison du risque élevé d'hématome.

IV directe: La phytonadione devrait être diluée dans 10 mL de NaCl 0,9 % ou de D5%E.

Vitesse d'administration: Si l'on doit absolument administrer la phytonadione par voie IV, il faut le faire très lentement, à un débit ne dépassant pas 1 mg/min.

Perfusion intermittente: La phytonadione peut aussi être diluée dans une solution de NaCl 0,9 %, de D5%E ou de D5%E/NaCl 0,9 %.

Vitesse d'administration: Si l'on doit absolument administrer la phytonadione par voie IV, il faut le faire très lentement, en 15 à 30 minutes, à un débit ne dépassant pas 1 mg/min.

Compatibilité (tubulure en Y): adrénaline ▪ ampicilline ▪ famotidine ▪ héparine ▪ hydrocortisone sodique, succinate d' ▪ potassium, chlorure de ▪ tolazoline ▪ vitamines du complexe B avec C.

Incompatibilité (tubulure en Y): dobutamine.

ENSEIGNEMENT AU PATIENT ET À SES PROCHES

- Conseiller au patient de respecter rigoureusement la posologie recommandée. S'il n'a pu prendre le médicament au moment habituel, il doit le prendre dès que possible à moins qu'il ne soit presque l'heure prévue pour la dose suivante. Lui conseiller de prévenir un professionnel de la santé s'il n'a pu prendre plusieurs doses.
- La cuisson ne détruit pas considérablement la vitamine K. Les patients qui prennent de la vitamine K ne doivent pas apporter des modifications importantes à leur alimentation. Les aliments riches en vitamine K sont indiqués à l'annexe J.
- Recommander au patient d'éviter les injections par voie IM et les activités pouvant entraîner des blessures. L'inciter à utiliser une brosse à dents à poils doux et un rasoir électrique et à ne pas se servir de soie dentaire jusqu'à ce que le trouble de coagulation soit corrigé.
- Recommander au patient de signaler les saignements ou les ecchymoses inhabituels: saignement des gencives, saignement de nez, selles noires et goudronneuses, hématurie, débit menstruel abondant.
- Conseiller au patient qui reçoit un traitement par la vitamine K de consulter un professionnel de la santé avant de prendre des médicaments en vente libre ou des produits naturels.
- Recommander au patient qui doit suivre un traitement ou subir une intervention chirurgicale d'informer

le professionnel de la santé qu'il suit un traitement avec ce médicament.
- Conseiller au patient de porter sur lui en tout temps une pièce d'identité où est inscrit son trouble de santé.
- Insister sur l'importance des tests fréquents permettant de mesurer les facteurs de coagulation.

VÉRIFICATION DE L'EFFICACITÉ THÉRAPEUTIQUE

L'efficacité du traitement peut être démontrée par: la prévention des hémorragies spontanées ou l'arrêt des saignements chez les patients souffrant d'hypoprothrombinémie secondaire due à une mauvaise absorption intestinale ou à un traitement par des anticoagulants oraux, des salicylates ou des antibiotiques ■ la prévention et le traitement des hémorragies du nouveau-né. ✳

PILOCARPINE (VOIE ORALE)

Salagen

CLASSIFICATION:

Cholinergique (à action directe)

Grossesse – catégorie C

Pour l'usage ophtalmique, voir l'annexe N.

P

INDICATIONS

Traitement de la sécheresse de la bouche (xérostomie) induite par la radiothérapie associée au cancer de la tête et du cou ■ Traitement de la sécheresse de la bouche (xérostomie) et des yeux (xérophtalmie) chez les patients atteints du syndrome de Sjögren.

MÉCANISME D'ACTION

Stimulation des récepteurs cholinergiques entraînant surtout un effet muscarinique incluant la stimulation des glandes exocrines ■ La pilocarpine entraîne aussi d'autres effets, dont les suivants: transpiration et sécrétions gastriques accrues ■ sécrétions bronchiques accrues ■ tonus et motilité accrus des voies urinaires, de la vésicule biliaire et du muscle lisse des canaux biliaires. ***Effets thérapeutiques:*** Augmentation des sécrétions des glandes salivaires.

PHARMACOCINÉTIQUE

Absorption: Bonne (PO).

Distribution: Inconnue.

Métabolisme et excrétion: Inactivation aux synapses neuronales et dans le plasma. Une certaine quantité de pilocarpine et de ses métabolites est excrétée dans l'urine.

Demi-vie: *Après une dose de 5 mg, pendant 2 jours* – 0,8 heure; *après une dose de 10 mg, pendant 2 jours* – 1,3 heure.

Profil temps-action

	DÉBUT D'ACTION	PIC	DURÉE
PO	20 min	1 h	3 – 5 h

CONTRE-INDICATIONS, PRÉCAUTIONS ET MISES EN GARDE

Contre-indications: Hypersensibilité ■ Asthme non maîtrisé ■ Glaucome à angle fermé ■ Iritis.

Précautions et mises en garde: Antécédents de maladie pulmonaire (asthme, bronchite ou bronchopneumopathie chronique obstructive) ■ Maladie des canaux biliaires ou calculs biliaires ■ Ulcère gastroduodénal évolutif ■ Maladie cardiovasculaire ■ Maladies de la rétine ■ Lithiase rénale ■ Antécédents de troubles psychiatriques ou cognitifs ■ Insuffisance rénale ou hépatique ■ **OBST., ALLAITEMENT, PÉD.:** L'innocuité du médicament n'a pas été établie.

RÉACTIONS INDÉSIRABLES ET EFFETS SECONDAIRES

SNC: étourdissements, céphalées, faiblesse.

ORLO: amblyopie, épistaxis, rhinite.

CV: œdème, hypertension, tachycardie.

GI: nausées, vomissements, dyspepsie, dysphagie.

GU: mictions fréquentes.

Tég.: bouffées vasomotrices, transpiration.

SN: tremblements.

Divers: frissons, changement de la voix.

INTERACTIONS

Médicament-médicament: L'administration concomitante d'**anticholinergiques** réduit l'efficacité de la pilocarpine ■ L'usage concomitant de **béthanéchol** ou d'**agents cholinergiques pour usage ophtalmique** peut entraîner des effets cholinergiques additifs ■ L'administration concomitante de **bêtabloquants** peut accroître le risque de réactions cardiovasculaires indésirables (troubles de la conduction).

VOIES D'ADMINISTRATION ET POSOLOGIE

- **PO (adultes):** 5 mg, 3 ou 4 fois par jour; on peut augmenter la dose jusqu'à concurrence de 30 mg/jour.

PRÉSENTATION

Comprimés: 5 mg[Pr].

SOINS INFIRMIERS

ÉVALUATION DE LA SITUATION

- Examiner à intervalles réguliers pendant toute la durée du traitement la muqueuse buccale du patient pour déceler la présence de sécheresse et d'aphtes.

DIAGNOSTICS INFIRMIERS POSSIBLES

- Atteinte à l'intégrité de la muqueuse buccale (Indications).
- Connaissances insuffisantes sur le traitement médicamenteux (Enseignement au patient et à ses proches).

INTERVENTIONS INFIRMIÈRES

- Lors du traitement d'entretien, administrer la plus faible dose efficace tolérée.

ENSEIGNEMENT AU PATIENT ET À SES PROCHES

- Conseiller au patient de respecter rigoureusement la posologie recommandée.
- Prévenir le patient que la pilocarpine peut entraîner des troubles de la vue, particulièrement le soir. Lui conseiller de ne pas conduire et d'éviter les activités qui exigent sa vigilance jusqu'à ce qu'on ait la certitude que le médicament n'entraîne pas cet effet chez lui.
- Recommander au patient de boire une quantité suffisante de liquides tous les jours (de 1 500 à 2 000 mL), particulièrement s'il transpire. Le prévenir que si sa consommation de liquides est insuffisante, il risque de se déshydrater.

VÉRIFICATION DE L'EFFICACITÉ THÉRAPEUTIQUE

L'efficacité du traitement peut être démontrée par: l'augmentation des sécrétions des glandes salivaires chez les patients souffrant de sécheresse de la bouche ■ la diminution de la sécheresse de la bouche chez les patients atteints du syndrome de Sjögren. Les pleins effets du médicament peuvent ne se manifester qu'après 12 semaines chez les patients atteints de cancer ou après 6 semaines chez les patients atteints du syndrome de Sjögren.

PIMÉCROLIMUS

Elidel

CLASSIFICATION:

Immunomodulateur topique, inhibiteur de la calcineurine

Grossesse – catégorie C

INDICATIONS

Traitement de deuxième intention à court terme ou intermittent à long terme de la dermatite atopique légère ou modérée, chez les patients non immunodéprimés chez qui l'emploi des traitements classiques est à proscrire en raison des risques qu'ils comportent, ou chez les patients qui n'ont pas répondu adéquatement aux traitements classiques ou qui ne les tolèrent pas.

MÉCANISME D'ACTION

Suppression de l'inflammation et de la réponse immunitaire normale par inhibition de l'activation des lymphocytes T. ***Effets thérapeutiques:*** Maîtrise de l'inflammation, des démangeaisons et des rougeurs reliées à la dermatite atopique.

PHARMACOCINÉTIQUE

Absorption: Faible.

Distribution: Inconnue.

Métabolisme et excrétion: Métabolisme hépatique. Le métabolisme cutané est négligeable. Excrétion dans les fèces.

Demi-vie: Inconnue.

Profil temps-action
(diminution de l'inflammation
et des symptômes de dermatite atopique)

	Début d'action	Pic	Durée
Topique	7 jours	8 jours	inconnue

CONTRE-INDICATIONS, PRÉCAUTIONS ET MISES EN GARDE

Contre-indications: Hypersensibilité au pimécrolimus ou à un ingrédient de la préparation.

Précautions et mises en garde: Maladie de Netherton (risque accru d'absorption systémique du pimécrolimus) ■ Surface cutanée atteinte d'une infection virale évolutive ■ Adénopathie ■ Mononucléose infectieuse ■ Patients immunodéprimés ■ **OBST., ALLAITEMENT:** Évaluer si les bienfaits escomptés dépassent les risques possibles ■ **PÉD.:** Enfants < 2 ans (utilisation déconseillée; on a signalé que certains effets indésirables étaient plus fréquents chez les patients traités avec le pimécrolimus qu'avec le placebo) ■ **GÉR.:** Patients âgés > 65 ans (l'efficacité et l'innocuité du pimécrolimus n'ont pas été étudiées) ■ Utilisation continue à long terme (l'innocuité de l'agent n'a pas été établie) ■ Néoplasie cutanée et lymphome (on en a signalé de rares cas, bien qu'aucun lien de cause à effet n'ait été établi).

RÉACTIONS INDÉSIRABLES ET EFFETS SECONDAIRES

SNC: céphalées.
Resp.: symptômes pseudogrippaux, toux, rhinite.
GI: nausée, diarrhée, douleurs abdominales.
Tég.: réaction allergique, sensation de brûlure, prurit, irritation locale de la peau, folliculite, infection cutanée, érythème cutané, éruptions maculopapuleuses, acné.
Divers: infections diverses, herpès, fièvre, lymphomes et néoplasmes cutanés (CARCINOME BASOCELLULAIRE, CARCINOME SPINOCELLULAIRE ET MÉLANOME).

INTERACTIONS

Médicament-médicament: Aucune interaction n'a été signalée (absence d'études) ■ La prudence est de mise lorsqu'on administre en concomitance des **inhibiteurs connus du CYP3A4** (p. ex., **érythromycine**, **itraconazole**, **kétoconazole**, **fluconazole**, **cimétidine**).

VOIES D'ADMINISTRATION ET POSOLOGIE

- **Usage topique (adultes et enfants ≥ 2 ans)**: Application topique d'une couche mince, 2 fois par jour, matin et soir.

PRÉSENTATION

Crème: 1 %[Pr].

P

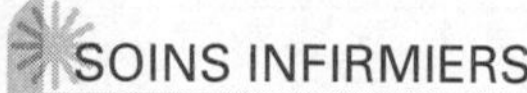

SOINS INFIRMIERS

ÉVALUATION DE LA SITUATION

- Examiner la peau affectée avant l'application de la préparation et, quotidiennement, pendant toute la durée du traitement. Noter le degré d'inflammation et de prurit. Prévenir le médecin ou un autre professionnel de la santé si les symptômes suivants d'infection se manifestent: douleur accrue, érythème, exsudats purulents.

DIAGNOSTICS INFIRMIERS POSSIBLES

- Risque d'atteinte à l'intégrité de la peau (Indications).
- Risque d'infection (Effets secondaires).
- Connaissances insuffisantes sur le traitement médicamenteux (Enseignement au patient et à ses proches).

INTERVENTIONS INFIRMIÈRES

- Suivre rigoureusement les consignes posologiques. La préparation topique est réservée à l'usage externe pour le traitement de l'eczéma (dermatite atopique). Elle ne doit être utilisée que si les autres traitements se sont avérés inefficaces ou inappropriés.
- Éviter l'utilisation continue à long terme de la préparation topique; son application devrait se limiter aux régions atteintes de dermatite atopique.
- Après l'application, bien se laver les mains s'il s'agit de régions qui ne doivent pas être traitées.
- Ne pas appliquer sur des régions présentant une infection active.
- Si la crème est appliquée après un bain ou une douche, s'assurer que la peau est bien séchée.
- Ne pas prendre de bain ni de douche et ne pas se baigner immédiatement après avoir appliqué le médicament, car on risque d'enlever la crème appliquée.
- Il n'est pas recommandé de recouvrir les régions traitées avec la crème de pimécrolimus d'un pansement occlusif, car les effets du produit sous un tel pansement n'ont pas fait l'objet d'études.

ENSEIGNEMENT AU PATIENT ET À SES PROCHES

- Montrer au patient comment appliquer le médicament. Appliquer la crème en une mince couche sur les régions touchées de la peau, y compris celles au niveau du visage, du cou et des paupières. Éviter tout contact direct avec les yeux. Ne pas avaler le produit. Si le patient n'a pas pu appliquer le médicament au moment habituel, il doit l'appliquer dès que possible, à moins que ce ne soit presque l'heure prévue pour l'application suivante.
- Conseiller au patient de respecter rigoureusement la posologie recommandée et d'éviter d'utiliser des cosmétiques, des bandages, des pansements ou d'autres produits topiques sur la région traitée, sauf sur recommandation d'un professionnel de la santé.
- Recommander au patient de cesser le traitement dès la disparition des signes et des symptômes de dermatite atopique (p. ex., prurit, inflammation et érythème). En l'absence d'amélioration après 3 semaines de traitement ou en cas d'exacerbation de la maladie, le patient devrait abandonner le traitement et consulter son médecin.
- Informer le patient que le pimécrolimus topique peut occasionner l'apparition de symptômes locaux de courte durée, tels qu'une sensation de brûlure cutanée (sensation de brûlure ou de chaleur) ou prurit. Les symptômes localisés, qui sont plus fréquents pendant les premiers jours d'application du produit, se résorbent de façon générale à mesure que se cicatrisent les lésions de la dermatite atopique.
- Informer le patient que les personnes atteintes de dermatite atopique sont particulièrement prédisposées aux infections superficielles de la peau. Le

traitement avec le pimécrolimus topique peut être associé à un risque accru d'infections par le virus varicelle-zona (varicelle ou zona), d'infections par le virus herpes simplex ou d'eczéma herpétiforme. Dans de tels cas, il faut évaluer les risques et les avantages de l'utilisation du produit, car son efficacité et son innocuité n'ont fait l'objet d'aucune étude.

- Conseiller au patient d'éviter autant que possible de s'exposer à la lumière du soleil ou à des lampes solaires (cabines de bronzage ou photothérapie par UVA/B).
- Informer le patient que la consommation d'alcool peut entraîner des rougeurs cutanées au niveau de la peau ou du visage, ou lui donner la sensation d'avoir chaud.
- Recommander à la patiente qui pense être enceinte ou qui souhaite le devenir d'informer le médecin qu'elle utilise ce médicament.
- Recommander au patient de prévenir un professionnel de la santé si les symptômes de la maladie sous-jacente ressurgissent ou s'aggravent ou si des symptômes d'infection se manifestent.
- Prévenir le patient que des cas d'adénopathie, généralement liée à des infections, ont été signalés dans les études cliniques. Le patient sous traitement par la préparation topique qui souffre d'une adénopathie ou de mononucléose infectieuse aiguë devrait consulter son médecin et subir des examens visant à en déterminer l'étiologie. L'utilisation de ce produit est déconseillée chez les personnes dont le système immunitaire est affaibli.
- Conseiller au patient de conserver le médicament à la température ambiante (de 15 °C à 30 °C).

VÉRIFICATION DE L'EFFICACITÉ THÉRAPEUTIQUE

L'efficacité du traitement peut être démontrée par: la résolution de l'inflammation, du prurit, de l'érythème ou des démangeaisons causés par la dermatite atopique.

PINDOLOL

Apo-Pindol, Gen-Pindolol, Novo-Pindol, PMS-Pindolol, Visken

CLASSIFICATION:

Antihypertenseur, antiangineux (bêtabloquant)

Grossesse – catégories B (1er trimestre) et D (2e et 3e trimestres)

INDICATIONS

Traitement de l'hypertension ■ Prophylaxie de l'angine de poitrine.

MÉCANISME D'ACTION

Inhibition de la stimulation des récepteurs bêta$_1$-adrénergiques (myocardiques) et bêta$_2$-adrénergiques (pulmonaires, vasculaires ou utérins) ■ Activité sympathomimétique intrinsèque (ASI) pouvant entraîner une bradycardie moindre. ***Effets thérapeutiques:*** Diminution de la fréquence cardiaque et abaissement de la pression artérielle.

PHARMACOCINÉTIQUE

Absorption: Bonne (PO).

Distribution: L'agent pénètre dans le SNC, traverse la barrière placentaire et passe dans le lait maternel.

Métabolisme et excrétion: Métabolisme hépatique. Excrétion rénale (40 % sous forme inchangée et 60 % sous forme de métabolites inactifs) et fécale (de 6 à 9 % sous forme de métabolites inactifs).

Demi-vie: De 3 à 4 heures.

Profil temps-action (effets cardiovasculaires)

	DÉBUT D'ACTION	PIC	DURÉE
PO	1 – 3 h	1 – 2 semaines	jusqu'à 24 h

CONTRE-INDICATIONS, PRÉCAUTIONS ET MISES EN GARDE

Contre-indications: Insuffisance cardiaque ■ Choc cardiogénique ■ Bradycardie sinusale ■ Bloc AV du 2e et du 3e degré ■ Insuffisance du ventricule droit secondaire à l'hypertension pulmonaire ■ Anesthésie à l'aide d'agents dépresseurs du myocarde ■ Bronchospasme, incluant asthme et bronchopneumopathie chronique obstructive grave.

Précautions et mises en garde: Insuffisance rénale ■ Insuffisance hépatique ■ **GÉR.**: Il est recommandé de réduire la dose chez les personnes âgées ou débilitées (sensibilité accrue aux bêtabloquants) ■ Arrêt brusque du traitement (risque d'aggravation de l'angine de poitrine, d'arythmies ventriculaires et d'infarctus du myocarde) ■ Diabète (le médicament peut masquer les signes d'hypoglycémie) ■ Thyrotoxicose (le médicament peut en masquer les symptômes) ■ Antécédents de réactions allergiques graves (les réactions peuvent être plus intenses) ■ **OBST., ALLAITEMENT**: L'innocuité du médicament n'a pas été établie chez la femme enceinte ou qui allaite (l'agent traverse la barrière placentaire et passe dans le lait maternel) ■ **PÉD.**: L'efficacité et l'innocuité du médicament n'ont pas été établies.

P

RÉACTIONS INDÉSIRABLES ET EFFETS SECONDAIRES

SNC: fatigue, faiblesse, anxiété, dépression, étourdissements, insomnie, perte de mémoire, modifications des opérations de la pensée, nervosité, cauchemars.
ORLO: vision trouble, xérophtalmie, congestion nasale.
Resp.: bronchospasme, respiration sifflante.
CV: ARYTHMIES, BRADYCARDIE, INSUFFISANCE CARDIAQUE CONGESTIVE, ŒDÈME PULMONAIRE, hypotension orthostatique, vasoconstriction périphérique.
GI: constipation, diarrhée, nausées.
GU: impuissance, baisse de la libido.
Tég.: démangeaisons, rash.
End.: hyperglycémie, hypoglycémie.
Loc.: arthralgie, douleurs lombaires, crampes musculaires.
SN: paresthésie.
Divers: syndrome lupique d'origine médicamenteuse.

INTERACTIONS

Médicament-médicament: Risque de dépression myocardique additive lors de l'administration concomitante d'une **anesthésie générale**, de **diltiazem** et de **vérapamil** ■ Risque de bradycardie additive lors de l'administration concomitante de **dérivés digitaliques** ■ Les **antihypertenseurs** et les **dérivés nitrés** ainsi que l'**alcool** pris en grandes quantités peuvent exercer des effets hypotenseurs additifs ■ Les **amphétamines**, la **cocaïne**, l'**éphédrine**, l'**adrénaline**, la **noradrénaline**, la **phényléphrine** ou la **pseudoéphédrine**, utilisés en concomitance, peuvent entraîner une réponse hypertensive excessive ■ Le médicament peut entraver l'efficacité de l'**insuline** ou des **hypoglycémiants oraux** (des adaptations de la posologie peuvent s'avérer nécessaires) ■ Le médicament peut réduire l'efficacité des **bronchodilatateurs bêta-adrénergiques** ■ Le médicament peut diminuer les effets cardiovasculaires bénéfiques de la **dopamine** ou de la **dobutamine** sur les récepteurs bêta-adrénergiques ■ Le pindolol doit être administré avec prudence dans les 14 jours précédant ou suivant un traitement par un **IMAO** (risque d'hypertension) ■ L'administration concomitante d'**AINS** peut réduire l'effet antihypertenseur du médicament.

P

VOIES D'ADMINISTRATION ET POSOLOGIE

Hypertension

- **PO (adultes)**: Initialement, 5 mg, 2 fois par jour; on peut augmenter la dose par paliers de 10 mg par jour, toutes les 1 ou 2 semaines, selon la réponse au traitement et la tolérance du patient. La dose d'entretien habituelle se situe entre 15 et 45 mg par jour. Ne pas dépasser 45 mg par jour.

Angine de poitrine

- **PO (adultes)**: Initialement, 5 mg, 3 fois par jour; on peut augmenter la dose toutes les 1 à 2 semaines. La dose d'entretien habituelle se situe entre 15 et 40 mg par jour, en 3 ou 4 prises. Ne pas dépasser 40 mg par jour.

PRÉSENTATION (version générique disponible)

Comprimés: 5 mg[Pr], 10 mg[Pr], 15 mg[Pr] ■ **En association avec**: hydrochlorothiazide (Viskazide).

SOINS INFIRMIERS

ÉVALUATION DE LA SITUATION

- Mesurer la pression artérielle et le pouls à intervalles fréquents au cours de la période d'adaptation de la posologie et à intervalles réguliers pendant la durée du traitement. Suivre de près l'hypotension orthostatique pendant qu'on aide le patient à se lever.
- Effectuer le bilan quotidien des ingesta et des excreta et peser le patient tous les jours. Évaluer, à intervalles réguliers, les signes et les symptômes suivants de surcharge liquidienne: œdème périphérique, dyspnée, râles ou crépitations, fatigue, gain pondéral, turgescence des jugulaires.

Angine: Noter la fréquence et les caractéristiques des épisodes de douleurs thoraciques à intervalles réguliers pendant toute la durée du traitement.

Tests de laboratoire:

- L'agent peut élever les concentrations d'urée et les concentrations sériques de lipoprotéines, de potassium, des triglycérides et d'acide urique.
- L'agent peut entraîner l'élévation de la glycémie.

DIAGNOSTICS INFIRMIERS POSSIBLES

- Débit cardiaque diminué (Effets secondaires).
- Connaissances insuffisantes sur le traitement médicamenteux (Enseignement au patient et à ses proches).
- Non-observance du traitement médicamenteux (Enseignement au patient et à ses proches).

INTERVENTIONS INFIRMIÈRES

- Mesurer le pouls avant d'administrer le médicament. Si le pouls est < 50 bpm ou si des arythmies se manifestent, ne pas administrer le pindolol et prévenir le médecin ou un autre professionnel de la santé.
- Le médicament doit être administré avec les repas.

ENSEIGNEMENT AU PATIENT ET À SES PROCHES

- Conseiller au patient de suivre rigoureusement la posologie recommandée et de prendre le médicament à la même heure, tous les jours, même s'il se sent mieux. L'avertir qu'il ne doit jamais sauter de dose, ni remplacer une dose manquée par une double dose. S'il n'a pu prendre le médicament au moment habituel, il doit le prendre aussitôt que possible jusqu'à 4 heures avant l'heure prévue pour la dose suivante. Le prévenir que le sevrage brusque peut provoquer des arythmies qui pourraient mettre sa vie en danger, l'hypertension ou l'ischémie du myocarde.
- Conseiller au patient d'avoir toujours à sa disposition une quantité suffisante de médicament pour les fins de semaine, les congés et les vacances. Il devrait garder dans son portefeuille une ordonnance pour parer à toute urgence.
- Montrer au patient et à ses proches comment mesurer le pouls et la pression artérielle. Leur recommander de noter le pouls tous les jours et la pression artérielle, 2 fois par semaine, et de communiquer avec un professionnel de la santé si le pouls < 50 battements par minute ou si la pression artérielle change de façon marquée.
- Prévenir le patient que le pindolol peut parfois provoquer des étourdissements. Lui conseiller de ne pas conduire et d'éviter les activités qui exigent sa vigilance jusqu'à ce qu'on ait la certitude que le médicament n'entraîne pas cet effet chez lui.
- Recommander au patient de changer lentement de position pour réduire le risque d'hypotension orthostatique, particulièrement au début du traitement ou lors de la majoration de la dose.
- Prévenir le patient que ce médicament peut le rendre plus sensible au froid.
- Avertir le patient qu'il ne doit pas prendre de médicaments en vente libre, particulièrement des préparations contre le rhume, ou un produit naturel sans avoir consulté au préalable un professionnel de la santé.
- Prévenir le patient diabétique qu'il doit suivre de près sa glycémie, particulièrement en cas de faiblesse, de malaise, d'irritabilité ou de fatigue. Le pindolol peut masquer certains signes d'hypoglycémie, mais la transpiration et les étourdissements peuvent continuer de se manifester.
- Recommander au patient de signaler à un professionnel de la santé les symptômes suivants: pouls ralenti, problèmes respiratoires, respiration sifflante, mains et pieds froids, étourdissements, confusion, dépression, rash, fièvre, maux de gorge, saignements ou ecchymoses inhabituels.
- Conseiller au patient qui doit suivre un autre traitement ou subir une intervention chirurgicale d'informer le professionnel de la santé qu'il suit un traitement par ce médicament.
- Conseiller au patient de porter sur lui en tout temps une pièce d'identité où sont inscrits son problème de santé et son traitement.

Hypertension: Encourager le patient à prendre d'autres mesures permettant de maîtriser l'hypertension: perdre du poids, consommer moins de sel, réduire le stress, faire régulièrement de l'exercice, diminuer sa consommation d'alcool et arrêter de fumer. Le prévenir que ce médicament stabilise la pression artérielle, mais ne guérit pas l'hypertension.

VÉRIFICATION DE L'EFFICACITÉ THÉRAPEUTIQUE

L'efficacité du traitement peut être démontrée par: la baisse de la pression artérielle ■ la diminution de la fréquence des crises d'angine ■ l'amélioration de la tolérance à l'effort.

PIOGLITAZONE

Actos

CLASSIFICATION:

Antidiabétique (thiazolidinedione)

Grossesse – catégorie C

INDICATIONS

Traitement d'appoint à la diétothérapie et à l'exercice lors de la prise en charge du diabète de type 2 ou traitement d'association avec la metformine ou une sulfonylurée, lorsque la diétothérapie et l'exercice, jumelés à la metformine ou à une sulfonylurée, n'ont pas réussi à équilibrer la glycémie.

MÉCANISME D'ACTION

Amélioration de la sensibilité à l'insuline par un effet agoniste au niveau des sites récepteurs jouant un rôle dans la réactivité de l'insuline et la production de glucose qui s'ensuit ■ Ces effets ne peuvent se manifester qu'en présence d'insuline. ***Effets thérapeutiques:*** Diminution de l'insulinorésistance entraînant l'équilibrage de la glycémie sans induire de l'hypoglycémie.

PHARMACOCINÉTIQUE

Absorption: Bonne (PO).

Distribution: Inconnue.

Liaison aux protéines: > 99 % (molécule mère et métabolites actifs).

Métabolisme et excrétion: Métabolisme hépatique; au moins 2 métabolites sont actifs. Excrétion fécale, sous forme inchangée ou de métabolites, et rénale, principalement sous forme de métabolites.

Demi-vie: *Pioglitazone* – de 3 à 7 heures; *Pioglitazone totale (pioglitazone et métabolites)* – de 16 à 24 heures.

Profil temps-action (effet sur la glycémie)

	DÉBUT D'ACTION	PIC	DURÉE
PO	4 semaines	inconnu	4 semaines

CONTRE-INDICATIONS, PRÉCAUTIONS ET MISES EN GARDE

Contre-indications: Hypersensibilité ▪ Insuffisance hépatique grave ▪ Insuffisance cardiaque aiguë.

Précautions et mises en garde: Œdème ▪ Femmes anovulatoires préménopausées (risque de rétablissement de l'ovulation et de grossesse) ▪ Acidocétose diabétique ▪ Preuve clinique de maladie hépatique évolutive ou élévation des concentrations d'ALT (plus de 2,5 fois la limite supérieure de la normale) ▪ **OBST., ALLAITEMENT:** L'innocuité du médicament n'a pas été établie chez la femme enceinte ou qui allaite; il est recommandé d'administrer de l'insuline à ces femmes ▪ **PÉD.:** L'innocuité et l'efficacité du médicament n'ont pas été établies chez les enfants < 18 ans ▪ Diabète de type 1 (le mode d'action du médicament est régi par la présence d'insuline) ▪ Œdème maculaire (risque d'apparition ou d'aggravation).

RÉACTIONS INDÉSIRABLES ET EFFETS SECONDAIRES

SNC: œdème.

Hémat.: anémie.

INTERACTIONS

Médicament-médicament: La pioglitazone peut réduire l'efficacité des **contraceptifs oraux** ▪ La pioglitazone est métabolisée par l'isoenzyme 3A4 du cytochrome P450; aucune étude n'a été menée pour évaluer l'effet de médicaments inhibiteurs ou inducteurs de ce cytochrome ou métabolisés par cette voie.

Médicament-produits naturels: La **glucosamine** peut entraver l'équilibrage de la glycémie ▪ Le **chrome** et le **coenzyme Q-10** peuvent augmenter le risque d'hypoglycémie.

VOIES D'ADMINISTRATION ET POSOLOGIE

- **PO (adultes):** De 15 à 30 mg, 1 fois par jour; on peut augmenter la dose jusqu'à concurrence de 45 mg par jour, selon la réponse au traitement et la tolérance du patient.

PRÉSENTATION

Comprimés: 15 mg[Pr], 30 mg[Pr], 45 mg[Pr].

SOINS INFIRMIERS

ÉVALUATION DE LA SITUATION

- Chez le patient qui prend simultanément une sulfonylurée, suivre à intervalles réguliers, pendant toute la durée du traitement, les signes et les symptômes d'hypoglycémie (transpiration, faim, faiblesse, étourdissements, tremblements, tachycardie, anxiété).

Tests de laboratoire:

- Pour évaluer l'efficacité du médicament, suivre la glycémie et les concentrations d'hémoglobine glyquée (HbA_{1c}) à intervalles réguliers, pendant toute la durée du traitement.
- Noter la numération globulaire et la formule leucocytaire à intervalles réguliers pendant toute la durée du traitement. La pioglitazone peut entraîner une baisse des concentrations d'hémoglobine et de l'hématocrite, habituellement au cours des 4 à 12 semaines qui suivent le début du traitement; ces concentrations se stabilisent par la suite.
- Noter les concentrations sériques d'ALT avant le traitement, puis tous les 2 mois pendant les 12 premiers mois de traitement et à intervalles réguliers par la suite ou en présence de jaunisse ou de signes de dysfonctionnement hépatique. On ne doit pas administrer la pioglitazone aux patients atteints d'une maladie hépatique évolutive ou présentant des concentrations d'ALT plus de 2,5 fois la limite supérieure de la normale. Les patients présentant des concentrations légèrement élevées d'ALT doivent être suivis de plus près. Si les concentrations d'ALT s'élèvent à plus de 3 fois la limite supérieure de la normale, il faut les mesurer rapidement de nouveau. Cesser le traitement par la pioglitazone si les concentrations d'ALT demeurent plus de 3 fois la limite supérieure de la normale.

DIAGNOSTICS INFIRMIERS POSSIBLES

- Alimentation excessive (Indications).
- Connaissances insuffisantes sur le traitement médicamenteux (Enseignement au patient et à ses proches).
- Non-observance du traitement médicamenteux (Enseignement au patient et à ses proches).

INTERVENTIONS INFIRMIÈRES

- Chez les patients dont la glycémie est stabilisée par une diétothérapie antidiabétique, le stress, la fièvre, un traumatisme, une infection ou une intervention chirurgicale peuvent dicter l'administration d'insuline.
- Le médicament peut être administré sans égard aux repas.

ENSEIGNEMENT AU PATIENT ET À SES PROCHES

- Conseiller au patient de respecter rigoureusement la posologie recommandée. S'il n'a pu prendre le médicament au cours d'une journée, il ne doit pas doubler la dose le lendemain.
- Expliquer au patient que ce médicament équilibre la glycémie, mais ne guérit pas le diabète. Le traitement est de longue durée.
- Revoir avec le patient les signes et les symptômes d'hypoglycémie et d'hyperglycémie. En cas d'hypoglycémie, conseiller au patient de prendre un verre de jus d'orange ou 2 ou 3 cuillerées à thé de sucre, de miel ou de sirop de maïs dissous dans de l'eau et d'en informer un professionnel de la santé.
- Encourager le patient à suivre sa diétothérapie, à prendre ses médicaments et à faire de l'exercice afin de prévenir les épisodes d'hyperglycémie ou d'hypoglycémie.
- Faire la démonstration du dosage de la glycémie et de la cétonémie. Ces résultats doivent être notés attentivement pendant des périodes de stress ou pendant une maladie. Il faut prévenir un professionnel de la santé si des modifications importantes surviennent.
- Conseiller au patient d'informer immédiatement un professionnel de la santé si des signes de dysfonctionnement hépatique (nausées, vomissements, douleurs abdominales, fatigue, anorexie, urines foncées, jaunisse) ou d'insuffisance cardiaque (œdème, difficultés respiratoires, gain de poids rapide) se manifestent.
- Informer la patiente que l'insuline est le médicament de prédilection permettant d'équilibrer la glycémie durant la grossesse. Lui expliquer que des doses plus élevées de contraceptifs oraux ou une autre forme de contraception peuvent être nécessaires. Lui recommander d'informer un professionnel de la santé si elle pense être enceinte ou si elle souhaite le devenir.
- Recommander au patient qui doit suivre un traitement ou subir une intervention chirurgicale de prévenir le professionnel de la santé qu'il suit un traitement par ce médicament.
- Inciter le patient souffrant de diabète à toujours garder sur lui du sucre (bonbons, sachets de sucre) et une pièce d'identité où sont inscrits sa maladie et son traitement médicamenteux.
- Insister sur l'importance des examens de suivi.

VÉRIFICATION DE L'EFFICACITÉ THÉRAPEUTIQUE

L'efficacité du traitement peut être démontrée par: l'équilibrage de la glycémie. ✳

PIPÉRACILLINE

Pipracil

PIPÉRACILLINE/ TAZOBACTAM

Tazocin

CLASSIFICATION:

Antibiotiques (pénicillines à très large spectre)

Grossesse – catégorie B

INDICATIONS

Pipéracilline: Traitement des infections graves dues aux microorganismes sensibles dont: les infections de la peau et de ses annexes ▪ les infections des os et des articulations ▪ la septicémie ▪ les infections des voies respiratoires ▪ les infections intra-abdominales ▪ les infections gynécologiques et urinaires ▪ Traitement d'association avec un aminoside (l'action contre *Pseudomonas* peut être synergique) ▪ Antécédents de traitement d'association avec d'autres antibiotiques en présence d'infections chez des patients immunodéprimés ▪ Prophylaxie périopératoire lors d'interventions abdominales ou génito-urinaires, ainsi que lors d'interventions au cou et à la tête ▪ **Pipéracilline/tazobactam:** infections intra-abdominales attribuables à l'appendicite et à la péritonite ▪ infections de la peau et de ses annexes ▪ infections gynécologiques ▪ pneumonie due à des bactéries productrices de bêtalactamases qui résistent à la pipéracilline, dont la pneumonie extrahospitalière.

MÉCANISME D'ACTION

Pipéracilline: Liaison à la membrane de la paroi cellulaire bactérienne induisant la destruction de la bactérie. Son spectre d'action est plus large que celui des autres pénicillines ▪ **Tazobactam:** Inhibition des bêtalactamases, enzymes capables de détruire les pénicillines.

Effets thérapeutiques: Effet bactéricide contre les bactéries sensibles. **Spectre d'action**: Spectre d'action semblable à celui des pénicillines, mais considérablement plus large, qui englobe plusieurs bactéries aérobies à Gram négatif importantes, dont: *Pseudomonas æruginosa* ■ *Escherichia coli* ■ *Proteus mirabilis* ■ *Providencia rettgeri* ■ *Neisseria gonorrhϾ* ■ La pipéracilline est également active contre certaines bactéries anaérobies comprenant les *Bacteroides* ■ La pipéracilline n'a pas d'effet sur les staphylocoques qui produisent des pénicillinases ni sur les *Enterobacteriaceæ* qui produisent des bêtalactamases ■ **Pipéracilline/tazobactam**: Cette association d'antibiotiques agit sur les bactéries suivantes productrices de bêtalactamases qui résistent à la pipéracilline: *Bacteroides fragilis* ■ *Escherichia coli* ■ *Staphylococcus aureus* ■ *Hæmophilus influenzæ*.

PHARMACOCINÉTIQUE

Absorption: 80 % (IM), 100 % (IV).

Distribution: Répartition dans tout l'organisme. L'agent ne pénètre suffisamment dans le liquide céphalorachidien qu'en présence d'une inflammation des méninges. Il traverse la barrière placentaire et passe à faibles concentrations dans le lait maternel.

Métabolisme et excrétion: *Pipéracilline* – excrétion majoritairement rénale (90 % sous forme inchangée); excrétion biliaire (10 %). *Tazobactam* – excrétion majoritairement rénale (80 %).

Demi-vie: de 0,7 à 1,2 heure.

Profil temps-action
(concentrations sanguines de pipéracilline)

	Début d'action	Pic	Durée
IM	rapide	30 - 50 min	4 - 6 h
IV	rapide	fin de la perfusion	4 - 6 h

CONTRE-INDICATIONS, PRÉCAUTIONS ET MISES EN GARDE

Contre-indications: Hypersensibilité aux pénicillines ou au tazobactam (risque de sensibilité croisée avec les céphalosporines).

Précautions et mises en garde: Insuffisance rénale (il est recommandé de réduire la dose ou de prolonger l'intervalle entre les doses si la Cl_{CR} < 40 mL/min) ■ Régimes hyposodés ■ **OBST., ALLAITEMENT**: L'innocuité du médicament n'a pas été établie.

RÉACTIONS INDÉSIRABLES ET EFFETS SECONDAIRES

SNC: CONVULSIONS (doses élevées), confusion, léthargie.

CV: arythmies, insuffisance cardiaque.

GI: COLITE PSEUDOMEMBRANEUSE, diarrhée, hépatite médicamenteuse, nausées.

GU: hématurie (enfants seulement), néphrite interstitielle.

Tég.: rash (risque accru chez les patients souffrant de fibrose kystique), urticaire.

HÉ: hypokaliémie, hypernatrémie.

Hémat.: saignements, leucopénie, neutropénie, dyscrasie sanguine, allongement du temps de saignement.

Locaux: douleur au point d'injection IM, phlébite au point d'injection IV.

Métab.: alcalose métabolique.

Divers: réactions d'hypersensibilité, incluant l'ANAPHYLAXIE et la MALADIE SÉRIQUE, surinfection, hyperthermie (risque accru chez les patients souffrant de fibrose kystique).

INTERACTIONS

Médicament-médicament: Le **probénécide** diminue l'excrétion rénale du médicament et en augmente les concentrations sanguines ■ Le médicament peut modifier l'excrétion du **lithium** ■ Les **diurétiques**, les **corticostéroïdes** ou l'**amphotéricine B**, administrés en concomitance, peuvent augmenter le risque d'hypokaliémie ■ Risque additif de toxicité hépatique lors de l'administration concomitante d'autres **agents hépatotoxiques** ■ Chez les patients souffrant d'insuffisance rénale, le médicament peut diminuer la demi-vie des **aminosides**.

VOIES D'ADMINISTRATION ET POSOLOGIE

Pipéracilline

La préparation contient 1,85 mmol de sodium par gramme de pipéracilline.

- **IM, IV (adultes et enfants > 12 ans)**: *La plupart des infections* – de 12 à 24 g/jour (de 200 à 300 mg/kg/jour), par voie IV, toutes les 4 à 6 heures (jusqu'à 24 g par jour). *Infections compliquées des voies urinaires* – de 8 à 16 g/jour (de 125 à 200 mg/kg/jour), par voie IV, toutes les 6 à 8 heures. *Infections non compliquées des voies urinaires et la plupart des pneumonies extrahospitalières* – de 6 à 8 g/jour (de 100 à 125 mg/kg/jour), par voie IV ou IM, toutes les 6 à 12 heures.
- ***INSUFFISANCE RÉNALE***

  IM, IV (ADULTES): *CL_{CR} DE 20 À 40 mL/MIN* – DE 3 À 4 g, TOUTES LES 8 HEURES; *CL_{CR} < 20 mL/MIN* – DE 3 À 4 g, TOUTES LES 12 HEURES.

Pipéracilline/tazobactam

La préparation contient 4,69 mmol de sodium par 2,25 g de pipéracilline/tazobactam.

- **IV (adultes):** *Infections de la peau et des structures cutanées, infections extrahospitalières des voies respiratoires inférieures, infections gynécologiques* – 3 g de pipéracilline et 0,375 g de tazobactam, toutes les 6 heures. *Infections intra-abdominales* – 4 g de pipéracilline et 0,5 g de tazobactam, toutes les 8 heures. *Pneumonie nosocomiale* – 4 g de pipéracilline et 0,5 g de tazobactam, toutes les 6 heures (en association avec un aminoside).
- ***INSUFFISANCE RÉNALE***

  IV (ADULTES): *TOUTES LES INFECTIONS À L'EXCEPTION DE LA PNEUMONIE NOSOCOMIALE: CL_{CR} DE 20 À 40 mL/MIN* – 2 g DE PIPÉRACILLINE ET 0,25 mg DE TAZOBACTAM, TOUTES LES 6 HEURES; *CL_{CR} < 20 mL/MIN* – 2 g DE PIPÉRACILLINE ET 0,25 mg DE TAZOBACTAM, TOUTES LES 8 HEURES. *PNEUMONIE NOSOCOMIALE: CL_{CR} DE 20 À 40 mL/MIN* – 3 g DE PIPÉRACILLINE ET 0,375 mg DE TAZOBACTAM, TOUTES LES 6 HEURES; *CL_{CR} < 20 mL/MIN* – 2 g DE PIPÉRACILLINE ET 0,25 mg DE TAZOBACTAM, TOUTES LES 6 HEURES.

PRÉSENTATION

- **Pipéracilline**

  Poudre pour injection: fioles de 2 g[Pr], de 3 g[Pr] et de 4 g[Pr].
- **Pipéracilline/tazobactam**

  Poudre pour injection: fioles contenant 2 g de pipéracilline et 0,25 g de tazobactam[Pr], 3 g de pipéracilline et 0,375 g de tazobactam[Pr], 4 g de pipéracilline et 0,5 g de tazobactam[Pr].

SOINS INFIRMIERS

ÉVALUATION DE LA SITUATION

- Au début du traitement et pendant toute sa durée, rester à l'affût des signes suivants d'infection: altération des signes vitaux, aspect de la plaie, des crachats, de l'urine et des selles, nombre de leucocytes.
- Recueillir les antécédents du patient avant d'amorcer le traitement afin de déterminer ses réactions à un traitement antérieur à une pénicilline ou à une céphalosporine. Même les personnes n'ayant jamais manifesté de sensibilité à la pénicilline peuvent présenter une réaction allergique.
- Prélever des échantillons pour les cultures et les antibiogrammes avant le début du traitement. La première dose peut être administrée avant même que les résultats soient connus.
- RESTER À L'AFFÛT DES SIGNES ET DES SYMPTÔMES SUIVANTS D'ANAPHYLAXIE: RASH, PRURIT, ŒDÈME LARYNGÉ, RESPIRATION SIFFLANTE. SI CES RÉACTIONS SE MANIFESTENT, ARRÊTER L'ADMINISTRATION DU MÉDICAMENT ET AVERTIR IMMÉDIATEMENT LE MÉDECIN OU UN AUTRE PROFESSIONNEL DE LA SANTÉ. GARDER À PORTÉE DE LA MAIN DE L'ADRÉNALINE, UN ANTIHISTAMINIQUE ET LE MATÉRIEL DE RÉANIMATION POUR PARER À UNE ÉVENTUELLE RÉACTION ANAPHYLACTIQUE.

Tests de laboratoire:

- Noter, avant le traitement et à intervalles réguliers pendant toute sa durée, les résultats des tests des fonctions hépatique et rénale, la numération globulaire, les concentrations sériques de potassium et le temps de saignement.
- Le médicament peut positiver les résultats du test de Coombs direct.
- Le médicament peut entraîner l'élévation des concentrations sériques d'urée, de créatinine, d'AST, d'ALT, de bilirubine, de phosphatase alcaline et de LDH.
- La pipéracilline peut induire la leucopénie et la neutropénie, particulièrement lors d'un traitement prolongé ou en présence d'une insuffisance hépatique.
- Le médicament peut allonger le temps de prothrombine et le temps de céphaline.
- La pipéracilline peut entraîner l'élévation des concentrations sériques de sodium et la diminution des concentrations sériques de potassium.
- L'association pipéracilline/tazobactam peut entraîner une chute de l'hémoglobine et de l'hématocrite ainsi que la thrombopénie, l'éosinophilie, la leucopénie et la neutropénie. Elle peut également provoquer la protéinurie, l'hématurie, la pyurie, l'hyperglycémie, la diminution des concentrations de protéines totales ou d'albumine et des anomalies au niveau des concentrations de sodium, de potassium et de calcium.

P

DIAGNOSTICS INFIRMIERS POSSIBLES

- Risque d'infection (Indications).
- Connaissances insuffisantes sur le traitement médicamenteux (Enseignement au patient et à ses proches).

INTERVENTIONS INFIRMIÈRES

IM:

- Pour reconstituer la solution destinée à la voie IM, ajouter 4 mL, 6 mL ou 8 mL d'eau stérile, d'eau bactériostatique ou de solution de NaCl 0,9% pour injection ou de chlorhydrate de lidocaïne pour injection (sans adrénaline) à 0,5 % ou à 1 % au contenu d'une fiole de 2 g, de 3 g et de 4 g, respectivement, afin d'obtenir une concentration de 1 g/2,5 mL ou de 0,4 g/mL. Consulter les directives de chaque fabricant avant de reconstituer la préparation.

- Injecter la préparation profondément dans une masse musculaire bien développée et bien masser. On ne devrait pas administrer plus de 2 g dans un même point d'injection.

Pipéracilline

- **IV**: La reconstitution initiale de la solution destinée à la voie IV doit se faire avec au moins 5 mL d'eau stérile pour injection, d'eau bactériostatique ou de solution de NaCl 0,9%. Consulter les directives de chaque fabricant avant de reconstituer la préparation. Bien mélanger jusqu'à dissolution complète. La solution reconstituée est stable pendant 24 heures à la température ambiante et pendant 12 jours au réfrigérateur.
- Changer de point d'injection IV toutes les 48 heures pour prévenir la phlébite.

IV directe: Injecter la préparation lentement, en 3 à 5 minutes, pour réduire l'irritation veineuse.

Perfusion intermittente: Diluer la pipéracilline dans au moins 50 mL de solution de NaCl 0,9 %, de D5%E, de D%5/NaCl 0,9 % ou de lactate de Ringer.

Vitesse d'administration: Administrer l'agent en 20 à 30 minutes chez les adultes et en 30 minutes chez les enfants.

Compatibilité (tubulure en Y): acyclovir ▪ amifostine ▪ aztréonam ▪ ciprofloxacine ▪ cyclophosphamide ▪ diltiazem ▪ énalaprilate ▪ esmolol ▪ famotidine fludarabine ▪ foscarnet gallium, nitrate de ▪ héparine ▪ hydromorphone ▪ labétalol ▪ lorazépam ▪ magnésium, sulfate de ▪ melphalan ▪ mépéridine ▪ midazolam ▪ morphine ▪ perphénazine ▪ ranitidine ▪ tacrolimus ▪ téniposide ▪ théophylline ▪ thiotépa ▪ vérapamil ▪ zidovudine.

Incompatibilité (tubulure en Y): filgrastim ▪ fluconazole ▪ ondansétron ▪ sargramostim ▪ vinorelbine. S'il faut administrer en même temps des aminosides et des pénicillines, les injecter à des points différents à au moins 1 heure d'intervalle.

Pipéracilline/tazobactam

Perfusion intermittente: Reconstituer avec une solution de NaCl 0,9%, d'eau stérile ou bactériostatique pour injection ou de solution de D5%E. Pour reconstituer les solutions, ajouter 10 mL à chaque fiole de 2,25 g (2 g - 0,25 g), 15 mL, à chaque fiole de 3,375 g (3 g - 0,375 g), et 20 mL, à chaque fiole de 4,5 g (4 g - 0,5 g). Consulter les directives de chaque fabricant avant de reconstituer la préparation. Ne pas utiliser de lactate de Ringer, car les deux agents sont incompatibles. Bien mélanger jusqu'à dissolution complète. Diluer de nouveau dans au moins 50 mL de diluant. Jeter toute portion inutilisée après 24 heures, si la solution a été gardée à la température ambiante, ou après 48 heures, si elle a été réfrigérée.

Vitesse d'administration: Administrer pendant au moins 30 minutes.

Compatibilité (tubulure en Y): aminophylline ▪ aztréonam ▪ bléomycine ▪ bumétanide ▪ buprénorphine ▪ butorphanol ▪ calcium, gluconate de ▪ carboplatine ▪ carmustine ▪ céfépime ▪ cimétidine ▪ clindamycine ▪ cyclophosphamide ▪ cytarabine ▪ dexaméthasone ▪ diphenhydramine ▪ dopamine ▪ énalaprilate ▪ étoposide ▪ floxuridine ▪ fluconazole ▪ fludarabine ▪ fluorouracil ▪ furosémide ▪ gallium, nitrate de ▪ héparine ▪ hydrocortisone ▪ hydromorphone ▪ ifosfamide ▪ leucovorine calcique ▪ lorazépam ▪ magnésium, sulfate de ▪ mannitol ▪ mépéridine ▪ mesna ▪ méthotrexate ▪ méthylprednisolone sodique, succinate de ▪ métoclopramide ▪ métronidazole ▪ morphine ▪ ondansétron ▪ plicamycine ▪ potassium, chlorure de ▪ ranitidine ▪ sargramostim ▪ sodium, bicarbonate de ▪ thiotépa ▪ triméthoprime/sulfaméthoxazole ▪ vinblastine ▪ zidovudine.

Incompatibilité (tubulure en Y): acyclovir ▪ amphotéricine B ▪ chlorpromazine ▪ cisplatine ▪ dacarbazine ▪ daunorubicine ▪ dobutamine ▪ doxorubicine ▪ doxycycline ▪ dropéridol ▪ famotidine ▪ ganciclovir ▪ halopéridol ▪ idarubicine ▪ miconazole ▪ minocycline ▪ mitomycine ▪ mitoxantrone ▪ nalbuphine ▪ prochlorpérazine, édisylate de ▪ prométhazine ▪ streptozocine ▪ vancomycine.

ENSEIGNEMENT AU PATIENT ET À SES PROCHES

- Conseiller au patient de signaler à un professionnel de la santé les signes de surinfection (excroissance pileuse sur la langue, pertes et démangeaisons vaginales, selles molles ou nauséabondes) et les allergies.
- RECOMMANDER AU PATIENT DE SIGNALER À UN PROFESSIONNEL DE LA SANTÉ LA FIÈVRE OU LA DIARRHÉE, PARTICULIÈREMENT EN PRÉSENCE DE SANG, DE PUS OU DE MUCUS DANS LES SELLES. CONSEILLER AU PATIENT DE NE PAS TRAITER LA DIARRHÉE AVANT D'AVOIR CONSULTÉ UN PROFESSIONNEL DE LA SANTÉ. CES EFFETS PEUVENT SE MANIFESTER ENCORE PENDANT PLUSIEURS SEMAINES APRÈS L'ARRÊT DU MÉDICAMENT.

VÉRIFICATION DE L'EFFICACITÉ THÉRAPEUTIQUE

L'efficacité du traitement peut être démontrée par: la disparition des signes et des symptômes d'infection. Le temps de résolution dépend du microorganisme infectant et du siège de l'infection. ✳

PIROXICAM

Alti-Piroxicam, Apo-Piroxicam, Dom-Piroxicam, Gen-Piroxicam, Novo-Pirocam, Nu-Pirox, PMS-Piroxicam, Pro-Piroxicam

CLASSIFICATION:

Anti-inflammatoire non stéroïdien, analgésique non opioïde

Grossesse – catégories D (1er et 3e trimestres) et B (2e trimestre)

INDICATIONS

Traitement des troubles inflammatoires dont: la polyarthrite rhumatoïde ■ l'arthrose ■ la spondylarthrite ankylosante ■ la dysménorrhée fonctionnelle.

MÉCANISME D'ACTION

Inhibition de la synthèse des prostaglandines. ***Effets thérapeutiques:*** Soulagement de la douleur et de l'inflammation.

PHARMACOCINÉTIQUE

Absorption: Bonne (PO).
Distribution: Inconnue. L'agent passe dans le lait maternel en faibles quantités.
Métabolisme et excrétion: Métabolisme hépatique. Excrétion rénale (petites quantités sous forme inchangée).
Demi-vie: 50 heures.

Profil temps-action (effets thérapeutiques)

	DÉBUT D'ACTION	PIC	DURÉE
PO (analgésie)	1 h	inconnu	48 - 72 h
PO (effet anti-inflammatoire)	7 - 12 jours	2 - 3 semaines†	inconnue

† Il faut parfois compter jusqu'à 12 semaines avant que le pic soit atteint.

CONTRE-INDICATIONS, PRÉCAUTIONS ET MISES EN GARDE

Contre-indications: Hypersensibilité ■ Risque d'hypersensibilité croisée avec d'autres anti-inflammatoires non stéroïdiens, incluant l'aspirine ■ Hémorragie digestive, atteinte inflammatoire du tube digestif ou ulcère en évolution ■ Antécédents récents d'hémorragie rectale ou anale ■ Contexte périopératoire en cas de pontage aortocoronarien.

Précautions et mises en garde: Maladie cardiovasculaire ou facteurs de risque de maladie cardiovasculaire (risque accru de complications thrombotiques, d'infarctus du myocarde ou d'accident vasculaire cérébral surtout lors d'un usage prolongé) ■ Maladie hépatique grave ■ Antécédents d'ulcère ■ **GÉR.:** Les personnes âgées sont plus à risque de souffrir d'hémorragies digestives, d'œdème et d'insuffisance rénale ■ Insuffisance rénale (il est recommandé de réduire la dose) ■ **OBST., ALLAITEMENT, PÉD.:** L'innocuité du médicament n'a pas été établie.

RÉACTIONS INDÉSIRABLES ET EFFETS SECONDAIRES

SNC: somnolence, céphalées, étourdissements.

ORLO: vision trouble, acouphènes.

CV: œdème.

GI: HÉPATITE MÉDICAMENTEUSE, HÉMORRAGIE DIGESTIVE, gêne gastro-intestinale, dyspepsie, nausées, vomissements, anorexie, constipation, diarrhée, flatulence.

GU: insuffisance rénale.

Tég.: DERMATITE EXFOLIATIVE, SYNDROME DE STEVENS-JOHNSON, ÉPIDERMOLYSE NÉCROSANTE SUBAIGUË, rash.

Hémat.: dyscrasie sanguine, allongement du temps de saignement.

Divers: réactions allergiques incluant l'ANAPHYLAXIE.

INTERACTIONS

Médicament-médicament: L'**aspirine**, administrée en concomitance, peut réduire les concentrations sanguines de piroxicam et en diminuer l'efficacité ■ Risque accru d'hémorragie lors de l'usage concomitant d'**anticoagulants**, de **céfamandole**, de **céfopérazone**, de **céfotétane**, d'**héparine**, de **ticlodipine**, de **clopidogrel**, d'**eptifibatide**, de **tirofiban**, d'**agents thrombolytiques**, d'**acide valproïque** ou de **plicamycine** ■ Effets nocifs additifs sur le tractus gastro-intestinal lors de l'usage concomitant d'**aspirine**, de **corticostéroïdes** et d'autres **AINS** ■ Le **probénicide**, administré en concomitance, élève les concentrations sanguines de piroxicam et peut en augmenter la toxicité ■ Le piroxicam peut diminuer la réponse aux **antihypertenseurs** ou aux **diurétiques** ■ Le piroxicam peut élever les concentrations sériques de **lithium** et le risque de toxicité ■ Risque accru d'hypoglycémie lors de l'usage concomitant d'**insuline** ou d'**hypoglycémiants oraux** ■ Risque accru d'effets nocifs sur les reins lors de l'administration concomitante de **sels d'or** ou de **cyclosporine** ou lors de l'usage prolongé d'**acétaminophène** ■ Les **antinéoplasiques** ou la **radiothérapie**, administrés en concomitance, peuvent augmenter le risque de toxicité hématologique.

Médicament-produits naturels: Risque accru de saignements en cas de consommation concomitante d'**ail**, d'**anis**, d'**arnica**, de **camomille**, de **dong quai**, de **fenugrec**, de **girofle**, de **gingembre**, de **ginkgo**, de **ginseng** et de certains **autres produits naturels**.

P

VOIES D'ADMINISTRATION ET POSOLOGIE

- **PO, IR (adultes)**: *Anti-inflammatoire* – de 10 à 20 mg/jour; administrer en 1 ou 2 doses fractionnées. *Traitement de la dysménorrhée* – initialement, 40 mg, puis 20 mg, 1 fois par jour.
- **PO, IR (personnes âgées)**: Initialement, 10 mg/jour.

PRÉSENTATION (version générique disponible)

Capsules: 10 mg^{Pr}, 20 mg^{Pr} ▪ **Suppositoires**: 10 mg^{Pr}, 20 mg^{Pr}.

SOINS INFIRMIERS

ÉVALUATION DE LA SITUATION

- LES PATIENTS SOUFFRANT D'ASTHME, D'ALLERGIE INDUITE PAR L'ASPIRINE OU DE POLYPES NASAUX SONT DAVANTAGE PRÉDISPOSÉS AUX RÉACTIONS D'HYPERSENSIBILITÉ. SUIVRE DE PRÈS LA RHINITE, L'ASTHME ET L'URTICAIRE.

Arthrite: Suivre de près la douleur et examiner la mobilité des articulations avant l'administration du piroxicam et de 1 à 2 heures plus tard.

***Tests de laboratoire*:**
- Le piroxicam peut allonger le temps de saignement pendant une période allant jusqu'à 2 semaines après l'arrêt du traitement.
- Le piroxicam peut diminuer l'hématocrite, les concentrations d'hémoglobine et le nombre de globules blancs et de plaquettes.
- Examiner à intervalles réguliers les résultats des tests de la fonction hépatique. Le piroxicam peut entraîner l'élévation des concentrations sériques de phosphatase alcaline, de LDH, d'AST et d'ALT.
- Mesurer, à intervalles réguliers pendant toute la durée du traitement, l'urée, la créatinine sérique et les électrolytes. Le piroxicam peut élever l'urée, la créatinine sérique et les concentrations sériques d'électrolytes et réduire les concentrations urinaires d'électrolytes.

DIAGNOSTICS INFIRMIERS POSSIBLES

- Douleur aiguë (Indications).
- Mobilité physique réduite (Indications).
- Connaissances insuffisantes sur le traitement médicamenteux (Enseignement au patient et à ses proches).

INTERVENTIONS INFIRMIÈRES

- L'administration de doses plus élevées que celles recommandées n'accroît pas l'efficacité du médicament, mais peut en intensifier les effets secondaires, particulièrement chez les personnes âgées. Utiliser la dose minimale efficace pendant le plus court laps de temps possible.
- Administrer le médicament dès que possible après le début des règles. L'administration en prophylaxie ne s'est pas révélée efficace.

PO: Administrer le piroxicam après les repas ou avec des aliments ou un antiacide renfermant du magnésium ou de l'aluminium afin de diminuer l'irritation gastrique.

ENSEIGNEMENT AU PATIENT ET À SES PROCHES

- Conseiller au patient de prendre le piroxicam avec un grand verre d'eau et de ne pas se coucher pendant les 15 à 30 minutes qui suivent.
- Conseiller au patient de respecter rigoureusement la posologie recommandée. S'il n'a pu prendre le médicament au moment habituel, il doit le faire dès que possible à moins que ce ne soit presque l'heure prévue pour la dose suivante. Le prévenir qu'il ne doit jamais remplacer une dose manquée par une double dose.
- Prévenir le patient que le piroxicam peut parfois provoquer de la somnolence ou des étourdissements. Lui conseiller de ne pas conduire et d'éviter les activités qui exigent sa vigilance jusqu'à ce qu'on ait la certitude que le médicament n'entraîne pas ces effets chez lui.
- Recommander au patient d'éviter de boire d'alcool pendant toute la durée du traitement et de consulter un professionnel de la santé avant de prendre de l'aspirine, de l'acétaminophène, d'autres médicaments en vente libre ou des produits naturels.
- Recommander au patient qui doit suivre un traitement ou subir une intervention chirurgicale d'avertir le professionnel de la santé qu'il suit un traitement par ce médicament.
- Conseiller au patient d'utiliser un écran solaire et de porter des vêtements protecteurs pour prévenir les réactions de photosensibilité (rares).
- Recommander au patient de consulter un professionnel de la santé en cas de rash, de démangeaisons, de troubles visuels, d'acouphènes, de gain pondéral, d'œdème, de selles noires, de céphalées persistantes ou d'un syndrome grippal (frissons, fièvre, douleurs musculaires, malaise).

VÉRIFICATION DE L'EFFICACITÉ THÉRAPEUTIQUE

***L'efficacité du traitement peut être démontrée par*:** la diminution de la douleur et l'amélioration de la mobilité des articulations. On observe habituellement un soulagement partiel de l'arthrite en l'espace de 2 semaines, mais le plein effet du médicament peut ne se manifester qu'après 12 semaines de traitement ininterrompu. Les patients qui ne répondent pas à un anti-inflammatoire non stéroïdien peuvent répondre à un autre.

POLYCARBOPHILE

Equalactin, Fibre Laxative, Prodiem Bulk Fibre Therapy

CLASSIFICATION:

Antidiarrhéique, laxatif (agent de masse)

Grossesse – catégorie inconnue

INDICATIONS

Traitement de la constipation ou de la diarrhée pouvant être associée à la diverticulose ou au syndrome du côlon irritable.

MÉCANISME D'ACTION

Effet laxatif par augmentation du volume du bol fécal grâce au maintien de l'eau dans la lumière intestinale ■ Effet antidiarrhéique par attraction de l'eau dans la lumière intestinale pour former des selles bien moulées. ***Effets thérapeutiques:*** Traitement de la diarrhée et de la constipation, grâce à la normalisation du contenu en eau des intestins et à l'augmentation du volume du bol fécal.

PHARMACOCINÉTIQUE

Absorption: Minimale (PO).
Distribution: Inconnue.
Métabolisme et excrétion: Le complexe et l'eau absorbée sont excrétés dans les fèces.
Demi-vie: Inconnue.

Profil temps-action (effet sur la fonction intestinale)

	DÉBUT D'ACTION	PIC	DURÉE
PO	12 – 24 h†	inconnu	inconnue

† Le début d'action peut ne se manifester qu'après 72 heures.

CONTRE-INDICATIONS, PRÉCAUTIONS ET MISES EN GARDE

Contre-indications: Hypersensibilité ■ Douleurs abdominales ■ Nausées ■ Vomissements (particulièrement lorsqu'ils s'accompagnent de fièvre ou d'autres signes d'abdomen aigu) ■ Adhérences intra-abdominales importantes ■ Dysphagie.

Précautions et mises en garde: OBST., ALLAITEMENT: Il existe, cependant, des antécédents d'administration sans danger.

RÉACTIONS INDÉSIRABLES ET EFFETS SECONDAIRES

GI: Sensation de plénitude.

INTERACTIONS

Médicament-médicament: Aucune interaction cliniquement significative n'a été signalée.

VOIES D'ADMINISTRATION ET POSOLOGIE

- **PO (adultes):** 1 g, de 1 à 4 fois par jour, ou selon les besoins (ne pas dépasser 6 g/24 h); en cas de diarrhée grave, répéter l'administration de cette dose toutes les 30 minutes (ne pas dépasser 4 g/24 h).
- **PO (enfants de 6 à 12 ans):** 500 mg, de 1 à 4 fois par jour, ou selon les besoins (ne pas dépasser 6 g/24 h); en cas de diarrhée grave, répéter l'administration de cette dose toutes les 30 minutes.

PRÉSENTATION (version générique disponible)

Comprimés: 652 mg (500 mg)[VL].

SOINS INFIRMIERS

ÉVALUATION DE LA SITUATION

- Suivre de près l'apparition de la fièvre, de nausées, de vomissements, d'une distension abdominale et de douleurs. En informer un professionnel de la santé, le cas échéant. Ausculter les bruits intestinaux. Interroger le patient sur son régime alimentaire habituel, sa consommation de liquides, ses activités physiques et sa fonction intestinale.
- Noter la couleur, la consistance et la quantité des selles éliminées.

Diarrhée: Suivre de près les signes suivants de déshydratation: sécheresse de la peau et des muqueuses, perte de poids, diminution du débit urinaire, tachycardie et hypotension.

DIAGNOSTICS INFIRMIERS POSSIBLES

- Constipation (Indications).
- Diarrhée (Indications).
- Connaissances insuffisantes sur le traitement médicamenteux (Enseignement au patient et à ses proches).

INTERVENTIONS INFIRMIÈRES

Diarrhée:

- Pour traiter la diarrhée grave, répéter l'administration toutes les 30 minutes. Ne pas dépasser la dose quotidienne totale prescrite.

P

- Les comprimés à croquer absorbent l'eau jusqu'à 60 fois leur poids.

Constipation: Pour traiter la constipation, administrer la préparation avec 240 mL d'eau ou de jus.

ENSEIGNEMENT AU PATIENT ET À SES PROCHES

- Encourager le patient à recourir à d'autres moyens de régulation de la fonction intestinale, par exemple, consommer plus de fibres alimentaires et de liquides et faire plus d'exercice. Expliquer au patient que la fréquence de l'élimination intestinale varie d'une personne à l'autre et qu'il est tout aussi normal de déféquer 3 fois par jour que 3 fois par semaine.
- Prévenir le patient que si la constipation survient brusquement, il faut en avertir un professionnel de la santé, car un examen médical pourrait s'avérer nécessaire.
- Recommander au patient souffrant de diarrhée de consulter un professionnel de la santé s'il a de la fièvre, si ses selles sont sanguinolentes ou si la diarrhée persiste ou s'aggrave. L'inciter à modifier sa consommation d'aliments et de liquides durant un épisode de diarrhée.

VÉRIFICATION DE L'EFFICACITÉ THÉRAPEUTIQUE

L'efficacité du traitement peut être démontrée par: l'émission de selles molles et bien moulées. Les résultats peuvent ne pas être manifestes avant 3 jours de traitement. ✳

P

POLYÉTHYLÈNE GLYCOL/ ÉLECTROLYTES

Colyte, GoLytely, Klean-Prep, Peglyte

CLASSIFICATION:

Laxatif (osmotique), préparation électrolytique de lavage du côlon

Grossesse – catégorie C

INDICATIONS

Évacuation des matières de l'intestin en vue d'un examen gastro-intestinal ■ Fécalome et constipation chez les personnes âgées (antécédents d'utilisation occasionnelle chez les enfants).

MÉCANISME D'ACTION

Le polyéthylène glycol en solution agit comme un agent osmotique en attirant l'eau dans la lumière intestinale. ***Effets thérapeutiques:*** Évacuation intestinale sans apparition d'un déséquilibre hydroélectrolytique.

PHARMACOCINÉTIQUE

Absorption: Les ions de la solution ne sont pas absorbés.
Distribution: Inconnue.
Métabolisme et excrétion: Excrétion fécale.
Demi-vie: Inconnue.

Profil temps-action (nettoyage du côlon)

	Début d'action	Pic	Durée
PO	1 h	inconnu	4 h

CONTRE-INDICATIONS, PRÉCAUTIONS ET MISES EN GARDE

Contre-indications: Iléus ■ Occlusion gastro-intestinale ■ Rétention gastrique ■ Colite toxique ■ Mégacôlon toxique ■ Perforation de l'intestin.

Précautions et mises en garde: Patients dont le réflexe pharyngé est absent ou réduit ■ Patients inconscients ou semi-comateux, chez lesquels il faut administrer la préparation par une sonde nasogastrique ■ Douleurs abdominales d'étiologie inconnue, particulièrement si elles s'accompagnent de fièvre ■ **Obst.**: L'innocuité du médicament n'a pas été établie chez la femme enceinte ■ **Péd.**: L'innocuité et l'efficacité de l'agent n'ont pas été établies.

RÉACTIONS INDÉSIRABLES ET EFFETS SECONDAIRES

GI: plénitude gastrique, diarrhée, ballonnement, crampes, nausées, vomissements.
Divers: réactions allergiques (rares).

INTERACTIONS

Médicament-médicament: La préparation peut entraver l'absorption des **médicaments administrés par voie orale**, en diminuant leur temps de transit.

VOIES D'ADMINISTRATION ET POSOLOGIE

Avant un examen

- **PO (adultes)**: 250 mL, toutes les 10 minutes. Le lavage est terminé quand les matières fécales évacuées sont claires (jusqu'à concurrence de 3 à 4 L). On peut administrer la préparation par sonde nasogastrique à raison de 20 à 30 mL/min (jusqu'à concurrence de 4 L).

Constipation chronique

- **PO (adultes)**: De 240 à 480 mL, en 1 ou 2 prises fractionnées, ou selon les recommandations du médecin.

Fécalomes

- **PO (adultes)**: De 2 à 3 L en l'espace de 3 à 4 heures (sur recommandation du médecin seulement).

PRÉSENTATION

Poudre pour solution orale[VL].

SOINS INFIRMIERS

ÉVALUATION DE LA SITUATION

- Suivre de près la distension abdominale, ausculter les bruits intestinaux, noter les habitudes normales d'élimination intestinale.
- Noter la couleur, la consistance et la quantité des selles éliminées.
- Si le médicament est administré par sonde nasogastrique, suivre de près les patients à demi conscients ou inconscients pour déceler la régurgitation.

DIAGNOSTICS INFIRMIERS POSSIBLES

- Diarrhée (Effets secondaires).
- Connaissances insuffisantes sur le traitement médicamenteux (Enseignement au patient et à ses proches).

INTERVENTIONS INFIRMIÈRES

- Ne pas ajouter d'aromatisants ou d'ingrédients supplémentaires à la solution avant de l'administrer.
- Le patient devrait être à jeun pendant 3 ou 4 heures avant l'administration du médicament et ne devrait pas consommer d'aliments solides dans les 2 heures qui suivent (lorsque l'agent est utilisé pour la préparation avant un examen).
- Après l'administration du médicament, le patient ne doit consommer que des liquides clairs (lorsque l'agent est utilisé pour la préparation avant un examen).
- La préparation peut être administrée le matin de l'examen si le patient a suffisamment de temps pour la boire (3 heures) et évacuer les matières de l'intestin (1 heure de plus). Dans le cas d'un lavement baryté, administrer la solution tôt en soirée (à 18 heures), la veille de l'examen, pour que le baryum puisse bien recouvrir les muqueuses.
- La solution peut être reconstituée avec l'eau du robinet. Agiter vigoureusement jusqu'à ce que la poudre soit dissoute.
- La solution peut être administrée par sonde nasogastrique à un débit de 20 à 30 mL/min.

ENSEIGNEMENT AU PATIENT ET À SES PROCHES

- Expliquer au patient qu'il doit boire 250 mL de préparation, toutes les 10 minutes, jusqu'à ce qu'il ait bu 4 L ou jusqu'à ce que le liquide éliminé soit transparent et qu'il ne contienne plus de matières solides. Lui expliquer qu'il est préférable de boire rapidement chaque verre de 250 mL plutôt que d'en avaler le contenu par petites gorgées (lorsque l'agent est utilisé pour la préparation avant un examen).

VÉRIFICATION DE L'EFFICACITÉ THÉRAPEUTIQUE

L'efficacité du traitement peut être démontrée par: la diarrhée, pour évacuer les matières de l'intestin en l'espace de 4 heures; la première défécation se produit habituellement dans l'heure qui suit l'administration du médicament. ✳

POLYSTYRÈNE SODIQUE, SULFONATE DE

Kayexalate, K-Exit, PMS-Sodium Polystyrene Sulfonate, Phl-Sodium Polystyrene Sulfonate, Resonium calcium

CLASSIFICATION:

Résine échangeuse de cations

Grossesse – catégorie C

INDICATIONS

Traitement de l'hyperkaliémie légère à modérée (dans les cas graves, il faudrait prendre des mesures immédiates, telles que l'administration de bicarbonate de sodium par voie IV, de calcium ou de glucose/insuline en perfusion).

MÉCANISME D'ACTION

Échange des ions sodium contre des ions potassium dans l'intestin (chaque gramme de sodium est échangé contre 0,5 à 1 mmol de potassium). ***Effets thérapeutiques:*** Réduction des concentrations sériques de potassium.

PHARMACOCINÉTIQUE

Absorption: Nulle.
Distribution: Aucune.
Métabolisme et excrétion: Élimination fécale.
Demi-vie: Inconnue.

Profil temps-action
(diminution des concentrations de potassium sérique)

	DÉBUT D'ACTION	PIC	DURÉE
PO	2 - 12 h	inconnu	6 - 24 h
IR	2 - 12 h	inconnu	4 - 6 h

P

CONTRE-INDICATIONS, PRÉCAUTIONS ET MISES EN GARDE

Contre-indications: Hypersensibilité ■ Hypersensibilité à la saccharine ou aux parabènes (certains produits en renferment) ■ Iléus ■ Patients dont le taux de potassium est inférieur à 5 mmol/L ■ Nouveau-nés ou patients qui présentent un ralentissement intestinal (voie orale).

Précautions et mises en garde: Hyperkaliémie menaçante pour la vie (prendre des mesures immédiates) ■ Intolérance connue à l'alcool (suspension seulement) ■ **GÉR.:** Risque de formation d'un fécalome en cas d'administration de doses élevées ■ Insuffisance cardiaque, hypertension, œdème ■ Régime hyposodé ■ Constipation ■ **OBST., ALLAITEMENT:** L'agent n'est pas absorbé dans le tractus gastro-intestinal. Néanmoins, son innocuité n'a pas été établie.

RÉACTIONS INDÉSIRABLES ET EFFETS SECONDAIRES

GI: constipation, fécalome, anorexie, irritation gastrique, nausées, vomissements.

HÉ: hypocalcémie, hypokaliémie, rétention sodique.

INTERACTIONS

Médicament-médicament: L'administration concomitante de **calcium** ou d'**antiacides contenant du magnésium** peut diminuer la capacité d'échange de la résine et augmenter ainsi le risque d'alcalose systémique ■ L'absorption du **lithium** et des **hormones thyroïdiennes** peut être diminuée ■ Les **inhibiteurs de l'enzyme de conversion de l'angiotensine**, les **diurétiques épargneurs de potassium** et les **suppléments de potassium** peuvent diminuer l'efficacité du polystyrène sodique ■ L'hypokaliémie peut accentuer la toxicité **digitalique**.

P

VOIES D'ADMINISTRATION ET POSOLOGIE

4 cuillerées à thé rases = 15 g (4,1 mmol de sodium/g).

- **PO (adultes):** 15 g, de 1 à 4 fois par jour dans de l'eau ou du sorbitol.
- **IR (adultes):** De 30 à 50 g dans de l'eau ou du D10%E, comme lavement à garder, 1 ou 2 fois par jour, à 6 heures d'intervalle.
- **PO, IR (enfants):** De 0,5 à 1 g/kg/dose.
- **IR (nouveau-nés):** De 0,5 à 1 g/kg (utiliser la dose minimale).

PRÉSENTATION (version générique disponible)

Suspension: 15 g de sulfonate de polystyrène sodique avec 14,1 g de sorbitol/60 mL[Pr] ■ **Lavement de rétention:** 30 g de sulfonate de polystyrène sodique avec 28,2 g de sorbitol/60 mL[Pr] ■ **Poudre:** 15 g/4 cuillerées à thé rases[Pr].

SOINS INFIRMIERS

ÉVALUATION DE LA SITUATION

- Observer le patient pour déceler les symptômes d'hyperkaliémie (fatigue, faiblesse musculaire, paresthésie, confusion, dyspnée, ondes T atteignant des pics, segments ST déprimés, allongement des segments QT, élargissement des complexes QRS, disparition des ondes P et arythmies cardiaques). Déceler l'apparition de l'hypokaliémie (faiblesse, fatigue, arythmies, ondes plates ou inversées, ondes U proéminentes).
- Effectuer le bilan quotidien des ingesta et des excreta et peser le patient tous les jours. Observer le patient à la recherche des symptômes suivants de surcharge liquidienne: dyspnée, râles ou crépitations, turgescence des jugulaires, œdème périphérique. On peut prescrire aux patients souffrant d'insuffisance cardiaque un régime hyposodé (voir l'annexe J).
- Chez le patient recevant un traitement concomitant par des glucosides cardiotoniques, déceler les symptômes de toxicité digitalique (anorexie, nausées, vomissements, troubles de la vision, arythmies).
- Examiner l'abdomen et noter la consistance des selles et la fréquence des défécations. On peut prescrire en concomitance du sorbitol ou des laxatifs pour prévenir la constipation ou la formation d'un fécalome. Certains produits renferment du sorbitol pour prévenir la constipation. Le patient devrait idéalement évacuer 1 ou 2 selles aqueuses chaque jour pendant toute la durée du traitement.

Tests de laboratoire:

- Mesurer quotidiennement tout au long du traitement les concentrations sériques de potassium. Prévenir le médecin si les concentrations de potassium s'abaissent jusqu'à 5 mmol/L.
- Noter, avant le traitement et à intervalles réguliers pendant toute sa durée, les résultats des tests de la fonction rénale et les concentrations d'électrolytes (particulièrement celles de sodium, de calcium, de bicarbonate et de magnésium).

DIAGNOSTICS INFIRMIERS POSSIBLES

- Constipation (Effets secondaires).
- Connaissances insuffisantes sur le traitement médicamenteux (Enseignement au patient et à ses proches).

INTERVENTIONS INFIRMIÈRES

- La solution est stable pendant 24 heures.
- Consulter le médecin au sujet de la possibilité d'arrêter la prise d'agents pouvant augmenter les concentrations sériques de potassium (inhibiteurs de l'enzyme de conversion de l'angiotensine, diurétiques épargneurs de potassium, suppléments de potassium, substituts de sel).

PO:

- On administre habituellement en concomitance un laxatif osmotique (sorbitol) pour prévenir la constipation.
- Pour l'administration par voie orale, ajouter la quantité prescrite de poudre à 3 à 4 mL d'eau/g de poudre. Bien mélanger. Pour améliorer le goût de la préparation, on peut aussi dissoudre la poudre dans un sirop.

Lavement à garder:

- Administrer un lavement évacuateur avant le lavement à garder par une sonde rectale ou une sonde de Foley numéro 28, munie d'un ballonnet de 30 mL. Introduire le tube sur une longueur d'au moins 20 cm et le fixer à l'aide d'un ruban adhésif.
- Lors de l'administration du lavement à garder, ajouter la poudre à 150 à 200 mL de la solution prescrite (habituellement de l'eau ordinaire, un mélange d'eau et de méthylcellulose 2% ou de D10%E). Bien mélanger pour dissoudre entièrement la poudre et pour que la solution soit très liquide. Demander au patient de se coucher sur le côté gauche et glisser un oreiller sous ses hanches pour les soulever, si la solution commence à fuir. Après le médicament, administrer de 50 à 100 mL de diluant pour s'assurer que le patient a reçu toute la dose. Encourager le patient à retenir le lavement aussi longtemps que possible, à savoir de 30 à 60 minutes.
- Après que le patient a retenu la solution pendant le laps de temps prévu, irriguer le côlon avec 1 à 2 litres de solution sans sodium. Le raccord en Y et la tubulure peuvent être reliés à la sonde de Foley ou à la sonde rectale; la solution d'évacuation est administrée par un orifice du raccord en Y et elle s'écoule en vertu de la pesanteur, par l'autre orifice.

ENSEIGNEMENT AU PATIENT ET À SES PROCHES

- Expliquer au patient le but du traitement et la méthode d'administration du médicament.
- Expliquer au patient l'importance des tests fréquents de laboratoire permettant de vérifier l'efficacité du traitement.

VÉRIFICATION DE L'EFFICACITÉ THÉRAPEUTIQUE

L'efficacité du traitement peut être démontrée par: la normalisation des concentrations sériques de potassium. ✳

POTASSIUM, PHOSPHATES DE

phosphate de potassium

K-Phos Neutral (disponible par l'intermédiaire du Programme d'accès spécial de Santé Canada). Phosphate de potassium

phosphate de potassium monobasique

Phosphate de potassium monobasique

CLASSIFICATION:

Minéraux et électrolytes, antiurolithiques (suppléments de phosphates)

Grossesse – catégorie C

INDICATIONS

Traitement et prévention de la carence en phosphates chez les patients incapables d'absorber une quantité suffisante de phosphate alimentaire. **Usages non approuvés:** Traitement d'appoint des infections urinaires en association avec l'hippurate ou le mandélate de méthénamine ■ Prévention de la formation de calculs calciques urinaires ■ Hypokaliémie s'accompagnant d'acidose métabolique ou d'une carence en phosphores.

MÉCANISME D'ACTION

Le phosphate est présent dans les os et participe au transport d'énergie et au métabolisme des glucides ■ Tampon pour l'excrétion rénale des ions hydrogène ■ Le phosphate de potassium dibasique est transformé dans les tubules rénaux en sel monobasique par les ions hydrogène, entraînant l'acidification de l'urine ■ L'acidification de l'urine est essentielle pour que l'hippurate ou le mandélate de méthénamine deviennent des anti-infectieux urinaires actifs ■ L'acidification de l'urine accroît la solubilité du calcium, diminuant ainsi la formation de calculs calciques. ***Effets thérapeutiques:*** Suppléments de phosphates en cas de carence ■ Acidification de l'urine ■ Augmentation de l'efficacité de la méthénamine ■ Diminution de la formation de calculs calciques dans les voies urinaires.

PHARMACOCINÉTIQUE

Absorption: Bonne (PO). La vitamine D favorise l'absorption gastro-intestinale des phosphates.

Distribution: Les phosphates pénètrent dans les liquides extracellulaires d'où ils parviennent à leur lieu d'action par transport actif.

Métabolisme et excrétion: Excrétion majoritairement rénale (90 %).

Demi-vie: Inconnue.

Profil temps-action
(effets sur les concentrations sériques de phosphate)

	DÉBUT D'ACTION	PIC	DURÉE
PO	inconnu	inconnu	inconnue
IV	rapide (quelques minutes ou heures)	fin de la perfusion	inconnue

CONTRE-INDICATIONS, PRÉCAUTIONS ET MISES EN GARDE

Contre-indications: Hyperkaliémie ▪ Hyperphosphatémie ▪ Hypocalcémie ▪ Insuffisance rénale grave ▪ Maladie d'Addison non traitée ▪ Traumatisme tissulaire grave ▪ Paralysie familiale périodique de forme hyperkaliémique.

Précautions et mises en garde: Hyperparathyroïdie ▪ Hyperphosphatémie ▪ Maladie cardiaque ▪ Insuffisance rénale.

RÉACTIONS INDÉSIRABLES ET EFFETS SECONDAIRES

Sauf indication contraire, les réactions indésirables et effets secondaires suivants sont reliés à l'hyperphosphatémie.

SNC: confusion, apragmatisme, faiblesse.

CV: ARYTHMIES, ARRÊT CARDIAQUE, modifications de l'ÉCG (absence d'ondes P, élargissement du complexe QRS avec courbe biphasique), hypotension; *hyperkaliémie* – ARYTHMIES, modifications de l'ÉCG (allongement des intervalles PR, dépression du segment ST, grandes ondes T pointues).

GI: diarrhée, douleurs abdominales, nausées, vomissements.

HÉ: hyperkaliémie, hyperphosphatémie, hypocalcémie, hypomagnésémie.

Locaux: irritation au point d'injection IV, phlébite.

Loc.: *hyperkaliémie* – crampes musculaires; *hypocalcémie* – tremblements.

SN: paralysie flasque, jambes lourdes, paresthésie.

INTERACTIONS

Médicament-médicament: Les **diurétiques épargneurs de potassium**, les **antagonistes des récepteurs de l'angiotensine II (ARA)** et les **inhibiteurs de l'enzyme de conversion de l'angiotensine (IECA)**, administrés en concomitance, peuvent entraîner une hyperkaliémie ▪ Les composés contenant du **calcium** ou de l'**aluminium**, administrés simultanément, diminuent l'absorption des phosphates par formation de complexes insolubles ▪ La **vitamine D**, administrée simultanément, favorise l'absorption des phosphates.

Médicament-aliments: Les **oxalates** (contenus dans les épinards et la rhubarbe) et les **phytates** (contenus dans le son et les grains entiers) peuvent diminuer l'absorption des phosphates en se liant à eux dans le tractus gastro-intestinal.

VOIES D'ADMINISTRATION ET POSOLOGIE

- **PO (adulte):** De 250 à 500 mg de phosphore, 4 fois par jour.
- **IV (adultes):** *Dose d'entretien en cas d'alimentation parentérale* – de 10 à 20 mmol de phosphore /L. *Hypophosphatémie légère* – de 0,08 à 0,16 mmol/kg de phosphate, et jusqu'à 15 à 30 mmol/dose. *Hypophosphatémie modérée* – de 0,16 à 0,32 mmol/kg de phosphate, et jusqu'à 15 à 45 mmol/dose. *Hypophosphatémie symptomatique grave* – de 0,24 à 0,64 mmol/kg de phosphate, et jusqu'à 30 à 60 mmol/dose.
- **IV (enfants):** De 1,5 à 2 mmol de phosphore par jour en perfusion.

PRÉSENTATION

- **Phosphate de potassium monobasique**
  Concentré pour injection: 1,29 mmol/mL de phosphore et 1,29 mmol/mL de potassium, en fioles de 10 mL[Pr].
- **Phosphates de potassium**
  Comprimés: 250 mg[Pr] (disponible par l'intermédiaire du Programme d'accès spécial de Santé Canada) ▪ **Concentré pour injection:** 3 mmol de phosphore/mL et 4,4 mmol/mL de potassium, en fioles de 10 mL[Pr] et de 50 mL[Pr].

SOINS INFIRMIERS

ÉVALUATION DE LA SITUATION

- PENDANT TOUTE LA DURÉE DU TRAITEMENT, SUIVRE DE PRÈS LES SIGNES ET LES SYMPTÔMES D'HYPOKALIÉMIE (FAIBLESSE, FATIGUE, ARYTHMIES, PRÉSENCE D'ONDES U SUR LE TRACÉ DE L'ÉCG, POLYURIE ET POLYDIPSIE) ET D'HYPOPHOSPHATÉMIE (ANOREXIE, FAIBLESSE, DIMINUTION DES RÉFLEXES, DOULEURS OSSEUSES, CONFUSION, DYSCRASIE SANGUINE).

- Mesurer le pouls et la pression artérielle et suivre de près l'ÉCG à intervalles réguliers pendant toute la durée du traitement par voie IV.
- Effectuer le bilan quotidien des ingesta et des excreta et peser le patient tous les jours. Signaler tout écart important.

Tests de laboratoire:

- Noter les concentrations sériques de phosphates, de potassium et de calcium avant le traitement et à intervalles réguliers pendant toute sa durée. L'élévation des concentrations de phosphates peut provoquer l'hypocalcémie.
- Examiner les résultats des tests de la fonction rénale avant le traitement et à intervalles réguliers pendant toute sa durée.
- Mesurer le pH de l'urine chez les patients recevant du phosphate de potassium pour acidifier l'urine.

TOXICITÉ ET SURDOSAGE:

- Les symptômes de toxicité sont ceux de l'hyperkaliémie (fatigue, faiblesse musculaire, paresthésie, confusion dyspnée, ondes T pointues, dépression du segment ST, élargissement du complexe QRS, absence des ondes P et arythmies) et de l'hyperphosphatémie ou de l'hypocalcémie (paresthésie, soubresauts musculaires, laryngospasme, coliques, arythmies ou signes de Chvostek ou de Trousseau).
- Le traitement inclut l'arrêt de la perfusion, la recharge en calcium et l'abaissement des concentrations sériques de potassium (administration de dextrose ou d'insuline, afin de faciliter le passage du potassium dans les cellules, de polystyrène de sodium à titre de résine échangeuse de cations et dialyse chez les insuffisants rénaux).

DIAGNOSTICS INFIRMIERS POSSIBLES

- Alimentation déficiente (Indications).
- Connaissances insuffisantes sur le traitement médicamenteux (Enseignement au patient et à ses proches).

INTERVENTIONS INFIRMIÈRES

PO: Les comprimés peuvent être administrés après les repas pour diminuer les effets secondaires gastro-intestinaux.

- Ne pas administrer avec des antiacides contenant du magnésium, de l'aluminium ou du calcium.

IV: N'administrer que le produit dilué. Cet agent est une composante courante de l'alimentation parentérale totale. Ne pas administrer par voie IM.

Perfusion continue: Diluer jusqu'à l'obtention d'une concentration ne dépassant pas 120 mmol/L avec une solution de NaCl 0,45 %, de NaCl 0,9 %, de D5%E, de D%10E, de D5%/NaCl 0,45 %, de D5%/NaCl 0,9 % ou avec une solution destinée à l'alimentation parentérale totale. Consulter les directives de chaque fabricant avant d'administrer la préparation.

Vitesse d'administration: Administrer lentement en perfusion continue. On ne devrait pas dépasser 7,5 mmol/h.

Compatibilité (tubulure en Y): ciprofloxacine ■ diltiazem ■ énalaprilate ■ esmolol ■ famotidine ■ labétalol.

Compatibilité en addition au soluté: sulfate de magnésium.

Incompatibilité en addition au soluté: solution de Ringer ou de lactate de Ringer pour injection ■ D10%/NaCl 0,9 % ■ D5%/solution de lactate de Ringer.

ENSEIGNEMENT AU PATIENT ET À SES PROCHES

- Expliquer au patient le but du traitement et lui conseiller de respecter rigoureusement la posologie recommandée. S'il n'a pas pu prendre le médicament au moment habituel, il doit le prendre aussitôt que possible à moins que ce ne soit presque l'heure prévue pour la dose suivante.
- Expliquer au patient qu'il est important de maintenir un apport suffisant de liquides (boire au minimum 250 mL d'eau à l'heure) pour prévenir la formation de calculs rénaux.
- Recommander au patient de prévenir rapidement un professionnel de la santé en cas de diarrhée, de faiblesse, de fatigue, de crampes musculaires ou de tremblements.

VÉRIFICATION DE L'EFFICACITÉ THÉRAPEUTIQUE

L'efficacité du traitement peut être démontrée par: la prévention et la correction d'une carence en phosphate et en potassium sériques ■ le maintien de l'acidité de l'urine ■ la diminution des concentrations de calcium dans les urines, prévenant ainsi la formation de calculs rénaux.

P

ALERTE CLINIQUE

POTASSIUM, SUPPLÉMENTS DE

acétate de potassium
Acétate de potassium

bicarbonate de potassium
Ce médicament n'est pas commercialisé au Canada.

bicarbonate de potassium/chlorure de potassium
Ce médicament n'est pas commercialisé au Canada.

bicarbonate de potassium/citrate de potassium
Polycitra-K

chlorure de potassium
Apo-K, Euro-K, Kaochlor, Kaon, K10, KCl Rougier, K-Dur, K-Lor, K-Long, K-Lyte/Cl, K-Med, Micro-K ExtenCaps, Novo-lente k, PMS-Potassium chloride, Pro-K, Riva-K 20 sr, Riva-K 8 sr, Roychlor, Slo Pot, Slow-K

chlorure de potassium/bicarbonate de potassium/ citrate de potassium
Ce médicament n'est pas commercialisé au Canada.

citrate de potassium
K-Lyte

gluconate de potassium
PMS-Potassium gluconate

gluconate de potassium/chlorure de potassium
Ce médicament n'est pas commercialisé au Canada.

gluconate de potassium/citrate de potassium
Ce médicament n'est pas commercialisé au Canada.

trikates (acétate de potassium/bicarbonate de potassium/citrate de potassium)
Ce médicament n'est pas commercialisé au Canada.

CLASSIFICATION:
Minéraux et électrolytes (traitement de remplacement)

Grossesse – catégorie C

P

INDICATIONS

PO, IV: Traitement ou prévention de la carence en potassium ■ Traitement de l'intoxication digitalique ■ **IV**: La voie IV est indiquée lorsque le patient est incapable de prendre le potassium par voie orale ou en cas d'hypokaliémie grave.

MÉCANISME D'ACTION

Maintien de l'équilibre acidobasique, de l'isotonicité et de l'équilibre électrophysiologique des cellules ■ Activation de nombreuses réactions enzymatiques ■ Élément essentiel à la transmission de l'influx nerveux ■ à la contraction des muscles cardiaque, squelettiques et lisses ■ aux sécrétions gastriques ■ au maintien de la fonction rénale ■ à la synthèse des tissus ■ au métabolisme des glucides. ***Effets thérapeutiques:*** Supplément de potassium en cas de carence ■ Prévention de la carence en potassium.

PHARMACOCINÉTIQUE

Absorption: Bonne (PO).

Distribution: L'agent pénètre dans le liquide extracellulaire d'où il parvient aux cellules par transport actif.

Métabolisme et excrétion: Excrétion rénale.

Demi-vie: Inconnue.

Profil temps-action
(élévation des concentrations sériques de potassium)

	DÉBUT D'ACTION	PIC	DURÉE
PO	inconnu	1 – 2 h	inconnue
IV	rapide	fin de la perfusion	inconnue

CONTRE-INDICATIONS, PRÉCAUTIONS ET MISES EN GARDE

Contre-indications: Hyperkaliémie ■ Insuffisance rénale grave ■ Fibrillation ventriculaire ■ Maladie d'Addison non traitée ■ Hyperplasie surrénalienne avec perte de sel ■ Traumatisme tissulaire grave ■ Déshydratation aiguë et crampes de chaleur ■ Sensibilité accrue au potassium (par exemple, paramyotonie congénitale ou adynamie épisodique héréditaire) ■ Hyperadrénalisme associé à un syndrome génitosurrénal ■ Hypomotilité gastro-intestinale, incluant la dysphagie ou la compression de l'œsophage due à l'hypertrophie auriculaire gauche (comprimés et capsules) ■ Hypersensibilité ou intolérance à la tartrazine (FDC jaune n° 5) ou à l'alcool (ne pas administrer dans ce cas les produits qui renferment ces additifs).

Précautions et mises en garde: Maladie cardiaque ■ Insuffisance rénale ■ Diabète (les préparations liquides peuvent contenir du sucre).

RÉACTIONS INDÉSIRABLES ET EFFETS SECONDAIRES

SNC: confusion, agitation, faiblesse.

CV: ARYTHMIES, modifications de l'ÉCG.

GI: douleurs abdominales, diarrhée, flatulence, nausées, vomissements; *comprimés et capsules seulement* – ulcère gastrique, lésions sténosées.

Locaux: irritation au point d'injection IV.

SN: paralysie, paresthésie.

INTERACTIONS

Médicament-médicament: Les **diurétiques épargneurs de potassium**, les **antagonistes des récepteurs de l'angiotensine II (ARA)** et les **inhibiteurs de l'enzyme de conversion de l'angiotensine (IECA)**, administrés en concomitance, peuvent entraîner une hyperkaliémie ■ Les **anticholinergiques**, administrés en concomitance, peuvent aggraver les lésions de la muqueuse gastro-intestinale chez les patients recevant les préparations de chlorure de potassium à matrice de cire.

VOIES D'ADMINISTRATION ET POSOLOGIE

Les doses sont exprimées en mmol de potassium. L'acétate de potassium en renferme 10,2 mmol/g; le chlorure de potassium, 13,4 mmol/g; le citrate de potassium, 9,3 mmol/g; le gluconate de potassium, 4,3 mmol/g.

- **PO (adultes)**: *Prévention de la carence* – de 20 à 40 mmol/jour; *traitement de la carence* – de 40 à 100 mmol/jour, en 2 ou 3 doses fractionnées.
- **PO (enfants)**: De 2 à 3 mmol/kg/jour ou de 20 à 40 mmol/m^2/jour, en doses fractionnées, avec surveillance des taux sériques.
- **IV (adultes)**: *Potassium sérique ≥ 2,5 mmol/L* – jusqu'à 200 mmol par jour sous perfusion; ne pas administrer plus de 10 mmol/h à une concentration maximale de 40 mmol/L par tubulure périphérique. (Pour obtenir des concentrations supérieures, administrer par un cathéter central.) *Potassium sérique < 2 mmol/L, accompagné de symptômes* – jusqu'à 400 mmol/jour en perfusion (en général, on ne doit pas dépasser 40 mmol/h).
- **IV (enfants)**: Jusqu'à 2 à 3 mmol/kg/jour en perfusion, avec surveillance des taux sériques.

PRÉSENTATION

- **Acétate de potassium**
  Préparation concentrée pour injection: 2 mmol/mL et 4 mmol/mL^{Pr}; plusieurs formats disponibles.
- **Bicarbonate de potassium**
  Ce médicament n'est pas commercialisé au Canada.
- **Bicarbonate de potassium/chlorure de potassium**
  Ce médicament n'est pas commercialisé au Canada.
- **Bicarbonate de potassium/citrate de potassium**
  Sachet pour solution orale effervescente: 30 mmol^{Pr} ■ **Solution orale**: 10 mmol/5 mL^{Pr}.
- **Chlorure de potassium**
  Comprimés à libération prolongée: 8 mmol^{VL}, 12 mmol^{VL}, 20 mmol^{VL} ■ **Capsules à libération prolongée**: 8 mmol^{VL}, 10 mmol^{VL} ■ **Solutions orales**: 10 mmol/15 mL^{VL}, 20 mmol/15 mL^{VL}, 40 mmol/15 mL^{VL} ■ **Poudre en sachets pour solution orale**: 20 mmol^{VL}, 25 mmol^{VL} ■ **Solutions concentrées pour injection**: 2 mmol/mL^{Pr}, en plusieurs concentrations et présentations ■ **Solutions prémélangées pour perfusion IV**: 10, 20, 30 et 40 mmol/L, diverses solutions pour injection et diverses présentations.
- **Chlorure de potassium/bicarbonate de potassium/citrate de potassium**
  Ce médicament n'est pas commercialisé au Canada.
- **Citrate de potassium**
  Comprimés: 99 mg^{VL} ■ **Comprimés pour solution orale effervescente**: 25 mmol^{VL}.
- **Gluconate de potassium**
  Comprimés: 550 mg^{VL}, 1 g^{VL} ■ **Élixir**: 20 mmol/15 mL^{VL}.
- **Gluconate de potassium/chlorure de potassium**
  Ce médicament n'est pas commercialisé au Canada.
- **Gluconate de potassium/citrate de potassium**
  Ce médicament n'est pas commercialisé au Canada.
- **Trikates (acétate de potassium/bicarbonate de potassium/citrate de potassium)**
  Ce médicament n'est pas commercialisé au Canada.

SOINS INFIRMIERS

ÉVALUATION DE LA SITUATION

- Suivre de près les signes et les symptômes d'hypokaliémie (faiblesse, fatigue, apparition d'ondes U sur le tracé de l'ÉCG, arythmies, polyurie, polydipsie) et d'hyperkaliémie (voir «Toxicité et surdosage»).
- MESURER LE POULS ET LA PRESSION ARTÉRIELLE ET SUIVRE L'ÉCG À INTERVALLES RÉGULIERS PENDANT TOUTE LA DURÉE DU TRAITEMENT PAR VOIE IV.

Tests de laboratoire: Examiner les concentrations sériques de potassium avant le traitement et à intervalles réguliers pendant toute sa durée. Suivre l'état de la fonction rénale, les concentrations sériques de bicarbonate et le pH. En cas d'hypokaliémie réfractaire, il faut déterminer les concentrations sériques de magnésium, car il faut corriger l'hypomagnésémie pour rendre les suppléments de potassium plus efficaces. Mesurer les concentrations sériques de chlorure en raison du risque d'hypochlorémie lors de l'administration de suppléments de potassium sans chlorure.

TOXICITÉ ET SURDOSAGE:

- LES SYMPTÔMES DE TOXICITÉ SONT LES MÊMES QU'EN CAS D'HYPERKALIÉMIE: BATTEMENTS CARDIAQUES LENTS ET IRRÉGULIERS, FATIGUE, FAIBLESSE MUSCULAIRE, PARESTHÉSIE, CONFUSION, DYSPNÉE, ONDES T POINTUES, DÉPRESSION DU SEGMENT ST, ALLONGEMENT DU SEGMENT QT, ÉLARGISSEMENT DU COMPLEXE QRS, DISPARITION DES ONDES P ET ARYTHMIES CARDIAQUES.
- Le traitement comprend l'arrêt de l'administration de potassium et l'administration de bicarbonate de sodium, pour corriger l'acidose, de dextrose et d'insuline, pour faciliter la pénétration du potassium dans les cellules, de sels de calcium, pour renverser les effets sur l'ÉCG (chez les patients ne recevant pas de dérivés digitaliques), de polystyrène de sodium comme résine échangeuse de cations et la dialyse, chez les patients souffrant d'insuffisance rénale.

DIAGNOSTICS INFIRMIERS POSSIBLES

- Alimentation déficiente (Indications).
- Connaissances insuffisantes sur le traitement médicamenteux (Enseignement au patient et à ses proches).

INTERVENTIONS INFIRMIÈRES

Alerte clinique: Des erreurs médicales sont survenues à la suite de l'administration de perfusions rapides ou de bolus intraveineux de chlorure de potassium. Ces erreurs ont mené au décès de certains patients. Voir la section concernant l'administration IV pour plus de détails.

- Dans la plupart des cas, on devrait administrer le chlorure de potassium, sauf en cas d'acidose tubulaire rénale (acidose hyperchlorémique), où d'autres sels sont plus appropriés (bicarbonate de potassium, citrate de potassium ou gluconate de potassium).
- Si l'hypokaliémie découle d'un traitement diurétique, il faudrait réduire la dose de diurétique, sauf en présence d'antécédents d'arythmies importantes ou d'un traitement concomitant par des dérivés digitaliques.

PO:

- Pour réduire l'irritation gastro-intestinale, administrer ces agents avec des aliments ou après les repas.
- Les comprimés et les capsules devraient être réservés aux patients qui ne tolèrent pas les préparations liquides.
- Dissoudre les comprimés effervescents dans 90 à 240 mL d'eau froide. S'assurer qu'ils sont totalement dissous. Diluer la poudre et la solution dans 90 à 240 mL d'eau froide ou de jus (ne pas utiliser de jus de tomates, si le patient suit un régime hyposodé). Recommander au patient de boire le mélange lentement, soit en 5 à 10 minutes.
- Il faut prendre les comprimés et les capsules avec des aliments et un grand verre d'eau. Prévenir le patient qu'il ne doit pas mâcher ni écraser les comprimés et les capsules à enrobage entérique ou à libération prolongée. On peut ouvrir les capsules Micro-K ExtenCaps, en saupoudrer le contenu sur des aliments mous (pouding, compote de pommes) et les avaler immédiatement avec un verre d'eau froide ou un jus.

IV: Éviter l'extravasation, car elle peut provoquer de fortes douleurs et la nécrose des tissus. **Alerte clinique:** Ne jamais administrer le chlorure de potassium en bolus rapide.

Acétate de potassium

Perfusion continue: Alerte clinique: Ne pas administrer le médicament sans le diluer. Diluer et bien mélanger chacune des doses avec 100 à 1 000 mL de dextrose, de soluté salin, de solution de Ringer ou de lactate de Ringer, de dextrose avec soluté salin, de dextrose avec solution de Ringer ou de dextrose avec solution de lactate de Ringer. Habituellement, la solution doit avoir une concentration maximale de 40 mmol/L, si elle est administrée par tubulure périphérique, ou de 100 mmol/L, si elle est administrée par cathéter central. Consulter les directives de chaque fabricant avant d'administrer la préparation.

Vitesse d'administration: Administrer lentement à une vitesse de 20 mmol/h. Ne pas dépasser un débit de 40 mmol/h, chez les adultes, et de 1 mmol/kg/h, chez les enfants (sous surveillance de l'ÉCG).

Chlorure de potassium

Perfusion continue: Alerte clinique: Ne pas administrer les préparations dont la concentration est de 1,5 mmol/mL ou de 2 mmol/mL, sans les diluer, en raison du risque de réactions mortelles. Les préparations concentrées sont présentées dans des fioles munies d'un bouchon noir ou dans des ampoules portant des stries noires sur leur extrémité supérieure et un avertissement concernant la dilution. Chaque dose doit être diluée et bien mélangée dans 100 à 1 000 mL de solution IV. Habituellement, la solution doit avoir une concentration maximale de 40 mmol/L, si elle est administrée par tubulure périphérique, ou de 100 mmol/L, si elle est administrée par cathéter central.

- Les concentrations de 0,01 mmol/mL et de 0,04 mmol/mL sont destinées à l'administration par un appareil à perfusion calibré et ne nécessitent pas de dilution. Consulter les directives de chaque fabricant avant d'administrer la préparation.

Vitesse d'administration: Administrer lentement à une vitesse de 20 mmol/h. Ne pas dépasser un débit de 40 mmol/h, chez les adultes, et de 1 mmol/kg/h, chez les enfants (sous surveillance de l'ÉCG).

Compatibilité avec diverses solutions: Le produit peut être dilué dans du dextrose, dans un soluté salin, dans une solution de Ringer, dans une solution de lactate de Ringer, dans des mélanges de dextrose et de soluté salin, de dextrose et de solution de Ringer ou de dextrose et de solution de lactate de Ringer. Il est commercialisé sous forme prémélangée avec bon nombre des solutions IV ci-dessus mentionnées.

Compatibilité (tubulure en Y): acyclovir ▪ adrénaline ▪ aldesleukine ▪ amifostine ▪ aminophylline ▪ amiodarone ▪ ampicilline ▪ amrinone ▪ atropine ▪ aztréonam ▪ bétaméthasone ▪ calcium, gluconate de ▪ céphalotine, sodium neutre de ▪ céphapirine ▪ chlordiazépoxide ▪ chlorpromazine ▪ ciprofloxacine ▪ cyanocobalamine ▪

P

dexaméthasone ■ digoxine ■ diltiazem ■ diphenhydramine ■ dobutamine ■ dopamine ■ dropéridol ■ dropéridol/fentanyl ■ édrophonium ■ énalaprilate ■ esmolol ■ éthacrynate sodique ■ famotidine ■ fentanyl ■ filgrastim ■ fludarabine ■ fluorouracile ■ furosémide ■ gallium, nitrate de ■ granisétron ■ hydralazine ■ idarubicine, potassique ■ indométhacine ■ insuline ■ isoprotérénol ■ kanamycine ■ labétalol ■ lidocaïne ■ lorazépam ■ magnésium, sulfate de ■ melphalan ■ ménadiol ■ mépéridine ■ méthicilline ■ méthoamine ■ méthylergonovine ■ midazolam ■ minocycline ■ morphine ■ néostigmine ■ noradrénaline ■ œstrogènes conjuguées ■ ondansétron ■ oxacilline ■ oxytocine ■ paclitaxel ■ pénicilline G potassique ■ pentazocine ■ phytonadione ■ pipéracilline/tazobactam ■ prednisolone ■ procaïnamide ■ prochlorpérazine, édisylate de ■ propranolol ■ pyridostigmine ■ sargramostim ■ scopolamine ■ sodium, bicarbonate de ■ succinylcholine ■ tacrolimus ■ téniposide ■ théophylline ■ thiotépa ■ triméthaphane ■ triméthobenzamide ■ vinorelbine ■ zidovudine.

Incompatibilité (tubulure en Y): diazépam ■ ergotamine, tartrate d' ■ phénytoïne.

Compatibilité en addition au soluté: calcium, gluconate de ■ cimétidine ■ lidocaïne ■ ranitidine ■ sodium, bicarbonate de ■ vitamines du complexe B avec C.

ENSEIGNEMENT AU PATIENT ET À SES PROCHES

- Expliquer au patient le but du traitement et lui conseiller de respecter rigoureusement la posologie recommandée, particulièrement s'il prend en concomitance des dérivés digitaliques ou des diurétiques. S'il n'a pu prendre le médicament au moment habituel, il devrait le prendre dès que possible dans les 2 heures, sinon il doit sauter cette dose et reprendre le schéma posologique habituel. Le prévenir qu'il ne faut jamais remplacer une dose manquée par une double dose.
- Expliquer au patient comment prendre le médicament. Si les préparations liquides ou la poudre ne sont pas suffisamment diluées ou si les comprimés à enrobage entérique sont mâchés, une ulcération ou une irritation gastro-intestinale peut survenir.
- Certains comprimés à libération prolongée sont enrobés d'une matrice de cire qui peut être excrétée dans les selles, mais ce fait n'a aucune conséquence clinique.
- Recommander au patient d'éviter les substituts de sel ou le lait et les aliments pauvres en sel, à moins qu'ils ne soient autorisés par un professionnel de la santé. Conseiller au patient de lire les étiquettes afin d'éviter un apport excessif en potassium.
- Expliquer au patient quelles sont les sources de potassium alimentaire (voir l'annexe J). L'inciter à suivre scrupuleusement le régime alimentaire recommandé.
- Prévenir le patient qu'il doit signaler à un professionnel de la santé la présence de selles foncées, goudronneuses ou sanguinolentes, la faiblesse, la fatigue inhabituelle ou les picotements dans les membres. Lui recommander également d'informer un professionnel de la santé si les nausées, les vomissements, la diarrhée ou la gêne gastrique persistent. Il peut s'avérer nécessaire de modifier la dose.
- Souligner l'importance des examens de suivi réguliers permettant de surveiller les concentrations sériques et d'évaluer l'efficacité du traitement.

VÉRIFICATION DE L'EFFICACITÉ THÉRAPEUTIQUE

L'efficacité du traitement peut être démontrée par: la prévention ou le traitement de la carence en potassium sérique ■ la disparition des arythmies dues à la toxicité attribuable aux glucosides digitaliques. ✳

PRAMIPEXOLE

Apo-Pramipexole, Mirapex, Novo-Pramipexole, PMS-Pramipexole

CLASSIFICATION:

Antiparkinsonien (agoniste de la dopamine)

Grossesse – catégorie C

INDICATIONS

Traitement de la maladie de Parkinson idiopathique, lors de la phase précoce, sans lévodopa, ou à titre de traitement d'appoint à la lévodopa ■ Traitement symptomatique du syndrome des jambes sans repos idiopathique modéré à grave.

MÉCANISME D'ACTION

Stimulation des récepteurs de la dopamine situés dans le striatum du cerveau. ***Effets thérapeutiques:*** Diminution des tremblements et de la rigidité associés à la maladie de Parkinson ■ Diminution des symptômes du syndrome des jambes sans repos.

PHARMACOCINÉTIQUE

Absorption: 90 % (PO).

Distribution: Tous les tissus de l'organisme.

P

Métabolisme et excrétion: 90 % est excrété sous forme inchangée dans l'urine (sécrétion tubulaire).
Demi-vie: 8 heures (prolongée chez les personnes âgées et les insuffisants rénaux).
Profil temps-action (concentrations sanguines)

	Début d'action	Pic	Durée
PO	inconnu	2 h	8 h

CONTRE-INDICATIONS, PRÉCAUTIONS ET MISES EN GARDE

Contre-indications: Hypersensibilité.
Précautions et mises en garde: Risque de narcolepsie (elle ne survient pas nécessairement au début du traitement; il faut également prévenir les patients que l'état de sommeil soudain peut survenir sans signe avant-coureur) ■ Risque de complications fibreuses (p. ex., fibrose péritonérale, fibrose pleurale et fibrose pulmonaire) ■ Intensification et rebond du syndrome des jambes sans repos ■ Risque d'aggravation des symptômes suivant l'interruption soudaine du traitement chez les patients prenant ce médicament pour traiter le syndrome des jambes sans repos ■ Risque d'une réaction de type syndrome malin des neuroleptiques (caractérisé par une augmentation de la température, une rigidité musculaire, des changements de l'état de conscience et une instabilité autonome), associé à une diminution rapide de la dose ou au retrait du pramipexole chez les patients atteints de la maladie de Parkinson ■ Risque de maladie rétinienne chez les patients albinos ■ Risque de mélanome (un suivi en dermatologie peut être indiqué) ■ **GÉR.**: Risque accru d'hallucinations ■ Insuffisance rénale (accroître l'intervalle posologique si la Cl_{Cr} est < 60 mL/min) ■ **OBST., ALLAITEMENT, PÉD.**: L'innocuité du médicament n'a pas été établie; il peut inhiber la lactation.

P

RÉACTIONS INDÉSIRABLES ET EFFETS SECONDAIRES

SNC: NARCOLEPSIE, amnésie, étourdissements, somnolence, hallucinations, faiblesse, rêves anormaux, confusion, dyskinésie, syndrome extrapyramidal, céphalées, insomnie.
CV: hypotension orthostatique.
GI: constipation, sécheresse de la bouche (xérostomie), dyspepsie, nausées, maladie des dents.
GU: mictions fréquentes.
Loc.: crampes dans les jambes.
SN: hypertonie, déséquilibre et chutes.

INTERACTIONS

Médicament-médicament: L'administration concomitante de **lévodopa** accroît le risque d'hallucinations et de dyskinésie ■ Les **médicaments qui inhibent la sécrétion tubulaire de bases organiques par l'entremise du système de transport cationique**, tels que l'**amantadine**, la **cimétidine**, la **ranitidine**, le **diltiazem**, le **triamtérène**, le **vérapamil**, la **quinidine** et la **quinine**, peuvent diminuer la clairance du pramipexole et augmenter les concentrations plasmatiques ■ Dépression additive du SNC lors de l'usage concomitant d'autres **dépresseurs du SNC**, tels que l'**alcool**, les **opioïdes** et les **hypnosédatifs** ■ L'efficacité du médicament peut être réduite par les **antagonistes dopaminergiques**, dont les **butyrophénones**, le **métoclopramide**, les **phénothiazines** ou les **thioxanthènes**.

VOIES D'ADMINISTRATION ET POSOLOGIE

Maladie de Parkinson

- **PO (adultes)**: *Dose initiale* – 0,125 mg, 3 fois par jour (0,375 mg/jour). On peut ensuite majorer la dose tous les 5 à 7 jours. *Traitement d'entretien* – écart posologique de 1,5 à 4,5 mg/jour, en 3 prises fractionnées, en monothérapie ou en association avec la lévodopa.
- ***INSUFFISANCE RÉNALE***
  PO (ADULTES): *CL_{CR} ≥ 60 mL/MIN* – COMME CI-DESSUS; *CL_{CR} DE 35 À 59 mL/MIN* – INITIALEMENT, 0,125 mg, 2 FOIS PAR JOUR. ON PEUT MAJORER LA DOSE TOUS LES 7 JOURS, JUSQU'À CONCURRENCE DE 1,5 mg, 2 FOIS PAR JOUR; *CL_{CR} DE 15 À 34 mL/MIN* – INITIALEMENT, 0,125 mg, 1 FOIS PAR JOUR. ON PEUT MAJORER LA DOSE TOUS LES 7 JOURS, JUSQU'À CONCURRENCE DE 1,5 mg, 1 FOIS PAR JOUR; *CL_{CR} < 15 mL/MIN* – USAGE DÉCONSEILLÉ.

Syndrome des jambes sans repos

- **PO (adultes)**: *Dose initiale* – 0,125 mg, une fois par jour, 2 à 3 heures avant le coucher. On peut ensuite majorer la dose tous les 4 à 7 jours. *Traitement d'entretien* – écart posologique de 0,125 à 0,75 mg/jour.
- ***INSUFFISANCE RÉNALE***
  PO (ADULTES): *CL_{CR} DE 20 À 60 mL/MIN* – PRÉVOIR UN INTERVALLE DE 14 JOURS ENTRE LES AUGMENTATIONS DE DOSE.

PRÉSENTATION

Comprimés: 0,25 mg^Pr^, 0,5 mg^Pr^, 1 mg^Pr^, 1,5 mg^Pr^.

SOINS INFIRMIERS

ÉVALUATION DE LA SITUATION

- Observer le patient avant le traitement et pendant toute sa durée à la recherche des signes et des symptômes parkinsoniens suivants: tremblements, faiblesse musculaire, rigidité et ataxie.

- Observer attentivement le patient pour déceler la confusion ou les hallucinations. Le cas échéant, en prévenir le médecin ou un autre professionnel de la santé.
- Noter l'ÉCG et mesurer la pression artérielle à intervalles fréquents pendant la période d'adaptation posologique et à intervalles réguliers pendant toute la durée du traitement.
- SUIVRE DE PRÈS LA SOMNOLENCE OU LA NARCOLEPSIE. LA SOMNOLENCE EST UN EFFET SECONDAIRE COURANT DU PRAMIPEXOLE, MAIS LA NARCOLEPSIE OU LES CRISES DE SOMMEIL DURANT DES ACTIVITÉS DEMANDANT UNE PARTICIPATION ACTIVE PEUVENT SURVENIR SPONTANÉMENT. VÉRIFIER SI LE PATIENT NE PREND PAS EN MÊME TEMPS D'AUTRES MÉDICAMENTS ENTRAÎNANT DES EFFETS SÉDATIFS OU POUVANT ACCROÎTRE LES CONCENTRATIONS SÉRIQUES DU PRAMIPEXOLE (VOIR « INTERACTIONS »). IL PEUT ÊTRE NÉCESSAIRE D'ARRÊTER LE TRAITEMENT.

DIAGNOSTICS INFIRMIERS POSSIBLES

- Mobilité physique réduite (Indications).
- Risque d'accident (Indications, Effets secondaires).
- Connaissances insuffisantes sur le traitement médicamenteux (Enseignement au patient et à ses proches).

INTERVENTIONS INFIRMIÈRES

- On peut essayer de réduire la dose de lévodopa pendant le traitement par le pramipexole.
- Administrer le médicament avec des aliments afin de réduire les nausées; cet effet diminue habituellement avec le temps, malgré la poursuite du traitement.

ENSEIGNEMENT AU PATIENT ET À SES PROCHES

- Conseiller au patient de respecter rigoureusement la posologie recommandée. S'il n'a pu prendre le médicament au moment habituel, il doit le prendre aussitôt que possible, mais pas s'il est presque l'heure de la dose suivante. Le prévenir qu'il ne doit pas remplacer une dose manquée par une double dose. Lui recommander de consulter un professionnel de la santé avant de réduire la dose ou de cesser de prendre le médicament.
- Prévenir le patient que le pramipexole peut provoquer la somnolence et la narcolepsie. Lui conseiller de ne pas conduire et d'éviter les activités qui exigent sa vigilance jusqu'à ce qu'on ait la certitude que le médicament n'entraîne pas ces effets chez lui. Conseiller au patient de signaler tout épisode de narcolepsie à un professionnel de la santé.
- Recommander au patient de changer lentement de position pour prévenir l'hypotension orthostatique, qui risque de survenir plus fréquemment au cours du traitement initial.
- Recommander à la patiente de prévenir un professionnel de la santé si elle pense être enceinte, si elle souhaite le devenir ou si elle allaite ou prévoit le faire.

VÉRIFICATION DE L'EFFICACITÉ THÉRAPEUTIQUE

L'efficacité du traitement peut être démontrée par: la diminution des tremblements et de la rigidité attribuables à la maladie de Parkinson ■ la diminution des symptômes du syndrome des jambes sans repos.

PRAVASTATINE,

voir Inhibiteurs de l'HMG-CoA réductase

PRAZOSINE

Apo-Prazo, Minipress, Novo-Prazin

CLASSIFICATION:

Antihypertenseur (antagoniste alpha$_1$-adrénergique à action périphérique)

Grossesse – catégorie C

INDICATIONS

Traitement de l'hypertension en association avec d'autres agents. **Usages non approuvés**: Traitement de l'occlusion des voies urinaires chez les patients atteints d'hyperplasie bénigne de la prostate (HBP).

MÉCANISME D'ACTION

Dilatation des artères et des veines par blocage des récepteurs alpha$_1$-adrénergiques postsynaptiques ■ Diminution des contractions des muscles lisses de la capsule prostatique. ***Effets thérapeutiques:*** Abaissement de la pression artérielle ■ Diminution de la précharge et de la postcharge cardiaque ■ Diminution des symptômes d'HBP (mictions impérieuses, retard à la miction, nycturie).

PHARMACOCINÉTIQUE

Absorption: 60 % (PO).
Distribution: Tout l'organisme.
Liaison aux protéines: 97 %.

Métabolisme et excrétion: Fort métabolisme hépatique. Excrétion rénale de 5 à 10 % sous forme inchangée.
Demi-vie: De 2 à 3 heures.

Profil temps-action (effets antihypertenseurs)

	DÉBUT D'ACTION	PIC	DURÉE
PO	2 h	2 - 4 h†	10 h

† Par suite de l'administration d'une seule dose. L'effet antihypertenseur maximal s'installe après 3 à 4 semaines de traitement.

CONTRE-INDICATIONS, PRÉCAUTIONS ET MISES EN GARDE

Contre-indications: Hypersensibilité aux dérivés de la quinazoline.
Précautions et mises en garde: Insuffisance rénale (sensibilité accrue aux effets du médicament; une réduction de la dose peut s'avérer nécessaire) ■ **ALLAITEMENT, OBST., PÉD.:** L'innocuité du médicament n'a pas été établie ■ Angine de poitrine ■ Administration concomitante de diurétiques (réduire la dose de prazosine).

RÉACTIONS INDÉSIRABLES ET EFFETS SECONDAIRES

SNC: étourdissements, céphalées, faiblesse, somnolence, dépression, syncope.
ORLO: vision trouble.
CV: hypotension orthostatique induite par la ou les premières doses, palpitations, angine, œdème.
GI: crampes abdominales, diarrhée, sécheresse de la bouche (xérostomie), nausées, vomissements.
GU: impuissance, priapisme.

INTERACTIONS

Médicament-médicament: Hypotension additive lors de l'administration concomitante de **sildénafil**, de **tadalafil**, de **vardénafil**, d'autres **antihypertenseurs** ou de **dérivés nitrés** ou lors de la consommation d'**alcool** ■ Les **anti-inflammatoires non stéroïdiens**, administrés simultanément, peuvent diminuer les effets antihypertenseurs de la prazosine.

VOIES D'ADMINISTRATION ET POSOLOGIE

Hypertension

- **PO (adultes):** *Première dose* – 0,5 mg (1/2 comprimé de 1 mg) au repas du soir, au moins 2 à 3 heures avant le coucher. *Dose de départ* – 0,5 mg, 2 ou 3 fois par jour, pendant les 3 premiers jours, puis majorer graduellement la posologie, selon les besoins, jusqu'à l'atteinte d'une dose d'entretien de 6 à 15 mg/jour, en 2 ou 3 prises fractionnées (ne pas dépasser 20 mg par jour).

Patients prenant des diurétiques, d'autres antihypertenseurs ou sujets atteints d'insuffisance rénale

- **PO (adultes):** Débuter à 0,5 mg, 1 fois par jour et augmenter graduellement la posologie, selon la réponse du patient.

PRÉSENTATION (version générique disponible)

Comprimés: 1 mgPr, 2 mgPr, 5 mgPr.

SOINS INFIRMIERS

ÉVALUATION DE LA SITUATION

- Effectuer le bilan quotidien des ingesta et des excreta et peser le patient tous les jours. L'observer quotidiennement, particulièrement au début du traitement, pour déceler la formation d'œdème. Signaler tout gain de poids important ou la présence d'œdème.

Hypertension:

- Mesurer la tension artérielle et le pouls à intervalles fréquents lors de l'adaptation posologique initiale et à intervalles réguliers pendant toute la durée du traitement. Signaler tout changement important.
- Vérifier le rythme de renouvellement des ordonnances pour évaluer l'observance au traitement.

Hyperplasie bénigne de la prostate: Suivre de près le patient à intervalles réguliers pendant toute la durée du traitement pour déceler l'apparition de symptômes urinaires: rétention urinaire, fuites postmictionnelles, retard à la miction, mictions impérieuses.

Tests de laboratoire:

- La prazosine peut élever les concentrations sériques de sodium.
- La prazosine peut élever les concentrations d'acide vanilmandélique; elle peut aussi entraîner des résultats faussement positifs aux tests de dépistage du phéochromocytome.

DIAGNOSTICS INFIRMIERS POSSIBLES

- Risque d'accident (Effets secondaires).
- Connaissances insuffisantes sur le traitement médicamenteux (Enseignement au patient et à ses proches).
- Non-observance du traitement médicamenteux (Enseignement au patient et à ses proches).

INTERVENTIONS INFIRMIÈRES

- Il y a risque d'hypotension orthostatique induite par la ou les premières doses, qui se produit, le plus souvent, de 30 à 90 minutes après l'administration de cette dose et qui peut se traduire par des étourdissements, la faiblesse et la syncope. Observer de près le patient durant cette période et prendre les précautions qui s'imposent pour prévenir les accidents. Les premières doses peuvent être administrées au coucher afin de réduire les risques auxquels une telle réaction pourrait exposer le patient.

- Pour traiter l'hypertension, la prazosine devrait toujours être administrée en association avec d'autres antihypertenseurs.

ENSEIGNEMENT AU PATIENT ET À SES PROCHES

- Inciter le patient à continuer à prendre ce médicament, même s'il se sent mieux.
- Expliquer au patient qu'il doit prendre la prazosine tous les jours, à la même heure. S'il n'a pu prendre le médicament au moment habituel, il doit le prendre aussitôt que possible, à moins que ce ne soit presque l'heure prévue pour la dose suivante. Le prévenir qu'il ne doit jamais remplacer une dose manquée par une double dose.
- Inciter le patient à suivre d'autres mesures de réduction de l'hypertension: perdre du poids, réduire sa consommation de sel, arrêter de fumer, boire de l'alcool avec modération, faire régulièrement de l'exercice et diminuer le stress.
- Montrer au patient et à ses proches comment mesurer la pression artérielle. Leur demander de prendre la pression artérielle au moins 1 fois par semaine et de signaler tout changement important à un professionnel de la santé.
- Prévenir le patient que la prazosine peut provoquer de la somnolence ou des étourdissements. Lui conseiller de ne pas conduire et d'éviter les activités qui exigent sa vigilance jusqu'à ce qu'on ait la certitude que le médicament n'entraîne pas ces effets chez lui.
- Recommander au patient de changer lentement de position pour diminuer le risque d'hypotension orthostatique.
- Conseiller au patient de consulter un professionnel de la santé avant de prendre tout médicament en vente libre ou produit naturel, particulièrement ceux contre la toux, le rhume ou les allergies.
- Insister sur l'importance des examens de suivi permettant d'évaluer les bienfaits du traitement.

VÉRIFICATION DE L'EFFICACITÉ THÉRAPEUTIQUE

L'efficacité du traitement peut être démontrée par: la baisse de la pression artérielle sans manifestation d'effets secondaires ■ la diminution des symptômes associés à l'hyperplasie bénigne de la prostate. ✳

PREDNICARBATE,

voir Corticostéroïdes (topiques)

PREDNISOLONE,

voir Corticostéroïdes (voie générale)

PREDNISONE,

voir Corticostéroïdes (voie générale)

PRÉGABALINE

Lyrica

CLASSIFICATION:

Analgésique

Grossesse – catégorie C

INDICATIONS

Traitement de la douleur neuropathique associée: à la neuropathie diabétique périphérique ■ aux névralgies postzostériennes.

MÉCANISME D'ACTION

Mécanisme d'action inconnu. Le médicament se lie à la protéine alpha$_2$-delta des canaux calciques dans les tissus cérébraux et freine la libération de plusieurs neurotransmetteurs. ***Effets thérapeutiques:*** Soulagement des douleurs neuropathiques diabétiques ou postzostériennes.

PHARMACOCINÉTIQUE

Absorption: 90 % (PO).

Distribution: L'agent traverse la barrière hématoencéphalique et la barrière placentaire et passe dans le lait maternel.

Métabolisme et excrétion: Métabolisme négligeable. Excrétion rénale sous forme inchangée (98 %).

Demi-vie: 6 heures.

Profil temps-action
(diminution des douleurs neuropathiques)

	Début d'action	Pic	Durée
PO	1 semaine	2 - 4 semaines	inconnue

P

CONTRE-INDICATIONS, PRÉCAUTIONS ET MISES EN GARDE

Contre-indications: Hypersensibilité.

Précautions et mises en garde: Insuffisance rénale (diminuer la dose quotidienne si la Cl_{Cr} est < 60 mL/min) ■ **GÉR.**: Il est recommandé de réduire la dose chez les personnes âgées ou débilitées (en raison de la détérioration de la fonction rénale) ■ Insuffisance cardiaque (œdème) ■ **OBST., ALLAITEMENT**: L'innocuité du médicament n'a pas été établie chez la femme enceinte ou qui allaite ■ **PÉD.**: L'innocuité et l'efficacité du médicament n'ont pas été établies chez les enfants < 18 ans.

RÉACTIONS INDÉSIRABLES ET EFFETS SECONDAIRES

SNC: étourdissements, somnolence, vertiges, confusion, céphalées, asthénie, euphorie, anomalies des opérations de la pensée, ataxie.

ORLO: sécheresse de la bouche (xérostomie), vision trouble, diplopie.

GI: nausées, douleurs abdominales, constipation, flatulence.

Loc.: démarche anormale.

Divers: œdème périphérique, gain pondéral.

INTERACTIONS

Médicament-médicament: Risque accru de dépression du SNC lors de la prise concomitante d'autres **dépresseurs du SNC**, incluant les **opioïdes**, l'**alcool**, les **benzodiazépines** et autres **hypnosédatifs** ■ L'emploi concomitant de prégabaline et d'un antidiabétique de la classe des **thiazolidinediones** peut se traduire par l'aggravation de l'œdème et par un gain de poids accru. Chez les patients atteints d'une maladie cardiaque, cette association peut accroître le risque d'insuffisance cardiaque.

P

VOIES D'ADMINISTRATION ET POSOLOGIE

- **PO (adultes) (fonction rénale normale ou Cl_{Cr} > 60 mL/min)**: Dose initiale de 150 mg par jour, fractionnée en 2 ou 3 prises, soit 75 mg, 2 fois par jour, ou 50 mg, 3 fois par jour. Après la première semaine de traitement et selon la réponse au traitement et la tolérance du patient, on peut porter la dose à 300 mg par jour, en 2 prises fractionnées. Si les douleurs restent intenses et tenaces et si le patient tolère bien la dose quotidienne de 300 mg, elle peut être portée à 600 mg par jour, en 2 prises fractionnées (dose maximale). Cependant, la dose de 600 mg par jour ne s'est pas révélée sensiblement plus efficace durant les études cliniques, tandis que les effets indésirables et les abandons du traitement ont augmenté de façon marquée.
- ***INSUFFISANCE RÉNALE***
  PO (ADULTES): IL FAUT ADAPTER LA POSOLOGIE CHEZ LES INSUFFISANTS RÉNAUX, SELON LA CLAIRANCE DE LA CRÉATININE. *CL_{CR} DE 30 À 59 mL/MIN* – DOSE INITIALE DE 75 mg PAR JOUR, DOSE INTERMÉDIAIRE DE 150 mg PAR JOUR, DOSE MAXIMALE DE 300 mg PAR JOUR, 2 OU 3 FOIS PAR JOUR; *CL_{CR} DE 15 À 29 mL/MIN* – DOSE INITIALE DE 25 À 50 mg PAR JOUR, DOSE INTERMÉDIAIRE DE 75 mg PAR JOUR, DOSE MAXIMALE DE 150 mg PAR JOUR, 1 OU 2 FOIS PAR JOUR; *CL_{CR} < 15 mL/MIN* – DOSE INITIALE DE 25 mg PAR JOUR, DOSE INTERMÉDIAIRE DE 25 À 50 mg PAR JOUR, DOSE MAXIMALE DE 75 mg PAR JOUR, 1 FOIS PAR JOUR.

  HÉMODIALYSE
  L'HÉMODIALYSE ÉLIMINE EFFICACEMENT LA PRÉGABALINE DU PLASMA, PUISQU'UNE SÉANCE DE 4 HEURES ABAISSE LA CONCENTRATION PLASMATIQUE D'ENVIRON 50 %. CHEZ LES PATIENTS DIALYSÉS, IL CONVIENT D'ADAPTER LA DOSE QUOTIDIENNE SELON LA FONCTION RÉNALE. IL FAUT, DE PLUS, ADMINISTRER UNE DOSE SUPPLÉMENTAIRE IMMÉDIATEMENT APRÈS CHAQUE SÉANCE D'HÉMODIALYSE DE 4 HEURES. DANS LE CAS DE LA PRISE D'UNE DOSE DE 25 mg, 1 FOIS PAR JOUR: DOSE SUPPLÉMENTAIRE DE 25 mg OU DE 50 mg. DANS LE CAS DE LA PRISE D'UNE DOSE DE 25 mg OU DE 50 mg, 1 FOIS PAR JOUR: DOSE SUPPLÉMENTAIRE DE 50 mg OU DE 75 mg. DANS LE CAS DE LA PRISE D'UNE DOSE DE 75 mg, 1 FOIS PAR JOUR: DOSE SUPPLÉMENTAIRE DE 100 mg OU DE 150 mg.

PRÉSENTATION

Capsules: 25 mg^{Pr}, 50 mg^{Pr}, 75 mg^{Pr}, 150 mg^{Pr}, 300 mg^{Pr}.

SOINS INFIRMIERS

ÉVALUATION DE LA SITUATION

Douleur chronique: Évaluer le siège, les caractéristiques et l'intensité de la douleur, à intervalles réguliers, pendant toute la durée du traitement.

Tests de laboratoire:

- Le médicament peut provoquer une baisse de la numération plaquettaire.
- Le taux de créatine kinase peut s'élever.

DIAGNOSTICS INFIRMIERS POSSIBLES

- Douleur chronique (Indications).
- Risque d'accident (Effets secondaires).
- Connaissances insuffisantes sur le traitement médicamenteux (Enseignement au patient et à ses proches).

INTERVENTIONS INFIRMIÈRES

- On peut administrer le médicament sans égard aux repas.
- Avant d'arrêter le traitement, il faudrait réduire graduellement la dose de prégabaline pendant au moins 1 semaine. Éviter le sevrage brusque, car des symptômes comme l'insomnie, les nausées, les céphalées et la diarrhée peuvent survenir.

ENSEIGNEMENT AU PATIENT ET À SES PROCHES

- Conseiller au patient de respecter rigoureusement la posologie recommandée. S'il n'a pas pu prendre le médicament au moment habituel, il doit le faire aussitôt que possible, à moins que ce ne soit l'heure prévue pour la dose suivante. Prévenir le patient qu'il ne doit pas remplacer une dose manquée par une double dose.
- Recommander au patient de prendre la prégabaline de façon régulière pour diminuer les douleurs chroniques. On ne doit pas la prendre seulement au besoin, lors d'un épisode de douleur. L'effet du traitement commence à se faire sentir en l'espace de 1 semaine.
- Conseiller au patient de signaler sans délai toute douleur, sensibilité ou faiblesse musculaire inexpliquée, surtout si ces symptômes s'accompagnent de malaises ou de fièvre. Abandonner le traitement en présence de myopathie diagnostiquée ou présumée, ou encore d'élévation marquée du taux de créatine kinase.
- Demander au patient de prévenir le médecin en cas de troubles de la vision.
- Prévenir le patient que la prégabaline peut provoquer la somnolence et des étourdissements. Lui conseiller de ne pas conduire et d'éviter les activités qui exigent sa vigilance jusqu'à ce qu'on ait la certitude que le médicament n'entraîne pas ces effets chez lui.
- Conseiller au patient d'éviter de consommer des boissons alcoolisées pendant le traitement par la prégabaline, à cause du risque de potentialisation de l'altération des capacités motrices et de la sédation liées à la consommation d'alcool.
- Conseiller au patient de signaler immédiatement à un professionnel de la santé l'œdème ou les difficultés respiratoires.
- Informer le patient qu'un gain de poids ou l'aggravation de l'œdème périphérique sont possibles lors de la prise de prégabaline, surtout s'il prend en même temps des antidiabétiques de la classe des thiazolidinediones, qui pourraient exacerber ou provoquer une insuffisance cardiaque.
- Recommander à la patiente d'informer un professionnel de la santé si elle pense être enceinte, si elle souhaite le devenir, si elle allaite ou prévoit le faire.
- Recommander au patient qui doit suivre un traitement ou subir une intervention chirurgicale d'avertir le professionnel de la santé qu'il suit un traitement avec ce médicament.

VÉRIFICATION DE L'EFFICACITÉ THÉRAPEUTIQUE

L'efficacité du traitement peut être démontrée par: la baisse d'intensité de la douleur neuropathique chronique. ✳

PRILOCAÏNE,

voir Lidocaïne/prilocaïne

PRIMIDONE

Apo-Primidone

CLASSIFICATION:

Anticonvulsivant (barbiturique)

Grossesse – catégorie D

P

INDICATIONS

Traitement prophylactique des crises partielles (simples ou complexes) avec ou sans généralisation secondaire.

MÉCANISME D'ACTION

Diminution de l'excitabilité des neurones ■ Élévation du seuil de stimulation électrique du cortex moteur. ***Effets thérapeutiques:*** Prévention des crises épileptiques.

PHARMACOCINÉTIQUE

Absorption: De 60 à 80 % (PO).

Distribution: Tout l'organisme. L'agent traverse la barrière placentaire et passe dans le lait maternel.

Métabolisme et excrétion: La primidone est transformée par le foie en phénobarbital et en un autre composé anticonvulsivant actif, le phényléthylmalonamide (PEMA).

Demi-vie: De 3 à 24 heures.

Profil temps-action (effets anticonvulsivants)

	DÉBUT D'ACTION	PIC	DURÉE
PO	4 - 7 jours	7 - 10 jours	8 - 12 h

CONTRE-INDICATIONS, PRÉCAUTIONS ET MISES EN GARDE

Contre-indications: Antécédents d'hypersensibilité à la primidone et au phénobarbital ■ Porphyrie.

Précautions et mises en garde: Insuffisance hépatique ou rénale (réduire la dose) ■ **OBST., ALLAITEMENT:** L'innocuité du médicament n'a pas été établie; risque d'hémorragie chez le nouveau-né.

RÉACTIONS INDÉSIRABLES ET EFFETS SECONDAIRES

SNC: somnolence, ataxie, vertige, léthargie, excitation (enfants).

ORLO: vision double (diplopie).

Resp.: dyspnée.

CV: œdème, hypotension orthostatique.

GI: nausées, anorexie, vomissements, hépatite.

Tég.: rash, alopécie.

Hémat.: dyscrasie sanguine, anémie mégaloblastique.

Divers: carence en acide folique.

INTERACTIONS

Médicament-médicament: La primidone induit les enzymes hépatiques et peut accélérer le métabolisme et diminuer l'efficacité d'autres **médicaments métabolisés par le foie** incluant les **contraceptifs oraux**, le **propranolol**, le **métoprolol**, la **doxycycline**, les **corticostéroïdes**, les **antidépresseurs tricycliques**, les **phénothiazines** et la **quinidine** ■ Dépression additive du SNC lors de l'usage concomitant d'autres **dépresseurs du SNC**, incluant l'**alcool**, les **antihistaminiques**, les **analgésiques opioïdes** et les **hypnosédatifs** ■ L'usage concomitant de **phénobarbital** peut provoquer une intoxication par cet agent.

Médicament-aliments: La primidone diminue l'absorption d'**acide folique**.

VOIES D'ADMINISTRATION ET POSOLOGIE

- **PO (adultes et enfants > 8 ans):** Initialement, de 100 à 125 mg au coucher, pendant 3 jours, puis de 100 à 125 mg, 2 fois par jour, pendant les 3 jours suivants, de 100 à 125 mg, 3 fois par jour pendant 3 jours de plus et, enfin, en dose d'entretien, 250 mg, 3 ou 4 fois par jour (jusqu'à concurrence de 2 g par jour).
- **PO (enfants < 8 ans):** Initialement, 50 mg au coucher pendant 3 jours, puis 50 mg, 2 fois par jour pendant les 3 jours suivants, 100 mg, 2 fois par jour, pendant 3 jours de plus et, enfin, en dose d'entretien, de 125 à 250 mg, 3 fois par jour (de 10 à 25 mg/kg par jour).

PRÉSENTATION

Comprimés: 125 mg^Pr, 250 mg^Pr.

SOINS INFIRMIERS

ÉVALUATION DE LA SITUATION

- Déterminer le siège, la durée et les caractéristiques des crises convulsives. Prendre les précautions qui s'imposent.
- Suivre de près l'allergie au phénobarbital puisqu'il s'agit d'un métabolite de la primidone.
- Suivre de près les signes suivants de carence en acide folique: troubles cognitifs, fatigue ou faiblesse inhabituelles, troubles psychiatriques, neuropathie, anémie mégaloblastique. La carence peut être traitée par l'administration d'acide folique.

Tests de laboratoire:

- Suivre à intervalles réguliers les concentrations sériques de primidone et de phénobarbital (principal métabolite de la primidone). Les concentrations sanguines thérapeutiques de primidone se situent entre 27 et 55 µmol/L, et celles du phénobarbital, entre 65 et 170 µmol/L.
- Évaluer les résultats de la numération globulaire tous les 6 mois pendant toute la durée du traitement. La primidone peut provoquer une leucopénie et une thrombopénie.

TOXICITÉ ET SURDOSAGE: Les signes d'une intoxication par la primidone incluent l'ataxie, la léthargie, les modifications de la vision, la confusion et la dyspnée.

DIAGNOSTICS INFIRMIERS POSSIBLES

- Risque d'accident (Réactions indésirables).
- Connaissances insuffisantes sur le traitement médicamenteux (Enseignement au patient et à ses proches).

INTERVENTIONS INFIRMIÈRES

- Lors de la substitution par la primidone d'un autre anticonvulsivant ou de l'ajout de la primidone au traitement médicamenteux, il faut augmenter graduellement la dose de primidone et diminuer la dose de l'autre anticonvulsivant ou continuer à l'administrer à la même dose afin d'assurer la maîtrise des crises épileptiques. Le passage du traitement antérieur à une monothérapie par la primidone devrait prendre au moins 2 semaines. On adapte habituellement les doses au coucher.
- La primidone peut être administrée avec des aliments afin de réduire l'irritation gastrique. Dans le cas des patients éprouvant des difficultés de déglutition, on peut écraser les comprimés et les mélanger avec des aliments ou des liquides.

P

ENSEIGNEMENT AU PATIENT ET À SES PROCHES

- Conseiller au patient de prendre le médicament chaque jour en respectant rigoureusement la posologie recommandée. S'il n'a pu prendre le médicament au moment habituel, il doit le prendre dès que possible à moins qu'il ne reste que 1 heure avant l'heure prévue pour la dose suivante. Le sevrage brusque peut déclencher l'état de mal épileptique.
- Prévenir le patient que la primidone peut provoquer la somnolence ou des étourdissements. Lui conseiller de ne pas conduire et d'éviter les activités qui exigent sa vigilance jusqu'à ce qu'on ait la certitude que le médicament n'entraîne pas ces effets chez lui. Ces symptômes diminuent habituellement en fréquence et en intensité lorsque le traitement est poursuivi sans interruption. Expliquer au patient qu'il ne doit reprendre la conduite automobile que si le médecin l'autorise à le faire après s'être assuré que le trouble convulsif a été maîtrisé.
- Recommander au patient d'éviter de boire de l'alcool ou de prendre d'autres dépresseurs du SNC en concomitance.
- Recommander au patient de changer lentement de position pour réduire le risque d'hypotension orthostatique.
- Recommander au patient qui doit suivre un autre traitement ou subir une intervention chirurgicale de prévenir le professionnel de la santé qu'il suit un traitement par ce médicament.
- Conseiller au patient de porter sur lui en tout temps une pièce d'identité où est inscrit son traitement médicamenteux.
- Inciter le patient à prévenir un professionnel de la santé si les symptômes suivants surviennent: rash, démarche chancelante, douleurs articulaires, fièvre, modifications dc la vision, dyspnée ou excitation paradoxale (particulièrement chez les enfants et les personnes âgées).
- Recommander à la patiente d'informer un professionnel de la santé si elle pense être enceinte.
- Insister sur l'importance des examens médicaux réguliers permettant d'évaluer l'efficacité du traitement.

VÉRIFICATION DE L'EFFICACITÉ THÉRAPEUTIQUE

L'efficacité du traitement peut être démontrée par: la diminution ou l'arrêt des crises sans sédation excessive. La réponse thérapeutique peut ne se manifester qu'après 1 semaine ou plus. ✳

PROBÉNÉCIDE

Benuryl

CLASSIFICATION:

Traitement de la goutte (uricosurique)

Grossesse – catégorie C

INDICATIONS

Traitement de l'hyperuricémie associée à la goutte. **Usages non approuvés:** Élévation et prolongation des concentrations sériques de pénicilline et d'antibiotiques apparentés ■ Prévention de la néphrotoxicité associée au cidofovir.

MÉCANISME D'ACTION

Inhibition de la réabsorption de l'acide urique par les tubules rénaux favorisant ainsi son excrétion par les reins. ***Effets thérapeutiques:*** Diminution des concentrations sériques d'acide urique.

PHARMACOCINÉTIQUE

Absorption: Bonne (PO).

Distribution: Le médicament traverse la barrière placentaire.

Liaison aux protéines: De 75 à 95 %.

Métabolisme et excrétion: Métabolisme majoritairement hépatique; 10 % excrété à l'état inchangé dans l'urine.

Demi-vie: De 4 à 17 heures.

Profil temps-action
(effets sur les concentrations sériques d'acide urique)

	Début d'action	Pic	Durée
PO	30 min	2 – 4 h	8 h

CONTRE-INDICATIONS, PRÉCAUTIONS ET MISES EN GARDE

Contre-indications: Hypersensibilité ■ Antécédents de lithiase rénale urique ■ Patients sous aspirine à fortes doses (> 325 mg/jour) ■ Enfants de < 2 ans ■ Patients sous traitement antinéoplasiques (ces médicaments augmentent les concentrations d'urate sérique et le probénécide augmente le risque de précipitation d'acide urique et de formation de calculs rénaux) ■ Insuffisance rénale (Cl_{Cr} < 50 mL/min).

Précautions et mises en garde: Le probénécide augmente la concentration urinaire d'acide urique et peut favoriser la formation de calculs rénaux, en particulier au début du traitement ■ Ulcère gastroduodénal ■ **Obst.,**

P

ALLAITEMENT: Précédents d'usage sans danger pendant la grossesse; l'innocuité du médicament durant l'allaitement n'a pas été établie.

RÉACTIONS INDÉSIRABLES ET EFFETS SECONDAIRES

SNC: céphalées, étourdissements.
GI: nausées, vomissements, douleurs abdominales, diarrhée, hépatite médicamenteuse, douleurs gingivales.
GU: calculs d'acide urique, mictions fréquentes.
Tég.: bouffées vasomotrices, rash.
Hémat.: ANÉMIE APLASIQUE, anémie.

INTERACTIONS

Médicament-médicament: Le probénécide entraîne l'élévation des concentrations sanguines d'**acétaminophène**, d'**acyclovir**, d'**allopurinol**, de **barbituriques**, de **benzodiazépines**, de **céphalosporines**, de **clofibrate**, de **dapsone**, de **fexofénadine**, de **furosémide**, d'**IECA**, de **mésalamine**, de **méthotrexate**, de **morphine**, d'**AINS**, d'**olanzapine**, d'**oseltamivir**, d'**acide pantothénique**, de **pénicillamine**, de **pénicillines**, de **pramipexole**, de **quinolones**, de **rifampine**, de **sulfamides**, d'**hypoglycémiants oraux (sulfonylurées)**, de **valacyclovir** et de **zidovudine** ■ Les doses importantes de **salicylates** peuvent réduire l'activité uricosurique ■ Le probénécide potentialise l'effet anticoagulant de l'**héparine** ■ Le **pyrazinamide** inhibe l'excrétion rénale de l'acide urique et réduit également le métabolisme du probénécide. Le probénécide, quant à lui, retarde l'élimination du pyrazinamide (ce qui entraîne la diminution de l'effet uricosurique du probénécide).

P

VOIES D'ADMINISTRATION ET POSOLOGIE

- **PO (adultes et adolescents)**: *Hyperuricémie et goutte* – 250 mg, 2 fois par jour pendant 1 semaine. On peut ensuite majorer la dose, en la faisant passer à 500 mg, 2 fois par jour, puis, si nécessaire, l'augmenter encore par paliers de 500 mg/jour, toutes les 4 semaines (ne pas dépasser 3 g/jour).

PRÉSENTATION

Comprimés: 500 mg^Pr^.

SOINS INFIRMIERS

ÉVALUATION DE LA SITUATION

Goutte:
- Examiner, pendant toute la durée du traitement, les articulations affectées pour évaluer leur mobilité et pour déceler les douleurs et l'œdème.
- Effectuer le bilan quotidien des ingesta et des excreta. Inciter le patient à boire beaucoup de liquides pour prévenir la formation de calculs d'acide urique (de 2000 à 3000 mL par jour). Pour contrer cet effet, on peut recommander l'alcalinisation de l'urine avec du bicarbonate de sodium, du citrate de potassium ou de l'acétazolamide.

Tests de laboratoire:
- IL FAUT ÉVALUER À INTERVALLES RÉGULIERS PENDANT TOUTE LA DURÉE D'UN TRAITEMENT DE LONGUE DURÉE LA NUMÉRATION GLOBULAIRE, LES CONCENTRATIONS SÉRIQUES D'ACIDE URIQUE ET LA FONCTION RÉNALE.
- Lorsque le probénécide est administré pour traiter l'hyperuricémie, il peut être utile de noter à intervalles réguliers les dosages sériques et urinaires d'acide urique.

DIAGNOSTICS INFIRMIERS POSSIBLES

- Douleur aiguë (Indications).
- Mobilité physique réduite (Indications).
- Connaissances insuffisantes sur le traitement médicamenteux (Enseignement au patient et à ses proches).

INTERVENTIONS INFIRMIÈRES

- Le probénécide n'est pas destiné au traitement de l'arthrite goutteuse, mais plutôt à sa prévention. Si des crises aiguës se produisent durant le traitement, on poursuit habituellement l'administration du probénécide à pleine dose et on administre en même temps de la colchicine ou des AINS.
- Administrer le probénécide avec des aliments ou des antiacides afin de réduire l'irritation gastrique.
- Si les concentrations d'acide urique demeurent stables après 6 mois de traitement, il faut tenter de réduire graduellement la dose.

ENSEIGNEMENT AU PATIENT ET À SES PROCHES

- Conseiller au patient de respecter rigoureusement la posologie recommandée et de ne pas arrêter le traitement sans consulter un professionnel de la santé au préalable. Le prévenir que s'il ne prend pas le médicament régulièrement, il y a risque d'élévation des concentrations d'acide urique et de crises de goutte.
- Expliquer au patient le but du traitement par le probénécide lorsque cet agent est administré en association avec la pénicilline.
- Inciter le patient à suivre les recommandations d'un professionnel de la santé concernant la perte de poids, le régime alimentaire et la consommation d'alcool.
- Recommander au patient de ne pas prendre en même temps de l'aspirine ou d'autres salicylates, car ces agents diminuent les effets du probénécide.

- Conseiller au patient de signaler immédiatement à un professionnel de la santé les nausées, les vomissements, la perte d'appétit, les douleurs abdominales, les saignements ou les ecchymoses inhabituels, les maux de gorge, la fatigue, les malaises ou le jaunissement de la peau ou des yeux.

VÉRIFICATION DE L'EFFICACITÉ THÉRAPEUTIQUE

L'efficacité du traitement peut être démontrée par: l'atténuation de la douleur et de l'enflure des articulations touchées et la diminution de la fréquence des crises de goutte (les pleins effets du médicament peuvent ne pas se manifester avant plusieurs mois de traitement continu) ■ la diminution des concentrations sériques d'acide urique ■ la présence prolongée de concentrations sériques thérapeutiques de pénicillines et d'autres antibiotiques apparentés. ✳

PROCAÏNAMIDE

Apo-Procaïnamide, Procaïnamide, Procan-SR

CLASSIFICATION:

Antiarythmique (classe IA)

Grossesse – catégorie C

INDICATIONS

Traitement d'une vaste gamme d'arythmies ventriculaires et auriculaires dont: la tachycardie ventriculaire ■ la fibrillation auriculaire ■ la tachycardie auriculaire paroxystique.

MÉCANISME D'ACTION

Diminution de l'excitabilité du myocarde ■ Ralentissement de la vitesse de conduction ■ Diminution possible de la contractilité du myocarde. ***Effets thérapeutiques:*** Suppression des arythmies.

PHARMACOCINÉTIQUE

Absorption: De 75 à 90 % (PO, IM). La préparation à libération prolongée destinée à la voie orale est absorbée plus lentement.

Distribution: Répartition rapide dans tout l'organisme.

Métabolisme et excrétion: Le procaïnamide est transformé par le foie en N-acétylprocaïnamide (NAPA), un composé antiarythmique actif. Excrétion rénale (de 40 à 70 % sous forme inchangée).

Demi-vie: De 2,5 à 4,7 heures (NAPA – 7 heures); prolongée en cas d'insuffisance rénale.

Profil temps-action (effets antiarythmiques)

	DÉBUT D'ACTION	PIC	DURÉE
PO	30 min	60 - 90 min	3 - 4 h
PO-LP†	inconnu	inconnu	6 - 12 h
IV	immédiat	25 - 60 min	3 - 4 h
IM	10 - 30 min	15 - 60 min	3 - 4 h

† LP = libération prolongée.

CONTRE-INDICATIONS, PRÉCAUTIONS ET MISES EN GARDE

Contre-indications: Hypersensibilité au médicament et risque de sensibilité croisée avec la procaïne et les substances apparentées ■ Bloc AV complet; bloc AV du 2e et du 3e degré (sauf en présence d'un stimulateur cardiaque) ■ Myasthénie grave ■ Lupus érythémateux aigu disséminé ■ Torsades de pointe.

Précautions et mises en garde: Dyscrasie sanguine ■ Infarctus du myocarde ou toxicité digitalique ■ Insuffisance cardiaque, rénale et hépatique ou personnes âgées (une surveillance des concentrations plasmatiques de procaïnamide et de NAPA et une réduction de la dose ou l'allongement des intervalles posologiques peuvent s'avérer nécessaires) ■ **OBST., ALLAITEMENT, PÉD.**: L'innocuité du médicament n'a pas été établie.

RÉACTIONS INDÉSIRABLES ET EFFETS SECONDAIRES

SNC: CONVULSIONS, confusion, étourdissements.

CV: ASYSTOLES, BLOC CARDIAQUE, ARYTHMIES VENTRICULAIRES, hypotension.

GI: diarrhée, anorexie, goût amer, nausées, vomissements.

Tég.: rash.

Hémat.: AGRANULOCYTOSE, éosinophilie, leucopénie, thrombopénie.

Divers: frissons, syndrome lupique d'origine médicamenteuse, fièvre.

INTERACTIONS

Médicament-médicament: Risque d'effets additifs ou antagonistes lors de l'administration concomitante d'autres **antiarythmiques** ■ Toxicité neurologique additive (confusion, convulsions) lors de l'administration concomitante de **lidocaïne** ■ Les **antihypertenseurs** et les **dérivés nitrés**, administrés simultanément, peuvent potentialiser l'effet hypotenseur du procaïnamide ■ Le procaïnamide potentialise les effets des **bloqueurs neuromusculaires** ■ Le médicament peut contrecarrer partiellement les effets thérapeutiques des **anticholinestérasiques** administrés pour traiter la myasthénie grave ■ Risque accru d'arythmies lors de l'administration concomitante de **pimozide** ■ Effets anticholinergiques additifs lors de l'administration concomitante d'autres **médicaments dotés de propriétés anticholinergiques**, incluant les **antihistaminiques**, les **antidépresseurs**, l'**atropine**, l'**halopéridol** et les **phénothiazines** ■ Risque d'intensification des effets du procaïnamide lors de l'administration concomitante de **cimétidine**, de **quinidine** ou de **triméthoprime**.

VOIES D'ADMINISTRATION ET POSOLOGIE

- **PO (adultes)**: Pour un traitement initial par voie orale, on conseille les préparations ordinaires de procaïnamide. Lorsque l'état du patient est stabilisé, il peut recevoir une préparation à libération prolongée à une posologie quotidienne équivalente. *Fibrillation auriculaire et tachycardie auriculaire paroxystique* – initialement 1,25 g, puis 750 mg, 1 heure plus tard et, ensuite, de 0,5 à 1 g, toutes les 2 heures; traitement d'entretien: de 0,5 à 1 g, toutes les 6 heures, sous forme de comprimés à libération prolongée. *Tachycardie ventriculaire* – dose d'attaque de 1 g, suivie par une dose d'entretien de 50 mg/kg/jour, en prises fractionnées, toutes les 3 heures; traitement d'entretien: de 0,5 à 1 g, toutes les 6 heures, sous forme de comprimés à libération prolongée. Il est recommandé d'administrer de plus faibles doses ou de prolonger l'intervalle posologique chez les personnes âgées ou chez les patients souffrant d'insuffisance rénale, hépatique ou cardiaque.
- **IM (adultes)**: 50 mg/kg/jour en doses fractionnées, toutes les 3 à 6 heures, jusqu'au moment où on peut commencer le traitement par voie orale.
- **IV (adultes)**: 100 mg, toutes les 5 minutes, jusqu'à la suppression des arythmies ou jusqu'à l'administration de 1 000 mg; pour maintenir les concentrations plasmatiques thérapeutiques, on peut administrer une perfusion d'entretien de 2 à 6 mg/min; *autre méthode* – perfusion d'une dose d'attaque de 500 à 600 mg, pendant 25 à 30 minutes, suivie d'une perfusion d'entretien de 2 à 6 mg/min. Voir le tableau des vitesses de perfusion à l'annexe C.

P

PRÉSENTATION

Comprimés à libération prolongée: 250 mg^{Pr}, 500 mg^{Pr}, 750 mg^{Pr} ■ **Capsules**: 250 mg^{Pr}, 375 mg^{Pr}, 500 mg^{Pr} ■ **Solution pour injection**: 100 mg/mL, en fioles de 10 mL^{Pr}.

SOINS INFIRMIERS

ÉVALUATION DE LA SITUATION

- MESURER LA PRESSION ARTÉRIELLE ET LE POULS ET EXAMINER L'ÉCG PENDANT TOUTE LA DURÉE DE L'ADMINISTRATION PAR VOIE INTRAVEINEUSE. IL FAUT SUIVRE DE PRÈS CES PARAMÈTRES À INTERVALLES RÉGULIERS PENDANT L'ADMINISTRATION DE LA PRÉPARATION PAR VOIE ORALE. IL FAUT HABITUELLEMENT CESSER L'ADMINISTRATION IV DANS LES CAS SUIVANTS: SUPPRESSION DES ARYTHMIES, ÉLARGISSEMENT DE 50 % DES COMPLEXES QRS, ALLONGEMENT DES INTERVALLES PR, CHUTE RAPIDE DE LA PRESSION ARTÉRIELLE OU APPARITION D'EFFETS TOXIQUES. AFIN DE RÉDUIRE LES RISQUES D'HYPOTENSION, LES PATIENTS DOIVENT DEMEURER EN POSITION COUCHÉE TOUT AU LONG DE L'ADMINISTRATION PAR VOIE IV.

Tests de laboratoire:

- EXAMINER LA NUMÉRATION GLOBULAIRE TOUTES LES 2 SEMAINES PENDANT LES 3 PREMIERS MOIS DU TRAITEMENT. LE PROCAÏNAMIDE PEUT DIMINUER LE NOMBRE DE LEUCOCYTES, DE PLAQUETTES ET DE POLYNUCLÉAIRES NEUTROPHILES. ON PEUT CESSER LE TRAITEMENT EN CAS DE LEUCOPÉNIE. LA NUMÉRATION GLOBULAIRE REVIENT HABITUELLEMENT AUX VALEURS NORMALES DANS LE MOIS SUIVANT L'ARRÊT DU TRAITEMENT.
- Examiner les titres d'anticorps antinucléaires à intervalles réguliers durant un traitement prolongé ou en présence de symptômes lupiques. Arrêter le traitement en présence d'une élévation constante des titres d'anticorps antinucléaires.
- Le procaïnamide peut entraîner l'élévation des concentrations d'AST, d'ALT, de phosphatase alcaline, de LDH et de bilirubine, et positiver le test de Coombs.

TOXICITÉ ET SURDOSAGE:

- Examiner les concentrations sériques de procaïnamide et de NAPA à intervalles réguliers durant la période d'adaptation de la posologie. Les concentrations sanguines thérapeutiques de procaïnamide sont de 17 à 42 µmol/L.
- Il y a risque de toxicité lorsque les concentrations sanguines de procaïnamide sont ≥ 42 à 54 µmol/L.
- Les signes de toxicité incluent la confusion, les étourdissements, la somnolence, la diminution des mictions, les nausées, les vomissements et les tachyarythmies.

DIAGNOSTICS INFIRMIERS POSSIBLES

- Débit cardiaque diminué (Indications).
- Connaissances insuffisantes sur le traitement médicamenteux (Enseignement au patient et à ses proches).

INTERVENTIONS INFIRMIÈRES

- Lorsqu'on substitue la voie orale à la voie IV, administrer la première dose par voie orale de 3 à 4 heures après la dernière dose par voie IV.

PO: Pour accélérer l'absorption du procaïnamide, l'administrer à jeun, 1 heure avant les repas ou 2 heures après, avec un grand verre d'eau. On peut administrer le procaïnamide avec des aliments ou immédiatement après les repas si l'irritation gastrique devient gênante. Dans le cas des patients qui éprouvent des difficultés de déglutition, on peut ouvrir les capsules ordinaires et en mélanger le contenu à des aliments ou à des liquides. IL NE FAUT PAS BRISER, ÉCRASER NI MÂCHER LES COMPRIMÉS À LIBÉRATION PROLONGÉE (PROCAN-SR). La matrice cireuse des comprimés à libération prolongée peut être éliminée dans les selles, mais ce fait n'a aucune conséquence clinique.

IM: Administrer le procaïnamide par voie IM seulement si l'administration par voie orale est impossible.

IV: N'utiliser qu'en cas d'urgence, sous surveillance électrocardiographique continue.

IV directe: Diluer 100 mg dans 10 à 20 mL de solution de D5%E.

Vitesse d'administration: Administrer la préparation à un débit ne dépassant pas 25 à 50 mg/min. L'administration rapide peut provoquer la fibrillation ventriculaire ou des asystoles.

Perfusion intermittente: Préparer la solution destinée à la perfusion IV en ajoutant de 200 mg à 1 g de procaïnamide à 50 à 500 mL de solution de D5%E pour obtenir une concentration de 2 à 4 mg/mL. Même si la solution prend une couleur jaune pâle, sa puissance n'est en rien altérée. Ne pas administrer une solution dont la couleur est plus foncée que l'ambre clair ou qui contient un précipité.

Vitesse d'administration: Administrer la perfusion initiale en 30 minutes. Pour maintenir l'effet antiarythmique du médicament, le débit de perfusion lors du traitement d'entretien doit être de 2 à 6 mg/min. Recourir à une pompe à perfusion afin d'assurer l'administration de la dose exacte (voir le tableau des vitesses de perfusion à l'annexe C).

Compatibilité (tubulure en Y): amiodarone ▪ famotidine ▪ héparine ▪ hydrocortisone sodique, succinate d' ▪ potassium, chlorure de ▪ ranitidine ▪ vitamines du complexe B avec C.

Incompatibilité (tubulure en Y): milrinone.

ENSEIGNEMENT AU PATIENT ET À SES PROCHES

- Expliquer au patient qu'il doit prendre le médicament, 24 heures sur 24, en respectant rigoureusement la posologie recommandée, même s'il se sent bien. Lui expliquer que s'il n'a pu prendre le médicament au moment habituel, il doit le prendre dès que possible dans les 2 heures qui suivent (4 heures pour les comprimés à libération prolongée), sinon il doit sauter cette dose. Le prévenir aussi qu'il ne doit jamais remplacer une dose manquée par une double dose. Recommander au patient de ne pas arrêter de prendre le médicament sans consulter au préalable un professionnel de la santé, car il peut s'avérer nécessaire de réduire graduellement la dose pour prévenir l'aggravation des arythmies.
- Montrer au patient ou à ses proches comment prendre le pouls. Conseiller au patient de signaler à un professionnel de la santé toute modification du rythme ou de la fréquence du pouls.
- Prévenir le patient que le procaïnamide peut provoquer des étourdissements. Lui conseiller de ne pas conduire et d'éviter les activités qui exigent sa vigilance jusqu'à ce qu'on ait la certitude que le médicament n'entraîne pas cet effet chez lui.
- Recommander au patient de communiquer immédiatement à un professionnel de la santé toute manifestation du syndrome lupique d'origine médicamenteuse (fièvre, frissons, douleurs ou enflure articulaires, respiration douloureuse, rash), de leucopénie (maux de gorge, de bouche ou des gencives) ou de thrombopénie (hémorragie ou ecchymoses inhabituelles). Parfois, il faut arrêter le traitement dans un tel cas.
- Recommander au patient de consulter un professionnel de la santé avant de prendre des médicaments en vente libre.
- Recommander au patient qui doit suivre un traitement ou subir une intervention chirurgicale d'avertir le professionnel de la santé qu'il suit un traitement par ce médicament.
- Recommander au patient de porter sur lui en tout temps une pièce d'identité où sont inscrits ses problèmes de santé et son traitement médicamenteux.
- Insister sur l'importance des examens de suivi permettant d'évaluer les bienfaits du médicament.

VÉRIFICATION DE L'EFFICACITÉ THÉRAPEUTIQUE

L'efficacité du traitement peut être démontrée par: la suppression des arythmies cardiaques sans effets secondaires nocifs. ✳

PROCARBAZINE

Matulane

CLASSIFICATION:

Antinéoplasique (alkylant)

Grossesse – catégorie D

P

INDICATIONS

Traitement de la maladie de Hodgkin de stade 3 ou 4 en association avec d'autres antinéoplasiques et d'autres interventions. **Usages non approuvés**: Traitement d'une variété de lymphomes et de gliomes malins réfractaires.

MÉCANISME D'ACTION

Inhibition de la synthèse de l'ADN, de l'ARN et des protéines (phase S du cycle cellulaire). ***Effets thérapeutiques:*** Destruction des cellules à croissance rapide, particulièrement des cellules malignes.

PHARMACOCINÉTIQUE

Absorption: Bonne (PO).

Distribution: Tout l'organisme. La procarbazine traverse la barrière hématoencéphalique.

Métabolisme et excrétion: Métabolisme hépatique. Excrétion rénale faible (< 5 % sous forme inchangée); excrétion possible par les voies respiratoires sous forme de méthane et de dioxyde de carbone.

Demi-vie: 1 heure.

Profil temps-action (effets sur la numération globulaire)

	DÉBUT D'ACTION	PIC	DURÉE
PO	14 jours	2 – 3 semaines (jusqu'à 8 semaines)	au moins 28 jours (jusqu'à 6 semaines)

P

CONTRE-INDICATIONS, PRÉCAUTIONS ET MISES EN GARDE

Contre-indications: Hypersensibilité ■ Réserve médullaire insuffisante révélée par aspiration de moelle osseuse (en tenir compte dans les cas de leucopénie, de thrombopénie ou d'anémie préexistantes).

Précautions et mises en garde: Grossesse ou allaitement ■ Alcoolisme ■ Insuffisance rénale ou hépatique ■ Phéochromocytome ■ Patientes en âge de procréer ■ Infections ■ Aplasie médullaire ■ Autres maladies chroniques débilitantes ■ Céphalées ■ Maladies psychiatriques ■ Insuffisance cardiaque ■ Maladie cardiovasculaire.

RÉACTIONS INDÉSIRABLES ET EFFETS SECONDAIRES

SNC: CONVULSIONS, confusion, étourdissements, somnolence, hallucinations, céphalées, manie, dépression, cauchemars, psychose, syncope, tremblements.

ORLO: nystagmus, photophobie, hémorragie rétinienne.

Resp.: toux, épanchements pleuraux, pneumonite.

CV: œdème, hypotension, tachycardie.

GI: nausées, vomissements, anorexie, diarrhée, sécheresse de la bouche (xérostomie), dysphagie, dysfonctionnement hépatique, stomatite.

GU: suppression de la fonction des gonades.

Tég.: alopécie, photosensibilité, prurit, rash.

End.: gynécomastie.

Hémat.: anémie, leucopénie, thrombopénie.

SN: neuropathie, paresthésie.

Divers: ascite, réactions d'hypersensibilité, néoplasies secondaires, saignements.

INTERACTIONS

Médicament-médicament: L'ADMINISTRATION CONCOMITANTE D'**AGENTS SYMPATHOMIMÉTIQUES**, INCLUANT LE **MÉTHYLPHÉNIDATE**, PEUT ENTRAÎNER UNE HYPERTENSION METTANT LA VIE DU PATIENT EN DANGER (NE PAS ADMINISTRER CES PRÉPARATIONS EN MÊME TEMPS QUE LA PROCARBAZINE NI DANS LES 14 JOURS SUIVANT L'ARRÊT DU TRAITEMENT PAR CET AGENT) ■ RISQUE DE COMA PROFOND ET DE DÉCÈS LORS DE L'ADMINISTRATION SIMULTANÉE D'**OPIOÏDES**; NE PAS ADMINISTRER LA PROCARBAZINE EN MÊME TEMPS QUE LA **MÉPÉRIDINE**; ADMINISTRER LES AUTRES AGENTS À UNE FAIBLE DOSE QU'ON MAJORERA GRADUELLEMENT JUSQU'À CE QUE L'ON OBTIENNE UN EFFET ■ APLASIE MÉDULLAIRE ADDITIVE LORS DE L'ADMINISTRATION CONCOMITANTE D'AUTRES **AGENTS ANTINÉOPLASIQUES** OU D'UNE **RADIOTHÉRAPIE** ■ RISQUE DE CONVULSIONS ET D'HYPERPYREXIE LORS DE L'USAGE CONCOMITANT D'**IMAO**, D'**ANTIDÉPRESSEURS TRICYCLIQUES**, D'**ISRS** (NE PAS ADMINISTRER LA PROCARBAZINE PENDANT LES 5 SEMAINES SUIVANT L'ARRÊT DE L'ADMINISTRATION DE **FLUOXÉTINE**) OU DE **CARBAMAZÉPINE** ■ La procarbazine peut réduire les concentrations sériques de **digoxine** ■ Risque de bouffées vasomotrices et d'hypertension lors de l'administration concomitante de **lévodopa** ■ Dépression additive du SNC lors de l'usage concomitant d'autres **dépresseurs du SNC**, incluant l'**alcool**, les **antidépresseurs**, les **antihistaminiques**, les **opioïdes**, les **phénothiazines** et les **hypnosédatifs** ■ La consommation simultanée d'**alcool** peut entraîner une réaction semblable à celle associée au disulfirame ■ Le **tabac** (**nicotine**) peut augmenter le risque de néoplasies pulmonaires secondaires.

Médicament-aliments: La consommation d'aliments riches en **tyramine** (voir l'annexe K) peut provoquer l'hypertension ■ L'ingestion d'aliments à haute teneur en **caféine** peut entraîner des arythmies.

VOIES D'ADMINISTRATION ET POSOLOGIE

Plusieurs schémas posologiques ont été utilisés.

- **PO (adultes)**: 100 mg/m^2 par jour, pendant 14 jours consécutifs, toutes les 4 semaines (dans le cadre d'un régime MOPP ou c-MOPP).

- **PO (enfants):** 100 mg/m², pendant 7 à 14 jours, toutes les 4 semaines, en association avec d'autres antinéoplasiques *(usage non approuvé)*.

PRÉSENTATION

Capsules: 50 mg[Pr].

SOINS INFIRMIERS

ÉVALUATION DE LA SITUATION

- Mesurer la pression artérielle, le pouls et la fréquence respiratoire à intervalles fréquents, pendant toute la durée du traitement. Signaler tout changement marqué à un professionnel de la santé.
- Évaluer l'état nutritionnel du patient (appétit, bilan des ingesta et des excreta, poids, fréquence et quantité des vomissements). On peut soulager l'anorexie et diminuer la perte de poids en servant au patient des repas légers mais fréquents. On peut réduire les nausées et les vomissements en administrant un antiémétique au moins 1 heure avant la dose de procarbazine. L'administration de phénothiazines à titre d'antiémétiques est à éviter.
- Noter l'apparition d'une aplasie médullaire. Suivre de près les saignements: saignement des gencives, ecchymoses, pétéchies, présence de sang dans les selles, l'urine et les vomissements. Éviter les injections IM et la prise de la température rectale si la numération plaquettaire est basse. Appliquer une pression sur les points de ponction veineuse pendant 10 minutes. Surveiller les signes d'infection en cas de neutropénie. Une anémie peut survenir. Suivre de près la fatigue accrue, la dyspnée et l'hypotension orthostatique.
- L'INGESTION CONCOMITANTE D'ALIMENTS RICHES EN TYRAMINE OU DE NOMBREUX MÉDICAMENTS PEUT ENTRAÎNER UNE CRISE HYPERTENSIVE METTANT LA VIE DU PATIENT EN DANGER. LES SIGNES ET LES SYMPTÔMES DE CRISE HYPERTENSIVE SONT LES DOULEURS THORACIQUES, LES CÉPHALÉES GRAVES, LES NAUSÉES ET LES VOMISSEMENTS, LA PHOTOPHOBIE ET LA DILATATION DES PUPILLES. LE TRAITEMENT COMPREND L'ADMINISTRATION DE PHENTOLAMINE IV.
- Il faut arrêter l'administration de la procarbazine jusqu'à la disparition des effets secondaires. On peut ensuite administrer une plus faible dose en cas de leucopénie, de thrombopénie, de stomatite (d'abord, une légère ulcération ou des douleurs persistantes), de diarrhée, d'hémorragie ou de prédisposition aux saignements.

Tests de laboratoire:

- Noter la concentration d'hémoglobine, l'hématocrite, le nombre de globules blancs, la formule leucocytaire, ainsi que le nombre de réticulocytes et de plaquettes, avant le traitement et tous les 3 ou 4 jours pendant toute sa durée. Informer le médecin si le nombre de globules blancs est $< 4 \times 10^9$/L ou si le nombre de plaquettes est $< 100 \times 10^9$/L. Il faut interrompre le traitement et le reprendre à une plus faible dose lorsque ces valeurs s'améliorent. Le nadir de la leucopénie et de la thrombopénie survient en l'espace d'environ 2 à 8 semaines et les valeurs se rétablissent habituellement en 4 à 6 semaines environ. L'anémie peut également survenir.
- Évaluer les fonctions rénale et hépatique avant le traitement. Noter le résultat de l'analyse des urines, ainsi que les concentrations d'AST, d'ALT, de phosphatase alcaline et d'urée au moins 1 fois par semaine pendant toute la durée du traitement.
- Suivre de près les concentrations de glucose sérique chez les patients diabétiques. Il peut s'avérer nécessaire de réduire les doses d'hypoglycémiants oraux ou d'insuline, car les effets hypoglycémiants sont accrus.
- Il est recommandé d'effectuer une ponction médullaire avant le traitement et au moment où la réponse hématologique est maximale pour s'assurer que la réserve médullaire est adéquate.

DIAGNOSTICS INFIRMIERS POSSIBLES

- Risque d'infection (Réactions indésirables).
- Alimentation déficiente (Réactions indésirables).
- Connaissances insuffisantes sur le traitement médicamenteux (Enseignement au patient et à ses proches).

INTERVENTIONS INFIRMIÈRES

- Administrer la procarbazine avec des aliments ou des liquides en cas d'irritation gastrique. Si le patient éprouve des difficultés de déglutition, demander au pharmacien si on peut ouvrir les capsules.

ENSEIGNEMENT AU PATIENT ET À SES PROCHES

- Insister sur la nécessité de prendre la procarbazine en respectant rigoureusement la posologie recommandée. Si le patient n'a pu prendre le médicament au moment habituel, il devrait le prendre dans les quelques heures qui suivent, mais non si plusieurs heures se sont écoulées ou s'il est presque l'heure prévue pour la dose suivante. Lui conseiller de consulter un professionnel de la santé si les vomissements se produisent peu après la prise du médicament.

- Recommander au patient de signaler immédiatement à un professionnel de la santé les signes d'infection suivants: fièvre, maux de gorge, frissons, toux, épaississement des sécrétions bronchiques, enrouement, douleurs lombaires ou aux flancs, mictions douloureuses ou difficiles, saignement des gencives, formation d'ecchymoses, pétéchies, présence de sang dans l'urine, les selles ou les vomissements. Inciter le patient à éviter les foules et les personnes contagieuses. Lui conseiller d'utiliser une brosse à dents à poils doux et un rasoir électrique et de prendre garde aux chutes. Il faut éviter les injections IM et la prise de température par voie rectale. Le prévenir qu'il ne doit pas prendre de boissons alcoolisées ni de préparations contenant de l'aspirine ou des AINS, en raison des risques d'hémorragie digestive.
- Recommander au patient d'éviter de boire de l'alcool et des boissons contenant de la caféine, de prendre des dépresseurs du SNC et des médicaments en vente libre, et de consommer des aliments ou des boissons contenant de la tyramine (la liste de ces aliments se trouve à l'annexe J) durant le traitement et pendant au moins 2 semaines après l'avoir arrêté, en raison du risque de crise hypertensive.
- Expliquer au patient que l'interaction alcool-procarbazépine peut aussi entraîner une réaction semblable à celle du disulfirame dont les symptômes sont les bouffées vasomotrices, les nausées et les vomissements, les céphalées et les crampes abdominales.
- Recommander au patient d'examiner sa muqueuse buccale à la recherche d'érythème et d'aphtes. En présence d'aphtes, conseiller au patient d'en informer un professionnel de la santé et lui conseiller de remplacer la brosse à dents par une brosse-éponge et de se rincer la bouche avec de l'eau après avoir bu et mangé. On pourrait lui prescrire des agents topiques si la douleur l'empêche de s'alimenter. La douleur entraînée par la stomatite peut dicter la prise d'opioïdes.
- Prévenir le patient que la procarbazine peut provoquer de la somnolence ou des étourdissements. Lui conseiller de ne pas conduire et d'éviter les activités qui exigent sa vigilance jusqu'à ce qu'on ait la certitude que le médicament n'entraîne pas ces effets chez lui.
- Expliquer à la patiente que la procarbazépine peut avoir des effets tératogènes. Lui recommander d'utiliser une méthode de contraception efficace durant le traitement et pendant au moins 4 mois après l'avoir arrêté.
- Expliquer au patient qu'il risque de perdre ses cheveux. Explorer avec lui les stratégies lui permettant de s'adapter à ce changement.
- Recommander au patient d'utiliser un écran solaire et de porter des vêtements protecteurs pour prévenir les réactions de photosensibilité.
- Prévenir le patient qu'il ne doit pas se faire vacciner sans recommandation expresse d'un professionnel de la santé.
- Recommander au patient d'informer les professionnels de la santé qu'il prend de la procarbazépine s'il doit suivre un autre traitement ou subir une intervention chirurgicale. Le traitement par la procarbazépine devrait être arrêté au moins 2 semaines avant une chirurgie.
- Recommander au patient de communiquer avec un professionnel de la santé si les douleurs musculaires ou articulaires, les nausées, les vomissements, la transpiration, la fatigue, la faiblesse, la constipation, les céphalées, les difficultés de déglutition ou la perte d'appétit s'aggravent.
- Conseiller au patient de porter sur lui en tout temps une pièce d'identité où sont inscrits ses problèmes de santé et le traitement qu'il suit.
- Insister sur l'importance des tests de laboratoire à intervalles réguliers permettant de déceler les effets secondaires du médicament.

VÉRIFICATION DE L'EFFICACITÉ THÉRAPEUTIQUE

L'efficacité du traitement peut être démontrée par: la diminution de l'atteinte et de la propagation des cellules malignes en cas de maladie de Hodgkin. ✳

PROCHLORPÉRAZINE

Apo-Prochlorazine, Nu-prochlor, PMS-Prochlorpérazine, Prochlorperazine mesylate inj., Sandoz Prochlorperazine

CLASSIFICATION:

Antiémétique, antipsychotique (phénothiazine)

Grossesse – catégorie C

INDICATIONS

Soulagement des nausées et vomissements ■ Traitement des manifestations des troubles psychotiques comme l'agitation, la confusion, le délire, la tension et l'anxiété ■ Traitement de l'hyperanxiété accompagnée de symptômes prononcés de tension et d'agitation et associée à un état psychonévrotique ou somatique.

MÉCANISME D'ACTION

Modification des effets de la dopamine dans le SNC ■ Action anticholinergique et blocage des récepteurs alpha-adrénergiques ■ Dépression de la zone gâchette chémoréceptrice du SNC. ***Effets thérapeutiques:*** Soulagement des nausées et des vomissements ■ Diminution des signes et des symptômes de psychose ou d'anxiété.

PHARMACOCINÉTIQUE

Absorption: Bonne (IM); variable (PO).

Distribution: Tout l'organisme. On retrouve l'agent en fortes concentrations dans le SNC. Il traverse la barrière placentaire et passe probablement dans le lait maternel.

Liaison aux protéines: ≥ 90 %.

Métabolisme et excrétion: Métabolisme hépatique et intestinal important. Transformation en certains composés exerçant un effet antipsychotique.

Demi-vie: Inconnue.

Profil temps-action (effet antiémétique)

	DÉBUT D'ACTION	PIC	DURÉE
PO	30 - 40 min	inconnu	3 - 4 h
IR	60 min	inconnu	3 - 4 h
IM	10 - 20 min	10 - 30 min	3 - 4 h
IV	rapide (min)	10 - 30 min	3 - 4 h

CONTRE-INDICATIONS, PRÉCAUTIONS ET MISES EN GARDE

Contre-indications: Hypersensibilité ■ Risque de réactions de sensibilité croisée avec d'autres phénothiazines ■ Collapsus circulatoire ■ Troubles de la conscience ■ État comateux ■ Dépression ■ Insuffisance rénale ■ Phéochromocytome ■ Encéphalopathie sous-corticale ■ Aplasie médullaire ■ Maladies hépatique ou cardiovasculaire graves ■ **PÉD.:** Avant une intervention chirurgicale.

Précautions et mises en garde: Glaucome ■ **GÉR.:** Personnes âgées ou patients débilités (réduire la dose) ■ Diabète ■ Maladie respiratoire ■ Hyperplasie bénigne de la prostate ■ Tumeurs du SNC ■ Épilepsie ■ Occlusion intestinale ■ **OBST.:** Grossesse ou allaitement (l'innocuité du médicament n'a pas été établie) ■ **PÉD.:** L'innocuité de l'agent n'a pas été établie chez les enfants âgés < 2 ans ou pesant < 9 kg ■ Usage concomitant de dépresseurs du SNC ou d'anticholinergiques ■ Troubles cardiovasculaires ■ Risque d'allongement de l'intervalle QT.

RÉACTIONS INDÉSIRABLES ET EFFETS SECONDAIRES

SNC: SYNDROME MALIN DES NEUROLEPTIQUES, réactions extrapyramidales, sédation, dyskinésie tardive.
ORLO: vision trouble, xérophtalmie, opacité du cristallin, glaucome.
CV: modifications de l'ÉCG, hypotension, tachycardie.
GI: constipation, sécheresse de la bouche (xérostomie), anorexie, hépatite médicamenteuse, occlusion intestinale.
GU: urine de couleur rose à brun rougeâtre, rétention urinaire.
Tég.: photosensibilité, rash, modification de la pigmentation.
End.: galactorrhée.
Hémat.: AGRANULOCYTOSE, leucopénie.
Métab.: hyperthermie, hyperprolactinémie.
Divers: réactions allergiques.

INTERACTIONS

Médicament-médicament: Effets hypotenseurs additifs lors de l'administration concomitante d'**antihypertenseurs** ou de **dérivés nitrés** ou de l'ingestion de grandes quantités d'**alcool** ■ Effets additifs sur la dépression du SNC lors de l'usage concomitant d'autres **dépresseurs du SNC**, incluant l'**alcool**, les **antidépresseurs**, les **antihistaminiques**, les **opioïdes**, les **hypnosédatifs** ou les **anesthésiques généraux** ■ Effets anticholinergiques additifs lors de l'administration concomitante d'autres **médicaments dotés de propriétés anticholinergiques** dont les **antihistaminiques**, certains **antidépresseurs**, l'**atropine**, l'**halopéridol** et les autres **phénothiazines** ■ Le **lithium**, administré simultanément, augmente le risque de réactions extrapyramidales ■ La prochlorpérazine peut masquer les signes précoces de l'intoxication au **lithium** ■ Risque accru d'agranulocytose lors de l'administration concomitante d'**agents antithyroïdiens** ■ La prochlorpérazine diminue les effets bénéfiques de la **lévodopa** ■ Les **antiacides**, administrés simultanément, peuvent diminuer l'absorption de la prochlorpérazine.

Médicament-produits naturels: La consommation concomitante de **kava**, de **valériane**, de **scutellaire**, de **camomille** ou de **houblon** peut augmenter la dépression du SNC ■ La consommation concomitante de **trompette des anges**, de **datura** et de **scopolia** peut augmenter les effets anticholinergiques.

VOIES D'ADMINISTRATION ET POSOLOGIE

Antiémétique

- **PO, IR (adultes):** De 5 à 10 mg, 3 ou 4 fois par jour (dose maximale: 40 mg/jour).

- **IM (adultes)**: De 5 à 10 mg, 2 ou 3 fois par jour. *Nausées et vomissements associés à une intervention chirurgicale* – de 5 à 10 mg, de 1 à 2 heures avant l'anesthésie; on peut répéter l'administration de cette dose 1 fois de plus pendant l'opération. Ensuite, de 5 à 10 mg, toutes les 3 ou 4 heures, selon les besoins (dose maximale: 40 mg/jour).
- **IV (adultes)**: De 2,5 à 10 mg (ne pas dépasser 40 mg/jour). *Nausées et vomissements associés à une intervention chirurgicale* – de 5 à 10 mg; on peut répéter l'administration de cette dose 1 fois.

Antipsychotique

- **PO, IR (adultes)**: 10 mg, 3 ou 4 fois par jour; on peut majorer la dose de 5 à 10 mg tous les 2 ou 3 jours (jusqu'à 150 mg/jour dans les cas graves).
- **IM (adultes)**: De 10 à 20 mg, toutes les 2 à 4 heures, selon les besoins; on administre habituellement 3 ou 4 doses.
- **IV (adultes)**: De 2,5 à 10 mg (jusqu'à 40 mg/jour).

Anxiolytique

- **PO, IR (adultes)**: De 5 à 10 mg, 3 ou 4 fois par jour.
- **IM (adultes)**: De 5 à 10 mg, 2 ou 3 fois par jour (jusqu'à 40 mg/jour).
- **IV (adultes)**: De 2,5 à 10 mg (jusqu'à 40 mg/jour).

Pédiatrie

Ne pas administrer aux enfants âgée < 2 ans ou pesant < 9 kg. Les doses destinées à l'usage pédiatrique ne doivent pas dépasser 10 mg, le premier jour, puis 20 mg par jour, chez les enfants de 2 à 5 ans, ou 25 mg par jour, chez les enfants de 6 à 12 ans.

P

- **PO, IR (enfants de 18 à 39 kg)**: 2,5 mg, 3 fois par jour, ou 5 mg, 2 fois par jour (ne pas dépasser 15 mg/jour).
- **PO, IR (enfants de 14 à 18 kg)**: 2,5 mg, 2 ou 3 fois par jour (ne pas dépasser 10 mg/jour).
- **PO, IR (enfants de 9 à 14 kg)**: 2,5 mg, 1 ou 2 fois par jour (ne pas dépasser 7,5 mg/jour).
- **IM (enfants)**: 0,13 mg/kg.

PRÉSENTATION (version générique disponible)

Comprimés: 5 mg^{Pr}, 10 mg^{Pr} ■ **Solution pour injection**: 5 mg/mL (mésylate) en 2 mL^{Pr} ■ **Suppositoires**: 10 mg^{Pr}.

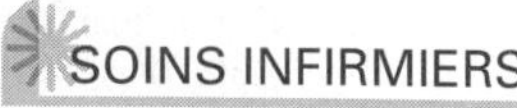

SOINS INFIRMIERS

ÉVALUATION DE LA SITUATION

- Mesurer la pression artérielle (en position assise, debout et couchée), le pouls et la fréquence respiratoire, surveiller l'ÉCG avant l'administration initiale et à intervalles fréquents pendant la période d'adaptation de la posologie. La prochlorpérazine peut entraîner des modifications des ondes Q et T sur l'ÉCG.
- Évaluer le degré de sédation après l'administration de ce médicament.
- Observer étroitement le patient pour déceler l'apparition d'une akathisie (agitation ou désir de bouger continuellement) et de symptômes extrapyramidaux (*symptômes parkinsoniens:* difficultés d'élocution ou de déglutition, perte d'équilibre, mouvements d'émiettement, faciès figé, démarche traînante, rigidité, tremblements; et *symptômes dystoniques:* spasmes musculaires, torsions, secousses musculaires, incapacité de bouger les yeux, faiblesse des bras ou des jambes), tous les 2 mois pendant toute la durée du traitement et de 8 à 12 semaines après l'avoir mené à terme. Signaler l'apparition de ces symptômes; il peut s'avérer nécessaire de réduire la dose ou de cesser le traitement. Il peut être utile d'administrer du trihexyphénidyle ou de la diphenhydramine pour maîtriser ces symptômes.
- Rester à l'affût des symptômes de dyskinésie tardive (mouvements rythmiques et incontrôlables de la bouche, du visage et des membres; émission de bruits secs avec les lèvres ou la langue; gonflement des joues; mouvements masticatoires incontrôlés; mouvements rapides de la langue). Signaler immédiatement ces symptômes, qui peuvent être irréversibles.
- SUIVRE DE PRÈS L'APPARITION DES SYMPTÔMES SUIVANTS DU SYNDROME MALIN DES NEUROLEPTIQUES: FIÈVRE, DÉTRESSE RESPIRATOIRE, TACHYCARDIE, CONVULSIONS, DIAPHORÈSE, HYPERTENSION OU HYPOTENSION, PÂLEUR, FATIGUE, RIGIDITÉ MUSCULAIRE MARQUÉE, PERTE DE CONTRÔLE DE LA VESSIE. INFORMER IMMÉDIATEMENT LE MÉDECIN OU UN AUTRE PROFESSIONNEL DE LA SANTÉ DE L'APPARITION DE CES SYMPTÔMES.
- Noter la consommation de liquides et l'élimination intestinale. Accroître l'apport en liquides et en aliments riches en fibres pour réduire la constipation.

Antiémétique: Suivre de près les nausées et les vomissements avant le traitement et de 30 à 60 minutes après l'administration du médicament.

Antipsychotique:

- Observer l'état mental du patient (orientation spatiotemporelle et comportement), avant le traitement et à intervalles réguliers pendant toute sa durée.
- Observer le patient de près lorsqu'on lui administre le médicament par voie orale pour s'assurer qu'il l'a bien avalé.

Anxiété: Évaluer le degré et les signes d'anxiété et l'état mental du patient avant le traitement et à intervalles réguliers pendant toute sa durée.

Tests de laboratoire:

- NOTER À INTERVALLES RÉGULIERS LA NUMÉRATION GLOBULAIRE ET LES RÉSULTATS DES TESTS DE LA FONCTION HÉPATIQUE. LE MÉDICAMENT PEUT ENTRAÎNER LA DYSCRASIE SANGUINE, PARTICULIÈREMENT ENTRE LA 4E ET LA 10E SEMAINE DE TRAITEMENT. L'HÉPATOTOXICITÉ RISQUE PLUS VRAISEMBLABLEMENT DE SE PRODUIRE ENTRE LA 2E ET LA 4E SEMAINE DE TRAITEMENT. ELLE PEUT RÉCIDIVER SI LE TRAITEMENT EST RECOMMENCÉ. LES ANOMALIES DES TESTS DE LA FONCTION HÉPATIQUE PEUVENT DICTER L'ARRÊT DU TRAITEMENT.
- La prochlorpérazine peut entraîner des résultats faussement positifs ou négatifs aux tests de grossesse et des résultats faussement positifs au dosage de la bilirubine urinaire.
- La prochlorpérazine peut entraîner l'élévation des concentrations sériques de prolactine et modifier les résultats des épreuves par la gonadolibérine.

DIAGNOSTICS INFIRMIERS POSSIBLES

- Déficit de volume liquidien (Indications).
- Opérations de la pensée perturbées (Indications).
- Connaissances insuffisantes sur le traitement médicamenteux (Enseignement au patient et à ses proches).

INTERVENTIONS INFIRMIÈRES

- NE PAS CONFONDRE LE PROCHLOPÉRAZINE AVEC LA CHLORPROMAZINE OU AVEC LE CHLORPROPAMIDE.
- Éviter les éclaboussures sur les mains, étant donné qu'il y a risque de dermatite de contact.
- Il faut interrompre le traitement aux phénothiazines 48 heures avant une myélographie et ne le reprendre que 24 heures plus tard, car ces médicaments abaissent le seuil de convulsion.

PO: Administrer le médicament avec des aliments, du lait ou un grand verre d'eau afin de diminuer l'irritation gastrique.

IM: Ne pas injecter par voie SC. Administrer lentement et en profondeur dans un muscle bien développé. Afin de réduire les effets hypotenseurs du médicament, demander au patient de rester en position couchée pendant au moins 30 minutes après l'injection. Même si la solution devient jaune pâle, sa puissance n'est en rien altérée. Ne pas administrer la solution si elle a fortement changé de couleur ou si elle renferme un précipité.

IV directe: Diluer jusqu'à l'obtention d'une concentration de 1 mg/mL.

Vitesse d'administration: Administrer à un débit de 1 mg/min; ne pas dépasser 5 mg/min.

Perfusion intermittente: Diluer 20 mg dans au maximum 1 L de dextrose, de soluté salin, de solution de Ringer ou de lactate de Ringer, de solution de dextrose/soluté salin, de dextrose/solution de Ringer ou de combinaisons de solutions de lactate de Ringer.

Incompatibilité dans la même seringue: Le fabricant ne recommande pas de mélanger la prochlorpérazine avec d'autres médicaments dans la même seringue.

Compatibilité (tubulure en Y): calcium, gluconate de ▪ cisatracurium ▪ cisplatine ▪ cyclophosphamide ▪ cytarabine ▪ doxorubicine ▪ doxorubicine liposomale ▪ fluconazole ▪ granisétron ▪ héparine ▪ hydrocortisone sodique, succinate d' ▪ melphalan ▪ méthotrexate ▪ ondansétron ▪ paclitaxel ▪ potassium, chlorure de ▪ propofol ▪ rémifentanil ▪ sargramostim ▪ sufentanil ▪ téniposide ▪ thiotépa ▪ vinorelbine ▪ vitamines du complexe B avec C.

Incompatibilité (tubulure en Y): aldesleukine ▪ allopurinol ▪ amifostine ▪ amphotéricine B, cholestéryle d' ▪ aztréonam ▪ céfépime ▪ filgrastim ▪ fludarabine ▪ foscarnet ▪ gallium, nitrate de ▪ pipéracilline/tazobactam.

ENSEIGNEMENT AU PATIENT ET À SES PROCHES

- Conseiller au patient de respecter rigoureusement la posologie recommandée. S'il n'a pu prendre le médicament au moment habituel, il doit le prendre aussitôt que possible, mais pas s'il est presque l'heure prévue pour la dose suivante. S'il doit prendre plus de 2 doses par jour, l'inciter à prendre la dose manquée en l'espace de 1 heure à partir du moment prescrit. Le sevrage brusque peut provoquer une gastrite, des nausées, des vomissements, des étourdissements, des céphalées, la tachycardie et l'insomnie.
- Informer le patient qu'il risque de manifester des symptômes extrapyramidaux ou une dyskinésie tardive. Lui recommander de signaler immédiatement ces symptômes au professionnel de la santé.
- Recommander au patient de changer lentement de position afin de réduire le risque d'hypotension orthostatique.
- Prévenir le patient que la prochlorpérazine peut provoquer de la somnolence. Lui conseiller de ne pas conduire et d'éviter les activités qui exigent sa vigilance jusqu'à ce qu'on ait la certitude que le médicament n'entraîne pas cet effet chez lui.
- Mettre en garde le patient contre la consommation d'alcool ou d'autres dépresseurs du SNC en même temps que ce médicament.
- Recommander au patient d'utiliser un écran solaire et de porter des vêtements protecteurs lors des expositions au soleil en raison des risques de photosensibilité.

Lui recommander également d'éviter les températures extrêmes, car ce médicament altère la thermorégulation.

- Conseiller au patient de se rincer fréquemment la bouche, de pratiquer une bonne hygiène buccale et de consommer de la gomme ou des bonbons sans sucre pour soulager la sécheresse de la bouche. Lui recommander de consulter un professionnel de la santé si la sécheresse de la bouche persiste pendant plus de 2 semaines.
- Expliquer au patient qu'il ne doit pas prendre la prochlorpérazine dans les 2 heures suivant la prise d'antiacides ou d'antidiarrhéiques.
- Recommander au patient d'augmenter sa consommation de fibres alimentaires et de liquides et de faire de l'exercice pour réduire les effets constipants de ce médicament.
- Informer le patient que la prochlorpérazine peut faire virer la couleur de l'urine au rose ou au rouge brun.
- Recommander au patient qui doit suivre un autre traitement ou subir une intervention chirurgicale d'avertir le professionnel de la santé qu'il prend ce médicament.
- Informer le patient qu'il doit prévenir sans délai un professionnel de la santé en cas de maux de gorge, de fièvre, de saignements ou d'ecchymoses inhabituels, de rash, de faiblesse, de tremblements ou de troubles de la vue ou, encore, si son urine prend une couleur foncée ou si ses selles deviennent grises.
- Insister sur l'importance des examens de suivi permettant d'évaluer la réponse au médicament et de déceler les effets secondaires. Des examens ophtalmiques sont également indiqués à intervalles réguliers. Inciter le patient à suivre une psychothérapie si le médecin la lui a prescrite.

P

VÉRIFICATION DE L'EFFICACITÉ THÉRAPEUTIQUE

L'efficacité du traitement peut être démontrée par: le soulagement des nausées et vomissements ■ la diminution de l'excitation, du comportement paranoïaque et du repli sur soi lorsque le médicament est utilisé à titre d'antipsychotique ■ la diminution de l'anxiété. ✳

PROCYCLIDINE

Kemadrin, PHL-Procyclidine, PMS-Procyclidine

CLASSIFICATION:

Antiparkinsonien (anticholinergique)

Grossesse – catégorie C

INDICATIONS

Traitement de la maladie de Parkinson ■ Prévention et traitement des symptômes extrapyramidaux induits par les médicaments.

MÉCANISME D'ACTION

Agent antimuscarinique synthétique qui entraîne une inhibition des centres moteurs du cerveau et un blocage des influx nerveux efférents. ***Effets thérapeutiques:*** Diminution des symptômes associés à la maladie de Parkinson et soulagement des symptômes de dysfonctionnement extrapyramidal (dystonie, akathisie et parkinsonisme).

PHARMACOCINÉTIQUE

Absorption: Bonne (PO). Biodisponibilité à 75 % (PO).

Distribution: Inconnue.

Liaison aux protéines: Élevée.

Métabolisme et excrétion: Métabolisme hépatique faible. Excrétion rénale minimale.

Demi-vie: De 7,7 à 16,1 heures.

Profil temps-action (effets antiparkinsoniens)

	Début d'action	Pic	Durée
PO	0,5 - 1 h	inconnu	4 - 6 h

CONTRE-INDICATIONS, PRÉCAUTIONS ET MISES EN GARDE

Contre-indications: Myasthénie grave ■ Glaucome à angle fermé ■ Colite ulcéreuse grave ou compliquée d'un mégacôlon ■ Uropathie obstructive.

Précautions et mises en garde: **Obst., allaitement:** L'innocuité du médicament n'a pas été établie ■ **Péd.:** L'innocuité et l'efficacité du médicament n'ont pas été établies ■ **Gér.:** Les personnes âgées sont particulièrement sensibles aux effets anticholinergiques de la procyclidine. Il est conseillé de commencer le traitement à petites doses et d'augmenter la posologie graduellement ■ Risque d'ahydrose et/ou d'hyperthermie pouvant mener à une issue fatale (les patients doivent donc éviter les circonstances où l'hyperthermie peut survenir) ■ Insuffisance rénale ou hépatique ■ Rétention urinaire ■ Hyperplasie bénigne de la prostate ■ Troubles mentaux (l'agent peut déclencher des épisodes psychotiques) ■ Colite ulcéreuse ■ Infection gastro-intestinale ■ Ulcère gastroduodénal ■ Reflux gastro-œsophagien ou hernie hiatale ■ Hypertension ■ Hypotension ■ Tachyarythmie ■ Insuffisance cardiaque ■ Cardiopathie ischémique ■ Dyskinésie tardive ■ Maladie pulmonaire obstructive chronique.

RÉACTIONS INDÉSIRABLES ET EFFETS SECONDAIRES

SNC: agitation, confusion, désorientation, étourdissements, hallucinations, incapacité de se concentrer, psychose toxique aiguë, sensations ébrieuses, somnolence, troubles de la mémoire, nervosité.
ORLO: mydriase, trouble de l'accommodation (vision brouillée), trouble de l'élocution.
CV: tachycardie, palpitations, hypotension orthostatique.
GI: constipation, dysphagie, épigastralgie, nausées, sécheresse de la bouche (xérostomie), vomissements, iléus paralytique.
GU: dysurie, rétention urinaire.
Tég.: éruptions cutanées, urticaire, diminution de la diaphorèse.
Mét.: hyperthermie.
Loc.: faiblesse musculaire.

INTERACTIONS

Médicament-médicament: Effets anticholinergiques additifs lors de l'administration concomitante d'autres **médicaments dotés de propriétés anticholinergiques**, tels que les **phénothiazines**, les **antidépresseurs tricycliques**, la **quinidine** et le **disopyramide** ■ Effets additifs sur la dépression du SNC lors de l'usage concomitant d'autres **dépresseurs du SNC** dont l'**alcool**, les **antihistaminiques**, les **analgésiques opioïdes** et les **hypnosédatifs** ■ La procyclidine pourrait contrecarrer l'effet des médicaments suivants: **donépézil**, **galantamine**, **rivastigmine** ■ Réduction possible de l'action de la **lévodopa**. Cet effet est probablement causé par la réduction de la motilité gastrique, ce qui entraîne la désactivation accrue de la lévodopa dans l'appareil digestif et la diminution de son absorption ■ La procyclidine peut potentialiser les effets indésirables sur le SNC de l'**amantadine**.

VOIES D'ADMINISTRATION ET POSOLOGIE

- **PO**: Initialement 2,5 mg, 3 fois par jour, puis augmenter la dose selon la réponse et la tolérance du patient.

PRÉSENTATION

Comprimés: 2,5 mg[Pr], 5 mg[Pr] ■ **Élixir**: 2,5 mg/5 mL[Pr].

SOINS INFIRMIERS

ÉVALUATION DE LA SITUATION

- Avant l'administration initiale du médicament et à intervalles réguliers pendant toute la durée du traitement, rester à l'affût des symptômes parkinsoniens et extrapyramidaux suivants: akinésie, rigidité, tremblements, mouvements d'émiettement, faciès figé, démarche traînante, spasmes musculaires, mouvements de torsion et bouche ouverte laissant s'échapper la salive (sialorrhée). À cause des fluctuations dans les réactions aux médicaments (effet *on-off*), les symptômes peuvent apparaître ou disparaître soudainement.

DIAGNOSTICS INFIRMIERS POSSIBLES

- Mobilité physique réduite (Indications).
- Risque d'accident (Indications).
- Connaissances insuffisantes sur le traitement médicamenteux (Enseignement au patient et à ses proches).

INTERVENTIONS INFIRMIÈRES

- Administrer le médicament 1 ou plusieurs fois par jour, avec des aliments. Éviter l'alcool.

ENSEIGNEMENT AU PATIENT ET À SES PROCHES

- Expliquer au patient qu'il doit respecter rigoureusement la posologie recommandée.
- Prévenir le patient que le médicament peut provoquer de la somnolence ou des étourdissements. Lui conseiller de ne pas conduire et d'éviter les activités qui exigent sa vigilance jusqu'à ce qu'on ait la certitude que le médicament n'entraîne pas ces effets chez lui.
- Conseiller au patient de pratiquer une bonne hygiène buccale, de se rincer la bouche avec de l'eau, de mâcher de la gomme ou de sucer des bonbons sans sucre pour diminuer la sécheresse de la bouche. Lui recommander de prévenir un professionnel de la santé si la sécheresse de la bouche persiste (on pourrait lui prescrire des substituts de salive). Lui recommander de consulter le dentiste si la sécheresse de la bouche gêne le port des prothèses dentaires.
- Prévenir le patient que le médicament peut diminuer la sécrétion de sueur et que la chaleur pourrait l'incommoder. Lui conseiller de rester dans une pièce climatisée par temps chaud.
- Recommander au patient de faire de l'exercice, si possible, et de consommer plus d'aliments riches en fibres et plus de liquides (si ce n'est pas contre-indiqué) pour réduire les effets constipants du médicament.

VÉRIFICATION DE L'EFFICACITÉ THÉRAPEUTIQUE

L'efficacité du traitement peut être démontrée par: la disparition des signes et symptômes parkinsoniens ■ la résolution des symptômes extrapyramidaux induits par les médicaments.

PROGESTÉRONE

Crinone, PMS-Progestérone, Progestérone inj, Prometrium

CLASSIFICATION:

Progestatif

Grossesse – catégorie D

INDICATIONS

Aménorrhée ▪ Saignement utérin anormal dû à un déséquilibre hormonal ▪ **Prometrium**: Femmes non hystérectomisées, comme traitement adjuvant à l'œstrogénothérapie substitutive postménopausique, pour réduire les risques d'hyperplasie endométriale et de cancer qui pourrait en résulter ▪ **Crinone gel**: Traitement de soutien de la phase lutéale lors de cycles induits, comme les cycles de fécondation *in vitro*, y compris les dons d'ovocytes. **Usages non approuvés**: Insuffisance fonctionnelle du corps jaune.

MÉCANISME D'ACTION

Modification des sécrétions de l'endomètre ▪ Élévation de la température corporelle basale ▪ Modification histologique de l'épithélium vaginal ▪ Relaxation des muscles lisses utérins ▪ Croissance des tissus alvéolaires mammaires ▪ Inhibition de l'hypophyse ▪ Hémorragie de privation lors d'une œstrogénothérapie parallèle. ***Effets thérapeutiques:*** Rétablissement de l'équilibre hormonal et répression des saignements utérins ▪ Résultats positifs lors de l'utilisation d'une technique de reproduction assistée.

P

PHARMACOCINÉTIQUE

Absorption: La micronisation augmente l'absorption orale et vaginale.

Distribution: L'agent passe dans le lait maternel.

Liaison aux protéines: ≥ 90 %.

Métabolisme et excrétion: Métabolisme hépatique. Excrétion rénale (de 50 à 60 %) et fécale (10 %).

Demi-vie: Plusieurs minutes.

Profil temps-action (concentrations sanguines)

	DÉBUT D'ACTION	PIC	DURÉE
PO	inconnu	2 – 4 h	inconnue
Voie vaginale	inconnu	34,8 – 55 h	inconnue
IM	inconnu	19,6 – 28 h	inconnue

CONTRE-INDICATIONS, PRÉCAUTIONS ET MISES EN GARDE

Contre-indications: Hypersensibilité ▪ Hypersensibilité aux arachides (les capsules de Prometrium contiennent de l'huile d'arachides) ▪ Hypersensibilité à l'huile de sésame (progestérone injectable seulement) ▪ Thrombophlébite ou maladie thromboembolique ▪ Maladie vasculaire cérébrale ▪ Maladie hépatique grave ▪ Cancer du sein ou des organes génitaux ▪ Néoplasie progestérone-dépendante ▪ Rétention fœtale ▪ Hyperplasie de l'endomètre ▪ Saignements génitaux anormaux inexpliqués ▪ **OBST.**: Grossesse avérée ou soupçonnée ▪ Migraine commune ▪ Perte partielle ou complète de la vue imputable à une maladie des vaisseaux oculaires ▪ Affection résultant d'une thromboembolie artérielle (accident vasculaire cérébral, infarctus du myocarde, coronaropathie), ou antécédents d'une telle affection.

Précautions et mises en garde: Antécédents de maladie hépatique ▪ Maladie rénale ▪ Maladie cardiovasculaire ▪ Troubles convulsifs ▪ Dépression ▪ **ALLAITEMENT**: La progestérone peut diminuer la production lactée; l'innocuité du médicament n'a pas été établie.

RÉACTIONS INDÉSIRABLES ET EFFETS SECONDAIRES

SNC: somnolence, étourdissements, dépression.

ORLO: thrombose de la rétine.

CV: EMBOLIE PULMONAIRE, THROMBOEMBOLIE, thrombophlébite.

GI: saignements des gencives, hépatite.

GU: érosion cervicale.

Tég.: chloasma, mélasme, rash.

End.: aménorrhée, pertes sanguines intermenstruelles, sensibilité mammaire, modification du débit de sang menstruel, galactorrhée, saignotements.

HÉ: œdème.

Locaux: irritation et douleur au point d'injection.

Divers: réactions allergiques incluant l'ANAPHYLAXIE et l'ŒDÈME ANGIONEUROTIQUE, gain de poids, perte de poids.

INTERACTIONS

Médicament-médicament: La progestérone peut diminuer l'efficacité de la **bromocriptine** administrée en concomitance dans le traitement de la galactorrhée et de l'aménorrhée.

VOIES D'ADMINISTRATION ET POSOLOGIE

- **PO (adultes)**: *Hormonothérapie substitutive* – 200 mg, 1 fois par jour, au coucher, pendant les 14 derniers jours de l'œstrogénothérapie, du 8e au 21e jour d'un cycle de 28 jours ou du 12e au 25e jour d'un cycle de 30 jours; si la patiente reçoit de fortes doses d'œstrogènes (soit l'équivalent de 1,25 mg/jour ou plus d'œstrogènes conjugués), 1 dose quotidienne de 300 mg de progestérone est nécessaire pendant les 12 à 14 derniers jours de l'œstrogénothérapie, dont 100 mg, 2 heures après le petit-déjeuner, et 200 mg, au coucher; il faut adapter la posologie selon les besoins.

- **Voie vaginale (adultes)**: *Traitement de l'infertilité et fertilisation* in vitro – 90 mg (le contenu d'un applicateur rempli de gel à 8 %), 1 ou 2 fois par jour, en commençant dans les 24 heures suivant le transfert de l'embryon (en cas de grossesse, le traitement doit être maintenu pendant 10 à 12 semaines).
- **IM (adultes)**: *Aménorrhée ou saignement utérin anormal* – de 5 à 10 mg par jour, pendant 6 à 10 jours. Lorsqu'on administre aussi des œstrogènes, administrer la progestérone 2 semaines après le début du traitement par les œstrogènes.

PRÉSENTATION

Capsules de progestérone micronisée (Prometrium): 100 mg[Pr] ■ **Gel vaginal de progestérone micronisée (Crinone)**: 8 %[Pr] ■ **Solution pour injection**: 50 mg/mL, en fioles de 10 mL[Pr].

SOINS INFIRMIERS

ÉVALUATION DE LA SITUATION

- Mesurer la pression artérielle à intervalles réguliers tout au long du traitement.
- Effectuer le bilan des ingesta et des excreta et peser la patiente toutes les semaines. Signaler toute modification importante ou un gain de poids constant.

Aménorrhée: Déterminer la durée habituelle du cycle menstruel de la patiente. On commence habituellement l'administration de progestérone de 8 à 10 jours avant la date prévue des règles. Les règles surviennent habituellement dans les 48 à 72 heures qui suivent la fin du traitement. Il faut arrêter le traitement si les règles surviennent durant le cycle d'injections.

Hémorragie utérine anormale: Déterminer les caractéristiques du flot sanguin et la quantité de sang perdu (nombre de serviettes hygiéniques utilisées). L'hémorragie devrait se terminer vers la 6e journée de traitement. Il faut arrêter le traitement si les règles surviennent durant le cycle d'injections.

Tests de laboratoire:

- Noter les résultats des tests de la fonction hépatique avant le traitement et à intervalles réguliers pendant toute sa durée.
- La progestérone peut entraîner l'élévation des concentrations plasmatiques d'acides aminés et de phosphatase alcaline.
- La progestérone peut diminuer l'excrétion de prégnandiol urinaire.
- La progestérone peut élever les concentrations de cholestérol LDL et abaisser celles de cholestérol HDL.
- Les doses élevées de progestérone peuvent augmenter l'excrétion urinaire de sodium et de chlorure.
- La progestérone peut modifier les résultats des tests de la fonction thyroïdienne.

DIAGNOSTICS INFIRMIERS POSSIBLES

- Dysfonctionnement sexuel (Indications).
- Connaissances insuffisantes sur le traitement médicamenteux (Enseignement au patient et à ses proches).

INTERVENTIONS INFIRMIÈRES

IM: Bien agiter la fiole avant l'administration de la solution. Administrer profondément dans le muscle. Assurer la rotation des points d'injection.

Voie vaginale: Administrer le gel à l'aide de l'applicateur fourni par le fabricant.

ENSEIGNEMENT AU PATIENT ET À SES PROCHES

- RECOMMANDER À LA PATIENTE DE SIGNALER À UN PROFESSIONNEL DE LA SANTÉ LES SIGNES ET SYMPTÔMES DE RÉTENTION HYDRIQUE (ŒDÈME DES CHEVILLES ET DES PIEDS, GAIN PONDÉRAL), DE TROUBLES THROMBOEMBOLIQUES (DOULEURS, ENFLURES, SENSIBILITÉ DES MEMBRES, CÉPHALÉES, DOULEURS THORACIQUES, VISION TROUBLE), de dépression mentale ou de dysfonctionnement hépatique (jaunissement de la peau ou des yeux, prurit, urine de couleur foncée, selles de couleur claire).
- Recommander à la patiente de signaler à un professionnel de la santé toute modification des caractéristiques des saignements vaginaux ou l'apparition de saignotements.
- Expliquer à la patiente qu'elle doit cesser de prendre le médicament et prévenir un professionnel de la santé si elle pense être enceinte.
- Recommander à la patiente d'utiliser un écran solaire et de porter des vêtements protecteurs afin de prévenir les réactions de photosensibilité.
- Recommander à la patiente qui doit suivre un autre traitement ou subir une intervention chirurgicale de prévenir le professionnel de la santé qu'elle suit un traitement par ce médicament.
- Insister sur l'importance d'un suivi médical régulier comprenant la prise de la pression artérielle, l'examen des seins, de l'abdomen et du pelvis, ainsi que le test de Papanicolaou.

Voie vaginale: Recommander à la patiente de ne pas utiliser simultanément le gel et un autre agent vaginal. Si de tels agents doivent être administrés en concomitance,

P

il faut le faire au moins 6 heures avant ou après l'application du gel.

VÉRIFICATION DE L'EFFICACITÉ THÉRAPEUTIQUE

L'efficacité du traitement peut être démontrée par: la normalisation du cycle menstruel.

PROMÉTHAZINE

Bioniche promethazine HCl inj, Histantil, Phenergan injectable, Phénergan crème, PMS-Promethazine syr, Promethazine HCl inj

CLASSIFICATION:

Antiémétique (phénothiazine), antihistaminique, anxiolytique et hypnosédatif

Grossesse – catégorie C

INDICATIONS

Réactions allergiques: rhume des foins ▪ urticaire ▪ rhinite vasomotrice ▪ allergies cutanées ▪ herbe à puce ▪ piqûres d'insectes ▪ prurit ▪ Nausées et vomissements d'étiologies diverses: mal des transports ▪ radiothérapie ▪ interventions chirurgicales ▪ anesthésie ▪ gastroentérite ▪ administration d'émétiques à action centrale ▪ troubles métaboliques ou endocriniens ▪ Usage à titre de sédatif, d'hypnotique et de tranquillisant en cas d'insomnie, de nervosité, d'anxiété, de tension ▪ Anesthésie locale pour soulager le prurit et les brûlures légères ou les irritations bénignes de la peau ▪ Adjuvant à l'anesthésie et à l'analgésie.

MÉCANISME D'ACTION

Inhibition des effets de l'histamine ▪ Effets inhibiteurs sur la zone gâchette chémoréceptrice dans le bulbe rachidien se traduisant par des propriétés antiémétiques ▪ Modification des effets de la dopamine dans le SNC ▪ Effets anticholinergiques importants ▪ Dépression du SNC par la diminution de la stimulation indirecte du système réticulé du SNC. ***Effets thérapeutiques:*** Soulagement des symptômes associés à un surplus d'histamine, habituellement observé chez les patients souffrant de maladies allergiques ▪ Diminution des nausées et vomissements ▪ Sédation.

PHARMACOCINÉTIQUE

Absorption: Bonne (PO et IM).

Distribution: Tout l'organisme. La prométhazine traverse les barrières hématoencéphalique et placentaire.

Liaison aux protéines: De 65 à 90 %.

Métabolisme et excrétion: Métabolisme hépatique.

Demi-vie: Inconnue.

Profil temps-action
(effets antihistaminiques; les effets sédatifs durent de 2 à 8 heures)

	DÉBUT D'ACTION	PIC	DURÉE
PO, IM	20 min	inconnu	4 – 12 h
IV	3 – 5 min	inconnu	4 – 12 h

CONTRE-INDICATIONS, PRÉCAUTIONS ET MISES EN GARDE

Contre-indications: Hypersensibilité aux phénothiazines ▪ Coma dû aux dépresseurs du SNC ▪ Glaucome ▪ **PÉD.:** L'innocuité du médicament n'a pas été établie chez les enfants < 2 ans.

Précautions et mises en garde: Hyperplasie de la prostate ▪ Obstruction du col de la vessie ▪ Antécédents d'intolérance à l'alcool (certaines préparations liquides contiennent cet ingrédient; en éviter l'administration dans ce cas) ▪ Hypertension ▪ Apnée du sommeil ▪ Épilepsie ▪ Aplasie médullaire sous-jacente ▪ **OBST.:** Le médicament a été utilisé sans danger durant le travail; éviter l'administration prolongée durant la grossesse ▪ **ALLAITEMENT:** L'innocuité du médicament n'a pas été établie; il peut provoquer la somnolence chez le nourrisson.

RÉACTIONS INDÉSIRABLES ET EFFETS SECONDAIRES

SNC: SYNDROME MALIN DES NEUROLEPTIQUES, confusion, désorientation, sédation, étourdissements, réactions extrapyramidales, fatigue, insomnie, nervosité.

ORLO: vision trouble, diplopie, acouphènes.

CV: bradycardie, hypertension, hypotension, tachycardie.

GI: constipation, hépatite médicamenteuse, sécheresse de la bouche (xérostomie).

Tég.: photosensibilité, rash.

Hémat.: dyscrasie sanguine.

INTERACTIONS

Médicament-médicament: Dépression additive du SNC lors de l'usage concomitant d'autres **dépresseurs du SNC**, incluant l'**alcool**, les autres **antihistaminiques**, les **opioïdes** et d'autres **hypnosédatifs** ▪ Effets anticholinergiques additifs lors de l'administration concomitante d'autres **médicaments dotés de propriétés anticholinergiques**, incluant les autres **antihistaminiques**, les **antidépresseurs**, l'**atropine**, l'**halopéridol**, d'autres **phénothiazines**, la **quinidine** et le **disopyra-**

mide ■ L'administration concomitante d'**IMAO** peut accroître la sédation et les effets secondaires anticholinergiques.

VOIES D'ADMINISTRATION ET POSOLOGIE

- **PO**: Ne pas dépasser 150 mg par jour.
- **IM, IV**: Ne pas dépasser 100 mg par jour.

Antihistaminique

- **PO (adultes)**: 12,5 mg, 4 fois par jour, ou 25 mg, au coucher, selon les besoins.
- **PO (enfants > 2 ans)**: 0,125 mg/kg (ou 3,75 mg/m^2) toutes les 4 à 6 heures, ou 0,5 mg/kg (ou 15 mg/m^2) au coucher, au besoin, ou de 5 à 12,5 mg, 3 fois par jour, ou 25 mg, au coucher, au besoin.
- **IM, IV (adultes)**: 25 mg; on peut répéter l'administration de cette dose 2 heures plus tard.
- **Voie topique**: Appliquer, au besoin, sur la région affectée. Éviter d'appliquer sur une grande surface de la peau. Ne pas dépasser 10 % de surface corporelle.

Sédation

- **PO, IM, IV (adultes)**: De 25 à 50 mg, au besoin.
- **PO, IM (enfants > 2 ans)**: De 0,5 à 1 mg/kg (ou de 15 à 30 mg/m^2), toutes les 6 heures, au besoin, ou de 12,5 à 25 mg, au besoin.

Antiémétique

- **PO, IM, IV (adultes)**: De 12,5 à 25 mg, toutes les 4 à 6 heures, selon les besoins; la dose initiale par voie orale doit être de 25 mg.
- **PO, IM (enfants > 2 ans)**: De 0,25 à 0,5 mg/kg (ou de 7,5 à 15 mg/m^2), toutes les 4 à 6 heures, selon les besoins.

PRÉSENTATION (version générique disponible)

Comprimés: 25 mg[Pr], 50 mg[Pr] ■ **Sirop**: 10 mg/5 mL[Pr] ■ **Solution pour injection**: 25 mg/mL[Pr], en ampoules de 1 mL et de 2 mL.

SOINS INFIRMIERS

ÉVALUATION DE LA SITUATION

- Mesurer la pression artérielle, le pouls et la fréquence respiratoire à intervalles fréquents tout au long de l'administration par voie IV.
- Déterminer le degré de sédation du patient après l'administration du médicament. Les risques de sédation et de dépression respiratoire sont accrus lors de l'administration concomitante de médicaments qui dépriment le SNC.
- Déceler l'apparition des effets secondaires extrapyramidaux suivants: *akathisie* – agitation; *dystonie* – spasmes musculaires et mouvements de torsion; *pseudoparkinsonisme* – faciès figé, rigidité, tremblements, bouche ouverte laissant échapper la salive, démarche traînante, dysphagie. Informer le médecin ou un autre professionnel de la santé de l'apparition de ces symptômes.

GÉR.: Rester à l'affût des effets secondaires anticholinergiques (délirium, confusion aigüe, somnolence, bouche sèche, vision trouble, rétention urinaire, constipation, tachycardie).

Allergie: Suivre de près, avant le traitement et à intervalles réguliers pendant toute sa durée, les symptômes allergiques suivants: rhinite, conjonctivite, urticaire.

Antiémétique: Suivre de près les nausées et les vomissements, avant et après l'administration du médicament.

Tests de laboratoire:

- La prométhazine peut entraîner des résultats faussement positifs ou faussement négatifs aux tests de grossesse.
- Examiner la numération globulaire à intervalles réguliers durant le traitement prolongé en raison des risques de dyscrasie sanguine.
- La prométhazine peut entraîner l'élévation des concentrations sériques de glucose.
- La prométhazine peut entraîner des résultats faussement négatifs aux tests cutanés avec des extraits allergènes. Arrêter l'administration de prométhazine 72 heures avant ces tests.

DIAGNOSTICS INFIRMIERS POSSIBLES

- Déficit de volume liquidien (Indications).
- Risque d'accident (Effets secondaires).
- Connaissances insuffisantes sur le traitement médicamenteux (Enseignement au patient et à ses proches).

INTERVENTIONS INFIRMIÈRES

- Lorsque la prométhazine est administrée en même temps qu'un analgésique opioïde, surveiller étroitement les déplacements du patient afin de prévenir les accidents imputables à une sédation accrue.

PO: Administrer le médicament avec des aliments, de l'eau ou du lait pour réduire l'irritation gastrique. Dans le cas des patients éprouvant des difficultés de déglutition, on peut écraser les comprimés et les mélanger avec des aliments ou des liquides.

IM: Administrer l'agent profondément dans un muscle bien développé. L'administration SC peut provoquer la nécrose tissulaire.

IV directe: Administrer l'agent sans le diluer ou diluer 1 mL avec 9 mL de NaCl 0,9%. Les doses ne devraient pas dépasser une concentration de 25 mg/mL. Même si la solution devient jaune pâle, sa puissance n'est en rien altérée. Ne pas utiliser la solution si elle renferme un précipité.

Vitesse d'administration: Administrer lentement à une vitesse minimale de 25 mg/min. L'administration rapide peut provoquer une chute transitoire de la pression artérielle.

Solutions compatibles: dextrose ■ soluté salin ■ solution de Ringer ou de lactate de Ringer ■ dextrose et soluté salin ■ dextrose et solution de Ringer ■ mélange de solutions de lactate de Ringer.

Compatibilité dans la même seringue: atropine ■ butorphanol ■ cimétidine ■ dropéridol ■ fentanyl ■ glycopyrrolate ■ hydromorphone ■ mépéridine ■ métoclopramide ■ midazolam ■ pentazocine ■ ranitidine ■ scopolamine.

Incompatibilité dans la même seringue: héparine ■ kétorolac ■ pentobarbital ■ thiopental.

Compatibilité (tubulure en Y): amifostine ■ aztréonam ■ ciprofloxacine ■ cisatracurium ■ cisplatine ■ cyclophosphamide ■ cytarabine ■ doxorubicine ■ filgrastim ■ fluconazole ■ fludarabine ■ melphalan ■ ondansétron ■ rémifentanil ■ sargramostim ■ téniposide ■ thiotépa ■ vinorelbine.

Incompatibilité (tubulure en Y): aldesleukine ■ amphotéricine B, cholestéryle d' ■ céfépime ■ céfopérazone ■ céfotétane ■ doxorubicine liposomale ■ foscarnet ■ méthotrexate ■ pipéracilline/tazobactam.

ENSEIGNEMENT AU PATIENT ET À SES PROCHES

P

- Expliquer au patient le schéma posologique. S'il doit prendre le médicament régulièrement et s'il n'a pas pu le prendre au moment habituel, il doit le prendre dès que possible à moins qu'il ne soit presque l'heure prévue pour la dose suivante.
- Prévenir le patient que la prométhazine peut provoquer de la somnolence. Lui conseiller de ne pas conduire et d'éviter les activités exigeant sa vigilance jusqu'à ce qu'on ait la certitude que le médicament n'entraîne pas cet effet chez lui.
- Conseiller au patient de se rincer fréquemment la bouche, de pratiquer une bonne hygiène buccale et de consommer de la gomme ou des bonbons sans sucre pour soulager la sécheresse de la bouche. Lui recommander de consulter un professionnel de la santé si la sécheresse de la bouche persiste pendant plus de 2 semaines.
- Recommander au patient d'utiliser un écran solaire et de porter des vêtements protecteurs pour prévenir les réactions de photosensibilité.
- Recommander au patient de changer lentement de position afin de réduire le risque d'hypotension orthostatique. **GÉR.:** Ce risque est plus élevé chez les personnes âgées.
- Mettre en garde le patient contre la consommation d'alcool ou d'autres dépresseurs du SNC avec ce médicament.
- Recommander au patient de prévenir un professionnel de la santé en cas de maux de gorge, de fièvre, de jaunisse ou de mouvements incontrôlés.

GÉR.: Expliquer les effets anticholinergiques au patient et à ses proches et leur demander de prévenir un professionnel de la santé si ces effets persistent.

Mal des transports: En prophylaxie du mal des transports, le patient doit prendre la prométhazine au moins 30 minutes et, de préférence, de 1 à 2 heures avant qu'il ne se trouve dans une circonstance où le mal des transports peut survenir.

VÉRIFICATION DE L'EFFICACITÉ THÉRAPEUTIQUE

L'efficacité du traitement peut être démontrée par: le soulagement des symptômes allergiques ■ la prévention du mal des transports ■ la sédation ■ le soulagement des nausées et vomissements. ✳

PROPAFÉNONE

Apo-Propafenone, Gen-Propafenone, PMS-Propafenone, Rythmol

CLASSIFICATION:

Antiarythmique (classe IC)

Grossesse – catégorie C

INDICATIONS

Traitement des arythmies ventriculaires mettant la vie du patient en danger, incluant la tachycardie ventriculaire soutenue ■ Traitement des arythmies ventriculaires symptomatiques confirmées, lorsque les symptômes sont suffisamment graves pour justifier la prise de ce médicament. **Usages non approuvés:** Prévention des tachyarythmies supraventriculaires dont: les tachycardies supraventriculaires paroxystiques, la fibrillation auriculaire paroxystique et le flutter auriculaire ■ Cardioversion médicamenteuse ambulatoire (approche «*pill in the pocket*»): Traitement des épisodes récidivants de fibrillation auriculaire paroxystique chez certains patients, à l'aide de 1 dose de charge unique.

MÉCANISME D'ACTION

Ralentissement de la conduction du tissu cardiaque par modification du transport des ions à travers la membrane cellulaire. ***Effets thérapeutiques:*** Suppression des arythmies ventriculaires.

PHARMACOCINÉTIQUE

Absorption: Bonne (PO). Biodisponibilité de 3 à 11 % (effet de premier passage important).

Distribution: Tout l'organisme; l'agent traverse la barrière placentaire.

Métabolisme et excrétion: Métabolisme majoritairement hépatique. Certains métabolites sont dotés d'une activité antiarythmique. On considère que chez plus de 90 % des patients, le métabolisme de la propafénone est très rapide. Chez les autres, le métabolisme est plus lent.

Demi-vie: De 2 à 10 heures («métabolisateurs» rapides); de 10 à 32 heures («métabolisateurs» lents).

Profil temps-action (effets antiarythmiques)

	DÉBUT D'ACTION	PIC	DURÉE
PO	plusieurs heures – jours	4 – 5 jours†	plusieurs heures

† Après un traitement prolongé.

CONTRE-INDICATIONS, PRÉCAUTIONS ET MISES EN GARDE

Contre-indications: Hypersensibilité ■ Choc cardiogénique ■ Troubles de conduction incluant le dysfonctionnement du nœud sinusal (maladie du sinus) et le bloc AV (en l'absence de stimulateur cardiaque) ■ Bradycardie importante (moins de 50 battements/min) ■ Hypotension grave ■ Bronchospasme non allergique ■ Déséquilibres électrolytiques ■ Insuffisance cardiaque marquée ou non maîtrisée ■ Insuffisance hépatique grave.

Précautions et mises en garde: Insuffisance hépatique ou rénale grave (il peut s'avérer nécessaire de réduire la dose) ■ **GÉR.:** Il peut s'avérer nécessaire de réduire la dose ■ **OBST., ALLAITEMENT, PÉD.:** L'innocuité du médicament n'a pas été établie.

RÉACTIONS INDÉSIRABLES ET EFFETS SECONDAIRES

SNC: étourdissements, tremblements, faiblesse.

ORLO: vision trouble.

CV: ARYTHMIES SUPRAVENTRICULAIRES, ARYTHMIES VENTRICULAIRES, troubles de conduction, angine, bradycardie, hypotension.

GI: altération du goût, constipation, nausées, vomissements, diarrhée, sécheresse de la bouche (xérostomie).

Tég.: rash.

Loc.: douleurs articulaires.

INTERACTIONS

Médicament-médicament: L'administration d'**inhibiteurs des isoenzymes CYP2D6, CYP1A2 et CYP3A4**, dont la **désipramine**, la **paroxétine**, le **ritonavir**, la **sertraline**, le **kétoconazole**, le **saquinavir** et l'**érythromycine**, peut entraîner une élévation des concentrations plasmatiques de propafénone ■ La propafénone est un inhibiteur de l'isoenzyme CYP2D6, pouvant entraîner une élévation des concentrations plasmatiques des **médicaments métabolisés par cet isoenzyme** (comme la **venlafaxine**, l'**halopéridol**, l'**imipramine** et la **désipramine**) ■ La propafénone élève les concentrations sériques de **digoxine** de 35 à 85 % (il peut s'avérer nécessaire de réduire la dose) ■ La propafénone élève les concentrations sanguines de **métoprolol** et de **propranolol**, administrés simultanément (il peut s'avérer nécessaire de réduire la dose) ■ Les **anesthésiques locaux**, administrés simultanément, peuvent augmenter le risque d'effets indésirables sur le SNC ■ La propafénone peut augmenter les effets de la **warfarine** (diminuer les doses de warfarine de 25 à 50 %) ■ La propafénone peut accroître les concentrations sanguines au creux de la **cyclosporine** et le risque de néphrotoxicité ■ La **rifampine** peut réduire les concentrations sériques et l'efficacité de la propafénone ■ L'administration concomitante d'**amiodarone** et de propafénone peut influer sur la conduction et la repolarisation et entraîner des effets proarythmiques ■ L'emploi concomitant de propafénone et de **lidocaïne** administrée par voie intraveineuse augmente la fréquence et la gravité des effets secondaires sur le SNC exercés par la lidocaïne.

Médicament-aliments: Le **jus de pamplemousse** peut élever considérablement les concentrations plasmatiques de propafénone.

VOIES D'ADMINISTRATION ET POSOLOGIE

- **PO (adultes):** 150 mg, toutes les 8 heures; on peut majorer la dose graduellement tous les 3 ou 4 jours, selon les besoins, jusqu'à 300 mg toutes les 12 heures. La posologie maximale est de 300 mg, toutes les 8 heures. Elle doit être individualisée selon la réponse et la tolérance du patient.
- **PO (adultes):** *Fibrillation auriculaire paroxystique* – cardioversion médicamenteuse ambulatoire (approche «*pill in the pocket*») – usage non approuvé. *Dose de charge unique – Patient < 70 kg:* 450 mg, immédiatement; *patient ≥ 70 kg:* 600 mg, immédiatement.

PRÉSENTATION

Comprimés: 150 mg^{Pr}, 300 mg^{Pr}.

P

SOINS INFIRMIERS

ÉVALUATION DE LA SITUATION

- SUIVRE DE PRÈS L'ÉCG OU LE TRACÉ HOLTER AVANT LE TRAITEMENT ET À INTERVALLES RÉGULIERS PENDANT TOUTE SA DURÉE. LA PROPAFÉNONE PEUT ALLONGER LES INTERVALLES PR ET QT.
- Mesurer la pression artérielle et le pouls à intervalles réguliers pendant toute la durée du traitement.
- Effectuer le bilan quotidien des ingesta et des excreta et peser le patient tous les jours. Observer le patient à la recherche des signes et des symptômes suivants d'insuffisance cardiaque: œdème périphérique, râles et crépitations, dyspnée, gain de poids, turgescence des jugulaires. Ce phénomène peut dicter l'arrêt du traitement ou la réduction de la dose.

Tests de laboratoire: La propafénone peut entraîner l'élévation des titres d'anticorps antinucléaires, phénomène habituellement asymptomatique, mais réversible.

TOXICITÉ ET SURDOSAGE: Les signes de toxicité sont l'hypotension, une somnolence excessive et un rythme cardiaque diminué ou anormal. Prévenir le médecin ou un autre professionnel de la santé si ces symptômes se manifestent.

DIAGNOSTICS INFIRMIERS POSSIBLES

- Débit cardiaque diminué (Indications).
- Connaissances insuffisantes sur le traitement médicamenteux (Enseignement au patient et à ses proches).

P

INTERVENTIONS INFIRMIÈRES

- Le traitement par la propafénone doit être amorcé dans un centre hospitalier doté du matériel nécessaire à la surveillance du rythme cardiaque. On observe les effets proarythmiques les plus graves durant les 2 premières semaines de traitement.
- Avant d'amorcer le traitement par la propafénone, il faut arrêter l'administration de tout autre médicament antiarythmique pendant un laps de temps entre 2 et 5 demi-vies.
- La posologie doit être adaptée à intervalles d'au moins 3 ou 4 jours en raison de la longue demi-vie de la propafénone.
- Il faut corriger toute hypokaliémie ou hyperkaliémie préexistante avant d'amorcer le traitement.

ENSEIGNEMENT AU PATIENT ET À SES PROCHES

- Expliquer au patient qu'il doit respecter rigoureusement la posologie recommandée et prendre le médicament à intervalles réguliers, 24 heures sur 24, même s'il se sent mieux. S'il n'a pas pu prendre le médicament au moment habituel, il doit le prendre aussitôt que possible dans les 4 heures suivantes; sinon, lui recommander de sauter cette dose. Une réduction graduelle de la dose peut s'avérer nécessaire.
- Prévenir le patient que la propafénone peut provoquer des étourdissements. Lui conseiller de ne pas conduire et d'éviter les activités qui exigent sa vigilance jusqu'à ce qu'on ait la certitude que le médicament n'entraîne pas cet effet chez lui.
- Recommander au patient qui doit suivre un traitement ou subir une intervention chirurgicale d'avertir le professionnel de la santé qu'il suit un traitement par ce médicament.
- Recommander au patient de prévenir un professionnel de la santé en cas de fièvre, de maux de gorge, de frissons, de saignements ou d'ecchymoses inhabituels ou de douleurs thoraciques, d'essoufflements, de diaphorèse, de palpitations ou de modifications de la vue.
- Conseiller au patient de porter sur lui en tout temps une pièce d'identité où sont inscrits son problème de santé et son traitement.
- Insister sur l'importance des examens de suivi permettant d'évaluer l'efficacité du traitement.
- **Cardioversion médicamenteuse ambulatoire (approche «*pill in the pocket*»)**: Expliquer au patient qu'il doit prendre la propafénone dans les 5 minutes qui suivent l'apparition subite de palpitations et rester en position couchée ou assise jusqu'à la disparition des palpitations ou pendant au moins 4 heures. Recommander au patient de se présenter à l'urgence si les symptômes persistent pendant plus de 6 à 8 heures après la prise du médicament ou si des symptômes tels que dyspnée, une syncope ou une élévation marquée de la fréquence cardiaque apparaissent.

VÉRIFICATION DE L'EFFICACITÉ THÉRAPEUTIQUE

L'efficacité du traitement peut être démontrée par: la diminution de la fréquence des arythmies ventriculaires.

PROPANTHÉLINE

Pro-Banthine

CLASSIFICATION:

Anticholinergique (antimuscarinique)

Grossesse – catégorie C

INDICATIONS

Traitement d'appoint de l'ulcère gastroduodénal ▪ Traitement symptomatique du syndrome d'irritabilité intestinale (côlon irritable, côlon spasmodique, colite mucomembraneuse) ▪ Colique rénale et hyperhydrose ▪ Traitement adjuvant de la colite ulcéreuse, de la diverticulite, de la cholécystite et de la pancréatite.

MÉCANISME D'ACTION

Inhibition compétitive de l'action muscarinique de l'acétylcholine, entraînant une réduction des sécrétions gastro-intestinales. ***Effets thérapeutiques:*** Diminution des signes et des symptômes d'ulcère gastroduodénal.

PHARMACOCINÉTIQUE

Absorption: < 50 % (PO).
Distribution: Inconnue. L'agent ne traverse pas la barrière hématoencéphalique.
Métabolisme et excrétion: La propanthéline est inactivée dans la partie haute de l'intestin grêle.
Demi-vie: Inconnue.

Profil temps-action (effets anticholinergiques)

	DÉBUT D'ACTION	PIC	DURÉE
PO	30 - 60 min	2 - 6 h	6 h

CONTRE-INDICATIONS, PRÉCAUTIONS ET MISES EN GARDE

Contre-indications: Hypersensibilité ▪ Glaucome ▪ Maladie occlusive du tractus gastro-intestinal (sténose pyloroduodénale, achalasie, iléus paralytique) ▪ Uropathie obstructive due au prostatisme ▪ Atonie intestinale ▪ Colite ulcéreuse grave ou mégacôlon toxique ▪ Instabilité cardiovasculaire en présence d'hémorragie aiguë ▪ Myasthénie grave.
Précautions et mises en garde: Personnes âgées ou patients de petite taille (réduire la dose) ▪ Hyperplasie de la prostate ▪ Maladies rénale, cardiaque ou pulmonaire chroniques ▪ Présence soupçonnée d'infections intra-abdominales ▪ **OBST., ALLAITEMENT, PÉD.**: L'innocuité du médicament n'a pas été établie.

RÉACTIONS INDÉSIRABLES ET EFFETS SECONDAIRES

SNC: confusion, étourdissements, somnolence, nervosité.
ORLO: vision trouble, mydriase, photophobie.
CV: tachycardie, hypotension orthostatique, palpitations.
GI: constipation, sécheresse de la bouche (xérostomie).
GU: hésitation avant ou pendant la miction, rétention urinaire.
Tég.: rash.
Divers: diminution de la diaphorèse.

INTERACTIONS

Médicament-médicament: Effets anticholinergiques additifs lors de l'administration simultanée d'autres **médicaments dotés de propriétés anticholinergiques**, incluant les **antihistaminiques**, les **antidépresseurs**, l'**atropine**, l'**halopéridol**, les **phénothiazines**, la **quinidine** et le **disopyramide** ▪ La propanthéline peut modifier l'absorption d'autres **médicaments administrés par voie orale** en ralentissant la motilité du tractus gastro-intestinal ▪ Les **antiacides** et les **antidiarrhéiques adsorbants**, administrés simultanément, diminuent l'absorption des anticholinergiques (ne pas administrer dans les 2 à 3 heures suivant l'administration de la propanthéline) ▪ La propanthéline peut aggraver les lésions de la muqueuse gastro-intestinale chez les patients prenant par voie orale des **préparations solides de chlorure de potassium**.

VOIES D'ADMINISTRATION ET POSOLOGIE

- **PO (adultes)**: *Dose d'attaque habituelle* – 15 mg, 3 fois par jour, avant chaque repas, et 30 mg, au coucher.
- **PO (personnes âgées ou de petite taille ou patients présentant des symptômes légers)**: 7,5 mg, 3 fois par jour. Pour certaines indications, on doit adapter la posologie selon chaque cas particulier; elle se situe entre 15 et 30 mg, 4 fois par jour.

PRÉSENTATION

Comprimés: 7,5 mg^{Pr}, 15 mg^{Pr}.

SOINS INFIRMIERS

ÉVALUATION DE LA SITUATION

- Suivre de près les douleurs abdominales avant le traitement et à intervalles réguliers pendant toute sa durée.

DIAGNOSTICS INFIRMIERS POSSIBLES

- Douleur aiguë (Indications).
- Constipation (Effets secondaires).
- Connaissances insuffisantes sur le traitement médicamenteux (Enseignement au patient et à ses proches).

INTERVENTIONS INFIRMIÈRES

- Administrer 30 minutes avant les repas. La dose qui doit être prise au coucher devrait être administrée au moins 2 heures après le dernier repas de la journée.

- Ne pas administrer la propanthéline dans l'heure précédant ou suivant la prise d'antiacides ou d'antidiarrhéiques.

ENSEIGNEMENT AU PATIENT ET À SES PROCHES

- Expliquer au patient qu'il doit respecter rigoureusement la posologie recommandée. S'il n'a pu prendre le médicament au moment habituel, il doit le prendre dès que possible à moins que ce ne soit presque l'heure prévue pour la dose suivante. Le prévenir qu'il ne doit jamais remplacer une dose manquée par une double dose.
- Prévenir le patient que la propanthéline peut provoquer de la somnolence et une vision trouble. Lui recommander de ne pas conduire et d'éviter les autres activités qui exigent sa vigilance jusqu'à ce qu'on ait la certitude que le médicament n'entraîne pas ces effets chez lui.
- Conseiller au patient de se rincer fréquemment la bouche, de pratiquer une bonne hygiène buccale et de consommer de la gomme ou des bonbons sans sucre pour soulager la sécheresse de la bouche. Si la sécheresse de la bouche persiste pendant plus de 2 semaines, lui conseiller de consulter un professionnel de la santé au sujet de la possibilité d'utiliser des substituts de salive.
- Expliquer au patient qu'en augmentant sa consommation de liquides et de fibres alimentaires, ainsi que ses activités physiques, il peut réduire les effets constipants du médicament.
- Recommander au patient âgé recevant la propanthéline de changer lentement de position pour réduire le risque d'hypotension orthostatique induite par le médicament.
- Recommander au patient d'éviter les températures extrêmes. Ce médicament diminue la sécrétion de sueur et peut augmenter le risque de coups de chaleur.
- Conseiller au patient de porter des verres fumés et de ne pas s'exposer à une lumière vive en raison du risque de photosensibilité.
- Conseiller au patient de prévenir un professionnel de la santé en cas de confusion, d'excitation, d'étourdissements, de rash, de difficultés de miction ou de douleurs oculaires. Le professionnel de la santé peut recommander des examens ophtalmiques à intervalles réguliers afin de mesurer la pression intraoculaire, particulièrement chez le patient âgé.

VÉRIFICATION DE L'EFFICACITÉ THÉRAPEUTIQUE

L'efficacité du traitement peut être démontrée par: la diminution des douleurs gastro-intestinales chez les patients présentant un ulcère gastro-intestinal. ✳

P

PROPOFOL

Diprivan EML, PMS-Propofol, Propofol

CLASSIFICATION:

Anesthésique et adjuvant anesthésique (à action générale)

Grossesse – catégorie B

INDICATIONS

Induction et maintien d'une anesthésie générale chez les enfants ≥ 3 ans et chez l'adulte ■ Élément d'une technique d'anesthésie équilibrée, y compris l'anesthésie IV totale, lors d'interventions chirurgicales chez des patients hospitalisés ou non ■ Sédation chez les patients soumis à une intubation et à une ventilation assistée dans une unité des soins intensifs ■ Sédation consciente lors de certaines interventions chirurgicales ou diagnostiques.

MÉCANISME D'ACTION

Effet hypnotique de courte durée. Le mécanisme d'action du propofol est inconnu ■ Induction de l'amnésie ■ Absence d'effets analgésiques. ***Effets thérapeutiques:*** Induction et maintien de l'anesthésie.

PHARMACOCINÉTIQUE

Absorption: Biodisponibilité à 100 %.

Distribution: Répartition rapide dans tout l'organisme. Le propofol traverse bien la barrière hématoencéphalique et il est rapidement transporté vers les autres tissus. Il traverse la barrière placentaire et passe dans le lait maternel.

Liaison aux protéines: De 95 à 99 %.

Métabolisme et excrétion: Métabolisme hépatique rapide.

Demi-vie: De 3 à 12 heures (demi-vie pour l'atteinte du point d'équilibre dans le compartiment hématoencéphalique: 2,9 minutes).

Profil temps-action (perte de conscience)

	DÉBUT D'ACTION	PIC	DURÉE†
IV	40 s	inconnu	3 – 5 min

† Le patient se réveille après 8 minutes (jusqu'à 19 minutes si on lui a aussi administré des opioïdes).

CONTRE-INDICATIONS, PRÉCAUTIONS ET MISES EN GARDE

Contre-indications: Cas où une anesthésie générale ou la sédation sont contre-indiquées ■ Hypersensibilité au propofol, à l'huile de soja, à la lécithine contenue dans l'œuf, au glycérol ou aux émulsions lipidiques ■ **PÉD.:**

Sédation chez les enfants ≤ 18 ans qui reçoivent des soins intensifs.

Précautions et mises en garde: Maladie cardiovasculaire ■ Dyslipidémies (l'émulsion peut avoir un effet délétère) ■ Pression intracrânienne accrue ■ Maladies vasculaires cérébrales ■ Personnes âgées (> 60 ans), débilitées ou hypovolémiques (il est recommandé de réduire la dose d'induction et d'entretien) ■ **PÉD., ALLAITEMENT**: L'innocuité du médicament n'a pas été établie ■ Travail et accouchement (césariennes comprises) ■ Patients des unités de soins intensifs qui présentent des troubles graves du métabolisme des lipides.

RÉACTIONS INDÉSIRABLES ET EFFETS SECONDAIRES

SNC: étourdissements, céphalées.

Resp.: APNÉE, toux.

CV: bradycardie, hypotension, hypertension.

GI: crampes abdominales, hoquet, nausées, vomissements.

Tég.: bouffées vasomotrices.

Locaux: sensation de brûlure ou de picotement, douleurs, sensation de froid, engourdissement et fourmillements au point d'injection IV.

Loc.: mouvements musculaires involontaires, myoclonie périopératoire.

Divers: fièvre.

INTERACTIONS

Médicament-médicament: Dépression additive du SNC et des respirations lors de l'usage concomitant d'**alcool**, d'**antihistaminiques**, d'**opioïdes** et d'**hypnosédatifs** (réduire la dose, au besoin) ■ Risque accru d'hypertriglycéridémie lors de l'administration d'une **émulsion lipidique intraveineuse** ■ Le propofol peut élever les concentrations sériques d'**alfentanil** ■ Risque de bradycardies graves chez les enfants lors de l'administration concomitante de **fentanyl**.

VOIES D'ADMINISTRATION ET POSOLOGIE

Anesthésie générale

- **IV (adultes < 55 ans)**: *Induction* – 40 mg (de 2 à 2,5 mg/kg), toutes les 10 secondes, jusqu'à induction de la sédation. *Maintien de l'anesthésie* – de 0,10 à 0,20 mg/kg/min. Il faut administrer habituellement de 0,15 à 0,20 mg/kg/min (de 9 à 12 mg/kg/h) durant les 10 à 15 premières minutes suivant l'induction, puis diminuer la dose de 30 à 50 % durant les 30 premières minutes pendant lesquelles l'anesthésie doit être maintenue. Une dose de 0,05 à 0,10 mg/kg/min assure un temps de réveil optimal. On peut également administrer des doses fractionnées de 25 à 50 mg, par paliers intermittents.
- **IV (personnes âgées, débilitées ou hypovolémiques)**: *Induction* – 20 mg (de 1 à 1,5 mg/kg) toutes les 10 secondes, jusqu'à l'induction de la sédation. *Maintien* – de 0,05 à 0,10 mg/kg/min.
- **IV (adultes soumis à une intervention neurologique)**: *Induction* – 20 mg (de 1 à 2 mg/kg) toutes les 10 secondes, jusqu'à l'induction de la sédation. *Maintien* – de 0,10 à 0,20 mg/kg/min (de 6 à 12 mg/kg/h).
- **IV (enfants > 8 ans)**: *Induction* – 2,5 mg/kg. *Maintien* – de 0,10 à 0,25 mg/kg/min (6 à 15 mg/kg/h).
- **IV (enfants de 3 à 8 ans)**: *Induction* – les enfants de cet âge peuvent avoir besoin d'une dose supérieure à 2,5 mg/kg.
- **IV (adultes soumis à une anesthésie cardiaque)**: *Induction* – 20 mg (de 0,5 à 1,5 mg/kg) toutes les 10 secondes, jusqu'à l'induction de la sédation. *Maintien* – de 0,1 mg/kg/min, dose à laquelle il faut ajouter une dose analgésique d'opioïdes en administration continue. Lorsqu'on administre un opioïde comme anesthésique principal, les vitesses d'administration ne doivent pas être inférieures à 0,05 mg/kg/min.

Sédation à des fins chirurgicales ou diagnostiques

- **IV (adultes < 55 ans)**: *Induction* – injection lente de 0,5 à 1 mg/kg, administrée en 3 à 5 minutes. *Maintien* – perfusion d'une dose de 0,025 à 0,075 mg/kg/min (de 1,5 à 4,5 mg/kg/h) ou bolus de 10 à 15 mg.
- **IV (personnes âgées, débilitées ou patients de classe ASA III ou IV)**: *Induction* – débit de perfusion et d'injection plus lent. *Maintien* – réduire la dose de propofol pour la passer à environ 70 à 80 % de la dose habituelle chez l'adulte; il faut éviter d'administrer des bolus rapides ou répétés.

Sédation dans les unités de soins intensifs

- **IV (adultes)**: *Induction* – 0,005 mg/kg/min pendant au moins 5 minutes. On peut augmenter la dose par paliers de 0,005 à 0,01 mg/kg/min (0,3 à 0,6 mg/kg/h), toutes les 5 à 10 minutes, jusqu'à l'obtention du niveau de sédation désiré (écart posologique de 0,005 à 0,05 mg/kg/min ou de 0,3 à 3 mg/kg/h). Il faut réévaluer la dose toutes les 24 heures.

PRÉSENTATION (version générique disponible)

Émulsion pour injection: 100 mg/mL, en ampoules de 20 mL[Pr] et fioles pour perfusion de 50 mL[Pr] et de 100 mL[Pr].

P

SOINS INFIRMIERS

ÉVALUATION DE LA SITUATION

- MESURER CONTINUELLEMENT LA FONCTION RESPIRATOIRE, LE POULS ET LA PRESSION ARTÉRIELLE TOUT AU LONG DE L'ADMINISTRATION DU MÉDICAMENT. LE PROPOFOL ENTRAÎNE FRÉQUEMMENT UNE APNÉE POUVANT DURER ≥ 60 SECONDES. MAINTENIR LA PERMÉABILITÉ DES VOIES RESPIRATOIRES ET LA VENTILATION. LE PROPOFOL NE DEVRAIT ÊTRE ADMINISTRÉ QUE PAR DES PERSONNES AYANT DE L'EXPÉRIENCE DANS L'INTUBATION ENDOTRACHÉALE. IL FAUT GARDER À PORTÉE DE LA MAIN LE MATÉRIEL NÉCESSAIRE À CETTE INTERVENTION.
- Noter le degré de sédation et le niveau de conscience du patient tout au long de l'administration du médicament et une fois qu'elle a pris fin.

TOXICITÉ ET SURDOSAGE: En cas de surdosage, mesurer continuellement le pouls, la fréquence respiratoire et la pression artérielle. Maintenir la perméabilité des voies aériennes et assister la ventilation, selon les besoins. En cas d'hypotension, administrer des liquides par voie IV, changer le patient de position et lui administrer des vasopresseurs.

DIAGNOSTICS INFIRMIERS POSSIBLES

- Mode de respiration inefficace (Réactions indésirables).
- Risque d'accident (Effets secondaires).
- Connaissances insuffisantes sur le traitement médicamenteux (Enseignement au patient et à ses proches).

P

INTERVENTIONS INFIRMIÈRES

- La dose de propofol doit être adaptée selon la réponse du patient.
- Le propofol n'exerce aucun effet sur le seuil de la douleur. On devrait *toujours* assurer une analgésie appropriée lorsque le propofol est administré comme adjuvant lors des interventions chirurgicales.

IV directe:

- Bien agiter l'émulsion avant de l'administrer. Si le propofol est dilué avant l'administration, n'utiliser qu'une solution de D5%E, afin d'obtenir une concentration d'au moins 2 mg/mL. L'émulsion est opaque, ce qui rend difficile la détection d'agents contaminants. Ne pas utiliser la préparation en présence de signes de séparation des phases de l'émulsion. L'émulsion ne contient aucun agent de conservation; utiliser une technique stérile et administrer immédiatement après la préparation. Jeter toute portion inutilisée du médicament ainsi que la tubulure IV à la fin de l'intervention ou dans les 6 heures suivant sa préparation. Lorsque l'agent est utilisé pour induire la sédation dans une unité de soins intensifs, jeter la préparation après 12 heures, si elle est administrée directement de la fiole, ou après 6 heures, si elle a été aspirée dans une seringue ou préparée dans un autre contenant. Consulter les directives de chaque fabricant avant de reconstituer la préparation.
- Il est essentiel d'utiliser une technique aseptique. L'émulsion est un milieu qui favorise la prolifération rapide de germes contaminants. On a signalé des cas d'infections d'issue fatale.
- L'administration du propofol provoque souvent des douleurs ou une sensation de brûlure ou de picotements au point d'injection. Injecter dans une grosse veine de l'avant-bras ou dans le pli du coude ou administrer par un cathéter IV déjà installé. On peut administrer de 10 à 20 mg de lidocaïne par voie IV avant l'injection afin de réduire la douleur.

Vitesse d'administration: Administrer en 3 à 5 minutes. Adapter la dose en vue d'obtenir le niveau de sédation souhaité.

Perfusion intermittente ou continue: On peut administrer le propofol en perfusion intermittente ou continue (les vitesses de perfusion sont indiquées à la rubrique «Voies d'administration et posologie»). Utiliser une pompe à perfusion pour pouvoir administrer le médicament au débit approprié. Il faut observer le patient pendant la période de réveil et évaluer le fonctionnement du SNC quotidiennement lors de la sédation continue chez les adultes soumis à une intubation et à une ventilation assistée dans les unités de soins intensifs, afin d'établir la dose minimale qui peut assurer la sédation. Maintenir la sédation à un faible niveau lors de ces évaluations; ne pas arrêter l'administration. L'arrêt brusque du traitement peut entraîner un réveil rapide s'accompagnant d'anxiété, d'agitation et de résistance à la ventilation artificielle.

Solutions compatibles: D5%E ■ solution de lactate de Ringer ■ D5%/solution de lactate de Ringer ■ D5%/NaCl 0,45 % ■ D5%/NaCl 0,2 %.

Incompatibilité (tubulure en Y): atracurium ■ plasma ■ sang.

Incompatibilité en addition au soluté: Le fabricant ne recommande pas de mélanger le propofol avec d'autres médicaments.

ENSEIGNEMENT AU PATIENT ET À SES PROCHES

- Expliquer au patient que ce médicament entraînera une perte de la mémoire et, de ce fait, ses souvenirs de l'intervention seront estompés.

- Prévenir le patient que le propofol peut provoquer de la somnolence ou des étourdissements. Lui conseiller de demander de l'aide lors de ses déplacements, de ne pas conduire et d'éviter les activités qui exigent sa vigilance pendant les 24 heures qui suivent l'administration de ce médicament.
- Recommander au patient d'éviter de boire de l'alcool et de prendre d'autres dépresseurs du SNC dans les 24 heures qui suivent l'administration du médicament.

VÉRIFICATION DE L'EFFICACITÉ THÉRAPEUTIQUE

L'efficacité du traitement peut être démontrée par: l'induction et le maintien de l'anesthésie ■ l'amnésie ■ la sédation chez les patients hospitalisés dans une unité de soins intensifs, sous ventilation artificielle. ✳

ALERTE CLINIQUE

PROPOXYPHÈNE

Darvon-N

CLASSIFICATION:

Analgésique opioïde (agoniste)

Grossesse – catégories C et D (en usage prolongé ou à doses élevées près du terme)

INDICATIONS

Soulagement de la douleur légère à modérée.

MÉCANISME D'ACTION

Liaison aux récepteurs des opioïdes du SNC ■ Modification de la perception de la douleur et de la réaction aux stimuli douloureux avec dépression généralisée du SNC. ***Effets thérapeutiques:*** Diminution de la douleur légère à modérée.

PHARMACOCINÉTIQUE

Absorption: Bonne (PO).

Distribution: Le médicament se répartit dans tout l'organisme. Il traverse probablement la barrière placentaire et passe en petites quantités dans le lait maternel.

Métabolisme et excrétion: Métabolisme majoritairement hépatique. Une fraction est transformée en norpropoxyphène, un métabolite toxique qui peut s'accumuler chez les personnes âgées et les personnes dont la fonction rénale est diminuée.

Demi-vie: De 6 à 12 heures; norpropoxyphène: de 30 à 36 heures.

Profil temps-action (effet analgésique)

	DÉBUT D'ACTION	PIC	DURÉE
PO	15 - 60 min	2 - 3 h	4 - 6 h

CONTRE-INDICATIONS, PRÉCAUTIONS ET MISES EN GARDE

Contre-indications: Hypersensibilité.

Précautions et mises en garde: Patients ayant des tendances suicidaires ou prédisposés à la toxicomanie ■ Traumatisme crânien ■ Pression intracrânienne accrue ■ Maladies rénale, hépatique ou pulmonaire graves ■ Hypothyroïdie ■ Insuffisance surrénalienne ■ Patients qui font usage de tranquillisants ou d'antidépresseurs ■ Alcoolisme ■ Personnes âgées ou débilitées (il est recommandé de réduire la dose) ■ Douleurs abdominales non diagnostiquées ■ Hyperplasie de la prostate ■ **ALLAITEMENT:** Précédents d'utilisation sans danger, éviter l'administration prolongée ■ **OBST., PÉD.:** L'innocuité du médicament n'a pas été établie ■ Risque de pharmacodépendance et d'abus.

RÉACTIONS INDÉSIRABLES ET EFFETS SECONDAIRES

SNC: étourdissements, faiblesse, dysphorie, euphorie, céphalées, insomnie, excitation paradoxale, sédation.

ORLO: vision trouble.

CV: hypotension.

GI: nausées, douleurs abdominales, constipation, vomissements.

Tég.: rash.

Divers: dépendance physique, dépendance psychologique, tolérance aux effets du médicament.

INTERACTIONS

Médicament-médicament: RISQUE DE RÉACTIONS IMPRÉVISIBLES GRAVES, QUI PEUVENT MÊME ÊTRE MORTELLES, LORS DE L'ADMINISTRATION SIMULTANÉE D'**IMAO** – UNE GRANDE PRUDENCE EST DE MISE LORS D'UN TRAITEMENT CONCOMITANT (RÉDUIRE LA DOSE INITIALE DE PROPOXYPHÈNE À 25 % DE LA DOSE HABITUELLE) ■ Dépression additive du SNC et du système respiratoire lors de l'usage concomitant d'**alcool**, d'**antihistaminiques**, de **phénothiazines**, de **barbituriques**, d'**antidépresseurs**, d'**hypnosédatifs** et d'autres **opioïdes** ■ L'administration d'**analgésiques opioïdes agonistes/antagonistes** (**nalbuphine**, **butorphanol**, **pentazocine**) peut diminuer l'analgésie ou déclencher des symptômes de sevrage chez les patients présentant une dépendance physique aux analgésiques opioïdes ■ Le **tabac** (**nicotine**) accélère le métabolisme du propoxyphène et peut en diminuer l'effet analgésique.

P

Médicament-produits naturels: Effets dépresseurs additifs sur le SNC lors de la consommation concomitante de **kava**, de **valériane**, de **scutellaire**, de **camomille** et de **houblon**.

VOIES D'ADMINISTRATION ET POSOLOGIE

- **PO (adultes):** 100 mg, 3 ou 4 fois par jour, selon les besoins (ne pas dépasser 600 mg/jour).

PRÉSENTATION

Capsules: 100 mg[N].

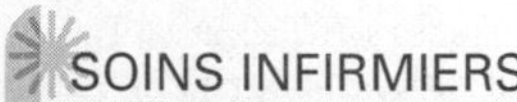

SOINS INFIRMIERS

ÉVALUATION DE LA SITUATION

- Évaluer le type de douleur, son siège et son intensité avant l'administration et 2 heures plus tard (pic). Lors de l'adaptation de la posologie, on devrait augmenter la dose par paliers de 25 à 50 % jusqu'à ce qu'on obtienne une réduction de 50 % de la douleur sur une échelle numérique ou analogique visuelle ou jusqu'à ce que le patient signale un soulagement adéquat de la douleur. On peut administrer sans danger une dose additionnelle lorsque la concentration de médicament atteint un pic, si la dose précédente s'est avérée inefficace et si les effets secondaires ont été minimes.
- On devrait se référer à un tableau des analgésiques équivalents (voir l'annexe A) lorsqu'on change de voie d'administration ou lorsqu'on substitue un type d'analgésique opioïde à un autre.
- Un traitement prolongé à des doses élevées peut entraîner la dépendance physique et psychologique ainsi que la tolérance aux effets du médicament. Cela ne doit cependant pas empêcher le patient de recevoir une quantité suffisante d'analgésique. La psychodépendance est rare chez la plupart des patients qui reçoivent le propoxyphène pour soulager la douleur. Lors d'un traitement prolongé, il faut parfois administrer des doses de plus en plus élevées ou recourir à un opioïde plus puissant pour soulager la douleur.
- ÉVALUER L'ÉTAT DE CONSCIENCE, MESURER LA PRESSION ARTÉRIELLE, LE POULS ET LA FRÉQUENCE DES RESPIRATIONS AVANT LE TRAITEMENT ET À INTERVALLES RÉGULIERS PENDANT TOUTE SA DURÉE. SI LA FRÉQUENCE RESPIRATOIRE EST INFÉRIEURE À 10 RESPIRATIONS PAR MINUTE, ÉVALUER LE NIVEAU DE SÉDATION. UNE STIMULATION PHYSIQUE PEUT SUFFIRE À PRÉVENIR L'HYPOVENTILATION. IL PEUT S'AVÉRER NÉCESSAIRE DE RÉDUIRE LA DOSE DE 25 À 50 %. LA SOMNOLENCE INITIALE S'ESTOMPERA LORS D'UN USAGE PROLONGÉ.

GÉR.: Évaluer les patients âgés à intervalles fréquents, car ils sont plus sensibles aux effets des analgésiques opioïdes que les adultes plus jeunes; chez eux, les effets indésirables et les complications respiratoires peuvent être plus fréquents.

- Évaluer le fonctionnement des intestins à intervalles réguliers. Pour prévenir la constipation, il faut accroître l'apport en liquides et en fibres et administrer des laxatifs. Il faudrait administrer systématiquement des laxatifs stimulants lorsque le traitement par les opioïdes dure plus de 2 ou 3 jours, à moins que leur usage ne soit contre-indiqué.

Tests de laboratoire:

- Le propoxyphène peut entraîner l'élévation des concentrations sériques d'amylase et de lipase.
- Le médicament peut entraîner l'élévation des concentrations d'AST, d'ALT, de phosphatase alcaline sérique, de LDH et de bilirubine.

TOXICITÉ ET SURDOSAGE: Si un opioïde antagoniste est nécessaire pour renverser la dépression respiratoire ou le coma, l'antidote est la naloxone (Narcan). Diluer le contenu d'une ampoule de 0,4 mg de naloxone dans 10 mL de solution de NaCl 0,9 % et administrer 0,5 mL (0,02 mg) par IV directe, toutes les 2 minutes. Dans le cas des patients < 40 kg, diluer 0,1 mg de naloxone dans 10 mL de solution de NaCl 0,9% pour obtenir une concentration de 10 µg/mL et administrer 0,5 µg/kg, toutes les 2 minutes. Adapter la dose pour prévenir les symptômes de sevrage, les convulsions et la douleur intense.

DIAGNOSTICS INFIRMIERS POSSIBLES

- Douleur aiguë (Indications).
- Trouble de la perception visuelle et auditive (Effets secondaires).
- Risque d'accident (Effets secondaires).

INTERVENTIONS INFIRMIÈRES

ALERTE CLINIQUE: DES SURDOSES ACCIDENTELLES D'ANALGÉSIQUES OPIOÏDES ONT CAUSÉ DES DÉCÈS. ÉVALUER L'UTILISATION ANTÉRIEURE D'ANALGÉSIQUES OPIOÏDES PAR LE PATIENT ET SES BESOINS COURANTS. AVANT L'ADMINISTRATION, CLARIFIER TOUTES LES AMBIGÜITÉS DE L'ORDONNANCE ET FAIRE VÉRIFIER L'ORDONNANCE D'ORIGINE ET LE CALCUL DES DOSES PAR UN AUTRE PROFESSIONNEL DE LA SANTÉ.

- Pour augmenter l'effet analgésique du propoxyphène, expliquer au patient la valeur thérapeutique du médicament avant de l'administrer.

P

- Les doses administrées selon un horaire fixe peuvent être plus efficaces que celles administrées sur demande. Le médicament s'avère plus efficace s'il est administré avant que la douleur ne devienne intense.
- Les analgésiques non opioïdes, administrés simultanément, peuvent exercer des effets analgésiques additionnels, ce qui permet parfois de diminuer les doses d'opioïde.
- Après un traitement prolongé, interrompre l'administration graduellement pour prévenir les symptômes de sevrage.

PO: On peut administrer le propoxyphène avec des aliments ou du lait pour réduire l'irritation gastrique.

ENSEIGNEMENT AU PATIENT ET À SES PROCHES

- Recommander au patient de prendre le médicament tel qu'il lui a été prescrit et de ne pas prendre une dose plus élevée que celle recommandée.
- Expliquer au patient comment et à quel moment il doit réclamer l'analgésique.
- Prévenir le patient que le propoxyphène peut parfois provoquer de la somnolence ou des étourdissements. Lui conseiller de ne pas conduire et d'éviter les activités qui exigent sa vigilance jusqu'à ce qu'on ait la certitude que le médicament n'entraîne pas ces effets chez lui.

GÉR.: Informer les personnes âgées du risque accru de chutes et d'effets indésirables sur le SNC.

- Recommander au patient de changer lentement de position pour diminuer le risque d'hypotension orthostatique.
- Recommander au patient d'éviter de boire de l'alcool ou de prendre d'autres dépresseurs du SNC en même temps que le propoxyphène.
- Recommander au patient de tourner dans le lit, de tousser et de faire des exercices de respiration profonde toutes les 2 heures pour prévenir l'atélectasie.
- Conseiller au patient de se rincer fréquemment la bouche, de pratiquer une bonne hygiène buccale et de consommer de la gomme à mâcher ou des bonbons sans sucre pour soulager la sécheresse de la bouche.
- Insister sur l'importance de la prévention de la constipation associée à la prise d'analgésiques opioïdes.

VÉRIFICATION DE L'EFFICACITÉ THÉRAPEUTIQUE

L'efficacité du traitement peut être démontrée par: la diminution de l'intensité de la douleur sans modification importante de l'état de conscience. ✳

ALERTE CLINIQUE

PROPRANOLOL

Apo-Propranolol, Dom-Propranolol, Inderal, Inderal LA, Novo-Pranol, Propranolol

CLASSIFICATION:

Antiangineux, antiarythmique (classe II), antihypertenseur (bêtabloquant)

Grossesse - catégories C (1er trimestre) et D (2e et 3e trimestres)

INDICATIONS

Traitement de l'hypertension ■ Prophylaxie de l'angine de poitrine ■ Traitement des arythmies ■ Traitement post-infarctus du myocarde ■ Prophylaxie de la migraine ■ Adjuvant dans le traitement du phéochromocytome ■ Traitement des tremblements essentiels ■ Traitement de la sténose sous-aortique hypertrophique. **Usages non approuvés**: Traitement de l'akathisie associée aux neuroleptiques ■ Traitement de l'anxiété réactionnelle ■ Prévention primaire ou secondaire des hémorragies variqueuses œsophagiennes.

MÉCANISME D'ACTION

Inhibition de la stimulation des récepteurs bêta$_1$-adrénergiques (myocardiques) et bêta$_2$-adrénergiques (pulmonaires, vasculaires et utérins). ***Effets thérapeutiques:*** Réduction de la fréquence cardiaque et de la pression artérielle ■ Suppression des arythmies ■ Prévention de l'infarctus du myocarde.

PHARMACOCINÉTIQUE

Absorption: Bonne, mais important métabolisme hépatique de premier passage (PO).

Distribution: L'agent pénètre dans le SNC. Il traverse la barrière placentaire et passe dans le lait maternel.

Liaison aux protéines: 93 %.

Métabolisme et excrétion: Métabolisme hépatique important (un métabolite est actif). Excrétion rénale (principalement sous forme de métabolites).

Demi-vie: De 3 à 6 heures.

Profil temps-action (effets cardiovasculaires)

	DÉBUT D'ACTION	PIC	DURÉE
PO	30 min	60 - 90 min†	6 - 12 h
PO-LP‡	inconnu	6 h	24 h
IV	immédiat	1 min	4 - 6 h

† Suivant l'administration d'une dose unique; l'effet maximal ne sera observé qu'après quelques semaines de traitement.

‡ LP = libération prolongée.

P

CONTRE-INDICATIONS, PRÉCAUTIONS ET MISES EN GARDE

Contre-indications: Hypersensibilité ■ Insuffisance cardiaque, à moins qu'elle ne soit secondaire à une tachyarythmie pouvant être traitée par le propranolol ■ Insuffisance ventriculaire droite secondaire à une hypertension pulmonaire ■ Œdème pulmonaire ■ Choc cardiogénique ■ Bradycardie sinusale ■ Bloc AV du 2e ou du 3e degré ■ Bronchospasme, incluant l'asthme et la bronchopneumopathie chronique obstructive ■ Rhinite allergique au cours de la saison pollinique ■ Maladie de Raynaud.

Précautions et mises en garde: Insuffisance rénale ■ Insuffisance hépatique ■ **GÉR.**: Il est recommandé de réduire la dose chez les personnes âgées ou débilitées (sensibilité accrue aux bêtabloquants) ■ Diabète (le médicament peut masquer les signes d'hypoglycémie) ■ Thyrotoxicose (le médicament peut en masquer les symptômes) ■ Antécédents de réactions allergiques graves (le médicament peut accroître l'intensité des réactions) ■ **OBST., ALLAITEMENT**: L'innocuité du médicament n'a pas été établie chez la femme enceinte ou qui allaite (l'agent traverse la barrière placentaire et passe dans le lait maternel) ■ **PÉD.**: L'efficacité et l'innocuité du médicament n'ont pas été établies.

RÉACTIONS INDÉSIRABLES ET EFFETS SECONDAIRES

SNC: fatigue, faiblesse, anxiété, étourdissements, somnolence, insomnie, perte de mémoire, dépression, modification des opérations de la pensée, nervosité, cauchemars.

ORLO: vision trouble, xérophtalmie, congestion nasale.

Resp.: bronchospasme, respiration sifflante.

CV: ARYTHMIES, BRADYCARDIE, INSUFFISANCE CARDIAQUE, ŒDÈME PULMONAIRE, hypotension orthostatique, vasoconstriction périphérique.

GI: constipation, diarrhée, nausées.

GU: impuissance, baisse de la libido.

Tég.: démangeaisons, rash.

End.: hyperglycémie, hypoglycémie.

Loc.: arthralgie, douleurs lombaires, crampes musculaires.

SN: paresthésie.

Divers: syndrome lupique d'origine médicamenteuse.

INTERACTIONS

Médicament-médicament: Une **anesthésie générale**, ainsi que le **diltiazem** et le **vérapamil**, administrés simultanément, peuvent provoquer une dépression additive du myocarde ■ Risque de bradycardie additive lors de l'administration concomitante de **dérivés digitaliques** ■ Risque d'hypotension additive lors de l'administration simultanée d'autres **antihypertenseurs** ou de **dérivés nitrés** ou lors de l'ingestion de grandes quantités d'**alcool** ■ Les **amphétamines**, la **cocaïne**, l'**éphédrine**, l'**adrénaline**, la **phényléphrine** ou la **pseudoéphédrine**, prises simultanément, peuvent entraîner une hypertension et une bradycardie excessive ■ Le médicament peut entraver l'efficacité de l'**insuline** ou des **hypoglycémiants oraux** (une adaptation posologique peut s'avérer nécessaire) ■ Le propanolol peut réduire l'efficacité des **bronchodilatateurs bêta-adrénergiques** ■ Le propranolol peut diminuer les effets bénéfiques sur les récepteurs bêtacardiaques de la **dopamine** ou de la **dobutamine** ■ La prudence est de mise lorsque le propranolol est administré dans les 14 jours suivant un traitement par un **IMAO** (risque d'hypertension) ■ La **cimétidine** peut accroître la toxicité associée au propranolol ■ Les **AINS** peuvent diminuer l'effet antihypertenseur du propranolol.

VOIES D'ADMINISTRATION ET POSOLOGIE

- **PO (adultes)**: *Antiangineux* – initialement, de 20 à 40 mg, 2 fois par jour. En présence d'une réponse satisfaisante après 7 jours, on peut porter la dose à 80 mg, 2 fois par jour (écart posologique habituel: de 80 à 320 mg par jour, en 2 à 4 doses fractionnées). *Antihypertenseur* – initialement 40 mg, 2 fois par jour ou 80 mg, 1 fois par jour sous forme de capsule à libération prolongée; on peut augmenter la dose en l'espace de 1 semaine, pour la passer à 80 mg, 2 fois par jour, ou à 160 mg, 1 fois par jour sous forme de capsule à libération prolongée (écart posologique habituel: de 160 à 320 mg par jour). *Antiarythmique* – de 10 à 30 mg, 3 ou 4 fois par jour. *Traitement post-infarctus du myocarde* – initialement, 40 mg, 3 fois par jour. Après 1 à 2 semaines, on peut porter la dose à 60 mg ou à 80 mg, 3 fois par jour (écart posologique habituel: de 180 à 240 mg par jour, en 2 à 4 doses fractionnées). *Sténose sous-aortique hypertrophique* – de 20 à 40 mg, 3 ou 4 fois par jour. *Phéochromocytome* – avant l'opération: 60 mg par jour, en doses égales en même temps qu'un alphabloquant qu'on commencera à administrer 3 jours avant la date prévue de l'intervention chirurgicale. *Prévention de la migraine* – initialement 40 mg, 2 fois par jour; on peut augmenter cette dose selon la réponse au traitement et la tolérance du patient jusqu'à concurrence de 160 mg par jour (écart posologique habituel: de 80 à 160 mg par jour, en 1 à 4 doses fractionnées). *Traitement des tremblements* – 40 mg, 2 fois par jour; on peut augmenter la dose selon la réponse au traitement et la tolérance du patient jusqu'à concurrence de 160 mg par jour (écart posologique habituel: de 120 à 320 mg par jour, en 3 doses fractionnées).

- **PO (enfants):** *Antiarythmique* – de 0,5 à 1 mg/kg par jour, en 3 ou 4 doses fractionnées; on peut augmenter la dose à intervalle de 3 à 7 jours selon la réponse au traitement et la tolérance du patient (écart posologique habituel: de 2 à 6 mg/kg par jour en doses fractionnées). Dose maximale: 16 mg/kg par jour, sans dépasser 60 mg, en 4 doses fractionnées. *Antihypertenseur* – de 0,5 à 1 mg/kg par jour, en 2 doses fractionnées; on doit adapter la dose selon l'efficacité du traitement et la tolérance du patient (écart posologique habituel: de 2 à 4 mg/kg par jour, en 2 doses fractionnées). Dose maximale: 16 mg/kg par jour. *Prévention de la migraine* – de 2 à 4 mg/kg par jour, ou de 10 à 20 mg, 3 fois par jour, si le poids ≤ 35 kg, ou de 20 à 40 mg, 3 fois par jour, si le poids > 35 kg.
- **IV (adultes):** *Antiarythmique* – de 1 à 3 mg; on peut répéter l'administration 2 minutes plus tard, puis 4 heures plus tard, si besoin est (posologie maximale: 1 mg/min).

PRÉSENTATION
(version générique disponible)

Comprimés: 10 mg^Pr^, 20 mg^Pr^, 40 mg^Pr^, 80 mg^Pr^, 120 mg^Pr^ ■ **Capsules à libération prolongée:** 60 mg^Pr^, 80 mg^Pr^, 120 mg^Pr^, 160 mg^Pr^ ■ **Solution pour injection:** 1 mg/mL^Pr^.

SOINS INFIRMIERS

ÉVALUATION DE LA SITUATION

- Mesurer la pression artérielle et le pouls à intervalles fréquents pendant la période d'adaptation de la posologie et à intervalles réguliers pendant toute la durée du traitement. Suivre de près l'hypotension orthostatique lorsqu'on aide le patient à se lever.
- CHEZ LES PATIENTS RECEVANT LE PROPANOLOL PAR VOIE IV, EXAMINER CONTINUELLEMENT LE TRACÉ DE L'ÉCG ET MESURER LA PRESSION CAPILLAIRE PULMONAIRE OU LA PRESSION VEINEUSE CENTRALE PENDANT L'ADMINISTRATION ET PENDANT PLUSIEURS HEURES APRÈS.
- EFFECTUER LE BILAN QUOTIDIEN DES INGESTA ET DES EXCRETA ET PESER LE PATIENT TOUS LES JOURS. OBSERVER RÉGULIÈREMENT LE PATIENT À LA RECHERCHE DES SIGNES ET DES SYMPTÔMES SUIVANTS DE SURCHARGE LIQUIDIENNE: ŒDÈME PÉRIPHÉRIQUE, DYSPNÉE, RÂLES OU CRÉPITATIONS, FATIGUE, GAIN PONDÉRAL, TURGESCENCE DES JUGULAIRES.

Angine: Noter la fréquence et la durée des épisodes de douleurs thoraciques à intervalles réguliers pendant toute la durée du traitement.

Prophylaxie des céphalées vasculaires: Noter la fréquence, la gravité, les caractéristiques et le siège des céphalées vasculaires à intervalles réguliers pendant toute la durée du traitement.

Tests de laboratoire:

- Le propranolol peut entraîner l'élévation de l'urée et des concentrations sériques de lipoprotéines, de potassium, de triglycérides et d'acide urique.
- Il peut provoquer une élévation ou une baisse de la glycémie. Chez les patients atteints de diabète labile, l'hypoglycémie peut s'accompagner d'une élévation soudaine de la pression artérielle.

TOXICITÉ ET SURDOSAGE:

- Suivre de près les patients recevant des bêtabloquants afin de déceler les signes suivants de surdosage: bradycardie, étourdissements graves ou évanouissements, somnolence prononcée, dyspnée, ongles ou paumes des mains bleutés, convulsions. Communiquer immédiatement avec un médecin ou un autre professionnel de la santé si ces signes se manifestent.
- On peut traiter l'hypotension en plaçant le patient en position de Tredelenberg et en lui administrant des liquides par voie IV, sauf contre-indication. On peut aussi administrer des vasopresseurs (adrénaline, noradrénaline, dopamine, dobutamine). L'hypotension ne répond pas aux agonistes bêta.
- On a déjà administré du glucagon pour traiter la bradycardie et l'hypotension.

P

DIAGNOSTICS INFIRMIERS POSSIBLES

- Débit cardiaque diminué (Effets secondaires).
- Connaissances insuffisantes sur le traitement médicamenteux (Enseignement au patient et à ses proches).
- Non-observance du traitement médicamenteux (Enseignement au patient et à ses proches).

INTERVENTIONS INFIRMIÈRES

ALERTE CLINIQUE: L'ADMINISTRATION PAR VOIE IV DES MÉDICAMENTS VASOACTIFS COMPORTE UN RISQUE PAR ELLE-MÊME. LES DOSES ADMINISTRÉES PAR VOIE ORALE ET PARENTÉRALE NE SONT PAS INTERCHANGEABLES. VÉRIFIER ATTENTIVEMENT LA DOSE À ADMINISTRER. LA DOSE PAR VOIE IV ÉQUIVAUT À $^1/_{10}$ DE LA DOSE PAR VOIE ORALE. ON PEUT L'ADMINISTRER SI LE PATIENT NE PEUT RIEN PRENDRE PAR LA BOUCHE. AVANT L'ADMINISTRATION, FAIRE VALIDER L'ORDONNANCE D'ORIGINE ET LE CALCUL DE LA DOSE PAR UN DEUXIÈME PROFESSIONNEL DE LA SANTÉ.

- NE PAS CONFONDRE LE PROPRANOLOL AVEC PRAVACHOL (PRAVASTATINE).
- NE PAS CONFONDRE INDERAL (PROPRANOLOL) AVEC ADDERALL (AMPHÉTAMINE/DEXTROAMPHÉTAMINE).

- NE PAS CONFONDRE INDERAL (PROPRANOLOL) AVEC IMDUR (MONONITRATE D'ISOSORBIDE).

PO:

- Mesurer le pouls à l'apex du cœur avant d'administrer le médicament. S'il est < 50 battements par minute ou s'il y a arythmie, ne pas administrer le propranolol et en avertir le médecin ou un autre professionnel de la santé.
- Administrer le médicament avec des aliments ou immédiatement après les repas pour améliorer l'absorption.
- LES CAPSULES À LIBÉRATION PROLONGÉE DOIVENT ÊTRE AVALÉES TELLES QUELLES; IL NE FAUT PAS LES ÉCRASER, LES OUVRIR OU LES MÂCHER. On peut écraser les *comprimés ordinaires* de propranolol et les mélanger à des aliments.

IV directe: Administrer le propranolol non dilué ou diluer chaque mg dans 10 mL de solution de D5%E pour injection.

Vitesse d'administration: Administrer en au moins 1 minute.

Perfusion intermittente: On peut aussi diluer le médicament destiné à la perfusion dans 50 mL de solution de NaCl 0,9 %, de D5%E, de D5%/NaCl 0,45 %, de D5%/NaCl 0,9 % ou de lactate de Ringer pour injection. Consulter les directives de chaque fabricant avant de reconstituer la préparation.

Vitesse d'administration: Perfuser en 10 à 15 minutes.

Compatibilité dans la même seringue: amrinone ■ milrinone.

Compatibilité (tubulure en Y): alteplase ■ amrinone ■ héparine ■ hydrocortisone sodique, succinate d' ■ mépéridine ■ milrinone ■ morphine ■ potassium, chlorure de ■ tacrolimus ■ vitamines du complexe B avec C.

Incompatibilité (tubulure en Y): diazoxyde.

ENSEIGNEMENT AU PATIENT ET À SES PROCHES

- Prévenir le patient qu'il doit prendre le propranolol tous les jours, à la même heure, en suivant rigoureusement les recommandations du médecin. Lui expliquer qu'il doit continuer à prendre le médicament même s'il se sent bien. L'avertir qu'il ne doit jamais sauter de dose ni remplacer une dose manquée par une double dose. S'il n'a pu prendre le médicament au moment habituel, il doit le prendre aussitôt que possible, mais au moins 4 heures avant l'heure prévue pour la dose suivante (8 heures, dans le cas du médicament à libération prolongée). LE PRÉVENIR ÉGALEMENT QUE LE SEVRAGE BRUSQUE PEUT PROVOQUER DES ARYTHMIES METTANT SA VIE EN DANGER, L'HYPERTENSION OU L'ISCHÉMIE DU MYOCARDE.
- Conseiller au patient de disposer d'une réserve suffisante de médicament pour les fins de semaine, les congés et les vacances. Lui conseiller également de conserver une ordonnance dans son portefeuille pour parer à toute urgence.
- Expliquer au patient et à ses proches comment prendre le pouls et la pression artérielle. Leur demander de mesurer le pouls tous les jours et la pression artérielle 2 fois par semaine. Si le pouls est inférieur à 50 battements par minute ou si la pression artérielle varie de façon importante, leur conseiller d'en informer un professionnel de la santé.
- Prévenir le patient que le propranolol peut parfois provoquer des étourdissements. Lui conseiller de ne pas conduire et d'éviter les activités qui exigent sa vigilance jusqu'à ce qu'on ait la certitude que le médicament n'entraîne pas cet effet chez lui.
- Conseiller au patient de changer lentement de position pour réduire le risque d'hypotension orthostatique, particulièrement au début du traitement ou lors de la majoration de la dose.
- Prévenir le patient que le médicament peut le rendre plus sensible au froid.
- Conseiller au patient de consulter un professionnel de la santé avant de prendre des médicaments en vente libre, particulièrement des préparations contre le rhume, ou des produits naturels en même temps que le propranolol.
- Recommander au patient diabétique de mesurer sa glycémie, particulièrement lorsqu'il se sent fatigué, faible ou irritable ou lorsqu'il ressent un malaise. Le propranolol peut masquer certains signes et symptômes d'hypoglycémie. Cependant, des étourdissements et des sueurs peuvent continuer de survenir.
- Recommander au patient de signaler à un professionnel de la santé les symptômes suivants: ralentissement du pouls, difficultés respiratoires, respiration sifflante, mains et pieds froids, étourdissements, sensation de tête légère, confusion, dépression, rash, fièvre, maux de gorge, saignements inhabituels ou formation d'ecchymoses.
- Recommander au patient qui doit suivre un autre traitement ou subir une intervention chirurgicale d'avertir le professionnel de la santé qu'il prend du propranolol.
- Conseiller au patient de porter sur lui en tout temps une pièce d'identité où sont inscrits son problème de santé et sa médication.

Hypertension: Inciter le patient à appliquer d'autres mesures de réduction de l'hypertension: perdre du poids, réduire sa consommation de sel, diminuer le stress, faire régulièrement de l'exercice, boire de l'alcool avec modération et cesser de fumer. Lui expliquer que le propranolol stabilise la pression artérielle, mais ne guérit pas l'hypertension.

Angine: Prévenir le patient qu'il ne doit pas faire d'efforts excessifs même si ses douleurs de poitrine diminuent.

Prophylaxie de la migraine: Informer le patient qu'il peut être dangereux de donner ce médicament à d'autres personnes.

VÉRIFICATION DE L'EFFICACITÉ THÉRAPEUTIQUE

L'efficacité du traitement peut être démontrée par: la baisse de la pression artérielle ▪ la maîtrise des arythmies, sans manifestation d'effets indésirables ▪ la diminution de la fréquence des crises d'angine ▪ une tolérance accrue à l'effort ▪ la prévention des infarctus du myocarde ▪ la prévention des migraines ▪ la maîtrise de l'hypertension et de la tachycardie associées au phéochromocytome ▪ la diminution des tremblements ▪ la maîtrise de la cardiomyopathie hypertrophique. ✳

PROPYLTHIOURACILE

Propyl-Thyracile

CLASSIFICATION:

Antithyroïdien

Grossesse – catégorie D

INDICATIONS

Pharmacothérapie de l'hyperthyroïdie ▪ Traitement d'appoint visant à maîtriser la thyrotoxicose en préparation à une thyroïdectomie ou à un traitement par de l'iode radioactif ▪ Traitement d'une crise thyroïdienne aiguë conjointement à d'autres mesures thérapeutiques.

MÉCANISME D'ACTION

Inhibition de la synthèse des hormones thyroïdiennes. ***Effets thérapeutiques:*** Diminution des signes et des symptômes d'hyperthyroïdie.

PHARMACOCINÉTIQUE

Absorption: Rapide (PO).

Distribution: Le médicament se concentre dans la glande thyroïde. Il traverse la barrière placentaire et passe dans le lait maternel en faibles concentrations.

Métabolisme et excrétion: Métabolisme hépatique.

Demi-vie: De 1 à 2 heures.

Profil temps-action (effets sur l'état clinique de la thyroïde)

	DÉBUT D'ACTION	PIC	DURÉE
PO	10 – 21 jours†	6 – 10 semaines	plusieurs semaines

† Les effets sur les concentrations sériques d'hormones thyroïdiennes peuvent se produire en l'espace de 60 minutes après l'administration d'une dose unique.

CONTRE-INDICATIONS, PRÉCAUTIONS ET MISES EN GARDE

Contre-indications: Hypersensibilité ▪ Allaitement.

Précautions et mises en garde: Aplasie médullaire ▪ OBST.: Grossesse (précédents d'administration sans danger; toutefois, des troubles thyroïdiens peuvent se manifester chez le fœtus).

RÉACTIONS INDÉSIRABLES ET EFFETS SECONDAIRES

SNC: somnolence, céphalées, vertiges.

GI: nausées, vomissements, diarrhée, hépatite médicamenteuse, perte du goût.

Tég.: rash, changement de couleur de la peau, urticaire.

End.: hypothyroïdie.

Hémat.: AGRANULOCYTOSE, leucopénie, thrombopénie.

Loc.: arthralgie.

Divers: fièvre, lymphadénopathie, parotidite.

INTERACTIONS

Médicament-médicament: Aplasie médullaire additive lors de l'administration simultanée d'**agents antinéoplasiques** ou d'une **radiothérapie** ▪ Le **lithium**, l'**iodure de potassium** ou l'**iodure de sodium**, administrés simultanément, intensifient l'effet antithyroïdien ▪ Risque accru d'agranulocytose lors de l'administration simultanée de **phénothiazines** ▪ Le propylthiouracile peut modifier l'effet de la **warfarine** et de la **digoxine**.

P

VOIES D'ADMINISTRATION ET POSOLOGIE

Le traitement peut durer de 6 mois à plusieurs années; habituellement, la durée moyenne est de 1 an.

- **PO (adultes)**: *Dose d'attaque* – de 50 à 100 mg, toutes les 8 heures, en augmentant la dose au besoin jusqu'à concurrence de 500 mg par jour. (On a déjà administré jusqu'à 900 mg/jour.) Lorsque la dose quotidienne est supérieure à 300 mg, on doit la fractionner et l'administrer toutes les 4 à 6 heures. *Dose d'entretien* – 50 mg, 2 ou 3 fois par jour, en prises également espacées.
- **PO (enfants > 10 ans)**: *Dose d'attaque* – 150 mg/m^2/jour. *Dose d'entretien* – de 150 à 300 mg par jour, en doses fractionnées également espacées.
- **PO (enfants de 6 à 10 ans)**: De 50 à 150 mg par jour, en doses fractionnées également espacées.

Insuffisance rénale

- Cl_{CR} *de 10 à 50 mL/min* – administrer 75 % de la dose; Cl_{CR} < *10 mL/min* – administrer 50 % de la dose.

PRÉSENTATION

Comprimés: 50 mg^Pr^, 100 mg^Pr^.

SOINS INFIRMIERS

ÉVALUATION DE LA SITUATION

- Suivre de près la réponse du patient pour déceler les symptômes suivants d'hyperthyroïdie ou de thyrotoxicose: tachycardie, palpitations, nervosité, insomnie, fièvre, diaphorèse, intolérance à la chaleur, tremblements, perte de poids, diarrhée.
- Suivre de près le patient pour déceler l'apparition de l'hypothyroïdie: intolérance au froid, constipation, peau sèche, céphalées, apragmatisme, fatigue ou faiblesse. Une adaptation de la posologie peut s'avérer nécessaire.
- Suivre de près l'apparition du rash ou d'une tuméfaction des ganglions lymphatiques du cou. Si ces symptômes se manifestent, il peut s'avérer nécessaire de cesser le traitement.

Tests de laboratoire:

- Examiner les résultats des tests de la fonction thyroïdienne avant le traitement, puis tous les mois au cours du traitement initial et, par la suite, tous les 2 à 3 mois pendant toute la durée du traitement.
- Noter le nombre de globules blancs et la formule leucocytaire à intervalles réguliers pendant toute la durée du traitement. L'agranulocytose peut survenir rapidement. Elle se manifeste habituellement au cours des 2 premiers mois. Le cas échéant, il faut arrêter le traitement.
- Le propylthiouracile peut élever les concentrations d'AST, d'ALT, de LDH, de phosphatase alcaline et de bilirubine sérique et allonger le temps de prothrombine.

P

DIAGNOSTICS INFIRMIERS POSSIBLES

- Connaissances insuffisantes sur le traitement médicamenteux (Enseignement au patient et à ses proches).
- Non-observance du traitement médicamenteux (Enseignement au patient et à ses proches).

INTERVENTIONS INFIRMIÈRES

- Le pharmacien peut intégrer le médicament dans un lavement ou dans un suppositoire lorsque le patient ne peut le prendre par voie orale.
- Administrer le médicament au même moment tous les jours par rapport à l'heure des repas. Les aliments peuvent augmenter ou diminuer l'absorption du médicament.

ENSEIGNEMENT AU PATIENT ET À SES PROCHES

- Conseiller au patient de suivre rigoureusement la posologie recommandée et de prendre le propylthiouracile à intervalles réguliers. S'il n'a pas pu prendre le médicament au moment habituel, il doit le prendre dès que possible; s'il est presque l'heure prévue pour la dose suivante, il devrait prendre les 2 doses ensemble. Conseiller au patient de consulter un professionnel de la santé s'il n'a pu prendre plus de 1 dose ou s'il veut arrêter le traitement.
- Conseiller au patient de se peser 2 ou 3 fois par semaine et de prévenir un professionnel de la santé si des changements importants surviennent.
- Prévenir le patient que le propylthiouracile peut parfois provoquer de la somnolence. Lui conseiller de ne pas conduire et d'éviter les activités qui exigent sa vigilance jusqu'à ce qu'on ait la certitude que le médicament n'entraîne pas cet effet chez lui.
- Recommander au patient de consulter un professionnel de la santé au sujet des sources alimentaires d'iode: sel iodé, crustacés.
- Recommander au patient de signaler rapidement à un professionnel de la santé les maux de gorge, la fièvre, les frissons, les céphalées, les malaises, la faiblesse, le jaunissement des yeux ou de la peau, les saignements ou les ecchymoses inhabituels, le rash ou les symptômes d'hyperthyroïdie ou d'hypothyroïdie.
- Conseiller au patient de consulter un professionnel de la santé avant de prendre un médicament en vente libre ou des produits naturels en même temps que cet agent.
- Inciter le patient à porter sur lui en tout temps une pièce d'identité où est inscrit son traitement médicamenteux. Recommander au patient qui doit suivre un autre traitement ou subir une intervention chirurgicale d'avertir le professionnel de la santé qu'il suit un traitement avec ce médicament.
- Insister sur l'importance des examens réguliers de suivi permettant d'évaluer l'évolution de la maladie et de vérifier les effets secondaires du traitement.

VÉRIFICATION DE L'EFFICACITÉ THÉRAPEUTIQUE

L'efficacité du traitement peut être démontrée par: la diminution de la gravité des symptômes d'hyperthyroïdie (diminution de la fréquence du pouls et gain de poids) ■ la normalisation des résultats des tests de la fonction thyroïdienne.

PROTAMINE, SULFATE DE

Protamine, sulfate de

CLASSIFICATION:

Antidote (antagoniste de l'héparine)

Grossesse – catégorie C

INDICATIONS

Traitement du surdosage en héparine. **Usages non approuvés**: Traitement du surdosage par des composés de type héparine.

MÉCANISME D'ACTION

Base forte formant un complexe avec l'héparine (acide). ***Effets thérapeutiques:*** Inactivation de l'héparine.

PHARMACOCINÉTIQUE

Absorption: Biodisponibilité à 100 % (IV).
Distribution: Inconnue.
Métabolisme et excrétion: Inconnus. Le complexe protamine-héparine finit par se décomposer.
Demi-vie: Inconnue.

Profil temps-action (renversement de l'effet de l'héparine)

	DÉBUT D'ACTION	PIC	DURÉE
IV	30 – 60 s	inconnu	2 h†

† Selon la température du corps.

CONTRE-INDICATIONS, PRÉCAUTIONS ET MISES EN GARDE

Contre-indications: Antécédents d'intolérance ou d'hypersensibilité à la protamine.
Précautions et mises en garde: Patients allergiques aux produits de poisson ▪ Patients ayant reçu précédemment de l'insuline contenant de la protamine ou hommes stériles ou ayant subi une vasectomie (risque accru de réactions d'hypersensibilité) ▪ Une administration trop rapide peut entraîner des réactions hypotensives et anaphylactoïdes ▪ **OBST., ALLAITEMENT, PÉD.**: L'innocuité du médicament n'a pas été établie.

RÉACTIONS INDÉSIRABLES ET EFFETS SECONDAIRES

Resp.: dyspnée.
CV: bradycardie, hypertension, hypotension, hypertension pulmonaire.
GI: nausées, vomissements.
Tég.: bouffées vasomotrices, sensation de chaleur.
Hémat.: saignements.
Loc.: douleurs lombaires.
Divers: réactions d'hypersensibilité, incluant l'ANAPHYLAXIE, l'ŒDÈME ANGIONEUROTIQUE et l'ŒDÈME PULMONAIRE.

INTERACTIONS

Médicament-médicament: Aucune interaction notable.

VOIES D'ADMINISTRATION ET POSOLOGIE

Surdosage de l'héparine

- **IV (adultes et enfants)**: Chaque mg de protamine neutralise environ 90 unités d'héparine provenant de tissus pulmonaires de bœuf et environ 115 unités d'héparine provenant de la muqueuse intestinale de porc. Si on administre le sulfate de protamine plus de 30 minutes après l'héparine, la moitié de la dose habituelle peut suffire. Les doses ultérieures doivent être établies d'après les études de coagulation. ***Surdosage de l'énoxapramine*** – 1 mg par mg d'énoxapramine à neutraliser *(usage non approuvé)*. ***Surdosage de daltéparine*** – 1 mg par 100 UI anti-Xa de daltéparine. Si une deuxième dose est nécessaire, on peut administrer 0,5 mg par 100 UI anti-Xa de daltéparine, de 2 à 4 heures plus tard, si les épreuves de laboratoire en indiquent la nécessité *(usage non approuvé)*.

PRÉSENTATION

Solution pour injection: 10 mg/mL, en fioles de 5 mL[Pr] et de 25 mL[Pr].

SOINS INFIRMIERS

ÉVALUATION DE LA SITUATION

- Suivre de près les saignements et les hémorragies pendant toute la durée du traitement. L'hémorragie peut récidiver de 8 à 9 heures après le traitement en raison des effets rebond de l'héparine. Les effets rebond peuvent se manifester jusqu'à 18 heures après la fin du traitement chez les patients héparinisés lors des interventions nécessitant l'établissement d'une circulation extracorporelle.
- DÉTERMINER SI LE PATIENT EST ALLERGIQUE AUX PRODUITS DE POISSON (SAUMON) OU S'IL A DES ANTÉCÉDENTS DE RÉACTION À L'INSULINE CONTENANT DE LA PROTAMINE OU DU SULFATE DE PROTAMINE. LES HOMMES VASECTOMISÉS OU STÉRILES SONT DAVANTAGE PRÉDISPOSÉS AUX RÉACTIONS D'HYPERSENSIBILITÉ.
- SUIVRE DE PRÈS LES SIGNES ET LES SYMPTÔMES SUIVANTS DE RÉACTIONS D'HYPERSENSIBILITÉ: URTICAIRE, ŒDÈME, TOUX, RESPIRATION SIFFLANTE. GARDER À LA PORTÉE DE LA MAIN DE L'ADRÉNALINE, UN

P

ANTIHISTAMINIQUE ET LE MATÉRIEL DE RÉANIMATION POUR POUVOIR PARER À TOUTE RÉACTION D'ANAPHYLAXIE.
- Déceler l'hypovolémie avant le début du traitement. Si l'hypovolémie n'est pas corrigée, il y a risque de collapsus cardiovasculaire en raison des effets vasodilatateurs périphériques du sulfate de protamine.

Tests de laboratoire: Mesurer les facteurs de coagulation, le temps de coagulation activée, le temps de céphaline activée (TCA) et le temps de thrombine (TT), de 5 à 15 minutes après la fin du traitement et à d'autres reprises, selon les besoins.

DIAGNOSTICS INFIRMIERS POSSIBLES

- Risque d'accident (Indications).
- Atteinte à l'intégrité des tissus (Indications).

INTERVENTIONS INFIRMIÈRES

- Arrêter la perfusion d'héparine. Lorsque le surdosage est léger, on peut traiter le patient en arrêtant simplement l'administration d'héparine.
- Pour juguler l'hémorragie en cas de fort surdosage, il faut parfois administrer également du plasma frais congelé ou du sang entier.
- Les doses varient selon le type d'héparine administrée, la voie d'administration de l'héparine et le temps écoulé depuis qu'on a arrêté l'administration de cet agent.
- Ne pas administrer plus de 100 mg en 2 heures sans vérifier à nouveau les résultats des études de coagulation, car le sulfate de protamine a ses propres propriétés anticoagulantes.

IV: Reconstituer le contenu d'une fiole de 50 mg, avec 5 mL, et le contenu d'une fiole de 250 mg, avec 25 mL d'eau stérile ou d'eau bactériostatique pour injection pour obtenir une concentration de 10 mg/mL. Agiter vigoureusement. On doit jeter toute portion inutilisée de la solution reconstituée dans de l'eau stérile pour injection. La solution reconstituée dans de l'eau bactériostatique est stable pendant 24 heures au réfrigérateur. Consulter les directives de chaque fabricant avant de reconstituer la préparation.

IV directe: La solution peut être administrée sans qu'on la dilue.

Vitesse d'administration: La solution peut être administrée par IV lente, en 1 à 3 minutes.

Perfusion intermittente: Diluer dans une solution de D5%E ou de NaCl 0,9 %.

Vitesse d'administration: Administrer à une vitesse inférieure ou égale à 50 mg/10 min. Une perfusion rapide peut provoquer de l'hypotension, de la bradycardie, des bouffées vasomotrices ou une sensation de chaleur. Si ces symptômes se manifestent, arrêter la perfusion et prévenir le médecin.

ENSEIGNEMENT AU PATIENT ET À SES PROCHES

- Expliquer le but du traitement au patient. Lui recommander de signaler immédiatement tout saignement récurrent.
- Recommander au patient d'éviter toute activité pouvant entraîner des saignements, comme le rasage, le brossage des dents, les injections ou la prise de la température par voie rectale, ou les déplacements, jusqu'à ce que le risque d'hémorragie soit écarté.

VÉRIFICATION DE L'EFFICACITÉ THÉRAPEUTIQUE

L'efficacité du traitement peut être démontrée par: la maîtrise de l'hémorragie ■ la normalisation des facteurs de coagulation chez les patients qui reçoivent de l'héparine.

PSEUDOÉPHÉDRINE

Eltor 120, Pseudofrin, Sudafed 12 heures

CLASSIFICATION:

Décongestionnant, traitement du rhume

Grossesse – catégorie C

INDICATIONS

Traitement symptomatique de la congestion nasale due à des infections virales aiguës des voies respiratoires supérieures, à la sinusite aiguë et subaiguë, à la rhinite allergique ou à la rhinite vasomotrice ■ Traitement des allergies en association avec des antihistaminiques ■ Ouverture des trompes d'Eustache obstruées en cas d'otite moyenne aiguë et d'inflammation ou d'infections auriculaires chroniques.

MÉCANISME D'ACTION

Stimulation des récepteurs alpha-adrénergiques et bêta-adrénergiques ■ Constriction des vaisseaux sanguins de la muqueuse des voies respiratoires (stimulation alpha-adrénergique) et bronchodilatation possible (stimulation bêta-adrénergique). ***Effets thérapeutiques:*** Réduction de la congestion nasale, de l'hyperémie et de l'œdème des fosses nasales.

PHARMACOCINÉTIQUE

Absorption: Bonne (PO).

Distribution: La pseudoéphédrine semble pénétrer dans le liquide céphalorachidien. Elle traverse probablement la barrière placentaire et passe dans le lait maternel.

Métabolisme et excrétion: Métabolisme hépatique partiel. Excrétion rénale de 55 à 75 % à l'état inchangé (selon le pH de l'urine).
Demi-vie: *Enfants:* 3,1 heures; *adultes:* de 9 à 16 heures (selon le pH de l'urine).

Profil temps-action (effets décongestionnants)

	DÉBUT D'ACTION	PIC	DURÉE
PO	15 – 30 min	inconnu	4 – 8 h
PO-LP†	60 min	inconnu	12 h

† LP = libération prolongée.

CONTRE-INDICATIONS, PRÉCAUTIONS ET MISES EN GARDE

Contre-indications: Hypersensibilité à la pseudoéphédrine, à l'un des composants de ce médicament ou aux amines sympathomimétiques ■ Hypertension grave ■ Maladie coronarienne grave ■ Traitement concomitant par un IMAO ou durant les 2 semaines précédentes ■ Intolérance connue à l'alcool (certains liquides en renferment).
Précautions et mises en garde: Hyperthyroïdie ■ Hypertension ■ Diabète ■ Hyperplasie de la prostate ou rétention urinaire ■ Maladie coronarienne ■ Insuffisance cardiaque congestive ■ Hyperthyroïdie ■ Glaucome ■ Insuffisance hépatique ou rénale (adapter la posologie selon la réponse du patient) ■ **GÉR.:** Risque accru d'effets indésirables ■ **OBST., ALLAITEMENT:** L'innocuité de l'agent n'a pas été établie ■ **PÉD.:** L'innocuité et l'efficacité de l'agent n'ont pas été établies chez les enfants < 2 ans.

RÉACTIONS INDÉSIRABLES ET EFFETS SECONDAIRES

SNC: CONVULSIONS, anxiété, nervosité, étourdissements, somnolence, excitabilité, peur, hallucinations, céphalées, insomnie, agitation, faiblesse.
Resp.: difficultés respiratoires.
CV: COLLAPSUS CARDIOVASCULAIRE, palpitations, hypertension, tachycardie.
GI: anorexie, sécheresse de la bouche (xérostomie).
GU: dysurie.
Divers: diaphorèse.

INTERACTIONS

Médicament-médicament: LES **IMAO**, ADMINISTRÉS SIMULTANÉMENT, PEUVENT DÉCLENCHER UNE CRISE HYPERTENSIVE ■ Effets sympathomimétiques additifs lors de l'administration concomitante d'autres **agents sympathomimétiques**, tels que autres **décongestionnants**, **anorexigènes** et **psychostimulants de type amphétaminique** ■ Risque d'hypertension lors de l'usage concomitant de **bêtabloquants** ou de **méthyldopa** ■ Les **phénothiazines** et les **antidépresseurs tricycliques** potentialisent les effets vasopresseurs de la pseudoéphédrine ■ Les **médicaments qui acidifient l'urine**, administrés simultanément, peuvent diminuer l'efficacité de la pseudoéphédrine ■ Les **médicaments qui alcalinisent l'urine** (**bicarbonate de sodium**, **doses élevées d'antiacides**), administrés simultanément, peuvent augmenter l'efficacité de la pseudoéphédrine.
Médicament-aliments: Les **aliments qui acidifient l'urine** peuvent diminuer l'efficacité de la pseudoéphédrine ■ Les **aliments qui alcalinisent l'urine** peuvent augmenter l'efficacité de la pseudoéphédrine (voir les listes de l'annexe K).

VOIES D'ADMINISTRATION ET POSOLOGIE

- **PO (adultes et enfants ≥ 12 ans):** de 30 à 60 mg, toutes les 4 à 6 heures, selon les besoins, ou 120 mg de la préparation à libération prolongée, toutes les 12 heures (ne pas dépasser 240 mg en 24 heures).
- **PO (enfants de 6 à < 12 ans):** 30 mg, toutes les 4 à 6 heures, selon les besoins. Il est aussi possible de donner 4 mg/kg/jour ou 125 mg/m^2/jour en 4 doses fractionnées (ne pas dépasser 120 mg/jour).
- **PO (enfants de 2 à < 6 ans):** 15 mg, toutes les 4 à 6 heures, selon les besoins. Il est aussi possible de donner 4 mg/kg/jour ou 125 mg/m^2/jour en 4 doses fractionnées (ne pas dépasser 60 mg/jour).

PRÉSENTATION (version générique disponible)

Comprimés: 30 mg[VL], 60 mg[VL], 120 mg[VL] ■ **Comprimés à libération prolongée:** 120 mg[VL] ■ **En association avec:** antihistaminiques, ibuprofène, acétaminophène, codéine, antitussifs et expectorants[VL].

SOINS INFIRMIERS

ÉVALUATION DE LA SITUATION

- Déterminer le degré de congestion (nez, sinus, trompes d'Eustache) avant le traitement et à intervalles réguliers par la suite.
- Mesurer le pouls et la pression artérielle avant le traitement et à intervalles réguliers par la suite.
- Ausculter le murmure vésiculaire et observer les caractéristiques des sécrétions bronchiques. Sauf en cas de contre-indication, maintenir l'apport de liquides de 1 500 à 2 000 mL par jour afin de réduire la viscosité des sécrétions.

Tests de laboratoire: La pseudoéphédrine peut entraîner un résultat faussement positif lors de certains tests de dépistage des amphétamines.

DIAGNOSTICS INFIRMIERS POSSIBLES

- Dégagement inefficace des voies respiratoires (Indications).
- Connaissances insuffisantes sur le traitement médicamenteux (Enseignement au patient et à ses proches).

INTERVENTIONS INFIRMIÈRES

- Administrer la pseudoéphédrine au moins 2 heures avant l'heure du coucher afin de réduire le risque d'insomnie.
- LES COMPRIMÉS ET LES CAPSULES À LIBÉRATION PROLONGÉE DEVRAIENT ÊTRE AVALÉS TELS QUELS, SANS ÊTRE ÉCRASÉS, BRISÉS NI MÂCHÉS.

ENSEIGNEMENT AU PATIENT ET À SES PROCHES

- Inciter le patient à respecter rigoureusement la posologie recommandée et à ne pas dépasser la dose prescrite. S'il n'a pu prendre le médicament au moment habituel, il doit le prendre dans l'heure qui suit, sinon, il doit sauter cette dose. L'avertir qu'il ne doit jamais remplacer une dose manquée par une double dose.
- Conseiller au patient de prévenir un professionnel de la santé en cas de nervosité, de fréquence cardiaque lente ou rapide, de difficultés respiratoires, d'hallucinations ou de convulsions, car ces symptômes peuvent indiquer un surdosage.
- Recommander au patient de prévenir un professionnel de la santé si les symptômes ne s'améliorent pas dans les 7 jours ou s'ils s'accompagnent de fièvre.

P

VÉRIFICATION DE L'EFFICACITÉ THÉRAPEUTIQUE

L'efficacité du traitement peut être démontrée par: la diminution de la congestion nasale ou sinusale ou de la congestion des trompes d'Eustache. ✳

PSYLLIUM

Metamucil, Novo-Mucilax, Prodiem, Psyllium

CLASSIFICATION:

Laxatif (agent de masse), hypocholestérolémiant

Grossesse – catégorie inconnue

INDICATIONS

Traitement adjuvant de l'hypercholestérolémie ■ Traitement de la constipation chronique, atonique, spasmodique et rectale ■ Traitement de la constipation accompagnant la grossesse, la convalescence et la vieillesse ■ Traitement adjuvant de la constipation causée par les colites mucomembraneuse et ulcéreuse, la diverticulite et le syndrome du côlon irritable ■ Prise en charge de la constipation, en facilitant une défécation régulière.

MÉCANISME D'ACTION

Le psyllium se mélange avec l'eau contenue dans les matières intestinales pour former un gel émollient ou une solution visqueuse favorisant le péristaltisme et réduisant le temps de transit. ***Effets thérapeutiques:*** Soulagement et prévention de la constipation.

PHARMACOCINÉTIQUE

Absorption: Aucune.

Distribution: L'agent ne se répartit pas dans l'organisme.

Métabolisme et excrétion: Excrétion dans les fèces.

Demi-vie: Inconnue.

Profil temps-action (effet laxatif)

	DÉBUT D'ACTION	PIC	DURÉE
PO	12 - 24 h	2 - 3 jours	inconnue

CONTRE-INDICATIONS, PRÉCAUTIONS ET MISES EN GARDE

Contre-indications: Hypersensibilité à l'un des composants du produit ■ Douleurs abdominales, nausées ou vomissements (particulièrement si ces symptômes s'accompagnent de fièvre) ■ Symptômes d'abdomen aigu, occlusion intestinale, fécalome ou saignement rectal non diagnostiqué ■ Dysphagie.

Précautions et mises en garde: PÉD.: L'innocuité et l'efficacité du médicament dans le traitement de l'hypercholestérolémie n'ont pas été établies chez les enfants ■ Patients suivant des régimes alimentaires particuliers, car certaines préparations contiennent du sucre ou de l'aspartame et ne devraient pas être administrées dans ce cas.

RÉACTIONS INDÉSIRABLES ET EFFETS SECONDAIRES

Resp.: bronchospasme (en cas d'inhalation de la poudre).

GI: crampes, occlusion intestinale ou œsophagienne, nausées, vomissements.

INTERACTIONS

Médicament-médicament: Le psyllium peut diminuer l'absorption d'**autres médicaments** administrés simultanément (ne pas prendre de psyllium dans les 2 heures suivant la prise d'un autre médicament).

VOIES D'ADMINISTRATION ET POSOLOGIE

- **PO (adultes):** *Hypocholestérolémiant* – de 3,4 à 5,1 g, 2 ou 3 fois par jour (jusqu'à 10,2 g par jour, au maximum). *Constipation* – 3,4 g, jusqu'à 3 fois par jour (jusqu'à 10,2 g par jour, au maximum). Dissoudre la poudre dans 240 mL de liquide, bien mélanger et boire immédiatement.
- **PO (enfants ≥ 6 ans):** La moitié de la dose recommandée chez l'adulte, de 1 à 3 fois par jour, dans 240 mL de liquide, bien mélanger et boire immédiatement.

PRÉSENTATION (version générique disponible)

Poudre: de 3,3 à 3,5 g/dose ou sachet[VL] ■ **Granules:** 2 g/dose[VL] ■ **Capsules:** 520 mg[VL] ou 625 mg[VL] par capsule ■ **Gaufrettes:** 3,4 g/gaufrette[VL].

SOINS INFIRMIERS

ÉVALUATION DE LA SITUATION

- Déceler la distension abdominale, ausculter les bruits intestinaux et observer les habitudes normales d'élimination.
- Noter la couleur, la consistance et la quantité des selles évacuées.

Tests de laboratoire: Le psyllium peut entraîner une élévation de la glycémie lors de l'administration prolongée de préparations contenant du sucre.

DIAGNOSTICS INFIRMIERS POSSIBLES

- Constipation (Indications).
- Connaissances insuffisantes sur le traitement médicamenteux (Enseignement au patient et à ses proches).

INTERVENTIONS INFIRMIÈRES

- Le volume contenu dans les sachets n'est pas standardisé, mais chaque sachet renferme de 3 à 3,5 g de psyllium.
- Administrer l'agent avec un grand verre d'eau ou de jus, suivi par un deuxième verre de liquide. La solution devrait être administrée immédiatement après avoir été mélangée, sinon elle fige. Ne pas administrer le médicament sans une quantité suffisante de liquide; il ne faut pas mâcher les granules.

ENSEIGNEMENT AU PATIENT ET À SES PROCHES

- Recommander au patient de prendre d'autres mesures qui favorisent l'élimination fécale: augmenter la consommation de fibres alimentaires, boire plus de liquides, bouger davantage. Lui expliquer que chaque personne a ses propres habitudes d'élimination et qu'il est tout aussi normal de déféquer 3 fois par jour que 3 fois par semaine.
- Expliquer au patient qu'il peut prendre le psyllium pendant une période prolongée pour traiter la constipation chronique.
- Recommander au patient souffrant de maladie cardiaque d'éviter les efforts associés à la défécation (manœuvre de Valsalva).
- Prévenir le patient que les laxatifs sont contre-indiqués si la constipation s'accompagne de douleurs abdominales, de nausées, de vomissements ou de fièvre.

VÉRIFICATION DE L'EFFICACITÉ THÉRAPEUTIQUE

L'efficacité du traitement peut être démontrée par: l'émission de selles molles bien moulées, habituellement dans les 12 à 24 heures. Les résultats peuvent ne pas se manifester avant 3 jours de traitement.

PYRAZINAMIDE

PMS-Pyrazinamide, Tebrazid

PYRAZINAMIDE/ ISONIAZIDE/RIFAMPINE

Rifater

CLASSIFICATION:

Antituberculeux

Grossesse – catégorie C

INDICATIONS

En association avec d'autres médicaments dans le traitement de la tuberculose en clinique.

MÉCANISME D'ACTION

Mécanisme d'action inconnu. ***Effets thérapeutiques:*** Effet bactériostatique ou bactéricide contre les mycobactéries sensibles, selon les concentrations du médicament aux sièges infectés. **Spectre d'action:** Le médicament n'est actif que contre les mycobactéries.

PHARMACOCINÉTIQUE

Absorption: Bonne (PO).

Distribution: Tout l'organisme. De fortes concentrations sont atteintes dans le SNC (équivalentes aux concentrations plasmatiques). Le pyrazinamide passe dans le lait maternel.

P

Métabolisme et excrétion: Métabolisme majoritairement hépatique. Le métabolite (acide pyrazinoïque) est doté d'une activité antimycobactérienne. Excrétion rénale (de 3 à 4 % sous forme inchangée).

Demi-vie: *Pyrazinamide* – 9,5 heures. *Acide pyrazinoïque* – 12 heures. La demi-vie de ces deux composés est prolongée en cas d'insuffisance rénale.

Profil temps-action

	DÉBUT D'ACTION	PIC	DURÉE
PO	inconnu	1 – 2 h (4 – 5 h†)	24 h

† Pour l'acide pyrazinoïque.

CONTRE-INDICATIONS, PRÉCAUTIONS ET MISES EN GARDE

Contre-indications: Hypersensibilité ■ Risque de sensibilité croisée avec l'éthionamide, l'isoniazide, la niacine ou l'acide nicotinique ■ Insuffisance hépatique grave.

Précautions et mises en garde: Goutte ■ Diabète ■ Porphyrie intermittente aiguë ■ **OBST., PÉD.**: L'innocuité de l'agent n'a pas été établie.

RÉACTIONS INDÉSIRABLES ET EFFETS SECONDAIRES

SNC: HÉPATOTOXICITÉ, anorexie, diarrhée, nausées, vomissements.

GU: dysurie.

Tég.: acné, démangeaisons, photosensibilité, rash.

Hémat.: anémie, thrombopénie.

Métab.: hyperuricémie.

Loc.: arthralgie, arthrite goutteuse.

INTERACTIONS

Médicament-médicament: Le pyrazinamide peut entraîner la diminution des concentrations sériques et de l'efficacité de la **cyclosporine** ■ Le médicament peut réduire l'efficacité des **agents uricosuriques**.

VOIES D'ADMINISTRATION ET POSOLOGIE

Le médicament doit toujours être administré avec un autre agent antituberculeux.

- **PO (adultes et adolescents)**: De 15 à 30 mg/kg/jour, en une seule dose (ne pas dépasser 2 g/jour, en une seule dose). On peut aussi administrer de 50 à 70 mg/kg, 2 ou 3 fois par semaine (ne pas dépasser 3 g par dose, si l'agent est administré 3 fois par semaine, ou 4 g par dose, si l'agent est administré 2 fois par semaine). *Patients infectés par le VIH* – de 20 à 30 mg/kg/jour, les 2 premiers mois de traitement; les doses ultérieures dépendent du schéma thérapeutique utilisé.
- **PO (enfants)**: 30 mg/kg/jour ou moins (ne pas dépasser 2 g par dose quotidienne, ou 3 g par dose, si l'agent est administré 3 fois par semaine, ou 4 g par dose, si l'agent est administré 2 fois par semaine).

Pyrazinamide/isoniazide/rifampine

- **PO (adultes dont le poids ≥ 55 kg)**: 6 comprimés par jour en une seule dose.
- **PO (adultes dont le poids se situe entre 45 et 54 kg)**: 5 comprimés par jour en une seule dose.
- **PO (patients dont le poids ≤ 44 kg)**: 4 comprimés par jour en une seule dose.

PRÉSENTATION (version générique disponible)

Comprimés: 500 mg^Pr ■ **Comprimés en association**: 300 mg de pyrazinamide avec 50 mg d'isoniazide et 120 mg de rifampine^Pr.

SOINS INFIRMIERS

ÉVALUATION DE LA SITUATION

Prélever des échantillons pour les cultures de mycobactéries et les épreuves de sensibilité, avant de commencer le traitement et à intervalles réguliers par la suite, afin de déceler une résistance éventuelle.

Tests de laboratoire:

- EXAMINER LES RÉSULTATS DES TESTS DE LA FONCTION HÉPATIQUE, AVANT LE TRAITEMENT ET TOUTES LES 2 À 4 SEMAINES, PAR LA SUITE. DES CONCENTRATIONS ACCRUES D'AST ET D'ALT NE RÉVÈLENT PAS NÉCESSAIREMENT UNE HÉPATITE CLINIQUE ET PEUVENT REVENIR À LA NORMALE DURANT LE TRAITEMENT. ON NE DOIT ADMINISTRER LE PYRAZINAMIDE AUX PATIENTS ATTEINTS D'INSUFFISANCE HÉPATIQUE QUE SI CE TRAITEMENT LEUR EST ABSOLUMENT NÉCESSAIRE.
- Noter les concentrations sériques d'acide urique tout au long du traitement. Le pyrazinamide peut entraîner l'élévation de ces concentrations, déclenchant une crise de goutte aiguë.
- Le pyrazinamide peut modifier les résultats du dosage des corps cétoniques dans l'urine.

DIAGNOSTICS INFIRMIERS POSSIBLES

- Risque d'infection (Indications).
- Connaissances insuffisantes sur le traitement médicamenteux (Enseignement au patient et à ses proches).
- Non-observance du traitement médicamenteux (Enseignement au patient et à ses proches).

P

INTERVENTIONS INFIRMIÈRES

Le pyrazinamide peut être administré en association avec l'isoniazide ou la rifampine.

ENSEIGNEMENT AU PATIENT ET À SES PROCHES

- Conseiller au patient de respecter rigoureusement la posologie recommandée. L'avertir qu'il ne doit jamais sauter de dose ni remplacer une dose manquée par une double dose. S'il n'a pu prendre le médicament au moment habituel, il doit le prendre dès que possible, à moins que ce ne soit presque l'heure prévue pour la dose suivante. Insister sur le fait qu'il est important de poursuivre le traitement même après la disparition des symptômes. La durée du traitement dépend du schéma thérapeutique utilisé et du stade de la maladie sous-jacente.
- Prévenir le patient diabétique que le pyrazinamide peut modifier le dosage des corps cétoniques dans l'urine.
- Conseiller au patient de prévenir un professionnel de la santé s'il ne note aucune amélioration en l'espace de 2 à 3 semaines ou si les symptômes suivants se manifestent: fièvre, anorexie, malaise, nausées, vomissements, urine foncée, coloration jaunâtre de la peau et des yeux, douleurs ou œdème articulaires.
- Inciter le patient à utiliser un écran solaire et à porter des vêtements protecteurs pour prévenir les réactions de photosensibilité.
- Insister sur l'importance des examens réguliers de suivi permettant d'évaluer les bienfaits du traitement et de déceler les effets secondaires.

VÉRIFICATION DE L'EFFICACITÉ THÉRAPEUTIQUE

L'efficacité du traitement peut être démontrée par: la résolution des signes et des symptômes de tuberculose ■ des résultats négatifs aux cultures des expectorations. ✳

PYRIDOSTIGMINE

Mestinon, Mestinon SR

CLASSIFICATION:

Cholinergique (inhibiteur de la cholinestérase), antimyasthénique

Grossesse – catégorie C

INDICATIONS

Augmentation de la force musculaire dans le cadre du traitement symptomatique de la myasthénie grave.

MÉCANISME D'ACTION

Inhibition de la décomposition de l'acétylcholine entraînant son accumulation et la prolongation de son effet ■ Effets: myosis ■ élévation du tonus des muscles intestinaux et locomoteurs ■ constriction bronchique et urétérale ■ bradycardie ■ salivation accrue ■ larmoiement ■ transpiration. ***Effets thérapeutiques:*** Amélioration de la fonction musculaire chez les patients souffrant de myasthénie grave.

PHARMACOCINÉTIQUE

Absorption: Faible (PO).

Distribution: Le médicament semble traverser la barrière placentaire.

Métabolisme et excrétion: La pyridostigmine est métabolisée par les cholinestérases plasmatiques et le foie.

Demi-vie: 3,7 heures.

Profil temps-action (effets cholinergiques)

	DÉBUT D'ACTION	PIC	DURÉE
PO	30 – 35 min	inconnu	3 – 6 h
PO-LP†	30 – 60 min	inconnu	6 – 12 h

† LP = libération prolongée.

CONTRE-INDICATIONS, PRÉCAUTIONS ET MISES EN GARDE

Contre-indications: Hypersensibilité à la pyridostigmine, aux inhibiteurs de la cholinestérase ou aux bromures ■ Occlusion mécanique du tractus gastro-intestinal ou génito-urinaire ■ Péritonite.

Précautions et mises en garde: Antécédents d'asthme ■ Ulcère gastroduodénal ■ Bradycardie ■ Vagotonie ■ Arythmies cardiaques ■ Occlusion récente d'une artère coronaire ■ Épilepsie ■ Hyperthyroïdie ■ Éviter les fortes doses chez les patients souffrant de mégacôlon ou de motilité gastro-intestinale diminuée; le médicament pourrait s'accumuler et donner lieu à une toxicité lors du rétablissement de la motilité gastro-intestinale ■ **OBST., ALLAITEMENT:** L'innocuité du médicament n'a pas été étudiée.

RÉACTIONS INDÉSIRABLES ET EFFETS SECONDAIRES

SNC: CONVULSIONS, étourdissements, faiblesse.

ORLO: larmoiement, myosis.

Resp.: bronchospasme, sécrétions excessives.

CV: bradycardie, hypotension.

GI: crampes abdominales, diarrhée, salivation excessive, nausées, vomissements.

Tég.: transpiration, rash.

P

INTERACTIONS

Médicament-médicament: Les **médicaments dotés de propriétés anticholinergiques**, dont les **antihistaminiques**, les **antidépresseurs**, l'**atropine**, l'**halopéridol**, les **phénothiazines**, le **procaïnamide**, la **quinidine** et le **disopyramide**, peuvent contrecarrer les effets cholinergiques de la pyridostigmine ■ La pyridostigmine prolonge l'effet des **relaxants musculaires du type dépolarisant** (**succinylcholine**) et des **inhibiteurs de la cholinestérase** ■ Toxicité additive lors de l'administration simultanée d'autres **inhibiteurs de la cholinestérase**, dont l'**écothiopate** ■ La **guanéthidine**, administrée simultanément, peut diminuer les effets de la pyridostigmine administrée dans le traitement de la myasthénie.

VOIES D'ADMINISTRATION ET POSOLOGIE

Myasthénie grave

Commencer le traitement à la pyridostigmine à une posologie inférieure à celle nécessaire pour obtenir l'effet maximal; augmenter graduellement la posologie quotidienne à des intervalles d'au moins 48 heures.

- **PO (adultes):** *Comprimés* – de 30 à 60 mg, toutes les 3 ou 4 heures, au départ. *Comprimés à libération prolongée* – de 180 à 540 mg, 1 ou 2 fois par jour (l'écart posologique est de 180 mg à 1,08 g par jour; risque accru de crises cholinergiques; il peut s'avérer nécessaire d'administrer simultanément une préparation à libération immédiate).

PRÉSENTATION

Comprimés: 60 mg[Pr] ■ **Comprimés à libération prolongée:** 180 mg[Pr].

SOINS INFIRMIERS

ÉVALUATION DE LA SITUATION

- Mesurer le pouls, la fréquence respiratoire et la pression artérielle avant l'administration de la pyridostigmine. Signaler tout changement marqué au niveau de la fréquence cardiaque.

Myasthénie grave:

- Examiner les réactions neuromusculaires, y compris la capacité vitale, le ptosis, la diplopie, la capacité de mastication, la capacité de déglutition, la préhension manuelle et la démarche avant l'administration du médicament et au moment de son effet maximal. Conseiller au patient de tenir un journal où il notera quotidiennement son état et les effets du médicament.
- Surveiller les signes suivants de surdosage, de dosage insuffisant ou de résistance au traitement: faiblesse musculaire, dyspnée, dysphagie. En cas de surdosage, les symptômes se manifestent habituellement dans l'heure qui suit l'administration alors que, en cas de dosage insuffisant, ils apparaissent 3 heures après l'administration ou plus tard. Les symptômes de surdosage (crise cholinergique) peuvent aussi inclure l'intensification des sécrétions pulmonaires et de la salivation, la bradycardie, les nausées, les vomissements, les crampes, la diarrhée et la diaphorèse. On peut distinguer le surdosage d'un dosage insuffisant par un test au Tensilon (chlorure d'édrophonium).

TOXICITÉ ET SURDOSAGE: En cas de surdosage, l'antidote est l'atropine.

DIAGNOSTICS INFIRMIERS POSSIBLES

- Mobilité physique réduite (Indications).
- Mode de respiration inefficace (Indications).
- Connaissances insuffisantes sur le traitement médicamenteux (Enseignement au patient et à ses proches).

INTERVENTIONS INFIRMIÈRES

- Chez les patients éprouvant des difficultés de mastication, la pyridostigmine peut être administrée 30 minutes avant les repas.

PO: Administrer le médicament avec du lait ou des aliments pour en réduire les effets secondaires. Les comprimés à libération prolongée doivent être avalés tels quels sans être écrasés, brisés ni mâchés. On peut administrer les comprimés ordinaires en même temps que les comprimés à libération prolongée pour mieux maîtriser les symptômes. Les tachetures sur les comprimés à libération prolongée n'altèrent en rien leur puissance.

ENSEIGNEMENT AU PATIENT ET À SES PROCHES

- Conseiller au patient de respecter rigoureusement la posologie recommandée. Le prévenir qu'il ne doit ni sauter de dose, ni remplacer une dose manquée par une double dose. Les patients présentant des antécédents de dysphagie devraient recourir en tout temps à un réveille-matin mécanique ou à piles afin de pouvoir prendre le médicament exactement à l'heure prévue. Les patients souffrant de dysphagie peuvent être incapables d'avaler le médicament, si la dose n'est pas prise à l'heure prévue. Si la dose est prise en retard, une crise myasthénique peut se déclencher. La prise prématurée du médicament peut entraîner une crise cholinergique. Les patients souffrant de myasthénie grave doivent suivre ce traitement pendant toute leur vie.
- Conseiller au patient de toujours porter sur lui une pièce d'identité où sont inscrits son problème de santé et son traitement médicamenteux.

P

- Conseiller au patient d'espacer ses activités afin d'éviter la fatigue.

VÉRIFICATION DE L'EFFICACITÉ THÉRAPEUTIQUE

L'efficacité du traitement peut être démontrée par: le soulagement du ptosis et de la diplopie, l'amélioration de la mastication, de la déglutition, de la force des membres et de la respiration, sans apparition de symptômes cholinergiques. ✳

PYRIDOXINE

Pyridoxine, Vitamine B_6

CLASSIFICATION:

Vitamine B (hydrosoluble)

Grossesse – catégorie A

INDICATIONS

Traitement et prévention des carences en pyridoxine (pouvant être associées à une alimentation inadéquate ou à des maladies chroniques débilitantes) ▪ Traitement et prévention de la neuropathie induite par l'isoniazide ▪ Correction d'un surdosage aigu par l'isoniazide ▪ Traitement de la toxicité aiguë associée à l'hydrazine contenue dans les champignons du genre *Gyromitra* ▪ Traitement de l'anémie sidéroblastique associée à des concentrations sériques de fer élevées ▪ Traitement des convulsions chez les nouveau-nés atteint du syndrome de dépendance à la pyridoxine. **Usages non approuvés:** Traitement et prévention de la neuropathie pouvant être attribuable à un traitement par la pénicillamine ▪ Empoisonnement à l'éthylène glycol.

MÉCANISME D'ACTION

Élément essentiel au métabolisme des acides aminés, des glucides et des lipides ▪ Élément nécessaire au transport des acides aminés, à la formation des neurotransmetteurs et à la synthèse des molécules d'hème. ***Effets thérapeutiques:*** Prévention des carences en pyridoxine ▪ Prévention ou renversement de la neuropathie attribuable au traitement par l'hydralazine, la pénicillamine ou l'isoniazide.

PHARMACOCINÉTIQUE

Absorption: Bonne (PO).

Distribution: La pyridoxine est emmagasinée dans le foie, les muscles et le cerveau. Elle traverse la barrière placentaire et passe dans le lait maternel.

Métabolisme et excrétion: La pyridoxine est transformée dans les globules rouges en phosphate et en un autre métabolite actif. Les quantités supérieures aux besoins quotidiens sont excrétées à l'état inchangé par les reins.

Demi-vie: De 15 à 20 jours.

Profil temps-action

	DÉBUT D'ACTION	PIC	DURÉE
PO, IM, IV	inconnu	inconnu	inconnue

CONTRE-INDICATIONS, PRÉCAUTIONS ET MISES EN GARDE

Contre-indications: Hypersensibilité à la vitamine B_6 ou à toute préparation pharmaceutique qui en contient.

Précautions et mises en garde: Maladie de Parkinson (traitement par la lévodopa seulement) ▪ **OBST.:** La prise prolongée de doses élevées peut provoquer le syndrome de dépendance à la pyridoxine chez le nouveau-né.

RÉACTIONS INDÉSIRABLES ET EFFETS SECONDAIRES

Les réactions indésirables énumérées ci-dessous ont été observées lors de l'administration de doses très élevées seulement.

SNC: neuropathie sensorielle, paresthésie.

Divers: syndrome de dépendance à la pyridoxine.

INTERACTIONS

Médicament-médicament: La pyridoxine entrave la réponse thérapeutique à la **lévodopa** (cette interaction est négligeable chez les patients prenant l'association lévodopa/carbidopa) ▪ L'**isoniazide**, l'**hydralazine**, le **chloramphénicol**, la **pénicillamine**, les **œstrogènes** et les **immunodépresseurs**, administrés simultanément, augmentent les besoins en pyridoxine.

VOIES D'ADMINISTRATION ET POSOLOGIE

Prévention des carences

- **PO (adultes et enfants > 14 ans):** De 1,2 à 1,7 mg par jour (administrer de plus fortes doses lors d'un traitement concomitant par des immunosuppresseurs, l'isoniazide, la pénicillamine et les contraceptifs oraux renfermant des œstrogènes).
- **PO (enfants de 4 à 13 ans):** De 0,6 à 1 mg par jour (administrer de plus fortes doses lors d'un traitement concomitant par des immunosuppresseurs, l'isoniazide et la pénicillamine).
- **PO (enfants de la naissance à 3 ans):** De 0,1 à 0,5 mg par jour (administrer de plus fortes doses lors d'un traitement concomitant par des immunosuppresseurs, l'isoniazide et la pénicillamine).

P

Traitement des carences

- **PO, IM, IV (adultes et enfants):** La dose doit être adaptée aux besoins individuels. Écart posologique: de 2,5 à 10 mg par jour. *Traitement d'entretien* – de 2 à 5 mg par jour.

Syndrome de dépendance à la pyridoxine

- **IM, IV (nourrissons):** De 10 à 100 mg par jour. Certains enfants auront besoin d'un apport complémentaire par voie orale de 2 à 100 mg par jour toute leur vie durant.

Anémie sidéroblastique héréditaire

- **PO:** De 200 à 600 mg par jour.

Surdosage par l'isoniazide

- **IM, IV (adultes):** Quantité en mg égale à la quantité d'isoniazide ingérée; si la dose d'isoniazide ingérée est inconnue, administrer 5 g par voie IV toutes les 30 minutes jusqu'à l'arrêt des convulsions.

Prévention de la neurotoxicité induite par l'isoniazide

- **PO (adultes):** De 10 à 50 mg par jour.

Empoisonnement par des champignons

- **IV (adultes):** *Dose initiale* – 2,5 mg/kg. Répéter au besoin afin de maîtriser les convulsions.

***Empoisonnement à l'éthylène glycol* – usage non approuvé**

- **IV (adultes):** 100 mg par voie IV, jusqu'à l'élimination de l'éthylène glycol et de son métabolite.

PRÉSENTATION (version générique disponible)

P

Capsules: 100 mg^{VL}, 200 mg^{VL}, 250 mg^{VL} ■ **Comprimés:** 10 mg^{VL}, 25 mg^{VL}, 50 mg^{VL}, 100 mg^{VL}, 200 mg^{VL}, 250 mg^{VL}, 500 mg^{VL} ■ **Solution pour injection:** 100 mg/mL, en fioles de 10 mL^{Pr} et de 30 mL^{Pr} ■ **En association avec:** vitamines, minéraux, oligoéléments dans diverses préparations vitaminiques^{VL}.

SOINS INFIRMIERS

ÉVALUATION DE LA SITUATION

- Observer le patient avant le traitement et à intervalles réguliers pendant toute sa durée, à la recherche de signes de carence en vitamine B_6: anémie, dermatite, chéilite, irritabilité, convulsions, nausées et vomissements. Prendre les précautions qui s'imposent en cas de convulsions chez les nourrissons présentant une dépendance à la vitamine B_6.

Tests de laboratoire: La pyridoxine peut entraîner des concentrations faussement élevées d'urobilinogène.

DIAGNOSTICS INFIRMIERS POSSIBLES

- Alimentation déficiente (Indications).
- Connaissances insuffisantes sur le traitement médicamenteux (Enseignement au patient et à ses proches).

INTERVENTIONS INFIRMIÈRES

- On administre habituellement la pyridoxine en association avec d'autres vitamines, car il est rare que le patient ne présente que ce seul type d'avitaminose.
- L'administration de la vitamine B_6 par voie parentérale est réservée aux patients qui sont incapables de prendre les comprimés par voie orale, qui souffrent de nausées ou de vomissements ou qui sont atteints d'un syndrome de malabsorption.
- Garder la solution parentérale à l'abri de la lumière, car elle peut se décomposer.

PO: LES CAPSULES ET LES COMPRIMÉS À LIBÉRATION PROLONGÉE DOIVENT ÊTRE AVALÉS TELS QUELS; IL NE FAUT PAS LES ÉCRASER, LES BRISER OU LES MÂCHER. CHEZ LES PATIENTS QUI SONT INCAPABLES D'AVALER, ON PEUT MÉLANGER LE CONTENU DES CAPSULES À DE LA CONFITURE OU À DE LA GELÉE.

IM: Assurer la rotation des points d'injection: une sensation de brûlure ou de picotement peut se produire au point d'injection.

IV:

- On peut administrer le médicament par IV directe ou par perfusion, dans des solutions IV standard. Consulter les directives de chaque fabricant avant de reconstituer la préparation.
- Les convulsions attribuables à la dépendance à la vitamine B_6 devraient cesser dans les 2 ou 3 minutes suivant l'administration IV de pyridoxine.

Vitesse d'administration: La perfusion a été administrée durant 15 à 30 minutes et même pendant un laps de temps allant jusqu'à 3 heures.

Associations incompatibles: riboflavine ■ solutions alcalines.

ENSEIGNEMENT AU PATIENT ET À SES PROCHES

- Conseiller au patient de prendre le médicament en respectant rigoureusement la posologie recommandée. S'il n'a pu le prendre au moment habituel, il peut sauter la dose, car la carence en vitamine B_6 ne survient qu'après un long laps de temps.
- Conseiller au patient de respecter rigoureusement les recommandations diététiques du professionnel de la santé. Lui expliquer que la meilleure source de vitamines est une alimentation bien équilibrée contenant des aliments provenant des 4 principaux groupes. Les aliments riches en vitamine B_6 comprennent les bananes, les céréales de grain entier, les pommes de terre, les haricots de Lima et la viande.

- Recommander au patient qui pratique l'automédication par des suppléments vitaminiques de ne pas dépasser les taux quotidiens recommandés (voir l'annexe K). L'efficacité de mégadoses dans le traitement de diverses affections n'a pas été prouvée. De telles doses peuvent entraîner des effets secondaires comme une démarche instable, l'engourdissement des pieds et des problèmes de coordination du mouvement des mains.
- Insister sur l'importance des examens de suivi permettant d'évaluer les bienfaits du traitement.

VÉRIFICATION DE L'EFFICACITÉ THÉRAPEUTIQUE

L'efficacité du traitement peut être démontrée par: la diminution des symptômes de carence en vitamine B_6. ✳

PYRIMÉTHAMINE

Daraprim

CLASSIFICATION:

Anti-infectieux (antiprotozoaire)

Grossesse – catégorie C

INDICATIONS

Traitement de la malaria résistant à la chloroquine, en association avec d'autres antipaludéens ▪ Traitement de la toxoplasmose en association avec des sulfamides. **Usages non approuvés:** Traitement de la pneumonie à *Pneumocystis carinii* en association avec d'autres agents (sulfamides, dapsone).

MÉCANISME D'ACTION

Liaison à une enzyme des protozoaires entraînant la déplétion de l'acide folique. ***Effets thérapeutiques:*** Destruction et arrêt de la croissance des microorganismes sensibles (protozoaires).

PHARMACOCINÉTIQUE

Absorption: Bonne (PO).

Distribution: Tout l'organisme; fortes concentrations dans les globules sanguins, les reins, les poumons, le foie et la rate. Une certaine fraction pénètre dans le liquide céphalorachidien (de 13 à 26 % des concentrations sériques). L'agent traverse la barrière placentaire et passe dans le lait maternel.

Métabolisme et excrétion: Métabolisme majoritairement hépatique. Excrétion rénale (de 20 à 30 % sous forme inchangée).

Demi-vie: 4 jours (plus courte chez les patients atteints du sida).

Profil temps-action

	DÉBUT D'ACTION	PIC	DURÉE
PO	inconnu	3 h	2 semaines†

† Concentrations entraînant la disparition des symptômes.

CONTRE-INDICATIONS, PRÉCAUTIONS ET MISES EN GARDE

Contre-indications: Hypersensibilité.

Précautions et mises en garde: OBST.: Risque théorique d'anomalies fœtales si l'agent est pris durant les 14 à 16 premières semaines de la grossesse. Après 16 semaines de grossesse, l'administration concomitante de leucovorine peut s'avérer nécessaire ▪ Anémie mégaloblastique attribuable à une carence en folate ▪ Traitement par des inhibiteurs des folates, administrés simultanément (risque d'anémie mégaloblastique) ▪ Antécédents de convulsions (doses élevées) ▪ Anémie ou aplasie médullaire sous-jacentes ▪ Insuffisance hépatique ▪ Carence en G-6-PD ▪ **ALLAITEMENT:** Des doses élevées, administrées à la mère, peuvent provoquer une carence en acide folique chez le nourrisson.

RÉACTIONS INDÉSIRABLES ET EFFETS SECONDAIRES

SNC: CONVULSIONS (doses élevées), céphalées, insomnie, sensation de tête légère, malaise, dépression.

Resp.: sécheresse de la gorge, éosinophilie pulmonaire.

CV: ARYTHMIES (doses élevées).

GI: glossite atrophique (doses élevées), anorexie, diarrhée, nausées.

GU: hématurie.

Tég.: pigmentation anormale, dermatite.

Hémat.: anémie mégaloblastique (doses élevées), pancytopénie, thrombopénie.

Divers: fièvre.

INTERACTIONS

Médicament-médicament: Risque accru d'aplasie médullaire lors de l'administration concomitante d'autres **dépresseurs de la moelle osseuse**, incluant les **antinéoplasiques** ou la **radiothérapie** ▪ Risque accru d'anémie mégaloblastique, lors de l'administration simultanée d'**inhibiteurs des folates** (**méthotrexate**); éviter l'administration concomitante.

VOIES D'ADMINISTRATION ET POSOLOGIE

Traitement de la malaria

- **PO (adultes):** 25 mg par jour, pendant 2 jours, en association avec des schizonticides à action rapide (chloroquine ou quinine).

P

- **Monothérapie**
  PO (adultes): 50 mg par jour, pendant 2 jours.
  PO (enfants de 4 à 10 ans): 25 mg par jour, pendant 2 jours.
- **Dose unique en association avec le sulfalène ou la sulfadoxine**
  PO (adultes et enfants > 14 ans): De 50 à 75 mg, avec 1 à 1,5 g de sulfalène ou de sulfadoxine.
  PO (enfants de 9 à 14 ans): 50 mg, avec 1 g de sulfalène ou de sulfadoxine.
  PO (enfants de 4 à 8 ans): 25 mg, avec 500 mg de sulfalène ou de sulfadoxine.
  PO (enfants < 4 ans): 12,5 mg, avec 250 mg de sulfalène ou de sulfadoxine.

Toxoplasmose
- **PO (adultes et enfants > 6 ans):** Initialement, 50 mg, suivis de 25 mg par jour, avec 150 mg/kg/jour de sulfadiazine (4 g au maximum), en 4 doses fractionnées.
- **PO (enfants de 2 à 6 ans):** Initialement, 25 mg, suivis de 12,5 mg par jour, avec 150 mg/kg/jour de sulfadiazine (2 g au maximum), en 4 doses fractionnées.
- **PO (enfants de 10 mois à < 2 ans):** 12,5 mg, avec 150 mg/kg/jour de sulfadiazine (1,5 g au maximum), en 4 doses fractionnées.
- **PO (nourrissons de 3 mois à 9 mois):** 6,25 mg, avec 100 mg/kg/jour de sulfadiazine (1 g au maximum), en 4 doses fractionnées.
- **PO (nourrissons < 3 mois):** 6,25 mg, tous les 2 jours, avec 100 mg/kg de sulfadiazine (750 mg au maximum), tous les 2 jours, en 4 doses fractionnées.

P

PRÉSENTATION

Comprimés: 25 mg[Pr].

SOINS INFIRMIERS

ÉVALUATION DE LA SITUATION

- Observer le patient tous les jours, pendant toute la durée du traitement, pour déceler une amélioration des signes et des symptômes d'infection.

Tests de laboratoire: Noter à intervalles réguliers, pendant toute la durée du traitement, la numération globulaire et la numération plaquettaire (2 fois par semaine, chez les patients atteints de toxoplasmose). La pyriméthamine peut diminuer le nombre de globules blancs et de plaquettes.

DIAGNOSTICS INFIRMIERS POSSIBLES

- Risque d'infection (Indications).
- Connaissances insuffisantes sur le traitement médicamenteux (Enseignement au patient et à ses proches).

INTERVENTIONS INFIRMIÈRES

- On peut administrer en concomitance de la leucovorine pour prévenir la carence en acide folique et pour normaliser l'hématopoïèse.
- Administrer le médicament avec du lait ou avec des aliments afin de réduire la gêne gastro-intestinale.
- Dans le cas des patients qui éprouvent des difficultés de déglutition, le pharmacien peut écraser les comprimés et les mélanger à un soluté salin ou à tout autre véhicule.

ENSEIGNEMENT AU PATIENT ET À SES PROCHES

- Conseiller au patient de respecter rigoureusement la posologie recommandée et de prendre toute la quantité de médicament qui lui a été prescrite même s'il se sent mieux. S'il saute une dose, il doit la prendre dès que possible à moins qu'il ne soit presque l'heure prévue pour la dose suivante. Le prévenir qu'il ne faut jamais remplacer une dose manquée par une double dose.
- Recommander au patient de prévenir rapidement un professionnel de la santé en cas de maux de gorge, de pâleur, de purpura ou de glossite. Lui recommander également d'arrêter de prendre la pyriméthamine et de consulter un professionnel de la santé dès que les premiers signes de rash cutané se manifestent, ou s'il ne note aucune amélioration de son état en l'espace de quelques jours.
- Insister sur l'importance des tests de laboratoire aux intervalles prévus, particulièrement dans le cas du patient prenant des doses élevées de médicament. Prévenir le patient qu'il ne devrait pas remettre ni annuler ces rendez-vous.

VÉRIFICATION DE L'EFFICACITÉ THÉRAPEUTIQUE

L'efficacité du traitement peut être démontrée par: la diminution des signes et des symptômes de malaria ■ la diminution des signes et des symptômes de toxoplasmose.

QUÉTIAPINE

Seroquel

CLASSIFICATION:
Antipsychotique

Grossesse – catégorie C

INDICATIONS

Traitement d'entretien des manifestations de la schizophrénie et des épisodes maniaques aigus, associés au trouble bipolaire.

MÉCANISME D'ACTION

Antagoniste dopaminergique et sérotoninergique ■ Également, effet antagoniste sur les récepteurs histaminergiques H_1 et les récepteurs alpha$_1$-adrénergiques. ***Effets thérapeutiques:*** Diminution des manifestations de psychose et de manie aiguë.

PHARMACOCINÉTIQUE

Absorption: Bonne (PO).
Distribution: Tout l'organisme.
Métabolisme et excrétion: Métabolisme majoritairement hépatique (principalement par l'isoenzyme CYP 3A4 du cytochrome P450); excrétion rénale faible (moins de 1 % sous forme inchangée).
Demi-vie: 6 heures.

Profil temps-action (effets antipsychotiques)

	DÉBUT D'ACTION	PIC	DURÉE
PO	inconnu	inconnu	8 - 12 h

CONTRE-INDICATIONS, PRÉCAUTIONS ET MISES EN GARDE

Contre-indications: Hypersensibilité à la quétiapine.
Précautions et mises en garde: Maladie cardiovasculaire ou accident vasculaire cérébral, déshydratation ou hypovolémie (risque accru d'hypotension) ■ **GÉR.:** Antécédents de convulsions, maladie d'Alzheimer ou personnes âgées ≥ 65 ans ■ Insuffisance hépatique (une réduction de la dose peut s'avérer nécessaire) ■ Hypothyroïdie (risque d'exacerbation) ■ Antécédents de tentatives de suicide ■ **OBST., ALLAITEMENT, PÉD.:** L'innocuité du médicament n'a pas été établie.

RÉACTIONS INDÉSIRABLES ET EFFETS SECONDAIRES

SNC: SYNDROME MALIN DES NEUROLEPTIQUES, CONVULSIONS, étourdissements, troubles cognitifs, symptômes extrapyramidaux, sédation, dyskinésie tardive.
ORLO: douleurs auriculaires, rhinite.
Resp.: toux, dyspnée, pharyngite.
CV: palpitations, œdème périphérique, hypotension orthostatique.
GI: anorexie, constipation, sécheresse de la bouche (xérostomie), dyspepsie.
Tég.: transpiration.
Hémat.: leucopénie.
Métab.: gain pondéral.
Divers: syndrome pseudogrippal.

INTERACTIONS

Médicament-médicament: Effets additifs sur la dépression du SNC lors de l'usage concomitant d'autres **dépresseurs du SNC**, incluant l'**alcool**, les **antihistaminiques**, les **analgésiques opioïdes** ou les **hypnosédatifs** ■ Risque accru d'hypotension lors de l'ingestion de grandes quantités d'**alcool** ou de la prise d'**antihypertenseurs** ■ La **phénytoïne** et la **thioridazine** augmentent la clairance de la quétiapine et en réduisent l'efficacité (il peut s'avérer nécessaire d'adapter la dose); des effets similaires peuvent survenir lors de l'administration de **carbamazépine**, de **barbituriques**, de **rifampicine** ou de **corticostéroïdes** ■ Les effets de la quétiapine peuvent être accrus par le **kétoconazole**, l'**itraconazole**, le **fluconazole** ou l'**érythromycine** ainsi que par d'autres **agents qui inhibent l'isoenzyme CYP 3A4 du cytochrome P450**.

VOIES D'ADMINISTRATION ET POSOLOGIE

- **PO (adultes):** *Schizophrénie* – dose initiale 25 mg, 2 fois par jour, majorée en l'espace de 4 à 7 jours par paliers de 25 à 50 mg, 2 fois par jour, jusqu'à concurrence de la dose cible de 300 mg par jour, en 2 prises fractionnées. Les doses doivent être adaptées selon la réponse clinique. Des doses plus élevées peuvent parfois s'avérer nécessaires. *Trouble bipolaire, manie* – 50 mg, 2 fois par jour, le premier jour; 100 mg, 2 fois par jour, le deuxième jour; 150 mg, 2 fois par jour, le troisième jour; 200 mg, 2 fois par jour, le quatrième jour; la dose peut être augmentée jusqu'à 300 mg, 2 fois par jour, le cinquième jour, et jusqu'à 400 mg, 2 fois par jour, le sixième jour.

Q

PRÉSENTATION

Comprimés: 25 mg^{Pr}, 100 mg^{Pr}, 200 mg^{Pr}, 300 mg^{Pr}.

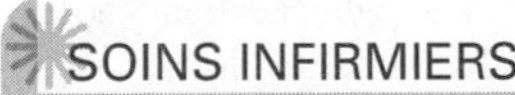

SOINS INFIRMIERS

ÉVALUATION DE LA SITUATION

- Évaluer l'état mental du patient (délire, hallucinations et troubles de comportement), avant le traitement et à intervalles réguliers pendant toute sa durée.

- Noter les sautes d'humeur du patient. Rester à l'affût des tendances suicidaires, particulièrement en début de traitement. Limiter la quantité de médicament dont le patient peut disposer.
- Mesurer la pression artérielle (en position assise, debout et couchée) et le pouls du patient avant le traitement et à intervalles fréquents pendant la période initiale d'adaptation de la posologie. En cas d'hypotension, revenir à la dose précédente.
- Observer le patient attentivement lorsqu'on lui administre le médicament pour s'assurer qu'il l'a bien avalé.
- Observer étroitement le patient pour déceler l'apparition d'effets secondaires extrapyramidaux (*akathisie:* besoin irrépressible de bouger; *dystonie:* spasmes musculaires, mouvements de torsion; ou *pseudoparkinsonisme:* faciès rigide, rigidité, tremblements, bouche ouverte laissant s'échapper la salive, démarche traînante, dysphagie). Signaler ces symptômes; il peut s'avérer nécessaire de réduire la dose ou de cesser le traitement. On peut administrer du trihexyphénidyle ou de la diphenhydramine pour maîtriser ces symptômes.
- Rester à l'affût des symptômes de dyskinésie tardive (mouvements involontaires rythmiques de la bouche, du visage et des membres). Signaler immédiatement ces symptômes, qui peuvent être irréversibles.
- SUIVRE DE PRÈS L'APPARITION DES SYMPTÔMES SUIVANTS DU SYNDROME MALIN DES NEUROLEPTIQUES: FIÈVRE, DÉTRESSE RESPIRATOIRE, TACHYCARDIE, CONVULSIONS, DIAPHORÈSE, HYPERTENSION OU HYPOTENSION, PÂLEUR, FATIGUE. SIGNALER IMMÉDIATEMENT AU MÉDECIN OU À UN AUTRE PROFESSIONNEL DE LA SANTÉ LA PRÉSENCE DE CES SYMPTÔMES.

Tests de laboratoire:

- La quétiapine peut entraîner des élévations asymptomatiques des taux d'AST et d'ALT.
- La quétiapine peut également entraîner l'anémie, la thrombopénie, la leucocytose et la leucopénie.
- Le médicament peut également élever les concentrations de cholestérol total et de triglycérides.

DIAGNOSTICS INFIRMIERS POSSIBLES

- Risque de violence (Indications).
- Opérations de la pensée perturbées (Indications).
- Risque d'accident (Effets secondaires).

INTERVENTIONS INFIRMIÈRES

- Si le traitement est repris après un arrêt de plus de 1 semaine, reprendre le processus d'adaptation de la posologie depuis le début.
- La quétiapine peut être administrée avec ou sans aliments.

ENSEIGNEMENT AU PATIENT ET À SES PROCHES

- Conseiller au patient de respecter rigoureusement la posologie recommandée.
- Informer le patient du risque d'apparition de symptômes extrapyramidaux. Lui recommander de signaler immédiatement ces symptômes à un professionnel de la santé.
- Recommander au patient de changer lentement de position afin de réduire le risque d'hypotension orthostatique.
- Prévenir le patient que la quétiapine peut provoquer de la somnolence. Lui conseiller de ne pas conduire et d'éviter les activités qui exigent sa vigilance jusqu'à ce qu'on ait la certitude que le médicament n'entraîne pas cet effet chez lui.
- Conseiller au patient d'éviter les écarts de température importants, étant donné que ce médicament altère la thermorégulation.
- Recommander au patient de ne pas consommer d'alcool et de ne pas prendre d'autres dépresseurs du SNC ou des médicaments en vente libre sans avoir consulté au préalable un professionnel de la santé.
- Inciter la patiente à prévenir un professionnel de la santé si elle pense être enceinte ou souhaite le devenir, ou si elle allaite ou prévoit le faire.
- Recommander au patient qui doit suivre un autre traitement ou subir une intervention chirurgicale d'avertir le professionnel de la santé qu'il suit un traitement par ce médicament.
- Recommander au patient d'informer un professionnel de la santé sans tarder en cas de maux de gorge, de fièvre, de saignements inhabituels, d'ecchymoses ou de rash.
- Insister sur l'importance d'un suivi constant, de la psychothérapie et de la surveillance des effets secondaires.
- Prévenir le patient que des examens ophtalmologiques devraient être réalisés avant le traitement et tous les 6 mois pendant toute sa durée étant donné le risque de modifications au niveau du cristallin.

VÉRIFICATION DE L'EFFICACITÉ THÉRAPEUTIQUE

L'efficacité du traitement peut être démontrée par: la diminution des symptômes psychotiques, tels que l'excitation, la manie, la paranoïa ou le repli sur soi.

QUINAGOLIDE

Norprolac

CLASSIFICATION:

Agoniste de la dopamine, inhibiteur de la prolactine

Grossesse – catégorie inconnue

INDICATIONS

Traitement de l'hyperprolactinémie (idiopathique ou secondaire à un adénome hypophysaire).

MÉCANISME D'ACTION

Inhibition de la sécrétion de prolactine par une action dopaminergique de type agoniste. ***Effets thérapeutiques:*** Diminution de la sécrétion de prolactine.

PHARMACOCINÉTIQUE

Absorption: Rapide et élevée. Biodisponibilité à 4 % en raison d'un métabolisme hépatique de premier passage important.

Distribution: Le volume de distribution est de 100 L.

Métabolisme et excrétion: Métabolisme hépatique important. Les métabolites sont éliminés par les reins (50 %) et dans les fèces (40 %).

Demi-vie: 17 h (à l'état d'équilibre).

Profil temps-action
(effet sur les concentrations sériques de prolactine)

	Début d'action	Pic	Durée
PO	moins de 2 h	4 – 6 h	24 h et plus

CONTRE-INDICATIONS, PRÉCAUTIONS ET MISES EN GARDE

Contre-indications: Hypersensibilité au quinagolide ■ Insuffisance rénale ou hépatique (on ne dispose pas de données cliniques à cet égard).

Précautions et mises en garde: **Obst.**: L'innocuité du médicament n'a pas été établie ■ **Allaitement**: L'administration est déconseillée, car l'agent inhibe la lactation ■ **Péd.**: L'innocuité et l'efficacité du médicament n'ont pas été établies ■ Psychose (active ou antécédents): La prudence est de mise en raison du risque de crise aiguë (réversible à l'arrêt de l'administration du quinagolide) ■ Le quinagolide peut rétablir la fertilité. Les femmes en âge de procréer devraient faire usage d'une méthode contraceptive fiable si elles ne souhaitent pas devenir enceintes.

RÉACTIONS INDÉSIRABLES ET EFFETS SECONDAIRES

SNC: étourdissements, céphalées, dépression, insomnie, somnolence, asthénie, fatigue, psychose.

CV: hypotension, syncope, bouffées vasomotrices.

GI: constipation, nausées, vomissements, diarrhée, douleurs abdominales, anorexie.

ORLO: congestion nasale.

Divers: œdème.

INTERACTIONS

Médicament-médicament: Aucune interaction cliniquement significative n'a été signalée. Cependant, l'utilisation concomitante d'**antagonistes puissants de la dopamine** (comme les **neuroleptiques**) pourrait théoriquement entraîner une diminution de l'action du quinagolide ■ Lors de l'administration concomitante d'un médicament **antihypertenseur**, le quinagolide peut exercer un effet hypotenseur additif.

Médicament-aliments: L'**alcool** peut diminuer la tolérabilité au quinagolide.

VOIES D'ADMINISTRATION ET POSOLOGIE

- **PO (adultes)**: *Hyperprolactinémie* – La stimulation dopaminergique provoquée par le quinagolide pouvant provoquer des symptômes orthostatiques, le traitement doit être amorcé graduellement, à l'aide d'une trousse de départ. Administrer pendant les 3 premiers jours 1 dose de 25 µg, 1 fois par jour, au coucher. Pendant les 3 jours qui suivent, administrer 1 dose de 50 µg, 1 fois par jour, au coucher, et, par la suite, 1 dose de 75 µg, 1 fois par jour, au coucher. Si nécessaire, on peut augmenter la dose progressivement selon la réponse clinique et en l'absence de signes d'intolérance, jusqu'à l'obtention de résultats optimaux. Les doses d'entretien habituelles se situent entre 75 et 150 µg par jour. Au besoin, augmenter la dose par paliers de 75 µg (jusqu'à concurrence de 150 µg, lorsque la dose est déjà de 300 µg par jour ou plus) à intervalles d'au moins 1 semaine (4 semaines dans le cas des doses de 300 µg et plus). La dose maximale qui a été évaluée lors des études d'efficacité est de 900 µg par jour.

PRÉSENTATION

Comprimés: 25 µg[Pr], 50 µg[Pr], 75 µg[Pr], 150 µg[Pr].

SOINS INFIRMIERS

ÉVALUATION DE LA SITUATION

- Mesurer la pression artérielle avant l'administration du médicament et à intervalles fréquents pendant le traitement initial. Faire preuve de prudence lors de l'administration concomitante d'autres médicaments qui abaissent la tension artérielle. Surveiller attentivement les déplacements du patient pendant la période initiale d'adaptation de la posologie pour éviter les accidents dus à l'hypotension.

Tests de laboratoire: Pour déterminer l'efficacité du traitement, on peut mesurer les concentrations plasmatiques de prolactine.

DIAGNOSTICS INFIRMIERS POSSIBLES

- Risque d'accident (Effets secondaires).
- Connaissances insuffisantes sur le traitement médicamenteux (Enseignement au patient et à ses proches).

INTERVENTIONS INFIRMIÈRES

- Administrer le médicament 1 fois par jour, au coucher, avec une collation.
- La prise de dompéridone pourrait permettre de maîtriser les nausées et les vomissements plus fréquents durant les quelques premiers jours de traitement. Administrer 1 heure avant la dose de quinagolide.

ENSEIGNEMENT AU PATIENT ET À SES PROCHES

- Conseiller au patient de respecter rigoureusement la posologie recommandée. S'il n'a pu prendre le médicament au moment habituel, il doit le prendre aussitôt que possible, sauf s'il est presque l'heure prévue pour la dose suivante. Lui expliquer qu'il ne faut jamais remplacer une dose manquée par une double dose.
- Conseiller au patient de prévenir un professionnel de la santé s'il souffre de nausées ou de vomissements.
- Prévenir le patient que le quinagolide peut provoquer de la somnolence et des étourdissements. Lui conseiller de ne pas conduire et d'éviter les activités qui exigent sa vigilance jusqu'à ce qu'on ait la certitude que le médicament n'entraîne pas ces effets chez lui.
- Recommander au patient de changer lentement de position pour prévenir le risque d'hypotension orthostatique.
- Recommander au patient d'éviter de boire de l'alcool pendant qu'il prend le quinagolide.
- Conseiller à la patiente d'utiliser une méthode contraceptive non hormonale et de prévenir un professionnel de la santé sans délai si elle pense être enceinte ou si elle souhaite le devenir.
- Recommander au patient qui prend le quinagolide pour traiter une tumeur hypophysaire de prévenir immédiatement un professionnel de la santé si les signes suivants qui évoquent l'accroissement de la taille de la tumeur se manifestent: vision trouble, céphalées soudaines, nausées graves et vomissements.
- Insister sur l'importance des examens de suivi permettant d'évaluer l'efficacité du traitement et de surveiller les effets secondaires.

VÉRIFICATION DE L'EFFICACITÉ THÉRAPEUTIQUE

L'efficacité du traitement peut être démontrée par: la diminution de la galactorrhée chez les patients souffrant d'hyperprolactinémie. On peut abandonner le traitement au quinagolide si les taux sériques normaux de prolactine se maintiennent pendant plus de 6 mois. On devrait mesurer ces taux à intervalles réguliers pour déterminer s'il est nécessaire de reprendre le traitement par le quinagolide.

QUINAPRIL,

voir Inhibiteurs de l'enzyme de conversion de l'angiotensine (IECA)

QUINIDINE

quinidine, bisulfate de
Biquin Durules

quinidine, gluconate de
Apo-Quin-G

quinidine, gluconate de, injectable
Ce médicament n'est pas commercialisé au Canada. Disponible par l'intermédiaire du Programme d'accès spécial de Santé Canada.

quinidine, sulfate de
Apo-Quinidine, Quinidine sulfate injectable

CLASSIFICATION:
Antiarythmiques (classe IA)

Grossesse – catégorie C

INDICATIONS

Traitement d'une vaste gamme d'arythmies ventriculaires et auriculaires dont: la tachycardie ventriculaire soutenue ■ la tachycardie auriculaire paroxystique ■ le maintien d'un rythme sinusal normal après cardioversion, en cas de fibrillation ou de flutter auriculaire ■ Traitement du paludisme (gluconate par voie IV seulement).

MÉCANISME D'ACTION

Diminution de l'excitabilité du myocarde ■ Diminution de la vitesse de conduction. ***Effets thérapeutiques:*** Suppression des arythmies.

PHARMACOCINÉTIQUE

Absorption: Bonne (PO), parfois erratique (IM). L'absorption des préparations par voie orale à libération prolongée de sulfate de quinidine ou de gluconate de quinidine est plus lente.

Distribution: Tout l'organisme. L'agent traverse la barrière placentaire et passe dans le lait maternel.

Métabolisme et excrétion: Métabolisme hépatique. Excrétion rénale (de 10 à 30 % sous forme inchangée).

Demi-vie: De 6 à 8 heures (prolongée en cas d'insuffisance cardiaque ou d'insuffisance hépatique grave).

Profil temps-action (effets antiarythmiques)

	DÉBUT D'ACTION	PIC	DURÉE
PO (sulfate)	30 min	1 - 1,5 h	6 - 8 h
PO-LP† (sulfate)	inconnu	4 h	8 - 12 h
PO (gluconate)	inconnu	3 - 4 h	6 - 8 h
IM	30 min	30 - 90 min	6 - 8 h
IV	1 - 5 min	rapide	6 - 8 h

† LP = libération prolongée.

CONTRE-INDICATIONS, PRÉCAUTIONS ET MISES EN GARDE

Contre-indications: Hypersensibilité ■ Bloc AV complet ou du 2e degré ■ Troubles de conduction nodale ou idioventriculaire ■ Insuffisance cardiaque non compensée ■ Toxicité digitalique ■ Prolongation de l'intervalle QT ■ Antécédents de torsades de pointes d'origine médicamenteuse ■ Myasthénie grave.

Précautions et mises en garde: Insuffisance cardiaque ou insuffisance hépatique grave (il est recommandé de réduire la dose) ■ Hypokaliémie ou hypomagnésémie (risque accru d'allongement des intervalles QT_C) ■ **OBST., ALLAITEMENT, PÉD.:** L'innocuité du médicament n'a pas été établie; il ne faudrait pas administrer aux enfants les préparations à libération prolongée.

RÉACTIONS INDÉSIRABLES ET EFFETS SECONDAIRES

SNC: étourdissements, céphalées, syncope.

ORLO: vision trouble, diplopie, mydriase, photophobie, acouphènes.

CV: HYPOTENSION, arythmies, tachycardie.

GI: anorexie, crampes, diarrhée, nausées, goût amer, hépatite médicamenteuse.

Tég.: rash.

Hémat.: anémie hémolytique, thrombopénie.

Divers: fièvre.

INTERACTIONS

Médicament-médicament: La quinidine élève les concentrations sériques de **digoxine** et peut mener à une toxicité (il est recommandé de réduire la dose de digoxine) ■ L'**amiodarone** élève les concentrations de quinidine et augmente le risque de toxicité ■ La **phénytoïne**, le **phénobarbital** et la **rifampine** peuvent accélérer le métabolisme de la quinidine et en réduire l'efficacité ■ La **cimétidine**, le **diltiazem** et le **vérapamil** ralentissent le métabolisme de la quinidine et peuvent en augmenter les concentrations sanguines ■ Les **inhibiteurs de l'anhydrase carbonique** retardent l'excrétion de la quinidine et en augmentent les effets ■ La quinidine accentue l'effet des **bloqueurs neuromusculaires** et de la **warfarine** ■ Risque d'hypotension additive lors de l'administration concomitante d'**antihypertenseurs** et de **dérivés nitrés** ainsi que de l'ingestion de grandes quantités d'**alcool** ■ La quinidine peut augmenter les concentrations de **procaïnamide**, de **propafénone** ou d'**antidépresseurs tricycliques** et accroître le risque de toxicité lié à ces médicaments ■ La quinidine peut contrecarrer les effets du **traitement anticholinestérasique** chez les patients souffrant de myasthénie grave ■ Les **médicaments qui alcalinisent l'urine**, incluant les **antiacides** à doses élevées ou le **bicarbonate de sodium**, élèvent les concentrations sanguines de quinidine et augmentent le risque de toxicité ■ Risque d'effets anticholinergiques accrus lors de l'administration concomitante d'**agents dotés de propriétés anticholinergiques**, incluant les **antihistaminiques** et les **antidépresseurs tricycliques** ■ Risque accru d'arythmies en cas d'administration concomitante de **pimozide**.

Médicament-aliments: Les **aliments qui alcalinisent l'urine** (voir l'annexe J) et le **jus de pamplemousse** peuvent élever les concentrations sériques de quinidine et augmenter le risque de toxicité.

Q

VOIES D'ADMINISTRATION ET POSOLOGIE

Bisulfate de quinidine (quinidine à 66 %)

Un comprimé de bisulfate à 250 mg équivaut à 200 mg de sulfate de quinidine.

- **PO (adultes):** De 500 mg à 1 250 mg de bisulfate de quinidine, toutes les 12 heures.

Gluconate de quinidine (quinidine à 62 %)

- **PO (adultes):** De 325 à 650 mg, 3 ou 4 fois par jour.

Sulfate de quinidine (quinidine à 83 %)

- **PO (adultes):** *Tachycardie supraventriculaire paroxystique* – de 400 à 600 mg, toutes les 2 ou 3 heures, jusqu'à ce que l'arythmie soit réprimée. *Cardioversion en cas de fibrillation auriculaire* – 200 mg, toutes les 2 ou 3 heures (de 5 à 8 doses); on peut augmenter la dose quotidienne selon les besoins (ne pas dépasser 4 g par jour). *Extrasystoles auriculaires ou ventriculaires* – de 200 à 300 mg, toutes les 6 à 8 heures (ne pas dépasser 4 g par jour).

PRÉSENTATION (version générique disponible)

- **Bisulfate de quinidine**
  Comprimés à libération prolongée: 250 mg[Pr].
- **Gluconate de quinidine**
  Comprimés: 325 mg[Pr].
- **Sulfate de quinidine**
  Comprimés: 200 mg[Pr] ■ **Solution pour injection IM:** 190 mg/mL[Pr].

SOINS INFIRMIERS

ÉVALUATION DE LA SITUATION

- MESURER LA PRESSION ARTÉRIELLE ET LE POULS ET EXAMINER L'ÉCG TOUT AU LONG DE L'ADMINISTRATION IV. CES PARAMÈTRES DOIVENT ÊTRE SUIVIS À INTERVALLES RÉGULIERS PENDANT TOUTE LA DURÉE DE L'ADMINISTRATION PO. IL FAUT HABITUELLEMENT INTERROMPRE L'ADMINISTRATION IV SI L'ARYTHMIE EST SUPPRIMÉE, SI LE COMPLEXE QRS S'ÉLARGIT DE 50 %, SI LES INTERVALLES PR OU QT S'ALLONGENT OU SI DES EXTRASYSTOLES VENTRICULAIRES FRÉQUENTES OU UNE TACHYCARDIE SURVIENNENT. POUR RÉDUIRE LES RISQUES D'HYPOTENSION, LE PATIENT DOIT RESTER COUCHÉ PENDANT TOUTE LA DURÉE DE L'ADMINISTRATION IV.

Tests de laboratoire: Examiner à intervalles réguliers, pendant toute la durée du traitement prolongé, les résultats des tests des fonctions rénale et hépatique, la numération globulaire et les concentrations sériques de potassium.

TOXICITÉ ET SURDOSAGE:

- On peut examiner à intervalles réguliers pendant toute la période d'adaptation de la posologie les concentrations sériques de quinidine. Les concentrations sériques thérapeutiques se situent entre 6 et 15 µmol/L. Les effets toxiques surviennent habituellement à des concentrations > 15 µmol/L.
- Les signes et les symptômes de toxicité ou de cinchonisme sont les suivants: acouphènes, perte auditive, troubles visuels, céphalées, nausées et étourdissements. Ces signes et symptômes peuvent survenir après l'administration d'une seule dose.
- Les signes cardiaques de toxicité sont: l'élargissement du complexe QRS, les asystoles cardiaques, les extrasystoles ventriculaires, les rythmes idioventriculaires (tachycardie ventriculaire, fibrillation ventriculaire), la tachycardie paroxystique et l'embolie artérielle.

DIAGNOSTICS INFIRMIERS POSSIBLES

- Débit cardiaque diminué (Indications).
- Connaissances insuffisantes sur le traitement médicamenteux (Enseignement au patient et à ses proches).

INTERVENTIONS INFIRMIÈRES

- NE PAS CONFONDRE LA QUINIDINE AVEC LA QUININE.
- Pour vérifier la tolérance du patient aux effets du médicament, on peut administrer avant le traitement par la quinidine un comprimé de sulfate de quinidine à 200 mg ou du gluconate de quinidine à 200 mg par voie IM, comme dose d'essai.
- Pour corriger les arythmies auriculaires, on doit parfois administrer des doses plus élevées que celles administrées habituellement pour supprimer les arythmies ventriculaires.

PO: Administrer le médicament à jeun, avec un grand verre d'eau, 1 heure avant ou 2 heures après les repas, pour en accélérer l'absorption. Si l'irritation gastrique devient gênante, administrer le médicament avec des aliments ou juste après les repas. LES PRÉPARATIONS À LIBÉRATION PROLONGÉE (BIQUIN DURULES) DOIVENT ÊTRE AVALÉES TELLES QUELLES, SANS ÊTRE BRISÉES, ÉCRASÉES NI MÂCHÉES.

ENSEIGNEMENT AU PATIENT ET À SES PROCHES

- Conseiller au patient de prendre le médicament à intervalles réguliers, 24 heures sur 24, en respectant rigoureusement la posologie recommandée, même s'il se sent mieux. S'il n'a pu prendre le médicament au moment habituel, il doit le prendre dès que possible, dans les 2 heures qui suivent. Sinon, il doit sauter cette dose. L'avertir qu'il ne faut jamais remplacer une dose manquée par une double dose.
- Montrer au patient ou à ses proches comment prendre le pouls. Leur conseiller de signaler à un professionnel de la santé tout changement de fréquence ou de rythme.
- Prévenir le patient que la quinidine peut provoquer des étourdissements ou une vision trouble. Lui conseiller de ne pas conduire et d'éviter les activités qui exigent sa vigilance jusqu'à ce qu'on ait la certitude que le médicament n'entraîne pas ces effets chez lui.
- Prévenir le patient que la quinidine peut le rendre plus sensible à la lumière. Lui conseiller de porter des lunettes de soleil pour réduire cet effet.
- Recommander au patient qui doit suivre un autre traitement ou subir une intervention chirurgicale

d'avertir le professionnel de la santé qu'il suit un traitement par ce médicament.

- Conseiller au patient de consulter un professionnel de la santé avant de prendre des médicaments en vente libre en même temps que la quinidine.
- Recommander au patient de communiquer avec un professionnel de la santé en cas de symptômes de cinchonisme (notamment acouphènes, céphalées, nausées et vision légèrement trouble), de rash, de dyspnée ou de diarrhée grave ou persistante.
- Recommander au patient de porter sur lui en tout temps une pièce d'identité où sont inscrits son problème de santé et son traitement médicamenteux.
- Insister sur l'importance des examens réguliers de suivi permettant d'évaluer les bienfaits du traitement.

VÉRIFICATION DE L'EFFICACITÉ THÉRAPEUTIQUE

L'efficacité du traitement peut être démontrée par: la suppression des arythmies sans effets secondaires nocifs. ✳

QUININE

Apo-Quinine, Novo-Quinine, Quinine-Odan

quinine, dihydrochlorate de, injectable

Ce médicament n'est pas commercialisé au Canada. Disponible par l'intermédiaire du Programme d'accès spécial de Santé Canada.

CLASSIFICATION:

Anti-infectieux (antiprotozoaire), antipaludéen

Grossesse – catégorie D

INDICATIONS

Traitement d'association du paludisme résistant à la chloroquine. **Usages non approuvés:** Prophylaxie et traitement des crampes musculaires nocturnes dans les jambes.

MÉCANISME D'ACTION

Inhibition du métabolisme de la phase érythrocytaire de *Plasmodium falciparum* ■ Prolongation de la phase réfractaire du muscle squelettique, augmentation de la distribution du calcium dans les fibres musculaires, diminution de l'excitabilité des plaques motrices, entraînant une diminution de la réponse à la stimulation répétée des nerfs et à l'acétylcholine. ***Effets thérapeutiques:*** Destruction de *P. falciparum* ■ Diminution de l'intensité des crampes dans les jambes.

PHARMACOCINÉTIQUE

Absorption: 80 % (PO).

Distribution: Variable d'un patient à l'autre, en fonction de son état; le médicament ne pénètre pas bien dans le liquide céphalorachidien. Il traverse la barrière placentaire et passe dans le lait maternel.

Liaison aux protéines: > 90 % chez les patients atteints de paludisme cérébral, les femmes enceintes et les enfants, de 85 à 90 % chez les patients atteints de paludisme non compliqué, 70 % chez les adultes en santé.

Métabolisme et excrétion: Métabolisme majoritairement hépatique (> 80 %). Excrétion rénale (sous forme de métabolites moins actifs que la quinine et 20 % sous forme inchangée). Le taux d'excrétion est accru si l'urine est acide.

Demi-vie: 11 heures (accrue chez les patients atteints de paludisme).

Profil temps-action

	DÉBUT D'ACTION	PIC	DURÉE
PO	inconnu	3,2 – 5,9 h	8 h

CONTRE-INDICATIONS, PRÉCAUTIONS ET MISES EN GARDE

Contre-indications: Hypersensibilité (une sensibilité croisée entre la quinine et la quinidine peut survenir) ■ Carence en glucose-6-phosphate-déshydrogénase (G-6-PD) ■ Acouphènes ■ Névrite optique ■ Myasthénie grave ■ Hypoglycémie ■ Antécédents de fièvre bilieuse hémoglobinurique ■ Antécédents de purpura thrombopénique.

Précautions et mises en garde: Traitement antipaludéen récurrent ou interrompu ■ Antécédents d'arythmies, particulièrement en cas d'allongement des intervalles QT ■ **OBST., ALLAITEMENT:** Administration à éviter, si possible, mais certaines patientes pourraient tirer profit de ce médicament.

RÉACTIONS INDÉSIRABLES ET EFFETS SECONDAIRES

CV: ARYTHMIES (RARES).

GI: douleurs et crampes abdominales, diarrhée, nausées, vomissements, hépatotoxicité.

Tég.: rash.

End.: hypoglycémie.

Hémat.: saignements, dyscrasie sanguine, purpura thrombopénique, thrombopénie.

Divers: cinchonisme, réactions d'hypersensibilité incluant la fièvre et le SYNDROME HÉMOLYTIQUE ET URÉMIQUE.

Q

INTERACTIONS

Médicament-médicament: La quinine peut élever les concentrations de **procaïnamide**, de **propafénone** ou d'**antidépresseurs tricycliques** et accroître le risque de toxicité lié à ces médicaments ▪ La **cimétidine** ralentit le métabolisme de la quinine et peut en augmenter les concentrations sanguines ▪ La **rifampine** peut accélérer le métabolisme de la quinine et en réduire l'efficacité ▪ Les antiacides peuvent diminuer l'absorption de la quinine ▪ La quinine accentue l'effet des **bloqueurs neuromusculaires** ▪ Le médicament peut accroître les concentrations sériques de **digoxine** ▪ La quinine peut accroître le risque de réactions hémolytiques, ototoxiques ou neurotoxiques, en cas d'administration concomitante d'**agents également associés à ces toxicités** ▪ Risque accru d'arythmies lors de l'administration concomitante de **quinidine**, de **procaïnamide**, de **disopyramide**, d'**antiarythmiques de classe III**, de **pimozide** et de **macrolides** ▪ La quinine peut accroître le risque de saignement en cas d'administration concomitante de **warfarine** ▪ La **méfloquine** augmente le risque de convulsions et de réactions cardiovasculaires indésirables ▪ Les **médicaments qui alcalinisent l'urine**, incluant l'**acétazolamide** et le **bicarbonate de sodium**, élèvent les concentrations sanguines de quinine et augmentent le risque de toxicité.

VOIES D'ADMINISTRATION ET POSOLOGIE

- **PO (adultes):** *Paludisme* – 600 mg, 3 fois par jour, pendant 3 à 7 jours, en association avec la doxycycline, la sulfadoxine/pyraméthamine ou la clindamycine; *crampes dans les jambes* – usage non approuvé: de 200 à 300 mg, au coucher; au besoin, on peut administrer une dose additionnelle de 200 à 300 mg avec le repas du soir.
- **PO (enfants):** 9 mg/kg, 3 fois par jour, pendant 3 à 7 jours, en association avec la doxycycline (si l'enfant est âgé > 8 ans) ou avec la sulfadoxine/pyraméthamine ou la clindamycine.

INSUFFISANCE RÉNALE

- **PO (ADULTES ET ENFANTS):** *Cl_{CR} DE 10 À 50 mL/MIN* – ADMINISTRER TOUTES LES 8 À 12 HEURES; *Cl_{CR} < 10 mL/MIN* – ADMINISTRER TOUTES LES 24 HEURES.

PRÉSENTATION

Capsules: 200 mg[Pr], 300 mg[Pr] ▪ **Comprimés:** 300 mg[Pr].

SOINS INFIRMIERS

ÉVALUATION DE LA SITUATION

Paludisme: Vérifier tous les jours, pendant toute la durée du traitement, si les signes et les symptômes diminuent.

Crampes nocturnes dans les jambes en décubitus: Évaluer la fréquence et l'intensité des crampes nocturnes dans les jambes. Si les crampes ne se manifestent pas pendant plusieurs nuits consécutives, le traitement peut être interrompu pour permettre de déterminer s'il est toujours nécessaire.

Tests de laboratoire: La quinine peut entraîner des concentrations urinaires élevées de 17-cétostéroïdes, si l'on utilise un test à la métyrapone ou la réaction de Zimmerman.

TOXICITÉ ET SURDOSAGE:

- Des concentrations plasmatiques de quinine > 3,2 µmol/L peuvent provoquer des acouphènes et des troubles auditifs.
- Les signes de toxicité ou de cinchonisme incluent les acouphènes, les céphalées, les nausées et une vision légèrement trouble; ces signes disparaissent habituellement rapidement si l'on arrête le traitement par la quinine.

DIAGNOSTICS INFIRMIERS POSSIBLES

- Risque d'infection (Indications).
- Douleur chronique (Indications).
- Connaissances insuffisantes sur le traitement médicamenteux (Enseignement au patient et à ses proches).

INTERVENTIONS INFIRMIÈRES

- NE PAS CONFONDRE LA QUININE AVEC LA QUINIDINE.
- Administrer la quinine avec ou après les repas pour réduire la gêne gastro-intestinale. Les antiacides à base d'aluminium diminuent l'absorption et la retardent; éviter l'usage concomitant.

ENSEIGNEMENT AU PATIENT ET À SES PROCHES

- Conseiller au patient de respecter rigoureusement la posologie recommandée et de mener le traitement à terme, même s'il se sent mieux. S'il n'a pu prendre le médicament au moment habituel, il doit le prendre dès que possible, à moins que ce ne soit presque l'heure prévue pour la dose suivante. L'avertir qu'il ne doit jamais remplacer une dose manquée par une double dose ni augmenter la posologie de son propre chef.
- En cas d'usage prophylactique, passer en revue les moyens de réduire l'exposition aux moustiques: utiliser un insectifuge, porter des chemises à manches longues et des pantalons, se protéger par une moustiquaire ou un filet.
- Prévenir le patient que la quinine peut modifier la vision. Lui conseiller de ne pas conduire et d'éviter les activités qui exigent sa vigilance jusqu'à ce qu'on

Q

ait la certitude que le médicament n'entraîne pas cet effet chez lui.

- Prévenir le patient que la quinine peut provoquer la diarrhée, des nausées, des crampes ou des douleurs d'estomac, des vomissements ou des acouphènes. Lui recommander de consulter rapidement un professionnel de la santé si ces signes deviennent marqués.
- Conseiller au patient de cesser de prendre la quinine et de consulter un professionnel de la santé en cas de symptômes pouvant être de nature allergique: bouffées vasomotrices, démangeaisons, rash, fièvre, douleurs d'estomac, troubles respiratoires, acouphènes, troubles visuels.
- Conseiller au patient de consulter un professionnel de la santé avant de prendre des produits naturels pouvant contenir de la quinine ou des médicaments en vente libre.
- Recommander à la patiente de prévenir immédiatement un professionnel de la santé si elle pense être enceinte ou si elle allaite.

VÉRIFICATION DE L'EFFICACITÉ THÉRAPEUTIQUE

L'efficacité du traitement peut être démontrée par: la prévention ou la diminution des signes et des symptômes de paludisme ■ la diminution de la fréquence et de l'intensité des crampes nocturnes dans les jambes.

QUINUPRISTINE/ DALFOPRISTINE

Synercid

CLASSIFICATION:

Antibiotique (streptogramine)

Grossesse - catégorie D

INDICATIONS

Traitement des infections graves ou mettant la vie du patient en danger, dues aux souches *Enterococcus fæcium* résistantes à la vancomycine ■ Infections compliquées de la peau et de ses annexes dues à *Staphylococcus aureus* (souches sensibles à la méthicilline) ou à *Streptococcus pyogenes,* et qui se prêtent à un traitement IV.

MÉCANISME D'ACTION

La quinupristine inhibe la phase tardive de la synthèse des protéines au niveau du ribosome bactérien; la dalfopristine en inhibe la phase précoce. ***Effets thérapeutiques:*** Effet bactériostatique contre les microorganismes sensibles. **Spectre d'action:** L'agent est actif contre les souches de *E. fæcium*, de *S. aureus* (souches sensibles à la méthicilline) et de *S. pyogenes* résistantes à la vancomycine et à plusieurs autres médicaments ■ Il n'exerce pas d'effet contre *E. fæcalis*.

PHARMACOCINÉTIQUE

Absorption: Biodisponibilité à 100 % (IV).

Distribution: Inconnue.

Liaison aux protéines: Modérée.

Métabolisme et excrétion: Les deux agents sont transformés en composés dotés d'une activité anti-infectieuse additionnelle; les molécules mères et les métabolites sont principalement excrétés dans les fèces (de 75 à 77 %); excrétion rénale (15 % pour la quinupristine et 17 % pour la dalfopristine).

Demi-vie: *Quinupristine* – 0,85 heure; *dalfopristine* – 0,7 heure.

Profil temps-action

	DÉBUT D'ACTION	PIC	DURÉE
IV	rapide	fin de la perfusion	8 - 12 h

CONTRE-INDICATIONS, PRÉCAUTIONS ET MISES EN GARDE

Contre-indications: Hypersensibilité à ce médicament ou aux autres agents de la classe des streptogramines.

Précautions et mises en garde: Usage concomitant d'autres agents métabolisés par le système enzymatique du cytochrome P450 3A4 (risque d'interactions graves; voir «Interactions médicament-médicament») ■ Ce médicament ne doit pas être administré par bolus intraveineux ■ Insuffisance hépatique (aucune adaptation posologique n'est nécessaire en présence d'insuffisance hépatique légère [classe A de Child-Pugh]; une diminution de la dose peut être envisagée en présence d'une insuffisance modérée [classe B de Child-Pugh]; ce médicament est déconseillé en cas d'insuffisance grave [classe C de Child-Pugh]) ■ Antécédents de maladie gastro-intestinale, particulièrement de colite ■ **OBST, ALLAITEMENT, PÉD. (ENFANTS < 16 ANS):** L'innocuité du médicament n'a pas été établie.

RÉACTIONS INDÉSIRABLES ET EFFETS SECONDAIRES

SNC: céphalées.

CV: thrombophlébite.

GI: COLITE PSEUDOMEMBRANEUSE, diarrhée, nausées, vomissements, hyperbilirubinémie.

Tég.: prurit, rash.

Loc.: myalgie, arthralgie.

Locaux: œdème, inflammation et douleur au point de perfusion, réactions au point de perfusion.
Divers: réactions allergiques, incluant l'ANAPHYLAXIE, douleur.

INTERACTIONS

Médicament-médicament: Puisque l'agent inhibe le cytochrome P450 3A4 (système enzymatique responsable du métabolisme de certains médicaments), il inhibe le métabolisme de la **cyclosporine**, du **midazolam** et de la **nifédipine** et augmente le risque de toxicité (une surveillance étroite est de mise) ■ Des effets similaires peuvent être prévus en cas d'administration concomitante de **délavirdine**, de **névirapine**, d'**indinavir**, de **ritonavir**, d'**alcaloïdes de la pervenche**, de **docétaxel**, de **paclitaxel**, de **diazépam**, de **vérapamil**, de **diltiazem**, d'**inhibiteurs de l'HMG-CoA réductase**, de **cisapride** (risque d'allongement de l'intervalle QT_c), de **tacrolimus**, de **méthylprednisolone**, de **carbamazépine**, de **quinidine** (risque d'allongement de l'intervalle QT_c), de **lidocaïne**(risque d'allongement de l'intervalle QT_c) et de **disopyramide** (risque d'allongement de l'intervalle QT_c) ■ L'utilisation concomitante de **rifampicine** dicte la surveillance des taux de bilirubine.

VOIES D'ADMINISTRATION ET POSOLOGIE

- **IV (adultes):** *Infection par* E. fæcium *résistant à la vancomycine* – 7,5 mg/kg, toutes les 8 heures, pendant une durée moyenne de 15 à 20 jours; *infections compliquées de la peau et de ses annexes* – 7,5 mg/kg, toutes les 12 heures, pendant au moins 7 jours.

Q

PRÉSENTATION

Poudre pour injection: 500 mg (150 mg de quinupristine et 350 mg de dalfopristine)[Pr].

SOINS INFIRMIERS

ÉVALUATION DE LA SITUATION

- Au début du traitement et pendant toute sa durée, rester à l'affût des signes suivants d'infection: altération des signes vitaux, aspect de la plaie, des crachats, de l'urine et des selles; accroissement du nombre de globules blancs.
- Prélever des échantillons pour les cultures et les antibiogrammes avant de commencer le traitement. On peut administrer la première dose avant que les résultats soient connus.
- Observer le patient à intervalles fréquents pour déceler la douleur ou l'inflammation au point de perfusion. Il peut s'avérer nécessaire d'augmenter le volume de diluant de 250 à 500 mL ou à 750 mL ou d'effectuer la perfusion à l'aide d'un cathéter central introduit dans la circulation périphérique, ou d'un cathéter veineux central.
- RESTER À L'AFFÛT DES SIGNES ET DES SYMPTÔMES SUIVANTS D'ANAPHYLAXIE: RASH, PRURIT, ŒDÈME LARYNGÉ, RESPIRATION SIFFLANTE. SI CES RÉACTIONS SE MANIFESTENT, ARRÊTER L'ADMINISTRATION DU MÉDICAMENT ET AVERTIR IMMÉDIATEMENT LE MÉDECIN OU UN AUTRE PROFESSIONNEL DE LA SANTÉ. GARDER À PORTÉE DE LA MAIN DE L'ADRÉNALINE, UN ANTIHISTAMINIQUE ET LE MATÉRIEL DE RÉANIMATION POUR PARER À UNE ÉVENTUELLE RÉACTION ANAPHYLACTIQUE.
- Déceler la présence de myalgie ou d'arthralgie après la perfusion, lesquelles pourraient être graves. Le fait de diminuer la fréquence des doses (toutes les 12 heures) peut réduire la douleur. Les symptômes disparaissent habituellement à l'arrêt de la médication.

Tests de laboratoire: L'agent peut entraîner une élévation des concentrations sériques de bilirubine totale.

DIAGNOSTICS INFIRMIERS POSSIBLES

- Risque d'infection (Indications, Effets secondaires).
- Diarrhée (Réactions indésirables).
- Connaissances insuffisantes sur le traitement médicamenteux (Enseignement au patient et à ses proches).

INTERVENTIONS INFIRMIÈRES

Perfusion intermittente: Reconstituer la solution en y ajoutant lentement 5 mL de solution de D5%E ou d'eau stérile pour injection pour obtenir une concentration de 100 mg/mL. Consulter les directives du fabricant avant de reconstituer la préparation. Faire tourner légèrement la solution pour la mélanger. Éviter d'agiter la fiole pour prévenir la formation de mousse. Laisser la solution au repos jusqu'à ce que toute la mousse ait disparu. La solution devrait être transparente. Diluer de nouveau en ajoutant la dose du médicament reconstitué à 250 mL de D5%E (on peut utiliser 100 mL, si on administre la préparation par une tubulure de perfusion centrale).

Vitesse d'administration: Administrer la solution en 60 minutes à l'aide d'un dispositif de perfusion contrôlée. Rincer la tubulure avant et après la perfusion avec une solution de D5%E. Ne pas utiliser de solution de NaCl 0,9 % ou d'héparine.

Compatibilité (tubulure en Y): aztréonam ■ ciprofloxacine ■ fluconazole ■ halopéridol ■ métoclopramide ■ potassium, chlorure de.

Incompatibilité en addition au soluté: Ne pas mélanger avec d'autres solutions ou médicaments.
Diluant incompatible: NaCl 0,9 %.

ENSEIGNEMENT AU PATIENT ET À SES PROCHES

- RECOMMANDER AU PATIENT DE COMMUNIQUER AVEC UN PROFESSIONNEL DE LA SANTÉ EN CAS DE FIÈVRE OU DE DIARRHÉE, PARTICULIÈREMENT SI SES SELLES RENFERMENT DU SANG, DU PUS OU DU MUCUS. LUI CONSEILLER DE NE PAS TRAITER LA DIARRHÉE SANS CONSULTER AU PRÉALABLE UN PROFESSIONNEL DE LA SANTÉ.

VÉRIFICATION DE L'EFFICACITÉ THÉRAPEUTIQUE

L'efficacité du traitement peut être démontrée par: la disparition des signes et des symptômes d'infection. Le temps de résolution dépend du microorganisme infectant et du siège de l'infection. ✱

RABÉPRAZOLE

Pariet

CLASSIFICATION:

Antiulcéreux (inhibiteur de la pompe à protons)

Grossesse – catégorie B

INDICATIONS

Traitement des affections nécessitant une réduction de la sécrétion d'acide gastrique dont le soulagement symptomatique et la cicatrisation de l'œsophagite érosive ou ulcéreuse liée au reflux gastro-œsophagien ■ Cicatrisation du reflux gastro-œsophagien (RGO) érosif ou ulcéreux ■ Traitement d'entretien pour maintenir la guérison du RGO érosif ou ulcéreux ■ Soulagement symptomatique et cicatrisation des ulcères duodénaux et gastriques ■ Traitement des états pathologiques associés à une hypersécrétion, dont le syndrome de Zollinger-Ellison ■ En association avec l'amoxicilline et la clarithromycine*:* Éradication de *H. pylori* chez les patients ayant des antécédents d'ulcère duodénal ■ Ulcère duodénal associé à *H. pylori*.

MÉCANISME D'ACTION

Inhibiteur spécifique de l'enzyme gastrique H^+, K^+-ATPase (pompe à protons), responsable des sécrétions acides des cellules pariétales de l'estomac, ce qui prévient l'entrée des ions hydrogène dans la lumière du tube gastrique. ***Effets thérapeutiques:*** Diminution de l'accumulation d'acide dans la lumière gastrique et réduction du reflux gastro-œsophagien ■ Cicatrisation des ulcères duodénaux et de ceux provoqués par l'œsophagite ■ Diminution des sécrétions acides caractérisant les états d'hypersécrétion.

R

PHARMACOCINÉTIQUE

Absorption: Le comprimé retard traverse l'estomac sans être modifié par les sucs gastriques. Par la suite, 52 % est absorbé.

Distribution: Inconnue.

Liaison aux protéines: 96,3 %.

Métabolisme et excrétion: Métabolisme majoritairement hépatique (par les isoenzymes du cytochrome P450 3A et 2C19); excrétion dans les fèces (10 %); le reste est excrété dans l'urine sous forme de métabolites inactifs.

Demi-vie: De 1 à 2 heures.

Profil temps-action (suppression des sécrétions acides)

	DÉBUT D'ACTION	PIC	DURÉE
PO	moins de 1 h	inconnu	24 h†

† La suppression des sécrétions continue de s'accroître au cours des premières semaines de traitement.

CONTRE-INDICATIONS, PRÉCAUTIONS ET MISES EN GARDE

Contre-indications: Hypersensibilité au rabéprazole ou aux médicaments apparentés (benzimidazoles).

Précautions et mises en garde: Insuffisance hépatique grave (une réduction de la dose peut s'avérer nécessaire) ■ **OBST., ALLAITEMENT, PÉD.:** L'allaitement est déconseillé; n'administrer au cours de la grossesse qu'en cas d'absolue nécessité; l'innocuité du médicament n'a pas été établie.

RÉACTIONS INDÉSIRABLES ET EFFETS SECONDAIRES

SNC: étourdissements, céphalées, malaise.

GI: douleurs abdominales, constipation, diarrhée, nausées.

Tég.: photosensibilité, rash.

Loc.: douleurs à la nuque.

Divers: réactions allergiques, frissons, fièvre.

INTERACTIONS

Médicament-médicament: Le rabéprazole est métabolisé par le cytochrome P450 et peut interagir avec d'autres **médicaments métabolisés par ce système** ■ Le rabéprazole diminue les concentrations sanguines de **kétoconazole** ■ Le rabéprazole élève les concentrations sanguines de **digoxine** ■ Le rabéprazole peut réduire l'absorption des **médicaments nécessitant un pH acide**, tels que le **kétoconazole**, l'**itraconazole**, les **esters d'ampicilline** et les **sels ferreux** ■ Risque accru de saignement lors de l'usage concomitant de **warfarine** (suivre le RNI et le temps de prothrombine).

VOIES D'ADMINISTRATION ET POSOLOGIE

■ **PO (adultes):** *Cicatrisation du RGO érosif ou ulcéreux* – 20 mg, 1 fois par jour, pendant 4 à 8 semaines; en l'absence de guérison en l'espace de 8 semaines, on peut envisager la poursuite du traitement pendant 8 semaines de plus. *Traitement d'entretien pour maintenir la guérison du RGO* – de 10 à 20 mg, 1 fois par jour. *Traitement des symptômes de RGO* – de 10 à 20 mg, 1 fois par jour. *Cicatrisation de l'ulcère duodénal* – 20 mg, 1 fois par jour, pendant 4 semaines; on peut envisager un traitement prolongé. *Cicatrisation de l'ulcère gastrique* – 20 mg, 1 fois par jour, pendant 6 semaines; on peut envisager un traitement prolongé. *États pathologiques associés à l'hypersécrétion* – initialement, 60 mg, 1 fois par jour; on peut adapter la dose, selon les besoins, et poursuivre le traitement tant qu'il est nécessaire; on a déjà administré des doses allant jusqu'à 60 mg, 2 fois par jour. *Ulcère duodénal* *évolutif associé à* H. pylori – 20 mg, 2 fois par jour, en association avec la clarithromycine et l'amoxicilline pendant 7 jours.

PRÉSENTATION

Comprimés à libération retard: 10 mg[Pr], 20 mg[Pr].

SOINS INFIRMIERS

ÉVALUATION DE LA SITUATION

- Observer le patient à intervalles réguliers afin de déceler les douleurs épigastriques ou abdominales ainsi que la présence de sang visible ou occulte dans les selles, les vomissures ou le liquide d'aspiration gastrique.

Tests de laboratoire: Noter, à intervalles réguliers pendant toute la durée du traitement, la numération globulaire et la formule leucocytaire.

DIAGNOSTICS INFIRMIERS POSSIBLES

- Douleur aiguë (Indications).
- Connaissances insuffisantes sur le traitement médicamenteux (Enseignement au patient et à ses proches).

INTERVENTIONS INFIRMIÈRES

PO: Administrer le médicament avant le repas, de préférence le matin. LES COMPRIMÉS DOIVENT ÊTRE AVALÉS TELS QUELS SANS QU'ILS SOIENT ÉCRASÉS, BRISÉS OU MÂCHÉS.

ENSEIGNEMENT AU PATIENT ET À SES PROCHES

- Conseiller au patient de suivre rigoureusement la posologie recommandée pendant toute la durée du traitement, même s'il se sent mieux. S'il n'a pu prendre le médicament au moment habituel, il doit le prendre aussitôt que possible, sauf s'il est presque l'heure prévue pour la dose suivante. Le prévenir qu'il ne doit jamais remplacer une dose manquée par une double dose.
- Prévenir le patient que le rabéprazole peut parfois provoquer de la somnolence ou des étourdissements. Lui conseiller de ne pas conduire et d'éviter les activités qui exigent sa vigilance jusqu'à ce qu'on ait la certitude que le médicament n'entraîne pas ces effets chez lui.
- Recommander au patient de ne pas prendre de médicaments à base d'aspirine ni d'AINS, sauf recommandation contraire du médecin, et de ne pas consommer d'alcool ni d'aliments pouvant aggraver l'irritation gastrique.
- Recommander au patient d'utiliser un écran solaire et de porter des vêtements protecteurs afin de prévenir les réactions de photosensibilité.
- Recommander au patient de signaler rapidement à un professionnel de la santé la présence de selles noires et goudronneuses, de diarrhée, de douleurs abdominales ou de céphalées persistantes.

VÉRIFICATION DE L'EFFICACITÉ THÉRAPEUTIQUE

L'efficacité du traitement peut être démontrée par: le soulagement de la douleur abdominale ou la prévention de l'irritation ou des saignements gastriques; on peut constater la guérison de l'ulcère gastroduodénal par radiographie ou endoscopie ■ la diminution des symptômes du reflux gastro-œsophagien (il faudrait poursuivre le traitement pendant 4 à 8 semaines après le premier épisode).

RALOXIFÈNE

Evista

CLASSIFICATION:

Inhibiteur de la résorption osseuse (modulateur sélectif des récepteurs des œstrogènes)

Grossesse – catégorie X

INDICATIONS

Traitement et prévention de l'ostéoporose chez les femmes ménopausées.

MÉCANISME D'ACTION

Liaison aux récepteurs des œstrogènes, exerçant des effets similaires à ceux des œstrogènes sur les os, ce qui entraîne une diminution de la résorption osseuse. ***Effets thérapeutiques:*** Prévention et traitement de l'ostéoporose chez les patientes à risque.

PHARMACOCINÉTIQUE

Absorption: 60 % (PO). Biodisponibilité à 2 % (PO) en raison d'un fort métabolisme hépatique de premier passage.

Distribution: Inconnue.

Liaison aux protéines: Forte.

Métabolisme et excrétion: Métabolisme hépatique important; l'agent subit un cycle entérohépatique et est excrété principalement dans les fèces.

Demi-vie: 27,7 heures.

R

Profil temps-action
(effet sur le renouvellement des cellules osseuses)

	DÉBUT D'ACTION	PIC	DURÉE
PO	inconnu	3 mois	inconnue

CONTRE-INDICATIONS, PRÉCAUTIONS ET MISES EN GARDE

Contre-indications: Hypersensibilité ■ Antécédents d'épisodes thromboemboliques veineux, tels que la thrombose veineuse profonde, l'embolie pulmonaire ou la thrombose des veines rétiniennes ■ Femmes en âge de procréer ■ Grossesse, allaitement.
Précautions et mises en garde: Périodes d'immobilisation prolongée (risque accru d'épisodes thromboemboliques) ■ Enfants ■ Insuffisance hépatique ■ Hommes ■ Hypertriglycéridémie.

RÉACTIONS INDÉSIRABLES ET EFFETS SECONDAIRES

CV: AVC, événement thromboembolique.
Loc.: crampes dans les jambes.
Divers: bouffées vasomotrices.

INTERACTIONS

Médicament-médicament: La **cholestyramine** diminue l'absorption du raloxifène (éviter l'administration concomitante) ■ Le raloxifène peut modifier les effets de la **warfarine** et d'autres **médicaments qui se lient fortement aux protéines** ■ Il n'est pas recommandé d'administrer en concomitance une **œstrogénothérapie** par voie systémique.

VOIES D'ADMINISTRATION ET POSOLOGIE

R

- **PO (adultes)**: 60 mg, 1 fois par jour.

PRÉSENTATION

Comprimés: 60 mg[Pr].

SOINS INFIRMIERS

ÉVALUATION DE LA SITUATION

- Déterminer, avant le traitement et à intervalles réguliers pendant toute sa durée, la densité minérale osseuse par des radiographies et par le dosage des marqueurs sériques et urinaires du renouvellement des cellules osseuses (phosphatase alcaline de l'os, ostéocalcine et produits de dégradation du collagène).

Tests de laboratoire:

- Le raloxifène peut entraîner une élévation des concentrations d'apolipoprotéine A-1 et une diminution des concentrations sériques de cholestérol total, de cholestérol LDL, de fibrinogène, d'apolipoprotéine B et de lipoprotéines.
- Le médicament peut entraîner une augmentation des globulines qui se fixent aux hormones (globuline qui se lie aux stéroïdes sexuels, globuline qui se lie à la thyroxine, globuline qui se lie aux corticostéroïdes), entraînant une élévation des concentrations totales d'hormones.
- Le raloxifène peut provoquer une légère diminution des concentrations sériques de calcium total, de phosphate inorganique, de protéines totales et d'albumine.
- L'agent peut également diminuer légèrement la numération plaquettaire.

DIAGNOSTICS INFIRMIERS POSSIBLES

- Risque d'accident (Indications).
- Connaissances insuffisantes sur le traitement médicamenteux (Enseignement au patient et à ses proches).

INTERVENTIONS INFIRMIÈRES

- Le raloxifène peut être administré sans égard aux repas.
- On devrait ajouter à l'alimentation un supplément de calcium et de vitamine D si l'apport alimentaire quotidien est insuffisant.

ENSEIGNEMENT AU PATIENT ET À SES PROCHES

- Conseiller à la patiente de respecter rigoureusement la posologie recommandée. Lui expliquer qu'il est important d'assurer un apport adéquat de calcium et de vitamine D ou, sinon, de prendre un supplément. Prévenir la patiente qu'elle doit cesser de fumer et de consommer de l'alcool.
- Insister sur le fait qu'il est important de faire régulièrement des exercices visant les articulations portantes. Prévenir la patiente qu'elle devrait arrêter de prendre le raloxifène au moins 72 heures avant une période d'immobilisation prolongée et pendant toute sa durée (convalescence à la suite d'une intervention chirurgicale, alitement prolongé). Conseiller à la patiente de bouger aussi souvent que possible pendant un voyage prolongé pour prévenir la thrombose veineuse.
- Prévenir la patiente que le raloxifène ne diminue pas les bouffées de chaleur ou les rougeurs du visage associées à une carence en œstrogènes et qu'il peut même en provoquer.
- Prévenir la patiente que le raloxifène peut exercer des effets tératogènes. Lui conseiller d'informer im-

médiatement un professionnel de la santé si elle pense être enceinte ou si elle souhaite le devenir.

- Recommander à la patiente de lire le dépliant de conditionnement du médicament avant de commencer le traitement et de le lire de nouveau chaque fois qu'elle renouvelle son ordonnance.

VÉRIFICATION DE L'EFFICACITÉ THÉRAPEUTIQUE

L'efficacité du traitement peut être démontrée par: la prévention ou le renversement de l'ostéoporose chez les femmes ménopausées.

RAMIPRIL,
voir Inhibiteurs de l'enzyme de conversion de l'angiotensine (IECA)

RANITIDINE,
voir Antagonistes des récepteurs H_2 de l'histamine

RASBURICASE

Fasturtec

CLASSIFICATION:

Agent anti-goutte, antihyperuricémique (enzyme)

Grossesse – catégorie C

INDICATIONS

Traitement et prévention de l'hyperuricémie chez les enfants et les adultes atteints de cancer.

MÉCANISME D'ACTION

Enzyme qui favorise la transformation de l'acide urique en allantoïne, un composé hydrosoluble inactif ■ Médicament produit par la technologie de l'ADN recombinant. ***Effets thérapeutiques:*** Diminution des séquelles de l'hyperuricémie (néphropathie, arthropathie).

PHARMACOCINÉTIQUE

Absorption: Biodisponibilité à 100 % (IV).

Distribution: Inconnue.

Métabolisme et excrétion: Inconnus.

Demi-vie: 18 heures.

Profil temps-action
(diminution des concentrations d'acide urique)

	DÉBUT D'ACTION	PIC	DURÉE
IV	rapide	inconnu	4 – 24 h

CONTRE-INDICATIONS, PRÉCAUTIONS ET MISES EN GARDE

Contre-indications: Déficit en G6PD ou anomalies du métabolisme cellulaire qui provoquent une anémie hémolytique ■ Antécédents de réactions allergiques au rasburicase, d'hémolyse ou de méthémoglobinémie dues à l'agent.

Précautions et mises en garde: Risque de réactions allergiques graves ou de réactions anaphylactiques ■ **OBST.:** N'administrer qu'en cas de besoin incontestable ■ **ALLAITEMENT:** L'innocuité du médicament n'a pas été établie.

RÉACTIONS INDÉSIRABLES ET EFFETS SECONDAIRES

SNC: céphalées.

Resp.: détresse respiratoire.

GI: douleurs abdominales, constipation, diarrhée, nausées, vomissements, mucosite.

Tég.: rash.

Hémat.: HÉMOLYSE, MÉTHÉMOGLOBINÉMIE, neutropénie.

Divers: réactions d'hypersensibilité comprenant l'ANAPHYLAXIE, fièvre, septicémie.

INTERACTIONS

Médicament-médicament: Aucune interaction connue.

VOIES D'ADMINISTRATION ET POSOLOGIE

- **IV (adultes et enfants > 1 mois):** 0,2 mg/kg, 1 fois par jour, pendant 7 jours au maximum.

PRÉSENTATION

Poudre lyophilisée à reconstituer: 1,5 mg/fiole, en cartons de 3 fioles avec un diluant spécial[Pr].

SOINS INFIRMIERS

ÉVALUATION DE LA SITUATION

- SUIVRE DE PRÈS LES SIGNES DE RÉACTIONS ALLERGIQUES ET D'ANAPHYLAXIE (DOULEURS THORACIQUES, DYSPNÉE, HYPOTENSION, URTICAIRE). SI CES SIGNES SURVIENNENT, IL FAUT ABANDONNER IMMÉDIATEMENT ET DE FAÇON PERMANENTE LE TRAITEMENT PAR LE RASBURICASE.

R

Tests de laboratoire:

- SUIVRE DE PRÈS L'HÉMOLYSE. DÉPISTER AVANT LE TRAITEMENT LES PATIENTS EXPOSÉS À UN RISQUE ÉLEVÉ DE DÉFICIT EN G6PD (PATIENTS D'ORIGINE AFRO-AMÉRICAINE OU MÉDITERRANÉENNE). EN CAS D'HÉMOLYSE, ARRÊTER L'ADMINISTRATION DU RASBURICASE ET NE PAS REPRENDRE LE TRAITEMENT.
- DÉPISTER LA MÉTHÉMOGLOBINÉMIE. SI ELLE SURVIENT, ARRÊTER L'ADMINISTRATION DU RASBURICASE ET NE PAS REPRENDRE LE TRAITEMENT.
- L'agent peut entraîner des concentrations d'acide urique faussement basses dans des échantillons de sang laissés à la température ambiante. Prélever les échantillons de sang destinés au dosage de l'acide urique dans des éprouvettes préréfrigérées contenant de l'héparine et les immerger immédiatement dans un bac d'eau glacée dans lequel il faudrait les laisser par la suite. Le dosage de l'acide urique doit se faire dans le plasma. Les échantillons de plasma doivent être analysés dans les 4 heures qui suivent le prélèvement.

DIAGNOSTICS INFIRMIERS POSSIBLES

- Connaissances insuffisantes sur le traitement médicamenteux (Enseignement au patient et à ses proches).

INTERVENTIONS INFIRMIÈRES

- Commencer la chimiothérapie dans les 4 à 24 heures qui suivent l'administration de la première dose de rasburicase.

Perfusion intermittente: Déterminer le nombre de fioles de rasburicase nécessaires en fonction du poids du patient et de la dose par kg. Reconstituer avec le diluant fourni. Ajouter 1 mL de ce diluant à chaque fiole et mélanger en faisant tourner la fiole dans les mains très délicatement. Ne pas agiter ni tourner vigoureusement la fiole. La solution doit être transparente et incolore. Ne pas utiliser de solutions qui ont changé de couleur ou qui contiennent des particules. Retirer la dose de la fiole contenant la solution reconstituée et l'injecter dans un sac de perfusion contenant du NaCl 0,9 % pour obtenir un volume total final de 50 mL. Administrer dans les 24 heures qui suivent la reconstitution. Garder les solutions reconstituées ou diluées au réfrigérateur pendant 24 heures au maximum.

Vitesse d'administration: Administrer en 30 minutes. Ne pas administrer sous forme de bolus.

Incompatibilité (tubulure en Y): Perfuser par une tubulure séparée. Ne pas utiliser de filtre. Si on ne dispose pas de tubulure séparée, rincer la tubulure avec au moins 15 mL de NaCl 0,9 % avant de perfuser le rasburicase.

ENSEIGNEMENT AU PATIENT ET À SES PROCHES

- Expliquer au patient et à ses proches le but de la perfusion de rasburicase.

VÉRIFICATION DE L'EFFICACITÉ THÉRAPEUTIQUE

L'efficacité du traitement peut être démontrée par: la diminution des concentrations plasmatiques d'acide urique chez les patients recevant des antinéoplasiques qui devraient entraîner la lyse de la tumeur et l'élévation ultérieure des concentrations plasmatiques d'acide urique. ✳

RÉPAGLINIDE

Gluconorm

CLASSIFICATION:

Antidiabétique (méglitinides)

Grossesse – catégorie C

INDICATIONS

Traitement du diabète de type 2 en association avec la diétothérapie et l'exercice; on peut aussi l'administrer en association avec la metformine ou la rosiglitazone.

MÉCANISME D'ACTION

Stimulation de la libération d'insuline depuis les cellules bêta du pancréas par la fermeture des canaux potassiques, ce qui entraîne l'ouverture des canaux calciques des cellules bêta. Il s'ensuit une libération d'insuline. L'action du médicament dépend du bon fonctionnement des cellules des îlots pancréatiques. ***Effets thérapeutiques:*** Abaissement de la glycémie.

PHARMACOCINÉTIQUE

Absorption: 56 % (PO).

Distribution: Inconnue.

Liaison aux protéines: > 98 %.

Métabolisme et excrétion: Métabolisme hépatique important. Excrétion fécale (90 %) et rénale (8 %), majoritairement sous forme de métabolites inactifs.

Demi-vie: 1 heure.

Profil temps-action (effet sur la glycémie)

	DÉBUT D'ACTION	PIC	DURÉE
PO	≤ 30 min	60 – 90 min	< 4 h

CONTRE-INDICATIONS, PRÉCAUTIONS ET MISES EN GARDE

Contre-indications: Hypersensibilité ■ Acidocétose diabétique avec ou sans coma ■ Diabète de type 1 ■ Administration concomitante de gemfibrozil (voir « Interactions »).

Précautions et mises en garde: Insuffisance hépatique de modérée à grave (il peut s'avérer nécessaire de prolonger les intervalles entre les adaptations posologiques pour permettre une évaluation complète de la réponse) ■ **OBST., ALLAITEMENT:** L'innocuité du médicament n'a pas été établie chez la femme enceinte ou qui allaite (il est recommandé d'administrer de l'insuline pour équilibrer le diabète pendant la grossesse et l'allaitement) ■ **PÉD.:** L'innocuité du médicament n'a pas été établie chez les enfants ■ **GÉR.:** Les personnes âgées ou débilitées sont davantage prédisposées au risque d'hypoglycémie.

RÉACTIONS INDÉSIRABLES ET EFFETS SECONDAIRES

CV: angine, douleurs thoraciques.
End.: HYPOGLYCÉMIE, hyperglycémie.

INTERACTIONS

Médicament-médicament: L'administration concomitante de **gemfibrozil** ralentit le métabolisme du répaglinide; on a signalé des épisodes d'hypoglycémie grave lors de l'emploi de cette association; l'administration concomitante de ces deux médicaments est contre-indiquée ■ Les effets du répaglinide peuvent être accrus par la **clarithromycine**, le **kétoconazole**, l'**itraconazole**, l'**érythromycine**, le **triméthoprime**, d'autres **agents hypoglycémiants**, les **IMAO**, les **bêtabloquants non sélectifs**, les **inhibiteurs de l'ECA**, les **salicylates**, les **AINS**, l'**octréotide**, l'**alcool** et les **stéroïdes anabolisants** ■ Les effets du répaglinide peuvent être diminués par les **contraceptifs oraux**, la **rifampicine**, les **barbituriques**, la **carbamazépine**, les **diurétiques thiazidiques**, les **corticostéroïdes**, le **danazol**, les **agents thyroïdiens**, l'**octréotide** et les **sympathomimétiques**.

Médicament-produits naturels: La **glucosamine** peut entraver l'équilibrage de la glycémie.

VOIES D'ADMINISTRATION ET POSOLOGIE

- **PO (adultes):** De 0,5 à 4 mg, au moment des repas, de 2 à 4 fois par jour. *Posologie initiale* – chez les patients dont l'hémoglobine glyquée < 0,08: 0,5 mg; chez les patients dont l'hémoglobine glyquée ≥ 0,08: de 1 à 2 mg. Ne pas dépasser 16 mg par jour.

PRÉSENTATION

Comprimés: 0,5 mg[Pr], 1 mg[Pr], 2 mg[Pr].

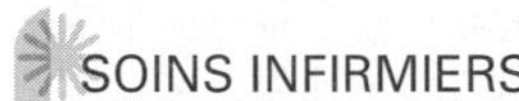

SOINS INFIRMIERS

ÉVALUATION DE LA SITUATION

- OBSERVER LE PATIENT À LA RECHERCHE DES SIGNES ET DES SYMPTÔMES SUIVANTS D'HYPOGLYCÉMIE: DOULEURS ABDOMINALES, TRANSPIRATION, FAIM, FAIBLESSE, ÉTOURDISSEMENTS, CÉPHALÉES, TREMBLEMENTS, TACHYCARDIE, ANXIÉTÉ. L'HYPOGLYCÉMIE PEUT ÊTRE DIFFICILE À DÉCELER CHEZ LES PERSONNES ÂGÉES ET CHEZ LES PATIENTS RECEVANT DES BÊTABLOQUANTS. L'HYPOGLYCÉMIE SURVIENT PLUS VRAISEMBLABLEMENT LORSQUE L'APPORT ÉNERGÉTIQUE EST INSUFFISANT, APRÈS UNE ACTIVITÉ PHYSIQUE INTENSE ET PROLONGÉE OU LORSQUE LE PATIENT CONSOMME DE L'ALCOOL OU PREND PLUSIEURS AGENTS HYPOGLYCÉMIANTS.

Tests de laboratoire: Suivre, à intervalles réguliers pendant toute la durée du traitement, la glycémie à jeun et la concentration d'hémoglobine glyquée afin d'évaluer l'efficacité du médicament.

DIAGNOSTICS INFIRMIERS POSSIBLES

- Alimentation excessive (Indications).
- Connaissances insuffisantes sur le traitement médicamenteux (Enseignement au patient et à ses proches).
- Non-observance du traitement médicamenteux (Enseignement au patient et à ses proches).

INTERVENTIONS INFIRMIÈRES

- Il peut s'avérer nécessaire d'administrer de l'insuline aux patients dont la glycémie a été stabilisée, mais qui font de la fièvre, qui sont exposés au stress, à un traumatisme ou à une infection ou qui doivent subir une intervention chirurgicale. Interrompre l'administration du répaglinide et attendre la fin de l'épisode aigu avant de reprendre le traitement.
- On devrait interrompre temporairement l'administration du répaglinide chez les patients qui doivent subir une intervention chirurgicale nécessitant une diminution de leur consommation d'aliments et de liquides.
- Le répaglinide n'est pas administré en doses fixes. La dose dépend des mesures de la glycémie, prises à intervalles réguliers; la réponse au traitement prolongé est démontrée par les concentrations d'hémoglobine glyquée. En l'absence d'une réponse satisfaisante, on peut ajouter au traitement de la metformine ou de la rosiglitazone. Si le traitement d'association échoue également, il peut s'avérer nécessaire de cesser l'administration d'hypoglycémiants oraux et de les remplacer par l'insuline.

- Lorsque le répaglinide remplace un autre hypoglycémiant oral, il peut être administré le jour suivant l'arrêt de l'ancien traitement. Suivre de près la glycémie. L'interruption du traitement par un hypoglycémiant oral à action prolongée peut dicter une surveillance étroite de la glycémie pendant au moins 1 semaine.
- On peut administrer un traitement de courte durée par le répaglinide aux patients dont le diabète est en général bien équilibré par la diétothérapie, mais qui connaissent des épisodes passagers de déséquilibre.
- Administrer le répaglinide jusqu'à 30 minutes avant le repas. Les patients qui sautent un repas ou qui en ajoutent un devraient aussi sauter une dose ou en ajouter une, selon le cas.

ENSEIGNEMENT AU PATIENT ET À SES PROCHES

- Conseiller au patient de prendre le médicament avant chaque repas, en suivant rigoureusement les recommandations du professionnel de la santé.
- Expliquer au patient que le répaglinide permet de normaliser la glycémie, mais ne peut guérir le diabète. Le traitement à l'aide de cet agent est habituellement de longue durée.
- Inciter le patient à suivre la diétothérapie, la pharmacothérapie et le programme d'exercices prescrits afin de prévenir les épisodes d'hypoglycémie ou d'hyperglycémie.
- Expliquer au patient les signes d'hypoglycémie et d'hyperglycémie. Si des symptômes d'hypoglycémie se manifestent, lui recommander de prendre un verre de jus d'orange ou un verre d'eau auquel il ajoute 2 ou 3 cuillerées à thé de sucre, de miel ou de sirop de maïs, et de prévenir un professionnel de la santé.
- Enseigner au patient la façon de mesurer sa glycémie. Lui recommander de surveiller étroitement les résultats de ces tests en période de stress ou de maladie et de prévenir immédiatement un professionnel de la santé si des modifications importantes surviennent.
- Conseiller au patient d'éviter de boire de l'alcool et de consulter un professionnel de la santé avant de prendre d'autres médicaments d'ordonnance ou en vente libre et des produits naturels en même temps que le répaglinide.
- Expliquer à la patiente que l'insuline est le médicament de prédilection pour équilibrer la glycémie au cours de la grossesse. Lui conseiller d'utiliser une méthode de contraception et d'informer rapidement un professionnel de la santé si elle pense être enceinte ou si elle souhaite le devenir.
- Recommander au patient qui doit suivre un autre traitement ou subir une intervention chirurgicale d'avertir le professionnel de la santé qu'il suit un traitement par ce médicament.
- Conseiller au patient de toujours avoir sur lui du sucre (sachets de sucre ou bonbons) et une pièce d'identité où sont inscrits son problème de santé et son traitement médicamenteux.
- Insister sur l'importance des examens de suivi et des dosages réguliers de la glycémie et de l'hémoglobine glyquée.

VÉRIFICATION DE L'EFFICACITÉ THÉRAPEUTIQUE

L'efficacité du traitement peut être démontrée par: l'équilibrage de la glycémie sans épisodes d'hypoglycémie ou d'hyperglycémie. ✷

RETÉPLASE,

voir Thrombolytiques

RIBAVIRINE

Virazole

CLASSIFICATION:

Antiviral

Grossesse – catégorie X

INDICATIONS

Inhalation: Chez les nourrissons et les jeunes enfants, traitement des infections graves des voies respiratoires inférieures dues au virus respiratoire syncytial (VRS) ■ **PO**: En association avec l'interféron alpha-2b ou le peginterféron alpha-2a, traitement des patients souffrant d'hépatite C chronique.

MÉCANISME D'ACTION

Inhibition de la synthèse de l'ADN et de l'ARN viraux et de la réplication ultérieure du virus ■ L'agent n'est activé qu'après phosphorylation à l'intérieur de la cellule. ***Effets thérapeutiques:*** **Inhalation**: Effet virostatique ■ **PO**: Ralentissement de l'évolution de l'hépatite C chronique et diminution des complications qu'elle entraîne.

PHARMACOCINÉTIQUE

Absorption: Bonne et rapide (PO) avec une biodisponibilité de 33 à 65 % à la suite d'un premier passage

hépatique. Une certaine absorption systémique se produit à la suite de l'inhalation par la bouche ou le nez.
Distribution: 70 % du médicament inhalé se dépose dans les voies respiratoires. L'agent semble se concentrer dans les voies respiratoires et dans les globules rouges. Il passe dans le lait maternel.
Métabolisme et excrétion: *Inhalation* – la ribavirine est éliminée des voies respiratoires par diffusion membranaire, par les macrophages, et par mouvement ciliaire; *voie orale* – métabolisme hépatique et excrétion urinaire des métabolites.
Demi-vie: *Inhalation* – 9,5 heures (40 jours dans les globules rouges); *voie orale* – 43,6 heures en moyenne (une seule dose) et de 270 à 300 heures (plusieurs doses).

Profil temps-action

	DÉBUT D'ACTION	PIC	DURÉE
Inhalation	inconnu	fin de l'inhalation	inconnue
PO	inconnu	1 - 3 h	12 h

CONTRE-INDICATIONS, PRÉCAUTIONS ET MISES EN GARDE

Contre-indications: Hypersensibilité ■ **OBST., ALLAITEMENT**: La ribavirine est tératogène (voie orale et inhalation) ■ Partenaires de sexe masculin des patientes enceintes (voie orale) ■ Traitement des hépatites auto-immunes ou cirrhose hépatique décompensée (voie orale) ■ Patients présentant une hémoglobinopathie comme la thalassémie ou la drépanocytose (voie orale) ■ **PÉD.**: L'innocuité et l'efficacité de l'agent n'ont pas été établies chez les enfants < 18 ans (voie orale).
Précautions et mises en garde: Antécédents de maladie cardiovasculaire; les symptômes peuvent être exacerbés par l'anémie (voie orale) ■ Anémie sous-jacente (une réduction de la dose ou l'arrêt du traitement peut être nécessaire) ■ Ventilation assistée ■ Insuffisance rénale avec une Cl_{Cr} < 50 mL/min ou une créatininémie > 177 µmol/L: l'arrêt du traitement doit être envisagé si des manifestations indésirables surviennent (voie orale) ■ Patientes en âge de procréer et leurs partenaires masculins: utilisation obligatoire de deux méthodes contraceptives efficaces (voie orale et inhalation).

RÉACTIONS INDÉSIRABLES ET EFFETS SECONDAIRES

Traitement par inhalation

SNC: étourdissements, évanouissement.
ORLO: vision trouble, conjonctivite, érythème de la paupière, irritation oculaire, photosensibilité.
Resp.: bronchospasme.
CV: ARRÊT CARDIAQUE, hypotension.
Tég.: rash.
Hémat.: réticulocytose.

Voie orale (en association ou non avec l'interféron)

SNC: labilité affective, fatigue, difficultés de concentration, insomnie, irritabilité.
Resp.: dyspnée.
GI: anorexie, dyspepsie, vomissements.
Hémat.: anémie, <u>anémie hémolytique</u>.
Tég.: prurit.
Loc.: arthralgie.
Divers: fièvre.

INTERACTIONS

Médicament-médicament: *Voie orale* – la ribavirine peut contrecarrer l'effet antiviral de la **stavudine** et de la **zidovudine** ■ La ribavirine peut intensifier la toxicité hématologique associée à la **zidovudine** ■ La ribavirine peut augmenter les concentrations et la toxicité de la **didanosine**.

VOIES D'ADMINISTRATION ET POSOLOGIE

- **Inhalation (nourrissons et jeunes enfants)**: Une dose de 300 mL d'une solution de 20 mg/mL, pulvérisée sous forme de brouillard. Administrer de façon continue, sauf pendant le temps nécessaire aux soins d'hygiène, pendant un minimum de 3 jours et un maximum de 7 jours, dans le cadre d'un programme thérapeutique global.
- **PO (adultes)**: De 800 à 1200 mg par jour (la dose varie selon le poids du patient et le génotype du virus de l'hépatite C), en 2 prises fractionnées, en association avec un interféron, pendant 24 à 48 semaines.

PRÉSENTATION

Poudre à reconstituer pour usage en aérosol: 6 g/fiole[Pr] ■ **Capsules**: 200 mg[Pr], avec de l'interféron alpha-2b péguylé (Pegetron) ou avec du peginterféron alpha-2a (Pegasys RBV).

R

SOINS INFIRMIERS

ÉVALUATION DE LA SITUATION

VRS:

- Au début du traitement et pendant toute sa durée, rester à l'affût des signes suivants d'infection: altération des signes vitaux, aspect des expectorations, accroissement du nombre de globules blancs.
- Suivre de près la fonction respiratoire (murmure vésiculaire, qualité et nombre de respirations) et l'équilibre hydrique avant le traitement et pendant toute sa durée.

Hépatite C chronique:

- Suivre les symptômes de l'hépatite tout au long du traitement.
- Les précautions suivantes concernent l'interféron utilisé en association pour le traitement de l'hépatite C chronique:
  - Rester à l'affût des signes de dépression tout au long du traitement.
  - RESTER À L'AFFÛT DES TROUBLES CARDIOVASCULAIRE (PRENDRE LE POULS ET LA PRESSION ARTÉRIELLE, ÉVALUER LES DOULEURS THORACIQUES). IL Y A RISQUE D'INFARCTUS DU MYOCARDE.
  - RESTER À L'AFFÛT DES SIGNES DE COLITE (DOULEURS ABDOMINALES, DIARRHÉES SANGUINOLENTES, FIÈVRE) ET DE PANCRÉATITE (NAUSÉES, VOMISSEMENTS, DOULEURS ABDOMINALES) TOUT AU LONG DU TRAITEMENT. ARRÊTER LE TRAITEMENT SI CES SIGNES SE MANIFESTENT; IL Y A RISQUE DE DÉCÈS.
  - Évaluer l'état de la fonction pulmonaire (murmure vésiculaire, respirations) à intervalles réguliers tout au long du traitement. Il peut s'avérer nécessaire d'arrêter le traitement.

Tests de laboratoire (hépatite C chronique):

- Noter la numération globulaire avec formule leucocytaire et la numération plaquettaire avant le traitement, aux deuxième et quatrième semaines et à intervalles réguliers, tout au long du traitement. Si les concentrations d'hémoglobine chutent en deçà de 100 g/L chez les patients sans antécédents de maladie cardiaque ou diminuent de plus de 20 g/L pendant n'importe lequel des cycles de 4 semaines de traitement chez les patients souffrant d'une maladie cardiaque stable, diminuer la dose de ribavirine à 600 mg (200 mg le matin et 400 mg le soir). Si, malgré la réduction de la dose, les concentrations d'hémoglobine chutent en deçà de 85 g/L, chez les patients sans antécédents de maladie cardiaque, ou en deçà de 120 g/L, chez les patients souffrant d'une maladie cardiaque stable, arrêter le traitement d'association. Lorsque l'anémie est corrigée, le traitement d'association peut être repris, si le médecin traitant le juge approprié.
- Suivre les résultats des tests de la fonction hépatique et de stimulation de la glande thyroïde avant le traitement et à intervalles réguliers pendant toute sa durée.
- Demander à la patiente en âge de procréer de se soumettre à un test de grossesse avant le traitement, tous les mois pendant toute sa durée et pendant 6 mois après l'avoir arrêté. Le traitement à la ribavirine ne doit être commencé que si le résultat du test initial est négatif.
- La ribavirine peut élever les concentrations de bilirubine sérique et d'acide urique.

DIAGNOSTICS INFIRMIERS POSSIBLES

- Risque d'infection (Indications, Effets secondaires).
- Échanges gazeux perturbés (Indications).
- Connaissances insuffisantes sur le traitement médicamenteux (Enseignement au patient et à ses proches).

INTERVENTIONS INFIRMIÈRES

Inhalation:

- Chez les nourrissons ayant besoin d'une ventilation assistée, on devrait effectuer des aspirations toutes les 1 ou 2 heures et vérifier la pression pulmonaire toutes les 2 à 4 heures.
- Pour que le traitement par la ribavirine soit efficace, il faudrait l'amorcer dans les 3 jours qui suivent l'apparition de l'infection à VRS.
- La ribavirine en aérosol ne devrait être administrée qu'à l'aide du générateur d'aérosol Viratek SPAG, modèle SPAG-2. Ne pas administrer la préparation à l'aide d'autres générateurs d'aérosol. L'agent est habituellement administré sous une tente à oxygène pour nourrissons, reliée au générateur d'aérosol SPAG-2. On peut également l'administrer par un masque si l'on ne peut se servir de la tente à oxygène.
- Reconstituer le contenu de la fiole de 6 g de ribavirine avec de l'eau stérile sans agent de conservation, destinée à l'injection ou à l'inhalation. Verser la solution dans le flacon Erlenmeyer propre et stérile du réservoir SPAG-2 et diluer jusqu'à un volume final de 300 mL. On recommande d'utiliser cette concentration (20 mg/mL) dans le réservoir pour assurer l'administration d'une dose de ribavirine en aérosol de 190 µg/L d'air par période de 12 heures. La solution doit être jetée et remplacée toutes les 24 heures. Consulter les directives de chaque fabricant avant de reconstituer la préparation.
- L'aérosolthérapie devrait être administrée de façon continue de 12 à 18 heures par jour, pendant 3 à 7 jours.

PO: Administrer avec de la nourriture. Les capsules doivent être avalées entières et ne doivent pas être ouvertes, brisées ou mâchées.

ENSEIGNEMENT AU PATIENT ET À SES PROCHES

VRS:

- Expliquer au patient et à ses parents l'objectif du traitement et la façon de l'administrer.
- Prévenir le patient et ses parents que la ribavirine peut entraîner une vision trouble et la photosensibilité.

- Insister sur le fait que le patient doit recevoir la ribavirine pendant toute la durée du traitement, selon un schéma posologique régulier et continu.

Hépatite C chronique:

- Recommander au patient de prendre la ribavirine pendant toute la période recommandée. Insister sur l'importance des tests de laboratoire permettant de déceler les effets secondaires.
- Il faut absolument obtenir un test de grossesse négatif juste avant le début du traitement par la ribavirine administrée par voie orale. Les femmes capables de procréer et les hommes ayant une partenaire qui prend de la ribavirine doivent être avertis des risques pour le fœtus et de la nécessité d'employer deux moyens de contraception efficaces (un moyen fiable par partenaire) durant le traitement et pendant au moins 6 mois après l'avoir mené à terme.
- Prévenir le patient que la ribavirine peut provoquer des étourdissements. Lui conseiller de ne pas conduire et d'éviter les activités qui exigent sa vigilance jusqu'à ce qu'on ait la certitude que le médicament n'entraîne pas cet effet chez lui.
- Informer le patient que la ribavirine ne réduit pas le risque de transmission de l'hépatite C à d'autres personnes et qu'elle peut ne pas prévenir la cirrhose, l'insuffisance hépatique ou le cancer du foie.

VÉRIFICATION DE L'EFFICACITÉ THÉRAPEUTIQUE

L'efficacité du traitement peut être démontrée par: la disparition des signes et des symptômes de l'infection à virus respiratoire syncytial ■ le ralentissement de l'évolution de l'hépatite C chronique et la diminution des complications qu'elle entraîne.

RIBOFLAVINE

Synonyme: vitamine B_2

CLASSIFICATION:

Vitamine B (hydrosoluble)

Grossesse – catégorie A

INDICATIONS

Traitement et prévention de la carence en riboflavine pouvant être attribuable à une alimentation inadéquate ou à une maladie débilitante chronique.

MÉCANISME D'ACTION

Coenzyme dans les réactions métaboliques qui se produisent lors du transport des ions hydrogène, incluant la respiration tissulaire ■ Élément indispensable au fonctionnement normal des globules rouges. ***Effets thérapeutiques:*** Traitement substitutif ou préventif d'un déficit vitaminique.

PHARMACOCINÉTIQUE

Absorption: Bonne (PO).

Distribution: Tout l'organisme. L'agent traverse la barrière placentaire et passe dans le lait maternel.

Métabolisme et excrétion: La riboflavine est transformée en ses coenzymes actives, le mononucléotide de flavine (MNF) et le dinucléotide d'adénine et de flavine (DAF). Les quantités supérieures aux besoins quotidiens sont excrétées à l'état inchangé par les reins.

Demi-vie: De 66 à 84 minutes.

Profil temps-action

	DÉBUT D'ACTION	PIC	DURÉE
PO	inconnu	inconnu	inconnue

CONTRE-INDICATIONS, PRÉCAUTIONS ET MISES EN GARDE

Contre-indications: Hypersensibilité à tout ingrédient des préparations de vitamine B_2.

Précautions et mises en garde: Aucune connue.

RÉACTIONS INDÉSIRABLES ET EFFETS SECONDAIRES

GU: coloration jaune de l'urine (doses élevées seulement).

INTERACTIONS

Médicament-médicament: Les **phénothiazines**, les **antidépresseurs tricycliques**, le **probénécide** ou l'**alcool** consommé en grandes quantités augmentent les besoins en riboflavine.

VOIES D'ADMINISTRATION ET POSOLOGIE

Traitement de la carence en vitamine B2

- **PO (adultes):** De 5 à 30 mg en doses fractionnées.
- **PO (enfants):** De 3 à 10 mg en doses fractionnées.

PRÉSENTATION (version générique disponible)

Comprimés ou capsules: 5 mg[VL], 25 mg[VL], 50 mg[VL], 100 mg[VL] ■ **Solution injectable:** 50 mg/mL[Pr] ■ **Poudre orale:** 0,083 mg/g[VL] ■ **En association avec:** plusieurs vitamines et minéraux, en diverses concentrations.

SOINS INFIRMIERS

ÉVALUATION DE LA SITUATION

- Avant le traitement et à intervalles réguliers pendant toute sa durée, suivre de près les signes suivants de carence en vitamine B_2: dermatose, stomatite, inflammation et irritation oculaires, photophobie et chéilite.

Tests de laboratoire: La riboflavine peut entraîner des concentrations faussement élevées de l'urobilinogène et des catécholamines urinaires.

DIAGNOSTICS INFIRMIERS POSSIBLES

- Alimentation déficiente (Indications).
- Connaissances insuffisantes sur le traitement médicamenteux (Enseignement au patient et à ses proches).

INTERVENTIONS INFIRMIÈRES

- On administre habituellement la riboflavine en association avec d'autres vitamines, car il est rare que le patient ne présente que ce seul type d'avitaminose.

ENSEIGNEMENT AU PATIENT ET À SES PROCHES

- Conseiller au patient de respecter la posologie recommandée. S'il n'a pas pu prendre la vitamine au moment habituel, il peut sauter cette dose, car la carence en riboflavine ne survient qu'après un long laps de temps.
- Encourager le patient à respecter rigoureusement les recommandations diététiques du professionnel de la santé. Lui expliquer que la meilleure source de vitamines est une alimentation bien équilibrée, contenant des aliments provenant des quatre principaux groupes. Les aliments riches en riboflavine comprennent les produits laitiers, la farine enrichie, les noix et les noisettes, la viande, les légumes-feuilles; la cuisson ne modifie pas les caractéristiques de la riboflavine.
- Recommander au patient qui pratique l'automédication par des suppléments vitaminiques de ne pas dépasser l'apport nutritionnel recommandé (ANR) (voir l'annexe K). L'efficacité des mégadoses dans le traitement de diverses affections n'a pas été prouvée; de plus, elles peuvent entraîner des effets secondaires.
- Conseiller au patient d'éviter de prendre des boissons alcoolisées, car l'alcool diminue l'absorption de la riboflavine.
- Expliquer au patient que la riboflavine peut rendre l'urine d'un jaune plus foncé, mais que cet effet n'a aucune signification sur le plan médical.
- Insister sur l'importance des examens de suivi permettant d'évaluer les bienfaits du traitement.

VÉRIFICATION DE L'EFFICACITÉ THÉRAPEUTIQUE

L'efficacité du traitement peut être démontrée par: la prévention ou la diminution des symptômes de carence en riboflavine.

RIFABUTINE

Mycobutin

CLASSIFICATION:

Antibiotique (mycobactéries atypiques)

Grossesse – catégorie B

INDICATIONS

Prévention des maladies disséminées du complexe *M. avium*, en présence d'infections par le VIH de stade avancé (numération CD4+ $\leq$ 200/mm^3 et diagnostic relié au sida, ou numération CD4+ $\leq$ 100/mm^3 sans diagnostic relié au sida).

MÉCANISME D'ACTION

Probablement, inhibition de l'ARN-polymérase dépendante de l'ADN des microorganismes sensibles. ***Effets thérapeutiques:*** Effet antimycobactérien sur les microorganismes sensibles. **Spectre d'action:** L'agent est actif contre *M. avium* et contre la plupart des souches de *M. tuberculosis*.

PHARMACOCINÉTIQUE

Absorption: De 50 à 85 % (PO). L'absorption est réduite chez les patients VIH positifs (biodisponibilité à 20 %).
Distribution: Tous les tissus et liquides physiologiques.
Métabolisme et excrétion: Métabolisme majoritairement hépatique. Excrétion rénale (5 % sous forme inchangée).
Demi-vie: 45 heures.

Profil temps-action

	Début d'action	Pic	Durée
PO	rapide	2 – 4 h	24 h

CONTRE-INDICATIONS, PRÉCAUTIONS ET MISES EN GARDE

Contre-indications: Hypersensibilité ■ Risque de sensibilité croisée avec d'autres rifamycines (rifampine).

Précautions et mises en garde: OBST., ALLAITEMENT, PÉD.: L'innocuité du médicament n'a pas été établie ■ Tuberculose évolutive.

RÉACTIONS INDÉSIRABLES ET EFFETS SECONDAIRES

ORLO: coloration brun-orangé des larmes, troubles oculaires.
Resp.: dyspnée.
CV: douleurs thoraciques, oppression thoracique.
GI: coloration brun-orangé de la salive, altération du goût, hépatite médicamenteuse.
GU: coloration brun-orangé de l'urine.
Tég.: rash, changement de la couleur de la peau.
Hémat.: hémolyse, neutropénie, thrombopénie.
Loc.: arthralgie, myosite.
Divers: coloration brun-orangé de tous les liquides physiologiques, syndrome pseudogrippal.

INTERACTIONS

Médicament-médicament: La rifabutine accélère le métabolisme et peut diminuer l'efficacité d'autres médicaments dont l'**éfavirenz**, l'**indinavir**, le **nelfinavir**, le **saquinavir**, les **corticostéroïdes**, le **disopyramide**, la **quinidine**, les **opioïdes**, les **hypoglycémiants oraux**, la **warfarine**, les **œstrogènes**, les **contraceptifs oraux à base d'œstrogènes**, la **phénytoïne**, le **vérapamil**, le **fluconazole**, la **théophylline**, la **zidovudine** et le **chloramphénicol** ■ Le **ritonavir**, l'**amprénavir**, l'**indinavir**, le **nelfinavir** et la **névirapine** élèvent les concentrations sanguines de rifabutine.

VOIES D'ADMINISTRATION ET POSOLOGIE

- **PO (adultes):** 300 mg, 1 fois par jour. En cas de gêne gastro-intestinale, administrer 150 mg, 2 fois par jour, avec des aliments.

PRÉSENTATION

Capsules: 150 mg^{Pr}.

SOINS INFIRMIERS

ÉVALUATION DE LA SITUATION

- Surveiller, avant le traitement et pendant toute sa durée, les signes de tuberculose évolutive à l'aide des tests suivants: fraction protéique purifiée (PPD), radiographie thoracique, mise en culture des échantillons d'expectorations, de globules sanguins et d'urines, biopsie des ganglions lymphatiques suspects. La rifabutine ne doit pas être administrée aux patients souffrant de tuberculose évolutive.

Tests de laboratoire: Suivre de près la numération globulaire à intervalles réguliers pendant tout le traitement. La rifabutine peut entraîner la neutropénie et la thrombopénie.

DIAGNOSTICS INFIRMIERS POSSIBLES

- Risque d'infection (Indications).
- Connaissances insuffisantes sur le traitement médicamenteux (Enseignement au patient et à ses proches).
- Non-observance du traitement médicamenteux (Enseignement au patient et à ses proches).

INTERVENTIONS INFIRMIÈRES

- On peut administrer la rifabutine sans égard aux repas. Les repas riches en matières grasses ralentissent l'absorption de la rifabutine, mais n'augmentent pas son absorption. La rifabutine peut être mélangée à des aliments tels que la purée de pommes. En cas d'irritation gastrique, administrer le médicament avec des aliments.

ENSEIGNEMENT AU PATIENT ET À SES PROCHES

- Conseiller au patient de respecter rigoureusement la posologie recommandée. L'avertir qu'il ne doit pas sauter de dose ni remplacer une dose manquée par une double dose. Insister sur le fait qu'il est important de poursuivre le traitement même après la disparition des symptômes.
- Conseiller au patient de signaler rapidement à un professionnel de la santé les signes et les symptômes de neutropénie (maux de gorge, fièvre, signes d'infection), de thrombopénie (saignements ou ecchymoses inhabituels) ou d'hépatite (jaunissement des yeux et de la peau, nausées, vomissements, anorexie, fatigue inhabituelle, faiblesse).
- Prévenir le patient qu'il doit éviter de boire de l'alcool pendant toute la durée du traitement en raison du risque accru d'hépatotoxicité.
- Recommander au patient de signaler à un professionnel de la santé les symptômes de myosite (myalgie, arthralgie) ou d'uvéite (inflammation intraoculaire).
- Prévenir le patient que la rifabutine peut rendre la salive, les crachats, la sueur, les larmes, l'urine et les selles rouge-orangé ou rouge-brun et peut modifier la couleur des verres de contact de façon permanente.
- Prévenir la patiente que ce médicament a des propriétés tératogènes et qu'il peut diminuer l'efficacité des contraceptifs oraux. Lui conseiller d'utiliser une méthode contraceptive non hormonale pendant toute la durée du traitement.
- Insister sur l'importance des examens réguliers de suivi permettant d'évaluer les bienfaits du traitement et de suivre les effets secondaires.

VÉRIFICATION DE L'EFFICACITÉ THÉRAPEUTIQUE

L'efficacité du traitement peut être démontrée par: la prévention des maladies disséminées du complexe *M. avium* en présence d'infections par le VIH de stade avancé.

RIFAMPINE

Rifadin, Rofact

CLASSIFICATION:

Antituberculeux

Grossesse - catégorie C

Voir aussi Pyrazinamide/isoniazide/rifampine

INDICATIONS

En association avec d'autres médicaments, traitement de la tuberculose active, à la phase primaire ou chronique ■ Prophylaxie chez certains sujets exposés à des personnes souffrant d'une maladie envahissante attribuable aux méningocoques (*N. meningitidis*) et à *Hæmophilus influenzæ* de type b ■ En association avec d'autres médicaments, traitement des infections dues au complexe *M. avium*, ainsi qu'à *M. kansasii, M. marinum, M. lepræ* (lèpre), *L. pneumophilia* (maladie du légionnaire) et à certaines bactéries à Gram positif et à Gram négatif.

MÉCANISME D'ACTION

R

Inhibition de la synthèse de l'ARN par blocage de la transcription de l'ARN chez les microorganismes sensibles. ***Effets thérapeutiques:*** Effet bactéricide contre les microorganismes sensibles. **Spectre d'action**: Large spectre d'action qui englobe les espèces: *Mycobacteria* ■ *Staphylococcus aureus* ■ *H. influenzæ* ■ *Legionella pneumophila* ■ *Neisseria meningitidis.*

PHARMACOCINÉTIQUE

Absorption: Bonne (PO).

Distribution: La plupart des tissus et des liquides physiologiques, incluant le liquide céphalorachidien. L'agent traverse la barrière placentaire et passe dans le lait maternel.

Métabolisme et excrétion: Métabolisme majoritairement hépatique; 60 % excrété dans les fèces par élimination biliaire.

Demi-vie: 3 heures.

Profil temps-action

	Début d'action	Pic	Durée
PO	rapide	2 - 4 h	12 - 24 h

CONTRE-INDICATIONS, PRÉCAUTIONS ET MISES EN GARDE

Contre-indications: Hypersensibilité aux rifamycines ■ Jaunisse ou ictère associé à une diminution de l'excrétion de bilirubine ■ Enfants prématurés et nouveau-nés dont la fonction hépatique n'est pas encore parvenue à maturité ■ Allaitement ■ Administration concomitante de ritonavir et de saquinavir.

Précautions et mises en garde: Antécédents de maladie hépatique ■ Administration concomitante d'autres agents hépatotoxiques ■ Grossesse.

RÉACTIONS INDÉSIRABLES ET EFFETS SECONDAIRES

SNC: ataxie, confusion, somnolence, fatigue, céphalées, faiblesse.

ORLO: coloration rouge des larmes.

GI: douleurs abdominales, diarrhée, flatulence, dyspepsie, nausées, vomissements, hépatite médicamenteuse, coloration rouge de la salive.

GU: coloration rouge de l'urine.

Hémat.: anémie hémolytique, thrombopénie.

Loc.: arthralgie, myalgie.

Divers: coloration rouge de tous les liquides physiologiques, syndrome pseudogrippal.

INTERACTIONS

Médicament-médicament: Risque accru d'hépatotoxicité lors de l'administration concomitante d'autres **agents hépatotoxiques**, dont l'**alcool**, le **kétoconazole**, l'**isoniazide** et le **pyrazinamide** ■ La rifampine réduit considérablement les concentrations sanguines de **delavirdine**, d'**éfavirenz**, d'**indinavir**, de **nelfinavir** et de **saquinavir** ■ La rifampine stimule les enzymes hépatiques, ce qui peut accélérer le métabolisme et diminuer l'efficacité d'autres médicaments, dont le **ritonavir**, la **névirapine**, l'**éfavirenz**, les **corticostéroïdes**, le **disopyramide**, la **quinidine**, les **analgésiques opioïdes**, les **hypoglycémiants oraux**, la **warfarine**, les **œstrogènes**, la **phénytoïne**, le **vérapamil**, le **fluconazole**, le **kétoconazole**, l'**itraconazole**, la **théophylline**, le **chloramphénicol** et les **contraceptifs oraux**.

VOIES D'ADMINISTRATION ET POSOLOGIE

Tuberculose

- **PO (adultes)**: 600 mg par jour ou 10 mg/kg/jour (jusqu'à 600 mg par jour) en une seule dose; on peut aussi administrer cette dose 2 ou 3 fois par semaine. En cas d'intolérance, la dose peut être réduite jusqu'à 450 mg.

- **PO (enfants > 5 ans)**: De 10 à 20 mg/kg/jour (ne pas dépasser 600 mg par jour); on peut aussi administrer cette dose 2 ou 3 fois par semaine.

INSUFFISANCE HÉPATIQUE
- **PO (ADULTES)**: 8 mg/kg/JOUR.

Patients âgés ou frêles
- **PO**: 10 mg/kg/jour.

Porteurs asymptomatiques de méningocoques
- **PO (adultes)**: 600 mg, toutes les 12 heures, pendant 2 jours.
- **PO (enfants ≥ 1 mois)**: 10 mg/kg, toutes les 12 heures, pendant 2 jours. Ne pas dépasser 600 mg par jour.
- **PO (nouveau-nés et nourrissons < 1 mois)**: 5 mg/kg, toutes les 12 heures, pendant 2 jours.

Prophylaxie de l'infection due à* H. influenzæ *de type b
- **PO (adultes)**: 600 mg par jour, pendant 4 jours.
- **PO (enfants)**: 20 mg/kg par jour, pendant 4 jours. Ne pas dépasser 600 mg par jour.
- **PO (nouveau-nés et nourrissons < 1 mois)**: 10 mg/kg, toutes les 24 heures, pendant 4 jours.

***Traitement des infections dues au complexe* M. avium *ou à* M. kansasii**
- **PO (adultes)**: 600 mg par jour, jusqu'à ce que les mises en culture donnent des résultats négatifs pendant 1 an.

Traitement des infections dues à* M. lepræ *(lèpre)
- **PO (adultes)**: 600 mg, 1 fois par mois, en association avec la dapsone.

***Traitement des infections dues à* M. marinum**
- **PO (adultes)**: 600 mg par jour, en association avec l'éthambutol pendant 3 mois, au moins.

PRÉSENTATION (version générique disponible)

Capsules: 150 mgPr, 300 mgPr ■ **En association avec**: isoniazide et pyrazinamide (Rifater)Pr.

SOINS INFIRMIERS

ÉVALUATION DE LA SITUATION

- Prélever des échantillons pour les cultures de mycobactéries et les épreuves de sensibilité avant de commencer le traitement et à intervalles réguliers par la suite afin de déceler une résistance éventuelle.
- Ausculter le murmure vésiculaire et noter les caractéristiques des crachats et la quantité expulsée, à intervalles réguliers, pendant toute la durée du traitement.

Tests de laboratoire:
- Examiner les résultats des tests de la fonction rénale et des analyses d'urine ainsi que la numération globulaire, à intervalles réguliers, pendant toute la durée du traitement.
- Noter les résultats des tests de la fonction hépatique au moins 1 fois par mois, pendant toute la durée du traitement. La rifampine peut entraîner l'élévation des concentrations d'urée, d'AST, d'ALT et des concentrations sériques de phosphatase alcaline, de bilirubine et d'acide urique.
- La rifampine peut entraîner des résultats faussement positifs au test direct de Coombs et peut modifier les résultats des dosages de l'acide folique et des vitamines du complexe B.
- La rifampine peut modifier les résultats de l'épreuve de freinage à la dexaméthasone; cesser l'administration de la rifampine 15 jours avant d'effectuer cette épreuve.
- La rifampine peut modifier les résultats des méthodes visant à déterminer les concentrations sériques de folates et de vitamine B et des tests urinaires (lorsque la réaction est fondée sur une modification de la couleur de l'urine).
- La rifampine peut retarder la captation hépatocytaire et l'excrétion de la bromesulfonephtaléine (BSP) lors des épreuves de captation et d'excrétion de la BSP; effectuer l'épreuve avant l'administration de la dose quotidienne de rifampine.

DIAGNOSTICS INFIRMIERS POSSIBLES

- Risque d'infection (Indications).
- Connaissances insuffisantes sur le traitement médicamenteux (Enseignement au patient et à ses proches).
- Non-observance du traitement médicamenteux (Enseignement au patient et à ses proches).

INTERVENTIONS INFIRMIÈRES

- Administrer le médicament à jeun, au moins 1 heure avant ou 2 heures après les repas, avec un grand verre d'eau (250 mL). Si l'irritation gastrique devient gênante, on peut administrer la rifampine avec des aliments. On peut également administrer des antiacides 1 heure avant la prise de la rifampine. Si le patient éprouve des difficultés de déglutition, on peut ouvrir les capsules et en mélanger le contenu à de la purée de pommes ou à de la gelée.
- Le pharmacien peut préparer un sirop pour les patients qui éprouvent des difficultés de déglutition.

R

ENSEIGNEMENT AU PATIENT ET À SES PROCHES

- Conseiller au patient de prendre la rifampine 1 fois par jour (à moins que le médecin n'ait prescrit la prise du médicament 2 fois par semaine), en respectant rigoureusement la posologie recommandée. Prévenir le patient qu'il ne doit pas sauter de dose ni remplacer une dose manquée par une double dose. Insister sur le fait qu'il est important de poursuivre le traitement même après la disparition des symptômes. La durée du traitement de la tuberculose dépend du type de traitement utilisé et du type de maladie sous-jacente. Expliquer au patient qui reçoit le médicament en prophylaxie de courte durée qu'il est essentiel d'observer rigoureusement le traitement prescrit.
- Conseiller au patient de prévenir rapidement un professionnel de la santé si des signes ou des symptômes d'hépatite (jaunissement des yeux et de la peau, nausées, vomissements, anorexie, fatigue inhabituelle ou faiblesse) ou de thrombopénie (saignements ou ecchymoses inhabituels) se manifestent.
- Mettre en garde le patient contre la consommation concomitante d'alcool qui peut accroître le risque d'hépatotoxicité.
- Recommander au patient de signaler rapidement à un professionnel de la santé l'apparition des symptômes pseudogrippaux (fièvre, frissons, myalgie, céphalées).
- Prévenir le patient que la rifampine peut parfois provoquer de la somnolence. Lui conseiller de ne pas conduire et d'éviter les activités qui exigent sa vigilance jusqu'à ce qu'on ait la certitude que le médicament n'entraîne pas cet effet chez lui.
- Prévenir le patient que la rifampine peut rendre la salive, les crachats, la sueur, les larmes, l'urine et les selles rouge-orangé ou rouge-brun, et peut modifier la couleur des verres de contact de façon permanente.
- Prévenir la patiente que la rifampine a des propriétés tératogènes et qu'elle peut diminuer l'efficacité des contraceptifs oraux. Lui conseiller d'utiliser une méthode contraceptive non hormonale pendant toute la durée du traitement.
- Insister sur l'importance des examens réguliers de suivi permettant d'évaluer les bienfaits du traitement et de suivre les effets secondaires.

VÉRIFICATION DE L'EFFICACITÉ THÉRAPEUTIQUE

L'efficacité du traitement peut être démontrée par: la diminution de la fièvre et des sueurs nocturnes ■ la diminution de la toux et de la production d'expectorations ■ des résultats négatifs après mise en culture des expectorations ■ un gain d'appétit ■ un gain de poids ■ une diminution de la fatigue ■ une sensation de bien-être chez les patients atteints de tuberculose ■ la prévention de la méningite à méningocoques ■ la prévention de l'infection à *Hæmophilus influenzæ* de type b; le traitement prophylactique est habituellement de courte durée ■ la guérison des infections dues au complexe *M. avium* ainsi que des maladies reliées à *M. kansasii*, *M. marinum*, *M. lepræ* (lèpre), *L. pneumophilia* (maladie du légionnaire) et à certaines bactéries à Gram positif et à Gram négatif. ✳

RISÉDRONATE

Actonel

CLASSIFICATION:

Régulateur du métabolisme osseux (bisphosphonate)

Grossesse – catégorie C

INDICATIONS

Traitement de la maladie osseuse de Paget chez les patients dont les concentrations sériques de phosphatase alcaline sont au moins le double des valeurs de la limite supérieure normale, qui manifestent des symptômes et qui sont exposés aux risques de complications ■ Traitement et prévention de l'ostéoporose (perte osseuse) postménopausique ■ Traitement et prévention de l'ostéoporose induite par les corticostéroïdes chez les hommes et les femmes.

MÉCANISME D'ACTION

Inhibition de la résorption osseuse par la liaison à l'hydroxyapatite osseuse qui bloque l'activité des ostéoclastes. ***Effets thérapeutiques:*** Diminution de la résorption osseuse et du remodelage osseux; normalisation des concentrations sériques de phosphatase alcaline, ce qui diminue les complications associées à la maladie de Paget.

PHARMACOCINÉTIQUE

Absorption: Rapide mais faible (biodisponibilité à 0,63 %).

Distribution: Répartition dans les os (60 % de la dose absorbée).

Métabolisme et excrétion: Excrétion rénale (40 % de la dose absorbée sous forme inchangée); la portion non absorbée est excrétée dans les fèces.

Demi-vie: *Phase initiale* – 1,5 heure; *phase terminale* – 220 heures (reflétant la dissociation d'avec l'os).

Profil temps-action
(effets sur les concentrations sériques de phosphatase alcaline)

	DÉBUT D'ACTION	PIC	DURÉE
PO	en quelques jours	30 jours	jusqu'à 16 mois

CONTRE-INDICATIONS, PRÉCAUTIONS ET MISES EN GARDE

Contre-indications: Hypersensibilité ■ Hypocalcémie ■ Insuffisance rénale grave (Cl_{Cr} < 30 mL/min).

Précautions et mises en garde: Antécédents de maladies des voies gastriques supérieures ■ Autres affections des os ou troubles du métabolisme des substances minérales (corriger les anomalies avant d'amorcer le traitement) ■ Troubles de l'alimentation (il peut s'avérer nécessaire d'administrer un supplément de vitamine D et de calcium) ■ **OBST., ALLAITEMENT, PÉD.:** L'innocuité du médicament n'a pas été établie.

RÉACTIONS INDÉSIRABLES ET EFFETS SECONDAIRES

SNC: faiblesse.
ORLO: amblyopie, xérophtalmie, acouphènes.
CV: douleurs thoraciques, œdème.
GI: douleurs abdominales, diarrhée, éructations, colite, constipation, dysphagie, œsophagite, ulcère œsophagien, ulcère gastrique, nausées.
Tég.: rash.
Loc.: arthralgie, douleurs osseuses, crampes dans les jambes, myasthénie.
Divers: syndrome pseudogrippal.

INTERACTIONS

Médicament-médicament: L'administration concomitante d'**AINS** ou d'**aspirine** augmente le risque d'irritation gastrique ■ L'absorption du risédronate est réduite lors de l'administration concomitante de **suppléments de calcium** ou d'**antiacides**.

Médicament-aliments: Les **aliments** diminuent l'absorption du risédronate (administrer le médicament au moins 30 minutes avant le petit-déjeuner). La **caféine** (**café**, **thé**, **cola**), l'**eau minérale** et le **jus d'orange** en diminuent également l'absorption.

VOIES D'ADMINISTRATION ET POSOLOGIE

Traitement et prévention de l'ostéoporose postménopausique

- **PO (adultes):** 5 mg, 1 fois par jour *ou* 35 mg, 1 fois par semaine; administrer 30 minutes avant le petit-déjeuner.

Traitement et prévention de l'ostéoporose induite par les corticostéroïdes

- **PO (adultes):** 5 mg, 1 fois par jour.

Maladie de Paget

- **PO (adultes):** 30 mg, 1 fois par jour, pendant 2 mois; administrer 30 minutes avant le petit-déjeuner. Après une période d'observation de 2 mois, on peut envisager une seconde cure.

PRÉSENTATION

Comprimés: 5 mg^{Pr}, 30 mg^{Pr}, 35 mg^{Pr}.

SOINS INFIRMIERS

ÉVALUATION DE LA SITUATION

Ostéoporose: Avant le traitement et à intervalles réguliers pendant toute sa durée, évaluer l'état du patient pour déceler une masse osseuse faible.

Maladie de Paget: Rester à l'affût des symptômes de la maladie osseuse de Paget (douleurs osseuses, céphalées, acuité visuelle et auditive réduite, augmentation du volume du crâne).

Tests de laboratoire:

- *Ostéoporose:* Évaluer les concentrations sériques de calcium avant le traitement et à intervalles réguliers pendant toute sa durée. Il faut traiter l'hypocalcémie et les carences en vitamine D avant d'amorcer le traitement par le risédronate. Le médicament peut entraîner une faible élévation passagère des concentrations de calcium et de phosphate.
- *Maladie osseuse de Paget:* Noter les concentrations de phosphatase alcaline avant le traitement et à intervalles réguliers pendant toute sa durée afin d'évaluer l'efficacité du traitement.

DIAGNOSTICS INFIRMIERS POSSIBLES

- Risque d'accident (Indications).
- Connaissances insuffisantes sur le traitement médicamenteux (Enseignement au patient et à ses proches).

INTERVENTIONS INFIRMIÈRES

- Administrer le médicament le matin dès le lever, avec 200 à 250 mL d'eau, 30 minutes avant la prise de tout autre médicament, boisson ou aliment.
- Les agents contenant du calcium, du magnésium ou de l'aluminium peuvent modifier l'absorption du risédronate; ils devraient donc être pris à un autre moment de la journée avec des aliments.

ENSEIGNEMENT AU PATIENT ET À SES PROCHES

- Expliquer au patient qu'il est essentiel de respecter rigoureusement la posologie recommandée, à savoir prendre le médicament le matin dès le lever, 30 minutes avant de prendre tout autre médicament, boisson ou aliment. Lui expliquer également que s'il attend plus de 30 minutes, l'absorption du médicament sera améliorée. Il devrait prendre le risédronate avec 200 à 250 mL d'eau ordinaire (l'eau minérale, le jus d'orange, le café et les autres boissons diminuent l'absorption du médicament). Prévenir le patient que s'il n'a pu prendre une dose, il doit la sauter et reprendre le traitement le lendemain matin. Le prévenir qu'il ne doit pas prendre une double dose ni prendre la dose plus tard dans la journée. Le prévenir également qu'il ne doit pas interrompre le traitement avant d'avoir consulté un professionnel de la santé.

- Expliquer au patient qu'il doit rester en position verticale pendant 30 minutes après la prise du médicament pour en faciliter le passage vers l'estomac et pour réduire le risque d'irritation œsophagienne.
- Conseiller au patient de suivre un régime alimentaire équilibré et de demander à un professionnel de la santé s'il a besoin de prendre un supplément de calcium et de vitamine D.
- Inciter le patient à participer à un programme d'exercices régulier et à modifier les comportements qui augmentent le risque d'ostéoporose (cesser de fumer, réduire la consommation d'alcool).
- Prévenir la patiente qu'elle doit informer un professionnel de la santé si elle pense être enceinte, si elle souhaite le devenir ou si elle allaite.

VÉRIFICATION DE L'EFFICACITÉ THÉRAPEUTIQUE

L'efficacité du traitement peut être démontrée par: le ralentissement de l'évolution de l'ostéoporose et la diminution des fractures et des autres séquelles ■ la diminution des concentrations sériques de phosphatase alcaline et le ralentissement de l'évolution de la maladie de Paget ■ la diminution des signes et des symptômes d'ostéoporose induite par les corticostéroïdes. ✳

RISPÉRIDONE

Apo-Risperidone, Co-Risperidone, Dom-Risperidone, Gen-Risperidone, Novo-Risperidone, PMS-Risperidone, Ratio-Risperidone, Riva-Risperidone, Risperdal, Risperdal Consta, Sandoz-Risperidone

CLASSIFICATION:
Antipsychotique

Grossesse – catégorie C

INDICATIONS

Traitement des manifestations de la schizophrénie et des troubles psychotiques apparentés ■ En présence de démence grave, traitement symptomatique à court terme des comportements inappropriés liés à l'agressivité ou à la psychose ■ Voie orale seulement: Traitement aigu des épisodes maniaques associés au trouble bipolaire.

MÉCANISME D'ACTION

Probablement, effets antagonistes sur la dopamine et la sérotonine au niveau du SNC. ***Effets thérapeutiques:*** Diminution des symptômes de psychose et de manie bipolaire.

PHARMACOCINÉTIQUE

Absorption: 70 % (PO – comprimés, solution ou comprimés à dissolution rapide). IM: faible libération initiale (< 1 % de la dose) suivie d'un temps de latence de 3 semaines. La libération du médicament débute après 3 semaines et se maintient durant 4 à 6 semaines.
Distribution: Inconnue.
Métabolisme et excrétion: Métabolisme hépatique important. Le métabolisme est déterminé génétiquement. Chez les personnes dont le métabolisme est rapide (la plupart des sujets), l'agent est rapidement transformé en 9-hydroxyrispéridone. Chez celles dont le métabolisme est plus lent (de 6 à 8 % des sujets de race blanche), cette transformation est moins rapide. La 9-hydroxyrispéridone est un composé antipsychotique. Excrétion rénale sous forme de métabolite et inchangée.
Demi-vie: *Personnes dont le métabolisme est rapide* – 3 heures pour la rispéridone et 21 heures pour la 9-hydroxyrispéridone. *Personnes dont le métabolisme est lent* – 20 heures pour la rispéridone et 30 heures pour la 9-hydroxyrispéridone.

Profil temps-action (effets antipsychotiques)

	DÉBUT D'ACTION	PIC	DURÉE
PO	1 – 2 semaines	inconnu	jusqu'à 6 semaines†
IM	3 semaines	4 – 6 semaines	jusqu'à 6 semaines†

† Après l'arrêt du traitement.

CONTRE-INDICATIONS, PRÉCAUTIONS ET MISES EN GARDE

Contre-indications: Hypersensibilité.
Précautions et mises en garde: **GÉR.**: Il est recommandé de réduire la dose initiale chez les personnes âgées ou chez les patients débilités et chez les insuffisants rénaux ou hépatiques; l'utilisation chez les personnes âgées atteint de psychoses reliées à la démence est associée à une augmentation du taux de mortalité et de morbidité par atteinte cardiovasculaire ■ Maladie cardiovas-

culaire sous-jacente (risque de plus grande prédisposition aux arythmies ou à l'hypotension) ■ Antécédents de convulsions ■ Antécédents de tentatives de suicide ou de toxicomanie ■ **OBST., ALLAITEMENT, PÉD.**: L'innocuité du médicament n'a pas été établie chez les femmes enceintes, chez celles qui allaitent et chez les enfants < 18 ans.

RÉACTIONS INDÉSIRABLES ET EFFETS SECONDAIRES

SNC: SYNDROME MALIN DES NEUROLEPTIQUES, comportement agressif, étourdissements, réactions extrapyramidales, céphalées, rêves plus intenses, sommeil prolongé, insomnie, sédation, fatigue, altération de la thermorégulation, nervosité, dyskinésie tardive.
ORLO: pharyngite, rhinite, troubles de la vision.
Resp.: toux, dyspnée, rhinite.
CV: arythmies, hypotension orthostatique, tachycardie.
GI: constipation, diarrhée, sécheresse de la bouche (xérostomie), nausées, douleurs abdominales, anorexie, dyspepsie, salivation accrue, vomissements.
GU: diminution de la libido, dysménorrhée et ménorragie, mictions difficiles, polyurie.
Tég.: démangeaisons et rash, peau sèche, pigmentation accrue, sécrétion accrue de sueur, photosensibilité, séborrhée.
End.: galactorrhée.
Loc.: arthralgie, douleurs lombaires.
Divers: gain pondéral, perte pondérale, polydipsie.

INTERACTIONS

Médicament-médicament: La rispéridone peut diminuer les effets antiparkinsoniens de la **lévodopa** ou d'autres **agonistes de la dopamine** ■ La **carbamazépine**, la **phénytoïne**, la **rifampicine**, le **phénobarbital** et autres **inducteurs enzymatiques** accélèrent le métabolisme de la rispéridone et peuvent en diminuer l'efficacité ■ La **fluoxétine** et la **paroxétine** peuvent augmenter les concentrations de risperidone et en augmenter ses effets; une adaptation posologique peut être nécessaire ■ La **clozapine** ralentit le métabolisme de la rispéridone et peut en augmenter les effets ■ Effets additifs sur la dépression du SNC lors de l'usage concomitant d'autres **dépresseurs du SNC**, dont l'**alcool**, les **antihistaminiques**, les **hypnosédatifs** et les **opioïdes**.
Médicament-produits naturels: L'administration concomitante de **kava**, de **valériane** ou de **camomille** peut augmenter les effets sur la dépression du SNC.

VOIES D'ADMINISTRATION ET POSOLOGIE

Schizophrénie et troubles psychotiques apparentés

- **PO (adultes)**: De 1 à 2 mg par jour, en 1 ou 2 prises; augmenter la dose graduellement, pendant plusieurs jours, jusqu'à l'atteinte d'une dose cible de 4 à 6 mg par jour. Par la suite, augmenter la dose par paliers de 1 mg ou moins, à intervalles de 1 semaine (ne pas dépasser 16 mg par jour). On peut également administrer le médicament en une seule dose quotidienne après la période d'adaptation posologique initiale (au maximum 8 mg en une seule prise).
- **PO (personnes âgées)**: Commencer le traitement par une dose de 0,25 mg, 2 fois par jour, et l'augmenter ensuite lentement, jusqu'à concurrence de 1,5 mg, 2 fois par jour.

  PO (adultes sujets à l'hypotension artérielle): On doit envisager des doses initiales plus faibles, soit de 0,25 à 0,5 mg, 2 fois par jour.
- **IM (adultes)**: 25 mg, toutes les 2 semaines; chez certains patients il faut administrer des doses allant jusqu'à 37,5 ou 50 mg, toutes les 2 semaines.

Manie bipolaire

- **PO (adultes)**: Commencer le traitement par une dose de 2 à 3 mg par jour, en une seule prise, qu'on pourra augmenter par paliers de 1 mg, à des intervalles de 24 heures minimum (dose maximale: 6 mg).

INSUFFISANCE HÉPATIQUE

- **PO (ADULTES)**: COMMENCER LE TRAITEMENT PAR UNE DOSE DE 0,25 À 0,5 mg, 2 FOIS PAR JOUR, ET L'AUGMENTER ENSUITE PAR PALIERS DE 0,5 mg, 2 FOIS PAR JOUR, JUSQU'À CONCURRENCE DE 1 À 2 mg, 2 FOIS PAR JOUR.

INSUFFISANCE RÉNALE

- **PO (ADULTES)**: COMMENCER LE TRAITEMENT PAR UNE DOSE DE 0,5 mg, 2 FOIS PAR JOUR, ET L'AUGMENTER ENSUITE PAR PALIERS DE 0,5 mg, 2 FOIS PAR JOUR, JUSQU'À CONCURRENCE DE 1,5 mg, 2 FOIS PAR JOUR. PAR LA SUITE, LES ADAPTATIONS DEVRAIENT SE FAIRE À DES INTERVALLES D'AU MOINS 1 SEMAINE.

Troubles comportementaux associés à la démence grave

- **PO (adultes)**: Commencer le traitement par une dose de 0,25 mg, 2 fois par jour (chez les personnes âgées, on peut débuter par une dose plus faible), et l'augmenter ensuite par paliers de 0,25 mg par jour, à des intervalles de 2 à 4 jours. Chez la plupart des patients, la dose optimale est de 0,5 mg, 2 fois par jour. Cependant, chez certains de ces patients, il peut être avantageux d'augmenter la dose jusqu'à un maximum de 1 mg, 2 fois par jour.

R

PRÉSENTATION

Comprimés: 0,25 mg^{Pr}, 0,5 mg^{Pr}, 1 mg^{Pr}, 2 mg^{Pr}, 3 mg^{Pr}, 4 mg^{Pr} ■ **Comprimés à dissolution rapide (M-tabs)**: 0,5 mg^{Pr}, 1 mg^{Pr}, 2 mg^{Pr}, 3 mg^{Pr}, 4 mg^{Pr} ■ **Solution orale**: 1 mg/mL^{Pr}, en flacons de 30 mL ■ **Microsphères pour injection (nécessitant un diluant spécial pour la suspension)**: 25mg/fiole[Pr], 37,5 mg/fiole[Pr], 50 mg/fiole[Pr].

SOINS INFIRMIERS

ÉVALUATION DE LA SITUATION

- Déterminer, avant le traitement et à intervalles réguliers pendant toute sa durée, l'état mental du patient (délire, hallucinations et troubles de comportement).
- Suivre les changements d'humeur du patient. Repérer les tendances suicidaires, particulièrement au cours du traitement initial. Limiter la quantité de médicament dont le patient peut disposer.
- Mesurer la pression artérielle du patient (en position assise, debout et couchée) et le pouls avant l'administration initiale et à intervalles fréquents pendant la période d'adaptation de la posologie. La rispéridone peut allonger l'intervalle QT et entraîner une tachycardie et une hypotension orthostatique. En cas d'hypotension, il peut s'avérer nécessaire de réduire la dose.
- Observer attentivement le patient pendant qu'il prend le médicament pour s'assurer qu'il l'a bien avalé.
- Rester à l'affût des effets secondaires extrapyramidaux (*akathisie* – besoin irrépressible de bouger; *dystonie* – spasmes musculaires et mouvements de torsion; *symptômes pseudoparkinsoniens* – faciès rigide, rigidité, tremblements, bouche ouverte laissant s'échapper la salive, démarche traînante, dysphagie). Signaler immédiatement ces symptômes; il peut s'avérer nécessaire de réduire la dose ou d'arrêter le traitement. On peut administrer du trihexyphénidyle ou de la diphenhydramine pour maîtriser ces symptômes.
- Suivre de près l'apparition d'une dyskinésie tardive qui se traduit par des mouvements rythmiques involontaires de la bouche, du visage et des membres. Signaler immédiatement ces symptômes, car ils peuvent être irréversibles.
- SUIVRE DE PRÈS L'APPARITION DES SYMPTÔMES SUIVANTS DU SYNDROME MALIN DES NEUROLEPTIQUES: FIÈVRE, DÉTRESSE RESPIRATOIRE, TACHYCARDIE, CONVULSIONS, DIAPHORÈSE, HYPERTENSION OU HYPOTENSION, PÂLEUR, FATIGUE. SIGNALER IMMÉDIATEMENT AU MÉDECIN OU À UN AUTRE PROFESSIONNEL DE LA SANTÉ L'APPARITION DE CES SYMPTÔMES.

Tests de laboratoire:

- La rispéridone peut élever les concentrations sériques de prolactine.
- La rispéridone peut élever les concentrations d'AST et d'ALT.
- Le médicament peut également entraîner l'anémie, la thrombopénie, la leucocytose et la leucopénie.

DIAGNOSTICS INFIRMIERS POSSIBLES

- Risque de violence (Indications).
- Opérations de la pensée perturbées (Indications).
- Risque d'accident (Effets secondaires).

INTERVENTIONS INFIRMIÈRES

- Lorsqu'on substitue la rispéridone à un autre antipsychotique, en arrêter l'administration au moment où l'on démarre le traitement par la rispéridone. Dans la mesure du possible, réduire la période pendant laquelle les deux traitements antipsychotiques se chevauchent.
- Si le traitement est amorcé de nouveau après une période sans traitement par la rispéridone, suivre le schéma initial d'adaptation posologique.
- Pour l'administration IM, établir la tolérance au traitement par les comprimés oraux avant d'utiliser la voie IM et poursuivre l'administration des comprimés durant les 3 premières semaines suivant l'injection IM. Ne pas augmenter les doses plus souvent que toutes les 4 semaines.

PO: Les comprimés à dissolution rapide doivent être manipulés avec précaution et avec les mains sèches. Détacher une alvéole de la plaquette en suivant le pointillé, et retirer la pellicule protectrice sans chercher à pousser le comprimé au travers de la pellicule. Soulever plutôt le comprimé en poussant le dessous de l'alvéole. En évitant de toucher le comprimé avec les mains, le placer directement dans la bouche. Le comprimé commence à se dissoudre dans la bouche en quelques secondes avec ou sans prise de liquide. Ne pas essayer de croquer ou de briser les comprimés. On ne doit pas conserver les comprimés une fois qu'on les a retirés de l'emballage.

- La solution orale peut être mélangée avec de l'eau, du café, du jus d'orange ou du lait écrémé. Ne pas mélanger avec du cola ou du thé.

IM: Reconstituer avec 2 mL du diluant fourni par le fabricant. Administrer dans le muscle fessier en utilisant l'aiguille de sécurité fournie. Alterner les points d'injection à chaque administration. Laisser reposer le matériel nécessaire à la reconstitution ainsi que la fiole de médicament à la température de la pièce avant de reconstituer la préparation. Administrer immédiatement (jusqu'à 6 heures) après la reconstitution avec le diluant; bien mélanger. Garder les trousses au réfrigérateur.

R

Consulter les directives de chaque fabricant avant d'administrer la préparation.

- Ne pas combiner différentes teneurs lors d'une même administration.

ENSEIGNEMENT AU PATIENT ET À SES PROCHES

- Inciter le patient à respecter rigoureusement la posologie recommandée.
- Mettre en garde le patient contre le risque de symptômes extrapyramidaux. Lui demander de prévenir immédiatement un professionnel de la santé si ces symptômes se manifestent.
- Recommander au patient de changer lentement de position afin de réduire le risque d'hypotension orthostatique.
- Prévenir le patient que la rispéridone peut provoquer de la somnolence. Lui conseiller de ne pas conduire et d'éviter les activités qui exigent sa vigilance jusqu'à ce qu'on ait la certitude que le médicament n'entraîne pas cet effet chez lui.
- Recommander au patient d'utiliser un écran solaire et de porter des vêtements protecteurs lorsqu'il s'expose au soleil pour prévenir les réactions de photosensibilité. Lui recommander également d'éviter les écarts importants de température, car ce médicament altère la thermorégulation.
- Prévenir le patient qu'il doit éviter de boire de l'alcool et de prendre d'autres dépresseurs du SNC, des médicaments en vente libre ou des produits naturels sans avoir consulté au préalable un professionnel de la santé.
- Conseiller à la patiente de prévenir un professionnel de la santé si elle pense être enceinte, si elle souhaite le devenir, si elle allaite ou si elle prévoit le faire.
- Recommander au patient qui doit suivre un autre traitement ou subir une intervention chirurgicale d'avertir le professionnel de la santé qu'il suit un traitement par ce médicament.
- Conseiller au patient d'informer rapidement un professionnel de la santé si les symptômes suivants se manifestent: maux de gorge, fièvre, saignements ou ecchymoses inhabituels, rash ou tremblements.
- Insister sur l'importance d'un suivi constant, de la psychothérapie et de la surveillance des effets secondaires de ce médicament.

VÉRIFICATION DE L'EFFICACITÉ THÉRAPEUTIQUE

L'efficacité du traitement peut être démontrée par: la diminution des symptômes psychotiques, tels que l'excitation, la paranoïa ou le repli sur soi ■ la diminution des symptômes de manie bipolaire.

RITONAVIR

Norvir, Norvir SEC

CLASSIFICATION:

Antirétroviral (inhibiteur de la protéase)

Grossesse – catégorie B

Voir également Lopinavir/ritonavir.

INDICATIONS

Traitement de l'infection par le VIH, en association avec d'autres antirétroviraux. **Usages non approuvés:** En association avec d'autres antirétroviraux, prophylaxie après une exposition accidentelle au VIH.

MÉCANISME D'ACTION

Inhibition de l'action de la protéase du VIH et prévention du clivage des polyprotéines virales. ***Effets thérapeutiques:*** Augmentation du nombre de cellules CD4 et diminution de la charge virale, ce qui se traduit par un ralentissement de l'évolution de l'infection par le VIH et de ses complications.

PHARMACOCINÉTIQUE

Absorption: Bonne (PO).

Distribution: Le ritonavir pénètre faiblement dans le SNC.

Liaison aux protéines: De 98 à 99 %.

Métabolisme et excrétion: Métabolisme hépatique important (par le système enzymatique du cytochrome P450 3A et 2D6); un des métabolites est doté d'une activité antirétrovirale. Excrétion urinaire à 3,5 % à l'état inchangé.

Demi-vie: De 3 à 5 heures.

Profil temps-action

	DÉBUT D'ACTION	PIC	DURÉE
PO	rapide	4 h†	12 h

† Lorsque le patient n'est pas à jeun.

CONTRE-INDICATIONS, PRÉCAUTIONS ET MISES EN GARDE

Contre-indications: Hypersensibilité ■ Traitement concomitant par l'amiodarone, le cisapride, les dérivés de l'ergot (comme la dihydroergotamine et l'ergotamine), le flécaïnide, le midazolam, le pimozide, la propafénone, la quinidine ou le triazolam ■ Hypersensibilité ou intolérance à l'alcool ou à l'huile de ricin (les capsules et la solution orale renferment ces ingrédients).

Précautions et mises en garde: Nombreuses interactions médicamenteuses ■ Insuffisance hépatique, antécédents d'hépatite ■ Diabète ■ Hémophilie (risque accru d'hémorragie) ■ **OBST., PÉD.**: Grossesse ou enfants < 2 ans (l'innocuité du médicament n'a pas été établie) ■ **ALLAITEMENT**: Déconseillé en raison du risque de transmission postnatale du VIH.

RÉACTIONS INDÉSIRABLES ET EFFETS SECONDAIRES

SNC: CONVULSIONS, altération des opérations de la pensée, faiblesse, étourdissements, céphalées, malaise, somnolence, syncope.
ORLO: pharyngite, irritation de la gorge.
Resp.: ŒDÈME ANGIONEUROTIQUE, bronchospasme.
CV: hypotension orthostatique, vasodilatation.
GI: douleurs abdominales, altération du goût, anorexie, diarrhée, nausées, vomissements, constipation, dyspepsie, flatulence, PANCRÉATITE.
GU: insuffisance rénale.
Tég.: rash, éruptions cutanées, transpiration, urticaire.
End.: hyperglycémie.
HÉ: déshydratation.
Métab.: hyperlipidémie, hypertriglycéridémie, modification de la distribution des tissus adipeux.
Loc.: concentrations accrues de créatine-phosphokinase (CK), myalgie.
SN: paresthésie péribuccale, paresthésie périphérique.
Divers: réactions d'hypersensibilité, incluant le SYNDROME DE STEVENS-JOHNSON et l'ANAPHYLAXIE, fièvre, syndrome de reconstitution immunitaire.

INTERACTIONS

Médicament-médicament: Le ritonavir est métabolisé par les P450 3A4 et 2D6; il inhibe également ces systèmes enzymatiques. L'effet de tout autre **médicament qui est métabolisé ou influencé par ces systèmes** peut être modifié lors d'un usage concomitant ■ L'administration concomitante d'**amiodarone**, de **cisapride**, de **dérivés de l'ergot** (comme la **dihydroergotamine** et l'**ergotamine**), de **flécaïnide**, de **midazolam**, de **pimozide**, de **propafénone**, de **quinidine** et de **triazolam** est contre-indiquée, car le ritonavir entraîne de fortes élévations de leurs concentrations sanguines et un risque accru d'effets toxiques graves ■ L'usage concomitant de **lovastatine** ou de **simvastatine** n'est pas recommandé (risque accru de myopathie et de rhabdomyolyse) ■ Risque accru de myopathie lors de l'usage concomitant d'**atorvastatine** (utiliser la plus petite dose de départ possible et assurer un suivi étroit) ■ Les concentrations sont diminuées par la **rifampine** (risque d'émergence d'une résistance virale, éviter l'usage concomitant) ■ Élévation des concentrations de **sildénafil**, de **vardénafil** et de **tadalafil** et augmentation possible de leurs effets indésirables, notamment l'hypotension, l'altération de la vue et le priapisme; faire preuve de prudence et diminuer la dose de **sildénafil** à 25 mg toutes les 48 heures, diminuer la dose de **tadalafil** à 10 mg toutes les 72 heures et éviter l'administration de **vardénafil** ■ Diminution des concentrations de **mépéridine** et augmentation des concentrations de **norméPéridine**, son métabolite neurotoxique (utiliser avec grande prudence) ■ Le ritonavir peut également élever les concentrations sanguines et intensifier les effets de nombreux médicaments (une réduction de la dose peut s'avérer nécessaire), dont certains **analgésiques opioïdes** (**alfentanil**, **fentanyl**, **hydrocodone**, **oxycodone**, **propoxyphène**), le **tramadol**, certains **antiarythmiques** (**disopyramide**, **lidocaïne**, **mexilétine**), certains **antibiotiques** (**clarithromycine** [réduire la dose seulement en présence d'insuffisance rénale], **érythromycine**, **rifabutine** [réduire la dose d'au moins 75 %], **triméthoprime**), certains **antirétroviraux** (**amprénavir**, **atazanavir**, **didanosine**, **éfavirenz**, **indinavir**, **nelfinavir**, **saquinavir**), certains **antifongiques** (**kétoconazole** [ne pas dépasser 200 mg/jour de kétoconazole], **itraconazole**), presque tous les **antidépresseurs**, certaines **benzodiazépines** (**alprazolam**, **clorazépate**, **diazépam**, **flurazépam**), certains **bêtabloquants** (**métoprolol**, **pindolol**, **propranolol**, **timolol**), les **bloqueurs des canaux calciques** (**amlodipine**, **diltiazem**, **félodipine**, **nifédipine**, **nimodipine**, **vérapamil**), certains **antinéoplasiques** (**étoposide**, **paclitaxel**, **tamoxifène**, **vinblastine**, **vincristine**), certains **corticostéroïdes** (**dexaméthasone**, **prednisone**, **fluticasone** [envisager une solution de rechange à la fluticasone]), certains **immunosuppresseurs** (**cyclosporine**, **tracrolimus**, **sirolimus**), certains **antipsychotiques** (**chlorpromazine**, **clozapine**, **halopéridol**, **olanzapine**, **perphénazine**, **rispéridone**) et également l'**alfuzosine**, la **buspirone**, la **digoxine**, la **carbamazépine**, l'**éthosuximide**, l'**ondansétron**, la **quinine**, la **méthamphétamine** et la **warfarine** (surveiller le RNI). ■ Le ritonavir diminue les concentrations sanguines et les effets des **contraceptifs oraux**, de l'**atovaquone**, de la **méthadone**, de la **phénytoïne**, de **l'acide valproïque**, de la **lamotrigine**, de la **zidovudine**, du **sulfaméthoxazole** et de la **théophylline**; une modification de la dose ou le recours à un traitement de rechange peut s'avérer nécessaire ■ La **fluoxétine** et la **delavirdine** peuvent élever les concentrations sanguines de ritonavir ■ Diminution des concentrations de **voriconazole**; éviter l'usage concomitant ■ La solution et les capsules contiennent de l'alcool et peuvent provoquer une intolérance si le patient prend du **disulfirame** ou du **métronidazole**.

Médicament-produits naturels: La consommation concomitante de **millepertuis** peut entraîner la diminution des concentrations sanguines et de l'efficacité du ritonavir, associée à l'émergence d'une résistance virale.

Médicament-aliments: Les **aliments** favorisent l'absorption du ritonavir.

VOIES D'ADMINISTRATION ET POSOLOGIE

Ces doses sont celles utilisées lorsque le ritonavir est utilisé comme inhibiteur de la protéase à part entière. Des doses plus faibles sont utilisées lorsque le ritonavir est utilisé seulement pour potentialiser l'effet d'un autre inhibiteur de la protéase.

- **PO (adultes):** 600 mg, 2 fois par jour. Cette dose de départ occasionne souvent des nausées. On peut débuter à 300 mg, 2 fois par jour, pendant la première journée, puis augmenter la dose par paliers de 100 mg, 2 fois par jour, jusqu'à concurrence de 600 mg, 2 fois par jour; la période d'adaptation posologique ne doit pas dépasser 14 jours.
- **PO (enfants):** Initialement, 250 mg/m^2, 2 fois par jour; augmenter par paliers de 50 mg/m^2, 2 fois par jour, tous les 2 ou 3 jours, jusqu'à concurrence de 400 mg/m^2 (600 mg au maximum), 2 fois par jour (dans l'impossibilité de monter la posologie jusqu'à 400 mg/m^2, 2 fois par jour, utiliser la dose tolérée la plus élevée comme traitement d'entretien en ajoutant un antirétroviral supplémentaire).

PRÉSENTATION

Capsules: 100 mg^{Pr} ▪ **Solution orale:** 80 mg/mL^{Pr} ▪ **En association avec:** lopinavir (Kaletra)^{Pr}.

SOINS INFIRMIERS

ÉVALUATION DE LA SITUATION

- Observer étroitement le patient tout au long du traitement pour déceler l'aggravation des symptômes de l'infection par le VIH et l'apparition d'infections opportunistes.
- Si une patiente enceinte est exposée à des antirétroviraux, l'inscrire dans le registre des femmes exposées aux antirétroviraux pendant leur grossesse, en composant le 1-800-258-4263.

Tests de laboratoire:

- Noter la charge virale et le nombre de CD4 à intervalles réguliers tout au long du traitement.
- Le médicament peut provoquer l'hyperglycémie.
- Le médicament peut entraîner une élévation des concentrations sériques d'AST, d'ALT, de GGT, de bilirubine totale, de CK, de triglycérides et d'acide urique.

DIAGNOSTICS INFIRMIERS POSSIBLES

- Risque d'infection (Indications).
- Connaissances insuffisantes sur le processus pathologique et sur le traitement médicamenteux (Enseignement au patient et à ses proches).
- Non-observance du traitement médicamenteux (Enseignement au patient et à ses proches).

INTERVENTIONS INFIRMIÈRES

- NE PAS CONFONDRE LE RITONAVIR AVEC RETROVIR (ZIDOVUDINE).
- Administrer le médicament au moment des repas ou avec une collation.
- Les capsules doivent être conservées au réfrigérateur et protégées de la lumière. Il n'est pas nécessaire de réfrigérer les capsules si elles sont utilisées dans les 30 jours et conservées dans leur flacon d'origine à une température inférieure à 25 °C. Garder le contenant hermétiquement fermé.
- Les patients peuvent améliorer le goût du ritonavir en solution buvable en le mélangeant à du lait au chocolat ou à Ensure, moins de 1 heure avant la prise. Il ne faut pas réfrigérer la solution orale. Administrer la solution orale à l'aide d'une seringue graduée destinée à cet usage.
- Si des nausées surviennent, lors de l'administration de la dose de 600 mg, 2 fois par jour, on peut essayer d'administrer 300 mg, 2 fois par jour, pendant la première journée, puis augmenter la dose par paliers de 100 mg, 2 fois par jour, jusqu'à concurrence de 600 mg, 2 fois par jour; la période d'adaptation posologique ne doit pas dépasser 14 jours.
- Les patients qui entreprennent un traitement d'association comprenant le ritonavir et d'autres antirétroviraux peuvent améliorer la tolérance gastro-intestinale en commençant par prendre le ritonavir seul, puis en ajoutant les autres antirétroviraux avant la fin des 2 semaines de monothérapie par le ritonavir.

ENSEIGNEMENT AU PATIENT ET À SES PROCHES

- Insister sur le fait qu'il est important de suivre rigoureusement la posologie recommandée et de prendre le ritonavir à des intervalles égaux tout au long de la journée. Recommander au patient de ne pas dépasser la dose prescrite et de ne pas cesser de prendre le médicament sans avoir consulté un professionnel de la santé au préalable. S'il n'a pas pu prendre le médicament au moment habituel, il doit le prendre aussitôt que possible. L'avertir qu'il ne doit jamais remplacer une dose manquée par une double dose.
- Informer le patient qu'il ne doit pas partager le ritonavir avec d'autres personnes.
- Conseiller au patient de consulter un professionnel de la santé avant de prendre d'autres médicaments,

sur ordonnance ou en vente libre, incluant les produits naturels, en même temps que le ritonavir.

- Expliquer au patient que ce médicament ne guérit pas le sida, ne prévient pas les infections associées au sida ou les infections opportunistes, et ne réduit pas le risque de transmission du VIH à autrui par les rapports sexuels ou par la contamination du sang. L'inciter à utiliser un condom et à éviter le partage d'aiguilles et les dons de sang afin de prévenir la transmission du VIH. Prévenir le patient que les effets de longue durée du ritonavir sont encore inconnus.
- Informer le patient que le ritonavir peut provoquer l'hyperglycémie. Lui conseiller de prévenir un professionnel de la santé si les symptômes suivants se manifestent: soif ou faim accrue, perte de poids inexpliquée, mictions plus fréquentes, fatigue et sécheresse de la peau ou démangeaisons.
- Recommander à la patiente prenant des contraceptifs oraux d'utiliser une méthode contraceptive non hormonale pendant la durée du traitement par le ritonavir.
- Expliquer au patient qu'il peut noter une modification de la répartition des tissus adipeux et leur accumulation, menant à l'obésité faciotronculaire, à l'empâtement de la nuque et du cou (bosse de bison), à l'atrophie des membres, à l'augmentation du volume des seins et à un aspect cushingoïde. La cause de ces changements et les effets de longue durée sont encore inconnus.
- Insister sur le fait qu'il est important de se soumettre à intervalles réguliers à des examens de suivi et à des tests hématologiques permettant de déceler les effets secondaires et les bienfaits du traitement.

R

VÉRIFICATION DE L'EFFICACITÉ THÉRAPEUTIQUE

L'efficacité du traitement peut être démontrée par: le ralentissement de l'évolution de l'infection par le VIH et de l'apparition de ses complications ■ l'augmentation du nombre de cellules CD4 et la diminution de la charge virale.

RITUXIMAB

Rituxan

CLASSIFICATION:

Antinéoplasique (anticorps monoclonal)

Grossesse – catégorie C

INDICATIONS

Traitement des lymphomes non hodgkiniens de type B, CD 20 positifs, de bas grade ou folliculaires réfractaires ou récidivants ■ Traitement des lymphomes non hodgkiniens diffus à grandes cellules B, CD 20 positifs, en association avec un protocole de chimiothérapie CHOP (cyclophosphamide, doxorubicine, vincristine et prednisone) ■ Traitement des lymphomes non hodgkiniens de type B, CD 20 positifs, folliculaires, de stade III/IV non traités auparavant, en association avec un protocole de chimiothérapie CVP (cyclophosphamide, vincristine et prednisone) ■ Traitement d'entretien des patients atteints d'un lymphome non hodgkinien folliculaire qui ont répondu au traitement d'induction par le protocole de chimiothérapie CHOP ou CHOP plus rituximab ■ En association avec le méthotrexate, soulagement des signes et des symptômes de la polyarthrite rhumatoïde évolutive modérée ou grave chez les adultes ayant présenté une réponse inadéquate ou une intolérance à un ou à plusieurs traitements par des inhibiteurs du facteur de nécrose tumorale (anti-TNF).

MÉCANISME D'ACTION

Liaison à l'antigène CD20 situé à la surface des lymphocytes B, prévenant le processus d'activation du début du cycle cellulaire et la différenciation. ***Effets thérapeutiques:*** Destruction des lymphocytes B.

PHARMACOCINÉTIQUE

Absorption: Biodisponibilité à 100 % (IV).

Distribution: Fixation sélective aux sites de liaison de l'antigène CD20 des lymphocytes B.

Métabolisme et excrétion: Inconnus.

Demi-vie: *Lymphome* – de 59,8 à 174 heures (selon la charge tumorale); *polyarthrite rhumatoïde* – 20,8 jours.

Profil temps-action (déplétion des lymphocytes B)

	DÉBUT D'ACTION	PIC	DURÉE
IV	en l'espace de 14 jours	3 – 4 semaines	6 – 9 mois†

† Durée de la déplétion après 4 semaines de traitement.

CONTRE-INDICATIONS, PRÉCAUTIONS ET MISES EN GARDE

Contre-indications: Hypersensibilité à l'agent, aux protéines murines (de souris) ou aux cellules ovariennes de hamster chinois.

Précautions et mises en garde: Dépression médullaire préexistante ■ Infection par le virus de l'hépatite B (l'infection peut se réactiver au cours du traitement et plusieurs mois après sa fin) ■ Infection par le VIH (risque accru d'infection) ■ **PÉD.:** L'innocuité de l'agent n'a pas été établie ■ **OBST.:** Grossesse ou allaitement ■

Prise d'antihypertenseurs (ne pas les administrer dans les 12 heures précédant la perfusion).

RÉACTIONS INDÉSIRABLES ET EFFETS SECONDAIRES

SNC: céphalées.
Resp.: bronchospasme, toux, dyspnée, PNEUMONITE, BRONCHIOLITE OBLITÉRANTE.
CV: ARYTHMIES, hypotension, œdème périphérique.
GI: douleurs abdominales, altération du goût, dyspepsie.
Tég.: RÉACTIONS MUCOCUTANÉES, rougeur de la peau, urticaire.
End.: hyperglycémie.
HÉ: hypocalcémie.
Hémat.: ANÉMIE, NEUTROPÉNIE, THROMBOPÉNIE.
Loc.: arthralgie, douleurs lombaires.
Divers: réactions allergiques comprenant l'ANAPHYLAXIE et l'ŒDÈME DE QUINCKE, RÉACTION À LA PERFUSION, SYNDROME DE LYSE TUMORALE, fièvre, frissons, rigidité, douleur au siège des lésions, bouffées vasomotrices (associées à la perfusion), infections.

INTERACTIONS

Médicament-médicament: Aucune interaction connue.

VOIES D'ADMINISTRATION ET POSOLOGIE

Lymphome non hodgkinien de faible grade ou folliculaire

- **IV (adultes)**: *Traitement initial – Monothérapie:* 375 mg/m^2, 1 fois par semaine, pendant 4 semaines; *association avec le protocole CVP:* 375 mg/m^2, toutes les 3 semaines (le 1er jour de chaque cycle), pendant 8 cycles. *Traitement d'entretien* – 375 mg/m^2, tous les 3 mois, jusqu'au moment où la maladie commence à évoluer ou pendant 2 ans au maximum.

Lymphome non hodgkinien diffus à grandes cellules B

- **IV (adultes)**: *Association avec le protocole CHOP* – 375 mg/m^2, toutes les 3 semaines (le 1er jour de chaque cycle).

Polyarthrite rhumatoïde

- **IV (adultes)**: 1 000 mg, suivis d'une 2e dose de 1 000 mg, 2 semaines plus tard.

PRÉSENTATION

Solution pour injection: 10 mg/mL, en fioles de 100 mg^{Pr} et de 500 mg^{Pr}.

SOINS INFIRMIERS

ÉVALUATION DE LA SITUATION

- Rester à l'affût de la fièvre, des frissons, de la rigidité, des nausées, de l'urticaire, de la fatigue, des céphalées, du prurit, du bronchospasme, de la dyspnée, de la sensation de tuméfaction de la langue ou de la gorge, des vomissements, de l'hypotension, des bouffées vasomotrices et de la douleur au siège du lymphome. Ces complications reliées à la perfusion se produisent souvent dans les 30 minutes à 2 heures qui suivent le début de la première perfusion et peuvent disparaître si on la ralentit ou on l'arrête et si on administre un soluté salin, de la diphenhydramine et de l'acétaminophène. LES PATIENTS EXPOSÉS À UN RISQUE ACCRU (FEMMES, PATIENTS PRÉSENTANT DES INFILTRATS PULMONAIRES OU CEUX ATTEINTS DE LEUCÉMIE LYMPHOÏDE CHRONIQUE OU DE LYMPHOMES DU MANTEAU) PEUVENT MANIFESTER DES RÉACTIONS PLUS GRAVES QUI RISQUENT DE MENER À UNE ISSUE FATALE. LES SIGNES DE RÉACTIONS GRAVES, NOTAMMENT L'HYPOTENSION, L'ŒDÈME DE QUINCKE, L'HYPOXIE OU LE BRONCHOSPASME, PEUVENT DICTER L'ARRÊT DE LA PERFUSION. CES RÉACTIONS PEUVENT ENTRAÎNER L'APPARITION D'INFILTRATS PULMONAIRES, UNE INSUFFISANCE RESPIRATOIRE AIGUË, UN INFARCTUS DU MYOCARDE, DE LA FIBRILLATION VENTRICULAIRE OU UN CHOC CARDIOGÉNIQUE. GARDER LE PATIENT SOUS ÉTROITE OBSERVATION. La fréquence de ces réactions diminue au cours des perfusions ultérieures.
- SUIVRE DE PRÈS LE SYNDROME DE LYSE TUMORALE, ENTRAÎNÉ PAR LA RÉDUCTION RAPIDE DU VOLUME DE LA TUMEUR (INSUFFISANCE RÉNALE AIGUË, HYPERKALIÉMIE, HYPOCALCÉMIE, HYPERURICÉMIE OU HYPOPHOSPHATÉMIE), QUI SE MANIFESTE HABITUELLEMENT DANS LES 12 À 24 HEURES QUI SUIVENT LA PREMIÈRE PERFUSION. LES RISQUES SONT PLUS ÉLEVÉS CHEZ LES PATIENTS AYANT UNE PLUS GRANDE CHARGE TUMORALE, ET CE SYNDROME PEUT METTRE EN JEU LE PRONOSTIC VITAL. CORRIGER LES ANOMALIES ÉLECTROLYTIQUES, SUIVRE DE PRÈS LA FONCTION RÉNALE ET L'ÉQUILIBRE HYDRIQUE ET ADMINISTRER UN TRAITEMENT DE SOUTIEN, DONT UNE DIALYSE, SI ELLE EST INDIQUÉE.
- SUIVRE DE PRÈS LES RÉACTIONS D'HYPERSENSIBILITÉ (HYPOTENSION, BRONCHOSPASME, ŒDÈME DE QUINCKE) TOUT AU LONG DE LA PERFUSION. ELLES PEUVENT ÊTRE PRISES EN CHARGE PAR LE RALENTISSEMENT DE LA VITESSE DE PERFUSION. ON RECOMMANDE UNE PRÉMÉDICATION AVEC DE LA DIPHENHYDRAMINE, UN CORTICOSTÉROÏDE ET DE L'ACÉTAMINOPHÈNE. ON ADMINISTRE COMME TRAITEMENT DE CES RÉACTIONS DE LA DIPHENHYDRAMINE, DE L'ACÉTAMINOPHÈNE, DES BRONCHODILATATEURS OU UNE SOLUTION SALINE, SELON LES BESOINS. GARDER À PORTÉE DE LA MAIN DE L'ADRÉNALINE, DES ANTIHISTAMINIQUES ET DES CORTICOSTÉROÏDES POUR PARER À TOUTE RÉACTION

R

GRAVE. SI DES RÉACTIONS MODÉRÉES À GRAVES SURVIENNENT, ARRÊTER LA PERFUSION. SI LA RÉACTION ÉTAIT LÉGÈRE À MODÉRÉE, ON PEUT REPRENDRE LA PERFUSION À 50 % DE LA VITESSE D'ADMINISTRATION L'AYANT PROVOQUÉE, UNE FOIS QUE LES SYMPTÔMES ONT COMPLÈTEMENT DISPARU. EN CAS DE RÉACTION GRAVE, CONSULTER LE MÉDECIN POUR SAVOIR SI LE TRAITEMENT PEUT ÊTRE POURSUIVI.

- SUIVRE L'ÉCG PENDANT LA PERFUSION ET IMMÉDIATEMENT APRÈS QU'ELLE A PRIS FIN, CHEZ LES PATIENTS ATTEINTS DE MALADIE CARDIAQUE PRÉEXISTANTE (ARYTHMIES, ANGINE) OU CHEZ CEUX QUI ONT DÉVELOPPÉ DES ARYTHMIES AU COURS DES PERFUSIONS ANTÉRIEURES PAR LE RITUXIMAB. DES ARYTHMIES MORTELLES PEUVENT SURVENIR.

Tests de laboratoire: SUIVRE À INTERVALLES RÉGULIERS LA NUMÉRATION GLOBULAIRE ET PLAQUETTAIRE TOUT AU LONG DU TRAITEMENT; ASSURER UN SUIVI PLUS FRÉQUENT EN CAS DE DYSCRASIE SANGUINE. L'AGENT PEUT PROVOQUER DE L'ANÉMIE, UNE THROMBOPÉNIE OU UNE NEUTROPÉNIE.

- Le rituximab entraîne souvent la déplétion des lymphocytes B. Cette déplétion est associée à une diminution des immunoglobulines sériques chez une minorité des patients; cependant, la fréquence des infections ne semble pas s'accroître.

DIAGNOSTICS INFIRMIERS POSSIBLES

- Risque d'infection (Effets secondaires).

INTERVENTIONS INFIRMIÈRES

- Une hypotension passagère peut survenir pendant la perfusion; ne pas administrer d'antihypertenseurs dans les 12 heures qui précèdent.

Perfusion intermittente: Diluer la solution pour obtenir une concentration de 1 à 4 mg/mL avec du NaCl 0,9 % ou du D5E. Mélanger le contenu du sac en le retournant délicatement. La solution est transparente et incolore; ne pas administrer de solutions qui ont changé de couleur ou qui contiennent des particules. Mettre au rebut la solution inutilisée qui reste dans la fiole. La solution est stable pendant 12 heures à la température ambiante et pendant 24 heures au réfrigérateur.

Vitesse d'administration: Ne pas administrer l'agent sous forme d'IV directe ou de bolus.

- *Première perfusion:* Administrer à une vitesse initiale de 50 mg/h. Si aucune réaction d'hypersensibilité ou de complication associée à la perfusion ne survient, on peut accélérer la perfusion, par paliers de 50 mg/h, à des intervalles de 30 minutes, jusqu'à concurrence de 400 mg/h.
- *Perfusions ultérieures*: On peut les administrer à une vitesse initiale de 100 mg/h qu'on augmentera par paliers de 100 mg/h, à des intervalles de 30 minutes, jusqu'à concurrence de 400 mg/h.

Incompatibilité en addition au soluté: Ne pas mélanger avec d'autres médicaments.

ENSEIGNEMENT AU PATIENT ET À SES PROCHES

- Informer le patient du but de ce traitement.
- Recommander au patient de signaler sans tarder les complications reliées à la perfusion ou les symptômes d'une réaction d'hypersensibilité.
- CONSEILLER AU PATIENT DE SIGNALER RAPIDEMENT À UN PROFESSIONNEL DE LA SANTÉ LES SIGNES ET LES SYMPTÔMES SUIVANTS: FIÈVRE, FRISSONS, TOUX, ENROUEMENT, MAUX DE GORGE, SIGNES D'INFECTION, DOULEURS DANS LE FLANC OU LE BAS DU DOS, MICTIONS DOULOUREUSES OU DIFFICILES, SAIGNEMENT DES GENCIVES, FORMATION D'ECCHYMOSES, PÉTÉCHIES, PRÉSENCE DE SANG DANS LES SELLES, L'URINE OU LES VOMISSURES, FATIGUE ACCRUE, DYSPNÉE OU HYPOTENSION ORTHOSTATIQUE. RECOMMANDER AU PATIENT D'ÉVITER LES FOULES ET LES PERSONNES AYANT CONTRACTÉ UNE INFECTION. LUI RECOMMANDER D'UTILISER UNE BROSSE À DENTS À POILS DOUX ET UN RASOIR ÉLECTRIQUE ET DE PRENDRE GARDE AUX CHUTES. LUI CONSEILLER DE NE PAS BOIRE DE BOISSONS ALCOOLISÉES ET DE NE PAS PRENDRE DE MÉDICAMENTS CONTENANT DE L'ASPIRINE OU UN AINS EN RAISON DU RISQUE DE SAIGNEMENTS GASTRIQUES.
- Recommander à la patiente d'utiliser une méthode de contraception efficace tout au long du traitement.

VÉRIFICATION DE L'EFFICACITÉ THÉRAPEUTIQUE

L'efficacité du traitement peut être démontrée par: le ralentissement de la dissémination des cellules cancéreuses. ✳

RIVASTIGMINE

Exelon

CLASSIFICATION:

Traitement de la maladie d'Alzheimer (inhibiteur de la cholinestérase)

Grossesse – catégorie B

INDICATIONS

Traitement symptomatique de la démence de type Alzheimer d'intensité légère ou modérée.

MÉCANISME D'ACTION

Amélioration de l'activité cholinergique par inhibition de l'acétylcholinestérase. Également inhibition de la butyrylcholinestérase. ***Effets thérapeutiques:*** Diminution passagère de certains symptômes de démence associés à la maladie d'Alzheimer ■ L'agent ne modifie pas l'évolution de la maladie.

PHARMACOCINÉTIQUE

Absorption: Bonne (PO).

Distribution: Liquide céphalorachidien, sang, plasma.

Liaison aux protéines: 40 %.

Métabolisme et excrétion: Métabolisme hépatique de premier passage. Transformation en un métabolite actif qui possède 10 % de l'activité de la molécule mère et en d'autres métabolites. Élimination rénale des métabolites. Les principales isoenzymes du cytochrome P450 n'interviennent pas dans le métabolisme de la rivastigmine.

Demi-vie: Molécule mère: de 1 à 2 heures, métabolite actif: de 2,5 à 4 heures.

Profil temps-action (diminution des symptômes)

	DÉBUT D'ACTION	PIC	DURÉE
PO	inconnu	jusqu'à 12 semaines	inconnue†

† Après l'arrêt du traitement, rétablissement des valeurs initiales.

CONTRE-INDICATIONS, PRÉCAUTIONS ET MISES EN GARDE

Contre-indications: Hypersensibilité à la rivastigmine, à d'autres carbamates ou à un des ingrédients de la préparation ■ Insuffisance hépatique grave (aucune étude n'a été réalisée chez cette population).

Précautions et mises en garde: Présence d'une maladie cardiaque sous-jacente, particulièrement le syndrome de dysfonctionnement sinusal ou des anomalies de conduction supraventriculaire (les cholinomimétiques peuvent exercer des effets vagotoniques sur la fréquence cardiaque, comme la bradycardie et un bloc cardiaque) ■ Antécédents de syncope ■ Antécédents d'ulcère, de saignements gastro-intestinaux ou traitement concomitant avec des anti-inflammatoires non stéroïdiens ■ Antécédents de convulsions ■ Antécédents d'asthme ou de bronchopneumopathie obstructive chronique ■ **OBST., ALLAITEMENT, PÉD.:** L'innocuité du médicament n'a pas été établie ■ Insuffisance rénale ■ Insuffisance hépatique ■ Anesthésie (augmentation possible de la relaxation musculaire causée par la succinylcholine) ■ Patients de petit poids (risque de perte de poids supplémentaire) ■ **GÉR.:** Patients > 85 ans ou présentant plusieurs maladies concomitantes (peu de données sur l'innocuité).

RÉACTIONS INDÉSIRABLES ET EFFETS SECONDAIRES

SNC: céphalées, dépression, étourdissements, somnolence, fatigue, asthénie, convulsions, insomnie, faiblesse.

CV: bradycardie, fibrillation auriculaire, palpitation, syncope, œdème, hypotension, insuffisance cardiaque.

GI: diarrhée, nausées, anorexie, vomissements, douleurs abdominales, dyspepsie, hémorragie digestive, constipation.

SN: tremblements.

Métab.: perte de poids, fièvre.

INTERACTIONS

Médicament-médicament: La rivastigmine accentue la relaxation musculaire induite par la **succinylcholine** au cours d'une anesthésie ■ La rivastigmine peut entraver les effets des **agents anticholinergiques** ■ Le médicament augmente les effets cholinergiques du **béthanéchol** ■ Risque accru d'hémorragie gastro-intestinale lors de l'administration concomitante d'**anti-inflammatoires non stéroïdiens** ■ L'usage concomitant de **nicotine** peut accélérer le métabolisme de la rivastigmine et en diminuer les concentrations plasmatiques.

VOIES D'ADMINISTRATION ET POSOLOGIE

- **PO (adultes):** Dose de départ: 1,5 mg, 2 fois par jour. Si le patient tolère bien cette dose, on peut l'augmenter pour la porter à 3 mg, 2 fois par jour, après un délai d'au moins 2 semaines. Toute augmentation supplémentaire doit être effectuée avec prudence. Il ne faut augmenter les doses pour les passer à 4,5 mg, 2 fois par jour, puis jusqu'à 6 mg, 2 fois par jour, que si le patient tolère bien la dose courante, et ce, après un minimum de 2 semaines de traitement à cette dose.

INSUFFISANCE RÉNALE OU HÉPATIQUE

- **PO (ADULTES):** COMMENCER LE TRAITEMENT À UNE POSOLOGIE PLUS FAIBLE (1,5 mg, 1 FOIS PAR JOUR), ET MAJORER LES DOSES MOINS RAPIDEMENT QUE CHEZ LES AUTRES ADULTES.

PRÉSENTATION

Capsules: 1,5 mg^Pr^, 3 mg^Pr^, 4,5 mg^Pr^, 6 mg^Pr^ ■ **Solution orale:** 2 mg/mL^Pr^.

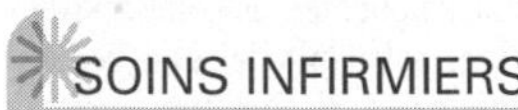

SOINS INFIRMIERS

ÉVALUATION DE LA SITUATION

- Évaluer le fonctionnement cognitif (mémoire, attention, raisonnement, langage, capacité à accomplir

R

des tâches simples) à intervalles réguliers pendant toute la durée du traitement.

- Mesurer la fréquence cardiaque à intervalles réguliers pendant toute la durée du traitement. La rivastigmine peut induire une bradycardie.
- Rester à l'affût des nausées, des vomissements, de l'anorexie ou d'une perte de poids. Prévenir un professionnel de la santé si un de ces effets se manifeste.

DIAGNOSTICS INFIRMIERS POSSIBLES

- Opérations de la pensée perturbées (Indications).
- Risque d'accident (Indications).
- Connaissances insuffisantes sur le traitement médicamenteux (Enseignement au patient et à ses proches).

INTERVENTIONS INFIRMIÈRES

- **PO**: Administrer la rivastigmine avec des aliments, en 2 doses, soit 1 le matin et l'autre le soir.
- La solution orale et les capsules de rivastigmine sont interchangeables à dose égale.

Solution orale: Prélever la quantité de solution prescrite à l'aide de la seringue fournie. Le contenu de la seringue peut être avalé directement ou être mélangé dans un verre avec un peu d'eau, de jus de fruits ou de boisson gazeuse. Ne pas mélanger à d'autres solutions. Brasser le mélange avant de le faire boire. S'assurer que le patient a avalé toute la solution. La solution orale est stable pendant 4 heures à la température de la pièce lorsqu'elle est mélangée avec du jus de fruits ou une boisson gazeuse froide.

ENSEIGNEMENT AU PATIENT ET À SES PROCHES

- Insister sur le fait qu'il est important de prendre la rivastigmine tous les jours, en suivant rigoureusement la posologie recommandée. Si le patient n'a pas pu prendre le médicament au moment habituel, il doit le prendre aussitôt que possible, à moins que ce ne soit presque l'heure prévue pour la dose suivante. Le prévenir qu'il ne doit jamais remplacer une dose manquée par une double dose. Lui expliquer qu'il peut être dangereux de donner ce médicament à une autre personne.
- Expliquer au patient et à ses proches comment utiliser la seringue pour mesurer la solution orale. Retirer la seringue de son emballage et ouvrir le flacon de rivastigmine en poussant le couvercle vers le bas tout en tournant. Introduire la seringue dans l'ouverture de l'obturateur du flacon. Tirer le piston de la seringue jusqu'à la dose prescrite. Éliminer les grosses bulles (les petites bulles ne modifient pas la dose) puis réajuster la dose au besoin. Enlever la seringue du flacon.
- Prévenir le patient qu'il ne doit pas prendre une dose plus élevée que celle prescrite; des doses plus élevées n'augmentent pas les effets bénéfiques du médicament, mais peuvent entraîner un plus grand nombre d'effets secondaires.
- Prévenir le patient et ses proches que, chaque fois qu'on interrompt le traitement durant plusieurs jours, il faut le recommencer à la dose quotidienne la plus faible qui soit (c'est-à-dire 1,5 mg, 1 fois par jour, ou 1,5 mg, 2 fois par jour, selon la recommandation du médecin, puis augmenter la posologie jusqu'à l'atteinte de la dose d'entretien).
- Prévenir le patient et ses proches que la rivastigmine peut provoquer des étourdissements.
- Recommander au patient et à ses proches de prévenir un professionnel de la santé en cas de nausées, de vomissements, de diarrhée, d'anorexie, de perte de poids ou de changement de la couleur des selles, ou encore si de nouveaux symptômes se manifestent ou si les symptômes déjà présents s'aggravent.
- Recommander au patient et à ses proches d'informer tous les professionnels de la santé avant tout autre traitement ou avant une intervention chirurgicale qu'il prend ce traitement médicamenteux.
- Insister sur l'importance des examens de suivi réguliers pour déterminer les effets du traitement.

VÉRIFICATION DE L'EFFICACITÉ THÉRAPEUTIQUE

L'efficacité du traitement peut être démontrée par: l'amélioration ou la stabilisation du fonctionnement cognitif (mémoire, attention, raisonnement, langage, capacité à accomplir des tâches simples) chez les patients souffrant de la maladie d'Alzheimer.

RIZATRIPTAN,

voir Agonistes de la sérotonine 5-HT_1

ROPINIROLE

Requip

CLASSIFICATION:

Antiparkinsonien (agoniste de la dopamine)

Grossesse – catégorie C

INDICATIONS

Traitement des signes et des symptômes de la maladie de Parkinson idiopathique en phase précoce, sans lévodopa, ou comme traitement d'appoint à la lévodopa.

MÉCANISME D'ACTION

Stimulation des récepteurs de la dopamine dans le cerveau. ***Effets thérapeutiques:*** Diminution des tremblements et de la rigidité qui caractérisent la maladie de Parkinson.

PHARMACOCINÉTIQUE

Absorption: 55 % (PO).

Distribution: Tout l'organisme.

Métabolisme et excrétion: Métabolisme majoritairement hépatique (par le système enzymatique du cytochrome P450 1A2); < 10 % est excrété à l'état inchangé dans l'urine.

Demi-vie: 6 heures.

Profil temps-action

	DÉBUT D'ACTION	PIC	DURÉE
PO	inconnu	inconnu	8 h

CONTRE-INDICATIONS, PRÉCAUTIONS ET MISES EN GARDE

Contre-indications: Hypersensibilité ■ Insuffisance rénale et hépatique graves.

Précautions et mises en garde: Risque de narcolepsie (qui ne survient pas nécessairement au début du traitement; les patients devraient également être prévenus que le sommeil soudain peut survenir sans signe avant-coureur) ■ Risque de complications fibreuses (p. ex., fibrose péritonérale, fibrose pleurale et fibrose pulmonaire) ■ Risque d'une réaction de type syndrome malin des neuroleptiques (caractérisée par l'élévation de la température, la rigidité musculaire, des changements de l'état de conscience et une instabilité autonome), associé à un diminution rapide de la dose ou le retrait du ropinirole chez les patient atteints de la maladie de Parkinson ■ **GÉR.:** Risque accru d'hallucinations chez les patients > 65 ans ■ Maladie cardiovasculaire grave ■ **OBST., ALLAITEMENT, PÉD.:** L'innocuité du médicament n'a pas été établie; il peut inhiber la lactation.

RÉACTIONS INDÉSIRABLES ET EFFETS SECONDAIRES

SNC: NARCOLEPSIE, étourdissements, syncope, confusion, somnolence, fatigue, hallucinations, céphalées, dyskinésie accrue, faiblesse.

ORLO: vision anormale.

CV: hypotension orthostatique, œdème périphérique.

GI: constipation, sécheresse de la bouche (xérostomie), dyspepsie, nausées, vomissements.

Tég.: sécrétion accrue de sueur.

INTERACTIONS

Médicament-médicament: Les **médicaments qui modifient l'activité du système enzymatique du cytochrome P450 1A2** peuvent modifier les effets du ropinirole ■ Les **œstrogènes** peuvent intensifier les effets du ropinirole ■ Les **phénothiazines**, les **butyrophénones**, les **thioxanthènes** ou le **métoclopramide** peuvent diminuer les effets du ropinirole ■ Le ropinirole peut intensifier les effets de la **lévodopa** (il peut s'avérer nécessaire de réduire la dose de lévodopa) ■ Dépression additive du SNC lors de l'usage concomitant d'autres **dépresseurs du SNC**, tels que l'**alcool**, les **opioïdes** et les **hypnosédatifs**.

VOIES D'ADMINISTRATION ET POSOLOGIE

- **PO (adultes):** 0,25 mg, 3 fois par jour, pendant 1 semaine, puis, 0,5 mg, 3 fois par jour, pendant 1 semaine, ensuite, 0,75 mg, 3 fois par jour, pendant 1 semaine et, enfin, 1 mg, 3 fois par jour, pendant 1 semaine; on peut ensuite augmenter la dose par paliers hebdomadaires de 0,5 mg à 1 mg par jour, jusqu'à concurrence de 24 mg par jour. Le traitement doit être arrêté graduellement en l'espace de 7 jours.

PRÉSENTATION

Comprimés: 0,25 mg[Pr], 1 mg[Pr], 2 mg[Pr], 5 mg[Pr].

SOINS INFIRMIERS

ÉVALUATION DE LA SITUATION

- Observer le patient avant le traitement et pendant toute sa durée à la recherche des signes et des symptômes parkinsoniens suivants: tremblements, faiblesse musculaire, rigidité, démarche tabétocérébelleuse.
- Mesurer la pression artérielle à intervalles fréquents pendant toute la durée du traitement.
- RESTER À L'AFFÛT DE LA SOMNOLENCE ET DE LA NARCOLEPSIE. LA SOMNOLENCE EST UN EFFET SECONDAIRE COURANT DU ROPINIROLE, MAIS LA NARCOLEPSIE OU DES ÉPISODES D'ENDORMISSEMENT AU COURS D'ACTIVITÉS QUI EXIGENT LA VIGILANCE DU PATIENT PEUVENT SURVENIR SANS SIGNE AVANT-COUREUR. DÉTERMINER LES MÉDICAMENTS PRIS EN CONCOMITANCE QUI EXERCENT DES EFFETS SÉDATIFS OU QUI PEUVENT AUGMENTER LES CONCENTRATIONS SÉRIQUES DE ROPINIROLE (VOIR «INTERACTIONS»). IL PEUT S'AVÉRER NÉCESSAIRE D'ARRÊTER LE TRAITEMENT.

Tests de laboratoire: Le médicament peut élever les concentrations d'urée.

R

DIAGNOSTICS INFIRMIERS POSSIBLES

- Mobilité physique réduite (Indications).
- Risque d'accident (Indications, Effets secondaires).
- Connaissances insuffisantes sur le traitement médicamenteux (Enseignement au patient et à ses proches).

INTERVENTIONS INFIRMIÈRES

- Administrer le ropinirole avec ou sans aliments. La prise concomitante d'aliments peut diminuer les nausées.

ENSEIGNEMENT AU PATIENT ET À SES PROCHES

- Conseiller au patient de respecter rigoureusement la posologie recommandée. S'il n'a pu prendre le médicament au moment habituel, il doit le prendre aussitôt que possible, à moins que ce ne soit presque l'heure prévue pour la dose suivante. Le prévenir qu'il ne doit pas remplacer une dose manquée par une double dose.
- Conseiller au patient de changer lentement de position afin de réduire le risque d'hypotension orthostatique.
- PRÉVENIR LE PATIENT QUE LE ROPINIROLE PEUT PROVOQUER DE LA SOMNOLENCE ET DES ÉPISODES D'ENDORMISSEMENT IMPRÉVUS. LUI CONSEILLER DE NE PAS CONDUIRE ET D'ÉVITER LES ACTIVITÉS QUI EXIGENT SA VIGILANCE JUSQU'À CE QU'ON AIT LA CERTITUDE QUE LE MÉDICAMENT N'ENTRAÎNE PAS CES EFFETS CHEZ LUI. LUI RECOMMANDER ÉGALEMENT DE PRÉVENIR UN PROFESSIONNEL DE LA SANTÉ SI DES ÉPISODES D'ENDORMISSEMENT SURVIENNENT.
- Prévenir le patient qu'il doit éviter de boire de l'alcool et de prendre d'autres dépresseurs du SNC en même temps que le ropinirole.
- Conseiller au patient de boire plus de liquides, de consommer de la gomme à mâcher ou des bonbons sans sucre, des glaçons ou des substituts de salive pour diminuer la sécheresse de la bouche et de consulter un professionnel de la santé si elle persiste pendant plus de 2 semaines.

VÉRIFICATION DE L'EFFICACITÉ THÉRAPEUTIQUE

L'efficacité du traitement peut être démontrée par: la diminution des tremblements et de la rigidité associés à la maladie de Parkinson. ✳

ROPIVACAÏNE,

voir Anesthésiques épiduraux à action locale

R

ROSIGLITAZONE

Avandia

CLASSIFICATION:

Antidiabétique (thiazolidinedione)

Grossesse – catégorie C

INDICATIONS

Traitement d'appoint à la diétothérapie et à l'exercice lors de la prise en charge du diabète de type 2 ou traitement d'association avec la metformine ou une sulfonylurée, lorsque la diétothérapie et l'exercice, jumelés à la metformine ou à une sulfonylurée, n'ont pas réussi à maîtriser la glycémie.

MÉCANISME D'ACTION

Amélioration de la sensibilité à l'insuline en raison d'un effet agoniste aux sites récepteurs intervenant dans la réponse à l'insuline et dans la production et l'utilisation ultérieures du glucose ▪ L'action du médicament ne peut s'exercer qu'en présence d'insuline. ***Effets thérapeutiques:*** Diminution de la résistance à l'insuline, permettant la maîtrise de la glycémie sans apparition de signes d'hypoglycémie.

PHARMACOCINÉTIQUE

Absorption: 99 % (PO).

Distribution: Inconnue.

Liaison aux protéines: 99,8 %.

Métabolisme et excrétion: Fort métabolisme hépatique. Élimination sous forme de métabolites dans l'urine (64 %) et dans les fèces (23 %).

Demi-vie: De 3 à 4 heures (plus longue en cas de maladie hépatique).

Profil temps-action (effet sur la glycémie)

	DÉBUT D'ACTION	PIC	DURÉE
PO	4 semaines	8 - 12 semaines	inconnue

CONTRE-INDICATIONS, PRÉCAUTIONS ET MISES EN GARDE

Contre-indications: Hypersensibilité ▪ Insuffisance cardiaque de classe III ou IV de la NYHA ▪ **OBST.:** Il est recommandé d'administrer de l'insuline pour équilibrer la glycémie durant la grossesse ▪ Dysfonction hépatique grave.

Précautions et mises en garde: Œdème ▪ Acidocétose diabétique ▪ Insuffisance cardiaque de classe I ou II de la NYHA ▪ Femmes préménopausées qui n'ovulent pas (le médicament peut rétablir le cycle ovulatoire et favoriser la grossesse) ■ Diabète de type 1 (le mode d'action du médicament est régi par la présence d'insuline) ■ Taux d'ALT accrus (> 2,5 fois la limite supérieure de la normale) ■ Œdème maculaire ■ **ALLAITEMENT**: On ignore si le médicament passe dans le lait maternel; il n'est donc pas recommandé chez les femmes qui allaitent ■ **PÉD.**: L'innocuité et l'efficacité du médicament n'ont pas été établies chez les enfants < 18 ans.

RÉACTIONS INDÉSIRABLES ET EFFETS SECONDAIRES

CV: INSUFFISANCE CARDIAQUE, œdème.
Tég.: urticaire.
Hémat.: anémie.
Métab.: élévation des taux de cholestérol total, de C-LDL et de C-HDL, gain pondéral.

INTERACTIONS

Médicament-médicament: L'administration concomitante d'**inhibiteurs du CYP2C8** (**gemfibrozil**, **montélukast**) peut entraîner une augmentation des concentrations sanguines de rosiglitazone ■ L'administration concomitante d'**inducteurs du CYP2C8** (**rifampicine**) peut entraîner une diminution des concentrations sanguines de rosiglitazone.
Médicament-produits naturels: La **glucosamine** peut entraver l'équilibrage de la glycémie ■ Le **chrome** et le **coenzyme Q-10** peuvent augmenter le risque d'hypoglycémie.

VOIES D'ADMINISTRATION ET POSOLOGIE

- **PO (adultes)**: 4 mg par jour, en 1 prise ou en 2 prises fractionnées; après 8 à 12 semaines, on peut majorer la dose, selon la réponse au traitement et la tolérance du patient, jusqu'à concurrence de 8 mg par jour, en 1 prise ou en 2 prises fractionnées.

PRÉSENTATION

Comprimés: 2 mg^{Pr}, 4 mg^{Pr}, 8 mg^{Pr} ■ **En association avec**: metformine (Avandamet) ou glimépiride (Avandaryl).

SOINS INFIRMIERS

ÉVALUATION DE LA SITUATION

- Rester à l'affût des signes et des symptômes suivants d'hypoglycémie, en cas d'administration concomitante d'une sulfonylurée: transpiration, faim, faiblesse, étourdissements, tremblements, tachycardie, anxiété.
- Évaluer la présence d'œdème et de signes d'insuffisance cardiaque: dyspnée, râles, crépitements, œdème périphérique, gain de poids, turgescence des jugulaires. Ils peuvent dicter l'arrêt du traitement par la rosiglitazone.

Tests de laboratoire:

- Suivre, à intervalles réguliers pendant toute la durée du traitement, la glycémie et la concentration d'hémoglobine glyquée, afin d'évaluer l'efficacité du médicament.
- Noter la numération globulaire et la formule leucocytaire à intervalles réguliers pendant toute la durée du traitement. La rosiglitazone peut réduire les concentrations d'hémoglobine, l'hématocrite et le nombre de globules blancs, habituellement au cours des 4 à 8 premières semaines de traitement; les concentrations se stabilisent par la suite.
- Suivre l'AST et l'ALT tous les 2 mois pendant les 12 premiers mois de traitement, et à intervalles réguliers par la suite ou en cas de jaunisse ou de symptômes de dysfonctionnement hépatique. La rosiglitazone peut entraîner des élévations irréversibles de l'AST et de l'ALT ou l'insuffisance hépatique (rare). Si la concentration d'ALT augmente à plus de 3 fois la limite supérieure de la normale, faire un nouveau test sans tarder. Si les résultats du deuxième test confirment ceux du premier, arrêter l'administration de la rosiglitazone.
- Le médicament peut entraîner des élévations des taux de cholestérol total, de C-LDL et de C-HDL, ainsi qu'une diminution des taux d'acides gras libres.

DIAGNOSTICS INFIRMIERS POSSIBLES

- Alimentation excessive (Indications).
- Connaissances insuffisantes sur le traitement médicamenteux (Enseignement au patient et à ses proches).

INTERVENTIONS INFIRMIÈRES

- Il peut s'avérer nécessaire d'administrer de l'insuline aux patients dont la glycémie a été stabilisée, mais qui font de la fièvre, qui sont exposés au stress, à un traumatisme ou à une infection ou à ceux qui doivent subir une intervention chirurgicale.
- Le médicament peut être administré avec ou sans aliments.

ENSEIGNEMENT AU PATIENT ET À SES PROCHES

- Conseiller au patient de respecter rigoureusement la posologie recommandée. S'il n'a pu prendre le médicament une journée, il ne doit pas doubler la dose le jour suivant.
- Expliquer au patient que la rosiglitazone permet de stabiliser la glycémie, mais ne peut guérir le diabète.

Le traitement à l'aide de cet agent est habituellement de longue durée.

- Expliquer au patient les signes d'hypoglycémie et d'hyperglycémie. Si des symptômes d'hypoglycémie se manifestent, lui recommander de prendre un verre de jus d'orange ou un verre d'eau auquel il ajoute 2 ou 3 cuillerées à thé de sucre, de miel ou de sirop de maïs et de prévenir un professionnel de la santé.
- Inciter le patient à suivre la diétothérapie, la pharmacothérapie et le programme d'exercices prescrits afin de prévenir les épisodes d'hypoglycémie ou d'hyperglycémie.
- Enseigner au patient la façon de mesurer sa glycémie et sa cétonurie. Lui recommander de surveiller étroitement les résultats de ces tests en période de stress ou de maladie et de prévenir immédiatement un professionnel de la santé si des modifications importantes surviennent.
- Recommander au patient de consulter immédiatement un professionnel de la santé si des signes d'insuffisance hépatique (nausées, vomissements, douleurs abdominales, fatigue, anorexie, urines foncées, jaunisse) ou d'insuffisance cardiaque (œdème, difficultés respiratoires, gain de poids rapide) se manifestent.
- Expliquer à la patiente que l'insuline est le médicament qu'il faut préférer pour équilibrer la glycémie au cours de la grossesse. L'informer que des doses plus élevées de contraceptifs oraux ou une autre méthode de contraception peuvent s'avérer nécessaires et lui conseiller d'informer rapidement un professionnel de la santé si elle pense être enceinte ou si elle souhaite le devenir.
- Recommander au patient qui doit suivre un autre traitement ou subir une intervention chirurgicale d'avertir le professionnel de la santé qu'il suit un traitement par ce médicament.
- Conseiller au patient de toujours avoir sur lui du sucre (sachets de sucre ou bonbons) et une pièce d'identité où sont inscrits son problème de santé et son traitement médicamenteux.
- Insister sur l'importance des examens de suivi.

R

VÉRIFICATION DE L'EFFICACITÉ THÉRAPEUTIQUE

L'efficacité du traitement peut être démontrée par : l'équilibrage de la glycémie. ✳

ROSUVASTATINE,

voir Inhibiteurs de l'HMG-CoA réductase

SALBUTAMOL

Synonyme: albutérol

Airomir, Apo-Salvent, Gen-Salbutamol, Nu-Salbutamol, Ratio-Salbutamol, Ventolin, Ventolin Diskus, Ventolin HFA

CLASSIFICATION:

Bronchodilatateur (agoniste bêta-adrénergique)

Grossesse – catégorie C

INDICATIONS

Traitement symptomatique et prévention du bronchospasme attribuable à l'asthme bronchique, à la bronchopneumopathie chronique obstructive (BPCO) ou à toute autre affection bronchopulmonaire chronique dans laquelle le bronchospasme constitue un facteur aggravant ■ **Inhalation**: Prévention du bronchospasme provoqué par l'effort ■ **PO**: Prévention et soulagement du bronchospasme ■ **IV**: Traitement du bronchospasme grave associé à des exacerbations aiguës de la BPCO et de l'asthme bronchique ■ Traitement de l'état de mal asthmatique.

MÉCANISME D'ACTION

Liaison aux récepteurs bêta$_2$-adrénergiques présents dans les muscles lisses des voies respiratoires, qui entraînent l'activation de l'adénylcyclase et une élévation des concentrations d'adénosine monophosphate-3′, 5′ cyclique (AMPc). Cette hausse des concentrations stimule les kinases, qui inhibent la phosphorylation de la myosine et abaissent les concentrations intracellulaires de calcium. La baisse de ces concentrations est associée à la relaxation des muscles lisses des voies respiratoires ■ Relaxation des muscles lisses des voies respiratoires entraînant la bronchodilatation ■ Spécificité relative pour les récepteurs bêta$_2$-adrénergiques (pulmonaires). ***Effets thérapeutiques:*** Bronchodilatation.

PHARMACOCINÉTIQUE

Absorption: Bonne (PO), mais l'agent subit rapidement un fort métabolisme. Faible (inhalation).

Distribution: L'agent, administré par voie générale, traverse la barrière placentaire.

Métabolisme et excrétion: Métabolisme hépatique (administration par voie générale). Excrétion rénale (administration par voie générale).

Demi-vie: De 3,8 à 7,1 heures.

Profil temps-action (bronchodilatation)

	DÉBUT D'ACTION	PIC	DURÉE
PO	30 min	2 - 3 h	6 h ou plus
Inhalation	5 - 15 min	60 - 90 min	3 - 6 h

CONTRE-INDICATIONS, PRÉCAUTIONS ET MISES EN GARDE

Contre-indications: Hypersensibilité ■ Hypersensibilité (à médiation IgE) au lactose ou au lait (Ventolin Diskus) ■ Tachyarythmie (PO, nébulisation et IV) ■ **OBST.**: Risque de fausse couche au cours du 1er ou du 2e trimestre de la grossesse (IV); ce médicament n'est pas indiqué pour prévenir ou arrêter le travail prématuré (risque d'œdème pulmonaire et d'ischémie myocardique) (IV).

Précautions et mises en garde: Maladie cardiaque (insuffisance coronarienne ou arythmie) ■ Sténose hypertrophique sous-aortique ■ Hypertension ■ Hyperthyroïdie ■ Diabète (lorsque le médicament est administré par nébulisation ou par perfusion) ■ Antécédents de réponse accrue aux amines sympathomimétiques ■ Troubles convulsifs ■ Bronchospasme paradoxal ■ **OBST., ALLAITEMENT**: L'innocuité du médicament n'a pas été établie chez la femme enceinte ou qui allaite (inhalation) ■ **PÉD.**: L'innocuité et l'efficacité du médicament n'ont pas été établies chez les enfants (IV), chez les enfants < 4 ans (inhalation), chez les enfants < 2 ans (PO) ■ Utilisation excessive, car elle peut entraîner un épuisement de l'effet et un bronchospasme paradoxal (inhalation).

RÉACTIONS INDÉSIRABLES ET EFFETS SECONDAIRES

SNC: nervosité, agitation, tremblements, céphalées, insomnie et hyperactivité chez les enfants.

CV: douleurs thoraciques, palpitations, angine, arythmies, hypertension.

GI: nausées, vomissements.

End.: hyperglycémie.

HÉ: hypokaliémie.

INTERACTIONS

Médicament-médicament: L'utilisation concomitante d'autres **agents adrénergiques (sympathomimétiques)** intensifie les effets secondaires adrénergiques ■ L'administration simultanée d'**IMAO** ou d'**antidépresseurs tricycliques** peut déclencher une crise hypertensive ■ Les **bêtabloquants** peuvent abolir l'effet thérapeutique ■ L'administration concomitante de **diurétiques non épargneurs de potassium** peut accroître le risque d'hypokaliémie ■ Le salbutamol peut diminuer les concentrations sanguines de **digoxine** ■ L'hypokaliémie accroît le risque de toxicité induite par la **digoxine**.

Médicament-produits naturels: L'administration concomitante de produits contenant de la caféine (**noix de cola**, **guarana**, **maté**, **thé**, **café**) augmente l'effet stimulant du salbutamol.

VOIES D'ADMINISTRATION ET POSOLOGIE

- **PO (adultes et enfants > 12 ans)**: De 2 à 4 mg, 3 ou 4 fois par jour (ne pas dépasser 32 mg par jour).

- **PO (personnes âgées)**: La dose initiale ne doit pas dépasser 2 mg; on peut administrer l'agent 3 ou 4 fois par jour (ne pas dépasser 32 mg par jour).
- **PO (enfants de 6 à 12 ans)**: 2 mg, 3 ou 4 fois par jour (ne pas dépasser 24 mg par jour).
- **PO (enfants de 2 à 6 ans)**: 0,1 mg/kg, 3 ou 4 fois par jour (ne pas dépasser 12 mg par jour).
- **Inhalation (adultes)**: *Aérosol doseur* – 1 ou 2 inhalations, toutes les 6 à 8 heures, ou 2 inhalations (100 µg/inhalation), 15 minutes avant l'effort; certains patients peuvent répondre à une seule inhalation (ne pas dépasser 8 inhalations par jour).
- **Inhalation (enfants ≥ 4 ans)**: 1 inhalation (100 µg), 4 fois par jour; au besoin, on peut passer à 2 inhalations. On peut administrer 1 inhalation, 15 minutes avant l'effort; au besoin, on peut passer à 2 inhalations (ne pas dépasser 4 inhalations par jour).
- **Inhalation (adultes et enfants ≥ 12 ans)**: *Nébuliseur ou respirateur à pression positive intermittente* – 2,5 mg ou 5 mg, jusqu'à 4 fois par jour.
- **Inhalation (enfants de 2 à 12 ans)**: *Nébuliseur ou respirateur à pression positive intermittente* – 1,25 mg ou 2,5 mg, jusqu'à 4 fois par jour. On peut administrer une dose unitaire de 5 mg s'il s'agit d'un cas réfractaire.
- **Inhalation (adultes et enfants ≥ 4 ans)**: *Inhalateur Diskus* – 1 inhalation (200 µg), 3 ou 4 fois par jour, ou 1 inhalation (200 µg), 15 minutes avant l'effort (ne pas dépasser 4 inhalations par jour).
- **IM (adultes)**: 500 µg (8 µg/kg de poids corporel), toutes les 4 heures, selon les besoins (ne pas dépasser 2 000 µg par jour).
- **IV (adultes)**: 5 µg/min; on peut porter la dose à 10 µg/min, puis à 20 µg/min, à intervalles de 15 à 30 minutes, au besoin.

PRÉSENTATION (version générique disponible)

Comprimés: 2 mg[Pr], 4 mg[Pr] ■ **Solution orale (sirop aromatisé à l'orange)**: 2 mg/5 mL[Pr] (0,4 mg/mL) ■ **Aérosol doseur**: 100 µg/vaporisation[Pr], 200 inhalations/aérosol-doseur ■ **Solution pour respirateur**: 5 mg/mL[Pr], en flacons de 10 mL ■ **Doses unitaires de solution de salbutamol pour respirateur**: une dose de solution isotonique stérile contient 1,25 mg[Pr], 2,5 mg[Pr] ou 5 mg[Pr] dans 2,5 mL ■ **Poudre pour inhalation (Ventolin Diskus)**: 200 µg[Pr], 60 doses/diskus ■ **Solution pour injection IM**: 500 µg/mL[Pr], ampoules de 1 mL ■ **Solution pour injection IV**: 1 000 µg/mL[Pr], ampoules de 5 mL.

SOINS INFIRMIERS

ÉVALUATION DE LA SITUATION

- Ausculter le murmure vésiculaire, mesurer le pouls et la pression artérielle avant l'administration du médicament et lorsque les concentrations atteignent un pic. Noter la quantité, la couleur et les caractéristiques des expectorations.
- Noter les résultats des tests de la fonction pulmonaire, avant le début du traitement et à intervalles réguliers pendant toute sa durée, pour déterminer l'efficacité du médicament.
- Suivre de près l'apparition du bronchospasme paradoxal (respiration sifflante). S'il survient, arrêter l'administration du médicament et prévenir immédiatement le médecin ou un autre professionnel de la santé.

Tests de laboratoire: Possibilité d'une réduction passagère des concentrations sériques de potassium lors de la nébulisation, du traitement IV ou de l'administration de doses plus élevées que celles qui sont recommandées.

DIAGNOSTICS INFIRMIERS POSSIBLES

- Dégagement inefficace des voies respiratoires (Indications).
- Connaissances insuffisantes sur le traitement médicamenteux (Enseignement au patient et à ses proches).

INTERVENTIONS INFIRMIÈRES

- NE PAS CONFONDRE LE SALBUTAMOL AVEC LE SALMÉTÉROL.

PO: Administrer le médicament par voie orale avec des aliments pour réduire l'irritation gastrique.

Inhalation:

- Bien agiter l'aérosol-doseur avant l'administration. Lors de la première utilisation, il faut activer le dispositif en vaporisant 4 fois dans l'air.
- Espacer d'au moins 1 minute les inhalations lorsque le médicament est pris en aérosol.
- L'utilisation d'une chambre d'espacement améliore l'efficacité du médicament. Toujours employer une chambre d'espacement chez les enfants.
- Le dispositif d'inhalation Diskus ne doit pas être agité ou activé. Il contient 60 doses mesurées. Pour l'utiliser, il suffit de l'ouvrir, de pousser le levier, d'inspirer et de le fermer.
- Il n'est pas nécessaire de diluer les solutions en doses unitaires lorsqu'elles sont administrées par un nébuliseur ou par un respirateur à pression positive intermittente. La solution à 5 mg/mL, destinée à l'inhalation, doit être diluée dans 2 à 5 mL d'une

solution de NaCl 0,9 %. Les solutions diluées sont stables pendant 24 heures à la température ambiante ou pendant 48 heures, au réfrigérateur. Consulter les directives de chaque fabricant avant de préparer ces solutions.

- Le débit d'oxygène ou l'air comprimé du nébuliseur devrait être de 6 à 10 L/min ; un seul traitement avec 3 mL dure environ 10 minutes.
- Le traitement par un respirateur à pression positive intermittente dure habituellement de 5 à 20 minutes.

IM:

- L'injection IM est réservée aux cas où la ponction veineuse n'est pas souhaitable ou pratique, ou bien lorsqu'elle est impossible à réaliser.

Perfusion IV: IL NE FAUT PAS INJECTER LA SOLUTION POUR PERFUSION IV NON DILUÉE. SA CONCENTRATION DOIT ÊTRE RÉDUITE DE 50 % AVANT L'ADMINISTRATION.

Perfusion continue: On peut préparer une solution pour perfusion en diluant 5 mL de la solution pour perfusion IV (à 1 mg/mL) dans 500 mL de NaCl 0,9 %, de dextrose 5 % ou de dextrose 5%/NaCl 0,9 % de manière à obtenir une concentration de 10 µg/mL. Consulter les directives de chaque fabricant avant de préparer ces solutions.

Incompatibilité (tubulure en Y): Ne jamais administrer en même temps qu'un autre médicament.

ENSEIGNEMENT AU PATIENT ET À SES PROCHES

- Conseiller au patient de respecter rigoureusement la posologie recommandée. Lorsque les doses doivent être prises à une heure précise, s'il a sauté une dose, il devra la prendre le plus rapidement possible et espacer les doses restantes de façon à pouvoir les prendre à intervalles réguliers. Le prévenir qu'il ne doit pas doubler les doses ni en accroître la fréquence. Avertir le patient qu'il ne doit pas dépasser la dose recommandée, car il s'expose au risque d'effets nocifs, de bronchospasme paradoxal (plus vraisemblablement lorsqu'il prendra la première dose d'un nouvel aérosol-doseur) ou d'une baisse d'efficacité du médicament. Informer le patient que tous les agents ne peuvent pas être utilisés pour traiter les crises aiguës.
- Conseiller au patient de prévenir immédiatement un professionnel de la santé si les essoufflements ne sont pas soulagés par le médicament ou s'ils s'accompagnent de diaphorèse, d'étourdissements, de palpitations ou de douleurs thoraciques.
- Recommander au patient d'amorcer l'aérosol avant de l'utiliser, en vaporisant 4 fois dans le vide, et de le jeter après 200 vaporisations. Le prévenir que les dispositifs d'administration ne sont pas interchangeables.
- Signaler au patient qu'il doit consulter un professionnel de la santé avant de prendre un médicament en vente libre et d'éviter de boire de l'alcool en même temps qu'il prend ce médicament. Mettre en garde le patient contre l'usage du tabac et d'autres agents irritants des voies respiratoires.
- Avertir le patient que le salbutamol peut donner un goût inhabituel ou mauvais dans la bouche.

Inhalation:

- Montrer au patient comment utiliser l'aérosol-doseur, le dispositif Diskus ou le nébuliseur (le mode d'emploi de ces dispositifs se trouve à l'annexe G).
- Prévenir le patient qui prend d'autres médicaments par inhalation qu'il doit commencer par le salbutamol et attendre 5 minutes avant d'inhaler les autres médicaments, sauf recommandation médicale contraire.
- Conseiller au patient d'avertir un professionnel de la santé si la dose habituelle de salbutamol n'est pas efficace ou si le contenu de l'aérosol est utilisé en moins de 2 semaines.

VÉRIFICATION DE L'EFFICACITÉ THÉRAPEUTIQUE

L'efficacité du traitement peut être démontrée par: la prévention ou le soulagement du bronchospasme. ✳

SALMÉTÉROL

Serevent Diskhaler, Serevent Diskus

CLASSIFICATION:

Bronchodilatateur (agoniste bêta-adrénergique)

Grossesse - catégorie C

INDICATIONS

Bronchodilatateur à action prolongée, destiné à la maîtrise de longue durée de l'asthme chez les patients ≥ 4 ans souffrant de maladie obstructive réversible des voies respiratoires, y compris les patients souffrant de l'asthme nocturne et ceux qui doivent utiliser régulièrement un bronchodilatateur à courte durée d'action, malgré un traitement optimal avec des corticostéroïdes ■ Traitement d'entretien à long terme des bronchospasmes et soulagement de la dyspnée associée à une bronchopneumopathie chronique obstructive incluant la bronchite chronique et l'emphysème.

MÉCANISME D'ACTION

Liaison aux récepteurs bêta$_2$-adrénergiques présents dans les muscles lisses des voies respiratoires, qui entraînent l'activation de l'adénylcyclase et une élévation des concentrations d'adénosine monophosphate-3′, 5′ cyclique (AMPc). Cette hausse des concentrations stimule les kinases, qui inhibent la phosphorylation de la myosine et abaissent les concentrations intracellulaires de calcium. La baisse de ces concentrations est associée à la relaxation des muscles lisses des voies respiratoires ■ Relaxation des muscles lisses des voies respiratoires entraînant la bronchodilatation ■ Spécificité relative pour les récepteurs bêta$_2$-adrénergiques (pulmonaires). ***Effets thérapeutiques:*** Bronchodilatation.

PHARMACOCINÉTIQUE

Absorption: Minime (inhalation).
Distribution: L'action est principalement locale.
Métabolisme et excrétion: Inconnus.
Demi-vie: 5,5 heures.

Profil temps-action (bronchodilatation)

	Début d'action	Pic	Durée†
Inhalation	10 - 25 min	3 - 4 h	12 h

† Chez les adolescents, 9 heures.

CONTRE-INDICATIONS, PRÉCAUTIONS ET MISES EN GARDE

Contre-indications: Hypersensibilité ■ Tachyarythmie ■ Patients allergiques au lactose ou au lait ■ Crise aiguë d'asthme (le début d'action est retardé).

Précautions et mises en garde: Maladie cardiovasculaire (incluant l'insuffisance coronarienne et l'hypertension) ■ Troubles convulsifs ■ Diabète ■ Bronchospasme paradoxal ■ Hyperthyroïdie ■ Usage excessif de l'inhalateur (risque d'apparition d'une tolérance aux effets du médicament et d'un bronchospasme paradoxal) ■ Antécédents de réponse accrue aux amines sympathomimétiques ■ **OBST., ALLAITEMENT:** L'innocuité du médicament n'a pas été établie chez la femme enceinte ou qui allaite ■ **PÉD.:** L'efficacité et l'innocuité du médicament n'ont pas été établies chez les enfants < 4 ans.

RÉACTIONS INDÉSIRABLES ET EFFETS SECONDAIRES

SNC: céphalées, nervosité.
CV: palpitations, tachycardie.
GI: douleurs abdominales, diarrhée, nausées.
Loc.: crampes ou douleurs musculaires.
SN: tremblements.
Resp.: bronchospasme paradoxal, toux.

INTERACTIONS

Médicament-médicament: L'utilisation concomitante d'autres **agents adrénergiques (sympathomimétiques)** intensifie les effets secondaires adrénergiques ■ L'administration simultanée d'**IMAO** ou d'**antidépresseurs tricycliques** peut déclencher une crise hypertensive ■ Les **bêtabloquants** peuvent abolir l'effet thérapeutique.

Médicament-produits naturels: L'administration concomitante de produits contenant de la caféine (**noix de cola**, **guarana**, **maté**, **thé**, **café**) augmente l'effet stimulant.

VOIES D'ADMINISTRATION ET POSOLOGIE

- **Inhalation (adultes et enfants ≥ 4 ans):** 50 µg, 2 fois par jour (espacer les inhalations d'environ 12 heures).

PRÉSENTATION

Poudre pour inhalation: Disques Diskhaler de 50 µg/coque^Pr^, Diskus de 50 µg/dose^Pr^.

SOINS INFIRMIERS

ÉVALUATION DE LA SITUATION

- Ausculter le murmure vésiculaire et mesurer le pouls et la pression artérielle avant l'administration et à intervalles réguliers pendant toute la durée du traitement.
- Noter les résultats des tests de la fonction pulmonaire avant le début du traitement et à intervalles réguliers pendant toute sa durée afin de déterminer l'efficacité du médicament.
- Suivre de près les signes de bronchospasme paradoxal (respiration sifflante, dyspnée, oppression thoracique) et les réactions d'hypersensibilité (rash, urticaire, œdème du visage, des lèvres et des paupières). S'ils surviennent, interrompre le traitement et en informer immédiatement le médecin ou un autre professionnel de la santé.

Tests de laboratoire:

- Le salmétérol peut entraîner une élévation de la glycémie; ce phénomène survient rarement aux doses recommandées et est plus marqué lors d'un usage fréquent de doses élevées.
- Le salmétérol peut entraîner une diminution des concentrations sériques de potassium, qui sont habituellement passagères et liées à la dose; ce phénomène survient rarement aux doses recommandées et est plus marqué lors d'un usage fréquent de doses élevées.

Toxicité et surdosage:

- Les symptômes du surdosage incluent l'agitation persistante, les douleurs ou l'oppression thoraciques, l'hypotension ou l'hypertension, les étourdissements, l'hyperglycémie, l'hypokaliémie, les convulsions, les tachyarythmies, les tremblements persistants et les vomissements.
- Le traitement inclut l'arrêt du traitement par le salmétérol ou par les agonistes bêta-adrénergiques, et un traitement symptomatique de soutien. On doit surveiller les fonctions cardiaque et pulmonaire, et recourir aux mesures de soutien appropriées. Les bêtabloquants cardiosélectifs doivent être utilisés avec prudence, puisqu'ils peuvent induire un bronchospasme.

DIAGNOSTICS INFIRMIERS POSSIBLES

- Dégagement inefficace des voies respiratoires (Indications).
- Connaissances insuffisantes sur le traitement médicamenteux (Enseignement au patient et à ses proches).

INTERVENTIONS INFIRMIÈRES

- NE PAS CONFONDRE LE SALMÉTÉROL AVEC LE SALBUTAMOL.

Inhalation:

- Ne pas utiliser de dispositif d'espacement (« Spacer ») lors de l'administration de la poudre pour inhalation.

ENSEIGNEMENT AU PATIENT ET À SES PROCHES

- Montrer au patient le mode d'emploi de la poudre pour inhalation et lui conseiller de respecter rigoureusement la posologie recommandée. Recommander au patient de ne pas dépasser la dose prescrite. S'il n'a pu prendre le médicament au moment habituel, il doit le prendre dès que possible et espacer les autres doses à intervalles réguliers. L'avertir qu'il ne doit jamais remplacer une dose manquée par une double dose. Si les symptômes se manifestent avant l'heure prévue pour la dose suivante, il devrait inhaler un bronchodilatateur à action rapide.
- Expliquer au patient utilisant la *poudre pour inhalation* à l'aide du dispositif d'inhalation qu'il ne doit jamais expirer dans le dispositif et qu'il doit toujours le tenir à l'horizontale. L'embout buccal devrait rester sec; il ne faut jamais le laver. Prévenir le patient qui utilise la poudre sèche sous forme de coques (4 coques/disque) qu'il faut jeter le disque 6 semaines après qu'on l'a retiré de sa surenveloppe d'aluminium ou une fois que toutes les coques du disque ont été vidées, selon la première éventualité.
- PRÉVENIR LE PATIENT QU'IL NE DOIT PAS PRENDRE LE SALMÉTÉROL POUR TRAITER LES SYMPTÔMES AIGUS. IL DEVRAIT PLUTÔT UTILISER UN BRONCHODILATATEUR BÊTA-ADRÉNERGIQUE À ACTION RAPIDE, PRIS PAR INHALATION, POUR SOULAGER LES CRISES AIGUËS D'ASTHME.
- Conseiller au patient suivant un traitement prolongé par le salmétérol de ne pas prendre des doses supplémentaires de ce médicament pour prévenir le bronchospasme d'effort.
- Conseiller au patient de prévenir immédiatement un professionnel de la santé si l'essoufflement n'est pas soulagé par le salmétérol, si son état s'aggrave, s'il doit inhaler plus souvent des bronchodilatateurs à action rapide pour soulager une crise aiguë ou s'il doit inhaler à 4 reprises et plus des bronchodilatateurs à action rapide pendant 2 jours consécutifs ou plus, ou encore s'il doit utiliser le contenu de plus de 1 aérosol-doseur pendant une période de 8 semaines.
- Recommander au patient suivant un traitement par des glucocorticoïdes systémiques ou par inhalation de consulter un professionnel de la santé avant d'interrompre son traitement ou de réduire les doses de médicaments.
- Insister sur l'importance des examens de suivi réguliers permettant de déterminer les bienfaits du traitement.

VÉRIFICATION DE L'EFFICACITÉ THÉRAPEUTIQUE

L'efficacité du traitement peut être démontrée par: la prévention du bronchospasme ou la diminution de la fréquence des crises aiguës d'asthme chez les patients souffrant d'asthme chronique. ✳

S

SAQUINAVIR

Fortovase, Invirase

CLASSIFICATION:

Antirétroviral (inhibiteur de la protéase)

Grossesse – catégorie B

INDICATIONS

Traitement de l'infection par le VIH en association avec d'autres antirétroviraux. **Usages non approuvés:** En association avec d'autres antirétroviraux, prophylaxie après une exposition accidentelle au VIH.

MÉCANISME D'ACTION

Inhibition de l'action de la protéase du VIH et prévention du clivage des polyprotéines virales. ***Effets thérapeutiques:*** Ralentissement de l'évolution de l'infection par le VIH et de l'apparition de ses complications ■ Augmentation du nombre de cellules CD4 et diminution de la charge virale.

PHARMACOCINÉTIQUE

Absorption: Faible (PO); fort métabolisme de premier passage hépatique. La nourriture augmente grandement l'absorption. Fortovase est mieux absorbé qu'Invirase; ils ne sont donc pas interchangeables.

Distribution: Le médicament se répartit dans les tissus, mais il ne pénètre que très peu dans le SNC.

Liaison aux protéines: 98 %.

Métabolisme et excrétion: Métabolisme hépatique à plus de 95 %, surtout par l'entremise du cytochrome P450 3A4. Excrétion de < 1 % à l'état inchangé dans l'urine.

Demi-vie: 13 heures.

Profil temps-action

	DÉBUT D'ACTION	PIC	DURÉE
PO	inconnu	inconnu	8 h

CONTRE-INDICATIONS, PRÉCAUTIONS ET MISES EN GARDE

Contre-indications: Hypersensibilité ■ Insuffisance hépatique grave ■ Traitement concomitant par des dérivés de l'ergot (comme la dihydroergotamine et l'ergotamine), le midazolam, le triazolam, le cisapride, l'amiodarone, la flécaïnide, la propafénone, la quinidine, le pimozide, la rifabutine (si le saquinavir est le seul inhibiteur de protéase utilisé) ou la rifampine ■ Insuffisance hépatique grave.

S

Précautions et mises en garde: Nombreuses interactions médicamenteuses ■ Diabète (risque d'aggravation de l'hyperglycémie; l'hyperglycémie peut évoluer vers l'acidocétose) ■ Hémophilie (risque accru d'hémorragie) ■ Insuffisance hépatique (risque d'exacerbation du dysfonctionnement hépatique dû à l'hépatite B ou C, ou à d'autres causes) ■ **OBST., PÉD.**: Grossesse ou enfants < 16 ans (l'innocuité du médicament n'a pas été établie) ■ **ALLAITEMENT**: Déconseillé en raison du risque de transmission postnatale du VIH.

RÉACTIONS INDÉSIRABLES ET EFFETS SECONDAIRES

SNC: CONVULSIONS, confusion, céphalées, insomnie, dépression, troubles psychiques, faiblesse, fatigue.

CV: thrombophlébite.

GI: douleurs abdominales, diarrhée, concentrations accrues d'enzymes hépatiques, ictère, nausées, dysgueusie.

Tég.: photosensibilité, réactions cutanées graves.

End.: hyperglycémie.

Hémat.: leucémie myéloblastique aiguë, anémie hémolytique, thrombopénie.

SN: ataxie.

Métab.: hyperlipidémie, modification de la distribution des tissus adipeux.

Divers: SYNDROME DE STEVENS-JOHNSON, syndrome de reconstitution immunitaire.

INTERACTIONS

Médicament-médicament: Le saquinavir est un inhibiteur et un substrat du **P450 3A4** et de la **P-glycoprotéine (P-gp)** ■ LA **RIFAMPINE** ET LA **RIFABUTINE** DIMINUENT DE FAÇON MARQUÉE LES CONCENTRATIONS DE SAQUINAVIR; L'USAGE CONCOMITANT DE CES MÉDICAMENTS EST DONC CONTRE-INDIQUÉ (ON PEUT ADMINISTRER LA RIFABUTINE SI LE SAQUINAVIR EST PRIS EN ASSOCIATION AVEC DU RITONAVIR) ■ LE SAQUINAVIR ÉLÈVE LES CONCENTRATIONS SANGUINES DES **DÉRIVÉS DE L'ERGOT**, COMME LA **DIHYDROERGOTAMINE** ET L'**ERGOTAMINE** (RISQUE ACCRU DE VASOCONSTRICTION), AINSI QUE CELLES DE **MIDAZOLAM** ET DE **TRIAZOLAM** (DÉPRESSION EXCESSIVE DU SNC) ET DU **CISAPRIDE**, DE L'**AMIODARONE**, DU **FLÉCAÏNIDE**, DE LA **PROPAFÉNONE**, DE LA **QUINIDINE** ET DU **PIMOZIDE** (RISQUE ACCRU D'ARYTHMIES CARDIAQUES GRAVES); L'USAGE CONCOMITANT EST DONC CONTRE-INDIQUÉ ■ L'usage concomitant de **lovastatine** ou de **simvastatine** n'est pas recommandé (risque accru de myopathie et de rhabdomyolyse) ■ Risque accru de myopathie lors de l'usage concomitant d'**atorvastatine** (utiliser la plus petite dose de départ possible et assurer un suivi étroit) ■ En cas d'usage concomitant de **clarithromycine**, les concentrations des deux médicaments s'élèvent ■ Les concentrations du saquinavir s'élèvent considérablement lors de l'administration concomitante d'**indinavir**, de **delavirdine**, de **nelfinavir**, de **ritonavir**, de **ranitidine** et de **kétoconazole** (des adaptations posologiques peuvent s'avérer nécessaires) ■ L'utilisation concomitante d'**itraconazole** ou de **voriconazole** peut augmenter les concentrations du saquinavir et de l'antifongique (suivre de près l'efficacité et la toxicité des deux agents) ■ La **carbamazépine**, le **phénobarbital**, la **phénytoïne**, la **névirapine** et la **dexaméthasone** peuvent diminuer les concentrations du saquinavir (des adaptations posologiques peuvent s'avérer nécessaires) ■ L'**éfavirenz** peut diminuer les concentrations de saquinavir (le saquinavir doit être administré dans ce cas avec du ritonavir) ■ Élévation des concentrations de **sildénafil**, de **vardénafil** et de **tadalafil**, et augmentation possible de leurs effets indésirables, notamment l'hypotension, l'altération de la vue et le priapisme; faire preuve de prudence et diminuer la dose de **sildénafil** à 25 mg, toutes les 48 h; diminuer la dose de **vardénafil** à 2,5 mg, toutes les 72 h; diminuer la dose de **tadalafil** à 10 mg, toutes les 72 h ■ Risque accru de saignements lors de l'administration concomitante de **warfarine** (surveiller le RNI) ■ Élévation possible des concentrations des **bloqueurs des canaux calciques** (la prudence s'impose et un suivi clinique du patient est recommandé) ■ Élévation des concentrations de **cyclosporine**, de **sirolimus** et de **tacrolimus** (surveiller les concentrations sanguines de l'immunosuppresseur) ■ Les concentrations sanguines et les effets de la **méthadone** peuvent être diminués (une modification de la dose peut s'avérer nécessaire).

Médicament-produits naturels: Le **millepertuis** et les **gélules d'ail** peuvent diminuer les concentrations sanguines de saquinavir et en réduire ainsi l'efficacité (l'usage concomitant n'est donc pas recommandé).

Médicament-aliments: Le **jus de pamplemousse** augmente les concentrations de saquinavir. Les **aliments** augmentent de façon marquée l'absorption du saquinavir.

VOIES D'ADMINISTRATION ET POSOLOGIE

Le saquinavir ne devrait pas être utilisé comme seul inhibiteur de la protéase en raison de sa faible biodisponibilité et de sa puissance antirétrovirale inférieure à celle des autres inhibiteurs de la protéase.

Fortovase

- **PO (adultes)**: 1 200 mg, 3 fois par jour, dans les 2 heures qui suivent un repas ou une collation substantielle.

Invirase

- **PO (adultes)**: 600 mg, 3 fois par jour, dans les 2 heures qui suivent un repas ou une collation substantielle.

PRÉSENTATION

- **Fortovase**
  Capsules molles de gélatine: 200 mg^{Pr}.
- **Invirase**
  Capsules dures de gélatine: 200 mg^{Pr}.

SOINS INFIRMIERS

ÉVALUATION DE LA SITUATION

- Rester à l'affût de toute modification au niveau de la gravité des symptômes de l'infection par le VIH et de l'apparition d'infections opportunistes pendant toute la durée du traitement.
- Invirase et Fortovase ne sont pas bioéquivalents et ne sont donc pas interchangeables.
- Si une patiente enceinte est exposée à des antirétroviraux, l'inscrire dans le registre des femmes exposées aux antirétroviraux pendant leur grossesse, en composant le 1 800 258-4263.

Tests de laboratoire:

- Noter la charge virale et le nombre de cellules CD4 à intervalles réguliers tout au long du traitement.
- Le saquinavir peut provoquer l'hyperglycémie, qui peut mener à une acidocétose diabétique.
- Suivre les valeurs hématologiques et les résultats des tests de la fonction hépatique avant le traitement et à intervalles réguliers pendant toute sa durée. Le saquinavir peut entraîner l'anémie, la thrombopénie et une élévation des concentrations d'enzymes hépatiques.

DIAGNOSTICS INFIRMIERS POSSIBLES

- Risque d'infection (Indications, Effets secondaires).
- Connaissances insuffisantes sur le traitement médicamenteux (Enseignement au patient et à ses proches).

INTERVENTIONS INFIRMIÈRES

- Administrer le médicament dans les 2 heures qui suivent un repas complet ou une collation substantielle afin d'en augmenter l'efficacité. Si le médicament n'est pas pris avec des aliments, les concentrations sanguines peuvent diminuer, ce qui peut se traduire par une absence d'effet antiviral.

Fortovase: Si elles sont conservées au réfrigérateur (entre 2 et 8 °C), les capsules sont stables jusqu'à leur date de péremption indiquée sur l'emballage. On peut les garder pendant 3 mois à la température ambiante.

Invirase: Conserver les capsules entre 15 et 30 °C.

ENSEIGNEMENT AU PATIENT ET À SES PROCHES

- Expliquer au patient qu'il doit suivre rigoureusement la posologie recommandée et prendre le saquinavir au même moment de la journée, dans les 2 heures qui suivent un repas complet ou une collation substantielle. S'il n'a pas pu prendre le médicament au moment habituel, il doit le prendre dès que possible à moins que ce ne soit presque l'heure prévue pour la dose suivante. Le prévenir qu'il ne doit jamais remplacer une dose manquée par une double dose. Lui conseiller de ne pas arrêter le traitement sans avoir consulté au préalable un professionnel de la santé. Le passage d'Invirase à Fortovase devrait se faire sous la surveillance d'un professionnel de la santé.
- Informer le patient qu'il ne doit pas donner le saquinavir à d'autres personnes.

- Expliquer au patient que le saquinavir ne guérit pas le sida, n'empêche pas l'apparition d'infections associées ou opportunistes et ne réduit pas le risque de transmission du VIH à autrui par les rapports sexuels ou par la contamination du sang. L'inciter à utiliser un condom, à ne pas se servir des mêmes aiguilles qu'une autre personne et à ne pas donner du sang afin de prévenir la transmission du VIH.
- Conseiller au patient de consulter un professionnel de la santé avant de prendre d'autres médicaments (sur ordonnance ou en vente libre, incluant les produits naturels), en même temps que le saquinavir.
- Informer le patient que le saquinavir peut provoquer l'hyperglycémie. Lui conseiller de prévenir un professionnel de la santé si les symptômes suivants se manifestent: soif ou faim accrue, perte de poids inexpliquée, mictions plus fréquentes, fatigue, sécheresse de la peau ou démangeaisons. Bien qu'elles soient rares, des éruptions cutanées bulleuses graves, accompagnées de polyarthrite, peuvent également se manifester.
- Informer le patient que les effets à long terme du saquinavir sont pour le moment inconnus.
- Prévenir le patient que le traitement antirétroviral l'expose au risque de redistribution ou d'accumulation de tissus adipeux dont les causes et les conséquences à long terme sur la santé sont pour le moment inconnues.
- Insister sur l'importance des examens de suivi et des analyses de sang, effectués à intervalles réguliers, permettant de déceler les effets secondaires et les bienfaits du traitement.

VÉRIFICATION DE L'EFFICACITÉ THÉRAPEUTIQUE

L'efficacité du traitement peut être démontrée par: le ralentissement de l'évolution de l'infection par le VIH et de l'apparition de ses complications ■ l'augmentation du nombre de cellules CD4 et la diminution de la charge virale. ✳

S

SCOPOLAMINE

Synonyme: hyoscine

scopolamine, bromhydrate de

Scopolamine, Transderm-V

scopolamine, butylbromure de

Buscopan

CLASSIFICATION:

Anticholinergique, antiémétique, antispasmodique

Grossesse – catégorie C

INDICATIONS

Timbre transdermique: Prévention des symptômes (nausées et vomissements) du mal des transports (bromhydrate de scopolamine) ■ **IM, IV, SC**: Induction de l'amnésie et de la sédation, et diminution de la salivation et des sécrétions excessives des voies respiratoires avant une intervention chirurgicale (bromhydrate de scopolamine) ■ **PO**: Soulagement des spasmes de la musculature lisse des voies gastro-intestinales et génito-urinaires (butylbromure de scopolamine) ■ **IM, IV, SC**: Soulagement des spasmes aigus des voies gastro-intestinales et génito-urinaires, et relâchement de la musculature lisse avant certains examens radiologiques (butylbromure de scopolamine). **Usages non approuvés – IM, IV, SC**: Diminution des sécrétions respiratoires chez les patients en phase terminale (bromhydrate de scopolamine).

MÉCANISME D'ACTION

Inhibition de l'activité muscarinique de l'acétylcholine ■ Correction du déséquilibre entre l'acétylcholine et la noradrénaline dans le SNC, qui peut être la cause du mal des transports. ***Effets thérapeutiques:*** Diminution des nausées et des vomissements ■ Induction de l'amnésie et diminution des sécrétions avant une intervention chirurgicale.

PHARMACOCINÉTIQUE

Absorption: Bonne (IM, SC et transdermique).
Distribution: La scopolamine traverse les barrières placentaire et hématoencéphalique.
Métabolisme et excrétion: Métabolisme majoritairement hépatique.
Demi-vie: 8 heures.

Profil temps-action (effets antiémétiques et sédatifs)

	Début d'action	Pic	Durée
PO, IM, SC	30 min	1 h	4 - 6 h
IV	10 min	1 h	2 - 4 h
Timbre transdermique	4 h	12 h	72 h

CONTRE-INDICATIONS, PRÉCAUTIONS ET MISES EN GARDE

Contre-indications: Hypersensibilité ■ Glaucome à angle fermé ■ Hyperplasie prostatique ■ Obstruction pylorique ■ Iléus paralytique ■ Tachycardie secondaire à l'insuffisance cardiaque ou à la thyrotoxicose ■ Sténose des voies gastro-intestinales (butylbromure de scopolamine) ■ Mégacôlon (butylbromure de scopolamine) ■ Myasthénie grave (butylbromure de scopolamine).
Précautions et mises en garde: GÉR., PÉD.: Prédisposition accrue à des réactions indésirables ■ Pression intra-

oculaire élevée ou glaucome à angle ouvert ■ Reflux gastro-œsophagien ■ Maladies gastro-intestinales occlusives ■ Risque d'occlusion intestinale ■ Maladies rénale, hépatique, pulmonaire ou cardiaque chroniques ■ **OBST., ALLAITEMENT**: L'innocuité du médicament n'a pas été établie ■ Hypersensibilité aux bromures (solution pour injection seulement) ■ Hémorragie aiguë.

RÉACTIONS INDÉSIRABLES ET EFFETS SECONDAIRES

SNC: somnolence, confusion.
ORLO: vision trouble, mydriase, photophobie.
CV: tachycardie, palpitations.
GI: sécheresse de la bouche (xérostomie), constipation.
GU: retard de la miction avec effort pour uriner, rétention urinaire.
Tég.: diminution de la sécrétion de sueur.

INTERACTIONS

Médicament-médicament: Effets anticholinergiques additifs lors de l'administration concomitante d'**antihistaminiques**, d'**antidépresseurs tricycliques**, d'**oxybutinine**, d'**IMAO**, d'**amantadine**, de **quinidine** ou de **disopyramide** ■ Effets additifs sur la dépression du SNC lors de l'usage concomitant d'**alcool**, d'**antidépresseurs**, d'**antihistaminiques**, de **phénothiazines**, de **barbituriques**, d'**analgésiques opioïdes** ou d'**hypnosédatifs** ■ La scopolamine peut modifier l'absorption d'autres **médicaments administrés par voie orale** en ralentissant la motilité du tractus gastro-intestinal ■ La scopolamine peut aggraver les lésions de la muqueuse gastro-intestinale chez les patients prenant des **préparations de chlorure de potassium à matrice de cire**.
Médicament-produits naturels: Effets anticholinergiques additifs lors de l'administration concomitante de **datura** et de **scopolia**.

VOIES D'ADMINISTRATION ET POSOLOGIE

Le bromhydrate de scopolamine et le butylbromure de scopolamine ne sont pas interchangeables.

Bromhydrate de scopolamine

- **Timbre transdermique (adultes)**: Le système Transderm-V libère 1 mg en 72 heures; l'effet antiémétique s'exerce 12 heures après l'application du timbre.
- **IM, IV, SC (adultes)**: De 0,3 à 0,6 mg; on peut répéter l'administration de cette dose 3 ou 4 fois par jour.
- **IM, IV, SC (enfants)**: 0,006 mg/kg ou 0,2 mg/m^2.

Butylbromure de scopolamine (soulagement des spasmes et relâchement de la musculature lisse des voies gastro-intestinale et génito-urinaire)

- **PO (adultes)**: 1 ou 2 dragées/jour, jusqu'à un maximum de 6 dragées/jour. En cas de maladie chronique nécessitant l'administration de doses répétées, la posologie est de 1 dragée, de 3 à 5 fois/jour.
- **IM, IV, SC (adultes)**: De 10 à 20 mg; la dose maximale quotidienne ne doit pas dépasser 100 mg.

PRÉSENTATION
(version générique disponible)

Timbre transdermique: *Transderm-V* – 1,5 mg de scopolamine/timbre, libérant 1 mg de scopolamine en 3 jours[Pr] ■ **Solution pour injection**: *Bromhydrate de scopolamine* – 0,4 mg/mL, en ampoules de 1 mL[Pr], 0,6 mg/mL, en ampoules de 1 mL[Pr]. *Butylbromure de scopolamine* – 20 mg/mL, en ampoules de 1 mL[Pr] ■ **Dragées**: *Butylbromure de scopolamine* – 10 mg[Pr].

SOINS INFIRMIERS

ÉVALUATION DE LA SITUATION

- Suivre de près les signes de rétention urinaire à intervalles réguliers pendant toute la durée du traitement.
- Mesurer la fréquence cardiaque à intervalles réguliers pendant toute la durée du traitement par voie parentérale.
- Déterminer la présence de douleurs avant l'administration du médicament. Si elle est administrée sans un analgésique opioïde, la scopolamine peut agir comme stimulant en présence de douleurs, entraînant le délire.

Antiémétique: Suivre de près les nausées et les vomissements à intervalles réguliers pendant toute la durée du traitement.

DIAGNOSTICS INFIRMIERS POSSIBLES

- Atteinte à l'intégrité de la muqueuse buccale (Indications, Effets secondaires).
- Risque d'accident (Effets secondaires).
- Connaissances insuffisantes sur le traitement médicamenteux (Enseignement au patient et à ses proches).

INTERVENTIONS INFIRMIÈRES

IV directe: On peut administrer l'agent non dilué ou dilué avec de l'eau stérile, du NaCl 0,9 % ou du D5%E pour injection avant l'administration IV. Injecter lentement en 1 minute au moins.
Associations compatibles dans la même seringue: butorphanol ■ chlorpromazine ■ cimétidine ■ diphenhydramine ■ dropéridol ■ fentanyl ■ hydromorphone ■ mépéridine ■ métoclopramide ■ midazolam ■ morphine ■ nalbuphine ■ pentazocine ■ pentobarbital ■ perphénazine ■ prochlorpérazine ■ promazine ■ prométhazine ■ ranitidine ■ sufentanil ■ thiopental.

S

Compatibilité (tubulure en Y): héparine ■ hydrocortisone sodique, succinate de ■ potassium, chlorure de ■ sufentanil ■ vitamines du complexe B avec C.

ENSEIGNEMENT AU PATIENT ET À SES PROCHES

- Conseiller au patient de respecter rigoureusement la posologie recommandée. S'il n'a pu prendre le médicament au moment habituel, il doit le prendre dès que possible, sans jamais remplacer une dose manquée par une double dose.
- Prévenir le patient que la scopolamine peut provoquer de la somnolence et une vision trouble. Lui conseiller de ne pas conduire et d'éviter les activités qui exigent sa vigilance jusqu'à ce qu'on ait la certitude que le médicament n'entraîne pas ces effets chez lui.
- Recommander au patient de faire preuve de prudence pendant les activités physiques ou lorsqu'il fait chaud, car la scopolamine peut augmenter le risque d'un coup de chaleur.
- Recommander au patient d'éviter de boire de l'alcool ou de prendre d'autres dépresseurs du SNC en même temps que la scopolamine.
- Conseiller au patient de se rincer fréquemment la bouche, de pratiquer une bonne hygiène buccale et de consommer de la gomme à mâcher ou des bonbons sans sucre pour soulager la sécheresse de la bouche.

Timbre transdermique:

- Montrer au patient comment appliquer le timbre transdermique. Pour prévenir le mal des transports, il faut appliquer le timbre suffisamment longtemps avant le départ, car l'effet antiémétique optimal ne se manifeste que 12 heures plus tard. Lui recommander de se laver les mains et de bien les sécher, avant et après l'application. Appliquer le timbre derrière l'oreille, sur la peau glabre, propre et sèche; éviter les régions éraflées ou irritées. Exercer une pression sur le timbre pour s'assurer qu'il a bien adhéré à la peau. Le timbre est efficace pendant 3 jours. S'il se détache, le remplacer par un nouveau timbre qu'on appliquera sur une autre partie de la peau, derrière l'oreille. Après avoir été retiré, le timbre devrait être jeté; il importe de bien nettoyer les mains et la région où le timbre a été appliqué, afin d'éviter que la moindre trace de scopolamine entre en contact avec les yeux. Le timbre est imperméable et son efficacité ne sera pas modifiée par l'eau, si le patient prend un bain ou une douche.
- Expliquer au patient qu'il doit retirer le timbre et prévenir immédiatement un professionnel de la santé si des symptômes de glaucome à angle fermé se manifestent (douleurs ou rougeurs des yeux avec dilatation de la pupille).
- Prévenir le patient qui pratique des sports sous-marins que la scopolamine peut provoquer la désorientation.

VÉRIFICATION DE L'EFFICACITÉ THÉRAPEUTIQUE

L'efficacité du traitement peut être démontrée par: la diminution de la salivation et des sécrétions des voies respiratoires avant une intervention chirurgicale ■ l'amnésie postopératoire ■ la prévention des symptômes du mal des transports ■ la diminution des sécrétions respiratoires chez les patients en phase terminale. ✳

SÉLÉGILINE

Apo-Selegiline, Dom-Selegiline, Eldepryl, Gen-Selegiline, Med-Selegiline, Novo-Selegiline, Nu-Selegiline, PMS-Selegiline

CLASSIFICATION:

Antiparkinsonien

Grossesse – catégorie C

INDICATIONS

Traitement de la maladie de Parkinson chez les patients qui ne répondent pas suffisamment à l'association lévodopa/carbidopa ou monothérapie chez les patients dont la maladie a été nouvellement diagnostiquée.

MÉCANISME D'ACTION

Après sa transformation par la monoamine-oxydase en son composé actif, la sélégiline inactive la monoamine-oxydase en se liant à elle de façon irréversible aux sites du type B (cerveau) ■ L'inactivation de la monoamine-oxydase entraîne une élévation des concentrations de dopamine dans le SNC. ***Effets thérapeutiques:*** Soulagement des symptômes de la maladie de Parkinson et réponse accrue au traitement par l'association lévodopa/carbidopa.

PHARMACOCINÉTIQUE

Absorption: Bonne (PO).

Distribution: Tout l'organisme.

Métabolisme et excrétion: Le métabolisme comporte une certaine transformation en amphétamine et en méthamphétamine; 45 % est excrété dans l'urine sous forme de métabolites.

Demi-vie: Inconnue.

S

Profil temps-action (effet antiparkinsonien)

	DÉBUT D'ACTION	PIC	DURÉE
PO	2 – 3 jours	inconnu	inconnue

CONTRE-INDICATIONS, PRÉCAUTIONS ET MISES EN GARDE

Contre-indications: Hypersensibilité ■ Traitement concomitant par la mépéridine ou par un analgésique opioïde (risque de réactions d'issue fatale) ■ Ulcère gastroduodénal évolutif ■ Troubles extrapyramidaux ou dyskinésie tardive ■ Psychose grave ou démence marquée.

Précautions et mises en garde: Administration de doses > 10 mg/jour (risque accru de réactions hypertensives en présence d'aliments contenant de la tyramine ou de certains médicaments) ■ Administration concomitante d'antidépresseurs tricycliques (ATC) ou d'inhibiteurs sélectifs du recaptage de la sérotonine (ISRS) (risque de syndrome sérotoninergique).

RÉACTIONS INDÉSIRABLES ET EFFETS SECONDAIRES

SNC: confusion, étourdissements, sensation de tête légère, évanouissement, confusion, hallucinations, insomnie, rêves saisissants.

GI: nausées, douleurs abdominales, sécheresse de la bouche (xérostomie).

INTERACTIONS

Médicament-médicament: Initialement, la sélégiline peut augmenter le risque d'effets secondaires entraînés par l'association **lévodopa/carbidopa** (réduire de 10 à 30 % la posologie de l'association lévodopa/carbidopa, le cas échéant) ■ L'ADMINISTRATION CONCOMITANTE DE **MÉPÉRIDINE** OU D'AUTRES **ANALGÉSIQUES OPIOÏDES** PEUT PROVOQUER UNE RÉACTION D'ISSUE FATALE (EXCITATION, TRANSPIRATION, RIGIDITÉ ET HYPERTENSION OU HYPOTENSION, ET COMA) ■ Risque d'apparition d'un syndrome sérotoninergique (confusion, agitation, hyperpyrexie, hypotension, convulsions) lors de l'administration concomitante d'**autres antidépresseurs du type ISRS** (arrêter l'administration de la **fluoxétine**, 5 semaines avant le début du traitement par la sélégiline, celle de la **venlafaxine**, 7 jours avant, et celle des autres agents, 2 semaines avant). Par ailleurs, il faut arrêter le traitement à la sélégiline 2 semaines avant le début du traitement par un ISRS ■ L'usage concomitant d'**antidépresseurs tricycliques** peut provoquer des asystolies, la diaphorèse, l'hypertension, des syncopes, des changements comportementaux, une baisse du niveau de conscience, l'hyperpyrexie, des tremblements, une rigidité musculaire et des convulsions (éviter l'usage concomitant; arrêter le traitement par la sélégiline 2 semaines avant le commencer celui par un antidépresseur tricyclique) ■ Risque accru d'hypertension, lors de l'usage concomitant d'**agonistes alpha/bêta** (p. ex., **pseudoéphédrine**, **éphédrine**), d'**agonistes alpha**$_1$ (p. ex., **midodrine**, **phényléphrine**), d'**amphétamines** (p. ex., **dextroamphétamine**), de **buspirone**, de **méthylphénidate** ou de **réserpine** ■ L'usage concomitant d'**atomoxétine** peut entraîner une neurotoxicité ■ Les **œstrogènes** peuvent intensifier les effets de la sélégiline.

Médicament-aliments: L'administration de doses > 10 mg/jour peut entraîner des réactions hypertensives lors de la consommation concomitante d'**aliments contenant de la tyramine** (voir l'annexe J).

VOIES D'ADMINISTRATION ET POSOLOGIE

- **PO (adultes):** 5 mg, 2 fois par jour (avec les repas du matin et du midi).

PRÉSENTATION

Comprimés: 5 mg[Pr].

SOINS INFIRMIERS

ÉVALUATION DE LA SITUATION

- Avant le traitement et pendant toute sa durée, suivre de près les signes et les symptômes parkinsoniens suivants: tremblements, faiblesse musculaire et rigidité, démarche ataxique.
- Mesurer la pression artérielle à intervalles réguliers pendant toute la durée du traitement.

DIAGNOSTICS INFIRMIERS POSSIBLES

- Mobilité physique réduite (Indications).
- Risque d'accident (Réactions indésirables).
- Connaissances insuffisantes sur le traitement médicamenteux (Enseignement au patient et à ses proches).

INTERVENTIONS INFIRMIÈRES

- NE PAS CONFONDRE LA SÉLÉGILINE AVEC LA SERTRALINE.
- Administrer le comprimé avec le repas du matin et du midi.
- On peut essayer de réduire la dose de l'association lévodopa/carbidopa de 10 à 30 %, après 2 ou 3 jours de traitement par la sélégiline.

S

ENSEIGNEMENT AU PATIENT ET À SES PROCHES

- Conseiller au patient de respecter rigoureusement la posologie recommandée. S'il n'a pu prendre le médicament au moment habituel, il doit le prendre aussitôt que possible, mais non en fin d'après-midi ou dans la soirée, ni si c'est presque l'heure prévue pour la dose suivante. Le prévenir qu'il ne doit pas remplacer une dose manquée par une double dose. Lui expliquer que la prise de doses plus élevées de médicament que celles qui sont prescrites peut augmenter les effets secondaires et le risque de crise hypertensive s'il mange des aliments contenant de la tyramine (voir l'annexe J).
- Expliquer au patient et à ses proches les signes et les symptômes d'une crise hypertensive déclenchée par un IMAO (céphalées graves, douleurs thoraciques, nausées, vomissements, photosensibilité, pupilles dilatées). Conseiller au patient de signaler immédiatement à un professionnel de la santé les céphalées graves ou tout autre symptôme inhabituel.
- Conseiller au patient de changer lentement de position afin de réduire le risque d'hypotension orthostatique.
- Conseiller au patient de boire plus de liquides, de consommer de la gomme à mâcher ou des bonbons sans sucre, des glaçons ou des substituts de salive pour diminuer la sécheresse de la bouche, et de consulter un professionnel de la santé si elle persiste pendant plus de 2 semaines.

VÉRIFICATION DE L'EFFICACITÉ THÉRAPEUTIQUE

L'efficacité du traitement peut être démontrée par: le soulagement des symptômes et l'amélioration de la réponse au traitement par l'association lévodopa/carbidopa, chez les patients souffrant de la maladie de Parkinson. ✳

S

SÉNÉ, SENNOSIDES

Ex-Lax Senne, Laxatif Sene, PMS-Sennoside, Riva-Senna, Sennatab, Sennosides, Senokot, X-Prep

CLASSIFICATION:
Laxatifs (stimulants)

Grossesse – catégorie C

INDICATIONS

Traitement de la constipation fonctionnelle (chronique ou occasionnelle).

MÉCANISME D'ACTION

Effet direct sur la muqueuse intestinale, augmentant la motilité du côlon, accélérant le transit au niveau du côlon et inhibant l'absorption de l'eau. ***Effets thérapeutiques:*** Effet laxatif.

PHARMACOCINÉTIQUE

Absorption: Minime (PO).
Distribution: Inconnue.
Métabolisme et excrétion: Inconnus.
Demi-vie: Inconnue.

Profil temps-action (effet laxatif)

	DÉBUT D'ACTION	PIC	DURÉE
PO	6 – 12 h†	inconnu	3 – 4 jours

† Le début d'action peut prendre jusqu'à 24 heures.

CONTRE-INDICATIONS, PRÉCAUTIONS ET MISES EN GARDE

Contre-indications: Hypersensibilité ■ Crises abdominales aiguës.
Précautions et mises en garde: Douleurs abdominales, nausées, vomissements ou fièvre ■ Usage prolongé ou abus (risque de dépendance).

RÉACTIONS INDÉSIRABLES ET EFFETS SECONDAIRES

GI: crampes, diarrhée, nausées.
GU: urine rose-rouge ou brun-noir.
HÉ: déséquilibres électrolytiques (usage prolongé ou dépendance).
Divers: dépendance aux laxatifs.

INTERACTIONS

Médicament-médicament: Le séné peut diminuer l'absorption d'autres **médicaments administrés par voie orale**, en raison de la diminution du temps de transit.

VOIES D'ADMINISTRATION ET POSOLOGIE

Des doses plus élevées de séné ont été administrées pour traiter ou prévenir la constipation induite par les opioïdes.

- **PO (adultes et enfants > 12 ans):** *Comprimés* – de 2 à 4 comprimés, 1 fois par jour au coucher, au besoin, et jusqu'à un maximum de 4 comprimés, 2 fois par jour. *Granules* – de 1 à 2 cuillerées à thé rases, 1 fois par jour au coucher, au besoin, sans dépasser 2 cuillerées à thé rases, 2 fois par jour. *Sirop* – de 10 à 15 mL, 1 fois par jour au coucher, au besoin; ne pas dépasser 15 mL, 2 fois par jour.
- **PO (grossesse et enfants de 6 à 12 ans):** *Comprimés* – 1 ou 2 comprimés, 1 fois par jour au coucher, au

besoin, sans dépasser 2 comprimés, 2 fois par jour. *Granules* – ½ à 1 cuillerée à thé rase, 1 fois par jour au coucher, au besoin, sans dépasser 1 cuillerée à thé rase, 2 fois par jour. *Sirop* – de 5 à 10 mL, 1 fois par jour au coucher, au besoin, jusqu'à un maximum de 10 mL, 2 fois par jour.

- **PO (enfants de 2 à 5 ans)**: *Sirop* – de 3 à 5 mL, 1 fois par jour, au coucher, au besoin; ne pas dépasser 5 mL, 2 fois par jour. *Granules* – de ¼ à ½ cuillerée à thé rase, 1 fois par jour au coucher, au besoin, sans dépasser ½ cuillerée à thé rase, 2 fois par jour.

PRÉSENTATION (version générique disponible)

Comprimés: 8,6 mg de sennosides standardisés[VL] ■ **Granules**: 15 mg de sennosides standardisés/3 g[VL] ■ **Sirop**: 1,7 mg/mL de sennosides standardisés[VL] ■ **En association avec**: docusate sodique (Senokot-S).

SOINS INFIRMIERS

ÉVALUATION DE LA SITUATION

- Suivre de près la distension abdominale, ausculter les bruits intestinaux et noter les habitudes normales d'élimination.
- Noter la couleur, la consistance et la quantité des selles produites.

DIAGNOSTICS INFIRMIERS POSSIBLES

- Constipation (Indications).
- Diarrhée (Effets secondaires).
- Connaissances insuffisantes sur le traitement médicamenteux (Enseignement au patient et à ses proches).

INTERVENTIONS INFIRMIÈRES

- Administrer le médicament avec un grand verre d'eau, au coucher, pour favoriser l'élimination de 6 à 12 heures plus tard. Pour obtenir des résultats plus rapides, administrer à jeun.
- Bien mélanger la solution orale avant de l'administrer.
- Les granules devraient être dissous ou mélangés dans de l'eau ou dans un autre liquide avant d'être administrés.

ENSEIGNEMENT AU PATIENT ET À SES PROCHES

- Prévenir le patient que les laxatifs devraient être pris pendant une courte période seulement. Un traitement prolongé peut provoquer des déséquilibres électrolytiques et la dépendance.
- Recommander au patient de prendre d'autres mesures qui favorisent l'élimination intestinale: p. ex., augmenter la consommation de fibres alimentaires et de liquides, et faire de l'exercice. Expliquer au patient que chaque personne a ses propres habitudes d'élimination et qu'il est tout aussi normal de déféquer 3 fois par jour que 3 fois par semaine.
- Prévenir le patient que ce médicament peut rendre ses urines rose-rouge ou brun-noir.
- Recommander au patient souffrant de cardiopathie d'éviter les efforts liés à la défécation (manœuvre de Valsalva).
- Conseiller au patient de ne pas prendre de laxatifs en présence de douleurs abdominales, de nausées, de vomissements ou de fièvre.

VÉRIFICATION DE L'EFFICACITÉ THÉRAPEUTIQUE

L'efficacité du traitement peut être démontrée par: l'émission de selles molles et bien moulées.

SENNOSIDES,

voir Séné

SERTRALINE

Apo-Sertraline, Gen-Sertraline, Novo-Sertraline, Ratio-Sertraline, Sertraline, Zoloft

CLASSIFICATION:

Antidépresseur (inhibiteur sélectif du recaptage de la sérotonine [ISRS])

Grossesse – catégorie C (risque durant le 3e trimestre; voir «Précautions et mises en garde»)

INDICATIONS

Traitement des affections suivantes (en association avec une psychothérapie): dépression ■ trouble panique ■ trouble obsessionnel-compulsif.

MÉCANISME D'ACTION

Inhibition du recaptage de la sérotonine par les neurones du SNC, ce qui en potentialise l'activité ■ Peu d'effet sur la noradrénaline ou sur la dopamine. ***Effets thérapeutiques:*** Effet antidépresseur ■ Incidence réduite d'attaques de panique ■ Diminution des comportements obsessionnels-compulsifs.

PHARMACOCINÉTIQUE

Absorption: Bonne (PO).

Distribution: Tous les tissus.

Liaison aux protéines: 98 %.

Métabolisme et excrétion: Métabolisme majoritairement hépatique; 14 % est excrété sous forme inchangée dans les fèces.

Demi-vie: 26 heures.

Profil temps-action (effet antidépresseur)

	DÉBUT D'ACTION	PIC	DURÉE
PO	en l'espace de 2 à 4 semaines	inconnu	inconnue

CONTRE-INDICATIONS, PRÉCAUTIONS ET MISES EN GARDE

Contre-indications: Hypersensibilité ■ Traitement concomitant par un IMAO (prévoir 14 jours entre l'arrêt de l'administration de l'IMAO et le début de l'administration de la sertraline, et vice versa. Risque de réactions graves pouvant mener à une issue fatale) ■ Traitement concomitant par le pimozide.

Précautions et mises en garde: Risque d'effets indésirables de type agitation grave, parallèlement à des blessures infligées à soi-même ou aux autres ■ Éviter de mettre fin abruptement au traitement, en raison du risque de symptômes de sevrage ■ Insuffisance hépatique ■ Antécédents de manie ou d'hypomanie ■ La surveillance des idées suicidaires est indiquée chez tous les patients recevant ce médicament ■ Antécédents de troubles épileptiques ■ Antécédents de maladie systémique concomitante, d'infarctus du myocarde récent ou de cardiopathie instable récente ■ **OBST.:** Risque de complications chez le nouveau-né lorsque la mère a pris ce médicament durant le 3e trimestre de la grossesse ■ **ALLAITEMENT:** Il est déconseillé d'administrer la sertraline chez la femme qui allaite, sauf si, de l'avis du médecin, les bienfaits escomptés pour la mère l'emportent sur les risques auxquels le fœtus pourrait être exposé ■ **PÉD.:** L'innocuité et l'efficacité de l'agent n'ont pas été établies ■ Risque d'hyponatrémie et de syndrome de sécrétion inappropriée d'hormone antidiurétique (SIADH), surtout chez les femmes âgées ■ Risque de saignements (la prudence est de mise chez les patients prédisposés ou prenant simultanément des médicaments qui accroissent le risque de saignements).

RÉACTIONS INDÉSIRABLES ET EFFETS SECONDAIRES

SNC: étourdissements, somnolence, fatigue, céphalées, insomnie, agitation, anxiété, confusion, labilité émotionnelle, difficultés de concentration, réactions maniaques, nervosité, faiblesse, bâillements.

ORLO: pharyngite, rhinite, acouphènes, troubles visuels.

CV: douleurs thoraciques, palpitations.

GI: diarrhée, sécheresse de la bouche (xérostomie), nausées, douleurs abdominales, altération du goût, anorexie, constipation, dyspepsie, flatulence, gain d'appétit, vomissements.

GU: dysfonctionnement sexuel, troubles menstruels, troubles urinaires, mictions fréquentes.

Tég.: sécrétion accrue de sueur, bouffées vasomotrices, rash.

Loc.: douleurs lombaires, myalgie.

SN: tremblements, hypertonie, hypoesthésie, paresthésie, soubresauts musculaires.

Divers: fièvre, soif.

INTERACTIONS

Médicament-médicament: LA SERTRALINE PEUT PROVOQUER DES RÉACTIONS GRAVES, POUVANT ÊTRE D'ISSUE FATALE (HYPERTHERMIE, RIGIDITÉ, MYOCLONIE, INSTABILITÉ DU SYSTÈME NERVEUX AUTONOME, ACCOMPAGNÉES DE FLUCTUATIONS DES SIGNES VITAUX ET D'UNE AGITATION EXTRÊME, QUI PEUVENT MENER AU DÉLIRE ET AU COMA) EN CAS D'ADMINISTRATION CONCOMITANTE D'**IMAO**; CESSER LE TRAITEMENT PAR L'IMAO AU MOINS 14 JOURS AVANT D'AMORCER CELUI PAR LA SERTRALINE. DE MÊME, L'ADMINISTRATION DE LA SERTRALINE DEVRAIT ÊTRE INTERROMPUE 14 JOURS AVANT D'ENTREPRENDRE UN TRAITEMENT PAR UN IMAO ■ L'utilisation concomitante de **pimozide** est contre-indiquée (risque de torsades de pointes) ■ L'usage concomitant de **médicaments sérotoninergiques** (p. ex., **tryptophane**, **linézolide**, **litium**, **tramadol**) augmente le risque de syndrome sérotoninergique ■ Risque de faiblesse, d'hyperréflexie et d'incoordination lors de l'utilisation concomitante de **tryptans,** tels que le **sumatriptan** ■ La sertraline peut ralentir le métabolisme et augmenter les effets de certains **médicaments métabolisés dans le foie par l'entremise du cytochrome P450 2D6**. L'usage concomitant de ces médicaments et de sertraline devrait s'accompagner de prudence ■ Il est recommandé de surveiller étroitement la glycémie des patients qui prennent la sertraline en concomitance avec un **hypoglycémiant oral** ou de l'**insuline** ■ L'administration concomitante de **cimétidine** peut inhiber la biotransformation de la sertraline et de son métabolite, la déméthylsertraline, ce qui peut entraîner une baisse de la clairance et de la biotransformation lors du premier passage de la sertraline, avec une augmentation possible des effets indésirables de ce médicament ■ La consommation concomitante d'**alcool** n'est pas recommandée ■ La sertraline peut intensifier les effets de la **warfarine**.

VOIES D'ADMINISTRATION ET POSOLOGIE

Dépression, trouble obsessionnel-compulsif

- **PO (adultes)**: Initialement, 50 mg par jour, en 1 seule dose, le matin ou au souper; on peut majorer la dose à intervalles hebdomadaires jusqu'à concurrence de 200 mg par jour, selon la réponse du patient.

Trouble panique

- **PO (adultes)**: Initialement, 25 mg par jour; on peut majorer la dose à intervalles hebdomadaires, jusqu'à concurrence de 200 mg par jour, selon la réponse du patient.

PRÉSENTATION

Capsules: 25 mg[Pr], 50 mg[Pr], 100 mg[Pr].

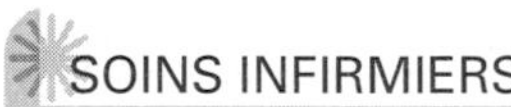

SOINS INFIRMIERS

ÉVALUATION DE LA SITUATION

- Suivre de près l'appétit du patient et son alimentation. Peser le patient toutes les semaines. Prévenir le médecin ou un autre professionnel de la santé en cas de perte constante de poids. Adapter le régime selon les aliments que le patient peut tolérer pour maintenir son état nutritionnel.

Dépression:

- Suivre de près les sautes d'humeur. Signaler au médecin ou à un autre professionnel de la santé l'aggravation de l'anxiété, de l'agitation ou de l'insomnie.
- Observer les tendances suicidaires, particulièrement durant le traitement initial. Réduire la quantité de médicament dont le patient peut disposer.

Trouble obsessionnel-compulsif: Observer la fréquence des comportements obsessionnels-compulsifs. Noter à quel point de telles pensées ou comportements empêchent le patient de poursuivre ses activités quotidiennes.

Attaques de panique: Évaluer la fréquence et la gravité des crises de panique.

DIAGNOSTICS INFIRMIERS POSSIBLES

- Stratégies d'adaptation inefficaces (Indications).
- Risque d'accident (Effets secondaires).
- Connaissances insuffisantes sur le traitement médicamenteux (Enseignement au patient et à ses proches).

INTERVENTIONS INFIRMIÈRES

- NE PAS CONFONDRE LA SERTRALINE AVEC LA SÉLÉGILINE.
- Réévaluer à intervalles réguliers la dose et le besoin de poursuivre le traitement.
- Administrer la sertraline en une seule dose, le matin ou au souper.

ENSEIGNEMENT AU PATIENT ET À SES PROCHES

- Conseiller au patient de respecter rigoureusement la posologie recommandée. S'il n'a pas pu prendre le médicament au moment habituel, lui conseiller de le prendre dès que possible et de revenir ensuite à son schéma posologique habituel. Lui recommander de ne jamais remplacer une dose manquée par une double dose.
- Prévenir le patient que la sertraline peut provoquer de la somnolence ou des étourdissements. Lui recommander de ne pas conduire et d'éviter les activités qui exigent sa vigilance jusqu'à ce qu'on ait la certitude que le médicament n'entraîne pas ces effets chez lui.
- Conseiller au patient d'éviter la consommation d'alcool ou la prise d'autres dépresseurs du SNC pendant le traitement et de consulter un professionnel de la santé avant de prendre d'autres médicaments en même temps que la sertraline.
- Expliquer au patient qu'il peut soulager la sécheresse de la bouche en se rinçant souvent la bouche, en pratiquant une bonne hygiène buccale et en consommant des bonbons ou de la gomme à mâcher sans sucre. Si la sécheresse de la bouche persiste pendant plus de 2 semaines, lui conseiller de consulter un professionnel de la santé, qui pourra lui recommander des substituts de salive.
- Recommander au patient d'utiliser des écrans solaires et de porter des vêtements protecteurs afin de prévenir les réactions de photosensibilité.
- Conseiller à la patiente de prévenir un professionnel de la santé si elle pense être enceinte ou désire le devenir ou, encore, si elle allaite.
- Conseiller au patient de prévenir un professionnel de la santé si les céphalées, la faiblesse, les nausées, l'anorexie, l'anxiété ou l'insomnie persistent.
- Insister sur l'importance des examens de suivi permettant de déterminer les bienfaits du traitement. Encourager le patient à s'engager dans une psychothérapie.

S

VÉRIFICATION DE L'EFFICACITÉ THÉRAPEUTIQUE

L'efficacité du traitement peut être démontrée par: une sensation de mieux-être ■ un regain d'intérêt pour l'entourage; les effets antidépresseurs peuvent ne pas se manifester avant 1 à 4 semaines ■ la diminution de la fréquence des comportements obsessionnels-compulsifs ■ la diminution de la fréquence et de la gravité des attaques de panique.

SEVELAMER

Renagel

CLASSIFICATION:

Modificateur électrolytique (chélateur de phosphate)

Grossesse – catégorie C

INDICATIONS

Traitement de l'hyperphosphatémie chez les patients hémodialysés souffrant d'insuffisance rénale terminale.

MÉCANISME D'ACTION

Polymère qui se lie aux phosphates dans le tractus gastro-intestinal, et qui en empêche l'absorption. ***Effets thérapeutiques:*** Diminution des concentrations sériques de phosphates et réduction des effets indésirables de l'hyperphosphatémie (calcification ectopique, hyperparathyroïdie secondaire associée à une ostéite fibreuse).

PHARMACOCINÉTIQUE

Absorption: Aucune, l'action est locale (dans les voies gastro-intestinales).
Distribution: Inconnue.
Métabolisme et excrétion: Élimination dans les fèces.
Demi-vie: Inconnue.

Profil temps-action
(diminution des concentrations sériques de phosphate)

	Début d'action	Pic	Durée
PO	5 jours	2 semaines	inconnue

CONTRE-INDICATIONS, PRÉCAUTIONS ET MISES EN GARDE

Contre-indications: Hypersensibilité ■ Hypophosphatémie ■ Occlusion intestinale.
Précautions et mises en garde: Dysphagie, troubles de déglutition, troubles graves de motilité gastro-intestinale ou chirurgie majeure des voies gastro-intestinales (l'innocuité et l'efficacité du médicament n'ont pas été établies) ■ **OBST., PÉD.:** Grossesse, allaitement ou enfants (l'innocuité du médicament n'a pas été établie).

RÉACTIONS INDÉSIRABLES ET EFFETS SECONDAIRES

GI: diarrhée, dyspepsie, vomissements, constipation, flatulence, nausées.

INTERACTIONS

Médicament-médicament: Administration concomitante d'**anticonvulsivants** ou d'**antiarythmiques** (le sevelamer peut modifier l'absorption de ces agents; administrer 1 heure avant ou 3 heures après) ■ Le sevelamer peut diminuer l'absorption d'autres médicaments et en réduire l'efficacité, particulièrement des **médicaments dont l'efficacité dépend de concentrations sanguines spécifiques** (administrer 1 heure avant ou 3 heures après).

VOIES D'ADMINISTRATION ET POSOLOGIE

- **PO (adultes):** De 800 à 1 600 mg, avant ou durant chaque repas. Toute dose oubliée doit être sautée.

PRÉSENTATION

Comprimés: 800 mg[Pr].

SOINS INFIRMIERS

ÉVALUATION DE LA SITUATION

- Observer le patient à intervalles réguliers pendant toute la durée du traitement à la recherche d'effets secondaires gastro-intestinaux.

Tests de laboratoire: Mesurer, à intervalles réguliers pendant toute la durée du traitement, les concentrations sériques de phosphore, de calcium, de bicarbonate et de chlorure.

DIAGNOSTICS INFIRMIERS POSSIBLES

- Connaissances insuffisantes sur le traitement médicamenteux (Enseignement au patient et à ses proches).

INTERVENTIONS INFIRMIÈRES

- Les doses des médicaments pris en concomitance, particulièrement des anticonvulsivants et des antiarythmiques, devraient être administrées au moins 1 heure avant ou 3 heures après le sevelamer.
- Administrer le sevelamer à chaque repas. Il ne faut pas croquer, mâcher ou couper les comprimés, car le sevelamer gonfle dans l'eau.

ENSEIGNEMENT AU PATIENT ET À SES PROCHES

- Expliquer au patient qu'il doit prendre le sevelamer au moment des repas, selon la posologie recommandée, et respecter la diétothérapie qui lui a été prescrite. Il ne doit pas croquer, mâcher ou couper les comprimés.
- Prévenir le patient qu'il doit prendre les autres médicaments au moins 1 heure avant ou 3 heures après le sevelamer.
- Conseiller au patient de prévenir un professionnel de la santé si les effets gastro-intestinaux indésirables sont graves ou prolongés.

VÉRIFICATION DE L'EFFICACITÉ THÉRAPEUTIQUE

L'efficacité du traitement peut être démontrée par: la diminution des concentrations sériques de phosphate jusqu'à ≤ 1,8 mmol/L. L'adaptation posologique est fondée sur les concentrations sériques de phosphate.

SIBUTRAMINE

Meridia

CLASSIFICATION:

Anorexigène (coupe-faim), agent antiobésité

Grossesse - catégorie C

INDICATIONS

Traitement d'appoint de l'obésité chez les patients dont l'indice de masse corporelle est ≥ 30 kg/m² (ou ≥ 27 kg/m² chez les patients souffrant de diabète de type 2 ou d'hypertension maîtrisée ou de dyslipidémie, ou chez ceux présentant d'autres facteurs de risque), en association avec d'autres interventions (régime amaigrissant, exercice).

MÉCANISME D'ACTION

Inhibition du recaptage de la sérotonine, de la noradrénaline et de la dopamine; impression accrue de satiété entraînée par la sérotonine. ***Effets thérapeutiques:*** Diminution de la faim, entraînant une perte de poids chez les patients obèses.

PHARMACOCINÉTIQUE

Absorption: 77 % (PO). L'agent subit rapidement un fort métabolisme de premier passage hépatique (par le système enzymatique du P450 3A4) et se transforme en 2 métabolites actifs (M1 et M2).

Distribution: Tout l'organisme; on en trouve des concentrations élevées dans le foie et dans les reins.

Métabolisme et excrétion: Les métabolites actifs subissent un fort métabolisme et se transforment en métabolites inactifs qui sont en grande partie excrétés par les reins.

Demi-vie: *Métabolite M1* - 14 heures; *métabolite M2* - 16 heures.

Profil temps-action (coupe-faim/perte pondérale)

	DÉBUT D'ACTION	PIC	DURÉE
PO	en quelques jours	4 semaines	inconnue

CONTRE-INDICATIONS, PRÉCAUTIONS ET MISES EN GARDE

Contre-indications: Hypersensibilité ■ Anorexie mentale ou boulimie ■ Maladie psychiatrique ■ Usage concomitant d'autres anorexigènes à action centrale, d'IMAO, d'antidépresseurs, d'antipsychotiques ou de millepertuis ■ Hypertension non maîtrisée ou instable ■ Antécédents de coronaropathie, d'insuffisance cardiaque, d'arythmies ou d'AVC.

Précautions et mises en garde: Antécédents de convulsions ■ Glaucome à angle étroit ■ **GÉR., PÉD. (< 18 ANS), OBST., ALLAITEMENT:** L'innocuité du médicament n'a pas été établie ■ Obésité de cause organique (hypothyroïdie non traitée) ■ Insuffisance rénale ou hépatique grave ■ Consommation excessive d'alcool.

RÉACTIONS INDÉSIRABLES ET EFFETS SECONDAIRES

SNC: CONVULSIONS, céphalées, insomnie, stimulation du SNC, étourdissements, somnolence, labilité émotionnelle, nervosité.

ORLO: laryngite/pharyngite, rhinite, sinusite.

CV: hypertension, palpitations, tachycardie, vasodilatation.

GI: anorexie, constipation, sécheresse de la bouche (xérostomie), altération du goût, dyspepsie, appétit accru, nausées.

GU: dysménorrhée.

Tég.: transpiration, rash.

INTERACTIONS

Médicament-médicament: L'ADMINISTRATION CONCOMITANTE D'AUTRES **ANOREXIGÈNES À ACTION CENTRALE**, D' **IMAO**, D'**ISRS**, DE **NARATRIPTAN**, DE **RIZATRIPTAN**, DE **ZOLMITRIPTAN**, DE **SUMATRIPTAN**, DE **DIHYDROERGOTAMINE**, DE **DEXTROMÉTHORPHANE**, DE **MÉPÉRIDINE**, DE **PENTAZOCINE**, DE **FENTANYL**, DE **LITHIUM** OU DE **TRYPTOPHANE** PEUT ENTRAÎNER UN « SYNDROME SÉROTONINERGIQUE » POUVANT ÊTRE D'ISSUE FATALE (ÉVITER L'ADMINISTRATION CONCOMITANTE; NE PAS ADMINISTRER LA SIBUTRAMINE PENDANT LES 2 SEMAINES QUI SUIVENT L'USAGE D'UN IMAO ET VICE VERSA) ■ L'usage concomitant de **décongestionnants** peut accroître le risque d'hypertension ■ Les **médicaments qui affectent le système enzymatique P450 3A4** peuvent modifier les effets de la sibutramine ■ Le **kétoconazole**, la **cimétidine** et l'**érythromycine** ralentissent le métabolisme de la sibutramine et peuvent en augmenter les concentrations sanguines et les effets.

VOIES D'ADMINISTRATION ET POSOLOGIE

- **PO (adultes):** 10 mg, 1 fois par jour; si la perte de poids est < 1,8 kg, après 4 semaines, on peut majorer la dose jusqu'à 15 mg par jour.

S

PRÉSENTATION

Capsules: 10 mg[Pr], 15 mg[Pr].

SOINS INFIRMIERS

ÉVALUATION DE LA SITUATION

- Suivre de près la perte pondérale et adapter la posologie des médicaments administrés en concomitance (antihypertenseurs, antidiabétiques, hypolipidémiants), en suivant les recommandations du médecin, et selon les besoins.
- Mesurer la pression artérielle et la fréquence cardiaque à intervalles réguliers pendant toute la durée du traitement. Une diminution de la dose de sibutramine ou même l'arrêt du traitement peuvent s'avérer nécessaires en cas d'élévation de la pression artérielle ou de la fréquence cardiaque, particulièrement au début du traitement.

DIAGNOSTICS INFIRMIERS POSSIBLES

- Image corporelle perturbée (Indications).
- Alimentation excessive (Indications).
- Connaissances insuffisantes sur le traitement médicamenteux (Enseignement au patient et à ses proches).

INTERVENTIONS INFIRMIÈRES

- Les capsules devraient être prises 1 fois par jour sans égard aux repas.

ENSEIGNEMENT AU PATIENT ET À SES PROCHES

- Conseiller au patient de respecter rigoureusement la posologie recommandée et de ne pas dépasser la dose prescrite de sibutramine. Au momen d'arrêter le traitement, il peut s'avérer nécessaire de diminuer la dose graduellement.
- Recommander au patient d'éviter de boire de l'alcool en grandes quantités ou de prendre d'autres dépresseurs du SNC en même temps que la sibutramine.

VÉRIFICATION DE L'EFFICACITÉ THÉRAPEUTIQUE

L'efficacité du traitement peut être démontrée par: une perte pondérale lente et constante lorsque le traitement est associé à un régime hypocalorique. Si on n'observe pas de perte de poids cliniquement notable (au moins 5 % du poids initial en 3 à 6 mois), on devrait réévaluer l'utilité du traitement.

SILDÉNAFIL

Revatio, Viagra

CLASSIFICATION:

Agent utilisé dans le traitement de l'impuissance ou de l'hypertension artérielle pulmonaire (inhibiteur de la phosphodiestérase de type 5)

Grossesse - catégorie B

INDICATIONS

Traitement du dysfonctionnement érectile (Viagra) ■ Traitement de l'hypertension artérielle pulmonaire (Revatio).

MÉCANISME D'ACTION

Amplification des effets du monoxyde d'azote libéré à la suite d'une stimulation sexuelle. Le monoxyde d'azote active l'enzyme guanylate cyclase, ce qui entraîne une élévation des concentrations de guanosine monophosphate cyclique (GMPc). La GMPc entraîne la relaxation des muscles lisses du corps caverneux, ce qui favorise l'afflux du sang dans le pénis et l'érection qui s'ensuit. Le sildénafil inhibe la phosphodiestérase de type 5 (PDE5), l'enzyme responsable de la biodégradation de la GMPc dans le corps caverneux (Viagra) ■ Vasodilatation sélective du réseau vasculaire pulmonaire par l'inhibition de la dégradation du GMPc, qui entraîne la relaxation des vaisseaux (Revatio). ***Effets thérapeutiques:*** Viagra: Augmentation du flux sanguin dans le corps caverneux, entraînant une érection suffisante pour permettre les rapports sexuels. Une stimulation sexuelle est nécessaire. ■ Revatio: Augmentation de la tolérance à l'effort.

PHARMACOCINÉTIQUE

Absorption: 40 % (PO).

Distribution: L'agent se répartit dans tous les tissus; une quantité négligeable est présente dans le sperme.

Liaison aux protéines: 96 %.

Métabolisme et excrétion: Métabolisme hépatique (cytochrome P450 3A4); un des métabolites est actif et responsable de 20 % des effets du médicament. Excrétion sous forme de métabolites dans les fèces (80 %) et dans l'urine (13 %).

Demi-vie: 4 heures (pour le sildénafil et son métabolite actif).

Profil temps-action (effet sur l'érection/vasodilatation)

	DÉBUT D'ACTION	PIC	DURÉE
PO (Viagra)	en moins de 1 h	30 - 120 min	jusqu'à 4 h
PO (Revatio)	1 - 2 h	inconnu	8 h

CONTRE-INDICATIONS, PRÉCAUTIONS ET MISES EN GARDE

Contre-indications: Hypersensibilité ■ TRAITEMENT CONCOMITANT PAR UN DÉRIVÉ NITRÉ ORGANIQUE (NITROGLYCÉRINE, MONONITRATE D'ISOSORBIDE, DINITRATE D'ISOSORBIDE) ■ Hommes chez lesquels l'activité sexuelle est déconseillée (Viagra).

Précautions et mises en garde: Maladie cardiovasculaire grave sous-jacente (incluant des antécédents d'infarctus du myocarde [IM], d'AVC ou d'arythmies graves au cours des 6 derniers mois), insuffisance cardiaque ou coronaropathie accompagnée d'angine instable ■ Sténose aortique ou cardiomyopathie hypertrophique ■ **GÉR.:** Personnes âgées (≥ 65 ans) ■ Insuffisance rénale (Cl_{Cr} < 30 mL/min) ou insuffisance hépatique; risque de concentrations sanguines accrues, donc une réduction de la dose s'avère nécessaire ■ Déformation pénienne (angulation, fibrose caverneuse, maladie de La Peyronie) ■ États associés au priapisme (drépanocytose, myélome multiple, leucémie) ■ Troubles hémorragiques ou ulcère gastroduodénal en évolution ■ Hypotension au repos (< 90/50 mm Hg) ou hypertension au repos (> 170/110 mm Hg) ■ Antécédents de neuropathie optique ischémique antérieure non artéritique (NOIANA) ■ Rétinite pigmentaire ■ **OBST., ALLAITEMENT, PÉD.:** Ce médicament n'est pas indiqué chez les femmes ou les enfants (Viagra); l'innocuité du médicament n'a pas été établie chez les femmes enceintes ou qui allaitent, ni chez les enfants (Revatio) ■ Maladie veino-occlusive pulmonaire (Revatio).

RÉACTIONS INDÉSIRABLES ET EFFETS SECONDAIRES

SNC: céphalées, étourdissements, insomnie (Revatio), paresthésies (Revatio).
ORLO: vision anormale (vision teintée, sensibilité accrue à la lumière, vision trouble), congestion nasale, épistaxis.
CV: INFARCTUS DU MYOCARDE, MORT SUBITE, COLLAPSUS CARDIOVASCULAIRE.
GI: diarrhée, dyspepsie.
GU: priapisme, infection des voies urinaires.
Tég.: bouffées vasomotrices, rash.
Loc.: arthralgie, myalgie.

INTERACTIONS

Médicament-médicament: RISQUE ACCRU D'HYPOTENSION LORS DE LA PRISE CONCOMITANTE DE **DÉRIVÉS NITRÉS**, SOUS QUELQUE FORME QUE CE SOIT; L'USAGE CONCOMITANT EST CONTRE-INDIQUÉ EN RAISON DU RISQUE D'HYPOTENSION GRAVE POUVANT ÊTRE D'ISSUE FATALE ■ Les concentrations sanguines du sildénafil et ses effets peuvent être accrus par la **cimétidine**, l'**érythromycine**, la **clarithromycine**, le **kétoconazole**, le **nelfinavir**, l'**indinavir**, le **ritonavir**, le **saquinavir** et l'**itraconazole** (la dose initiale devrait être réduite jusqu'à 25 mg) ■ Risque accru d'hypotension lors de l'administration concomitante d'**antihypertenseurs** ■ Risque accru d'hypotension lors de l'administration concomitante de **doxazosine,** de **prazosine** et de **térazosine** ■ L'administration concomitante d'**inducteurs puissants du CYP3A4** (**bosentan**, **barbituriques**, **carbamazépine**, **phénytoïne**, **éfavirenz**, **névirapine**, **rifampicine**, **rifabutine**) peut entraîner une diminution des concentrations sanguines (Revatio).

VOIES D'ADMINISTRATION ET POSOLOGIE

Dysfonction érectile (Viagra)

- **PO (adultes):** 50 mg, de 30 à 60 minutes avant les rapports sexuels (écart posologique: de 25 à 100 mg, de 30 minutes à 4 heures avant les rapports sexuels); ne pas administrer plus souvent que 1 fois par jour.
- **PO (personnes âgées ≥ 65 ans, insuffisance hépatique, ou traitement concomitant par des inhibiteurs enzymatiques du CYP3A4 [érythromycine, saquinavir, ritonavir, kétoconazole, itraconazole, etc.]):** Dose initiale: 25 mg, de 30 à 60 minutes avant les rapports sexuels (écart posologique: de 25 à 100 mg, de 30 minutes à 4 heures avant les rapports sexuels); ne pas administrer plus souvent que 1 fois par jour.
- ***INSUFFISANCE RÉNALE***
  PO (ADULTES): *CL_{CR} < 30 mL/MIN* – DOSE INITIALE: 25 mg, DE 30 À 60 MINUTES AVANT LES RAPPORTS SEXUELS (ÉCART POSOLOGIQUE: DE 25 À 100 mg, DE 30 MINUTES À 4 HEURES AVANT LES RAPPORTS SEXUELS); NE PAS ADMINISTRER PLUS SOUVENT QUE 1 FOIS PAR JOUR.

Hypertension artérielle pulmonaire (Revatio)

- **PO (adultes):** 20 mg, 3 fois par jour, toutes les 6 à 8 heures; une adaptation posologique peut être nécessaire lors de l'administration concomitante d'inducteurs du CYP3A4 (bosentan, barbituriques, carbamazépine, phénytoïne, éfavirenz, névirapine, rifampicine, rifabutine).

S

PRÉSENTATION

Comprimés: 25 mg[Pr], 50 mg[Pr], 100 mg[Pr] (Viagra) ■ **Comprimés:** 20 mg[Pr] (Revatio).

SOINS INFIRMIERS

ÉVALUATION DE LA SITUATION

Viagra: Déterminer la présence d'un dysfonctionnement érectile avant l'administration du médicament.

Le sildénafil n'a aucun effet si une stimulation sexuelle n'est pas présente.

Revatio: Évaluer les paramètres hémodynamiques et la tolérance à l'effort avant de commencer le traitement et à intervalles réguliers par la suite.

DIAGNOSTICS INFIRMIERS POSSIBLES

- Dysfonctionnement sexuel (Indications).
- Connaissances insuffisantes sur le traitement médicamenteux (Enseignement au patient et à ses proches).

INTERVENTIONS INFIRMIÈRES

- Dans le traitement de la dysfonction érectile, la dose de sildénafil doit habituellement être prise 1 heure avant les rapports sexuels. Toutefois, le patient peut la prendre de 30 minutes à 4 heures avant de s'engager dans des rapports sexuels.
- Dans le traitement de l'hypertension artérielle pulmonaire, la dose de sildénafil est administrée 3 fois par jour, toutes les 6 à 8 heures, sans égard aux repas.

ENSEIGNEMENT AU PATIENT ET À SES PROCHES

- Expliquer au patient traité pour une dysfonction érectile qu'il devrait prendre le sildénafil environ 1 heure avant les rapports sexuels et qu'il ne doit pas prendre le médicament plus de 1 fois par jour.
- Prévenir le patient que le sildénafil (Viagra) est contre-indiqué chez les femmes.
- Avertir le patient qu'il ne doit pas prendre en même temps le sildénafil et des dérivés nitrés.
- Conseiller au patient prenant le sildénafil pour le traitement de l'hypertension artérielle pulmonaire de consulter un professionnel de la santé avant de prendre un médicament de vente libre ou un produit naturel.
- Conseiller au patient de prévenir rapidement un professionnel de la santé si l'érection dure plus que 4 heures ou s'il remarque une perte de vision rapide ou graduelle affectant un œil ou les deux yeux.
- Informer le patient que le sildénafil n'assure aucune protection contre les maladies transmissibles sexuellement. Lui conseiller de prendre les mesures de protection nécessaires contre les maladies transmissibles sexuellement et les infections par le VIH.

VÉRIFICATION DE L'EFFICACITÉ THÉRAPEUTIQUE

L'efficacité du traitement peut être démontrée par: une érection suffisante pour que le patient puisse s'engager dans des rapports sexuels (Viagra) ■ une augmentation de la tolérance à l'effort (Revatio). ✳

S

SIMÉTHICONE

Gas-X, Ovol, Phazyme, Simethicone

CLASSIFICATION:

Antiflatulent

Grossesse – catégorie C

INDICATIONS

Soulagement des symptômes douloureux entraînés par les excès de gaz dans le tractus gastro-intestinal qui peuvent se former après une intervention chirurgicale ou à cause de: l'aérophagie ■ la dyspepsie ■ l'ulcère gastroduodénal ■ la diverticulite ■ Soulagement des coliques infantiles.

MÉCANISME D'ACTION

Stimulation de la coalescence des bulles de gaz ■ L'agent ne prévient pas la formation de gaz. ***Effets thérapeutiques:*** Évacuation des gaz du tractus gastro-intestinal par la bouche (éructation) ou par l'anus.

PHARMACOCINÉTIQUE

Absorption: Aucune (PO).

Distribution: Aucune distribution systémique.

Métabolisme et excrétion: Excrétion à l'état inchangé dans les fèces.

Demi-vie: Inconnue.

Profil temps-action (effet antiflatulent)

	Début d'action	Pic	Durée
PO	immédiat	inconnu	3 h

CONTRE-INDICATIONS, PRÉCAUTIONS ET MISES EN GARDE

Contre-indications: ■ Hypersensibilité ■ Occlusion ou perforation intestinale ■ Coliques du nourrisson (usage déconseillé, à l'exception des gouttes pédiatriques destinées à cet usage).

Précautions et mises en garde: Douleurs abdominales d'étiologie inconnue, particulièrement en présence de fièvre ■ Grossesse et allaitement (cependant, la siméthicone a déjà été administrée sans problèmes dans ce cas).

RÉACTIONS INDÉSIRABLES ET EFFETS SECONDAIRES

Aucune réaction importante.

INTERACTIONS

Médicament-médicament: Aucune interaction notable.

VOIES D'ADMINISTRATION ET POSOLOGIE

- **PO (adultes)**: De 40 à 160 mg, 4 fois par jour, après les repas et au coucher (jusqu'à 540 mg par jour).
- **PO (enfants de 2 à 12 ans)**: 40 mg, 4 fois par jour.
- **PO (enfants < 2 ans)**: De 10 à 20 mg, pendant ou après les repas (jusqu'à 60 mg par jour).

PRÉSENTATION (version générique disponible)

Comprimés à croquer: 40 mg^{VL}, 80 mg^{VL}, 160 mg^{VL} ■ **Comprimés**: 80 mg^{VL}, 180 mg^{VL} ■ **Capsules**: 95 mg^{VL}, 125 mg^{VL}, 166 mg^{VL}, 180 mg^{VL} ■ **Liquide**: 125 mg/10 mL^{VL} ■ **Gouttes pédiatriques**: 40 mg/1 mL^{VL} ■ **En association avec**: antiacides^{VL}, lopéramide^{VL}.

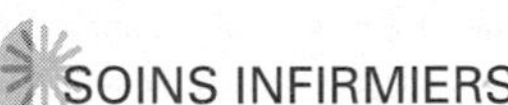

SOINS INFIRMIERS

ÉVALUATION DE LA SITUATION

- Suivre de près, avant le traitement et à intervalles réguliers pendant toute sa durée, la distension et les douleurs abdominales ainsi que la présence de bruits intestinaux. Noter également la fréquence des éructations ou de l'expulsion de gaz par l'anus.

DIAGNOSTICS INFIRMIERS POSSIBLES

- Douleur aiguë (Indications).
- Connaissances insuffisantes sur le traitement médicamenteux (Enseignement au patient et à ses proches).

INTERVENTIONS INFIRMIÈRES

- Pour obtenir des résultats optimaux, administrer le médicament après les repas et au coucher. Bien mélanger les préparations liquides avant de les administrer. Pour obtenir un effet plus rapide et plus complet, demander au patient de bien mâcher les comprimés à croquer.
- Les gouttes peuvent être mélangées à 30 mL d'eau tiède, de préparation pour nourrissons ou d'autres liquides, selon les recommandations. Bien mélanger la solution avant de l'utiliser.

ENSEIGNEMENT AU PATIENT ET À SES PROCHES

- Expliquer au patient qu'une alimentation appropriée et l'exercice l'aideront à prévenir la formation de gaz intestinaux. Lui expliquer également que ce médicament ne prévient pas la formation des gaz.
- Conseiller au patient de prévenir un professionnel de la santé si les symptômes persistent.

VÉRIFICATION DE L'EFFICACITÉ THÉRAPEUTIQUE

L'efficacité du traitement peut être démontrée par: la diminution de la distension abdominale et le soulagement de la gêne gastro-intestinale.

SIMVASTATINE,

voir Inhibiteurs de l'HMG-CoA réductase

SIROLIMUS

Rapamune

CLASSIFICATION:
Immunosuppresseur

Grossesse – catégorie C

INDICATIONS

Prévention du rejet d'une greffe à la suite d'une transplantation d'un rein allogénique (en association avec des corticostéroïdes et la cyclosporine). **Tuteur coronarien libérant du sirolimus (Cypher)**: prévention de la resténose à la suite de l'implantation d'un tuteur coronarien.

MÉCANISME D'ACTION

Inhibition de l'activation et de la prolifération des lymphocytes T, qui survient en réponse à une stimulation des antigènes et des cytokines; également, inhibition de la production d'anticorps. ***Effets thérapeutiques:*** Diminution de l'incidence et de la gravité des réactions de rejet d'organe.

PHARMACOCINÉTIQUE

Absorption: Rapide (PO). Biodisponibilité à 14 % (PO).
Distribution: Concentration dans les érythrocytes; concentrations élevées dans le cœur, les intestins, les reins, le foie, les poumons, les muscles, la rate et les testicules.
Liaison aux protéines: 92 %.
Métabolisme et excrétion: Métabolisme hépatique important en partie par le système enzymatique P4503A4. Excrétion fécale importante (91 %).
Demi-vie: 62 heures.

Profil temps-action (concentrations sanguines)

	DÉBUT D'ACTION	PIC	DURÉE
PO	rapide	1-2 h	24 h

S

CONTRE-INDICATIONS, PRÉCAUTIONS ET MISES EN GARDE

Contre-indications: Hypersensibilité ■ Intolérance ou sensibilité à l'alcool (les solutions renferment de l'éthanol).

Précautions et mises en garde: Insuffisance hépatique ■ **PÉD.**: L'innocuité du médicament n'a pas été établie chez les enfants < 13 ans ■ Usage concomitant de kétoconazole, d'un inhibiteur ou d'un inducteur puissant du CYP3A4 ou de jus de pamplemousse ■ **OBST.**: Femmes en âge de procréer, grossesse et allaitement.

RÉACTIONS INDÉSIRABLES ET EFFETS SECONDAIRES

Effets signalés lors du traitement d'association avec des corticostéroïdes et la cyclosporine.

SNC: insomnie.

CV: œdème, hypotension, hypertension, tachycardie.

Resp.: PNEUMOPATHIE INTERSTITIELLE, HÉMORRAGIE PULMONAIRE.

GI: HÉPATOTOXICITÉ, diarrhée, anomalies révélées par le bilan hépatique.

GU: insuffisance rénale.

Tég.: acné, rash, hirsutisme, purpura thrombopénique.

HÉ: hypokaliémie.

Hémat.: leucopénie, thrombopénie, anémie.

Métab.: hyperlipidémie.

Loc.: arthralgie.

SN: tremblements.

Divers: risque accru d'infection, risque accru de lymphome, lymphocèle, infections herpétiques des muqueuses, ralentissement de la cicatrisation des plaies, RÉACTIONS ANAPHYLACTIQUES, RÉACTIONS ANAPHYLACTOÏDES.

INTERACTIONS

S

Médicament-médicament: La **cyclosporine** élève considérablement les concentrations sanguines de sirolimus (administrer le sirolimus 4 heures après la cyclosporine et administrer des doses légèrement plus faibles de cyclosporine) ■ Le **kétoconazole,** l'**itraconazole**, le **voriconazole**, la **clarithromycine**, l'**érythromycine** et la **télithromycine** élèvent de façon marquée les concentrations sanguines de sirolimus (l'usage concomitant est contre-indiqué) ■ Les concentrations sanguines de sirolimus sont également élevées par le **diltiazem** (mesurer les concentrations de sirolimus et adapter la dose si cela s'avère nécessaire) et peuvent être accrues par le **vérapamil**, le **clotrimazole**, le **fluconazole**, le **métoclopramide**, la **cimétidine**, le **danazol** et les **antirétroviraux inhibiteurs de la protéase**, administrés en concomitance ■ La **rifampine** et la **rifabutine** accélèrent le métabolisme du sirolimus et en diminuent fortement les concentrations sanguines (il faudrait envisager un traitement de rechange) ■ Les concentrations sanguines de sirolimus peuvent être également réduites lors de l'administration concomitante de **carbamazépine**, de **phénobarbital** et de **phénytoïne** ■ Le risque d'insuffisance rénale peut être accru lors de l'administration concomitante d'autres **agents néphrotoxiques** ■ L'administration concomitante de **tacrolimus** et de **corticostéroïdes** chez les patients ayant subi une transplantation pulmonaire peut augmenter le risque de déhiscence de l'anastomose bronchique; des décès sont survenus (le sirolimus n'est pas approuvé pour cette indication) ■ L'administration concomitante de **tacrolimus** et de **corticostéroïdes** chez les patients ayant subi une transplantation hépatique peut augmenter le risque de thrombose de l'artère hépatique; des décès sont survenus (le sirolimus n'est pas approuvé pour cette indication) ■ Le sirolimus peut diminuer la réponse des anticorps aux **vaccins à virus vivants** et augmenter le risque de réactions indésirables.

Médicament-aliments: La consommation concomitante de **jus de pamplemousse** ralentit le métabolisme par l'isoenzyme CYP3A4 et élève les concentrations de sirolimus; il ne faut donc pas servir ce jus au patient qui prend le sirolimus ni l'utiliser pour des dilutions.

Médicament-produits naturels: La consommation concomitante d'**échinacée** et de **mélatonine** peut entraver l'effet du sirolimus. Le **millepertuis** peut accélérer le métabolisme du sirolimus et en diminuer fortement les concentrations sanguines, entraînant une diminution de l'efficacité.

VOIES D'ADMINISTRATION ET POSOLOGIE

En association avec la cyclosporine et un corticostéroïde en traitement initial. Chez les patients à risque immunologique faible ou modéré, l'abandon du traitement par la cyclosporine est recommandé de 2 à 4 mois après la transplantation.

- **PO (adultes et enfants ≥ 13 ans, pesant ≥ 40 kg)**: Administrer une dose d'attaque de 6 mg, suivie d'une dose d'entretien de 2 mg par jour. Si l'on arrête l'administration de cyclosporine de 2 à 4 mois après la transplantation, les doses de sirolimus doivent être réajustées en fonction des concentrations sanguines.
- **PO (enfants ≥ 13 ans, pesant < 40 kg)**: Administrer une dose d'attaque de 3 mg/m^2, suivie d'une dose d'entretien de 1 mg/m^2 par jour.

INSUFFISANCE HÉPATIQUE

- **PO (ADULTES ET ENFANTS)**: RÉDUIRE LA DOSE D'ENTRETIEN DE 33 %; LA DOSE D'ATTAQUE DEMEURE INCHANGÉE.

PRÉSENTATION

Comprimés: 1 mg^{Pr}, 2 mg^{Pr}, 5 mg^{Pr}. **Solution orale**: 1 mg/mL^{Pr} avec adaptateur de seringue, en flacons de 60 mL, avec 30 seringues ambrées à usage unique.

SOINS INFIRMIERS

ÉVALUATION DE LA SITUATION

- Suivre de près la pression artérielle pendant toute la durée du traitement. L'hypertension étant une complication courante du traitement par le sirolimus, elle devrait être traitée.

Tests de laboratoire:

- On devrait mesurer les concentrations sanguines de sirolimus chez les patients dont le métabolisme des médicaments risque d'être altéré, chez les patients ≥ 13 ans qui pèsent < 40 kg, chez les insuffisants hépatiques et chez les personnes qui prennent des médicaments qui peuvent mener à des interactions avec le sirolimus, de 1 à 2 semaines après une modification de dose ainsi que de 1 à 2 semaines après un changement de préparation (substitution de la suspension par des comprimés). Des concentrations minimales (creux) ≥ 15 ng/mL sont associées à un nombre accru de réactions indésirables.
- Suivre de près les concentrations sanguines de cholestérol et de triglycérides, car ce médicament peut entraîner l'hyperlipidémie. Il peut s'avérer nécessaire de recourir à des interventions supplémentaires pour traiter ce trouble.
- Le sirolimus peut entraîner l'anémie, la leucopénie, la thrombopénie et l'hypokaliémie.

DIAGNOSTICS INFIRMIERS POSSIBLES

- Risque d'infection (Réactions indésirables).
- Connaissances insuffisantes sur le traitement médicamenteux (Enseignement au patient et à ses proches).

INTERVENTIONS INFIRMIÈRES

- Le traitement par le sirolimus devrait être amorcé aussitôt que possible après la transplantation. Il est recommandé d'administrer en concomitance de la cyclosporine et des corticostéroïdes. Le sirolimus devrait être pris 4 heures après la cyclosporine.
- Le sirolimus ne devrait être prescrit que par des médecins expérimentés dans les traitements immunosuppresseurs et qui disposent d'un personnel qualifié et d'installations appropriées pour traiter les patients ayant reçu une greffe de rein.
- Après la transplantation, il est recommandé d'administrer un traitement prophylactique antimicrobien contre la pneumonie à *Pneumocystis carinii* pendant 1 an et contre le cytomégalovirus pendant 3 mois.
- Administrer toujours à la même heure, avec ou sans aliments, à condition de toujours conserver la même habitude. Ne pas servir au patient de jus de pamplemousse ni ne mélanger la solution avec ce jus.
- Pour diluer, retirer la quantité prescrite de médicament du flacon à l'aide de la seringue couleur ambre destinée à l'administration par voie orale. Évacuer le sirolimus de la seringue dans un récipient de verre ou de plastique contenant 60 mL d'eau ou de jus d'orange; ne pas utiliser d'autres liquides. Mélanger vigoureusement pendant 1 minute et demander au patient de boire la préparation immédiatement. Remplir le verre de nouveau avec au moins 120 mL de liquide, mélanger vigoureusement et demander au patient de boire immédiatement le contenu de ce deuxième verre également.
- Garder les flacons au réfrigérateur. La solution peut devenir un peu trouble lorsqu'elle est réfrigérée. Avant de l'utiliser, la laisser reposer à la température ambiante et la mélanger délicatement jusqu'à ce qu'elle redevienne transparente. Le sirolimus peut rester dans la seringue à la température ambiante ou être réfrigéré pendant 24 heures au maximum. La seringue est uniservice; la jeter après usage.

ENSEIGNEMENT AU PATIENT ET À SES PROCHES

- Expliquer au patient qu'il doit prendre le médicament à la même heure tous les jours en respectant rigoureusement la posologie recommandée. Le prévenir qu'il ne doit pas sauter de dose ni remplacer une dose manquée par une double dose. Prévenir le patient qu'il ne doit pas cesser le traitement sans avoir consulté un professionnel de la santé au préalable.
- Expliquer au patient qu'il est possible qu'il doive suivre ce traitement toute sa vie durant pour prévenir le rejet de l'organe transplanté. Passer en revue les symptômes de rejet d'un organe greffé et insister sur le fait qu'il faut prévenir un professionnel de la santé dès que ces symptômes apparaissent.
- Insister sur l'importance des tests de laboratoire, effectués à intervalles fréquents, tout au long du traitement par le sirolimus.
- Expliquer à la patiente le risque de prendre le sirolimus pendant la grossesse. Prévenir la patiente en âge de procréer qu'elle doit utiliser une méthode de contraception efficace avant et pendant le traitement ainsi qu'au cours des 12 semaines qui suivent la fin du traitement.

VÉRIFICATION DE L'EFFICACITÉ THÉRAPEUTIQUE

L'efficacité du traitement peut être démontrée par: la prévention du rejet du rein greffé. ✳

SODIUM, BICARBONATE DE

Bicarbonate de sodium

CLASSIFICATION:

Minéraux et électrolytes (alcalinisant), antiacide

Grossesse – catégorie C

INDICATIONS

PO, IV: Traitement de l'acidose métabolique ■ Alcalinisation de l'urine et stimulation de l'excrétion de certains médicaments en cas de surdosage (phénobarbital, aspirine) ■ Traitement adjuvant de l'hyperkaliémie ■ Prévention de l'insuffisance rénale associée à l'utilisation d'agents de contraste ■ Arrêt cardiaque ■ **PO:** Antiacide ■ Maladies, comme l'insuffisance rénale chronique, nécessitant un traitement prolongé par un agent alcalinisant.

MÉCANISME D'ACTION

Effet alcalinisant grâce à la libération d'ions bicarbonate ■ Par suite de l'administration par voie orale, libération de bicarbonate pouvant neutraliser l'acide gastrique. ***Effets thérapeutiques:*** Alcalinisation ■ Neutralisation de l'acide gastrique.

PHARMACOCINÉTIQUE

Absorption: Par suite de l'administration par voie orale, le bicarbonate en excès est absorbé, ce qui entraîne une alcalose métabolique et l'alcalinisation de l'urine.

S

Distribution: Tous les liquides extracellulaires.

Métabolisme et excrétion: Excrétion rénale.

Demi-vie: Inconnue.

Profil temps-action

(effets thérapeutiques [PO = effet antiacide; IV = alcalinisation])

	Début d'action	Pic	Durée
PO	immédiat	30 min	1 – 3 h
IV	immédiat	rapide	inconnue

CONTRE-INDICATIONS, PRÉCAUTIONS ET MISES EN GARDE

Contre-indications: Alcalose métabolique ou respiratoire ■ Hypocalcémie ■ Perte excessive de chlorure ■ Ingestion d'acides minéraux forts (éviter l'utilisation à titre d'antidote) ■ Régime hyposodé (voie orale, à titre d'antiacide seulement) ■ Insuffisance rénale (voie orale, à titre d'antiacide seulement) ■ Douleurs abdominales graves d'étiologie inconnue, surtout en présence de fièvre (voie orale, à titre d'antiacide seulement).

Précautions et mises en garde: Insuffisance cardiaque ■ Insuffisance rénale ■ Traitement concomitant par des glucocorticoïdes ■ Utilisation prolongée à titre d'antiacide (risque d'alcalose métabolique et de surcharge sodique).

RÉACTIONS INDÉSIRABLES ET EFFETS SECONDAIRES

CV: œdème.

GI: *PO* – flatulence, distension abdominale.

HÉ: alcalose métabolique, hypernatrémie, hypocalcémie, hypokaliémie, rétention hydrosodée.

Locaux: irritation au point d'injection.

SN: tétanie.

INTERACTIONS

Médicament-médicament: Par suite de l'administration par voie orale, le bicarbonate de sodium peut diminuer l'absorption du **kétoconazole** ■ Les **antiacides à base de calcium**, administrés simultanément, peuvent provoquer le syndrome du lait et des alcalins ■ L'alcalinisation de l'urine peut entraîner la diminution des concentrations sanguines de **salicylates** ou de **barbituriques** et l'élévation des concentrations sanguines de **quinidine**, de **mexilétine**, de **flécaïnide** ou d'**amphétamines** ■ Risque accru de cristallurie lors de l'administration concomitante de **fluoroquinolones** ■ Le bicarbonate de sodium diminue l'efficacité de la **méthénamine** ■ Le bicarbonate de sodium peut inhiber les effets protecteurs des **médicaments entérosolubles** (espacer l'administration de ces médicaments de 1 ou 2 heures).

VOIES D'ADMINISTRATION ET POSOLOGIE

84 mg de bicarbonate de sodium = 1 mmol.

Alcalinisation de l'urine

- **PO (adultes):** Initialement, 48 mmol (4 g); puis de 12 à 24 mmol (de 1 à 2 g), toutes les 4 heures (jusqu'à 48 mmol, toutes les 4 heures).
- **PO (enfants):** De 1 à 10 mmol/kg (de 12 à 120 mg/kg) par jour, en doses fractionnées.

Effet antiacide

- **PO (adultes):** *Comprimés ou poudre* – de 325 mg à 2 g, de 1 à 4 fois par jour, ou ½ cuillerée à thé, toutes les 2 heures, selon les besoins. *Poudre effervescente* – de 3,9 à 10 g dans de l'eau, après les repas; les patients > 60 ans ne devraient prendre que de 1,9 à 3,9 g, après les repas.

Alcalinisation par voie systémique/arrêt cardiaque

- **IV (adultes et enfants > 2 ans):** *Arrêt cardiaque et situations d'urgence* – 1 mmol/kg; on peut administrer une dose de 0,5 mmol/kg, toutes les 10 minutes. *Situations moins urgentes* – de 2 à 5 mmol/kg, en perfusion pendant 4 à 8 heures.

Prévention de l'insuffisance rénale associée à l'administration d'agents de contraste

- IV (adultes): 150 mmol dans 850 mL D5%E, à un débit de 3 mL/kg, pendant l'heure qui précède l'examen, puis 1 mL/kg, pendant les 6 heures qui suivent l'examen.

PRÉSENTATION (version générique disponible)

Nombreuses préparations de concentrations différentes destinées à l'administration orale et parentérale.

SOINS INFIRMIERS

ÉVALUATION DE LA SITUATION

IV:

- Suivre de près, pendant toute la durée du traitement, l'équilibre hydrique, incluant le bilan des ingesta et des excreta; mesurer le poids du patient; rechercher la présence d'un œdème et d'un murmure vésiculaire. Signaler les symptômes suivants de surcharge liquidienne: hypertension, œdème, dyspnée, râles et crépitations, crachats mousseux.
- Observer le patient pendant toute la durée du traitement pour déceler les signes et les symptômes d'acidose (désorientation, céphalées, faiblesse, dyspnée, hyperventilation), d'alcalose (confusion, irritabilité, paresthésie, tétanie, mode de respiration inefficace), d'hypernatrémie (œdème, gain pondéral, hypertension, tachycardie, fièvre, rougeurs de la peau, irritabilité) ou d'hypokaliémie (faiblesse, fatigue, apparition d'ondes U sur le tracé de l'ÉCG, arythmies, polyurie, polydipsie).
- Observer attentivement le point d'injection IV. Éviter l'extravasation en raison des risques d'irritation tissulaire ou de cellulite. En cas d'infiltration, demander au médecin ou à un autre professionnel de la santé si l'on peut appliquer des compresses chaudes et infiltrer le point d'injection avec de la lidocaïne ou de l'hyaluronidase.

Antiacide: Suivre de près les douleurs épigastriques et abdominales, et la présence de sang franc ou occulte dans les selles, les vomissements ou les échantillons prélevés par aspiration gastrique.

Tests de laboratoire:

- Noter, avant le traitement et à intervalles réguliers pendant toute sa durée, les concentrations de sodium, de potassium, de calcium et de bicarbonate, l'osmolarité sérique, l'équilibre acidobasique ainsi que les résultats des tests de la fonction rénale.
- Dans les situations d'urgence et lors de l'administration parentérale, déterminer à intervalles fréquents les concentrations de gaz artériels.
- Noter à intervalles fréquents le pH urinaire lorsque le bicarbonate de sodium est administré pour alcaliniser l'urine.
- Le bicarbonate de sodium inhibe les effets de la pentagastrine et de l'histamine lors des tests d'exploration de la sécrétion gastrique. En éviter l'administration dans les 24 heures qui précèdent ce test.

DIAGNOSTICS INFIRMIERS POSSIBLES

- Échanges gazeux perturbés (Indications).
- Excès de volume liquidien (Effets secondaires).
- Connaissances insuffisantes sur le traitement médicamenteux (Enseignement au patient et à ses proches).

INTERVENTIONS INFIRMIÈRES

- Le bicarbonate de sodium peut entraîner la dissolution prématurée des comprimés à enrobage entérique dans l'estomac.

PO:

- Les comprimés doivent être pris avec un grand verre d'eau.
- Lorsque le bicarbonate de sodium est administré dans le cadre du traitement de l'ulcère gastroduodénal, le patient peut le prendre 1 et 3 heures après les repas et au coucher.

S

IV directe: En cas d'arrêt cardiaque, administrer par IV directe. Afin d'administrer la dose exacte, utiliser des ampoules prédosées ou des seringues préremplies. Les doses doivent être établies d'après les concentrations des gaz artériels. On peut répéter l'administration toutes les 10 minutes.

Vitesse d'administration: On peut aussi administrer le médicament par bolus intraveineux rapide. Rincer la tubulure IV avant et après l'administration pour prévenir la formation d'un précipité par les médicaments incompatibles, administrés pour le traitement de l'arrêt cardiaque.

Perfusion continue: On peut diluer le médicament dans une solution de dextrose, dans du soluté salin ou dans une association de dextrose et de soluté salin.

Vitesse d'administration: On peut administrer le médicament pendant 4 à 8 heures. Consulter les directives du fabricant avant d'administrer la préparation.

Compatibilité (tubulure en Y): acyclovir ■ amifostine ■ asparaginase ■ aztréonam ■ céfépime ■ ceftriaxone ■ cyclophosphamide ■ cytarabine ■ daunorubicine ■ dexaméthasone ■ doxorubicine ■ étoposide ■ famotidine ■ filgrastim ■ fludarabine ■ gallium, nitrate de ■ granisétron ■ héparine ■ ifosfamide ■ indométhacine ■ insuline ■ melphalan ■ mesna ■ morphine ■ paclitaxel ■ pipéracilline/tazobactam ■ potassium, chlorure de ■ tacrolimus ■ téniposide ■ thiotépa ■ tolazoline ■ vancomycine ■ vitamines du complexe B avec C.

Incompatibilité (tubulure en Y): amiodarone ■ amrinone ■ calcium, chlorure de ■ idarubicine ■ imipénem/cilastatine ■ leucovorine calcique ■ midazolam ■ nalbuphine ■ ondansétron ■ oxacilline ■ sargramostim ■ vérapamil ■ vincristine ■ vinorelbine.

Incompatibilité en addition au soluté: Ne pas ajouter à une solution de Ringer ou de lactate de Ringer ni à des produits Ionosol, car la compatibilité varie selon les concentrations.

ENSEIGNEMENT AU PATIENT ET À SES PROCHES

- Conseiller au patient de respecter rigoureusement la posologie recommandée. S'il n'a pas pu prendre le médicament au moment habituel, il doit le prendre aussitôt que possible à moins que ce ne soit presque l'heure prévue pour la dose suivante.
- Expliquer au patient qui suit un traitement prolongé les symptômes d'un déséquilibre électrolytique; lui conseiller de prévenir un professionnel de la santé si ces symptômes se manifestent.
- Recommander au patient de ne pas consommer de produits laitiers en même temps que ce médicament afin de prévenir la formation de calculs rénaux ou l'hypercalcémie (syndrome du lait et des alcalins).
- Insister sur l'importance des examens de suivi réguliers pour déterminer les concentrations sériques d'électrolytes et l'équilibre acidobasique, et pour évaluer les bienfaits du traitement.

Antiacide:

- Recommander au patient d'éviter l'utilisation régulière de bicarbonate de sodium en cas d'indigestion. La dyspepsie qui persiste pendant plus de 2 semaines devrait faire l'objet d'un examen mené par un professionnel de la santé.
- Recommander au patient qui suit un régime hyposodé d'éviter de prendre du bicarbonate de soude pour traiter l'indigestion.
- Conseiller au patient de prévenir un professionnel de la santé si l'indigestion s'accompagne de douleurs thoraciques, de difficultés respiratoires ou de diaphorèse, ou si ses selles deviennent foncées et goudronneuses.

VÉRIFICATION DE L'EFFICACITÉ THÉRAPEUTIQUE

L'efficacité du traitement peut être démontrée par: l'élévation du pH urinaire ■ l'amélioration de l'acidose sur le plan clinique ■ l'augmentation de l'excrétion des substances nocives en cas d'empoisonnement ou de surdosage ■ la diminution de la gêne gastrique. ✳

ALERTE CLINIQUE

SODIUM, CHLORURE DE

Chlorure de sodium

CLASSIFICATION:

Minéraux et électrolytes (solution de remplissage vasculaire)

Grossesse – catégorie C

INDICATIONS

IV: Hydratation et apport de NaCl en cas de carence ■ Maintien de l'équilibre hydroélectrolytique en cas de pertes marquées (diurèse excessive ou régime hyposodé strict) ■ La solution à 0,45 % (« soluté demi-salin ») est plus souvent utilisée pour l'hydratation et pour le traitement du diabète hyperosmolaire ■ La solution à 0,9 % (« soluté normal ») est utilisée dans les cas suivants: solution de remplissage vasculaire ■ traitement de l'alcalose métabolique ■ liquide d'amorce lors des hémodialyses ■ liquide de remplacement au début et à la fin des transfusions sanguines ■ Petits volumes de chlorure de sodium à 0,9 % (sans agent de conservation ni agent bactériostatique) – reconstitution ou dilution d'autres médicaments ■ La solution hypertonique (à 3 % ou à 5 %) peut être administrée lorsqu'une réplétion sodique rapide s'avère nécessaire, comme dans les cas suivants: hyponatrémie ■ hypochlorémie ■ insuffisance rénale ■ insuffisance cardiaque ■ **PO:** Prévention ou traitement de la déplétion volémique attribuable à une restriction sodée ou à un coup de chaleur en cas de transpiration excessive lors de l'exposition à des températures très élevées ■ **Solutions d'irrigation:** Les solutions à 0,9 % et à 0,45 % peuvent être utilisées comme solutions d'irrigation ■ **Préparations nasales:** Traitement de la congestion, de la sécheresse ou de l'irritation des voies nasales.

MÉCANISME D'ACTION

Le sodium, principal cation du liquide extracellulaire, permet de maintenir la distribution de l'eau dans l'organisme, l'équilibre hydroélectrolytique, l'équilibre acidobasique et la pression osmotique ■ Le chlorure, principal anion du liquide extracellulaire, favorise le maintien de l'équilibre acidobasique. Les solutions de NaCl ressemblent au liquide extracellulaire ■ Diminution de l'œdème cornéen par effet osmotique. **Effets thérapeutiques - IV, PO**: Traitement de substitution en cas de carence et maintien de l'homéostasie.

PHARMACOCINÉTIQUE

Absorption: Bonne (PO). Les solutions de remplacement à base de chlorure de sodium (NaCl) sont réservées à l'administration IV.

Distribution: Répartition rapide dans tout l'organisme.

Métabolisme et excrétion: Excrétion principalement rénale.

Demi-vie: Inconnue.

Profil temps-action (effets cliniques)†

	DÉBUT D'ACTION	PIC	DURÉE
PO	inconnu	inconnu	inconnue
IV	rapide (quelques min)	fin de la perfusion	inconnue

† Effets sur les électrolytes.

CONTRE-INDICATIONS, PRÉCAUTIONS ET MISES EN GARDE

Contre-indications: Solution IV - Les solutions hypertoniques (à 3 % et à 5 %) ne devraient pas être utilisées chez les patients présentant des concentrations sériques de sodium élevées, légèrement réduites ou normales ■ Rétention hydrique ou hypernatrémie.

Précautions et mises en garde: IV - Patients prédisposés à des anomalies métaboliques ou à des déséquilibres acidobasiques ou hydroélectrolytiques, incluant: les personnes âgées ■ les patients intubés (aspiration gastrique par voie nasale) ■ les patients qui vomissent ■ les patients qui ont la diarrhée ■ les patients qui suivent un traitement par des diurétiques ■ les patients prenant des glucocorticoïdes ■ les patients qui présentent des fistules ■ les insuffisants cardiaques ■ les patients souffrant d'insuffisance rénale grave ■ les patients atteints de maladies hépatiques graves (l'administration d'électrolytes supplémentaires peut s'avérer nécessaire) ■ **PÉD.**: Ne pas administrer les solutions de NaCl bactériostatiques contenant de l'alcool benzylique aux nouveau-nés ■ **PO -** Hydratation inadéquate (l'eau et les autres électrolytes doivent être remplacés).

RÉACTIONS INDÉSIRABLES ET EFFETS SECONDAIRES

Les effets sont observés principalement au cours de l'administration par voie PO et IV.

CV: INSUFFISANCE CARDIAQUE, ŒDÈME PULMONAIRE, œdème.

HÉ: hypernatrémie, hypervolémie, hypokaliémie.

Locaux: *IV* – extravasation, irritation au point d'injection IV.

INTERACTIONS

Médicament-médicament: Les quantités excessives de NaCl peuvent contrecarrer partiellement les effets des **antihypertenseurs** ■ L'utilisation concomitante de **corticostéroïdes** peut entraîner une rétention sodique excessive.

VOIES D'ADMINISTRATION ET POSOLOGIE

- **IV (adultes)**: *NaCl 0,9 % (isotonique)* – 1 L (contient 150 mmol de sodium par litre); déterminer la vitesse d'administration et la quantité à administrer compte tenu de la maladie qu'il faut traiter. *NaCl 0,45 % (hypotonique)* – de 1 à 2 L (contient 75 mmol de sodium par litre); déterminer la vitesse d'administration et la quantité à administrer compte tenu de la maladie à traiter. *NaCl 3 % ou 5 % (hypertonique)* – 100 mL pendant 1 heure (la solution à 3 % contient 50 mmol de sodium par 100 mL; la solution à 5 % contient 83,3 mmol de sodium par 100 mL).
- **PO (adultes)**: De 1 à 2 g, 3 fois par jour, selon les besoins.
- **Voie intranasale (adultes)**: De 1 à 3 vaporisations ou 2 ou 3 gouttes, de 1 à 3 fois par jour.
- **Voie intranasale (enfants)**: 1 vaporisation ou 1 goutte, de 1 à 3 fois par jour.

S

PRÉSENTATION
(version générique disponible)

Nombreuses préparations de concentrations différentes pour irrigation, inhalation, administration orale et parentérale.

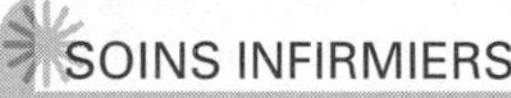

SOINS INFIRMIERS

ÉVALUATION DE LA SITUATION

- EFFECTUER LE BILAN HYDROÉLECTROLYTIQUE (INGESTA ET EXCRETA, POIDS QUOTIDIEN, PRÉSENCE D'ŒDÈME, MURMURE VÉSICULAIRE) PENDANT TOUTE LA DURÉE DU TRAITEMENT.

- Observer le patient pendant toute la durée du traitement pour déceler les signes et les symptômes d'hyponatrémie (céphalées, tachycardie, lassitude, sécheresse des muqueuses, nausées, vomissements, crampes musculaires) ou d'hypernatrémie (œdème, gain pondéral, hypertension, tachycardie, fièvre, rougeur de la peau, irritabilité). On mesure le sodium en fonction de sa concentration dans les liquides organiques; les symptômes peuvent donc changer selon le degré d'hydratation du patient.

Tests de laboratoire:

- Noter à intervalles réguliers, pendant toute la durée du traitement prolongé au chlorure de sodium, les concentrations sériques de sodium, de potassium, de bicarbonate et de chlorure ainsi que l'équilibre acidobasique.
- Noter l'osmolarité sérique chez les patients recevant des solutés salins hypertoniques.

DIAGNOSTICS INFIRMIERS POSSIBLES

- Déficit de volume liquidien (Indications).
- Excès de volume liquidien (Effets secondaires).

INTERVENTIONS INFIRMIÈRES

ALERTE CLINIQUE: L'ADMINISTRATION ACCIDENTELLE DE SOLUTIONS HYPERTONIQUES A ENTRAÎNÉ DE SÉRIEUX DÉSÉQUILIBRES ÉLECTROLYTIQUES. NE PAS CONFONDRE LES FIOLES DE CHLORURE DE SODIUM CONCENTRÉ (23,4 %) AVEC LES FIOLES DE CHLORURE DE SODIUM DESTINÉ À LA DILUTION (0,9 %).

- La concentration de NaCl à utiliser dépend de l'âge du patient, de son poids, de son état et de l'équilibre hydroélectrolytique et acidobasique.

PÉD.: Ne pas administrer à des nouveau-nés une solution de chlorure de sodium bactériostatique contenant de l'alcool benzylique comme agent de conservation. Ne pas utiliser une telle solution pour reconstituer ou diluer une autre solution, ou pour rincer les cathéters intravasculaires destinés aux nouveau-nés.

S

- La solution de NaCl 0,45 % pour perfusion est hypotonique; la solution de NaCl 0,9 % pour perfusion est isotonique et les solutions à 3 % et à 5 % sont hypertoniques.

Perfusion intermittente: Administrer la solution de NaCl 3 % ou 5 % dans une grosse veine et prévenir l'infiltration. Après la perfusion des 100 premiers millilitres, réévaluer les concentrations de sodium, de chlorure et de bicarbonate afin de déterminer s'il est nécessaire de poursuivre l'administration. Consulter les directives du fabricant avant d'administrer la préparation.

Vitesse d'administration: La vitesse de perfusion des solutions de NaCl hypertoniques ne devrait pas dépasser 100 mL/h.

Compatibilité en addition au soluté: D5%E ▪ D10%E ▪ solution de Ringer ou de lactate de Ringer pour injection ▪ solution de dextrose et de lactate de Ringer en association ▪ solution de dextrose et de soluté salin en association ▪ solution de lactate de sodium à 1/6 M.

ENSEIGNEMENT AU PATIENT ET À SES PROCHES

- Expliquer au patient le but de la perfusion.
- Prévenir le patient qu'il s'expose au risque de se déshydrater par temps très chaud; lui expliquer à quel moment et de quelle façon il doit prendre les comprimés de NaCl. Prévenir aussi le patient que des comprimés non digérés peuvent se retrouver dans les selles. Lui recommander d'utiliser plutôt des solutions d'électrolytes à prendre par voie orale.

VÉRIFICATION DE L'EFFICACITÉ THÉRAPEUTIQUE

L'efficacité du traitement peut être démontrée par: la prévention de la déshydratation ou le rétablissement de l'équilibre hydrique ▪ la normalisation des concentrations sériques de sodium et de chlorure ▪ la prévention des coups de chaleur en cas d'exposition à des températures très élevées.

SODIUM, CITRATE DE, ET ACIDE CITRIQUE

PMS-Dicitrate

CLASSIFICATION:

Antiurolithique, minéraux et électrolytes (alcalinisant)

Grossesse – catégorie C

INDICATIONS

Traitement de l'acidose métabolique chronique associée à l'insuffisance rénale chronique ou à l'acidose tubulaire rénale ▪ Alcalinisation de l'urine ▪ Prévention de la formation de calculs de cystine et de calculs d'urate dans l'urine ▪ Prévention de la pneumonie d'aspiration au cours d'une intervention chirurgicale ▪ Tampon neutralisant.

MÉCANISME D'ACTION

Transformation en bicarbonate dans l'organisme, ce qui entraîne une élévation du pH sanguin ▪ Alcalinisation de l'urine par suite de l'excrétion rénale du bicarbonate, ce qui augmente la solubilité de la cystine et de l'acide urique ▪ Neutralisation de l'acide gastrique.

Effets thérapeutiques: Apport de bicarbonate en cas d'acidose métabolique ▪ Alcalinisation de l'urine ▪ Prévention de la formation de calculs de cystine et de calculs d'urate dans l'urine ▪ Prévention de la pneumonie d'aspiration.

PHARMACOCINÉTIQUE

Absorption: Bonne (PO).

Distribution: Répartition rapide dans tout l'organisme.

Métabolisme et excrétion: L'agent est rapidement transformé en bicarbonate par oxydation; le bicarbonate est excrété principalement par les reins. Excrétion pulmonaire faible (5 % à l'état inchangé).

Demi-vie: Inconnue.

Profil temps-action (effets sur le pH sérique)

	DÉBUT D'ACTION	PIC	DURÉE
PO	rapide (quelques min à quelques h)	inconnu	4-6 h

CONTRE-INDICATIONS, PRÉCAUTIONS ET MISES EN GARDE

Contre-indications: Insuffisance rénale grave ▪ Régime hyposodé strict ▪ Insuffisance cardiaque, hypertension non traitée, œdème ou toxémie de la grossesse.

Précautions et mises en garde: **OBST., ALLAITEMENT:** L'innocuité du médicament n'a pas été établie.

RÉACTIONS INDÉSIRABLES ET EFFETS SECONDAIRES

GI: diarrhée.

HÉ: surcharge liquidienne, hypernatrémie (insuffisance rénale grave), hypocalcémie, alcalose métabolique (doses élevées seulement).

Loc.: tétanie.

INTERACTIONS

Médicament-médicament: L'agent peut contrecarrer partiellement les effets des **antihypertenseurs** ▪ L'alcalinisation de l'urine peut entraîner la diminution des concentrations sanguines de **salicylates** ou de **barbituriques**, ou l'élévation des concentrations sanguines de **quinidine**, de **flécaïnide** ou d'**amphétamines**.

VOIES D'ADMINISTRATION ET POSOLOGIE

Adapter la dose selon le pH de l'urine. PMS-Dicitrate contient 1 mmol de sodium et est équivalent à 1 mmol de bicarbonate par mL de solution.

Alcalinisation

- **PO (adultes):** De 10 à 30 mL (de 1 à 3 g) de solution diluée dans de l'eau, 4 fois par jour.
- **PO (enfants):** De 5 à 10 mL (de 0,5 à 1 g) de solution diluée dans de l'eau, 4 fois par jour.

Effet antiurolithique

- **PO (adultes):** De 10 à 30 mL (de 1 à 3 g) de solution diluée dans de l'eau, 4 fois par jour.

Tampon neutralisant

- **PO (adultes):** De 15 à 30 mL (de 1,5 à 3 g) de solution diluée dans 15 à 30 mL d'eau.

PRÉSENTATION

Solution orale: 500 mg de citrate de sodium/334 mg d'acide citrique/5 mL[Pr].

SOINS INFIRMIERS

ÉVALUATION DE LA SITUATION

- Observer le patient pendant toute la durée du traitement pour déceler les signes et les symptômes d'alcalose (confusion, irritabilité, paresthésie, tétanie, mode de respiration inefficace) ou d'hypernatrémie (œdème, gain pondéral, hypertension, tachycardie, fièvre, rougeur de la peau, irritabilité).
- Suivre de près le patient souffrant d'insuffisance rénale pour déceler les signes et les symptômes suivants de surcharge liquidienne: écart entre les ingesta et les excreta, gain pondéral, œdème, râles et crépitations, hypertension.

Tests de laboratoire:

- Noter, avant l'administration et tous les 4 mois pendant toute la durée d'un traitement prolongé, l'hématocrite, les concentrations d'hémoglobine et d'électrolytes, le pH, les concentrations de créatinine, le résultat de l'analyse des urines ainsi que celui de l'analyse des urines de 24 heures, pour déterminer les concentrations de citrate.
- Déterminer le pH urinaire lorsque l'agent est utilisé pour l'alcalinisation de l'urine.

DIAGNOSTICS INFIRMIERS POSSIBLES

- Connaissances insuffisantes sur le traitement médicamenteux (Enseignement au patient et à ses proches).

INTERVENTIONS INFIRMIÈRES

- La solution a meilleur goût si elle est froide. Il faut l'administrer avec 30 à 90 mL d'eau glacée, 30 minutes après les repas ou avec la collation que le patient prend avant de se coucher afin de réduire l'effet laxatif du soluté salin.

- Lorsque l'agent est administré avant l'anesthésie, demander au patient de prendre de 15 à 30 mL de citrate de sodium avec 15 à 30 mL d'eau glacée.

ENSEIGNEMENT AU PATIENT ET À SES PROCHES

- Conseiller au patient de respecter rigoureusement la posologie recommandée. S'il n'a pas pu prendre le médicament au moment habituel, il doit le prendre dans les 2 heures qui suivent. Le prévenir qu'il ne doit jamais remplacer une dose manquée par une double dose.
- Montrer au patient qui suit un traitement prolongé au citrate de sodium comment mesurer le pH urinaire et comment maintenir l'alcalinité de l'urine. Lui recommander d'augmenter sa consommation de liquides jusqu'à 3 000 mL par jour. Lorsque le traitement est arrêté, le pH commence à diminuer et finit par revenir aux valeurs notées avant le traitement.
- Recommander au patient recevant un traitement prolongé d'éviter de consommer des aliments salés.

VÉRIFICATION DE L'EFFICACITÉ THÉRAPEUTIQUE

L'efficacité du traitement peut être démontrée par: la correction de l'acidose métabolique ■ le maintien de l'alcalinité de l'urine, diminuant ainsi la formation de calculs ■ la neutralisation du pH des sécrétions gastriques, ce qui permet de prévenir la pneumonie d'aspiration associée à l'intubation et à l'anesthésie. ✳

SODIUM (NITROPRUSSIATE DE),

voir Nitroprusside

SODIUM, PHOSPHATE DE

Phosphate de sodium

CLASSIFICATION:

Minéraux et électrolytes (supplément de phosphate)

Grossesse – catégorie C

INDICATIONS

Traitement et prévention du déficit en phosphate chez les patients incapables d'absorber une quantité suffisante de phosphate d'origine alimentaire.

MÉCANISME D'ACTION

Élément présent dans les os et participant au transport d'énergie et au métabolisme des glucides ■ Tampon servant à l'excrétion des ions hydrogène par les reins. ***Effets thérapeutiques:*** Supplément de phosphore en cas de carence.

PHARMACOCINÉTIQUE

Absorption: Biodisponibilité à 100 % (IV).
Distribution: Le phosphore pénètre dans les liquides extracellulaires d'où il est acheminé vers son lieu d'action par transport actif.
Métabolisme et excrétion: *IV* – excrétion rénale (> 90 %).
Demi-vie: Inconnue.

Profil temps-action (effets thérapeutiques:
IV – effets sur les concentrations sériques de phosphate)

	DÉBUT D'ACTION	PIC	DURÉE
IV	rapide (de quelques min à quelques h)	fin de la perfusion	inconnue

CONTRE-INDICATIONS, PRÉCAUTIONS ET MISES EN GARDE

Contre-indications: Hyperphosphatémie ■ Hypocalcémie ■ Insuffisance rénale grave.
Précautions et mises en garde: Hyperparathyroïdie ■ Maladie cardiaque ■ Hypernatrémie ■ Hypertension.

RÉACTIONS INDÉSIRABLES ET EFFETS SECONDAIRES

Sauf indication contraire, les réactions indésirables et les effets secondaires suivants sont liés à l'hyperphosphatémie.
SNC: confusion, apragmatisme, faiblesse.
Resp.: *hypernatrémie* – essoufflement.
CV: ARYTHMIES, ARRÊT CARDIAQUE, modifications de l'ÉCG (absence des ondes P, élargissement du complexe QRS avec courbe biphasique), hypotension; *hypernatrémie* – œdème.
GI: <u>diarrhée</u>, <u>douleurs abdominales</u>, nausées, vomissements.
HÉ: hypernatrémie, hyperphosphatémie, hypocalcémie, hypomagnésémie.
Locaux: irritation au point d'injection IV, phlébite.
Loc.: *hypocalcémie* – tremblements.
SN: paralysie flasque, jambes lourdes, paresthésie des membres.

INTERACTIONS

Médicament-médicament: Les **corticostéroïdes**, administrés simultanément, peuvent entraîner une hypernatrémie.

VOIES D'ADMINISTRATION ET POSOLOGIE

- **IV (adultes)**: De 12 à 15 mmol de phosphore/L de solution d'alimentation, administrés par voie parentérale.

Hypophosphatémie

- **IV (adultes)**: De 0,025 à 0,5 mmol/kg, en perfusion, pendant 4 à 6 heures (selon la gravité de l'état).

PRÉSENTATION (version générique disponible)

Injection IV pour dilution: 3 mmol de phosphate et 4 mmol de sodium/mL, en fioles de 10 mL[Pr].

SOINS INFIRMIERS

ÉVALUATION DE LA SITUATION

- Observer le patient pendant toute la durée du traitement pour déceler les signes et les symptômes suivants d'hypophosphatémie: anorexie, faiblesse, diminution des réflexes, douleurs osseuses, confusion, dyscrasie sanguine.
- Effectuer le bilan quotidien des ingesta et des excreta, et peser le patient tous les jours. Signaler tout écart important à un autre professionnel de la santé.

Tests de laboratoire:

- Noter les concentrations sériques de phosphate, de potassium, de sodium et de calcium, avant le traitement et à intervalles réguliers pendant toute sa durée. L'élévation des concentrations de phosphate peut entraîner l'hypocalcémie.
- Examiner les résultats des tests de la fonction rénale, avant le traitement et à intervalles réguliers pendant toute sa durée.

Toxicité et surdosage: Les symptômes de toxicité sont les mêmes qu'en cas d'hyperphosphatémie ou d'hypocalcémie (paresthésie, soubresauts musculaires, laryngospasme, coliques, arythmies cardiaques, signe de Chvostek ou de Trousseau) ou d'hypernatrémie (soif, sécheresse et rougeur de la peau, fièvre, tachycardie, hypotension, irritabilité, diminution du débit urinaire).

DIAGNOSTICS INFIRMIERS POSSIBLES

- Alimentation déficiente (Indications).
- Connaissances insuffisantes sur le traitement médicamenteux (Enseignement au patient et à ses proches).

INTERVENTIONS INFIRMIÈRES

- Le phosphate de sodium est présenté sous forme orale en association avec le phosphate de potassium pour acidifier l'urine et pour prévenir la formation de calculs rénaux (voir aussi Potassium, phosphate de).

IV: Administration réservée à la voie IV; diluer les solutions et perfuser lentement. Consulter les directives du fabricant avant d'administrer la préparation.

Vitesse d'administration: Administrer à une vitesse maximale de 7,5 mmol/h de phosphate.

Incompatibilité en addition au soluté: calcium ■ magnésium.

ENSEIGNEMENT AU PATIENT ET À SES PROCHES

- Expliquer au patient le but du traitement et lui conseiller de respecter rigoureusement la posologie recommandée. S'il n'a pas pu prendre le médicament au moment habituel, il doit le prendre aussitôt que possible à moins que ce ne soit presque l'heure prévue pour la dose suivante.

VÉRIFICATION DE L'EFFICACITÉ THÉRAPEUTIQUE

L'efficacité du traitement peut être démontrée par: la prévention et la correction des déficits en phosphate sérique.

SOLIFÉNACINE

Vesicare

CLASSIFICATION:

Anticholinergique (antispasmodique urinaire)

Grossesse – catégorie C

INDICATIONS

Traitement de l'hyperactivité vésicale chez l'adulte qui présente des symptômes d'incontinence urinaire par impériosités vésicales, d'urgence mictionnelle et de pollakiurie (mictions fréquentes).

MÉCANISME D'ACTION

Antagoniste compétitif des récepteurs muscariniques, doté d'une sélectivité pour les récepteurs de la vessie ■ Effets antagonistes sur la contraction des muscles lisses de la vessie. ***Effets thérapeutiques:*** Diminution des symptômes d'hyperactivité vésicale.

PHARMACOCINÉTIQUE

Absorption: Biodisponibilité à 90 % (PO).

Distribution: Distribution importante dans les tissus autres que ceux du SNC.

S

Liaison aux protéines plasmatiques: 98 %.

Métabolisme et excrétion: Métabolisme hépatique important, principalement sous l'effet de l'isoenzyme CYP3A4 du cytochrome P450. Élimination rénale (69 %) et fécale (22,5 %).

Demi-vie: De 45 à 68 heures.

Profil temps-action (amélioration clinique)

	DÉBUT D'ACTION	PIC	DURÉE
PO	2 semaines	au moins 4 semaines	moins de 2 semaines après l'arrêt du traitement

CONTRE-INDICATIONS, PRÉCAUTIONS ET MISES EN GARDE

Contre-indications: Hypersensibilité ▪ Rétention urinaire ▪ Insuffisance rénale nécessitant une dialyse ▪ Gastroparésie ▪ Glaucome à angle fermé.

Précautions et mises en garde: Obstruction vésicale (aggravation possible des symptômes de rétention urinaire) ▪ Patients ayant de la difficulté à transpirer (risque de prostration due à la chaleur) ▪ Patients présentant un allongement congénital ou acquis de l'intervalle QT/QT_c ou des troubles électrolytiques, ceux qui prennent des médicaments pouvant allonger cet intervalle (p. ex., plusieurs antiarythmiques) ou ceux qui utilisent des inhibiteurs puissants du CYP3A4 ▪ Motilité gastro-intestinale ralentie ▪ Troubles digestifs occlusifs (p. ex., sténose du pylore), constipation grave et colite ulcéreuse en raison du risque d'occlusion gastro-intestinale ▪ Insuffisance hépatique modérée (limiter la dose à 5 mg par jour) ▪ Insuffisance hépatique grave (usage déconseillé) ▪ Insuffisance rénale grave – $Cl_{Cr} < 30$ *mL/min* (limiter la dose à 5 mg par jour) ▪ **OBST., ALLAITEMENT:** L'innocuité du médicament n'a pas été établie ▪ **PÉD.:** L'innocuité et l'efficacité du médicament n'ont pas été établies ▪ Myasthénie grave.

S

RÉACTIONS INDÉSIRABLES ET EFFETS SECONDAIRES

SNC: fatigue.

ORLO: sécheresse oculaire, vision trouble.

GI: constipation, sécheresse de la bouche (xérostomie), nausées, vomissements, dyspepsie, douleurs abdominales, élévation des enzymes hépatiques (rare), FÉCALOME, OBSTRUCTION DU CÔLON, OBSTRUCTION INTESTINALE.

GU: infection des voies urinaires, RÉTENTION URINAIRE AIGUË.

Métab.: œdème des membres inférieurs.

INTERACTIONS

Médicament-médicament: L'administration de la solifénacine avec d'autres médicaments **dotés de propriétés anticholinergiques** pourrait donner lieu à des effets thérapeutiques plus prononcés et à des réactions indésirables. Un intervalle d'environ 1 semaine doit être prévu entre l'arrêt du traitement par la solifénacine et le début d'un autre traitement anticholinergique ▪ L'effet thérapeutique de la solifénacine peut être atténué par l'administration concomitante d'**agonistes des récepteurs cholinergiques** ▪ La solifénacine peut réduire l'effet des agents qui stimulent la motilité du tractus gastro-intestinal, comme le **métoclopramide** ▪ La biotransformation de la solifénacine dépend principalement de l'isoenzyme CYP3A4 du cytochrome P450. Par conséquent, les **médicaments qui induisent ou qui inhibent le CYP3A4** peuvent modifier la pharmacocinétique de la solifénacine ▪ Le **kétoconazole**, la **clarithromycine**, l'**érythromycine**, le **diclofénac**, le **vérapamil** et d'autres **inhibiteurs puissants du CYP3A4** augmentent le niveau d'exposition à la solifénacine (limiter la dose quotidienne de cette dernière à 5 mg) ▪ Les **médicaments pouvant allonger l'intervalle QT** (p. ex., plusieurs **antiarythmiques**), administrés en concomitance, peuvent allonger encore plus cet intervalle et provoquer des arythmies ▪ Aucun effet notable n'a été signalé avec les médicaments suivants: **digoxine**, **contraceptifs oraux**, **warfarine**.

Médicament-aliments: Le **jus de pamplemousse** pourrait élever les concentrations sériques de solifénacine.

VOIES D'ADMINISTRATION ET POSOLOGIE

▪ **PO (adultes):** 5 mg, 1 fois par jour. La dose peut être portée à 10 mg, 1 fois par jour, selon la réponse du patient.

INSUFFISANCE RÉNALE GRAVE

▪ **PO (ADULTES):** $CL_{CR} < 30$ *mL/MIN* – NE PAS DÉPASSER 5 mg, 1 FOIS PAR JOUR.

INSUFFISANCE HÉPATIQUE

▪ **PO (ADULTES):** *MODÉRÉE (STADE B DE CHILD-PUGH)* – NE PAS DÉPASSER 5 mg, 1 FOIS PAR JOUR; *GRAVE (STADE C DE CHILD-PUGH)* – USAGE DÉCONSEILLÉ.

PRÉSENTATION

Comprimés: 5 mg[Pr], 10 mg[Pr].

SOINS INFIRMIERS

ÉVALUATION DE LA SITUATION

▪ Noter le mode d'élimination urinaire, les symptômes de vessie hyperactive (mictions impérieuses, incontinence urinaire, pollakiurie), faire le bilan des ingesta et des excreta, examiner l'abdomen afin de déceler la distension de la vessie, avant le début du traitement et pendant toute sa durée. Pour évaluer les résidus postmictionnels, on peut procéder à des cathétérismes. La cystométrie permettant de diagnostiquer le type de dysfonctionnement vésical est habituellement effectuée avant que la solifénacine soit prescrite.

Toxicité et surdosage: Le surdosage d'agents anticholinergiques peut provoquer des effets anticholinergiques graves (p. ex., pupilles fixes et dilatées, vision trouble, échec du test talon-orteils, tremblements et sécheresse de la peau). On doit administrer un traitement symptomatique sous étroite surveillance médicale et prendre, au besoin, des mesures de soutien, comme le lavage gastrique, le but visé étant de faire disparaître les symptômes anticholinergiques.

DIAGNOSTICS INFIRMIERS POSSIBLES

- Élimination urinaire altérée (Indications).
- Connaissances insuffisantes sur le traitement médicamenteux (Enseignement au patient et à ses proches).

INTERVENTIONS INFIRMIÈRES

- La solifénacine doit être administrée 1 fois par jour, dans la mesure du possible à la même heure, avec ou sans aliments. Les comprimés doivent être avalés entiers avec des liquides.

ENSEIGNEMENT AU PATIENT ET À SES PROCHES

- Conseiller au patient de respecter rigoureusement la posologie recommandée. Lui conseiller de lire l'information destinée au patient avant de commencer le traitement par ce médicament ainsi qu'à chaque renouvellement d'ordonnance. S'il n'a pas pu prendre le médicament au moment habituel, il doit le prendre dès que possible, à moins que ce ne soit presque l'heure prévue pour la dose suivante. Le prévenir qu'il ne doit pas prendre 2 doses dans la même journée.
- Prévenir le patient qu'il ne doit pas partager son médicament avec d'autres personnes, car cela pourrait être dangereux.
- Conseiller au patient de se rincer fréquemment la bouche, de pratiquer une bonne hygiène buccale et de consommer de la gomme à mâcher ou des bonbons sans sucre pour soulager la sécheresse de la bouche. Lui recommander de consulter un professionnel de la santé si la sécheresse de la bouche persiste pendant plus de 2 semaines.
- Conseiller au patient d'éviter de faire de l'exercice par temps chaud, car la solifénacine peut diminuer sa capacité à transpirer.
- Conseiller au patient de prévenir un professionnel de la santé en cas de rétention urinaire ou de constipation persistante. Lui expliquer qu'il peut prévenir la constipation en adoptant un régime alimentaire riche en fibres, en buvant plus de liquides (si son état le permet) et en faisant de l'exercice.
- Insister sur la nécessité d'un suivi médical constant. On peut effectuer des cystométries à intervalles réguliers, afin d'évaluer l'efficacité du traitement, et des examens ophtalmiques, à intervalles réguliers, afin de déceler tout signe de glaucome, particulièrement chez les patients > 40 ans.
- Prévenir le patient que la solifénacine peut provoquer une vision trouble. Lui conseiller de ne pas conduire et d'éviter les activités qui exigent sa vigilance jusqu'à ce qu'on ait la certitude que le médicament n'entraîne pas cet effet chez lui.
- Recommander au patient de ne pas prendre de médicaments en vente libre, ni de commencer à prendre de nouveaux médicaments ou de cesser la prise de ceux qui lui ont été prescrits sans consulter au préalable un professionnel de la santé.

VÉRIFICATION DE L'EFFICACITÉ THÉRAPEUTIQUE

L'efficacité du traitement peut être démontrée par: le soulagement du spasme de la vessie et des symptômes connexes (mictions fréquentes, mictions impérieuses, nycturie et incontinence) chez les patients présentant une hyperactivité vésicale. ✷

SOMATOTROPHINE (RECOMBINANTE),

voir Hormones de croissance

SOMATREM (RECOMBINANT),

voir Hormones de croissance

SOTALOL

Apo-Sotalol, Gen-Sotalol, Novo-Sotalol, PMS-Sotalol, Ratio-Sotalol, Sotacor

CLASSIFICATION:

Antiarythmique (classes II et III), bêtabloquant

Grossesse – catégories B (1er trimestre) et D (2e et 3e trimestres)

S

INDICATIONS

Traitement des arythmies supraventriculaires et ventriculaires mettant la vie du patient en danger.

MÉCANISME D'ACTION

Inhibition de la stimulation des récepteurs bêta$_1$-adrénergiques (myocardiques) et bêta$_2$-adrénergiques (pulmonaires, vasculaires et utérins). ***Effets thérapeutiques:*** Suppression des arythmies.

PHARMACOCINÉTIQUE

Absorption: De 60 à 100 % (PO).
Distribution: L'agent traverse la barrière placentaire et passe dans le lait maternel.
Métabolisme et excrétion: Excrétion rénale sous forme inchangée.
Demi-vie: De 7 à 18 heures (prolongée en présence d'insuffisance rénale).

Profil temps-action (effets antiarythmiques)

	Début d'action	Pic	Durée
PO	quelques heures	2-3 jours	8-12 h

CONTRE-INDICATIONS, PRÉCAUTIONS ET MISES EN GARDE

Contre-indications: Hypersensibilité ▪ Insuffisance cardiaque non maîtrisée ▪ Œdème pulmonaire ▪ Asthme ▪ Bronchopneumopathie chronique obstructive ▪ Choc cardiogénique ▪ Syndrome congénital ou acquis de l'allongement de l'intervalle QT ▪ Dysfonctionnement grave du nœud sinoauriculaire ▪ Bradycardie sinusale ou bloc AV du 2e ou du 3e degré (à moins qu'un stimulateur cardiaque ne soit installé) ▪ Insuffisance rénale (il est recommandé d'augmenter l'intervalle entre les doses si la Cl_{Cr} est < 60 mL/min).

Précautions et mises en garde: Insuffisance rénale (il est recommandé d'augmenter l'intervalle entre les doses si la Cl_{Cr} est < 60 mL/min) ▪ Patients ayant subi une anesthésie avec des agents qui dépriment le myocarde ▪ **GÉR.**: Il est recommandé de réduire la dose initiale chez les personnes âgées (sensibilité accrue aux bêtabloquants) ▪ Hypokaliémie ou hypomagnésémie (risque accru d'arythmies graves) ▪ Autres maladies pulmonaires ▪ Diabète (le médicament peut masquer les signes d'hypoglycémie) ▪ Thyrotoxicose (le médicament peut en masquer les symptômes) ▪ Antécédents de réactions allergiques graves (le médicament peut accroître l'intensité des réactions) ▪ **OBST., ALLAITEMENT**: L'innocuité du médicament n'a pas été établie chez les femmes enceintes ou qui allaitent ▪ **PÉD.**: L'innocuité et l'efficacité du médicament n'ont pas été établies chez les enfants.

RÉACTIONS INDÉSIRABLES ET EFFETS SECONDAIRES

SNC: fatigue, faiblesse, anxiété, étourdissements, somnolence, insomnie, perte de mémoire, dépression, modification des opérations de la pensée, nervosité, cauchemars.
ORLO: vision trouble, xérophtalmie, congestion nasale.
Resp.: bronchospasme, respiration sifflante.
CV: ARYTHMIES, BRADYCARDIE, INSUFFISANCE CARDIAQUE, ŒDÈME PULMONAIRE, hypotension orthostatique, vasoconstriction périphérique.
GI: constipation, diarrhée, nausées.
GU: impuissance, baisse de la libido.
Tég.: démangeaisons, rash.
End.: hyperglycémie, hypoglycémie.
Loc.: arthralgie, douleurs lombaires, crampes musculaires.
SN: paresthésie.
Divers: syndrome lupique d'origine médicamenteuse.

INTERACTIONS

Médicament-médicament: Il n'est pas recommandé d'administrer en concomitance des **antiarythmiques de la classe 1A** en raison du risque accru d'arythmies ▪ Les **anesthésiques par voie générale**, le **diltiazem** et le **vérapamil**, administrés simultanément, peuvent provoquer une dépression additive du myocarde ▪ Risque de bradycardie additive lors de l'administration concomitante de **glucosides cardiotoniques** ▪ Risque d'hypotension additive lors de l'administration simultanée d'autres **antihypertenseurs** ou de **dérivés nitrés**, ou lors de l'ingestion de grandes quantités d'**alcool** ▪ Les **amphétamines**, la **cocaïne**, l'**éphédrine**, l'**adrénaline**, la **noradrénaline**, la **phényléphrine** ou la **pseudoéphédrine**, prises simultanément, peuvent entraîner une stimulation alpha-adrénergique à laquelle rien ne s'oppose (hypertension et bradycardie excessive) ▪ Risque de perte de l'efficacité de l'**insuline** ou des **hypoglycémiants oraux** (une adaptation posologique peut s'avérer nécessaire) ▪ Le sotalol peut réduire l'efficacité des **bronchodilatateurs bêta-adrénergiques** ▪ Le sotalol peut diminuer les effets bénéfiques sur les récepteurs bêta$_1$-cardiaques de la **dopamine** ou de la **dobutamine** ▪ L'arrêt du traitement par la **clonidine** chez les patients recevant le sotalol peut entraîner une hypertension rebond excessive ▪ La prudence est de mise lorsque le sotalol est administré dans les 14 jours suivant un traitement par un **IMAO** (risque d'hypertension) ▪ Les médicaments qui allongent l'intervalle QT (**amiodarone**, **amitriptyline**, **clarithromycine**, **désipramine**, **dropéridol**, **érythromycine**, **fluconazole**, **gémifloxacine**, **moxifloxacine**, **nortriptyline**, **quétiapine**, **rispé-**

ridone, **télithromycine**), administrés en concomitance, peuvent entraîner des arythmies graves et même mortelles.

VOIES D'ADMINISTRATION ET POSOLOGIE

- **PO (adultes)**: 80 mg, 2 fois par jour; on peut augmenter graduellement la dose selon la réponse au traitement et la tolérance du patient (dose d'entretien habituelle: de 160 à 320 mg par jour, en 2 doses).

INSUFFISANCE RÉNALE

- **PO (ADULTES)**: *Cl_{CR} DE 30 À 59 mL/MIN* – DOSE INITIALE DE 80 mg; ADMINISTRER LES DOSES ULTÉRIEURES TOUTES LES 24 HEURES; *Cl_{CR} DE 10 À 29 mL/MIN* – DOSE INITIALE DE 80 mg; ADMINISTRER LES DOSES ULTÉRIEURES TOUTES LES 36 À 48 HEURES.

PRÉSENTATION

Comprimés: 80 mg[Pr], 160 mg[Pr], 240 mg[Pr].

SOINS INFIRMIERS

ÉVALUATION DE LA SITUATION

- Mesurer la pression artérielle et le pouls à intervalles fréquents pendant la période d'adaptation de la posologie et à intervalles réguliers pendant toute la durée du traitement. Suivre de près l'hypotension orthostatique pendant qu'on aide le patient à se lever.
- EFFECTUER LE BILAN QUOTIDIEN DES INGESTA ET DES EXCRETA, ET PESER LE PATIENT TOUS LES JOURS. OBSERVER LE PATIENT À INTERVALLES RÉGULIERS À LA RECHERCHE DES SIGNES ET DES SYMPTÔMES SUIVANTS DE SURCHARGE LIQUIDIENNE: ŒDÈME PÉRIPHÉRIQUE, DYSPNÉE, RÂLES OU CRÉPITATIONS, FATIGUE, GAIN PONDÉRAL, TURGESCENCE DES JUGULAIRES.

Tests de laboratoire:

- Le sotalol peut entraîner l'élévation de l'urée et des concentrations sériques de lipoprotéines, de potassium, de triglycérides et d'acide urique.
- Il peut provoquer une élévation de la glycémie.

TOXICITÉ ET SURDOSAGE:

- Suivre de près les patients recevant des bêtabloquants afin de déceler les signes suivants de surdosage: bradycardie, étourdissements graves ou évanouissements, somnolence prononcée, dyspnée, ongles ou paumes des mains bleutés, convulsions. Communiquer immédiatement avec un médecin si ces signes se manifestent.
- On a déjà administré du glucagon pour traiter la bradycardie et l'hypotension.

DIAGNOSTICS INFIRMIERS POSSIBLES

- Débit cardiaque diminué (Effets secondaires).
- Connaissances insuffisantes sur le traitement médicamenteux (Enseignement au patient et à ses proches).
- Non-observance du traitement médicamenteux (Enseignement au patient et à ses proches).

INTERVENTIONS INFIRMIÈRES

- LORS DE LA PHASE INITIALE DU TRAITEMENT ET DES MAJORATIONS DE LA DOSE, LE PATIENT DEVRAIT ÊTRE HOSPITALISÉ ET SUIVI POUR QU'ON PUISSE DÉCELER L'APPARITION DES ARYTHMIES.
- MESURER LE POULS À L'APEX DU CŒUR AVANT D'ADMINISTRER LE MÉDICAMENT. S'IL EST INFÉRIEUR À 50 BATTEMENTS PAR MINUTE OU SI DES ARYTHMIES SURVIENNENT, NE PAS ADMINISTRER LE SOTALOL ET EN AVERTIR LE MÉDECIN.
- Administrer le sotalol à jeun, 1 heure avant ou 2 heures après les repas. L'administration du médicament avec des aliments, particulièrement avec du lait ou des produits laitiers, en réduit l'absorption d'environ 20 %.
- Éviter l'administration d'antiacides renfermant de l'aluminium ou du magnésium dans les 2 heures précédant ou suivant l'administration du sotalol.

ENSEIGNEMENT AU PATIENT ET À SES PROCHES

- Prévenir le patient qu'il doit prendre le sotalol tous les jours, à la même heure, en suivant rigoureusement les recommandations du médecin. Lui expliquer qu'il doit continuer à prendre le médicament même s'il se sent bien. L'avertir qu'il ne doit jamais sauter de dose ni remplacer une dose manquée par une double dose. S'il n'a pu prendre le médicament au moment habituel, il doit le prendre aussitôt que possible, mais au moins 8 heures avant l'heure prévue pour la dose suivante. Le prévenir également que le sevrage brusque peut provoquer des arythmies mettant sa vie en danger, l'hypertension ou l'ischémie du myocarde.
- Conseiller au patient d'avoir une réserve suffisante de médicament pour les fins de semaine, les congés et les vacances. Lui conseiller également de conserver une ordonnance dans son portefeuille pour parer à toute urgence.
- Enseigner au patient et à ses proches la façon de prendre le pouls et la pression artérielle. Leur demander de mesurer le pouls tous les jours et la pression artérielle, 2 fois par semaine. Si le pouls est inférieur à 50 battements par minute ou si la pression artérielle varie de façon importante, conseiller

au patient de ne pas prendre le sotalol et d'en informer un médecin ou un autre professionnel de la santé.

- Prévenir le patient que le sotalol peut parfois provoquer des étourdissements. Lui conseiller de ne pas conduire et d'éviter les activités qui exigent sa vigilance jusqu'à ce qu'on ait la certitude que le médicament n'entraîne pas ces effets chez lui.
- Conseiller au patient de changer lentement de position pour réduire le risque d'hypotension orthostatique, particulièrement au début du traitement ou lors de la majoration de la dose.
- Prévenir le patient que le médicament peut le rendre plus sensible au froid.
- Conseiller au patient de consulter un professionnel de la santé avant de prendre des médicaments en vente libre, particulièrement des préparations contre le rhume, ou un produit naturel en même temps que le sotalol.
- Recommander au patient diabétique de mesurer sa glycémie, surtout lorsqu'il se sent fatigué, faible ou irritable, ou lorsqu'il ressent un malaise. Le sotalol peut masquer certains symptômes d'hypoglycémie. Cependant, des étourdissements et des sueurs peuvent toujours survenir.
- Recommander au patient de signaler à un professionnel de la santé les symptômes suivants: ralentissement du pouls, difficultés respiratoires, respiration sifflante, mains et pieds froids, étourdissements, confusion, dépression, rash, fièvre, maux de gorge, saignements inhabituels ou formation d'ecchymoses.
- Recommander au patient qui doit suivre un autre traitement ou subir une intervention chirurgicale d'avertir le professionnel de la santé qu'il prend du sotalol.
- Conseiller au patient de porter sur lui en tout temps une pièce d'identité où sont inscrits son problème de santé et sa médication.

S

VÉRIFICATION DE L'EFFICACITÉ THÉRAPEUTIQUE

L'efficacité du traitement peut être démontrée par: la maîtrise des arythmies, sans manifestation d'effets indésirables. ✱

SPIRONOLACTONE,

voir Diurétiques (épargneurs de potassium)

STABILISATEURS DES MASTOCYTES

cromolyn (cromoglycate)†
Apo-Cromolyn, Cromolyn, Nalcrom, Opticrom†

nédocromil†
Alocril†

CLASSIFICATION:
Antihistaminique, anti-inflammatoire bronchique

Grossesse – catégorie B

† Pour l'usage ophtalmique, voir l'annexe N.

INDICATIONS

Traitement prophylactique d'appoint (maîtrise au long cours) d'affections allergiques incluant la rhinite allergique saisonnière et l'asthme ■ Prévention des bronchospasmes induits par des facteurs déclenchants connus: l'effort, l'air froid, les allergènes et les polluants atmosphériques ■ **PO**: Allergie gastro-intestinale.

MÉCANISME D'ACTION

Prévention de la libération de l'histamine et d'autres médiateurs de l'inflammation des mastocytes sensibilisés. L'agent ne possède pas d'activité antihistaminique ou anti-inflammatoire intrinsèque. ***Effets thérapeutiques:*** Diminution de la fréquence et de l'intensité des réactions allergiques.

PHARMACOCINÉTIQUE

Absorption: *Cromolyn* – faible (PO), l'action est locale. Après l'inhalation, on peut retrouver de petites quantités de médicament dans la circulation générale.
Distribution: Puisque seules de petites quantités sont absorbées, la distribution de ces agents demeure inconnue. Ils traversent difficilement les membranes biologiques et agissent surtout localement.
Métabolisme et excrétion: Les petites quantités absorbées sont excrétées à l'état inchangé dans la bile et l'urine.
Demi-vie: *Cromolyn* – 80 minutes; *nédocromil* – de 1,5 à 2,3 heures.

Profil temps-action (effets sur les symptômes)

	DÉBUT D'ACTION	PIC	DURÉE
Cromolyn – inhalation	< 1 semaine	2 – 4 semaines	inconnue
Cromolyn – préparation nasale	< 1 semaine	2 – 4 semaines	inconnue
Cromolyn – PO	en l'espace de 2 semaines	2 – 3 semaines	inconnue

CONTRE-INDICATIONS, PRÉCAUTIONS ET MISES EN GARDE

Contre-indications: Hypersensibilité au médicament ou au gaz propulseur ■ Crises aiguës d'asthme.

Précautions et mises en garde: Crises aiguës de bronchospasme (la préparation destinée à l'inhalation ne peut pas soulager ces crises et ne remplace pas les bronchodilatateurs) ■ **PÉD.:** L'innocuité du médicament n'a pas été établie chez les enfants < 2 ans ■ **ALLAITEMENT, OBST.:** L'innocuité du médicament n'a pas été établie.

RÉACTIONS INDÉSIRABLES ET EFFETS SECONDAIRES

SNC: céphalées, insomnie.

ORLO: *voie intranasale* – irritation nasale, éternuements.

Resp.: *inhalation* – irritation de la gorge et de la trachée, bronchospasme, toux.

GI: dysgueusie, nausées.

Tég.: érythème, rash, urticaire.

Divers: réactions allergiques, incluant l'ANAPHYLAXIE ou l'aggravation des affections traitées.

INTERACTIONS

Médicament-médicament: Aucune interaction notable.

VOIES D'ADMINISTRATION ET POSOLOGIE

Cromolyn

- **Inhalation (adultes et enfants > 2 ans):** 20 mg, en solution pour nébuliseur, 4 fois par jour, à intervalles de 4 à 6 heures. Pour les cas graves ou en période d'exposition intense aux allergènes, l'intervalle peut être de 3 heures. Lorsque les symptômes sont maîtrisés, les doses peuvent être espacées à des intervalles de 8 à 12 heures. En traitement prophylactique du bronchospasme, administrer de 15 à 30 minutes avant que le patient s'engage dans l'une des activités qui déclenchent le trouble.
- **Solution nasale (adultes et enfants > 5 ans):** 1 vaporisation dans chaque narine, de 4 à 6 fois par jour. Lorsque les symptômes sont maîtrisés, la dose peut être portée à 1 vaporisation dans chaque narine, 2 ou 3 fois par jour.
- **PO (adultes):** *Maladie chronique inflammatoire des intestins* – 200 mg, 4 fois par jour, avant les repas et au coucher. *Allergie alimentaire* – ***Dose d'attaque:*** 200 mg, 4 fois par jour, de 15 à 30 minutes avant les repas et au coucher. ***Dose d'entretien:*** Une fois la réponse thérapeutique obtenue, la dose pourra être réduite jusqu'au minimum nécessaire pour maîtriser les symptômes. Les patients qui, dans certaines circonstances, se trouvent dans l'impossibilité d'éviter les aliments allergènes pourront prévenir les effets délétères de ces aliments en prenant une dose unique, 15 minutes avant le repas.
- **PO (enfants de 2 à 14 ans):** *Maladie chronique inflammatoire des intestins* – 100 mg, 4 fois par jour, avant les repas et au coucher. *Allergie alimentaire* – ***Dose d'attaque:*** 100 mg, 4 fois par jour, de 15 à 30 minutes avant les repas et au coucher. Si les symptômes ne sont pas maîtrisés de façon satisfaisante en l'espace de 2 à 3 semaines, on pourrait doubler la dose sans toutefois dépasser 40 mg/kg/jour. ***Dose d'entretien:*** Une fois la réponse thérapeutique obtenue, la dose pourra être réduite jusqu'au minimum nécessaire pour maîtriser les symptômes. Les patients qui, dans certaines circonstances, se trouvent dans l'impossibilité d'éviter les aliments allergènes pourront prévenir les effets délétères de ces aliments en prenant une dose unique, 15 minutes avant le repas.

PRÉSENTATION (version générique disponible)

- **Cromolyn**

  Capsules: 100 mg^{Pr} **Solution pour nébulisation:** 1 %, en stérules de 2 mL (20 mg)^{Pr} ■ **Solution nasale:** 2 %, en flacons de 13 mL ou de 26 mL^{VL} ■ **Gouttes ophtalmiques:** 2 %, en flacons de 5 mL^{VL}, de 10 mL^{VL} ou de 15 mL^{VL} (voir l'annexe N).
- **Nédocromil**

  Gouttes ophtalmiques: 2 %, en flacons de 5 mL^{Pr} (voir l'annexe N).

SOINS INFIRMIERS

ÉVALUATION DE LA SITUATION

Inhalation:

- Chez les patients asthmatiques, examiner les résultats des tests de la fonction pulmonaire avant d'amorcer le traitement.
- Noter le murmure vésiculaire et la fonction respiratoire avant le début du traitement et à intervalles réguliers pendant toute sa durée.

Vaporisateur nasal: Rechercher les symptômes suivants de rhinite: congestion nasale, rhinorrhée.

DIAGNOSTICS INFIRMIERS POSSIBLES

- Dégagement inefficace des voies respiratoires (Indications).
- Connaissances insuffisantes sur le traitement médicamenteux (Enseignement au patient et à ses proches).

S

INTERVENTIONS INFIRMIÈRES

- On peut envisager de diminuer la dose des autres médicaments destinés au traitement de l'asthme après 2 à 4 semaines de traitement.

Inhalation:

- Le médicament doit être utilisé en prophylaxie et non pour le traitement des crises aiguës d'asthme ou de l'état de mal asthmatique.
- Le traitement ne doit pas être arrêté subitement, particulièrement chez les patients dont les symptômes se sont améliorés. L'arrêt brusque peut causer une exacerbation aiguë de l'asthme; le traitement devrait donc être interrompu graduellement en l'espace de 1 semaine.
- Le médecin peut recommander un traitement préalable par un bronchodilatateur pour accroître l'effet du produit inhalé.
- Ne pas utiliser une solution qui est trouble ou qui renferme un précipité. La solution est compatible avec l'acétylcystéine, le salbutamol, l'adrénaline, l'isoprotérénol, l'ipratropium exempt d'agent de conservation et les solutions de terbutaline, pendant un maximum de 60 minutes.

PO: Il faut avaler les capsules entières ou en dissoudre le contenu dans une petite quantité d'eau très chaude à laquelle on ajoute de l'eau froide pour permettre au patient de boire le mélange. L'administration sous cette forme de solution est probablement la meilleure méthode pour contrer les allergies alimentaires.

ENSEIGNEMENT AU PATIENT ET À SES PROCHES

- Recommander au patient de prendre le médicament à intervalles réguliers, sans augmenter la fréquence des prises. S'il n'a pu prendre le médicament au moment habituel, il doit le faire dès que possible et espacer les autres prises à intervalles réguliers. Il ne faut jamais doubler la dose ni interrompre le traitement sans avoir consulté un professionnel de la santé, car les symptômes pourraient s'intensifier.
- Recommander au patient de ne pas interrompre le traitement concomitant par un corticostéroïde ou un bronchodilatateur sans avoir consulté un professionnel de la santé.
- Si le cromolyn est prescrit avant le contact avec un allergène connu ou avant l'effort, expliquer au patient qu'il doit prendre le médicament de 15 à 30 minutes avant cette exposition ou cet effort, et pas plus de 60 minutes avant pour tirer profit de tous ses bienfaits.

Inhalation:

- Montrer au patient comment utiliser le nébuliseur.
- Recommander au patient de faire des gargarismes et de se rincer fréquemment la bouche après chaque inhalation afin de réduire la sécheresse de la bouche, l'irritation de la gorge et l'enrouement.
- Recommander au patient de consulter un professionnel de la santé si les symptômes d'asthme ne s'améliorent pas dans les 2 à 4 semaines, s'ils s'aggravent ou s'ils réapparaissent.

Préparation nasale: Expliquer au patient qu'il doit se dégager les narines avant l'administration et inhaler le médicament par le nez.

VÉRIFICATION DE L'EFFICACITÉ THÉRAPEUTIQUE

L'efficacité du traitement peut être démontrée par: la réduction des symptômes d'asthme ▪ la prophylaxie du bronchospasme induit par l'effort ▪ la diminution des symptômes de rhinite. L'amélioration peut ne pas être notable avant 2 à 4 semaines. ✳

STAVUDINE

Synonyme: d4T

Zerit

CLASSIFICATION:

Antirétroviral (inhibiteur nucléosidique de la transcriptase inverse)

Grossesse – catégorie C

INDICATIONS

Traitement de l'infection par le VIH (avec d'autres antirétroviraux). **Usages non approuvés:** En association avec d'autres antirétroviraux, prophylaxie après une exposition accidentelle au VIH.

MÉCANISME D'ACTION

Après la transformation intracellulaire de la stavudine en triphosphate de stavudine, inhibition de la synthèse et de la réplication de l'ADN viral. ***Effets thérapeutiques:*** Effet virostatique contre le VIH ▪ Diminution de la charge virale et augmentation du nombre de cellules CD4 ▪ L'agent ne guérit pas l'infection par le VIH, mais peut en ralentir l'évolution et diminuer l'incidence et la gravité de ses complications.

PHARMACOCINÉTIQUE

Absorption: Bonne (de 78 à 80 % PO).

Distribution: La stavudine traverse la barrière hématoencéphalique; elle pénètre dans les globules rouges et dans le plasma en proportions égales.

Métabolisme et excrétion: L'agent est transformé à l'intérieur des cellules en triphosphate de stavudine, qui est la substance active. Excrétion rénale (40 % sous forme inchangée) et non rénale (50 %).

Demi-vie: *Adultes:* de 1 à 1,6 heure; *enfants:* de 0,9 à 1,1 heure; *insuffisants rénaux:* jusqu'à 8 heures; demi-vie intracellulaire: 3,5 heures.

Profil temps-action

	DÉBUT D'ACTION	PIC	DURÉE
PO	inconnu	0,5 – 1,5 h	12 h

CONTRE-INDICATIONS, PRÉCAUTIONS ET MISES EN GARDE

Contre-indications: Hypersensibilité.

Précautions et mises en garde: Antécédents d'alcoolisme ■ Antécédents de maladie hépatique ou d'insuffisance hépatique ■ Insuffisance rénale (si la Cl_{Cr} < 50 mL/min, il est recommandé de réduire la dose ou d'espacer l'intervalle entre les doses) ■ Obésité, femmes, prise prolongée d'un inhibiteur nucléosidique (il peut s'agir de facteurs de risque d'acidose lactique ou d'hépatomégalie) ■ Antécédents de neuropathie périphérique ■ **OBST.:** L'innocuité du médicament n'a pas été établie ■ **ALLAITEMENT:** Les mères séropositives ne devraient pas allaiter, car le VIH passe dans le lait maternel ■ Traitement concomitant par la didanosine chez des femmes enceintes (précédents d'acidose lactique d'issue fatale).

RÉACTIONS INDÉSIRABLES ET EFFETS SECONDAIRES

SNC: céphalées, insomnie, faiblesse.

GI: TOXICITÉ HÉPATIQUE, anorexie, diarrhée, PANCRÉATITE.

HÉ: ACIDOSE LACTIQUE.

Hémat.: anémie.

Loc.: arthralgie, myalgie.

SN: neuropathie périphérique.

Métab.: modification de la distribution du tissu adipeux.

Divers: syndrome de reconstitution immunitaire.

INTERACTIONS

Médicament-médicament: Administrer la stavudine avec prudence lors d'un traitement par des **médicaments entraînant une neuropathie périphérique (chloramphénicol, cisplatine, dapsone, éthambutol, éthionamide, hydralazine, isoniazide, lithium, métronidazole, nitrofurantoïne, phénytoïne, vincristine ou zalcitabine)** ■ L'administration concomitante d'**hydroxyurée** augmente le risque d'hépatotoxicité, qui peut être d'issue fatale ■ L'administration concomitante de **didanosine** augmente le risque d'acidose lactique, d'hépatotoxicité, de neuropathie périphérique et de pancréatite (éviter l'usage concomitant sauf si d'autres options ne sont pas envisageables) ■ L'administration concomitante de **zidovudine** n'est pas recommandée en raison du risque d'effets antirétroviraux antagonistes.

VOIES D'ADMINISTRATION ET POSOLOGIE

- **PO (adultes ≥ 60 kg):** 40 mg, toutes les 12 heures.
- **PO (adultes < 60 kg):** 30 mg, toutes les 12 heures.
- **PO (enfants ≥ 30 kg):** La même dose que chez l'adulte.
- **PO (nouveau-nés, de la naissance à 13 jours):** 0,5 mg/kg, toutes les 12 heures.
- **PO (enfants ≥ 14 jours et < 30 kg):** 1 mg/kg, toutes les 12 heures.

INSUFFISANCE RÉNALE

- **PO (ADULTES ≥ 60 kg):** *CL_{CR} DE 26 À 50 mL/MIN* – 20 mg, TOUTES LES 12 HEURES; *CL_{CR} DE 10 À 25 mL/MIN* – 20 mg, TOUTES LES 24 HEURES.
- **PO (ADULTES < 60 kg):** *CL_{CR} DE 26 À 50 mL/MIN* – 15 mg, TOUTES LES 12 HEURES; *CL_{CR} DE 10 À 25 mL/MIN* – 15 mg, TOUTES LES 24 HEURES.

PRÉSENTATION

Capsules: 15 mg[Pr], 20 mg[Pr], 30 mg[Pr], 40 mg[Pr].

SOINS INFIRMIERS

ÉVALUATION DE LA SITUATION

- Examiner le patient pendant toute la durée du traitement pour déceler toute aggravation des symptômes de l'infection par le VIH ou l'apparition de symptômes d'infections opportunistes.
- L'AGENT PEUT PROVOQUER UNE ACIDOSE LACTIQUE ET UNE HÉPATOMÉGALIE GRAVE AVEC STÉATOSE. CES COMPLICATIONS SONT PLUS PROBABLES CHEZ LES PATIENTS DE SEXE FÉMININ, CHEZ LES PERSONNES OBÈSES ET CHEZ CELLES QUI PRENNENT DES ANALOGUES NUCLÉOSIDIQUES PENDANT UN LAPS DE TEMPS PROLONGÉ. SUIVRE DE PRÈS LES SIGNES DE CES COMPLICATIONS (TAUX ACCRUS DE LACTATE SÉRIQUE, CONCENTRATIONS ÉLEVÉES D'ENZYMES HÉPATIQUES, HYPERTROPHIE DU FOIE DÉCELÉE À LA PALPATION). ARRÊTER LE TRAITEMENT DÈS L'APPARITION DE SIGNES CLINIQUES OU DÈS L'OBTENTION DE RÉSULTATS DE TESTS DE LABORATOIRE QUI ÉVOQUENT UN TEL PROBLÈME.
- OBSERVER LE PATIENT À LA RECHERCHE DES SYMPTÔMES SUIVANTS DE PANCRÉATITE: DOULEURS ABDOMINALES, NAUSÉES, VOMISSEMENTS, CONCENTRATIONS

ACCRUES D'AMYLASE, DE LIPASE OU DE TRIGLYCÉRIDES. SI LE PATIENT MANIFESTE DES SIGNES ET DES SYMPTÔMES DE PANCRÉATITE, LE TRAITEMENT PAR LA STAVUDINE DEVRAIT ÊTRE INTERROMPU. LA PANCRÉATITE PEUT METTRE LA VIE DU PATIENT EN DANGER.

- Rester à l'affût des signes et des symptômes suivants de neuropathie périphérique: engourdissement, sensation de brûlure, fourmillements ou douleurs au niveau des pieds ou des mains. Il peut s'avérer difficile de distinguer cette neuropathie de celle accompagnant une infection grave par le VIH. Ces symptômes peuvent disparaître si l'on arrête rapidement le traitement par la stavudine ou ils peuvent s'aggraver passagèrement après l'arrêt de la médication. Si les symptômes disparaissent entièrement, on peut reprendre le traitement par la stavudine à 50 % de la dose habituelle.
- Si une patiente enceinte est exposée à des antirétroviraux, l'inscrire dans le registre des femmes exposées aux antirétroviraux pendant leur grossesse, en composant le 1 800 258-4263.

Tests de laboratoire:

- Suivre de près la charge virale et le nombre de cellules CD4, avant le traitement et à intervalles réguliers pendant toute sa durée.
- NOTER À INTERVALLES RÉGULIERS PENDANT TOUTE LA DURÉE DU TRAITEMENT LES CONCENTRATIONS SÉRIQUES D'AMYLASE, DE LIPASE ET DE TRIGLYCÉRIDES. DES CONCENTRATIONS ÉLEVÉES PEUVENT RÉVÉLER LA PRÉSENCE DE PANCRÉATITE ET DICTENT L'ARRÊT DU TRAITEMENT.
- SUIVRE DE PRÈS LA FONCTION HÉPATIQUE. LA STAVUDINE PEUT ENTRAÎNER UNE ÉLÉVATION DES CONCENTRATIONS D'AST, D'ALT ET DE PHOSPHATASE ALCALINE, MAIS ELLES REVIENNENT HABITUELLEMENT À LA NORMALE APRÈS L'ARRÊT DU TRAITEMENT. L'ACIDOSE LACTIQUE PEUT SURVENIR EN PRÉSENCE D'UNE TOXICITÉ HÉPATIQUE ENTRAÎNANT UNE STÉATOSE HÉPATIQUE QUI PEUT ÊTRE D'ISSUE FATALE, PARTICULIÈREMENT CHEZ LES FEMMES.
- La stavudine peut entraîner une élévation des concentrations sériques d'amylase et de lipase.

DIAGNOSTICS INFIRMIERS POSSIBLES

- Risque d'infection (Indications).
- Connaissances insuffisantes sur le traitement médicamenteux (Enseignement au patient et à ses proches).

INTERVENTIONS INFIRMIÈRES

- La stavudine peut être administrée avec ou sans aliments.

ENSEIGNEMENT AU PATIENT ET À SES PROCHES

- Demander au patient de prendre la stavudine, exactement comme elle lui a été prescrite, toutes les 12 heures. Insister sur le fait qu'il est important d'observer rigoureusement le traitement tout au long, de ne pas prendre plus de médicament que la quantité exacte qui lui a été prescrite, et de consulter un professionnel de la santé avant d'arrêter la prise de la stavudine. Expliquer au patient que s'il n'a pu prendre le médicament au moment habituel, il doit le prendre aussitôt que possible, à moins que ce ne soit presque l'heure prévue pour la dose suivante. Le prévenir qu'il ne doit jamais remplacer une dose manquée par une double dose. Insister sur le fait qu'il ne faut pas donner ce médicament à d'autres personnes.
- Expliquer au patient que la stavudine ne guérit pas l'infection par le VIH ni ne réduit le risque de transmission du VIH par les rapports sexuels ou par la contamination du sang. Conseiller au patient d'éviter les contacts sexuels non protégés et d'utiliser un condom lors des rapports sexuels, de ne pas utiliser les mêmes seringues qu'une autre personne et de ne pas faire de dons de sang afin de prévenir la transmission du virus à autrui.
- RECOMMANDER AU PATIENT DE PRÉVENIR UN PROFESSIONNEL DE LA SANTÉ IMMÉDIATEMENT SI DES SIGNES D'ACIDOSE LACTIQUE (FATIGUE OU FAIBLESSE, DOULEURS MUSCULAIRES INHABITUELLES, DIFFICULTÉS RESPIRATOIRES, DOULEURS D'ESTOMAC AVEC DES NAUSÉES ET DES VOMISSEMENTS, SENSATION DE FROID, SURTOUT AU NIVEAU DES EXTRÉMITÉS, ÉTOURDISSEMENTS OU BATTEMENTS CARDIAQUES RAPIDES ET IRRÉGULIERS) OU D'HÉPATOTOXICITÉ (JAUNISSEMENT DE LA PEAU OU DU BLANC DES YEUX, URINE DE COULEUR FONCÉE, SELLES DE COULEUR PÂLE, PERTE D'APPÉTIT PENDANT PLUSIEURS JOURS DE SUITE, NAUSÉES OU DOULEURS ABDOMINALES) SE MANIFESTENT. Ces symptômes peuvent se présenter plus fréquemment chez les sujets de sexe féminin, les personnes obèses ou celles qui prennent des médicaments comme la stavudine pendant un laps de temps prolongé.
- Recommander au patient de signaler immédiatement à un professionnel de la santé tout signe de neuropathie périphérique: engourdissements, fourmillements ou douleurs au niveau des mains ou des pieds.
- Informer le patient du risque d'accumulation ou de redistribution des tissus adipeux, pouvant entraîner une obésité centrale, une infiltration de graisse dans la région dorsocervicale (bosse de bison), l'atrophie

des tissus périphériques, l'augmentation du volume des seins et un aspect cushinoïde. Les causes et les effets à long terme de ce phénomène sont inconnus.

- Conseiller au patient de ne pas prendre d'autres médicaments en vente libre ou sur ordonnance ni de produits naturels en même temps que la stavudine sans consulter au préalable un professionnel de la santé.
- Insister sur l'importance des examens réguliers de suivi et des analyses sanguines permettant de déceler l'évolution de la maladie et les effets secondaires de la stavudine.

VÉRIFICATION DE L'EFFICACITÉ THÉRAPEUTIQUE

L'efficacité du traitement peut être démontrée par: le ralentissement de l'évolution de l'infection par le VIH et de l'apparition de ses complications ■ l'augmentation du nombre de cellules CD4 et la diminution de la charge virale.

STREPTOKINASE,
voir Thrombolytiques

STREPTOMYCINE,
Voir Aminosides

SUCCIMER

Ce médicament n'est pas commercialisé au Canada. Il est disponible par l'intermédiaire du Programme d'accès spécial de Santé Canada.

CLASSIFICATION:
Antidote (chélateur du plomb)

Grossesse – catégorie C

INDICATIONS

Usages non approuvés: Traitement de l'intoxication par le plomb, lorsque les concentrations sanguines de plomb sont supérieures à 2,2 μmol/L.

MÉCANISME D'ACTION

Formation d'un complexe hydrosoluble qui favorise l'élimination des quantités excessives de plomb dans les urines. ***Effets thérapeutiques:*** Diminution des concentrations sanguines de plomb et réduction des lésions des organes cibles en cas d'intoxication par le plomb.

PHARMACOCINÉTIQUE

Absorption: Rapide, mais variable.

Distribution: Inconnue.

Métabolisme et excrétion: Fort métabolisme; 10 % est excrété à l'état inchangé par les reins.

Demi-vie: 2 jours.

Profil temps-action (excrétion du plomb dans l'urine)

	DÉBUT D'ACTION	PIC	DURÉE
PO	moins de 2 h	2 – 4 h	8 – 12 h

CONTRE-INDICATIONS, PRÉCAUTIONS ET MISES EN GARDE

Contre-indications: Hypersensibilité ou allergie au succimer ■ Allaitement (à déconseiller pendant le traitement par le succimer).

Précautions et mises en garde: Insuffisance rénale (les chélateurs ne sont pas dialysables) ■ Insuffisance hépatique ■ **PÉD.:** Enfants (risque accru de bradyarythmies). Enfants souffrant de myopathie des muscles squelettiques (prédisposition accrue à des réactions indésirables rares, mais graves). Enfants < 1 an (l'innocuité du médicament n'a pas été établie) ■ **GÉR.:** Administrer des doses plus faibles, compte tenu de la diminution de la fonction rénale, hépatique et cardiaque ■ Grossesse.

RÉACTIONS INDÉSIRABLES ET EFFETS SECONDAIRES

SNC: étourdissements, somnolence, céphalées.

ORLO: opacités cornéennes, otite moyenne, oreilles bouchées, larmoiement des yeux.

Resp.: toux, congestion nasale, rhinorrhée, maux de gorge.

CV: arythmies.

GI: nausées, vomissements, crampes abdominales, anorexie, diarrhée, résultats élevés aux tests de la fonction hépatique, symptômes hémorroïdaux, goût métallique.

GU: oligurie, protéinurie, mictions difficiles.

Tég.: éruptions mucocutanées, prurit, rash.

Hémat.: éosinophilie, thrombocytose.

Loc.: douleurs dans le dos, les côtes, le flanc et les jambes.

SN: paresthésie, neuropathie sensorimotrice.

Divers: frissons, fièvre, syndrome pseudogrippal, candidose.

INTERACTIONS

Médicament-médicament: L'administration d'autres **chélateurs** n'est pas recommandée.

VOIES D'ADMINISTRATION ET POSOLOGIE

- **PO (adultes et enfants)**: 10 mg/kg (350 mg/m^2), toutes les 8 heures, pendant 5 jours, puis réduire la dose jusqu'à 10 mg/kg (350 mg/m^2), toutes les 12 heures, pendant 2 semaines de plus. Avant d'administrer un nouveau traitement, observer une période d'arrêt de la médication de 2 semaines.

PRÉSENTATION

Ce médicament n'est pas commercialisé au Canada.

ÉVALUATION DE LA SITUATION

- Observer le patient et les membres de sa famille pour déceler les signes d'intoxication par le plomb, avant le traitement et à intervalles réguliers pendant toute sa durée. L'intoxication aiguë par le plomb est caractérisée par les symptômes suivants: goût métallique, coliques, vomissements, diarrhée, oligurie et coma. Les symptômes d'intoxication chronique varient selon la gravité du cas et comprennent l'anorexie, l'apparition d'une ligne bleu foncé le long des gencives, des vomissements intermittents, la paresthésie, l'encéphalopathie, les convulsions et le coma.
- Effectuer un bilan quotidien rigoureux des ingesta et des excreta, et peser le patient tous les jours. Prévenir le médecin si les valeurs changent. Les patients qui suivent un traitement par le succimer doivent être adéquatement hydratés.
- Examiner attentivement l'état neurologique: état de conscience, réactions pupillaires et mouvements. Prévenir immédiatement le médecin en cas de modification de l'état du patient.
- Suivre de près les signes d'allergie ou autres réactions mucocutanées, particulièrement lors de l'administration répétée du succimer.

S

Tests de laboratoire:

- Noter les concentrations de plomb dans le sang et dans l'urine, avant le traitement et à intervalles réguliers pendant toute sa durée. Après le traitement, suivre, au moins une fois par semaine, les concentrations sanguines jusqu'à ce que les valeurs se stabilisent pour pouvoir déceler un rebond éventuel. L'administration du succimer est indiquée si les concentrations sanguines de plomb sont supérieures à 2,2 μmol/L.
- Le succimer peut entraîner l'élévation des concentrations sériques de transaminases, de phosphatase alcaline et de cholestérol; noter ces concentrations avant le traitement et au moins hebdomadairement pendant toute sa durée.
- Le succimer peut fausser les résultats des épreuves sériques et urinaires.

DIAGNOSTICS INFIRMIERS POSSIBLES

- Risque d'intoxication (Enseignement au patient et à ses proches).
- Entretien inefficace du domicile (Indications).
- Connaissances insuffisantes sur le traitement médicamenteux (Enseignement au patient et à ses proches).

INTERVENTIONS INFIRMIÈRES

- L'administration du succimer en association avec d'autres chélateurs n'est pas recommandée. Les patients ayant reçu un traitement par de l'EDTA (acide éthylènediamine tétracétique) ou du dimercaprol (British anti-lewisite [BAL]) peuvent recevoir le succimer 4 semaines plus tard.
- Chaque cure dure 19 jours. Les doses sont administrées toutes les 8 heures, pendant 5 jours, puis toutes les 12 heures, pendant 14 jours. À moins que les concentrations sanguines ne dictent un traitement rapide, il est recommandé d'espacer les cures d'au moins 2 semaines.

PO: Si le patient ne peut pas avaler la capsule, l'ouvrir et en verser le contenu sur une petite quantité d'aliments mous et le faire prendre à la cuillère, puis donner un verre de jus de fruits.

ENSEIGNEMENT AU PATIENT ET À SES PROCHES

- Insister sur l'importance des examens de suivi permettant de mesurer les concentrations de plomb. Des traitements supplémentaires peuvent s'avérer nécessaires.
- Inciter le patient à boire des quantités adéquates de liquide pendant toute la durée du traitement.
- Recommander au patient de prévenir un professionnel de la santé en cas de rash.
- Recommander au patient de consulter les services de santé publics pour déterminer les sources possibles d'intoxication par le plomb à domicile, au travail, à l'école ou ailleurs. Le traitement par un chélateur ne peut être utilisé comme prophylaxie de l'intoxication par le plomb.

VÉRIFICATION DE L'EFFICACITÉ THÉRAPEUTIQUE

L'efficacité du traitement peut être démontrée par: la diminution des symptômes d'intoxication par le plomb ■ la diminution des concentrations sanguines de plomb au-dessous de 2,2 μmol/L, bien que la limite normale supérieure soit de 1,4 μmol/L.

SUCRALFATE

Apo-Sucralfate, Novo-Sucralate, Nu-Sucralfate, Sulcrate

CLASSIFICATION:
Anti-ulcéreux (cytoprotecteur gastroduodénal)

Grossesse – catégorie B

INDICATIONS

Comprimés: Traitement de l'ulcère duodénal et de l'ulcère gastrique non malin ■ Traitement d'entretien (prophylactique) de l'ulcère duodénal. **Suspension:** Traitement de l'ulcère duodénal et prophylaxie des hémorragies gastro-intestinales provoquées par les ulcères de stress. **Usages non approuvés:** Traitement du reflux gastro-œsophagien ■ Prévention des lésions de la muqueuse gastrique lors de l'administration de doses élevées d'aspirine ou d'anti-inflammatoires non stéroïdiens aux patients qui souffrent de polyarthrite rhumatoïde ■ Traitement des mucosites, des stomatites et des ulcérations buccales d'étiologies variées.

MÉCANISME D'ACTION

Formation d'une pâte épaisse en réaction avec l'acide gastrique; cette pâte adhère sélectivement aux surfaces ulcérées. ***Effets thérapeutiques:*** Protection des ulcères et leur cicatrisation par la suite.

PHARMACOCINÉTIQUE

Absorption: Minime (PO < 5 %).
Distribution: Inconnue.
Métabolisme et excrétion: Élimination dans les fèces (> 90 %).
Demi-vie: De 6 à 20 heures.

Profil temps-action (effet protecteur des muqueuses)

	DÉBUT D'ACTION	PIC	DURÉE
PO	30 min	inconnu	5 h

CONTRE-INDICATIONS, PRÉCAUTIONS ET MISES EN GARDE

Contre-indications: Hypersensibilité.
Précautions et mises en garde: Insuffisance rénale chronique grave avec ou sans recours à la dialyse (risque d'accumulation d'aluminium) ■ **PÉD.:** Enfants (l'innocuité du médicament n'a pas été établie) ■ Grossesse.

RÉACTIONS INDÉSIRABLES ET EFFETS SECONDAIRES

SNC: étourdissements, somnolence.
GI: constipation, diarrhée, sécheresse de la bouche (xérostomie), gêne gastrique, indigestion, nausées.
Tég.: prurit, rash.

INTERACTIONS

Médicament-médicament: Le sucralfate diminue l'absorption de la **phénytoïne**, des **vitamines liposolubles**, des **tétracyclines,** de la **digoxine**, de la **warfarine** et des **fluoroquinolones** (espacer d'au moins 2 heures l'administration de ces médicaments) ■ Les **antiacides**, administrés simultanément, diminuent l'efficacité du sucralfate (espacer les prises d'au moins 30 minutes).

VOIES D'ADMINISTRATION ET POSOLOGIE

Traitement des ulcères
- **PO (adultes):** 1 g, 4 fois par jour, 1 heure avant les repas et au coucher, ou 2 g, 2 fois par jour, au réveil et au coucher.

Prévention de l'ulcère duodénal
- **PO (adultes):** 1 g, 2 fois par jour, 1 heure avant un repas.

Ulcère duodénal
- **Suspension:** 2 g, 2 fois par jour, à jeun.

Prophylaxie des hémorragies gastro-intestinales causées par les ulcères de stress
- **Suspension:** 1 g, de 4 à 6 fois par jour.

PRÉSENTATION (version générique disponible)

Comprimés: 1 g[Pr] ■ **Suspension orale:** 1 g/5 mL[Pr].

SOINS INFIRMIERS

ÉVALUATION DE LA SITUATION

- Suivre à intervalles réguliers les douleurs abdominales et la présence de sang franc ou occulte dans les selles.

DIAGNOSTICS INFIRMIERS POSSIBLES

- Douleur aiguë (Indications).
- Constipation (Effets secondaires).
- Connaissances insuffisantes sur le traitement médicamenteux (Enseignement au patient et à ses proches).

INTERVENTIONS INFIRMIÈRES

- Administrer le médicament à jeun, 1 heure avant les repas et au coucher. Bien agiter la suspension avant de l'administrer.
- S'il faut administrer le sucralfate par sonde nasogastrique, consulter le pharmacien; puisque le sucralfate

se lie aux protéines, il peut former un bézoard avec d'autres médicaments ou avec une préparation pour alimentation entérale.

- Si le patient doit également prendre un antiacide contre la douleur gastrique, ne pas le lui administrer dans les 30 minutes qui précèdent ou qui suivent l'administration du sucralfate.

ENSEIGNEMENT AU PATIENT ET À SES PROCHES

- Recommander au patient de poursuivre le traitement pendant 4 à 12 semaines, même s'il se sent mieux, pour assurer la guérison complète de l'ulcère. S'il n'a pas pu prendre le médicament au moment habituel, il doit le prendre dès que possible à moins que ce ne soit presque l'heure prévue pour la dose suivante. Le prévenir qu'il ne doit jamais remplacer une dose manquée par une double dose.
- Recommander au patient d'augmenter sa consommation de liquides et d'aliments riches en fibres, et de faire de l'exercice pour essayer de prévenir la constipation induite par le médicament.
- Insister sur l'importance des examens réguliers permettant de déterminer les bienfaits du traitement.

VÉRIFICATION DE L'EFFICACITÉ THÉRAPEUTIQUE

L'efficacité du traitement peut être démontrée par: la diminution des douleurs abdominales ■ la prévention et la cicatrisation des ulcères gastroduodénaux, révélées par des examens radiologiques et l'endoscopie.

S

ALERTE CLINIQUE

SUFENTANIL

Sufenta

CLASSIFICATION:

Analgésique opioïde (agoniste), anesthésique et adjuvant anesthésique (à action générale)

Grossesse – catégories C et D (usage prolongé ou doses élevées prises près du terme)

INDICATIONS

IV: Adjuvant analgésique dans le maintien de l'anesthésie générale équilibrée lors d'interventions chirurgicales majeures ■ Anesthésique principal avec de l'oxygène pur lors d'interventions chirurgicales majeures ■ **Voie épidurale:** Analgésie postopératoire lors de certaines interventions chirurgicales ■ Adjuvant analgésique à la bupivacaïne épidurale pendant le travail et l'accouchement par voie vaginale.

MÉCANISME D'ACTION

Liaison aux récepteurs opioïdes du SNC modifiant ainsi la perception de la douleur et la réaction à celle-ci, et entraînant une dépression généralisée du SNC. ***Effets thérapeutiques:*** Diminution de l'intensité de la douleur modérée à grave ■ Anesthésie.

PHARMACOCINÉTIQUE

Absorption: Biodisponibilité à 100 % (IV).

Distribution: Le sufentanil pénètre lentement dans les tissus adipeux. Il traverse la barrière placentaire et passe dans le lait maternel.

Métabolisme et excrétion: Métabolisme majoritairement hépatique. Un certain métabolisme a lieu dans l'intestin grêle.

Demi-vie: 2,7 heures (prolongée pendant le pontage cardiopulmonaire).

Profil temps-action (analgésie)

	DÉBUT D'ACTION	PIC	DURÉE
IV	en 1 min	inconnu	5 min
Voie épidurale	5 – 10 min	inconnu	4 – 6 h

CONTRE-INDICATIONS, PRÉCAUTIONS ET MISES EN GARDE

Contre-indications: Hypersensibilité au fentanyl ou à d'autres agents morphinomimétiques ■ Intolérance connue ■ **Voie IV seulement**: durant le travail ou avant le clampage du cordon ombilical au cours d'une césarienne ■ **Voie épidurale seulement**: hémorragie grave ■ état de choc ■ septicémie ■ infection locale au point d'injection envisagé ■ troubles de la morphologie sanguine ou traitement anticoagulant.

Précautions et mises en garde: Personnes âgées ■ Patients débilités ou très malades ■ Patients diabétiques ■ Maladie pulmonaire grave ■ Insuffisance rénale ■ Insuffisance hépatique ■ Tumeurs du SNC ■ Pression intracrânienne accrue ■ Traumatisme crânien ■ Insuffisance surrénalienne ■ Douleurs abdominales non diagnostiquées ■ Hypothyroïdie ■ Alcoolisme ■ Maladie cardiaque (arythmies) ■ **OBST.**: Grossesse (précédents d'administration au cours d'une césarienne; risque de somnolence chez le nouveau-né) ■ Travail et accouchement (voie IV déconseillée; voie épidurale – la prudence est de mise en cas de souffrance fœtale) ■ **ALLAITEMENT**: L'innocuité du médicament n'a pas été établie.

RÉACTIONS INDÉSIRABLES ET EFFETS SECONDAIRES

SNC: étourdissements, torpeur, somnolence.

ORLO: vision trouble.

Resp.: apnée, DÉPRESSION RESPIRATOIRE.

CV: bradycardie, tachycardie, hypotension, hypertension, arythmies.

GI: nausées, vomissements.

Tég.: démangeaisons, érythème.

Loc.: rigidité des muscles thoraciques, mouvements musculaires pendant l'intervention chirurgicale.

Divers: frissons.

INTERACTIONS

Médicament-médicament: Dépression additive du SNC et du système respiratoire lors de l'usage concomitant d'**alcool**, d'**antihistaminiques,** de **phénothiazines**, de **barbituriques**, d'**antidépresseurs**, d'**hypnosédatifs** et d'**autres opioïdes** ■ Éviter l'administration d'**IMAO** pendant les 14 jours qui précèdent le traitement avec ce médicament ■ Les inhibiteurs du CYP450 3A4, comme la **cimétidine**, le **kétaconazole**, le **ritonavir** ou l'**érythromycine**, peuvent prolonger la durée de la récupération ■ Risque accru d'hypotension lors de l'administration simultanée de **benzodiazépines** ■ L'administration d'**analgésiques opioïdes agonistes/antagonistes (nalbuphine, butorphanol, pentazocine)** peut diminuer l'analgésie et/ou déclencher des symptômes de sevrage chez les patients présentant une dépendance physique aux analgésiques opioïdes.

VOIES D'ADMINISTRATION ET POSOLOGIE

Adjuvant anesthésique (anesthésie d'au moins 1 heure)

- **IV (adultes)**: *Dose initiale* – minimum 0,5 µg/kg. *Dose d'entretien* – de 10 à 25 µg, selon les besoins. *Dose cumulative* – de 0,5 à 2 µg/kg (ne pas dépasser 1 µg/kg/h lors de l'administration en association avec du protoxyde d'azote et de l'oxygène).

Adjuvant anesthésique (anesthésie d'au moins 2 heures)

- **IV (adultes)**: *Dose d'entretien* – de 25 à 50 µg, selon les besoins. *Dose cumulative* – de 2 à 8 µg/kg (ne pas dépasser 1 µg/kg/h lors de l'administration en association avec du protoxyde d'azote et de l'oxygène).

Anesthésique principal (avec de l'oxygène pur)

- **IV (adultes)**: *Dose d'entretien* – de 25 à 50 µg, selon les besoins. *Dose cumulative* – de 8 à 30 µg/kg.
- **IV (enfants < 12 ans)**: *Chirurgie cardiovasculaire* – initialement, de 10 à 25 µg/kg; on administre par la suite des doses d'entretien de 25 à 50 µg.

Analgésie postopératoire

- **Voie épidurale (adultes)**: Initialement, de 30 à 60 µg. On peut administrer des doses supplémentaires de 25 µg, à des intervalles d'au moins 1 heure, selon les besoins.

Adjuvant analgésique à la bupivacaïne épidurale

- **Voie épidurale (adultes)**: Initialement, 10 µg (avec 0,125 à 0,25 % de bupivacaïne). On peut administrer 2 doses supplémentaires, à des intervalles d'au moins 1 heure, selon les besoins (ne pas dépasser une dose totale de 30 µg).

PRÉSENTATION

Solution injectable: 50 µg/mL[N].

SOINS INFIRMIERS

ÉVALUATION DE LA SITUATION

- SUIVRE DE PRÈS LES SIGNES VITAUX, PARTICULIÈREMENT LA FONCTION RESPIRATOIRE, LA PRESSION ARTÉRIELLE ET L'ÉCG DURANT ET APRÈS L'ADMINISTRATION. SIGNALER IMMÉDIATEMENT AU MÉDECIN TOUTE MODIFICATION IMPORTANTE.
- Les effets dépresseurs du sufentanil sur la respiration durent plus longtemps que ses effets analgésiques. Suivre de près l'état du patient.

Tests de laboratoire: Le sufentanil peut entraîner l'élévation des concentrations sériques d'amylase et de lipase.

TOXICITÉ ET SURDOSAGE: Les symptômes de toxicité comprennent la dépression respiratoire, l'hypotension, les arythmies, la bradycardie et l'asystolie. On peut renverser la dépression respiratoire avec de la naloxone. La bradycardie peut être traitée avec de l'atropine.

DIAGNOSTICS INFIRMIERS POSSIBLES

- Douleur aiguë (Indications).
- Mode de respiration inefficace (Réactions indésirables).
- Risque d'accident (Réactions indésirables).
- Connaissances insuffisantes sur le traitement médicamenteux (Enseignement au patient et à ses proches).

INTERVENTIONS INFIRMIÈRES

ALERTE CLINIQUE: DES SURDOSES ACCIDENTELLES D'ANALGÉSIQUES OPIOÏDES ONT CAUSÉ DES DÉCÈS. AVANT D'ADMINISTRER L'AGENT, CLARIFIER TOUS LES POINTS AMBIGUS ET FAIRE VÉRIFIER L'ORDONNANCE D'ORIGINE ET LE CALCUL DES DOSES PAR UN AUTRE PROFESSIONNEL DE LA SANTÉ.

- NE PAS CONFONDRE LE SUFENTANIL AVEC L'ALFENTANIL OU LE FENTANYL.

- On peut administrer des benzodiazépines avant le sufentanil pour réduire la dose d'induction et pour écourter le temps qui s'écoule avant la perte de conscience. Cette association peut augmenter le risque d'hypotension.

Alerte clinique: Au cours de l'administration du sufentanil, garder à portée de la main un antagoniste des opioïdes, de l'oxygène et les appareils de réanimation. Le sufentanil ne doit être administré que dans un milieu où l'anesthésie est surveillée de près (salle d'opération, unité de soins intensifs) et où l'on dispose d'appareils de maintien des fonctions vitales. L'administration est réservée au personnel dûment formé en réanimation et en prise en charge des urgences en cas de troubles respiratoires.

Voie épidurale:

- Vérifier si l'aiguille ou le cathéter sont bien placés dans l'espace épidural avant d'injecter le sufentanil, pour éviter d'administrer par inadvertance par voie intravasculaire ou intrathécale.
- Si l'analgésie est insuffisante, vérifier l'emplacement et l'état du cathéter avant de continuer à administrer le médicament par voie épidurale.

IV directe: L'administration IV lente peut réduire l'incidence ou la gravité de la rigidité musculaire, de la bradycardie ou de l'hypotension.

Vitesse d'administration: Administrer lentement en au moins 1 ou 2 minutes.

Perfusion continue: Lorsque le sufentanil est utilisé comme anesthésique principal, on peut l'administrer sous forme de perfusion continue en même temps que la dose initiale ou après celle-ci pour obtenir des effets immédiats et soutenus tout au long d'une intervention chirurgicale prolongée.

S

ENSEIGNEMENT AU PATIENT ET À SES PROCHES

- Avant l'intervention chirurgicale, expliquer au patient le mode d'administration des agents anesthésiques et les sensations auxquelles il doit s'attendre.
- Conseiller au patient de changer lentement de position pour réduire le risque d'hypotension orthostatique.
- Prévenir le patient que le sufentanil provoque des étourdissements et de la somnolence. Lui conseiller de demander de l'aide lorsqu'il se déplace, de ne pas conduire et d'éviter les activités qui exigent sa vigilance pendant au moins 24 heures suivant l'administration du sufentanil lors d'une intervention chirurgicale de courte durée (chirurgie d'un jour) et jusqu'à ce qu'on ait la certitude que le médicament n'entraîne pas ces effets chez lui.
- Conseiller au patient d'éviter de boire de l'alcool ou de prendre des dépresseurs du SNC dans les 24 heures qui suivent l'administration du sufentanil lors d'une intervention chirurgicale de courte durée (chirurgie d'un jour).

VÉRIFICATION DE L'EFFICACITÉ THÉRAPEUTIQUE

L'efficacité du traitement peut être démontrée par: l'apaisement généralisé ■ le ralentissement de l'activité motrice ■ une analgésie prononcée. ✳

SULFAMÉTHOXAZOLE,

voir Triméthoprime/sulfaméthoxazole

SULFASALAZINE

Apo-Sulfasalazine, PMS-Sulfasalazine, PMS-Sulfasalazine E.C., Ratio-Sulfasalazine, Ratio-Sulfasalazine EN, Salazopyrin, Salazopyrin Entabs

CLASSIFICATION:

Agent antirhumatismal modificateur de la maladie (AARMM), anti-inflammatoire (effet gastro-intestinal local)

Grossesse – catégorie B (D si fin de grossesse)

INDICATIONS

Traitement des maladies inflammatoires de l'intestin, incluant: la rectocolite hémorragique grave ■ la rectocolite hémorragique distale ■ la rectite ■ la maladie de Crohn ■ **Comprimés à enrobage entérique:** Traitement de la polyarthrite rhumatoïde active, lorsque le traitement par les médicaments de première intention habituellement prescrits s'avère inefficace.

MÉCANISME D'ACTION

Action anti-inflammatoire locale au niveau du côlon, due probablement à l'inhibition de la synthèse des prostaglandines. ***Effets thérapeutiques:*** Réduction des symptômes de la maladie inflammatoire de l'intestin.

PHARMACOCINÉTIQUE

Absorption: De 10 à 15 % (PO).

Distribution: Tout l'organisme. La sulfasalazine traverse la barrière placentaire et passe dans le lait maternel.

Liaison aux protéines: 99 %.

Métabolisme et excrétion: La sulfasalazine est clivée en sulfapyridine et en acide 5-aminosalicylique (synonyme: mésalamine) sous l'effet des bactéries de l'intestin. Une fraction de la sulfasalazine est excrétée par la bile dans l'intestin, sinon l'excrétion est surtout rénale (15 % à l'état inchangé).

Demi-vie: 6 heures.

Profil temps-action (concentrations sanguines)

	Début d'action	Pic	Durée
PO	1 h	1,5 - 6 h	6 - 12 h

CONTRE-INDICATIONS, PRÉCAUTIONS ET MISES EN GARDE

Contre-indications: Hypersensibilité aux sulfamides, aux salicylates ou à la sulfasalazine ▪ Patients présentant des crises d'asthme aiguës, de l'urticaire, une rhinite ou d'autres manifestations allergiques dues à l'administration d'acide acétylsalicylique (AAS) ou d'autres anti-inflammatoires non stéroïdiens (AINS) ▪ Occlusion des voies urinaires ou des intestins ▪ Porphyrie ▪ **Péd.**: Enfants âgés de moins de 2 ans; enfants atteints de polyarthrite juvénile.

Précautions et mises en garde: Insuffisance rénale ou hépatique ▪ Patients ayant des antécédents de dyscrasie sanguine ou d'asthme bronchique grave ▪ Carence en glucose-6-phosphate-déshydrogénase (G-6-PD) ▪ Risque de réactions de sensibilité croisée avec le furosémide, les hypoglycémiants de type sulfonylurée ou les inhibiteurs de l'anhydrase carbonique ▪ **Obst.**: Précédents d'usage sans danger; administration possible en cas de nécessité absolue ▪ **Allaitement**: L'innocuité du médicament n'a pas été établie.

RÉACTIONS INDÉSIRABLES ET EFFETS SECONDAIRES

SNC: céphalées.

Resp.: pneumonite.

GI: anorexie, diarrhée, nausées, vomissements, hépatite médicamenteuse.

GU: cristallurie, oligospermie, coloration jaune orangé de l'urine.

Tég.: rash, érythrodermie, photosensibilité, jaunissement de la peau.

Hémat.: AGRANULOCYTOSE, ANÉMIE APLASIQUE, dyscrasie, éosinophilie, anémie mégaloblastique, thrombopénie.

SN: neuropathie périphérique.

Divers: réactions d'hypersensibilité, incluant la MALADIE SÉRIQUE et le SYNDROME DE STEVENS-JOHNSON, fièvre.

INTERACTIONS

Médicament-médicament: La sulfasalazine peut intensifier les effets des **hypoglycémiants oraux**, de la **phénytoïne**, du **méthotrexate**, de la **zidovudine** ou de la **warfarine**, et augmenter le risque de toxicité ▪ Risque accru d'hépatite médicamenteuse lors de l'administration concomitante d'autres **agents hépatotoxiques** ▪ Risque accru de cristallurie lors de l'administration concomitante de **méthénamine** ▪ La sulfasalazine peut diminuer l'absorption de la **digoxine** ▪ Le **probénécide** peut augmenter la toxicité de la sulfasalazine.

Médicament-aliments: La sulfasalazine peut diminuer l'absorption du **fer** et de l'**acide folique**.

VOIES D'ADMINISTRATION ET POSOLOGIE

- **PO (adultes)**: *Maladies inflammatoires de l'intestin (crise aiguë)* – de 1 à 2 g, 3 ou 4 fois par jour. *Prophylaxie* – 1 g, 2 ou 3 fois par jour. *Polyarthrite rhumatoïde* – majoration graduelle de la dose pour atteindre 1 g, 2 fois par jour (sous forme de comprimés à enrobage entérique).
- **PO (enfants)**: *Maladies inflammatoires de l'intestin (crise aiguë)* – **(enfants de 25 à 35 kg)**: 500 mg, 3 fois par jour; **(enfants de 35 à 50 kg)**: 1 g, 2 ou 3 fois par jour. *Prophylaxie* – **(enfants de 25 à 35 kg)**: 500 mg, 2 fois par jour; **(enfants de 35 à 50 kg)**: 500 mg, 2 ou 3 fois par jour.

PRÉSENTATION (version générique disponible)

Comprimés: 500 mg^Pr ▪ **Comprimés à enrobage entérique**: 500 mg^Pr.

S

SOINS INFIRMIERS

ÉVALUATION DE LA SITUATION

- Déterminer si le patient n'est pas allergique aux sulfamides et aux salicylates. Le traitement devrait être interrompu en cas de rash ou de fièvre.
- Effectuer le bilan quotidien des ingesta et des excreta. L'apport de liquides doit être suffisant pour maintenir un débit urinaire d'au moins 1 200 à 1 500 mL par jour, afin de prévenir la cristallurie et la formation de calculs.

Maladie inflammatoire de l'intestin: Suivre de près la douleur abdominale et noter la fréquence, la quantité et la consistance des selles au début du traitement et pendant toute sa durée.

Polyarthrite rhumatoïde: Évaluer l'amplitude des mouvements ainsi que l'enflure et la douleur des articulations touchées, avant le traitement et à intervalles réguliers pendant toute sa durée.

Tests de laboratoire: Suivre de près les résultats de l'analyse des urines, l'urée et les concentrations sériques de créatinine avant le traitement et à intervalles réguliers pendant toute sa durée. La mésalamine (5-ASA) peut entraîner une toxicité rénale. La sulfasalazine peut entraîner une cristallurie et la formation de calculs urinaires. NOTER LA NUMÉRATION GLOBULAIRE AVANT L'ADMINISTRATION ET TOUS LES 3 À 6 MOIS EN CAS DE TRAITEMENT PROLONGÉ. INTERROMPRE L'ADMINISTRATION DE LA SULFASALAZINE EN CAS DE DYSCRASIE SANGUINE.

DIAGNOSTICS INFIRMIERS POSSIBLES

- Douleur aiguë (Indications).
- Diarrhée (Indications).
- Connaissances insuffisantes sur le traitement médicamenteux (Enseignement au patient et à ses proches).

INTERVENTIONS INFIRMIÈRES

- NE PAS CONFONDRE LA SULFASALAZINE AVEC LE SULFISOXAZOLE.
- Pour diminuer les effets secondaires gastro-intestinaux, on peut modifier la posologie ou administrer les comprimés à enrobage entérique.
- Pour réduire l'irritation gastro-intestinale, on peut administrer la sulfasalazine avec des aliments ou après les repas. Servir ensuite au patient un grand verre d'eau. SIGNALER AU PATIENT QU'IL NE DOIT PAS ÉCRASER NI CROQUER LES COMPRIMÉS À ENROBAGE ENTÉRIQUE.

S

ENSEIGNEMENT AU PATIENT ET À SES PROCHES

- Expliquer au patient la méthode d'administration du médicament. Lui conseiller de respecter rigoureusement la posologie recommandée, même s'il se sent mieux. S'il n'a pu prendre le médicament au moment habituel, il doit le prendre dès que possible, à moins que ce ne soit presque l'heure prévue pour la dose suivante.
- Prévenir le patient que le médicament peut provoquer des étourdissements. Lui conseiller de ne pas conduire et d'éviter les activités qui exigent sa vigilance jusqu'à ce qu'on ait la certitude que le médicament n'entraîne pas cet effet chez lui.
- Recommander au patient de signaler à un professionnel de la santé le rash, les maux de gorge, la fièvre, les aphtes, les saignements ou les ecchymoses inhabituels, la respiration sifflante, la fièvre ou l'urticaire.
- Inciter le patient à utiliser des écrans solaires et à porter des vêtements protecteurs pour prévenir les réactions de photosensibilité.
- Prévenir le patient que ce médicament peut teinter sa peau et ses urines en jaune orangé; cet effet n'a aucune signification clinique. Le médicament peut jaunir les lentilles cornéennes de façon permanente.
- Recommander au patient de consulter un professionnel de la santé si les symptômes s'aggravent ou ne s'améliorent pas. Lui conseiller d'interrompre le traitement et de consulter un professionnel de la santé immédiatement si des symptômes d'intolérance aiguë se manifestent (crampes, douleurs abdominales aiguës, diarrhée contenant du sang, fièvre, céphalées, rash).
- Informer le patient qu'il devrait peut-être se soumettre à une rectoscopie et à une sigmoïdoscopie à intervalles réguliers pour que sa réponse au traitement puisse être évaluée.
- Conseiller au patient de communiquer avec un professionnel de la santé si les symptômes ne s'améliorent pas après 1 à 2 mois de traitement.

VÉRIFICATION DE L'EFFICACITÉ THÉRAPEUTIQUE

L'efficacité du traitement peut être démontrée par: la diminution de la diarrhée et des douleurs abdominales ▪ le rétablissement d'un mode normal d'élimination intestinale chez les patients souffrant d'une maladie inflammatoire de l'intestin; les effets peuvent se manifester dans les 3 à 21 jours; la durée habituelle du traitement est de 3 à 6 semaines ▪ la rémission chez les patients souffrant d'une maladie inflammatoire de l'intestin ▪ la diminution de la douleur et de l'inflammation, et une augmentation de la mobilité chez les patients souffrant de polyarthrite rhumatoïde. ✳

ALERTE CLINIQUE

SULFONYLURÉES

chlorpropamide

Apo-Chlorpropamide, Diabinèse, Novo-Propamide

gliclazide

Apo-Gliclazide, Diamicron, Diamicron MR, Gen-Gliclazide, Novo-Gliclazide, Sandoz-Gliclazide

glimépiride

Amaryl, Novo-Glimépiride, Ratio-Glimépiride, Sandoz-Glimépiride

glyburide

Apo-Glyburide, DiaBeta, Gen-Glybe, Novo-Glyburide, Nu-Glyburide, PMS-Glyburide, Ratio-Glyburide, Sandoz-Glyburide

tolbutamide

Apo-Tolbutamide, Mobenol

CLASSIFICATION:

Antidiabétiques (sulfonylurées)

Grossesse – catégories C (chlorpropamide, glimépiride, glyburide, tolbutamide) et X (gliclazide)

INDICATIONS

PO: Traitement d'appoint à l'exercice physique et à la diétothérapie dans le traitement du diabète de type 2, en monothérapie ou en association avec d'autres agents oraux ou avec l'insuline. Une certaine fonction pancréatique doit cependant subsister.

MÉCANISME D'ACTION

Diminution de la glycémie par la stimulation des sécrétions d'insuline par les cellules bêta fonctionnelles du pancréas. À long terme, les sulfonylurées augmentent la sensibilité à l'insuline aux sites récepteurs et diminuent la production de glucose hépatique. ***Effets thérapeutiques:*** Diminution de la glycémie chez les patients diabétiques.

PHARMACOCINÉTIQUE

Absorption: Bonne (PO).

Distribution: Le *glyburide* atteint des concentrations élevées dans la bile. Il traverse la barrière placentaire.

Liaison aux protéines: Tous les agents sont fortement liés aux protéines plasmatiques (> 90 %).

Métabolisme et excrétion: Tous les agents sont presque entièrement métabolisés par le foie. Les métabolites sont ensuite éliminés dans l'urine et les fèces.

Demi-vie: *Chlorpropamide* – 36 heures; *gliclazide* – 10 heures; *glimépiride* – 5 heures; *glyburide* – 10 heures; *tolbutamide* – de 4,5 à 6,5 heures.

Profil temps-action (effets hypoglycémiants)

	DÉBUT D'ACTION	PIC	DURÉE
Chlorpropamide	12 h	3 - 6 h	24 h
Gliclazide	inconnu	4 - 6 h	12 - 24 h
Glimépiride	inconnu	2 - 3 h	24 h
Glyburide	45 - 60 min	1,5 - 3 h	24 h
Tolbutamide	60 min	5 - 8 h	12 h

CONTRE-INDICATIONS, PRÉCAUTIONS ET MISES EN GARDE

Contre-indications: Hypersensibilité ■ Risque de sensibilité croisée avec les sulfamides (incluant les diurétiques thiazidiques) ■ Diabète de type 1 ■ Coma diabétique ou acidocétose ■ Insuffisance rénale ou hépatique grave ■ Maladie thyroïdienne grave ■ États de stress, tels une infection non maîtrisée, des brûlures graves, un traumatisme ou une intervention chirurgicale ■ **OBST.**: Les sulfonylurées ne sont pas recommandées pour équilibrer le diabète de type 1 ou le diabète gravidique (l'insuline est recommandée pendant la grossesse) ■ **ALLAITEMENT**: Risque d'hypoglycémie chez le nourrisson.

Précautions et mises en garde: **GÉR.**: Il est recommandé de réduire la dose chez les personnes âgées ou débilitées (risque accru d'hypoglycémie) ■ Maladie rénale (risque accru d'hypoglycémie) ■ Modification de l'alimentation (modification de la glycémie) ■ Insuffisance thyroïdienne, hypophysaire ou surrénalienne ■ Malnutrition, forte fièvre, nausées prolongées ou vomissements.

RÉACTIONS INDÉSIRABLES ET EFFETS SECONDAIRES

SNC: étourdissements, somnolence, céphalées, faiblesse.

GI: constipation, crampes, diarrhée, hépatite, brûlures d'estomac, gain d'appétit, nausées, vomissements.

Tég.: photosensibilité, rash.

End.: hypoglycémie.

HÉ: hyponatrémie.

Hémat.: ANÉMIE APLASIQUE, agranulocytose, leucopénie, pancytopénie, thrombopénie.

INTERACTIONS

Médicament-médicament: L'ingestion simultanée d'**alcool** peut entraîner une réaction semblable à celle au disulfirame ■ Les **diurétiques**, les **corticostéroïdes**, les **phénothiazines**, les **contraceptifs oraux**, les **œstrogènes**, les **préparations thyroïdiennes**, la **phénytoïne**, l'**acide nicotinique**, les **agents sympathomimétiques** et l'**isoniazide** peuvent diminuer l'efficacité des sulfonylurées ■ L'**alcool**, les **hormones androgènes** (**testostérone**), le **chloramphénicol**, les **IMAO**, les **anti-inflammatoires non stéroïdiens** (sauf le **diclofénac**), les **salicylates**, le **fluconazole**, les **sulfamides** et la **warfarine** peuvent accroître le risque d'hypoglycémie ■ L'administration concomitante de **warfarine** peut modifier la réponse aux deux agents (initialement, intensification des effets des deux agents, puis diminution); on recommande une surveillance étroite lors des adaptations posologiques ■ Les **bêtabloquants** peuvent

S

modifier la réponse aux hypoglycémiants oraux (augmentation ou diminution des besoins; des agents non spécifiques peuvent entraîner une hypoglycémie prolongée).

Médicament-produits naturels: La **glucosamine** peut entraver l'équilibrage glycémique ■ Le **chrome** et le **coenzyme Q-10** peuvent entraîner des effets hypoglycémiants additifs.

VOIES D'ADMINISTRATION ET POSOLOGIE

Chlorpropamide

- **PO (adultes)**: Initialement, 250 mg, 1 fois par jour avec le premier repas de la journée (dose habituelle de 100 à 500 mg par jour). La dose quotidienne maximale est de 500 mg.

Gliclazide

- **PO (adultes)**: *Comprimés à libération immédiate* – initialement, 80 mg par jour, 2 fois par jour, avec le déjeuner et le souper (dose habituelle de 80 à 320 mg par jour). La dose quotidienne maximale est de 320 mg. *Comprimés à libération modifiée* – initialement, 30 mg, 1 fois par jour avec le premier repas de la journée (dose habituelle de 30 à 120 mg par jour). La dose quotidienne maximale est de 120 mg.

Glimépiride

- **PO (adultes)**: Initialement, 1 mg, 1 fois par jour, avec le premier repas de la journée (dose habituelle de 1 à 4 mg par jour). La dose quotidienne maximale est de 8 mg.

Glyburide

- **PO (adultes)**: Initialement, 5 mg, 1 fois par jour (dose habituelle de 1,25 à 20 mg par jour). Si une dose de plus de 10 mg par jour est nécessaire, administrer le surplus avec le repas du soir. La dose quotidienne maximale est de 20 mg.
- **PO (personnes âgées)**: Initialement, 2,5 mg par jour; on peut augmenter la dose de 2,5 mg par jour, toutes les semaines.

Tolbutamide

- **PO (adultes)**: Initialement, 1 000 mg par jour, en 1 à 3 prises fractionnées (dose habituelle de 500 à 2 000 mg par jour). La dose quotidienne maximale est de 3 000 mg.

S

PRÉSENTATION

- **Chlorpropamide** (version générique disponible)
  Comprimés: 100 mg^{Pr}, 250 mg^{Pr}.
- **Gliclazide** (version générique disponible)
  Comprimés à libération immédiate: 80 mg^{Pr} ■ **Comprimés à libération modifiée**: 30 mg^{Pr}.
- **Glimépiride** (version générique disponible)
  Comprimés: 1 mg^{Pr}, 2 mg^{Pr}, 4 mg^{Pr} ■ **En association avec**: rosiglitazone (Avandaryl^{Pr}).
- **Glyburide** (version générique disponible)
  Comprimés: 2,5 mg^{Pr}, 5 mg^{Pr}.
- **Tolbutamide** (version générique disponible)
  Comprimés: 500 mg^{Pr}.

SOINS INFIRMIERS

ÉVALUATION DE LA SITUATION

- Observer les signes et les symptômes suivants de réactions d'hypoglycémie: transpiration, faim, faiblesse, étourdissements, tremblements, tachycardie, anxiété.
- Déterminer si le patient n'est pas allergique aux sulfamides.

Tests de laboratoire:

- Mesurer à intervalles réguliers tout au long du traitement les concentrations sériques de glucose et d'hémoglobine glyquée pour déterminer l'efficacité du traitement.
- SUIVRE LA NUMÉRATION GLOBULAIRE À INTERVALLES RÉGULIERS TOUT AU LONG DU TRAITEMENT. PRÉVENIR IMMÉDIATEMENT LE MÉDECIN EN CAS DE DIMINUTION DU NOMBRE DE GLOBULES SANGUINS.
- Le médicament peut élever les concentrations d'AST, de LDH, d'urée et de créatinine sérique.

TOXICITÉ ET SURDOSAGE: Le surdosage se manifeste par des symptômes d'hypoglycémie. En cas d'hypoglycémie légère, administrer du glucose par voie orale. En cas d'hypoglycémie grave, administrer par voie IV une solution de D50%E, suivie de la perfusion continue d'une solution de dextrose plus diluée, à un débit suffisant pour maintenir la glycémie à environ 5,6 mmol/L.

DIAGNOSTICS INFIRMIERS POSSIBLES

- Alimentation excessive (Indications).
- Connaissances insuffisantes sur le traitement médicamenteux (Enseignement au patient et à ses proches).
- Non-observance du traitement médicamenteux (Enseignement au patient et à ses proches).

INTERVENTIONS INFIRMIÈRES

- **ALERTE CLINIQUE**: L'ADMINISTRATION ACCIDENTELLE DE SULFONYLURÉES À DES ADULTES NON DIABÉTIQUES ET À DES ENFANTS A ENTRAÎNÉ DES DOMMAGES IMPORTANTS OU LA MORT. TOUJOURS CONFIRMER QUE LE PATIENT EST DIABÉTIQUE AVANT D'ADMINISTRER LE MÉDICAMENT.
- Chez les patients dont la glycémie a été équilibrée grâce aux sulfonylurées, mais qui ont de la fièvre ou

qui sont exposés au stress, aux traumatismes, à l'infection ou à une intervention chirurgicale, administrer de l'insuline, si besoin est.

- Il n'est pas nécessaire d'ajuster graduellement la posologie lors du passage d'une sulfonylurée à une autre. Chez les patients qui prennent moins de 20 unités d'insuline par jour, on peut substituer le traitement aux sulfonylurées à l'insulinothérapie sans devoir ajuster graduellement la posologie. Chez les patients qui prennent 20 unités par jour ou plus, la substitution devra se faire graduellement : on leur administrera l'agent oral et on réduira la dose d'insuline de 25 à 30 % tous les jours ou tous les 2 jours, selon leur tolérance. On devra mesurer la glycémie et la cétonurie au moins 3 fois par jour pendant cette période.
- On peut administrer le médicament en une seule dose, le matin, ou en 2 doses fractionnées. Administrer la plupart des sulfonylurées avec des repas pour assurer un meilleur équilibrage de la glycémie et pour réduire l'irritation gastrique et le risque d'hypoglycémie. Ne pas administrer le médicament après le dernier repas de la journée.
- Dans le cas des patients qui éprouvent des difficultés de déglutition, on peut écraser les comprimés et les administrer dans des liquides. LES COMPRIMÉS À LIBÉRATION MODIFIÉE DE GLICLAZIDE (DIAMICRON MR) DOIVENT ÊTRE AVALÉS ENTIERS ; NE PAS LES ÉCRASER NI LES MÂCHER.

ENSEIGNEMENT AU PATIENT ET À SES PROCHES

- Conseiller au patient de prendre le médicament tous les jours à la même heure. S'il n'a pas pu prendre le médicament au moment habituel, il doit le prendre aussitôt que possible à moins que ce ne soit presque l'heure prévue pour la dose suivante. Ne pas administrer le médicament si le patient est incapable de manger.
- Expliquer au patient que le médicament maîtrise l'hyperglycémie, mais ne peut guérir le diabète. Le traitement est de longue durée.
- Expliquer au patient les signes d'hypoglycémie et d'hyperglycémie. En cas d'hypoglycémie, recommander au patient de prendre un verre de jus d'orange ou de 2 à 3 cuillérés à thé de sucre, de miel ou de sirop de maïs dans de l'eau et de prévenir un professionnel de la santé.
- Encourager le patient à suivre le régime alimentaire, la pharmacothérapie et le programme d'exercices prescrits afin de prévenir les épisodes d'hypoglycémie ou d'hyperglycémie.
- Enseigner au patient les méthodes appropriées de dosage du glucose sanguin et des corps cétoniques urinaires. Ces résultats doivent être notés attentivement pendant les périodes de stress ou pendant une maladie. Il faut prévenir immédiatement un professionnel de la santé si des modifications importantes surviennent.
- Prévenir le patient que les sulfonylurées peuvent parfois provoquer des étourdissements ou des faiblesses. Lui conseiller de ne pas conduire et d'éviter les activités qui exigent sa vigilance jusqu'à ce qu'on ait la certitude que le médicament n'entraîne pas ces effets chez lui.
- Conseiller au patient de consulter un professionnel de la santé avant de prendre d'autres médicaments ou de l'alcool, en même temps que ces médicaments.
- Prévenir le patient que la consommation simultanée d'alcool peut entraîner une réaction semblable à celle provoquée par le disulfirame : crampes abdominales, nausées, rougeurs du visage, céphalées et hypoglycémie.
- Informer la patiente que l'insuline est l'agent recommandé pour équilibrer la glycémie pendant la grossesse. Lui conseiller de ne pas prendre des contraceptifs oraux, mais d'utiliser une autre méthode de contraception et d'informer rapidement un professionnel de la santé si elle pense être enceinte ou si elle souhaite le devenir.
- Conseiller au patient d'utiliser un écran solaire et de porter des vêtements de protection pour prévenir les réactions de photosensibilité.
- Recommander au patient qui doit suivre un traitement ou subir une intervention chirurgicale de prévenir le professionnel de la santé qu'il suit un traitement par ce type de médicaments.
- Conseiller au patient d'avoir toujours sur lui du sucre (sachets de sucre ou bonbons) et de porter en tout temps un bracelet d'identité où sont inscrits son problème de santé et son traitement médicamenteux.
- Recommander au patient d'informer rapidement un professionnel de la santé en cas de gain de poids inhabituel, d'œdème des chevilles, de somnolence, d'essoufflement, de crampes musculaires, de faiblesse, de maux de gorge, de rash, de saignements ou d'ecchymoses inhabituels.
- Insister sur l'importance d'un suivi médical régulier.

VÉRIFICATION DE L'EFFICACITÉ THÉRAPEUTIQUE

L'efficacité du traitement peut être démontrée par: l'équilibrage de la glycémie sans survenue d'épisodes d'hypoglycémie ou d'hyperglycémie.

SULINDAC

Apo-Sulin, Novo-Sundac, Nu-Sulindac

CLASSIFICATION:

Anti-inflammatoire non stéroïdien, analgésique non opioïde

Grossesse – catégorie inconnue

INDICATIONS

Traitement des maladies inflammatoires, incluant: la polyarthrite rhumatoïde ■ l'arthrose ■ la spondylarthrite ankylosante ■ l'arthrite goutteuse aiguë ■ la périarthrite aiguë de l'épaule (bursite, tendinite).

MÉCANISME D'ACTION

Inhibition de la synthèse des prostaglandines. ***Effets thérapeutiques:*** Suppression de la douleur et de l'inflammation.

PHARMACOCINÉTIQUE

Absorption: Bonne (PO).

Distribution: Inconnue. L'agent passe dans le lait maternel en petites quantités.

Métabolisme et excrétion: Métabolisme hépatique (formation d'un métabolite actif). Excrétion rénale (en petites quantités sous forme inchangée).

Demi-vie: 7,8 heures (métabolite actif: 16,4 heures).

Profil temps-action (effets thérapeutiques)

	DÉBUT D'ACTION	PIC	DURÉE
PO (effet analgésique)	1 – 2 jours	inconnu	12 h
PO (effet anti-inflammatoire)	de quelques jours à 1 semaine	2 semaines ou plus	inconnue

CONTRE-INDICATIONS, PRÉCAUTIONS ET MISES EN GARDE

Contre-indications: Hypersensibilité ■ Risque de réactions de sensibilité croisée avec d'autres anti-inflammatoires non stéroïdiens, incluant l'aspirine ■ Hémorragie digestive manifeste ou ulcère évolutif, ou inflammation évolutive du tractus gastro-intestinal ■ Contexte périopératoire en cas de pontage aortocoronarien.

Précautions et mises en garde: Maladie cardiovasculaire ou facteurs de risque de maladie cardiovasculaire (risque accru de complications thrombotiques, d'infarctus du myocarde, d'AVC, surtout lors d'un usage prolongé) ■ Maladies rénale ou hépatique graves (il est recommandé de modifier la dose) ■ **GÉR.:** Les personnes âgées sont davantage prédisposées aux hémorragies digestives ■ Antécédents d'ulcère ■ **OBST., ALLAITEMENT, PÉD.:** Usage déconseillé.

RÉACTIONS INDÉSIRABLES ET EFFETS SECONDAIRES

SNC: étourdissements, céphalées, somnolence.

ORLO: vision trouble, acouphènes.

CV: œdème.

GI: HÉMORRAGIE DIGESTIVE, HÉPATITE, constipation, diarrhée, gêne gastro-intestinale, dyspepsie, nausées, vomissements, anorexie, flatulence, pancréatite.

GU: insuffisance rénale.

Tég.: DERMATITE EXFOLIATIVE, SYNDROME DE STEVENS-JOHNSON, ÉPIDERMOLYSE NÉCROSANTE SUBAIGUË, rash, photosensibilité.

Hémat.: dyscrasie sanguine, allongement du temps de saignement.

Divers: réactions allergiques, incluant l'ANAPHYLAXIE et le SYNDROME D'HYPERSENSIBILITÉ.

INTERACTIONS

Médicament-médicament: L'**aspirine**, administrée simultanément, peut diminuer l'efficacité du sulindac ■ Risque accru de saignements lors de l'administration concomitante d'**anticoagulants**, d'**agents thrombolytiques**, de **tirofiban**, d'**eptifibatide**, de **clopidogrel**, de **ticlopidine**, de **céfamandole**, de **céfopérazone**, de **céfotétane**, d'**acide valproïque** ou de **plicamycine** ■ Effets gastro-intestinaux indésirables additifs lors de l'administration concomitante d'**aspirine**, de **corticostéroïdes** et d'autres **agents anti-inflammatoires non stéroïdiens** ■ Le sulindac peut diminuer la réponse thérapeutique aux **diurétiques** ou aux **antihypertenseurs** ■ Le sulindac peut élever les concentrations sériques de **lithium** et augmenter le risque de toxicité ■ Risque accru de réactions hématologiques indésirables lors de l'administration simultanée d'**agents antinéoplasiques** ou d'une **radiothérapie** ■ Risque accru de réactions rénales indésirables lors de l'administration concomitante de **sels d'or**, de **cyclosporine** ou d'un traitement prolongé par l'**acétaminophène** ■ Les **antiacides**, administrés simultanément, abaissent les concentrations sanguines de sulindac et en diminuent l'efficacité ■ Risque accru de photosensibilité lors de l'administration simultanée d'autres **médicaments photosensibilisants** ■ Risque accru d'hypoglycémie en cas d'administration simultanée d'**insuline** ou d'**hypoglycémiants oraux** ■ Le sulindac ne devrait pas être administré en même temps que le **diméthylsulfoxyde**

en raison du risque accru de neuropathie périphérique et de réduction des concentrations de sulindac et de son métabolite.

VOIES D'ADMINISTRATION ET POSOLOGIE

- **PO (adultes):** De 150 à 200 mg, 2 fois par jour, avec des aliments (ne pas dépasser 400 mg par jour).

PRÉSENTATION (version générique disponible)

Comprimés: 150 mg^{Pr}, 200 mg^{Pr}.

SOINS INFIRMIERS

ÉVALUATION DE LA SITUATION

- LES PATIENTS SOUFFRANT D'ASTHME, D'ALLERGIE INDUITE PAR L'ASPIRINE ET DE POLYPES NASAUX SONT DAVANTAGE PRÉDISPOSÉS À DES RÉACTIONS D'HYPERSENSIBILITÉ. SUIVRE DE PRÈS LES SYMPTÔMES DE RHINITE, D'ASTHME ET D'URTICAIRE.
- Évaluer la douleur et l'amplitude des mouvements, avant l'administration et après 1 ou 2 semaines de traitement.

Tests de laboratoire:

- Examiner à intervalles réguliers, tout au long du traitement prolongé, les concentrations sériques d'urée et de créatinine ainsi que la numération globulaire et les résultats des tests de la fonction hépatique.
- Le sulindac peut entraîner l'élévation des concentrations sériques de potassium, de glucose, de phosphatase alcaline, d'AST et d'ALT.
- Le sulindac peut allonger le temps de saignement pendant 24 heures après l'arrêt du traitement.

DIAGNOSTICS INFIRMIERS POSSIBLES

- Douleur aiguë (Indications).
- Mobilité physique réduite (Indications).
- Connaissances insuffisantes sur le traitement médicamenteux (Enseignement au patient et à ses proches).

INTERVENTIONS INFIRMIÈRES

- L'administration de doses plus élevées que celles qui sont recommandées n'accroît pas l'efficacité du sulindac, mais peut entraîner des effets indésirables accrus. Utiliser la dose la plus faible efficace, pendant le moins de temps possible.
- On peut administrer le sulindac avec des aliments, du lait ou des antiacides pour réduire l'irritation gastrique. Les aliments ralentissent l'absorption du médicament, mais ne réduisent pas la quantité totale absorbée. Les comprimés peuvent être écrasés et mélangés à des liquides ou à des aliments.

ENSEIGNEMENT AU PATIENT ET À SES PROCHES

- Conseiller au patient de prendre le sulindac avec un grand verre d'eau et de ne pas s'allonger pendant les 15 à 30 minutes qui suivent.
- Conseiller au patient de respecter rigoureusement la posologie recommandée. S'il n'a pu prendre le médicament au moment habituel, il doit le prendre dès que possible, à moins que ce ne soit presque l'heure prévue pour la dose suivante. L'avertir qu'il ne doit jamais remplacer une dose manquée par une double dose.
- Prévenir le patient que le sulindac peut provoquer des étourdissements. Lui conseiller de ne pas conduire et d'éviter les activités qui exigent sa vigilance jusqu'à ce qu'on ait la certitude que le médicament n'entraîne pas cet effet chez lui.
- Conseiller au patient d'éviter de boire de l'alcool et de ne pas prendre de l'aspirine, d'autres AINS, de l'acétaminophène ou tout autre médicament en vente libre, en même temps que le sulindac, sans consulter au préalable un professionnel de la santé.
- Recommander au patient qui doit suivre un autre traitement ou subir une intervention chirurgicale d'avertir le professionnel de la santé qu'il suit un traitement par ce médicament.
- Conseiller à la patiente d'informer un professionnel de la santé si elle pense être enceinte ou désire le devenir ou, encore, si elle allaite.
- Inciter le patient à utiliser un écran solaire et à porter des vêtements protecteurs pour prévenir les réactions de photosensibilité.
- Recommander au patient de signaler à un professionnel de la santé le rash, les démangeaisons, les troubles visuels, les acouphènes, le gain de poids, l'œdème, les selles noires, les céphalées persistantes ou le syndrome pseudogrippal (frissons, fièvre, douleurs musculaires, douleurs).

S

VÉRIFICATION DE L'EFFICACITÉ THÉRAPEUTIQUE

L'efficacité du traitement peut être démontrée par: le soulagement de la douleur et une mobilité accrue des articulations. Le soulagement partiel des douleurs arthritiques survient habituellement dans les 7 jours qui suivent le début du traitement, mais le plein effet du médicament peut ne se manifester qu'après 2 ou 3 semaines. Les patients qui ne répondent pas à un anti-inflammatoire non stéroïdien peuvent répondre à un autre.

SUMATRIPTAN,

voir Agonistes de la sérotonine 5-HT_1

TACROLIMUS

Prograf

tacrolimus (topique)

Protopic

CLASSIFICATION:

Immunosuppresseur

Grossesse – catégorie C

INDICATIONS

Prévention du rejet d'une greffe, à la suite de la transplantation d'un foie, d'un rein ou d'un cœur allogénique (en traitement concomitant avec des glucocorticoïdes ou d'autres immunosuppresseurs) ■ Traitement du rejet réfractaire chez les receveurs d'allogreffe rénale ou hépatique ■ Traitement de la polyarthrite rhumatoïde évolutive chez les adultes, lorsqu'un traitement antirhumatismal modifiant la maladie est inefficace ou contre-indiqué ■ **Topique**: Traitement intermittent à court et à long terme chez les patients atteints de dermatite atopique modérée à grave, lorsque les traitements classiques sont jugés inopportuns à cause des risques possibles, ou que les patients ne répondent pas adéquatement ou sont intolérants aux traitements classiques. **Usages non approuvés**: Prévention du rejet d'autres types d'organes greffés ■ Maladies auto-immunes ■ Psoriasis grave, réfractaire au traitement.

MÉCANISME D'ACTION

Inhibition de l'activation des lymphocytes T. ***Effets thérapeutiques:*** Prévention du rejet de l'organe greffé ■ Diminution des lésions articulaires en présence de polyarthrite rhumatoïde ■ Diminution de l'étendue et de la gravité des lésions de la dermatite atopique (voie topique).

PHARMACOCINÉTIQUE

Absorption: Variable (PO); biodisponibilité de 14,4 à 21,8 % (PO). Minimale (topique).

Distribution: Le tacrolimus traverse la barrière placentaire et passe dans le lait maternel.

Liaison aux protéines: De 75 à 99 %.

Métabolisme et excrétion: Métabolisme hépatique important (99 %).

Demi-vie: *Greffés du foie* – 11,7 heures; *greffés du rein* – 18,8 heures; *volontaires en santé* – 34,2 heures.

Profil temps-action (immunosuppression)

	DÉBUT D'ACTION	PIC	DURÉE
PO	rapide	1,3 – 3,2 h†	12 h
IV	rapide	inconnu	8 – 12 h
Topique	inconnu	1 – 2 semaines‡	inconnue

† Concentrations sanguines.

‡ Amélioration de l'état des lésions entraînées par la dermatite atopique.

CONTRE-INDICATIONS, PRÉCAUTIONS ET MISES EN GARDE

Contre-indications: Hypersensibilité au tacrolimus ou à l'huile de ricin qui entre dans la composition de la solution pour injection.

Précautions et mises en garde: Insuffisance rénale ou hépatique (il peut s'avérer nécessaire de réduire la dose; en cas d'oligurie, attendre l'amélioration de la fonction rénale avant de commencer le traitement par le tacrolimus) ■ Ne pas administrer la cyclosporine en même temps ■ Exposition au soleil (risque accru de néoplasies cutanées) ■ **PÉD.**: Il est nécessaire d'administrer les doses les plus élevées recommandées pour maintenir des concentrations sanguines adéquates; risque accru de cardiomégalie ■ **OBST.**: Grossesse (risque d'hyperkaliémie et d'insuffisance rénale chez le nouveau-né; administrer l'agent seulement si les bienfaits pour la mère justifient le risque pour le fœtus). Allaitement déconseillé ■ **Topique**: **PÉD.**: N'utiliser que si les autres traitements possibles n'ont pas été efficaces; l'innocuité de l'agent chez les enfants < 2 ans n'a pas été établie ■ Infections de la peau.

RÉACTIONS INDÉSIRABLES ET EFFETS SECONDAIRES

SNC: CONVULSIONS, céphalées, insomnie, tremblements, rêves bizarres, agitation, anxiété, confusion, étourdissements, labilité émotionnelle, dépression, hallucinations, psychose, somnolence.

ORLO: vision anormale, amblyopie, rhinite, sinusite, acouphènes, modification de la voix.

Resp.: asthme, bronchite, toux, pharyngite, pneumonie, œdème pulmonaire.

CV: ascite, hypertension, œdème périphérique.

GI: HÉMORRAGIE GASTRO-INTESTINALE, douleurs abdominales, anorexie, diarrhée, nausées, vomissements, cholangite, ictère cholestatique, dyspepsie, dysphagie, flatulence, gain d'appétit, élévation des résultats des tests de la fonction hépatique, muguet, péritonite.

GU: néphrotoxicité, infection des voies urinaires.

Tég.: prurit, rash, alopécie, herpès, hirsutisme, photosensibilité, transpiration.

End.: hyperglycémie.

T

HÉ: hyperkaliémie, hypomagnésémie, acidose, alcalose, hyperlipidémie, hyperphosphatémie, hyperuricémie, hypocalcémie, hypokaliémie, hyponatrémie, hypophosphatémie.

Hémat.: anémie, lymphocytose, thrombopénie, troubles de la coagulation, leucopénie.

Loc.: arthralgie, hypertonie, crampes dans les jambes, spasmes musculaires, myalgie, myasthénie, ostéoporose.

Locaux: douleurs, démangeaisons, brûlures.

SN: paresthésie, neuropathie.

Divers: réactions allergiques incluant l'ANAPHYLAXIE, douleurs généralisées, cicatrisation anormale des plaies, frissons, fièvre, risque accru de lymphome, risque accru de cancer de la peau (topique).

INTERACTIONS

Médicament-médicament: Le risque de néphrotoxicité est accru lors de l'usage concomitant d'**aminosides**, d'**amphotéricine B**, de **cisplatine** ou de **cyclosporine** (administrer le tacrolimus 24 heures après avoir arrêté le traitement par la cyclosporine) ■ Les **diurétiques d'épargne potassique** ou les **inhibiteurs de l'enzyme de conversion de l'angiotensine (IECA)**, administrés en concomitance, augmentent le risque d'hyperkaliémie ■ Les concentrations sanguines de tacrolimus peuvent être augmentées lors de l'administration concomitante de plusieurs médicaments comme les **antifongiques de type azole**, la **bromocriptine**, les **bloqueurs des canaux calciques**, la **cimétidine**, la **clarithromycine**, la **cyclosporine**, le **danazol**, l'**érythromycine**, l'**hydroxyde de magnésium/aluminium**, la **méthylprednisolone,** les **inhibiteurs de la protéase** et le **métoclopramide** ■ Les concentrations sanguines du tacrolimus peuvent s'abaisser en cas d'administration concomitante de **phénobarbital**, de **phénytoïne**, de **carbamazépine**, de **caspofongine**, de **sirolimus** et de **rifampicine** ■ Le tacrolimus peut diminuer l'efficacité des **vaccins** (les vaccins à virus vivants sont déconseillés) ■ Les **AINS**, administrés en concomitance, augmentent le risque d'hypertension artérielle et d'insuffisance rénale.

Médicament-aliments: Les **aliments** diminuent la vitesse et le taux d'absorption gastro-intestinale du tacrolimus ■ Le **jus de pamplemousse** diminue le métabolisme du tacrolimus.

Médicament-produits naturels: La consommation concomitante d'**astragale**, d'**échinacée** et de **mélatonine** peut modifier les effets immunosuppresseurs ■ La consommation concomitante de **millepertuis** peut diminuer l'efficacité du tacrolimus.

T

VOIES D'ADMINISTRATION ET POSOLOGIE

- **PO (adultes)**: *Transplantation rénale* – de 0,1 à 0,15 mg/kg, toutes les 12 heures. *Transplantation hépatique* – de 0,05 à 0,075 mg/kg, toutes les 12 heures. *Transplantation cardiaque* – 0,0375 mg/kg, toutes les 12 heures. *Polyarthrite rhumatoïde* – 3 mg, 1 fois par jour.
- **PO (enfants)**: *Traitement initial* – De 0,15 à 0,2 mg/kg/jour.
- **IV (adultes, enfants)**: *Transplantation rénale ou hépatique* – de 0,03 à 0,05 mg/kg/jour en perfusion continue. *Transplantation cardiaque* – 0,01 mg/kg/jour en perfusion continue.
- **Topique (adultes)**: *Onguent à 0,03 % ou à 0,1 %* – appliquer 2 fois par jour une couche mince sur les régions touchées. Cesser l'application 1 semaine après la résolution des lésions.
- **Topique (enfants > 2 ans)**: *Onguent à 0,03 %* – appliquer 2 fois par jour une couche mince sur les régions touchées. Cesser l'application 1 semaine après la résolution des lésions.

PRÉSENTATION

Capsules: 0,5 mg[Pr], 1 mg[Pr], 5 mg[Pr] ■ **Solution pour injection**: 5 mg/mL, en ampoules de 1 mL[Pr] ■ **Onguent topique**: 0,03 %[Pr], 0,1 %[Pr].

SOINS INFIRMIERS

ÉVALUATION DE LA SITUATION

- Suivre de près la pression artérielle pendant toute la durée du traitement. L'hypertension est une complication courante du traitement par le tacrolimus et devrait être traitée.
- OBSERVER ÉTROITEMENT LE PATIENT QUI REÇOIT LE TACROLIMUS PAR VOIE IV, PENDANT AU MOINS 30 MINUTES ET À INTERVALLES FRÉQUENTS PAR LA SUITE, EN RAISON DU RISQUE D'ANAPHYLAXIE (RASH, PRURIT, ŒDÈME LARYNGÉ, RESPIRATION SIFFLANTE). SI DES SIGNES SE MANIFESTENT, CESSER LA PERFUSION ET DÉMARRER LE TRAITEMENT QUI S'IMPOSE.

Dermatite atopique: Examiner les lésions de la peau avant le traitement et à intervalles réguliers pendant toute sa durée. Utiliser seulement pendant une courte période, de façon intermittente et à la dose la plus faible possible pour diminuer le risque de cancer de la peau.

Tests de laboratoire:

- La détermination des concentrations sanguines de tacrolimus permet d'évaluer le risque de rejet et de toxicité, les adaptations posologiques qui pourraient être nécessaires et l'observance au traitement.

On a constaté que la concentration de tacrolimus dans le sang entier, lorsque le dosage est effectué par la méthode immuno-enzymatique (test ELISA), varie le plus au cours de la première semaine suivant la greffe. Après la première semaine, la moyenne des concentrations sanguines minimales (creux) se situe entre 9,8 et 19,4 ng/mL.

- Suivre de près les concentrations sériques de créatinine et de potassium ainsi que la glycémie. Des concentrations sériques élevées de créatinine et un débit urinaire réduit peuvent être des signes de néphrotoxicité. L'administration de tacrolimus peut entraîner l'hyperglycémie; il peut s'avérer nécessaire d'administrer de l'insuline ou un hypoglycémiant oral.
- Le tacrolimus peut aussi provoquer l'hyperuricémie, l'hypokaliémie, l'hypomagnésémie, l'acidose, l'alcalose, l'hyperlipidémie, l'hyperphosphatémie, l'hypophosphatémie, l'hypocalcémie et l'hyponatrémie.
- Suivre de près les numérations globulaire et plaquettaire. Le tacrolimus peut provoquer l'anémie, la lymphocytose et la thrombopénie.

Toxicité et surdosage: Des tremblements et des céphalées ont été associés à des concentrations élevées de tacrolimus dans le sang entier; on peut diminuer ces effets secondaires en réduisant les doses de médicament.

DIAGNOSTICS INFIRMIERS POSSIBLES

- Risque d'infection (Réactions indésirables).
- Connaissances insuffisantes sur le traitement médicamenteux (Enseignement au patient et à ses proches).

INTERVENTIONS INFIRMIÈRES

- Le traitement par le tacrolimus ne devrait être amorcé que 6 heures après la transplantation. Au début de la période postopératoire, il est recommandé d'administrer en concomitance des glucocorticoïdes.
- Il est préférable d'administrer le tacrolimus par voie orale en raison du risque de réactions anaphylactiques qui accompagne l'administration par voie intraveineuse. Il faudrait donc remplacer le plus tôt possible le traitement intraveineux par celui par voie orale.
- Chez les adultes, on devrait amorcer le traitement par la dose thérapeutique la plus faible. Les enfants ont besoin de doses plus élevées et ils les tolèrent bien. Dans leur cas, il faudrait donc amorcer le traitement par la dose thérapeutique la plus élevée possible.

PO: On peut administrer les doses par voie orale de 8 à 12 heures après l'arrêt du traitement par voie IV.

Perfusion continue: Diluer l'agent dans une solution de NaCl 0,9 % ou de D5%E, pour obtenir une concentration de 0,004 à 0,02 mg/mL. La solution peut être gardée dans des récipients de polyéthylène ou de verre pendant 24 heures après la dilution. Ne pas la conserver dans des récipients en PVC et ne pas utiliser de tubulure en PVC.

Vitesse d'administration: Administrer la dose quotidienne sous forme de perfusion continue pendant 24 heures.

Compatibilité (tubulure en Y): acyclovir ■ aminophylline ■ amphotéricine B ■ ampicilline ■ ampicilline/sulbactam ■ benztropine ■ calcium, gluconate de ■ céfazoline ■ céfotétane ■ ceftazidime ■ ceftriaxone ■ céfuroxime ■ chloramphénicol ■ cimétidine ■ ciprofloxacine ■ clindamycine ■ dexaméthasone ■ digoxine ■ diphenhydramine ■ dobutamine ■ dopamine ■ doxycycline ■ érythromycine, lactobionate d' ■ esmolol ■ fluconazole ■ furosémide ■ ganciclovir ■ gentamicine ■ halopéridol ■ héparine ■ hydrocortisone sodique, succinate d' ■ imipénem/cilastatine ■ insuline ■ isoprotérénol ■ leucovorine ■ lorazépam ■ méthylprednisolone ■ métoclopramide ■ métronidazole ■ mezlocilline ■ multivitamines ■ nitroglycérine ■ oxacilline ■ pénicilline G potassique ■ perphénazine ■ phénytoïne ■ pipéracilline ■ potassium ■ propranolol ■ ranitidine ■ sodium, bicarbonate de ■ tobramycine ■ triméthoprime/sulfaméthoxazole ■ vancomycine.

ENSEIGNEMENT AU PATIENT ET À SES PROCHES

- Prévenir le patient qu'il doit prendre le médicament à la même heure tous les jours, en respectant rigoureusement la posologie recommandée. Le prévenir également qu'il ne doit pas sauter de dose ni remplacer une dose manquée par une double dose, et qu'il ne doit pas cesser le traitement sans avoir consulté un professionnel de la santé au préalable.
- Expliquer au patient qu'il doit suivre ce traitement toute sa vie durant pour prévenir le rejet de l'organe transplanté. Passer en revue les symptômes de rejet d'un organe greffé et insister sur le fait qu'il faut prévenir un professionnel de la santé dès que ces symptômes apparaissent.
- Insister sur l'importance de tests de laboratoire répétés au cours du traitement par le tacrolimus.
- Expliquer au patient qu'il doit éviter de consommer des huîtres ou des fruits de mer crus; s'assurer qu'ils sont bien cuits avant de les consommer.
- Expliquer au patient qu'il doit éviter d'être exposé à la varicelle, aux oreillons, à la rubéole et à la rougeole. Lui conseiller de consulter un professionnel

de la santé au sujet d'un traitement prophylactique en cas d'exposition.

- Expliquer à la patiente les risques que comporte un traitement par le tacrolimus pendant la grossesse.
- Informer le patient du risque de lymphome associé au traitement par le tacrolimus.

VÉRIFICATION DE L'EFFICACITÉ THÉRAPEUTIQUE

L'efficacité du traitement peut être démontrée par: la prévention du rejet de l'organe greffé ■ la diminution des lésions entraînées par la dermatite atopique ■ la diminution des symptômes et des lésions articulaires en présence de polyarthrite rhumatoïde.

TADALAFIL

Cialis

CLASSIFICATION:

Agent utilisé dans le traitement de l'impuissance (inhibiteur de la phosphodiestérase de type 5)

Grossesse – catégorie inconnue

INDICATIONS

Traitement du dysfonctionnement érectile.

MÉCANISME D'ACTION

Amplification des effets du monoxyde d'azote libéré à la suite d'une stimulation sexuelle. Le monoxyde d'azote active l'enzyme guanylate cyclase, ce qui entraîne une élévation des concentrations de guanosine monophosphate cyclique (GMPc). La GMPc entraîne la relaxation des muscles lisses du corps caverneux, ce qui favorise l'afflux du sang dans le pénis et l'érection qui s'ensuit. Le tadalafil inhibe la phosphodiestérase de type 5 (PDE5), l'enzyme responsable de la biodégradation de la GMPc dans le corps caverneux. ***Effets thérapeutiques:*** Augmentation du flux sanguin dans le corps caverneux entraînant une érection suffisante pour permettre les rapports sexuels. Une stimulation sexuelle est nécessaire.

PHARMACOCINÉTIQUE

Absorption: Rapide (PO).

Distribution: Dans les tissus.

Liaison aux protéines: 94 %.

Métabolisme et excrétion: Métabolisme hépatique par le cytochrome P450 3A4. Élimination fécale (61 %) et rénale (36 %).

Demi-vie: 17,5 heures en moyenne (chez des sujets en bonne santé).

Profil temps-action (effet sur l'érection)

	DÉBUT D'ACTION	PIC	DURÉE
PO	30 - 45 min	inconnu	jusqu'à 36 h

CONTRE-INDICATIONS, PRÉCAUTIONS ET MISES EN GARDE

Contre-indications: Hypersensibilité ■ TRAITEMENT CONCOMITANT PAR UN DÉRIVÉ NITRÉ ORGANIQUE (NITROGLYCÉRINE, MONONITRATE D'ISOSORBIDE, DINITRATE D'ISOSORBIDE).

Précautions et mises en garde: Hommes chez lesquels l'activité sexuelle est déconseillée ■ Maladie cardiovasculaire grave sous-jacente (incluant des antécédents d'infarctus du myocarde [IM] au cours des 90 derniers jours, d'angine instable ou de crises d'angine pendant les rapports sexuels, d'accident vasculaire cérébral au cours des 6 derniers mois) ou insuffisance cardiaque ■ Sténose aortique ou cardiomyopathie hypertrophique ■ Troubles hémorragiques ou ulcère gastroduodénal en évolution ■ États associés au priapisme (drépanocytose, myélome multiple, leucémie) ■ Déformation anatomique du pénis (angulation, fibrose caverneuse, maladie de La Peyronie) ■ Insuffisance rénale (Cl_{Cr} < 30 mL/min), insuffisance hépatique (classe C de Child-Pugh); risque de concentrations sanguines accrues, donc une réduction de la dose s'avère nécessaire ■ Hypotension au repos (< 90/50 mm Hg) ou hypertension au repos (> 170/100 mm Hg) ■ Antécédents de neuropathie optique ischémique antérieure non artéritique (NOIANA) ■ Maladies touchant la rétine, incluant la rétinite pigmentaire ■ **OBST., ALLAITEMENT, PÉD.:** Le médicament n'est pas indiqué chez les femmes et les enfants.

RÉACTIONS INDÉSIRABLES ET EFFETS SECONDAIRES

SNC: céphalées, étourdissements.

GI: dyspepsie.

CV: tachycardie, hypotension, hypertension, DOULEURS THORACIQUES, ANGINE DE POITRINE, INFARCTUS DU MYOCARDE.

GU: priapisme.

Loc.: lombalgies, myalgies.

ORLO: congestion nasale, vision anormale (vision teintée, sensibilité accrue à la lumière, vision trouble).

Divers: bouffées vasomotrices.

INTERACTIONS

Médicament-médicament: RISQUE ACCRU D'HYPOTENSION LORS DE LA PRISE CONCOMITANTE DE **DÉRIVÉS**

NITRÉS, SOUS QUELQUE FORME QUE CE SOIT; L'USAGE CONCOMITANT EST CONTRE-INDIQUÉ EN RAISON DU RISQUE D'HYPOTENSION GRAVE POUVANT ÊTRE D'ISSUE FATALE ■ Les concentrations sanguines du tadalafil et ses effets peuvent être accrus par la **cimétidine**, l'**érythromycine**, le **kétoconazole**, le **nelfinavir**, l'**indinavir**, le **ritonavir**, le **saquinavir** et l'**itraconazole**, de puissants inhibiteurs du CYP3A4 (la dose initiale devrait être réduite jusqu'à 5 mg). Des effets similaires peuvent être observés avec d'autres **inhibiteurs du CYP3A4** ■ Risque accru d'hypotension lors de l'administration concomitante d'**antihypertenseurs** ■ Risque accru d'hypotension lors de l'administration concomitante de **doxazosine**, de **prazosine** et de **terazosine** ■ L'ingestion de quantités importantes d'**alcool** peut entraîner une hypotension.

VOIES D'ADMINISTRATION ET POSOLOGIE

- **PO (adultes)**: 20 mg, 30 minutes avant des rapports sexuels prévus; ne pas prendre plus souvent que 1 fois par jour.

INSUFFISANCE HÉPATIQUE OU RÉNALE, OU TRAITEMENT CONCOMITANT PAR DES INHIBITEURS ENZYMATIQUES DU CYP3A4 (ÉRYTHROMYCINE, SAQUINAVIR, RITONAVIR, KÉTONAZOLE, ITRACONAZOLE, ETC.)

- **PO (ADULTES)**: DOSE INITIALE DE 10 mg, MAIS PAS PLUS SOUVENT QUE TOUS LES 2 JOURS ET AU MAXIMUM 3 FOIS PAR SEMAINE. SI LA DOSE DE 10 mg EST TOLÉRÉE, MAIS SI ELLE N'EST PAS SUFFISAMMENT EFFICACE, ELLE PEUT ÊTRE PORTÉE À 20 mg. NE PAS DÉPASSER 20 mg PAR DOSE.

PRÉSENTATION

Comprimés: 10 mg^{Pr}, 20 mg^{Pr}.

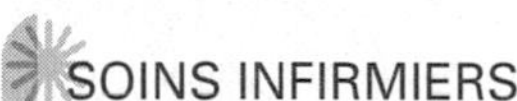

SOINS INFIRMIERS

ÉVALUATION DE LA SITUATION

- Déterminer la présence d'un dysfonctionnement érectile avant l'administration du médicament. Le tadalafil n'a aucun effet si une stimulation sexuelle n'est pas présente.

DIAGNOSTICS INFIRMIERS POSSIBLES

- Dysfonctionnement sexuel (Indications).
- Connaissances insuffisantes sur le traitement médicamenteux (Enseignement au patient et à ses proches).

INTERVENTIONS INFIRMIÈRES

- La dose de tadalafil doit habituellement être prise au moins 30 minutes avant les rapports sexuels; l'effet du médicament peut se maintenir pendant 36 heures. La fréquence d'administration maximale recommandée est de 1 fois par jour. Le tadalafil peut être pris avec ou sans aliments.

ENSEIGNEMENT AU PATIENT ET À SES PROCHES

- Expliquer au patient qu'il devrait prendre le tadalafil au moins 30 minutes avant les rapports sexuels et qu'il ne doit pas prendre le médicament plus de 1 fois par jour. Informer le patient qu'une stimulation sexuelle est nécessaire afin d'obtenir une érection.
- Prévenir le patient que le tadalafil est contre-indiqué chez les femmes.
- Avertir le patient qu'il ne doit pas prendre en même temps le tadalafil et des dérivés nitrés. Conseiller au patient de consulter rapidement un professionnel de la santé si des douleurs thoraciques apparaissent après la prise du médicament.
- Conseiller au patient d'éviter la prise concomitante de quantités importantes d'alcool, car il y a un risque accru d'hypotension et d'hypotension orthostatique.
- Conseiller au patient de prévenir rapidement un professionnel de la santé si l'érection dure plus de 4 heures ou s'il remarque une perte de vision rapide ou graduelle affectant un œil ou les deux yeux.
- Conseiller au patient de consulter un professionnel de la santé avant de prendre un médicament de vente libre ou un produit naturel.
- Informer le patient que le tadalafil n'assure aucune protection contre les maladies transmissibles sexuellement. Lui conseiller de prendre les mesures de protection nécessaires contre les maladies transmissibles sexuellement et les infections par le VIH.

VÉRIFICATION DE L'EFFICACITÉ THÉRAPEUTIQUE

L'efficacité du traitement peut être démontrée par: une érection suffisante pour que le patient puisse avoir des rapports sexuels.

T

TAMOXIFÈNE

Apo-Tamox, Gen-Tamoxifen, Nolvadex-D, Novo-Tamoxifen, PMS-Tamoxifen, Tamofen, Tamone, Tamoxifen

CLASSIFICATION:

Antinéoplasique (bloqueur des œstrogènes)

Grossesse – catégorie D

INDICATIONS

Traitement adjuvant du cancer du sein ou traitement du cancer du sein localement avancé ou métastatique chez les patientes dont les tumeurs sont œstrogéno-dépendantes. **Usages non approuvés**: Prévention du cancer du sein chez les patientes à risque élevé.

MÉCANISME D'ACTION

Liaison compétitive aux sites récepteurs œstrogéniques des tissus mammaires et des autres tissus ▪ Diminution de la synthèse de l'ADN et de la réponse œstrogénique. ***Effets thérapeutiques:*** Inhibition de la croissance tumorale ▪ Réduction de l'incidence du cancer du sein chez les patientes à risque élevé.

PHARMACOCINÉTIQUE

Absorption: Lente (PO).

Distribution: Tout l'organisme.

Métabolisme et excrétion: Métabolisme principalement hépatique; élimination lente dans les fèces.

Demi-vie: 7 jours.

Profil temps-action (réponse tumorale)

	DÉBUT D'ACTION	PIC	DURÉE
PO	4 - 10 semaines	plusieurs mois	plusieurs semaines

CONTRE-INDICATIONS, PRÉCAUTIONS ET MISES EN GARDE

Contre-indications: Hypersensibilité ▪ Grossesse.

Précautions et mises en garde: Réserve médullaire réduite ▪ Antécédents de thromboembolie ▪ Femmes en âge de procréer ▪ Allaitement.

RÉACTIONS INDÉSIRABLES ET EFFETS SECONDAIRES

T

SNC: confusion, dépression, céphalées, faiblesse.

ORLO: vision trouble, rétinopathie.

CV: EMBOLIE PULMONAIRE, AVC, œdème, thrombose veineuse.

GI: nausées, vomissements, augmentation des enzymes hépatiques.

GU: CANCER DE L'ENDOMÈTRE, saignements vaginaux, écoulement vaginal, prurit vulvaire.

HÉ: hypercalcémie.

Hémat.: leucopénie, thrombopénie.

Tég.: alopécie, rash.

Métab.: bouffées de chaleur, hypertriglycéridémie.

Loc.: douleurs osseuses.

Divers: réaction d'hypersensibilité, croissance de la tumeur.

INTERACTIONS

Médicament-médicament: Les **œstrogènes** et l'**aminoglutéthimide**, administrés en concomitance, peuvent diminuer l'efficacité du tamoxifène ▪ La **bromocriptine** pourrait élever les concentrations sanguines de tamoxifène ▪ Le tamoxifène peut intensifier l'effet anticoagulant de la **warfarine** ▪ Risque accru d'épisodes thromboemboliques lors de l'administration concomitante d'autres **antinéoplasiques**.

VOIES D'ADMINISTRATION ET POSOLOGIE

Traitement du cancer du sein

- **PO (adultes)**: De 20 à 40 mg par jour, en prise unique ou fractionnée. En cas de traitement adjuvant, l'utilisation doit se prolonger pendant au moins 5 ans.

Prophylaxie du cancer du sein

- **PO (adultes)**: 20 mg, 1 fois par jour; pendant 5 ans *(usage non approuvé)*.

PRÉSENTATION (version générique disponible)

Comprimés: 10 mg[Pr], 20 mg[Pr].

SOINS INFIRMIERS

ÉVALUATION DE LA SITUATION

Suivre de près l'intensification de la douleur osseuse ou tumorale. Demander au médecin ou à un autre professionnel de la santé s'il y a lieu d'administrer des analgésiques. Cette douleur passagère disparaît habituellement même si le traitement est poursuivi.

Tests de laboratoire:

- Noter la numération globulaire et plaquettaire ainsi que les concentrations de calcium, avant le traitement et pendant toute sa durée. Le tamoxifène peut provoquer une hypercalcémie passagère chez les patientes présentant des métastases osseuses. Il faut évaluer la présence des récepteurs d'œstrogènes avant d'amorcer le traitement.
- Mesurer les concentrations sériques de cholestérol et de triglycérides en cas d'hyperlipidémie préexistante. Le tamoxifène peut entraîner une élévation de ces concentrations.
- Suivre les résultats des tests de la fonction hépatique et les concentrations de thyroxine (T_4), à intervalles réguliers pendant toute la durée du traitement. Le tamoxifène peut entraîner une élévation des concentrations sériques des enzymes hépatiques et de la thyroxine.

- Des examens gynécologiques devraient être effectués à intervalles réguliers; le tamoxifène peut modifier les résultats du test de Papanicolaou et les frottis vaginaux.

DIAGNOSTICS INFIRMIERS POSSIBLES

- Connaissances insuffisantes sur le traitement médicamenteux (Enseignement au patient et à ses proches).

INTERVENTIONS INFIRMIÈRES

- Administrer le tamoxifène avec des aliments ou des liquides si l'irritation gastrique devient gênante. Consulter le médecin ou un autre professionnel de la santé si la patiente vomit peu après l'administration du médicament, afin de déterminer s'il y a lieu d'administrer de nouveau cette dose.
- IL NE FAUT PAS ÉCRASER, BRISER OU MÂCHER LES COMPRIMÉS.

ENSEIGNEMENT AU PATIENT ET À SES PROCHES

- Expliquer à la patiente qu'elle doit prendre le médicament en respectant rigoureusement la posologie recommandée. Si elle n'a pu le prendre au moment habituel, elle doit sauter cette dose.
- Expliquer à la patiente qui présente des lésions cutanées que la taille et le nombre de ces lésions peuvent augmenter passagèrement et que l'érythème pourrait s'aggraver.
- Recommander à la patiente de signaler rapidement à un professionnel de la santé les douleurs osseuses. La prévenir que ces douleurs peuvent être fortes, mais qu'elles pourraient constituer un indice de l'efficacité du médicament et qu'elles se résorberont avec le temps. On peut prescrire des analgésiques pour soulager la douleur.
- Recommander à la patiente de se peser toutes les semaines et de signaler à un professionnel de la santé tout gain pondéral ou la présence d'un œdème périphérique.
- Prévenir la patiente que le tamoxifène peut induire l'ovulation et qu'il pourrait avoir des effets tératogènes. Lui conseiller d'utiliser une méthode de contraception non hormonale durant le traitement et pendant au moins 1 mois après l'avoir arrêté.
- Prévenir la patiente que le tamoxifène peut entraîner des bouffées de chaleur. Lui conseiller de consulter un professionnel de la santé si elles deviennent gênantes.
- Recommander à la patiente de signaler immédiatement à un professionnel de la santé les symptômes suivants: douleur et enflure des jambes, essoufflements, faiblesse, somnolence, confusion, nausées, vomissements, gain pondéral, étourdissements, céphalées, perte d'appétit ou vision trouble, tout comme un cycle menstruel irrégulier, des saignements vaginaux ou des douleurs ou une pression au niveau du pelvis.

VÉRIFICATION DE L'EFFICACITÉ THÉRAPEUTIQUE

L'efficacité du traitement peut être démontrée par: la diminution de la taille de la tumeur mammaire ou le ralentissement de la propagation des cellules malignes. Les effets observables du médicament peuvent ne pas être manifestes pendant les 4 à 10 premières semaines qui suivent le début du traitement. ✻

TAMSULOSINE

Flomax CR, Novo-Tamsulosine

CLASSIFICATION:

Antagoniste sélectif des récepteurs alpha$_{1A}$-adrénergiques de la prostate

Grossesse – catégorie B

INDICATIONS

Traitement des signes et des symptômes de l'hyperplasie bénigne de la prostate.

MÉCANISME D'ACTION

Diminution des contractions des muscles lisses de la capsule prostatique par liaison préférentielle aux récepteurs alpha$_{1A}$-adrénergiques. ***Effets thérapeutiques:*** Diminution des symptômes d'hyperplasie prostatique (mictions impérieuses, retard à la miction, nycturie).

PHARMACOCINÉTIQUE

Absorption: Lente (PO).
Distribution: Tout l'organisme.
Liaison aux protéines: De 94 à 99 %.
Métabolisme et excrétion: Fort métabolisme hépatique. Excrétion rénale (< 10 %).
Demi-vie: 14 heures.

Profil temps-action (augmentation du débit urinaire)

	DÉBUT D'ACTION	PIC	DURÉE
PO	inconnu	2 semaines	inconnue

CONTRE-INDICATIONS, PRÉCAUTIONS ET MISES EN GARDE

Contre-indications: Hypersensibilité.

Précautions et mises en garde: Patients exposés à un risque de cancer de la prostate (les symptômes peuvent être similaires).

RÉACTIONS INDÉSIRABLES ET EFFETS SECONDAIRES

SNC: étourdissements, céphalées.
ORLO: rhinite.
CV: hypotension orthostatique.
GU: éjaculation rétrograde ou réduite.

INTERACTIONS

Médicament-médicament: La **cimétidine** peut augmenter les concentrations sanguines de la tamsulosine et le risque de toxicité ■ Risque accru d'hypotension lors de l'administration simultanée d'autres **adrénolytiques à action périphérique** (**doxazosine**, **prazosine**, **térazosine**); en éviter l'usage concomitant.

VOIES D'ADMINISTRATION ET POSOLOGIE

- **PO (adultes):** 0,4 mg, 1 fois par jour, après un repas (capsules à libération prolongée) ou sans égard aux repas (comprimés à libération contrôlée); on peut majorer la dose après 2 à 4 semaines jusqu'à concurrence de 0,8 mg par jour.

PRÉSENTATION

Capsules à libération prolongée: 0,4 mg^Pr ■ **Comprimés à libération contrôlée (Flomax CR):** 0,4 mg^Pr.

SOINS INFIRMIERS

ÉVALUATION DE LA SITUATION

- Suivre de près le patient, avant le traitement et à intervalles réguliers pendant toute sa durée, pour déceler l'apparition des symptômes suivants d'hyperplasie de la prostate: retard à la miction, sensation d'évacuation incomplète de la vessie, interruption du jet, puissance du jet et quantités d'urine éliminées insuffisantes, fuites post-mictionnelles, effort à la miction, dysurie, mictions impérieuses.
- Après l'administration de la première dose de tamsulosine, observer le patient pour déceler des signes d'hypotension et la syncope. L'incidence de ces effets peut être reliée à la dose. Suivre le patient de près pendant cette période et prendre les mesures qui s'imposent pour prévenir les accidents.
- Effectuer le bilan quotidien des ingesta et des excreta et peser le patient tous les jours. L'observer quotidiennement, particulièrement au début du traitement, pour déceler la formation d'un œdème. Signaler tout gain de poids ou la présence d'un œdème.

DIAGNOSTICS INFIRMIERS POSSIBLES

- Risque d'accident (Effets secondaires).
- Élimination urinaire altérée (Indications).
- Connaissances insuffisantes sur le traitement médicamenteux (Enseignement au patient et à ses proches).

INTERVENTIONS INFIRMIÈRES

- NE PAS CONFONDRE FLOMAX (TAMSULOSINE) AVEC FOMASAX (ALENDRONATE).
- Capsules à libération prolongée: Administrer la dose quotidienne 30 minutes après le même repas de la journée.
- Comprimés à libération contrôlée: Administrer la dose quotidienne sans égard aux repas.
- Si l'administration est interrompue pendant plusieurs jours, qu'il s'agisse de la dose de 0,4 mg ou de 0,8 mg, reprendre le traitement à la dose de 0,4 mg par jour.

ENSEIGNEMENT AU PATIENT ET À SES PROCHES

- Expliquer au patient qu'il doit prendre la tamsulosine tous les jours, à la même heure, même s'il se sent mieux. S'il n'a pu prendre le médicament au moment habituel, il doit le prendre aussitôt que possible, à moins que ce ne soit presque l'heure prévue pour la dose suivante. Le prévenir qu'il ne doit jamais remplacer une dose manquée par une double dose.
- Prévenir le patient que la tamsulosine peut provoquer des étourdissements. Lui conseiller de ne pas conduire et d'éviter les activités qui exigent sa vigilance jusqu'à ce qu'on ait la certitude que le médicament n'entraîne pas cet effet chez lui.
- Recommander au patient de changer lentement de position pour diminuer le risque d'hypotension orthostatique.
- Conseiller au patient de consulter un professionnel de la santé avant de prendre un médicament en vente libre contre la toux, le rhume ou les allergies.
- Insister sur l'importance des examens de suivi permettant d'évaluer les bienfaits du traitement.

VÉRIFICATION DE L'EFFICACITÉ THÉRAPEUTIQUE

L'efficacité du traitement peut être démontrée par: la diminution des symptômes urinaires associés à l'hyperplasie bénigne de la prostate.

TAZOBACTAM,
voir Pipéracilline

TÉLITHROMYCINE
Ketek

CLASSIFICATION:
Antibiotique (kétolide)

Grossesse – catégorie C

INDICATIONS
Traitement de la pneumonie extrahospitalière (légère ou modérée) attribuable à *Streptococcus pneumoniæ*, à *Hæmophilus influenzæ*, à *Moraxella catarrhalis*, à *Chlamydophila (Chlamydia) pneumoniæ*, à *Mycoplasma pneumoniæ* ou à *Staphylococcus aureus*.

MÉCANISME D'ACTION
Inhibition de la synthèse des protéines au niveau de la sous-unité 50S des ribosomes bactériens, tout comme de l'assemblage de nouveaux ribosomes. ***Effets thérapeutiques:*** Effet bactériostatique contre les bactéries sensibles. **Spectre d'action:** *Staphylococcus aureus* ■ *Streptococcus pneumoniæ* (y compris les souches multirésistantes) ■ *Streptococcus pyogenes* (du groupe A) ■ *Hæmophilus influenzæ* ■ *Moraxella catarrhalis* ■ *Mycoplasma pneumoniæ* ■ *Chlamydophila (Chlamydia) pneumoniæ*.

PHARMACOCINÉTIQUE
Absorption: 57 % (PO) avec ou sans prise d'aliments.
Distribution: Répartition importante dans tout l'organisme. Les concentrations dans les tissus sont considérablement plus élevées que dans le plasma.
Liaison aux protéines: De 60 à 70 %.
Métabolisme et excrétion: Métabolisme majoritairement hépatique (70 %) (50 % par l'entremise du CYP3A4). Excrétion rénale (13 % sous forme inchangée), excrétion biliaire et intestinale (7 % sous forme inchangée).
Demi-vie: 10 heures.

Profil temps-action (concentrations sériques)

	DÉBUT D'ACTION	PIC	DURÉE
PO	rapide	1 h	24 h

CONTRE-INDICATIONS, PRÉCAUTIONS ET MISES EN GARDE
Contre-indications: Hypersensibilité à la télithromycine, à tout autre ingrédient inactif du médicament ou à tout antibiotique de type macrolides (azithromycine, clarythromycine, érythromycine) ■ Traitement concomitant par le cisapride, le pimozide, l'astémizole, la terfénadine ou les alcaloïdes de l'ergot de seigle ■ Antécédents d'hépatite et/ou d'ictère induits par la télithromycine.
Précautions et mises en garde: Antécédents ou troubles favorisant l'allongement de l'intervalle QTc ou les arythmies (hypokaliémie ou hypomagnésémie non corrigée), bradycardie, traitement avec des médicaments antiarythmiques de classe IA ou III ■ Colite pseudomembraneuse ■ Myasthénie grave (des cas d'exacerbation de la maladie ont été signalés) ■ Insuffisance rénale grave (Cl_{Cr} < 30 mL/min) ■ **OBST., ALLAITEMENT:** On ne doit administrer le médicament que si les avantages escomptés pour la mère l'emportent sur tout risque éventuel pour le nouveau-né ■ **PÉD.:** L'innocuité de l'agent n'a pas été établie chez les enfants < 18 ans.

RÉACTIONS INDÉSIRABLES ET EFFETS SECONDAIRES
SNC: somnolence, étourdissements, céphalées, insomnie, anxiété.
ORLO: vision trouble, anomalie de la vision, diplopie.
CV: ARYTHMIE SINUSALE, BRADYCARDIE, BLOC DE BRANCHE, ALLONGEMENT DE L'INTERVALLE QT, palpitations, bouffées vasomotrices, hypotension.
GI: diarrhée, nausées, vomissements, selles molles, dyspepsie, douleur abdominale, flatulence, sécheresse de la bouche (xérostomie), COLITE PSEUDOMEMBRANEUSE, constipation, gastroentérite, candidose buccale, hépatite.
GU: irritation vaginale, candidose vaginale, modification de la couleur de l'urine, polyurie.
HÉ: hypokaliémie, hyperkaliémie.
Tég.: éruptions cutanées, prurit, eczéma, intensification de la sudation, sécheresse de la peau, urticaire.
Hémat.: thrombocythémie, éosinophilie, leucopénie, anémie, neutropénie, lymphopénie, troubles de la coagulation.
Métab.: élévation des taux des enzymes hépatiques (ALT, AST), troubles hépatobiliaires (lésion hépatocellulaire) avec ou sans ictère, cholestase.
Loc.: crampes musculaires.
Divers: anorexie, fatigue, asthénie, vertiges, hypersensibilité.

INTERACTIONS
Médicament-médicament: La télithromycine est principalement métabolisée par le CYP3A4 et dans une moindre mesure par le CYP1A. Elle inhibe l'activité du CYP3A4 et, dans une moindre mesure, celle du CYP2D6 ■ **Inhibiteurs du CYP3A4 (itraconazole, ritonavir,**

T

kétoconazole): élévation des concentrations plasmatiques de télithromycine (et diminution de celles de kétoconazole) ▪ **Inducteurs du CYP3A4 (rifampine, phénytoïne, carbamazépine, phénobarbital, millepertuis)**: diminution probable des concentrations plasmatiques de télithromycine ▪ **Substrats du CYP3A4 (midazolam, simvastatine, lovastatine, atorvastatine, cisapride, ergotamine ou dihydroergotamine, pimozide)**: élévation des concentrations de ces médicaments (car la télithromycine inhibe l'activité du CYP3A4) ▪ **Substrat du CYP2D6 (métoprolol)**: élévation des concentrations de métoprolol; utiliser avec prudence chez les insuffisants cardiaques ▪ **Digoxine**: élévation des concentrations ▪ **Sotalol**: diminution des concentrations ▪ **Carbamazépine, cyclosporine, disopyramide, hexobarbital, phénytoïne, quinidine, triazolam**: même si aucune étude particulière n'a été menée à cet égard sur la télithromycine, les concentrations plasmatiques de ces médicaments pourraient s'élever lors d'une prise concomitante, car on a observé des interactions médicamenteuses avec les **macrolides**.

VOIES D'ADMINISTRATION ET POSOLOGIE

- **PO (adultes)**: 800 mg, 1 fois par jour, pendant 10 jours.

INSUFFISANCE RÉNALE GRAVE (CL_{CR} < 30 mL/MIN)

- **PO (ADULTES)**: 400 mg, 1 FOIS PAR JOUR.

PRÉSENTATION

Comprimés: 400 mg[Pr].

SOINS INFIRMIERS

ÉVALUATION DE LA SITUATION

- Au début du traitement et pendant toute sa durée, rester à l'affût des signes suivants d'infection: altération des signes vitaux, aspect de la plaie, des crachats, de l'urine et des selles, accroissement du nombre de leucocytes.
- Prélever des échantillons pour les cultures et les antibiogrammes avant le début du traitement. La première dose peut être administrée avant que les résultats soient connus.
- Déterminer s'il y a des antécédents familiaux d'allongement de l'intervalle QTc ou présence d'un trouble proarythmique (hypokaliémie, bradycardie).
- SUIVRE DE PRÈS LES RÉACTIONS D'HYPERSENSIBILITÉ: FRISSONS, FIÈVRE, URTICAIRE, ENFLURE DES LÈVRES, DIFFICULTÉS RESPIRATOIRES, ETC. Signaler ces réactions au médecin.

Tests de laboratoire: Risque d'élévation de la numération plaquettaire.

DIAGNOSTICS INFIRMIERS POSSIBLES

- Risque d'infection (Indications).
- Connaissances insuffisantes sur le traitement médicamenteux (Enseignement au patient et à ses proches).
- Non-observance du traitement médicamenteux (Enseignement au patient et à ses proches).

INTERVENTIONS INFIRMIÈRES

- On peut administrer les comprimés avec ou sans aliments.

ENSEIGNEMENT AU PATIENT ET À SES PROCHES

- Expliquer au patient qu'il est important de respecter rigoureusement la posologie recommandée et de suivre le traitement jusqu'à la fin, même s'il se sent mieux. S'il n'a pu prendre le médicament au moment habituel, il doit le prendre aussitôt que possible, à moins que ce ne soit presque l'heure prévue pour la dose suivante. Le prévenir qu'il ne doit jamais remplacer une dose manquée par une double dose, ni prendre plus d'une dose par période de 24 heures. Lui expliquer qu'il peut être dangereux de donner ce médicament à une autre personne.
- Prévenir le patient que le médicament peut parfois provoquer des troubles visuels (vision trouble, difficulté de focalisation, diplopie). Lui conseiller de ne pas conduire et d'éviter les activités qui exigent une bonne acuité visuelle jusqu'à ce qu'on ait la certitude que le médicament n'entraîne pas cet effet chez lui. Prévenir un professionnel de la santé si les troubles visuels rendent difficile l'accomplissement des activités journalières.
- Prévenir le patient que le médicament peut parfois provoquer de la somnolence et des étourdissements. Lui conseiller de ne pas conduire et d'éviter les activités qui exigent sa vigilance jusqu'à ce qu'on ait la certitude que le médicament n'entraîne pas ces effets chez lui. Lui recommander de prendre le médicament à l'heure du coucher.
- Conseiller au patient de prévenir un professionnel de la santé si une syncope survient.
- Conseiller au patient de signaler à un professionnel de la santé les signes suivants de surinfection: excroissance pileuse sur la langue, pertes et démangeaisons vaginales, selles molles ou nauséabondes.
- CONSEILLER AU PATIENT DE CONSULTER IMMÉDIATEMENT UN PROFESSIONNEL DE LA SANTÉ EN CAS DE FIÈVRE ET DE DIARRHÉE, PARTICULIÈREMENT SI SES SELLES CONTIENNENT DU SANG, DU PUS OU DU MUCUS. LUI RECOMMANDER DE NE PAS TRAITER LA DIARRHÉE AVANT D'AVOIR CONSULTÉ UN PROFESSIONNEL DE LA SANTÉ.

T

- Recommander à la patiente d'informer le médecin qui lui prescrit ce médicament si elle pense être enceinte ou si elle souhaite le devenir.
- Conseiller au patient de consulter un professionnel de la santé avant de prendre un médicament d'ordonnance, un médicament en vente libre ou un produit naturel.
- Conseiller au patient de prévenir un professionnel de la santé si aucune amélioration des symptômes n'est notée après quelques jours.

VÉRIFICATION DE L'EFFICACITÉ THÉRAPEUTIQUE

L'efficacité du traitement peut être démontrée par: la disparition des signes et des symptômes d'infection. Le temps de résolution dépend du microorganisme infectant et du siège de l'infection.

TELMISARTAN,

voir Antagonistes des récepteurs de l'angiotensine II

TÉMAZÉPAM

Apo-Témazépam, Dom-Témazépam, Gen-Témazépam, Novo-Témazépam, Nu-Témazépam, PMS-Témazépam, Ratio-Témazépam, Restoril

CLASSIFICATION:

Anxiolytique et hypnosédatif (benzodiazépine)

Grossesse – catégorie X

INDICATIONS

Traitement de courte durée de l'insomnie.

MÉCANISME D'ACTION

Dépression du SNC, probablement par potentialisation de l'activité neuro-inhibitrice de l'acide gamma-aminobutyrique (GABA). ***Effets thérapeutiques:*** Amélioration du sommeil.

PHARMACOCINÉTIQUE

Absorption: Bonne (PO).

Distribution: L'agent se répartit dans tout l'organisme et traverse la barrière hématoencéphalique. Il traverse probablement la barrière placentaire et passe dans le lait maternel. Lors d'une administration prolongée, le médicament s'accumule dans les tissus.

Liaison aux protéines: 96 %.

Métabolisme et excrétion: Métabolisme hépatique avec transformation en composés inactifs. Excrétion rénale (principalement sous forme de métabolites inactifs).

Demi-vie: De 10 à 20 heures.

Profil temps-action (sédation)

	Début d'action	Pic	Durée
PO	30 min	2-3 h	6-8 h

CONTRE-INDICATIONS, PRÉCAUTIONS ET MISES EN GARDE

Contre-indications: Hypersensibilité ■ Risque de réactions de sensibilité croisée avec d'autres benzodiazépines ■ Glaucome à angle fermé ■ Myasthénie grave ■ Insuffisance pulmonaire grave ou apnée du sommeil.

Précautions et mises en garde: Dysfonctionnement hépatique ■ Dépression majeure ou psychose lorsque l'anxiété n'est pas un facteur prédominant ■ Comportement suicidaire ou antécédents de tentatives de suicide, de toxicomanie ou de pharmacodépendance ■ **GÉR.:** Il est recommandé de réduire la dose initiale chez les personnes âgées ou débilitées ■ Coma ou dépression préexistante du SNC ■ **OBST., ALLAITEMENT:** L'usage de cet agent chez la femme enceinte ou qui allaite n'est pas recommandé ■ **PÉD.:** L'efficacité et l'innocuité du médicament n'ont pas été établies chez les enfants < 18 ans.

RÉACTIONS INDÉSIRABLES ET EFFETS SECONDAIRES

SNC: sensation de tête légère, étourdissements, somnolence, léthargie, excitation paradoxale.

ORLO: vision trouble.

GI: constipation, diarrhée, nausées, vomissements.

Tég.: rash.

Divers: dépendance physique, dépendance psychologique, tolérance aux effets du médicament.

INTERACTIONS

Médicament-médicament: Dépression additive du SNC lors de l'usage concomitant d'autres **dépresseurs du SNC**, y compris l'**alcool**, les **antihistaminiques**, les **antidépresseurs**, les **opioïdes** et les autres **hypnosédatifs** (incluant d'autres **benzodiazépines**) ■ La **phénytoïne**, administrée en concomitance, peut diminuer l'efficacité du témazépam ■ La **théophylline** peut réduire les effets sédatifs du témazépam.

Médicament-produits naturels: Le **kava**, le **houblon**, la **scutellaire**, la **valériane** et la **camomille** peuvent accentuer la dépression du SNC.

VOIES D'ADMINISTRATION ET POSOLOGIE

- **PO (adultes):** Initialement, de 15 à 30 mg, 1 fois par jour, au coucher, selon la réponse au traitement et la tolérance du patient.
- **PO (personnes âgées ou débilitées):** 15 mg, 1 fois par jour, au coucher.

PRÉSENTATION

Capsules: 15 mg^T\C^, 30 mg^T\C^.

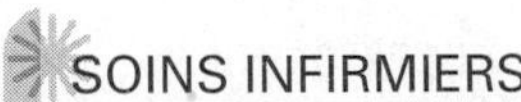

SOINS INFIRMIERS

ÉVALUATION DE LA SITUATION

- Suivre de près les habitudes de sommeil avant le traitement et à intervalles réguliers pendant toute sa durée.

GÉR.: Évaluer les effets au niveau du SNC et le risque de chutes et mettre en place les mesures préventives.

- Le traitement prolongé avec des doses élevées peut entraîner une dépendance psychologique ou physique. Limiter la quantité de médicament dont peut disposer le patient, particulièrement s'il est déprimé ou suicidaire ou s'il a des antécédents de toxicomanie.

DIAGNOSTICS INFIRMIERS POSSIBLES

- Habitudes de sommeil perturbées (Indications).
- Risque d'accident (Effets secondaires).
- Connaissances insuffisantes sur le traitement médicamenteux (Enseignement au patient et à ses proches).

INTERVENTIONS INFIRMIÈRES

- Après l'administration du témazépam, surveiller le patient lors de ses déplacements ou des transferts. Retirer les cigarettes. Remonter les ridelles du lit et installer la sonnette d'appel à portée de la main.
- Administrer le témazépam avec des aliments si l'irritation gastrique devient gênante.

T

ENSEIGNEMENT AU PATIENT ET À SES PROCHES

- Conseiller au patient de respecter rigoureusement la posologie recommandée. Lui expliquer qu'il est important de préparer un cadre propice au sommeil: la pièce doit être sombre et calme, la nicotine et la caféine sont à proscrire. Le prévenir qu'il ne doit pas augmenter la dose si elle devient moins efficace après quelques semaines sans consulter au préalable un professionnel de la santé.
- Prévenir le patient que le témazépam peut entraîner de la somnolence ou des étourdissements pendant la journée. Lui conseiller de ne pas conduire et d'éviter les activités qui exigent sa vigilance jusqu'à ce qu'on ait la certitude que le médicament n'entraîne pas ces effets chez lui.

GÉR.: Enseigner au patient et à ses proches les mesures préventives visant à réduire le risque de chutes.

- Recommander au patient de ne pas boire d'alcool, d'éviter de prendre d'autres dépresseurs du SNC et de consulter un professionnel de la santé avant de prendre des préparations en vente libre contenant des antihistaminiques ou de l'alcool.
- Conseiller à la patiente d'informer le professionnel de la santé si elle pense être enceinte ou si elle souhaite le devenir.
- Insister sur l'importance des examens de suivi permettant d'évaluer l'efficacité du médicament.

VÉRIFICATION DE L'EFFICACITÉ THÉRAPEUTIQUE

L'efficacité du traitement peut être démontrée par: l'amélioration des habitudes de sommeil; cet effet bénéfique peut ne pas être manifeste avant le troisième jour de traitement.

TÉMOZOLOMIDE

Temodal

CLASSIFICATION:

Antinéoplasique (alkylant)

Grossesse – catégorie D

INDICATIONS

Traitement du glioblastome multiforme nouvellement diagnostiqué, en association avec la radiothérapie, puis en traitement d'entretien ■ Traitement du glioblastome multiforme ou de l'astrocytome anaplasique réfractaire, qui évolue malgré un traitement type.

MÉCANISME D'ACTION

Le témozolomide n'est pas actif avant d'être transformé au pH physiologique en MTIC; ce métabolite entraîne l'alcoylation de l'ADN, en inhibant sa synthèse. ***Effets thérapeutiques:*** Destruction des cellules à réplication rapide, particulièrement, les cellules malignes, ce qui entraîne la régression ou le ralentissement de la croissance tumorale.

PHARMACOCINÉTIQUE

Absorption: Rapide et complète (PO).

Distribution: Inconnue. L'agent traverse la barrière hématoencéphalique.
Métabolisme et excrétion: Transformation rapide en MTIC, le métabolite actif. Transformation ultérieure en d'autres métabolites.
Demi-vie: 1,8 heure.

Profil temps-action
(effets sur les numérations globulaires)

	DÉBUT D'ACTION	PIC	DURÉE
PO	inconnu	21 - 28 jours	14 jours

CONTRE-INDICATIONS, PRÉCAUTIONS ET MISES EN GARDE

Contre-indications: Hypersensibilité au témozolomide ou à la dacarbazine (DTIC) ■ Aplasie médullaire grave.
Précautions et mises en garde: Insuffisance hépatique ou rénale ■ **GÉR.**: Risque accru d'aplasie médullaire ■ Infections actives ■ Autres maladies chroniques débilitantes ou faible indice corporel ■ Patientes en âge de procréer ■ **OBST., ALLAITEMENT**: L'innocuité du médicament n'a pas été établie ■ **PÉD.**: L'innocuité du médicament n'a pas été établie chez les enfants de 3 à 18 ans.

RÉACTIONS INDÉSIRABLES ET EFFETS SECONDAIRES

SNC: CONVULSIONS, fatigue, céphalées, manque de coordination, anxiété, dépression, étourdissements, somnolence, modifications de l'état mental, faiblesse.
ORLO: vision anormale, diplopie.
Resp.: toux.
CV: œdème périphérique.
GI: nausées, vomissements, douleurs abdominales, anorexie, constipation, diarrhée, dysphagie.
Tég.: prurit, rash.
End.: hypercorticisme surrénalien.
Hémat.: leucopénie, thrombopénie, anémie.
Métab.: gain pondéral.
Loc.: démarche titubante, douleurs lombaires.
SN: hémiparésie, myalgie.
Divers: douleurs mammaires (femmes), fièvre, néoplasie secondaire (rare).

INTERACTIONS

Médicament-médicament: Les autres **antinéoplasiques** ou la **radiothérapie** peuvent aggraver l'aplasie médullaire ■ Le témozolomide peut réduire la réponse des anticorps aux **vaccins à virus vivants** et augmenter le risque de réactions indésirables ■ L'administration concomitante d'**acide valproïque** a été associée à une légère diminution de l'élimination du témozolomide.

VOIES D'ADMINISTRATION ET POSOLOGIE

- **PO (adultes)**: *Gliomes malins récidivants ou évolutifs* – de 150 à 200 mg/m²/jour, pendant 5 jours consécutifs, lors de chaque cycle de traitement de 28 jours; les doses doivent être adaptées en fonction des numérations globulaires. *Glioblastome multiforme – traitement initial:* 75 mg/m²/jour, pendant 42 jours en association avec la radiothérapie, suivi d'un traitement d'entretien. *Glioblastome multiforme – traitement d'entretien:* débuter 4 semaines après la fin du traitement initial: 1ᵉ cycle: 150 mg/m²/jour, pendant 5 jours, suivis d'une période de 23 jours sans traitement; cycles 2 à 6: porter la dose à 200 mg/m²/jour, pendant 5 jours, selon les effets secondaires observés lors du 1ᵉ cycle.

PRÉSENTATION

Capsules: 5 mg^Pr^, 20 mg^Pr^, 100 mg^Pr^, 250 mg^Pr^.

SOINS INFIRMIERS

ÉVALUATION DE LA SITUATION

- Suivre de près les convulsions.

Tests de laboratoire: Noter la numération globulaire, la formule leucocytaire et le nombre de plaquettes. Le patient doit présenter un nombre absolu de polynucléaires neutrophiles $\geq 1,5 \times 10^9$/L et un nombre de plaquettes $\geq 100 \times 10^9$/L avant chaque cycle. On devrait noter la numération globulaire le 22ᵉ jour du cycle (21 jours après l'administration de la première dose) ou dans les 48 heures qui suivent, et toutes les semaines par la suite, jusqu'à ce que le nombre absolu de polynucléaires neutrophiles soit supérieur à $1,5 \times 10^9$/L, et le nombre de plaquettes, supérieur à 100×10^9/L. Si le nombre absolu de polynucléaires neutrophiles est $< 1,0 \times 10^9$/L ou si le nombre de plaquettes est $< 50 \times 10^9$/L au cours d'un cycle de traitement, la dose administrée lors du cycle suivant devrait être réduite de 50 mg/m², sans qu'elle soit inférieure à 100 mg/m², qui est la dose la plus faible recommandée. Les personnes âgées sont exposées à un risque plus élevé d'aplasie médullaire. Le nadir de la thrombopénie et de la neutropénie survient habituellement entre le 21ᵉ et le 28ᵉ jour. Les valeurs se rétablissent généralement dans les 14 jours suivant le nadir.

DIAGNOSTICS INFIRMIERS POSSIBLES

- Risque d'accident (Réactions indésirables).
- Connaissances insuffisantes sur le traitement médicamenteux (Enseignement au patient et à ses proches).

T

INTERVENTIONS INFIRMIÈRES

- Les capsules devraient être prises, 1 à la fois, avec un grand verre d'eau, à la même heure tous les jours. Prendre le médicament à jeun ou à l'heure du coucher. Les capsules devraient être avalées telles quelles, sans qu'elles soient mâchées ou ouvertes. Si, par inadvertance, les capsules sont ouvertes ou brisées, il faut éviter d'inhaler la poudre. Il faut également éviter qu'elle entre en contact avec les muqueuses du nez ou de la bouche.
- Il faut administrer un traitement prophylactique contre *P. carinii* (PCP) chez tous les patients traités en même temps par radiothérapie.
- L'administration concomitante d'antiémétiques peut être nécessaire.

ENSEIGNEMENT AU PATIENT ET À SES PROCHES

- Expliquer au patient qu'il doit prendre le médicament à la même heure tous les jours, en respectant rigoureusement la posologie recommandée. Les capsules devraient être emballées dans 5 sachets séparés ou dans de petits flacons portant une étiquette avec la mention « 1er jour », « 2e jour », « 3e jour », « 4e jour » et « 5e jour ». La couleur et la taille des capsules de chaque sachet peuvent être différentes. Conseiller au patient de communiquer avec le pharmacien ou le médecin prescripteur s'il a des doutes au sujet de l'emballage.
- Informer le patient qu'il peut prendre un antiémétique en cas de nausées et de vomissements.
- Recommander au patient de signaler à un professionnel de la santé la dyspnée, les maux de gorge, la fièvre, les frissons, les saignements ou ecchymoses inhabituels et la fatigue. Le prévenir qu'il doit éviter les foules et les personnes contagieuses. Lui conseiller d'utiliser une brosse à dents à poils doux et un rasoir électrique et de prendre garde aux chutes. Le prévenir également qu'il ne doit pas prendre de boissons alcoolisées ni de préparations contenant de l'aspirine ou des AINS, en raison du risque d'hémorragie gastro-intestinale.
- Conseiller à la patiente de prendre des mesures contraceptives non hormonales pendant toute la durée du traitement.
- Recommander au patient de ne pas se faire vacciner sans recommandation expresse d'un professionnel de la santé.
- Insister sur l'importance des examens de suivi permettant d'évaluer les bienfaits du traitement et les effets secondaires.

T

VÉRIFICATION DE L'EFFICACITÉ THÉRAPEUTIQUE

L'efficacité du traitement peut être démontrée par: le ralentissement de l'évolution du glioblastome multiforme ou de l'astrocytome réfractaire. Le traitement peut être poursuivi tant et aussi longtemps que la maladie n'évolue pas. ✳

TENECTEPLASE,

voir Thrombolytiques

TÉNOFOVIR DISOPROXIL

Viread

CLASSIFICATION:

Antirétroviral (inhibiteur nucléosidique de la transcriptase inverse [INTI])

Grossesse – catégorie B

INDICATIONS

Traitement de l'infection par le VIH (en association avec d'autres antirétroviraux). **Usages non approuvés:** En association avec d'autres antirétroviraux, prophylaxie après une exposition accidentelle au VIH.

MÉCANISME D'ACTION

L'ingrédient actif (ténofovir) subit une phosphorylation intracellulaire; le diphosphate de ténofovir inhibe la transcriptase inverse du VIH, interrompant la synthèse de l'ADN viral. ***Effets thérapeutiques:*** Ralentissement de l'évolution de l'infection par le VIH et diminution de ses complications ▪ Augmentation du nombre de CD4 et diminution de la charge virale.

PHARMACOCINÉTIQUE

Absorption: 25 % (PO); 40 % (avec des aliments). Le ténofovir disoproxil est un promédicament qui se transforme en ténofovir, qui est l'ingrédient actif.

Métabolisme et excrétion: Excrétion majoritairement rénale (de 70 à 80 % sous forme inchangée).

Demi-vie: Inconnue.

Profil temps-action

	DÉBUT D'ACTION	PIC	DURÉE
PO	inconnu	1 h (à jeun) 2 h†	24 h

† Lorsque l'agent est pris avec des aliments.

CONTRE-INDICATIONS, PRÉCAUTIONS ET MISES EN GARDE

Contre-indications: Hypersensibilité.

Précautions et mises en garde: Hépatite B chronique intercurrente (l'arrêt du traitement par le ténofovir peut provoquer une exacerbation aiguë de l'hépatite B) ■ Obésité, femmes, prise prolongée d'inhibiteur nucléosidique (il peut s'agir de facteurs de risque d'acidose lactique ou d'hépatomégalie) ■ Insuffisance rénale (utiliser prudemment si la Cl_{Cr} est < 50 mL/min) ■ **OBST.:** Grossesse (utiliser pendant la grossesse seulement si les bienfaits possibles chez la mère dépassent les risques auxquels est exposé le fœtus) ■ **PÉD.:** Enfants (l'innocuité du médicament n'a pas été établie) ■ **ALLAITEMENT:** Les femmes infectées par le VIH ne devraient pas allaiter.

RÉACTIONS INDÉSIRABLES ET EFFETS SECONDAIRES

SNC: céphalées, faiblesse.

GI: HÉPATOMEGALIE (avec stéatose), nausées, douleurs abdominales, anorexie, diarrhée, vomissements, flatulence, pancréatite.

GU: insuffisance rénale, syndrome de Fanconi.

HÉ: ACIDOSE LACTIQUE, hypophosphatémie.

Loc.: diminution de la densité minérale osseuse.

Métab.: modification de la distribution du tissu adipeux.

Divers: syndrome de reconstitution immunitaire.

INTERACTIONS

Médicament-médicament: L'usage concomitant de **didanosine** entraîne une élévation des concentrations sanguines et du risque de toxicité de cette dernière (suivre de près les effets indésirables de la didanosine) ■ L'**atazanavir** et le **lopinavir/ritonavir** augmentent les concentrations et le risque d'effets indésirables du ténofovir (notamment des troubles rénaux) ■ Le ténofovir réduit les concentrations d'**atazanavir**, ce qui peut entraîner la diminution de la réponse virologique et l'émergence d'une résistance à l'atazanavir (on peut ajouter une faible dose de **ritonavir** pour en élever les concentrations sanguines) ■ Les concentrations sanguines peuvent être élevées par le **cidofovir**, l'**acyclovir**, le **ganciclovir** ou le **valganciclovir** ■ Risque accru de toxicité rénale lors de l'usage concomitant d'autres **agents néphrotoxiques**.

VOIES D'ADMINISTRATION ET POSOLOGIE

- **PO (adultes):** 300 mg, 1 fois par jour.
- ***INSUFFISANCE RÉNALE***

  PO (ADULTES ≥ 18 ANS): *CL_{CR} DE 30 À 49 mL/MIN* – 300 mg, TOUTES LES 48 HEURES; *CL_{CR} DE 10 À 29 mL/MIN* – 300 mg, 2 FOIS PAR SEMAINE.

PRÉSENTATION

Comprimés: 300 mg ■ **En association avec:** emtricitabine (Truvada[Pr]) (voir l'annexe U).

SOINS INFIRMIERS

ÉVALUATION DE LA SITUATION

- Suivre de près l'aggravation des symptômes de l'infection par le VIH et l'apparition de symptômes d'infections opportunistes, avant le traitement et pendant toute sa durée.
- L'AGENT PEUT PROVOQUER UNE ACIDOSE LACTIQUE ET UNE HÉPATOMÉGALIE GRAVE AVEC STÉATOSE. CES COMPLICATIONS SONT PLUS PROBABLES CHEZ LES PATIENTS DE SEXE FÉMININ, CHEZ LES PERSONNES OBÈSES ET CHEZ CELLES QUI PRENNENT DES ANALOGUES NUCLÉOSIDIQUES PENDANT UN LAPS DE TEMPS PROLONGÉ. SUIVRE DE PRÈS LES SIGNES DE CES COMPLICATIONS (TAUX ACCRUS DE LACTATE SÉRIQUE, CONCENTRATIONS ÉLEVÉES D'ENZYMES HÉPATIQUES, HYPERTROPHIE DU FOIE DÉCELÉE À LA PALPATION). ARRÊTER LE TRAITEMENT DÈS L'APPARITION DE SIGNES CLINIQUES OU DE RÉSULTATS DE TESTS DE LABORATOIRE QUI ÉVOQUENT UN TEL PROBLÈME.
- Si une patiente enceinte est exposée à des antirétroviraux, l'inscrire dans le registre des femmes exposées aux antirétroviraux pendant leur grossesse, en composant le 1-800-258-4263.

Tests de laboratoire:

- Suivre de près la charge virale et la numération des CD4 avant le traitement et à intervalles réguliers pendant toute sa durée pour déterminer la réponse au traitement.
- NOTER À INTERVALLES RÉGULIERS PENDANT TOUTE LA DURÉE DU TRAITEMENT LES CONCENTRATIONS SÉRIQUES D'AMYLASE, DE LIPASE ET DE TRIGLYCÉRIDES. DES CONCENTRATIONS ÉLEVÉES PEUVENT RÉVÉLER LA PRÉSENCE D'UNE PANCRÉATITE ET DICTENT L'ARRÊT DU TRAITEMENT.
- L'AGENT PEUT ÉLEVER LES CONCENTRATIONS D'AST, D'ALT, DE PHOSPHATASE ALCALINE, DE CRÉATINE KINASE, D'AMYLASE ET DE TRIGLYCÉRIDES. IL Y A RISQUE D'ACIDOSE LACTIQUE ET DE TOXICITÉ HÉPATIQUE PROVOQUANT UNE STÉATOSE HÉPATIQUE, LAQUELLE PEUT MENER À UNE ISSUE FATALE, SURTOUT CHEZ LES FEMMES.
- L'agent peut provoquer une hypophosphatémie chez les insuffisants rénaux.
- L'agent peut aussi provoquer une hyperglycémie et une glycosurie.

T

DIAGNOSTICS INFIRMIERS POSSIBLES

- Risque d'infection (Indications, Effet secondaires).
- Risque d'accident (Effets secondaires).

INTERVENTIONS INFIRMIÈRES

- Si le ténofovir est administré en même temps que la didanosine, l'administrer 2 heures avant ou 1 heure après celle-ci.

PO: Administrer 1 fois par jour avec un repas.

ENSEIGNEMENT AU PATIENT ET À SES PROCHES

- Expliquer au patient qu'il est important de prendre le ténofovir en respectant rigoureusement les recommandations du médecin, même s'il se sent mieux. Lui conseiller de ne pas prendre une dose plus grande que celle qui lui a été prescrite ni d'arrêter le traitement sans avoir consulté un professionnel de la santé au préalable. Lui recommander de prendre toute dose manquée dès que possible, mais de ne jamais la remplacer par une double dose. Le prévenir qu'il ne faut pas donner ce médicament à d'autres personnes.
- Informer le patient que le ténofovir peut provoquer l'hyperglycémie. Lui conseiller de prévenir un professionnel de la santé en cas de soif ou de faim accrue, d'une perte de poids inexpliquée, d'une augmentation de la fréquence des mictions, de fatigue, ou de sécheresse ou de démangeaison de la peau.
- Recommander au patient de ne pas prendre d'autres médicaments d'ordonnance ou en vente libre ni de produits naturels sans consulter un professionnel de la santé au préalable.
- Conseiller au patient d'éviter les foules ou les personnes ayant contracté une infection.
- Prévenir le patient que le ténofovir ne guérit pas l'infection par le VIH ni ne réduit le risque de transmission du VIH à d'autres personnes par les rapports sexuels ou le sang. Inciter le patient à utiliser un condom et à éviter le partage d'aiguilles ou les dons de sang pour prévenir la propagation du VIH.
- RECOMMANDER AU PATIENT DE PRÉVENIR UN PROFESSIONNEL DE LA SANTÉ IMMÉDIATEMENT, SI DES SIGNES D'ACIDOSE LACTIQUE (FATIGUE OU FAIBLESSE, DOULEURS MUSCULAIRES INHABITUELLES, DIFFICULTÉS RESPIRATOIRES, DOULEURS D'ESTOMAC AVEC DES NAUSÉES ET DES VOMISSEMENTS, SENSATION DE FROID, SURTOUT AU NIVEAU DES EXTRÉMITÉS, ÉTOURDISSEMENTS OU BATTEMENTS CARDIAQUES RAPIDES ET IRRÉGULIERS) OU D'HÉPATOTOXICITÉ (JAUNISSEMENT DE LA PEAU OU DU BLANC DES YEUX, URINE DE COULEUR FONCÉE, SELLES DE COULEUR PÂLE, PERTE D'APPÉTIT PENDANT PLUSIEURS JOURS DE SUITE, NAUSÉES OU DOULEURS ABDOMINALES) SE MANIFESTENT. Ces symptômes peuvent se présenter plus fréquemment chez les sujets de sexe féminin, les personnes obèses ou celles qui prennent des médicaments comme le ténofovir pendant un laps de temps prolongé.
- Informer le patient du risque d'accumulation ou de redistribution des tissus adipeux, pouvant entraîner une obésité centrale, une infiltration de graisse dans la région dorsocervicale (bosse de bison), l'atrophie des tissus périphériques, l'augmentation du volume des seins et un aspect cushinoïde. Les causes et les effets à long terme sont inconnus.
- Insister sur l'importance des examens réguliers permettant de suivre de près les effets secondaires.

VÉRIFICATION DE L'EFFICACITÉ THÉRAPEUTIQUE

L'efficacité du traitement peut être démontrée par: la diminution de la fréquence des infections opportunistes et le ralentissement de l'évolution de l'infection par le VIH ■ la diminution de la charge virale et l'augmentation du nombre de CD4. ✳

TÉRAZOSINE

Apo-Térazosin, Hytrin, Novo-Térazosin, PMS-Térazosin, Ratio-Térazosin

CLASSIFICATION:

Antihypertenseur (antagoniste alpha$_1$-adrénergique à action périphérique), traitement symptomatique de l'hyperplasie bénigne de la prostate

Grossesse – catégorie C

INDICATIONS

Traitement de l'hypertension en association avec d'autres agents ■ Traitement de l'occlusion des voies urinaires chez les patients atteints d'hyperplasie bénigne de la prostate (HBP).

MÉCANISME D'ACTION

Dilatation des artères et des veines par blocage des récepteurs alpha$_1$-adrénergiques postsynaptiques ■ Diminution des contractions des muscles lisses de la capsule prostatique. ***Effets thérapeutiques:*** Abaissement de la pression artérielle ■ Diminution des symptômes d'HBP (mictions impérieuses, retard à la miction, nycturie).

PHARMACOCINÉTIQUE

Absorption: Bonne (PO).
Distribution: Inconnue.
Métabolisme et excrétion: Important métabolisme hépatique et excrétion majoritairement biliaire. Excrétion rénale sous forme inchangée à 10 %.
Demi-vie: 12 heures.

Profil temps-action

	DÉBUT D'ACTION	PIC	DURÉE
PO - hypertension	15 min†	6 - 8 semaines‡	24 h§
PO - hyperplasie de la prostate	2 - 6 semaines	inconnu	inconnue

† Par suite de l'administration d'une seule dose.
‡ Par suite de l'administration de plusieurs doses par voie orale.
§ Par suite de l'administration d'une seule dose.

CONTRE-INDICATIONS, PRÉCAUTIONS ET MISES EN GARDE

Contre-indications: Hypersensibilité.
Précautions et mises en garde: Déshydratation, déplétion volémique ou sodique, risque accru d'hypotension ■ Insuffisance rénale (risque accru d'hypotension) ■ **GÉR.**: Les personnes âgées sont exposées à un risque accru d'hypotension orthostatique ■ **OBST., ALLAITEMENT, PÉD.**: L'innocuité du médicament n'a pas été établie.

RÉACTIONS INDÉSIRABLES ET EFFETS SECONDAIRES

SNC: étourdissements, céphalées, faiblesse, somnolence, nervosité.
ORLO: congestion nasale, vision trouble, conjonctivite, sinusite.
Resp.: dyspnée.
CV: hypotension orthostatique induite par la ou les premières doses, arythmies, douleurs thoraciques, palpitations, œdème périphérique, tachycardie.
GI: nausées, douleurs abdominales, diarrhée, sécheresse de la bouche (xérostomie), vomissements.
GU: impuissance, mictions fréquentes.
Tég.: prurit.
Métab.: gain pondéral par rétention liquidienne.
Loc.: arthralgie, douleurs lombaires, douleurs dans les membres.
SN: paresthésie.
Divers: fièvre.

INTERACTIONS

Médicament-médicament: Hypotension additive lors de l'administration concomitante de **sildénafil**, de **tadalafil**, de **vardénafil**, d'autres **antihypertenseurs** ou de **dérivés nitrés** ou lors de la consommation de grandes quantités d'**alcool** ■ Les **anti-inflammatoires non stéroïdiens**, les **agents sympathomimétiques** ou les **œstrogènes** peuvent diminuer les effets antihypertenseurs de la térazosine ■ Le **vérapamil** peut accroître les concentrations et les effets hypotenseurs de la térazosine.

VOIES D'ADMINISTRATION ET POSOLOGIE

Les premières doses doivent être prises au coucher.

Hypertension

- **PO (adultes)**: Initialement, 1 mg, au coucher, puis augmenter lentement la dose jusqu'à concurrence de 5 mg par jour (écart posologique habituel de 1 à 5 mg par jour, mais la dose peut être augmentée jusqu'à 20 mg par jour, qui est la dose maximale); on peut administrer le médicament en une seule dose ou en 2 doses fractionnées. Si le traitement est interrompu pendant quelques jours ou davantage, il faut le reprendre dès le début, en administrant la dose initiale.

Hyperplasie bénigne de la prostate

- **PO (adultes)**: 1 mg, au coucher; on peut augmenter la dose graduellement, à intervalles de 1 semaine, jusqu'à concurrence de 5 à 10 mg par jour. Si le traitement est interrompu pendant quelques jours ou davantage, il faut le reprendre dès le début, en administrant la dose initiale.

PRÉSENTATION

Comprimés: 1 mg^{Pr}, 2 mg^{Pr}, 5 mg^{Pr}, 10 mg^{Pr}.

SOINS INFIRMIERS

ÉVALUATION DE LA SITUATION

- Mesurer la pression artérielle (en position couchée et debout) et le pouls à intervalles fréquents lors de l'adaptation posologique initiale et à intervalles réguliers pendant toute la durée du traitement. Signaler au médecin ou à un autre professionnel de la santé tout changement important.
- Observer le patient pour déceler les symptômes d'hypotension orthostatique et de syncope induits par les premières doses. Ces symptômes peuvent se manifester de 30 minutes à 2 heures après l'administration de la dose initiale et à l'occasion, par la suite. L'incidence des symptômes peut être reliée à la dose. Les patients présentant une déplétion volémique ou suivant un régime hyposodé peuvent être davantage prédisposés à ces effets.
- Effectuer le bilan quotidien des ingesta et des excreta et peser le patient tous les jours. L'observer quotidiennement, particulièrement au début du traitement, pour déceler la formation d'un œdème.

T

Hypertension: Vérifier la fréquence des renouvellements des ordonnances pour s'assurer que le patient observe son traitement.

Hyperplasie bénigne de la prostate:

- Suivre de près le patient avant le traitement et à intervalles réguliers pendant toute sa durée, pour déceler l'apparition des symptômes suivants d'HBP: retard à la miction, sensation d'évacuation incomplète de la vessie, interruption du jet, puissance diminuée du jet et quantités d'urine éliminées insuffisantes, fuites postmictionnelles, effort à la miction, dysurie, mictions impérieuses.
- Écarter la possibilité d'un cancer de la prostate avant d'amorcer le traitement; les symptômes sont similaires.

DIAGNOSTICS INFIRMIERS POSSIBLES

- Risque d'accident (Effets secondaires).
- Connaissances insuffisantes sur le traitement médicamenteux (Enseignement au patient et à ses proches).
- Non-observance du traitement médicamenteux (Enseignement au patient et à ses proches).

INTERVENTIONS INFIRMIÈRES

- La térazosine peut être administrée en association avec un diurétique ou un bêtabloquant afin de réduire la rétention sodique et hydrique. Si ces médicaments sont ajoutés au traitement par la térazosine, réduire initialement la dose de cette dernière, puis l'adapter pour obtenir l'effet souhaité.
- Administrer la dose quotidienne au coucher. Au besoin, on peut administrer l'agent 2 fois par jour.

ENSEIGNEMENT AU PATIENT ET À SES PROCHES

- Expliquer au patient qu'il doit prendre la térazosine tous les jours, à la même heure. S'il n'a pu prendre le médicament au moment habituel, il doit le prendre aussitôt que possible, mais s'il ne l'a pas pris jusqu'au lendemain, il doit sauter cette dose. Le prévenir qu'il ne doit jamais remplacer une dose manquée par une double dose.
- Recommander au patient de se peser 2 fois par semaine et d'examiner ses pieds et ses chevilles pour déceler les signes de rétention hydrique.
- Prévenir le patient que la térazosine peut provoquer des étourdissements ou de la somnolence. Lui conseiller de ne pas conduire et d'éviter les activités qui exigent sa vigilance jusqu'à ce qu'on ait la certitude que le médicament n'entraîne pas ces effets chez lui.
- Recommander au patient de changer lentement de position pour diminuer le risque d'hypotension orthostatique. Le prévenir qu'il devrait éviter de boire de l'alcool, de prendre des dépresseurs du SNC, de rester debout pendant de longues périodes, de prendre des douches chaudes et de faire de l'exercice par temps chaud en raison du risque d'effets orthostatiques accrus.
- Conseiller au patient de consulter un professionnel de la santé avant de prendre un médicament en vente libre contre la toux, le rhume ou les allergies.
- Recommander au patient qui doit subir une intervention chirurgicale d'avertir le professionnel de la santé qu'il suit un traitement par ce médicament.
- Prévenir le patient qu'il doit signaler à un professionnel de la santé les symptômes suivants: étourdissements fréquents, évanouissements, œdème des pieds ou de la partie inférieure des jambes.
- Insister sur l'importance des examens de suivi permettant d'évaluer l'efficacité du traitement.

Hypertension:

- Expliquer au patient qu'il est important de poursuivre le traitement en respectant rigoureusement les recommandations du médecin, même s'il se sent mieux. La térazosine normalise la pression artérielle, mais ne guérit pas l'hypertension.
- Inciter le patient à suivre d'autres mesures de réduction de l'hypertension: perdre du poids, réduire sa consommation de sel, arrêter de fumer, boire de l'alcool avec modération, faire régulièrement de l'exercice et diminuer le stress.
- Montrer au patient et à ses proches comment mesurer la pression artérielle. Leur demander de prendre la pression artérielle au moins 1 fois par semaine et de signaler tout changement important à un professionnel de la santé.

VÉRIFICATION DE L'EFFICACITÉ THÉRAPEUTIQUE

L'efficacité du traitement peut être démontrée par: la baisse de la pression artérielle sans apparition d'effets secondaires ■ la diminution des symptômes associés à l'hyperplasie bénigne de la prostate. Les effets du médicament peuvent ne pas être manifestes pendant les 2 à 6 semaines qui suivent le début du traitement.

TERBINAFINE

Apo-Terbinafine, Gen-Terbinafine, Lamisil, Novo-Terbinafine, PMS-Terbinafine

CLASSIFICATION:

Antifongique (par voie générale)

Grossesse – catégorie B

Pour l'usage topique, voir Antifongiques topiques.

T

INDICATIONS

Traitement de l'onychomycose (infection fongique de l'ongle) due aux dermatophytes ■ La voie orale peut être indiquée pour le traitement des dermatophyties (*Tinea corporis, Tinea cruris* et *Tinea pedis*), compte tenu du foyer, de la gravité ou de l'étendue de l'infection.

MÉCANISME D'ACTION

Altération de la synthèse de la paroi cellulaire fongique (biosynthèse de l'ergostérol) par inhibition de l'enzyme squalène-époxydase. ***Effets thérapeutiques:*** Destruction des cellules fongiques. **Spectre d'action:** Le médicament agit contre les dermatophytes et d'autres champignons.

PHARMACOCINÉTIQUE

Absorption: De 70 à 80 % (PO).

Distribution: Le médicament se répartit dans tout l'organisme; il pénètre dans le derme et l'épiderme et se concentre dans la couche cornée, les poils, le cuir chevelu et les ongles. Il passe dans le lait maternel.

Liaison aux protéines: 99 %.

Métabolisme et excrétion: Métabolisme majoritairement hépatique.

Demi-vie: *Plasma* – 22 jours; prolongée dans la peau et les ongles.

Profil temps-action
(concentrations antifongiques dans les tissus)

	DÉBUT D'ACTION	PIC	DURÉE
PO	plusieurs jours	plusieurs jours – semaines	plusieurs semaines

CONTRE-INDICATIONS, PRÉCAUTIONS ET MISES EN GARDE

Contre-indications: Hypersensibilité ■ Maladie hépatique chronique ou évolutive ■ Insuffisance rénale (Cl_{Cr} < 50 mL/min).

Précautions et mises en garde: Antécédents d'alcoolisme ■ Risque de toxicité hépatique chez les patients atteints ou non d'une maladie hépatique ■ **OBST., ALLAITEMENT, PÉD.:** L'innocuité du médicament n'a pas été établie.

RÉACTIONS INDÉSIRABLES ET EFFETS SECONDAIRES

CV: insuffisance cardiaque.

GI: HÉPATOTOXICITÉ, <u>anorexie</u>, <u>diarrhée</u>, <u>nausées</u>, <u>douleurs gastriques</u>, <u>vomissements</u>, altération du goût, hépatite médicamenteuse, modification de la perception gustative.

Tég.: NÉCROLYSE ÉPIDERMIQUE TOXIQUE, démangeaisons, rash.

Hémat.: neutropénie, pancytopénie.

Divers: SYNDROME DE STEVENS-JOHNSON.

INTERACTIONS

Médicament-médicament: L'**alcool** ou les autres **agents hépatotoxiques**, pris en concomitance, peuvent accentuer le risque d'hépatotoxicité ■ La **rifampine** et les autres **agents qui induisent les enzymes hépatiques métabolisant les médicaments** peuvent diminuer l'efficacité de la terbinafine ■ La **cimétidine** et les autres **agents qui inhibent les enzymes hépatiques métabolisant les médicaments** peuvent accroître l'efficacité de la terbinafine ■ La terbinafine augmente les concentrations plasmatiques de **théophylline**.

Médicament-produits naturels: Augmentation de la concentration plasmatique et de la toxicité de la **caféine** lors de la consommation concomitante de produits naturels qui en contiennent (**noix de cola**, **guarana**, **maté**, **thé**, **café**).

VOIES D'ADMINISTRATION ET POSOLOGIE

- **PO (adultes):** *Infection des ongles (sauf du gros orteil):* 250 mg, 1 fois par jour, pendant 6 semaines à 3 mois. *Infection de l'ongle du gros orteil:* 250 mg, 1 fois par jour, pendant 3 à 6 mois. *Tinea pedis:* 250 mg, 1 fois par jour, pendant 2 à 6 semaines. *Tinea corporis, Tinea cruris:* 250 mg, 1 fois par jour, pendant 2 à 4 semaines.

PRÉSENTATION

Comprimés: 250 mg[Pr].

ÉVALUATION DE LA SITUATION

- Suivre de près le patient à la recherche des signes et des symptômes d'infection (observer le lit de l'ongle) avant le traitement et à intervalles réguliers pendant toute sa durée.
- Prélever des échantillons pour la mise en culture avant d'amorcer le traitement. On peut commencer le traitement avant même que les résultats soient connus.

Tests de laboratoire:

- Noter la numération globulaire et les résultats des tests de la fonction hépatique chez les patients recevant le traitement pendant plus de 6 semaines. Interrompre le traitement en cas de résultats anormaux.
- MESURER L'AST ET L'ALT AVANT LE TRAITEMENT ET À INTERVALLES RÉGULIERS PENDANT TOUTE SA DURÉE. LE TRAITEMENT À LA TERBINAFINE DEVRAIT ÊTRE ARRÊTÉ SI UNE ÉLÉVATION SYMPTOMATIQUE DE CES CONCENTRATIONS SURVIENT.
- Si des signes d'infection secondaire se manifestent, suivre la numération des polynucléaires neutrophiles.

T

Si le nombre de polynucléaires neutrophiles est < 1 × 10^9/L, interrompre le traitement.

- La terbinafine peut entraîner la diminution du nombre absolu de lymphocytes.
- Mesurer les concentrations de potassium. La terbinafine peut entraîner l'hypokaliémie.

DIAGNOSTICS INFIRMIERS POSSIBLES

- Risque d'infection (Indications).
- Connaissances insuffisantes sur le traitement médicamenteux (Enseignement au patient et à ses proches).
- Non-observance du traitement médicamenteux (Enseignement au patient et à ses proches).

INTERVENTIONS INFIRMIÈRES

- NE PAS CONFONDRE LAMISIL (TERBINAFINE) AVEC LAMICTAL (LAMOTRIGINE).
- On peut administrer la terbinafine sans égard aux repas.

ENSEIGNEMENT AU PATIENT ET À SES PROCHES

- Expliquer au patient qu'il doit respecter rigoureusement la posologie recommandée et prendre la terbinafine tous les jours, à la même heure, pendant toute la durée du traitement, même si les symptômes s'améliorent.
- Expliquer au patient qu'il doit prévenir un professionnel de la santé en cas de signes et de symptômes de dysfonctionnement hépatique (fatigue inhabituelle, anorexie, nausées, vomissements, ictère, urine foncée ou selles blanchâtres). Le traitement par la terbinafine devrait être interrompu dans ce cas.
- Recommander au patient de consulter un professionnel de la santé avant de prendre des médicaments d'ordonnance ou des préparations en vente libre pendant le traitement par la terbinafine.

VÉRIFICATION DE L'EFFICACITÉ THÉRAPEUTIQUE

L'efficacité du traitement peut être démontrée par: la disparition des signes cliniques de l'infection fongique des ongles, confirmée par les résultats des tests de laboratoire. Une durée de traitement insuffisante peut entraîner la récurrence de l'infection. ✳

TERBUTALINE

Bricanyl

CLASSIFICATION:

Bronchodilatateur (agoniste bêta-adrénergique)

Grossesse – catégorie B

INDICATIONS

Bronchodilatation en cas d'obstruction réversible des voies respiratoires attribuable à l'asthme ou à la bronchopneumopathie chronique obstructive (BPCO).

MÉCANISME D'ACTION

Liaison aux récepteurs bêta$_2$-adrénergiques, présents dans les muscles lisses des voies respiratoires, entraînant l'activation de l'adénylcyclase et l'élévation des concentrations d'adénosine monophosphate-3', 5' cyclique (AMPc). Cette hausse des concentrations stimule les kinases, qui inhibent la phosphorylation de la myosine et abaissent les concentrations intracellulaires de calcium. La baisse de ces concentrations est associée à la relaxation des muscles lisses des voies respiratoires ■ Relaxation des muscles lisses des voies respiratoires entraînant la bronchodilatation ■ Spécificité relative pour les récepteurs bêta$_2$-adrénergiques (pulmonaires). ***Effets thérapeutiques:*** Bronchodilatation.

PHARMACOCINÉTIQUE

Absorption: Minime (inhalation).
Distribution: L'action est principalement locale. L'agent passe dans le lait maternel.
Métabolisme et excrétion: Inconnus.
Demi-vie: Inconnue.

Profil temps-action (bronchodilatation)

	DÉBUT D'ACTION	PIC	DURÉE
Inhalation	5 - 30 min	1 - 2 h	3 - 6 h

CONTRE-INDICATIONS, PRÉCAUTIONS ET MISES EN GARDE

Contre-indications: Hypersensibilité aux amines adrénergiques ■ Tachyarythmie.
Précautions et mises en garde: Maladie cardiaque (insuffisance coronarienne ou arythmies) ■ Hypertension ■ Hyperthyroïdie ■ Diabète ■ Troubles convulsifs ■ Antécédents de réponse accrue aux amines sympathomimétiques ■ **GÉR.:** Il est recommandé de réduire la dose chez les personnes âgées ou débilitées (davantage prédisposées aux réactions indésirables) ■ Usage excessif pouvant entraîner la tolérance aux effets du médicament et un bronchospasme paradoxal (inhalateur) ■ **OBST., ALLAITEMENT:** L'innocuité du médicament n'a pas été établie chez la femme enceinte ou qui allaite ■ **PÉD.:** L'innocuité et l'efficacité du médicament n'ont pas été établies chez les enfants < 6 ans.

RÉACTIONS INDÉSIRABLES ET EFFETS SECONDAIRES

SNC: nervosité, agitation, tremblements, céphalées, insomnie.

Resp.: BRONCHOSPASME PARADOXAL (usage excessif des inhalateurs).
CV: angine, arythmies, hypertension, tachycardie.
GI: nausées, vomissements.
End.: hyperglycémie.

INTERACTIONS

Médicament-médicament: Risque accru d'effets adrénergiques additifs lors de l'administration simultanée d'autres **agents adrénergiques (sympathomimétiques)** ■ Risque de crise hypertensive lors de l'administration concomitante d'**IMAO** ou d'**antidépresseurs tricycliques** ■ Les **bêtabloquants** peuvent contrecarrer les effets du médicament.
Médicament-produits naturels: La consommation concomitante de produits contenant de la **caféine** (**noix de cola**, **guarana**, **maté**, **thé**, **café**) augmente l'effet stimulant de la terbutaline.

VOIES D'ADMINISTRATION ET POSOLOGIE

- **Inhalation (adultes et enfants ≥ 6 ans)**: 1 inhalation (500 µg/dose), toutes les 4 à 6 heures, au besoin; si nécessaire, une 2e inhalation peut être prise 5 minutes après la 1e (ne pas dépasser 6 inhalations/24 h).

PRÉSENTATION

Turbuhaler pour inhalation: 500 µg/dose[Pr].

SOINS INFIRMIERS

ÉVALUATION DE LA SITUATION

- Ausculter le murmure vésiculaire; déterminer les caractéristiques des respirations et mesurer la pression artérielle et le pouls avant d'administrer le médicament et pendant le pic de son effet. Noter la quantité, la couleur et les caractéristiques des expectorations produites et signaler au médecin ou à un autre professionnel de la santé tout résultat anormal.
- Noter les résultats des tests de la fonction pulmonaire, avant le début du traitement et à intervalles réguliers pendant toute sa durée pour déterminer l'efficacité du médicament.
- Suivre de près l'apparition d'un bronchospasme paradoxal (respiration sifflante). S'il survient, arrêter l'administration du médicament et prévenir immédiatement le médecin ou un autre professionnel de la santé.
- OBSERVER LE PATIENT POUR DÉCELER LE BRONCHOSPASME PARADOXAL (RESPIRATION SIFFLANTE). EN CAS DE BRONCHOSPASME PARADOXAL, CESSER LE TRAITEMENT ET PRÉVENIR IMMÉDIATEMENT LE MÉDECIN OU UN AUTRE PROFESSIONNEL DE LA SANTÉ.
- Observer le patient pour déceler tout signe de tolérance ou de bronchospasme rebond. Suivre de près les patients qui ont besoin de plus de 3 inhalations en 24 heures. Si le soulagement est mineur ou absent après 3 à 5 inhalations en 6 à 12 heures, il n'est pas recommandé de suivre le traitement par le Turbuhaler seul.

Tests de laboratoire:

- La terbutaline peut entraîner une diminution passagère des concentrations sériques de potassium lors de l'administration de doses supérieures à celles recommandées.

TOXICITÉ ET SURDOSAGE:

- Les symptômes de surdosage incluent l'agitation persistante, la gêne ou des douleurs thoraciques, l'abaissement de la pression artérielle, des étourdissements, l'hyperglycémie, l'hypokaliémie, les convulsions, les tachyarythmies, des tremblements persistants et des vomissements.
- Le traitement inclut l'interruption de l'administration des agonistes bêta-adrénergiques et du traitement de soutien. Il faut administrer les bêtabloquants cardiosélectifs avec prudence, car ils peuvent déclencher des bronchospasmes.

DIAGNOSTICS INFIRMIERS POSSIBLES

- Dégagement inefficace des voies respiratoires (Indications).
- Connaissances insuffisantes sur le traitement médicamenteux (Enseignement au patient et à ses proches).

INTERVENTIONS INFIRMIÈRES

Inhalation:

- Ne jamais expirer dans l'embout buccal.
- Ne pas utiliser l'inhalateur Turbuhaler s'il est endommagé ou si l'embout buccal s'est détaché.
- Étant donné que la quantité de poudre libérée est très petite, il se peut qu'on ne sente pas le goût du médicament après l'inhalation. Toutefois, si les instructions ont été rigoureusement suivies, la dose a été inhalée.

Nettoyage: Nettoyer la partie extérieure de l'embout buccal chaque semaine à l'aide d'un linge sec. Ne jamais utiliser d'eau ni un autre liquide pour le nettoyer. Si du liquide entre dans l'inhalateur, cela peut nuire à son fonctionnement.

ENSEIGNEMENT AU PATIENT ET À SES PROCHES

- Conseiller au patient de respecter rigoureusement la posologie recommandée. S'il doit prendre le médicament à intervalles réguliers et s'il a sauté une dose, il devra la prendre le plus rapidement possible et espacer les doses restantes de façon à pouvoir les prendre à intervalles égaux. Le prévenir qu'il ne doit pas remplacer une dose manquée par une double dose ni dépasser la dose recommandée, car il s'expose au risque d'effets nocifs, de bronchospasme paradoxal ou d'une baisse de l'efficacité du médicament.

- Conseiller au patient de prévenir immédiatement un professionnel de la santé si les essoufflements ne sont pas soulagés par le médicament ou s'ils s'accompagnent de diaphorèse, d'étourdissements, de palpitations ou de douleurs thoraciques.
- Signaler au patient qu'il doit consulter un professionnel de la santé avant de prendre un médicament en vente libre et d'éviter de consommer de l'alcool en même temps qu'il prend ce médicament. Mettre en garde le patient contre l'usage du tabac et d'autres agents irritants des voies respiratoires.

Inhalation:

- Faire une démonstration de l'utilisation correcte de Turbuhaler (le mode d'emploi est expliqué à l'annexe G). Attendre de 1 à 5 minutes avant d'administrer la dose suivante. Il faut nettoyer la partie extérieure de l'embout buccal chaque semaine avec un linge sec. Si du liquide entre dans l'inhalateur, son fonctionnement peut être entravé.
- Prévenir le patient qui prend d'autres médicaments par inhalation qu'il doit commencer par le bronchodilatateur et attendre 15 minutes avant d'inhaler les autres médicaments, sauf recommandation contraire.
- Recommander au patient de se rincer la bouche avec de l'eau après chaque inhalation pour réduire la sécheresse buccale.
- Recommander au patient de boire suffisamment de liquides (de 2 000 à 3 000 mL/jour) pour diminuer la viscosité des sécrétions tenaces.
- Conseiller au patient de consulter un professionnel de la santé si les symptômes respiratoires ne sont pas soulagés ou s'ils s'aggravent après le traitement ou, encore, s'il manifeste des douleurs thoraciques, des céphalées, des étourdissements graves, des palpitations, de la nervosité ou de la faiblesse.
- Conseiller au patient d'informer un professionnel de la santé s'il vide un flacon de Turbuhaler en moins de 2 semaines.

VÉRIFICATION DE L'EFFICACITÉ THÉRAPEUTIQUE

L'efficacité du traitement peut être démontrée par: la prévention ou le soulagement du bronchospasme ■ une respiration plus facile.

T

TERCONAZOLE,

voir Antifongiques vaginaux

TÉRIPARATIDE

Forteo

CLASSIFICATION:

Agent ostéoformateur (parathormone [de source ADNr])

Grossesse – catégorie C

INDICATIONS

Traitement de l'ostéoporose grave chez les femmes ménopausées, exposées à un risque élevé de fracture ou chez lesquelles un autre traitement a échoué ou n'a pas été toléré ■ Augmentation de la masse osseuse chez les hommes atteints d'ostéoporose grave, chez lesquels un autre traitement a échoué ou n'a pas été toléré.

MÉCANISME D'ACTION

Régulation du métabolisme du calcium et du phosphate dans les os et les reins par liaison à des récepteurs cellulaires particuliers ■ Stimulation de l'activité des ostéoblastes. ***Effets thérapeutiques:*** Augmentation de la densité minérale osseuse avec réduction du risque de fractures (démontrée chez la femme seulement).

PHARMACOCINÉTIQUE

Absorption: Biodisponibilité à 95 % (SC).

Distribution: Inconnue.

Métabolisme et excrétion: Métabolisme hépatique; excrétion rénale (sous forme de métabolites).

Demi-vie: SC: 1 heure.

Profil temps-action (concentration sérique de calcium)

	DÉBUT D'ACTION	PIC	DURÉE
SC	2 h	4-6 h	16-24 h

CONTRE-INDICATIONS, PRÉCAUTIONS ET MISES EN GARDE

Contre-indications: Hypersensibilité ■ Maladie osseuse de Paget ou autre maladie métabolique touchant les os ■ Élévation inexpliquée de la phosphatase alcaline ■ Antécédents de radiothérapie, de métastases osseuses ou de cancer des os ■ Hypercalcémie préexistante ■ Insuffisance rénale grave.

Précautions et mises en garde: Usage concomitant de digoxine ■ **PÉD.:** Enfants et jeunes adultes (l'innocuité du médicament n'a pas été établie) ■ **OBST., ALLAITEMENT:** L'innocuité du médicament n'a pas été établie ■ Lithiase urinaire active ou récente.

RÉACTIONS INDÉSIRABLES ET EFFETS SECONDAIRES

CV: hypotension orthostatique.
GI: nausées.
Métab.: hypercalcémie.
Loc.: crampes aux jambes.
Divers: réaction d'hypersensibilité.

INTERACTIONS

Médicament-médicament: L'hypercalcémie transitoire peut accroître le risque d'intoxication par la **digoxine**.

VOIES D'ADMINISTRATION ET POSOLOGIE

- **SC (adultes):** 20 µg, 1 fois par jour.

PRÉSENTATION

Dispositif d'injection prérempli (stylo-injecteur FORTEO): 20 µg/dose (28 doses)[Pr].

SOINS INFIRMIERS

ÉVALUATION DE LA SITUATION

- Évaluer la densité minérale osseuse avant le traitement et à intervalles réguliers pendant toute sa durée.

Tests de laboratoire: L'agent élève transitoirement les concentrations sériques de calcium et diminue les concentrations sériques de phosphore. L'effet maximal se manifeste en l'espace de 4 à 6 heures. Environ 16 heures après l'administration de la dose, les concentrations sériques de calcium retournent près des valeurs initiales. Si l'hypercalcémie persiste, arrêter l'administration du tériparatide et évaluer la cause de l'hypercalcémie.

- Le tériparatide peut causer des élévations asymptomatiques de la concentration sérique d'acide urique.

DIAGNOSTICS INFIRMIERS POSSIBLES

- Risque d'accident (Indications).

INTERVENTIONS INFIRMIÈRES

- Ne pas utiliser le tériparatide pendant plus de 18 mois.

SC: Administrer par voie sous-cutanée dans la cuisse ou la paroi abdominale, 1 fois par jour. On peut l'administrer à n'importe quel moment de la journée, sans égard aux repas. La solution doit être transparente et incolore. Ne pas utiliser de solution contenant des particules solides, trouble ou colorée. Garder le stylo-injecteur dans le réfrigérateur; ne pas le conserver au congélateur et ne pas l'utiliser s'il a été congelé. Le garder hors du réfrigérateur pendant le moins longtemps possible; s'en servir dès qu'on l'a sorti du réfrigérateur et l'y remettre aussitôt. Le stylo-injecteur *Forteo* peut être utilisé pendant 28 jours après la première injection. Après 28 jours d'utilisation, jeter le stylo-injecteur *Forteo* même s'il contient encore de la solution.

ENSEIGNEMENT AU PATIENT ET À SES PROCHES

- Recommander au patient de s'autoadministrer le médicament tous les jours à la même heure. S'il n'a pas pu s'injecter le médicament au moment habituel, l'injecter dès que possible le même jour. Le prévenir qu'il ne faut pas s'administrer plus de 1 injection par jour.
- Enseigner au patient la technique appropriée d'administration et de mise au rebut des aiguilles. Lui recommander de lire les renseignements destinés au patient et le manuel de l'utilisateur avant de commencer le traitement et de les relire à chaque renouvellement d'ordonnance. Prévenir le patient qu'il faut jeter le stylo-injecteur après 28 jours d'utilisation et qu'il ne faut pas le partager avec d'autres personnes.
- Expliquer au patient l'importance des autres traitements de l'ostéoporose (suppléments de calcium et de vitamine D, exercices des articulations portantes, modification d'autres facteurs comportementaux, comme le tabagisme et la consommation d'alcool).
- Prévenir le patient qu'il y a risque d'hypotension orthostatique au cours des premières journées de traitement. Lui conseiller de s'autoadministrer le médicament en position couchée ou assise. En cas de sensation de tête légère, d'étourdissements ou de palpitations, lui recommander de rester couché jusqu'à ce que les symptômes disparaissent. Si les symptômes persistent ou s'aggravent, l'inciter à en informer un professionnel de la santé.
- Conseiller au patient de prévenir un professionnel de la santé si des symptômes d'hypercalcémie persistante (nausées, vomissements, constipation, léthargie, faiblesse musculaire) se manifestent.
- Insister sur l'importance des tests de suivi qui évaluent la densité minérale osseuse.

VÉRIFICATION DE L'EFFICACITÉ THÉRAPEUTIQUE

L'efficacité du traitement peut être démontrée par: l'augmentation de la densité minérale osseuse et la réduction du risque de fractures.

T

TESTOSTÉRONE

cypionate de testostérone
Depo-Testostérone, Testostérone cypionate

énanthate de testostérone
Delatestryl, PMS-Testostérone

propionate de testostérone
Testostérone propionate

timbre transdermique de testostérone
Androderm

undécanoate de testostérone
Andriol

gel topique de testostérone
AndroGel, Testim

CLASSIFICATION:
Hormone androgène et stéroïde anabolisant

Grossesse – catégorie X

INDICATIONS

Traitement de l'hypogonadisme chez les hommes présentant un déficit en androgènes ■ Traitement du retard pubertaire chez les hommes ■ Traitement palliatif du cancer du sein sensible aux androgènes ■ Traitement androgénique adjuvant chez la femme.

MÉCANISME D'ACTION

Hormone responsable de la croissance et du développement normal des organes sexuels masculins ■ Maintien des caractères sexuels secondaires chez l'homme: croissance et maturation de la prostate, des vésicules séminales, du pénis et du scrotum ■ développement de la pilosité et répartition caractéristique des poils chez l'homme ■ épaississement des cordes vocales ■ modification de la musculature corporelle et de la répartition des tissus adipeux. ***Effets thérapeutiques:*** Correction du déficit hormonal caractérisant l'hypogonadisme ■ Déclenchement de la puberté chez l'homme ■ Suppression de la croissance des tumeurs dans le cas de certaines formes de cancer du sein.

PHARMACOCINÉTIQUE

Absorption: Bonne (IM). Les sels de cypionate, de propionate et d'énanthate sont absorbés lentement. Bonne absorption par la peau (la peau du scrotum est de 5 à 30 fois plus perméable que les autres emplacements).

Distribution: L'agent traverse probablement la barrière placentaire et passe dans le lait maternel.

Métabolisme et excrétion: Métabolisme hépatique.

Demi-vie: *Cypionate* – 8 jours.

Profil temps-action (effets androgènes)†

	DÉBUT D'ACTION	PIC	DURÉE
IM – cypionate, énanthate	inconnu	inconnu	2 – 4 semaines
IM – propionate	inconnu	inconnu	1 – 3 jours
Timbre transdermique	inconnu	2 – 4 h‡	2 h§

† La réponse individuelle varie fortement; les effets peuvent survenir après plusieurs mois de traitement.

‡ Concentrations plasmatiques de testostérone après l'application de timbres (les plateaux sont atteints après 3 à 4 semaines).

§ Après le retrait du timbre.

CONTRE-INDICATIONS, PRÉCAUTIONS ET MISES EN GARDE

Contre-indications: Hypersensibilité ■ Grossesse et allaitement ■ Patients de sexe masculin atteints de cancer du sein ou de la prostate ■ Hypercalcémie ■ Maladies hépatique, rénale ou cardiaque graves.

Précautions et mises en garde: Diabète ■ Coronaropathie ■ Antécédents de maladie hépatique ■ Prépuberté masculine.

RÉACTIONS INDÉSIRABLES ET EFFETS SECONDAIRES

ORLO: approfondissement ou enrouement de la voix.

CV: œdème.

GI: modifications de l'appétit, hépatite médicamenteuse, nausées, vomissements.

GU: irritation de la vessie, irrégularités menstruelles, hyperplasie de la prostate.

End.: *femmes* – modifications de la libido, hyperplasie du clitoris, diminution du volume des seins; *hommes* – acné, croissance de la pilosité faciale, gynécomastie, impuissance, oligospermie, priapisme.

HÉ: hypercalcémie.

Locaux: irritation chronique de la peau (timbres transdermiques), douleurs au point d'injection.

INTERACTIONS

Médicament-médicament: La testostérone augmente le métabolisme de certains facteurs de coagulation, ce qui peut augmenter l'effet de la **warfarine** ■ La testostérone administrée en concomitance avec l'**insuline** ou des **hypoglycémiants oraux** augmente le risque d'hypoglycémie ■ Hépatotoxicité additive lors de l'administration simultanée d'autres **agents hépatotoxiques** ■ Risque accru d'œdème en cas d'administration concomitante de **corticostéroïdes à activité minéralocorticoïde**.

VOIES D'ADMINISTRATION ET POSOLOGIE

Hormonothérapie substitutive

- **IM (adultes):** De 25 à 50 mg, 2 ou 3 fois par semaine (propionate), *ou* de 200 à 400 mg, toutes les 4 semaines (énanthate), *ou* de 200 à 400 mg, toutes les 3 ou 4 semaines (cypionate).

Hypogonadisme

- **IM (adultes):** De 200 à 400 mg, toutes les 4 semaines (cypionate ou énanthate), *ou* de 10 à 25 mg, de 2 à 5 fois par semaine (propionate).
- **Timbre transdermique (adultes):** *Androderm* (hommes) – 5 mg, à appliquer toutes les 24 heures.
- **Gel topique (adultes):** *AndroGel* (hommes) – 5 g, à appliquer toutes les 24 heures.

Retard de la puberté chez l'homme

- **IM (enfants > 12 ans):** Jusqu'à 100 mg par mois pendant une période pouvant aller jusqu'à 6 mois.

Traitement palliatif du cancer du sein

- **IM (adultes):** De 50 à 100 mg, 3 fois par semaine (propionate), *ou* de 200 à 400 mg, toutes les 2 à 4 semaines (énanthate).

Traitement par voie orale (sauf cancer du sein)

- **PO (adultes et adolescents):** *Undécanoate* – initialement, de 120 à 160 mg en 2 doses fractionnées, pendant 2 ou 3 semaines; par la suite, 1 dose d'entretien de 40 à 120 mg par jour.

PRÉSENTATION (version générique disponible)

Cypionate de testostérone en injection (dans de l'huile de graines de coton): 100 mg/mL, en fioles de 10 mL[C] ■ **Énanthate de testostérone en injection (dans de l'huile de sésame):** 200 mg/mL, en fioles de 5 mL[C] ■ **Propionate de testostérone en injection (dans de l'huile):** 100 mg/mL, en fioles de 10 mL[C] ■ **Timbres transdermiques de testostérone:** *Androderm* – 2,5 mg/jour, 60 par paquet[C] et 5 mg/jour, 30 par paquet[C] ■ **Undécanoate de testostérone (capsules):** 40 mg[C] ■ **Gel topique de testostérone:** *AndroGel* – 2,5 g, 5 g par sachet[C]; pompes à doses mesurées (1,25 g de gel par actionnement[C]).

SOINS INFIRMIERS

ÉVALUATION DE LA SITUATION

- Effectuer le bilan des ingesta et des excreta, peser le patient 2 fois par semaine et suivre de près l'apparition d'un œdème. Signaler toute modification importante traduisant une rétention hydrique.

Hommes:

- Suivre de près l'apparition de la puberté précoce chez les garçons (acné, couleur foncée de la peau, développement des caractères sexuels secondaires masculins – augmentation de la taille du pénis, érections fréquentes, croissance de la pilosité corporelle). On devrait effectuer tous les 6 mois des examens radiologiques permettant d'évaluer l'âge osseux et de déterminer la vitesse de maturation des os et les effets de l'hormone sur la soudure des épiphyses.
- Suivre de près l'augmentation du volume des seins, les érections persistantes et le besoin accru d'uriner. Déceler les difficultés de miction chez les patients âgés, en raison du risque d'hyperplasie de la prostate.

Femmes:

- Déceler les signes de virilisation: raucité de la voix, croissance ou chute exagérée des poils, hypertrophie du clitoris, acné, irrégularités menstruelles.
- Chez les femmes souffrant de cancer métastatique du sein, suivre de près l'apparition des symptômes d'hypercalcémie: nausées, vomissements, constipation, léthargie, perte de tonus musculaire, soif, polyurie.

Tests de laboratoire:

- Noter les concentrations d'hémoglobine et l'hématocrite à intervalles réguliers pendant toute la durée du traitement. La testostérone peut entraîner la polycythémie.
- Évaluer les résultats des tests de la fonction hépatique et les concentrations sériques de cholestérol à intervalles réguliers pendant toute la durée du traitement; la testostérone peut entraîner l'élévation des concentrations d'AST et de bilirubine, l'élévation ou la diminution des concentrations de cholestérol et la suppression des facteurs de coagulation II, V, VII et X.
- Examiner les concentrations sériques et urinaires de calcium et les concentrations sériques de phosphatase alcaline en cas de cancer métastatique.
- La testostérone peut modifier la glycémie à jeun, les résultats des tests de tolérance au glucose, des tests de la fonction thyroïdienne et des tests à la méthyrapone. L'augmentation des concentrations de créatine et la diminution de la clairance de la créatinine peuvent se poursuivre jusqu'à 2 semaines après l'arrêt du traitement. La testostérone peut entraîner l'élévation des concentrations sériques de chlorure, de potassium, de phosphate et de sodium.
- La testostérone peut entraîner l'élévation des concentrations du 17-cétostéroïde dosé dans les urines de 24 heures.

T

- La testostérone peut entraîner la diminution de la quantité de globulines liées aux corticostéroïdes et celle de globulines liées aux hormones stéroïdes sexuelles; les concentrations d'hormones libres restent inchangées. La testostérone peut également entraîner une diminution des concentrations de l'hormone folliculostimulante (FSH), de l'hormone lutéinisante (LH) et de la quantité de sperme.
- *Timbre transdermique:* Mesurer les taux d'antigène prostatique spécifique à intervalles réguliers pendant toute la durée du traitement par un timbre transdermique. On devrait mesurer les concentrations sériques de testostérone de 2 à 4 heures après l'application du timbre, après 3 à 4 semaines d'utilisation.
- Déterminer les concentrations de LH et les concentrations sériques d'ALT tous les 6 mois au cours d'un traitement androgène visant le changement de sexe pour évaluer l'issue du traitement et ses effets secondaires.

DIAGNOSTICS INFIRMIERS POSSIBLES

- Dysfonctionnement sexuel (Indications, Effets secondaires).
- Connaissances insuffisantes sur le traitement médicamenteux (Enseignement au patient et à ses proches).

INTERVENTIONS INFIRMIÈRES

- On devrait inciter tous les patients alités à faire des exercices d'amplitude du mouvement, afin de prévenir la résorption osseuse du calcium.

IM: Administrer la solution profondément dans le muscle fessier. À une basse température, des cristaux peuvent se former dans la solution; pour les dissoudre, réchauffer et agiter la fiole. Si l'on utilise une seringue ou une aiguille humide, la solution devient trouble, mais sa puissance n'est pas modifiée pour autant.

Timbre transdermique:

- Appliquer les timbres sur une peau glabre, propre et sèche. La peau peut être rasée à sec; ne pas utiliser de produits dépilatoires. On peut appliquer de nouveau le timbre après le bain, la douche ou la natation. *Androderm* est appliqué sur la peau du dos, de l'abdomen, des avant-bras ou des cuisses.
- En cas d'irritation cutanée, retirer le timbre et appliquer une petite quantité de crème d'hydrocortisone topique en vente libre; on peut appliquer une petite quantité de crème de triamcinolone à 0,1 %[Pr] sur la peau située sous la partie centrale du timbre *Androderm*, sans que cela affecte l'absorption de la testostérone. Ne pas appliquer d'onguent en prétraitement, car l'absorption de la testostérone peut être considérablement réduite.

Gel topique:

- Appliquer le gel 1 fois par jour, de préférence le matin sur une peau sèche, propre et intacte. *AndroGel* est appliqué sur les épaules, la partie supérieure des bras ou l'abdomen. Ne pas appliquer sur les parties génitales. Consulter le feuillet d'instruction pour connaître le mode d'emploi de la pompe à doses mesurées.

ENSEIGNEMENT AU PATIENT ET À SES PROCHES

- Recommander au patient de signaler rapidement les signes et les symptômes suivants: chez les hommes, le priapisme (érection prolongée et souvent douloureuse) ou la gynécomastie; chez les femmes, la virilisation (pouvant être renversée si le traitement est arrêté dès que de tels changements deviennent notables), l'hypercalcémie (nausées, vomissements, constipation et faiblesse), l'œdème (gain pondéral inattendu, enflure des pieds), l'hépatite (jaunissement de la peau ou des yeux et douleurs abdominales) ou les saignements ou ecchymoses inhabituels.
- Expliquer au patient la raison pour laquelle l'usage de ce médicament dans le but d'augmenter la performance athlétique est déconseillé. Dans ce cas, la testostérone n'est ni sûre ni efficace, et elle peut provoquer des effets secondaires graves.
- Recommander à la patiente de prévenir immédiatement un professionnel de la santé si elle pense être enceinte ou si elle souhaite le devenir.
- Recommander au patient diabétique de suivre de près sa glycémie afin de déceler toute modification.
- Insister sur l'importance des examens physiques, diagnostiques, biochimiques et radiologiques à intervalles réguliers permettant d'évaluer les bienfaits du traitement.
- Prévenir les parents que l'enfant prépubertaire doit se soumettre tous les 6 mois à des examens radiologiques permettant d'évaluer l'âge osseux et de déterminer la vitesse de maturation des os et les effets de l'hormone sur la soudure des épiphyses.

Timbre transdermique: Recommander au patient de prévenir un professionnel de la santé si certains signes de virilisation apparaissent chez sa partenaire sexuelle.

VÉRIFICATION DE L'EFFICACITÉ THÉRAPEUTIQUE

L'efficacité du traitement peut être démontrée par: la disparition des signes de déficit en androgènes sans apparition d'effets secondaires; le traitement doit habituellement se limiter à une période de 3 à 6 mois et être suivi d'une évaluation de l'âge osseux ou de la maturation des os ■ la diminution de la taille des tumeurs et le ralentissement de la propagation des métastases en cas de cancer du sein chez les femmes ménopausées. En cas de traitement antinéoplasique, la réponse peut ne survenir que 3 mois plus tard; si l'on note des signes d'évolution de la maladie, il faut arrêter ce traitement. ✳

TÉTRACYCLINES

doxycycline
Apo-Doxy, Doxycin, Novo-Doxylin, Nu-Doxycycline, Ratio-Doxycycline, Periostat, Vitra-Tabs

minocycline
Apo-Minocycline, Enca, Gen-Minocycline, Minocin, Novo-Minocycline, PMS-Minocycline, Ratio-Minocycline, Sandoz-Minocycline

tétracycline
Apo-Tetra, Nu-Tetra

CLASSIFICATION:
Antibiotiques

Grossesse – catégorie D

INDICATIONS

Traitement d'infections des voies respiratoires, gastro-intestinales, génito-urinaires, de la peau et des tissus mous ainsi que de diverses infections attribuables à des microorganismes inhabituels, notamment: *Mycoplasma* ■ *Chlamydia* ■ *Rickettsia* ■ *Borellia burgdorferi* (maladie de Lyme) ■ Traitement de la gonorrhée et de la syphilis chez les patients allergiques à la pénicilline ■ Traitement de l'acné inflammatoire ■ **Doxycycline**: Prophylaxie de la malaria ■ Traitement d'appoint de la parodontite chronique ■ **Tétracycline**: En association, traitement de l'ulcère à *H. pylori.* **Usages non approuvés: Doxycycline**: Traitement de l'anthrax.

MÉCANISME D'ACTION

Inhibition de la synthèse des protéines bactériennes au niveau de la sous-unité 30S du ribosome ■ La préparation à faible dose utilisée pour le traitement de la parodontite inhibe la collagénase. ***Effets thérapeutiques:*** Effet bactériostatique contre les bactéries sensibles ■ Diminution des complications de la parodontite. **Spectre d'action**: Les tétracyclines sont actives contre certains agents pathogènes à Gram positif incluant: *Bacillus anthracis* ■ *Clostridium perfringens* ■ *Clostridium tetani* ■ *Listeria monocytogenes* ■ *Nocardia* ■ *Propionibacterium acnes* ■ *Actinomyces israelii* ■ certaines souches de staphylocoques et de streptocoques (la résistance est cependant en train de s'accroître) ■ Elles sont actives contre certains agents pathogènes à Gram négatif incluant: *Hæmophilus influenzæ* ■ *Legionella pneumophila* ■ *Yersinia enterocolitica* ■ *Yersinia pestis* ■ *Neisseria gonorrhœæ* ■ *Neisseria meningitidis* ■ Elles sont également actives contre plusieurs autres agents pathogènes incluant: *Mycoplasma* ■ *Treponema pallidum* ■ *Chlamydia* ■ *Rickettsia* ■ *Borellia burgdorferi.*

PHARMACOCINÉTIQUE

Absorption: *Tétracycline* – de 60 à 80 % (PO). *Doxycycline, minocycline* – de 90 à 100 % (PO).

Distribution: Les tétracyclines se répartissent dans tout l'organisme et pénètrent en faible quantité dans le liquide céphalorachidien. Elles traversent la barrière placentaire et passent dans le lait maternel.

Métabolisme et excrétion: *Doxycycline* – excrétion urinaire à l'état inchangé de 20 à 40 %; partiellement inactivée dans l'intestin; une certaine fraction entre dans la circulation entérohépatique, puis est excrétée dans la bile et les fèces. *Minocycline* – métabolisme hépatique avec circulation entérohépatique et excrétion dans la bile et les fèces; excrétion à l'état inchangé dans l'urine de 5 à 20 %. *Tétracycline* – excrétion à l'état inchangé par les reins à 60 % et excrétion dans les fèces.

Demi-vie: *Doxycycline* – de 14 à 24 heures (prolongée en présence d'une insuffisance rénale grave). *Minocycline* – de 11 à 23 heures. *Tétracycline* – de 6 à 12 heures.

Profil temps-action

	DÉBUT D'ACTION	PIC	DURÉE
Doxycycline - PO	1 - 2 h	1,5 - 4 h	12 h
Minocycline - PO	rapide	1 - 4 h	6 - 12 h
Tétracycline - PO	1 - 2 h	2 - 4 h	6 - 12 h

T

CONTRE-INDICATIONS, PRÉCAUTIONS ET MISES EN GARDE

Contre-indications: Hypersensibilité ■ **OBST.**: Risque de coloration sombre (jaune, gris, brun) permanente des dents chez les nourrissons, si le médicament est administré durant la dernière moitié de la grossesse ■ **ALLAITEMENT, PÉD.**: Coloration sombre (jaune, gris, brun) permanente des dents chez les enfants < 9 ans ■ Myasthénie grave.

Précautions et mises en garde: Patients cachectiques ou débilités ■ Maladie rénale (réduire la dose de tétracycline uniquement) ■ Insuffisance hépatique (doxycycline, minocycline) ■ Diabète insipide néphrogénique ■

Minocycline – Lupus érythémateux (risque d'aggravation des symptômes).

RÉACTIONS INDÉSIRABLES ET EFFETS SECONDAIRES

SNC: hypertension intracrânienne bénigne (plus élevée chez les enfants); *minocycline* – céphalées, étourdissements, vertiges.

ORLO: acouphènes; *minocycline* – réactions vestibulaires.

GI: diarrhée, nausées, vomissements, œsophagite, hépatotoxicité, pancréatite, COLITE PSEUDOMEMBRANEUSE; *doxycycline* – œsophagite, ulcération de l'œsophage.

Tég.: photosensibilité, rash; *minocycline* – pigmentation de la peau et des muqueuses.

Hémat.: dyscrasie sanguine.

Divers: réactions d'hypersensibilité, surinfection.

INTERACTIONS

Médicament-médicament: Les tétracyclines peuvent intensifier l'effet de la **warfarine** (surveiller le RNI) ■ Les tétracyclines peuvent diminuer l'efficacité des **contraceptifs oraux à base d'œstrogènes** ■ Les **antiacides**, l'**aluminium**, le **calcium**, le **fer** et le **magnésium** forment avec les tétracyclines un chélate insoluble en diminuant ainsi l'absorption (espacer les prises d'au moins 2 heures); l'effet est moindre dans le cas de la doxycycline ■ Le **sucralfate**, administré simultanément, peut se lier aux tétracyclines et empêcher son absorption depuis le tractus gastro-intestinal ■ La **cholestyramine** ou le **colestipol**, administrés simultanément, diminuent l'absorption des tétracyclines administrées par voie orale ■ Les **antidiarrhéiques adsorbants** (**attapulgite**, **sous-salicylate de bismuth**) peuvent diminuer l'absorption des tétracyclines ■ Les **barbituriques**, la **carbamazépine** ou la **phénytoïne** peuvent diminuer l'activité de la doxycycline ■ Risque accru d'hépatotoxicité lors de l'administration concomitante de **médicaments hépatotoxiques** ■ L'usage concomitant risque d'entraver l'action bactéricide des **pénicillines**.

Médicament-aliments: Le **calcium** contenu dans les aliments ou les produits laitiers diminue l'absorption des tétracyclines en formant avec elles des chélates insolubles (espacer les prises d'au moins 2 heures).

VOIES D'ADMINISTRATION ET POSOLOGIE

Doxycycline

D'autres schémas posologiques que les suivants peuvent être utilisés.

- **PO (adultes)**: *La plupart des infections* – 100 mg, toutes les 12 heures, *ou* 200 mg en 1 dose, le premier jour, puis 100 mg, 1 fois par jour, *ou* de 100 à 200 mg par jour, en 1 ou 2 prises. *Chlamydia* – 100 mg, toutes les 12 heures, pendant 7 à 10 jours. *Prophylaxie de la malaria* – 100 mg, 1 fois par jour; commencer 1 ou 2 jours avant l'entrée dans la région impaludée et continuer pendant 4 semaines après l'avoir quittée. *Maladie de Lyme* – 100 mg, 2 fois par jour pendant 14 à 21 jours. *Parodontite* – 20 mg, 2 fois par jour (durée jusqu'à 9 mois).
- **PO (enfants ≥ 9 ans)**: De 2 à 4 mg/kg/jour, toutes les 12 à 24 heures (ne pas dépasser la dose administrée chez l'adulte).

Minocycline

- **PO (adultes)**: Initialement, 100 ou 200 mg en dose d'attaque, puis 100 mg, toutes les 12 heures, *ou* 50 mg, toutes les 6 heures. *Traitement de l'acné* – initialement, 100 mg par jour, puis 50 mg par jour en dose d'entretien.
- **PO (enfants ≥ 9 ans)**: Initialement, 4 mg/kg, puis 2 mg/kg, toutes les 12 heures.

Tétracycline

- **PO (adultes)**: De 250 à 500 mg, toutes les 6 heures. *Traitement prolongé de l'acné* – au début, 500 mg, 2 fois par jour, puis diminuer à la dose d'entretien de 250 à 500 mg par jour. *Traitement de l'ulcère à* H. pylori – 500 mg, 4 fois par jour, en association avec le métronidazole, le sous-salicylate de bismuth et un inhibiteur de la pompe à protons pendant 7 à 14 jours.
- **PO (enfants ≥ 9 ans)**: De 25 à 50 mg/kg/jour, en 2 à 4 doses fractionnées.

INSUFFISANCE RÉNALE

- *CL_{CR} DE 50 À 80 mL/MIN* – DIMINUER L'INTERVALLE D'ADMINISTRATION DE LA TÉTRACYCLINE (TOUTES LES 8 À 12 HEURES). *CL_{CR} DE 10 À 49 mL/MIN* – DIMINUER L'INTERVALLE D'ADMINISTRATION (TOUTES LES 12 À 24 HEURES). *CL_{CR} < 10 mL/MIN* – DIMINUER L'INTERVALLE D'ADMINISTRATION (TOUTES LES 24 HEURES).

PRÉSENTATION

- **Doxycycline (version générique disponible)**
  Comprimés: 100 mg^{Pr} ■ **Capsules**: 100 mg^{Pr} ■ **Gélules**: 20 mg^{Pr} ■ **Poudre pour injection**: disponible par l'intermédiaire du Programme d'accès spécial de Santé Canada.
- **Minocycline (version générique disponible)**
  Capsules: 50 mg^{Pr}, 100 mg^{Pr}.
- **Tétracycline (version générique disponible)**
  Capsules: 250 mg^{Pr}.

T

SOINS INFIRMIERS

ÉVALUATION DE LA SITUATION

Infection:

- Observer le patient au début du traitement et pendant toute sa durée pour déceler les signes suivants d'infection: altération des signes vitaux, aspect de la plaie, des crachats, de l'urine et des selles, numération leucocytaire.
- Prélever des échantillons pour la mise en culture et les antibiogrammes avant le début du traitement. La ou les premières doses peuvent être administrées avant que les résultats soient connus.

Tests de laboratoire:

- Examiner les résultats des tests des fonctions hépatique et rénale et la numération globulaire à intervalles réguliers tout au long du traitement prolongé.
- Les tétracyclines peuvent entraîner l'élévation des concentrations d'AST et d'ALT ainsi que des concentrations sériques d'urée, de phosphatase alcaline, de bilirubine et d'amylase.
- Les tétracyclines peuvent entraîner une fausse élévation des concentrations urinaires des catécholamines.

DIAGNOSTICS INFIRMIERS POSSIBLES

- Risque d'infection (Indications, Effets secondaires).
- Connaissances insuffisantes sur le traitement médicamenteux (Enseignement au patient et à ses proches).
- Non-observance du traitement médicamenteux (Enseignement au patient et à ses proches).

INTERVENTIONS INFIRMIÈRES

- Les tétracyclines peuvent rendre les dents d'une couleur jaune-brune-grise ou ramollir les dents et les os des enfants si elles sont administrées pendant la période prénatale ou au début de l'enfance. Il est déconseillé d'administrer ces médicaments chez les enfants < 9 ans et au cours de la grossesse ou de l'allaitement, à moins que les avantages possibles pour la mère ne l'emportent sur les risques pour le fœtus ou l'enfant.
- Administrer ces médicaments à intervalles réguliers, au moins 1 heure avant ou 2 heures après les repas. La doxycycline et la minocycline peuvent être prises avec des aliments si une irritation gastrique survient. Il faut les prendre avec un grand verre d'eau et éviter de se coucher dans l'heure qui suit afin de prévenir l'ulcération de l'œsophage. Espacer de 1 à 3 heures l'administration d'autres médicaments.
- Éviter d'administrer du calcium, des antiacides, des médicaments contenant du magnésium, du bicarbonate de sodium ou des suppléments de fer dans les 2 à 3 heures qui suivent ou qui précèdent l'administration des tétracyclines.

ENSEIGNEMENT AU PATIENT ET À SES PROCHES

- Expliquer au patient qu'il doit prendre le médicament à intervalles réguliers et utiliser toute la quantité qui lui a été prescrite, en respectant rigoureusement la posologie recommandée, même s'il se sent mieux. S'il n'a pu prendre le médicament au moment habituel, il doit le prendre dès que possible, à moins que ce ne soit presque l'heure prévue pour la dose suivante. Le prévenir qu'il ne doit jamais remplacer une dose manquée par une double dose. Insister sur le fait qu'il peut être dangereux de donner ce médicament à une autre personne.
- Expliquer au patient qu'il doit éviter de prendre du lait ou d'autres produits laitiers en même temps que les tétracyclines. Le prévenir qu'il doit aussi éviter de prendre des antiacides, du calcium, des médicaments contenant du magnésium, du bicarbonate de sodium ou des suppléments de fer dans les 2 à 3 heures qui suivent ou qui précèdent la prise des tétracyclines.
- Conseiller à la patiente d'utiliser une méthode de contraception non hormonale pendant le traitement par une tétracycline et jusqu'au cycle menstruel suivant.
- Prévenir le patient que la minocycline peut provoquer des étourdissements et de la somnolence. Lui conseiller de ne pas conduire et d'éviter les activités qui exigent sa vigilance jusqu'à ce qu'on ait la certitude que le médicament n'entraîne pas ces effets chez lui et de communiquer avec un professionnel de la santé si l'un ou l'autre de ces effets se produit.
- Conseiller au patient d'utiliser un écran solaire avec un FPS d'au moins 15 et de porter des vêtements protecteurs afin d'éviter les réactions de photosensibilité.
- Conseiller au patient de communiquer avec un professionnel de la santé si les signes suivants de surinfection se manifestent: excroissance noire et pileuse sur la langue, démangeaisons ou pertes vaginales, selles molles ou nauséabondes. Lui conseiller de signaler également le rash, le prurit et l'urticaire.
- Recommander au patient qui doit suivre un autre traitement ou subir une intervention chirurgicale de prévenir le professionnel de la santé qu'il suit un traitement par ces médicaments.

- Recommander au patient de prévenir un professionnel de la santé si les symptômes ne s'améliorent pas en l'espace de quelques jours.
- Recommander au patient de jeter toute tétracycline périmée ou décomposée étant donné qu'elle peut être toxique.

VÉRIFICATION DE L'EFFICACITÉ THÉRAPEUTIQUE

L'efficacité du traitement peut être démontrée par: la disparition des signes et des symptômes d'infection; le temps de résolution dépend du microorganisme infectant et du siège de l'infection ■ la diminution des lésions acnéiques. ✳

THALIDOMIDE

Ce médicament n'est pas commercialisé au Canada. Disponible par l'intermédiaire du Programme d'accès spécial de Santé Canada.

CLASSIFICATION:
Immunomodulateur

Grossesse – catégorie X

INDICATIONS

Traitement du myélome multiple en association avec la dexaméthasone ■ Traitement de courte durée des manifestations cutanées de l'érythème noueux lépreux modéré à grave ■ Prévention et suppression de l'érythème noueux lépreux récurrent (traitement d'entretien).
Usages non approuvés: Syndrome de Behçet ■ Syndrome cachectique associé à l'infection au VIH ■ Stomatite aphteuse (incluant celle associée au VIH) ■ Maladie de Crohn.

MÉCANISME D'ACTION

Suppression possible des concentrations excessives du facteur de nécrose tumorale alpha (TNF-alpha) chez les patients souffrant d'un érythème noueux lépreux et modification de la migration des leucocytes par la modification des caractéristiques des surfaces cellulaires.
Effets thérapeutiques: Diminution des lésions cutanées en cas d'érythème noueux lépreux et prévention des épisodes récurrents ■ Ralentissement de l'évolution du myélome multiple.

PHARMACOCINÉTIQUE

Absorption: De 67 à 93 % (PO).
Distribution: Le médicament traverse la barrière placentaire.
Liaison aux protéines: De 55 à 66 %.
Métabolisme et excrétion: Le médicament est hydrolysé dans le plasma pour former plusieurs métabolites.
Demi-vie: De 5 à 7 heures.

Profil temps-action (effets dermatologiques)

	DÉBUT D'ACTION	PIC	DURÉE
PO	48 h	1 - 2 mois	inconnue

CONTRE-INDICATIONS, PRÉCAUTIONS ET MISES EN GARDE

Contre-indications: OBST., ALLAITEMENT: Grossesse, femmes en âge de procréer (sauf si certains critères particuliers sont remplis) et allaitement ■ Hommes ayant atteint la maturité sexuelle (sauf si certains critères particuliers sont remplis) ■ Hypersensibilité.
Précautions et mises en garde: PÉD.: L'innocuité du médicament n'a pas été établie chez les enfants âgés < 12 ans.

RÉACTIONS INDÉSIRABLES ET EFFETS SECONDAIRES

SNC: étourdissements, somnolence, convulsions.
CV: bradycardie, œdème, hypotension orthostatique, complications thromboemboliques.
GI: constipation.
Tég.: rash, photosensibilité.
Hémat.: neutropénie.
SN: neuropathie périphérique.
Divers: MALFORMATIONS CONGÉNITALES GRAVES, réactions d'hypersensibilité incluant le SYNDROME DE STEVENS-JOHNSON et la NÉCROLYSE ÉPIDERMIQUE TOXIQUE, charge de VIH accrue.

INTERACTIONS

Médicament-médicament: Risque accru de dépression du SNC lors de la prise de **barbituriques**, d'**hypnosédatifs**, de **chlorpromazine** ou d'autres **dépresseurs du SNC** ou lors de l'usage concomitant d'**alcool** ■ L'usage concomitant d'**agents qui peuvent entraîner une neuropathie périphérique** peut accroître le risque de cette maladie.
Médicament-produits naturels: La consommation concomitante d'**échinacée** et de **mélatonine** peut modifier l'effet immunomodulateur de la thalidomide.

VOIES D'ADMINISTRATION ET POSOLOGIE

Érythème noueux lépreux

- **PO (adultes ≥ 50 kg):** *Traitement initial* – de 100 à 300 mg par jour, au coucher; on a déjà administré jusqu'à 400 mg par jour. Une fois les symptômes résolus (généralement après au moins 2 semaines), il faudrait essayer d'arrêter la prise de ce médicament en réduisant la dose par paliers de 50 mg, toutes les 2 à 4 semaines. *Traitement d'entretien* – à des intervalles de 3 à 6 mois, il faudrait essayer d'arrêter la prise de ce médicament en réduisant la dose par paliers de 50 mg, toutes les 2 à 4 semaines.

- **PO (adultes < 50 kg)**: *Traitement initial* – 100 mg par jour, au coucher; on a déjà administré jusqu'à 400 mg par jour. Une fois les symptômes résolus (généralement après au moins 2 semaines), il faudrait essayer d'arrêter la prise de ce médicament en réduisant la dose par paliers de 50 mg, toutes les 2 à 4 semaines. *Traitement d'entretien* – à des intervalles de 3 à 6 mois, il faudrait essayer d'arrêter la prise de ce médicament en réduisant la dose par paliers de 50 mg, toutes les 2 à 4 semaines.

Myélome multiple

- **PO (adultes)**: 200 mg par jour, au coucher en association avec la dexaméthasone.

PRÉSENTATION

Ce médicament n'est pas commercialisé au Canada.

SOINS INFIRMIERS

ÉVALUATION DE LA SITUATION

- Évaluer l'état du patient mensuellement pendant les 3 premiers mois et à intervalles réguliers pendant toute la durée du traitement pour déceler les signes précoces de neuropathie périphérique (engourdissements, picotements ou douleurs au niveau des mains et des pieds). La neuropathie périphérique survient habituellement lors d'un traitement prolongé, mais on en a déjà signalé la présence après un traitement de courte durée ou après la fin du traitement. Elle peut être grave et irréversible. Des analyses électrophysiologiques peuvent être faites au début du traitement et tous les 6 mois par la suite pour déceler une neuropathie périphérique asymptomatique. Si des symptômes se manifestent, arrêter le traitement immédiatement pour limiter l'atteinte. Ne reprendre le traitement qu'au moment où l'état du patient se rétablit.
- Suivre de près le patient à la recherche des signes de réactions d'hypersensibilité (rash maculaire érythémateux, fièvre, tachycardie, hypotension). Il peut s'avérer nécessaire d'interrompre le traitement en présence de symptômes graves. Si les réactions se manifestent de nouveau lorsqu'on recommence à administrer l'agent, cesser le traitement.

Tests de laboratoire:

- Suivre de près la numération et la formule leucocytaires pendant toute la durée du traitement. La thalidomide peut entraîner une diminution du nombre de globules blancs. Ne pas entreprendre de traitement par la thalidomide si la numération absolue de neutrophiles est $< 0,75 \times 10^9$/L. Si, au cours du traitement, cette valeur diminue jusqu'à $< 0,75 \times 10^9$/L, réévaluer la posologie; si la neutropénie persiste, il faudrait envisager l'abandon du traitement.
- La thalidomide peut accroître la charge virale chez les patients séropositifs.

DIAGNOSTICS INFIRMIERS POSSIBLES

- Atteinte à l'intégrité de la peau (Indications).
- Risque d'accident (Réactions indésirables).
- Connaissances insuffisantes sur le traitement médicamenteux (Enseignement au patient et à ses proches).

INTERVENTIONS INFIRMIÈRES

- EN RAISON DE SES EFFETS TÉRATOGÈNES, LA THALIDOMIDE PEUT ÊTRE PRESCRITE UNIQUEMENT PAR DES MÉDECINS QUI EN CONNAISSENT BIEN L'UTILISATION. ON NE DEVRAIT COMMENCER L'ADMINISTRATION QUE 24 HEURES APRÈS UN TEST DE GROSSESSE NÉGATIF AYANT UNE SENSIBILITÉ D'AU MOINS 50 mUI/mL. UN TEST DE GROSSESSE DOIT ÊTRE EFFECTUÉ CHAQUE SEMAINE PENDANT LE PREMIER MOIS DE TRAITEMENT, PUIS MENSUELLEMENT CHEZ LES PATIENTES AYANT UN CYCLE MENSTRUEL RÉGULIER. CHEZ LES PATIENTES AYANT UN CYCLE MENSTRUEL IRRÉGULIER, UN TEST DE GROSSESSE DOIT ÊTRE EFFECTUÉ TOUTES LES 2 SEMAINES. SI UN TEST DE GROSSESSE EST POSITIF, L'ADMINISTRATION DE LA THALIDOMIDE DOIT ÊTRE ARRÊTÉE IMMÉDIATEMENT. TOUTE EXPOSITION FŒTALE SUSPECTÉE DOIT ÊTRE SIGNALÉE AU FABRICANT ET LA PATIENTE DOIT ÊTRE ADRESSÉE À UN OBSTÉTRICIEN AYANT DE L'EXPÉRIENCE EN MATIÈRE DE TOXICITÉ FŒTALE.
- Pour prévenir l'exposition à la thalidomide, le port des gants est obligatoire tout au long des interactions avec le patient. Si un professionnel de la santé ou un autre soignant est exposé aux liquides corporels d'un patient recevant de la thalidomide, les précautions d'usage doivent être appliquées pour prévenir l'exposition cutanée à la thalidomide (soit le lavage de la région exposée avec de l'eau et du savon).
- On peut administrer des glucocorticoïdes en même temps que la thalidomide chez les patients souffrant d'une névrite modérée à grave, associée à une réaction grave d'érythème noueux lépreux. On peut commencer à réduire les doses de glucocorticoïdes

en vue d'arrêter ce traitement lorsque la névrite disparaît.

- Administrer la thalidomide 1 fois par jour avec de l'eau, de préférence au coucher, au moins 1 heure après le repas du soir. Si le patient doit prendre des doses fractionnées, les lui administrer au moins 1 heure après les repas.

ENSEIGNEMENT AU PATIENT ET À SES PROCHES

- Conseiller au patient de respecter rigoureusement la posologie recommandée. Le prévenir qu'il ne doit jamais arrêter le traitement sans avoir consulté au préalable un professionnel de la santé; la dose de thalidomide devrait être réduite graduellement.
- Insister sur le fait qu'il peut être dangereux de donner ce médicament à une autre personne.
- INSISTER AUPRÈS DU PATIENT SUR LE FAIT QU'IL EST EXTRÊMEMENT IMPORTANT D'UTILISER UNE MÉTHODE DE CONTRACEPTION EFFICACE DURANT LE MOIS QUI PRÉCÈDE LE TRAITEMENT, PENDANT TOUTE SA DURÉE ET PENDANT LE MOIS QUI SUIT LA DERNIÈRE PRISE DU MÉDICAMENT. *Les femmes en âge de procréer* devraient utiliser parallèlement 2 méthodes de contraception fiables, à moins qu'elles ne pratiquent l'abstinence. *Les hommes* devraient utiliser un condom, même s'ils sont vasectomisés. Les patients doivent recevoir des mises en garde verbales et écrites à propos des effets tératogènes possibles de la thalidomide.
- Recommander au patient de consulter un professionnel de la santé avant de consommer d'autres médicaments prescrits, des médicaments en vente libre ou des produits naturels. Prévenir la patiente qu'il y a risque de diminution de l'efficacité des contraceptifs oraux tout au long de leur utilisation et pendant le mois qui suit l'arrêt de cette prise, lors de l'utilisation concomitante de certains agents, comme les inhibiteurs de la protéase, le modafinil, les pénicillines, la rifampine, la rifabutine, la phénytoïne, la carbamazépine ou certains produits naturels, comme le millepertuis. Les femmes qui prennent ces médicaments doivent utiliser 2 autres méthodes de contraception fiables ou pratiquer l'abstinence de rapports hétérosexuels pendant la prise de la thalidomide et pendant le mois qui suit l'arrêt de ce traitement.
- Prévenir le patient que la thalidomide entraîne fréquemment de la somnolence ou des étourdissements. Lui conseiller de ne pas conduire et d'éviter les activités qui exigent sa vigilance jusqu'à ce qu'on ait la certitude que le médicament n'entraîne pas ces effets chez lui.
- Recommander au patient de changer lentement de position afin de réduire le risque d'hypotension orthostatique.
- Inciter le patient à utiliser un écran solaire et à porter des vêtements protecteurs pour prévenir les réactions de photosensibilité.
- Recommander au patient des deux sexes de ne pas donner de sang et au patient de sexe masculin de ne pas faire de dons de sperme pendant toute la durée du traitement par la thalidomide.
- Recommander au patient de signaler immédiatement à un professionnel de la santé la présence de douleurs, d'engourdissements, de picotements ou d'une sensation de brûlure au niveau des mains ou des pieds.

VÉRIFICATION DE L'EFFICACITÉ THÉRAPEUTIQUE

L'efficacité du traitement peut être démontrée par: la disparition des signes et des symptômes d'une réaction d'érythème noueux lépreux évolutif; les effets ne se manifestent qu'après au moins 2 semaines de traitement ■ la prévention d'épisodes récurrents d'érythème noueux lépreux ■ l'amélioration des paramètres sanguins en cas de myélome multiple.

THÉOPHYLLINE,

voir Bronchodilatateurs (xanthines)

THIAMINE

Betaxin, Thiamiject, Thiamine, Vitamine B_1

CLASSIFICATION:

Vitamine B (hydrosoluble)

Grossesse – catégorie A

INDICATIONS

Traitement des carences en thiamine (béribéri) ■ Prévention de l'encéphalopathie de Wernicke ■ Supplément diététique en cas de maladie gastro-intestinale, d'alcoolisme ou de cirrhose.

MÉCANISME D'ACTION

Élément essentiel au métabolisme des glucides. ***Effets thérapeutiques:*** Supplément diététique en cas de carence.

PHARMACOCINÉTIQUE

Absorption: Bonne (PO) par un processus actif. Les quantités excessives ne sont pas complètement absorbées. L'agent est également bien absorbé depuis les points d'injection IM.
Distribution: Tout l'organisme. L'agent passe dans le lait maternel.
Métabolisme et excrétion: Métabolisme hépatique. Les quantités excessives sont excrétées à l'état inchangé par les reins.
Demi-vie: Inconnue.

Profil temps-action
(temps de résolution des symptômes de carence: œdème, insuffisance cardiaque)†

	DÉBUT D'ACTION	PIC	DURÉE
PO, IM, IV	plusieurs heures	plusieurs jours	plusieurs jours – semaines

† La confusion et la psychose répondent plus lentement au traitement.

CONTRE-INDICATIONS, PRÉCAUTIONS ET MISES EN GARDE

Contre-indications: Hypersensibilité à la vitamine B_1 ou à tout autre ingrédient d'une préparation contenant de la vitamine B_1.
Précautions et mises en garde: Encéphalopathie de Wernicke (l'état du patient peut s'aggraver si la thiamine n'est pas administrée avant le glucose).

RÉACTIONS INDÉSIRABLES ET EFFETS SECONDAIRES

Les réactions indésirables et les effets secondaires énumérés sont extrêmement rares et ils surviennent habituellement par suite de l'administration IV ou de l'administration de doses très élevées.
SNC: agitation, faiblesse.
ORLO: sensation de constriction du pharynx.
Resp.: œdème pulmonaire, détresse respiratoire.
CV: COLLAPSUS VASCULAIRE, hypotension, vasodilatation.
GI: hémorragie digestive, nausées.
Tég.: cyanose, prurit, transpiration, picotements, urticaire, sensation de chaleur.
Divers: œdème angioneurotique.

INTERACTIONS

Médicament-médicament: Aucune interaction significative sur le plan clinique.

VOIES D'ADMINISTRATION ET POSOLOGIE

Carence en thiamine (béribéri)

- **PO (adultes)**: De 5 à 10 mg, 3 fois par jour, pendant 1 mois.
- **PO (enfants)**: De 10 à 50 mg par jour, en doses fractionnées pendant 2 semaines; puis de 5 à 10 mg par jour pendant 1 mois.
- **IM, IV (adultes)**: De 50 à 100 mg par jour.
- **IM, IV (enfants)**: De 10 à 25 mg par jour.

Supplément diététique

- **PO (adultes)**: De 0,9 à 1,2 mg par jour.
- **PO (enfants de 4 à 10 ans)**: De 0,6 à 1 mg par jour.
- **PO (enfants de la naissance à 3 ans)**: De 0,2 à 0,5 mg par jour.

PRÉSENTATION (version générique disponible)

Comprimés: de nombreuses teneurs sont disponibles ■ **Solution pour injection**: 100 mg/mL, en ampoules de 1 mL et en fioles de 10 mL[Pr] ■ **En association avec**: autres vitamines, minéraux, oligoéléments, dans diverses préparations vitaminiques[VL].

SOINS INFIRMIERS

ÉVALUATION DE LA SITUATION

- Surveiller les signes et les symptômes de carence en thiamine: anorexie, détresse gastro-intestinale, irritabilité, palpitations, tachycardie, œdème, paresthésie, faiblesse et douleurs musculaires, dépression, perte de mémoire, confusion, psychose, troubles visuels, concentrations sériques élevées d'acide pyruvique.
- Évaluer l'état nutritionnel du patient (alimentation, poids) avant le traitement et pendant toute sa durée.
- Suivre de près le patient recevant de la thiamine par voie IV pour déceler tout signe d'anaphylaxie (respiration sifflante, urticaire, œdème).

Tests de laboratoire: La thiamine peut fausser les résultats de certains tests permettant de mesurer les concentrations sériques de théophylline, d'acide urique et d'urobilinogène.

T

DIAGNOSTICS INFIRMIERS POSSIBLES

- Alimentation déficiente (Indications).
- Connaissances insuffisantes sur le traitement médicamenteux (Enseignement au patient et à ses proches).

INTERVENTIONS INFIRMIÈRES

- On administre habituellement la thiamine en association avec d'autres vitamines, car il est rare que le patient ne présente que ce seul type d'avitaminose.

IM et IV: L'administration par voie parentérale est réservée aux patients qui sont incapables de prendre les comprimés par voie orale.

IM: L'administration de la préparation par voie IM peut entraîner la sensibilité et l'induration au point d'injection. L'application de compresses froides peut diminuer la douleur.

IV: Des réactions d'hypersensibilité et des décès sont survenus par suite de l'administration IV. Il est recommandé d'administrer une dose d'épreuve intradermique aux patients chez lesquels on soupçonne une hypersensibilité. Rester à l'affût d'un érythème et d'une induration au point d'injection.

IV directe: Administrer la préparation sans la diluer.

Vitesse d'administration: Administrer à raison de 100 mg en au moins 5 minutes.

Perfusion continue: On peut diluer la thiamine dans une préparation associant une solution de dextrose et une solution de Ringer ou de lactate de Ringer ou une solution de dextrose et de soluté salin, dans une solution de D5%E ou de D10%E, dans une solution de Ringer ou de lactate de Ringer pour injection ou dans une solution de NaCl 0,9 % ou de NaCl 0,45 %. La thiamine est habituellement administrée avec d'autres vitamines. Consulter les directives de chaque fabricant avant d'administrer la préparation.

Compatibilité (tubulure en Y): famotidine.

Incompatibilité en addition au soluté: solutions dont le pH est neutre ou alcalin, telles que les carbonates, les bicarbonates, les citrates et les acétates.

ENSEIGNEMENT AU PATIENT ET À SES PROCHES

- Conseiller au patient de respecter rigoureusement les recommandations diététiques du professionnel de la santé. Lui expliquer que la meilleure source de vitamines est une alimentation bien équilibrée contenant des aliments provenant des 4 principaux groupes.
- Expliquer au patient que les aliments riches en thiamine comprennent les céréales (de grain entier ou enrichies), les viandes (particulièrement, le porc) et les légumes frais; la perte de thiamine durant la cuisson est variable.
- Recommander au patient qui pratique l'automédication par des suppléments vitaminiques de ne pas dépasser les apports quotidiens recommandés (voir l'annexe K). L'efficacité de mégadoses dans le traitement de diverses affections n'a pas été prouvée. De telles doses peuvent entraîner des effets secondaires.

VÉRIFICATION DE L'EFFICACITÉ THÉRAPEUTIQUE

L'efficacité du traitement peut être démontrée par: la prévention ou la diminution des signes et des symptômes de carence en vitamine B_1 ■ la diminution des symptômes de névrite, des signes oculaires, de l'ataxie, de l'œdème et de l'insuffisance cardiaque, notables dans les quelques heures qui suivent l'administration de la thiamine (les symptômes disparaissent après quelques jours) ■ la disparition de la confusion et de la psychose (parfois, ces symptômes sont plus longs à disparaître et peuvent même persister en cas de lésions nerveuses).

ALERTE CLINIQUE

THROMBOLYTIQUES

alteplase
Activase, Activase-rt-PA, Cathflo

retéplase
Retavase

streptokinase
Streptase

tenecteplase
TNKase

CLASSIFICATION:
Thrombolytiques (activateurs du plasminogène)

Grossesse – catégorie C

INDICATIONS

Traitement d'urgence de la thrombose coronarienne associée à un infarctus du myocarde (ces agents favorisent la lyse des thrombus) ■ **Alteplase:** Traitement de l'accident vasculaire cérébral (AVC) ischémique aigu ■ Désobstruction des cathéters veineux centraux ■ **Streptokinase:** Traitement de la thrombose veineuse profonde ou de la thromboembolie artérielle (sauf en cas d'embolies artérielles survenant du côté gauche du cœur) ■ Traitement d'une embolie pulmonaire massive ■ Désobstruction des canules artérioveineuses partiellement ou complètement obstruées. **Usages non approuvés – Alteplase:** Traitement d'une embolie pulmonaire massive ■ Traitement de la thrombose veineuse profonde ou de la thromboembolie artérielle.

MÉCANISME D'ACTION

Transformation du plasminogène en plasmine, ce qui permet la dégradation de la fibrine contenue dans les caillots. L'alteplase, la retéplase et la tenecteplase activent directement le plasminogène. La streptokinase se fixe au plasminogène pour former des complexes activateurs, qui transforment ensuite le plasminogène en plasmine. ***Effets thérapeutiques:*** Lyse des thrombus coronaires et préservation de la fonction ventriculaire ■ Lyse des caillots en cas d'embolie pulmonaire ou de thrombose veineuse profonde ■ Diminution des séquelles neurologiques d'un accident vasculaire cérébral ■ Désobstruction des canules artérioveineuses et des cathéters centraux.

PHARMACOCINÉTIQUE

Absorption: Complète (IV). L'administration intracoronarienne ou celle par une canule ou un cathéter bouché entraîne un effet plus localisé.

Distribution: La streptokinase semble traverser la barrière placentaire en quantités infimes, sinon nulles. Le reste de la distribution de la streptokinase ou des autres agents est inconnu.

Métabolisme et excrétion: L'*alteplase* est rapidement métabolisée par le foie. La *retéplase* est éliminée principalement par le foie et les reins. La *streptokinase* est rapidement éliminée de la circulation. La *tenecteplase* est métabolisée par le foie.

Demi-vie: *Alteplase* – de 26 à 46 minutes; *retéplase* – de 13 à 16 minutes; *complexe activateur de la streptokinase* – 83 minutes; *tenecteplase* – de 90 à 130 minutes.

Profil temps-action (fibrinolyse)

	DÉBUT D'ACTION	PIC	DURÉE
Alteplase IV	inconnu	20 min – 2 h	inconnue
Retéplase IV	rapide	en l'espace de 2 h	48 h
Streptokinase IV	immédiat	rapide	4 h (jusqu'à 12 h)
Tenecteplase IV	rapide	inconnu	inconnue

CONTRE-INDICATIONS, PRÉCAUTIONS ET MISES EN GARDE

Contre-indications: Hémorragie interne active ■ Antécédents d'accident vasculaire cérébral, de traumatismes intracrâniens ou intraspinaux ou de chirurgie du SNC au cours des 2 derniers mois ■ Néoplasme intracrânien ou malformation artérioveineuse ou anévrisme ■ Hypertension grave non maîtrisée ■ Réanimation cardiorespiratoire traumatique récente ■ Diathèse hémorragique connue ■ Rétinopathie hypertensive au stade III ou IV (sauf la reteplase et la tenecteplase) ■ Hypersensibilité.

AVC – À ces contre-indications s'ajoutent les suivantes: chirurgie intracrânienne ou intrarachidienne, traumatisme crânien grave ou AVC au cours des 3 derniers mois ■ symptômes survenus depuis plus de 3 heures ■ signe d'hémorragie intracrânienne lors de l'anamnèse ■ hémorragie sous-arachnoïdienne soupçonnée lors de l'anamnèse ■ antécédents d'hémorragie intracrânienne ■ crise épileptique lors de la survenue de l'AVC ■ prise de warfarine ■ RNI ≥ 1,7 ou temps de Quick > 15 secondes ■ administration d'héparine dans les 48 heures précédant la survenue de l'AVC et l'allongement du TCA à l'arrivée du patient à l'hôpital ■ plaquettes < 100×10^9/L.

Précautions et mises en garde: Chirurgie majeure, biopsie, ponction de vaisseaux non compressibles, traumatisme, hémorragie gastro-intestinale ou génito-urinaire au cours des 10 derniers jours ■ Thrombus au niveau du cœur gauche ■ Maladie vasculaire cérébrale ■ Hypertension: TAS ≥ 180 mm Hg ou TAD ≥ 110 mm Hg ■ Forte probabilité de thrombus formé dans le cœur gauche ■ Administration récente d'inhibiteurs des récepteurs GP IIb/IIIa ■ Maladies hépatique ou rénale graves ■ Affections ophtalmiques hémorragiques ■ Phlébite septique ou occlusion d'une canule artérioveineuse installée dans un site fortement infecté ■ Antécédents de ponction d'un vaisseau qui ne peut être comprimé ■ Endocardite bactérienne subaiguë ■ Péricardite aiguë ■ Pancréatite aiguë ■ Tout autre cas où un saignement représente un risque important ou serait particulièrement difficile à arrêter compte tenu de son emplacement ■ Infection récente aux streptocoques ou traitement préalable par la streptokinase (de 5 jours à 6 mois): risque d'apparition d'une résistance en raison de la production d'anticorps; il peut s'avérer nécessaire d'augmenter la dose (streptokinase seulement) ■ **GÉR.**: Risque accru d'hémorragie intracrânienne chez les patients > 75 ans ■ **OBST., ALLAITEMENT, PÉD.**: L'innocuité de ces médicaments n'a pas été établie.

AVC – À ces précautions et mises en garde s'ajoutent les suivantes: preuves cliniques ou antécédents d'ischémie cérébrale transitoire ■ glycémie < 2,8 ou > 22 mmol/L (risque d'erreur de diagnostic).

EXTRÊME PRUDENCE: PATIENTS RECEVANT UN TRAITEMENT PAR LA WARFARINE ■ PHASE INITIALE DU POST-PARTUM (10 JOURS).

RÉACTIONS INDÉSIRABLES ET EFFETS SECONDAIRES

SNC: HÉMORRAGIE INTRACRÂNIENNE, céphalées.

ORLO: épistaxis, hémorragie gingivale; *streptokinase* – œdème périorbital.

Resp.: bronchospasmes, hémoptysie.

CV: arythmies par suite du rétablissement de l'irrigation du tissu cardiaque, hypotension.

GI: HÉMORRAGIE DIGESTIVE, HÉMORRAGIE RÉTROPÉRITONÉALE.

GU: HÉMORRAGIE DES VOIES URINAIRES.

Tég.: ecchymoses, rougeurs du visage, urticaire.

Hémat.: HÉMORRAGIE.

Locaux: hémorragie aux points d'injection, phlébite aux points d'injection IV.

T

Loc.: douleurs musculosquelettiques.
Divers: réactions allergiques incluant l'ANAPHYLAXIE, fièvre, EMBOLISATION PAR LE CHOLESTÉROL.

INTERACTIONS

Médicament-médicament: Risque accru d'hémorragie lors de l'usage concomitant d'**aspirine**, d'**AINS**, de **warfarine**, d'**héparine** et d'**agents de type héparine**, d'**abciximab**, d'**eptifibatide**, de **tirofiban**, de **clopidogrel**, de **ticlopidine** ou de **dipyridamole**, bien que ces agents aient été souvent administrés ensemble ou en séquence ■ Le risque d'hémorragie peut aussi être accru lors de l'administration concomitante d'**acide valproïque** ■ Les effets des agents thrombolytiques peuvent être contrecarrés par les **agents antifibrinolytiques**, incluant l'**acide aminocaproïque**, l'**aprotinine** ou l'**acide tranexamique**.
Médicament-produits naturels: Risque accru de saignements lors de la prise concomitante d'**ail**, d'**arnica**, de **camomille**, de **clous de girofle**, de **dong quai**, de **fenugrec**, de **grande camomille**, de **gingembre**, de **ginkgo**, de **ginseng** et d'**autres produits**.

VOIES D'ADMINISTRATION ET POSOLOGIE

Alteplase

- *Infarctus du myocarde (perfusion accélérée)*
  La perfusion de 90 minutes n'est recommandée que pendant un laps de temps allant jusqu'à 6 heures après l'apparition des symptômes d'infarctus.
  IV (adultes): Initialement, 15 mg en bolus en 2 minutes, puis 0,75 mg/kg (jusqu'à 50 mg), en perfusion pendant 30 minutes, enfin, 0,5 mg/kg (jusqu'à 35 mg), en perfusion au cours des 60 minutes suivantes; l'administration de ce médicament est souvent associée à un traitement par l'héparine.
- *Infarctus du myocarde (traitement classique ou perfusion de 3 heures)*
  La perfusion de 3 heures n'est recommandée que pendant un laps de temps allant jusqu'à 12 heures après l'apparition des symptômes d'infarctus.
  IV (adultes > 65 kg): Dose totale de 100 mg répartie comme suit: 60 mg au cours de la 1re heure (dont 6 à 7 mg seront administrés sous forme de bolus intraveineux pendant les 1 ou 2 premières minutes), puis 20 mg au cours de la 2e heure et 20 mg durant 1 à 4 heures, par la suite.
  IV (adultes < 65 kg): Dose totale de 1,25 mg/kg (ne pas dépasser 100 mg au total) répartie comme suit: 0,75 mg/kg au cours de la 1re heure (de 0,075 à 0,087 5 mg/kg, administrés sous forme de bolus intraveineux pendant les 1 ou 2 premières minutes), puis 0,25 mg/kg au cours de la 2e heure et 0,25 mg/kg au cours de la 3e heure.
- *AVC ischémique aigu*
  Le traitement doit être amorcé dans les 3 heures qui suivent le début des symptômes d'AVC.
  IV (adultes): 0,9 mg/kg (ne pas dépasser 90 mg), en perfusion d'une durée de 1 heure; 10 % de cette dose est administrée sous forme de bolus intraveineux au cours de la première minute.
- *Désobstruction des cathéters veineux centraux*
  Injection dans le cathéter (poids ≥ 30 kg): 2 mg, dans un volume de 2 mL. On ne possède aucune donnée sur l'efficacité et l'innocuité de doses supérieures à 2 mg. Si une dose de 2 mg ne suffit pas à rétablir la perméabilité du cathéter, une seconde dose de 2 mg peut être instillée. Aucune étude n'a été réalisée sur des doses totalisant plus de 4 mg (2 doses de 2 mg).
  Injection dans le cathéter (poids < 30 kg): La dose recommandée est égale à 110 % du volume interne de la lumière du cathéter, jusqu'à concurrence de 2 mL.

Retéplase

- *Infarctus du myocarde*
  IV (adultes): 10 unités, suivies 30 minutes plus tard de 10 unités de plus.

Streptokinase

- *Infarctus du myocarde*
  IV (adultes): 1,5 million UI en 60 minutes.
  Voie intracoronarienne (adultes): 20 000 UI, sous forme de bolus intraveineux, suivies d'une perfusion de 2 000 à 4 000 UI à la minute pendant 30 à 90 minutes.
- *Thrombose veineuse profonde, embolie pulmonaire, embolie artérielle ou thrombose*
  IV (adultes): Dose d'attaque de 250 000 UI pendant 30 minutes, suivie de 100 000 UI à l'heure, pendant 24 heures (embolie pulmonaire ou artérielle et thrombose) ou pendant 72 heures (embolie pulmonaire récurrente ou thrombose veineuse profonde).
- *Désobstruction des canules artérioveineuses*
  Injection dans la canule (adultes): Instiller lentement 250 000 UI de streptokinase dissoute dans 2 mL de solution pour injection IV; clamper pendant 2 heures, puis aspirer le contenu de la canule, rincer avec une solution saline et rétablir la circulation dans la canule.

Tenecteplase

- *Infarctus du myocarde*
  IV (adultes): La dose totale recommandée dépend du poids du patient et ne doit pas dépasser 50 mg. La dose sous forme de bolus doit être administrée pendant 5 secondes. Posologie en fonction du poids: *< 60 kg:* 30 mg ou 6 mL ■ *de 60 à < 70 kg:* 35 mg ou 7 mL ■ *de 70 à < 80 kg:* 40 mg ou 8 mL ■ *de*

T

80 à < 90 kg: 45 mg ou 9 mL ▪ ≥ *90 kg:* 50 mg ou 10 mL.

PRÉSENTATION

- **Alteplase**
  Poudre pour injection: 2 mg/fiole[Pr], 50 mg/fiole[Pr], 100 mg/fiole[Pr].
- **Retéplase**
  Poudre pour injection: 10,4 UI/fiole[Pr].
- **Streptokinase**
  Poudre pour injection: 250 000 UI/fiole[Pr], 750 000 UI/fiole[Pr], 1 500 000 UI/fiole[Pr].
- **Tenecteplase**
  Poudre pour injection: 50 mg/fiole[Pr].

SOINS INFIRMIERS

ÉVALUATION DE LA SITUATION

- Amorcer le traitement dès que possible après l'apparition des symptômes.
- Noter les signes vitaux et prendre la température de façon continue en cas de thrombose coronarienne et au moins toutes les 4 heures au cours du traitement pour d'autres indications. Ne pas mesurer la pression artérielle au niveau des membres inférieurs. Prévenir le médecin si la pression artérielle systolique > 180 mm Hg ou si la pression artérielle diastolique > 110 mm Hg. Le prévenir également en cas d'hypotension, qui peut être due au thrombolytique, à une hémorragie ou à un choc cardiogénique.
- SUIVRE L'ÉTAT DU PATIENT POUR DÉCELER LES SIGNES D'HÉMORRAGIE, TOUTES LES 15 MINUTES AU COURS DE LA PREMIÈRE HEURE DU TRAITEMENT, TOUTES LES 15 À 30 MINUTES AU COURS DES 8 HEURES SUIVANTES ET AU MOINS TOUTES LES 4 HEURES, PENDANT LA DURÉE RESTANTE DU TRAITEMENT. UNE HÉMORRAGIE FRANCHE PEUT SURVENIR À L'EMPLACEMENT D'UNE INTERVENTION EFFRACTIVE OU AU NIVEAU DES ORIFICES DU CORPS. UNE HÉMORRAGIE INTERNE PEUT ÉGALEMENT SURVENIR (DÉTÉRIORATION DE L'ÉTAT NEUROLOGIQUE, DOULEURS ABDOMINALES ACCOMPAGNÉES DE VOMISSURES AYANT L'ASPECT DU MARC DE CAFÉ OU DE SELLES NOIRES ET GOUDRONNEUSES, HÉMATURIE, DOULEURS ARTICULAIRES). SI UNE HÉMORRAGIE QU'ON NE PEUT RÉPRIMER SURVIENT, ARRÊTER LE TRAITEMENT ET PRÉVENIR IMMÉDIATEMENT LE MÉDECIN.
- DEMANDER AU PATIENT S'IL A DÉJÀ FAIT DES RÉACTIONS AU TRAITEMENT PAR LA STREPTOKINASE. SURVEILLER LES RÉACTIONS D'HYPERSENSIBILITÉ (RASH, DYSPNÉE, FIÈVRE, MODIFICATION DE LA COULEUR DU TEINT, ŒDÈME PÉRIORBITAL, RESPIRATION SIFFLANTE). SI CES SYMPTÔMES SE MANIFESTENT, EN INFORMER RAPIDEMENT LE MÉDECIN. GARDER À PORTÉE DE LA MAIN DE L'ADRÉNALINE, UN ANTIHISTAMINIQUE ET LE MATÉRIEL DE RÉANIMATION POUR PARER À TOUTE RÉACTION ANAPHYLACTIQUE.
- Demander au patient s'il a contracté depuis peu une infection aux streptocoques. La *streptokinase* peut s'avérer moins efficace si elle est administrée durant une période allant de 5 jours à 6 mois après une telle infection.
- ÉVALUER L'ÉTAT NEUROLOGIQUE DU PATIENT PENDANT TOUTE LA DURÉE DU TRAITEMENT. DES MODIFICATIONS SENSORIELLES OU NEUROLOGIQUES PEUVENT INDIQUER LA PRÉSENCE D'UNE HÉMORRAGIE INTRACRÂNIENNE.

Thrombose coronarienne:

- Suivre continuellement l'ÉCG. Prévenir le médecin en cas d'arythmies importantes. On peut prescrire en prophylaxie de la lidocaïne ou du procaïnamide par voie IV. On devrait mesurer souvent les concentrations des enzymes cardiaques. De 7 à 10 jours après la fin du traitement, on peut effectuer une scintigraphie myocardique ou une angiographie coronarienne, ou les deux, pour déterminer l'efficacité du traitement.
- Déterminer l'intensité, les caractéristiques et l'emplacement des douleurs thoraciques ainsi que le territoire où elles se propagent. Noter la présence de symptômes associés (nausées, vomissements, diaphorèse). Administrer des analgésiques selon les recommandations du médecin et le prévenir si les douleurs thoraciques ne sont pas soulagées ou si elles se manifestent de nouveau.
- Ausculter les bruits cardiaques et les murmures vésiculaires à intervalles fréquents. Informer le médecin si des signes d'insuffisance cardiaque (râles et crépitations, dyspnée, bruits cardiaques B3, turgescence des jugulaires, diminution de la pression veineuse centrale) se manifestent.

Embolie pulmonaire: Mesurer le pouls, la pression artérielle et les paramètres hémodynamiques; évaluer l'état respiratoire (fréquence respiratoire, gravité de la dyspnée, gazométrie du sang artériel [GSA]).

Thrombose veineuse profonde ou occlusion artérielle aiguë: Observer les membres et palper le pouls des membres affectés toutes les heures. Prévenir immédiatement le médecin en cas d'altération de la circulation. Pour vérifier si le flux sanguin s'est rétabli et pour déterminer la durée du traitement, on peut utiliser une des techniques suivantes: tomographie assistée par ordinateur, phléthysmographie par impédance, mesure quantitative par Doppler, par angiographie ou par phlébographie.

Toutefois, les phlébographies à répétition sont déconseillées.

Occlusion d'une canule artérioveineuse ou d'un cathéter central: Aspirer du sang pour déterminer si la canule ou le cathéter sont perméables. S'assurer que le patient expire et qu'il retient sa respiration pendant l'installation ou le retrait de la tubulure IV afin d'éviter tout risque d'embolie (ne s'applique pas à tous les cathéters ou canules).

AVC ischémique aigu: Évaluer l'état neurologique du patient. Déterminer à quel moment les symptômes ont commencé à se manifester. L'alteplase doit être administrée dans les 3 heures qui suivent l'apparition des symptômes.

Tests de laboratoire:

- On peut déterminer avant le traitement et à intervalles fréquents pendant toute sa durée l'hématocrite, les concentrations d'hémoglobine, la numération plaquettaire, les concentrations des produits de dégradation de la fibrine (PDF), les concentrations de fibrinogène, le temps de prothrombine, le temps de thrombine et le temps de céphaline activée. Le temps de saignement peut être évalué avant le traitement si le patient a reçu des agents antiplaquettaires.
- Déterminer le groupe sanguin du patient et effectuer une épreuve de compatibilité croisée; garder à portée de la main du sang en cas d'hémorragies.
- Analyser les selles, à intervalles réguliers pendant la durée du traitement, pour déterminer la présence de sang occulte, et les urines, pour déceler la présence d'une hématurie.

Toxicité et surdosage: **Alerte clinique:** En cas de saignement localisé, exercer une pression sur le point de saignement. En cas de saignements graves ou internes, arrêter la perfusion. On peut rétablir les facteurs de coagulation et le volume sanguin par des perfusions de sang complet, de concentrés de globules rouges, de plasma frais congelé ou par cryoprécipitation. Ne pas administrer de dextran, car cet agent exerce des effets antiplaquettaires. On peut utiliser comme antidote l'acide tranexamique (Cyklokapron) ou l'aprotinine (Trasylol).

DIAGNOSTICS INFIRMIERS POSSIBLES

- Irrigation tissulaire inefficace (Indications).
- Risque d'accident (Effets secondaires).
- Connaissances insuffisantes sur le traitement médicamenteux (Enseignement au patient et à ses proches).

INTERVENTIONS INFIRMIÈRES

Alerte clinique: Des surdoses ou des doses insuffisantes de thrombolytiques ont nui aux patients ou ont entraîné des décès. Avant l'administration, clarifier tous les points ambigus sur les ordonnances et faire vérifier l'ordonnance d'origine, les calculs de doses et le réglage de la pompe à perfusion par un autre professionnel de la santé.

- Ne pas confondre l'abréviation t-PA pour l'alteplase (Activase) avec l'abréviation TNK t-PA pour la tenecteplase (TNKase). Clarifier cette ambiguïté sur les ordonnances qui contiennent ces abréviations.
- Dans le cas du traitement thrombolytique d'un AVC ischémique aigu, il **ne** faut **pas** commencer l'administration d'anticoagulants avant 24 heures.
- On administre habituellement un traitement anticoagulant systémique par l'héparine non fractionnée (ou un autre anticoagulant comme une héparine de faible poids moléculaire) pendant le traitement thrombolytique et plusieurs heures après qu'il a pris fin. Lors de l'utilisation de streptokinase, l'administration d'héparine est recommandée chez les patients à haut risque d'embolie artérielle ou veineuse (infarctus de la paroi antérieure, défaillance de la pompe cardiaque, antécédents d'embolie, fibrillation auriculaire ou thrombus dans le ventricule gauche). En l'absence de ces facteurs de risque, l'héparine n'a pas donné les mêmes bénéfices que les autres thrombolytiques. Si on l'administre, on doit utiliser une dose plus faible ou commencer la perfusion plusieurs heures après la perfusion de streptokinase.
- Ce type de médicament ne devrait être utilisé que dans des centres où on peut suivre de près la fonction hématologique et la réponse clinique.
- Il est recommandé de mettre en place 2 tubulures de perfusion IV avant d'amorcer le traitement: une pour l'agent thrombolytique et l'autre pour une perfusion additionnelle, si elle s'avère nécessaire.
- Éviter toute intervention effractive, telle qu'une injection par voie IM ou une ponction artérielle, pendant l'administration de ces agents. Si de telles interventions doivent être effectuées, exercer une pression sur tous les points de ponction artérielle et veineuse pendant au moins 30 minutes. Éviter les ponctions veineuses sur des points qui ne peuvent être comprimés (veine jugulaire, veine sous-clavière).
- Le médecin peut prescrire de l'acétaminophène pour abaisser la fièvre.

Alteplase

Perfusion intermittente: L'emballage des fioles contient également de l'eau stérile pour injection (sans agent de conservation) qu'on peut utiliser comme diluant. Reconstituer seulement avec de l'eau stérile pour injection ne contenant aucun agent de conservation. Reconstituer la solution contenue dans les fioles de 50 mg avec 50 mL et celle contenue dans les fioles de 100 mg avec 100 mL d'eau stérile à l'aide d'une aiguille de calibre 18. Ne pas agiter la fiole pendant la dilution; la faire tourner ou la renverser délicatement pour en mélanger le contenu. La solution reconstituée peut mousser. Les bulles disparaîtront si on laisse reposer la solution pendant quelques minutes. La solution est transparente ou jaune pâle. Elle est stable pendant 8 heures à la température ambiante. On peut l'administrer sous sa forme reconstituée (1 mg/mL) ou la diluer davantage juste avant l'utilisation dans un volume égal de solution de NaCl 0,9 % ou de D5%E. Consulter les directives de chaque fabricant avant de reconstituer la préparation.

Vitesse d'administration:

- Rincer la tubulure avec 20 à 30 mL de soluté physiologique à la fin de la perfusion pour s'assurer que toute la dose a été administrée.
- La dose standard pour le traitement de l'*infarctus du myocarde* doit être administrée en 3 heures (jusqu'à 12 heures après le début des symptômes) ou en perfusion accélérée d'une durée de 90 minutes (seulement pendant 6 heures après le début des symptômes).
- En cas d'*AVC ischémique aigu*, administrer 10 % de la dose totale sous forme de bolus intraveineux en 1 minute, et le reste en perfusion en l'espace de 60 minutes.

Désobstruction des cathéters veineux centraux (Cathflo): Diluer le contenu de la fiole avec 2,2 mL d'eau stérile pour injection, en dirigeant le jet de solvant sur la poudre. Reconstituer seulement avec de l'eau stérile pour injection ne contenant aucun agent de conservation. Il n'est pas rare qu'une mousse légère se forme; laisser reposer la solution pour permettre la dissipation des grosses bulles. Imprimer un léger mouvement de rotation à la fiole jusqu'à dissolution complète du contenu. Ne pas agiter. La reconstitution donne une solution transparente, incolore ou jaune pâle, d'une concentration de 1 mg/mL. Reconstituer la solution juste avant de l'utiliser, car elle ne contient pas d'agent de conservation. La solution peut être administrée dans les 8 heures suivant la reconstitution si elle est conservée entre 2 °C et 30 °C. Consulter les directives de chaque fabricant avant de reconstituer la préparation. Instiller la dose appropriée dans le cathéter obstrué. Après 30 minutes, évaluer la perméabilité du cathéter en essayant d'aspirer du sang. Si le cathéter est perméable, aspirer de 4 à 5 mL de sang pour retirer l'alteplase recombinante et le caillot résiduel, jeter le produit qui a été aspiré et rincer doucement le cathéter avec une solution de NaCl 0,9%. Si le cathéter n'est pas perméable après 30 minutes, attendre 90 minutes de plus avant d'en réévaluer la perméabilité. Si le cathéter n'est pas perméable après 120 minutes, une seconde dose peut être donnée.

Compatibilité (tubulure en Y): lidocaïne ■ métoprolol ■ propranolol.

Incompatibilité (tubulure en Y): dobutamine ■ dopamine ■ héparine ■ nitroglycérine.

Retéplase

IV directe: Reconstituer à l'aide du diluant, de l'aiguille, de la seringue et de l'embout de transfert fournis dans l'emballage. Reconstituer avec 10 mL d'eau stérile pour injection. Reconstituer seulement avec de l'eau stérile pour injection ne contenant aucun agent de conservation. Remuer délicatement la fiole d'un mouvement circulaire jusqu'à ce que toute la solution soit complètement dissoute. Ne pas agiter. La solution est incolore. Ne pas administrer de solutions qui ont changé de couleur ou qui contiennent un précipité. Un peu de mousse peut se former; laisser reposer la fiole pendant plusieurs minutes pour que les bulles disparaissent. Reconstituer la solution juste avant de l'utiliser. Elle est stable pendant 4 heures à la température ambiante ou au réfrigérateur. Consulter les directives de chaque fabricant avant de reconstituer la préparation.

Vitesse d'administration: Administrer chaque bolus intraveineux en 2 minutes dans une tubulure IV contenant une solution de NaCl 0,9 % ou de D5%E; rincer la tubulure avant et après l'administration du bolus.

Incompatibilité (tubulure en Y): héparine ■ aucun autre médicament ne devrait être perfusé ou injecté dans la tubulure utilisée pour l'administration de la retéplase.

Streptokinase

Voie intracoronarienne: Diluer une fiole de 250 000 UI pour obtenir un volume total de 125 mL avec une solution de NaCl 0,9 % ou de D5%E. Administrer 20 000 UI (10 mL) par bolus intracoronaire.

Vitesse d'administration: Le bolus intracoronaire doit être administré dans un laps de temps qui va de 15 secondes à 2 minutes.

Perfusion intermittente: Reconstituer le médicament avec 5 mL d'une solution de NaCl 0,9 % ou de D5%E (injectée directement sur la paroi de la fiole) et mélanger délicatement; ne pas secouer la fiole. Diluer davantage avec une solution de NaCl 0,9 % pour obtenir un volume total de 50 mL en cas d'infarctus du myocarde ou de 45 mL en cas de thrombose veineuse profonde ou d'embolie pulmonaire. Au besoin, on peut augmenter le volume total jusqu'à concurrence de 500 mL en accélérant la vitesse de perfusion en conséquence. La solution est de couleur jaune pâle. Si un filtre est utilisé pour l'administration, les pores du filtre doivent être d'au moins 0,8 µm (filtre de cellulose) ou de 0,22 µm s'il s'agit d'un filtre en PVC (polymère acrylique). Utiliser la solution dans les 24 heures qui suivent sa reconstitution. La solution diluée jusqu'à 50 mL est stable pendant 24 heures à la température ambiante ou au réfrigérateur. La solution diluée au-delà de 50 mL est stable pendant 24 heures au réfrigérateur ou pendant 12 heures à la température ambiante. Consulter les directives de chaque fabricant avant de reconstituer la préparation.

Vitesse d'administration:

- Administrer la dose destinée au traitement de l'infarctus du myocarde en 60 minutes.
- L'administration du bolus intracoronaire doit être suivie par une perfusion intracoronarienne d'entretien de 2 000 à 4 000 UI à la minute, pendant 30 à 90 minutes.
- La dose d'attaque en cas de *thrombose veineuse profonde* ou d'*embolie pulmonaire* doit être administrée en 30 minutes; elle sera suivie d'une perfusion de 100 000 UI à l'heure.
- Utiliser une pompe de perfusion pour s'assurer qu'on administre des doses exactes.

Compatibilité (tubulure en Y): dobutamine ■ dopamine ■ héparine ■ lidocaïne ■ nitroglycérine.

Incompatibilité en addition au soluté: Ne pas mélanger avec aucun autre médicament.

Désobstruction des canules artérioveineuses: Diluer 250 000 UI dans 2 mL de solution de NaCl 0,9 % ou de D5%E.

Vitesse d'administration: Injecter lentement, dans chaque branche bouchée de la canule et, ensuite, clamper pendant au moins 2 heures. Aspirer délicatement le contenu et rincer les tubulures avec une solution de NaCl 0,9 %.

Tenecteplase

IV directe: Reconstituer à l'aide du diluant et du matériel fournis dans l'emballage. Reconstituer avec 10 mL d'eau stérile pour injection en dirigeant le jet de solvant sur la poudre. Reconstituer seulement avec de l'eau stérile pour injection ne contenant aucun agent de conservation. Remuer délicatement la fiole d'un mouvement circulaire jusqu'à ce que tout le médicament soit complètement dissous. Ne pas agiter. La solution reconstituée est incolore à jaune pâle. Ne pas administrer de solutions qui ont changé de couleur ou qui contiennent un précipité. Un peu de mousse peut se former; laisser reposer la fiole pendant quelques minutes pour que les bulles disparaissent. Reconstituer la solution juste avant de l'utiliser, car elle ne contient pas d'agent de conservation. Si la solution reconstituée n'est pas utilisée immédiatement, elle est stable pendant 8 heures au réfrigérateur entre 2 °C et 8 °C. Consulter les directives de chaque fabricant avant de reconstituer la préparation.

Vitesse d'administration: Administrer en un seul bolus intraveineux en 5 secondes.

Incompatibilité (tubulure en Y): Un précipité peut se former lorsque la tenecteplase est administrée par une tubulure contenant du dextrose. Rincer les tubulures contenant du dextrose avec une solution saline avant et après le bolus de tenecteplase ■ Aucun autre médicament ne devrait être perfusé ou injecté dans la tubulure utilisée pour l'administration de la tenecteplase.

ENSEIGNEMENT AU PATIENT ET À SES PROCHES

- Expliquer au patient et à ses proches le but du traitement et la nécessité d'un suivi étroit. Conseiller au patient de signaler au médecin les réactions d'hypersensibilité (rash, dyspnée), les saignements et les ecchymoses.
- Expliquer au patient qu'il doit rester allongé et bouger le moins possible pendant toute la durée du traitement afin de prévenir les accidents. Éviter toute intervention qui n'est pas essentielle comme le rasage et le brossage vigoureux des dents.

VÉRIFICATION DE L'EFFICACITÉ THÉRAPEUTIQUE

L'efficacité du traitement peut être démontrée par: la lyse des thrombus et le rétablissement de la circulation sanguine ■ la prévention des séquelles neurologiques, en cas d'AVC ischémique aigu ■ la perméabilité de la canule artérioveineuse ou du cathéter central. ✳

THYROÏDIENNES, PRÉPARATIONS

lévothyroxine

Eltroxin, Euthyrox, Synthroid

liothyronine

Cytomel

extrait thyroïdien lyophilisé

Thyroid

CLASSIFICATION:

Hormones thyroïdiennes

Grossesse – catégorie A

INDICATIONS

Hormonothérapie substitutive en présence d'une insuffisance thyroïdienne partielle ou complète de diverses étiologies ■ **Lévothyroxine**: Suppression de l'hormone thyréotrope hypophysaire (TSH) lors du traitement préventif de divers goitres euthyroïdiens ■ Traitement de certains types de cancer de la thyroïde conjointement avec la chirurgie et un traitement à l'iode radioactif ■ **Liothyronine**: Goitre simple (non toxique) – à utiliser à titre d'essai pour réduire le volume du goitre ■ Diagnostic différentiel entre une hyperthyroïdie soupçonnée et une euthyroïdie.

MÉCANISME D'ACTION

Accélération de la vitesse du métabolisme tissulaire (effet principal): activation de la gluconéogenèse ■ augmentation de l'utilisation et de la mobilisation des réserves de glycogène ■ stimulation de la synthèse des protéines ■ stimulation de la croissance et de la différenciation cellulaires ■ effet favorable sur le développement du cerveau et du SNC. ***Effets thérapeutiques:*** Hormonothérapie substitutive en cas de carence et rétablissement de l'équilibre hormonal normal ■ Suppression des cancers thyroïdiens dépendant de la thyrotrophine.

PHARMACOCINÉTIQUE

Absorption: *Lévothyroxine* et *extrait thyroïdien lyophilisé* – variable (PO de 50 à 80 %); *liothyronine* – bonne (PO).

Distribution: La plupart des tissus de l'organisme. L'hormone thyroïdienne ne traverse pas facilement la barrière placentaire; des quantités minimes passent dans le lait maternel.

Liaison aux protéines: > 99 %.

Métabolisme et excrétion: Métabolisme par le foie et d'autres tissus. Les hormones thyroïdiennes subissent plusieurs cycles entérohépatiques et sont excrétées dans les fèces par la bile (de 20 à 40 %).

Demi-vie: T_3 *(liothyronine)* – de 1 à 2 jours; T_4 *(thyroxine)* – de 6 à 7 jours.

Profil temps-action
(effets sur les résultats des tests de la fonction thyroïdienne)

	DÉBUT D'ACTION	PIC	DURÉE
Lévothyroxine – PO	inconnu	1 – 3 semaines	1 – 3 semaines
Lévothyroxine – IV	6 – 8 h	24 h	inconnue
Liothyronine – PO	inconnu	24 – 72 h	72 h
Thyroid (extrait thyroïdien) – PO	plusieurs jours – semaines	1 – 3 semaines	plusieurs jours – semaines

CONTRE-INDICATIONS, PRÉCAUTIONS ET MISES EN GARDE

Contre-indications: Hypersensibilité ■ Infarctus aigu du myocarde ■ Thyrotoxicose ■ Hypersensibilité aux protéines porcines (Thyroid) ■ Troubles corticosurrénaux non corrigés ■ Les hormones thyroïdiennes, prises seules ou en association avec d'autres agents thérapeutiques, ne doivent pas être utilisées pour le traitement de l'obésité ni pour la perte de poids.

Précautions et mises en garde: Maladie cardiovasculaire (amorcer le traitement par des doses plus faibles) ■ Insuffisance rénale grave ■ **GÉR.**: Personnes âgées et patients myxœdémateux (sensibilité accrue aux hormones thyroïdiennes; il faut réduire considérablement la dose initiale).

RÉACTIONS INDÉSIRABLES ET EFFETS SECONDAIRES

Ces effets ont été observés la plupart du temps lors de l'administration de doses excessives.

SNC: insomnie, irritabilité, nervosité, céphalées.

CV: COLLAPSUS CARDIOVASCULAIRE, arythmies, tachycardie, angine de poitrine, hypotension, pression artérielle accrue, débit cardiaque accru.

GI: crampes, diarrhée, vomissements.

Tég.: alopécie, excrétion accrue de sueur.

End.: hyperthyroïdie, irrégularités du cycle menstruel.

Métab.: perte de poids, intolérance à la chaleur.

Loc.: maturation accélérée de la substance osseuse chez les enfants, réduction de la densité minérale osseuse.

INTERACTIONS

Médicament-médicament: La **cholestyramine**, le **colestipol**, les **antiacides**, le **sucralfate**, la **siméthicone**, le **calcium**, le **magnésium**, le **fer**, les **résines échangeuses d'ions** (comme le **sulfonate de polystyrène sodique**), administrés simultanément, réduisent l'absorption des préparations thyroïdiennes destinées à l'administration par voie orale (administrer à au moins 4 heures d'intervalle) ■ L'hormone thyroïdienne peut modifier l'efficacité de la **warfarine** ■ L'hormone thyroïdienne peut accroître les besoins en **insuline** ou en **hypoglycémiants oraux** chez les diabétiques ■ Effets cardiovasculaires additifs lors de l'administration concomitante d'**agents adrénergiques (sympathomimétiques)** ■ L'hormone thyroïdienne peut diminuer la réponse aux **bêtabloquants** ■ L'administration concomitante de **kétamine** peut provoquer l'hypertension et la tachycardie ■ L'administration concomitante d'**antidépresseurs tricycliques** peut amplifier les effets thérapeutiques et toxiques des deux médicaments et accélérer le début d'action des agents tricycliques ■ Les taux plasmatiques de **digoxine** peuvent varier selon l'état thyroïdien ■ L'administration concomitante d'**œstrogènes**, de **carbamazépine**, de **phénytoïne**, de **phénobarbital** ou de **rifampine** peut accroître les besoins en hormone thyroïdienne ■ Un traitement par le **lithium** peut entraîner l'apparition d'un goitre et d'une hypothyroïdie subclinique ou d'une hypothyroïdie manifeste ■ Un traitement par l'**amiodarone** peut entraîner l'apparition d'une hypothyroïdie ou d'une hyperthyroïdie.

Médicament-aliments: La **farine de soya** peut diminuer l'absorption des hormones thyroïdiennes.

VOIES D'ADMINISTRATION ET POSOLOGIE

Remarque: 60 mg d'extrait thyroïdien lyophilisé équivalent généralement à 100 μg ou moins de lévothyroxine (T_4) ou à 25 μg de liothyronine (T_3). Dans tous les cas, la posologie doit être individualisée en fonction du patient, de la réponse clinique et des résultats des épreuves de laboratoire.

Lévothyroxine

- **PO (adultes):** *Hypothyroïdie* – initialement, 50 μg en une seule dose; on peut augmenter la dose de 12,5 à 25 μg par jour, toutes les 6 à 8 semaines (toutes les 2 à 3 semaines dans les cas d'hypothyroïdie grave); la dose d'entretien habituelle se situe entre 75 et 125 μg par jour (1,7 μg/kg/jour). La plupart des patients n'ont pas besoin de plus de 200 μg par jour. *Suppression de la TSH dans le traitement du cancer thyroïdien et des goitres* – la dose doit être individualisée en fonction de la gravité de la maladie, de l'état du patient, de la réponse clinique et des résultats des épreuves de laboratoire. Il faut administrer habituellement des doses supérieures à 2 μg/kg/jour.
- **PO (personnes âgées et patients présentant une sensibilité accrue aux hormones thyroïdiennes):** Initialement, de 12,5 à 25 μg, en une seule dose; on peut augmenter la dose de 12,5 à 25 μg toutes les 3 à 6 semaines; la dose d'entretien habituelle est de 75 μg par jour (peut être < 1 μg/kg/jour).
- **PO (enfants > 12 ans, mais qui poursuivent encore leur croissance et qui n'ont pas encore atteint la puberté):** De 2 à 3 μg/kg/jour.
- **PO (enfants de 6 à 12 ans):** De 4 à 5 μg/kg/jour.
- **PO (enfants de 1 à 5 ans):** De 5 à 6 μg/kg/jour.
- **PO (enfants de 6 à 12 mois):** De 6 à 8 μg/kg/jour.
- **PO (nourrissons de 3 à 6 mois):** De 8 à 10 μg/kg/jour.
- **PO (nourrissons de 0 à 3 mois):** De 10 à 15 μg/kg/jour.
- **IM, IV (adultes):** *Hypothyroïdie* – la moitié de la posologie par voie orale, en une seule dose quotidienne. *Coma myxœdémateux/stupeur* – de 300 à 500 μg par voie IV le 1er jour, suivis de l'administration quotidienne de doses de 75 à 100 μg jusqu'à ce que l'état du patient se stabilise et que l'administration PO soit possible.
- **IM, IV (enfants):** *Hypothyroïdie* – De 50 à 75 % de la posologie par voie orale, en une seule dose quotidienne.

Liothyronine

- **PO (adultes):** *Hypothyroïdie légère* – 25 μg, 1 fois par jour; on peut augmenter la dose à intervalles de 1 à 2 semaines de 12,5 à 25 μg par jour; la dose d'entretien habituelle se situe entre 25 et 75 μg. *Myxœdème* – initialement, 5 μg, 1 fois par jour; augmenter la dose de 5 à 10 μg par jour, toutes les 1 à 2 semaines, jusqu'à concurrence de 25 μg par jour, puis de 12,5 à 25 μg par jour, toutes les 1 à 2 semaines; la dose d'entretien habituelle se situe entre 50 et 100 μg par jour. *Goitre simple* – initialement, 5 μg, 1 fois par jour; augmenter la dose de 5 à 10 μg par jour, toutes les 1 à 2 semaines, jusqu'à concurrence de 25 μg par jour, puis de 12,5 à 25 μg par jour, toutes les 1 à 2 semaines, jusqu'à l'obtention de l'effet souhaité; la dose d'entretien habituelle est de 75 μg par jour. *Test de suppression de la T_3* – de 75 à 100 μg par jour, pendant 7 jours. On administre l'iode radioactif (I^{131}) avant et après une cure de 7 jours.
- **PO (personnes âgées, patients souffrant de maladie cardiovasculaire ou enfants):** Initialement, 5 μg par jour; augmenter par paliers de 5 μg par jour au maximum, toutes les 2 semaines.
- **PO (enfants):** *Crétinisme* – initialement, 5 μg/jour, on peut augmenter la dose de 5 μg par jour, à intervalles de 3 ou 4 jours, jusqu'à ce que la réponse souhaitable soit obtenue. La thérapie doit s'amorcer le plus tôt possible après la naissance afin d'éviter tout changement physique et mental permanent.

Extrait thyroïdien lyophilisé

- **PO (adultes et enfants):** *Hypothyroïdie* – initialement, 60 mg par jour; augmenter de 30 mg tous les mois; la dose d'entretien habituelle se situe entre 30 et 125 mg par jour. L'écart posologique est de 60 à 300 mg par jour. *Myxœdème/hypothyroïdie accompagnée d'une maladie cardiovasculaire*– initialement, 15 mg; augmenter de 30 mg par jour, toutes les 2 semaines, puis de 30 à 60 mg, toutes les 2 semaines; la dose d'entretien habituelle se situe entre 60 et 180 mg par jour.

PRÉSENTATION

- **Lévothyroxine (version générique disponible)**
  Comprimés: 25 μg^Pr^, 50 μg^Pr^, 75 μg^Pr^, 88 μg^Pr^, 100 μg^Pr^, 112 μg^Pr^, 125 μg^Pr^, 137 μg^Pr^, 150 μg^Pr^, 175 μg^Pr^, 200 μg^Pr^, 300 μg^Pr^ ■ **Poudre pour injection:** 500 μg/fiole, en fioles de 10 mL^Pr^.
- **Liothyronine**
  Comprimés: 5 μg^Pr^, 25 μg^Pr^.
- **Extrait thyroïdien lyophilisé**
  Comprimés (extrait porcin): 30 mg^Pr^, 60 mg^Pr^, 125 mg^Pr^.

T

SOINS INFIRMIERS

ÉVALUATION DE LA SITUATION

- MESURER LA PRESSION ARTÉRIELLE ET LE POULS À L'APEX DU CŒUR AVANT LE TRAITEMENT ET À INTERVALLES RÉGULIERS PENDANT TOUTE SA DURÉE. ÉVALUER LES DOULEURS THORACIQUES ET LES TACHYARYTHMIES.

Enfants: Mesurer la taille et le poids et évaluer le développement psychomoteur.

Tests de laboratoire:

- Examiner les résultats des tests de la fonction thyroïdienne avant le traitement et pendant toute sa durée.
- Mesurer la glycémie et la glycosurie chez les patients diabétiques. Il peut s'avérer nécessaire d'augmenter les doses d'insuline et d'hypoglycémiants oraux.

TOXICITÉ ET SURDOSAGE: Le surdosage se manifeste sous forme d'hyperthyroïdie (tachycardie, douleurs thoraciques, nervosité, insomnie, diaphorèse, tremblements, perte de poids). Pour contrer ces symptômes, on interrompt habituellement l'administration d'hormone pendant 2 à 6 jours. On traite un surdosage aigu par induction de vomissements ou par lavage gastrique, suivis par l'administration de charbon activé. La surstimulation sympathique peut être maîtrisée par des médicaments adrénolytiques (bêtabloquants), tels que le propranolol. On utilise également l'oxygène et on prend des mesures de soutien pour maîtriser des symptômes tels que la fièvre.

DIAGNOSTICS INFIRMIERS POSSIBLES

- Connaissances insuffisantes sur le traitement médicamenteux (Enseignement au patient et à ses proches).

INTERVENTIONS INFIRMIÈRES

- Administrer le médicament en une seule dose, de préférence avant le petit-déjeuner, pour prévenir l'insomnie.
- La dose initiale doit être faible, particulièrement chez les personnes âgées et les patients cardiaques. Il faut augmenter la dose graduellement, selon les résultats des tests de la fonction thyroïdienne. Les effets secondaires se manifestent plus rapidement lors du traitement par la liothyronine, en raison de son début d'action rapide.

Lévothyroxine

IV directe: Diluer le contenu des fioles de 500 µg avec 5 mL de solution de NaCl 0,9 % sans agent de conservation, pour obtenir une concentration de 100 µg/mL. Bien secouer la fiole pour dissoudre complètement la solution. Administrer la solution immédiatement après l'avoir préparée; jeter toute portion inutilisée. Consulter les directives de chaque fabricant avant de reconstituer la préparation.

Vitesse d'administration: Administrer à un débit de 100 µg par minute. Ne pas ajouter cet agent à des perfusions IV; on peut administrer le médicament par une tubulure en Y.

Incompatibilité (tubulure en Y): Ne pas administrer avec d'autres médicaments.

ENSEIGNEMENT AU PATIENT ET À SES PROCHES

- Inciter le patient à respecter rigoureusement la posologie recommandée et à prendre le médicament à la même heure chaque jour. Lui expliquer que s'il n'a pu prendre le médicament au moment habituel, il doit le prendre dès que possible, à moins que ce ne soit presque l'heure prévue pour la dose suivante. S'il n'a pu prendre plus de 2 ou 3 doses, il doit prévenir un professionnel de la santé. L'avertir qu'il est déconseillé d'arrêter le traitement sans consulter au préalable un professionnel de la santé.
- Montrer au patient et à ses proches comment prendre le pouls. Conseiller au patient de ne pas prendre l'hormone thyroïdienne et de prévenir un professionnel de la santé si le pouls au repos est supérieur à 100 bpm.
- Expliquer au patient que le médicament ne guérit pas l'hypothyroïdie, il ne fait que remplacer les hormones thyroïdiennes; le traitement doit être poursuivi toute la vie durant.
- Prévenir le patient qu'il ne doit pas substituer une marque de préparation thyroïdienne à une autre, car la biodisponibilité de chaque médicament peut être différente.
- Conseiller au patient de prévenir un professionnel de la santé si les symptômes suivants se manifestent: céphalées, nervosité, diarrhée, transpiration abondante, intolérance à la chaleur, douleurs thoraciques, fréquence accrue du pouls, palpitations, perte de poids > 0,9 kg par semaine. L'inciter également à signaler tout autre symptôme inhabituel.
- Prévenir le patient qu'il ne doit pas prendre d'autres médicaments ni des produits naturels en même temps que les préparations thyroïdiennes, sauf sur recommandation d'un professionnel de la santé.
- Recommander au patient qui doit consulter un professionnel de la santé de le prévenir qu'il suit un traitement par des hormones thyroïdiennes.
- Insister sur l'importance des examens de suivi permettant d'évaluer l'efficacité du traitement. Les tests

de la fonction thyroïdienne doivent être effectués au moins 1 fois par année.

PÉD.:

- Expliquer aux parents que les examens de suivi sont importants puisqu'ils permettent au médecin de surveiller la croissance de l'enfant. Les prévenir du risque d'alopécie partielle auquel sont exposés les enfants qui suivent un traitement par des hormones thyroïdiennes. Cet effet est habituellement passager.
- On peut faire prendre les comprimés de lévothyroxine aux enfants qui ne peuvent les avaler tels quels en les écrasant et en les mettant aussitôt en suspension dans une petite quantité d'eau (de 5 à 10 mL), de lait maternel ou de préparation pour nourrissons ne renfermant pas de soya. La suspension peut être donnée avec une cuiller ou un comptegouttes. **Ne pas conserver cette suspension pour quelque durée que ce soit.** On peut aussi saupoudrer le comprimé écrasé sur une petite quantité de nourriture, comme de la compote de pommes.

VÉRIFICATION DE L'EFFICACITÉ THÉRAPEUTIQUE

L'efficacité du traitement peut être démontrée par: la disparition des symptômes d'hypothyroïdie. La réponse inclut: la diurèse ■ la perte de poids ■ une sensation de mieux-être ■ un regain d'énergie, l'accélération du pouls, un gain d'appétit et l'augmentation de l'activité psychomotrice ■ la normalisation de la texture de la peau et des cheveux ■ la suppression de la constipation ■ l'élévation des concentrations de T_3 et de T_4 ■ Chez les enfants, l'efficacité du traitement est déterminée par un développement physique et psychomoteur approprié. ✳

TICARCILLINE

Ce médicament n'est pas commercialisé au Canada.

TICARCILLINE/ CLAVULANATE

Timentin

CLASSIFICATION:

Antibiotique (pénicilline à très large spectre), inhibiteur des bêtalactamases

Grossesse – catégorie B

INDICATIONS

Traitement des infections suivantes: infections de la peau et de ses annexes ■ infections des os et des articulations ■ septicémie ■ infections des voies respiratoires ■ infections intra-abdominales, gynécologiques et urinaires.

MÉCANISME D'ACTION

Liaison à la membrane de la paroi cellulaire bactérienne provoquant la destruction de la bactérie ■ L'ajout du clavulanate améliore la résistance aux bêtalactamases, enzymes capables de détruire les pénicillines. ***Effets thérapeutiques:*** Effet bactéricide contre les bactéries sensibles. **Spectre d'action:** Spectre d'action semblable à celui des pénicillines, mais considérablement plus large, qui englobe plusieurs agents pathogènes aérobies à Gram négatif importants, dont: *Pseudomonas æruginosa* ■ *Escherichia coli* ■ *Proteus mirabilis* ■ *Providencia rettgeri* ■ La ticarcilline est également active contre certaines bactéries anaérobies comprenant les *Bacteroides*.

PHARMACOCINÉTIQUE

Absorption: 100 % (IV).

Distribution: Tout l'organisme. L'agent ne pénètre suffisamment dans le liquide céphalorachidien qu'en présence d'une inflammation des méninges. Il traverse la barrière placentaire et on le retrouve dans le lait maternel à faible concentration.

Métabolisme et excrétion: Métabolisme hépatique faible (10 %). Excrétion majoritairement rénale (90 % sous forme inchangée). Le clavulanate est métabolisé par le foie.

Demi-vie: *Ticarcilline* – de 0,9 à 1,3 heure (prolongée en présence d'insuffisance rénale); *clavulanate* – de 1,1 à 1,5 heure.

Profil temps-action (concentrations sériques)

	DÉBUT D'ACTION	PIC	DURÉE
IV	rapide	fin de la perfusion	4-6 h

CONTRE-INDICATIONS, PRÉCAUTIONS ET MISES EN GARDE

Contre-indications: Hypersensibilité aux pénicillines (risque de sensibilité croisée avec les céphalosporines), aux céphalosporines ou à l'acide clavulanique.

Précautions et mises en garde: Insuffisance rénale (il est recommandé de réduire la dose ou de prolonger l'intervalle entre les doses si la clairance de la créatinine est < 60 mL/min) ■ **OBST., ALLAITEMENT:** L'innocuité du médicament n'a pas été établie ■ Maladie hépatique grave.

RÉACTIONS INDÉSIRABLES ET EFFETS SECONDAIRES

SNC: CONVULSIONS (doses élevées), confusion, léthargie.

CV: INSUFFISANCE CARDIAQUE, arythmies.
GI: COLITE PSEUDOMEMBRANEUSE, diarrhée, nausées.
GU: hématurie (enfants seulement).
Tég.: rash, urticaire.
HÉ: hypokaliémie, hypernatrémie.
Hémat.: saignements, dyscrasie sanguine, allongement du temps de saignement.
Locaux: phlébite.
Métab.: alcalose métabolique.
Divers: réactions d'hypersensibilité incluant l'ANAPHYLAXIE, surinfection.

INTERACTIONS

Médicament-médicament: Le **probénécide** diminue l'excrétion rénale de la ticarcilline et en augmente les concentrations sanguines ■ La ticarcilline peut modifier l'excrétion du **lithium** ■ Les **diurétiques thiazidiques**, les **diurétiques de l'anse**, l'**amphotéricine B** ou les **corticostéroïdes** peuvent augmenter le risque d'hypokaliémie.

VOIES D'ADMINISTRATION ET POSOLOGIE

L'association ticarcilline/clavulanate contient 4,75 mmol de sodium par gramme de ticarcilline et 0,15 mmol de potassium par 100 mg de clavulanate.

Ticarcilline/clavulanate

La préparation contient 3 g de ticarcilline et 100 mg de clavulanate donnant une teneur combinée de 3,1 g.

- **Traitement**

  IV (adultes ≥ 60 kg): 3,1 g, toutes les 4 à 6 heures.

  IV (enfants > 1 mois et adultes < 60 kg): De 200 à 300 mg/kg/jour de l'équivalent de ticarcilline en doses fractionnées, toutes les 4 à 6 heures.

  INSUFFISANCE RÉNALE: POSOLOGIE QUOTIDIENNE DANS LES INFECTIONS PAR DES BACTÉRIES SENSIBLES (SELON LE TENEUR EN TICARCILLINE): *CL_{CR} > 60 mL/MIN* – 3 g, TOUTES LES 4 HEURES, *CL_{CR} DE 30 À 60 mL/MIN* – 2 g, TOUTES LES 4 HEURES, *CL_{CR} DE 10 À 30 mL/MIN* – 2 g, TOUTES LES 8 HEURES, *CL_{CR} < 10 mL/MIN* – 2 g, TOUTES LES 12 HEURES, *CL_{CR} < 10 mL/MIN AVEC INSUFFISANCE HÉPATIQUE* – 2 g, TOUTES LES 24 HEURES. *PATIENTS SOUS DIALYSE PÉRITONÉALE:* 3 g TOUTES LES 12 HEURES; *PATIENTS SOUS HÉMODIALYSE:* 2 g TOUTES LES 12 HEURES (EN PLUS DE 3 g APRÈS CHAQUE DIALYSE).

- **Prophylaxie avant la chirurgie**

  IV (adultes): 3,1 g dès que le cordon ombilical est clampé (césarienne) *ou* de 30 à 60 minutes avant l'incision initiale (chirurgie colorectale ou hystérectomie); ensuite, 2 doses de plus à des intervalles de 4 heures. Ne pas dépasser 3 doses.

PRÉSENTATION

- **Ticarcilline**

  Ce médicament n'est pas commercialisé au Canada.

- **Ticarcilline/clavulanate**

  Poudre pour injection: 3,1 g/fiole[Pr] ou 31 g/fiole[Pr].

SOINS INFIRMIERS

ÉVALUATION DE LA SITUATION

- Au début du traitement et pendant toute sa durée, rester à l'affut des signes suivants d'infection: altération des signes vitaux, aspect de la plaie, des crachats, de l'urine et des selles, accroissement du nombre de globules blancs.
- Recueillir les antécédents du patient avant d'amorcer le traitement afin de déterminer ses réactions à un traitement antérieur à une pénicilline ou à une céphalosporine. Même les personnes n'ayant jamais manifesté de sensibilité à la pénicilline peuvent présenter une réaction allergique.
- Prélever des échantillons pour les cultures et les antibiogrammes avant le début du traitement. La première dose peut être administrée avant que les résultats soient connus.
- RESTER À L'AFFÛT DES SIGNES ET DES SYMPTÔMES SUIVANTS D'ANAPHYLAXIE: RASH, PRURIT, ŒDÈME LARYNGÉ, RESPIRATION SIFFLANTE. SI CES RÉACTIONS SE MANIFESTENT, ARRÊTER L'ADMINISTRATION DU MÉDICAMENT ET AVERTIR IMMÉDIATEMENT LE MÉDECIN. GARDER À PORTÉE DE LA MAIN DE L'ADRÉNALINE, UN ANTIHISTAMINIQUE ET LE MATÉRIEL DE RÉANIMATION POUR PARER À UNE ÉVENTUELLE RÉACTION ANAPHYLACTIQUE.

Tests de laboratoire:

- Noter, avant le traitement et à intervalles réguliers pendant toute sa durée, les résultats des tests des fonctions hépatique et rénale, la numération globulaire, les concentrations sériques de potassium et le temps de saignement.
- La ticarcilline peut entraîner des résultats faussement positifs au dosage des protéines dans l'urine ainsi que l'élévation des concentrations d'urée, de créatinine, d'AST, d'ALT, de bilirubine sérique, de phosphatase alcaline, de LDH et d'acide urique. Elle peut également allonger le temps de saignement.
- Lors de l'administration de doses élevées de ticarcilline, une hypokaliémie et une hypernatrémie peuvent survenir.

DIAGNOSTICS INFIRMIERS POSSIBLES

- Risque d'infection (Indications, Effets secondaires).

- Connaissances insuffisantes sur le traitement médicamenteux (Enseignement au patient et à ses proches).

INTERVENTIONS INFIRMIÈRES

- **IV**: Changer de point d'injection IV toutes les 48 heures pour prévenir la phlébite.

Ticarcilline/clavulanate

- Ce médicament doit être administré sous forme diluée, par perfusion IV; il ne doit **jamais** être administré par voie IM ou par bolus IV.

Perfusion intermittente: Ajouter 13 mL d'eau stérile pour injection au contenu de la fiole de 3,1 g pour obtenir une concentration de ticarcilline de 200 mg/mL et d'acide clavulanique de 6,7 mg/mL. Diluer une fois de plus dans une solution de NaCl 0,9 %, de D5%E, de lactate de Ringer ou d'eau stérile pour injection. La solution est stable pendant 6 heures à la température ambiante et pendant 72 heures au réfrigérateur.

Vitesse d'administration: Administrer en 30 minutes par une tubulure en Y ou par IV directe. Consulter les directives de chaque fabricant avant d'administrer la préparation.

Compatibilité (tubulure en Y): amifostine ■ aztréonam ■ céfépime ■ cyclophosphamide ■ diltiazem ■ famotidine ■ filgrastim ■ fludarabine ■ foscarnet ■ gallium, nitrate de ■ granisétron ■ héparine ■ insuline ■ melphalan ■ mépéridine ■ morphine ■ ondansétron ■ perphénazine ■ sargramostim ■ téniposide ■ théophylline ■ thiotépa ■ vinorelbine.

Incompatibilité (tubulure en Y): S'il faut administrer en même temps des aminosides et des pénicillines, les injecter à des points différents à au moins 1 heure d'intervalle.

T

ENSEIGNEMENT AU PATIENT ET À SES PROCHES

- Conseiller au patient de signaler à un professionnel de la santé les signes de surinfection (excroissance pileuse sur la langue, pertes et démangeaisons vaginales, selles molles ou nauséabondes) et les allergies.
- RECOMMANDER AU PATIENT DE SIGNALER À UN PROFESSIONNEL DE LA SANTÉ LA FIÈVRE OU LA DIARRHÉE, PARTICULIÈREMENT EN PRÉSENCE DE SANG, DE PUS OU DE MUCUS DANS LES SELLES. CONSEILLER AU PATIENT DE NE PAS TRAITER LA DIARRHÉE AVANT D'AVOIR CONSULTÉ UN PROFESSIONNEL DE LA SANTÉ. CES EFFETS PEUVENT SE MANIFESTER PENDANT PLUSIEURS SEMAINES APRÈS L'ARRÊT DU TRAITEMENT.

VÉRIFICATION DE L'EFFICACITÉ THÉRAPEUTIQUE

L'efficacité du traitement peut être démontrée par: la disparition des signes et des symptômes d'infection. Le temps de résolution dépend du microorganisme infectant et du siège de l'infection. ✳

TICLOPIDINE

Apo-Ticlopidine, Gen-Ticlopidine, Novo-Ticlopidine, Nu-Ticlopidine, Sandoz Ticlopidine, Ticlid

CLASSIFICATION:
Antiplaquettaire

Grossesse – catégorie B

INDICATIONS

Prévention primaire ou secondaire d'un accident vasculaire cérébral (AVC) thromboembolique constitué, d'un AVC mineur, d'un déficit neurologique ischémique réversible ou d'une ischémie cérébrale transitoire (ICT), y compris une cécité monoculaire transitoire. **Usages non approuvés**: Prévention d'une resténose précoce chez le porteur d'une endoprothèse intracoronarienne.

MÉCANISME D'ACTION

Inhibition de l'agrégation plaquettaire par modification de la fonction des membranes plaquettaires ■ Allongement du temps de saignement. ***Effets thérapeutiques:*** Diminution de la fréquence des accidents vasculaires cérébraux chez les patients exposés à un risque élevé.

PHARMACOCINÉTIQUE

Absorption: Bonne (> 80 % PO).

Distribution: Inconnue.

Liaison aux protéines: 98 %.

Métabolisme et excrétion: Métabolisme hépatique important. Une quantité minime (< 1 %) est excrétée à l'état inchangé par les reins.

Demi-vie: *Dose unique* – 12,6 heures; *plusieurs doses* – de 4 à 5 jours.

Profil temps-action (effet sur la fonction plaquettaire)

	DÉBUT D'ACTION	PIC	DURÉE
PO	en l'espace de 2 – 4 jours	8 – 11 jours	10 – 14 jours

CONTRE-INDICATIONS, PRÉCAUTIONS ET MISES EN GARDE

Contre-indications: Hypersensibilité ■ Troubles hémostatiques ■ Saignements actifs ■ Maladie hépatique grave ■ Présence ou antécédents de troubles hématopoïétiques (p. ex., neutropénie, thrombopénie ou agranulocytose).

Précautions et mises en garde: Risque d'hémorragie (traumatisme, intervention chirurgicale, antécédents d'ulcère) ■ En cas de chirurgie non urgente ou d'extraction dentaire, on doit envisager l'arrêt du traitement de 10 à 14 jours avant l'intervention pour que l'effet du médicament ait le temps de disparaître ■ Insuffisance hépatique ou rénale (une adaptation posologique peut s'avérer nécessaire) ■ **GÉR.**: Sensibilité accrue ■ **ALLAITEMENT, OBST., PÉD. (enfants < 18 ans)**: L'innocuité du médicament n'a pas été établie.

RÉACTIONS INDÉSIRABLES ET EFFETS SECONDAIRES

SNC: étourdissements, céphalées, faiblesse.

ORLO: épistaxis, acouphènes.

GI: diarrhée, résultats anormaux aux tests de la fonction hépatique, anorexie, plénitude gastro-intestinale, douleurs gastro-intestinales, nausées, vomissements.

GU: hématurie.

Tég.: rash, ecchymoses, prurit, urticaire.

Hémat.: AGRANULOCYTOSE, HÉMORRAGIE CÉRÉBRALE, NEUTROPÉNIE, saignements, thrombopénie, purpura thrombopénique thrombotique (PTT).

Métab.: hypercholestérolémie, hypertriglycéridémie.

INTERACTIONS

Médicament-médicament: L'**aspirine**, administrée en concomitance, potentialise l'effet de la ticlopidine sur les plaquettes (l'administration concomitante n'est pas recommandée) ■ Risque accru d'hémorragie lors de l'administration concomitante d'**héparine**, de **warfarine**, d'**abciximab**, de **tirofiban**, d'**eptifibatide**, d'**AINS** ou d'**agents thrombolytiques** ■ La **cimétidine**, administrée simultanément, ralentit le métabolisme de la ticlopidine et peut augmenter le risque de toxicité ■ La ticlopidine ralentit le métabolisme de la **théophylline** et peut augmenter le risque de toxicité.

Médicament-produits naturels: Risque accru de saignements lors de la consommation concomitante d'**ail**, d'**anis**, d'**arnica**, de **camomille**, de **clous de girofle**, de **fenugrec**, de **grande camomille**, de **gingembre**, de **ginkgo**, de **ginseng** et d'**autres produits**.

Médicament-aliments: L'absorption de la ticlopidine est accrue si elle est prise avec des **aliments**.

VOIES D'ADMINISTRATION ET POSOLOGIE

- **PO (adultes)**: 250 mg, 2 fois par jour, avec des aliments.

PRÉSENTATION

Comprimés: 250 mg^{Pr}.

SOINS INFIRMIERS

ÉVALUATION DE LA SITUATION

- Rester à l'affût d'un AVC; suivre le patient à intervalles réguliers pendant toute la durée du traitement.

Tests de laboratoire:

- SUIVRE DE PRÈS LE TEMPS DE SAIGNEMENT PENDANT TOUTE LA DURÉE DU TRAITEMENT. LA TICLOPIDINE ALLONGE LE TEMPS DE SAIGNEMENT (DE 2 À 5 FOIS LA LIMITE NORMALE). CET EFFET DÉPEND DE LA DURÉE DU TRAITEMENT ET DE LA DOSE ADMINISTRÉE.
- NOTER LA NUMÉRATION GLOBULAIRE, LA FORMULE LEUCOCYTAIRE ET LA NUMÉRATION PLAQUETTAIRE, TOUTES LES 2 SEMAINES, À PARTIR DE LA 2e SEMAINE ET JUSQU'À LA FIN DU 3e MOIS DE TRAITEMENT; DES ANALYSES PLUS FRÉQUENTES SONT NÉCESSAIRES SI LE NOMBRE ABSOLU DE POLYNUCLÉAIRES NEUTROPHILES DIMINUE OU S'IL EST < 30 % DES VALEURS INITIALES. EN CAS DE NEUTROPÉNIE (NEUTROPHILES $< 1,2 \times 10^9$/L), IL FAUT ARRÊTER LE TRAITEMENT PAR LA TICLOPIDINE. LE NOMBRE DE POLYNUCLÉAIRES NEUTROPHILES REVIENT HABITUELLEMENT À LA NORMALE DANS LES 1 À 3 SEMAINES SUIVANT L'ARRÊT DU TRAITEMENT. ÉTANT DONNÉ LA LONGUE DEMI-VIE DE LA TICLOPIDINE, IL FAUT EFFECTUER CHEZ TOUS LES PATIENTS QUI ARRÊTENT DE LA PRENDRE, POUR QUELQUE RAISON QUE CE SOIT AU COURS DES 90 PREMIERS JOURS DU TRAITEMENT, UNE NUMÉRATION GLOBULAIRE ADDITIONNELLE AVEC UNE FORMULE LEUCOCYTAIRE ET UNE NUMÉRATION PLAQUETTAIRE, 2 SEMAINES APRÈS L'ARRÊT DU TRAITEMENT. APRÈS LES 3 PREMIERS MOIS DE TRAITEMENT, LA NUMÉRATION GLOBULAIRE DEVRAIT ÊTRE MESURÉE SEULEMENT CHEZ LES PATIENTS PRÉSENTANT DES SIGNES ET DES SYMPTÔMES D'INFECTION.
- La ticlopidine peut entraîner la thrombopénie, habituellement dans les 3 à 12 semaines suivant le début du traitement. Si le nombre de plaquettes est $< 80 \times 10^9$/L, arrêter le traitement.
- La ticlopidine peut entraîner l'élévation des concentrations sériques de cholestérol total et de triglycérides. Les concentrations augmentent habituellement de 8 à 10 % durant le premier mois de traitement et restent à ce niveau.

T

- La ticlopidine peut entraîner l'élévation des concentrations de phosphatase alcaline, de bilirubine, d'AST et d'ALT durant les 4 premiers mois de traitement.

Toxicité et surdosage: Le temps de saignement allongé revient à la normale dans les 2 heures qui suivent l'administration de méthylprednisolone par voie IV. On peut également effectuer des transfusions de plaquettes pour renverser les effets de la ticlopidine sur le temps de saignement.

DIAGNOSTICS INFIRMIERS POSSIBLES

- Risque d'accident (Indications, Effets secondaires).
- Connaissances insuffisantes sur le traitement médicamenteux (Enseignement au patient et à ses proches).

INTERVENTIONS INFIRMIÈRES

- Administrer la ticlopidine avec des aliments ou immédiatement après les repas afin de réduire la gêne gastro-intestinale et d'augmenter l'absorption du médicament.
- En cas de chirurgie non urgente ou d'extraction dentaire, on doit envisager l'arrêt du traitement de 10 à 14 jours avant l'intervention pour que l'effet du médicament ait le temps de disparaître.

ENSEIGNEMENT AU PATIENT ET À SES PROCHES

- Inciter le patient à respecter rigoureusement la posologie recommandée. S'il n'a pu prendre le médicament au moment habituel, il doit le prendre dès que possible, à moins que ce ne soit presque l'heure prévue pour la dose suivante. L'avertir qu'il ne doit jamais remplacer une dose manquée par une double dose.
- Recommander au patient de signaler à un professionnel de la santé la fièvre, les frissons, les maux de gorge, les saignements ou les ecchymoses inhabituels, la diarrhée grave ou persistantc, le rash, la jaunisse, l'urine de couleur foncée ou les selles de couleur pâle.
- Recommander au patient qui doit subir une intervention chirurgicale, une extraction dentaire ou un autre traitement effractif de prévenir le professionnel de la santé qu'il suit un traitement par ce médicament. Il peut s'avérer nécessaire d'arrêter le traitement pendant les 10 à 14 jours précédant une intervention chirurgicale.
- Insister sur le fait qu'il est important d'effectuer des tests de laboratoire au cours des 3 premiers mois de traitement pour pouvoir déceler les effets secondaires.

VÉRIFICATION DE L'EFFICACITÉ THÉRAPEUTIQUE

L'efficacité du traitement peut être démontrée par: la prévention des AVC. ✳

TIGÉCYCLINE

Tygacil

CLASSIFICATION:

Antibiotique (glycylcycline)

Grossesse – catégorie D

INDICATIONS

Traitement des infections compliquées de la peau et des tissus mous ou des infections intra-abdominales compliquées, dues aux bactéries sensibles.

MÉCANISME D'ACTION

Inhibition de la synthèse de la protéine bactérienne par liaison à la sous-unité ribosomale 30S. ***Effets thérapeutiques:*** Guérison de l'infection. **Spectre d'action:** L'antibiotique englobe dans son spectre d'activité les bactéries à Gram positif suivantes: *Enterococcus fæcalis* (souches sensibles à la vancomycine seulement), *Staphylococcus aureus* (souches sensibles ou résistantes à la méthicilline), *Streptococcus agalactiæ*, *Streptococcus anginosus* et *Streptococcus pyogenes*. Il agit également contre les microorganismes à Gram négatif suivants: *Citrobacter freundii*, *Enterobacter cloacæ*, *Escherichia coli*, *Klebsiella oxytoca* et *Klebsiella pneumoniæ*. De plus, il est actif contre les microorganismes anaérobies suivants: *Bacteroides fragilis*, *Bacteroides thetaiotaomicron*, *Bacteroides uniformis*, *Bacteroides vulgatus*, *Clostridium perfringens* et *Peptostreptococcus micros*.

PHARMACOCINÉTIQUE

Absorption: Biodisponibilité totale (IV).

Distribution: L'agent se répartit dans tous les tissus, avec une bonne pénétration dans la vésicule biliaire, les poumons et le côlon; il traverse la barrière placentaire.

Métabolisme et excrétion: Faible métabolisme; excrétion du médicament sous forme inchangée et des métabolites par voie biliaire et fécale (59 %) et par voie rénale (33 %).

Demi-vie: 27,1 heures (après une seule dose); 42,4 heures après plusieurs doses.

Profil temps-action

	DÉBUT D'ACTION	PIC	DURÉE
IV	rapide	fin de la perfusion	12 h

CONTRE-INDICATIONS, PRÉCAUTIONS ET MISES EN GARDE

Contre-indications: Hypersensibilité au médicament ou aux tétracyclines.

Précautions et mises en garde: Infections intra-abdominales compliquées dues à une perforation ■ Insuffisance hépatique grave (classe C selon la classification de Child-Pugh: il est recommandé de réduire la dose d'entretien) ■ **GÉR.:** Les personnes âgées peuvent être plus sensibles aux effets indésirables ■ **OBST.:** L'utilisation chez la femme enceinte n'est justifiée que si les bienfaits possibles chez la mère dépassent les risques auxquels est exposé le fœtus ■ L'administration pendant l'allaitement doit s'accompagner de prudence ■ **PÉD.:** Enfants < 18 ans (l'innocuité et l'efficacité de l'agent n'ont pas été établies). La tigécycline ne doit pas être administrée à des enfants < 8 ans à cause du risque de changement de la couleur des dents.

RÉACTIONS INDÉSIRABLES ET EFFETS SECONDAIRES

SNC: somnolence.

CV: modification de la fréquence cardiaque, vasodilatation.

GI: COLITE PSEUDOMEMBRANEUSE, nausées, vomissements, diarrhée, altération du goût, anorexie, sécheresse de la bouche (xérostomie), jaunisse, PANCRÉATITE.

GU: vaginite, candidose génitale, élévation des taux de créatinine.

End.: hyperglycémie.

HÉ: hypocalcémie, hyponatrémie.

Locaux: réactions au point d'injection.

Divers: réactions allergiques.

INTERACTIONS

Médicament-médicament: L'agent peut diminuer l'efficacité des **contraceptifs hormonaux** ■ Ses effets sur la **warfarine** sont inconnus (une surveillance est recommandée).

VOIES D'ADMINISTRATION ET POSOLOGIE

- **IV (adultes ≥ 18 ans):** 100 mg, initialement; ensuite, 50 mg toutes les 12 heures pendant 5 à 14 jours.

INSUFFISANCE HÉPATIQUE

- **IV (ADULTES ≥ 18 ANS):** *SCORE DE CHILD PUGH C* – 100 mg, INITIALEMENT; ENSUITE 25 mg, TOUTES LES 12 HEURES.

PRÉSENTATION

Poudre lyophilisée à reconstituer: 50 mg^{Pr}, en fioles de 5 mL.

SOINS INFIRMIERS

ÉVALUATION DE LA SITUATION

- Rechercher les signes d'infection (altération des signes vitaux, aspect de la plaie, des expectorations, de l'urine et des selles, accroissement du nombre de leucocytes) en début de traitement et pendant toute sa durée.
- Prélever des échantillons pour les cultures et les antibiogrammes avant le début du traitement. On peut administrer la première dose avant que les résultats soient connus.
- Recueillir les antécédents du patient quant à une hypersensibilité aux tétracyclines avant de commencer le traitement; les patients ayant manifesté une sensibilité à ces agents peuvent être allergiques à la tigécycline.

Tests de laboratoire:

- La tigécycline peut provoquer une anémie, une leucocytose et une thrombocythémie.
- L'agent peut élever les concentrations sériques de phosphatase alcaline, d'amylase, de bilirubine, de LD, d'AST et d'ALT.
- Il peut provoquer une hyperglycémie, une hypokaliémie, une hypoprotéinémie, une hypocalcémie, une hyponatrémie et élever les concentrations d'urée.

DIAGNOSTICS INFIRMIERS POSSIBLES

- Risque d'infection (Indications).

INTERVENTIONS INFIRMIÈRES

Perfusion intermittente: Reconstituer le contenu de chaque fiole avec 5,3 mL de NaCl 0,9 % ou de D5E pour obtenir une concentration de 10 mg/mL. Tourner délicatement la fiole pour en dissoudre le contenu. Retirer immédiatement 5 mL de solution reconstituée et l'ajouter à un sac de 100 mL de NaCl 0,9 % ou de D5E pour administration IV. La concentration maximale de la solution dans le sac pour administration IV doit être de 1 mg/mL. La couleur de la solution reconstituée doit aller de jaune à orange. Si la solution a changé de couleur ou contient des particules, la jeter. On peut la garder dans le sac pendant 6 heures au maximum à la température ambiante et pendant 6 heures au réfrigérateur. On peut administrer la solution par une tubulure IV séparée ou par une tubulure en Y. Rincer la tubulure avant et après utilisation avec du NaCl 0,9 %

ou du D5E. Consulter les directives de chaque fabricant avant de reconstituer la préparation.

Vitesse d'administration: Administrer toutes les 12 heures, pendant 30 à 60 minutes.

Compatibilité (tubulure en Y): dobutamine ▪ dopamine ▪ LR ▪ lidocaïne ▪ potassium, chlorure de ▪ ranitidine ▪ théophylline.

ENSEIGNEMENT AU PATIENT ET À SES PROCHES

- Prévenir le patient qu'il doit prendre toute la quantité de médicament qui lui a été prescrite, même s'il se sent mieux. Lui expliquer que des doses manquées ou l'arrêt du traitement avant la fin prévue peuvent diminuer l'efficacité de l'antibiothérapie et accroître le risque d'émergence d'une résistance bactérienne.
- Conseiller à la patiente d'utiliser une méthode contraceptive non hormonale pendant toute la durée du traitement à la tigécycline et jusqu'aux premières règles qui suivent l'arrêt de l'antibiothérapie.
- Recommander au patient de prévenir un professionnel de la santé en cas de fièvre ou de diarrhée, particulièrement si ses selles contiennent du sang, du pus ou du mucus. Conseiller au patient de ne pas traiter la diarrhée sans consulter un professionnel de la santé au préalable.
- Recommander au patient de prévenir un professionnel de la santé si des signes de surinfection (excroissance noire et pileuse sur la langue, démangeaisons ou pertes vaginales, selles molles et nauséabondes) se manifestent. Lui conseiller de signaler également le rash, le prurit et l'urticaire.

VÉRIFICATION DE L'EFFICACITÉ THÉRAPEUTIQUE

L'efficacité du traitement peut être démontrée par: la résolution des signes et des symptômes d'infection. ✳

T

TIMOLOL

Apo-Timol, Blocadren, Novo-Timol

CLASSIFICATION:

Antihypertenseur, antiangineux (bêtabloquant)

Grossesse – catégories C (1er trimestre) et D (2e et 3e trimestres)

INDICATIONS

Traitement de l'hypertension ▪ Traitement de l'angine de poitrine attribuable à une cardiopathie ischémique ▪ Prévention de l'infarctus du myocarde ▪ Prophylaxie des migraines. **Usages non approuvés:** Traitement des arythmies ventriculaires ▪ Traitement des tremblements essentiels ▪ Traitement de l'anxiété.

MÉCANISME D'ACTION

Inhibition de la stimulation des récepteurs adrénergiques bêta$_1$ (myocardiques) et bêta$_2$ (pulmonaires, vasculaires ou utérins). ***Effets thérapeutiques:*** Diminution de la fréquence cardiaque et abaissement de la pression artérielle ▪ Prévention de l'infarctus du myocarde ▪ Diminution de la fréquence des crises migraineuses.

PHARMACOCINÉTIQUE

Absorption: Bonne (PO).

Distribution: L'agent passe dans le lait maternel.

Métabolisme et excrétion: Métabolisme hépatique important (50 % de la dose absorbée subit un effet de premier passage hépatique). Excrétion rénale (principalement sous forme de métabolites).

Demi-vie: De 2 à 4 heures.

Profil temps-action (effets cardiovasculaires)

	Début d'action	Pic	Durée
PO	30 min	1 – 2 h†	12 h

† Après une seule dose; le plein effet du médicament ne se manifeste qu'après plusieurs semaines de traitement.

CONTRE-INDICATIONS, PRÉCAUTIONS ET MISES EN GARDE

Contre-indications: Hypersensibilité ▪ Insuffisance cardiaque non compensée ▪ Choc cardiogénique ▪ Bradycardie sinusale ▪ Cardiomégalie importante ▪ Bloc AV du 2e et du 3e degré ▪ Œdème pulmonaire ▪ Insuffisance du ventricule droit secondaire à l'hypertension pulmonaire ▪ Anesthésie à l'aide d'agents dépresseurs du myocarde ▪ Bronchospasme, incluant asthme et bronchopneumopathie chronique obstructive grave.

Précautions et mises en garde: Insuffisance rénale ▪ Insuffisance hépatique ▪ **Gér.:** Il est recommandé de réduire la dose initiale chez les personnes âgées ou débilitées (sensibilité accrue aux bêtabloquants) ▪ Diabète (le médicament peut masquer les signes d'hypoglycémie) ▪ Thyrotoxicose (le médicament peut en masquer les symptômes) ▪ Antécédents de réactions allergiques graves (le médicament peut accroître l'intensité des réactions) ▪ **Obst.:** Risque de toxicité fœtale si le médicament est pris au cours du 2e et du 3e trimestre; ce risque serait absent s'il est pris au cours du 1er trimestre ▪ **Allaitement:** L'innocuité du médicament n'a pas été établie chez la femme qui allaite ▪ **Péd.:**

L'innocuité et l'efficacité du médicament n'ont pas été établies chez les enfants.

RÉACTIONS INDÉSIRABLES ET EFFETS SECONDAIRES

SNC: fatigue, faiblesse, anxiété, dépression, étourdissements, somnolence, insomnie, perte de mémoire, modification des opérations de la pensée, nervosité, cauchemars.
ORLO: vision trouble, xérophtalmie, congestion nasale.
Resp.: bronchospasme, respiration sifflante.
CV: ARYTHMIES, BRADYCARDIE, INSUFFISANCE CARDIAQUE, ŒDÈME PULMONAIRE, hypotension orthostatique, vasoconstriction périphérique.
GI: constipation, diarrhée, nausées.
GU: impuissance, baisse de la libido.
Tég.: démangeaisons, rash.
End.: hyperglycémie, hypoglycémie.
Loc.: arthralgie, douleurs lombaires, crampes musculaires.
SN: paresthésie.
Divers: ANAPHYLAXIE (rare).

INTERACTIONS

Médicament-médicament: L'**anesthésie générale**, le **diltiazem** et le **vérapamil** peuvent provoquer une dépression additive du myocarde ■ Risque de bradycardie additive lors de l'administration concomitante de **dérivés digitaliques** ■ Risque d'hypotension additive lors de la prise d'autres **antihypertenseurs** ou de **dérivés nitrés** ou lors de l'ingestion de grandes quantités d'**alcool** ■ Les **amphétamines**, l'**adrénaline**, la **noradrénaline**, la **cocaïne**, l'**éphédrine**, la **phényléphrine** ou la **pseudoéphédrine**, prises en concomitance, peuvent entraîner une stimulation alpha-adrénergique à laquelle rien ne s'oppose (hypertension et bradycardie excessives) ■ Risque de diminution de l'efficacité de l'**insuline** ou des **hypoglycémiants oraux** (une adaptation posologique peut s'avérer nécessaire) ■ Le timolol peut réduire l'efficacité des **bronchodilatateurs** ■ Le timolol peut diminuer les effets bénéfiques de la **dopamine** ou de la **dobutamine** sur les récepteurs bêtacardiaques ■ La prudence est de mise lorsque le timolol est administré dans les 14 jours suivant un traitement par un **IMAO** (risque d'hypertension) ■ La **cimétidine** peut accroître la toxicité associée au timolol ■ Les **AINS**, pris en concomitance, peuvent diminuer l'effet antihypertenseur du timolol.

VOIES D'ADMINISTRATION ET POSOLOGIE

- **PO (adultes)**: *Antihypertenseur* – initialement, de 5 à 10 mg, 2 fois par jour; on peut augmenter la dose de 5 mg, 2 fois par jour, tous les 7 jours, selon la réponse au traitement et la tolérance du patient (la dose d'entretien habituelle est de 10 à 20 mg, 2 fois par jour, jusqu'à concurrence de 60 mg par jour). *Angine* – initialement, 5 mg, 2 fois par jour; on peut augmenter la dose à intervalles de 7 jours, à raison de 10 mg par jour, en doses fractionnées, jusqu'à concurrence de 60 mg par jour. *Prévention de l'infarctus du myocarde* – 10 mg, 2 fois par jour; il faut commencer le traitement de 1 à 4 semaines après la survenue de l'infarctus. *Prévention des céphalées vasculaires* – initialement, 10 mg, 2 fois par jour; on peut administrer le médicament en une seule dose quotidienne; on peut majorer la dose jusqu'à 10 mg, le matin, et jusqu'à 20 mg, le soir.

PRÉSENTATION
(version générique disponible)

Comprimés: 5 mg^{Pr}, 10 mg^{Pr}, 20 mg^{Pr}.

SOINS INFIRMIERS

ÉVALUATION DE LA SITUATION

- Mesurer la pression artérielle et le pouls à intervalles fréquents pendant la période d'adaptation de la posologie et à intervalles réguliers pendant toute la durée du traitement. Suivre de près l'hypotension orthostatique pendant qu'on aide le patient à se lever.
- Effectuer le bilan quotidien des ingesta et des excreta et peser le patient tous les jours. Observer régulièrement le patient à la recherche des signes et des symptômes suivants de surcharge liquidienne: œdème périphérique, dyspnée, râles ou crépitations, fatigue, gain pondéral, turgescence des jugulaires.

Prophylaxie des céphalées vasculaires: Noter la fréquence, la gravité, les caractéristiques et le siège des céphalées vasculaires à intervalles réguliers pendant toute la durée du traitement.

Tests de laboratoire:

- Le timolol peut élever l'urée et les concentrations sériques de lipoprotéines, de potassium, de triglycérides et d'acide urique.
- Il peut élever la glycémie.

TOXICITÉ ET SURDOSAGE:

- Suivre de près les patients recevant des bêtabloquants afin de déceler les signes suivants de surdosage: bradycardie, étourdissements graves ou évanouissements, somnolence prononcée, dyspnée, bleuissement des ongles ou des paumes de la main, convulsions. Communiquer immédiatement avec un médecin ou un autre professionnel de la santé si ces signes se manifestent.

- On a déjà administré du glucagon pour traiter la bradycardie et l'hypotension.

DIAGNOSTICS INFIRMIERS POSSIBLES

- Débit cardiaque diminué (Effets secondaires).
- Connaissances insuffisantes sur le traitement médicamenteux (Enseignement au patient et à ses proches).
- Non-observance du traitement médicamenteux (Enseignement au patient et à ses proches).

INTERVENTIONS INFIRMIÈRES

- Mesurer le pouls à l'apex du cœur avant d'administrer le médicament. S'il est inférieur à 50 battements par minute ou s'il y a arythmie, ne pas administrer le timolol et en avertir le médecin ou un autre professionnel de la santé.
- Administrer le médicament avec des aliments ou à jeun.
- On peut écraser les comprimés de timolol et les mélanger à des aliments.

ENSEIGNEMENT AU PATIENT ET À SES PROCHES

- Prévenir le patient qu'il doit prendre le timolol tous les jours, à la même heure, en suivant rigoureusement les recommandations du médecin. Lui expliquer qu'il doit continuer à prendre le médicament même s'il se sent bien. L'avertir qu'il ne doit jamais sauter de dose ni remplacer une dose manquée par une double dose. S'il n'a pu prendre le médicament au moment habituel, il doit le prendre aussitôt que possible, mais au moins 4 heures avant l'heure prévue pour la dose suivante. Le prévenir également que le sevrage brusque peut provoquer des arythmies mettant sa vie en danger, l'hypertension ou l'ischémie du myocarde.
- Conseiller au patient d'avoir une réserve suffisante de médicament pour les fins de semaine, les congés et les vacances. Lui conseiller également de conserver une ordonnance dans son portefeuille pour parer à toute urgence.
- Enseigner au patient et à ses proches la méthode de prise du pouls et de la pression artérielle. Leur demander de mesurer le pouls tous les jours et la pression artérielle 2 fois par semaine. Si le pouls est inférieur à 50 battements par minute ou si la pression artérielle varie de façon importante, conseiller au patient d'en informer un professionnel de la santé.
- Prévenir le patient que le timolol peut parfois provoquer des étourdissements. Lui conseiller de ne pas conduire et d'éviter les activités qui exigent sa vigilance jusqu'à ce qu'on ait la certitude que le médicament n'entraîne pas cet effet chez lui.
- Conseiller au patient de changer lentement de position pour réduire le risque d'hypotension orthostatique, particulièrement au début du traitement ou lors de la majoration des doses.
- Prévenir le patient que le médicament peut le rendre plus sensible au froid.
- Conseiller au patient de consulter un professionnel de la santé avant de prendre des médicaments en vente libre, particulièrement des préparations contre le rhume, ou des produits naturels en même temps que le timolol.
- Recommander au patient diabétique de mesurer sa glycémie, particulièrement lorsqu'il se sent fatigué, faible ou irritable ou lorsqu'il ressent un malaise. Le timolol peut masquer la tachycardie ou les tremblements, qui sont des signes d'hypoglycémie. Cependant, des étourdissements et des sueurs peuvent toujours survenir.
- Recommander au patient de signaler à un professionnel de la santé les symptômes suivants: ralentissement du pouls, difficultés respiratoires, respiration sifflante, mains et pieds froids, étourdissements, confusion, dépression, rash, fièvre, maux de gorge, saignements inhabituels ou formation d'ecchymoses.
- Recommander au patient qui doit suivre un autre traitement ou subir une intervention chirurgicale d'avertir le professionnel de la santé qu'il prend du timolol.
- Conseiller au patient de porter sur lui en tout temps une pièce d'identité où sont inscrits son problème de santé et sa médication.

Hypertension: Inciter le patient à appliquer d'autres mesures de réduction de l'hypertension: perdre du poids, réduire sa consommation de sel, diminuer le stress, faire régulièrement de l'exercice, boire de l'alcool avec modération et cesser de fumer. Lui expliquer que le timolol stabilise la pression artérielle, mais ne guérit pas l'hypertension.

Prophylaxie des céphalées vasculaires: Informer le patient qu'il ne doit pas donner ce médicament à d'autres personnes.

VÉRIFICATION DE L'EFFICACITÉ THÉRAPEUTIQUE

L'efficacité du traitement peut être démontrée par: la baisse de la pression artérielle ■ la réduction des symptômes d'angine de poitrine ■ la prévention des infarctus du myocarde ■ la prévention des céphalées vasculaires. ✱

TINZAPARINE,
voir Héparines de faible poids moléculaire/héparinoïdes

TIOTROPIUM (INHALATION)
Spiriva

CLASSIFICATION:
Bronchodilatateur (anticholinergique)

Grossesse – catégorie inconnue

INDICATIONS
Traitement d'entretien uniquotidien prolongé du bronchospasme associé à la bronchopneumopathie chronique obstructive (BPCO), y compris la bronchite chronique et l'emphysème.

MÉCANISME D'ACTION
Antagoniste des récepteurs muscariniques des muscles lisses des bronches (longue durée d'action). ***Effets thérapeutiques:*** Bronchodilatation sans effets anticholinergiques systémiques.

PHARMACOCINÉTIQUE
Absorption: 19,5 % (inhalation).
Distribution: Inconnue.
Métabolisme et excrétion: Métabolisme hépatique (25 % du médicament absorbé). Excrétion rénale sous forme inchangée (75 %).
Demi-vie: de 5 à 7 jours.

Profil temps-action (bronchodilatation)

	DÉBUT D'ACTION	PIC	DURÉE
Inhalation	30 min	1,5 - 3 h	prolongée, au moins 24 h

CONTRE-INDICATIONS, PRÉCAUTIONS ET MISES EN GARDE
Contre-indications: Hypersensibilité à l'atropine ou à ses dérivés (ipratropium), ou au lactose (utilisé comme excipient).
Précautions et mises en garde: Glaucome à angle fermé ▪ Hyperplasie de la prostate ▪ Obstruction du col de la vessie ▪ Usage déconseillé en présence de bronchospasme aigu ▪ **OBST., ALLAITEMENT**: L'innocuité du médicament n'a pas été établie chez la femme enceinte ou qui allaite ▪ **PÉD.**: L'innocuité et l'efficacité du médicament n'ont pas été établies chez les enfants < 18 ans.

RÉACTIONS INDÉSIRABLES ET EFFETS SECONDAIRES
SNC: céphalées.
ORLO: sécheresse de la bouche (xérostomie), vision trouble, glaucome, irritation oropharyngée.
Resp.: toux, symptômes pseudogrippaux, bronchospasme paradoxal.
GI: constipation.
GU: miction difficile, rétention urinaire.
Loc.: arthrite.
Divers: réactions allergiques.

INTERACTIONS
Médicament-médicament: Risque d'effets anticholinergiques additifs lors de l'administration concomitante d'autres **médicaments dotés de propriétés anticholinergiques**.

VOIES D'ADMINISTRATION ET POSOLOGIE
- **Inhalation (adultes)**: Inhalation du contenu d'une capsule de 18 µg, 1 fois par jour.

PRÉSENTATION
Capsules pour inhalation: 18 µg[Pr], avec dispositif d'inhalation HandiHaler.

SOINS INFIRMIERS

ÉVALUATION DE LA SITUATION
- Déterminer si le patient est allergique à l'atropine ou à ses dérivés (ipratropium) puisque les sujets souffrant de ce type d'allergie peuvent également être sensibles au tiotropium.
- Suivre de près la fonction respiratoire: ausculter le murmure vésiculaire, mesurer la fréquence respiratoire et le pouls, évaluer la gravité de la dyspnée, avant l'administration et pendant le traitement. Consulter le médecin ou un autre professionnel de la santé au sujet des solutions de rechange en présence d'un bronchospasme grave, puisque le début d'action du tiotropium est trop lent en cas de crise aiguë. En cas de bronchospasme paradoxal (respiration sifflante), arrêter l'administration de ce médicament et prévenir immédiatement le médecin ou un autre professionnel de la santé.

Tests de laboratoire: Noter à intervalles réguliers, pendant toute la durée du traitement, les paramètres de la fonction respiratoire.

DIAGNOSTICS INFIRMIERS POSSIBLES
- Dégagement inefficace des voies respiratoires (Indications).

T

- Intolérance à l'activité (Indications).
- Connaissances insuffisantes sur le traitement médicamenteux (Enseignement au patient et à ses proches).

INTERVENTIONS INFIRMIÈRES

- Enseigner au patient l'utilisation du dispositif d'inhalation HandiHaler.

ENSEIGNEMENT AU PATIENT ET À SES PROCHES

- Conseiller au patient de respecter rigoureusement la posologie recommandée. S'il n'a pu prendre le médicament au moment habituel, il doit le prendre dès que possible à moins que ce ne soit presque l'heure prévue pour la dose suivante. Lui dire qu'il doit prendre une seule dose par jour.
- Prévenir le patient que la capsule ne doit pas être avalée.
- Expliquer au patient qu'il doit inhaler le contenu de la capsule 1 fois par jour, à la même heure tous les jours, uniquement à l'aide du dispositif d'inhalation HandiHaler. Le prévenir qu'il ne doit pas prendre les capsules de tiotropium avec un autre type d'inhalateur, ni utiliser le dispositif d'inhalation HandiHaler pour prendre d'autres capsules.
- Recommander au patient de bien lire les explications et de se familiariser avec le dispositif avant de l'utiliser.
- Conseiller au patient de ne retirer qu'une seule capsule à la fois de l'emballage d'aluminium, et de garder le médicament à l'abri de l'humidité, des températures extrêmes et de la lumière du soleil.
- Faire la démonstration du mode d'emploi: insérer la capsule dans la chambre centrale du dispositif, bien refermer l'embout buccal jusqu'à ce qu'un déclic se fasse entendre, tout en laissant le capuchon protecteur ouvert. Perforer la capsule en enfonçant complètement le bouton vert une fois, puis le relâcher. La capsule est maintenant prête à être inhalée.
- Expliquer au patient le mode d'auto-administration: serrer les lèvres autour de l'embout buccal, et inspirer lentement et profondément jusqu'à ce que la capsule se mette à vibrer. Inspirer ensuite jusqu'à ce que les poumons soient remplis, puis retenir son souffle aussi longtemps que possible pendant qu'on retire le dispositif de la bouche. Par la suite, respirer normalement. Répéter l'opération pour s'assurer qu'on a inhalé tout le contenu de la capsule.

Mise au rebut: Ouvrir l'embout buccal à nouveau. Jeter la capsule à la poubelle, sans la toucher. En cas de contact fortuit, se laver les mains à fond.

- Conseiller au patient de se rincer la bouche après l'inhalation du médicament afin de prévenir la sécheresse buccale. Cet effet tend à disparaître avec le temps.

Entretien: Nettoyer le dispositif HandiHaler 1 fois par mois, selon les recommandations contenues dans le feuillet d'informations.

- Prévenir le patient qu'il ne doit pas utiliser ce médicament comme traitement de secours, lors d'une crise aiguë de bronchospasme, car le début d'action est trop lent.
- Recommander au patient d'arrêter de fumer, le cas échéant.
- Prévenir le patient que si la poudre a été en contact avec les yeux, il y a risque de douleurs ou de gêne oculaires, de vision trouble passagère, d'images colorées se formant sur la rétine et de rougeur oculaire.
- Conseiller à la patiente d'informer rapidement un professionnel de la santé si elle pense être enceinte, si elle souhaite le devenir ou si elle allaite.

VÉRIFICATION DE L'EFFICACITÉ THÉRAPEUTIQUE

L'efficacité du traitement peut être démontrée par: la diminution de la dyspnée. ✳

TIPRANAVIR

Aptivus

CLASSIFICATION:

Antirétroviral (inhibiteur de la protéase)

Grossesse – catégorie C

INDICATIONS

Infection par le VIH à un stade avancé qui résiste aux autres traitements anti-VIH (il faut toujours administrer le tipranavir en association avec le ritonavir).

MÉCANISME D'ACTION

Inhibition de la synthèse des polyprotéines virales, prévenant la formation de virions matures. ***Effets thérapeutiques:*** Réduction de la charge virale et des complications de l'infection par le VIH.

PHARMACOCINÉTIQUE

Absorption: Bonne (PO).
Distribution: Inconnue.
Liaison aux protéines: > 99,9 %.
Métabolisme et excrétion: Métabolisme rapide et complet en l'absence de ritonavir (surtout par le système

enzymatique du CYP3A4), ce qui dicte l'administration simultanée de ritonavir, à titre d'inhibiteur du métabolisme, permettant d'atteindre des concentrations sanguines thérapeutiques. Le tipranavir est surtout excrété par les fèces; l'excrétion rénale est minime.

Demi-vie: De 5,5 à 6 heures.

Profil temps-action†

	DÉBUT D'ACTION	PIC	DURÉE
PO	rapide	2 h	12 h

† Avec le ritonavir.

CONTRE-INDICATIONS, PRÉCAUTIONS ET MISES EN GARDE

Contre-indications: Hypersensibilité ■ Insuffisance hépatique de modérée à grave (classification de Child-Pugh B ou C) ■ Usage concomitant de certains antiarythmiques (amiodarone, flécaïnide, propafénone, quinidine), de dérivés de l'ergot, de pimozide, de cisapride, de vardénafil, de midazolam ou de triazolam.

Précautions et mises en garde: Nombreuses interactions médicamenteuses ■ Allergie aux sulfamides (le tipranavir contient un groupement sulfamide) ■ Intolérance connue à l'alcool (les capsules contiennent de l'alcool) ■ Maladie hépatique préexistante (risque accru de toxicité hépatique) ■ Antécédents ou facteurs de risque de diabète (risque d'hyperglycémie) ■ Hémophilie (risque accru de saignements) ■ Hypersensibilité au Cremophor EL (solvant utilisé dans les capsules) ■ **PÉD.**: L'innocuité du médicament chez les enfants < 18 ans n'a pas été établie ■ **OBST.**: Grossesse (n'utiliser qu'en cas de besoin incontestable) ■ **ALLAITEMENT**: L'allaitement est déconseillé aux patientes infectées par le VIH.

RÉACTIONS INDÉSIRABLES ET EFFETS SECONDAIRES

SNC: céphalées, fatigue.

GI: TOXICITÉ HÉPATIQUE, diarrhée, nausée, vomissement.

Tég.: rash (risque accru chez la femme).

End.: hyperglycémie.

Métab.: élévation des taux de cholestérol, élévation des taux de triglycérides.

Divers: réactions allergiques, modification de la distribution du tissu adipeux, syndrome de reconstitution immunitaire, HÉMORRAGIE INTRACRÂNIENNE.

INTERACTIONS

Médicament-médicament: L'usage concomitant de tipranavir et de certains **antiarythmiques** (**amiodarone**, **flecaïnide**, **propafénone**, **quinidine**), de **dérivés de l'ergot** (**dihydroergotamine**, **ergotamine**, **ergonovine**), de **pimozide**, de **cisapride**, de **vardénafil**, de **midazolam** et de **triazolam** est contre-indiqué en raison du risque d'élévation des concentrations sanguines de ces agents et de leur toxicité ■ Le tipranavir, administré avec une faible dose de ritonavir, entraîne des réductions importantes des concentrations plasmatiques d'**abacavir**, d'**amprénavir**, d'**atazanavir**, de **lopinavir**, de **saquinavir** et de **zidovudine** (l'usage concomitant n'est pas recommandé) ■ L'usage concomitant d'**atorvastatine**, de **simvastatine** ou de **lovastatine** augmente le risque de rhabdomyolyse (éviter l'usage concomitant de simvastatine ou de lovastatine; administrer la plus faible dose possible d'atorvastatine et suivre de près l'état du patient) ■ L'usage concomitant de **sildénafil**, de **vardénafil** ou de **tadalafil** doit s'accompagner d'une extrême prudence, en raison du risque d'hypotension, de syncope, de changements visuels et d'érection prolongée (suivre de près l'état du patient et réduire la dose de sildénafil à 25 mg, toutes les 48 heures, et de tadalafil à 10 mg, toutes les 72 heures; éviter l'usage de vardénafil) ■ Le médicament peut diminuer les concentrations et les effets de la **méthadone** (augmenter, au besoin, la dose de méthadone) ■ Les capsules contiennent de l'alcool et peuvent provoquer une intolérance si le patient prend du **disulfirame** ou du **métronidazole** ■ Les concentrations sont considérablement diminuées par la **rifampine** (risque d'émergence d'une résistance virale, éviter l'usage concomitant) ■ Le ritonavir élève les concentrations de **fluticasone**; envisager une solution de rechange ■ Élévation des concentrations de **trazodone**; diminuer la dose de trazodone ■ Élévation des concentrations d'**itraconazole** et de **kétoconazole** (ne pas administrer plus de 200 mg par jour de ces **antifongiques**) ■ Élévation des concentrations de tipranavir lors d'administration concomitante de **fluconazole** (ne pas administrer plus de 200 mg par jour de fluconazole) ■ Risque de diminution des concentrations de **voriconazole** (éviter l'usage concomitant) ■ Élévation des concentrations de **clarithromycine** (il est recommandé de réduire la dose de clarithromycine chez les patients dont la Cl_{Cr} est ≤ 60 mL/min) ■ Élévation des concentrations de **rifabutine** (il est recommandé de réduire la dose de rifabutine) ■ Élévation possible des concentrations des **bloqueurs des canaux calciques** (une surveillance clinique est de mise) ■ Variations possibles des concentrations et du risque de toxicité des **immunosuppresseurs**, comme la **cyclosporine** ou le **tacrolimus** (il est recommandé de suivre de près les concentrations sanguines) ■ Risque de modification des concentrations et de l'effet de la **warfarine** (surveiller le RNI) ■ Risque de diminution des concentrations de **théophylline** (il pourrait être nécessaire d'augmenter la dose de théophylline et d'assurer une surveillance thérapeutique) ■ Diminution des concentrations de **didanosine** (administrer à au moins 2 heures d'intervalle) ■ Les **antiacides** peuvent diminuer l'absorption du tipranavir (espacer les prises) ■ Les **contraceptifs oraux** pris en concomitance peuvent élever le risque de rash ■ Le tipranavir peut diminuer l'efficacité des **contraceptifs oraux**.

Médicament-produits naturels: L'usage concomitant de **millepertuis** peut diminuer les concentrations sanguines et l'efficacité du tipranavir, entraînant le risque d'émergence d'une résistance virale.

VOIES D'ADMINISTRATION ET POSOLOGIE

- **PO (adultes)**: 500 mg, 2 fois par jour; il faut toujours prendre le tipranavir en association avec le ritonavir à 200 mg, 2 fois par jour.

PRÉSENTATION

Capsules: 250 mg[Pr].

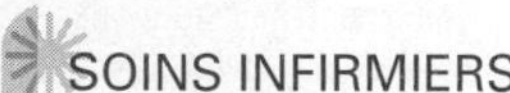

SOINS INFIRMIERS

ÉVALUATION DE LA SITUATION

- Évaluer le patient pendant toute la durée du traitement pour déceler tout changement au niveau de l'aggravation des symptômes de l'infection par le VIH ainsi que l'apparition des symptômes d'infections opportunistes.
- Dépister l'apparition de l'hépatite (fatigue, malaises, anorexie, nausées, jaunisse, urine foncée [bilirubinurie], selles pâles, sensibilité au toucher au niveau du foie, hépatomégalie).
- Rester à l'affût des allergies aux sulfamides. Il y a risque de sensibilité croisée.
- Si une patiente enceinte est exposée à des antirétroviraux, l'inscrire dans le registre des femmes exposées aux antirétroviraux pendant leur grossesse, en composant le 1-800-258-4263.

T

Tests de laboratoire:

- Suivre la charge virale et le nombre de cellules CD4 à intervalles réguliers tout au long du traitement.
- L'agent peut élever les taux d'AST et d'ALT; mesurer ces taux en début du traitement et à intervalles réguliers par la suite.
- Le tipranavir peut élever les taux de cholestérol et de triglycérides; mesurer ces taux en début du traitement et à intervalles réguliers par la suite.
- L'agent peut provoquer l'hyperglycémie. Suivre attentivement la glycémie, particulièrement chez les patients diabétiques.

DIAGNOSTICS INFIRMIERS POSSIBLES

- Risque d'infection (Indications).
- Non-observance du traitement médicamenteux (Enseignement au patient et à ses proches).

INTERVENTIONS INFIRMIÈRES

PO: Il faut administrer l'agent avec du ritonavir, 2 fois par jour, avec des aliments. La biodisponibilité est accrue si l'agent est pris avec un repas riche en graisses.

- Garder les capsules au réfrigérateur. Une fois le flacon ouvert, le médicament peut être conservé à une température ambiante pendant 60 jours. Inscrire la date d'ouverture sur l'étiquette; ne pas administrer après la date de péremption. Si le patient doit prendre le médicament hors de chez lui, lui recommander de le garder à la température ambiante dans un endroit frais.

ENSEIGNEMENT AU PATIENT ET À SES PROCHES

- Expliquer au patient qu'il est important de prendre le tipranavir en suivant rigoureusement les recommandations du médecin et d'espacer également les prises durant la journée. Lui recommander de lire les renseignements destinés au patient avant de commencer le traitement et à chaque renouvellement d'ordonnance. Prévenir le patient qu'il ne doit prendre que la quantité de médicament qui lui a été prescrite et qu'il ne doit pas arrêter de prendre le tipranavir sans avoir consulté un professionnel de la santé au préalable. Lui expliquer qu'il doit prendre toute dose manquée aussitôt que possible et revenir ensuite à son horaire habituel. L'informer qu'il ne faut jamais remplacer une dose manquée par une double dose.
- Prévenir le patient qu'il ne doit pas donner le tipranavir à d'autres personnes.
- Conseiller au patient de ne pas prendre de médicaments d'ordonnance ou en vente libre ni de produits naturels sans avoir consulté un professionnel de la santé au préalable.
- Informer le patient que l'agent ne guérit pas le sida ni ne prévient les infections associées ou opportunistes. Il ne réduit pas le risque de transmission du VIH à d'autres personnes par les rapports sexuels ou le sang. Inciter le patient à utiliser un condom et à éviter le partage d'aiguilles ou les dons de sang pour prévenir la propagation du VIH.
- Conseiller au patient d'arrêter de prendre le tipranavir et le ritonavir et de prévenir un professionnel de la santé si des signes d'hépatite (fatigue, malaise, anorexie, nausées, jaunisse, urine foncée, selles pâles) se manifestent. Ces signes pourraient dicter l'abandon du traitement.

- Prévenir le patient que le tipranavir peut provoquer l'hyperglycémie. Lui conseiller d'informer un professionnel de la santé en cas de soif ou de faim accrues, de perte de poids inexpliquée, d'une augmentation du nombre de mictions, de fatigue, de démangeaisons ou de dessèchement de la peau.
- Prévenir la patiente que l'agent peut diminuer l'efficacité des contraceptifs hormonaux; lui conseiller d'utiliser une méthode de contraception non hormonale tout au long du traitement. L'informer également que les femmes qui prennent des contraceptifs hormonaux sont exposées à un risque accru de rash.
- Informer le patient du risque d'accumulation ou de redistribution des tissus adipeux, pouvant entraîner une obésité centrale, une infiltration de graisse dans la région dorsocervicale (bosse de bison), l'atrophie des tissus périphériques, l'augmentation du volume des seins et un aspect cushinoïde. Les causes et les effets à long terme sont inconnus.
- Insister sur l'importance des numérations globulaires et des examens de suivi réguliers permettant de déterminer les progrès du traitement et de surveiller les effets secondaires.

VÉRIFICATION DE L'EFFICACITÉ THÉRAPEUTIQUE

L'efficacité du traitement peut être démontrée par: le ralentissement de l'évolution de l'infection par le VIH et un moindre risque de contracter des infections opportunistes ▪ la diminution de la charge virale et l'augmentation du nombre de CD4.

ALERTE CLINIQUE

TIROFIBAN

Aggrastat

CLASSIFICATION:

Antiplaquettaire (inhibiteur des récepteurs des glycoprotéines IIb/IIIa)

Grossesse – catégorie B

INDICATIONS

Traitement, en association avec l'aspirine et l'héparine, du syndrome coronarien aigu (angine instable, IM sans ondes Q), chez les patients sous pharmacothérapie et chez ceux qui subiront une angioplastie coronarienne transluminale percutanée (ACTP).

MÉCANISME D'ACTION

Diminution de l'agrégation plaquettaire par inhibition de façon réversible de la liaison du fibrinogène aux sites de fixation des glycoprotéines IIb/IIIa, situés à la surface des plaquettes. ***Effets thérapeutiques:*** Inhibition de l'agrégation plaquettaire entraînant une diminution de l'incidence d'un nouvel IM, de décès ou d'une ischémie rebelle au traitement, dictant le recours à des interventions cardiaques répétées.

PHARMACOCINÉTIQUE

Absorption: Biodisponibilité totale (IV).

Distribution: Inconnue.

Métabolisme et excrétion: Excrétion rénale sous forme inchangée (65 %) et fécale sous forme inchangée (25 %).

Demi-vie: 2 heures.

Profil temps-action (effets sur la fonction plaquettaire)

	Début d'action	Pic	Durée
IV	rapide	30 min†	brève‡

† Inhibition de l'agrégation plaquettaire > 90 % à la fin de la perfusion initiale de 30 minutes.

‡ L'inhibition est réversible après l'arrêt de la perfusion.

CONTRE-INDICATIONS, PRÉCAUTIONS ET MISES EN GARDE

Contre-indications: Hypersensibilité ▪ Hémorragie interne active ou antécédents de diathèse hémorragique ▪ Antécédents d'hémorragie ou de néoplasme intracrâniens, de malformation artérioveineuse ou d'anévrisme ▪ Antécédents de thrombopénie au cours d'un traitement antérieur par le tirofiban ▪ Accident vasculaire cérébral dans les 30 jours précédents ou antécédents d'AVC hémorragique ▪ Intervention chirurgicale majeure ou traumatisme physique grave dans les 30 jours précédents ▪ Antécédents ou présence de symptômes d'anévrisme aortique ou autres signes connexes ▪ Hypertension grave (pression systolique > 180 mm Hg ou pression diastolique > 110 mm Hg) ▪ Usage concomitant d'autres antagonistes des récepteurs des glycoprotéines IIb/IIIa ▪ Péricardite aiguë ▪ Coagulopathie connue, thrombopathie ou antécédents de thrombopénie ▪ Cirrhose ou maladie hépatique cliniquement significative ▪ Angine de poitrine consécutive à des facteurs déclenchants évidents (p. ex., arythmie, anémie grave, hyperthyroïdie ou hypotension) ▪ Intervention épidurale ou péridurale récente.

Précautions et mises en garde: Nombre de plaquettes $< 150 \times 10^9$/L ▪ Rétinopathie hémorragique ▪ Hémorragie au cours de la dernière année ▪ AVC au cours de la dernière année ▪ Administration concomitante d'autres médicaments qui agissent sur l'hémostase (augmentation

T

du risque d'hémorragie) ■ Femmes ou personnes âgées (risque accru de saignements) ■ Insuffisance rénale grave (diminuer de 50 % la vitesse de perfusion, si la Cl_{Cr} est < 30 mL/min) ■ **OBST., ALLAITEMENT, PÉD.**: Grossesse ou enfants (l'innocuité du médicament n'a pas été établie; l'administrer pendant la grossesse seulement si ce traitement s'avère réellement nécessaire); allaitement (il faut interrompre l'allaitement durant le traitement et éliminer le lait retiré durant cette période; l'allaitement peut être repris 24 heures après la fin du traitement par le tirofiban).

RÉACTIONS INDÉSIRABLES ET EFFETS SECONDAIRES

Effets signalés chez les patients recevant de l'héparine et de l'aspirine en plus du tirofiban.

SNC: étourdissements, céphalées.

CV: bradycardie, dissection coronarienne, œdème, réaction vasovagale.

GI: nausées.

Tég.: urticaire, rash.

Hémat.: SAIGNEMENTS, thrombopénie.

Loc.: douleurs au niveau des jambes.

Divers: fièvre, réactions d'hypersensibilité, douleurs pelviennes, transpiration.

INTERACTIONS

Médicament-médicament: Risque accru de saignements lors de l'administration concomitante d'autres **médicaments qui affectent l'hémostase** (**héparine** et **composés de type héparinique**, **warfarine**, **AINS**, **agents thrombolytiques**, **abciximab**, **eptifibatide**, **lepirudine**, **dipyridamole**, **ticlodipine**, **clopidogrel**, **valproates**).

Médicament-produits naturels: Risque accru de saignements lors de la consommation des produits naturels suivants: **ail**, **arnica**, **camomille**, **clous de girofle**, **dong quai**, **grande camomille**, **gingembre**, **ginkgo**, **ginseng** et **autres**.

T

VOIES D'ADMINISTRATION ET POSOLOGIE

- **IV (adultes)**: 0,4 µg/kg/min, en 30 minutes, puis 0,1 µg/kg/min; poursuivre l'administration pendant toute la durée de l'angiographie et pendant les 12 à 24 heures qui suivent l'angioplastie. Chez les patients qui ne présentent pas de signes ou de symptômes d'ischémie rebelle et qui ne seront pas soumis à une angiographie ou à une angioplastie, la perfusion devrait durer au moins 48 heures.

INSUFFISANCE RÉNALE

- **IV (ADULTES)**: *CL_{CR} < 30 ML/MIN* – ADMINISTRER 50 % DE LA DOSE RECOMMANDÉE.

PRÉSENTATION

Solution prémélangée pour injection, prête à l'emploi: 50 µg/mL, en sacs de 250 mL[Pr].

SOINS INFIRMIERS

ÉVALUATION DE LA SITUATION

- RESTER À L'AFFÛT DES SAIGNEMENTS. LE SIGNE LE PLUS FRÉQUENT EST UN SUINTEMENT À L'EMPLACEMENT DE LA PONCTION ARTÉRIELLE PRATIQUÉE EN VUE DU CATHÉTÉRISME CARDIAQUE. ON DEVRAIT ÉVITER AUTANT QUE POSSIBLE LES PONCTIONS ARTÉRIELLES ET VEINEUSES, LES INJECTIONS PAR VOIE IM ET L'USAGE DES SONDES URINAIRES ET DES TUBES NASOTRACHÉAUX ET NASOGASTRIQUES, TOUT COMME LES INJECTIONS IV DANS DES POINTS DE PONCTION SUR LESQUELS ON NE PEUT EXERCER DE PRESSION. SI LES SAIGNEMENTS NE PEUVENT ÊTRE RÉPRIMÉS EN EXERÇANT UNE PRESSION SUR LE POINT D'INJECTION, ARRÊTER IMMÉDIATEMENT LE TRAITEMENT PAR LE TIROFIBAN ET L'HÉPARINE.
- Pendant l'accès vasculaire, éviter de ponctionner la paroi postérieure de l'artère fémorale. Demander au patient de rester allongé et placer la tête du lit à un angle de 30°. Lui expliquer qu'il doit garder la jambe affectée tendue aussi longtemps que la gaine vasculaire est en place. Avant de retirer la gaine, on devrait interrompre l'administration de l'héparine pendant 3 à 4 heures; le temps de coagulation activée devrait être < 180 secondes ou le temps de céphaline activée < 45 secondes. Utiliser des méthodes de compression pour obtenir l'hémostase et surveiller attentivement le patient. L'hémostase devrait être maintenue pendant plus de 4 heures, avant que le patient ne puisse sortir de l'hôpital.
- Suivre les signes de thrombopénie (frissons, faible fièvre), pendant toute la durée du traitement.

Tests de laboratoire:

- Mesurer les concentrations d'hémoglobine et l'hématocrite et noter la numération plaquettaire avant d'amorcer le traitement par le tirofiban, dans les 6 heures qui suivent la perfusion d'attaque et au moins 1 fois par jour, pendant la durée du traitement (plus souvent si on observe une diminution de ces paramètres). Le tirofiban peut entraîner une diminution de l'hématocrite et des concentrations d'hémoglobine.
- Si le nombre de plaquettes diminue pour atteindre < 90×10^9/L, effectuer de nouveau une numération plaquettaire pour écarter la possibilité d'une pseudothrombopénie. Si la thrombopénie est confirmée,

on devrait interrompre l'administration du tirofiban et de l'héparine, observer étroitement le patient et lui administrer le traitement approprié.

- Pour suivre adéquatement le patient qui reçoit une perfusion à l'héparine non fractionnée, évaluer le temps de céphaline activée, 6 heures après le début de la perfusion. Adapter la dose d'héparine de façon à maintenir un temps de céphaline activée qui soit approximativement le double des valeurs normales.
- Lors de l'administration du tirofiban, on peut retrouver du sang occulte dans les urines et les fèces.

DIAGNOSTICS INFIRMIERS POSSIBLES

- Irrigation tissulaire inefficace (Indications).
- Connaissances insuffisantes sur le traitement médicamenteux (Enseignement au patient et à ses proches).

INTERVENTIONS INFIRMIÈRES

Alerte clinique: Des surdoses accidentelles d'inhibiteur des récepteurs des glycoprotéines IIb/IIIa ont causé des réactions indésirables graves ou des décès par hémorragie interne ou saignements intracrâniens. Avant l'administration, clarifier toutes les ambiguïtés sur l'ordonnance et faire vérifier l'ordonnance d'origine, les calculs de doses et la programmation de la pompe à perfusion par un autre professionnel de la santé.

- La plupart des patients reçoivent en même temps que le tirofiban de l'héparine et de l'aspirine.
- Ne pas administrer les solutions qui ont changé de couleur ou qui contiennent un précipité. Jeter toute portion inutilisée.

Perfusion intermittente:

- Pour ouvrir, déchirer l'enveloppe protectrice d'aluminium à partir de l'une des encoches situées sur les côtés, puis retirer le sac IntraVia. Si les parois du sac sont légèrement opaques, c'est qu'elles ont absorbé de l'humidité au cours de la stérilisation. Ce phénomène est normal et ne compromet nullement la qualité ni l'innocuité de la solution. L'opacité s'estompera graduellement. Comprimer fermement le sac pour vérifier s'il y a des fuites. Le cas échéant, jeter la solution, car elle n'est peut-être plus stérile. Ne pas utiliser la solution si elle n'est pas limpide ou si l'emballage n'est pas parfaitement étanche. Ne pas ajouter d'autres médicaments ni retirer de solution directement du sac au moyen d'une seringue.
- Jeter toute solution inutilisée.

Vitesse d'administration: Le débit est réglé en fonction du poids du patient. Administrer à un débit initial de 0,4 µg/kg/min pendant 30 minutes, puis continuer à un débit de 0,1 µg/kg/min.

Compatibilité (tubulure en Y): adrénaline ■ atropine ■ dobutamine ■ dopamine ■ famotidine ■ furosémide ■ héparine ■ lidocaïne ■ midazolam ■ morphine ■ nitroglycérine ■ potassium, chlorure de ■ propranolol.

ENSEIGNEMENT AU PATIENT ET À SES PROCHES

- Expliquer au patient le but du traitement par le tirofiban.
- Recommander au patient de prévenir immédiatement un professionnel de la santé en cas de saignement.

VÉRIFICATION DE L'EFFICACITÉ THÉRAPEUTIQUE

L'efficacité du traitement peut être démontrée par: l'inhibition de l'agrégation plaquettaire entraînant une incidence moindre de nouveaux IM, de décès ou d'ischémies rebelles, dictant le recours à des interventions cardiaques répétées. ✳

TIZANIDINE

Apo-Tizanidine, Gen-Tizanidine, Zanaflex

CLASSIFICATION:

Relaxant musculosquelettique (à action centrale), antispasmodique

Grossesse - catégorie C

INDICATIONS

Traitement de la spasticité associée à des maladies comme la sclérose en plaques ou à des lésions de la moelle épinière.

MÉCANISME D'ACTION

Effet agoniste au niveau des sites centraux des récepteurs alpha-adrénergiques ■ Diminution de la spasticité par augmentation de l'inhibition présynaptique des neurones moteurs. ***Effets thérapeutiques:*** Soulagement de la spasticité favorisant un meilleur fonctionnement moteur.

PHARMACOCINÉTIQUE

Absorption: Bonne (PO). Biodisponibilité à 40 % (PO) en raison d'un important métabolisme de premier passage hépatique.

Distribution: Tout l'organisme.

Métabolisme et excrétion: Métabolisme majoritairement hépatique (95 %).

Demi-vie: 2,5 heures.

Profil temps-action (réduction du tonus musculaire)

	Début d'action	Pic	Durée
PO	inconnu	1-2 h	3-6 h

CONTRE-INDICATIONS, PRÉCAUTIONS ET MISES EN GARDE

Contre-indications: Hypersensibilité.

Précautions et mises en garde: Insuffisance rénale ■ Personnes âgées ■ Traitement antihypertenseur concomitant ■ **Obst., allaitement, péd.:** L'innocuité du médicament n'a pas été établie.

Extrême prudence: Dysfonctionnement hépatique.

RÉACTIONS INDÉSIRABLES ET EFFETS SECONDAIRES

SNC: anxiété, dépression, étourdissements, somnolence, faiblesse, dyskinésie, hallucinations, nervosité.

ORLO: vision trouble, pharyngite, rhinite.

CV: hypotension, bradycardie.

GI: douleurs abdominales, diarrhée, sécheresse de la bouche (xérostomie), dyspepsie, constipation, lésions hépatocellulaires, concentrations accrues d'enzymes hépatiques, vomissements.

GU: mictions fréquentes.

Tég.: rash, ulcération de la peau, transpiration.

Loc.: douleurs lombaires, myasthénie, paresthésie.

Divers: fièvre, troubles d'élocution.

INTERACTIONS

Médicament-médicament: Les concentrations sanguines de tizanidine et les effets du médicament peuvent être accrus lors de la prise concomitante de **contraceptifs oraux** ou d'**alcool** ■ Risque de dépression additive du SNC lors de l'ingestion concomitante d'**alcool** ou de la prise d'autres **dépresseurs du SNC**, incluant certains **antidépresseurs**, les **hypnosédatifs**, les **antihistaminiques** et les **opioïdes** ■ Risque accru d'hypotension ou d'hypotension orthostatique lors de la prise concomitante d'**agents antihypertenseurs**.

T

VOIES D'ADMINISTRATION ET POSOLOGIE

- **PO (adultes):** Initialement, 4 mg, toutes les 6 à 8 heures (ne pas dépasser 3 doses en 24 heures); augmenter graduellement de 2 à 4 mg par dose pendant 2 à 4 semaines jusqu'à concurrence de 8 mg par dose ou de 24 mg par jour (ne pas dépasser 36 mg par jour).

PRÉSENTATION

Comprimés: 4 mg[Pr].

SOINS INFIRMIERS

ÉVALUATION DE LA SITUATION

- Noter le degré de spasticité musculaire avant le début du traitement et à intervalles réguliers pendant toute sa durée.
- Mesurer la pression artérielle et le pouls, particulièrement pendant la période d'adaptation de la posologie. La tizanidine peut entraîner l'hypotension orthostatique, la bradycardie, des étourdissements et, rarement, la syncope. Les effets sont habituellement reliés à la dose.
- Suivre de près la somnolence, les étourdissements et l'asthénie (faiblesse, fatigue et/ou lassitude). Une modification de la dose peut soulager ces troubles.

Tests de laboratoire: Noter les résultats des tests de la fonction hépatique avant l'administration du médicament et après 1, 3 et 6 mois de traitement. La tizanidine peut entraîner l'élévation de la glycémie et des concentrations sériques de phosphatase alcaline, d'AST et d'ALT.

DIAGNOSTICS INFIRMIERS POSSIBLES

- Mobilité physique réduite (Indications).
- Risque d'accident (Réactions indésirables).
- Connaissances insuffisantes sur le traitement médicamenteux (Enseignement au patient et à ses proches).

INTERVENTIONS INFIRMIÈRES

- Pour prévenir les effets secondaires, les doses devraient être majorées avec prudence.
- La tizanidine peut être prise sans égard aux repas.

ENSEIGNEMENT AU PATIENT ET À SES PROCHES

- Expliquer au patient qu'il doit respecter rigoureusement la posologie recommandée. Le traitement par la tizanidine devrait être arrêté graduellement.
- Prévenir le patient que la tizanidine peut parfois provoquer des étourdissements et de la somnolence; lui conseiller de ne pas conduire et d'éviter les activités qui exigent sa vigilance jusqu'à ce qu'on ait la certitude que le médicament n'entraîne pas ces effets chez lui.
- Recommander au patient de changer lentement de position afin de diminuer le risque d'hypotension orthostatique.
- Recommander au patient d'éviter de boire de l'alcool ou de prendre d'autres dépresseurs du SNC en même temps que la tizanidine.

VÉRIFICATION DE L'EFFICACITÉ THÉRAPEUTIQUE

L'efficacité du traitement peut être démontrée par: la diminution de la spasticité musculaire, accompagnée d'une capacité accrue de mener à bien les activités de la vie quotidienne.

TOBRAMYCINE,
voir Aminosides

TOLBUTAMIDE,
voir Hypoglycémiants (oraux)

TOLMÉTINE

Novo-Tolmetin, Tolectin

CLASSIFICATION:

Anti-inflammatoire non stéroïdien, analgésique non opioïde.

Grossesse – catégories D (1er et 3e trimestres) et B (2e trimestre)

INDICATIONS

Traitement des troubles inflammatoires dont ■ la polyarthrite rhumatoïde ■ la polyarthrite juvénile ■ l'arthrose ■ la spondylarthrite ankylosante.

MÉCANISME D'ACTION

Inhibition de la synthèse des prostaglandines. ***Effets thérapeutiques:*** Suppression de la douleur et de l'inflammation.

PHARMACOCINÉTIQUE

Absorption: Bonne (PO).
Distribution: Inconnue.
Liaison aux protéines: > 99 %.
Métabolisme et excrétion: Métabolisme majoritairement hépatique. Excrétion rénale (20 % sous forme inchangée).
Demi-vie: 1 heure.

Profil temps-action (effets anti-inflammatoires)

	DÉBUT D'ACTION	PIC	DURÉE
PO	en l'espace de 7 jours	1 – 2 semaines	inconnue

CONTRE-INDICATIONS, PRÉCAUTIONS ET MISES EN GARDE

Contre-indications: Hypersensibilité ■ Risque d'hypersensibilité croisée avec d'autres anti-inflammatoires non stéroïdiens, dont l'aspirine ■ Contexte périopératoire en cas de pontage aortocoronarien ■ Hémorragie digestive, ulcère en poussée évolutive ou autre affection inflammatoire évolutive du système digestif.

Précautions et mises en garde: Maladie cardiovasculaire ou facteurs de risque de maladies cardiovasculaires (risque accru de complications coronariennes, d'infarctus du myocarde ou d'accidents vasculaires cérébraux, surtout lors d'un usage prolongé) ■ Maladies rénale ou hépatique graves ■ Antécédents d'ulcère ■ Insuffisance hépatique ou rénale grave (il est recommandé de réduire la dose) ■ **GÉR.:** Les personnes âgées sont davantage prédisposées aux saignements gastro-intestinaux ■ **OBST., ALLAITEMENT:** L'innocuité du médicament n'a pas été établie; en éviter l'administration au cours de la deuxième moitié de la grossesse.

RÉACTIONS INDÉSIRABLES ET EFFETS SECONDAIRES

SNC: étourdissements, céphalées, somnolence, dépression, troubles du sommeil.
ORLO: acouphènes, troubles de la vision.
CV: œdème, hypertension.
GI: HÉPATITE MÉDICAMENTEUSE, HÉMORRAGIE DIGESTIVE, diarrhée, gêne gastrique, dyspepsie, nausées, vomissements, constipation, flatulence.
GU: insuffisance rénale.
Tég.: DERMATITE EXFOLIATIVE, SYNDROME DE STEVENS-JOHNSON, ÉPIDERMOLYSE NÉCROSANTE SUBAIGUË, rash.
Hémat.: allongement du temps de saignement.
Loc.: faiblesse musculaire.
Divers: réactions allergiques incluant l'ANAPHYLAXIE.

INTERACTIONS

Médicament-médicament: Risque accru d'hémorragie lors de l'usage concomitant de **warfarine**, d'**héparine** ou d'**héparinoïdes**, de **céfamandole**, de **céfopérazone**, de **céfotétane**, d'**acide valproïque**, d'**agents thrombolytiques**, de **clopidogrel**, de **ticlopidine**, d'**abciximab**, de **tirofiban**, d'**eptifibatide** ou de **plicamycine** ■ Effets nocifs additifs sur le tractus gastro-intestinal lors de l'usage concomitant d'**aspirine**, de **corticostéroïdes** et d'autres **AINS** ■ La tolmétine peut diminuer la réponse aux **antihypertenseurs** ou aux **diurétiques** ■ La tolmétine peut élever les concentrations sériques de **lithium** et le risque de toxicité associé à cet agent ■ Les **antinéoplasiques** ou la **radiothérapie**, administrés en concomitance, peuvent augmenter le risque de toxicité hématologique ■ Risque accru d'effets nocifs sur les reins lors de l'administration de **sels d'or** ou de **cyclosporine** ou lors de l'usage prolongé d'**acétaminophène** ■ Risque accru d'hypoglycémie lors de l'usage concomitant d'**insuline** ou d'**hypoglycémiants oraux**.

Médicament-produits naturels: Risque accru de saignements en cas de la consommation concomitante **d'ail**, d'**anis**, d'**arnica**, de **camomille**, de **dong quai**, de **girofle**, de **gingembre**, de **ginkgo** et de **ginseng**.

VOIES D'ADMINISTRATION ET POSOLOGIE

Polyarthrite rhumatoïde et spondylarthrite ankylosante

- **PO (adultes)**: Initialement, 400 mg, 3 fois par jour, puis une dose d'entretien de 600 à 1 800 mg par jour, en 3 ou 4 prises fractionnées (ne pas dépasser 2 000 mg par jour).
- **PO (enfants > 2 ans)**: Initialement, 20 mg/kg/jour, en 3 ou 4 prises fractionnées, puis une dose d'entretien de 15 à 30 mg/kg/jour, en 3 ou 4 prises fractionnées.

Arthrose

- **PO (adultes)**: Initialement, de 800 à 1 200 mg par jour, en 3 ou 4 prises fractionnées; la dose d'entretien se situe entre 600 et 1 600 mg par jour, en 3 ou 4 prises fractionnées.

PRÉSENTATION
(version générique disponible)

Comprimés: 600 mg[Pr] ■ **Capsules**: 400 mg[Pr].

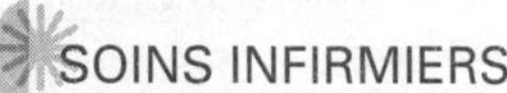

SOINS INFIRMIERS

ÉVALUATION DE LA SITUATION

- LES PATIENTS SOUFFRANT D'ASTHME, D'ALLERGIE INDUITE PAR L'ASPIRINE OU DE POLYPES NASAUX SONT DAVANTAGE PRÉDISPOSÉS AUX RÉACTIONS D'HYPERSENSIBILITÉ. SUIVRE DE PRÈS LA RHINITE, L'ASTHME ET L'URTICAIRE.
- Suivre de près la douleur et examiner la mobilité des articulations avant l'administration de la tolmétine et toutes les semaines, tout au long du traitement.

Tests de laboratoire:

- Chez les patients qui suivent un traitement prolongé, examiner à intervalles réguliers les résultats des tests de la fonction hépatique, la numération globulaire, les concentrations d'urée et de créatinine sérique.
- La tolmétine peut entraîner l'élévation des concentrations sériques de potassium, d'urée, d'AST et d'ALT.
- La tolmétine peut diminuer l'hématocrite et les concentrations d'hémoglobine. Elle peut également allonger le temps de saignement pendant une période allant jusqu'à 2 jours après l'arrêt du traitement.
- La tolmétine peut entraîner des résultats faussement positifs au dosage des protéines urinaires.

DIAGNOSTICS INFIRMIERS POSSIBLES

- Douleur aiguë (Indications).
- Mobilité physique réduite (Indications).
- Connaissances insuffisantes sur le traitement médicamenteux (Enseignement au patient et à ses proches).

INTERVENTIONS INFIRMIÈRES

- L'administration de doses plus élevées que celles recommandées n'accroît pas l'efficacité du médicament, mais peut en intensifier les effets secondaires.
- On peut administrer la tolmétine avec des aliments, du lait ou des antiacides pour diminuer l'irritation gastrique. On peut écraser les comprimés ou ouvrir les capsules, et les mélanger avec des liquides ou des aliments.

ENSEIGNEMENT AU PATIENT ET À SES PROCHES

- Conseiller au patient de prendre la tolmétine avec un grand verre d'eau et de ne pas se coucher pendant 15 à 30 minutes.
- Conseiller au patient de respecter rigoureusement la posologie recommandée. S'il n'a pu prendre le médicament au moment habituel, il doit le faire dès que possible à moins que ce ne soit presque l'heure prévue pour la dose suivante. Le prévenir qu'il ne doit jamais remplacer une dose manquée par une double dose.
- Prévenir le patient que la tolmétine peut parfois provoquer de la somnolence ou des étourdissements. Lui conseiller de ne pas conduire et d'éviter les activités qui exigent sa vigilance jusqu'à ce qu'on ait la certitude que le médicament n'entraîne pas ces effets chez lui.
- Recommander au patient d'éviter de boire de l'alcool pendant toute la durée du traitement et de consulter un professionnel de la santé avant de prendre de l'aspirine, un AINS, de l'acétaminophène, d'autres médicaments en vente libre ou des produits naturels, en même temps que la tolmétine.
- Conseiller au patient d'utiliser un écran solaire et de porter des vêtements protecteurs pour prévenir les réactions de photosensibilité.
- Recommander au patient qui doit suivre un traitement ou subir une intervention chirurgicale d'avertir le professionnel de la santé qu'il suit un traitement par ce médicament.
- Recommander au patient de consulter un professionnel de la santé en cas de rash, de démangeaisons, de troubles visuels, d'acouphènes, de gain pondéral, d'œdème, de selles noires, de céphalées persistantes ou d'un syndrome pseudogrippal (frissons, fièvre, douleurs musculaires, douleurs).

T

VÉRIFICATION DE L'EFFICACITÉ THÉRAPEUTIQUE

L'efficacité du traitement peut être démontrée par: la diminution de la douleur ▪ l'amélioration de la mobilité des articulations. On observe habituellement un soulagement partiel de l'arthrite en l'espace de 7 jours, mais le plein effet du médicament peut ne se manifester qu'après 1 ou 2 semaines de traitement ininterrompu. Les patients qui ne répondent pas à un anti-inflammatoire non stéroïdien peuvent répondre à un autre. ✳

TOLNAFTATE,
voir Antifongiques topiques

TOLTÉRODINE

Detrol, Detrol LA

CLASSIFICATION:
Anticholinergique (antispasmodique urinaire)

Grossesse – catégorie C

INDICATIONS

Traitement des symptômes associés à une vessie hyperactive, se manifestant sous la forme de mictions fréquentes, de mictions impérieuses, d'incontinence urinaire par besoin impérieux ou d'une combinaison de ces symptômes.

MÉCANISME D'ACTION

Action compétitive à titre d'antagoniste des récepteurs muscariniques, entraînant l'inhibition des contractions de la vessie par médiation cholinergique. ***Effets thérapeutiques:*** Diminution du besoin impérieux d'uriner, de la fréquence des mictions et des épisodes d'incontinence.

PHARMACOCINÉTIQUE

Absorption: 77 % (PO).

Distribution: Inconnue.

Liaison aux protéines: 96,3 %.

Métabolisme et excrétion: Métabolisme hépatique important; l'un des métabolites (5-hydroxyméthyltoltérodine) est actif, les autres sont excrétés dans l'urine.

Demi-vie: *Toltérodine* – de 1,9 à 3,7 heures; *5-hydroxyméthyltoltérodine* – de 2,9 à 3,1 heures.

Profil temps-action (effet sur le fonctionnement de la vessie)

	DÉBUT D'ACTION	PIC	DURÉE
PO	inconnu	inconnu	12 h (24 h pour les capsules à action prolongée)

CONTRE-INDICATIONS, PRÉCAUTIONS ET MISES EN GARDE

Contre-indications: Hypersensibilité ▪ Rétention urinaire ▪ Rétention gastrique ▪ Glaucome à angle fermé non corrigé.

Précautions et mises en garde: Troubles reliés à l'occlusion gastro-intestinale incluant la sténose du pylore (risque accru de rétention gastrique) ▪ Occlusion importante de l'écoulement de l'urine (risque accru de rétention urinaire) ▪ Glaucome à angle fermé corrigé ▪ Insuffisance hépatique grave (il est recommandé d'administrer des doses plus faibles) ▪ Dysfonctionnement rénal ▪ **OBST.:** L'innocuité du médicament n'a pas été établie; ne l'administrer que si les bienfaits pour la mère justifient les risques pour le fœtus ▪ Allaitement ▪ **PÉD.:** L'innocuité du médicament n'a pas été établie ▪ Allongement de l'intervalle QT.

RÉACTIONS INDÉSIRABLES ET EFFETS SECONDAIRES

SNC: céphalées, étourdissements.

ORLO: vision trouble, xérophtalmie.

GI: sécheresse de la bouche (xérostomie), constipation, dyspepsie.

INTERACTIONS

Médicament-médicament: L'**érythromycine**, la **clarithromycine**, le **kétoconazole**, l'**itraconazole**, la **cyclosporine** et le **miconazole**, administrés en concomitance, peuvent inhiber le métabolisme et augmenter les effets de la toltérodine ▪ Les **médicaments pouvant allonger l'intervalle QT**, pris en concomitance, peuvent augmenter le risque d'arythmies.

VOIES D'ADMINISTRATION ET POSOLOGIE

- **PO (adultes):** 2 mg, 2 fois par jour (préparation ordinaire); 4 mg, 1 fois par jour (préparation à action prolongée); on peut réduire la dose selon la réponse du patient.
- **PO (adultes atteints de dysfonctionnement hépatique ou rénal ou recevant un traitement concomitant par des inhibiteurs enzymatiques):** 1 mg, 2 fois par jour (préparation ordinaire); 2 mg, 1 fois par jour (préparation à action prolongée).

PRÉSENTATION

Comprimés: 1 mg[Pr], 2 mg[Pr] ■ **Capsules à action prolongée:** 2 mg[Pr], 4 mg[Pr].

ÉVALUATION DE LA SITUATION

- Suivre à intervalles réguliers pendant toute la durée du traitement les mictions impérieuses, les mictions fréquentes et l'incontinence urinaire par besoin impérieux.

DIAGNOSTICS INFIRMIERS POSSIBLES

- Élimination urinaire altérée (Indications).
- Incontinence urinaire par besoin impérieux (Indications).
- Connaissances insuffisantes sur le traitement médicamenteux (Enseignement au patient et à ses proches).

INTERVENTIONS INFIRMIÈRES

- Administrer la toltérodine sans égard aux repas.
- LES CAPSULES À ACTION PROLONGÉE DOIVENT ÊTRE AVALÉES TELLES QUELLES, SANS ÊTRE OUVERTES OU MÂCHÉES.

ENSEIGNEMENT AU PATIENT ET À SES PROCHES

- Conseiller au patient de respecter rigoureusement la posologie recommandée.
- Prévenir le patient que la toltérodine peut provoquer des étourdissements et rendre la vision trouble. Lui conseiller de ne pas conduire et d'éviter les activités qui exigent sa vigilance jusqu'à ce qu'on ait la certitude que le médicament n'entraîne pas ces effets chez lui.

VÉRIFICATION DE L'EFFICACITÉ THÉRAPEUTIQUE

L'efficacité du traitement peut être démontrée par: la diminution de la fréquence des mictions, des mictions impérieuses et de l'incontinence urinaire par besoin impérieux.

TOPIRAMATE

Apo-Topiramate, Gen-Topiramate, Novo-Topiramate, PMS-Topiramate, Topamax

CLASSIFICATION:

Anticonvulsivant

Grossesse – catégorie C

INDICATIONS

Traitement en monothérapie des patients (adultes et enfants ≥ 6 ans) atteints d'une épilepsie de diagnostic récent ■ Traitement adjuvant chez les patients (adultes et enfants ≥ 2 ans) atteints d'épilepsie, dont l'état n'est pas maîtrisé de façon satisfaisante par un traitement classique ■ Prophylaxie de la migraine chez l'adulte.

MÉCANISME D'ACTION

L'action de l'agent peut être attribuable: au blocage des canaux sodiques situés dans les neurones ■ à la stimulation de l'activité de l'acide gamma-aminobutyrique (GABA), un neurotransmetteur inhibiteur ■ à la prévention de l'activation des récepteurs excitateurs. ***Effets thérapeutiques:*** Diminution de la fréquence des crises.

PHARMACOCINÉTIQUE

Absorption: Bonne (80 %).

Distribution: Inconnue.

Métabolisme et excrétion: Excrétion majoritairement rénale (70 % sous forme inchangée).

Demi-vie: 21 heures.

Profil temps-action†

	DÉBUT D'ACTION	PIC	DURÉE
PO	inconnu	2 h	12 h

† Après une seule dose.

CONTRE-INDICATIONS, PRÉCAUTIONS ET MISES EN GARDE

Contre-indications: Hypersensibilité.

Précautions et mises en garde: Insuffisance rénale (il est recommandé de réduire la dose si la Cl_{Cr} est < 70 mL/min/1,73 m^2) ■ Insuffisance hépatique ■ Déshydratation ■ **OBST., ALLAITEMENT, PÉD. (enfants < 2 ans):** L'innocuité du médicament n'a pas été établie ■ **GÉR.:** Commencer le traitement à faible dose et surveiller la fonction rénale.

RÉACTIONS INDÉSIRABLES ET EFFETS SECONDAIRES

SNC: FRÉQUENCE ACCRUE DES CRISES ÉPILEPTIQUES, étourdissements, somnolence, fatigue, altération de la concentration et perte de mémoire, nervosité, ralentissement psychomoteur, troubles d'élocution, agressivité, agitation, anxiété, troubles cognitifs, confusion, dépression, malaises, troubles thymiques.

ORLO: vision anormale, diplopie, nystagmus, myopie aiguë et glaucome secondaire à angle fermé.

GI: nausées, douleurs abdominales, anorexie, constipation, sécheresse de la bouche (xérostomie).

GU: calculs rénaux.

Tég.: oligohydrose (diminution de la transpiration), surtout chez les enfants.
Hémat.: leucopénie.
Métab.: perte de poids, hyperthermie (surtout chez les enfants).
SN: ataxie, paresthésie, tremblements.
Divers: TENTATIVES DE SUICIDE, fièvre.

INTERACTIONS

Médicament-médicament: La **phénytoïne**, la **carbamazépine** ou l'**acide valproïque**, administrés en concomitance, diminuent les concentrations sanguines de topiramate et en réduisent les effets ■ Le topiramate peut élever les concentrations sanguines de **phénytoïne** et en intensifier les effets ■ Le topiramate peut abaisser les concentrations sanguines des **contraceptifs oraux** et en diminuer les effets ■ Risque accru de dépression du SNC lors de l'ingestion d'**alcool** ou de la prise concomitante d'autres **dépresseurs du SNC** ■ L'utilisation concomitante d'**inhibiteurs de l'anhydrase carbonique** (**acétazolamide**) peut élever le risque de formation de calculs rénaux ■ L'administration concomitante de topiramate et d'**acide valproïque** peut augmenter le risque d'encéphalopathie avec ou sans hyperammoniémie.

VOIES D'ADMINISTRATION ET POSOLOGIE

Épilepsie (monothérapie)

- **PO (adultes et enfants ≥ 6 ans)**: Initialement, 25 mg par jour; majorer graduellement la dose hebdomadairement, à raison de 25 mg/jour, jusqu'à concurrence de 50 mg, 2 fois par jour (ne pas dépasser 400 mg par jour).

Épilepsie (adjuvant)

- **PO (adultes et enfants ≥ 17 ans)**: Initialement, 50 mg par jour; majorer graduellement la dose hebdomadairement, à raison de 50 mg/jour, jusqu'à concurrence de 200 mg, 2 fois par jour (ne pas dépasser 800 mg par jour).
- **PO (enfants de 2 à 16 ans)**: De 5 à 9 mg/kg/jour en 2 doses fractionnées; amorcer le traitement par 1 dose de 25 mg (moindre si l'on administre de 1 à 3 mg/kg), le soir, pendant 7 jours, puis augmenter par paliers de 1 à 3 mg/kg par jour, en 2 prises fractionnées, à des intervalles de 1 ou 2 semaines; l'adaptation de la posologie devrait être fondée sur les résultats cliniques.

Migraine (prophylaxie)

- **PO (adultes)**: Amorcer le traitement par 1 dose de 25 mg, le soir, pendant 7 jours, puis augmenter par paliers de 25 mg, en 2 prises fractionnées, à des intervalles de 1 semaine jusqu'à concurrence de 50 mg, 2 fois par jour (ne pas dépasser 100 mg par jour).

INSUFFISANCE RÉNALE

- **PO (ADULTES)**: CL_{CR} < *70 mL/MIN* – 50 % DE LA DOSE HABITUELLE.

PRÉSENTATION

Capsules à saupoudrer: 15 mg[Pr], 25 mg[Pr] ■ **Comprimés**: 25 mg[Pr], 100 mg[Pr], 200 mg[Pr].

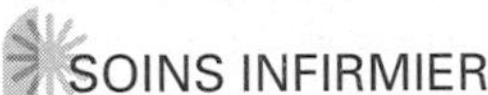

SOINS INFIRMIERS

ÉVALUATION DE LA SITUATION

Épilepsie: Déterminer le siège, la durée et les caractéristiques des convulsions.
Migraine: Déterminer le siège, l'intensité et la durée de la douleur lors d'une crise de migraine et les symptômes qui sont reliés (photophobie, phonophobie, nausées, vomissements).

Tests de laboratoire:

- Suivre de près la numération globulaire; examiner la formule leucocytaire et la numération plaquettaire avant l'administration du médicament, afin de déterminer les valeurs initiales, et à intervalles réguliers pendant toute la durée du traitement. Le topiramate induit souvent l'anémie.
- Noter les résultats des tests de la fonction hépatique à intervalles réguliers pendant toute la durée du traitement. Le topiramate peut entraîner l'élévation des concentrations d'AST et d'ALT.
- Mesurer le taux sérique de bicarbonate au départ et à intervalles réguliers tout au long du traitement. Si une acidose métabolique apparaît et persiste, on devrait envisager de réduire la dose ou d'arrêter de façon graduelle le traitement par le topiramate.

T

DIAGNOSTICS INFIRMIERS POSSIBLES

- Risque d'accident (Indications, Effets secondaires).
- Connaissances insuffisantes sur le traitement médicamenteux (Enseignement au patient et à ses proches).

INTERVENTIONS INFIRMIÈRES

- Prendre les précautions de mise en cas de crises épileptiques.
- On peut administrer le topiramate sans égard aux repas.
- Ne pas briser les comprimés car ils ont un goût amer.
- Le contenu des capsules peut être saupoudré sur une petite quantité (une cuillerée à thé) d'aliments mous,

comme la compote de pommes, la crème anglaise, la crème glacée, le gruau, le pouding ou le yogourt. Pour ouvrir la capsule, la tenir en position verticale de façon à ce que le mot «TOP» puisse être lu. Dévisser délicatement la partie transparente de la capsule. Il est préférable d'effectuer cette opération au-dessus de l'aliment choisi; saupoudrer tout le contenu de la capsule. S'assurer que le patient avale tout le contenu de la cuiller, sans mâcher, et qu'il boit tout de suite après des liquides afin que tout le mélange soit avalé. Ne jamais conserver ce mélange en vue d'une utilisation ultérieure.

ENSEIGNEMENT AU PATIENT ET À SES PROCHES

- Expliquer au patient qu'il doit prendre le topiramate en suivant rigoureusement la posologie recommandée. S'il n'a pu prendre le médicament au moment habituel, il doit le prendre aussitôt que possible, sauf s'il est presque l'heure prévue pour la dose suivante. Le prévenir qu'il ne doit jamais remplacer une dose manquée par une double dose et qu'il doit informer un professionnel de la santé s'il n'a pu prendre plus de 1 dose. Le sevrage devrait être graduel afin d'éviter les convulsions et l'état de mal épileptique.
- Expliquer au patient et aux parents, s'il s'agit d'un enfant, qu'il faut surveiller les signes de diminution de la transpiration et d'augmentation de la température corporelle, surtout par temps chaud. Recommander une hydratation adéquate avant et pendant des activités telles que l'exercice physique ou l'exposition à la chaleur.
- Prévenir le patient que le topiramate peut provoquer des étourdissements, de la somnolence, de la confusion et des difficultés de concentration. Lui conseiller de ne pas conduire et d'éviter les activités qui exigent sa vigilance jusqu'à ce qu'on ait la certitude que le médicament n'entraîne pas ces effets chez lui.
- Recommander au patient de maintenir un apport hydrique de 2 000 à 3 000 mL par jour pour prévenir la formation de calculs rénaux.
- Prévenir le patient qu'il doit informer un professionnel de la santé immédiatement si une diminution rapide de l'acuité visuelle et/ou une douleur oculaire se présentent. Le traitement par le topiramate devrait être interrompu le plus rapidement possible, si le médecin traitant le juge nécessaire. Faute d'une prise en charge adéquate, les conséquences peuvent être graves, notamment la perte permanente de la vue.
- Recommander au patient de changer lentement de position pour diminuer le risque d'hypotension orthostatique.
- Recommander au patient d'éviter de boire de l'alcool ou de prendre d'autres dépresseurs du SNC en même temps que le topiramate.
- Recommander à la patiente d'utiliser une méthode contraceptive non hormonale pendant qu'elle suit le traitement par le topiramate.
- Recommander au patient qui doit suivre un autre traitement ou subir une intervention chirurgicale d'avertir le professionnel de la santé qu'il suit un traitement par ce médicament.
- Conseiller au patient d'utiliser un écran solaire et de porter des vêtements protecteurs pour prévenir les réactions de photosensibilité.
- Conseiller au patient de porter sur lui en tout temps un bracelet d'identité où sont inscrits son problème de santé et son traitement médicamenteux.

VÉRIFICATION DE L'EFFICACITÉ THÉRAPEUTIQUE

L'efficacité du traitement peut être démontrée par: la suppression des convulsions ou la réduction de leur fréquence. ✳

ALERTE CLINIQUE

TOPOTÉCAN

Hycamtin

CLASSIFICATION:

Antinéoplasique (inhibiteur enzymatique)

Grossesse – catégorie D

INDICATIONS

Traitement du cancer métastatique des ovaires n'ayant pas répondu à une chimiothérapie antérieure ▪ Traitement du cancer du poumon non à petites cellules n'ayant pas répondu au traitement de première intention.

MÉCANISME D'ACTION

Altération de la synthèse de l'ADN par inhibition de l'enzyme topoisomérase. ***Effets thérapeutiques:*** Destruction des cellules à réplication rapide, particulièrement des cellules malignes.

PHARMACOCINÉTIQUE

Absorption: Biodisponibilité à 100 % (IV).
Distribution: Inconnue.

Métabolisme et excrétion: Excrétion rénale (de 20 à 60 %) et biliaire; de petites quantités sont métabolisées par le foie.

Demi-vie: De 2 à 3 heures.

Profil temps-action (effet sur la numération leucocytaire)

	DÉBUT D'ACTION	PIC	DURÉE
IV	en l'espace de quelques jours	12 jours	7 jours

CONTRE-INDICATIONS, PRÉCAUTIONS ET MISES EN GARDE

Contre-indications: Hypersensibilité ■ Grossesse ou allaitement ■ Aplasie médullaire grave préexistante (neutrophiles < 1,5 × 10^9/L ou plaquettes < 100 × 10^9/L) ■ Insuffisance rénale grave (Cl_{Cr} < 20 mL/min) ■ **PÉD.**: L'innocuité et l'efficacité du médicament n'ont pas été établies.

Précautions et mises en garde: Dysfonctionnement rénal (il est recommandé de réduire la dose si la Cl_{Cr} est < 40 mL/min) ■ Femmes en âge de procréer.

RÉACTIONS INDÉSIRABLES ET EFFETS SECONDAIRES

SNC: céphalées, fatigue, faiblesse.

Resp.: dyspnée.

GI: douleurs abdominales, diarrhée, nausées, vomissements, anorexie, constipation, concentrations accrues d'enzymes hépatiques, stomatite.

Tég.: alopécie.

SN: paresthésies.

Hémat.: anémie, leucopénie, thrombopénie.

Loc.: arthralgie, réactions d'hypersensibilité.

INTERACTIONS

Médicament-médicament: La neutropénie est prolongée lors de l'administration concomitante de **filgrastim** (ne pas administrer avant le 6ᵉ jour de traitement; attendre 24 heures après l'arrêt du traitement par le topotécan) ■ Aplasie médullaire additive lors de l'administration d'autres **antinéoplasiques** (particulièrement, le **cisplatine**) ou d'une **radiothérapie** ■ Risque de diminution de la réponse des anticorps aux **vaccins à virus vivants** et risque accru de réactions indésirables.

VOIES D'ADMINISTRATION ET POSOLOGIE

- **IV (adultes):** 1,5 mg/m²/jour, pendant 5 jours, toutes les 3 semaines.

INSUFFISANCE RÉNALE

- **IV (ADULTES):** *Cl_{CR} DE 20 À 39 mL/MIN* – 0,75 mg/m²/JOUR, PENDANT 5 JOURS, TOUTES LES 3 SEMAINES.

PRÉSENTATION

Poudre lyophilisée pour injection: 4 mg/fiole[Pr].

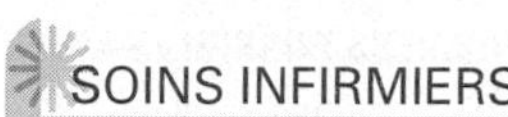

SOINS INFIRMIERS

ÉVALUATION DE LA SITUATION

- Prendre les signes vitaux à intervalles fréquents tout au long de l'administration.
- Déceler l'apparition d'une aplasie médullaire. Suivre de près les saignements (saignement des gencives, formation d'ecchymoses, pétéchies, présence de sang occulte dans les selles, l'urine et les vomissements). Éviter les injections IM et la prise de la température par voie rectale si le nombre de plaquettes est bas. Appliquer une pression sur les points de ponction veineuse pendant 10 minutes. Évaluer les signes d'infection en présence d'une neutropénie. Une anémie peut survenir. Suivre de près la fatigue accrue, la dyspnée et l'hypotension orthostatique.
- Le topotécan entraîne souvent des nausées et des vomissements. On devrait envisager l'administration en prophylaxie d'un antiémétique.
- Observer fréquemment les points d'injection IV pour déceler les signes d'extravasation pouvant entraîner un léger érythème et des ecchymoses.

Tests de laboratoire:

- Suivre de près la numération globulaire, la formule leucocytaire et la numération plaquettaire, avant l'administration du médicament et à intervalles fréquents pendant toute la durée du traitement. Avant d'administrer la première dose, le nombre de polynucléaires neutrophiles doit être ≥ 1,5 × 10^9/L, et celui des plaquettes, ≥ 100 × 10^9/L. Le nadir de la neutropénie se produit en l'espace de 12 jours et dure 7 jours. Le nadir de la thrombopénie se produit en l'espace de 15 jours et dure 5 jours. Le nadir de l'anémie se produit en l'espace de 15 jours. Ne pas administrer de doses ultérieures tant que le nombre de polynucléaires neutrophiles n'est pas revenu à une valeur > 1 × 10^9/L, que le nombre de plaquettes n'est pas > 100 × 10^9/L et que les concentrations d'hémoglobine n'ont pas atteint 90 g/L. Si une neutropénie grave survient au cours d'un cycle, on devrait réduire les doses administrées par la suite de 0,25 mg/m² ou on peut administrer du filgrastim après la cure suivante, en commençant le 6ᵉ jour, 24 heures après avoir arrêté le traitement par le topotécan.

- Noter les résultats des tests de la fonction hépatique. Le topotécan peut élever passagèrement les concentrations d'AST, d'ALT et de bilirubine.

DIAGNOSTICS INFIRMIERS POSSIBLES

- Risque d'infection (Réactions indésirables).
- Connaissances insuffisantes sur le traitement médicamenteux (Enseignement au patient et à ses proches).

INTERVENTIONS INFIRMIÈRES

- **ALERTE CLINIQUE:** DES DÉCÈS SONT SURVENUS LORS DE CERTAINES CHIMIOTHÉRAPIES. AVANT D'ADMINISTRER L'AGENT, CLARIFIER TOUS LES POINTS AMBIGUS. VÉRIFIER UNE FOIS DE PLUS LA LIMITE DES DOSES UNITAIRES ET QUOTIDIENNES AINSI QUE CELLE DES DOSES À ADMINISTRER PENDANT LE TRAITEMENT. DEMANDER À UN AUTRE PROFESSIONNEL DE LA SANTÉ DE VÉRIFIER L'ORDONNANCE D'ORIGINE, LE CALCUL DES DOSES ET LE RÉGLAGE DE LA POMPE À PERFUSION.
- Préparer la solution sous une hotte à flux laminaire. Porter un masque, un vêtement protecteur et des gants pendant la manipulation de ce médicament. Mettre au rebut le matériel dans des contenants réservés à cette fin (voir l'annexe H).

Perfusion intermittente: Reconstituer le contenu de chaque fiole avec 4 mL d'eau stérile pour injection. Diluer de nouveau avec 50 à 100 mL d'une solution de NaCl 0,9 % ou de D5%E pour obtenir une concentration se situant entre 20 et 500 µg/mL. Utiliser la solution immédiatement après l'avoir préparée. Elle est de couleur jaune à jaune-vert. Elle est stable pendant 24 heures au réfrigérateur. Consulter les directives de chaque fabricant avant de reconstituer la préparation. ***Vitesse d'administration:*** Administrer la dose en 30 minutes.

Incompatibilité en addition au soluté: On ne dispose d'aucune donnée à cet égard. Ne pas mélanger avec d'autres solutions ou médicaments.

T

ENSEIGNEMENT AU PATIENT ET À SES PROCHES

- Conseiller au patient de signaler à un professionnel de la santé les symptômes suivants: fièvre, frissons, maux de gorge, signes d'infection, saignement des gencives, formation d'ecchymoses, pétéchies ou présence de sang dans les urines, les selles ou les vomissements. L'inciter à éviter les foules et les personnes contagieuses. Lui recommander d'utiliser une brosse à dents à poils doux et un rasoir électrique, de ne pas consommer de boissons alcoolisées et de ne pas prendre de médicaments contenant de l'aspirine ou des anti-inflammatoires non stéroïdiens.
- Expliquer au patient qu'il risque de perdre ses cheveux. Explorer avec lui les stratégies lui permettant de s'adapter à ces changements.
- Prévenir la patiente que le topotécan peut exercer des effets tératogènes. Lui recommander d'utiliser une méthode contraceptive efficace pendant toute la durée du traitement.
- Expliquer au patient qu'il ne doit pas se faire vacciner sans recommandation expresse d'un professionnel de la santé.
- Insister sur l'importance des tests de laboratoire à intervalles réguliers permettant de suivre de près les effets secondaires.

VÉRIFICATION DE L'EFFICACITÉ THÉRAPEUTIQUE

L'efficacité du traitement peut être démontrée par: la diminution de la taille de la tumeur et le ralentissement de la propagation des cellules malignes. ✳

TORÉMIFÈNE

Ce médicament n'est pas commercialisé au Canada. Disponible par l'intermédiaire du Programme d'accès spécial de Santé Canada.

CLASSIFICATION:

Antinéoplasique (bloqueur des œstrogènes)

Grossesse – catégorie D

INDICATIONS

Traitement du cancer métastatique du sein chez les femmes ménopausées présentant des tumeurs œstrogénodépendantes ou de statut hormonal inconnu.

MÉCANISME D'ACTION

Médicament exerçant des effets anti-œstrogéniques; il entre en compétition avec les œstrogènes pour accaparer leurs sites de fixation. ***Effets thérapeutiques:*** Régression ou stabilisation du cancer du sein.

PHARMACOCINÉTIQUE

Absorption: Bonne (PO).

Distribution: Tout l'organisme.

Liaison aux protéines: 99,5 %.

Métabolisme et excrétion: Métabolisme hépatique important par le biais du cytochrome P450 3A4; l'agent subit une circulation entérohépatique.

Demi-vie: 5 jours.

Profil temps-action (concentration sanguine)

	DÉBUT D'ACTION	PIC	DURÉE
PO	inconnu	3 h	4 – 6 semaines†

† Les concentrations sanguines à l'état d'équilibre sont atteintes après 4 à 6 semaines.

CONTRE-INDICATIONS, PRÉCAUTIONS ET MISES EN GARDE

Contre-indications: Hypersensibilité ▪ Grossesse ou allaitement ▪ Antécédents de maladie thromboembolique.

Précautions et mises en garde: Métastases osseuses (risque accru d'hypercalcémie) ▪ Hyperplasie endométriale préexistante (on devrait éviter le traitement prolongé) ▪ **PÉD.:** L'innocuité de l'agent n'a pas été établie.

RÉACTIONS INDÉSIRABLES ET EFFETS SECONDAIRES

SNC: dépression, étourdissements, céphalées, léthargie.

ORLO: vision trouble, cataractes, kératopathie cornéenne, xérophtalmie, glaucome.

CV: INSUFFISANCE CARDIAQUE, INFARCTUS DU MYOCARDE, EMBOLIE PULMONAIRE, angine, arythmies, œdème, thrombophlébite.

GI: nausées, concentrations élevées d'enzymes hépatiques, vomissements.

GU: pertes vaginales, saignements vaginaux.

Tég.: transpiration.

HÉ: hypercalcémie.

Hémat.: anémie.

Divers: bouffées vasomotrices, croissance de la tumeur.

INTERACTIONS

Médicament-médicament: L'administration concomitante d'**agents qui diminuent l'excrétion urinaire de calcium** (**diurétiques thiazidiques**) peut augmenter le risque d'hypercalcémie ▪ Le torémifène peut intensifier l'effet de la **warfarine** ▪ Les **inhibiteurs du cytochrome P450 3A4** (p. ex., le **kétoconazole**, l'**itraconazole**, la **clarithromycine**, l'**érythromycine**) peuvent augmenter les concentrations sanguines de torémifène ▪ Les **inducteurs du cytochrome P450 3A4** (p. ex., la **rifampine**, le **phénobarbital**, la **phénytoïne**) peuvent diminuer les concentrations sanguines de torémifène.

VOIES D'ADMINISTRATION ET POSOLOGIE

- **PO (adultes):** 60 mg, 1 fois par jour.

PRÉSENTATION

Ce médicament n'est pas commercialisé au Canada.

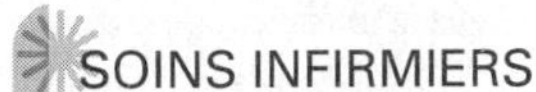

SOINS INFIRMIERS

ÉVALUATION DE LA SITUATION

- Suivre de près l'intensification de la douleur osseuse ou tumorale. Demander au médecin ou à un autre professionnel de la santé s'il y a lieu d'administrer des analgésiques. Cette douleur passagère disparaît habituellement même si le traitement est poursuivi.
- La patiente devrait se soumettre à intervalles réguliers à des examens gynécologiques; le torémifène peut modifier les résultats du test de Papanicolaou et les frottis vaginaux.

Tests de laboratoire:

- Noter la numération globulaire et plaquettaire ainsi que les concentrations de calcium avant le traitement et pendant toute sa durée. Le torémifène peut provoquer une hypercalcémie passagère chez les patientes présentant des métastases osseuses. Chez ces patientes, il faudrait effectuer un dosage des récepteurs des œstrogènes avant d'amorcer le traitement.
- Suivre les résultats des tests de la fonction hépatique à intervalles réguliers pendant toute la durée du traitement. Le torémifène peut entraîner une élévation des concentrations sériques d'AST, de phosphatase alcaline et de bilirubine.

DIAGNOSTICS INFIRMIERS POSSIBLES

- Douleur aiguë (Réactions indésirables).
- Connaissances insuffisantes sur le traitement médicamenteux (Enseignement au patient et à ses proches).

INTERVENTIONS INFIRMIÈRES

- Administrer le torémifène 1 fois par jour.

ENSEIGNEMENT AU PATIENT ET À SES PROCHES

- Expliquer à la patiente qu'elle doit prendre le médicament en respectant rigoureusement la posologie recommandée. Si elle n'a pu prendre le médicament au moment habituel, elle doit sauter cette dose.
- Recommander à la patiente de signaler rapidement à un professionnel de la santé les douleurs osseuses. La prévenir que ces douleurs peuvent être fortes, mais qu'elles pourraient constituer un indice de l'efficacité du médicament et qu'elles se résorberont avec le temps. Lui conseiller de demander au médecin de lui prescrire des analgésiques pour soulager la douleur.

T

- Prévenir la patiente que le torémifène peut induire l'ovulation, mais qu'il peut être doté de propriétés tératogènes. Lui conseiller d'utiliser une méthode de contraception non hormonale durant le traitement et pendant au moins 1 mois après l'avoir arrêté.
- Prévenir la patiente que le torémifène peut entraîner des bouffées vasomotrices. Lui conseiller d'informer un professionnel de la santé si elles deviennent gênantes.
- Recommander à la patiente de signaler immédiatement à un professionnel de la santé les symptômes suivants : enflure ou douleur au niveau des jambes, essoufflements, faiblesse, insomnie, confusion, nausées, vomissements, étourdissements, céphalées, perte d'appétit ou vision trouble. Elle devrait également signaler les irrégularités du cycle menstruel, les saignements vaginaux ainsi que les douleurs ou une pression pelviennes.

VÉRIFICATION DE L'EFFICACITÉ THÉRAPEUTIQUE

L'efficacité du traitement peut être démontrée par : la diminution de la taille de la tumeur et le ralentissement de la propagation du cancer du sein. ✳

TRAMADOL

Ralivia, Tridural, Zytram XL

TRAMADOL/ ACÉTAMINOPHÈNE

Tramacet

CLASSIFICATION :

Analgésique opioïde

Grossesse – catégorie C

T

INDICATIONS

Soulagement de la douleur d'intensité moyenne chez les adultes qui ont besoin d'un traitement pendant plusieurs jours ou plus longtemps ■ **Tramadol/acétaminophène :** Traitement de courte durée (5 jours ou moins) de la douleur aiguë.

MÉCANISME D'ACTION

Liaison aux récepteurs mu des opioïdes ■ Inhibition du recaptage de la sérotonine et de la noradrénaline dans le SNC. ***Effets thérapeutiques :*** Diminution de la douleur.

PHARMACOCINÉTIQUE

Absorption : De 70 à 75 % (PO).

Distribution : L'agent traverse la barrière placentaire et passe dans le lait maternel.

Métabolisme et excrétion : Métabolisme majoritairement hépatique ; un des métabolites exerce des effets analgésiques. Excrétion rénale sous forme inchangée (30 %).

Demi-vie : *Tramadol* – de 5 à 9 heures ; *métabolite actif* – de 5 à 9 heures (les deux demi-vies sont prolongées en présence d'une insuffisance hépatique ou rénale).

Profil temps-action (analgésie)

	DÉBUT D'ACTION	PIC	DURÉE
PO	1 h	2 - 3 h	4 - 6 h
PO libération contrôlée	inconnu	4 - 8 h	24 h

CONTRE-INDICATIONS, PRÉCAUTIONS ET MISES EN GARDE

Contre-indications : Hypersensibilité ■ Risque de sensibilité croisée avec les opioïdes ■ Intoxication aiguë par l'alcool, les hypnosédatifs, les analgésiques à action centrale, les analgésiques opioïdes ou les psychotropes ■ Traitement concomitant par les IMAO ou au cours des 14 jours précédents ■ Insuffisance hépatique grave (Child-Pugh classe C) ■ *Tramadol à libération contrôlée* – Insuffisance rénale grave (Cl_{Cr} < 30 mL/min).

Précautions et mises en garde : GÉR. : Personnes âgées > 75 ans (risque accru d'effets indésirables) ■ Antécédents d'épilepsie ou risques de convulsions ■ *Tramadol/acétaminophène* – Insuffisance rénale (il est recommandé d'allonger l'intervalle posologique si la Cl_{Cr} est < 30 mL/min) ■ Traitement concomitant par des dépresseurs du SNC ■ Pression intracrânienne accrue ou traumatisme crânien ■ Abdomen aigu (une évaluation clinique précise devient impossible) ■ Patients qui courent un risque de dépression respiratoire ■ Antécédents de dépendance aux opioïdes ou d'un traitement récent par des doses élevées d'opioïdes (le tramadol ne peut pas supprimer les symptômes de sevrage aux opioïdes, même si c'est un agoniste opioïde) ■ **OBST. :** Grossesse ou allaitement (l'innocuité du médicament n'a pas été établie). ■ **PÉD. :** Enfants < 18 ans (l'innocuité du médicament n'a pas été établie) ■ Risque de pharmacodépendance et d'abus.

RÉACTIONS INDÉSIRABLES ET EFFETS SECONDAIRES

SNC : CONVULSIONS, étourdissements, céphalées, somnolence, anxiété, stimulation du SNC, confusion, troubles de la coordination, euphorie, malaise, nervosité, troubles du sommeil, faiblesse.

ORLO : troubles visuels.

CV: vasodilatation.
GI: constipation, nausées, douleurs abdominales, anorexie, diarrhée, sécheresse de la bouche (xérostomie), dyspepsie, flatulence, vomissements.
GU: rétention urinaire et mictions fréquentes.
Tég.: rash, prurit, transpiration.
SN: hypertonie.
Divers: réactions allergiques, dépendance physique, dépendance psychologique, tolérance aux effets du médicament.

INTERACTIONS

Médicament-médicament: Risque accru de dépression du SNC et du système respiratoire lors de l'usage concomitant d'autres **dépresseurs du SNC**, incluant l'**alcool**, les **antihistaminiques**, les **hypnosédatifs**, les **opioïdes**, les **anesthésiques** ou les **psychotropes** ■ Risque accru de convulsions lors de l'administration concomitante de doses élevées de **pénicillines** ou de **céphalosporines**, de **neuroleptiques**, d'**opioïdes**, d'**antidépresseurs** ou d'**IMAO** ■ Risque de survenue d'un syndrome sérotoninergique lors de l'administration concomitante d'**agents sérotoninergiques**, comme les **ISRS**, les **IMAO** et la majorité des autres **antidépresseurs** ■ La **carbamazépine** accélère le métabolisme du tramadol et en diminue ainsi l'efficacité (l'usage concomitant n'est pas recommandé) ■ Les **inhibiteurs du CYP2D6** comme la **quinidine**, la **fluoxétine**, la **paroxétine** et l'**amytriptyline**, administrés en concomitance, peuvent modifier l'efficacité du tramadol ■ Le **ritonavir** peut augmenter les concentrations de tramadol ainsi que le risque d'effets indésirables.
Médicament-produits naturels: Effets dépresseurs additifs sur le SNC lors de l'usage concomitant de **kava**, de **valériane** et de **camomille**.

VOIES D'ADMINISTRATION ET POSOLOGIE

- **PO (adultes)**: *Comprimés à libération contrôlée* – commencer avec 100 ou 150 mg, 1 fois par jour. La dose peut être augmentée à intervalles de 7 jours, jusqu'à un maximum de 400 mg par jour.
- **PO (adultes)**: *Tramadol/acétaminophène* – 1 ou 2 comprimés, toutes les 4 à 6 heures, jusqu'à un maximum de 8 comprimés par jour.

INSUFFISANCE RÉNALE (CL_{CR} < 30 mL/MIN)

- **PO (ADULTES)**: *TRAMADOL/ACÉTAMINOPHÈNE* – 1 OU 2 COMPRIMÉS, TOUTES LES 12 HEURES.

PRÉSENTATION

Comprimés à libération contrôlée: 100 mg[Pr], 150 mg[Pr], 200 mg[Pr], 300 mg[Pr], 400 mg[Pr] ■ **En association avec**: acétaminophène (Tramacet[Pr]) (voir l'annexe U).

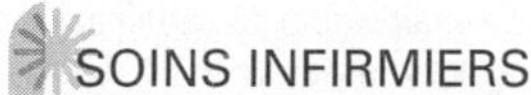

SOINS INFIRMIERS

ÉVALUATION DE LA SITUATION

- Évaluer le type de douleur, son siège et son intensité avant l'administration du médicament et au moment de l'effet maximal après la prise de la dose.
- Mesurer la pression artérielle et la fréquence respiratoire avant l'administration du médicament et à intervalles réguliers pendant toute la durée du traitement. On n'a pas signalé de dépression respiratoire lorsque le médicament a été administré aux doses recommandées.
- Évaluer la fonction intestinale à intervalles réguliers. On devrait prendre les mesures qui s'imposent pour réduire les effets constipants du tramadol: augmenter l'apport de liquides et de fibres, administrer des laxatifs.
- Interroger le patient au sujet d'un traitement préalable aux analgésiques. Il n'est pas recommandé d'administrer le tramadol à des patients présentant une dépendance aux opioïdes ou qui ont déjà reçu des opioïdes pendant plus de 1 semaine; le médicament peut déclencher des symptômes de sevrage aux opioïdes.
- L'utilisation prolongée du tramadol peut mener à une dépendance physique et psychologique et à la tolérance aux effets du médicament, bien que ces réactions soient plus bénignes que celles aux opioïdes. Cependant, ce n'est pas pour autant qu'on devrait priver le patient d'un traitement analgésique adéquat. La plupart des patients qui ont pris le tramadol pour soulager la douleur n'ont pas développé de dépendance psychologique. En cas de tolérance aux effets du médicament, il peut s'avérer nécessaire d'administrer un agoniste opioïde pour soulager la douleur. L'arrêt brusque du traitement par le tramadol peut donner lieu à des symptômes de sevrage. Les patients sous traitement prolongé devraient être sevrés graduellement du médicament, s'il n'est plus nécessaire pour maîtriser la douleur.
- RESTER À L'AFFÛT DES CONVULSIONS, QUI PEUVENT SURVENIR MÊME AUX DOSES RECOMMANDÉES. LE RISQUE AUGMENTE AVEC LES DOSES PLUS ÉLEVÉES ET LORS DE L'ADMINISTRATION CONCOMITANTE D'ANTIDÉPRESSEURS (P. EX., ISRS, IMAO, TRICYCLIQUES), D'ANALGÉSIQUE OPIOÏDES ET D'AUTRES MÉDICAMENTS QUI ABAISSENT LE SEUIL CONVULSIF.

Tests de laboratoire: Le tramadol peut élever les concentrations de créatinine sérique et d'enzymes hépatiques et diminuer les concentrations d'hémoglobine et la protéinurie.

T

Toxicité et surdosage: Le surdosage peut entraîner une dépression respiratoire et des convulsions. La naloxone (Narcan) peut inverser certains des symptômes de surdosage, mais pas tous. En cas de surdosage, il faut prendre en charge les symptômes, administrer un traitement de soutien et assurer la perméabilité des voies respiratoires. L'hémodialyse n'est pas utile, car elle ne retire qu'une petite portion de la dose administrée. On peut traiter les convulsions avec des barbituriques ou des benzodiazépines. L'administration de naloxone en cas de surdosage peut accroître le risque de convulsions.

DIAGNOSTICS INFIRMIERS POSSIBLES

- Douleur aiguë (Indications).
- Risque d'accident (Effets secondaires).
- Connaissances insuffisantes sur le traitement médicamenteux (Enseignement au patient et à ses proches).

INTERVENTIONS INFIRMIÈRES

- NE PAS CONFONDRE LE TRAMADOL AVEC TORADOL (KÉTOROLAC).
- Expliquer au patient la valeur thérapeutique du traitement avant de lui administrer le tramadol, afin d'intensifier l'effet analgésique du médicament.
- Les doses administrées à intervalles réguliers peuvent s'avérer plus efficaces que celles administrées au besoin. L'analgésique est plus efficace s'il est administré avant que la douleur ne devienne intense.
- En cas de traitement prolongé, on devrait réduire graduellement la dose de tramadol afin de prévenir les symptômes de sevrage.
- Le tramadol peut être administré sans égard aux repas.
- Les comprimés à libération contrôlée doivent être avalés entiers et ne doivent pas être brisés, mâchés ou écrasés, car cela peut entraîner une libération rapide de tramadol et l'absorption d'une dose potentiellement mortelle.

ENSEIGNEMENT AU PATIENT ET À SES PROCHES

- Expliquer au patient à quel moment il doit réclamer un analgésique.
- Prévenir le patient que le tramadol peut parfois provoquer des étourdissements et de la somnolence. Lui conseiller de ne pas conduire et d'éviter les activités qui exigent sa vigilance jusqu'à ce qu'on ait la certitude que le médicament n'entraîne pas ces effets chez lui.
- Recommander au patient de changer lentement de position afin de réduire le risque d'hypotension orthostatique.
- Mettre en garde le patient contre la consommation d'alcool ou d'autres dépresseurs du SNC en même temps que le tramadol.
- Inciter le patient à tourner dans le lit, à tousser et à prendre de grandes respirations toutes les 2 heures, afin de prévenir l'atélectasie.

VÉRIFICATION DE L'EFFICACITÉ THÉRAPEUTIQUE

L'efficacité du traitement peut être démontrée par: la diminution de l'intensité des douleurs sans une altération importante du degré de conscience ou de l'état respiratoire. ✳

TRANDOLAPRIL,

voir Inhibiteurs de l'enzyme de conversion de l'angiotensine (IECA)

TRANYLCYPROMINE,

voir Inhibiteurs de la monoamine-oxydase (IMAO)

ALERTE CLINIQUE

TRASTUZUMAB

Herceptin

CLASSIFICATION:

Antinéoplasique (anticorps monoclonal, immunomodulateur)

Grossesse – catégorie B

INDICATIONS

Traitement du cancer métastatique du sein chez les femmes présentant des tumeurs avec surexpression de la protéine du récepteur 2 du facteur de croissance épidermique humain (HER2).

MÉCANISME D'ACTION

Anticorps monoclonal qui se lie aux sites du récepteur 2 du facteur de croissance épidermique humain, situés dans les tissus mammaires cancéreux, et qui inhibe la prolifération des cellules qui surexpriment la protéine de ce facteur de croissance. ***Effets thérapeutiques:*** Régression du cancer du sein et des métastases.

PHARMACOCINÉTIQUE

Absorption: Biodisponibilité à 100 % (IV).

Distribution: Liaison aux protéines du récepteur 2 du facteur de croissance épidermique humain.

Métabolisme et excrétion: Inconnus.

Demi-vie: Dose de 10 mg – 1,7 jour; dose de 500 mg – 12 jours.

Profil temps-action

	DÉBUT D'ACTION	PIC	DURÉE
IV	inconnu	inconnu	inconnue

CONTRE-INDICATIONS, PRÉCAUTIONS ET MISES EN GARDE

Contre-indications: Hypersensibilité connue au trastuzumab, aux protéines des cellules ovariennes de hamsters chinois ou à tout ingrédient qui entre dans la composition du médicament.

Précautions et mises en garde: Hypersensibilité à l'alcool benzylique (utiliser de l'eau stérile pour injection plutôt que l'eau bactériostatique fournie dans le conditionnement) ▪ **GÉR.**: Risque accru de dysfonctionnement cardiaque ▪ **OBST.**: N'utiliser pendant la grossesse qu'en cas de besoin réel ▪ **ALLAITEMENT**: L'utilisation de l'agent est déconseillé ▪ **PÉD.**: L'innocuité du médicament n'a pas été établie ▪ Affections pulmonaires préexistantes.

EXTRÊME PRUDENCE: DYSFONCTIONNEMENT CARDIAQUE PRÉEXISTANT.

RÉACTIONS INDÉSIRABLES ET EFFETS SECONDAIRES

SNC: étourdissements, céphalées, insomnie, faiblesse, dépression.

Resp.: dyspnée, toux accrue, pharyngite, rhinite, sinusite, bronchospasme.

CV: INSUFFISANCE CARDIAQUE, tachycardie, hypotension.

GI: douleurs abdominales, anorexie, diarrhée, nausées, vomissements.

Tég.: rash, acné, herpès.

HÉ: œdème.

Hémat.: anémie, leucopénie.

Loc.: douleurs lombaires, arthralgie, douleurs osseuses.

SN: neuropathie, paresthésie, névrite périphérique.

Divers: RÉACTIONS D'HYPERSENSIBILITÉ, frissons, fièvre, infection, douleurs, syndrome pseudogrippal.

INTERACTIONS

Médicament-médicament: Le traitement concomitant par une **anthracycline** (**daunorubicine**, **doxorubicine** ou **idarubicine**) peut augmenter le risque de cardiotoxicité ▪ Le **paclitaxel**, administré en concomitance, peut élever les concentrations sanguines de trastuzumab.

VOIES D'ADMINISTRATION ET POSOLOGIE

- **IV (adultes)**: La dose de charge est de 4 mg/kg; elle peut être suivie d'une dose d'entretien de 2 mg/kg/semaine.

PRÉSENTATION

Poudre lyophilisée pour injection: 440 mg/fiole, avec une fiole de 20 mL d'eau stérile bactériostatique pour injection (renferme de l'alcool benzylique à 1,1 %)[Pr].

SOINS INFIRMIERS

ÉVALUATION DE LA SITUATION

- Lors de la première perfusion du trastuzumab, observer la patiente à la recherche des symptômes reliés à la perfusion (frissons, fièvre). On peut traiter ces symptômes par l'acétaminophène, la diphenhydramine ou la mépéridine. Ils dictent rarement l'abandon du traitement.
- NOTER, À INTERVALLES FRÉQUENTS PENDANT TOUTE LA DURÉE DU TRAITEMENT, LES SIGNES ET LES SYMPTÔMES SUIVANTS DE DYSFONCTIONNEMENT CARDIAQUE: DYSPNÉE, TOUX ACCRUE, DYSPNÉE NOCTURNE PAROXYSTIQUE, ŒDÈME PÉRIPHÉRIQUE, BRUIT DE GALOP B_3, FRACTION D'ÉJECTION RÉDUITE. EFFECTUER UNE ÉVALUATION CARDIAQUE INITIALE INCLUANT LA PRISE DES ANTÉCÉDENTS, L'EXAMEN PHYSIQUE ET AU MOINS UNE DES INTERVENTIONS SUIVANTES: ÉCG, ÉCHOCARDIOGRAPHIE OU SCINTIGRAPHIE SÉQUENTIELLE SYNCHRONISÉE. L'INSUFFISANCE CARDIAQUE CONGESTIVE ASSOCIÉE AU TRASTUZUMAB PEUT ÊTRE GRAVE, ET MENER À UNE DÉFAILLANCE CARDIAQUE, À UN ACCIDENT VASCULAIRE CÉRÉBRAL OU À LA MORT. ON DEVRAIT ABANDONNER LE TRAITEMENT PAR LE TRASTUZUMAB DÈS L'APPARITION D'UNE INSUFFISANCE CARDIAQUE CONGESTIVE MARQUÉE.
- SURVEILLER L'APPARITION D'UNE RÉACTION PULMONAIRE D'HYPERSENSIBILITÉ POUVANT SE MANIFESTER PAR DE LA DYSPNÉE, DES INFILTRATS PULMONAIRES, UN ÉPANCHEMENT PLEURAL, UN ŒDÈME PULMONAIRE NON CARDIOGÉNIQUE, UNE INSUFFISANCE PULMONAIRE, L'HYPOXIE OU UN SYNDROME DE DÉTRESSE RESPIRATOIRE. LES PATIENTS PRÉSENTANT UNE MALADIE PULMONAIRE SYMPTOMATIQUE OU UNE TUMEUR PULMONAIRE ÉTENDUE SONT DAVANTAGE PRÉDISPOSÉS À CES MANIFESTATIONS. LA PERFUSION DEVRAIT ÊTRE ARRÊTÉE SI DES SYMPTÔMES GRAVES SURVIENNENT.

Tests de laboratoire: La surexpression de la protéine HER2 est utilisée pour déterminer si le trastuzumab est indiqué. La surexpression de la protéine HER2 peut être détectée par une méthode de coloration immunohistochimique (comme le HercepTest) ou un test de FISH.

- Le trastuzumab peut entraîner l'anémie et la leucopénie.

DIAGNOSTICS INFIRMIERS POSSIBLES

- Diarrhée (Réactions indésirables).
- Risque d'infection (Réactions indésirables).
- Connaissances insuffisantes sur le traitement médicamenteux (Enseignement au patient et à ses proches).

INTERVENTIONS INFIRMIÈRES

ALERTE CLINIQUE: DES DÉCÈS SONT SURVENUS LORS DE CERTAINES CHIMIOTHÉRAPIES. AVANT D'ADMINISTRER L'AGENT, CLARIFIER TOUS LES POINTS AMBIGUS. VÉRIFIER UNE FOIS DE PLUS LA LIMITE DES DOSES UNITAIRES ET QUOTIDIENNES AINSI QUE CELLE DES DOSES À ADMINISTRER PENDANT LE TRAITEMENT. DEMANDER À UN AUTRE PROFESSIONNEL DE LA SANTÉ DE VÉRIFIER L'ORDONNANCE D'ORIGINE, LE CALCUL DES DOSES ET LE RÉGLAGE DE LA POMPE À PERFUSION.

- Le trastuzumab peut être administré en consultation externe.

Perfusion intermittente: Reconstituer le contenu de chaque fiole avec 20 mL d'eau stérile bactériostatique pour injection fournie avec le produit, en dirigeant directement le jet de diluant sur la poudre lyophilisée. On obtient ainsi une solution multidose à une concentration de 21 mg/mL. Faire tourner délicatement la fiole sans la secouer. La solution peut mousser légèrement; laisser reposer la fiole pendant 5 minutes. La solution devrait être transparente à légèrement opalescente et d'incolore à jaune pâle, mais exempte de toute particule. Étiqueter immédiatement la fiole et inscrire à la section portant la mention «Ne pas utiliser après le ...» la date qui correspond au 28e jour qui suit la reconstitution de la solution. La solution est stable pendant 24 heures à la température ambiante ou pendant 28 jours au réfrigérateur. En cas d'allergie à l'alcool benzylique, reconstituer la solution avec de l'eau stérile pour injection sans agent bactériostatique; utiliser immédiatement la solution et jeter toute portion inutilisée. Calculer le volume nécessaire pour obtenir la dose souhaitée, retirer cette quantité de la fiole et l'ajouter au sac de perfusion renfermant 250 mL de solution de NaCl 0,9 %. Renverser délicatement le sac pour bien mélanger.

Vitesse d'administration: Perfuser la dose d'attaque de 4 mg/kg en 90 minutes, et la dose hebdomadaire de 2 mg/kg, en 30 minutes si la dose d'attaque a été bien tolérée. Ne pas administrer par IV directe ou sous forme de bolus.

Incompatibilité en addition au soluté: Ne pas diluer le trastuzumab avec une solution de dextrose ni l'ajouter à des solutions qui en contiennent. Ne pas mélanger le trastuzumab à d'autres médicaments ni le diluer avec d'autres agents.

ENSEIGNEMENT AU PATIENT ET À SES PROCHES

- Recommander à la patiente de communiquer rapidement avec un professionnel de la santé en présence de symptômes d'insuffisance cardiaque congestive, de fièvre, de maux de gorge, de signes d'infection, de douleurs lombaires ou aux flancs ou de mictions difficiles ou douloureuses. L'inciter à éviter les foules et les personnes contagieuses.
- Expliquer à la patiente qu'elle ne doit pas se faire vacciner sans recommandation expresse d'un professionnel de la santé.

VÉRIFICATION DE L'EFFICACITÉ THÉRAPEUTIQUE

L'efficacité du traitement peut être démontrée par: la régression du cancer du sein et des métastases.

TRAZODONE

Apo-Trazodone, Desyrel, Dom-Trazodone, Gen-Trazodone, Novo-Trazodone, Nu-Trazodone, PMS-Trazodone, Trazorel

CLASSIFICATION:
Antidépresseur

Grossesse – catégorie C

INDICATIONS

Traitement de la dépression majeure, souvent en association avec une psychothérapie. **Usages non approuvés:** Traitement de l'insomnie et des syndromes de douleur chronique, incluant la neuropathie diabétique.

MÉCANISME D'ACTION

Modification des effets de la sérotonine dans le SNC. ***Effets thérapeutiques:*** Effet antidépresseur qui peut ne se manifester qu'après plusieurs semaines de traitement.

PHARMACOCINÉTIQUE

Absorption: Bonne (PO).

Distribution: Le médicament se répartit dans tout l'organisme.

Liaison aux protéines: De 89 à 95 %.

Métabolisme et excrétion: Métabolisme majoritairement hépatique (cytochrome P450-3A4); faible excrétion rénale à l'état inchangé.

Demi-vie: De 5 à 9 heures.

Profil temps-action (effet antidépresseur)

	DÉBUT D'ACTION	PIC	DURÉE
PO	1 - 2 semaines	2 - 4 semaines	plusieurs semaines

CONTRE-INDICATIONS, PRÉCAUTIONS ET MISES EN GARDE

Contre-indications: Hypersensibilité.

Précautions et mises en garde: Risque de priapisme (les patients de sexe masculin ayant des érections prolongées ou inappropriées devraient cesser immédiatement la prise du médicament et consulter un médecin) ■ Maladie cardiovasculaire ■ Période de convalescence après un infarctus du myocarde ■ Électrochocs concomitants ■ La surveillance des idées suicidaires est indiquée chez tous les patients recevant ce médicament ■ Antécédents de convulsions ■ Maladie hépatique ou rénale grave (il est recommandé de réduire la dose) ■ **GÉR.:** Amorcer le traitement à des doses plus faibles ■ **OBST., ALLAITEMENT, PÉD.:** L'innocuité du médicament n'a pas été établie.

RÉACTIONS INDÉSIRABLES ET EFFETS SECONDAIRES

SNC: somnolence, confusion, étourdissements, fatigue, hallucinations, céphalées, insomnie, cauchemars, troubles de l'élocution, syncope, faiblesse.

ORLO: vision trouble, acouphènes.

CV: hypotension, arythmies, douleurs thoraciques, hypertension, palpitations, tachycardie.

GI: sécheresse de la bouche (xérostomie), altération du goût, constipation, diarrhée, salivation excessive, flatulence, nausées, vomissements.

GU: hématurie, impuissance, priapisme, mictions fréquentes.

Tég.: rash.

Hémat.: anémie, leucopénie.

Loc.: myalgie.

SN: tremblements.

INTERACTIONS

Médicament-médicament: La trazodone peut élever les concentrations sériques de **digoxine** ou de **phénytoïne** ■ Dépression additive du SNC lors de l'usage concomitant d'autres **dépresseurs du SNC**, tels que l'**alcool**, les **opioïdes** et les **hypnosédatifs** ■ Effets hypotenseurs additifs lors de l'administration concomitante d'**antihypertenseurs** ou de **dérivés nitrés** ou de la consommation d'**alcool** ■ La **fluoxétine**, administrée en concomitance, élève les concentrations de trazodone et accroît le risque de toxicité associé à cet agent ■ Les **médicaments inhibiteurs du cytochrome P450-3A4**, tels que le **ritonavir**, l'**indinavir** et le **kétoconazole**, augmentent les concentrations plasmatiques du trazodone et le risque de toxicité ■ Les **médicaments qui induisent le cytochrome P450-3A4**, tels que la **carbamazépine**, diminuent les concentrations plasmatiques de la trazodone et peuvent en diminuer l'efficacité ■ Risque de diminution du RNI lors de l'administration concomitante de **warfarine**.

VOIES D'ADMINISTRATION ET POSOLOGIE

- **PO (adultes):** De 150 mg à 200 mg par jour, en 2 ou 3 doses fractionnées; majorer par paliers de 50 mg par jour, tous les 3 ou 4 jours, jusqu'à l'obtention de la réponse souhaitée (ne pas dépasser 400 mg par jour, chez les patients en consultation externe ou 600 mg par jour, chez les patients hospitalisés).
- **PO (personnes âgées):** La dose ne devrait pas dépasser la moitié de celle recommandée chez les adultes.

PRÉSENTATION (version générique disponible)

Comprimés: 50 mg^{Pr}, 100 mg^{Pr}, 150 mg^{Pr}.

SOINS INFIRMIERS

ÉVALUATION DE LA SITUATION

- Mesurer la pression artérielle et le pouls avant l'administration et pendant toute la durée du traitement initial. Chez les patients souffrant de maladie cardiaque, on devrait suivre l'ÉCG, avant le traitement et à intervalles réguliers pendant toute sa durée pour déceler les arythmies.

Dépression: Suivre de près l'état mental du patient et ses sautes d'humeur. Observer les tendances suicidaires, particulièrement au début du traitement. Réduire la quantité de médicament dont le patient peut disposer.

Douleur: Noter la durée, l'intensité, les caractéristiques et le siège des douleurs avant le traitement et à intervalles réguliers pendant toute sa durée.

Tests de laboratoire: Noter la numération globulaire et les résultats des tests de la fonction hépatique ou rénale avant le traitement et à intervalles réguliers pendant toute sa durée. La trazodone peut entraîner une légère

T

diminution, sans signification clinique, du nombre de globules blancs et de polynucléaires neutrophiles.

DIAGNOSTICS INFIRMIERS POSSIBLES

- Stratégies d'adaptation inefficaces (Indications).
- Connaissances insuffisantes sur le traitement médicamenteux (Enseignement au patient et à ses proches).

INTERVENTIONS INFIRMIÈRES

- Administrer la trazodone avec des aliments ou immédiatement après les repas pour réduire les effets secondaires (nausées, étourdissements) et pour favoriser une absorption maximale du médicament. On peut administrer une plus grande portion de la dose quotidienne totale au coucher afin de diminuer la somnolence diurne et les étourdissements.

ENSEIGNEMENT AU PATIENT ET À SES PROCHES

- Conseiller au patient de respecter rigoureusement la posologie recommandée. S'il n'a pas pu prendre le médicament au moment habituel, il doit le faire dès que possible, mais pas plus tard que 4 heures avant l'heure prévue pour la dose suivante. Le prévenir qu'il ne doit jamais remplacer une dose manquée par une double dose. Conseiller au patient de consulter un professionnel de la santé avant d'arrêter le traitement. Il faut réduire la posologie graduellement pour prévenir une aggravation de son état.
- Prévenir le patient que la trazodone peut provoquer de la somnolence et une vision trouble. Lui conseiller de ne pas conduire et d'éviter les activités qui exigent sa vigilance jusqu'à ce qu'on ait la certitude que le médicament n'entraîne pas ces effets chez lui.
- Recommander au patient de changer lentement de position afin de réduire le risque d'hypotension orthostatique.
- Mettre en garde le patient contre la consommation d'alcool ou d'autres dépresseurs du SNC en même temps que la trazodone.
- Expliquer au patient qu'il peut soulager la sécheresse de la bouche en se rinçant souvent la bouche, en pratiquant une bonne hygiène orale et en consommant des bonbons ou de la gomme à mâcher sans sucre. Si la sécheresse de la bouche persiste pendant plus de 2 semaines, lui recommander de consulter un professionnel de la santé. Conseiller au patient d'augmenter sa consommation de liquides et de fibres alimentaires et de faire de l'exercice pour prévenir la constipation.
- Recommander au patient qui doit suivre un autre traitement ou subir une intervention chirurgicale d'avertir le professionnel de la santé qu'il suit un traitement par ce médicament.
- Recommander au patient de communiquer avec un professionnel de la santé en cas de priapisme, de battements cardiaques irréguliers, d'évanouissement, de confusion, de rash ou de tremblements ou encore si les symptômes suivants s'aggravent: sécheresse de la bouche, nausées et vomissements, étourdissements, céphalées, douleurs musculaires, constipation ou diarrhée.
- Insister sur l'importance des examens de suivi permettant de déterminer les bienfaits du traitement.

VÉRIFICATION DE L'EFFICACITÉ THÉRAPEUTIQUE

L'efficacité du traitement peut être démontrée par: la disparition des symptômes de dépression ■ une sensation de mieux-être ■ un regain d'intérêt pour l'entourage ■ un gain d'appétit ■ un regain d'énergie ■ un sommeil amélioré ■ la diminution de l'intensité des douleurs en présence d'un syndrome de douleur chronique ■ Les effets thérapeutiques sont habituellement notables en l'espace de 1 semaine, bien que parfois 4 semaines puissent s'écouler avant d'obtenir des résultats thérapeutiques importants.

TRIAMCINOLONE,

voir Corticostéroïdes (topiques), Corticostéroïdes (voie générale) et Corticostéroïdes (voie intranasale)

TRIAMTÉRÈNE/ HYDROCHLOROTHIAZIDE,

voir Diurétiques (épargneurs de potassium)

TRIAZOLAM

Apo-Triazo, Gen-Triazolam, Halcion

CLASSIFICATION:

Anxiolytique et hypnosédatif (benzodiazépine)

Grossesse – catégorie X

INDICATIONS

Traitement de courte durée de l'insomnie.

MÉCANISME D'ACTION

Dépression du SNC, probablement par potentialisation de l'activité neuro-inhibitrice de l'acide gamma-aminobutyrique (GABA). ***Effets thérapeutiques:*** Amélioration du sommeil.

PHARMACOCINÉTIQUE

Absorption: Bonne (PO).
Distribution: L'agent se répartit dans tout l'organisme et traverse la barrière hématoencéphalique. Il traverse probablement la barrière placentaire et passe dans le lait maternel.
Liaison aux protéines: De 89 à 94 %.
Métabolisme et excrétion: Métabolisme hépatique, dont un métabolite, l'alphahydroxytriazolam, est actif. Excrétion rénale (principalement sous forme de métabolites inactifs).
Demi-vie: De 1 à 5 heures.

Profil temps-action (sédation)

	Début d'action	Pic	Durée
PO	15 - 30 min	inconnu	6 - 7 h

CONTRE-INDICATIONS, PRÉCAUTIONS ET MISES EN GARDE

Contre-indications: Hypersensibilité ■ Risque de réactions de sensibilité croisée avec d'autres benzodiazépines ■ Glaucome à angle fermé ■ Myasthénie grave ■ Insuffisance pulmonaire grave ou apnée du sommeil ■ **Obst.**: L'usage du médicament chez la femme enceinte accroît le risque de malformations congénitales.
Précautions et mises en garde: Dysfonctionnement hépatique ■ Dépression majeure ou psychose lorsque l'anxiété n'est pas un facteur prédominant ■ Comportement suicidaire ou antécédents de tentatives de suicide, de toxicomanie ou de pharmacodépendance ■ **Gér.**: Il est recommandé de réduire la dose initiale chez les personnes âgées ou débilitées ■ Coma ou dépression préexistante du SNC ■ **Péd.**: L'innocuité et l'efficacité du médicament n'ont pas été établies chez les enfants < 18 ans ■ **Allaitement**: Le médicament passe dans le lait maternel, son utilisation n'est donc pas recommandée chez la femme qui allaite.

RÉACTIONS INDÉSIRABLES ET EFFETS SECONDAIRES

SNC: étourdissements, sédation excessive, sensation de tête légère, céphalées, amnésie antérograde, confusion, léthargie, dépression, excitation paradoxale.
ORLO: vision trouble.
GI: constipation, diarrhée, nausées, vomissements.
Tég.: rash.
Divers: dépendance physique, dépendance psychologique, tolérance aux effets du médicament.

INTERACTIONS

Médicament-médicament: LA **CIMÉTIDINE**, LA **CLARITHROMYCINE**, L'**ÉRYTHROMYCINE**, LE **FLUCONAZOLE**, L'**ITRACONAZOLE**, LE **KÉTOCONAZOLE**, L'**INDINAVIR**, LE **NELFINAVIR**, LE **RITONAVIR** OU LE **SAQUINAVIR**, ADMINISTRÉS EN CONCOMITANCE, PEUVENT DIMINUER LE MÉTABOLISME DU TRIAZOLAM ET EN ACCROÎTRE LES EFFETS ; L'ASSOCIATION DE CES MÉDICAMENTS DEVRAIT ÊTRE ÉVITÉE ■ Dépression additive du SNC lors de l'ingestion d'**alcool** ou de la prise concomitante d'**antidépresseurs**, d'**antihistaminiques** et d'**opioïdes** ■ La **théophylline** peut diminuer les effets sédatifs du triazolam.
Médicament-produits naturels: Le **kava**, le **houblon**, la **scutellaire**, la **valériane** et la **camomille** peuvent accentuer la dépression du SNC.
Médicament-aliments: Le **jus de pamplemousse** augmente les concentrations sanguines et les effets du médicament.

VOIES D'ADMINISTRATION ET POSOLOGIE

- **PO (adultes)**: De 0,125 à 0,25 mg (jusqu'à 0,5 mg chez certains patients), 1 fois par jour, au coucher.
- **PO (personnes âgées débilitées)**: 0,125 mg, 1 fois par jour, au coucher (jusqu'à 0,25 mg chez certains patients).

PRÉSENTATION (version générique disponible)

Comprimés: 0,125 mg$^{T/C}$, 0,25 mg$^{T/C}$.

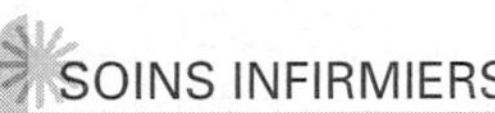

SOINS INFIRMIERS

ÉVALUATION DE LA SITUATION

- Noter les habitudes de sommeil avant le traitement et à intervalles réguliers pendant toute sa durée.

Gér.: Évaluer les effets au niveau du SNC et le risque de chutes et mettre en place les mesures préventives.

- Le traitement prolongé à des doses élevées peut entraîner une dépendance psychologique ou physique. Réduire la quantité du médicament dont le patient peut disposer, particulièrement s'il est déprimé ou suicidaire, ou s'il a des antécédents de toxicomanie.

DIAGNOSTICS INFIRMIERS POSSIBLES

- Habitudes de sommeil perturbées (Indications).
- Risque d'accident (Effets secondaires).
- Connaissances insuffisantes sur le traitement médicamenteux (Enseignement au patient et à ses proches).

T

INTERVENTIONS INFIRMIÈRES

- Après l'administration du médicament, surveiller le patient lors de ses déplacements ou des transferts. Retirer les cigarettes. Remonter les ridelles du lit et installer la sonnette d'appel à portée de la main.
- Administrer le triazolam avec des aliments si l'irritation gastrique devient gênante.

ENSEIGNEMENT AU PATIENT ET À SES PROCHES

- Conseiller au patient de respecter rigoureusement la posologie recommandée. Lui expliquer qu'il est important de préparer un cadre propice au sommeil: la pièce doit être sombre et calme, la nicotine et la caféine sont à proscrire. Lui recommander de consulter un professionnel de la santé si le traitement devient moins efficace après quelques semaines. Le prévenir qu'il ne doit pas augmenter la dose de sa propre initiative.
- Prévenir le patient que le triazolam peut provoquer des étourdissements ou de la somnolence diurne. Lui conseiller de ne pas conduire et d'éviter les activités qui exigent sa vigilance jusqu'à ce qu'on ait la certitude que le médicament n'entraîne pas ces effets chez lui.

GÉR.: Enseigner au patient et à ses proches les mesures préventives visant à réduire le risque de chutes.

- Recommander au patient d'éviter de boire de l'alcool ou de prendre d'autres dépresseurs du SNC et de consulter un professionnel de la santé avant de prendre des préparations en vente libre contenant des antihistaminiques ou de l'alcool.
- Conseiller à la patiente d'informer un professionnel de la santé si elle pense être enceinte ou si elle souhaite le devenir.
- Recommander au patient de signaler à un professionnel de la santé la confusion, la dépression ou les céphalées persistantes. Recommander aux proches ou au soignant de communiquer avec un professionnel de la santé s'il survient des changements de personnalité.
- Demander au patient de signaler à un professionnel de la santé l'aggravation de l'anxiété diurne, qui peut survenir dès le 10e jour de traitement. Il peut s'avérer nécessaire de cesser le traitement par le triazolam.
- Insister sur l'importance des examens de suivi permettant d'évaluer l'efficacité du médicament.

VÉRIFICATION DE L'EFFICACITÉ THÉRAPEUTIQUE

L'efficacité du traitement peut être démontrée par: l'amélioration des habitudes de sommeil; cet effet bénéfique peut ne pas être manifeste avant le 3e jour de traitement. ✳

T

TRIFLUOPÉRAZINE

Apo-Trifluopérazine, Novo-Flurazine, PMS-Trifluopérazine, Terfluzine, Trifluopérazine

CLASSIFICATION:

Antipsychotique, anxiolytique, antiémétique (phénothiazine)

Grossesse – catégorie C

INDICATIONS

Traitement des psychoses aiguës et chroniques ■ Traitement de l'anxiété ■ Prévention et traitement des nausées et des vomissements.

MÉCANISME D'ACTION

Modification des effets de la dopamine dans le SNC ■ Fort effet anticholinergique et blocage marqué des récepteurs alpha-adrénergiques. ***Effets thérapeutiques:*** Diminution des signes et des symptômes psychotiques.

PHARMACOCINÉTIQUE

Absorption: Variable (comprimés); l'absorption des préparations liquides destinées à la voie orale pourrait être meilleure.

Distribution: Tout l'organisme. On retrouve l'agent en fortes concentrations dans le SNC. Il traverse la barrière placentaire et passe dans le lait maternel.

Liaison aux protéines: ≥ 90 %.

Métabolisme et excrétion: Métabolisme majoritairement hépatique.

Demi-vie: De 7 à 18 heures.

Profil temps-action (effets antipsychotiques)

	DÉBUT D'ACTION	PIC	DURÉE
PO	inconnu	inconnu	12 - 24 h

CONTRE-INDICATIONS, PRÉCAUTIONS ET MISES EN GARDE

Contre-indications: Hypersensibilité ■ État comateux ou dépression grave du SNC en raison de la prise de grandes quantités de dépresseurs de SNC ■ Dyscrasie sanguine ou aplasie médullaire ■ Maladies hépatiques.

Précautions et mises en garde: **GÉR.**: Il est recommandé de réduire la dose chez les personnes âgées ou débilitées ■ Diabète ■ Maladie respiratoire ■ Hyperplasie de la prostate ■ Tumeurs du SNC ■ Épilepsie ■ Occlusion intestinale ■ **OBST., ALLAITEMENT**: L'innocuité du médicament n'a pas été établie; risque d'effets indésirables chez le nouveau-né ■ Hypersensibilité aux bisulfites (concentré oral seulement) ■ Glaucome à angle fermé ■ Maladie cardiovasculaire grave ■ Risque de réactions de sensibilité croisée avec d'autres phénothiazines.

RÉACTIONS INDÉSIRABLES ET EFFETS SECONDAIRES

SNC: SYNDROME MALIN DES NEUROLEPTIQUES, réactions extrapyramidales, sédation, dyskinésie tardive.
ORLO: xérophtalmie, vision trouble, opacité du cristallin.
CV: hypotension, tachycardie.
GI: constipation, anorexie, sécheresse de la bouche (xérostomie), hépatite, occlusion intestinale.
GU: rétention urinaire.
Tég.: photosensibilité, modification de la pigmentation, rash.
End.: galactorrhée.
Hémat.: AGRANULOCYTOSE, leucopénie.
Métab.: hyperthermie.
Divers: réactions allergiques.

INTERACTIONS

Médicament-médicament: Effets hypotenseurs additifs lors de l'administration concomitante d'**antihypertenseurs** ou de **dérivés nitrés** ou de la consommation d'**alcool** ■ Effets additifs sur la dépression du SNC lors de l'usage concomitant d'autres **dépresseurs du SNC**, incluant l'**alcool**, les **antihistaminiques**, les **opioïdes**, les **hypnosédatifs** et les **anesthésiques généraux** ■ Effets anticholinergiques additifs lors de l'administration concomitante d'autres **médicaments ayant des propriétés anticholinergiques**, dont les **antihistaminiques**, les **antidépresseurs**, la **quinidine**, le **disopyramide** et d'autres **phénothiazines** ■ Risque d'encéphalopathie aiguë lors de l'administration concomitante de **lithium** ■ La trifluopérazine peut contrer l'effet vasopresseur de l'**adrénaline** ■ La trifluopérazine peut diminuer les effets bénéfiques de la **lévodopa** ■ Risque accru d'agranulocytose lors de l'administration concomitante d'**agents antithyroïdiens** ■ Le **lithium**, administré en association avec la trifluopérazine peut augmenter le risque de réactions extrapyramidales ■ L'administration concomitante de **phénothiazines** et d'autres **agents qui peuvent également allonger l'intervalle QTc** est déconseillée.
Médicament-produits naturels: Effets additifs sur la dépression du SNC lors de l'usage concomitant de **kava**, de **centella asiatique**, de **valériane** ou de **millepertuis**. Le **dong-quai** peut augmenter les effets photosensibilisants.

VOIES D'ADMINISTRATION ET POSOLOGIE

- **PO (adultes)**: *Médecine générale et médecine psychiatrique extrahospitalière* – de 1 à 2 mg, 2 fois par jour (jusqu'à 6 mg par jour).
- **PO (enfants de 6 à 12 ans)**: *Médecine générale et médecine psychiatrique extrahospitalière* – 1 mg, 1 ou 2 fois par jour.
- **PO (adultes)**: *Patients psychiatriques hospitalisés* – de 2 à 5 mg, 2 ou 3 fois par jour. La posologie se situe entre 15 et 20 mg/jour, bien que l'état d'un petit nombre de patients puisse dicter l'administration d'une dose allant jusqu'à 40 mg/jour ou plus.
- **PO (enfants de 6 à 12 ans)**: *Patients psychiatriques hospitalisés* – 1 mg, 1 ou 2 fois par jour, jusqu'à un maximum de 15 mg/jour.
- **PO (adultes)**: *Antiémétique* – de 1 à 2 mg, 1 ou 2 fois par jour, si besoin est.

PRÉSENTATION (version générique disponible)

Comprimés: 1 mg[Pr], 2 mg[Pr], 5 mg[Pr], 10 mg[Pr], 20 mg[Pr] ■ **Sirop**: 1 mg/mL[Pr], 10 mg/mL[Pr].

SOINS INFIRMIERS

ÉVALUATION DE LA SITUATION

- Évaluer l'état mental du patient (orientation, humeur et comportement) et le degré d'anxiété, avant le traitement et à intervalles réguliers pendant toute sa durée.
- Mesurer la pression artérielle (en position assise, debout et couchée), le pouls et la fréquence respiratoire, et surveiller l'ÉCG avant l'administration initiale et à intervalles fréquents pendant la période d'adaptation de la posologie. La trifluopérazine peut entraîner la modification des ondes Q et T sur l'ÉCG.
- Observer le patient attentivement pendant qu'on lui administre le médicament par voie orale pour s'assurer qu'il l'a bien avalé.
- Évaluer le degré de sédation après l'administration de ce médicament.
- Effectuer le bilan des ingesta et des excreta et peser le patient tous les jours. Signaler au médecin ou à un professionnel de la santé toute modification importante.
- Observer étroitement le patient pour déceler l'apparition d'une akathisie (agitation ou désir de bouger continuellement) et des effets secondaires extrapyramidaux (*symptômes parkinsoniens:* difficultés d'élocution ou de déglutition, perte d'équilibre, mouvements d'émiettement, faciès figé, démarche traînante, rigidité, tremblements; *symptômes dystoniques:* spasmes musculaires, torsions, secousses musculaires, incapacité de bouger les yeux, faiblesse

T

des bras ou des jambes), tous les 2 mois pendant toute la durée du traitement et de 8 à 12 semaines après qu'il a pris fin. Signaler l'apparition de ces symptômes au médecin ou à un professionnel de la santé, car il peut s'avérer nécessaire de réduire la dose ou de cesser le traitement. Il peut être utile d'administrer du trihexyphénidyle ou de la diphenhydramine pour maîtriser ces symptômes.

- Rester à l'affût des symptômes de dyskinésie tardive (mouvements rythmiques et incontrôlables de la bouche, du visage et des membres; émission de bruits secs avec les lèvres ou la langue; gonflement des joues; mouvements masticatoires incontrôlables; mouvements rapides de la langue). Informer immédiatement le médecin ou un autre professionnel de la santé de l'apparition de ces symptômes, qui peuvent être irréversibles.
- SUIVRE DE PRÈS L'APPARITION DES SYMPTÔMES SUIVANTS DU SYNDROME MALIN DES NEUROLEPTIQUES: FIÈVRE, DÉTRESSE RESPIRATOIRE, TACHYCARDIE, CONVULSIONS, DIAPHORÈSE, HYPERTENSION OU HYPOTENSION, PÂLEUR, FATIGUE, RIGIDITÉ MUSCULAIRE MARQUÉE, PERTE DE CONTRÔLE DE LA VESSIE. INFORMER IMMÉDIATEMENT LE MÉDECIN OU UN AUTRE PROFESSIONNEL DE LA SANTÉ DE L'APPARITION DE CES SYMPTÔMES.

Tests de laboratoire:

- Noter à intervalles réguliers, pendant toute la durée du traitement, la numération globulaire et les résultats des tests de la fonction hépatique et des examens ophtalmologiques. La trifluopérazine peut entraîner la diminution de l'hématocrite, des concentrations d'hémoglobine et du nombre de globules blancs, de granulocytes et de plaquettes ainsi que l'élévation des concentrations de bilirubine, d'AST, d'ALT et de phosphatase alcaline. L'AGRANULOCYTOSE SURVIENT ENTRE LA 4e ET LA 10e SEMAINE DE TRAITEMENT ET DISPARAÎT 1 OU 2 SEMAINES APRÈS QU'IL A PRIS FIN. ELLE PEUT RÉCIDIVER SI LE TRAITEMENT EST RECOMMENCÉ. Des résultats anormaux aux tests de la fonction hépatique peuvent dicter l'arrêt du traitement.
- La trifluopérazine peut entraîner des résultats faussement positifs ou négatifs aux tests de grossesse et des résultats faussement positifs au dosage de la bilirubine urinaire.
- La trifluopérazine peut entraîner l'élévation des concentrations sériques de prolactine et modifier les résultats des épreuves à la gonadolibérine.

DIAGNOSTICS INFIRMIERS POSSIBLES

- Stratégies d'adaptation inefficaces (Indications).
- Opérations de la pensée perturbées (Indications).
- Connaissances insuffisantes sur le traitement médicamenteux (Enseignement au patient et à ses proches).

INTERVENTIONS INFIRMIÈRES

- Éviter les éclaboussures sur les mains, étant donné qu'il y a risque de dermatite de contact chez les patients qui ont une hypersensibilité connue aux phénothiazines. En cas d'éclaboussures, bien se laver les mains.
- Il faut interrompre le traitement aux phénothiazines 48 heures avant une myélographie et ne le reprendre que 24 heures plus tard, car ces médicaments abaissent le seuil des convulsions.
- La solution peut être jaune pâle. Ne pas utiliser une solution de couleur brune ou qui contient un précipité. La garder à l'abri de la lumière.
- Administrer le médicament par voie orale avec des aliments, de l'eau ou du lait afin de diminuer l'irritation gastrique. Chez les patients éprouvant des difficultés de déglutition, on peut écraser les comprimés et les mélanger avec des aliments ou des liquides.
- Diluer la solution concentrée juste avant de l'administrer, dans au moins 120 mL de jus de tomate ou de fruits, de lait, de boisson gazéifiée, de café, de thé ou d'eau. On peut également l'administrer avec des aliments semi-solides (soupes, poudings).

ENSEIGNEMENT AU PATIENT ET À SES PROCHES

- Conseiller au patient de respecter rigoureusement la posologie recommandée. L'avertir qu'il ne doit jamais sauter de dose ni remplacer une dose manquée par une double dose. S'il n'a pu prendre le médicament au moment habituel, il doit le prendre aussitôt que possible, à moins que ce ne soit presque l'heure prévue pour la dose suivante. S'il doit prendre plus de 2 doses par jour, lui expliquer qu'il doit prendre la dose manquée dans les 60 minutes qui suivent l'heure prévue, sinon il doit sauter cette dose. Le sevrage brusque peut provoquer une gastrite, des nausées, des vomissements, des étourdissements, des céphalées, la tachycardie et l'insomnie.
- Informer le patient qu'il risque de manifester des symptômes extrapyramidaux ou une dyskinésie tardive. Lui recommander de signaler immédiatement ces symptômes au médecin ou à un autre professionnel de la santé.
- Prévenir le patient que la trifluopérazine peut provoquer de la somnolence. Lui conseiller de ne pas conduire et d'éviter les activités qui exigent sa vigilance

jusqu'à ce qu'on ait la certitude que le médicament n'entraîne pas cet effet chez lui.

- Recommander au patient de changer lentement de position afin de réduire le risque d'hypotension orthostatique.
- Recommander au patient d'utiliser un écran solaire et de porter des vêtements protecteurs lors des expositions au soleil en raison des risques de photosensibilité. Lui recommander également d'éviter les températures extrêmes, car ce médicament altère la thermorégulation.
- Mettre en garde le patient contre la consommation d'alcool ou d'autres dépresseurs du SNC en même temps que ce médicament.
- Conseiller au patient de se rincer fréquemment la bouche, de pratiquer une bonne hygiène buccale et de consommer de la gomme ou des bonbons sans sucre pour soulager la sécheresse de la bouche. Lui recommander de consulter un professionnel de la santé si la sécheresse de la bouche persiste pendant plus de 2 semaines.
- Recommander au patient d'augmenter sa consommation de fibres alimentaires et de liquides et de faire de l'exercice pour réduire les effets constipants de ce médicament.
- Informer le patient que la trifluopérazine peut faire virer la couleur de l'urine au rose ou au rouge brun.
- Recommander au patient qui doit suivre un autre traitement ou subir une intervention chirurgicale d'avertir le professionnel de la santé qu'il suit un traitement par ce médicament.
- Informer le patient qu'il doit prévenir sans délai un professionnel de la santé en cas de maux de gorge, de fièvre, de saignements ou d'ecchymoses inhabituels, de rash, de faiblesse, de tremblements ou de troubles de la vue ou encore si son urine prend une couleur foncée ou si ses selles deviennent grises.
- Insister sur l'importance des examens de suivi permettant d'évaluer la réponse au médicament et de déceler les effets secondaires. Des examens ophtalmologiques sont également indiqués à intervalles réguliers. Inciter le patient à suivre une psychothérapie si le médecin la lui a prescrite.

VÉRIFICATION DE L'EFFICACITÉ THÉRAPEUTIQUE

L'efficacité du traitement peut être démontrée par: la diminution de l'excitation, du comportement paranoïaque et du repli sur soi ■ la diminution de l'anxiété accompagnant la dépression. Les effets thérapeutiques du médicament administré par voie orale peuvent ne pas être manifestes avant 2 ou 3 semaines. ✳

TRIHEXYPHÉNIDYLE

Apo-Trihex, Artane, PMS-Trihexyphenidyl, Trihexyphen

CLASSIFICATION:

Antiparkinsonien (anticholinergique)

Grossesse – catégorie C

INDICATIONS

Traitement de la maladie de Parkinson ■ Prévention et traitement des symptômes extrapyramidaux induits par les médicaments.

MÉCANISME D'ACTION

Agent antimuscarinique synthétique qui entraîne une inhibition des centres moteurs du cerveau et un blocage des influx nerveux efférents. ***Effets thérapeutiques:*** Diminution des symptômes associés à la maladie de Parkinson et soulagement des symptômes de dysfonctionnement extrapyramidal (dystonie, akathisie et parkinsonisme).

PHARMACOCINÉTIQUE

Absorption: Bonne (PO).

Distribution: Inconnue.

Métabolisme et excrétion: Excrétion majoritairement rénale.

Demi-vie: 3,7 heures.

Profil temps-action (effets antiparkinsoniens)

	DÉBUT D'ACTION	PIC	DURÉE
PO	1 h	2 - 3 h	6 - 12 h

CONTRE-INDICATIONS, PRÉCAUTIONS ET MISES EN GARDE

Contre-indications: Hypersensibilité ■ Glaucome à angle fermé ■ Colite ulcéreuse grave.

Précautions et mises en garde: Personnes âgées et patients très jeunes (risque accru de réactions indésirables) ■ Occlusion ou infection intestinales ■ Colite ulcéreuse ■ Ulcère gastroduodénal ■ Reflux gastro-œsophagien ou hernie hiatale ■ Hyperplasie bénigne de la prostate ■ Rétention urinaire ■ Maladies rénale, hépatique, pulmonaire ou cardiaque chroniques ■ Risque d'anhydrose et/ou d'hyperthermie pouvant mener à une issue fatale (les patients doivent donc éviter de s'exposer à toute occasion d'hyperthermie) ■ **OBST., ALLAITEMENT, PÉD.**: L'innocuité du médicament n'a pas été établie ■ Hémorragie aiguë ■ Arythmies cardiaques ■ Hypertension ■ Hypotension ■ Thyrotoxicose ■ Dyskinésie tardive ■ Troubles mentaux (l'agent peut déclencher des épisodes psychotiques) ■ Intolérance connue à l'alcool (élixir seulement).

RÉACTIONS INDÉSIRABLES ET EFFETS SECONDAIRES

SNC: étourdissements, nervosité, confusion, somnolence, céphalées, psychoses, faiblesse.
ORLO: vision trouble, mydriase, hypertension intraoculaire, cycloplégie, photophobie, xérophtalmie.
CV: hypotension orthostatique, tachycardie, palpitations.
GI: sécheresse de la bouche (xérostomie), nausées, constipation, vomissements.
GU: retard de la miction avec difficultés d'uriner, rétention urinaire.
Tég.: diminution de la sécrétion de sueur, éruptions cutanées.
Métab.: hyperthermie.
Loc.: faiblesse musculaire.

INTERACTIONS

Médicament-médicament: Effets anticholinergiques additifs lors de l'administration concomitante d'autres **médicaments dotés de propriétés anticholinergiques**, tels que les **phénothiazines**, les **antidépresseurs tricycliques**, la **quinidine** et le **disopyramide** ■ Le trihexyphénidyle peut accroître l'efficacité de la **lévodopa**, mais peut augmenter le risque de psychoses ■ Effets additifs sur la dépression du SNC lors de l'usage concomitant d'autres **dépresseurs du SNC**, incluant l'**alcool**, les **antihistaminiques**, les **opioïdes** et les **hypnosédatifs** ■ Les anticholinergiques peuvent modifier l'absorption d'autres **médicaments administrés par voie orale** en ralentissant la motilité du tractus gastro-intestinal ■ Le trihexyphénidyle pourrait contrecarrer l'effet des médicaments suivants: **donépézil**, **galantamine**, **rivastigmine** ■ Le trihexyphénidyle peut potentialiser les effets indésirables de l'**amantadine** sur le SNC.

T

VOIES D'ADMINISTRATION ET POSOLOGIE

- **PO (adultes)**: *Maladie de Parkinson* – 1 mg, le premier jour; augmenter la dose par paliers de 2 mg, tous les 3 à 5 jours, jusqu'à 6 à 10 mg/jour répartis en 3 doses fractionnées. *Réactions extrapyramidales d'origine médicamenteuse* – initialement, 1 mg 1 fois par jour; la dose quotidienne se situe entre 5 et 15 mg.

PRÉSENTATION (version générique disponible)

Comprimés: 2 mg^{Pr}, 5 mg^{Pr} ■ **Élixir (parfum de lime et menthe)**: 2 mg/5 mL^{Pr}.

SOINS INFIRMIERS

ÉVALUATION DE LA SITUATION

- Observer le patient, avant le traitement et pendant toute sa durée, à la recherche des symptômes parkinsoniens et extrapyramidaux suivants: agitation ou besoin de bouger, rigidité, tremblements, mouvements d'émiettement, faciès figé, démarche traînante, spasmes musculaires, mouvements de torsion, troubles d'élocution ou de déglutition, perte d'équilibre.
- Effectuer le bilan quotidien des ingesta et des excreta et observer le patient à la recherche des signes de rétention urinaire (dysurie; distension abdominale; mictions peu fréquentes, avec élimination de petites quantités d'urine; incontinence par regorgement).
- Chez les patients souffrant de maladie mentale, le risque d'exacerbation des symptômes de ce type de maladie est accru au début du traitement par le trihexyphénidyle. Interrompre l'administration et prévenir le médecin ou un autre professionnel de la santé si des changements de comportement importants se produisent.

DIAGNOSTICS INFIRMIERS POSSIBLES

- Mobilité physique réduite (Indications).
- Risque d'accident (Indications).
- Connaissances insuffisantes sur le traitement médicamenteux (Enseignement au patient et à ses proches).

INTERVENTIONS INFIRMIÈRES

- On administre habituellement le trihexyphénidyle après les repas. On peut l'administrer avant les repas, si le patient souffre de sécheresse de la bouche, ou avec des aliments, si l'irritation gastrique devient gênante. Utiliser un récipient gradué pour mesurer les doses d'élixir.

ENSEIGNEMENT AU PATIENT ET À SES PROCHES

- Conseiller au patient de respecter rigoureusement la posologie recommandée. S'il n'a pas pu prendre le médicament au moment habituel, il doit le prendre dès que possible, mais pas plus tard que 2 heures avant l'heure prévue pour la dose suivante. L'avertir qu'il ne doit jamais remplacer une dose manquée par une double dose.
- Prévenir le patient qu'avant d'arrêter le traitement par le trihexyphénidyle, il faut diminuer graduellement la dose pour éviter les réactions suivantes de

sevrage: anxiété, tachycardie, insomnie, symptômes parkinsoniens ou extrapyramidaux rebond.

- Prévenir le patient que le trihexyphénidyle peut provoquer de la somnolence ou des étourdissements. Lui conseiller de ne pas conduire et d'éviter les activités qui exigent sa vigilance jusqu'à ce qu'on ait la certitude que le médicament n'entraîne pas ces effets chez lui.
- Conseiller au patient de changer lentement de position afin de réduire le risque d'hypotension orthostatique.
- Conseiller au patient de se rincer fréquemment la bouche, de pratiquer une bonne hygiène buccale et de consommer de la gomme à mâcher ou des bonbons sans sucre pour diminuer la sécheresse de la bouche. Lui recommander de consulter un professionnel de la santé si la sécheresse de la bouche persiste (on pourrait lui prescrire des substituts de salive). Lui recommander également de prévenir le dentiste si la sécheresse de la bouche l'empêche de porter sa prothèse dentaire.
- Conseiller au patient de consulter un professionnel de la santé avant de prendre un médicament en vente libre, particulièrement des préparations contre le rhume, et avant de consommer des boissons alcoolisées.
- Avertir le patient que ce médicament peut diminuer les sécrétions de sueur et qu'il y a risque d'hyperthermie par temps chaud. Lui recommander de rester par temps chaud dans une pièce climatisée.
- Recommander au patient d'augmenter sa consommation de fibres alimentaires et de liquides et de faire de l'exercice pour réduire les effets constipants de ce médicament.
- Conseiller au patient de ne pas prendre des antiacides ou des antidiarrhéiques dans l'heure ou les 2 heures qui suivent la prise de ce médicament.
- Recommander au patient de prévenir un professionnel de la santé en cas de confusion, de rash, de rétention urinaire, de constipation grave ou de troubles visuels.
- Insister sur l'importance des examens de suivi réguliers.

VÉRIFICATION DE L'EFFICACITÉ THÉRAPEUTIQUE

L'efficacité du traitement peut être démontrée par: la diminution des tremblements et de la rigidité et l'amélioration de la démarche et de l'équilibre; les effets thérapeutiques se manifestent habituellement dans les 2 ou 3 jours qui suivent le début du traitement ■ la disparition des symptômes extrapyramidaux induits par les médicaments. ✳

TRIMÉTHOPRIME

Apo-Trimethoprim, Proloprim

CLASSIFICATION:

Antibiotique

Grossesse - catégorie C

INDICATIONS

Traitement des infections non compliquées des voies urinaires. **Usages non approuvés:** Prophylaxie des infections urinaires chroniques récurrentes ■ En association avec la dapsone, traitement de la pneumonie légère à modérée, attribuable à *Pneumocystis carinii* (PPC).

MÉCANISME D'ACTION

Altération de la synthèse bactérienne de l'acide folique. ***Effets thérapeutiques:*** Action bactéricide contre les microorganismes sensibles. **Spectre d'action:** Le triméthoprime agit contre certains agents pathogènes à Gram positif dont: *Streptococcus pneumoniæ* ■ les streptocoques bêtahémolytiques du groupe A ■ certains staphylocoques ■ Le spectre d'action contre les bactéries à Gram négatif englobe les souches *Enterobacteriaceæ* suivantes: *Acinetobacter* ■ *Citrobacter* ■ *Enterobacter* ■ *Escherichia coli* ■ *Klebsiella pneumoniæ* ■ *Proteus mirabilis* ■ *Salmonella* ■ *Shigella* ■ D'autres souches de *Proteus*, certaines bactéries *Providencia* et *Serratia* ainsi que *Pneumocystis carinii* sont également sensibles à cet agent (en traitement d'association).

PHARMACOCINÉTIQUE

Absorption: Bonne (PO).

Distribution: Le médicament se répartit dans tout l'organisme. Il traverse la barrière placentaire et on le retrouve à de fortes concentrations dans le lait maternel.

Métabolisme et excrétion: Métabolisme hépatique à 20 % et excrétion rénale à l'état inchangé à 80 %.

Demi-vie: De 8 à 11 heures (prolongée en cas d'insuffisance rénale).

Profil temps-action

	DÉBUT D'ACTION	PIC	DURÉE
PO	rapide	1 - 4 h	12 - 24 h

CONTRE-INDICATIONS, PRÉCAUTIONS ET MISES EN GARDE

Contre-indications: Hypersensibilité ■ Anémie mégaloblastique secondaire à une carence en folate ■ Insuffisance

T

rénale grave (administration déconseillée si la Cl_{Cr} est < 15 mL/min) ■ Allaitement ■ Grossesse.

Précautions et mises en garde: Insuffisance rénale (une réduction de la dose s'avère nécessaire si la Cl_{Cr} est < 30 mL/min) ■ Patients débilités ■ Insuffisance hépatique grave ■ Carence en folate ■ **PÉD.**: L'efficacité du médicament utilisé en monothérapie n'a pas été établie chez les enfants < 12 ans.

RÉACTIONS INDÉSIRABLES ET EFFETS SECONDAIRES

GI: altération du goût, gêne épigastrique, glossite, nausées, vomissements, hépatite médicamenteuse.

Tég.: prurit, rash, photosensibilité.

Hémat.: anémie mégaloblastique, neutropénie, thrombopénie.

Divers: réactions allergiques incluant l'ÉRYTHÈME POLYMORPHE et le SYNDROME DE STEVENS-JOHNSON, fièvre.

INTERACTIONS

Médicament-médicament: Le triméthoprime augmente les concentrations de **phénytoïne** et peut exacerber la carence en folate qu'elle entraîne ■ Risque accru d'une carence en folate lors de l'administration concomitante de **méthotrexate** ■ Risque accru d'aplasie médullaire lors de l'administration concomitante d'**antinéoplasiques** ou d'une **radiothérapie** ■ La **rifampine**, administrée en concomitance, peut diminuer l'efficacité du triméthoprime en augmentant son élimination.

VOIES D'ADMINISTRATION ET POSOLOGIE

Traitement des infections urinaires

T

- **PO (adultes)**: 100 mg, toutes les 12 heures, ou 200 mg, toutes les 24 heures, pendant 10 jours.

INSUFFISANCE RÉNALE

- **PO (ADULTES)**: *CL_{CR} DE 15 À 30 mL/MIN* – 50 mg, TOUTES LES 12 HEURES. *CL_{CR} < 15 mL/MIN* – L'ADMINISTRATION DU TRIMÉTHOPRIME N'EST PAS RECOMMANDÉE.

PRÉSENTATION (version générique disponible)

Comprimés: 100 mg^Pr^, 200 mg^Pr^ ■ **En association avec**: sulfaméthoxazole^Pr^ (voir Triméthoprime/sulfaméthoxazole).

SOINS INFIRMIERS

ÉVALUATION DE LA SITUATION

- Observer le patient au début du traitement et pendant toute sa durée à la recherche des signes d'infection urinaire (fièvre, urine trouble, mictions fréquentes, besoin impérieux d'uriner, mictions qui s'accompagnent de douleurs ou de brûlures) et d'autres signes d'infection.
- Prélever des échantillons pour la mise en culture et les antibiogrammes avant l'administration du médicament. Les premières doses peuvent être administrées avant que les résultats soient connus.
- Effectuer le bilan des ingesta et des excreta. Sauf contre-indication, le patient devrait consommer suffisamment de liquides pour maintenir un débit urinaire d'au moins 1 200 à 1 500 mL par jour.

Tests de laboratoire:

- Le triméthoprime peut entraîner l'élévation des concentrations sériques de bilirubine, de créatinine, d'urée, d'AST et d'ALT.
- Noter la numération globulaire et les résultats de l'analyse des urines à intervalles réguliers pendant toute la durée du traitement. Le traitement devrait être arrêté en cas de dyscrasie sanguine.

DIAGNOSTICS INFIRMIERS POSSIBLES

- Risque d'infection (Indications, Effets secondaires).
- Connaissances insuffisantes sur le traitement médicamenteux (Enseignement au patient et à ses proches).

INTERVENTIONS INFIRMIÈRES

- Administrer le triméthoprime à jeun avec un grand verre d'eau, au moins 1 heure avant les repas ou 2 heures après. On peut l'administrer avec des aliments en cas d'irritation gastrique.

ENSEIGNEMENT AU PATIENT ET À SES PROCHES

- Inciter le patient à respecter rigoureusement la posologie recommandée et à prendre toute la quantité de médicament qui lui a été prescrite, même s'il se sent mieux. S'il n'a pas pu prendre le médicament au moment habituel, il doit le faire dès que possible et espacer également les autres prises de la journée. Insister sur le fait qu'il peut être dangereux de donner ce médicament à une autre personne.
- Inciter le patient à utiliser un écran solaire avec un FPS d'au moins 15 et à porter des vêtements protecteurs pour prévenir les réactions de photosensibilité.

- Sauf contre-indication, recommander au patient de consommer au moins 1,5 L de liquides par jour.
- Recommander au patient de signaler rapidement à un professionnel de la santé les éruptions cutanées, les maux de gorge, la fièvre, les aphtes buccaux, les arthralgies, la pâleur, la toux, l'essoufflement inhabituel, le purpura, la jaunisse, l'urine foncée et les selles pâles ainsi que les ecchymoses ou les saignements inhabituels.
- Recommander au patient d'informer un professionnel de la santé si les symptômes ne s'améliorent pas.
- Insister sur l'importance des examens de suivi réguliers permettant d'évaluer les bienfaits du traitement.

VÉRIFICATION DE L'EFFICACITÉ THÉRAPEUTIQUE

L'efficacité du traitement peut être démontrée par: la disparition des signes et des symptômes d'infection (il faut habituellement compter de 10 à 14 jours de traitement avant que l'infection des voies urinaires ne disparaisse). ✳

TRIMÉTHOPRIME/ SULFAMÉTHOXAZOLE

Apo-Sulfatrim, Bactrim, Novo-Trimel, Nu-Cotrimox, Septra

CLASSIFICATION:

Antibiotique (sulfamide et antiprotozoaire)

Grossesse – catégories C et D (usage près du terme)

INDICATIONS

Traitement des infections suivantes: infections des voies respiratoires supérieures et inférieures ▪ infections des voies gastro-intestinales notamment choléra, dysenterie bacillaire, typhoïde, paratyphoïde ▪ infections des voies urinaires ▪ urétrite gonococcique non compliquée ▪ infections de la peau et des tissus mous ▪ brucellose ▪ mycétome ▪ nocardiose ▪ blastomycose sud-américaine ▪ ostéomyélite aiguë et chronique ▪ Traitement de la pneumonie à *Pneumocystis carinii* (PPC). **Usages non approuvés:** Diarrhée du voyageur ▪ Prévention des infections opportunistes, dont la PPC, chez les patients immunosupprimés, incluant les patients séropositifs.

MÉCANISME D'ACTION

L'association médicamenteuse inhibe le métabolisme de l'acide folique, nécessaire à la biosynthèse des acides nucléiques de la bactérie, à deux étapes différentes. ***Effets thérapeutiques:*** Action bactéricide contre les bactéries sensibles. **Spectre d'action:** L'association agit contre de nombreuses souches d'agents pathogènes aérobies à Gram positif dont: *Streptococcus pneumoniæ* ▪ *Staphylococcus aureus* ▪ les streptocoques bêtahémolytiques du groupe A ▪ *Nocardia* ▪ Elle est également active contre de nombreux agents pathogènes aérobies à Gram négatif dont: *Acinetobacter* ▪ *Enterobacter* ▪ *Klebsiella* ▪ *Escherichia coli* ▪ *Proteus mirabilis* ▪ *Neisseria gonorhoeæ* ▪ *Vibrio choleræ* ▪ *Shigella* ▪ Salmonella ▪ *Hæmophilus influenzæ*, incluant les souches résistantes à l'ampicilline ▪ Le médicament agit aussi contre *Pneumocystis carinii* (un protozoaire), *Stenotrophomonas maltophilia* et *Toxoplasma gondii* ▪ L'association n'exerce aucun effet sur *Pseudomonas æroginosa* et *Mycoplasma*.

PHARMACOCINÉTIQUE

Absorption: Bonne et rapide (PO).

Distribution: Le médicament se répartit dans tout l'organisme. Il traverse la barrière hématoencéphalique et placentaire et passe dans le lait maternel.

Métabolisme et excrétion: Métabolisme hépatique à 20 %; le reste est excrété à l'état inchangé par les reins.

Demi-vie: *Triméthoprime* – de 8 à 11 heures; *sulfaméthoxazole* – de 9 à 13 heures. Les deux sont prolongées en présence d'insuffisance rénale.

Profil temps-action

	DÉBUT D'ACTION	PIC	DURÉE
PO	rapide	2-4 h	6-12 h
IV	rapide	fin de la perfusion	6-12 h

CONTRE-INDICATIONS, PRÉCAUTIONS ET MISES EN GARDE

Contre-indications: Hypersensibilité aux sulfamides ou au triméthoprime ▪ Anémie mégaloblastique consécutive à une carence en folate ▪ Dyscrasie sanguine ▪ Atteinte importante du parenchyme hépatique ▪ Porphyrie ▪ Insuffisance rénale grave (Cl_{Cr} < 15 mL/min) ▪ **ALLAITEMENT, OBST., PÉD.:** Grossesse, allaitement ou enfants < 2 mois (risque d'ictère et d'anémie hémolytique chez le nouveau-né).

Précautions et mises en garde: Dysfonctionnement hépatique ou rénal (une réduction de la dose s'avère nécessaire si la Cl_{Cr} est < 30 mL/min) ▪ Patients séropositifs (risque accru de réactions indésirables, en particulier la fièvre et des réactions hématologiques et dermatologiques) ▪ Déficit en glucose-6-phosphate déshydrogénase (risque accru d'hémolyse) ▪ Patients chez qui le

T

risque de carence en folate est élevé : personnes âgées, alcooliques, patients sous anticonvulsivants, patients dénutris et patients qui souffrent du syndrome de malabsorption).

RÉACTIONS INDÉSIRABLES ET EFFETS SECONDAIRES

SNC : fatigue, hallucinations, céphalées, insomnie, dépression.

GI : NÉCROSE HÉPATIQUE, nausées, vomissements, diarrhée, stomatite, COLITE PSEUDOMEMBRANEUSE.

GU : cristallurie.

HÉ : hyperkaliémie.

Tég. : NÉCROLYSE ÉPIDERMIQUE TOXIQUE, rash, photosensibilité.

Hémat. : AGRANULOCYTOSE, ANÉMIE APLASIQUE, anémie hémolytique, leucopénie, anémie mégaloblastique, thrombopénie.

Locaux : phlébite au point d'injection IV.

Divers : réactions allergiques incluant l'ÉRYTHÈME POLYMORPHE et le SYNDROME DE STEVENS-JOHNSON, fièvre.

INTERACTIONS

Médicament-médicament : L'association triméthoprime/sulfaméthoxazole augmente les concentrations de **phénytoïne** et peut exacerber la carence en acide folique qu'elle entraîne ▪ L'association triméthoprime/sulfaméthoxazole peut accentuer les effets des **agents antidiabétiques oraux de type sulfonylurée** et de la **warfarine** ▪ Le médicament peut accroître la toxicité du **méthotrexate**, du **dofétilide** et de la **zidovudine** ▪ Le médicament élève le risque de thrombopénie attribuable aux **diurétiques thiazidiques**, administrés en concomitance (risque accru chez les personnes âgées) ▪ L'association triméthoprime/sulfaméthoxazole diminue l'efficacité de la **cyclosporine** et élève le risque de néphrotoxicité.

VOIES D'ADMINISTRATION ET POSOLOGIE

(TMP = triméthoprime ; SMX = sulfaméthoxazole)

Infections bactériennes

- **PO (adultes et enfants > 12 ans)** : 160 mg TMP/800 mg SMX, toutes les 12 heures.
- **PO (enfants > 2 mois à 12 ans)** : De 5 à 10 mg/kg/jour de TMP et de 25 à 50 mg/kg/jour de SMX, en doses fractionnées toutes les 12 heures.
- **IV (adultes)** : De 160 à 240 mg/dose de TMP et de 800 à 1 200 mg/dose de SMX, toutes les 6, 8 ou 12 heures.
- **IV (enfants)** : De 5 à 10 mg/kg/jour de TMP et de 25 à 50 mg/kg/jour de SMX, en doses fractionnées.
- ***INSUFFISANCE RÉNALE***

  CL_{CR} DE 15 À < 30 mL/MIN – ADMINISTRER LA MOITIÉ DE LA DOSE.

Pneumonie à* Pneumocystis carinii *(traitement)

- **PO (adultes et enfants)** : De 15 à 20 mg/kg/jour de TMP et de 75 à 100 mg/kg/jour de SMX, en 3 ou 4 doses fractionnées.
- **IV (adultes et enfants)** : De 15 à 20 mg/kg/jour de TMP et de 75 à 100 mg/kg/jour de SMX, en doses fractionnées, toutes les 6 heures.
- ***INSUFFISANCE RÉNALE***

  CL_{CR} DE 15 À < 30 mL/MIN – ADMINISTRER LA MOITIÉ DE LA DOSE.

PRÉSENTATION (version générique disponible)

Comprimés : 20 mg TMP/100 mg SMX[Pr], 80 mg TMP/400 mg SMX[Pr], 160 mg TMP/800 mg SMX[Pr] ▪ **Suspension pédiatrique** : 40 mg TMP/200 mg SMX par 5 mL[Pr] ▪ **Solution pour injection** : 80 mg TMP/400 mg SMX par 5 mL[Pr].

SOINS INFIRMIERS

ÉVALUATION DE LA SITUATION

- DES DÉCÈS SONT SURVENUS EN RAISON D'EFFETS SECONDAIRES HÉMATOLOGIQUES, DERMATOLOGIQUES ET HÉPATIQUES GRAVES CAUSÉS PAR LE TRIMÉTHOPRIME/SULFAMÉTHOXAZOLE. IL EST IMPORTANT DE SURVEILLER LES SIGNES ET SYMPTÔMES ÉVOCATEURS DE TELLES RÉACTIONS : ÉRUPTIONS CUTANÉES, MAUX DE GORGE, FIÈVRE, PÂLEUR, ARTHRALGIES, TOUX, ESSOUFFLEMENT, PURPURA, JAUNISSE, URINE FONCÉE ET SELLES PÂLES. SI DE TELS SIGNES SE MANIFESTENT, LE TRAITEMENT DOIT ÊTRE INTERROMPU SUR-LE-CHAMP.
- Évaluer l'état du patient au début du traitement et pendant toute sa durée à la recherche des signes d'infection (signes vitaux, aspect de la plaie, des expectorations, de l'urine et des selles, numération leucocytaire). Prélever des échantillons pour la mise en cultures et les antibiogrammes avant l'administration du médicament. Les premières doses peuvent être administrées avant que les résultats soient connus.
- Examiner fréquemment le point d'injection IV. La phlébite est courante.
- DÉTERMINER SI LE PATIENT EST ALLERGIQUE AUX SULFAMIDES.
- Effectuer le bilan des ingesta et des excreta. Sauf contre-indication, le patient devrait consommer suffisamment de liquides pour maintenir un débit

urinaire d'au moins 1 200 à 1 500 mL par jour afin de prévenir la cristallurie et la formation de calculs.

Tests de laboratoire:

- NOTER LA NUMÉRATION GLOBULAIRE ET LES RÉSULTATS DE L'ANALYSE DES URINES À INTERVALLES RÉGULIERS PENDANT TOUTE LA DURÉE DU TRAITEMENT.
- L'association triméthoprime/sulfaméthoxazole peut entraîner l'élévation des concentrations sériques de bilirubine, de créatinine, de potassium et de phosphatase alcaline.

DIAGNOSTICS INFIRMIERS POSSIBLES

- Risque d'infection (Indications, Effets secondaires).
- Connaissances insuffisantes sur le traitement médicamenteux (Enseignement au patient et à ses proches).
- Non-observance du traitement médicamenteux (Enseignement au patient et à ses proches).

INTERVENTIONS INFIRMIÈRES

- NE PAS CONFONDRE LA PRÉPARATION DS (DOUBLE CONCENTRATION, 160 mg/800 mg) AVEC LA PRÉPARATION SS (SIMPLE CONCENTRATION, 80 mg/400 mg).
- Ne pas administrer le médicament par voie IM.

PO: Administrer le triméthoprime/sulfaméthoxazole à intervalles réguliers, avec un grand verre d'eau. Utiliser un récipient gradué pour mesurer les doses de préparation liquide.

Perfusion intermittente: Diluer le contenu de chaque ampoule de 5 mL avec 100 à 125 mL de solution de D5%E ou de NaCl 0,9 % ou de solution de Ringer. On peut réduire la quantité de diluant jusqu'à 75 mL si l'apport liquidien doit être limité. Ne pas utiliser la solution si elle est trouble ou si elle contient un précipité. À la température ambiante, la solution est stable pendant 24 heures en dilution standard, mais seulement pendant 12 heures si elle est plus concentrée. Ne pas la réfrigérer. Consulter les directives de chaque fabricant avant de reconstituer la préparation.

Vitesse d'administration: Perfuser pendant 30 à 90 minutes. Ne pas administrer à un débit rapide ni sous forme de bolus.

Compatibilité (tubulure en Y): acyclovir ▪ aldesleukine ▪ amifostine ▪ amphotéricine B, cholestéryle d' ▪ atracurium ▪ céfépime ▪ cyclophosphamide ▪ diltiazem ▪ doxorubicine, liposome de ▪ énalaprilate ▪ esmolol ▪ filgrastim ▪ fludarabine ▪ gallium, nitrate de ▪ hydromorphone ▪ labétalol ▪ lorazépam ▪ magnésium, sulfate de ▪ melphalan ▪ mépéridine ▪ morphine ▪ pancuronium ▪ perphénazine ▪ pipéracilline/tazobactam ▪ rémifentanil ▪ tacrolimus ▪ téniposide ▪ thiotépa ▪ vécuronium ▪ zidovudine.

Incompatibilité (tubulure en Y): fluconazole ▪ midazolam ▪ vinorelbine.

Incompatibilité en addition au soluté: Le fabricant recommande de ne pas mélanger avec un autre médicament ou solution.

ENSEIGNEMENT AU PATIENT ET À SES PROCHES

- Inciter le patient à respecter rigoureusement la posologie recommandée et à prendre toute la quantité de médicament prescrite, à intervalles réguliers, même s'il se sent mieux. S'il n'a pas pu prendre le médicament au moment habituel, il doit le faire dès que possible à moins que ce ne soit presque l'heure prévue pour la dose suivante. Insister sur le fait qu'il peut être dangereux de donner ce médicament à une autre personne.
- Inciter le patient à utiliser un écran solaire avec un FPS d'au moins 15 et à porter des vêtements protecteurs pour prévenir les réactions de photosensibilité.
- Sauf contre-indication, recommander au patient de consommer au moins 1,5 L de liquides par jour.
- Recommander au patient de signaler rapidement à un professionnel de la santé les éruptions cutanées, les maux de gorge, la fièvre, les aphtes buccaux, les arthralgies, la pâleur, la toux, l'essoufflement inhabituel, le purpura, la jaunisse, l'urine foncée et les selles pâles ainsi que les ecchymoses ou les saignements inhabituels.
- Recommander au patient d'informer un professionnel de la santé si les symptômes ne s'améliorent pas en quelques jours.
- Insister sur l'importance des examens de suivi réguliers permettant de noter les numérations globulaires chez les patients qui suivent un traitement prolongé.

VÉRIFICATION DE L'EFFICACITÉ THÉRAPEUTIQUE

L'efficacité du traitement peut être démontrée par: la disparition des signes et des symptômes d'infection. Le temps de résolution dépend du microorganisme infectant et du siège de l'infection ▪ la prévention des infections opportunistes, dont la PPC, chez les patients immunosupprimés. ✳

T

TROSPIUM

Trosec

CLASSIFICATION:

Antispasmodique urinaire (antimuscarinique)

Grossesse – catégorie C

INDICATIONS

Traitement symptomatique de la vessie hyperactive (incontinence urinaire avec besoin impérieux d'uriner, mictions fréquentes et incontinence urinaire mixte).

MÉCANISME D'ACTION

L'agent contrecarre les effets de l'acétylcholine au niveau des récepteurs muscariniques de la vessie; son action parasympatholytique réduit le tonus du muscle lisse de la vessie. ***Effets thérapeutiques:*** Augmentation de la capacité de la vessie et diminution des symptômes de vessie hyperactive.

PHARMACOCINÉTIQUE

Absorption: Moins de 10 % (PO); la consommation simultanée d'aliments diminue fortement l'absorption.
Distribution: Répartition principalement dans le plasma.
Métabolisme et excrétion: Métabolisme 40 % (voie métabolique inconnue). Faible excrétion rénale (6 %).
Demi-vie: 20 heures.

Profil temps-action (effets anticholinergiques)

	DÉBUT D'ACTION	PIC	DURÉE
PO	inconnu	5 - 6 h	24 h

CONTRE-INDICATIONS, PRÉCAUTIONS ET MISES EN GARDE

Contre-indications: Hypersensibilité ■ Rétention gastrique ou urinaire, glaucome à angle fermé non traité ou risque d'apparition de ces affections.
Précautions et mises en garde: Obstruction vésicale ■ Maladies obstructives du tractus gastro-intestinal (rectocolite hémorragique, atonie intestinale, myasthénie grave) ■ Glaucome à angle fermé traité (n'administrer le médicament qu'en cas de besoin incontestable et sous surveillance attentive) ■ Cl_{Cr} < 30 mL/min (il est recommandé de réduire la dose) ■ Insuffisance hépatique de modérée à grave ■ **GÉR.**: Plus grande sensibilité aux effets anticholinergiques; il peut s'avérer nécessaire de réduire les doses ■ **OBST., ALLAITEMENT**: N'administrer l'agent que si les bienfaits chez la mère justifient les risques auxquels est exposé le fœtus ou le nouveau-né ■ **PÉD.**: L'innocuité de l'agent n'a pas été établie.

T

RÉACTIONS INDÉSIRABLES ET EFFETS SECONDAIRES

SNC: céphalées, étourdissements, somnolence, fatigue.
ORLO: vision trouble.
GI: constipation, sécheresse de la bouche (xérostomie), dyspepsie.
GU: rétention urinaire, infections urinaires.
Divers: fièvre, coup de chaleur.

INTERACTIONS

Médicament-médicament: Risque d'interaction avec d'autres **médicaments qui entrent en compétition pour la sécrétion tubulaire** ■ Risque accru d'effets anticholinergiques lors de l'administration concomitante d'autres **médicaments ayant des propriétés anticholinergiques**.

VOIES D'ADMINISTRATION ET POSOLOGIE

- **PO (adultes)**: 20 mg, 2 fois par jour.
- **PO (adultes ≥ 75 ans)**: Selon la tolérabilité, on peut administrer 20 mg, 1 fois par jour, au coucher.

INSUFFISANCE RÉNALE

- **PO (ADULTES)**: *CL_{CR} DE 15 À 30 mL/MIN* – 20 mg, 1 FOIS PAR JOUR, AU COUCHER.

PRÉSENTATION

Comprimés: 20 mg.

SOINS INFIRMIERS

ÉVALUATION DE LA SITUATION

- Suivre de près les habitudes d'élimination urinaire ainsi que les ingesta et les excreta.

DIAGNOSTICS INFIRMIERS POSSIBLES

- Élimination urinaire altérée (Indications).

INTERVENTIONS INFIRMIÈRES

- Administrer 1 heure avant les repas ou à jeun.

ENSEIGNEMENT AU PATIENT ET À SES PROCHES

- Recommander au patient de suivre rigoureusement les recommandations du médecin. S'il n'a pas pu prendre le médicament à l'heure habituelle, lui conseiller de prendre la dose suivante 1 heure avant le repas suivant.
- Expliquer au patient qu'il y a risque d'épuisement par la chaleur (fièvre et coup de chaleur dus à une sécrétion moindre de sueur) s'il prend le trospium par temps très chaud.
- Prévenir le patient que le trospium peut provoquer des étourdissements, de la somnolence, des vertiges et une vision trouble. Lui recommander de ne pas conduire et d'éviter les activités qui exigent sa vigilance jusqu'à ce qu'on ait la certitude que le médicament n'entraîne pas ces effets chez lui. Conseiller au patient de ne pas boire de l'alcool à cause du risque accru de somnolence.

VÉRIFICATION DE L'EFFICACITÉ THÉRAPEUTIQUE

L'efficacité du traitement peut être démontrée par: l'augmentation de la capacité de la vessie et la diminution des symptômes de vessie hyperactive. ✳

VACCIN CONTRE LE VIRUS DU PAPILLOME HUMAIN

Gardasil

CLASSIFICATION:

Vaccin recombinant quadrivalent contre le virus du papillome humain (types 6, 11, 16 et 18)

Grossesse – catégorie B

INDICATIONS

Prévention de l'infection par les virus du papillome humain (VPH) de types 6, 11, 16 et 18 ainsi que d'autres maladies causées par les VPH de ces types, soit le cancer de l'utérus, le cancer de la vulve et du vagin, les verrues génitales (condylomes acuminés), l'adénocarcinome in situ (AIS) du col de l'utérus, les néoplasies intraépithéliales cervicales (CIN) de grade 2 et 3, les néoplasies intraépithéliales vulvaires (VIN) de grade 2 et 3, les néoplasies intraépithéliales vaginales (VaIN) de grade 2 et 3 et les néoplasies intraépithéliales cervicales (CIN) de grade 1, chez les filles et les femmes âgées de 9 à 26 ans.

MÉCANISME D'ACTION

Le vaccin est préparé à partir de pseudoparticules virales (PPV) hautement purifiées de la principale protéine (L1) recombinante de la capside des VPH des types 6, 11, 16 et 18. Ces PPV ressemblent aux protéines du virion sauvage, mais ne contiennent pas d'ADN viral. Elles ne peuvent donc ni infecter les cellules ni se reproduire. Le vaccin procure une immunisation active contre le VPH. ***Effets thérapeutiques:*** Protection contre le VPH.

PHARMACOCINÉTIQUE

Absorption: Inconnue.
Distribution: Inconnue.
Métabolisme et excrétion: Inconnus.
Demi-vie: Inconnue.

V

Profil temps-action (immunisation)

	DÉBUT D'ACTION	PIC	DURÉE
IM	inconnu	7 mois	inconnue

CONTRE-INDICATIONS, PRÉCAUTIONS ET MISES EN GARDE

Contre-indications: Hypersensibilité aux ingrédients actifs ou à l'un des excipients du vaccin ■ Patientes présentant des symptômes révélateurs d'une hypersensibilité après avoir reçu une dose de vaccin.

Précautions et mises en garde: PÉD.: L'innocuité et l'efficacité de ce vaccin n'ont pas été établies chez les enfants < 9 ans ■ Adultes > 26 ans (l'efficacité et l'innocuité de l'agent n'ont pas été établies) ■ **OBST.:** L'innocuité de l'agent n'a pas été établie chez la femme enceinte (les femmes qui deviennent enceintes avant d'avoir reçu les trois doses de vaccin prévues au calendrier devraient recevoir les doses manquantes après la naissance du bébé) ■ Épisode actuel ou récent de fièvre (compte tenu de la gravité des symptômes et de leur cause) ■ Thrombopénie ou troubles de la coagulation (administrer seulement si les bienfaits dépassent les risques de saignements) ■ Patientes présentant une réponse immunitaire altérée en raison d'un traitement immunosuppresseur, d'une anomalie génétique, d'une infection par le virus de l'immunodéficience humaine (VIH) ou d'autres causes (la production d'anticorps en réponse à une immunisation active peut être diminuée).

RÉACTIONS INDÉSIRABLES ET EFFETS SECONDAIRES

SNC: étourdissements, insomnie, céphalées.
GI: nausées, diarrhées, vomissements, douleurs abdominales, gastroentérite, APPENDICITE.
Resp.: ASTHME, BRONCHOSPASME, toux.
ORLO: congestion nasale, maux de dents.
GU: MALADIES INFLAMMATOIRES PELVIENNES.
Loc.: arthralgie, ARTHRITE JUVÉNILE, ARTHRITE, POLYARTHRITE RHUMATOÏDE, LUPUS ÉRYTHÉMATEUX DISSÉMINÉ.
Locaux: douleurs, œdème, érythème, prurit.
Divers: fièvre.

INTERACTIONS

Médicament-médicament: Les patientes recevant des immunosuppresseurs à des doses ayant une action générale (**corticostéroïdes**, **antimétabolites**, **agents alkylants** ou **agents cytotoxiques**) risquent de ne pas présenter de réponse optimale à l'immunisation active.
Remarque: Le vaccin contre le virus du papillome humain peut être administré en même temps (à des points d'injection différents) que le **vaccin contre l'hépatite B (recombinant)**.
Médicament-aliments: Interactions inconnues.
Médicament-produits naturels: Interactions inconnues.

VOIES D'ADMINISTRATION ET POSOLOGIE

- **IM:** 0,5 mL à la date choisie, puis 0,5 mL, 2 mois plus tard, et 0,5 mL, 6 mois après la première dose. Si on ne peut respecter le calendrier de vaccination indiqué, il est recommandé d'administrer la deuxième dose au moins 1 mois après la première dose, et la troisième au moins 3 mois après la deuxième dose.

Les trois doses doivent être administrées en l'espace de 1 an. Le vaccin doit être administré dans la région du deltoïde, à la partie supérieure du bras ou dans la région antérolatérale supérieure de la cuisse.

PRÉSENTATION

Fioles à usage unique: 0,5 mL[Pr] ■ **Seringues préremplies à dose unique:** 0,5 mL[Pr]. Une dose de 0,5 mL contient environ 20 µg de protéine L1 du VPH-6, 40 µg de protéine L1 du VPH-11, 40 µg de protéine L1 du VPH-16 et 20 µg de protéine L1 du VPH-18.

SOINS INFIRMIERS

ÉVALUATION DE LA SITUATION

- S'informer des vaccinations antérieures de la patiente et des réactions d'hypersensibilité observées, le cas échéant.

DIAGNOSTICS INFIRMIERS POSSIBLES

- Risque d'infection (Indications).
- Connaissances insuffisantes sur le traitement médicamenteux (Enseignement au patient et à ses proches).

INTERVENTIONS INFIRMIÈRES

- Administrer chaque vaccin par la voie d'administration appropriée.
- Conserver le vaccin au réfrigérateur à une température se situant entre 2 °C et 8 °C. Ne pas congeler. Garder à l'abri de la lumière. Après agitation, la suspension homogène prend la forme d'un liquide blanc trouble. Jeter tout produit qui change de couleur ou qui contient des particules étrangères.

ENSEIGNEMENT AU PATIENT ET À SES PROCHES

- Informer la patiente des réactions indésirables et des effets secondaires possibles. Lui conseiller d'informer le médecin si l'un des symptômes suivants se manifeste: fièvre supérieure à 39,4 °C, difficultés respiratoires, urticaire, démangeaisons, enflure des yeux, du visage ou de l'intérieur du nez, fatigue et faiblesse soudaines et intenses, convulsions.
- Recommander à la patiente de prendre rendez-vous pour la prochaine séance de vaccination, s'il y a lieu.

VÉRIFICATION DE L'EFFICACITÉ THÉRAPEUTIQUE

L'efficacité du traitement peut être démontrée par: la prévention de l'infection au VPH par la vaccination.

VALACYCLOVIR

Valtrex

CLASSIFICATION:

Antiviral

Grossesse – catégorie B

INDICATIONS

Traitement du zona ■ Traitement et suppression des infections génitales herpétiques récurrentes chez les patients immunocompétents ■ Suppression de l'herpès génital récurrent chez les personnes infectées par le VIH ■ Réduction du risque de transmission de l'herpès génital dans le cadre d'un traitement suppressif ■ Traitement de l'herpès labial.

MÉCANISME D'ACTION

Le valacyclovir est rapidement transformé en acyclovir. L'acyclovir entrave la synthèse de l'ADN viral. ***Effets thérapeutiques:*** Inhibition de la réplication virale, raccourcissement de la période d'excrétion virale et accélération de la cicatrisation des lésions.

PHARMACOCINÉTIQUE

Absorption: Biodisponibilité de l'acyclovir – 54 % (après administration PO du valacyclovir).

Distribution: La concentration de l'acyclovir dans le liquide céphalorachidien correspond à 50 % de la concentration plasmatique. L'acyclovir traverse la barrière placentaire et passe dans le lait maternel.

Métabolisme et excrétion: Le valacyclovir est rapidement transformé en acyclovir par métabolisme intestinal et hépatique.

Demi-vie: De 2,5 à 3,3 heures; jusqu'à 14 heures en présence d'insuffisance rénale (acyclovir).

Profil temps-action (concentrations sanguines d'acyclovir)

	Début d'action	Pic	Durée
PO	inconnu	1,5 – 2,5 h	8 – 24 h

CONTRE-INDICATIONS, PRÉCAUTIONS ET MISES EN GARDE

Contre-indications: Hypersensibilité ou intolérance au valacyclovir ou à l'acyclovir.

Précautions et mises en garde: Insuffisance rénale (réduire la posologie ou allonger l'intervalle posologique, si la Cl_{Cr} est < 30 mL/min) ■ **Gér.:** Réduire la dose au besoin ■ **Obst., allaitement, péd.:** L'innocuité de l'agent n'a pas été établie.

V

RÉACTIONS INDÉSIRABLES ET EFFETS SECONDAIRES

SNC: céphalées, étourdissements, faiblesse.
GI: nausées, douleurs abdominales, anorexie, constipation, diarrhée.
Hémat.: PURPURA THROMBOPÉNIQUE THROMBOTIQUE, SYNDROME HÉMOLYTIQUE ET URÉMIQUE (lorsque le médicament est utilisé à très hautes doses chez les patients immunosupprimés).

INTERACTIONS

Médicament-médicament: Le **probénécide** et la **cimétidine** augmentent les concentrations sanguines du médicament.

VOIES D'ADMINISTRATION ET POSOLOGIE

Zona aigu
- **PO (adultes):** 1 g, 3 fois par jour, pendant 7 jours. Amorcer le traitement dans les 72 heures suivant l'apparition des lésions.
- ***INSUFFISANCE RÉNALE***
  PO (ADULTES): *CL_{CR} DE 15 À 30 mL/MIN* – 1 g, TOUTES LES 12 HEURES; *CL_{CR} < 15 mL/MIN* – 1 g, TOUTES LES 24 HEURES.

Épisode initial d'herpès génital
- **PO (adultes):** 1 g, 2 fois par jour, pendant 10 jours. Amorcer le traitement dans les 72 heures (idéalement en moins de 48 heures) suivant l'apparition des lésions.
- ***INSUFFISANCE RÉNALE***
  PO (ADULTES): *CL_{CR} DE 15 À 30 mL/MIN* – 1 g, TOUTES LES 24 HEURES; *CL_{CR} < 15 mL/MIN* – 500 mg, TOUTES LES 24 HEURES.

Herpès génital récurrent
- **PO (adultes):** 500 mg, 2 fois par jour, pendant 3 jours. Le traitement doit être commencé au premier signe ou symptôme de récurrence.
- ***INSUFFISANCE RÉNALE***
  PO (ADULTES): *CL_{CR} < 15 mL/MIN* – 500 mg, TOUTES LES 24 HEURES.

V

Suppression de l'herpès génital chez les patients immunocompétents
- **PO (adultes):** – 1 g, 1 fois par jour, ou 500 mg, 1 fois par jour, chez les patients présentant moins de 10 infections récurrentes par année.
- ***INSUFFISANCE RÉNALE***
  PO (ADULTES): *SUPPRESSION DES INFECTIONS RÉCURRENTES (≥ 10 RÉCURRENCES/ANNÉE): CL_{CR} < 30 mL/MIN* – 500 mg, TOUTES LES 24 HEURES. *SUPPRESSION DES INFECTIONS RÉCURRENTES (< 10 RÉCURRENCES/ANNÉE): CL_{CR} < 15 mL/MIN* – 500 mg, TOUTES LES 48 HEURES.

Suppression de l'herpès génital chez les patients infectés par le VIH dont le nombre de cellules CD_4 est > 100/mm³
- **PO (adultes):** 500 mg, 2 fois par jour. L'innocuité et l'efficacité du traitement pendant plus de 6 mois n'ont pas été évaluées.
- ***INSUFFISANCE RÉNALE***
  PO (ADULTES): *CL_{CR} < 30 mL/MIN* – 500 mg, TOUTES LES 24 HEURES.

Réduction de la transmission de l'herpès génital (patients présentant < 10 infections récurrentes par année)
- **PO (adultes):** 500 mg, 1 fois par jour.

Herpès labial
- **PO (adultes):** 2 g, 2 fois par jour, pour 2 doses. Il est recommandé de prendre la deuxième dose environ 12 heures, mais pas moins de 6 heures, après la première. Le traitement doit être amorcé au tout premier symptôme d'herpès labial.
- ***INSUFFISANCE RÉNALE***
  PO (ADULTES): *CL_{CR} DE 30 À 49 mL/MIN* – 1 g, 2 FOIS PAR JOUR, POUR 2 DOSES; *CL_{CR} DE 10 À 29 mL/MIN* – 500 mg, 2 FOIS PAR JOUR, POUR 2 DOSES; *CL_{CR} < 10 mL/MIN* – 500 mg, POUR 1 DOSE.

PRÉSENTATION

Comprimés: 500 mg[Pr], 1 000 mg[Pr].

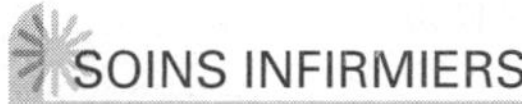

SOINS INFIRMIERS

ÉVALUATION DE LA SITUATION

- Examiner les lésions avant le début du traitement et quotidiennement pendant toute sa durée.
- Rester à l'affût des signes de purpura thrombopénique thrombotique ou d'un syndrome urémique hémolytique (thrombopénie, anémie hémolytique microangiopathique, signes neurologiques, dysfonction rénale, fièvre). Un traitement rapide s'impose en raison du risque de décès.

DIAGNOSTICS INFIRMIERS POSSIBLES

- Risque d'atteinte à l'intégrité de la peau (Indications).
- Risque d'infection (Indications, Enseignement au patient et à ses proches).
- Connaissances insuffisantes sur le traitement médicamenteux (Enseignement au patient et à ses proches).

INTERVENTIONS INFIRMIÈRES

- NE PAS CONFONDRE LE VALACYCLOVIR AVEC LE VALGANCICLOVIR.
- Le valacyclovir peut être administré sans égard aux repas.

Herpès zoster: Le valacyclovir devrait être administré dès que possible après l'apparition des signes ou des symptômes d'herpès zoster; son efficacité est maximale s'il est administré dans les 48 heures qui suivent l'apparition de l'éruption. L'efficacité du traitement amorcé après 72 heures est inconnue.

Herpès génital et labial: Amorcer le traitement de l'herpès génital et labial dès que possible après l'apparition des symptômes.

ENSEIGNEMENT AU PATIENT ET À SES PROCHES

- Inciter le patient à suivre rigoureusement la posologie recommandée pendant toute la durée du traitement. S'il n'a pu prendre le médicament au moment habituel, il doit le prendre le plus rapidement possible sauf si c'est presque l'heure prévue pour la dose suivante.

Herpès zoster: Prévenir le patient que le médicament ne prévient pas la transmission de l'infection à d'autres personnes. Jusqu'à la formation de croûtes sur toutes les lésions, il faut éviter tout contact avec les personnes qui n'ont pas eu la varicelle, qui n'ont pas reçu de vaccin contre la varicelle ou qui sont immunodéprimées.

Herpès génital et labial: Prévenir le patient que le médicament ne prévient pas la transmission de l'herpès labial à d'autres personnes. Lui conseiller de ne pas toucher les lésions et de ne pas avoir de rapports sexuels pendant que des lésions ou des symptômes sont présents. Le valacyclovir réduit le risque de transmission de l'herpès génital à d'autres personnes. Conseiller au patient de ne pas s'engager dans des rapports sexuels non protégés (éviter les rapports sexuels aussi longtemps que les lésions sont présentes et porter un préservatif en latex ou en polyuréthane pendant tout contact génital).

VÉRIFICATION DE L'EFFICACITÉ THÉRAPEUTIQUE

L'efficacité du traitement peut être démontrée par: l'accélération de la cicatrisation complète des lésions, la disparition des vésicules et des ulcères et la formation de croûtes chez les patients atteints d'herpès zoster (zona) ▪ l'accélération de la cicatrisation complète des lésions, la disparition des vésicules et des ulcères et la formation de croûtes chez les patients atteints d'herpès génital ▪ la diminution de la fréquence des récurrences chez les patients atteints d'herpès génital ▪ la diminution de la transmission de l'herpès génital ▪ l'accélération de la cicatrisation complète des lésions, la disparition des vésicules et des ulcères et la formation de croûtes chez les patients atteints d'herpès labial. ✳

VALGANCICLOVIR

Valcyte

CLASSIFICATION:

Antiviral

Grossesse – catégorie C

INDICATIONS

Traitement de la rétinite à cytomégalovirus (CMV) chez les personnes atteintes du sida ▪ Prévention de l'infection à CMV chez les patients ayant reçu une greffe de rein, de rein et pancréas, de foie ou de cœur, qui sont exposés au risque de contracter ce type d'infection.

MÉCANISME D'ACTION

Le valganciclovir est un promédicament qui est rapidement transformé en ganciclovir par les enzymes hépatiques et intestinales. Le CMV transforme le ganciclovir en sa forme active (phosphate de ganciclovir) à l'intérieur de la cellule hôte où il inhibe l'ADN polymérase virale. ***Effets thérapeutiques:*** Effet antiviral dirigé surtout contre les cellules infectées par le cytomégalovirus.

PHARMACOCINÉTIQUE

Absorption: 59,4 % (PO).

Distribution: Inconnue.

Métabolisme et excrétion: Transformation rapide en ganciclovir, lequel est surtout excrété par les reins.

Demi-vie: 4,1 heures (la demi-vie intracellulaire du phosphate de ganciclovir est de 18 heures).

Profil temps-action (concentrations sanguines de ganciclovir)

	Début d'action	Pic	Durée
PO	rapide	2 h	12 - 24 h

CONTRE-INDICATIONS, PRÉCAUTIONS ET MISES EN GARDE

Contre-indications: Hypersensibilité au valganciclovir ou au ganciclovir ▪ Risque d'allergie croisée avec le valacyclovir ou l'acyclovir ▪ **Obst.**: Ce médicament est contre-indiqué chez la femme enceinte. Les femmes en âge de procréer doivent utiliser une méthode contraceptive efficace. Conseiller aux hommes de porter un préservatif durant le traitement et au moins 90 jours après qu'il a pris fin ▪ Hémodialyse ▪ Ne pas administrer aux patients qui présentent un nombre absolu de neutrophiles (NAN) inférieur à $0,5 \times 10^9$/L, un nombre de plaquettes inférieur à 25×10^9/L ou un taux d'hémoglobine inférieur à 80 g/L.

Précautions et mises en garde: Risque de toxicité hématologique ■ Risque de néoplasie ■ Insuffisance rénale (il est recommandé de réduire la dose si la Cl_{Cr} est < 60 mL/min) ■ Dépression médullaire préexistante ■ Radiothérapie ou traitement myélosuppresseur antérieurs ou concomitants ■ **GÉR.**: La diminution de la fonction rénale due au vieillissement dicte une réduction de la dose ■ Stérilité temporaire ou permanente probable chez l'homme. Risque de stérilité chez la femme ■ **PÉD., ALLAITEMENT**: L'innocuité de l'agent n'a pas été établie.

RÉACTIONS INDÉSIRABLES ET EFFETS SECONDAIRES

SNC: CONVULSIONS, céphalées, insomnie, agitation, confusion, étourdissements, hallucinations, psychose, sédation.

GI: douleurs abdominales, diarrhée, nausées, vomissements.

GU: insuffisance rénale.

Hémat.: NEUTROPÉNIE, THROMOCYTOPÉNIE, anémie, anémie aplasique, dépression médullaire, pancytopénie.

SN: ataxie, paresthésie, neuropathie périphérique.

Divers: fièvre, réactions d'hypersensibilité, infections.

INTERACTIONS

Médicament-médicament: Risque accru de toxicité hématologique lors de l'administration concomitante de **zidovudine**, d'**agents antinéoplasiques** ou d'une **radiothérapie** ■ Les concentrations sanguines et les effets peuvent être accrus par le **probénécide** ■ Les insuffisants rénaux risquent que des métabolites de **mycophénolate** et de valganciclovir s'accumulent dans leur organisme ■ Risque accru de néphrotoxicité lors de l'administration concomitante d'autres **agents néphrotoxiques**, de **cyclosporine** ou d'**amphotéricine B** ■ L'agent peut élever les concentrations sanguines et les effets toxiques de la **didanosine** ■ L'administration concomitante d'**imipénem/cilastatine** peut augmenter le risque de convulsions.

Médicament-aliments: Les aliments augmentent l'absorption.

VOIES D'ADMINISTRATION ET POSOLOGIE

Traitement de la rétinite à CMV

- **PO (adultes)**: *Induction* – 900 mg, 2 fois par jour, pendant 21 jours; *traitement d'entretien ou patients atteints de rétinite à CMV inactive* – 900 mg, 1 fois par jour. Si la rétinite s'aggrave, on peut envisager de répéter le traitement d'induction.
- ***INSUFFISANCE RÉNALE***
  PO (ADULTES): *CL_{CR} DE 40 À 59 mL/MIN: INDUCTION* – 450 mg, 2 FOIS PAR JOUR, PENDANT 21 JOURS; *TRAITEMENT D'ENTRETIEN OU PATIENTS ATTEINTS DE RÉTINITE À CMV INACTIVE* – 450 mg, 1 FOIS PAR JOUR. *CL_{CR} DE 25 À 39 mL/MIN: INDUCTION* – 450 mg, 1 FOIS PAR JOUR, PENDANT 21 JOURS; *TRAITEMENT D'ENTRETIEN OU PATIENTS ATTEINTS DE RÉTINITE À CMV INACTIVE* – 450 mg, TOUS LES 2 JOURS. *CL_{CR} DE 10 À 24 mL/MIN: INDUCTION* – 450 mg, TOUS LES 2 JOURS PENDANT 21 JOURS; *TRAITEMENT D'ENTRETIEN OU PATIENTS ATTEINTS DE RÉTINITE À CMV INACTIVE* – 450 mg, 2 FOIS PAR SEMAINE.

Prévention de l'infection à CMV chez les receveurs de greffe

- **PO (adultes)**: 900 mg, 1 fois par jour, en commençant 10 jours avant la greffe et en continuant pendant 100 jours, par la suite.
- ***INSUFFISANCE RÉNALE***
  PO (ADULTES): *CL_{CR} DE 40 À 59 mL/MIN* – 450 mg, 1 FOIS PAR JOUR; *CL_{CR} DE 25 À 39 mL/MIN* – 450 mg, TOUS LES 2 JOURS; *CL_{CR} DE 12 À 24 mL/MIN* – 450 mg, 2 FOIS PAR SEMAINE.

PRÉSENTATION

Comprimés: 450 mg.

SOINS INFIRMIERS

ÉVALUATION DE LA SITUATION

- Avant d'administrer le valganciclovir, il faut confirmer le diagnostic de rétinite à CMV par ophtalmoscopie.
- Avant d'administrer l'agent, prélever des échantillons d'urine, de sang et de sécrétions de la gorge pour une mise en culture permettant de déceler la présence de CMV. Cependant, il n'est pas justifié d'écarter une rétinite à CMV, même si les résultats sont négatifs. Si les symptômes ne disparaissent pas après plusieurs semaines, il se peut qu'une résistance au valganciclovir se soit développée. Il faut effectuer des examens ophtalmiques toutes les semaines, pendant le traitement d'induction et toutes les 2 semaines pendant le traitement d'entretien ou à intervalles plus fréquents si la région maculaire ou le nerf optique sont menacés. La rétinite à CMV peut continuer d'évoluer pendant ou après le traitement au valganciclovir.
- Rester à l'affût des signes suivants d'infection: fièvre, frissons, toux, enrouement, douleurs lombaires ou aux flancs, mictions douloureuses. Prévenir le médecin ou un professionnel de la santé si ces symptômes se manifestent.

- Rechercher les saignements: saignement des gencives, formation d'ecchymoses, pétéchies, présence de sang dans les selles, l'urine ou les vomissures, relevée par l'épreuve au gaïac. Éviter les injections IM et la prise de la température par voie rectale. Appliquer une pression sur les points de ponction veineuse pendant 10 minutes.

Tests de laboratoire:

- Le valganciclovir peut induire une granulopénie, une anémie et une thrombopénie. Suivre de près le compte de granulocytes neutrophiles et de plaquettes tout au long du traitement. Ne pas administrer le médicament si le nombre absolu de neutrophiles (NAN) est inférieur à $0,5 \times 10^9$/L, si le nombre de plaquettes est inférieur à 25×10^9/L ou si la concentration d'hémoglobine est inférieure à 80 g/L. Les valeurs se rétablissent dans les 3 à 7 jours qui suivent l'arrêt du traitement.
- Mesurer l'urée et le taux sérique de créatinine au moins 1 fois toutes les 2 semaines. Le valganciclovir peut élever les taux de créatinine sérique.

DIAGNOSTICS INFIRMIERS POSSIBLES

- Risque d'infection (Indications, Enseignement au patient et à ses proches).
- Connaissances insuffisantes sur le traitement médicamenteux (Enseignement au patient et à ses proches).

INTERVENTIONS INFIRMIÈRES

- NE PAS CONFONDRE LE VALGANCICLOVIR AVEC LE VALACYCLOVIR.
- Le valganciclovir et le ganciclovir ne sont pas interchangeables. On ne doit pas les substituer l'un à l'autre.
- IL FAUT MANIPULER AVEC SOIN LES COMPRIMÉS DE VALGANCICLOVIR. ON NE DOIT PAS LES CASSER NI LES ÉCRASER. ILS PEUVENT ÊTRE TÉRATOGÈNES: ÉVITER TOUT CONTACT AVEC UN COMPRIMÉ CASSÉ OU ÉCRASÉ. EN CAS DE CONTACT AVEC LA PEAU OU UNE MUQUEUSE, BIEN LES LAVER AVEC DE L'EAU ET DU SAVON ET RINCER LES YEUX À GRANDE EAU.

PO: Administrer les capsules avec des aliments.

ENSEIGNEMENT AU PATIENT ET À SES PROCHES

- Recommander au patient de prendre le valganciclovir avec des aliments, en suivant rigoureusement les consignes du médecin.
- Expliquer au patient que le valganciclovir ne guérit pas la rétinite à CMV. La rétinite peut continuer d'évoluer pendant et après le traitement chez les patients présentant un déficit immunitaire. Conseiller au patient de se soumettre à des examens ophtalmiques réguliers au moins à des intervalles de 4 à 6 semaines. La durée du traitement préventif de l'infection à CMV dépend de la durée et de la gravité de l'immunosuppression.
- Le valganciclovir peut provoquer des convulsions, de la somnolence, des étourdissements, de l'ataxie et de la confusion. Conseiller au patient de ne pas conduire et de ne pas s'engager dans d'autres activités qui exigent sa vigilance jusqu'à ce qu'on ait la certitude que le médicament n'entraîne pas ces effets chez lui.
- Recommander au patient de prévenir un professionnel de la santé en cas de fièvre, de frissons, de maux de gorge ou d'autres signes d'infection, tout comme en cas de saignements des gencives, de formation d'ecchymoses, de pétéchies ou de présence de sang dans les selles, l'urine ou les vomissures. L'inciter à éviter les foules ou les personnes ayant contracté une infection. Lui conseiller d'utiliser une brosse à dents à poils doux et un rasoir électrique et de ne pas consommer de boissons alcoolisées ni de produits contenant de l'AAS ou d'AINS.
- Prévenir le patient que le valganciclovir peut avoir des effets tératogènes. Recommander à la patiente d'utiliser une méthode contraceptive non hormonale, et au patient, un condom pendant le traitement et pendant au moins 90 jours par la suite.
- Recommander au patient d'utiliser un écran solaire et de porter des vêtements protecteurs pour prévenir les réactions de photosensibilité.
- Insister sur l'importance des analyses sanguines fréquentes permettant de suivre de près les numérations globulaires.

VÉRIFICATION DE L'EFFICACITÉ THÉRAPEUTIQUE

L'efficacité du traitement peut être démontrée par: le soulagement des symptômes de rétinite à CMV chez les patients atteints du sida. ✳

VALPROATES

acide valproïque

Apo-Valproic, Depakene, Deproic, Dom-Valproic acid, Gen-Valproic, Novo-Valproic, Nu-Valproic, PMS-Valproic acid, Ratio-Valproic, Valproic acid

divalproex sodique

Apo-Divalproex, Divalproex, Epival, Epival ER, Novo-Divalproex, Nu-Divalproex, PMS-Divalproex

valproate sodique
Epiject
CLASSIFICATION:
Anticonvulsivants
Grossesse – catégorie D

INDICATIONS

Traitement des absences épileptiques à symptomatologie simple ou complexe ■ Traitement des crises tonicocloniques ■ **Divalproex seulement**: Épisodes maniaques associés au trouble bipolaire. **Usages non approuvés**: Prévention des migraines (Divalproex seulement).

MÉCANISME D'ACTION

Élévation des concentrations d'acide gamma-aminobutyrique (GABA), neurotransmetteur inhibiteur du SNC. ***Effets thérapeutiques:*** Suppression des épisodes d'absence épileptique ■ Diminution des comportements maniaques ■ Réduction de la fréquence des migraines.

PHARMACOCINÉTIQUE

Absorption: Bonne (PO); les comprimés de divalproex sont recouverts d'un enrobage entérique, ce qui en retarde l'absorption. Biodisponibilité à 100 % (IV).
Distribution: Répartition rapide dans le plasma et les liquides extracellulaires. L'agent traverse la barrière hématoencéphalique et placentaire et passe dans le lait maternel.
Liaison aux protéines: De 90 à 95 %.
Métabolisme et excrétion: Métabolisme majoritairement hépatique. Excrétion rénale (minime sous forme inchangée).
Demi-vie: *Nouveau-nés (≤ 10 jours)*: de 10 à 67 heures; *nourrissons (≥ 2 mois)*: de 7 à 13 heures; adultes: de 6 à 16 heures.

Profil temps-action
(début d'action = effet anticonvulsivant;
pic = concentrations sanguines)

	DÉBUT D'ACTION	PIC	DURÉE
PO – liquide	2 – 4 jours	15 – 120 min	6 – 24 h
PO – capsules	2 – 4 jours	1 – 4 h	6 – 24 h
PO – LP†	2 – 4 jours	3 – 5 h	12 – 24 h
IV	2 – 4 jours	fin de la perfusion	6 – 24 h

† LP = libération prolongée.

CONTRE-INDICATIONS, PRÉCAUTIONS ET MISES EN GARDE

Contre-indications: Hypersensibilité ■ Insuffisance hépatique ■ Hypersensibilité connue à la tartrazine (certains produits en contiennent) ■ Anomalies connues du cycle de l'urée.
Précautions et mises en garde: Troubles hémorragiques ■ Antécédents de maladie hépatique ■ Syndrome cérébral organique ■ Aplasie médullaire ■ Insuffisance rénale ■ **PÉD.** (surtout ≤ 2 ans): Risque accru d'hépatotoxicité ■ **ALLAITEMENT**: L'innocuité de l'agent n'a pas été établie ■ **OBST.**: Des effets tératogènes, des anomalies congénitales et des retards de croissance ont été signalés. Le rapport risques-avantages doit être soigneusement évalué.

RÉACTIONS INDÉSIRABLES ET EFFETS SECONDAIRES

SNC: confusion, étourdissements, céphalées, somnolence.
ORLO: troubles visuels.
GI: HÉPATOTOXICITÉ, indigestion, nausées, vomissements, anorexie, constipation, diarrhée, gain d'appétit, PANCRÉATITE.
Tég.: rash.
Hémat.: leucopénie, allongement du temps de saignement, thrombopénie.
Métab.: hyperammoniémie.
SN: ataxie, paresthésie.

INTERACTIONS

Médicament-médicament: Risque accru de saignements lors de l'administration d'**antiagrégants plaquettaires** (dont l'**aspirine** et les **AINS**, le **tirofiban**, l'**eptifibatide** et l'**abciximab**), d'**héparine** ou d'**héparinoïdes**, d'**agents thrombolytiques** ou de **warfarine** ■ Les valproates diminuent le métabolisme des **barbituriques** et de la **primidone** et en augmentent ainsi le risque de toxicité ■ La **carbamazépine**, la **cimétidine** et l'**érythromycine**, administrés en concomitance, peuvent augmenter les concentrations sanguines de ces agents et accroître le risque de toxicité associée ■ Dépression additive du SNC lors de l'usage concomitant d'autres **dépresseurs du SNC**, incluant l'**alcool**, les **antihistaminiques**, les **antidépresseurs**, les **opioïdes**, les **IMAO** et les **hypnosédatifs** ■ Les doses élevées de **salicylates** (chez les enfants) intensifient les effets de l'acide valproïque ■ Ces agents peuvent augmenter ou diminuer les effets et la toxicité de la **phénytoïne** ■ Les **IMAO** et d'autres **antidépresseurs** peuvent abaisser le seuil des convulsions et diminuer l'efficacité des valproates ■ La **carbamazépine**, la **rifampine** et la **lamotrigine** peuvent diminuer les concentrations sanguines d'acide valproïque ■ L'acide valproïque peut accroître le risque de toxicité associé à la **carbamazépine**, à l'**amitriptyline**, à la **nortriptyline**, à l'**éthosuximide**, à la **lamotrigine** et à la **zidovudine**.

VOIES D'ADMINISTRATION ET POSOLOGIE

Doses exprimées en mg d'acide valproïque.

Anticonvulsivant

- **PO (adultes et enfants):** *Monothérapie* – dose initiale de 15 mg/kg/jour; majorer de 5 à 10 mg/kg/jour, toutes les semaines, jusqu'à l'atteinte des concentrations thérapeutiques (ne pas dépasser 60 mg/kg/jour); lorsque la dose quotidienne est supérieure à 250 mg, il faut la fractionner.
- **IV (adultes et enfants ≥ 2 ans):** Administrer la même dose quotidienne que la dose par voie orale; si la dose est supérieure à 250 mg, administrer en doses fractionnées, toutes les 6 heures (ne pas dépasser 2 000 mg/jour; administrer pendant 48 heures, au maximum).

Agent antimaniaque

- **PO (adultes):** *Divalproex* – initialement, 750 mg/jour en doses fractionnées (ne pas dépasser 60 mg/kg/jour).

PRÉSENTATION

Doses exprimées en mg d'acide valproïque.

- **Acide valproïque (version générique disponible)**
  Capsules: 250 mg[Pr] ■ **Capsules entérosolubles:** 500 mg[Pr] ■ **Sirop:** 250 mg/5 mL[Pr].
- **Valproate sodique**
  Solution pour injection: 100 mg/mL, en fioles de 5 mL[Pr].
- **Dilvaproex sodique**
  Comprimés à libération prolongée: 500 mg[Pr] ■ **Comprimés entérosolubles:** 125 mg[Pr], 250 mg[Pr], 500 mg[Pr].

SOINS INFIRMIERS

ÉVALUATION DE LA SITUATION

Convulsions: Déterminer le siège, la durée et les caractéristiques des convulsions. Prendre les précautions qui s'imposent.

Trouble bipolaire: Évaluer l'humeur, l'idéation et le comportement à intervalles fréquents.

Prophylaxie de la migraine: Noter la fréquence des migraines.

GÉR.: Rester à l'affût des signes de somnolence.

Tests de laboratoire:

- Noter avant le traitement et à intervalles réguliers pendant toute sa durée la numération globulaire, la numération plaquettaire et le temps de saignement. Ces agents peuvent provoquer la leucopénie et la thrombopénie.
- EXAMINER LES RÉSULTATS DES TESTS DE LA FONCTION HÉPATIQUE (LDH, AST, ALT ET BILIRUBINE) ET LES CONCENTRATIONS SÉRIQUES D'AMMONIAQUE AVANT LE TRAITEMENT ET À INTERVALLES RÉGULIERS PENDANT TOUTE SA DURÉE. CES MÉDICAMENTS PEUVENT PROVOQUER UNE TOXICITÉ HÉPATIQUE, IL FAUT DONC SUIVRE DE PRÈS LE PATIENT PENDANT LES 6 PREMIERS MOIS DE TRAITEMENT, CAR ON A SIGNALÉ DES CAS D'ISSUE FATALE. IL FAUT ARRÊTER LE TRAITEMENT EN PRÉSENCE D'HYPERAMMONIÉMIE.
- Ces agents peuvent fausser les résultats des tests de la fonction thyroïdienne et diminuer la réaction au test à la métyrapone.
- Ces agents peuvent entraîner des résultats faussement positifs au dosage de la cétonurie.

TOXICITÉ ET SURDOSAGE: Les concentrations sériques thérapeutiques sont de 350 à 700 µmol/L. Il faut majorer graduellement la dose jusqu'à l'atteinte d'une concentration sérique avant l'administration de la dose d'au moins 350 µmol/L. Toutefois, on n'a pas établi une bonne corrélation entre la dose quotidienne, les concentrations sériques et les effets thérapeutiques. Il faut suivre de près les signes de toxicité chez les patients qui reçoivent une dose s'approchant de la dose maximale de 60 mg/kg/jour.

DIAGNOSTICS INFIRMIERS POSSIBLES

- Risque d'accident (Indications).
- Connaissances insuffisantes sur le traitement médicamenteux (Enseignement au patient et à ses proches).

INTERVENTIONS INFIRMIÈRES

- En raison des effets sédatifs de ces agents, on administre habituellement les doses quotidiennes uniques au coucher.

PO:

- Administrer le médicament pendant ou immédiatement après les repas afin de réduire l'irritation gastrique. LE PATIENT DOIT AVALER LES CAPSULES ET LES COMPRIMÉS À ENROBAGE ENTÉRIQUE TELS QUELS, SANS LES ÉCRASER NI LES MÂCHER, EN RAISON DU RISQUE D'IRRITATION DE LA BOUCHE OU DE LA GORGE. Ne pas administrer les comprimés avec du lait afin d'en prévenir la dissolution prématurée. Les préparations de divalproex sodique à libération prolongée peuvent entraîner moins d'irritation que les comprimés d'acide valproïque.
- Bien mélanger les préparations liquides avant de les verser. Utiliser un récipient gradué pour mesurer les doses et s'assurer qu'elles sont exactes. On peut mélanger le sirop à des aliments ou à d'autres liquides pour en masquer le goût.

- Pour passer d'une préparation d'acide valproïque à une préparation de divalproex sodique, amorcer le traitement par le divalproex sodique à la même dose quotidienne et selon le même schéma posologique que celui par l'acide valproïque. Une fois que l'état du patient s'est stabilisé, tenter d'administrer le divalproex sodique 2 ou 3 fois par jour.

Perfusion intermittente: Le médicament doit être dilué dans une solution de D5%E, de NaCl 0,9% ou de lactate de Ringer, pour obtenir une concentration finale de 2 mg/mL. La solution est stable pendant 24 heures à la température ambiante.

Vitesse d'administration: Perfuser en 60 minutes sans dépasser un débit de 10 mg/min. Une perfusion rapide risque d'intensifier les effets secondaires.

ENSEIGNEMENT AU PATIENT ET À SES PROCHES

- Inciter le patient à respecter rigoureusement la posologie recommandée. S'il doit prendre le médicament 1 fois par jour et s'il n'a pu le prendre au moment habituel, il doit le faire dès que possible. S'il doit prendre plus de 1 dose par jour, il doit la prendre dans les 6 heures suivant l'heure prévue et espacer ensuite les doses restantes de la journée. Le sevrage brusque peut déclencher l'état de mal épileptique.
- Prévenir le patient que ces agents peuvent provoquer de la somnolence ou des étourdissements. Lui conseiller de ne pas conduire et d'éviter les activités qui exigent sa vigilance jusqu'à ce qu'on ait la certitude que le médicament n'entraîne pas ces effets chez lui. Prévenir le patient qu'il ne doit pas conduire avant que le médecin ne lui en donne l'autorisation, une fois les convulsions maîtrisées.
- Recommander au patient d'éviter de boire de l'alcool ou de prendre d'autres dépresseurs du SNC ou des médicaments en vente libre en concomitance, sans consulter au préalable un professionnel de la santé.
- Recommander au patient qui doit suivre un traitement ou subir une intervention chirurgicale d'avertir le professionnel de la santé qu'il suit un traitement par ces médicaments.
- Conseiller au patient de porter sur lui en tout temps une pièce d'identité où est inscrit son traitement médicamenteux.
- INCITER LE PATIENT À PRÉVENIR UN PROFESSIONNEL DE LA SANTÉ SI LES SYMPTÔMES SUIVANTS SURVIENNENT: ANOREXIE, NAUSÉES ET VOMISSEMENTS GRAVES, JAUNISSEMENT DE LA PEAU OU DES YEUX, FIÈVRE, MAUX DE GORGE, MALAISES, FAIBLESSE, ŒDÈME DU VISAGE, LÉTHARGIE, SAIGNEMENTS OU ECCHYMOSES INHABITUELS. LUI CONSEILLER ÉGALEMENT DE PRÉVENIR UN PROFESSIONNEL DE LA SANTÉ SI LE MÉDICAMENT NE PERMET PLUS DE MAÎTRISER LES CONVULSIONS. RECOMMANDER À LA PATIENTE DE COMMUNIQUER AVEC UN PROFESSIONNEL DE LA SANTÉ SI ELLE EST ENCEINTE. PRÉVENIR LES PARENTS QUE LES ENFANTS < 2 ANS SONT PARTICULIÈREMENT PRÉDISPOSÉS À UNE TOXICITÉ HÉPATIQUE D'ISSUE FATALE.
- INSISTER SUR L'IMPORTANCE DES EXAMENS MÉDICAUX RÉGULIERS PERMETTANT D'ÉVALUER L'EFFICACITÉ DU TRAITEMENT.

VÉRIFICATION DE L'EFFICACITÉ THÉRAPEUTIQUE

L'efficacité du traitement peut être démontrée par: la diminution ou la suppression des convulsions sans sédation excessive ■ la diminution de l'incidence des sautes d'humeur chez les patients atteints d'un trouble bipolaire ■ la diminution de la fréquence des migraines.

VALSARTAN,

voir Antagonistes des récepteurs de l'angiotensine II

VANCOMYCINE

PMS-Vancomycin, Vancocin, Vancomycine

CLASSIFICATION:

Antibiotique

Grossesse – catégorie B

INDICATIONS

IV: Traitement des infections staphylococciques graves ou pouvant mettre la vie du patient en danger, dont l'endocardite, la pneumonie, l'ostéomyélite, la septicémie et les infections des tissus mous, lorsque des anti-infectieux moins toxiques sont contre-indiqués, chez les patients allergiques aux pénicillines ou à leurs dérivés et lorsque les antibiogrammes font état d'une résistance à la méthicilline. **PO**: Traitement de l'entérocolite staphylococcique et de la colite pseudomembraneuse due à *Clostridium difficile*.

MÉCANISME D'ACTION

Liaison à la paroi cellulaire bactérienne entraînant la destruction de la bactérie. ***Effets thérapeutiques:*** Effet bactéricide contre les bactéries sensibles. **Spectre d'action**: La vancomycine est active contre les microorganismes à Gram positif dont: les staphylocoques (incluant les souches de *Staphylococcus aureus* résistantes à la méthicilline (SARM)) ■ les streptocoques bêtahémolytiques du groupe A ■ *Streptococcus pneumoniæ* ■ *Corynebacterium* ■ *Clostridium difficile* ■ *Enterococcus fæcalis* ■ *Enterococcus fæcium*.

PHARMACOCINÉTIQUE

Absorption: Négligeable (PO).

Distribution: Tout l'organisme. De 20 à 30 % pénètre dans le liquide céphalorachidien lorsque les méninges sont enflammées. La vancomycine traverse la barrière placentaire.

Métabolisme et excrétion: Excrétion dans les fèces (PO). Excrétion rénale sous forme inchangée (IV).

Demi-vie: *Nouveau-nés:* de 6 à 10 heures; *enfants de 3 mois à 3 ans:* 4 heures; *enfants > 3 ans:* de 2,2 à 3 heures; *adultes:* de 4 à 6 heures (prolongée en cas d'insuffisance rénale).

Profil temps-action

	Début d'action	Pic	Durée
IV	rapide	fin de la perfusion	12 - 24 h

CONTRE-INDICATIONS, PRÉCAUTIONS ET MISES EN GARDE

Contre-indications: Hypersensibilité.

Précautions et mises en garde: Insuffisance rénale (réduire la dose si la Cl_{Cr} est < 80 mL/min) ■ Troubles auditifs ■ Occlusion ou inflammation intestinale (absorption systémique accrue lors de l'administration par voie orale) ■ Patients brûlés (taux de clairance totale de l'organisme plus élevés, d'où la nécessité d'administrer des doses plus fréquentes et plus élevées) ■ **Obst., allaitement**: L'innocuité de la vancomycine n'a pas été établie.

RÉACTIONS INDÉSIRABLES ET EFFETS SECONDAIRES

ORLO: ototoxicité.

CV: hypotension.

GI: nausées, vomissements.

GU: <u>néphrotoxicité</u>.

Tég.: rash.

Hémat.: éosinophilie, leucopénie.

Locaux: <u>phlébite</u>.

Loc.: douleurs lombaires et cervicales.

Divers: réactions d'hypersensibilité, incluant l'ANAPHYLAXIE, la fièvre, les frissons, le « syndrome du cou rouge » (relié à une vitesse de perfusion trop rapide), la surinfection.

INTERACTIONS

Médicament-médicament: Risque d'effets ototoxiques et néphrotoxiques additifs lors de l'administration concomitante d'autres **médicaments dotés de propriétés ototoxiques et néphrotoxiques** (**aspirine**, **aminosides**, **cyclosporine**, **cisplatine**, **diurétiques de l'anse**) ■ La vancomycine peut intensifier l'effet de blocage neuromusculaire exercé par les **bloqueurs neuromusculaires de type non dépolarisant** ■ Risque accru de rougeurs induites par l'histamine lors de l'administration concomitante d'**anesthésiques généraux** chez les enfants.

VOIES D'ADMINISTRATION ET POSOLOGIE

Modifier la posologie chez les insuffisants rénaux pour prévenir l'atteinte de taux sériques toxiques.

Infections systémiques graves

- **IV (adultes)**: 500 mg, toutes les 6 heures, ou 1 g, toutes les 12 heures (jusqu'à 3 ou 4 g par jour).
- **IV (enfants > 1 mois)**: 10 mg/kg, toutes les 6 heures.
- **IV (nouveau-nés de 1 semaine à 1 mois)**: Initialement, 15 mg/kg, puis 10 mg/kg, toutes les 8 heures.
- **IV (nouveau-nés < 1 semaine)**: Initialement, 15 mg/kg, puis 10 mg/kg, toutes les 12 heures.

Colite pseudomembraneuse et entérocolite staphylococcique

- **PO (adultes)**: De 125 à 500 mg, toutes les 6 à 8 heures.
- **PO (enfants)**: 40 mg/kg/jour, en 3 ou 4 prises (ne pas dépasser 2 g/jour).

INSUFFISANCE RÉNALE

- **IV (ADULTES)**: *DOSE D'ATTAQUE:* 15 mg/kg; CHEZ LES PATIENTS ATTEINTS D'INSUFFISANCE RÉNALE, LA MESURE DES CONCENTRATIONS SÉRIQUES CONSTITUE LA MÉTHODE OPTIMALE POUR ÉTABLIR LA DOSE D'ENTRETIEN.

PRÉSENTATION (version générique disponible)

- **Capsules**: 125 mg^{Pr}, 250 mg^{Pr} ■ **Poudre pour injection**: fioles de 500 mg, de 1 g^{Pr}, de 5 g^{Pr} et de 10 g^{Pr}.

SOINS INFIRMIERS

ÉVALUATION DE LA SITUATION

- Au début du traitement et pendant toute sa durée, rester à l'affût des signes suivants d'infection: altération des signes vitaux; aspect de la plaie, des crachats,

V

de l'urine et des selles; accroissement du nombre de leucocytes.

- Prélever des échantillons pour les cultures et les antibiogrammes avant le début du traitement. La première dose peut être administrée avant que les résultats soient connus.
- Suivre de près le point d'injection IV. La vancomycine irrite les tissus et peut entraîner la nécrose et une douleur intense en cas d'extravasation. Assurer la rotation des points de perfusion.
- Mesurer la pression artérielle pendant toute la durée de la perfusion IV.
- Chez les patients prédisposés à un dysfonctionnement rénal et chez ceux > 60 ans, déterminer les concentrations sériques de vancomycine ainsi que le fonctionnement de la VIIIe paire de nerfs crâniens par audiométrie avant le début du traitement et pendant toute sa durée. Pour prévenir les lésions permanentes, un diagnostic et une intervention rapides sont essentiels.
- Effectuer le bilan quotidien des ingesta et des excreta et peser le patient tous les jours. Une urine trouble ou rosée peut être un signe de toxicité rénale.
- Suivre de près les signes suivants de surinfection: excroissance noire pileuse sur la langue, démangeaisons ou pertes vaginales, selles molles ou nauséabondes. Signaler ces signes, le cas échéant.

Colite pseudomembraneuse: Évaluer tout au long du traitement l'état de la fonction intestinale: ausculter les bruits intestinaux; déterminer la fréquence des défécations et la consistance des matières fécales ainsi que la présence de sang ou de mucus dans les selles.

Tests de laboratoire:

- Noter le nombre de cylindres et de cellules ainsi que la concentration d'albumine dans l'urine. Rester à l'affût d'une diminution de la gravité spécifique de l'urine; vérifier la numération globulaire et les résultats des tests de la fonction rénale à intervalles réguliers, pendant toute la durée du traitement.
- La vancomycine peut entraîner l'élévation des concentrations d'urée.

TOXICITÉ ET SURDOSAGE: Les concentrations pic de la vancomycine ne devraient pas dépasser de 25 à 40 µg/mL. Habituellement, les creux sanguins visés sont de 5 à 10 µg/mL, mais selon le type de bactérie, le siège de l'infection et la présence ou non de matériel prosthétique infecté, on peut viser des creux de 10 à 15 µg/mL ou même allant jusqu'à 15 à 20 µg/mL ou plus.

DIAGNOSTICS INFIRMIERS POSSIBLES

- Risque d'infection (Indications).
- Trouble de la perception auditive (Effets secondaires).
- Connaissances insuffisantes sur le traitement médicamenteux (Enseignement au patient et à ses proches).

INTERVENTIONS INFIRMIÈRES

PO: Chez les patients qui ne peuvent avaler les capsules de vancomycine, on peut diluer les préparations destinées à la voie IV dans 30 mL d'eau et les administrer par voie orale ou par sonde nasogastrique, car le contenu des capsules est très dur et très difficile à faire sortir. Cette solution a un goût amer et désagréable. Elle est stable pendant 14 jours au réfrigérateur.

Perfusion intermittente: Diluer le contenu d'une fiole de 500 mg avec 10 mL d'eau stérile pour injection. Diluer une fois de plus dans 100 à 250 mL de solution de NaCl 0,9 % ou de D5%E. Les solutions obtenues après la reconstitution et les solutés préparés doivent être utilisés dans les 24 heures s'ils sont conservés à la température ambiante ou dans les 96 heures s'ils sont conservés au réfrigérateur. Consulter les directives du fabricant avant de reconstituer la préparation.

Vitesse d'administration: Administrer en au moins 60 minutes, à un débit maximum de 10 mg/min. Ne pas administrer rapidement ou sous forme de bolus afin de réduire le risque de thrombophlébite, d'hypotension et de « syndrome du cou rouge » (hypotension soudaine et grave; rougeur ou rash maculopapulaire au niveau du visage, du cou, de la poitrine et des membres supérieurs). Il peut s'avérer nécessaire de perfuser les doses plus lentement (en 1,5 à 2 heures ou plus) en cas d'apparition du « syndrome du cou rouge ». On peut réduire le risque de thrombophlébite en utilisant des solutions diluées de 2,5 à 5 mg/mL et en assurant la rotation des points d'injection.

Compatibilité (tubulure en Y): acyclovir ▪ amifostine ▪ amiodarone ▪ atracurium ▪ cyclophosphamide ▪ diltiazem ▪ énalaprilate ▪ esmolol ▪ filgrastim ▪ fluconazole ▪ fludarabine ▪ gallium, nitrate de ▪ hydromorphone ▪ insuline ▪ labétalol ▪ lorazépam ▪ magnésium, sulfate de ▪ melphalan ▪ mépéridine ▪ midazolam ▪ morphine ▪ ondansétron ▪ paclitaxel ▪ pancuronium ▪ perphénazine ▪ sodium, bicarbonate de ▪ tacrolimus ▪ téniposide ▪ théophylline ▪ thiotépa ▪ tolazoline ▪ vécuronium ▪ vinorelbine ▪ zidovudine.

Incompatibilité (tubulure en Y): albumine ▪ céfépime ▪ héparine ▪ idarubicine ▪ pipéracilline/tazobactam.

ENSEIGNEMENT AU PATIENT ET À SES PROCHES

- Inciter le patient qui doit prendre la vancomycine par voie orale à respecter rigoureusement la posologie recommandée. S'il n'a pu prendre le médicament au moment habituel, il doit le prendre aussitôt que possible, mais pas s'il est presque l'heure de la dose suivante. Le prévenir qu'il ne doit pas remplacer une dose manquée par une double dose.

- Recommander au patient de signaler les signes d'hypersensibilité, les acouphènes, les vertiges ou une perte auditive.
- Inciter le patient à communiquer avec un professionnel de la santé si les symptômes ne s'améliorent pas en l'espace de quelques jours.

VÉRIFICATION DE L'EFFICACITÉ THÉRAPEUTIQUE

L'efficacité du traitement peut être démontrée par: la disparition des signes et des symptômes d'infection; le temps nécessaire à une résolution complète dépend du microorganisme infectant et du siège de l'infection.

VARDÉNAFIL

Levitra

CLASSIFICATION:

Agent utilisé dans le traitement de l'impuissance (inhibiteur de la phosphodiestérase de type 5)

Grossesse – catégorie inconnue

INDICATIONS

Traitement du dysfonctionnement érectile.

MÉCANISME D'ACTION

Amplification des effets du monoxyde d'azote libéré à la suite d'une stimulation sexuelle. Le monoxyde d'azote active l'enzyme guanylate cyclase, ce qui entraîne une élévation des concentrations de guanosine monophosphate cyclique (GMPc). La GMPc entraîne la relaxation des muscles lisses du corps caverneux, ce qui favorise l'afflux du sang dans le pénis et l'érection qui s'ensuit. Le vardénafil inhibe la phosphodiestérase de type 5 (PDE5), l'enzyme responsable de la biodégradation de la GMPc dans le corps caverneux. ***Effets thérapeutiques:*** Augmentation du flux sanguin dans le corps caverneux entraînant une érection suffisante pour permettre les rapports sexuels. Une stimulation sexuelle est nécessaire.

PHARMACOCINÉTIQUE

Absorption: 15 % (PO).

Distribution: Tissus.

Liaison aux protéines: 95 %.

Métabolisme et excrétion: Métabolisme hépatique principalement par l'enzyme 3A4 du cytochrome P450 et, accessoirement, par les enzymes 2C9 et 3A5. Élimination sous forme de métabolites dans les fèces (de 91 à 95 %) et dans les urines (de 2 à 6 %).

Demi-vie: De 4 à 5 heures.

Profil temps-action (effet sur l'érection)

	DÉBUT D'ACTION	PIC	DURÉE
PO	25 min	inconnu	jusqu'à 4 h

CONTRE-INDICATIONS, PRÉCAUTIONS ET MISES EN GARDE

Contre-indications: Hypersensibilité ■ TRAITEMENT CONCOMITANT PAR UN DÉRIVÉ NITRÉ ORGANIQUE (NITROGLYCÉRINE, MONONITRATE D'ISOSORBIDE, DINITRATE D'ISOSORBIDE) ■ Traitement concomitant avec l'indinavir, le ritonavir, le kétoconazole ou l'itraconazole.

Précautions et mises en garde: Hommes chez lesquels l'activité sexuelle est déconseillée ■ Maladie cardiovasculaire grave sous-jacente (notamment des antécédents d'infarctus du myocarde [IM] au cours des 6 derniers mois, d'angine instable, d'accident vasculaire cérébral au cours des 6 derniers mois ou d'arythmies non maîtrisées), insuffisance cardiaque ou coronaropathie accompagnée d'angine instable ■ Antécédents d'hypertension (> 140/90 mm Hg) ou d'hypotension (< 90/50 mm Hg) non maîtrisée ■ Sténose aortique ou cardiomyopathie hypertrophique ■ Allongement congénital de l'espace Q-T (syndrome du Q-T long) ou prise d'un antiarythmique de classe IA ou III ■ Troubles hémorragiques ou ulcère gastroduodénal en évolution ■ Troubles associés au priapisme (drépanocytose, myélome multiple, leucémie) ■ Déformation anatomique du pénis (angulation, fibrose caverneuse, maladie de La Peyronie) ■ Insuffisance rénale exigeant une dialyse, insuffisance hépatique modérée à grave ■ Antécédents de neuropathie optique ischémique antérieure non artéritique (NOIANA) ■ Troubles héréditaires dégénératifs connus de la rétine, tels que la rétinite pigmentaire ■ **OBST., ALLAITEMENT, PÉD.:** Le médicament n'est pas indiqué chez les femmes et chez les enfants < 18 ans ■ **GÉR.:** Il est recommandé de diminuer la dose chez les patients > 65 ans.

RÉACTIONS INDÉSIRABLES ET EFFETS SECONDAIRES

SNC: céphalées, étourdissements.

GI: nausées, dyspepsie.

CV: tachycardie, hypotension, hypertension, INFARCTUS DU MYOCARDE, ANGINE DE POITRINE.

GU: priapisme (plus de 4 heures).

Hémat.: hausse des taux de créatinine kinase.

Loc.: lombalgies, myalgies.
ORLO: rhinite, sinusite, symptômes pseudogrippaux, troubles de vision colorée, PERTE DE VISION SOUDAINE.
Tég.: bouffées vasomotrices.

INTERACTIONS

Médicament-médicament: RISQUE ACCRU D'HYPOTENSION LORS DE LA PRISE CONCOMITANTE DE **DÉRIVÉS NITRÉS**, SOUS QUELQUE FORME QUE CE SOIT; L'USAGE CONCOMITANT EST CONTRE-INDIQUÉ EN RAISON DU RISQUE D'HYPOTENSION GRAVE POUVANT ÊTRE D'ISSUE FATALE ▪ L'ADMINISTRATION CONCOMITANTE D'**ANTIARYTHMIQUES DE CLASSE IA** (**QUINIDINE** OU **PROCAÏNAMIDE**) **OU DE CLASSE III** (**AMIODARONE** OU **SOTALOL**) AUGMENTE LE RISQUE D'ARYTHMIES POUVANT METTRE LA VIE DU PATIENT EN DANGER ▪ Augmentation des concentrations sanguines du vardénafil et diminution de sa clairance lors de l'administration concomitante de **kétoconazole**, d'**indinavir**, de **ritonavir** et d'**itraconazole** (une utilisation simultanée est donc contre-indiquée) ▪ Risque accru d'hypotension lors de l'administration concomitante d'**antihypertenseurs** ▪ La prise concomitante d'**érythromycine** augmente considérablement les concentrations sanguines de vardénafil; il est recommandé de ne pas administrer une dose supérieure à 5 mg de vardénafil ▪ Risque accru d'hypotension lors de l'administration concomitante de **doxazosine**, de **prazosine** et de **terazosine**.
Médicament-aliments: La consommation de **pamplemousse** (ou de jus de pamplemousse), même espacée de plusieurs heures de la prise de vardénafil, est susceptible d'en augmenter les concentrations plasmatiques. Il est recommandé de ne pas consommer de pamplemousse durant le traitement par le vardénafil.

VOIES D'ADMINISTRATION ET POSOLOGIE

- **PO (adultes)**: 10 mg, de 25 à 60 minutes avant des rapports sexuels prévus; ne pas administrer plus souvent que 1 fois par jour. La dose peut être ajustée à la baisse (5 mg) ou à la hausse (20 mg), en fonction de la réponse au traitement et de la tolérance du patient. La dose maximale quotidienne est de 20 mg.
- **PO (personnes âgées)**: Dose initiale de 5 mg, de 25 à 60 minutes avant des rapports sexuels prévus; ne pas administrer plus souvent que 1 fois par jour. La dose pourra être portée à 10 mg ou à 20 mg en fonction de la réponse au traitement et de la tolérance du patient.
- ***INSUFFISANCE HÉPATIQUE***

  PO (ADULTES): *INSUFFISANCE HÉPATIQUE MODÉRÉE (CHILD-PUGH B)* – DOSE INITIALE DE 5 mg, DE 25 À 60 MINUTES AVANT DES RAPPORTS SEXUELS PRÉVUS; NE PAS ADMINISTRER PLUS SOUVENT QUE 1 FOIS PAR JOUR. LA DOSE PEUT ÊTRE AUGMENTÉE JUSQU'À CONCURRENCE DE 10 mg, SELON LA TOLÉRANCE DU PATIENT ET SA RÉPONSE AU TRAITEMENT.

PRÉSENTATION

Comprimés: 5 mg^{Pr}, 10 mg^{Pr}, 20 mg^{Pr}.

SOINS INFIRMIERS

ÉVALUATION DE LA SITUATION

- Déterminer la présence d'un dysfonctionnement érectile avant l'administration du médicament. Le vardénafil n'a aucun effet en l'absence d'une stimulation sexuelle.

DIAGNOSTICS INFIRMIERS POSSIBLES

- Dysfonctionnement sexuel (Indications).
- Connaissances insuffisantes sur le traitement médicamenteux (Enseignement au patient et à ses proches).

INTERVENTIONS INFIRMIÈRES

- La dose de vardénafil doit habituellement être prise de 25 à 60 minutes avant les rapports sexuels. La fréquence d'administration maximale recommandée est de 1 fois par jour. Le vardénafil peut être pris avec ou sans aliments. La consommation d'un repas riche en matières grasses peut retarder de 1 heure l'atteinte des concentrations plasmatiques maximales.

ENSEIGNEMENT AU PATIENT ET À SES PROCHES

- Expliquer au patient qu'il devrait prendre le vardénafil de 25 à 60 minutes avant les rapports sexuels et qu'il ne doit pas prendre ce médicament plus souvent que 1 fois par jour. Le prévenir qu'une stimulation sexuelle est nécessaire afin d'obtenir une érection.
- Prévenir le patient que le vardénafil est contre-indiqué chez la femme.
- Prévenir le patient qu'il ne doit pas prendre en même temps le vardénafil et des dérivés nitrés.
- Conseiller au patient de prévenir rapidement un professionnel de la santé si l'érection dure plus de 4 heures ou s'il remarque une perte de vision rapide ou graduelle affectant un œil ou les deux yeux.
- Conseiller au patient de consulter un professionnel de la santé avant de prendre un médicament en vente libre ou un produit naturel.

- Informer le patient que le vardénafil n'assure aucune protection contre les maladies transmissibles sexuellement. Lui conseiller de prendre les mesures de protection nécessaires contre ces maladies et l'infection par le VIH.

VÉRIFICATION DE L'EFFICACITÉ THÉRAPEUTIQUE

L'efficacité du traitement peut être démontrée par: une érection suffisante pour que le patient puisse s'engager dans des rapports sexuels. ✳

VENLAFAXINE

Effexor XR, Novo-Venlafaxine XR

CLASSIFICATION:

Antidépresseur, traitement de l'anxiété généralisée, de la phobie sociale et du trouble panique

Grossesse – catégorie C (risque durant le 3e trimestre; voir «Précautions et mises en garde»)

INDICATIONS

Dépression ▪ anxiété généralisée ▪ phobie sociale ▪ trouble panique. **Usages non approuvés:** Trouble dysphorique prémenstruel.

MÉCANISME D'ACTION

Inhibition du recaptage de la sérotonine et de la noradrénaline dans le SNC. ***Effets thérapeutiques:*** Diminution des symptômes de la dépression avec moins de rechutes et de récurrences ▪ Diminution de l'anxiété ▪ Diminution de la fréquence des crises de panique ou des épisodes de phobie sociale.

PHARMACOCINÉTIQUE

Absorption: De 92 à 100 % (PO).

Distribution: Tous les tissus de l'organisme.

Métabolisme et excrétion: Premier passage hépatique important. Un métabolite, la O-déméthylvenlafaxine (ODV), exerce une activité antidépressive; 5 % de la venlafaxine est excrété à l'état inchangé dans l'urine; 30 % du métabolite actif est excrété dans l'urine.

Demi-vie: *Venlafaxine* – de 3 à 5 heures; *ODV* – de 9 à 11 heures (la demi-vie est prolongée en présence d'une insuffisance hépatique ou rénale).

Profil temps-action (effets antidépresseurs)

	Début d'action	Pic	Durée
PO	en 2 semaines	2 - 4 semaines	inconnue

CONTRE-INDICATIONS, PRÉCAUTIONS ET MISES EN GARDE

Contre-indications: Hypersensibilité ▪ Traitement concomitant par un IMAO (prévoir 14 jours entre l'arrêt de l'administration l'IMAO et le début de l'administration de la venlafaxine, et vice versa; risque de réactions graves pouvant mener à une issue fatale).

Précautions et mises en garde: Risque d'effets indésirables de type agitation grave, parallèlement à des blessures infligées à soi-même ou aux autres ▪ Éviter de mettre fin abruptement au traitement, en raison du risque de symptômes de sevrage ▪ La surveillance des idées suicidaires est indiquée chez tous les patients recevant ce médicament ▪ Une élévation des valeurs tensionnelles reliée à la dose a été constatée chez certains patients traités par la venlafaxine. Des rapports de pharmacovigilance font également état de rares cas de crise hypertensive ou d'hypertension maligne chez des patients normotendus ou des patients sous traitement antihypertenseur ▪ Maladie cardiovasculaire, incluant l'hypertension ▪ Risque d'élévation de la cholestérolémie ▪ Risque d'hyponatrémie, le plus souvent chez des patients présentant une déplétion volumique ou une déshydratation, dont ceux sous diurétiques. L'hyponatrémie semble être réversible à l'arrêt du traitement; dans la majorité des cas, il s'agit de personnes âgées ▪ Risque de syndrome de sécrétion inappropriée d'hormone antidiurétique (SIADH) ▪ Risque de saignements anormaux ▪ Insuffisance hépatique (il est recommandé de réduire la dose) ▪ Insuffisance rénale (il est recommandé de réduire la dose) ▪ Antécédents de convulsions ou de troubles neurologiques ▪ Antécédents de manie et d'hypomanie ▪ Antécédents de pharmacodépendance ▪ **Obst.:** Risque de complication chez le nouveau-né lorsque la mère a pris ce médicament durant le 3e trimestre ▪ **Allaitement:** La femme qui allaite ne devrait pas prendre de la venlafaxine. Si son médecin juge cependant que ce traitement est essentiel, il doit envisager la possibilité que le nourrisson présente, à l'arrêt de l'allaitement, des symptômes de sevrage ▪ **Péd.:** L'innocuité et l'efficacité de l'agent n'ont pas été établies.

V

RÉACTIONS INDÉSIRABLES ET EFFETS SECONDAIRES

SNC: CONVULSIONS, rêves bizarres, anxiété, étourdissements, céphalées, insomnie, nervosité, faiblesse, modification des opérations de la pensée, agitation, confusion, dépersonnalisation, somnolence, labilité émotionr[illegible], aggravation de la dépression.

ORLO: rhinite, troubles visuels, acouphènes.

CV: douleurs thoraciques, hypertension, pal[illegible] tachycardie.

GI: douleurs abdominales, altération du goût, anorexie, constipation, sécheresse de la bouche (xérostomie), dyspepsie, nausées, vomissements, perte de poids.
GU: dysfonctionnement sexuel, mictions fréquentes, rétention urinaire.
Tég.: ecchymoses, démangeaisons, photosensibilité, rash.
SN: paresthésie, mouvements brefs et saccadés.
Divers: frissons, bâillements.

INTERACTIONS

Médicament-médicament: LA VENLAFAXINE PEUT PROVOQUER DES RÉACTIONS GRAVES, POUVANT ÊTRE D'ISSUE FATALE, EN CAS D'ADMINISTRATION CONCOMITANTE D'**IMAO** (NE PAS ADMINISTRER EN MÊME TEMPS; CESSER L'ADMINISTRATION DE L'IMAO AU MOINS 2 SEMAINES AVANT D'AMORCER LE TRAITEMENT PAR LA VENLAFAXINE ET VICE VERSA) ■ L'usage concomitant d'**alcool** et d'autres **dépresseurs du SNC**, comme les **antihistaminiques**, l'**alcool**, les **opioïdes** et les **hypnosédatifs**, chez les patients déprimés, est déconseillé ■ Risque d'effets sérotoninergiques additifs lors de l'administration concomitante de **lithium**; administrer ce dernier agent avec prudence chez les patients qui prennent la venlafaxine ■ Risque d'interaction avec les **médicaments inhibiteurs du cytochrome P450 2D6,** car la venlafaxine est métabolisée par ce système enzymatique et une augmentation de ses concentrations plasmatiques peut survenir ■ Risque de syndrome sérotoninergique lors de l'utilisation concomitante de **trazodone**, de **sibutramine**, le **linézolide**, d'**ISRS** (comme la **paroxétine** et la **fluoxétine**) et d'**antimigraineux de la classe des agonistes des récepteurs 5-HT_1**, tels que le **sumatriptan** ■ Risque d'intensification des effets de la venlafaxine lors de l'administration concomitante de **cimétidine** (l'effet peut être plus prononcé chez les personnes âgées, les insuffisants rénaux ou hépatiques ou les patients hypertendus).
Médicament-produits naturels: La consommation concomitante de **kava**, de **valériane**, de **véronique en écusson**, de **camomille** ou de **houblon** peut augmenter l'effet dépresseur du SNC ■ La consommation concomitante de **millepertuis** ou de **SAMe** augmente le risque d'effets secondaires sérotoninergiques, incluant le syndrome sérotoninergique.

V

VOIES D'ADMINISTRATION ET POSOLOGIE

Dépression

- **PO (adultes)**: Initialement, 75 mg, 1 fois par jour pendant 4 à 7 jours (certains patients peuvent commencer le traitement avec 37,5 mg/jour); on peut augmenter la dose de 75 mg par jour, à des intervalles de 4 jours (écart posologique: de 75 à 225 mg).

Anxiété généralisée

- **PO (adultes)**: Initialement, 37,5 mg/jour, 1 fois par jour pendant 4 à 7 jours; on peut augmenter la dose de 75 mg par jour, à des intervalles de 4 jours (écart posologique: de 75 à 225 mg).

Phobie sociale

- **PO (adultes)**: Initialement, 75 mg, 1 fois par jour pendant 4 à 7 jours (certains patients peuvent commencer le traitement avec 37,5 mg/jour); on peut augmenter la dose de 75 mg par jour, à des intervalles de 4 jours (écart posologique: de 75 à 225 mg).

Trouble panique

- **PO (adultes)**: 37,5 mg/jour, 1 fois par jour pendant 7 jours; on peut augmenter la dose de 75 mg par jour, à des intervalles de 7 jours (écart posologique: de 75 à 225 mg).

INSUFFISANCE HÉPATIQUE

- **PO (ADULTES)**: RÉDUIRE LA DOSE QUOTIDIENNE DE MOITIÉ CHEZ LES PATIENTS PRÉSENTANT UNE INSUFFISANCE HÉPATIQUE MODÉRÉE.

INSUFFISANCE RÉNALE

- **PO (ADULTES)**: *INSUFFISANCE RÉNALE LÉGÈRE À MODÉRÉE* – RÉDUIRE LA DOSE QUOTIDIENNE DE 25 À 50 %.

PRÉSENTATION

Capsules à libération prolongée: 37,5 mg[Pr], 75 mg[Pr], 150 mg[Pr].

SOINS INFIRMIERS

ÉVALUATION DE LA SITUATION

- Suivre de près l'état mental du patient et ses changements d'humeur. Signaler au médecin ou à un autre professionnel de la santé l'aggravation de l'anxiété, de l'agitation ou de l'insomnie.
- Observer les tendances suicidaires, particulièrement durant le traitement initial. Réduire la quantité de médicament dont le patient peut disposer.
- Mesurer la pression artérielle avant le début du traitement et à intervalles réguliers, pendant toute sa durée. Une hypertension soutenue peut être reliée à la dose; réduire la dose ou arrêter le traitement dans ce cas.
- Suivre de près l'appétit et l'apport nutritionnel. Peser le patient toutes les semaines. Signaler toute perte de poids continue. Adapter le régime alimen-

taire selon les aliments que le patient peut tolérer pour maintenir son état nutritionnel.

Tests de laboratoire:

- Noter la numération globulaire, la formule leucocytaire et le nombre de plaquettes à intervalles réguliers pendant toute la durée du traitement. La venlafaxine peut entraîner l'anémie, la leucocytose, la leucopénie, la thrombopénie, la basophilie et l'éosinophilie.
- La venlafaxine peut élever les concentrations sériques de phosphatase alcaline, de bilirubine, d'AST, d'ALT, d'urée et de créatinine.
- Ce médicament peut aussi élever les taux sériques de cholestérol.
- La venlafaxine peut entraîner des anomalies électrolytiques, telles que l'hyperglycémie ou l'hypoglycémie, l'hyperkaliémie ou l'hypokaliémie, l'hyperuricémie, l'hyperphosphatémie ou l'hypophosphatémie et l'hyponatrémie.

DIAGNOSTICS INFIRMIERS POSSIBLES

- Stratégies d'adaptation inefficaces (Indications).
- Risque d'accident (Réactions secondaires).
- Connaissances insuffisantes sur le traitement médicamenteux (Enseignement au patient et à ses proches).

INTERVENTIONS INFIRMIÈRES

- Administrer la venlafaxine avec des aliments.
- LES COMPRIMÉS À LIBÉRATION PROLONGÉE DOIVENT ÊTRE AVALÉS TELS QUELS. IL NE FAUT PAS LES ÉCRASER, LES BRISER OU LES MÂCHER.
- On peut aussi ouvrir les comprimés à libération prolongée et en saupoudrer avec le contenu d'une cuillérée de compote de pommes. Demander au patient de l'avaler immédiatement et de boire ensuite un verre d'eau. Ne pas conserver le mélange en vue d'une utilisation ultérieure.

ENSEIGNEMENT AU PATIENT ET À SES PROCHES

- Conseiller au patient de respecter rigoureusement la posologie recommandée. S'il n'a pas pu prendre le médicament au moment habituel, il doit le faire dès que possible à moins que ce ne soit presque l'heure prévue pour la dose suivante. Lui recommander de ne jamais remplacer une dose manquée par une double dose ou de cesser brusquement le traitement. Prévenir le patient qui prend ce médicament depuis plus de 6 semaines, qu'il faut réduire la dose graduellement avant de cesser le traitement.
- Prévenir le patient que la venlafaxine peut parfois provoquer de la somnolence ou des étourdissements. Lui conseiller de ne pas conduire et d'éviter les activités qui exigent sa vigilance jusqu'à ce qu'on ait la certitude que le médicament n'entraîne pas ces effets chez lui.
- Mettre en garde le patient contre la consommation d'alcool ou d'autres dépresseurs du SNC en même temps que cet agent et lui conseiller de consulter un professionnel de la santé avant de prendre un autre médicament sur ordonnance ou en vente libre en même temps que la venlafaxine.
- Conseiller à la patiente de prévenir un professionnel de la santé si elle pense être enceinte, si elle souhaite le devenir ou si elle allaite.
- Recommander au patient d'informer un professionnel de la santé en cas de signes d'allergie (rash, urticaire).
- Insister sur l'importance des examens de suivi permettant de déterminer les bienfaits du traitement. Encourager le patient à s'engager dans une psychothérapie.

VÉRIFICATION DE L'EFFICACITÉ THÉRAPEUTIQUE

L'efficacité du traitement peut être démontrée par: une sensation de mieux-être ■ un regain d'intérêt pour l'entourage; l'utilité du traitement devrait être réévaluée à intervalles réguliers; habituellement, il doit être poursuivi pendant plusieurs mois ■ la diminution de l'anxiété ■ la diminution de la fréquence et de la gravité des crises de panique ■ la diminution de la fréquence et de la gravité des épisodes de phobie.

VÉRAPAMIL

Apo-Verap, Covera-HS, Gen-Verapamil, Isoptin SR, Novo-Veramil SR, Nu-Verap, Verapamil

CLASSIFICATION:

Antiangineux (bloqueur des canaux calciques), antiarythmique (classe IV), antihypertenseur

Grossesse – catégorie C

V

INDICATIONS

Traitement de l'hypertension essentielle légère à modérée ■ Traitement de l'angine de poitrine d'effort stable, chronique ■ Traitement de l'angine provoquée par des spasmes coronariens (préparation à libération immédiate) ■ Traitement des tachycardies supraventriculaires paroxystiques (préparation à libération immédiate et IV) ■ Maîtrise du rythme ventriculaire rapide en cas de flutter ou de fibrillation auriculaire (préparation à libération immédiate et IV) ■ Traitement de la cardiomyopathie hypertrophique lorsqu'une chirurgie n'est pas indiquée (préparation à libération immédiate).

MÉCANISME D'ACTION

Inhibition du transport du calcium dans les cellules du myocarde et des muscles lisses vasculaires, entraînant l'inhibition du couplage excitation-contraction et de la contraction qui suit ■ Diminution de la conduction dans le nœud SA et le nœud AV et prolongation des périodes réfractaires effectives dans les tissus de conduction. ***Effets thérapeutiques:*** Vasodilatation systémique entraînant l'abaissement de la pression artérielle ■ Vasodilatation coronarienne et diminution, par la suite, de la fréquence et de la gravité des crises d'angine ■ Ralentissement de la fréquence cardiaque ■ Suppression des tachycardies supraventriculaires.

PHARMACOCINÉTIQUE

Absorption: 90 % (PO), mais la majorité est métabolisée, donnant lieu à une biodisponibilité allant de 20 à 25 %.
Distribution: L'agent traverse la barrière placentaire et passe dans le lait maternel.
Liaison aux protéines: 90 %.
Métabolisme et excrétion: Métabolisme hépatique. Excrétion rénale (70 % de la dose administrée est excrété sous forme de métabolites, de 3 à 4 % sous forme inchangée) et fécale (16 % de la dose administrée).
Demi-vie: De 4,5 à 12 heures.

Profil temps-action (effets cardiovasculaires)

	DÉBUT D'ACTION	PIC	DURÉE
PO	30 - 90 min	1 - 2 h†	6 - 8 h
PO-LP‡	4 - 5 h	5 - 7 h	24 h
IV	1 - 5 min§	10 min	0,5 - 6 h§

† Une seule dose; les effets de doses multiples peuvent ne pas être manifestes avant 24 à 48 heures.
‡ LP = libération prolongée.
§ Effets antiarythmiques; les effets hémodynamiques se manifestent de 3 à 5 minutes après l'injection et se maintiennent pendant 10 à 20 minutes.

CONTRE-INDICATIONS, PRÉCAUTIONS ET MISES EN GARDE

Contre-indications: Hypersensibilité ■ Infarctus compliqué du myocarde (insuffisance ventriculaire secondaire) ■ Syndrome de dysfonctionnement sinusal ■ Bloc AV du 2e ou du 3e degré (sauf en présence d'un stimulateur cardiaque) ■ Hypotension grave ■ Insuffisance cardiaque, dysfonctionnement ventriculaire gauche grave, sauf en présence d'une tachyarythmie ventriculaire curable par le vérapamil ■ Choc cardiogénique ■ Bradycardie importante ■ Flutter ou fibrillation auriculaire présentant une voie de conduction accessoire.
Précautions et mises en garde: Insuffisance hépatique grave (il est recommandé de réduire la dose) ■ **GÉR.:** Il est recommandé de réduire la dose et de perfuser le médicament plus lentement chez les personnes âgées ou débilitées (risque accru d'hypotension) ■ Insuffisance rénale ■ Antécédents d'arythmies ventriculaires graves ou d'insuffisance cardiaque ■ **OBST., ALLAITEMENT:** L'innocuité du médicament n'a pas été établie chez la femme enceinte ou qui allaite (l'agent traverse la barrière placentaire et passe dans le lait maternel) ■ **PÉD.:** L'efficacité et l'innocuité du médicament n'ont pas été établies chez les enfants.

RÉACTIONS INDÉSIRABLES ET EFFETS SECONDAIRES

SNC: rêve anormaux, anxiété, confusion, étourdissements/sensation de tête légère, somnolence, céphalées, agitation, nervosité, troubles psychiatriques, faiblesse.
ORLO: vision trouble, déséquilibre, épistaxis, acouphènes.
Resp.: toux, dyspnée, essoufflement.
CV: ARYTHMIES, INSUFFISANCE CARDIAQUE, bradycardie, douleurs thoraciques, hypotension, palpitations, œdème périphérique, syncope, tachycardie.
GI: résultats anormaux aux tests de la fonction hépatique, anorexie, constipation, diarrhée, sécheresse de la bouche (xérostomie), dysgueusie, dyspepsie, nausées, vomissements.
GU: dysurie, nycturie, polyurie, dysfonctionnement sexuel, mictions fréquentes.
Tég.: dermatite, érythème polymorphe, rougeurs du visage, sécrétion accrue de sueur, photosensibilité, prurit et urticaire, rash.
End.: gynécomastie, hyperglycémie.
Hémat.: anémie, leucopénie, thrombopénie.
Métab.: gain pondéral.
Loc.: raideurs articulaires, crampes musculaires.
SN: paresthésie, tremblements.
Divers: SYNDROME DE STEVENS-JOHNSON, hyperplasie gingivale.

INTERACTIONS

Médicament-médicament: Risque d'hypotension additive lors de l'administration concomitante de **fentanyl**, d'autres **antihypertenseurs**, de **dérivés nitrés** ou de **quinidine** et de la consommation d'**alcool** ■ Risque de diminution de l'effet antihypertenseur lors de l'administration concomitante d'**AINS** ■ Risque d'augmentation des concentrations sériques de **digoxine** ■ Risque accru de bradycardie, de troubles de la conduction et d'insuffisance cardiaque lors de l'administration de **bêtabloquants**, de **digoxine**, de **disopyramide** ou de **phénytoïne** ■ Le vérapamil peut ralentir le métabolisme de la **cyclosporine**, de la **prazosine**, de la **quinidine** ou du **carbamazépine** et augmenter le risque de toxicité associée à ces médicaments ■ Le vérapamil intensifie les effets myorelaxants des **bloqueurs neuromusculaires de type non dépolarisant** ■ Le vérapamil peut modifier les concentrations sériques de **lithium** ■ Les **médicaments qui inhibent le cytochrome P450** (**itraconazole, fluconazole**, **kétoconazole**, **cimétidine**, **érythromycine**, **clarithromycine**, **terfénadine**), administrés en concomitance, peuvent intensifier l'effet du vérapamil ■ Les **médicaments qui induisent le cytochrome P450** (**phénobarbital**, **phénytoïne**, **rifampicine**), administrés en concomitance, peuvent diminuer l'effet du vérapamil.

VOIES D'ADMINISTRATION ET POSOLOGIE

- **PO (adultes)**: De 80 à 120 mg, 3 ou 4 fois par jour; majorer la dose selon la réponse au traitement et la tolérance du patient jusqu'à un maximum de 480 mg par jour. *Patients présentant une insuffisance hépatique et personnes âgées* – initialement 40 mg, 3 fois par jour. *Préparations à libération prolongée* – de 120 à 240 mg par jour, en une seule dose; majorer la dose selon la réponse au traitement et la tolérance du patient (écart posologique: de 240 à 480 mg par jour). En présence de cardiomyopathie hypertrophique, il peut s'avérer nécessaire d'administrer des doses quotidiennes de 600 à 720 mg.
- **IV (adultes)**: De 5 à 10 mg (de 75 à 150 µg/kg), en bolus IV, administré pendant au moins 2 minutes; si la réponse initiale n'est pas adéquate, on peut administrer 10 mg (150 µg/kg), 30 minutes plus tard.
- **IV (enfants de 1 à 15 ans)**: De 2 à 5 mg (de 100 à 300 µg/kg) en bolus IV, administré pendant au moins 2 minutes (la dose initiale ne doit pas dépasser 5 mg); on peut administrer une nouvelle dose, 30 minutes plus tard (sans dépasser 10 mg).
- **IV (enfants < 1 ans)**: De 0,75 à 2 mg (de 100 à 200 µg/kg) en bolus IV, administré pendant au moins 2 minutes et sous surveillance stricte de l'ÉCG; on peut administrer une nouvelle dose, 30 minutes plus tard.

PRÉSENTATION
(version générique disponible)

Comprimés: 80 mg[Pr], 120 mg[Pr] ■ **Comprimés à libération prolongée**: 120 mg[Pr], 180 mg[Pr], 240 mg[Pr] ■ **Capsules à libération prolongée**: 120 mg[Pr], 180 mg[Pr], 240 mg[Pr] ■ **Solution pour injection**: 2,5 mg/mL, en fioles et ampoules de 2 mL ou de 4 mL ■ **En association avec**: trandolapril (Tarka).

SOINS INFIRMIERS

ÉVALUATION DE LA SITUATION

- Mesurer la pression artérielle avant l'administration du médicament, pendant l'adaptation posologique et à intervalles réguliers pendant toute la durée du traitement. SUIVRE L'ÉCG À INTERVALLES RÉGULIERS LORS D'UN TRAITEMENT PROLONGÉ. LE VÉRAPAMIL PEUT ALLONGER LES INTERVALLES PR.
- EFFECTUER LE BILAN QUOTIDIEN DES INGESTA ET DES EXCRETA ET PESER LE PATIENT TOUS LES JOURS. SUIVRE DE PRÈS LES SIGNES SUIVANTS D'INSUFFISANCE CARDIAQUE: ŒDÈME PÉRIPHÉRIQUE, RÂLE OU CRÉPITATIONS, DYSPNÉE, GAIN PONDÉRAL, TURGESCENCE DES JUGULAIRES.
- Noter régulièrement les concentrations sériques de digoxine et suivre les signes et les symptômes de toxicité cardiaque chez les patients prenant des dérivés digitaliques en même temps que le vérapamil.

Angine: Déterminer le siège, la durée et l'intensité des douleurs angineuses et les facteurs qui les déclenchent.

Arythmies: SUIVRE CONTINUELLEMENT L'ÉCG DURANT L'ADMINISTRATION IV. PRÉVENIR RAPIDEMENT LE MÉDECIN EN CAS DE BRADYCARDIE OU D'HYPOTENSION PROLONGÉE. GARDER À PORTÉE DE LA MAIN LE MATÉRIEL DE RÉANIMATION ET LES MÉDICAMENTS À ADMINISTRER EN CAS D'URGENCE. MESURER LA PRESSION ARTÉRIELLE ET LE POULS AVANT L'ADMINISTRATION ET À INTERVALLES FRÉQUENTS PENDANT TOUTE SA DURÉE.

Tests de laboratoire:

- Les concentrations sériques totales de calcium ne sont pas modifiées par les bloqueurs des canaux calciques.
- Mesurer les concentrations sériques de potassium à intervalles réguliers. L'hypokaliémie accroît le risque d'arythmies et devrait être corrigée.
- Évaluer les fonctions hépatique et rénale à intervalles réguliers pendant un traitement qui est de longue durée. Le vérapamil peut entraîner une élévation des enzymes hépatiques après quelques jours de traitement; les concentrations devraient revenir à la normale après l'arrêt du traitement.

DIAGNOSTICS INFIRMIERS POSSIBLES

- Débit cardiaque diminué (Indications).
- Douleur aiguë (Indications).
- Connaissances insuffisantes sur le traitement médicamenteux (Enseignement au patient et à ses

INTERVENTIONS INFIRMIÈRES

- NE PAS CONFONDRE COVERA (VÉRAPAMIL) AVEC PROVERA (MÉDROXYPROGESTÉRONE).

PO:

- Administrer le médicament avec des aliments ou du lait afin de réduire l'irritation gastrique.
- ON NE DOIT PAS OUVRIR, ÉCRASER, BRISER OU MÂCHER LES COMPRIMÉS ET LES CAPSULES À LIBÉRATION PROLONGÉE. Il ne faut pas s'inquiéter de la présence de capsules vides dans les selles.

IV: Le patient doit rester en position couchée pendant au moins 1 heure après l'administration IV pour que les effets hypotenseurs du médicament puissent diminuer.

IV directe: Administrer le vérapamil par voie IV, sans le diluer, dans une tubulure en Y, à un débit de 2 minutes par dose. Administrer la préparation en 3 minutes chez les patients âgés. Consulter les directives de chaque fabricant avant d'administrer la préparation.

Compatibilité dans la même seringue: amrinone ■ héparine ■ milrinone.

Compatibilité (tubulure en Y): ampicilline ■ amrinone ■ ciprofloxacine ■ dobutamine ■ dopamine ■ famotidine ■ hydralazine ■ mépéridine ■ méthicilline ■ milrinone ■ pénicilline G potassique ■ pipéracilline ■ ticarcilline.

Incompatibilité (tubulure en Y): albumine ■ amphotéricine B, cholestéryl d' ■ mezlocilline ■ nafcilline ■ oxacilline ■ sodium, bicarbonate de.

ENSEIGNEMENT AU PATIENT ET À SES PROCHES

- Conseiller au patient de respecter rigoureusement la posologie recommandée, même s'il se sent mieux. S'il n'a pu prendre le médicament au moment habituel, il doit le prendre dès que possible à moins que ce ne soit presque l'heure de la dose suivante. L'avertir qu'il ne doit jamais remplacer une dose manquée par une double dose. Il peut s'avérer nécessaire de réduire graduellement la dose.
- Enseigner au patient la façon de prendre son pouls. Lui recommander d'informer un professionnel de la santé si le pouls est < 50 battements par minute.

- Recommander au patient de changer lentement de position afin de réduire le risque d'hypotension orthostatique.
- Prévenir le patient que le vérapamil peut provoquer des étourdissements. Lui conseiller de ne pas conduire et d'éviter les activités qui exigent sa vigilance jusqu'à ce qu'on ait la certitude que le médicament n'entraîne pas ces effets chez lui.
- Expliquer au patient qu'il est important de maintenir une bonne hygiène buccale et de consulter le dentiste à intervalles réguliers pour se faire nettoyer les dents afin de prévenir le saignement, la sensibilité et l'hyperplasie des gencives.
- Conseiller au patient d'éviter de boire de l'alcool et de prendre des médicaments en vente libre, tout particulièrement des préparations contre le rhume, ou des produits naturels en même temps que le vérapamil sans consulter au préalable un professionnel de la santé.
- Recommander au patient de consulter un professionnel de la santé en cas de battements de cœur irréguliers, de dyspnée, d'œdème des mains et des pieds, d'étourdissements marqués, de nausées, de constipation, d'hypotension ou de céphalées graves ou persistantes.
- Inciter le patient à utiliser un écran solaire et à porter des vêtements protecteurs pour prévenir les réactions de photosensibilité.

Angine:

- Expliquer au patient qui suit en même temps un traitement par un dérivé nitré ou un bêtabloquant qu'il doit prendre les 2 médicaments comme ils lui ont été prescrits et utiliser la nitroglycérine sublinguale, selon les besoins, si une crise d'angine de poitrine survient.
- Recommander au patient de prévenir un professionnel de la santé si la douleur thoracique ne diminue pas, si elle s'aggrave après le traitement, si elle s'accompagne de diaphorèse ou d'essoufflements ou si des céphalées graves et persistantes se manifestent.
- Recommander au patient de consulter un professionnel de la santé à propos d'une restriction d'activités physiques.

Hypertension:

- Inciter le patient à appliquer d'autres mesures de réduction de l'hypertension: perdre du poids, réduire sa consommation de sel, cesser de fumer, boire modérément, faire régulièrement de l'exercice et diminuer le stress. Lui expliquer que le vérapamil stabilise la pression artérielle, mais ne guérit pas l'hypertension.
- Enseigner au patient et à ses proches la façon de mesurer la pression artérielle et leur conseiller de la prendre 1 fois par semaine. Leur recommander d'informer immédiatement un professionnel de la santé de tout changement important.

VÉRIFICATION DE L'EFFICACITÉ THÉRAPEUTIQUE

L'efficacité du traitement peut être démontrée par: la baisse de la pression artérielle ■ la diminution de la fréquence et de la gravité des crises d'angine ■ un moindre recours aux dérivés nitrés ■ l'augmentation de la tolérance à l'effort et une sensation de mieux-être ■ la suppression et la prévention des tachycardies supraventriculaires. ✳

ALERTE CLINIQUE

VINBLASTINE

Vinblastine

CLASSIFICATION:

Antinéoplasique (alcaloïde extrait de la pervenche)

Grossesse – catégorie D

INDICATIONS

Chimiothérapie ■ des lymphomes ■ du cancer des testicules sans séminome ■ du cancer du sein avancé ■ du sarcome de Kaposi ■ du choriocarcinome ■ de l'histiocytose X ■ du mycosis fongoïde (souvent utilisé en association).

MÉCANISME D'ACTION

Liaison aux protéines du fuseau achromatique entraînant l'arrêt de la métaphase et, par conséquent, la réplication cellulaire (phase M du cycle cellulaire). ***Effets thérapeutiques:*** Destruction des cellules à croissance rapide, particulièrement des cellules malignes ■ Médicament doté de propriétés immunosuppressives.

PHARMACOCINÉTIQUE

Absorption: Biodisponibilité à 100 % (IV).

Distribution: L'agent traverse difficilement la barrière hématoencéphalique.

Métabolisme et excrétion: Transformation dans le foie en plusieurs métabolites dont un composé antinéoplasique actif. Élimination dans les fèces par excrétion biliaire; faible excrétion rénale (moins de 1 % sous forme inchangée).

Demi-vie: 24 heures.

Profil temps-action (effet sur la numération leucocytaire)

	DÉBUT D'ACTION	PIC	DURÉE
IV	5 – 7 jours	4 – 10 jours	7 – 14 jours (jusqu'à 21 jours)

CONTRE-INDICATIONS, PRÉCAUTIONS ET MISES EN GARDE

Contre-indications: Hypersensibilité ■ Aplasie médullaire ■ Infections actives (on doit d'abord traiter l'infection) ■ Administration intrathécale (risque d'issue fatale).

Précautions et mises en garde: Patientes en âge de procréer ■ Infections ■ Grossesse ou allaitement ■ Autres maladies chroniques débilitantes ou personnes âgées (risque accru d'effets indésirables) ■ Insuffisance hépatique (diminuer la dose) ■ Maladie cardiovasculaire ischémique ■ Dysfonction pulmonaire préexistante (risque accru de bronchospasme).

RÉACTIONS INDÉSIRABLES ET EFFETS SECONDAIRES

SNC: CONVULSIONS, dépression, neurotoxicité, faiblesse.

CV: hypertension, phénomène de Raynaud, angine.

Resp.: BRONCHOSPASME.

GI: nausées, vomissements, anorexie, constipation, diarrhée, stomatite, crampes abdominales, goût métallique.

GU: suppression de la fonction des gonades, rétention urinaire.

Tég.: alopécie, dermatite, vésication.

End.: syndrome d'antidiurèse inappropriée.

Hémat.: anémie, leucopénie, thrombopénie.

Loc.: douleur à la mâchoire, myalgie.

Locaux: phlébite au point d'injection.

Métab.: hyperuricémie.

SN: névrite, paresthésie, neuropathie périphérique.

INTERACTIONS

Médicament-médicament: Effet additif sur l'aplasie médullaire lors de l'administration concomitante d'autres **antinéoplasiques** ou d'une **radiothérapie** ■ Risque de bronchospasme chez les patients ayant été traités auparavant par la **mitomycine** ■ La vinblastine peut diminuer la réponse des anticorps aux **vaccins à virus vivants** et augmenter le risque de réactions indésirables ■ La vinblastine peut réduire les concentrations sériques de **phénytoïne** ■ La **carbamazépine** peut diminuer les concentration plasmatiques et l'efficacité de la vinblastine ■ Les **inhibiteurs du CYP P450 3A4**, comme l'**érythromycine** et l'**itraconazole**, peuvent augmenter les concentrations plasmatiques de vinblastine et sa toxicité ■ Les **agents ototoxiques**, comme le **cisplatine**, les **aminosides** ou le **furosémide**, administrés en concomitance, peuvent augmenter le risque d'ototoxicité.

Médicament-produits naturels: Le **millepertuis** peut diminuer l'efficacité de la vinblastine.

VOIES D'ADMINISTRATION ET POSOLOGIE

Les doses peuvent varier considérablement selon la tumeur, le schéma posologique, l'état du patient et la numération globulaire. On ne doit pas administrer la vinblastine par voie intrathécale.

- **IV (adultes)**: *Initialement* – 3,7 mg/m², en une seule dose; augmenter la dose à intervalles hebdomadaires, selon la tolérance du patient, par palier de 1,8 mg/m², jusqu'à concurrence de 18,5 mg/m² (dose habituelle: de 5,5 à 7,4 mg/m²). *Dose d'entretien* – administrer la dose maximale n'entraînant pas de leucopénie, tous les 7 jours.

- **IV (enfants):** *Initialement* – 2,5 mg/m², en une seule dose; augmenter la dose à intervalles hebdomadaires, selon la tolérance du patient, par paliers de 1,25 mg/m², jusqu'à concurrence de 7,5 mg/m². *Dose d'entretien* – administrer la dose maximale n'entraînant pas de leucopénie, tous les 7 jours.
- ***INSUFFISANCE HÉPATIQUE***

  IV (ADULTES ET ENFANTS): *BILIRUBINE DE 25 À 50 µmol/L* – 50 % DE LA DOSE HABITUELLE. *BILIRUBINE > 50 µmol/L* – 25 % DE LA DOSE HABITUELLE.

PRÉSENTATION
(version générique disponible)

Solution pour injection: 1 mg/mL, en fioles de 10 mL[Pr].

SOINS INFIRMIERS

ÉVALUATION DE LA SITUATION

- MESURER LA PRESSION ARTÉRIELLE, LE POULS ET LA FRÉQUENCE RESPIRATOIRE PENDANT TOUTE LA DURÉE DU TRAITEMENT. SIGNALER IMMÉDIATEMENT AU MÉDECIN L'APPARITION D'UNE DÉTRESSE RESPIRATOIRE. LE BRONCHOSPASME PEUT METTRE LA VIE DU PATIENT EN DANGER; IL PEUT SURVENIR PENDANT LA PERFUSION OU PLUSIEURS HEURES OU SEMAINES APRÈS.
- Surveiller les signes d'aplasie médullaire. Suivre de près les saignements: saignement des gencives, formation d'ecchymoses, pétéchies, présence de sang occulte dans les selles, l'urine et les vomissements. Éviter les injections IM et la prise de température par voie rectale si le nombre de plaquettes est bas. Appliquer une pression pendant 10 minutes sur les points de ponction veineuse. Évaluer les signes d'infections pendant qu'une neutropénie est présente. La vinblastine peut provoquer l'anémie. Suivre de près la fatigue accrue, la dyspnée et l'hypotension orthostatique.
- La vinblastine peut entraîner des nausées et des vomissements. Effectuer le bilan des ingesta et des excreta. Noter l'appétit et l'état nutritionnel du patient. On peut avoir recours à un antiémétique administré en prophylaxie. Modifier le régime alimentaire en fonction des aliments que le patient peut tolérer.
- Observer les points d'injection à intervalles réguliers pour déceler la rougeur, l'irritation ou l'inflammation. En cas d'extravasation, arrêter la perfusion et la recommencer à un point différent afin d'éviter la lésion des tissus sous-cutanés. Le traitement classique consiste en l'application de chaleur.
- Rester à l'affût des symptômes de goutte: concentrations accrues d'acide urique, douleurs articulaires, œdème. Inciter le patient à boire au moins 2 litres de liquides par jour si son état le permet. On peut lui prescrire de l'allopurinol ou l'alcalinisation de l'urine afin de réduire les concentrations d'acide urique.

Tests de laboratoire:

- Noter la numération globulaire avant le traitement et à intervalles réguliers pendant toute sa durée. Si le nombre de leucocytes est $< 2 \times 10^9$/L, interrompre le traitement jusqu'à ce qu'il soit $\geq 4 \times 10^9$/L. Le nadir de la leucopénie survient en l'espace de 4 à 10 jours; les valeurs se rétablissent habituellement de 7 à 14 jours plus tard. Une thrombopénie peut également survenir chez les patients ayant reçu une radiothérapie ou d'autres agents chimiothérapeutiques.
- Noter les résultats des tests des fonctions hépatique (AST, ALT, LDH, bilirubine) et rénale (urée, créatinine), avant le traitement et à intervalles réguliers pendant toute sa durée.
- La vinblastine peut entraîner l'élévation des concentrations d'acide urique. Noter ces concentrations à intervalles réguliers pendant toute la durée du traitement.

DIAGNOSTICS INFIRMIERS POSSIBLES

- Risque d'infection (Réactions indésirables).
- Alimentation déficiente (Réactions indésirables).
- Connaissances insuffisantes sur le traitement médicamenteux (Enseignement au patient et à ses proches).

INTERVENTIONS INFIRMIÈRES

ALERTE CLINIQUE: DES DÉCÈS SONT SURVENUS LORS DE CERTAINES CHIMIOTHÉRAPIES. AVANT D'ADMINISTRER L'AGENT, CLARIFIER TOUS LES POINTS AMBIGUS. VÉRIFIER UNE FOIS DE PLUS LA LIMITE DES DOSES UNITAIRES ET QUOTIDIENNES AINSI QUE CELLE DE LA DOSE À ADMINISTRER PENDANT LE TRAITEMENT. DEMANDER À UN DEUXIÈME PROFESSIONNEL DE LA SANTÉ DE VÉRIFIER DE NOUVEAU L'ORDONNANCE D'ORIGINE, LES CALCULS ET LE RÉGLAGE DE LA POMPE À PERFUSION. NE PAS ADMINISTRER PAR VOIE SC, IM OU INTRATHÉCALE (IT). L'ADMINISTRATION IT PEUT MENER À UNE ISSUE FATALE. L'EMBALLAGE DOIT CONTENIR LA MENTION: « ATTENTION – POUR UTILISATION IV SEULEMENT. N'ENLEVEZ L'EMBALLAGE QU'AU MOMENT DE L'INJECTION. ADMINISTRATION INTRATHÉCALE MORTELLE. »

- NE PAS CONFONDRE LA VINBLASTINE AVEC LA VINORELBINE OU LA VINCRISTINE.

V

- La solution devrait être préparée sous une hotte à flux laminaire. Porter des gants, une blouse et un masque lors de la manipulation de ce médicament. Mettre au rebut tout le matériel destiné à l'administration IV dans les contenants réservés à cet usage (voir l'annexe H).
- Ne pas administrer la vinblastine dans les bras ou les jambes en présence d'un trouble de la circulation, en raison du risque de thrombophlébite.

IV directe: La vinblastine est diluée et prête à être utilisée. Consulter les directives de chaque fabricant avant de diluer la préparation.

Vitesse d'administration: Administrer chaque dose unique en 1 minute dans le raccord en Y d'une tubulure par laquelle s'écoule une solution de NaCl 0,9 % ou de D5%E.

Perfusion intermittente: La dilution dans des volumes importants (de 100 à 250 mL) ou la perfusion prolongée (> 30 minutes) élèvent le risque d'irritation veineuse et d'extravasation.

Compatibilité dans la même seringue: bléomycine ▪ cisplatine ▪ cyclophosphamide ▪ dropéridol ▪ fluorouracile ▪ leucovorine calcique ▪ méthotrexate ▪ métoclopramide ▪ mitomycine ▪ vincristine.

Comptabilité (tubulure en Y): amifostine ▪ aztréonam ▪ bléomycine ▪ céfépime ▪ cisplatine ▪ cyclophosphamide ▪ doxorubicine ▪ dropéridol ▪ fludarabine ▪ fluorouracile ▪ héparine ▪ leucovorine calcique ▪ méphalan ▪ méthotrexate ▪ métoclopramide ▪ mitomycine ▪ ondansétron ▪ paclitaxel ▪ pipéracilline/tazobactam ▪ sargramostim ▪ téniposide ▪ thiotépa ▪ vincristine ▪ vinorelbine.

Incompatibilité (tubulure en Y): furosémide.

ENSEIGNEMENT AU PATIENT ET À SES PROCHES

- Inciter le patient à signaler à un professionnel de la santé la fièvre, les frissons, les maux de gorge, les signes d'infections, le saignement des gencives, les ecchymoses, les pétéchies ou la présence de sang dans les selles, l'urine ou les vomissements. Lui recommander d'éviter les foules et les personnes contagieuses. Lui recommander aussi d'utiliser une brosse à dents à poils doux et un rasoir électrique. Prévenir le patient qu'il ne doit pas consommer de boissons alcoolisées, ni prendre d'AINS ou de préparations contenant de l'aspirine.
- Recommander au patient d'examiner sa muqueuse buccale à la recherche d'érythème ou d'aphtes. En présence d'aphtes, lui conseiller d'éviter les aliments épicés, de remplacer la brosse à dents par une brosse-éponge et de se rincer la bouche avec de l'eau après avoir bu et mangé. On peut lui prescrire des agents topiques si la douleur l'empêche de s'alimenter. La douleur associée à la stomatite pourrait dicter l'administration d'opioïdes.
- Recommander au patient de signaler les symptômes suivants de neurotoxicité: paresthésie, douleurs, problèmes liés à la marche, constipation persistante.
- Prévenir le patient que des douleurs aux mâchoires ou aux organes touchés par la tumeur, ainsi que des nausées et des vomissements peuvent se manifester. Lui recommander de prévenir la constipation et de signaler toutes les réactions indésirables.
- Prévenir la patiente que la vinblastine peut avoir des effets tératogènes. Lui conseiller d'utiliser une méthode de contraception efficace durant le traitement et pendant au moins 2 mois après l'avoir arrêté.
- Prévenir le patient qu'il risque de perdre ses cheveux. Explorer avec lui les stratégies lui permettant de s'adapter à ce changement.
- Expliquer au patient qu'il ne doit pas se faire vacciner sans recommandation expresse d'un professionnel de la santé.
- Insister sur le fait qu'il est nécessaire d'effectuer des examens de suivi à intervalles réguliers afin de déceler les effets secondaires du médicament.

VÉRIFICATION DE L'EFFICACITÉ THÉRAPEUTIQUE

L'efficacité du traitement peut être démontrée par: la diminution de la taille de la tumeur maligne sans apparition d'effets secondaires délétères. ✳

ALERTE CLINIQUE

VINCRISTINE

Vincristine

CLASSIFICATION:

Antinéoplasique (alcaloïde extrait de la pervenche)

Grossesse - catégorie D

V

INDICATIONS

En monothérapie ou en association avec d'autres modalités thérapeutiques (agents antinéoplasiques, chirurgie ou radiothérapie) en présence des troubles suivants: maladie de Hodgkin ▪ leucémies ▪ neuroblastor ▪ lymphomes malins ▪ cancer colorectal ▪ cance ovaires ▪ cancer du poumon à petites cellules ▪ r myosarcome ▪ sarcome du tissu osseux ▪ tu Wilms ▪ cancer du sein et du col de l'utérus ▪ r malin. **Usages non approuvés**: Traitement du purpura thrombopénique idiopathique réfractaire à la splénectomie et aux corticostéroïdes.

MÉCANISME D'ACTION

Liaison aux protéines du fuseau achromatique entraînant l'arrêt de la métaphase et, par conséquent, de la réplication cellulaire (phase M du cycle cellulaire) ■ L'agent a peu ou pas d'effet sur la réserve médullaire. ***Effets thérapeutiques:*** Destruction des cellules à croissance rapide, particulièrement des cellules malignes ■ Médicament doté de propriétés immunosuppressives.

PHARMACOCINÉTIQUE

Absorption: Biodisponibilité à 100 % (IV).
Distribution: Répartition rapide dans tout l'organisme; forte liaison aux tissus.
Métabolisme et excrétion: Métabolisme hépatique; élimination dans les fèces par excrétion biliaire.
Demi-vie: De 10,5 à 37,5 heures.

Profil temps-action (effet sur la numération globulaire)†

	DÉBUT D'ACTION	PIC	DURÉE
IV	inconnu	4 jours	7 jours

† Habituellement léger.

CONTRE-INDICATIONS, PRÉCAUTIONS ET MISES EN GARDE

Contre-indications: Hypersensibilité ■ Radiothérapie administrée dans diverses régions du corps, dont le foie ■ Poliomyélite de l'enfance ou amyotrophie péronière de Charcot-Marie-Tooth de forme démyélinisante (aggravation possible de la maladie neurologique sous-jacente) ■ Administration intrathécale (risque d'issue fatale).

Précautions et mises en garde: Grossesse, allaitement, patientes en âge de procréer ■ Infections ■ Aplasie médullaire ■ Autres maladies chroniques débilitantes ■ Insuffisance hépatique (diminuer la dose) ■ Administration concomitante de médicaments ototoxiques (risque d'ototoxicité additive) ■ **PÉD., GÉR.**: Enfants < 16 ans et personnes âgées (sensibilité accrue aux effets neurotoxiques).

RÉACTIONS INDÉSIRABLES ET EFFETS SECONDAIRES

SNC: agitation, insomnie, dépression, modification de l'état de la conscience.
ORLO: cécité corticale, diplopie, vision brouillée, ptosis.
Resp.: bronchospasme.
GI: nausées, vomissements, crampes abdominales, anorexie, constipation, iléus, stomatite.
GU: suppression de la fonction des gonades, nycturie, oligurie, rétention urinaire.
Tég.: alopécie.
End.: syndrome d'antidiurèse inappropriée.
Hémat.: anémie, leucopénie, thrombopénie (légère et brève).
Locaux: phlébite au point d'injection IV, nécrose tissulaire (due à l'extravasation).
Métab.: hyperuricémie.
SN: neuropathies périphériques ascendante, centrale et autonome, douleur à la mâchoire, ataxie.

INTERACTIONS

Médicament-médicament: Risque de bronchospasme chez les patients ayant été traités auparavant par la **mitomycine** ■ La **L-asparaginase** peut diminuer le métabolisme hépatique de la vincristine (administrer la vincristine de 12 à 24 heures avant l'asparaginase) ■ La vincristine peut diminuer la réponse des anticorps aux **vaccins à virus vivants** et augmenter le risque de réactions indésirables ■ Les **inducteurs** (comme le **phénobarbital**, la **carbamazépine**, **phénytoïne**) et les **inhibiteurs** (comme l'**érythromycine**, l'**isoniazide**, les **antifongiques azolés**, le **vérapamil**) du **CYP P450 3A4** peuvent modifier les concentrations sériques et donc l'efficacité ou la toxicité de la vincristine ■ Les **médicaments ototoxiques** (comme le **furosémide**, les **aminosides**, le **cisplatine**), administrés en concomitance, peuvent entraîner une ototoxicité additive.

VOIES D'ADMINISTRATION ET POSOLOGIE

LA DOSE DOIT ÊTRE ÉTABLIE AVEC BEAUCOUP D'ATTENTION, CAR UNE TROP FORTE DOSE PEUT MENER À UNE ISSUE FATALE. Ne pas administrer par voie intrathécale. De nombreux autres protocoles sont utilisés.

- **IV (adultes)**: De 0,4 à 1,4 mg/m^2; on peut répéter l'administration toutes les semaines (la dose habituelle est de 1,4 mg/m^2). La dose peut être limitée à 2 mg, quelle que soit la surface corporelle, pour diminuer la neurotoxicité. Toute dose supérieure à 3 mg devrait être remise en question.
- **IV (enfants > 10 kg)**: De 1 à 2 mg/m^2, en une seule dose; on peut répéter l'administration toutes les semaines.
- **IV (enfants < 10 kg)**: De 0,03 à 0,05 mg/kg, en une seule dose; on peut répéter l'administration toutes les semaines.
- ***INSUFFISANCE HÉPATIQUE***

  IV (ADULTES ET ENFANTS): *BILIRUBINE DE 25 À 50 μmol/L* –50 % DE LA DOSE HABITUELLE. *BILIRUBINE > 50 μmol/L* – 25 % DE LA DOSE HABITUELLE.

PRÉSENTATION
(version générique disponible)

Solution pour injection: 1 mg/mL, en fioles de 1 mL[Pr], de 2 mL[Pr] et de 5 mL[Pr].

SOINS INFIRMIERS

ÉVALUATION DE LA SITUATION

- Mesurer la pression artérielle, le pouls et la fréquence respiratoire pendant toute la durée du traitement. Signaler tout changement notable.
- Évaluer l'état neurologique du patient. Déceler les signes de paresthésie (engourdissements, picotements, douleurs), la perte des réflexes tendineux profonds (le réflexe achilléen est habituellement le premier touché), la faiblesse (poignet ou pied tombant, problèmes liés à la marche), la paralysie des nerfs crâniens (douleurs aux mâchoires, raucité de la voix, ptosis, modifications visuelles), le dysfonctionnement du système nerveux autonome (iléus, mictions difficiles, hypotension orthostatique, modification des sécrétions de sueur) et le dysfonctionnement du SNC (diminution de l'état de conscience, agitation, hallucinations). Informer le médecin si ces symptômes apparaissent, car ils peuvent persister pendant plusieurs mois.
- Effectuer le bilan des ingesta et des excreta et noter le poids du patient tous les jours; signaler tout changement important. La diminution du débit urinaire s'accompagnant d'hyponatrémie peut indiquer la présence du syndrome d'antidiurèse inappropriée, lequel répond habituellement à une restriction hydrique.
- Observer les points d'injection à intervalles réguliers pour déceler la rougeur, l'irritation ou l'inflammation. En cas d'extravasation, arrêter la perfusion et la recommencer à un point différent afin d'éviter la lésion des tissus sous-cutanés. Le traitement de l'extravasation consiste en l'application immédiate de compresses chaudes sur la région touchée pendant 30 à 60 minutes; on arrête ensuite de les appliquer pendant 15 minutes et on les applique de nouveau pendant 15 minutes et ainsi de suite pendant 24 heures, pour accroître l'absorption systémique du médicament.
- Noter l'état nutritionnel du patient. On peut avoir recours à l'administration d'un antiémétique pour réduire les nausées et les vomissements.
- Rester à l'affût des symptômes de goutte: concentrations accrues d'acide urique, douleurs articulaires, œdème. Inciter le patient à boire au moins 2 litres de liquides par jour si son état le permet. On peut lui prescrire de l'allopurinol ou l'alcalinisation de l'urine afin de réduire les concentrations d'acide urique.

Tests de laboratoire:

- Noter la numération globulaire avant le traitement et à intervalles réguliers pendant toute sa durée. La vincristine peut provoquer une légère leucopénie 4 jours après l'arrêt du traitement, laquelle se résorbe habituellement en l'espace de 7 jours. Le nombre de plaquettes peut augmenter ou diminuer.
- Vérifier les résultats des tests des fonctions hépatique (AST, ALT, LDH, bilirubine) et rénale (urée, créatinine) avant le traitement et à intervalles réguliers pendant toute sa durée.
- La vincristine peut entraîner l'élévation des concentrations d'acide urique. Noter ces concentrations à intervalles réguliers pendant toute la durée du traitement.

DIAGNOSTICS INFIRMIERS POSSIBLES

- Risque d'accident (Réactions indésirables).
- Alimentation déficiente (Réactions indésirables).
- Connaissances insuffisantes sur le traitement médicamenteux (Enseignement au patient et à ses proches).

INTERVENTIONS INFIRMIÈRES

ALERTE CLINIQUE: DES DÉCÈS SONT SURVENUS LORS DE CERTAINES CHIMIOTHÉRAPIES. AVANT D'ADMINISTRER L'AGENT, CLARIFIER TOUS LES POINTS AMBIGUS. VÉRIFIER UNE FOIS DE PLUS LA LIMITE DES DOSES UNITAIRES ET QUOTIDIENNES AINSI QUE CELLE DE LA DOSE À ADMINISTRER PENDANT LE TRAITEMENT. DEMANDER À UN DEUXIÈME PROFESSIONNEL DE LA SANTÉ DE VÉRIFIER DE NOUVEAU L'ORDONNANCE D'ORIGINE, LES CALCULS ET LE RÉGLAGE DE LA POMPE À PERFUSION. NE PAS ADMINISTRER PAR VOIE SC, IM OU INTRATHÉCALE. L'ADMINISTRATION PAR VOIE INTRATHÉCALE PEUT MENER À UNE ISSUE FATALE. LA VINCRISTINE DOIT SE TROUVER DANS DES CONTENANTS RECOUVERTS D'UNE SURENVELOPPE SUR LAQUELLE EST INSCRITE LA MISE EN GARDE SUIVANTE: «ADMINISTRER PAR VOIE IV SEULEMENT.» CETTE SURENVELOPPE DOIT DEMEURER SUR LE CONTENANT JUSQU'AU MOMENT DE L'ADMINISTRATION DE LA PRÉPARATION.

- NE PAS CONFONDRE LA VINCRISTINE AVEC LA VINBLASTINE OU AVEC LA VINORELBINE.
- La solution devrait être préparée sous une hotte à flux laminaire. Porter des gants, une blouse et un masque lors de la manipulation du médicament. Mettre au rebut tout le matériel destiné à l'admini[illegible]tration IV dans les contenants réservés à cet usa[illegible] (voir l'annexe H).

V

IV directe: Solution pour injection prête à l'emploi d'une concentration de 1 mg/mL. Administrer la solution sans la diluer.

Vitesse d'administration: Administrer chaque dose unique en 1 minute dans le raccord en Y d'une tubulure par laquelle s'écoule une solution de NaCl 0,9% ou de D5%E. Consulter les directives de chaque fabricant avant d'administrer la préparation.

Compatibilité dans la même seringue: bléomycine ■ cisplatine ■ cyclophosphamide ■ doxapram ■ doxorubicine ■ dropéridol ■ fluorouracile ■ héparine ■ leucovorine calcique ■ méthotrexate ■ métoclopramide ■ mitomycine ■ vinblastine.

Incompatibilité dans la même seringue: furosémide.

Compatibilité (tubulure en Y): allopurinol sodique ■ amifostine ■ aztréonam ■ bléomycine ■ cisplatine ■ cyclophosphamide ■ doxorubicine ■ dropéridol ■ filgrastim ■ fludarabine ■ fluorouracile ■ granisétron ■ héparine ■ leucovorine calcique ■ melphalan ■ méthotrexate ■ métoclopramide ■ mitomycine ■ ondansétron ■ paclitaxel ■ pipéracilline/tazobactam ■ sargramostim ■ téniposide ■ thiotépa ■ vinblastine ■ vinorelbine.

Incompatibilité (tubulure en Y): céfépime ■ furosémide ■ idarubicine ■ sodium, bicarbonate de.

ENSEIGNEMENT AU PATIENT ET À SES PROCHES

- Recommander au patient de signaler immédiatement à un professionnel de la santé la présence de rougeurs, d'œdème ou de douleur au point d'injection.
- Recommander au patient de signaler les symptômes suivants de neurotoxicité: paresthésie, douleurs, difficultés à se déplacer, constipation persistante. L'informer qu'un apport liquidien accru, la consommation de fibres alimentaires et l'exercice peuvent diminuer la constipation. Il peut aussi recourir à des laxatifs émollients ou autres. L'inciter à communiquer avec un professionnel de la santé en cas de constipation grave ou de gêne abdominale, puisqu'il pourrait s'agir de signes de neuropathie.

- Inciter le patient à signaler à un professionnel de la santé la fièvre, les frissons, les maux de gorge, les signes d'infection, le saignement des gencives, les ecchymoses, les pétéchies ou la présence d'aphtes ou de sang dans les selles, l'urine ou les vomissements. Lui recommander d'éviter les foules et les personnes contagieuses.
- Prévenir la patiente que la vincristine peut avoir des effets tératogènes. Lui conseiller d'utiliser une méthode de contraception efficace durant le traitement et pendant au moins 2 mois après l'avoir arrêté.
- Prévenir le patient qu'il risque de perdre ses cheveux. Explorer avec lui les stratégies lui permettant de s'adapter à ce changement.
- Expliquer au patient qu'il ne doit pas se faire vacciner sans recommandation expresse d'un professionnel de la santé.
- Insister sur le fait qu'il est nécessaire d'effectuer des examens de laboratoire à intervalles réguliers afin de déceler les effets secondaires du médicament.

VÉRIFICATION DE L'EFFICACITÉ THÉRAPEUTIQUE

L'efficacité du traitement peut être démontrée par: la diminution de la taille de la tumeur maligne sans apparition d'effets secondaires délétères.

ALERTE CLINIQUE

VINORELBINE

Navelbine

CLASSIFICATION:

Antinéoplasique (alcaloïde extrait de la pervenche)

Grossesse – catégorie D

INDICATIONS

Monothérapie ou traitement d'association avec le cisplatine chez les patients atteints d'un cancer du poumon non à petites cellules ayant atteint un stade avancé ■ Traitement du cancer métastatique du sein lorsque la chimiothérapie classique a échoué.

MÉCANISME D'ACTION

Liaison à une protéine (tubuline) des microtubules cellulaires entravant l'assemblage des microtubules et entraînant l'arrêt de la réplication cellulaire (phase M du cycle cellulaire). ***Effets thérapeutiques***: Destruction des cellules à croissance rapide, particulièrement des cellules malignes.

PHARMACOCINÉTIQUE

Absorption: Biodisponibilité à 100 % (IV).

Distribution: Forte liaison aux plaquettes et aux lymphocytes.

Métabolisme et excrétion: Métabolisme principalement hépatique. Au moins un des métabolites est actif. Élimination importante dans les fèces. Faible élimination rénale (11 %).

Demi-vie: De 28 à 44 heures.

Profil temps-action (effet sur la numération leucocytaire)

	DÉBUT D'ACTION	PIC	DURÉE
IV	inconnu	7 - 10 jours	7 - 15 jours

CONTRE-INDICATIONS, PRÉCAUTIONS ET MISES EN GARDE

Contre-indications: Hypersensibilité ■ Granulopénie ou thrombopénie iatrogène grave.

Précautions et mises en garde: Insuffisance hépatique (diminuer la dose lorsque la bilirubine est > 35 µmol/L) ■ Patients débilités (risque accru d'hyponatrémie) ■ **PÉD.**: L'innocuité de l'agent n'a pas été établie ■ Grossesse, allaitement ou patientes en âge de procréer ■ Infections actives ■ Aplasie médullaire ■ Autres maladies chroniques débilitantes ■ Neuropathie préexistante.

RÉACTIONS INDÉSIRABLES ET EFFETS SECONDAIRES

SNC: fatigue.

Resp.: essoufflements.

CV: douleur à la poitrine.

GI: constipation, nausées, douleurs abdominales, anorexie, élévation transitoire des enzymes hépatiques, vomissements, stomatite.

Tég.: alopécie, rash, vésication.

HÉ: hyponatrémie (avec ou sans syndrome d'antidiurèse inappropriée).

Hémat.: anémie, neutropénie, thrombopénie.

Locaux: irritation au point d'injection, réactions cutanées, phlébite.

Loc.: arthralgie, douleurs lombaires, douleur à la mâchoire, myalgie.

SN: neurotoxicité.

Divers: douleurs dans les tissus envahis par la tumeur.

INTERACTIONS

Médicament-médicament: Effet additif sur l'aplasie médullaire lors de l'administration concomitante d'autres **antinéoplasiques** ou d'une **radiothérapie** ■ L'administration concomitante de **cisplatine** accroît le risque d'aplasie médullaire et sa gravité ■ La **mitomycine** ou les **radiations thoraciques** accroissent le risque de réactions pulmonaires aiguës ■ L'administration concomitante ou séquentielle de **paclitaxel** peut augmenter le risque de neuropathies.

VOIES D'ADMINISTRATION ET POSOLOGIE

- **IV (adultes)**: 30 mg/m², 1 fois par semaine.

Adaptations posologiques en fonction du nombre de granulocytes

- **IV (adultes)**: ≥ *1,5 × 10⁹/L* - 30 mg/m², 1 fois par semaine; *de 1 à 1,499 × 10⁹/L* - 15 mg/m², 1 fois par semaine; < *1 × 10⁹/L* - ne pas administrer le médicament.

INSUFFISANCE HÉPATIQUE

- **IV (ADULTES)**: *BILIRUBINE TOTALE DE 36 À 50 µmol/L* - 15 mg/m², 1 FOIS PAR SEMAINE; *BILIRUBINE TOTALE > 50 µmol/L* - 7,5 mg/m², 1 FOIS PAR SEMAINE.

PRÉSENTATION (version générique disponible)

Solution pour injection: 10 mg/mL[Pr], en fioles de 1 mL et de 5 mL.

SOINS INFIRMIERS

ÉVALUATION DE LA SITUATION

- Mesurer la pression artérielle, le pouls et la fréquence respiratoire pendant toute la durée du traitement. Noter tout changement important. L'essoufflement aigu et des bronchospasmes graves peuvent se manifester, quoique rarement, peu après l'administration du médicament. L'administration de corticostéroïdes, de bronchodilatateurs et d'oxygène peut s'avérer nécessaire, particulièrement chez les patients ayant des antécédents de maladies pulmonaires.
- Évaluer le patient à intervalles fréquents à la recherche de signes d'infection (maux de gorge, fièvre, toux, modification de l'état mental), particulièrement à l'approche du nadir de la granulopénie.
- Évaluer l'état neurologique du patient. Déceler les signes de paresthésie (engourdissements, picotements, douleurs), la perte des réflexes tendineux profonds (le réflexe achilléen est habituellement le premier touché), la faiblesse (poignet ou pied tombant, problèmes liés à la marche), la paralysie des nerfs crâniens (douleurs aux mâchoires, raucité de la voix, ptosis, modifications visuelles), le dysfonctionnement du système nerveux autonome (constipation, iléus, mictions difficiles, hypotension orthostatique, modification des sécrétions de sueur) et le dysfonctionnement du SNC (diminution de l'état de conscience, agitation, hallucinations). Ces symptômes peuvent persister pendant plusieurs mois. L'incidence de la neurotoxicité associée à cet agent est moins élevée que dans le cas des autres alcaloïdes extraits de la pervenche.

V

- Effectuer le bilan des ingesta et des excreta et noter le poids du patient tous les jours pour déceler tout écart.
- Évaluer l'état nutritionnel du patient. Les nausées légères à modérées sont courantes. On peut administrer un antiémétique pour réduire les nausées et les vomissements.
- Rester à l'affût des symptômes de goutte: concentrations accrues d'acide urique, douleurs articulaires, œdème. Inciter le patient à boire au moins 2 litres de liquides par jour si son état le permet. On peut lui prescrire de l'allopurinol ou l'alcalinisation de l'urine afin de réduire les concentrations d'acide urique.

Tests de laboratoire:

- Noter la numération globulaire avant l'administration de chaque dose et à intervalles réguliers pendant toute la durée du traitement. Le nadir de la granulopénie survient habituellement en l'espace de 7 à 10 jours après l'administration de la vinorelbine; les valeurs se rétablissent habituellement de 7 à 15 jours plus tard. Si le nombre de granulocytes est < 1,5 × 10^9/L, il peut s'avérer nécessaire d'interrompre temporairement le traitement ou de réduire la dose de médicament. En cas de fièvre ou de septicémie récurrente pendant la granulopénie, il faut adapter la posologie de la vinorelbine. Le médicament peut aussi entraîner une anémie légère à modérée. La thrombopénie survient rarement.
- Vérifier les résultats des tests des fonctions hépatique (AST, ALT, LDH, bilirubine) et rénale (urée, créatinine), avant le traitement et à intervalles réguliers pendant toute sa durée. La vinorelbine peut entraîner l'élévation des concentrations d'acide urique. Noter ces concentrations à intervalles réguliers pendant toute la durée du traitement.

DIAGNOSTICS INFIRMIERS POSSIBLES

- Risque d'accident (Réactions indésirables).
- Risque d'infection (Réactions indésirables).
- Connaissances insuffisantes sur le traitement médicamenteux (Enseignement au patient et à ses proches).

V

INTERVENTIONS INFIRMIÈRES

ALERTE CLINIQUE: DES DÉCÈS SONT SURVENUS LORS DE CERTAINES CHIMIOTHÉRAPIES. AVANT D'ADMINISTRER L'AGENT, CLARIFIER TOUS LES POINTS AMBIGUS. VÉRIFIER UNE FOIS DE PLUS LA LIMITE DES DOSES UNITAIRES ET QUOTIDIENNES AINSI QUE CELLE DE LA DOSE À ADMINISTRER PENDANT LE TRAITEMENT. DEMANDER À UN DEUXIÈME PROFESSIONNEL DE LA SANTÉ DE VÉRIFIER DE NOUVEAU L'ORDONNANCE D'ORIGINE, LES CALCULS ET LE RÉGLAGE DE LA POMPE À PERFUSION.

- NE PAS CONFONDRE LA VINORELBINE AVEC LA VINBLASTINE OU AVEC LA VINCRISTINE.
- La solution devrait être préparée sous une hotte à flux laminaire. Porter des gants, une blouse et un masque lors de la manipulation du médicament. Mettre au rebut tout le matériel destiné à l'administration IV dans les contenants réservés à cet usage (voir l'annexe H).
- Observer fréquemment le point de perfusion pour déceler les rougeurs, l'inflammation ou l'infiltration. La vinorelbine est un agent vésicant. En cas d'extravasation, arrêter immédiatement la perfusion et la reprendre dans une autre veine afin d'éviter la lésion des tissus sous-cutanés. Le traitement de l'extravasation consiste en l'application immédiate de compresses chaudes sur la région touchée pendant 30 à 60 minutes; on arrête ensuite de les appliquer pendant 15 minutes et on les applique de nouveau pendant 15 minutes et ainsi de suite pendant 24 heures pour accroître l'absorption systémique du médicament.

IV directe: Pour obtenir une concentration de 1,5 à 3 mg/mL, diluer la vinorelbine dans une solution de NaCl 0,9 % ou de D5%E. Consulter les directives de chaque fabricant avant d'administrer la préparation.

Vitesse d'administration: Perfuser en 6 à 10 minutes dans le raccord en Y le plus près du sac de la solution IV ou dans un cathéter central pendant que le soluté coule librement. Après la perfusion, purger la veine avec au moins 75 à 125 mL d'une solution de NaCl 0,9 % ou de D5%E, administrés pendant 10 minutes ou plus.

Perfusion intermittente: Pour obtenir une concentration de 0,5 à 2 mg/mL, diluer la vinorelbine dans une solution de NaCl 0,9 %, de D5%E, de NaCl 0,45 %, de D5%/NaCl 0,45 %, de Ringer ou de lactate de Ringer. La solution peut être d'incolore à jaune pâle. Ne pas administrer les solutions qui ont changé de couleur ou qui renferment des particules. La solution diluée est stable pendant 24 heures à la température ambiante. Consulter les directives de chaque fabricant avant d'administrer la préparation.

Vitesse d'administration: Perfuser en 6 à 10 minutes dans le raccord en Y le plus près du sac de la solution IV ou dans un cathéter central pendant que le soluté coule librement. Après la perfusion, purger la veine avec au moins 75 à 125 mL d'une solution de NaCl 0,9 % ou de D5%E, administrés pendant 10 minutes ou plus.

Compatibilité (tubulure en Y): amikacine ■ aztréonam ■ bléomycine ■ bumétanide ■ buprénorphine ■ butorphanol ■ calcium, gluconate de ■ carboplatine ■ carmustine ■ céfotaxime ■ ceftazidime ■ ceftizoxime ■ ceftriaxone ■ chlorpromazine ■ cimétidine ■ cisplatine ■ clindamycine ■ cyclophosphamide ■ cytarabine ■

dacarbazine ■ dactinomycine ■ daunorubicine ■ dexaméthasone sodique, phosphate de ■ diphenhydramine ■ doxorubicine ■ doxycycline ■ dropéridol ■ énalaprilate ■ étoposide ■ famotidine ■ floxuridine ■ fluconazole ■ fludarabine ■ gallium, nitrate de ■ gentamycine ■ halopéridol ■ héparine ■ hydrocortisone ■ hydromorphone ■ idarubicine ■ ifosfamide ■ imipénem/cilastatine ■ lorazépam ■ mannitol ■ méchloretamine ■ melphalan ■ mépéridine ■ mesna ■ méthotrexate ■ métoclopramide ■ métronidazole ■ miconazole ■ minocycline ■ mitoxantrone ■ morphine ■ nalbuphine ■ nétilmicine ■ ondansétron ■ plicamycine ■ streptozocine ■ téniposide ■ ticarcilline/clavulanate ■ tobramycine ■ vancomycine ■ vinblastine ■ vincristine ■ zidovudine.

Incompatibilité (tubulure en Y): acyclovir ■ aminophylline ■ amphotéricine B ■ ampicilline ■ céfazoline ■ céfopérazone ■ céforanide ■ céfotétane ■ ceftriaxone ■ céfuroxime ■ fluorouracile ■ furosémide ■ ganciclovir ■ méthylprednisolone ■ mitomycine ■ pipéracilline ■ sodium, bicarbonate de ■ thiotépa ■ triméthoprime/sulfaméthoxazole.

ENSEIGNEMENT AU PATIENT ET À SES PROCHES

- Recommander au patient de signaler les symptômes suivants de neurotoxicité: paresthésie, douleur, difficultés à se déplacer, constipation persistante.
- Informer le patient qu'un apport liquidien accru, la consommation de fibres alimentaires et l'exercice peuvent diminuer la constipation. Il peut aussi prendre des laxatifs émollients ou autres. Lui conseiller de communiquer avec un professionnel de la santé en cas de constipation grave ou de gêne abdominale, puisqu'il pourrait s'agir de signes d'iléus attribuable à la neuropathie.
- Inciter le patient à signaler à un professionnel de la santé la fièvre, les frissons, les maux de gorge, les signes d'infection, le saignement des gencives, les ecchymoses, les pétéchies ou la présence d'aphtes ou de sang dans les selles, l'urine ou les vomissements.
- Recommander au patient d'éviter les foules et les personnes contagieuses.
- Prévenir la patiente que la vinorelbine peut avoir des effets tératogènes. Lui conseiller d'utiliser une méthode de contraception efficace durant le traitement et pendant au moins 2 mois après l'avoir arrêté.
- Prévenir le patient qu'il risque de perdre ses cheveux. Explorer avec lui les stratégies lui permettant de s'adapter à ce changement.
- Expliquer au patient qu'il ne doit pas se faire vacciner sans recommandation expresse d'un professionnel de la santé.
- Insister sur le fait qu'il est nécessaire d'effectuer des examens de laboratoire à intervalles réguliers afin de déceler les effets secondaires du médicament.

VÉRIFICATION DE L'EFFICACITÉ THÉRAPEUTIQUE

L'efficacité du traitement peut être démontrée par: la diminution de la taille de la tumeur maligne sans apparition d'effets secondaires délétères.

VITAMINE B_2,
voir Riboflavine

VITAMINE B_{12} (PRÉPARATIONS)

cyanocobalamine
Bedoz, Cobex, Cyanocobalamine, Vitamin B_{12}

hydroxocobalamine
Acti-B12, Hydro Cobex, Hydroxocobalamine, Hydroxy-Cobal, Vitamine B_{12}

CLASSIFICATION:
Vitamines B (hydrosolubles), hématopoïétique

Grossesse – catégories A (doses dans les limites des apports nutritionnels recommandés [ANR]) et C (doses > ANR)

INDICATIONS

Traitement et prévention des carences en vitamine B_{12} ■ Traitement de l'anémie pernicieuse ■ Test de Schilling (agent diagnostique).

MÉCANISME D'ACTION

Coenzyme nécessaire à de nombreux processus métaboliques incluant le métabolisme des lipides et des glucides et la synthèse des protéines ■ Élément indispensable à la formation de globules rouges. ***Effets thérapeutiques:*** Correction des manifestations d'anémie pernicieuse (indices mégaloblastiques, lésions gastro-intestinales et atteinte neurologique) ■ Prévention des carences en vitamine B_{12}.

PHARMACOCINÉTIQUE

Absorption: L'absorption depuis le tractus gastro-intestinal ne peut se faire en l'absence de facteur intrinsèque et de calcium (seulement 5 µg/jour pourraient être absorbés). Bonne (IM, SC).

V

Distribution: Ces vitamines sont emmagasinées dans le foie. Elles traversent la barrière placentaire et passent dans le lait maternel.
Métabolisme et excrétion: Les quantités excessives sont éliminées à l'état inchangé dans l'urine.
Demi-vie: 6 jours (400 jours dans le foie).

Profil temps-action (réticulocytose)

	DÉBUT D'ACTION	PIC	DURÉE
Cyanocobalamine, IM, SC, voie nasale	inconnu	3 – 10 jours	inconnue
Hydroxocobalamine, IM, SC	inconnu	3 – 10 jours	Inconnue

CONTRE-INDICATIONS, PRÉCAUTIONS ET MISES EN GARDE

Contre-indications: Hypersensibilité.
Précautions et mises en garde: Atrophie héréditaire du nerf optique (accélération des lésions) ■ Urémie, carences en acide folique, infection concomitante, carences en fer (altération de la réponse à la vitamine B_{12}).

RÉACTIONS INDÉSIRABLES ET EFFETS SECONDAIRES

GI: diarrhée.
Tég.: démangeaisons, urticaire.
HÉ: hypokaliémie.
Locaux: douleur au point d'injection IM.
Divers: réactions d'hypersensibilité incluant l'ANAPHYLAXIE.

INTERACTIONS

Médicament-médicament: Le **chloramphénicol** et les **antinéoplasiques** peuvent diminuer la réponse hématologique à la vitamine B_{12} ■ Les **aminosides**, la **colchicine**, les **suppléments potassiques à libération prolongée**, l'**acide para-aminosalicylique**, les **anticonvulsivants**, la **cimétidine**, ainsi que les quantités excessives d'**alcool** ou de **vitamine C** peuvent diminuer l'absorption ou l'efficacité de la vitamine B_{12}.

V

VOIES D'ADMINISTRATION ET POSOLOGIE

Carence en cyanocobalamine

- **PO (adultes et enfants):** La dose dépend de la gravité de la carence; jusqu'à 1 000 µg/jour.
- **IM, SC (adultes):** De 30 à 100 µg/jour, pendant 5 à 10 jours, puis de 100 à 200 µg/mois. On a déjà administré des doses allant jusqu'à 1 000 µg. La dose pour l'injection administrée dans le cadre du test de Schilling est de 1 000 µg.
- **IM, SC (enfants):** 100 µg/jour, jusqu'à l'atteinte d'une dose cumulative totale de 1 à 5 mg, puis 60 µg/mois. On a déjà administré des doses allant jusqu'à 1 000 µg. La dose pour l'injection administrée dans le cadre du test de Schilling est de 1 000 µg.

Carence en hydroxocobalamine

- **IM, SC (adultes):** De 30 à 100 µg/jour, pendant 5 à 10 jours, puis de 100 à 200 µg/mois. La dose pour l'injection administrée dans le cadre du test de Schilling est de 1 000 µg.
- **IM, SC (enfants):** 100 µg/jour, jusqu'à l'atteinte d'une dose cumulative totale de 1 à 5 mg, puis 60 µg/mois.

PRÉSENTATION

- **Cyanocobalamine**
  Capsules: 1 000 µg[VL] ■ **Comprimés:** 25 µg[VL], 50 µg[VL], 100 µg[VL], 250 µg[VL], 500 µg[VL], 1 000 µg[VL] ■ **Comprimés à libération prolongée:** 100 µg[VL], 200 µg[VL], 500 µg[VL], 1 000 µg[VL], 1 200 µg[VL] ■ **Solution pour injection:** 100 µg/mL, en ampoules de 1 mL[VL], 1 000 µg/mL, en ampoules de 1 mL[VL] et en fioles de 10 mL[VL] et de 30 mL[VL].
- **Hydroxocobalamine**
  Solution pour injection: 1 000 µg/mL, en fioles de 30 mL[Pr].

SOINS INFIRMIERS

ÉVALUATION DE LA SITUATION

- Avant le traitement et pendant toute sa durée, rechercher les signes suivants de déficit en vitamine B_{12}: pâleur, neuropathie, psychose, langue rougie et tuméfiée.

Tests de laboratoire: Examiner les concentrations plasmatiques d'acide folique, la numération des réticulocytes et les concentrations plasmatiques de vitamine B_{12} avant l'administration initiale et entre le 5e et le 7e jour de traitement. Chez les patients recevant de la vitamine B_{12} pour le traitement de l'anémie mégaloblastique, il faut déterminer les concentrations sériques de potassium au cours des 48 premières heures de traitement en raison des risques d'hypokaliémie. Il faut suivre les patients atteints d'anémie pernicieuse tous les 5 à 6 mois.

DIAGNOSTICS INFIRMIERS POSSIBLES

- Alimentation déficiente (Indications).
- Intolérance à l'activité (Indications).
- Connaissances insuffisantes sur le traitement médicamenteux (Enseignement au patient et à ses proches).

INTERVENTIONS INFIRMIÈRES

- On administre habituellement la vitamine B_{12} en association avec d'autres vitamines, car il est rare que le patient ne présente que ce seul type de carence vitaminique.

- L'administration de la vitamine B_{12} par voie orale n'est utile qu'en cas de carences nutritionnelles. Le médicament doit être administré par voie parentérale en présence d'une maladie de l'intestin grêle, d'un syndrome de malabsorption, d'une gastrectomie ou d'une iléoctomie.

PO:

- Administrer ces vitamines aux repas afin d'en accroître l'absorption.
- On peut mélanger la cyanocobalamine à des jus de fruits. Demander au patient de boire la préparation aussitôt que le mélange a été fait puisque l'acide ascorbique en diminue la stabilité.

IV: La voie IV n'est pas recommandée. Toutefois, on peut mélanger de petites quantités de cyanocobalamine à une solution destinée à l'alimentation par voie parentérale totale.

Compatibilité (tubulure en Y): héparine ▪ hydrocortisone sodique, succinate d' ▪ potassium, chlorure de ▪ vitamines du complexe B avec C.

Compatibilité en addition au soluté: D5%E ▪ D10%E ▪ dextrose et solution de Ringer ou de lactate de Ringer ▪ dextrose et solution saline ▪ NaCl 0,45 % ▪ NaCl 0,9 % ▪ solution de Ringer ou de lactate de Ringer ▪ vitamines du complexe B avec C.

ENSEIGNEMENT AU PATIENT ET À SES PROCHES

- Encourager le patient à respecter rigoureusement les recommandations diététiques du professionnel de la santé. Lui expliquer que la meilleure source de vitamines est une alimentation bien équilibrée. Lui recommander de suivre un régime comprenant des aliments des quatre principaux groupes alimentaires.
- Expliquer au patient que les aliments riches en vitamine B_{12} comprennent les viandes, les fruits de mer, le jaune d'œuf et les fromages fermentés; une petite quantité seulement est perdue lors de la cuisson normale des aliments.
- Recommander aux patients prenant des suppléments vitaminiques de ne pas dépasser l'apport quotidien recommandé (voir l'annexe K). L'efficacité des mégadoses dans le traitement de diverses affections n'a pas été démontrée et leur administration peut entraîner des effets secondaires.
- Expliquer au patient ayant subi une gastrectomie ou une iléoctomie qu'il doit prendre des suppléments de vitamine B_{12} tout au long de sa vie.
- Insister sur l'importance des examens de suivi permettant d'évaluer les bienfaits du traitement.

VÉRIFICATION DE L'EFFICACITÉ THÉRAPEUTIQUE

L'efficacité du traitement peut être démontrée par: la résolution des symptômes de carence en vitamine B_{12} ▪ l'augmentation du nombre de réticulocytes ▪ l'amélioration des symptômes d'anémie pernicieuse. ✳

VITAMINE D (COMPOSÉS DE)

alfacalcidol (1α-hydroxycholécalciférol, métabolite de la vitamine D_3)

One-Alpha

calcitriol (1,25-dihydroxycholécalciférol, métabolite de la vitamine D_3)

Calcijex, Calcitriol, Rocaltrol

cholécalciférol (vitamine D_3)

D-Pro, D-400, D-Vi-Sol, Euro-D, Odan-D, Pediavit-D, Riva-D, Vitamine D_3

doxercalciférol

Hectorol

ergocalciférol (vitamine D_2)

Drisdol, Ostoforte

paricalcitol

Zemplar

CLASSIFICATION:

Vitamines D (liposolubles)

Grossesse – catégories A (cholécalciférol aux doses ≤ aux apports nutritionnels recommandés [10 µg/jour]), B (doxercalciférol) et C (calcitriol, paricalcitol)

INDICATIONS

Alfacalcidol: Traitement de l'hypocalcémie, de l'hyperparathyroïdie secondaire et de l'ostéodystrophie chez les patients souffrant d'insuffisance rénale chronique ▪ **Calcitriol**: Traitement de l'hypocalcémie et de l'ostéodystrophie chez les patients souffrant d'insuffisance rénale chronique soumis à la dialyse ▪ Traitement de l'hypoparathyroïdie postchirurgicale ou idiopathique ou de la pseudohypoparathyroïdie ▪ Traitement du rachitisme vitaminorésistant (hypophosphatémie familiale) ▪ **Cholécalciférol**: Prévention de la carence chez les nourrissons allaités au sein ▪ Prévention et traitement de la carence en vitamine D ▪ **Doxercalciférol**: Traitement de l'hyperparathyroïdie secondaire chez les patients atteints d'insuffisance rénale chronique ▪ **Ergocalciférol**: Prévention et traitement de la carence en vitamine D ▪ Traitement de l'hypophosphatémie ou de l'hypocalcémie ▪ Traitement

V

de l'ostéodystrophie ■ Traitement du rachitisme vitaminorésistant (hypophosphatémie familiale) et de l'hypoparathyroïdie ■ **Paricalcitol**: Prévention et traitement de l'hyperparathyroïdie secondaire associée à l'insuffisance rénale chronique. **Usages non approuvés pour les agents précédents**: Traitement et prévention de l'ostéoporose primaire ou provoquée par les corticostéroïdes, en association avec des suppléments de calcium.

MÉCANISME D'ACTION

Le dihydrotachystérol et l'ergocalciférol sont des formes inactives de vitamine D; ils sont transformés en une forme active par le foie et les reins. Le calcitriol est la forme active ■ La vitamine D favorise l'absorption du calcium et du phosphore ■ Elle régularise l'homéostasie calcique en association avec la parathormone et la calcitonine. ***Effets thérapeutiques:*** Traitement et prophylaxie des maladies de carence, particulièrement des manifestations osseuses ■ Amélioration de l'homéostasie du calcium et du phosphore chez les patients atteints d'insuffisance rénale chronique.

PHARMACOCINÉTIQUE

Absorption: *Calcitriol* - Bonne (PO). *Ergocalciférol* - Cet agent, sous forme inactive, est bien absorbé. *Doxercalciférol* - Cet agent est un promédicament qui est bien absorbé (PO). *Paricalcitol* - Biodisponibilité à 100 % (IV).

Distribution: Ces vitamines sont emmagasinées dans le foie et dans les autres tissus adipeux; le calcitriol traverse la barrière placentaire.

Métabolisme et excrétion: *Calcitriol* - recyclage entérohépatique. Excrétion majoritairement biliaire. *Ergocalciférol* - transformation en une forme active par le soleil, le foie et les reins. *Doxercalciférol* - transformation par le foie en 1α,25-$(OH)_2D_2$ (métabolite majeur) et en 1,24-dihydroxyvitamine D_2 (métabolite mineur). *Paricalcitol* - métabolisme majoritairement hépatique et élimination par voie hépatobiliaire.

Demi-vie: *Calcitriol* - de 3 à 8 heures. *Métabolites du doxercalciférol* - de 32 à 37 heures (jusqu'à 96 heures). *Paricalcitol* - 15 heures.

V

Profil temps-action
(effets sur les concentrations sériques de calcium)

	DÉBUT D'ACTION	PIC	DURÉE
Calcitriol - PO	2 - 6 h	2 - 6 h	3 - 5 jours
Calcitriol - IV	inconnu	inconnu	inconnue
Doxercalciférol - PO	inconnu	8 semaines	1 semaine
Ergocalciférol - PO	12 - 24 h†	inconnu	jusqu'à 6 mois
Paricalcitol - IV	inconnu	jusqu'à 2 semaines	inconnue

† L'effet thérapeutique peut ne pas se manifester avant 10 à 14 jours.

CONTRE-INDICATIONS, PRÉCAUTIONS ET MISES EN GARDE

Contre-indications: Hypersensibilité ■ Hypercalcémie, hyperphosphatémie ■ Toxicité associée à la vitamine D ou sensibilité anormale aux effets de la vitamine D ■ **Ergocalciférol**: Diminution de la fonction rénale, syndrome de malabsorption.

Précautions et mises en garde: Hyperparathyroïdie ■ Traitement par des dérivés digitaliques ■ **OBST., ALLAITEMENT**: L'innocuité de ces vitamines administrées à des doses élevées n'a pas été établie ■ **Doxercalciférol**: Administration concomitante d'antiacides renfermant du magnésium ou d'autres suppléments de vitamine D.

RÉACTIONS INDÉSIRABLES ET EFFETS SECONDAIRES

Ces réactions et ces effets sont surtout des manifestations de toxicité (hypercalcémie).

SNC: céphalées, somnolence, faiblesse; *doxercalciférol* - étourdissements, malaise, troubles du sommeil.

ORLO: conjonctivite (calcifiante), photophobie, rhinorrhée.

Resp.: *doxercalciférol* - dyspnée.

CV: arythmies, hypertension; *doxercalciférol* - bradycardie; *paricalcitol* - œdème, palpitations.

GI: anorexie, constipation, sécheresse de la bouche (xérostomie), goût métallique, nausées, polydipsie, vomissements, perte de poids.

GU: albuminurie, baisse de la libido, nycturie, polyurie.

Tég.: prurit.

End.: *doxercalciférol* - suppression excessive de la parathormone.

HÉ: hypercalcémie; *doxercalciférol* - hypercalciurie, hyperphosphatémie.

Métab.: hyperthermie.

Loc.: douleurs osseuses, douleurs musculaires; *doxercalciférol* - maladie osseuse adynamique, arthralgie; *paricalcitol* - calcification métastatique.

Divers: *paricalcitol* - réactions allergiques, frissons, fièvre.

INTERACTIONS

Médicament-médicament: L'absorption des analogues de la vitamine D est diminuée par l'administration concomitante de **cholestyramine**, de **colestipol** ou d'**huile minérale** ■ L'administration de **diurétiques thiazidiques** chez des patients atteints d'hypoparathyroïdie peut entraîner l'hypercalcémie ■ Les **corticostéroïdes** peuvent réduire l'efficacité des analogues de la vitamine D ■ L'administration concomitante de **dérivés digitaliques** augmente le risque d'arythmies ■ La **phénytoïne** et d'autres **anticonvulsivants hydantoïnes**, le **sucralfate**, les **barbituriques** et la **primidone** augmentent les besoins en vitamine D ■ Administrer avec prudence aux patients qui reçoivent des **antiacides contenant du magnésium** ou des **médicaments renfermant du calcium** ■ L'administration concomitante d'**antiacides renfermant du magnésium** peut entraîner l'hypermagnésémie ■ L'administration concomitante d'autres **suppléments de vitamine D** peut accroître le risque d'hypercalcémie.

Médicament-aliments: La consommation d'**aliments riches en calcium** (voir l'annexe J) peut mener à une hypercalcémie.

VOIES D'ADMINISTRATION ET POSOLOGIE

Alfacalcidol

- **PO (adultes)**: *Posologie initiale* – 0,25 µg/jour, pendant 2 mois. Chez les patients dialysés, la dose de départ devrait être de 1 µg/jour. Si on n'obtient pas l'effet désiré après 4 semaines, on doit augmenter la dose de 0,5 µg, à intervalles de 2 ou de 4 semaines. (Écart posologique: entre 1 et 2 µg/jour; ne pas dépasser 3 µg/jour). *Dose d'entretien* – de 0,25 à 1 µg/jour. Le patient doit bénéficier en même temps d'un apport quotidien suffisant de calcium (de 800 à 1 000 mg).
- **IV**: *Traitement intermittent: Posologie initiale* – 1 µg par dialyse (2 ou 3 fois/semaine); la dose peut être augmentée à raison de 1 µg par dialyse, jusqu'à un maximum de 12 µg/semaine. *Dose d'entretien* – 6 µg/semaine (de 1,5 à 12 µg/semaine).

Calcitriol

- **PO (adultes)**: *Hypocalcémie et ostéodystrophie chez les patients atteints d'insuffisance rénale* – de 0,25 à 1 µg/jour (des doses plus élevées ont déjà été utilisées). On peut parfois administrer 0,25 µg, 1 jour sur 2. *Hypoparathyroïdie* – de 0,25 à 2,0 µg/jour. *Hypoparathyroïdie et rachitisme vitaminorésistant* – 0,25 µg/jour (des doses plus élevées ont déjà été utilisées).
- **PO (enfants)**: *Rachitisme vitaminorésistant et hypophosphatémique* – de 0,01 à 0,02 µg/kg/jour (dose moyenne: 0,018 µg/kg/jour). *Rachitisme vitaminorésistant de type I* – de 0,010 à 0,025 µg/kg/jour (dose moyenne: 0,017 µg/kg/jour). *Hypoparathyroïdie* – de 0,03 à 0,05 µg/kg/jour (dose moyenne: 0,04 µg/kg/jour). *Traitement intermittent (à doses élevées)* – L'administration intermittente de doses élevées de calcitriol par voie orale, 2 ou 3 fois par semaine, s'est révélée efficace même dans les cas réfractaires au traitement continu.
- **IV (adultes)**: *Dose initiale* – 0,5 µg, en bolus IV dans le cathéter, à la fin de l'hémodialyse, 3 fois par semaine. On peut majorer la dose de 0,25 à 0,5 µg, toutes les 2 à 4 semaines. *Dose d'entretien* – de 0,5 à 3 µg, 3 fois par semaine (de 0,01 à 0,05 µg/kg, 3 fois par semaine).

Cholécalciférol

- **PO (nourrissons)**: 400 unités, 1 fois par jour.
- **PO (adulte)**: 800 unités, 1 fois par jour.

Ergocalciférol

- **PO (adultes)**: *Carence en vitamine D* – 5 000 unités (125 µg)/jour, selon la gravité de la carence. *Rachitisme résistant à la vitamine D* – de 12 000 à 500 000 UI/jour (de 0,3 à 12,5 mg). *Hypoparathyroïdie* – de 50 000 à 200 000 unités (de 1,25 à 5 mg)/jour. Le patient doit recevoir en même temps un supplément de calcium approprié.
- **PO (enfants)**: *Carence en vitamine D* – 5 000 unités (125 µg)/jour, selon la gravité de la carence. *Dose d'entretien* – 400 unités/jour.

PRÉSENTATION

- **Alfacalcidol**
  Capsules: 0,25 µg[Pr], 1 µg[Pr] ■ **Gouttes orales**: 2 µg/mL, en flacons de 10 mL[Pr] ■ **Solution pour injection**: 2 µg/mL, en ampoules de 0,5 mL[Pr].
- **Calcitriol**
  Capsules: 0,25 µg[Pr], 0,5 µg[Pr] ■ **Solution orale**: 1 µg/mL, en flacons de 15 mL[Pr] ■ **Solution pour injection**: 2 µg/mL, en fioles de 0,5 mL[Pr] ou de 1 mL[Pr].
- **Cholécalciférol**
  Gouttes orales: 400 unités/mL, en flacons de 50 mL[VL] ■ **Comprimés**: 400 mg[VL] ■ **En association avec**: multivitamines et minéraux[VL].
- **Doxercalciférol**
  Capsules: 2,5 µg[Pr].
- **Ergocalciférol**
  Solution liquide: 8 288 unités/mL, en flacons de 60 mL[VL] ■ **Capsules**: 50 000 unités[Pr].
- **Paricalcitol**
  Solution pour injection: 5 µg/mL, en ampoules de 1 mL[Pr].

SOINS INFIRMIERS

ÉVALUATION DE LA SITUATION

- Suivre de près les symptômes de carence vitaminique avant l'administration et à intervalles réguliers tout au long du traitement.
- Avant l'administration de ces vitamines et pendant toute la durée du traitement, rester à l'affût de la faiblesse ou des douleurs osseuses.
- Observer attentivement le patient pour déceler les signes suivants d'hypocalcémie: paresthésie, soubresauts musculaires, laryngospasme, coliques, arythmies

cardiaques et signe de Chvostek ou de Trousseau. Pour protéger les patients qui manifestent ces symptômes, remonter et rembourrer les ridelles du lit; garder le lit en position basse.

Enfants: Suivre de près la taille et le poids; il y a risque d'interruption de la croissance lors de l'administration prolongée de doses élevées.

Rachitisme, ostéomalacie: Avant l'administration de ces vitamines et pendant toute la durée du traitement, rester à l'affût de la faiblesse ou des douleurs osseuses.

Tests de laboratoire: Au cours du traitement initial, il faut doser la calcémie hebdomadairement. Durant le traitement au *doxercarciférol*, maintenir le produit calcium sérique × phosphore sérique (Ca × P) inférieur à 5,7 mmol/L. Déterminer à intervalles réguliers les taux de parathormone sérique ou plasmatique, les taux de calcium et de phosphore sériques ainsi que la phosphatase alcaline. Si on constate une hypercalcémie, une hyperphosphatémie ou un Ca × P ≥ 5,7 mmol/L, on doit arrêter immédiatement le traitement jusqu'à ce que ces paramètres s'abaissent de façon appropriée. Puis, on peut recommencer le traitement à une dose de 2,5 µg plus faible.

- Examiner à intervalles réguliers les concentrations sériques d'urée, de créatinine, de phosphatase alcaline et de parathormone, ainsi que le ratio des concentrations de calcium/créatinine urinaires de 24 heures.
- Noter les concentrations sériques de phosphate avant l'administration et à intervalles réguliers pendant toute la durée du traitement. La phosphatémie doit être normalisée avant le début du traitement par le calcitriol. C'est la raison pour laquelle on administre du carbonate de calcium ou de l'hydroxyde d'aluminium aux patients dialysés.
- Une chute des concentrations de phosphatase alcaline peut indiquer l'apparition d'une hypercalcémie. Le surdosage est associé au produit de la multiplication de la concentration sérique de calcium par celle du phosphate (Ca × P) ≥ 5,7 mmol/L et à des concentrations élevées d'urée, d'AST et d'ALT.
- Ces vitamines peuvent entraîner des concentrations faussement élevées de cholestérol.

TOXICITÉ ET SURDOSAGE: La toxicité se manifeste sous forme d'hypercalcémie, d'hypercalciurie ou d'hyperphosphatémie. Observer l'apparition des symptômes suivants: nausées, vomissements, anorexie, faiblesse, constipation, céphalées, douleurs osseuses et goût métallique. Les symptômes tardifs sont la polyurie, la polydipsie, la photophobie, la rhinorrhée, le prurit et les arythmies cardiaques. Signaler immédiatement au médecin ou à un autre professionnel de la santé ces signes d'excès de vitamine D. Pour traiter ce type d'hypervitaminose, il faut habituellement interrompre l'administration du calcitriol, servir un régime alimentaire pauvre en calcium, n'utiliser que des dialysats à faible teneur en calcium chez les patients sous dialyse péritonéale et administrer un laxatif. On peut prescrire l'hydratation par voie IV et des diurétiques de l'anse pour augmenter l'excrétion urinaire du calcium. On peut également soumettre le patient à l'hémodialyse.

DIAGNOSTICS INFIRMIERS POSSIBLES

- Alimentation déficiente (Indications).
- Connaissances insuffisantes sur le traitement médicamenteux (Enseignement au patient et à ses proches).

INTERVENTIONS INFIRMIÈRES

- Étant donné que les carences en une seule vitamine sont rares, on doit souvent administrer des associations vitaminiques.

PO: Ces vitamines peuvent être administrées sans égard aux repas. Mesurer la solution avec le compte-gouttes gradué fourni par le fabricant. On peut mélanger ces vitamines à du jus, à des céréales ou à des aliments ou les déposer directement dans la bouche.

IV directe: Injecter rapidement le *calcitriol* dans une tubulure à la fin de l'hémodialyse.

ENSEIGNEMENT AU PATIENT ET À SES PROCHES

- Conseiller au patient de respecter rigoureusement la posologie recommandée. S'il n'a pu prendre la vitamine au moment habituel, il doit la prendre aussitôt que possible sauf s'il est presque l'heure de prendre la dose suivante. Le prévenir qu'il ne doit jamais remplacer une dose manquée par une double dose.
- Revoir avec le patient les modifications qu'il doit apporter à son régime alimentaire. Consulter l'annexe J pour connaître les aliments riches en calcium et en vitamine D. Les patients souffrant d'insuffisance rénale doivent choisir des aliments en fonction du régime approprié. Le professionnel de la santé peut prescrire la prise simultanée de suppléments calciques.
- Inciter le patient à suivre rigoureusement les recommandations diététiques du professionnel de la santé. Lui expliquer que la meilleure source de vitamines est un régime bien équilibré, composé d'aliments des quatre groupes, et qu'il lui est conseillé de s'exposer au soleil.
- Recommander au patient qui pratique l'automédication par des suppléments vitaminiques de ne pas dépasser les apports quotidiens recommandés d'éléments nutritifs (voir l'annexe K). Rien ne permet

d'affirmer que les mégadoses sont efficaces pour traiter les divers problèmes de santé. Elles peuvent par contre provoquer des réactions indésirables.

- Recommander au patient de ne pas prendre en même temps un antiacide à base de magnésium.
- Passer en revue avec le patient les symptômes de surdosage et l'inciter à signaler immédiatement ces symptômes au professionnel de la santé, le cas échéant.
- Insister sur l'importance des examens de suivi permettant de déterminer les bienfaits du traitement.

VÉRIFICATION DE L'EFFICACITÉ THÉRAPEUTIQUE

L'efficacité du traitement peut être démontrée par: la normalisation des concentrations sériques de calcium et de parathormone ■ la diminution de la faiblesse et des douleurs osseuses chez les patients souffrant d'ostéodystrophie rénale ■ l'amélioration des symptômes de rachitisme résistant à la vitamine D. ✳

VITAMINE E

acétate de d-α-tocophérol

acétate de d-α-tocophéryl

Aquasol-E, Vitamin E Naturelle, Webber Vitamine E

acétate de dl-α-tocophérol

acétate de dl-α-tocophéryl

E-200, E-400, E-800

dl-tocophérol

d-α-tocophérol

succinate acide de d-α-tocophérol

succinate acide de dl-α-tocophérol

α-tocophérol

CLASSIFICATION:

Vitamine E (liposoluble)

Grossesse – catégories A (doses dans les limites des apports nutritionnels recommandés [ANR]) et C (doses > ANR)

INDICATIONS

PO: Supplément diététique ■ Prévention et traitement de la carence en vitamine E ■ **Préparation topique**: Traitement de la peau irritée, gercée ou sèche. **Usages non approuvés**: Prévention des coronaropathies.

MÉCANISME D'ACTION

Prévention de l'oxydation d'autres substances (antioxydant) ■ Protection de la membrane érythrocytaire contre l'hémolyse, particulièrement chez les nouveau-nés de faible poids à la naissance. ***Effets thérapeutiques:*** Prévention et traitement des carences chez les patients exposés à un risque élevé.

PHARMACOCINÉTIQUE

Absorption: De 20 à 80 % (PO). L'absorption ne peut se faire en l'absence de lipides et de sels biliaires.

Distribution: Tout l'organisme. La vitamine est emmagasinée dans les tissus adipeux (réserve pour 4 ans).

Métabolisme et excrétion: Métabolisme hépatique et excrétion biliaire.

Demi-vie: Inconnue.

Profil temps-action

	DÉBUT D'ACTION	PIC	DURÉE
PO	inconnu	inconnu	inconnue

CONTRE-INDICATIONS, PRÉCAUTIONS ET MISES EN GARDE

Contre-indications: Hypersensibilité aux ingrédients de la préparation (parabènes, propylène glycol).

Précautions et mises en garde: Anémie attribuable à une carence en fer ■ Nourrissons de faible poids à la naissance (l'administration PO peut entraîner une entérocolite nécrosante) ■ Carence en vitamine K (risque accru d'hémorragie).

RÉACTIONS INDÉSIRABLES ET EFFETS SECONDAIRES

Les réactions indésirables et les effets secondaires sont surtout observés lors de l'administration de doses élevées pendant de longues périodes de temps.

SNC: fatigue, céphalées, faiblesse.

ORLO: vision trouble.

GI: ENTÉROCOLITE NÉCROSANTE (administration PO chez les nourrissons de faible poids à la naissance), crampes, diarrhée, nausées.

Tég.: rash.

End.: dysfonction gonadique.

INTERACTIONS

Médicament-médicament: La **cholestyramine**, le **colestipol**, l'**huile minérale** et le **sucralfate** diminuent l'absorption de la vitamine E ■ La vitamine E peut diminuer la réponse hématologique aux **suppléments de fer** ■ La vitamine E peut augmenter le risque de saignements lors de l'administration concomitante de **warfarine**.

VOIES D'ADMINISTRATION ET POSOLOGIE

Traitement de la carence en vitamine E

- **PO (adultes)**: De 60 à 75 UI par jour.
- **PO (enfants)**: Selon l'apport nutritionnel et la gravité de la carence.
- **Préparation topique (adultes et enfants)**: Appliquer sur les régions touchées, selon les besoins.

On peut utiliser d'autres schémas posologiques.

PRÉSENTATION

Capsules: 25 unités^{VL}, 100 unités^{VL}, 200 unités^{VL}, 400 unités^{VL}, 800 unités^{VL}, 1 000 unités^{VL} ■ **Solution orale**: 50 unités/mL^{VL}, 77 unités/mL^{VL} ■ **Comprimés**: 100 unités^{VL}, 200 unités^{VL}, 400 unités^{VL}, 800 unités^{VL} ■ **Comprimés à croquer**: 400 unités^{VL} ■ **Onguent**: 30 unités/g^{VL} ■ **Crème**: 250 unités/mL^{VL} ■ **Lotion**: ^{VL} ■ **Huile**: ^{VL}.

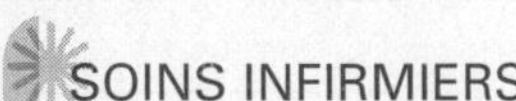

SOINS INFIRMIERS

ÉVALUATION DE LA SITUATION

- Observer le patient, avant le traitement et à intervalles réguliers pendant toute sa durée, pour déceler les signes suivants de carence en vitamine E: *nouveau-nés* – irritabilité, œdème, anémie hémolytique, excès de créatine dans les urines; *adultes et enfants (rares)* – faiblesse musculaire, dépôts de céroïdes dans les muscles, anémie, excès de créatine dans les urines.
- Évaluer l'état nutritionnel par le bilan de l'alimentation de 24 heures. Déterminer la fréquence de la consommation d'aliments riches en vitamine E.

Tests de laboratoire: Des doses élevées de vitamine E peuvent entraîner l'élévation des concentrations de cholestérol, de triglycérides et de CPK.

DIAGNOSTICS INFIRMIERS POSSIBLES

- Alimentation déficiente (Indications).
- Connaissances insuffisantes sur le traitement médicamenteux (Enseignement au patient et à ses proches).

INTERVENTIONS INFIRMIÈRES

PO:

- Administrer la vitamine E pendant ou après les repas.
- Il faut bien mâcher ou écraser les comprimés à croquer avant de les avaler. On peut déposer la solution directement dans la bouche ou la mélanger avec des céréales, des jus de fruits ou d'autres aliments. Utiliser le compte-gouttes fourni par le fabricant pour mesurer la solution.

ENSEIGNEMENT AU PATIENT ET À SES PROCHES

- Recommander au patient de respecter rigoureusement la posologie recommandée. S'il n'a pu prendre le médicament au moment habituel, il doit sauter cette dose, car les vitamines liposolubles sont emmagasinées dans l'organisme pendant de longues périodes.
- Inciter le patient à respecter les recommandations diététiques du professionnel de la santé. Lui expliquer que la meilleure source de vitamines est une alimentation bien équilibrée comprenant des aliments provenant des quatre principaux groupes alimentaires.
- Expliquer au patient que les aliments riches en vitamine E incluent les huiles végétales, le germe de blé, les céréales de blé entier, le jaune d'œuf et le foie. La teneur en vitamine E des aliments n'est pas modifiée considérablement par la cuisson.
- Recommander au patient qui pratique l'automédication par des suppléments vitaminiques de ne pas dépasser les apports quotidiens recommandés d'éléments nutritifs (voir l'annexe K). Rien ne permet d'affirmer que les mégadoses sont efficaces pour traiter les divers problèmes de santé. Elles peuvent par contre provoquer des effets secondaires et toxiques.
- Passer en revue avec le patient les symptômes du surdosage: troubles gastro-intestinaux, léthargie et céphalées. Lui recommander de signaler rapidement ces symptômes à un professionnel de la santé.
- Prévenir le patient que l'huile minérale peut entraver l'absorption des vitamines liposolubles et qu'il ne devrait par conséquent pas en prendre en même temps.

VÉRIFICATION DE L'EFFICACITÉ THÉRAPEUTIQUE

L'efficacité du traitement peut être démontrée par: la prévention ou la diminution des symptômes d'avitaminose E ■ le soulagement des problèmes de peau sèche ou gercée.

VITAMINE K,

voir Phytonadione

VORICONAZOLE

Vfend

CLASSIFICATION:

Antifongique par voie générale (de type azole)

Grossesse – catégorie D

INDICATIONS

Traitement de l'aspergillose invasive ■ Traitement de la candidémie (chez les patients non neutropéniques) et des infections à Candida suivantes: infections disséminées de la peau et infections de l'abdomen, du rein, de la paroi vésicale et des plaies.

MÉCANISME D'ACTION

Inhibition de la synthèse des stérols fongiques, un élément essentiel de la paroi cellulaire. ***Effets thérapeutiques:*** Activité fongicide contre les microorganismes sensibles. **Spectre d'action**: espèces *Aspergillus*, espèces *Candida*, espèces *Fusarium*, espèces *Cryptococcus neoformans*, espèces *Bipolaris*, *Pseudallescheria boydii*, *Histoplasma capsulatum*, *Saccahromyces cerevisiæ*, etc. Aucun effet sur les espèces de *Zygomycete in vitro*. L'activité globale *in vitro* du voriconazole est supérieure à celle du fluconazole, similaire ou supérieure à celle de l'itraconazole et de l'amphotéricine B ordinaire et comparable ou inférieure à celle de l'amphotéricine B liposomale.

PHARMACOCINÉTIQUE

Absorption: Bonne et rapide. Biodisponibilité à 96 % (PO) et 100 % (IV).

Distribution: Distribution tissulaire importante. D'après certains rapports de cas, le voriconazole pénètre dans le liquide céphalorachidien et dans le liquide pleural. On ignore s'il passe dans le lait maternel.

Liaison aux protéines plasmatiques: Environ 58 %.

Métabolisme et excrétion: Métabolisme majoritairement hépatique (par l'intermédiaire des isoenzymes 2C19, 2C9 et 3A4 du cytochrome P450). Excrétion majoritairement rénale (plus de 80 % sous forme de métabolites et moins de 2 % sous forme inchangée).

Demi-vie: Dépendante de la dose. Environ 6 heures (à la suite d'une dose de 3 mg/kg IV ou de 200 mg PO). La pharmacocinétique n'est pas linéaire, de sorte que la demi-vie terminale ne permet pas de prédire l'accumulation ni l'élimination du voriconazole.

Profil temps-action (concentrations plasmatiques)

	DÉBUT D'ACTION	PIC (T_{MAX})	DURÉE
PO	rapide	1 - 2 h	12 h
IV	rapide	fin de la perfusion	12 h

CONTRE-INDICATIONS, PRÉCAUTIONS ET MISES EN GARDE

Contre-indications: Hypersensibilité au voriconazole ou à ses excipients ■ Risque de réactions de sensibilité croisée avec d'autres antifongiques de type azole (miconazole, itraconazole, kétoconazole) ■ Le voriconazole est un substrat et un inhibiteur des isoenzymes CYP2C19, CYP2C9 et CYP3A4 du cytochrome P450. Par conséquent, l'administration concomitante de voriconazole et de médicaments dont la clairance dépend fortement de ces isoenzymes et dont l'augmentation des concentrations plasmatiques est associée à des manifestations graves ou à une issue fatale est contre-indiquée. L'administration de voriconazole en même temps que des médicaments qui en diminuent considérablement les concentrations plasmatiques en raison de l'induction de ces isoenzymes est également contre-indiquée ■ Administration concomitante de substrats du CYP3A4 (cisapride, pimozide, quinidine), en raison du risque d'allongement de l'intervalle QTc entraînant des torsades de pointes pouvant être mortelles ■ Administration concomitante de rifampicine, de carbamazépine, de barbituriques à longue durée d'action et de ritonavir (400 mg, toutes les 12 heures), en raison du risque de réduction marquée des concentrations plasmatiques de voriconazole ■ Administration concomitante d'éfavirenz, en raison d'une diminution marquée des concentrations plasmatiques de voriconazole et d'une élévation marquée des concentrations plasmatiques d'éfavirenz ■ Administration concomitante de sirolimus, en raison d'une élévation importante des concentrations de sirolimus induite par le voriconazole ■ Administration concomitante de rifabutine, en raison d'une élévation marquée des concentrations plasmatiques de rifabutine et d'une diminution marquée des concentrations plasmatiques de voriconazole ■ Administration concomitante de dérivés de l'ergot (ergotamine et dihydroergotamine), en raison d'une élévation possible des concentrations plasmatiques des dérivés de l'ergot, pouvant mener à l'ergotisme.

Précautions et mises en garde: On ne dispose d'aucune donnée concernant une hypersensibilité croisée entre le voriconazole et les autres antifongiques azolés. La prudence est donc de rigueur ■ Risque d'allongement de l'intervalle QTc induit par le voriconazole, ce qui peut accroître le risque d'arythmies (p. ex., torsades de pointes). Donc, la prudence est de mise chez les patients présentant des affections pouvant être proarythmiques (p. ex., hypokaliémie, bradycardie cliniquement notable, ischémie myocardique aiguë, insuffisance cardiaque, allongement congénital de l'intervalle QT); la prudence est également de mise lors de l'administration de médicaments susceptibles d'allonger l'intervalle QT (p. ex., antipsychotiques, antidépresseurs tricycliques, érythromycine, antiarythmiques de la classe IA [p. ex., le procaïnamide] et de la classe III [p. ex., l'amiodarone et le sotalol]). Les médicaments métabolisés par les isoenzymes CYP2C19, CYP2C9 et CYP3A4 (p. ex., le tacrolimus, les inhibiteurs de la protéase du VIH et les antibiotiques de la classe des macrolides) peuvent modifier les concentrations de voriconazole, et vice versa, ce qui peut se répercuter sur l'intervalle QT ■ Troubles visuels (vue brouillée, photophobie, altération ou amélioration de la perception visuelle ou modification de la vision des couleurs). La plupart de ces troubles semblent se résorber spontanément en l'espace de 60 minutes. L'effet du voriconazole sur la vision n'est pas connu si le traitement se poursuit au-delà de 28 jours. Le cas échéant, la vision devrait être surveillée au moyen d'examens (vérification de l'acuité visuelle, du champ visuel et de la perception des couleurs) ■ Insuffisance rénale (Cl_{Cr} < 50 mL/min; éviter d'administrer la préparation intraveineuse) ■ Risque de toxicité hépatique importante même chez les patients ne souffrant pas d'insuffisance hépatique. Un suivi de la fonction hépatique est indiqué ■ Insuffisance hépatique (une adaptation de la dose est nécessaire) ■ Risque de réaction de type anaphylactoïde reliée à la perfusion ■ Risque de réactions cutanées exfoliatives (il faut suivre de près les patients présentant des éruptions cutanées dès qu'elles apparaissent, et cesser l'administration de voriconazole si les lésions s'aggravent) ■ Femmes en âge de procréer (la patiente doit adopter une méthode contraceptive pendant le traitement) ■ **OBST., ALLAITEMENT:** N'utiliser que si les avantages dépassent les risques ■ **PÉD.:** Enfants < 12 ans (l'innocuité et l'efficacité du médicament n'ont pas été établies) ■ Intolérance au galactose (les comprimés contiennent du lactose).

RÉACTIONS INDÉSIRABLES ET EFFETS SECONDAIRES

SNC: céphalées, étourdissements, hallucinations.

ORLO: troubles visuels (altération ou amélioration de la perception visuelle, vue brouillée, modification de la vision des couleurs ou photophobie), hémorragie oculaire. Se référer à la section « Précautions et mises en garde ».

Resp.: troubles respiratoires.

CV: INFARCTUS DU MYOCARDE, ACCIDENT VASCULAIRE CÉRÉBRAL, tachycardie, FIBRILLATION VENTRICULAIRE, TORSADES DE POINTES, SYNCOPE.

GI: nausées, vomissements, diarrhée, douleurs abdominales, ictère, CHOLESTASE, HÉPATITE, INSUFFISANCE HÉPATIQUE FULMINANTE.

GU: anurie, cystite hémorragique, incontinence urinaire, rétention urinaire.

HÉ: œdème périphérique, hypokaliémie, hypomagnésémie.

Tég.: éruptions cutanées, photosensibilité (surtout en cas de traitement prolongé), SYNDROME DE STEVENS-JOHNSON, ÉRYTHRODERMIE BULLEUSE AVEC ÉPIDERMOLYSE, RASH.

Hémat.: AGRANULOCYTOSE, ANÉMIE, ANÉMIE APLASIQUE, ANÉMIE HÉMOLYTIQUE, THROMBOCYTOPÉNIE, LEUCOPÉNIE, PANCYTOPÉNIE.

Métab.: albuminurie, INSUFFISANCE RÉNALE AIGUË, élévation des résultats des tests de la fonction hépatique (AST, ALT, bilirubine, phosphatase alcaline), RÉACTIONS ANAPHYLACTOÏDES (bouffées vasomotrices, fièvre, transpiration, tachycardie, oppression thoracique, dyspnée, etc.) lors de l'administration de la solution de voriconazole injectable.

Loc.: arthralgie, myalgie, myasthénie.

Divers: fièvre, septicémie, frissons.

INTERACTIONS

Médicament-médicament: Le voriconazole est métabolisé par les isoenzymes CYP2C19, CYP2C9 et CYP3A4 du cytochrome P450. Les **inhibiteurs ou les inducteurs de ces isoenzymes** peuvent accroître ou abaisser les concentrations plasmatiques de voriconazole, respectivement ■ L'exposition au voriconazole est *considérablement réduite* si ce médicament est administré en concomitance avec les agents suivants: **rifampine**, **ritonavir**, **carbamazépine** et **barbituriques à longue durée d'action** (associations contre-indiquées) ■ L'emploi concomitant de voriconazole et des agents suivants est contre-indiqué: **cisapride**, **pimozide** et **quinidine** (en raison d'un allongement possible de l'intervalle QT pouvant entraîner des torsades de pointes), **sirolimus** (très forte élévation des concentrations plasmatiques de ce dernier), **dérivés de l'ergot** (risque d'ergotisme) ■ Les interactions entre le voriconazole et les agents énumérés ci-dessous peuvent *accroître* l'exposition à ces agents. Par conséquent, une surveillance étroite et l'adaptation de la posologie doivent être envisagées en cas d'administration concomitante de **certains bloqueurs des canaux calciques** (p. ex., **amlodipine**, **diltiazem**, **vérapamil**, **félodipine** et **nifédipine**), de certains **inhibiteurs de l'enzyme HMG-CoA réductase**, de **cyclosporine**, de **méthadone**, de **tacrolimus**, de **warfarine**, de **sulfamides hypoglycémiants** (risque d'hypoglycémie), de **statines**, de **benzodiazépines**, d'**alcaloïdes de la pervenche** (p. ex., **vincristine** et **vinblastine**) ■ L'administration concomitante de voriconazole et d'**éfavirenz** est contre-indiquée (diminution marquée des concentrations plasmatiques de voriconazole et élévation marquée des concentrations plasmatiques d'éfavirenz) ■ L'administration concomitante de voriconazole et de **rifabutine** est contre-indiquée (élévation marquée des concentrations plasmatiques de rifabutine et diminution marquée des concentrations plasmatiques de voriconazole) ■ L'administration concomitante de voriconazole et de **phénytoïne** entraîne une diminution des concentrations plasmatiques de voriconazole et une élévation des concentrations plasmatiques de phénytoïne ■ L'administration concomitante de voriconazole et d'**oméprazole** entraîne l'élévation des concentrations plasmatiques d'oméprazole (cette interaction peut aussi se produire avec d'autres **inhibiteurs de la pompe à protons**). Lorsqu'un traitement au voriconazole est amorcé chez des patients qui prennent déjà de l'oméprazole, il est recommandé de réduire de moitié la dose de cet agent ■ L'usage concomitant d'**inhibiteurs de la protéase** risque d'augmenter les concentrations plasmatiques de voriconazole ■ L'usage concomitant d'**inhibiteurs non nucléosidiques de la transcriptase inverse** peut augmenter ou diminuer les concentrations plasmatiques de voriconazole.

VOIES D'ADMINISTRATION ET POSOLOGIE

Compte tenu de la biodisponibilité élevée du médicament pris par voie orale, on peut substituer le traitement par voie orale au traitement intraveineux lorsque le tableau clinique le permet.

Aspergillose invasive

- **PO (adultes)**: *Dose d'attaque – patients > 40 kg:* 400 mg, toutes les 12 heures; *patients < 40 kg:* 200 mg, toutes les 12 heures. *Dose d'entretien (après les 24 premières heures) – patients > 40 kg:* 200 mg, toutes les 12 heures; *patients < 40 kg:* 100 mg, toutes les 12 heures.
- **IV (adultes)**: *Dose d'attaque* – 6 mg/kg, toutes les 12 heures. *Dose d'entretien (après les 24 premières heures)* – 4 mg/kg, toutes les 12 heures. Le traitement continu par voie intraveineuse ne doit pas durer plus de 6 mois. La durée du traitement est en fonction de la réponse clinique et mycologique des patients.

Candidémie et candidose invasive

- **PO (adultes)**: *Dose d'attaque* – 400 mg, toutes les 12 heures. *Dose d'entretien (après les 24 premières heures) – patients > 40 kg:* 200 mg, toutes les 12 heures; *patients < 40 kg:* 100 mg, toutes les 12 heures.
- **IV (adultes)**: *Dose d'attaque* – 6 mg/kg, toutes les 12 heures. *Dose d'entretien (après les 24 premières heures)* – de 3 à 4 mg/kg, toutes les 12 heures. Le traitement continu par voie intraveineuse ne doit pas durer plus de 6 mois. La durée du traitement est en fonction de la réponse clinique et mycologique des patients.

INSUFFISANCE HÉPATIQUE

- **PO, IV (ADULTES)**: *INSUFFISANCE HÉPATIQUE LÉGÈRE À MODÉRÉE (CLASSES A ET B DE CHILD-PUGH):* DOSE D'ATTAQUE HABITUELLE, MAIS RÉDUCTION DE MOITIÉ DE LA DOSE D'ENTRETIEN. L'INNOCUITÉ ET L'EFFICACITÉ D'UNE DOSE RÉDUITE DE VORICONAZOLE CHEZ CES PATIENTS N'ONT PAS ÉTÉ ÉTABLIES. *INSUFFISANCE HÉPATIQUE GRAVE (CLASSE C DE CHILD-PUGH):* ÉVALUER LE RAPPORT AVANTAGES-RISQUES, CAR LES EFFETS DU VORICONAZOLE N'ONT PAS ÉTÉ ÉTUDIÉS CHEZ CE TYPE DE PATIENTS. UNE SURVEILLANCE ÉTROITE DOIT ÊTRE EXERCÉE AFIN DE DÉCELER TOUT SIGNE DE TOXICITÉ MÉDICAMENTEUSE.

INSUFFISANCE RÉNALE

- **PO (ADULTES)**: LA PHARMACOCINÉTIQUE DU VORICONAZOLE, LORSQU'IL EST ADMINISTRÉ PAR VOIE ORALE, NE SEMBLE PAS SE MODIFIER EN PRÉSENCE D'INSUFFISANCE RÉNALE. PAR CONSÉQUENT, AUCUNE ADAPTATION POSOLOGIQUE N'EST NÉCESSAIRE EN CAS D'ADMINISTRATION PAR VOIE ORALE CHEZ LES PATIENTS ATTEINTS D'INSUFFISANCE RÉNALE LÉGÈRE À GRAVE.
- **IV (ADULTES)**: CHEZ LES PATIENTS PRÉSENTANT UN DYSFONCTIONNEMENT RÉNAL MODÉRÉ À GRAVE (CL_{CR} < 50 mL/MIN), IL SE PRODUIT UNE ACCUMULATION DE SBECD, LE VÉHICULE UTILISÉ DANS LA PRÉPARATION POUR PERFUSION. LE VORICONAZOLE DOIT ÊTRE ADMINISTRÉ À CES PATIENTS PAR VOIE ORALE, À MOINS QUE LE RAPPORT AVANTAGES-RISQUES NE JUSTIFIE L'USAGE DU VORICONAZOLE PAR VOIE INTRAVEINEUSE. DANS CE DERNIER CAS, IL FAUT SURVEILLER DE PRÈS LA FONCTION RÉNALE (Y COMPRIS LA CRÉATININÉMIE ET LA CLAIRANCE DE LA CRÉATININE) ET SI DES CHANGEMENTS IMPORTANTS SURVIENNENT, ENVISAGER D'ADMINISTRER LE VORICONAZOLE PAR VOIE ORALE PLUTÔT QUE PAR VOIE INTRAVEINEUSE.

PRÉSENTATION

Comprimés: 50 mg[Pr], 200 mg[Pr] ■ **Poudre lyophilisée pour injection**: fioles de 200 mg[Pr].

ÉVALUATION DE LA SITUATION

- Inspecter la région infectée et analyser les cultures fongiques des prélèvements, avant le traitement et à intervalles réguliers pendant toute sa durée.
- Avant le traitement et à intervalles réguliers pendant toute sa durée, rester à l'affût des signes et des symptômes d'infection: altération des signes vitaux, accroissement du nombre de globules blancs, aspect des muqueuses de la bouche, etc.

- Prélever des échantillons destinés à la mise en culture avant d'amorcer le traitement. On peut cependant démarrer le traitement sans attendre les résultats.
- Évaluer la vision (acuité visuelle, champ visuel, perception des couleurs) chez les patients qui reçoivent le traitement pendant plus de 28 jours. La vision revient habituellement à la normale dans les 14 jours suivant l'arrêt du traitement.
- Observer le patient à la recherche de symptômes reliés à la perfusion (bouffées vasomotrices, fièvre, forte diaphorèse, tachycardie, serrement de la poitrine, dyspnée, évanouissements, nausées, prurit, érythème). Les symptômes peuvent se manifester dans les quelques instants qui suivent le début de la perfusion. Il peut s'avérer nécessaire d'arrêter le traitement.

Tests de laboratoire:

- SUIVRE DE PRÈS LES RÉSULTATS DES TESTS DE LA FONCTION HÉPATIQUE AVANT LE DÉBUT DU TRAITEMENT ET PENDANT TOUTE SA DURÉE. EN CAS DE RÉSULTATS ANORMAUX, RESTER À L'AFFÛT DE LA FORMATION D'UNE LÉSION HÉPATIQUE GRAVE. ARRÊTER LE TRAITEMENT EN CAS D'APPARITION DE SIGNES ET DE SYMPTÔMES DE MALADIE HÉPATIQUE.
- Les troubles électrolytiques, comme l'hypokaliémie, l'hypomagnésémie et l'hypocalcémie, doivent être maîtrisés avant le début du traitement par le voriconazole (risque de torsades de pointes).
- La prise en charge des patients doit comprendre aussi une évaluation à intervalles réguliers de la fonction rénale (en particulier, la mesure de la créatininémie).

TOXICITÉ ET SURDOSAGE: Il n'existe aucun antidote connu du voriconazole; en cas de surdosage, il est recommandé de recourir à un traitement axé sur le soulagement des symptômes et le maintien des fonctions vitales. L'administration de charbon activé peut aider à éliminer le médicament non absorbé.

DIAGNOSTICS INFIRMIERS POSSIBLES

- Risque d'infection (Indications).
- Connaissances insuffisantes sur le traitement médicamenteux (Enseignement au patient et à ses proches).
- Non-observance du traitement médicamenteux (Enseignement au patient et à ses proches).

INTERVENTIONS INFIRMIÈRES

- Dès que le patient est en mesure de prendre un médicament par voie orale, il faudrait privilégier le traitement par les comprimés de voriconazole.

PO: Les comprimés devraient être pris au moins 1 heure avant ou 2 heures après un repas.

Perfusion intermittente:
Reconstituer le contenu d'une fiole de 200 mg avec 19 mL d'eau stérile pour injection. La concentration obtenue sera de 10 mg/mL. Bien mélanger la solution jusqu'à ce qu'elle devienne claire. Pour l'administration par perfusion, le volume nécessaire de solution reconstituée doit être ajouté à l'une des solutions compatibles recommandées (NaCl 0,9 %, solution de lactate de Ringer, D5%E/solution de lactate de Ringer, D5%E/NaCl 0,45 %, D5%E, NaCl 0,45 %, D5%E/NaCl 0,9 %) pour que la solution finale de voriconazole ait une concentration de 2 à 5 mg/mL, selon les besoins. La préparation diluée doit être utilisée dans les 24 heures suivant la reconstitution du contenu initial du flacon de poudre. Les préparations diluées doivent être conservées au réfrigérateur (entre 2 °C et 8 °C). Les flacons de poudre non reconstituée doivent être conservés à la température ambiante (entre 15 °C et 30 °C). Il est recommandé de jeter toute portion inutilisée. Consulter les directives de chaque fabricant avant de reconstituer la préparation.

Vitesse d'administration: Débit maximal de 3 mg/kg à l'heure, pendant 1 à 2 heures. Le voriconazole ne doit pas être donné en bolus rapide.

Incompatibilité: Ne pas perfuser en même temps que des produits sanguins. Le voriconazole ne doit pas être perfusé dans la même tubulure ou canule que d'autres médicaments, y compris les préparations pour nutrition parentérale. Le médicament ne doit pas être dilué avec une solution pour perfusion de bicarbonate de sodium à 4,2 %. La compatibilité avec des solutions de concentrations différentes est inconnue.

ENSEIGNEMENT AU PATIENT ET À SES PROCHES

- Expliquer au patient qu'il doit respecter rigoureusement la posologie recommandée et continuer à prendre le médicament même s'il se sent mieux. Lui conseiller de prendre le médicament au même moment, tous les jours. S'il n'a pas pu le prendre au moment habituel, il doit le prendre aussitôt que possible à moins que ce ne soit presque l'heure prévue pour la dose suivante, sans jamais remplacer une dose manquée par une double dose.
- Demander au patient de prévenir un professionnel de la santé s'il manifeste les signes et symptômes suivants de dysfonctionnement hépatique: fatigue inhabituelle, anorexie, nausées, vomissements, jaunisse, urine foncée ou selles de couleur pâle, ou encore s'il ne note aucune amélioration après quelques jours de traitement.
- Expliquer au patient que le voriconazole peut causer des troubles visuels dont une vue brouillée ou

une photophobie. La plupart des troubles visuels semblent se résorber spontanément en l'espace de 60 minutes. Les patients traités par le voriconazole doivent éviter les tâches qui peuvent s'avérer dangereuses, telles que la conduite d'une automobile ou l'utilisation de machines, s'ils perçoivent un changement de leur vision, quel qu'il soit. La conduite nocturne est déconseillée pendant le traitement.

- Expliquer au patient que le voriconazole peut entraîner des réactions de photosensibilité. Il vaut mieux éviter de s'exposer à la lumière vive du soleil.
- Déconseiller à la patiente de prendre le voriconazole si elle est enceinte, si elle pense l'être ou si elle souhaite le devenir. Une contraception adéquate est de rigueur pendant le traitement.
- Conseiller au patient de s'informer auprès d'un professionnel de la santé avant de consommer tout autre médicament vendu avec ou sans ordonnance, y compris des produits naturels, en raison des interactions médicamenteuses graves qui peuvent survenir.

VÉRIFICATION DE L'EFFICACITÉ THÉRAPEUTIQUE

L'efficacité du traitement peut être démontrée par: la résolution des signes cliniques et l'amélioration des résultats des tests indiquant une infection fongique. Le traitement peut parfois durer plusieurs semaines ou plusieurs mois après la résolution des symptômes. Un traitement d'une durée inadéquate peut provoquer l'apparition d'une infection récurrente.

V

ALERTE CLINIQUE

WARFARINE

Apo-Warfarin, Coumadin, Taro-Warfarin

CLASSIFICATION:

Anticoagulant

Grossesse – catégorie X

INDICATIONS

Prophylaxie et traitement des troubles suivants: thrombose veineuse ▪ embolie pulmonaire ▪ fibrillation auriculaire accompagnée d'embolisation ▪ Traitement complémentaire dans le cadre de la prophylaxie de l'embolie généralisée à la suite d'un infarctus du myocarde, des accidents vasculaires cérébraux, des récidives d'infarctus et du décès ▪ Prévention de la formation de thrombus et de l'embolisation après la mise en place d'une prothèse valvulaire.

MÉCANISME D'ACTION

Inhibition de la synthèse hépatique des facteurs de coagulation dépendant de la vitamine K (II, VII, IX et X). ***Effets thérapeutiques:*** Prévention des épisodes thromboemboliques.

PHARMACOCINÉTIQUE

Absorption: Bonne (PO).

Distribution: La warfarine traverse la barrière placentaire, mais ne passe pas dans le lait maternel.

Liaison aux protéines: 99 %.

Métabolisme et excrétion: Métabolisme hépatique.

Demi-vie: De 0,5 à 3 jours.

Profil temps-action
(effets sur les résultats des tests de coagulation)

	DÉBUT D'ACTION	PIC	DURÉE
PO, IV	36 – 72 h	5 – 7 jours	2 – 5 jours

CONTRE-INDICATIONS, PRÉCAUTIONS ET MISES EN GARDE

Contre-indications: Hypersensibilité ▪ Tendances hémorragiques ou dyscrasies ▪ Ulcère gastroduodénal évolutif ▪ Intervention chirurgicale récente ou prévisible ▪ Ponction lombaire et autres procédés thérapeutiques et diagnostiques présentant un risque d'hémorragie qui pourrait être impossible à maîtriser ▪ Anesthésie locale majeure ou lombaire ▪ Hypertension non maîtrisée ou due à une tumeur maligne ▪ Grossesse ▪ Risque d'avortement ▪ Éclampsie, prééclampsie ▪ Services de laboratoire inadéquats ▪ Patients non supervisés, atteints de sénilité, d'alcoolisme ou de psychose ou qui sont incapables de collaborer.

Précautions et mises en garde: Tumeur ▪ Antécédents d'ulcère gastroduodénal ▪ Insuffisance hépatique ▪ Insuffisance rénale ▪ Insuffisance cardiaque ▪ Carence héréditaire ou acquise en protéine C ou en protéine S ▪ Hypertension artérielle modérée à grave ▪ Sondes à demeure ▪ Maladies infectieuses ou déséquilibres de la flore intestinale, tels que la sprue ou ceux observés lors d'une antibiothérapie ▪ Traumatisme pouvant entraîner une hémorragie interne ▪ Maladies affectant le réseau des petits vaisseaux ou la microcirculation, telles que la polycythémie vraie, la vasculite et le diabète grave ▪ Thrombopénie induite par l'héparine ▪ Allaitement ▪ Antécédents de non-observance du traitement ▪ Changement dans le régime alimentaire ▪ Femmes en âge de procréer.

RÉACTIONS INDÉSIRABLES ET EFFETS SECONDAIRES

GI: crampes, nausées.

Tég.: nécrose dermique.

Hémat.: SAIGNEMENTS.

Divers: fièvre.

INTERACTIONS

Médicament-médicament: Les interactions avec la warfarine sont très nombreuses. En voici les principales: L'**abciximab**, l'**amiodarone**, les **hormones androgènes**, la **céfazoline**, la **ceftriaxone**, la **cholestyramine**, l'**hydrate de chloral**, le **clarithromycine**, le **clopidogrel**, le **diclofénac**, le **fluconazole**, les **fluoroquinolones**, l'**itraconazole**, le **métronidazole**, le **naproxène**, les **agents thrombolytiques**, l'**eptifibatide**, le **tirofiban**, la **ticlodipine**, les **sulfamides**, la **quinidine**, la **quinine**, les **AINS**, les **valproates**, le **triméthoprime/sulfaméthoxazole** et l'**aspirine** peuvent accroître la réponse à la warfarine et augmentent le risque d'hémorragie ▪ L'usage prolongé d'**acétaminophène** peut augmenter les risques de saignements ▪ La consommation prolongée d'**alcool** peut diminuer l'effet de la warfarine; si cette consommation prolongée provoque des lésions hépatiques importantes, l'effet de la warfarine peut être intensifié à la suite d'une diminution de la production de facteurs de coagulation ▪ La consommation rapide de grandes quantités d'**alcool** peut augmenter l'effet de la warfarine ▪ Les **barbituriques**, la **carbamazépine** et les **contraceptifs oraux contenant des œstrogènes** peuvent diminuer les effets anticoagulants de la warfarine.

Médicament-produits naturels: Les interactions entre la warfarine et les produits naturels sont très nombreuses. En voici les principales: Risque accru de saignements lors de la consommation concomitante de **dong quai**,

W

de **poivre de Cayenne**, de **grande camomille**, d'**ail**, de **ginkgo biloba** ou de **gingembre** ■ La prise simultanée de **ginseng** ou de **luzerne** peut réduire l'efficacité de la warfarine.

Médicament-aliments: La consommation de quantités importantes d'**aliments riches en vitamine K** peut contrecarrer l'effet anticoagulant de la warfarine.

VOIES D'ADMINISTRATION ET POSOLOGIE

- **PO, IV (adultes)**: Initialement, de 2 à 5 mg, 1 fois par jour; adapter la dose quotidienne en fonction du rapport normalisé international (RNI). Amorcer le traitement à une dose plus faible chez les personnes âgées ou débilitées (écart habituel de 2 à 10 mg/jour).

PRÉSENTATION (version générique disponible)

Comprimés: 1 mg[Pr], 2 mg[Pr], 2,5 mg[Pr], 3 mg[Pr], 4 mg[Pr], 5 mg[Pr], 6 mg[Pr], 7,5 mg[Pr], 10 mg[Pr] ■ **Solution pour injection**: 5,4 mg/fiole[Pr].

SOINS INFIRMIERS

ÉVALUATION DE LA SITUATION

- SUIVRE DE PRÈS LES SIGNES SUIVANTS D'HÉMORRAGIE OU DE SAIGNEMENT: SAIGNEMENT DES GENCIVES ET DU NEZ, FORMATION INHABITUELLE D'ECCHYMOSES, SELLES NOIRES GOUDRONNEUSES, HÉMATURIE, CHUTE DE L'HÉMATOCRITE OU DE LA PRESSION ARTÉRIELLE, PRÉSENCE DE SANG OCCULTE DANS LES SELLES, L'URINE OU LES ÉCHANTILLONS PRÉLEVÉS PAR ASPIRATION NASOGASTRIQUE.
- Observer le patient pour déceler les signes qui révèlent que la thrombose s'aggrave ou qu'elle s'étend. Les symptômes dépendent du territoire touché.

GÉR.: Chez les personnes > 60 ans, le RNI et le temps de prothrombine peuvent être plus élevés que les valeurs prévisibles. Suivre de près les effets secondaires à la suite de l'administration d'une posologie inférieure à celle qui s'inscrit dans l'intervalle thérapeutique.

PÉD.: L'atteinte et le maintien d'un RNI ou d'un temps de prothrombine qui s'inscrivent dans l'intervalle thérapeutique peuvent s'avérer plus difficiles chez l'enfant. Suivre plus fréquemment le RNI et le temps de prothrombine.

Tests de laboratoire:

- Noter le RNI à intervalles fréquents pendant toute la durée du traitement.
- Examiner avant le traitement et à intervalles réguliers pendant toute sa durée les résultats des tests de la fonction hépatique et la numération globulaire.
- Examiner les selles et l'urine avant le traitement et à intervalles réguliers pendant toute sa durée pour déceler la présence de sang occulte.

TOXICITÉ ET SURDOSAGE: Dans le cas d'un RNI excessivement allongé ou d'un saignement mineur, il est habituellement suffisant de sauter 1 ou plusieurs doses de médicament. En cas de surdosage ou d'une anticoagulation qui doit être immédiatement renversée, l'antidote est la vitamine K (phytonadione, AquaMEPHYTON). Il peut également s'avérer nécessaire d'administrer du plasma ou du sang entier en cas d'hémorragie grave, en raison du début d'action tardif de la vitamine K.

DIAGNOSTICS INFIRMIERS POSSIBLES

- Irrigation tissulaire inefficace (Indications).
- Risque d'accident (Effets secondaires).
- Connaissances insuffisantes sur le traitement médicamenteux (Enseignement au patient et à ses proches).

INTERVENTIONS INFIRMIÈRES

ALERTE CLINIQUE: DES ERREURS DE MÉDICATION IMPLIQUANT DES ANTICOAGULANTS ONT ENTRAÎNÉ DES PROBLÈMES GRAVES DE SANTÉ ET DES DÉCÈS. AVANT D'ADMINISTRER LA WARFARINE, ÉVALUER LES DERNIERS RNI ET TEMPS DE PROTHROMBINE ET DEMANDER À UN AUTRE PROFESSIONNEL DE LA SANTÉ DE VÉRIFIER UNE FOIS DE PLUS L'ORDONNANCE D'ORIGINE.

- En raison du grand nombre de médicaments qui peuvent modifier de façon marquée les effets de la warfarine, il faut suivre de près le patient lorsqu'on lui administre de nouveaux agents ou lorsqu'on cesse l'administration d'autres agents. Il faut évaluer le risque d'interactions avec tout nouveau médicament (médicaments sur ordonnance ou en vente libre, produits naturels).
- Administrer la warfarine à la même heure chaque jour.

PO:

- Il faut compter de 3 à 5 jours avant que des concentrations médicamenteuses efficaces puissent être atteintes. On commence habituellement le traitement pendant que le patient reçoit encore de l'héparine.
- Il ne faut pas substituer une marque à une autre, car la puissance peut ne pas être équivalente.

IV directe: Reconstituer la solution avec 2,7 mL d'eau stérile pour injection. Il ne faut pas utiliser les solutions qui ont changé de couleur ou qui renferment des particules. La solution est stable pendant 4 heures à la température ambiante.

Vitesse d'administration: Administrer sous forme de bolus lent, en 1 ou 2 minutes, dans une veine périphérique.

Compatibilité (tubulure en Y): céfazoline ■ ceftriaxone ■ dopamine ■ héparine ■ lidocaïne ■ morphine ■ nitroglycérine ■ potassium, chlorure de ■ ranitidine.

Incompatibilité (tubulure en Y): aminophylline ■ brétylium ■ ceftazidime ■ cimétidine ■ ciprofloxacine ■ dobutamine ■ esmolol ■ gentamicine ■ labétalol ■ métronidazole ■ vancomycine.

ENSEIGNEMENT AU PATIENT ET À SES PROCHES

- Conseiller au patient de respecter rigoureusement la posologie recommandée. S'il n'a pu prendre le médicament au moment habituel, il doit le prendre dès que possible le jour même. Lui expliquer qu'il ne faut jamais remplacer une dose manquée par une double dose. Lui conseiller de signaler au professionnel de la santé, au moment de l'examen de routine ou des tests de laboratoire, le nombre de doses qu'il n'a pas pu prendre.
- Revoir avec le patient les aliments riches en vitamine K. Lui recommander de consommer une quantité limitée de ces aliments, car la vitamine K est l'antidote de la warfarine. Des changements radicaux dans la consommation de ces aliments entraînent des fluctuations du RNI.
- Expliquer au patient qu'il doit éviter les injections par voie IM et les activités pendant lesquelles il peut se blesser. Lui recommander d'utiliser une brosse à dents à poils doux, de ne pas utiliser de soie dentaire et de se servir d'un rasoir électrique durant le traitement par la warfarine. Lui expliquer que pour prévenir l'hémorragie ou la formation d'hématomes, il doit appliquer une pression sur les points d'injection et de ponction veineuse.
- Conseiller au patient de signaler à un professionnel de la santé tout saignement ou ecchymose inhabituels: saignement des gencives ou du nez, selles noires goudronneuses, hématurie, écoulement menstruel excessif.
- RECOMMANDER AU PATIENT DE NE PAS PRENDRE PENDANT LE TRAITEMENT PAR LA WARFARINE DE MÉDICAMENTS EN VENTE LIBRE, PARTICULIÈREMENT CEUX QUI CONTIENNENT DE L'ASPIRINE ET DES AINS, NI DE COMMENCER À PRENDRE DE NOUVEAUX MÉDICAMENTS OU DE CESSER LA PRISE DE CEUX QUI LUI ONT ÉTÉ PRESCRITS ET DE NE PAS CONSOMMER D'ALCOOL, SANS CONSULTER AU PRÉALABLE UN PROFESSIONNEL DE LA SANTÉ.
- INSISTER SUR L'IMPORTANCE DES TESTS DE LABORATOIRE PERMETTANT DE MESURER LES FACTEURS DE COAGULATION.
- Conseiller au patient de toujours porter sur lui une pièce d'identité où est inscrit son traitement et d'informer tous les membres de l'équipe soignante qu'il prend un anticoagulant avant de se soumettre à des tests de laboratoire ou à un traitement ou avant de subir une intervention chirurgicale.

VÉRIFICATION DE L'EFFICACITÉ THÉRAPEUTIQUE

L'efficacité du traitement peut être démontrée par: l'élévation du RNI (de 2 à 3,5 fois plus élevé que les valeurs de référence), sans signes d'hémorragie. Les valeurs cibles du RNI peuvent varier selon l'indication. ✳

ZAFIRLUKAST

Accolate

CLASSIFICATION:

Bronchodilatateur (antagoniste des récepteurs des leucotriènes)

Grossesse – catégorie B

INDICATIONS

Traitement au long cours de l'asthme.

MÉCANISME D'ACTION

Inhibition des effets des leucotriènes, qui entrent dans la composition de la substance à réaction différée de l'anaphylaxie (SRD-A) ■ Médiation des réactions suivantes: œdème des voies aériennes ■ constriction des muscles lisses ■ modification de l'activité cellulaire ■ Diminution du processus inflammatoire faisant partie des manifestations de l'asthme. ***Effets thérapeutiques:*** Diminution de la fréquence et de la gravité des crises d'asthme.

PHARMACOCINÉTIQUE

Absorption: Rapide (PO).
Distribution: L'agent passe dans le lait maternel.
Liaison aux protéines: 99 %.
Métabolisme et excrétion: Métabolisme hépatique. Excrétion rénale (10 %) et fécale (90 %).
Demi-vie: 10 heures.

Profil temps-action
(diminution des symptômes d'asthme)

	DÉBUT D'ACTION	PIC	DURÉE
PO	30 min	3,5 h	12 h

CONTRE-INDICATIONS, PRÉCAUTIONS ET MISES EN GARDE

Contre-indications: Hypersensibilité ■ Insuffisance hépatique ■ **ALLAITEMENT:** Le médicament passe dans le lait maternel et ne doit pas être administré aux femmes qui allaitent.
Précautions et mises en garde: Crises aiguës d'asthme ■ Réduction de la dose des corticostéroïdes administrés par voie orale (risque accru de troubles éosinophiliques) ■ **GÉR.:** Les personnes âgées > 65 ans sont davantage prédisposées aux effets indésirables, incluant des infections des voies respiratoires supérieures ■ **OBST.:** L'innocuité du médicament n'a pas été établie chez la femme enceinte ■ **PÉD.:** L'efficacité et l'innocuité du médicament n'ont pas été établies chez les enfants < 12 ans.

RÉACTIONS INDÉSIRABLES ET EFFETS SECONDAIRES

SNC: céphalées, étourdissements, faiblesse.
GI: douleurs abdominales, diarrhée, hépatite médicamenteuse, dyspepsie, nausées, vomissements.
Loc.: arthralgie, douleurs lombaires, myalgie.
Divers: SYNDROME DE CHURG ET STRAUSS, fièvre, infection (personnes âgées > 65 ans), douleurs.

INTERACTIONS

Médicament-médicament: L'**aspirine** élève les concentrations sanguines ■ L'**érythromycine** et la **théophylline** abaissent les concentrations sanguines ■ Augmentation des effets et du risque de saignements associés à la **warfarine**.
Médicament-aliments: Les **aliments** réduisent l'absorption du zafirlukast.

VOIES D'ADMINISTRATION ET POSOLOGIE

- **PO (adultes et enfants ≥ 12 ans):** 20 mg, 2 fois par jour.

PRÉSENTATION

Comprimés: 20 mg[Pr].

SOINS INFIRMIERS

ÉVALUATION DE LA SITUATION

- Évaluer le murmure vésiculaire et la fonction respiratoire avant le traitement et à intervalles réguliers pendant toute sa durée.

Tests de laboratoire: Vérifier les résultats des tests de la fonction hépatique avant de commencer le traitement et à intervalles réguliers pendant toute sa durée. Le zafirlukast peut élever les concentrations d'ALT. Si une dysfonction hépatique survient, le traitement doit être interrompu.

DIAGNOSTICS INFIRMIERS POSSIBLES

- Dégagement inefficace des voies respiratoires (Indications).
- Connaissances insuffisantes sur le traitement médicamenteux (Enseignement au patient et à ses proches).

INTERVENTIONS INFIRMIÈRES

- Administrer le médicament à jeun, à intervalles réguliers, 1 heure avant ou 2 heures après les repas.

ENSEIGNEMENT AU PATIENT ET À SES PROCHES

- Recommander au patient de prendre ce médicament à jeun, à intervalles réguliers, même s'il ne présente pas de symptômes d'asthme. S'il n'a pu prendre le médicament au moment habituel, il doit le faire dès que possible sauf s'il est presque l'heure de prendre la dose suivante. L'avertir qu'il ne doit jamais remplacer une dose manquée par une double dose, ni cesser le traitement sans consulter un professionnel de la santé.

- Conseiller au patient de ne pas interrompre la prise des autres médicaments contre l'asthme ni d'en réduire la dose sans consulter un professionnel de la santé au préalable.
- Informer le patient que le zafirlukast n'est pas destiné au traitement des crises aiguës d'asthme, mais qu'on peut continuer de le prendre lors d'une exacerbation aiguë.
- RECOMMANDER AU PATIENT DE SIGNALER À UN PROFESSIONNEL DE LA SANTÉ LA MANIFESTATION DES SYMPTÔMES SUIVANTS DU SYNDROME DE CHURG ET STRAUSS : SYNDROME GÉNÉRALISÉ DE TYPE GRIPPAL, FIÈVRE, DOULEURS MUSCULAIRES, PERTE DE POIDS, AGGRAVATION DES SYMPTÔMES RESPIRATOIRES. CES SYMPTÔMES, BIEN QUE RARES, PEUVENT METTRE LA VIE DU PATIENT EN DANGER. ILS SONT PLUS SUSCEPTIBLES DE SURVENIR LORS DU SEVRAGE DES CORTICOSTÉROÏDES ADMINISTRÉS PAR VOIE ORALE.

VÉRIFICATION DE L'EFFICACITÉ THÉRAPEUTIQUE

L'efficacité du traitement peut être démontrée par: la prévention et la réduction des symptômes d'asthme.

ZANAMIVIR

Relenza

CLASSIFICATION:

Antiviral (inhibiteur sélectif de la neuraminidase)

Grossesse – catégorie C

INDICATIONS

Traitement de la grippe aiguë sans complications, due aux virus de la grippe de type A et de type B chez les adultes et les enfants > 7 ans qui présentent des symptômes depuis 2 jours au maximum ▪ Prévention de la grippe chez les adultes et les enfants > 7 ans, après un contact étroit avec une personne infectée (cas primaire) ▪ Le zanamivir ne s'est pas avéré efficace en prophylaxie de la grippe chez les personnes âgées hébergées dans des centres de soins ▪ Le zanamivir ne remplace pas la vaccination antigrippale, qui reste la méthode de prévention privilégiée contre la grippe.

MÉCANISME D'ACTION

Inhibition de l'enzyme neuraminidase, ce qui modifie l'agrégation et la libération des particules virales. ***Effets thérapeutiques:*** Soulagement des symptômes grippaux et diminution de leur durée (lorsque l'agent est utilisé en traitement) ou diminution de l'incidence de la grippe fébrile (lorsque l'agent est utilisé en prévention).

PHARMACOCINÉTIQUE

Absorption: De 4 à 17 % (par inhalation).
Distribution: Inconnue.
Liaison aux protéines: < 10 %.
Métabolisme et excrétion: Excrétion majoritairement rénale sous forme inchangée; la fraction non absorbée du médicament est excrétée dans les fèces.
Demi-vie: De 2,5 à 5,1 heures.

Profil temps-action (concentrations sanguines)

	DÉBUT D'ACTION	PIC	DURÉE
Inhalation	rapide	1 – 2 h	12 h

CONTRE-INDICATIONS, PRÉCAUTIONS ET MISES EN GARDE

Contre-indications: Hypersensibilité au zanamivir ou à l'un des ingrédients entrant dans la composition de la poudre pour inhalation (dont le lactose).
Précautions et mises en garde: Bronchopneumopathie chronique obstructive ou asthme grave ou décompensé (risque accru d'altération de la fonction pulmonaire et de bronchospasmes) ▪ Insuffisance rénale grave ▪ Grossesse, allaitement ou enfants < 7 ans (l'innocuité et l'efficacité de l'agent n'ont pas été établies).

RÉACTIONS INDÉSIRABLES ET EFFETS SECONDAIRES

Resp.: Bronchospasme.
Divers: ANAPHYLAXIE.

INTERACTIONS

Médicament-médicament: Aucune interaction n'a été signalée.

VOIES D'ADMINISTRATION ET POSOLOGIE

Traitement de la grippe

- **Inhalation (adultes et enfants ≥ 12 ans)**: 2 inhalations (à l'aide du DISKHALER), de 5 mg chacune, pour une dose totale de 10 mg, 2 fois par jour, pendant 5 jours. Le traitement doit commencer au plus tard 2 jours après le début des symptômes de la grippe.

Prévention de la grippe en milieu familial

Le traitement doit commencer au plus tard 1,5 jour après l'exposition au cas primaire (personne infectée) présentant déjà des symptômes, et se poursuivre pendant 10 jours.

- **Inhalation (adultes et enfants ≥ 12 ans)**: 2 inhalations (à l'aide du DISKHALER), de 5 mg chacune, pour une dose totale de 10 mg, 1 fois par jour.

Prévention de la grippe lors d'éclosions dans les collectivités

Le traitement doit commencer au plus tard 5 jours après la déclaration de l'éclosion et se poursuivre pendant 28 jours.

- **Inhalation (adultes et enfants ≥ 12 ans)**: 2 inhalations (à l'aide du DISKHALER), de 5 mg chacune, pour une dose totale de 10 mg, 1 fois par jour.

PRÉSENTATION

Poudre pour inhalation: 5 mg/coque[Pr].

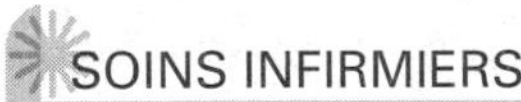

SOINS INFIRMIERS

ÉVALUATION DE LA SITUATION

- Évaluer le patient à la recherche de signes et symptômes de grippe (fièvre, céphalées, myalgie, toux, maux de gorge) avant l'administration. Déterminer la durée des symptômes. N'administrer ce médicament qu'aux patients qui présentent des symptômes depuis 2 jours ou moins.

DIAGNOSTICS INFIRMIERS POSSIBLES

- Risque d'infection (Indications).
- Connaissances insuffisantes sur le traitement médicamenteux (Enseignement au patient et à ses proches).

INTERVENTIONS INFIRMIÈRES

- **Inhalation**: Administrer, dans la mesure du possible, 2 doses le premier jour de traitement, pourvu qu'il y ait un intervalle de 2 heures entre les doses. Les jours suivants, administrer les doses à intervalles d'environ 12 heures.

ENSEIGNEMENT AU PATIENT ET À SES PROCHES

- Prévenir le patient qu'il doit respecter rigoureusement la posologie recommandée et qu'il doit prendre toute la quantité de médicament qui lui a été prescrite (pendant 5 jours), même s'il se sent mieux.
- Montrer au patient comment se servir du DISKHALER. Lui recommander de lire le mode d'emploi destiné aux patients.
- Avertir le patient que le zanamivir ne remplace pas la vaccination contre la grippe. Il devrait recevoir chaque année le vaccin contre la grippe suivant les recommandations gouvernementales.
- Recommander au patient ayant des antécédents d'asthme d'avoir sous la main un bronchodilatateur à action rapide pour parer à un bronchospasme induit par le zanamivir. Lors de l'administration concomitante du zanamivir et d'un bronchodilatateur, il faut administrer d'abord le bronchodilatateur.

VÉRIFICATION DE L'EFFICACITÉ THÉRAPEUTIQUE

L'efficacité du traitement peut être démontrée par: la diminution des signes et des symptômes de grippe (fièvre, céphalées, myalgie, toux, maux de gorge).

ZIDOVUDINE

Synonyme: AZT

Apo-Zidovudine, Retrovir

CLASSIFICATION:

Antirétroviral (inhibiteur nucléosidique de la transcriptase inverse)

Grossesse – catégorie C

INDICATIONS

Traitement des infections dues au VIH en association avec d'autres antirétroviraux ▪ Diminution du risque de transmission du VIH de la mère à l'enfant. **Usages non approuvés**: En association avec d'autres antirétroviraux, prophylaxie après exposition accidentelle au VIH.

MÉCANISME D'ACTION

Par suite de la transformation intracellulaire en une forme active, blocage de la synthèse virale par inhibition de l'ADN-polymérase (transcriptase inverse) ▪ Prévention de la réplication virale. ***Effets thérapeutiques:*** Action virostatique contre certains rétrovirus ▪ Ralentissement de l'évolution de l'infection par le VIH et diminution de ses complications ▪ Diminution de la charge virale et augmentation du nombre de cellules CD4 ▪ Diminution de la transmission du VIH aux nourrissons nés d'une mère infectée par le VIH.

PHARMACOCINÉTIQUE

Absorption: Bonne (PO).

Distribution: Tout l'organisme. La zidovudine pénètre dans le SNC et traverse la barrière placentaire.

Métabolisme et excrétion: Métabolisme hépatique à 75 %. Excrétion urinaire sous forme inchangée de 15 à 20 %.
Demi-vie: 1,1 heure.

Profil temps-action

	Début d'action	Pic	Durée
PO	inconnu	0,5 – 1,5 h	4 h
IV	rapide	fin de la perfusion	4 h

CONTRE-INDICATIONS, PRÉCAUTIONS ET MISES EN GARDE

Contre-indications: Hypersensibilité ■ Neutrophiles < 0,75 × 10^9/L ■ Hémoglobine < 75 g/L.
Précautions et mises en garde: Diminution de la réserve médullaire (administrer avec une extrême prudence en cas d'anémie [hémoglobine < 95 g/L] ou de granulopénie < 1 × 10^9/L) ■ Maladies hépatique ou rénale graves (une modification de la dose peut s'avérer nécessaire) ■ Obésité, femmes, prise prolongée d'un inhibiteur nucléosidique (il peut s'agir de facteurs de risque d'acidose lactique ou d'hépatomégalie) ■ **ALLAITEMENT**: Les mères séropositives ne devraient pas allaiter, car le VIH pénètre dans le lait maternel.

RÉACTIONS INDÉSIRABLES ET EFFETS SECONDAIRES

SNC: CONVULSIONS, céphalées, faiblesse, anxiété, confusion, diminution de l'acuité mentale, étourdissement, insomnie, dépression, agitation, évanouissement.
GI: douleurs abdominales, diarrhée, nausées, anorexie, hépatite médicamenteuse, HÉPATOMÉGALIE GRAVE AVEC STÉATOSE, dyspepsie, vomissements, pigmentation de la muqueuse orale, PANCRÉATITE.
HÉ: ACIDOSE LACTIQUE.
Tég.: pigmentation des ongles.
End.: gynécomastie.
Hémat.: anémie, granulopénie, thrombocytose, thrombopénie.
Loc.: douleurs lombaires, myopathie.
SN: tremblements.
Métab.: modification de la distribution des tissus adipeux.
Divers: syndrome de reconstitution immunitaire.

Z

INTERACTIONS

Médicament-médicament: Toxicité médullaire additive lors de l'administration d'autres **agents entraînant l'aplasie médullaire**, d'**antinéoplasiques**, de **ganciclovir**, d'**interféron alpha** ou d'une **radiothérapie** ■ Risque de neurotoxicité additive lors de l'administration concomitante d'**acyclovir** ■ Augmentation des concentrations de zidovudine et risque de toxicité accrue lors de l'administration concomitante d'**acide valproïque**, de **probénicide** ou de **fluconazole** ■ La **clarithromycine** abaisse les concentrations de zidovudine ■ L'administration concomitante de **stavudine** ou de **ribavirine** n'est pas recommandée en raison du risque d'effets antirétroviraux antagonistes.

VOIES D'ADMINISTRATION ET POSOLOGIE

Traitement de l'infection par le VIH

- **PO (adultes et enfants > 12 ans)**: 200 mg, toutes les 8 heures, ou 300 mg, toutes les 12 heures.
- **PO (enfants de 3 mois à 12 ans)**: 180 mg/m², toutes les 6 heures (ne pas dépasser 200 mg par dose).
- **IV (adultes et enfants > 12 ans)**: De 1 à 2 mg/kg, en perfusion pendant 1 heure, toutes les 4 heures (6 fois par jour). Passer à l'administration par voie orale dès que possible.
- **IV (enfants de 3 mois à 12 ans)**: 120 mg/m², en perfusion pendant 1 heure, toutes les 6 heures (ne pas dépasser 160 mg/dose).

Prévention de la transmission de l'infection par le VIH de la mère au fœtus

- **PO (mères – grossesse > 14 semaines)**: 100 mg, 5 fois par jour, jusqu'au déclenchement du travail.
- **IV (mères – pendant le travail et l'accouchement)**: 2 mg/kg, en 1 heure, puis 1 mg/kg/h en perfusion continue jusqu'à ce que le cordon ombilical soit clampé.
- **IV (nourrissons)**: 1,5 mg/kg, en perfusion pendant 30 minutes, toutes les 6 heures, jusqu'à ce que la prise de zidovudine par voie orale soit possible.
- **PO (nourrissons)**: 2 mg/kg, toutes les 6 heures, à amorcer dans les 12 heures suivant la naissance; maintenir ce traitement pendant 6 semaines.

PRÉSENTATION

Capsules: 100 mg^Pr ■ **Gélules**: 100 mg^Pr ■ **Sirop**: 50 mg/5 mL^Pr ■ **Solution pour injection**: 200 mg/20 mL^Pr ■ **En association avec**: lamivudine (Combivir), abacavir et lamivudine (Trizivir).

SOINS INFIRMIERS

ÉVALUATION DE LA SITUATION

- Observer le patient pendant toute la durée du traitement pour déceler l'aggravation des symptômes de l'infection par le VIH ou les symptômes d'infections opportunistes.
- L'AGENT PEUT PROVOQUER UNE ACIDOSE LACTIQUE ET UNE HÉPATOMÉGALIE GRAVE AVEC STÉATOSE. CES COMPLICATIONS SONT PLUS PROBABLES CHEZ LES

PATIENTS DE SEXE FÉMININ, CHEZ LES PERSONNES OBÈSES ET CHEZ CELLES QUI PRENNENT DES ANALOGUES NUCLÉOSIDIQUES PENDANT UN LAPS DE TEMPS PROLONGÉ. SUIVRE DE PRÈS LES SIGNES DE CES COMPLICATIONS (TAUX ACCRUS DE LACTATE SÉRIQUE, CONCENTRATIONS ÉLEVÉES D'ENZYMES HÉPATIQUES, HYPERTROPHIE DU FOIE DÉCELÉE À LA PALPATION). ARRÊTER LE TRAITEMENT DÈS L'APPARITION DE SIGNES CLINIQUES OU DÈS QUE LES RÉSULTATS DE TESTS DE LABORATOIRE ÉVOQUENT UN TEL PROBLÈME.

- OBSERVER LE PATIENT À LA RECHERCHE DES SYMPTÔMES SUIVANTS DE PANCRÉATITE : DOULEURS ABDOMINALES, NAUSÉES, VOMISSEMENTS, CONCENTRATIONS ACCRUES D'AMYLASE, DE LIPASE OU DE TRIGLYCÉRIDES. SI LES CONCENTRATIONS D'AMYLASE S'ÉLÈVENT DE 1,5 À 2 FOIS LA LIMITE SUPÉRIEURE DE LA NORMALE OU SI LE PATIENT MANIFESTE DES SYMPTÔMES DE PANCRÉATITE, LE TRAITEMENT PAR LA ZIDOVUDINE DEVRAIT ÊTRE INTERROMPU. LA PANCRÉATITE PEUT METTRE LA VIE DU PATIENT EN DANGER.
- Si une patiente enceinte est exposée à des antirétroviraux, l'inscrire dans le registre des femmes exposées aux antirétroviraux pendant leur grossesse, en composant le 1-800-258-4263.

***Tests de laboratoire*:**

- Suivre de près la charge virale et le nombre de cellules CD4 avant le traitement et à intervalles réguliers pendant toute sa durée.
- Chez les patients atteints d'une infection par le VIH à un stade avancé, suivre la numération globulaire toutes les 2 semaines, pendant les 8 premières semaines de traitement, et toutes les 4 semaines par la suite si la zidovudine est bien tolérée. Chez les patients asymptomatiques ou chez ceux présentant des symptômes précoces, suivre la numération globulaire 1 fois par mois, pendant les 3 premiers mois et tous les 3 mois par la suite ou plus fréquemment si cela est indiqué. La granulopénie et l'anémie surviennent couramment lors du traitement par la zidovudine. L'anémie peut survenir dans les 2 à 4 semaines qui suivent le début du traitement. La granulopénie survient habituellement dans les 6 à 8 semaines suivant le début du traitement. Il faut envisager la réduction de la dose, l'arrêt du traitement ou des transfusions sanguines, si l'hémoglobine est inférieure à 75 g/L ou si elle chute de plus de 25 % par rapport aux valeurs initiales, ou encore si le nombre de granulocytes est inférieur à $0,75 \times 10^9$/L ou s'il chute de plus de 50 % par rapport aux valeurs initiales. L'anémie peut répondre à l'administration d'une érythropoïétine recombinante et la granulopénie à l'administration de filgrastim. Le traitement peut être repris graduellement lorsqu'on a la certitude que les réserves médullaires sont rétablies.
- Noter à intervalles réguliers pendant toute la durée du traitement, les concentrations sériques d'amylase, de lipase et de triglycérides. Des concentrations élevées peuvent révéler la présence de pancréatite et dictent l'arrêt du traitement.
- SUIVRE DE PRÈS LA FONCTION HÉPATIQUE. LA ZIDOVUDINE PEUT ENTRAÎNER UNE ÉLÉVATION DES CONCENTRATIONS D'AST, D'ALT, DE BILIRUBINE ET DE PHOSPHATASE ALCALINE, MAIS ELLES REVIENNENT HABITUELLEMENT À LA NORMALE APRÈS INTERRUPTION DU TRAITEMENT. L'ACIDOSE LACTIQUE PEUT SURVENIR EN PRÉSENCE D'UNE TOXICITÉ HÉPATIQUE ENTRAÎNANT UNE STÉATOSE HÉPATIQUE, QUI PEUT ÊTRE D'ISSUE FATALE, PARTICULIÈREMENT CHEZ LES FEMMES.

DIAGNOSTICS INFIRMIERS POSSIBLES

- Risque d'infection (Indications, Effets secondaires).
- Connaissances insuffisantes sur le traitement médicamenteux (Enseignement au patient et à ses proches).

INTERVENTIONS INFIRMIÈRES

- NE PAS CONFONDRE RETROVIR (ZIDOVUDINE) AVEC RITONAVIR.
- Administrer le médicament à intervalles réguliers.

IV: Le patient devrait recevoir la perfusion IV seulement jusqu'à ce que le traitement PO puisse lui être administré.

Perfusion intermittente: Retirer la dose calculée de la fiole et la diluer dans une solution de D5%E ou de NaCl 0,9 % pour obtenir une concentration inférieure à 4 mg/mL. Ne pas utiliser une solution qui a changé de couleur. La solution diluée est stable pendant 8 heures à la température ambiante et pendant 24 heures au réfrigérateur.

***Vitesse d'administration*:** Administrer la solution par perfusion à un débit constant pendant 1 heure. Éviter la perfusion rapide ou l'injection de bolus.

Compatibilité (tubulure en Y): acyclovir ■ amifostine ■ amikacine ■ amphotéricine B céfépime ■ ceftazidime ■ ceftriaxone ■ cimétidine ■ clindamycine ■ dexaméthasone ■ dobutamine ■ dopamine ■ érythromycine, lactobionate d' ■ filgrastim ■ fluconazole ■ fludarabine ■ gentamicine ■ héparine ■ imipénem/cilastatine ■ lorazépam ■ melphalan ■ métoclopramide ■ morphine ■ ondansétron ■ oxacilline ■ paclitaxel ■ pentamidine ■ phényléphrine ■ pipéracilline ■ pipéracilline/tazobactam ■ potassium, chlorure de ■ ranitidine ■ thiotépa ■ tobramycine ■ triméthoprime/sulfaméthoxazole ■ vancomycine ■ vinorelbine.

Incompatibilité en addition au soluté: produits du sang et solutions protéiques.

ENSEIGNEMENT AU PATIENT ET À SES PROCHES

- Inciter le patient à respecter rigoureusement la posologie recommandée et à prendre la zidovudine à intervalles réguliers, même s'il doit interrompre son sommeil. Souligner le fait qu'il est important d'observer ce traitement, de ne pas prendre une quantité plus grande de médicament que celle qui a été prescrite et de ne pas abandonner le traitement sans consulter un professionnel de la santé au préalable. Prévenir le patient que s'il n'a pu prendre le médicament au moment habituel, il doit le prendre dès que possible à moins que ce ne soit presque l'heure prévue pour la dose suivante. Lui conseiller de ne jamais remplacer une dose manquée par une double dose. L'informer que les effets à long terme de la zidovudine demeurent inconnus.
- Expliquer au patient qu'il ne doit pas donner ce médicament à d'autres personnes.
- Prévenir le patient que la zidovudine peut provoquer des étourdissements ou des évanouissements. Lui conseiller de ne pas conduire et d'éviter les activités qui exigent sa vigilance jusqu'à ce qu'on ait la certitude que le médicament n'entraîne pas ces effets chez lui.
- Expliquer au patient que la zidovudine ne guérit pas l'infection par le VIH et qu'elle ne réduit pas le risque de transmission du VIH à d'autres personnes par les rapports sexuels ou par la contamination du sang. Inciter le patient à utiliser un condom durant les rapports sexuels, à éviter le partage d'aiguilles et les dons de sang afin de prévenir la propagation du VIH.
- Recommander au patient de signaler rapidement à un professionnel de la santé la fièvre, les maux de gorge ou les signes d'infections. Lui conseiller d'éviter les foules et les personnes contagieuses, de se servir d'une brosse à dents à poils doux et d'utiliser avec prudence les cure-dents ou la soie dentaire. L'inciter à se soumettre à tout traitement dentaire avant de commencer le traitement par la zidovudine ou de le retarder jusqu'à ce que la numération globulaire revienne à la normale. Inciter le patient à communiquer avec un professionnel de la santé en cas d'essoufflements, de douleurs musculaires, de symptômes de pancréatite ou de toute autre manifestation inattendue.
- RECOMMANDER AU PATIENT DE PRÉVENIR UN PROFESSIONNEL DE LA SANTÉ IMMÉDIATEMENT SI DES SIGNES D'ACIDOSE LACTIQUE (FATIGUE OU FAIBLESSE, DOULEURS MUSCULAIRES INHABITUELLES, DIFFICULTÉS RESPIRATOIRES, DOULEURS D'ESTOMAC AVEC DES NAUSÉES ET DES VOMISSEMENTS, SENSATION DE FROID, SURTOUT AU NIVEAU DES EXTRÉMITÉS, ÉTOURDISSEMENTS OU BATTEMENTS CARDIAQUES RAPIDES ET IRRÉGULIERS) OU D'HÉPATOTOXICITÉ (JAUNISSEMENT DE LA PEAU OU DU BLANC DES YEUX, URINE DE COULEUR FONCÉE, SELLES DE COULEUR PÂLE, PERTE D'APPÉTIT PENDANT PLUSIEURS JOURS DE SUITE, NAUSÉES OU DOULEURS ABDOMINALES) SE MANIFESTENT. Ces symptômes peuvent se présenter plus fréquemment chez les sujets de sexe féminin, les personnes obèses ou celles qui prennent des médicaments comme la zidovudine pendant un laps de temps prolongé.
- Recommander au patient d'éviter de prendre des médicaments en vente libre ou sur ordonnance ou des produits naturels sans consulter au préalable un professionnel de la santé.
- Insister sur le fait qu'il est important de se soumettre à intervalles réguliers à des examens de suivi et à des analyses de sang permettant de déceler les effets secondaires et les bienfaits du traitement.

VÉRIFICATION DE L'EFFICACITÉ THÉRAPEUTIQUE

L'efficacité du traitement peut être démontrée par: la diminution de la charge virale et l'augmentation du nombre de cellules CD4 chez les patients infectés par le VIH ■ le ralentissement de l'évolution de l'infection par le VIH et la diminution du nombre d'infections opportunistes chez les patients infectés par le VIH. ✳

ZINC, SULFATE DE

Egozinc, Micro Zn

CLASSIFICATION:

Minéral et électrolyte (oligoélément)

Grossesse – catégorie C (voie parentérale)

INDICATIONS

Traitement de substitution et supplément diététique chez les patients prédisposés à une carence en zinc, incluant les patients recevant une nutrition parentérale à long terme. **Usages non approuvés:** Traitement du retard de la cicatrisation des plaies dû à la carence en zinc.

MÉCANISME D'ACTION

Cofacteur dans de nombreuses réactions enzymatiques ■ Élément essentiel à la croissance normale et à la réparation des tissus, à la cicatrisation des plaies et au maintien du goût et du sens de l'odorat. ***Effets thérapeutiques:*** Traitement de substitution en cas de carence.

PHARMACOCINÉTIQUE

Absorption: De 20 à 30 % (PO).
Distribution: Le sulfate de zinc se répartit dans tout l'organisme. On le retrouve à fortes concentrations dans les muscles, les os, la peau, le pancréas, la rétine, les cheveux, les ongles et les spermatozoïdes.
Métabolisme et excrétion: Excrétion dans les fèces (90 %), l'urine et la sueur.
Demi-vie: Inconnue.
Profil temps-action (concentrations sanguines)

	Début d'action	Pic	Durée
PO	inconnu	2 h	inconnue
IV	inconnu	inconnu	inconnue

CONTRE-INDICATIONS, PRÉCAUTIONS ET MISES EN GARDE

Contre-indications: Hypersensibilité ou allergie à l'un des ingrédients de la préparation ■ **Péd.**: Ne pas administrer les préparations contenant de l'alcool benzylique chez les nouveau-nés.
Précautions et mises en garde: Insuffisance rénale ■ **Obst., allaitement**: L'apport quotidien recommandé est plus élevé chez les femmes enceintes ou qui allaitent (voir l'annexe K).

RÉACTIONS INDÉSIRABLES ET EFFETS SECONDAIRES

GI: irritation gastrique (PO seulement), nausées, vomissements.

INTERACTIONS

Médicament-médicament: Le zinc administré par voie orale peut diminuer l'absorption des **tétracyclines** ou des **fluoroquinolones**.
Médicament-aliments: La **caféine**, les **produits laitiers** et le **son** peuvent diminuer l'absorption du zinc administré par voie orale.

VOIES D'ADMINISTRATION ET POSOLOGIE

AQR (adultes) = 15 mg. Sauf indication contraire, les doses sont exprimées en mg de zinc élémentaire. Le sulfate de zinc contient 23 % de zinc.

Carence

- **PO (adultes)**: *Prévention de la carence* – de 15 à 19 mg par jour; *traitement de la carence* – dose adaptée à la gravité de la carence.

Supplément nutritionnel par voie IV – patients ayant un métabolisme stable

- **IV (adultes)**: De 2,5 à 4 mg par jour; une dose plus élevée peut être nécessaire chez les patients accusant des pertes excessives.
- **IV (nourrissons et enfants ≤ 5 ans)**: 100 µg/kg/jour.
- **IV (nourrissons prématurés pesant jusqu'à 3 kg)**: 300 µg/kg/jour.

PRÉSENTATION (version générique disponible)

Comprimés: 220 mg[VL] ■ **Solution pour injection**: 1 mg/mL, en fioles de 10 mL[Pr], 5 mg/mL, en fioles de 10 mL[Pr].

SOINS INFIRMIERS

ÉVALUATION DE LA SITUATION

- Observer pendant toute la durée du traitement l'évolution des symptômes de carence en zinc: retard de la cicatrisation des plaies, retard de la croissance, perte du goût, perte du sens de l'odorat.

Tests de laboratoire:

- Les concentrations sériques de zinc peuvent ne pas refléter avec précision une carence.
- Le traitement prolongé par des doses élevées de zinc peut entraîner une baisse des concentrations sériques de cuivre.
- Surveiller mensuellement les concentrations sériques de phosphatase alcaline, lesquelles peuvent s'élever lorsqu'il y a un apport en zinc.
- Mesurer les concentrations de cholestérol HDL, 1 fois par mois chez les patients recevant des doses élevées de zinc pendant une période prolongée, en raison du risque de diminution de ces taux.

DIAGNOSTICS INFIRMIERS POSSIBLES

- Alimentation déficiente (Indications).
- Connaissances insuffisantes sur le traitement médicamenteux (Enseignement au patient et à ses proches).

Z

INTERVENTIONS INFIRMIÈRES

PO: Administrer les doses PO avec des aliments afin de réduire l'irritation gastrique. La caféine, les produits laitiers ou le son peuvent entraver l'absorption du zinc.
IV: Le zinc est souvent inclus sous forme d'oligoélément dans les préparations destinées à la nutrition parentérale faites par le pharmacien.

ENSEIGNEMENT AU PATIENT ET À SES PROCHES

- Inciter le patient à respecter rigoureusement les recommandations diététiques du professionnel de la santé. Lui expliquer que la meilleure source d'oligoéléments est une alimentation bien équilibrée comprenant des aliments des quatre principaux groupes alimentaires. Les aliments riches en zinc sont les fruits de mer, les abats et le germe de blé.
- Prévenir le patient qui s'autoadministre des suppléments vitaminiques qu'il ne doit pas dépasser l'apport quotidien recommandé (voir l'annexe K). L'efficacité des mégadoses dans le traitement de divers troubles médicaux reste à prouver; par contre, elles peuvent entraîner des effets secondaires.
- Recommander au patient recevant le zinc par voie orale de signaler au professionnel de la santé les nausées et les vomissements graves, les douleurs abdominales ou les selles goudronneuses.
- Insister sur l'importance des examens de suivi permettant d'évaluer les bienfaits du traitement.

VÉRIFICATION DE L'EFFICACITÉ THÉRAPEUTIQUE

L'efficacité du traitement peut être démontrée par: Une cicatrisation plus rapide des plaies ■ l'amélioration du goût et du sens de l'odorat. De 6 à 8 semaines de traitement peuvent s'avérer nécessaires avant que les pleins effets du médicament puissent être observés. ✳

ZOLMITRIPTAN,

voir Agonistes de la sérotonine 5-HT_1

ZOPICLONE

Apo-Zopiclone, Gen-Zopiclone, Imovane, Novo-Zopiclone, PMS-Zopiclone, Ratio-Zopiclone, Rhovane

CLASSIFICATION:

Hypnosédatif

Grossesse – catégorie C

INDICATIONS

Traitement des symptômes de l'insomnie transitoire et de courte durée, caractérisée par des difficultés d'endormissement, des réveils nocturnes fréquents ou un réveil précoce.

MÉCANISME D'ACTION

Dérivé de la cyclopyrrolone appartenant à une nouvelle famille chimique non reliée par sa structure aux autres hypnotiques existants. Toutefois, le profil pharmacologique de la zopiclone est semblable à celui des benzodiazépines. ***Effets thérapeutiques:*** Réduction du délai d'endormissement, diminution du nombre de réveils nocturnes et augmentation de la durée du sommeil.

PHARMACOCINÉTIQUE

Absorption: > 75 % (PO).

Distribution: Rapide. L'agent passe dans le lait maternel.

Métabolisme et excrétion: Métabolisme hépatique important (CYP3A4 et CYP2C8). Excrétion rénale (75 %), principalement sous forme de métabolites, et fécale (16 %).

Demi-vie: De 3,8 à 6,5 heures (environ 5 heures).

Profil temps-action (effet hypnotique)

	DÉBUT D'ACTION	PIC	DURÉE†
PO	15 – 30 min	60 – 90 min	24 h (dose unique)

† Concentrations sanguines.

CONTRE-INDICATIONS, PRÉCAUTIONS ET MISES EN GARDE

Contre-indications: Hypersensibilité ■ Perturbation importante de la fonction respiratoire (p. ex., syndrome d'apnée du sommeil).

Précautions et mises en garde: Insuffisance hépatique ■ Insuffisance rénale ■ Insuffisance pulmonaire grave ■ Myasthénie ■ Antécédents de réactions paradoxales consécutives à l'ingestion d'alcool ou de sédatifs ■ Antécédents d'alcoolisme, de toxicomanie ou de troubles marqués de la personnalité ■ Patients dépressifs ■ **OBST.:** L'innocuité du médicament n'a pas été établie chez la femme enceinte ■ **ALLAITEMENT:** L'agent passe dans le lait maternel à des concentrations pouvant atteindre 50 % des taux plasmatiques ■ **PÉD.:** L'innocuité et l'efficacité du médicament n'ont pas été établies chez les enfants < 18 ans ■ **GÉR.:** Il est recommandé d'utiliser la dose minimale efficace afin d'éviter une sédation excessive chez les personnes âgées ou débilitées.

RÉACTIONS INDÉSIRABLES ET EFFETS SECONDAIRES

SNC: agitation, amnésie antérograde ou troubles de la mémoire, anomalies de la coordination, anxiété ou nervosité, asthénie, cauchemars, céphalées, confusion, dépression, diminution de la libido, étourdissements, euphorie, hostilité, hypotonie, paresthésie, sensation ébrieuse, somnolence, spasmes musculaires, tremblements, trouble de l'élocution.

Z

ORLO: amblyopie.
Resp.: dyspnée.
CV: palpitations.
GI: anorexie ou gain d'appétit, constipation, diarrhée, dyspepsie, langue saburrale, mauvaise haleine, nausées, sécheresse de la bouche (xérostomie), vomissements.
End.: frissons.
Loc.: lourdeur des membres.
Locaux: éruptions cutanées, taches sur la peau, transpiration.
Divers: élévation des taux d'AST, d'ALT ou de phosphatase alcaline (rare), goût amer, perte pondérale.

INTERACTIONS

Médicament-médicament: Potentialisation de la dépression du SNC lors de l'usage concomitant d'autres **dépresseurs du SNC**, y compris l'**alcool**, les **antihistaminiques à action sédative**, certains **antiépileptiques**, les **opioïdes**, les **analgésiques**, les **anesthésiques** et les **psychotropes** ▪ Les **composés qui inhibent la production de certaines enzymes hépatiques (en particulier le CYP3A4 du cytochrome P450)** peuvent accroître l'activité de la zopiclone (p. ex., **clarithromycine**, **kétoconazole**, **itraconazole**, **ritonavir**, **cimétidine** et **érythromycine**).

VOIES D'ADMINISTRATION ET POSOLOGIE

- **PO (adultes)**: De 5 à 7,5 mg, 1 fois par jour, avant le coucher. Le traitement ne devrait pas durer plus de 7 à 10 jours consécutifs. L'emploi de ce médicament pendant plus de 2 ou 3 semaines de suite exige une réévaluation complète du cas.
- **PO (personnes âgées ou débilitées)**: Initialement, 3,75 mg, 1 fois par jour, avant le coucher. On peut augmenter la dose jusqu'à concurrence de 5 mg ou de 7,5 mg, 1 fois par jour, avant le coucher, selon la réponse au traitement et la tolérance du patient.

INSUFFISANCE HÉPATIQUE OU RESPIRATOIRE CHRONIQUE

- **PO (ADULTES)**: INITIALEMENT, 3,75 mg, 1 FOIS PAR JOUR, AU COUCHER. ON PEUT AUGMENTER LA DOSE JUSQU'À CONCURRENCE DE 5 mg OU DE 7,5 mg, 1 FOIS PAR JOUR, AU COUCHER, SELON LA RÉPONSE AU TRAITEMENT ET LA TOLÉRANCE DU PATIENT.

INSUFFISANCE RÉNALE

- **PO (ADULTES)**: INITIALEMENT, 3,75 mg, 1 FOIS PAR JOUR, AU COUCHER. ON PEUT AUGMENTER LA DOSE JUSQU'À CONCURRENCE DE 5 mg OU DE 7,5 mg, 1 FOIS PAR JOUR, AU COUCHER, SELON LA RÉPONSE AU TRAITEMENT ET LA TOLÉRANCE DU PATIENT.

PRÉSENTATION

Comprimés: 5 mg[Pr], 7,5 mg[Pr].

SOINS INFIRMIERS

ÉVALUATION DE LA SITUATION

- Noter les habitudes de sommeil du patient avant le traitement et à intervalles réguliers pendant toute sa durée.
- Le traitement prolongé peut entraîner une dépendance psychologique ou physique. Réduire la quantité du médicament dont le patient peut disposer, particulièrement si ce dernier est dépressif ou suicidaire ou s'il a des antécédents de toxicomanie.

Tests de laboratoire: Vérifier les résultats des tests de la fonction hépatique, car on a signalé quelques rares cas isolés d'élévation des taux d'AST, d'ALT ou de phosphatase alcaline.

DIAGNOSTICS INFIRMIERS POSSIBLES

- Habitudes de sommeil perturbées (Indications).
- Risque d'accident (Effets secondaires).
- Connaissances insuffisantes sur le traitement médicamenteux (Enseignement au patient et à ses proches).

INTERVENTIONS INFIRMIÈRES

- Administrer immédiatement avant le coucher.
- Surveiller le patient lors de ses déplacements ou de son transport après l'administration du médicament. Retirer les cigarettes. Remonter les ridelles du lit et laisser la sonnette d'alarme à portée de sa main en tout temps.

ENSEIGNEMENT AU PATIENT ET À SES PROCHES

- Conseiller au patient de respecter rigoureusement la posologie recommandée. Le prévenir qu'il ne doit pas augmenter la dose si elle devient moins efficace après quelques semaines, sans consulter au préalable un professionnel de la santé.
- Expliquer au patient qu'il est important de préparer un cadre propice au sommeil: la pièce doit être sombre et calme; la nicotine et le café sont à proscrire.
- Prévenir le patient que le médicament peut affecter la vigilance et la mémoire. Lui conseiller de ne pas conduire et d'éviter les activités qui exigent sa vigilance jusqu'à ce qu'on ait la certitude que le médicament n'entraîne pas ces effets chez lui.
- Prévenir le patient qu'il ne doit pas consommer d'alcool ni prendre de dépresseurs du SNC en même temps que la zopiclone.
- Prévenir le patient qu'il est possible qu'à l'arrêt du traitement il éprouve des difficultés à s'endormir (insomnie rebond) ou qu'il ressente une plus grande

anxiété durant la journée (anxiété rebond) pendant 1 ou 2 jours.

- Recommander au patient de ne pas cesser brusquement de prendre la zopiclone, car des symptômes de sevrage semblables à ceux qui sont attribués à l'usage de barbituriques et d'alcool ont été observés (convulsions, tremblements, crampes abdominales et musculaires, vomissements, transpiration, dysphorie, troubles de la perception et insomnie). Par conséquent, chez tout patient ayant pris ce genre de médicament pendant plusieurs semaines, il ne faut pas interrompre le traitement abruptement, mais plutôt réduire les doses graduellement. Chez le patient ayant des antécédents de convulsions, la réduction graduelle des doses est particulièrement importante.
- Conseiller à la patiente d'informer immédiatement un professionnel de la santé si elle pense être enceinte ou si elle souhaite le devenir.

VÉRIFICATION DE L'EFFICACITÉ THÉRAPEUTIQUE

L'efficacité du traitement peut être démontrée par: l'amélioration du sommeil. ✳

PRODUITS NATURELS

MISE EN GARDE

Dans les monographies qui suivent nous présentons certains produits naturels d'usage courant. Puisque la teneur en ingrédients actifs de ces agents n'est pas normalisée et que, dans ses lignes directrices actuelles, Santé Canada ne fait aucune recommandation à cet égard, les auteurs du *Guide des médicaments*, bien que respectueux du droit du patient de choisir parmi une variété d'options thérapeutiques, n'avalisent pas leur usage systématique, à moins qu'il ne soit surveillé par un professionnel de la santé bien informé. Les consommateurs doivent tenir compte du risque de réactions indésirables et d'interactions et prendre en considération le fait qu'on ne dispose que de peu de données qui appuient l'usage de ces produits. Les doses ne sont pas normalisées, raison pour laquelle nous conseillons au consommateur de lire attentivement l'étiquette de l'emballage afin de s'assurer que son utilisation du produit comporte le moins de dangers possible.

ACIDE OMÉGA 3

AUTRES APPELLATIONS:
Acide gras oméga-3, oméga-3, ω-3, huiles de poisson

CLASSIFICATION:
Hypolipidémiant

USAGES COURANTS

Traitement de problèmes divers dont les suivants: hypertriglycéridémie ■ hypercholestérolémie ■ hypertension ■ coronaropathie ■ maladies inflammatoires de l'intestin ■ dépression ■ fatigue chronique ■ lupus érythémateux ■ polyarthrite rhumatoïde ■ asthme.

MÉCANISME D'ACTION

Source d'acides gras essentiels au bon fonctionnement cellulaire ■ Inhibition de la synthèse des triglycérides et du cholestérol ■ Inhibition de la synthèse des prostaglandines et des leucotriènes. ***Effets thérapeutiques:*** Abaissement du taux de triglycérides ■ Effets anti-inflammatoires.

PHARMACOCINÉTIQUE

Absorption: Bonne.
Distribution: Inconnue.
Métabolisme et excrétion: Avec les phospholipides.
Demi-vie: Inconnue.

Profil temps-action (abaissement des taux de triglycérides)

	DÉBUT D'ACTION	PIC	DURÉE
PO	inconnu	2 mois	inconnue

CONTRE-INDICATIONS, PRÉCAUTIONS ET MISES EN GARDE

Contre-indications: Hypersensibilité.
Précautions et mises en garde: Allergie/hypersensibilité au poisson ■ Diabète (l'agent peut entraver l'équilibrage glycémique) ■ **OBST.:** N'utiliser que si les bienfaits chez la mère justifient le risque auquel est exposé le fœtus pendant la gestation ■ **ALLAITEMENT:** L'usage doit s'accompagner de prudence ■ **PÉD.:** L'innocuité chez les enfants < 18 ans n'a pas été établie.

RÉACTIONS INDÉSIRABLES ET EFFETS SECONDAIRES

GI: altération du goût, éructations, halitose.
ORLO: épistaxis.
Tég.: rash.

INTERACTIONS

Produit naturel-médicaments: Risque de potentialisation des effets des **anticoagulants** et des **antiplaquettaires**, avec risque accru de saignements ■ Risque de potentialisation des effets des **antihypertenseurs**, avec risque accru d'hypotension.
Produit naturel-produits naturels: Les plantes médicinales ayant des propriétés anticoagulantes ou antiplaquettaires utilisées en concomitance peuvent accroître le risque de saignements; il s'agit notamment des plantes suivantes: **angélique**, **anis**, **trèfle d'eau**, **boldo**, **piment**, **céleri**, **camomille**, **clou de girofle**, **danshen**, **dong quai**, **fenugrec**, **grande camomille**, **gingembre**, **ginkgo**, **ginseng**, **marronnier d'Inde**, **raifort**, **réglisse**, **reine des près**, **poivre du Sichuan**, **oignon**, **papaïne**, **passiflore**, **peuplier blanc**, **quassia**, **trèfle rouge**, **curcuma**, **frêne épineux**, **laitue sauvage**, **saule** et **autres**.

VOIES D'ADMINISTRATION ET POSOLOGIES COURANTES

- **PO (adultes)**: *Hypertriglycéridémie* – 4 g/jour; on peut administrer la pleine dose en une seule fois, ou à raison de 2 g par dose, 2 fois par jour. *Autres indications* – de 1 à 4 g/jour.

PRÉSENTATION

Capsules de gélatine (remplies d'huile)[VL].

SOINS INFIRMIERS

ÉVALUATION DE LA SITUATION

- Recueillir les antécédents concernant l'alimentation, particulièrement en ce qui a trait à la consommation de graisses.

DIAGNOSTICS INFIRMIERS POSSIBLES

- Non-observance du traitement médicamenteux (Enseignement au patient et à ses proches).

INTERVENTIONS INFIRMIÈRES

- Le patient doit suivre avant le traitement et pendant toute sa durée une diétothérapie hypolipémiante.

ENSEIGNEMENT AU PATIENT ET À SES PROCHES

- Inciter le patient à suivre rigoureusement les recommandations du médecin, à ne pas sauter de doses et à ne pas remplacer une dose manquée par une double dose. Lui expliquer que cet agent permet de régulariser les taux élevés de triglycérides sériques mais qu'il ne peut les normaliser.
- Recommander au patient de prendre cet agent en association avec une diétothérapie (restriction de la consommation de graisses, de cholestérol, de lipides et d'alcool), un programme d'exercice, la perte de poids (en cas d'obésité) et la prise en charge des maladies (comme le diabète ou l'hypothyroïdie) qui contribuent au maintien de l'hypertriglycéridémie.
- Insister sur l'importance des examens de suivi qui permettent de déterminer l'efficacité du traitement.

VÉRIFICATION DE L'EFFICACITÉ THÉRAPEUTIQUE

L'efficacité du traitement peut être démontrée par: l'abaissement des taux de triglycérides sériques. Les patients qui ne répondent pas adéquatement à cet agent après 2 mois de traitement devront l'abandonner.

ACTÉE À GRAPPES NOIRES

AUTRES APPELLATIONS:

Cimicaire, chasse-punaises, cierge à grappes

CLASSIFICATION:

Phytoestrogène

Ne pas confondre l'actée à grappes noires avec l'actée à grappes blanches ou à grappes bleues.

USAGES COURANTS

Prise en charge des symptômes de la ménopause ■ Gêne prémenstruelle ■ Dysménorrhée ■ Sédation légère.

MÉCANISME D'ACTION

Les effets thérapeutiques sont dus aux glycosides extraits du rhizome frais ou séché et des racines attachées ■ Le mécanisme d'action n'a pas été élucidé. ***Effets thérapeutiques:*** Possibilité de diminution des symptômes de la ménopause, notamment des bouffées de chaleur, des sueurs, des troubles du sommeil et de l'anxiété ■ Sans effet sur l'épithélium vaginal.

PHARMACOCINÉTIQUE

Absorption: Inconnue.

Distribution: Inconnue.

Métabolisme et excrétion: Inconnus.

Demi-vie: Inconnue.

Profil temps-action

	DÉBUT D'ACTION	PIC	DURÉE
PO	inconnu	inconnu	inconnue

CONTRE-INDICATIONS, PRÉCAUTIONS ET MISES EN GARDE

Contre-indications: Grossesse et allaitement.

Précautions et mises en garde: Les effets de cette plante prise en association avec une hormonothérapie substitutive n'ont pas été étudiés ■ Les effets en présence d'un cancer de l'endomètre ou de l'ovaire n'ont pas été étudiés ■ L'usage peut s'avérer dangereux chez les femmes ayant des antécédents de cancer du sein, puisqu'il pourrait accroître le risque de formation de métastases ■ Usage au-delà de 6 mois ■ L'usage des préparations contenant de l'alcool doit s'accompagner de prudence chez les patientes dont l'intolérance est connue ou qui souffrent d'une maladie hépatique.

RÉACTIONS INDÉSIRABLES ET EFFETS SECONDAIRES

SN: CONVULSIONS (en association avec l'onagre et le poivre sauvage), céphalées, étourdissements.

GI: gêne gastrique.

Tég.: rash.

Divers: gain pondéral, crampes.

INTERACTIONS

Produit naturel-médicaments: Effets inconnus en association avec une **hormonothérapie substitutive** et des **anti-œstrogènes** (p. ex., le **tamoxifène**) ■ L'usage concomitant de **médicaments hépatotoxiques** peut accroître le risque de lésions hépatiques ■ L'**alcool** contenu dans certaines préparations peut interagir avec le **disulfirame** et le **métronidazole** ■ Risque de diminution des effets cytotoxiques du **cisplatine** ■ Risque d'hypotension lors de l'usage en association avec des **antihypertenseurs**.

VOIES D'ADMINISTRATION ET POSOLOGIES COURANTES

- **PO (adultes):** *Comprimés* – 20 mg, 2 fois par jour. *Extrait liquide* – de 0,3 à 2 mL, 2 ou 3 fois par jour. *Teinture* – de 2 à 4 mL, 2 ou 3 fois par jour. *Rhizome séché* – de 0,3 à 2 g, 3 fois par jour. Ne pas utiliser au-delà de 6 mois.

PRÉSENTATION

En monothérapie ou en association avec d'autres produits à base de plantes médicinalesVL**:** ComprimésVL ■ Extrait liquideVL ■ TeintureVL ■ Rhizome séché.

SOINS INFIRMIERS

ÉVALUATION DE LA SITUATION

- Déterminer la fréquence et la gravité des symptômes de la ménopause.
- Mesurer la pression artérielle des patientes sous traitement antihypertenseur, car l'actée à grappes noires peut intensifier les effets du médicament et provoquer l'hypotension.
- Rester à l'affût des nausées et des vomissements.
- Se renseigner sur la consommation d'alcool et sur les antécédents de convulsions et de maladie hépatique.
- S'assurer que la patiente dont les règles sont irrégulières n'est pas enceinte, avant de lui recommander ce produit, car des doses importantes d'actée à grappes noires peuvent provoquer une fausse couche.

DIAGNOSTICS INFIRMIERS POSSIBLES

- Privation de sommeil (Indications).

INTERVENTIONS INFIRMIÈRES

- L'administration avec des aliments peut aider à réduire les nausées.

ENSEIGNEMENT AU PATIENT ET À SES PROCHES

- Expliquer à la patiente qu'elle ne doit pas prendre ce produit naturel si elle est enceinte, car il peut provoquer une fausse couche.
- Recommander à la patiente d'arrêter de prendre ce produit si elle pense être enceinte et d'en prévenir un professionnel de la santé.
- Prévenir la patiente que l'actée à grappes noires peut potentialiser les effets des antihypertenseurs et, par conséquent, provoquer l'hypotension. Recommander à la patiente qui prend des antihypertenseurs de ne pas prendre ce produit naturel sans consulter au préalable un professionnel de la santé.
- Conseiller à la patiente qui consomme des quantités excessives d'alcool ou qui souffre de convulsions, de dysfonctionnement hépatique, de cancer ou d'autres troubles de santé de consulter un professionnel de la santé avant de commencer à prendre ce produit naturel.
- Si les nausées commencent à poser problème, recommander à la patiente de ne pas prendre l'actée à grappes noires à jeun.
- Recommander à la patiente de ne pas prendre cet agent si elle suit une œstrogénothérapie substitutive, sans avoir consulté un professionnel de la santé au préalable.
- Insister sur l'importance d'une surveillance médicale continue, notamment test de Papanicolaou, mammographie, examen pelvien et mesure de la pression artérielle aux intervalles recommandés par le professionnel de la santé.

VÉRIFICATION DE L'EFFICACITÉ THÉRAPEUTIQUE

L'efficacité du traitement peut être démontrée par: la résolution des symptômes vasomoteurs de la ménopause.

AIL

AUTRE APPELLATION:
Allium sativum

CLASSIFICATION:
Hypolipidémiant

USAGES COURANTS

PO: Hypertension, hyperlipidémie, prévention des maladies cardiovasculaires, prévention du cancer colorectal et gastrique ■ **Préparation topique**: infections fongiques de la peau.

MÉCANISME D'ACTION

Inhibition possible de l'HMG-CoA réductase pouvant abaisser les taux de cholestérol, mais moins efficacement que les statines ■ Propriétés vasodilatatrices et antiplaquettaires.

PHARMACOCINÉTIQUE

Absorption: L'huile d'ail est bien absorbée.
Distribution: Inconnue.
Métabolisme et excrétion: Reins et poumons.
Demi-vie: Inconnue.

Profil temps-action

	Début d'action	Pic	Durée
PO	4 – 25 semaines	inconnu	inconnue

CONTRE-INDICATIONS, PRÉCAUTIONS ET MISES EN GARDE

Contre-indications: Troubles de saignement.
Précautions et mises en garde: Diabète, inflammation ou infections gastro-intestinales ■ Arrêter la consommation 1 ou 2 semaines avant une intervention chirurgicale.

RÉACTIONS INDÉSIRABLES ET EFFETS SECONDAIRES

SNC: étourdissements.
GI: irritation de la bouche, de l'œsophage et de l'estomac, nausées, mauvaise haleine, vomissements.
Tég.: dermatite de contact et autres réactions allergiques (asthme, rash, anaphylaxie [rare]), diaphorèse.
Hémat.: l'usage prolongé ou en quantités excessives peut entraîner la diminution de la production d'hémoglobine et la lyse des érythrocytes, un dysfonctionnement plaquettaire ou la prolongation du temps de saignement.
Divers: odeur corporelle.

INTERACTIONS

Produit naturel-médicaments: L'utilisation de l'ail avec des **anticoagulants**, des **antiplaquettaires** et des **thrombolytiques** peut accroître le risque de saignements ■ Risque de diminution de l'effet des **contraceptifs** et de la **cyclosporine** ■ Risque de diminution des concentrations plasmatiques de **saquinavir**, de **névirapine**, de **délavirdine** et d'**éfavirenz**.

Produit naturel-produits naturels: Les **plantes médicinales ayant des propriétés anticoagulantes ou antiplaquettaires** consommées en concomitance peuvent accroître le risque de saignements; il s'agit notamment des plantes suivantes: **angélique**, **anis**, **ase fétide**, **trèfle d'eau**, **boldo**, **piment**, **céleri**, **camomille**, **clou de girofle**, **danshen**, **dong quai**, **fenugrec**, **grande camomille**, **gingembre**, **ginkgo**, **ginseng**, **marronnier d'Inde**, **raifort**, **réglisse**, **reine des prés**, **poivre du Sichuan**, **oignon**, **papaïne**, **passiflore**, **peuplier blanc**, **quassia**, **trèfle rouge**, **curcuma**, **frêne épineux**, **laitue sauvage**, **saule** et **autres**.

VOIES D'ADMINISTRATION ET POSOLOGIES COURANTES

- **PO (adultes)**: De 200 à 400 mg, 3 fois par jour d'extrait standardisé de poudre d'ail avec 1,3 % d'alline. *Ail frais* – de 1 à 7 gousses par jour.

PRÉSENTATION

Capsules[VL] ■ **Comprimés**[VL] ■ **Ail frais**[VL].

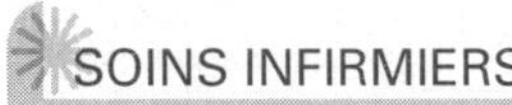

SOINS INFIRMIERS

ÉVALUATION DE LA SITUATION

- Déterminer l'apport alimentaire habituel, surtout pour ce qui est de la consommation de graisses.
- Déterminer la raison pour laquelle le patient consomme ce produit naturel et ses connaissances en ce qui concerne l'hyperlipidémie.
- Déterminer la quantité d'ail que le patient consomme régulièrement.

DIAGNOSTICS INFIRMIERS POSSIBLES

- Connaissances insuffisantes sur le traitement médicamenteux (Enseignement au patient et à ses proches).
- Non-observance (Enseignement au patient et à ses proches).

INTERVENTIONS INFIRMIÈRES

- Administrer par voie orale sous forme d'ail frais, de capsules ou de comprimés.
- Ne pas dépasser la posologie recommandée.

ENSEIGNEMENT AU PATIENT ET À SES PROCHES

- Expliquer au patient qu'il est important de suivre un régime alimentaire sain (pauvre en graisses et riche en légumes et en fruits) en même temps qu'il consomme de l'ail dans un but thérapeutique. Lui recommander d'autres stratégies de réduction des

taux de lipides, comme l'exercice et l'abandon de la cigarette.
- Informer le patient sur les agents hypolipidémiants plus efficaces.
- Insister sur l'importance des examens de suivi par un professionnel de la santé qui pourra déterminer l'efficacité du traitement.
- Mettre en garde le patient contre le risque de saignements. Lui recommander de ne pas prendre ce produit naturel s'il prend d'autres médicaments, sans consulter au préalable un professionnel de la santé. Inciter le patient qui doit subir une chirurgie non urgente d'arrêter de consommer de l'ail pendant les 2 semaines qui précèdent l'intervention et de prévenir le chirurgien qu'il prend de l'ail s'il doit subir une intervention chirurgicale d'urgence.
- Prévenir le patient qu'il y a risque d'allergie. Lui recommander d'arrêter de prendre de l'ail si des symptômes se manifestent.

VÉRIFICATION DE L'EFFICACITÉ THÉRAPEUTIQUE

L'efficacité du traitement peut être démontrée par: la normalisation des taux de lipides ■ la prévention de la maladie cardiaque.

ARNICA

AUTRES APPELLATIONS:
Herbe au loup, herbe vulnéraire, herbe à éternuer, tabac des Vosges, tabac des Savoyards, etc.

CLASSIFICATION:
Anti-infectieux

USAGES COURANTS

Traitement topique des piqûres d'insectes, des ecchymoses, de l'acné, des furoncles, des entorses et des douleurs musculaires et articulaires.

MÉCANISME D'ACTION

Les polysaccharides contenus dans l'arnica peuvent exercer un léger effet anti-inflammatoire et analgésique. On note certains effets antibactériens en plus d'un effet révulsif, qui pourrait accélérer la cicatrisation des plaies.

PHARMACOCINÉTIQUE

Absorption: Risque d'absorption par voie générale après application sur une peau éraflée.
Distribution: Inconnue.
Métabolisme et excrétion: Inconnus.
Demi-vie: Inconnue.
Profil temps-action

	DÉBUT D'ACTION	PIC	DURÉE
Préparation topique	inconnu	inconnu	inconnue

CONTRE-INDICATIONS, PRÉCAUTIONS ET MISES EN GARDE

Contre-indications: Usage par voie orale (sauf dans le cas des préparations homéopathiques très diluées) ■ Application sur une plaie ouverte ■ Allergie à l'arnica ■ Application sur une peau fissurée ■ Maladies gastro-intestinales infectieuses ou inflammatoires.

RÉACTIONS INDÉSIRABLES ET EFFETS SECONDAIRES

Tég.: dermatite œdémateuse avec pustules (traitement chronique des lésions de la peau), eczéma (usage prolongé).
Divers: réactions allergiques locales.

INTERACTIONS

Produit naturel-médicaments: L'**alcool** contenu dans certaines préparations peut interagir avec le **disulfirame** et le **métronidazole** ■ Risque de perte de l'efficacité des **antihypertenseurs** ■ Risque de potentialisation des effets des **anticoagulants** et des **antiplaquettaires**, avec risque accru de saignements.

VOIES D'ADMINISTRATION ET POSOLOGIES COURANTES

Usage topique (adultes): *Préparation topique* – frotter ou masser avec la teinture, la crème ou le gel d'arnica la région atteinte, seulement si la peau n'est pas éraflée. *Compresse* – diluer une cuillérée de teinture d'arnica dans 0,5 L d'eau. Imbiber une compresse de gaze avec la solution et appliquer sur la région atteinte pendant 15 minutes. Pour utiliser sous forme de cataplasme, diluer la teinture dans 3 à 10 fois son volume d'eau.

PRÉSENTATION

Crème[VL] ■ **Teinture**[VL] ■ **Pommade**[VL] ■ **Onguent**[VL] ■ **Gel**[VL] ■ **Huile**[VL] ■ **Préparation topique** (les préparations ne doivent pas contenir plus de 20 à 25 % de teinture d'arnica ou 15 % d'huile d'arnica)[VL] ■ **Préparations homéopathiques**[VL].

SOINS INFIRMIERS

ÉVALUATION DE LA SITUATION

- Inspecter la peau avant l'utilisation de la préparation pour s'assurer qu'on n'applique l'arnica que sur une surface intacte. Noter la taille, les caractéristiques et l'emplacement de la région atteinte avant d'appliquer l'arnica.

- Après application, observer la région atteinte pour déceler les signes d'une réaction allergique.

Toxicité et surdosage: L'absorption par voie générale peut entraîner des nausées, des vomissements, des lésions organiques, de l'hypertension, une toxicité cardiaque, des arythmies, de la faiblesse musculaire, un collapsus, des vertiges, le dysfonctionnement rénal, le coma et la mort. En cas d'ingestion, provoquer des vomissements et faire un lavage gastrique pour éliminer la fraction non digérée. Un traitement de soutien peut s'avérer nécessaire. Ne pas administrer par voie orale ni appliquer sur une peau éraflée pour prévenir l'absorption par voie générale.

DIAGNOSTICS INFIRMIERS POSSIBLES

- Douleur aiguë (Indications).

INTERVENTIONS INFIRMIÈRES

- Avant d'appliquer l'arnica, nettoyer la peau avec une préparation ne contenant pas d'alcool. Appliquer sur la région atteinte ou sur le siège de la lésion, en s'assurant que la peau est intacte.
- NE PAS ADMINISTRER PAR VOIE ORALE NI APPLIQUER SUR UNE PLAIE OUVERTE, EN RAISON DU RISQUE D'ABSORPTION PAR VOIE GÉNÉRALE ET D'INTOXICATION.
- Éviter l'usage prolongé en raison du risque de réactions allergiques ou d'hypersensibilité.

ENSEIGNEMENT AU PATIENT ET À SES PROCHES

- Recommander au patient d'inspecter la région atteinte pour y déceler les fissures ou les éraflures cutanées et de n'appliquer l'arnica que sur une peau intacte.
- Prévenir le patient que l'application sur une peau qui n'est pas intacte ou la prise par voie orale peuvent provoquer une intoxication mortelle.
- INFORMER LE PATIENT QUE BIEN QUE CERTAINS ORGANISMES RÉGLEMENTAIRES COMME LA COMMISSION E D'ALLEMAGNE AIENT TROUVÉ QUE CE SUPPLÉMENT NATUREL EST UN ANTI-INFLAMMATOIRE, UN ANALGÉSIQUE ET UN ANTIBACTÉRIEN EFFICACE, D'AUTRES, COMME LA FDA DES ÉTATS-UNIS, ONT CLASSÉ L'ARNICA PARMI LES PLANTES MÉDICINALES **DANGEREUSES**.
- Conseiller au patient de n'utiliser l'arnica que pendant une courte période de temps, pour traiter des douleurs ou des gênes mineures, associées à une atteinte musculaire, articulaire ou cutanée locale. L'usage prolongé peut provoquer des réactions allergiques ou d'hypersensibilité.
- Recommander au patient qui prend des antihypertenseurs d'éviter l'usage concomitant d'arnica.

VÉRIFICATION DE L'EFFICACITÉ THÉRAPEUTIQUE

L'efficacité du traitement peut être démontrée par: le soulagement ou la diminution de la gêne ou des douleurs mineures associées à une surutilisation des muscles ou des articulations ou à une foulure ■ le soulagement de l'irritation locale de la peau, due aux piqûres d'insectes, aux ecchymoses, aux furoncles ou à l'acné. ✳

AUBÉPINE DORÉE
(espèces *Cratægus*)

AUTRES APPELLATIONS:

Aubépine officinale, *Cratægus lævigate*

CLASSIFICATION:

Antihypertenseur, inotrope

USAGES COURANTS

Hypertension ■ Insuffisance cardiaque de légère à modérée ■ Angine ■ Spasmolytique ■ Sédatif.

MÉCANISME D'ACTION

Les principaux ingrédients actifs de l'aubépine sont les flavonoïdes et les procyanidines ■ Augmentation du débit coronarien ■ Effets chronotropes et inotropes positifs en raison d'une perméabilité accrue au calcium et l'inhibition de la phosphodiestérase. ***Effets thérapeutiques:*** Débit cardiaque accru ■ Abaissement de la pression artérielle, du travail du myocarde et de la consommation d'oxygène.

PHARMACOCINÉTIQUE

Absorption: Inconnue.
Distribution: Inconnue.
Métabolisme et excrétion: Inconnus.
Demi-vie: Inconnue.

Profil temps-action

	DÉBUT D'ACTION	PIC	DURÉE
PO	inconnu	6 – 8 semaines	inconnue

CONTRE-INDICATIONS, PRÉCAUTIONS ET MISES EN GARDE

Contre-indications: Grossesse (risque d'effets sur le tonus utérin) ■ Allaitement.

Précautions et mises en garde: Usage concomitant d'inhibiteurs de l'ECA et de digoxine ■ Ne pas arrêter le traitement abruptement.

RÉACTIONS INDÉSIRABLES ET EFFETS SECONDAIRES

SNC: agitation, étourdissements, fatigue, vertiges, céphalées, sédation (doses élevées), insomnie, transpiration.
CV: hypotension (doses élevées), palpitations.
GI: nausées.

INTERACTIONS

Produit naturel-médicaments: Risque de potentialisation des effets de la **digoxine**, des **bloqueurs des canaux calciques** et des **bêtabloquants** ■ Risque de potentialisation des effets cardiovasculaires indésirables lors de l'usage concomitant de **théophylline**, de **caféine**, d'**adrénaline**, d'**inhibiteurs de la 5-phosphodiestérase** (**sildénafil**, **tadalafil**, **vardénafil**) et de **dérivés nitrés** ■ Risque de dépression additive du SNC lors d'usage concomitant d'autres **dépresseurs du SNC**.
Produit naturel-produits naturels: Lors de l'usage concomitant d'autres **plantes médicinales contenant des glycosides cardiotoniques** (**feuilles de digitaline**, **hellébore noire**, **feuilles de laurier** et **autres**), les effets peuvent être additifs ■ Effets hypotenseurs additifs lors de l'usage concomitant de **plantes médicinales qui abaissent la pression artérielle**, comme le **gingembre**, le **ginseng** et la **valériane** ■ Effets additifs lors de l'usage concomitant d'autres **plantes qui stimulent le cœur** (**griffe du diable**, **fenugrec** et **autres**).

VOIES D'ADMINISTRATION ET POSOLOGIES COURANTES

- **PO (adultes):** *Insuffisance cardiaque* – de 160 à 1 800 mg par jour d'extrait standardisé de feuilles et de fleurs d'aubépine en 2 ou 3 doses fractionnées. *Extrait liquide d'aubépine (1:1 dans 25 % d'alcool)* – de 0,5 à 1 mL, 3 fois par jour. *Teinture de fruits d'aubépine (1:5 dans 45 % d'alcool)* – 1 ou 2 mL, 3 fois par jour. *Baies séchées d'aubépine* – de 300 à 1 000 mg, 3 fois par jour.

PRÉSENTATION

Fruits séchés[VL] ■ **Extrait liquide de fruits ou de feuilles**[VL] ■ **Teinture de fruits ou de feuilles**[VL].

SOINS INFIRMIERS

ÉVALUATION DE LA SITUATION

- Ausculter les bruits pulmonaires pour déceler des signes d'insuffisance cardiaque (râles, crépitations, sifflements).
- Peser le patient tous les jours et rester à l'affût des signes de surcharge volémique (œdème des chevilles, essoufflement, besoin de dormir sur plusieurs oreillers).
- Mesurer la pression artérielle à intervalles réguliers tout au long du traitement.
- Prendre la fréquence du pouls et en évaluer la régularité.

DIAGNOSTICS INFIRMIERS POSSIBLES

- Débit cardiaque diminué (Indications).
- Connaissances insuffisantes sur le traitement médicamenteux (Enseignement au patient et à ses proches).

INTERVENTIONS INFIRMIÈRES

- Administrer en 2 ou 3 doses fractionnées, aux mêmes moments de la journée.
- On peut prendre l'agent sans égard aux repas.

ENSEIGNEMENT AU PATIENT ET À SES PROCHES

- Prévenir le patient qu'il existe d'autres traitements de l'insuffisance cardiaque qui ont fait leurs preuves et qu'il faudrait les mettre à l'essai avant de prendre de l'aubépine.
- Conseiller au patient de ne pas prendre de l'aubépine sans la recommandation d'un professionnel de la santé.
- Expliquer au patient les symptômes d'infarctus du myocarde (douleurs rétrosternales, ainsi que douleurs aux mâchoires, dans le bras et dans la partie supérieure de l'abdomen; transpiration; sensation de serrement dans la poitrine) et de l'insuffisance cardiaque (essoufflement, enflure des chevilles, gain de poids [surcharge liquidienne], étourdissements, fatigue, diminution de l'appétit). Lui recommander d'en informer rapidement un professionnel de la santé, le cas échéant.
- Conseiller au patient de signaler à un professionnel de la santé le gain pondéral ou l'enflure persistante des chevilles.
- Recommander au patient qui pratique l'automédication de consulter un professionnel de la santé en l'absence d'améliorations en l'espace de 6 à 8 semaines. Les effets de l'aubépine pourraient ne pas être notables avant 3 mois.
- Conseiller au patient de changer de position lentement pour réduire le risque d'hypotension orthostatique.
- Inciter le patient à ne pas combiner l'aubépine à des antihypertenseurs ou à des médicaments destinés au traitement des maladies cardiaques s'il n'est pas suivi par un professionnel de la santé, en raison du risque d'effets additifs.

- Prévenir le patient que cette plante peut provoquer de la somnolence. Lui conseiller de ne pas conduire et de ne pas s'engager dans d'autres activités qui exigent sa vigilance jusqu'à ce qu'on ait la certitude que l'aubépine n'entraîne pas cet effet chez lui.
- Recommander au patient de ne pas prendre d'alcool ou d'autres dépresseurs du SNC s'il n'est pas suivi par un professionnel de la santé.
- Prévenir le patient qu'une forte transpiration et la déshydratation en cas de chaleur extrême peuvent accroître les effets hypotenseurs de l'aubépine, provoquant une hypotension grave. Lui recommander d'éviter l'effort par temps chaud pour réduire le risque d'effets secondaires.
- Prévenir le patient que l'aubépine aide à maîtriser les symptômes de l'insuffisance cardiaque, mais ne guérit pas la maladie. Lui recommander de maintenir les changements apportés à son mode de vie (diminuer la consommation de liquides et de sel, maîtriser son poids, faire de l'exercice selon sa tolérance, rester fidèle à son traitement médicamenteux).
- EXPLIQUER AU PATIENT QUE BIEN QU'ON AIT ÉVALUÉ EN EUROPE LES BIENFAITS DE L'AUBÉPINE DANS LA PRISE EN CHARGE DE L'INSUFFISANCE CARDIAQUE, AUCUNE ÉTUDE N'A CONSTATÉ DES EFFETS DÉTERMINANTS PERMETTANT D'EN RECOMMANDER L'UTILISATION.
- Recommander au patient de consulter un professionnel de la santé avant de prendre d'autres médicaments d'ordonnance ou en vente libre en même temps que l'aubépine.

VÉRIFICATION DE L'EFFICACITÉ THÉRAPEUTIQUE

L'efficacité du traitement peut être démontrée par: la diminution des symptômes d'insuffisance cardiaque ▪ l'amélioration du débit cardiaque, prouvée par l'augmentation de la tolérance à l'effort. ✳

CHARDON-MARIE

AUTRES APPELLATIONS:

Sylibum marial, chardon de Notre-Dame, lait de Notre-Dame, artichaut sauvage

CLASSIFICATION:

Antidote

USAGES COURANTS

Cirrhose ▪ Hépatite chronique ▪ Calculs biliaires ▪ Psoriasis ▪ Nettoyage et détoxication du foie ▪ Traitement de l'intoxication du foie due à l'alcool ▪ Empoisonnement par le champignon amanite (préparation IV, commercialisée en Europe seulement) et par des produits chimiques.

MÉCANISME D'ACTION

L'ingrédient actif, la silymarine, a des effets antioxydants et hépatoprotecteurs. La silymarine aide à prévenir la pénétration des toxines et stimule la régénération des hépatocytes.

PHARMACOCINÉTIQUE

Absorption: De 23 à 47 % (PO).

Distribution: Inconnue.

Métabolisme et excrétion: Métabolisme hépatique par le cytochrome P450 3A4.

Demi-vie: 6 heures.

Profil temps-action

	DÉBUT D'ACTION	PIC	DURÉE
PO	5 – 30 jours ou plus	inconnu	inconnue

CONTRE-INDICATIONS, PRÉCAUTIONS ET MISES EN GARDE

Contre-indications: Grossesse et allaitement (données insuffisantes) ▪ Allergie à la camomille, à l'herbe à poux, aux asters, aux chrysanthèmes et aux autres membres de la famille des composées.

Précautions et mises en garde: Cancers ou maladies hormonosensibles (certaines parties de la plantes peuvent avoir des effets œstrogéniques).

RÉACTIONS INDÉSIRABLES ET EFFETS SECONDAIRES

GI: effets laxatifs, nausées, ballonnements, anorexie.

Divers: réactions allergiques.

INTERACTIONS

Produit naturel-médicaments: *In vitro*, l'extrait de chardon-Marie a inhibé le cytochrome P450 3A4, une voie métabolique importante pour plusieurs médicaments. Bien qu'on n'ait pas signalé d'interactions chez l'humain, il faudrait faire preuve de prudence si on consomme le chardon-Marie en même temps que des **médicaments métabolisés par la voie du 3A4**, comme la **cyclosporine**, la **carbamazépine**, les **inhibiteurs de l'HMG-CoA réductase**, le **kétoconazole**, l'**alprazolam** et de nombreux **autres**.

VOIES D'ADMINISTRATION ET POSOLOGIES COURANTES

- **PO (adultes)**: *Cirrhose du foie* – 420 mg/jour d'extrait contenant de 70 à 80 % de silymarine. *Hépatite chronique évolutive* - 240 mg de silibinine, 2 fois par jour. *Infusion* – 3 ou 4 fois par jour, 30 minutes avant les repas. On déconseille cependant les infusions, puisque la silymarine n'est pas suffisamment soluble dans l'eau.

PRÉSENTATION

Capsules[VL] ■ **Comprimés**[VL] ■ **Plante brute**[VL] ■ **Infusion**[VL] ■ **Extrait**[VL].

SOINS INFIRMIERS

ÉVALUATION DE LA SITUATION

- Suivre de près les signes d'insuffisance hépatique, comme la jaunisse, les changements de l'état mental, la distension abdominale (ascite) et l'œdème généralisé.
- Suivre de près les résultats des tests de la fonction hépatique à intervalles réguliers pendant toute la durée du traitement.
- Évaluer la consistance et la fréquence des selles.

DIAGNOSTICS INFIRMIERS POSSIBLES

- Connaissances insuffisantes sur le traitement médicamenteux (Enseignement au patient et à ses proches).

INTERVENTIONS INFIRMIÈRES

- Administrer par voie orale, sous forme d'extrait, de capsules ou de comprimés, ou sous forme de fruit séché, en une seule dose quotidienne ou en 3 doses fractionnées.
- La consommation du chardon-Marie sous forme d'infusion n'est pas recommandée, puisque ses composantes actives ne sont pas solubles dans l'eau.

ENSEIGNEMENT AU PATIENT ET À SES PROCHES

- Expliquer au patient les symptômes de l'insuffisance hépatique et lui recommander de signaler rapidement à un professionnel de la santé toute aggravation de la symptomatologie.
- Insister sur la nécessité des analyses sanguines permettant de suivre la fonction hépatique.
- Recommander au patient de ne pas boire d'alcool et de suivre un régime alimentaire adapté à la maladie du foie ou de la vésicule biliaire qui fait l'objet du traitement.

VÉRIFICATION DE L'EFFICACITÉ THÉRAPEUTIQUE

L'efficacité du traitement peut être démontrée par: la normalisation des résultats des tests de la fonction hépatique ■ la diminution de la jaunisse, de la distension abdominale, de la fatigue et d'autres symptômes associés à la maladie hépatique.

CHONDROÏTINE

AUTRES APPELLATIONS:

Polysulfate de chondroïtine, CDS

CLASSIFICATION:

Analgésique non opioïde

USAGES COURANTS

Arthrose ■ Cardiopathie ischémique ■ Hyperlipidémie ■ Ostéoporose.

MÉCANISME D'ACTION

Effets possibles découlant du mécanisme d'action: élément constitutif du cartilage articulaire ■ protection du cartilage contre la destruction ■ effets anti-athérogènes. ***Effets thérapeutiques:*** Amélioration des symptômes d'arthrose.

PHARMACOCINÉTIQUE

Absorption: Inconnue.
Distribution: Inconnue.
Métabolisme et excrétion: Inconnus.
Demi-vie: Inconnue.

Profil temps-action

	DÉBUT D'ACTION	PIC	DURÉE
PO	inconnu	inconnu	inconnue

CONTRE-INDICATIONS, PRÉCAUTIONS ET MISES EN GARDE

Contre-indications: Grossesse et allaitement.
Précautions et mises en garde: Asthme (risque d'exacerbation des symptômes) ■ Troubles de la coagulation (risque accru de saignements) ■ Cancer de la prostate (risque accru de formation de métastases ou de récurrence).

RÉACTIONS INDÉSIRABLES ET EFFETS SECONDAIRES

GI: brûlures d'estomac, nausées, diarrhée.

Hémat.: saignements (effet antiplaquettaire).
Divers: réactions allergiques, œdème, chute des cheveux.

INTERACTIONS

Produit naturel-médicaments: L'utilisation de la chondroïtine avec des **anticoagulants** et des **antiplaquettaires**, des **thrombolytiques**, des **AINS** ou des **valproates** peut accroître le risque de saignements.
Produit naturel-produits naturels: Les produits naturels suivants ayant des propriétés anticoagulantes ou antiplaquettaires peuvent accroître le risque de saignements lors de l'usage concomitant de chondroïtine: **anis**, **arnica**, **camomille**, **clou de girofle**, **dong quai**, **fenugrec**, **grande camomille**, **gingembre**, **ginkgo**, **ginseng**, **réglisse** et **autres**.

VOIES D'ADMINISTRATION ET POSOLOGIES COURANTES

- **PO (adultes)**: *Arthrose* – de 200 à 400 mg, 2 ou 3 fois par jour, ou de 1 000 à 1 200 mg, 1 fois par jour.

PRÉSENTATION

Comprimés[VL] ■ **Capsules**[VL].

SOINS INFIRMIERS

ÉVALUATION DE LA SITUATION

- Recueillir des renseignements sur la pharmacothérapie courante du patient avant d'administrer cet agent. S'il prend des anticoagulants ou des antiplaquettaires, ne pas lui administrer la chondroïtine.
- Évaluer constamment la douleur (type, siège et intensité) et l'amplitude des mouvements, qui sont des indices de l'efficacité de l'agent.
- Suivre de près la gêne gastrique.
- Suivre de près les signes de saignement.

DIAGNOSTICS INFIRMIERS POSSIBLES

- Douleur aiguë (Indications).
- Mobilité physique réduite (Indications).

INTERVENTIONS INFIRMIÈRES

- Administrer la chondroïtine avec des aliments.

ENSEIGNEMENT AU PATIENT ET À SES PROCHES

- Expliquer au patient que la chondroïtine se prend habituellement en association avec la glucosamine.
- Recommander au patient de ne pas prendre de l'aspirine, des AINS, des antiplaquettaires, des anticoagulants ou d'autres médicaments en vente libre en même temps que la chondroïtine sans avoir consulté au préalable un professionnel de la santé.
- Prévenir la patiente qu'elle doit arrêter de prendre la chondroïtine si elle pense être enceinte et ne pas en prendre si elle allaite.
- En cas de saignements, inciter le patient à arrêter immédiatement la prise de chondroïtine et à consulter sans tarder un professionnel de la santé qui devrait assurer un suivi.
- Recommander au patient de demander conseil à un professionnel de la santé en cas de gêne gastrique persistante.
- Expliquer au patient que la chondroïtine favorise la formation et la réparation du cartilage et qu'il faut la prendre régulièrement pendant un laps de temps donné pour qu'elle soit efficace. Elle n'est pas recommandée à titre d'analgésique à prendre au besoin seulement.

VÉRIFICATION DE L'EFFICACITÉ THÉRAPEUTIQUE

L'efficacité thérapeutique peut être démontrée par: la diminution de la douleur et l'amélioration de l'amplitude des mouvements articulaires ■ un recours moindre à des analgésiques.

DONG QUAI

AUTRES APPELLATIONS:
Angélique (officinale) chinoise, dang gui, danggui, dong qua, ligustilide, angélique géante, herbe aux anges, tang kuei, tan ke bai zhi

CLASSIFICATION:
Phytoestrogène

USAGES COURANTS

Prise en charge des crampes menstruelles, des cycles menstruels irréguliers et des symptômes de la ménopause ■ Usages variés à titre de purificateur du sang ■ Usage topique en association avec d'autres ingrédients pour prévenir l'éjaculation précoce.

MÉCANISME D'ACTION

Propriétés vasodilatatrices et antispasmodiques possibles ■ Liaison aux récepteurs des œstrogènes. ***Effets thérapeutiques:*** Prolongation de latence de l'éjaculation ■ Possibilité de diminution des symptômes de la ménopause.

PHARMACOCINÉTIQUE

Absorption: Inconnue.
Distribution: Inconnue.
Métabolisme et excrétion: Inconnus.
Demi-vie: Inconnue.

Profil temps-action

	Début d'action	Pic	Durée
PO	inconnu	inconnu	inconnue

CONTRE-INDICATIONS, PRÉCAUTIONS ET MISES EN GARDE

Contre-indications: Grossesse et allaitement.
Précautions et mises en garde: Cancers ou maladies hormonosensibles (risque de stimulation de la croissance des cellules cancéreuses ou d'exacerbation de la maladie).

RÉACTIONS INDÉSIRABLES ET EFFETS SECONDAIRES

Tég.: photosensibilité.
Divers: certaines composantes de la plante sont carcinogènes et mutagènes.

INTERACTIONS

Produit naturel-médicaments: L'**alcool** contenu dans certaines préparations peut interagir avec le **disulfirame** et le **métronidazole** ■ L'utilisation du dong quai avec des **anticoagulants** et des **antiplaquettaires**, des **thrombolytiques**, des **AINS** ou des **valproates** peut accroître le risque de saignements.
Produit naturel-produits naturels: Les produits naturels ayant des propriétés anticoagulantes ou antiplaquettaires peuvent accroître le risque de saignements lors de l'usage concomitant de dong quai (**arnica**, **camomille**, **clou de girofle**, **danshen**, **ail**, **gingembre**, **ginkgo**, **ginseng** et **saule**).

VOIES D'ADMINISTRATION ET POSOLOGIES COURANTES

- **PO (adultes)**: *Feuilles ou racines* – de 3 à 4,5 g par jour en doses fractionnées, à prendre avec les repas; *extrait* – 1 mL (de 20 à 40 gouttes), 3 fois par jour.

PRÉSENTATION

Feuilles ou racines[VL] ■ **Extrait**[VL].

SOINS INFIRMIERS

ÉVALUATION DE LA SITUATION

- Suivre de près les douleurs avant et après le cycle menstruel, ainsi que les caractéristiques des règles, pour déterminer l'efficacité de cette plante médicinale.
- S'assurer que la patiente n'est pas enceinte avant de lui recommander d'utiliser cette plante médicinale et lui expliquer qu'elle doit arrêter d'en consommer si elle pense être enceinte.
- S'assurer que la patiente n'a pas d'antécédents de cancer ou de maladie hormonosensible; si de tels antécédents existent, lui expliquer que ce produit lui est déconseillé.
- Évaluer le traitement médicamenteux courant de la patiente contre les douleurs menstruelles (médicaments d'ordonnance et en vente libre, tels que l'aspirine et les AINS, comme l'ibuprofène).

DIAGNOSTICS INFIRMIERS POSSIBLES

- Douleur aiguë (Indications).
- Connaissances insuffisantes sur le traitement médicamenteux (Enseignement au patient et à ses proches).

INTERVENTIONS INFIRMIÈRES

- Administrer cet agent avec les repas.

ENSEIGNEMENT AU PATIENT ET À SES PROCHES

- Mettre en garde la patiente contre l'utilisation de ce produit naturel pendant la grossesse et l'allaitement.
- Mettre en garde le patient contre l'usage concomitant d'aspirine ou d'autres AINS en raison du risque de saignements.
- Prévenir la patiente qu'aucune étude n'a confirmé l'utilité de cette plante médicinale dans le traitement des symptômes de la ménopause.
- Conseiller au patient qui prend des médicaments d'ordonnance de consulter un professionnel de la santé avant de prendre le dong quai.
- Recommander au patient d'arrêter de prendre cet agent en cas de diarrhée ou de saignements anormaux et de consulter un professionnel de la santé si les symptômes persistent.
- Prévenir le patient que l'agent peut le rendre photosensible. Lui conseiller d'utiliser un écran solaire et de porter des vêtements protecteurs s'il prévoit s'exposer au soleil.

VÉRIFICATION DE L'EFFICACITÉ THÉRAPEUTIQUE

L'efficacité du traitement peut être démontrée par: la réduction des douleurs et des crampes menstruelles et la régularisation du cycle menstruel avec normalisation du débit sanguin menstruel.

PRODUITS NATURELS

ÉCHINACÉE

(*Echinacea purpurea*)

AUTRES APPELLATIONS:

Échinacée pourpre, rudbeckia pourpre, *Echinacea angustifolia, Echinacea pallida*

CLASSIFICATION:

Anti-infectieux, antipyrétique

USAGES COURANTS

Infections bactériennes et virales ■ Prévention et traitement des rhumes, de la toux, de la grippe et de la bronchite ■ Fièvre ■ Plaies et brûlures ■ Inflammation de la bouche et du pharynx ■ Infections des voies urinaires ■ Infections aux levures.

MÉCANISME D'ACTION

Echinacea purpurea herba pourrait favoriser la cicatrisation des plaies, phénomène qui pourrait s'expliquer par l'augmentation du nombre de leucocytes et de cellules spléniques et par l'intensification de l'activité des granulocytes, ainsi que par l'augmentation du nombre de lymphocytes T auxiliaires et des cytokines. *E. purpurea radix* pourrait exercer des effets antibactériens, antiviraux, anti-inflammatoires et immunomodulateurs. ***Effets thérapeutiques:*** Résolution des infections des voies respiratoires et urinaires ■ Diminution de la durée et de l'intensité du rhume ■ Accélération de la cicatrisation des plaies ■ Stimulation de la phagocytose: inhibition de l'activité de la hyaluronidase (sécrétée par les bactéries), enzyme qui leur permet d'attaquer des cellules saines ■ *Usage externe:* propriétés antifongiques et bactériostatiques.

PHARMACOCINÉTIQUE

Absorption: Inconnue.

Distribution: Inconnue.

Métabolisme et excrétion: Inconnus.

Demi-vie: Inconnue.

Profil temps-action

	DÉBUT D'ACTION	PIC	DURÉE
PO	inconnu	inconnu	inconnue

CONTRE-INDICATIONS, PRÉCAUTIONS ET MISES EN GARDE

Contre-indications: Sclérose en plaques, leucose, collagénose, sida, tuberculose, maladies auto-immunes ■ Hypersensibilité et sensibilité croisée chez les patients allergiques à la famille des astéracées/composées (marguerite, chrysanthème, tagète, etc.) ■ Grossesse et allaitement.

Précautions et mises en garde: Diabète ■ Patients alcooliques ou atteints de maladie hépatique (la prudence est de mise lors de l'utilisation des teintures) ■ Usage au-delà de 8 semaines (risque de suppression de la fonction immunitaire).

RÉACTIONS INDÉSIRABLES ET EFFETS SECONDAIRES

SNC: étourdissements, fatigue, céphalées, somnolence.

ORLO: sensation de picotement au niveau de la langue, maux de gorge.

GI: nausées, vomissements, brûlures d'estomac, constipation, douleurs abdominales, diarrhée.

Tég.: réactions allergiques, rash (plus courant chez les enfants).

Divers: fièvre.

INTERACTIONS

Produit naturel-médicaments: Risque de modification des effets des **immunosuppresseurs** en raison des effets immunostimulants de la plante ■ Les **stéroïdes anabolisants**, le **méthotrexate** et le **kétoconazole** peuvent interagir avec l'échinacée.

VOIES D'ADMINISTRATION ET POSOLOGIES COURANTES

- **PO (adultes):** *Comprimés* – 2 comprimés, 3 fois par jour. *Extrait liquide* – 1 ou 2 mL, 3 fois par jour; *forme solide* (6,5:1) – de 150 à 300 mg, 3 fois par jour; ne pas prendre pendant plus de 8 semaines. *Infusion* – ½ cuillérée de racine fragmentée, qu'il faut laisser macérer et filtrer après 10 minutes; boire 5 ou 6 tasses, le premier jour, à diminuer graduellement jusqu'à une seule tasse, le cinquième jour. *Jus des parties aériennes d'Echinacea purpurea* – de 6 à 9 mL/jour. *Liquide* – 20 gouttes toutes les 2 heures, le jour de l'apparition des symptômes, ensuite 3 fois par jour jusqu'à 10 jours au maximum.
- **Préparation topique (adultes):** *Onguent, lotion, teinture pour usage externe* – de 1,5 à 7,5 mL de teinture ou de 2 à 5 g de racine séchée.

PRÉSENTATION

Capsules[VL] ■ **Comprimés**[VL] ■ **Racine séchée**[VL] ■ **Extrait liquide**[VL] ■ **Teinture**[VL] ■ **Infusion**[VL].

SOINS INFIRMIERS

ÉVALUATION DE LA SITUATION

- Évaluer la taille et l'aspect de la plaie ainsi que la quantité de l'écoulement avant le début du traitement et à intervalles réguliers pendant toute sa durée.
- Évaluer la fréquence de l'apparition des maladies bénignes (comme le rhume) à la suite de la prise de cette plante médicinale.

DIAGNOSTICS INFIRMIERS POSSIBLES

- Atteinte à l'intégrité de la peau (Indications).

INTERVENTIONS INFIRMIÈRES

- Les teintures peuvent contenir des quantités non négligeables d'alcool et pourraient ne pas convenir aux enfants, aux alcooliques, aux patients atteints d'une maladie hépatique ou à ceux prenant du disulfirame, du métronidazole, certaines céphalosporines ou des sulfonylurées (une classe d'hypoglycémiants oraux).
- L'usage prolongé de cet agent peut entraîner une surstimulation du système immunitaire, raison pour laquelle il est déconseillé de l'utiliser pendant plus de 8 semaines. Un traitement de 10 à 14 jours est habituellement considéré comme suffisant.
- On peut prendre cet agent avec ou sans aliments.

ENSEIGNEMENT AU PATIENT ET À SES PROCHES

- La plante est plus efficace en traitement qu'en prévention du rhume. Conseiller au patient de prendre cet agent dès l'apparition des premiers symptômes.
- Inciter le patient à consulter le médecin sans tarder si son état ne s'améliore pas après la prise de cette plante médicinale.
- Prévenir le patient que le traitement dure habituellement de 8 à 10 jours jusqu'à 8 semaines au maximum.
- Informer le patient que l'utilisation de cette plante médicinale est déconseillée en cas de maladie grave (comme le sida ou la tuberculose) ou de maladie auto-immune (comme la sclérose en plaques, les maladies du collagène, etc.).
- Prévenir le patient que l'usage prolongé de cette plante médicinale peut provoquer une surstimulation du système immunitaire, avec des effets immunosuppresseurs ultérieurs.
- Conseiller à la patiente enceinte ou qui allaite de ne pas prendre ce produit naturel.
- Conseiller au patient de consulter un professionnel de la santé avant de prendre un médicament en vente libre en même temps que l'échinacée.
- Conseiller au patient de garder la teinture dans un flacon de couleur foncée, à l'abri des rayons du soleil. Lui recommander d'en prendre plusieurs fois par jour.
- Conseiller au patient de garder l'herbe séchée dans un contenant hermétiquement fermé, à l'abri des rayons du soleil.

VÉRIFICATION DE L'EFFICACITÉ THÉRAPEUTIQUE

L'efficacité du traitement peut être démontrée par: l'accélération de la cicatrisation des plaies ■ une fréquence moindre de maladies bénignes ■ une durée et une gravité moindres des maladies.

ESPÈCES *CRATAEGUS*,

voir Aubépine dorée.

GINGEMBRE

(*Zingiber officinale*)

AUTRES APPELLATIONS

Gingembre de Jamaïque, racine de gingembre

CLASSIFICATION:

Antiémétique

USAGES COURANTS

Prévention et traitement des nausées et des vomissements provoqués par le mal des transports, la perte d'appétit, la grossesse, une intervention chirurgicale et la chimiothérapie ■ Prévention des nausées et des vomissements postopératoires ■ Usage possible pour soulager la dyspepsie, la flatulence, les douleurs articulaires de la polyarthrite rhumatoïde, les crampes et la diarrhée ■ Effets tonifiants et revigorants pouvant s'avérer bénéfiques en présence de goutte, de gaz, d'infections respiratoires ■ Effets anti-inflammatoires ■ Effets tonifiants et stimulants (tonifiant des intestins, augmentation de la production de salive, effets anticoagulants, abaissement de la cholestérolémie).

MÉCANISME D'ACTION

Effet antiémétique par intensification de la motilité et du transport GI; effet possible sur les récepteurs sérotoninergiques ■ Agent hypoglycémiant, hypotenseur ou hypertenseur et inotrope positif ■ Inhibition des prostaglandines et des plaquettes, abaissement des taux de cholestérol, amélioration de l'appétit et de la digestion. ***Effets thérapeutiques:*** Diminution des nausées et des vomissements provoqués par le mal des transports, une intervention chirurgicale ou la chimiothérapie ■ Diminution de la douleur articulaire et amélioration des mouvements articulaires en présence de polyarthrite rhumatoïde ■ Antioxydant.

PHARMACOCINÉTIQUE

Absorption: Inconnue.
Distribution: Inconnue.
Métabolisme et excrétion: Inconnus.
Demi-vie: Inconnue.

Profil temps-action

	DÉBUT D'ACTION	PIC	DURÉE
PO	inconnu	inconnu	inconnue

CONTRE-INDICATIONS, PRÉCAUTIONS ET MISES EN GARDE

Contre-indications: Grossesse et allaitement (consommation en quantités excessives) ■ Calculs biliaires.
Précautions et mises en garde: Patients exposés à un risque accru de saignements ■ Diabète ■ Anticoagulothérapie ■ Maladie cardiovasculaire.

RÉACTIONS INDÉSIRABLES ET EFFETS SECONDAIRES

GI: légères brûlures d'estomac.
Tég.: dermatite (usage topique).

INTERACTIONS

Produit naturel-médicaments: L'utilisation du gingembre avec des **anticoagulants**, des **antiplaquettaires** et des **thrombolytiques** peut accroître le risque de saignements ■ Risque d'effets additifs avec les **antidiabétiques** (provoquant une hypoglycémie) et les **bloqueurs des canaux calciques** (provoquant une hypotension).
Produit naturel-produits naturels: Risque accru de saignements lors de l'usage concomitant d'autres **plantes médicinales ayant des effets anticoagulants et antiplaquettaires.**

VOIES D'ADMINISTRATION ET POSOLOGIES COURANTES

■ **PO (adultes):** *Mal des transports* – 1 000 mg de racine de gingembre séchée, à prendre de 30 minutes à 4 heures avant le voyage, ou 250 mg, 4 fois par jour. *Prévention des nausées postopératoires* – 1 000 mg, à prendre 1 heure avant l'induction de l'anesthésie. *Nausées induites par la chimiothérapie* – de 2 à 4 g/jour. On a utilisé jusqu'à 2 g de gingembre fraîchement réduit en poudre à titre d'antiémétique (ne pas dépasser 4 g/jour). *Polyarthrite rhumatoïde (extrait de gingembre)* – 170 mg, 3 fois par jour, ou 225 mg, 2 fois par jour. *Rhizome entier* – de 0,25 à 1 g, pour la prise en charge d'autres maladies. *Infusion* – verser 150 mL d'eau bouillante sur 0,5 à 1 g de gingembre et laisser macérer pendant 5 minutes. *Teinture* – de 0,25 à 3 mL.

PRÉSENTATION

En monothérapie ou en association avec d'autres plantes médicinales[VL]: Racine sèche réduite en poudre[VL] ■ Sirop[VL] ■ Teinture[VL] ■ Comprimés[VL] ■ Capsules[VL] ■ Épice[VL] ■ Infusion[VL].

SOINS INFIRMIERS

ÉVALUATION DE LA SITUATION

- Suivre de près les nausées, les vomissements, la distension abdominale et la douleur avant l'administration, si le gingembre est utilisé à titre d'antiémétique.
- Suivre de près la douleur et la tuméfaction articulaires et l'amplitude des mouvements des articulations touchées, avant et après l'administration, lorsque le gingembre est utilisé pour le traitement de l'arthrite.
- Rester à l'affût de la douleur épigastrique, avant et après l'administration, lorsque le gingembre est utilisé à titre d'agent gastroprotecteur.
- Suivre de près la pression artérielle en présence de maladies cardiovasculaires, dont l'hypertension.

DIAGNOSTICS INFIRMIERS POSSIBLES

- Douleur aiguë (Indications).
- Connaissances insuffisantes sur le traitement médicamenteux (Enseignement au patient et à ses proches).

INTERVENTIONS INFIRMIÈRES

- Administrer le gingembre avant des circonstances où des nausées ou des vomissements pourraient survenir (p. ex., pour prévenir le mal des transports).
- La présentation et les teneurs varient en fonction de la maladie à traiter. S'assurer qu'on administre la préparation et la posologie appropriées.
- Administrer pour stimuler le péristaltisme.

ENSEIGNEMENT AU PATIENT ET À SES PROCHES

- Recommander au patient qui reçoit des anticoagulants de ne pas prendre du gingembre sans avoir consulté un professionnel de la santé au préalable (risque accru de saignements).

- Conseiller au patient d'arrêter de prendre l'agent immédiatement en cas de palpitations et d'en informer un professionnel de la santé.
- Recommander au patient de rester à l'affût de la formation d'ecchymoses et d'autres signes de saignements. Si de tels signes se manifestent, lui recommander d'arrêter de prendre l'agent immédiatement et d'en informer un professionnel de la santé.
- Recommander au patient ayant des antécédents de calculs biliaires de ne consommer de gingembre que sous la surveillance d'un professionnel de la santé.
- Conseiller au patient de consulter un professionnel de la santé avant de prendre d'autres médicaments d'ordonnance ou en vente libre en même temps que du gingembre.
- Expliquer au patient que le gingembre est un agent tonifiant et qu'il n'est pas destiné à un usage prolongé.

VÉRIFICATION DE L'EFFICACITÉ THÉRAPEUTIQUE

L'efficacité du traitement peut être démontrée par: la prévention des nausées et des vomissements ■ le soulagement des douleurs épigastriques ■ l'amélioration de la mobilité articulaire et le soulagement de la douleur.

GINKGO

AUTRES APPELLATIONS:

Noyer du Japon, arbre aux quarante écus, arbre aux mille écus, arbre du sel, ginkgo biloba

CLASSIFICATION:

Antiplaquettaire, stimulant du système nerveux central

USAGES COURANTS

Soulagement des symptômes d'un dysfonctionnement cérébral organique (syndrome de démence, déficience de la mémoire à court terme, incapacité de se concentrer, dépression) ■ Claudication intermittente ■ Vertiges et acouphènes d'origine vasculaire ■ Amélioration de la circulation périphérique ■ Dysfonctionnement sexuel.

MÉCANISME D'ACTION

Amélioration de la tolérance à l'hypoxémie, particulièrement dans le tissu cérébral ■ Inhibition de la formation d'un œdème cérébral et accélération de sa régression ■ Amélioration de la mémoire, de la microcirculation et des propriétés rhéologiques du sang ■ Amélioration de l'équilibre en cas de vertiges ■ Inactivation des radicaux libres toxiques générés par l'oxygène ■ Effets antagonistes sur le facteur d'activation plaquettaire ■ Blocage de la bronchoconstriction et inhibition de la chimiotaxie des phagocytes. ***Effets thérapeutiques:*** Soulagement des symptômes de démence ■ Inhibition des spasmes artériels, diminution de la fragilité des capillaires et de la viscosité du sang ■ Amélioration du tonus veineux, relaxation du muscle lisse vasculaire.

PHARMACOCINÉTIQUE

Absorption: de 70 à 100 %.
Distribution: Inconnue.
Métabolisme et excrétion: Inconnus.
Demi-vie: Inconnue.

Profil temps-action

	DÉBUT D'ACTION	PIC	DURÉE
PO	inconnu	inconnu	inconnue

CONTRE-INDICATIONS, PRÉCAUTIONS ET MISES EN GARDE

Contre-indications: Hypersensibilité ■ Grossesse et allaitement.
Précautions et mises en garde: Maladies du sang ■ Enfants (les graines fraîches ont provoqué des convulsions et la mort) ■ Diabète ■ Épilepsie ■ Chirurgie (arrêter l'utilisation 2 semaines avant l'intervention).

RÉACTIONS INDÉSIRABLES ET EFFETS SECONDAIRES

SNC: HÉMORRAGIE CÉRÉBRALE, étourdissements, céphalées, vertiges, convulsions.
CV: palpitations.
GI: flatulence, indigestion.
Tég.: réactions cutanées de nature allergique.
Hémat.: saignements.
Divers: réactions d'hypersensibilité.

INTERACTIONS

Produit naturel-médicaments: En théorie, le ginkgo peut potentialiser les effets des **anticoagulants**, des **antiplaquettaires**, des **thrombolytiques** et des **inhibiteurs de la MAO** ■ Il pourrait également accroître le risque de saignements lors de l'administration concomitante d'**acide valproïque** et d'**AINS** ■ Il pourrait réduire l'efficacité des **anticonvulsivants** ■ Il pourrait modifier le métabolisme de l'**insuline**, ce qui pourrait dicter des adaptations posologiques.
Produit naturel-produits naturels: Le ginkgo pourrait accroître le risque de saignements lorsqu'il est pris en

concomitance avec d'autres plantes ayant des effets antiplaquettaires (dont l'**angélique**, l'**arnica**, la **camomille**, la **grande camomille**, l'**ail**, le **gingembre** et la **réglisse**).

VOIES D'ADMINISTRATION ET POSOLOGIES COURANTES

Syndrome organique cérébral

- **PO (adultes):** De 120 à 240 mg d'extrait de feuilles de ginkgo par jour, en 2 ou 3 doses.

Dysfonctionnement sexuel

- **PO (adultes):** De 60 à 240 mg d'extrait de feuilles de ginkgo, 2 fois par jour.

Claudication intermittente

- **PO (adultes):** De 120 à 240 mg d'extrait de feuilles de ginkgo par jour, en 2 ou 3 doses.

Vertiges et acouphènes

- **PO (adultes):** De 120 à 160 mg d'extrait de feuilles de ginkgo par jour, en 2 ou 3 doses.

Amélioration de la fonction cognitive

- **PO (adultes):** De 120 à 600 mg par jour.

PRÉSENTATION

Extrait de feuilles de ginkgo (acétone/eau): De 22 à 27 % de glycosides flavonoïdes, de 5 à 7 % de terpène lactone, de 2,6 à 3, 2 % de bilobalide, < 5 ppm d'acides ginkgoliques.

SOINS INFIRMIERS

ÉVALUATION DE LA SITUATION

- Exclure toutes les autres causes traitables de la démence avant de commencer un traitement par le ginkgo.
- Évaluer la fonction cognitive (mémoire, attention, raisonnement, langage, capacité d'accomplir des tâches simples) à intervalles réguliers pendant toute la durée du traitement.
- Évaluer la fréquence, la durée et la gravité des crampes musculaires (claudication) dont souffre le patient, avant le traitement et à intervalles réguliers pendant toute sa durée.
- Rester à l'affût des céphalées et des modifications au niveau du système nerveux (thromboembolie).

DIAGNOSTICS INFIRMIERS POSSIBLES

- Opérations de la pensée perturbées (Indications).
- Douleur aiguë (Indications).
- Connaissances insuffisantes sur le traitement médicamenteux (Enseignement au patient et à ses proches).

INTERVENTIONS INFIRMIÈRES

- Commencer le traitement par une dose de 120 mg par jour et l'accroître selon les besoins pour réduire les effets secondaires.
- Le patient doit prendre 1 dose de 80 mg (3 fois par jour) pendant 6 à 8 semaines au moins (pas moins de 6 semaines) avant que sa réponse au traitement puisse être déterminée.
- On peut administrer l'agent sans égard aux repas.
- Il n'est pas recommandé d'utiliser les préparations de feuilles séchées sous forme d'infusion, en raison de la quantité insuffisante d'ingrédients actifs qu'elles contiennent.
- Conseiller au patient de ne pas manipuler ou consommer la plante crue en raison du risque de réactions allergiques graves.
- Administrer l'agent tous les jours à la même heure.
- Garder la plante hors de l'atteinte des enfants en raison du risque de convulsions en cas de consommation de doses importantes de graines.

ENSEIGNEMENT AU PATIENT ET À SES PROCHES

- Recommander au patient de rester à l'affût des ecchymoses et des autres signes de saignements inexplicables et d'en informer un professionnel de la santé le cas échéant.
- Prévenir le patient qu'il doit garder cette plante médicinale hors de la portée des enfants, car sa consommation peut provoquer des convulsions.
- Conseiller au patient d'éviter de toucher la pulpe ou l'enveloppe des graines en raison du risque de dermatite de contact. En cas de contact par inadvertance, lui recommander de se laver la peau à l'eau courante.
- Conseiller au patient de ne pas dépasser les doses recommandées, car les doses importantes peuvent être toxiques (les signes de toxicité sont l'agitation, la diarrhée, les nausées et les vomissements, et les maux de tête).
- Expliquer au patient qui prend des anticoagulants ou des antiplaquettaires qu'il ne doit prendre cet agent que s'il lui est recommandé par un professionnel de la santé et s'il reste sous surveillance étroite.
- Conseiller au patient de consulter un professionnel de la santé avant de prendre un médicament d'ordonnance ou en vente libre en même temps que du ginkgo.

VÉRIFICATION DE L'EFFICACITÉ THÉRAPEUTIQUE

L'efficacité du traitement peut être démontrée par: l'allongement de la distance parcourue à la marche sans éprouver de douleurs ■ le soulagement des acouphènes et du vertige ■ l'amélioration de la mémoire à court terme, ainsi que de la capacité de se concentrer et d'accomplir des tâches simples ■ l'amélioration de la fonction sexuelle.

GINSENG (*Panax ginseng*)

AUTRES APPELLATIONS:

Ginseng asiatique, ginseng chinois, hong shen, ginseng japonais, ginseng coréen, ginseng rouge, renshen, ginseng blanc

CLASSIFICATION:

Non attribuée

USAGES COURANTS

Amélioration de la résistance physique et de l'état mental ■ Effets énergisants pendant les périodes de fatigue et de difficultés de concentration ■ Effets sédatifs (amélioration du sommeil) et antidépresseurs ■ Diabète ■ Aphrodisiaque et stimulant de la libido ■ Prolongation de l'espérance de vie ■ Traitement du cancer ■ Traitement d'appoint du cancer ■ Amélioration de la réponse immunologique ■ Stimulation de l'appétit.

MÉCANISME D'ACTION

Le principal ingrédient actif est le ginsenoside dérivé de la racine séchée ■ Stimulation et dépression du SNC ■ Amélioration de la fonction immunitaire ■ Inhibition de la coagulation et de l'agrégation plaquettaire ■ Effets analgésiques et anti-inflammatoires, ainsi qu'effets ressemblant à ceux des œstrogènes. ***Effets thérapeutiques:*** Amélioration des capacités mentales et physiques ■ Effets bénéfiques possibles sur l'appétit, la mémoire et le sommeil ■ Abaissement possible de la glycémie à jeun chez les patients diabétiques.

PHARMACOCINÉTIQUE

Absorption: Inconnue.
Distribution: Inconnue.
Métabolisme et excrétion: Inconnus.
Demi-vie: Inconnue.

Profil temps-action

	DÉBUT D'ACTION	PIC	DURÉE
PO	inconnu	inconnu	inconnue

CONTRE-INDICATIONS, PRÉCAUTIONS ET MISES EN GARDE

Contre-indications: Grossesse (androgénisation fœtale) ■ Allaitement ■ Enfants ■ Troubles maniacodépressifs et psychoses ■ Hypertension ■ Asthme ■ Infection ■ Receveurs de greffe (risque d'interaction avec le traitement immunosuppresseur) ■ Cancers hormonosensibles.

Précautions et mises en garde: Maladie cardiovasculaire ■ Diabète (risque d'effets hypoglycémiants) ■ Patients sous anticoagulants ■ Troubles de saignement.

RÉACTIONS INDÉSIRABLES ET EFFETS SECONDAIRES

SNC: agitation, dépression, étourdissements, euphorie, céphalées, insomnie, nervosité.
CV: hypertension, tachycardie.
GI: diarrhée.
GU: aménorrhée, saignements vaginaux.
Tég.: éruptions cutanées.
End.: effets ressemblant à ceux des œstrogènes.
Divers: fièvre, mastalgie, SYNDROME DE STEVENS-JOHNSON.

INTERACTIONS

Produit naturel-médicaments: Risque de modification des effets anticoagulants de la **warfarine** ■ L'agent peut entraver les effets des **inhibiteurs de la MAO** et provoquer des symptômes comme des céphalées ou des trémulations, ainsi que des épisodes de manie ■ Risque d'élévation des effets hypoglycémiants des **hypoglycémiants oraux** et de l'**insuline** ■ Risque d'interaction avec les **immunosuppresseurs** ■ La prudence est de mise en cas de traitement par des **œstrogènes**.

Produit naturel-produits naturels: Risque accru de saignements lors de l'usage concomitant de **plantes médicinales ayant des propriétés antiplaquettaires ou anticoagulantes** ■ Risque d'allongement de l'intervalle QT et d'arythmies mortelles lors de la prise concomitante de **mauve des champs** et d'**orange amère** ■ Risque de potentialisation des effets de la **caféine**, du **café** ou du **thé** et des effets de stimulation du SNC du **maté**.

VOIES D'ADMINISTRATION ET POSOLOGIES COURANTES

- **PO (adultes):** *Capsule* – de 200 à 600 mg/jour. *Extrait* – de 100 à 300 mg, 3 fois par jour. *Racine brute* – de 1 à 2 g/jour. *Infusion ou thé* – de 1 à 2 g de racine par jour (½ c. à table dans une tasse d'eau) jusqu'à 3 fois par jour (les sachets de thé de *P. ginseng* contiennent habituellement 1 500 mg de racine de ginseng). Ne pas consommer pendant plus de 3 mois. *Prévention du rhume et de la grippe* –

100 mg par jour, 4 semaines avant la vaccination contre la grippe; poursuivre pendant 8 semaines, par la suite. *Bronchite chronique* – 100 mg, 2 fois par jour, pendant 9 jours en association avec une antibiothérapie. *Dysfonctionnement érectile* – 900 mg, 3 fois par jour. *Diabète de type 2* – 200 mg par jour.

PRÉSENTATION

Poudre de racine[VL] ■ Extrait dans de l'alcool[VL] ■ Capsules[VL] ■ Sachets de tisane[VL].

SOINS INFIRMIERS

ÉVALUATION DE LA SITUATION

- Évaluer le niveau d'énergie, la durée de l'attention et le niveau de fatigue du patient avant le traitement et à intervalles réguliers pendant toute sa durée.
- Évaluer l'appétit, la durée du sommeil et sa qualité perçue par le patient, la labilité affective et le rendement au travail avant le traitement et à intervalles réguliers pendant toute sa durée.
- Les patients atteints de maladies chroniques ne devraient prendre cette plante médicinale que sur recommandation d'un professionnel de la santé.
- Rester à l'affût des effets toxiques du ginseng (nervosité, insomnie, palpitations et diarrhée).
- Mesurer à intervalles plus fréquents la glycémie chez les patients diabétiques jusqu'au moment où leur réponse à cet agent est connue.
- Rester à l'affût du syndrome d'abus de ginseng (qui peut apparaître lorsque des doses importantes de cet agent sont prises en même temps que d'autres stimulants psychomoteurs, comme le café et le thé). Le syndrome se caractérise par les effets suivants: diarrhée, hypertension, agitation, insomnie, éruptions cutanées, dépression, perte d'appétit, euphorie et œdème.

DIAGNOSTICS INFIRMIERS POSSIBLES

- Champ énergétique perturbé (Indications).
- Habitudes de sommeil perturbées (Indications).

INTERVENTIONS INFIRMIÈRES

- On peut prendre le ginseng avec ou sans aliments.
- Administrer le ginseng au même moment de la journée; ne pas administrer une dose supérieure à celle recommandée en raison du risque d'effets toxiques.

ENSEIGNEMENT AU PATIENT ET À SES PROCHES

- Recommander au patient atteint de maladie cardiovasculaire, d'hypertension ou d'hypotension ou à celui qui est sous corticothérapie d'éviter la consommation de ginseng.
- Conseiller à la patiente enceinte ou allaitante de ne pas prendre de ginseng.
- Expliquer au patient les symptômes d'une intoxication au ginseng; lui recommander de réduire les doses ou de cesser d'en prendre s'il manifeste de tels symptômes.
- Recommander au patient de réduire sa consommation de caféine.
- Conseiller au patient diabétique de mesurer souvent sa glycémie jusqu'à ce que sa réponse à cet agent soit connue.
- Prévenir le patient que la durée recommandée du traitement est de 3 semaines. Il peut répéter le traitement par la suite. Lui recommander de ne pas prendre de ginseng pendant plus de 3 mois.
- Expliquer au patient les signes et les symptômes de l'hépatite et lui conseiller de cesser de consommer du ginseng et d'en informer rapidement un professionnel de la santé, le cas échéant. (Cette plante protège le foie, si elle est prise à faible dose, mais peut lui nuire, si elle est consommée à doses élevées.)
- Recommander au patient de ne pas dépasser la dose recommandée en raison du risque d'effets secondaires et de toxicité.
- Recommander au patient d'arrêter de prendre le ginseng en cas de diarrhée.
- Recommander au patient de consulter un professionnel de la santé avant de prendre des médicaments d'ordonnance ou en vente libre en même temps que du ginseng.

VÉRIFICATION DE L'EFFICACITÉ THÉRAPEUTIQUE

L'efficacité du traitement peut être démontrée par: un regain d'énergie et une sensation de mieux-être ■ l'amélioration de la qualité du sommeil ■ l'amélioration de la concentration et du rendement au travail ■ un gain d'appétit. Le plein effet de ce produit naturel pourrait ne se manifester qu'après plusieurs semaines.

GLUCOSAMINE

AUTRES APPELLATIONS:

2-amino-2-deoxyglucose sulfate, chitosamine

CLASSIFICATION:

Antirhumatismal

USAGES COURANTS

Arthrose ▪ Arthrite temporomaxillaire.

MÉCANISME D'ACTION

Inhibition ou ralentissement possible de l'évolution de l'arthrose par stimulation du métabolisme du cartilage et du tissu synovial. ***Effets thérapeutiques:*** Diminution de la douleur et amélioration du fonctionnement des articulations.

PHARMACOCINÉTIQUE

Absorption: 0,9 %.

Distribution: Inconnue.

Métabolisme et excrétion: La glucosamine est éliminée à 74 % lors d'un métabolisme de premier passage.

Demi-vie: Inconnue.

Profil temps-action

	Début d'action	Pic	Durée
PO	inconnu	inconnu	inconnue

CONTRE-INDICATIONS, PRÉCAUTIONS ET MISES EN GARDE

Contre-indications: Allergie aux crustacés et aux coquillages (la glucosamine est souvent dérivée de l'exosquelette de crustacés marins) ▪ Grossesse et allaitement.

Précautions et mises en garde: Diabète (risque de déséquilibres glycémiques) ▪ Asthme (risque d'exacerbation des symptômes).

RÉACTIONS INDÉSIRABLES ET EFFETS SECONDAIRES

GI: nausées, brûlures d'estomac, diarrhée, constipation.

SNC: céphalées, étourdissements.

Tég.: réactions cutanées.

INTERACTIONS

Produit naturel-médicaments: La glucosamine peut diminuer les effets des **antidiabétiques** ▪ Elle peut induire une résistance à certains **médicaments administrés dans le cadre d'une chimiothérapie**, comme l'**étoposide**, le **téniposide** et la **doxorubicine**.

VOIES D'ADMINISTRATION ET POSOLOGIES COURANTES

- **PO (adultes):** 500 mg, 3 fois par jour.

PRÉSENTATION

Comprimés[VL] ▪ **Capsules**[VL].

SOINS INFIRMIERS

ÉVALUATION DE LA SITUATION

- Avant de commencer le traitement, s'assurer que le patient n'est pas allergique aux crustacés.
- Évaluer la douleur (type, siège et intensité) ainsi que l'amplitude des mouvements articulaires à intervalles fréquents, puisqu'elles sont de bons indices de l'efficacité du traitement.
- Suivre de près la glycémie chez les patients diabétiques qui utilisent un glucomètre à domicile pour assurer un équilibrage approprié jusqu'à ce qu'on soit assuré que la glucosamine n'entraîne aucun effet à cet égard.
- Évaluer la gêne gastrique et recommander au patient de demander conseil à un professionnel de la santé en cas de problèmes gastriques persistants.
- Suivre de près la fonction intestinale et traiter la constipation, le cas échéant, en augmentant l'apport de liquides et de fibres alimentaires et en administrant des laxatifs mucilagineux, si nécessaire.

DIAGNOSTICS INFIRMIERS POSSIBLES

- Douleur aiguë (Indications).
- Mobilité physique réduite (Indications).

INTERVENTIONS INFIRMIÈRES

- Administrer la glucosamine avant les repas.

ENSEIGNEMENT AU PATIENT ET À SES PROCHES

- Informer le patient allergique aux crustacés que la glucosamine lui est déconseillée.
- Expliquer au patient que les effets de ce médicament découlent de la stimulation du métabolisme du cartilage et du tissu synovial et qu'il faut le prendre régulièrement pour profiter de ses bienfaits. Lui expliquer que la glucosamine n'est pas un produit à prendre par intermittence.
- Recommander au patient de communiquer avec un professionnel de la santé en cas de gêne gastrique avec symptômes persistants.
- Conseiller au patient diabétique de suivre de près sa glycémie pour assurer un équilibrage glycémique approprié.

VÉRIFICATION DE L'EFFICACITÉ THÉRAPEUTIQUE

L'efficacité du traitement peut être démontrée par: le soulagement de la douleur et l'amélioration de l'amplitude des mouvements.

PRODUITS NATURELS

GRANDE CAMOMILLE

AUTRES APPELLATIONS:

Chrysanthème-matricaire, matricaire, malherbe, grand chrysanthème, *Chrysanthemum parthenium, Tanacetum parthenium*, quinine sauvage

CLASSIFICATION:

Soulagement des céphalées vasculaires

USAGES COURANTS

PO: Prophylaxie des migraines ■ **Préparation topique**: Rages de dents ■ Antiseptique.

MÉCANISME D'ACTION

Les effets antimigraineux prophylactiques de la grande camomille pourraient lui être conférés par le parthénolide, une lactone sesquiterpène ■ La plante pourrait aussi exercer des effets antiplaquettaires et vasodilatateurs et bloquer la synthèse des prostaglandines. ***Effets thérapeutiques:*** Réduction possible des symptômes et de la fréquence des migraines.

PHARMACOCINÉTIQUE

Absorption: Inconnue.

Distribution: Inconnue.

Métabolisme et excrétion: Inconnus.

Demi-vie: Inconnue.

Profil temps-action

	DÉBUT D'ACTION	PIC	DURÉE
PO	2 - 4 mois	inconnu	inconnue

CONTRE-INDICATIONS, PRÉCAUTIONS ET MISES EN GARDE

Contre-indications: Grossesse et allaitement ■ Hypersensibilité ou allergie aux plantes de la famille des astéracées/composées (herbe à poux, marguerite, chrysanthème et tagète).

Précautions et mises en garde: Utilisation au-delà de 4 mois (l'innocuité et l'efficacité n'ont pas été établies).

RÉACTIONS INDÉSIRABLES ET EFFETS SECONDAIRES

SNC: « syndrome post-grande camomille » (anxiété, céphalées, insomnie, douleurs musculaires et articulaires).

CV: *usage prolongé* – tachycardie.

GI: nausées, vomissements, diarrhée, brûlures d'estomac, douleurs et aphtes buccaux.

Tég.: dermatite de contact (usage topique).

INTERACTIONS

Produit naturel-médicaments: La prise concomitante de grande camomille et d'**anticoagulants,** d'**antiplaquettaires**, de **thrombolytiques**, d'**AINS** ou de **valproates** peut accroître le risque de saignements ■ L'usage concomitant d'**AINS** peut aussi réduire l'efficacité de la grande camomille.

Produit naturel-produits naturels: L'usage concomitant d'**anis**, d'**arnica**, de **camomille**, de **clou de girofle**, de **dong quai**, de **fenugrec**, d'**ail**, de **gingembre**, de **ginkgo**, de **ginseng** et de **réglisse** peut accroître l'effet anticoagulant de la grande camomille.

VOIES D'ADMINISTRATION ET POSOLOGIES COURANTES

- **PO (adultes)**: De 50 à 100 mg d'extrait de grande camomille par jour (normalisé pour contenir de 0,2 à 0,35 % de parthénolide) ou de 50 à 125 mg de feuilles lyophilisées par jour, à prendre avec des aliments ou après un repas.

PRÉSENTATION

Extrait de grande camomille^{VL}: normalisé pour contenir de 0,2 à 0,35 % de parthénolide ■ **Feuilles fraîches**^{VL} ■ **Feuilles lyophilisées**^{VL}.

SOINS INFIRMIERS

ÉVALUATION DE LA SITUATION

- Déterminer la fréquence, l'intensité et la durée des migraines avant le traitement et pendant toute sa durée.
- Suivre de près les aphtes buccaux et les ulcérations de la peau tout au long du traitement.

DIAGNOSTICS INFIRMIERS POSSIBLES

- Douleur aiguë (Indications)
- Connaissances insuffisantes sur le traitement médicamenteux (Enseignement au patient et à ses proches).

INTERVENTIONS INFIRMIÈRES

- Prendre l'agent avec des aliments ou après un repas.

ENSEIGNEMENT AU PATIENT ET À SES PROCHES

- Expliquer au patient qu'il doit prendre ce produit naturel de façon constante pour prévenir les migraines. Lui expliquer qu'il n'est pas destiné au traitement des migraines.
- Mettre en garde le patient contre le risque de douleurs et d'aphtes buccaux. L'inciter à consulter un profes-

sionnel de la santé s'il en souffre et à maintenir une bonne hygiène buccale.

- Recommander au patient de ne pas arrêter brusquement de prendre cet agent en raison du risque d'apparition du « syndrome post-grande camomille ». Lui expliquer que l'anxiété, les maux de tête, l'insomnie et les douleurs musculaires peuvent représenter des symptômes de sevrage. La prise de cet agent doit être interrompue graduellement.
- Revoir l'alimentation et la pharmacothérapie du patient pour déceler les interactions possibles. Renseigner le patient sur les autres plantes médicinales qui peuvent interagir avec la grande camomille.
- Conseiller au patient sous anticoagulothérapie de ne pas prendre de grande camomille sauf si un professionnel de la santé le lui recommande expressément.
- Conseiller au patient d'éviter de prendre des AINS, car ils peuvent réduire l'efficacité de la grande camomille.
- Conseiller au patient de rester à l'affût des signes de saignements (formation inhabituelle d'ecchymoses ou retard de cicatrisation d'une coupure) et de consulter un professionnel de la santé, le cas échéant.
- Informer le patient que la grande camomille devrait réduire le nombre de migraines et la gravité des symptômes, mais qu'elle pourrait ne pas agir sur leur durée.

VÉRIFICATION DE L'EFFICACITÉ THÉRAPEUTIQUE

L'efficacité du traitement peut être démontrée par: la réduction de la fréquence et de la gravité des migraines.

HYPERICUM PERFORATUM,

voir Millepertuis

KAVA-KAVA

(*Piper methysticum*)

AUTRES APPELLATIONS:

Poivre de Kava, kawa-kawa

CLASSIFICATION:

Anxiolytique, hypnosédatif

USAGES COURANTS

Anxiété ■ Stress ■ Agitation ■ Insomnie ■ Sevrage des benzodiazépines ■ Douleurs musculaires légères ■ Crampes menstruelles et syndrome prémenstruel.

MÉCANISME D'ACTION

Modulation des processus émotionnels par le système limbique ■ Relaxation des muscles squelettiques par une action au niveau du système nerveux central. ***Effets thérapeutiques:*** Soulagement de l'anxiété ■ Sédation.

PHARMACOCINÉTIQUE

Absorption: Le pic plasmatique se produit environ 1,8 heure après la prise de la dose par voie orale.

Distribution: L'agent passe dans le lait maternel.

Métabolisme et excrétion: Excrétion majoritairement rénale (sous forme inchangée et sous forme de métabolites) et fécale. Métabolisme hépatique (par réduction ou déméthylation).

Demi-vie: Environ 9 heures.

Profil temps-action

	Début d'action	Pic	Durée
PO	1,8 h	inconnu	8 h

CONTRE-INDICATIONS, PRÉCAUTIONS ET MISES EN GARDE

Contre-indications: Grossesse (risque d'effets sur le tonus utérin) et allaitement ■ Dépression endogène (risque accru de suicide) ■ Enfants < 12 ans ■ Hépatite ou autres maladies hépatiques.

Précautions et mises en garde: Usage concomitant d'autres agents hépatotoxiques ■ Dépression et maladie de Parkinson (risque d'aggravation des symptômes) ■ Risque de dépendance psychologique (ne pas utiliser pendant plus de 3 mois).

RÉACTIONS INDÉSIRABLES ET EFFETS SECONDAIRES

SNC: étourdissements, céphalées, somnolence, troubles sensoriels, effets extrapyramidaux.

ORLO: dilatation des pupilles, rougeurs oculaires, problèmes d'accommodation visuelle.

GI: TOXICITÉ HÉPATIQUE, troubles gastro-intestinaux.

Tég.: réactions cutanées allergiques, jaunissement de la peau, érythème pellagroïde.

Hémat.: lymphopénie, thrombopénie.

Métab.: perte de poids (usage prolongé de doses élevées).

SN: ataxie, faiblesse musculaire.

INTERACTIONS

Produit naturel-médicaments: Potentialisation des effets des **dépresseurs du SNC** (p. ex., **éthanol**, **barbituriques**, **benzodiazépines**, **analgésiques opioïdes**) ■ Diminution de l'efficacité de la **lévodopa** dans certains cas ■ En théorie, effets additifs possibles lors de la prise d'**agents antiplaquettaires** ■ L'usage concomitant

d'autres substances hépatotoxiques, p. ex., **DHEA, coenzyme Q-10 (doses élevées)** et **niacine** peut accroître le risque de lésions hépatiques.
Produit naturel-produits naturels: En théorie, effets sédatifs additifs possibles lors de l'usage concomitant d'autres **plantes médicinales ayant des propriétés sédatives**.

VOIES D'ADMINISTRATION ET POSOLOGIES COURANTES

- **PO (adultes):** *Anxiolytique* - 100 mg (70 mg de kavalactones), 3 fois par jour. *Sevrage des benzodiazépines* - de 50 à 300 mg/jour pendant 1 semaine, en diminuant graduellement la dose de benzodiazépines pendant 2 semaines (utiliser l'extrait de kavalactone à 70 %). *Insomnie* - de 180 à 210 mg de kavalactones. *Usage habituel:* sous forme d'infusion de la racine dans de l'eau chaude et filtrage de la solution.

PRÉSENTATION

Extraits de racine séchée (dans de l'alcool ou l'acétone): contenant de 30 à 70 % de kavapyrone.

SOINS INFIRMIERS

ÉVALUATION DE LA SITUATION

- Évaluer les spasmes musculaires, la douleur associée et la limitation des mouvements avant le traitement et à intervalles réguliers pendant toute sa durée.
- Évaluer le degré d'anxiété et de sédation (les troubles visuels et les modifications des réflexes moteurs sont des effets indésirables) avant le traitement et à intervalles réguliers pendant toute sa durée.
- Suivre de près les habitudes de sommeil et le degré de sédation au lever.
- L'usage prolongé peut entraîner la diminution du nombre de plaquettes et de lymphocytes.

DIAGNOSTICS INFIRMIERS POSSIBLES

- Anxiété (Indications).
- Mobilité physique réduite (Réactions indésirables).
- Risque d'accident (Effets secondaires).

INTERVENTIONS INFIRMIÈRES

- Préparer une boisson avec la racine pulvérisée, les comprimés, les capsules ou l'extrait.

ENSEIGNEMENT AU PATIENT ET À SES PROCHES

- Prévenir le patient que l'usage prolongé peut entraîner des effets secondaires graves. Lui expliquer qu'il n'est pas recommandé de prendre cet agent pendant plus de 1 mois sans la surveillance d'un professionnel de la santé.
- Prévenir le patient qu'il ne doit pas prendre d'alcool et d'autres dépresseurs du SNC en même temps que cette plante médicinale, car cette association peut potentialiser les effets sédatifs du kava-kava.
- Conseiller au patient de ne pas conduire et de ne pas s'engager dans d'autres activités qui exigent sa vigilance jusqu'à ce que sa réponse au traitement soit connue.
- PRÉVENIR LE PATIENT QU'IL DOIT ARRÊTER DE CONSOMMER LE KAVA-KAVA SANS TARDER EN CAS D'ESSOUFFLEMENTS OU DE SIGNES DE MALADIE HÉPATIQUE (JAUNISSEMENT DE LA PEAU OU DU BLANC DES YEUX, URINE DE COULEUR BRUNE, SELLES DE COULEUR CLAIRE, NAUSÉES, VOMISSEMENTS, FATIGUE INHABITUELLE, FAIBLESSE, DOULEURS D'ESTOMAC OU D'ABDOMEN, PERTE D'APPÉTIT) ET EN INFORMER UN PROFESSIONNEL DE LA SANTÉ.
- Conseiller au patient qui souffre d'affections hépatiques ou qui prend des médicaments qui agissent sur le foie de ne pas prendre de kava-kava sans consulter au préalable un professionnel de la santé.
- Expliquer au patient que bien qu'il n'existe pas de preuves de dépendance physiologique, un risque de dépendance psychologique subsiste.
- Conseiller à la femme enceinte ou allaitante de ne pas consommer cette plante médicinale.
- Conseiller au patient de consulter un professionnel de la santé avant de prendre d'autres médicaments d'ordonnance ou en vente libre en même temps que du kava-kava.

VÉRIFICATION DE L'EFFICACITÉ THÉRAPEUTIQUE

L'efficacité du traitement peut être démontrée par: la diminution de l'anxiété ■ la diminution des spasmes musculaires ■ le soulagement de l'insomnie.

MILLEPERTUIS

(*Hypericum perforatum*)

AUTRES APPELLATIONS:
Herbe de la Saint-Jean, herbe à mille trous, herbe percée, herbe aux piqûres, millepertuis perforé

CLASSIFICATION:
Antidépresseur

USAGES COURANTS

PO: Prise en charge de la dépression légère ou modérée et du trouble obsessionnel compulsif (inefficace en présence de dépression majeure). **Préparation topique**: Inflammation de la peau, contusions, plaies et brûlures ■ **Autres usages**: Diminution des saignements utérins et réduction de la taille des tumeurs.

MÉCANISME D'ACTION

L'ingrédient actif est l'hypéricine, extraite de *Hypericum perforatum*. **PO**: Effet antidépresseur dû probablement à la capacité de recaptage de la sérotonine et d'autres neurotransmetteurs. **Préparation topique**: Propriétés anti-inflammatoires, antifongiques, antivirales et antibactériennes. ***Effets thérapeutiques* – PO**: Diminution des signes et des symptômes de dépression. **Préparation topique**: Diminution de l'inflammation en présence de brûlures et autres lésions.

PHARMACOCINÉTIQUE

Absorption: Inconnue

Distribution: Inconnue.

Métabolisme et excrétion: Inconnus.

Demi-vie: Composants de *Hypericum* – de 24,8 à 26,5 heures.

Profil temps-action

	DÉBUT D'ACTION	PIC	DURÉE
PO	10 – 14 jours	en l'espace de 4 à 6 semaines	inconnue

CONTRE-INDICATIONS, PRÉCAUTIONS ET MISES EN GARDE

Contre-indications: Grossesse, allaitement, enfants.

Précautions et mises en garde: Antécédents de réactions phototoxiques ■ Maladie d'Alzheimer (risque de psychose) ■ Patients soumis à une anesthésie générale (risque de collapsus cardiovasculaire) ■ Antécédents de tentatives de suicide, de dépression grave, de schizophrénie ou de trouble bipolaire (risque d'épisodes d'hypomanie ou de psychose).

RÉACTIONS INDÉSIRABLES ET EFFETS SECONDAIRES

SNC: étourdissements, agitation, troubles du sommeil.

CV: hypertension.

GI: douleurs abdominales, ballonnements, constipation, sécheresse de la bouche (xérostomie), sensation de plénitude, flatulence, nausées, vomissements.

Tég.: réactions allergiques (urticaire, démangeaison, rash), réactions phototoxiques.

INTERACTIONS

Produit naturel-médicaments: Le millepertuis est un inducteur du cytochrome P450 3A4. Il peut diminuer les concentrations plasmatiques et diminuer l'efficacité de nombreux médicaments comme la **cyclosporine**, la **carbamazépine**, la **phénytoïne**, les **inhibiteurs de l'HMG-CoA réductase** et le **kétoconazole** ■ Ne pas prendre cet agent en même temps que des **antidépresseurs**, la **mépéridine**, la **pentazocine**, le **tramadol**, le **dextrométhorphane** ou d'autres **agents sérotoninergiques** (risque de déclenchement d'un syndrome sérotoninergique) ■ L'**alcool** ou les **antidépresseurs** pris en même temps peuvent accroître le risque d'effets indésirables sur le SNC ■ Le millepertuis peut diminuer l'efficacité et les concentrations sériques de **digoxine** ■ Prévoir un intervalle de 2 semaines entre l'administration du millepertuis et celle d'**inhibiteurs de la MAO**.

VOIES D'ADMINISTRATION ET POSOLOGIES COURANTES

- **PO (adultes)**: *Dépression légère* – 300 mg de millepertuis (extrait normalisé d'hypéricine à 0,3 %), 3 fois par jour ou 250 mg d'extrait d'hypéricine à 0,2 %. *Trouble obsessionnel compulsif* – 450 mg de préparation à libération prolongée, 2 fois par jour.
- **Préparation topique (adultes)**: De 0,2 à 1 mg d'hypéricine totale par jour.

PRÉSENTATION

Préparations par voie orale: Herbe séchée^{VL} ■ Extrait sec hydroalcoolique^{VL} ■ Huile^{VL} ■ Teinture^{VL}.

Préparations topiques: Liquide^{VL} ■ Semi-solide^{VL}.

SOINS INFIRMIERS

ÉVALUATION DE LA SITUATION

Dépression: Évaluer l'état du patient à intervalles réguliers pendant toute la durée du traitement.

Inflammation: Évaluer la peau et les lésions cutanées à intervalles réguliers pendant toute la durée du traitement.

DIAGNOSTICS INFIRMIERS POSSIBLES

- Stratégies d'adaptation inefficaces (Indications).
- Anxiété (Indications).
- Connaissances insuffisantes sur le traitement médicamenteux (Enseignement au patient et à ses proches).

INTERVENTIONS INFIRMIÈRES

- **PO**: Administrer 2 ou 3 fois par jour selon l'indication.

PRODUITS NATURELS

ENSEIGNEMENT AU PATIENT ET À SES PROCHES

- Conseiller au patient de prendre le millepertuis en suivant rigoureusement les recommandations du médecin.
- Recommander au patient atteint de dépression de faire évaluer son état par un professionnel de la santé. Lui expliquer que le traitement classique pourrait être plus efficace en présence de dépression modérée ou grave.
- Conseiller au patient de prévenir le professionnel de la santé avant un traitement ou une intervention chirurgicale qu'il prend du millepertuis.
- Mettre en garde le patient contre l'exposition au soleil et l'inciter à utiliser un écran solaire pour réduire le risque de réactions de photosensibilité.
- Informer le patient que le traitement par le millepertuis dure habituellement de 4 à 6 semaines. Si aucune amélioration n'est constatée, il faudrait envisager un autre traitement.
- Conseiller au patient d'acheter le millepertuis d'un fournisseur ayant bonne réputation, car la qualité du produit et sa teneur ne sont pas uniformes.
- Recommander au patient de ne pas consommer d'alcool pendant qu'il prend du millepertuis.
- PRÉVENIR LE PATIENT QUE LE MILLEPERTUIS PEUT RÉDUIRE L'EFFICACITÉ DE PLUSIEURS MÉDICAMENTS.
- Expliquer au patient que le millepertuis peut potentialiser les effets des sédatifs et les effets secondaires d'autres antidépresseurs. Lui recommander de ne pas en prendre dans les 2 semaines qui précèdent ou qui suivent un traitement par des inhibiteurs de la MAO.
- Recommander au patient de consulter un professionnel de la santé avant de prendre un médicament d'ordonnance ou en vente libre en même temps que du millepertuis.

VÉRIFICATION DE L'EFFICACITÉ THÉRAPEUTIQUE

L'efficacité du traitement peut être démontrée par: la diminution des signes et des symptômes de dépression ou d'anxiété ■ le soulagement de l'inflammation de la peau. ✳

PALMIER NAIN

AUTRES APPELLATIONS:

Sabal, *Sabal palmetto*, chou palmiste, *Serenoa repens*

CLASSIFICATION:

Non attribuée

USAGES COURANTS

Hyperplasie bénigne de la prostate (HBP) ■ Cancer de la prostate (en association avec 7 autres plantes, sous la forme de PC-SPES).

MÉCANISME D'ACTION

Les propriétés anti-androgènes, anti-inflammatoires et antiprolifératives qui s'exercent sur les tissus prostatiques entraînent l'amélioration des symptômes de l'HBP, comme les mictions fréquentes, le retard à la miction, les mictions impérieuses et la nycturie ■ Efficacité comparable à celle du finastéride, mais efficacité moindre que celle de la prazosine. ***Effets thérapeutiques:*** Diminution des symptômes urinaires qui caractérisent l'HBP.

PHARMACOCINÉTIQUE

Absorption: Inconnue

Distribution: Inconnue.

Métabolisme et excrétion: Inconnus.

Demi-vie: Inconnue.

Profil temps-action

	DÉBUT D'ACTION	PIC	DURÉE
PO	1 - 2 mois	inconnu	48 semaines (la durée de traitement la plus longue étudiée)

CONTRE-INDICATIONS, PRÉCAUTIONS ET MISES EN GARDE

Contre-indications: Grossesse et allaitement.

Précautions et mises en garde: Avant une intervention chirurgicale (arrêter l'administration 2 semaines avant pour prévenir les saignements).

RÉACTIONS INDÉSIRABLES ET EFFETS SECONDAIRES

SNC: étourdissements, céphalées.

GI: nausées, vomissements, constipation et diarrhée.

INTERACTIONS

Produit naturel-médicaments: L'effet hormonal peut entraver celui des autres **hormonothérapies** (**testostérone**, **contraceptifs oraux**) ■ Éviter l'usage concomitant d'**antiplaquettaires** ou d'**anticoagulants** (risque accru de saignements).

VOIES D'ADMINISTRATION ET POSOLOGIES COURANTES

- **PO (adultes):** *Extrait lipophile (de 80 à 90 % d'acides gras)* – 160 mg, 2 fois par jour ou 320 mg, 1 fois par jour. *Baies entières* – de 1 à 2 g par jour. *Extrait* *liquide* - de 0,6 à 1,5 mL par jour. *Infusion (l'efficacité est remise en question en raison de la lipophilie des ingrédients actifs)* - 1 tasse, 3 fois par jour. Pour préparer l'infusion, on laisse macérer de 0,5 à 1 g de fruits secs dans 150 mL d'eau bouillante pendant 5 à 10 minutes.

PRÉSENTATION

Extrait lipophile (80-90 % d'acides gras)[VL] ■ Baies entières[VL] ■ Extrait liquide[VL].

SOINS INFIRMIERS

ÉVALUATION DE LA SITUATION

- Évaluer les signes d'HBP (retard à la miction, sensation de vessie incomplètement vidée, interruption du jet, modification du volume et de la force du jet urinaire, « gouttes retardataires », effort pour amorcer le jet, dysurie, envie impérieuse d'uriner) avant le traitement et à intervalles réguliers pendant toute sa durée.
- On recommande des touchers rectaux avant le traitement et pendant toute sa durée pour évaluer la taille de la prostate.

DIAGNOSTICS INFIRMIERS POSSIBLES

- Élimination urinaire altérée (Indications).
- Connaissances insuffisantes sur le traitement médicamenteux (Enseignement au patient et à ses proches).

INTERVENTIONS INFIRMIÈRES

- Administrer cet agent après les repas pour réduire les effets GI.

ENSEIGNEMENT AU PATIENT ET À SES PROCHES

- Recommander au patient de commencer le traitement par cet agent seulement après évaluation de son état par un professionnel de la santé qui assurera un suivi constant.
- Informer le patient que le palmier nain ne modifie pas la taille de la prostate, mais qu'il devrait soulager les symptômes de l'HBP.
- Conseiller au patient de prendre cet agent avec des aliments pour une réduction des effets GI et une meilleure tolérance.

VÉRIFICATION DE L'EFFICACITÉ THÉRAPEUTIQUE

L'efficacité du traitement peut être démontrée par: la diminution des symptômes urinaires de l'HBP.

PANAX GINSENG,

voir Ginseng.

PIPER METHYSTICUM,

voir Kava-kava.

SAMe

AUTRES APPELLATIONS:

Adémétionine, S-adénosylméthionine

CLASSIFICATION:

Antidépresseur

Grossesse – catégorie inconnue

USAGES COURANTS

Traitement de la dépression. **Autres usages**: prise en charge de l'arthrose, de la fibromyalgie, des maladies hépatiques et des migraines.

MÉCANISME D'ACTION

L'agent pourrait contribuer à la production, l'activation et le métabolisme de divers acides aminés, phospholipides, hormones et neurotransmetteurs ■ Il pourrait stimuler la croissance et la réparation du cartilage articulaire. ***Effets thérapeutiques:*** Soulagement de la dépression ■ Effets analgésiques et anti-inflammatoires pouvant améliorer les symptômes d'arthrose.

PHARMACOCINÉTIQUE

Absorption: Inconnue.

Distribution: Inconnue.

Métabolisme et excrétion: Métabolisme hépatique.

Demi-vie: 100 minutes.

Profil temps-action

	Début d'action	Pic	Durée
PO (dépression)	1 - 2 semaines	inconnu	inconnue
PO (arthrose)	30 jours	inconnu	inconnue

CONTRE-INDICATIONS, PRÉCAUTIONS ET MISES EN GARDE

Contre-indications: Hypersensibilité.

Précautions et mises en garde: Grossesse, allaitement ou enfants (l'innocuité de l'agent n'a pas été établie) ■ Trouble bipolaire (risque d'induction d'accès de manie)

- Maladie de Parkinson (risque d'aggravation des symptômes).

RÉACTIONS INDÉSIRABLES ET EFFETS SECONDAIRES

SNC: agitation, étourdissements, légère insomnie, réactions maniaques (chez les patients atteints de trouble bipolaire).

GI: vomissements, diarrhée, flatulence.

INTERACTIONS

Produit naturel-médicaments: Ne pas prendre cet agent en même temps que des **antidépresseurs**, la **mépéridine**, la **pentazocine**, le **tramadol** et le **dextrométhorphane** ou d'autres **agents sérotoninergiques** (risque d'effets sérotoninergiques additifs) ▪ L'usage concomitant risque de réduire l'efficacité de la **lévodopa** et d'aggraver les symptômes de la maladie de Parkinson ▪ Ne pas prendre l'agent en même temps que des **inhibiteurs de la MAO** (ne pas prendre le SAMe dans les 2 semaines qui précèdent ou qui suivent).

Produit naturel-produits naturels: Ne pas prendre l'agent en même temps que des produits naturels qui élèvent les concentrations de sérotonine, comme le **l-tryptophane** et le **millepertuis**.

VOIES D'ADMINISTRATION ET POSOLOGIES COURANTES

- **PO (adultes)**: *Dépression* – 200 mg, 1 ou 2 fois par jour, en augmentant la dose en l'espace de 2 semaines (intervalle: de 400 à 1 600 mg/jour). *Maladie hépatique* – de 1 200 à 1 600 mg/jour. *Arthrose* – 200 mg, 3 fois par jour. *Fibromyalgie* – 800 mg/jour.

PRÉSENTATION

Comprimés [VL].

SOINS INFIRMIERS

ÉVALUATION DE LA SITUATION

- Évaluer l'état mental du patient avant le traitement et pendant toute sa durée pour déceler les symptômes de dépression; recommander au patient atteint de dépression de consulter un professionnel de la santé.
- Évaluer les douleurs et la fatigue avant le traitement et pendant toute sa durée.

DIAGNOSTICS INFIRMIERS POSSIBLES

- Stratégies d'adaptation inefficaces (Indications).
- Connaissances insuffisantes sur le traitement médicamenteux (Enseignement au patient et à ses proches).

INTERVENTIONS INFIRMIÈRES

- Seules les préparations à enrobage entérique sont recommandées en raison de problèmes de biodisponibilité.

PO: La dose initiale devrait être de 200 mg, 1 ou 2 fois par jour, pour réduire les troubles gastro-intestinaux. On peut augmenter la dose en l'espace de 1 ou 2 semaines, selon la réponse du patient et sa tolérance.

ENSEIGNEMENT AU PATIENT ET À SES PROCHES

- Inciter le patient à prendre le SAMe en respectant rigoureusement les recommandations du médecin.
- Conseiller au patient de choisir de préférence le sel butane-disulfonate de SAMe, car cette préparation est plus stable.

VÉRIFICATION DE L'EFFICACITÉ THÉRAPEUTIQUE

L'efficacité du traitement peut être démontrée par: la diminution des symptômes de dépression ▪ le soulagement des symptômes d'arthrose.

VALÉRIANE

AUTRES APPELLATIONS:
Herbe de Saint-Georges, valériane sauvage, herbe aux chats, herbe à la meurtrie, valériane officinale

CLASSIFICATION:
Anxiolytique, hypnosédatif

USAGES COURANTS

Insomnie ▪ Anxiété.

MÉCANISME D'ACTION

Augmentation possible des concentrations de GABA, un neurotransmetteur qui inhibe le SNC. ***Effets thérapeutiques:*** Amélioration de la qualité du sommeil.

PHARMACOCINÉTIQUE

Absorption: Inconnue

Distribution: Inconnue.

Métabolisme et excrétion: Inconnus.

Demi-vie: Inconnue.

Profil temps-action

	DÉBUT D'ACTION	PIC	DURÉE
PO	30 - 60 min	2 h	inconnue

CONTRE-INDICATIONS, PRÉCAUTIONS ET MISES EN GARDE

Contre-indications: Grossesse et allaitement.
Précautions et mises en garde: Consommation d'alcool (risque d'effets sédatifs additifs).

RÉACTIONS INDÉSIRABLES ET EFFETS SECONDAIRES

SNC: étourdissements, céphalées.
Divers: symptômes de sevrage ressemblant à ceux du sevrage des benzodiazépines lors de l'arrêt du traitement après un usage prolongé.

INTERACTIONS

Produit naturel-médicaments: Dépression additive du SNC en cas d'usage concomitant d'**alcool**, d'**antihistaminiques**, d'**hypnosédatifs** et d'autres **dépresseurs du SNC** ▪ Les préparations contenant de l'alcool peuvent interagir avec le **disulfirame** et le **métronidazole**.
Produit naturel-produits naturels: Risque d'effets sédatifs additifs lors de l'usage concomitant d'autres **produits naturels ayant des effets sédatifs**, comme le **kava**, le **l-tryptophane,** la **mélatonine,** le **SAMe** et le **millepertuis.**

VOIES D'ADMINISTRATION ET POSOLOGIES COURANTES

- **PO (adultes):** *Infusion* – 1 tasse, de 1 à 5 fois par jour. Pour préparer l'infusion, laisser macérer de 2 à 3 g de racine dans 150 mL d'eau bouillante pendant 5 à 10 minutes et filtrer. *Teinture* – de 1 à 3 mL, de 1 à 5 fois par jour. *Extrait* – de 400 à 900 mg, jusqu'à 2 heures avant l'heure du coucher, ou de 300 à 450 mg, en 3 doses fractionnées.

PRÉSENTATION

Capsules^{VL} ▪ Extrait^{VL} ▪ Infusion^{VL} ▪ Teinture^{VL}.

SOINS INFIRMIERS

ÉVALUATION DE LA SITUATION

- Évaluer le degré d'anxiété et de sédation avant le traitement et à intervalles réguliers pendant toute sa durée.
- Évaluer la structure du sommeil.
- Évaluer la réponse chez les patients âgés, car la somnolence et la perte d'équilibre peuvent les exposer à un risque important d'accidents.

DIAGNOSTICS INFIRMIERS POSSIBLES

- Anxiété (Indications).
- Risque d'accident (Effets secondaires).

INTERVENTIONS INFIRMIÈRES

- Si le patient prend la valériane en raison de ses propriétés d'hypnosédatif, l'administrer 1 ou 2 heures avant l'heure du coucher.
- Administrer par voie orale, de 3 à 5 fois par jour pour soulager l'anxiété.

ENSEIGNEMENT AU PATIENT ET À SES PROCHES

- Conseiller au patient de ne pas prendre d'autres médicaments ou plantes médicinales ayant des effets sédatifs, car une telle association augmentera la somnolence et la sédation.
- Conseiller au patient de ne pas conduire et de ne pas faire fonctionner de machines lourdes après avoir pris de la valériane.
- Conseiller à la patiente de ne pas prendre de la valériane si elle est enceinte ou si elle allaite.
- Conseiller au patient de ne pas s'engager dans des activités qui exigent sa vigilance jusqu'à ce que sa réponse à cette plante médicinale soit connue.
- Prévenir le patient qu'il y a risque de dépendance et de symptômes de sevrage en cas d'usage prolongé.
- Recommander au patient de ne pas consommer d'alcool pendant qu'il prend de la valériane.
- Encourager le patient d'éliminer les stimulants comme la caféine et de dormir dans un environnement propice à un sommeil réparateur.

VÉRIFICATION DE L'EFFICACITÉ THÉRAPEUTIQUE

L'efficacité du traitement peut être démontrée par: la diminution de l'anxiété ▪ l'amélioration du sommeil, avec le sentiment de s'être bien reposé, sans somnolence au réveil.

ZINGIBER OFFICINALE,

voir Gingembre.

PRODUITS NATURELS

IBLIOGRAPHIE

American Hospital Formulary Service. *Drug Information 2007*, American Society of Hospital Pharmacists, Bethesda, MD, 2007.

American Pain Society. *Principles of Analgesic Use in the Treatment of Acute Pain and Cancer Pain*, 5e éd., American Pain Society, Skokie, IL, 2003.

Association des pharmaciens du Canada. *Compendium des produits et spécialités pharmaceutiques* (CPS), en ligne. www.e-therapeutics.com

Bédard, M., M. Guidice, J. Mackenzie *et al. Manuel sur la pharmacothérapie parentérale.* 27e éd., Hôpital d'Ottawa, 2006.

Blumenthal, M., *et al. The Complete German Commission E Monographs: Therapeutic Guide to Herbal Medicines*, Integrative Medical Communications, Boston, 1998.

Briggs, G.G., R.K. Freeman et S.J. Yaffe. *Drugs in Pregnancy and Lactation: A Reference Guide to Fetal and Neonatal Risk*, 7e éd., Lippincott Williams & Wilkins, Philadelphia, PA, 2005.

Drug Facts and Comparisons. Facts and Comparisons, a Wolters Kluwer Company, St. Louis, 2005.

Fetrow, C.W., et J.R. Avila. *Professional's Handbook of Complementary & Alternative Medicines*, 3e éd., Lippincott Williams & Wilkins, Philadelphia, PA, 2004.

Furger, P. *Médecine interne. Du symptôme au diagnostic*, Éditions D & F, Québec, 2005.

Jellin, J.M., F. Batz et K. Hitchens. *Pharmacist's Letter/Prescriber's Letter Natural Medicines Comprehensive Database*, Therapeutic Research Faculty, Stockton, CA, 1999.

Jonas, W.B., J.S. Levin (dir.). *Essentials of Complementary and Alternative Medicine*, Lippincott Williams & Wilkins, a Wolters Kluwer Company, Baltimore and Philadelphia, 1999.

Kuhn, M.A., et D. Winston. *Herbal Therapy and Supplements: A Scientific and Traditional Approach*, Lippincott, Philadelphia, 2001

Lacy, C.F., L.L. Armstrong, M.P. Goldman et L.L. Lance. *Drug Information Handbook*, 15e éd., Hudson, Lexi-Comp et American Pharmaceutical Association, 2007.

Mahan, L.K., et S. Escott-Stump. *Krause's Food, Nutrition, and Diet Therapy*, 9e éd., W.B. Saunders, Philadelphia, 1996.

McCaffery, M., et C. Pasero. *Pain: Clinical Manual*, 2e éd., Mosby-Yearbook, St Louis, 1999.

MICROMEDEX® Healthcare Series. www.thomsonhc.com

Monographies officielles des médicaments ne figurant pas dans le CPS ni dans le CNP.

NANDA International. *Diagnostics infirmiers — Définitions et classification 2005-2006*, Paris, Masson, 2006.

National Institutes of Health Warren Grant Magnuson Clinical Center. *Drug—Nutrient Interactions*, Bethesda, MD, 2003. http://www. cc.nih.gov/ccc/supplements/intro.html

National Kidney Foundation. *A-Z Guide for High Potassium Foods*, National Kidney Foundation, 2005.

Phelps, S.J., et E.B. Hak. *Pediatric Injectable Drugs*, 7e éd., American Society of Health-System Pharmacists, Bethesda, MD, 2004.

Panel on Antiretroviral Guidelines for Adult and Adolescents. *Guidelines for the use of antiretroviral agents in HIV-infected adults and adolescents*, Department of Health and Human Services. 10 octobre 2006; 1-113. Disponible à l'adresse http://www.aidsinfo.nih.gov/ContentFiles/AdultandAdolescentsGL.pdf. Consulté le 1er février 2007.

PDR for Herbal Medicines, Medical Economics Company, Montvale, NJ, 1998.

Physicians' Desk Reference (PDR). Medical Economics Company, Montvale, NJ, 2005.

Polovich, M., J.M. White et L.O. Kelleher. *Chemotherapy and Biotherapy Guidelines and Recommendations for Practice*, 2e éd., Oncology Nursing Society, Pittsburgh, 2005.

Regroupement des pharmaciens en soins palliatifs. *Guide pratique de soins palliatifs : gestion de la douleur et autres symptômes*, 3e éd., APES, Montréal, 2002.

Schnell, Z., A.M.Van Leewan et T. Kranpitz. *Davis's Comprehensive Book of Laboratory and Diagnostic Tests with Nursing Implications*, FA Davis Company, Philadelphia, PA, 2003.

Taketomo, C.K., J.H. Hodding et D.M. Kraus. *Pediatric Dosage Handbook,* 12e éd., Hudson, Lexi-Comp et American Pharmaceutical Association, 2005.

Trissel, L.A. *Handbook on Injectable Drugs*, 13e ed., American Society of Hospital Pharmacists, Bethesda, MD, 2005.

USP Dispensing Information (USP-DI). *Advice for the Patient*, Volume II, 25e éd., United States Pharmacopeial Convention, Rockville, MD, 2005.

USP Dispensing Information (USP-DI). *Drug Information for the Health Care Professional,* Volume I, 25e éd., Micromedex, Rockville, MD, 2005.

ANNEXES

ANNEXE A
Analgésiques opioïdes

Les doses équianalgésiques ci-dessous sont données à titre indicatif, car l'effet peut varier d'une personne à l'autre. Noter que pour obtenir un soulagement équivalent de la douleur, la dose par voie orale doit être environ 2 ou 3 fois plus élevée que la dose parentérale. Ce rapport est surtout valable en cas d'administrations répétées, mais il peut aussi servir de référence en présence d'une douleur aiguë.

DOSES ÉQUIANALGÉSIQUES DES ANALGÉSIQUES OPIOÏDES

MÉDICAMENT	VOIE	DOSE ÉQUIANALGÉSIQUE[1] (mg)	DURÉE (h)	DEMI-VIE PLASMATIQUE (h)	REMARQUES
AGONISTES					
MORPHINE	IM PO IR	10 20 – 30 30	4 – 5 4 – 5	2 – 4 (adultes)	Agent de référence. Le premier choix dans plusieurs circonstances.
CODÉINE	IM PO	120 200	4 4	2,5 – 4	
OXYCODONE	PO	10 – 15	3 – 6	2 – 4	Présentation parentérale inexistante.
HYDROMORPHONE	IM PO	2 4 – 6	4 – 5 4 – 5	2 – 4	
MÉPÉRIDINE	IM PO	75 – 100 200	2 – 5 2 – 5	3 – 5 (adultes)	**Mise en garde :** USAGE DÉCONSEILLÉ POUR SOULAGER LA DOULEUR CANCÉREUSE OU CHRONIQUE, en raison de l'accumulation du métabolite actif toxique, la norméperidine, qui entraîne la stimulation du SNC.
MÉTHADONE	PO	Voir les références spécialisées en soins palliatifs ou en traitement de la douleur chronique	jusqu'à 24	15 – 30	Préparation orale très puissante ; il faut adapter très soigneusement la dose initiale pour éviter l'accumulation du médicament. Agent utilisé aussi pour les désintoxications.

AGONISTES-ANTAGONISTES					
PENTAZOCINE	IM PO	60 180	2 - 3 2 - 3	2 - 5	Usage déconseillé pour le soulagement de la douleur cancéreuse ou chronique ; les effets psychosomimétiques augmentent avec la dose ; risque de symptômes de sevrage chez les patients physicodépendants.
NALBUPHINE	IM	10	3 - 6	5	Effets psychosomimétiques moins graves que ceux entraînés par la pentazocine ; risque de symptômes de sevrage chez les patients physicodépendants.
BUTORPHANOL	nasale				Ce médicament est commercialisé seulement en préparation nasale au Canada. Effets psychosomimétiques ; risque de symptômes de sevrage chez les patients physicodépendants.

1. Selon des études qui visaient à établir la puissance relative de chacun des médicaments énumérés, en comparant les effets d'une seule dose à ceux de la morphine. Par exemple, 10 mg de **morphine** IM procure une analgésie approximativement équivalente à 200 mg de **codéine** PO.

Attention : certaines doses PO équianalgésiques sont beaucoup trop élevées pour être administrées en une seule fois. Consulter la monographie de chaque produit pour connaître la dose initiale à administrer sans danger.

Ce tableau ne tient pas compte de la tolérance croisée incomplète entre les différents opioïdes : certains ajustements de doses seront nécessaires.

Source : Adaptation de P.G. Fine, « Cancer Pain : Assessment and Management », *Hospital Formulary*, vol. 22, n° 936, 1987.

Source complémentaire : *Guide pratique de soins palliatifs : gestion de la douleur et autres symptômes*, 3e édition, APES, Montréal, 2002.

Les doses équianalgésiques du fentanyl transdermique peuvent être calculées à l'aide du tableau suivant.

QUANTITÉ TOTALE DE MORPHINE PAR JOUR		TIMBRE DE FENTANYL
Voie orale	Voie parentérale	(µg/h)
50	25	25

Le tableau fourni avec les timbres transdermiques est peu utilisé en pratique, car il est moins précis. En effet, il permet seulement de passer de la morphine au fentanyl en timbre, car il n'a pas été conçu pour déterminer les doses de morphine chez une personne recevant le fentanyl transdermique.

Ces méthodes sont données à titre indicatif et des adaptations sont souvent nécessaires, car les doses équivalentes de fentanyl transdermique varient beaucoup d'une personne à l'autre. On doit donc observer plus étroitement les personnes chez lesquelles on substitue le fentanyl à la morphine afin d'évaluer l'intensité de la douleur et de déceler les effets indésirables.

ANNEXE B

Résumé des règlements concernant les stupéfiants, drogues contrôlées, benzodiazépines et autres substances ciblées

CLASSIFICATION ET DESCRIPTION	FORMALITÉS LÉGALES
Stupéfiants[1] ■ 1 stupéfiant (p. ex., cocaïne, codéine, hydromorphone, kétamine, morphine) ■ 1 stupéfiant + 1 ingrédient actif non stupéfiant (p. ex., Cophylac, Empracet-30, Tylenol No. 4) ■ Toutes formes injectables de stupéfiants (p. ex., fentanyl, péthidine) ■ Tout produit contenant: diamorphine (hôpitaux seulement), hydrocodone, oxycodone, méthadone ou pentazocine ■ Dextropropoxyphène, propoxyphène (seul) (p. ex., Darvon-N, 642)	■ Ordonnances écrites obligatoires. ■ Ordonnances verbales interdites. ■ Renouvellements interdits. ■ Les ordonnances écrites peuvent être exécutées partiellement si le médecin l'indique. ■ Pour les ordonnances exécutées partiellement, on devra en rédiger des copies avec référence à l'ordonnance originale. Indiquer sur l'ordonnance originale: le nouveau numéro de l'ordonnance, la date de l'exécution partielle, la quantité fournie et les initiales du pharmacien. ■ Aucun transfert d'ordonnances n'est autorisé. ■ Maintenir les registres nécessaires et conserver tous les documents relatifs à toutes les transactions pendant un minimum de 2 ans, de manière à en permettre la vérification. ■ Rapports de ventes obligatoires, sauf pour le dextropropoxyphène et le propoxyphène. ■ Signaler dans les 10 jours toute perte ou vol de stupéfiants au Bureau des substances contrôlées, à l'adresse indiquée sur les formulaires fournis à cette fin.
Préparations de stupéfiants[1] ■ Stupéfiants d'ordonnance verbale: 1 stupéfiant + 2 ingrédients actifs non stupéfiants ou plus dans une dose thérapeutique reconnue (p. ex., Fiorinal-C1/4, Fiorinal-C1/2, Robitussin AC, 282, 292, 692, Tylenol No. 2 et No. 3) ■ Composés de codéine exonérés: contiennent jusqu'à 8 mg de codéine/ dose solide ou 20 mg/ 30 mL de liquide + 2 ingrédients actifs non stupéfiants ou plus (p. ex., Atasol-8)	■ Ordonnances écrites ou verbales autorisées. ■ Renouvellements interdits. ■ Les ordonnances écrites ou verbales peuvent être exécutées partiellement si le médecin l'indique. ■ Pour les ordonnances exécutées partiellement, on devra en rédiger des copies avec référence à l'ordonnance originale. Indiquer sur l'ordonnance originale: le nouveau numéro de l'ordonnance, la date de l'exécution partielle, la quantité fournie et les initiales du pharmacien. ■ Aucun transfert d'ordonnances n'est autorisé. ■ Pour l'exécution des ordonnances de composés exonérés, suivre les mêmes règlements que pour les stupéfiants d'ordonnance verbale. ■ Maintenir les registres nécessaires et conserver tous les documents relatifs à toutes les transactions pendant un minimum de 2 ans, de manière à en permettre la vérification. ■ Rapports de ventes non sollicités. ■ Signaler dans les 10 jours toute perte ou vol de stupéfiants au Bureau des substances contrôlées, à l'adresse indiquée sur les formulaires fournis à cette fin.
Drogues contrôlées[1] ■ Partie I p. ex., amphétamines (Dexedrine, Adderall XR) méthylphénidate (Biphentin, Concerta, Ritalin) pentobarbital (Nembutal) préparations: 1 drogue contrôlée + 1 drogue active non contrôlée ou plus (Bellergal Spacetabs)	■ Ordonnance écrites ou verbales autorisées. ■ Renouvellements des ordonnances verbales interdits. ■ Renouvellements des ordonnances écrites autorisés, si le médecin a inscrit le nombre de renouvellements et les dates ou les intervalles entre les renouvellements. ■ Les ordonnances écrites ou verbales peuvent être exécutées partiellement si le médecin l'indique. ■ Pour les renouvellements et pour les ordonnances exécutées partiellement, on devra en rédiger des copies avec référence à l'ordonnance originale. Indiquer sur l'ordonnance originale: le nouveau numéro de l'ordonnance, la date du renouvellement ou de l'exécution partielle, la quantité fournie et les initiales du pharmacien.

Drogues contrôlées[1] (suite)	▪ Aucun transfert d'ordonnances n'est autorisé. ▪ Maintenir les registres nécessaires et conserver tous les documents relatifs à toutes les transactions pendant un minimum de 2 ans, de manière à en permettre la vérification. ▪ Rapports de ventes obligatoires, sauf pour les préparations. ▪ Signaler dans les 10 jours toute perte ou vol de stupéfiants au Bureau des substances contrôlées, à l'adresse indiquée sur les formulaires fournis à cette fin.
▪ Partie II p. ex., barbituriques (phénobarbital) butorphanol diéthylpropion (Tenuate) nalbuphine (Nubain) phentermine (Ionamin) préparations: 1 drogue contrôlée + 1 ingrédient actif non contrôlé ou plus (Fiorinal) ▪ Partie III p. ex., stéroïdes anabolisants androgènes (méthyltestostérone, décanoate de nandrolone)	▪ Ordonnances écrites ou verbales autorisées. ▪ Renouvellements autorisés pour les ordonnances écrites ou verbales si le médecin indique, par écrit ou verbalement (au moment d'émettre l'ordonnance), le nombre de renouvellements et les dates ou les intervalles entre les renouvellements. ▪ Les ordonnances écrites ou verbales peuvent être exécutées partiellement si le médecin l'indique. ▪ Pour les renouvellements ou pour les ordonnances exécutées partiellement, on devra en rédiger des copies avec référence à l'ordonnance originale. Indiquer sur l'ordonnance originale: le nouveau numéro de l'ordonnance, la date du renouvellement ou de l'exécution partielle, la quantité fournie et les initiales du pharmacien. ▪ Aucun transfert d'ordonnances n'est autorisé. ▪ Maintenir les registres nécessaires et conserver tous les documents relatifs à toutes les transactions pendant un minimum de 2 ans, de manière à en permettre la vérification. ▪ Rapports de ventes non sollicités. ▪ Signaler dans les 10 jours toute perte ou vol de drogues contrôlées au Bureau des substances contrôlées, à l'adresse indiquée sur les formulaires fournis à cette fin.
Benzodiazépines et autres substances ciblées[1] p. ex., alprazolam (Xanax) bromazépam (Lectopam) chlordiazépoxide (Librium) clobazam (Frisium) lorazépam (Ativan) méprobamate oxazépam (Serax)	▪ Ordonnances écrites et verbales autorisées. ▪ Renouvellements autorisés pour les ordonnances verbales si le médecin l'indique et si moins de 1 an s'est écoulé depuis la date d'émission de l'ordonnance. ▪ Exécutions partielles autorisées selon les instructions du médecin. ▪ Lors de renouvellements ou d'exécutions partielles, inscrire sur le registre les renseignements suivants: la date du renouvellement ou de l'exécution partielle, le numéro de l'ordonnance, la quantité fournie et les initiales du pharmacien. ▪ Transfert d'ordonnances autorisé, sauf s'il s'agit d'un deuxième transfert. ▪ Maintenir les registres nécessaires et conserver tous les documents relatifs à toutes les transactions pendant un minimum de 2 ans, de manière à en permettre la vérification. ▪ Rapports de ventes non sollicités. ▪ Signaler dans les 10 jours toute perte ou vol de benzodiazépines et autres substances ciblées au Bureau des substances contrôlées, à l'adresse indiquée sur les formulaires fournis à cette fin.

1. Les produits sont indiqués à titre d'exemple.

Source: Association des pharmaciens du Canada, *Compendium des produits et spécialités pharmaceutiques (CPS)*, 42e édition, 2007, p. A1-A2.

ANNEXE C
Tableaux des vitesses de perfusion de certains médicaments

DOBUTAMINE

Exemples de dilutions possibles: 250 mg/1 000 mL = 250 µg/mL
250 mg/500 mL = 500 µg/mL
250 mg/250 mL = 1 000 µg/mL

Pour calculer la vitesse de perfusion en mL/min, multiplier le poids (kg) du patient par la vitesse en mL/kg/min.
Pour calculer la vitesse de perfusion en mL/h, multiplier le poids (kg) du patient par la vitesse en mL/kg/min × 60.

Vitesses de perfusion de la dobutamine (mL/kg/min) à diverses concentrations

	Concentrations		
Dose (µg/kg/min)	**250 µg/mL**	**500 µg/mL**	**1 000 µg/mL**
2,5 µg/kg/min	0,01 mL/kg/min	0,005 mL/kg/min	0,0025 mL/kg/min
5 µg/kg/min	0,02 mL/kg/min	0,01 mL/kg/min	0,005 mL/kg/min
7,5 µg/kg/min	0,03 mL/kg/min	0,015 mL/kg/min	0,0075 mL/kg/min
10 µg/kg/min	0,04 mL/kg/min	0,02 mL/kg/min	0,01 mL/kg/min
12,5 µg/kg/min	0,05 mL/kg/min	0,025 mL/kg/min	0,0125 mL/kg/min
15 µg/kg/min	0,06 mL/kg/min	0,03 mL/kg/min	0,015 mL/kg/min

DOPAMINE

Exemples de dilutions possibles: 200 mg/500 mL = 400 µg/mL
400 mg/500 mL = 800 µg/mL
800 mg/500 mL = 1 600 µg/mL

Pour calculer la vitesse de perfusion en mL/min, multiplier le poids (kg) du patient par la vitesse en mL/kg/min.
Pour calculer la vitesse de perfusion en mL/h, multiplier le poids (kg) du patient par la vitesse en mL/kg/min × 60.

Vitesses de perfusion de la dopamine (mL/kg/min) à diverses concentrations

	Concentrations		
Dose (µg/kg/min)	**400 µg/mL**	**800 µg/mL**	**1 600 µg/mL[1]**
2 µg/kg/min	0,005 mL/kg/min	0,0025 mL/kg/min	0,00125 mL/kg/min
5 µg/kg/min	0,0125 mL/kg/min	0,00625 mL/kg/min	0,003125 mL/kg/min
10 µg/kg/min	0,025 mL/kg/min	0,0125 mL/kg/min	0,00625 mL/kg/min
20 µg/kg/min	0,05 mL/kg/min	0,025 mL/kg/min	0,0125 mL/kg/min
30 µg/kg/min	0,075 mL/kg/min	0,0375 mL/kg/min	0,01875 mL/kg/min
40 µg/kg/min	0,1 mL/kg/min	0,05 mL/kg/min	0,025 mL/kg/min
50 µg/kg/min	0,125 mL/kg/min	0,0625 mL/kg/min	0,03125 mL/kg/min

1. Concentration appropriée chez les patients dont l'apport hydrique est restreint.

ESMOLOL

Dilution : 5 g/500 mL ou autre pour obtenir une concentration finale de 10 mg/mL.

	Poids du patient					
	50 kg	60 kg	70 kg	80 kg	90 kg	100 kg
Dose d'attaque (mL) (administrer en 1 min)	2,5 mL	3 mL	3,5 mL	4 mL	4,5 mL	5 mL

Vitesses de perfusion de l'esmolol
Concentration = 10 mg/mL

	Poids du patient					
Dose de perfusion	**50 kg**	**60 kg**	**70 kg**	**80 kg**	**90 kg**	**100 kg**
50 µg/kg/min	15 mL/h	18 mL/h	21 mL/h	24 mL/h	27 mL/h	30 mL/h
75 µg/kg/min	22,5 mL/h	27 mL/h	31,5 mL/h	36 mL/h	40,5 mL/h	45 mL/h
100 µg/kg/min	30 mL/h	36 mL/h	42 mL/h	48 mL/h	54 mL/h	60 mL/h
125 µg/kg/min	37,5 mL/h	45 mL/h	52,5 mL/h	60 mL/h	67,5 mL/h	75 mL/h
150 µg/kg/min	45 mL/h	54 mL/h	63 mL/h	72 mL/h	81 mL/h	90 mL/h
175 µg/kg/min	52,5 mL/h	63 mL/h	73,5 mL/h	84 mL/h	94,5 mL/h	105 mL/h
200 µg/kg/min	60 mL/h	72 mL/h	84 mL/h	96 mL/h	108 mL/h	120 mL/h

HÉPARINE

Exemple de dilution possible : 20 000 unités/1 000 mL = 20 unités/mL.

Dose d'attaque : de 5 000 à 10 000 unités sous forme de bolus IV (chez l'adulte).

Vitesses de perfusion de l'héparine (mL/h)
Concentration = 20 unités/mL

Dose (unités/h)	Dose (mL/h)
500 unités/h	25 mL/h
750 unités/h	37,5 mL/h
1 000 unités/h	50 mL/h
1 250 unités/h	62,5 mL/h
1 500 unités/h	75 mL/h
1 750 unités/h	87,5 mL/h
2 000 unités/h	100 mL/h

LIDOCAÏNE

Exemples de dilutions possibles: 1 g/1 000 mL = 1 mg/mL
1 g/500 mL = 2 mg/mL
1 g/250 mL = 4 mg/mL
2 g/250 mL = 8 mg/mL

Dose d'attaque: de 50 à 100 mg à une vitesse de 25 à 50 mg/min.

Vitesses de perfusion de la lidocaïne (mL/h)

	Concentrations			
Dose (mg/min)	**1 mg/mL**	**2 mg/mL**	**4 mg/mL**	**8 mg/mL**
1 mg/min	60 mL/h	30 mL/h	15 mL/h	7,5 mL/h
2 mg/min	120 mL/h	60 mL/h	30 mL/h	15 mL/h
3 mg/min	180 mL/h	90 mL/h	45 mL/h	22,5 mL/h
4 mg/min	240 mL/h	120 mL/h	60 mL/h	30 mL/h

MILRINONE

Dilutions possibles: 20 mg/200 mL (soit 180 mL de diluant + 20 mL de milrinone) = 100 µg/mL
20 mg/133 mL (soit 113 mL de diluant + 20 mL de milrinone) = 150 µg/mL
20 mg/100 mL (soit 80 mL de diluant + 20 mL de milrinone) = 200 µg/mL

Dose d'attaque: 50 µg/kg, administrée en 10 minutes.

Pour calculer la vitesse de perfusion en mL/min, multiplier le poids (kg) du patient par la dose en mL/kg/min.

Pour calculer la vitesse de perfusion en mL/h, multiplier le poids (kg) du patient par la dose en mL/kg/min × 60.

Dose d'attaque administrée en 10 minutes

	Poids du patient					
Dose	**50 kg**	**60 kg**	**70 kg**	**80 kg**	**90 kg**	**100 kg**
Dose d'attaque (mg)	2,5 mg	3,0 mg	3,5 mg	4,0 mg	4,5 mg	5,0 mg

Vitesses de perfusion de la milrinone (mL/kg/min)

	Concentrations		
Dose (µg/kg/min)	**100 µg/mL**	**150 µg/mL**	**200 µg/mL**
0,375 µg/kg/min	0,00375 mL/kg/min	0,0025 mL/kg/min	0,001875 mL/kg/min
0,4 µg/kg/min	0,004 mL/kg/min	0,00267 mL/kg/min	0,002 mL/kg/min
0,5 µg/kg/min	0,005 mL/kg/min	0,0033 mL/kg/min	0,0025 mL/kg/min
0,6 µg/kg/min	0,006 mL/kg/min	0,004 mL/kg/min	0,003 mL/kg/min
0,7 µg/kg/min	0,007 mL/kg/min	0,00467 mL/kg/min	0,0035 mL/kg/min
0,75 µg/kg/min	0,0075 mL/kg/min	0,005 mL/kg/min	0,00375 mL/kg/min

NITROGLYCÉRINE

Dilutions possibles : 5 mg/100 mL (25 mg/500 mL, 50 mg/1 000 mL) = 50 µg/mL
25 mg/250 mL (50 mg/500mL, 100 mg/1 000mL) = 100 µg/mL
50 mg/250 mL (100 mg/500 mL, 200 mg/1 000 mL) = 200 µg/mL

Remarque : puisque les divers produits sont présentés dans des solutions à diverses concentrations, il faudrait les administrer par les tubulures de perfusion appropriées. Les nécessaires de perfusion standard en chlorure de polyvinyle (PVC) peuvent adsorber jusqu'à 80 % de la nitroglycérine en solution. Utiliser exclusivement des flacons en verre ou des sacs de plastique et des tubulures conçues pour l'administration de la nitroglycérine.

Vitesses de perfusion de la nitroglycérine (mL/h)

	Concentrations		
Dose (µg/min)	**50 µg/mL**	**100 µg/mL**	**200 µg/mL**
2,5 µg/min	3 mL/h	1,5 mL/h	0,75 mL/h
5 µg/min	6 mL/h	3 mL/h	1,5 mL/h
10 µg/min	12 mL/h	6 mL/h	3 mL/h
15 µg/min	18 mL/h	9 mL/h	4,5 mL/h
20 µg/min	24 mL/h	12 mL/h	6 mL/h
30 µg/min	36 mL/h	18 mL/h	9 mL/h
40 µg/min	48 mL/h	24 mL/h	12 mL/h
50 µg/min	60 mL/h	30 mL/h	15 mL/h
60 µg/min	72 mL/h	36 mL/h	18 mL/h

NITROPRUSSIATE

Dilutions possibles : 50 mg/1 000 mL = 50 µg/mL
100 mg/1 000 mL = 100 µg/mL
200 mg/1 000 mL = 200 µg/mL

Pour calculer la vitesse de perfusion en mL/min, multiplier le poids (kg) du patient par la dose en mL/kg/min.
Pour calculer la vitesse de perfusion en mL/h, multiplier le poids (kg) du patient par la dose en mL/kg/min x 60.

Vitesses de perfusion du nitroprussiate (mL/kg/min)

	Concentrations		
Dose (µg/kg/min)	**50 µg/mL**	**100 µg/mL**	**200 µg/mL**
0,5 µg/kg/min	0,01 mL/kg/min	0,005 mL/kg/min	0,0025 mL/kg/min
1 µg/kg/min	0,02 mL/kg/min	0,01 mL/kg/min	0,005 mL/kg/min
2 µg/kg/min	0,04 mL/kg/min	0,02 mL/kg/min	0,01 mL/kg/min
3 µg/kg/min	0,06 mL/kg/min	0,03 mL/kg/min	0,015 mL/kg/min
4 µg/kg/min	0,08 mL/kg/min	0,04 mL/kg/min	0,02 mL/kg/min
5 µg/kg/min	0,1 mL/kg/min	0,05 mL/kg/min	0,025 mL/kg/min
6 µg/kg/min	0,12 mL/kg/min	0,06 mL/kg/min	0,03 mL/kg/min
7 µg/kg/min	0,14 mL/kg/min	0,07 mL/kg/min	0,035 mL/kg/min
8 µg/kg/min	0,16 mL/kg/min	0,08 mL/kg/min	0,04 mL/kg/min

PROCAÏNAMIDE

Dilutions possibles : 1 000 mg/500 mL = 2 mg/mL
1 000 mg/250 mL = 4 mg/mL

Dose d'attaque : 100 mg, toutes les 5 minutes jusqu'à la répression de l'arythmie, la survenue d'une réaction indésirable ou l'administration d'une dose de 1 000 mg ; on peut aussi administrer de 500 à 600 mg sous forme de perfusion d'attaque en l'espace de 25 à 30 minutes.

Vitesses de perfusion du procaïnamide (mL/h)

Concentrations			
2 mg/mL		**4 mg/mL**	
Dose (mg/min)	**Dose (mL/h)**	**Dose (mg/min)**	**Dose (mL/h)**
2 mg/min	60 mL/h	2 mg/min	30 mL/h
3 mg/min	90 mL/h	3 mg/min	45 mL/h
4 mg/min	120 mL/h	4 mg/min	60 mL/h
5 mg/min	150 mL/h	5 mg/min	75 mL/h
6 mg/min	180 mL/h	6 mg/min	90 mL/h

ANNEXE D
Médicaments et grossesse : catégories[1]

Puisque la Direction générale des produits de santé et des aliments (DGPSA) n'a pas publié de règles concernant l'administration des médicaments pendant la grossesse, nous avons retenu, à titre indicatif, la classification américaine établie par la Food and Drug Administration (FDA). Les monographies du *Guide* contiennent les mentions de catégories qui indiquent le risque rattaché à la prise de chaque médicament pendant la grossesse.

CATÉGORIE A

Lors d'études adéquates et dûment contrôlées, menées chez des femmes enceintes, aucun risque pour le fœtus n'a été observé au cours du premier trimestre. Aucun risque apparent n'a été observé non plus au cours des deuxième et troisième trimestres. Les effets nocifs chez le fœtus sont probablement très faibles.

CATÉGORIE B

Les études menées sur les animaux n'ont démontré aucun risque pour le fœtus, mais on ne dispose pas d'étude contrôlée chez la femme enceinte OU les études menées sur les animaux ont fait état de l'existence de certains risques (autre qu'une diminution de la fertilité). Toutefois, les études contrôlées menées chez l'humain n'ont fait état d'aucun risque semblable lors du premier trimestre (et il n'y a pas de preuve de risque pour les deux autres trimestres).

CATÉGORIE C

On a noté des réactions indésirables chez les animaux, mais on ne dispose pas d'étude contrôlée chez les femmes enceintes OU il n'y a pas de données chez les animaux et on ne dispose pas d'étude controlée chez les femmes enceintes. Le médicament devrait être administré seulement si ses bienfaits chez la mère dépassent les risques possibles pour le fœtus.

CATÉGORIE D

Il existe un risque connu pour le fœtus humain. Le médicament pourrait être administré dans certaines circonstances, si ses bienfaits chez la mère dépassent les risques possibles pour le fœtus (par exemple, si le médicament est nécessaire dans une circonstance menaçant la vie de la mère ou pour traiter une maladie grave pour laquelle des médicaments plus inoffensifs ne peuvent être utilisés ou sont inefficaces).

CATÉGORIE X

Les études menées chez l'humain ou sur les animaux ou encore des observations faites chez l'humain ont clairement établi le risque auquel est exposé le fœtus humain. Les risques auxquels le fœtus est exposé sont beaucoup plus importants que les bienfaits possibles du traitement en question pour la femme enceinte. L'administration du médicament est contre-indiquée chez les femmes enceintes et les femmes en âge de procréer.

1. Ces catégories ont été établies par la Food and Drug Administration (FDA) des États-Unis.

ANNEXE E
Formules mathématiques utilisées pour calculer les doses

RAPPORT ET PROPORTION

Un rapport est l'équivalent d'une fraction; il peut donc être exprimé sous forme de fraction (½) ou sous forme algébrique (1:2). Il s'agit ici d'un rapport de 1 pour 2.

Par exemple:

$$\frac{1}{2} = \frac{4}{8}$$

Pour calculer les doses, on applique la règle de trois. Cette méthode permet de trouver le quatrième terme d'une proportion quand les trois autres sont connus. Pour commencer le calcul, on écrit d'un côté de l'équation les deux valeurs connues, par exemple 10 milligrammes = 2 millilitres (concentration disponible). On doit ensuite s'assurer que les unités de mesure du côté opposé de l'équation sont les mêmes que les unités des valeurs connues et qu'elles sont placées au même niveau de l'équation.

$$\frac{10\text{ mg}}{2\text{ mL}} = \frac{5\text{ mg}}{x\text{ mL}}$$

Une fois que la proportion est écrite correctement, on multiplie les valeurs opposées de la proportion.

$$\frac{10\text{ mg}}{2\text{ mL}} \times \frac{5\text{ mg}}{x\text{ mL}}$$

$$10x = 10$$

Par la suite, pour trouver la réponse, il faut diviser les deux côtés de l'équation par le nombre accompagnant la valeur inconnue (x). On indique ensuite l'unité de mesure correspondant à x dans l'équation d'origine.

$$\frac{10x}{10} = \frac{10}{10}$$

$$x = 1\text{ mL}$$

CALCUL DE LA VITESSE D'ÉCOULEMENT D'UNE SOLUTION ADMINISTRÉE EN PERFUSION IV

Afin de calculer la vitesse d'écoulement d'une solution administrée en perfusion intraveineuse (en gouttes/min), on doit connaître trois valeurs:

1. La quantité de solution et la durée de la perfusion. Le médecin peut prescrire:

   1 000 mL en 8 heures
   ou
   125 mL/h

2. Le nombre de minutes en 1 heure:

   1 h = 60 minutes

3. Le nombre de gouttes contenues dans 1 mL de liquide (ce renseignement est indiqué sur le conditionnement des tubulures IV):

   10 gouttes = 1 mL

Pour résoudre le problème, on écrit les trois valeurs sous forme de proportion.

$$\frac{125\text{ mL}}{1\text{ h}} \times \frac{1\text{ h}}{60\text{ min}} \times \frac{10\text{ gouttes}}{1\text{ mL}} = \frac{x\text{ gouttes}}{\text{min}}$$

On peut réduire le membre de gauche à sa plus simple expression.

Les chiffres annulés sont les suivants:

$$\frac{125\ \text{mL}}{1\ \text{h}} \times \frac{1\ \text{h}}{\cancelto{6}{60}\ \text{min}} \times \frac{\cancelto{1}{10}\ \text{gouttes}}{1\ \text{mL}}$$

Les unités annulées sont les suivantes:

$$\frac{125\ \cancel{\text{mL}}}{1\ \cancel{\text{h}}} \times \frac{1\ \cancel{\text{h}}}{6\ \text{min}} \times \frac{1\ \text{goutte}}{1\ \cancel{\text{mL}}}$$

Pour obtenir la réponse, on multiplie tous les numérateurs entre eux et tous les dénominateurs entre eux et on fait ensuite la division.

$$\frac{125}{1} \times \frac{1}{6\ \text{min}} \times \frac{1\ \text{goutte}}{1} = \frac{125\ \text{gouttes}}{6\ \text{min}}$$

$$125 \div 6 = 20{,}8 \text{ ou } 21\ \text{gouttes/min}$$

CALCUL DE LA CLAIRANCE DE LA CRÉATININE (Cl_{Cr}) CHEZ LES ADULTES À PARTIR DES CONCENTRATIONS DE CRÉATININE SÉRIQUE

Hommes: $Cl_{Cr}(\text{mL/s}) = \dfrac{\text{poids (kg)} \times (140 - \text{âge})}{50 \times \text{créatine sérique } (\mu\text{mol/L})}$

Femmes: $Cl_{Cr}(\text{mL/s}) = 0{,}85 \times \text{valeur calculée chez l'homme}$

Pour convertir le résultat obtenu de mL/s en mL/min, multiplier la valeur en mL/s par 60.

CALCUL DU POIDS IDÉAL (kg) CHEZ LES ADULTES

Hommes: 50 kg + (0,91 × [taille (cm) – 152])

Femmes: 45,5 kg + (0,91 × [taille (cm) – 152])

CALCUL DE LA SURFACE CORPORELLE (SC) CHEZ LES ADULTES ET LES ENFANTS

Méthode de Dubois: $SC\ (\text{m}^2) = \dfrac{\text{poids (kg)}^{0{,}425} \times \text{taille (cm)}^{0{,}725} \times 71{,}84}{10\,000}$

Méthode pour les enfants: $SC\ (\text{m}^2) = \dfrac{4 \times \text{poids (kg)} + 7}{\text{poids} + 90}$

INDICE DE MASSE CORPORELLE (IMC)

IMC = poids (kg) ÷ taille^2 (m)

ANNEXE F
Nomogrammes de la surface corporelle

Pour trouver la surface corporelle, on place l'extrémité d'une règle sur la graduation qui correspond à la taille du patient (colonne de gauche), et l'autre extrémité, sur la graduation qui correspond à son poids (colonne de droite). Le point où la règle croise la colonne du centre correspond à la surface corporelle.

CALCUL DE LA SURFACE CORPORELLE CHEZ LES ENFANTS

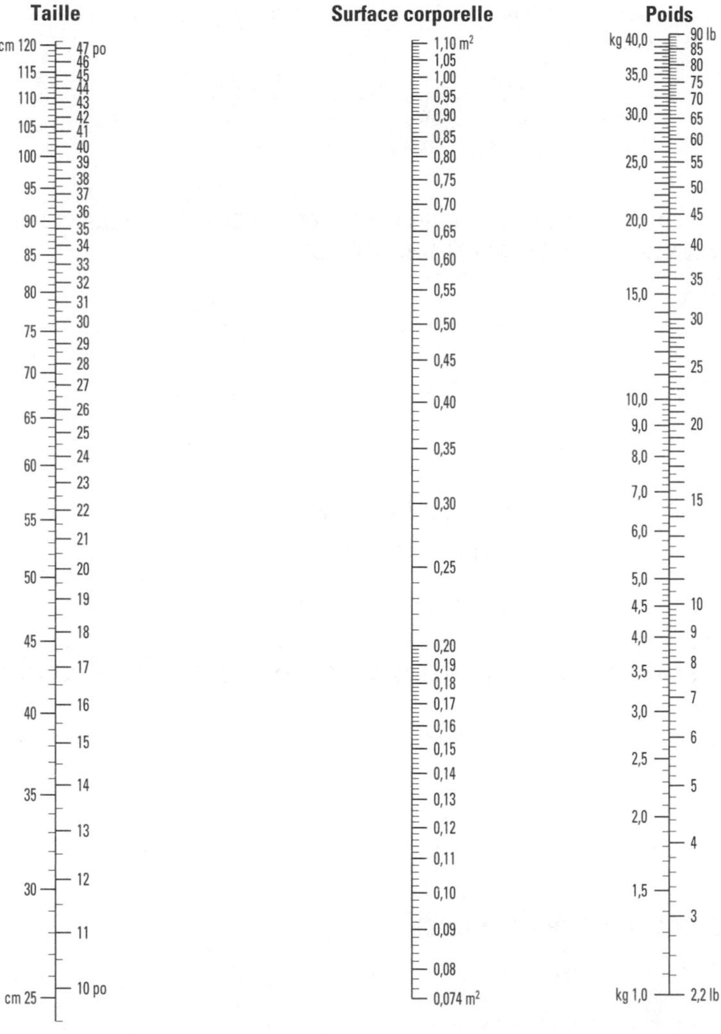

CALCUL DE LA SURFACE CORPORELLE CHEZ LES ADULTES

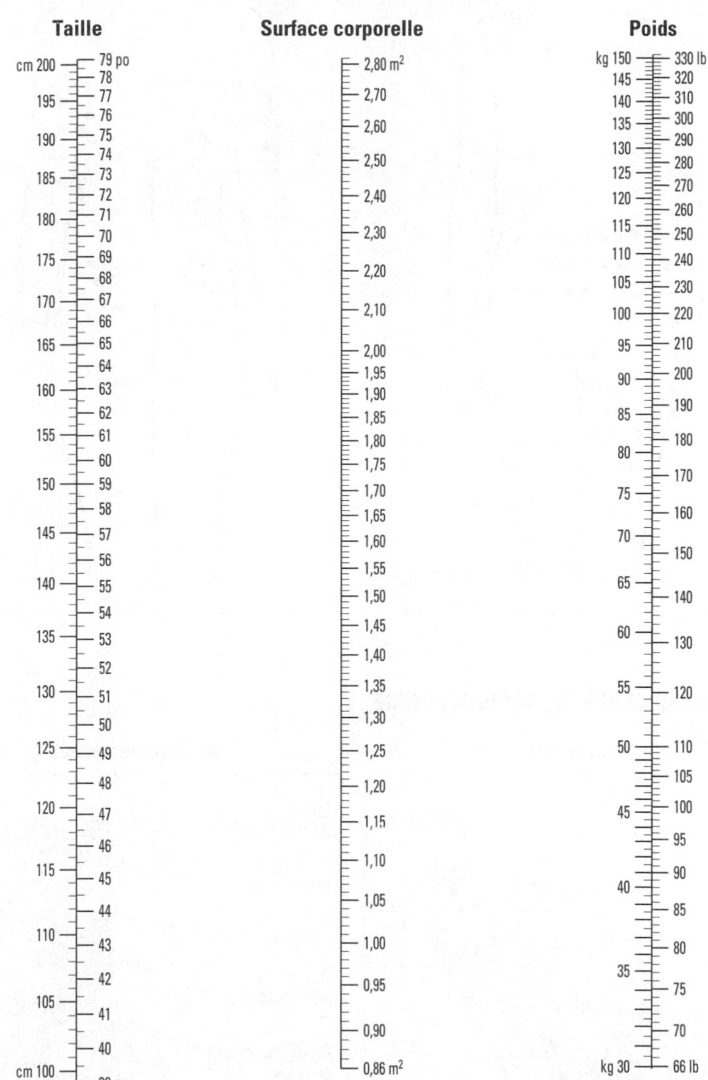

Source : Dubois D, Dubois EF. A formula to estimate the approximate surface area, if height and weight be known. *Archives of Internal Medicine.* 1916 : 17 ; 863-71,

ANNEXE G
Méthodes d'administration

POINTS D'INJECTION SOUS-CUTANÉE

POINTS D'INJECTION INTRAMUSCULAIRE

Muscle deltoïde

Muscle fessier postérieur

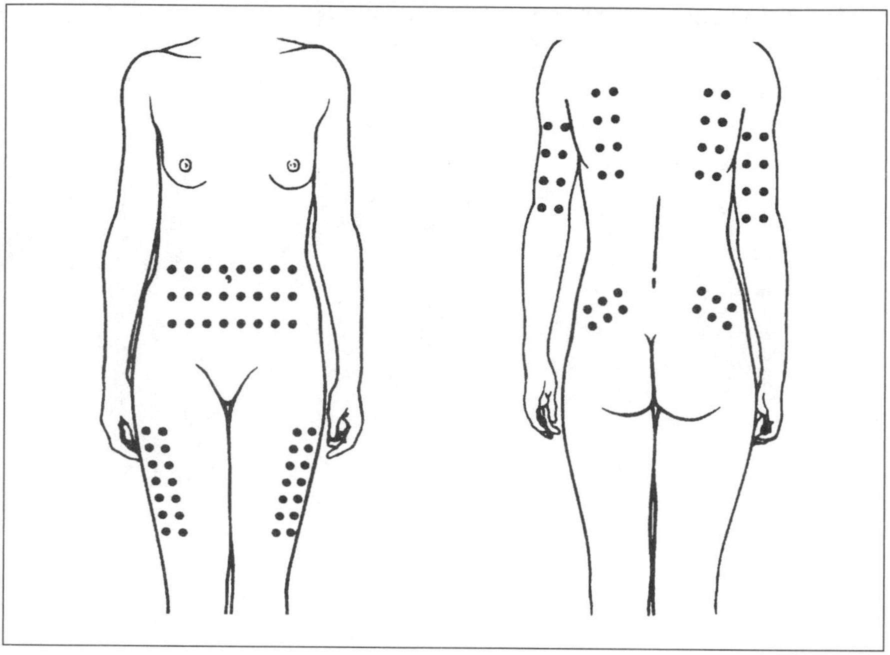

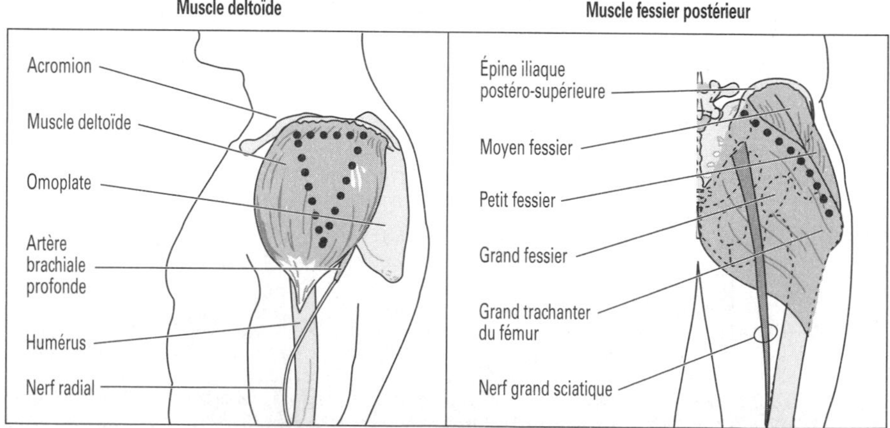

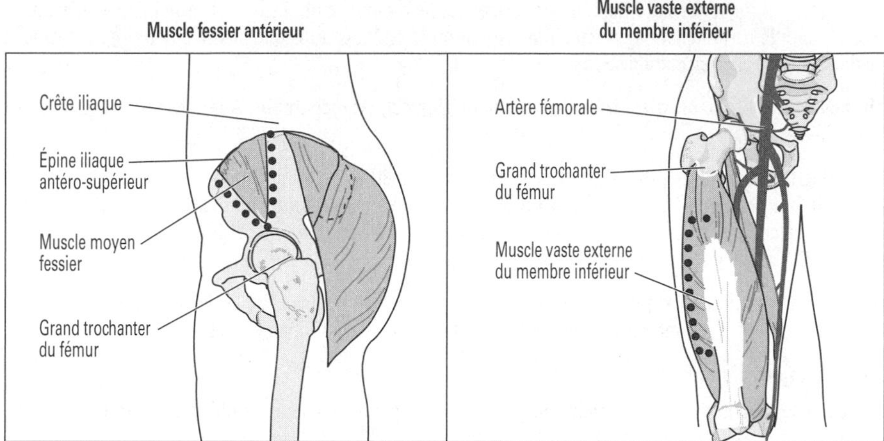

ADMINISTRATION DES PRÉPARATIONS OPHTALMIQUES

Bien se laver les mains avant d'administrer les préparations ophtalmiques.

Éviter tout contact entre le bouchon ou l'extrémité du tube ou de la bouteille et les yeux, les doigts ou toute autre surface.

Si plusieurs médicaments ophtalmiques doivent être administrés en même temps, commencer par la solution, administrer ensuite la suspension et finir par les onguents.

Pour instiller une **solution ophtalmique**, se coucher sur le dos ou pencher la tête vers l'arrière et regarder vers le haut. Ensuite, abaisser la paupière inférieure pour former un petit sac et y verser la solution. Fermer doucement les yeux et avec un doigt maintenir une légère pression sur le canthus interne (commissure des paupières) pendant 1 ou 2 minutes afin de réduire l'absorption systémique. Attendre au moins 5 minutes avant d'instiller une deuxième goutte du médicament ou toute autre solution ophtalmique.

Pour la **suspension ophtalmique**, suivre les indications données pour la solution ophtalmique, mais, au préalable, agiter le flacon afin de bien disperser le principe actif dans la suspension.

Dans le cas des **onguents et des gels ophtalmiques**, comprimer le tube pour faire sortir un petit ruban d'onguent (0,62 à 1,25 cm ou ¼ à ½ po) ou une goutte de gel, et l'appliquer à l'intérieur de la paupière inférieure. Fermer doucement les yeux et bouger les globes oculaires dans toutes les directions en gardant les paupières fermées pour permettre au médicament de se répartir sur toute la surface de l'œil. Attendre 10 minutes avant d'appliquer tout autre onguent (ou gel) ophtalmique.

ADMINISTRATION DES MÉDICAMENTS EN INHALATION

Il existe trois méthodes d'utilisation d'un **aérosol-doseur**.

Méthode A: Bouche ouverte: Boire un peu d'eau pour humidifier la gorge. Placer l'embout buccal à une distance de deux doigts de la bouche, pencher la tête légèrement vers l'arrière et expirer. Pendant qu'on actionne l'aérosol-doseur, inspirer lentement et profondément pendant 3 à 5 secondes, retenir sa respiration pendant 10 secondes et expirer lentement.

Méthode B: Bouche fermée: Expirer et refermer les lèvres sur l'embout buccal. Administrer pendant la seconde moitié de l'inhalation, et retenir la respiration aussi longtemps que possible pour s'assurer que le médicament a pénétré profondément.

Méthode C: Utiliser un **dispositif d'espacement** (Spacer, Aérochambre, Aérochambre avec masque, Vent-ah-aler, etc.).

Se renseigner auprès d'un professionnel de la santé sur la méthode d'administration préconisée. Dans tous les cas, il faut d'abord bien agiter l'aérosol-doseur. Attendre 1 ou 2 minutes entre les inhalations. Se rincer la bouche avec de l'eau ou un rince-bouche après chaque utilisation afin de réduire les effets indésirables du médicament (p. ex. sécheresse de la bouche, muguet, enrouement, etc.).

Si on utilise un **inhalateur à poudre sèche**, tourner la tête pour ne pas souffler dedans, et expirer. Ne pas agiter le dispositif. Bien refermer les lèvres sur l'embout buccal de l'inhalateur et inspirer rapidement.

Mode d'emploi d'un inhalateur

1. Retirer le bouchon et tenir l'inhalateur à la verticale (aérosol-doseur, handihaler et turbuhaler) ou à l'horizontale (diskus et autres dispositifs à poudre sèche).
2. Agiter l'aérosol-doseur ou charger la dose de l'inhalateur à poudre sèche.
3. Pencher légèrement la tête vers l'arrière et expirer lentement.
4. Placer l'inhalateur dans l'une des positions suivantes (les positions A et C sont celles qu'il faudrait privilégier, mais la position B est aussi acceptable si on n'est pas à l'aise avec les deux premières; les inhalateurs à poudre sèche doivent être placés en position D):

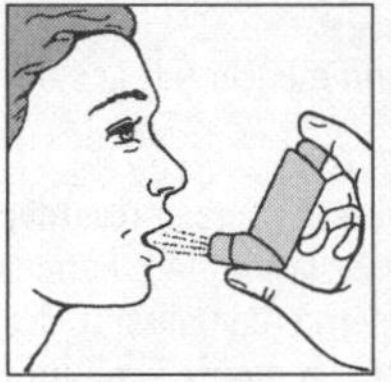

A. Ouvrir la bouche et placer l'inhalateur près des lèvres (de 2,5 à 5 cm).

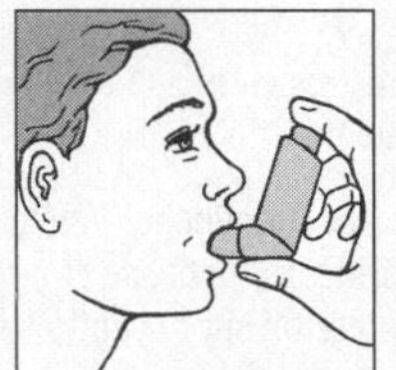

B. Placer l'inhalateur dans la bouche. Ne pas le placer dans cette position pour l'inhalation de corticostéroïdes.

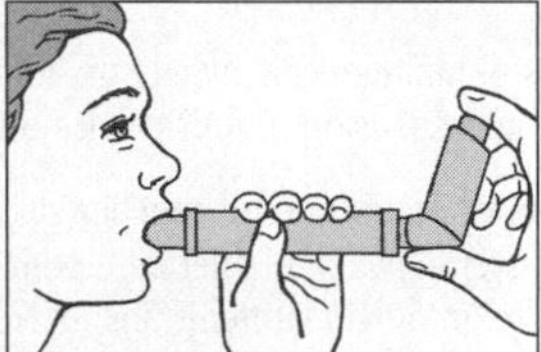

C. Utiliser le dispositif d'espacement (particulièrement chez les jeunes enfants et les personnes qui reçoivent des corticostéroïdes).

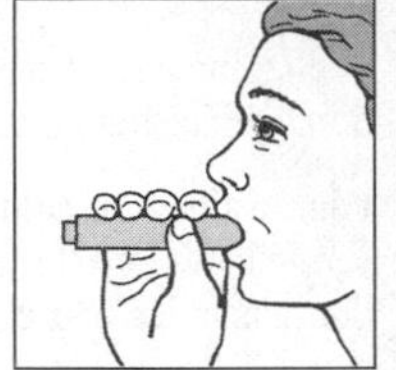

D. REMARQUE: lorsqu'on utilise un inhalateur à poudre sèche, bien fermer les lèvres sur l'embout buccal et inspirer rapidement.

5. Comprimer l'aérosol-doseur pour libérer le médicament tout en inspirant lentement.
6. Inspirer lentement (pendant 3 à 5 secondes).
7. Retenir la respiration pendant 10 secondes pour que le médicament puisse pénétrer profondément dans les poumons.
8. Répéter les inhalations selon les recommandations du professionnel de la santé. Espacer les inhalations d'au moins 1 minute pour que la deuxième dose de médicament puisse également bien pénétrer dans les poumons.
9. Les dispositifs d'espacement sont utiles pour tous les patients. Ils sont particulièrement recommandés chez les jeunes enfants et chez les personnes âgées et lorsqu'il faut prendre des corticostéroïdes par inhalation.

Pour éviter les erreurs courantes d'utilisation d'un inhalateur, suivre les conseils suivants:

- Expirer **avant** de comprimer l'inhalateur.
- Inspirer lentement.
- Inspirer par la bouche, non pas par le nez.
- Comprimer l'inhalateur au début de l'inhalation (ou au cours de la première seconde d'inhalation).
- Continuer d'inspirer tout en comprimant l'inhalateur.
- Comprimer l'inhalateur une seule fois pendant l'inhalation (une respiration par vaporisation).
- Prendre des respirations profondes et uniformes.

Il existe actuellement sur le marché d'autres modèles d'inhalateurs que celui illustré ici. Le mode d'emploi peut différer selon le modèle. Pour plus d'informations, voir la monographie de chaque produit.

ADMINISTRATION DES MÉDICAMENTS PAR NÉBULISEUR

Administrer le médicament dans un endroit où le patient peut rester confortablement assis pendant 10 à 15 minutes. Brancher le compresseur. Mélanger le médicament selon les recommandations ou vider le contenu d'une fiole à dose unitaire dans le nébuliseur. Ne pas mélanger différents types de médicaments sans demander conseil à un professionnel de la santé. Assembler le masque ou l'embout buccal et en relier la tubulure à l'orifice du compresseur. Demander au patient de s'asseoir le dos bien droit. S'assurer que le masque couvre parfaitement le nez et la bouche et que le médicament ne pénètre pas dans les yeux, ou placer l'embout buccal dans la bouche du patient. Mettre en marche le compresseur. Demander au patient de respirer lentement et profondément. S'il peut le faire, il devrait retenir sa respiration pendant 10 secondes avant d'expirer lentement. Continuer ce processus jusqu'à ce que le compartiment qui renferme le médicament soit vide. Laver le masque dans de l'eau chaude savonneuse; bien rincer et laisser sécher à l'air en attendant l'utilisation suivante.

ADMINISTRATION DES MÉDICAMENTS PAR VAPORISATEUR NASAL

Voici les conseils à donner au patient:

1. Agiter légèrement le flacon. Enlever le capuchon protecteur de l'embout nasal.
2. Si on utilise le vaporisateur pour la première fois, charger la pompe en pressant sur l'appuie-doigt plusieurs fois jusqu'à ce qu'une fine vaporisation apparaisse.
3. Se moucher délicatement. Tenir le vaporisateur en plaçant l'index et le majeur de chaque côté de l'embout nasal et le pouce sous le flacon.
4. Boucher une narine en appuyant avec un doigt, et introduire délicatement l'embout nasal dans l'autre narine. Pencher la tête légèrement vers l'avant tout en tenant le vaporisateur bien droit.
5. Inspirer par le nez et du même coup appuyer une fois sur la collerette avec les doigts afin de libérer une vaporisation.
6. Expirer par la bouche.

Si une deuxième vaporisation dans cette même narine est nécessaire, répéter les étapes 5 et 6.

7. Répéter les étapes 4, 5 et 6 pour l'autre narine.

Après utilisation:

8. Essuyer l'embout nasal à l'aide d'un papier mouchoir ou d'un linge propre et remettre le capuchon.

Entretien:

9. Soulever délicatement la collerette blanche pour libérer l'embout nasal et laver celui-ci à l'eau froide.
10. Enlever l'excès d'eau et laisser sécher l'embout à l'air ambiant, sans le chauffer.
11. Remettre délicatement l'embout sur le flacon et replacer le capuchon protecteur.
12. Si l'embout nasal est obstrué, l'enlever et le laisser tremper dans de l'eau tiède. Le rincer ensuite à l'eau froide, le laisser sécher puis le replacer. Ne pas essayer de libérer l'embout nasal en y introduisant un quelconque objet pointu.

Il existe plusieurs types de préparations pharmaceutiques (par exemple, solution, suspension, poudre sèche) et de dispositifs pour l'administration intranasale. Voir les recommandations du fabricant pour chacun des produits.

PULVÉRISATEUR LINGUAL DE NITROGLYCÉRINE

Voir les recommandations du fabricant pour les explications détaillées et les illustrations.

Idéalement, pour prendre ce médicament, le patient devrait être au repos, en position assise.

1. En tenant le flacon à la verticale, retirer le couvercle de plastique. **NE PAS AGITER LE PRODUIT.**
2. Certains types de flacons de nitroglycérine doivent être amorcés avant une première utilisation. Pour ce faire, diriger le jet loin du visage et appuyer fermement sur l'appuie-doigt avec l'index pour libérer l'équivalent d'une pulvérisation. Répéter 3 fois. Le flacon est maintenant amorcé et prêt à l'emploi. On ne doit réamorcer le flacon que s'il n'a pas été utilisé pendant plus de 14 jours. Dans ce cas, libérer l'équivalent de 1 pulvérisation en procédant de la façon indiquée ci-dessus. Il n'est pas nécessaire de réamorcer le flacon entre des utilisations plus fréquentes.
3. Pour utiliser le médicament, tenir le flacon à la verticale, avec l'index posé sur l'appuie-doigt nervuré. Il n'est pas nécessaire d'agiter le flacon.
4. Ouvrir la bouche et y rapprocher le flacon le plus possible.
5. Appuyer fermement sur l'appuie-doigt avec l'index pour libérer le médicament dans la bouche ou sur ou sous la langue. **NE PAS INHALER LE PRODUIT.**
6. Relâcher l'appuie-doigt et fermer la bouche.
7. Si une deuxième dose est nécessaire, répéter les étapes 4, 5 et 6.
8. Remettre le capuchon en plastique.

Avant d'utiliser l'aérosol pour la première fois, il est recommandé de se familiariser avec son mode d'emploi, en pulvérisant le médicament dans l'air (loin de soi et des autres personnes). Il est conseillé d'apprendre la façon correcte de placer l'index sur l'appuie-doigt pour pouvoir bien utiliser le pulvérisateur pendant la nuit.

Dose habituelle: Pendant une crise d'angine, vaporiser 1 ou 2 doses sur ou sous la langue, **sans inhaler**. Le médecin établira la dose exacte qui convient dans chaque cas particulier. On devrait prendre le médicament au repos, de préférence en position assise. On peut répéter l'administration 2 fois, à des intervalles de 5 minutes. Si la douleur persiste, il faut obtenir de l'aide médicale sans tarder.

RECOMMANDER AU PATIENT DE TOUJOURS AVOIR UNE POMPE DE RECHANGE (POUR ÉVITER D'EN MANQUER EN CAS DE BESOIN).

ANNEXE H
Recommandations relatives à la manipulation des produits pharmaceutiques dangereux[1,2]

INTRODUCTION ET CATÉGORISATION

Voici un résumé des lignes directrices révisées sur la santé et la sécurité au travail portant sur la manipulation des produits pharmaceutiques dangereux. Auparavant, ces lignes directrices ne contenaient que des recommandations sur la manipulation des antinéoplasiques (cytotoxiques), mais elles ont été révisées et englobent maintenant tous les produits pharmaceutiques dangereux, tels que certains antiviraux et certaines hormones qui ont aussi un potentiel toxique, carcinogène, mutagène ou tératogène. Ces agents peuvent aussi entraîner une irritation de la peau, des yeux et des muqueuses de même que l'ulcération et la nécrose des tissus.

En raison de la toxicité des produits pharmaceutiques dangereux, les professionnels de la santé doivent s'exposer le moins possible à ce type de médicaments, quelles que soient les circonstances, et s'assurer en même temps que les exigences relatives au maintien d'un milieu aseptique pour la plupart des agents sont respectées.

PRODUITS PHARMACEUTIQUES DANGEREUX ET RISQUES PROFESSIONNELS

Il faut s'exposer le moins possible aux produits pharmaceutiques dangereux puisqu'ils se lient au matériel génétique et peuvent affecter la synthèse des protéines cellulaires. De plus, ils peuvent s'attaquer autant aux cellules normales qu'aux cellules cancéreuses. Des études menées chez l'humain et les animaux ont documenté ces risques.

Durant la préparation et l'administration de ces produits, c'est par l'inhalation de poussières ou de particules projetées par les aérosols, par l'absorption par la peau et par l'ingestion qu'on risque de s'exposer le plus souvent à leurs effets nocifs. Le risque d'exposition à ces produits dangereux est présent à tout moment lors de leur manipulation. Les sources d'exposition ont été documentées par des études qui ont révélé la présence de produits pharmaceutiques dangereux ou de leurs métabolites dans le sang ou les urines des professionnels de la santé les ayant manipulés, ainsi que des cas de toxicité des organes ou d'effets nocifs sur la reproduction. Ces suites peuvent être encore plus marquées chez les professionnels de la santé qui fument.

PRÉPARATION

Les produits pharmaceutiques dangereux doivent être préparés sous une hotte à flux laminaire de classe IIb ou III. Dans les hôpitaux, la préparation incombe généralement à la pharmacie. Toutefois, dans certains cabinets ou cliniques médicaux, ces produits ne sont pas préparés sous une hotte à flux laminaire. Pendant la préparation des produits pharmaceutiques dangereux, même lorsqu'on prend d'énormes précautions, il y a toujours un risque d'éclaboussures, de pulvérisation et de dispersion lors du retrait de l'aiguille de la fiole, du transvasement du médicament, de l'ouverture des ampoules et de l'expulsion de l'air des seringues. En l'absence d'une telle hotte, l'employé devrait porter un respirateur doté d'un filtre à rendement élevé, un masque qui recouvre le visage tout entier ou la moitié du visage et des lunettes de sécurité, une blouse à manches longues et deux paires de gants approuvés pour la manipulation de produits cytotoxiques.

Même si les hottes à flux laminaire de type IIb ou III permettent une préparation dans des conditions d'asepsie ainsi que l'évacuation de l'air directement vers l'extérieur, le risque d'exposition pour le personnel est

---

1. Controlling occupational exposure to hazardous drugs. *Am J Health Syst Pharm*, 1996; 53:1669-85.
2. E. Clyde Buchanan, Philip J. Schneider. *Compounding Sterile Preparation*, American Society of Health-system pharmacists, 2e édition, 2005.

réel. Il est interdit de fumer, de boire, de se maquiller ou de manger dans les aires de préparation, d'entreposage ou d'administration de tels produits pour préserver l'asepsie et diminuer le risque d'exposition. Il faut aussi éviter toutes les tâches qui peuvent accroître le risque d'exposition (par exemple, le personnel devrait s'abstenir de casser les aiguilles ou d'écraser les seringues). La hotte devrait être régulièrement entretenue et décontaminée.

Habillement

Le personnel qui manipule les produits pharmaceutiques dangereux doit porter un équipement de protection individuelle (gants, blouse, bonnet, couvre-chaussures). On recommande d'enfiler deux paires de gants approuvés pour la manipulation de produits cytotoxiques et de changer de gants toutes les 30 minutes ou, plus souvent, s'ils sont déchirés ou contaminés. On recommande, par ailleurs, de porter des vêtements protecteurs approuvés pour les produits cytotoxiques et de glisser les manches entre la première et la deuxième paire de gants. Il faut aussi enseigner aux employés la façon correcte de retirer l'équipement de protection individuelle. Ces employés doivent aussi porter un respirateur certifié par un organisme reconnu et des lunettes de sécurité formant une barrière de protection contre les substances chimiques, chaque fois qu'il y a risque d'éclaboussures, de vaporisation ou de dispersion, et avoir accès à des postes de rinçage oculaire. Tout l'équipement protecteur doit être mis au rebut adéquatement ou nettoyé avant d'être réutilisé, lorsque les conditions s'y prêtent.

Techniques stériles

Durant la manipulation de produits pharmaceutiques dangereux, il faut protéger la surface de travail sous la hotte par une feuille de papier plastifié qui doit être changée régulièrement. Pour la préparation des produits pharmaceutiques dangereux, on devrait utiliser des seringues et des tubulures IV munies d'un embout Luer-Lock. Le calibre des seringues doit être adapté aux volumes à prélever et les solutions en excès doivent être mises au rebut dans des contenants couverts destinés à cette fin. On doit également mettre à la disposition des employés des contenants destinés à la mise au rebut des objets pointus et tranchants. Tous les produits pharmaceutiques dangereux doivent être jetés dans des sacs adéquatement étiquetés.

On doit utiliser une technique aseptique adaptée au travail sous une hotte à flux laminaire. Avant de commencer le travail, le personnel doit enfiler l'équipement de sécurité et déposer tout le matériel nécessaire sous la hotte. Toutes les seringues et les sacs IV devraient être munis d'une étiquette additionnelle de mise en garde, en plus de l'étiquette standard. Il faut jeter les aiguilles dans les contenants destinés aux objets pointus et tranchants (sans les casser ni les couper) et éviter les pressions positives dans les fioles. Pour ce genre de travail, les dispositifs à usages multiples munis d'un filtre pourraient s'avérer plus appropriés que de simples aiguilles. Il faut aussi prendre toutes les précautions de rigueur afin de réduire le risque d'éclaboussures ou de fuites. Une fois que la solution a été préparée, on essuiera le sac ou le flacon avec une gaze humide. On emballera l'unité dans un sac de plastique scellé, qui sera placé dans un contenant de protection.

PROTECTION DES UTILISATEURS

Des recommandations écrites concernant la préparation des produits pharmaceutiques dangereux doivent être mises à la disposition du personnel dans toutes les aires de préparation. Elles devraient porter sur les points suivants:

- Les précautions à prendre pour assurer la sécurité et pour préserver la santé du personnel exposé aux produits pharmaceutiques dangereux.
- Les mesures visant à réduire l'exposition aux produits pharmaceutiques dangereux.
- Les consignes relatives à la présence de dispositifs de ventilation et à l'entretien.

- Les directives concernant l'information et la formation.
- La marche à suivre lors de la manipulation de produits pharmaceutiques dangereux faisant l'objet d'une recherche.
- Les dispositions relatives aux soins médicaux prodigués au personnel exposé aux produits pharmaceutiques dangereux.
- Le nom des employés qui ont la responsabilité de faire respecter ces recommandations.

ADMINISTRATION DES PRODUITS PHARMACEUTIQUES DANGEREUX

Dans la mesure du possible, la manipulation des produits pharmaceutiques dangereux devrait être centralisée dans des aires d'accès réservé où toute activité pouvant accroître le risque d'exposition devrait être défendue. Il est recommandé d'afficher dans ces aires les directives concernant les déversements et les mesures d'urgence.

Pour administrer des produits pharmaceutiques dangereux, il faut porter un équipement de sécurité comprenant une paire de gants et une blouse certifiés par un organisme reconnu, plus un respirateur et des lunettes de sécurité lorsqu'il a un risque d'inhalation et d'éclaboussures. On devrait aussi garder à portée de la main le matériel suivant, utilisé lors de l'administration : carrés de gaze pour divers nettoyages, serviettes humides imbibées d'alcool, tissus absorbants jetables plastifiés, contenant pouvant accueillir des objets pointus ou tranchants (pour les aiguilles et les seringues), sacs de plastique qu'on peut fermer hermétiquement et qui portent une étiquette de mise en garde et des étiquettes additionnelles.

Il faut observer les consignes suivantes :

- Bien se laver les mains avant d'enfiler les gants et après les avoir enlevés. Mettre au rebut tout l'équipement contaminé et le remplacer immédiatement.
- Utiliser des techniques aseptiques et manipuler le matériel avec attention afin d'éviter les éclaboussures, les fuites de médicament ou toute autre exposition au médicament.
- S'assurer que toutes les pompes à perfusion et tubulures IV sont munies d'un embout Luer-Lock et vérifiées régulièrement. Placer sous la tubulure des tissus absorbants plastifiés. Recouvrir de gaze les points d'injection IV et coller les raccords avec du ruban adhésif.
- Amorcer les dispositifs et effectuer l'expulsion de l'air sous la hotte à flux laminaire. Lorsque cela n'est pas possible, on amorcera les tubulures avec une solution non médicamenteuse ou à l'aide d'un dispositif fermé antireflux. L'utilisation de dispositifs à évent devrait être défendue.
- Essuyer les seringues, les flacons IV, les sacs et les pompes avec de la gaze. Les aiguilles et les seringues doivent être placées dans les contenants destinés aux objets pointus ou tranchants, puis dans un sac de mise au rebut des produits pharmaceutiques dangereux. Il faudrait jeter les tubulures utilisées telles quelles sans les débrancher du sac. Suivre les directives relatives à la mise au rebut des sacs de déchets dans lesquels on jette des produits pharmaceutiques dangereux et retourner à la pharmacie tous les produits inutilisés. Suivre les consignes de mise au rebut du matériel jetable et les consignes de nettoyage du matériel réutilisable.
- Dans les aires où l'on administre des produits pharmaceutiques dangereux, garder à portée de la main les trousses d'urgence pour parer aux éclaboussures ou à la contamination des yeux et de la peau.
- Porter l'équipement de sécurité, s'il y a risque d'éclaboussures pendant qu'on administre des médicaments en solution par voie orale.
- Réserver l'administration des produits pharmaceutiques dangereux destinés à la recherche aux personnes expérimentées.

Il faut observer aussi scrupuleusement que possible ces directives lorsque de tels produits sont administrés au domicile du patient. Les patients et les soignants devraient pouvoir rejoindre facilement les professionnels de la santé et bien connaître les plans d'urgence.

L'administration des médicaments en aérosol doit se faire sous surveillance pour prévenir l'exposition à des produits dangereux de toute autre personne se trouvant à proximité. On peut utiliser des méthodes d'isolement et de ventilation particulières.

SOINS DES PATIENTS RECEVANT UN PRODUIT PHARMACEUTIQUE DANGEREUX

Il faut prendre des précautions universelles pour prévenir le contact avec tout matériel ou tout fluide corporel pouvant être dangereux ou infecté. Les fluides corporels des patients recevant des produits pharmaceutiques dangereux peuvent contenir des concentrations nocives de ces agents ou de leurs métabolites, raison pour laquelle il faudrait les manipuler prudemment. Lorsqu'on doit manipuler une matière contaminée par un produit pharmaceutique dangereux, il faut que le personnel soit dûment formé à cette tâche, qu'il porte des gants et une blouse et qu'il jette les déchets dans des contenants bien étiquetés, scellés et recouverts, réservés à cette fin. Les employés devraient aussi prendre des précautions s'il y a eu contamination par du sang ou des liquides organiques.

Le personnel qui se rend au chevet d'un patient ayant reçu un produit dangereux doit porter des vêtements protecteurs et des gants pendant les 48 heures qui suivent l'administration d'un tel produit et il doit remplacer ces vêtements en cas de contamination. S'il y a risque d'éclaboussures, il faut porter des lunettes de sécurité. Le linge contaminé doit être mis dans un sac spécial et lavé séparément avant d'être lavé avec le reste du linge. Le personnel travaillant à la buanderie doit porter des vêtements protecteurs et des gants lorsqu'il manipule du linge contaminé. Les articles réutilisables doivent être lavés à deux reprises avec du détergent et le personnel chargé de cette tâche doit porter pendant cette opération des vêtements protecteurs et une double paire de gants.

Le matériel mis au rebut doit être introduit dans des sacs portant l'étiquette « cytotoxique ». Les aiguilles, les seringues et les articles fragiles, contaminés par du sang ou d'autres matières injectées, doivent être mis au rebut dans un contenant spécial destiné aux objets tranchants ou pointus contaminés. Ce contenant devrait être gardé hermétiquement fermé en tout temps et remplacé à intervalles réguliers. Il faudrait aussi protéger ses parois externes de la contamination et le placer, s'il venait à être contaminé, dans un autre contenant non contaminé. Conformément aux règlements en vigueur, les déchets de produits pharmaceutiques dangereux ne doivent pas être mis au rebut dans les mêmes contenants que les autres déchets.

DÉVERSEMENT DE PRODUIT PHARMACEUTIQUE DANGEREUX

Les déversements doivent être nettoyés par des employés qui portent un équipement protecteur approprié et qui suivent les directives de l'établissement à cet égard. Lorsque la quantité de produit dangereux déversé est faible (moins de 5 mL ou de 5 g), il peut être nettoyé par des membres du personnel portant des vêtements protecteurs, des gants, des lunettes de sécurité et un respirateur, au besoin. On essuiera les liquides avec une gaze absorbante, les solides avec une gaze humidifiée, puis on lavera la surface avec du détergent à trois reprises et on la rincera à l'eau. Les tessons seront ramassés à l'aide d'une cuillère et mis au rebut de façon appropriée.

On devrait isoler les aires où une grande quantité de produit dangereux a été déversée. Pour le nettoyage, on utilisera dans ce cas des draps ou des chiffons absorbants. Pour nettoyer de la poudre déversée, on utilisera des chiffons humides. Si on a déversé plus de 150 mL de liquide (ou le contenu d'une fiole) sous une hotte à flux laminaire, il faut la décontaminer complètement si le déversement n'a pas été contenu. Si le filtre de la hotte à flux laminaire est contaminé, il faut la fermer jusqu'à ce que le personnel d'entretien qualifié puisse le nettoyer ou le remplacer. Dans les aires où l'on manipule des produits pharmaceutiques dangereux, on devrait disposer en tout temps d'une trousse de nettoyage des déversements, facilement accessible. Cette trousse doit renfermer des lunettes de sécurité, deux paires de gants, des gants tout usage, des vêtements protecteurs, deux carrés de tissu absorbant, des coussins de nettoyage des déversements (deux tailles), un contenant destiné à la mise au rebut des objets pointus et tranchants et deux grands sacs destinés à la mise au rebut de produits pharmaceutiques dangereux.

En cas de contamination du personnel, voici la marche à suivre :

- Retirer immédiatement les gants et les vêtements protecteurs.
- Nettoyer la peau atteinte avec de l'eau et du savon.
- Rincer l'œil touché au poste de secours pour le lavage des yeux ou le rincer avec de l'eau stérile ou une solution isotonique spéciale pendant 15 minutes au moins.
- Consulter un médecin et suivre les directives qui s'appliquent à chaque cas particulier.
- Documenter l'incident.

SUIVI MÉDICAL

Tout employé doit se soumettre à un examen avant l'embauche et après une exposition accidentelle. Il faut accorder une attention particulière aux questions reliées à la reproduction. L'employeur doit élaborer et implanter un programme de communications sur les produits pharmaceutiques dangereux. Les employés doivent être mis au courant des risques associés à la manipulation de tels produits. Il faut aussi assurer leur formation pour minimiser les risques d'exposition et garder dans les archives de l'établissement des documents qui attestent que de telles séances ont été suivies.

ANNEXE I

Valeurs normales des résultats des tests de laboratoire courants

Les valeurs normales des résultats des tests de laboratoire peuvent varier d'un laboratoire à l'autre, selon les méthodes d'analyse utilisées.

TESTS SÉROLOGIQUES

Hématologie	Hommes	Femmes
Hémoglobine	140 - 170 g/L	120 - 155 g/L
Hématocrite	0,42 - 0,52 (valeur relative)	0,35 - 0,47 (valeur relative)
Globules rouges (érythrocytes)	4,2 - 5,7 × 10^{12}/L	3,8 - 5,0 × 10^{12}/L
Volume globulaire moyen (VGM)	81 - 99 fL	81 - 99 fL
Teneur globulaire moyenne en hémoglobine (TGMH)	28 - 33 pg	28 - 33 pg
Concentration globulaire moyenne en hémoglobine (CGMH)	320 - 365 g/L	320 - 365 g/L
Vitesse de sédimentation globulaire	0 - 15 mm/h	0 - 20 mm/h
Globules blancs (leucocytes)	4,5 - 11 × 10^9/L	4,5 - 11 × 10^9/L
Neutrophiles	0,45 - 0,73 (valeur relative)	0,45 - 0,73 (valeur relative)
Éosinophiles	0 - 0,04 (valeur relative)	0 - 0,04 (valeur relative)
Basophiles	0 - 0,01 (valeur relative)	0 - 0,01 (valeur relative)
Monocytes	0,02 - 0,1 (valeur relative)	0,02 - 0,1 (valeur relative)
Lymphocytes	0,2 - 0,4 (valeur relative)	0,2 - 0,4 (valeur relative)
Lymphocytes T	60 - 80 % des lymphocytes	60 - 80 % des lymphocytes
Lymphocytes B	10 - 20 % des lymphocytes	10 - 20 % des lymphocytes
Plaquettes	140 - 500 × 10^9/L	140 - 500 × 10^9/L
Temps de prothrombine (PT)	9 - 12 s	9 - 12 s
Temps de céphaline (PTT)	20 - 39 s	20 - 39 s
Temps de saignement	2,5 - 9,5 min	2,5 - 9,5 min
RNI (patient sous anticoagulant oral)	variable selon l'indication et la protection voulue (2,0 - 3,0 à 2,5 - 3,5)	variable selon l'indication et la protection voulue (2,0 - 3,0 à 2,5 - 3,5)

Biochimie	Hommes	Femmes
Sodium	135 - 145 mmol/L	135 - 145 mmol/L
Potassium	3,5 - 5,1 mmol/L	3,5 - 5,1 mmol/L
Chlorure	97 - 107 mmol/L	97 - 107 mmol/L
Bicarbonate (HCO_3)	22 - 28 mmol/L	22 - 28 mmol/L
Calcium total	2,13 - 2,56 mmol/L	2,13 - 2,56 mmol/L
Calcium ionise	1 - 1,15 mmol/L	1 - 1,15 mmol/L
Phosphore/phosphate	0,8 - 1,6 mmol/L	0,8 - 1,6 mmol/L
Magnésium	0,8 - 1,2 mmol/L	0,8 - 1,2 mmol/L
Glucose (à jeun)	3,9 - 6,1 mmol/L	3,9 - 6,1 mmol/L

TESTS SÉROLOGIQUES (SUITE)

Hématologie	Hommes	Femmes
Osmolalité (plasma)	275 – 300 mmol/kg	275 – 300 mmol/kg
Ammoniaque (NH_{4+})	5 – 50 µmol/L	5 – 50 µmol/L
Amylase	23 – 85 U/L	23 – 85 U/L
Créatine-kinase totale (CPK ou CK)	40 – 150 U/L	40 – 150 U/L
Lactate-déshydrogénase (LDH ou LD)	98 – 192 U/L	98 – 192 U/L
Protéines totales	60 – 80 g/L	60 – 80 g/L
Albumine	40 – 60 g/L	40 – 60 g/L
Exploration hépatique	**Hommes**	**Femmes**
AST	10 – 47 U/L	10 – 47 U/L
ALT	7 – 56 U/L	7 – 56 U/L
Bilirubine totale	7 – 34 µmol/L	7 – 34 µmol/L
Bilirubine conjuguée	1,7 – 8,6 µmol/L	1,7 – 8,6 µmol/L
Phosphatase alcaline	30 – 120 U/L	30 – 120 U/L
Exploration rénale	**Hommes**	**Femmes**
Urée	2 – 8 mmol/L	2 – 8 mmol/L
Créatinine	50 – 110 µmol/L	50 – 110 µmol/L
Acide urique	220 – 480 µmol/L	140 – 380 µmol/L

GAZOMÉTRIE ARTÉRIELLE

	Hommes	Femmes
pH	7,35 – 7,45	7,35 – 7,45
pO_2	75 – 100 mm Hg	75 – 100 mm Hg
pCO_2	35 – 45 mm Hg	35 – 45 mm Hg
Saturation en O_2	0,96 – 1	0,96 – 1
Bicarbonate (HCO_3)	22 – 26 mmol/L	22 – 26 mmol/L

ANALYSE DES URINES

Urine	Hommes	Femmes
pH	4,6 – 8,0	4,6 – 8,0
Densité	1,01 – 1,025	1,01 – 1,025

ANNEXE J
Guide alimentaire

Aliments riches en potassium		
fruits frais et leur jus	légumes cuits et leur jus	poissons
fruits secs	légumineuses	viandes
lait	noix et graines	

Aliments riches en sodium		
aliments enrobés de sel : arachides, amandes, craquelins, croustilles	glutamate monosodique	sauce à spaghetti ou chili en conserve
beurre, margarine	ketchup	sauces barbecue, chili, Worcestershire et soja
choucroute	légumes en conserve et leur jus	sels de table, au céleri, à l'oignon, à l'ail
eau minérale	marinades	soupes en sachet ou en conserve
extraits de bouillon (cube, poudre ou concentré liquide)	plats préparés pour four à micro-ondes	viandes salées, séchées ou fumées
fruits de mer en conserve	plats surgelés	vinaigrettes préparées
	poissons salés ou en conserve	

Aliments riches en calcium		
amandes	jus de fruits enrichi en calcium	saumon rose et sardines en conserve avec os
boissons de soya enrichies en calcium	lait et produits laitiers	soupes-crèmes
brocoli cuit	mélasse noire	tofu ferme
chou cuit	noix du Brésil	
épinards cuits	rhubarbe cuite	

Aliments riches en vitamine K		
avocat	fines herbes fraîches	pistaches
brocoli	fraises	pommes de terre avec la pelure
chou	haricots	riz sauvage
choux de Bruxelles	huiles de soja et de canola	thon à chair pâle (en conserve) dans l'huile
concombre avec la pelure	kiwi	viande de porc
épinards	laitue	yogourt

Aliments riches en vitamine D		
boissons de soya enrichies	jaune d'oeuf	margarine molle (soya, tournesol, maïs)
huile de foie de poisson	lait enrichi	saumon

Aliments riches en fer		
abats	fruits secs	légumes verts en feuilles
céréales	légumineuses	viandes rouges maigres

Aliments qui acidifient l'urine		
canneberges	œufs	prunes
fromages	poisson	viandes
grains entiers (pains et céréales)	pruneaux	volailles

Aliments qui alcalinisent l'urine		
lait	tous les fruits à l'exception des canneberges, des pruneaux et des prunes	tous les légumes

Aliments contenant de la tyramine		
avocats (particulièrement trop mûrs)	fromage fondu	saucissons et autres charcuteries (bologne, salami, pepperoni, salami d'été)
bananes	fromages vieillis (bleu, brie, camembert, cheddar, emmental, gruyère, mozzarella, parmesan, romano, roquefort, stilton, suisse)	soupe à base de miso
bières et ales	fruits trop mûrs	spiritueux distillés
boissons à base de caféine (café, thé, colas)	levure	tofu
bouillons de bœuf, poulet et légumes	pâte aux crevettes	viandes préparées avec un sel attendrisseur
caviar	pois mange-tout	vin rouge (particulièrement le chianti) et blanc
chocolat	poissons fumés ou marinés	vermouth
choucroute	raisins secs	yogourt
figues	sauce soya	xérès
foie		

RÉFÉRENCES

Brault Dubuc, M. et L. Caron Lahaie, *Valeur nutritive des aliments*, 8e édition, Société Brault-Lahaie, Québec, 1998.

Locong, A. et D. Ruelle, *Guide des interactions médicaments, nutriments et produits naturels*, Les Presses de l'Université Laval, Québec, 2004.

Ordre professionnel des diététistes du Québec (OPDQ). *Manuel de nutrition clinique*, www.opdq.org. (consulté en avril 2007).

ANNEXE K
Apports nutritionnels de référence

RECOMMANDATIONS D'APPORTS INDIVIDUELS POUR LES CANADIENS ET LES AMÉRICAINS (1998-2000)[1]

Âge (années) et sexe	Calcium (mg/jour)	Phosphore (mg/jour)	Magnésium (mg/jour)	Vitamine D (µg/jour)[2]	Fluorure (mg/jour)	Thiamine (mg/jour)	Riboflavine (mg/jour)	Niacine (mg/jour)[3]	Vitamine B_6 (mg/jour)	Acide folique (µg/jour)[4]	Vitamine B_{12} (µg/jour)	Acide pantothénique (mg/jour)	Biotine (µg/jour)	Choline[8] (mg/ jour)
Nourrissons														
0,0 – 0,5	210*	100*	30*	5*	0,01*	0,2*	0,3*	2*	0,1*	65*	0,4*	1,7*	5*	125*
0,6 – 1,0	270*	275*	75*	5*	0,5*	0,3*	0,4*	4*	0,3*	80*	0,5*	1,8*	6*	150*
Enfants														
1 – 3	500*	460	80	5*	0,7*	0,5	0,5	6	0,5	150	0,9	2*	8*	200*
4 – 8	800*	500	130	5*	1*	0,6	0,6	8	0,6	200	1,2	3*	12*	250*
Hommes														
9 – 13	1 300*	1 250	240	5*	2*	0,9	0,9	12	1	300	1,8	4*	20*	375*
14 – 18	1 300*	1 250	410	5*	3*	1,2	1,3	16	1,3	400	2,4	5*	25*	550*
19 – 30	1 000*	700	400	5*	4*	1,2	1,3	16	1,3	400	2,4	5*	30*	550*
31 – 50	1 000*	700	420	5*	4*	1,2	1,3	16	1,3	400	2,4	5*	30*	550*
51 – 70	1 200*	700	420	10*	4*	1,2	1,3	16	1,7	400	2,4[7]	5*	30*	550*
71 +	1 200*	700	420	15*	4*	1,2	1,3	16	1,7	400	2,4[7]	5*	30*	550*
Femmes														
9 – 13	1 300*	1 250	240	5*	2*	0,9	0,9	12	1	300	1,8	4*	20*	375*
14 – 18	1 300*	1 250	360	5*	3*	1	1	14	1,2	400[5]	2,4	5*	25*	400*
19 – 30	1 000*	700	310	5*	3*	1,1	1,1	14	1,3	400[5]	2,4	5*	30*	425*
31 – 50	1 000*	700	320	5*	3*	1,1	1,1	14	1,3	400[5]	2,4	5*	30*	425*
51 – 70	1 200*	700	320	10*	3*	1,1	1,1	14	1,5	400	2,4[7]	5*	30*	425*
71 +	1 200*	700	320	15*	3*	1,1	1,1	14	1,5	400	2,4[7]	5*	30*	425*
Femmes enceintes														
≤ 18	1 300*	1 250	400	5*	3*	1,4	1,4	18	1,9	600[6]	2,6	6*	30*	450*
19 – 30	1 000*	700	350	5*	3*	1,4	1,4	18	1,9	600[6]	2,6	6*	30*	450*
31 – 50	1 000*	700	360	5*	3*	1,4	1,4	18	1,9	600[6]	2,6	6*	30*	450*
Femmes allaitantes														
≤ 18	1 300*	1 250	360	5*	3*	1,4	1,6	17	2	500	2,8	7*	35*	550*
19 – 30	1 000*	700	310	5*	3*	1,4	1,6	17	2	500	2,8	7*	35*	550*
31 – 50	1 000*	700	320	5*	3*	1,4	1,6	17	2	500	2,8	7*	35*	550*

1. Ce tableau présente les Apports nutritionnels recommandés (ANR) en caractère gras, et les apports suffisants (AS) en caractère ordinaire, suivis d'un astérisque (*). Les ANR et les AS peuvent servir d'objectif pour les apports individuels. Les ANR couvrent les besoins de 97 à 98 % de la population. Chez les enfants âgés de moins de 1 an, les AS correspondent aux apports moyens des nourrissons allaités et sont censés couvrir les besoins des autres groupes d'âge bien que l'information disponible ne permette pas de préciser ce point. Veuillez vous reporter aux monographies pour prendre connaissance des apports et des nutriments qui ne sont pas énumérés ici.
2. Sous forme de cholécalciférol; 1 µg de cholécalciférol = 40 UI de vitamine D. En l'absence d'une exposition appropriée au soleil.
3. Sous forme d'équivalents en niacine; 1 mg de niacine = 60 mg de tryptophane; de 0 à 6 mois = niacine préformée.
4. Sous forme d'équivalents alimentaires en folate; 1 équivalent alimentaire en folate = 1 µg de folate alimentaire = 0,6 µg d'acide folique (d'aliments enrichis ou de suppléments) pris avec des aliments = 0,5 µg d'acide folique synthétique (supplément) pris à jeun.
5. Compte tenu des liens connus entre l'apport de folate et les anomalies du tube neural fœtal, il est recommandé que toutes les femmes en âge de procréer consomment 400 µg d'acide folique de synthèse, provenant d'aliments enrichis ou de suppléments, en plus des apports alimentaires de folate.
6. On présume que les femmes continueront à consommer 400 µg d'acide folique jusqu'à ce que leur grossesse soit confirmée et qu'elles bénéficieront de soins prénataux, ce qui survient habituellement à la fin de la période périconceptionnelle, laquelle est critique pour la formation du tube neural.
7. L'absorption de la vitamine B_{12} liée aux aliments serait réduite chez 10 à 30% des personnes âgées. Il est suggéré que les personnes âgées de plus de 50 ans tirent la plus grande partie de cette vitamine d'aliments enrichis ou de suppléments de B_{12}.
8. Bien qu'on ait recommandé l'apport de choline, il existe peu de données indiquant la nécessité d'un apport alimentaire à toutes les étapes de la vie; il est possible que les besoins en choline soient comblés à certaines de ces étapes par une synthèse endogène.

RÉFÉRENCES

Institute of Medicine and Food and Nutrition Board. Dietary Reference Intakes for Calcium, Magnesium, Phosphorus Fluorine, and Vitamin D. Washington DC: National Academy of Sciences, 1998.

Institute of Medicine and Food and Nutrition Board. Dietary Reference Intakes for Thiamine, Riboflavin, Niacin, Vitamin B_6, Folate, Vitamin B_{12}, Pantothenic Acid, Biotin, and Choline. Washington, DC: National Academy of Sciences, 2000.

Ordre professionnel des diététistes du Québec (OPDQ). *Manuel de nutrition clinique*, www.opdq.org. (consulté en avril 2007).

ANNEXE L
Calendrier d'immunisation régulier du Québec

Les informations présentées dans cette annexe sont tirées du Protocole d'immunisation du Québec, qui est une référence incontournable pour les professionnels de la santé de cette province qui administrent des vaccins. Ce protocole fait l'objet de mises à jour à intervalles réguliers. Le lecteur est donc invité à consulter la version la plus récente avant d'administrer un vaccin. Le Protocole de même que ses mises à jour peuvent être obtenus en s'adressant à la direction de la Santé publique de sa région ou en consultant le site Internet officiel (www.msss.gouv.qc.ca/publications).

CALENDRIER RÉGULIER

Âge	Vaccins			
2 mois[1]	DCaT	Polio inactivé	Hib	Pneumocoque conjugué
4 mois[1]	DCaT	Polio inactivé	Hib	Pneumocoque conjugué
6 mois[1]	DCaT	Polio inactivé[2]	Hib	Grippe[3]
1 an	RRO[4]	Méningocoque conjugué de sérogroupe C[4]	Varicelle[4]	Pneumocoque conjugué[4]
18 mois[1]	DCaT	Polio inactivé	Hib	RRO
4 - 6 ans[5]	DCaT	Polio inactivé		
4e année du primaire[6]	Hépatite B			
14 - 16 ans	dCaT[7]			
50 ans[8]	d_2T_5[7] ou dCaT			
60 ans	Grippe[9]			
65 ans	Pneumocoque polysaccharidique			

Légende: DCaT : diphtérie-coqueluche-tétanos;
Hib : *Hæmophilus influenzæ* de type B;
RRO : rougeole-rubéole-oreillons;
d_2T_5 : diphtérie-tétanos.

1. Un vaccin combiné est utilisé pour la vaccination DCT-Polio-Hib à 2, à 4, à 6 et à 18 mois.
2. Cette 3e dose est administrée en raison de l'utilisation d'un produit d'association. Toutefois, elle n'est pas obligatoire pour assurer la protection.
3. Le vaccin est recommandé durant la saison de la grippe chez les enfants âgés de 6 à 23 mois. Chez les enfants qui n'ont jamais reçu de vaccin contre la grippe, administrer 2 doses à 4 semaines d'intervalle. Toutefois, la 2e dose est inutile si l'enfant a reçu une dose dans le passé.
4. Il faut administrer ce vaccin le jour du 1er anniversaire ou le plus tôt possible après ce jour.
5. Un vaccin combiné est utilisé pour la vaccination contre DCT-Polio entre 4 et 6 ans.
6. Un programme de vaccination contre l'hépatite B est suivi par le réseau des CLSC en milieu scolaire pendant la 4e année du primaire.
7. Par la suite, rappel de d_2T_5 tous les 10 ans. À noter qu'il existe une différence de concentration de la composante diphtérique entre les versions DCaT et dCaT.
8. Comme la majorité des adultes ne reçoit pas l'injection de rappel tous les 10 ans, il est recommandé, à cet âge, de mettre à jour le statut vaccinal. Les adultes qui n'ont jamais reçu de dose du vaccin acellulaire contre la coqueluche devraient recevoir une seule dose de dCaT.
9. Il faut administrer ce vaccin annuellement.

CARACTÉRISTIQUES DES VACCINS INSCRITS DANS LE CALENDRIER D'IMMUNISATION RÉGULIER DU QUÉBEC

Vaccin contre la DIPHTÉRIE, la COQUELUCHE, le TÉTANOS, la POLIOMYÉLITE et les INFECTIONS À *HÆMOPHILUS INFLUENZÆ* DE TYPE B (Pentacel, Pediacel et Infanrix-IPV/Hib)

VOIE D'ADMINISTRATION ET POSOLOGIE: Tout le contenu de la fiole, à administrer par voie IM. La vaccination débute généralement à l'âge de 2 mois. Répéter la dose, 2 mois après la 1re dose, 2 mois après la 2e dose et 12 mois après la 3e dose. On peut administrer le vaccin dans le muscle deltoïde, dès l'âge de 12 mois, si la masse musculaire le permet.

CONTRE-INDICATIONS: Maladie fébrile aiguë ▪ Allergie de type anaphylactique tant à l'une des composantes du vaccin qu'à une dose antérieure soit du même vaccin, soit d'un autre vaccin ayant la composante acellulaire de la coqueluche, soit d'un vaccin ayant la composante à cellule entière de la coqueluche.

PRÉCAUTIONS ET MISES EN GARDE: Le vaccin combiné $D_{15}CaT_5$-Polio ne doit pas être administré aux personnes ≥ 7 ans, en raison des risques de réactions indésirables liées à l'administration de concentrations plus élevées d'anatoxine diphtérique ▪ Le syndrome de Guillain et Barré (SGB) a déjà été associé à la composante tétanique. Les études qui ont analysé les cas de syndrome de Guillain et Barré chez des adultes et des enfants permettent de conclure que si un tel risque existe, il est très rare. La décision de donner des doses additionnelles de vaccin contenant la composante tétanique à des personnes qui ont développé un SGB dans les 6 semaines suivant une dose antérieure doit être basée sur l'évaluation des bienfaits de la poursuite de la vaccination et du faible risque de récurrence d'un SGB. Par exemple, il est justifié de mener à terme la primovaccination chez l'enfant.

RÉACTIONS INDÉSIRABLES ET EFFETS SECONDAIRES: Sensibilité ▪ Nodule ≥ 2 cm ▪ Érythème ≥ 2 cm ▪ Fièvre ≥ 38 °C ▪ Pleurs persistants ≥ 1 heure ▪ Épisode d'hypotonie et d'hyporéactivité ▪ Réaction anaphylactique (rare) ▪ Névrite brachiale (rare) survenue après l'administration d'autres vaccins comprenant la composante tétanique ▪ La fréquence des réactions locales a tendance à augmenter avec le nombre de doses administrées.

Remarques: On ne connaît aucune interaction entre les vaccins.

Vaccin conjugué contre le PNEUMOCCOQUE (Prevnar)

VOIE D'ADMINISTRATION ET POSOLOGIE: 0,5 mL, administré par voie IM, à 2 et à 4 mois et à 1 an.

CONTRE-INDICATIONS: Maladie aiguë modérée ou grave, avec ou sans fièvre ▪ Allergie de type anaphylactique tant à l'une des composantes du vaccin qu'à une dose antérieure soit du même vaccin, soit d'un autre vaccin ayant une composante identique, incluant l'anatoxine diphtérique.

PRÉCAUTIONS ET MISES EN GARDE: La réponse immunitaire peut être sous-optimale chez les personnes immunocompromises. Dans la mesure du possible, il est recommandé de vacciner la personne de 10 à 14 jours au moins avant le traitement immunosuppresseur ou une chirurgie élective de type splénectomie ou visant un implant cochléaire ▪ Allergie au latex (le bouchon de la fiole du vaccin Prevnar contient du latex naturel).

RÉACTIONS INDÉSIRABLES ET EFFETS SECONDAIRES: Réactions locales: Sensibilité ▪ Érythème ▪ Induration. **Réactions systémiques:** Fièvre entre 38 °C et 39 °C ▪ Irritabilité et changements dans l'appétit et le sommeil ▪ Vomissements et diarrhée ▪ En général, les réactions systémiques sont plus intenses après la 2e ou la 3e dose ▪ Le vaccin entraîne rarement des convulsions fébriles (moins de 1 par 7 000 doses) lorsqu'il est administré en même temps qu'un vaccin du calendrier régulier ▪ Réactions anaphylactiques (rares).

Remarques: S'il est indiqué d'administrer le vaccin conjugué et un vaccin polysaccharidique 23-valent contre le pneumocoque, on doit, dans la mesure du possible, administrer le vaccin conjugué en premier. L'intervalle recommandé entre l'administration de ces 2 produits est d'au moins 8 semaines. L'usage du vaccin polysaccharidique dans ce contexte ne constitue pas une revaccination.

Vaccin contre la ROUGEOLE, la RUBÉOLE et les OREILLONS (MMR-II et Priorix)

VOIE D'ADMINISTRATION ET POSOLOGIE: Tout le contenu de la fiole à administrer par voie SC à 1 an et à 18 mois.

CONTRE-INDICATIONS: Maladie fébrile aiguë ■ État d'immunosuppression secondaire à toute affection néoplasique généralisée pouvant altérer le mécanisme immunitaire, à une radiothérapie, à une chimiothérapie, à une corticothérapie immunosuppressive ou à un déficit immunitaire héréditaire ■ Grossesse ■ Allergie de type anaphylactique tant à une dose antérieure qu'à l'une ou l'autre des composantes du vaccin, autre que l'allergie aux œufs.

PRÉCAUTIONS ET MISES EN GARDE: Tout sujet ayant des antécédents personnels ou familiaux de convulsions devrait être informé des précautions à prendre pour atténuer une réaction fébrile postvaccinale ■ Sujets infectés par le VIH ■ Il est conseillé d'éviter la grossesse au cours du mois suivant la vaccination ■ Toute personne qui présente une thrombopénie dans le mois suivant l'administration du vaccin RRO ne devrait être revaccinée qu'après une évaluation médicale. Toutefois, un épisode antérieur de thrombopénie non lié au vaccin n'empêche pas la vaccination, car on estime que les avantages de celle-ci sont supérieurs aux risques encourus. On doit préciser que la rougeole et la rubéole naturelles entraînent beaucoup plus souvent cette complication que le vaccin.

RÉACTIONS INDÉSIRABLES ET EFFETS SECONDAIRES: **Réactions locales**: Rougeur ■ Gonflement ■ Sensibilité habituellement de courte durée. **Réactions systémiques**: Fièvre légère et éruption passagère non contagieuse, parfois entre le 5e et le 12e jour après la vaccination ■ Fièvre modérée à forte (entre 38,5 et 39,5 °C) pouvant entraîner, quoique rarement, des convulsions fébriles (ce risque diminue avec l'âge) ■ La composante antirubéoleuse peut causer une lymphadénopathie, une arthrite ou une arthralgie transitoire survenant de 1 à 3 semaines après l'injection. De rares cas d'arthrite aiguë, récurrente ou chronique, ont été signalés. La maladie entraîne beaucoup plus souvent ces complications ■ La composante des oreillons peut occasionnellement causer une parotidite ■ Thrombopénie transitoire (rare) signalée à la suite de l'administration du vaccin RRO ■ Réaction allergique de type anaphylactique (très rare) ■ Problèmes neurologiques (encéphalite) (rare).

Remarques: Il ne faut pas vacciner l'enfant avant son 1er anniversaire, même pas la veille. La protection contre ces trois maladies serait durable. Si l'épreuve de Mantoux (tuberculine) est indiquée, elle doit être faite avant, le même jour ou au moins 6 semaines après la vaccination, parce que le vaccin contre la rougeole peut diminuer la réaction à l'épreuve. Le vaccin RRO doit être administré 2 semaines avant l'administration d'immunoglobulines humaines, de sang ou de dérivés du sang. Après l'administration d'immunoglobulines ou de produits sanguins, on devra respecter un intervalle pouvant aller jusqu'à 10 mois avant d'administrer le RRO (consulter le Protocole). Les produits sanguins ou les immunoglobulines anti-Rh_0 (D) qui sont administrés avant le vaccin ou en même temps que lui n'entravent généralement pas la réponse immunitaire au vaccin contre la rubéole présent dans le RRO. Lorsque c'est le cas, le Comité consultatif national de l'immunisation (CCNI) conseille quand même une analyse sérologique entre 6 et 8 semaines après la vaccination afin de déterminer la réponse au vaccin. Toutefois, cette recommandation ne doit pas remettre en question la vaccination des femmes en post-partum immédiat. Le vaccin RRO peut être administré le même jour qu'un autre vaccin à virus vivants ou à 4 semaines d'intervalle.

Vaccin conjugué contre le MÉNINGOCOQUE DE SÉROGROUPE C (Meningitec, Menjugate et NeisVac-C)

VOIE D'ADMINISTRATION ET POSOLOGIE: 0,5 mL, à administrer par voie IM à l'âge de 1 an. La nécessité de doses de rappel pour ce vaccin n'a pas été établie. On peut administrer le vaccin dans le muscle deltoïde dès l'âge de 12 mois, si la masse musculaire le permet.

CONTRE-INDICATIONS: Maladie fébrile aiguë ▪ Allergie de type anaphylactique tant à l'une des composantes du vaccin, incluant l'anatoxine diphtérique (Meningitec et Menjugate) et l'anatoxine tétanique (NeisVac-C), qu'à une dose antérieure soit du même vaccin, soit d'un autre vaccin ayant une composante analogue.

PRÉCAUTIONS ET MISES EN GARDE: Les études animales n'ont pas démontré de risque pour le fœtus (Menjugate). L'innocuité des vaccins conjugués contre le méningocoque de sérogroupe C chez la femme enceinte n'a pas été évaluée. Ces vaccins étant inactivés, il n'est pas contre-indiqué de les administrer à la femme enceinte s'il existe un risque élevé d'infection méningococcique.

RÉACTIONS INDÉSIRABLES ET EFFETS SECONDAIRES: Érythème > 2,5 cm ▪ Fièvre ▪ Irritabilité ▪ Pleurs ▪ Céphalées ▪ Nausées ▪ Vomissements ▪ Éruptions cutanées mineures ▪ Fatigue ▪ Étourdissements ▪ Douleurs abdominales.

Remarques: Ne pas confondre avec le vaccin polysaccharidique contre le méningocoque de sérogroupes A, C, Y et W-135 (Menomune). Dans la mesure du possible, s'il est indiqué d'utiliser les deux types de vaccin (conjugué et polysaccharidique) chez la même personne (p. ex., asplénie, déficience en complément, manipulation de *Neisseria meningitidis* dans un laboratoire), le vaccin conjugué devrait être administré avant le vaccin polysaccharidique (minimum 2 semaines). Le vaccin conjugué entraîne une meilleure réponse immunitaire au sérogroupe C et permet d'éviter l'induction d'une tolérance immunitaire. Pour les cas où le vaccin polysaccharidique aurait été administré en premier, on recommande d'attendre 6 mois (minimum 2 semaines dans un contexte épidémiologique à haut risque) avant d'administrer le vaccin conjugué. Par ailleurs, il n'y a aucune autre interaction vaccinale connue. Le vaccin conjugué peut être administré en même temps qu'un autre vaccin, mais dans un autre point d'injection.

Vaccin contre la VARICELLE (Varivax III et Varilrix)

VOIE D'ADMINISTRATION ET POSOLOGIE: 0,5 mL, à administrer par voie SC à l'âge de 1 an.

CONTRE-INDICATIONS: Maladie aiguë modérée ou grave, avec ou sans fièvre ▪ Allergie de type anaphylactique tant à l'une des composantes du vaccin qu'à une dose antérieure soit du même vaccin, soit d'un autre vaccin ayant une composante identique ▪ Tuberculose active non traitée ▪ Grossesse ▪ États d'immunosuppression graves.

PRÉCAUTIONS ET MISES EN GARDE: Plusieurs types de personnes immunocompromises pourraient tirer profit d'une vaccination contre la varicelle (p. ex., certaines personnes atteintes de leucémie aiguë ou étant sous traitement immunosuppresseur, certains enfants infectés par le VIH). La décision de vacciner sera prise après consultation avec un spécialiste connaissant la maladie et le vaccin. Dans ce contexte, la vaccination se fera suivant une évaluation médicale. Les personnes en attente d'une greffe ou d'un traitement immunosuppresseur devraient être vaccinées, dans la mesure du possible, de 6 à 8 semaines avant l'intervention ou le début du traitement. Il existe un très faible risque de transmission du virus vaccinal à l'entourage des personnes vaccinées qui présentent une éruption varicelliforme; cette éruption peut survenir dans les 6 semaines suivant la vaccination. Toutefois, l'éruption causée par le virus vaccinal est moins grave que celle causée par le virus sauvage. Par mesure de prudence, il est conseillé aux personnes vaccinées ayant développé une éruption cutanée d'éviter, pendant la durée de l'éruption, tout contact étroit avec des personnes non immunes présentant un risque élevé de complications (p. ex., personnes immunocompromises, prématurés). Cependant, un tel contact, s'il survenait, ne justifierait pas l'administration systématique d'immunoglobulines ■ La majorité des enfants et des adolescents qui ont présenté le syndrome de Reye après avoir contracté la varicelle de façon naturelle avaient pris des salicylates. Le risque de développer ce syndrome après la vaccination est inconnu. Toutefois, les fabricants recommandent aux enfants et aux adolescents de ne pas prendre de salicylates au cours des 6 semaines suivant la vaccination contre la varicelle. Bien qu'aucun cas de syndrome de Reye n'ait été signalé en rapport avec la prise de salicylates après l'administration du vaccin contre la varicelle, le professionnel de la santé qui administre le vaccin doit tenir compte de ce risque théorique à la lumière du risque réel de syndrome de Reye après une infection par le virus sauvage chez les enfants recevant un traitement prolongé aux salicylates ■ On ne sait pas si le vaccin comporte un risque pour le fœtus lorsqu'il est administré à une femme enceinte. Par mesure de prudence, il faut conseiller aux femmes en âge de procréer d'éviter la grossesse au cours du mois suivant la vaccination. Cependant, la vaccination d'une femme qui ne savait pas qu'elle était enceinte, ou qui l'est devenue dans le mois suivant l'administration du vaccin, ne justifie pas d'envisager l'interruption de la grossesse.

RÉACTIONS INDÉSIRABLES ET EFFETS SECONDAIRES: Réactions locales: Douleur ■ Rougeurs ■ Éruption varicelliforme au point d'injection (dans les 3 semaines suivant la vaccination). **Réactions systémiques:** Éruption varicelliforme (dans les 4 semaines suivant la vaccination) ■ Fièvre ■ Zona (chez les patients ayant présenté une éruption varicelliforme).

Remarques: Le vaccin contre la varicelle peut être administré le même jour qu'un autre vaccin à virus vivants injectable ou à au moins 4 semaines d'intervalle. Cela s'applique en particulier dans le cas du vaccin combiné contre la rougeole, la rubéole et les oreillons (RRO). Une étude américaine a montré que la protection contre la varicelle diminuait lorsque le vaccin avait été administré à des enfants dans un intervalle de moins de 4 semaines après le vaccin RRO: le risque de contracter la varicelle était augmenté de 2,5 fois ■ L'effet de l'administration du vaccin contre la varicelle sur la réaction au test cutané à la tuberculine (TCT) est inconnu. Comme il s'agit d'un vaccin à virus vivants, il est possible qu'il fausse l'interprétation des résultats. En l'absence de données, il est recommandé de respecter dans le cas du vaccin contre la varicelle les mêmes délais qu'entre l'administration du vaccin contre la rougeole et ce test. Ainsi, lorsqu'il est indiqué, le TCT doit être administré avant, en même temps ou au moins 4 semaines après la vaccination contre la varicelle ■ Le vaccin contre la varicelle doit être administré 2 semaines avant l'administration d'immunoglobulines humaines, de sang ou de dérivés du sang. L'effet de l'administration de produits sanguins sur la réponse au vaccin contre la varicelle est inconnu. Comme il s'agit d'un vaccin à virus vivants, la réponse immunitaire pourrait être inhibée si le vaccin est administré après une transfusion de sang ou de plasma ou après l'administration d'immunoglobulines. En l'absence de données, il est recommandé de respecter dans le cas du vaccin contre la varicelle les mêmes délais qu'entre l'administration de ces produits et le vaccin contre la rougeole.

Vaccin contre la DIPHTÉRIE, la COQUELUCHE, le TÉTANOS et la POLIOMYÉLITE (Quadracel et Infanrix-IPV)

VOIE D'ADMINISTRATION ET POSOLOGIE: 0,5 mL, à administrer par voie IM entre l'âge de 4 et de 6 ans (si Pentacel a été administré antérieurement comme le recommande le Protocole).

CONTRE-INDICATIONS: Voir plus haut, le vaccin combiné contre *Hæmophilus influenzæ* de type B (Pentacel).

PRÉCAUTIONS ET MISES EN GARDE: Voir plus haut, le vaccin combiné contre *Hæmophilus influenzæ* de type B (Pentacel).

RÉACTIONS INDÉSIRABLES ET EFFETS SECONDAIRES: Voir plus haut, le vaccin combiné contre *Hæmophilus influenzæ* de type B (Pentacel).

Remarques: On ne connaît aucune interaction entre les vaccins.

Vaccin contre l'HÉPATITE B (Engerix-B et Recombivax HB)

VOIE D'ADMINISTRATION ET POSOLOGIE: Calendrier régulier (4e année du primaire): Engerix-B – à administrer par voie IM ■ **Recombivax HB** – 0,25 mL, à administrer par voie IM ■ **Engerix-B et Recombivax HB** – répéter 1 mois après la 1re dose et 5 mois après la 2e dose. Injecter dans le muscle deltoïde chez l'enfant et l'adulte et dans le muscle vaste externe chez le nouveau-né et le nourrisson. Ne pas administrer dans le muscle dorsofessier.

CONTRE-INDICATIONS: Maladie fébrile aiguë ■ Allergie de type anaphylactique tant à l'une des composantes du vaccin qu'à une dose antérieure soit du même vaccin, soit d'un autre vaccin ayant une composante analogue.

PRÉCAUTIONS ET MISES EN GARDE: Les personnes dialysées ou immunocompromises répondent moins bien à la vaccination et doivent recevoir des doses plus élevées de vaccin (voir les calendriers d'immunisation qui les concernent). Pour établir leur calendrier vaccinal, on devrait considérer les personnes infectées par le VIH et les utilisateurs de drogues par injection qui ignorent leur statut immunitaire comme des sujets immunocompromis.

RÉACTIONS INDÉSIRABLES ET EFFETS SECONDAIRES: Dans la majorité des cas, le vaccin ne provoque aucune réaction ■ Réactions signalées: réactions locales, fièvre, céphalées, problèmes digestifs, étourdissements, fatigue et réactions allergiques anaphylactiques (rares).

Remarques: Les vaccins contre l'hépatite B sont interchangeables. Il est donc possible de substituer un vaccin à l'autre à condition de respecter la dose de chacun d'entre eux. L'administration systématique de doses de rappel à des personnes immunocompétentes n'est pas recommandée puisque la protection persiste pendant au moins 15 ans. Chez une personne ayant déjà présenté des anticorps anti-HBs au-delà du seuil protecteur (≥ 10 UI/L), l'absence d'anticorps ne signifie pas l'absence de protection en raison de la persistance de la mémoire immunologique.

Vaccin contre la DIPHTÉRIE et le TÉTANOS (d2T5) (Td Adsorbées)

VOIE D'ADMINISTRATION ET POSOLOGIE: Après la primo-immunisation, une dose de rappel (0,5 mL, administrée par voie IM) devrait être administrée tous les 10 ans. Un premier rappel peut être administré entre l'âge de 14 et de 16 ans, en respectant un intervalle minimal de 5 ans depuis la dernière dose. Dans des circonstances exceptionnelles (p. ex., un long séjour dans une région où l'accès aux soins de santé est limité), un vaccin de rappel peut être donné si plus de 5 ans se sont écoulés depuis la dernière dose.

CONTRE-INDICATIONS: Maladie fébrile aiguë ■ Allergie de type anaphylactique à une dose antérieure du même vaccin ou à l'une ou l'autre de ses composantes ■ Réaction locale grave, accompagnée ou non d'une forte fièvre, à la suite d'une dose antérieure d'un vaccin antitétanique ■ Névrite brachiale à la suite d'une dose antérieure du vaccin ■ Syndrome de Guillain et Barré à la suite d'une dose antérieure du vaccin.

PRÉCAUTIONS ET MISES EN GARDE: Les personnes chez qui l'administration d'une dose d'anatoxine tétanique a entraîné des réactions locales graves, accompagnées ou non d'une forte fièvre, ne doivent pas recevoir une autre dose avant au moins 10 ans, et cette dernière ne sera administrée que sur ordonnance médicale individuelle. Cette manifestation pourrait être une réaction d'hypersensibilité de type Arthus.

RÉACTIONS INDÉSIRABLES ET EFFETS SECONDAIRES: Réactions locales: Douleur ■ Érythème ■ Induration au point d'injection ■ Abcès stérile. **Réactions systémiques:** Fièvre ■ Myalgies ■ Céphalées ■ Rarement, réaction allergique importante ■ Névrite brachiale ■ Des réactions d'hypersensibilité de type Arthus et des réactions locales graves peuvent survenir chez les personnes dont les taux d'anticorps contre le tétanos sont élevés avant la vaccination ■ L'intensité des réactions à l'anatoxine tétanique augmente avec le nombre de doses administrées.

Remarques: En ce qui concerne les mesures à prendre lors de la prophylaxie du tétanos en cas de blessures, se référer au Protocole. On ne connaît aucune interaction entre les vaccins.

Vaccin contre la GRIPPE (Fluviral S/F, Influvac et Vaxigrip)

VOIE D'ADMINISTRATION ET POSOLOGIE: Enfants âgés de 6 à 35 mois: 0,25 mL ▪ **enfants âgés ≥ 3 ans et adultes:** 0,5 mL. Administrer par voie IM. Injecter dans le muscle deltoïde chez les adultes et les enfants plus âgés, et dans le muscle vaste externe chez les jeunes enfants et les nourrissons. Sur le plan de l'immunisation, le muscle dorsofessier est réservé à l'injection des immunoglobulines; pour plusieurs vaccins, ce territoire est moins immunogène. Chez les enfants de moins de 9 ans qui n'ont jamais reçu de vaccin contre la grippe, administrer 2 doses à 4 semaines d'intervalle. Toutefois, la seconde dose est inutile si un enfant a reçu au moins une dose du vaccin au cours d'une saison grippale antérieure.

CONTRE-INDICATIONS: Maladie fébrile aiguë ▪ Allergie de type anaphylactique à l'une ou l'autre des composantes du vaccin, incluant les œufs, ou antécédents de réaction anaphylactique lors de l'administration d'un vaccin antigrippal.

PRÉCAUTIONS ET MISES EN GARDE: Les personnes qui ont présenté un syndrome oculorespiratoire sévère qui comportait des symptômes graves au niveau des voies respiratoires inférieures (p. ex., difficultés respiratoires, respiration sifflante, oppression thoracique) lors de leur dernière vaccination contre la grippe doivent être vaccinées sur ordonnance médicale individuelle, afin de permettre l'évaluation des risques et des bienfaits de la vaccination dans chaque cas particulier ▪ Le vaccin contre la grippe n'est pas recommandé chez les enfants âgés de moins de 6 mois parce qu'il est moins immunogène à cet âge ▪ Les personnes présentant des troubles de la coagulation devraient être vaccinées en prenant des précautions particulières ▪ Il serait prudent d'éviter de redonner le vaccin à une personne ayant développé un syndrome de Guillain et Barré dans les 6 semaines suivant une vaccination antérieure contre la grippe.

RÉACTIONS INDÉSIRABLES ET EFFETS SECONDAIRES: Réactions locales (le plus souvent douleur) au point d'injection, pouvant durer jusqu'à 2 jours ▪ Fièvre, malaises ou myalgies survenant dans les 6 à 12 heures et pouvant persister 1 ou 2 jours après la vaccination, particulièrement chez les sujets qui sont vaccinés pour la première fois contre la grippe ▪ Réaction allergique de type anaphylactique (très rare) ▪ Syndrome de Guillain et Barré ▪ Vascularite systémique (rare) ▪ Syndrome oculorespiratoire (yeux rouges, symptômes respiratoires [toux, mal de gorge, difficultés respiratoires, oppression dans la poitrine] et œdème facial).

Remarques: On ne connaît aucune interaction entre les vaccins. Le vaccin contre la grippe peut être administré en même temps que d'autres vaccins, mais dans des points d'injection différents. Les vaccins contre la grippe à virion fragmenté sont interchangeables.

Vaccin polysaccharidique 23-valent contre les PNEUMOCOQUES (Pneumovax 23, Pnu-Imune 23 et Pneumo 23)

VOIE D'ADMINISTRATION ET POSOLOGIE: Enfants âgés de 2 ans: 0,5 mL, par voie SC ou IM. En général, on ne devrait pas administrer plus d'une dose de ce vaccin. Toutefois, une revaccination est recommandée dans certaines circonstances (p. ex., asplénie ou problème médical lié à une immunosuppression).

CONTRE-INDICATIONS: Maladie fébrile aiguë ▪ Allergie de type anaphylactique tant à l'une des composantes du vaccin qu'à une dose antérieure soit du même vaccin, soit d'un autre vaccin ayant une composante analogue.

PRÉCAUTIONS ET MISES EN GARDE: Ce vaccin est déconseillé chez les enfants âgés < 24 mois, car il est très peu immunogène avant cet âge ▪ La réponse immunitaire peut être sous-optimale chez les personnes immunocompromises. Il est recommandé de vacciner au moins 10 à 14 jours avant le début d'un traitement immunosuppresseur ■ L'innocuité du vaccin pendant le 1er trimestre de la grossesse n'a pas été évaluée; cependant, les vaccins contre le pneumocoque étant inactivés, le risque est considéré comme négligeable. Ne vacciner une femme enceinte qu'en cas d'indication claire ■ La vaccination des personnes atteintes d'une infection à VIH (symptomatique ou non) au moyen d'un vaccin polysaccharidique 23-valent doit être entreprise sur recommandation médicale individuelle.

RÉACTIONS INDÉSIRABLES ET EFFETS SECONDAIRES: Sensibilité locale, érythème et gonflement, pendant moins de 48 heures ■ Fièvre légère à modérée et myalgies, pendant moins de 24 heures ■ Rares réactions systémiques (p. ex., fièvre élevée, céphalées, malaise, adénite, myalgie, arthralgie, arthrite, éruption cutanée ou urticaire) ■ Phénomènes d'Arthus ■ Réactions de type anaphylactique (très rares).

Remarques: Si possible, il faut administrer le vaccin au moins 10 à 14 jours avant une splénectomie ■ Ne pas confondre avec le vaccin conjugué 7-valent contre le pneumocoque (Prevnar). S'il est indiqué d'administrer le vaccin conjugué et un vaccin polysaccharidique 23-valent contre le pneumocoque chez un enfant, on doit, dans la mesure du possible, administrer le vaccin conjugué en premier. L'intervalle recommandé entre l'administration de ces deux produits est d'au moins 8 semaines. L'usage du vaccin polysaccharidique dans ce contexte ne constitue pas une revaccination ■ Aucune autre interaction entre vaccins n'est soupçonnée ■ Le vaccin polysaccharidique 23-valent contre le pneumocoque peut être administré en même temps que tout autre vaccin, mais à un autre point d'injection.

SOINS INFIRMIERS

ÉVALUATION DE LA SITUATION

- S'informer de la vaccination antérieure du patient et des réactions d'hypersensibilité observées s'il y a lieu.

DIAGNOSTICS INFIRMIERS POSSIBLES

- Risque d'infection (Indications).
- Connaissances insuffisantes sur le traitement médicamenteux (Enseignement au patient et à ses proches).

INTERVENTIONS INFIRMIÈRES

- Administrer chaque vaccin par la voie d'administration appropriée.

ENSEIGNEMENT AU PATIENT ET À SES PROCHES

- Informer les patients des réactions indésirables et des effets secondaires possibles. Le médecin devrait être informé si le patient présente un des symptômes suivants: fièvre supérieure à 39,4 °C, difficultés respiratoires, urticaire, démangeaisons, enflure des yeux, du visage ou de l'intérieur du nez, fatigue et faiblesse soudaines et intenses, convulsions.
- Prévoir la prochaine séance de vaccination avec les parents.

VÉRIFICATION DE L'EFFICACITÉ THÉRAPEUTIQUE

L'efficacité du traitement peut être démontrée par: la prévention des maladies par la vaccination.

ANNEXE M
Prévention de l'endocardite bactérienne

Un bon nombre de professionnels de la santé croient que l'administration prophylactique d'un antibiotique avant une intervention pouvant entraîner une bactériémie passagère pourrait prévenir l'endocardite bactérienne chez les patients à risque. Toutefois, l'utilité de cette pratique courante n'est pas confirmée systématiquement par des études contrôlées chez l'humain.

En 2007, les recommandations de l'American Heart Association sur la prévention de l'endocardite bactérienne ont été révisées et concernent maintenant un nombre de patients plus restreint. Les principales raisons justifiant ces changements sont qu'une éventuelle bactériémie découlant des activités de la vie quotidienne prédispose davantage à l'endocardite bactérienne que la bactériémie associée aux interventions dentaires et que seul un nombre extrêmement petit de cas d'endocardite bactérienne pourrait être prévenu par une antibiothérapie prophylactique, même si la prophylaxie était à 100 % efficace.

On trouve au tableau 1, les problèmes cardiaques pour lesquels une antibiothérapie prophylactique est acceptable, au tableau 2, les types d'interventions pour lesquelles une antibiothérapie prophylactique est acceptable, et au tableau 3, les antibiotiques recommandés.

TABLEAU 1
Problèmes cardiaques associés au risque le plus élevé d'une issue défavorable de l'endocardite bactérienne, pour lesquels une antibiothérapie prophylactique lors d'interventions dentaires est acceptable[1]

- Présence d'une prothèse valvulaire ou de matériel prothétique utilisé pour la réparation d'une valve cardiaque
- Antécédents d'endocardite bactérienne
- Cardiopathie congénitale[2]
  - Cardiopathie congénitale cyanogène non corrigée, y compris les conduits et les déviations réalisées à titre d'interventions palliatives
  - Cardiopathie congénitale complètement corrigée par une prothèse ou du matériel prothétique, installés par une intervention chirurgicale ou par cathétérisme au cours des 6 premiers mois qui suivent l'intervention[3]
  - Cardiopathie congénitale corrigée, avec défauts résiduels au siège de la pièce prothétique ou de la prothèse ou dans la région avoisinante (qui inhibent l'endothélialisation)
- Receveurs d'une greffe cardiaque qui développent une valvulopathie

1. **Les patients qui ne nécessitent plus d'antibiothérapie prophylactique contre l'endocardite** sont les sujets présentant un prolapsus de la valve mitrale, une cardiopathie rhumatismale, une maladie mitrale, une sténose aortique calcifiée ou des cardiopathies congénitales comme une malformation congénitale du septum interventriculaire ou auriculaire, et la myocardiopathie hypertrophique.
2. À l'exception des problèmes ci-dessus, une antibiothérapie prophylactique n'est plus recommandée en présence d'aucune autre forme de cardiopathie congénitale.
3. Une intervention prophylactique est acceptable, car l'endothélialisation du matériel prothétique se produit durant les 6 premiers mois qui suivent l'intervention.

TABLEAU 2[4]

Types d'interventions pour lesquelles une antibiothérapie prophylactique est acceptable chez les patients présentant l'un des problèmes cardiaques mentionnés au tableau 1

Dentaires	Prophylaxie recommandée pour toutes les interventions dentaires qui touchent le tissu gingival ou la région périapicale de la dent ou qui comportent la perforation de la muqueuse buccale (comprenant les nettoyages de routine, les extractions dentaires, les biopsies, le retrait de points de suture et l'installation de bagues d'orthodontie). Les interventions ou épisodes suivants ne dictent pas la prise de mesures prophylactiques : injections anesthésiques ordinaires administrées dans un tissu non infecté, radiographies dentaires, installation d'appareils orthodontiques et de prothèses dentaires amovibles, ajustement des appareils orthodontiques, installation de broches, extraction de dents de lait et saignements à la suite d'une blessure aux lèvres ou à la muqueuse buccale.
Interventions effractives au niveau des voies respiratoires comportant une incision ou une biopsie de la muqueuse, comme l'amygdalectomie ou la polypectomie	Prophylaxie recommandée. Utiliser les mêmes antibiotiques que dans le cas des interventions dentaires. Prophylaxie non recommandée pour la bronchoscopie, à moins que cette intervention comporte une incision des voies respiratoires.
Interventions au niveau du tractus génito-urinaire ou gastro-intestinal, y compris l'œsophago-gastroduodénoscopie et la coloscopie	La prophylaxie dans le seul but de prévenir l'endocardite n'est pas recommandée.

4. Ce tableau n'inclut pas les recommandations en cas d'infection active des voies respiratoires, gastro-intestinales, génito-urinaires ou de la peau, des structures cutanées et musculosquelettiques.

TABLEAU 3

Antibiotiques recommandés[5]

	Posologie – adultes **1 dose, de 30 à 60 minutes avant l'intervention**	**Posologie – enfants[6]** **1 dose, de 30 à 60 minutes avant l'intervention**
VOIE ORALE		
amoxicilline[7]	2 g	50 mg/kg
Allergie à la pénicilline :		
clindamycine **OU**	600 mg	20 mg/kg
céphalexine[8] **OU**	2 g	50 mg/kg
azithromycine ou clarithromycine	500 mg	15 mg/kg
VOIE PARENTÉRALE		
ampicilline **OU**	2 g, IM ou IV	50 mg/kg, IM ou IV
céfazoline ou ceftriaxone[9]	1 g, IM ou IV	50 mg/kg, IM ou IV
Allergie à la pénicilline :		
clindamycine **OU**	600 mg, IM ou IV	20 mg/kg, IM ou IV
céfazoline ou ceftriaxone[9]	1 g, IM ou IV	50 mg/kg, IM ou IV

5. Les médicaments et les posologies indiqués correspondent à ceux recommandés par l'American Heart Association.
6. Ne pas dépasser la dose recommandée chez l'adulte.
7. L'amoxicilline est recommandée en première intention en raison de son excellente biodisponibilité et de ses concentrations plasmatiques élevées et soutenues.
8. Ou une autre céphalosporine par voie orale de première ou de deuxième génération en doses équivalentes chez l'adulte et l'enfant.
9. Agent déconseillé chez les patients ayant des antécédents de réaction allergique immédiate à la pénicilline (urticaire, œdème angioneurotique, anaphylaxie).

Source : Wilson W., Taubert K.A., Gewitz M, *et al.* Prevention of infective endocarditis : guidelines from the American Heart Association : A guideline from the American Heart Association Rheumatic Fever, Endocarditis, and Kawasaki Disease Committee, Council on Cardiovascular Disease in the Young, and the Council on Clinical Cardiology, Council on Cardiovascular Surgery and Anesthesia, and the Quality of Care and Outcomes Research Interdisciplinary Working Group, Circulation. 9 octobre 2007 ; 116(15) : 1736-54 ; e-pub 19 avril 2007, Erratum in : Circulation, 9 octobre 2007 ; 116(15) : e376-7.
Aussi disponible à l'adresse : http://circ.ahajournals.org/cgi/content/full/116/15/1736. Site consulté le 18 octobre 2007.

ANNEXE N
Médicaments ophtalmiques

Renseignements généraux:

- Les méthodes d'administration des préparations ophtalmiques sont indiquées à l'annexe G.
- La plupart des médicaments ophtalmiques doivent être jetés 4 semaines après l'ouverture du flacon en raison du risque de contamination.
- Une petite quantité de médicaments ophtalmiques peut toujours être absorbée par voie générale, d'où le risque de réactions systémiques, notamment d'allergies.

Consulter un professionnel de la santé au sujet:

- du port de lentilles cornéennes (certains médicaments ou additifs peuvent être absorbés par les lentilles);
- de l'administration simultanée d'autres préparations ophtalmiques (l'ordre d'administration ainsi que les intervalles à respecter entre les administrations sont importants).

AGONISTES DES PROSTAGLANDINES $F_{2\alpha}$

Indications: Réduction de la pression intraoculaire chez les patients souffrant de glaucome à angle ouvert ou d'hypertension oculaire.

Précautions et mises en garde: Risque d'augmentation graduelle de la pigmentation de l'iris, des paupières et des cils, ainsi qu'une modification des cils; ne pas utiliser en présence d'inflammation intraoculaire évolutive; *latanoprost* – formation d'un précipité lors de l'utilisation simultanée de produit renfermant du thimérosal (espacer les instillations d'au moins 5 minutes); on peut l'utiliser en association avec d'autres agents afin d'abaisser la pression intraoculaire.

Réactions indésirables et effets secondaires: Irritation locale, hyperémie conjonctivale, sensation de présence d'un corps étranger, œdème maculaire.

■ BIMATOPROST (Lumigan)

POSOLOGIE

Adultes: 1 goutte de solution à 0,03 %, 1 fois par jour, le soir.

■ LATANOPROST (Xalatan)

POSOLOGIE

Adultes: 1 goutte de solution à 0,005 %, 1 fois par jour, le soir.

Remarques: Conserver le flacon qui n'a pas été ouvert au réfrigérateur. Après ouverture du flacon, le conserver au frais (si possible au réfrigérateur) pendant un maximum de 6 semaines.

■ TRAVOPROST (Travatan)

POSOLOGIE

Adultes: 1 goutte de solution à 0,004 %, 1 fois par jour, le soir.

ANESTHÉSIQUES LOCAUX

Indications: Anesthésie locale de courte durée permettant de mesurer la pression intraoculaire, de retirer les corps étrangers ou d'entreprendre toute autre intervention superficielle.

Précautions et mises en garde: L'usage répété retarde la guérison des lésions cornéennes et peut accroître le risque de toxicité cardiovasculaire et du SNC. Risque d'allergie croisée avec certains anesthésiques locaux. Éviter de frotter l'œil après l'administration, en raison du risque accru de lésions au niveau de l'œil anesthésié.

Réactions indésirables et effets secondaires: *Ophtalmiques* – irritation; *systémiques (rares)* – arythmies, dépression ou stimulation du SNC.

■ PROPARACAÏNE (Alcaine)

POSOLOGIE

Adultes et enfants: 1 ou 2 gouttes de solution à 0,5 % (une seule dose).

Remarques: Conserver au réfrigérateur • Aucune interaction avec les inhibiteurs de la cholinestérase destinés à l'usage ophtalmique.

■ TÉTRACAÏNE (Pontocaine, Minims Tetracaine)

POSOLOGIE

Adultes: 1 ou 2 gouttes de solution à 0,5 % ou à 1 % (une seule dose).

Remarques: Interaction possible avec les inhibiteurs de la cholinestérase destinés à l'usage ophtalmique, ce qui pourrait en prolonger la durée d'action et accroître le risque de toxicité.

ANTIALLERGIQUES OPHTALMIQUES

Indications: Conjonctivite allergique.

Précautions et mises en garde: Les effets ne se manifestent qu'après plusieurs jours de traitement.

■ CROMOGLYCATE (Cromolyn, Opticrom)

Synonyme: cromolyn

POSOLOGIE

Adultes et enfants > 5 ans: 2 gouttes de solution à 2 %, 4 fois par jour dans chaque œil.

Remarques: Le port de lentilles cornéennes pendant le traitement est déconseillé.

Réactions indésirables et effets secondaires: Chémosis, irritation oculaire.

■ KÉTOTIFÈNE (Zaditor)

POSOLOGIE

Adultes et enfants > 3 ans: 1 goutte de solution à 0,025 % dans l'œil affecté, toutes les 8 à 12 heures.

Réactions indésirables et effets secondaires: Hyperémie conjonctivale, céphalées.

■ LODOXAMIDE (Alomide)

Posologie

Adultes et enfants > 4 ans: 1 ou 2 gouttes de solution à 0,1 %, 4 fois par jour, pendant 3 mois au maximum.

Réactions indésirables et effets secondaires: Vision trouble, sensation de présence d'un corps étranger, irritation.

■ NÉDOCROMIL (Alocril)

Posologie

Adultes et enfants > 3 ans: 1 goutte de solution à 2 % dans chaque œil, 2 fois par jour, pendant toute la période d'exposition.

Remarques: Le port de lentilles cornéennes pendant le traitement est déconseillé.

Réactions indésirables et effets secondaires: Céphalées, brûlures oculaires, altération du goût.

ANTIBIOTIQUES

Indications: Infections ophtalmiques superficielles et localisées.

Précautions et mises en garde: Risque d'absorption de petites quantités pouvant entraîner une réaction d'hypersensibilité systémique, comme dans le cas de tous les médicaments ophtalmiques.

■ CHLORAMPHÉNICOL (Pentamycetin)

Posologie

Adultes et enfants: 1 goutte de solution ou un petit ruban d'onguent, toutes les 3 heures pendant les 48 premières heures, après quoi la fréquence d'administration peut être réduite.

Remarques: Risque rare de toxicité hématologique systémique en cas de traitement prolongé ou d'administration prolongée de doses très élevées.

■ CIPROFLOXACINE (Ciloxan)

Posologie

Adultes et enfants > 1 an (solution) et enfants > 2 ans (onguent): *Conjonctivite bactérienne - solution:* 1 ou 2 gouttes de solution à 0,3 %, dans l'œil atteint, toutes les 2 heures pendant 48 heures, lorsque le patient est éveillé, puis 2 gouttes, toutes les 4 heures pendant 5 jours; *onguent:* un petit ruban d'onguent, 3 fois par jour, pendant 48 heures, puis 2 fois par jour, pendant 5 jours.

Adultes et enfants > 12 ans: *Ulcère de la cornée - solution:* 2 gouttes dans l'œil atteint, toutes les 15 minutes, pendant 6 heures, puis toutes les 30 minutes, pendant le reste de la journée, puis toutes les heures, pendant les 24 heures suivantes, puis, toutes les 4 heures, jusqu'à la ré-épithélisation de la cornée; *onguent:* un petit ruban d'onguent toutes les 1 à 2 heures (nuit et jour) pendant 48 heures, puis toutes les 4 heures.

Remarques: Risque de formation d'un précipité blanc cristallin, inoffensif, qui disparaît avec le temps.

Réactions indésirables et effets secondaires: Altération du goût, réaction allergique généralisée, photophobie.

■ ÉRYTHROMYCINE (Ilotycin, PMS-Érythromycine)

POSOLOGIE

Adultes et enfants: *Traitement des infections* – un petit ruban, jusqu'à 6 fois par jour, au maximum, selon la gravité de l'infection.

Nourrissons: *Prophylaxie de la conjonctivite gonococcique ou à Chlamydia du nouveau-né* – un petit ruban dans chaque œil (une seule dose).

Réactions indésirables et effets secondaires: irritation.

■ GATIFLOXACINE (Zymar)

POSOLOGIE

Adultes et enfants > 1 an: 1 goutte de solution à 0,3 % dans l'œil atteint, toutes les 2 heures (jusqu'à 8 fois par jour) pendant 48 heures, lorsque le patient est éveillé, puis 1 goutte, 4 fois par jour pendant 5 jours, pendant 7 jours au total.

Réactions indésirables et effets secondaires: Altération du goût, irritation, sensation de brûlure, réaction allergique généralisée, photophobie.

■ GENTAMICINE (Garamycin, PMS-Gentamicin, Ratio-Gentamicin)

POSOLOGIE

Adultes et enfants > 6 ans: 1 ou 2 gouttes de solution à 0,3 %, 3 ou 4 fois par jour, ou un petit ruban d'onguent à 0,3 %, 3 ou 4 fois par jour.

Réactions indésirables et effets secondaires: Irritation, sensation de brûlure, vision trouble (onguent).

Remarques: Risque de ralentissement de la guérison de la cornée.

■ MOXIFLOXACINE (Vigamox)

POSOLOGIE

Adultes et enfants > 1 an: 1 goutte de solution à 0,5 %, 3 fois par jour, pendant 7 jours.

Réactions indésirables et effets secondaires: Altération du goût, irritation, sensation de brûlure, réaction allergique généralisée, photophobie.

■ OFLOXACINE (Ocuflox)

POSOLOGIE

Adultes: 1 ou 2 gouttes, toutes les 2 à 4 heures, pendant 2 jours, puis 4 fois par jour, pendant 8 jours.

Réactions indésirables et effets secondaires: Altération du goût, irritation, sensation de brûlure, réactions allergiques systémiques, photophobie.

■ TOBRAMYCINE (Sandoz Tobramycin, Tobrex)

POSOLOGIE

Adultes et enfants > 2 ans: 1 ou 2 gouttes de solution à 0,3 %, toutes les 1 à 4 heures, selon la gravité de l'infection, ou un petit ruban d'onguent à 0,3 %, 2 ou 3 fois par jour.

Remarques: Risque de ralentissement de la guérison de la cornée ■ Le port de lentilles cornéennes durant le traitement est déconseillé.

Réactions indésirables et effets secondaires: Irritation, sensation de brûlure, vision trouble (onguent).

ANTIHISTAMINIQUES

Indications: Diverses formes de conjonctivite allergique.

■ ÉMÉDASTINE (Emadine)

POSOLOGIE

Adultes: 1 goutte de solution à 0,05 % dans l'œil atteint, de 2 à 4 fois par jour.

Réactions indésirables et effets secondaires: Irritation locale, céphalées, somnolence, malaise.

■ LÉVOCABASTINE (Livostin)

POSOLOGIE

Adultes et enfants > 12 ans: 1 goutte de suspension à 0,05 %, de 2 à 4 fois par jour.

Réactions indésirables et effets secondaires: Légère sensation passagère de brûlure ou de picotement, céphalées, œdème de la paupière, somnolence, xérostomie.

■ OLOPATADINE (Patanol)

POSOLOGIE

Adultes et enfants > 3 ans: 1 ou 2 gouttes de solution à 0,1 %, 2 fois par jour.

Remarques: Une petite fraction est absorbée et excrétée dans l'urine.

Réactions indésirables et effets secondaires: Irritation de la conjonctive, céphalées, altération du goût.

ANTI-INFLAMMATOIRES NON STÉROÏDIENS

Précautions et mises en garde: Risque de sensibilité croisée avec les autres anti-inflammatoires non stéroïdiens ou l'aspirine, administrés par voie générale; ces agents peuvent masquer les signes d'infection; risque accru d'hémorragie lors de l'administration concomitante d'anticoagulants, d'autres AINS, d'antiplaquettaires, de thrombolytiques et de valproate.

■ DICLOFÉNAC (Voltaren Ophtha)

Indications: Inflammation à la suite d'une chirurgie de la cataracte et inflammation post-traumatique non chronique des plaies non pénétrantes.

POSOLOGIE

Adultes: *États inflammatoires* – 1 goutte de solution à 0,1 %, 4 ou 5 fois par jour; *chirurgie de la cataracte* – avant l'intervention, 1 goutte, jusqu'à 5 fois durant les 3 heures qui précèdent l'intervention; après l'intervention, 1 goutte, 15, 30 et 45 minutes après l'intervention, et ensuite de 3 à 5 fois par jour.

Remarques: Le port de lentilles souples pendant le traitement est déconseillé.

Réactions indésirables et effets secondaires: Irritation, hyperémie conjonctivale, vision trouble.

■ KÉTOROLAC (Acular, Acular LS)

Indications: Inflammation à la suite d'une chirurgie du cristallin et diminution de la douleur et des symptômes oculaires à la suite d'une chirurgie réfractive.

POSOLOGIE

Adultes: 1 ou 2 gouttes de solution à 0,5 %, toutes les 6 à 8 heures, en commençant le traitement 24 heures avant l'intervention chirurgicale du cristallin et en le poursuivant pendant 3 à 4 semaines, pour prévenir et pour soulager l'inflammation oculaire postopératoire OU 1 goutte de solution à 0,4 %, 4 fois par jour, pendant un maximum de 4 jours.

Réactions indésirables et effets secondaires: Irritation, hyperémie conjonctivale, sensation de présence d'un corps étranger.

ANTIVIRAUX

Indications: Kératoconjonctivite primaire et kératite épithéliale récurrente, causées par les virus de l'herpès simplex de types 1 et 2.

Précautions et mises en garde: Ne pas dépasser la posologie ni la fréquence recommandées en raison du risque de toxicité oculaire.

■ TRIFLURIDINE (Viroptic)

POSOLOGIE

Adultes: 1 goutte de solution à 1 %, toutes les 2 heures (jusqu'à 9 gouttes par jour), lorsque le patient est éveillé, jusqu'à la ré-épithélisation de la cornée, puis 1 goutte, toutes les 4 heures (jusqu'à 5 fois par jour), pendant 7 jours.

Réactions indésirables et effets secondaires: Sensation de brûlure, kératopathie (rare).

BÊTABLOQUANTS

Indications: Réduction de la pression intraoculaire chez les patients présentant un glaucome à angle ouvert ou une hypertension oculaire (diminution de la formation d'humeur aqueuse).

Contre-indications: Asthme bronchique ou antécédents d'asthme bronchique; bronchopneumopathie chronique obstructive grave; bradycardie; bloc auriculoventriculaire des 2e et 3e degrés; insuffisance cardiaque; choc cardiogénique.

Précautions et mises en garde: Absorption systémique possible, laquelle peut intensifier les effets cardiovasculaires indésirables (bradycardie, hypotension), particulièrement lors de l'administration concomitante d'agents cardiovasculaires (antihypertenseurs, antiarythmiques). D'autres réactions systémiques peuvent survenir, dont les bronchospasmes et la confusion (patients âgés).

■ BÉTAXOLOL (Betoptic S)

POSOLOGIE

Adultes: 1 goutte de suspension à 0,25 %, 2 fois par jour.

Réactions indésirables et effets secondaires: Conjonctivite, baisse de l'acuité visuelle, sensation de brûlure, rash (risque moindre de bronchospasmes en cas d'absorption systémique que lors de l'usage d'autres bêtabloquants).

■ LÉVOBUNOLOL (Apo-Levobunolol, Betagan, Novo-Levobunolol, PMS-Levobunolol, Ratio-Levobunolol)

POSOLOGIE

Adultes: 1 goutte de solution à 0,25 %, 2 fois par jour, ou 1 goutte de solution à 0,5 %, 1 ou 2 fois par jour.

Réactions indésirables et effets secondaires: Conjonctivite, baisse de l'acuité visuelle, sensation de brûlure, rash.

■ **TIMOLOL** (Apo-Timop, Gen-Timolol, PMS-Timolol, Sandoz Timolol, Timoptic, Timoptic-XE)

POSOLOGIE

Adultes: 1 goutte, 2 fois par jour, de solution à 0,25 % ou à 0,5 % ; 1 goutte, 1 fois par jour, le soir, de solution gélifiante (XE) à 0,25 % ou à 0,5 %.

Réactions indésirables et effets secondaires: Conjonctivite, baisse de l'acuité visuelle, sensation de brûlure, rash.

CHOLINERGIQUES (À ACTION DIRECTE)

Indications: Traitement du glaucome à angle ouvert (pour favoriser l'écoulement de l'humeur aqueuse) ; également, facilitation du myosis après une chirurgie ou un examen oculaire (pour contrer l'effet des mydriatiques).

Contre-indications: Toute affection au cours de laquelle il faut éviter la constriction de la pupille.

Précautions et mises en garde: Les effets indésirables systémiques comprennent la bradycardie, la transpiration et la salivation accrue, l'asthme, les nausées et les vomissements, les étourdissements, la diarrhée et les crampes abdominales.

■ **CARBACHOL** (Isopto Carbachol, Miostat)

POSOLOGIE

Adultes: 1 goutte de solution à 1,5 % ou à 3 %, 2 ou 3 fois par jour, ou solution à 0,01 % pendant l'intervention chirurgicale.

Réactions indésirables et effets secondaires: Vision trouble, altération de la vue, brûlures et douleurs oculaires, céphalées.

■ **PILOCARPINE** (Isopto Carpine, Minims Pilocarpine, Miocarpine, Pilopine HS)

POSOLOGIE

Adultes: 1 goutte de solution de 1 à 6 %, de 2 à 4 fois par jour, ou un petit ruban de gel à 4 %, au coucher.

Remarques: Chez les nourrissons, utiliser la solution à 1 % ou une quantité moins importante des autres teneurs ■ Une solution plus concentrée peut s'avérer nécessaire chez les patients dont l'iris est foncé.

Réactions indésirables et effets secondaires: Vision trouble, altération de la vue, brûlures et douleurs oculaires, céphalées, douleur aux sourcils.

CORTICOSTÉROÏDES

Indications: Traitement des inflammations du segment antérieur de l'œil dont la conjonctivite allergique, la kératite superficielle non spécifique, la conjonctivite infectieuse (avec des anti-infectieux) ; traitement des lésions de la cornée ; suppression du rejet du greffon après une kératoplastie, prévention de l'inflammation postopératoire.

Contre-indications: Infections oculaires fongiques ou virales ou tuberculose ophtalmique.

Précautions et mises en garde: Infections oculaires (les symptômes risquent d'être masqués, administrer l'anti-infectieux approprié) ; diabète ; glaucome.

Réactions indésirables et effets secondaires: Amincissement de la cornée, pression intraoculaire accrue, irritation.

Remarques: Diminuer la fréquence des applications au fil du traitement.

■ DEXAMÉTHASONE (AK-Dex, Diodex, Maxidex)

Posologie

Adultes: 1 ou 2 gouttes de solution à 0,1 %, de 4 à 6 fois par jour (au cours des 24 à 48 premières heures, on peut administrer cette dose toutes les heures), ou un petit ruban d'onguent à 0,1 %, 3 ou 4 fois par jour.

■ FLUOROMÉTHOLONE (Flarex, FML, FML Forte, PMS-Fluorometholone)

Posologie

Adultes: 1 ou 2 gouttes de suspension à 0,1 % ou à 0,25 %, de 2 à 4 fois par jour (au cours des 24 à 48 premières heures, on peut administrer cette dose toutes les heures).

Remarques: Bien agiter le contenant avant l'emploi.

■ PREDNISOLONE (AK-Tate, Diopred, Pred Forte, Pred Mild, Ratio-Prednisolone, Sandoz Prednisolone)

Posologie

Adultes: 1 ou 2 gouttes de la solution ou de la suspension à 0,12 % ou à 1 %, de 2 à 4 fois par jour (au cours des 24 à 48 premières heures, on peut administrer cette dose toutes les heures).

Remarques: Bien agiter le contenant avant l'emploi.

■ RIMEXOLONE (Vexol)

Posologie

Adultes: *Inflammation postopératoire* – 1 ou 2 gouttes de suspension à 1 %, 4 fois par jour; *uvéite antérieure* – 1 ou 2 gouttes de suspension à 1 %, toutes les heures lorsque le patient est éveillé pendant la 1re semaine; 1 goutte, toutes les 2 heures lorsque le patient est éveillé pendant la 2e semaine; 1 goutte, 4 fois par jour, durant la 3e semaine; 1 goutte, 3 fois par jour, durant les 4 premiers jours de la 4e semaine; et 1 goutte, 2 fois par jour, durant les 3 derniers jours de la 4e semaine.

Remarques: Bien agiter le contenant avant l'emploi.

DÉCONGESTIONNANTS ET VASOCONSTRICTEURS OCULAIRES

Indications: Diminution de la congestion oculaire due à l'irritation par vasoconstriction des vaisseaux sanguins de la conjonctive.

Précautions et mises en garde: Risque d'effets mydriatiques; l'absorption systémique peut entraîner des effets cardiovasculaires indésirables; l'usage prolongé ou excessif peut entraîner une hyperémie rebond; faire preuve de prudence chez les patients exposés à un risque de glaucome aigu par fermeture de l'angle; risque d'intensification des effets cardiovasculaires lors de l'administration simultanée de bêtabloquants, d'IMAO ou d'antidépresseurs tricycliques; risque accru d'arythmies lors de l'administration d'anesthésiques par inhalation.

■ NAPHAZOLINE (AK Con, Albalon, Allergy Drops, Clear Eyes, Collyre Bleu Laiter, Diopticon, Naphcon Forte)

Posologie

Adultes: 1 ou 2 gouttes de solution à 0,012 %[VL], 2 ou 3 fois par jour, selon les besoins, ou 1 ou 2 gouttes de solution à 0,1 %[Pr], toutes les 3 ou 4 heures, selon les besoins.

Réactions indésirables et effets secondaires: *Ophtalmiques* – irritation, vision brouillée; *systémiques* – étourdissements, céphalées, nausées, transpiration, faiblesse.

■ OXYMÉTAZOLINE (Claritin Soulagement des yeux irrités par les allergies, Visine Au travail)

Posologie

Adultes et enfants > 6 ans: 1 ou 2 gouttes de solution à 0,025 %, 3 ou 4 fois par jour, selon les besoins.

Réactions indésirables et effets secondaires: *Ophtalmiques* – irritation; *systémiques* – céphalées, insomnie, nervosité, tachycardie.

■ TÉTRAHYDROZOLINE (Visine Originale)

Posologie

Adultes et enfants > 6 ans: 1 ou 2 gouttes de solution à 0,05 %, de 2 à 4 fois par jour.

Réactions indésirables et effets secondaires: *Ophtalmiques* – irritation; *systémiques* – tachycardie, hypertension.

INHIBITEURS DE L'ANHYDRASE CARBONIQUE

Indications: Traitement du glaucome à angle ouvert et d'autres formes d'hypertension oculaire (diminution de la formation d'humeur aqueuse).

Précautions et mises en garde: Risque d'allergie croisée avec les sulfamides; risque d'exacerbation de la lithiase rénale; ne pas administrer aux patients dont la Cl_{Cr} est < 30 mL/min.

■ BRINZOLAMIDE (Azopt)

Posologie

Adultes: 1 goutte de solution à 1 %, 2 ou 3 fois par jour.

Réactions indésirables et effets secondaires: Goût amer, irritation oculaire ou allergie.

■ DORZOLAMIDE (Trusopt)

Posologie

Adultes: *Monothérapie* – 1 goutte de solution à 2 %, 3 fois par jour; *traitement d'appoint avec un bêtabloquant* – 1 goutte, 2 fois par jour.

Réactions indésirables et effets secondaires: Goût amer, irritation oculaire ou allergie.

LARMES ARTIFICIELLES, LUBRIFIANTS OCULAIRES (solutions isotoniques ou onguents tamponnés et stériles, pellet oculaire)

(Artificial Tears, Celluvisc, Duolube, Duratears Naturale, Eyelube, Genteal, HypoTears, Lacri-Lube, Lacrisert, Liquifilm Forte, Liquifilm Tears, Moisture Drops, Murine Supplemental Tears, Refresh, Refresh Plus, Refresh Tears, Tear Drops, Tear-Gel, Tears Naturale, Tears Naturale Free, Tears Naturale II, Tears Plus, Visine True Tears)

Chaque produit peut contenir, entre autres, les ingrédients actifs suivants: alcool polyvinylique, carboxyméthylcellulose sodique, dextran 70, hydroxypropylméthylcellulose, glycérine, huile minérale, hyaluronate sodique, hydroxypropylcellulose, lanoline, polysorbate 80, vaseline.

Indications: *Larmes artificielles* – traitement de la xérophtalmie (solutions isotoniques et agents mouillants); lubrification des yeux. *Lubrifiants oculaires* – lubrification et protection, en présence de diverses affections dont la kératite, la sensibilité réduite de la cornée, l'érosion de la cornée, la kératite sèche, ou pendant ou après une chirurgie oculaire ou le retrait d'un corps étranger.

Posologie

Adultes et enfants: *Larmes artificielles et lubrifiants oculaires* – 1 ou 2 gouttes, 3 ou 4 fois par jour, ou au besoin; *pellets* (Lacrisert) – 1 ou 2 fois par jour; *onguents* – un petit ruban d'onguent, au besoin.

Remarques: Risque de modification des effets d'autres médicaments ophtalmiques administrés en même temps.

Réactions indésirables et effets secondaires: Photophobie, œdème de la paupière, sensation de brûlure (pellets seulement), vue passagèrement brouillée (surtout avec l'onguent), gêne oculaire.

MYDRIATIQUES CYCLOPLÉGIQUES

Indications: Préparation à la réfraction cycloplégique; traitement de l'uvéite (à l'exception du tropicamide).

Contre-indications: Glaucome (atropine et homatropine), glaucome à angle fermé (cyclopentolate et tropicamide).

Précautions et mises en garde: Faire preuve de prudence chez les patients ayant des antécédents de glaucome à angle ouvert (cyclopentolate, phényléphrine et tropicamide); l'absorption systémique peut entraîner des effets anticholinergiques tels que la confusion, un comportement inhabituel, des rougeurs du visage, des hallucinations, des troubles de l'élocution, la somnolence, le gonflement d'estomac (nourrissons), la tachycardie, la xérostomie.

Remarques: Une solution plus concentrée ou plusieurs applications peuvent s'avérer nécessaires chez les patients dont l'iris est foncé.

■ ATROPINE (Atropine AK, Dioptic's Atropine, Isopto Atropine, Minims Atropine)

Posologie

Adultes et enfants > 6 ans: *Réfraction cycloplégique* – 1 goutte de solution à 1%, la veille de l'examen, répéter 1 heure avant l'examen; *uvéite* – 1 goutte de solution à 1%, 3 fois par jour.

Remarques: Ne pas administrer aux enfants ayant des antécédents de réactions graves à l'atropine ■ Les effets sur l'accommodation peuvent durer jusqu'à 6 jours; la mydriase peut durer jusqu'à 12 jours.

Réactions indésirables et effets secondaires: Irritation, vision trouble, photophobie, pression intraoculaire accrue.

■ CYCLOPENTOLATE (AK-Pentolate, Cyclogyl, Diopentolate, Minims Cyclopentolate, PMS-Cyclopentolate)

Posologie

Adultes et enfants: 1 goutte de solution de 0,5 à 1 %; répéter après 5 minutes, au besoin.

Remarques: Le pic de la cycloplégie est atteint dans les 25 à 75 minutes et l'effet dure de 6 à 24 heures ■ Le pic de la mydriase est atteint dans les 30 à 60 minutes et l'effet peut durer plusieurs jours.

Réactions indésirables et effets secondaires: Irritation, vision trouble, photophobie, pression intraoculaire accrue.

■ HOMATROPINE (Isopto Homatropine)

Posologie

Adultes et enfants: *Réfraction cycloplégique* – 1 ou 2 gouttes de solution à 2 % ou à 5 %; répéter après 10 à 20 minutes, au besoin; *uvéite* – 1 goutte de solution à 2 % ou à 5 %, 2 ou 3 fois par jour (on peut administrer à une plus grande fréquence, soit toutes les 3 ou 4 heures).

Remarques: La cycloplégie et la mydriase peuvent persister pendant 24 à 72 heures.

Réactions indésirables et effets secondaires: Irritation, vision trouble, photophobie, pression intraoculaire accrue.

■ PHÉNYLÉPHRINE (Mydfrin)

POSOLOGIE

Adultes et enfants: 1 goutte de solution à 2,5 %, à répéter au besoin, selon l'intervention ou la chirurgie.

Remarques: Une absorption systémique peut entraîner un risque de réactions cardiovasculaires et d'effets sur le SNC (particulièrement chez les patients atteints de cardiopathie) ■ L'effet maximal se manifeste dans les 15 à 60 minutes ■ La mydriase dure jusqu'à 3 heures.

Réactions indésirables et effets secondaires: *Ophtalmiques* – vision trouble, douleur aux sourcils, irritation, photophobie; *systémiques* – étourdissements, tachycardie, hypertension, pâleur, transpiration, tremblements.

■ TROPICAMIDE (Diotrope, Minims Tropicamide, Mydriacyl, Tropicacyl)

POSOLOGIE

Adultes: 1 ou 2 gouttes de solution à 0,5 % ou à 1%; répéter après 5 minutes.

Remarques: L'effet maximal se manifeste dans les 20 à 40 minutes ■ La cycloplégie dure de 2 à 6 heures et la mydriase jusqu'à 7 heures.

Réactions indésirables et effets secondaires: Irritation, vision trouble, photophobie, pression intraoculaire accrue.

SYMPATHOMIMÉTIQUES (agonistes alpha$_2$-adrénergiques spécifiques)

Indications: Réduction de la pression intraoculaire chez les patients souffrant de glaucome à angle ouvert ou d'hypertension oculaire et agent destiné à maîtriser ou à prévenir les hausses postopératoires de la pression intraoculaire, qui apparaissent après les chirurgies ophtalmiques au laser du segment antérieur (apraclonidine).

Précautions et mises en garde: Ne pas administrer en concomitance avec un IMAO; l'absorption systémique peut entraîner un risque de réactions cardiovasculaires et d'effets sur le SNC (particulièrement chez les patients atteints de cardiopathie).

Remarques: Risque de réduction de l'efficacité lors de l'administration simultanée d'antidépresseurs tricycliques; risque de dépression accrue du SNC lors de la prise simultanée d'alcool et d'autres dépresseurs du SNC; risque d'effets cardiovasculaires indésirables additifs lors de l'usage simultané d'autres agents cardiovasculaires.

■ APRACLONIDINE (Iopidine)

POSOLOGIE

Adultes: *Glaucome* – 1 ou 2 gouttes de solution à 0,5 %, 2 ou 3 fois par jour; *usage préopératoire* – 1 goutte de solution à 1 %, 1 heure avant l'intervention chirurgicale, et une seconde goutte immédiatement après l'opération.

Réactions indésirables et effets secondaires: *Ophtalmiques* – irritation, hyperémie conjonctivale, sensation de présence d'un corps étranger, mydriase, réactions allergiques; *systémiques* – réactions allergiques, arythmies, bradycardie, somnolence, sécheresse nasale, évanouissement, céphalées, nervosité, faiblesse.

Remarques: Vérifier le pouls et la pression artérielle.

■ BRIMONIDINE (Alphagan, Alphagan P, Apo-Brimonidine, PMS-Brimonidine, Ratio-Brimonidine)

POSOLOGIE

Adultes: 1 goutte de solution à 0,15 % ou 0,2 %, 2 fois par jour (à 12 heures d'intervalle).

Réactions indésirables et effets secondaires: *Ophtalmiques* – irritation; *systémiques* – somnolence, étourdissements, xérostomie, céphalées, faiblesse, douleurs musculaires.

ANNEXE O
Notification d'un effet indésirable d'un produit pharmaceutique

Santé Canada Health Canada

Canada Vigilance

Direction générale des produits de santé et des aliments
Health Products and Food Branch

Le formulaire doit être imprimé, ensuite envoyé par télécopie à : **1 866 678-6789** ou par courrier selon les instructions fournies.

Notification concernant un effet indésirable soupçonné dû à **des produits de santé commercialisés*** au Canada

PROTÉGÉ B**
(lorsque complété)

The English version of this document is available at: http://www.hc-sc.gc.ca/dhp-mps/medeff/report-declaration/ar-ei_form_e.html

A. Données relatives au patient (voir section «confidentialité»)

1. Identification

2. Age au moment de la réaction

3. Sexe ☐ Homme ☐ Femme

4. Taille ______ pi ou ______ cm

5. Poids ______ lb ou ______ kg

B. Effet indésirable

1. Suites de l'effet indésirable (cocher toutes les cases pertinentes)

☐ Décès__________ (aaaa/mm/jj)
☐ Met la vie en danger
☐ Hospitalisation
☐ Hospitalisation prolongée
☐ Incapacité
☐ Malformation congénitale
☐ Besoin d'intervention pour prévenir lésion / invalidités permanentes
☐ Autre : ______________

2. Date de l'effet AAAA | MM | JJ

3. Date de la présente notification AAAA | MM | JJ

4. Description de l'effet ou du problème

C. Produit(s) de santé commercialisé(s) (voir section «Comment déclarer un EI»)

1. Nom (préciser la teneur indiquée sur l'étiquette et le nom du fabricant, si connus)
N°1
N°2

2. Dose, fréquence et voie d'administration
N°1
N°2

3. Date du traitement (si inconnues, donner la durée)
N°1 Du (aaaa/mm/jj) - Au (aaaa/mm/jj)
N°2

4. Indications relatives au produit de santé suspect
N°1
N°2

5. Effet disparu après arrêt de l'administration ou réduction de la dose
N°1 ☐ Oui ☐ Non ☐ Ne s'applique pas
N°2 ☐ Oui ☐ Non ☐ Ne s'applique pas

6. N° de lot (si connu)
N°1
N°2

7. Date d'exp(si connue)
N°1 (aaaa/mm/jj)
N°2

8. Effet réapparu après réadministration
N°1 ☐ Oui ☐ Non ☐ Ne s'applique pas
N°2 ☐ Oui ☐ Non ☐ Ne s'applique pas

9. Produit de santé concomitante (nom, dose, fréquence et voie d'administration) et dates du traitement (aaaa/mm/jj) (exclure le traitement de l'effet)

5. Données (tests, analyses de laboratoire) pertinentes (avec les dates (aaaa/mm/jj))

6. Histoire médicale pertinente, y compris les facteurs pré-existants
(p. ex. allergies, grossesse, consommation de tabac et d'alcool, dysfonctionnement hépatique / rénal)

10. Traitement de l'effet indésirable (médicaments et / ou traitement), avec les dates (aaaa/mm/jj)

D. Déclarant (voir section «confidentialité»)

1. Nom, adresse et numéro de téléphone

2. Professionnel de la santé? ☐ Oui ☐ Non	**3. Profession**	**4. Également déclaré au fabricant?** ☐ Oui ☐ Non

Une déclaration n'équivaut pas à reconnaître que le personnel médical ou le produit a causé ou contribué à causer l'effet indésirable.
*** Utilisez ce formulaire pour déclarer les effets indésirables soupçonnés dûs aux produits pharmaceutiques, biologiques (incluant les dérivés plasmatiques ainsi que les vaccins thérapeutiques et diagnostiques), produits de santé naturels et produits radiopharmaceutiques.**
**** Selon les Politiques sur la Sécurité du Sécrétariat du Conseil du Trésor du Canada.**
SC/HC 4016 (10/07)

Canada

Expédiez ce formulaire au bureau de Canada Vigilance de votre région (voir la liste ci-dessous)

DIRECTIVES CONCERNANT LA NOTIFICATION VOLONTAIRE DES EFFETS INDÉSIRABLES (EI)

Confidentialité de l'information concernant les effets indésirables
Toute information relative à l'identité du patient ou du déclarant des effets indésirables sera protégée selon la *Loi sur la protection des renseignements personnels*. Pour la case «Identification», indiquez un code d'identification quelconque qui vous permettra, à vous le déclarant, de trouver le cas facilement si l'on communique avec vous pour obtenir davantage de renseignements; n'employez pas le nom du patient.
Énoncé de confidentialité: L'information relative à l'identité du patient ou du déclarant sera protégée sous la *Loi sur la protection des renseignements personnels,* même lors d'une demande d'accès à l'information. Les renseignements sur les effets indésirables présumés attribuables à un produit de santé commercialisé sont fournis volontairement et sont maintenus dans une base de données informatisée. Ces données sont utilisées dans le cadre de l'évaluation des produits de santé commercialisés et peuvent contribuer à la détection de problèmes potentiels en matière de sécurité ainsi qu'à l'évaluation de leurs bienfaits et de leurs risques. Pour obtenir plus d'information sur les renseignements personnels recueillis dans le cadre de ce programme, veuillez consulter le document suivant : Fichier de renseignements personnels; Santé Canada; Direction générale des produits de santé et des aliments; Système de déclaration des incidents; SCan PPU 088, qui est disponible à l'adresse Internet suivante: http://infosource.gc.ca/inst/shc/fed07_f.asp

Quoi signaler?
Les effets indésirables associés à des produits de santé commercialisés d'ordonnance et sans ordonnance, à des produits biologiques (incluant les dérivés plasmatiques ainsi que les vaccins thérapeutiques et diagnostiques), à des produits de santé naturels et à des produits radiopharmaceutiques sont recueillies par le Programme Canada Vigilance. Un effet non voulu, l'abus de médicaments, la surdose de médicaments, les interactions médicamenteuses et les interactions entre les médicaments et les aliments et l'absence inhabituelle d'efficacité thérapeutique sont également considérés comme des EI qui doivent être déclarés.

Les effets indésirables signalés sont, dans la plupart des cas, uniquement des associations soupçonnées. Une simple association temporelle ou possible peut justifier une déclaration, laquelle n'implique pas nécessairement un lien de cause à effet.

Nous voulons être informés de tous les effets indésirables présumés, surtout s'ils sont:
- **imprévus** (compte tenu des renseignements sur le produit ou de l'étiquetage), peu importe leur gravité;
- **graves**, qu'ils soient prévus ou non;
- **liés à des produits récemment mis sur le marché** (commercialisés depuis moins de 5 ans), peu importe leur nature ou leur gravité.

Qu'entend-on par effet grave?
Un effet indésirable grave est une réaction qui nécessite ou prolonge l'hospitalisation, une malformation congénitale ou une invalidité ou incapacité persistante ou importante, met la vie en danger ou entraîne la mort. Les effets indésirables qui nécessitent une intervention médicale importante pour éviter l'un des autres effets signalés plus haut sont aussi jugés graves.

Comment déclarer un EI?
Pour signaler un effet indésirable soupçonné dû à des produits de santé commercialisés au Canada, les professionels de la santé ou les consommateurs (de préférence en collaboration avec leur professionnel de la santé afin d'inclure les renseignements concernant leurs antécédents médicaux pour que les notifications soient complètes et valides sur le plan scientifique) doivent remplir la Notification concernant un effet indésirable soupçonné dû à des produits de santé commercialisés au Canada (SC/HC 4016). Vous pouvez obtenir le formulaire sur l'Internet, à http://www.hc-sc.gc.ca/dhp-mps/medeff/report-declaration/ar-ei_form_f.html; vous pouvez aussi le procurer en vous adressant à votre Bureau régional de Canada Vigilance (voir ci-dessous les renseignements concernant les personnes-ressources), ou encore en consultant les annexes du *Compendium des produits et spécialités pharmaceutiques* (CPS).

Il s'agit de remplir le Formulaire de déclaration de Canada Vigilance en fournissant le plus de détails possible et en utilisant un formulaire distinct pour chaque patient. On peut déclarer jusqu'à deux produits de santé soupçonnés sur un même formulaire. S'il y a plus de deux produits présumés responsable de l'effet indésirable, il faut joindre un autre formulaire. Des pages supplémentaires peuvent être jointes au formulaire au besoin. Le succès du programme dépend de la qualité et de l'exactitude des données fournies.

Les critères des présentes lignes directrices s'appliquent également pour les effets secondaires suivant l'immunisation (ESSI) de vaccins administrés pour prévenir des maladies infectieuses. Les professionnels de la santé doivent remplir *Le formulaire de rapport des effets secondaires suivant l'immunisation*. Vous pouvez obtenir ce formulaire sur l'Internet, à http://www.phac-aspc.gc.ca/im/aefi-form_f.html, ou dans les annexes du CPS. Il existe aussi des formulaires propres aux provinces et territoires, qu'on peut se procurer auprès des services de santé publique locaux ou des autorités sanitaires des provinces ou territoires.

Pour obtenir des renseignements supplémentaires sur le Programme Canada Vigilance ou d'autres exemplaires du Formulaire de déclaration de Canada Vigilance, ou pour déclarer un EI, les professionnels de la santé et les consommateurs sont invités à communiquer avec les Bureaux régionaux de Canada Vigilance (voir la liste d'adresses ci-après). Les professionnels de la santé et les consommateurs peuvent utiliser les numéros suivant sans frais. Les appels seront automatiquement dirigés vers le Bureau régional de Canada Vigilance approprié en fonction de l'indicatif régional d'où provient l'appel.

Téléphone sans frais : 1 866 234-2345 **Télécopieur sans frais : 1 866 678-6789**

Colombie-Britannique et Yukon : Bureau régional de Canada Vigilance - C.-B. et Yukon, 400-4595, Canada Way, Burnaby (Colombie-Britannique.) V5G 1J9
CanadaVigilance_BC@hc-sc.gc.ca

Alberta et Territoires du Nord-Ouest : Bureau régional de Canada Vigilance - Alberta et Territoires du Nord-Ouest, 9700, ave Jasper, pièce 730, Edmonton (Alberta) T5J 4C3
CanadaVigilance_AB@hc-sc.gc.ca

Saskatchewan : Bureau régional de Canada Vigilance - Saskatchewan, 101 - 22e rue Est, 4e étage, pièce 412, Saskatoon (Saskatchewan) S7K 0E1
CanadaVigilance_SK@hc-sc.gc.ca

Manitoba : Bureau régional de Canada Vigilance - Manitoba, 510, boulevard Lagimodière, Winnipeg (Manitoba), R2J 3Y1
CanadaVigilance_MB@hc-sc.gc.ca

Ontario et Nunavut : Bureau régional de Canada Vigilance - Ontario et Nunavut, 2301, avenue Midland, Toronto (Ontario), M1P 4R7
CanadaVigilance_ON@hc-sc.gc.ca

Québec : Bureau régional de Canada Vigilance - Québec, 1001, rue Saint-Laurent Ouest, Longueuil (Québec), J4K 1C7
CanadaVigilance_QC@hc-sc.gc.ca

Atlantique : Bureau régional de Canada Vigilance - Atlantique, pour Nouveau-Brunswick, Nouvelle-Écosse, île-du-Prince-Édouard, Terre-Neuve/Labrador
Maritime Centre, 1505, rue Barrington, 16e étage, pièce 1625, Halifax (Nouvelle-Écosse), B3J 3Y6
CanadaVigilance_ATL@hc-sc.gc.ca

Que faire si l'on obtient des renseignements additionnels sur un EI déjà déclaré?
Tout renseignement concernant le suivi d'un EI qui a déjà été signalé peut être communiqué sur un autre formulaire. Ce suivi peut être également communiqué par téléphone, par télécopieur ou par courriel à l'adresse du Bureau régional de Canada Vigilance (voir la liste d'adresses ci-haut). Afin que l'on puisse faire le lien entre cette information et la déclaration initiale, il importe de signaler qu'il s'agit d'un suivi, d'indiquer la date de la déclaration initiale et le numéro de référence fournis dans l'accusé de réception, si vous les connaissez. Il est très important que les données de suivi soient clairement désignées comme telles et soient rattachées à la déclaration initiale.

Peut-on signaler les EI au détenteur d'une autorisation de mise en marché (fabricant)?
Les professionels de la santé et les consommateurs peuvent également signaler les EI au détenteur d'une autorisation de mise en marché. Veuillez indiquer, dans votre déclaration faite à Santé Canada, si le cas a également été signalé au détenteur d'une autorisation de mise en marché pour le produit.

ANNEXE O (suite)
Notification d'un effet indésirable d'un vaccin

ACHEMINER À : (COORDONNÉES DE LA DIRECTION RÉGIONALE DE SANTÉ PUBLIQUE)

Santé et Services sociaux Québec

RAPPORT DE MANIFESTATIONS CLINIQUES SURVENUES APRÈS UNE VACCINATION

À L'USAGE DE LA DSP : NO « ESPRI »

IDENTIFICATION DE LA PERSONNE VACCINÉE — NUMÉRO RAMQ :

NOM, PRÉNOM	# TÉLÉPHONE	DATE DE NAISSANCE (ANNÉE / MOIS / JOUR)	SEXE	DATE DE VACCINATION (ANNÉE / MOIS / JOUR)
			❑[1] Masculin ❑[2] Féminin	

VACCINS

VACCIN(S) ADMINISTRÉS	DOSE (1e, 2e, 3e…)	SITE	VOIE (IM, SC, ID)	QUANTITÉ	FABRICANT	NUMÉRO DE LOT

INTERVALLE ENTRE LA VACCINATION ET LE DÉBUT DE LA MANIFESTATION CLINIQUE PRINCIPALE MOTIVANT LA DÉCLARATION — MIN | HEURES | JOURS

MANIFESTATIONS CLINIQUES

Ne pas signaler les manifestations cliniques qui sont clairement attribuables à une infection ou à une autre étiologie concomitante.

Les manifestations cliniques marquées d'un astérisque (*) doivent être diagnostiquées par un médecin.

Fournir tout autre renseignement, dont la durée et la sévérité, au verso (RENSEIGNEMENTS COMPLÉMENTAIRES)

FIÈVRE

Température la plus élevée enregistrée

❑[1] ≥40,5° C (105° F)
❑[2] 39,0-40,4° C (102,2-104,9° F)
❑[3] Température jugée très élevée mais non mesurée (doit être accompagnée d'autres symptômes)

RÉACTIONS LOCALES AU SITE D'ADMINISTRATION

❑[1] **ABCÈS INFECTÉ** (cocher un ou deux des éléments ci-dessous)
- Coloration de gram ou culture positive ____ ❑[1]
- Écoulement purulent avec signes d'inflammation ____ ❑[2]
- Sans écoulement, avec signes d'inflammation ____ ❑[3]

❑[2] **ABCÈS STÉRILE/NODULE** (aucun signe d'infection)
Durant plus d'un mois et mesurant plus de 2,5 cm de diamètre
Culture non faite ❑[1] Culture négative ❑[2]

❑[3] **RÉACTION LOCALE IMPORTANTE** (cocher un ou plusieurs éléments ci-dessous)
- Qui dure 4 jours ou plus ____ ❑[1]
- Qui s'étend au-delà de l'articulation la plus proche ____ ❑[2]
- Autre (décrire dans la case « renseignements complémentaires ») ____ ❑[3]

SIGNES NEUROLOGIQUES

❑[2] **CONVULSIONS** *
Fébriles ❑[1] Afébriles ❑[2] Ne sait pas ❑[3]
Ne pas tenir compte des évanouissements, convulsions qui surviennent en dedans des 30 minutes qui suivent l'immunisation, ni des convulsions qui entrent dans le cadre d'une encéphalopathie ou d'une méningite/encéphalite

Antécédents personnels de convulsions :
Non ❑[1] Antécédents inconnus ❑[2] Fébriles ❑[3]
Afébriles ❑[4] Type inconnu ❑[5]

❑[3] **ENCÉPHALOPATHIE** *
Apparition rapide d'une condition neurologique grave caractérisée par au moins deux des signes suivants :
i : Convulsions
ii : Changement marqué dans le niveau de conscience ou l'état mental (comportement et/ou personnalité) qui dure 24 heures ou plus
iii : Signes neurologiques en foyer qui persistent pendant plus de 24 heures

❑[4] **MÉNINGITE ET/OU ENCÉPHALITE** *
Résultats anormaux du LCR et installation rapide de :
i : Fièvre avec raideur de la nuque ou signes d'atteinte méningée OU
Signes et symptômes d'encéphalopathie (voir ENCÉPHALOPATHIE ci-dessus)
(inscrire le résultat de l'analyse du LCR dans la case « renseignements complémentaires ») (VERSO)

☐4 **CELLULITE ***
Infection cutanée avec prescription d'antibiotiques

MANIFESTATIONS CLINIQUES SYSTÉMIQUES

☐1 **ADÉNOPATHIE GRAVE** (cocher l'un des éléments ci-dessous)
- Tuméfaction ganglionnaire sans écoulement ______ ☐1
- Tuméfaction ganglionnaire avec écoulement ______ ☐2

(s.v.p. décrire dans la case « renseignements complémentaires ») (VERSO)

☐2 **ALLERGIE** (cocher un ou plusieurs éléments ci-dessous)
- Difficulté respiratoire due à un bronchospasme ______ ☐1
- Oedème au niveau de la bouche ou de la gorge ______ ☐2
- Oedème au visage ou généralisé ______ ☐3
- Manifestations cutanées prurigineuses (décrire dans la case « renseignements complémentaires »)
  - Urticaire ______ ☐4
  - Autre (décrire dans la case « renseignements complémentaires ») (VERSO) ______ ☐5

☐3 **ÉRUPTION CUTANÉE** (sans prurit)
Qui dure 4 jours ou plus
(décrire dans la case « renseignements complémentaires »)
- Généralisée ______ ☐1
- Localisée ______ ☐2

Qui dure < 4 jours
(décrire dans la case « renseignements complémentaires »)
- Généralisée ______ ☐3
- Localisée ______ ☐4

☐4 **CHOC ANAPHYLACTIQUE ***
Dans les 30 minutes suivant l'immunisation, associé habituellement à une réaction allergique et évoluant rapidement vers un collapsus cardio-vasculaire. Requiert l'administration d'adrénaline

☐5 **ÉPISODE D'HYPOTONIE-HYPORÉACTIVITÉ** (enfant < 2 ans seulement)
Présence de toutes les caractéristiques suivantes :
i : Diminution/perte généralisée du tonus musculaire ET
ii : baisse du niveau de conscience ou perte de conscience ET
iii : pâleur ou cyanose. Ne devrait pas être confondu avec un évanouissement, un choc vagal, un état post-convulsif, une anaphylaxie ou un état léthargique dû à la fièvre

☐6 **ARTHRALGIE/ATHRITE**
Douleur ou inflammation articulaire qui dure au moins 24 heures
S'il s'agit d'une poussée évolutive d'une maladie pré-existante, fournir les détails dans la case « renseignements complémentaires » (VERSO)

☐7 **VOMISSEMENTS ET/OU DIARRHÉES SÉVÈRES**
Doivent être assez sévères pour nuire aux activités quotidiennes

☐8 **ÉPISODE DE CRIS OU PLEURS PERSISTANTS**
Inconsolable pendant 3 heures ou plus ; ou type de pleurs vraiment anormal pour l'enfant et jamais observé antérieurement par les parents

☐5 **ANESTHÉSIE/PARESTHÉSIE ***
Qui dure plus de 24 heures
(décrire dans la case « renseignements complémentaires ») (VERSO)
- Généralisée ______ ☐1
- Localisée ______ ☐2

☐6 **PARALYSIE *** (Ne pas cocher si syndrome de Guillain-Barré déjà coché)
- Paralysie des membres ______ ☐1
- Paralysie faciale ou des nerfs crâniens ______ ☐2

☐7 **SYNDROME DE GUILLAIN-BARRÉ ***
Diminution progressive et subaiguë de la force musculaire de plus d'un membre (habituellement symétrique) avec hyporéflexie/aréflexie

DIVERS

☐1 **PAROTIDITE**
Glande(s) parotide(s) tuméfié(es) douloureuse(s) ou sensible(s)

☐3 **THROMBOCYTOPÉNIE ***
(inscrire le résultat de l'analyse dans la case « renseignements complémentaires »)

☐4 **SYNDROME OCULO-RESPIRATOIRE (SOR)** (Selon les définitions de surveillance)

AUTRES MANIFESTATIONS CLINIQUES GRAVES OU INHABITUELLES

☐ Inclure toute manifestation clinique susceptible d'être associée à l'immunisation, qui ne peut être classée dans aucune des catégories énumérées ci-dessus ni être clairement reliée à une autre cause.
Signaler les manifestations cliniques présentant un intérêt clinique et pour lesquelles il faut consulter un médecin, en particulier celles qui (une seule est suffisante) :
i : sont mortelles
ii : menacent le pronostic vital
iii : requièrent une hospitalisation
iv : entraînent une incapacité permanente

FORMULER SOUS FORME DE DIAGNOSTIC :

______

NOM DU PARENT : ______

NO. TÉL. TRAVAIL : ______

Ce formulaire s'inspire essentiellement du formulaire canadien (HC/SC 4229 (03-96)-PQ).

Septembre 2005

Pour obtenir des exemplaires de ce formulaire, s'adresser à sa direction régionale de santé publique. MSSS, septembre 2005

ÉVOLUTION DES MANIFESTATIONS CLINIQUES AU MOMENT DU RAPPORT PERSONNE VACCINÉE (Veuillez transmettre toute information subséquente)

RÉCUPÉRATION ☐[1]	SÉQUELLES (Décrire) ☐[2]	NE SAIT PAS ☐[4]	DÉCÈS ☐[5]	DATE DE DÉCÈS	ANNÉE	MOIS	JOUR

CONSULTATION MÉDICALE (Urgence, Clinique externe, Clinique médicale, Etc.)

OUI ☐[1] NON ☐[2] NE SAIT PAS ☐[3] (Si OUI, inscrire les détails pertinents du traitement dans la case « renseignements complémentaires » ci-dessous)

HOSPITALISATION SUITE À L'APPARITION DES MANIFESTATIONS CLINIQUES

OUI ☐[1]	NON ☐[2]	NE SAIT PAS ☐[3]	DATE D'ADMISSION	ANNÉE	MOIS	JOUR	DATE DE SORTIE	ANNÉE	MOIS	JOUR

RENSEIGNEMENTS COMPLÉMENTAIRES Indiquer toute information pertinente dans cette section, en particulier la durée de l'incident et sa sévérité, médications pertinentes, antécédents, etc. en précisant la date de mise à jour (An/Mois/Jour)

DURÉE TOTALE DES MANIFESTATIONS : MIN ☐ HRS ☐ JRS ☐ SÉVÉRITÉ DU CAS : LÉGER ☐ MODÉRÉ ☐ SÉVÈRE ☐

CONSIGNES POUR REMPLIR LE RAPPORT DE MANIFESTATIONS CLINIQUES

1. Signaler uniquement les manifestations cliniques survenues après l'administration d'un vaccin et qui ne peuvent être clairement attribuées à une ou des conditions co-existantes et tenir compte des définitions proposées. **Il n'est pas nécessaire d'établir une relation de cause à effet entre l'immunisation et les manifestations cliniques. La soumission d'un rapport ne met pas nécessairement en cause le vaccin**. Inscrire **tous les vaccins** administrés lors de la séance de vaccination, sauf dans le cas de réaction locale clairement attribuable à 1 seul vaccin.

2. Les manifestations cliniques marquées d'un astérisque (*) doivent être diagnostiquées par un médecin.

3 Inscrire l'intervalle entre l'administration du ou des vaccins et l'apparition de la manifestation clinique principale motivant la déclaration (en minutes, heures ou jours). Noter la DURÉE de la manifestation clinique principale dans la case RENSEIGNEMENTS COMPLÉMENTAIRES.

4 Fournir au besoin tous les renseignements pertinents dans la case RENSEIGNEMENTS COMPLÉMENTAIRES, notamment : détails des diagnostics du médecin, résultats des tests diagnostiques ou de laboratoire, traitements à l'hôpital et diagnostics au moment du congé lorsque la personne vaccinée a été hospitalisée à cause des manifestations cliniques rapportées. Si on le juge indiqué, des photocopies des dossiers originaux peuvent être soumises. On précisera la sévérité des manifestations (LÉGER : ne nuit pas aux occupations régulières, MODÉRÉ : nuit aux occupations régulières, SÉVÈRE : empêche les occupations régulières).

5 Fournir des renseignements pertinents sur les antécédents médicaux qui se rapportent aux manifestations cliniques signalées, par exemple : antécédents d'allergie, épisodes antérieurs ou maladies concomitantes.

REMPLI PAR (S.V.P. compléter en lettres moulées)

NOM, PRÉNOM			# TÉLÉPHONE ( ) -
ÉTABLISSEMENT, ADRESSE (Établissement, N°. rue, etc.)	VILLE	PROVINCE	CODE POSTAL
PROFESSION INF ☐[1] MD ☐[2] AUTRE ☐[3]	SIGNATURE	DATE ANNÉE MOIS JOUR	

NOTES (Réservé à la direction de santé publique)

SUIVI : OUI ☐[1] TERMINÉ ☐[2]	REGISTRE DÉCISIONNEL : ☐[1] OUI ☐[2] NON ☐[3] INACTIVÉ

NOM DE LA PERSONNE RESSOURCE À LA DSP	SIGNATURE	DATE ANNÉE MOIS JOUR

Septembre 2005

ANNEXE O (suite)
Rapport d'accident relié à la pharmacothérapie

Exemple de rapport. Chaque centre de soins (hôpital, CHSLD, etc.) devrait avoir un formulaire semblable.

RAPPORT D'INCIDENT / ACCIDENT N° 3612901

Ce rapport doit être rempli selon les politiques et procédures en vigueur dans l'établissement

Nom de l'établissement ____________

Usager ☐ Visiteur ☐ Autre : ____________ ☐

Sexe : ☐ M ☐ F

Curatelle : { oui ☐ non ☐ } { Privée ☐ Publique ☐ }

Année Mois Jour
Date ___ Heure ___ : ___

Date de naissance (Année, Mois, Jour) | N° chambre | N° de dossier
Nom et prénom à la naissance
Nom usuel ou nom du conjoint
Adresse
Code postal | Téléphone | Sexe M ☐ F ☐
N° d'assurance maladie | Nom du médecin traitant

1- ENDROIT

SALLES :

Accueil ☐	Escaliers ☐	à manger ☐	de réveil ☐
Ascenseurs ☐	Laboratoires ☐	collective ☐	de thérapie ☐
Chambre ☐	Local/sport ☐	d'isolement ☐	d'examen ☐
Corridor ☐	Stationnement ☐	d'opération ☐	
Cour ☐	Terrain ☐	de bain/toilette ☐	de cours /atelier ☐

Préciser (unité, département, etc...) ____________

Autre endroit : ____________ ☐

2- OBJET

A- Services cliniques/soins

Complications ☐ Fugue ☐
Consentement ☐ Identification ☐

B- Médication

Heure d'administration ☐
Identification de l'usager ☐
Médicament ☐

3- SITUATION PRÉALABLE

A- État de la personne

Normal ☐ Somnolent ☐
Désorienté/confus ☐ Comateux ☐
Agité ☐ Inconnu ☐
Agressif/violent ☐
Autre : ____________ ☐

B- Capacité de déplacement

Autonomie totale ☐
Autonomie partielle ☐
Dépendance totale ☐

C- Surveillance requise

Usuelle ☐
Étroite ☐
Continuelle ☐

D- Considérations cliniques

Médication (prémédication, etc...) ☐
Préciser ____________
Altérations physiologiques (drainage, trachéo) ☐
Préciser ____________
Autre : ____________ ☐

E- Environnement

Plancher/rampe, etc... ☐

F- Lit

Décompte (compresses, instruments) ☐ Refus de traitement ☐ Report/retard ☐
Autre : ☐

Posologie ☐
Voie d'administration ☐
Autre : ☐

Contention, type : ☐
Autre : (Particularité) ☐

Position élevée ☐ Position baissée ☐
Freins enclenchés ☐ Freins non-enclenchés ☐
Ridelles levées : gauche ☐ droite ☐

C- Chute

Chaise ☐
Lit ☐
Civière ☐
En circulant ☐
Trouvé par terre ☐
Autre : ☐

D- Équipement/matériel

Choc électrique ☐ Fonctionnement ☐
Disponibilité ☐ Stérilité ☐
Autre : ☐
Identification et n° d'inventaire, le cas échéant

E- Divers

Agression ☐ Incendie ☐
Automutilation ☐ Inondation ☐
Bris de matériels/objets pers. ☐ Tentative de suicide ☐
Disparition de matériel/objets pers. ☐ Autre : ☐

F- Description des faits

Pas d'analyse, ni jugement, ni accusation

4- MESURES PRISES

A- Description brève des gestes posés

B- Personnes avisées

Nom	Titre	Heure	Visite faite
		:	☐
		:	☐
		:	☐

5- DIAGNOSTIC CONSÉCUTIF *(versé au dossier par le médecin)*

6- TÉMOINS IDENTIFIÉS

oui ☐ non ☐

7- PLAINTE PRÉVISIBLE

oui ☐ non ☐

8- SIGNATAIRE DU RAPPORT

Nom	Titre	Direction

Signature	Poste tél.	Date du rapport Année / Mois / Jour

AH-223-2 (rév. 99-10) **RAPPORT D'INCIDENT / ACCIDENT** **DOSSIER DE L'USAGER**

ANNEXE P

Diagnostics infirmiers – Classification de NANDA International, taxinomie II

PROMOTION DE LA SANTÉ

CONNAISSANCE DE L'ÉTAT DE SANTÉ

PRISE EN CHARGE DE LA SANTÉ

- Prise en charge efficace du programme thérapeutique
- Prise en charge inefficace du programme thérapeutique
- Prise en charge inefficace du programme thérapeutique par la famille
- Prise en charge inefficace du programme thérapeutique par une collectivité
- Recherche d'un meilleur niveau de santé (préciser les comportements)
- Maintien inefficace de l'état de santé
- Entretien inefficace du domicile
- Motivation à améliorer la prise en charge de son programme thérapeutique
- Motivation à améliorer son alimentation

NUTRITION

INGESTION

- Mode d'alimentation inefficace chez le nouveau-né/nourrisson
- Trouble de la déglutition
- Alimentation déficiente
- Alimentation excessive
- Risque d'alimentation excessive

DIGESTION

ABSORPTION

MÉTABOLISME

HYDRATATION

- Déficit de volume liquidien
- Risque de déficit de volume liquidien
- Excès de volume liquidien
- Risque de déséquilibre de volume liquidien
- Motivation à améliorer son équilibre hydrique

ÉLIMINATION

SYSTÈME URINAIRE

- Élimination urinaire altérée
- Rétention urinaire
- Incontinence urinaire complète (vraie)
- Incontinence urinaire fonctionnelle
- Incontinence urinaire à l'effort
- Incontinence urinaire par besoin impérieux
- Incontinence urinaire réflexe
- Risque d'incontinence urinaire par besoin impérieux
- Motivation à améliorer son élimination urinaire

SYSTÈME GASTRO-INTESTINAL

- Incontinence fécale
- Diarrhée
- Constipation
- Risque de constipation
- Pseudo-constipation

SYSTÈME TÉGUMENTAIRE

SYSTÈME RESPIRATOIRE

- Échanges gazeux perturbés

ACTIVITÉ ET REPOS

SOMMEIL ET REPOS

- Habitudes de sommeil perturbées
- Privation de sommeil
- Motivation à améliorer son sommeil

ACTIVITÉ ET EXERCICE

- Risque de syndrome d'immobilité
- Mobilité physique réduite
- Mobilité réduite au lit
- Mobilité réduite en fauteuil roulant
- Difficulté lors d'un transfert
- Difficulté à la marche
- Activités de loisirs insuffisantes
- Rétablissement postopératoire retardé
- Mode de vie sédentaire

ÉQUILIBRE ÉNERGÉTIQUE

- Champ énergétique perturbé
- Fatigue

RÉPONSES CARDIO-VASCULAIRES OU RESPIRATOIRES

- Débit cardiaque diminué
- Respiration spontanée altérée
- Mode de respiration inefficace

- Intolérance à l'activité
- Risque d'intolérance à l'activité
- Intolérance au sevrage de la ventilation assistée
- Irrigation tissulaire inefficace (préciser: cardiopulmonaire, cérébrale, gastro-intestinale, périphérique, rénale)

Soins personnels

- Déficit de soins personnels: se vêtir et soigner son apparence
- Déficit de soins personnels: se laver et effectuer ses soins d'hygiène
- Déficit de soins personnels: s'alimenter
- Déficit de soins personnels: utiliser les toilettes

PERCEPTIONS ET COGNITION

Attention

- Négligence de l'hémicorps

Orientation

- Syndrome d'interprétation erronée de l'environnement
- Errance

Sensation et perception

- Trouble de la perception sensorielle (préciser: visuelle, auditive, kinesthésique, gustative, tactile, olfactive)

Cognition

- Connaissances insuffisantes (préciser)
- Confusion aiguë
- Confusion chronique
- Troubles de la mémoire
- Opérations de la pensée perturbées

Communication

- Communication verbale altérée
- Motivation à améliorer sa communication

PERCEPTION DE SOI

Conception de soi

- Identité personnelle perturbée
- Sentiment d'impuissance
- Risque de sentiment d'impuissance
- Perte d'espoir
- Risque de sentiment de solitude
- Motivation à améliorer le concept de soi

Estime de soi

- Diminution chronique de l'estime de soi
- Diminution situationnelle de l'estime de soi
- Risque de diminution situationnelle de l'estime de soi

Image corporelle

- Image corporelle perturbée

RELATIONS ET RÔLE

Rôles de l'aidant naturel

- Tension dans l'exercice du rôle de l'aidant naturel
- Risque de tension dans l'exercice du rôle de l'aidant naturel
- Exercice du rôle parental perturbé
- Risque de perturbation dans l'exercice du rôle parental

Relations familiales

- Dynamique familiale perturbée
- Motivation à améliorer la dynamique familiale
- Dynamique familiale dysfonctionnelle: alcoolisme
- Risque de perturbation de l'attachement parent-enfant

Performance dans l'exercice du rôle

- Allaitement maternel efficace
- Allaitement maternel inefficace
- Allaitement maternel interrompu
- Exercice inefficace du rôle
- Conflit face au rôle parental
- Interactions sociales perturbées

SEXUALITÉ

Identité sexuelle

Fonction sexuelle

- Dysfonctionnement sexuel
- Habitudes sexuelles perturbées

Reproduction

ADAPTATION ET TOLÉRANCE AU STRESS

Réactions post-traumatiques

- Syndrome d'inadaptation à un changement de milieu
- Risque de syndrome d'inadaptation à un changement de milieu
- Syndrome de traumatisme de viol
- Syndrome de traumatisme de viol: réaction silencieuse
- Syndrome de traumatisme de viol: réaction mixte

- Syndrome post-traumatique
- Risque de syndrome post-traumatique

Stratégies d'adaptation

- Peur
- Anxiété
- Angoisse face à la mort
- Chagrin chronique
- Déni non constructif
- Deuil anticipé
- Deuil dysfonctionnel
- Inadaptation à un changement dans l'état de santé
- Motivation à améliorer ses stratégies d'adaptation
- Motivation d'une collectivité à améliorer ses stratégies d'adaptation
- Motivation d'une famille à améliorer ses stratégies d'adaptation
- Stratégies d'adaptation inefficaces
- Stratégies d'adaptation familiale invalidantes
- Stratégies d'adaptation familiale compromises
- Stratégies d'adaptation défensives
- Stratégies d'adaptation inefficaces d'une collectivité

Réactions neuro-comportementales au stress

- Dysréflexie autonome
- Risque de dysréflexie autonome
- Désorganisation comportementale chez le nouveau-né/nourrisson
- Risque de désorganisation comportementale chez le nouveau-né/nourrisson
- Réceptivité du nouveau-né/nourrisson à progresser dans son organisation comportementale
- Capacité adaptative intra-crânienne diminuée

PRINCIPES DE VIE

Valeurs

Croyances

- Motivation à améliorer son bien-être spirituel

Congruence entre les valeurs, les croyances et les actes

- Détresse spirituelle
- Risque de détresse spirituelle
- Conflit décisionnel (préciser)
- Non-observance (préciser)
- Risque de perturbation de la pratique religieuse
- Pratique religieuse perturbée
- Motivation à améliorer sa pratique religieuse

SÉCURITÉ ET PROTECTION

Infection

- Risque d'infection

Lésions

- Atteinte de la muqueuse buccale
- Risque d'accident
- Risque de blessure en périopératoire
- Risque de chute
- Risque de trauma
- Atteinte à l'intégrité de la peau
- Risque d'atteinte à l'intégrité de la peau
- Atteinte à l'intégrité des tissus
- Dentition altérée
- Risque de suffocation
- Risque d'aspiration (de fausse route)
- Dégagement inefficace des voies respiratoires
- Risque de dysfonctionnement neurovasculaire périphérique
- Mécanismes de protection inefficaces
- Risque de syndrome de mort subite du nourrisson

Violence

- Risque d'automutilation
- Automutilation
- Risque de violence envers les autres
- Risque de violence envers soi-même
- Risque de suicide

Dangers environnementaux

- Risque d'intoxication

Processus défensifs

- Réaction allergique au latex
- Risque de réaction allergique au latex

Thermorégulation

- Risque de température corporelle anormale
- Thermorégulation inefficace
- Hypothermie
- Hyperthermie

BIEN-ÊTRE

Bien-être physique

- Douleur aiguë
- Douleur chronique
- Nausée

Bien-être dans l'environnement

Bien-être au sein de la société

- Isolement social

CROISSANCE ET DÉVELOPPEMENT

CROISSANCE

- Retard de la croissance et du développement
- Risque de croissance anormale
- Perte d'élan vital chez l'adulte

DÉVELOPPEMENT

- Retard de la croissance et du développement
- Risque de retard du développement

Source : Élaboré à partir de NANDA International, *Diagnostics infirmiers - Définitions et classification 2005-2006*, Paris, Masson, 2006.

ANNEXE Q
Administration des médicaments aux enfants

Lignes directrices

L'administration de médicaments en pédiatrie représente parfois un défi. Le professionnel de la santé devrait prescrire une forme pharmaceutique appropriée à l'âge de l'enfant. Si l'enfant est incapable de prendre une forme pharmaceutique particulière, il faut demander au pharmacien s'il peut fournir une autre forme ou s'il peut suggérer d'autres possibilités.

Liquides par voie orale

On peut administrer les médicaments sous forme liquide à l'aide d'un gobelet gradué, d'un compte-gouttes gradué, d'une seringue destinée à la voie orale ou d'une cuillère en plastique graduée. Il faut recommander aux parents d'utiliser un de ces dispositifs gradués plutôt que des cuillères ou des gobelets ordinaires. Si un dispositif est fourni avec un médicament particulier, il ne faut pas s'en servir pour administrer d'autres médicaments. Chez les jeunes enfants, il est préférable de faire gicler le médicament petit à petit à l'intérieur de la joue, loin des papilles gustatives du fond de la langue qui réagissent au goût amer.

Gouttes et onguents ophtalmiques

Incliner la tête de l'enfant vers l'arrière et tirer délicatement la peau de la paupière inférieure vers le bas jusqu'à ce qu'une petite poche se forme. Instiller l'onguent ou les gouttes (une à la fois) et fermer l'œil pendant quelques minutes pour que le médicament reste dans l'œil.

Gouttes otiques

Agiter les suspensions otiques avant de les administrer. Pour les enfants < 3 ans, tirer l'oreille externe vers l'arrière et vers le bas avant d'instiller les gouttes. Pour les enfants ≥ 3 ans, tirer l'oreille externe vers l'arrière et vers le haut. Garder l'enfant couché sur le côté pendant 2 minutes et placer une boule de coton (ouate) dans l'oreille.

Gouttes nasales

Retirer les sécrétions du nez avant d'instiller les gouttes. On peut utiliser une poire ou un coton-tige chez les nourrissons et les jeunes enfants. On demande aux enfants plus âgés de se moucher. Utiliser un oreiller pour incliner la tête de l'enfant vers l'arrière et éviter de toucher la narine avec le bout du compte-gouttes. Garder l'enfant couché avec la tête inclinée vers l'arrière pendant 2 minutes.

Suppositoires

Garder les suppositoires au réfrigérateur pour faciliter l'administration. Mettre des gants et humecter l'extrémité du suppositoire avec un peu d'eau ou y appliquer un peu de gel lubrifiant. Avec le petit doigt chez les enfants < 3 ans et l'index chez les enfants ≥ 3 ans, introduire le suppositoire dans le rectum jusqu'à 1 à 2 cm après le sphincter. Si le suppositoire glisse vers l'extérieur, l'introduire de nouveau en le poussant un peu plus loin. Tenir les fesses de l'enfant ensemble pendant quelques minutes, puis faire garder à l'enfant la même position pendant 20 minutes, si possible.

Produits topiques

Nettoyer la région atteinte et bien la sécher avant l'application. Étendre une mince couche du médicament sur la peau et faire pénétrer en frottant délicatement. Ne pas couvrir la région, sauf si le médecin l'a prescrit.

Aérosol-doseurs

La méthode d'administration est la même que chez les adultes. On recommande l'utilisation d'un dispositif d'espacement chez les jeunes enfants.

ANNEXE R
Calcul des doses pédiatriques[1]

En général, les médicaments sont prescrits pour les enfants en fonction du poids (mg/kg) ou de la surface corporelle (mg/m^2). Il faut veiller à utiliser le poids en kilogrammes; convertir les livres en kilogrammes (1 kg = 2,2 lb), le cas échéant.

Les médicaments chimiothérapeutiques sont souvent dosés selon la surface corporelle; il faut donc établir celle-ci avant de calculer la dose. Les médicaments sont disponibles en plusieurs concentrations. Par conséquent, les ordonnances en « mL » plutôt qu'en « mg » demandent une clarification.

Les doses varient également selon l'indication. Par conséquent, il est utile de connaître le diagnostic au moment du calcul de la dose. Les exemples suivants représentent des situations courantes lors du calcul des doses destinées aux enfants.

EXEMPLE 1

Calcul de la dose de suspension d'amoxicilline en mL pour traiter une otite moyenne chez un enfant de 1 an qui pèse 22 lb. La dose prescrite est de 40 mg/kg/jour en doses fractionnées, à administrer 2 fois par jour (2 f.p.j.). La suspension est disponible dans une concentration de 400 mg/5 mL.

Étape 1. Convertir les livres en kg: 22 lb × 1 kg/2,2 lb = 10 kg

Étape 2. Calculer la dose en mg: 10 kg × 40 mg/kg/jour = 400 mg/jour

Étape 3. Diviser la dose par la fréquence d'administration: 400 mg/jour ÷ 2 (f.p.j.) = 200 mg/dose, 2 f.p.j.

Étape 4. Convertir en mL la dose en mg: 200 mg/dose ÷ 400 mg/5 mL = **2,5 mL, 2 f.p.j.**

EXEMPLE 2

Calcul de la dose de ceftriaxone en mL pour traiter une méningite chez un enfant de 5 ans qui pèse 18 kg. La dose prescrite est de 100 mg/kg/jour par voie IV, 1 fois par jour (1 f.p.j.) et le médicament est disponible dans une solution prédiluée de 40 mg/mL.

Étape 1. Calculer la dose en mg: 18 kg × 100 mg/kg/jour = 1 800 mg/jour

Étape 2. Diviser la dose par la fréquence: 1 800 mg/jour ÷ 1 (1 f.p.j.) = 1 800 mg/dose

Étape 3. Convertir en mL la dose en mg: 1 800 mg/dose ÷ 40 mg/mL = **45 mL, 1 f.p.j.**

EXEMPLE 3

Calcul de la dose de vincristine en mL pour traiter la leucémie chez un enfant de 4 ans qui pèse 37 lb et mesure 97 cm. La dose prescrite est de 2 mg/m^2 et le médicament est disponible en concentration de 1 mg/mL.

Étape 1. Convertir les livres en kg: 37 lb × 1 kg/2,2 lb = 16,8 kg

Étape 2: Calculer la surface corporelle (annexe E): $\sqrt{(16{,}8 \times 97 \text{ cm}/3\,600)} = 0{,}67 \text{ m}^2$

Étape 3. Calculer la dose en mg: 2 mg/m^2 × 0,67 m^2 = 1,34 mg

Étape 4. Calculer la dose en mL: 1,34 mg ÷ 1 mg/mL = **1,34 mL**

1. Voir le chapitre consacré au calcul des doses de médicaments destinés aux nourrissons et aux enfants dans *La dose exacte*, de Lorrie N. Hegstad et Wilma Hayek, adaptation française de Monique Guimond, Saint-Laurent, ERPI, 2004.

ANNEXE S
Besoins hydriques et électrolytiques de l'enfant

CALCUL DES BESOINS HYDRIQUES DE L'ENFANT

1. **Méthode de la surface corporelle** (souvent utilisée chez les enfants > 10 kg)

   1 500 – 2 000 mL/m^2/jour ÷ 24 h = débit des liquides en mL/h

   Exemple: Calcul de l'apport liquidien en mL/h chez un enfant dont la surface corporelle est de 0,8 m^2.

   Réponse: 1 500 mL/m^2/jour × 0,8 m^2 = 1 200 mL/jour ÷ 24 h = 50 mL/h
   2 000 mL/m^2/jour × 0,8 m^2 = 1 600 mL/jour ÷ 24 h = 66,6 mL/h

   Intervalle possible: de 50 à 66,6 mL/h.

2. **Méthode du poids corporel**

< 10 kg	100 mL/kg/jour
11 – 20 kg	1 000 mL + 50 mL/kg pour chaque kg > 10
> 20 kg	1 500 mL + 20 mL/kg pour chaque kg > 20

   Exemple: Calcul de l'apport liquidien en mL/h chez un enfant pesant 25 kg.

   Réponse: 1 500 mL + 20 mL/kg × 5 kg = 1 500 mL + 100 mL = 1 600 mL
   1 600 mL ÷ 24 h = 66,6 mL/h

BESOINS EN ÉLECTROLYTES CHEZ LES ENFANTS

Sodium	2 à 6 mmol/kg/jour
Potassium	2 à 4 mmol/kg/jour
Calcium	0,5 à 2 mmol/kg/jour[1]
Magnésium	0,15 à 0,25 mmol/kg/jour
Phosphore	0,5 à 2,0 mmol/kg/jour[1]

SITUATIONS QUI PEUVENT MODIFIER LES BESOINS HYDRIQUES DES ENFANTS

Fièvre	**Transpiration**	**Insuffisance rénale**
Hyperventilation	**Hyperthyroïdie**	**Diarrhée**

RÉHYDRATATION PAR VOIE ORALE

La réhydratation par voie orale est aussi efficace que le traitement intraveineux pour répondre aux besoins des enfants présentant une déshydratation de légère à modérée à cause de la diarrhée. Les solutions orales de réhydratation vendues dans le commerce contiennent habituellement une faible concentration de glucose (de 2 à 3 %), de 45 à 75 mmol/L de sodium, de 20 à 25 mmol/L de potassium et de 30 à 35 mmol/L de citrate (source de bicarbonate). Leur faible concentration en glucose ne constitue pas un apport énergétique significatif, mais facilite l'absorption intestinale du sodium et de l'eau. Toutes les solutions orales de réhydratation vendues dans le commerce sont sûres et efficaces, et on les préfère aux remèdes maison (comme les colas, les jus et le bouillon de poulet) qui ne sont pas préparés en tenant compte de la physiologie de la diarrhée aiguë.

1. Les nouveau-nés peuvent avoir besoin de l'apport maximal de calcium et de phosphore, étant donné que leurs os de développent rapidement.

ANNEXE T
Médicaments à utiliser avec prudence chez la personne âgée

LISTE DE BEERS (ADAPTÉE AU CONTEXTE CANADIEN)

La liste de Beers est une compilation de médicaments et de classes de médicaments qui accroissent le risque de réactions indésirables chez les personnes âgées, qui sont souvent plus sensibles aux médicaments et plus susceptibles de présenter des réactions indésirables. Celles-ci entraînent des dépenses pour la société et réduisent la qualité de vie des patients. Elles peuvent provoquer des hospitalisations plus fréquentes, des séquelles permanentes ou même la mort. Il est possible de réduire le risque de réactions indésirables en choisissant des médicaments qui n'apparaissent pas sur la liste ou en prescrivant la dose efficace la plus faible possible. La liste suivante apparaît dans *Archives of Internal Medicine*, volume 163, publié en décembre 2003. Il s'agit d'une mise à jour de la liste originale, publiée en 1991 par le Dr Mark H. Beers.

acide éthacrynique
agents anorexigènes
alcaloïdes de la belladone
alprazolam
amiodarone
amitriptyline
amphétamines
barbituriques
bisacodyl
cascara sagrada
chlordiazépoxide
chlorphéniramine
chlorpropamide
chlorzoxazone
cimétidine
clonidine
clorazépate
cyclobenzaprine
cyproheptadine
diazépam
dicyclomine
digoxine
diphénhydramine
dipyridamole
disopyramide
doxazosine
doxépine
fluoxétine
flurazépam
huile minérale
hydroxyzine
mépéridine
mésyloïdes de l'ergot
méthocarbamol
méthyldopa
méthyltestostérone
naproxen
nifédipine
nitrofurantoïne
œstrogènes
orphénadrine
oxaprozine
oxazépam
oxybutynine
pentazocine
piroxicam
prométhazine
propoxyphène et associations
sulfate ferreux (fer)
témazépam
thioridazine
thyroïde lyophilisée
ticlopidine
triazolam

MÉDICAMENTS ASSOCIÉS À UN RISQUE ACCRU DE CHUTE CHEZ LES PERSONNES ÂGÉES

De nombreux facteurs prédisposent les personnes âgées aux chutes. Parmi eux, on compte la faiblesse, la maladie, les troubles de la vision, la polypharmacie et la prise de certains médicaments. On trouve ci-dessous une liste non exhaustive des médicaments qui peuvent prédisposer les patients âgés aux chutes. Il faut évaluer le risque de chutes chez les patients âgés qui prennent ces médicaments; l'infirmière devrait mettre en place des mesures de prévention des chutes.

ANTIDÉPRESSEURS
amitriptyline
bupropion
citalopram
clomipramine
désipramine
doxépine
fluoxétine
fluvoxamine
imipramine
mirtazapine
moclobémide
nortriptyline
paroxétine
sertraline
trazodone
venlafaxine

BENZODIAZÉPINES (ACTION PROLONGÉE)
chlordiazépoxide
clonazépam
diazépam
flurazépam

BENZODIAZÉPINES (ACTION INTERMÉDIAIRE)
alprazolam
lorazépam
nitrazépam
oxazépam
témazépam

BENZODIAZÉPINES (ACTION BRÈVE)
midazolam
triazolam

ANTICONVULSIVANTS
carbamazépine
gabapentine
lamotrigine
phénobarbital
phénytoïne

topiramate
valproate

ANTAGONISTES DES RÉCEPTEURS DE L'ANGIOTENSINE II

candésartan
éprosartan
irbesartan
losartan
telmisartan
valsartan

INHIBITEURS DE L'IECA

bénazépril
captopril
cilazapril
énalapril
fosinopril
lisinopril
perindopril
quinapril
ramipril

BÊTABLOQUANTS

acébutolol
aténolol
bisoprolol
carvédilol
labétalol
métoprolol
propranolol
sotalol
timolol

BLOQUEURS DES CANAUX CALCIQUES

amlodipine
diltiazem
félodipine
nifédipine
vérapamil

VASODILATATEURS

doxazosine
hydralazine
isosorbide
nitroglycérine
prazosine
térazosine

DIURÉTIQUES

amiloride/hydrochlorothiazide
furosémide
hydrochlorothiazide
triamtérène/hydrochlorothiazide

AGENTS ANTI-ALZHEIMER

donépézil
galantamine
rivastigmine

ANTIPSYCHOTIQUES (CLASSIQUES)

chlorpromazine
halopéridol
loxapine
méthotriméprazine
perphénazine
prochlorpérazine
rispéridone
trifluopérazine

ANTIPSYCHOTIQUES (ATYPIQUES)

clozapine
olanzapine
quétiapine
rispéridone

ANTIHISTAMINIQUES ET ANTINAUSÉEUX

dimenhydrinate
diphénhydramine
méclizine
métoclopramide
prochlorpérazine
prométhazine
scopolamine (timbre)

ANTIPARKINSONIENS

amantadine
bromocriptine
entacapone
lévodopa/bensérazide
lévodopa/carbidopa
pramipexole
ropinirole
sélégiline

OPIOÏDES

codéine
fentanyl
hydromorphone
mépéridine
morphine
oxycodone
pentazocine

MÉDICAMENTS EN VENTE LIBRE

Antitussifs
Médicaments contre le rhume
Médicaments contre les allergies
Relaxants musculaires
Somnifères

American Geriatrics Society (AGS). Panel on Falls in Older Persons, Guideline for the Prevention of Falls in Older Persons. *JAGS* 49:664-672, 2001.

Frick DM, *et al.* Potentially Inappropriate Medications for Use in Older Adults (Beers List. Updating the Beers criteria for potentially inappropriate medication use in older adults: results of a US consensus panel of experts. *Arch Intern Med.* 2003; 163:2716-2724.

ANNEXE U
Associations médicamenteuses

N.B.: Cette liste n'est pas exhaustive. Elle donne un échantillon des nombreux produits disponibles en association sur le marché. Les noms et les compositions de chaque association peuvent varier au fil du temps.

Remarque: Les médicaments sont énumérés par ordre alphabétique selon leur nom commercial. Si le nom commercial ne précise pas la forme galénique, il s'agit de comprimés ou de capsules. Après chaque nom commercial, on indique la dénomination commune et les doses de chaque ingrédient actif contenu dans la préparation. Pour obtenir des informations sur ces médicaments, prière de se référer à la monographie de chacune des dénominations communes qui entrent dans l'association. Pour ce qui est des ingrédients inactifs, prière de se référer à l'étiquette du produit.

222 – 375 mg d'aspirine, 15 mg de caféine et 8 mg de codéine

Accuretic 10/12,5 – 10 mg de quinapril et 12,5 mg d'hydrochlorothiazide

Accuretic 20/12,5 – 20 mg de quinapril et 12,5 mg d'hydrochlorothiazide

Accuretic 20/25 – 20 mg de quinapril et 25 mg d'hydrochlorothiazide

Acetazone Forte – 250 mg de chlorzoxazone et 300 mg d'acétaminophène

Acetazone Forte C8 – 250 mg de chlorzoxazone, 300 mg d'acétaminophène et 8 mg de codéine

Actifed – 60 mg de pseudoéphédrine et 2,5 mg de triprolidine

Actifed Plus Extra Puissant – 60 mg de pseudoéphédrine, 2,5 mg de triprolidine et 500 mg d'acétaminophène

Advair 100 Diskus – Par inhalation: 100 µg de fluticasone et 50 µg de salmétérol

Advair 125 (en aérosol-doseur) – Par inhalation: 125 µg de fluticasone et 25 µg de salmétérol

Advair 250 (en aérosol-doseur) – Par inhalation: 250 µg de fluticasone et 25 µg de salmétérol

Advair 250 Diskus – Par inhalation: 250 µg de fluticasone et 50 µg de salmétérol

Advair 500 Diskus – Par inhalation: 500 µg de fluticasone et 50 µg de salmétérol

Advicor 500/20 mg – 500 mg de niacine à libération prolongée et 20 mg de lovastatine

Advicor 750/20 mg – 750 mg de niacine à libération prolongée et 20 mg de lovastatine

Advicor 1 000/20 mg – 1 000 mg de niacine à libération prolongée et 20 mg de lovastatine

Advicor 1 000/40 mg – 1 000 mg de niacine à libération prolongée et 40 mg de lovastatine

Advil Rhume et Sinus - 200 mg d'ibuprofène et 30 mg de chlorhydrate de pseudoéphédrine

Aggrenox – 25 mg d'aspirine et 200 mg de dipyridamole à libération prolongée

Aldactazide 25 – 25 mg d'hydrochlorothiazide et 25 mg de spironolactone

Aldactazide 50 – 50 mg d'hydrochlorothiazide et 50 mg de spironolactone

Alka-Seltzer – 325 mg d'aspirine, 1 916 mg de bicarbonate de sodium et 1 000 mg d'acide citrique

Allegra-D – 60 mg de fexofénadine et 120 mg de pseudoéphédrine

Allergy Sinus Headache – 500 mg d'acétaminophène, 25 mg de diphenhydramine et 30 mg de pseudoéphédrine

Altace HCT 2,5/12,5 – 2,5 mg de ramipril et 12,5 mg d'hydrochlorothiazide

Altace HCT 5/12,5 – 5 mg de ramipril et 12,5 mg d'hydrochlorothiazide

Altace HCT 5/25 – 5 mg de ramipril et 25 mg d'hydrochlorothiazide

Altace HCT 10/12,5 – 10 mg de ramipril et 12,5 mg d'hydrochlorothiazide

Altace HCT 10/25 – 10 mg de ramipril et 25 mg d'hydrochlorothiazide

Anacin – 325 mg d'aspirine et 32 mg de caféine

Anacin Extra Forte – 500 mg d'aspirine et 32 mg de caféine

Anodan-HC, onguent – Par 1 g: 0,5 % d'hydrocortisone et 0,5 % de zinc

Anugesic-HC, onguent – 1 % de pramoxine, 0,5 % d'hydrocortisone et 0,5 % de zinc

Anusol-HC, onguent – Par 1 g: 0,5 % d'hydrocortisone et 0,5 % de zinc

Apo-Amilzide – 50 mg d'hydrochlorothiazide et 5 mg d'amiloride

Apo-Peram 2-25 – 25 mg d'amitriptyline et 2 mg de perphénazine

Apo-Peram 3-15 – 15 mg d'amitriptyline et 3 mg de perphénazine

Apo-Triacomb, crème – Par 1 g: 0,25 mg de gramicidine, 2,5 g de néomycine, 100 000 U de nystatine et 1 mg de triamcinolone

Apo-Triazide – 25 mg d'hydrochlorothiazide et 50 mg de triamtérène

Arthrotec – 50 mg de diclofénac et 200 µg de misoprostol

Atacand Plus – 16 mg de candésartan et 12,5 mg d'hydrochlorothiazide

Atasol-30 – 30 mg de codéine et 325 mg d'acétaminophène

Avalide 150/12,5 mg – 150 mg d'irbésartan et 12,5 mg d'hydrochlorothiazide

Avalide 300/12,5 mg – 300 mg d'irbésartan et 12,5 mg d'hydrochlorothiazide

Avalide 300/25 mg – 300 mg d'irbésartan et 25 mg d'hydrochlorothiazide

Avandamet 1 mg/500 mg – 1 mg de rosiglitazone et 500 mg de metformine

Avandamet 2 mg/500 mg – 2 mg de rosiglitazone et 500 mg de metformine

Avandamet 2 mg/1 000 mg – 2 mg de rosiglitazone et 1 000 mg de metformine

Avandamet 4 mg/500 mg – 4 mg de rosiglitazone et 500 mg de metformine

Avandamet 4 mg/1 000 mg – 4 mg de rosiglitazone et 1 000 mg de metformine

Avandaryl 4 mg/1 mg – 4 mg de rosiglitazone et 1 mg de glimépiride

Avandaryl 4 mg/2 mg – 4 mg de rosiglitazone et 2 mg de glimépiride

Avandaryl 4 mg/4 mg – 4 mg de rosiglitazone et 4 mg de glimépiride

Balminil Codéine + Décongestionnant + Expectorant, sirop – Par 5 mL: 3,33 mg de codéine, 30 mg de pseudoéphédrine et 100 mg de guaifénésine

Balminil DM + Décongestionnant + Expectorant, sirop – Par 5 mL: 15 mg de dextrométhorphane, 30 mg de pseudoéphédrine et 100 mg de guaifénésine

Balminil Night-Time – Par 5 mL: 125 mg de chlorure d'ammonium, 15 mg de dextrométhorphane et 12,5 mg de diphenhydramine

Balminil Toux et Grippe, sirop – Par 15 mL: 15 mg de dextrométhorphane, 30 mg de pseudoéphédrine, 100 mg de guaïfénésine et 325 mg d'acétaminophène

Barrière HC, crème – 1 % d'hydrocortisone dans une base de crème à la silicone

Bellergal Spacetabs – 0,6 mg d'ergotamine, 0,2 mg d'alcaloïdes de belladone et 40 mg de phénobarbital

Benadryl Allergy & Sinus – 500 mg d'acétaminophène, 12,5 mg de diphenhydramine et 30 mg de pseudoéphédrine

Benadryl Total – 500 mg d'acétaminophène, 25 mg de diphenhydramine et 30 mg de pseudoéphédrine

Benylin 1 Tout-en-un Rhume et grippe, sirop – Par 5 mL: 15 mg de dextrométhorphane, 30 mg de pseudoéphédrine, 100 mg de guaifénésine et 500 mg d'acétaminophène

BenzaClin, gel topique – 1 % de clindamycine et 5 % de peroxyde de benzoyle

Benzamycin, gel topique – Par 1 g: 30 mg d'érythromycine et 50 mg peroxyde de benzoyle

Blephamide, suspension ophtalmique – 10 % de sulfacétamide et 0,2 % de prednisolone

Caduet 5 mg/10 mg – 5 mg d'amlodipine et 10 mg d'atorvastatine

Caduet 5 mg/20 mg – 5 mg d'amlodipine et 20 mg d'atorvastatine

Caduet 5 mg/40 mg – 5 mg d'amlodipine et 40 mg d'atorvastatine

Caduet 5 mg/80 mg – 5 mg d'amlodipine et 80 mg d'atorvastatine

Caduet 10 mg/10 mg – 10 mg d'amlodipine et 10 mg d'atorvastatine

Caduet 10 mg/20 mg – 10 mg d'amlodipine et 20 mg d'atorvastatine

Caduet 10 mg/40 mg – 10 mg d'amlodipine et 40 mg d'atorvastatine

Caduet 10 mg/80 mg – 10 mg d'amlodipine et 80 mg d'atorvastatine

Cafergot – 100 mg de caféine et 1 mg d'ergotamine

Caltrate Plus – 1 500 mg de carbonate de calcium, 1 mg de cuivre, 50 mg d'oxyde de magnésium, 1,8 mg de manganèse, 200 UI de vitamine D et 7,5 mg de zinc

Chlor-Tripolon ND SRT – 5 mg de loratadine et 120 mg de pseudoéphédrine

Choledyl Expectorant Sirop – Par 5 mL: 100 mg d'oxtriphylline et 50 mg de guaifénésine

Ciprodex, suspension otique – 0,3 % de ciprofloxacine et 0,1 % de dexaméthasone

Cipro HC, suspension otique – 0,2 % de ciprofloxacine et 1 % d'hydrocortisone

Claritin Allergies et Sinus – 5 mg de loratadine et 120 mg de pseudoéphédrine

Clindasol, crème topique – 1 % de clindamycine, 7,5 % de Parsol MCX et 2 % de Parsol 1789 (FPS 15)

Clindoxyl, gel topique – 1 % de clindamycine et 5 % de peroxyde de benzoyle

Combigan, solution ophtalmique – 2 % de brimonidine et 0,5 % de timolol

Combivir – 150 mg de lamivudine et 300 mg de zidovudine

Contac Congestion des Bronches, sans somnolence, ordinaire – 5 mg de phényléphrine, 250 mg d'acétaminophène et 100 mg de guaifénésine

Cortisporin, onguent – Par 1 g: 5 000 UI de polymyxine B, 400 UI de bacitracine, 5 mg de néomycine et 10 mg d'hydrocortisone

Cosopt, solution ophtalmique – 2 % de brinzolamide et 0,5 % de timolol

Coversyl Plus – 4 mg de perindopril et 1,25 mg d'indapamide

Coversyl Plus LD – 2 mg de perindopril et 0,625 mg d'indapamide

Dalmacol, sirop – Par 1 mL: 0,33 mg d'hydrocodone, 3,33 mg d'étafédrine et 1,2 mg de doxylamine

Dimetane expectorant DC, sirop – Par 5 mL: 1,8 mg d'hydrocodone, 2 mg de bromphéniramine, 5 mg de phényléphrine et 100 mg de guaifénésine

Diophenyl-T, solution ophtalmique – 5 % de phényléphrine et 0,8 % de tropicamide

Diovan-HCT 80 mg/12,5 mg – 80 mg de valsartan et 12,5 mg d'hydrochlorothiazide

Diovan-HCT 160 mg/12,5 mg – 160 mg de valsartan et 12,5 mg d'hydrochlorothiazide

Diovan-HCT 160 mg/25 mg – 160 mg de valsartan et 25 mg d'hydrochlorothiazide

Diovol – 200 mg d'hydroxyde d'aluminium et 200 mg d'hydroxyde de magnésium

Diovol Plus – 300 mg d'hydroxyde d'aluminium, 100 mg d'hydroxyde de magnésium et 25 mg de siméthicone

Diovol Plus AF, suspension – Par 5 mL: 200 mg de carbonate de calcium, 200 mg d'hydroxyde de magnésium et 25 mg de siméthicone

Diovol plus, comprimés – 300 mg d'hydroxyde d'aluminium/carbonate de magnésium, 100 mg d'hydroxyde de magnésium et 25 mg de siméthicone

Diovol Plus, suspension – Par 5 mL: 165 mg d'hydroxyde d'aluminium, 200 mg d'hydroxyde de magnésium et 25 mg de siméthicone

Diprosalic, lotion – Par 1 g: 0,5 mg de dipropionate de bétaméthasone et 20 mg d'acide salicylique

Diprosalic, pommade – Par 1 g: 0,5 mg de dipropionate de bétaméthasone et 30 mg d'acide salicylique

Dovobet, onguent – Par 1 g: 50 µg de calcipotriol et 0,5 mg de dipropionate de bétaméthasone

Dristan – 5 mg de phényléphrine, 2 mg de chlorphéniramine et 325 mg d'acétaminophène

Dristan N.D. – 30 mg de pseudoéphédrine et 325 mg d'acétaminophène

DuoTrav, solution ophtalmique – 0,004 % de travoprost et 0,5 % de timolol

EMLA, crème – Par 1 g: 25 mg de lidocaïne et 25 mg de prilocaïne

EMLA, timbre – Par timbre: 25 mg de lidocaïne et 25 mg de prilocaïne

Empracet-30 – 30 mg de codéine et 325 mg d'acétaminophène

Empracet-60 – 60 mg de codéine et 325 mg d'acétaminophène

Emtec-30 – 30 mg de codéine et 325 mg d'acétaminophène

Entex LA – 120 mg de pseudoéphédrine et 600 mg de guaifénésine

Excedrin Extra-Fort – 500 mg d'acétaminophène et 65 mg de caféine

Fiorinal – 330 mg d'aspirine, 40 mg de caféine et 50 mg de butalbital

Fiorinal C1/4 – 330 mg d'aspirine, 40 mg de caféine, 50 mg de butalbital et 15 mg de codéine

Fiorinal C1/2 – 330 mg d'aspirine, 40 mg de caféine, 50 mg de butalbital et 30 mg de codéine

Flagystatin, crème vaginale – Un applicateur rempli de crème fournit 500 mg de métronidazole et 100 000 UI de nystatine

Flagystatin, ovules vaginaux – 500 mg de métronidazole et 100 000 UI de nystatine

Fucidin H, crème – 2 % d'acide fucidique et 1 % d'hydrocortisone

Garasone, pommade ophtalmique – Par 1 g: 3,0 mg (0,3 %) de gentamicine et 1 mg de bétaméthasone

Garasone, solution oto-ophtalmique – Par 1 mL: 3,0 mg (0,3 %) de gentamicine et 1 mg de bétaméthasone

Gaviscon – 40 mg de carbonate de magnésium et 200 mg d'alginate de sodium

Gaviscon Extra-Fort – 63 mg de carbonate de magnésium et 313 mg d'alginate de sodium

Gaviscon, suspension – Par 5 mL: 100 mg d'aluminium et 250 mg d'alginate de sodium

Gelusil – 200 mg d'hydroxyde d'aluminium et 200 mg d'hydroxyde de magnésium

Gelusil Extra-Puissant – 400 mg d'hydroxyde d'aluminium et 400 mg d'hydroxyde de magnésium

Gen-Amilazide – 50 mg d'hydrochlorothiazide et 5 mg d'amiloride

Gentlax-S – 5 mg de bisacodyl et 50 mg de docusate sodique

Gravergol – 50 mg de dimenhydrinate, 100 mg de caféine et 1 mg d'ergotamine

Hycomine, sirop – Par 5 mL: 5 mg d'hydrocodone, 12,5 mg de pyrilamine, 10 mg de phényléphrine et 60 mg de chlorure d'ammonium.

Hycomine-S, sirop – Par 5 mL: 2,5 mg d'hydrocodone, 6,25 mg de pyrilamine, 5 mg de phényléphrine et 30 mg de chlorure d'ammonium.

Hyzaar 50 mg/12,5 mg – 50 mg de losartan et 12,5 mg d'hydrochlorothiazide

Hyzaar 100 mg/12,5 mg – 100 mg de losartan et 12,5 mg d'hydrochlorothiazide

Hyzaar DS 100 mg/25 mg – 100 mg de losartan et 25 mg d'hydrochlorothiazide

Imodium avancé – 125 mg de siméthicone et 2 mg de lopéramide

Inhibace Plus – 5 mg de cilazapril et 12,5 mg d'hydrochlorothiazide

Kivexa – 600 mg d'abacavir et 200 mg de lamivudine

Liberator – 10 mg de loratadine et 240 mg de pseudoéphédrine

Librax – 5 mg de chlordiazépoxide et 2,5 mg de clidinium (génériques disponibles: Apo-Chlorax et Pro-Chlorax)

Lomotil – 2,5 mg de diphénoxylate et 0,025 mg de sulfate d'atropine

Lotriderm, crème – Par 1 g: 10 mg de clotrimazole et 0,5 mg de dipropionate de bétaméthasone

Malarone – 250 mg d'atovaquone et 100 mg de proguanil

Malarone Pédiatrique – 62,5 mg d'atovaquone et 25 mg de proguanil

Maxitrol, pommade ophtalmique – Par 1 g: 6 000 UI de sulfate de polymyxine B, 3,5 mg de néomycine et 1 mg (0,1 %) de dexaméthasone

Maxitrol, suspension ophtalmique – Par 1 mL: 6 000 UI de sulfate de polymyxine B, 3,5 mg de néomycine et 1 mg (0,1 %) de dexaméthasone

Medrol, lotion contre l'acné – Par 1 mL: 2,5 mg de méthylprednisolone, 100 mg de complexe de chlorhydrate d'aluminium et 50 mg de soufre colloïdal

Methoxacet – 400 mg de méthocarbamol et 325 d'acétaminophène

Methoxacet-C1/8 – 400 mg de méthocarbamol, 325 d'acétaminophène et 8 mg de codéine

Methoxacet Extra Fort – 400 mg de méthocarbamol et 500 d'acétaminophène

Methoxisal – 400 mg de méthocarbamol et 325 mg d'AAS

Methoxisal-C 1/8 – 400 mg de méthocarbamol, 500 mg d'AAS et 8 mg de codéine

Methoxisal-C 1/4 – 400 mg de méthocarbamol, 500 mg d'AAS et 16,2 mg de codéine

Methoxisal-C 1/2 – 400 mg de méthocarbamol, 500 mg d'AAS et 32,4 mg de codéine

Methoxisal Extra Fort – 400 mg de méthocarbamol et 500 mg d'AAS

Micardis Plus – 80 mg de telmisartan et 12,5 mg d'hydrochlorothiazide

Moduret – 50 mg d'hydrochlorothiazide et 5 mg d'amiloride

Naphcon-A, solution ophtalmique – 0,025 % de naphazoline et 0,3 % de phéniramine

Neo-Medrol, lotion contre l'acné – Par 1 mL: 2,5 mg de méthylprednisolone, 2,5 mg de néomycine, 100 mg de complexe de chlorhydrate d'aluminium et 50 mg de soufre colloïdal

Neosporin, crème – Par 1 g: 10 000 UI de polymyxine B, 3,5 mg de néomycine et 250 µg de gramicidine

Neosporin, onguent topique – Par 1 g: 3,5 mg de néomycine, 400 UI de bacitracine zinc et 5 000 UI de polymyxine B

Neosporin, solution oto-ophtalmique – Par 1 mL: 10 000 UI de polymyxine B, 1,75 mg de néomycine et 0,025 mg de gramicidine

Neosporin, solution pour irrigation – Par 1 mL: 40 mg de néomycine et 200 000 UI de polymyxine B

Nerisalic, crème – 0,1 % de diflucortolone et 3 % d'acide salicylique

Novahistex DH, sirop – Par 5 mL: 5 mg d'hydrocodone et 20 mg de phényléphrine

Novahistine DH, sirop – Par 5 mL: 1,7 mg d'hydrocodone et 10 mg de phényléphrine

Novamilor – 50 mg d'hydrochlorothiazide et 5 mg d'amiloride

Novo-Spirozine – 25 mg d'hydrochlorothiazide et 25 mg de spironolactone

Novo-Triazide – 25 mg d'hydrochlorothiazide et 50 mg de triamtérène

Nu-Amilzide – 50 mg d'hydrochlorothiazide et 5 mg d'amiloride

Nu-Triazide – 25 mg d'hydrochlorothiazide et 50 mg de triamtérène

Optimyxin Plus, solution oto-ophtalmique – Par 1 mL: 10 000 UI de polymyxine B, 0,025 mg de gramicidine et 1,75 mg de néomycine

Palafer CF – 300 mg de fumarate ferreux, 200 mg d'acide ascorbique et 0,5 mg d'acide folique

Parafon Forte – 250 mg de chlorzoxazone et 300 mg d'acétaminophène

Pédiazole, suspension – Par 5 mL: 200 mg d'érythromycine et 600 mg d'acétylsulfisoxazole

Pegasys RBV – Boîtes contenant: 1 flacon de 180 µg/mL OU 1 seringue préremplie de 180 µg/0,5 mL d'interféron alfa-2a pégylé et 1 flacon de 28 comprimés de 200 mg de ribavirine

Pegetron – Boîtes contenant: interféron alfa-2b pégylé injectable et 1 flacon de capsules de 200 mg de ribavirine (quantité de médicament selon le poids du patient)

Penta/3b + C – 250 mg de vitamine B_1, 125 mg de vitamine B_6, 250 µg de vitamine B_{12} et 250 mg de vitamine C

Pepcid complet – 800 mg de carbonate de calcium, 10 mg de famotidine et 165 mg d'hydroxyde de magnésium

Percocet – 5 mg d'oxycodone et 325 mg acétaminophène

Percocet-Demi – 2,5 mg d'oxycodone et 325 mg d'acétaminophène

Percodan – 5 mg d'oxycodone et 325 mg d'aspirine

Pico-Salax – Par sachet: 3,5 g d'oxyde de magnésium, 12 g d'acide citrique et 10 mg de picosulfate de sodium

PMS-Levazine 2 -25 – 25 mg d'amitriptyline et 2 mg de perphénazine

PMS-Levazine 3 -15 – 15 mg d'amitriptyline et 3 mg de perphénazine

Prinzide 10 mg/12,5 mg – 10 mg de lisinopril et 12,5 mg d'hydrochlorothiazide

Prinzide 20 mg/12,5 mg – 20 mg de lisinopril et 12,5 mg d'hydrochlorothiazide

Prinzide 20 mg/25 mg – 20 mg de lisinopril et 25 mg d'hydrochlorothiazide

Proctodan-HC, onguent – 1 % de pramoxine, 0,5 % d'hydrocortisone et 0,5 % de zinc

Proctol, onguent – Par 1 g: 5 mg d'hydrocortisone, 5 mg de cinchocaïne, 10 mg de framycétine et 10 mg d'esculine

Proctosedyl, pommade – Par 1 g: 5 mg d'hydrocortisone, 5 mg de cinchocaïne, 10 mg de framycétine et 10 mg d'esculine

Ratio-Hemcort-HC, onguent – 0,5 % d'hydrocortisone et 0,5 % de zinc

Ratio-Oxycocet – 5 mg d'oxycodone et 325 mg d'acétaminophène

Ratio-Oxycodan – 5 mg d'oxycodone et 325 mg d'aspirine

Ratio-Proctosone, pommade – Par 1 g: 5 mg d'hydrocortisone, 5 mg de cinchocaïne, 10 mg de framycétine et 10 mg d'esculine

Ratio-Topisalic, lotion – Par 1 g: 0,5 mg de dipropionate de bétaméthasone et 20 mg d'acide salicylique

Ratio-Triacomb, crème – Par 1 g: 1 mg de triamcinolone, 100 000 unités de nystatine, 2,5 mg de néomycine et 0,25 mg de gramicidine

Réactine Allergy & Sinus – 5 mg de cétirizine et 120 mg de pseudoéphédrine

Rectogel HC, onguent – 0,5 % de zinc, 10 % de benzocaïne et 1 % d'hydrocortisone

Rifater – 120 mg de rifampine, 50 mg d'isotamine et 300 mg de pyrazinamide

Rivasol-HC, onguent – 0,5 % d'hydrocortisone et 0,5 % de zinc

Robaxacet – 325 mg d'acétaminophène et 400 mg de méthocarbamol

Robaxacet Extra Fort – 400 mg de méthocarbamol et 500 d'acétaminophène

Robaxacet-8 – 325 mg d'acétaminophène, 400 mg de méthocarbamol et 8 mg de codéine

Robaxisal Extra Fort– 400 mg de méthocarbamol et 500 mg d'AAS

Robax platinum – 200 mg d'ibuprofène et 400 mg de méthocarbamol

Robitussin Toux et Rhume Liqui-Gels – 200 mg de guaifénésine, 10 mg de dextrométhorphane et 30 mg de pseudoéphédrine

Robitussin-Toux et Rhume, sirop – Par 5 mL : 100 mg de guaifénésine, 30 mg de pseudoéphédrine et 15 mg de dextrométhorphane

Rosasol, crème topique – 1 % de métronidazole, 7,5 % de Parsol MCX et 2 % de Parsol 1789

Royvac (trousse) – 3 comprimés de 5 mg et 1 suppositoire de 10 mg de bisacodyl, 296 mL de citrate de magnésium

SAB-Anuzinc HC, onguent – Par 1 g : 5 mg d'hydrocortisone et 5 mg de zinc

SAB-Anuzinc HC Plus, onguent – Par 1 g : 10 mg de pramoxine, 5 mg d'hydrocortisone et 5 mg de zinc

SAB-Proctomyxin HC – Par 1 g : 5 mg d'hydrocortisone, 5 mg de cinchocaïne, 10 mg de framycétine et 10 mg d'esculine

Senokot-S – 8,6 mg de sennosides et 50 mg de docusate sodique

Sinutab Sinus et allergies – 325 mg d'acétaminophène, 2 mg de chlorphéniramine et 30 mg de pseudoéphédrine

Sinutab Sinus et allergies Extra-puissant – 500 mg d'acétaminophène, 2 mg de chlorphéniramine et 30 mg de pseudoéphédrine

Sofracort, solution oto-ophtalmique – 0,5 % de framycétine, 0,005 % de gramicidine et 0,05 % de dexaméthasone

Stievamycin gel – 0,025 % de trétinoïne et 4 % d'érythromycine

Stresstabs + Fer – 0,4 mg d'acide folique, 27 mg de fumarate ferreux, 500 mg d'acide ascorbique, complexe de vitamine B et 30 UI de vitamine E

Stresstabs Régulier – 0,6 mg d'acide folique, 15 mg de vitamine B_1, 15 mg de vitamine B_2, 20 mg de niacine, 10 mg de vitamine B_6, 25 µg de vitamine B_{12}, 30 µg de biotine, 20 mg d'acide pantothénique, 500 mg de vitamine C et 30 UI de vitamine E

Sudafed Rhume de cerveau et sinus, extra-puissant – 500 mg d'acétaminophène et 60 mg de pseudoéphédrine.

Sudafed Rhume et grippe – 250 mg d'acétaminophène, 10 mg de dextrométhorphane, 100 mg de guaifénésine et 30 mg de pseudoéphédrine

Symbicort 100 Turbuhaler – 100 µg de budésonide et 6 µg de formotérol

Symbicort 200 Turbuhaler – 200 µg de budésonide et 6 µg de formotérol

Tarka 2/240 mg – 2 mg de trandolapril et 240 mg de vérapamil

Tarka 4/240 mg – 4 mg de trandolapril et 240 mg de vérapamil

Tecnal – 330 mg d'aspirine, 40 mg de caféine et 50 mg de butalbital

Tecnal C1/4 – 330 mg d'aspirine, 40 mg de caféine, 50 mg de butalbital et 15 mg de codéine

Tecnal C1/2 – 330 mg d'aspirine, 40 mg de caféine, 50 mg de butalbital et 30 mg de codéine

Tenoretic 50/25 – 50 mg d'aténolol et 25 mg de chlorthalidone

Tenoretic 100/25 – 100 mg d'aténolol et 25 mg de chlorthalidone

Teveten Plus – 600 mg d'éprosartan et 12,5 mg d'hydrochlorothiazide

Theraderm – Par 1 g : 0,25 mg de gramicidine, 2,5 g de néomycine, 100 000 U de nystatine et 1 mg de triamcinolone

Tobradex, onguent ophtalmique – Par 1 g : 3 mg de tobramycine et 0,1 % de dexaméthasone

Tobradex, suspension ophtalmique – Par 1 mL : 3 mg de tobramycine et 0,1 % de dexaméthasone

Tramacet – 37,5 mg de tramadol et 325 mg d'acétaminophène

Trinalin – 1 mg de maléate d'azatadine et 60 mg de pseudoéphédrine

Trizivir – 300 mg d'abacavir, 150 mg de lamivudine et 300 mg de zidovudine

Truvada – 200 mg d'emtricitabine et 300 mg de ténofovir

Tussionex, comprimé – 5 mg d'hydrocodone et 10 mg de phényltoloxamine

Tussionex, sirop – Par 5 mL: 5 mg d'hydrocodone et 10 mg de phényltoloxamine

Tylenol Douleurs musculaires – 250 mg de chlorzoxazone et 500 mg d'acétaminophène

Tylenol Extra Fort douleur et congestion sinusales pour la nuit – 500 mg d'acétaminophène, 30 mg de pseudoéphédrine et 2 mg de chlorphéniramine

Tylenol Extra Fort douleur et congestion sinusales pour le jour – 500 mg d'acétaminophène et 30 mg de pseudoéphédrine

Tylenol Rhume et Grippe pour la nuit – Par 30 mL: 1 000 mg d'acétaminophène, 60 mg de pseudoéphédrine, 30 mg de dextrométhorphane et 12,5 mg de doxylamine

Tylenol Rhume et Grippe pour le jour – Par 30 mL: 1 000 mg d'acétaminophène, 60 mg de pseudoéphédrine et 30 mg de dextrométhorphane

Tylenol Ultra-efficace – 500 mg d'acétaminophène et 65 mg de caféine

Uremol HC, crème et lotion – 1 % d'hydrocortisone et 10 % d'urée

Valisone-G, crème et lotion – Par 1 g: 1 mg de valérate de bétaméthasone et 1 mg de gentamicine

Valisone-G, crème et pommade topique – Par 1 g: 1 mg (0,1 %) de valérate de bétaméthasone et 1 mg (0,1 %) de gentamicine

Vaseretic 5 mg/12,5 mg – 5 mg d'énalapril et 12,5 mg d'hydrochlorothiazide

Vaseretic 10 mg/25 mg – 10 mg d'énalapril et 25 mg d'hydrochlorothiazide

Viaderm-K.C., crème et onguent – Par 1 g: 1 mg de triamcinolone, 100 000 unités de nystatine, 2,5 mg de néomycine et 0,25 mg de gramicidine

Visine Allergie, solution ophtalmique – 0,05 % de tétrahydrozoline et 0,25 % de sulfate de zinc

Visine Lubrifiant, solution ophtalmique – 0,05 % de tétrahydrozoline et 1 % de polyéthylèneglycol 400

Visine Plus Allergies, solution ophtalmique – 0,025 % de naphazoline à et 0,3 % de phéniramine

Viskazide 10/25 – 10 mg de pindolol et 25 mg d'hydrochlorothiazide

Viskazide 10/50 – 10 mg de pindolol et 50 mg d'hydrochlorothiazide

Vita 3B + C – 250 mg de vitamine B_1, 125 mg de vitamine B_6, 250 µg de vitamine B_{12} et 250 mg de vitamine C

Vitathion-A.T.P. – Par sachet: 500 mg d'acide ascorbique, 2 mg de thiamine et 18 mg d'inositol

Xalacom, solution ophtalmique – 0,005 % de latanoprost et 0,5 % de timolol

Zestoretic 10/12,5 – 10 mg de lisinopril et 12,5 mg d'hydrochlorothiazide

Zestoretic 20/12,5 – 20 mg de lisinopril et 12,5 mg d'hydrochlorothiazide

Zestoretic 20/25 – 20 mg de lisinopril et 25 mg d'hydrochlorothiazide

INDEX

Les **NOMS GÉNÉRIQUES** sont en **PETITES MAJUSCULES NOIRES**.
Les noms commerciaux sont en caractères ordinaires.
Les CLASSES DE MÉDICAMENTS sont en PETITES MAJUSCULES.

A

C

G

H

I

K

N

O

P

S

NOTES

NOTES

NOTES

NOTES

Acclaim and Laurels for David Robinson's
CHAPLIN: His Life and Art

"In all, one of the great cinema books; a labor of love, and a splendid achievement."
—*Variety*

"I cannot imagine how anyone could write a better book on the great complex subject. . . . It is movingly entertaining, awesomely thorough and profoundly respectful."
—*Sunday Telegraph*

"Mr. Robinson explores Chaplin's many troubles and adventures along his Dickensian journey from England to America and records them so trenchantly that the reader must wonder how all this activity could have been crowded into a mere 88 years. It is a massive work and reflects a massive talent. . . . In his painstaking and brilliantly researched book . . . Mr. Robinson has given us a valuable and important chronicle."
—*New York Times Book Review*

"His account of Chaplin the artist at work is unlikely ever to be surpassed. . . . David Robinson has written a marvelous book on Chaplin and a fascinating biography of the man. . . . One is grateful for the lucidity of his writing and for the enormous amount of information carefully sifted and expertly presented." —*Spectator*

"An indispensable work for all concerned with the history of the cinema."
—London *Sunday Times*

"This is one of those addictive biographies in which you start by looking in the index for items that interest you, then find that each item has a knock-on effect into the next and as dawn breaks you're reading the book from cover to cover."
—*Financial Times*

"A classic piece of film biography which is also the fascinating story of a brilliant, perverse, courageous man, indisputably one of the great artists of the twentieth century."
—*Tatler*

"Robinson has given us . . . the life, complete with a chronology and filmography, that we've long needed, . . . a combination of warmth towards its subject and judicious setting straight of the records. . . . This book increases one's respect for Chaplin's craftsmanship and sharpens one's understanding of his art."
—*The Observer*

"This book will surely do all that is needed to restore Charlie Chaplin not just to the academic pantheon but to the hearts of living, laughing people."
—*Times Literary Supplement*

About the Author

David Robinson is one of the most widely respected film critics and historians in the world. He has been for ten years film critic of the *Times* and before that for fifteen years wrote about cinema for the *Financial Times*. His special areas of study are the pre-history of motion pictures, film comedy and East European cinema; he is also an authority on English music hall and popular entertainment in general. His collections of pre-cinema apparatus and film posters have been the subject of a number of exhibitions in Europe, and his books include *World Cinema*, *Hollywood in the Twenties*, *The Great Funnies*, *Buster Keaton*, *Chaplin—The Mirror of Opinion*, *The Illustrated History of the Cinema* (co-editor), *Music of the Shadows*, *Masterpieces of Animation, 1833-1908*, *Richard Attenborough*, and *George Melies*.

DAVID ROBINSON

Chaplin

His Life and Art

DA CAPO PRESS
New York

Library of Congress Cataloging in Publication Data

Robinson, David, 1930–
Chaplin, his life and art / David Robinson.—1st Da Capo Press ed.
p. cm.
Includes bibliographical references and index.
ISBN 0-306-80600-2
1. Chaplin, Charlie, 1889–1977. 2. Comedians—United States—Biography. 3. Motion picture actors and actresses—United States—Biography. I. Title.
PN2287.C5R56 1994
791.43'028'092—dc20
[B] 94-21593
CIP

First Da Capo Press edition 1994

This Da Capo Press paperback edition of *Chaplin* is an unabridged republication of the edition first published in London in 1985, with minor revisions added in 1992. It is reprinted by arrangement with HarperCollins Publishers, Ltd.

Published by Da Capo Press, Inc.
A Subsidiary of Plenum Publishing Corporation
233 Spring Street, New York, N.Y. 10013

Manufactured in the United States of America

CONTENTS

ILLUSTRATIONS

All photographs unless otherwise specifically acknowledged are the copyright of the Roy Export Company Establishment.

Section 1, between pages 72 and 73

Section 2, between pages 232 and 233

Page 1
The Keystone Studios. (Bison Archives: Marc Wanamaker Collection)
Mack Sennett. (Bison Archives: Marc Wanamaker Collection)

Page 2
The Essanay Studio. (Bison Archives: Marc Wanamaker Collection)
The Majestic Studio. (Bison Archives: Marc Wanamaker Collection)

Page 3
Mabel Normand. (Author's collection)
Making a Living. (Bison Archives: Marc Wanamaker Collection)

Page 4
Essanay publicity, 1915. (Bison Archives: Marc Wanamaker Collection)

Page 5
Essanay picture postcards, 1915. (Author's collection)

Pages 6 and 7
The cast and crew of *The Bank*, 1915. (Author's collection)

Page 8
Chaplin's first day at the Lone Star Studios. (Bison Archives: Marc Wanamaker Collection)
Filming *The Vagabond*, 1916.

Page 9
Edna Purviance. (Author's collection)
Edna's star hat, *The Count.*

Page 10
The old mansion in the grounds of the Chaplin Studio.
Chaplin and Sydney visit the site of the projected studio.

Page 11
Building the studio, 1918.
Chaplin on the studio site.

Pages 12 and 13
Cartoon by Cami, 1917.
Anticipation of *Shoulder Arms*, 1918.
Aerial views of Chaplin Studio.

Page 14
A Dog's Life, 1918.

Page 15
A Dog's Life: Chaplin with Mut.
A rehearsal at the studio, posed for *How to Make Movies*, 1918.

Page 16
Visitors to the studio: Helen Keller with Annie Sullivan (*above*); Douglas Fairbanks and Harry Lauder (*below*).

Section 3, between pages 328 and 329

Page 1
Chaplin addressing a Bond rally in Wall Street, 1918.
Chaplin at a Bond rally in Washington, 1918.

Page 2
Shoulder Arms: sets for the abandoned prologue and epilogue.
Shoulder Arms: Chaplin getting into his tree costume.

Page 3
Chaplin with Dorothy Rosher during the making of *The Bond.*
The Bond: Chaplin and Edna.
A break during filming of *The Bond.*

Pages 4 and 5
Douglas Fairbanks vaults the gate of the Chaplin Studio.
Tea break during shooting of *Sunnyside*.
Mildred Harris Chaplin. (Author's collection)

Illustrations

Page 6
A Days Pleasure: between shots. (Author's collection: Jack Wilson Archive)
The Kid: Chaplin practises flying.
The Freak. (Jean-Baptiste Thierrée)

Page 7
The Professor. (Both author's collection: Jack Wilson Archive)

Pages 8 and 9
The Kid: Chaplin with Jackie Coogan, Edith Wilson and her baby. (Author's collection: Jack Wilson Archive)
Handing over the negative of *The Kid*.

Pages 10 and 11
Aboard the *Olympic*, 1921. (National Film Archive)
Chaplin leaving the *Olympic* at Southampton. (National Film Archive)

Page 12
Portrait of Max Linder.
Chaplin directs Lord Mountbatten in *Nice and Friendly*.

Page 13
Chaplin in his cutting room, c. 1920.
Lady Mountbatten in *Nice and Friendly*.

Pages 14 and 15
Pola Negri. (Author's collection)
A Woman of Paris, 1923.
A Woman of Paris: Lydia Knott, Carl Miller, Edna Purviance. (Inman Hunter Collection)

Page 16
The United Artists. (Author's collection: Jack Wilson Archive)
Jack Wilson photographs the four United Artists. (Author's collection: Jack Wilson Archive)
Chaplin rehearsing with Abe Lyman's orchestra, 1925.

Section 4, between pages 424 and 425

Page 1
The Gold Rush: Lita Grey with Chaplin at the signing of her contract.
Chaplin on set.

Pages 2 and 3
The Gold Rush: on location at Truckee.
Chaplin performs the Dance of the Rolls out of costume.
Preparing to film a travelling shot.
Between takes on location.

Pages 4 and 5
The Gold Rush: Lita Grey as leading lady.
Georgia Hale as leading lady.

Page 6
Chaplin's first Hollywood home. (Author's collection)
His house on Summit Drive. (Author's collection)

Page 7
The Circus: Merna Kennedy.
Chaplin succumbs to exhaustion. (Author's collection: Jack Wilson Archive).

Page 8
The Lita Grey divorce: Lita takes the oath. (Author's collection)

Page 9
After the studio fire.

Page 10
Sea Gulls (A Woman of the Sea): the cast and crew on location. (Inman Hunter Collection)
Edna Purviance. (Inman Hunter Collection)

Page 11
Sea Gulls: Edna Purviance and Gayne Whitman. (Inman Hunter Collection)

Pages 12 and 13
City Lights: Chaplin at the camera.
The studio back lot during the shooting of *City Lights*.
Chaplin with Ralph Barton on the set.
Chaplin in the costume of the Duke.
Al Jolson visits Chaplin on the set.

Pages 14 and 15
Hannah Chaplin in 1921. (Pauline Mason)
Hannah Chaplin in Hollywood.
Hannah Chaplin's grave in the Hollywood Cemetery. (Author's collection)
Chaplin's sons, Sydney (*left*) and Charles Jr.
Chaplin at home, 1930.

Page 16
Chaplin with Mr and Mrs Albert Einstein at the première of *City Lights*.
The première of *City Lights* at the Los Angeles Theatre, 30 January 1931.

Section 5, between pages 552 and 553

Page 1
The 1931 world tour. Chaplin at the Majestic Hotel, Nice.
Sydney with May Reeves at St Moritz.

Page 2
Paulette Goddard.
Chaplin with Paulette Goddard at the première of *Modern Times*.

Page 3
Paulette Goddard, photographed by Hurrell.

Page 4
Modern Times: principal members of the Chaplin unit at this period.
Set design for the department store skating sequence.

Page 5
Chaplin as Napoleon, 1925. (Bison Archives: Marc Wanamaker Collection)
Chaplin as Napoleon, mid-1930s.

Page 6
The Great Dictator.
Chaplin and Roland Totheroh.
The last meeting with Douglas Fairbanks, on the set of *The Great Dictator*.

Page 7
The Great Dictator: Chaplin at a music recording session.
Chaplin at the New York press conference for *The Great Dictator*.

Pages 8 and 9
Chaplin with Oona in Hollywood, 1944.
Monsieur Verdoux: Chaplin and Marilyn Nash
Chaplin and Margaret Hoffmann.

Page 10
Chaplin directing at the Circle Theatre, Hollywood. (Jerry Epstein)
Limelight: Chaplin with Wheeler Dryden and Claire Bloom.

Page 11
Limelight: the screen debuts of Geraldine, Josephine and Michael Chaplin.
The flea circus routine.

Page 12
Chaplin and Oona backstage at the Comedie Française, Winter 1952.

Page 13
Chaplin and Sophia Loren at a press conference to announce *The Countess from Hong Kong* at the Savoy Hotel, London, November 1, 1965.
The Countess from Hong Kong: Chaplin on the set with Sophia Loren and Margaret Rutherford.

Pages 14 and 15
Chaplin, Oona and Christopher, c. 1967.
Chaplin and Oona in 1974.
Chaplin, with Oona and Geraldine.
Manoir de Ban, Corsier-sur-Vevey, Switzerland.

Page 16
The Chaplin Studio, 1983. (Author's collection)
The last official portrait, 1977.

PREFACE

> The world is not composed of heroes and villains,
> but of men and women with all the passions that God
> has given them.
>
> The ignorant condemn, but the wise pity.
>
> CHARLES CHAPLIN, prefatory title to
> *A Woman of Paris*, 1923.

> Those big shoes are buttoned with 50,000,000 eyes.
>
> GENE MORGAN, Chicago newsman, 1915.

Charles Chaplin's autobiography appeared in 1964. He was then seventy-five years old. The book ran to more than five hundred pages and represented a prodigious feat of memory, for it was in large part done without reference to documentation. At the time, indeed, the feat seemed too prodigious to some reviewers, who were incredulous that anyone could remember in such detail events that had taken place a long lifetime before.

Since Chaplin's death, I have had the privilege of examining the great mass of his working papers – some of them unseen for more than half a century. In the public archives of London and in old theatrical records I have been able to uncover many long-forgotten traces of the young Chaplin and his family. In addition, a number of people in England and America have generously shared their memories and papers.

Sifting this mass of documentation has only served to heighten regard for the powers of Chaplin's memory and the honesty of his record. An instance of the kind of detail which is constantly corroborated by the archives is the recollection, from his thirteenth year, that when his brother first went to sea he sent home thirty-five shillings from his pay packet: Sydney Chaplin's seaman's papers – which were not available to Chaplin when he wrote – exactly confirm the sum. Even small inaccuracies attest to rather than discredit his memory. He remembers a childhood ogre, one of his schoolmasters, as 'Captain Hindrum', an old vaudeville friend of his mother's as 'Dashing Eva Lestocq' and the friendly stage manager at the Duke of York's Theatre as 'Mr Postant'. In fact their names turn out to have been Hindom, Dashing Eva Lester and William Postance. Chaplin probably never saw any of the names written down, and no doubt he recalled them simply as he heard them as a child. In themselves the slips clearly show that Chaplin's record is the result of a phenomenal memory rather than the product of *post facto* research and reconstruction. So regularly is his memory vindicated by other evidence that where there are discrepancies without proof one way or the other, the benefit of the doubt seems best given to Chaplin.

The present volume, written twenty years after Chaplin's own account of his life, serves in part to complement *My Autobiography*. Subsequent research makes it possible to add further documentation and detail to the subject's sometimes random recollections. In their study *Chaplin: Genesis of a Clown*, Raoul Sobel and David Francis complained of the lack of hard facts and dates in the early chapters of *My Autobiography*. 'To try to keep a running time scale while reading *My Autobiography* is rather like having to navigate by the stars on an overcast night. By the time one reaches the next break in the clouds, the boat may be miles off course.' This is true, perhaps: the special charm of those first chapters of *My Autobiography* is the free range of memory, unrestrained by the cold collaboration of any ghostly researcher. It is hardly to be wondered at if, at six or seven years old, the infant Chaplin was a trifle confused about the order of the workhouses and charity schools into which he was thrust. The importance of the autobiography is that it recorded his feelings in the face of these misadventures. The present volume can, at risk of pedantry, tidy up the facts and chronology.

While *My Autobiography* is a strikingly truthful record of things witnessed, Chaplin might sometimes have been misled in the case of things reported to him. Like any mother, Mrs Chaplin must have tried to shield her children from unpleasant facts when she was able to do so. Some critics of the autobiography doubted whether Chaplin's childhood could really have been as awful as he described. New discoveries suggest that Mrs Chaplin kept the worst from her children. The Chaplin boys seem never to have known, for example, of the sad fate of his maternal grandmother as she declined into alcoholism and vagrancy. Charles always believed that this grandmother was a gypsy, whereas the gypsy blood came with his *paternal* grandmother. Again it was a natural misunderstanding for a child. Grandma Chaplin died years before his birth. Told that his grandmother was a gypsy, he could only assume it to mean the grandmother he had known.

Chaplin was an accurate and truthful chronicler of what he had seen. He was not always a comprehensive one. There are large and deliberate areas of omission from the autobiography. His description of friends, acquaintances and affairs was selective. Some relationships are described in the autobiography with great frankness and humour, while other people who at one time or another were very close to him are not even mentioned. To an extent, gallantry may have played a part in the selection. Most of the people left out were still living: Chaplin may have felt that they would have been too easily hurt or offended. As it happened, a lot were offended by being left out.

His reticence about his own work was more disappointing. He discussed very few of his films, and then had little to say about the way he made them. Later in his career, visitors to his sets were discouraged, and he would explain his reluctance to let people into his working secrets by saying, "If people know how it's done, all the magic goes." This, though, was probably only a small factor in Chaplin's secretiveness. It may be that he came to feel more and more that he was unable to unveil the mysteries, simply because the essential part of the mysteries remained veiled for him, too. How could he ever explain, to himself or to anyone else, how it was that he was able, one afternoon in 1914, to walk into the Keystone wardrobe hut, pick out a costume, and on the spot create a character which was so soon to become the most universally recognized representation of a human being in the history of mankind? In later years, Chaplin and his apologists would rationalize the appeal of the Tramp; but no one could ever figure why it was he, and that moment, that were chosen for the mystical birth of Charlie.

There were more practical reasons for leaving his work out of the autobiography. Chaplin wrote the book in the spirit of the entertainer that, his whole life, he was. Like most people, he saw no particular glamour in his job: he once told someone that his working life was no more exciting than that of a bank clerk. He probably felt that it would simply be boring to tell people how his films were made. If genius is computed at 10 per cent inspiration and 90 per cent perspiration, that 90 per cent should be reckoned much higher in Chaplin's case. No one was ever more dogged in the pursuit of the best of which he was capable.

Ironically, considering his legendary secrecy during his lifetime, Chaplin has left a more comprehensive record of the processes of his creativity than any other film maker of his generation (or generations, for Chaplin's whole working life spanned eight decades). For this reason alone, it has seemed important to explore these at length in this book. The reader must judge if Chaplin was justified in his fears that the daily work even of a comic genius was too humdrum to be interesting.

The worknotes, the studio records and the out-takes and rushes that have survived tell us what Chaplin was reluctant to reveal about his methods and his indefatigable application to the quest for perfection. Part of this book is devoted to reconstructing the way that Chaplin created his comic visions – the long and painful processes of refining and polishing plots and gags; the mechanical problems involving resources, studios, apparatus, sets; the choice of collaborators and working relations with them; the endless repetitions, trials, rehearsals, shooting, reshooting, rejection, revision; and finally the months of editing until the finished product should betray nothing of the labour, but seem as simple and natural (in the phrase of Alistair Cooke) 'as water running over stones'.

When I began this book, I intended to deal only with Chaplin's work. The private biography seemed to have been recorded more than enough times, and at first sight the two elements of his life appeared clearly distinguishable. Chaplin himself described the way he divided his life: when he was at work on a film, his creative concentration left him no time for other pursuits. It quickly appeared, however, that Chaplin's life was not in fact so easily divisible. His mind, said one collaborator, was like an attic, in which everything that might one day come in handy was stored away for future use. He may have forgotten about his private life when he was at work; but he never forgot work at the other times. Again and again we can recognize the people and incidents and feelings of his personal life transposed into incidents in the films.

Readers who like biographers to supply post-Freudian interpretations for every action and incident may be frustrated. I have no personal liking for that genre of biography; I do not feel qualified for psychoanalysis; and finally I think that Chaplin's singular life story would defy the process. The childhood, for a start, made up of experiences that few people can even comprehend, let alone share, and felt through a sensibility that was already out of the ordinary, had to leave its impression upon his attitudes to people, work, money, wives, families, politics, himself. Then he was an actor, with the actor's ability to stay ahead, to adapt his personality to suit the occasion and the company. His protean quality was often puzzling. People who knew him well enough to record their impressions have described him as modest, vain, prodigal, mean, generous, shy, show-off, ruthless, timid, kind, patient, impatient . . . Most likely he was all these things, since he was human. Perhaps the most remarkable achievement of his life, in fact, was to stay fallibly, recognizably human, despite the adulation amounting to apotheosis at the peak of his fame; despite experiencing public revilement as passionate as the affection he had known; despite having lived the most dramatic of all the rags to riches stories ever told. There is no wonder if he was a complex creature. For all we can learn about Chaplin's life and thought, it will still not be easy to explain him. But we can try to understand.

ACKNOWLEDGEMENTS

My principal thanks are of course to the late Lady Chaplin, who gave me full access to Sir Charles's working papers, without seeking to impose the restraints implied in an "authorized" biography, which this assuredly is not. I am also grateful to her children for their kindness and patience. It was in large part due to the urging of Victoria Chaplin, her husband Jean-Baptiste Thierrée and their friend David Gothard that I first undertook the book. Nor could it have been possible without the wholehearted cooperation of Miss Rachel Ford, who has been responsible for ordering and maintaining the Chaplin archives, and her successor Madame Pam Paumier. I was very conscious of the courtesies and warmth of the household staff at Vevey – Renato, Gino, Mirella, Fernanda and "Kay-Kay" McKenzie – during my stays there.

An important personal link with Chaplin was Jerry Epstein. He had been Chaplin's producer and assistant, and became my agent. Even more important was his great gift of friendship which, like Chaplin himself, I was privileged to share. He urged me to embark upon this book for several years before I was finally persuaded to attempt it.

In sharing the mass of material they assembled during the years of research for their incomparable film series *Unknown Chaplin*, Kevin Brownlow and David Gill have far exceeded any ordinary calls of friendship or scholarship. Not a week has gone by without an envelope in the post addressed in Brownlow's meticulous hand, containing some new discovery turned up in his monumental files. My friends Al and Candy Reuter have shown equal generosity in finding for me rare stills and posters not represented in the Chaplin collection. The late Inman Hunter freely made available the treasures of his own collection, including the papers of Edna Purviance, which since his death have passed to the Museum of the Moving Image, London.

I am particularly indebted to the pioneer researches of Harold Manning and David Clegg, who have spent years combing public archives and the volumes of *The Era* in the Birmingham Public Library. Mr Manning is the most vital nonagenarian of my acquaintance, with a store of vivid theatrical memories that go back to his first Christmas pantomime in 1899. He is, in addition, a scrupulous and indefatigable scholar, whose advice has been invaluable. David Clegg's own listings have made a major contribution to the record of Chaplin's theatrical appearances which appears in the appendices.

Research in the archives of the Greater London Record Office has produced much new evidence of Chaplin's childhood years; and here I owe a particular debt to Mr Alan Neate, the former Record Keeper for the Director-General, who has over the years carefully noted every Chaplin reference. Mr Neate also drew my attention to the discovery by Mrs Weston of the record of Hannah Chaplin's and her father's adult baptisms.

Others in this country to whom I am especially grateful are Roy Waters, who has helped me with research on *Sherlock Holmes* and has lent or given me rare photographs from his collection; Peter Cotes, whose *The Little Fellow*, written with the late Thelma Niklaus, remains one of the best appreciations; Colin Sorenson of the Museum of London who has passed on a note of any Chapliniana that has come under his eye; Tony Barker, for music hall references; John Whitehorn of Francis, Day and Hunter for dating the songs of Charles Chaplin Senior; Bill Douglas and Peter Jewell for advice and pictures; Ken Wlaschin, whose eagle eye has often spotted a reference, a postcard or a music sheet; Miss Kathleen Saintsbury for memories of her father; Mrs Fred Karno Junior for her recollections of the Karno troupes; I am also grateful to the Garrick Club and its former librarian, the late Dr Geoffrey Ashton, for access to their files of *The Era*; and especially Pauline Mason (*née* Chaplin) for her family recollections.

In the United States my first debt is to Mark Stock, the most dedicated Chaplinian of my acquaintance, who gave me every possible help in Hollywood. Marc Wanamaker was also of inestimable assistance in driving me around the wildernesses of California, giving helpful leads and supplying photographs. Paul and Betty Tetrick were generous hosts and wonderful informants about life at the Chaplin Studio; they also loaned me rare and precious photographs. Moreover they introduced me to Wyn Ray Evans, with her precise and fascinating reminiscences of her parents' days with Karno and her own meetings with Hannah Chaplin.

Of those who worked with Chaplin, I enjoyed long conversations with Hans Koenekamp, who photographed the first film in which Chaplin appeared in the famous costume; with Georgia Hale, the exquisite leading lady of *The Gold Rush*; with Eugene Lourié, the great designer who was art director on *Limelight*. I spent a memorable day with Dan James at his cliff-edge eyrie at Carmel. Anthony Coogan talked to me of his father, and Steve Totheroh of his grandfather. I was also able to speak to Virginia Cherrill Martini, Chaplin's leading lady in *City Lights*; to Lita Grey Chaplin; to David Raksin; to Tim Durant; to Dean Riesner (once the Horrid Child in *The Pilgrim*) and to the nonagenarian Nellie Bly Baker, Chaplin's first studio secretary.

A special debt of gratitude is due to Charles Mandelstam in New York, for obtaining the FBI files on Chaplin in time to make use of them in this book. I would also like to record with particular appreciation the support I have received, in friendship, interest and encouragement, from Alexander Walker; from Mo and Lynn Rothman; from Peter Rose and Albert Gallichan; and from my endlessly patient friends Roger Few and Harry Ogle who gave invaluable help in laborious proofreading. Finally, at Collins I must thank Christopher MacLehose and Roger Schlesinger who nursed the book along, Ronald Clark and Marian Morris who designed it, and my editor, Ariane Goodman.

Embleton, Northumberland
June 1984.

London
August 1992.

The Chaplin Family

Table 1

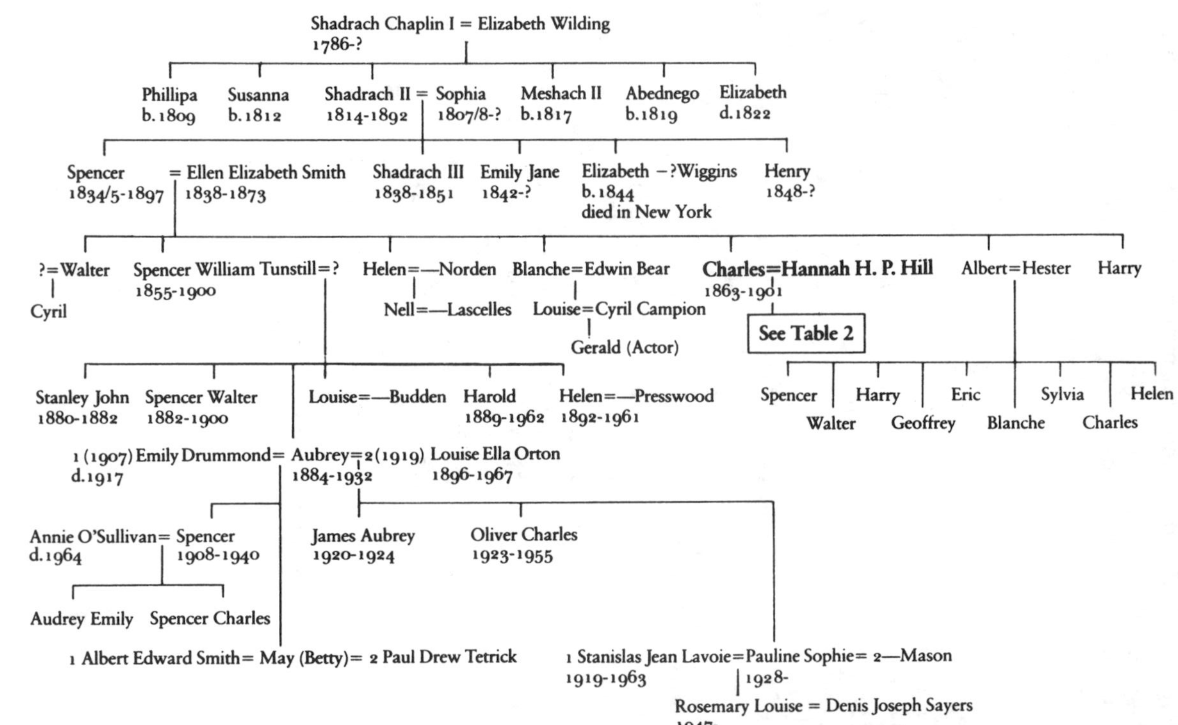

Shadrach Chaplin I = Elizabeth Wilding
1786-?
Phillipa
b.1809
Susanna
b.1812
Shadrach II = Sophia
1814-1892
1807/8-?
Meshach II
b.1817
Abednego
b.1819
Elizabeth
d.1822
Spencer = Ellen Elizabeth Smith
1834/5-1897
1838-1873
Shadrach III
1838-1851
Emily Jane
1842-?
Elizabeth –?Wiggins
b.1844
died in New York
Henry
1848-?
?=Walter
Cyril
Spencer William Tunstill=?
1855-1900
Helen=—Norden
Nell=—Lascelles
Blanche=Edwin Bear
Louise=Cyril Campion
Gerald (Actor)
Charles=Hannah H. P. Hill
1863-1901
See Table 2
Albert=Hester
Harry
Spencer
Walter
Harry
Geoffrey
Eric
Blanche
Sylvia
Charles
Helen
Stanley John
1880-1882
Spencer Walter
1882-1900
Louise=—Budden
Harold
1889-1962
Helen=—Presswood
1892-1961
1 (1907) Emily Drummond= Aubrey=2(1919) Louise Ella Orton
d.1917
1884-1932
1896-1967
Annie O'Sullivan= Spencer
d.1964
1908-1940
James Aubrey
1920-1924
Oliver Charles
1923-1955
Audrey Emily
Spencer Charles
1 Albert Edward Smith= May (Betty)= 2 Paul Drew Tetrick
1 Stanislas Jean Lavoie=Pauline Sophie= 2—Mason
1919-1963
1928-
Rosemary Louise = Denis Joseph Sayers
1947-

Table 2

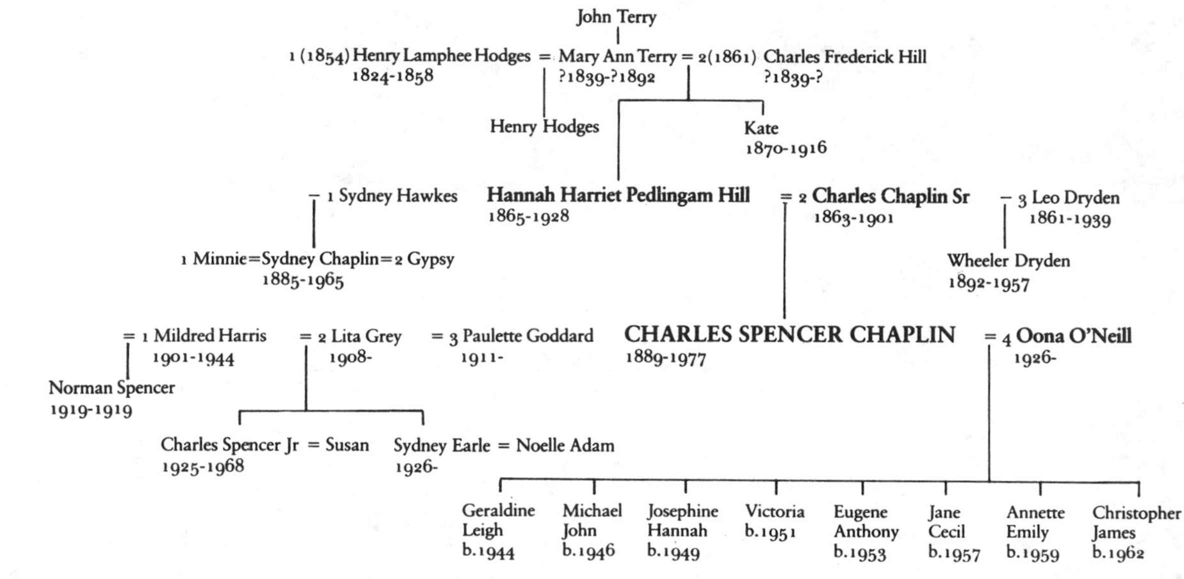

John Terry
1 (1854) Henry Lamphee Hodges = Mary Ann Terry = 2(1861) Charles Frederick Hill
1824-1858
?1839-?1892
?1839-?
Henry Hodges
Kate
1870-1916
1 Sydney Hawkes
Hannah Harriet Pedlingam Hill
1865-1928
= 2 Charles Chaplin Sr
1863-1901
3 Leo Dryden
1861-1939
1 Minnie=Sydney Chaplin=2 Gypsy
1885-1965
Wheeler Dryden
1892-1957
= 1 Mildred Harris
1901-1944
= 2 Lita Grey
1908-
= 3 Paulette Goddard
1911-
CHARLES SPENCER CHAPLIN
1889-1977
= 4 Oona O'Neill
1926-
Norman Spencer
1919-1919
Charles Spencer Jr = Susan
1925-1968
Sydney Earle = Noelle Adam
1926-
Geraldine Leigh b.1944
Michael John b.1946
Josephine Hannah b.1949
Victoria b.1951
Eugene Anthony b.1953
Jane Cecil b.1957
Annette Emily b.1959
Christopher James b.1962

The London of Chaplin's Youth

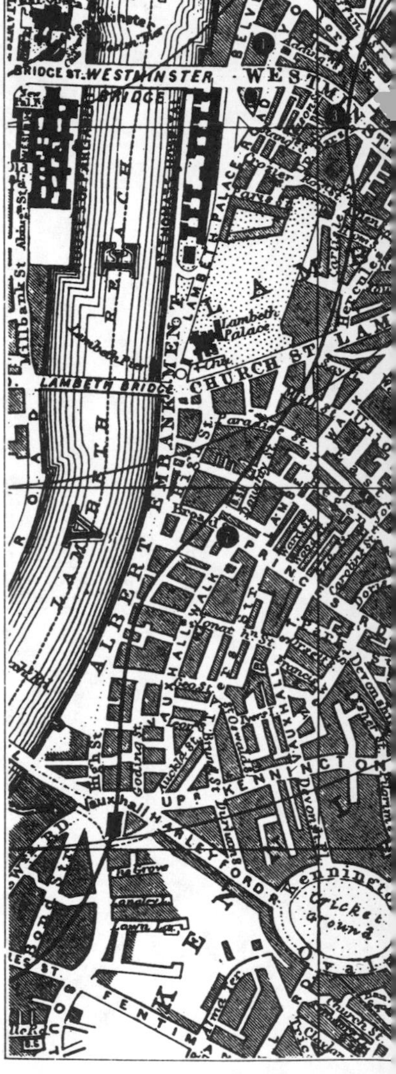

● *York Road*
CC lived at number 164 with Hodges family, 1895.

● *14 Lambeth Square*
CC's mother lived here, May 1890.

● *Canterbury Music Hall, Westminster Bridge Road.*
CC recalled seeing father perform here.

● *Christchurch, Westminster Bridge Road.*
CC's mother and paternal grandfather baptized here as adults, 10 January 1898.

● *South London Palace, 92 London Road, Lambeth.*
Hannah appeared in a benefit performance here on 27 May 1886, and Charles Chaplin Senior frequently performed. Chaplin also remembered that this was where he first saw a Karno company, about 1903.

● *West Square*
CC's parents lived together here, c.1890.

● *Broad Street, (now Black Prince Road)*
Spencer Chaplin, CC's uncle, landlord of Queen's Head, c.1890-1900.

● *3 Pownall Terrace*
CC lived here with mother, early 1903.

● *Kennington Road*
CC lived with Mr and Mrs Alfred Jackson at 5 Kennington Mansions, April 23 - May 3, 1900.

● *Renfrew Road*
Lambeth Workhouse.

● *Chester Street*
CC lived here with mother, and worked in barber's shop, c.1901.

● *289 Kennington Road*
CC and Sydney stayed here with father and 'Louise', September-November(?) 1898.

● *39 Methley Street.*
CC's mother lived here, November 1898 - August 1899 and subsequently.

● *Kennington Park*
Mrs Chaplin and her sons spent the day of their 'escape' from the Lambeth Workhouse here, in August 1898.

● *10 Farmer's Road (now Kennington Park Gardens)*
CC's mother lodging here, July 1898.

● *Brixton Road*
CC and Sydney rented a flat here, in Glenshaw Mansions, 1906 - 1912.

● *57 Brandon Street*
CC's parents living here at time of Sydney Chaplin's birth (16 March 1885) and their marriage (22 June 1885).

St John's Church, Larcom Street
CC's parents married here 22 June 1885; Sydney baptized here.

11 Camden Street
(now Morecambe Street)
CC's maternal grandparents living here at time of Hannah Chaplin's birth, 1865.

68 Camden Street
CC's parents living here, March 1890.

East Street
CC believed he was born here 16 April 1889.

The Cradle.

On the 15th ultimo, the wife of Mr Charles Chaplin (*nee* Miss Lily Harley), of a beautiful boy. Mother and son both doing well. Papers please copy.

Chaplin's first press notice -
The Magnet, 11 May 1889. Contrary
to this announcement, Chaplin always
celebrated his birthday on 16 April.

I

A London boyhood

The Chaplin family lived for generations in Suffolk. The name suggests that they were descended from Huguenots, who had settled in great numbers in East Anglia. Chaplin's great-great-grandfather, Shadrach Chaplin, was born in 1786 and became the village bootmaker in Great Finborough, Suffolk. Shadrach inherited the taste for Old Testament names, so that the Chaplin family descent has the appearance of a biblical genealogy. Shadrach, as well as three daughters, begat Shadrach II (1814), Meshach (1817) and Abednego (1819). Shadrach II married a woman named Sophia, seven years older than himself, who came from Tunstall, Staffordshire: it became a Chaplin family tradition to give children the middle name 'Tunstall', though, depending on the parish clerk, it sometimes became 'Tunstill'.[1]

In 1851 Shadrach II was described as a 'master brewer'. He lived in Carr Street, Ipswich,[2] where he established an inn and eating house and conducted a pork butchery. Perhaps these enterprises did not prosper, however, for in the early 1870s he had given up the catering business altogether and taken up his father's trade of boot- and shoemaker. He seems still to have been in this business at the time of his death in 1892, when he bequeathed his stock-in-trade, his shoemaker's tools and his estate of £144 to his widow.[3] Poor Sophia had very temporary benefit from her bequest, since she died the day after her husband.

Shadrach II inevitably begat Shadrach III, but his eldest son – the great Charles Chaplin's grandfather, who was born in 1834 or 1835 – had been named, for a change, Spencer. Spencer was trained to the trade of butcher. It is with Spencer that the first touch of poetry enters the Chaplin history, for on 30 October 1854, still a minor, he married a seventeen-year-old gypsy girl called Ellen Elizabeth Smith, in the parish church of St Margaret, Ipswich.[4] The witnesses to the marriage included the girl's father, who was illiterate, but no Chaplin, so perhaps the family were not happy with the match. Ellen Elizabeth died in 1873, at thirty-five,[5] and no photograph of her survives, so we can only speculate that it might have been she who originated the striking looks, jet hair and fine eyes that became the Chaplin heritage.

The marriage may have been precipitated, for only eight months later, in June 1855, the couple's first child, Spencer William Tunstill (*sic*), was born in Ipswich.[6] Shortly after this event the young Chaplins moved to London. Spencer continued to work as a journeyman butcher, though he was later, in the 1890s, to become a publican and the landlord of the Davenport Arms, Radnor Place, Paddington. On 18 March 1863 a second son, Charles, was born at 22 Orcus Street, Marylebone.[7] This Charles was the future father of the more famous Charles Chaplin.

Towards the end of Sir Charles Chaplin's life, an admirer sent him an old poetry book she had found which bore a school prize label. It had been awarded at St Mark's Schools, Notting Hill in 1874 to Charles Chaplin in Standard 4.[8] The registers of the school no longer exist, so we can discover no more details about this Charles Chaplin to confirm that he was, indeed, Chaplin's father. However the St Mark's Schools in Lancaster Road were only a mile or so from the only addresses we know for Grandfather Spencer Chaplin. In 1874 Charles Chaplin Senior would have been ten or eleven, the appropriate age for Standard 4. Moreover, the registrations of births in the years 1862–1864 indicate no likely contender of that name for the prize in the London area. The balance of evidence seems to confirm Charles Chaplin as the diligent scholar thus rewarded.

Apart from this brief tantalizing glimpse, the elder Charles's early life is shrouded in obscurity until the age of twenty-two, when he met and married Chaplin's mother, Hannah Hill.[9] The Hills appear to have been if anything more humble people than the Chaplins. Hannah's father, Charles Frederick Hill, the son of a bricklayer, was born on 16 April 1839 – fifty years to the day before his famous grandson. There was a family tradition that he had come from Ireland, though in this respect it may be remarked that he seems to have been and remained a Protestant. His whole working life was spent as a journeyman shoe-maker: considering that Charlie Chaplin would come to be symbolized by a pair of disintegrating boots, it is curious that the making and mending of footwear should appear so often as an occupation of his ancestors.

With the Hills the Chaplin story moves to South London. On 16 August 1861 Charles Hill, then living in Lambeth Walk, married Mary Ann Hodges.[10] Both had been married before. There is no record of Charles Hill's first wife; but Mary Ann's previous marriage was to have some relevance to the early years of the younger Charles Chaplin. Socially, Mary Ann seems to have been a cut above her second husband. Her father was John Terry, a mercantile clerk. On 15 May 1854 she had married Henry Lamphee Hodges, a sign-writer and grainer.[11] After four and a half years of marriage however, poor young Hodges fell off an omnibus and suffered a fatal concussion.[12]

When she married Charles Hill, Mary Ann brought with her a five-year-old son by Hodges, also called Henry. Four years later a daughter was born at 11 Camden Street and christened Hannah Harriet Pedlingham Hill.[13] A second daughter, Chaplin's Aunt Kate, followed on 18 January 1870.[14]

Charles Hill's boot-making appears not to have given the family much stability, and they moved from lodging to lodging – always in Lambeth or Southwark – with bewildering frequency. The census of 1871 records them at 77 Beckway Street, Walworth. They are described as Charles Hill, boot riveter, aged thirty-two; his wife, Mary Ann Hill, boot binder, aged thirty-two; their son Henry, boot-maker, aged fifteen; and their daughters Harriett (Hannah), aged five, and Kate, aged one.[15]

While their step-brother, known as young Harry, stuck to the boot business, Hannah and Kate grew up into strikingly attractive women. As the music hall songs of the time delighted to relate, the streets of London were full of perils for young girls. Hannah became pregnant. In later years she told her sons that she had run off to South Africa with a rich bookmaker called Hawkes, but it is now impossible to verify either the trip or Mr Hawkes. All that is certain is that on 16 March 1885 Hannah gave birth to a boy, who was named Sidney John. When the birth was registered and again when he was baptized at St John's Church, Larcom Street, the father's name was not entered.

Sidney John was not to remain fatherless for long.*

The accouchement took place at 57 Brandon Street,[16] the premises of Joseph Hodges, trading as a general dealer and most likely the brother of the unfortunate Hodges who fell off the omnibus.[17] It seems probable that Hannah had left the paternal home and taken refuge with her mother's former brother-in-law. At some point Charles Chaplin Senior took up residence in Joseph Hodges' house, and less than fourteen weeks after Sydney's birth Charles Chaplin and Hannah Hill were married. Both gave their address as 57 Brandon Street. One of the two witnesses at the ceremony at St John's Church, Larcom Street, Walworth, was Mary Ann Hill, the mother of the bride.[18]

Charles Chaplin described himself on the registration of the marriage as 'professional singer'. In fact, however, there is no evidence that either Charles or Hannah had begun a career as professional entertainer until after their marriage. Certainly *The Era*, the weekly

1885. Marriage solemnized at St John's Church in the Parish of St John Walworth in the County of Surrey

No.	When Married.	Name and Surname.	Age.	Condition.	Rank or Profession.	Residence at the time of Marriage.	Father's Name and Surname.	Rank or Profession of Father.
289	June 29 1885	Charles Chaplin Hannah Harriett Hill	22 19	Bachelor Spinster	Professional Singer	57 Brandon Street 57 Brandon Street	Spencer Chaplin Charles Hill	Butcher Boot maker

Married in the Parish Church according to the Rites and Ceremonies of the Established Church, by ______ after Banns by me, G. T. Cotham Vicar

This Marriage was solemnized between us, Charles Chaplin, Hannah Harriett Hill — in the Presence of us, George Bailey, Mary Ann Hill

1885 - Marriage certificate of Charles Chaplin Senior and Hannah Harriett Hill.

* The correct spelling of the name of the elder Chaplin brother can not be resolved. He was baptized 'Sidney', but the records of the local authorities and institutions generally spell the name as 'Sydney'. During his days with Karno the forms Sidney, Sydney, Sid and Syd all occur. As an adult Sydney-Sidney himself used the 'y' form, but Charles consistently used the 'i' in writing his brother's name. (It was said that Chaplin and his then wife Lita Grey disagreed over the spelling of the name of their son, Sydney Earle Chaplin, because Chaplin thought the 'y' was pretentious. The present Chaplin family consider that uncle and nephew are differentiated as, respectively, 'Sidney' and 'Sydney'.) The solution adopted for this book is to adopt the 'y' form in the main text, but to retain whatever form is adopted by the writers in quoted texts.

journal of the British theatrical profession, which provided exhaustive records of theatrical presentations, lists no appearances by either of them before 1886 (Hannah) and 1887 (Charles). There is no record or family tradition to suggest what lured these two young people, with no previous connexion with show business, into the theatre.

Still, it was not surprising that the music halls should beckon young people with looks and even a small talent. This was the start of the great era of the British music hall. In London, the London Pavilion had just been handsomely reconstructed, the Alhambra had recently established itself as a variety house, and the Empire, Leicester Square was to be opened in 1887. In all, London boasted thirty-six music halls of varying class in 1886, while throughout the rest of the country, from Aberdeen to Plymouth, there were no less than 234 halls with weekly bills to fill. Dublin alone had nine music halls, Liverpool eight and Birmingham six. The opportunities were immense, and perhaps more apparent in Lambeth than in any other quarter of London. The first music hall agent, Ambrose Maynard, had set up his offices in Waterloo Road in 1858, and shortly afterwards moved to York Road, where he was soon followed by rival firms. York Road ran into Westminster Bridge Road, where the Canterbury and Gatti's Music Halls stood. Proceeding further south from Westminster Bridge Road was Kennington Road, with a parade of public houses – The Three Stags, The White Horse, The Tankard and above all The Horns – which were favourite resorts of the music hall professionals. Large numbers of performers lived in Kennington, though the more successful preferred the somewhat smarter Brixton, immediately to the south. No doubt Charles and Hannah Chaplin were as dazzled by the glamour of the élite of the music halls, at their Sunday morning get-togethers in the Kennington pubs, as their son was to be fifteen years later.

Both Hannah and Charles were evidently talented. Chaplin's descriptions of his mother's gifts for observation and mimicry are certainly not inspired by sentiment alone; and he was a shrewd judge of talent. Hannah may simply have been unlucky: perhaps her particular talent was out of tune with the time. Her career was brief and not triumphant. Her recorded performances were all in small provincial music halls, and at the bottom of the bill – 'among the wines and spirits' as they said in a day when music halls were still often also drinking places, and the artists' names were followed on the printed programme by the tariff of refreshments. Still, Hannah's brief time as a music hall artist was sufficient to supply glamorous memories with which to stir the imagination of her worshipping young sons in later years.

Debutants like Hannah and Charles would in those days have gained their experience of entertaining audiences with one-night engagements in the 'free-and-easies' and public houses which provided nightly entertainment for their guests. Hannah's first advertised professional engagements were at the end of 1885, when she appeared at The Star, Dublin. By this time she had acquired an agent, Frank Albert, and by the start of the new year was sufficiently encouraged to place her 'professional card' in *The Era*. These 'cards' have been an almost unchanging feature of British theatrical journals for well over a century: they serve to announce a performer's success, his availability, even his mere existence.

When Hannah placed her first card, to appear on 2 January 1886, there was still apparently some doubt as to the spelling of her professional name. The announcement read:

That Charming little Chanter.
LILLIE HARLEY,
just finished a most successful Engagement Star, Dublin. Now appearing with great success in BELFAST.
Agent, Frank Albert.

The following week's card read:

New Song, "He might have sent on the gloves," J. Bowess.
LILLIE HARLEY,
just finished, grand success Nightly, Star, Dublin, and Buffalo, Belfast. SCOTIA, GLASGOW, Monday next.
Booking dates fast. Sole Agent, Frank Albert.

Next week Hannah's stage name appeared in its definitive form:

The Refined and Talented Artist
LILY HARLEY
complimented by Proprietors, the Public and Press
Heaps of notices in different papers every week
Pleasing success SCOTIA GLASGOW
A few good songs required. Agent, F. Albert

Perhaps something more than a few good songs was required, for after this Lily Harley's card vanished for periods of several weeks, and her engagements seem to have been sporadic. On 27 May 1886 she appeared (as 'Miss Lilly Harley') in London at a benefit concert for William Bishop at the South London Palace. On this occasion she figured rather low on a bill whose stars were Vesta Tilley, The Great Vance and Chirgwin. Below her, however, at the very bottom of the bill, was the sixteen-year-old Marie Lloyd, soon destined to become the greatest star of British music hall. In the autumn there was a run of bookings ('Lily Harley – The Essence of Refinement') at M'Farland's Music Hall, Aberdeen, M'Farland's, Dundee and The Folly, Glasgow. After this, both 'cards' and bookings cease altogether.

The disappointments of Hannah's own career must have been aggravated by watching the success of a friend, 'Dashing Eva Lester', with whom for a while she shared the same agent. Billed as 'The California Queen and England's Queen of Song', Eva had a brashness which Hannah lacked. *The Era* wrote of her performance at the Metropolitan in September 1886: 'Miss Eva Lester, one of the prettiest and most fascinating serio-comic songstresses we have. In a delineation of a romp, Miss Lester, by her piquancy, won much applause . . .' In his autobiography Chaplin recalls how a dozen or so years later, when they were themselves upon hard times, they found poor Eva in the street, a sick, dirty, shaven-headed derelict. The boy Charlie was horrified and ashamed to be seen with her but kindly Hannah took her in for the night and cleaned her up.

Charles's career had a slower start than Hannah's but a more promising progression. His first recorded professional engagement was in the week of Queen Victoria's Golden Jubilee, 20 June 1887, at the Poly Variety Theatre.[19]

At first he worked as a mimic, but soon developed into what was called a 'dramatic and descriptive singer' with a strong attraction for his audiences. He was a pleasant-looking man, with no very evident facial similarity to his son. Chaplin described him as a quiet, brooding man with dark eyes, and said that Hannah thought he looked like Napoleon. The portraits that appear on the sheet music of his song successes show him with dark eyes that seem somewhat melancholy despite the broad prop grin.

Charles sang songs in the character of a masher, a man about town, or an ordinary husband and father, bedevilled by problems all too familiar to his audiences such as mothers-in-law, landladies who

LONDON ROAD, S.E.

Proprietors ... ... POOLE & ULPH, Jun.

MR. WILLIAM

BISHOP'S

COMPLIMENTARY

BENEFIT CONCERT

WILL TAKE PLACE, ON

THURSDAY, MAY 27th, 1886.

The following Powerful Array of Talent will appear

VESTA TILLEY, London Idol.

Great VANCE · T. W. BARRETT

Brothers Horne and Nelly Clairette

Jessie ACTON Hyram TRAVERS

Miss Pattie Heywood. TOM BASS.

Wm. Jas Strip and James Stephens.

Yank-hoe & Ormene Scully & Morrell.

MEDLEY SLADE MURRAY

Walter Blount and Sadlier.

Fred Harrington. Miss Lottie Dittmar

Miss Lilly Harley. Miss Bertie Stokes

EDGAR GRANVILLE

Miss Birdie Brightling The Sisters Bilton

Masters Courtney & Cross.

Mr. WALTER JOYCE F. W. Stephens

CHIRGWIN.

Alex. Gerard. Geo Vokes W. F. Moss

FELICE NAPOLI, Italian Hercules.

CAPTAIN FOWLER,

Champion Stage Shot of the World assisted by Miss Nelly Frezell

LIEUT. WALTER COLE.

Maud & Charley Ross McCall Chambers

Marie Lloyd. George Ripon.

The Chair will be taken by several Influential Gentlemen including Baron [illegible]

Private Boxes, 1 & 2 Guineas. Reserved Stalls, 3s. Stalls, 1s. 6d. Balcony, 1s. Hall, 6d. Gallery, 3d. Open at 7. Commence at 7.15.

Manager - - Mr. Harry Ulph, Jun.

1886 - Handbill for benefit concert at the South London Palace, including Hannah Chaplin (as Miss Lilly Harley).

wanted to be paid, nagging wives and crying babies. The clearest sign of his success is that between 1890 and 1896 the music publishers Francis, Day and Hunter issued several of his song successes, with

1893 – Illustrated cover of song sung by Charles Chaplin Sr.

his portrait prominent on the cover. This honour was accorded only to artists whose reputation the publishers were certain would sell copies. These years were the peak of Chaplin's career. Without ever achieving the rank of contemporaries like Herbert Campbell, Dan Leno, Arthur Roberts, Charles Coborn or Charles Godfrey (to whom he was considered to have a striking physical resemblance), he was a star: as late in his career as 1898 he could share (with the 'Beograph' moving pictures) top billing at the New Empire Palace Theatre of Varieties, Leicester:

VERY IMPORTANT AND WELCOME RETURN OF
ONE OF LEICESTER'S GREATEST FAVOURITES, MR
CHARLES CHAPLIN
STAR DESCRIPTIVE VOCALIST AND CHORUS COMEDIAN
IN HIS LATEST SUCCESSES AND OLD FAVOURITES
"DEAR OLD PALS"

All this, however, and much unhappiness besides, was before him on Tuesday 16 April 1889, when his first son, Charles Spencer Chaplin was born. At that moment he was playing a week's engagement at 'Professor' Leotard Bosco's Empire Palace of Varieties, Hull.[20] Perhaps in later years the elder Chaplin told his son stories of the colourful Professor Bosco, because Chaplin was twice to use the name for characters in his films. The expectant Hannah had, presumably, stayed at home in London to await her baby.

Charles and Hannah were not so meticulous in registering Charles's birth as Sydney's; and it has tormented historians and biographers for decades that there is no official record of the birth of London's most famous son. The fact is not especially remarkable. It was easy enough, particularly for music hall artists, constantly moving (if they were lucky) from one town to another, to put off and eventually to forget this kind of formality; at that time the penalties were not strict or efficiently enforced. In the early days of his cinema fame, Chaplin said that he was born at Fontainebleau, in France. This may have been one of the colourful stories with which Hannah seems to have endeavoured to brighten her sons' lives. Later Chaplin was certain that he was born in East Lane, Walworth, just round the corner from Sydney's birthplace in Brandon Street.

It is a certain mark of a Walworth native that Chaplin refers to the street as 'East Lane'. On the map it has never appeared otherwise than as 'East Street', but the locals, like Chaplin, have never known it as other than 'East Lane'. For Londoners a street with a market is characteristically described as a 'Lane' (as with Petticoat Lane, the other side of the river). East Lane market is still as flourishing now as when Chaplin was a child. For some reason the East Lane traders seem to have a greater bent for drama, and the food that is cooked there has more variety and pungency than in any other London market. Practically nothing survives from the time of Chaplin's childhood, apart from one or two ruinous shops at the west end and The Mason's Arms, a building whose theatrical flamboyance must have been thrilling to a small boy. Even so, the colour and vitality, the tumult of fruit and fish and pop music and old clothes still evoke an atmosphere as close, perhaps, as we may come to Chaplin's London.

Chaplin recalled that soon after his birth, the family moved to much smarter lodgings in West Square. West Square has somehow survived the destruction of the little streets and community life of the area by insensitive urban development. In 1890, as today, it must have been a strange oasis in a perennially depressed region: an elegant Georgian square of tall brick houses, with gardens in the centre. The move was made possible by Charles Chaplin's growing success. In the months after his son's birth, he was getting regular engagements, and in the year 1890–1 the music publishers Francis, Day and Hunter regarded him as such a 'comer' that they published no less than three of his song successes – 'As the Church Bells Chime', 'Everyday Life' and 'Eh, Boys?', which was written by John P. Harrington and George Le Brunn, 'the Gilbert and Sullivan of the halls' who wrote most of Marie Lloyd's greatest successes, including 'Oh Mr Porter'.

The portrait that appears on the cover of 'Eh, Boys?', with the singer in silk hat, frock coat and floppy orange bow tie, shows some resemblance between the elder and the younger Charles Chaplin. One of the verses – illustrated by a comic vignette on the cover – ominously touches upon one of the real-life domestic troubles of the Chaplin family:

When you're wed, and come home 'late-ish'
  Rather *too* late – boozy, too,
Wifey dear says, 'Oh, you *have* come!'
  And then turns her back on you;
Only gives you 'noes' and 'yesses',
  Until, with a sudden bound,
She quite fiercely pokes the fire up,
  And then spanks the kids all round.

CHORUS

  We all of us know what *that* means – Eh, boys? Eh, boys?
We all of us know what that means, – Eh, boys? Eh?
    When first she starts to drat you,
    And then throws something at you,
We all of us know what that means – it's her playful little way.

Drink was the endemic disease of the music halls. The halls had evolved from drinking establishments and the sale of liquor still made up an important part of the managers' incomes. When they were not on stage the artists were expected to mingle with the audiences in the bars, to encourage conviviality and consumption – which inevitably was best achieved by example. Poor Chaplin was only one of many who succumbed to alcoholism as an occupational hazard.

In 1890, however, he was still leaping from success to success. In the summer he was invited to sign for an American tour, and in August and September was appearing in New York at the Union Square Theatre.[21] The stay appears to have been pleasant and sociable. Charles's aunt Elizabeth had married a Mr Wiggins and now lived in New York. Through her he met and made friends with Dr Charles Horatio Shepherd, who had a dentist's practice, and Mrs Shepherd. 'We had some delightful hours together,' recalled Dr Shepherd, a quarter of a century later.[22]

J. P. Harrington, the song-writer, recalled an incident that occurred just before Chaplin's departure for America:

> One of our first clients was Charlie Chaplin, father of the famous film 'star'. Chaplin was a good, sound performer of the Charles Godfrey type, although he, of course, lacked the latter's wonderful talent and versatility. We wrote the majority of Charlie's songs for some considerable time: in fact at one period, all three of the songs he was nightly singing were from our pens.
>
> In this connexion, an incident which strikes me as far more amusing now than when it happened, occurs to me. We had made an appointment with Mr David Day, head of Francis, Day and Hunters, the music publishers, to hear the three songs played over and sung in his office, with a view to their publication. In due course, Chaplin, Le Brunn and I arrived: the songs were played over by George and were sung by Charlie, and David was delighted with all three.
>
> The cheque book appeared on the scene. 'Terms? The usual, I suppose?'
>
> Trio of course, in delightful unanimity: 'Certainly, Mr Day.'
>
> The cheque book is opened – the pen is raised – then, George Le Brunn, anxious to paint the lily and gild refined gold, says: 'You know, he'll sing all these songs in America as well, Mr Day.'
>
> Pen suspended in mid-air.
>
> 'Ah, yes?' murmurs Mr Day, softly. 'And when do you go to America, Mr Chaplin?'
>
> 'Week after next,' says Charlie.

'How long for?'

'Four months.'

'Snap!' Cheque book returned to its little nest in the desk-drawer; pen carefully laid aside.

'Come and see me again, when you come back from America. It won't be any use publishing the songs while you're singing them on the other side of the Atlantic!'

The things Charlie Chaplin and deponent said to George Le Brunn when we got outside that office would not look well if set down in this veracious narrative.[23]

The American trip, however, seemed to mark the final break-up of the Chaplins' marriage. No doubt Hannah had been making new friends in Charles's absence. Certainly she had a new friend by the autumn of 1891, another music hall singer who over the years frequently appeared on the same bill as Charles Chaplin. He was Leo Dryden.

Dryden's real name was George Dryden Wheeler, and he was born in Limehouse, London, on 6 June 1861. He had first gone on the halls in 1881 but had little success for several years until one of the great stars of Victorian variety, Jenny Hill, noticed him and introduced him to her own agent, Hugh Didcott. From then onwards his career prospered. His greatest hit came early in 1891 when he presented his sentimental ballad 'The Miner's Dream of Home', depicting the nostalgia of an emigrant in the Australian gold fields. From this time on, Dryden, with his square-jawed, handsome face, was established as the minstrel of England, Empire and patriotism. His later songs included 'The Miner's Return', 'India's Reply', 'Bravo, Dublin Fusiliers', 'Freedom and Japan', 'The Great White Mother', 'The Only Way' and 'Love and Duty'. Unfortunately the stoic nobility of the characters he presented on stage does not seem to have distinguished his private life. He was from all accounts erratic and given to violence. He is said to have given each of his three wives a rough time. In 1919, irked at finding his star fading, he sought publicity by singing his songs in the streets.

In October 1891 he was engaged at the Cambridge, a large music hall in Shoreditch. The popularity of 'The Miner's Dream of Home' obliged the management to extend his engagement week by week until Christmas. During these twelve weeks in London Dryden brought his affair with Hannah Chaplin to fruition. We have comic evidence of his courtship. As he became more successful, Dryden took to inserting flamboyant advertising in the professional papers. A typical example reads:

OCTOBER 31, 1891

MR. LEO DRYDEN,
"Love and Duty," Published by Maynard.
"Struck 'Ile," "Struck 'Ile," "Struck 'Ile" again.
"Love and Duty," the Premier Descriptive Song, but
I have "Struck 'Ile" with a Song that will be the Song,
a Song that will be Sung in every home,
where the "Mother Tongue" is spoken.
On Tuesday, Oct. 20th, I produced at the Cambridge
"The Miner's Dream,"
Written and Composed by Will Godwin and L. D.
I was to have finished on the following Saturday, but directly
Mr E. Page the Manager, saw and heard
"The Miner's Dream,"
he immediately rescinded the Notice, and made arrangements for me to stay on, and took me from 8 10 Turn and put me "Star Turn." 10 20. Such facts speak volumes
On Monday next I produce "The Miner's Dream" at the
Foresters', with Special Scenery and Effects.
Managers are cordially invited to see and hear
"The Miner's Dream."
ALHAMBRA (Second Week) 8 20
FORESTERS' (Second Week).... 9 20
CAMBRIDGE (Fifth Week).. ... 10 20
Messrs Francis, Day, and Hunter have Paid the Highest Price they have ever paid for any Song for
"The Miner's Dream of Home"
Owing to certain unprincipled Artistes (?) taking mean advantage of my knowledge of the Law of Copyright, the Song I Reconstructed and made so Popular in Birmingham, Liverpool, Birkenhead, Newcastle, and Sunderland, I have entirely discarded
Remember, it was the Singer, not the Song.
"The Miner's Dream"
is both Singer and Song, and will eclipse all previous productions. I shall shortly produce a Descriptive Monologue,
in Three Scenes, entitled "Hard Times,"
in which I shall introduce the success of successes,
"The Miner's Dream,"
which will ensure the success of the Monologue.
Representatives, Messrs Healy and Cooke.

It was a feature of these advertisements that Dryden aggressively asserted his rights in his songs, offering licences for performances outside London, and threatening legal proceedings against anyone who infringed his rights. One exceptional announcement in November 1891, however, introduced, for those who could recognize it, a romantic touch:

In answer to many letters received, I beg to inform those ladies who have written that I intend to retain the London Right for myself. Re "Opportunity," Artistes wishing to secure the Pantomime Rights (£1 1s.) may apply to me for same.
Middlesbrough Right Secured by Miss Kittie Fairdale.
No other Artiste has my permission to Sing the above but
Miss Kittie Fairdale and Miss Lillie Harley.
Proprietors and Managers kindly note.

Miss Kittie Fairdale had, of course, paid her guinea. Miss Lillie Harley – Hannah Chaplin – had presumably not; nor was she very likely to take advantage of her rights, since she had no apparent engagements at which she could sing 'Opportunity'. Still, the announcement must have found her vulnerable indeed. This was the first time for more than five years that her name had appeared in the professional press, and now it was linked with the star of the day. Dryden was thirty and handsome, and the flattery of his announcement must have been irresistible. The advertisement appeared on Friday 28 November. Nine months and three days later, on 31 August 1892, Hannah gave birth to Leo Dryden's son, also George Dryden Wheeler.

Thus the young Charles Chaplin found himself fatherless, but with another half-brother. He was three and a half; Sydney was four years older. In his autobiography he recalls that at this time the children and their mother were still living in some affluence. He attributed the cause to his mother's work on the stage, and recalled that she would tuck the two boys in bed and leave them in the care of a house-maid while she went to the theatre. Since there is no record of Hannah working at this period, and since Charles's payments for the support of his sons seem to have stopped quite early, it can only be supposed that Leo Dryden was providing this temporary prosperity. What were the domestic arrangements of Leo and Hannah is not clear. Years later their son – he had adopted the professional name of Wheeler Dryden – said that according to information he had received from his father, they lived 'for a year or two as man and wife',[24] but neither Charles nor Sydney recorded any recollection of Leo Dryden.

The comfort which sheltered Chaplin's first three or four years was soon to end. Hannah's liaison with Leo did not long survive the birth of their child. Hannah seems to have been a devoted, affectionate and protective mother, and to have loved the new baby as fiercely as she did her older sons. It is then easy to appreciate the shock that she must have suffered in the spring of 1893 when the appalling Dryden entered her lodgings and snatched away their six-month-old son. The baby was to vanish from the lives of the Chaplins for almost thirty years.

Poor Hannah had only wanted to be Lily Harley and to dream of the glamour of the stage. Now her life became a nightmare. Other troubles came on her at exactly the moment that her baby was stolen from her. Her mother, Chaplin's Grandma Hill, had apparently left

Grandfather Hill: family tradition said that her husband had caught her in a compromising situation with another man. Since the separation, Grandma Hill had gone from bad to worse. She had taken to drinking heavily, and supported herself by hawking old clothes. She became more and more eccentric and, in the village-like community of Lambeth and Southwark, must have been a grave embarrassment to her family. Eventually, in February 1893, she was taken off the streets into the Newington Workhouse, and from there transferred to the Infirmary.

The doctors recorded: 'She is incoherent. She says that she sees beetles, rats, mice and other things about the place. She thinks that the doctors at the Infy. tried to poison her. She makes a lot of rambling statements and frequently contradicts herself.'[25] After some days she was 'much more noisy and troublesome', and on 23 February she was certified insane and committed to the London County Asylum at Banstead.[26] Dr Williams, who signed the certificate, found her still imagining rats and mice, and beetles in her bed. He noted that her condition had been deteriorating for several months, and attributed her madness to drink and worry. Cheap gin was a perilous liquor. Mary Ann was now fifty-four years old. Her husband was ordered to pay four shillings a week towards her support.

The collapse of her mother must have been appalling for Hannah, even if she had no foreboding of her own eventual fate. Yet she appears to have kept the catastrophe from her boys – hard as that must have been in the gossipy intimacy of the Lambeth streets. Chaplin only remembered his grandmother as 'a bright little old lady who always greeted me effusively with baby talk'. Mary Ann survived in Banstead Asylum for two more years.

Hannah now found herself without any means of livelihood. Leo had gone out of her life and Charles appears to have contributed little or nothing to the support of his sons. Chaplin remembered that she earned a little money by nursing and by dressmaking for other members of the congregation of Christchurch, Westminster Bridge Road: she had turned to religion in search of some kind of spiritual comfort. She seems also to have tried to take up her stage career again. As autobiographer, Chaplin generally proves phenomenally accurate in reporting those events in which he was personally involved, so there is no reason to question his version of his own first appearance on the stage, which he described more than once. It appears to have been in about 1894. Hannah had succeeded in getting an engagement at the Canteen, Aldershot. Her health had already begun to deteriorate, and during the performance her voice failed her. The Aldershot audience – mostly soldiers – was notoriously rough, and became vocally hostile. When Hannah left the stage, the manager, who had seen little Charlie do turns to amuse Hannah's friends backstage, led him on as an *extempore* replacement. Unabashed, the child obliged with a song which the coster comedian Gus Elen had made a hit in 1893, ''E Dunno Where 'E Are', and which described the dismay of his former pals at the airs put on by a coster who had come into an inheritance:

Since Jack Jones come into a little bit of splosh,
Why 'E dunno where 'E are!

The performance was a great success and to Charlie's delight the audience threw money on to the stage. His business sense was born that night: he announced that he would resume the performance when he had retrieved the coins. This produced still greater appreciation and more money; and Chaplin continued to sing, dance and do impersonations until his mother carried him off into the wings. He noted that this night marked his first appearance on the stage and his mother's last, but this is not quite accurate (unless he much misjudged his own age at the time) since in his later book *My Life in Pictures* he illustrates a handbill advertising a one-night appearance of 'Miss Lily Chaplin, Serio and Dancer' at the Hatcham Liberal Club on 8 February 1896.

Hannah's financial situation must have been desperate, but her sons were to remember more vividly than the privations her efforts to bring gaiety and small pleasures into their lives: the weekly comic, bloater breakfasts and an unforgettable day at Southend after Sydney had providentially found a purse containing seven guineas but no means of identifying its owner. She was, when well, a constantly amusing companion. She would sing and dance her old music hall numbers and act out plays to them. In his old age Chaplin still recalled the emotion aroused in him by her account of the Crucifixion and of Christ as the fount of love, pity and humanity.

The music halls may not have appreciated her gifts, but she had the greatest of audiences in her young sons. She undoubtedly had a talent, and – consciously or not – she applied herself to cultivating the innate gifts of observation that both children seemed to share. Chaplin recalled in 1918:

> If it had not been for my mother I doubt if I could have made a success of pantomime. She was one of the greatest pantomime artists I have ever seen. She would sit for hours at a window, looking down at the people on the street and illustrating with her hands, eyes and facial expression just what was going on below. All the time, she would deliver a running fire of comment. And it was through watching and listening to her that I learned not only how to express my emotions with my hands and face, but also how to observe and study people.
>
> She was almost uncanny in her observations. For instance, she would see Bill Smith coming down the street in the morning, and I would hear her say: 'There comes Bill Smith. He's dragging his feet and his shoes are polished. He looks mad, and I'll wager he's had a fight with his wife, and come off without his breakfast. Sure enough! There he goes into the bake shop for a bun and coffee!'
>
> And inevitably during the day, I would hear that Bill Smith had had a fight with his wife.[27]

He had paid touching tribute to his mother in an earlier press statement, an 'autobiography' published by *Photoplay* in 1915:

> It seems to me that my mother was the most splendid woman I ever knew . . . I have met a lot of people knocking around the world since, but I have never met a more thoroughly refined woman than my mother. If I have amounted to anything, it will be due to her.

Soon after Charlie's sixth birthday, the family's situation reached a new crisis. Hannah became ill – it is not certain with what, but Chaplin recalls that she suffered from acute headaches. On 29 June she was admitted to the Lambeth Infirmary, where she stayed until the end of July. On 1 July Sydney was taken into Lambeth Workhouse,[28] and four days later placed in the West Norwood Schools, which accommodated the infant poor of Lambeth. As Poor Law institutions went, Norwood was pleasant enough. It stood on the slope of a hill facing green fields, on the boundary of Croydon and Streatham, which were then still quite rural. The building, in which Sydney shared a dormitory with thirty-five other boys between nine and sixteen, had been erected only ten years before. There was a steam-heated swimming bath, and the children were not uniformed. Under each bed was a wicker basket for the children to store their clothes at night. Each child had his own towel, brush and comb, but at an inspection a year or two after Sydney's stay there, it was noted that 'only a few of them are provided with tooth-brushes'. Sydney remained at Norwood until 17 September: he was lucky not to stay longer than the autumn, for the inspectors were gravely concerned about the inadequate heating arrangements in the Schools. Strangely, when Sydney was discharged, he was given into the care of his step-father, so perhaps Hannah was still not well enough to care for the boys.[28]

In Charlie's case, the Hodges – Grandma Hill's relations by her first marriage – came to the rescue: and Charlie was lodged, at 164 York Road, with John George Hodges, son of the Joseph Hodges from whose house Charles and Hannah had married, and nephew of the unfortunate Henry Lamphee Hodges who fell from the omnibus. He had, as it happened, taken up the same profession as his deceased uncle, and was a master sign-writer. John George entered Charlie into Addington Road Schools, along with his own son, who was a year or so younger. Charlie appears to have stayed in the school only a week or two: he was never to undergo any prolonged period of day-school attendance.[29]

Only eight months after Sydney's discharge from Norwood Schools, both Chaplin boys were to experience in earnest life in charity institutions. Hannah was again taken into the Infirmary, and Sydney and Charlie, now eleven and seven, were admitted to the workhouse, 'owing to the absence of their father and the destitution and illness of their mother'.[30] Charles Chaplin Senior was traced and reluctantly appeared before the District Relief Committee. Somewhat heartlessly, he told them that while he was willing to take Charlie, he would not accept responsibility for Sydney, who was born illegitimate. The Committee retorted that since Chaplin had married the boy's mother, he was now legally liable for Sydney's maintenance. At this stage, however, Hannah intervened to reject the idea of the boys living with their father as wholly repugnant, since he was living with another woman. Charles was not slow to point out her own adultery. No doubt somewhat bewildered by the family bickering, the Relief Committee decided that it was desirable to keep the boys together and that the best solution would be to place them in the Central London District Poor Law School at Hanwell. It was ruled that Chaplin should pay the sum of fifteen shillings a week towards the cost of keeping them: 'The man is a Music Hall singer, ablebodied and is in a position to earn sufficient to maintain his children.' On 1 July, a fortnight after the boys had been transferred to Hanwell, the Board of Guardians reported to the Local Government Board that Chaplin had consented to this arrangement.

It was one thing to get Chaplin to consent; quite another to get

C Chaplin	✓	3. Your Committee recommend that the Collector be instructed to collect the sum of 15/- per week from Charles Chaplin of 15 Gunters Grove, Fulham, in respect of the maintenance of his two children, Sydney aged 12 and Charles aged 7 about to be sent to Hanwell School Dated this 9th day of June 1896 C G Hamel On behalf of the Committee

17th June 6

My Lords & Gentlemen,

In accordance with article 10 of the Outdoor Relief Regulation Order, 21 December 1852 I beg to report what appears to be a departure from the regulations therein contained.

Two children, Sydney Chaplin, 10, and Charles Chaplin, 7, were admitted to the Workhouse owing to the absence of their father and to the destitution and illness of their mother who was residing with them in this Union.

Enquiries were made for the father and eventually he appeared before the District Relief Committee. On that occasion he stated he was willing to take the younger boy but wanted the Guardians to keep the elder, who was born illegitimate. As however Chaplin married the boys' mother he is legally liable for the boys' maintenance.

Subsequently to the admission of the boys to the Workhouse the mother became chargeable in the Guardians' Infirmary. The idea of the boys being given up to her husband was most repugnant to her as it was alleged he was now living with another woman and this the man did not deny. It was also stated that the mother herself had committed adultery in the absence of her husband.

1896 – Extracts from minutes of
Southwark Board of Guardians.

him to pay. Throughout the following year the Board of Guardians was receiving regular reports of Chaplin's non-payment.

The boys, however, knew nothing of this. On 18 June 1896 they were driven the twelve miles to Hanwell in a horse-drawn bakery van, and Chaplin always recalled with a pleasant nostalgia the adventurous drive through the then beautiful countryside on the way. He thought Hanwell less sombre than Norwood, though it was not so up-to-date. Part of the buildings had been adapted from a much older institution; others were one-storeyed corrugated iron structures; but it had a swimming pool and large play areas, and the heating arrangements were at least efficient. In one respect Sydney and Charles were fortunate. Only six or seven years earlier massive reform and reorganization had taken pace at Hanwell. Before that it had long been notorious as a forcing ground for the contagion of ophthalmia: many children who had entered the school healthy left it either wholly or partially blind from the disease.

By 1896 modern treatments and the isolation of sick children had checked the spread of the most infectious diseases. It was harder to control vermin, and Charlie had the misfortune to be one of the thirty-five children who picked up ringworm in the course of the year. He retained bitter memories of having his head shaved, iodined and wrapped in a bandana. Remembering the contempt of the other boys for the ringworm sufferers, he carefully avoided being seen by them looking out of the window of the first-floor ward where those so afflicted were confined.

Life at the school was healthy, with games and exercises, country walks and emphasis on hygiene. The administration was by and large humane and the food sufficient. (Charlie recalled that Sydney worked in the kitchen and was able to smuggle out rolls and butter, but that for all his pleasure in the thrill of stolen fruits he had no actual need for extra nutrition.) The boys remembered with a thrill of horror the weekly punishments by cane or birch administered to infant malefactors by 'Captain' Hindom, the school drill master.[31] Once Charlie found himself, quite unjustly, included in the punishment list: he had been innocently using the lavatory at the moment it was discovered some boys had set fire to some paper there, and received three strokes of the cane from Hindom as presumed arsonist.

The worst part of institutional life was separation from Sydney. The adversities of their childhood had created an unusually close bond of understanding between them, which was to survive throughout their lives. Writing not long before her death in 1916, their Aunt Kate Mowbray wrote: 'It seems strange to me that anyone can write about Charlie Chaplin without mentioning his brother Sydney. They have been inseparable all their lives, except when fate intervened at intervals. Syd, of quiet manner, clever brain and steady nerve, has been father and mother to Charlie. Charlie always looked up to Syd, and Sydney would suffer anything to spare Charlie.'[32] For his own part, Sydney wrote to his brother, almost forty years after their Hanwell days, 'It has always been my unfortunate predicament or should I say fortunate predicament? to concern myself with your protection. This is the result of my fraternal or rather paternal instinct. . .'[33]

Charlie was very soon to be deprived, at least temporarily, of this protection. In November 1896 Sydney was transferred to the Training Ship *Exmouth*, moored at Grays, in Essex. The *Exmouth* was an old wooden-walled, line-of-battle ship which had seen service at Balaclava, and since 1876 had been used by the Metropolitan Asylums Board 'for training for sea-service poor boys chargeable to metropolitan parishes and unions'.[34] The children came from all parts of London and the Board were selective about entrants. There was, indeed, some difficulty in maintaining the full complement of six hundred boys since there was 'not unnaturally, a disinclination on the part of the various school authorities to part with *all* their finest "show" boys'.[35] Boys became eligible at the age of twelve, and Sydney's selection was a tribute to his physique, intelligence and athletic prowess. Life on the *Exmouth* was tough but varied. The boys' first task 'is to learn how to mend and patch their clothes, and thus acquire the deftness of using their fingers, which every real sailor displays. They also learn to wash their own clothes and to keep their lockers (one of which is set apart for each lad) and their contents in good order and condition. Each boy has his own hammock, which is neatly stowed away during the day, leaving the decks free from all encumbrance, in the shape of bedding.'[36] The general schooling was good, and the boys learned seamanship, gunnery and first aid. Sydney was to turn to his subsequent advantage the emphasis in the *Exmouth*'s curriculum upon gymnastics and band training. He learned to be a bugler. Sydney left the *Exmouth* with generous enough memories of the ship and its veteran captain-superintendent, Staff-Commander W. S. Bourchier. Years afterwards, he took the trouble to arrange and finance special treats and entertainments for later generations of youthful crewmen.

The two boys stayed in their respective institutions throughout 1897. There is little trace of how or where Hannah lived during this period, though at one point she was resident at 133 Stockwell Park Road. Meanwhile the Southwark Board of Guardians wrestled with the problem of extracting from Charles Chaplin Senior the weekly contribution of fifteen shillings he had agreed to pay towards the maintenance of his sons. The first problem was to find him, though had the guardians been more assiduous readers of the music hall professional press they would have been aware that he was still in good work around the provinces and occasionally in London.[37]

Early in 1897 Dr Shepherd, the New York dentist with whom Charles had become friendly on his 1890 American tour, visited London and recalled that he was given 'a very, very Royal time' during his three months' stay, not only by Charles but also by Charles's brother Spencer and their father, also Spencer. When Dr Shepherd left London, they presented him with several pieces of Doulton ware, which was produced locally, and for those days was comparatively costly. Charles was clearly not in want of money at this period.[38]

Very soon after Dr Shepherd's visit Charles's father died. He drew up a will one week before his death on 29 May 1897. It contained a curious provision, requiring 'that my son, Charles Chaplin, doth carry on the business of The Davenport Arms, Radnor Place, Paddington for a period of 12 months, during which time he is to find a home for Mrs Machell. At the expiration of 12 months, the business is to be sold and the proceeds equally divided amongst my children unless an amicable arrangement can be made amongst themselves.'[39] Grandfather Chaplin's intention may have been to try to introduce some stability into the life of his undeniably feckless son. If that was the intention, however, it was frustrated, for Charles managed, through some technical flaw in the will, to evade responsibility for the paternal pub and the mysterious Mrs Machell.

The Southwark Board of Guardians, however, was not to permit him so easily to shuffle off his family responsibilities. After more than a year during which he had not paid one penny of the agreed contribution,[40] the Guardians applied for a warrant for Chaplin, for neglecting to maintain his children, and offered a reward of one pound for information leading to his arrest. Happily there seemed to be the same kind of fraternal bond between Charles Chaplin Senior and his brother Spencer, eight years his senior, as there was between his two sons. Spencer stepped in with the back payments – amounting to the then very considerable sum of £44 8s – and averted Charles's arrest. The Guardians had clearly had enough of Chaplin, and at their meeting on 11 November 1897, it was moved that the two boys should be returned to their father within fourteen days. Again the problem was to find him. On 16 November the Clerk to the Guardians wrote to the long-suffering Spencer:

> Dear Sir,
> I shall esteem it a favour if you will kindly inform your brother Charles Chaplin that the Guardians desire him to relieve them of the future maintenance of his two children Sydney and Charles within 14 days from this date: – I am compelled to write to you not knowing his address.[41]

Evidently Spencer was unable or unwilling on this occasion to help, and again, two days before Christmas, the Guardians applied for a warrant for Charles's arrest. A helpful citizen named Charles Creasy supplemented his Christmas budget by informing on poor Charles, and claiming the one pound reward. This time Charles paid up £5. 6s. 3d, but passed on future responsibility to Hannah, by requesting that the boys should be discharged to the care of his wife. So on 18 January 1898 Charlie came home again. He had been an inmate of Hanwell Schools for exactly eighteen months. Sydney's return from the *Exmouth* two days later completed the family reunion.

Charlie later remembered that they moved from one back room to another: 'It was like a game of draughts: the last move was back to the workhouse.' In the early summer they were living in a room at 10 Farmers Road, a little row of cottages directly behind Kennington Park. It was from here that on 22 July 1898 the three of them trundled three quarters of a mile up Kennington Park Road, to the Lambeth Workhouse in Renfrew Road, to throw themselves once more on the mercy of the parish authorities. They stayed ten days in the workhouse, then Sydney and Charles – now thirteen and nine – were sent off to Norwood Schools. This time however they stayed only a fortnight, for Hannah announced her intention of taking herself and the boys away from the workhouse. Sydney and Charles were duly brought back from Norwood and on Friday 12 August the three of them were discharged.[42] It was only a ruse of Hannah's to see her sons again. Charles vividly remembered that day, and the joy of meeting his mother at the workhouse gates in the early morning. Their own clothes had been returned to them, rumpled and unpressed after obligatory steam-disinfection by the workhouse authorities. With nowhere else to go they spent the day in Kennington Park – a rather cheerless patch of green, though it had recently been glorified with a fountain by Doultons' popular sculptor-ceramist George Tinworth.

The resourceful Sydney had saved ninepence, which they spent on half a pound of black cherries to eat in the park, and a lunch of two halfpenny cups of tea, a teacake and a bloater which they shared between them. They played catch with a ball which Sydney improvised out of newspaper and string, and after lunch Hannah sat crocheting in the sun while her children played. Finally she announced that they would be just in time for tea in the workhouse, and they set off again up Kennington Park Road. The workhouse authorities, Charles recalled, were very indignant when Hannah demanded their readmission, since it involved not only paperwork but also a fresh disinfection of their clothes. An added bonus of the day out was that Sydney and Charles had to remain in the workhouse during the weekend, and so spend more time with their mother. On Monday they were sent back to the Norwood Schools.

This adventure which Hannah had devised for them remained a joyous memory for her sons to the end of their lives.* Ironically, the courage to carry it out was probably a sign of her growing mental instability. On 6 September – just three weeks after the outing to Kennington Park—she was taken from the workhouse to the Infirmary. The intervening period in the workhouse had left her in poor physical condition. She had dermatitis, and her body was covered in bruises. No one troubled or dared to inquire into the cause of her injuries; they were most likely explained by violent encounters with

* This account is based on Chaplin's version of the event. Sydney's recollection of it, related to an interviewer in the 1920s, did not materially differ, although he suggests that the idea had originated with the boys rather than with Hannah:

> Finally we hit upon a plan. I had made ninepence doing odd jobs and had carefully hoarded it.
>
> I got word to our mother and we all checked out of the institution. They gave us back our clothes all wrinkled up from having been packed away. Hand in hand, we went out. I spent the ninepence for some cakes and cherries and we sat all day together in the park. When night came, we all went back to the workhouse and went thru all the formalities of entering again – greatly to the disgust of the officials.[43]

other patients as a result of her mental condition. She was committed to Cane Hill Asylum, the doctors reporting:

> Has been very strange in manner – at one time abusive & noisy, at another using endearing terms. Has been confined in P[added] R[oom] repeatedly on a/c of sudden violence – threw a mug at another patient. Shouting, singing and talking incoherently. Complains of her head and depressed and crying this morning – dazed and unable to give any reliable information. Asks if she is dying. States she belongs to Christ Church (Congregation) which is Ch. of E. She was sent here on a mission here by the Lord. Says she wants to get out of the world.[44]

When she was admitted to the hospital she had given her occupation as 'machinist' – so she was still apparently supporting the family by sewing whilst in Farmers Road – and gave her first name as 'Lily'. The workhouse authorities corrected it to Hannah Harriett. As a true theatrical, she had had the presence of mind to tell them that she was twenty-eight: her real age at that time was just over thirty-three.

When Hannah and her children re-entered the workhouse in July, the Board of Guardians had resumed their pursuit of Charles Chaplin Senior. He was now living at 289 Kennington Road*, a few minutes away from Spencer's pub, The Queen's Head, on the corner of Broad Street and Vauxhall Walk. A fortnight after Hannah was committed to the asylum, Sydney and Charles were discharged from Norwood Schools to the care of their father.

When they were delivered – again in a bakery van – to the house, Charles remembered seeing his father only twice before. Once, he said, was on stage at the Canterbury Music Hall in Westminster Bridge Road; another time Charles had actually addressed him when they had met outside the house in Kennington Road. On that occasion Charles Chaplin Senior was accompanied by the woman with whom he was still living, and who is only identified in Chaplin's autobiography as 'Louise'. 289 Kennington Road was (and remains) a large, handsome late Georgian terraced house, set back behind a small front garden. Charles Senior occupied the two first-floor rooms with Louise and their four-year-old son (another half-brother for Charlie). The arrival of the two boys cannot have been convenient. In fact Sydney and Charles lived with their father for no more than two months,

* This is the address in the records of the Board of Guardians. Chaplin, whose memory was generally reliable, thought it was 287, not 289, and a commemorative plaque placed there in 1980 marks No. 287.

but it clearly seemed like years to them. Louise was surly and resentful and took particular dislike to Sydney (who on one occasion took his revenge by threatening her with a sharpened button-hook). When she drank she only became more morose. Yet in retrospect Chaplin felt a kind of sympathy for her. She had the remains of beauty, and sad, doe-like eyes; Chaplin sensed that she and his father were genuinely in love. Life with the elder Chaplin could not have been easy. He was drinking heavily by this time, and rarely came home sober. There were moments when he was attentive and charming and full of amusing stories about the music halls, but more often Charlie remembered the fights between Charles and Louise, and the occasions when he himself was locked out of the house. One of these occasions led to a visit by the Society for the Prevention of Cruelty to Children.

At this period Hannah's illness was subject to periods of remission. On 12 November 1898 she was discharged from Cane Hill Asylum,[45] and soon afterwards gathered up her sons from 289 Kennington Road. The three of them moved into a room at 39 Methley Street, behind Haywards' pickle factory which exuded a pungent atmosphere throughout the neighbourhood. Their home was next to a slaughterhouse; and Chaplin remembered the horror with which he realized that a merry slapstick chase after a runaway sheep was destined to end in tragedy and the slaughter of the entertaining animal.

Apart from this, life in Methley Street appears not to have been too uncomfortable. Charles Chaplin Senior was making occasional contributions to his sons' support, presumably to ensure that they did not return to disrupt the dubious harmony of Kennington Road. Hannah had returned to church and sewing, putting together blouses that were already cut out for a sweat shop which paid her a penny-halfpenny apiece. (In early versions of Chaplin's script for *Limelight* he describes Terry's mother as a worn but still beautiful woman, bent over a sewing machine in their attic room.) About this time Sydney took a job as a telegraph boy at the Strand Post Office. Louise, at the insistence of the Board of Guardians, had sent Charlie back to the Kennington Road Schools. He did not enjoy it very much, and to the end of his life complained of the failure of so many teachers to stir the imagination and curiosity of their pupils.

He spent his last day at Kennington Road Schools on Friday 25 November 1898.[46] Charlie Chaplin was now to become a professional entertainer. In early interviews he occasionally gave rather romantic accounts of his discovery by William Jackson, the founder of the Eight Lancashire Lads:

> One day I was giving an exhibition of the ordinary street Arab's contortions, the kind so common in the London streets, when I saw a man watching me intently. 'That boy is a born actor!' I heard him say, and then to me, 'Would you like to be an actor?' I scarcely knew what an actor was in those days, though my mother and father had both been connected with the music hall stage for years, but anything that promised work and the rewards of work as a means of getting out of the dull rut in which I found myself was welcome, and I listened to the tempter with the result that a few days later I was making my appearances in London suburban music halls with the variety artists known as the Eight Lancashire Lads.[47]

This was the kind of story newspaper reporters and readers loved in the 1920s. In his autobiography Chaplin explained, more mundanely but more credibly, that his father knew Mr Jackson and persuaded him to take on his son. Hannah was convinced: the arrangement was that Charlie would get board and lodging on tour, and Hannah would receive half a crown a week. William Jackson and his wife were evidently reliable people to whom to entrust her son. They were devout Catholics; they allowed their own children to perform in the troupe; and they proved conscientious about enrolling the Lads in schools in the towns where they appeared – though Charlie was only too well aware that these weekly attendances did not greatly benefit his education. Mr Jackson's least appealing habit was to pinch the boys' cheeks if they looked pale before they went on: he liked to boast that they did not need make-up since they had naturally rosy cheeks. A writer in a music hall paper, *The Magnet*,[48] described the act at the time that Charlie was a part of it:

> A bright and breezy turn, with a dash of true 'salt' in it, is contributed to the Variety stage by that excellent troupe, the Eight Lancashire Lads, whose speciality act we cannot speak too highly of. Mr William Jackson presents to the public eight perfectly drilled lads, who treat the audience to some of the finest clog dancing it is possible to imagine. The turn is a good one, because it gets away from the usual, and plunges boldly into the sea of novelty. The Lancashire Lads are fine specimens of boys and most picturesque do they look in their charming continental costumes: indeed, they are useful as well as ornamental, and treat us to a most enjoyable ten minutes' entertainment. The head of the troupe is William Jackson, and with this gentleman I had an interview recently. Mr Jackson

> some years ago commenced his career in Liverpool where he acquired a thorough knowledge of dancing. I was advised, he said to me, to go in for it professionally, so I gave up my work as a sculptor, and devoted myself to the stage. [Chaplin understood that Jackson had originally been a school teacher.]

Mr Jackson told the interviewer that the Lads

> made their first appearance at Blackpool, achieving a big success there, and afterwards going to the chief halls in the provinces. You see, the turn was quite new and caught on at once . . . and we are always endeavouring to improve the show. After this we were engaged for pantomime at the Newcastle Grand, and scored again in a most satisfactory way . . . After the run of this engagement I brought the lads to London, and they made their appearance at Gatti's [Westminster Bridge Road]; this being followed by other halls and also the Moss and Thornton tour.

Asked if any of his own sons appeared in the act he replied, 'Yes, two of them are included in it; and the other six are pupils. They have all been trained under my personal supervision, and in this direction my wife gives me much assistance.' Again Chaplin's recollection was slightly different: he believed that four of the Lads were Jackson offspring, though one of these was a girl with her hair cut like a boy's. In any event, the *Magnet* correspondent concluded: 'Jackson's Eight Lancashire Lads are all charming little fellows, well cared for, and an inspection of them was sufficient to satisfy me that they are all endowed with that which is most delightful to youth – good health and spirits. They take as much interest in their work as does [*sic*] Mr and Mrs Jackson themselves; and the public need never fear of having their interests neglected by the eight boys from Lancashire.'

Charlie remembered that he had to rehearse his clog dancing for six weeks before he was allowed to appear – almost paralysed with stage fright. His debut may then have been at the Theatre Royal, Manchester, where the troupe appeared in the Christmas pantomime *Babes in the Wood* which opened on Christmas Eve. If so, Charles Chaplin Senior would have been on hand to watch his son's first steps: he opened on Boxing Day at the Manchester Tivoli. Certainly Charlie was working with the troupe by 9 January 1899, when he was enrolled by Mrs Jackson at the Armitage Street School, Ardwick, Manchester.[49]

William Jackson's youngest son, Alfred, a year older than Charlie, remembered the new boy, not quite ten, being taken on.

> He was living with an aunt and his brother Sydney above a barber's shop [now a draper's] in Chester Street, off the Kennington-road. He was a very quiet boy at first, and, considering that he didn't come from Lancashire, he wasn't a bad dancer. My first job was to take him to have his hair, which was hanging in matted curls about his shoulders, cut to a reasonable length.
>
> He came to stay with us at 267 Kennington-road, and slept with me in the attic under the tiles. While we were in London we all went to the Sancroft-street Schools [opposite Kennington Cross], and he began to brighten up as he got to know us better. He was a great mimic, but his heart was set on tragedy. For weeks he would imitate Bransby Williams in 'The Old Curiosity Shop' wearing an old grey wig and tottering with a stick, until we others were sick of him.[50]

Charlie himself had vivid memories of his Bransby Williams impersonation. Mr Jackson had seen him entertaining the other boys with imitations of Williams in his 'Death of Little Nell, from *The Old Curiosity Shop*', and had decided it should go into the act, but it was disastrous. Charlie wore his regular Lancashire Lads costume of blouse, knickerbockers, lace collar and red dancing shoes, with an ill-fitting old man's wig, and his inaudible stage whisper irritated the audience into stamping and cat-calls. The solo experiment was not repeated.

Charlie had, in fact, a number of opportunities to study Bransby Williams. The Eight Lancashire Lads got engagements at the major London and provincial halls and shared the bill with Williams and other top artists of the time. Chaplin clearly remembered seeing Marie Lloyd and remarking how seriously she approached her work, though he felt he had not seen Dan Leno, who was on the same bill at the Tivoli in April 1900, in his prime.

Chaplin, however, made the acquaintance of the English music halls at their zenith. In the years since his father's debut, new civic organization and safety regulations had closed many of the innumerable tiny fleapit theatres, and in every urban centre opulent new Empires and Palaces had sprung up. These grander theatres and a conscious move towards respectability by the highly organized new managements, had begun to attract a more discerning middle class audience. The huge salaries that star artists could earn attracted a lot of talented people from the legitimate theatre, Bransby Williams and Albert Chevalier among them. In 1897 Charles Douglas Stuart and A. J. Park, the first historians of the music halls, could write:

> The position occupied by the variety stage today is as conspicuous everywhere as it is unique. Neither drama nor opera has had erected to its service more numerous or more palatial temples, and neither branches of art can count so many professors and supporters as those devoted to the cause of this peculiar and popular form of entertainment. But if the music hall has a glowing and interesting past, it has a still more golden and attractive future.
>
> Keeping, as before, in close and sympathetic touch with the great beating heart of the people and enlisting in its service, as its sphere of usefulness extends and broadens, the active and artistic co-operation of the best authors, the best artistes and the keenest intelligence of its day, it will necessarily yield still better and brighter results, and the cultured audience of the twentieth century – when, melancholy prospect! the present writers have been gathered to their fathers – may sit through a programme in which Shakespeare and the Henry Irvings of the future may collaborate to glorify and adorn.[51]

Even to a ten-year-old in a troupe of clog dancers, the music halls of those times must have provided an incomparable schooling in method, technique and discipline. A music hall act had to seize and hold its audience and to make its mark within a very limited time – between six and sixteen minutes. The audience was not indulgent, and the competition was relentless. The performer in the music hall could not rely on a sympathetic context or build-up: Sarah Bernhardt might find herself following Lockhart's Elephants on the bill. So every performer had to learn the secrets of attack and structure, the need to give the act a crescendo – a beginning, a middle and a smashing exit – to grab the applause. He had to learn to command every sort of audience, from a lethargic Monday first-house to the Saturday rowdies.

The best of music hall was invariably rooted in character. There were the eccentrics, such as Nellie Wallace or W. C. Fields (who as a tramp juggler was popular on both sides of the Atlantic), who always presented the same well-loved character; or there were the singers like Marie Lloyd, Albert Chevalier, George Robey or Charles Chaplin Senior himself, who would create an entire and individual character within each song. Hetty King, who was beginning her career at this time, was to bill her act as 'Song Characters True to Life'. The 'true to life' was important. The audience was keenly alive to falsehood, and comedy had to observe its own laws of dramatic and psychological integrity.

Charlie seems to have toured with the Eight Lancashire Lads

throughout 1899 and 1900. The registers of St Mary the Less School, Lambeth, reveal that Mrs Jackson enrolled him there during the Lads' engagement at the Tivoli. He was evidently still with them at the end of the year, when the pantomime season came round. Alfred Jackson remembered, 'Charlie accompanied us on tour and played in the first Cinderella pantomime at the Hippodrome as one of the cats. Finally, he left the Lancashire Lads for the "legitimate".'[52] This confirms Chaplin's own very circumstantial memories of *Cinderella*, although William Jackson's boys do not appear on the programme. Such a popular act might be expected to receive advertisement, but it is not entirely surprising that it did not on this occasion. The cast of a spectacular pantomime presentation at this time could be huge, with scores of extras and speciality acts. Mr Jackson too may have felt that work as pantomime animals, though profitable, was slightly demeaning. The cast list ends: 'Members of the Prince's Hunting Party, Guests at the Bar, Foreign Ambassadors and their Retinues, etc. etc.' Charlie and the Lads may have been the etceteras.

Opened in January 1900, the Hippodrome was London's latest theatrical marvel. The impresario Sir Edward Moss had set out to give Londoners 'a circus show second to none in the world, combined with elaborate stage spectacles impossible in any other theatre'. The building was the masterpiece of a genius of theatrical architecture, Frank Matcham. The centrepiece of this palace of marble, mosaic, gilt and terracotta was the great arena, which could be flooded with 100,000 gallons of water, or converted within sixty seconds to a dry performing space by raising up platforms which lay at the bottom of the artificial lake. For animal acts, shimmering grilles could be automatically raised in moments around the whole area. In its first years the Hippodrome presented a unique combination of variety, circus and aquatic spectacle. As time went on seats were built over the arena, and a more conventional style of variety took over.

There is a persistent but unlikely legend that Charlie was an extra in the first production at the Hippodrome, *Giddy Ostend*, which opened on 15 January 1900. At that time the Eight Lancashire Lads were playing in *Sinbad the Sailor* at the Alexandra, Stoke Newington. The Hippodrome *Cinderella* which was produced by Frank Parker and ran from Christmas Eve 1900 until 13 April 1901, was more like one of the spectacular ballet spectacles that made up the second half of the programmes at the Alhambra and the Empire Music Halls. The first half of the programme was made up of eleven variety acts including Captain Woodward's Seals and Sea Lions, Lockhart's Elephants, Leon Morris's Educated and Comedy Ponies, the Aquamarinoff troupe of Russian Dancers, equestrian acts, trapeze artists, Captain Kettle and Stepsons (comical acrobats), and Gobert, Belling and Filpe, 'The Famous Continental Grotesques'. The ninth act on the bill was Gibbons' 'Phono-Bio-Tableaux', an early attempt to combine sound with moving pictures.

Cinderella was perhaps more a fairy play than a conventional pantomime. It was written by W. H. Risque, with music by George Jacobi, formerly the Alhambra's Director of Music, and dances arranged by Will Bishop. It was in five scenes and an aquatic display; and the setting for the ball was so elaborate that even with the Hippodrome's stage machinery it required a pause of several minutes. The cats and dogs provided by the Lancashire Lads presumably figured in the scene 'The Baron's Kitchen'.

Buttons was played by the French clown Marceline, who was to remain a favourite on Hippodrome bills for some four years, billed as 'Continental Auguste' or simply 'The Droll'. Chaplin never forgot the impression made on him by this young clown, and the description in his autobiography is one of the rare accounts we have of Marceline, who subsequently faded into obscurity and committed suicide in 1927, when he was fifty-four. Chaplin recalled how Marceline would perch on a camp stool beside the flooded arena, and fish with a rod for the chorus girls who had disappeared under the waves – anticipating Busby Berkeley musicals of later years. For bait he used diamond necklaces and bracelets. There is something perfectly Chaplinesque about the impertinence of angling in the Hippodrome's grand arena, as there seems also to have been in the little poodle who shadowed Marceline's every movement.

Chaplin also recalled from *Cinderella* his own first comic improvisations. He played a cat (which had the privilege of tripping up Marceline in the kitchen scene) and at one of the children's matinées introduced some very unfeline comic business, sniffing at a dog and raising its leg against the proscenium. According to Chaplin's own account the laughs were gratifying but repetitions were strictly forbidden. The Lord Chamberlain in those days was very watchful for any impropriety in music hall performances.

Chaplin's explanation of his departure from the Eight Lancashire Lads was that William Jackson became tired of Hannah behaving like a stage mother, and constantly complaining that her son looked peaky. If this were so, it would most likely have happened during the troupe's prolonged London season at the Hippodrome. Perhaps there was some justice in Hannah's fears. In 1912 Chaplin, then starring with the Karno troupe, told a Winnipeg reporter:[53]

> Those were tough days sure enough. Sometimes we would almost fall asleep on the stage, but, casting a glance at Jackson in the wings, we would see him making extraordinary grimaces, showing his teeth, pointing to his face and making other contortions, indicating that he wanted us to brace up and smile. We would promptly respond, but the smile would slowly fade away again until we got another glance at Jackson. We were only kids and had not learned the art of forcing energy into listless nerves.
>
> But it was good training, fitting us for the harder work that comes before the goddess of success began to throw her favors around.

Despite Jackson's grimaces and his way of massaging roses into small boys' cheeks, Chaplin retained a feeling of wry gratitude towards him. In 1931 when he was in Paris Chaplin met the Jacksons – William and his son Alfred – again. The old man was then over eighty, but in very good form. Chaplin was touched when he told him, 'You know, Charlie, the outstanding memory I have of you as a little boy was your gentleness.'

Hannah's life as usual had not been easy during her son's frequent absences from London. Her father, Grandfather Hill, was now sixty and had not been doing well since Grandma Hill had left him to go to the dogs. Gout and rheumatism had made it hard to work at his cobbling, and for some years he had been moving from lodging to lodging almost as frequently as his daughter. In July 1899 he was homeless, and moved into Hannah's little room in Methley Street. After five days he was admitted to Lambeth Infirmary, and after that spent a month or so in the workhouse.[54] The return of Grandfather Hill into their lives could have its compensations. Charlie remembered that during one of his infirmary periods, Grandfather worked in the kitchen and was able to smuggle bags of stolen eggs to his nervous grandson when he came to visit him.

While Charlie was appearing in *Cinderella* Sydney decided to go to sea, taking advantage of the qualifications he had acquired aboard the *Exmouth*. He was still only sixteen, and seems to have added three years to his age, to improve his prospects: throughout his seagoing career, his personal documents invariably gave his date of birth as 1882, instead of the correct 1885. On 6 April 1901 he joined the Union Castle Mail Steamship Company Line's SS *Norman*, embarking on the Cape Mail run. He was engaged as an assistant steward and bandsman, on the strength of his aptitude with the bugle. Sydney was to make seven voyages in all, and from each his work and conduct were recorded on his Continuous Certificate of Discharge as 'Very Good'.[55] Throughout his life Sydney seems to have undertaken everything he did with the same conscientious zeal. More than thirty years after his first voyage, he recalled:

> When I first went away to sea as a steward and was seventeen years old, they put me to scrub a stairway that led down to the hold of the ship, and was used merely for the purpose of carrying down empty bottles and all waste matter used on the ship. These stairs were filthily black and with the aid of silver sand and holystone, I succeeded in getting these stairs so white that you could eat your meals off them. It was noticed by the captain, who sent for me, and told me that he had been captain for nineteen years and had never seen those stairs look so clean. He congratulated me, and told me that if I was always as conscientious in all my work, that I was bound to make a success in life and I have never forgotten that lesson, and the captain's praise.

Evidently such industry also brought more immediate rewards. When the Master of the *Norman* transferred to the *Kinfairns Castle*, Sydney was engaged for four successive voyages on that ship.

Before sailing, Sydney sent £1. 15s. out of his first pay instalment to his mother.[56] The officer making out the Seaman's Allotment Note entered her name as 'Annie' – a misinterpretation no doubt resulting from the weak aspirates of London speech.*

It was apparently on the strength of this very small fortune that Hannah and Charlie improved their conditions and moved into two rooms over a barber's shop in Chester Street.** This must have been at Number 24, where Frederick Clarke had the only hairdressing business in the street. Chester Street (now Chester Way) is a turning off Kennington Road, very close to the house where the boys had

* On more than one occasion Hannah's name appeared thus as 'Anna' or 'Annie' in official documents, presumably because of weak Hs. In the London *Star* of 3 September 1921, a childhood acquaintance of Charlie's recalled: 'Charlie's mother always struck me as being very refined, quiet and sad. He always said her name was Lily, so I don't know how 'Annie' got in the school register.' (A school register which the newspaper had traced but which has since disappeared.)

** Presumably the rooms previously rented by Aunt Kate *c.f.* p. 30.

lived with Charles and Louise. Chaplin's memories of Chester Street were still apparently vivid in 1943, when he made a transatlantic broadcast to Britain, and could still remember the names of the shops: Edward Ash the grocer at Number 18; Francis William Healey, the greengrocer, on the other side of Clarke's barber's shop, at Number 27; and round the corner, at 225 Kennington Road, Jethro Waghorn, who had only recently taken over the butcher's shop.

Charles Chaplin Senior was dying. He was only thirty-seven, but his constitution had been undermined by his drinking. He was suffering from cirrhosis of the liver and dropsy.* When, ultimately and inevitably, he succumbed, *The Era* wrote that its readers 'will hear with regret but without surprise of the death of poor Charles Chaplin, the well-known mimic and music-hall comedian . . . Of late years poor Chaplin was not fortunate, and good engagements, we are afraid, did not often come his way . . .' His last recorded engagement was the week of September 1900, at the Granville Theatre of Varieties, Walham Green.** Charlie remembered seeing him a few weeks before his death in The Three Stags, a public house at the northern end of Kennington Road, and being shocked at his changed appearance. On that occasion, he remembered, his father was very pleased to see him, and for the first time in his life took him in his arms and kissed him.

At the end of Charles's life he and Hannah may have drawn close again. When he was taken to St Thomas's Hospital on 29 April, it was from 16 Golden's Place, a lane of mean houses just off Chester Street; and when Hannah gave her own address, as informant on her husband's death certificate, that, too, was 16 Golden's Place. Charles died on 9 May 1901.

Hannah, of course, had no money for a funeral, and the Lambeth parish authorities, perhaps at the instigation of the hospital, granted a pauper's grave in the cemetery at Tooting. Hannah proposed to go to the Variety Artists' Benevolent Fund to ask for the other costs of the funeral: no doubt she employed the Chester Street undertaker, Albert Mummery, who shared his premises at Number 34 with his relation Thomas Alfred Mummery, a maker of wine casks. The

* The cause of death is given on the death certificate as 'cirrhosis of the liver', but both Chaplin and *The Era* speak only of dropsy. At this time the cause of 'hob-nail liver' was too familiar, and perhaps cirrhosis was not considered a polite disease to acknowledge.

** Built by Frank Matcham in 1898 as a 'try-out' theatre for the great comedians Dan Leno and Herbert Campbell.

Chaplin family, however, were opposed to a charity funeral. Fortunately Charles's younger brother Albert, who had done well for himself in South Africa, was visiting London at the time. *The Era* reported: 'Poor Charles Chaplin was buried at Tooting on Monday [13 May 1901] at 12.30. The chief mourners were the widow and only child [*sic*], his brother and sister and sister-in-law. Mr and Mrs Harry Clarke also followed. At the graveside were Mr R. Voss, the song-writer, and Mr Fredericks of De Voy, Hurst and Fredericks. The coffin was of polished oak. The expense of the funeral was borne by Mr Albert Chaplin, from South Africa, the brother of the deceased comedian.' Afterwards, Charlie remembered, the Chaplins stopped for lunch at one of the public houses they owned, after dropping off Hannah and himself to go home to an empty larder and no immediate prospects of filling it. Fortunately on 31 May Sydney docked at Southampton; his pay and more than three pounds he had earned in tips ensured the three Chaplins a comparatively luxurious summer, with bloaters, crumpets, cake and ice-cream, that Charlie was never to forget.

On 1 September Sydney returned to sea. This time he was a fully-fledged steward on the *Haverford*, and signed on for the voyage to New York and back. Much to the alarm of his mother and brother, this voyage lasted much longer than the anticipated three weeks. Sydney appears to have been put ashore in New York on account of sickness; and had to wait until 5 October before he could get another boat for his return. He signed on as steward on the *St Louis* out of New York on a North Atlantic voyage, and arrived back in England on 23 October.[57]

The chronology of the next year and a half of Charles Chaplin's life is somewhat unclear: even he admitted that 'my memory of this period goes in and out of focus'. During much of the time Hannah, with Charlie and sometimes Sydney, was living at 3, Pownall Terrace, though there were interludes during which they stayed with one of Hannah's fellow church members, a devout lady called Mrs Taylor, and with a less austere friend who was being kept in style in Stockwell by an old military gentleman, though she still kept up her younger gentleman caller.

For some reason Chaplin always had more vivid memories of the garret in Pownall Terrace than of any other of the many houses of his childhood. Perhaps it was simply that he spent longer there than anywhere else. When he made his triumphal return to Britain in 1921, he made a sentimental visit to the place one night. It was then occupied by a war widow called Mrs Reynolds, who told the newspaper reporters,

> He said, 'Many's the time I've banged my head on that sloping ceiling, and got thrashed for making so much noise.'
>
> He asked me where I did my cooking, and I showed him my old fireplace, and said if it wasn't so late I'd show him the loft. Charlie said, 'I know it. I've often hidden in there. I'd like to spend just one night here.' I said he could spend two if he liked, and I'd go somewhere else.
>
> One of the gentlemen said, 'It's not like your hotel, Charlie,' and he said, 'Never mind my hotel. This is my old room, where I used to sleep twelve years ago [*sic*].' And they went on laughing and talking and smoking cigarettes. He asked me what I paid for rent, and I said five shillings a week, though eight years ago, when I took it, it was only half a crown. He said when he was living here he paid 3s. 6d.[58]

More than twenty years later, in his 1943 transatlantic broadcast to Lambeth, Chaplin said:

> Although I left Lambeth thirty-five years ago, I shall always remember the top room at 3, Pownall Terrace, where I lived as a boy; I shall always remember climbing up and down those three flights of narrow stairs to empty those troublesome slops. Yes, and Healey's the greengrocer's in Chester Street, where one could purchase fourteen pounds of coal and a pennorth of pot herbs and a pound of tuppeny pieces at Waghorn's the butcher's; and Ash's the grocer's where one bought a pennyworth of mixed stale cake, with all its pleasant and dubious surprises.
>
> Yes, I went back and visited that little top room in Pownall Terrace, where I had to lug the slops and fourteen pounds of coal. It was all there, the same Lambeth I had left, the same squalor and poverty. Now they tell me that Pownall Terrace is in ruins, blasted out of existence by the German blitz.
>
> I remember the Lambeth streets, the New Cut and the Lambeth Walk, Vauxhall Road. They were hard streets, and one couldn't say they were paved with gold; nevertheless the people who lived there are made of pretty good metal.

In one respect Chaplin was misinformed. It was not the Germans who destroyed Pownall Terrace, but the urban developers, and not until 1966. In 1984 the site still remained empty and unused.

After the ill-fated New York voyage, Sydney appears to have remained in London for more than ten months, during which his savings must have dwindled away. On 6 September 1902 he embarked on the first of four Cape Mail voyages on the SS *Kinfairns Castle*. Each trip lasted seven weeks, with a fortnight's shore leave between. Charlie, having clearly by this time given up all thought of school, turned his mind to ways of earning a little money. While he still had a mourning band on his arm following the death of his father, he tried selling flowers round the Kennington pubs, successfully but briefly since Hannah did not approve. He worked as a barber's boy (presumably for Mr Clarke in Chester Street) and a chandler's boy. He worked as a doctor's boy for a partnership called Hool and Kinsey-Taylor at 10, Throgmorton Avenue. This must have been quite early in 1901, since the doctors moved from that address during the course of the year.[59] He lost the job because he was too small to cope with cleaning the windows, but the Kinsey-Taylors took him on as a page boy in their house in Lancaster Gate. As he reflects, he might eventually have achieved a long career as a butler, if Mrs Kinsey-Taylor had not sacked him for fooling around, improvising an alpenhorn from a length of drain pipe. He lost a job with W. H. Smith when they discovered he was under age, and lasted only one day in a glass factory. A period with Strakers the stationers, feeding an enormous Wharfedale printing press, seems to have been an augury of his battles with machinery in *Modern Times*. Two odd jobs from this period seem particularly to have caught his imagination. He first described his efforts as a hawker of old clothes, in 1916:

> I conceived the idea of wanting to earn money to support the members of the family. I had observed the street merchants in Petticoat Lane* raking in the shekels, so I ransacked the house for all the discarded garments I could find and hurried to the famous street and, mounting on a box, began in a thin, boyish voice to auction off my wares.
>
> The pedestrians stopped in amazement and watched me for a short time and then out of kindness purchased my meagre stock. I returned home that night with a shilling and sixpence for the afternoon's work; but small as the sum was, it helped out.[60]

Fifty years later, his version of the experience had not changed greatly, except that he remembered the takings as only sixpence, the price of a pair of gaiters which Hannah declared should have realized more.

He was always fascinated by his memory of the two Scots who

* Petticoat Lane sounded better for the press. In *My Autobiography* Chaplin says it was Newington Butts.

made penny toys out of old shoe-boxes, grape cork, tinsel and scrap wood. Charlie helped them in the mews behind Kennington Road where they worked, and afterwards set up in business making toy boats on his own account. The experiment did not last long: Hannah found the odour and hazards of the glue too great when she was working at sewing her blouses. He told May Reeves, in 1931: 'If I were to lose everything one day and not be able to work any more, I would make toys . . . When I was a child I made little boats out of newspaper and sold them on the streets so as not to die of hunger.' 'How often,' Miss Reeves added, 'he repeated, during our friendship, "If I were one day to lose all my money . . ."'[61]

Ill fortune had not done buffeting the Chaplins. On 24 March 1903 Sydney embarked on what was to be the last of his voyages on the *Kinfairns Castle*. By the beginning of May Charles was aware that his mother was sick again. She had grown listless, seemed unconcerned when the sweat shop for whom she sewed stopped giving her work and took back the sewing machine, and neglected the little room. On Tuesday 5 May Charlie arrived home to be told by other children around the door that his mother had gone insane. He had the job of leading her to the Infirmary in Renfrew Road, and then, as her nearest known relative, reporting the case to the authorities. He had just turned fourteen. The medical certificate records: 'Charles Chaplin, son, 3 Pownall Terrace, Kennington Road, states she keeps on mentioning a lot of people who are dead and fancies she can see them looking out of the window and talking to imaginary people – going into strangers' rooms etc.' Hannah's delightful window entertainments had moved into the region of madness.[62]

Charlie remembered being dealt with by a kindly young doctor at the Infirmary. This was probably Dr M. H. Quarry, who examined Hannah: 'She is very noisy and incoherent, praying and swearing by turns – crying & shouting – She says the floor is the river Jordan and she cannot cross it. At times violent and destructive.' The relieving officer stated that she was dangerous to others, since she was inclined to strike people. After interviewing Charlie, he recorded on Hannah's documents that it was not known whether any near relative had been afflicted with insanity, which seems to confirm that Hannah had successfully concealed the matter of Grandma Hill's certification from her sons. Again Hannah's occupation appears on her documents as 'machinist'; and again, even in these straits, she had the presence of mind to subtract five years from her age. She is recorded as being thirty-three years old; she was in fact nearing thirty-eight.

1. Facts indicating Insanity observed by myself at the time of examination, viz: She is very noisy and incoherent praying & swearing, by turns – crying & shouting – She says the floor is the river Jordan and she cannot cross it at times. Violent and destructive

2. Other facts (if any) indicating Insanity communicated to me by others: Charles Chaplin son. 3 Pownall Terrace Kennington Road states she keeps on mentioning a lot of people who are dead and fancies she can see them looking out of the window and talking to them – giving people – going into strangers rooms etc.

I give this certificate having first read the section of the Act of Parliament printed below.

Signed, Name JMH Quarry

Place of Abode Lambeth Infirmary

Dated this 9th day of May 1903.

1. Names, residences, and occupations of relatives; also state how far each is able to contribute

1903 – Part of the 'Order for the Reception of a Pauper Lunatic' relating to Hannah Chaplin, 9 May 1903, including the evidence given to Dr Quarry by the fourteen-year-old Charles Chaplin.

Dr Quarry asked Charlie what he would do now; and terrified of being sent back to Norwood he quickly replied that he would be living with his aunt. In fact there is some evidence that he did at some periods stay with Aunt Kate; but on this occasion he went back to 3, Pownall Terrace to wait for Sydney's return. The autobiography eloquently describes the misery and anguish of these days, how he cried in the solitude of the wretched and now lonely little room, and the kindness of the landlady who allowed him to stay on and gave him food when he was not too proud or shy to take it. Six days after entering the Infirmary, Hannah was sent back to Cane Hill Asylum. This time she was to stay for almost eight months.

Sydney was due back in England on 9 May but his return to

London seems to have been delayed. (Chaplin believed that this was the voyage during which Sydney was kept abroad by his illness, but this is not corroborated by Sydney's personal documents.) While waiting for Sydney's return, Charlie remembered making friends with some wood-choppers – also working in a mews behind Kennington Road – and that one of them treated him to a gallery seat at the South London Music Hall in London Road, Lambeth. The star act was Fred Karno's *Early Birds*. This was his first encounter with the company in which he was first to achieve fame.

Sydney finally arrived home, and Charlie at last could share his troubles. They went to Cane Hill to visit Hannah and were shocked at how ill she looked. Charlie was long and deeply troubled by her reproach, 'If only you had given me a cup of tea that afternoon I would have been all right.'

Sydney announced that he had come home for good. He had saved enough to live on for the next few months, and had determined to go on the stage. It was an ambition which his younger brother shared. Many years later he was to tell his son (a third Charles Chaplin): 'Even when I was in the orphanage, when I was roaming the streets trying to find enough to eat to keep alive, even then I thought of myself as the greatest actor in the world. I had to feel that exuberance that comes from utter confidence in yourself. Without that you go down to defeat.'[63]

2

The young professional

Even at eleven or twelve, touring with William Jackson's Lancashire Lads, Chaplin's ambition to be a star was formed. 'I would have liked to be a boy comedian – but that would have taken nerve, to stand on the stage alone.'[1] With another of the Lancashire Lads, Tommy Bristol, he planned a double act, which they would call 'Bristol and Chaplin, the Millionaire Tramps'. The idea never came to anything, but more than a decade later Chaplin was impressed to meet Tommy Bristol in New York, where he and a partner were earning $300 a week as comedians.[2]

Bert Herbert, a minor English variety comedian, remembered another project from this period, and there is enough circumstantial detail in his account to give it credibility:

> After Charlie had left the Lancashire Lads my uncle brought him to our house (Thrush Street, Walworth), and asked my parents if they would agree to my brother and I joining another boy to tour as a dancing trio.
>
> My people agreed, and Charlie took over his duties straight away. Charlie was an excellent dancer and teacher, but I am afraid we did more larking about than dancing – we were between ten and fourteen years.
>
> Eventually we mastered six steps (the old six Lancashire steps) and got a trial show at the Montpelier, in Walworth, at that time, I believe a Mr Ben Weston was the proprietor.
>
> I remember that we had no stage dresses, and went on in our street clothes. Charlie and my brother wore knickerbockers, and as I had long trousers I had to tie them up underneath at the knee to make them look like knickers.
>
> How Charlie laughed when I went wrong, because one leg of my trousers started to come down as soon as I commenced to dance.

My uncle then went to America, and as we had no money to carry on, we had to let the Trio fall through. It was to have been called 'Ted Prince's Nippers'.

I lost sight of Charlie for some time, but I met him again when he was with Mr Murray in 'Casey Court' [*sic*] (a troupe of lads).

At the time I am speaking of Charlie lived in the buildings in Munton-road, off New Kent-road, and I rather fancy he went to Rodney-road school.

He certainly was not a 'gutter snipe'. My mother used to admonish my brother and I with the remark, 'Why aren't you good like little Charlie? See how clean he keeps himself and how well behaved he is.'

Of course, I could have told her that he was as bad as us when she was out of the way, but then, as now, he could pull the innocent face at a moment's notice.

I have heard it said that Charlie was always funny as a boy but, on the contrary, I found him just the reverse. I think he himself would bear out my statement.

His one ambition was to be a villain in drama. We often used to set a drama in the kitchen, and Charlie always wanted to be a villain. He certainly did not have awkward feet, as some people have suggested.

He was an ingenious kid. I remember often going to his house in Munton-road and playing with a farthing-in-the-slot machine, which he had made. It was an exact miniature model of the 'penny-in-the-slot' machines seen at fairs, etc., and worked admirably.[3]

Munton Road is not recorded anywhere else as an address for the Chaplins, but it is well within that small area of Lambeth and Southwark where all Chaplin's childhood was spent. If Bert Herbert's recollection about 'a Mr Ben Weston' is accurate, it would place these incidents somewhere around Chaplin's fourteenth birthday, in the early part of 1903, when Benjamin Dent Weston took over management of the Montpelier Palace in Montpelier Street, Newington, from Francis Albert Pinn.[4]

Quite suddenly young Charlie Chaplin's luck changed. In fact initiative and determination must have had as much to do with it as luck. It must have required some nerve for the shy and shabby fourteen-year-old to register with one of the better-known theatrical agencies, H. Blackmore's in Bedford Street, Strand. He clearly already had the looks, vivacity and charm of later years, and made an impression: within a short time of his registering, the Blackmore agency sent a postcard asking him to come in about a job. He was seen by Mr Blackmore himself, and sent off to the offices of Charles Frohman, whose wide-ranging interests as an impresario included management of the Duke of York's Theatre in London; later Frohman was also to lease the Aldwych and the Globe and at one time had five London theatres under his control. He was to die in the sinking of the *Lusitania* in 1915. Frohman's manager, C. E. Hamilton, engaged Chaplin on the spot to play Billy the pageboy in a tour of William C. Gillette's *Sherlock Holmes* due to start in October. His salary would be £2. 10s. a week.

Meanwhile, Mr Hamilton advised him, there was a likely part for him in a new play, *Jim, A Romance of Cockayne*, written by H. A. Saintsbury, who was to play Holmes in the forthcoming tour. Hamilton gave the boy a note to take to Saintsbury at the Green Room Club. To present himself in those august premises must have tested the boy's courage.

Saintsbury was a dedicated professional of the old Victorian repertory school. Born in Chelsea on 18 December 1869 he came from a good middle-class background and was educated at St John's College, Hurstpierpoint. He started his working life as a clerk in the Bank of England, but he was irretrievably stage-struck. At eighteen he was in Kate Vaughan's revival of *Masks and Faces*, and soon afterwards became a professional. He toured in the standard repertory of Victorian melodrama – *The Silver King, The Harbour Lights, The Lights o' London*, and *Under the Red Robe*, and a repertoire of classic parts. His great role, however, was Sherlock Holmes. Chaplin thought he looked just like the *Strand Magazine* illustrations of the great detective. Saintsbury was to play Holmes for almost thirty years, and for some 1400 performances. His own plays and adaptations reveal his romantic streak: as well as *Jim*, they included *The Eleventh Hour, Romance* (after Dumas), *The Four Just Men, Anna of the Plains, King of the Huguenots* and *The Cardinal's Collation.*

Saintsbury clearly took to Charlie on sight, and handed him the part there and then. The boy was much relieved that he was not asked to read on the spot, because he still found it very difficult to make out words on the page. Sydney read the part for him, however, and in three days he was word-perfect. The brothers were amazed and moved at their good fortune. Sydney said that it was the turning point of their lives – and promptly went off to Frohman's office in an unsuccessful attempt to up Charlie's salary.

Chaplin admired Saintsbury, and learned much about stagecraft working in his companies. Saintsbury, for his part, encouraged the boy. No doubt thanks to Saintsbury's interest, Master Chaplin was generally mentioned in the press copy which the company sent each week to *The Era*. Unfortunately *Jim, A Romance of Cockayne* was not a success. Its author described it as 'an original modern play', but it was very like Jones and Hermans' old warhorse, *The Silver King*, written twenty years before. Mr Saintsbury himself played Royden Carstairs, a young man of aristocratic lineage, inconveniently given to going off into cataleptic fits, who is down on his luck and sharing a garret with Sammy, a newsboy – Chaplin's part – and Jim, a flower girl who sleeps, for decorum's sake, in a cupboard. The play is packed with dramatic incident, improbable coincidences, a stolen sweetheart, a long-lost child, a murder, false accusations, and a lot of self-sacrifice.

As Sammy, Chaplin had a meaty supporting comedy role. His best scene is where he returns to the garret to find a detective searching the cupboard which is Jim's quarters:

SAMMY: Oi, you. Don't you know that's a lady's bedroom?

DETECTIVE: What! That cupboard? Come here!

SAMMY: The cool cheek of him!

DETECTIVE: Stow that. Come in and shut the door.

SAMMY: Polite, ain't you, inviting blokes to walk into their own drawing rooms?

DETECTIVE: I'm a detective.

SAMMY: What – a cop? I'm off.

DETECTIVE: I'm not going to hurt you. All I want is a little information that will help to do someone a good turn.

SAMMY: A good turn indeed! If a bit of luck comes to anyone here, it won't be through the cops!

DETECTIVE: Don't be a fool. Would I have started by telling you I was in the force?

SAMMY: Thanks for nothing. I can see your boots.

The critic of *The Era* praised the play ('The dialogue is polished and epigrammatic, and the story of remarkable interest.') but neither his fellow critics nor the audience shared his enthusiasm. *Jim* opened at the Royal County Theatre, Kingston-upon-Thames on 6 July 1903, moved to the Grand Theatre, Fulham for the following week, and closed finally on 18 July.

Chaplin, however, had earned his first press notices. Reviewing the first week, the *Era* critic wrote: '. . . mention should be made of . . . Master Charles Chaplin, who, as a newsboy known as Sam, showed promise.' Reviewing the Fulham performance, the critic praised him again: 'Master Charles Chaplin is a broth of a boy as Sam the newspaper boy, giving a most realistic picture of the cheeky, honest, loyal, self-reliant, philosophical street Arab who haunts the regions of Cockayne.'

His best notice though was in *The Topical Times* which ended its slaughter of poor Saintsbury's play with:

> But there is one redeeming feature, the part of Sammy, a newspaper boy, a smart London street Arab, much responsible for the comic part. Although hackneyed and old-fashioned, Sammy was made vastly amusing by Master Charles Chaplin, a bright and vigorous child actor. I have never heard of the boy before, but I hope to hear great things of him in the near future.

The premature demise of *Jim* seems to have hastened *Sherlock Holmes* into rehearsal, and provided for one or two extra dates prior to commencing the main tour. Chaplin played Billy for the first time on Monday 27 July 1903 at the Pavilion Theatre, Whitechapel Road. Seating an audience of 2650, it was an awe-inspiring place for a small, fourteen-year-old actor. The first provincial engagement was in Newcastle on 10 August 1903.

The management and Mr Saintsbury were concerned about the well-being of the youngest member of the company, and decided that Mr and Mrs Tom Green, the stage carpenter and wardrobe mistress, should be his guardians whilst on tour. In his autobiography Chaplin said that by mutual agreement they abandoned this arrangement after three weeks: it was not, he said, 'very glamorous', the Greens sometimes drank, and it was tiresome to eat what and when they ate. He felt it was probably more irksome to them than it was to him. In fact the shyness which was to remain characteristic may have led him to underestimate Mrs Green's concern for him. Almost thirty years later she recorded her recollections of the period, and though she was a year out on her dating, in all other respects, where her anecdotes can be checked against verifiable facts, she proves a remarkably accurate witness. At the time she was interviewed, in 1931, she was living in Scarborough as Miss Edith Scales. Mrs Tom Green, she said, was her 'stage name', so the liaison with Tom the carpenter may have been just temporary and informal.

> We opened our tour at the Pavilion Theatre, Mile End Road in July 1904 [*sic*]. I became his guardian a week later when we went to Newcastle to play at the Theatre Royal.* Charlie was all right when we were in London because he was at home, but when we started touring he had no one to look after him. There was a matinée on the Saturday, but Charlie, who had failed to leave his address, knew nothing about this matinée, and when he did not turn up for the opening, we had to get his understudy into his clothes. The show had started when up came Charlie proudly carrying under his arm a five-shilling camera he had just bought. Poor boy, he started to cry when he heard he was late for the matinée, but I told him to dry his eyes and rushed off to get the understudy out of his clothes again. Charlie was not due on until the second act, and so I rushed him off into the ladies' dressing room and we got him ready in time.[5]

The five-shilling camera which Chaplin had bought with his first week's wages from *Sherlock Holmes* remained an interest for some time. He had retained the mercantile spirit of the hard times of his first search for work in London, and set up as a part-time street photographer – it was a common itinerant trade at that time – taking portraits for threepence and sixpence a time. The sixpenny ones were framed: he had found a shop where he could buy cardboard frames for a penny. Miss Scales said that he generally sought out the working class streets for his trade.

Miss Scales remembered that Charlie did his own processing and printing:

> Whenever we went to new rooms, Charlie would ask the landlady, 'Have you got a dark room, ma?' One landlady asked Miss Scales to fetch Charlie for his dinner, but she could not find him anywhere in their rooms upstairs, so she called out. There was a knocking from inside the wardrobe, and Charlie's voice: 'Don't open the door! You'll spoil my plates if you do.'
>
> I was very much annoyed, then he came out and I discovered he had burnt the bottom of the landlady's wardrobe with his candle.
>
> 'It will be jolly fine if she charges you for the damage before we go,' I told him. 'Don't worry, she won't notice it,' said Charlie. 'I'll put a piece

* A Newcastle magazine, *Northern Gossip*, noted: 'Other characters are in very capable hands, but a special word of praise is due to Master C. Chaplin, for his wonderfully clever acting as Billy.' (15 August 1903)

of clean paper in the bottom and cover it over.' He did, and we heard no more about it.[6]

The Frohman tour proper began on 26 October 1903 at the Theatre Royal, Bolton. In the third week of the tour Miss Scales and Charlie found themselves in the magistrates' court and the local papers, as witness of a fracas that sounds like a try-out for *Dough and Dynamite*.

They were playing at the Theatre Royal, Ashton-under-Lyne, and lodging with Mrs Emma Greenwood in Cavendish Street. On Tuesday 10 November Mrs Greenwood was baking in the kitchen. Charlie was hovering: 'Charlie was an expert at getting round landladies,' Miss Scales remembered. 'When it was baking day, they could never resist his appeals for hot cakes.' Suddenly there was a loud knocking on the front door: it was a drunken chimney sweep called Robert Birkett who was notorious in the district for his violence and foul language. When Mrs Greenwood opened the door, he began to swear at her, told her her chimney was on fire, and insisted upon seeing it for himself.

> Complainant said he came into the house and when he saw the fire he said, 'Give me a lading can full of water.' She said she had not a can, and gave him a jugfull. He threw the water on the fire to put it out. He said, 'Give me another,' and she did, which he also threw on the fire. He then said, 'I will make you pay for this.' She told him if she had to pay she would do so. He then said, 'I want one shilling,' and came out with bad language. She opened the door and told him he had to go out, as she would give him no shilling. The defendant then caught hold of her and pulled her into the backyard where he thrashed her shamefully. He got hold of her arms in front and kicked her legs. – Defendant: I never lifted my foot up. – The Clerk: How was he for drink? – Complainant: He was not sober and was not drunk. – Defendant: Didn't you hit me with the poker? – Complainant: No. – Charles Chapman [*sic*], a boy, said he saw it all, and the complainant's evidence was quite true.[7]

As Miss Scales recalled the incident, she had been resting in her room when Charlie rushed in, woke her, told her a man was attacking him, and rushed out again. 'Of course, thinking a lot about the boy, I was off like a shot.' She arrived in time to see Mrs Greenwood putting Bob Birkett out, ably asisted by Charlie who was threatening him with a poker.

> We were at Stockport the following Monday when they sent for us to appear in court, and we had to return to give evidence. Charlie first went into the witness box, but no one could understand his cockney accent.

The sergeant kept touching him on the shoulder and saying, 'Will you speak a little more clearly please.' But Charlie was very excited and indignant about the man kicking the landlady. After a lot of fun he got his story out, however, and the man was sent to prison, I believe for about three months.

Then Charlie asked the sergeant, what about our expenses? The sergeant replied, there's no fine and so there's no pay. Charlie was very vexed, but despite his indignation at such treatment, the court allowed us no expenses. Charlie chattered and grumbled all the way to the station about this, and it took him a long time to forget it. 'To think we have had to come all this way and pay our own fares,' he complained.[8]

The week before this excitement in Ashton-under-Lyne, when the *Sherlock Holmes* company was playing in Wigan, Charlie had bought two tame rabbits, and Miss Scales' Tom – 'a very kind-hearted man' – had made him a box covered over with canvas to keep them in.

Charlie had a great affection for his two pets, and kept them for several months. When one got worried, he vowed vengeance and searched all over for the cat or dog that had done it, walking through all the streets in the district, but of course he did not find it. He took the rabbits wherever we went, and when we were travelling he used to put them on the luggage rack and take the cover off the box to give them plenty of air. Once he let his rabbits run away in the landlady's sitting room and of course they made a mess and annoyed the landlady. That was the only time I really had to chastise him. He could make those pets do all sorts of tricks.[9]

This story of the rabbits corroborates Chaplin's own autobiographical recollections, though he records only one of them, presumably the survivor of the worrying, which ultimately met its own fate at the hands of a landlady with a cryptic smile. He remembered that this was in Tonypandy, which the *Holmes* tour did not hit until 3–8 April 1905, so the rabbit had retained his affection for seventeen months. The following week they played at Ebbw Vale, where the landlady's son was a pathetic, legless human frog. Charlie concealed his revulsion and bravely shook the poor thing's hand when he left the house.

Miss Scales was constantly impressed by young Charlie's financial acumen. On a later tour, in August 1905, she remembered:

One day, while we were at the Market Hotel, Blackburn, he went into the sitting room and delighted all the farmers by singing to them. It was market day and the place was full. He finished up by showing them the clog dance, and he could do that dance too. But the farmers had to pay for the entertainment. Yes, Charlie went round with the hat when he had finished. I got hauled over the coals for allowing him to do that, but I wasn't there to stop him. But everyone liked Charlie. He was a wonderfully clever boy and had wonderfully perfect teeth and hair. We had Robert Forsyth playing as Professor Moriarty in the company. He was a great friend of Charlie's. Another friend of Charlie's was H. A. Saintsbury . . .[10]

When the time came to settle with the landlady, Charlie would carefully inspect the bill and knock out any item he had not had. 'He allowed no overcharging. If he had been out to tea, for instance, he would deduct the amount chargeable for one tea from the bill.'[11]

This kind of touring must have been an extraordinary schooling in life for a bright boy to whom Hannah Chaplin had passed on her gift of observation. They toured all over Britain, from London to Dundee, from Wales to East Anglia. Mostly, though, they travelled through the sooty industrial towns of the Midlands and North – Sheffield, Blackburn, Huddersfield, Manchester, Bolton, Stockport, Rochdale, Jarrow, Middlesbrough, Sunderland, Leeds. At the time, even the smallest town had its theatre: if you included the Co-op halls and corn exchanges, there were well over five hundred active professional theatres in the British Isles.

Despite Mr and Mrs Green, Chaplin remembered that he became melancholy and solitary, and began to neglect his personal appearance. Meanwhile Sydney, whose theatrical aspirations had long predated his brother's but who had not yet succeeded in finding stage work, had taken a job as bar tender at the Coal Hole in the Strand (one of London's first song-and-supper rooms, it had by this time long since reverted to the role of an ordinary pub). In December 1903, however, Charlie persuaded the *Sherlock Holmes* management to give his brother a part as Count Von Stalberg; and for the remainder of the 1903–4 tour, which closed on 11 June at the Royal West London Theatre in Church Street, Edgware Road, the brothers were together.

The casting of Sydney in an aristocratic – albeit foreign – role raises the question of the Chaplin brothers' diction at this time. We have seen that Charlie's cockney accent was so pronounced that he was hardly comprehensible in Ashton-under-Lyne (before the days of radio, people were generally less accustomed to regional accents different from their own). Even after his arrival in Hollywood, interviewers occasionally referred in passing to his 'cockney' accent. Later, as we know from the talking films, there was no trace of such an accent.* Sydney's speech, however, retained evidence of his London origins to the end of his life. It might be supposed that an accent would be a handicap in a theatre committed to 'correct' English diction. Both in the music hall and the legitimate theatre, however, there was a formal 'Thespian' style of speech, which the ordinarily accomplished performer could adopt as readily as he put on make-up. A good example of stage accents was Gus Elen, whose song "'E Dunno Where 'E Are' is supposed to have been Chaplin's debut performance. Born in London, Elen retained a South London accent to the end of his life. He performed his coster songs with quite different diction, which still kept the Dickensian cockney's interchange of 'W' and 'V'. A gramophone record made at the time of a come-back in 1930, however, includes a speech of thanks to his public declaimed in full 'Thespian formal'. No doubt the Chaplin boys would have been thus equipped to rise to any role on the stage. The music hall style of 'Thespian formal' is admirably demonstrated in Chaplin's flea circus number in *Limelight*. The diction of the song that he sings as the circus proprietor is remarkably like that of the famous music hall star George Bastow, performing 'Captain Gingah' or 'Beauty of the Guards'.

For part of the tour the whole Chaplin family was reunited. Hannah had had one of the periodic remissions characteristic of her illness, and on 2 January 1904 was discharged from Cane Hill. For a week or two she joined her sons on tour. Charlie was touched and saddened. Their relationship had changed. Her sons had ceased to be children, and she in her way had become a child. On the tour she did the shopping and cooking, and bought flowers for their rooms: Chaplin remembered that even at their poorest she would manage to save a penny for a bunch of wallflowers. But, he said, 'She acted more like a guest than our mother.' After a month, Hannah decided she should go back to London, and rented the apartment over the hairdresser's in Chester Street again. The boys helped her furnish it, and sent her twenty-five shillings out of their weekly earnings.

Some time before Hannah's discharge from Cane Hill, the brothers had moved their London base from Pownall Terrace to smarter rooms

* Georgia Hale recalls that Chaplin was upset when Ivor Montagu referred to his 'cockney' accent around 1929.

in Kennington Road. Now that Hannah had a home again, they seem to have given up the new rooms. Chaplin confessed with slight shame and regret that when they stayed with her in Chester Street in the summer of 1904, after the close of the *Sherlock Holmes* tour, he secretly looked forward to the extra comforts they were able to enjoy in theatrical lodgings.

On 20 August 1904, just over two months after the end of the *Holmes* tour, the following advertisement appeared in *The Era*:

MR ERNEST STERN presents
"FROM RAGS TO RICHES."
"FROM RAGS TO RICHES."
"FROM RAGS TO RICHES."
Now running with enormous success in America.
Specially Selected Cast, including
Master CHARLIE CHAPLIN,
as NED NIMBLE, the Newsboy.
Everything carried.
Magnificent Plant of Printing
by the Best American and English Firms.
New York Times says:—Most exciting melodrama seen locally for a long time. Interest never flags.
Cleveland Daily World says:—Last night's audience went into paroxysms of delight at the heroic work of Ned Nimble, the gutter boy, who works his way from gutter to palace.
Vacant Dec. 26 and onwards, with exceptions.
Also First-class Suburban Theatre for Production.
Apply, JOHN A. ATKIN,
Bramcote Lodge, Sunbury-on-Thames.

The critical quotes refer somewhat misleadingly to the play's original American presentation. This British production, promising young Charles his first starring role, was apparently still only in the planning. The advertisement continued to appear through the rest of August and September and during the first two weeks of October, but there was no announcement of any engagements, so perhaps the production never progressed beyond rehearsals – for which, in 1904, the artists would almost certainly have been unpaid. In his later days, however, Chaplin spoke with some pleasure of the role.

He was next offered his old role as Billy in a new tour of *Sherlock Holmes*, starting on 31 October 1904. Sydney's part was filled, so he went back to sea, as assistant steward and bugler on the *Dover Castle* to Natal. He sailed from Southampton on 10 November, and did not return until 19 January 1905.[12] It was on this voyage that he discovered his gifts as a solo comedian. On 2 December he wrote home:

Union Castle Line
SS 'Dover Castle'
2nd Dec 04

Dear Mama,

I hope you received my last letter from Las Palmas. I have had a most enjoyable trip up till now. The weather has been splendid, not too hot, but just like an English summer. I am afraid I shall not make the money on these boats like I did on the Mail boats. I have done all right up till now. I had three passengers to Las Palmas. They gave me half sovereign between them, & when they had gone ashore, I had four more passengers

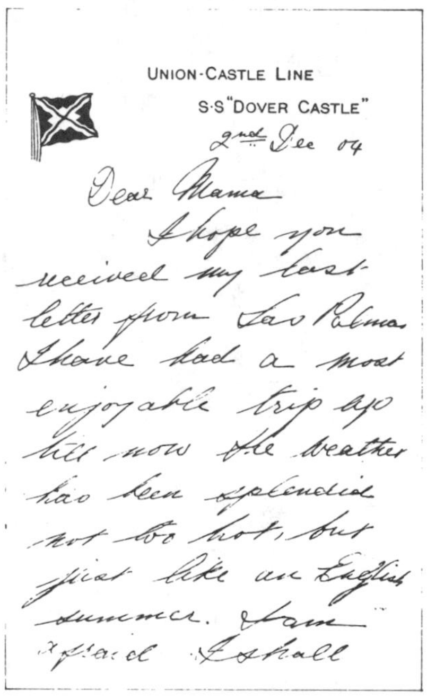

UNION-CASTLE LINE
S·S "DOVER CASTLE"
2nd Dec 04
Dear Mama
I hope you
received my last
letter from Las Palma
I have had a most
enjoyable trip up
till now the weather
has been splendid
not too hot, but
just like an English
summer. I am
afraid I shall

1904 - Letter from Sydney Chaplin to his mother, written while at sea on the Cape mail run.

3 to Cape Town & one to Natal. I think they will all give me half sovereign each. I had to march in front of the Fancy dress ball procession with the Bugle & play a march, & then a couple of days after the Scotchmen all dressed in kilts & I had to blow them round the deck, so

the sports committee have just called me into the smoking room & gave me 10/– not so bad is it? I have also made half a crown on the afternoon tea table, so altogether I can consider I have made £3 - 2 - 6. I have still got coast passengers to come yet besides my passengers home again so I may clear over £5. Thank God my health has been splendid & I do so hope your leg is better. Whatever you do take great care of yourself. I suppose the weather is getting very cold in London. I hope you will enjoy your Xmas. Try and get invited out somewhere. You don't want to be too much alone. How is little Charlie getting on? I hope he is in the best of health and taking great care of himself. Give him my love tell him so. I hope he will have an enjoyable Xmas & send him heaps of Kisses for me and heaps for yourself. You will be pleased to hear that I made a terrific success at the concert on board. I gave an impersonation of George Mozart* as the 'Dentist'. They simply roard and would not let me off the platform until I had sung them 'Two Eyes of Blue'. There is another concert on tonight and why [while] I am writing this they have sent down three people to ask me to oblige. They tell me the audience are shouting for the Bugler and the boy who has just got up to recite 'The Boy stood on the Burning Deck' has been hissed off. Fancy the quiet old Syd becoming a comedian. I have told them to tell the chairman I don't feel up to it tonight. The fact is I have undressed. I am lying on my bunk in my pyjamas. It is best to leave them wanting. My histrionic [word illegible] have become the talk of the boat the last two days. Give my love to Grandfather. I shall go & see him when I come home. Remember me to Miss Turnbull give her my Xmas Greetings. Best Love and Kisses to your own dear little self,

From your loving son,
Sydney

Charlie's new tour of *Sherlock Holmes* began at the end of October. At this time Frohman had three *Holmes* companies on the road, designated as 'Northern', 'Midland' and 'Southern'. Charlie was with the Midland Company, with Kenneth Rivington in the role of Holmes.

Chaplin was appearing in Hyde during the week of 6 March 1905 when news came of Hannah's relapse. Neighbours had taken her to Lambeth Infirmary on 6 March. Three days later Dr Marcus Quarry examined her and concluded that she was 'a Lunatic and a proper person to be taken charge of and detained under care and treatment . . . She is very strange in manner and quite incoherent. She dances

* George Mozart (1864–1947) was a popular English character comedian.

sings and cries by turns. She is indecent in conduct & conversation at times and again at times praying and saying she has been born again.'[13]

One week later a Justice of the Peace, Charles William Andrews, signed the necessary Lunatic Reception Order, and two days after

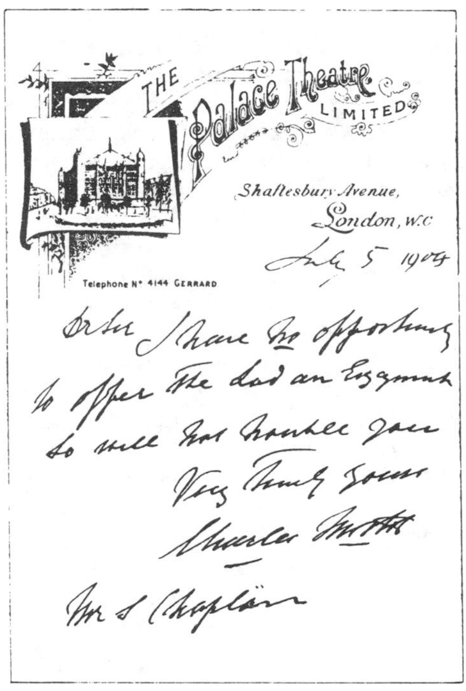

THE Palace Theatre LIMITED

Shaftesbury Avenue,
London, W.C.

Telephone Nº 4144 Gerrard

July 5 1904

Dear Sir I have no opportunity
to offer the lad an engagement
so will not trouble you

Very truly yours
Charles Morton

Mr S Chaplin

1904 – Letter from the great pioneer music hall manager Charles Morton in reply to Sydney's application for an audition for Charles.

that Hannah was returned to Cane Hill. She was never to recover. On the statement of her particulars she was described as a widow and a stage artist (the boys' success must have revived the old dreams) and her age was given as thirty-five – she was of course forty. Sydney must have been away from home, as the only name of a relative entered on the forms was that of her sister, Kate Hill, then living at

27 Montague Place, Russell Square. Charlie was unable to visit Hannah until the tour ended on 22 April.[14] The homecoming must have been bleak.

In Hannah's lucid moments she would write to her children, and it is not hard to imagine the pain that her pathetic pleas must have

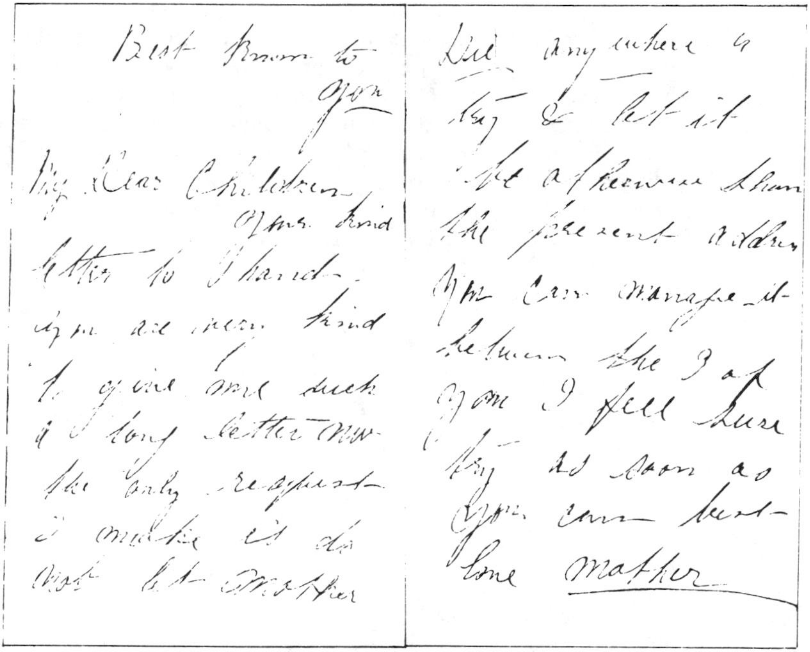

1905 – Letter from Hannah Chaplin to her sons written from the Cane Hill Lunatic Asylum. Instead of an address she writes, 'Best known to you'.

given them. In one letter, she could not even bring herself to write the name of the asylum.

This was evidently written soon after her arrival in Cane Hill. A few weeks later she seems more resigned, even jocular: the uncharacteristic mis-spelling of the address may itself be an Old Testament joke:

Cain Hill Asylum
Purley
Surrey.
3/7/05

My Dear Boys,

— for I presume you are both together by this time, altho Charlie has not written. Never mind, I expect you are both very busy, so I must forgive you. Oh, I do wish you had gone and seen about my ('Ta – yeithe') I mention this word as [illegible] know what I mean. *Do* see what you can do about *them*, as I am most uncomfortable without them, & if W.G.* should pay me a visit on this coming Monday, I am afraid he will not renew his offer of a few years back & I shall be 'on the shelf' for the rest of my life, now don't smile.

But joking apart you might have attended to small matter like that whilst you were in Town. Now I must draw to a close as it is Bedtime & broad daylight. Guess how I feel? Anyhow, good wishes & God Bless & prosper you both is always the Prayer of

your Loving Mother,
H. H. P. Chaplin.

Send me a few stamps and if possible *The Era*. Do not forget this, there's a dear.

Mum

Tons of Love & Kisses, for you both.

Hannah's request for *The Era* shows that she still liked to read about her old music hall acquaintances.

Charlie was out of work for fifteen weeks, but no doubt he had saved enough on his tours to support himself until August, when he was on the road again. The new tour was a distinct come-down. The touring rights of *Sherlock Holmes* had been taken over by Harry Yorke, lessee of the Theatre Royal, Blackburn, who had got together a pick-up company with one H. Lawrence Layton in the title role. Charlie was obliged to accept a reduced salary of thirty-five shillings a week, but had the consolation of being the seasoned pro of the troupe, laying down the law about the way things were done in the Frohman Company. He was aware that this precocity did not endear him to the rest of the cast.

* The significance of this reference is lost.

The tour opened in Blackburn at Mr Yorke's own theatre, then went on to Hull, Dewsbury, Huddersfield, Queen's at Manchester and the Rotunda at Liverpool. In the seventh week, when they were playing at the Court Theatre, Warrington, there came a miraculous reprieve in the form of a telegram from William Postance, stage manager to the celebrated American actor-manager William Gillette (1855–1937). Gillette was not only co-author, with Arthur Conan Doyle, of the dramatic version of *Sherlock Holmes*, but was also the greatest interpreter of the role. He had first played Holmes in New York at the Garrick Theatre on 6 November 1899, and scored a tremendous success with the play in London at Irving's Lyceum, in September 1901.

Gillette had just returned to London with a new comedy, *Clarice*, in which his leading lady was the exquisite Marie Doro, who had played opposite him in New York the year before in *The Admirable Crichton* and had made her mark in January 1905 with her London debut in *Friquet*. *Clarice* opened in London at the Duke of York's Theatre on 13 September 1905. It was not a success. The London critics not only disliked the play but they disapproved of Gillette's American accent. Gillette decided to reply with a joke, a little afterpiece to be called *The Painful Predicament of Sherlock Holmes*, 'a fantasy in about one-tenth of an act', in which he would appear, but not speak. The playlet had only three characters: Holmes, his page Billy and a mad woman. The idea was that despite the efforts of Billy to keep her away from Holmes, the mad lady bursts into his room and talks incessantly and incoherently for twenty minutes, defeating all his efforts to get a word in. Holmes, however, manages to ring the bell and slip a note to Billy. Shortly afterwards two attendants come in and carry the lady off, leaving the last line to Billy: 'You were right, sir – it was the right asylum.' The unfortunate mad lady, Gwendolen Cobb, was to be played by one of the most gifted young actresses on the London stage, Irene Vanbrugh, wife of Dion Boucicault. Gillette required a Billy, and the Frohman office, who ran the Duke of York's and were managing Gillette, had the very boy. Hence the telegram from Mr Postance.

After his last Saturday performance in Lancashire, Charlie hurried to London, and after a couple of days of rehearsals was a West End actor. *The Painful Predicament of Sherlock Holmes* went onto the programme on 3 October. Unfortunately Gillette's good-humoured little joke still failed to save the day, and the double bill ended its short run on 14 October, to be replaced after three days by a revival of the infallible *Sherlock Holmes*. Charlie, who had clearly made the same hit with Gillette as with everyone else with whom he worked, was kept on as Billy. Another veteran of the Frohman tours, Kenneth Rivington, who had played Watson to Saintsbury's Holmes and taken over the title role for the 1904–5 tour, was cast as Gillette's Watson. Marie Doro played Alice Faulkner for the first time; and the sixteen-year-old Chaplin fell desperately and agonizingly in love with this radiant young woman, seven years older than himself. The play repeated its original success: on 20 November there was a Royal Gala performance in honour of the King of Greece, who attended the show with Queen Alexandra, Prince Nicholas and Princess Victoria. Chaplin remembered that in a tense moment in the third act, when he and Gillette were alone on stage, the Prince was evidently explaining the plot to the King whose strongly accented voice boomed out in agitation, 'Don't tell me! Don't tell me!'

Saintsbury had taught the young Chaplin something of his stagecraft (one of his lessons, Chaplin recalled, was not to 'mug'* or move his head too much when he talked). Working with Gillette provided other valuable lessons. Gillette was highly intelligent and very successful. His father was a senator and he was himself educated at Harvard, the University of Boston and the Massachusetts Institute of Technology. Though his whole background was intellectual, he brought an aggressively populist approach to the theatre, both as actor and playwright. The dramatist, he said, should not study dramaturgy, but the public. He held that the drama should be derived from observation of life and not from concerns about correctness of grammar, diction and aesthetics. He reacted against current melodramatic, declamatory conventions of acting, adopting a casual, down-played style which suited light comedy rather better than love scenes. His guiding principle was that the actor must always strive to convince the audience that what he is doing he is doing for the first time. He set out this principle in an essay published in 1915, 'Illusion of First Time Acting'.

Someone in the company or the Frohman office at this time very clearly had Chaplin's interests at heart: it may have been Gillette himself, or Mr Hamilton or even William Postance, whom Chaplin remembered long afterwards with affection. (He was to call the kindly

* 'Mug. *v. slang . . . threat.* To "make a face"; to grimace' – Oxford English Dictionary.

impresario played by Nigel Bruce in *Limelight* Mr Postant: this seems to be intended as a tribute to Mr Postance, whose name is similarly misremembered as 'Postant' in the autobiography.) Two privileges which Chaplin enjoyed during the Duke of York's run of *Sherlock Holmes* were certainly exceptional for a small-part child actor in the West End. He was procured a seat at the funeral of Henry Irving, which took place two days after *Sherlock Holmes* opened.

GAUTIER'S
FAMOUS
COGNAC.

The Popular American Whisky
HUNTER
BALTIMORE
RYE.
Sold at the Bars of this Theatre.

H. L. SAVORY & Co.,
47, PICCADILLY, W.
Cigarette Manufacturers
By Special Appointment to
His Majesty King Edward VII.

TOM SMITH'S CRACKERS.

Fuller's
209, REGENT ST., W.
AMERICAN CONFECTIONERY.
Table d'Hote Luncheons.
Afternoon Teas.

Duke of York's Theatre

ST MARTIN'S LANE WC

Proprietors ... Mr & Mrs Frank Wyatt

Sole Lessee and Manager ... CHARLES FROHMAN

CHARLES FROHMAN PRESENTS
A DRAMA IN FOUR ACTS
BY A. CONAN DOYLE
AND WILLIAM GILLETTE
ENTITLED

SHERLOCK HOLMES

BEING A HITHERTO UNPUBLISHED EPISODE
IN THE CAREER OF THE GREAT DETECTIVE
AND SHOWING HIS CONNECTION WITH THE

STRANGE CASE OF MISS FAULKNER

CHARACTERS IN THE PLAY	COMPANY APPEARING IN THE CAST
SHERLOCK HOLMES	WILLIAM GILLETTE
DOCTOR WATSON	KENNETH RIVINGTON
JOHN FORMAN	EUGENE MAYEUR
SIR EDWARD LEIGHTON	REGINALD DANCE
COUNT VON STAHLBURG	FREDERICK MORRIS
PROFESSOR MORIARTY	GEORGE SUMNER
JAMES LARRABEE	FRANCIS CARLYLE
SIDNEY PRINCE	QUINTON McPHERSON
ALFRED BASSICK	WILLIAM H. DAY
JIM CRAIGIN	CHRIS WALKER
THOMAS LEARY	HENRY WALTERS
"LIGHTFOOT" MCTAGUE	WALTER DISON
JOHN	THOMAS QUINTON
PARSONS	G. MERTON
BILLY	CHARLES CHAPLIN
ALICE FAULKNER	MARIE DORO
MRS. FAULKNER	DE OLIA WEBSTER
MADGE LARRABEE	ADELAIDE PRINCE
THERESE	SYBIL CAMPBELL
MRS. SMEEDLEY	ETHEL LORRIMORE

THE PLACE IS LONDON
THE TIME TEN YEARS AGO

FIRST ACT–DRAWING ROOM AT THE LARRABEES'–EVENING

SECOND ACT–Scene I–PROFESSOR MORIARTY'S UNDERGROUND OFFICE–MORNING

Scene II–SHERLOCK HOLMES' APARTMENTS IN BAKER STREET–EVENING

THIRD ACT–THE STEPNEY GAS CHAMBER–MIDNIGHT

FOURTH ACT–DOCTOR WATSON'S CONSULTING ROOM KENSINGTON–THE FOLLOWING EVENING

Scenery by Ernest Gros   Incidental Music by William Furst

INTERMISSIONS

MATINEE every Saturday at 2.15 o'clock

BUSINESS MANAGER–JAMES W MATHEWS   ACTING MANAGER ROBERT M EBERLE
STAGE MANAGER–WILLIAM POSTANCE   MUSICAL DIRECTOR–JOHN CROOK

Hooper, Struve & Co's
Royal German Spa
Table Waters.
LONDON & BRIGHTON

MACKIE'S
WHITE HORSE
SCOTCH WHISKY
10 YEARS OLD
Obtainable at all the bars of this Theatre. Est'd 1742

MACMINN'S
"CLUBLAND"
Highland Liqueur Whisky
MACMINN RICHARDSON & Co.

The Cream of Cocoa.
EPPS'S
Contains all the nutriment
COCOA
of the Choicest Nibs.

SUPPORT HOME INDUSTRIES.
BRYANT & MAY'S
MATCHES.

1905 - Programme for *Sherlock Holmes*
at the Duke of York's Theatre.

The funeral took place on October 19th, and a vast concourse assembled outside Westminster Abbey from an early hour, the signs of public mourning being as general as they were sincere and deep-seated. The Abbey itself was filled with a great and distinguished assemblage, including representatives of the King and Queen, eminent statesmen, and men and women renowned in art, literature and science, as well as in the profession of which Sir Henry Irving had long been the acknowledged head. The ceremony itself, with all the aids of a superb musical service, was profoundly impressive, and was conducted by the Dean and Canon

> Duckworth. The pall-bearers, who were assembled with the chief mourners round the coffin, included Sir Squire Bancroft, Lord Aberdeen, Sir A. C. Mackenzie, Sir George Alexander, Mr Beerbohm Tree, Sir L. Alma-Tadema, Professor Sir James Dewar, Mr J. Forbes-Robertson, Mr A. W. Pinero and Mr Burdett-Coutts, MP.[15]

And so among the great and distinguished sat sixteen-year-old Charles Chaplin, who within a decade would have won far greater fame even than the departed actor-knight. He was seated, he recalled, between another celebrated actor-manager, Lewis Waller, and 'Dr' Walford Bodie, the current sensation of the music halls as hypnotist, healer and miracle worker. Chaplin was shocked by Dr Bodie's unseemly behaviour, 'stepping on the chest of a supine duke' to get a better view as the ashes were lowered into the crypt.

A more remarkable achievement was that Chaplin managed to secure an entry in the first edition of *The Green Room Book, or Who's Who on the Stage*. This was the forerunner of *Who's Who in the Theatre*, but contained many fewer entries and so was more selective and prestigious. Hence it is remarkable to find listed among the aristocracy of the Edwardian stage:

> CHAPLIN, Charles, impersonator, mimic and sand dancer; b. London, April 16th 1889; *s.* of Charles Chaplin; brother of Sidney Chaplin; cradled in the profession, made first appearance at the Oxford as a speciality turn, when ten years of age; has fulfilled engagements with several of Charles Frohman's companies (playing Billy in 'Sherlock Holmes', &c.), and at many of the leading variety theatres in London and provinces; won 20-miles walking championship (and £25 cash prize) at Nottingham. *Address:* c/o Ballard Macdonald, 1, Clifford's Inn, E.C.

There are other mysteries about this brief biography, apart fom how Chaplin managed to make his way into *The Green Room Book* at all. The 'impersonator, mimic and sand dancer' presumably refers to talents acquired with the Eight Lancashire Lads; but does his 'first appearance' really mean his 'first London appearance', since he seems to have been with the lads for at least three months before their seven-week season at the Oxford in April–May 1899 when Chaplin did, indeed, pass his tenth birthday. This, too, is the only known reference to the very substantial prize allegedly won in Nottingham, where Chaplin's sole recorded appearance was in the week of 17 July 1899, again with the Lancashire Lads.

Sherlock Holmes might have settled in for a long run at the Duke of York's, but that the theatre was booked for the first revival of Sir James Barrie's *Peter Pan*, with Cissie Loftus this year in the leading role. In the 1950s Chaplin finally squashed the long-standing legend that he played a wolf in this second production of the popular Christmas entertainment after *Sherlock Holmes* closed on 2 December. Instead, on 1 January he was on the road again with Harry Yorke's touring *Holmes* company.

This was to be Chaplin's farewell to the play after more than two and a half years. The tour opened at the Grand Theatre, Doncaster, then played Cambridge and four weeks around London – at the Pavilion, East, where Chaplin had played Billy for the first time, the Dalston Theatre, the Carlton, Greenwich and the Crown, Peckham. After a further week at Crewe and a week at Rochdale, the tour ended. Chaplin placed a 'card' in *The Stage*:

Master Charles Chaplin
SHERLOCK HOLMES CO.
Disengaged March 5th
Coms. 9 Tavistock Place, Tele., 2 187 Hop.

Chaplin might have continued in the legitimate theatre but for a display of pride in the foyer of the St James's Theatre, just before the end of the London run of *Sherlock Holmes*. Irene Vanbrugh's husband Dion Boucicault gave him a letter of introduction to Mr and Mrs Kendal, who needed a boy actor for their 1906 tour of *A Tight Corner*. Madge Kendal swept in imperious and late, and asked him to come back the next day at the same time, whereupon young Chaplin coolly retorted that he could not accept anything out of town and swept out, dignified but unemployed.

Fortunately Sydney was able to find him a job. Intoxicated by his success at ships' smoking concerts, Sydney had decided that his future lay in the music halls, and joined the Charles Manon sketch company as a comedian. In March 1906 he joined a new company set up under the management of one Fred Regina to tour a sketch, *Repairs*, written by the popular author and playwright, Wal Pink. It was advertised as 'A New Departure – A Novel Item. WAL PINK'S WORKMEN IN *REPAIRS*. A brilliant example of "How NOT to do it".' The setting represented 'The interior of Muddleton Villa, in the hands of those eminent house decorators, Messrs Spoiler and Messit.' The idea of a gang of inefficient painters, paperhangers and plumbers was to be affectionately recalled in the slapstick paperhanger sketch in *A King in New York*. The plot, with Sydney as a heavily moustachioed and beery agitator endeavouring to get the slow-witted workmen to strike, looked forward to several two-reeler plots including *Dough and Dynamite* and *Behind the Screen*.

Sydney secured the part of plumber's mate for his brother. He wore a green tam o'shanter which was an object of unreasonable irritation to the plumber. When instructed by the latter to hang it up, Charlie would knock a nail into a water pipe and soak himself. In exasperation, the plumber would seize the offending headgear, throw it to the ground and trample it in fury. Sydney told the journalist R. J. Minney that the sketch went well until they reached Ireland, where there was fury at the trampling of a green tam o'shanter. For subsequent performances a hat of different hue was substituted. A rare photograph of the sketch exists, which seems to show the plumber in the act of seizing a hat from Charlie. The seventeen-year-old Charlie himself stands with a red nose, clown-like make-up, short trousers, a hammer in his hand and a look of blank idiocy on his face.

Repairs opened at the Hippodrome, Southampton, on 19 March. It was extravagantly advertised with a full column in *The Era*, predicting a brilliant future for the act with a tour that would continue at The Duchess, Balham, the Zoo Hippodrome, Glasgow, and subsequently Boscombe, Belfast, Manchester, Wolverhampton, Liverpool, Portsmouth etc. In fact the show seems not to have lived up to expectations. Not all of these engagements can be traced and the advertisement was never repeated. After the week of 7 May, when *Repairs* was playing at the Grand Palace, Clapham, Chaplin left the troupe and his act was taken over by another youth, Horace Kenney (1890–1955), who was subsequently to become a music hall star in his own right.

Chaplin had answered an advertisement in *The Era* announcing that boy comedians were required for *Casey's Court Circus, or the Caseydrome* which was shortly to be produced. It was a follow-up to a show, *Casey's Court*, that had already proved successful. The setting for this was an alley, and the central figure, around whom a dozen or so juvenile comedians clowned, was 'Mrs Casey' – played in pantomime style by the comedian Will Murray (1877–1955), who continued to tour with the act until he was well into his seventies. Harry Cadle, the creator and impresario of the troupe, encouraged by the success of the original turn, had now decided to establish and tour a second company with Will Murray again as leading artist and general director. *Casey's Court Circus* was described as 'a street urchin's idea of producing circus'.

11		
	Ferndale	
	Mrs Mason 38 Rhondda Ter	
	Garstone	
	Mrs Lewstone 1 Beaconsfield Terrace	
	" Whitehead 1 Hastings Terrace	3 V.G. 14/-
	Gt Grimsby	
V.G.	Mrs Pearson 31 Newmarket St	G.
	Glasgow	
(com)	Mrs Chatham 12 Rutherglen Rd	
Excellent	Mrs Welby 166 Main St	
18/- for 3	Combined room 10/- for 1 12/- for 2	
	Gravesend	
	Mrs Strickland 36 Wakefield St	V.G.
V.G.	" Mountain 18 Cowcaddens	

c1906 - Page from Sydney's directory of good cheap theatrical lodgings. The invaluable information was shared by both brothers.

Chaplin appeared with *Casey's Court Circus* in its opening week at the Olympia Theatre, Liverpool, from 21 to 26 May 1906. There is a story, without documentary corroboration, that he did a tryout with the original *Casey's Court* at the Bradford Empire the previous week. There is, too, some uncertainty about the terms of his contract. In October 1927 the magazine *Picturegoer* claimed,

> There is an interesting document still in existence dated May 26th 1906 which is the first legal document Charlie ever had. It is signed by his brother Sydney, as his guardian. In it he agrees to accept 45/= per week and his travelling expenses for his assistance in 'anything connected with the performance of "Casey's Court" that may be a reasonable request'.

A recent Chaplin biographer (Denis Gifford: *Chaplin*) quotes another circumstantial version of this alleged contract, without providing a source:

> I, the guardian of Charles Chaplin, agree for him to appear in *Casey's Court* wherever it may be booked in the British Isles only, the agreement to commence May 14th, 1906, at a salary weekly of £2. 5. 0. (two pounds five shillings) increasing to £2. 10. 0. the week commencing July 1906.

Will Murray, for his part, reminisced fifteen years later:

> I first met Charlie when I was running the sketch 'Casey's Court (Circus)'. These sketches, which were pure burlesque, met with a great measure of success throughout the country,
>
> To carry out a second edition of the sketch, I found it necessary to advertise for a number of boys between fourteen and nineteen years of age.
>
> Amongst the applicants was one little lad who took my fancy at once. I asked him his name and what theatrical experience he had had.
>
> 'Charlie Chaplin, sir,' was the reply. 'I've been one of the Eight Lancashire Lads, and just now [*sic*] I've got a part in the sketch [*sic*] 'Sherlock Holmes'.
>
> I put him through his paces. He sang, danced, and did a little of practically everything in the entertaining line. He had the makings of a 'star' in him, and I promptly took him on salary, 30s per week.[16]

Chaplin, whose memory for sums of money seemed infallible, remembered his salary as £3 a week. He also remembered that he was the star of the show and though the individual boys' names were not billed, this seems to be confirmed by his placing, seated beside Mr Murray, in a group photograph of the troupe in 1906. Certainly he was given the two plum turns in the Circus. The act included a number of burlesques of current music hall favourites. 'I particularly wanted a good thing made of Dr Bodie,' remembered Murray. 'Chaplin seemed the likeliest of the lot for the part and he got it.'

'Dr' Walford Bodie, whose indecorous curiosity had shocked Chaplin at the funeral of Sir Henry Irving, was at the peak of his celebrity. He was born plain Sam Brodie in Aberdeen in 1870, was apprenticed as an electrician with the National Telephone Company, but soon took to the variety stage as a conjuror and ventriloquist. By the time of his London debut, in 1903, at the Britannia, Hoxton, he had developed a new and original act, billed as 'The most remarkable man on Earth, the great healer, the modern miracle worker, demonstrating nightly "Hypnotism, Bodie force and the wonders of bloodless surgery".' He claimed among other benefits to mankind to have cured nine hundred cases of paralysis judged incurable by the medical profession. Those who revered him as a miracle man and those who regarded him as a fake, alike acknowledged he was a great showman. He was a handsome man with a fine head of hair, an upswung waxed moustache and penetrating eyes. He appeared in a frock coat of exquisite cut and a gleaming silk hat. Chaplin studied his make-up from the photograph in Bodie's advertisement in *The Era*, and had a studio portrait taken of himself adopting the identical pose. 'Rehearsals were numerous,' remembered Will Murray,

> and Charlie always showed a keen desire to learn. He had never seen Bodie's turn, but I endeavoured to give him an idea of the Doctor's little mannerisms.
>
> For hours he would practise these in front of a mirror. He would walk for long spells backwards and forwards cultivating the Bodie manner.
>
> Then he would ring the changes with a characteristic twist to the Bodie moustache, the long flowing adornment which the 'Electric Spark' affected, not the now world-famous tooth-brush variety . . .[17]

Dan Lipton, a writer of comic songs who befriended the young Chaplin confirmed that Chaplin had never seen Bodie in performance: 'The way that boy burlesqued Dr Bodie was wonderful. I tell you he had never *seen* the man. He just put on an old dress suit and bowler hat, and as he marched onto the stage he swelled with pride.'[18]

When the act came south to the Richmond Theatre, *The Era* commented that 'the fun reaches its height when a burlesque imitation of "lightning cures on a poor working man" is given'. Six weeks later, when the *Casey's Court Circus* company played at the Stratford Empire, *The Era* noted that 'an extravagant skit on Dick Turpin's ride to York concludes the turn'. Chaplin was the star of this number also. Will Murray recalled:

> . . . he 'got' the audience right away with 'Dr Bodie'.
>
> Then came 'Dick Turpin', that old invincible evergreen standby of the circus. It all went well, but the climax was the flight after the death of 'Bonnie Black Bess'.
>
> You can imagine the position of poor Mr Turpin. He had to run, hide, do anything to get out of the way of the runners, and yet he had nowhere to go except round the circus track.
>
> Nevertheless, Charlie started to run – and run – and run. He had to turn innumerable corners, and as he raised one foot and hopped along a

> little way on the other in getting round a nasty 'bend' the audience simply howled.
>
> I think I can justly say that I am the man who taught Charlie to turn corners. Yes, that peculiar run, and still more weird one-leg turnings of corners, which seems so simple when you see it carried out in the pictures, is the very same manoeuvre that I taught Chaplin to go through in the burlesque of Dick Turpin. It took many, many weary hours of monotonous rehearsals, but I am sure Charlie Chaplin, in looking back over those hours of rehearsals, will thank me for being so persistent in my instructions as to how I wanted the thing done.[19]

The *Casey's Court Circus* tour ended on 20 July 1907, and Chaplin left the company. Young though he looked, he was probably considered already too old for a further season with a juvenile troupe. He was to remain three months without a job. Sydney however was now in regular work. After leaving *Repairs* he had signed a contract with Fred Karno's Silent Comedians. In July 1907, by this time a major Karno star, he signed a new contract for a second year at £4 per week. No doubt, as he had done before, he helped his younger brother over a lean period.

In this period between jobs, Charles lodged with a family in Kennington Road, and on his own admission lived a solitary, harum-scarum, boyishly dissolute life. He decided to work up a solo act as a Jewish comedian. Towards the end of the *Casey's Court Circus* tour, in June 1907, he had played the Foresters' Music Hall in Cambridge Road (formerly Dog Row), Bethnal Green. The management remembered his success as Dr Bodie and Dick Turpin, and agreed to let him do a week's unpaid try-out. His material – he later realized that it was not only poor but anti-Semitic – make-up and accent were not well calculated for the predominantly Jewish audience of the neighbourhood. The first – and only – night was a disaster, and Charles fled from the theatre and the catcalls and pelted orange peel. This nightmare experience undoubtedly helped to instill in him an eventual dislike of working before a live audience. He was to have triumphant successes with the Karno Company, but it was evidently a tremendous relief when he was finally able to abandon the live theatre. Nothing would ever again persuade him to perform in front of an audience. In 1915 he told the actor Fred Goodwins, who was then working with him at the Essanay Studios: 'Back to the stage! I'll never go back to the stage again as long as I live. No. Unless my money leaves me, not ten thousand dollars would tempt me back behind the footlights again.'[20] Very soon he was to be offered much larger sums than $10,000 but his decision was still unshakeable. More than fifty years later he told Richard Meryman: 'On the stage I was a very good comedian in a way. In shows and things like that. [But] I hadn't got that come-hither business that a comedian should have. Talk to an audience – I could never do that. I was too much of an artist for that. My artistry is a bit austere – it is austere.'[21]

Many great artists whose work depended upon the precision of a highly polished technique shared this mistrust of the unpredictable element offered by the audience. In the 1950s the great music hall artist Hetty King, after almost sixty years' stage experience, disliked following the still rumbustious Ida Barr in the veterans' programme in which they were appearing: 'I hate to follow that old woman. She gets the audience so unruly. I'm always terrified they will shout to me, talk to me. It throws me.' Max Miller, too, could be thrown off balance when audience reaction was not entirely predictable. It is possible that Chaplin had also inherited anxieties about audience reaction from his mother; fear of the public is a possible explanation of the lack of success of her career, despite her evident talents.

Not entirely daunted by the Foresters' fiasco, however, he wrote a comedy sketch *The Twelve Just Men*, the title probably suggested by his friend Mr Saintsbury's adaptation of *The Four Just Men*. The twelve men of Chaplin's plot, however, were the jury deliberating a breach of promise case. Their discussions were complicated by the presence in their number of a deaf-mute, a drunk, and other unlikely personages. Chaplin sold the sketch for £3 and was hired to direct it, but the backer pulled out after two or three days. Sydney had to break the bad news to the cast for him; in later years, when he was in command of his own studios, Chaplin could never bring himself to deliver bad tidings, like sackings and reprimands, in person, but always did it through intermediaries.

The Twelve Just Men was to come back and haunt him a quarter of a century later. Either Chaplin or his backer, a stage hypnotist called Charcoate, had subsequently managed to sell the sketch to the comedian Ernie Lotinga (one of the Six Brothers Luck and the first husband of Hetty King) for £5. Lotinga forgot about it until he came upon the manuscript again in 1932, and announced that he would produce this sketch written by Charlie Chaplin. Chaplin was distressed at the prospect and offered to buy back the rights for $5000. Lotinga, reckoning he was on to a good thing, refused, whereupon the offer was raised to $7500. Lotinga still refused but proposed that he and Chaplin should go into partnership in the production, and that Chaplin should play the drunk. When this proposal aroused no enthusiasm, Lotinga announced that he would produce the sketch in the form of a musical revue and play the leading role himself. No more was heard of it.

3

With the Guv'nor

The comedy sketch was a staple of the music halls in the early years of the century. Harry Tate's *Motoring*, *Golfing*, *Flying*, *Billiards* and *Fishing*; Will Evans' *Building a Chicken House*, *Harnessing a Horse*, *Papering the Parlour*; Joe Boganny's *Lunatic Bakers*, Charlie Baldwin's *Bank Clerks,* the Six Brothers' *Luck*, the Boisset and Manon troupes were only the more celebrated acts of the kind. Fred Karno's Speechless Comedians, though, were supreme of their kind. They were the conjuncture and end of several traditions of English pantomime. There was, first, the clowning of the pantomime proper, that singular British theatrical institution. Chaplin recalled in 1917:

> Christmas in London in the old days, when it was hard scratching for me to get sixpence so that I might see the Christmas pantomime spectacle at Drury Lane, *Jack and the Beanstalk*, *Puss in Boots* or *Cinderella.* I used to watch the clowns in the pantomimes breathlessly. They were clever fellows. There were Montgomery, Laffin, Feefe, Brough, Cameron – all high-class performers. Every move they made registered on my young brain like a photograph. I used to try it all over when I got home. But what I think of now is the rapt attention with which six or seven thousand boys and girls would watch the clowns work.* It was slapstick stuff. Everybody used to say that sort of thing would be dead in another ten years. What has happened is that pantomime, through motion picture developments, has taken the lead in the world's entertainment. My early

* Chaplin may not have been accurately reported. Drury Lane in the years when he could have known it had a capacity of three thousand: even for the famous children's matinées, twice that number could hardly have been squeezed in. The names he quotes, also, are not familiar from Drury Lane programmes of the period.

> study of the clowns in the London pantomimes has been of tremendous value to me. What I learned from them has been supplemented by original research.[1]

Pantomime, in the more general sense, was stimulated by the licensing laws of the eighteenth century which forbade dialogue except on the stages of the two Theatres Royal. Hence the unlicensed theatres developed styles of wordless spectacle, with music and mime to explain the plot. These entertainments became so popular at Sadler's Wells and the Royal Circus, that the Theatres Royal in Covent Garden and Drury Lane were obliged to adopt the genre themselves for afterpieces. In the music halls, the prohibition of dialogue lingered much longer, and so in consequence did the mime sketches. Perhaps the finest pantomimist of the later nineteenth century was Paul Martinetti (1851–1924), born to French parents in the United States. Making his first appearance on the British music hall stage in the late 1870s, he formed a pantomime troupe with his brother Alfred, performing highly melodramatic sketches like *Robert Macaire*, *A Duel in the Snow*, *After the Ball*, *A Terrible Night*, *Remorse* and *The Village Schoolmaster* right up to the time of the First World War.

The circus also made its contribution with a genre of spectacles which combined acrobatics, scenic effects, narrative and comedy. Out of this tradition developed troupes like the Ravels and the Hanlon-Lees. The Hanlon-Lees, who toured in Britain, France and the United States from the 1860s to the 1880s, consisted of the six Hanlon Brothers and a celebrated acrobat, 'Professor' John Lees. The description of their entertainment *Voyage en Suisse* at the Gaiety Theatre, London, in March 1880 sounds like the prototype for Karno or Keystone chaos: 'It included a bus smash, a chaotic scene on board a ship in a storm, an exploding Pullman car, a banquet transformed into a wholesale juggling party after one of the Hanlons had crashed through the ceiling on to the table, and one of the cleverest drunk scenes ever presented on the stage.'[2]

Fred Karno was heir to all these traditions; in turn he contributed his own gifts for organization, for invention, for spotting and training talent, for *mise-en-scène* and direction. Like most of the great figures of the English music hall, his origins were humble. He was born in Exeter on 26 March 1866. His father was a cabinet maker called Westcott, who moved around the country a good deal during the boyhood of Frederick, his eldest son. Eventually the family settled in

Photograph, c.1870, believed to be Spencer Chaplin, grandfather of Charles and Sydney Chaplin.

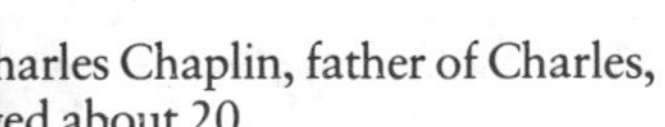

harles Chaplin, father of Charles, ged about 20.

Hannah Chaplin, mother of Charles and Sydney, c.1885.

Illustrated cover for Charles Chaplin Senior's song, "Pals That Time Cannot Alter!" c. 1892.

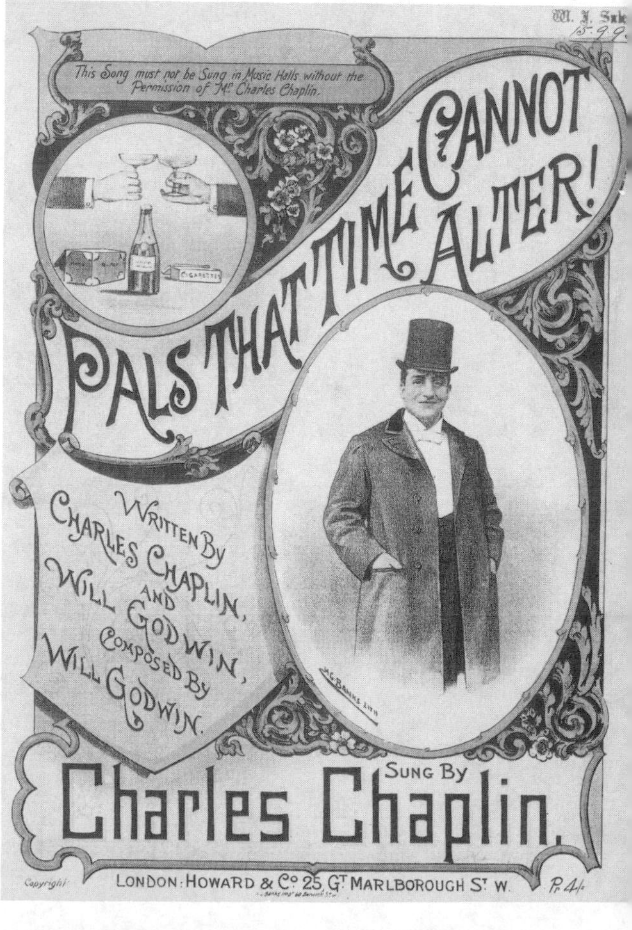

Leo Dryden's 'card' in *The Era*, 1902.

Cuckoo Schools, Hanwell.

Charles Chaplin at the time he was touring with the Eight Lancashire Lads.

Left: Charles Chaplin at the Hanwell Schools, 1897.

Right: Chaplin as Sammy the Newsboy in *Jim, A Romance of Cockayne,* 1903.

Chaplin as Billy the Page in *Sherlock Holmes*, 1903.

aplin's two Sherlock Holmes –
lliam Gillette (left) and
A.Saintsbury (below).

Sydney, aged 18, c.1903.

Below left: Chaplin in *Repairs*, 1906, with hammer and offensiv tam-o'-shanter.

Casey's Court Circus, 1906. Chaplin (in bowler) at Will Murray's left. Others in the group are Hal Jones (back row, third from left), George Doonan (back row, extreme right), Tom Brown (? left of centre row), Eddie Emerson (next to Murray), Herbert Kirk (next to Chaplin), Fred Hawes, Hal Cheryl and Billy Leonard.

The real Dr Walford Bodie, from an advertisement in *The Era*.

Chaplin's impersonation of Dr Walford Bodie, 1906, clearly based on the *Era* advertisement.

Fred Karno in his office.

Workers leaving the Karno Fun Factory, 1905.

Chaplin, c.1909.

Sydney as Archibald in *Skating* with his wife, Minnie.

Chaplin as Archibald in *Skating*.

Chaplin as The Inebriate, c.1910.

CAR

Left: The Karno troupe en route for America, 1910, photographed aboard the *SS Cairnrona* by Alf Reeves. Chaplin is framed in life belt; the others in the group are, back row, left to right, Albert Austin, Bert Williams, Fred Palmer, unknown, Frank Melrose; front row, left to right, Stan Laurel, Fred Karno Jr, Mickey Palmer, (Chaplin), Arthur Dando (behind), Mike Asher, Amy Reeves

Below left: On tour in USA Chaplin is at right in right-hand train window. A note on the back says 'Charlie at $75 a week.'

Below: On tour with the Karno troupe. About to leave Solano railway depot, Philadelphia.

Chaplin in front of Karno poster, Spokane.

On tour with the Karno troupe: with an Indian pedlar.

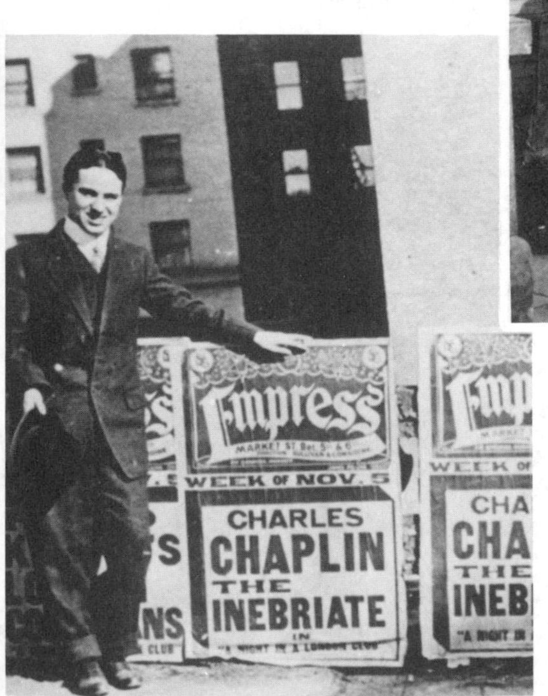

Chaplin with posters at Exeter (California) railway depot.

Nottingham where Fred started work in a lace factory when he was about fourteen, attending school in the afternoons. He moved on to work as a barber's boy, a costermonger, a bricklayer and a chemist's shop boy. Eventually he was apprenticed to a plumber. When this work took him to a gymnasium he was intrigued by the place, enrolled, and was soon a good enough gymnast to make his stage debut in an amateur competition at the Alhambra Theatre, Nottingham. Very soon he was partnering a professional gymnast, as the second half of Olvene and Leonardo. After a spell as a solo gymnast in north-country fairground shows, he toured for a year with Harry Manley's Circus. As luck would have it, Manley's was one of the last circuses still presenting pantomime sketches. Its repertory included *Dick Turpin*, *Mazeppa*, *The Bear and Sentinel*, *Love in a Tub*, *The Statue Blanche*, *Gregory's Blunder*, *The Prince and the Tinker*, *Black and White, or Tea for Two*, *The Wig Makers*, *Swiss Lovers*, *Where's Your Ticket?* and *The Copper Ballet*. Karno seems to have played in a good many of these.

Karno had varied fortunes in fairgrounds and music halls with different partners, and was obliged for a while to abandon show business and earn his living as a glazier (he claimed to have employed a boy to go ahead breaking windows – an idea which would reappear in Chaplin's film *The Kid*). In 1888 he put together an impromptu act with two other acrobats, Bob Sewell and Ted Tysall, to substitute for an act that had failed to turn up for their booking at the Metropolitan, Edgware Road. Shamelessly, they adopted the name of the absent act, The Three Carnos, but soon afterward adopted the spelling Karno, as more stylish (in 1914 Karno changed his name officially, by deed poll). The Karnos were a modest success, and Karno augmented his earnings with a solo act in which he demonstrated the Edison phonograph – still a comparative novelty – which he impertinently renamed the Karnophone. Always brash and energetic, he earned money by busking in the streets in the weeks when the act had no booking.

The Three Karnos presented their first sketch about 1894. Again it was an impromptu, to fill in for the pugilist Jem Mace in Portsmouth. The sketch was one of the old Manley's Circus standbys, *Love in a Tub*, but it was successful enough to give Karno the idea of creating original sketches and a company to play them. In 1895 he presented *Hilarity* at the Gaiety, Birmingham. It was to tour continuously for five years and to provide the prototype for the long succession of Karno pantomime comedies. In 1901 he presented *Jail Birds* at the Paragon, Mile End Road, and pulled off the first of the extravagant publicity stunts for which he was to become famous by carrying the company around in a Black Maria, which he even took to the Derby. *Early Birds* was a 'tale of slumland', in which Karno himself played a glazier. In *The New Woman's Club* which satirized the early feminist movement, he played a lady cyclist: it was his last stage appearance. His early productions were generally launched at the Paragon, Mile End Road. Subsequently the sketches were premièred as annual Christmas attractions at the Palace, Manchester, among them *His Majesty's Guests, Saturday to Monday*, *The Football Match* and *Skating*. A contemporary advertisement for *The Football Match* announces:

Grand Christmas Production

Of FRED KARNO'S latest Burlesque

"THE FOOTBALL MATCH."

Over 100 Auxiliaries. Catchy Music.

Clever Comedians. Wonderful Scenery.

Realistic Football Match—in the rain—with real Football Champions contesting, and the usual High-class Variety Entertainment.

Special Matinees Xmas Week—See future announcements.

TWICE NIGHTLY.

The *Pantomime Annual* described it as 'an entertainment that shall be unique in the history of amusements', vividly depicting 'the desperate struggle for supremacy between the Middleton Pie-Cans and the Midnight Wanderers'. *The Football Match* was characteristic of the elaborate scenic effects in which Karno specialized. The settings included a huge panoramic cloth with a great crowd of people painted on it. The painted figures had loose arms and hats which were activated by electric fans hidden behind a raked ground row. In front of these were supers, with very small people arranged behind larger ones, to produce an effect of perspective. In *The Wontdetainia*, presented at the Paragon, Mile End Road on 11 April 1910, and satirizing public enthusiasm for the great new luxury liners like the recently launched *Lusitania* and *Mauretania,* the effects were even more elaborate, with a practicable liner so huge that when it was made to move across the stage it was built up section by section in the wings. For *Mumming Birds*, which was to be closely linked to the fate and future of Charles Chaplin, a stage was built within the theatre stage, complete with boxes, proscenium and tabs. *Mumming Birds* grew out of a quickly concocted entertainment devised for a charity performance called *Entertaining the Shah* at the London Pavilion in 1904. It was extended and developed, and presented at the Star, Bermondsey, as *Twice Nightly, or a Stage upon a Stage*. In its second week at the Canterbury, it was finally renamed *Mumming Birds*.

Karno's publicity methods were as colourful, unconventional and ambitious as his sketches. He had his companies travel about in a bizarre collection of vehicles boldly painted with the words 'Karno's Speechless Comedians'. His own car was similarly inscribed in large letters and odious hues – to the grave embarrassment of his young son on parents' days at his smart boarding school. On the death of the Duke of Cambridge, Karno bought his state coaches; and there was some official embarrassment when the Karno comics galloped around London in them with the royal arms blazoned. Other Karno publicity methods included bands, balloons, advertising leaflets bearing testimonials wrung from audiences, and stunts like fake police chases through the towns in which the companies appeared.

Among Karno's first stars was Fred Kitchen, who had played Harlequin in the Drury Lane pantomime of 1896, *Aladdin*, which starred Dan Leno and Herbert Campbell. He was famous for his catch-line from Karno's *The Bailiffs:* 'Meredith – we're in!' Billie Reeves, who created the role of the drunk in *Mumming Birds* which Chaplin was later to take over and make famous, was the brother of Alfred Reeves, who managed Karno companies for many years before becoming general manager of the Chaplin film studios. Reeves had joined Karno in 1900, and since 1905 had spent a large part of his time in the United States. At the time that Sydney Chaplin joined him, in 1906, Karno had as many as ten companies regularly on tour. They were managed and serviced from Karno's 'Fun Factory', established in three houses at 26, 28a and 28 Vaughan Road, Coldharbour Lane, Camberwell. In 1906 Karno advertised a

> Magnificent NEW WING just added to the above, comprising a Paint Room, Rehearsal Room and Storage Dock . . . The new Paint Room is furnished with Two Frames capable of carrying any Cloths. The new Rehearsal Room, splendidly lighted, ventilated, and heated, is 72 feet long, 21 feet wide, and owing to the exceptional height (28 feet 6 inches) can be used as a Practice Room for any Gymnastic or Aerial Acts. The huge Storage Dock, thoroughly ventilated and dry, covers an area of 316 square yards, and has a cubic space of 32,648 feet.

Sydney's first contract with Karno was dated 9 July 1906. He was engaged as a 'pantomimist' at £3 a week, with a provision that he should be paid £6 a week if called upon to tour in the United States. He clearly made a rapid impression, because less than three months later he was selected for one of the two companies sent to America for Karno's second season there. Sydney played the drunk in *Mumming Birds* in a company managed by Arthur Forest; Billie Reeves was the star of the other company, playing *Early Birds*, under the management of Alf Reeves. Sydney was back in time for Christmas, to play in *The Football Match* in Manchester. The star role of Stiffy the Goalkeeper was played by Harry Weldon, a slow-talking Lancashire comedian. On 17 July 1907, when Charlie's tour with *Casey's Court Circus* was coming to an end, Sydney appeared in a brand new sketch, *London Suburbia*, at the Canterbury.

Sydney tried hard to persuade Karno to give Charlie, now unemployed, a job; but Karno showed no interest. In February 1908 he relented so far as to give Charlie a two-week trial with the chance of a contract if he proved satisfactory. He thought him, however, 'a pale, puny, sullen-looking youngster. I must say that when I first saw him, I thought he looked much too shy to do any good in the theatre, particularly in the knockabout comedies that were my speciality.' The try-out was in the vast London Coliseum, which had reopened a few weeks before. Charlie was to play the role of the comic villain who attempts to bribe Stiffy to throw the game. Ordinarily the character's appearance served only to prepare an entrance for Harry Weldon as Stiffy; but Chaplin, schooled in *Casey's Court Circus*, had worked out some laughs. He entered with his back to the audience, wearing a silk hat and opera cloak, and elegantly handling a cane.

The first laugh came when he rounded suddenly on the audience, and the svelte figure turned out to have a shocking crimson nose. He did a funny trip, got entangled with his cane and collided with a punching ball (the scene represented the team's training quarters). Weldon was surprised and disconcerted, particularly when Chaplin topped the laughs the star earned for improvised lines with his own quick ripostes. Chaplin had quite clearly earned his contract: it was signed on 21 February 1908, eighteen days after his first appearance with Karno. The agreement provided for one year at a weekly salary of £3 10s, a second year at £4 and a third year's option. For the first time in their lives the Chaplin brothers had security, and £7 10s a week between them since Sydney's salary had risen to £4. When Sydney returned to London from a provincial tour, they rented a flat in Brixton Road, at 15 Glenshaw Mansions, and furnished it from a second-hand store, comfortably and with a touch of florid luxury provided by a Moorish screen and coloured lamps.

Chaplin felt that Weldon, eight years older than himself, was jealous of his success with the audience and his favour with Karno; this seems to be confirmed by the distinctly ungenerous tone of an article Weldon contributed some years later to *Pearson's Weekly*, a magazine run by Frank Harris:

> Charlie had undoubtedly a flair for pantomime, but in a speaking part he was rather out of it. Fred Karno, who always had an eye to new talent, was exceedingly impressed by him, and I know that Fred used to tell all the managers what a great find he had got.
>
> I know on one occasion when we were playing at the Olympic, Liverpool, I did Stiffy at the first house, and Chaplin, on the instructions of Karno, took on the part in the second house.
>
> I had the unique experience of sitting in a box and seeing my understudy perform. I cannot say that either the audience or myself were very impressed with the show that Charlie made. He did his best, but his slight physique prevented him from looking the part, and the audience were so cold to his Stiffy that he never appeared in gaol – at least while I was in the company.
>
> Although Karno had such a high opinion of Chaplin, no one else in the company paid him much attention, but regarded him as one of the boys.

Other colleagues recorded impressions of the nineteen-year-old Chaplin. Karno himself said, 'He wasn't very likeable. I've known him go whole weeks without saying a word to anyone in the company.

Occasionally he would be quite chatty, but on the whole he was dour and unsociable. He lived like a monk, had a horror of drink, and put most of his salary in the bank as soon as he got it.' A young Karno-ite from Lancashire, called Stanley Jefferson, who was eventually to change his name to Stan Laurel, remembered on the other hand:

> To some of the company I know he appeared stand-offish and superior. He wasn't, he wasn't at all. And this is something a lot of people through the years don't know or refuse to believe about Charlie: he is a very, very shy man. You could even say he is a desperately shy man. He was never able to mix easily unless people came to him and volunteered friendship or unless he was among people who didn't know him. Then he wasn't so shy.[3]

Fred Goodwins, who knew him in the vaudeville days and worked with him in a few films in 1915, said that Chaplin always struck him as a dreamer

> – a builder of castles in the air – and I used to watch him interestedly and note the way he acted in the varying conditions into which his life brought him. He was ambitious, I think, in his own peculiar way. He has told me since how he used to wonder what it was like to be at the top of things and how he scoffed at himself for ever supposing that fame and fortune would come his way.
>
> He seemed to have some realization that a big bank balance was an invaluable aid in the battle of life and so he lived steadily and saved a goodly percentage of his salary. He was never mean or close – just thrifty. Neither was he ever an habitual drinker; in fact nothing but cheap scandal has ever held him otherwise than as the most abstemious of men. In all my experience of him I don't think I have found him addicted to a vice of any kind. He seldom smokes or drinks and, strangely enough, he has not even the vice of vainglory. True, he loves his success, and fights hard to retain and hold it, but only because he feels it is his due. He hates ostentation, and does not want to be lionised for the mere sake of it.
>
> Yet Charles is one of the lightest-hearted men I have ever known.
>
> He is very highly strung and given to extravagant expressions of delight when things go aright with him and his work; yet a little incident, the merest mishap to a fellow-actor, for example, will crumple him up completely and render further work impossible for the rest of the day. Sympathy, light-heartedness and his amazing common sense are perhaps his strongest characteristics . . .
>
> There is nothing stand-offish about Charlie; his preoccupied state of mind and his peculiar way of looking vaguely at his interlocutors, as he

> does oftentimes, have misled many casual acquaintances into thinking his success has given him a 'swollen head'.
>
> There never was a greater mistake in this world. Charlie is essentially 'one of the boys', a democrat, a staunch believer in the spirit of born camaraderie and fraternity.[4]

In his own account of himself at this time in *My Autobiography*, Chaplin gives the impression of a solitary, reclusive youth, but from the testimony of former Karno colleagues, it cannot have been always so. 'I have often thought,' Bert Weston (by this time a single act, 'The Mat Man'), wrote to him in 1918, 'of the time when you first came with the football match at Newcastle-on-Tyne, and we all travelled down to Blackburn together, and young Will Poluski had his 21st birthday, and we had the party.' Clifford Walton, then an officer in the Royal Air Force, just awaiting demobilization, wrote to him in March 1919:

> It must be at least eight [years] since I left you outside your flat after coming back with you from the Holborn Empire. I remember my friend was very inebriated and insisted on reminding us every few minutes that he was very worried. Anyhow, the poor fellow has since died, after a short and very merry life. Well, old boy, I must first of all congratulate you upon your enormous success . . . You always did amuse me especially in the various digs we shared. I often go over those days in my mind again; after all we did not have such a bad time. Do you remember the week in Belfast and the little girl you were so keen on, also the incident with reference to Will Poluski and your box camera . . . My ideas of life have quite changed since those days although I still possess that roving spirit. Do you play poker nowadays? We used to have some very good games on Sundays, but usually rather disastrous to my financial resources, do you remember? I believe Harry Weldon was usually the lucky one. Am now going to turn into my campbed, so Cheerio Charlie. Hope to run across you somewhere again one day – Best of luck.
>
> Your old pal
> Clifford Walton.[5]

These memories give the impression of a young man who was not by any means unsociable, even though

> People who were with Chaplin in the old Karno days tell all sorts of stories of his self-absorption in those times. On long train journeys when the other boys in the company were playing ha'penny nap, or reading the Sunday papers, or discussing football, or racing, or the girls, Charlie

would sit in a corner by himself, gazing, not at the scenery, but into space . . . They thought he was moonstruck.[6]

Then, in the late summer of 1908, Chaplin fell in love. For anyone else it would have been an adolescent infatuation, a temporary heartbreak forgotten in a week. But Chaplin was not like anyone else, and something in his sensibilities or rooted in the deprivations of his childhood caused this encounter to leave a deep and ineradicable impression upon him. The object of his feeling was a girl called Henrietta Florence Kelly. She was born in Bristol, where her father was an upholsterer, in October 1893.[7] It is not known what became of her father, William Henry Kelly, but her mother Eliza Kelly had arrived in London with her son and three beautiful daughters, for whom she planned stage careers. Hetty was a dancer with Bert Coutts' Yankee Doodle Girls when Chaplin met her. The act was on the bill with the Karno troupe at the Streatham Empire. He saw her when he was standing in the wings – 'a slim gazelle, with a shapely oval face, a bewitching full mouth, and beautiful teeth'. When she came off the stage she asked him to hold a mirror for her. The following night, Wednesday, he asked her if she would meet him on Sunday afternoon. He took her to the Trocadero (he had drawn £3 from his bank), but the evening was a mild fiasco since Hetty had eaten and Charlie had no appetite. Walking her home to Camberwell he experienced a new sense of joy – 'I was walking in Paradise with inner blissful excitement.'

On Monday morning he was up in time to call for her at seven and walk her up Camberwell Road and Walworth Road to the underground: she was rehearsing that week in Shaftesbury Avenue. He collected and escorted her again on Tuesday and Wednesday, but on Thursday when he met her, Hetty was cool and nervous and would not hold his hand. She told him that she was too young, and that he was asking too much of her. He was nineteen, she was fifteen. Talk of love puzzled and alarmed her.

Chaplin could not resist walking to Camberwell Road the next morning, but instead of Hetty he met her mother, who said that Hetty had come home crying. He asked to see her, but Eliza Kelly at first refused to let him. When she relented, and he went with her to the house, he found Hetty cold and unfriendly. He remembered, more than sixty years later, that she had just washed her face with Sunlight soap, and the fresh smell of it.

Chaplin did not understand what had happened, and we can never know. The answer may be that Eliza Kelly did not intend her beautiful daughter to be wasted on a little vaudeville comedian with no prospects. Certainly she was, within a very few years, to see her three daughters married to husbands with money and position. From first sight to farewell, the affair had lasted eleven days, and apart from the Sunday meeting, they had never been together for more than twenty minutes. Chaplin never forgot; and both in his life and art he seemed for many years to be trying to recapture the ecstasy he had felt in the company of Hetty Kelly. Thirteen years afterwards, in 1921, he wrote:

> Kennington Gate. That has its memories. Sad, sweet, rapidly recurring memories.
>
> 'Twas here, my first appointment with Hetty (Sonny's sister). How I was dolled up in my little tight-fitting frock coat, hat, and cane! I was quite the dude as I watched every street car until four o'clock waiting for Hetty to step off, smiling as she saw me waiting.
>
> I get out and stand there for a few moments on Kennington Gate. My taxi driver thinks I am mad. But I am forgetting taxi drivers. I am remembering a lad of nineteen, dressed to the pink, with fluttering heart, waiting, waiting for the moment of the day when he and happiness walked along the road. The road is so alluring now. It beckons for another walk, and as I hear a street car approaching I turn eagerly, for the moment almost expecting to see the same trim Hetty step off, smiling.
>
> The car stops. A couple of men get off. An old woman. Some children. But no Hetty.
>
> Hetty is gone. So is the lad with the frock coat and cane.[8]

He was to describe the encounter again, in more detail, ten years later, adding, 'What happened was the inevitable. After all, the episode was but a childish infatuation to her, but to me it was the beginning of a spiritual development, a reaching out for beauty.'[9]

The life of a touring vaudevillian left little time for repining. In the autumn of 1909 he was sent with a Karno company to Paris, where they played at the Folies Bergères. Karno's pantomime sketches were eminently exportable, since they presented no language problems. Off stage the performers did experience some difficulties of communication, but Chaplin was not perturbed by them and was impressed and excited by all he saw in Paris. By his own account he toyed in a boyish way with the traditional carnal pleasures of the city. In the theatre he seems to have been performing the role which was to establish his fame in America, the Inebriate Swell in *Mumming Birds*, which had previously been played by Billy Ritchie, Billie Reeves and Sydney Chaplin.

The setting for *Mumming Birds* represents the stage of a small music hall, with two boxes at either side. The sketch opens with *fortissimo* music as a girl shows an elderly gentleman and his nephew – an objectionable boy, armed with peashooter, tin trumpet and picnic hamper – into the lower O.P. box. The Inebriated Swell is settled into the prompt side box, and instantly embarks upon some business of a very Chaplinesque character. He peels the glove from his right hand, tips the waiting attendant, and then, forgetting that he has already removed his glove, absently attempts to peel it off again. He tries to light his cigar from the electric light beside the box. The boy holds out a match for him, and in gracefully inclining to reach it, the Swell falls out of the box.

The show within the show consisted of a series of abysmal acts. (Chaplin told a reporter that in some more benighted towns they visited – he instanced Lincoln – the public believed the acts were offered seriously, and received them with critical disapproval rather than laughter.) The acts changed over the years, but some remained invariable: ballad singer, a male voice quartet, and the Saucy Soubrette, delighting the Swell with her rendering of 'You Naughty, Naughty Man!' The finale was always 'Marconi Ali, the Terrible Turk – the Greatest Wrestler Ever to Appear Before the British Public'. The Terrible Turk was a poor, puny little man weighed down by an enormous moustache, who would leap so voraciously upon a bun thrown to him by the Boy that the Stage Manager had to cry out, 'Back, Ali! Back!' The Turk's offer to fight any challenger for a purse of £100 provided the excuse for a general scrimmage to climax the act.

There were clearly elements in the business and character which Chaplin was later to use in films; descriptions of his glare of mute distaste and the dismissive wave of the hand to indicate boredom anticipate the screen character. Chaplin played other leading roles in the Karno companies. Despite Weldon's contempt, he eventually took on the part of Stiffy with success, even though he had another unlucky experience with it. He was excited when Karno announced that he was to do the role at the Oxford, a major London music hall – perhaps too excited, because as the night approached he lost his voice. Since *The Football Match* was one of the dialogue sketches which now increasingly figured alongside the mimed pieces in the Karno repertory, Chaplin, to his bitter disappointment, was replaced by an understudy. By the spring of 1909, however, he was playing Stiffy in the provinces, and on the last day of the year he was finally billed in the role at the Oxford.

Sydney was now originating material for Karno, as well as starring in leading roles in the sketches. He was co-writer with Karno and a well-known pantomime author, J. Hickory Wood,* of *Skating*, which was presented in 1909 as 'A New and Original Pantomimical Absurdity on the Latest Craze'. Sydney created the role of Archibald Binks. A representative dialogue exchange between Archibald and his friend Bertie at the Olympia Rink runs:

'There we stood with our retreat cut off.'

'Our what cut off?'

'Our retreat cut off.'

'Oh stop it.'

'There we stayed for three days without food or water, think of it, not even a drop of water. What did we do?'

'We drank it neat . . .'

'How are your brothers getting along?'

'Do you remember my brothers?'

'I should say so. Two of 'em are bandy and the other knock-kneed.'

'Do you remember when they used to go out? The two bandy ones would walk on the outside and the knock-kneed one in the centre.'

'Yes, and when they walked down the street they spelt Oxo.'

'How's the world been treating you?'

'Oh, up and down.'

'Are you working?'

'Now and then.'

'Where are you working?'

'Oh, here and there.'

'Do you like it?'

'Well, yes and no.'

'What do you work at?'

'Oh, this and that.'

'You're always in work I suppose?'

'Well, in and out.'

* In 1905 Wood had written the biography of the great music hall and pantomime comedian Dan Leno.

'Do you work hard?'
'On and off.'
'How much do you earn?'
'That and half as much again.'
'Who do you work for?'
'Mr So-and-So.'
'Well – are you looking for work?'
'I'm afraid to, in case I find it.'[10]

Years later Chaplin was to commemorate this style of nonsense in the cross-talk scene in *Limelight*. While Sydney toured with the No. 1 *Skating* company, with Jimmy Russell in the part of 'Zena Flapper', a roller-skating flirt, Charlie toured with a second company performing the same sketch, with Johnny Doyle as the lady.

In April 1910 Karno offered Chaplin the leading role in a brand new act, *Jimmy the Fearless, or The Boy 'Ero*. It was planned in four scenes, with spectacular transformations. The sketch opens in a working-class parlour where mother and father are waiting up for Jimmy who arrives home late, brazenly explaining that he has been out 'with a bit o' skirt'. Mother dresses him down and leaves him to eat his supper by the light of the candle. As he eats he takes a penny dreadful out of his pocket and reads it avidly. After supper he draws his chair up to the fire and continues to read until he nods off to sleep.

In his dreams he wanders in the Rocky Mountains, encounters desperadoes in Dead Man's Gulch but overcomes them after a ferocious hand-to-hand struggle, and rescues the heroine. He is next seen with heroine and new-found riches in a palatial home, is about to save his poor old parents from eviction when . . . he awakens in the kitchen, with Father about to lay about him with his belt. 'It probably owes its inspiration,' guessed one reviewer, 'to Dickens. In *A Christmas Carol*, a superabundance of liquor produced the horrible nightmare which made of Scrooge a teetotaller [*sic*] but Jimmy's undoing was a too substantial supper allied to an orgy of "penny dreadfuls".'[11]

Chaplin for some reason turned the part down, and Karno gave it instead to a new boy, Stanley Jefferson:

> I thought it was a wonderful sketch, so I jumped at the chance to play Jimmy . . . Charlie was out front the opening night, and right after the show he told Karno he had made a mistake. He wanted to play Jimmy.

> And he did. No, I didn't feel bitter about it. For me, Charlie was, is, and will be always the greatest comedian in the world. I thought he should have played it to begin with. But after that I used to kid him – always very proudly – that for once in my life Charlie Chaplin was my replacement. Charlie loved to play Jimmy, and the memory of that role and of that production stayed with him all his life, I think. You can see *Jimmy the Fearless* all over some of his pictures – dream sequences, for instance. He was fond of them, especially in his early pictures. And when it comes down to it, I've always thought that poor, brave, dreamy Jimmy one day grew up to be Charlie the Tramp.[12]

Jimmy the Fearless, or The Boy 'Ero was an immediate success for Karno ('another winner – in which line of business he is as successful as Frohman') and for Chaplin. At the start of the tour he was not billed by name, but the critics noticed him: 'A word is due to the very capable comedian who played the dreamer, but whose modesty keeps his name off the programme'; 'The piece is capitally played by a strong company, including a comedian of original method in the role of the "'Ero".' By the time they reached Swansea his photograph was published in the local papers, with a brief biography:

> Charles Chaplin, who plays the title role in *Jimmy the Fearless* at Swansea Empire this week, is only 21 years of age, and comes of an old stage stock, his father having been the late Charles Chaplin, a well-known comedian a few years back, and he started his own career when only nine years of age with the Eight Lancashire Lads. He is the youngest principal comedian in the Karno Companies, and has played 'Perkins' in *The G.P.O.* and *The Bailiffs*; 'Stiffy' in *The Football Match*; 'Archibald' in *Skating*; and the Inebriated Swell in *Mumming Birds*.[13]

The *Yorkshire Evening Post of* 23 July 1910 devoted a whole paragraph to him:

> A RISING ACTOR
>
> To assume the roles made famous by Fred Kitchen is no small task for a stripling of twenty-one, yet Mr Chas. Chaplin, who has caused so much laughter at the Leeds Empire this week as Jimmy the Fearless in Fred Karno's latest sketch, has done so with vast credit to himself. Mr Chaplin has only been three years with Mr Karno, yet he has played all the principal parts, and he fully realises the responsibility of following so consummate an artist as Fred Kitchen. He is ambitious and painstaking, and is bound to get on . . . Young as he is he has done some good work on the stage, and his entrance alone in *Jimmy the Fearless* sets the house in a roar and stamps him as a born comedian.

It was a sure sign of Chaplin's versatility and standing that he could take over the role of the bumbling and middle-aged Perkins in *The G.P.O.* and *The Bailiffs* which had been created by Karno's hitherto unrivalled star Fred Kitchen. Chaplin had clearly developed his gifts in his three years with Karno. A crude, ignorant and sadistic man, Karno had a touch of genius in the creation of comedy and comedians. He had an unerring instinct for what was funny. He understood the value of tempo and rhythm (his sketches always had special musical accompaniments). He strove for finesse and for faultless ensemble work. Until a company had been playing together for half a year he reckoned them unskilled, 'a scratch company'. Each player had to be perfect in his part, or rather in several parts, for it was necessary to be able to replace individual members of a cast like the parts of a precision machine.

Karno knew how to get the best out of his artists even if his methods of doing it sometimes lacked charm: a below-standard performance would be criticized with humiliating insults or simply a loud 'raspberry' blown from the wings. His treatment even of his stars could be brutish. Chaplin recalled that when he went to negotiate a new contract, Karno had arranged a plant at the other end of the telephone to pose as the manager of a theatre and confirm his view that Chaplin had no appeal and so was not worth any more money.

Another feature of the Karno style was to remain dominant in Chaplin's work. 'I do not remember if he was the one who originated the idea of putting a bit of sentiment right in the middle of a funny music hall turn,' Stan Laurel told John McCabe,

> but I know he did it all the time. I recall one or two instances of that. I forget the Karno sketch, but there was one in which a chap got all beat up – deservedly. He was the villain, a terrible person, and the audience was happy to see him get his [just deserts]. Then Karno added this little bit after the man was knocked down. He had the hero – who, mind you, had *rightfully* beaten up this bad man – walk over to the villain and make him feel easier. Put a pig's bladder under his head or what the hell have you. It got a laugh, and at the same time it was a bit touching. Karno encouraged that sort of thing. 'Wistful' for him I think meant putting in that serious touch once in a while. Another thing I seem to recall: you would have to look sorry, really sorry, for a few seconds after hitting someone on the head. Karno would say, 'Wistful, please, wistful.' It was only a bit of a look, but somehow it made the whole thing funnier. The audience didn't expect that serious look. Karno really knew how to sharpen comedy in that way.[14]

Karno taught his comedians other principles of comedy: that a slow delivery can often be more effective than hectic speed, but that in any event pace must be varied to avoid monotony; that humour lies in the unexpected, so it is funnier if the man is not expecting the pie that hits him in the face. The serious absurdity and the bizarre comic transpositions of the Karno sketches must often have resembled Chaplin gags. In one of them a man picks up a passing dog to wipe his hat. (Dogs figured in Karno sketches as they did in Chaplin films. Sydney's scenario for *Flats* contains the direction, 'This row outside wants to be a succession of shrieks, yells and noise. A dog can be obtained for the purpose or even two. It only requires their master to set them off in the first place and the shouts of the people will keep the dogs going.')

For the sixth successive year, Karno was to send a company on an American tour, with Alf Reeves as manager. 'The adroitness with which he has met the altered conditions of business,' noted *Variety*, 'so different from the methods obtaining in England, has won him the respect and friendship of the managers.' In the winter of 1910 he returned to London, and set about organizing a company for the next American season. Amy Minister, a charming soubrette in one of the Karno companies* told him, 'Al, there's a clever boy in the Karno troupe at the Holloway Empire. His name's Charlie Chaplin. He's a wonderful kid and a marvellous actor.' Reeves remembered in later years that on a foggy night he took a bus to Holloway, where Chaplin was playing *Jimmy the Fearless*.

> Just as I popped in he was putting great dramatic fire into the good old speech, 'Another shot rang out, and another redskin bit the dust!' . . .
>
> He looked the typical London street urchin, who knows every inch of the town as he darts through hurrying throngs and dodges in and out of rushing traffic, managing by some miracle to escape with his life. He had a cap on the back of his head and wore a shabby old suit, short in the sleeves and frayed at the cuffs – a suit he had long since outgrown.
>
> But it was not until he did something strikingly characteristic that I realised he was a real find. His father in the skit was ordering him to drop his novel and eat his supper. 'Get on with it now, m'lad,' and jabbing a loaf of bread at him. Charlie, I noticed, cut the bread without once taking his eyes off his book. But what particularly attracted my attention was

* In January 1911, during the Karno company's American tour, Reeves and Amy slipped off to the Cupid Bureau of New York City Hall to marry. Amy was at the time playing the Saucy Soubrette in *Mumming Birds*.

that while he absentmindedly kept cutting the bread, he held the knife in his left hand. Charlie's left-handed, but I didn't know it then. The next thing I knew, he had carved that loaf into the shape of a concertina.[15]

A few years later, Chaplin would use the same gag in his film *A Jitney Elopement*. Reeves went round to the dressing room after the act and asked Chaplin if he would like to go to America. 'Only too gladly, if you'll take me on,' he replied.

I told him I'd have a talk with Karno. At hearing this he wiped the smudge of make-up off his face to give his smile full play, and I saw he was a very good-looking boy. I had made up my mind about him before leaving his dressing room.

'Well,' considered Karno, 'you can have him for the American company if you think he's old enough for the parts.' We were then giving *A Night in an English Music Hall, A Night in a London Club* and *A Night in a London Secret Society*.

'He's old enough,' I told Karno, 'and big enough and clever enough for anything.'[16]

Karno appears to have been happy to send Charlie in preference to Sydney because previous tours had resulted in a number of defections to the American vaudeville stage, and Sydney was too valuable to risk losing. Before he left, Chaplin solemnly assured the Guv'nor that there was no fear of his not returning. His contract was not due for renewal until March 1911, but a new one was drawn up and signed on 19 September 1910, just before the company set sail on the SS *Cairnrona*. The new agreement was to take effect from 6 March 1911, and provided for three years' engagement at £6 a week in the first year, £8 in the second and £10 in the third. After that there would be an option for a further three years.

The American company that year also included Stan Jefferson, Fred and Muriel Palmer, George Seaman, who doubled as stage carpenter, and his wife Emily, Albert Austin, who in later years worked in many Chaplin films, Fred Westcott, Karno's nineteen-year-old-son, and Mike Asher, who played the awful boy in *Mumming Birds*.

The *Cairnrona* docked at Quebec, and the troupe travelled by train via Toronto to New York, where they were to open on 3 October at the Colonial Theatre. Karno had insisted that they present a new sketch, *The Wow-Wows, or A Night in a London Secret Society*. The first scene was set in a summer camp, where the campers resolve to get even with the tight-wadded Archie by creating a phoney secret society. The second scene satirized the absurd initiation ceremonies of such arcane organizations. The cast were dismayed to open with a piece which they all regarded as silly and ineffective. As we can judge from the notices, only Chaplin's performance saved it from total disaster. *Variety* prophetically wrote that 'Chaplin will do all right for America, but it is too bad that he didn't first appear in New York with something with more in it than this piece.' Another reviewer wrote:

> Now Charles Chaplin is so arriving a comedian that Mr Karno will be forgiven for whatever else the act may lack. The most enthusiastic Karnoite will surely admit, too, the act lacks a great deal that might help to make it vastly more entertaining. Still, Mr Chaplin heads the cast, so the people laughed and were content.
>
> He plays Archibald, a chappie with one end of his moustache turned up and the other turned down, a chappie with spots on his face betokening many a bad night, a chappie who declared himself in on everything though never paying his or any share.
>
> His first appearance is made from a tent, one of several occupied by a camping party. He looks more than seedy, despite his dress being immaculate.
>
> 'How are you, Archie?' inquires a woman visitor, decidedly attractive, and of whom Archie appeared to be enamoured.
>
> 'Not well,' he responds. 'I just had a terrible dream.'
>
> 'Very terrible?' she asks solicitously.
>
> 'Oh, frightful!' says Archie. 'I dreamed I was being chased by a caterpillar.'
>
> Archie makes such remarks as this in an exceedingly droll, ludicrous fashion. Outside Archie the company is composed of the most remarkable collection of blithering, blathering Englishmen New York has seen in many a day.[17]

After a month or two on tour, Chaplin and the company evidently built the business up until the sketch was tolerable. A rather later review noted that 'Nothing funnier has been seen in some time than the scene when Charles Chaplin, the fancy "souse", is initiated into the mysteries of the Wow-Wows. Chaplin is a real comedian. He is actually funny and *The Wow-Wows* might have been made to order for him.'[18]

During their three months around the New York circuit, the company dutifully played *The Wow-Wows*, but despite the improvement they wrought in it they were eager to be rid of it. At the

American Music Hall, Chicago, in the week of 30 January 1911 they offered a seventeen-minute sketch, in a single set, entitled *A Night in a London Club*. Some mystery surrounds this presentation, since it

If the Public demand an act, you must give them it.
The real PEOPLE'S FAVORITE

FRED KARNO'S LONDON Company

Under the Personal Direction of Alf Reeves

SIXTH YEAR IN U. S. A.

Opened this season Oct. 3rd, 1910, playing absolutely continuous time and booked solid until June 26th.

"NIGHT IN ENGLISH MUSIC HALL"

"NIGHT IN A LONDON CLUB," "THE WOW WOWS," and others, all copyrighted and protected.
ESTABLISHED HEADLINERS and never fail to get the money back for the proprietors.

These are the acts in demand.
Now open to consider PROPOSITIONS FOR NEXT SEASON.

Address direct to ALF REEVES, Manager, Karno Co., care VARIETY, New York

1910 - Karno advertisement.

was apparently not repeated, and only briefly figured in Karno publicity. The most likely explanation was that, with the resourcefulness in which Karno players were trained, they had simply improvised a completely new act, using the club set from *The Wow-Wows*. It was related to an old Karno sketch, *The Smoking Concert*, but with elements taken from *Mumming Birds* and *The Wow-Wows*:

> The offering somehow suggests Dickens. Seeing it one is reminded of the gatherings of the Pickwick club. The caricatures of the individual members of the club are with a graveness which makes the comedy stand out. The comedy is rough but the characters are well drawn. Various members of the club are called upon to entertain. There is a woman singer who gets her key repeatedly but cannot strike it when she begins to sing, a precious daughter of one of them, who offers a childish selection to the plaudits of admiring friends and among others an ambitious tragedian who, after reminding the master of ceremonies several times, is at length permitted

to start a scene of a play, only to be interrupted by the 'drunk' (played by Charles Chaplin) which has come to be recognized as the leading comedy character of the Karno offerings. As seen Monday afternoon the only shortcoming of the farce was the lack of a big laugh at the finish.[19]

1911 - Cartoon of Chaplin in *A Night in a London Club*, in USA.

It is not too imaginative to suppose that, as the leading comedian, Chaplin would have played a major role in devising a new act of this sort, as he must also have done in an intriguing entertainment which the company put on as an extra turn at the American Music Hall in New York for their six-week Christmas season. It was billed as *A Harlequinade in Black and White: An Old Style Christmas Pantomime.* It was entirely played as a shadow show, behind a large white screen.

It brought forth our old friends, the Clown, Pantaloon, Harlequin and Columbine. The pantomime was much more interesting than one would imagine it to be by merely hearing about it, for the pantomimists were funny in their extravagant make-up and actions. There was plenty of action to it, a diversity of ideas shown, and much pleasure derived by the audience, judging by the way they received it.

> First the characters indulged in a little general knockabout fooling, then they had fun with a stolen bottle, after which the policeman was relieved of his clothes, and another 'cop' was knocked out and laid upon a table to be dissected, his internal organs being brought forth one by one. The baby was stolen from the carriage of the nurse-maid, and all the characters had a 'rough house' experience while seeking lodgings. A droll duel brought forth two characters who grew and diminished in size rapidly as they fought, the phantom army appeared and paraded, and all the characters leaped 'up to the moon', the silhouettes showing them apparently jumping away up into the air and out of sight. They all jumped back again, and the act closed. It was quite a happy little idea for the holiday season, occupying about eleven minutes.[20]

Years later Chaplin was to use the same shadow technique for a wonderful scene which he in the end discarded from *Shoulder Arms*. In this case an antiquated form of entertainment was given such vitality that 'in a programme that embraces the best of every branch of vaudeville an astonishing hit was made by an act that may set the managers constantly striving . . .'[21] Within a few weeks the idea was borrowed by Gus Hill's *Vanity Fair*, for a number with shadow show-girls wearing strip tights and nighties.*

During the months in New York Chaplin lived in a brownstone house off 43rd Street, over a dry cleaner's. At first he found the city unfriendly and intimidating; in time he was stimulated by the energy of American life and the apparent classlessness of the country. After New York came a twenty-week tour, doing three shows a day on the Sullivan and Considine circuit. It provided a thrilling revelation of the country, from East to West – Chicago, St Louis, Minneapolis, St Paul, Kansas City, Denver, Butte, Billings, Tacoma, Seattle, Portland, San Francisco and Los Angeles, which Chaplin did not like. In Canada they played in Winnipeg and Vancouver, where they felt they were back among English audiences.

Stan Laurel told John McCabe:

> We were thrilled at the excitement of New York, but seeing the whole country, mile and mile, was really the way to see America. I was Charlie's roommate on that tour and he was fascinating to watch. People through the years have talked about how eccentric he became. He was a very eccentric person *then*. He was very moody and often very shabby in

* Among the few dozen press cuttings which Chaplin kept from this tour, several deal with this Christmas shadow show. His particular interest in it can reasonably be taken to indicate at the least a significant creative contribution to the turn.

appearance. Then suddenly he would astonish us all by getting dressed to kill. It seemed that every once in a while he would get an urge to look very smart. At these times he would wear a derby hat (an expensive one), gloves, smart suit, fancy vest, two-tone side button shoes, and carry a cane. I have a lot of quick little memories of him like that. For instance, I remember that he drank only once in a while, and then it was always port.

He read books incessantly. One time he was trying to study Greek, but he gave it up after a few days and started to study yoga. A part of this yoga business was what was called the 'water cure' – so for a few days after that he ate nothing, just drank water for his meals. He carried his violin wherever he could. Had the strings reversed so he could play left-handed, and he would practice for hours. He bought a cello once and used to carry it around with him. At these times he would always dress like a musician, a long fawn-coloured overcoat with green velvet cuffs and collar and a slouch hat. And he'd let his hair grow long at the back. We never knew what he was going to do next. He was unpredictable.[22]

Other members of the Karno companies confirmed Laurel's account of Chaplin's sartorial unpredictability. An anonymous columnist noted too that 'the world's greatest impersonator of inebriates and the biggest laughmaker on the vaudeville stage' (a striking encomium in 1911)

is one of the quietest and most non-committal of men – except just before, during and just after each performance. On these thrice-daily occasions he seems to enter heart and soul into the spirit of the impersonation and he's the most genial fellow one could meet. Then he lapses into a reserved state of mind during which he either sits quite still and thinks – thinks – thinks, or delves into the pages of the heaviest kind of literature he can find – philosophy preferred. It is said of him that, when in a small town where he could not secure a book to his liking, he purchased a Latin grammar and satisfied his peculiar mood for a time by devouring the dry contents as though it was a modern novel.[23]

Still, he was not unsociable. A gymnastic act called Lohse and Sterling was on the tour with them, and Chaplin struck up a warm friendship with Ralph Lohse, a big, handsome young Texan with ambitions to become a prize-fighter. They used to spar together, and became enthusiastic about a plan to quit show business and raise hogs in a big way. Chaplin lost his enthusiasm after reading up on techniques of castrating hogs, but Ralph Lohse was more dogged, and four years later wrote to Chaplin that though he was still in vaudeville – now with his wife in the act – he had a flourishing farm in Arkansas:

> I sold my first one and bought a second one and I have it running in great shape. I have in the neighbourhood of 600 hogs on it now and if conditions get better this fall I am going to put home-sugar-cured hams and bacon on the market, also pure pork farm sausage in little pound cartons. There is a great demand for such goods. My grandfather was considered one of the best sausage makers in the country and I know his process. And you was the durn fool that put all these notions in my head.
>
> Charlie I am glad to see you doing so well in pictures. We never go to a picture show unless you are in them and we manage to see nearly all of the pictures you are in. You will remember that all those Englishmen used to say that you would never amount to much if you ever lost out with Karno. Losing Karno was the best thing you ever done.[24]

1910 - Cartoon of Chaplin as the Inebriate in *A Night in an English Music Hall*, in USA.

Charlie had not lost all his chances of raising hogs, and making sausages: Ralph said that if ever he wanted 'to go in at round about $1800, let me know . . .'

Once out on the tour, the company thankfully revived the old faithful *Mumming Birds*, retitled for America *A Night in an English Music Hall*. Audiences had seen it before but welcomed it back joyously. Chaplin won his usual praise at every theatre. In Butte, Montana, he was said to prove himself 'one of the best pantomime artists ever seen here'. 'Charles Chaplin as the inebriated swell is a revelation and is given a big hand many times during the act.' 'Charles Chaplin, as the polite drunk, is an artist and even though doing the broadest burlesque, never gets out of the part for an instant. His falls in and out of the boxes are wonderful, and were he not a skilled acrobat, he would break his neck.'[25]

After the Sullivan and Considine tour, the company was booked for another six-week New York season by the William Morris Agency; then sent out for a further twenty-week Sullivan and Considine tour, which finally ended in May 1912 in Salt Lake City.

When the company arrived back in England in June 1912, they had been away for twenty-one months. For Charlie the homecoming was not particularly happy. He was met at the station by Sydney who

1910 - *A Night in an English Music Hall*: The Inebriate meets the Terrible Turk.

told him that he had married Minnie Constance, a Karno actress, and had given up the flat in Glenshaw Mansions. To be suddenly deprived like this of the first place he had recognized as his own home was a sharp blow to Charlie; for the first time in their lives there was a distance between the brothers. Hannah was still in Cane Hill, and not in any way improved. Now that they could afford it, Sydney and Charlie arranged for her to be moved to a private nursing home, Peckham House, Peckham Road. It was the place where Dan Leno had been cared for after his mental collapse.

Karno put the American company on the road, in suburban halls. Their year and a half together had polished them and sharpened their comedy, and they were very successful with the English audiences, but England seemed flat after the excitements of America, and Chaplin was glad to leave again for a new American tour. The company sailed from Southampton on 2 October 1912 on the SS *Oceanic*. (In his autobiography Chaplin refers to the ship as the *Olympic*, but the *Olympic* was laid up at this time, undergoing modifications following the sinking of the *Titanic*.) The only members of the last American company to remain with him were Alf and Amy Reeves, Stan Jefferson and Edgar and Ethel Hurley. One new member of the troupe was 'Whimsical Walker', the famous Drury Lane clown, who at this time was sixty-one years old. According to Walker he was engaged the night before sailing to fill a vacancy in the company, having met Alf Reeves and some members of the company by accident in a bar. He complained that he had not worked for such a low salary for years, but he was out of work and glad to take it.

They were again stuck with *The Wow-Wows* for much of the tour, which was not in any way a lucky one. Poor Walker's diction proved to be very bad. When they reached Butte, Montana, they found that the theatre had burnt down since their last visit and they had to play in a public hall. A number of the cast fell ill, and poor old Walker developed erysipelas and had to be hospitalized in Seattle. He did not rejoin the company.[26]

The third time round the Sullivan and Considine circuit, the sight-seeing had lost its novelty. Chaplin was growing tired of audiences which could be remarkably unsophisticated in the American sticks, as he discovered:

> . . . we had been heavily billed as vaudeville, because vaudeville was a new thing there at the time. That fact was evident the first night, for the

people did not seem to understand that our work was merely burlesque. This was plainly brought home to us after the show. We were playing *A Night in an English Music Hall* during which a quartette renders a song in the most awful manner possible – the worse it is sung, the greater the fun produced.

Well, we had returned to the hotel and were compelled to listen to many uncomplimentary remarks. 'What do you think of the big act?' one Pennsylvania man asked another Pennsylvania man. 'Which big act?' was the reply. 'The Karno act,' responded the first speaker. 'Absolutely rotten,' snapped the other. 'Why,' he added, 'that quartette couldn't sing for sour apples. In fact, our local quartette could beat them in seven different ways!'[27]

Still, success brought economic consolations. On 8 October 1913 Chaplin was able to acquire $200 worth of shares in the Vancouver Island Oil Company: he was always preparing for a rainy day. It was time to be moving on, too. The week of 4 August, when the Karno company were playing in Winnipeg, Chaplin wrote one of his infrequent letters to his brother, from the La Claire Hotel:

My Dear Sid,

I hope you received my letter all right. I know there wasn't much news in it – 'they say no news is good news' but not in this case. I have quite a lot of good news to tell you this time. Did I tell you I met Sonny Kelly in New York? Yes, I met him and had a grand time – he took me all over the place. He has a lovely apartment on Madison Avenue which you know is the swell part of New York. Hetty was away at the time – so I never saw her but still I am keeping correspondence with Sonny and he tells me I am always welcome to his place when in New York. I do nothing else but meet people and old friends – right here in Winnipeg I met one of the old boys who use to be in the Eight Lancashire Lads. I dont know wether you would know him or not – Tommy Bristol – he use to be my bigest pal – now he's working the Orpheum turns with a partner getting about 300 dollars per – I tell you they are all doing well, even me. I have just to sign a contract for *150 Dollars a week*. 'Now comes the glad news.' Oh' Sid I can see you!! beaming now as you read this, those sparkling eyes of yours scanning this scrible and wondering what coming next. I'll tell you how the land lyes. I have had an offer from a moving picture company for quite a long time but I did not want to tell you untill the whole thing was confirmed and it practically is settled now – all I have to do is to mail them my address and they will forward contract. It is for the New York Motion Picture Co., a most reliable firm in the States – they have about four companies, the 'Kay Bee' and

'Broncho' [and] 'Keystone' which I am to joyne, the Keystone is the Comedy Co. I am to take Fred Mace place. He is a big man in the movies. So you bet they think a lot of me – it appears they saw me in *Los Angeles, Cal.* playing the Wow-Wows then they wrote to me in Philadelphia which was a long time after. I could have told you before but I wanted the thing settled. We had a week's lay-of in Phili so I went over to New York and saw them personaly. I had no idea they would pay any money but a pal of mine told me that Fred Mace was getting four hundred a week well I ask them for two hundred. They said they would have to put it before the board of Directors ('dam this pen!') Well we hagled for quite a long time and then I had to do all my business by writing them and you bet I put a good business letter together with the help of the dictionary. Finaly we came to this arrangement i.e. A year's contract. Salary for the first three months 150 per week and if I make good after three months 175 per week with no expences at all and in Los Angeles the whole time. I don't know whether you have seen any Keystone pictures but they are very funny, they also have some nice girls ect. Well that's the whole strength, so now you know. Of course I told them I would not leave this company until we finished the S.C.* circuit, so I will join them by about the beginning of Dec that will be about the time we get through. I have told Alf and of course he doesn't want me to leave but he says I am certainly bettering myself and he can't say otherwise. Mr Kessel tells me there is no end of advancement for me if I make good. Just think Sid £35 per week is not to be laugh at and I only want to work about five years at that and then we are independent for life. I shall save like a son of a gun. Well I am getting tired now so will draw to a close. Don't tell anybody about what Alf said because it may get to the Guvnor's ears and he will think Alf had been advising me. And if you know of any little Ideas in the way of synaros ect. don't forget to let me have them. Hoping you are in good health and Mother improving also I would love her and you to be over hear. Well we may some day when I get in right.

Love to Minnie
and yourself
Your loving Brother,
Charlie.

Chaplin left the Karno company in Kansas City on 28 November 1913. 'I missed him, I must say,' Stan Laurel told John McCabe.

Arthur Dandoe, a chap in the Karno company with whom I teamed one time in a vaudeville act, didn't like Charlie. Arthur didn't like him because he considered him haughty and cold. So in Kansas City on our last night

* Sullivan and Considine.

with Charlie, Arthur announced to everybody that he was going to present a special goodbye present. He told me what it was – about five pieces of old brown Leichner grease paint, looking just like turds, all wrapped up in a very fancy box. 'Some shit for a shit,' is the way Arthur put it. This was Arthur's idea of a joke.

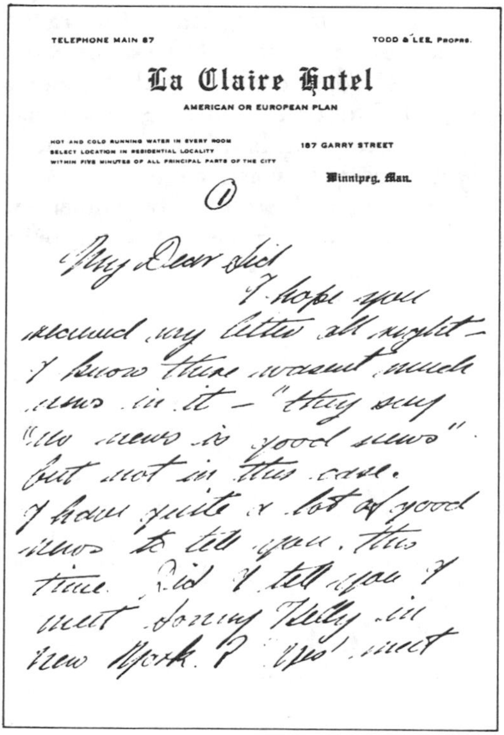

TELEPHONE MAIN 87 TODD & LEE, PROPRS.

La Claire Hotel

AMERICAN OR EUROPEAN PLAN

HOT AND COLD RUNNING WATER IN EVERY ROOM
SELECT LOCATION IN RESIDENTIAL LOCALITY
WITHIN FIVE MINUTES OF ALL PRINCIPAL PARTS OF THE CITY

187 GARRY STREET

Winnipeg, Man.

(1)

My Dear Sid
I hope you received my letter all right – I know there wasn't much news in it – "they say "no news is good news" but not in this case. I have quite a lot of good news to tell you, this time. Did I tell you I met Jonny Kelly in New York? Yes! met

1913 - Charles Chaplin's letter to Sydney announcing he is going into films.

I tried to argue him out of it but all Arthur said was, 'It'll serve the superior bastard right.'

The so-called presentation never took place however and later Arthur told me why. First of all, Charlie stood the entire company drinks after the show. That fazed Arthur a bit but the thing that really shamed him into not going through with the so-called gag was this:

> just after his final curtain with us, Charlie hurried off to a deserted spot backstage. Curious, Arthur followed, and he saw haughty, cold, unsentimental Charlie crying.[29]

This story has a sad footnote. When Chaplin made his triumphal return to his native city in 1921, Arthur Dandoe, down on his luck, was working as a pavement artist in Trafalgar Square.[30]

Alf Reeves saw Charlie off at the Kansas City railroad depôt. As he stepped into the train he handed Alf a small package and said, 'Merry Christmas, Alf.' When the train had carried Charlie off, Alf opened the package and found a handsome pocket book, and inside it a $100 bill, with a note: 'A little tribute to our friendship. To Alf, from Charlie.' Not wanting to waste good money on something he might not like, Charlie wanted Alf to choose something for himself; but Alf kept the pocket book with the note intact for many years.

4

In Pictures

Accounts of how Chaplin came to be discovered by the Keystone Film Company vary. Mack Sennett, who ran Keystone for Adam Kessel and Charles Baumann, owners of the parent company, New York Motion Pictures, claimed that he had spotted Chaplin while spending a week in New York with his leading lady and girlfriend, Mabel Normand, 'late in 1912'. Chaplin was playing *A Night in an English Music Hall* at the American Theatre on 42nd Street and 8th Avenue.

> 'Feller's pretty funny,' Mabel said.
>
> 'Think he'd be good enough for pictures?' I said.
>
> 'He might be,' Mabel said . . .
>
> 'I don't know,' I said to Mabel. 'He has all the tricks and routines and he can take a fall, and probably do a 108, but that limey make-up and costume – I don't know.'[1]

By the time he came to write his autobiography, Chaplin was himself satisfied that Sennett's version was true, though his letter of 1913 to Sydney indicates that any of the motion picture people might have seen him with the Karno company at the Empress Theatre, Los Angeles. Other accounts allege that it was Adam Kessel or his brother Charles who had seen Chaplin in New York, at Hammerstein's Theatre. A more recent, and persuasive, version of events appears in a letter from T. K. (Kim) Peters to Kevin Brownlow. Peters had been interested in films since 1899 when he had shot some moving pictures in Paris; in 1913 he was in Hollywood. His letter, written in 1973, suggests it was another N.Y.M.P. executive who discovered Chaplin:

> Harry Aitken . . . gave Charlie Chaplin his first job in movies . . . I had been moonlighting by painting some murals for the Pantage Theatre. In one of the murals I painted a beautiful semi-nude woman, after the fashion of Mucha . . . The manager of Pantage called me up shortly after they opened and asked me to come down as he had had several criticisms on the lady, as her breasts were bare. I went down and painted a veil over her breasts, and had stepped out into the lobby to go home when a well-dressed man who was looking at the billing photos . . . asked me if I was connected with the show . . . He said that he had heard that the show was interesting . . . The show was Karno's *Night in an English Music Hall* . . . He said that he was going to attend the matinée . . . He told me he was just in from New York . . .
>
> I did not give it much thought, but he was Harry Aitken, owner of the major stock in the Keystone Comedies, and the actor was Charlie Chaplin. Harry hired Chaplin away from Karno . . . and it was my first meeting with Harry, which ripened into a life-long friendship.[2]

In any event, in the spring of 1913 Kessel and Baumann sent Alf Reeves a telegram which allegedly read (accounts of it vary in textual detail):

> MAY 12 1913
>
> ALF REEVES MANAGER
> KARNO LONDON COMEDIANS
> NIXON THEATRE, PHILADELPHIA
>
> IS THERE A MAN NAMED CHAFFIN IN YOUR COMPANY OR SOMETHING LIKE THAT IF SO WILL HE COMMUNICATE WITH KESSEL AND BAUMANN 24 LONGACRE BUILDING BROADWAY NEW YORK.[3]

It was in response to this that Chaplin returned to New York for a day. He supposed that Kessel and Baumann must be lawyers, like most of the tenants of Longacre Building, and he speculated that perhaps his great-aunt, Mrs Wiggins, had died in New York and left him a fortune. Instead he was asked if he would consider signing up with the Keystone Company. From his letter to Sydney it is clear that Chaplin was told that he was to replace Fred Mace, the heavyweight star of the earliest Keystone comedies. In his autobiography, however, Mack Sennett says that his reason for asking Chaplin to join his company was the ever-growing demands of Keystone's other male star, Ford Sterling, and his fears that Sterling might at any time give in his notice. Sennett's version has been generally accepted by subsequent historians, but Chaplin's original understanding of the circumstances seems more likely. Tact, on the part of Kessel and Baumann, of course, would have made it more likely for Chaplin to be told that he was to replace a departing star than that he was required to stand by in case of the defection of a current leading player. But the date of the telegram is significant: Mace left Keystone at the end of April 1913: it would seem most likely that the company would be urgently seeking a successor a couple of weeks later. Moreover, Ford Sterling was only just coming into his own as the company's leading star with the removal of Mace's competition; and he was in fact to remain at Keystone for a further nine months, until February 1914.

Chaplin, tired of touring, was ready for a change. By July a contract was drawn up to engage Charles Chaplin of the City, County and State of New York 'as a moving picture actor to enact roles in the moving picture productions of the party of the first part in its companies, and such other companies as the party of the first part may hereafter form, for a period of one year commencing November 1st 1913 (unless sooner terminated by either party as hereinafter provided), for a salary of One Hundred and Fifty Dollars weekly.'

A remarkably uncomplicated, two-page document, the contract was signed in New York by Adam and Charles Kessel, as President and Secretary respectively of the Keystone Film Company, witnessed by a notary public and despatched to Chaplin on tour. Chaplin, however, evidently refused to sign: and a new version was drawn up, omitting the parenthetical phrase '(unless sooner terminated by either party as hereinafter provided)' and the associated provision that the contract was terminable by two weeks' written notice by either party. Chaplin at this stage of his career was not prepared to throw up security with Karno to run the risk of unforeseen unemployment within the year. The commencing date of the contract was changed to 16 December 1913.[4]

The signatures of the two Kessels were witnessed on 15 September 1913, and the revised contract was sent to Chaplin, who signed it in Portland, Oregon, on 25 September. Curiously the contract makes no mention of the arrangement to raise Chaplin's weekly salary by $25 at the end of three months. Since Chaplin was equally certain in 1913 and in 1964 that these were the terms (and his memory was almost faultless in matters of business) this must have been the subject of a separate verbal agreement.

The origins and history of the Keystone Film Company have been fogged by the chronic mythomania of its presiding genius, the Canadian-Irish Mack Sennett, whose highly-coloured recollections were published long after the events they related. Among the few certain facts are that Sennett was born Michael Sinnott, to Irish parents, in Richmond, Quebec on 17 January 1880. While working

in writing, scenarios or in any other manner engage or assist others in any branch of the moving picture business, and that he will not, during the term of his employment hereunder, or at any time thereafter, enact for any others than the party of the first part, any of the roles to which he may have been assigned by the party of the first part during his employment, and that he will not, at any time during the continuance of his employment hereunder, appear in any public or private performance as an actor, lecturer, or entertainer, except with the written consent of the party of the first part.

This contract may be terminated by either par upon two (2) weeks written notice to the other party hereto.

IN WITNESS WHEREOF, the party of the first part has caused these presents to be signed by its President and Secretary, and its corporate seal to be hereunto affixed, and the party of the second part has hereunto set his hand and seal, the day and year first above written.

THE KEYSTONE FILM CO.

By ______________
President

____
Secretary

______________ (L.S.)

1913 - Chaplin's first film contract: the first draft (above) which he did not sign, and the second (right) with his signature.

in an iron foundry in Northampton, Connecticut, he obtained from the local attorney – Calvin Coolidge – an introduction to the famous comedienne, Marie Dressler, who was appearing in town. Miss Dressler, in turn, sent him to David Belasco, the most prominent actor-manager of the day, who counselled burlesque as the proper *métier* for the raw-boned youth. Sennett, however, did not at once

in writing, scenarios or in any other manner engage or assist others in any branch of the moving picture business, and that he will not, during the term of his employment hereunder, or at any time thereafter, enact for any others than the party of the first part, any of the roles to which he may have been assigned by the party of the first part during his employment, and that he will not, at any time during the continuance of his employment hereunder, appear in any public or private performance as an actor, lecturer, or entertainer, except with the written consent of the party of the first part.

IN WITNESS WHEREOF, the party of the first part has caused these presents to be signed by its President and Secretary, and its corporate seal to be hereunto affixed, and the party of the second part has hereunto set his hand and seal, the day and year first above written.

THE KEYSTONE FILM CO.

THE KEYSTONE FILM CO. CORPORATE SEAL 1912

By

A Kessel Jr
President

Chas Kessel
Secretary

Charles Chaplin (L.S.)

abandon ambitions to exploit his powerful baritone voice, and divided his time between touring burlesque and the chorus of musical comedy.

In 1908, like many another disappointed actor, Sennett was reduced to seeking work in 'the galloping tintypes', as movies were disparagingly styled. He claimed that it was on his twenty-eighth birthday, in January 1908, that he joined the Biograph Company at 11 East 14th Street, New York. With Irish luck, Sennett had chanced upon a time and place that were to prove historic. David Wark Griffith had arrived at Biograph a few months before, and was already embarked upon the period of prodigal creation which, in barely five years, was to explore and reveal the whole expressive possibilities of motion pictures, and to turn them into an art.

Sennett was inquisitive, ambitious, imitative, ingenious. He studied Griffith's work and determined to be a director himself. Soon he began to augment his income by writing scenarios. He recognized his natural bent for comedy, and he took note of the success of the anarchic, knockabout comedy films imported from France, where they were produced by the Pathé and Gaumont companies. In 1909 he played the leading role in a comedy directed by Griffith, *The Curtain Pole*. Humour was not Griffith's strong point, yet here too he applied his innate gift for discovering first principles. The farce was slight: Sennett played a tipsy Frenchman whose efforts to carry home a curtain pole wreak havoc in the streets of an unoffending township. Griffith however brought to the service of comedy all his discoveries of editing, suspense and timing.

In 1910 Sennett was appointed Biograph's principal director of comic productions, and between March 1911 and July 1912 directed upwards of eighty one-reel comedies. When Kessel and Baumann were looking for a man to run their new comedy studio, Sennett was the ideal candidate.* Keystone was established in the summer of 1912, and by early September Sennett had moved into the former Bison

* Sennett's characteristically highly-coloured version of events is that he conned Kessel and Baumann, 'two bookmakers', into going into partnership with him as a means of settling a $100 gambling debt. In fact Kessel and Baumann had given up bookmaking some four years earlier, and by this time were major film producers. Their prospering New York Motion Picture Company was the parent company for 101 Bison Films, producing Thomas Ince's western and historical spectacles, and for Reliance, specializing in dramas. Kessel and Baumann naturally now wanted to establish a comedy arm.

Studio at 1712 Allessandro Street, Edendale, California (the Edendale Studios). He brought with him Fred Balshofer as manager; Mabel Normand, Fred Mace and Ford Sterling as his stars; and Henry Lehrman who was to direct Keystone's second unit while Sennett directed the first. All had worked together at Biograph. The first Keystone releases were announced for 23 September 1912 and by February 1913 the studio was maintaining a steady production of eight reels a month.

As producer and director, Sennett shared many of Fred Karno's characteristics. He was a rough, tough, intelligent, uneducated man. He had an instinctive feeling for physical comedy. Because he was easily bored himself, he could tell what would keep the audience's attention happily engaged, and what would not. He could maintain discipline in his troupe of high-spirited and unruly clowns. At Biograph he had mastered film craft, and he passed on his lessons. The Keystone cameramen were dexterous in following the free flight of the clowns, and the dynamism of 'Keystone editing', adapted from Griffith's innovatory montage methods, soon became a byword.

Keystone films derived from vaudeville, circus, comic strips, and at the same time from the realities of early twentieth-century America. It was a world of wide, dusty streets with one-storey clapboard houses, grocery and hardware stores, dentists' surgeries and saloon bars; kitchens and parlours; the lobbies of cheap hotels; bedrooms with iron beds and rickety washstands; railroad tracks and angular automobiles that were just overtaking the horse and buggy; men in bowler hats and heavy whiskers; ladies in feathered hats and harem skirts; spoiled children and stray dogs. The stuff of comedy was wild caricature of the ordinary joys and terrors of daily life. At all events, the guiding principle at Keystone was to keep things moving, to leave no pause for breath or critical reflection. No excess of make-up or mugging was too great. In time the original group of comedians who had come west with Sennett was augmented by the recruitment of Roscoe 'Fatty' Arbuckle, cross-eyed Ben Turpin, gangling Charley Chase, the walrus-whiskered Chester Conklin and Billy Bevan, giant Mack Swain, Tom and Edgar Kennedy, Slim Summerville, Louise Fazenda, Polly Moran, Alice Davenport and others who could contribute acrobatic skill or outrageous characterization to the troupe. These were Chaplin's future colleagues.

He reached Los Angeles in early December 1913 and took a modest room at the Great Northern Hotel on Bunker Hill, close to the

Empress Theatre, where he had played. His first meeting with his new boss was accidental. On his first night in Los Angeles, very lonely, he went to the Empress. There he ran into Sennett, with Mabel Normand. Chaplin sensed Sennett's misgivings on seeing how young he appeared without stage make-up. Karno had had the same reaction, and received the same reassuring reply: 'I can make up as old as you like.'

The following day (according to his own recollections) Chaplin set out for the studio. Edendale was a district of shanty buildings and lumber yards and the studio itself was a strange-looking place. An area 150 feet square was surrounded by a green board fence. At the centre stood the stage, overhung with white linen to diffuse the sunlight. An old bungalow housed the offices and the women's dressing rooms; some converted agricultural buildings served as dressing rooms for the men. Chaplin arrived at lunchtime, was intimidated by the sight of the high-spirited actors surging out of the bungalow in quest of food, and fled back to his hotel. The same thing happened the next day; and only an anxious telephone call from Sennett got him beyond the gates on the third.

Sennett explained to Chaplin the Keystone method. There was no scenario; 'we get an idea, then follow the natural sequence of events until it leads up to a chase which is the essence of our comedy.' This did not entirely reassure Chaplin, accustomed to the months of polishing that perfected the team work of a Karno sketch. His first weeks at Keystone were far from happy: sometimes he began to think that he had made a mistake, and he was certain that Sennett felt the same. He came to films a complete novice, and had to master the basic notions: cutting; the shooting of scenes in discontinuity; the actor's problem of staying within the camera's range; the importance of sight lines, so that the direction of the actor's gaze in one shot will convincingly link with the object of that gaze in another shot. He felt that his own subtle and carefully paced comedy was going to be lost here, since the tempo of all the films seemed to be matched to the leaping and mugging of Ford Sterling's comedy. He was irked by enforced idleness: Sennett – perhaps intending him to watch and learn the techniques of film making – did not use him in a film until the end of January.

By this time, however, Chaplin already knew enough to doubt the competence of the director assigned to his first film. Henry Lehrman was born in Vienna in 1886 and had emigrated to the United States at the age of nineteen. He was working as a tram conductor when he first presented himself to D. W. Griffith at the Biograph Studios, claiming to have been a director with the Pathé Company in France. Griffith, no doubt seeing through the fraud, nicknamed him Pathé and passed him on to Sennett. Sennett, as we have seen, thought well enough of him to make him his second unit director when he opened his own studios. 'Pathé' Lehrman was to continue directing films until the mid-1930s, but he remained a mediocre man-of-all-work. History remembers him only as Chaplin's first director, and as the chief prosecution witness in the trial that ruined Roscoe Arbuckle seven years later.

Chaplin's first film, *Making a Living*, was one of Keystone's more elaborate productions. It had a comparatively well-developed story line, and was shot partly on the stage, partly in the gardens of a nearby house, and partly in the street, on Glendale Avenue. Chaplin's costume, make-up and character resembled Archibald Binks in *The Wow-Wows* and *A Night in a London Club*, with nothing as yet of the Charlie figure to come. He wore a grey top hat, check waistcoat, stiff collar, spotted cravat and monocle. Most surprising was the long, drooping moustache of a rather dejected stage villain. At the start of the film he established the fraudulence of his elegant pretensions by touching a passing friend (played by Lehrman) for a loan. The first characteristically Chaplin gag is where he disdainfully rejects the proffered coin as too mean, but then hastily grabs it before the friend can change his mind. In return for this favour, the Dude decides to steal his benefactor's girl, and sets to flirting with both the girl (Virginia Kirtley) and her mother (Alice Davenport) in the garden.

Lehrman plays a reporter, and most of the action is concerned with the Dude's attempts to muscle in on the job and scoop him. It all ends with a chase, a contretemps in a lady's bedroom (an almost indispensable incidental to Keystone films) and a grand finale on the cow-catcher of a moving train. The American critic Walter Kerr has pointed out that one small but striking gag established a permanent and productive pattern of Chaplin's screen personality, of 'adjusting the rest of the universe to his merely reflexive needs'.[5] The Dude is explaining his own merits to the newspaper editor, emphasizing his argument by banging him on the knee. When the editor withdraws his knee, the Dude pulls it back again so that he can continue his pummelling.

Chaplin hated the film. He was outraged when he saw the finished thing and discovered that in the cutting Lehrman had excised or mangled good gags which he had introduced. He was certain that Lehrman had deliberately tried to destoy his work, out of pique because Chaplin had been too free with suggestions for comic business during the shooting. In fact there was nothing to be ashamed of for a first film. It is a rough little effort, but so were most of the Keystone products. True, we can see in it very little of the Karno comedian of whom three years before one critic had written: 'Chaplin has been described, by some critics, as a genius. To say the least he carries the hallmarks of genius . . .' Nor was there as yet much, except these one or two little gags, to hint at the character he would ultimately create. But he emerges as a defined and dominant figure, already with a more consistent character, in his bland and airy malefactions, than was common in Keystone films. The trade press picked him out at once: 'The clever player who takes the part of a sharper . . . is a comedian of the first water.' If there is any truth in the legends passed on for seventy years that Sennett and his Keystone colleagues were convinced that the film and the new comedian were destined to flop, it can only be assumed either that they were startlingly unperceptive, or had pitched their expectations on some miracle.

Despite the appearance of chaos at the Keystone Studios, the films were made to a production-line formula. There were four main kinds of production. The simplest and probably the cheapest were the 'park' films, always shot in Westlake Park, and using park benches, promenades, a refreshment stand and (for the inevitable aquatic finale) Echo Lake as the setting for improvised mix-ups between courting couples. Another variety of production also used locations: Sennett would take advantage of some public occasion – a military parade, speedway event or horse-race meeting – and send a unit to film the comedians fooling and playing out some impromptu farce, with the crowd and the spectacle of the event as free background. More formal films were shot in sets which seem to have stood more or less permanently on the stage. The quintessential Keystone set, which Chaplin himself was to use and elaborate during the next few years, consisted of a hallway with a room on either side. This arrangement would variously represent a domestic setting, with parlour (always to the left) and kitchen (to the right); a hotel, with rooms facing each other across the corridor, ideally placed for nocturnal mix-ups; neighbouring offices; or perhaps a doctor's or dentist's surgery and waiting room, with the indispensable hall in between. Special settings might represent a restaurant, bar, hotel lobby, cinema or boxing booth; or the studio buildings might provide off-the-cuff sets. The fourth category of film, like *Making a Living*, combined location and studio sets.

Whatever the plan of the film, the director would restrict himself to no more than ten camera set-ups – a moving camera was practically unknown at Keystone. So far as possible all the material required in each set-up was filmed together: the ingenuity of a Keystone film lay in making, with as little waste as possible, a collection of shots which would join neatly together in the cutting room to make a coherent narrative. The usual number of shots for a one-reel film was between fifty and sixty. (Sennett did not recognize the principle of retakes – material once shot had to be used.)

It is too simple to dismiss these Sennett farces, machine-made at the rate of two a week, as crude and primitive, appealing to a naïve audience to whom all novelty was wonder. Walter Kerr, bringing to them the cultivated perceptions of seventy years later (perhaps too cultivated and too far removed in time) speculated:

> Perhaps we might have laughed too in 1914. At least we would have felt excitement.
>
> I say 'perhaps' we might have laughed, because I'm not entirely sure – though I'm certain we'd have felt the excitement. There is very little in the Sennett films, for all their breakneck pace and bizarre manhandling of the universe, that one would care to call humour under analytic examination. Normally it is possible to understand a joke that has faded, to recapture the principle that once provoked laughter while being unable to capture the laughter itself . . . Not so with Sennett for the most part. The jokes, as jokes, are rarely there . . . and all the activity is so headlong that there is scarcely time to pause for the 'constructed' quality of a jest . . . The films are successful agitations, successful explorations of elaborate visual possibilities; if laughter once accompanied them, it has to have been the laughter of breathlessness.[6]

It is true that to our unaccustomed vision, a Keystone comedy at first presents only a blurred impression of breakneck speed, running, jumping and wild gesticulation. If we take the trouble to view these films patiently, more times than once, and try to adjust to their pace, much more emerges. First the apparently senseless gesturing resolves itself into a quite deliberate and precise system of mime, not unlike that of classical ballet, and at certain moments as formal. One of the most striking instances appears in *Mabel's Married Life*, when Mabel Normand with a shrug of her shoulders, a gesture of pointing with her right index finger to the ring on her left hand, a quick and brilliant impersonation of the Chaplin waddle and an appeal to the camera with her big expressive eyes asks us, 'Why ever did I marry that man?'

A notable demonstration of this all but lost language is the fourth film which Chaplin made at Keystone, *Between Showers*. Henry Lehrman directed, and by this time Chaplin had adopted his definitive costume and was on the way to perfecting a screen character. At first sight it is one of the fastest, wildest, and most inexplicable Keystones. If we make the effort to penetrate its language, however, it presents quite a different appearance: a little story like the anecdote of a comic strip, yet even more (and the comparison is inevitable, not pretentious) like the scenario of the *commedia dell'arte*.

There are five main characters: Charlie and Ford Sterling, rival mashers; a pretty but faithless girl (Emma Clifton); a policeman (Chester Conklin) and the policeman's lady friend (Sadie Lampe). While the policeman is making love to his lady friend, Ford 'borrows' her umbrella, since it is raining and his own is broken. After the shower is over, he hands the umbrella to Emma for safe-keeping, while he goes to find a plank of wood to help her cross a large puddle. By the time he has returned, Emma has already found a new suitor to help her across the puddle, and now refuses to hand back the umbrella. Charlie arrives on the scene and defends Emma from Ford's wrath. Emma flounces off, leaving Charlie in firm possession of the umbrella. Ford goes off in search of assistance, and returns with a policeman. Unfortunately the policeman turns out to be Chester, who recognizes the stolen umbrella. Too late Ford attempts to disown the umbrella. Chester hauls Ford off to jail, leaving a happy Charlie to thumb his nose at both of them.

It is a neatly-turned little anecdote, but it only emerges after two or three viewings and careful study of the mime. We have no means of knowing whether the audience of the day, by familiarity and enthusiasm, had developed more acute perceptions of the form than we are able to apply. Were they able to see, instantly and at first viewing, beyond the initial impression of aimless running, jumping, assult and mugging? Was this why they found the Keystone pictures funnier than Walter Kerr could half a century later, and followed them with such enthusiasm?

The enigma ceases to be relevant with the arrival of Chaplin. In a film like *Between Showers* Chaplin still conforms more or less to the Keystone style, though already there are irrepressible touches of a different kind of character comedy, like his child-like pride in the eventual possession of the disputed umbrella. The traditional historical view of Chaplin's innovations at Keystone is that, despite the doubt and resistance of Sennett and the Keystone comedians, he succeeded in slowing down the helter-skelter pace, and introduced new subtlety to the gag comedy. This is true so far as it goes, but the difference lay deeper. Keystone comedy was created from without; anecdote and situations were *explained* in pantomime and gesture. Chaplin's comedy was created from within. What the audience saw in him was the expression of thoughts and feelings, and the comedy lay in the relation of those thoughts and feelings to the things that happened around him. The crucial point of Chaplin's comedy was not the comic occurrence itself, but Charlie's relationship and attitude to it. In the Keystone style, it was enough to bump into a tree to be funny. When Chaplin bumped into a tree, however, it was not the collision that was funny, but the fact that he raised his hat to the tree in a reflex gesture of apology. The essential difference between the Keystone style and Chaplin's comedy is that one depends on *exposition*, the other on *expression*. While the expository style may depend upon such codes as the Keystone mime, the expressive style is instantly and universally understood; that was the essential factor in Chaplin's almost instant and world-wide fame.

In his second film, Chaplin created the costume and make-up which were to become universally recognized. For many years it has been accepted that that second film, and the first appearance of Chaplin's tramp character, was *Kid Auto Races at Venice, California*. It now seems much more likely that the film was *Mabel's Strange Predicament*. In order of release, *Kid Auto Races* was certainly the first of the two. It was issued on 7 February 1914. *Mabel's Strange Predicament* came out two days later. Yet Chaplin clearly remembered that it was in *Mabel's Strange Predicament* that he first wore the costume, and his memory on such details rarely failed him. Hans Koenekamp, who was cameraman on *Mabel's Strange Predicament*, also remembers this as being the first appearance of the costume. The answer most likely is that *Mabel's Strange Predicament* was *shot* first. *Kid Auto Races* was one of Sennett's location films, said to have been filmed in forty-five minutes during a soap-box car rally, and consisting of no more than twenty shots. It could have been shot, cut, printed and slipped into the release schedule while the more elaborate film, *Mabel's Strange Predicament*, was being assembled.

The tramp costume, which was to be little modified in its twenty-two-year career, was apparently created almost spontaneously, without premeditation. The legend is that it was concocted one rainy afternoon in the communal male dressing room at Keystone, where Chaplin borrowed Fatty Arbuckle's voluminous trousers, tiny Charles Avery's jacket, Ford Sterling's size fourteen shoes which he was obliged to wear on the wrong feet to keep them from falling off, a too-small derby belonging to Arbuckle's father-in-law, and a moustache intended for Mack Swain's use, which he trimmed to toothbrush size. This neat and colourful version of the genesis of the tramp seems to have originated in the Keystone Studio, and was certainly never endorsed by Chaplin. In his autobiography he states that he decided on the style of the costume 'on the way to the wardrobe'. His idea was to create an ensemble of contrasts – tiny hat and huge shoes, baggy pants and pinched jacket.

It is easy enough to find precedents for the costume in the English music halls. Grotesquely ill-fitting clothes, tiny hats, distasteful moustaches and wigger-wagger canes were the necessary impedimenta of the comedian. Some of Dan Leno's stage costumes hint at Chaplin's; and Chaplin's old Karno colleague, Fred Kitchen, used to complain gently that it was he who had first originated the costume and the splay-footed walk. Elements of the character had been predicted in Chaplin's own stage career. His make-up in the single surviving photograph of Wal Pink's sketch *Repairs* somewhat resembles that of Charlie; and there is said to have been much of the costume in his get-up as a rag-and-bone man in Karno's *London Suburbia*.

Whatever its origins, the costume and make-up created that day in early February 1914 were inspired. Chaplin recalled how the costume induced the character, so that 'by the time I walked on to the stage he was fully born'.[7] We know from the films that this was not strictly true; the character was to take a year or more to evolve its full dimensions and even then – which was its particular strength – it would evolve during the whole of the rest of his career. It is a fair guess that the symbolic interpretations that Chaplin and his publicity staff gave to the individual elements of the Tramp's ensemble were the fruits of the hindsight of later years. From the first, though, certain traits were obvious: the derby, the cane, the bow-tie and close-trimmed moustache indicated brave but ineffectual pretensions to the dignity of the *petit bourgeoisie*.

The characteristic motions of the character had other origins. In 1916 Chaplin told an interviewer from *McClure's* magazine that he had based his characteristic shuffling walk on that of an old man called 'Rummy' Binks, who used to hold the horses for coachmen outside Uncle Spencer Chaplin's pub, The Queen's Head, at the corner of Broad Street and Vauxhall Walk.

> There was a cab stand near by and an old character they called 'Rummy' Binks was one of the landmarks. He had a bulbous nose, a crippled, rheumatic body, a swollen and distorted pair of feet, and the most extraordinary trousers I ever saw. He must have got them from a giant, and he was a little man.
>
> When I saw Rummy shuffle his way across the pavement to hold a cabman's horse for a penny tip, I was fascinated. The walk was so funny to me that I imitated it. When I showed my mother how Rummy walked, she begged me to stop because it was cruel to imitate a misfortune like that. But she pleaded while she had her apron stuffed into her mouth. Then she went into the pantry and giggled for ten minutes.
>
> Day after day I cultivated that walk. It became an obsession. Whenever I pulled it, I was sure of a laugh. Now, no matter what else I may do that is amusing, I can never get away from the walk.

We have already seen that Will Murray took credit for Chaplin's distinctive technique of rounding corners pivoting on one leg, with the other leg stuck out horizontally and revolving into the new direction of the run. According to Murray it had been developed for the grand chase in *Dick Turpin*. Billy Danvers, a fellow member of the Karno company, however, recalled that this mode of turning was in fairly general use in the company as an effective and laughable means of coping with the limited run permitted by small out-of-town stages.

Sennett took a hand in the direction of *Mabel's Strange Predicament*, no doubt because it starred his girlfriend, Mabel Normand. Mabel was born Mabel Ethelreid Normand in Providence, Rhode Island, the youngest of the three surviving children of Claude G. Normand, a Frenchman who played the piano in pit orchestras in small theatres, and his Irish-Catholic wife Mary Drury. Accounts of her birth date vary, but her family state that she was born on 9 November 1892. Her family, according to Sennett, 'was temperamental, improvident, and often in transit'. He also recalled that though she had had little formal education, Mabel was a great reader and had acquired a particular aptitude for geography. She was also an athlete, a fine swimmer and had been taught by her father to play the piano.

In her early teens she took a job in the pattern-making department of the Butterick Company in Manhattan, but was soon finding regular work as a model for illustrators. Among the popular magazine artists of the time for whom she is said to have sat were Carl F. Kleinschmidt, Henry Hutt, Penrhyn Stanlaws, Charles Dana Gibson and James Montgomery Flagg. In 1910 another model, Alice Joyce, encouraged her to try her luck in the movies, and Mabel began to get small roles in Vitagraph pictures. Soon afterwards she was recruited by Biograph where she met the aspiring young director Mack Sennett. When Sennett opened up the Keystone Studios he naturally chose her as his star.

Mabel was petite, beautiful, infectiously vivacious and exquisitely funny. Like Chaplin she was one of the rare artists who could establish a direct rapport between screen and spectator: more than half a century after her death her screen presence retains its immediacy and vivacity. After Chaplin achieved fame, she became known as 'the female Chaplin', which is an underestimation of the individuality of her own comedy. Certainly in this year at Keystone Mabel was to provide Chaplin with a very worthy foil and partner. Although after difficult beginnings they were to become good friends, the partnership was confined to work. Mabel had exceptional charms, but at this time in her life they were exclusively reserved for Mack Sennett.

In 1984 there still survived a witness of Chaplin's first scene in his tramp costume and character – perhaps, indeed, the most significant witness, since he was the cameraman who actually filmed it. Hans Koenekamp had arrived at Keystone in 1913 and stayed until 1918 or 1919; he retained the happiest memories of his days at the studio. He remembered Sennett as 'the mastermind' and Mabel as 'the nicest person I ever met. She was great.' He also recalled how the units would load all their equipment onto public streetcars to go on location in Westlake Park or elsewhere. 'Finally we got transportation of our own.' Half a dozen cameramen worked between as many units, turning out as many as three films a week. 'Sometimes we'd go out into a park and shoot and by the end of the day we came back, we had the film.' Working like this, it was often difficult to remember what films a cameraman had worked on and with whom. Even so, though he had forgotten the title, Hans Koenekamp very clearly remembered the film: 'Can't think of the title. Tried to remember it. I can still see the scene he's in though. It was a hotel lobby, and he acted like a half drunk with that cockiness with his foot and the hat and the cane. I shot him.'[8]

Before shooting the scene Hans Koenekamp had watched Chaplin come on the set:

> I can still see the little shack where he came out the dressing room. He'd come out and he'd kind of rehearse *himself* – that walk, the cane, the hat and things like that, you know.
>
> I can still see him when he came onto the set. He was supposed to be half drunk or something like that. He came into the lobby and tried to make eyes at women, and women ignored him and all that kind of stuff . . . I can remember that. Never forget that. So I really photographed the first scene he played in . . .
>
> Did it look funny there and then? Yes, it did. Well it was, because it was *fresh* . . . And his movements too. Wiggle the mouth and that moustache would kinda work. And the cane flapping around, swinging on his arm . . . and going around on one leg like he was skating.[9]

Mabel's Strange Predicament revolved around a standard Keystone theme – bedroom mix-ups in a small hotel. Sennett introduced Chaplin in a sequence in the hotel lobby. He enters, mildly inebriated, becomes entangled with the leash of Mabel's dog, takes some falls with a cuspidor, and evinces a flirtatious interest in every passing female. The humour lies in the air of precarious dignity with which he carries off both his tipsiness and the evident imposture of his presence in the hotel, down-at-heel as he is. Chaplin recalled with satisfaction how the rest of the Keystone players and technicians gathered round to watch rehearsals for the scene, and reassured him with their laughter. In subsequent sequences Charlie encounters Mabel, who has locked herself out of her room, wearing only her nightgown, and gives lecherous chase through the hotel corridors. When, ultimately and inevitably, there is a confrontation between Mabel, her admirer, the gentleman under whose bed Mabel has somehow found herself and the man's jealous wife, the bemused Charlie gets in the way of most of the blows. With this film, Chaplin won his first major point at Keystone. Sennett was so impressed with Chaplin's business in the lobby scene, and the favourable reactions of the bystanders, that he over-rode Lehrman's objections and let it run on for the full minute of the take, without the usual busy Keystone-after-Griffith intercutting.

Mabel's Strange Predicament was one of the company's more elaborate productions. *Kid Auto Races at Venice, California* was the most elementary type of impromptu shot in the course of a public event. The Kid Auto Races were held on a specially made track at the seaside resort of Venice. The competitors were boys in soap-box cars, which were laboriously pushed by the drivers and their team up a steep ramp erected at the beginning of the course. The run down this incline provided the momentum for the race. The film which Henry Lehrman shot against the background of the race and the crowds had only one joke: Lehrman is a film director; Chaplin is a nuisance who wants to get in the picture and constantly spoils the cameraman's shots. Chaplin later said that it was his idea, and had been suggested by an incident he had witnessed when he was touring with the Karno Company in Jersey. During the filming of the carnival procession there a fussy local official kept pushing himself into the picture.

Bits of business are already recognizable. Twirling his cane, he knocks off his own hat or injures his ankle. He pertly tips his hat to an official he has annoyed. The principal quality of the character Chaplin creates here is infantilism. He is a mischievous child, grimacing at a car that almost runs him down and sticking out his tongue at Lehrman. There is a long shot of him running, leaping and skipping down the track in crazed abandon. The final shot of the film is a huge close-up of a frightful grimace. Yet, as Walter Kerr wrote with admirable perception,

> He is elbowing his way into immortality, both as a 'character' in the film and as a professional comedian to be remembered. And he is doing it by calling attention to the camera as camera.
>
> He would do this throughout his career, using the instrument as a means of establishing a direct and openly acknowledged relationship between himself and his audience. In fact he is, with this film, establishing himself as *one among the audience*, one among those who are astonished by this new mechanical marvel, one among those who would like to be photographed by it, and – he would make the most of the implication later – one among those who are invariably chased away. He looked at the camera and went through it, joining the rest of us. The seeds of his subsequent hold upon the public, the mysterious and almost inexplicable bond between the performer and everyman, were there.[10]

The skirmishes of the film director and the persistent camera hog were a comic echo of the behind-the-screen relationship of Lehrman and Chaplin. After one more film, *Between Showers*, Sennett recognized that the partnership was unprofitable and assigned Chaplin to another director, George Nichols, a veteran from the pioneering days, now approaching sixty. Chaplin seems to have got on no better with him: he repulsed all the comedian's suggestions for business with the cry 'No time, no time!' and complained to Sennett when Chaplin talked back. Sennett responded by more closely supervising the films himself. *A Film Johnnie* was an elementary affair, shot around the studio and, like Chaplin's later films *The Masquerader*, *His New Job* and *Behind the Screen*, giving us evocative glimpses of life in the early American studios. Charlie goes to the cinema and falls for the star of the film. He therefore pursues her to the Keystone Studios, where he causes havoc among the productions. Fire breaks out and he is squirted by the fire brigade. In a crazy, funny little gag, he twists his ears and thereby gives the fireman a retaliatory squirt.

In *His Favorite Pastime* Chaplin plays the drunk again. He gets into a fight in a bar, follows a pretty young woman home, pays court to her coloured maid and ends up in a fracas with a jealous husband. Chaplin was able to introduce some virtuoso gags – the first of many *contretemps* with a swing door; and a memorable feat in which he somersaults from a balcony to land in sitting position on a sofa, his cigar still lit. The film had a special significance in Chaplin's personal life at the time. The girl is eighteen-year-old Peggy Pearce, Chaplin's first recorded Hollywood love. Peggy was an impregnably virtuous girl and lived with her parents. Chaplin felt that he was not yet ready to contemplate marriage and the affair was not of long duration. There is a touching, tangible memento of it, though: more than sixty years later Mrs Walter Matthau found in a Hollywood antique shop a plated cup won by Chaplin and Peggy in a dance contest.

Cruel, Cruel Love gave Chaplin the opportunity for parody melodrama: as a spurned aristocratic suitor he swallows a glass of water under the impression that it is poison and in his supposed death throes has hallucinations of hell. *The Star Boarder*, the most charming of this group of films supervised by Sennett, was partly shot in gardens and orchards, and has the verve and simplicity of a comic strip. Charlie is the pet of the landlady (Minta Durfee), carrying on a flirtation under the nose of her husband (Edgar Kennedy) who has his own extra-marital interests. All this is enthusiastically recorded by their mischievous son who possesses – just like the boy Chaplin in his *Sherlock Holmes* days – a box camera.

These four films occupied Chaplin throughout March and the beginning of April. During the same period Sennett took his male stars – Chaplin, Arbuckle, Sterling and Conklin – to a dance hall, where they improvised a knockabout film, *Tango Tangles*, on the theme of the rivalry of the first three over the hat-check girl (Minta Durfee). Except for Conklin, who put on Keystone Kop uniform, they are in their natty everyday clothes and without make-up. Sterling is the band leader, Arbuckle one of his musicians, and the handsome Chaplin a tipsy and smooth-shaven lounge lizard. The real patrons look on with unfeigned amusement and, to set the scene, the film opens with real demonstration dancers. Chaplin does an eccentric tango and in the fight scenes, menacingly twitching his protruded bottom, he looks forward to the pugilistic efforts of *The Knockout*, *The Champion* and *City Lights*.

Recognizing that Chaplin was getting on no better with Nichols than with Lehrman, and seeing that Chaplin and Mabel had struck up an amiable relationship, Sennett now made the mistake of assigning Mabel to direct the next film in which she and Chaplin were to co-star, *Mabel at the Wheel*. Chaplin from the start was not happy about taking direction from a girl several years younger than himself and with none of his stage experience. The happy working relationship evaporated rapidly as Mabel swept aside Chaplin's suggestions just as Lehrman and Nichols had done.

During the previous few months Pearl White had established herself as the heroine of dramatic adventure films, and the week before *Mabel at the Wheel* was begun had appeared on American screens in the first episode of the most famous of all serial thrillers, *The Perils of Pauline*. *Mabel at the Wheel* was a take-off of the Pearl White style, with Mabel as a race-track driver's girlfriend who takes over her boyfriend's car and wins the race when he is kidnapped by the villain. The villain, uncharacteristically, is Chaplin, dressed in a grey frock coat and silk hat, and with tufts of whisker on his chin in the style of Ford Sterling. He also has a magnificent new prop in the shape of a motor-cycle; in the first scene of the film he uses it to compete with Harry McCoy, as the racing driver, for Mabel's affection. Mabel unfortunately falls off the pillion into a puddle and there is a fine comic moment when Charlie feels behind him and finds her gone.

When Mabel, affronted by the incident with the puddle, abandons Charlie for Harry, Charlie and a couple of shady confederates kidnap

Harry and lock him in a hut. They then attempt to sabotage Mabel who has taken the car out herself. In one scene Charlie and his friends throw water on the track in front of Mabel's car. The trouble between them came to a head when they were shooting this scene. Chaplin suggested a bit of business to liven it up: he would step on the hose, peer into it to see why it had stopped, and then release his foot and soak himself. Perhaps Mabel was aware that this was, in historic fact, the oldest joke in the cinema: it was used by the Lumière Brothers (who had got it from a comic strip) in *L'Arroseur Arrosé*, for their first film programme in 1896. Mabel brushed the suggestion aside, Chaplin refused to work and sat down on the roadside. Mabel, the pet of the studio, was bewildered and the men in the crew were ready to beat up Charlie for upsetting her. Chaplin had himself grown attached to Mabel but, as he recalled in a significant phrase, '*this was my work*'. Nothing in his life was ever to take prior place to that.

They packed up for the day (it was already after five) and returned to the studio. Sennett, acutely sensitive to any hurt to Mabel (his turbulent and frustrated love affair with her was to survive her death, to his own) was furious. It was assumed on both sides that Chaplin's days at Keystone were finished, contract or no contract. Chaplin was therefore surprised the following day to find both Sennett and Mabel conciliatory; later he discovered that Sennett had had orders from the east for more Chaplin films, since sales of the first were already booming. Chaplin agreed to finish *Mabel at the Wheel* with Sennett's supervision, and took the opportunity to announce to Sennett that he was now ready and anxious to direct his own pictures. According to Chaplin Sennett was dubious, but accepted Chaplin's guarantee of $1500 – the money he had saved since his arrival in California – in case the film proved unshowable.

There is some doubt which film should be regarded as Chaplin's directorial debut. In his 1964 autobiography Chaplin said that it was *Caught in the Rain*. On 9 August 1914, however, he sent Sydney a list of the films in which he had appeared during his seven months at Keystone. On it he very deliberately marked as 'My Own' six films which he had already directed; these, in order of release, are *Twenty Minutes of Love* (released 20 April), *Caught in the Rain* (4 May), *Mabel's Married Life* (20 June), *Laughing Gas* (9 July), *The Property Man* (1 August) and *The Face on the Bar Room Floor* (released 10 August – the day after he sent the list to Sydney).

From this time to the end of his year at Keystone, Chaplin directed all the films in which he appeared except the feature *Tillie's Punctured Romance*, directed by Mack Sennett. It is notable that Chaplin does not include in the list of his own films three which existing filmographies record as collaborations with Mabel Normand: *Caught in a Cabaret* (27 April), *Her Friend the Bandit* (4 June), (Chaplin does not list this film at all and no existing copy is known) and *Mabel's Busy Day* (13 June). On the other hand he *does* include the fourth of these alleged collaborations, *Mabel's Married Life*.

Hear is a list of some of
my pictures.
Making a living
Kid Auto Races
Mable Strange predicament
Between showers
Film Johnny
His favorite pastime
Cruel Cruel love
Star border
my own Twenty minutes of love
Caught in a Cabaret
my own Caught in the rain
Knock out
Mable at the wheel
Mable busy day.
my own Mable married life
The fatal mallet
my own Laughing Gas
my own The property man
my own The face on the bar room floor

1914 - Chaplin's first filmography,
written by himself, August 1914.

Chaplin might understandably have forgotten fifty years later that he directed *Twenty Minutes of Love*, or have simply written it off as apprentice practice, since it is the first and one of the slightest of the 'park' films. Nevertheless there are developing traits of the later Charlie character. There is a sweetness about his mischief and flirtations, and a touch of the romantic.

There was no danger of Chaplin's having to pay up the guarantee against the failure of *Caught in the Rain*. It proved one of the best and most successful Keystones up to that time. The film shows all the care of an apprentice's demonstration piece. Chaplin had made good use of his months at Keystone. In particular he had studied the work of the cutting room, and the jigsaw method of film construction that Sennett had inherited from Griffith. In addition, of course, he brought from Karno a highly developed skill in stagecraft. Already in his first film the *mise-en-scène* of each shot excels, or at least equals, the best work of the Keystone directors. This first effort shows him particularly conscious of the shot-by-shot method of narrative and assembly. The one reel contains far more shots than the average Keystone production, and though Chaplin would never again revert to this Griffith style of rapid montage, the logic and fluidity of the narrative are admirable.

The anecdote is absurd, but the telling is exemplary, and this remains one of the most accomplished films of Chaplin's year at Keystone. The film has clarity, verve, a musical or balletic rhythm in the rapid cutting; it is still entertaining and amusing after seventy years. He follows the ground rules of the studio, but he already has a special mastery of telling a story in images. Titles are used only for extra laughs, and as the action speeds up they are dispensed with altogether. As his own director, he is able to place and pace his gags as he wants and to introduce virtuoso comedy turns. He had chosen excellent supporting comedians in Mack Swain, who after this first partnership was to remain for more than a decade a favourite foil, and Alice Davenport.

Chaplin's next release, *A Busy Day*, has long been assumed to have been directed by him though he did not include it in the list of his films which he sent to Sydney in August 1914. Since it had been made only three months before, he clearly did not rate it very highly. Certainly it is one of Sennett's throwaways – it is only half a reel in length – but it is a curiosity for all that. It is one of the films in which Sennett has taken advantage of a local event – in this case a military parade – to provide a spectacular background, and the comic action takes place around a bandstand and grandstand.

Chaplin, for the first of three times in his film career, is dressed as a woman. In *The Masquerader* and *A Woman* the plots would call for him to disguise himself as a seductive and fashionable lady. Here he goes through the whole film as an angry little working-class termagant – almost a pantomime dame as she lays about her with her brolly, blows her nose very rudely on her skirt, and gives a preparatory hitch of her clothing and a wild leap in the air before setting off in pursuit of some victim. She and her husband Mack are spectators at the parade. Mack wanders off in the train of a prettier woman. The wife gives chase, on the way battling with several policemen, and getting in the way of a film cameraman, much as Charlie did in *Kid Auto Races*. Afer a lot of skirmishes and rough-houses, Mack very sensibly shoves the creature into the harbour, where she sinks in a flurry of bubbles. Apart from Chaplin's unwonted disguise, the film is curious for its technique. Whether Chaplin himself directed it or not, it has all the look of a study exercise in shot relations. Again and again the same effect of someone being thrown out of one shot and landing in another shot is repeated, for example:

8 Director throws wife off screen left.

9 Rear of bandstand. Wife is thrown into screen from right, and knocks over a policeman. The policeman throws her back off screen right.

10 As 8. Wife is thrown in from screen left. She picks herself up and starts to pose in front of movie camera. The director again throws her off screen left.

11 Rear of bandstand. Wife is thrown in, screen right, and lands on bandstand.

Fifty years later he regarded it as a serious shortcoming in old George Nichols that the only movie trick he knew was this one of throwing people out of one shot and into another. Still, for a comedy director, shot relationship was a useful lesson to learn.

In *The Knockout*, directed by Charles Avery, Chaplin played a two-minute supporting role as referee to a boxing bout between Roscoe Arbuckle and Edgar Kennedy. It is a lively little performance that anticipates *The Champion* and *City Lights*. Chaplin's refereeing is balletic, and introduces gags of a sophistication alien to the rest of the film. Worse hit than the pugilists, he lies down and drags himself around the ring by the ropes; then counts the loser out from a sitting position.

Chaplin's name was by this time already a sufficient draw for Keystone to advertise *The Knockout* as a Chaplin film. It is no longer clear whether he was deliberately added to the cast for his box-office value, or whether it was just part of the Keystone method of using any available talent at any time. More than fifty years later Chaplin told an interviewer that he had actually played bit roles as a Kop in Keystone films, though so far none of these appearances has been identified.

If we accept Chaplin's identification of his films in the letter to Sydney, we can discount *Mabel's Busy Day*, a rough and rowdy little piece, matching material shot at a race track with studio shots, which has generally been credited as a collaboration between Chaplin and Mabel. The film provides evidence of the growth of Chaplin's popularity. In *Kid Auto Races* the ordinary public at the sporting event show little interest in the proceedings of the film unit. In *Mabel's Busy Day* the crowds in the background are huge, and roped off from the performers. Clearly with Chaplin on hand the Sennett unit did not need to borrow the audience assembled for the sports event. Chaplin's very presence attracted all the audience they needed to provide a spectacular background.

In the succeeding six months Chaplin directed sixteen films, four of them two-reelers, running for half an hour. They are uneven; some are throwaways, some are sketches of ideas he will later elaborate and refine; but the speed with which he masters his craft is astounding.

Mabel's Married Life is as expert as *Caught in the Rain*, but with less tension in the cutting and more leisure for gags and character touches. Partly filmed in a park and partly on sets, the picture is concerned with the irritation inflicted by Mack, a hefty Don Juan, who taunts Charlie and pursues Charlie's wife Mabel. Mabel buys a punch-dummy to get Charlie into condition. Returning home drunk, Charlie takes it for his rival and fights it. The film contains much character comedy: Charlie's look of ineffable disapproval rudely cut short when the spring doors of the saloon knock him down; the *connaissance* with which he sizes up Mack's ample bottom before belabouring it with boot and cane; his panic when faced with an unexplained odour.

His next three films harked back in different ways to vaudeville. Dentists were a rich source for music hall jokes, and *Laughing Gas* explores the comic possibilities when the dentist's assistant substitutes for him. In *The Property Man* he is property man in a vaudeville theatre peopled by grotesque and unreasonably temperamental artists. Contemporary critics were shocked by the cruelty of the prop man's treatment of his aged and decrepit assistant; and shocked by the nursery rudeness of a scene in which, having concealed a glass of beer down the front of his trousers, he inadvisedly bends over. With a quick appeal of his eyes for the audience's understanding, he gingerly shakes the water down his leg. *The Face on the Bar Room Floor* is a parody in the *Casey's Court Circus* vein, and technically the least interesting of Chaplin's films – for the most part simply alternating lengthy titles with tableaux in comic illustration of Hugh Antoine d'Arcy's pathetic and then popular ballad of love betrayed. This and the two films that followed look like marking time: *Recreation* is a fast-improvised 'park' film. *The Masquerader* is simple knockabout set in a film studio, mainly notable for its behind-the-screen glimpses of the Keystone lot and for Chaplin's second female impersonation.

In his last three months at Keystone, Chaplin directed ten films which alternated improvisations like these (*His New Profession*, *Those Love Pangs*, *Gentlemen of Nerve*, *Getting Acquainted*) with more elaborately staged films which look like sketches for films to come. *The Rounders*, in which he was teamed with Roscoe Arbuckle, looks back over Chaplin's whole gallery of inebriates from Karno to Keystone, and forward to *A Night Out* and ultimately to the Tramp's nights on the town with the millionaire in *City Lights*. *The New Janitor* is the prototype for *The Bank*. Only seventeen days separated the releases of *The Rounders* and *The New Janitor*, yet in that short space of time, Chaplin's art seemed to take a massive leap forward both in approach to film narrative and in appreciation of the character that was developing within the tramp make-up and costume. The film conforms to the basic Keystone rules, using only eight static camera set-ups, yet out of his material Chaplin fashions a brilliant little narrative, clear, precise, with drama, suspense and an element of sentiment that goes deeper than the flirtations of Westlake Park. The animated strip cartoon of *Caught in the Rain* has developed into comic drama. The editing creates a real dynamic in the Griffith manner rather than simply providing a step-by-step progression of narrative incidents. Gags and character touches are developed without the Keystone rush and integrated into the story. Chaplin reveals his gift for observing behaviour: the secretary's brief, loving look at the manager's straw boater hanging in the hall intimates a whole past relationship. (See Appendix 5)

Chaplin's ambition led him to overspend his $1000 budget for

Dough and Dynamite. A worried Sennett withheld the $25 due to Chaplin as his director's fee, and decided that the only way to retrieve the loss was to release the film as a two-reeler. His anxiety was unfounded: it proved one of the most profitable of all Keystone pictures. The story is simple: Charlie and Chester are waiters in a teashop who take over the bakery when the bakers go on strike. The dastardly strikers secrete dynamite in a loaf before it goes into the oven, thus blowing the place up. The story is mostly an excuse for variations on the fun to be had from sticky dough and clouds of flour, but the film shows Chaplin developing new sophistication in his deployment of studio sets and restricted camera set-ups.

Chaplin at this time had not committed himself to a fixed method of film making. His technique in *His Musical Career*, an attractive film which provided the model for Laurel and Hardy's *The Music Box*, sixteen years later, is in marked stylistic contrast to *Dough and Dynamite*. The single reel consists of a mere twenty-seven shots; usually Chaplin and the other Keystone directors used up to ninety shots in a film of the same length. Here, as Buster Keaton was later to do, he bypassed the current fashion in editing, recognizing that each shot needed to be a stage for his own extended comedy routines. He declared this early that cutting was not an obligation but a convenience.

The last film which Chaplin directed and played in at Keystone was *His Prehistoric Past*, released on 7 December 1914. The discovery of the so-called Piltdown Man in 1912 and of some Neanderthal bits and pieces around the same time had aroused intense popular interest in man's ancient ancestors, and the subject was taken up by every popular cartoonist and not a few film comedians. Chaplin's film, recalling *Jimmy the Fearless*, was cast in the form of a dream. Charlie falls asleep on a park bench and dreams that he is Weakchin, a cave man. Weakchin runs into trouble when he starts up a flirtation with the favourite of the harem of King Lowbrow (Mack Swain). When the king finally catches up with him, he is forcibly struck on the head with a large rock – and wakes up again on the park bench where a policeman is roughly shaking him.

Tillie's Punctured Romance, which was released three weeks previously, was the last film in which Chaplin would appear under the direction of anyone else (if we exclude two or three brief guest appearances in the 1920s). It was also the first and only time in his film career that he played a supporting role to another star. Perhaps these factors explain his laconic dismissal of the film in his autobiography, even though it was his first feature picture, and a landmark in establishing him with the public. 'It was pleasant working with Marie [Dressler] but I do not think the picture had much merit. I was more than happy to get back to directing myself.'

The film was the first feature-length comedy. Before it no comic film made anywhere in the world had exceeded one third of its length of six reels (ninety minutes' running time). Sennett may have been stirred to this ambitious venture by a spirit of rivalry: his partner in Triangle Film Corporation, D. W. Griffith, was at the time embarking on *The Birth of a Nation*. The project was also undertaken under the influence of the current 'famous players in famous plays' policy of bringing stars and properties from the New York stage. It was natural enough that in looking for a theatrical success to film, Sennett should turn to *Tillie's Nightmare*. Written in 1910, the comedy had had a long and triumphant run on Broadway and its star, Marie Dressler, was America's greatest comic personality in the days before the First World War. Moreover Sennett may have felt a personal attachment to Dressler, remembering her counsel, discouraging though it may have been, in his own early days.

Sennett may, in fact, originally have intended to devise a new vehicle to star Miss Dressler. His unreliable memoirs mention that his writers spent some weeks struggling with a scenario, with Marie on the payroll at $2500 a week, before they decided to go ahead and film *Tillie's Nightmare* with a new title. After this, he recalled, the work went swiftly, though the fourteen-week production period was unprecedented at the studio.

It was natural enough, as box-office insurance, to use the two top stars of the studio, Chaplin and Mabel, to support Marie Dressler. Already there was a vast, international audience quite unfamiliar with even the greatest luminaries of Broadway. Marie, in her own memoirs, offered a rather different (and patently mistaken) view of things: 'I went up on the lot and looked around until I found Charlie Chaplin who was then unknown. I picked him out and also Mabel Normand . . . I think the public will agree that I am a good picker for it was the first real chance Charlie Chaplin ever had.' Marie was clearly not a picturegoer. Even so the enormous success of the film did make it a landmark in Chaplin's career. It was released on 14 November 1914 to a favourable press and ecstatic public acclaim, and it was constantly revived and still turns up fom time to time in cinemas in truncated, doctored and sound-synchronized versions.

Parts of the film betray its stage origin – the characters mouth conversations and soliloquies – but when the story gets under way and particularly in the final chase Sennett's direction exploits the vulgar, earthy knockabout with assurance. From the stage text, too, the film acquires some narrative and character strength: behind the slapstick and extravagant farce, there is a realistic and quite affecting theme of a stupid, good-natured country girl duped by a ne'er-do-well sharper. Dressler's warm personality wins through even though Chaplin and Normand's screen experience gives them an undoubted advantage. At moments Chaplin's characterization of the deft, funny, heartless adventurer anticipates Verdoux – even though Verdoux could never insult the footmen and an effeminate guest at a party as Chaplin does.

From the time he began to direct until his departure from Keystone, there is practically no record of Chaplin's private life. The reason is that he had virtually no life outside his work. He was fascinated by the new medium and absorbed in the task of mastering it. 'This was my work,' indeed. Throughout his career the pattern was to be repeated: committed to a job of work, a film, the private Charlie all but disappeared.

A modest private life was not entirely strange in Hollywood at that time. Publicists were already helping to promote, for the delight of avid fans, stories of the gaiety and high living of the movie world, but life in Hollywood must, a lot of the time, have been more sedate than the legend. At Keystone, as at every other successful studio, the film people worked long hours and six days a week: time for play was limited. We know of Chaplin's Sunday calls on Peggy Pearce. Once, he remembered, when they were on their way to a charity appearance, he kissed Mabel Normand but nothing came of it: Mabel told him they were not each other's type. In any case both had their loyalties to Sennett. Chaplin and Sennett undoubtedly grew fond of each other. Chaplin recalled that Sennett practically adopted him and that they ate together every night.

Certainly during his first months at Keystone he grew gregarious enough to surprise himself. It would indeed have been hard to resist the evident high spirits and good nature of the Keystone people. Hans Koenekamp remembers, 'A whole bunch of 'em, actors as well, would pitch in if they had to build the set or something.' Chaplin shared the general habit of dropping into the Alexandria Bar on the way back to his hotel. In his early Hollywood days, too, he enjoyed going with the rest to see fights.

Later in the year, though, concentration on the work must have taken over. As in the Karno Company, some of his colleagues saw his abstractedness as a sign that he was unsociable and stand-offish. Even Hans Koenekamp felt that towards the end of his Keystone time 'he got to be a big shot. And he was a bit off-colour in politics.' Suspicion of Chaplin's libertarian instincts began this early, it seems.

Chaplin continued to live in a hotel and his thrift was marked. His only notable expenditure was when he signed an agreement on 10 February with the English Motor Car Company for the hire, for five months, of a 1912 Kissell Kar Roadster. This cost him $300 down and $100 per month.

Neither Sennett, nor the Keystone executives, nor Chaplin himself can have anticipated the effect of the first releases upon the public. We can only look back at the first few Keystone films and see a crude, unfinished form, and the earliest tentative search for a screen character. To the audiences of the time they arrived like rockets. Chaplin, from the very start, had created a new relationship with the audience, a new response that no one before in films or in any other medium had elicited.

In Britain the first Chaplin films were released in June 1914. Having already observed the phenomenon in America, the Keystone Company advertised:

ARE YOU PREPARED FOR THE CHAPLIN BOOM?

There has never been so instantaneous a hit as that of Chas Chaplin, the famous Karno comedian in Keystone Comedies. Most first-rank exhibitors have booked every film in which he appears, and after the first releases there is certain to be a big rush for copies.

The first seven films were shown to the trade press, and on 25 June, Keystone were able proudly to reprint their reviews. *Kine Weekly* reported:

> We have seen seven Chaplin releases, and every one has been a triumph for the one-time hero of 'Mumming Birds' who has leapt into the front rank of film comedians at a bound.

The Cinema's opinion was as favourable:

> *Kid Auto Races* struck us as about the funniest film we have seen. When we subsequently saw Chaplin in more ambitious subjects our opinion that the Keystone Company has made the capture of their career was strengthened. Chaplin is a born screen comedian; he does things we have never seen done on the screen before.

Both Sennett and Chaplin were aware of Chaplin's fast growing value. Chaplin recalled that it was around the time of the outbreak of war in Europe that he and Sennett discussed the renewal of their contract. Chaplin announced that he would require $1000 a week for a further year, at which Sennett protested that that was more than he earned himself. Chaplin reminded him that it was not for Sennett's name that the public lined up outside cinemas, but for his. Sennett countered by pointing out that Ford Sterling was already regretting his decision to leave Keystone, to which Chaplin in turn replied that all *he* needed to make a comedy was a park, a policeman and a pretty girl.

Sennett apparently sought the advice of Kessel and Baumann, and came back with a counter-offer to Chaplin's demand for $1000 a week. He offered a three-year contract, at $500 a week for the first year, $750 for the second and $1500 for the third, the contract to become operative immediately. Chaplin said that he would agree if the terms were reversed – $1500 for the first year, $750 for the second and $500 for the third. Evidently baffled by Chaplin's economics, Sennett let the matter drop.

It was clear to Chaplin that the time had come to move on; and on Sunday 9 August – five days after the outbreak of the European War and presumably immediately after his conversation with Sennett – he sat down to write one of his very rare letters, to Sydney, in London:

> Los Angeles Athletic Club,
> Los Angeles, Calif.
> Sunday Aug 9th
>
> My Dear Sid,
>
> You are doubtless realising who is addressing you. Yes. It really is your brother Chas. after all these years, but you must forgive me. The whole of my time is taken up with the movies. I write, direct, and play in them and believe me it keeps you busy. Well, Sid, I have made good. All the theatres feature my name in big letters i.e. 'Chas Chaplin hear today'. I tell you in this country I am a big box office attraction. All the managers

tell me that I have 50 letters a week from men and women from all parts of the world. It is wonderfull how popular I am in such a short time and next year I hope to make a bunch of dough. I have had all kinds of offers at 500 a week with 40% stock which would mean a salary of or about 1000 a week. Mr Marcus Lowe [*sic*]*, the big theatre man over hear, has made me a proposition which is a certainty and wants me to form a comedy company and give me either a salary per week or 50% stock. This is a sure thing, any way, the whole matter is in the hands of my Lawyers, of course I shall finish out my contract with the Keyst. people, and if they come through with something better I shall stay where I am. This Marcus Lowe business is a sure I have a guarantee sale at all his theaters and then sell to the outside people. Anyway, I will let you know all about it in my next letter. He will finance the whole thing if it comes through it means thoullions to us. Mr Sennett is in New York. He said he would write to you and make you an offer. I told him you would do great for pictures of course he has not seen you and he is only going by what I say. He said he would give you 150 to start with. I told him you are getting that now and would not think of coming over hear for that amount. If you do consider it, don't sign for any length of time, because I will want you with me when I start. I could get you 250 as easy as anything but of course you would have to sign a contract. It will be nice for you to come over for three months with the Keystone and then start for ourselves. You will hear from Sennet [*sic*] but don't come for *less than 175 understand?* You will like it out hear it is a beautiful country and the fresh air is doing me the world of good. I have made a heap of good friends hear and go to all the partys ect. I stay at the best Club in the city where all the millionairs belong in fact I have a good sane, wholsome time. I am living well. I have my own valet, some class to me eh what? I am still saving my money and since I have been hear I have 4000 dollars in one bank, 1200 in another, 1500 in London not so bad for 25 and still going strong thank God. Sid, we will be millionaires before long. My health is better than it ever was and I am getting fatter. Well you must tell me how Mother is and don't forget to write me before you sign any contract because there is another firm who will pay you 250. They wanted me and I told them about you, as I could not break my contract of course. Mr Sennett is a lovely man and we are great pals but business is business. Of course he does not know I am leaving or that I have had these offeres, so don't say anything in case it gets back hear, you never know. I would not like to heart Sennet feelings he thinks the world of me. Now about that money for mother do you think it is safe for me to send you it while the war is on, or do you think it better for

* Marcus Loew (1870–1927). American exhibition magnate and co-founder of Metro Goldwyn Mayer, which was long controlled by Loews Inc.

you to pay my share and then we will arrainge things later on. So long as I know the money will get there I will send it. Anyway tell me in your next letter what to do. I hope they don't make you fight over there. This war is terrible. Well that about all the important news. I have just finished a six real picture with Marie Dressler the American star and myself. It cost 50,000 to put [?] and I have hog the whole picture. It is the best thing I ever did. I must draw to a close now as I am getting hungry. Just this second my valet tells me I have friends to take me out Automobiling so am going to the beach to dine. Good night Sid, Love to Minnie

Your loving brother
Charlie

5

Essanay

Sydney arrived to start work at Keystone early in November 1914. He invented for himself a character called 'Gussle'; padded out to a grotesque pear shape, he wore a curious little boat-shaped hat and a moustache, tight jacket and cane which seemed like homage to his younger brother. His first film, to be released in December, was *Gussle the Golfer*. As for Charlie, the Loew proposal which he had outlined in his letter to Sydney had eventually come to nothing. By the time of Sydney's arrival in California he had still no firm offer from any other studio, and he was nervous. The apparent lack of interest may in fact confirm the oft-repeated stories that Sennett made strenuous efforts to prevent representatives of other film companies from reaching Chaplin, hoping that he would eventually come, by attrition, to accept Keystone's offer of $400 a week. Chaplin considered setting up his own production unit, but Sydney – to whom the film business as well as his own $200 salary was a startling novelty – opposed the idea.

Eventually, however, Chaplin received an emissary from the Essanay Film Manufacturing Company of Chicago, in the person of Jesse Robbins, a producer and director with the firm. The name 'Essanay' was made up from the initial letters of the names of the founders, George K. Spoor and G. M. Anderson. Spoor had started in the film business as an exhibitor and renter in Chicago; Anderson (1882–1971), born Max Aronson, made his acting debut in *The Great Train Robbery* (1903) and later, as Broncho Billy, became the cinema's first cowboy star. Spoor and Anderson went into partnership in Essanay in February 1907, taking as their trade-mark an Indian head, borrowed from the copper one-cent piece. Anderson established a little studio at Niles, near San Francisco, in 1908, where he set an unbeatable record by producing and starring in a series of *Broncho Billy* films, turned out at the rate of one each week.

Anderson and Robbins had been greatly impressed by rumours that Chaplin was demanding $1250 per week and a bonus on signing of $10,000. Though the idea of the bonus was quite novel to him when Robbins mentioned it, Chaplin thought it best not to turn it down. Anderson agreed to the arrangement without consulting Spoor, who was greatly alarmed to learn that they would be paying about fifteen times the going rate for Essanay-featured players to a comedian he personally had never heard of. Chaplin signed, but became more and more suspicious when the $10,000 bonus failed to materialize, and it was poor Anderson who was left to placate him since Spoor, who was supposed to hand the money over, had tactically disappeared from the Chicago studios.

Fortunately Chaplin liked Anderson, an amiable if taciturn westerner. With him he visited Essanay's little glasshouse studio at Niles, and decided he did not care for it. In the last days of December 1914 therefore Anderson accompanied him by train to Chicago, Essanay's eastern headquarters, where the company had a studio at 1333 Argyle Street. Anderson returned to California on New Year's Day, 1915, leaving Chaplin to discover, with no small dismay, the chilliness of a Chicago January and the indifferent amenities of the studio. It still belonged to the era of 'film factories'. After the creative chaos of Keystone, Chaplin found the cold, production-line style of the Chicago studio inimical. The worst affront was when he was told to collect his script from the scenario department, whose chief at that time was the future queen of Hearst columnists, Louella Parsons.

Other irritations were in store. Neither Spoor, bonus nor salary turned up. He found that the Essanay staff had little or no concern for the quality of their product, while with the absurd, penny-pinching, pound-foolish bookkeeper mentality of the place, they recklessly screened and edited the negatives rather than pay the few dollars needed for proper positive rushes and working material. Some compensation was provided by the acting talent on hand in Chicago. Ben Turpin, a wizened little man rather like a prematurely hatched bird, with permanently crossed eyes and a prominent adam's-apple dancing up and down his scrawny neck, was one of the best comedy partners Chaplin ever found. Leo White was a lean, fierce, volatile little man who originally came from Manchester but had worked in operetta and specialized in characterizing comic Frenchmen in goatees and silk hats. Bud Jamison – a former vaudeville performer, baby-faced, six feet tall and weighing nineteen stone – provided the same grotesque physical contrast to Chaplin that Mack Swain had done at Keystone. Two pretty extras in Chaplin's first Essanay film, Gloria Swanson and Agnes Ayres, were to become major Hollywood stars. Swanson plays a stenographer: Chaplin was disappointed when he gave her a try-out for a more ambitious role, only to find her wooden and unresponsive. Years later Swanson told him she had been deliberately unco-operative as she wanted to be a dramatic actress, not a comedienne.

We have a rare glimpse of Chaplin on the eve of starting work in Chicago. He was interviewed by Gene Morgan, a local reporter who was uncommonly perceptive and accurate in detail. One of his more striking revelations is that the legendary costume was at this period bought off the peg. Chaplin told him he had been shopping on State Street for a fresh costume and had had difficulty in getting boots large enough. He had also bought trousers. He told Morgan that he often followed people for miles to study character: 'Fortunately my types are all small men. I would hate to be found following a big man and imitating him behind his back.'

Morgan's summing up of the Chaplin personality deserves to be remembered if only for the haunting final phrase:

> You know him as a human gatling gun of laughs. He makes you chortle once every second. He has lots of flying black hair, and, do you know, it sort of grows on you. He wears an eloquent little moustache, which bounces on top of the funniest smile put on celluloid. He sports an unsteady derby hat, which he never fails to tip after kicking friends in the face. And he twirls a cane as if it were a blackthorn, Sousa's baton, a carpet beater and a lightning rod, all in one.
>
> And his feet –
>
> You can't keep your eyes off his feet.
>
> Those big shoes are buttoned with 50,000,000 eyes.

Chaplin's first film at Essanay was appropriately titled *His New Job*. As he had done in *A Film Johnnie*, he chose to set the action in a film studio. If nothing else this had the advantage that sets and props were ready to hand: at least he could limit his dependence on the Essanay scenic staff.

Chaplin is still the incorrigible Keystone Charlie, cheerfully causing chaos by his insouciant incompetence, tittering gleefully behind his hand at the spectacle of the destruction he has provoked, ever ready to apply a boot to the behind or a hammer to the head of anyone who presumes to protest. Chaplin clearly never worked out a scenario for the film. He adopts comedy props as they come to hand – cigarettes, matches, a pipe, a soda syphon, a saw and mallet, a swing door, a recalcitrant scenic pillar, an officer's uniform many sizes too large and with accompanying shako and exceedingly bendy sword. He goes through favourite routines with his cane (especially handy for hooking Ben Turpin's feet from under him) and hat. He was several times later to repeat and elaborate the business of being reprimanded for failing to remove his hat, which he here introduces. With child-like insolence he makes to replace the hat on his head and then at the last moment causes it to spring up into the air. He conscientiously searches the fur of the shako for fleas; and sizes up a piece of nude statuary with the affectation of disinterested connoisseurship he would later bring to the contemplation of the nude in the art shop window in *City Lights*.

After two weeks' work, *His New Job* was ready for release on 1 February. By this time Spoor was back in Chicago, now happily reconciled to the idea of his new star. To his surprise, business colleagues had rushed to congratulate him on his good fortune; and now *His New Job* chalked up more advance sales than any previous Essanay picture. Chaplin finally received his bonus, but neither that nor Spoor's strenuous efforts to make up for his previous offhandedness endeared him to his star. Unhappy with conditions in the Chicago factory, Chaplin announced that after all he would prefer to work in the company's Californian studio. Niles was the lesser of two evils.

Since the historian Theodore Huff compiled the first Chaplin filmography in the late 1940s, Chaplin chroniclers have trustingly followed his assertion that the Essanay films were photographed by Roland Totheroh. In fact Totheroh was not to become Chaplin's cameraman until 1916. His most regular cameraman at Essanay was Harry Ensign. Totheroh himself was wholly occupied on Broncho films. He nevertheless remembered his first meeting with Chaplin at Niles: 'We thought he was a little Frenchman.'[1] Broncho Billy Anderson suggested that Chaplin might like to live in one of the studio bungalows as he did. Chaplin was appalled however by the mean and squalid style in which the millionaire star lived, and soon moved to the Stoll Hotel nearby. Totheroh's description of his arrival affords a vivid picture of the informal and rural character of film studios of the period, as well as the austerity of Chaplin's own style of living in 1915:

> We had a bungalow in the studio. I had a corner one, and later on Ben Turpin had the next one . . . And Anderson had one about a block down the road further, his own bungalow, you know. It was anything but a palace, he had an old wood stove in the kitchen and everything. So Charlie had one handbag with him – just a little old one of those canvas-like handbags, you know. Jim said, Charlie's room will be this one here, and of course my room's in front, whatever it was. And they were saying, 'We've got the old wood stove going in the kitchen, and we heated up some tea or something. We had Joe heat up some tea, you know. Charlie was an Englishman . . . So we opened his bag to put the things out. All he had in it was a pair of socks with the heels worn out and an old couple of dirty undershirts, and an old mess shirt and an old worn out toothbrush. He had hardly nothing in that thing. So we didn't say anything. Joe said, Jeez, he hasn't got much in this thing, has he? . . . I'll never forget down there, nothing, he said, no bed and all this and that, and I felt like saying, yeah, and what the hell did you have? Jesus. Nothing in his handbag or anything.[2]

Years later visitors to the Chaplin studio would be no less surprised by the austerity of the star's quarters.

Chaplin began to build up his own little stock company. From Chicago he brought Ben Turpin, Leo White and Bud Jamison. He also recruited a former Karno comedian, Billy Armstrong, and another English artist, Fred Goodwins, who had been on the legitimate stage after an early career as a newspaperman. Paddy McGuire came from New Orleans via burlesque and musical comedy but typed well as an Irish bucolic. The essential task,however, was to find a leading lady. One of Broncho Billy Anderson's cowboys, either Carl Strauss or Fritz Wintermeyer, recommended a girl who frequented Tate's Café on Hill Street, San Francisco. The girl was traced and proved to be called Edna Purviance. Born in Lovelock, Nevada, she had trained as a secretary but (at least according to later publicity biographies) had done some amateur stage work. She was blonde, beautiful, serious and Chaplin was instantly captivated by her. Only after he had engaged her did he have some qualms as to whether or not she had any gift for comedy. Edna convinced him of her sense of humour at a party the night before she started work, when she bet him $10 that he could not hypnotize her, and then played along with the gag, pretending to fall under his spell. She was to appear with him in thirty-five films during the next eight years and to prove his most enchanting leading lady, with a charm exceeding even that of Mabel Normand. For some time their association, both professional and private, was to be the happiest of Chaplin's youth.

Chaplin's first film at Niles was *A Night Out*. If stuck for an idea, he could always rely upon a restaurant for inspiration: he ordered the construction crew to build a large café set, complete with a fountain in the foyer as an extra source of havoc. In this film Chaplin and Ben Turpin form a beautiful double act, sharing a solemn, unselfconscious, childlike air of mischief. It is an interesting variation on the partnership of Chaplin and Arbuckle in *The Rounders*. Charlie and Ben are a couple of drunks, absorbed in the tricky business of staying upright to the exclusion of all other proprieties. They are aggressive, whether loyally defending each other against interfering policemen, waiters and other hostile strangers, or fighting between themselves, with fists and bricks.

Unlike *His New Job*, this comic pantomime depends upon comedy situations rather than comic incidents and props. It is so close to the Karno style that it is easy to imagine how it would have appeared on a theatre programme:

Prologue: Outside the Bar-Room
Scene 1: The Restaurant
Scene 2: The Hotel
Scene 3: The Other Hotel

In the prologue Charlie and Ben have an altercation with Leo White, as a Frenchified man-about-town. In Scene 1, much the worse for drink, they meet Leo again in a restaurant and proceed to harass him and his lady friend until they are thrown out by a gigantic waiter (Bud Jamison). In Scene 2, Charlie flirts with a pretty girl in the room across the hall, until he discovers that her husband is the same hostile waiter. He decides to move to another hotel, but the couple have the same idea; and Scene 3 is the kind of hotel room mix-up (very piquant for 1915) that did service in *Mabel's Strange Predicament* and *Caught in the Rain*.

Chaplin and Essanay still did not fully understand each other. Having completed shooting, Chaplin announced that he was going to San Francisco for the weekend. In his absence, Anderson, worried that they were behind schedule, asked Totheroh to help him edit

Chaplin's picture. According to Totheroh, Anderson's notion of editing his own pictures was to take a close-up of himself rolling his eyes around, and 'use it in any place. He just measured it at the tip of his nose to the length of his arm, and then he'd tear it off, and that was his close-up. He'd shove it in.'[3] Anderson and Totheroh had just started on the film when Chaplin, having changed his mind about the weekend, walked into the cutting room, and told them, very forthrightly, to take their hands off his picture.

He took this opportunity to tell them also that in future he would not conform to the studio practice of cutting the negative, but would insist on proper positive rushes. This required sending to Chicago for a new printer to be installed in the studio's laboratory. When the new machine arrived and was installed, it proved to be missing a vital part, so this in turn had to be sent for. Anderson fretted at the delay in starting the third Chaplin film, but the director-star was adamant. Evidently the cutting-room incident did not permanently injure relations with Totheroh; a year later, when Chaplin took charge of his own studios, he invited him to join his staff.

Chaplin next set to work on *The Champion*. The studio lot served admirably as the setting for a boxing training establishment. Much of the action takes place in front of the board fence surrounding the studio, and we also glimpse Essanay's glass-house stage, the bungalows and the dusty, open countryside. As interiors, Chaplin needed only rough, hut-like rooms for the gymnasium. Like other Essanay films, this seems a deliberate effort to retrieve opportunities lost at Keystone. Chaplin at this time loved boxing – going to prize-fights with members of his staff was his favourite leisure occupation – and he evidently found much satisfaction in developing the business of *The Knockout*.

Charlie is here quite firmly established as a vagrant: in the opening scene we see him on a doorstep, sharing his hot dog with his bulldog, a choosy pooch, who won't touch the sausage until it has been properly seasoned. He decides to try his luck as a sparring partner, and to enhance his chances slips a horse-shoe in his glove. The characters include a silk-hatted and moustachioed villain, straight from Karno's *The Football Match*, who tries to bribe him; and the *pièce de résistance* is the championship bout that ends the film. Running for six minutes, it is balletic in composition, with Charlie devising a series of exquisite choreographic variations. At one moment the opponents fall into each other's arms in a fox trot.

The delay in getting the new printing apparatus prolonged the production of *The Champion* to three weeks. To make up, Chaplin dashed off *In the Park* within a week. Having found a park at Niles that looked very like Westlake, he reverted to the reliable old Keystone formula, with Charlie intervening in the affairs of two distinctly star-crossed lovers. The Tramp is here at his least ingratiating. He is not only a pickpocket, but a cad as well. Having immobilized big Bud Jamison with a brick, he uses his victim's open mouth as an ashtray. He even makes awful grimaces behind Edna's back. Only one moment looks forward to the gallant Charlie of mature years. When Edna kisses him, he cavorts madly off under the trees in a satyr dance that anticipates *Sunnyside* and *Modern Times*.

Though Chaplin was never happy in the glass-covered studio at Niles, the open country around provided admirable locations for his next two films, *A Jitney Elopement* and *The Tramp*. The first was a conventional situation comedy with Charlie and Leo White competing for Edna's hand. (Leo purports to be a French count and Charlie masquerades in the same role.) The film ends with a spectacular and imaginative car chase: at one point the cars, shown in extreme long shot, waltz with one another. Chaplin also recorded for posterity the ingenious gag which Alf Reeves had admired when he saw him on stage as *Jimmy the Fearless*, and decided to recruit him for America. Attempting to take a slice from a French roll, Charlie continues in a spiral cut which turns the roll, in one of his most witty comic transpositions, into a concertina.

With this film, genuine romance begins to emerge in the love scenes. At our first sight of Charlie he is caressing a flower, as tenderly as the romantic vagabond of *City Lights*. Perhaps this new romantic element owed much to Chaplin's growing relationship with Edna. A charming note has survived, dated 1 March 1915, when they were at work on *The Champion*. Chaplin addresses his leading lady as 'My Own Darling Edna' and tells her that she is 'the cause of my being the happiest person in the world'. He was replying to a note which she had written to him: 'My heart throbbed this morning when I received your sweet letter. It could be nobody else in the world that could have given me so much joy. Your language, your sweet thoughts and the style of your love note only tends to make me crazy over you. I can picture your darling self sitting down and looking up wondering what to say, that little pert mouth and those bewitching eyes so thoughtful. If I only had the power to express my sentiments I would be afraid you'd get vain . . .'

The romantic element is still more pronounced in *The Tramp*. Made in only ten days, this remarkable film shows a staggering leap forward in its sense of structure, narrative skill, use of location, and

1915 - Two picture postcards:
'Charlie Chaplin in the Post Office'.

emotional range. Charlie is now clearly defined as a tramp. He saves a farmer's daughter from some ruffians, and subsequently foils the ruffians' plot to rob the farm. The pet of the place, he falls in love with Edna, but his happiness is crushed by the appearance of her handsome young fiancé. Charlie is disconsolate: his back alone expresses utter dejection. He departs from the farm, leaving a note:

> I thort your kindness was love but it aint cause
> I seen him good bye
>
> x x

For the first time, he makes his classic exit: he waddles sadly away from the camera up a country road, his shoulders drooped, the picture of defeat. Suddenly he shakes himself, and perks into a jaunty step as the screen irises in upon him.

Chaplin was anxious to get back to Los Angeles, and Anderson was hardly less anxious for his departure, since the Niles studio was proving too small to accommodate the productions of both of them. The move caused a break in the flow of production, and the next film, *By the Sea*, has all the appearance of having been shot in a day – on the breezy sea-front around Crystal Pier – to catch up on the schedule while the new studio was being made ready. It is the kind of scenario which would equally have served the *commedia dell'arte* or Keystone – a series of slapstick and situation variations skilfully managed within the restrictions of only nine camera set-ups.

Until this time Chaplin had respected the production-line methods of the time and maintained a steady rate of output. Now he declared his independence by taking much longer over his films. Twenty-seven days had elapsed between the release of *A Night Out* and *The Champion*; Essanay had to be content to wait still longer for subsequent releases. *By the Sea* was issued on 29 April 1915; *Work* did not appear until 21 June. The delay may in part be attributable to moving studios. For *Work* Chaplin temporarily took over the converted Bradbury Mansion at 147 North Hill Street, whose imposing approach serves for the exterior of the house seen in the film.

Some aspects of *Work* place it among the most remarkable comedies made up to that time. It apeared four months after D. W. Griffith's revolutionary *Birth of a Nation*, and within its circumscribed form and ambitions is as original. Painters, plumbers and paperhangers had been the stuff of slapstick on the music halls for years –

> When Father papered the parlour,
> You couldn't see him for paste.
> Dabbing it here,
> Dabbing it there –
> Paste and paper everywhere.
> Mother was stuck to the ceiling,
> Kids were stuck to the floor.
> You never saw a blooming fam'ly
> So stuck up before.

Sydney and Charlie had appeared in Wal Pink's *Repairs*, and Karno toured a sketch called *Spring Cleaning*. Chaplin would later introduce paperhanging sketches into *The Circus* and *A King in New York*.

The basic notion of *Work* is that Charlie and his boss (Charles Insley) are decorators come to do over a middle class home. This gives rich scope for all the traditional business with planks, ladders, paste and paint. Charlie wrestles with sticky and disintegrating wallpaper and transforms a peaceful parlour into a quagmired battlefield. The situation is the richer since the household consists of a tetchy little husband (Billy Armstrong), angrily protesting because his breakfast is late, a flamboyant wife (Marta Golden), *en déshabillé* and rocketing around the house giving artistic instruction to the glazed-eyed workman, a pretty but inactive maid (Edna) and a gas stove given to periodic explosions. The mistress has also a secret lover (Leo White in French count style) who comes calling with flowers at the most awkward moment and has to be passed off, improbably, as one of the workmen. No opportunity for insult or assault with all the tools of the decorator's trade is allowed to pass. The grand finale is a massive explosion which leaves the heads of the ménage showing out of the rubble, Charlie's boss submerged in the bath, and Charlie himself feebly emerging from the guilty oven.

It is the introduction to this delirium of destruction that makes the film most memorable. Our first sight of Charlie is as he advances towards the camera down a busy city street, harnessed to a cart piled high with ladders, boards and buckets. The boss sits on the driver's seat, flicking at him with a whip. The cart gets stuck on the tramlines: Charlie drags it clear in the nick of time. He attempts a hill, but the cart again slides back into the path of an oncoming tram. In silhouette we see Charlie hauling the cart up the side of a 45-degree incline. The weight of the cart raises the shafts in front, with poor Charlie dangling helplessly in the air. The boss thoughtfully offers a heavyweight friend a lift, and Charlie must now drag the two of them. He disappears down an open manhole, but is hauled back, hanging on to the shafts and counterweighted by the cart.

It is a series of haunting, grotesque, horror-comedy images of slavery, with a degree of audacity and invention in the visualization that was hardly to be challenged until the Soviet avant-garde (idolaters of Chaplin) a decade later. The closest approximation to these first scenes of *Work* is to be found in Alexander Medvedkin's 1934 production, *Happiness*. Chaplin's aims in inventing the sequence were no doubt uncomplicated enough: it is funny; and it prepares the audience to accept as his proper deserts the ill-treatment that the boss will later receive at Charlie's hands. Yet, almost incidentally to his purposes, he has created a masterly and unforgettable image of the exploitation and humiliation of labour, the reverse of the Victorian ideal of the salutary virtues of work.

It was such aspects of Chaplin's vision that found the hearts of the great mass audience of the early twentieth century. There is another memorable moment of comic irony in a gag that sums up the ineradicable mistrust between middle and working classes. The lady of the house, having left the workmen alone in her dining room, suddenly remembers 'My silver!'. She rushes back and fixes them beadily with her eyes as she hastily gathers up her treasures and packs them into the safe. They watch her in cool amazement. Then, without a word, they carefully remove their watches and money from their pockets. These valuables are carefully placed in Charlie's right-hand trouser pocket. With his gaze mistrustfully fixed all the time on the woman, Charlie takes a safety pin and firmly secures the pocket.

Chaplin now moved into the old Majestic Studio on Fairview Avenue. Here he performed his third, last and best female impersonation in *A Woman*. It was a tempting exercise: female attire suited him disturbingly well; the role gave scope for a whole new range of character mime; and moreover Julian Eltinge's sophisticated female impersonations had brought the genre into vogue and respectability.

The female impersonation is remarkable: it was no small tribute that the film was banned in Scandinavia until the 1930s. Perhaps the most memorable image of the film however, is Charlie without moustache, hat or trousers suddenly transformed by the 'woman's' fox fur (= a ruffle), long pants (= tights) and striped underclothing (= knickerbockers) into a traditional clown figure – a guise in which he was to appear briefly again, many years later, in *Limelight*. Critics of the time were distracted from the charm and unforeseen poetry of the image by their disapproval of the film's improprieties. The pincushion bosom and the defrocking stirred a good deal of prudish protest, as did a throwaway scene in *Work* where Charlie puritanically covers the nakedness of a statuette with a lampshade, but then wiggles the lampshade to turn the figurine into a hula dancer. Chaplin was stung by charges of 'vulgarity'. Fred Goodwins wrote at the time:

> His fame was at its zenith here in America when suddenly the critics made a dead set at him . . . They roasted his work wholesale; called it crude, ungentlemanly and risqué, even indecent . . . the poor little fellow was knocked flat. But he rose from his gloomy depths one day, and came out of his dressing room rubbing his hands. 'Well boys,' he said, with his funny little twinkly smile, 'let's give them something to talk about, shall we? Something that has no loopholes in it!' Thus began the new era in Chaplin comedies – clean, clever, dramatic stories with a big laugh at the finish.[4]

The Bank was not only a response to adverse criticism, however. Chaplin had been greatly struck by the praise he had received for *The Tramp* with its strong injection of sentiment and the ambivalence of the fade-out. Now he set out to emphasize the sentimental element still further. Working with Edna required no pretending in the love story. Again *The Bank* gave him an opportunity to rework an idea only partially realized in the hurly-burly of Keystone. The essential story of *The Bank* is the same as *The New Janitor*. Chaplin once more introduced the dream device from *Jimmy the Fearless*. Charlie's dreams of adventure and romantic success must remain merely dreams; the reality of the Little Fellow allows of no such escape from poverty.

The film opens with a surprise twist: Charlie enters the great city bank, descends to the vaults, makes great play with the combinations of a giant safe which he opens to produce – a pail, a mop and a janitor's uniform. Charlie the janitor is hopelessly in love with the pretty secretary, Edna, but her heart is set on another Charlie, the suave cashier. The janitor falls asleep and dreams that he rescues the fair Edna from a gang of bank robbers: he presses her to his side and caresses her hair, but wakes to find it is the mop he has in his arms. The reawakened Charlie, spurned, wanders back into his vaults, past Edna and her cashier, who are oblivious to his presence. He still holds in his hand the rejected bouquet he brought her. He tosses it down, gives it a kick, shrugs his shoulders and quickens his funny walk as he leaves us and the camera irises in.

A comedy with a sad end was something new. The scenes in which Charlie, with tragedy in his wide eyes, watches Edna contemptuously throw aside his declaration of love touched depths of pathos quite unfamiliar in film comedy. It was from this time that serious critics and audiences began to discover what the common public had long ago recognized, that Chaplin was not like anyone else before him.

Fred Goodwins recorded a rare, brief impression of Chaplin at work with his actors on *The Bank*:

> We had a scene in the vault – a burglary, with a creeping, noiseless entrance. All the time Chaplin sat beside the cameraman, whispering, almost inaudibly, 'Hush. Gently boys: they'll hear us upstairs!' It is infectious, it gets into the actors' systems and so 'gets over' on the screen.[5]

It was far from easy to discover new ideas for films, but Chaplin knew that a good setting or prop would at once set his imagination working. For *Shanghaied* he rented a boat, the *Vaquero*, which suggested a neat plot and a lot of funny business. Charlie is hired to shanghai a crew, but finds himself shanghaied as well. Moreover his loved one, Edna, has stowed away, and the owner, Edna's father, has plotted to sink the ship for the sake of the insurance.

The ship proved a marvellous prop. To simulate its rocking motion, the cameraman, Harry Ensign, developed a pivot on which the camera could swing, controlled by a heavy counterweight. Chaplin also had a cabin built on rockers so that he could realistically recreate the hazards of a storm-tossed ship. *Mal de mer* was to remain a favourite joke: it figured in Chaplin's very last appearance on the screen, more than half a century later. The shipboard gags were also to provide prototypes for the first half of *The Immigrant*.

A good idea, he decided, will never wear out, so next he adapted his old Karno success *Mumming Birds* to the screen, as *A Night in the Show*. There is no evidence of any formal arrangement with Karno over the copyright, which is surprising since Karno was notoriously jealous of his properties. The *Mumming Birds* scenario is followed closely, with Chaplin in his old role of the drunk, here called Mr Pest.

Chaplin added new material, set in the foyer and auditorium of the theatre, to the original Karno scenario: a flirtation with Edna, altercations with the orchestra, much changing of seats, and the precipitation of a fat lady into the foyer fountain. Chaplin moreover plays a second role, Mr Rowdy, an outrageous tipsy working man in the gallery. This new character is forever needing to be rescued by his neighbours from tumbling into the pit below, and enthusiastically pelts the performers with rotten tomatoes. Finally, anticipating King Shahdov in *A King in New York*, he turns the fire hose on the fire-eater.

In his last days at Essanay Chaplin was reported to be working on a feature film called *Life* which was apparently to mark a new stage of realism in his comedy. The project was abandoned, but the time Chaplin spent on it may explain the long delays between the release of *The Bank* and *Shanghaied* (fifty-six days) and between *Shanghaied* and *A Night in the Show* (forty-seven days). Some ideas and material from *Life*, notably a fragmentary sequence in a dosshouse, were incorporated into *Police*.

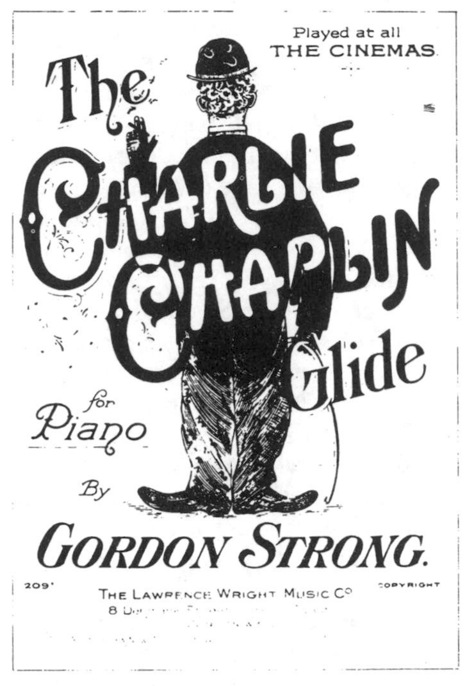

1915 - Chaplin music sheet:
The Charlie Chaplin Glide.

Chaplin's critics had confirmed his own growing recognition that the Charlie character acquired definition and dimension from the reality of his situations and milieu. Charlie belongs to the dirt roads and mean urban streets, and the solitude of vagrancy. The dosshouse scene is a tantalizing glimpse of what Chaplin may have intended in *Life*. There is a Cruickshankian touch of the macabre about the place. A remarkable troupe of derelicts includes a befogged old drunk, an unshaven heavyweight whose first menacing appearance is belied by a display of mincing effeminacy, a broken-down actor and a lean consumptive whose sunken cheeks and hacking cough Charlie callously impersonates when he perceives that such suffering is good for a free bed.

There is also a new irony. *Police* opens with Charlie coming out of prison. The title 'Once again into the cruel, cruel world' looks forward to *Modern Times* and Charlie's efforts in that film to get back to the security and protection of jail. There is a foretaste too of later scepticism in the face of formal religion and its bigotries. Outside the prison gates Charlie meets a clergyman who begs him to 'go straight'. Within moments the man of the cloth has not only filched Charlie's last cent, but also pocketed the watch of a drunk which Charlie had passed up – easy pickings as it was – on account of his newfound, if temporary, Christian morality. The next cleric who offers help in going straight is swiftly seen off for his pains.

Chaplin's last film for Essanay was his sole essay in a style of parody then current. It was eventually released as *Charlie Chaplin's Burlesque on Carmen. Carmen* was the current rage of Hollywood. Sam Goldwyn (then still Sam Goldfish) and his brother-in-law Jesse Lasky had lured the beautiful, 33-year-old star of the Metropolitan Opera, Geraldine Farrar, to Hollywood with a salary of $20,000 for eight weeks, plus motor car, house, servants and groceries. Her extravagantly publicized first film was *Carmen*, directed by Cecil B. De Mille and adapted from Merimée and Bizet by De Mille's brother William.

De Mille's film was ready in October 1915, and was swiftly followed by a rival version directed by Raoul Walsh for William Fox, and starring the sultry Theda Bara. In the Essanay version, Don José, as played by Chaplin, became Darn Hosiery, with Edna as Carmen, sent by the smuggler chief, Lilias Pasta (Jack Henderson), to seduce this strutting Captain of the Guard. The film was due for release in December 1915, but after Chaplin's departure the company decided it would be more profitable as a feature than as a two-reeler. Leo White was called in to direct some completely new scenes with a new character, Don Remendado, played by Ben Turpin; Chaplin's scenes were extended by salvaging his out-takes, and by the time of its release on 22 April 1916 the film had grown to four reels. The horror of it sent Chaplin to bed for two days. The rambling, shambling knockabout of the film shows, by contrast, how taut and well-edited

Chaplin's own films had become. Some good things of Chaplin remain: the duel between Darn Hosiery and his rival of the Civil Guard (Leo White), though clearly longer and untidier than Chaplin intended it, contains some wonderful balletic passages. Audiences and serious critics were equally startled by the death scene, in which the hero stabs Carmen and then kills himself, and which was a good deal more realistically and movingly played than most genuine tragic death scenes of the period. Having shocked and silenced his audience with this scene, Chaplin then revealed how they had been fooled. His bottom suddenly twitches back to life, and he and Edna get up, laughing, to demonstrate the collapsing prop dagger with which the deed had been done.

These odd moments did not vindicate the film, and Chaplin looked for a remedy in the courts. In May 1916 Chaplin, through his lawyer Nathan Burkan, appealed for an injunction to prevent Essanay from distributing *Charlie Chaplin's Burlesque on Carmen*, claiming that he had not approved of the play; that his author's rights had been infringed; that it was a fraud upon the public; that his own role in the film had been garbled and distorted; and that he would be damaged by the production. The plea was heard on Monday 22 May before Justice Hotchkiss of the Supreme Court, State of New York. Chaplin's application for an injunction was dismissed; Justice Hotchkiss said:

> Whether plaintiff will suffer any damage from the production is problematical, while an injunction is certain to work loss for defendants.

While Nathan Burkan threatened that Chaplin would appeal to the Supreme Court and ask for a further $100,000 in damages, Essanay claimed for the recovery of half a million dollars' damages against Chaplin. The grounds of this counter-suit were that in July 1915 Chaplin agreed to 'aid in the production of' ten two-reel comedies before 1 January 1916. For each of them he was to receive a bonus of $10,000 over and above his salary of $1250 a week. One of the number was already completed: the company nevertheless retrospectively gave Chaplin his $10,000 bonus. (This must refer to *Work*.) Chaplin himself had decided that these comedies could be produced at the rate of one every three weeks. However he completed only five two-reel pictures before leaving the company, receiving the $10,000 bonus on each. 'The remaining four Chaplin failed to appear in, although the Essanay Company was prepared and still is ready to proceed with the making of these pictures. Under this arrangement the *Burlesque on Carmen* was produced and paid for.' The company's claim of $500,000 dollars was based on the estimated lost profit of $125,000 on each of the four films not made.

Justice Hotchkiss's ruling was encouraging enough for Essanay to prepare a further 'new' Chaplin comedy, three years after he had left the company. Two sections from the unfinished *Life* were retrieved. In one Edna is a down-trodden house maid, desperately scrubbing floors, while Charlie is the kitchen boy. The second is evidently a continuation of the dosshouse scene in *Police*: the old drunk has now become vocal and requires to be sedated with a bottle expertly applied to his cranium; a mad, vampiric sneak-thief filches from the other inmates. The scene has a wonderfully sinister quality, but it counts for little in the hotchpotch which Essanay concocted and called (for no good reason) *Triple Trouble*. Leo White was again engaged to direct additional scenes: a framing story about German spies, led by White himself, endeavouring to steal an inventor's powerful new explosive device. White was not without style: he enjoyed using groups of people moving in formal, geometrical fashion, and he quite ingeniously welds the old and new material. In one scene Charlie the kitchen boy throws a pail of garbage over a fence in sunny California, 1915; it lands on the other side, in wintry Chicago, 1918. The film was a travesty. Chaplin had learned his lesson, however, and this time did not seek legal remedy.

Essanay continued until 1922 to press their claim on account of the alleged revised agreement of July 1915. In 1921 Spoor brashly proposed that he would settle the case in exchange for distribution rights in *The Kid* – an arrangement which would have required Chaplin to break his current contract with First National. Sydney curtly answered, 'nothing doing'. Chaplin's initial dislike of Spoor seemed vindicated when Spoor threatened that if necessary he would start a scandal relating to poor Hannah, still in the care of the Peckham House nursing home. Spoor claimed that his brother in England had advanced money to Aunt Kate Mowbray to pay the Peckham House bills, and that the money had not been returned. Kate was dead by this time, and so could not deny Spoor's charges. Sydney wrote to his brother on 1 April 1922 to confirm that Kate had borrowed money from Spoor's brother, but that it had been returned and that he had receipts to prove it. The situation had arisen in May 1915, when payments to Peckham House became so overdue that the nursing home threatened to send Mrs Chaplin back to Cane Hill at the charge of the Board of Guardians. The Lambeth Settlement Examination Book recorded:

> Chaplin, Hannah Harriet, Widow. Has been Private Patient in Peckham House since 9th Sept 1912. Sent to Cane Hill by Lambeth 18th March 1905. 2 Sons, Sidney and Charles Chaplin were subsequently discovered earning large salaries as Music Hall Artists – with motor cars of their own &c.
>
> Owing to payments lapsing at Peckham House where the sons had their mother transferred as above, Peckham House apply under Sec 19 for the woman to be placed on Parish Class.
>
> Mrs Mowbray, sister, now of 4 Coram Street Bloomsbury states that possibly owing to the war and sons Charles and Sidney moving about America, they have not been able to send.
>
> These sons are now prominent Cinema Artists Charles earning about £70 per week with the Essanay and Keystone Producers and Sidney about £40 per week and no difficulty will be experienced if patient again sent to Cane Hill. Patient has expressed a wish to go there . . .[6]

The Peckham House receipts have survived and show that Hannah's sons were conscientious but irregular in remitting their weekly thirty shillings. The pressure of their work and the uncertain wartime mails across the Atlantic were contributory causes. So Kate, desperate to prevent her sister being sent back to Cane Hill, had sought the then willing help of the Spoors. She could hardly have foreseen the mean advantage Spoor would later seek from the incident.

Chaplin was, during this period, so tied up in his work at Essanay that he was almost the last to realize the extent of his phenomenal popularity. The year 1915 had seen the great Chaplin explosion. Every newspaper carried cartoons and poems about him. He became a character in comic strips and in a new Pat Sullivan animated cartoon series. There were Chaplin dolls, Chaplin toys, Chaplin books. In the revue *Watch Your Step* Lupino Lane sang 'That Charlie Chaplin Walk':

> Since Charlie Chaplin became all the craze,
> Ev'ryone copies his funny old ways;
> They copy his hat and the curl in his hair,
> His moustache is something you cannot compare!
> They copy the ways he makes love to the girls,
> His method is a treat;
> There's one thing about Charlie they never will get,
> And that is the shoes on his feet.

It doesn't matter anywhere you go
Watch 'em coming out of any cinema show,
Shuffling along, they're acting like a rabbit,
When you see Charlie Chaplin you can't help but get the habit.
First they stumble over both their feet,
Swing their sticks then look up and down the street,
Fathers, mothers, sisters, brothers,
All your wife's relations and a half dozen others,
In London, Paris or New York
Ev'rybody does that Charlie Chaplin Walk!

There was a 'new fox-trot song' of the same title, a 'Charlie Chaplin Glide', 'Charlie Chaplin – March Grotesque', 'Those Charlie Chaplin Feet', 'Charlie Chaplin, the Funniest of them All', and 'The Funniest Man in Pictures' with words by Marguerite Kendall:

He tips his hat and twirls his cane,
His moustache drives the girls insane . . .

In France there was a popular 'Charlot One-Step'.

By the autumn of 1915 Sydney had worked out his Keystone contract and now proposed to devote himself whole-time to the management of his brother's affairs. He persuaded Chaplin that they should themselves undertake the commercial exploitation of the various Chaplin by-products, and accordingly the Charles Chaplin Music Company and the Charles Chaplin Advertising Service Company were incorporated. Neither seems to have lasted very long: the administrative cost and problems of chasing royalties on ephemeral productions selling for a few cents proved uneconomic. In October 1915 James Pershing, who had been appointed to run the advertising service, reported to Sydney:

We find that things pertaining to royalties are in a very chaotic state. There seems to be hundreds of people making different things under the name of Charlie Chaplin. First we have to find out where they are, what they are making, and are notifying them as fast as possible to stop or arrange with us for royalties, which is about all we can do.

Sydney suggested that Aunt Kate would be an ideal English representative for the Advertising Service, and accordingly Mr Pershing wrote:

In regard to the English rights, we have attended to that by writing to your aunt, asking her to look us up an attorney and engage him on a commission basis, and are suggesting the various things that may be made over the name of Charlie and endeavouring to get her to place these rights

> herself, or have it done by some competent party. It is impossible for any of us to go over at the present time, although we realize that this should be done . . .

Evidently Aunt Kate entered into the arrangement with an enthusiasm worthy of her nephews, for a month later the President of the Advertising Service indignantly reported to Sydney:

> Miss Kate Mowbray cabled that she had been appointed agent and insisted upon 25% royalties. We did not appoint her, as you know, and I hardly believed that you have assumed the authority. If you have, we are going to back you up, but we cannot, from our end, give her 25%. Let me hear from you in this connection so that we can write her intelligently.

Almost from the moment of Chaplin's arrival in the United States, there was a bizarre fascination with his racial origins. Even during the Karno tours, interviewers and reporters frequently reported that he was the child of Jewish vaudeville artists. Yet in the four generations that we can confidently trace back his ancestry – through the Chaplins, Hills, Terrys, and Hodges, and certainly through the gypsy Smiths – there is no positive evidence of Jewish blood. All these forbears seem to have regularly performed the family rituals within the Church of England, until Hannah sought solace with the Baptists in later years.

Chaplin's first recorded statement on the question dates from 1915, when a reporter asked him, if, as was supposed, he was Jewish. With the grace he so often mustered in the face of the press, Chaplin replied 'I have not that good fortune.' This was not an empty courtesy: throughout his life Chaplin would continue to express a profound admiration for the race (which in itself would certainly have led him to acknowledge any Jewish origins). On a boat returning from Europe in 1921 (see page 290) he told a small girl who was a fellow-passenger: "All great geniuses have Jewish blood in them. No, I am not Jewish . . . but I am sure there must be some somewhere in me. I hope so'. This feeling for the race did not imply uncritical approval of everything Jewish. He always suspected, for instance, that circumcision must be dangerous psychologically as well as undesirable aesthetically and physically.

A fragment of film in the Chaplin Archive, showing Sydney and the studio staff seeing Chaplin off on an east-bound train, provides charming and curious evidence of his own conviction that he was not, to his regret, Jewish. The family tradition was that Sydney's father, the putative Mr Hawkes, *was* Jewish – even though Sydney was baptized according to the rites of the Church of England. Fooling for the cameras, Chaplin puts his arm around Sydney and mimes, with beautiful clarity of expression: 'We're brothers. Aren't we alike?' He thereupon answers his own question in the negative, explaining the lack of familial resemblance by pointing a finger at Sydney and doing a stage-Jew impersonation, all shrugs and raised hands, to indicate that Sydney is Jewish and he is not. Another odd visual comment appears in a shot of Chaplin with Harry Lauder in 1918. Lauder draws a crude caricature of Chaplin on a blackboard. Chaplin pointedly alters the unmistakable hook nose of a caricature Jew.

Chaplin, the supposed Jew, was an early target for Nazi anti-Semitism. *The Gold Rush* was banned from the early years of the Third Reich, and Chaplin figured in a hideous publication attacking prominent international Jewish intellectuals. Along with Einstein, Mann, Reinhardt and others, Chaplin's portrait, crudely retouched to emphasize its 'Hebraic' features, was printed with an accompanying caption which dismissed him as 'a little Jewish acrobat, as disgusting as he is tedious'. Chaplin's riposte, in *The Great Dictator*, was to play an overtly Jewish character, and to say, 'I did this film for the Jews of the world.' By this time he was adamant in his refusal ever to contradict any statement that he was a Jew. He explained to Ivor Montagu, 'Anyone who denies this in respect of himself plays into the hands of the anti-Semites.'

6

Mutual

Chaplin only became aware of the extent of his fame in February 1916 when he took a train east to join Sydney in New York. To his astonishment, when they stopped at Amarillo, Texas, the station was hung with bunting, there was a civic deputation to greet him and a huge crowd mobbed the train. In Kansas City and Chicago the crowds were even greater and before they arrived in New York the Chief of Police requested him by cable to alight at 125th Street station instead of Grand Central to avoid trouble with the throng that had been assembling since early morning. News of his itinerary had been leaked to the press by the telegraphists who had relayed his telegram to Sydney announcing his time of arrival.

Sydney had gone ahead to canvass offers for Chaplin's future services. While relations were still tolerable, Spoor had gone from Chicago to Los Angeles with an offer of $350,000 for twelve two-reelers, but would not meet Chaplin's demand of a bonus on signature of $150,000. Chaplin knew his value, and Sydney was determined to get the right price. Sydney found himself wooed on all sides. Universal, Mutual, The Triangle, Famous Players, Fox and Vitagraph were all bidding optimistically; even Spoor and Anderson followed Charlie to New York in an effort to gain a new contract. In the end none of them could better the proposition of John R. Freuler, President of the Mutual Film Corporation, which had been incorporated only three years before by Freuler and Harry Aitken, and now set the seal on its success with the acquisition of the biggest star in motion pictures. Freuler agreed to pay Chaplin $10,000 a week, with a bonus of $150,000 on signing.

Mutual, as it happened, had just engaged the most gifted publicist in motion pictures, Terry Ramsaye (1885–1954) who a decade later was to write the first and classic history of the motion picture industry in the United States.* It was Ramsaye who wrote the account of the contract in Mutual's publicity magazine, *Reel Life* (4 March 1916):

> Charles Chaplin has signed a contract to appear exclusively in the releases of the Mutual Film Corporation.
>
> Chaplin will receive a salary of $670,000 for his first year's work under the contract. The total operation in forming the Chaplin producing company involved the sum of $1,530,000. This stands as the biggest operation centered about a single star in the history of the motion picture industry.
>
> AN EXPRESSION OF POLICY
>
> Following close on this announcement from President John R. Freuler of the Mutual, comes his declaration that the signing of Chaplin is but the beginning of a dominating policy on the part of the corporation and the suggestion that the expiration of certain contracts held by other famous stars now working for other concerns will result in further announcements rivaling that of the Mutual's achievement this week.
>
> The game of 'button, button, who's got Chaplin?' which had been engaging the attention of the photoplay world so long was brought to an abrupt end in President Freuler's office late last Saturday night, at the close of the last of the weighty series of conferences and negotiations.
>
> Next to the war in Europe Chaplin is the most expensive item in contemporaneous history.
>
> Every hour that goes by brings Chaplin $77.55 and if he should need a nickel for a carfare it only takes two seconds to earn it.
>
> COMPETITORS' GUESSES ALL TOO LOW
>
> Mr Chaplin will be twenty-seven years old the 16th of April. He is doing reasonably well for his age.
>
> The closing of the contract ends a war of negotiations involving unending conferences and diplomatic exchanges for weeks. In this time five or six motion picture concerns and promoters have claimed Chaplin and audibly whispered figures – with every guess too low. A week ago Mr Freuler put Chaplin under a tentative contract or option, pending the completion of arrangements for the organization of a special producing company. At that time the negotiations were entirely personal between President Freuler and Chaplin.

* *A Million and One Nights*, New York, 1926.

Saturday night the final conference was held and the ceremony of signing up with the Mutual proceeded, with all due array of attorneys, notaries, etc., including, of course, a battery of arc lamps and a motion picture camera, since the motion picture does its own reporting these days.

Charles Chaplin was accompanied as usual by his brother, Sidney Chaplin, who conducts the younger comedian's business affairs and salary negotiations.

The lawyers for everybody looked over all the papers for the last tedious time and announced that everything was correct. The ponderous seal was brought forth from a vault by a law clerk and placed with precise care on the president's mahogany office table.

FILM SIGNING FOR MUTUAL WEEKLY

The lights flared up under the pressure of 'more juice' and the office shimmered with the rippling glare of a studio.

Charles Chaplin was draped over the edge of the table in one of his characteristic off-stage attitudes, eyeing the proceedings with a casual air of shocking disinterestedness.

'What's the action in this scene?' he inquired of his brother, spreading the expensive [*sic*] Chaplin smile.

'Sign here and here,' explained Sid, indicating the neat and beckoning dotted lines on the last page of the ponderous twenty-thousand word contract evolved by the Mutual's astonishingly industrious legal department.

President Freuler handed over his pet fountain pen, with which all the stars sign. Sidney Chaplin called 'camera' and the action started.

In five minutes the deed was done and the camera man reported 'three hundred feet' as President Freuler handed Chaplin a check for $150,000 bonus payment.

Chaplin looked over the check critically, then with gingery fingers passed it on. 'Take it, Sidney, take it away from me please, my eyes hurt.'

In addition to the bonus paid Mr Chaplin on the signing of the contract, he receives a salary of $10,000 a week.

TO MAKE FILMS IN LOS ANGELES

The new Mutual Chaplins will be produced in studios now being equipped in Los Angeles, Cal., where the comedian will begin work March 20, or at an earlier date if conditions permit. One two-part comedy will be produced each month.

The Chaplin contract is one of the most ponderous and intricate documents ever evolved for the employment of a motion picture star. It contains something more than 20,000 words and provides conditions and clauses to cover anything that might happen and a lot of things that can not. An element of 'war risk' enters into the contract. Mr Chaplin is a British subject. It is stipulated that he shall not leave the United States within the life of the contract without the permission of the corporation. Incidentally, Mr Freuler has insured the costly comedian's life for $250,000.

'This contract,' observed Mr Freuler yesterday, 'is only a new token of the bigness of the motion picture and the motion picture industry, a combination of art, amusement and business. The figures are all business,' he added with a dry smile.

'We can afford to pay Mr Chaplin this large sum annually because the public wants Chaplin and will pay for him. I consider this contract a very pleasing bargain for everybody concerned – including this corporation, Mr Chaplin and the fun-loving American public.'

Chaplin himself made a skilful and disarming statement to the press:

A great many people are inclined to make wide eyes at what is called my salary. Honestly, it is a matter I do not spend much time thinking about.

Money and business are very serious matters and I have to keep my mind off of them. In fact I do not worry about money at all.

It would get in the way of my work. I do not think that life is all a joke to me, but I do enjoy working on the sunny side of it.

What this contract means is simply that I am in business with the worry left out and with the dividends guaranteed.

It means that I am left free to be just as funny as I dare, to do the best work that is in me and to spend my energies on the thing that the people want. I have felt for a long time that this would be my big year and this contract gives me my opportunity. There is inspiration in it. I am like an author with a big publisher to give him circulation.

The Chaplin contract was capitalized from a newly floated company, the Lone Star Film Corporation; and Mr Freuler was able to give his stockholders a rosy forecast of results from the Chaplin films. According to the President's calculations the average cost of the twelve features would be $10,000 each, or a total of $120,000, which when added to the comedian's salary made an overall outlay of $790,000. The revenue was calculated on an income of $25 a day for each copy of a two-reeler for a period of at least thirty days. The company aimed to make at least one hundred prints of each film, so that there would be a minimum daily income of $2500, or $75,000 a month. Multiplied by twelve months, at a film per month, the total came to $900,000 – already $110,000 over the outlay. The life of the prints, however, would in fact be considerably longer than thirty days: the 'sixties' and 'nineties' as the more used prints were known, could go on earning $20 and $10 per day in smaller cinemas. Freuler told his stockholders that his estimate of the potential profits was conservative: it did not take into account the possibility of distributing many more than one hundred prints of each subject, or the foreign sales which, even in war conditions, remained huge. Freuler was soon to discover how much even he had underestimated his prize. He would no doubt have been even more surprised to learn that films whose life expectancy he estimated at sixty days would still be entertaining millions (with no advantage to Mutual) sixty *years* later.

The press and the public were thrilled and even sceptical at the size of Chaplin's earnings. $670,000 a year meant $12,884 a week, $1840 a day, $76.70 an hour, $1.27 a minute. No person in the world other than a king or an emperor – unless perhaps Charlie Schwab of the US Steel Corporation – had ever received even half that salary. Mary Pickford was to ensure that Chaplin's record salary did not go unchallenged for long, but for the moment it was the topic of the day. On one hand it triumphantly realized the American dream of success; on the other it offended a puritan reverence for money. The Reverend Frederick E. Heath, preaching at the Warren Avenue Baptist Church in Boston, took as his text 'Charlie Chaplin's Half Million': 'Had Chaplin lived in the old Puritanical days they would have believed him a witch and taken his life . . . I believe in a good laugh . . . The great mistake in American life today is this wicked and immoral manner of throwing away money.'

Chaplin, as it happened, somewhat disappointed New York during his visit. For Easterners, the stars of motion pictures had already become a strange and exotic species, given to high living and reckless spending. Chaplin did not at all conform to this image. He was serious, quiet and retiring. Worse, he did not throw his money around. Memories of poverty were too close; and he was for long to consider, quite philosophically, the possibility that one day the public would tire of him. He respected money as those who have been without it must, but he was not mean. While he was in New York he gave a cheque for $1300 to Sam Goldfish's actors' fund – it was half the fee he had received for a personal appearance at a Sunday show at the Hippodrome. The myth of Chaplin's tightwaddedness however started from this time; notably in an interesting portrait of Chaplin at the age of twenty-six by Karl K. Kitchen:

> Charlie is enjoying his riches with becoming modesty. He spent a month in New York before he signed his contract, and it was a dizzy month, up and down and across Broadway, dining, wining, playgoing and dancing and having the time of his young life, but – keeping his bankroll exclusively to himself.
>
> For at the age of 26 and with an annual income of $670,000 Charlie Chaplin has the finance idea developed to 100 per cent efficiency. The only thing he spent on Broadway in a month of gay life was four weeks. Not since Harry Lauder astonished and then amused New York with his Scotch thrift, to use a pleasant word, has Broadway known such a frugal celebrity.

To be fair, the writer conceded, Chaplin had had no need to spend money. He was the most sought-after man in New York. With every motion picture magnate trying to get him under contract, 'he was fêted as no actor who ever visited New York was fêted before.' Innumerable dinners were given in his honour and he took back with him to California a trunk full of costly presents.

> His only extravagance is a 12-cylinder automobile. He does not even allow himself the luxury of a wife. Jewelry, slow horses and fast company, country homes, *objets d'art* and other expensive fads of the predatory rich do not appeal to this slender young movie actor, who has risen in less than five years from obscurity to the distinction of being the highest-paid employee in the world . . .
>
> His personal expenses last year were considerably less than $500 and there are no indications that his new contract has turned his head. If anything it has caused him to be even more tight-fisted. Chaplin's theory of life may not be plain living and high thinking – he is more interested in prize fights than art or literature – but the fact remains that he lives plainly – except when someone else foots the bill.
>
> Instead of a secretary he has his brother Sidney . . . to look after his social and business arrangements. He is without a valet for the reason that he has less than half a dozen suits of clothes. Unless he is specially requested to wear evening dress he appears at the theatre or even a more formal function in a tweed suit . . .
>
> In flesh he is entirely different from the gelatine. He is of surprisingly small stature – he weighs less than 125 pounds – and he possesses a perfectly ordinary face – a face that would not attract attention in a crowd of five, let alone 500. To be sure, he has black eyes of more than ordinary brilliance and a mass of coal black hair inclined to curl, but all

> in all his appearance is absolutely undistinguished. His manner too is in striking contrast to his picture antics. For in private life he is unusually shy, quiet and reserved. When he talks, his cockney speech betrays his origin. Strangely enough, he speaks without gestures, a remarkable thing for an actor of any brand.[1]

Chaplin tried to explain his own position: 'No one realizes more than I do that my services may not be worth $100 a week five years from now. I'm simply making hay while the sun shines.'[2] Another interview statement was at once prophetic and an accurate self-analysis: 'I have been a worker all my life. It is true that I could quit the screen today if I wished and live the rest of my life in ease and comfort. I'm still a young man – just twenty-six years old but you will find me working just as hard fifty years from now. Money is not everything. One can find more happiness in work than in anything else I know of.'[3] As he anticipated, exactly fifty years from that time he was working on a new film, *A Countess from Hong Kong*. He also gave his views on marriage: 'When I wanted to marry I didn't have the money. Now that I have the money I don't care to marry. Besides, there's plenty of time for that sort of thing when I quit work.'[4]

For all that he had not been able to forget Hetty Kelly. He recalled half a century later that when he was in New York, believing that Hetty was living with her sister on Fifth Avenue, he had loitered near the house, hoping to meet her. It was a vain hope: Hetty was in England where, six months earlier, she had married Lieutenant Alan Horne, son of the MP for Guildford.

This was the first time since they had met almost a year before, that Chaplin and Edna had been apart. While Chaplin was in New York, Edna had gone home to her family in Lovelock, Nevada. Chaplin promised to write to her, but he was never a good correspondent, and Edna wrote to reproach him gently:

> I really don't know why you don't send me some word. Just one little telegram so unsatisfactory. Even a night letter would be better than nothing. You know 'Boodie' you promised faithfully to write. Is your time so taken up that you can't even think of me. Every night before I go to bed I send out little love thoughts wishing you all the success in the world and counting the minutes until you return. How much longer do you expect to stay. Please, Hon, don't forget your 'Modie' and hurry back. Have been home for over a week and believe me my feet are itching to get back.
>
> Have you seen Mable and the Bunch? I suppose so. Am so sorry that

> you couldn't have taken me. Have you been true to me? I'm afraid not. Oh, well, do whatever you think is right. I really do trust you to that extent . . .

After 'Lots of love and kisses' Edna signs herself, charmingly, 'Yours faithfully'.

Chaplin, from his own account, passed a rather quiet time in New York, trying to avoid the crowds, and somewhat depressed by a sense of loneliness. He went to the opera and was induced against his better judgement to go backstage and meet Caruso. Slightly confused as to whether he was seeing *Carmen* or *Rigoletto*, blithely introduced as 'the Caruso of the moving pictures' and aware that Caruso was not particularly interested to meet him, Chaplin was triply mortified. The conversation, according to a contemporary news report, ran: 'Caruso: "I read you make gooda contract." Chaplin: "Yes, I've made a fine contract." Caruso: "That's gooda. I geta gooda contract too. I am very glada to meet you." And there the interview ended.' Afterwards Chaplin remarked, 'I'm sorry I didn't call him the Chaplin of opera. I intended to, but I lost my nerve.' He was to have happier encounters with other stars of the musical world. Later in the year Dame Nellie Melba visited him in his new studios during her Los Angeles season, and revealed promising gifts for comedy. Fooling for the camera, Chaplin walked down a flight of stairs with her and did a comic fall. Melba jerked him to his feet, slammed his hat on his head and said: 'Charlie, behave yourself. This is not a place of amusement.' Paderewski also visited the studio, watched Chaplin at work, clapped his hands in delight and exclaimed enigmatically: 'Bravo! What a grand piano player has the motion picture lost. What a great pie thrower has the music world gained in the fine Mr Chaplin.'

On 10 March the Chaplin brothers, in company with Henry P. Caulfield who had been appointed by Mutual as general manager of Chaplin's new studio, boarded the *Twentieth Century* for their return journey to the West coast. The party stopped off for a couple of days in Chicago. Chaplin was induced to do his funny walk outside a cinema where one of his films was playing, but the publicity stunt fell flat. No one recognized him and the cashier, bored to death with would-be Chaplin imitators, only sniffed haughtily. In the lobby of the Sherman Hotel, Chaplin gave an interview while Sydney strove to keep the curious onlookers at bay and to deal with the excited bellboys forever bringing more letters for the comedy king. He spoke of his plans for the forthcoming films:

> One can be just as artistic in shoes that flap as in a dress suit. It isn't how one is dressed, but what one does and how. Slapstick comedy has as much artistic possibility as the best tailored efforts from the stage . . .
>
> This year has a large inspiration . . . I'm going to make better pictures than I did last. I am doing my own scenarios and my own directing. We're to have a little bit more legitimate plots. I like a little story, with maybe an idea in it, not too much, not to teach anything, but some effect, like in *The Bank* for instance. I think *Police* (to be released in a few weeks by Essanay) is the best thing I've ever done. One must consider the kiddies, not to go over their heads, and remember the grown-ups too . . .
>
> I'll keep the moustache, but won't stick so closely to the other clothes. It'll depend on what the circumstances demand. And it doesn't matter what one is funny in so [long as] one is funny. That's why I can't take things too seriously. This salary is just figures, figures to me. It doesn't mean anything. If I took things seriously I couldn't make pictures.
>
> Some time, when they don't care about me in pictures any more, and I hope I know it in time before it happens . . . oh yes, some time that will happen. It won't be my fault, it will be the public's. It will get tired of seeing the same figure, you know. Well, then I hope to accomplish something bigger. Not that pictures aren't big, but I want to work on the stage a little, to feel my audience.[5]

Shortly after they returned to California, the Chaplin brothers learned that Aunt Kate, whose beauty and gaiety was one of the happiest memories of their boyhood, had died. She had died among strangers in her lodgings at 99 Gower Street; no one there even knew her real name, and her death was registered in her professional name of Kate Mowbray. Her death certificate, which gives her occupation as Actress, states that she died of cancer. She would no doubt have been delighted that they put down her age as thirty-five: in fact she was forty-one. The Hill sisters, whatever else befell them, kept their youthful looks. With Kate's death there was no near relative left to watch over Hannah, or to take action when the fees at Peckham House fell into arrears.

The new Lone Star Studio was opened on 27 March, only a week later than Mutual had hoped. Formerly the Climax Studios, the lot stood on the corner of Lillian Way and Eleanor Avenue in the Colegrave district of Los Angeles. In the centre of the property was the stage, said to be the largest of any single producing unit in California. It was open, but surrounded by canvas side walls, with linen diffusers draped overhead. There was plenty of space for the erection of large exterior sets like the street scene for *Easy Street*, and it was rarely necessary for the unit to go out on location except where water was needed. There were few administration buildings: the largest was the laboratory where all the studio's films were to be developed and printed. The offices were contained in a four-room bungalow with a projection room in an annexe. To the south and west there were twenty dressing rooms, also in bungalow style. Scene docks, property rooms and the scenic workshops adjoined the stage on the west side.

Caulfield was production manager; William C. Foster was chief cameraman, and Roland Totheroh became his assistant. Totheroh had left Essanay, and was without a job when Chaplin arrived back from New York.

> I went to see him. Charlie said, 'Sure we can use you.' He said we'd get started the next week. The cameraman was Bill Foster, later head cameraman at Universal. I met Bill and told him I'd been shooting comedies and everything else, and I knew about the speed. At that time they had no motors on the cameras and we changed the speed for chases. Foster had always shot dramas and things like that. We started together, Bill and I, as camera one and two. When it came to selecting scenes and that, pretty near all of my scenes were selected. When Charlie would do something like kick his feet, we had to be all prepared and crank.[6]

Foster left the Lone Star Studio after four films, leaving Totheroh as chief cameraman.

> Bill Foster had heard about some cameraman who was going to do a film at Fox, so he left to work over there. Now I was on my own. I did all the Mutuals, the First Nationals, and all the rest.[7]

With his first film, Chaplin built up his little stock company of players. Edna, naturally, remained his leading lady. From Essanay he brought Leo White (whose involvement in the *Carmen* affair seems not to have been held against him), Charlotte Mineau, Lloyd Bacon, John Rand, Frank J. Coleman, and James T. Kelley, an elderly Irish actor with a fine line in ruinous old men. Two invaluable Essanay colleagues, Bud Jamison and Billy Armstrong, had departed to pursue independent careers; in their place Chaplin engaged three new actors who would make a significant contribution to his future films. Albert Austin, born in Birmingham in 1885, was an old Karno trouper who had played in *Mumming Birds*. Lean and lugubrious, with a sort of bewildered irritability, he was the only player to appear alongside Chaplin in each of the twelve Mutual comedies. In Eric Stuart

Campbell, Chaplin found the ideal Goliath to his own David. Campbell looked much older than his thirty-seven years, and much more fearsome than he was in real life: he seems in fact to have been a jolly and sociable man. Six-foot-four and almost twenty stone, he made an even more striking contrast to Charlie's slight figure than Bud Jamison or Mack Swain.

Roland Totheroh described Chaplin's method of work at the time he moved to the Lone Star Studio:

> When Charlie was working on an idea, often he would call me in. There were always a lot of his own people around. He'd hit on a certain situation where there was something he was building on, and he'd want conversation more or less. If someone came up with an idea that sounded as if he could dovetail it and it would build up his situation, it would sink back in his head and he'd chew it over . . .
>
> He didn't have a script at the time, didn't have a script girl or anything like that, and he never checked whether the scene was in its right place or that continuity was followed. The script would develop as it went along. A lot of times after we saw the dailies the next morning, if it didn't warrant what he thought the expectation was, he'd put in some other sort of a sequence and work on that instead of going through with what he started out to do. We never had a continuity. He'd have an idea and he'd build up. He had sort of a synopsis laid out in his mind but nothing on paper. He'd talk it over and come in and do a sequence. In a lot of his old pictures, he'd make that separation by using titles about the time: 'next day' or 'the following day' or 'that night' – these would cover the script gaps in between.
>
> Every picture that he made always had one particular highlight, a good built-up spot to rock the house with it. Of course, everyone would contribute a little bit to the ideas and the script. But no one'd dare butt in and say, 'Oh, you should do this and you should do that.' I would never leave that camera when they were rehearsing, always right behind them, watching every move, everything that he did. When the scene was taken, if I saw something in there, I was around that camera in a wink. In a nice way I'd say, 'Gee, Charlie, you could do this,' or 'Aren't you going to do that?' and he'd agree to it. But you couldn't go out and say to him things like some of them did, like Albert Austin . . . he'd say something to Charlie, and then tell everybody all around the lot: 'I gave Charlie that gag.'
>
> Charlie would rehearse them. He'd rehearse everybody and even in silents, we had dialogue. It came to a little woman's part, and he'd go out there and he'd play it. He'd change his voice and he'd be in the character that he wanted the little old woman to play. He'd build their

lines up and rehearse them, even before he rehearsed himself in it. He rehearsed so many darn different ways with them that when he came in there, it'd be changed all around with what he put down. You had to be on the alert for him.

I never got away from that camera, looking through that lens. And all those rehearsals, I sat right there, watching every move he made. Then if he came along and something spontaneous hit him, you had to be ready there to take it and get it.

As a director, Mr Chaplin didn't have anything to say as far as exposures, things like that [were concerned]. Otherwise, I used to say, 'Take a look through here.' The idea of that was that if he was directing, he'd have to know the field that I was taking in. Of course, in the early days, the role of the cameraman was much bigger than it is now. It was up to the cameraman to decide what angle to shoot for lighting; or outside, which is the best angle on a building or whatever it is. Then you have to figure what time of the day it would be better to shoot that shot, whether you want back-light or cross-light or whatever on your set.

On a typical day, we'd shoot from around eight or nine in the morning right straight through till lunch. Of course, this was before unions. And a lot of times he'd want to shoot two hours after dinner. After we'd break for lunch or for dinner, we'd start up again. I could always tell my set-ups because I was smoking Bull Durhams and I used so many matches. You could see all those matches all over the floor.

While Charlie was working, rehearsing or filming or whatever, lots of his people would stand around and watch. He used to use their reactions to see how his stuff was going over. But later on he got so that if they stood there gawking at him, he'd stop and say, 'Get out of here! What are you standing there glaring at me for?' But prior to that, anything he'd do on location or anything, the crowds around, they'd laugh their heads off at his antics.

A lot of times we'd get through a sequence and run it maybe three or four days later. And he'd figure, 'No, that's not it.' So he'd go on to something else. Then if that was worthy of carrying on and adding and building to it, then he'd go and do it. He finished a lot of times a sequence and then he'd blame it on somebody else. He didn't want people to think that he didn't know what he was doing. He'd turn around and think overnight, 'Jesus Criminy, this is what I should have done. I didn't do it.' Now he'd dismissed all the people and had sets torn down. But it was his own money, so what the devil – 'Call the people back.' . . .

Lots of times he'd start building sets before he was really set on his story. Once they double-crossed him after he pulled this once or twice. He'd have an idea but it wasn't really set. Then for a stall, he'd say, 'I don't want the window in the back there or the door in this side.' So it would take a few couple of days to make that changeover. Then they got tired of that, and they put casters on the set . . .

Charlie was always so proud when he was building a set. We had the lousiest looking sets I ever saw, a side wall and a back wall. He'd build something with a little balcony or something and he'd get ahold of Doug Fairbanks or somebody and say, 'I want you to see this set I'm building.' He'd make his little sketches for these set guys . . . Fairbanks had the most spectacular sets of anybody. And Doug used to say, 'Oh, gee, that's swell, Charlie.' He always wanted to encourage Charlie in whatever he did.[8]

There is evidence of Chaplin's methods of work at this time far more detailed than exists for any other director of the silent films. Sydney, always provident, carefully kept and stored all the out-takes, every piece of film that Chaplin exposed in the course of making the Mutual films. Totheroh, who had the problem of accommodating all this material, was distinctly irritated:

Syd kept all the out-takes of Charlie's early films. He held those in reserve. He thought at the time when Charlie passed away that there'd be nobody to object: he had all sorts of cuttings from Mutual, but they didn't belong to Charlie – a lot of scenes and sequences we didn't use. I had them there in the vault, and Syd knew it. And he'd want to cut into them, and I'd say, 'Oh, no – that's not our property.' And he knew that I knew, too. I said, 'That belongs to Mutual.'[9]

Mutual in time vanished, but the out-takes were preserved. When Chaplin closed down his studio in 1952, Totheroh was ordered to destroy the great mass of material. He was no longer young, and not well and, perhaps fortunately, did not do the job very efficiently. Several hundred reels survived, and eventually came into the possession of the distributor Raymond Rohauer. In 1982 they were to provide the basis for a remarkable series of three television programmes, *Unknown Chaplin*, directed by Kevin Brownlow and David Gill. Brownlow and Gill demonstrated that the analysis of Chaplin's rushes, with a comparison of the shot numbers, provided an incomparable insight into his methods.

The out-takes reveal, first of all, that Chaplin rehearsed, practised, perfected and refined his gags in front of the camera. We can see him, for example, tentatively trying out and then developing the best ways to use a wonderful new prop he had had built for his first Mutual film, *The Floorwalker* – a moving staircase. Terry Ramsaye described the genesis of the film:

Firstly – Chaplin comedies are not made. They occur . . .

The comedian had only three weeks in which to decide upon the plot which would enable him to kick somebody in the addenda to the satisfaction of the expectant millions waiting, dime in hand, at the box office.

Two weeks and six days Mr Chaplin wandered about New York between breakfast at the Plaza and dinner all over town . . .

One day when time was desperately short he was walking up Sixth Avenue at Thirty-third Street when an unfortunate pedestrian slipped and skidded down the escalator serving the adjacent elevated station. Everybody but Chaplin laughed. But Mr Chaplin's eyes lit up. Also he lit out – for the studio in Los Angeles.

Thus was *The Floorwalker* born. Mr Chaplin did not care a whoop about the floorwalker person as a type – what he sought were the wonderful possibilities of the escalator as a vehicle upon which to have a lot of most amusing troubles. *The Floorwalker* was built about the escalator not the floorwalker.

This history of *The Floorwalker* is in a diagnostic sense typical of the building of a Chaplin comedy. Every one of them is built *around* something.[10]

Around this particular something Chaplin created a whole department store. On the ground floor are toiletries, travel goods, shoes and ladies' hosiery, all watched over by Albert Austin as a suspicious assistant. On the first floor are the offices where the manager, played by a heavily whiskered Eric Campbell, is planning large-scale embezzlement with the floorwalker (Lloyd Bacon). The store's customers are shop-lifters to a man, or woman, and much assisted by the concentration of Austin's baleful gaze upon the innocent Charlie. Ultimately pursued by Austin, Charlie flees upstairs and bumps into the floorwalker who happens to be his near double. The floorwalker, having just double-crossed his confederate, the manager, offers Charlie the chance to change places with him, to which Charlie, with innocent gratitude, agrees. When the manager comes to, his pursuit of Charlie culminates in a final, fade-out scrum.

The Floorwalker reverts to pure physical comedy, with little of the irony and none of the romance that had became increasingly evident in the Essanay films. Edna plays only a minor role as the manager's secretary. The gag sequences are developed with virtuosity. The pursuits on the escalator are miraculously timed and choreographed. Charlie's confrontation with the angry giant manager produces bizarre moments of comedy: Charlie suddenly breaks away, to divert him with a passage of classical ballet; later the manager picks Charlie up by his neck and carries him across the room. The elaborate mechanism to produce this effect – Chaplin was in fact suspended on a wire to make Campbell's support of him seem effortless – is entirely effaced by the dexterity of the execution. Chaplin also provides a virtuoso performance of an old music hall routine – already done in films by Max Linder. Entering the floorwalker's office, he sees in front of him a figure so like himself that he can only suppose it is a mirror. The two men continue so exactly to reproduce each other's actions that both continue in their illusion until Charlie suddenly notices that while he is holding a cane in his hand the floorwalker has a satchel (containing the embezzled funds).

An early scene in the toiletries department provides an extended sequence of character comedy. Charlie fills a mug with water from a drinking fountain and ambles with it to the counter, where he proceeds to borrow the goods on display to shave and perfume himself, all under the outraged eyes of Albert Austin. As he finishes with each of the expensive cosmetics, Charlie throws them back on the counter with the exaggerated disdain of a dissatisfied customer. In other scenes he works new variations on favourite themes. Serving in the shoe department, he arranges an electric fan to deflect the fumes from the clients' hot feet. The recurrent homosexual motif appears in the scene where he and the floorwalker begin to realize that they are looking at each other, and not into the mirror. The shopwalker stretches out a hand to stroke Charlie's cheek and Charlie, misunderstanding, responds to the supposed caress with an amiable kiss. Later he also plants a kiss upon the withered brow of James Kelley, playing the oldest lift-boy in the world.

Casting around for another everyday occupation that might be food for comedy, Chaplin next hit upon *The Fireman*. Again the film has pretensions to little but light-hearted slapstick. It is strung together with an anecdote rather like *Shanghaied* or a Keystone plot. Fireman Charlie and his brutish chief (Eric Campbell) are both in love with Edna. Edna's father promises the chief the girl, so long as he agrees not to bring the brigade when the old man burns down his house for the sake of the insurance. Unknowingly he sets fire to the house while his daughter is upstairs. In a thrilling finale Charlie climbs the ladder to rescue the girl, and win her hand and heart. A subsidiary intrigue has Leo White as an excitable man who is quite unable to interest the firemen in the conflagration of his house.

Invention was sacrificed to elaborate production. The film was shot in a real fire station and its stables where the magnificent engine-horses nervily watch the proceedings. Two condemned houses were burnt down to provide the spectacular conflagrations. The horsedrawn engine, with its inclination to strew firemen and parts of itself along the road, suggested possibilities for comic chases. Otherwise Chaplin's most characteristic gag constructions in this film are in the styles of transposition (the fire engine's boilers become a coffee urn, as Charlie draws coffee and cream from its taps) and disproportion, as when Charlie, cleaning up the firehouse, sets about the horses with a dainty feather duster. There is a touch of irony when the firemen arrive at the scene of the blaze and, before setting to work, perform their drill exercises rather in the style of a musical comedy chorus.

From these uncomplicated scenarios *The Vagabond* marks a huge leap forward. It is a well-turned miniature drama, in which Charlie's adoption of a friendless girl anticipates *The Circus*, *Modern Times*, *City Lights* and *Limelight*. Gag comedy is skilfully juxtaposed with a subtler comedy of character and with a sentimental theme which, though it may seem a trifle heavy to modern tastes, is handled with a delicacy and judgement superior to most dramatic cinema of the period.

Charlie is a street musician and we are able to see, if not to hear, his accomplishment as a left-handed violinist. Out in the country, he rescues a little blonde drudge from villainous gypsies. Their life together in a stolen caravan is a (very chaste) idyll until a handsome young artist chances along and wins the heart of the girl. The artist's portrait of her is exhibited and recognized (thanks to the inevitable birthmark) by her long-lost mother. The girl is whisked off to a new life, leaving Charlie alone and disconsolate, unable even to manage the usual recuperative flip of his heels.

For the release version of the film, Chaplin imposed an improbable happy ending, in which the girl turns back the car in which she is being driven away, to take Charlie along. The viewer is left to speculate on the little Tramp's chances of co-existence with rich Mama and handsome artist. There is a legend, unsubstantiated by any existing footage, that Chaplin shot an alternative ending, in which the despairing Charlie throws himself into a river. He is fished out by a passing maiden, but since the maiden proves to be the hatchet-faced Phyllis Allen, he plunges back into the water to face a kinder fate.

Chaplin's sentiment is invariably saved from mawkishness by comedy and the belligerence that always underlies his despair. His jealousy as he watches the girl dancing with the artist is not entirely impotent: he maliciously flicks a fly in the man's direction, and later manages to drop an egg on his shoes. After the girl's elegant mother condescendingly shakes hands with him, he suspiciously sniffs the perfume left on his fingers. He uses his favourite trick of deflating his own dramatic despair with farce: in *The Vagabond* the anguish of a lover rejected is quite eclipsed by the agonies of the same man accidentally sitting on a stove.

One A.M. was a daring display of virtuosity – so daring that Chaplin afterwards confided to his collaborators: 'One more like that and it's goodbye Charlie.' It is a solo performance, played for most of its two reels in a single set. The tramp costume is abandoned for elegant evening dress, silk hat and opera cloak. This might be the inebriate returning home from *Mumming Birds*. An introductory scene shows the drunken swell arriving at his house in a taxi driven by Albert Austin, whose role is to sit in the cab displaying impervious lack of concern at the accidents which befall his vulnerable passenger as he endeavours to disentangle himself from the vehicle. After this Chaplin is alone on the screen, in what might be an elaborated vaudeville solo; in fact Billie Reeves had performed a very similar routine called 'The Clubman' not many months before. Unable to find his key, Charlie, with gravity and difficulty, enters through the window. Having made his way in, falling into a goldfish bowl *en route*, he discovers his key with delight and solemnly makes his way back through the window in order to enter with greater decorum through the door. The succeeding battles with the furnishings of a stylishly over-dressed house of the period become a comic nightmare, a series of variations of beautifully structured escalation.

Surviving out-takes from the film reveal Chaplin's pains to perfect some tiny and apparently simple piece of business like a slide on a slithery mat, and how many failures were sometimes necessary to achieve the perfect take. *One A.M.* is one of the best and most sustained film records of Chaplin's inebriate, who perfectly illustrates the principle set out in an article credited to Chaplin in *American Magazine* of November 1918:

> Even funnier than the man who has been made ridiculous . . . is the man who, having had something funny happen to him, refuses to admit that anything out of the way has happened, and attempts to maintain his

> dignity. Perhaps the best example is the intoxicated man who, though his tongue and walk will give him away, attempts in a dignified manner to convince you that he is quite sober.
>
> He is much funnier than the man who, wildly hilarious, is frankly drunk and doesn't care a whoop who knows it. Intoxicated characters on the stage are almost always 'slightly tipsy' with an attempt at dignity, because theatrical managers have learned that this attempt at dignity is funny.

A considerable quantity of out-takes from Chaplin's next film, *The Count*, have survived to reveal the way he constructed and developed his stories in the course of shooting. In its completed form, *The Count* opens with Charlie as assistant to an ill-tempered and grotesquely bearded tailor played, inevitably, by Eric Campbell. The tailor masquerades as a Count at a party given by Miss Moneybags (Edna) and here he again encounters his troublesome former assistant, who is competing with the local police force for the cook's affections. For a while they collaborate in imposture, but inevitably set to fighting for the favours of the lovely Miss Moneybags. The film ends in a general mêlée, a ferocious battle with shotgun and iced cake.

We know that at this time Chaplin, working without a written script, tried as nearly as possible to shoot his films in exact order of story sequence. So by examining the out-takes and comparing the shot numbers, we can make a fairly accurate guess at how his original plan for the film was modified in the course of shooting. The earliest shot numbers are all found on the kitchen scenes so it may have been that Chaplin started the film with the idea of making a comedy of below-stairs intrigue: both the butler and the policeman are promising characters who vanish after the present kitchen episode. The numbering progresses to show that Chaplin next intended to go into the fake Count plot that had already served, in rudimentary form, for *Caught in a Cabaret*, *Her Friend the Bandit* and *A Jitney Elopement*. The scenes in the tailor's shop, which established the prior relationship of Charlie and the tailor, appear to have been shot as an afterthought, when all the other scenes of the film had been completed. The out-takes include one attractive little scene shot for this sequence but in the end abandoned: Charlie sits cross-legged, industriously sewing a garment, only to discover that he has firmly attached it to his own trousers.

The Count was one of Chaplin's most elaborate productions of that time, with three quite ambitious settings for the shop, the kitchen and Miss Moneybags' opulent home, complete with ballroom. Chaplin seems to have spent a considerable amount of the production time on the brilliantly choreographed dance sequence, for which he hired an entire dance orchestra. Chester Courtney, an old music hall acquaintance who had been given a job at the studio and recalled his impressions in an article in *Film Weekly* in 1931, remembered that most of the time they played 'They Call it Dixieland'. Chaplin's routine is a masterpiece of eccentric dancing, involving a lot of splits, from one of which he retrieves himself by hooking his cane to the chandelier and pulling himself to his feet. A recurrently dislocating hip joint anticipates the leg-shortening gag in the vaudeville finale of *Limelight*. Another detail which looks forward to later years is the star-shaped hat which Edna wears for the party. Its form clearly stuck in Chaplin's strange memory for fifteen years, until he found a comic use for it in a party scene in *City Lights*, in which a rather tipsy Charlie mistakes a bald head framed in exactly such a hat for a pink blancmange on a frilly plate.

Of all Chaplin's films *The Pawnshop* is the richest in gag invention. The setting is a back-street pawnbroker establishment, and both it and its eccentric customers smack more of Chaplin's boyhood London than of California. Chaplin maintains constant hostilities with his fellow assistant (John Rand), asphyxiating him with dust, engulfing him in a snowstorm of feathers by absentmindedly dusting the electric fan with a feather duster, assaulting him with ladders, fists and the three balls of the shop sign. When he is dismissed by the fat old pawnbroker Charlie pleads, in a celebrated flash of mime, the plight of his large family. He is reinstated, and so is able to continue his courtship of the pawnbroker's pretty daughter, Edna. His claim to her hand is vindicated when his prompt and ingenious action accomplishes the capture of a burglar (Eric Campbell).

It is as if in this film Chaplin were exploring every possible use of the comedy of transposition which had appeared fairly frequently in his preceding work. Here every object seems to suggest some other thing and other use to his ingenious mind. In Edna's kitchen, her freshly baked doughnuts are wielded as if they were heavy dumb bells; a roll of dough becomes a leg and a ladle a Hawaiian guitar; cups and saucers, Charlie's own hands and eventually a wad of dough are briskly rolled through the mangle. Comic transposition is brought to its utmost refinement in the lengthy scene in which Charlie examines an alarm clock brought in by a dusty and dejected customer

(Albert Austin). Charlie becomes a doctor and the clock his patient as he sounds it with a stethoscope and tests its reflexes. Suddenly it is a rare piece of porcelain as he deftly rings it with his finger tips. He drills it like a safe. He opens it up with a can-opener and then dubiously smells the contents with a look that declares them putrid. Momentarily the clock becomes a clock again as Charlie unscrews the mouthpiece of the telephone and transforms *that* into a jeweller's eye-glass. Having oiled the springs, he produces a pair of forceps and becomes a dentist as he ferociously pulls out the contents. Extracting the spring, he measures it off like ribbon from nose to fingertip. He snips off lengths, then tips out the rest of the clock's contents onto the counter. When they start wriggling like a basket of worms he squirts them with oil. Having now demolished the alarm clock, he sweeps the contents back into the empty case and hands it back to the dazed Austin with a shake of the head and a look of grave distaste.

The pawnbroker was played by Henry Bergman, a new recruit who was to become an indispensable member of the Chaplin entourage for the next thirty years. Bergman was born in 1868 and claimed to be a third-generation Californian. His father was a horse-breeder and his mother a former Grand Opera singer, known in Europe as Aeolia. Henry inherited his mother's vocal talent, and studied in Italy and Germany, making his operatic debut in a small role in *Faust*. He told an interviewer in 1931:

> I got my histrionic training in Wagnerian roles. Twenty years ago I came into pictures. Before that I had been with Augustin Daly's company for nine years in New York. I was catapulted from stage to screen by a musical comedy flop. I had been rehearsing for it for many weeks without pay, and when it closed a few days after it opened I was disgusted. 'This is no business for me,' I said. One day I ran into a player I had known in Germany. When I asked him what he was doing he said, 'Shh. Don't let anybody know. I'm working in pictures. Doing pretty well too – making five dollars a day.' He suggested he might be able to fix me up at the studio . . . So I went to Pathé. There I got my first job with Pearl White in *The Perils of Pauline*. An introduction by Paul Panzer led to my association with Henry Lehrman, with whom I came to Hollywood with the L-Ko Company in 1914. We did a series of pictures, after which I went to Mr Chaplin to play with him. I had known Mr Chaplin personally. We used to be quite friendly at dinners etc, and when I mentioned to him that I was looking for a job he said, 'Why don't you come with me? You

can work with me when I start a company of my own.' That's the way it was.[11]

A bachelor, Bergman's single-minded, adoring dedication to Chaplin was to become his ruling passion. He assumed the role of assistant, confidant and indulgent aunt. Chaplin was happy to rely on an amanuensis, helper and foil as loyal as Henry, as well as using him as an actor in every one of his films up to *Modern Times*. Henry's pride in sharing Chaplin's confidences, and in his own ability to play any role, tended to spark jealousies among the rest of the studio staff. Totheroh, ordinarily a generous man, said: 'Some of the make-ups were terrible, especially Henry Bergman. He always thought he was a great make-up artist. He'd put on a beard and you'd see the glue sticking through it. He thought he was the greatest make-up man in the world. He used to brag about it.'[12] Edward Sutherland's view of Henry was: 'He was a great big fat actor who played in all of Charlie's pictures and revered and adored Charlie, to the extent that he was a detriment at times, because Charlie, like everybody else, made mistakes from time to time, and with Henry he could make no mistakes. Everything he did was great.'[13]

In *Behind the Screen* Henry was cast as a film director. This was Chaplin's fourth comedy set in a film studio. At Keystone he had made *A Film Johnnie* and *The Masquerader*, and at Essanay, *His New Job*. *Behind the Screen* is in fact merely a refinement of the same business. Charlie is the put-upon assistant of the idle, bullying property man (Eric Campbell), whose earnest efforts manage to disrupt all three of the productions being shot side by side. Edna plays a would-be actress who disguises herself as a boy and gets a job as a stage hand when the regular crew go on strike. (The strikers, and their plot to blow up the studio, are inherited from *Dough and Dynamite*.) Most of the business is unremarkable, some of it lifted almost directly from *His New Job*.

The surviving out-takes show that one gag whose ingenuity probably exceeded its comic effectiveness was cut out of the film altogether. It seems to have been a running joke: every time Charlie pushed his sack barrow past the set for the costume picture where a beheading was taking place, a heavy and evidently very sharp axe would crash to the ground within millimetres of his feet. Kevin Brownlow and David Gill, working on *Unknown Chaplin*, discovered that the effect was achieved by a camera trick: Totheroh *reversed* the camera,

Charlie went backwards, and the axe was heaved out of the floor and into the air. The number of takes of the scene shows that it was only achieved with much effort, yet the effect was convincing. Chaplin must nevertheless have estimated that it would not get the laugh that he wanted. Elsewhere, however, the out-takes show that though he was prepared to shoot a scene innumerable times to get it right, it was very rare for him to eliminate a scene or idea entirely, as he did in this case, and with the sewing scene in *The Count*. Film was cheap, but ideas came hard. (Chaplin often told his collaborators that 'film is cheap' when they marvelled at the number of times that he was prepared to shoot a scene. It was characteristic of his economic caprices, however, that he always insisted that Totheroh cut the shot exactly when told: film was not so cheap that he wanted to waste six inches at the shot-ends.)

In *Behind the Screen* Chaplin adds two more notable gags to his collection of comic transpositions. Doubled up beneath the weight of a dozen bentwood chairs, all looped around his person with their legs sticking into the air, he is metamorphosed into a porcupine. He becomes a coiffeur as he dresses a bearskin rug, combing it, sprinkling on tonic, applying a finger massage, parting the hair and finally applying hot towels to the face. Chaplin's preoccupation with nasty eaters and smelly food recurs in the lunch-hour scene in which he is seated beside Albert Austin who is devouring onions. Charlie uses a bellows to deflect the fumes, then puts on a helmet, stuffing his own food through the briefly-opened visor. He is not, however, too proud to steal an occasional bite from the end of Austin's meat-bone, clamping it between his own slices of bread.

The most surprising element in the film is a sequence that was to remain the most overt representation of a homosexual situation anywhere in the Anglo-Saxon commercial cinema before the 1950s. Edna has disguised herself in workman's overalls and a large cloth cap which conceals her hair. Charlie comes upon the 'boy' sitting playing a guitar (in the first takes Edna had a harp, but this was clearly discarded as being too obviously feminine). Charlie teases the 'boy' when he catches him powdering 'his' face. At that moment Bergman, who has split the seat of his trousers in a prior encounter with Charlie, enters and asks the 'boy' to sew them up for him. Edna promptly faints away and her cap falls off, releasing her hair. She comes to, begs Charlie not to expose her, and replaces her cap. The brutish property man (Campbell) enters just in time to catch them kissing. 'Oh you naughty boys!' he exclaims in a title; and teases them by doing a little 'fairy' dance, finally turning his back and offering his huge bottom – which Charlie obligingly kicks.

The Rink must have been suggested by the old Karno sketch *Skating*, though the resemblance remains fairly superficial. The *raison d'être* of the piece is the actual rink scene and Chaplin's spectacular and supremely graceful demonstration of his roller-skating skills. The opening sequence shows Charlie as a waiter, making up Eric Campbell's bills by checking off the stains on his lapels, and shaking a remarkable cocktail, topped with a carnation. There is a park-style amorous quadrangle with Mr Stout (Campbell) importuning Edna while Mrs Stout (Henry Bergman in the first of several amusing female impersonations) flirts with Edna's father (James T. Kelley). There is even an element of the bogus count theme, since Charlie makes a hit at the evening skating party by introducing himself as 'Sir Cecil Seltzer'.

The Rink occasioned some critical stir thanks to the terms in which Heywood Broun discussed it in his review in the *New York Tribune*, which was headed

NIETZSCHE HAS GRIP ON CHAPLIN
'The Rink' Strong Plea for Acceptance of Master Morality
FERMENT AT WORK ON POPULAR FILMS
Discussion of Education To Be Derived by Visit to Rialto

After summarizing the action, Broun concluded:

> This is the play, barring a few diversions of no particular importance. It is interesting to note that Chaplin falls only twice during the picture, both times of his own volition, and that not once is he kicked. Is it not obvious, then, what ferment is at work in the philosophy of the Chaplin comedies? Gone is the old comedy of submission, as emphasized in *The Bank*, *The Tramp*, *Shanghaied* and others, and in its place there has grown up a comedy of aggression. One cannot overlook the influence of Nietzsche and the 'Will to Power' here.
>
> Was it in 'Menschliches, Allzumenschliches' or in 'Also Sprach Zarathustra' that the sage declared it was comic to kick, but never to be kicked? At any rate 'master morality' has set its mark upon Charlie Chaplin and his comedies. The old Chaplin of whom it was said, 'Here is the head upon which all the ends of the world are come and the eyelids are a little weary' is done. 'Welcome' has been erased from his shoulder-blades. The new Chaplin is a superman, and though the hordes

of fat villains may rage against him, with pie and soup and siphons they shall not prevail.

Broun, we may take it, was not wholly serious; but a lot of his readers took him to be so. A day or two later the following anonymous poem appeared:

TO CHARLIE CHAPLIN,
AFTER READING THURSDAY'S TRIBUNE

Triply distilled octessence of the vulgar,
Puller of chairs from overweighty women,
Hurler of pies into aged person's faces,
Cinema lowbrow -

Wreaker of wrongs that rouse the careless giggle,
Skater that skateth but to lose his balance,
Walking with steps unutterably comic,
How I detest thee!

How (though in years of profitless adventure
Crowded with wasted afternoons and evenings
Not even once – no, never – have I seen thee)
Scornful I'm of thee!

Scorn and contempt have I for all thine antics,
Menace are they, say I, to little children
Yet there is that which urges me to write thee
Words of laudation.

These are the words, then, Menace of the Movies,
Thanks for thy coarse and pseudo-comic antics,
For they produce those peerless things about thee
Old Heywood Broun writes.[14]

Here was another detractor who boasted he had never actually seen the artist he was attacking.

The Rink was released on 4 December 1916, and was Chaplin's last film of the year. Chaplin had kept very nearly to the schedule of one film every four weeks he had agreed with Mutual. Only *Behind the Screen* had come out late, and the press reported that in this case Chaplin had telegraphed the company with the request 'It's the best idea I ever had. Give me two weeks more and I will make it the funniest comedy I ever produced.' *The Rink*, issued only three weeks later, caught up at least one week of the schedule. For the remaining films under the Mutual contract, however, Chaplin was to demand

and take more time: he would in fact take a total of ten months to make four two-reelers.

The year that was ending had brought some irritations, not the least of which was the book called *Charlie Chaplin's Own Story*. Despite Chaplin's strenuous efforts to suppress it, this spurious publication has continued to this day to confuse and falsify the record of Chaplin's career. It is useful to disentangle the story of this curious publication.

With the start of the great Chaplin mania in 1915 there was keen competition between publishers of books and periodicals to secure the biography of Charlie Chaplin. Unauthorized versions appeared in many less reputable journals. On 15 November 1915, the dismayed editor of the *Detroit News* telegraphed Chaplin at Essanay:

> WE ARE RUNNING YOUR LIFE STORY PURCHASED FROM THE DAVID SWING RICHES SYNDICATE. THE DETROIT JOURNAL HAS STARTED ANOTHER STORY VARYING GREATLY IN CHARACTER AND CLAIMING TO BE AUTHORIZED BY YOURSELF CAN YOU WIRE US OUR EXPENSE WHICH IS THE AUTHORIZED STORY OF YOUR LIFE.

In March or April 1915 Chaplin had given an interview to a representative of the *San Francisco Bulletin*, Rose Wilder Lane at the Niles Essanay studio. Subsequently to publication in the newspaper, Mrs Lane's manuscript was acquired by an entrepreneur called Guy Mayston. The original story was augmented with colourful invented detail. Mayston's agent interested the New York publishers, Bobbs Merrill, in the book, and they went ahead with publication. The only notification that reached Chaplin was a telegram so casual in tone that little note was taken of it in the studio office, though the photographs requested in it were duly supplied. The telegram was dated 10 July 1916:

> WE HAVE ACCEPTED AND SHALL PUBLISH AS QUICKLY AS POSSIBLE THE STORY OF YOUR LIFE CAN YOU SEND US PHOTOGRAPHS OF YOURSELVES AS A BOY YOUR FATHER MOTHER AND BROTHER ALSO OF THE STUDIO IN WHICH YOU ARE NOW WORKING ANY ASSISTANCE YOU WILL GIVE WILL BE APPRECIATED.

Within two months of this, and without any further word passing between publisher and alleged 'author', *Charlie Chaplin's Own Story* was printed and ready for publication. As early as 20 September however it was clear that Bobbs Merrill were girding themselves for some kind of trouble. An official of the company called D. L. Chambers telegraphed a colleague, Samuel Dorsey, in Los Angeles:

> CONTRACT FOR CHARLIE CHAPLIN'S STORY WAS SIGNED BY GUY MAYSTON OF SAN FRANCISCO AS OWNER OF THE MANUSCRIPT IT GUARANTEES US AGAINST ALL CLAIMS CURTIS BROWN MAYSTONE'S AGENT IN NEW YORK SAYS WE ARE FULLY PROTECTED IN OUR RIGHTS NOTICE OF AN ACCEPTANCE OF THE STORY AND INTENTION TO PUBLISH WAS WIRED CHARLIE CHAPLIN JULY 10TH.[15]

This might be thought a rather broad interpretation of the July telegram. Towards the end of September Chaplin came by a copy of the book, and both he and Sydney were outraged, not least by the plain untruths of the title page: 'The faithful recital of a romantic career, beginning with early recollections of boyhood in London and closing with the signing of his latest motion picture contract . . . The subject of this biography takes great pleasure in expressing his obligations and his thanks to Mrs Rose Wilder Lane for invaluable editorial assistance.' The subject was anything but grateful, in fact. The book began with an account of Chaplin's birth in a small town in France. (It may be that in his early days in movies Chaplin himself had laid claim to a French birthplace to satisfy reporters who wanted something more romantic for their public than the hard realities of Kennington.) Mrs Chaplin was described kindly, but Charles Chaplin Senior was depicted as a drunken brute. Chaplin's early employers were as unjustly dealt with. The eminently respectable John William Jackson was transformed into a kind of Fagin, who pursued little Charlie with dogs when he ran away to London. *Casey's Court Circus* became 'fifteen ragged, hungry-looking, sallow-faced boys desperately being funny under the direction of a fat greasy-looking manager who smelt strongly of ale'. Presumably intended to represent poor Will Murray, he was named 'Mr Casey' (who, of course, had never existed). Inevitably the *Casey's Court Circus* company rehearsed in 'a very dirty dark room', and dressed in 'a dirty makeshift dressing room in a cheap East End music hall', where the audience threw vegetables. So much for the Moss and Thornton tour.

Karno, in his turn, became Carno; and Dr Walford Bodie, the toast of the halls, became

> Doctor Body, a patent-medicine faker, who was drawing big crowds on the London street corners and selling a specific for all the ills of man and beast at a shilling a bottle. Watching him one afternoon I was seized with the great idea – I would let the manager rehearse me all he jolly well liked, but when the opening night came I would play Doctor Body as he really was – I would put on such a marvellous character delineation that even the lowest music-hall audience would recognize it as great acting and I would be rescued by some good manager and brought back to a West End theater . . .

The book is full of such romantic and misleading nonsense, which has nevertheless continued to supply and confuse gullible Chaplin historians for seven decades.

On 1 October Chaplin's New York lawyer, Nathan Burkan, wrote to Bobbs Merrill's lawyers, Lockwood and Jeffery, informing them that Chaplin had instructed him to institute proceedings

> to prevent the publication and sale of this work on the grounds that it is not his autobiography, as the work is advertised, that it is purely a work of fiction, holding him to public ridicule and contempt, and that it reflects upon the memory of his late lamented father and is libel on several men of excellent reputation.
>
> Mr Chaplin informs me that he has never authorized or consented to the use of his name, picture or portrait in connexion with this work and that he never acknowledged the publication thereof.

The same day Burkan wrote in a similar vein to Bobbs Merrill themselves, adding: 'Mr Chaplin's father, who was a lovable character and devoted husband and kind father, is depicted in the work as a drunken sot who brutalized and neglected his wife and family. Several characters represented as being employers of Mr Chaplin in his early days are purely fictitious and are not known to Mr Chaplin.' Burkan perhaps exaggerated the domestic virtues of the elder Charles Chaplin. He threatened an injunction to prevent publication but was evidently cautious, for he wrote to Sydney, also on 1 October:

> Please ask Charlie to communicate to the best of his recollections what he told to the lady who called upon him in Niles for an interview.
>
> Will you please get me a copy of the article that appeared in the *San Francisco Bulletin* purporting to be a biography of Charlie. You say this biography was syndicated to a number of papers as an autobiography of Charlie Chaplin. Will you get me a copy of this biography as it appeared in the Harmsworth papers?

On 6 October Mrs Lane herself reappeared in the affair, addressing a lengthy letter to Chaplin in a vein which suggests remarkable ingenuousness:

> It won't require any effort on your part to imagine that the news fell upon me like a thunderbolt, in one way at least . . . You were so very courteous in giving me a great deal of time, and all the information on which to base the story, while I was in Los Angeles, that I have been assuming that your attitude toward me was quite friendly . . .
>
> I'm sure you will feel, in recalling the information you gave me, that this is true, and that I made the best possible use of it in writing the story. Its appeal to the public was tremendous. It not only disposed of any number of wild rumors which, as you know, were afloat about you, but in addition the sympathetic interest of the public in the little boy who had such a hard time to get started in London was greater than that of any of the other successful men whose life stories I have written. Not even excepting Henry Ford or Art Smith, who was the idol of San Francisco during the Exposition.
>
> Your mother, too, made a wonderful appeal, as well as your brother. Truly, I don't believe you realize how very well that story was written, how real you and she and your brother were for the people who read it, and how much it increased your own interest in the eyes of the public here . . .
>
> Your present attitude of course puts me in a perfectly frightful position with the Bobbs Merrill people. I suppose I deserve it for not making sure that the arrangement would be all right with you . . .
>
> I suppose that your feeling is simply that you should have some money from the book if it should appear. It is natural enough to want money, but I wonder if you are not exaggerating the possible profits to be made from book publication? My own profits from it, even if it sold up to the very limit of our expectations, would be only a few hundred dollars – perhaps worth half a day of your time. As matters now stand, it appears that your action will result merely in my losing the amount – which I need not say would make much more of an impression on my bank account than on yours – and also in your losing publicity value of the book, a publicity which even Theodore Roosevelt in his palmiest days was glad to utilize.

Having, however unwittingly, added insult to the injuries committed, Mrs Lane goes on to a rather endearing assessment of her work:

> You've lived a life which makes a corking book. I have written the book – and really, it is no more than true to say that it is a book whose popular appeal is greater than that of a book any other hack writer is apt to write . . .

> It is in the interest of both of us to have the book published. I admit it's more to my interest than yours . . . But it is to the interest of neither of us to stop the publication of the book. And if the situation is allowed to develop into a real scrap, we'll both be in the position of the two men who fought over a nut and brought the matter to a judge who ate the nut and divided the shell. I don't see a bit of use in the world in letting the lawyers have the nut, do you?
>
> Yours very sincerely,
> Rose Wilder Lane.

Chaplin, not surprisingly, was unmoved by Mrs Lane's appeal. Burkan had meanwhile received a reply from John L. Lockwood of Lockwood and Jeffery, saying that he was waiting for documentation but considered that since Bobbs Merrill had acted in good faith, believing that Chaplin had authorized what Mrs Lane wrote, the rights as sold by Mayston were good. It was Lockwood's view that the remarks about Charles Chaplin Senior were 'quite respectful'.

By the end of November, Bobbs Merrill were seeking a compromise. Burkan telegraphed to Sydney on the 29th:

> BOBBS MERRILL WILL NOT PUBLISH CHARLIE CHAPLIN'S OWN STORY WITHOUT HIS WRITTEN CONSENT THEY ARE WILLING TO ELIMINATE HAWKINS AND [MARCUS] LOEW'S NAME AND PAY CHARLIE FIVE PER CENT OF THE RETAIL SELLING PRICE OF BOOK TO BE RAISED TO ONE DOLLAR FIFTY I PERSONALLY THINK IT BAD FORM FOR CHARLIE TO GIVE HIS PERMISSION TO PUBLISH BOOK ON ACCOUNT OF REFLECTION ON YOUR FATHER HOWEVER YOU AND CHARLIE ARE THE BEST JUDGES OF THAT PLEASE WIRE ME WHETHER I SHOULD GO AHEAD AND POSTPONE CONTRACT BOBBS MERRILL UNWILLING TO ACCEPT YOUR PROPOSITION FOR CHARLIE AND MISS WILDER [*sic*] TO COLLABORATE ON WRITING A NEW BOOK REGARDS TO CHARLIE.

The entrepreneur Mayston now attempted to act as go-between, but was as unsuccessful in his attempts to persuade Bobbs Merrill to undertake the cost of a completely new book as he was in persuading Chaplin to allow publication and split the royalties with himself. The matter was settled quite precipitately in mid-December. A New York police magistrate was awarded damages of $35,000 in a libel action against Bobbs Merrill. The firm saw no merit in risking trouble on other fronts, and Lockwood forthwith gave Burkan an undertaking that the book would not be sold without the prior consent of Chaplin.

Valueless as its content is, the book is now rated the greatest rarity in the Chaplin bibliography. The stock was suppressed but not before one or two copies had leaked out to be the bane of film historians. Stan Laurel possessed a copy, which he annotated with corrections and subsequently gave to a Chaplin biographer, John McCabe.

Chaplin still had not finished with the troubles brought by *Charlie Chaplin's Own Story*. As Burkan mentioned in his letter, syndication rights in Mrs Lane's original articles had been acquired by the Harmsworth Press; plans for English newspaper publication were already advanced when Burkan stepped in to prevent it. The campaign which now began, to discredit Chaplin for failure to enlist in the British services, appears to have been stimulated by Lord Northcliffe's consequent personal pique. It is true that as early as March 1916 there had been adverse comment in the *Daily Mail* about the war risks clause in the Mutual contract, which specified that Chaplin should not return to Britain for the duration of hostilities and so run the risk of being mobilized in the British armed forces: 'We have received several letters protesting against the idea of Freuler or any other American making a profit on the exhibition in this country of a man who binds himself not to come home to fight for his native land.' In June 1917 Northcliffe went onto the offensive, with an editorial in the *Weekly Despatch*:

> Charles Chaplin, although slightly built, is very firm on his feet, as is evidenced by his screen acrobatics. The way he is able to mount stairs suggests the alacrity with which he would go over the top when the whistle blew.
>
> During the thirty-four months of the war it is estimated by Charlie's friends that he has earned well over £125,000. He is contracted for next year's pictures for a sum exceeding £1,000,000 with the First National Exhibitors, a newly formed and wealthy syndicate. Under the contract, Charlie will produce his own pictures and have his own company.
>
> Cable messages have sought to show that Chaplin has invested £25,000 of his earnings in the British war loan, but this has not been confirmed. Chaplin can hardly refuse the British Nation both his money and his services.
>
> If Charlie joined up, as is his duty, if he is fit, at least thirty other British cinema performers of military age who are now performing in the United States would have no excuse for withholding from the British Army . . .
>
> Nobody would want Charlie Chaplin to join up if the Army doctors pronounced him unfit, but until he has undergone medical examination

> he is under the suspicion of regarding himself as specially privileged to escape the common responsibilities of British citizenship. This thought may not have occurred to the much-boomed film performer, and he will no doubt be thankful that an opportunity for reminding him has been presented by the course of events.
>
> Charlie in khaki would be one of the most popular figures in the Army. He would compete in popularity even with Bairnsfather's 'Old Bill'. If his condition did not warrant him going into the trenches he could do admirable work by amusing troops in billets.
>
> In any case, it is Charlie's duty to offer himelf as a recruit and thus show himself proud of his British origin. It is his example which will count so very much, rather than the difference to the war that his joining up will make. We shall win without Charlie, but (his millions of admirers will say) we would rather win with him.

A *Daily Express* article in the same vein carried the headline:

> FIGHTING – FOR MILLIONS
>
> Charlie Chaplin Still Faces the Deadly Films.

Chaplin issued a statement to the press:

> I am ready and willing to answer the call of my country to serve in any branch of the military service at whatever post the national authorities may consider I might do the most good. But, like thousands of other Britishers, I am awaiting word from the British Embassy in Washington. Meanwhile I have invested a quarter of a million dollars in the war activities of America and England . . .
>
> I registered for the draft here, and asked no exemption or favours. Had I been drawn I would have gone to the front like any other patriotic citizen. As it is I shall wait for orders from the British Government through its Ambassador in Washington.

The British Embassy confirmed:

> We would not consider Chaplin a slacker unless we received instructions to put the compulsory service law into effect in the United States and unless after that he refused to join the colours . . .
>
> Chaplin could volunteer any day he wanted to, but he is of as much use to Great Britain now making big money and subscribing to war loans as he would be in the trenches, especially when the need for individual men is not extremely pressing.
>
> There are various ways for one to do one's bit. Certainly the man who subscribes liberally to war loans and the Red Cross could not be said to be a slacker, especially when he follows his subscriptions with an

announcement that he will serve in the trenches when called. Obviously, when the compulsory law is not in operation here, where Chaplin has made his home for a number of years, he could not be considered a slacker.

Such statements did not immediately put a stop to the 'slacker' charges. The Draft Board received anonymous reports that Sydney had falsified his age and was eligible for the draft. Sydney was in consequence called before the Board to satisfy them that he was, in fact, over thirty-one. The campaign finally abated when it was reported that Charlie had actually gone to a recruiting office but been turned down by the doctors because he was underweight. For years afterwards Chaplin continued to receive white feathers and anonymous invective for his failure to fight.

These attacks certainly did not come from servicemen. When Chaplin visited England in 1921, one ex-soldier wanted to give him his medals, because, he said, of all he had done for the men at war. 'Charlie is a prime favourite with our gallant soldiers and sailors,' wrote Essanay's English publicist, Langford Reed, 'who feel that the brightness and joy he has brought into their lives outweighs, a million times, any services he might have been able to render as an asthenic little castigator of Huns.'[16] In military hospitals special projectors were fitted up so that Chaplin's films could be projected onto the ceilings for patients unable to sit up. Dr Lewis Coleman Hall, attached to a US Army neurological unit in France, appealed to Chaplin for autographed pictures of himself: 'Please write your name on the photos, the idea being that nearly everyone has seen you in pictures. I will show your picture to a poor fellow and it may arrest his mind for a second. He may say, "Do you know Charlie?" and then begins the first ray of hope that the boy's mind can be saved.'[17] Miracle cures were attributed to the effect of Chaplin's image on the screen. Sam Leonard, General Manager of the United Picture Company of St Helens, Lancashire, wrote:

Since the war it has been my greatest pleasure to entertain wounded soldiers at my hall. Last week I was showing a 'Charlie Chaplin', and a wounded soldier laughed so much he got up and walked to the end of the hall, and quite forgot he had left his crutches behind. My assistant went after him, and he said, 'That fellow Chaplin would make anyone forget his head. I never laughed so much in my life.'[18]

'If Chaplin had done what was expected of him and answered his country's call to the colours in August 1914, the chances of his surviving the war would have been slight. Chaplin would have been a footnote in film history,' commented Kevin Brownlow, sixty years after the end of the First World War.[19] The smears of Northcliffe and his followers in no way affected Chaplin's popularity with his audience, but they were to hurt him deeply and for many years.

Towards the end of 1916 Chaplin began to change his way of life. He hired a valet-secretary, Tom Harrington, who became, he said, 'the *sine qua non*' of my existence. Harrington was a New Yorker, who had been dresser and handyman to an English comedian, Bert Clark, who worked for a while at Keystone. In 1915 Clark became a partner in the short-lived Chaplin Music Corporation, and brought Harrington with him to take charge of the office. When the office was closed and Clark returned East, Harrington offered to stay on and work for Chaplin. Harrington is glimpsed once or twice in Chaplin films: he was a lean, solemn, ascetic-looking man, who proved not only the ideal gentleman's gentleman, but also helped Chaplin with his choice of reading. It was Harrington who introduced him, as he remembered, to Lafcadio Hearn, Frank Harris and James Boswell.

Sydney persuaded Chaplin that he should have another car, and at the beginning of December Chaplin bought a standard Locomobile tourer, with blue body and white wire wheels. Harrington engaged a chauffeur, a 28-year-old Japanese, Toraichi Kono. Kono came from a well-off middle-class family in Hiroshima, but had emigrated to the United States to avoid a career in the family business after several commercial ventures of his own failed. In the United States he had been dissuaded from a career as an aviator by his young wife, so reconciled himself to working as chauffeur. Kono's efficiency and discretion impressed Chaplin and gave him a preference for Japanese servants: there was to be a succession of them until the outbreak of hostilities with Japan in the Second World War, when the Chaplin domestic staff was interned. Kono himself remained with Chaplin for eighteen years and assumed the role of special confidant and emissary.

Along with the acquisition of a *ménage*, Chaplin's social life was changing. He had continued to be regarded as something of a solitary in Hollywood. Most evenings he would dine with Edna at the Los

Angeles Athletic Club, where he had set up a permanent residence. Occasionally everyone from the studio would go off to a fight after work was done. Totheroh remarked that the unit began to feel him growing away from them socially:

> In the evenings he'd go maybe to Levy's Café or some of those places. He always attended the prize fights, every Tuesday night at Doyle's out in Vernon. All the bunch got together and we used to meet there and afterwards we'd go some place for a glass of beer and a sandwich. He more or less mingled, went to the baseball games; he had the spirit of everybody around him and they did, too. But as soon as he got out of that character of the tramp, making these features, a big change came over him. He didn't mingle around with the bunch any more. He more or less entertained up at his house. And the people that he had associated with no doubt were people of reputation – authors and writers and maybe actors. But he had well-known columnists and different ones up at his house. He'd throw these parties up at his house because he was the center of attraction. He was a great entertainer and he had the floor. He'd entertain them and he just drifted away from the old bunch.
>
> When he went to fights, he had tickets set up. I didn't sit right with the bunch, but I sat a lot of times a couple of rows behind him. It was set up for three tickets: it was Albert Austin, Eric Campbell and Charlie; there might have been a fourth one, but Charlie was the center of attraction there, too. Especially among the fighters; he got to think the world of a bunch of these fighters. Before the fight would start, the first thing they'd go over there – they knew where he sat – and they'd reach out and shake hands with him. They all got to know who he was. Even at baseball games, they'd spot him and you'd see everybody looking down in the box seat – Charlie's there. He was one of the bunch, meeting down at Barney Oldfield's or any place where they all hung out after. Charlie coined a phrase, he'd say, 'How's the light, Rollie?' And I would say, 'Well, maybe we can shoot another scene, couple of scenes. I think the light is better down at Barney Oldfield's.' Meaning that the light beer is better. Maybe he might have been tired or he ran out of ideas, then he'd dismiss the crew.

Dining one evening at Levy's Café, Chaplin was thrilled to be invited to her table by Constance Collier, who had arrived in the United States to appear opposite Sir Herbert Tree in Triangle's film of *Macbeth*. Miss Collier had been one of Chaplin's boyhood heroines when she was Tree's leading lady at His Majesty's Theatre, and he, in his early teens, watched them from the gallery between his own modest theatrical engagements. They took to each other at once, and were to remain friends until Constance's death in 1955. It is possible that it was she who helped him improve his elocution during these early years in Hollywood. She recalled in her own memoirs that he dined with her very often,

> and we would talk about London, and the Lambeth Road, and Kennington, and all the places we had known in our youth. He was a strange, morbid, romantic creature, seemingly totally unconscious of the greatness that was in him. How he loved England! And yet the years he had spent there had been so bitter and full of poverty and sorrow. America had given him all, and his allegiance belonged to her, but in our talks one felt his longing, sometimes, to see the twisted streets and misty days and hear Big Ben chiming over London . . .
>
> Sometimes we would steal down to Los Angeles and have a meal at a cafeteria, and Charlie would wait on me, fetch my coffee and thick sandwiches, or bread and cheese, and we would talk for hours. He was happier this way. It was impossible to go to the big restaurants, as the minute he appeared he was mobbed. Besides, he said he couldn't bear the masses of knives and forks on the table, and the magnificence of the head waiters gave him a feeling of inferiority.
>
> He didn't like luxury in those days. He hated to drive in a car – he said it made him feel nervous – but I expect he has got used to it by this time.
>
> He remembered all the plays and every actor he had seen in England, and described to me how he used to sit in the gallery at His Majesty's whenever he could spare a shilling or two, and would give up his meal for his seat.
>
> He worshipped the theatre and had the same reverence for it as had that other great comedian I had once met – Dan Leno.
>
> One would never have thought of Charlie Chaplin as funny in those long, serious talks we had.
>
> Then – some nights – his mood would quite change, and he would be ridiculous and make me laugh until I was ill. He would pretend to be a German or a Frenchman or an Italian and invent an imaginary language, and keep it up so wonderfully that he really looked like the part he was assuming. He would keep up this mood for hours and insist on answering serious questions with that same absurd accent.[20]

Constance Collier took the young Chaplin's social life in hand, and introduced him to Tree and his young daughter Iris, both of whom initially awed him somewhat, though later they would all go off together on jaunts to Venice beach. Chaplin, noted Constance, 'had the greatest admiration for Herbert Tree, whose eccentricities in the unusual environment of the picture world were more marked than ever.' It was Constance, too, who insisted that he should meet another Triangle player, Douglas Fairbanks, who had just arrived in pictures after some success on the stage. 'They had never met, and one night I took Charles to dinner at Douglas Fairbanks' house. They were a bit shy and self-conscious during the early part of the evening, but from that day on their friendship never wavered.' Near the end of his life, Chaplin said that Fairbanks had been perhaps the only really close friend he had ever known. He was to be an intimate witness to the romance between Fairbanks and Mary Pickford – both at this time in the process of divorcing their previous partners – which resulted in 1920 in the most celebrated of all Hollywood marriages.

Another friendship at this time was with Julian Eltinge, who had come to stardom as a female impersonator and arrived in Hollywood in early 1917 to make three films for Jesse Lasky. Eltinge was amusing, cultured, and five years older than Chaplin, and seems also to have had some influence in broadening his social life.[21]

Chaplin's last four films for Mutual, all made in 1917, remain among his finest. Two, certainly, were masterworks. The first of these was *Easy Street* – 'an exquisite short comedy,' wrote Walter Kerr; 'humor encapsulated in the regular rhythms of light verse.'[22] At the impressive cost of $10,000 Chaplin built the first of those T-junction street sets that were to prove his ideal theatre. The setting has the unmistakable look of South London. Even today Methley Street, where Hannah Chaplin and her younger son lodged, between Hayward's pickle factory and the slaughterhouse, presents the same arrested vista, the cross-bar of the 'T' leading to the grimier mysteries on either side.

The story is a comic parody of Victorian 'reformation' melodramas. The vagrant Charlie wanders into a mission, where he is moved – less by the hymn-singing than by the charms of missionary Edna – to turn over a new leaf. Joining the police force, he is at once posted to the perilous beat of Easy Street, terrorized by the Herculean Eric Campbell. The most effective of Charlie's ploys to conquer the bully and restore peace to Easy Street results when Campbell proves his strength by bending a street lamp in two. Charlie seizes the opportunity thus offered to fit the lamp over the man's head, and operates the gas tap with the expertise of a dentist's anaesthetist.

The production was not without its troubles. On 16 December 1916 the prop lamppost prepared for Campbell's strong-man act buckled of its own accord and injured Chaplin's nose, preventing him from wearing make-up for several days. The Californian rains were particularly persistent that year. The least of the problems to be coped with was that the baby which Charlie nurses in the mission scene stole his moustache. By 1 February, Mutual were obliged to issue a statement explaining the postponed release:

> Owing to the unusual character of the latest Charlie Chaplin production, *Easy Street*, involving so many big scenes which, while they appear to be 'interiors' are 'exteriors', necessitating sun for their success, Mr Chaplin has been compelled to announce the postponement of release of No 9 of the Chaplin series from January 22 to February 5, preferring to delay completion of the comedy until conditions for its successful filming are perfect.
>
> With this announcement of the postponement, Mr Chaplin, while expressing regret at the delay, points out that it is his determination to permit nothing but the best to be released, and he would prefer producing nothing at all to assuming responsibility for poor photography. He remarks incidentally that 30,000 feet of negative have already been used in the effort to perfect 2000 feet of laughs.[23]

Just before the film's release, Chaplin published his reflections upon it:

> If there is one human type more than any other that the whole wide world has it in for, it is the policeman type. Of course the policeman isn't really to blame for the public prejudice against his uniform – it's just the natural human revulsion against any sort of authority – but just the same everybody loves to see the 'copper' get it where the chicken got the axe.
>
> So, to begin with, I make myself solid by letting my friends understand that I am not a real policeman except in the sense that I've been put on for a special job – that of manhandling a big bully. Of course I have my work cut out tackling a contract like that and the sympathy of the audience is with me, but I have also the element of suspense which is invaluable in a motion picture plot. The natural supposition is that the policeman is going to get the worst of it and there is an intense interest in how I am to come out of my apparently unequal combat with 'Bully' Campbell.
>
> There is further contrast between my comedy walk and general funny business and the popular conception of dignity that is supposed to hedge a uniformed police officer.[24]

For his next subject Chaplin settled on *The Cure*, for which he chose a setting similar to Sydney's old Karno hit, *The Hydro*. Chaplin warned the Mutual office, in the same terms as the press release for *Easy Street*, 'Owing to the incessant rains on the coast and because I do not care to risk the chance of a single Chaplin release being in any way below quality, it is impossible to complete *The Cure* according to schedule.'[25]

We can learn more about the genesis of *The Cure*, thanks to the survival of most of the rushes and out-takes, which were analyzed first by Kevin Brownlow and David Gill for the *Unknown Chaplin*. Take 1 shows Chaplin's first conception of the hydro. The forecourt is full of patients; in the centre is a fountain, all ready for future fun. The staff of this 'health' resort are a crumbling bunch, so decrepit that it takes four of them to lift a cane chair. The proprietor of the hydro, played by the diminutive Loyal Underwood, is a pathetic wreck with a hacking cough. By take 17 or earlier Chaplin has made his appearance, at this stage of the game dressed as a bellboy and pushing with difficulty a wheelchair containing Eric Campbell, his gouty foot bound up in a monstrous bandage.

By take 23 he has decided to shift the action originally planned in the forecourt of the hydro to the lobby. Fourteen takes later he has changed his own costume from a bellboy to that of a spa attendant in a white jacket; and the patient in the wheelchair from the volcanic Eric Campbell to a comatose Albert Austin. At this stage, too, Chaplin introduces a wonderful gag. Despairing at the confusion of wheelchairs being pushed all over the place, he sets himself up as a traffic cop, and imposes order on the chaos. At one moment he stops both streams of traffic to permit an excruciatingly decrepit bellhop (played by James T. Kelley, a specialist in such roles) to cross the 'road'.

By take 77 the whole set has been changed. The fountain in the forecourt has been replaced by a well, which clearly provides more comic perils for unwary walkers and in particular for a drunk, played by John Rand with very evident instruction from Chaplin himself. Only seven takes later, Chaplin has been unable to resist the drunk's part, and has taken over Rand's role and costume himself. By this time he has discovered one of those props which always stimulated his invention – a revolving door. One take in particular shows the part that chance could play in his comic creation. The take is spoiled when he inadvertently catches his cane in the revolving door, and jams it. Soon afterwards he begins to introduce the caught cane as a deliberate piece of business.

After the first hundred or so takes Chaplin is into his narrative stride, and the shooting follows very much the progression of the finished film. Charlie, the inebriate, arrives at the hydro and in no time at all has made an enemy of the gouty-legged Eric Campbell, following an encounter in the revolving door, and a friend of Edna, Eric's companion. While the staff interest themselves in Charlie's luggage, which consists of a cabin trunk exclusively stocked with liquor, Charlie unenthusiastically samples the amenities of the place – the massage parlour, the swimming pool and the sauna. Meanwhile the director has ordered his staff to get rid of Charlie's liquor store. It is emptied by accident into the pool, which considerably raises the spirits of the entire establishment.

The highest slate number on the surviving out-takes is 677 and since this shot, though it was never used, was evidently an intended fade-out for the film – Charlie falls into the pool and sinks amid a flurry of bubbles – it is most likely one of the final takes for the film. We can consequently assume that take 622 was made quite late in the shooting period, yet at this stage we find Chaplin once more trying the traffic cop gag. As one of his collaborators said, 'Chaplin had a mind like an attic. Everything was stored away in case it ever came in handy.' Clearly this was too good a piece of business to waste. This time he filmed it wearing his costume of white blazer, slacks and boater. As it survives in the out-takes it is a scene of great comic brilliance, but again it was rejected. As Brownlow and Gill speculate in their commentary to *Unknown Chaplin*, he must have recognized that it could never be in character for Charlie to create, rather than disrupt, order.

The production was held up when Chaplin caught a chill after shooting the swimming pool scenes, but was eventually ready for release on 16 April 1917. The following day's issue of *Photoplay News* declared,

> As the Chaplin specials are unfolded to the public gaze it becomes increasingly apparent that the great comedian is a master of innumerable arts. For instance it was not known until he produced *The Rink* that Charlie could skate like a professional, and it was not until he devised the swimming bath scene in *The Cure* that anyone realized what an expert swimmer he is. In that scene Chaplin dives under the vast bulk of Campbell with the speed and agility of an otter, circles him in the water, sits on his head and nearly drowns him and in other ways disports himself as an expert waterman.

Altogether *The Cure* is certain to enhance Chaplin's popularity for he has never produced anything funnier.

On 24 April Chaplin received a telegram:

CHARLES CHAPLIN,
LOS ANGELES ATHLETIC CLUB.

WE THE UNDERSIGNED BRING SUIT AGAINST YOU FOR SORE RIBS WE SAW THE CURE.
MARY PICKFORD
DOUGLAS FAIRBANKS
MRS CHARLOTTE PICKFORD
TED HAMMER

In the case of *The Immigrant*, the surviving out-takes enable us to follow in even greater detail the progression of Chaplin's conception. This comic masterpiece, whose qualities of irony and satire and pity survive intact after almost seventy years, took from start to finish a bare two months to make. *The Cure* had been released on Chaplin's twenty-eighth birthday, and he began his new film immediately in an effort to catch up on his production schedule. He had probably already begun production when he told an interviewer,

> I have also long been ambitious to produce a serio-comedy, the action of which is set in the Parisian *Quartier Latin*.
>
> This theme offers unbounded scope for the sentimental touch which somehow always creeps into my stories. But the trouble is to prevent that touch from smothering the comedy end. There's so much pathos back of the lives of all true bohemians that it is hard to lose sight of it even for a moment and the real spirit of that community is far too human and deeply respected by the world at large for me to even think of burlesquing it.[26]

The Immigrant clearly started out to be this film. Among the first few takes are some establishing scenes representing an artists' café populated by bizarre and extravagant types – men in cloaks and broad-brimmed hats, aquiline women in mannish suits. In a corner of the café, beside the arch that leads to the kitchens, is an unlikely guest, Charlie. He is sitting beside Albert Austin, who was always to be his favourite partner for eating scenes. In this case Austin is a well-dressed diner who is having some trouble with a plate of hot beans. Every time he puts the fork to his mouth he burns himself and starts violently, to the distress of the fastidious Charlie. By take 46, Edna has been introduced into the film and the bean-eating business.

At this time Chaplin averaged around twenty shots a day, so that we can assume that this was at the start of the third day of shooting. Edna was shot sitting alone and disconsolate at a table across the other side of the archway, then side by side with Charlie, having supplanted Albert Austin. The principal business on which they worked at this time involved Charlie's sharing his plate of beans with the apparently impecunious Edna. Edna was still eating beans more than a hundred takes later, and this was reckoned good for a publicity story, which appeared in the newspaper towards the end of production:

CONTINUOUS DIET OF BEANS CAUSES A REAL GAGGING

Edna Purviance Forced to Consume This Viand in Latest Chaplin Comedy

Edna Purviance, Charlie Chaplin's vis-a-vis running mate, hopes something happens to the bean crop this year. The reason is this: the play on which they are now working opens in a cheap restaurant and shows her a famished orphan whom Charlie is regaling with copious plates of beans.

So far so good, but there were so many trying gags to be worked out that retake after retake was necessary and, as the days follow close upon each other without a cessation of the eternal bean diet, Miss Purviance began to experience difficulty in even getting the succulent Boston viand up to her mouth.

'It's no use, Charlie,' she announced. 'I simply can't swallow another one.'

'Great Scott!' exclaimed Charlie. 'How am I going to get my gagging over, then?'

'I give it up,' replied Edna. 'If you'd been gagging as much as I have for the past five days you wouldn't want to gag any more.'[27]

The out-takes reveal that Chaplin began shooting these scenes with James T. Kelley playing the decrepit waiter who served Charlie and Edna. By around the fourth day, however, he had devised some new comedy business which required a heavyweight, so he recast Henry Bergman in the role of waiter. The sequence involves Charlie's inability to pay his bill. He and Edna look on in alarm as a tipsy diner who has failed to pay his bill is set upon and mercilessly pummelled by the restaurant staff, led by Bergman. Charlie feels in his own pocket, and discovers in mounting panic that his one and only coin has slipped through a hole. By the time he spies it on the floor, the waiter has firmly planted his foot on it and is already writing out the bill. Charlie succeeds in retrieving his coin from the floor and grandly hands it to the waiter, who promptly bends it between his teeth to establish that it is a particularly pliable counterfeit.

Chaplin continued to shoot, re-shoot and vary these scenes for more than a week before he discovered what was wrong with them. Bergman clearly lacked the menace necessary to give the dramatic-comic motive for Charlie's fear. Chaplin scrapped all the previous material and recast Eric Campbell in the role, wearing his most diabolic false eyebrows. According to conventional standards and economies of film production in 1917 this kind of decision, the courage to scrap a week's work (when many producers were making entire two-reel comedies in that time) was without precedent. Indeed Chaplin's whole approach of making take after take until he was totally satisfied with the result was something new in Hollywood. For most directors, shots were only retaken if something had gone noticeably wrong. More than two years after *The Immigrant*, D. W. Griffith made his ambitious *Broken Blossoms* practically without a second take. For a director like Griffith to shoot any scene more than once would have been an admission of inadequate rehearsal and error. For Chaplin it was an assertion that it was always possible to do better.

Having cast Campbell as the waiter Chaplin discovered a new role for Bergman, as a flamboyant artist. This new character offered a perfect denouement to Charlie's drama of paying the bill. The artist notices Edna, is instantly taken by her beauty, and joins the couple at their table to ask if he may paint her portrait. Magnanimously he attempts to pay their bill along with his own, but Charlie declines the offer – politely and too insistently, since the artist takes him at his word and contents himself with paying his own bill. Charlie deftly solves the problem. The waiter brings a plate with the change, which the artist disdainfully pushes aside as a tip. Charlie niftily slips his bill under the coins and airily pushes it to the waiter, who is baffled to see his tip thus diminished to pennies. The scene neatly wrapped up the sequence, but the artists' café had not provided enough material for a full two-reeler.

Chaplin needed something else for his story, and evidently found it by asking himself where Edna has come from, and how it is that she and Charlie recognize each other in the restaurant. He found his answer: they are both migrants, and have met on an immigrant ship. The ship immediately set his comic imagination whirling. He revived the rocker idea he had used for *Shanghaied*, and created a convincing rolling deck and steerage-class mess room. Some scenes were actually taken on a boat at sea; for these Rollie Totheroh devised a pivot so that the camera could swing on the tripod, controlled by a heavy pendulum. The storm-tossed vessel was peopled by a weird and sorry lot of migrants: Albert Austin as a sea-sick Russian, Henry Bergman as a stout peasant woman and Loyal Underwood as her diminutive spouse, whom she dandles like a child and sticks over the side of the ship when he, too, is sick. Charlie also falls in with a murderous bunch of card-sharpers; the out-takes show that he originally intended a dice game, but changed his mind since the card game offers the opportunity for an amusing gag of high-speed shuffling which anticipates Monsieur Verdoux's dexterity in counting bank notes.

Among the passengers, Charlie meets Edna and her aged mother, played by Kitty Bradbury, a sweet-faced old character actress. Mother is robbed of all their savings while she is sleeping, but Charlie consoles the weeping Edna by stuffing into her purse all the money he has won at cards – all, that is, except for one note which he providently retrieves for his own needs. A passing purser, inevitably, sees him taking the note back, and threatens to put him in irons until Edna intercedes.

The café scenes represent takes numbers 1 to 384; the boat scenes numbers 385 to approximately 730. Knowing Chaplin's method of work in subsequent films, we can safely assume that there would have been a pause of a week or two between the two stages of the shooting, while he edited together the first sequence or 'faction', as the usage was on the Chaplin unit. There would have been a comparable break for editing after the complexity of the boat shooting. A final group of some thirty takes reveals Chaplin dexterously tying up his narrative into the beautifully structured two-act whole that *The Immigrant* was to become.

First (takes 737 *et seq.*) he films the exterior of the café, and Charlie finding a coin on the pavement. This provides an ideal transition between the ship and the city scenes, and motivates the hitherto broke Charlie's entrance into the café. Next (743 *et seq.*) he re-shoots the scene inside the café, where he first sees and recognizes Edna at the opposite table. He has added one detail: Charlie now observes that

Edna's handkerchief is edged with black. Nothing more is needed to tell us that since the boat trip Edna's mother has died. Chaplin also took the opportunity to temper sentiment with comedy: as Charlie gazes rapt and blissful into Edna's eyes, his beans fall from his knife into his coffee cup.

In a few takes around number 763 Chaplin invented a scene which was outrageous in its irony, and remains to this day astounding. As the sequence appears in the finished film, we see a distant view of the Statue of Liberty. A title announces 'Arrival in the Land of Liberty'. On the deck of the boat the huddled masses stand – and the immigration authorities suddenly arrive to throw a rope around them, as if they were so many cattle. (One of the out-takes for this last shot contains an unrehearsed moment: the extras are clearly not acting to order, and Charlie the Tramp is suddenly transformed into Chaplin the director, turning on them in sudden rage.)

After this there remained only a couple more shots to be made. In a charming little scene, Charlie drags the bashful Edna to the registry office. On the doorstep Charlie's ebullience provokes the unspoken rebuke of a solemn clerk, played by Chaplin's new valet, Tom Harrington.

At this time, at the beginning of June 1917, there were some changes at the Lone Star Studio. John Jasper succeeded Henry Caulfield as general manager, and in turn Jasper recruited Carlyle T. Robinson, whom he had known when they both worked at the Horsley Studios in 1915, as publicity director. Originally a journalist, Robinson was one of the first generation of Hollywood publicists. He was to remain with Chaplin for the next fourteen years. Before Robinson's appointment any publicity stories had been written by Fred Goodwins, an old English vaudeville acquaintance of Chaplin's who had some newspaper experience and appeared in several Essanay and Mutual films.

When Robinson reported for work at the Lone Star Studio he found that Chaplin was away for a few days while a new set was being built.

> This allowed me to familiarize myself meanwhile with my new job. One of the first things I discovered was that Chaplin was a very difficult person to meet, even within his own studio. I learned also that it was absolutely forbidden for strangers to penetrate into the studio, that the star did not

> like journalists, and did not at all wish to be bothered by old friends, even those who had known Charlie Chaplin when he played in the English music halls.
>
> I discovered that he liked to be called Charlie and hated to hear himself called 'Mr'. I discovered that his hours were very irregular, and most of his demands impossible to satisfy, that he had very strong likings and even stronger hatreds, that anyone whom he seemed to prefer among the studio employees was always the most disliked by the rest, that he had not the least idea of time, that although he was theoretically an employee his prestige was such that he had the real right to decide ultimately who would work or who would not work at the studio.[28]

Robinson was struck – as others were later to be – by the jealousies among the male members of the unit, and was surprised that Chaplin himself appeared unaware of them. He was also astounded by the daily ceremonial attending Chaplin's arrival at the studio, which began with the cry, 'He's here!'

> Instantly everyone stopped whatever they were doing. Actors, stage-hands, electricians, everybody stood in line, at attention. Then Chaplin entered the studio gates.
>
> All this comedy seemed to me quite absurd. They might just as well have blown a trumpet or fired a cannon, I thought.
>
> He arrived in a big sports car with black coachwork, very luxurious. Two men were seated in front: one, tall and thin, jumped out of the car first. The other was a Japanese. The tall thin man ran round the car and opened the door. Chaplin stepped out, dressed in a long overcoat with an astrakhan collar. He was hatless. He slowly crossed the studio yard, with the tall man at his heels, while the Japanese chauffeur put the car away.[29]

Robinson asked the studio typist, Miss Roberts, if the same ceremony happened every day. 'Oh yes,' she told him, 'the whole gang does that for a gag. Charlie has no illusions, but he adores it!'[30]

The first day that Chaplin was back at the studio, Robinson was asked to join a screening of the 'Land of Liberty' scene from *The Immigrant* in the studio projection room.

> I had a curious impression when I entered the room. From the people scattered around the screening room there emanated such an absence of friendliness that it verged on hostility. I was instantly aware of their dislike. There were two rows, each of half a dozen chairs. In one corner a man stood at a table with a pencil and paper.

I chose a chair near the door. No one introduced me to my new boss. I felt very embarrassed . . .

When the lights went on again, Charlie addressed me:

'What do you think of all that?' he asked me, with a pronounced Cockney accent.

'Very funny and very realistic,' I answered.

'Do you find anything shocking in it?'

'Not that I can recall.'

Chaplin thereupon turned to the man on his left, who spoke with a strong accent similar to his own. From his remarks I understood that he was the one who had criticized the scene. Charlie pointed to me: 'So you see, he didn't find anything wrong with it. It shocks you because you see too much in it. But I'm sure there will not be any difficulties with the public.'

Of course I had no idea what they were talking about. Later I learned that the one who had criticized Chaplin had claimed that the public would not like his showing the Statue of Liberty in this way. The scene was kept in the final version of the film, and there was never the least complaint.[31]

Robinson was to be embarrassed in the early days of his employment by his new boss's quirks. The same night as this screening Robinson saw Chaplin with Edna in a restaurant and greeted him amiably, only to be cut dead (much to his embarrassment since he had been boasting to his table companions of his prestigious new job). Some days later some English trade unionists were guests at the studio. One of them was whistling while Chaplin was trying to work, whereupon Chaplin turned angrily on Robinson, accusing *him* of being the whistler. Afterwards Robinson asked him if he really believed him to be the culprit. 'Oh, of course not. But I had to use that little trick. I couldn't tell off my guest myself, and that's why I made it your responsibility!'

Robinson hardened himself against such embarrassments, and at the same time developed a high regard for his employer's dedication:

I was only really able fully to appreciate the little man's energy after the final scene of *The Immigrant* had been shot. It was then a matter of eliminating the thousands of metres of excess film that had been exposed.

The Immigrant had to be reduced to a length of 1800 feet before being handed over to the distributors. Now he had shot more than 40,000 feet of film! For four days and four nights, wihout taking any rest, Chaplin cut the film. He would view the same scene fifty times in succession, cutting four inches here, a foot there! One collaborator assisted him,

> another simply watched. Rollie Totheroh, his cameraman, was the assistant, and I was the 'observer'.
>
> By the time the film had been definitively brought to the requisite length, and was wholly approved by Chaplin, the great comedian's best friends would certainly not have recognized him. His beard had grown several centimetres. His hair was tangled. He was dirty, haggard and collarless. But his film was finished.[32]

The Immigrant was released on 17 June. Four months were to elapse before the next Chaplin release – the longest interval between pictures since the start of his film career. After completing *The Immigrant* Chaplin and Sydney went to San Francisco for a holiday. On their return the unit moved to location on the Sierra Madre coast, where most of the first two hundred takes of *The Adventurer* were made. Shooting there must have extended into August, since it was reported in the press that on 11 August Chaplin dived into the rough seas off Topanga Canyon to save a seven-year-old girl from drowning. The child, Mildred Morrison, daughter of a stockbroker, had been swept off a rock by a wave whilst watching the Chaplin company at work. There was a more serious interruption to production a week or so later, when Edna was admitted to the Good Samaritan Hospital with an unspecified illness.

The scenes shot on the coast, which were to provide the opening sequence of the film, were of inspired comic virtuosity; a series of complex and beautiful variations as Charlie, in prison stripes, attempts to elude the pursuit of a troupe of prison warders. After this, and after Edna's recovery, Chaplin spent some weeks and more than 300 takes on a sequence of a party in a rich house where Charlie, now in elegant evening dress, flirts with the daughter of the house, Edna, under the angry eyes of her jealous suitor, Eric Campbell. To judge from the unavailing effort to work out a gag involving a seductive Spanish dancer, and another with a hot steam radiator – neither of which remain except as hints in the finished film – Chaplin was going through a period of comparative creative block.

One gag in this sequence is of particular interest since Chaplin himself analyzed it in detail in an article in *American Magazine* (most likely, to judge from the style, transcribed by his friend Rob Wagner from Chaplin's ideas):

> . . . all my pictures are built around the idea of getting me into trouble and so giving me the chance to be desperately serious in my attempt to

appear as a normal little gentleman. That is why, no matter how desperate the predicament is, I am always very much in earnest about clutching my cane, straightening my derby hat and fixing my tie, even though I have just landed on my head.

I am so sure of this point that I not only try to get myself into embarrassing situations, but I also incriminate the other characters in the picture. When I do this, I always aim for economy of means. By this I mean that when one incident can get two big, separate laughs, it is much better than two individual incidents. In *The Adventurer* I accomplished this by first placing myself on a balcony, eating ice cream with a girl. On the floor directly underneath the balcony, I put a stout, dignified, well-dressed woman at a table. Then, while eating the ice cream, I let a piece drop off my spoon, slip through my baggy trousers, and drop from the balcony onto this woman's neck.

The first laugh came at my embarrassment over my own predicament. The second, and the much greater one, came when the ice cream landed on the woman's neck and she shrieked and started to dance around. Only one incident had been used, but it had got two people into trouble and had also got two big laughs.

Simple as this trick seems, there were two real points of human nature involved in it. One was the delight the average person takes in seeing wealth and luxury in trouble. The other was the tendency of the human being to experience within himself the emotions he sees on the stage or screen.

One of the things most quickly learned in theatrical work is that people as a whole get satisfaction from seeing the rich get the worst of things. The reason for this, of course, lies in the fact that nine tenths of the people in the world are poor, and secretly resent the wealth of the other tenth.

If I had dropped the ice cream, for example, on a scrubwoman's neck, instead of getting laughs sympathy would have been aroused for the woman. Also, because a scrubwoman has no dignity to lose, that point would not have been funny. Dropping ice cream down a rich woman's neck, however, is, in the minds of the audience, just giving the rich what they deserve.

By saying that human beings experience the same emotions as the people in the incidents they witness, I mean that – taking ice cream as an example – when the rich woman shivered the audience shivered with her. A thing that puts a person in an embarrassing predicament must always be perfectly familiar to an audience, or else the people will miss the point entirely. Knowing that the ice cream is cold, the audience shivers. If something was used that the audience did not recognize at once, it would not be able to appreciate the point as well. On this same fact was based the throwing of custard pies in the early pictures. Everyone knew that custard pie is squashy and so was able to appreciate how the actor felt when one landed on him.

Chaplin completed shooting the material for his party sequence by take 550, and devoted the next 150 takes to filming a sequence in which, his imposture having been discovered, he is chased around the house by prison warders and eventually makes his escape. The sequence provided an exciting climactic finish to the film. As with *The Immigrant* Chaplin left to the end the problem of tying up the separate parts of the film – the opening chase and escape of Charlie the convict, and Charlie's subsequent appearance as an imposter in a grand house. His solution was a sequence in which Charlie, having swum around the coast to safety, comes upon a catastrophe at a jetty. Edna's mother has fallen into the sea. When the cowardly Campbell refuses to go in after her, Edna dives in. Charlie arrives at the opportune moment to rescue Edna and, with rather less enthusiasm, her mother. Campbell has meanwhile himself tumbled into the water, but when Charlie far too gallantly rescues him too, he brutally pushes Charlie under the water. Unconscious, Charlie is fished from under the jetty by Edna's Japanese chauffeur, who drives him back to Edna's house. Charlie wakes next morning in a luxurious bed, though he is momentarily alarmed to find himself wearing striped pyjamas and gazing through the bars of an iron bedstead.

The car used in the sequence was Chaplin's own new Locomobile, and the handsome young chauffeur was Kono. This was to be Kono's only appearance on the screen. When his wife saw the film she protested. To work as a chauffeur was one thing but to play the movie actor was altogether too demeaning for a Japanese of respectable family.

The out-takes from *The Adventurer* provide a lively glimpse of the way that, even on the Chaplin set, there were unforeseen hazards. A gag in the jetty scene involves the unconscious Campbell being placed on a stretcher laid with one end to the edge of the jetty. Charlie busily takes up the other end of the stretcher, unaware that he is precipitating Campbell over the edge and into the sea. They had reckoned without Campbell's massive belly, which wedged firmly beneath the lowest rail of the fence and refused to budge.

The Adventurer was to be the last screen appearance of Eric Campbell, who has taken his place in screen history as Chaplin's ideal heavy opponent. Campbell's life during the period of production had been eventful. On 9 July his wife died. While travelling to make arrangements for the funeral, the actor and his daughter Una were injured in a car accident – Campbell had a weakness for fast cars. On or about 1 August, Carlyle Robinson introduced him to a young woman called Pearl Gilman, whose sister Mabelle was a *Floradora* sextet girl and married to a millionaire steel magnate, W. E. Corey. After a five-day courtship, Campbell and Pearl were married at the home of Mrs Elsie Hardy.

The couple planned a honeymoon in Honolulu in December, following completion of *The Adventurer*, but a few weeks after the wedding Pearl was suing her husband for separation maintenance. On 20 December Campbell was driving with two girls in his car, allegedly at sixty miles an hour, when it collided with another vehicle at the corner of Wilshire Boulevard and Vermont Avenue. Campbell was killed instantly. Belying his looks, this massive, kindly, child-like Scot was only thirty-seven.

We have a revealing glimpse of Chaplin's personal life at this period in an article that was syndicated in the press at the time he was at work on *The Vagabond*. The article is unsigned, but it reveals a fairly privileged insight and was probably the work of Terry Ramsaye in his role as Mutual's press chief:

> What are his diversions, his hobbies, his amusements when he leaves the studio? If you were to drop into Chaplin's home in Los Angeles some evening, you might be surprised to find him playing a selection from *Carmen* or *La Bohème* on his violin. Not only is Chaplın an exceptionally good violinist, but he is a composer of music as well. A number of his pieces have already found favor with the music loving public, particularly the march song he composed especially for the benefit performance held some time ago at the Hippodrome in New York City.
>
> Off the screen Chaplin is a serious-minded young fellow, whose entire time is spent in seeking to better himself in other lines. He doesn't want to remain a funny man in the cinema all his life. He wants to make a name for himself in some other field that will win him just as much fame – and money – as he has earned on the screen. Chaplin is, to some extent, a dreamer.
>
> 'No man or woman,' said the Mutual comedian recently, 'should be satisfied with having won a fortune or fame in one particular line of endeavour. The field is large, and there are opportunities everywhere for the young man of today. But he must work if he expects to climb to the top. Otherwise I am afraid there is not much hope.'

DAY BEGINS AT 6.30

Chaplin is just as busy a young man away from the studio as he is in it. He is what may be classed as a systematic worker and a systematic liver. His day begins promptly at 6.30 o'clock every morning. And every night at 10 o'clock, with an exception here and there, he turns off the electric light and gives himself into the hands of Morpheus.

While Chaplin's salary received from the Mutual Film Corporation aggregates $670,000 and his income from various other investments totals many additional thousands a year, he is by no means what may be termed a spender. He lives well but quietly, dresses well, owns several automobiles,* employs a chauffeur, valet and several secretaries. Chaplin believes in [getting] the best and most out of life.

As previously stated, Chaplin's day begins at 6.30 o'clock. At that hour his valet wakes him. Five minutes later he is in his bath. This over with, he places himself in the hands of his barber, sits down to breakfast, spends a half hour with the morning papers and then – a visit to his chiropodist!

HIS OWN CHIROPODIST

It is not generally known that Chaplin employs the service of a chiropodist. Nevertheless such is a fact. Violinists, pianists and others of similar professions have experts who care for their fingers and hands, so why shouldn't Chaplin, whose feet help earn him a princely income each year, have the services of a chiropodist?

This visit over, Chaplin takes a whirl through the Los Angeles park in his car, provided, of course, he has the time. He reaches the studio every morning when he is working, which is practically every day of the year, at 10 o'clock. Once in the studio, Chaplin confers with his studio manager, members of his company and other officials and then doffs his street clothes for his make-up.

A PROLIFIC WORKER

In the studio Chaplin is a prolific worker, for he directs as well as acts. Every set, regardless of its size, is placed under his personal direction. He is an expert in lighting effects and sees to it that everything in this respect is in proper shape before starting work. This completed, he summons his company, rehearses the scenes about to be staged and then becomes the busiest young man imaginable.

Chaplin's day at the studio comprises anywhere from eight to ten hours, depending on the importance of the production he is working on. In many respects Chaplin is a hard taskmaster. He is a great believer in

* This is the only indication that Chaplin had *several* cars at this time. In spring 1917, however, Sydney bought a car for his wife, Minnie – a Mitchell sedan 'which did not have a lot of complicated devices unknown and hard to operate by a woman'.

details and sees to it that every member of his company, from himself all the way down the line, do their parts and do them well.

His day at the studio generally ends about 4 o'clock. A half hour later he is again in his street clothes. But this does not mean that he rushes away from the studio to seek some amusement. Far from it. When the day has closed, so far as the actual work is concerned, Chaplin enters a little private office and lays out the routine for the following day.

Then he leaves for a short spin in his car, generally with his studio manager or some other intimate, and winds up at the Los Angeles Athletic Club, where he is domiciled during his stay in Los Angeles. Until time to dine, Chaplin lounges about the corridors, talking with friends or reading the afternoon papers. Dinner over, Chaplin goes immediately to his room, where he dons his 'gym' suit and repairs to the club's gymnasium. Here he spends an hour each evening boxing, wrestling, tussling with the weight machines and bag punching, followed by a plunge in the pool.

HUNDREDS OF LETTERS

Following this, unless he has an engagement to spend the evening with friends, at a theater, Chaplin remains in his suite, answering the mass of correspondence that reaches him every day from admirers in every section of the universe. Chaplin does not pay much attention to business for most of that is handled by one of his secretaries, whose duties consist of nothing else. Although the letters run into the hundreds on some occasions, Chaplin replies each day to as many as he possibly can.

A letter from a little boy far off in Australia, or from a little girl in equally far off Scotland, receives just as much consideration as does one from his personal representative in New York. If the writer asks for his photograph, Chaplin invariably sends it.*

Chaplin devotes almost two hours every night to his correspondence and the business affairs he must personally take care of, aside from those handled by one of his secretaries. Ten o'clock finds him ready for bed. His valet prepares his bath again and after a cold shower, Chaplin ducks in between the sheets. Within the space of a very few minutes he is fast asleep.**

* This is a surprising statement, since Chaplin was throughout his life a reluctant letter-writer, and very few letters in his hand have survived. However some rough drafts, apparently for letters to be subsequently worked up by a secretary, exist; this may have been the nature of his evening work on correspondence.

** This conflicts with reports that at this period he tended to suffer from insomnia. At the time he began producing for Mutual, he had already installed a dictaphone by his bed at the Athletic Club so that he could record any sudden inspiration in the night. He seems to have retained the dictaphone for many years. Luis Buñuel humorously reported that while preparing *City Lights* Chaplin awoke one morning to find that he had composed Padilla's 'La Violetera' (see page 418).

OUTDOOR RECREATIONS

Chaplin does not smoke nor drink. To be exact, he smoked but one time in his life. He never cared to make another attempt.

The comedian is an expert tennis player and an exceedingly clever dancer.

Of late he has taken up golf and is mastering the intricate points of the game. Motoring is one of his hobbies, but he prefers to let his chauffeur do the driving. Chaplin does not believe in speed – while motoring, of course – rather preferring to move along at a fair rate and drinking in plenty of fresh air. When opportunity permits, Chaplin likes nothing better than to steal off for an hour or so for a little walk by himself in the park.

Like all red-blooded young men, Chaplin delights in the latest of light fiction. He is not what one might call a heavy reader, rather preferring to read slowly and thoughtfully. He has read Shakespeare from beginning to end, is familiar with the works of George Eliot and other noted writers and is a stickler for poetry.

His chief hobby, however, is found in his violin. Every spare moment away from the studio is devoted to this instrument. He does not play from notes excepting in a very few instances. He can run through selections of popular operas by ear and if in the humor, can rattle off the famous Irish jig or some negro selection with the ease of a vaudeville entertainer.

Chaplin admits that as a violinst he is no Kubelik or Elman but he hopes, nevertheless, to play in concerts some day before very long.

The delicacy in omitting any mention of Chaplin's leading lady perhaps confirms that this account originated in Mutual's publicity department. Throughout the Mutual years the affair with Edna was conducted with the utmost discretion. While Chaplin lived at the Athletic Club, Edna stayed at the Engstrom Hotel. They were seen dining together most nights, and most mornings Chaplin would drive past her hotel and pick her up to take her to the studio. The relationship with Edna was the happiest of his early life. Although she was younger, she provided a protective, encouraging and maternal presence in his life. Years afterwards he remembered with affection how, when he was about to go in front of the camera for a scene, she would say to him, 'Go on. Be cute!' Partly out of total confidence in Edna's devotion and partly out of the constant need to test it, Chaplin often treated her in an inconsiderate manner. He later told a friend that she only rebelled once, but that the occasion was alarming. He had been rude to her on the set in some way, and she suddenly flew at him with such fury that he fled to his dressing room and locked himself in. Only after some time did he emerge and make his way apologetically to Edna's dressing room. She had forgotten her anger and only laughed.

At this period Chaplin would still go to boxing matches or ball games with Totheroh, Bergman and others from the studio. Reporting the excitement of the crowd at the bout between Little Eddie Miller and Young Kitchell at Jack Doyle's, on 19 November 1916, one newspaper observed, 'Even Charlie Chaplin rose on top of his chair and advised the pugilists to "get together".'

In March 1917, too, he was a participant in a memorable ball game played in Washington Park, Los Angeles, beween the Tragics and the Comics. The Tragics were Wallace Reid, William Desmond, George Walsh, 'Gene (Eugene) Pallette, Antonio Moreno, Franklyn Farnum, Jack Pickford, Hobart Bosworth and George Behan; the Comics, apart from Chaplin, were Eric Campbell, Charlie Murray, Slim Summerville, Bobby Dunn, Hank Mann, Lonesome Luke (better known in later years as Harold Lloyd), Ben Turpin and Chester Conklin. The umpires were two famous sportsmen of the period, the motor racer Barney Oldfield and the boxer James J. Jeffries.

The medium which Chaplin had made his own was still regarded as a pretty common and low-class thing. True, a few prestigious works like *La Reine Elisabeth* with Bernhardt, *Cabiria*, *Quo Vadis* and recently the D. W. Griffith epics *Birth of a Nation* and *Intolerance* had turned the attention of a more serious-minded audience to the moving pictures, but comedy was still for the people. On 6 May 1916, however, *Harper's Weekly* published an article that was to have far-reaching influence. Entitled 'The Art of Charles Chaplin' it was written by a distinguished stage actress of the day, Minnie Maddern Fiske:

> It will surprise numbers of well-meaning Americans to learn that a constantly increasing body of cultured, artistic people are beginning to regard the young English buffoon, Charles Chaplin, as an extraordinary artist, as well as a comic genius. To these Americans one may dare only to whisper that it is dangerous to condemn a great national figure thoughtlessly. First, let us realize that at the age of twenty-six Charles Chaplin (a boy with a serious, wistful face) has made the whole world laugh. This proves that his work possesses a quality more vital than mere clowning. Doubtless, before he came upon the scene there were many

'comedians' who expressed themselves in grotesque antics and grimaces, but where among them was there one who at twenty-six made his name a part of the common language of almost every country, and whose little, baggy-trousered figure became universally familiar? To the writer Charles Chaplin appears as a great comic artist, possessing inspirational powers and a technique as unfaltering as Réjane's. If it be treason to Art to say this, then let those exalted persons who allow culture to be defined only upon their own terms make the most of it.

Apart from the qualified critics, many thoughtful persons are beginning to analyze the Chaplin performances with a serious desire to discover his secret for making irresistible entertainment out of more or less worthless material. They seek the elusive quality that leavens the lump of the usually pointless burlesques in which he takes part. The critic knows his secret. It is the old, familiar secret of inexhaustible imagination, governed by the unfailing precision of a perfect technique.

Chaplin is vulgar. At the present stage of his career he is frankly a buffoon, and buffoonery is and always has been tinctured with the vulgar. Broad comedy all the way through history has never been able to keep entirely free from vulgarity. There is vulgarity in the comedies of Aristophanes, and in those of Plautus and Terence and the Elizabethans, not excluding Shakespeare. Rabelais is vulgar, Fielding and Smollett and Swift are vulgar. Among the great comedians there is vulgarity without end. Vulgarity and distinguished art can exist together . . .

Mrs Fiske returned some months later to the subject of Chaplin's art, when she rebuked a drama critic for speaking slightingly of the comedian. Not as well known as her earlier essay, her letter is no less eloquent:

Until I read your article in Sunday's paper I was unaware of the existence of anyone who failed to appreciate the art of Charlie Chaplin. Your passing depreciation is difficult to answer on account of its vagueness. And, of course, I feel the absurdity of my taking up cudgels in defense of an artist whose name and mannerisms are familiar to, and whose art is appreciated by, the people of every nation where moving pictures are shown. If it is true that the test of an artist's greatness is the width of his human appeal, then Charlie Chaplin must be entitled to a place amongst the foremost of all living artists. It is almost unprecedented that a comedian can appeal to the widely different senses of humor possessed by the Anglo-Saxon, Latin, Teutonic, Slavonic and Mongolian races.

Like all true artists, he is a master of light and shade, merriment and pathos, smiles and tears. The manner in which he approaches the object of his affections, realizing the futility of his devotion, is very pathetic. It reminds one of a mongrel who, half boldly, half diffidently, licks one's hand, hoping for a caress but fearing a kick. Nevertheless, Charlie Chaplin's is a brave, dauntless philosophy, for no matter what vicissitudes he may have undergone, he squares his shoulders and walks bravely into the future, ignoring his past troubles. Surely he serves a worthy cause who makes the world brighter and preaches optimism, and I am a unit of the vast multitude grateful for Charlie Chaplin.

In conclusion, let me beg you to reinstate yourself in the estimation of the playgoing public, which I trust you enjoyed before the publication of last Sunday's article. I would suggest, as a preliminary step, a speedy visit to the nearest picture house where a Chaplin picture is being shown. For, obviously, you have never seen him!

Hard on the heels of Mrs Fiske came the playwright Harvey O'Higgins with an article in *The New Republic* of 3 February 1917, entitled 'Charlie Chaplin's Art'. O'Higgins compared Chaplin to a great though little-known circus clown, Slivers, a comedian of 'a penetrating imagination':

He would see the shoelace as anything from an angleworm to a string of spaghetti, and see it and relate himself to it so convincingly that he made you see it as he did. Chaplin performs the same miracle with a walking stick. He will see it – outrageously – as a toothpick, but he will use it exactly as you see toothpicks used at a lunch counter, looking at you with an air of sad repletion, with a glazed eye from which all intelligence has withdrawn, inwardly, to brood over the internal satisfaction of digestive process – absurdly, but with unimpeachable realism. Or he is a clerk in a pawnshop, and a man brings in an alarm clock to pledge it. Chaplin has to decide how much it is worth. He sees it first as a patient to be examined diagnostically. He taps it, percusses it, puts his ear to its chest, listens to its heartbeat with a stethoscope, and, while he listens, fixes a thoughtful medical eye on space, looking inscrutably wise and professionally self-confident. He begins to operate on it – with a can-opener. And immediately the round tin clock becomes a round tin can whose contents are under suspicion. He cuts around the circular top of the can, bends back the flap of tin with a kitchen thumb gingerly, scrutinizes the contents gingerly, and then, gingerly approaching his nose to it, sniffs with the melancholy expression of an experienced housekeeper who believes the worst of the packing-houses. The imagination is accurate. The acting is restrained and naturalistic. The result is a scream.

And do not believe that such acting is a matter of crude and simple means. It is as subtle in its naturalness as the shades of intonation in a really tragic speech.

Chaplin, concluded O'Higgins,

> is on a stage where the slapstick, the 'knockabout', the gutta-percha hammer and the 'rough-house' are accepted as the necessary ingredients of comedy, and these things fight against the finer qualities of his art, yet he overcomes them. In his burlesque of Carmen he commits suicide with a collapsible dagger, and the moment of his death is as tragic as any of Bernhardt's. His work has become more and more delicate and finished as the medium of its reproduction has improved to admit of delicate and finished work. There is no doubt, as Mrs Fiske has said, that he is a great artist. And he is a great lesson and encouragement to anyone who loves an art or practises it, for he is an example of how the best can be the most successful, and of how a real talent can triumph over the most appalling limitations put upon its expression, and of how the popular eye can recognize such a talent without the aid of the pundits of culture and even in spite of their anathemas.

Chaplin had become and was to remain a name among the intelligentsia. Reviewing Dukas's *L'Apprenti Sorcier*, Edwin Stone, music critic of the *Los Angeles Times*, compared it complimentarily to Chaplin. So did Heywood Broun reviewing a production of *Gammer Gurton's Needle*, in the *New York Tribune*. Robert Benchley, already a widely syndicated journalist, devoted a humorous column to comparing Chaplin's Tramp with Falstaff. A writer in the *Kansas City Star*, in an article headed 'Have you the Chaplinitis? – Kansas City in the Throes of a Movie Mania Epidemic', attempted seriously to analyze Chaplin's appeal:

> Why should a comedian, whose work is of the broadest slapstick variety, attain such a vogue? Why should a film actor, without the aid of the comedian's chief asset, humorous lines, be able to send his audiences into near hysterics and draw those to the picture houses who will not look at other films? Why is Charlie Chaplin so funny to the great majority of the public?
>
> To which it must be answered first of all that he is a master of pantomime. Seldom, if ever, does he utter a word in the picture. Emotions, thoughts and lines are expressed by his universal power of facial and bodily expression. His feet are most eloquent of all.
>
> In addition to this, he uses every clown trick in the calendar. Every device developed by the funny men of the sawdust ring in the years since circuses began is employed by Chaplin at some time or other on the screen. This in connexion with the agility of an acrobat is another great help to his art of laugh creating.
>
> Another reason may be psychological. Chaplin is such a nonchalant,

> happy-go-lucky fellow. His are the same sort of deeds, grotesque and somewhat distorted, maybe, that endear D'Artagnan and his fellow musketeers to the reader, that cause the tales of swashbuckling heroes to stir the blood; and that have fired the imagination and the sympathies since knights errant went forth in search of adventures with lances instead of a bamboo cane and plumed helmets instead of a battered derby.

Commentators of the time were not unanimous in enthusiasm. The *Yale Magazine* was inclined to blame Chaplin for the dearth of good men on the athletic field: 'It is in the upper classes that the lapses begin to occur and students equipped for serious competition for varsity teams are too often lured by that growing indoor sport, the motion-picture show. We find them lingering with Mr Chaplin in *Easy Street*.' Mrs Lillian W. Betts, executive secretary of the Brooklyn Parks and Playgrounds Committee, went further when she told the members of the Womens' Alliance of the Fourth Unitarian Church at Beverley Road, East 19th Street, that Charlie Chaplin was 'a moral menace. His is the low type of humor that appeals only to the lowest type of intellect. I cannot understand how any resident of Flatbush can go to see [him].' (Mrs Betts was at the time crusading for a municipal bath in Flatbush, 'not only for the health of those who need washing, but for the health of those who must necessarily at one time or another come in contact with them.')

Not all the efforts of such zealots could stop the spread of Chaplinitis. Costume balls were in great vogue in 1917 but magazine writers constantly complained that they were spoiled because most of the girls came as Annette Kellerman, and nine out of ten men as Charlie Chaplin. In February 1917 a Charlie Chaplin costume was used as a disguise by a hold-up man in Cincinnati.[33] About the same time the Boston Society for Psychical Research was investigating 'certain phenomena connected with the simultaneous paging of Mr Charles Chaplin, motion picture comedian, in more than 800 large hotels of the United States'. This surprising psycho-pathological phenomenon was supposed to have been observed on 12 November 1916 across the country from the Atlantic to the Pacific coasts, and from the Canadian boundary to the Gulf. Professor Bamfylde More Carew, a member of the society and author of the paper on the phenomenon, pointed out that Chaplin with his 'singular brand of humor' had become an American obsession, and that among young and active minds of the country, Chaplin was a subject of constantly recurrent thought – in fact, the inspiration of widely registered impulse waves plainly to be noted on charts of the society which are perfected from local charts submitted from widely separated localities.

We find beyond peradventure that on the date mentioned, November 12, there existed for some inexplicable reason a Chaplin impulse, which extended through the length and breadth of the continent. In more than 800 of the principal hotels Mr Chaplin was being paged at the same hour. In hundreds of smaller towns people were waiting at stations to see him disembark from trains upon which he was supposed to arrive.

There is no reason to doubt the correctness of scientific proof that constant reiteration of a certain fact or idea will or may precipitate precisely such a phenomenon as that which has resulted from the wide display of Chaplin absurdities in motion picture theatres – a sudden mental impulse manifesting itself simultaneously practically throughout the length and breadth of the land. It is therefore important though the incident in itself appears trivial, to establish the exact extent of the Chaplin wave and, so far as it may be traced, local causerie.[34]

We have two vivid glimpses of how audiences of the time received Chaplin's films. At Christmas 1916 an unprecedented experiment was undertaken at the New Jersey State Prison. A film – inevitably a Charlie Chaplin comedy – was shown to 1200 prisoners in the prison chapel.

Of course there were some among the more recent arrivals at the prison who were more or less familiar with Charlie and his movements and those who knew him only by reputation. There was a great number, however, to whom he was entirely an unknown personage, and for these the film held the largest measure of delight.

It is doubtful if merriment was ever before in the institution's history unloosed in such abundant stores within its grim walls. Men whose faces had become set and hardened through constant contact with the harsh phases of life gave way to smiles when Charlie and his million dollar feet and funny hat and cane ambled into their visions, and they made no effort to subdue their mirth . . .[35]

The *Memphis Tennessee Appeal* (17 June 1917) reported,

The boy or girl who has not picked his or her favourite of the film world is lost forever in the estimation of his friends. Mary Pickford and Charlie Chaplin are household companions. Boys speak to Charlie like he had for years been a companion in arms. It is interesting to hear the conversation carried on with Charlie at some of the suburban picture theatres. The boys call to him and express their approval over certain things that he

> does and their disapproval of the things that he does not do. They bid him goodnight as though he was present in person. His astral body does the same work on the screen that his physical personality is expected to do.

There was still more concrete evidence of Chaplin's unique appeal in *Photoplay News* on 3 March 1917: several cinema managements reported that after two weeks' run of Chaplin comedies it was necessary to tighten up the bolts in the theatre seats, since the audience laughed so hard that the vibration had loosened them.

A more irksome kind of flattery was the surge of Chaplin imitators at this time. They even included Chaplin's old Karno colleague Stan Jefferson (later Stan Laurel) who was touring the vaudeville circuits with an act called 'The Keystone Trio' in which he imitated Chaplin while two other old Karnoites impersonated Mabel Normand and Chester Conklin. Counterfeit Charlies in films were more damaging. The most persistent Chaplin imitator was the Russian-born Billy West (1883–1975) who made some fifty one- and two-reelers of quite competent quality.

Billy Ritchie (1879–1921) was an old Karno colleague who had originated the part of the drunk in *Mumming Birds* in 1903. Arriving in America in 1905, he continued to specialize in comedy drunk roles, and had a successful stage career for eight years. In July 1914, however, he had the ill luck to fall in with Chaplin's old Keystone enemy, Henry Lehrman, who had just seceded from Sennett to set up the L-Ko Motion Picture Company. Lehrman engaged Ritchie as principal comedian, and persuaded him to adopt a character which, though not an exact imitation of Chaplin, was undeniably Chaplinesque. Ritchie defended his prior right to this character; a letter from his lawyers dated 2 January 1915 states: 'Ritchie in his statement says that he first used the present make-up (of which he affirms "I am the originator; also of this kind of comedy") in the year 1887.'[36]

The association with Lehrman was unfortunate. Ritchie twice received severe injuries while working on the lot (the second time he was attacked by an ostrich) and died as a result in 1921. He had trusted his financial affairs to Lehrman and had told his widow Winifred and his young daughter Wyn that they would be provided for when he died. In fact they found themselves penniless. Chaplin seems to have had no lasting animus against Ritchie as he had against his other imitators, and the comedian's dependents found a helpful friend in Alfred Reeves, who by the time of Ritchie's death was Chaplin's general manager. Winifred Ritchie supported herself by her skill in making costumes and was to work from time to time at the Chaplin Studio.

In November 1917 Chaplin found himself obliged to file a suit against a number of his imitators. His suit was decribed as 'the most sweeping known to motion picture circles'. Against the Otis Lithograph Company, the Motion Picture Film Company, the Big A Film Company and several individuals he sought a permanent injunction against Chaplin imitations, the suppression of pictures in which he supposedly appeared, and damages amounting to $250,000. Another action against the F.F.F. Amusement Corporation sought the suppression of a spurious Chaplin picture called *The Fall of the Rummy-Nuffs*. A third was directed against the New Apollo Feature Film Company and sought to restrain them from releasing *Charlie in a Harem* and *Charlie Chaplin in a Son of the Gods*. The injunctions were granted in all three cases.

> Chaplin's managers have found a new way to insure the authenticity of his pictures. He will be the first screen artist to sign his plays and his signature will appear at the start of each one.
>
> If Charlie gets his damages, and he certainly appears to deserve them, it will be rather a good thing for the motion picture industry. For where is the incentive for an actor to work and establish a type, if imitators can wait until the type is perfected and appropriate it for their own?[37]

While Chaplin was still at Mutual, there was a startling reminder of his boyhood. In the autumn of 1917, Edna received a letter from Hannah Chaplin's long-lost son by Leo Dryden:

> Royal Opera House,
> Bombay, INDIA.
> September 8th 1917
>
> Dear Miss Purviance,
>
> Kindly excuse the liberty I take in writing to you, but I am sending you this letter in the hope that you will assist me in my hitherto futile attempts to obtain recognition and acknowledgement from my half-brother, Charles Chaplin, for whose Company I believe you are Leading Lady. Now do not throw this letter aside, but kindly read every word very carefully and pay attention to my story, which I will tell you as shortly as possible.
>
> My father is Leo Dryden, the famous British Music Hall Star. I came

out to India in January 1912 with his Vaudeville Company, and on his return to England I stayed in India and have been here, in Burma, China, Japan, Straits Settlements, Philippine Islands, Federated Malay States, etc. ever since, touring with various travelling theatrical companies. I am at present the Principal Comedian of the Charles Howitt and A. Phillips Dramatic and Comedy Repertoire Company, which position I have occupied for the last three years or thereabouts. When the Company was in Singapore (Straits Settlements) in September 1915, that is to say, two years ago, I heard from my father for the first time since his return to England from India, and in his letter he mentioned that my half-brother, Charlie Chaplin, had been making a great name for himself in Cinema work in America. Well, when I read this you can imagine my surprise, for my father had always kept the secret of my birth unknown to me, and had always evaded any questions on the subject that I had put to him when a boy. I immediately wrote to my Dad and asked him for further particulars of my birth and of my relationship to Charlie Chaplin, which he sent me in a letter received at Calcutta a few months later. He explained how my mother was a certain Lily Harley, an impersonator of Variety Artistes in her day, with whom he had lived as man and wife, and to whom I had been born, an illegitimate child! He told me how she had been the wife of Charles Chaplin (Senior) who was the father of the present Charlie Chaplin, and how she had lived with another man previously, a certain Sidney Hawke, who was the father of her other son, the eldest, who now calls himself Sid Chaplin! In this way you will see, Miss Purviance, Charlie Chaplin is my mother's only legitimate son, and that Sid and myself are both illegitimate. All this I have since had corroborated by my Aunts Jessie, Ada and Louie, and my Grandfather, who is still alive. They all remember my mother, and Charlie and Sid, so you see I am no imposter, Miss Purviance.

On receipt of Dad's letter I wrote a nice long letter to Charlie (he was with the Essanay Company in Chicago at the time) and sent him my photograph, and told him all about myself and what I was doing in India and the Far East, and of my work with the Howitt-Phillips Company, and congratulated him on his great success in America, and told him that it was not my fault that I had not acknowledged him years ago when he was a poorly paid Comedian in Fred Karno's Company in England, but that I had always been kept in ignorance of the circumstances of my birth, and that I hoped he would be glad to hear from me, but judge my surprise when I didn't get a reply from Charlie. I wrote again, and again, and again, from various places in the Far East when the Company was touring, but still failed to get any acknowledgement from him. Then I wrote to Sid and told him to explain to Charlie, what I had already explained to him time after time, and that was, that it was not my fault that I had not acknowledged him in the old days, and that I did not write to him now that he had made such a success because I wanted any of his money, but because I wanted his FRIENDSHIP and brotherly interest in my work. Sid did not reply either! This was curious, for I had previously heard from a friend of mine in London that when Sid had been playing at the Empress Theatre, Brixton, London, in one of Fred Karno's Companies, he had particularly asked after me, and had wondered where I was.

And so, Miss Purviance, this ridiculous farce has continued for two solid years! Neither Charlie or Sid will acknowledge me as their own flesh and blood! For Charlie there might be some excuse, for LEGALLY I am nothing to him, except an illegitimate half-brother. But I am surprised at Sid's conduct, for HE IS IN THE SAME POSITION AS REGARDS HIS RELATIONSHIP TO CHARLIE AS MYSELF! If Charlie has seen it fit to publicly acknowledge Sid as not only his half-brother, but his BROTHER, and allowed him to use his name too, then surely he can at least ACKNOWLEDGE me, his other half-brother? I don't want his money, I only want his friendship and brotherly interest and encouragement. Surely I am not asking much?

And so, Miss Purviance, I am asking you to intercede with Charlie on my behalf, and let me know what he says. I am sure that I have acted in a perfectly honourable and straightforward manner throughout the whole proceedings, and I am only asking for a little courteous treatment. I am enclosing you a couple of photographs of myself impersonating Charlie, in which you will see the striking family resemblance, although on account of my nose being rather longer than Charlie's, I am more like Sid in features, though not so stout, for I gauge that he is stout by some of his 'Keystone' pictures that I have seen. I also send you one of my private photos, which I hope you will accept with my very best wishes and sincere regards. All three of us have good teeth, you will notice, though Charlie's are better than Sid's and mine.

I celebrated the twenty-fifth anniversary of my birthday last month (August the thirty-first – last day) and begin to feel quite old and responsible. I am like my father in disposition, very ambitious and determined, and like him have made what little reputation I have amongst the theatrical world in India and the East, entirely on my own merits. My Dad is not ashamed to acknowledge that he started as a singer in the streets, and has had to work his way up to the top. Of course he is getting on in years now (fifty-four or thereabouts) and cannot command the high salary he once used to. No doubt you have heard some of his famous songs: The Miner's Dream of Home, which all Britishers sing on New Year's Eve throughout the world where the English language is spoken: India's Reply: Bravo! Dublin Fusiliers (written at the time of the Boer War); Josephine (written on the famous Napoleonic play 'A Royal Divorce');

The Skipper's Daughter; Mercia (written on the famous play 'The Sign of the Cross') and a host of others, most of his own writing and composition.

Well, My Dear Miss Purviance, I will not bore you further with my letter but leave myself entirely in your hands. Please do your best for me in your chat with Charlie. Explain things as I have explained them to you, and then write and tell me what he has to say on the matter.

Trusting to be favoured with your friendship,

Believe me,

Very Sincerely Yours,

Wheeler Dryden

(Son of the famous Leo Dryden and half-brother of Charlie Chaplin).

P.S. Send your reply to:- c/o Thos. Cook & Son, Calcutta, India. It will be re-directed to where I am at the time.

It is unlikely that the gentle and generous Edna failed to respond to so touching an appeal. Certainly Chaplin and Sydney were eventually to recognize their long-lost half-brother. In the mid 1920s he visited Hollywood and was reunited with the mother from whom he had been snatched more than thirty years before. Subsequently he assisted Sydney on an abortive project to establish a production organization in England. In 1939 he was to become a regular member of the staff of the Chaplin Studio, where he remained until Chaplin's final departure from the USA.

It was about this time that Chaplin and Edna began to drift apart. They had been so close and dependent that it is hard to see what led Edna, apparently so loyal and loving, to be unfaithful. Was it perhaps that like other women after her she eventually succumbed to jealousy over the one insuperable rival, the ruling passion in Chaplin's life, his work; and wanted to retaliate? Reflecting on the matter in his autobiography, nearly half a century after the event, Chaplin recalled, 'I blamed myself for having neglected her at times.'

The autobiography makes clear the pain he felt at the break, and his forlorn hope of a reconciliation – difficult as that was with his need for exclusive and undivided love. Even so he could see an element of comedy in the circumstances in which he discovered Edna's infidelity. In 1917 they had begun to enter more into the social life of Hollywood, with the unavoidable dinners and galas in aid of the Red Cross and other war charities. Unused to this kind of gathering,

Edna tended to become jealous when other women monopolized Chaplin, and devised an innocent if eventually rather irritating ruse. She would disappear, stage a faint and on coming round ask for Chaplin. One night however, at a party given by the beautiful actress Fanny Ward, she asked instead for Thomas Meighan, a Hollywood actor just coming into vogue at that moment. Ten years older than Chaplin and married, Meighan had trained as a doctor, but then embarked on a long stage career before arriving in pictures. Chaplin was not unreasonably suspicious and jealous. There was a showdown (during which Edna hurt him by saying there was nothing that need prevent them from being 'good friends') and a reconciliation, but subsequently Chaplin found that Edna was still seeing Meighan. From this time the most fulfilling love of Chaplin's early life was at an end.

The loss was no less to Edna herself. The affair with Meighan, such as it was, was brief. Afterwards, though their working relationship apparently continued as cordial and fruitful as before, Edna never again sought to obtrude upon Chaplin's private life. Her devotion, though, undoubtedly revived and survived. She never married. To the end of her life she continued painstakingly to collect every newspaper item about Chaplin's activities, and this touching archive and testimony of affection, which also includes Wheeler's letter, survives in the collection of Inman Hunter.

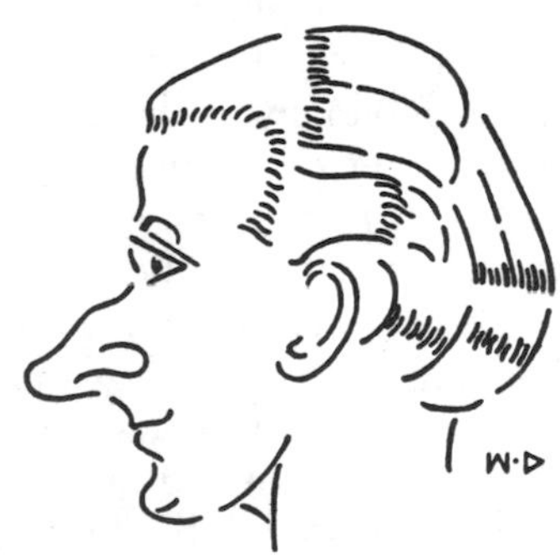

Alphabeticature Self-portrait by Wheeler Dryden

7

Penalties and rewards of independence

The Adventurer concluded the contract with Mutual. Unlike the Essanay relationship, it ended amicably on both sides: the company had sagely remained patient through the increasingly lengthy delays between releases. Mutual in fact offered a million dollars for eight more films, but Chaplin realized that he needed still greater independence if he was to achieve the standards of which he knew he was capable. Sydney was again sent off shopping for a new contract. On the way to New York in April he stopped off in Chicago and spoke to the press:

> All the big film companies are now negotiating with me for Charlie's services, and I am just waiting for the best offer. We are in no hurry but I hope to be able to sign him up before leaving New York this time.
>
> The best offer we have had so far is $1,000,000 for eight pictures. We are also considering forming our own producing company, but haven't been able to arrange satisfactory releasing arrangements, so probably will not enter the field as producers for several months.
>
> There is one thing that will be stipulated in the articles of all Charlie Chaplin contracts hereafter, and that is that Charlie be allowed all the time he needs and all the money for producing them the way he wants. No more of this sixty-mile-an-hour producing stuff will be seen in the Chaplin films from now on. Charlie has made enough money now so that he doesn't have to worry. He is able to either dictate his own terms or sit back and bide his time.
>
> Hereafter the Chaplin pictures will take from two to three times longer to produce than they do now. The settings and stage properties will be the finest. It is quality, not quantity that we are after. After we have made a scene and it isn't up to the new Chaplin quality, it will be made over.

And then, if the whole reel doesn't satisfy Charlie, it will not be released, no matter what money is offered, but thrown into the discard where it belongs.

A close observer of late probably has noticed the increased quality of Chaplin pictures. Charlie has been bringing out more and more new stuff, and he has a great deal more to bring out. The new pictures will be surprises even for the most ardent Chaplin fans.

Also the films hereafter, instead of being just a series of comical stunts or humorous situations, will have a continuous story running through them, with a beginning gradually rising to a climax and winding up with the catastrophe.

We are in the field now for real scenarios. We want the best, and are now negotiating with some of the finest writers in the country to prepare them for us. We have the money to buy what we want, and will be most discriminating in selecting from what is offered.

The next Chaplin series will be wonders. They will be improved upon in every way from those that have gone before. The supporting casts will be greatly strengthened.

Either in this next series, or in those that we plan producing ourselves, I myself will play with Charlie. I have a great many things that are new and will go big, and the two of us, with a strong supporting cast, good stories and good directing and scenery, will be unbeatable.

Charlie and I talked it over before I left Los Angeles on this trip, and we concluded that it was up to us to make the name Chaplin stand for all that there is in true and wholesome comedy, no matter what some of the producing companies want. That is why I am going to take plenty of time before signing the next contract.[1]

Strategically, Sydney could not have chosen a better moment to go to New York. The film industry was on the point of a revolution, and Chaplin was to be a significant factor in it. The most influential figure in industry politics was, and was long to remain, Adolph Zukor. Zukor had arrived in the United States as an immigrant the year before Chaplin was born. He had gone into the fur trade, made a killing by inventing a patent clip for fox furs, and then early in the century entered the nickelodeon business. In 1973, on his hundredth birthday, he was still around to pass judgement on the movies: 'There is nothing wrong with Hollywood that good pictures will not cure.'

Zukor was the first to perceive that the key to domination of the industry lay with the stars. Having captured the unchallenged sweetheart of the box office, Mary Pickford, by the beginning of 1917 Zukor's Paramount Pictures Corporation was on the way to achieving a monopoly of the nation's first-run theatrical outlets. This would enable him to raise his rental rates without restraint. A group of prominent exhibitors, led by Thomas L. Tally and John D. Williams, decided to fight Zukor by creating an organization to buy, or make, and distribute pictures of its own. The new organization, First National Exhibitors' Circuit, had its inaugural meeting in April 1917. The timing was perfect. Nothing could have given First National a finer send-off than the announcement two months later that they had captured Chaplin, and that their arrangement with him was of a kind likely to be much more attractive to other stars than any which Zukor's Paramount-Artcraft could offer.

Chaplin was to become his own producer, contracted to make for First National eight two-reel comedies a year. First National would advance $125,000 to produce each negative, with the star's salary included in the sum. If the films were longer than two reels, First National would advance $15,000 for each additional reel. First National were also to pay for positives, trade advertising and various other incidentals. The cost of distribution was set at thirty per cent of the total rentals, and after all costs were recouped, First National and Chaplin were to divide net profits equally.

The contract involved protracted negotiations between First National and Sydney, aided by Charlie's lawyer, Nathan Burkan, and was completed late in June. Sydney's doggedness in fighting for Charlie's advantage at this time was the more remarkable since he was having troubles of his own. His wife Minnie had undergone a dangerous operation in Sterns Hospital in New York. In the second month of pregnancy a growth was discovered in her stomach, and its removal involved the loss of the child. She was told that she would be able to have future pregnancies; in fact the couple were to remain childless. Moreover, Sydney was fighting to gain for Charlie an independence which privately made him nervous. Whatever he might say to the press about his brother's perfectionism, as long as they worked together he would be uneasy at Charlie's disregard of cost in his single-minded pursuit of the best.

On 3 July Sydney wrote:

> Well Charlie, I hope you were satisfied with the contract. Burkan and I tried to think of every little thing we could to put in, and I think everything of importance has been covered. During the discussion of the terms of the contract, the subject of a second negative came up. The other side were of opinion that you should include a second negative for the sum

arranged as only a limited number of prints could be obtained from the one negative, besides the risk of losing some in the event it would be necessary to ship it abroad. I tried to evade the provision of a second negative, but as they had been very lenient with all our other clauses in the contract and had raised very few objections I did not wish to appear too grabbing, so offered to provide a second negative if they would pay half the cost which they agreed to. I told them the cost of film and cameraman would be about $1000 per picture, but I very much doubt whether it will cost so much as that. Anyway they agreed to pay an extra $500 a picture, so under the circumstances, if you will take my advice, you will use three cameras on your pictures in the future. I certainly think it is worth the added cost to have a brand new negative locked away for the future, especially as the rights to the pictures revert to you after five years, and I feel sure they have a great future value.

There was one other point that was discussed strongly during the framing of the contract, and that was that instead of them paying you the $200,000 in advance, the money should be deposited in escrow until you had carried out your contract. Even Burkan agreed with them in this but I stood pat and insisted that the cash should be paid without any restrictions. I had mother's old saying well in mind, that 'possession is nine points of the law' so they eventually agreed after a long discussion. How did you like the clause about the extra reel? Getting that by pleased me more than anything. I was racking my brains all the way up in the train trying to think how I could raise the price of your pictures even more than I had agreed upon, and yet not break my word with them, when the thought occurred to me, why not make them pay for extra footage. I remembered how difficult it was for you to cut your picture down to footage, and how in doing so you were often compelled to sacrifice a lot of good business and sometimes whole factions.* Here was a chance to not only get them to accept a picture if by chance it should run over two thousand feet, but at the same time make them pay for it. Of course I did not tell them that you had great difficulty in cutting your pictures to two thousand feet. On the contrary I said that many a time you had a story that would make an excellent three-reel picture, but you were compelled to make it a mediocre two reeler, due to the restrictions of your past contracts, but I also impressed them strongly with the fact that by making a three reeler, it would naturally take a great deal more money and time, so with that I raised the price another fifteen thousand dollars per picture which should pay for the cost of your production, and if you are wise, every picture will run about 2500 feet.

* 'Faction' was a word that came into use (apparently exclusively) at the Chaplin Studio to indicate a complete story episode.

Well Charlie, everyone in town here seems to be remarking about the much better class work you are turning out now. I am glad to hear it and I hope you will keep it up and above all refrain from any vulgarity. We must try and frame up a bunch of good stories for the next year and above all, decide and know exactly what you are going to do before the sets are ordered. Have you decided where you are going for your holiday? Marcus Loew I think would be glad to take a trip with you somewhere . . .[2]

There is a hint of reproach in Sydney's remark about Charlie's need to make up his mind what he is going to do before building his sets, and an optimism that was quickly to be dashed in his hope that the films could be made at a cost within the supplementary advance for an extra reel. Though he never adopted Sydney's wily but somewhat impractical advice about shooting with three cameras, Charlie profited by First National's demand that he make two negatives. Throughout the rest of his career in silent films he always shot with two cameras. The wisdom of this precaution was proved when the second negative of *The Kid* was accidentally destroyed by fire in the late summer of 1938.

Marcus Loew did not have the pleasure of taking a trip with Chaplin. Having finished *The Adventurer* Charlie took off for Hawaii in company with Edna, his secretary-valet Tom Harrington, and Rob Wagner, who had become a regular member of the immediate entourage. A teacher of Greek and art, Wagner became fascinated by Chaplin, and on this trip hoped to write a biography. Instead he worked for a period as press representative, and wrote a number of very perceptive articles on Chaplin's art persona.

The party left in August, and stayed five weeks. The affair with Edna seems already to have ended, but perhaps there was some forlorn hope on one side or the other that the holiday might retrieve it. Chaplin, though, was eager to get back. Before he left he had approved the plans for his new studio, and was impatient to start the actual construction. The site was a five-acre plot which had been the home of a Mr R. S. McClennan, on the corner of Sunset Boulevard and La Brea Avenue. At the north side of the property stood a handsome ten-roomed house in colonial style, and initially Chaplin intended to make this his own residence. Instead Sydney and Minnie lived there for a time. The site was then a good mile away from the usual studio quarter, in one of Hollywood's best residential districts; and at first there was considerable local alarm at this encroachment by the movie folk. Film studios of that period tended to be no asset to a community: mostly they were dreadful agglomerations of tumble-down outhouses, corrugated iron, flapping canvas diffusers supported on crazy structures of girders, the whole protected by flimsy timber fences. Chaplin's Lone Star Studio had been one of the more presentable examples of the kind.

Chaplin's plans however completely won over the élite of La Brea and De Longpre Avenues. The exposed elevations were designed to look like a row of English cottages. The local aesthetes were bound to admit that the irruption of an Olde English village street on Sunset 'was not only conferring distinction on the neighborhood, but was considerably improving it'. The cottages served as offices, dressing rooms and work rooms, and the elevation that faced into the studio was more functionally designed in the style of Californian bungalows. The grounds were laid out with lawns and gardens, and there was a large swimming pool. The production facilities were the best that money could buy.

> The stage will be unusually large, and for months Mr Chaplin has been studying a new diffusing system which will dispense with the old coverings and at the same time will cope with all the climatic conditions of the Pacific coast.
>
> The site of the new studio was purchased for the sum of $30,500*, but Mr Chaplin plans the investment of $500,000 in beautifying his property.

Charlie and Sydney broke the first sod in November, with an informal and unpublicized ceremony witnessed by the permanent cast and unit. During the three months it took to build the studio Rollie Totheroh filmed a record of the progress. His shots of the daily growth of the cottage façades, when cut together as stop-action, provided an amusing effect of a magical mushroom growth. When everything was more or less ready, Chaplin shot more film to show off the facilities of the studio. He was filmed arriving in his car and going to his dressing room, to get into his costume and make-up. Tom Harrington is seen solemnly opening a safe and taking out the studio's 'most priceless possessions', Charlie's derby and boots, and then being reprimanded for failing to treat them with the proper reverence. The dreadful boots are delicately placed on a cushion. On the stage (at this time almost bare of sets or scenery) the company, including Henry Bergman, Albert Austin and the diminutive Loyal

* The freehold seems in fact to have cost $34,000.

Underwood, hide their playing cards and leap into suitably industrious attitudes. Chaplin takes a rehearsal, and delicately and repeatedly instructs a gigantic actor how to strangle Loyal Underwood. Other scenes show Chaplin attending to the hair-dressing of an actress, and fun and games at the pool.

At some point in the First National contract Chaplin seems to have had the idea of putting this material together as a two-reeler to be called *How To Make Movies*, but perhaps First National would not accept it as a substitute for regular comedy. Parts of the material were used by Chaplin as introduction to a later re-issue of a compilation of First National films, *The Chaplin Revue*. In 1982 Kevin Brownlow and David Gill edited the whole film together, using the continuity provided by a title list surviving in the Chaplin archives.

In January 1918 Alf Reeves arrived from England to join the studio staff. Since the start of the War he had been touring Britain with the Karno companies, 'thrashing the old horse *Mumming Birds* to pieces still'. He had kept up a fairly regular correspondence with the Chaplin brothers, giving them news of Karno and all their old colleagues, and reporting on the reception of Chaplin's new fame. In January 1916 he wrote to Chaplin, 'I always, as you know, expected big things of you, but never dreamed of the extent of the popularity you would enjoy.' In August 1917 he congratulated the brothers on Charlie's new contract: 'Everyone's breath is taken away.'

Alf's health had not been good, and he had nostalgic memories of California:

> I have to be careful, and these winters here are rather trying – you know the old digs – sitting room just warm as long as you keep around the fires – cold when you leave them, and as for the bedrooms – wow. I really miss the good old steam heat in those nice hotel rooms there, where the warmth is equable and distributed all over the house . . . The little hotel room with its bath, its running water, its elevator, and up to date comfort of it springs to my memory . . .

When Sydney suggested that there might be a job for him at the new studios Alf leapt at the chance:

> When you tell me there is a probability of Charlie embarking on his own account next year, and that he might think of a way to fix me up you fill me full of good hopes. There is nothing I should like more than a long sojourn in the land of Sun. Warm weather and I agree. Venice, Los Angeles, is one of my ideal spots on this earth. Your suggestion, even, of

> the bungalow, with its car ride to town, is far too good to be true I am afraid – especially the Automobile part of it, but then, say I, what's the matter with the streetcar . . .?
>
> So when you are again conversing with Charlie, and thoughts turn this far – if there is anything to suit me – you know about the extent of my humble qualifications – here we are all ready and willing – two of us. Amy is a good cook – Charlie knows – ask him . . . We used to indulge in beefsteak and kidney puddings, and used to do *some* scoffing . . . There are no bones in a beefsteak and kidney pudding. If there had been – I'm sure we would have eaten them. It was Charlie's favourite dinner.

At the end of August 1917 Chaplin offered Reeves a job at the studio, and he at once handed his resignation to Karno and set about making arrangements for sailing. Even though he was forty-eight and so well over military service, there was some difficulty in obtaining the necessary visas from the foreign office; but at last, just after Christmas 1917, Alf and Amy set sail. They arrived in time for Alf to appear before the cameras for *How To Make Movies*: he is seen alerting the company with the cry of 'He's here!' which was part of the daily ritual at the studio. He also made brief appearances in *A Dog's Life* and *Shoulder Arms*: after that Alf's brief acting career came to an end.

When the studio was completed Chaplin decided that it would be good for public relations to open it up to the public, and 2000 people signed the visitors' book in January 1918. A disagreeable incident which resulted from this undoubtedly contributed to Chaplin's secrecy and suspicion in later years. Two people who had represented themselves as journalists spent three days in the studio before they were detected, eavesdropping outside a production meeting. When they were searched they turned out to be in possession of a series of eight sketches of the completed sets for *A Dog's Life*, stenograph notes of story discussions, and descriptions of characters and costumes. In view of the extent to which Chaplin's films were improvised and altered until the very last day of production, his claim that it had cost an estimated $10,000 to scrap the material already planned must be regarded as exaggeration. However the incident was taken seriously enough for all visitors to be banned for the future.

Everything was ready for shooting to start on 15 January 1918. The first production was provisionally titled *I Should Worry*. Only when it was completed did Chaplin decide on the title *A Dog's Life*. It remains one of his most perfect films. Louis Delluc called it 'the cinema's first total work of art'. It is as fast and prodigal of gags as a Karno sketch; its individual scenes cohere into a purposeful structure; at the same time it has a harder core of reality than any film that Chaplin had made before. It is about street life, low life, poverty and hunger, prostitution and exploitation. Without pretension and without sacrificing anything of its comic verve, Chaplin drives home the parallel between the existence of a stray dog, Scraps, and two human unfortunates – Charlie the Tramp and Edna, the bar singer. *A Dog's Life*, said *Photoplay* 'though only a grimy little backyard tableau, ranks with the year's few real achievements.'

Charlie's battle with other applicants for the few available jobs at the Employment Office is compared with Scraps' furious struggle over a bone with a horde of bigger and fiercer dogs. The two strays adopt each other and prove an effective partnership in filching a meal from Syd Chaplin's lunch-wagon. They chance into The Green Dragon, described by a critic of the day as 'a dance hall of the character for which Coney Island, New York's Bowery and the Tenderloin of Chicago were famous some twenty years ago, where the "celebrities" of the underworld gave and took fractured skulls as nightly souvenirs.' It is there that they meet Edna, and become rich by outwitting a couple of crooks who have stolen the wallet of a passing drunk.

A Dog's Life has a strange and charming little coda. The last image of Charlie's escape from the crooks ends on an iris-out. This is followed by an iris-in on a vast ploughed field. Charlie, in a big straw hat, astride a ridge between the furrows, waddles along, dibbing holes with his forefinger and planting a seed in each. He looks up and waves happily towards the camera and to Edna, awaiting him in their idyllic little cottage, all cretonne and Home Sweet Home. A cradle stands beside the fire, and the couple gaze into it with pride. The audience is permitted to jump to the obvious conclusion before the interior of the cradle is revealed: within lies a proud Scraps amongst a litter of puppies. The pride is not unjustified – in earlier scenes Scraps' male sex has been more than evident.

Charlie had perceived the comic possibilities of dogs at least as early as *The Champion* – and Sydney had introduced canine comedy into Karno's *Flats* sketch years earlier. More than a year before he began *A Dog's Life*, in December 1916, the newspapers were carrying the headline 'Chaplin Wants A Dog with Lots of Comedy Sense'. Chaplin told the reporters:

> For a long time I've been considering the idea that a good comedy dog would be an asset in some of my plays, and of course the first that was offered me was a dachshund. The long snaky piece of hose got on my nerves. I bought him from a fat man named Ehrmentraut, and when Sausages went back to his master I made no kick.
>
> The second was a Pomeranian picked up by Miss Purviance, who had him clipped where he ought to have worn hair and left him with whiskers where he didn't need 'em. I got sick of having 'Fluffy Ruffles' round me so I traded the 'Pom' for Helene Rosson's poodle. That moon-eyed snuffling little beast lasted two days.

After this he was reported to have tried a Boston bull terrier, and in March 1917 he was said to have been seen in the company of a pedigree English bulldog called Bandy, whose grandmother, appropriately, was Brixton Bess.

'What I really want,' he said, 'is a mongrel dog. The funniest "purps" I ever set eyes on were mongrels. These studio beasts are too well kept. What I want is a dog that can appreciate a bone and is hungry enough to be funny for his feed. I'm watching all the alleys and some day I'll come home with a comedy dog that will fill the bill.' If the news reports are to be believed, after starting work on *A Dog's Life* Chaplin had taken into the studio twenty-one dogs from the Los Angeles pound. In response to complaints from the neighbours, however, the city authorities insisted that he reduce the number to twelve. The studio petty cash accounts show entries for dogs' meat starting from the second week of production and continuing until the end of shooting. The star of the film, a charming little mongrel called Mut (or Mutt), certainly became resident and remained on staff until his untimely death.

Even at this critical early period of his career as an independent, Chaplin was apparently always ready for extemporization or distraction. He had to be, for his studio was to become a place of pilgrimage for the famous in all walks of life who chanced to be in Los Angeles. Harry Lauder, the great Scottish comedian who had rocketed to stardom in the British music hall about the time that Chaplin was touring with Eight Lancashire Lads, was playing the Empress Theatre. He came to call on 22 January. All work stopped while the two comedians fraternized. Over lunch they decided to make a short film together, there and then, in aid of the Million Pound War Fund to which Lauder had dedicated his efforts following the death of his son at the front in December 1916.*

In the afternoon the two cameras were set up and 745 feet of film (approximately eight and a half minutes) were exposed on each while the two comedians fooled before them. Lauder put on Chaplin's derby and twirled his cane, while Chaplin adopted Lauder's tam o'shanter and knobbly walking stick; each impersonated the other's characteristic comedy walk – Chaplin a good deal more successfully than Lauder. There was more business with a bottle of whisky and a blackboard on which they drew each other's caricature. The *pièce de résistance* was the old music hall 'William Tell' gag. Chaplin placed an apple on Lauder's head and then prepared to shoot it with a pistol. Each time Chaplin's back was turned, however, Lauder would take a great bite out of the apple, reducing it to an emaciated core before Chaplin had a chance to take aim. Each time Chaplin turned to throw a suspicious glance, Lauder's face would freeze into blank, immobile innocence. The two comedians optimistically told the press that they anticipated the film would raise a million dollars for the fund. They were disappointed: it is not certain whether the public even saw the film.

The T-shaped street set first seen in *Easy Street*, which, variously redressed to suit the current needs, was to remain for twenty years the central and essential location for Chaplin's comic world, was erected in the new studio. In *A Dog's Life* Chaplin fixes on this little plot of ground all the mean streets of every city in the world. Methley Street and all the other back ways of Kennington which he had wandered as a boy are clearly the originals, just as they were for *Easy Street*. Yet Chaplin discovers here something universal, in the mysterious doorways, the loitering bums, the loungers at corners, the sitters on doorsteps, the traders with their flimsy stalls only waiting for pilferers or for the small daily catastrophe which will upend them with avalanches of fruit and vegetables. The locale and atmosphere were to prove as recognizable to audiences in London as in Paris, Chicago, Rio or Manila. Yet it is not an abstraction: there is such a local reality in the setting that Chaplin was able to cut from studio shots to scenes filmed on location in the city (there was a day's

* The Harry Lauder Million Pound Fund For Maimed Men, Scottish Soldiers and Sailors, launched 17–18 September 1917. In April 1919 Lauder was knighted by George V for his fund-raising activities.

shooting of dog scenes in front of the Palace Market) without the difference being evident.

Little pre-planning was possible with the dog scenes. The animals and Charlie were set off on the run, and Rollie Totheroh and Jack Wilson, the resourceful cameramen, followed them as best they could. The canine extras were fearsome brutes, and things evidently became somewhat boisterous. After one or two days of work with the dogs, the studio prop people sent out for a large syringe and sixty-five cents' worth of ammonia to separate the dogs when they became too rough.

After a couple of weeks Chaplin suddenly became dissatisfied with the entire story. His staff had become too accustomed to these abrupt switches of mood to be unduly disconcerted by them. Returning to the studio on Monday morning, 11 February, he announced that they would start on an entirely new film to be called *Wiggle and Son*. He took a few shots, ordered the property department to buy ant paste, salts and half a dozen snails, for comic purposes which will never now be divined. The next day, however, *Wiggle and Son* was forgotten, and Chaplin returned with fresh enthusiasm to *I Should Worry*, as the film was still officially known.*

For the crowd scenes in the dance hall thirty extras were hired to supplement the stock company, and as usually happened on Chaplin productions, friends and studio staff were recruited from time to time. Alf Reeves and Rob Wagner may be glimpsed, and Sydney's wife, Minnie Chaplin, played a role. The tough proprietor of the dance hall was played by another new acquaintance of Chaplin's, Granville Redmond, a successful landscape painter. Redmond was a deaf-mute, but he and his director established a perfect pantomime communication, as his performances in *A Dog's Life* and *The Kid* testify.

Grace Kingsley, a keenly observant journalist of the day, visited the studio during the filming of the dance hall sequence, and recorded her impressions:

> It's coming to be quite the fad to visit the Chaplin Studio – that is, if you can get in. Of course nobody is allowed to visit there. Nobody, that is, except picture magnates and newspaper and magazine representatives and their friends, and fellow artists – of whom there are always some thousands in the city – and all the soldiers and sailors and–

* According to a contemporary report, however, (*The Bioscope*, Scottish edition, 18 April 1918) the final title was suggested by a remark of Harry Lauder's who told Chaplin, 'It's a dog's life you're leadin' these days, Charlie.'

The Keystone Studios around 1913.

Mack Sennett on the set, about the time that Chaplin joined the studio.

DEALEY
FOTO

ft: The Essanay Studio at Niles,
lifornia, 1915.

low left: The Majestic Studio
rmerly the Bradbury Mansion)
here *Work* was filmed.

ght: Mabel Normand.

low: *Making a Living*, Chaplin's
t film. The other actor is
enry 'Pathé' Lehrman, who also
ected the film.

Right: Group of picture postcards issued in 1915, with scenes from Essanay films.

Essanay publicity, 1915.

LETTER PHOTOCARD.

"Shanghaied."

RED LETTER PHOTOCARD.

(Charles Chaplin.) "I've come aboard, sir." (Shanghaied

LETTER PHOTOCARD.

Spoons.

RED LETTER PHOTOCARD.

(Champion Charlie.)

Charlie and the Bulldog.

LETTER PHOTOCARD.

Making Love to the Queen. (Charlie's New Job)

(Charles Chaplin).

LETTER PHOTOCARD.

(Charles Chaplin.)

Charlie's Flirtation.

(Charlie by the Sea.)

Panoramic group photograph of Chaplin's Essanay unit taken on the set of *The Bank*, 1915. Each person in the picture has signed the photograph, but many of the signatures are now illegible. A note at the foot of the picture says that the dotted cross indicates the British members of the unit. From left to right: 1 (unknown), 2 Chaplin, 3 Edna Purviance, 4 (unknown), 5 Charles Insley, 6 Leo White, 7 Billy Armstrong, 8 Carl Stockdale, 9 Fred Goodwins, 10 Lawrence A. Bowes, 11 Harold (?), 12 Paddy McQuire (*sic*), 13 John L. Crizer, 14 (?) Easterday, 15 Jack Roach, 16 (?) Stockdale, 17 (unknown), 18 George Cleethorpes, 19 Harry Ensign (cameraman), 20 (unknown), 21 (unknown), 22 Shortie Wilson, 23 (unknown), 24 (?) Charlie Gordon Jr, 25 (unknown), 26 (unknown), 27 (unknown), 28 George Green, 29 (unknown), 30 (unknown), 31 William Gorham, 32 Lee Hall, 33 Jesse Robbins. The set for the bank vault is clearly visible; to the left is part of the set of the manager's office. At the right of the picture are the dressing rooms and overhead are the muslin light diffusers.

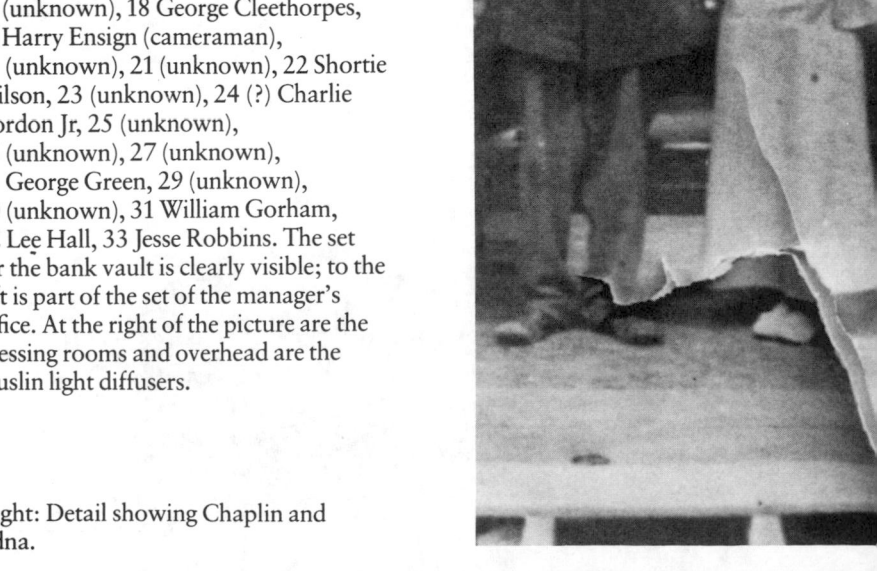

Right: Detail showing Chaplin and Edna.

Details showing Jesse Robbins, the producer, and Harry Ensign, Chaplin's cameraman at Essanay.

Below: Filming *The Vagabond*, 1916.

ft: Chaplin's first days at e Lone Star Studios. Chaplin can seen at the front of the stage. ound him are the uncompleted ts for *The Floorwalker*, including e escalator.

ght: Edna Purviance, 1918. previously unpublished photograph by ck Wilson, Chaplin's second cameraman.

Edna's star hat, *The Count*, 1916.

Above left: The old mansion in the grounds of the Chaplin Studio. Sydney Chaplin, Kono Toraichi and Wheeler Dryden lived here at various times. It was eventually demolished, and the site is now occupied by a Safeway supermarket.

Left: Chaplin and Sydney visit the site of the projected studio.

Above: Building the studio, 1918.

Right: *How to Make Movies:* Chaplin offers a lemon from the grove on the studio site.

1917 cartoon by the French artist Cami, showing Chaplin in a German helmet.

Anticipation of *Shoulder Arms*: 'advertisement' for a putative film, probably sketched by Chaplin in April-May 1918.

Left: Aerial view of Chaplin Studio taken by Jack Wilson, 1918 and showing the extent of the citrus groves in Hollywood.

Below: Aerial views of studio during shooting of *A Woman of Paris* (1922-3) and *Modern Times* (1935-6) showing the urban encroachment. The film sets may be distinguished on the back lot.

A Dog's Life (1918).
The 'lady' at top right is Henry Bergman.

Dog's Life: Chaplin with Mut.

elow: A rehearsal at the studio,
osed for *How To Make Movies*, 1918.
rom left to right: (unknown),
oyal Underwood, Chaplin, Henry
ergman, Edna Purviance; standing:
ıck Wilson.

Visitors to the studio. Above (1918): Helen Keller with Annie Sullivan. Miss Keller 'saw' *Shoulder Arms* on this occasion.

Below: Douglas Fairbanks and Harry Lauder. Sydney is on the left.

But that's enough to show you what one of Charlie's days must be like. And he's the most astonishing combination of busy artist and gracious, good-natured host . . .

Catch Charlie in the right mood and he'll do $10,000 worth of acting for you while you wait. So that, though following Charlie Chaplin around all day is as strenuous as following a soldier at drill, the similarity ends there.

After Charlie has drawn on his funny trousers and shoes and his old shirt, in the privacy of his luxurious dressing room, he finishes making up at a little dressing table on the stage, where he can keep an eye on the dressing of the sets. This happens around 9 o'clock, when the sun encourages photography.

'If I don't get this moustache on right, it's all off,' grinned Charlie as he carefully combed the crêpe and cut it, pasting it on his lip first as a big wad. 'Got to trim that down, or Chester Conklin will think I'm trying to steal his stuff!'

I'm only one of the many interviewers who call on Charlie, so he talks as he makes up: 'The day of sausage pictures is over,' he said. Then he made an important announcement. 'I shall never again bind myself to the making of two-reel comedies. You must have a story, and it's got to be a clear story. Otherwise quite naturally the public doesn't get it. Also you've got to have the gags and the jokes and the jazz. You've got to grab these out of the air as it were. You don't know just when or where the ideas come from – and sometimes they don't!'

Charlie's make-up being on straight by now and his hat on crooked, he took a peep in his glass and descrying over his shoulders a bunch of soldiers, of course, he had to go over and say 'Hello'. Some dear ladies of the Red Cross just then entered, and a candy company having contributed a whole shop full of chocolates for Charlie to auction off, he had to pause to be photographed before the collection with some of the Red Cross ladies.

I think Charlie gets most of his inspiration when he is 'kidding'. He wanted some special idea for that photograph, and he took a dozen different comical poses before, grasping a broom which lay on the set, he hit upon the right idea.

'The Chocolate Soldier!' he grinned, as he fell into a funny attitude with the broom as a gun.

Then the comedian went over to the dance hall set and called out to Miss Purviance and the other members of the company. He sat down beside the two cameras that are always ranged on the action, and he shut his eyes and put his fingers in his ears.

'That's the way he visualizes an idea,' explained Brother Sid. 'He sees it on the screen that way.'

A rehearsal – a long and careful rehearsal with Chaplin playing all the parts in turn – followed . . .

It was lunch time then. So we all went to lunch in Sid's beautiful house, Charlie and Edna Purviance still in their make-up. After lunch it was discovered that there was one of those awful – what Charlie calls 'brick walls' – a dead stop, until a minor snarl in the story and its action was straightened out. For this, Charlie called Charles Lapworth into consultation. Then out came Charlie and kidded around a bit – he does that while he's waiting for an idea to pop, kept everyone laughing, while in the back of his head all the while was that awful question – the brick wall. Presently it came, the longed-for idea.

He had just started once more for the stage when Carlyle Robinson, his publicity man, came forward, announcing in a fairly awe-struck whisper: 'The Earl of Dunmore!'

Of course one cannot overlook a real Earl on the busiest day, so Mr Chaplin paused and chatted a few moments. And though the Earl was an Earl, he realized that a comedian is a hard-working person, and so insisted Charlie should go back to work. Anyhow, Earl or no Earl he was probably dying, just like everybody else, to see Charlie at work. So Charlie hopped onto the stage, and, having at last got possession of the longed-for idea, and having escaped all visitors, he set briskly to work. Half an hour, an hour, two hours passed, with no let-up to the filming of scenes. Somebody brought him some mail, which, after opening, he dropped as carelessly as the hero of a motion picture does when thickening the plot with 'the papers'.

'He'll be working like this until he finishes all the scenes he has in mind,' said Brother Sid, 'until 6, 7, or even 8 o'clock. And when the cutting begins, he will work all night and all day too.'

You'd think to see him acting out there on the stage, that he was still kidding. Maybe he doesn't quite know himself, you think.

Charles Lapworth was an emigré English journalist who had arrived to interview Chaplin, and briefly found a niche in the studio. His own impressions of Chaplin in his dressing room and on the set fill out Grace Kingsley's description:

He will permit you to sit in his dressing room, and let you do the talking while he affixes the horsehair to make up his moustache. You will notice a violin near at hand, also a cello. And it will be unusual if Charlie does not pick up the fiddle and the bow, and accompany your remarks with an obligato from the classics, what time he will fix you with a far-away stare and keep you going with monosyllabic responses.

If you run out of remarks before the violinist has come back to earth, and you are curious enough to glance round the luxuriously furnished room, you may judge a little of Charlie's literary tastes by observing cheek by jowl with Thomas Burke's *Limehouse Nights*, Sigmund Freud's *Psychoneurosis* and Lafcadio Hearn's *Life and Literature*; not on the shelves, but lying around as if they are really being read. On the desk, perhaps, Mark Twain's *Mysterious Stranger*, an allegory that sometimes Charlie will get enthusiastic about; while in the bookcase one may notice that the man who first introduced custard pie into polite argument has not failed to acquaint himself with what the philosophers from way back down to Bergson have had to say about the underlying causes of laughter . . .

No matter how competent any member of his company may be, he has to acknowledge that when he responds to Charlie's direction he achieves better results. It is interesting, for instance, to watch him show the big heavy how to be 'tough', or a girl, obviously at the moral crossroads, how to look the part. His variety of facial gestures is amazing: he is a king of burlesque.

Sometimes, of course, he strikes a snag, and then he will just disappear off the 'lot'. The whole works are at a standstill, and there is a hue and cry around the neighboring orange groves. Perhaps two hours afterwards the comedian steals back to the studio, and his return is made known by the soul-stirring strains from his cello. A little later work is resumed, and Charlie will confess that after much prayerful wrestling he has ironed out the kinks . . .

He frequently interrupts the 'shooting' with an impromptu clog dance. He may close his eyes, and with his hands make weird passes of a geometrical character. But nobody gets alarmed. The chief is just inwardly visualizing the camera shots and when he has got the angles worked out to his own satisfaction he gives instructions for the necessary modifications of the set. Like as not he will order it burned; he has changed his mind, and the carpenters have to tear down an elaborate and costly set, unused.

Chaplin is at once the joy and despair of all managers. If he does not feel like work, he won't work. And he can always fall back on the public for support of his argument that the public are entitled to the best. If he does not feel he is doing his best, he quits and hang the expense. And the thousands of feet of film that he shoots go to waste. Again, that's nobody's business but his. He pays for it, and he will declare that if a picture costs him every penny he makes (it took him three months to make his last one), he is still determined to make it as perfect as he can. And, oh the travail of the cutting! Sometimes sixty thousand feet to get two thousand. Only a rewrite man on a newspaper knows what such a boiling down means. Yet Charlie, and Charlie alone, does the cutting. And he ruthlessly condemns to the scrap-heap miles of excellent comedy that would make the fortunes of other comedians.[3]

For all Chaplin's extravagance in the pursuit of perfection, the book-keeping of this first independent production was meticulous; and the daily record of petty cash disbursements is often as amusing as revealing. Everything is detailed, down to the last five cents for 'beans', seemingly used by Charlie to represent seeds in the final sequence. A wastage of thirty-five feet of film stock (with a running time of about thirty seconds) calls for detailed explanation in the accounts. There are daily entries for dog meat and for gas and oil for the studio Ford (at nineteen cents a gallon). Prop food and drink – pies, sausages, rolls, 'tamalies', chewing gum, beer, near-beer and ginger-ale – figure large also. Henry Bergman played several roles in the film, but his favourite was clearly that of the stout, gum-chewing old lady in the dance hall, whose tears on hearing Edna's plaintive song drench Charlie. Entries for 'fur for Bergman – $2.34' and 'elastic for Bergman – 30¢' show that he started preparing his costume well ahead of time. On 26 February there is a disconcerting item: 'Whiskey (Mut) – 60¢'. The explanation is a scene in which Charlie and the dog sleep together on their plot of waste ground. Charlie uses the suspiciously compliant animal as a pillow, energetically plumping him into shape before settling down, and then agitatedly searching the immobile dog for fleas. ('There are strangers in our midst,' says one of the film's very few titles.) The item in the petty cash account reveals the secret of Mut's docility: he was dead drunk.

Shooting was completed on 22 March, when Chaplin used 1792 feet of film to round off one thousand takes and 35,887 feet of film exposed on each camera. This time Chaplin was forced to accept help with the editing. From 26 to 29 March he stayed night and day in the cutting room with Bergman, the two cameramen and two assistants, Brown and Depew, to help him. Between times he had a last-minute inspiration and shot a charming little scene in which Charlie sits on the steps of a second-hand store and feeds the dog with milk from a near-empty bottle he has found there. When the dog cannot reach the milk with his tongue, Charlie obligingly dips Mut's tail into the bottle and gives it to him to suck like a pacifier.

With a superhuman effort the cutting was completed late on 31 March, and Chaplin was ready to depart on a Liberty Bond tour the following day. The staff worked on to prepare the negatives. While Chaplin was off on the Bond tour, the staff were instructed to prepare ideas for submission on his return. Mut, sad to say, did not live to see Charlie's return to California. He had apparently grown so attached to his master that he pined during his absence, refused to eat, and died. He was buried in the studio ground under a little memorial composed of artistically arranged garbage, and with the epitaph: 'Mut, died April 29th – a broken heart'. His single film role had earned him his small piece of immortality.

The trip east was made in company with Douglas Fairbanks, Mary Pickford, and Rob Wagner. The plan was for the three stars to take part in the official launching of the Third Liberty Bond campaign in Washington, to go on together to New York, and then to split up, Doug and Mary taking on the northern states and Chaplin the southern. Chaplin slept during the first two days of the rail journey. Recovering from his exhaustion, he set to writing his speech and confided to the others his nervousness about making a serious address to a crowd. Doug suggested that he practise on the crowd that gathered around the train at a stop *en route* but, as the last speaker, he found the train moving off just as he got into his stride, enthusiastically addressing a rapidly receding audience.

In Washington the party made a triumphal progress through the streets to a football field where a vast crowd had come to hear them. Marie Dressler was on the platform as well, and when Chaplin was carried away by his own eloquence, and fell off the platform, he managed to take the ample Marie with him. They fell on top of the young Assistant Secretary of the Navy, Franklin D. Roosevelt. Later they were formally presented to President Wilson at the White House; Chaplin felt that he and the President were mutually unimpressed by the encounter.

In New York the excitement was even greater. Crowds began to gather at the junction of Broad and Wall Streets during the morning, and by the time the party arrived around noon, on 8 April 1918, it was estimated that between twenty and thirty thousand people were waiting, many clinging to the Morgan Building, the Stock Exchange and the pillars of the Sub-Treasury. Their speeches were greeted with applause, laughter and shouting; and the crowd went wild when Fairbanks lifted Chaplin onto his shoulders. Chaplin was wearing a wasp-waisted blue suit, light-top shoes and a black derby.

'Now listen –' he began, only to be interrupted by cheers and laughter from the thousands of bankers, brokers, office boys and stenographers. 'I never made a speech before in my life –' he continued, and was interrupted again, '— but I believe I can make one now!' The next few words were inaudible; then the crowd settled down, and most of the rest of his words, screamed through a megaphone, were heard:

> You people out there – I want you to forget all about percentages in this third Liberty Loan. Human life is at stake, and no one ought to worry about what rate of interest the bonds are going to bring or what he can make by purchasing them.
>
> Money is needed – money to support the great army and navy of Uncle Sam. This very minute the Germans occupy a position of advantage, and we have got to get the dollars. It ought to go over so that we can drive that old devil the Kaiser, out of France!

The cheers for this sentiment resounded through several blocks of the city. When he could again get silence, Chaplin concluded: 'How many of you men – how many of you boys, out there, have bought or are willing to buy Liberty Bonds?' The hand-stretching that followed, said the *Wall Street Journal*, 'suggested vividly the latter part of the seventh innings at the Polo Grounds during a world series'.

The New York trip brought one personal bonus. Marie Doro, the beautiful star of the London production of *Sherlock Holmes* thirteen years ago, was playing in *Barbara* at the Klaw Theatre, and Chaplin was able to arrange an intimate dinner with her. The impossible dream of the sixteen-year-old who played Billy the pageboy had come true.

Chaplin's tour began at Petersburg, Virginia, and took him through North Carolina, Kentucky, Tennessee and Mississippi. He arrived in New Orleans exhausted, and was forced to rest for a few days before completing the tour, and returning home via Texas. In Memphis he found waiting for him a letter from his exasperated studio manager, John Jasper, resigning his post. Chaplin had departed California leaving Jasper's drawing account for running the studio three weeks in arrears. In reply to Jasper's protests, he had arranged by cable for a weekly payment of $2000, even though it was previously agreed that the minimum average budget was $3000. 'I expected of course that I would have the money every week,' wrote Jasper. 'The only way any Manager can ever give satisfaction in this job is to have a drawing account. Why don't you put sufficient funds in the Citizen's National Bank and stop all this confusion? It is not as if you did not have the money like so many others.'

CHARLIE CHAPLIN STUDIOS

DAILY PRODUCTON REPORT

NUMBER OF DAYS ON PICTURE INCLUDING TO-DAY		
IDLE	WORK	TOTAL
1	11	12

DIRECTOR

DATE January 28th 1918

CAMERAMAN

PICTURE No. 1

WORKING TITLE "I Should Worry"

NUMBER OF REELS

CAST	RATE	SCENES PLAYED IN
CHARLIE CHAPLIN	*	
HENRY BERGMAN	STOCK	
ALBERT AUSTIN	STOCK	
FRED STARR	STOCK	
TOM WILSON	STOCK	
SLIM COLE	STOCK	
JAMES T. KELLEY	GUAR	
TED EDWARDS	GUAR	

PETTY CASH EXPENDITURES — ARTICLE	AMOUNT
BALANCE OF HAND	11 90
Meat for Dogs	34
" " "	20
" " "	36
Gasoline	20
Fur for Bergman	2 34
Rent of 2 Dogs	2 00
	6 46
STILLS TAKEN TO-DAY:	2
NUMBER BROUGHT FORWARD	2
TOTAL STILLS TO DATE	5

SCENES TAKEN TO-DAY: No	FEET	SCENE No.	FEET	SCENE No.	FEET
		FORWARD		FORWARD	
TOTAL		TOTAL		GRAND TOT.	

FILM USED	FOOTAGE
TO-DAY	1200
BAL. FORWD	4877
TOTAL TO DATE	6077

STARTED WORK A. M.	P. M.
10:30	

AUTO USED	STARTED TIME A. M.	P. M.	FINISHED TIME A. M.	P. M.

MEMO. Mr Chaplin arrived at 9:40 A M Started shooting dog no tract kept of scenes. Fight was unsatisfactory.

WEATHER { FAIR ~~CLOUDY~~ ~~RAIN~~ }

O. K. M W Brown

CLERK

1918 - Production report on *A Dog's Life* (at first called *I Should Worry*).

CHARLIE CHAPLIN STUDIOS

DAILY PRODUCTON REPORT

NUMBER OF DAYS ON PICTURE INCLUDING TO-DAY		
IDLE	WORK	TOTAL
1	18	19

DIRECTOR

CAMERAMAN

WORKING TITLE

DATE February 4hh 1918

PICTURE No. 1

NUMBER OF REELS 2

CAST	RATE		SCENES PLAYED IN
CHARLIE CHAPLIN	*		Shot only dog scenes today
HENRY BERGMAN	STOCK		
ALBERT AUSTIN	STOCK		
FRED STARR	STOCK		
TOM WILSON	STOCK		
SLIM COLE	STOCK		
JAMES KELLEY	GUAR		
TED EDWARDS	GUAR		Made up.
LOUIS FITZROY	GUAR		
THOMAS RILEY	GUAR		
DAVE ANDERSON	GUAR		
JANET SULLEY	GUAR		
MISS PITTS	STOCK		
JAMES McCORMICK	2	50	
GRACE WILSON	2	50	
MARGARET DRACUP	2	50	
OLIVER HALL	2	50	
JERRY FARRAGAMA	2	50	
LOYAL UNDERWOOD	2	50	
CHAS. GEE (Dog)	5	00	

PETTY CASH EXPENDITURES		
ARTICLE	AMOUNT	
BALANCE OF HAND	6	38
Advanced	10	00
Gas & Oil		45
Radiator Cap		50
Sausagc		75
Rolls		12
Sausage compound		50
Casters		90
Pies & Eggs	1	22
Hot dogs		60
	11	34

STILLS TAKEN TO-DAY:

NUMBER BROUGHT FORWARD 8

TOTAL STILLS TO DATE

SCENES TAKEN TO-DAY					
No.	FEET	SCENE No.	FEET	SCENE No.	FEET
3	12	FORWARD	46	FORWARD	128
4	8	320	12	326	12
5	5	321	10	327	10
6	8	322	12	328	7
7	3	323	15	320	6
8	3	324	15	330	62
9	7	325	18	331	23
TOTAL		TOTAL		GRAND TOT.	

FILM USED		STARTED WORK	
FOOTAGE		A. M.	P. M.
TO-DAY	1256	10:00	
BAL FORWD	12837		
TOTAL TO DATE	13093		

MEMO. Shooting dogs in street scene.

AUTO USED	STARTED TIME		FINISHED TIME	
	A. M.	P. M.	A.	P M

WEATHER { FAIR ~~CLOUDY~~ ~~RAIN~~

O. K. MWBrown

CLERK

— Over —

1918 - Production report on *A Dog's Life* (at first called *I Should Worry*).

Chaplin appears not to have been gravely inconvenienced by the departure of Jasper. Alf Reeves was immediately appointed as his successor, and for the next twenty-eight years proved an ideal manager, seemingly never surprised or discomposed by his employer's caprices.

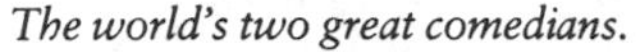

The world's two great comedians.

1917 - Spanish cartoon showing Chaplin with the Kaiser.

Chaplin was back in Hollywood in early May and by the end of the month was ready to start his new film, tentatively recorded as 'Production No 2. *Camouflage.* 2 reels'. The notion of Charlie at war was irresistible. From the time of the 'slacker' campaign against him, newspaper cartoonists in every country had delighted in speculating on the possibilities of a confrontation beween Charlie and the Kaiser. Late in 1917, Chaplin had amused himself by drawing on a post-card – still preserved in one of his scrap books – an advertisement for a putative film, *Private Chaplin U.S.A.*: 'Ladies and Gentlemen – Charlie in this picture lies down his cane and picks up the sword to fight for Democracy. Picture produced by Charlie Chaplin Film Corp. released through First National Exhibitors' Circuit.' Chaplin's collaborators and friends shook their heads about the wisdom of making comedy out of so dreadful an event as the War, whose full effect Americans had so recently begun to experience. Chaplin, however, always growing more aware of the proximity of comedy, drama and tragedy, was confident.

He seems to have begun the film with a more determined idea of its structure than was customary, though in the event this idea was to be modified. Originally he planned three acts. The first would show Charlie in civilian life, at the mercy of a virago wife and the father of several children. After a bridging sequence in the recruiting office, the film would show his adventures at the front. The third part was to be 'the banquet', with the crowned heads of Europe gratefully toasting Charlie for his gallant capture of the Kaiser. At the end, like Jimmy the Fearless or Charlie in *The Bank*, he would wake up to the cold reality of the training camp.

When his plans were as certain as this, Chaplin liked to shoot his stories in sequence. He began with the scenes of civilian life, using three child actors, True Boardman Jr, Frankie Lee and Marion Feducha. The angry wife was to remain off screen, her presence indicated only by the occasional flying plate, frying-pan or other missile. As finally assembled, the sequence shows Charlie coming along the street with his three sons. Without a sign he turns into the door of a saloon, leaving them to wait patiently outside. When he rejoins them they all troop home where he docilely sets about making soup for lunch amidst the bombardments of his unseen spouse. The arrival of the postman with his draft papers comes as a happy release.

The next sequence, which took two weeks to prepare and shoot, shows Charlie's arrival at the recruiting office for his medical examination. He is told to enter the office and disrobe. Partially stripped, he opens the wrong door and finds himself trapped in a maze of glass partitioned offices occupied by lady clerks. After much trouble Charlie evades the women. He reads on a door, 'Dr. Francis Maud'. The name makes him still more apprehensive; the doctor turns out to be no lady, however, but the lugubrious Albert Austin, heavily bearded. The examination is seen only in silhouette through the frosted glass panel of the office door. The doctor appears and sticks a gigantic probe into Charlie's throat, only to have it repeatedly and violently shot back at him. Eventually Charlie swallows the thing entirely, and the doctor is obliged to resort to a line and hook to retrieve it. No doubt suggested by memories of the Karno *Harlequinade* of Christmas 1910, in essence it is a hoary old routine of the vaudeville 'shadowgraphist'. Chaplin was a master at giving new life to old jokes, though, and when, sixty-five years on, the rediscovered sequence was included in the *Unknown Chaplin* television series, it proved to have lost none of its verve.

Yet Chaplin was to discard all that he had shot in this first month of work. Such rigorous self-censorship would seem remarkable at any time in the history of the cinema. In 1918, when a month was reckoned time enough to shoot a first-class feature film, it was astounding. Moreover, under the contract with First National, Chaplin bore all the production costs. It was his own money that he was prepared to throw away in the cause of perfection. Rightly, though, he knew that he could do better.

The first week of July was devoted to revising the story and building new sets. When shooting was resumed, Chaplin filmed from beginning to end, practically without the breaks to talk over and revise the story which had become and were to remain customary. The most substantial interruption to shooting came on 11 July when Marie Dressler visited the studio, accompanied by the actress Ina Claire. As usual, Chaplin abandoned work with surprising cheerfulness to entertain his old co-star. They posed together for photographs which show the formidable Marie in Hun-scaring mood in the trench set.

The trench and dug-out are a remarkable abstraction of the reality of the Western Front. When Chaplin reissued *Shoulder Arms* more than half a century later, he proudly prefaced it with actuality shots of the war, to show how well his set-builders had done. The trench scenes, showing Charlie, Sydney and their companions adapting to front-line conditions – vermin, bad food, homesickness, snipers, rain, mud, floods and fear – took four weeks to shoot. By this time it was high summer. One day the heat was so great that it was impossible to film at all. Chaplin spent four days of this heatwave sweating inside a camouflage tree. His discomfort was rewarded by one of the most deliriously surreal episodes of his work. Charlie scuttles around no-man's-land in his tree disguise, freezing into arboreal immobility at the approach of a German patrol, and coping ingeniously with a great German soldier with an axe who is bent on chopping him down for firewood. In our last memorable vision of the Charlie-tree it is skipping and hopping off towards a distant horizon. The expanses of no-man's-land were provided, in those days of a still-rural Hollywood, by the back of Beverly Hills, while Wilshire Boulevard and the back of Sherman provided the forest. Back of Sherman, too, they found a half-buried pipe which suggested a piece of comic business. Charlie bolts, rabbit-like into the pipe; his German pursuers grab his legs, but capture only his boots and his disguise which he has shed like a snake-skin. Following this, rotund Henry Bergman, playing a German officer, gets stuck in the pipe as he goes after Charlie, and has to be broken out. It is not recorded if the Los Angeles sewage authorities ever discovered how their property came to be shattered.

Dedicated to his patriotic commitments, Chaplin had agreed to donate a short film to the Liberty Bond drive, and now realized that to deliver it on time he would have to interrupt production of *Camouflage*, which had inevitably already overrun its anticipated schedule. On 14 August the unit worked on until 1 a.m., to complete the scenes of Private Charlie's encounter with Edna, playing a French peasant, in her ruined home. The next day the studio was turned over to making what was identified only as 'propaganda film'. Eventually titled *The Bond*, it ran 685 feet (about ten minutes) and was completed in six working days. Sydney appeared as the Kaiser in the costume and make-up he used for *Camouflage*. Besides Chaplin the rest of the cast was made up of Edna, Albert Austin and a child called Dorothy Rosher. The film had four episodes, introduced by the title, 'There are different kind of Bonds: the Bond of Friendship; the Bond of Love; the Marriage Bond; and most important of all – the Liberty Bond.' The use of simple, stylized white properties against a plain black back-drop gave this curious little film a proto-Expressionist look. It was donated to the Government, and distributed without charge to all theatres in the United States in the Autumn of 1918.

With *The Bond* out of the way, Chaplin rapidly finished off *Camouflage*. By 16 September the film was cut and re-titled *Shoulder Arms*.

Chaplin, tired, dispirited and depressed by personal troubles, suddenly lost confidence in the film, and later claimed that he had seriously thought of scrapping it and was incredulous when Douglas Fairbanks, having demanded to see it, laughed till the tears ran down his cheeks. Better than any other clown in history, Chaplin was able to prove that comedy is never so rich as when it is poised on the edge of tragedy. He had metamorphosed the real-life horrors of war into a cause for laughter; and in the event there was no audience more appreciative of *Shoulder Arms* than the men who had seen and suffered the reality. Soldier Charlie includes in his kit a mousetrap and a grater which serves as a back-scratcher when the lice grow too assertive. His food parcel from home includes biscuits as hard as ration issue, and a Limburger cheese so high that he uses it like a grenade to bomb and gas the enemy. He takes advantage of passing bullets to open a bottle and light a cigarette. As a sniper, he chalks up his hits – then rubs out the last mark in acknowledgement of a return shot that clips his tin helmet. Even the nightmare of the flooded trenches of the Somme is turned into laughter: Charlie fishes out his submerged pillow to plump it up ineffectually before settling down for the night, and blows out the candle as it floats by on the flood water. One title became a classic joke of the First World War. Asked how he has captured thirteen Germans single-handed, Charlie replies simply and mystifyingly: 'I surrounded them.'

As memorable is the scene where Charlie is the only soldier to receive no letter or parcel in the mail delivery. With misguided pride he refuses an offer of cake from a luckier comrade, and wanders from the dugout into the trench. There a soldier on guard duty is reading a letter from home. Charlie reads over his shoulder, and echoes all the emotions that are passing over the soldier's face. Though he might make comedy from it, the folly and tragedy and waste of war were always to bewilder and torment Chaplin. One apparently light-hearted scene in *Shoulder Arms* already hints at a more serious drift of thought. Charlie, having 'surrounded' and captured his German prisoners, offers them cigarettes. The common soldiers accept them gratefully, but the diminutive Prussian officer takes a cigarette only to throw it away with contempt. Charlie instantly seizes the little man, lays him across his knee and spanks him soundly. The German soldiers delightedly gather round and applaud. There is a comradeship of ordinary men that transcends the warring of governments and armies.

Shoulder Arms was one of the greatest successes of Chaplin's career. His marriage to Mildred Harris was not. When he met Mildred at a party given by Samuel Goldwyn, probably in the early part of 1918, she was rising sixteen. Already established as a child actress before she was ten, she was at this time employed at Paramount under the direction of Lois Weber. She still radiated a child-like quality which charmed Chaplin: his feminine ideal had been definitively fixed, it seemed, by his first infatuation with the fifteen-year-old Hetty Kelly. For her part, Mildred seems to have made knowing use of her golden hair, blue eyes and flirtatious prattle. She was presumably not discouraged by her mother, who as wardrobe mistress at the Ince

Studios could not but be aware of Chaplin as the most eligible and the most handsome bachelor in Hollywood. Harriette Underhill described his appearance at this time: 'He talks humorously, he thinks seriously, he dresses quietly and he looks handsome. He has the whitest teeth we ever saw, the bluest eyes and the blackest eye-lashes . . .'

Soon both Chaplin and the Harrises were coyly fending off enquiries from the press, who were not however to be easily put off. On 25 June the *Los Angeles Times* reported rumours of an engagement, and the subsequent denials. The following day the *Los Angeles Examiner* had a fuller and more circumstantial report:

CHAPLIN MARRIAGE RUMOR IS DENIED

Despite rumors that will not die down to the effect that Mildred Harris, the dainty screen favorite, has won the heart of Charlie Chaplin and soon is to be his bride, both the petite actress and her mother Mrs A. F. Harris denied last night the last half of the double-barrelled allegation.

'No, Mr Chaplin and I are not engaged,' Miss Harris said last night when she returned to her quarters in the Wilshire Apartments after an evening at his studio. 'We're just very dear friends. Why, we've only known each other two months and we've only been going together a month or so. I'm sure, too, Mr Chaplin will deny the report. We have not discussed the rumor as we have not seen each other for about a week.'

Mrs Harris was much surprised by the report, she said, and added that her daughter was only seventeen years of age and too young to think of marrying.

According to the circulated report in motion picture circles, Chaplin recently conferred with Philip Smalley of the Lois Weber Studio, where Miss Harris is employed, and asked how her contract would be affected if they should be married. It was said, according to the report, that the marriage would not affect the contract.

Philip Smalley denied that this reported conference took place.

Mrs Harris stopped her denials shortly after the completion of *Shoulder Arms*, when Mildred announced that she was pregnant. Chaplin was trapped: he could not possibly risk the scandal of this kind of involvement with a seventeen-year-old. Tom Harrington, his valet, secretary, confidant and general factotum, was told to arrange a registry office marriage for 23 September 1918, after studio working hours. Harrington arranged the affair with the discretion for which Chaplin valued him, and Chaplin found himself, without any pleasure, a married man. Leaving the Los Angeles Athletic Club, which had been his home practically since he arrived in Hollywood, he rented a house at 2000 De Mille Drive. The lease was only for six months, but long tenancies were hardly appropriate to the marriage. His reaction on seeing the bride awaiting his arrival at the registry office was, to say the least, not promising: 'I felt a little sorry for her.'

Edna only knew about the marriage when she read the newspapers the following day, but she faced the fact with dignity and outward calm. Chaplin recalled that when he went to the studio the morning after, she appeared at the door of her dressing room. 'Congratulations' , she said softly. 'Thank you,' he replied, and went on his way to his dressing room. 'Edna made me feel embarrassed.' Edna did not see *Shoulder Arms* in the studio projection room with Chaplin; but when he was about to embark for a week of honeymoon on Catalina Island, she wrote to him:

Hotel Alexandria
Los Angeles

Dear Charlie:-

Saw the picture this afternoon at the Iris theatre in Hollywood - I cannot tell you how good it was - Everybody was thrilled, although there were not many people there. I know you were just a "wee" bit discouraged, but please forget that, as it is wonderful and <u>very</u> <u>pathetic</u> when you did not receive

Hotel Alexandria
Los Angeles

a package - A "lump" came in my throat as it did with everyone else around me - Just one thing I did not like especially - When the German shook your hand in the trenches and you accepted it - they might not be liked in foreign countries - Of course no one else noticed it, but I being one of your most true and sincere critics tell you this -

The time spent on the picture was well worth while, so have a good time and catch lots of <u>fishes</u>. Always

Edna

1918 - Letter written by Edna Purviance after seeing *Shoulder Arms*.

To her other qualities Edna added that of being a noble loser. Poor Mildred was, as Chaplin gently put it, 'no mental heavyweight'. She bored him, and in her turn resented the exclusive single-mindedness of his concentration when he was working. She was annoyed because he would not concern himself in her career, which enjoyed a brief stimulus from the celebrity of being Mildred Harris Chaplin. The worst irony for Chaplin was that the pregnancy which had shot-gunned him into marriage turned out to be a false alarm.

Chaplin was convinced that the marriage debilitated his creative ability, and the acute difficulties he experienced with his next film, *Sunnyside*, begun under the working title *Jack of All Trades*, seemed to confirm his fears. Chaplin's ideas seemed much less clear than usual. He had decided on a rural subject, had turned the studio's regular street setting into the main thoroughfare of an old world village and built a set for the lobby of a seedy hotel, in which he himself was to play the man of all work who gave the film its (provisional) title. The first few days of shooting were spent on location at the Phelps ranch; and the petty cash disbursements that survive from this period are evocative of that far-off, rustic California. Mrs Phelps was paid $3 a day for the use of her ranch, a dollar a day for the hire of a cow, a dollar for repairs to a fence, and thirty cents a head for lunch for the unit in the ranch cook-house. Cowboys and horses were hired from a neighbouring rancher, Joe Floris.

Production began on 4 November, five weeks behind the scheduled starting date, but Chaplin's desperate lack of a guiding idea was evident from the number of days he took off to 'talk the story' with Bergman and the others, and his readiness to seize on any distraction which offered itself. Work was abandoned so that Charlie, Sydney and Minnie Chaplin could lunch with the Bishop of Birmingham, whose visit to the studio was duly filmed. Another day Chaplin reported to the studio but then went off motoring with Carter De Haven in a 'juvenile racer'. Later in the production the whole company took three days off to go to the air circus in San Diego, vaguely justifying the trip by shooting two thousand feet of film of the event, which was never used. In mid-December Chaplin cut together what he had already shot, but was so dispirited that he absented himself from the studio altogether. Christmas came but Chaplin did not. Neither he nor Edna was seen at the studio in the first weeks of the new year, and on 19 January 1919 the studio closed down altogether. In all Chaplin stayed away from the studio for six weeks. None of his colleagues had ever witnessed such a severe creative crisis in him.

Chaplin returned to the studio on 29 January, and announced that the 21,053 feet of film that had been exposed for *Jack of All Trades* was to be abandoned, and that he intended embarking on a new production to be called *Putting It Over*. Matters proceeded no better: and the situation was aggravated by a series of rainy days that prevented shooting. Chaplin tested some new actresses, hired a couple of cowboys and horses, a cow, a bull and a stunt man; then, after a few more days, he announced that they would after all resume work on *Jack of All Trades*, once more called *Sunnyside*.

The studio daily reports tell their own story:

February 21	Did not shoot. Mr Chaplin cutting
February 22	Did not shoot. Mr Chaplin cutting
February 23	Did not shoot. Mr Chaplin cutting
February 25	Did not shoot. Looking for locations
February 26	Did not shoot. Mr Chaplin not feeling well
February 27	Did not shoot. Mr Chaplin cutting
February 28	Did not shoot
March 1	Did not shoot. Filmed sunset, 100 feet.
March 2	Did not shoot. Talked story
March 4	Did not shoot. Talked story
March 5	Did not shoot. Mr Chaplin sick
March 6	Did not shoot. Mr Chaplin absent
March 7	Shot 376 feet
March 8	Did not shoot. Talked story

Suddenly, in the middle of March, Chaplin was seized either by desperation or by inspiration. He had by this time spent 150 days on the production, two thirds of them idle. Now however, for three weeks he shot day in and day out, filming well over a thousand feet of film most days, and putting together the elements of a rough and ready but cohesive story. He developed a love interest, between Edna and himself, and a rival in the shape of a dashing city slicker who arrives to turn her head with his natty clothes and gallant manners. (Was he turning life into art?)

Sunnyside betrays the strain that went into its completion, and Chaplin and his contemporaries regarded it as one of his least successful pictures. Certainly the comedy is neither so tightly structured nor so firmly motivated as in his other films of this period, but there are interesting departures from Chaplin's usual manner, quite apart from the experiment of showing Charlie in a bucolic setting. He indulges a peculiarly macabre strain with his device to get rid of the village idiot, while he is courting Edna. Blindfolding the youth under the pretext of a game of hide-and-seek, he gently guides him to the middle of the road where the wretched creature stays for the rest of the film, threatened by on-rushing traffic. There is, too, Charlie's strange homage to *L'Après-midi d'un Faune*. The sequence begins with the cattle chase through the village after cowherd Charlie has allowed his charges to stray. He is tossed by the most ferocious of the beasts, lands on her back and is borne out of the village to be thrown, unconscious, into a ditch beside a little bridge.

He dreams that he is awakened by four nymphs, who draw him into an arcadian dance with them. Charlie's ballet becomes decidedly more animated after he has fallen backwards on a cactus. A brilliant if eccentric dancer, as he was often to demonstrate, Chaplin had been fascinated by the Ballets Russes on their recent appearances in Los Angeles, and flattered by the dancers' admiration of his own mimetic gifts. Nijinsky and his company visited the studios, and when Chaplin went to see them in the theatre, the great dancer – who had recently left Diaghilev and was himself experiencing the problems of independence – kept the audience waiting for half an hour while he chatted to Chaplin in the interval.

The ending is more enigmatic than any other in Chaplin's films. Seeing that he has lost Edna to the city slicker, he places himself deliberately in the path of an on-coming car. Abruptly the scene cuts to a swift and happy dénouement, in which a truculent Charlie sends the city slicker packing in his automobile, and wins back his Edna. In sixty-five years, critics have failed to agree whether it is the suicide itself which is the dream, or whether the happy end is itself the wish-dream of the dying suicide. *Sunnyside* was finished, to Chaplin's intense relief, on 15 April 1919, and premièred two months later.

There were other causes for Chaplin's anxiety besides his cheerless marriage. As early as 1917 Sydney had been making efforts to bring Hannah to California. Since Aunt Kate's death, Aubrey Chaplin, Charlie's cousin, had kept an eye on Hannah in Peckham House. It seemed an ideal opportunity to bring Hannah to America when Alf Reeves came over in the autumn of 1917, and Sydney cabled him: 'Have obtained American Government permission for my mother's admission here for special treatment. Can you bring her over with two special nurses? See Aubrey Chaplin 47 Hereford Road.Bayswater he has full particulars. If satisfactory will cable money for fare, clothes.'

Aubrey found however that the necessary permits were not forthcoming at the English end, and poor Hannah remained in the home. In March 1919, however, Aubrey was able to write to Chaplin that he hoped that arrangements for her journey would be completed by mid-May. Plagued by his marriage and his creative crisis, Chaplin suddenly realized that he could not at this time face the pain of seeing his mother in her current condition. On 21 April he cabled Sydney, who was at the Claridge Hotel, New York: 'SECOND THOUGHTS CONSIDER WILL BE BEST MOTHER REMAIN IN ENGLAND SOME GOOD SEASIDE RESORT. AFRAID PRESENCE HERE MIGHT DEPRESS AND AFFECT MY WORK. GOOD MAY COME ALONE.' Loyal Aubrey set about finding a suitable haven on the coast, and suggested she might be settled, preferably under an assumed name, at Margate, with a nurse and a companion; but for the time being she continued at Peckham House, her dull days varied by occasional rides out and visits from an old friend, Marie Thorne.

After a month's break, Chaplin started on a new production – and the trouble began all over again. The title, *Charlie's Picnic*, suggested all sorts of gag possibilities. Chaplin tried out a number of children and chose five, True Boardman Jr, Marion Feducha, Raymond Lee, Bob Kelly and Dixie Doll, who were kept on the payroll for the next four weeks. During the whole time Chaplin managed only to shoot a few desultory scenes on two days. A sweltering summer was not conducive to inspiration. One day the studio clerk recorded 'Hot as the devil'. On 16 June Chaplin gave up, dismissed the children and went out riding with Clement Shorter. A fortnight later he tried again. For four days at the beginning of July he struggled to film something – anything. He dragged in Kono, his chauffeur, to drive his car, and put Alf Reeves and a friend, Elmer Ellsworth, into a scene. Then the studio relapsed into inactivity. One day all the studio clerk could find to enter on his daily report sheet was 'Note: Willard took a nap today'. History has left no clue to the identity of Willard – perhaps he was the studio cat – but the comment indicates the general desperation in face of the inactivity at Sunset and La Brea.

Not the least of Chaplin's problems were domestic worries. Mildred was now really pregnant, and on 7 July gave birth to a malformed boy. Three days later, on 10 July 1919 the studio report laconically records, 'Norman Spencer Chaplin passed on today – 4 p.m.' and the next day: '11 July. Cast all absent . . . Did not shoot. Norman Spencer Chaplin buried today 3 p.m. Inglewood Cemetery.' It was Mildred's idea to inscribe on his gravestone 'The Little Mouse'. Many years later Mildred recalled, 'Charlie took it hard . . . that's the only thing I can remember about Charlie . . . that he cried when the baby died.' Chaplin told a friend bitterly that the undertakers had manipulated a prop smile on the tiny dead face, though the baby had never smiled in life.

It would be presumptuous to trace connexions between this emotional shock and the sudden startling resurgence of creativity in Chaplin that followed it; or between the death of his first child and the subject of the film he was about to make, and which for many remains his greatest work. Ten days after Norman Chaplin's death, Charlie was auditioning babies at the studio. He had meanwhile already found a co-star. In the depressed period which followed the completion of *Sunnyside* he had gone to the Orpheum, and seen there an eccentric dance act, Jack Coogan. For the finish of his act Coogan brought on his four-year-old son who took a bow, gave an impersonation of his father's dancing, and made his exit with an energetic shimmy. Chaplin was delighted – perhaps it reminded him of his own first appearance on the stage when he was not much older than Jackie Coogan.

A night or two later, Chaplin met Jackie for the first time. He entered the dining room of the Alexandria Hotel with Sid Grauman, just as Jackie and his parents were leaving. They stopped and spoke: Grauman had known both Coogan parents in vaudeville, when he was managing theatres for his father; Mrs Coogan had toured the circuit as a child performer known as Baby Lillian. While Grauman and the Coogans were talking, Chaplin sat down beside Jackie so that he was on his level, and began to talk to him. Then he asked Mrs Coogan if he could borrow him for a few moments. Mrs Coogan was surprised, but Charlie Chaplin was Charlie Chaplin. As she later remembered, for an hour and forty-five minutes Chaplin and Coogan played together in the corner of the lobby on the Alexandria's famous 'million-dollar carpet' (so called because of all the movie deals that had been made on it).

Eventually Chaplin brought the child back, and said, 'This is the most amazing person I ever met in my life.' The moment of enchantment for Chaplin, it appeared, was when he asked Jackie what he did, and Jackie serenely replied: 'I am a prestidigitator who works in a world of legerdemain.' The phrase must have been one of the brilliant little mimic's show pieces, but it could not fail to touch Chaplin with his own keen delight in words. Charmed as he was, however, Chaplin had still no thought of using Jackie in a picture.

During the period of sitting around in the studio, waiting for inspiration for *Charlie's Picnic*, Chaplin began to talk about the Coogan act. Somebody in the unit said that he had heard that Roscoe Arbuckle had just signed up Coogan. At once Chaplin kicked himself for not having the idea of putting the boy into films himself. Wretchedly he began to think of all the gags he might have done with the child. The publicity man, Carlyle Robinson, made the happy discovery that it was the father and not the son who had been signed up by Arbuckle. The studio secretary, Mr Biby, was sent to see Jack Coogan, who agreed to let his son work for Chaplin. 'Of course you can have the little punk,' he said.

On 30 July Chaplin happily laid aside the 6570 feet of film he had already shot for *Charlie's Picnic*, decided that the best of the infant aspirants he had auditioned was Baby Hathaway, and started to work on *The Waif*. Now he seemed inspired. Throughout August and September he worked in a fury of enthusiasm. There were no absences from the studio, no days off to 'talk the story' or to make outings to San Diego. Some days the unit would shoot more than four thousand feet of film, the footage of two two-reelers.

As usual Chaplin filmed the story in continuity; and the scenes he shot during these prolific weeks were to appear almost without revision in the definitive version of *The Kid*. Edna is seen leaving the charity hospital, a child in her arms, under the scornful gaze of a nurse and a gateman: in the completed film a title succinctly explains her situation: 'The woman – whose sin was motherhood'. Edna – probably intending suicide – leaves the baby in the back of an opulent car,* with a note asking the finder to protect and care for him. Ironically the car is thereupon stolen by two murderous-looking crooks. Finding the baby in the back, they roughly dump him in an alley.

In the studio Charles D. Hall had created the attic setting which indelibly defines our vision of *The Kid*. It might be an illustration to *Oliver Twist*, with its sloping ceiling under the eaves, its peeling walls, bare boards, maimed furniture and a door giving onto a precipice of

* The car used for the scene belonged to D. W. Griffith.

stairs. It might – must – also be a recollection of the attic at 3 Pownall Terrace, where Charlie had bumped his head on the ceiling when he sat up in bed.

Here, in four days of shooting, Chaplin created the memorable sequence with Baby Hathaway, in which the Tramp, having unwillingly become the guardian of Edna's mislaid child, teaches himself the crafts of child care. He improvises a hammock-cradle, a feeding bottle made from an old coffee pot and (when with some concern he feels the moist underside of the hammock) a handy device consisting of a chair with a hole cut in the seat and a cuspidor placed beneath it. These homely details caused offence to a few more puritanical spectators of the period, but the audience at large loved them.

Chaplin moved on to the scenes in the same attic supposed to take place some five years later, when the baby has grown into Jackie Coogan. Jackie proved such a natural actor and apt pupil that most of this sequence was shot within a week. One or other of the Coogan parents was always on the set – Mrs Coogan during the early period while Jack Senior was still under contract to Arbuckle; later Jack Senior himself. They watched with delighted fascination Chaplin's relationship with their son. It was a very real and close friendship. The two of them would disappear together to walk and play in the orange groves. They might spend hours watching ants at work, and Chaplin would enjoy explaining to Jackie the marvels of nature. For his part Jackie was not really aware of Chaplin's importance: he simply regarded him as the most remarkable man he had ever met.

Mrs Coogan, as she explained much later to her grandson, Anthony Coogan, felt that the relationship was one of great complexity. On one level Chaplin, in Jackie's company, became a child. A large part of his gift, and of the character of the Tramp, was his ability to see life from a child-like viewpoint. In his association with Jackie he was able to exhibit and extend this child-like behaviour. On another level Chaplin, off screen as well as on, adopted a paternal role to Jackie. It was impossible for people at the studio to resist the feeling that Jackie represented the child that he had just lost.

Above all Jackie provided Chaplin with the most perfect actor with whom he was ever to work. For Chaplin, the complete protean, actors were necessary tools. Ideally he would have played every part in his films himself. Because he could not, he needed actors who could reproduce his own performances. What he looked for in his actors was a perfect imitation of the looks and gestures and, later, intonations he would show them. This was why more independently creative players were often irked; and why in some of the best performances we seem to be seeing Chaplin himself in someone else's skin – it could be man or woman.

Jackie's genius was as a mimic. When Chaplin showed him something, he could do it. Three or four rehearsals were usually enough; and Chaplin said he was a one-take player. He could undertake scenes of complexity that might defeat grown-ups. 'The mechanics,' Chaplin noted, 'induced the emotion.' It cannot have invariably gone so easily but, as Lita Grey remembered, 'his patience was limitless with the child, even when Jackie muffed one take after another. "We've plenty of time," he said, soothing the confused child. "The most difficult scenes are the simplest to do. The simplest bits of business are usually the hardest . . ."'[4] No child actor, whether in silent or in sound pictures, has ever surpassed Jackie Coogan's performance as The Kid, in its truthfulness and range of sentiment.

Little could stem Chaplin's tremendous creative surge, though there were interruptions. One day in that very different Hollywood, the smoke from a nearby forest fire spoilt the pictures. There was a day of rain; and one day Jackie disgraced himself by going missing. The incident is tersely recorded in the daily report for 17 September: 'Jackie Coogan – lost and licked'.* At the end of September, however, the surge ended. Chaplin moved into a new set, and a dead end. The scene was a dosshouse, for which he was later to find the right use in *The Kid*. For the moment though he was evidently unclear how best to use it. He spent three days and upwards of seven thousand feet of film for an elaborate gag about a flea circus and the inconveniences attendant on the escape of artistes. This footage was later to play a part in one of the more intriguing mysteries of Chaplin's creative life. For the moment it was abandoned. Then work on *The Waif* came to a halt.

One reason was that Chaplin had realized that *The Waif* was going to prove much bigger than anything he had previously attempted, and was likely to take many months to complete. First National, however, were impatient for a new release. The only way to gain the breathing space necessary to work at his own pace on *The Waif* was

* This minimizes the anxiety of the event. Jackie had fallen asleep behind some scenery. When he woke up he stayed in his hiding place watching with detached curiosity the hue and cry for him, as a nearby lake was dragged. It was Jack Coogan Senior who administered the ultimate licking.

to knock out a film as fast as possible. He had, after all, made two-reelers in a month for Mutual and in a week at Keystone.

With such a strong incentive to produce a film, Chaplin had little trouble with his 'quickie'. The material with the cars and the children already shot for *Charlie's Picnic* was reconsidered. It cut together well enough, and the title was changed to *The Ford Story*. Chaplin hired a featured comedienne, ample Babe London (enthusiastically described on the daily studio reports as 'great'), along with fifteen extras and four coloured musicians. The whole unit was bussed to San Pedro, where a pleasure boat, the *Ace*, was rented from the San Pedro Transportation Company for $5 an hour. The boat was the kind of prop that had never failed to ignite his imagination in the old Mutual days, and he set to inventing variations on the themes of dancing, sea-sickness, collapsing deckchairs, jealous husbands and the perils of storm-tossed boats. In seven consecutive working days he had shot some twenty-five thousand feet of film. The editing was finished in a fortnight, and the film, now called *A Day's Pleasure*, was shipped to First National on 3 November.

The film was a cheerful throw-back to Mutual days and earlier. As Chaplin originally planned the editing, it would have been even more like the old style of Essanay and Mutual two-act two-reeler than in the event it turned out. His first idea was simply to precede the boat sequence with the motor car material, involving Charlie's efforts to start his temperamental Ford, and his encounters on the road with angry fellow-motorists, hostile speed cops and newly-spread tar. In the end, however, the car material was divided to provide neat framing sequences for the central boat material. The film now ends with a title, 'The end of a perfect day', as Charlie's car shimmies off towards the horizon amidst clouds of smoke.

Chaplin was quite aware that the film was a makeshift, and neither audiences nor reviewers of the time concealed their disappointment with *A Day's Pleasure*, as with *Sunnyside*. Chaplin was confident enough in his current project to ignore criticisms. On 14 November he resumed work on the film which was now definitively re-titled *The Kid*. The next sequence on which he embarked was destined to be removed from the film, on the grounds of its excessive sentimentality, when Chaplin re-edited the film and added a musical accompaniment, fifty years later. As it appeared in the original release version of the film, the scene followed Edna's discharge from the charity hospital and a brief sequence introducing the father of her child, an artist.

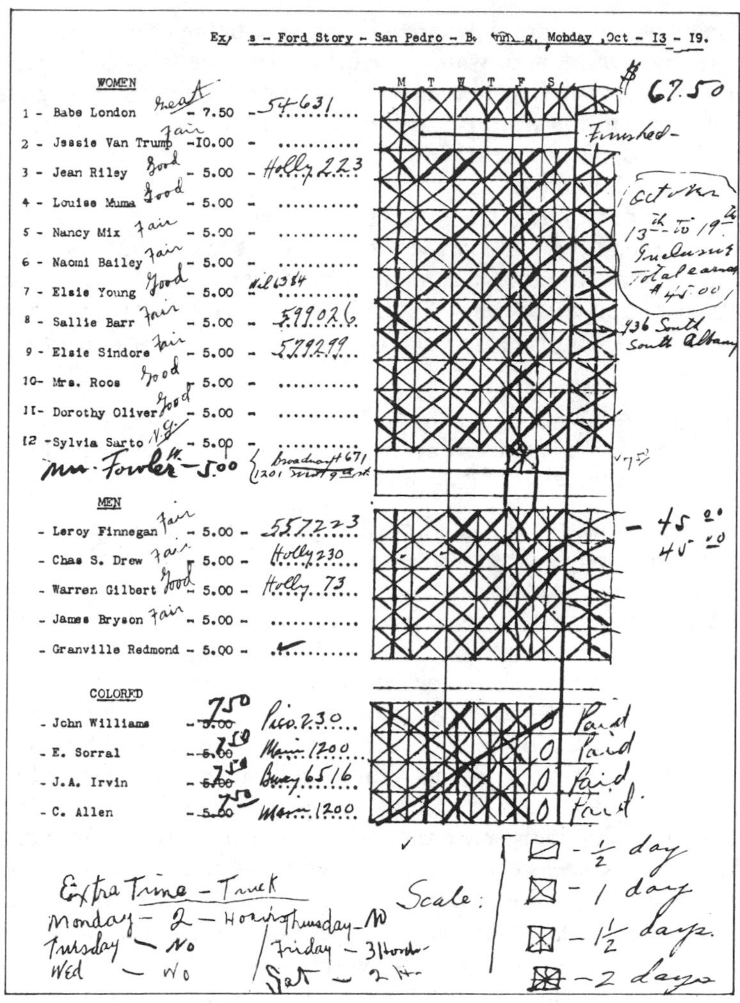

Ex, s - Ford Story - San Pedro - B, g, Mohday ,Oct - 13 - 19.

	WOMEN				M T W T F S
1 -	Babe London	Great	- 7.50	- 54631	$67.50
2 -	Jessie Van Trump	Fair	-10.00	-	Finished-
3 -	Jean Riley	Good	- 5.00	- Holly 223	
4 -	Louise Muma	Good	- 5.00	-	October 13th to 19th Inclusive Total earned $45.00
5 -	Nancy Mix	Fair	- 5.00	-	
6 -	Naomi Bailey	Fair	- 5.00	-	
7 -	Elsie Young	Good	- 5.00	- Wil 1384	
8 -	Sallie Barr	Fair	- 5.00	- 599026	436 South
9 -	Elsie Sindore	Fair	- 5.00	- 579299	South Albany
10-	Mrs. Roos	Good	- 5.00	-	
11-	Dorothy Oliver	Good	- 5.00	-	
12 -	Sylvia Sarto	V.G.	- 5.00	-	
	Mrs. Fowler		- 5.00	Broadway 671 / 1201 West 9th st.	

	MEN				
-	Leroy Finnegan	Fair	- 5.00 -	557223	- 45.00
-	Chas S. Drew	Fair	- 5.00 -	Holly 230	45.00
-	Warren Gilbert	Good	- 5.00 -	Holly 73	
-	James Bryson	Fair	- 5.00 -	....	
-	Granville Redmond		- 5.00 -	✓..........	

	COLORED			
-	John Williams	~~5.00~~ 7.50	Pico 230	Paid
-	E. Sorral	~~5.00~~ 7.50	Main 1200	Paid
-	J.A. Irvin	~~5.00~~ 7.50	Bway 6516	Paid
-	C. Allen	~~5.00~~ 7.50	Main 1200	Paid

Extra Time - Truck
Monday - 2 - Hours
Tuesday - No
Wed - No
Thursday - No
Friday - 3 Hours
Sat - 2 Hrs

Scale:
- ½ day
- 1 day
- 1½ days
- 2 days

1919 - Record of employment and payment of actors while shooting the boat scenes of *A Day's Pleasure*.

Edna arrives at a church where a marriage is being celebrated. As she pauses by a window to watch, the bride's corsage falls to the ground and is accidentally crushed under the feet of the elderly bridegroom. A reflection in the window appears momentarily like a halo around Edna's head. The scene preceded that of the mother abandoning her child in the limousine.

One incident during the filming of this sequence is a reminder that these were still very much the infant days of the film industry. One of the extras hired was a man called Edgar Sherrod, so much a specialist in playing priests that he brought along his own vestments. There was an ugly scene over this, however. The studio paysheet records:

> Edgar Sherrod and vestments. Paid $25. Paid under protest. Note: After being established in picture at rate of $12.50, Edgar Sherrod held out for $25.00. Reported to M.P.P.S for Black List.

For Christmas 1919 Chaplin asked Jackie what he would like as a present. The boy told him that most of all he would like to visit his grandmother in San Francisco. To make this possible, Chaplin closed the studio for a week – perhaps the most singular mark of his feeling for his small co-star. With only this interruption, the whole of December and the first week of the New Year were spent on the sequence which remains the most extraordinary in the film, and indeed one of the most memorable in the whole history of the cinema. The Kid falls sick, and the Tramp calls in a curmudgeonly old physician. When the doctor asks if he is the boy's father, the Tramp inadvisedly shows the note that was attached to the foundling, and which he now keeps carefully preserved between the pages of a worn and dusty copy of the *Police Gazette*. The doctor says that the child needs proper care and attention. Proper care and attention soon arrive – in the form of a self-important representative of the orphan asylum and his toadying aide. Despite the heroic struggles of the Tramp and the Kid – armed with a hammer as big as himself – the child is carried off and thrown, like a stray dog, into the back of a wagon. With a fierce cop in hot pursuit, the Tramp blunders across the slum roof-tops to intercept the wagon, hurls the orphanage official into the road, and rescues the Kid. This astonishing scene never loses its impact, however often it is seen. There is passion, despair, madness in the Tramp's desperate trajectory across the roofs, and the absurd, waddling little figure is elevated to heroic pathos. Few screen embraces are as affecting as the kiss which the Tramp plants on the quivering lips of the terrified child.

The ebullient Jackie was not too easily subdued to the emotional temper of the scene. Chaplin could not bear to make Jackie cry himself. The direction of Jackie in this scene was left to his father. Jack Senior quite simply whispered to Jackie that if he did not cry to order he would be taken off the film and sent to a real workhouse. Jackie was no fool. He cried so hard that Chaplin was alarmed and anxiously reassured him that nobody would take him away. 'I knew Daddy was fooling,' he replied, conspiratorially. Jack Coogan Senior was a useful man to have about the set. He played several roles in the film: the skid row bum who picks the Tramp's pocket, the Devil, and a guest at the artists' party at which Edna, now become a famous opera star, meets again the father of her child. Chaplin removed this scene from his 1970 re-issue of *The Kid*.

At this stage of production, Chaplin's domestic troubles began to obtrude once more. After the lease on their first home expired, Chaplin had moved the household – it now included Mildred's mother, which did not help matters – to 674 South Oxford Drive, Beverly Hills. In the months of creative exaltation Chaplin had been able to forget the frustrations and irritations of his marriage but Mildred did not relish being forgotten. The estrangement which now occurred was inevitable. Chaplin moved back to the Los Angeles Athletic Club. Mildred retained the house.

At first the separation was fairly amicable and dignified. Then the press latched on to the story and provoked the talkative Mildred into attacks on her estranged husband. Irritation and anxiety made it more and more difficult for Chaplin to concentrate. Towards the end of February 1920 the pace of work at the studio began to slow down and Chaplin was increasingly absent. From 15 March filming stopped completely, and two days later the newspapers across the country published the news that Mrs Chaplin was filing a suit for divorce. The announcement followed very soon after the news that Douglas Fairbanks and Mary Pickford, Chaplin's friends and peers as million dollar stars, were divorcing their respective partners. At first Mildred merely accused her husband of desertion, said she still 'loved him to death' and that she did not want a divorce or money. A day or two later, on 22 March 1920, her lawyers had changed the charges to cruelty, and Mildred now announced that she proposed to 'tell everything. I shall let the world know how he failed to provide for me and how he sent an employee to my house and took away certain of my private papers. He humiliated me before the servants. Isn't that cruelty?' Chaplin replied with a brief press statement:

> On account of my reputation, which I have spent eighteen years in building up, I am compelled to refute Mrs Chaplin's statement as to non-support, for I have over $50,000 in cancelled cheques which have been paid out during our short married life on her behalf. And this has been spent in addition to her own salary which is $1000 a week. Until this outbreak of hers I have not refused payment of one solitary request or bill which she has presented to me. With reference to legal proceedings I wish to remain absolutely silent. I have tried to be gentlemanly and to act with dignity under the unfortunate circumstances, and have nothing further to say.

The circumstances of Hollywood made it hard to remain dignified, however, and on 7 April 1920 Chaplin was involved in one of the scandals which thrilled the motion picture fans and were throughout his life deeply repugnant to his naturally reserved temper. He was dining at the Alexandria Hotel with some friends; Louis B. Mayer, who had Mildred Harris under contract, was with a party at a neighbouring table. Notes were exchanged (Roland Totheroh alleged however that Mayer's supposed note, which sparked the affair, was in fact fabricated as a prank by one of Chaplin's own party, Jack Pickford). Chaplin was still resentful of Mayer for having rushed Mildred into a contract immediately following the marriage and the attendant publicity, against Chaplin's advice. Now Chaplin told Mayer to take off his glasses, and aimed a punch at him. Mayer, after a youth spent in the scrap metal business, was no weakling and hit back. Both men fell, the hotel staff intervened, Chaplin was escorted to his room and Mayer left the hotel.

Mildred at the time was dancing fox-trots with the Prince of Wales and Lord Louis Mountbatten at a dance given by the Mayor of San Diego at Coronado Beach, eight hundred miles from Hollywood. When told by eager reporters what had occurred, she showed only mild concern and was keener to tell them that 'The Prince is a nice, clean-cut boy, and he is certainly a clever dancer. I enjoyed every minute of our dance together.'

Work at the studio had briefly resumed soon after this, on 17 April, but only to pose some stills of Christ bearing the cross (they were shot on Eagle Rock Hill) which were eventually to be inserted in the opening scenes of the film as a commentary upon the sufferings of the unwed mother. An additional factor in the break-down of production may have been difficulties with Edna. During the shooting of the film, she had begun to drink, 'not heavily', said Lita Grey, who worked on the film, 'but enough to displease Chaplin, who viewed drinking during working hours as unprofessional and therefore intolerable.' However the difficulties, whatever they were, were smoothed over, and Edna remained in the film.

Eventually Chaplin sought distraction from private annoyances in a return to work. He made tests for the last sequence of the film, reshot some of the attic material and in May had the dosshouse set rebuilt. Now he had a narrative purpose for it: Tramp and Kid seek refuge there from the orphanage officials, but are betrayed by the housekeeper (Henry Bergman). The dosshouse scenes were finished by the end of May, and the next two months were spent on the last major sequence of the film – one of the most elaborate and certainly the strangest of the many dream sequences in Chaplin's films. Alone, wretched and locked out, the Tramp falls asleep on the doorstep and dreams that the alley is transformed into paradise. All the characters of the film – even the Bully, the Cop and the orphanage officials – become genial winged angels. He is reunited with the Kid; but when all seems bliss, Sin creeps in. The Devil tempts the Tramp with a pretty girl, which arouses the jealousy of her boyfriend, the Bully. He takes out a gun and shoots the Tramp. The Kid cries over his bleeding and lifeless body . . . at which point the Tramp is wakened by the Cop.

The dream puzzled contemporary spectators and critics; Chaplin was disappointed when Sir James Barrie, king of whimsy, accused him of being too whimsical and said the sequence was a mistake. Francis Hackett in *The New Republic* was more perceptive:

> The dream of Heaven I thought highly amusing. What amused me was its limitedness, its meagreness. It was like a simple man's version of the Big Change, made up from the few properties with which a simple man would be likely to be acquainted. The lack of inventiveness seemed to me to be its best point. Others tell me that it was a failure of inventiveness. Mayhap. But after suffering the success of movie-inventiveness so many times, with the whole apparatus of the factory employed to turn out some sort of slick statement or other, I rejoice over this bit of thin and faltering fantasy. And I venture to believe that it represents exactly what Chaplin intended. It was the simplified Heaven of the antic sprite whom Chaplin

has created and whose inner whimsicality is here so amusingly indulged.

Not the least intriguing aspect of the dream sequence in *The Kid* is the casting. One of the children who appears in it is Esther Ralston, who was to become a major star in the later 1920s. The minx who vamps and tempts the Tramp was a twelve-year-old called Lillita McMurray who had been introduced to the studio by Chaplin's assistant, Chuck Riesner, a neighbour of the child's mother and grandparents. Her prettiness intrigued Chaplin, and he put her under contract. Lillita believed that the dream sequence in the film was actually inspired by her arrival at the studio. Four years later Lillita, as Lita Grey, was to become the second Mrs Chaplin, a marriage that was to bring more bitterness to Chaplin's life even than his time with Mildred.

Mildred, however, was giving her husband a great deal of trouble, spurred on, rather unexpectedly, by Chaplin's business associates at First National. Chaplin was in dispute with the company over the way they intended to deal with him over *The Kid*. They were determined to pay him for its seven reels on the basis of three two-reelers. Having expended $500,000 and eighteen months of his life on the film, he was asking for a special arrangement which would give him something more than the $405,000 this would have produced. When Mildred suddenly reneged on her previous agreement to a divorce settlement of $100,000 Chaplin realized that First National was behind her, meaning to make use of her divorce suit to attach his business assets – which included the negative of *The Kid*.

Chaplin had in fact been aware of such a danger for several months. As early as 9 April he had telegraphed to Sydney in New York: 'IMPENDING TROUBLE WILL I SHIP NEGATIVE TO YOU FOR SAFETY WIRE ADVISE IMMEDIATELY.' For the moment, however, no such precaution had seemed necessary. At the beginning of August 1920 Totheroh was awakened at three o'clock one morning by Alf Reeves, who told him that they had to get out of town. In turn Totheroh got hold of his assistant, Jack Wilson, and the studio carpenter and together they worked to pack the negative – it amounted to some 400,000 feet – in twelve crates. Inside the crates the film was in 200-foot rolls, enclosed for safety in coffee tins. At Santa Fe railroad depot they were met by Chaplin and his secretary Tom Harrington, with the tickets. There was a moment of thoroughly

Chaplinesque comedy: Chaplin was confident that no one would recognize him behind his dark glasses, but no sooner had they entered the station restaurant than a small boy began to shriek 'Charlie Chaplin! Charlie Chaplin!'[5]

The conspirators arrived at Salt Lake City, and put up at a hotel where they turned a bedroom into an improvised cutting room. Handling the highly inflammable nitrate film in a public place of this sort was against all regulations, but somehow they managed to keep their operations and the vast quantities of film secret. When the editing was completed, they risked a trial preview in a local cinema. Chaplin was greatly reassured by the enthusiasm of the audience. With the cut negative, they took the train to New York and found a vacant studio in New Jersey to complete the editing and laboratory work. To evade awkward inquiries they erected a notice outside the place saying 'Blue Moon Film Company'.

Chaplin moved into the Ritz where he stayed in hiding for fear of process servers. He was bored, however, and badly wanted to meet the writer Frank Harris, so borrowed a dress, hat and veil from Minnie Chaplin and swept through the Ritz lobby in drag. He was rewarded: he and Harris got on famously, and Chaplin stayed until the small hours after which, having resumed his own clothes, he did not dare to return to the Ritz. Unable to find a hotel, he was obliged to stay in the home of a sympathetic taxi driver. During the evening Chaplin acted out for Harris his own version of the divorce settlement negotiations, as Harris later described:

> Every morning in the paper a fresh appeal appeared from Mildred Chaplin: the injured lady wept, protested, cajoled, threatened all in a breath. One morning a change: she published the following:
>
> 'My final statement: Mr Chaplin is not a Socialist. He is a great artist, a very serious personality, and a real intellectual.' Yes, those are her very words; and she continues: 'The world will be amazed at the intensity of his mind.' What can have happened? I ask myself. Has Charlie weakened and paid without counting?
>
> I read on: 'I have no desire to obtain half of his fortune. (No?) I will not hinder the sale of his latest moving picture.' (Whew, the wind sets in that quarter, does it?)
>
> And then: 'I am entitled to a settlement. (Eh?) I am too ill, physically and mentally, to work at present, and this notoriety and exposition of my personal affairs is very disagreeable to me.' (Really? You needn't indulge in it, Madame, unless you want to.)
>
> Finally: 'He is a great artist, a brilliant man, plays the violin, 'cello,

piano, and so forth . . . I have already filed papers against him.' Well, well, and again well.

Here is Charlie's story of talks with his wife on the 'phone about their divorce.

'Is that you, Charlie? It's me. Mildred. I'm ill and have no money. Won't you give me fifty thousand dollars, and settle all this disagreeable law business? You will? You're a dear; I knew a great artist like you couldn't be mean. If you knew how I hate to quarrel and dispute. Let us meet at my lawyer's in an hour, eh? Goodbye till then.'

Quarter of an hour later:

'Is that you, Charlie? Oh, I'm so sorry, but my lawyer won't let me take fifty thousand; he says it's ridiculous. Won't you give me a hundred thousand, and I can satisfy him? Please; I'm so nervous and ill. You will? Oh you –! Well, you're just you – the one man in the world. I can't say more. Now for that dreadful lawyer, and then we'll meet and just sign. How are you? Well! Oh, I'm so glad. In half an hour, dear.'

Quarter of an hour later:

'Charlie! What can I say? I'm just heart-broken, and I've such a headache. That lawyer says I mustn't settle for a hundred thousand. His fee is goodness knows how much. I must have at least a hundred and fifty thousand. What am I to do? Mamma says – You will? Oh, my! I'm so glad. I don't know how to thank you. It's the last word, you say? All right, Charlie, I'm satisfied. In half an hour, then.'

Ten minutes later:

'It's no good, Charlie. I can't settle for that; it's really too little. You see, Charlie! Charlie! Did you ring off? Or is it the filthy exchange? Oh, dear! Damn!'

Charlie Chaplin is a master of comedy in life, as he is on the stage; an artist in refined humour, he can laugh even at himself and his own emotions. On the point of leaving Pasadena for a trip to New York, he rang his wife up.

'Mildred, it's me, Charlie. Will you take half a million dollars, and settle this ridiculous claim? You will? No, I'm not a darling; but meet me at my lawyer's in an hour, and we can sign.'

A quarter of an hour later:

'Mildred, dear, I'm sorry, but my lawyer won't let me give half a million; he says a year's earnings for a week's marriage is too much. He says a hundred thousand is more than generous. Will I listen to you? Of course I will. Talk away . . .'

A woman's voice, high pitched: 'You're no man. Again you've let me down, and made a fool of me. You've no character. I'll teach you . . .' (Left talking).

Charlie Chaplin strolls away from the 'phone with a smile on his lips

> and a little sub-acid contempt for human, and especially for feminine, nature.[6]

The divorce suit commenced in August. Chaplin's lawyer announced that he would not contest it provided that Mildred's lawyers withdrew an order restraining him from selling *The Kid*. The divorce was granted on 19 November: Mildred was awarded $100,000 and a share of community property.

Chaplin was now free to negotiate *The Kid* with First National. Emboldened by the enthusiasm at the first showing in Salt Lake City, he asked them for an advance of $1,500,000, and 50 per cent of the net after the company had recovered the advance. The company demurred, and affected an insulting lack of enthusiasm when Chaplin showed them the film, but he stuck it out until even the executives of First National recognized that in *The Kid* he had an untrumpable card. The film finally opened in New York on 6 January 1921 to instant and huge success. Within the next three years *The Kid* was distributed in some fifty countries across the world from Norway to Malaya, Egypt to Australia. By 1924 the Soviet Union, Yugoslavia and Colombia were practically the only places where it had not been shown. Everywhere its reception was enthusiastic.

The Kid made little Jackie Coogan into a world figure. Chaplin himself was among those who felt that the vast, universal response to Jackie's image was in part due to his function as a symbol of all the orphans of the recent war. Jackie provided something that the world needed, as he himself had done. He also saw that they could not continue to work together. He told the Coogans, 'I am not going to hold him back,' and gave them the option he held on Jackie's services.

Jackie went on to make a score of feature films for First National and Metro. One or two, like *Peck's Bad Boy* and *Oliver Twist*, caught something of the great child actor of *The Kid*; but for the most part the rest suffered from sentimental scripts and insensitive direction. By 1927 Jackie's film career had virtually finished. 'Senility,' it was said in Hollywood, 'hit him at thirteen.' In the half dozen years of his fame, however, he had mixed with great celebrities of the world. In 1924 he undertook a World Crusade in aid of Near East Relief. It raised more than a million dollars' worth of food and clothing: the Coogan family would accept no fees or expenses. The crusade became a royal progress. Jackie met Mussolini and was decorated by the Pope in special audience. Only Clemenceau declined to meet him, cabling his regret to Jackie's father that, 'I am not celebrity enough to meet your illustrious son.' Jackie received the adoration of the public everywhere he went, and somehow managed to stay natural, unspoilt, the perfect child.

His parents had meanwhile become estranged, though their Catholicism and concern for their son's career kept them from making the matter public. Jack Coogan Senior devoted himself to the management of Jackie's business affairs, and Jackie confidently believed that the $4 million he had earned in the good years were held in trust for him and would be his when he reached his majority. Five months before Jackie's twenty-first birthday, however, his father was killed when the car in which they were driving crashed. His father's estate went to his mother, who was subsequently to deny the existence of a trust fund and to assert, on the contrary, the legal right of parents to all moneys earned by their children while minors. In 1938 Jackie brought a suit against his mother and his former business manager, Arthur L. Bernstein, whom she had by this time married.

The suit dragged on until most of the fortune was eaten away. Finally, in March 1939 a settlement was agreed.* Not long afterwards Jackie was reconciled with his mother, who clearly had exerted a dominating influence over him and would continue to do so until her death. At the time of the suit, he was married to Betty Grable. It was to be the first of a number of somewhat turbulent marriages. He served in the United States forces during the war, and afterwards had an uneven career as entertainer and actor. There was a special irony in the most celebrated role of his later career – as Uncle Fester in the television series *The Addams Family*. The most wonderful child in the world had become the nastiest of all old men. The older Coogan took pleasure in this kind of irony: at the end of his life he drove a car whose registration plate carried the letters K-I-D, but with the order reversed.

Chaplin had little contact with his child friend in later years: he appears not even to have included him on his Christmas card list.

* The single positive outcome of the Coogan case was that it led to the passage of the Child Actor's Bill (4 May 1939), which has always since been known as The Coogan Act. This provides that the guardian of a child artist shall set aside half the earnings for a trust fund or equivalent form of savings for the child's benefit, and account to the court for the remainder of the earnings.

When Jackie in a moment of particular financial crisis asked him for assistance, however, Chaplin handed him $1,000 without hesitation.

After his disillusion with First National over *The Kid*, Chaplin was eager to be done with the contract as quickly as possible. His partners in a new distribution venture were also impatient. In January 1919 United Artists had been incorporated with Douglas Fairbanks, Mary Pickford, D. W. Griffith and Chaplin as partners. The seeds of the plan had been sown in the course of the Liberty Bond tours, when Chaplin, Fairbanks and Pickford had met Oscar Price, press agent of William Gibbs McAdoo, Secretary of the Treasury, in Washington. 'Why,' Price asked them, 'don't you folks get together and distribute your own pictures?' They began to consider the idea more seriously at the end of 1918, when their suspicions were aroused by the behaviour of their various employers. First National were adamant in their refusal to better Chaplin's existing contract; Paramount showed no interest at all in renewing the contracts of Pickford and Fairbanks, which were due to expire. The three stars got together with Griffith and William S. Hart, the stone-faced Western hero, and speculated that the film companies were planning a strategy to put a stop to the astronomical salaries that the major stars were commanding. The idea, they rightly guessed, was to organize a great merger of the producing companies and a monopoly of distribution outlets, and in this way bring the stars to heel once more. The producers' move was imminent: during the first week in January the heads of the industry met for a convention in the Alexandria Hotel.

Fairbanks and Chaplin decided to hire private detectives to spy on the delegates to the convention. The reports of Pinkertons' Operator 5 and Operator 8 read like operetta, as they describe their ruses of paging and shadowing Adolph Zukor, Sam Goldfish (later Goldwyn) and the rest of the boardroom *dramatis personae*. Operator 8 was an attractive young woman, and used her charms to advantage:

> While gentleman was waiting for 'Jim' to return he looked at me and smiled. I did not return the smile but looked at said gentleman at different times.
>
> Later, after this gentleman had left Parlor A. and went downstairs, he sent me a card asking me to call him at 8 p.m. in Room 1157. Later, at 4.30 p.m. gentleman met me on the mezzanine and asked me my room number, which I gave him. At 5 p.m. this gentleman knocked on my

door. I answered door and was rather surprised to find said gentleman. He stated his name was Mr Harry, and that he would try and see me later in the p.m. Within five hours, 10 p.m., this gentleman came to my door, stating he had to go up to the twelfth floor to see Mr Zukor and that Clara Kimball Young was up there, but that he would be back in a few minutes. At 10.35 he returned and sat in a chair and smoked. He asked if my home was in Los Angeles. I told him no, that I was from Kentucky, but that I came from San Francisco here. He then asked me if I was interested in the pictures. I said no, but that I always enjoyed looking at a good picture. He then stated he was here from Detroit, Mich., and that they were holding a meeting in regard to the releasing of pictures. He then asked me who my favourite actress was. I told him Clara Kimball Young and Norma Talmadge. He asked me if I liked Mary Pickford. I told him yes and I liked Clara. He asked me if I knew how much Mary made. I told him no. He said that she got the biggest salary of any moving picture actress or actor. I remarked that I had heard that Charlie Chaplin received the highest salary, and he said no indeed. I then said that I did not think it right for Mary and Charlie to receive such salary when there were others that are just as good. He said, 'That's so, too, and their salary will have to be cut for we picture men cannot pay the price that is being asked for the releasing of their pictures. I then asked if that was the reason he came to Los Angeles and he said yes. I asked if he thought they would succeed and he said, 'Surely they will have to come to our terms.' About this time the House Officer came to my door. I went to door and he stated he was sorry but that the house would not allow any lady that's alone to have company in her room. Officer said he realized there was no harm done but that it was the rules of the house. I told the officer that I was sorry. Gentleman assured Officer that there was no harm meant. Officer said that he could see that, but it was merely the rules of the house. Gentleman left, saying he would call me the next day in the p.m.[7]

Despite this frustrating interruption at the most exciting part of her Mata Hari effort, Operator 8 managed more meetings with 'Mr Harry', and used her charms (precisely how we shall never know) to extract from him the information that Fairbanks and Chaplin needed. Fairbanks, Pickford, Hart and Chaplin made sure that the moguls were aware of their presence around the Alexandria Hotel, and on 15 January 1919 called a press conference to announce their intention of setting up a company to distribute their own independent productions, which they would call United Artists. Now committed to their idea, they drew up contracts of incorporation for the company on 5 February (by this time Hart had withdrawn from the scheme).

Certificates of incorporation were filed in Delaware on 17 April. At once they were besieged by offers from prominent producers – including Zukor himself – who wanted to resign their jobs to run United Artists. The Artists however invited McAdoo to be President. He declined, but said that if they appointed Oscar Price, the first begetter of the idea, he would help them organize and act as general counsel. Hiram Abrams, a former President of Paramount who had seceded from Zukor after disagreements, became General Manager. (Benjamin B. Hampton's authoritative *History of the American Film Industry* credits Abrams and his colleague Benjamin P. Schulberg with the original concept of United Artists. Abrams remained General Manager until his death in 1928.)

The corporation operated as a distributor for films which the four partners – and other film makers who wished to join in the plan – produced independently. The arrangement was revolutionary. Until this time producers and distributors – with the exception of First National – had been employers, and the stars salaried employees. Now the stars became their own employers. They were their own financiers, and they received the profits that had hitherto gone to their employers. Each in addition received his share of the profits of the distributing organization.

Fairbanks and Pickford built a fine modern studio on Santa Monica Boulevard to make their pictures for United Artists' release. Fairbanks had already released five films through United Artists, including the spectacular *Robin Hood*. Griffith brought *Broken Blossoms* (which he bought back from Paramount for $250,000) and *Way Down East*. Pickford's *Dorothy Vernon of Haddon Hall* was less successful with the public. Chaplin meanwhile was stuck with First National: at the time of the formation of United Artists he was still entangled with *Sunnyside*, with four films to go after that.

Now, at the start of 1921, he had still three films to deliver, and his partners were understandably impatient. *The Idle Class*, though it took five months to complete, gave him few problems. Although much more opulent in its production, it was a story simple enough for an Essanay or early Mutual film: some elements recall the early 'bogus Count' stories. Ironically, the story centres upon an unhappy marriage. Chaplin plays a dual role: as Edna's inebriate and neglectful husband; and as Charlie the Tramp, his double, who is mistaken for her husband by Edna, her father and friends. Completed at the end of June, *The Idle Class* was not released until 25 September.

Chaplin now felt that he could face the strain of having his mother near him, and fresh application for a visa was made to the State Department. On 3 March 1921 the State Department informed the Justice Deparment, 'Referring to your desire to have Mrs Hannah Chaplin, mother of Charles Chaplin, come to this country from England, you are informed that telegraphic authorization is now being sent to the American Consul General at London to grant a visa to the above-mentioned person.' Mr Hughes of the Solicitor General's office passed on the message to Charles and Sydney, expressing his hope that 'the matter has been satisfactorily adjusted and that the old lady will soon be on her way over.'

Tom Harrington was sent to England to bring her back to California. Hannah was astonished and delighted when Harrington, with

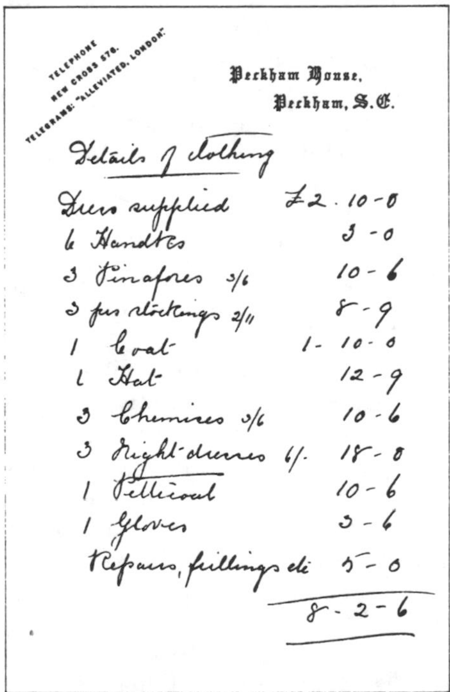

TELEPHONE NEW CROSS 570.
TELEGRAMS: "ALLEVIATED, LONDON."

Peckham House,
Peckham, S.E.

Details of clothing

Dress supplied		£2.10-0
6 Handkfs		3-0
3 Pinafores	3/6	10-6
3 prs stockings	2/11	8-9
1 Coat		1-10-0
1 Hat		12-9
3 Chemises	3/6	10-6
3 Night-dresses	6/-	18-0
1 Petticoat		10-6
1 Gloves		3-6
Repairs, fittings etc		5-0
		8-2-6

1920 - Bill from Peckham House
for Hannah Chaplin's clothing.

the help of Aubrey Chaplin and his wife, spent more than £100 on a new wardrobe for her, including hats, coats, a dressing gown and a toilet case. On the journey she behaved quite normally, but on her arrival in New York there was a slight contretemps when she mistook an immigration official for Jesus Christ. Harrington smoothed over the incident. Hannah was settled in a bungalow with a pleasant garden near the sea, with a couple to keep house and a trained nurse, Mrs Carey. Chaplin found it painful to visit her too often, but Sydney and Minnie, Amy Reeves and (during the period of her marriage with Chaplin) Lita Grey were among her visitors. They remembered that she would seem perfectly normal for long periods, and entertain them with stories and songs from the music hall days. Sometimes she would talk affectionately about her husband, and would discuss the Zeppelin raids on London. (The Chaplin publicity office announced that her health had been affected by the air raids.) People noticed that she was more subdued and quiet when she was with her son; and Chaplin was sometimes startled by enigmatic insights. 'If you weren't so diffident, I might be able to give you a little advice,' she told him at the time of his marital problems; and then said no more.

She enjoyed sewing, and playing draughts – which she always won. She also liked to go out in her car on shopping expeditions. Konrad Bercovici recounted how on one such spree she came back with hundreds of yards of coloured silk, costing some thousands of dollars. Chaplin was about to send the silk back, but suddenly said, 'Let her have all that and more, and all that she wants of the frippery. The poor soul has been longing for such things all her life.' Only occasionally did her whims, like handing ice cream to startled passers-by, result in embarrassment.

Sometimes she seemed indifferent to her sons' prosperity; at other times she was puzzled and embarrassed by it. Chaplin once or twice brought her to the studio to try to make her understand what his work consisted of. Edward Sutherland was there on one such occasion.

> I remember we were making tests one day, I think for *The Gold Rush*, and we were shooting indoors. In the old days, we had Cooper-Hewitt lighting, the grandfather of the neon light. This was a kind of ghastly blue which washed all the colour out of one's face – the lips were green or purplish. Klieg lights were carbon arc lights . . . These were hard lights encased. Mrs Chaplin, Charlie's mother, came in to the lot. Charlie was made up in character. She said, 'Charlie, I have to get you a new suit.'

He said, 'Now look, Mother. You've seen me in character a million times. You've seen me in pictures. I don't need a new suit.'

She said, 'I've got to get you a new suit – and you have a ghastly colour. You ought to go out in the sunlight.'

He took her out in the sunlight and said, 'Now look, Mother, this is the part I play. This is the character I play.' But he couldn't get it through to her; this day, it wouldn't penetrate to her intelligence. I don't know that he was particularly devoted to her: he felt under obligation to her. I don't think Charlie is what I would call devoted to anybody.[8]

The people chosen to visit Mrs Chaplin in her house in the valley were family friends whose discretion could be relied upon. Winifred Ritchie often went with Alf or Amy Reeves, and sometimes took young Wyn, their daughter.

I was only a schoolgirl, but they knew I wouldn't talk about such things. I never did speak of my visits to Nan till after she died and after Charlie died. She had a very nice house in the valley, with a companion and a nurse. We would go out with Amy and have lunch or dinner with Nan. Sometimes she was brilliant. She would do old songs and sketches. She was like Charlie. She would do wonderful imitations. She could do whole plays from beginning to end. And then all of a sudden, she wouldn't be right.

One day I was sitting beside her at lunch, and I noticed a mark on her arm. And innocently I said, 'Nan, what's that?' And immediately she drew her arm away and hid it; and then started putting bits of bread all about herself, and on her head. The nurse, Mrs Carey, said 'Come with me, Nan,' and took her off into another room. When Mrs Carey came back she said that the mark was a tattoo from the workhouse. She said it brought back the days when they had not had enough to eat; and she was putting the bread away for Sydney and Charlie.[9]

During her days in Hollywood, Hannah was at last reunited with her youngest son, Wheeler Dryden, whom she had not seen since he was snatched away by his father, Leo Dryden, at the age of six months. Wheeler, given to histrionic postures, staged his entrance and asked her dramatically, 'Do you know who I am?' 'Of course I do,' Hannah replied pleasantly. 'You're my son. Sit down and have a cup of tea.'

8
Escape

After finishing *The Idle Class* Chaplin started directly into a new picture, which was provisionally called *Come Seven*, and was to feature himself and Mack Swain as a pair of rich plumbers given to arriving at their work in a chauffeur-driven limousine. He spent the latter part of July at Catalina with Edward Knoblock and Carlyle Robinson working on ideas for the scenario, and returned to the studio at the beginning of August to start work. Sets were built, locations were found and the cast was assembled: Edna, Sydney, Mack Swain, Henry Bergman, Loyal Underwood, John Rand and two bit players, Pete Griffin and Jos Kedian. On 22 August Chaplin began to shoot. But after only 348 feet of film had been exposed he took a sudden decision to go to Europe. Carlyle Robinson was told to make the arrangements and five days later* Chaplin, accompanied by Robinson and Tom Harrington, was seen off at the Los Angeles railway depot by 'most of Hollywood . . . and . . . their sisters and their cousins and their aunts'. As the train pulled out, Sydney called to Robinson, 'For God's sake don't let him get married.' 'It gave the crowd a laugh and me a scare,' Chaplin commented.

A number of circumstances had led to this apparently capricious decision. A bout of influenza and the symptomatic depression had brought home to Chaplin how tired he was after seven years of almost continuous work, during which he made seventy-one films. Growing nostalgia for England had crystallized when Montague Glass, the

* In his own account of the 1921 trip, *My Trip Abroad* (in the English edition *My Wonderful Visit*) Chaplin says that he stopped work one day and left for New York the next. This was dramatic licence.

author of *Potash and Perlmutter*, had invited him to dinner and served a very English steak-and-kidney pie. He had started a correspondence with H. G. Wells after Wells had written solicitously to him on reading a much exaggerated account of burns he had suffered while filming *The Idle Class*, and was curious to meet an author whom he much admired. *The Kid* was about to open in London, and he wanted for the first time to be present at a première of his own and enjoy the applause. 'I wanted to grab it while it was good. Perhaps *The Kid* might be my last picture. Maybe there would never be another chance for me to bask in the spotlight . . .'[1] He had still the feeling that one day, like Jimmy the Fearless, he would have to wake up.

England, too, meant Hetty Kelly. The slim gazelle with the oval face and bewitching mouth still haunted his memory. He had seen her once since the parting at her home in Camberwell Road. She was seventeen, and was just about to leave for America to join her sister.

He had found her silly and coquettish, and the charm had faded for the moment. In his new bachelorhood, however, he found his curiosity stirring. In August 1915 Hetty, then twenty-one, had married Lieutenant Alan Edgar Horne, serving with the Surrey Yeomanry. His father was the MP for Guildford, subsequently Sir William Edgar Horne, Bt. Hetty by this time called herself Henriette, and was described on the marriage certificate as 'Spinster, of Independent means'. After the marriage the couple moved into Alan Horne's home at 5 Tilney Street, Mayfair.

One day in July 1918, out of the blue, Chaplin received a letter from Hetty. We do not know what it contained, except that it began, 'Do you remember a silly young girl . . .?' Chaplin's reply to Hetty, however, dated 18 July 1918, has survived. It is a mixture of enthusiasm and reserve, pleasure and embarrassment:

> Dear Hetty,
>
> It is always the unexpected that happens, both in moving pictures and in real life. You can imagine what an unexpected pleasure it was for me when I discovered your letter on my desk this morning. At first, when I caught sight of the envelope, my pulse quickened, then there was the recognition of a familiar 'E' I had not seen for a number of years. Something in my subconscious mind said 'Hetty'. I quickly tore open the envelope and – Lo and Behold! – it was from you. *You*, above all people, to hear from and after so many years! I was certainly thrilled, and yet I half expected you would write some time or other because of the interest-

ing events that have taken place in our lives; and, after all, to hear from one's old friends is a great pleasure.

Well, Hetty, you have not changed a particle. By that I mean your personality – it is manifest on every page of your letter. Of course, environment and association may have improved your viewpoint, but your charming personality is evident – which, to my way of thinking, is one's biggest asset. In your letter you ask how I am, etc., etc., Well, physically I am perfect; morally? – well, I am all that could be desired for a young man of twenty-nine years. I am still a bachelor, but that is not my fault. And now, philosophically – like yourself, my environment has given me a particular outlook on life. I suppose I have arrived at the pessimistic age of youth, but still there is hope, for I have that priceless quality of being curious about life and things which keeps up my enthusiasm.

Do you remember, Hetty, I once told you that money and success were not everything. At the time I had not had the experience of either, but I felt it was so, and now I have experienced both. I find that the pursuit of happiness can only be had from within ourselves and the interest of others.

But enough of this philosophy. How about yourself? I sincerely hope you have fully recovered by now, and are in the pink of condition. You must take greater care of yourself. Don't forget to remember me to Sonney [*sic*] and give Edie my best wishes. As for yourself – I shall be anxiously counting the days until I hear from you, so please write and let me know that you are well and smiling again.

Yours ever,
Charlie

Chaplin rarely wrote letters. Carlyle Robinson marvelled that the man who received more letters than anyone else wrote so few. He estimated that in his whole life Chaplin had written no more than a dozen. This one was obviously composed with great care; and the literary style of *My Autobiography* is already quite recognizable. It was evidently typed by a secretary, since it reveals none of the persistent idiosyncrasies of Chaplin's orthography: he always wrote 'ect' for 'etc', for instance.

He seems to have received no reply. It is possible that Hetty never read it, for transatlantic mails in the last year of the war could be delayed for weeks, and on 4 November 1918, a week before the Armistice, Henriette Florence Horne, née Hetty Kelly, died.

The concern for her health which Chaplin expresses in his letter suggests that she had already been ill, perhaps following the birth of her only child, a daughter. On 18 October she fell ill with the influenza then epidemic in Europe. On the 27th the sickness was complicated by pneumonia, and only a week afterwards, Hetty died.

Chaplin knew nothing of this when he set out on his European trip more than three years after he had written to Hetty. He, Robinson and Harrington amused themselves on the train journey with solitaire, and stopped for a night in Chicago, where Chaplin was a judge in a scenario competition and where he attempted to meet Carl Sandburg. It was there, too, that he had his first taste of the reporters who were going to dog him throughout the trip. Their questions, he found, varied little wherever he met them:

> 'Mr Chaplin, why are you going to Europe?'
> 'Just for a vacation!'
> 'Are you going to make pictures while you are there?'
> 'No.'
> 'What do you do with your old moustaches?'
> 'Throw them away.'
> 'What do you do with your old canes?'
> 'Throw them away.'
> 'What do you do with your old shoes?'
> 'Throw them away.'
> That lad did well. He got in all those questions before he was shouldered aside and two black eyes boring through lenses surrounded by tortoise-shell frames claimed an innings. I restored the 'prop grin' which I had decided was effective for interviews.
> 'Mr Chaplin, have you your cane and shoes with you?'
> 'No.'
> 'Why not?'
> 'I don't think I'll need them.'
> 'Are you going to get married while you are in Europe?'
> 'No . . .'
> 'Mr Chaplin, do you ever expect to get married?'
> 'Yes.'
> 'To whom?'
> 'I don't know.'
> 'Do you want to play Hamlet?'
> 'Why, I don't know. I haven't thought much about it, but if you think there are any reasons why –'
> But she was gone. Another district attorney had the floor.
> 'Mr Chaplin, are you a Bolshevik?'
> 'No.'
> 'Then why are you going to Europe?'

'For a holiday.'

'What holiday?'

'Pardon me, folks, but I did not sleep well on the train and I must go to bed.'

In New York he was met by Douglas Fairbanks and Mary Pickford who were there for the première of *The Three Musketeers*. Before the première they screened the film for him, as well as Mary's *Little Lord Fauntleroy*, and solemnly asked for his criticisms and suggestions. He gave them as solemnly, knowing that they would be politely heard and ignored. The première was a nightmare: Fairbanks and Pickford managed to enter the theatre unscathed, but Chaplin lost his hat and tie in the crowd, had a piece cut from his trousers by a lady souvenir-hunter, and was repeatedly pummelled and punched in the face by policemen. Eventually he was handed in, over the heads of the crowds, and felt that his companions were shocked by his sartorial disarray.

Chaplin shared his time in New York between his lawyer, Nathan Burkan, and new and old friends among the East Coast intelligentsia – Alexander Woollcott, Heywood Broun, the radical Max Eastman, Edward Knoblock, Harrison Rhodes and Madame Maurice Maeterlinck. Eastman gave a party for Chaplin, at which he met a young IWW worker on parole from a twenty-year prison sentence because of ill health, who made a great impression on him. Chaplin in turn gave a dinner party, at which they played games and did turns of various kinds:

> I acted with Mme Maeterlinck. We played a burlesque on the great dying scene of *Camille*. But we gave it a touch that Dumas overlooked.
>
> When she coughed, I got the disease immediately, and was soon taken with convulsions and died instead of Camille.

He went to see *Liliom* and afterwards met Joseph Schildkraut and Eva le Gallienne, who were starring in it; and suddenly had an uncharacteristic yearning to go back on the stage. Despite the crowds and the reporters, New York society was a great relief after California:

> No one asked me to walk funny, no one asked me to twirl a cane. If I wanted to do a tragic bit, I did, and so did everyone else. You were a creature of the present, not a production of the past, not a promise of the future. You were accepted as is, *sans* 'Who's Who' labels and income-tax records.

The trio left New York on the *Olympic* on the morning of 3 September. Edward Knoblock was also travelling to England on the ship. Many friends, including Fairbanks and Pickford, came to see them off, but

> Somehow I don't seem interested in them very much . . . I am trying to make a conversation, but am more interested in the people and the boat and those who are going to travel with me.
>
> Many of the passengers on the boat are bringing their children that I may be introduced . . .
>
> I find myself smiling at them graciously and pleasantly, especially the children.
>
> I doubt if I am really sincere in this, as it is too early in the morning. Despite the fact that I love children, I find them difficult to meet. I feel rather inferior to them. Most of them have assurance, have not yet been cursed with self-consciousness.
>
> And one has to be very much on his best behaviour with children because they detect our insincerity . . .

Chaplin's account of the visit is disarmingly frank and self-critical. It is as if this unaccustomed experience of relaxation permitted him to stand back and take a detached, amused view of his reactions to every experience. The days on board ship were a mixture of excitements and annoyances. He enjoyed the luxury. ('There is nothing like money. It does make life so easy.') He was both annoyed and flattered by the people who forced their attentions and their opinions on him. After a conversation with some of them he decided, 'I am, indeed, a narrow-minded little pinhead.' Inhibited about speaking to Marguerite Namara, the opera singer and wife of the dramatist Guy Bolton, he decided, 'I just do not know how to meet people.' He was uncertain as to which members of the crew he ought to tip.

There is an odd discrepancy about an incident on the voyage. Carlyle Robinson claimed that Chaplin declined to appear in a ship's concert, and was as a result insulted by the chairman, Herman Metz, who told the audience that Chaplin had refused to appear (it was in aid of a seamen's charity) but that it hardly mattered since they could see him on the screen for a nickel any time they pleased. Guy Bolton, however, recalled that

> at the ship's concert Marguerite sang and Chaplin did a pantomime act in which he portrayed an out-of-work actor applying for a job. As the manager, played by Knoblock, described each aspect of the character, Chaplin became successively humble, aggressive, charming, ultra-

> aristocratic. Told he was too short for the role, he seemingly grew several inches taller. Questioned as to his romantic qualification, he hurled himself into the manager's lap. Finally he is asked to run through a scene in which he is supposed to come home and find his wife in the arms of his best friend. In a frenzy of jealous rage he is called on to kill his betrayer. The manager shakes his head and says he fears Charlie can never be sufficiently convincing in the scene, whereupon the actor, determined to win the coveted role, seizes the manager by the throat. When he at last relaxes his grip and turns away to get his hat and stick, the manager is a corpse on the floor. Charlie, turning back with an ingratiating smile to receive his applause, was Chaplin at his best. His surprise on seeing the empty chair, his consternation on discovering the body that has slipped down under the desk were done as only Chaplin can do it. And then his famous shuffling exit, looking back over his shoulder and raising his hat to the corpse. It made a perfect finish.

Daily bulletins on the ship's noticeboard reported the excitement already being echoed in the British press. Long before his departure the newspapers had begun to sustain a running commentary on his Eastward progress. Now cables from correspondents aboard the *Olympic* described in detail his life aboard:

> Charlie rests in his suite on the promenade deck until eleven, when he takes his breakfast, consisting of a glass of hot water with a pinch of salt. He then starts at a brisk walk round the deck in the company of one or two friends. Four laps on the deck equal one mile. His next occupation is a further spell of rest in a steamer chair, reading or watching games of volley ball, deck tennis, shuffleboard or quoits. Occasionally he joins the children in the gymnasium on the boat deck, delightedly romping with them in their games. He is a great favourite with the children, although they listen, wide-eyed with amazement, when you tell them that this
>
> DAPPER YOUNG MAN
>
> who so successfully plays uncle is Charlie Chaplin. Noon finds Charlie in the gymnasium beginning a bout of systematic exercise. Then to the Turkish bath and the swimming pool. Luncheon follows.
>
> In the afternoon he watches the card games – but does not play himself – until it is time for a second turn round the deck. Towards evening he will be found on the forward deck playing cricket with the deck hands. Later he often appears in the smoke room listening to the bids at the auction pool on the ship's daily run. The passengers have identified their unassuming young fellow voyager.[2]

The *Olympic* was due at Cherbourg at 1 p.m. on 9 September but fog delayed the arrival until 5 p.m. Fifty or more newsmen, cameramen and network photographers instantly invaded the ship and ran Chaplin to earth behind the navigator's bridge. 'This is far, far worse than New York,' he said, and in reply to the barrage of questions – this time mostly in French – he made an impromptu speech:

> This is my first holiday for years, and there is only one place to spend a holiday, long overdue, and that is at home. That is why I intend to go to London. I want to walk the streets, see all the many changes, and feel the good old London atmosphere again.
>
> My trip across has been the result of a last-minute decision the day before the *Olympic* sailed [*sic*]. I felt I had to come home and here I am. After England I mean to go to Paris and then Russia.
>
> 'Why Russia?' you say. Because I am immensely interested in that great country and its efforts towards social reconstruciton after chaos. After Russia I have plans for seeing Spain. There is a great desire in my heart for the romance of Seville, and besides, I want to see a bullfight.
>
> I mean to enjoy myself thoroughly, and to go to all the old corners that I knew when I was a boy. I want to be a Londoner among Londoners, not a sort of comic hero to be stared at.[3]

To the inevitable 'Are you a Bolshevik?' he replied, 'I am an artist, not a politician.' Asked whether he thought Lenin or Lloyd George the greater man he answered mischievously and enigmatically, 'One works, the other plays.' Such moments were anxious for Robinson as his press representative. After this, somewhat to the surprise of the reporters, Chaplin vanished through a handy doorway.

The ship crawled through the fog to Southampton, where they had been warned there would be a civic reception. Chaplin was unreasonably nervous at the prospect of making a speech of thanks, sat up half the night drafting it, and then left his notes behind in the confusion. In the event it was considered he gave a better performance than the flustered Mayor. Chaplin confessed to slight disappointment that the crowds in Southmpton were not larger. It was explained that this was because of their delayed arrival. 'This explanation relieves me tremendously, though it is not so much for myself that I feel this, but for my companions and my friends, who expect so much. I feel that the whole thing should go off with a bang for their sake. Yes I do.' He was relieved to find familiar faces to greet him: Tom Geraghty, Fairbanks's sometime script writer, Donald Crisp, the Scottish-born actor who had played Battling Burrows in Griffith's *Broken Blossoms*,

Abe Breman, the London representative of United Artists, and Hetty's brother, Arthur Kelly, known as 'Sonny', who had independently found his way into the film business.* There was also Chaplin's cousin Aubrey, Uncle Spencer Chaplin's son, who had helped care for Hannah during her stay in Peckham House. 'I feel that Aubrey is a nice, simple soul and quite desirous of taking me in hand.' He found himself wanting to pose a little in front of Aubrey, 'I want to shock him; no, not exactly shock him, but surprise him . . . I shall have a long talk with Aubrey later and explain everything . . .'

On the train journey to London he found everything different and irresistibly beautiful: the girls, the countryside – despite the parching and the new buildings – the crowds that waited to see his train pass

Charlie's Rest Cure

1921 – Low's comment on Chaplin's visit to London.

* Edith Kelly, sister of Hetty and Arthur, had married Frank Jay Gould, the American millionaire. When Gould added films to his many business interests, Arthur was found a post in his New York office. Arthur was subsequently to work in United Artists as Chaplin's representative. Later he became Vice President of the company. It was at this meeting with Kelly that Chaplin first learned of Hetty's death, almost three years before.

at every station. As it drew towards Waterloo, it passed through the streets of his boyhood: he could even glimpse Uncle Spencer's old pub, the Queen's Head in Broad Street, Lambeth. The scenes that awaited him in London were astonishing. His homecoming was a triumph hardly paralleled in the twentieth century outside a few great royal or national events.

From Waterloo to the Ritz the streets were thronged with people all waiting for a glimpse of their idol and a chance to cheer.

> I feel like doing something big. What an opportunity for a politician to say something and do something big!
>
> Then, as we approach, the tide comes in towards the gates of the hotel. They have been kept locked to prevent the crowd from demolishing the building. I can see one intrepid motion-picture camera man at the door as the crowd starts to swarm. He begins to edge in, and starts grinding his camera frantically as he is lifted into the whirlpool of humanity. But he keeps turning, and his camera and himself are gradually turned up to the sky, and his lens is registering nothing but clouds as he goes down turning – the most honorable fall a camera man can have, to go down grinding. I wonder if he really got any pictures.
>
> In some way my body has been pushed, carried, lifted, and projected into the hotel. I can assure you that through no action of mine was that accomplished.

The crowd insisted on his showing himself at the window of his suite, but the management of the Ritz asked him to desist from throwing flowers to the people below for fear of causing a riot.

Chaplin now felt a desperate urge to see the places of his youth without delay. With Geraghty and Crisp he managed to make his way out of the service entrance of the hotel. Then he left his companions, to go alone in a taxi to Kennington. From his own description there seems to have been a real passion of hunger in this search for the scenes and impressions remembered from his childhood. Much remained: an old, blind, Bible-reading beggar under the arches by the Canterbury Music Hall; Christchurch, where Hannah worshipped when religion took her; Baxter Hall, 'where we used to see magic lantern shows for a penny . . . You could get a cup of coffee and a piece of cake there and see the Crucifixion of Christ all at the same time'; Kennington Police Station; Kennington Baths, 'reason for many a day's hookey'; Kennington Cross. In Chester Street he recognized the shop where he had once worked as lather boy, though the barber had gone, and an old tub where he himself once used to wash in the morning. He saw himself in the children who played in the street. He thought them lovely, and was thrilled to hear them speak: 'They seem to talk from their souls.' Proceeding to Lambeth Walk he met a girl who had been the servant in a cheap lodging house where he had once stayed, and whom he remembered losing her job, because she had 'fallen'.

His clothes made him conspicuous in Lambeth Walk. He was recognized, and a crowd began to follow him, though at a respectful distance. He felt ashamed after he asked a policeman for help and the policeman reassured him, 'That's all right, Charlie. These people won't hurt you.' They called 'Goodbye, Charlie. God bless you!' as he drove off in his taxi. He drove to Kennington Gate, where he had had his rendezvous with Hetty, to the Horns, and to Kennington Cross, where he had heard the clarinetist play 'The Honeysuckle and the Bee', and 'music first entered my soul'. He reflected that he was seeing all this 'through other eyes. Age trying to look back through the eyes of youth.' Yet, after all, he was only thirty-two.

A couple of nights later he decided to return to Lambeth, this time in the company of Robinson, Geraghty, Crisp and Kelly. He noticed Sharps the photographers in Westminster Bridge Road, and went in and asked if he could buy prints of some photographs they took of him when he was with *Casey's Court Circus*. The assistant replied that the negatives would have been destroyed long ago. He pointed out that they had still a photograph of Dan Leno, who had died seventeen years before, in the window.

> 'Have you destroyed Mr Leno's negative?' I asked him.
>
> 'No,' was the reply, 'but Mr Leno is a famous comedian.'
>
> Such is fame.

There were other landmarks he remembered: an old bottle-nosed tomato seller, ten years more decrepit; the coffee stall at Elephant and Castle which was the focus of the nightlife of the neighbouring streets, and where Chaplin noticed among the loungers a number of men maimed by the war. Then Chaplin took his friends to 3 Pownall Terrace. Mrs Reynolds, the aging war widow who now lived in the Chaplins' former garret, was astonished to be got out of bed at 10.30 p.m. by the celebrity of the moment, but not nonplussed:

> The place was in darkness . . . and when I heard a scuffling outside, I shouted, 'Who is there!'
>
> 'It is Charlie Chaplin,' I heard a voice say.

Never dreaming it was really Mr Chaplin, I shouted from the bed, 'Oh, don't you try and play any jokes on me. Charlie won't come at this hour.'

But the knocking went on, so I got out of bed. I had to take a picture away before I could open the door, as it has no key and I have to wedge it up.

Then I saw four gentlemen on the stairs, and one of them, slightly built and wearing a grey lounge suit said in a gentle voice, 'I really am Charlie Chaplin. Were you asleep?' he asked, and I said, 'No' as I had been listening to the [news] boys calling the results of the great fight.

'Oh,' said Charlie, 'I was supposed to be there.'

Then he looked round the room – I was glad that the sheets on the bed were clean . . . and said, 'This is my old room. I have bumped my head many times on that ceiling' – pointing to the slope above the bed – 'and got thrashed for it. I should like to sleep here again for a night.'

I said, 'It's not like your hotel,' and he answered merrily, 'Never you mind about my hotel. This is my old room, and I am much more interested in that than my hotel!'

Having had their fill of drabness for the night, the friends went back to Park Lane to visit the American film director George Fitzmaurice. There Chaplin quarrelled with another guest, an American actor who had gone sightseeing in Limehouse in search of the tough and highly coloured world of Thomas Burke's *Limehouse Nights*, and was disappointed that nobody there wanted to pick a fight.

That was enough. It annoyed.

I told him that it was very fine for well-fed, overpaid actors flaunting toughness at these deprived people, who are gentle and nice and, if ever tough, only so because of environment. I asked him just how tough he would be if he were living the life that some of these unfortunate families must live. How easy for him with five meals a day beneath that thrust-out chest with his muscles trained and perfect, trying to start something with these people. Of course they were not tough, but when it comes to four years of war, when it comes to losing an arm or a leg, then they are tough. But they are not going around looking for fights unless there is a reason.

It rather broke up the party, but I was feeling so disgusted that I did not care.

On the way back to the Ritz they fell into conversation with three very young prostitutes; Chaplin was rather sad that having gaily hailed them, 'Hello, boys', as soon as they recognized him they became solemn and respectful and called him 'Mr Chaplin'. They helped a driver, on his way to Covent Garden with a load of apples, to push his wagon up a slippery street, and Chaplin was touched that the man 'did not belay the tired animal with a whip and curse and swear at him in his helplessness. He saw the animal was up against it, and instead of beating him he got out and put his shoulder to the wheel, never for the moment doubting that the horse was doing his best.'

The derelicts huddled at night under the arches of the Ritz, the newest and most glamorous hotel in London at that time, seemed to symbolize the two poles of Chaplin's life: the privations of boyhood and the triumph of this homecoming. Chaplin woke the sleepers to give them money. He never ceased observing behaviour: 'There was an old woman about seventy. I gave her something. She woke up, or stirred in her sleep, took the money without a word of thanks – took it as though it was her ration from the bread line and no thanks were expected, huddled herself up in a tighter knot than before, and continued her slumber. The inertia of poverty had long since claimed her.'

Chaplin's search for his past, at first so urgent, seems now to have been satisfied – though to the end of his life he was to return to Kennington and Lambeth and regret the disappearance of the places he had known. Now he was quite content to be a celebrity, an immortal among (as he called them) the immortals. Knoblock took him to meet Bernard Shaw, but at Shaw's flat at 10 Adelphi Terrace Chaplin held back. Every visiting movie actor called upon Shaw and he did not want to be like the rest. He was not to meet Shaw until ten years later. E. V. Lucas gave a dinner in his honour at the Garrick, where he sat between Sir James Barrie, who told him he would like him to play Peter Pan, and Sir Squire Bancroft. Sir Squire, then in his eightieth year, had broken his rule that day and gone to the pictures to see *Shoulder Arms*. Chaplin was overjoyed when he praised the letter-reading scene. He disputed Barrie's criticism that the Heaven scene in *The Kid* was 'entirely unnecessary', but generally felt that he was not making sufficient contribution to the conversation of the party which also included the extrovert Edwin Lutyens (whom Chaplin thought rather common), George Frampton, Harry Graham and Knoblock. Afterwards Chaplin and Knoblock went with Barrie to his flat in Robert Street, Adelphi, close to Shaw's, and there met Gerald du Maurier who had come from playing in *Bulldog Drummond* at Wyndham's Theatre.

The most significant encounters in London were H. G. Wells and Thomas Burke. Chaplin had come to London with the intention of meeting Wells, but their first meeting was engineered by the publicists of the Stoll Picture Corporation, who got each man to a screening of a new film of *Kipps* by telling him that the other wished to meet him there. George K. Arthur, who made his film début in the title role,

1921 – Will Owen on Chaplin's visit to London.

was at the showing, and Chaplin was impressed by Wells's kindliness when he whispered to him, 'Say something nice to the boy,' even though he knew Wells was not impressed by the film. (Some years later Arthur would be instrumental in bringing together Chaplin and Josef von Sternberg – a meeting which resulted in the ill-fated *Sea*

Gulls.) Later they had a pleasant dinner at which Rebecca West was present. Wells complimented him on his turn of phrase when, a bit for the sake of effect, Chaplin apostrophized 'The indecent moon!' He was obliged to confess that the phrase was not original, but was Knoblock's. A quarter of a century later he used it again, in *Monsieur Verdoux*, but without acknowledgement to the originator.

Later in the trip, after his return from Paris and Berlin, Chaplin spent a weekend at Wells's house in the country. It was a carefree visit. Chaplin relaxed and slept a lot and they talked and played games with Wells's two young sons. St John Ervine came to visit and talked about the possibility of talking pictures. Chaplin told him that he didn't think the voice was necessary, that it would spoil the art as much as painting statuary. 'I would as soon rouge marble cheeks. Pictures are pantomimic art. We might as well have the stage. There would be nothing left to the imagination.' Even when he was most comfortable with people, Chaplin still questioned his relationship with them: 'As I speed into town I am wondering if Wells wants to know me or whether he wants me to know him.'

Chaplin found an immediate sympathy with Thomas Burke, who had had a great success with his stories of the darker aspects of East London. A small, silent man, Burke accompanied him on a tour of the places that provided the settings for his books, speaking little but pointing things out with his walking stick. Burke was later to write perhaps the most perceptive analysis of Chaplin's character. The source of their understanding came from their similar backgrounds. As Burke described it:

> He didn't know then, nor did I, that when he was young, and I was young, we were walking the same side-streets of Kennington, living a similar shabby, makeshift kind of life, and loathing it with equal intensity. He was mixed up with red-nose comedians of the minor music halls; I was mixed up with futile clerks. But our backgrounds were much the same. We grew and played in the same streets; we knew the same experiences in the same settings, and took them through a common temperament. In our teens each of us was recoiling from the drab, draggled Kennington in which we lived; each of us, in a crude, undirected way, was yearning towards the things of decency and the things of the mind, and each of us was hopeless of ever attaining them. I discovered literature by picking up a copy of *T.P.'s Weekly* in a tea-shop; he discovered the inwardness of music on hearing a man playing a clarinet outside a Kennington pub – playing *The Honeysuckle and the Bee!*[4]

Impetuously Chaplin decided to go to France, taking Robinson with him. The boat trip was one of his own *mal de mer* gags in real life. He had just decided to take advantage of the offer of a charming young woman to teach him French when he was immobilized by seasickness. On the train to Paris he was impressed by the service and the cheapness of the lunch, but on arrival in Paris to find rain and reporters awaiting him, nausea struck again.

He was eager to meet the caricaturist Cami, with whom he had been in a correspondence – or rather an exchange of drawings and photographs – since Cami had written him a fan letter in 1914. It came as a shock to find that the two, reckoning themselves friends, had no common language. Cami's account is charming, though perhaps over-coloured; Chaplin's own account however in part confirms it. When they met they at first chattered to each other in their own languages, not troubling too much that the other could not understand. Then, when they were having lunch together in Chaplin's hotel, Chaplin suddenly became depressed and left the table with tears in his eyes. The English hotel manager explained to Cami, 'He is overcome by the thought that there is a greater barrier than the ocean between you – the barrier of language.' Later, Cami said, they developed a deaf-and-dumb pantomime, and got on well enough. They went together to the Folies Bergères, which Chaplin found grubbier and less glamorous than when he had played there with the Karno troupe. He dealt with the French-speaking reporters as best he could, and among the Americans and British in Paris met Dudley Field Malone, Waldo Frank, Lady Astor and Sir Philip Sassoon, Lloyd George's private secretary, who invited him for the weekend when he returned to England, and was to become and remain a friend for many years. Of the local celebrities he met Georges Carpentier and Jacques Copeau, and had supper with the Copeau Company. He was excited by the ambience and the performers of the Quartier Latin, and was clearly storing up impressions which would later be useful when he came to make *A Woman of Paris*.

Chaplin and Robinson next took the train to Berlin. Chaplin's films had not been shown in Germany, so his face was unknown. At first he enjoyed relief from the crowds and the reporters; later he began to feel mildly resentful, missing the celebrity treatment and finding himself placed at the worst tables in restaurants. Things looked up when he met the spectacular star Pola Negri, who showed an immediate and lively interest in him. Negri was born Apollonia Chalupiec in

Yanowa, near Lipnia in Poland. She was a dancer at the Imperial Theatre in St Petersburg, and acted on stage and screen in Poland before being invited to Berlin by Max Reinhardt to play in *Sumurun*.

> Pola Negri is really beautiful. She is Polish and really true to the type. Beautiful jet-black hair, white, even teeth and wonderful coloring. I think it such a pity that such coloring does not register on the screen.
>
> She is the centre of attraction here. I am introduced. What a voice she has! Her mouth speaks so prettily the German language. Her voice has a soft, mellow quality, with charming inflection. Offered a drink, she clinks my glass and offers her only English words, 'Jazz boy Charlie.'

Returning briefly to Paris, Chaplin was impressed by a young Russian emigrée called Moussia Sodskaya whom he saw singing in a Montmartre restaurant, and talked of putting her into pictures. The following day he flew from Le Bourget. In those less formal days of passenger transport, the pilot obligingly put him off at Lympne in Kent, where he was to attend Sir Philip Sassoon's garden party. The next day they attended the unveiling of a war memorial in the local school, and Chaplin was embarrassed and upset to find that he, rather than the ceremony, was the centre of attention. 'I wished I hadn't come.' Sassoon also took him to a hospital for the war wounded, and he was greatly shocked and depressed by what he saw. 'What is to become of them?' he asked. 'That is up to you and me.'

Then followed his weekend with Wells, after which he intrepidly flew back to Paris for a charity première of *The Kid* at the Trocadero. He had been persuaded to attend by the daughter of J. P. Morgan, with the promise of an award. In the outcome the award itself was not very impressive – Officier de l'Instruction Publique – but the event was. The audience included Prince George of Greece and Princess Xenia, an assortment of dukes, duchesses, marquis, marquises, Stuyvesants and Vanderbilts. There were also Elsa Maxwell, Georges Carpentier, Cecile Sorel and Henri Letellier, a prominent Parisian publisher who was to provide the original for the character of Pierre Revel in *A Woman of Paris*. Chaplin dined with Carpentier and Letellier the following evening.

With an appointment for lunch with Sassoon to meet Lloyd George and other celebrities, Chaplin decided to fly back to London, but the plane was lost in the fog and the cross-channel journey took seven hours. He missed Lloyd George and was disappointed. 'I love to meet interesting personages. I would love to meet Lenin, Trotsky and the Kaiser.'

Despite this, Chaplin refused Wells's invitation to dinner with Chaliapin, since he had promised to spend his last evening in England with cousin Aubrey. Uncharacteristically, and despite Aubrey's own objections, Chaplin insisted on visiting Aubrey's pub and behaving flamboyantly because, 'I must get him more custom.' He stayed with Aubrey until four in the morning, learning about his Chaplin forbears; then hitched a lift back to the Ritz in a Ford truck driven by an ex-officer who was now in the grocery business, and on his way from Bayswater to Covent Garden. Chaplin revelled in those casual encounters.

It was now the second week in October, and Chaplin set off for Southampton 'dejected and sad'. He felt that he was going to miss the crowds more than the friends who had come to see him off, like Arthur Kelly, who brought him a picture of Hetty. He even forgave reporters – 'After all, it's their job to ask questions and they have been merely doing their job with me.' On the boat back to America he struck up a pleasant friendship with an eight-year-old girl. He describes a fragment of their conversation:

> 'You like smashing windows? You must be Spanish,' I tell her.
>
> 'Oh! no, not Spanish; I'm Jewish,' she answers.
>
> 'That accounts for your genius.'
>
> 'Oh, do you think Jewish people are clever?' she asks eagerly.
>
> 'Of course. All great geniuses have Jewish blood in them. No, I am not Jewish,' as she is about to put that question, 'but I am sure there must be some somewhere in me. I hope so.'

On the boat he also befriended the English producer-director Cecil Hepworth and his star Alma Taylor who were making their first visit to the States. On their arrival he took them to dinner with Sam Goldwyn, and invited them to his home.

In New York he met Claude McKay, the negro poet, and the educationalist Marguerite Naumberg. Frank Harris took him to Sing Sing where he met the Irish nationalist and labour leader Jim Larkin, was appalled by the death chamber, and made an impromptu speech which went down well:

> Brother criminals and fellow sinners: Christ said, 'Let him who is without sin cast the first stone.' I cannot cast the stone, though. I have compromised and thrown many a pie. But I cannot cast the first stone.

'Some got it,' he remarked, 'others never will.'

Chaplin's record of the trip was mostly written in the course of the train journey back to California, and was taken down at his dictation by a young newspaperman, Monta Bell, who was subsequently to be an assistant on *A Woman of Paris* and to go on to become a very competent director in his own right. Some Chaplin biographers have suggested that the text was 'ghosted' by Bell, but the style is too distinctive and the analysis of Chaplin's reactions and sensations far too personal for that. The account originally appeared as a series of articles in *Photoplay* before publication in book form as *My Trip Abroad* (*My Wonderful Visit*, for the English edition). 'Going over it all,' Chaplin's account concluded,

> it has all been worth while and the job ahead of me looks worth while. If I can bring smiles to the tired eyes in Kennington and Whitechapel, if I have absorbed and understood the virtues and problems of those simpler people I have met, and if I have gathered the least bit of inspiration from those greater personages who were kind to me, then this has been a wonderful trip, and somehow I am eager to get back to work and begin paying for it.

He was not to return to work instantly, however. He arrived back in Los Angeles at noon on 31 October, and that evening dined with some friends, Mr and Mrs Abraham Lehr. There was only one other guest, Clare Sheridan, the sculptor, painter, traveller and writer. She and Chaplin struck up an instant friendship. Mrs Sheridan was a niece of Winston Churchill. Her husband had been killed in France, leaving her with a daughter and a small son, Dick, who was in California with her. She had been commissioned by the Soviet Government to make portrait busts of Lenin, Trotsky, Dzerzhinsky and other Bolshevik leaders, and her subsequent articles and interviews had created a furore. Americans, Chaplin pointed out in his autobiography, were confused by the phenomenon of an English aristocrat writing pro-Bolshevik articles. Chaplin was fascinated by all she had to tell him about the Soviet Union; she was interested in his impressions of Britain. 'A good country to belong to, we agreed, but not a country to live in – not for the creative artist, and he advised me to remain where I am.'

Mrs Sheridan said that in the United States she was becoming a writer rather than a sculptor because American men were self-conscious about being portrayed in sculpture. 'I'm vain, thank goodness,' said Chaplin; and there and then they decided that she would make his bust. As he accompanied her back to the Hollywood Hotel they had an argument about marriage, and Chaplin put her in mind of Francis Thompson's essay on Shelley in which he said that Shelley tired not so much of a woman's arms as of her mind. 'It seemed to me that it is more spiritual than a physical companionship that Charlie is subconsciously searching for in his heart.'

Two days later on Monday 2 November they met again, this time with little Dick. At noon they went to the studio where Chaplin showed them *The Kid*. In the pathetic parts he would tiptoe to the harmonium in the screening room and play an accompaniment. Dick sobbed so hysterically that Chaplin was alarmed and kept reassuring him, 'It's only a play, Dick! It will come right in the end.' They lunched at Chaplin's home. He was somewhat apologetic about his rented house on Beechwood Drive and Argyle, 'the tortuous unsimplicity' of whose Moorish architecture greatly disturbed him though he liked the panoramic view of the city below. After lunch they went for a walk and talked about art and the satisfaction it gives, suicide and immortality. Chaplin became quite carried away:

> There is nothing so beautiful that it will make people forget their eggs and bacon for breakfast – as for admiration of the world – it's not worth anything – there is in the end but oneself to please: – you make something because it means something to you. You work – because you have a superabundance of vital energy. You find that not only can you make children but you can express yourself in other ways. In the end it is you – all you – your work, your thought, your conception of the beautiful, yours the happiness, yours the satisfaction. Be brave enough to face the veil and lift it, and see and know the void it hides, and stand before that void and know that within yourself is your world . . .[5]

Then they laughed at themselves for being so serious. After tea they took Dick home and then Chaplin and Mrs Sheridan dined and danced at the Ambassador Hotel, where most of the other guests knew Chaplin and hurried to welcome him back and to speculate about Mrs Sheridan.

The following day they began work on the bust. Chaplin insisted it must be finished by Saturday because he wanted to go to Catalina to fish. Mrs Sheridan found it an amusing and productive day. Chaplin started the morning in a brown silk dressing gown and was serious. After a while he seized his violin and walked about the room playing it. Then, clearly in a gayer mood, he disappeared to change into an orange and primrose robe. Occasionally they would stop for tea. Chaplin 'would either philosophize or impersonate'; or he might put on a gramophone record and conduct an imaginary band. Between times he confided that when he was a young man in London he longed to know people, but that now he knew many, he felt lonelier than ever.

The bust was finished in three days. Friends were amazed that Chaplin had stayed patient so long; and Mrs Sheridan congratulated herself on her foresight in making it in his own home and specifying that he should be bare-throated. 'A man in his dressing gown does not suddenly get a notion to order his motor car and go off to some place. I had him fairly anchored. Nevertheless he has been difficult to do. There is so much subtlety in the face, and sensitiveness, and varying personality.'

Chaplin was pleased with it, said it might be the head of a criminal, and at once concocted a theory that criminals and artists were psychologically akin, that 'on reflection we all have a flame, a burning flame of impulse, a vision, a sidetracked mind, a deep sense of unlawfulness.' Jean de Limur arrived as the bust was finished and commented slyly: 'I see it is Pan . . . *on ne peut jamais tromper une femme.*'

Chaplin changed his mind about Catalina, since he had discovered that the fishing season had closed on 1 November. He decided instead that he and the Sheridans would go camping on Sunday morning. They set off in Chaplin's car, followed by a van with the tents and paraphernalia and a Ford containing the chef. The Sunday roads were thick with cars and exhaust fumes, and they began to despair of finding a camping site. Eventually they struck off across country and found an idyllic seaside spot, designated with a sign 'Private Property. No trespassing. No camping. No hunting'. For Charlie Chaplin, however, the owner made an exception.

> Late into the night I sat with him over the camp fire. A sea mist rose and little veils of sea mist swept like gossamer over the dunes and the naked, shiny eucalyptus stems cast black shadows. Mingling with the nightbird cries, the rhythmical sound of the sea and the shore.
>
> One by one the lanterns in the camp flickered and went out. Charlie sat huddled up before the flame, an elfin, elemental creature with gleaming eyes and tousled hair, his little nervous hands raking the embers with a stick. His voice was very deep, the voice of a much bigger man. He ruminated moodily. He said it was 'Too much – too great – too beautiful – there are no words –'[6]

They stayed in the camp through the week. Chaplin played with Dick, and entertained them with imitations of Nijinsky and Pavlova which he did so well and so gracefully that Mrs Sheridan did not know whether to 'laugh or silently appreciate'. On Friday the seaside idyll was broken with the arrival of five motors full of children wanting to see him, and two reporters. They returned to Hollywood. Back at the house, taking tea, Mrs Sheridan wrote,

> We found ourselves making conversation to one another with difficulty. He looked at me as strangely as I looked at him, and then he said:
>
> 'You know what's the matter – we don't know each other.'
>
> And it was true. I was talking not with the elemental, wild-haired Charlie of the camp fire, nor yet with Charlie Chaplin of the films, but with a neatly dressed, smooth-haired young man I didn't even know by sight. Civilization and its trappings had changed us both. The past seemed tinged with unreality. 'I think it has all been a dream,' I said.[7]

This stimulating friendship ended rather abruptly. The newspapers were eager to sniff out a love affair, and Carlyle Robinson emphasized his denial by adding rather tactlessly 'Mrs Sheridan is old enough to be Mr Chaplin's mother.' The Sheridans thereupon returned to New York. Dick Sheridan was to die at the age of nineteen, and his mother spent her later years in North Africa. Her powerful bust portrait of Chaplin still stands in the Manoir de Ban at Corsier sur Vevey.

Since the divorce the Hollywood gossip columns had eagerly watched every feminine social liaison. The names of Thelma Morgan Converse, Lila Lee and Anna Q. Nilsson were from time to time connected with Chaplin's. Rumours of an engagement to a New York actress, May Collins, were admitted, then denied. Enthusiasm for a beautiful film actress, Claire Windsor, waned after she pulled the kind of stunt which always offended Chaplin's sense of dignity and propriety: she staged a 'disappearance'. Chaplin joined in the search in the nearby hills, and offered a reward for the discovery of Miss Windsor whom the headlines now described as his 'fiancée'. She was found apparently unconscious: Robinson was the first to notice how clean her riding boots were. When a young couple claimed the reward, there was closer investigation into the 'disappearance', and the hoax was exposed.

His picnic over, Chaplin was soon back in the studio and working with a will to finish the two films still due under the First National contract. *Pay Day* and *The Pilgrim* were completed in eight months.

Pay Day took thirty working days; *The Pilgrim*, in four reels, took forty-two and was by far the most economically made of all Chaplin's feature productions. *Pay Day* was to be the last Chaplin two-reeler released. Visually it marks a considerable advance. During Chaplin's absence, Totheroh seems to have been experimenting with the new lights installed in the studio, and the night scenes with rain are lit with sophistication.

Chaplin is cast as a working man and hen-pecked husband, and the comedy is derived from the ordinary frustrations of daily life. The opening section of the film has Charlie at work as a labourer on a building site; the middle section shows the effects of an inebriate night out as Charlie endeavours to make his way home – eventually strap-hanging in a lunch-wagon under the mistaken impression that it is a moving bus. In the last sequence he returns home, oiling his boots in a vain hope of creeping to bed unobserved by his virago wife who sleeps with a rolling pin at her side. He ends the night seeking repose in the bath – as in *A Night Out* and *One A.M.* Too late he finds the bath is full of cold water. There is a notably articulate piece of mime in the payday scene. Charlie is seen arguing with some person off-screen, pleading that he has been underpaid. As he calculates on his fingers, his mime betrays the gradual realization that he has in fact been paid too much.

There was only one pause during shooting for story preparation, which indicates that Chaplin had begun the film with a more fully developed scenario than was his usual habit. This degree of pre-planning was no doubt the reason why he was able to depart from his normal practice up to this time of shooting in narrative continuity. The second part of *Pay Day*, filmed in the studio, was shot first, during the last five days of November and most of December. Chaplin was ill with a cold in the first week of the New Year; when he returned he shot in the space of four working weeks the first part of the film, on the building site. Material filmed on location at La Brea and De Longpre where a large new building was in construction, was matched with studio material shot 'by natural light', as the studio records now specify, indicating the growing adoption of artificial lighting.

Pay Day was despatched to First National on 23 February 1922, and Chaplin began to prepare the story that was to be *The Pilgrim*. By the time shooting began on 10 April, the narrative continuity seems to have been largely worked out. Monta Bell, having finished his work on *My Trip Abroad*, was taken on as a general assistant and bit player. It is possible that his advent introduced a new method for the preparation of the Chaplin pictures. *The Pilgrim* is the first film for which there survives a quantity of written scenario and gag notes. It is possible, though not likely, that this kind of preparatory writing did take place on earlier films, but has simply not survived. The reduction of the periods during which production was halted for 'working on story' and the extent of these notes would seem rather to indicate that Chaplin was moving away from his earlier method of creating and improvising on the set and even on film, towards a greater degree of advance planning on paper.

The film was originally intended as a Western comedy – it would have had some similarities to *The Gold Rush* – and for a first working title was simply designated *Western.** The earliest scenario was clearly modified because it would at that time have been judged too sophisticated and ironic for a comic subject; aspects of it look directly forward to *Monsieur Verdoux*.

Charlie was to have been one of four desperate escaped convicts who waylay a minister and steal his clothes. Disguised as a man of the cloth, Charlie arrives in the Wild West town of Hell's Hinges, a sink of immorality. He is taken for the new young reformer sent to replace the town's old minister, helpless in the face of the immorality of the place:

> Show a Chinaman or two shot down by the rough element in casual fashion . . . Show scene in saloon which is also combination gambling house, lunchroom and dance hall. Men rough with women. Gold dust for dance hall girls. Card game that ends in a fight and there is gun play.

With the same kind of fortuity that made him master of Easy Street, Charlie overcomes the town bullies and falls in love with Edna, the Minister's beautiful daughter. His programme for reform is to replace the church organ with a jazz band, to perform the hymns in ragtime and to introduce other attractions such as motion pictures and dice games for the collection. As a result the saloon empties while the church fills up.

> Charlie begins to preach a peculiar sort of preaching based on common sense rather than religion. He goes through all sorts of gestures. He is a lousy talker and they go to sleep on him in spots. But when they do he

* When shooting began the working title became *The Tail End*, a jocular reference to the anticipated conclusion of the First National contract.

> waves for the band and with the jazz they awaken and listen as Charlie goes on . . .

At the end of the service, Charlie amiably shakes hands with his congregation, finally holding out his hands absently to a sheriff who immediately claps a pair of handcuffs on him. The congregation

> demand that Charlie be released and threaten sheriff. With eloquent gesture Charlie bids them do no violence. Tells them to stick by the church and the old man. He shakes old man's hand and bids him build new church. There are tears in girl's eyes as he bids her goodbye and with the crowd shouting his praise he goes up the aisle and out with the sheriff into fadeout.

This curious moral fable was never made: the eventual film was in more conventional comedy style, with the Wild West element replaced by lightly satirical treatment of the manners and hypocrisies of small-town religion. Charlie is still an escaped convict. Stealing the clothes of a bathing parson, he arrives thus disguised in the town of Dead Man's Gulch, where he is mistaken for the new minister. Called upon to deliver a sermon, he pantomimes the story of David and Goliath. He experiences such hazards of the clerical life as a parochial tea party where he is tormented by a horrid spoilt child. Having fallen in love with his landlady's beautiful daughter, he foils the attempt of a former cell-mate to rob the women.

The local sheriff realizes his identity and reluctantly arrests him. Touched by his gallantry and the girl's pleas, he takes him to the Mexican border to give him a chance to escape. He orders Charlie to pick some flowers on the other side of the border and – unable to take the hint – Charlie obediently returns with a bouquet. The exasperated sheriff is finally obliged to kick him over the border to freedom. On the Mexican side however a bunch of bandits spring out of the bushes, wildly shooting at one another. Caught between two hostile countries, Charlie waddles off into the distance with one foot in Mexico and one in the United States. It is an image open to any number of symbolic interpretations.

One of the most polished and charming of the films of Chaplin's middle period, and with admirable scenes of sustained comedy such as the tea party, *The Pilgrim* seems to have been shot with few problems. Chaplin made extensive use of locations for the shooting, and there are evocative scenes of still-rural Saugus, Sawtella, Newhall, Rosoc, South Pasadena, Ventura Road and Eagle Rock.

Dinky Dean, who played the horrid little boy in the tea party scene, was in real life not at all horrid. He was the son of Chuck Riesner; sixty years later as Dean Riesner, a prominent Hollywood scriptwriter, he recalled how difficult it had been for him to pummel two men whom he knew as Uncle Sydney and Uncle Charlie. He was finally persuaded to do it only when Charles and Sydney spent some time slapping each other and laughing wildly to prove to the sceptical child that it really was fun after all.

In some quarters *The Pilgrim* ran into trouble with censors and church authorities. In Atlanta the Evangelical Ministers' Association demanded its withdrawal as 'an insult to the Gospel'. In South Carolina the Daniel Morgan Klan of the Knights of the Ku Klux Klan protested at the showing of the film on the grounds that it held the Protestant ministry up to ridicule. The Pennsylvania Board of Censors eliminated so many scenes that it virtually constituted a ban on the film. Elsewhere, however, churchmen as well as laity agreed with P. W. Gallico, writing in the *New York Daily News*:

> Now Mr Chaplin's picture is not without satire. But the shaft is not directed at the clergy. It is aimed at the narrow mind, the bigot, the person who can see no farther than the written word. In fact it seems to travel on dead line and smite the very people who in this case had the power to condemn, to shut off from others, laughter which might be directed at them.

Arrangements for the distribution of *The Pilgrim* were the source of much acrimony between Chaplin and First National. Chaplin was already roused to fury at the beginning of September, when he was still cutting the film, by an article in the *Exhibitor's Herald* which quoted Harry Schwalbe of First National accusing him of not fulfilling his contracts over *The Kid*. 'I INTEND SUING SCHWALBE AND FIRST NATIONAL FOR TEN MILLION DOLLARS,' Chaplin cabled Sydney; but the affair was smoothed over. Chaplin had no intention of letting First National have *The Pilgrim* under the terms applying to a normal two-reeler supplied under the contract. Like *The Kid* it was a feature of altogether more ambitious scope than had been anticipated by the original agreement with the distributors. Sydney was sent to New York to negotiate with Schwalbe, and was given a memorandum on the matter by Alf Reeves:

IDEA

> The idea is, Chief wishes to deliver No. 8 'Pilgrim' as a feature four reeler to terminate the contract. He thinks to let them have it on a 70–30 basis same as 'Kid'. This for U.S., Canada and all Foreign Countries, with a guarantee from them of $400,000.00 in advance of his share, payable $200,000.00 on delivery of the two negatives and one Positive print, and a note for $200,000.00 due in three or six months, at their convenience . . .
>
> Failing their acceptance of these terms, it is proposed you will deliver picture No. 8 as per contract, a two-reeler entitled 'The Professor' for which he has received full contract price.
>
> Before delivery to First National of either, Mr Burkan and yourself will see that his interests are protected in regard to any question that may arise in the future.
>
> *Before exhibiting* 'Pilgrim' or 'Professor' to First National (there being no compulsion on our part to give them a preview) they should agree that if they do not come to terms for 'Pilgrim' as a feature, they are to accept 'The Professor' as picture No. 8 in full termination of all Chief's obligations to them under the Contract.

The remarkable aspect of this document is its discussion of *The Professor*. No Chaplin film of this title was ever shown or released, and nowhere in the comprehensive daily records of the Chaplin studio is there any reference to its production. Yet the subsequent correspondence between Chaplin in Los Angeles and Sydney in New York seems to establish beyond doubt that such a film actually existed in 1922. On 13 November Sydney sent a long telegram to Chaplin reporting the results of a meeting with Harry Schwalbe. Schwalbe, he said, was very friendly, sympathetic to the Chaplin proposition and eager to conclude the contract amicably. Schwalbe felt however that it would be easier to negotiate if his executive committee could see the films. He further suggested that Chaplin should offer First National both films: *The Professor* could conclude the contract, and *The Pilgrim* could be handled as an independent production, though he insisted that Chaplin's 70–30 proposition left no profit for the company.

Sydney recommended that Chaplin permit him to show both pictures to First National without getting a written release in advance; and that he increase the distribution allowance to the distributors for release of *The Pilgrim*.

Chaplin replied the following day that he would on no account allow First National to have both films. He waived his objection to showing them *The Pilgrim* but not in the case of the two-reeler. He was willing to modify the distribution arrangement to 65–35, but in other respects the contract had to be the same as for *The Kid.* 'IN THE EVENT FIRST NATIONAL DO NOT WANT PILGRIM AFTER VIEWING SAME, THEN DELIVER TWO-REELER AS PER CONTRACT.' First National, via Sydney, made a counter-proposal of 50 per cent of the gross over $280,000 for *The Pilgrim.* Chaplin wired back on November 21st: PROPOSITION RIDICULOUS STOP DELIVER TWO REELER AND MAKE IMMEDIATE ARRANGEMENTS WITH ABRAMS* TO DISTRIBUTE PILGRIM. He confirmed these instructions in a further telegram sent both to Sydney and to Burkan on 7 December:

> FIRST NATIONAL EXECUTIVES HAVING FAILED TO OFFER SUITABLE CONDITIONS FOR PRODUCTION OF SPECIAL FOUR REEL FEATURE PILGRIM IT NOW OK COURSE FOR YOU AND MR BURKAN TO DELIVER TWO REELS PROFESSOR IN ACCORDANCE WITH CONTRACTS AND THEIR ACCEPTANCE OF THIS AS NUMBER EIGHT TERMINATES THE SERIES STOP REGARDS.

On 15 December Chaplin cabled Sydney:

> WILL ACCEPT THEIR PROPOSITIONS AS OUTLINED IN YOUR TELEGRAM OF DECEMBER THIRTEEN PROVIDING THEIR GUARANTEE FURTHER SEVENTY-FIVE THOUSAND DOLLARS CASH IN SIX MONTHS STOP USE YOUR JUDGMENT IF YOU CAN GET ANY BETTER TERMS BY JUDICIOUS APPROACH STOP HAVING NEGATIVE PILGRIM HERE WILL DELIVER WHEN FIRST CASH PAYMENT IS MADE STOP ON NO ACCOUNT RELEASE TWO REEL PROFESSOR STOP REGARDS.

After a few more telegrams of indignation, conciliation and threats to let United Artists distribute *The Pilgrim* after all, amicable arrangements were finally concluded with First National. *The Professor* was never mentioned again and for the moment remains the major mystery in the Chaplin canon. The film must have existed, unless we predicate some outlandish bluff between the two brothers to convince the telegraph operators between California and New York of the existence of a purely imaginary film. A partial solution was suggested when Kevin Brownlow and David Gill, preparing their *Unknown*

* of United Artists

Chaplin, found in the Chaplin archives a complete and cut five-minute sequence in a can labelled *The Professor*. The sequence begins in a slum street, down which waddles Chaplin in a quite unfamilar costume and make-up. He wears a heavy and dejected moustache and is dressed in a long coat and battered silk hat. He carries a suitcase labelled 'PROFESSOR BOSCO. FLEA CIRCUS'. Bosco enters a dosshouse, and before retiring to sleep inspects his fleas. Chaplin's mime creates a whole world of the busy but invisible creatures (the act was to be recreated in *Limelight*, thirty years later*). While Bosco sleeps, a dog of disgustingly mangy appearance wanders into the dormitory and knocks over the box of fleas. The dog starts to scratch desperately. So, very shortly, do the other inmates of the dormitory. Bosco wakes up and frantically runs about the place, retrieving his pets from the whiskers of his neighbours. He takes his case and leaves the doss house and the sequence ends with him trotting down the road where we first saw him.

The sequence gives all the appearance of a section cut out of a completed film. Among the out-takes which Brownlow and Gill examined is a series of shots taken in the same dosshouse set, but with Chaplin costumed as a very shabby bellboy who goes about the now empty dormitory, preparing the beds with all the aplomb and dexterity of an employee of the Ritz. The dosshouse set is the same in both the cut sequence and the out-takes, but is quite different from the dosshouse scenes in both *Police* and *The Kid*. Three years earlier, however, when he reached a block with *The Kid* Chaplin spent three days, 30 September and 1–2 October 1919, shooting some 7500 feet of film merely described in the daily shooting reports as 'Flophouse set – Flea bus.' or 'Trained fleas – bunkhouse bus.' Two snapshots taken at the time by Jack Wilson** (see plates in section 3) confirm that this is the material found by Brownlow and Gill. But of what did the rest of *The Professor* consist, if a two-reel version really existed? Had Chaplin or his cutter in fact assembled a new film out of rejected scenes, perhaps from the Mutual as well as the First National series? There is no one living who can give us the answer, and unless the film itself one day comes to light, the mystery of *The Professor* will remain unsolved.

* Chaplin clearly had a particular affection for this flea circus gag. Before managing to use it in *Limelight* he had tried to work it into both *The Circus* and *The Great Dictator*.

** Discovered in London in 1984.

9

A WOMAN OF PARIS

With the completion of *The Pilgrim*, Chaplin was at last free to make his first film for the United Artists. This was a considerable relief to his partners Douglas Fairbanks, Mary Pickford and D. W. Griffith, who were fretting because Chaplin had not yet made any contribution to the profits of the corporation. As it turned out, his first United Artists picture was, in this respect at least, to prove a disappointment.

Chaplin decided that he would use his new independence to fulfil an old ambition. He would make a serious dramatic film. He had already moved in that direction with *The Kid*, of course, and the unfinished Essanay picture *Work* was clearly a good deal more sombre than the general run of comedy at that time. In 1917 he had made another move towards drama when he attempted to buy the film rights to Hall Caine's play *The Prodigal Son*, in which he saw a serious role for himself.

He was moreover concerned to launch Edna in an independent starring role. Even though they had remained, as he put it, 'emotionally estranged', he retained an affectionate concern for her. She was no longer an ideal comic partner. Totheroh remembered that 'by this time Edna was getting pretty heavy but her little face still had charm in it. And she got to drinking pretty heavy. One day we were looking at rushes and Charlie could see it.' Chaplin tried to think of suitably mature roles. He considered an adaptation of *The Trojan Women*, then considered casting Edna as Josephine to his own Napoleon – a role which would continue to fascinate him. The idea for *A Woman of Paris* came to him as a result of his meetings with the notorious

Peggy Hopkins Joyce. The term 'gold digger' was coined in honour of Peggy around 1920. Born Margaret Upton in Virginia, she arrived in Chicago at the time of the First World War, changed her name to Hopkins, and landed her first millionaire husband, Stanley Joyce. Divorced and with a million-dollar settlement, she became a Ziegfeld girl, from which strategic launching she went on to net four more millionaire husbands in rapid succession. In 1922 she arrived in Hollywood, bent on a film career.

Marshall Neilan found himself threatened with the prospect of directing Peggy's first picture. Neilan was a colourful and erratic Hollywood figure. Born in 1891, he had left school at eleven, drifted into films as an actor, and seen service at Biograph Studios as D. W. Griffith's chauffeur. He graduated to directing and by the age of twenty-six he was Mary Pickford's favourite director. In addition Neilan was one of Hollywood's most colourful playboys: his high-living and marathon drinking bouts cut short his career. Temperamentally he was no doubt well matched to Peggy; professionally he probably saw the hazards of trying to turn her into an actress. It may not have been without some ulterior motive that he brought her on a visit to the Chaplin studios one afternoon in the high summer of 1922.

Peggy was at all times a flamboyant dresser and that afternoon she was weighed down with jewels and exuded costly and exotic perfumes. Faced with a new and highly eligible millionaire divorcé, she determined to impress, and played the lady with a fine excess of airs and graces. Chaplin was amused, not least when the *noblesse oblige* role collapsed rather suddenly. After an hour or so of liquid hospitality Neilan said he thought they should be going, and emphasized the fact by playfully slapping Peggy's bottom. Her dignity thus assaulted, Peggy turned on him with an impressive tirade of profanities. Chaplin was intrigued by this former country girl and self-made woman of the world. For a couple of weeks they were inseparable. They took a trip together to Catalina Island, and Hollywood gossip marked Chaplin as Peggy's sixth conquest.

Peggy was soon to recognize that Chaplin was not to be one of her more profitable ventures, and moved on to more promising quarry in the shape of the young Irving Thalberg. It was Chaplin who gained from the liaison, which he was to describe as 'bizarre but brief'. Peggy had given him the idea for his next film. During their meetings she had regaled Chaplin with her colourful reminiscences. She had described her affair with the rich and famous Parisian publisher and man-about-town, Henri Letellier, whom Chaplin had met during his European trip the previous year. She told him also about a young man who had committed suicide out of desperate love for her, giving her the excuse for some very stylish mourning outfits. He was no less amused by her protestations that she was really a simple girl at heart, and desired only a home and babies.

A story based on Peggy's Parisian encounters had the added attraction of the setting. Paris had intrigued Chaplin since he first went there with the Karno company. Even at Mutual he had talked of a story set in the Bohemian quarter of Paris: *The Immigrant*, as we have seen, was begun as such. For weeks Chaplin wrestled with the story, for which he chose the working title *Destiny*. Many pages of notes survive from this stage, ranging from sketchy memoranda scribbled on the backs of Western Union telegraph forms to elaborate directions for the sets that would be required. These notes reveal the way that Chaplin built his story, elaborating and eliminating, inventing and refining, developing complex emotional situations and then analyzing them in order to isolate an essence that could be expressed by visual means. *A Woman of Paris* was to represent a very conscious stage in his development. Through eight years of film work he had discovered and developed his ability to reveal the inner workings of the mind and heart through external signs. In his new film he wanted to explore the limits of that expressiveness – the range, subtlety and sophistication of the sentiments and motives that could be revealed in pictures.

In the earliest stages of the story development the characters are called Peggy and Letellier, and it seems likely that some incidents in the first versions of the plot are just as Peggy related them. As the characters become more and more Chaplin's own creatures, though, they acquire fictional names – at first Marie Arnette and Poiret; later, and definitively, Marie St Clair and Pierre Revel. It is interesting however that much later, as the identification of the role and the character becomes more important, the notes frequently refer to them by the players' names, Edna and [Adolphe] Menjou.

Chaplin possessed the gift of just selection. Here, as always in the preparatory stages of his films, the notes show him exploring a great mass of ideas and incidents, and then eliminating and paring them away to arrive at a story progression.

Although at this stage the plot remained unclear the tone of irony that would characterize the film was already marked, as suggestions for incidents and details show:

> Peggy wants marriage and kids. Let. gives her elaborate doll . . .
> Mentions fact, 'If we were only married.' He laughs at it . . .
> Girl tells Let. she is going to leave him – He laughs at it – But humours her – Tells her that she will be back – She emotional about 'Goodbyes' – Goes home starts to send back jewelry. Then keeps it.

In outline the final plot could serve any old melodrama, and in other hands it might well have been no more. Marie lives with her tyrannical father in a little French village. Her boyfriend Jean helps her escape from the house for an evening, but on their return her father will not let her in. Nor will Jean's father allow her to remain in his house. Marie and Jean decide to elope to Paris, but Jean fails to arrive for the *rendezvous* at the station: his father has died suddenly of a stroke. Marie sets off for Paris alone . . .

A year later Marie St Clair is the glittering but discontented mistress of a rich man-about-town, Pierre Revel. By chance she once more meets Jean, who has come to Paris with his mother and is now a struggling artist. Marie commissions him to paint her portrait. They fall in love once again, and Jean proposes marriage. Marie decides to leave Pierre but then overhears the weak-willed Jean reassuring his possessive mother that his proposal of marriage is not serious. Marie returns to Pierre, and refuses to see the now distraught and remorseful Jean. In despair, he shoots himself. His mother sets out with his gun to avenge herself on Marie, but is touched when she finds the disconsolate girl weeping over the body of Jean. The two women are reconciled.

Chaplin agonized week after week before he found the right ending, eventually an ironic anti-climax. Marie and the mother of Jean have together found redemption and consolation in the service of others – raising orphans in a country home. In the final shot Marie is cheerfully riding with her charges on the back of a haycart. A limousine flashes by. Inside it, Pierre Revel's secretary asks him, 'By the way, whatever happened to Marie St Clair?' Pierre shrugs with indifference.

Chaplin's directions for sets to his designer, Arthur Stibolt, show that even when this story line was worked out he had ideas for elaborations and other scenes that were not finally to be filmed. He asked for a race track, for an art gallery and a jewellery store. He proposed that they should rent facilities at Universal Studios for scenes of a church and church bazaar, and a poor hotel. A whole group of Canadian settings relates to one of several alternative ends proposed for the film. He asked Stibolt to provide exteriors of a Canadian street, a railway station, a hospital and a preacher's house, and interiors of the same preacher's house.

Chaplin's instructions to Stibolt show his concern for the sets and their relationship to the characters. Edna's Parisian apartment must be 'elaborate and costly looking'. Letellier's house 'must be beautiful . . . every means must be taken to make this set very elaborate and still in good taste.' The café was 'supposed to be the most expensive café in Paris'. Of the boy's Parisian studio apartment: 'while it is not a "poor" set it should get over the atmosphere of the Latin Quarter . . . It must be artistically furnished, so make preparations for this in your construction . . . this set is not elaborate but must be comfortable and suggest the home of an artist in Paris who is fairly successful.' (In the outcome, Jean was shown as being poor.) The jewellery store, Chaplin suggested, might be shot on actual location, perhaps Nordlingers. At this point his idea was to match up the studio sets with locations which he would film in Paris:

FRENCH EXTERIORS

Entrance to First Café
Driving away to Theatre
Driving to Jazz Café
Driving home in front of church
In front of Edna's Apt.
Front of Boy's Studio
Front of Menjou Home
Front of Menjou Office
Along Seine (Boy's Scene)
Streets for driving

For *A Woman of Paris*, Chaplin hired four young assistants, each of whom was soon afterwards to become a capable director in his own right. Edward Sutherland already knew Chaplin socially, and had just written off his chances of making good as an actor when he met Chaplin in a restaurant.

He said, 'What are you doing, Eddie?'
I said, 'Well, I just changed my life.'
He said, 'What are you going to do?'

I said, 'I'm going to be your assistant.'
He said, 'You are?'
I said, 'Yes, I want to be your assistant, Charlie.'
He said, 'Why?'
I said, 'Well, I admire you greatly, and I want to be a director, and I think the best way I can do that is to study under you.'
He said, 'Well, we might be able to fix it. How much money are you getting?'
I told him the largest amount, $500.
He said, 'Oh, I couldn't pay anything like that.'
I said, 'I don't care what you pay me as long as I get the job.'
Charlie was very frugal. He had a great fear of poverty.[1]

Sutherland, who was briefly married to Louise Brooks, was later to have a successful career as a director: he was responsible for two of the best W. C. Fields comedies, *It's The Old Army Game* and *Poppy.* A second American assistant, Monta Bell, who had helped Chaplin with his book *My Trip Abroad*, was to become a prolific director and supervisor of Paramount's sound studios in New York. Among his most notable films was *The Torrent*, Garbo's first American picture.

Two young Frenchmen were engaged as research assistants, to ensure correct Parisian atmosphere. Comte Jean de Limur had arrived in Hollywood, after war service as a flyer, to try his luck as an actor, and played in Fairbanks' *The Three Musketeers*. After *A Woman of Paris* he worked as assistant to De Mille and Rex Ingram before becoming a director in his own right. Two early sound films in which he directed Jeanne Eagels, *The Letter* and *Jealousy*, were supervised by Monta Bell: there was clearly a camaraderie of Chaplin alumni. Returning to France, de Limur's work included co-direction with G. W. Pabst on *Don Quixote*.

Henri d'Abbadie d'Arrast was born in Argentina in 1897 and trained as an architect. For many years after *A Woman of Paris* he retained the friendship of Chaplin, who was attracted by his sharp intelligence and amused by his volatile and irascible temperament. Irascibility in the end limited his career as a director in Hollywood, which was a pity because he made a group of films distinguished by wit that still glitters after more than half a century; they include two of Adolphe Menjou's best silent films, *Service for Ladies* and *A Gentleman of Paris*.

These two young experts competed fiercely to establish who was the more expert on taste and other matters Parisian. They seldom agreed on anything, as Menjou recalled:

One day Chaplin decided that he wanted some rare dish to be served and discussed in a dinner scene. The technical experts racked their minds to remember some of the exotic and expensive dishes served in Parisian restaurants. Finally one of them had an inspiration – truffle soup with champagne! The second expert refused to sanction such a dish. He had eaten at the best restaurants in Paris but never once had he been served such a *potage* as truffle soup!

But expert number one only curled his lip. 'You have probably failed to dine at the finest restaurant of all,' he replied. 'It is a very small place where a very select clientèle is allowed to dine by invitation only. It is called *La Truffe d'Or* and it is the one place in the world where they serve truffle soup with champagne.'

Expert number two was sure he was being out-experted by sheer imagination, but despite his protests, Chaplin decided that he liked the idea of truffle soup with champagne and ordered the prop man to prepare such a dish. The prop man was stumped. He didn't even know what a truffle was. He refused to admit his ignorance, however, and called up several chefs in the town's best restaurants to try to get a special order of truffle soup. But there were no truffles in all Los Angeles nor was there a chef who would attempt to make imitation truffle soup.

Prop men are always ingenious, however, so we ended up with a horrible concoction that looked like clear soup with several withered objects floating in it. They might even have been truffles, but they were probably some sort of deadly fungi grown in the shade of a *nux vomica* tree. No one ever had nerve enough to taste the truffle soup with champagne, but it was in the picture.[2]

Edward Sutherland remembered that Jim Tully* was already employed at the Chaplin studio:

Jim always thought of himself as kind of an American Gorki. He was an awfully nice man, but having taken an awful beating in his youth, never quite got over the inferiority that this gave him, in spite of the fact that he wrote powerfully. It has been said, I think with some degree of truth, that his subject matter was never up to his talent. He was having an awful time, and Charlie gave him fifty bucks a week so he could eat, and gave him an office at the studio, really to do nothing, just to give him a chance to write . . . There were always people coming in and out, on jobs. Charlie was supposed to be very tough with a buck, but he was always befriending anybody who was really in trouble.[3]

* Tully became a celebrity in the 1920s as the 'hobo' author of *Beggars of Life*, which was filmed in 1928. He also acted in *Way for a Sailor* (1930).

The entourage for *A Woman of Paris* included an artist who was kept on the payroll for most of the film simply to provide the painting of Edna which was to figure in the plot, but he never actually came up with a usable likeness.

The film was not, in the end, to make a great star of Edna; in fact it virtually marked the end of her career. Her role as sophisticated woman of the world destroyed her old image for the public without giving her a new one. It was, however a milestone for Adolphe Menjou, whom Chaplin chose for the role of Pierre Revel. The son of a French-born restaurateur and his Irish wife, Menjou had been acting in films since 1912, but it was only after his return from the war that he began to establish himself as a character actor. He played Louis XIII in Fairbanks' *The Three Musketeers*, the confidant of Rudolph Valentino in *The Sheik*, and was undergoing the colourful experience of playing alongside Pola Negri in *Bella Donna*, when he heard rumours that Chaplin was preparing *A Woman of Paris*. He seemed destined for the part. During Chaplin's brief liaison with Peggy Hopkins Joyce, Peggy had pointed Menjou out to him in a restaurant as having the Parisian style of Henri Letellier. Menjou was friendly with both Sutherland and Bell, both of whom recommended him to Chaplin. For his own part, Menjou was especially attracted to the job after Bell told him that the character 'goes all through the story, and you know what that means on a Chaplin picture. You will have a steady job for months and months.'

Bell warned Menjou that there were other candidates for the part but Menjou determined to have it, and prepared his strategy with care. He discovered that Chaplin was in the habit of lunching on Hollywood Boulevard, at Armstrong-Carlton's or at Musso and Frank's. Menjou made a point of arriving for lunch at the same restaurant and the same time as Chaplin, always wearing an elegant outfit he reckoned would give the impression of a *boulevardier* – morning suit, cutaway, hunting tweeds with Alpine hat, white flannels, white tie and tails. This in itself did not surprise anyone: Hollywood restaurants at lunchtime were regularly filled with movie actors in make-up and costume. It was more conspicuous when he asked a nonplussed waiter, loud enough for Chaplin to hear, for fresh *escargots* in white wine sauce. Either this play-acting or a reel of a Menjou film which Sutherland showed him persuaded Chaplin to interview Menjou. This in itself was unusual: Chaplin usually hated to interview actors because he felt so bad afterwards if he could not give them the job. He found Menjou perfect for the part but was somewhat startled by his salary demands, as Sutherland recalled:

> Chaplin had never paid more than $250 a week in his life, but Mr Menjou insisted on $500 or no contract, and he would not budge an inch, and Charlie finally, reluctantly, gave in. It nearly killed all of us.
>
> We were supposed to start this on a certain date, and time marched on. I had given Menjou a starting date three months hence – perfectly safe to my opinion or anybody's opinion – but we didn't start for another month after that. Menjou came around and said, 'I'm ready,' and I said, 'Well, we're not.'
>
> He said, 'I've got to have my money.'
>
> 'Oh, no, no . . .'
>
> Not an inch would he budge. He had the courage of a lion. We had to pay him, and it's a good thing we did, because it got us started eventually.[4]

Menjou also remembered the incident vividly:

> When I think of it now, my brassiness frightens me. There I was quibbling about a week's salary and my career was hanging in the balance. But Sutherland went to Chaplin and told him what I had said. According to Eddie, Chaplin called me some very unpleasant names, but finally ordered a voucher sent through for my salary. Every week I went down and drew my pay cheque, even though I was not called to work until January 11.[5]

It was still quite usual at that time for actors to provide their own wardrobe, so Menjou spent the interim with his tailors. Chaplin was still planning a scene on a racecourse, so Menjou ordered an expensive grey cutaway and topper. He was greatly irked when it was not used, and three years later had a racetrack scene written into one of his pictures so that he could use the outfit. He also spent half of one week's salary on an opera cloak which was not in the end required.

Shooting began on 27 November 1922 and continued for seven months. Even in this elaborate feature Chaplin worked without a script, a fact which surprised commentators at the time. In fact, by the time he came to shoot the film the scenario, worked out over the preceding months in masses of notes, was so precise in Chaplin's mind that a normal screenplay would have been superfluous, even a distraction. This method of working demanded a very careful documentation of the shooting continuity, and this has survived. It shows that Chaplin, once on the set, worked with confidence and precision. There was nothing tentative or improvisational about the shooting. In a few scenes he shot variants of the action, so that in editing he could select the most effective version. Though he made many takes to get any particular shot right, there was very little outright wastage: only three minor scenes were actually shot but not used. 'Charlie shot pictures as we went along,' said Sutherland.

> We had a basic idea of the story, then we would do the incident every day. We'd shoot for three or four days, then lay off for two weeks and rewrite and perfect it and rehearse it and rarify it. Charlie had the patience of Job. Nothing is too much trouble. A real perfectionist.
>
> With this basis of working, it took us about a year to shoot the picture, because Charlie had another theory that he really believed. He said, 'I shoot a sequence and if I'm not completely happy with it, I shoot it over the next day. That only puts me one day behind schedule.' Well, he didn't figure it put him one day behind schedule every day. That's the way he worked and that's the way he did good pictures, because he could afford to and he was a great perfectionist.[6]

On one occasion after watching the daily rushes Chaplin expressed himself satisfied with one of Menjou's scenes but asked the actor how he liked it. 'I think I can do better,' Menjou replied. 'Great!' said Chaplin. 'Let's go!' and the rest of the day was spent reshooting the scene.

Chaplin's method involved shooting his film in the exact order of the story. It was a method as singular (because so costly) in 1922 as it would be now. Thus the very first shot filmed is the opening shot of the finished film: a long-shot of the house in the little French village where Edna lives, and Edna herself looking out of the window of the bedroom where her stern father has locked her to prevent her seeing her boyfriend Jean.

The brief sequence in the railway station, which has a major place in film history, was filmed between 11 p.m. and 6 a.m. on the night of 29/30 November. The innovation which aroused so much admiring comment when the film appeared was in fact dictated by economy. The scene required Marie to stand on the station as the fateful train for Paris arrives. In order to save the trouble and expense of simulating a French train, Rollie Totheroh simply cut apertures to represent the windows of a train in a ten-foot piece of board, then drew it across the front of a powerful spotlight. The light cast upon Marie's face appeared like the reflection from the lights of a moving train. The effect was done in eight takes.

In this scene Chaplin made a brief appearance as a clumsy porter.

He was not listed as an actor on the credit titles of the film, and in fact he prefaced the film with a title emphasizing that he did not appear. He was heavily disguised and muffled up. Nevertheless audiences found the scene so funny, according to Menjou, that it was necessary to abbreviate it so as not to destroy the mood of the film. Even in its cut form, one reviewer of the time picked it out:

> People laugh at an incident which may occupy three seconds. A baggage smasher enters with a trunk, drops it, and goes out. It is the simplest, unexaggerated incident of a station platform. Its effectiveness is so great as to suggest that the comedian himself was the baggage smasher, although he announces that he took no part in the play. Possibly not, but he knew how to get that baggage smasher to drop a trunk, get a laugh, and be out of it in three seconds.[7]

For four more months the work went on, creating the story, scene after scene, in the exact order in which it would appear on the screen. As the plot progressed to deal with the relationship between Revel and Marie, Chaplin demanded an altogether new style of acting from his players. Adolphe Menjou was never to forget what he learnt from Chaplin at that time:

> Not until we started shooting did I begin to realize that we were making a novel and exciting picture. It was Chaplin's genius that transformed the very ordinary story. Aside from his own great talent as an actor he had the ability to inspire other actors to perform their best. Within a few days I realized that I was going to learn more about acting from Chaplin than I had ever learned from any director. He had one wonderful, unforgettable line that he kept repeating over and over throughout the picture. 'Don't sell it!' he would say. 'Remember, they're peeking at you.'
>
> It was a colourful and concise way to sum up the difference between the legitimate stage and the movies – a reminder that in pictures, when one has an important emotion or thought to express, the camera moves up to his face and there he is on the screen with a head that measures six feet from brow to chin. The audience is peeking at him under a microscope, so he can't start playing to the gallery 200 feet away, because there is no gallery in a movie theatre; the audience is sitting in his lap.
>
> From my early days in movies I had been schooled in the exaggerated gestures and reactions that were thought necessary to tell a story in pantomime. But when I, or any other actor, would give out with one of those big takes, Chaplin would just shake his head and say,'They're peeking at you.' That did it. I knew that I had just cut myself a large slice of ham and had tossed the scene out of the window.

> Since then I have never played a scene before a camera without thinking to myself, 'They're peeking at you; don't sock it.'
>
> Another pet line of Chaplin's was, 'Think the scene! I don't care what you do with your hands or your feet. If you think the scene, it will get over.'
>
> And we had to keep shooting every scene until we *were* thinking it – until we believed it and were playing it with our brains and not just with our hands or our feet or our eyebrows.[8]

The novel style and the expressive restraint which Chaplin sought from his actors was not achieved without pain. Two days and ninety takes were necessary to get the right reactions in a tiny scene, in which Marie, bored, throws down her cigarette and says she will not go out.

Menjou also remembered with mixed feelings shooting a scene with Edna in which they were required to kiss. Menjou had to express passion and yet make it clear that he was not in love with Marie; Edna had to show that the kiss was not objectionable to her, but that she was unhappy and bored. 'It was like engraving the Constitution on the head of a pin – much to be told in a very confined space. To achieve this required so many takes that affectionate proximity to Edna had lost all its charm.' Yet 'it was remarkable how much Chaplin made us tell with just a look, a gesture, a lifted eyebrow.'[9]

Sometimes things went easily. Seen today, the finest moment of Edna's impeccable performance is a scene in which her girlfriends, too gleefully, show her a magazine with an announcement that Revel is to marry a rich heiress. She laughs it off and only the nervy irregularity with which she taps her cigarette indicates the emotion she is repressing. This scene, which seems as remarkable on every re-viewing, was swiftly shot in half a dozen takes at the end of a February afternoon.

The new style of acting which Chaplin demanded was easier for the younger artists than for older and more seasoned performers. For the role of Jean's mother Chaplin cast Lydia Knott who, though she was at the time only forty-eight years old, had made a speciality of playing sweet old ladies ever since her entry into films in 1917. She remained a very busy character player in the 1930s.

> She was a beautiful Madonna-faced old lady with a will of steel. We had a scene where she found out that Carl Miller, her son, was killed, and the Sûreté was asking her the normal questions: 'What was his name?', 'Age?' etc. We wanted a complete, dead, no-reaction from her – wanted

> the audience to supply the emotion, not the actress. I can't tell you how many times we shot it, and she would always do it feeling sorry for herself and smiling sweetly. I don't know how many times we shot it, then finally Charlie determined to get it the way he wanted it – and we were all with him – and he shot it 110 times, and then said 'You shoot it for a while' so I shot it about 100 times, and finally the old lady got so angry that she swore at us and just went through this scene in such a temper that we got it. And I venture to say we shot that scene 500 times. I don't know how many days it took us, about a week, to get that one reaction. I would think that took the record for retakes. In dollars and cents I don't know whether that pays off, but certainly in quality it did.[10]

Unfortunately for legend, Sutherland considerably exaggerates the number of takes. In fact Charlie shot the scene thirty-nine times on Friday 4 May, then brought Miss Knott back on Saturday morning for forty-one more takes. For a single brief shot, however, eighty takes is a lot. Chaplin was not satisfied even then: fifty years later he still shuddered at Lydia Knott's over-acting whenever he saw *A Woman of Paris*.

Non-professional actors could be much more malleable. One of the most memorable figures in *A Woman of Paris* is the stony-faced lady who gives Edna a massage, as Edna's *demi-mondaine* friends (played by Betty Morrissey and Malvina Polo) discuss the latest gossip with her. The camera rises to the face and upper half of the masseuse. From the movement of her arms we can sense which portion of Edna's voluptuous body is receiving attention: her face is set in perpetual disapproval, impassive yet all too evidently soaking in the gossip like blotting paper. The lady was not an actress at all but the studio secretary, Nellie Bly Baker, yet the set of her features and every move is exactly Chaplin; he had schooled her to a perfect imitation. Like little Jackie Coogan, Nellie Bly Baker, as a perfect mimic, provided Chaplin with the acting material most ideal for his purposes: bodies through whom he could convey his own performance. Nellie's performance made such an impression that she left her work at the studio to become a character actress in a few films for other directors.

Chaplin's comedy had always been built upon visual suggestion, metaphor, simile. In the comedies an alarm clock could become a can of gone-off fish, a cow's tail a pump handle, or a man a bird. Adolphe Menjou described how he extended his range of visual symbolism to meet the needs of drama.

> Because of the censorship boards in various states Chaplin had to indicate [the relationship between Pierre Revel and Marie] in a way that would not be obvious or offensive. He accomplished it in a manner that was, at that time, amazingly subtle.
>
> This is the way the scene was developed: Revel came to the girl's luxurious apartment and was admitted by a maid. The audience had no idea who or what this man was in her life. Apparently he was just an admirer calling to take her out to dinner. Chaplin wanted to find some casual piece of business that would suddenly reveal that Revel was a frequent and privileged caller. A good many devices were discussed. First Chaplin had me pick up a pipe from the table and light it, but that was no good because Revel was not the pipe-smoking type. Then he considered having the maid bring me a pair of slippers, but that was out of key because I had called to take Marie out to dinner.
>
> Finally Chaplin thought of the handkerchief business, which solved the problem. I went to a liquor cabinet, took out a bottle of sherry and poured a drink, then sipped it. But when I started to take a handkerchief from my pocket I discovered that I had none, so I turned casually and walked into the bedroom. Edna was at her dressing table, fully dressed but still fussing with her coiffure. I didn't look at her and she paid no attention to me as I crossed to a chiffonier. There I opened a top drawer and took out a large gentleman's handkerchief, put it in my pocket, and walked out. Immediately the relationship was established: we were living together and had been for some time.
>
> It happened that when Chaplin thought of this piece of business, the property man had not dressed the drawers of the chiffonier because he didn't know that they would be used. So I went to my dressing room and brought back several handkerchiefs and one of my dress collars and it fell out of the drawer. This gave Charlie an idea for a later scene in which the maid accidentally dropped a collar and thus disclosed to the girl's former sweetheart that she was living with Revel.
>
> Little touches like this gave the picture a flavour that was new to picturemaking.[11]

Right up until the beginning of June 1923, Chaplin was still puzzled as to how to end the film. He considered letting Marie marry Revel, or alternatively having her return to the village to nurse her now widowed and failing mother. There are notes for a version in which she emigrates to America, and for another where she goes to Canada and devotes herself to Christian works. He considered a railway accident which would give Marie the opportunity to redeem herself by heroism. Both Sutherland and Menjou remembered with unseemly glee a day when Chaplin arrived at the studio with a new solution:

Marie should give up Revel to consecrate herself to a life of penance as a nurse in a leper colony. Chaplin all too accurately sensed the adverse reactions of Bell, Sutherland, Menjou and others of his entourage. Huffily he left the studio and stayed away for several days. When he returned the leper colony was forgotten.

Even without the mute distaste of his collaborators, Chaplin with his gift for selection, rejection, simplification would undoubtedly have quickly seen the faults of his solution. It is illuminating to see how the eventual swift, ironic ending of the film was refined out of a much more elaborate sequence in which Revel was to seek out Marie in her country retreat. Revel was to propose marriage; Marie was to refuse; then,

> 'You know where you can find me. I shall always love you. Goodbye'. They shake hands and look into each other's eyes and the souls of both of them are in that look. Menjou then gets into the car and drives off in the direction he had come, passing on the way a rustic looking farm cart carrying several workers from the fields, one of them playing an accordion and the rest singing a homely folk song to the accompaniment.
>
> Edna looks after Menjou's car and as the farm cart comes abreast the kiddie begs to ride back to the picnic grounds. The workers also urge it and Edna lifting the kid on the cart, gets on it herself and they drive down the road to the tune of the worker's song as Menjou and his fancy car pass out of the picture in the other direction.[12]

By avoiding a sentimental reunion of Marie and Pierre in favour of a scene in which two very different vehicles carry the pair to their separate destinies, Chaplin arrived at the essence.

Unusually intelligent and perceptive men themselves, both Sutherland and Menjou were impressed by Chaplin's talent for selection:

> Chaplin listened to everybody's ideas and evaluated them with an unerring instinct for those that were good. He had no academic knowledge of proper dramatic structure, only an innate comprehension of good theatre and how to portray either simple or complex ideas in pantomime without the aid of dialogue or subtitles. I remember hearing him say in an argument about a certain scene, 'I don't know why I'm right about the scene. I just know I'm right.' And it was true.[13]

'While Chaplin is supposed to be a great intellectual', said Sutherland, '(this will make him furious if he ever hears it) I think that Charlie's intellect is mostly emotion. I think his instincts are magnificent, and

I think his knowledge is perception, feeling, rather than anything else . . .'[14]

The daily studio staff conferences, with their interchange of ideas, were important to Chaplin's creative activity. They were not always fruitful. On one occasion they sat for hours trying to decide whether the better title for the gigolo scene would be 'Who is it?' or 'Who is he?' When everyone was beginning to think that perfectionism can be carried too far, the conference was brought to an end by an Airedale dog which Chaplin kept at the studio and which wandered into the room, listened for a while with its head cocked on one side, and then vomited on the floor.

Nor was Chaplin always right, particularly towards the end of shooting when nerves became frayed. One day the unit was shooting exteriors near Westlake Park (of Keystone days) when it was recognized that in shooting a scene of two actors walking past a building Chaplin was breaking the basic, practical rule that you must never cut to a reverse shot of an actor or group of actors crossing the screen, since it reverses the direction of the action, changes the background and generally confuses the viewer. Sutherland pointed out the error to Chaplin, who was embarrassed to be corrected in front of bystanders and rebuked his critic so forcefully that Sutherland instantly threatened to quit. Next day the rushes revealed the mistake all too clearly, and the chagrined Chaplin had to go out and take the scenes again. On another occasion even the gentle Rollie rebelled when Chaplin, in a mood of irritation, insisted that some shots were out of focus when they quite clearly were not. 'Well, if you can say that is lousy, you'd better get yourself another boy,' Rollie told him. 'I will,' replied Chaplin, and Rollie stormed off.

> The next morning I was sitting on the bench and instead of Charlie driving in through the gates the way he always did, he came into his office through the screen door and I was sitting on the bench outside. He motioned me to come down to him and he turned around and put his behind up in the air and said, 'Kick me in the ass, Rollie.' And I did. And he said, 'You know, I wanted to take that shot over anyhow.'[15]

His moods were a byword. The regular studio staff insisted that they knew his mood at once from the colour of the suit he was wearing, and would telephone his home to find out from the valet what clothes he had put on that morning. His green suit was notorious. 'Every time he wore it all hell broke loose,' said Sutherland. The blue suit with pin stripes portended a jovial, productive day. The grey suit was in between, 'so we would feel our way for a while until a definite mood developed.' As Menjou remarked:

> One or two of the staff had this suit-to-match-the-mood theory developed to a very fine degree. I think they were exaggerating; the only thing I noticed about Charlie's wardrobe was that it was deplorable. His clothes did not fit properly and there was no style to the way he wore them. I inquired one day who his tailor was, thinking that I would take great pains to avoid the fellow. To my horror Charlie confessed that he had no tailor, that he hated tailors. He had never had a tailored suit in his life![16]

Chaplin explained that he could not bear to waste time being fitted, so just walked into a good men's store and ordered half a dozen ready-made suits for convenience. 'I believe him. He looked terrible in his clothes. That was a long time ago. Since then he has outgrown this attitude.'[17]

The final scene of the film, with Revel and his secretary speeding down the country road,was shot on Monday 25 June. The editing was completed one year, one month and fourteen days after Chaplin had first begun work on the scenario. He had shot a total of 3,862 takes, amounting to 130,115 feet, which were reduced in the finished film to 7,557 feet. The total cost of the production was $351,853.

In the course of production the title had changed from *Destiny* to *Public Opinion*. Alternative titles considered before the choice eventually fell on *A Woman of Paris* included *Melody of Life*, *The Joy Route*, *Social Customs*, *Human Nature*, *Love, Ladies and Life* and *The Stars Incline*. Chaplin prefaced the film with a title which might have been the motto of many of his films: 'The world is not composed of heroes and villains, but of men and women with all the passions that God has given them. The ignorant condemn but the wise pity.'

The première on 26 September 1923 was the opening attraction of the Criterion Theatre on Grand Avenue and 7th Street in Hollywood. 'The most aristocratic showplace in Hollywood', the theatre had been decorated and furnished without regard to cost. 'The inside resembles a Byzantine jewel box. Walls of antique stone in colours of gray and silver, with bolder hues like mellow sunlight caught without.' The première was one of the most glittering occasions of the era. The guests included Fairbanks, Pickford, Irving Thalberg, the De Milles, Will Rogers and most of the other ruling stars of Hollywood as well as the Mayor, fire chief and civic dignitaries of Los Angeles. Old acquaintances of the star included Mack Sennett, Mabel Normand, Jackie Coogan and Mildred Harris. The musical accompaniment was conducted by Adolf Tandler, former director of the Los Angeles Symphony Orchestra; and Chaplin had himself devised a special live mimed prologue entitled *Nocturne*. Menjou was convinced of the film's success when he heard loud stage whispers of 'Wonderful! Terrific!' from the Irish-born director Herbert Brenon, and when outside the theatre Harold Lloyd, whom he had never met, clasped his hands above his head in a congratulatory handshake and grinned his compliments across the heads of the crowd that separated them.

Chaplin and Edna did not attend the première: they were already on the train for New York where the film was to be premièred at the Lyric Theatre on 1 October. For that show Chaplin had written a special programme note which revealed his growing anxiety about the public's reaction to the film: it was certainly not his usual style to ask for comments from his audiences:

> No doubt while you are waiting I can have a little heart to heart talk with you. I've been thinking that the public wants a little more realism in pictures, whereby a story is pursued to the logical ending. I would like to get your ideas on the subject, for I am sure that those of us who are producing pictures do not know – we only guess.
>
> In my first serious drama, *A Woman of Paris*, I've striven for realism, true to life. What you will see is life as I personally see it – the beauty – the sadness – the touches – the gaiety, all of which are necessary to make life interesting. However, it is not for me to say that I am right. My first thoughts have been to entertain you. The story is intimate, simple and human, presenting a problem as old as the ages – showing it with as much truth as I am allowed to put into it – giving it a treatment as near realism as I have been able to devise.
>
> I do not wish that *A Woman of Paris* should appear as a preachment, nor am I expounding a sort of philosophy, unless it be an appeal for a better understanding of human frailties.
>
> After all, you are the judge, and your taste must be served. To some it may look as though I have not taken full advantage of dramatic possibilities, while others may see good taste in the strength of repression, and by your reception will I guide myself in the future.
>
> I was over seven months making *A Woman of Paris* and I enjoyed every moment of the time. However, if I have failed in my effort to

entertain you, I feel it will be my loss. Nevertheless I enjoyed making it, and sincerely hope you will enjoy seeing it.

Sincerely,
CHARLES CHAPLIN

Few films have ever enjoyed such unanimous enthusiasm from the press. Chaplin was freely compared to Hardy, to de Maupassant and to Ibsen, though generally they thought him a good deal better than Ibsen because, having long demonstrated that comedy is never far removed from tragedy, Chaplin now showed that tragedy could have its share of gaiety. Robert Sherwood in the *New York Herald* wrote:

> There is more real genius in Charles Chaplin's *A Woman of Paris* than in any picture I have ever seen . . . Charles Chaplin has proved many times that he understands humanity; he has leavened his hilariously broad comedy with elements of poignant tragedy. He has caught and conveyed the contrast between joy and sorrow which makes existence on this terrestrial ball as interesting as it is.

The critic of *Exceptional Photoplays* wrote that

> Mr Chaplin . . . has not done anything radical or anything esoteric. He has merely used his intelligence in the highest degree, an act which has ceased to be expected of motion picture people for many years. He has written and directed a story in which all the characters act upon motives which the spectator immediately recognizes as natural and sincere, and therefore *A Woman of Paris* breathes an atmosphere of reality, and thereby holds the attention of any perceptive audience in thrall . . .
>
> *A Woman of Paris* has the one quality almost every other motion picture that has been made to date lacks – restraint. The acting is moving without ever being fierce, the story is simple and realistic without ever being inane, the settings are pleasing and adequate without ever being colossally stupid. The result is a picture of dignity and intelligence and the effect is startling because it is so unusual.

When the film reached Britain, the critic of the *Manchester Guardian* called it 'the greatest modern story that the screen has yet seen . . .

> He has had the courage to throw the sum total of screen convention on the scrap heap.'

As most critics pointed out, there was nothing very new about the plot: when Chaplin first recounted it to Menjou, he thought it 'a trite bit of schmaltz'. What made it so startling for audiences of its own time was the novelty of its characters, who observed none of the rules of screen drama. The heroine was no better than she should be; the villain was likeable, charming, generous and considerate; the hero was a mother-dominated weakling; and all the tragedy was precipitated by the folly, blindness and selfishness of parents – who as a class the screen had hitherto held in superstitious reverence.

After sixty years it is difficult to appreciate the first surprise of Chaplin's new methods of story telling, new style of acting and new sophistication of the expressive means of pantomime; his innovations were all rapidly assimilated to become part of the common practice of film craft. Chaplin's own approach to his discoveries, too, had been so simple in its logic: 'As I have noticed life in its dramatic climaxes,' he told an interviewer in New York, 'men and women try to hide their emotions rather than seek to express them. And that is the method I have pursued in an endeavour to become as realistic as possible.'

Inaugurating a whole new style of comedy of manners, *A Woman of Paris* opened the way for the director Ernst Lubitsch, who confessed himself overwhelmed by the film, which he saw just as he was embarking on his own satirical masterpiece, *The Marriage Circle*. Every film maker studied Chaplin's discoveries: the future work of Sutherland, Bell, de Limur and d'Arrast all bears the clear mark of their experience with Chaplin. Menjou summed up his own impressions:

> To him motion pictures were a new art form and required the painstaking care that any art requires. Of course he happened also to be an artist. Everyone who has worked with Chaplin the actor or with Chaplin the director seems to agree on that point, regardless of what he may think of him personally.
>
> The word 'genius' is used very carelessly in Hollywood, but when it is said of Chaplin, it is always with a special note of sincerity. If Hollywood has ever produced a genius, Chaplin is certainly first choice.[18]

The éclat of the New York première made up for missing the Hollywood gala. Two days afterwards Chaplin made his first radio broadcast, from L. Bamberger's WOR Studio in Newark, under the sponsorship of the *Morning Telegraph*. 'My friends,' he began, 'this is all way beyond me. I'm glad you can't see me – I am nervous as a witch.' In the course of the broadcast, which lasted half an hour, he told the listeners that he was experimenting with the possibilities of voice on the air. He then played the violin and saxophone and did some impersonations.

On 5 October he went to hear Lloyd George speak at City Hall, and was deeply embarrassed when his own presence completely stole the audience's attention from the great British politician. He even stole the thunder of three bandits who robbed the jewellery store at the Ritz Carlton where he was staying: just because he happened to walk through the lobby a few minutes after the crime, it was Chaplin who made the headlines in all the newspaper reports. On the way back he stopped at Detroit. Again poor Herbert Hoover, who was on the same train, was upstaged and even found difficulty getting someone to carry his bags, so taken up was everyone with the excitement of seeing Chaplin.

Later Chaplin went on the platform with Hoover and the President of the Rockefeller Foundation at the first Annual General Meeting of the American Child Health Association, and gave a message to the children of the nation: 'Brush your teeth every day so that you'll always be proud to laugh. And remember that as long as you can laugh you're happy and happiness means much towards good health.' The two hundred children in the audience needed some convincing that he really was Chaplin, since they did not recognize him without his moustache and big boots. He received a visit from Henry and Edsel Ford. 'I have come twenty miles from Dearborn to see you,' grunted Ford. 'That's nothing,' Chaplin told him, 'I came all the way from Los Angeles to see you.'[19]

The euphoria of the premières, the press and this royal progress was soon to be dashed. The Hollywood run of *A Woman of Paris* ended after only four weeks. After the first few days, Chaplin's film proved to be a failure at the box office. The New York run actually lost money. In Hollywood and London the film barely covered its guarantee. Such a thing had never happened to a Chaplin film before. Ironically, it was probably the enthusiasm of the press that had killed the film. The critics told the public that the picture was great art, but Chaplin's audience were not interested in him as a great artist: they liked him because he was funny. Moreover, they were clearly not disposed to pay money to see a Chaplin film in which he didn't appear, except heavily disguised in a walk-on part of two or three seconds. Chaplin's disappointment was intense and lasting. As soon as he was able, he withdrew the picture from circulation and hid it in his vaults, unseen, for more than half a century. He loved *A Woman of Paris* and was proud of it, and was not inclined to expose himself again to this snub from his public.

COMING: Cynthia Stockley's "PONJOLA" with James Kirkwood and Anna Q. Nilsson

A NATIONAL INSTITUTION

Direction of JOSEPH PLUNKETT

MOE MARK, President and General Manager

FIRE NOTICE.—Look around now and choose the nearest exit to your seat. In case of fire, walk, not run, to the exit. Do not try to beat your neighbor to the street.

THOS. J. DRENNAN, Fire Commissioner.

PROGRAM

WEEK COMMENCING SUNDAY, NOVEMBER 4th, 1923

CHAPLIN WEEK

1. PRELUDE
   MARK STRAND SYMPHONY ORCHESTRA
   CARL EDOUARDE, Conductor
   John Ingram, Associate Conductor

2. MARK STRAND TOPICAL REVIEW
   Pictorial News of the World, presented as fast as modern equipment can deliver.
   (At 1:55, 3:52, 7:25 and 9:34 P. M.)

3. PROLOGUE to "A WOMAN OF PARIS"
   (a) "Fascination" (Valse) .... Marchetti
   Mlles. Ames, Hixon, Bawn, Loraine, Dickson and Mahurin.
   (b) "Aime Moi" .... Bemberg
   Estelle Carey, Soprano
   (c) "Celebrated Minuet" .... Boccherini
   Mlle. Klementowicz and M. Bourmann
   (d) "Meditation" .... Massenet
   Madeleine MacGuigan, Violinist
   Anatole Bourmann, Ballet Master
   (Premier Piano Used).
   (At 4:00, 7:33 and 9:42 P. M.)

PROGRAM SUBJECT TO CHANGE WITHOUT NOTICE.

PROGRAM (Continued)

The Mark Strand takes great pleasure in presenting

"A WOMAN OF PARIS"

A Drama of Fate

Featuring

EDNA PURVIANCE

Written and Directed by

CHARLES CHAPLIN

Released by United Artists Corp.

CAST

Marie St. Clair	Edna Purviance
Pierre Revel	Adolphe Menjou
John Millet	Carl Miller
His Mother	Lydia Knott
His Father	Charles French
Marie's Father	Clarence Geldert
Fifi and Paulette, Friends of Marie	Betty Morrissey and Malvina Polo

(At 2:03, 4:12, 5:58, 7.43 and 9:52 P. M.)

5. A Chaplin Revival
   CHARLES CHAPLIN
   in one of his funniest pictures
   "PAY DAY"
   A First National Attraction

ORGAN SOLO

PERCY J. STARNES, Mus. Doc. } Organists
RALPH S. BRAINARD

The Entire Program Arranged and Produced by JOSEPH PLUNKETT

COMING: "FLAMING YOUTH" with Colleen Moore, Milton Sills, Elliott Dexter

MAURICE TOURNEUR'S PRODUCTION "JEALOUS HUSBANDS"

1923 - Programme for *A Woman of Paris*.

To exacerbate the pain there was the activity of the official guardians of the nation's morals. New York's Board of Censors approved the film without changes, but in Kansas, where cigarette smoking was regarded with the same horror as Dreiser's novels and bootleg liquor, all scenes that showed people smoking were excised. The Pennsylvania censors, who had a not unreasonable aversion to firearms, cut out the scene of Jean's suicide, thus confusing the plot somewhat. Ohio achieved most notoriety, as a result of the action taken by the State Director of Education and Head of the Board of Censors, a Vernon M. Riegel. Mr Riegel admitted the artistic merits of the film but regretted that the leading characters behaved in a fashion so unacceptable. He therefore set about making them conduct themselves 'as a lady and gentleman should conduct themselves toward one another', by cutting out a number of scenes and adding a title to explain that Marie's opulent style of living in Paris was made possible only by a bequest from a wealthy aunt. Maryland took up the idea, restoring Marie's respectability by attributing her luxurious accessories to her earnings as a popular actress.

Work on a film ordinarily left Chaplin no time for private life, but the period of *A Woman of Paris* was exceptional, thanks to the irruption into Hollywood of Pola Negri. Her screen career had flourished in Germany thanks to her association with the director Ernst Lubitsch. Lubitsch's *Madame Dubarry* – retitled for America *Passion* – brought international celebrity and offers from Hollywood. Paramount won her, and she arrived in September 1922 to begin work. Immediately she informed the press of her eagerness to be reunited with 'Sharlee', whom she had met briefly in Berlin the previous year. As Negri was to remember:

> We spent four delightful days together in Berlin on the occasion of his first visit to Germany.
>
> I was completely captivated by his gaiety, but as he did not speak more than three words of German and at that time I did not speak more than three words of English, our conversation was rather limited. In fact, I don't think we thought of love.
>
> But now, as I look back on our meeting, I know that my love for him began on that fateful night at the Palais Heinroth.[20]

Chaplin too admitted:

> It began in Berlin, a year and a half ago. I fell in love with Pola the instant I met her and the only reason I didn't tell her so was because I was too bashful to confess it. I did tell her she was the loveliest lady I had ever met and I'm sure she must have guessed the secret of my heart.
>
> But for nearly a year an ocean separated us – and an ocean is an awful bar to a successful love affair.[21]

Despite such touching protestations, Chaplin managed to avoid meeting Pola during her first weeks in Hollywood. Later he explained gallantly: 'I have purposely avoided her when she first arrived in Hollywood for I felt that it would result exactly as it has. Isn't it strange how we instinctively feel the fate that is about to overtake us?'[22]

The fateful meeting eventually could be postponed no longer: it took place at the Actors' Fund Pageant at the Hollywood Ball in October 1922. Pola was playing Cleopatra and Chaplin was conducting the orchestra. Even at this stage he must have been putting off the moment, because Pola recalled,

> Strangely enough we missed each other at rehearsals – it was not until the actual performance that I saw him wielding his baton. And as I walked toward him I looked into his face.
>
> It was then that I realized that I had been in love with him for more than a year – without being aware of it. I could hardly wait until the pageant was over to see him. And later he confided to me that he had experienced the same feeling at exactly the same time.
>
> Of course, after the performance we met. The following day he called at my home and since then, except when business or social duties prevented, we have been inseparable.
>
> We understand each other perfectly, and I am sure we will be happy. For my Charlie is not only the dearest boy in the world, but the cleverest. He is a genius.[23]

Chaplin, with not much alternative, corroborated Pola's story:

> . . . when I saw Pola in all her glorious beauty as she swept toward me that fateful day of the great pageant I could not resist her any longer. Something I can't describe surged all over inside of me. I felt like a drowning man – yet excited as I had never been before.
>
> And it was not long before I confessed my love, and, to my happiness and surprise, I learned that Pola felt the same way about me.[24]

From this time the two stars were inseparable and for the next nine months news and rumours of the on-and-off romance were to delight American newspaper readers and embarrass poor Chaplin. By the end of November the press were asking him to confirm whether they were going to marry. 'I can't say yes,' he replied cagily; 'any such announcement must of necessity come from her. Neither can I say no: think of the position that would put her in.' On 25 January 1923 Jesse Lasky, on behalf of Paramount Studios, announced that there was nothing in Pola's contract which presented any obstacle to her marrying Chaplin. He did not add that such a marriage would be exceedingly advantageous for the star's publicity. Three days later, on 28 January, Chaplin and Pola invited the press to the Del Monte Lodge suite of the Countess Domaska – Pola's title by a marriage just ended by special Vatican dispensation. Chaplin was reported to be looking rather ill when he arrived by train, but Pola was pronounced 'exquisite . . . exotic . . . Her paleness, comparable only to the creamy texture of the leaf of a camellia blossom, contrasted sharply with the vivid crimson of her lips. Happiness burned in her expressive eyes of greenish gray. She was clad in a simple black velvet suit with a vestee of old lace and a black velvet tam.'

When the press were admitted to Pola's drawing room, they found her snuggling on the shoulder of Chaplin, whom they described as 'squirming' with embarrassment and confusion. He was tongue-tied, but Pola's volubility made up for that:

> 'I am a European woman. I do not understand zee custom but I am – we are – what you say? – Mr Chaplin and I are engaged. We are to be married.'
>
> In these words, Pola, in hesitant and dulcet words, for the first time officially announced the engagement.
>
> Charlie blushed, swallowed hard and affirmed the marriage compact in answer to a little shake and Pola's question:
>
> 'Eez zat not so, Sharlie?'
>
> 'Sharlie' gulped. A bridegroom blush swept up to his gray temples. He opened his lips. He was speechless. Another gulp.
>
> 'Yes,' was his sole historical utterance.
>
> Then Pola buried her face on his shoulder. 'Sharlie's' arm stole protectively about her. The gorgeous diamond on Pola's ring finger sparkled happily . . .[25]

Pola kept on talking. When the press men asked Chaplin when the happy event would take place, he referred the question to his fiancée:

> We are to marry – when I do not know. Perhaps after my contract has feenished. Perhaps before. We do not know and have not decided . . .
>
> We have been engaged for a long time, but we decided to say nossing about it. We felt it was our affair and not zee world's. But newspaper men have been so-o-o persistent, and since we wanted this one day together without being haunted we decided to tell you so that you could all tell zee people.[26]

Rumour and speculation only increased after the announcement. It was said that the couple had actually married a year before in Europe, and that Pola had signed a telegram 'Pola Negri Chaplin'. The rumours were denied. Five weeks later zee people read that the engagement was broken off and that Pola was prostrate with grief. The cause was a newspaper report that Chaplin had said that he was 'too poor to marry just now. This is a workaday world and we've all got to stay busy and keep away from the climaxes of sentiment' – which seemed a rather apt description of Pola. Pola countered with much-photographed tears and a typewritten statement declaring that she was 'too poor to marry Charles Chaplin; he needs a wealthy woman.' Orally she added, 'There were a thousand things. It was another experience. I have learned. Now I will live only for my work. As for the rest, the happy days are dead for me. It is all over.'

Six hours afterwards it was all on again. Chaplin denied that he had said anything of the sort and drove to Pola for a conference of reconciliation. Afterwards, in the small hours of 2 March, Pola told newsmen that she was 'too happy to sleep' and that Chaplin had told her 'he loved me and could not live without me'.

Chaplin corroborated his repentance in an interview with one of the best Hollywood reporters, Karl K. Kitchen. His assessment of Pola's matrimonial assets and likely domestic virtues might seem, given all the evidence, a trifle exaggerated. His statement is more interesting for his very realistic view of his own ambitions and potential shortcomings as a husband:

> I have always wanted to be married, to have a real home, with children. I have wanted this more than anything in the world. And for years I had hoped that I would meet the right woman – a woman with sympathy, understanding, affection and at the same time possessed of beauty, charm and intelligence.
>
> Until I met Pola this ideal woman remained a dream. Today she is a reality.
>
> I can understand my love for Pola, for she is everything I have ever dreamed of. But why she should love me is something I will never understand. I lack the physique, the physical strength that a beautiful woman admires. However, perhaps it is best that I do not question the gifts of the gods.
>
> I will be a difficult husband to live with – for when I am at work I give every ounce of myself to my task. My wife will have to show great understanding – great sympathy. And my wife must trust me – there must be mutual trust, mutual freedom from suspicion, or there can be no happiness. Understanding – that's the great thing in married life. And that is what Pola and I have in common.[27]

Chaplin's assessment of the desiderata and difficulties of marriage might be ideally applied to his last and brilliantly successful union. It is fascinating however to find it stated at this period of his life and strange to find it applied to Pola, who seems not to have been the marrying kind, as Chaplin was to recognize in the course of the succeeding months.

The next disruption in the relationship came with the Marina Varga affair. Marina was a somewhat disturbed young Mexican woman with a desire to go into pictures and an excessive fan-worship of Chaplin. Having run away from her husband in Vera Cruz and crossed the border without papers, disguised as a boy, she presented herself at the studio, where she was sent off by Kono. The same night, however, she managed somehow to make her way to Chaplin's bedroom and to enter not only his bed but also his pyjamas. She was discovered by Kono while Chaplin and Pola were dining downstairs with Chaplin's friends and neighbours, Dr and Mrs Reynolds. (Dr Reynolds was a good conversationalist, a poor amateur actor and a brain surgeon. It was a standing joke that there was not much material in Hollywood for him to work on in this professional capacity.) Kono persuaded Marina to dress, with the promise that Chaplin would then speak to her; after Chaplin had talked kindly to her under the unfriendly gaze of Pola, Marina was persuaded to leave the house.

Next day Marina was again seen around the Chaplin grounds. According to her own account, she subsequently despaired of winning her idol, went to a neighbouring drug store, asked for arsenic, and swallowed whatever it was the store clerk gave her. She then took herself to Chaplin's garden to lie down and die, having first scattered an offering of roses around the front steps. She was discovered and carried into a laundry room where Dr Reynolds examined her and concluded that her distressed state was due to hysteria rather than poison. Chaplin and Pola again met her. This time however Chaplin's rival admirers, volatile Mexican and temperamental Pole, started an altercation. It quickly became so ferocious that Chaplin (so it was said) had to cool them down with a pail of cold water. Marina was removed to the Receiving Hospital where the physicians could discover no symptoms of poisoning. At the Alexandria Hotel, where she was staying, her luggage was found to consist of little more than copies of telegrams to the Mexican Secretary of War and the Inspector General of Police asking them for financial aid. On being discharged from the hospital, Marina went directly to the offices of the *Los Angeles Examiner*, where she co-operatively posed for photographs. She was rewarded next day with front-page headlines: 'GIRL TRIES TO DIE FOR LOVE IN CHARLIE CHAPLIN'S HOUSE'.

Chaplin addressing a Bond rally in Wall Street, 1918.

Chaplin at a Bond rally in Washington, 1918.
Also in the group are Franklin D. Roosevelt,
Secretary of the Navy, Douglas Fairbanks and
Mary Pickford, and (next to Chaplin), Marie Dressler.

Above: *Shoulder Arms*: Set for the abandoned prologue.

Centre: *Shoulder Arms*: Set for the abandoned epilogue, 'The Banquet'.

Right: *Shoulder Arms*: Chaplin getting into his tree costume.

ıaplin with Dorothy Rosher during the
aking of *The Bond*.

ght: *The Bond* (1918): Chaplin and Edna. This
ot shows particularly clearly the remarkable
:pressionist style of the decors.

break during filming of *The Bond*. In the
reground Henry Bergman, as John Bull, is
atting to Sydney, as the Kaiser.

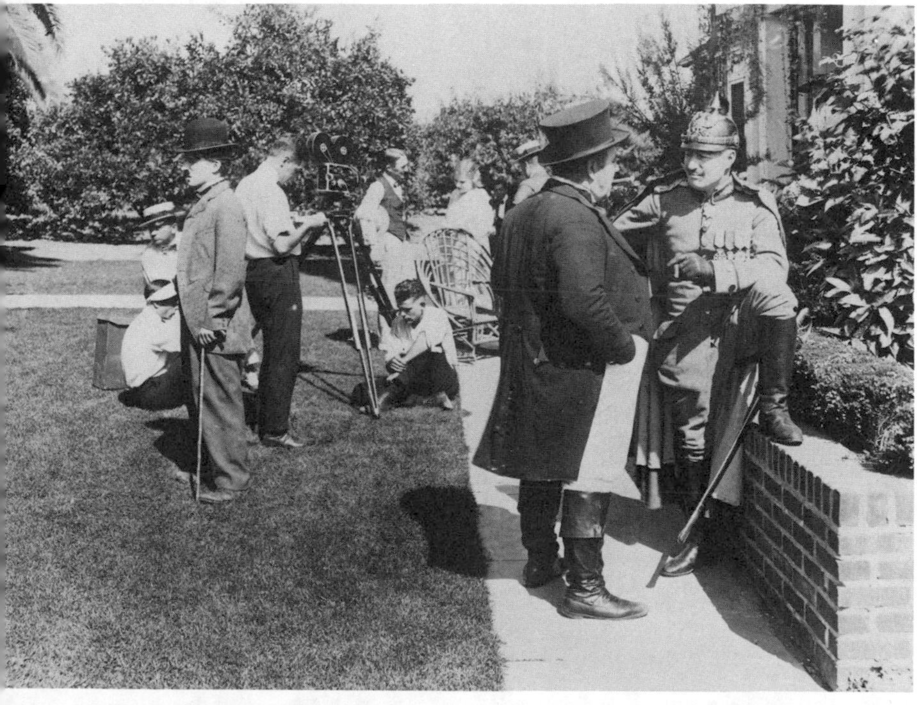

An impetuous visitor: Douglas Fairbanks vaults the gate of the Chaplin Studio.

Below left: Tea break during shooting of *Sunnyside*.

Mildred Harris Chaplin, 1918.

A Day's Pleasure: Edna sits on the pavement outside the studio chatting to the children in the cast. At this point she had no role in the film: the part of Chaplin's wife was to be played by Tom Wood, who can be glimpsed wearing a woman's straw hat, behind Chaplin.

The Kid: Chaplin, with wings, practices flying.

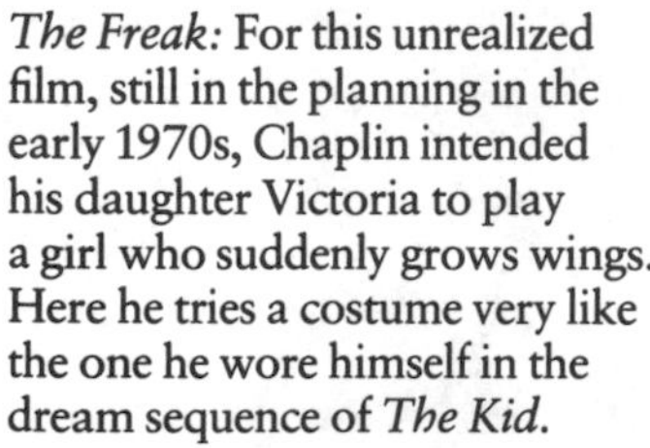

The Freak: For this unrealized film, still in the planning in the early 1970s, Chaplin intended his daughter Victoria to play a girl who suddenly grows wings. Here he tries a costume very like the one he wore himself in the dream sequence of *The Kid.*

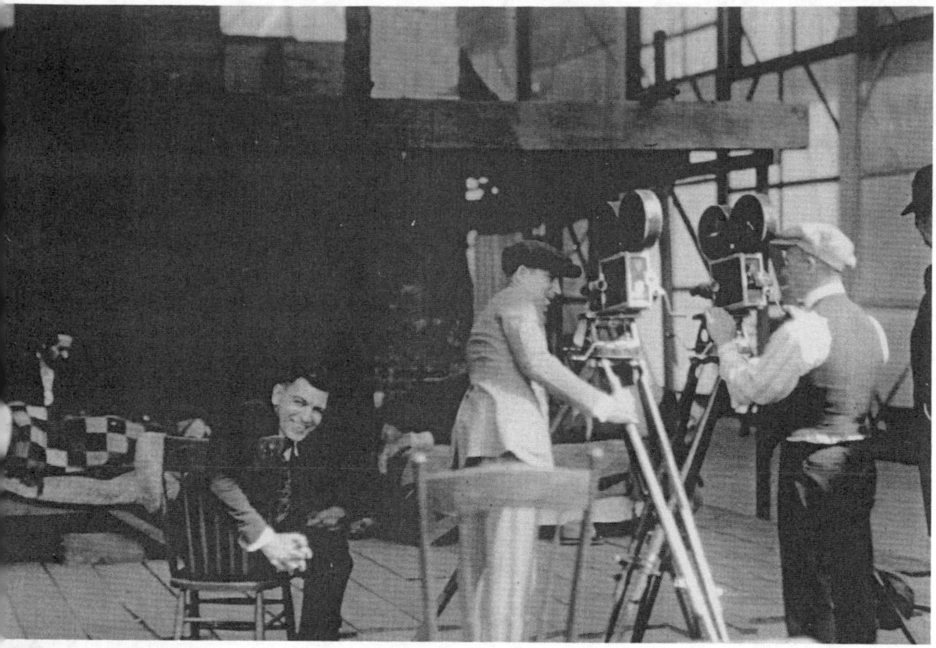

The Professor: Hitherto unknown photographs taken during the shooting of the dosshouse scene.

The Kid: Chaplin with Jackie Coogan, Edith Wilson and her baby. Edith Wilson was the wife of Jack Wilson, the second cameraman, who wrote on the back of this photograph: 'Charlie thanking Edith for taking part in his picture. She was paid $15 for 4 hours work. Not bad, eh?'

Handing over the negative of *The Kid*: left to right: A First National executive; Sol Lesser; Alf Reeves, with cheque; Chaplin; another First National executive; Sydney. The First National men show every sign of having come off worse in the financial negotiations.

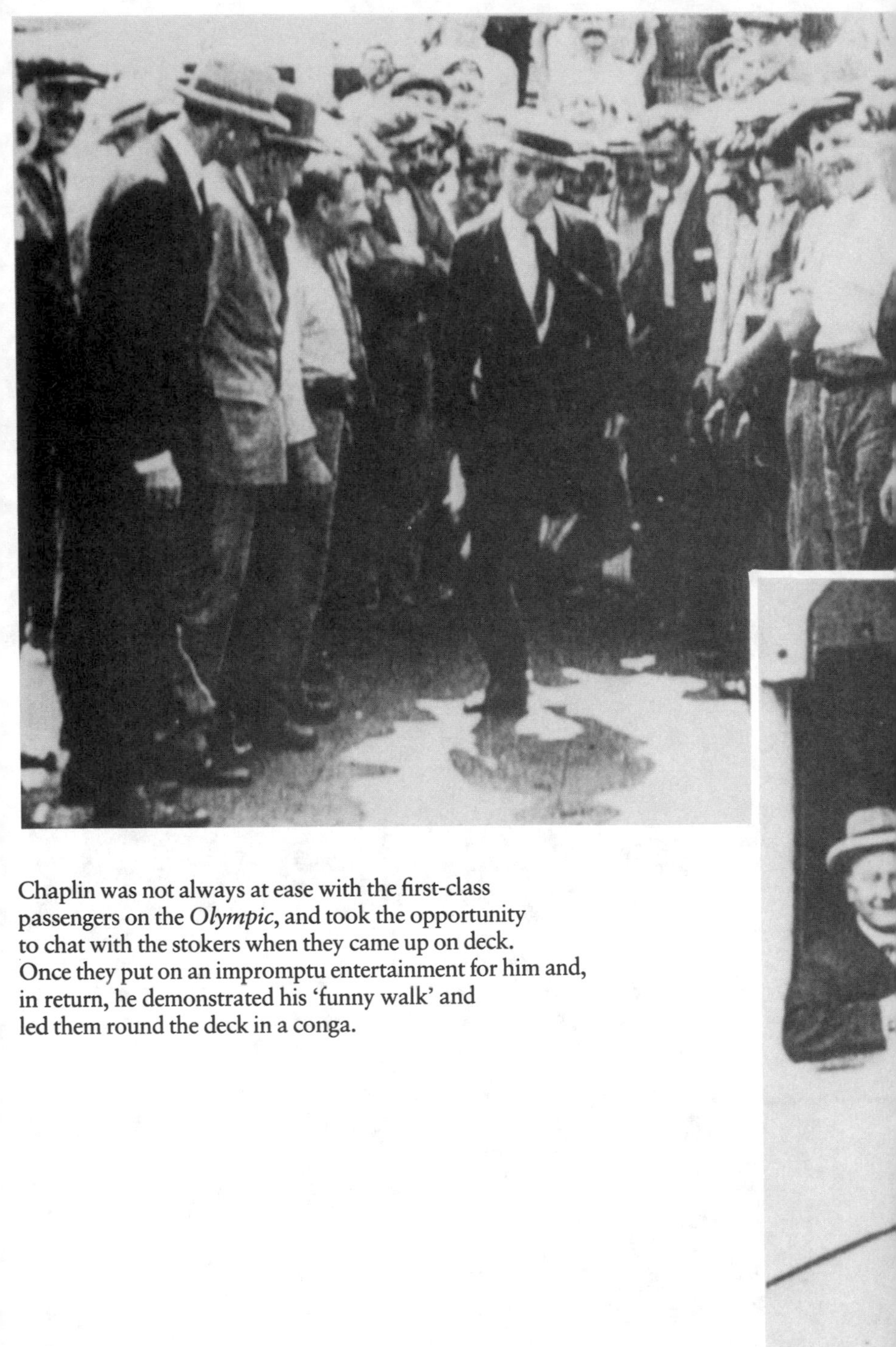

Chaplin was not always at ease with the first-class passengers on the *Olympic*, and took the opportunity to chat with the stokers when they came up on deck. Once they put on an impromptu entertainment for him and, in return, he demonstrated his 'funny walk' and led them round the deck in a conga.

Chaplin leaving the *Olympic* at Southampton.
He was mobbed by crowds as he arrived.

Portrait of Max Linder dedicated by Linder to 'The King of All Directors'.

Chaplin directs Lord Louis Mountbatten in an improvised film – *Nice and Friendly*.

Chaplin in his cutting room, c. 1920.

Lady Mountbatten in *Nice and Friendly*.

Pola Negri

Above right: *A Woman of Paris* (1923): A Bohemian party.

Right: *A Woman of Paris* (1923): Lydia Knott, Carl Miller, Edna Purviance.

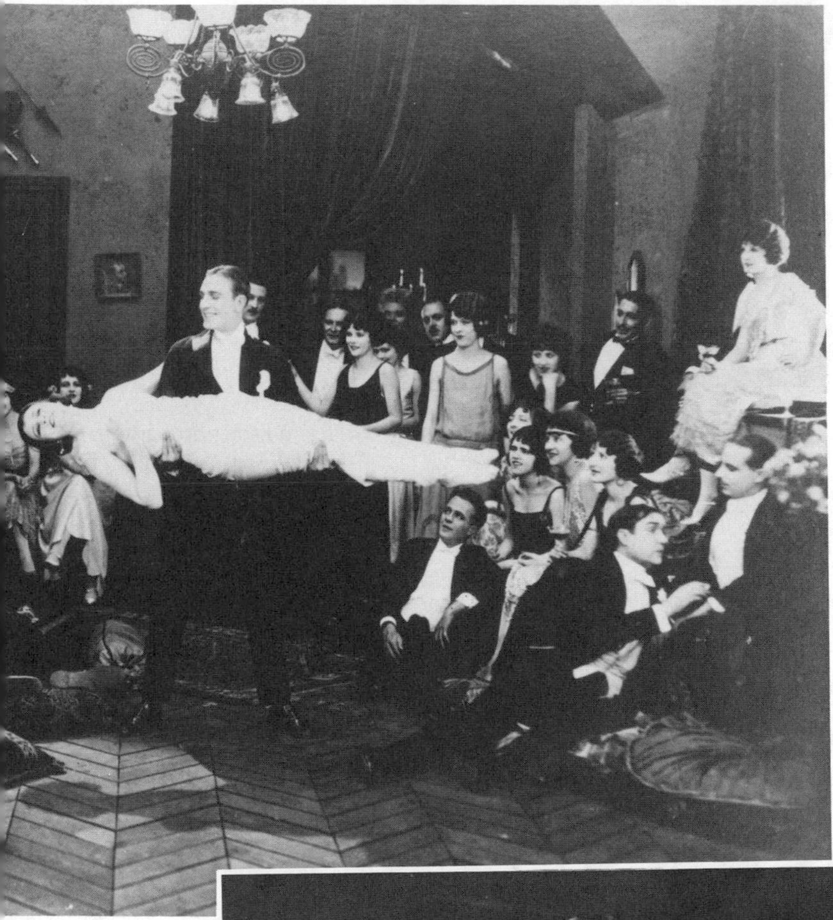

The United Artists: Douglas Fairbanks, Mary Pickford, Chapli and D.W. Griffith with Mr Price.

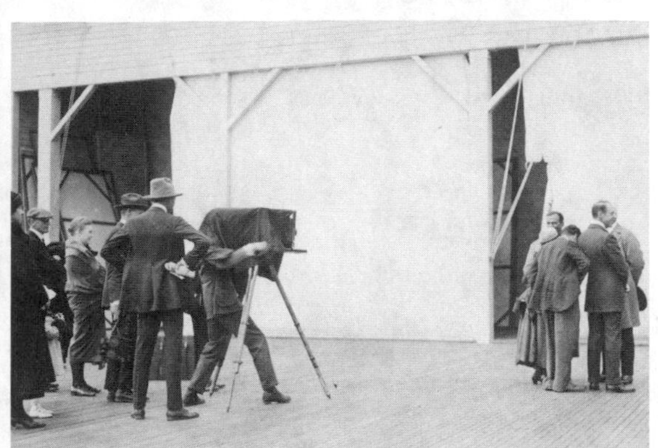

Jack Wilson photographs the four United Artists (Chaplin, Fairbanks Pickford and Griffith). Mr Biby, the studio manager, is beside the camera; Edna in shawl behind.

Below: Chaplin rehearsing for a recording with Abe Lyman's orchestra, 1925.

Pola was highly displeased with the whole incident. There were clearly other rifts in the harmony. As Rodney Ackland wrote years later. 'She had a blind and uncritical admiration of her own genius in the blaze of which her sense of humour evaporated like a dew-drop on a million-watt arc lamp.' Chaplin's sense of humour however was not to be quenched. Menjou, a generally reliable witness, described an incident which cannot have furthered the romance, given the temperaments involved. At a party Pola, overcome by some passing emotion, swooned decorously. The rest of the guests ran for water to revive her but Chaplin, not to be upstaged, lay down on the hearth rug and calmly swooned beside her. Pola, reviving swiftly, did not appreciate it.

On 28 July the comedy was officially pronounced ended. A night or two before, at the reopening of the Ambassador's Coconut Grove, Chaplin and Pola had sat at separate tables. He was with the young actress Leonore Ulric; she was with the tennis star William Tilden. They did not acknowledge each other. The loyal *Examiner* interviewed Pola:

> 'I realized five weeks ago that it was an impossibility. He's a charming fellow. We're still friends. I say "hello" to him but I realize now I could never have married him – he is too temperamental – as changing as the wind – he dramatizes everything – he experiments in love.
>
> 'In my opinion Mr Chaplin should never marry. He has not any quality for matrimony. I am glad it is over for it was interfering with my life, my work. I have great ambitions and I am sure that I could not be a great actress as Mrs Chaplin.
>
> 'I am glad it is over and I have profited by the experience.'
>
> Here she wrote 'finis' on Mr Chaplin, her 'Sharlie' of other days, by assailing a peach. It takes perfect self control for a screen star to attack a juicy peach when she has her make-up on, but she did it daintily. Actresses, especially Europeans, are great two-handed eaters, but here Pola excels them as well. She disposed of each peach as surely, as completely as she had disposed of Charlie Chaplin.

For the newspapers and their readers the Chaplin–Negri romance had been a delectable farce. The statements of the principals, however, at moments seem to intimate genuine feeling and genuine pain. We can now never know how much love there was between these two exceptional and certainly irreconcilable temperaments. They were, after all, the King of Comedy and the Tragedy Queen. In later years both monarchs tended to disclaim their own roles in the affair. Negri, in her memoirs, said that the persistence was all on Chaplin's side: she was not really attracted to him, though she enjoyed his conversation. Chaplin said that the party most interested in the match was the Paramount publicity department, who pressed him to marry her because the bad publicity of broken engagements might be injurious to the company's investment in her. Chaplin drily replied that since he held no Paramount stock, he saw no reason why he should marry her. Pola's subsequent marriage to Prince Serge Mdivani was one of the great social events of twenties Hollywood. She returned to Europe in the thirties but was back to the United States in 1943. After retiring to San Antonio, Texas, she made only one further screen appearance, in Walt Disney's *The Moonspinners* (1964).

The colourful and comic Negri affair was a singular episode in Chaplin's life. It was the only time that he was voluntarily involved in a relationship that attracted to his private life the kind of publicity he ordinarily abhorred; and it was the only time in his career that he permitted himself to be simultaneously engaged in the production of a film and the entanglements of a dramatic romance. Since there is no doubt about Chaplin's concern with and concentration on *A Woman of Paris* during this period, an attractive possibility suggests itself to explain Chaplin's susceptibility to the distractions of Pola. Perhaps they were not in fact distractions. Whether Chaplin was conscious of it or not, Pola may have served to provide the atmosphere of 'contintental' sophistication which he needed for his film, which he certainly achieved in it and which could not have been supplied by Peggy Hopkins Joyce, the country girl from Virginia. It would not have been the only time an artist combined or confused romance and research.

During the period of their romance, Pola had taken a keen interest in the preparations of Chaplin's new house on Summit Drive, no doubt anticipating the day when she would be its mistress. Chaplin had finally yielded to the pleas of Douglas Fairbanks and Mary Pickford that he should build a permanent home after eight years of living in hotels and rented houses. The site he chose, with their help, was a six-and-a-half-acre plot on the hillside immediately below Pickfair. Below it again lay Harold Lloyd's house. Beside these mansions, Chaplin's fourteen-room house was comparatively modest, though it shared their view of the Pacific Ocean, with Catalina Island just visible on a clear day. On the lower side the lawns sloped away to a tennis court and swimming pool. Behind the house were the

POLA DROPS "SHARLIE"

Tennis Champion Ace-High Now

Celebrated Actress Asserts Chaplin "Got the Gate" Five Weeks Ago

She Still Says "Hello" to Him, but Thinks He's Too Temperamental

BY H. B. K. WILLIS

The king is dead! Long live the king!

The tennis racket has supplanted the mask of comedy as the omen of domestic bliss in Pola Negri's demesne. Yesterday the gorgeous tragedy queen, with a laugh on her lips, admitted that Charlie Chaplin, clowndom's king, received his conge five weeks ago, thus ending the match which has kept kings and caddies on the qui vive for almost a year.

green slopes of the Santa Monica Mountains. Pola made one lasting contribution by supervising the planting of fir, cedar, pine, spruce and hemlock on three sides of the house. Today these trees, a memorial to a long-ago and short-lived Hollywood sensation, hide the house from the road.

Pola's interest tended somewhat to complicate the building of the house. Chaplin had designed it himself in what he jokingly called 'Californian Gothic'. He had originally planned huge windows looking towards the ocean but Pola persuaded him to reduce their size. After Pola's reign was over, Mary Pickford persuaded him to revert to the large windows.

Inside, a large hall extended the full length and height of the house, with a balustraded balcony at first floor level. In a high arched vestibule to the left of the hall, Chaplin installed a massive pipe organ.

The vestibule also served as a projection room, with a screen which dropped down in front of the organ. Down the hall was the living room which, until a study was added in the corner of the house, gave onto terraced lawns at the back. In the 1920s the living room was cosy, cluttered with books and mementoes and containing a rather heterogeneous collection of furniture, mostly in the English style, which Chaplin had gradually acquired in his previous residences. It had an open fire, a Steinway grand and, as Charles Chaplin Junior remembered 'close by was the big Webster dictionary, which Dad consulted so often, and the table he used when he worked downstairs.' Across the hall was the dining room, which also gave on to the lawns and which made greater concessions to modernity and design in its planning. Beyond it lay the kitchen and staff quarters.

The stairs were at the front of the hall. Some years later, Charles Chaplin Junior remembered that an oriental gong stood on the bend. 'There seemed to be a secret rapport between Dad and that gong. Sometimes when he was passing by deep in thought he would turn and lightly tap it with one finger and then wait quietly to hear the muted tone come softly back to him as though in reply to some question he had asked.'

Upstairs were three bedrooms, each with its bathroom. Chaplin's son remembered that his father's bathroom seemed 'always permeated with the odor of Mitsouko, my father's favourite cologne'. (This was in the 1930s. Chaplin was evidently already using the perfume in 1922, since it was one of Peggy Hopkins Joyce's more annoying quirks, during her friendship with him, to sprinkle his Mitsouko around the house on Beechwood Drive to improve the atmosphere. Kono was outraged both by the extravagance and by the resulting spots on the upholstery.) His bedroom was a large, bright room with a fine fireplace that was never used, but it was simply furnished with a writing table and chair, twin beds and night stands, and another Webster dictionary. However worn and disreputable it became Chaplin would never part with the Persian rug on the floor, which he was sure brought him luck.

> My father usually slept in the far bed, the one by the windows. I recall the pulp detective magazines that were always stacked by this bed. My father might read Spengler and Schopenhauer and Kant for edification, but for sheer relaxation he chose murder mysteries. Tired from a hard day's work, he liked to read them in bed for they put him to sleep.
>
> In the drawer of the night stand beside his bed, my father kept a

> thirty-eight caliber automatic with its bullets. He would sometimes show it to Syd and me, though we never saw him fire it.[28]

Two more things in their father's room were to delight and intrigue his sons in their boyhood. One was the little closet that led off the bedroom and which contained the pipes of the organ below: 'It took a lot of work to get them all in there. A lot of work,' Chaplin would tell them proudly. The other was a powerful telescope which he had installed to study the heavens. His sons noticed, though, that he was far more interested in watching what went on on the earth below. It is hard to know whether he was consciously passing on the childhood lessons in observation he had learned from Hannah, looking out at the Kennington streets, when he would train a telescope on some far-off pedestrian and say to his sons, 'You see that man? He must be going home after a day's work. Look at his gait, so slow, so tired. His head's bent. Something's on his mind. What could it be?'[29]

10

THE GOLD RUSH

Chaplin was now to embark upon the film by which, he often said, he would most like to be remembered; and a marriage which for the rest of his life he would try vainly to forget. Chaplin recalled very clearly the moment when the inspiration for *The Gold Rush* had come to him. One Sunday morning in September or October 1923 he had been invited to breakfast by Douglas Fairbanks and Mary Pickford who, as his partners in United Artists, were anxious to see him start on a new film. After breakfast he amused himself looking at stereograms and was particularly struck by one showing an endless line of prospectors in the 1898 Klondike gold rush, toiling up the Chilkoot Pass. A caption on the back described the hardships the men suffered in their search for gold.

His imagination was further stimulated by reading a book about the disasters which befell a party of immigrants – twenty-nine men, eighteen women and forty-three children – on the trail to California in 1846. Led by George Donner, their misfortunes multiplied, until eventually they found themselves snowbound in the Sierra Nevada. Of a party of ten men and five women who set out to cross the mountains to bring help, eight men died and the rest survived by eating their bodies. Before relief could be brought to those who had remained in camp, many of them also had died, and the survivors had resorted to eating the corpses of their comrades, as well as dogs, cowhides and, it was said, their own moccasins.

Out of this unlikely material Chaplin was to create one of the cinema's great comedies. 'It is paradoxical,' he wrote, 'that tragedy stimulates the spirit of ridicule . . . ridicule, I suppose, is an attitude of defiance; we must laugh in the face of our helplessness against the forces of nature – or go insane.'[1] Although he was as usual to work without a conventional script, improvising and developing new incidents as the shooting progressed, Chaplin seems to have had a much clearer sense of the eventual story line than at the start of most of his previous films. He worked fast on the first draft story, and on 3 December 1923 – only two months after the première of *A Woman of Paris*, he was able to deposit for copyright a 'play in two scenes' provisionally entitled *The Lucky Strike*.

Throughout December and January Chaplin whipped along activity in the studio in preparation for what they now called 'the northern story'. Chaplin continued to tinker with the scenario while his assistants – Eddie Sutherland, Henri d'Abbadie d'Arrast and Chuck Riesner, as well as the indispensable Henry Bergman – compiled research data about Alaska. Props and costumes were meanwhile prepared; dog-sleighs and fur coats were not readily come by in southern California. Danny Hall's staff were feverishly building the elaborate sets required for the opening scenes of the film. Chaplin asked for a huge scenic cyclorama of a mountain backgound with a 'snowfield' of salt and flour in front of it. Hall also built the prospectors' hut, arranged on a pivoted rocker and operated by an elaborate system of pulleys, for the scene in which it is supposed to have slid to the edge of a ravine where it teeters perilously with each movement of the men within. The cameramen were, as usual, to be Rollie Totheroh and Jack Wilson.

The first actor engaged was Fred Karno Junior. The only players on regular contract were Henry Bergman and Edna, but it soon became evident that Edna was not to be Chaplin's leading lady. Even before *A Woman of Paris* Chaplin had observed that she had grown too 'matronly' for comedy roles. Her drinking had made her weight unpredictable and her acting unreliable. Josef von Sternberg, who was to direct her last American film a couple of years later, said that she 'was still charming, though she had not appeared in pictures for a number of years and had become unbelievably timid and unable to act in even the simplest scene without great difficulty.' Moreover, just as work was starting on *The Gold Rush* Edna was involved in one of the scandals that shadowed Hollywood's brightest years like nightmares.

By coincidence the scandal also involved Chaplin's previous leading lady, the unhappy Mabel Normand. The incident was never wholly explained. On New Year's Day 1924 Edna was the guest of an oil magnate, Courtland Dines. She had spent the day in his apartment. In the afternoon they were joined by Mabel Normand and some time later Mabel's chauffeur arrived, apparently to take her home. There was an altercation between Dines and the chauffeur, who produced a revolver belonging to Mabel and fired. Dines was not killed, but Edna's reputation was. All the parties claimed to recall nothing of the events: Dines, who at the time was wearing only an undershirt and knee-length silk dressing gown, said he had been drinking all night and day. After inconclusive courtroom hearings a number of cities banned *A Woman of Paris*, and Edna withdrew from the limelight to her little apartment on the outskirts of the city.

Though there was no longer a deep emotional involvement, Chaplin retained his affection for Edna and his concern for her career. Certainly he was too loyal, too gallant, and too scornful of Hollywood gossip to let the scandal affect his decision not to use her. But the incident cannot have helped Edna's failing confidence and competence. When it was announced that he would choose a new leading lady, Chaplin emphasized in his press statements that there was no truth in rumours that Edna was no longer associated with his studios, and no long-term significance in her absence from the cast of *The Gold Rush*. 'Miss Purviance is still under contract and receives her weekly salary as though she were actively engaged in production . . . Miss Purviance will again appear under the Chaplin banner, in a dramatic production supervised by Charles Spencer Chaplin.'

Chaplin now had to find a replacement for his leading lady. The news reached the ears of Lillita McMurray, the Angel of Temptation in *The Kid*. Lillita was now fifteen years and nine months old. On Saturday 3 February 1924 she presented herself in the studio reception office accompanied by her best friend, Merna Kennedy, who was five months younger but had acquired a store of worldly wisdom as child dancer in touring vaudeville. They asked to see Chuck Riesner, who had been a neighbour of the McMurrays, and Riesner allowed them to go on to the set and watch Chaplin doing tests of himself and Mack Swain in the rocking cabin. Lillita no doubt made sure that Chaplin noticed her and Chaplin was impressed with the way her looks had matured since the expiry of her original one-year contract to the studio. He invited her to make a screen test, which Alf Reeves arranged at some point during the subsequent four weeks.

After satisfying himself with tests of the moving hut and the wind machines which were to provide the blizzard effects, Chaplin began to shoot *The Gold Rush* on 8 February. The first scenes were for the sequence where Charlie, lost in the white wilderness, chances into the hut, is menaced by the villainous Black Larson but is unable to obey Larson's orders to leave the hut as he is coninually blown back inside by the blizzard. Larson was played with great energy by Tom Murray, a vaudevillian who had long toured throughout the English-speaking world with a blackface song-and-dance-act, Gillihan and Murray. When the scenes were completed and cut, Chaplin prepared to embark on a preliminary reconnaissance of Truckee, near the Donner Pass, where the location scenes were to be shot. He took with him Riesner, Totheroh and Hall.

Truckee stands beside Lake Tahoe high in the Sierra Nevada, almost four hundred miles north of Hollywood and just over twenty miles from Reno. At that time it boasted only one hotel, of awful modesty – Lita Grey noted that the appointments of the room she later shared with her mother there included one chamber pot and three cuspidors. The winter climate was bitterly cold; Chaplin could rely on all the snow he needed until the end of April.

Chaplin and his reconnaissance party stayed at Truckee from 20 to 24 February. When they returned to the studio the following week, there was a new addition to the cast – a large and sleek brown bear accompanied by its keeper, Bud White. The studio began to look like a menagerie when a Mr Niemayer and ten husky dogs were signed up a couple of days later. The bear had the privilege of two scenes with Chaplin. In the opening sequence of the film he pads silently after Charlie who, unaware, makes his way along a precarious cliff path. In the hut scene Charlie, blinded by a blanket that has become entangled about his head, grapples with the bear under the impression that it is big Mack Swain in his bearskin coat.

Meanwhile Chaplin had run Lillita McMurray's tests a number of times. Rollie Totheroh and Jim Tully – who was engaged to work on the script and on publicity copywriting, were bold enough to express their dismay. Lita was a big-boned, heavy-faced girl – cheerful enough but hardly sparkling. Chaplin disregarded his colleagues' adverse views, and on 2 March Lillita McMurray signed a contract to appear as leading lady of *The Gold Rush* at $75 per week. It was agreed that she should adopt the professional name of Lita Grey. Whatever his misgivings about her talent, Tully did a valiant job on the press. During the succeeding weeks American newspaper readers were constantly regaled with Lita's slightly squinting portrait and fulsome stories of her beauty, talent, charm, innocence and aristocratic lineage.

> Her talent [runs a typical example, in the florid prose of the popular press of the time] is as yet in its formative period. Chaplin claims, however, that a rare spark is there and that with training she will develop a splendid talent. Of Lita personally there is little to say, for she knows so much less of life than does the average jazzy, effervescent flapper.
>
> No love affairs have ever brought a quick beating to her heart, a flush to her cheeks. She idolizes Chaplin, but much as a child feels for some much older man who has shown her a great kindness. Romances constitute her favorite reading – and the glamorous deeds of yesterday's heroes who walk across the pages of her history books.
>
> One is conscious of an awakened something in her, as though some glow were breathing back of her large brown eyes, lurking upon her half-curved lips. She is so quiet, with that Spanish slumberous quality seeming to hold back her fires of expression until some moment of great feeling will liberate them to flame, one imagines, into beauty. Even her sports – swimming, horseback riding, tennis – she enjoys in leisurely fashion until that inherent dominant streak makes itself felt through her languor and gives her an animated grace.
>
> It is as if she expresses two forces – the slumberous calm of her Spanish heritage that suggests dreamy, sunlit days of unhurried beauty, and a vitality that quivers beneath her tranquillity. Perhaps it is the spirit of those gallant Dons who braved the dangers of the new world for the glory of conquest, perhaps merely modern feminine independence struggling beneath the placid ivory loveliness of her. Whatever its origin, I have an idea that it is likely some day to make itself felt, to establish her as one of the unique personalities of the shadow-screen.
>
> She dreams with her capabilities not yet fully awakened. When she speaks of the possibilities ahead, her eyes grow luminous and there is fire in them, and her pale face becomes mobile with her thoughts and feelings. She has a charming voice, of soft, musical cadence, rising in inflection when she becomes keenly interested, vibrant with what she is saying . . .[2]

When she signed her contract, it was reported, Lillita–Lita jumped up and down, clapping her hands and crying 'Goody, goody.' The view of another journalist, Jack Junsmeyer, reveals a little more:

> Schooling in the dance and the arts, supplemented by business college education and dramatic training has occupied the four-year interval following her only [*sic*] appearance on the screen in *The Kid*.

> 'I have held firm to my ambition to go into pictures,' says Miss Grey, 'but I felt that I didn't want to work with anyone except Mr Chaplin. Patience has its reward.'
>
> Her first interview at the Chaplin studio revealed the new leading lady as a peculiarly shy, reticent and far from loquacious girl. She seemed phlegmatic.
>
> But a few minutes later, in the presence of Chaplin on the set where his Alaska gold rush comedy is under way, the girl underwent a remarkable transformation. She bloomed with animation. She became galvanic.
>
> Observation indicated that Chaplin wields a powerful professional sway over his new protégée – that almost hypnotic influence which the more masterful directors exert upon sensitive players before the camera.[3]

Every newspaper report said that Lita was nineteen. Clearly the studio publicity department felt it prudent not to publicize the employment of a minor as the star of the film. Lita was sufficiently well-developed to make the subterfuge convincing.

During her first fortnight at the studio, Lita had nothing to do but watch. Chaplin moved on to his scenes in the cabin with Mack Swain as Big Jim McKay. The two men are snow-bound and starving Jim takes it badly, in old-time melodrama style, clutching his head and declaiming 'Food! I must have food!' Charlie, with the flair of a Brillat-Savarin, stews his boot but it proves a less than satisfying meal and Big Jim, suffering hallucinations from hunger, imagines that Charlie is a plump hen and almost eats him. Shooting the scenes of cooking and eating the boot took three shooting days and sixty-three takes. Chaplin was as usual constantly refining and elaborating his business during this time. Only on the afternoon of the third day of shooting, for instance, did he arrive at two of his most memorable transposition gags. Charlie's dainty handling of the sole of the boot – he has graciously given Big Jim the more tender upper – transforms it into a *filet*; then, coming upon a bent nail, he crooks it on his little finger and invites Jim to break it with him as if it were a wishbone. The boots and laces used for the scene were made from liquorice and it is said that both actors experienced its inconvenient laxative effects.

The scene of Charlie's metamorphosis, under Mack's crazed eyes, into a chicken, was similarly evolved during shooting. For several days the unit shot a version of the scene in which Mack simply sees the vision of a fine fat turkey sitting on the cabin table. When he grabs for it, it disappears only to reappear in Charlie's person, whereupon Mack chases him around the hut with a knife. When Mack comes to himself a little, Charlie gives him a book to take his mind off food. On the Saturday however (15 March 1924) Chaplin had a better idea; and when work resumed the following Monday the costume department had provided him with a man-size chicken costume. Now Big Jim would not imagine that he saw a turkey, but that Charlie actually became a chicken.

The film cameramen of those days had to be resourceful. Their cameras were technically excellent, but had few refinements compared to present-day apparatus. Much effects-work, like fades, dissolves or irises which in later years were done in the laboratories, had still to be achieved in the camera. So it was with the chicken transformations in *The Gold Rush*. Chaplin would start the scene in his ordinary costume. At a given moment the camera would be faded out and stopped. The scene and camera position would be kept unchanged while Chaplin rapidly changed into his chicken costume. At the same time the camera was wound back to the start of the fade, the place where the transformation was to begin. While the camera started up and faded in, Chaplin would precisely retrace the action he had just filmed. In this way the two images of Charlie and the chicken, would be exactly superimposed so that the two figures would seem to dissolve into one another. Precisely the same technique was needed to turn the chicken back into Charlie. During the pause for the costume change Mack Swain, who was also in the scene, had to stay absolutely motionless. To help him, he was seated at a table with his head firmly supported on his elbows. The precision and faultless matching of the effect is a remarkable tribute to the technicians* as well as to the actors. The whole thing is made to seem quite effortless. As Chaplin would have wished, the magic remains intact.

The peculiar genius for perceiving in any object the properties of another object, which was the basis of a life-time of 'transposition' gags, is here seen at its most developed as Chaplin discovers the chickenish properties in his own person. The 'dissolve' is not only in the camera but in his own mind and physique. He discerns, in the manner that Charlie flaps his arms and in his toes-out waddle, those characteristics which exactly coincide with the movements of the chicken. Eddie Sutherland recalled that for another scene, another

* The elaborate technical feat had to be accomplished, of course, by *two* cameras, simultaneously.

actor was substituted in the chicken costume. It did not work. Chaplin had to take over. The actor was only able to be a man in a chicken costume. Chaplin, at will, could *be* a chicken.

For use in the publicity matter of the film, Jim Tully wrote a description of Chaplin at work on the starvation scenes in the cabin:*

> There are present neither mobs nor megaphones. There is a minimum of noise. The cameramen, property men, electricians all speak amongst themselves in hushed whispers when they speak at all. For the most part they look into the center of the set in much the same way as the Sunday flock looks at its pastor. For there gesticulates Charlie Chaplin.
>
> 'Great! Now just one more for luck . . .'
>
> Only three scenes were taken in the entire afternoon, but the proof that Mr Chaplin is without doubt the hardest working individual in Hollywood is that each scene is shot at least twenty times. Any one of the twenty would transport almost any director other than Charlie; he does them over and over again, seeking just the shade to blend with the mood. And his moods are even more numerous than his scenes.
>
> 'Just once more – we'll get it this time!' It is his continual cry, ceaseless as the waves of the sea. And each additional 'take' means just three times as much work for him as for anyone else.
>
> Perhaps in the middle of a scene when everything seems to be superlative, he will stop the action with a gesture, 'Cut' – he walks over to a little stool beside one of the cameras and leans his head upon the tripod. The cameramen stand silently beside their cranks; everyone virtually holds his breath until Charlie jumps up with an enthusiastic yell:
>
> 'I've got it, Mack; you should cry: "Food! Food! l I must have food!" You're starving and you are going to pieces. See – like this!'**
>
> Mr Swain, a veteran trooper, watches intently as Charlie goes through every detail of the action.
>
> 'Let's take it!' Charlie suddenly exclaims. 'What do you say, Mack?'
>
> 'Sure,' answers Mack.
>
> And again the scene is re-enacted and recorded by the tireless cameras.[4]

* In the publicity brochure for the film the article appears as 'On the Set with Charlie' by Sid Grauman. (Grauman was the Hollywood showman who built Grauman's Chinese and Grauman's Egyptian Theatres.) In the Chaplin archives, however, there is a typescript of the article, with a manuscript note discussing who might be the most suitable person to whom to attribute authorship.

** The continuity reports show that Mack Swain actually spoke these words on the set. In the original version of the film they appeared as a sub-title. When Chaplin made a version with synchronized soundtrack, he retained them in his own commentary.

Now, finally, it was time to shoot Lita's first scene. It was in fact to be the only scene for *The Gold Rush* which she shot in the studio. Chaplin seemed sometimes to have an eerie gift of presentiment. In *The Kid* Lita had appeared in a dream sequence, as the Angel of Temptation whose blandishments (in his dream) bring about his death. In *The Gold Rush*, too, she was to appear in a dream. As first conceived, the scene had Charlie sleeping in the cabin. He dreams that he is awakened by a beautiful girl (Lita) who brings him a great plate of roast turkey.

The scene, the setting for which was a dream kitchen, was begun on Saturday 22 March. When he returned to the studio on the following Monday, however, Chaplin had quite a new idea. The turkey was replaced by a big, beautiful strawberry shortcake. The new action is described in the day's continuity reports. The final take, completed at 6.30 p.m., was thus:

> Scene 14: Close-up. Dissolve. C. asleep in kitchen on couch. Lita standing over him with cake – wakens him – he sits up – she sits down beside him – smiles – takes berry – gives it to him – he turns forward – eats it – smiles – she takes another berry – starts to give it to him. She says: Close your eyes and open your mouth. He does so and she throws whole cake in his face and laughs. C. takes cake off – face all smeared with cream – Fade out and fade into close-up in cabin with C. asleep in cot – blanket over body but not on head – snow on neck and face – snow drops down from roof five times – he wakes up then sits up – and looks around room – brushes snow off – gets up – comes forward left of camera. O.K.

The scene, which was never to reach the screen, was to prove a vivid metaphor for the sad story of Charlie's future relationship with Lita.

The succeeding fortnight was spent in cutting and re-shooting the cabin scenes with Mack Swain: it was probably at this time that Tully wrote the description of Chaplin at work just quoted. Now preparations began for the great trek to Truckee to shoot the scenes on the locations already selected by the February advance party. The first party, consisting of Eddie Sutherland, Danny Hall, seven carpenters, four electricians and Mr Wood the painter, left on 9 April. The following day the camera crew and a Mexican labourer, Frank Antunez, followed. A week later they were joined by the main party: Chaplin attended by Kono, Lita chaperoned by her mother Mrs Spicer, Henri d'Arrast, Jim Tully, Tom Murray, Mack Swain, Della

Steele (the clerk who made up the daily continuity reports) several assistants and handymen, and Bud White and his bear. The journey, though long, was not uncomfortable: the party travelled in private cars, with drawing rooms and dining rooms. Despite (or perhaps because of) Mrs Spicer's watchful presence, Lita sensed a growing mutual interest between herself and her employer that was more than professional.

Eddie Sutherland had efficiently prepared everything so that the morning after his arrival Chaplin could direct the opening scene of the film, which remains one of the most memorable visions in the whole of cinema. Again, Tully has left a colourful description of the occasion:

> . . . To make the pass, a pathway of 2300 feet long was cut through the snows, rising to an ascent of 1000 feet at an elevation of 9850 feet. Winding through a narrow defile to the top of Mount Lincoln, the pass was only made possible because of the drifts of eternal snow against the mountainside. The exact location of this feat was accomplished in a narrow basin, a natural formation known as the 'Sugar Bowl'.
>
> To reach this spot, trail was broken through the big trees and deep snows, a distance of nine miles from the railroad, and all paraphernalia was hauled through the immense fir forest. There a construction camp was laid for the building of the pioneers' city. To make possible the cutting out of the pass, a club of young men, professional ski-jumpers, were employed to dig steps in the frozen snows, at the topmost point, as there the pass is perpendicular and the ascent was made only after strenuous effort.
>
> With the building of the mining camp, and the pass completed, special agents of the Southern Pacific Railway were asked to round up 2500 men for this scene . . . On two days a great gathering of derelicts had assembled. They came with their own blanket packs on their backs, the frayed wanderers of the western nation. It was beggardom on holiday.
>
> A more rugged and picturesque gathering of men could hardly be imagined. They arrived at the improvised scene of Chilkoot Pass in special trains; and, what is more, special trains of dining cars went ahead of them. It was thought best to keep the diners in full view of the derelicts . . .
>
> They trudged through the heavy snows of the narrow pass as if gold were actually to be their reward, and not just a day's pay. To them what mattered [was]: they were to be seen in a picture with Chaplin, the mightiest vagrant of them all. It would be a red-letter day in their lives, the day they went over Chilkoot Pass with Charlie Chaplin.[5]

Tully is guilty here of some exaggeration. The studio records show that 600 men were brought from Sacramento, not the 2500 he claims. They were supplemented by every member of the unit not otherwise occupied. Both Sutherland and Lita joined the trail.

Chaplin was very concerned to sustain morale in the discomfort, bitter cold and tedium of Truckee. On Monday he shot one scene of the cabin sliding down the mountainside. Then, while the carpenters were making changes to the cabin set, he joined the unit in bob-sledding and ski racing. As a result, the following day he was confined to bed with a chill. Two feet of snow had fallen in the night, and the snowstorm continued. The storm was an opportunity too good to be missed, so in Chaplin's absence Eddie Sutherland shot some effective scenes of Tom Murray as Black Larson, battling through the blizzard with his sledge.

Chaplin was up and about again next day: he was eager not to prolong the costly and uncomfortable stay in Truckee. Material was shot for some action that was not to figure in the final film, involving Tom Murray's partner, played by Eddie Sutherland. In one scene they were filmed together outside the cabin; in another they rescue Lita from the assault of a villainous prospector played by Joseph Van Meter, for many years a general assistant at the Chaplin studios and blessed with a mean face which came in handy whenever Chaplin needed an extra for a criminal role. Other scenes shot in the Truckee snow showed Charlie finding a grave marked 'Here lies Jim Sourdough'; Bud White's bear prowling around the cabin; and Big Jim chasing the Charlie-chicken across the snowy wastes. Mack Swain had by this time succumbed to 'flu, so Sid Swaney stood in for him in these scenes. The last day of location shooting was 28 April. The four cameras were again used for a shot of Charlie sliding down 'Chilkoot Pass'. Then Chaplin, with Kono, Bergman, d'Arrast and Mack Swain entrained for Los Angeles via San Francisco. The unit stayed behind to tear down the sets: on the evening of the 29th what remained was burned after dark and Sutherland filmed the conflagration in case it came in handy. That night Lita and her mother,* the camera crew, Danny Hall and some others boarded the train home. Everyone was back by 2 May.

* In her own account, *My Life With Chaplin*, Lita described conversations with Chaplin on this return journey. The transportation records show that her memory is at fault.

Having captured his snow, Chaplin shot nothing more throughout May and June, and the company grew restive. While Chaplin worked over script and gag material with Bergman, d'Arrast and Tully, and Lita was photographed for stills in different costumes and coiffures, the scenic department were occupied in recreating Alaska in the studio during a California summer. Even though extra labour was brought in (Tully's publicity claimed that 500 scenic craftsmen had been employed) they were hard pressed to complete the sets in the eight or nine weeks allotted to them. A small-scale mountain range was built. Its 'snow'-capped peaks, glistening in the sun, were visible miles off, and brought hundreds of curious sightseers for a closer view. Tully published some statistics on the making of the mountains. The framework required 239,577 feet of timber, which was covered with 22,750 linear feet of chicken wire, and over that 22,000 feet of burlap. The artificial ice and snow required 200 tons of plaster, 285 tons of salt and one hundred barrels of flour. The blizzard scenes called for an additional four cart-loads of confetti.

Other miscellaneous items from the hardware bills on *The Gold Rush* included 300 picks and shovels, 2000 feet of garden hose, 7000 feet of rope, four tons of steel, five tons of coke, four tons of asbestos, thirty-five tons of cement, 400 kegs of nails, 3000 bolts and several tons of smaller items.

Shooting resumed on 1 July, with more scenes of Chaplin and Mack Swain hungry in the cabin. A pleasant gag sequence which was ultimately rejected had the two of them playing cards. Mack falls asleep over the game, but with his elbow too firmly planted on his own cards to permit Charlie to take advantage with a little cheating. Instead, Charlie constructs a toy windmill, and playfully powers it with Mack's windy snores. These scenes finished, he moved on to the sequence in which the cabin slides to the edge of the chasm where it delicately balances, responding to every move and cough of the two men inside. This required work with miniature models. In the early 1920s there were as yet no special effects firms in Hollywood to entrust with this kind of work; all depended on the skills of cameramen, production designers, set builders and property men. The miniature work in *The Gold Rush* is exemplary. The cuts from the full-size hut to the model are barely perceptible: sometimes when the viewer thinks he has detected the model, he is suddenly made aware of his error. The continuity reports of the shots made with models suggest that Chaplin contemplated a scene – anticipating the opening of *The*

Wizard of Oz – in which the hut and its occupants would whirl through the blizzard:

> Scene 2175: L.S. camera on moving platform – l. to r. – trees in foreground moving l. to r. – backgound storm effect – panorama for insert where C.C. looks out window house going 90 m.p.h.

In the last days of September 1924 Chaplin shot a few more scenes of the cabin in the snowstorm, but by the end of the month all work had come to a halt. Chaplin was to shoot nothing in his studio for the rest of that year. He had been stopped dead in his tracks by the bombshell delivered by Lita. Some time in the last days of September she announced that she was pregnant. She had a mother aflame with outrage, a grandfather who literally toted a shotgun and an uncle who was a lawyer in San Francisco. Where minors were concerned, the Californian law afforded a charter to shotgun weddings: for a man to have relations with an under-age girl constituted, *de facto*, rape, carrying penalties of up to thirty years in jail. The McMurrays held the trump card and would hear of no solution but an immediate marriage. Chaplin had again trapped himself with a hopelessly incompatible partner.

The press for once suspected nothing. Chaplin and his young leading lady had been seen in public a good deal, but always chaperoned by Lita's mother or by Thelma Morgan Converse, the sister of Gloria Vanderbilt, whom the gossips had decided was Chaplin's secret fiancée. At this moment too they were off following another scent. On 16 November Grace Kingsley, the columnist of the *New York Daily News* commented : 'Charlie Chaplin continues to pay ardent attention to Marion Davies. He spent the evening at Montmartre dining and dancing with the fair Marion the other night. There was a lovely young dancer entertaining that evening. And Charlie applauded but with his back turned. He never took his eyes off Marion's blonde beauty.'

This kind of item in a publication of a rival newspaper group was not likely to please William Randolph Hearst, who by this time had been for almost nine years Marion Davies' devoted and jealously possessive lover. Both Hearst and his wife had known and admired Chaplin for several years, and Hearst can not have been unaware that the friendship between Chaplin and Marion was closer than with most of the men with whom she flirted. Marion was shooting a circus story, *Zander the Great*, at the same time as Chaplin was making

The Gold Rush, and he would often pick her up after he had finished the day's work. Marion's biographer Fred Laurence Guiles' view is that 'All of the cast and crew of *Zander* were aware that something was going on, but Marion was far too much like Chaplin for it to have been a meaningful affair. In the presence of others, they clowned together like an affectionate brother and sister, and it is difficult to imagine them being very different when they were alone together.'

Hearst was nevertheless, in Guiles' words, 'wounded in spirit and fretting what he should do'. In fact he returned to California from New York and on 18 November – two days after the appearance of Grace Kingsley's squib – set off on a trip on his yacht the *Oneida* with a party of invited guests. Principal among these was the producer Thomas Harper Ince, whom Hearst was attempting to persuade to become an active producer for his own Cosmopolitan Pictures. Others on board, apart from Hearst and Marion, were the columnist Louella Parsons, the actress Seena Owen, the dancer Theodore Kosloff, the writer Elinor Glyn, Hearst's secretary Joseph Willicombe, a publisher, Frank Barham with his wife, Marion's sisters Ethel and Reine and her niece Pepi, and Hearst's studio manager, Dr Daniel Goodman. According to Hollywood mythology, Chaplin also was on the boat. In Guiles' account, 'Hearst also invited Chaplin. Perhaps he thought that it was safe to do so, if he believed that he had broken up the romance; or he may have wanted to clarify Marion's status a bit with Chaplin, since Chaplin seemed to have some doubts about it.'

What happened next is one of the great unsolved mysteries of Hollywood. On 19 November Ince was carried unconscious from the yacht at San Diego, and died a few hours afterwards. The official story was that Ince died of a heart attack brought on by ptomaine poison or acute indigestion. The persistent rumour was that Hearst had discovered Ince and Marion together in the dimly lit lower galley and had pulled out a pistol and shot Ince. The question is whether or not the shooting (if it actually happened) was a case of mistaken identity: Ince was a small man with similar head shape and hair colour to Chaplin from the back view.

With time the rumour might have died but for the startling contradictions in the evidence of all those concerned. With blatant untruth, the Hearst press at first gave out a story that Ince was taken ill at his ranch. Marion said that there were no firearms aboard. Hearst's biographer, John Tebbel, recorded that Hearst kept a gun aboard to pot the occasional seagull. There is great doubt as to whether or not Ince's girlfriend, the actress Margaret Livingston, was aboard. Chaplin consistently declared to his intimates that he was not aboard the yacht, and in his autobiography is so hazy about the chronology that he asserts Ince survived for three more weeks, and received a visit from Hearst, Marion and Chaplin. (There exist, however, photographs of Chaplin at Ince's cremation, which took place forty-eight hours after the death.) Kono, according to Eleanor Boardman, then Mrs King Vidor, said that when he was meeting the boat, he saw Ince being carried off with a bullet wound in his head. Others said that the blood that was visible had been vomited from a perforated ulcer.

Elinor Glyn told Eleanor Boardman that everyone aboard the yacht had been sworn to secrecy, which would hardly have seemed necessary if poor Ince had died of natural causes. There was no inquest to settle the matter, though the San Diego District Attorney, the Los Angeles Homicide Chief and the proprietor of the mortuary where Ince's body was taken all declared themselves satisfied that there had been no foul play. Sixty years after the events, there is little hope that we shall ever satisfactorily explain the mystery which remains, casting a shadow on all those who were, however remotely, concerned.

Three days after attending Ince's funeral, Chaplin sent Lita and her mother off to Guaymas, Mexico. He had decided that the wedding, if there must be one, should at least be discreet. He devised an elaborate cover to avoid publicity, and left the ingenious Kono to mastermind the details. A nucleus of the *Gold Rush* unit was marshalled, and on 25 November entrained for Guaymas. Two newsmen, sensing a story, boarded the train and quizzed Chaplin, who successfully fobbed them off with the implausible story that he was setting some of the scenes of *The Gold Rush* in Mexico. 'I'm very odd when I make pictures,' he told them humorously. The following day, to lend conviction to his story, he hired a fishing boat and sent the camera crew out in it to shoot sea scenes. (The 1600 feet of film they shot that day still survive.) That evening Chaplin, Riesner, Lita and her mother drove to neighbouring Empalme, a dismal railway junction with sea on one side and desert on the other, on the edge of Yaqui Indian territory. There the marriage ceremony was performed by a stout civil magistrate in his shabby parlour. Afterwards they returned to the little hotel in Guaymas. That night Chaplin left the bridal suite to Lita and her mother.

Returning to Los Angeles next day, Chaplin planned to avoid the reporters. It was arranged that while the main part of the unit would travel back to the Southern Pacific station, he and Lita, accompanied by Kono, would get off at the little whistle-stop station of Shorb, near Alhambra, where they would be met by the Japanese chauffeur, Frank Kawa.

> Turning up his overcoat and pulling a derby hat over his ears, Chaplin, surrounded by a few close friends, helped his bride from the rear platform of the private car in which they travelled on their return from Empalme, Mexico, where they were married last Tuesday [*sic*].
>
> Everything, it appeared, was working to a carefully scheduled plan whereby Chaplin was to return to his home in Beverly Hills with a degree of privacy rarely sought by film stars.
>
> The comedian and his bride skirted a fence, looking for their limousine and Japanese driver. Just as they rounded a corner, they met 'the press'. A movie camera, to which Charlie owes so much of his fame, commenced grinding away. Chaplin displayed impatience.
>
> 'Can't a man have a little privacy? I've been trying to avoid this. It's awful!' was the actor's only comment to the reporters, who immediately began firing questions at him.
>
> The limousine was sighted about a block away and Chaplin's Japanese secretary was despatched to summon it. Meanwhile the comedian only turned up his overcoat further and with his bride tried to avoid facing the battery of cameras which were trained on him, and grumbled loudly at the fact that his Japanese chauffeur had apparently not understood his directions to run his machine as close to the tracks as possible.
>
> 'Home,' said Chaplin, and as a parting farewell to the newspaper men who had paid him so much attention, 'I don't want any publicity.'
>
> A large group of studio friends, of the mistaken opinion that a royal welcome would please the comedian, had gathered at the Southern Pacific station, but were disappointed to find only the lesser lights of the Chaplin party who had remained aboard the private car as a supposed decoy for the newspaper men who were aboard the train.
>
> After the newlyweds reached Chaplin's new home in Beverly Hills, they were seen no more during the day.[6]

To reach the door of their home they had to run the gauntlet of a siege party at the gates of the house.

A leading article in the *New York Daily News* offered peculiarly wry congratulations to the newlyweds:

> SPOILING A GOOD CLOWN
>
> One of Charlie Chaplin's screen comedies ended with the comedian doing a wild dash among the cactuses (or cacti) along the Mexican border.

> Then he was uncertain upon which side of the boundary lay safety. Now he has made a decision, but whether he considered safety in making it is a question.
>
> The other day the comedian dashed across the border into Mexico aboard a train. His destination was Guaymas and his purpose was to wed Lita Grey, his leading lady. Marrying leading ladies seems to be a weakness among male screen and stage stars. Why, we don't know.
>
> But the practice seems to give weight to the old saying that 'while absence makes the heart grow fonder, presence is a darned sight more effective'. Leading ladies are usually present – and unusually effective.
>
> We hope Charlie finds what he is supposed to be looking for – happiness. But he and his leading lady are about to tackle the toughest cross word puzzle of the ages – married life. So often there are more cross words than there are solutions; and frequently a synonym of four letters meaning 'love' is set down on the matrimonial patchwork as 'bunk'.
>
> We wish Mr Chaplin and Miss Grey the conventional quota of joy. But if they have to give up the puzzle we have this consolation. The best clowns have broken hearts. And no tragedy could be as great as spoiling the best clown of the screen by making him too happy.

The liaison threatened no such danger. One of the incidental compensations of the marriage was that Chaplin threw himself feverishly back into work at the studio – no doubt to avoid spending time at home with his child bride, who forlornly realized that her position in her husband's house was that of an unwanted guest. It may have been comforting to her when her mother moved in with them a few weeks after the marriage, though it cannot have made life easier for Chaplin. He remained impeccably courteous in his dealings with his wife's family, however.

Lita's pregnancy also gave Chaplin an excuse to find a new leading lady for *The Gold Rush*, the production of which was clearly likely to go on for several more months. For the moment the press were necessarily kept in ignorance of Lita's condition. Tully imaginatively told the press that the former Miss Lita Grey had given up her role as the dance hall girl because now that she was married she wished 'to devote every moment of her time to her husband.'

Just before Christmas it was announced that the actress who would replace Lita was Georgia Hale, still quite unknown to the public. She was eighteen. Born into a working class family in St Joseph, Missouri, she had spent most of her life in Chicago. A striking, delicate beauty, at sixteen she won the title of Miss Chicago, which brought with it a cash prize and a chance to compete in the Miss America contest in

Atlantic City. She was knocked out of the competition, but her prize money enabled her to reach Hollywood in July 1923. Her hopes of work as a dancer were dashed by a fall in which she badly sprained her ankle; when her money ran out she settled for work as an extra. One of her first jobs was in a film directed by Roy William Neill, called *By Divine Right*. The star, by chance, was Mildred Harris. The writer and assistant director was the young Josef von Sternberg, who was greatly impressed when he discovered the girl reading his own translation of Karl Adolph's novel *Daughters of Vienna*, and much more impressed to notice that she had dropped a mascara-stained tear on the page. A few months later when von Sternberg embarked on his own first film, a shoe-string experiment in an expressionist manner, *The Salvation Hunters*, he remembered Georgia Hale and cast her in the lead, paying her the same as her daily salary as an extra.

Von Sternberg's partner and leading man, the English actor George K. Arthur, somehow succeeded in getting Chaplin to see the film (Sternberg claimed that he had bribed Kono to smuggle it into the projection box of the screening room at Chaplin's home).

> George K. Arthur was a little devil. You couldn't understand him: he had such a funny accent from some place in England [*sic*: Arthur was born in Aberdeen]. He was so cute. He was a promoter. He got Kono to put it on. Charlie fell in love with that picture. He thought it was a little gem. Von Sternberg was not a genius, but he had talent.[7]

Chaplin at once called up the Fairbankses, who came from next door to see the picture the same night. A day or two later he showed the film to Nazimova, and it was at this showing that he first met Georgia.

> We met in the screening room at FBO Studios. He wanted Joe and me to be there for the show. I sat behind him and Nazimova. After the screening Joe said, 'This is Georgia, the girl.' He said, 'Oh, I'm so happy to meet you.' And then he lost interest in Nazimova and everyone else, and wanted to take me for tea. He asked me what I was doing, and I said I was doing fine. I had a regular daily understanding with Sennett. If I didn't have anything else I could work there any day. He said, 'Keep that up. That's fine. But I want to keep in touch. I like your work.'
>
> Then Douglas Fairbanks signed me to play the Queen in *Don Q, Son of Zorro*. I'd done a test and it turned out fine. All the costumes were ready, but then Charlie went to Doug and said: 'You've signed the girl I need. I want her for *The Gold Rush*.' However, they got together and agreed, and Douglas Fairbanks released me.

> Now, he'd tested lots of people for the part. Everybody tested. One of them was Jean Peters – she became Carole Lombard. He invited me to see the tests, and I said to him, 'But *they're* wonderful!' Because I thought I was terrible. In my test I just stood there looking mad and doing nothing. And they were all laughing and such. And he said, 'That's what I want. That's the quality.'[8]

For Georgia it was a dream come true. She had idolized Chaplin long before she thought of Hollywood. As a child and adolescent in Chicago, psychologically bruised by her father's insensitive discouragement of all her ambitions, she had discovered reassurance in the Tramp's defiant resilience and had convinced herself of some mystical affinity with him. Working with him in no way disillusioned her.

> You just knew you were working with a genius. He's the greatest genius of all times for motion picture business. He was so wonderful to work with. You didn't mind that he told you what to do all the time, every little thing. He was infinitely patient with actors – kind. He knew exactly what to say and what to do to get what he wanted.
>
> One thing was that everything in his pictures was for real. Take the scene where I slap the boy [Malcolm Waite]. That slap was really for real. Charlie had had us doing that scene, and him pawing me, for so long, that I got really mad with him. I really did slap him – good and hard. And of course that was what Charlie wanted.[9]

The change of leading lady was not too disruptive since the character of the dance hall girl does not appear until half-way through the film – it is one of the odd aspects of its structure, but in the outcome perfectly satisfactory. Since Chaplin was as usual shooting in story continuity, he had not yet arrived at the heroine's scenes. The brief sequences which he had already shot with Lita were possibly intended as tests, and in the end had no place in the story. The rest of December was spent reworking the story, testing and costuming Georgia and organizing her publicity and photographs. Meanwhile Danny Hall and his staff were building the big dance hall and bar where Charlie first meets Georgia.

The bar room scenes were difficult and costly, involving paying – and worse, keeping under control – as many as a hundred extras, who included Mexicans, Indians and, the pride of the unit, a proven centenarian, 'Daddy' Taylor, who was already over forty when he saw service in the Civil War. Chaplin was so delighted by the old man's energy as a dancer, that he gave him a brief scene of his own in the New Year party scene. Extra rates had gone up since First

National days. The base rate was now $7.50 a day, while some received as much as twice that sum. 'Tiny' Sanford, as the barman, was paid $20 a day. The highest daily rate on the unit, however, was paid to the dog which appears with Chaplin in the dance hall scene – seizing a handy length of rope to support his sinking trousers, Charlie fails to notice that it is attached to the collar of this heavy-weight but docile animal. The dog was on hire from the Hal Roach studios and cost $35 a day.

Perhaps it was the celebrations of New Year 1925 that suggested to Chaplin setting the Tramp's most poignant scenes on New Year's Eve, when everyone else is celebrating, leaving the lonely prospector lonelier than ever. The dance hall scenes were finished on 19 January, when Chaplin filmed the comic-pathetic moment where the Tramp retrieves a torn and discarded picture of Georgia from the floor under the disconcerting gaze of a prospector of somewhat demented mien.

By the beginning of February the set-builders had completed the cabin supposed to be in the same township as the dance hall, where Charlie finds a home with the kindly engineer Hank Curtis (played by Henry Bergman). This was to be the setting for the New Year party which Charlie, with his meagre savings, prepares for Georgia and her friends. The girls forget all about him and fail to turn up. Waiting for them, Charlie falls asleep and dreams that the dinner party is a brilliant social success. The English music hall artist Wee Georgie Wood, who knew Chaplin both in England and the United States, said that the scene was suggested by an incident in the young Chaplin's days on tour when he invited the members of another juvenile troupe, working another theatre, to tea. The manager of the troupe would not let them go, but nobody informed Chaplin, who vainly waited for his guests.

Chaplin seems to have been conscious that this sequence had to be something out of the ordinary. At most other studios in the silent period it was customary to employ instrumental groups, even small orchestras, to inspire the actors with mood music. At the Chaplin studios this was not considered necessary. For these hut scenes, however, musicians were employed on the set. The first week or so it was the Hollywood String Quartet, at $50 a day; after that the studio replaced them with Abe Lyman and a trio of players who did the job for $37.50 plus overtime. The famous 'Dance of the Rolls' which is the climax of the sequence was clearly filmed to music; every one of the eleven takes Chaplin made of the sequence was uniform in length, and when he subsequently added a music track to the film the turn synchronized perfectly to 'The Oceana Roll'.

Famous though it was, this was not the first time that the 'Dance of the Rolls' had been filmed. In *The Cook*, made in 1918, Roscoe Arbuckle also speared two bread rolls with forks and made the miniature booted legs thus formed perform a little dance. Quite possibly Arbuckle had picked up the gag from Chaplin during their days together at Sennett. With Arbuckle it is an ingenious gag; with Chaplin it is touched with genius, in the dexterity, the timing, the expressiveness and reality of the dancing legs. The bread-roll feet become a living extension, their every move reflected in the face above them. The scene was initially shot quite casually, in the middle of a miscellaneous series of takes made late in the afternoon of 19 February:

> Scene 3653: Great close-up – C.C. at head of table – doing dance with rolls on forks.
>
> Scene 3655: Retake
>
> Scene 3656: Retake

Chaplin evidently liked the rushes, and the following day did eight retakes of the scene.

After more than a year, the end of shooting was in sight. The last big set to be constructed was the street of the mining town. The cheerful scene in which Charlie earns money for Georgia's party by clearing snow, ensuring continued custom by shifting it from one door to the next, was finished in two swift days of shooting. On 10 April Chaplin, Georgia and Mack Swain left for San Diego with a camera crew to film the final scenes with Big Jim and Charlie, now millionaires as a result of Jim's lucky strike, on the boat returning home. The scenes were shot on a boat called *The Lark* while it plied its regular route between San Diego, Los Angeles and San Francisco. Chaplin was clearly feeling relaxed; Georgia recalls, 'Coming back, we went to a nightclub. When we went in they started to play "Charlie, My Boy". Then the band started to play a tango, and we danced, and everybody else got off the floor. He really loved that. You'd have thought it would have made him a million dollars, he was so pleased.'[10]

The last scene (apart from some retakes on the miniatures) was shot on 14–15 May 1925. This was to be one of the most spectacular and surprising moments in the film – the end of the villainous Black

Larson, when a chasm opens up in the ice and snow and he plummets to his death. Partly it was done with miniatures, though how the shots done to full scale and with the actor Tom Murray were made has never been explained. The collapse of a huge cliff-edge of snow and ice may have been arranged in connexion with the dismantling of the mountain sets.

For nine weeks, from 20 April almost to the day of the première on 26 June, Chaplin was cutting the film. Meanwhile his domestic affairs were again impinging. The couple had put a brave public face on their marriage. Cornered by the correspondent of the London *People*, Chaplin said, 'I am the happiest married man in the whole world, and but for these malignant rumours, quite content.' Asked about stories of a marriage settlement Chaplin replied, 'The marriage settlement is just a wedding present to my wife, a present any man would give to the woman he loved.' Lita in her turn said that she was 'as happy as the day is long', and that she had given up her role as leading lady to become the mistress of the nursery. She denied a rumour that Chaplin had moved back to his old quarters in the Los Angeles Athletic Club.

On 5 May 1925 Lita gave birth to a boy. Chaplin's concern over the final stages of her pregnancy and his pride in the baby seemed to achieve a temporary rapprochement. He even reconsidered his earlier objection to naming a son Charles: hitherto he had declared that to give a child the name of a famous parent was to give it a cross to bear. In order to give no ammunition to Hollywood gossips, it was thought prudent to keep the child's birth a secret for a while; it was still less than six months since the marriage in Mexico. So Lita, with her baby and her mother, remained hidden, at first in a cabin in the San Bernardino Mountains belonging to the doctor who attended the birth and now (for a monetary consideration) falsified the birth registration. Subsequently they moved to a house at Manhattan Beach rented for them by Alf Reeves, whose wife Amy helped care for Lita when she suffered a post-natal illness. It was agreed that the baby's official birthday should be 28 June – two days after the Los Angeles première of *The Gold Rush*.

While Lita fretted because he had no time to visit his first son, Chaplin laboured in the cutting room. In a shooting period that had spread over a year and three months, with 170 days of actual filming, he had shot 231,505 feet of film. From this mass he edited a finished film of 8555 feet. The longest comedy he had yet made, *The Gold*

Rush was edited with unchecked narrative fluidity. The harmony of the scenes and the images betrayed nothing of the interruptions, the irritations, the technical effort. When Chaplin came to reissue the film with a sound track seventeen years later, the only significant (and inexplicable) change he made, apart from leaving out the titles, was to the ending. The original version ended with Charlie and Georgia in a long and loving embrace. In the reissue Chaplin substituted a more chaste fade-out, with the two simply walking out of view.

'A Chaplin première,' said the *Los Angeles Evening Herald*, the day after the gala showing of *The Gold Rush* on 26 June 1925, 'is always an outstanding event. Other stars and pictures attract great throngs, but a certain significance which attaches to the first presentations of films bearing the comedian's hallmark makes his première just a little more important or, at least, it would seem so judging by the avidity shown by profession as well as public. There was not a vacant seat at the opening. If any ticket-holder preferred to stay away, he could have disposed of his coupons at a fancy figure . . .'

The court in front of Grauman's Egyptian Theatre was 'a veritable fairyland of color and light. The most skilled decorators in the realm of make-believe had been at work for a week dressing the enclosure for the occasion.' Inside, the celebrities were announced as they entered the auditorium by a stentorian voice, and each was applauded according to his or her degree of popularity. 'The house rang with applause as favorites sauntered along behind attentive ushers.' These announcements were an innovation, as was the chilled punch served by pretty usherettes in the interval. The film was preceded by a prologue 'of matchless beauty . . . Grauman has actually outdone himself in this achievement and *The Gold Rush* première probably never will be surpassed. If it is, only a genius like Grauman can do it.' The curtain rose on a panorama of the frozen north, revealing a school of seals mounting a jagged crag of ice. The seals were quickly joined by a group of Eskimo dancing girls. They were followed by a series of 'impressively artistic dances by fascinatingly pretty young women wearing astoundingly rich and beautiful gowns all blending with the Arctic atmosphere and bespeaking the moods of the barren white country.' The numbers which followed included ice skating, a balloon act presented by Miss Lillian Powell and a Monte Carlo dance hall scene.

After the film, the director-star was led down to the stage. 'He was too emotional, he explained, to make much of a speech and then, characteristically, he proceeded to deliver a fairly good one.' Georgia noted that this was one of the rare occasions when Chaplin had no self-doubts about his work: 'He was confident about that. He really felt it was the greatest picture he had made. He was quite satisfied.'[11]

Chaplin spent the next week refining the cutting of the film, and then a fortnight after that preparing a new musical score. Once there was no more work to be done, he was clearly eager to get away from

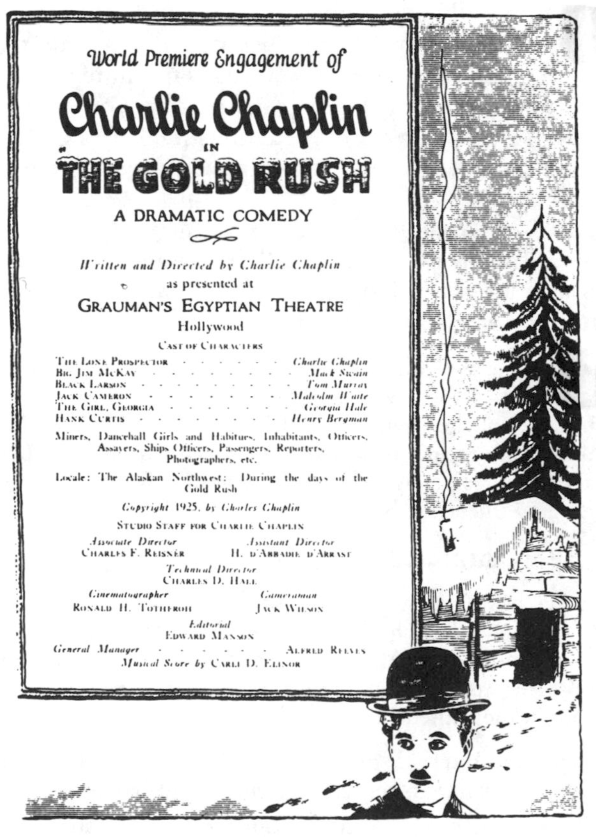

1925 - Première programme for *The Gold Rush*.

Los Angeles and the house and on 29 July left for New York by train with Kono and Henri d'Arrast, though the New York première was not until 16 August. Edna, who was on the way to Europe, joined Chaplin briefly in New York between 17 August and her sailing for Cherbourg on 22 August.

In the big cities *The Gold Rush* was an instant success, but business was slower in the sticks. In January Arthur Kelly of United Artists wrote to Sydney that *The Gold Rush* had 'proved to be a flop in all the small cities. In fact it is rather disastrous to some of the exhibitors. Apparently they do not want to see Charlie in any dramatic work, which is proved by analyzing his gross receipts. On every engagement the opening broke all records, but immediately flopped on the second and subsequent days, proving that they had all made up their minds to go for a big laugh in which they were disappointed, and naturally a reaction set in. Perhaps this will be a tip to you on your future productions . . .' Kelly's fears proved unjustified. *The Gold Rush* had cost Chaplin $923,886.45; in time it would gross more than six million dollars.

In Britain *The Gold Rush* opened at the Tivoli, Strand, which Chaplin had known as a music hall and which had recently been converted into a luxury cinema. It made broadcasting history, or at least a rather bizarre fragment of it:

> Next Saturday at 7.30 an attempt will be made to broadcast the laughter of the audience at the Tivoli Theatre during the ten most uproariously funny minutes of the new Charlie Chaplin film *The Gold Rush*. I hear that a preliminary experiment has been successful, but the BBC will not guarantee good results on the night itself, for this sort of transmission is a difficult and uncertain business.[12]

Evidently all went off well, however:

> What so far has been the most original experiment in radio work was carried out by the British Broadcasting Company on Saturday evening last (26 September) when there was broadcasted to every station throughout the British Isles what was announced badly [?baldly] enough in every newspaper in the United Kingdom thus:
>
> '7.30 p.m. Interlude of Laughter. Ten Minutes with Charlie Chaplin and his audience at the Tivoli.'
>
> 'Uncle Rex', the broadcasting announcer, prefaced the item by stating that the B.B.C. were trying a unique experiment – that of broadcasting 'a storm of uncontrolled laughter, inspired by the only man in the world

who could make people laugh continually for the space of five minutes, viz., Charlie Chaplin!' The episode chosen was that which forms the climactic scene of *The Gold Rush* when Charlie and his partner awake to discover their log cabin is resting perilously on the edge of a precipice.

This experiment, as reported by one listener-in, proved highly successful. The first outburst of laughter from the audience sounded like big crested waves breaking in fury against huge butting crags, and slowly dissolving in a thousand ripples and cascades that dropped like sea-pearls in an angry sea.

This was succeeded by a sound that echoed like the rolling of jam jars in an express train. Followed sounds of vague, whimsical crescendoes of delirious delight, which culminated in torrential laughter that finally broke out into a terrific uproar – a perfect storm of uncontrollable guffaws. Then shrieks of shrill but helpless laughter – and above them all the piercing silver-toned laugh of a woman which overtopped the thousand and one outbursts.

The climax came when one mighty outburst of laughter broke out in fullest fury, and sounding like salvoes of a thousand guns making the Royal salute. Gradually the laughter died away with sounds like an exhaust-valve, stuttering away its strength into thin air.

So ended what may be regarded as a historic event in film history – ten minutes of laughter with Charlie Chaplin at the Tivoli, London.[13]

The film's première at the Capitol in Berlin was distinguished by the perhaps unique occurrence of an encore within a film. At the Dance of the Rolls the audience went wild with enthusiasm. The manager of the theatre, with admirable presence of mind, rushed up to the projection box and instructed the projectionist to roll the film back and play the scene again. The orchestra picked up their cue and the *reprise* was greeted with even more tumultuous applause.[14]

11

THE CIRCUS

California and the house on Summit Drive now held little attraction, and Chaplin remained more than two months in New York after the première of *The Gold Rush*. He eventually returned on 15 October 1925, and was very soon at work on *The Circus*. It was to be a production dogged by persistent misfortune. The most surprising aspect of the film is not that it is as good as it is, but that it was ever completed at all.

After *The Gold Rush*, Chaplin considered a version of Stevenson's *The Suicide Club* and *The Dandy*. He was always toying with an idea for a Napoleon film. In March Sydney had cabled him from New York:

> SHERWOOD OF LIFE WRITTEN MOVIE STORY CALLED SKY-SCRAPER FOR BUSTER KEATON STOP KEATON CONSIDERS STORY GOOD BUT HAS NOT AS YET DEFINITELY PURCHASED IT STOP HAVE READ IT AND THINK IT OKAY SHERWOOD WRITING ANOTHER ONE SUITABLE FOR YOU STOP WIRE ME IF YOU WANT ME TO TRY AND CLOSE THE DEAL FOR YOU.

Sherwood was one of Chaplin's most appreciative critics, but Chaplin seems not to have responded to the proposition.

Henry Bergman, a modest man who recorded few impressions of his many years with Chaplin, described the genesis of the new film:

> Before he had made *The Circus* he said to me one night, 'Henry, I have an idea I would like to do a gag placing me in a position I can't get away from for some reason. I'm on a high place troubled by something else, monkeys or things that come to me and I can't get away from them.' He

> was mulling around in his head a vaudeville story. I said to him, 'Charlie, you can't do anything like that on a stage. The audience would be uncomfortable craning their necks to watch a vaudeville actor. It would be unnatural. Why not develop your idea in a circus tent on a tightrope. I'll teach you to walk a rope.'[1]

Clearly there were other arguments against setting a film in a vaudeville theatre so soon after E. A. Dupont's German production *Variety* which was currently the talk of the film world.

'Many of his ideas are built on one gag,' Bergman added. Nightmare has often been the essence of comedy. Harold Lloyd's most famous film *Safety Last* is centred on his perils on the top of a skyscraper. James Agee described a sequence in a Laurel and Hardy film 'simple and real . . . as a nightmare. Laurel and Hardy are trying to move a piano across a narrow suspension bridge. The bridge is slung over a sickening chasm, between a couple of Alps. Midway they meet a gorilla.'[2]

The nightmare that Chaplin invented – to what extent might it have been an unconscious metaphor for his troubles? – was to place himself on a tightrope, high above the ring of a circus. He has no net. His safety harness comes loose. He is attacked by monkeys. They rip off his trousers. He has forgotten to put on his tights.,

The story which eventually grew around this climactic incident of farcical horror is a neat comic-romantic melodrama. Charlie the Tramp chances upon a travelling circus which is doing bad business. He is chased into the ring by police, and his accidents there prove a tremendous hit with the audience. He is consequently taken on as a clown: the problem is that he is funny only when he does not intend to be. He falls in love with the daughter of the proprietor, and defends her from her father's cruelties. The idyll is ended when a new star, Rex the High Wire Walker, arrives in the show and steals the girl's heart. It is in consequence of his efforts to emulate his rival that he finds himself in the disastrous predicament on the tightrope. He finally faces defeat, helps the couple to elope, and at the end is left alone in the ring of trodden grass which is all that remains of the circus.

Chaplin had a new assistant, who was also eventually to be chosen to play the part of Rex. Harry Crocker was a new favourite in the San Simeon set, and it was through Hearst and Marion Davies that Chaplin first met him. Crocker at this time was thirty years old, slightly over six feet tall and conventionally handsome. He came from a prominent San Francisco banking family, had been through Yale and had started his working life in the brokerage business. Yearning for something more glamorous he had thrown brokerage up in the autumn of 1924 to come to Hollywood, where his good looks and taste for practical jokes attracted Marion Davies. Having acted with the Los Angeles Playhouse Company and done a bit part as a soldier in *The Big Parade*, he was given a leading role by Marion in her film *Tillie the Toiler*. Since then he had landed three other film roles, and when Chaplin suggested he might work with him had just begun work as an extra in King Vidor's *La Bohème*. Chaplin told Crocker to make the necessary arrangements with Alf Reeves; but when Crocker reported to Reeves' office, the latter knew nothing about it. 'Don't let that bother you,' he said. 'He is very vague.'[3] When Eddie Sutherland heard that Crocker had joined Chaplin in his own former capacity as assistant director, he advised him: 'If you're smart you enter Chaplin on your books as a son-of-a-bitch. He isn't always one, but he can be one on occasion. I thought it better to start off with that appellation of him in mind, then when he behaves badly it doesn't come as quite the shock it might otherwise be, and all his good behaviour comes as quite a pleasant surprise.'

Another former Chaplin assistant, Henri d'Abbadie d'Arrast, also warned him, 'Charlie has a sadistic streak in him. Even if he's very fond of you he'll try and lick you mentally, to cow you, to get your goat. He can't help it. You'll be surprised how many friends he's alienated through that one trait.' Crocker's experiences of Chaplin were happier, and his affection and admiration lasted through the years, even though on occasion their fights could be bitter, and a disagreement led to his departure from *City Lights*. On *The Circus* he found he had been engaged as assistant, writer-actor and companion. His first job was to work with Chaplin on story ideas, which essentially meant acting as sounding board and stenographer. Chaplin and Crocker took off for ten days (9–18 November 1925) to Del Monte to work on the story, leaving the studio staff, under the supervision of Danny Hall, to start building a circus tent and menagerie on the studio lot. The trip provided a further escape from the household at Summit Drive. It was also necessary to get away from the now regular distractions of evenings in the company of Hearst and Marion.

Chaplin's chauffeur, Frank Kawa, drove them in the black Locomobile, with Kono following in his own car. Crocker later recalled his bewilderment at the variety of Chaplin's conversation on the leisurely journey. He outlined a scheme for taxing industry by a kind of 25 per cent tithe on its products; he talked of his horror at working conditions in factories and the pressure to succeed exerted upon employees by American business; about customs of breakfast time gastronomy; about time and space and light.

A lot of their thinking was done in the course of long walks around Del Monte. Crocker recalled how Chaplin, oblivious of the surrounding traffic, suddenly acted out a piece of business he had thought up himself. The spieler in front of a side show would point at the banners advertising a giant and a midget. Charlie would pause on his way out of the door of the tent, reach up to shake hands with the unseen giant, then turn to the other side and stoop to say goodbye to the midget.

When these creative sessions had gone well Chaplin would sing music hall songs on the way back to Pearl Lodge, where they stayed, or launch upon discussions of international finance or the transmigration of souls. Then he might suddenly propose games of betting on the length of each straight stretch of road to the next curve. One night in the Lodge, Crocker recalled, they competed to make bad puns, after which Chaplin performed all the parts in a performance of the third and fourth acts of *Sherlock Holmes*.

The notes which they brought back from their scenario trip still exist and clearly illustrate Chaplin's method of starting the construction of a film by assembling a disparate mass of potential gags, scenes or hazy notions. He collected together a mass of fabrics; only later did he settle upon the pattern of the material and cut of the garment. At this time Chaplin was still undecided as to whether to call the film *The Circus* or *The Traveller*. The notes are presented as a series of 'suggestions'. Some are for whole sequences:

> *Suggestion:* Charlie notices the dog trainer is ill-treating animals – one dog especially. He takes trainer to task and fight ensues. As the 2 men are struggling, the dog that Charlie has tried to save comes into the fight and bites Charlie. Charlie finally flees. He is angered at dog, but dog sits up and begs. Charlie forgives him and goes to pat him and dog almost bites his hand off.

The last is a parable of ingratitude worthy of Luis Buñuel. Chaplin had a characteristic afterthought:

> *Suggestion:* At end of episode with cruel trainer, have Charlie present him with whip to replace one he has broken.

This sequence, like others, was to be rejected. Other 'suggestions' remained intact in the eventual scenario:

> *Suggestion:* Charlie mistaken for pickpocket. Cop chases him through funhouse. Charlie takes place on outside of fun house beside dummies, imitating their wooden action. Maybe introduce crook – also in fight with police – hiding as dummy when Charlie socks him as part of act – crook being forced to take it as cop is watching.

Some 'suggestions' are for individual gags:

> *Suggestions:* Charlie is standing near camel. Tactlessly he asks fellow workman for a 'Lucky Strike'* and the incensed camel bites him.
>
> *Suggestion:* Charlie at work with hose, accidentally hits boss, blames it on elephant and spanks elephant's trunk. Tells elephant 'Put that away.'

Often in this kind of preliminary work on a film we find Chaplin reverting to ideas which seem almost obsessive with him, but then – perhaps recognizing a too persistent preoccupation – rejecting them. The lurking fear of the audience – particularly an audience in a live theatre – which was to be most completely expressed in *Limelight*, is ever present:

> Suggestion: During the efforts of Charlie to be funny as clown, there is a tough guy in the audience who fails to appreciate his efforts, making it exceedingly difficult for Charlie to work.

One gag idea echoes, whether consciously or not, Chaplin's current efforts to keep his domestic worries from a suspicious and prying press:

> *Suggestion:* An acrobat fights violently with wife or partner off-stage and is very suave and loving on.

Chaplin's first idea for the beginning was never used: his eventual solution was certainly much neater. It nevertheless showed his reluctance ever to waste a good idea, for here once more was the stuff of the abandoned film, *The Professor*:

> *Suggestion for opening:* Under the archway of a bridge is a jungle of hoboes. Some asleep – some sitting around – one stirring food in a can over the fire. Charlie comes into camp. He looks around fastidiously –

* 'Lucky Strike' and 'Camel' were rival brands of cigarettes.

> takes out a handkerchief – dusts off a rock and sits down. One bum looks up and inquires: 'What's your line?' Charlie answers: 'I am a circus man.' Bum looks at him incredulously. He notices look and takes from under his arm a small box labelled 'Flea Circus'. Business ad lib with fleas.
>
> In putting fleas away for night, Charlie discovers one gone – goes over to bum with long beard – picks up flea from beard, regards it and puts it back. It is evidently not one of the circus.
>
> All asleep. In movements in sleep, flea circus is overturned and fleas escape. Scratching commences among bums but fleas concentrate on dog. Dog finally gets up in agony and whines, waking Charlie. He notices overturned flea circus – watches dog and jumps at the right conclusion. Pursuit of dog which goes into the lake, drowning circus. Charlie in despair.

The surviving sequence of *The Professor* also ends with the Professor giving chase to the dog. The tragic finale indicated in his 'suggestion' perhaps tells us how the sequence might have ended in the earlier film. The idea for the opening of *The Circus* continues with a wonderful gag which was unfortunately never used – by Chaplin or any other comedian:

> Next morning bums prepare to board train. They will ride brakebeams. Charlie spies mail-sack in brackets – removes same and stands in brackets – is caught in arm of mail-car. Mail clerk is asleep. Charlie rides at ease, enjoying view, while bums gaze enviously from underneath car. Passenger in car in front of Charlie throws cigarette out of window. Charlie catches same and smokes it – dropping butt with gesture to one of the bums underneath car. Arrives in town to discover circus in progress.

Although much would be changed in the course of the lengthy production of *The Circus* there was plenty for the unit to work on when Chaplin and Crocker returned from Del Monte on 18 November.

Henry Bergman carried out his promise to teach Chaplin to walk the tightrope: it is not clear at what point in his career this man of so many parts had learned a skill not evidently suited to a man of his large girth. 'I taught Charlie to walk a rope in one week . . . We stretched the rope this high from the floor [he indicated a foot high to the interviewer] then raised it as high as the ceiling with a net under it, but Charlie never fell. He walked it all day long. You didn't see anything in the picture of what he did on that rope.' Crocker, for the role of Rex, also had to learn to walk the rope convincingly, and day after day, right up to Christmas, he and Chaplin practised for hours while below and around them the sets were decorated and the costumes prepared. They were only briefly interrupted by the first of the catastrophes which hit the production. The tent was almost ready when, on Sunday 6 December, an exceptionally rough storm of wind and rain badly damaged it.

As the use of her name in the story suggestions indicates, Georgia Hale was expected to be Chaplin's leading lady once more. Her contract however came to an end on 31 December. It is not certain why it was not renewed. Her work in *The Gold Rush* had been good and Chaplin seems to have been genuinely fond of her; their friendship continued intermittently for years after the film. Perhaps Georgia was impatient for a faster-moving career. As it was she had appeared in five films before *The Circus* eventually emerged. She made half a dozen more films by 1928 and then retired from the screen: her voice and diction were not as pleasing as her looks and her career was doomed by talking pictures. Her most memorable performances were those in *The Salvation Hunters*, *The Gold Rush* and *The Last Moment*, directed by the gifted Paul Fejös – apparently confirming von Sternberg's view that Georgia Hale was an actress whose on-screen qualities depended to a great extent upon the gifts of her directors.

Chaplin's new leading lady was Merna Kennedy, the childhood friend of Lita Grey who had accompanied her to the studio on the day she secured her test for *The Gold Rush*. The studio publicity for the release of the film related how Merna got the part:

> . . . Charlie was about to make *The Circus*. He was to walk a tightrope and frolic about in the sideshows and seek to win the fluff-skirted girl who rides the circling white Arabian in the middle ring. Who was to be the girl?
>
> 'Merna Kennedy is playing in a musical show at the Mason Opera House here in Los Angeles.'
>
> 'Let's look at her tonight,' was the answer.
>
> So Charlie Chaplin went to the Mason and saw the musical show *All For You*.
>
> Merna Kennedy was picked. Screen tests followed, of course, and the vivaciousness and charm of the red-haired lady with the screen eyes registered with Charlie. He chose a leading lady whom none knew, whom none had seen on the screen.[4]

Merna Kennedy had in fact been suggested for the role by her childhood friend Lita, who had met Merna again after more than a year, while Chaplin was in New York. Chaplin appears initially to have been less enthusiastic about the suggestion than the press story suggests, but he was persuaded. Lita herself came to regret her initiative: she had already been jealous of Georgia Hale and came to realize that her husband was more attentive to the leading lady she had proposed than he was to herself. Merna Kennedy's contract was dated to start on 2 January 1926. There was little other casting to be done. Chaplin wanted Henry Bergman to be Merna's step-father, the mean circus proprietor, 'but I said, "No, Charlie, I'm a roly-poly kind-faced man, not the dirty heavy who would beat a girl." So I was cast as the fat old clown.' Instead Allan Garcia, making his first appearance in a major role, was put under contract to play the part.

Shooting began on Monday 11 January. The first two weeks were spent on the scenes on the tightrope. This was contrary to Chaplin's usual method of shooting in story sequence, but he was in training, and in any case this was the one scene of the film which was so far fully worked out in his head. On 17 January – a Sunday, which showed that Chaplin was particularly engrossed in the scene – he began work with the monkeys. On 27 January he steeled himself to shooting material of the audience in the circus tent. He was never happy with crowd scenes, and the cost – even in 1926 – was worrying if crowd shooting went on too long. For the circus audience the studio hired 185 extras at $5 for the day, 114 at $7.50, seventy-seven at $10, and one at $15. Chaplin made eighteen long takes with the crowd to be subsequently cut up for inserts, and ensured that the crowd shots were finished that day. Three days later there was a more costly extra on the lot – an elephant whose day's hire was $150, with $15 for its trainer.

The first week in February, no doubt somewhat depressed by a cold, Chaplin edited the scenes already shot on the tightrope and decided he wanted to retake them, which took up the rest of the week. The following week he and Crocker shot the scenes in which they rode the bicycle on the tightrope, with Charlie making his 'ride for life'. Thereupon catastrophe struck again. The unit realized that the rushes they had seen so far were marred by scratches. Faults or errors were discovered in the studio laboratory. There is no record of precisely what happened, but it is not hard to guess Chaplin's reaction. The laboratory staff was changed, but Chaplin had to face the fact that all the work of the past month would have to be redone. Throughout the week of 16 February he was back on the tightrope again. By the time he had finished, he had done more than 700 takes on the wire. It is hardly surprising that he was, as Crocker remembered, often exhausted. 'Nobody has ever noticed that my legs doubled for Charlie's when he needed a rest.' The retakes were completed by the end of February and the first week in March Merna Kennedy was put to work. She apparently worked well under Chaplin's tutelage: the daily shooting records indicate few problems with her scenes.

Work on the film was a welcome distraction from the wretchedness of Summit Drive. In the autumn of 1925 Lita discovered that she was again pregnant. Chaplin was furious to find he had created yet another snare for himself (or so he felt) and the pregnancy led, if it were possible, to further deterioration of relations between the couple. Lita found it impossible to please her husband and was wretchedly jealous of his attentions to Marion Davies, Merna Kennedy and Georgia Hale. Chaplin for his part was tormented by the situation; he began to suffer from acute insomnia, and would prowl the house at night with a shotgun, fearing intruders. He would bathe or shower a dozen times a day. He had the studio electricians fix bugging devices in Lita's room, but there was nothing to hear and the equipment was in any case technically inadequate. Even efforts at conciliation went wrong. Chaplin acceded to Lita's pleas to meet people of her own age, and paid for her to give a party for eight of her young friends in a restaurant. Rashly, Lita took them home to Summit Drive afterwards. When Chaplin returned unexpectedly he flew into a rage and threw the guests out of the house. The incident was to be cited by both parties in the subsequent divorce action. In this fraught atmosphere Lita's second child, Sydney Earle Chaplin, was born five weeks prematurely, on 30 March 1926. Lita's single consolation was that the birth, unlike that of her first son, was easy.

Certainly the new child did nothing to improve the unhappy marriage. Again the choice of name was a matter of dispute but Lita agreed to name the boy after her brother-in-law. After the break-up of the marriage, Lita called the boy 'Tommy'. There was disagreement over baptism: Chaplin always believed that children should be allowed to choose their own religion when they reached a sufficiently mature age.

Home life was merely a distraction, with work on *The Circus* resuming at full tilt. The day after the birth Chaplin was rehearsing the mirror maze, which required some ingenious camera placement by Totheroh. The exteriors of the carnival were shot at Venice Beach, not far from the spot where *Kid Auto Races* had been filmed. The location scenes, which involved up to thirty extras and a bus to take them to the shooting, were shot in the mornings, before the regular crowds arrived. Among the scenes filmed in the studio in the afternoons was the business where the hungry Charlie eats a hot dog clutched by a babe in arms, solicitously wiping the child's mouth when its father turns round. The incident was perhaps suggested by a favourite yarn of Fred Karno, who related how he and some young friends from the circus stole jam sandwiches from school children when they had no money to buy breakfast.

Throughout the succeeding five months work continued steadily. There was a brief but notable interruption on 16 June when Raquel Meller visited the set. Chaplin had conceived great enthusiasm for the petite and colourful Spanish actress and *chanteuse*. For a while he felt that he had at last found the ideal Josephine for the Napoleon film that continued to obsess him. On 7 September the studio was closed for the day to mark the funeral of Rudolph Valentino. Chaplin, who was one of the Great Screen Lover's pall-bearers, said graciously that his death was 'one of the greatest tragedies that has occurred in the history of the motion picture industry'.

The work with the lions caused concern. Two animals were hired (at a cost of $150 a day, including the trainer). One was docile, but the other was a spirited creature. In at least one scene that appears in the finished film, as Chaplin would unashamedly point out in later years, the fear on his face was not pretence. Despite the risk, Chaplin went back into the cage day after day. By the time the sequence was completed he had made more than 200 takes with the lions.

One of the inconveniences of working with the lions was that the unit had to fit in with their meal hours, and the lions preferred to eat around three in the afternoon. Between the nervous strain and the change of routine, Chaplin suffered from indigestion, and the doctor prescribed Epsom salts taken in regular small doses in hot water for two or three days. Crocker recalled how he would pace the floor in story conferences, interspersing his oratory with belches, each of which would be followed by a relieved sigh of 'Ah! That's better.' Crocker remembered a typical example: 'Now, what I want in this story is not only love and romance, but magic. There must be *magic*. The audience must be enthralled – burp – ah, that's better!'

Apart from gas on the director's heart, all seemed for the moment to be going well. Then, on 28 September a fire suddenly broke out, sweeping through the closed stage. Before it could be brought under control, the set had been completely destroyed. Props and equipment were damaged by fire and water. Thousands of panes of glass in the roof and walls were broken. The electrical equipment was put out of action. The stills photographer captured a few shots of Chaplin, still in his costume, gazing in dismay at the wreckage. These unposed shots are some of the most poignant images of the Tramp. Totheroh was as resourceful, and filmed 250 feet of the catastrophe and his bemused boss. It was slight compensation that this piece of impromptu film could be exploited as pre-publicity for *The Circus*.

The studio was rapidly put back into partial operation; and in only ten working days, between 3 and 14 October, Chaplin had completed a lengthy and complicated sequence in the café set. For reasons known only to himself, he was not to use the sequence in the film, though it is a faultlessly constructed and self-contained comic sketch. Charlie, his nose much out of joint, reluctantly accompanies Rex and Merna to the café. At a neighbouring table sit two prize fighters, twin brothers. (Both 'twins' are played by the same actor, 'Doc' Stone: Totheroh and his fellow cameramen performed the magic with double exposure.) One of the two brothers amuses himself by insulting and annoying Charlie. This gives Charlie an idea for winning back Merna's admiration. He takes the fighter aside, and pays him $5 to pretend to be beaten in a fight. The ruse works successfully, and Rex and Merna see Charlie with fresh eyes – until the fighter's twin, who had earlier left the restaurant, returns to take his brother's place. Charlie, expecting to repeat his earlier performance, attacks him, but is dismayed when the fighter starts hitting back. A series of happy accidents save the day, and Rex knocks out Charlie's opponent. As the party departs from the restaurant, Charlie leaves Rex and Merna for a moment to retrieve $5 from the pocket of the opponent whom he believes to have reneged on the contract.

In early November Chaplin shot an amusing sequence to lead in to this café episode. It was filmed on Sunset Boulevard, which still retained a pleasantly rural look. Charlie is proudly walking Merna out, despite the tiresome attentions of a stray dog which snaps about his ankles. To his chagrin however they meet Rex, who joins them in their walk. Merna is touched by Rex's gallantry when he picks up the purse a lady has dropped. Charlie determines to show himself as gallant, but unhappily the distressed damsel who falls to his lot is a stalwart woman laden with indequately wrapped parcels of fish. Charlie attempts to pick up a single fish she has dropped but his efforts only result in an endless scaly avalanche, as he struggles desperately to rewrap them. The lady becomes more and more angry and Charlie more and more helpless until he retreats with the embarrassed hint of a shrug.

At the end of November, while Chaplin was rehearsing a new roller-skating routine, Lita walked out of the house on Summit Drive, taking their two children with her. Life can have been no easier for the unwelcome child bride than for her exasperated husband. Lita was jealous and fearful of the more sophisticated, beautiful and intelligent women who, she felt, exerted a much more powerful attraction than she herself could ever do. She must have understood, however, that the single rival with which she could never compete was Chaplin's work. Chaplin knew also that this was where he was most vulnerable. He remembered the adventures involved in spiriting *The Kid* to safety, a mere five years ago; as soon as Lita's lawyers began to gather (her lawyer uncle, Edwin McMurray, moved from San Francisco to an office in Los Angeles so that he could be near the case), Chaplin took action to protect *The Circus* in the event of trouble. On 3 December stock was taken of the film already shot; nine reels of cut positive and thirteen reels of essential uncut scenes were carefully packed into two boxes ready for removal to safety. On Sunday 5 December notice was posted that studio operations were temporarily suspended. The studio staff was cut down to the minimum. All the actors were laid off, with the exception of Merna Kennedy, Henry Bergman, Harry Crocker and Allan Garcia. As if all this were not enough, the US Government chose this moment to decide that Chaplin's income tax for the preceding years was underpaid by $1,113,000.

It was at about this time that Robert Florey, a French idolater of Chaplin who was later to become a director in his own right and was to be Chaplin's assistant on *Monsieur Verdoux*, wrote a haunting pen portrait of his hero:

> Often in the evening, around eleven, when I go to Henry's, the actors' restaurant in Hollywood run by the excellent Henry Bergman (whom you have seen in all Chaplin's films) I meet, walking alone or sometimes with his devoted assistant Harry Crocker, the popular Charlie, the great Charles Spencer Chaplin, unrecognizable beneath his big, shapeless felt hat. To protect himself against the evening mists – the night can be

perilous in California – he wraps himself in a big grey overcoat, and his trousers, quite wide, according to the current fashion, hide his tiny feet, shod in buttoned boots with beige cloth tops. So it was that one night last December, coming out of Grauman's Egyptian, I was striding the short distance between the theatre and our favourite restaurant when I recognized, a few steps ahead of me, the familiar outline of Charlie. Instinctively I slowed my pace, and I cannot express what melancholy overwhelmed me in recognizing the total solitude of the most popular man in the world. He was walking slowly, close to the darkened shop windows; the fog was thick, and Charlie, his hands in the pockets of his raglan, was making a slight, regular movement of his elbows. His footsteps made no sound; his collar was turned up, and he was so slight in his big coat that he might have been taken for a child dressed up in his father's clothes. This man whose cinematic masterpieces had been shown that very night on screens all across the world, this man who had made people laugh that night in all the continents, was there, walking in front of me in the fog. There was infinite sadness in the spectacle of Charlie, alone in the night. A man whom the smartest *salons* in the world would have fought to entertain, was quietly walking, alone in the shadows, his hands in his pockets and the brim of his hat pulled down over his eyes. It is true that the life of artists in Hollywood, especially in the evening, when the day's work is finished, cannot be compared to existence in Paris or London, but to see Charlie Chaplin, alone on the boulevard, like some little extra without a job or a place to live, wrung my heart.

At the corner of Cherokee Street an important event occurred – important for Charlie at least . . . he met a dog. A fat, common, mongrel who was sitting waiting for who knew what. And Charlie stopped, abruptly. He had found someone to talk to. And he started to question the dog, who probably recognized in him a comrade, because it offered him its paw. I couldn't hear Charlie's words, but as I caught up with him he said to me: 'Are you going to Henry's? Let's go together.' Two minutes later we arrived at the café-restaurant. But instead of entering the front door on Hollywood Boulevard, he went through the kitchen, because Charlie had a guest with him – the fat dog, who had followed him. Charlie ordered a copious dinner for his friend from the Filipino cook, and the dog once more offered his paw to be shaken. We left the kitchen, and as we were going into the restaurant Charlie said, 'That dog knows me. He often waits on the corner of Cherokee, and I realized tonight that he hadn't eaten again . . . so you see I couldn't do anything else but invite him!' And that sweet, large-hearted little man talked of other things.[5]

On 10 January 1927, a day after Chaplin had left for New York, Lita's lawyers filed the divorce complaint. It was an exceptional document of its kind. In the first place Chaplin was joined as defendant with his studio, his company, Kono, Reeves, the National Bank of Los Angeles, the Bank of Italy, and various other banks and corporations. Again, it was unprecedented among divorce complaints for its length. Normally such complaints run to three or four pages: this one had fifty-two. For the most part it was the awful tittle-tattle of who said

Charlie and 'the Kid'- BY HUNGERFORD

1927 - A cartoonist's view of the Chaplin - Grey divorce.

and did what, a wretched reprise of the abuses and recriminations of a marriage fast repented. Then there was an innuendo of infidelity with 'a certain prominent film actress'. The lawyers' biggest gun, though, was their demonstration that things which are done in the dark privacy of the bedroom take on a lurid and shocking aspect in the light of print and the spotlight of the courtroom. They had moreover discovered an obscure corner of the Californian Statute

Book – a certain section 288a – which whimsically forbade areas of commonplace sexual practice.

The style of the complaint made clear its dual purpose. The joining of Chaplin's business associates and interests indicated the lawyers' intention of securing as large a proportion of his material goods as possible. The grubbing detail of the rest was intended, quite simply, to destroy his reputation in the eyes of the public. The Fatty Arbuckle and William Desmond Taylor scandals were still recent in memory. Arbuckle had been acquitted of the manslaughter of Virginia Rappe, but the associations of the trials were enough to ruin him and end his career. The lawyers must have been confident that so much innuendo would ensure Chaplin's fall.

The document was demeaning and humiliating to everyone concerned. What pain it must have caused to a man who so prized his privacy and public dignity can hardly be imagined. Chaplin was reported to be in a state of nervous breakdown in New York, where he was with his lawyer, Nathan Burkan. It would hardly have been surprising. Meanwhile pirated copies of the divorce complaint became best sellers in the shadier areas of the book trade: the paperback was titled: *The Complaint of Lita*. The reporters were insatiable and the Chaplin case supplanted Teapot Dome, the American landings in Nicaragua, Aimée Semple McPherson and the Hall-Mills murder case in the headlines.

Chaplin's foresight in removing *The Circus* to safety was swiftly vindicated. Lita's lawyers asked for, and were granted, the exceptional remedy of a temporary restraining order to secure not only the community property but also his personal assets, pending litigation. On 12 January the receivers put the studio under guard: in charge of the operation were an attorney, W. I. Gilbert, and a real-estate agent, Herman Spitzel. Alfred Reeves had conveniently taken leave of absence, taking the keys with him, but on 18 January, for no very evident purpose, the receivers opened up the safe and vault. Chaplin talked vaguely of continuing work on *The Circus* in New York but even he must have had fears that it would never be completed.

Almost more degrading than the complaint was the wrangling over money that now commenced. The court awarded Lita temporary occupation of the house and provisional alimony of $3000 a month. The house brought her little joy: the servants had left it; the cost of upkeep was enormous; and since the Federal Tax Authorities had placed a lien on Chaplin's financial assets, the temporary alimony payments were not forthcoming.

Chaplin's Californian lawyers, with a very poor sense of public relations, proposed a permanent settlement of $25 a week for Lita and the children. Uncle Edwin made nation-wide propaganda with this: one women's club started a milk fund for the Chaplin babies before the Chaplin lawyers agreed to the adjudicated temporary alimony.

> Suddenly [Robert Florey recorded] Charlie disappeared . . . Overnight, *Charlie's house is empty.*
>
> The other day, when I was working with Douglas in his Beverly Hills drawing room, I was surprised to see the interpreter of *Zorro* stop abruptly in front of the window and gaze at something which, from where I sat, I could not see. I didn't interrupt his meditation, thinking that he was working out some idea for his new film . . . but after a few moments of silence, Doug exclaimed:
>
> 'Look at the house with the blind windows!'
>
> And, in my turn, I looked and saw the sad spectacle of Charlie's house, two hundred yards away, standing in the misty first light of the Californian December; Charlie had been gone two months and all that remained were thirty-eight big black eyes. The house was deserted, no light, no curtains at the windows; thirty-eight blind eyes which wept for the sentimental and lamentable existence of the greatest of screen comedians . . . And Douglas added: 'How well that house reflects the existence of the great Chaplin.'
>
> The house with thirty-eight blind windows was truly melancholy, surrounded by its pines and cypresses.[6]

Contrary to the expectations of Lita's lawyers, the complaint did not ruin Chaplin; though it would have ruined almost any other man in America. Neither the lawyers nor anyone else could have conceived how deep was the love the public held for him, or that it would survive even smears so black. Some women's clubs agitated for the boycott of Chaplin's films, and in a few backwoods cities and states they succeeded. News of these boycotts produced a strong counter-reaction, which greatly heartened Chaplin, in the form of a protest signed by French intellectuals including Louis Aragon, René Clair, Germaine Dulac and (French by adoption) Man Ray. When Chaplin began to emerge from his seclusion, East Coast society, as if in demonstration, courted and entertained him. He was invited to the Old Timers' Night of the New York Newspaper Club, and delighted them by performing a pantomime about an ill-fated toreador. It was no waste of effort to win over an influential section of the Eastern press in this way.

Among the innumerable letters of encouragement and support from friends and collaborators, one of the most touching was from the un-named, plain-faced woman who had worked with him for a day on a scene with tumbling fish, just before the studio close-down:

> All I can say is I think you are wonderful and don't let them break your heart.

Even in the letter, she did not reveal her name: she signed herself simply: 'Your Fishwoman'.

Sydney was in California and keeping an eye on the studio; careful about money as he was, he was troubled to see that there were still 'several people walking around the studio – such as publicity men etc., and I am wondering if you know they are still on salary and if you want to keep up this big expense as your future actions are so indefinite.' His letter to Chaplin is full of fraternal concern and anxiety:

> Dear Charlie:
>
> Because I have not written to you is not that I lack sympathy – you are continually in my thoughts. I hate to imagine how you must have felt when you were on that train, alone, and the news broke. It was like a bomb-shell to me. I did not believe that she could be so vindictive as to actually try to ruin you. She was cutting her own throat. I only just learned the result of the last conference Wright* had with her attorneys – I certainly would not pay her a million nor for that matter make any settlement until the government suit was out of the way. Certainly if worse comes to worse the government will take so much there will be nothing left for her any way. She would have a tough time collecting, especially if you go to England for your future work. The more I think of England the more I believe it will be the best thing.
>
> It all seems to me that some one must have a personal grudge against you – I have heard from several people that there has been considerable talk about your socialist tendencies – and as this is a capitalistic government it does not help under the circumstances. I do hate to paint GLOOM but it does seem to me that we should be prepared to go to the other side if things do not shape themselves to our satisfaction . . .

Thoughts of England touchingly stirred old memories:

* Loyd Wright, Chaplin's lawyer.

> Do not get too despondent, Charlie, remember there is more in life than great wealth – as long as you know you are comfortably fixed for the future and your health is good it would help to maintain a philosophical attitude toward your troubles. When I am feeling sort of worried, myself, I always think of the great joy, happiness and elated feeling I had when I signed on the dotted line for Fred Karno – just think, the great sum of three pounds a week – why I ran all the way to Kennington Road to send you the glad news. So it seems, after all, that happiness is a matter of comparison and dependent upon our own viewpoint or way of thinking. So CHEER UP OLD KID it will be interesting reading in your biography.

In this, Sydney was mistaken. Almost forty years afterwards, when Chaplin did finally write his memoirs, the recollection of these desolate times was still too painful to touch on beyond a bare mention: 'For two years we were married and tried to make a go of it, but it was hopeless and ended in a great deal of bitterness.'

On 2 June Chaplin's lawyers filed an answer to the complaint. In general this was simply a denial of the charges. It was admitted that the defendant had not visited the plaintiff on occasions when she had left home to holiday in Coronado, but that 'the plaintiff well knew that, because of the fact that at that time the defendant had from two hundred to three hundred people actually working, it would be impossible for this defendant to leave his work and go to Coronado.'

One charge evokes special sympathy for the defendant:

> 3(h) That on several occasions during the past year, defendant had said to plaintiff: 'Go away some place for a while; I can't work or create when you are here. You are ruining my career.' That on one such occasion plaintiff replied to defendant: 'Why, Charlie, I don't understand how I interfere with your work. I never see you or annoy you.' And he replied in a tone of exasperation; 'That isn't it. It is just the fact that you are here, and I am supposed to give the usual attention to a home and family. It annoys me, and irritates me, and I cannot work.'

The answer specifically denied this charge, but added significantly in this connexion:

> this defendant alleges that during said time, the plaintiff well knew that the defendant was busily engaged in the work of his profession and she at all times well knew of the demands and requirements made upon this defendant, and of the necessity of his devoting his undivided attention to the work of his profession; that the plaintiff was aware that in order for this defendant successfully to produce a good picture, that it was necessary

> and important that he concentrate upon his work and devote his every attention to it. That during said time this defendant explained to the plaintiff that it was vitally important that he give his undivided attention to his motion picture production.

One week after the answer was filed, the guards were removed from the studio and the receivers left. In August Lita's lawyers decided to precipitate matters by announcing that they were ready to name 'five prominent women' with whom, they would allege, Chaplin had been intimate during the period of his marriage. Rightly, they estimated that Chaplin was not the man to allow other people's careers to be ruined as, in the prevailing temper, they certainly would be. To make quite sure, however, Lita herself went to Marion Davies to tell her that she was at the top of the list (the others were Merna Kennedy, Edna Purviance, Claire Windsor and either Pola Negri or Peggy Hopkins Joyce). Marion, fearful of the possible effect the incident would have upon Hearst, conveyed her terror to Chaplin. The Chaplin lawyers agreed on a cash settlement and the case was settled with a brief, anti-climactic court hearing on 22 August 1927. The judge declined to hear all the unseemly stuff of the complaint. Lita withdrew her charges and asked for an interlocutory decree on the single charge of cruelty. She was awarded a settlement of $600,000, with a trust fund of $100,000 for each child. It was the largest such settlement in American legal history to that time. Chaplin was granted access to his sons. His legal costs amounted to almost one million dollars.

Lita was to find a generous portion of her settlement going to her lawyers, and the case they made for her would in the end ricochet harmfully on her own reputation. The last unsporting gesture of smearing the five women had not helped. Chaplin's popularity on the contrary seemed almost unaffected. One of many similar leading articles in the daily press stated:

> CHARLIE IS A REAL HERO
>
> Charlie Chaplin, who has entertained millions on the screen, has never been as satisfying as when he declines to entertain the thrill seekers by refusing to fight the divorce suit of his 'girl wife'. Charlie 'stands and delivers' to the tune of nearly a million dollars, thus depriving his public of another opportunity to determine whether where a film star lives is a home or a night club.
>
> There have been enough lurid stories to last for a while . . . Whether

> Charlie was actuated by good taste or good business sense is beside the point. His popularity, which is his capital, might seriously have been impaired had Lita been granted the opportunity to 'tell all' on the stand. The 'unnamed actresses' whom Lita was to have named are as well left in the obscurity of the screen as to the publicity of the printed page. We prefer to see them on the silver sheet showing high emotion by feverish undulation of the diaphragm, to placing them in the witness box to 'deny the allegation' with real tears.
>
> It is also a coincidence that Fatty Arbuckle, trying a comeback from a scandal years old, is denied a hearing in Washington, which would have none of him even at this late date. There has been enough washing of movie dirty linen in public to have a depressing effect on more than one reputation which lost its earning capacity.
>
> Whatever the reason, a rising vote of thanks to Charlie for sparing us the minute details of life, liberty, and the pursuit of happiness with the little woman.

The great comedian Will Rogers was as usual more succinct: 'Good joke on me. I left Hollywood to keep from being named in the Chaplin trial and now they go and name nobody. Not a name was mentioned but Charlie's bank. Charlie is not what I would call a devoted husband, but he certainly is worth marrying.'

The Circus was almost finished at the time of the suspension, and the material shot in the few weeks after work was resumed was mostly to fill out what had already been shot. Further scenes were taken in the circus ring, again entailing bringing back extras – about 250 of them this time – for two days' work. The fates had not quite done with *The Circus*. Months before, a location (a squat one-storeyed store on the corner of Lankershim and Hill, in Sawtelle) had been selected for the scene where Charlie is shot right out of the circus tent after his ride for life from the tightrope. One day in early October the crew was loaded into seven cars and set out for the location to shoot retakes. Unfortunately Sawtelle was a mushrooming suburb. In the long months since the spot had been selected, the one-storey building had been replaced by an ornate new hotel. A witness of Chaplin's reaction noted: 'A crowd of the curious surge about the big blue car and Charlie is somewhat embarrassed. The tramp atmosphere disappears as a soft English voice remonstrates: "You see, things like this are responsible for the delay."' The Lankershim and Hill scene, with its grocery store, was faithfully reconstructed on the studio lot.

At the beginning of October, Chaplin and Crocker were searching Glendale for a suitably deserted and melancholy location for the final scenes of the film. The same reporter described the scene in the small hours of 10 October 1927:

Perspiring men rush about the Chaplin studio. Carpenters, painters, electricians, technical minds, laborers. Charlie must not be held up. A caravan of circus wagons are hitched on behind four huge motor trucks. They start for Cahuenga Pass. A long and hard pull to Glendale. The location is flooded with light. It comes from all directions. The dynamo wagon hums. So the men work through the night.

Daylight breaks. The morning is cold. Crackings echo from a dozen fires. It is an unusual Californian crispness. Cars begin to arrive. The roar of exhausts signals their coming. There is an extra-loud rumbling. The big blue limousine comes to a stop. *The Circus* must be finished. Everyone is on time. Cameras are set up. Now the sun is holding things up. Why doesn't it hurry and come up over the mountains? It is long shadows the Tramp wants.

Six o'clock and half the morning wasted. The edge of the circus ring is too dark. It doesn't look natural. The tramp refuses to work artificially. Men start to perspire again. Thirty minutes later the soft voice speaks, 'Fine! That's fine! Let's shoot!'

Cameras grind. Circus wagons move across the vast stretch of open space. There is a beautiful haze in the background. The horses and the wagon wheels cause clouds of dust. The picture is gorgeous. No artist would be believed should he paint it. Twenty times the scene is taken.

The cameras move in close to the ring. Carefully the operators measure the distance. From the lens to the tramp. He is alone in the center of the ring.

He rehearses. Then action for camera. Eighty feet. The business is done again. And again! And again! Fifty persons are looking on. All members of the company. There are few eyes that are not moist. Most of them know the story. They knew the meaning of this final 'shot'.

'How was that?' came inquiring from the Tramp. Fifty heads nodded in affirmation. 'Then we'll take it again; just once more,' spoke the man in the baggy pants and derby hat and misfit coat and dreadnought shoes. The sun was getting high. The long shadows became shorter and shorter. 'Call it a day,' said the Tramp, 'we'll be here again tomorrow at four.'

At three the following morning Chaplin was watching the day's rushes:

The little fellow in the big black leather chair was no longer the Tramp. But he was watching him on the screen. Charlie Chaplin was passing

> judgement. 'He should do that much better.' 'He doesn't ring true.' 'He has his derby down too far over his eyes.' 'They have burned his face up with those silver reflectors.' A severe critic, this Chaplin. The Tramp doesn't please him. The stuff must be retaken. A leap from the leather chair. Speed, dust, location.

Now followed the last of the misfortunes of *The Circus*. In the night the wagons had disappeared. The sheriff had his deputies on the job, but there was to be no shooting that day: all that the company could do was to rehearse for retakes, should the wagons ever be recovered.

They were, that night. They had been taken by some students who planned to burn them at their fire celebration. An entire freshman class was arrested, but Chaplin declined to prosecute: anything to avoid a further delay. The retakes were made on 14 October.

Even those who worked for years with Chaplin were often mystified by his constant retakes. He might rebuke Totheroh if he heard the camera crank a couple of turns after he had called 'Cut', but he would use hundreds of feet retaking some apparently insignificant piece of business. It was sometimes suggested by his colleagues that when he was stuck for an idea as to what to do next, he would just go on retaking the last thing to hide his indecision. Yet that could not explain the retakes of such a scene as this, taken at the end of a shooting session, when time and light were pressing. The answer must be sought elsewhere. Charlie Chaplin had a compulsion to seek perfection, and equally a conviction that he could never achieve it. He just went on trying.

So much of the film had been cut as the work went along that the final cutting and titling took barely a fortnight. On 28 October the working print of the film was previewed at the Alexandra Theatre, Glendale. (The audience must have been delighted to glimpse the Glendale courthouse used as the scene of the marriage of Rex and Merna.) It was well received, but the reactions suggested some cuts and retakes. For four days Chaplin and Crocker were back on the tightrope for retakes. The close-ups presented some difficulties when it came to matching shots made almost two years before. The anguish of the divorce had left its mark on Chaplin's features. At the height of the troubles with Lita his hair had gone white overnight: Henry Bergman remembered the shock when the changed Chaplin arrived at the studio one morning. When he began the film his naturally black hair was touched with silver. Now it had to be dyed for the screen.

The revised print was previewed again at Bard & West Adams

Theatre on West Adams and Crenshaw, and Miss Steele recorded in the daily studio reports that it 'went over great'. Chaplin could at last relax. He went on a fishing trip with Harry Crocker.

In the 1920s, even in a small independent organization like Chaplin's, all the work towards the release and exploitation of films was done within the studio. There were as yet no independent outside laboratories and publicity organizations to undertake the work. So the period between the completion and release of a film was one of the busiest for the staff. The cameramen under Totheroh had to cut two negatives, made on two cameras, for domestic and European release. The laboratory then had to make the release prints – fifteen copies of the film were required for the initial release of *The Circus*. The press department had to prepare press books, programmes, releases and to supervise the distribution of the stills that were printed in great numbers by the stills department. Meanwhile the last sets had to be struck and cleared, the costumes, properties and electrical equipment carefully renovated, and the studio made ready for the next production.

Chaplin had more than once declared his views on the importance of the musical accompaniment to films. The preview of *The Circus* had been accompanied by stock themes chosen *ad hoc* by the theatre's musical arrangers. For the première performances, however, Arthur Kay was commissioned to compile a special score. Chaplin worked closely with Kay in the final stages.

The world première was held on 6 January 1928 at the Strand Theatre, New York: perhaps Chaplin felt that he owed that city a debt for the refuge it had provided during the troubles of the preceding year. The Los Angeles opening was three weeks later, on 27 January, at Grauman's Chinese. Sid Grauman provided a spectacular showcase for his friend's picture. Patrons were greeted on the forecourt of the theatre by a full-scale menagerie and sideshows including Alice from Dallas, the 503-pound fat girl and Major Mite and Lady Ruth, respectively twenty-five inches tall and twenty-one pounds, and thirty-two inches tall and fifty-two pounds. On the stage a live Prologue starred Poodles Hannaford, the Ace of Riding Clowns and his troupe, Pallenberg's Performing Bears on their bicycles, a lion tamer, and Samaroff and Sona's performing dogs.

Chaplin had no cause to be dissatisfied with his press: the reviews were hardly less enthusiastic than for *The Gold Rush*. Some critics indeed welcomed a film in which, they felt, the drama and pathos did not eclipse the slapstick element. The Lita affair seemed all but forgotten, barely six months later. Only the ever-faithful Alexander Woollcott touched on it with irony: the film, he said, was overdue 'because it was interrupted in the making. I now only vaguely recall the circumstances, but I believe it was because thanks to the witless clumsiness of the machinery of our civilization, someone (a wife I think it was, or something like that) was actually permitted to have the law on Chaplin as though he were a mere person and not such a bearer of healing laughter as the world had never known.' Woollcott's uncritical devotion was a byword among his contemporaries, though this romantic move to place the artist above the law might well have invited scepticism. The thought, though, was kind.

It was while working on *The Circus* that Chaplin embarked for the first and last time on the adventure of producing a film by another director. The most likely reason for this venture was to launch Edna – for whom he evidently no longer saw a place in his own studio – on a new phase of her career, as a dramatic actress. He had been immoderately enthusiastic over Josef von Sternberg's shoe-string production *The Salvation Hunters* and even more enthusiastic about its star Georgia Hale. Now he invited von Sternberg to direct a film tentatively titled *Sea Gulls*. 'This was quite a distinction' wrote von Sternberg forty years later in his autobiography, *Fun in a Chinese Laundry*:

> as he had never honored another director in this fashion, but it only resulted in an unpleasant experience for me.
>
> The film was to revolve around Edna Purviance, a former star of his, with whom, among other notable films, he had made the impressive *Woman of Paris*. She was still charming, though she had not appeared in pictures for a number of years and had become unbelievably timid and unable to act in even the simplest scene without great difficulty. Aware of this, Mr Chaplin credited me with sufficient skill to overcome such handicaps, and in the completed film she actually seemed at ease.
>
> The tentative title of the film was *The Sea-Gull* [*sic*] (no relation to the Anton Chekhov tragedy) and it was based on a story of mine about some fishermen on the Californian coast. When the filming had ended I showed it exactly once at one theatre, then titled *A Woman of the Sea* and that was the end of that. The film was promptly returned to Mr Chaplin's vaults and no one has ever seen it again. We spent many idle hours with each other, before, during, and after the making of this film, but not once was this work of mine discussed, nor have I ever broached the subject of

> its fate to him. He charged off its cost against his formidable income tax, and I charged it off to experience.
>
> Though it did me a great deal of harm at the time, I bore Mr Chaplin no ill will for repressing my work. I have always been fond of him though for a few hours his arbitrary action placed a great strain on my affection.

Chaplin did not even mention the film in his own autobiography, and the story of *Sea Gulls* has hitherto been shrouded in myth and mystery. Neither the film itself nor any scenario survives; but the daily shooting records and the title list still preserved in the Chaplin archive enable us to recreate something of its history.

There seems no foundation for the often repeated assertion that the story of the film was Chaplin's: the credit titles clearly stated 'written and directed by Josef von Sternberg'. It was in essence a commonplace melodrama about the two daughters of a fisherman: Edna played Joan, the good sister; Eve Southern was Magdalen, the bad one. Magdalen abandons Peter, her simple fisherman fiancé to go off to the big city with a playboy novelist. Years later, when Joan and Peter are happily married, Magdalen returns to trifle once more with Peter's affections and disrupt the marriage. Peter and Joan are finally reconciled however, and the mischievous Magdalen gets her just deserts.

Work on the film began in January 1926, almost simultaneously with *The Circus* and continued without break until the end of shooting on 2 June. Cutting was completed three weeks later. The story that Chaplin ordered some retakes is not borne out by the shooting records. Certainly there can be no truth in the frequent assertion that Chaplin himself shot some material on the film, since throughout the production period he was working full out and every day on *The Circus*.

The production – part of which took place on location at Carmel and Monterey – may well have been fraught with difficulties. Von Sternberg seems frequently to have returned to scenes with which he was apparently dissatisfied. When work began the photographer was Edward Gheller, who had filmed *The Salvation Hunters*, but on 26 April he was replaced by the 25-year-old, Russian-born Paul Ivano, who had previously co-directed *Seven Years' Bad Luck* with Max Linder, acted as technical director on *The Four Horsemen of the Apocalypse* and been one of the forty-two cameramen who shot the chariot race in *Ben Hur*. Ivano was to be the credited cinematographer, though the bulk of the film was shot by Gheller.

Von Sternberg's statements about Edna's condition seem to be confirmed by the daily shooting records. For the most part he was shooting with considerable economy, generally printing the second or third take of a shot. Scenes which demanded work of the slightest complication from Edna, however, seem often to have required nine, ten or more takes. It was said that Sternberg endeavoured to assist her by having two kettle-drums on the set to establish a rhythm for the performance.

Speculation about Chaplin's reasons for suppressing the film have included the notion – less than likely, given Chaplin's commercial sense – that he was jealous because von Sternberg had directed Edna so successfully; and, alternatively and ever so slightly more possibly, that he was distressed by the quality of Edna's performance. Privately Chaplin himself said later that the film was simply not good enough to release. Von Sternberg was a man of strong opinions, and the mild tone of his protests might well be taken to imply his own sense of the film's shortcomings.

John Grierson claimed to have seen the film, and as a good journalist made a good story out of this exclusive privilege; but his rather misleading references to the narrative cast some doubt on the rest of his evidence:

> The story was Chaplin's, and humanist to a degree; with fishermen that toiled, and sweated, and lived and loved as proletarians do. Introspective as before, Sternberg could not see it like Chaplin. Instead, he played with the symbolism of the sea* till the fishermen and the fish were forgotten. It would have meant something just as fine in its different way as Chaplin's version, but he went on to doubt himself. He wanted to be a success, and here plainly and pessimistically was the one way to be unsuccessful. The film was as a result neither Chaplin's nor Sternberg's. It was a strangely beautiful and empty affair – possibly the most beautiful I have ever seen – of net patterns, sea patterns and hair in the wind. When a director dies he becomes a photographer.

* The last title in the film runs: 'And the sea – made of all the useless tears that have ever been shed – grows neither less nor more.' Compared with Chaplin's films, *A Woman of the Sea* made excessive use of titles – more than 160 of them in seven reels.

The only person now living* who saw *A Woman of the Sea* – as *Sea Gulls* was eventually retitled – is Georgia Hale; and her opinion corroborates Chaplin's view that the film was commercially unshowable. It was, she said, wonderfully beautiful to look at;** but the narrative was incomprehensible. Nor does she feel that von Sternberg had wholly overcome the problems of Edna's nervous state. The eventual fate of *A Woman of the Sea* is dealt with in Chapter 14.

* Paul Ivano died on 20 April 1984.

** The shooting records suggest that there was no stills photographer on the production; and no stills of *A Woman of the Sea* were known until several photographs turned up in Edna Purviance's private archive, now in the possession of Inman Hunter, by whose courtesy four are reprinted for the first time in this volume.

12

CITY LIGHTS

Even before the Los Angeles première of *The Circus*, Chaplin was at work on a new scenario—in part spurred on, no doubt, by the financial demands of the divorce and the Federal Tax Authorities. During the two years that *The Circus* had been in production, the sound film had not only arrived, but made clear its intention of staying. It is a hitherto unknown curiosity of film history that Chaplin could have been the one to effect the revolution, almost a decade earlier. On 9 December 1918, when Chaplin was working on *Sunnyside*, Eugène Augustin Lauste, the pioneer of sound-on-film recording, wrote to him from New York:

To Mr Charlie Chaplin
California Studio.

Dear Sir,

I have just returned from England, on at my arrival I heard that you have started a new moving pictures studio on your own, for which I am very pleased to congratulate you as a wonder artist who by your cleverness and your ingenuity you have been able to conquer the whole world. I am myself one of your admirer at the time that you have been engaged with Fred. Karno. Since that time, you have rapidly progressed with enormous success, so, let me take the liberty to present to you my most hearty congratulations for the great achievement you have already done in the history of the cinematograph.

My self, I am an inventor, I was first working with Mr T. A. Edison, at his private laboratory at Orange N.J. for many years. Then in 1894, I had design, build, and exhibited the first projecting moving pictures machine, called the (Eidoloscope) so I claim that I was the first one who bring out this great invention, which is not my last one. However, I am very please to say that my invention has been favorable to you, and my other one, if you are interested in it, would bring to you an enormous fortune . . .

Referring to my invention, kindly allow me few seconds of your attention to explain the great future of it. As you know, the present machines will in a short time, come at end. For years and years, the public want to see the realism, that means the real talking pictures which up to now has never been accomplished practically and commercially. Many inventors they have already tried to synchronize the gramophone or phonograph in connection with the cinematograph, which has been a failure, and always will be. The only way which that could be done satisfactory, is my own principle on which I have working on, for over 25 years.

I do not want that you think I come to you and bring to you an invention which is an imaginary or dreaming idea which is in the air, but the truth. So before I will engage myself with a party which I have in view, I like to give you the opportunity to take in your hands this wonderful discovery which I believe you will be surprise to hear that a such machine was in existence. The fact, that I had giving in London, several demonstrations to the press, and also to scientists experts, which their opinions was very satisfactory from the reports which I will prove to you by the originals.

In few words, I will explain the principle of my invention, which after his completion will certainly revolutionize the cinematograph industry. The idea which has already accomplished, is to photograph pictures and sounds simultaneously on the same film, and in one operation, and reproduce same without any contact on the film, or the use of a gramophone or phonograph. The sounds is absolutely clear, no scratching whatever or distortion in the voice or music, I am certain that you will be very surprise to hear it.

However, if you think you will be interested, let me know as soon as possible, then I will send to you more particular regarding same, and also a copies of the reports and documents . . .

Notwithstanding the strong French accent in Monsieur Lauste's letter, Chaplin was clearly intrigued by the idea, and Sydney replied on his behalf: 'Regarding your invention, it sounds very interesting to Mr Chaplin and he would be glad to receive further details concerning same if you will be so good as to send them on.' Lauste seems never to have replied, and Chaplin was too taken up with his current productions to follow the matter up. Lauste's claims were not exaggerated: Merritt Crawford, an authority on Lauste's work on sound films, considers that but for war conditions and lack of capital he would have brought forward the sound era by a decade.

The chance slipped by in 1918. Warners presented their first Vitaphone programme, featuring John Barrymore and Mary Astor in *Don Juan*, on 6 August 1926: it was Hannah Chaplin's sixty-first birthday, and Chaplin was just then flinching in the lions' cage. The feature in the second Vitaphone show, at Christmas 1926, was *The Better 'Ole*. Since the star of the film was Sydney Chaplin himself, the Chaplin brothers must have been keenly aware of the new technique and its implications. A year later, on 6 October 1927, *The Jazz Singer* had demonstrated voice synchronization; and by 8 July 1928, when Chaplin was still in the preparatory stages for *City Lights*, Warner Brothers had shown the first all-talking picture *Lights of New York*.

Hollywood for the most part was on the defensive. Like everyone else, Chaplin was very conscious of the technical shortcomings of the first sound films and – in the early stages – of the unimaginative and inartistic use of the new medium. As late as 1931 he was still declaring: 'I'll give the talkies three years, that's all.' He may not have believed this, but he knew how much he had to lose if he were forced into talking pictures. Chaplin had made the silent pantomime into an international language. He had proved that the gestures, the expressions, the quirks, the thoughts, the feelings of his little Tramp were as readily comprehensible to Japanese, Chinese, Bantu tribesmen or Uzbekhs as to the great cinema audiences of America or Europe. Speech would instantly rob the figure of this universality. In any case, how would he speak? What kind of voice and accent could be conceived to suit the Tramp? This was a conundrum that was still puzzling him more than thirty years after he parted from the character.

Chaplin had no doubt that he must continue to make silent films; even so, the decision left him in a state of anxiety which, as his unit was well aware, stayed with him throughout the new production. Chaplin and Harry Crocker started work on the story in Chaplin's bungalow at the studio. Chaplin's first notion was for another circus story: a clown has lost his sight in an accident but is obliged to conceal the fact from his frail and nervous little daughter. The pathos and comedy would have come from the clown's efforts to pretend that his errors and stumbles are done for fun. He also thought of having two rich men conduct the experiment of giving a wretched tramp a night of luxury and pleasure and then dumping him back on the Embankment where they found him. He was thinking on other lines also: 'How would people like to see me with a companion?' he asked Crocker. 'Would they laugh to see me, a character laughed at by the world, discover someone of even less education, someone over whom I could lord it, someone to whom I would be a great person. I can see lots of fun in that idea.'

'Given the germ of an idea,' commented Crocker,

> from it a dozen stories will grow. Charlie does not concern himself at once with concrete action, the story merely grows as he goes along. If fifty different people were to inquire about his story, he tells fifty different stories. The underlying feeling is always the same, but he emphasizes the particular sequence which happens to be uppermost in his mind at the moment as the main theme of the current story. Thus Chaplin and I launched into the writing of *City Lights* and it was to bring to the screen another facet of the Chaplin genius. Our personal relationship was as close during the preparation of *City Lights* and its shooting [as on *The Circus*].[1]

Many years later, Chaplin was to describe the process of constructing a film as like being in a labyrinth, challenged to find the way out: 'I've got into the proposition, how do I get out?' Again his working notes illustrate the process, and how Chaplin threaded this particular labyrinth to arrive, from an unlikely starting point, at the story of *City Lights*. The brevity and simplicity with which the eventual plot can be told is a mark of its structural excellence.

A tramp, wandering a large and hostile city, meets a fellow waif, a blind flower girl. He also makes the acquaintance of an eccentric millionaire when he saves him from suicide in a moment of alcoholic depression. When drunk the millionaire entertains and treats him lavishly. When sober he has no recollection of him and turns him out of the house.

The Tramp learns that the girl's sight can be cured if she goes to Vienna for an operation. He tries various methods – as street cleaner and prize fighter – to earn the money for her trip; but then chances on the millionaire, in expansive mood once more. Unfortunately the millionaire's gift of money coincides with a burglary of his house. Sobered up, he forgets his gift and the Tramp (having meanwhile given the money to the girl) is suspected of the theft and jailed.

The Tramp comes out of prison a sorrier creature than before but the flower girl, now cured, has a flower shop of her own. She longs to meet the benefactor whom she never saw, and whom she imagines must be rich and handsome. The Tramp chances on her shop and gazes with joy at the cured girl. When she approaches him – to give him a coin and a flower, out of pity – he attempts to flee, however, ashamed and afraid to speak to her. But she touches his hand – and recognizes it. They gaze at each other. 'You?' she asks. He nods. 'You can see now?'

Although Chaplin abandoned the idea of the blind clown as too sticky with sentiment, the possibilities of blindness as a theme caught his imagination, and he decided almost from the start to place the blind flower girl at the centre of his story. The city, at this stage, was to be Paris. After juggling with various ideas for scenes, characters and gags, they were still far from having a real story to work on; but about this time, Chaplin hit upon the ending for the film which was to prove the key to the whole:

> Charlie meets blind girl trying to cross street.
>
> Punctuate story with his buying flowers. Eventually she is cured and Charlie finds her in little shop. As she laughs at him, Charlie does not dare disclose identity. Girl finally recognizes him – takes him by hand and leads him into flower shop.

From the moment of this discovery, Chaplin's invention seemed to be liberated. Now pages are covered with propositions, suggestions, plot devices, gags. Most of the ideas focus on the theme of blindness which provided possibilities both for pathos and for gags about Charlie's discomfiture and the scope for irony in the contrasts between what the blind girl imagines and the reality. So false would be the poor girl's illusions about her tramp friend that she would know him as 'the Duke'. The essence of their relationship at this time was that

> the two of them are driven towards each other – she by her physical disability – he by his being ridiculed by all but her. She may fall wildly in love with him as the Duke, and refuses to believe other stories and descriptions of him.

Already Chaplin had the germ of the scene of their first meeting:

> Might have first meeting with girl in helping her across the street. Might have her fixing flowers under parasol and hail him. 'Flower, sir?' He thinks quickly how to get coin for flower and comes back to get one. Plays he is wealthy person. 'Nice day,' he remarks as she puts flower in his buttonhole. Slams automobile door as taxi drives off, to make her believe that it is his.

Thursday, Oct. 23, 1930.
Time 1 P.M.
of C.C.

Scene 4537. - Exterior. Ext. Closeup/ New Flower shop. A retake of finish of picture.
Focus 6' (C.C. with collar turned up, no collar, tie or shirt, derby on,
Speed 18. coat buttoned top button and ragged trousers, no cane) C.C. standing with rose in right hand and biting finger of same hand - looks at (Virginia - partly in shot as she holds his left hand in hers and then runs right hand up his coat sleeve and to coat lapel as she recognises him) C.C. nods as she asks if he is the duke - smiles then points to right eye and says: "You can see now?" - tries to smile, bites finger nervously and looks at her. O.K.-44

Scene 4538. - Retake. Fade out.
Focus 6'
Speed 18. O.K.-44

Scene 4539. - Retake. Fade out.
6'
Speed 18. O.K.-41

Scene 4540. - Retake. Fade out.
6'
Speed 18. O.K.-38

Scene 4541. - Retake. Fade out. C.C. has both buttons on coat buttoned and
6' large safety pin in trousers.
Speed 18. O.K.-41

Scene 4542. - Retake. Fade out.
6'
Speed 18. O.K.-40

Scene 4543. - Retake. Fade out.
6'
Speed 18. O.K.-44

Time 1:30 P.M.

1930 - Shooting continuity for
final scene of *City Lights*.

There is also the germ of that part of the plot which involves the girl's need of money:

> On one occasion the Duke passes the girl's stand and sees the sign 'For Rent' which indicates to him that the girl is in desperate straits. On another occasion the Duke makes his visit to the flower girl's stand and finds the place in possession of an elderly woman and after his inquiry as to the whereabouts of the blind girl, he learns that she no longer has the stand because she was unable to meet the cost of her licence.

He had still not wholly solved the problem of integrating the story of the millionaire:

> The desire [to see] the blind flower girl prosper causes him to bring her in contact with the millionaire, while the latter is having one of his orgies and it so develops that thereafter the millionaire, when under the influence

> of drink, craves both the companionship of the Tramp and the flower girl. The Tramp gains the knowledge of the millionaire's devotion for the flower girl when the two men are out on one of their sprees and it is because of this knowledge that the Tramp realizes that now that the girl has regained her sight and because of everything the millionaire is in a position to offer her, he sees that it would be futile for him to make known his identity to the girl.
>
> The rich man calls Charlie 'the Duke' and sells that idea to the girl.

An ending in which the girl went off with the millionaire would, however, have interfered with the last scene of which Chaplin had now an even clearer conception.

> Ext. of Flower Shop. It is late afternoon. In front of the shop there is a mass of flowers and the flower girl with several others are trimming and watering the various plants. As they throw some of the withered flowers into the gutter the Tramp comes into view. He stops to bend down and pick up a flower and as he places it in his coat lapel, the girls laugh at him. He fixes his eyes on the flower girl and smiles at her. With a gesture of laughter, she turns to the other girls and remarks, 'He's flirting with us,' and they all laugh.
>
> She is unaware of the Tramp's identity but he is of the knowledge that she had dreamed of the day of his return as her ideal. She suddenly plucks a beautiful rose and with extended hand offers it to him while she is still amused at his ridiculous appearance. The Tramp still continues to smile and his gaze is fixed on her and he slowly moves toward her and takes the flower from her hand without turning his gaze from her and places it in his buttonhole and slowly walks away, looking back smiling as though through tears while the flower girl and the others are shown in a hearty laugh.

Chaplin had rarely before begun a film with an idea of how it would end. Certainly never before had he described a final scene in such detail, almost like a shooting script, long before he had begun to shoot. But he knew already that this scene was to be the climax, perhaps the very *raison d'être* of *City Lights*.

There was a host of ideas for additional elaborations and complications of the plot. Perhaps the Tramp could take a room in the same lodging house as the girl, and perhaps the girl and the other lodgers could take him for a rich and well-known author who is reported to be living in disguise in a poor quarter to get material for a novel. Or perhaps he could be mistaken for a kidnapper when he accidentally picks up a package of ransom money that has been thrown from a passing car. Perhaps the girl might have a ne'er-do-well brother who takes her money for crap games, and a sick little sister. Several pages are filled with possible schemes to exploit the comedy, irony and pathos in the girl's illusions about her friend and benefactor:

> When Charlie calls for girl, her friends are hiding to get a peek at him. 'He doesn't like to meet people,' she confides to them, 'but, my, he's grand.' When they see him they roar then one girl weeps. 'We should tell her,' they say. 'Don't laugh, it's tragic,' says weeping girl. 'And don't tell her, it would break her heart.' Charlie overhears the friends discussing him as a comic figure and looks disconsolately at his big feet. Charlie overhears Virginia [the flower girl] inquire from her friends what he looks like. He waits tensely for the girl's answer. 'Oh, he's wonderful,' says Virginia's friend. Charlie relaxes and two tears come into his eyes.
>
> There is a child in neighbourhood who laughs at Charlie at every appearance. 'Why are they laughing?' she asks Charlie. Charlie is invariably laughed at in street scenes with girl. Girl gradually notices that people all laugh.

The girl's blindness could also provoke gags of inappropriate reaction. The couple could go out boating: when Charlie is knocked out by a low bridge, the girl comments dreamily, 'It's so nice here.' There might be a complex variation on the shame gag-nightmares: Charlie could lose his trousers, but then realize that there is no cause for shame since the girl cannot see. One characteristic piece of business involving the abrupt termination of sentiment was to reach the finished film, with some variation, to provide one of the most memorable moments:

> Another time Virginia comes home with Charlie. Charlie looks back and sees her watering the plants in the window – sneaks back and gets water in face. Sneaks away . . .

The old nightmares of thirty years before also briefly recur:

> Blind girl's living room – The Tramp has departed on an errand for the girl. At his departure the landlady enters and confronts the girl with a demand for her back rent. When it is not forthcoming the landlady suggests that the girl give herself over to an institution for the blind and that she send her younger sister to the almshouse . . .

Chaplin seems already at this stage to have anticipated the addition of a synchronized track of some sort:

> The blind girl shall own a phonograph which she operates at her flower stand. Her favorite record shall be 'Bright Eyes' or some other semi-jazzy number. The Duke becomes haunted by the melody and whistles the tune as he strolls. In a penny arcade he seeks the number and listens to it through the old-fashioned ear receivers and his mannerisms attract attention by onlookers. This means is also suggested for a love-making scene between the Duke and the girl through his answering her song with another of significance. The Duke also buys or gets in some manner new records for the girl.

Jean Cocteau said that when they met in the course of Chaplin's 1936 world tour, Chaplin told him that he felt a film was like a tree: you shook it, and all that was loose and unnecessary fell away, leaving only the essential form.[2] In Chaplin's case most of his elimination took place at the story stage. Even though he might shoot fifty times the quantity of raw film that appeared in the finished picture, he rarely filmed material for any scene that was not eventually used in the final film. There would, however, be two such discarded sequences in *City Lights*.

By the beginning of May Chaplin was sure enough of his story to set the studio staff to work on sets and props and to order costumes. Still given to sudden enthusiasms for interesting people, he had taken up an Australian artist, Henry Clive, and invited Clive to prepare sketches for the sets and costumes. Clive was working on these sketches throughout June, July and August, though eventually Danny Hall was to take responsibility. Then Chaplin decided that Clive would be ideal for the role of the millionaire, and he was recruited as the first member of the supporting cast.

Robert Sherwood was later to write about the mythical city which eventually became the setting for *City Lights*, 'It is a weird city, with confusing resemblances to London, Los Angeles, Naples, Paris, Tangier and Council Bluffs. It is no city on earth and it is also all cities.' Practically everything was shot within the studio. At the rear of the open stage, a high concrete wall was built, and on it the scenic men painted a cyclorama of huge buildings. A T-shaped set in front of this followed the old plan of the intersecting streets that had done service in so many of the two-reelers. On one side of the T was the entrance to a theatre and a cabaret; opposite were one or two shops, including an art store, and just round the corner from them the flower shop. The monument to 'Peace and Prosperity' which figures in the opening scene of the film, stood at the crossing of the T. On a corner a park was planted up, with a railing surrounding it. On the outside of this stood the blind girl's flower stand. The inside served as the garden of the millionaire's house. The sets for the millionaire's house were erected on the closed stage. From these elements Chaplin created his own mythical city.

On 28 August 1928 Hannah Chaplin died. Chaplin had continued to find frequent visits to his mother distressing but when, a week or so before her death, she was taken into Glendale Hospital suffering from an infected gall-bladder, he visited her every day, and forced himself to joke with her: the day before she died nurses at the hospital heard them laughing together. A few hours before the end she fell into a coma, and Chaplin was advised not to see her. He drove away from the hospital, but then turned back. He decided to go to her after all. She momentarily recovered consciousness, and took his hand. When he tried to reassure her that she would get well, she wearily murmured 'Perhaps', and lapsed into unconsciousness.

Chaplin was at work at the studio the following day when a message came that she had died. Harry Crocker went with him to the hospital and waited outside while Chaplin went into the room, with the sunlight filtering through the half-drawn curtains. It was the first time he had seen someone close to him in death. Twenty-seven years before he had been taken to see his dead father but 'I couldn't see my father in his coffin. I shrugged, I turned away, frightened like a child . . .' With his mother it was different, 'because it was natural. She wasn't incarcerated in a coffin. I didn't see her in a coffin. I couldn't. Afterwards at the burial they wanted me to see her before they put the lid on. I said no: I couldn't . . . on the bed there was . . . relief. You see, she'd been in pain, and there was a relief. Before she had looked puzzled, as though . . . and then there was a release. You could see that she suffered no more . . . I suppose when life tortures, death is very welcome. She was still in hospital on a bed. I had seen her the day before and she was in agony. But then the following day, suddenly seeing somebody beloved and small, you think of all the events of life . . . It's really moving . . . I couldn't . . . I couldn't touch her. No, I couldn't touch her.'[3] He remembered that as he looked at the little figure he thought of the battles she had fought in her life, and wept. Afterwards he drove home in silence with Crocker. Chaplin sent telegrams to Sydney, who was ill in Europe, and to Wheeler Dryden in New York. Hannah was buried in the Hollywood Cemetery. Her simple gravestone lies in the shadow of the great mausoleum erected for Marion Davies and the rest of her family, and close to the graves of Henry Lehrman and his fiancée Virginia Rappe. Lita arrived at the funeral with the two children, but to the relief of Chaplin's friends he was too upset to notice her. Friends said that it was several weeks before he overcame his distress at his mother's death. Throughout her lifetime, Hannah had consistently subtracted a few years from her age. She might have been pleased that her gravestone gives the year of her birth as 1866 instead of 1865.

A note dated 10 September 1928 shows that Chaplin was then still far from the final narrative form of *City Lights*. A negro newsboy still figured prominently in the incidents planned – apparently the character which Chaplin had discussed with Crocker: 'someone of even less education, someone over whom I could lord it, someone to whom I would be a great person.' Their adventures together would have produced chaos in a theatre and a public library.

Since *The Bank* a recurrent motif had been the dream of bliss and the subsequent awakening to cold reality. Most likely this owed more to childhood escape dreams when he was away from home in institutions than to *Jimmy the Fearless*. At this period of his work on *City Lights* Chaplin was determined to open the film with a dream, from which the Tramp would be rudely awakened. In the dream he would have been a prince, wooing and winning a princess. The princess 'seizes and kisses him madly' but he awakes to find himself still a tramp, and being licked by a stray dog. Stills survive showing Chaplin wearing the resplendent white uniform intended for the prince role. A variant of the scene was set in Venice, so that the prince could arrive by gondola for his rendezvous with the princess.

An alternative dream opening had Charlie the Tramp being summoned into a house by a mysterious femme fatale:

> Charlie enters and finds woman on settee. She holds out her arms toward him and as music sounds she says: 'My adorable one, come to me.' Charlie at once gives her a passionate kiss and as he kisses the woman's hand, grasps and crushes an orange. As they stand and continue their kiss, the curtains are thrown back and the butler brings in a feast – a turkey and champagne. As Charlie continues to press the lips of the woman, he swings her around so that his hungry eyes can follow the feast to its destination. As he releases her he makes gracious gesture towards the table and says: 'Shall we eat?' The woman, swooning from his kiss, says: 'One more – one more.'

> Charlie kisses her beside the table and as she puts her head forward on his shoulder he picks up a drumstick from the table and eats it, then kisses her again. A conflict between his desire for love and food has put him in a quandary. As he is again kissing her passionately, we lap dissolve into the dog licking his face and the police, who chase him off the bench.

Chaplin seems to have been very much taken by this theme of the competing claims of love and hunger. Other comedy business contemplated included the confusion of two chicken drumsticks and two roses, and a moment in which Chaplin passionately bends the woman back over the table – so that he can reach the salt.

When shooting finally began on 27 December 1928, Chaplin had been working for almost a year on the story, and was still far from the eventual structure. He had found a leading lady, however. There is some disagreement over how Chaplin first encountered Virginia Cherrill. The contemporary publicity for the film said that during the summer of 1928 Virginia, then just twenty, 'ventured to Hollywood. Her mission was to tour California and spend some time with friends.' In fact she was recuperating from her first divorce, from Irving Adler. Chaplin, having interviewed applicants for the role of the flower girl all day, noticed her one night when they were both in ringside seats for a prizefight at the Hollywood American Legion Stadium. He instantly saw in her something of the young Edna Purviance. She was invited to the studios, where she took a screen test the following day. In his autobiography, however, Chaplin said that he had met her previously, having noticed her when she was working with a film company on Santa Monica beach, wearing a blue bathing suit. He called her for a screen test, he said, 'out of sheer desperation'. Virginia was beautiful, photographed well, and had no acting experience, which in the past Chaplin had already proved could be a considerable advantage. The decisive factor was that she was the only actress he tested who could 'look blind without being offensive, repulsive – the others all turned their eyes up to show the whites.' Chaplin, with his gift for giving his actors the right instruction, simply advised her to look at him but 'to look inwardly and not to see me'. Virginia's family, who belonged to the Chicago social set, were not at first happy about a career for her in the movies. Her contract was signed, however, to run from 1 November 1928, and Mrs Cherrill moved to Los Angeles to set up house in the Hancock Park district and to watch over her daughter.

Chaplin still liked to surround himself with known and trusted people. Allan Garcia had done good work as the proprietor in *The Circus*. With no very clear idea for a part for him as yet, Chaplin hired him as casting director of the new film: in time Garcia would play two roles in the picture. As Christmas passed, with the sets more or less ready, Chaplin felt forced to make some effort to start shooting, though he was aware he had not yet properly worked out the story. Work during the first three weeks was desultory, general shots establishing Charlie about the city streets. The week of 21 January Chaplin left with Crocker and the new favourite, Henry Clive, for San Simeon – ostensibly to do more work on the story, though Hearst's pleasure-dome can hardly have been conducive to concentration. Before he left he gave orders to call extras for 28 February. Two scenes were firmly fixed in his plans: the first meeting of Charlie and the flower girl, and the closing scene. The closing scene was too difficult to begin with an untried actress, so he settled to start on the flower stand.

As it turned out this was to give him more trouble than any other sequence he had attempted. From the start he began to have doubts about Virginia. It has become legendary how Chaplin spent shot after shot, hour after hour, day after day, trying to get her to hand a flower with the line and rhythm he wanted, and to speak to his satisfaction a line – 'Flower, sir?' – which was never to be heard. The fault was not all Virginia's inexperience. One problem, undoubtedly was that for the first time Chaplin was working with a leading lady with whom he felt no personal contact of affection or even liking. 'I never liked Charlie and he never liked me,' said Virginia more than half a century later.[4] He never met her outside the studio or invited her to his home. Many years later, when he wrote his autobiography, Chaplin admitted it was not Virginia's fault, but 'partly my own, for I had worked myself into a neurotic state of wanting perfection'. His state was aggravated no doubt by his anxiety over the arrival of sound films. He was bothered too by the necessary presence of the extras when he was working on a scene requiring such delicate handling. His friend the artist and cartoonist Ralph Barton recorded some moments of the work with a 16mm camera, and captured a moment of sudden fearsome anger as Chaplin rounds on an assistant who is apparently responsible for the extras.

Along with his 'neurotic state of wanting perfection', Chaplin had a very clear idea of what he wanted from this scene, as he described, almost forty years later, to Richard Meryman:

> Everything I do is a dance. I think in terms of dance. I think more so in *City Lights*. The blind girl – beautiful dance there. I call it a dance. Just purely pantomime. The girl extends her hand. And the Tramp doesn't know she's blind. And he says, 'I'll take this one.' 'Which one?' He looks incredulous – what a stupid girl . . . Then the flower falls to the ground; and she goes to feel for where it is. I pick it up and hold it there for a moment. And then she says, 'Have you found it sir?' And then he looks, and realizes. He holds it in front of her eyes – just makes a gesture. Not much. That is completely dancing . . . It took a long time. We took this day after day after day . . .
>
> She'd be doing something which wasn't right. Lines. A line. A contour hurts me if it's not right. And she'd say, 'Flower, sir?' I'd say, 'Look at that! Nobody says "flower" like that.' She was an amateur . . .
>
> I'd know in a minute when she wasn't there, when she'd be searching, or looking up just too much or too soon . . . Or she waited a second. I'd know in a minute.[5]

The minutes went by, and the days, from 29 January to 14 February. On 20 February they tried again, changing the action of the scene. Then on 25 February Chaplin fell ill, apparently with ptomaine poisoning, though acute anxiety may have had something to do with it. The stomach infection passed into influenza, and Chaplin did not return to the studio, except for a couple of conferences with the staff, during the whole of March. He returned on 1 April determined to start the flower stand scene all over again. After ten days he was still not satisfied, but decided to set it aside and start on another sequence.

By this time he had decided – it was to prove a stroke of genius – to open the film with a scene which, in a single stroke of comic irony, sums up the economic and social inequalities of modern urban life. In its completed form the scene opens on a large crowd assembled for the unveiling of a monument, 'Peace and Prosperity'. A stout civic dignitary and a hawk-like club woman make speeches, and the monument is unveiled. There, cradled in the lap of the central female figure, is the disreputable and calmly sleeping figure of the Tramp. When ordered to descend by the angry and embarrassed officials, he does his best, but manages to get the sword of Peace (!) entangled in his trousers. Thus suspended he loyally attempts to maintain a position of attention throughout the playing of the national anthem. The sequence ends with a mêlée and the Tramp's retreat.

This elaborate scene was finished, apart from some of Chaplin's close-ups, in a week: the presence and cost of a crowd of extras (one day 380 people were called for this sequence) was always an effective goad to Chaplin. Alf Reeves, who as manager of the studios saw his role as being to worry quietly, wrote to Sydney Chaplin with some satisfaction on 28 April:

> Charlie is working on his picture as usual but of course sound effects, if required, can be added afterwards.
>
> He is just in the midst of a sequence which looks to me as if it will be one of the greatest moments in motion picture comedy when it is finally cut. We are using four hundred extras in the scene.

The scene did, indeed, benefit from one of Chaplin's happiest aural gags, asserting right at the start of the film his hostility to sound films. The speeches of the dignitary and the lady were rendered by jabbering saxophones which burlesqued the metallic tones of early talkie voices. Adept lip-readers, however, are able to observe that Henry Bergman conscientiously mouths an actual speech:

> Ladies and Gentlemen – It is with great pleasure and admiration that I introduce these charming ladies who have done so much to make this moment possible. Miss-ess Fill-ber-nut! Also Miss-ess Oscar Beedell-Bottom. And last, but not least, Miss-ess Putt. Ladies and Gentlemen, I am only too happy to be able to do anything for this occasion, but I am sure you will know who is really responsible for this great moment. It is the artist himself, Mr Hugo Frothingham-Grimthorpe-Shafe-Shaferkee . . .

Poor Chaplin's already frayed nerves were not helped by major structural work that had now to be done on the studio. The city authorities had decided as part of a modernization scheme to widen La Brea Avenue, which meant that the studio buildings on that side, including office accommodation, dressing rooms and laboratories, had to be bodily moved back fifteen feet. Chaplin was at least able to move his shooting as far as possible from the building work, to the studio swimming pool where the suicide sequence was to be filmed. This was the sort of knockabout with which he anticipated no problems. The sequence had been fully worked out a month before: a note dated 24 May described the action:

> . . . At midnight we find Charlie wandering along the embankment searching for a place to sleep. As he is about to curl up in the darkness, we see the drunk arriving in evening dress clothes in a taxi-cab. He gets out with a large, heavy bundle under his arm – tosses a roll of bills to the taxi-cab driver – and staggers with his parcel to the edge of the river. From the package he takes a large stone with a rope tied round it. As he

> commences to knot the rope around his neck, Charlie rushes out to stop him from suicide. In the argument Charlie gets the rope around his own neck and as the drunk heaves the stone into the river to take his own life, Charlie is thrown in. The drunk rescues him and takes him home where he confides to Charlie as he is feeding the latter brandy in front of a fire that he is bored with life. He points to a photograph of a beautiful woman and indicates that he is bored with her. To show how little anything means to him he throws a roll of bills into the fire . . .

Henry Clive, as the millionaire, did his scenes admirably; but on the third day of shooting, when it was his turn to fall into the water, he demurred. He explained he had bronchial trouble and had not been well recently, and asked if they could wait until the sun had been on the water for a while. Chaplin left the set in a fury and Carl Robinson was sent back to tell Clive that he was dismissed. The friendship ended then and there. Four days later Chaplin resumed work with a new actor, Harry Myers, in the role. Myers was a veteran who had started his career in vaudeville and joined the Biograph Company about the same time as Mack Sennett. Since then he had played leading roles in over fifty films (including *Up in Mabel's Room* and *Getting Gertie's Garter*), and was too much the professional to be bothered by a little cold water, or even a pool-full. After the conclusion of the water-suicide scene and a few location exteriors shot at Pasadena Bridge in the small hours of 11 July, the building operations at the studio, added to the extreme heat of the summer of 1929, brought work to a total halt.

Not until the middle of August was the laboratory reconstructed and the other buildings that had suffered from the removal redecorated and refurnished. The enforced lay-off had at least given Chaplin leisure to work out an entirely new piece of business, which he now spent seven days shooting. This seven-minute sequence is one of the most fascinating creations of Chaplin's *oeuvre*, not least because it was in the end never used. As a series of variations, escalating in absurdity, on a single theme, it might have been a Karno sketch; but Chaplin makes it one of the great peaks of his comic invention and execution.

All that happens is that the Tramp, walking past the window of a dress shop, spies a piece of wood wedged between the bars of a grating in the pavement. Idly he prods it with his stick to try to release it, but it only pivots in position and stays there. He becomes intrigued, engrossed, and involves the spectator in his mounting frustration. A crowd gathers and the inevitable cop has to disperse them, with accusatory glances at Charlie, who pretends of course that he has nothing to do with it. When he returns to the problem of the stick, innocent bystanders become involved. A messenger boy of dim and soporific mien which gives the lie to the message 'EXPRESS' emblazoned on his cap, stops to gaze with contempt. He is chewing an orange and absently spits his peel at Charlie, whose natural fastidiousness is affronted. The boy is paid out next moment when he squirts himself in the eye with juice. When he has passed on, two women stop to look in the window. Charlie is far too engrossed to notice the interruption, and with his stick fumbles between the stouter lady's feet, below her skirts. The ladies walk on in understandable huff. Then a display artist in the shop window (Harry Crocker) involves himself, mouthing and signalling his increasingly testy advice through the sound-barrier of the plate glass window. Inattention brings troubles for him too: he absently sticks a price tag not onto the dummy as intended, but onto the rear of a stout manageress. The sketch ends with a fine anti-climactic dénouement when the stick, unnoticed by Charlie and the entourage he has collected, simply slips away.

The messenger boy – a haunting figure whose malevolent, wooden-faced idiocy gives him the look of a distant and mentally retarded cousin of Buster Keaton – was played by Charles Lederer, Marion Davies's favourite nephew, the son of her sister Reine Douras. Eighteen or thereabouts at this time, he was already a favourite – even with Hearst himself – at San Simeon, for his intelligence, wit and outrageous pranks. In later years he was to become a successful Hollywood writer and less successful director. He was also co-writer, with Luther Davis, of the stage musical *Kismet*. No doubt Marion Davies or Harry Crocker – often Lederer's co-conspirator in practical jokes – had recommended him to Chaplin; or Chaplin may have met him and been taken with him, like the rest of the circle at San Simeon.

Almost forty years later, when Richard Meryman interviewed him, Chaplin recalled the sequence with enormous pleasure: 'a beautiful sequence . . . It was marvellous.' He remembered it all and could still act it out, and thought that Lederer's messenger boy was 'very well acted'. The decision in the end not to use it shows that however prolix Chaplin's invention in the stages of inventing a story, his rigour in eliminating the inessential or distracting – 'shaking the tree' – was extreme. The sequence – as Chaplin said, 'a whole story in itself' – was not seen publicly for more than fifty years, until it was included by Kevin Brownlow and David Gill in their *Unknown Chaplin.*

Chaplin went on to film a solo gag that does remain in the final film. The Tramp pauses in front of the window of an art store, in the centre of which is a voluptuous nude statuette. He legitimizes his interest by affecting the poses of a connoisseur, sizing up the art works with a fine critical detachment. As he steps backwards and forwards for the sake of better perspective, he does not notice an elevator in the pavement which is moving constantly up and down, its arrival at ground level always luckily coinciding with the moment he chooses to step upon it. When, finally, he takes too sudden a step and almost falls into the hole, he upbraids the workman whose head alone is seen protruding from the hole. The elevator rises and rises, gradually revealing the full seven feet (as it seems) of the powerful figure. Charlie's indignation is somewhat tempered by the revelation of his opponent's stature.

The trick with the elevator was simply done, by having the camera in the shop window looking out, and someone behind the camera keeping watch on the elevator and signalling to Chaplin its position. He rehearsed the effect on film, wearing smart everyday clothes, and the rehearsal scene still survives (it is also included in *Unknown Chaplin*). The comparison between the graceful gymnastics of the handsome, elegant man in white flannels and sweater and the comical cuts of the little Tramp are perhaps the most vivid illustration we have of the way the costume and make-up wholly metamorphosed the personality of the man within.

Chaplin's moods remained very erratic. One morning early in September 1929, when he had just begun rehearsing the scene in which the millionaire takes the Tramp to a night club, he telephoned Alf Reeves from his home and told him, 'I will not set foot in the studio as long as Crocker stays there.' He then hung up. Reeves found Crocker preparing the day's schedule, and passed on the message.

'What does that mean?' asked Crocker.

'I don't know,' replied Reeves, 'but in your place I would hand in my resignation.'[6]

Crocker did so. The reasons for the rift must have been extremely personal, since neither Chaplin nor Crocker spoke of them, and no one else at the studio could guess at them. Henry Bergman and Carlyle Robinson were no doubt delighted to be reinstated to the roles of Chaplin's confidants: they had felt somewhat eclipsed by the friendships with Clive and Crocker.

The next month went by calmly enough, with rehearsals and the filming of the night club scene, in which the drunken millionaire and a tipsy Charlie introduce a touch of chaos with cigars, matches, seltzer water, and spaghetti that gets mixed up with the party streamers. Charlie has unfortunate encounters with a stout lady dancer, an over-loaded waiter and an apache floorshow act.

Chaplin now prepared to resume work with Virginia Cherrill. Though she had reported daily to the studio, she had not been required in front of the cameras for more than six months. During that time Chaplin's feelings towards her had not improved. The other members of the unit were puzzled by his evident coolness, but perhaps it was not so surprising. Virginia was not, and could not be, a worker in the sense that Chaplin understood the term. She was not a career actress, nor dependent upon her job at the studio. She probably showed clearly that she was bored with the months of inactivity. She went to parties at night, and showed the effects of tiredness the day after. Chaplin throughout his career desperately needed collaborators who could share in his enthusiasm.

Many years later Chaplin explained to Richard Meryman how the essential impetus of his creation was enthusiasm: 'An idea will generate enthusiasm, and then you're off! The enthusiasm only lasts for a little while, and then you wait for another day. It replenishes itself, and you start again. If something is right, and I think it is right, then it will generate enthusiasm.' The problem was that enthusiasm was vulnerable to the mood of those around. 'If I get an idea and someone tries to dampen my enthusiasm, then I'm lost. That's what it is. It's a fact that my enthusiasm is the thing that makes me mad and everything else.' Virginia's inability to reflect his enthusiasm undoubtedly made him mad. She went before the cameras again on Monday 4 November 1929. He worked her in with an easy scene, then he wanted to attempt the crucial final scene of the film. By Saturday they were ready to try a few close-ups and Chaplin announced that they would continue the scene on the following Monday. It is not quite certain what happened on that day: the version related by Chaplin's son Sydney is that just when his father was keyed up for this most emotional and difficult scene, Virginia innocently if tactlessly asked if she could leave early because she had a hair appointment. Chaplin, who always needed an intermediary for such unpleasant jobs, instructed Carlyle Robinson to tell Virginia that she would not be required for work in the near future. Georgia Hale, who had not worked in films for more than a year, was called in that same day, and was overjoyed to be put on the payroll. Two days later Chaplin began to test Georgia in the role of the girl, in the last scene of the film. Every writer on Chaplin has marvelled at the recklessness of his decision to replace his leading lady after almost a year's shooting. In fact during that time he had used Virginia in only two sequences, neither of which had been completed to his satisfaction. Similarly the replacement of Henry Clive had represented only three lost shooting days. Many directors – including Chaplin himself – were often more prodigal.

Those tests of Georgia survive. She would have been a very beautiful flower girl, and her work on *The Gold Rush* proved that she could be tender as well as crisply gay. She loved the part and longed to play it:

> Oh, that *City Lights*. That's what I would have loved to do. And I had it, you know. We went to dinner at the Double Eagle on Sunset afterwards and he told me 'You've got the part. You're going to do it. Now I'll get what I want.'[7]

The following morning Chaplin ran the tests. The others in the projection room all agreed that she could do the part, but Carlyle Robinson, who appears to have liked Virginia more than the others, was highly critical. He told Chaplin that Georgia could no more do this part than Virginia could have played the dance hall girl in *The Gold Rush*. Chaplin was disturbed and annoyed, but Robinson followed up this attack skilfully. Knowing Chaplin's sensitivity in this area, he warned him that Georgia would certainly sue him if he did not give her the part. It was always a weakness of the Chaplin brothers that suspicion once planted in their minds rapidly grew to seem reality. Chaplin was persuaded. Next time he met Georgia he was chilly.

> Then he told me what a terrible person I was, and he raved and raved and raved. He only calmed down when he realized I had no idea what he was talking about. Then he said, 'But I thought you were going to sue me.' Oh, I wanted to do that part. I loved that part so.[8]

Chaplin, however, was not to change his mind again.

Next he tested a beautiful and clever sixteen-year-old blonde called Violet Krauth, who had taken the professional name of Marilyn

Morgan, and arrived at the studio with her mother. Chaplin was enthusiastic at her tests, and decided to draw up a contract there and then. Reeves and Robinson, however, knew his indecisive state of mind at the time, and moreover felt nervous at the arrival of yet another sixteen-year-old with a mother in tow. It was late in the afternoon: Reeves and Robinson tactically sent the secretary home, so that they were obliged to tell Chaplin that the contract could not be prepared that night as there was no one to type it. As they had anticipated, Chaplin's enthusiasm had faded somewhat the next morning, and Robinson was instructed to break it gently to Miss Morgan and her mother that he had changed his mind. The girl accepted the rejection with good grace which considerably impressed the two conspirators, Robinson and Reeves. Under a new name of Marion Marsh she went on to enjoy a small but bright career as a leading lady of the 1930s; among other films she starred in Josef von Sternberg's *Crime and Punishment*.

A week after she had left, Virginia was asked to return to the studio. As she remembers the events, she had in the meantime discussed the business with Marion Davies. On Marion's advice, she now told Chaplin that she would not come back unless he doubled her previous salary of $75 a week. Chaplin protested, but she pointed out that their agreement had been signed when she was under age and so had never been legally valid. Chaplin, says Virginia, gave in. While he probably felt that insult was added to injury, it may be that this show of spirit, or even spite, on Virginia's part actually raised her in his estimation. According to Carlyle Robinson, when Virginia returned to the studio Chaplin sent for her to go to his dressing room, and she emerged after an hour's interview chastened and tearful. From this time on, Chaplin seems to have had no serious difficulties in working with her. Perhaps he began to realize that a professional Hollywood actress could not have done the part better. Perhaps precisely because she *was* so phlegmatic about her work, her interpretation wholly resists all the obvious pitfalls of sentimentality. After fifty years the performance that resulted from the eventual mutual patience (or forbearance) of director and actress remains pure and charming.

For the role of the girl's mother (when the film was finished the role was re-named as her grandmother) Chaplin hired an experienced old character actress, Florence D. Lee, who gave none of the problems of the stage-trained matriarch, Lydia Knott, in *A Woman of Paris*. For five weeks Chaplin worked with Virginia and Mrs Lee on the uncomplicated scenes in their home. In the final days of 1929 he took the plunge and started out again on the flower stand sequence. None of the material he had shot before satisfied him: for the new takes he even decided on a different costume for Virginia. This time, in only six days' shooting he seems to have achieved his 'dance': except for one or two minor retakes, this troublesome, marvellous scene was done at last. After all the agonies, it would, as Alistair Cooke remarked of it, flow as easily as water over pebbles.

The reinstatement of Virginia Cherrill and the successful completion of the flower stand scene were a turning point in the film. The shooting had gone on for over a year and there were still nine months to go but after this, though Chaplin must often have been exhausted, his anxieties had dissipated. There is no more record of quarrels and sackings. Virginia had three more months of idleness – her job must have seemed quite boring sometimes – while Chaplin went back to work with Harry Myers on the millionaire scenes. Allan Garcia was cast as the millionaire's butler, required to act, straight-faced, according to the whims of his master as he now clutches the tramp to his bosom, now orders him to be thrown out. The 'whoopee party' in the millionaire's house at which a tipsy Charlie commits various faux-pas like mistaking an old gentleman's bald head for a blancmange, and swallowing a whistle which chirps as he hiccups, involved thirty extras and an orchestra which cost $80 a day. Sometimes Chaplin could indulge in extravagance. The singer whose soulful ballad is constantly interrupted by the cheeps of Charlie's whistle was not just another extra, but a *real* singer, whose fee was $50 a day, even though his voice would not be heard from the screen. No doubt Chaplin felt that an extra could not convincingly mime the style of the professional performer.

Throughout most of March and April Chaplin was working on the various sequences that take place in the millionaire's house. When he needed an exterior for this he found it on location, at Town House, Wilshire Boulevard. In the roles of the burglars who break into the house he cast Joe Van Meter and Albert Austin – the last time that an old Karno colleague would appear in a Chaplin film.

Only one major comedy sequence now remained to be shot. Chaplin had left the prize-fight scenes to the end. The speed and concentration with which they were filmed reveals that they represented one of Chaplin's greatest bursts of 'enthusiasm'. To the end of his life the sequence continued to give him immense pleasure and satisfaction.

For his opponent he engaged the hang-dog giant Hank Mann, with whom he had worked in his third Keystone film and often afterwards, and who had since made a considerable career in Hollywood. The dignified referee was Eddie Baker, an actor who had been seen in only one or two small parts. A dozen extras had sufficed for a previous Chaplin bout in *The Champion*. For the fight scenes in *City Lights* more than a hundred extras were hired for the audience. The fight was rehearsed in four days and shot in six, and proved the apogee of Chaplin's 'dance' in slapstick mode.

By the end of July 1930 the shooting of *City Lights* was all but finished, but for six weeks more Chaplin nervously continued with innumerable retakes before the various artists' engagements should come to an end. On 25 August he shot some scenes in which two cheeky newsboys on a street corner mock the Tramp. They were to appear twice – once at the beginning of the film where the Tramp affects a contemptuous insouciance in reply to their mockery; the second time immediately before the final scene, where, in his wretchedness after a jail sentence, he is as miserably vulnerable as a mangy stray. Chaplin seems to have worked easily with children, perhaps because they were simply required to copy his own actions; and the shots required only half a day. One of the newsboys, a pretty, round-faced, insolent child, was Robert Parrish, who in time would become a prominent Hollywood editor and director. In his memoirs he recalled:

> He would blow a pea [from Parrish's peashooter] and then run over and pretend to be hit by it, then back to blow another pea. He became a kind of dervish, playing all the parts, using all the props, seeing and cane-twisting as the Tramp, not seeing and grateful as the blind girl, peashooting as the newsboys. Austin [the other boy actor] and I and Miss Cherrill watched while Charlie did his show. Finally, he had it all worked out and reluctantly gave us back our parts. I felt that he would much rather have played all of them himself.[9]

Chaplin had left to the end the retakes on the final scene. He spent six days on the general action inside and outside the flower shop, then on 22 September 1930 once more attempted the critical final close-ups with Virginia. This time there were no problems, no anxieties, no hair appointments. They worked from 2.30 to 5.30 that afternoon, and made seventeen takes. Whatever it was – enthusiasm, inspiration, magic – this time it worked, as Chaplin remembered four decades later:

> Sometimes it comes through with a great deal of that magic. I've had that once or twice . . . I had one close-up once, in *City Lights*, just the last scene. One could have gone overboard . . . I was looking more at her and interested in her, and I detached myself in a way that gives a beautiful sensation. I'm not acting . . . almost apologetic, standing outside myself and looking, studying her reactions and being slightly embarrassed about it. And it came off. It's a beautiful scene, beautiful; and because it isn't over-acted.[10]

Richard Meryman said to Chaplin that he thought the ending of *City Lights* was one of the greatest moments in films ever. Chaplin replied simply: 'Well, I know it was *right*.' James Agee, less restrained, wrote that 'It is enough to shrivel the heart to see, and it is the greatest piece of acting and the highest moment in movies.'[11]

Among the pick-up shots that were all that now remained to be done, Chaplin had a pleasant afterthought, and devised a piece of slapstick nonsense to play with Albert Austin, a nostalgic tribute to their many adventures together with Karno, Essanay and Mutual. A corner of the public market at Vine and Melrose did service as the public street-cleaners' yard, and Chaplin and Austin, as sweepers, sat down to one of the odorous and onion-scented packed lunches that had so often figured in the early shorts. In this case Charlie, blinded by suds as he is washing his face, seizes poor Austin's cheese in mistake for the soap, while myopic Austin takes a hearty bite from a soap sandwich. The sequence ends with Austin attempting to bawl out Charlie, but only managing to erupt in clouds of soap bubbles. It was the last appearance before the cameras of this loyal old collaborator.

The cutting and titling of *City Lights* took from mid-October to mid-December. The film was finished, but it was a *silent* film. By this time, however, after *Broadway Melody*, *All Quiet on the Western Front*, *Hallelujah!*, *Sous les Toits de Paris* and *The Blue Angel*, the silent cinema was an anachronism. Chaplin, though he may still have hoped, had evidently foreseen the possibility: such gags as the swallowed whistle and the incidents that ensue from it must have been conceived in anticipation of sound synchronization. In April 1929, as we have seen, Alf Reeves had written to Sydney that 'sound effects, if required, can be added afterwards'. On 16 May 1930 he wrote again, confirming: '. . . he intends to synchronize it for sound and music . . . no dialogue.'

Chaplin was to surprise his collaborators, and all Hollywood into the bargain. Other directors, having completed their films, simply handed them over to the musical arrangers who had descended upon Hollywood since 1927 – many of them former directors of cinema orchestras whose jobs had been taken from them by the advent of synchronized films. Chaplin, who since *A Woman of Paris* had taken a keen interest in the musical accompaniments for his silent films, determined that he would create his own musical accompaniment.

Chaplin had no musical training, but he had an irrepressible musical gift. In 1915 his Aunt Kate considered that

> If Charles Chaplin remains a picture actor, the musical world will be a genius less . . . As a baby, he would stop playing with his toys the instant he heard music of any description, and would beat time with his tiny hand and nod his head until the music ceased. In later years I have seen him sit for hours at the piano, composing as he went along.
>
> The 'cello was the instrument I think he loved best, 'because it was so plaintive', he said. I took a delight in watching his changing expression and his small hand quivering as he touched the chords. It was almost a caress.
>
> It was only when he caught my eyes glistening that he would laugh, and suddenly do some funny little movement or dash off a gay air. This would immediately change my sad mood to one scream of laughter . . .

In 1921, seeing Kennington Cross again had awakened strange memories for Charlie:

> It was here that I first discovered music, or where I first learned its rare beauty, a beauty that has gladdened and haunted me from that moment. It all happened one night when I was there, about midnight. I recall the whole thing so distinctly.
>
> I was just a boy, and its beauty was like some sweet mystery. I did not understand. I only knew that I loved it and I became reverent as the sounds carried themselves through my brain *via* my heart.
>
> I suddenly became aware of a harmonica and a clarinet playing a weird, harmonious message. I learned later that it was 'The Honeysuckle and the Bee'. It was played with such feeling that I became conscious for the first time of what melody really was. My first awakening to music.
>
> I remembered how thrilled I was as the sweet sounds pealed into the night. I learned the words the next day. How I . . . would love to hear it now, that same tune, that same way!
>
> Kennington Cross, where music first entered my soul. Trivial, perhaps, but it was the first time.[12]

Chaplin acquired his 'cello and violin when he was about sixteen, and painstakingly heaved them about on his various tours, taking lessons from the musical directors of the theatres where he played and practising from four to six hours a day. He played left-handed, which meant that his violin had to be strung with the bass bar and sounding post reversed from normal mode. He would improvise for hours on the piano, and when he built his own home, installed a costly pipe organ. In 1916 he started the Charles Chaplin Music Corporation which was short-lived but published three of his compositions, 'There's Always One You Can't Forget', 'Oh, That 'Cello' and 'The Peace Patrol'. He conducted Sousa's Band in a performance of the last of these, along with the 'Poet and Peasant' overture at a benefit concert at the New York Hippodrome on 20 February 1916. In 1921 he composed special themes for *The Kid* and *The Idle Class*; and in 1925 published two more compositions, 'Sing a Song' and 'With You Dear in Bombay' of which he also made a recording with Abe Lyman's orchestra.

Something of the universal appeal of Chaplin's screen character emerged in his composition also: the themes of *Modern Times* and *Limelight* were to win a place among perennial favourites of popular music. In method (the use of recurrent *leitmotifs* and strong emotional themes) and power, Chaplin's film scores were akin to the musical accompaniments of nineteenth-century drama which still occasionally lingered in his boyhood. It cannot be without significance that among Chaplin's working papers for the score to accompany *A Woman of Paris* was a copy of André Wormser's music for *L'Enfant Prodigue*, the most famous nineteenth-century mime play. It was revived several times during Chaplin's youth, and it seems unlikely, with his already conscious interest in pantomime, that he would have failed to see it.

After the première of *City Lights*, Chaplin told a reporter from the *New York Telegram*: 'I really didn't write it down. I la-laed and Arthur Johnson wrote it down, and I wish you would give him credit, because he did a very good job. It is all simple music, you know, in keeping with my character.'

Chaplin's work on the score with Arthur Johnson lasted six weeks. The score had almost a hundred musical cues: the principal original themes created by Chaplin included a trumpet fanfare, a kind of fate theme which introduced the film and various subsequent sequences, a 'cello theme for the Tramp, a mixture of operatic burlesque and Al Jolson laughing-through-tears melodies for the suicide scenes, a jazz motif for the nightclub, and a combination of comic tango and 'hurry' music for the boxing match. The blind girl had several variant themes, though the principal motif was Padilla's 'La Violetera', which had made a great impression on Chaplin when he had first heard it sung by Raquel Meller in 1926. Other musical quotations used for comic effect included a snatch of *Scheherezade*, 'I Hear You Calling Me' and 'How Dry Am I'. Chaplin always had difficulties with arrangers who wanted to make the music funny. 'I wanted no competition. I wanted the music to be a counterpoint of grace and charm . . . I tried to compose elegant and romantic music to frame my comedies . . .' In the same way he disliked the 'mickey-mousing' technique of directly pointing gags with sound effects and snare drums. In *City Lights* the effects are sparingly used: mainly for the whistle gag, for the saxophone voices of the officials at the unveiling, for pistol shots and the bells in the boxing ring.

The music was recorded over a period of five days under the direction of Alfred Newman, United Artists' musical director, and Ted Reed, who was in charge of sound and recording. Only Henry Bergman, with his musical background, was deeply disappointed in the results: 'It is interesting, the terrible deficiencies of the medium are too apparent. I don't think they will ever overcome them. Thirty-five of the very finest artists played the score for *City Lights* so beautifully on the set. Through the mechanics of the microphone it became something else.'

Chaplin was deeply depressed by the preview at the Tower Theatre, Los Angeles. The theatre was only half full and the audience, who had gone expecting to see the adventure drama which had been billed, was apathetic. As a result of the reactions he trimmed the film a little, though re-cutting, which had been a regular practice in silent films, was not so cheap or easy with sound. The notices which appeared on the day of the première, following the previous day's press show, were distinctly more heartening. A veteran critic on the *Los Angeles Examiner* recalled happily that 'not since I reviewed the first Chaplin comedy way back in the two-reel days has Charlie given us such an orgy of laughs.' *The Record* said:

> Nobody in the world but Charlie Chaplin could have done it. He is the only person that has that peculiar something called 'audience appeal' in sufficient quantity to defy the popular penchant for pictures that talk. *City Lights*, though it was received with whole-hearted delight and punctuated with innumerable bursts of applause from the audience, is no menace for the talkies. It is the exception that proves the rule. It is sure

to be an immense box-office attraction. He has made a picture that the world will want to see. Charlie Chaplin is an institution.

Even institutions have first-night nerves. Henry Bergman remembered that on the afternoon of the première, 'I was just leaving the studio in my car when Charlie drove up. At once he came to me and said in all seriousness, "Henry, I don't know so much about that picture. I'm not sure." And I said to him, "I'm telling you Charlie, I've never failed you yet, have I? If this isn't right, you'll quit the business and go to live abroad on what you've got. Nobody could do what you've done."'

The première, on 30 January 1931, went down to legend as the greatest Hollywood had ever seen – though it was not in fact held in Hollywood. Until this time premières had always been held in the handful of Hollywood picture palaces; but Chaplin decided to show *City Lights* in the brand new Los Angeles Theatre on Broadway, between 6th and 7th Streets. It was equipped with restaurant, soda fountain, art gallery, 'crying-room' for mothers with babies, ballroom, shoeshine parlour, broadcasting room, playroom, French cosmetics room and practically anything else the Californian heart might yearn for. From early afternoon the Los Angeles police were out to try to control the crowds that congested the city centre in the hope of glimpsing some small flash of the evening's glamour. The traffic was halted, and department store windows broken by the sheer pressure of the crowds. At one point the police threatened to use tear gas. The guests who made their slow progress through the crush included the aristocracy of Hollywood – the Vidors, the De Milles, the Zanucks, the Schencks, the John Barrymores, the Jack Warners, Hedda Hopper, Gloria Swanson. The press were also pleased to point out the presence of Marion Davies, Claire Windsor, Merna Kennedy and Georgia Hale. Chaplin's personal guests were Professor and Mrs Albert Einstein, in whose honour the entire house rose. The Einsteins were still rather too overcome at battling their way through the crowds fully to appreciate the gesture.

Chaplin was accompanied to the première by Georgia. 'Going down in the car, all the way he was like a little mouse. "I don't think it's going to go over," he said. "I don't think they're going to like it . . . No, I just feel it." He was like a shy little kid. He was always that way about his work.'

From the first shot the audience were delighted. All went well until the end of the third reel, when the film was stopped, the houselights turned on, and a bland voice announced that the show would be interrupted so that the audience could admire the beautiful features of the new theatre. The glittering audience forgot decorum and started to boo and whistle. Their indignation was as nothing compared to Chaplin's fury as he charged off in search of the management. The film was resumed; the audience was instantly recaptured. The ovation at the end vindicated all the months of work and anxiety.

The next day Chaplin left to make preparations for the New York opening. This resulted in a major row with United Artists. Chaplin found that pre-publicity in the East was negligible, while United Artists questioned his policy of raising seat prices to $1.50 (15¢ over the normal top price) for a film which they no doubt now regarded as out-dated. Moreover they were outraged by his demand for a rental of 50 per cent of the gross. Chaplin decided to exhibit his picture independently, and took whole-page advertisements in the trade press to announce the fact. The première took place in the old George M. Cohan Theatre, somewhat off the beaten track of major moving picture theatres. Chaplin's gamble paid off well: in its twelve weeks at the Cohan, the film grossed $400,000. Two months later, while Chaplin was in Europe, Alf Reeves was despatched to New York to inform Arthur Kelly, who had represented Chaplin's interests in United Artists, that his services were no longer needed.

The years of *City Lights* had left Chaplin with little time or inclination for social life. When shooting he worked a six- and sometimes seven-day week; evenings and Sundays were for rest and recuperation. In 1968 he recalled, with feeling, 'I had to correct and act and write and produce a film, cut it . . . and I did it all, which very few in my day did, you know. They didn't do it all, you see . . . And that's why I was so exhausted.' He told Richard Meryman: 'The evening is rather a lonesome place, you know, in California, especially Hollywood.'[13]

It was a measure of the quiet social life that Chaplin was leading at this time that during the entire production of *City Lights*, and indeed since the divorce, the gossip columnists had failed to sniff out or invent any romantic liaisons for him. At this period his most constant companion was Georgia Hale, loyal, worshipping and undemanding. Sometimes in the evening he would still stop in at Henry's restaurant, where he liked the lentil soup and coleslaw. Ivor Montagu, who met Chaplin about this time, greatly admired Georgia's qualities of character:

> She was a fine person, and, I firmly believe, one of the few women in Charlie's early life who cared for him frankly and unselfishly.
>
> One evening, returning from the Hollywood Bowl with a girlfriend she went for a late bite to Henry's . . . Henry Bergman came over to their table and they grew sentimental together.
>
> 'Ah,' said Georgia, 'three hearts that beat as one – yours, mine and Charlie's.'
>
> 'Yes,' replied Henry, 'and they're all thinking of the same thing, Charlie.'
>
> When we retold the tale to Charlie in Georgia's presence, Charlie considered, then admitted: 'Yes, it's true.'[14]

Montagu was in Hollywood with Sergei Eisenstein and Grigori Alexandrov who were there studying American sound techniques and hoping to set up productions of their own. When finally they reached Chaplin, thanks to Montagu's letters of introduction from Shaw and Wells, he was warm in his hospitality. 'Charlie's house and garden became our second home. We would always ring up and ask Kono before dropping in, but Kono who, when he wished, could be an impenetrable wall, treated inquiry from us as a polite formality. Sometimes we would be rung up and asked over.' The party was especially welcome because they played tennis – Montagu well, Alexandrov conscientiously.

> Even Sergei Mikhailovich [Eisenstein] bought ducks and tried pursuing the ball with a sort of savage spite. He spoiled all by wearing braces and scarlet ones at that, as well as a belt for security. When I told him this was improper he was downcast, but reassured when I added that braces for tennis were a practice of the late Lord Birkenhead.[15]

Since Georgia had introduced Chaplin to tennis in the late 1920s, the game had become a passion. He developed unusual skill and always liked to challenge professionals. He told Konrad Bercovici – who was astonished at the rejuvenation it had produced in Chaplin – that he played tennis for several hours every day, and found that it exorcized his prime fears. He loved its form and grace; it was not important, he said, if you hit the ball or not, provided that you moved gracefully and 'in form'. (This was not strictly true: he was distinctly displeased to lose at any time.) It was for him not only recreation but an experience of beauty. Other friends too remarked on the therapeutic value the game had for him. He continued to play with pleasure and skill until late in his life. As soon as the Chaplins had settled down in their Swiss home in 1953 a tennis court was built.

Sunday tennis parties broadened Chaplin's social life. In the ordinary way he had never much cared for big parties: he preferred the intimacy of small dinners. The absence of an official hostess at the Summit Drive house gave him the excuse to do little formal entertaining. 'It wasn't that he was stingy,' Georgia recalls, 'but it wasn't easy for him. He wasn't at ease. Sometimes though he would do a big party, to pay back all the people who had entertained him.' The Montagu-Eisenstein troupe's first visit was to a rather formal, English-style garden party at the house:

> Chaplin afterwards confessed to us that this was an 'occasional garden party' when enough people had piled up to whom he owed hospitality. From time to time he would nerve himself to hold one and rid himself of all the accumulated obligations in one fell swoop.[16]

Generally he allowed Mary Pickford and Douglas Fairbanks to organize his social life for him. He was an indispensable guest when there were distinguished visitors at Pickfair. Fairbanks' fondness for fellow-celebrities, particularly if they had a European title, was a byword. One day Chaplin asked him, 'How's the Duke, Doug?' 'What Duke?' asked Fairbanks, puzzled. 'Oh, any Duke,' replied Chaplin.

There were other foreign visitors to the Chaplin home in the summer of 1930. One day when Eisenstein and Ivor Montagu were at the house, two young Spaniards, Luis Buñuel and the writer Eduardo Ugarte were deposited there by a mutual friend. Buñuel, having achieved notoriety with the Surrealist masterpieces *Un Chien Andalou* and *L'Age d'Or*, had been whimsically offered a kind of traineeship by Metro Goldwyn Mayer, and as whimsically accepted it. The conversation when they arrived at the house was an embarrassed struggle in sign language: too late did Montagu and Eisenstein discover that Buñuel's French was faultless. Buñuel became a visitor at the house, and recalled in his autobiography how Chaplin had obligingly arranged an 'orgy' for him and two of his compatriots. Alas, 'when the three ravishing young women arrived from Pasadena, they immediately got into a tremendous argument over which one was going to get Chaplin, and in the end all three left in a huff.'

At Christmas 1930, Chaplin and Georgia were invited to a dinner party given by some of the Spanish colony. Buñuel, Ugarte and an actor named Pena decided to liven things up with a Surrealist incident, and leapt up from the dinner table to set about hacking down the Christmas tree. Buñuel admitted that 'it's not easy to dismember a Christmas tree. In fact, we got a great many scratches for some rather pathetic results, so we resigned ourselves to throwing the presents on the floor and stomping on them.' The other guests were shocked. Nevertheless Chaplin ('a forgiving man') invited the Spaniards to his New Year's Eve party. They arrived to find an enormous Christmas tree. Chaplin took Buñuel aside before dinner and said, 'Since you're so fond of tearing up trees, Buñuel, why don't you get it over with now, so we won't be disturbed during dinner?'

'I replied,' said Buñuel, 'that I really had nothing against trees . . .'[17]

Buñuel remembered other visits to Chaplin's home. Several times he screened *Un Chien Andalou*: the first time Kono, who was running the projector, fainted away when he saw the opening scene of a razor blade slicing an eye. Years later Buñuel was delighted to learn from Carlos Saura that according to Geraldine Chaplin her father used to frighten the children by describing scenes from Buñuel's films.[18]

One day Buñuel was invited to see some rushes from *City Lights* with the writer Edgar Neville, who seems to have been officially attached to the unit for a while. Buñuel was too timid to declare his opinion, but Neville suggested that the scene with the swallowed whistle went on too long. Chaplin later cut it. 'Curiously, he seemed to lack self-confidence and had a good deal of trouble making decisions.' Georgia remarked the same when she watched rushes with Chaplin. 'He was real humble about some things. At rushes he'd ask, "Which one did you like?" And I'd tell him; and he would consider it. Then I got that I didn't want to see the rushes. It disturbed me seeing it out of continuity. When he *directed* you the continuity was there, because he would tell you before all that had happened up to that moment.'[19]

One of Buñuel's stories is engaging but inaccurate in detail: 'He also had strange work habits, which included composing the music for his films while sleeping. He'd set up a complicated recording device at his bedside and used to wake up partway, hum a few bars, and go back to sleep. He composed the entire score of "La Violetera" that way, a plagiarism that earned him a very costly trial.'[20] Although Chaplin may have re-composed the piece in his dreams, he was never in any doubt about its origins in his waking hours. Although there was some costly wrangling over copyright fees, there was certainly no plagiarism suit.

13

Away from it all

When Chaplin left Hollywood the day following the première of *City Lights*, neither he nor any of his entourage and friends could have guessed that it would be a year and four months before he returned. His immediate plans were to attend the New York and London premières of the film, and thereafter take a brief European holiday, perhaps of the duration of the 1921 trip. Writing just after his return Chaplin himself explained, 'The disillusion of love, fame and fortune left me somewhat apathetic . . . I needed emotional stimulus . . . like all egocentrics I turn to myself. I want to live in my youth again.'[1]

After two disastrous marriages and a succession of inconclusive love affairs, he was without doubt emotionally unsettled. Some of those nearest to him suspected that he was at this time eager to evade the perilous affections of Marion Davies, who by 1931 was a great deal more interested in Chaplin than Chaplin was in her. Certainly he felt disoriented professionally. Four years after the definitive establishment of sound films, he had got away with making what was virtually a silent film; but could he do it again? 'I was obsessed by a depressing fear of being old-fashioned,' he later admitted.

No doubt the holiday was a matter of playing for time and a search for new roles in his private life. 'He is,' wrote Thomas Burke, who by intuition probably knew Chaplin better than anyone else,

> first and last an actor, possessed by this, that or the other. He lives only in a role, and without it he is lost . . . He can be anything you expect him to be, and anything you don't expect him to be, and he can maintain the role for weeks . . .
>
> From time to time this imagined life changes. When he was in England

ten years ago, he was with every conviction the sad, remote Byronic figure – the friend of unseen millions and the loneliest man in the world. That period has passed. On his last visit to England* his role was that of the playboy, the Tyl Eulenspiegel of today.

In New York he was met by the usual crowd of reporters. Among the interviews he granted was one by transatlantic telephone to London. He much regretted this ordeal and adamantly refused to do the same for an Australian newspaper. It was at this time too that he refused an offer of $670,000 for twenty-six weekly radio broadcasts – which would have been the highest fee paid to any broadcaster up to that time. Apart from that his brief time in New York was taken up in social engagements on Fifth or Park Avenue, arrangements for the independent exhibition of *City Lights*, and a visit to Sing Sing, where he showed his new film to an audience of inmates, and was deeply touched by their enthusiasm. Carlyle Robinson had received a tip-off which made him fear an impending kidnap attempt, and he and Arthur Kelly arranged for Chaplin to be shadowed by two hefty detectives.

It had been decided that Robinson and Kono would accompany Chaplin to Europe, and Robinson was as usual entrusted with the arrangements. Unfortunately by this period Chaplin had conceived a growing dislike of Robinson, which was to come to a head during the impending trip and result in Robinson's dismissal after fourteen years' service. The explanation may have been that Robinson had by this time become more opinionated than Chaplin liked the people around him to be. Robinson was accustomed to joke that his job was less often that of 'press agent' than of 'sup-press agent'; and his constant anxiety to anticipate, forestall or cover up any indiscretions, *faux pas* or unintentional discourtesies on Chaplin's part threw him into a nannyish role which cannot have made relations with his boss especially easy.

It may have been partly to avoid being thrown too much upon Robinson's companionship that Chaplin at the last moment recruited an extra member of the touring entourage. This was his friend Ralph Barton, a well-known cartoonist and illustrator. Chaplin invited him along in the hope that it might allay the acute depression which had already resulted in one suicide attempt. Eccentric and hypersensitive, Barton was in deep despair after being deserted by the actress Carlotta

* i.e. 1931.

Monterey, who had left him to live with the playwright Eugene O'Neill. O'Neill was to become, a dozen years later, Chaplin's unwilling father-in-law. Coincidence always played a large role in Chaplin's life.

This last-minute change of plan caused Robinson some embarrassment. Having already negotiated special rates for three berths on the *Mauretania*, less than an hour before sailing he was now obliged to plead for an extra place on the ship, which was in theory fully booked. The problem was solved only by a shipping line official agreeing to share his cabin with Robinson, so that Barton could take Robinson's place in Chaplin's personal suite. During the voyage Chaplin finally yielded to the exhaustion that followed the years of work on *City Lights*. He rarely left his cabin, except for midnight walks on deck with Barton. Out of the mass of radiograms conveying good wishes and pressing invitations which he received, he responded only to three: from Lady Astor, Sir Phillip Sassoon and Alistair MacDonald, son of the Prime Minister, Ramsay MacDonald.

The *Mauretania* docked at Portsmouth, and Chaplin was delighted to find a private coach had been provided for the journey to Paddington. The rest of the train was full of journalists, but Chaplin pleaded tiredness and left Robinson to deal with them. Robinson was surprised therefore when the train made an unscheduled stop at a wayside station, and Chaplin energetically set to signing autographs for the large crowd of locals who had collected merely in the hope of seeing his train pass by. 'Weren't they nice people!' he murmured placidly as the train drew away again. At Paddington the crowds were as vast and enthusiastic as they had been at Waterloo ten years before, but the police were better prepared to deal with them; Chaplin obligingly mounted the roof of his car and waved his hat and stick, to the general delight.

An enormous suite had been reserved at the Carlton to accommodate Chaplin, Barton, Robinson and Kono; and Chaplin himself was impressed with its splendour: 'The saddest thing I can imagine is to get used to luxury. Each day I stepped into the Carlton was like entering a golden paradise. Being rich in London made life an exciting adventure every moment. The world was an entertainment. The performance started first thing in the morning.'

The performance involved a heady social whirl among the intellectual and political élite of London, mainly organized for him by Sassoon, Lady Astor and his old friend Edward Knoblock. At lunch

CARLTON HOTEL
LONDON, S.W. 1
Feb. 28.. 1931.

MR. CHARLES CHAPLIN begs to acknowledge the receipt of your communication. Because of the enormous volume of mail received by him, it is impossible at this time to undertake to be more thorough in writing Will you therefore kindly accept this means of acknowledgment in place of a personal letter.

1931 - Form of acknowledgement sent to correspondents during Chaplin's stay in London.

at Lady Astor's he had a lively debate on the world economy with Maynard Keynes, and met Bernard Shaw for the first time. Initially somewhat awed by Shaw, Chaplin decided after an argument or two on the nature of art that he was 'just a benign old gentleman with a great mind who uses his piercing intellect to hide his Irish sentiment'. He frequently met H. G. Wells, who was now an established friend. He was invited to Chartwell for the weekend by Winston Churchill, whom he was to continue to admire deeply despite their apparent political polarity. (Paradoxical and unpredictable as he was in this respect, he even took the platform at one of Lady Astor's meetings at the October 1931 election, though he had some difficulty in explaining both to himself and his auditors this support for a Tory candidate.) As guest of honour at a dinner party at Lady Astor's home at Cliveden, Chaplin startled the guests – a carefully chosen political spectrum, including Lloyd George – with an after-dinner speech in which he launched into a diatribe against complacent acceptance of the growth of the machine age. They could hardly have known that they were witnesses to the genesis of *Modern Times*.

Despite efforts to keep it from the press, Chaplin's visit to Chequers was much publicized. He seems to have been somewhat disappointed in the dour Labour premier, Ramsay MacDonald. A private meeting with Lloyd George arranged by Sassoon, who had served Lloyd George as secretary during his premiership, appears to have been at least more lively, with Chaplin enthusiastically developing a plan for clearance of the London slums.

Chaplin steeled himself to do something he had not brought himself to do in 1921: he visited the Hanwell Schools, where he had spent the loneliest months of his boyhood. Carlyle Robinson believed that he took Ralph Barton with him, but contemporary news reports suggest that he arrived alone and without any announcement. As soon as his arrival was known, however, the excitement in the school was intense.

> . . . He entered the dining hall, where four hundred boys and girls cheered their heads off at the sight of him – and he entered in style.
>
> He made to raise his hat, and it jumped magically into the air! He swung his cane and hit himself in the leg! He turned out his feet and hopped along inimitably. It was Charlie! Yells! Shrieks of joy! More yells!
>
> And he was enjoying himself as much as the children.
>
> He mounted the dais and announced solemnly that he would give an imitation of an old man inspecting some pictures. He turned his back and moved along, peering at the wall. Marvel of marvels – as he moved the old man grew visibly! A foot, two feet! A giant of an old man!
>
> The secret was plain if you faced him. His arms were stretched above his head; his overcoat was supported on his fingertips; his hat was balanced on the coat-collar.
>
> He saw the 'babies' bathed and in their night attire, sitting for a final warming round the fire, and the babies gave him another ovation, and he laughed like a baby.
>
> The children will never forget his visit.[2]

The experience seems to have made a great impression on Chaplin. Robinson alleged that Chaplin wept when he returned to the Carlton. A day or so later, however, Chaplin told Thomas Burke that it had been 'the greatest emotional experience of his life . . . He said excitedly that it *had* been fearful, but that he liked being hurt, and I

The Gold Rush: Lita Grey (Lillita McMurray) with Chaplin at the signing of her contract. Chaplin on the set (below); evidently things are not going quite right.

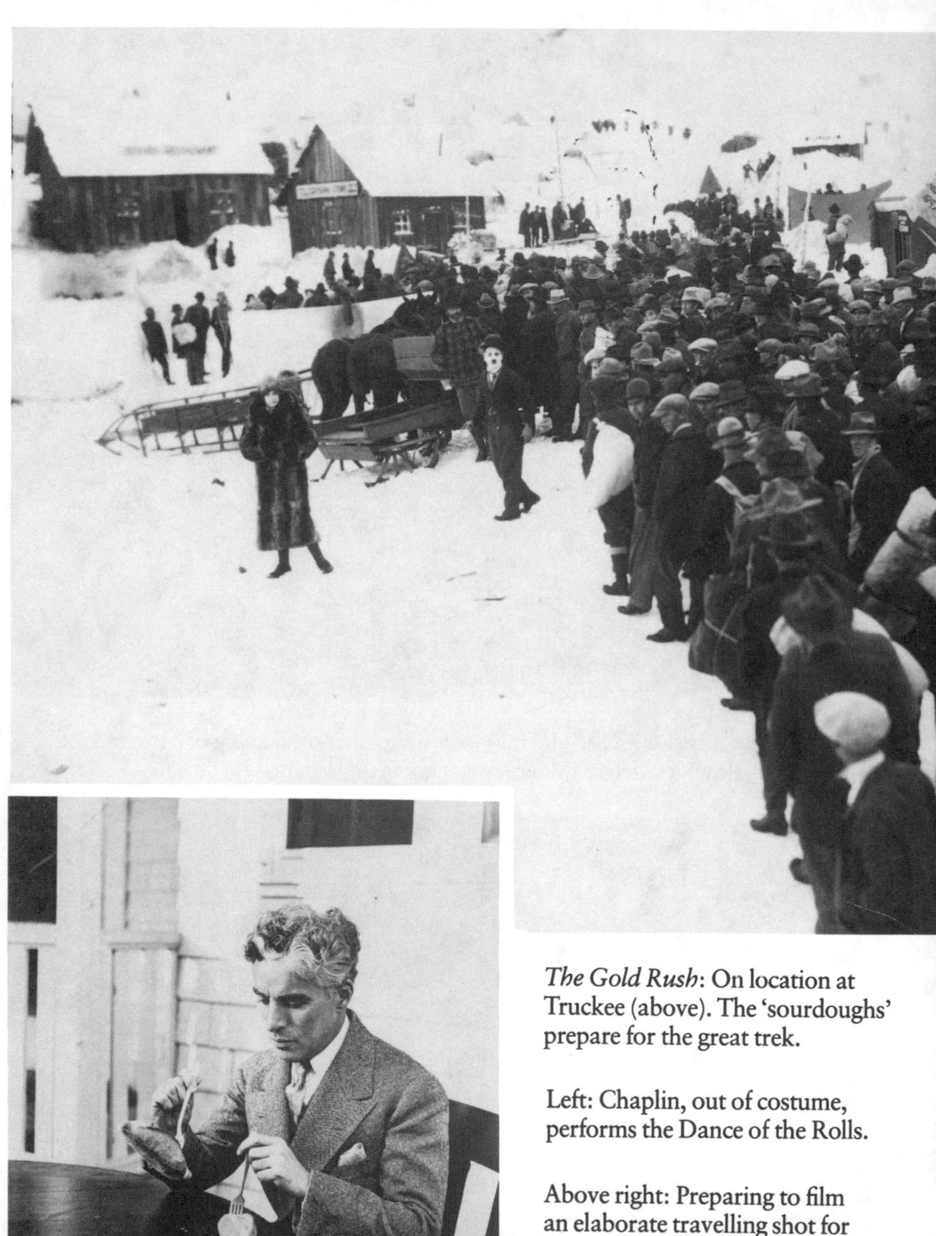

The Gold Rush: On location at Truckee (above). The 'sourdoughs' prepare for the great trek.

Left: Chaplin, out of costume, performs the Dance of the Rolls.

Above right: Preparing to film an elaborate travelling shot for a sequence which was never used. The scene was to have shown the hut being whirled at 100 miles an hour through the storm.

Right: Between takes on location. Chaplin as a chicken, with Mack Swain and Kono Toraichi.

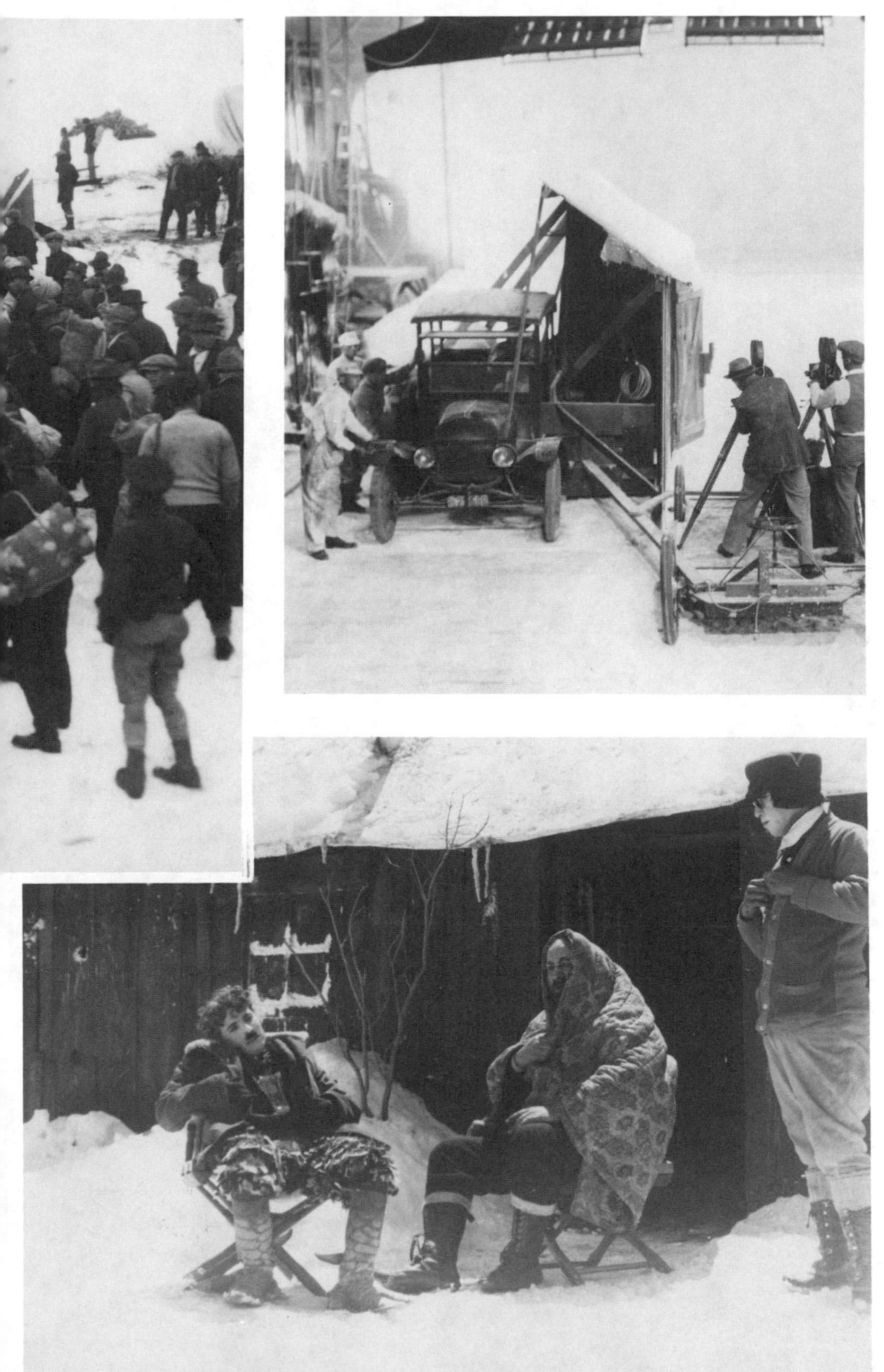

The Gold Rush: Lita Grey (below) as leading lady and Georgia Hale (right) as leading lady.

Chaplin's first Hollywood home (above)
and his house on Summit Drive (below).

he Circus: Merna ennedy (right).

elow: Chaplin uccumbs to xhaustion. A photo- raph taken by ack Wilson.

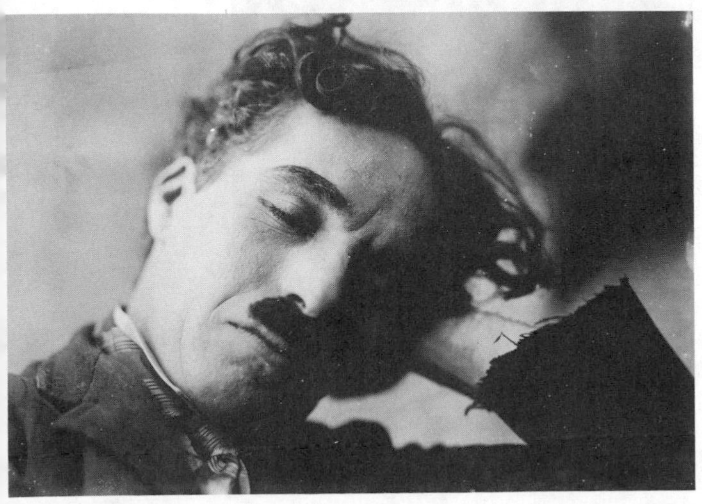

Left: The Lita Grey divorce. Lita takes the oath in court.

Right: After the studio fire.

Edna Purviance in two scenes from Josef von Sternberg's *Sea Gulls* (*A Woman of the Sea*)

Sea Gulls (*A Woman of the Sea*): The cast and crew on location (left). Flanking Edna Purviance are the director Josef von Sternberg (on rock) and Gayne Whitman. Standing behind Whitman is Eve Southern, and to the right of her, Raymond Bloomer and Charles French.

Below: Edna Purviance and Gayne Whitman.

City Lights: Chaplin at the camera (left) and (right) on the set, with Ralph Barton by the fountain. When the film was finished, Barton accompanied Chaplin on the first stage of his world tour, but returned to New York and committed suicid

Below: The studio back lot durin the shooting of *City Lights*. The *trompe l'oeil* painted buildings can be clearly seen in the background. Chaplin can be seen at left of centre.

City Lights: Chaplin (above) in the costume of the Duke for the projected dream sequence.
Below: Al Jolson, an important force in launching 'talkies', visits Chaplin, the last director to resist them.

Above: Hannah Chaplin in 1921, while still in the nursing home in Peckham.

Right: Hannah in Hollywood, playing checkers with Amy Reeves.

Below: Hannah's grave in the Hollywood Cemetery, photographed in 1983.

Above right: Chaplin's sons, Sydney and Charles Jr, c. 1930.
Right: Chaplin, the bachelor, at home, c.1930.

The première of *City Lights*: Chaplin stands between Mr and Mrs Albert Einstein

realized that his cold-blooded nature was interested in the throbbing of the neuralgia and the effects of the throbbing. He loves studying himself.'[3]

Chaplin told Burke,

> I wouldn't have missed it for all I possess. It's what I've been wanting. God, you feel like the dead returning to earth. To smell the smell of the dining hall, and to remember that was where *you* sat, and that scratch on the pillar was made by *you*. Only it wasn't you. It was you in another life – your soul-mate – something you were and something you aren't now. Like a snake that sheds its skin every now and then. It's one of the skins you've shed, but it's still got your odour about it. O-o-oh, it was wonderful. When I got there, I knew it was what I'd been wanting for years. Everything had been leading up to it, and I was ripe for it. My return to London in 1921, and my return this year, were wonderful enough, but they were nothing to that. Being among those buildings and connecting with everything – with the misery and something that wasn't misery . . . The shock of it, too. You see, I never really believed that it'd be *there*. It was thirty years ago when I was there, and thirty years – why, nothing in America lasts that long. I wanted it to be, Oh God, how I wanted it to be, but I felt it couldn't be.
>
> Well, I got a taxi, and told him the direction, and we started out for it. And when we got near the place it was all streets – and shops – and houses. And I guessed it was gone. I don't know what I'd have done if it was gone. I reckon I'd have gone right back to Hollywood. Because it was what I'd come for. I told the driver to go on, though I didn't think it was any good, because I'd always remembered that the place was in the country, with fields all round it. And then the taxi stopped . . . and then turned off the main road into something that looked like country fields and bushes. And then, all of a sudden, *th-ere* it was. O-o-oh, it was there – just as I'd left it. I've never had a moment like that in my life. I was almost physically sick with emotion.[4]

Burke chided him for his sentimentality in trying to recapture the past he had forever left behind. 'But one can pick it up and look at it,' he replied. 'One can think that one was happy once, or intensely miserable – perhaps it's the same thing as long as it's intense – and one can get something by looking at the setting where it happened . . . And anyway,' he added, 'I like being morbid. It does me good, I thrive on it.'

Moved as he was by their excitement, Chaplin promised the children that he would come back and see them, and bring them a cinema projector as a gift. Robinson was instructed to procure, with the help of United Artists, the most suitable equipment. For each child a present was prepared, consisting of a bag of sweets, an orange and a new shilling in an envelope inscribed 'A Present from Charlie Chaplin'.

On the day planned for his visit, however, Chaplin lunched with Lady Astor instead. Either the emotional effect of the first visit had proved too powerful, or it had worn off: in either event, no pleas from Robinson could persuade Chaplin to abandon the luncheon. Robinson and Kono were obliged to deliver the gifts, greatly embarrassed to find themselves driving in a limousine through huge crowds who had gathered for a glimpse of their idol. The press, who had also turned out in numbers, did not fail to point out the echoes of *The Gold Rush* in the tea table set out in the school dining hall for the guest who did not arrive.

The incident attracted the first less than favourable publicity which Chaplin had received since his arrival in England, but for the moment he was too busy with arrangements for the première of *City Lights* to worry. The show took place at the Dominion, Tottenham Court Road on 27 February. The vast crowds who assembled outside the theatre in pouring rain hoping for a sight of the star were disappointed: Chaplin and Robinson had been smuggled into the theatre during the afternoon before the show. There had been great competition for seats near Chaplin. In the event he was flanked by Lady Astor and Bernard Shaw and he was somewhat nervous in anticipation of Shaw's reaction to the film. Shaw, however, laughed and cried with the rest. Later a reporter asked him what he thought of the idea of Chaplin playing Hamlet. 'Why not?' he replied. 'Long before Mr Chaplin became famous, and had got no further than throwing bricks or having them thrown at him, I was struck with his haunting, tragic expression, remarkably like Henry Irving's, and Irving made a tremendous success as Hamlet – or rather of an invention of his own which he called Hamlet.'

Chaplin had planned a small private supper party after the show; but the invitation list rapidly expanded to more than two hundred, and the affair became the social event of the season. Thomas Burke who, like Wells and Barrie, cautiously declined to attend, remarked that 'Tyl Eulenspiegel himself never achieved so superb a prank as Charles did when he set the whole Mayfair mob struggling for invitations to his *City Lights* supper party, and made them give him all the amusement that his films gave them.' Titles and talent, the great, the good, and the gifted of London met; and Chaplin broke the ice with an endearing faux pas when he referred to Churchill, in the course of his speech as "the *late* Chancellor of the Exchequer".'

From this evening Chaplin threw himself energetically into the role of playboy, which it was to amuse him to fill for the next year or so. As if in reaction to the lonely years of work on *City Lights*, from the moment that the film was launched he embarked with almost adolescent enthusiasm on a series of flirtations and adventures. Contrary to his usual distaste for personal publicity, he appeared to welcome the attention as the world's press delightedly photographed him in the company of a succession of beautiful women, and speculated recklessly on future marriages and leading ladies. The first of the series was Sari Maritsa, who with her friend Vivian Gaye (later Mrs Ernst Lubitsch) had gone to the première and party as Carlyle Robinson's guests. Chaplin intimated his interest, was delighted to find that Miss Maritsa was an accomplished dancer, and thrilled his guests by performing a stylish tango with her. During the rest of this British visit Sari (whose real name seems to have been Patricia Deterring, and who was later to have a brief Hollywood career) was constantly in Chaplin's company. Robinson, in his role of 'sup-press agent', attempted to put reporters off the track by claiming that Sari was in fact his own girlfriend; but it did not prevent the British newspapers speculating that she would be the star of Chaplin's next film.

Both in Britain and abroad the press now began to assert confidently that Ramsay MacDonald had recommended Chaplin for a knighthood. Several papers published cartoons celebrating the forthcoming honour; a headline in the Boise (Idaho) *Statesman* trumpeted inelegantly, 'Charlie will get Cracked on Dome with King's Sword'. Suddenly, however, the press declared that the honour would not after all be accorded. The general opinion, openly published, was that the knighthood had been vetoed by the personal intervention of Queen Mary herself, who felt that the Royal Family would be party to some kind of publicity stunt in honouring a motion picture comedian.

More than forty years later, when Chaplin finally received his knighthood from the granddaughter of George V and Queen Mary, a press leak from the Prime Minister's office revealed that the only explanation for withholding the honour recorded in 1931 was the unfavourable publicity generated by the Northcliffe press during the

First World War. Ramsay MacDonald may not have been encouraged by Chaplin's last-minute refusal of an invitation to a dinner the Prime Minister had arranged in his honour at the House of Commons, to meet a select party of Members. Chaplin, who had clearly not taken to MacDonald, became less and less enthusiastic over the idea; and finally decided that it was imperative that he travel to Berlin the day

Knighthood proposed for Chaplin (News Item)

before the appointment. The Premier's son Alistair MacDonald and Chaplin's own entourage were additionally embarrassed by Chaplin's refusal to telephone his apologies. He would prefer to write, he said; and then, predictably, did not write either. Finally Sir Philip Sassoon was obliged to follow the party to Europe in order to draft a suitable letter to extricate all concerned from grave embarrassment. The embarrassment was indeed almost compounded at the very moment of Chaplin's departure, when Sari endeavoured to persuade him to stay in London rather than face the rigours of a stormy channel crossing. Realizing the affront to the Prime Minister that would be committed if Chaplin remained in London after having declined the invitation, his friends hurried him unwillingly off to Liverpool Street, where they had taken the precaution of arranging for the train to be delayed for fifteen minutes.

Barton had meanwhile left the group. Having arrived in apparently high spirits, he had declined once more into acute depression. After the first week or so he could not be persuaded to leave the hotel, but wandered the suite and the public corridors. On one occasion Robinson found him fingering a revolver, and was terrified that he might take Chaplin's life along with his own. Chaplin was alarmed and irritated to discover that Barton had cut the wires on the electric clocks, for reasons known only to himself. The party at the Carlton were positively relieved when Barton announced his intention to return home. Robinson booked him a passage on the *Europa* to New York and Chaplin gave him £25 for his expenses, since he was by this time penniless. Two or three weeks after his return, Ralph Barton shot himself in the head in his New York apartment.

In the decade since his last visit, Chaplin's fame had become as great in Germany as in the rest of the world, and the usual dense crowds lined the route from the railway station – where he was met by Marlene Dietrich – to the Hotel Adlon. He was entertained by members of the Reichstag and given a guided tour of Potsdam (which he did not like, but he never approved of palaces) by Prince Henry of Prussia. He visited the Einsteins and was much impressed by the modesty of their apartment and delighted when Einstein concluded a lively debate on world economics with the compliment, 'You are not a comedian, Charlie, but an economist.'

Even at this time the political atmosphere in Germany was ominous. The Nazi press railed against the Berlin populace for losing its head over a 'Jewish' comedian from America. Then, on a day when Chaplin had an audience with Chancellor Wirth, ten men claiming to represent unemployed cinema workers arrived at the Adlon demanding an interview with Chaplin. Robinson said that it was useless for them to see him, but they threatened a 10,000-strong demonstration outside the hotel if they did not. Finally three of them were admitted, and Chaplin told them that he was very sorry for their plight but that

To Ralph
From the author
of this dastardly crime
Charlie Chaplin

1931 - Ralph Barton, caricatured
by Chaplin.

there were 75,000 unemployed in Hollywood also. An hour later, the Berlin Communist daily newspaper was out with a report that Chaplin had received a delegation of its editors and had expressed deep sympathy with the young Communist cause. The incident clearly annoyed and embarrassed Wirth at the subsequent audience.

Chaplin had the consolation of further romantic encounters, with the Viennese dancer La Jana and the American-born actress Betty Amann. Delightful as these flesh and blood acquaintances were, he was more permanently impressed by his first sight of Nefertiti in the Pergamon Museum. He at once ordered a facsimile of the bust by the artist who had made a copy for the museum at Munich, and it was to retain a permanent place of honour in his homes.

The party next moved on to Vienna, where the crowds which greeted his arrival were perhaps the most astounding of either of his

European trips. Fortunately news film of the event still survives, showing Chaplin being carried over the heads of the crowd, as he was all the way from the railway station to the Hotel Imperial. On this occasion, too, Chaplin spoke his first words before a sound film camera, five years before *Modern Times*. They consisted only of '*Gute tag! Gute tag!*' repeated rather nervously as he clung tightly to his hat and cane lest they be lost in the sea of faces on which he floated. The romantic encounters of Berlin were forgotten as he discovered shared artistic enthusiasms with the pianist Jennie Rothenstein. The ebullience of the beautiful operetta star Irene Palasthy proved too much for him, however, and he decided not to travel on to Budapest, fearing that the city's much vaunted female beauties might all prove as demonstrative.

Chaplin and his party then moved to Venice, which made a deep impression upon him although he found it too melancholy to spend more than a couple of days sightseeing there. He arrived somewhat fearful that Marion Davies might have arrived there on one of her European tours. In fact she descended on Venice a couple of months later when Chaplin was elsewhere and able thankfully to decline an invitation to a sumptuous party at her palazzo.

From Venice Chaplin travelled by train to Paris, where he was to lunch with Aristide Briand, and to receive the Légion d'Honneur. Unknown to Chaplin the decision to make the award was the outcome of representations by a group of his French admirers, led by his first and most faithful Parisian friend, the cartoonist Cami. Cami had in fact come to London during Chaplin's stay at the Carlton; but Chaplin had been too busy to do more than shake his hand hurriedly as he left the hotel for Liverpool Street on the final night of his stay.

As the train approached Paris the French police came aboard to warn Chaplin that because of the huge crowds he would be advised to leave the train before it arrived at the terminus. They had taken it upon themselves to change his hotel reservation to the Crillon in order to avoid the worst of the mob. Chaplin was irritated by this interference with his plans, and refused to leave the train before the terminus, though he agreed to the change of hotel. Despite the crowds and the twelve-strong police guard put around Chaplin, Cami somehow managed to reach his side. This however irritated rather than pleased Chaplin, who became positively furious when he suspected that Cami was involved in a plot to make him speak into a microphone that was thrust before him. (Cami had only been guilty of yelling in his ear that it would please the mob if he said something like '*Bonjour Paris*'.) Cami accompanied the Chaplin party to the Crillon, but Chaplin, still angry, insisted on his being ejected. This was, so far as can be discovered, the last time the two men met, though the sentimental Cami never wavered in his adoration of his youthful idol.

Apart from the Briand lunch, there were two memorable social occasions in France. For a rather uneasy audience with King Albert of the Belgians, Chaplin was seated on a very low chair while the tall King occupied a much higher one. The incident later gave Chaplin the idea for the meeting of the rival heads of state in *The Great Dictator*.

On the train to Venice, Chaplin had met the Duke and Duchess of Westminster and had unwisely accepted their invitation to a boar hunt at their estate at Saint-Saëns in Normandy. The rigours of the ride left him in need of days of massage. Moreover, ordinarily so careful of his appearance, Chaplin was chagrined to be photographed by press men while wearing an unbecoming hunting outfit made up of items borrowed from the Duke and various guests of assorted sizes. There was to be a memory of this, too, in the 'animal trainer' costume in *Limelight*.

It was now the end of March, and Chaplin decided to move on to the South of France. Sydney had been settled in Nice for six months: when a variety of causes, both financial and personal, frustrated his plans to set up production in England, he decided that he was sufficiently well off to retire to a life of leisure. Sydney's apartment was too small for guests, and Chaplin gratefully accepted the invitation of the American millionaire Frank Jay Gould to stay at the Majestic Hotel in Nice, which he owned along with the Casino. Gould had formerly been married to Edith Kelly, sister of Hetty and of Arthur Kelly, who had arranged the invitation.

Chaplin quickly realized that Gould's eagerness to have him as a guest was not entirely disinterested. Chaplin's presence at the Majestic and Gould's other Nice hotel, the Palais de la Méditerranée, was a big draw to the rich and curious local clientèle. On the evening of Chaplin's arrival Gould gave a dinner party in his honour at the Palais, and introduced an admission charge of five francs to the *terrasse*, from which guests could have a view of Chaplin. The charm of the latest Mrs Gould (there was even talk of Chaplin making her into an actress) dissuaded Chaplin from giving vent to his anger, but a number of social activities which Gould had optimistically planned for him were promptly cancelled. Both Charles and Sydney however seem to have been taken by Gould's busy press agent, an engaging, mischievous White Russian called Boris Evelinoff, who combined his work for Gould with a job as correspondent for *Le Soir*. Evelinoff became a regular member of the Chaplin entourage on the Riviera, and after Chaplin's return to America was for a while his official representative in Paris until it became evident that the size of his expense accounts somewhat outweighed the value of his services. Apart from the Gould circle, Chaplin mingled with the Riviera set, including Elsa Maxwell, Mary Garden and the Duke of Connaught. He was especially delighted to meet Emil Ludwig, the biographer of Napoleon, in whom Chaplin always envisioned an ideal part for himself.

The most significant Riviera encounter was with May Reeves, alias Mizzi Muller, who was to remain for eleven months the exclusive romantic involvement in his life and, more durably, was to provide much of the inspiration for the character of Natascha in the script *Stowaway*, eventually to become *A Countess from Hong Kong*. May's past was somewhat shadowy. She appears to have been Czech, and had won prizes in national beauty contests in Czechoslovakia. Arriving on the Riviera she had won a dancing contest, and had made the acquaintance of Sydney.

Robinson, since the arrival of the party in the South of France, had been overwhelmed by the bulk of Chaplin's correspondence, a large part of which was in languages he could not read. He asked Sydney if he could help him find a multi-lingual secretary and one evening at the Casino Sydney presented May as an ideal candidate for the job, since she spoke six languages fluently. Elegant and beautiful, with the look of a sophisticated adventuress, May did not give the appearance of the perfect secretary that night. Robinson was pleasantly surprised however the following morning when she arrived on the stroke of nine and buckled to to sort the letters and inscribe them with neat little *précis* translations.

He enjoyed the perfect secretary for a mere three hours, however. The moment that Chaplin set eyes on May he was struck by her beauty and charm. The same night she was invited to dinner with Chaplin, Sydney and Robinson and from that moment was Chaplin's inseparable companion. Chaplin seemed positively stimulated by the intense disapproval of the liaison evinced by everyone around him apart from Kono, who took warmly to the young woman, particularly after she nursed him capably through a severe bout of ptomaine poisoning. The Goulds were outraged that Chaplin should be seen in their establishment with this *déclassée* person; Sydney and Minnie were terrified that a new Lita Grey situation would ensue; Robinson gritted his teeth in his role of 'sup-press' agent.

Chaplin and his hosts both realized that it was time they parted company, but neither found it easy to make the first move. Mrs Gould found the most courteous way out of the impasse: one morning she arrived at Chaplin's suite, presented him with an exquisite pair of platinum cufflinks, and said graciously how lovely it had been having him there. Chaplin blithely announced that the party, including May and Sydney, would travel to Algeria. He was with difficulty persuaded that it would be better if May travelled on a different boat.

Such ruses did not entirely put the press off the scent, and articles continued to proliferate about Chaplin and 'the mysterious Mary' as May was for some reason generally identified. Back at the studios, Alf Reeves did his best to keep the Californian press happy. He told Kathlyn Hayden, whom the studio had trusted slightly more than most journalists:

> Charlie has fallen madly in love . . . but it's not what you think! He managed to withstand the charms of all the beautiful ladies of London, Berlin, Paris and Vienna – only to succumb to the allure of – Algiers. And Algiers it is which will be Charlie's habitat for the next two or three years – or however long it may take him to complete his next film, which will be made *entirely* in that country.
>
> I understand that reports have been circulated in English and European newspapers to the effect that Charlie's next film will be made either in London, Paris or Berlin – but the truth is that every scene in the new picture will be shot in Algiers.
>
> Charlie is now at work developing the story. From the sketchy outline which he has cabled me I gather that he will repeat a trick which made a great hit in two of his earlier films – completely altering his appearance at some stage in the story for purposes of disguise. In *The Pilgrim* old-timers will remember that he dressed up as a clergyman, and in a still earlier film he donned a wig and woman's clothes. Of course, in the new film, he will be the same little tramp that he always has been, but at some stage of the action circumstances will compel him to disguise himself in the flowing robes of a sheik!

Nothing more was ever heard of Chaplin's sheik film. There can be little doubt however that one of the Chaplin brothers had given this information to Reeves, who was notoriously cautious in statements to the press. To squash other rumours that had filtered back from Europe, Reeves emphasized to Miss Hayden:

> Charlie's leading lady in the new film will most assuredly *not* be any of the fair ones of London, Berlin and Paris whose names have been mentioned in this connection. She will definitely come from Hollywood.

Bored with inactivity, Sydney now began to take an interest once more in his brother's business affairs, and succeeded in convincing Chaplin that distribution arrangements both in America and France should be more closely overseen. This gave Chaplin an excuse to rid himself temporarily of the irksome Robinson, who was despatched to New York with a list of embarrassing investigatory instructions. On Robinson's return he and Sydney went together to Paris to look into the distribution arrangements of *City Lights* there. No sooner had they arrived than they began to receive a stream of letters from Minnie Chaplin in Nice, gravely alarmed by the mounting publicity being given to the May Reeves affair. Sydney despatched Robinson back to the South of France with unequivocal instructions to put a stop to the affair, even though it meant telling Chaplin that Sydney had had an affair with the girl himself: he was acutely aware of his brother's need for monopoly in matters of the heart.

Apprehensively but dutifully, Robinson carried out his commission. He arrived in Marseilles in time to meet the boat bringing Chaplin and May from Algiers. Rushing onto the vessel ahead of the reporters, he managed to persuade the couple to leave the vessel separately, escorting May himself so that there were no compromising newspaper pictures. The results of his subsequent efforts to disillusion Chaplin with May were predictable. The relationship of the couple was no doubt impaired, but Robinson's relationship with Chaplin was ended, permanently and bitterly. Already irritated by Robinson's constant presence, Chaplin became furious over the wretched part he was now playing. So, in his turn, did Sydney when he discovered that Robinson had taken him at his word in revealing his own relationship with May.

Robinson was swiftly despatched to New York, where he was appointed the studio's East Coast representative. At the end of the year Robinson received a letter from Alf Reeves explaining that his services would no longer be required since work on *City Lights* contracts had more or less finished and Chaplin's future production plans remained vague. He was given a fortnight's notice. Robinson was subsequently to publish an embittered but verifiable account of his fifteen years as a Chaplin employee.

Robinson left France at the end of May 1931, and, despite some periods of separation, May remained close to Chaplin. She had fallen deeply in love with him. It is impossible to know what were his feelings for her after the first infatuation had worn off, but there seems no doubt that she was a jolly, affectionate, undemanding holiday companion. From Nice they moved on to Juan-les-Pins which was at the height of fashion at that time. It was there that Kono had his severe attack of ptomaine poisoning, to the great alarm of Chaplin who was sure that his indispensable attendant was about to die. Henri d'Abbadie d'Arrast, the former assistant on *A Woman of Paris*, devised motor trips to Paris and to his own family home. On one of the trips they were involved in an accident, but Chaplin was unharmed. D'Arrast next persuaded Chaplin to move to Biarritz, where he was entertained to lunch by Winston Churchill. In Biarritz, too, he first met Edward, Prince of Wales, through the introduction of Lady Furness, the former Thelma Morgan Converse. Lady Furness (who had done service as chaperone in the early Lita Grey days) was evidently important in arranging the Prince's social affairs: it was she who first introduced him to Mrs Wallis Simpson. From Biarritz it was a short trip to Spain, where Chaplin witnessed a bullfight. He was observed to flinch when the bull attacked the horse. Asked afterwards if he had enjoyed the fight he answered cautiously, 'I would rather not say anything.' In later years, following the rise of Franco, Chaplin was adamant in his refusal to return to Spain, even though his daughter Geraldine made her home there.

At the end of August Chaplin returned through Paris to spend the autumn in London. He was both relieved and disturbed to find his reception cooler than the previous winter. It was partly a case of novelty wearing off, but without the protection of a press agent, Chaplin had begun to attract some unfavourable notice in the English newspapers. A lady called May Shepherd, who had been hired by Robinson to remain in England to deal with the continuing avalanche of correspondence, demanded an increase of the weekly £5 to which she had originally agreed, since the job proved much more onerous than originally anticipated. United Artists and Chaplin's immediate friends and advisers urged him to agree to her request but he stood firm, regarding it as a matter of principle to hold her to the original agreement. Only after weeks of anxiety for everyone, considerable legal expenses and a good deal of press furore did Chaplin abruptly agree to settle with Miss Shepherd in full.

The newspapers took more malicious delight in the Royal Variety Performance fracas. While Chaplin was in Juan-les-Pins, he received a telegram from George Black inviting him to take part in the Royal Variety Performance the following month. There are two different versions of what happened next. One is that, lacking a secretary to deal with his correspondence, Chaplin simply overlooked the invitation. Most papers however reported that he had declined to appear, saying that he never appeared on the stage. (In one interview he said that it would be 'bad taste' for him to do so.) Instead he sent a donation of $1000 with the rather acid comment that this represented his earnings in his last two years of residence in England.

The popular press, perversely ignoring the fact that the Variety Performance is a Royal, but not a Royal Command performance, represented Chaplin's refusal as an insult to the King. Chaplin was, quite reasonably, incensed. Unfortunately he compounded his problems by pouring out his indignation to a young man he met on the tennis court in Juan, without being aware that he was a reporter – he was missing his 'sup-press' agent:

> They say I have a duty to England. I wonder just what that duty is. No one wanted me or cared for me in England seventeen years ago. I had to go to America for my chance and I got it there.
>
> . . . Then down here (at Juan-les-Pins) I sat one night patiently waiting for the Prince of Monaco, and it appears that I was insulting the Duke of Connaught.
>
> Why are people bothering their heads about me? I am only a movie comedian and they have made a politician out of me.

He went on to express some forthright opinions on the subject of patriotism:

> Patriotism is the greatest insanity the world has ever suffered. I have been all over Europe in the past few months. Patriotism is rampant everywhere, and the result is going to be another war. I hope they send the old men to the front the next time, for it is the old men who are the real criminals in Europe today.

More than thirty years afterwards Chaplin had found no reason to modify his views: 'How can one tolerate patriotism, when six million

Jews were murdered in its name?' Prescient as his opinion was, however, it was far from fashionable in the England of 1931.

The fickleness of the press had no effect upon Chaplin's social life in England. He saw the Prince of Wales several times, and was invited for the weekend to Fort Belvedere. This opened up to him a good many more doors than he cared to enter. Among the celebrated London hostesses who entertained him were Margot Asquith, Lady Oxford, Sibyl Lady Colefax and Lady Cunard. Late in September there was a much publicized meeting with Gandhi who was then visiting England and lodging in a modest house in East India Dock Road. The interview had a special piquancy since Gandhi was one of the very small handful of people in the world who did not know who Charlie Chaplin was, and had certainly never seen one of his films. The Mahatma was affable and gracious however, and politely exchanged economic ideas with his guest before inviting him to stay and watch him at prayers. Chaplin left with the impression of 'a realistic, virile-minded visionary with a will of iron'.

Chaplin also witnessed the autumn election, which resulted in a Conservative landslide, and accompanied some of his politician friends to election meetings. He made a sentimental journey to Lancashire in search of scenes he remembered from days on tour with *Sherlock Holmes* and in variety. He found Manchester on a Sunday 'cataleptic' and so drove on to Blackburn, which had been one of his favourite towns on tour. He found the pub where he used to lodge for fourteen shillings a week, and had a drink in the bar, unrecognized.

He was now ready to return to the United States, but the holiday was to be prolonged. Douglas Fairbanks invited him to join him in St Moritz. Chaplin went there in company with Lady Cholmondeley. In Switzerland they were joined by May Reeves and Sydney. Having hitherto always expressed an aversion to mountains in general and Switzerland in particular, Chaplin stayed on throughout January and February, until the season was coming to an end and Syd, Douglas and Lady Cholmondeley had all returned home. Chaplin now decided to prolong the holiday still further with a visit to Japan, a country in which his interest had been excited two years earlier when he had become enthusiastic over the visit of the Japanese Kengeki theatre to California.

Chaplin wired an invitation to Sydney who had meanwhile returned to Nice, and it was arranged that they would meet in Naples. Chaplin, Kono and May travelled through Italy via Milan and Rome, where a planned audience with Mussolini failed to take place. On the quayside at Naples Chaplin bade his final farewell to the devoted May. His last sight of her as the ship pulled out was on the dock, bravely attempting to smile and doing an imitation of his tramp walk.

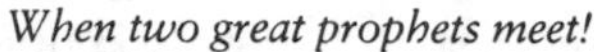
When two great prophets meet!

GANDHI

1931 – Gandhi and Chaplin.

Sydney, fiercely protective of his brother and constitutionally suspicious of the rest of the world, continued to worry that there would be some bad aftermath to the affair. His fears became more acute a year later when it became necessary to dispense with the services of Boris Evelinoff as Paris representative. Sydney confided to Alf Reeves his fears that Evelinoff might have entered into some sort of league with May:

> I would not be surprised if a story broke in the *Paris Midi* relating the whole history of that affair, although Robinson has taken the edge off.

> The reason I mention this is because Evelinoff came to Cannes and hit upon a story of a girl who had been the mistress of a certain Balkan king. I met the girl and heard the proposition made to her to spew up all she knows. The king having given her up, she agreed to do so, and now the story is appearing in the *Paris Midi* under the glaring headlines 'From the Folies Bergère to the Throne'. At the time Evelinoff was arranging this, May was living in the same hotel as Boris at exceptionally low terms arranged by him. She left Cannes about the same time as he did. The other day in Paris Minnie phoned Boris at his house, the secretary answered, and Minnie feels sure it was May's voice, so perhaps she is also writing her life story.

Poor Sydney must have felt his nightmares were to be realized in 1935 when May actually published her recollections of those eventful months in book form, as *Charlie Chaplin Intime*, edited by Claire Goll. Any such fears were unfounded. May's memoirs proved that she was no sophisticated and scheming adventuress but the cheerful, somewhat naïve young woman who had provided the ideal Riviera playmate. Her book was a touching, tedious declaration of affection, forgiveness and regret.

Chaplin and Sydney embarked on the *Suwa Maru* on 12 March 1932. Their first stop was Singapore, where they were delayed by Chaplin's succumbing to a fever. When he recovered they moved on to Bali whose people and culture thrilled and astonished Chaplin. The brothers shot some 400 metres of film on the island, and were rather proud of it: unfortunately the best parts were lost through some rather dubious activity on the part of a Dutch cameraman, Hank Alsem, whom they entrusted with the editing.

In the second week of May they arrived in Tokyo to crowds and a welcome as spectacular as they were accustomed to encounter in Europe. Chaplin responded with enthusiasm and excitement to every aspect of Japanese culture – the geishas, the tea ceremony, wood-block prints and drama. The visit was shadowed however by a series of sinister events connected with the activities of an ultra-rightist group, the Black Dragon Society, which for a moment considered Chaplin as a likely assassination target. There were vague and not so vague menaces, of which poor Kono, as interpreter, bore the brunt. Then one night while the party was in the company of the young son of the Premier, Tsuyoshi Inugai, the Premier himself was murdered by six extremists.

Finally, on 2 June 1932, Chaplin with Kono set sail on the *Hikawa*

Maru from Yokohama to Seattle. The day before they sailed, Sydney, who was to make his separate way to Nice, wrote to Alf Reeves, 'Charlie is returning home with the solution to the world's problems, which he hopes to have put before the League of Nations. He has been working very hard on this solution and I must say that he has hit upon an exceptionally good idea.'

During the homeward voyage Chaplin continued to work on his economic theory as well, apparently, as on some preliminary notes for *Modern Times*. Perhaps this contemplation of the world's problems provided distractions from the problems of his own studio, which he had so soon now to face. Since the completion of *City Lights* the establishment on La Brea and Sunset had had its share of the general depression in the film industry. Knowing Chaplin's life-long habit of delegating to others any unpleasant or graceless duties, it is possible to suppose that one factor in his prolonged absence was the desire not to witness or to be seen as responsible for the current situation at the studio. On 23 April 1931 Alf Reeves had reported to Carl Robinson, who was then in Paris,

> You can tell the Chief the staff here is reduced to the minimum. Rollie, Mark, Morgan, Ted Miner, Anderson and Val Lane are all gone. I have retained Jack Wilson as a librarian and laboratory man. The carpenters, electric and paint shops are closed. The small staff we have here is very busy, and we have plenty to do. Most of the people who have left are out and things look pretty bad. The stock market is all to pieces but we are hoping for the best.
>
> P.S. General conditions are still bad here. The picture business is going down generally.

Henry Bergman seems to have been kept on a retainer, because in August 1932 it was widely reported in the press that he had declined to accept his weekly salary of $75 any longer, unless the studio was in active production. Bergman at that time had an income from his restaurant. For the others laid off, life could be difficult. Rollie Totheroh's son Jack remembers having to take along food and other necessities for his father; Rollie himself published a couple of cartoons urging Chaplin to get back to work so that the studio might reopen.

These were hard times for everyone. Since leaving the studio, Edna had resolutely refrained from asking for any help from Chaplin apart from the monthly retainer she was paid, and remained anxious not to impinge in any way upon his life. During the period of his holiday, however, things had become so difficult for her that she was finally forced to seek assistance, in a poignant letter:

Dear Charlie,

Fearing I might bother you and trouble you, I have hesitated writing, but finding it absolutely necessary I am doing so, hoping you will not be angry and misconstrue my real thoughts toward you, as they are constantly for you and with you on your so long and interesting travels. However you said many years ago (perhaps you have forgotten) what you were going to do, have been doing and are doing, and though you may not know I have been [watching] very silently and with the greatest pride your most every act.

Am just recuperating from severe illness, which almost terminated with the *final* rest. But to my great joy and gladness am feeling better than ever before in my life. On [*illegible*] 29 I was stricken with a perforated ulcer . . . which caused haemorrhage in my stomach and was rushed to hospital. The first day four doctors worked constantly on me with the result of no result what-so-ever. Being unconscious but with apparently subconscious determination I rallied with the aid of every known heart stimulant and one good doctor. Saline was administered into the blood stream for one week as I was unable to take any other form of nourishment. I was in a run down condition to begin with from a bad cold. So to add to all I almost had pneumonia. All told it was a battle . . .

The same night I was stricken, my father died, but I was too ill to be told of it. He was 84 years old, and of course not able to support himself for years. I have been sending him a small check every month to live on. So when friends notified us of his death, they wanted me to send the money for burial expenses. My mother in desperation went to see Alf Reeves and asked if he could lend the financial aid needed, as I only had about $300 in cash in the bank at the time, and money was needed every day at the hospital, so she knew we could not send that for burial purposes. I like others lost $2300 in the Fidelity Loan and Trust Co. So perhaps you can see why I was and am short of money. Mother again appealed to Alf, and he kindly let her have $750.00 – $350 for burial of my father and the rest for hospital and nurses. On top of this my Drs bill is $700 and $50 for heart specialist. So all in all I am in a most difficult and needy situation.

Charlie *I know* it is bothersome and a dam nuisance to have to read of or listen to anyone's troubles, and I feel that you know well enough *I would not* take up your time, not even for a second, unless I simply had to. Please forgive me.

Will be so happy to see you back here, But I wonder how long you will be interested enough to stay?

All my love,
Edna

April 3 1932

P.S. Saw by the papers that Minnie was here – Am going to telephone her.

In 1932 Chaplin was nearing the mid-point of both his actual and his professional life. We are fortunate to possess from this moment the most searching and perceptive portrait ever written of him. It is an essay under the title 'A Comedian' in Thomas Burke's *City of Encounters*, published in 1933. Burke's life started at the same period, in the same social background and the same part of London as Chaplin. They had first met in 1921 (Chaplin had been very excited by reading Burke's *Nights in Town*), kept up their acquaintance over the years, and met again during Chaplin's 1931 holiday. Chaplin invited him to take the unhappy Barton's place as his travelling companion on the trips to Berlin and Spain, but Burke refused: 'I knew that a fortnight of proximity to that million-voltage battery would have left me a cinder.'

Burke loved Chaplin without idolatry (he called him 'this hard, bright, icy creature') and understood him perhaps better than any other man in his lifetime. Burke's fifty-page essay is essential to the discovery of Chaplin. He compares his character to that of Dickens:

> a man of querulous outlook, self-centred, moody, and vaguely dissatisfied with life. That is the kind of man he is.
>
> Or nearly. For to get at him is not easy. It is impossible to see him straight. He dazzles everybody – the intellectual, the simple, the cunning, and even those who meet him every day. At no stage can one make a firm sketch and say: 'This is Charles Chaplin.' One can only say: 'This is Charles Chaplin, wasn't it?' He's like a brilliant, flashing now from this facet and now from that – blue, green, yellow, crimson by turns. A brilliant is the apt simile; he's as hard and bright as that, and his lustre is as erratic. And if you split him you would find, as with the brilliant, and as with Charles Dickens, that there was no personal source of those charging lights; they were only the flashings of genius. It is almost impossible to locate him. I doubt if he can locate himself; genius seldom can . . .

Burke attempts it, nonetheless:

> For the rest he is all this and that. He is often as kind and tender as any man could be, and often inconsiderate. He shrinks from the limelight, but misses it if it isn't turned upon him. He is intensely shy, yet loves to be the centre of attention. A born solitary, he knows the fascination of the crowd. He is really and truly modest, but very much aware that there is nobody quite like Charles Chaplin. He expects to get his own way in everything, and usually gets it. Life hampers him; he wants wings. He wants to eat his cake and have it. He wants a *peau de chagrin* for the granting of all his wishes, but the *peau de chagrin* must not diminish. He makes excessive demands upon life and upon people, and because these demands cannot always be answered he is perplexed and irritated. He commands the loyalty of friends while being casual himself. He takes their continuing friendship for granted. He likes to enjoy the best of the current social system, while at heart he is the reddest of Reds. Full of impulsive generosities, he is also capable of sudden changes to the opposite . . . He takes himself seriously, but he has a sharp sense of humour about himself and his doings. He has a genuine humility about the position he has won, but, like most other really humble artists, he doesn't always like you to take the humility as justified. For two hours he will be the sweetest fellow you have ever sat with; then, without apparent cause, he will be all petulance and asperity. Like a child, his interest is quickly caught and he is quickly bored. In essence he is still a Cockney, but he is no longer English – if he ever was. In moments of excitement, and in all his work, the Cockney appears. At other times he is, in manners, speech and attitude, American. He is not at all in sympathy with the reserved English character, and he cares little for England and English things.
>
> . . . He is by no means contemptuous of money, but the possession of a very large sum means little to him. It represents economic safety, nothing else. He likes plain bourgeois foods – on his visit to England he was babbling to me of kippers, bloaters, tripe, sheep's heart – and, although he has a large wardrobe, he prefers old clothes and no fuss. Drink doesn't interest him, and he smokes one or none to my twenty.
>
> He is one of the most honest of men. If you ask his opinion on anything or anybody you get it straight and clear. Most of us have some touch of humbug about us, but Charles has none. You can accept anything he says for the truth as he sees it. A point of his honesty is his selfishness. Most of us are selfish, in one way or another, but are annoyed if people bring the accusation . . . Yet selfish people are usually the more agreeable. By pleasing themselves they maintain a cheerful demeanour to those about them. Charles lives as most of us would if we had the necessary nerve to face ourselves as we really are – however disturbing the 'really' might be to our self-esteem. He will only do what he wants to do. If any engagement

is in opposition to his mood of the moment he breaks it, and if asked why he didn't keep it he will blandly answer – Because he didn't want to. In whatever company he may be, he is simple and spontaneous. He may be always living in a part, but he never poses; he has a hatred of sham . . .

His life at home, despite the Japanese valets and cooks and chauffeurs, is not the glamorous, crowded affair that some people imagine it to be. He told me that he leads almost as humdrum a life as a London clerk. He is not over-popular in that lunatic asylum – one could hardly expect Hollywood to know what to make of a poet – and they leave him pretty much to himself . . .

His mind is extraordinarily quick and receptive; retentive, too. He reads very little, but with a few elementary facts on a highly technical subject, his mind can so work upon them that he can talk with an expert on that subject in such a way as to make the expert think. He thus appears a very well-read and cultivated man when, in fact, his acquaintance with books is slight. With little interest in people, he yet has a swifter and acuter eye than any novelist I know for their oddities and their carefully hidden secrets. It is useless to pose before him; he can call your bluff in the moment of being introduced . . .

He is now (1931) forty-two in years, but he cannot live up to that age, and never will. His attitude and his interest are always towards youth and young things. He takes no concern in the historical past; his spiritual home is his own period. He is intensely a child of these times, and his mind finds nothing to engage it farther back than his own boyhood. 'I always feel such a kid,' he told me once, 'among grown-ups . . .'

14

MODERN TIMES

Chaplin arrived back in Hollywood on 10 June 1932. He had left on the last day of January 1931. Returning, he felt confused, disorientated and above all lonely. The house on Summit Drive was empty except for the servants. The first person he called was Georgia, and they spent the evening of his return together, but it was not a success. They dined by the fire. Chaplin had brought back two trunks full of souvenirs of the trip for Georgia. Late in the evening, as they ate cornflakes in the kitchen, she told him rather forcefully that all his presents did not make up for seventeen months without a word or a postcard. She refused his presents and left, telling him he need not trouble to telephone. He did not, and they were not to meet again for ten years. Like Edna, Georgia gave Chaplin disinterested friendship, loyalty and affection. There were incompatibilities between them. Georgia had her own mind and opinions. She was also religious. 'He used to say to me "Don't start talking to me about God."' He was more than half in earnest.[1]

Chaplin no longer felt at home in Hollywood. The place had changed since the age of golden silence, which was coming to an end when he began *City Lights*. During his absence, Douglas Fairbanks and Mary Pickford had separated, 'so that world was no more'.[2] There were new people and new techniques, and a new streamlined industrialization had supplanted artisan methods and pioneering enthusiasm. Chaplin was in no mood to take up battle with the talkies. In the empty moments of his return, he thought of selling up everything, retiring and going to live in China. (He never made clear why this was his choice.)

In his memoirs he admitted that he had had a vague hope of meeting someone in Europe who might orient his life. He did not, but there was soon to be a meeting on his doorstep in Hollywood. In July 1932, Joseph Schenck invited Chaplin for a weekend on his yacht. Schenck was accustomed to decorate his parties with pretty girls, and on this occasion they included Paulette Goddard. Paulette had been born in New York, most likely in 1911. Her real name was Pauline Levy. At fourteen she was a Ziegfeld girl, then appeared in the chorus of *No Foolin'* and *Rio Rita*, and landed a small part in Archie Selwyn's *The Conquering Male*. At sixteen she married a rich playboy, Edgar James, but divorced him in the same year, whereupon she made her way to Hollywood. By the time she met Chaplin she had played bit parts in *The Girl Habit*, *The Mouthpiece* and *The Kid From Spain*, and had signed a contract with the Hal Roach studio.

Paulette was beautiful, radiant, vivacious, ambitious and uncomplicated. She and Chaplin enjoyed an immediate rapport. There were similarities in their backgrounds – Paulette too came from a broken home and was the family breadwinner while still a child. They were both alone. Chaplin was delighted at this first meeting to give Paulette some financial counsel. She was still naïve enough in Hollywood ways to be contemplating 'investing' $50,000 of her alimony in a dubious film project. Chaplin was just in time to prevent her signing the documents.

Soon they were seeing a great deal of each other. Chaplin persuaded Paulette to revert from platinum blonde to her natural dark hair; he also bought up her Roach contract. The press were soon hard on their heels, describing Paulette as a 'mysterious blonde'. She did not long remain mysterious. When Chaplin saw her off on the plane to New York on 19 September – he had stayed up with her all night at Glendale Airport – their farewell kiss made headlines across the continent. Both denied rumours of an engagement. The kiss was only friendly, said Paulette, adding that she was to be his next leading lady.

Meanwhile there were irritating reminders that Chaplin was still, in a way, a family man. In the years immediately following the divorce he had made little effort to contact his sons. They were still babies, and the associations were still too painful. Now, however, Charles was seven and Sydney six. Before his departure he appears to have seen them a few times, mostly on the initiative of Lita's grandmother. With their upbringing left largely to Lita's mother, since Lita was trying to make a career for herself as a singer, they had grown into irresistibly attractive children. Ida Zeitlin, one of the most intelligent and perceptive of the great generation of Hollywood 'sob-sisters', interviewed them for *Screenland* in the summer of 1932 and her shrewd assessment of their contrasting personalities might serve, with very little change, to characterize them in their maturer years:

> Tommy [i.e. Sydney] is lively and venturesome, where Charlie is reflective and reserved. With Tommy, to have an idea is to act on it, but Charlie will think twice before he moves. Tommy is restless, turbulent, independent – Charlie is sensitive, high-strung and craves affection. Nothing is safe with Tommy – his toys have a habit of breaking apart in his hands. Charlie's clothes are always folded at night and his small shoes placed carefully side by side. Tommy would sleep sweetly, says his grandmother, through an explosion, but there aren't many nights when she isn't awakened by an apprehensive little voice from Charlie's bed: 'Are you there, Nana?' And only on being reassured does Charlie fall asleep again. Charlie has his father's troubled temperament – Tommy, like his mother, is equable; and if signs mean anything, life is going to be considerably harder on Charlie than on his little brother Tommy.[3]

Miss Zeitlin cannot have known how accurate a prophet time would prove her.

While their father was away on his travels, Sydney and Charlie had also been in Europe. They had spent almost a year in and around Nice, where their still youthful grandmother had a gentleman friend, and where the boys learned French (they already spoke Spanish fluently, as well as English). Although they must often have been very near their father on the Côte d'Azur, there appears to have been no contact. In France, however, the children discovered with delight that being Chaplin's sons made them, too, celebrities. Charlie learned that he could infallibly gain attention by imitating his father's screen walk – a feat which Sydney, slightly pigeon-toed, could not master.

A week or so before Chaplin arrived back in America, Lita summoned the boys and Nana home: she had fixed up a film contract with David Butler to appear together with her sons in *The Little Teacher*. In New York the children were met by a battery of cameramen and reporters, but they were by this time professionals with the press. Charlie modestly told them that he was going to be a great actor and would like to play cowboys. Sydney said that he was going to be Mickey Mouse. 'I am wondering,' speculated Louella Parsons with evident glee, 'just how Charles Chaplin Senior will react to this.'

She was soon to discover. On 25 August, Loyd Wright, Chaplin's attorney, filed a petition objecting to the boys working in motion pictures. Chaplin appeared in court on 27 August, but a further hearing was set for 2 September. On this occasion Alf Reeves represented Chaplin. When Lita refused to accept Judge H. Parker Wood's decision in Chaplin's favour, a new hearing was set for the following day. Again Reeves represented Chaplin. Judge Wood's decision was upheld. Lita announced she would appeal.

Lita's persistence showed bad judgement in public relations. Opinion was unanimously with Chaplin. 'A good mother,' said the *Boston Globe*, 'prefers a normal childhood for her children.' Support for Chaplin came from unexpected quarters. Mildred Harris, who had now a six-year-old son of her own, Johnny McGovern, told the press:

> I can understand Lita Grey Chaplin's reluctance to decline a $65,000 contract which she probably reasons would mean a geat deal to her boys' future.
>
> But I'd rather my child didn't do anything till he's old enough to know what he wants to do. I've been on the screen since I was eight. Child actors don't have a hard life. It isn't that. Quite the contrary. The danger is that they will be spoiled.[4]

The boys cried in understandable disappointment; but their father explained:

> If you're really in earnest about wanting to act, going into it now would be the worst thing in the world for you boys. You'd be typed as child actors. When you reached the gawky stage they'd drop you. Then you would have to make a complete comeback and you'd have a hard time of it, because everyone would remember you as those cute little juveniles. But if after you've grown up you still want to act, then I won't interfere.[5]

In later years they appreciated his wisdom. At the time they were less convinced, partly because their playmates included Shirley Temple.

On 15 September a new hearing was granted, and Lita wrote a ten-page letter to Chaplin appealing for his permission to allow the boys to work. Her letter reveals how keenly aware she was of the backlash of all the publicity. She said she had taken up a theatrical career 'in the hope that I might by such a contact with the public be able to remove the impression that I was coarse, vulgar and uneducated.'[6]

One happy outcome of the business was that Chaplin had begun to see much more of his sons. From now on he tried to arrange some meeting or trip every Saturday. On 15 October he called for them as usual, but on entering the house was served with a subpoena to appear in court on 26 October: Lita's lawyers were still a little short on delicacy. The case was again and finally decided in Chaplin's favour. In court he found himself face to face with Lita's lawyer uncle, Edwin T. McMurray, who asked him 'What do you mean by the word exploitation?' Chaplin had no hesitation in his reply: 'You exploit something when you sell it, and you're trying to sell the services of these little children. I want them to lead a natural existence of normal play.'[7] Chaplin knew well enough, from memories of his own childhood, what the alternatives could be.

The former husband and wife were to be in conflict once more the following February when Chaplin questioned the administration of the boys' trust fund. He insisted that a weekly savings account be set up for them – an arrangement for which they were duly grateful when they grew up and reaped the benefits. After this there was little contact between the couple except through the boys. Lita made a brief career as a vaudeville singer ('She must like work, for it is four-a-day at the least,' wrote Alf Reeves to Sydney) and drifted into an alcoholic breakdown, from which she was happily to recover. In 1936 she was playing at the Café de Paris in London at the same time as Mildred Harris, now an acute alcoholic, was singing in a bottle club. For some reason she decided to go and see Mildred in the club; for the first and only time these two former wives of Chaplin faced each other. Lita remembered Mildred's last words to her: 'Go home, Lady; go do your slumming some place else.'[8]

Chaplin had come back to other troubles. The national economic situation had led to a general tightening up of taxation and the federal tax authorities were taking a keen interest in Chaplin's affairs. They had estimated his taxable assets as the highest in the country, with taxable securities assessed at $7,687,570. Chaplin countered that the real value was only $1,657,316, and that the assessors' investigators had used old values instead of actual prices. 'They even charged me with $25,000 worth of old machinery which isn't worth $500 today and film paraphernalia that they list at $25,000 would bring about $558.'[9] The hearing was set for 14 July 1932. Sydney, in the South of France, was much concerned over his brother's troubles and characteristically worried that not all possible economies were being made in the studios.

Alf tried to reassure him but they were unlucky in having been alloted a ferret-like, relentlessly probing inspector. Alf had to break it to Sydney that he had started inquiries about a transaction in which some prop furniture had been written off the books and shipped to Sydney for use in his home. The inspector was charging that not only was the furniture improperly written off, but that it had been shipped under false declarations to avoid payment of French duty. The inspector was further demanding why no rental had been charged on the Chaplin home – reckoned as a studio asset – during his eighteen-month absence in Europe. 'And to add one more they are questioning Edna Purviance's place on the corporation payroll and want to make it a personal charge.'

The Federal inspectors were pushing the studios hard. Some stocks were sold on poor terms – Alf reckoned a $200,000 loss – but stock losses were no longer admissible. They sought relief on the losses incurred in 1926 on the production of *Sea Gulls*. The condition on which the inspectors allowed this were that the film must be shown, by destruction, to be utterly devoid of possible future value. Hence on 21 June 1933 the 'original and only negative' of von Sternberg's film was destroyed by fire in the presence of Alf Reeves, Jack Wilson, Sylvia Sobol, Lois G. Watt and Charles Bigelow, of Consolidated Film Inc., each of whom signed the affidavit to that effect.

Sydney was also worried because Chaplin showed no signs of settling down to make a new film. He was for the moment otherwise occupied. Willa Roberts, the managing editor of *Woman's Home Companion*, had trailed him to Europe and persuaded him to write a 50,000-word serialization of his European adventures for a fee of the same number of dollars. Chaplin was certainly more tempted by the challenge of writing than by the fee: he had after all just turned down the offer of $670,000 from the Blaine-Thompson advertising agency for a series of twenty-six fifteen-minute radio programmes which he would be free to use in any way he liked. At that time the highest fee ever paid for a broadcast was $15,000, paid to Heifetz for a one-hour recital. Theodore Huff, in his 1951 biography of Chaplin, said that the 'article' (*sic*) was 'ghost-written by his secretary, Catherine Hunter'; and the statement has been uncritically accepted by subsequent writers. It was quite inaccurate: Chaplin was too proud and too perfectionist to allow someone else to write under his name. It is true that in the early days Rob Wagner may have shaped his thoughts on comedy into literary form, but there is a consistency of

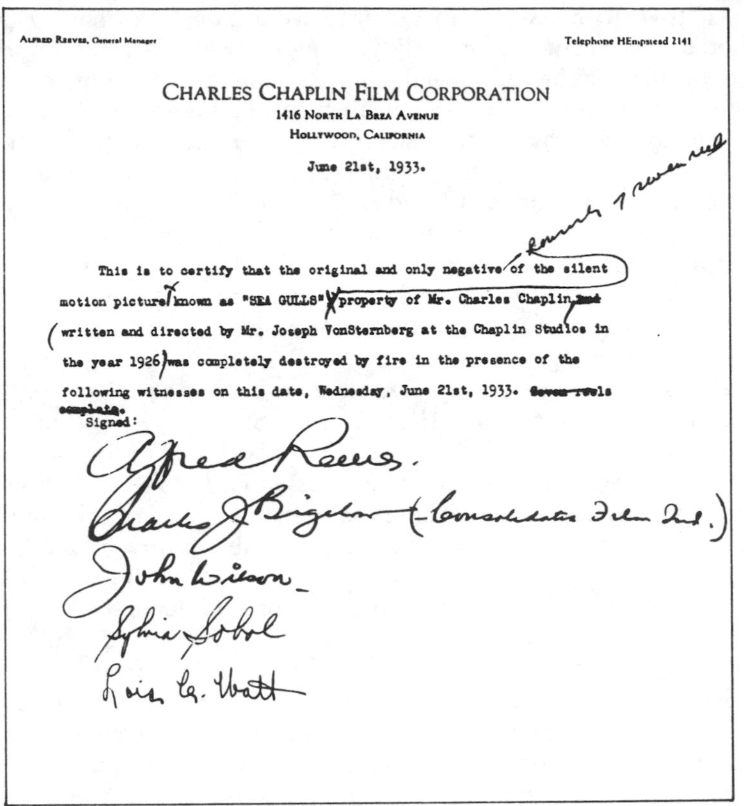

ALFRED REEVES, General Manager

Telephone HEmpstead 2141

CHARLES CHAPLIN FILM CORPORATION
1416 NORTH LA BREA AVENUE
HOLLYWOOD, CALIFORNIA

June 21st, 1933.

This is to certify that the original and only negative of the silent motion picture known as "SEA GULLS" property of Mr. Charles Chaplin (written and directed by Mr. Joseph VonSternberg at the Chaplin Studios in the year 1926) was completely destroyed by fire in the presence of the following witnesses on this date, Wednesday, June 21st, 1933.

Signed:

1933 - Certificate of destruction
of *Sea Gulls*.

style, phrasing and vocabulary from *My Wonderful Visit (My Trip Abroad)* through *A Comedian Sees the World* – the title given to the *Woman's Home Companion* series – to *My Autobiography*.

Chaplin found writing laborious – which is why he practically never wrote personal letters – and remained cavalier about spelling. But he loved words and was fascinated by them. In his youth he had made a practice of learning one new word from the dictionary every day, and in both his speech and writing he used words vividly and with the freshness of new discovery. When Richard Meryman interviewed him, at the age of seventy-five, he had grown attached to the word 'atavistic'. Meryman asked him what it meant and Chaplin explained, adding disarmingly: 'I do like big words sometimes.'

His method was the same whether writing conventional prose or his later scripts. He would first write everything out in longhand, and then dictate it to his secretary. Afterwards he would work over the typescript, and successive secretaries were astonished at how he would labour over a word, trying different positions or variations. The typing and correcting process could be repeated many times: he was as tireless in writing as in making films. He worked solidly on the *Woman's Home Companion* articles from his return in July 1932 until late February 1933. Sydney, down in Nice, was exasperated, and Alf Reeves attempted to reassure him:

> Just a few remarks without the aid of the typist. Of course I understand your intent in commenting on time taken by C. in writing up his story – but you (*knowing him as well as you do*) realize that while he works hard – he works spasmodically – and all work and no play not being good for the health, he naturally plays quite a bit – possibly being in no great hurry in view of everything to make the government a present of the fruits of his labors whilst they are just sitting on the receiving end and making it hard for him at that – as far as they can. We know he could earn more by picturemaking and that the price he gets for the book whilst a lot in some people's ideas is nothing compared to what he commands as an actor.

Despite the attentions of the Federal tax agents, this was one of the happiest periods Chaplin had yet experienced in his private life. He saw his sons regularly, and they delighted him as much as he delighted them. 'Oh, those wonderful weekends,' Charlie Junior reminisced:

> That wonderful magical house on the hill, with the man who lived there, the man who was so many men in one. We were to see them all now: the strict disciplinarian, the priceless entertainer, the taciturn, moody dreamer, the wild man of Borneo with his flashes of volcanic temper. The beloved chameleon shape was to weave itself subtly through all my boyhood and was never to stop fascinating me.[10]

Paulette was essential to it all and the boys fell in love with her the moment their father introduced her:

> We lost our hearts at once, never to regain them through all the golden years of our childhood. Have you ever realized, Paulette, how much you

meant to us? You were like a mother, a sister, a friend all in one. You lightened our father's spells of sombre moodiness and you turned the big house on the hill into a real home. We thought you were the loveliest creature in the whole world. And somehow I feel, looking back today, that we meant as much to you, that we satisfied some need in your life too.[11]

Alf Reeves, who had watched Chaplin falling in and out of love for more than twenty years, was a trifle less romantic in his approval. 'Charlie,' he informed Sydney, 'is still quite "chummy" with Paulette, who is a nice little "cutie".' Some time later, about the time that *Modern Times* was being finished, Reeves wrote to Sydney:

I spent a day with Charlie on a recent trip I made to the coast. It was a Sunday and the two boys were there. I have never seen such attractive kids in my life, and Charlie is positively fascinated by them. They are terribly fond of Paulette and in her shorts she looks like a little girl and the boys look upon her as a sister and expect her to come out and play with them. I am afraid they have the adventurous spirit of one Sydney Chaplin.

When I was there they were on the roof of the house, exploring the innermost parts under the roof. Young Syd is turning out to be an artist and Charlie is a musician. Daddy Charlie gave Charlie Jr his first accordion on which he has been practising and he does quite well; and it would have made you very happy to see Daddy Charlie playing the accordion and young Charlie's expression totally fascinated by his daddy's movements over the notes and of course the minor tones that Charlie drags out of that instrument. You would be happy to see your namesake. They are lovely boys and I was terribly thrilled because it was the first time I had the opportunity of seeing Charlie *au famille*.

We had a regular English Tea with muffins and crumpets and cake and to make it thoroughly English, Paulette had a little drop of rum in her tea. I missed both you and Minnie. With you it would have made one grand happy family.

Charlie Junior remembered this Sunday tea (with marmalade on the crumpets) as an unchanging ritual. '"It's four o'clock, boys," he [their father] would religiously inform us on the weekends we spent with him. "Time for tea and crumpets as it's done in England just at this hour."'

That spring of 1933 Chaplin acquired a new toy, which was for years to provide him with therapeutic recreation. Disregarding financial stringencies, he ordered from Chris-Craft a 1932 model

38-foot commuting cruiser, with an 8-cylinder, 250 h.p. motor and a speed of 26 knots. It slept four, would ride twenty people, and had a one-man crew – Andy Anderson, a one-time Keystone Kop. It had luxurious cabin, galley and dining quarters and, provided with bedding, linen, stove, refrigerator and cooking utensils cost $13,950 at the Michigan factory. Sydney, between his usual advice about contracts and investments, wrote to Alf Reeves: 'I hear he has bought a yacht. Tom Harrington sent me a photograph of it. It is certainly a good looking boat, and he must be having a great time. It is a good place to concentrate on a story, provided he has not too many distractions aboard.' For the first few weeks of course the boat was nothing but distraction. On 25 March the two boys were taken to Wilmington to see it for the first time; after that Chaplin and Paulette spent every free moment in it, with trips to Catalina, Santa Cruz and Santa Barbara. Chaplin called the boat *Panacea*.

Sydney was right that a boat was a good place for writing; almost as soon as he had acquired it, Chaplin set to work on the scenario that was to become *Modern Times*.

It was in the 1930s that Chaplin's critics – often the best-disposed of them – began to complain that he was getting above his station. The clown was setting himself up as a philosopher and statesman. He had mingled so much with world leaders (they said) that he had begun to think of himself as one. They regretted the lost, innocent purity of the old slapstick and shook their heads at the arrogance, conceit and self-importance of the man. If this had been true, it would have been less surprising than that Chaplin had remained as human and as conscious of reality as he did. No one before or since had ever had such a burden of idolatry thrust upon him. It was not he or his critics, but the crowds that mobbed him everywhere on his world tour that cast him in the role of symbol of all the little men of the world. To survive this, still sane and human, was something of a miracle. Chaplin felt the burden and the responsibility deeply. In a sudden outburst, in 1931, he told Thomas Burke:

> But, Tommy, isn't it pathetic, isn't it awful that these people should hang around me and shout 'God bless you Charlie!' and want to touch my overcoat, and laugh and even shed tears. I've seen 'em do that – if they can touch my hand. And why? Why? Simply because I cheered 'em up. God, Tommy, what kind of a filthy world is this – that makes people lead such wretched lives that if anybody makes 'em laugh they want to kneel down and touch his overcoat, as though he was Jesus Christ raising

> 'em from the dead. There's a comment on life. There's a pretty world to live in. When those crowds come round me like that – sweet as it is to me personally – it makes me sick spiritually, because I know what's behind it. Such drabness, such ugliness, such utter misery, that simply because someone makes 'em laugh and helps 'em to forget, they ask God to bless him.[12]

Burke felt that Chaplin had failed to understand. It was not the world that was wrong ;

> It's Charlie himself. He asks too much. If only he could be as tolerant as 'Charlie' he would be happier. A little melting of that icy detachment; a little something that helped him see the world clearly as a world, instead of through his own temperament, a view of that world as a place not entirely given over to the breaking of the noble and the beautiful, and he would come to that understanding by which men as acutely sensitive as himself manage to live happily in this pigstye. Much of the trouble in his private life, and he has had a lot, has arisen from this very lack of patience with human nature. With a wide experience of life, he seems not to have profited by it. He knows people and is a quick judge of character, but he cannot adjust his ideals to meet them. He has intellectual perception, but it is unwarmed by the rays of tolerance, and is therefore sterile. But whatever he is, generous, cold, capricious, he calls out all my affection as a man and all my admiration as an artist . . .[13]

If, from time to time, Chaplin felt impelled to set down his views on the state of the world and the path it should take, it was not from any overwhelming self-importance, but because he felt it was somehow his due to those billions who had appointed him their idol and their symbolic representative. He was a reasoning, reading, pensive man. He was realistically aware of his ability to gain a swift, superficial understanding of practically any subject. As a man in command of considerable personal wealth, he was particularly fascinated by economics. He had read Major H. Douglas's *Social Credit* and was so impressed by its theory of the direct relationship of unemployment to failure of profit and capital, that – taking warning from growing unemployment in the United States – he had in 1928 turned his stocks and bonds into liquid capital, and so been spared at the time of the Wall Street crash. Douglas's theory was enshrined in the opinions Chaplin gave forth to Flora Merrill of the *New York World* when she interviewed him in New York in February 1931, on the first stage of his world tour:

If America is to have sustained prosperity, the American people must have sustained ability to spend. If we continue to view the present condition as inevitable, the whole structure of our civilization may crumble. The present deplorable conditions certainly cannot be charged against the five million men out of work, ready to work, anxious to work, and yet unable to get jobs. If capital represents the genius of America it would seem obvious that for its own sake the present conditions should not continue or ever again be repeated. While crossing the continent I have been talking to all sorts of men – railroad men, workers, fellow travellers – and I heard that times are even harder than before the end of the old year. The country is talking about prohibition which, as Will Rogers says, you cannot feed to the hungry. Unemployment is the vital question, not prohibition. Machinery should benefit mankind. It should not spell tragedy and throw it out of work.

Labor-saving devices and other modern inventions were not really made for profit, but to help humanity in the pursuit of happiness. If there is to be any hope for the future it seems to me that there must be some radical change to cope with these conditions. Some people who are sitting comfortable do not want the present state of affairs changed. This is hardly the way to stave off bolshevistic or communistic ideas which may become prevalent.

Something is wrong. Things have been badly managed when five million men are out of work in the richest country in the world. I don't think you can dismiss this very shocking fact with the old-time argument that these are the inevitable hard times which are the reaction of prosperity. Nor do I think the present economic conditions should be blamed on current events. I personally doubt it. I think there is something wrong with our methods of production and systems of credit. Of course I speak as a layman, like many thousands of others who are anxious at this very serious state of affairs.

I am not in a position to go into world economics, but it seems to me that the question is not whether the country is wet or dry, but whether the country is starved or fed. Also, it doesn't seem to me that there is any doubt but that a shorter working day would take care of the unemployed. Mr Ford has urged for shorter hours for labor and innovations in our credit system. I think such changes might avert serious future national catastrophes.

Miss Merrill asked him what changes he most wanted to see. He replied:

Shorter hours for the working man, and a minimum wage for both skilled and unskilled labor, which will guarantee every man over the age of twenty-one a salary that will enable him to live decently.

Chaplin spent the whole of the first week after his return home working on the Economic Solution he had begun in Japan. As it finally emerged, it was an ingenious scheme to promote the movement of money in Europe, and to keep purchasing power abreast of production potential. It involved creating a new international currency, in which the former Allies would pay themselves the money owed them in war reparations, but which Germany was not in a position to pay. Each of the Allies would put up a bond to guarantee the currency. 'It only remains for the Allies to ratify this currency as having the value of gold, and it shall have the value of gold.' Whether Chaplin's Economic Solution could ever have been practical or not, it serves to illustrate the range and ingenuity of his intellectual effort. In political terms it probably represents capitalist utopianism rather than the socialism with which he was so regularly charged. Chaplin was full of enthusiasm for Roosevelt (who like himself was charged with dangerous socialist ideas) and the New Deal. He was delighted to make a broadcast on 23 October 1933 on station KHJ of the Columbia Broadcasting System in support of the National Recovery Act.

Undoubtedly these concerns and preoccupations underlay Chaplin's thinking on *Modern Times*, but it was not his concern now or at any other time to make a didactic or satirical film – a fact which, unreasonably perhaps, disappointed many critics of the picture. He told Miss Merrill in her February 1931 interview:

> I leave humanity to humanity. Achievement is more than propaganda. I am always suspicious of a picture with a message. Don't say that I'm a propagandist. The world at the moment is in such a turmoil of change that there are no signs of stability anywhere on which to speculate sensibly concerning the future, but I am sure it will be a good enough world to want to live in for a while. I want to live for ever. I find that life is very interesting, not from the point of view of success but from the changing conditions, if only people would meet them and accept them and go along with them. It is so much better to go with the change, I think, than to go against. As I grow older I find it is better to go with the tide.

Modern Times is an emotional response, based always in comedy, to the circumstances of the times. In the Keystone and Essanay films the Tramp was knocked around in a pre-war society of underprivilege among the other immigrants and vagrants and petty miscreants. In *Modern Times* he is one of the millions coping with poverty, unemployment, strikes and strike-breakers, and the tyranny of the machine.

A remarkable and revealing note by Chaplin on the characterization in *Modern Times* shows that he did not intend the Tramp and the Waif – 'the Gamin' as she was called, though in later years Chaplin was inclined to correct this to 'Gamine' – as either rebels or victims. They were rather spiritual escapees from a world in which he saw no other hope:

> The only two live spirits in a world of automatons. They really live. Both have an eternal spirit of youth and are absolutely unmoral.
>
> Alive because we are children with no sense of responsibility, whereas the rest of humanity is weighted down with duty.
>
> We are spiritually free.
>
> There is no romance in the relationship, really two playmates – partners in crime, comrades, babes in the woods.
>
> We beg, borrow or steal for a living. Two joyous spirits living by their wits.

The Tramp, then, is finally a self-confessed anarchist.

Modern Times has not the integrated and organic structure of Chaplin's previous features. The critic Otis Ferguson, not unjustly, said that it was really a collection of two-reelers which might have been called *The Shop*, *The Jailbird*, *The Watchman* and *The Singing Waiter*. The unifying theme is the battle for survival, ultimately a joint battle waged by the two main characters. The scenes of the Gamin's troubles before her meeting with the Tramp are among the very rare instances in Chaplin's films (another is Edna's scenes in *The Kid*) where there is an independent secondary and parallel line of action running alongside the narrative of the Tramp's misadventures.

The finished film opens with a symbolic juxtaposition of sheep being herded and workers streaming out of a factory. Charlie is seen at work on a conveyor belt in a great factory. He is caught up in the cogs of a giant machine, is used as guinea pig for an automatic feeder, and finally runs amok. Released from the mental hospital, he quickly lands in prison on a charge of being a Red agitator (he has merely helpfully picked up a red flag that has fallen off a lorry). After he inadvertently prevents a jail-break, life in prison becomes so plesant that he is heartbroken to be pardoned. He does his best to get arrested again, but changes his mind after he meets the Gamin, a gutsy little orphan on the run from the juvenile officers. They set up home together in a waterfront shack, where Charlie sleeps in the doghouse outside.

Now that he values freedom, Charlie is soon sent back to prison after some of his former prison friends burgle the department store where he works as night-watchman. On his release, he finds the Gamin working as a dancer in a low cabaret, where she finds him a job as a singing waiter. Called upon to substitute for the romantic tenor, Charlie writes the words on his cuffs, which inconveniently fly off at his first dramatic gesture. He retrieves the situation by performing the song in a make-believe jabberwock language. Before he can take his bow, however, the juvenile officers arrive to carry off the Gamin. The pair make a quick escape. On a country road, they jerk themselves out of their dejection. 'We'll get along,' says the title. Arm in arm they go off towards the horizon.

As usual, Chaplin's ideas went through many metamorphoses and permutations before the story took its final form. An early series of notes suggests a possible opening:

> Large city – early morning rush of commerce – showing subway street traffic – newspaper printing office – factory whistles – ferry boats – ambulance, fire engine – motor traffic – introducing a comedian in complete contrast – calm, nothing to do – business crossing the road – klaxon – policeman belching – mistaken for klaxon – stick business and grating outside store window – search for work – different jobs and fired from each . . .

It is interesting to find the stick business cut out of *City Lights* figuring here; later the notes also suggest, 'work the twin fighter gag in a café'. Chaplin never wasted anything. There are suggestions for nice ironic gags. The factory boss, nursing his ulcers on clear soup, crackers and pills looks out of his window and sees his workers gobbling huge lunches while listening to an agitator lamenting that the poor working man must starve while the bosses live on the fat of the land. The infuriated boss empties his soup out of the window onto the orator's head. Two tramps on a park bench solemnly discuss the world crisis and their fears of going off the gold standard: 'This means the end of our prosperity – we shall have to economize.' They replace their cigarette butts in their tins and one puts his lighted match into his pocket. The tone is ribald:

> Second tramp: 'Are you carrying anything?' First tramp: 'Yes, I am loaded up with consolidated gas but I am afraid I shall have to let it go.' Second tramp, gives him look of concern: 'I would try and hold onto it for a while if I were you.'

Another idea is for a factory where heavy machinery is developed for such trivial tasks as cracking nuts or knocking the ash off cigars. After this the story takes off on a quite different tack as the Tramp or tramps stow away on a ship and land up in a series of Crusoe-like gag adventures on a tropical island – adventures evidently inspired as much by the possibility of parodying *King Kong* and *Tarzan* as by Chaplin's own recent oriental sightseeing.

Alf Reeves, who rarely sought to make a contribution to the creative side of the studio work, was this time responsible for a good idea, very similar to one used much later by Woody Allen in *Sleeper* (1973). Charlie would find his way into the locked room where the factory's management are experimenting with a robot which can fly an aircraft. Surprised by the bosses, Charlie is obliged to disguise himself as the robot, and must then go through the robot's actions, including flying the plane. 'If more thrills were required,' wrote Reeves enthusiastically in his memorandum, 'it could be worked up with the effects mechanism they use now and it should be an incident which could be worked up for a big gag.' The suggestion was never taken up, however. Chaplin was rejecting and refining his ideas, and at the next stage wrote out a list of the gag suggestions he now felt germane:

Stomach rumbling
Steam shovel
Kidnapping
City environment
Museum and public gallery
Dry goods store
Street fair
Docks
Dives
Cabarets
Band parade
Street fire
Police raid
Street riots
Strikes
Telephone wire repairing
Dock working

Baggage staircase
Labor exchange
Bread line . . .

The earliest scenario draft which is clearly identifable as the prototype for *Modern Times* has the title *Commonwealth*. The episodes are more numerous and less closely linked than in the finished film, though the relationship of Charlie and the Gamin and the general progression in search of work are already defined. Some incidents of the finished film are already present: the red flag, the accidental launch of a liner, the jail-break, Charlie's efforts to get himself newly arrested, the meeting with the Gamin in the police wagon and subsequent escape. The factory is in part developed, with a world of push-button gadgets for the boss. Charlie's conveyor-belt mental breakdown is now the motive for pathos.

Among the sequences that were to be rejected was a long scene of slapstick action when Charlie pretends he is a qualified steam shovel operator in order to get a job. In another sequence Charlie and the Gamin take shelter in an empty house, unaware that it is in the process of being demolished. Chaplin's politico-economic preoccupations surface in a scene in which Charlie and the girl are punished for eating eggs which are being dumped in the sea as surplus. There is an echo of *The Kid* in one of their ruses to make a little money: the Gamin steals purses and wallets, which Charlie then politely returns hoping for (but not demanding) a reward from the grateful owners. The café sequence in this draft is very different: it is Charlie who first gets a job as waiter, and in turn gets a place for the girl – in blissful innocence that the place is also used as a bawdy house.

The major divergence, however, is the ending of the film. At this stage Chaplin was evidently looking for something to surpass *City Lights* in pathos. Following a breakdown brought on by nut-tightening, Charlie is put in hospital. As he is recuperating, he is told he has a visitor: it is the Gamin, who has become a nun. They part with sad smiles.

The 'nun' ending was fully elaborated:

> The full moon has changed to a crescent, and from a crescent to a full moon again.
>
> The scene changes to the hospital. Fully recovered, the Tramp, who is about to be discharged, is informed that a visitor is waiting to see him in the reception room. He makes his way, laboriously, towards it. When he

arrives there, to his surprise, he finds the Gamin, attired as a nun. She is standing, and beside her is a Mother Superior. The Gamin greets him, smiling wistfully. The Tramp looks bewildered. Somehow a barrier has risen up between them. He tries to speak but can say nothing. Smiling sympathetically, she takes his hand. 'You have been very ill,' she says, 'and now you are going out into the world again. Do take care of yourself, and remember I shall always like to hear from you.'

He tries to speak again but, with a gesture, gives it up. As she smiles, tears well up in her eyes while she holds his hand and he becomes embarrassed; then she stands [*sic*] as a final gesture that they must part.

The Mother Superior leads them to the door and at the entrance of the hospital she says her last 'goodbye', while the Mother Superior waits in the reception room.

He releases his hand and walks slowly down the hospital steps, she gazing after him. He turns and waves a last farewell and goes towards the city's skyline. She stands immobile, watching him as he fades away.

There is something inscrutable in her expression, something of resignation and regret. She stands as though lost in a dream, watching after him and her spirit goes with him, for out of herself the ghost of the Gamin appears and runs rampant down the hospital steps, dancing and bounding after him, calling and beckoning as she runs toward him. Along that lonely road she catches up to him, dancing and circling around him, but he does not see her, he walks alone.

She is standing on the hospital steps. She is awakened from her revelry [reverie?] by a light touch, the hand of the Mother Superior. She starts, then turns and smiles wistfully at the kindly old face and together they depart into the portals of the hospital again. FADE OUT

During the year that the story was in preparation, life went on practically without incident. At the studio the stages were repaired and made ready for the moment that Chaplin chose to start production, and a bathroom was added to the dressing room that was to be Paulette's. In September 1933 Carter De Haven was taken on to the staff, to be a general assistant to Chaplin, and in particular to help on the story. At the beginning of January 1934 Henry Bergman was put back on the payroll. De Haven and Henry sat in on most of Chaplin's script sessions. Chaplin had decided to keep the eventual title of the film secret. In November 1933 a sealed envelope containing the title was sent by registered mail to Will H. Hays, President of the Motion Picture Producers' and Distributors' Association in New York, with instructions not to open it but to register the unknown title as of 11 November 1933, and to place the envelope in safekeeping until publication should be announced.

At the house, too, life followed its routine, with trips on the boat when the weather was good and regular outings or visits for the boys. In April their father took them to the circus, and they were thrilled to be photographed with Poodles Hannaford and Chaplin's old Keystone colleague, Charlie Murray. Chaplin went to a party and to a drill demonstration at the Black-Foxe Military Academy where the boys had been enrolled. Charles Junior remembered 'that I marched straighter, that I was more alert, that I saluted with a snappier gesture and clicked my heels more sharply when I saw those ice-blue eyes upon me.'[14]

There was one major domestic revolution during this period. Kono, who had served Chaplin with discreet devotion for eighteen years, first as chauffeur, later as private secretary and major domo, announced his intention of leaving. Paulette was not content to be a guest at Summit Drive as Mildred and Lita had been, and as she gave more and more attention to the running of the house, Kono felt he was being gradually usurped. Chaplin and Paulette both ridiculed his fears, but he was adamant and resigned. Chaplin was distressed but arranged a job for Kono with the United Artists exchange in Tokyo, and sent him and his wife on their way with a present of $1000 each. Kono found no consolation in the job and made no better success when, his United Artists contract having run out, he tried distributing the Chaplin films in Japan. He returned to California but never rejoined the Chaplin staff.

By the end of August Chaplin was satisfied with his story. According to the studio records he spent a week or so at Lake Arrowhead with De Haven, Bergman and Miss Steele, the secretary, 'to put story into script form'. If there ever were a script in conventional form, however, no copy has survived; this note may be a reference to a dialogue script, which will be discussed later. Throughout September and the early part of October the studio went into full operation. Danny Hall had been preparing sketches for some time and now set his construction crew to build the factory sets in the studio. The films had outgrown the old studio street, and four acres of land at Wilmington were rented on which to build a big street set. The Chaplin studio was one of the last in Hollywood still to have a stage open to the sky, and preparations were finally begun to enclose it and bring it up to modern, sound-era standards. On 4 September Paulette signed her contract. On 20 September Alf Reeves wrote to Sydney: 'Looks like shooting next week. Some factory interiors are being built on the stage, and he has found some splendid locations. In view of the fact that he has practically eliminated the worry during production of thinking out his story, he expects to have the picture finished by January. However, this, as you know, is not definite.' Alf's doubts about the January finish were reasonable and justified: the final shot of the picture was not taken until 30 August 1935. Even so, the shooting period of ten and a half months was the shortest for a Chaplin film since *A Woman of Paris*.

Shooting finally began on 11 October with a scene in the office of the factory boss, played by Allan Garcia. The next sequence was set in the dynamo room, and on 15 October the unit worked through the night from 7.30 p.m. to 4.45 a.m. This seemed like prescience because the following evening, just as they were coming to the end of work on the sequence, a heavy rainstorm penetrated the tarpaulins laid over the set on the still open stage, and severely damaged it.

The rest of the factory scenes were shot in six weeks, uninterrupted except for a day in December when Douglas Fairbanks brought Lady Edwina Mountbatten and her party to visit the set. Working hours now tended to be longer than in silent days, when frequently no shooting began before lunch. Now Chaplin was generally at the studio by 10.30, although on days when he was playing alone he still preferred a shorter, afternoon session of work, perhaps to avoid exhaustion.

Even at this stage Chaplin remained undecided about sound. In public statements on the matter he was unequivocal. Early in 1931 he had made several statements to the press: 'I give the talkies six months more. At the most a year. Then they're done.' Three months later, in May 1931, he had modified his opinion slightly: 'Dialogue may or may not have a place in comedy . . . What I merely said was that dialogue does not have a place in the sort of comedies I make . . . For myself I know that I cannot use dialogue.' The interviewer asked him if he had tried:

> I never tried jumping off the monument in Trafalgar Square, but I have a definite idea that it would be unhealthful . . . For years I have specialized in one type of comedy – strictly pantomime. I have measured it, gauged it, studied. I have been able to establish exact principles to govern its reactions on audiences. It has a certain pace and tempo. Dialogue, to my way of thinking, always slows action, because action must wait upon words.

However firm his public statements on the issue, in the privacy of his studio Chaplin was clearly less convinced. At the end of November he and Paulette did sound tests: since both had pleasant voices which recorded well, it is unlikely Chaplin was dissatisfied with them. It is now clear that Chaplin at this time had steeled himself to shoot the film, including his own scenes with dialogue. A dialogue script was prepared for all scenes up to and including the department store sequence, and still survives.

The dialogue which Chaplin gives to the Tramp is staccato, quippy, touched with nonsense; in the Dream House fantasy sequence it is remarkably similar to the cross-talk act between Calvero (Chaplin) and Terry (Claire Bloom), as Tramp and Pretty Girl, in Calvero's dream in *Limelight*.

GAMIN: 'What's your name?'

TRAMP: 'Me? oh, mine's a silly name. You wouldn't like it. It begins with an "X".'

GAMIN: 'Begins with an "X"?'

TRAMP: 'See if you can guess.'

GAMIN: 'Not eczema?'

TRAMP: 'Oh, worse than that – just call me Charlie.'

GAMIN: 'Charlie! There's no "X" in that!'

TRAMP: 'No – oh, well, where d'ya live?'

GAMIN: 'No place – here – there – anywhere.'

TRAMP: 'Anywhere? That's near where I live.'

The first dialogue which Chaplin began to rehearse was for the scenes in the jail and warden's office. Much of the dialogue was concerned with confusions over the name of the curate and his wife – Stumbleglutz, Stumblerutz, Glumblestutz, Rumbleglutz. Stumblestutz and, as the inevitable climax, Grumblegutz. Chaplin was evidently deeply dissatisfied with the results. The unit had been told that the Dream House sequence would be shot the following day with sound. In fact no more dialogue scenes were to be shot for *Modern Times*.

Chaplin did proceed with sound effects, however, and used the recording apparatus set up to create the stomach rumbles for the scene. He created the noise himself by blowing bubbles into a pail of water. As Totheroh warned him, the noises were much too explosive;

eventually they were re-shot. The fact that Chaplin was sufficiently keen to create the effects personally indicates the extent to which he was intrigued by sound problems at this time. A memorandum about possible musical effects notes: 'Natural sounds part of composition, i.e. Auto horns, sirens, and cowbells worked into the music.'

Chester Conklin, who had worked with Chaplin so many times since *Making a Living*, was engaged for three weeks' work as the walrus-moustached old workman who gets caught up in the cog wheels of a gigantic machine of doubtful purpose. When he becomes completely stuck, Charlie considerately feeds lunch to his protruding head. Two other reliable old allies from two-reeler days – Hank Mann and an escalator – were introduced for the department store scenes which, including retakes, took five weeks to shoot. Eight working days of this time were taken up by Chaplin's brilliant roller-skating routine: the skating was quickly shot but time was needed to prepare the trick 'glass shots' to give the illusion that he was skating at the edge of a high balcony with no balustrade.

Charlie was still intent on ending the film with the Gamin as a nun. The sentiment was perilous, but Chaplin had attempted perilous things before: the ending of *City Lights*, seen set down on paper, could be cause for nerviness. He also planned to prepare for the ending with a recurrent theme of a kindly nun, and her effect upon the Gamin.

THEME

1. On one of our adventures we come into contact with a nun. It's just a momentary feeling or sense of beauty and the Gamin is moved by it.

Gamin: 'She makes me want to cry.'

The nun is always very tender and nice to the Gamin – a pat on the head, etc.

2. We encounter her in the street again. The Gamin imitates her headgear and admires it. Each time the Gamin sees her she stops short in the midst of the comedy and her eyes fill and she says:

Gamin: 'She makes me feel wicked.'

3. We are in the street and the Gamin has just pinched something. The nun comes around the corner and the Gamin puts it back.

Charlot:* 'What in blazes is wrong with you?'
Gamin: (Gulp) 'I dunno.'

The nun sequence was shot in late May and early June. On Friday 25 July 1935 Chaplin and his assistants ran the film and, noted the studio secretary at the time, discussed a new ending. No one concerned has left any account of the discussion, so we shall never know if the decision to change was spontaneously Chaplin's or whether, as sometimes happened, he made his judgement from watching the reactions of his colleagues. Whatever the temper of the meeting, Chaplin went off on his yacht the following day for the weekend.

The final sequence to be shot on *Modern Times* was the café scene. It took twelve days, and involved a large number of extras: 250 were called for the day when Chaplin shot the business of carrying a roast duck across the jam-packed dance floor. This was to be the historic scene in which the Tramp, for the first and only time, found his voice on the screen. When the Tramp opened his mouth and sang it was in a language of his own invention, expressive of everything and nothing:

Se bella piu satore, je notre so catore,
Je notre qui cavore, je la qu', la qui, la quai!
Le spinash or le busho, cigaretto toto bello,
Ce rakish spagoletto, si la tu, la tu, la tua!
Senora pelafima, voulez-vous le taximeter,
La zionta sur le tita, tu le tu le tu le wa!

and so on, for several more verses. The accompanying pantomime elaborates a tale of a seducer and a coyly yielding maiden.

At some point during late July or early August, the decision was finally taken to change the ending. The last shots taken on the café set, on 20 August, were those involving the detectives who arrive at the café to take the Gamin away. Since this action, and the subsequent getaway of Charlie and the Gamin, provide the link with the present ending of the film, the clear assumption is that the decision was made during the shooting of the café scenes.

The last retakes were taken on 30 August, and after the Labour Day holiday Chaplin began cutting. On 10 September the film was

* A curious aspect of this series of story notes is the alternation of 'Charlie' and 'Charlot' in referring to the Tramp character. Elsewhere in the same notes Chaplin, exceptionally, refers to his character in the first person, styling Tramp and Gamin as 'We'.

in a sufficiently assembled form for Chaplin to run it for two of his most valued critics: Charles Junior and Sydney, who had just arrived back after three months with their mother in New York. At ten years old, Charles Junior observed with astonishment the extent of the physical and emotional strain to which Chaplin submitted himself in the course of making a picture. After the day's work, during which he would astound and irritate his staff with his apparent inexhaustibility, he would arrive home, still in make-up and costume, already half asleep and so tired that he had to be helped from his car. The exhaustion, young Charles remembered years later, was worse when the day had not gone well. Chaplin's therapy for his weariness was in itself punishing. He would shut himself in his steam room for three quarters of an hour, after which he might well emerge sufficiently restored to go out for dinner. Sometimes, though, he would simply retire to bed for the evening, and have his meal sent up.

In the last stages of shooting *Modern Times* he had worked with such concentration that he had actually lived at the studio, and brought George, the Japanese cook, there to see to his meals. Paulette, like Chaplin's previous wives, discovered that at such critical times Chaplin's work left no room for personal life, even his most precious relationships. More easily than the previous women she ultimately acknowledged this insuperable rival. When she was seen around the town without Chaplin, however, there was speculation about a break-up; though what was to be broken up was unclear, since Chaplin and Paulette, with admirable disdain for the gossips, refused to clarify their marital or non-marital status merely to satisfy other people's curiosity.

Work on the music began in August 1935. Alfred Newman, whose collaboration on *City Lights* had given Chaplin great satisfaction, was again to be musical director, and Edward Powell was engaged as orchestrator. Powell wired to the East Coast to invite a talented colleague from his days with the music publishers Harms, David Raksin, to join him. Raksin, who has vividly and sensitively recorded his impressions of working with Chaplin,* recalls that Powell's telegram arrived on 8 August 1935, four days after his twenty-third birthday. Chaplin, having been promised a musician who was 'brilliant, experienced, a composer, orchestrator and arranger with several big shows in his arranging cap' confided that he was somewhat

* *Quarterly Journal of the Library of Congress*, Summer, 1983.

disconcerted when 'this infant shows up'. Raksin for his part was captivated by Chaplin, loved *Modern Times* and laughed at it so hard that Chaplin for a time wondered whether he was exaggerating for his benefit. After only a week and a half, however, Raksin was summarily fired:

> Like many self-made autocrats, Chaplin demanded unquestioning obedience from his associates; years of instant deference to his point of view had persuaded him that it was the only one that mattered. And he seemed unable, or unwilling, to understand the paradox that this imposition of will over his studio had been achieved in a manner akin to that which he professed to deplore in *Modern Times*. I, on the other hand, have never accepted the notion that it is my job merely to echo the ideas of those who employ me; and I had no fear of opposing him when necessary, because I believed he would recognize the value of an independent mind close at hand.
>
> When I think of it now, it strikes me as appallingly arrogant to have argued with a man like Chaplin about the appropriateness of the thematic material he proposed to use in his own picture. But the problem was real. There is a specific kind of genius that traces its ancestry back to the magpie family, and Charlie was one of those. He had accumulated a veritable attic full of memories and scraps of ideas, which he converted to his own purposes with great style and individuality. This can be perceived in the subject matter, as well as the execution of his story lines and sequences. In the area of music, the influence of the English music hall was very strong, and since I felt that nothing but the best would do for this remarkable film, when I thought his approach was a bit vulgar, I would say 'I think we can do better than that.' To Charlie this was insubordination, pure and simple – and the culprit had to go.

Raksin was heartbroken, but Newman told him, 'I've been looking at your sketches, and they're marvellous – what you're doing with Charlie's little tunes. He'd be crazy to fire you.' As Raksin was packing to leave, Alf Reeves called him and asked him to come back. Raksin agreed, after first explaining to Chaplin that he could always hire a musical secretary if that was what he wanted, 'but if he needed someone who loved his picture and was prepared to risk getting fired every day to make sure that the music was as good as it could possibly be, then I would love to work with him again.' This was the beginning of 'four and a half months of work and some of the happiest days of my life.'

Raksin feels that previous commentators have given at once too much and too little credit to Chaplin's musical abilities.

Charlie and I worked hand in hand. Sometimes the initial phrases were several phrases long, and sometimes they consisted of only a few notes, which Charlie would whistle, or hum, or pick out on the piano . . . I remained in the projection room, where Charlie and I worked together to extend and develop the musical ideas to fit what was on the screen. When you have only a few notes or a short phrase with which to cover a scene of some length, there must ensue considerable development and variation – what is called for is the application of the techniques of composition to shape and extend the themes to the desired proportions. (That so few people understand this, even those who may otherwise be well informed, makes possible the common delusion that composing consists of getting some kind of microflash of an idea, and that the rest of it is mere artisanry; it is this misconception that has enabled a whole generation of hummers and strummers to masquerade as composers.)

Theodore Huff and others to the contrary, no informed person has claimed that Charlie had any of the essential techniques. But neither did he feed me a little tune and say, 'You take it from there.' On the contrary: we spent hours, days, months in that projection room running scenes and bits of action over and over, and we had a marvellous time shaping the music until it was exactly the way we wanted it. By the time we were through with a sequence we had run it so often that we were certain the music was in perfect sync. Very few composers work this way . . . the usual procedure is to work from timing sheets, with a stop clock, to coordinate image and music . . .

Chaplin had picked up an assortment of tricks of our trade and some of the jargon and took pleasure in telling me that some phrase should be played 'vrubato', which I embraced as a real improvement upon the intended Italian word, which was much the poorer for having been deprived of the *v*. Yet, very little escaped his eye or ear, and he had suggestions not only about themes and their appropriateness, but also about the way in which the music should develop . . .

Sometimes in the course of our work, when the need for a new piece of thematic material arose, Charlie might say, 'A bit of "Gershwin" might be nice there.' He meant that the Gershwin style would be appropriate for that scene. And indeed there is one phrase that makes a very clear genuflection toward one of the themes in *Rhapsody in Blue*. Another instance would be the tune that later became a pop song called 'Smile'. Here, Charlie said something like, 'What we need here is one of those "Puccini" melodies.' Listen to the result, and you will hear that although the notes are not Puccini's, the style and feeling are.

The ten-year-old Charles Chaplin Junior observed that 'if the people in his own studio had suffered from Dad's perfectionist drive, the musicians . . . endured pure torture.'

> Dad wore them all out. Edward Powell concentrated so hard writing the music down that he almost lost his eyesight and had to go to a specialist to save it. David Raksin, working an average of twenty hours a day, lost twenty-five pounds and sometimes was so exhausted that he couldn't find strength to go home but would sleep on the studio floor. Al Newman saw him one day in the studio street walking along with tears running down his cheeks.

Chaplin would work with Raksin on the transcription of his compositions night after night until long after midnight, and did not even spare him at the weekends, though on one of these there was the consolation of working on the *Panacea* while Paulette took the children to Palm Springs to keep them out of their busy father's way. Raksin recalls not only the killing round-the-clock work, but also the gags and jokes and high spirits. Unfortunately it was to end unhappily. Newman liked to work in the small hours of the night. At one of these nocturnal sessions on 4 December, when Raksin was taking a night off at Chaplin's suggestion, Chaplin and the volatile Newman had a fierce argument. After a bad take, Chaplin accused the musicians of 'dogging it' (lying down on the job). Newman exploded, hurled his baton across the studio, addressed a string of curses to Chaplin and stalked off to his suite to revive himself with a whiskey before calling Sam Goldwyn to tell him that on no account would he ever work again with Chaplin. Nor did he. From loyalty to Newman, Raksin would not take over the conducting, and the outcome was an estrangement from Chaplin that lasted for many years. Powell was coerced on the strength of his contract to conduct. 'With Eddie conducting, I did most of the remaining orchestration, and the recordings concluded in a rather sad and indeterminate spirit.' The music was finally completed on 22 December 1935. Years later the former cordiality between Chaplin and Raksin was resumed: the musician last visited the studio the day before Chaplin's final departure from America in 1952.

To add to his anxieties, Chaplin had a distinguished house guest: H. G. Wells arrived in Hollywood on 27 November for a four-week stay; and the evening of the Newman row, he and Chaplin were guests of honour at a Motion Picture Academy dinner. With Paulette's help Wells was somehow entertained. Alf Reeves wrote to Sydney that he had not even seen the great man during his visit, because Chaplin only brought him to the studio at nights. With the music finished, however, his host at least had time to see Wells off on his flight back to the East.

Chaplin finally previewed *Modern Times*, with great secrecy ahead of the show, in San Francisco. Alf Reeves was able to report to Sydney the following day: 'audience applauded "Titine" (and "encored" it!) and cheered at the end.' Chaplin nevertheless decided on a few cuts and there were more after a second preview at the Alexander Theatre, Glendale. Generally the launching of this film was effected more quietly than that of *City Lights*. The film opened at the Rivoli, New York to capacity business on 5 February 1936, and at the Tivoli, London on 11 February. The following day there was a gala première at Grauman's Chinese Theatre in Hollywood, but it was a quieter event. Perhaps Chaplin was more confident this time. Certainly the public reaction was all he could have hoped for. The press was mixed. One section disapproved because he had attempted socio-political satire; another part regretted that he had not, though he seemed to promise it with the opening title of the film: 'the story of industry, of individual enterprise – humanity crusading in the pursuit of happiness'.

Private matters from time to time obtruded upon Chaplin's concentration. The Lindbergh case was still very much in people's minds in autumn 1934, and there were kidnap threats against the Chaplin children. Chaplin announced to the press that he had hired bodyguards and armed the house and studio; a few weeks earlier he had given his opinions on the possibility of his own kidnap. 'Not one cent for ransom! I've given positive orders to my associates that under no condition is one cent to be paid anyone trying to extort money from me. If I should be kidnapped – and I'm not worrying any that it's going to happen – I'd fight at the first opportunity. They'd either have to let me go or do murder.'

In April 1935 Minnie Chaplin became seriously ill in the South of France. She was operated upon but shortly afterwards died. The telegram of sympathy which Chaplin sent to his brother during Minnie's last illness vividly illustrates how even genuine fraternal concern could not supersede his preoccupation with work. He advises Sydney to be 'philosophical' and to 'buck up':

> I HAVE BEEN WORKING HARD ON THE PICTURE WHICH WILL BE READY FOR FALL RELEASE AND FROM ALL INDICATIONS WE SHALL HAVE A SENSATIONAL SUCCESS STOP IN TREATMENT IT WILL BE SIMILAR TO CITY LIGHTS WITH SOUND EFFECTS AND AUDIBLE TITLES SPOKEN BY ONE PERSON HOW-

EVER WE ARE GOING TO EXPERIMENT WITH THIS IDEA STOP I INTEND TO WORK RIGHT ON AFTER FINISHING THIS PICTURE AS I FEEL I AM IN MY STRIDE AND INTEND TO MAKE HAY WHILE THE SUN SHINES STOP WHAT YOU NEED IS A CHANGE YOU SHOULD COME HERE WHERE YOUR ABILITY WOULD BE OF GREAT SERVICE AND VALUE STOP WHEN MINNIE GETS WELL YOU MIGHT CONSIDER COMING TO HOLLYWOOD IT WOULD DO YOU BOTH GOOD STOP.

No doubt between his personal troubles Sydney was both cheered and sceptical about Chaplin's intentions to go straight back to work. Perhaps Chaplin had in mind a project which he had somehow found time to continue preparing during the whole production period of *Modern Times* – apparently the only time that he worked on another feature project when he was already occupied with a film. Chaplin commentators with a psychoanalytical bent have made much of his persistent ambition to make a film about Napoleon. His interest is probably quite simply explained. Napoleon offers a uniquely rich role for an actor of small stature. Chaplin had been fascinated by the character ever since childhood, when his mother had told him that his father resembled the Emperor. In 1922, when looking for a vehicle to launch Edna Purviance as a dramatic actress (the eventual choice was *A Woman of Paris*) he had thought of a story to team the two of them as Napoleon and Josephine. When he first showed an interest in Lita Grey he spoke of creating the role of Josephine for her. Chaplin and Lita went to a fancy dress party given by Marion Davies costumed as Napoleon and Josephine. Subsequently Lita began to worry when she found that he had offered the role in turn to Merna Kennedy. In 1926, much impressed by the Spanish singer Raquel Meller, Chaplin had spoken of working with her in a Napoleon film; but a year later the appearance of Abel Gance's spectacular *Napoleon* temporarily discouraged him, even though it was shown in the United States only in a version cut by Metro Goldwyn Mayer from the original six hours to little more than sixty minutes.

The idea of a Napoleon film became serious again soon after the completion of *City Lights*. In the course of his 1931 world tour, Chaplin met Comte Jean de Limur, who had been one of his young assistants on *A Woman of Paris*, and who recommended to him Jean Weber's novel *La Vie Secrète de Napoleon Ier*. Negotiations for the film rights began but foundered when Weber tried to impose restrictive conditions upon the adaptation.

Word of Chaplin's plans reached Sydney in Nice after his brother's return to Hollywood. His letter reflects his relief at the idea of a subject not likely to pose such problems and expense as *City Lights*:

> There has been considerable publicity over here concerning your next picture. They say you are thinking of doing a Napoleonic story. Of course I know that this publicity has broken before but if you are really serious in the matter I think that a dramatic picture coming from you would be a great box-office attraction at this time, as so many millions of people are waiting to hear you in the talkies. Then again it might be a great advantage from the cost point of view as the scenario of the dramatic production would have to be almost complete in detail before you started to shoot, in which case the shooting would not take you so very long. It is also a great idea because it would leave your present character in its present pantomimic form. If you do decide upon this subject I would certainly advise that you make it more the domestic side of Napoleon's life as this offers great possibilities with good human comedy, and a side of Napoleon which so far, I think, has not been presented. Besides, it would save a tremendous outlay of money which would be required in portraying the spectacular or militaristic side of the Napoleonic period . . . In any case whatever you decide to do I would strongly advise that you do not gamble too much of your fortune in your next picture as conditions are very unsettled and the film business is trending [*sic*] towards large combines with the small independent exhibitors being frozen out. This will make the booking situation a little more difficult . . .

Back in California after his tour, Chaplin continued to ponder the project, but for the time being was too occupied with his *Woman's Home Companion* articles and the legal wrangles over the employment of Charles Junior and Sydney Junior. In the summer of 1933, however, Chaplin met Alistair Cooke. Cooke was then twenty-five and in the United States on a Commonwealth Fund Fellowship. When he arrived at the studio to interview Chaplin for the *Manchester Guardian* Chaplin was immediately taken by the attractive, intelligent and witty young Englishman. Invitations to dinner and then to the yacht followed. In the winter of 1933, after Cooke had returned to the East, Chaplin wrote to suggest that he might like to return to Hollywood the following summer to help him research and write a *Napoleon* script.

Cooke duly returned in the early summer of 1934 and began with historical research in the public library, using Las Cases' *Memorial of St Helena* as the principal source. The research notes still survive in the Chaplin archive, though nothing of the script remains. Cooke recalls long working sessions generally with Henry Bergman in attendance, and sometimes with Carter De Haven who was meanwhile working with Chaplin on *Modern Times*. Chaplin at the outset explained his method: 'We look for some little incident, some vignette that fixes the other characters. With them the audience must never be in any doubt. We have to fix them on sight. Nobody cares about *their* troubles. They stay the same. You know them every time they appear. This is no different from the characters who surround "the little fellow". *He's* the one we develop.'

The script sessions continued into August 1934 and Cooke thought they 'were coming along well' when Chaplin abruptly informed him that it was a beautiful idea, but for somebody else. Cooke married (Chaplin agreed to be best man, but since Cooke tactlessly failed to invite Paulette, did not make an appearance), declined Chaplin's offer to put him into *Modern Times* as a light comedian, and returned to London to be the BBC's film critic.

In fact, however, even though he was now hard at work on *Modern Times*, Chaplin had by no means abandoned the Napoleon project. In 1934 negotiations for the rights of *La Vie Secrète de Napoleon Ier* were reopened. Sydney now took an active interest, and was very suspicious of de Limur's procrastination in the affair. Weber, the author, was now more amenable – partly because he was having alimony problems. After a good deal of haggling and back-tracking by Weber and his agent, a price of 78,650 francs was agreed, though Weber, on account of his marital problems, requested that any publicity given to the arrangement should declare the sum as no more than 30,000 francs.

The Chaplin Film Corporation acquired rights to the book in December 1935 for a period of eight years; in January 1936 Jean de Limur delivered a film treatment based on the novel. The treatment had a fatal weakness: it did not provide a suitably prominent part for Paulette. Chaplin had meanwhile been working on an independent treatment of the Napoleon subject. In July 1935 John Strachey stayed with Chaplin and Paulette at their Beverly Hills house. It is not certain when or how they first met, though it was most likely during the 1931 European holiday.

Strachey was a sympathetic spirit. At thirty-four, he was already one of the most prominent left-wing intellectuals in Britain, and had recently published *The Coming Struggle for Power* and *The Nature of Capitalist Crisis*. Since breaking away from Oswald Mosley's New Party in 1931, he had become increasingly drawn to Communism, though he was never to become a member of the Communist Party. Like Chaplin, he admired both Roosevelt and Keynes. Here was someone with whom Chaplin could enjoy sympathetic discussion of his own newly-formulated Economic Solution and his pacifism. Strachey was amusing and charming as well as intelligent. Moreover, though he was tall and somewhat ungainly, he was an enthusiastic tennis player.

Together Chaplin and Strachey developed their ideas for a new scenario, and Strachey returned to England to write it. The script was completed early in 1936 and registered for copyright on 9 April as

NAPOLEON'S RETURN FROM ST HELENA,*

> written by Charles Chaplin of Great Britain, domiciled in United States, at Los Angeles, California, in collaboration with John Strachey of Great Britain.

The Chaplin–Strachey script, which possibly incorporated the work already done with Cooke, was in several ways an advance on the de Limur treatment. There is a much stronger political and pacifist moral, it has more action and, most important, there is a well-tailored role for Paulette. The only significant element retained from the Weber novel is the initial premise of Napoleon's escape from St Helena with the help of a self-sacrificing double who takes his place. The script has many typical Chaplin elements, in particular a sustained tone of irony and the theme of love between an older man and a young girl which is frustrated by her romantic illusions. Chaplin also intended to develop some of his own notions on peace and politics through Napoleon. A draft annotated in Chaplin's handwriting sketches a discussion between Napoleon and Montholon at St Helena:

> NAPOLEON: There is something wrong with the whole political structure of Europe . . . Governments and Constitutions are old-fashioned, obsolete . . . mechanical science is running away with us . . . steamboats, railroads, iron barges . . . all these things spell revolution and we must prepare for the future . . . The man of the future will be a scientist . . . Future Governments will realize that the religious and moral prin-

* Alternative titles suggested were *The Return*, *The Return From St Helena*, *The Return of the Emperor*, *Napoleon's Return* and *The Return of Napoleon*.

ciples are problems for the individual, but the economic problems of the individual are the business of the State, and the Governments of the future will separate these two factors . . . Countries will combine forces for the protection of their trades . . . The statesman of the future will be the Nation's book keeper, not a dispenser of moral principles, and politics will become mathematics . . . Montholon, one hears words like 'Socius' . . .

MONTHOLON: You have me swimming . . . I don't know what it is all about.

NAPOLEON: I mean the day of war and aggression will be a thing of the past . . . One can accomplish more by treaties, friendship, commercial understanding . . . If I could live my life again, I'd use the power of my victories to unite all nations of Europe into one solid State . . . Evolution tends towards these things . . .

This was only a first sketch of course – with much like it the audience would have been swimming along with poor Montholon. Still, in the Napoleon of 1936, with his prophecies of the EEC, we can already sense something of the final speech of *The Great Dictator* and anticipate the diatribes of young Macabee in *A King in New York*.

A device in the script concerning the theft of a treaty was suggested by a notorious adventure of Marion Davies which had occurred a few years earlier. In the summer of 1928 William Randolph Hearst, Marion and their entourage – including Harry Crocker – were touring in Europe and were entertained to lunch by the French Foreign Minister, Aristide Briand. Shortly afterwards Hearst's suite at the Crillon was searched and he was ordered to leave the country within an hour. Someone had stolen from the Ministry a pact concerning Anglo-French naval deployments, and Hearst was the prime suspect since the theft had occurred at the time of the lunch. Despite the search, Hearst, it seems, successfully concealed the document on his person when he left for London.

Subsequently, after a number of arrests in Paris, considerable diplomatic embarrassment and maximum use of the document's headline value in the Hearst press, Marion regaled her friends with a story that was tall even by her standards in an effort to exculpate Hearst. Her version was that during the dinner she excused herself to go to the ladies' room, and on the way noticed a half-open door to a room inside which there stood an unlocked safe. Unable to resist her curiosity, she had opened the safe, and merely out of mischief removed a document which she had stuck into the elastic of her 'sissy-britches'. This last detail makes all the less credible her claim that she then forgot about the deed – a document in one's underclothes is not exactly comfortable – until she was taking her bath, whereupon she confessed what she had done to the suitably shocked Hearst. Few people believed Marion's version of the story, but it clearly amused Chaplin sufficiently for him to adapt it for his Napoleon plot.

At some point Chaplin had still photographs made of himself in the role of Napoleon, with Harry Crocker as (presumably) Las Cases. His own costume is the one in which he attended Marion Davies' fancy-dress ball. Since Crocker already looks slightly older and heavier than he appeared in *The Circus*, the stills may have been taken some years after the party, and before Crocker's departure from the studio during the shooting of *City Lights*. The project of a Napoleon film seems to have been finally abandoned almost as soon as the Strachey script was finished, having remained a preoccupation with Chaplin for at least fourteen years. By the time *Napoleon's Return from St Helena* was registered for copyright, Chaplin and Paulette had embarked on a tour of the Far East, and were to return full of new ideas.

On Monday 17 February, five days after the gala première of *Modern Times* at Grauman's Chinese Theatre in Hollywood, Chaplin, together with Paulette, her mother and his valet, Frank Yonamori, sailed from Wilmington on the SS *Coolidge* for a holiday in Honolulu. Frank had previously made reservations at the Royal Hawaiian Hotel, but when the ship arrived in Honolulu the Chaplin party stayed aboard. Having noticed that the cargo was labelled for Hong Kong, Chaplin impetuously decided that he would take Paulette to the Far East. She protested that she was unprepared and had nothing suitable to wear for the trip, but he told her that they would buy anything they needed *en route*. The decision taken, Chaplin wired Alf Reeves, 'PLANNING TO BE ON "COOLIDGE" TO HONG KONG – WILL BE AWAY THREE MONTHS.' Alf had learned to accept Chaplin's caprices with equanimity.

Another passenger on the *Coolidge* was Jean Cocteau who, as a form of convalescence from illness, was retracing the steps of Phileas Fogg in company with his Moroccan lover, Marcel Khill. In his published account of the journey Cocteau coyly called Marcel his

'Passepartout'; Chaplin discreetly described him as Cocteau's 'secretary'. It is fascinating to compare Chaplin's account of their meetings with Cocteau's. Chaplin describes how the enthusiasm of their first encounter and a stirring philosophical conversation interpreted by Marcel, which went on far into the night, was quickly dispelled by the barrier and embarrassments of language. According to his version the rest of the journey was spent in dodging each other and diligently missing appointments. When they found they were both to make the return trip on the *Coolidge*, 'we became resigned, making no further attempts at enthusiasm.'

This is markedly different from Cocteau's account. The explanation of the disparity may be that Chaplin was too shy and in a certain sense too modest to believe that a stranger could feel so enthusiastic an affection for him as did Cocteau. 'My meeting with Charlie Chaplin,' the latter recalled, 'remains the delightful miracle of this voyage.' When he discovered Chaplin was on board, Cocteau with diffidence sent a note to his cabin. At dinner that night Chaplin showed no sign of recognition, and Cocteau reluctantly decided that he wished to remain incognito and undisturbed. Later that evening, however, as Cocteau was undressing for bed, Chaplin and Paulette knocked at Cocteau's door: they had only received his note after dinner, and had then cautiously checked with the purser to make sure it was not an imposture.

Cocteau felt none of Chaplin's embarrassment over their means of communication:

> I do not speak English; Chaplin does not speak French. Yet we talked without the slightest difficulty. What is happening? What is this language? It is *living* language, the most living of all and springs from the will to communicate at all costs in the language of mime, the language of poets, the language of the heart. Chaplin detaches every word, stands it on the table as it were on a plinth, walks back a step, turns it where it will catch the best light. The words he uses for my benefit are easily transported from one language to the other. Sometimes the gesture precedes the words and escorts them. He announces each word first before pronouncing it and comments on it afterwards. No slowness, or only the apparent slowness of balls when a juggler is juggling with them. He never confuses them, you can follow their flight in the air.[15]

Cocteau was delighted by Paulette's intelligence in refusing to intervene as interpreter, which she was equipped to do: 'If I help them they will lose themselves in details. Left to their own devices, they only say the essentials.'

Chaplin spoke to Cocteau with enthusiasm about his future projects. He was thinking of making a film in Bali, and seriously proposed that Marcel might play a part in it. (Marcel was thrilled, but Cocteau said he could not spare him.) His own next role, he said, was to be that of a clown torn between the contrasts of real life and the theatre – a foreshadowing, perhaps, of *Limelight*. Cocteau wished that he would one day play Prince Myshkin. They talked of *The Gold Rush* and Chaplin complained: 'The dance of the bread rolls. That's what they all congratulate me on. It is a mere cog in the machine. A detail. If that was what they specially noticed, they must have been blind to the rest!'[16] Of his most recent film Chaplin told Cocteau, 'I worked too long on *Modern Times*. When I had worked a scene up to perfection, it seemed to fall from the tree. I shook the branches and sacrificed the best episodes. They existed in their own right. I could show them separately, one by one, like my early two-reelers.'[17] Chaplin thereupon mimed two of his favourite cut scenes: the scene of the stick in the grating from *City Lights* and a street-crossing scene from *Modern Times*.

Cocteau was fascinated by Chaplin. Although, according to his account, 'we joined forces, shared our meals and the journey alike; to such an extent did we form the habit of living together that we found it painful to part company in San Francisco,' Cocteau nevertheless recognized Chaplin's shyness and withdrawal. 'Even friendship is suspect; the duties and inconveniences it entails. His instant taking to me was, it seems, unique, and it produced a kind of panic in him. I felt him withdraw into himself again, and close up after his expansiveness.'[18] Most of all he was delighted to observe Chaplin's relationship with Paulette:

> Paulette went off for a few minutes. Charlie bent over and whispered in a mysterious voice, 'And then I feel such pity.' What? Pity for this thousand-spiked cactus, this little lioness with her mane and superb claws, this great sports Rolls with its shining leatherwork and metal? The whole of Chaplin is in that remark: that is what his heart is like.
>
> Pity for himself, the tramp, pity for us, pity for her – the poor waif whom he drags after him to make her eat because she is hungry, put her to bed because she is sleepy, snatch her away from the snares of city life because she is pure, and suddenly I no longer see a Hollywood star in her silver satin page-boy outfit nor the rich impresario with his white curls

> and salt and pepper tweeds – but a pale little man, curly-haired, with his comic cane, dragging away a victim of the ogre of capital cities and police-traps, as he stumbles along through the world on one leg.
>
> I find it extremely difficult to fit the two pictures together. The florid-complexioned man who is talking to me and the pale little ghost who is his multiple angel whom he can divide up like quicksilver. I gradually succeed in superimposing the two Chaplins. A grimace, a wrinkle, a gesture, a wink and the two silhouettes coincide, that of the fool of the Bible, the little saint in a bowler hat who tugs at his cuffs and straightens his shoulders as he enters paradise, and that of the impresario pulling his own strings.[19]

Cocteau reported that Chaplin was working energetically during the course of the trip, 'shut up in his cabin . . . unshaved, in a suit which is too tight, his hair untidy, he stands fidgeting his glasses in those very small hands of his, setting in order sheets of paper covered in writing.' He may have been working on the Bali script that he mentioned to Cocteau, but Shanghai gave him a completely new idea. A party from the ship including Cocteau, Chaplin and Paulette went slumming to a dance hall called the 'Venus', where they watched American sailors dancing with 'taxi-girls'. Out of this and certain memories of May Reeves came the idea for *Stowaway*. By the time he arrived back in California on 11 June 1936 Chaplin was able to report that he had already written ten thousand words of a story with a Far Eastern setting for Paulette.

The story told of a White Russian countess, now earning her living as a Shanghai taxi-girl, who stows away in the cabin of an American millionaire diplomat. Chaplin continued to work energetically at the script for the next four months and by the end of October had completed a fairly polished draft. At this point, like the *Napoleon* idea, it was shelved. Unlike *Napoleon*, however, it was to be revived more than thirty years later and, with comparatively little revision apart from geographical relocation, to serve as the scenario for *A Countess From Hong Kong*.

In August work began on an alternative project. The London office of United Artists had purchased on behalf of the Chaplin Film Corporation film rights in D. L. Murray's period novel *Regency*, and a writer, Major Ronald Bodley, was hired to work on it. Bodley prepared a synopsis and treatment, and from October to February Chaplin also worked on the script, making copious manuscript emendations and notes. In March 1937 Major Bodley's engagement with the studio came to an end, and on 26 May, while dictating an introduction to Gilbert Seldes' book *Movies for the Millions*, Chaplin informed his secretary, Catherine Hunter, that *Regency* had been laid aside in favour of the contemporary story on which he was already working.

It is now rather unclear what recommended D. L. Murray's costume romance about the adventures of a high spirited and unconventional young girl of aristocratic blood in Regency England. True, it offered a lively part for Paulette. Moreover Chaplin gave it a political tinge by having the girl, Regency, torn between loyalty to the hedonist Regent and to a young highwayman of radical tendency. Chaplin's manuscript notes show a fascination with the central character; perhaps he saw in Regency something of Paulette herself.

> Regency has a dominant will. It manifests itself at a very early age . . . She was not popular among her own sex, but certain men, even young men, were irresistibly drawn to her . . . When men fell in love with her, they were so completely under her domination that she lost interest in them. On the other hand, anyone that tried to dominate her she immediately repelled. So long as no man stood in the path of her will, she was a friend to him. What stood out uppermost in her character was her firm sense of justice.

Years later Chaplin revealed that he and Paulette had been married in Canton during the course of their Far Eastern holiday. Although he maintained a genuine and loyal concern for Paulette's career, their professional and personal lives were by now already beginning to drift irresistibly apart. Paulette was too ambitious and impatient to wait for the next Chaplin project. Along with every other Hollywood leading lady, she longed for the role of Scarlett O'Hara in *Gone With The Wind*. Chaplin helped her in every way he could to equip herself for the role. He even arranged special tuition with his friend Constance Collier, the distinguished British stage actress. No one at the studio liked to tell him that Paulette was inclined to cut the lessons short in favour of other current interests. She eventually took her screen test on 1 October 1937. She did not get the part, though whether for want of tuition or too much of it, will never be known.

15

THE GREAT DICTATOR

Quite apart from any particular merits of the film, *The Great Dictator* remains an unparalleled phenomenon, an epic incident in the history of mankind. The greatest clown and best-loved personality of his age directly challenged the man who had instigated more evil and human misery than any other in modern history.

There was, to begin with, something uncanny in the resemblance between Chaplin and Hitler, representing opposite poles of humanity. On 21 April 1939, a year and a half before the release of *The Great Dictator*, an unsigned article in the *Spectator* noted:

> Providence was in an ironical mood when, fifty years ago this week, it was ordained that Charles Chaplin and Adolf Hitler should make their entry into the world within four days of each other . . . Each in his own way has expressed the ideas, sentiments, aspirations of the millions of struggling citizens ground between the upper and the lower millstone of society; the date of their birth and the identical little moustache (grotesque intentionally in Mr Chaplin) they well might have been fixed by nature to betray the common origin of their genius. For genius each of them undeniably possesses. Each has mirrored the same reality – the predicament of the 'little man' in modern society. Each is a distorting mirror, the one for good, the other for untold evil. In Chaplin the little man is a clown, timid, incompetent, infinitely resourceful yet bewildered by a world that has no place for him. The apple he bites has a worm in it; his trousers, remnants of gentility, trip him up; his cane pretends to a dignity his position is far from justifying; when he pulls a lever it is the wrong one and disaster follows. He is a heroic figure, but heroic only in the patience and resource with which he receives the blows that fall upon his bowler. In his actions and loves he emulates the angels. But in Herr Hitler

the angel has become a devil. The soleless boots have become *Reitstieffeln*; the shapeless trousers, riding breeches; the cane, a riding crop; the bowler, a forage cap. The Tramp has become a storm trooper; only the moustache is the same.

There were even those who believed that Hitler had at first adopted the moustache in a deliberate attempt to suggest a resemblance to the man who had attracted so much love and loyalty in the world.

Konrad Bercovici brought a plagiarism suit against Chaplin, claiming that he had first proposed that Chaplin should play Hitler in the mid-1930s. A good many newspaper cartoonists, notably David Low, might equally have claimed the idea as their own; after all, it was inevitable. Much later Chaplin admitted, 'Had I known of the actual horrors of the German concentration camps, I could not have made *The Great Dictator*; I could not have made fun of the homicidal insanity of the Nazis.'[1] Hitler, true, turned out to be no laughing matter; but there was nothing light-hearted in Chaplin's deeper intentions in making the film. He suffered very real and acute pain and revulsion at the horrors and omens of world politics in the 1930s. We have seen, in his 1931 diatribe against the myth of patriotism, that he already foresaw with dread another war. His recent Far Eastern tour had made him more alert than most to the perils of the China Incident of July 1937 and the escalation of the Sino–Japanese conflict.

He was no less disturbed by events in Spain. In April 1938 the French film magazine *Cinémonde* published a translation of a remarkable short story by Chaplin himself, entitled 'Rhythme'.* It describes the execution of a Spanish Loyalist, a popular humorous writer. The officer in charge of the firing squad was formerly a friend of the condemned man; 'their divergent views were then friendly, but they had finally provoked the unhappiness and disruption of the whole of Spain.' Both the officer and the six men of the firing squad privately hope that a reprieve may still come. Finally, though, the officer must give the rhythmic orders: 'Attention! . . . Shoulder arms! . . . Present arms! . . . Fire!' The officer gives the first three orders. Hurried footsteps are heard: all realize that it is the reprieve. The officer calls out 'Stop!' to his firing squad, but,

> Six men each held a gun. Six men had been trained through rhythm. Six men, hearing the shout 'Stop!' fired.

The story at once embodies those fears of seeing men turned into machines which Chaplin had expressed in *Modern Times*, and looks forward to some grim, ironic gags in *The Great Dictator*.[2]

There is more evidence of Chaplin's feelings about Spain in a poem which he scribbled in a folio notebook among some memoranda on the development of *Regency*, presumably in the winter of 1936–7. The poem was quite clearly never meant for publication, or even for other eyes. It was a private attempt to express his sentiments.

To a dead Loyalist soldier
on the battlefields of Spain

Prone, mangled form,
Your silence speaks your deathless cause,
Of freedom's dauntless march.
Though treachery befell you on this day
And built its barricades of fear and hate
Triumphant death has cleared the way
Beyond the scrambling of human life
Beyond the pale of imprisoning spears
To let you pass.

There was, he said euphemistically, 'a good deal of bad behaviour in the world'. Feeling as deeply as he did, he felt impelled to do whatever he could to correct it, or at least to focus attention upon it. His only weapon, as he knew, was comedy.

In the latter part of the 1930s Chaplin was very friendly with the

* No original English text for the story has been traced.

director King Vidor and his family, and it was through the Vidors, some time in 1938, that he met Tim Durant. Like Harry Crocker, Durant was a tall, good-looking, patrician, university-educated young man: Chaplin seemed to have a penchant for the type among his friends and assistants. Durant had the added merits of being sympathetic, amusing, discreet, and very good at tennis. Through Durant he was introduced into the society of Pebble Beach and Carmel, one hundred miles south of San Francisco. Chaplin called Pebble Beach 'the abode of lost souls'. He was fascinated, charmed and attracted by the collection of Californian millionaires who still made their homes there, and no less by the abandoned mansions that now lay in decay. The more Bohemian colony at nearby Carmel, a section of coast much favoured by artists and writers, had a different but potent attraction. He was especially pleased by his meetings there with the famous Californian poet Robinson Jeffers.

Tim Durant remembered that at first Chaplin was reluctant to become involved with the Pebble Beach set:

> I knew a girl who was married to one of the Crockers in San Francisco, and she heard I was there and called me up and asked me to come over for dinner and bring Charlie. But Charlie said to me, 'Listen, Tim, I don't want to get into this group at all . . .' I said, 'Look, Charlie, will you do this just as a personal favour – I don't ask you to do anything. Will you just go over and have dinner with them, and we can say honestly that we have to get back and do some work, and you can leave immediately.'
>
> He said, 'All right, Tim; but get me out of there, remember; don't let me spend the evening there.'
>
> So we went over there. We walked in and everybody congregated around him, you know, and he was a hero. He had an audience, and he couldn't leave – wanted to stay until three o'clock in the morning. After that he wanted to go out every night, because they accepted him as a great artist and a wonderful person. They loved him and he entertained them, and we went out all the time. He wrote many stories – I took notes of stories about the characters there. He had an idea of making a story about the people there.[3]

One of his hosts was D. L. James, who lived in a Spanish-style mansion perched on the cliff-edge at Carmel, one of northern California's architectural monuments. (James's parents actually had him baptized 'D.L.' with the idea that he could choose names to suit the initials when he grew up. In fact he remained simply 'D,L.' though occasionally he intimated that he might consider 'Dan' as a first name.) At the James house Chaplin met D.L.'s son Dan, who was then twenty-six, an aspiring writer and ardent Marxist, and rather unsettled: 'My writing was getting nowhere; I was separating from my wife; and I was just then thinking of going to New York.' They met on several occasions and Dan would hold forth on films and about the war against Fascism. Chaplin in turn outlined his ideas for a Hitler film.

When Chaplin returned from Pebble Beach to Hollywood at the end of the summer, Dan James took a chance and wrote to him saying that he was enthusiastic about the idea of the Hitler film, and would be very happy to be able to work on it in any capacity. 'I went on packing my bags for the East, though.' Somewhat to his surprise a telephone call came from the Chaplin studio a few days later, and he was invited to call and see Alf Reeves. Reeves warned him that Chaplin was very 'changeable', but that he liked him and was prepared to employ him on a salary of $80 a week, and to put him up at the Beverly Hills Hotel until he could find somewhere to live. 'My first evening he took me to Ciro's Trocadero Oyster bar; then we dined and he told me the outline of the story. The next day I went up and started to make notes . . . I think Charlie took me on because of my height, because my family had a castle out here, and because he knew pretty quickly I was a declared Communist, so that my background and political preoccupations would keep me from selling him out for money.'

This was presumably at the end of September 1938. The Jameses knew John Steinbeck, whom Chaplin was eager to meet; Dan James made the necessary arrangements. On 1 October Dan accompanied Chaplin for a weekend at Steinbeck's ranch at Los Gatos. He was impressed by Chaplin's perspicuity: 'Even then he said, "There's a lot that's phoney in Steinbeck," and I think time has proved him right.'

For three months James reported daily to the house in Beverly Hills, where he would make notes as Chaplin discussed ideas for the plot and gags. From time to time James would go to the studio to dictate the notes to Kathleen Pryor: the first of these dictation sessions seems to have taken place on 26 October 1938. During these three months James was able to assess Chaplin's own political thinking:

> He did not read deeply, but he *felt* deeply everything that happened. The end of *Modern Times*, for instance, reflected perfectly the optimism of

the New Deal period: already by 1934 and 1935 he had a sense of that. He had probably never read Marx, but his conception of the millionaire in *City Lights* is an exact image for Marx's conception of the business cycle. Marx wrote of the madness of the business cycle once it began to roll, the veering from one extreme to another. Chaplin presents a magnificent metaphor. Whether he was aware of the social meaning of this I do not know, but *he got it.*

He had a sixth sense about a lot of things. In 1927 and 1928, for instance, he began to feel that the stock market was going mad, and he took everything he had and put it into Canadian gold.

Charlie called himself an anarchist. He was always fascinated with people of the left. One of the people he wanted to meet was Harry Bridges of the Longshoremen's Union. I fixed up a meeting, and they took to each other immediately. Chaplin talked about the beauty of labor, and described how in the islands he had heard the fishermen sing as they went out in their boats. Harry said, 'I think you would have found that it was the old men on the shore, the ones who had given up going to sea, who did the singing.'[4]

Whatever his exact politics, Charlie had a position of revolt against wealth and stuffiness. He had a real feeling for the underdog . . . He was certainly a libertarian. He saw Stalin as a dangerous dictator very early, and Bob [Meltzer] and I had difficulty getting him to leave Stalin out of the last speech in *The Great Dictator*. He was horrified by the Soviet–German pact.

His description of himself as an anarchist is as good as any. He believed in human freedom and human dignity. He hated and suspected the machine, even though it was the motion picture machine that gave him his life. I would say that he was anti-capitalist, anti-organization. And dammit, that's the way people ought to be.

When it came to Hitler it is easy to say, with hindsight, that Chaplin made too light of him. You have to remember that the film was conceived before Munich, and that Chaplin had undoubtedly had it in his head a couple of years before that. And the thought then was that this monster was not so awe-inspiring as he appeared. He was a big phoney, and had to be shown up as such. Of course by the time the film appeared, France had fallen and we knew much more; so that a lot of the comedy had lost its point.

The Great Dictator marked an inevitable revolution in Chaplin's working methods. This was to be his first dialogue film, and for the first time he was to begin a picture with a complete script. The old method had been to work out each sequence in turn, alternating periods of story preparation with shooting – changing, selecting and discarding ideas as the work proceeded. Now these processes had to be transferred to the preparatory period, the work on a definitive script. The notes which Dan James periodically dictated to Miss Pryor reveal the metamorphoses through which the story progressed during his preparatory work.

The original and basic premise was the physical resemblance of the Dictator and the little Jew. All the early treatments of the story begin with the return of Jewish soldiers, many maimed, from the war to the ghetto. They are all welcomed back by wives and families, except 'the little Jew' (clearly returning from service in *Shoulder Arms*). He 'is alone walking down the ghetto street. In his hunger for companionship he embraces a lamppost.'

One early idea was for a flophouse sequence which

> can be used for the setting of our inflation material. The little Jew will return to pay his bill. The sign will read,'Beds, $1,000,000 a night – baths $500,000 extra.' Someone will send out for a package of cigarettes: 'You'll have to carry the money yourself,' or perhaps the little Jew goes out balancing a huge basket of currency on his head. $10,000,000 for cigars. The tobacco dealer insists that the money be counted. It is all in $1.00 bills.

Never willing to waste a good comedy idea, Chaplin planned to use the flea circus business, just as it appears in *The Professor*, for this scene. It stayed in through several successive treatments, but was finally abandoned. Having been frustrated in his efforts to introduce the business into *The Circus* and *The Great Dictator*, Chaplin would eventually manage to squeeze it into *Limelight*.

Chaplin early conceived the idea of two rival dictators competing to upstage one another. He was to abandon an idea for the Great Dictator's wife, a role intended for the famous Jewish comedienne Fanny Brice. A scene sketched out, with a lot of revision in Dan James's handwriting, indicates the kind of relationship Chaplin had in mind, and suggests that it might have encountered serious problems with the Breen Office and other censorship groups:

> SCENE: Mrs Hinkle alone – boredom and sex starvation with Freudian fruit symbols. Enter Hinkle from speech. She's mad at him – orders him about. He's preoccupied about matters of State.
>
> MRS: I'm a woman. I need affection, and all you think about is the State! THE STATE! What kind of state do you think I'm in?

HINKLE: You've made me come to myself. I'm not getting any younger. Sometimes I wonder. (good old melo)

MRS: Life is so short and these moments are so rare . . . Remember, Hinkle, I did everything for you. I even had an operation . . . on my nose. If you don't pay more attention to me I'll tell the whole world I'm Jewish!

HINKLE: Shhh!

FANNY: [*sic*] And I'm not so sure you aren't Jewish, too. We're having gefüllte fish for dinner.

HINKLE: Quiet! Quiet!

FANNY: Last night I dreamt about blimps.

HINKLE: Blimps?

FANNY: Yes, I dreamt we captured Paris in a big blimp and we went right through the Arc de Triomphe. And then I dreamed about a city all full of Washington monuments.

(She presses grapes in his mouth, plays with a banana)

By 13 December 1938 Chaplin had decided on much of the story, including the idea of the ending. Charlie and the father of the Girl from the ghetto with whom he has fallen in love are put in a concentration camp. They escape, and on the road run into Hinkle's troops, preparing to invade the neighbouring country of Ostrich. The general in command mistakes Charlie for Hinkle. Hinkle himself, out shooting ducks while trying to make up his mind about the invasion, is meanwhile mistaken for Charlie and thrown into prison.

Charlie and the Girl's father are carried along on the invasion of Ostrich and finally find themselves in the palace square of Vanilla, the capital:

> Hinkle's soldiers are drawn up before the platform from which the conqueror is about to speak. Charlie walks out on it. He can't say a word. The Girl's father is at his shoulder. 'You've got to talk now! It's our only chance! For God's sake, say something.' Herring (Hinkle's Prime Minister) first addresses the crowd – and through microphones the whole world, which is listening in. He calls for an end to democracies. He introduces Hinkle, the new conqueror who must be obeyed or else. In the crowd we show dozens of Ostrich patriots ready to kill Hinkle. Charlie steps forward. He begins slowly – scared to death. But his words give him power. As he goes on, the clown turns into the prophet.

By the middle of January 1939 Chaplin clearly felt confident with his story, though it was to undergo much subsequent revision. Dan James was set to adapt it into a dramatic composition in five acts and an epilogue, in order to register it for copyright. Copyright was also sought in the title *The Dictator*, but it was discovered that Paramount Pictures and the estate of Richard Harding Davies already owned the title and were unwilling to relinquish it. In June therefore the title *The Great Dictator* was registered, but Chaplin was not entirely convinced that it was right: having already registered *Ptomania*, he subsequently registered as alternatives *The Two Dictators*, *Dictamania* and *Dictator of Ptomania*.

After 16 January Dan James no longer went to the Beverly Hills house, since Chaplin now worked at the studio, where he could supervise preparations for shooting. The stage was being soundproofed; there were contracts to be negotiated with outside organizations like RCA who were to be responsible for the sound; and work was already in hand on miniatures for special effects. Now the daily script conferences took place in Chaplin's bungalow on the lot. On 21 January Sydney returned to work at the studio for the first time in almost twenty years: with conditions in Europe as they were, he and his new French wife, Gypsy, had decided that they were likely to be safer in America. The daily script conferences were now augmented, as Sydney and Henry Bergman joined Chaplin and Dan James, who recalled:

> I don't remember Henry contributing anything to the meetings except enthusiasm and laughter – and that was very important. Sydney, though, was immensely ingenious with gags. Very few of them had any relevance to what we were doing, but that didn't matter. It was stimulating. A bad gag is always a challenge to do better . . .
>
> Sydney was always asking me to remind Charlie how much it was all costing, and that we didn't need all those extras and things, and that it wasn't necessary to do so much overtime. He was very much the older brother. You would never have taken them for brothers though – they seemed so different. I think Charlie had outgrown Sydney. Sydney would rarely go to Charlie's parties, with all his smart intellectual friends . . . If you saw Sydney you would never even have taken him for an actor . . .

By the late summer of 1939 when the script was finished and Chaplin was ready to start shooting, he was able to reassure Sydney: 'This time, Syd, I have the script totally visualized. I know where every close-up comes.' 'Of course,' said Dan James, 'it didn't work out quite like that.'

During the weeks of preparation, Chaplin ran films for the staff in the studio projection room, among them *Shoulder Arms* and the mysterious *The Professor*. He also screened all the newsreels of Hitler on which he could lay hands. He later returned often to a particular sequence showing Hitler at the signing of the French surrender. As Hitler left the railway carriage, he seemed to do a little dance. Chaplin would watch the scene with fascination, exclaiming, 'Oh, you bastard, you son-of-a-bitch, you swine. I know what's in your mind.' According to Tim Durant, 'He said, "this guy is one of the greatest actors I've ever seen"...Charlie admired his acting. He really did.' Dan James commented forty-five years later, 'Of course he had in himself some of the qualities that Hitler had. He dominated his world. He created his world. And Chaplin's world was not a democracy either. Charlie was the dictator of all those things.'

The script, which was completed by 1 September, remains one of the most elaborate ever made for a Hollywood film. It runs to the extraordinary length of almost 300 pages (the average feature film script varies from 100 to 150 pages). It was divided into twenty-five sections, each designated by a letter of the alphabet and separately paginated; throughout shooting every take was identified by the letter and number of the relevant script page. Despite the doubt Dan James casts on Chaplin's assertion that everything was visualized, the system seems, to judge from the shooting records, to have served pretty well in the 168 days of a very complicated production.

Throughout the spring and early summer of 1939 Chaplin was collecting his crew around him. Henry Bergman was nominated 'co-ordinator'. Dan James was joined by two more assistant directors. One was Chaplin's half-brother Wheeler Dryden, who arrived at La Brea in March, overjoyed to be given a job on Chaplin's permanent studio staff. Wheeler had continued to pick up a living as an actor and in 1923 had had a play, *Suspicion*, co-written with George Appell, produced at the Egan Theatre in Los Angeles.* He was to remain at the studio until Chaplin's departure from the United States in 1952. A slight man, Wheeler retained the air and diction of an old-style stage actor. Though he adored Chaplin, Wheeler could

* In the late 1920s Sydney expressed a high regard for Wheeler and proposed taking him on as an assistant in his abortive British production venture.

sometimes madden him as well as the rest of the studio staff with his finicky attention to detail.

The amusing and devil-may-care Robert Meltzer, like James an avowed Communist, was in striking contrast to the solemn and nervy Wheeler. He had also been recruited in Pebble Beach. During the summer there the gossip writers had linked Chaplin's name with several women, notably the sugar heiress Geraldine Spreckels and a striking young red-headed actress called Dorothy Comingore, whom Chaplin saw on stage in Carmel. Dorothy Comingore was then living with Bob Meltzer, and when Chaplin convinced her that she should try her luck in Los Angeles, Meltzer came too. In the end it was Meltzer who worked for Chaplin and not Miss Comingore, who joined Orson Welles' Mercury Theatre and made her most striking impact as Susan Alexander – the role transparently based on Marion Davies – in *Citizen Kane*. After *The Great Dictator* Meltzer himself was to work briefly with Welles. With the outbreak of hostilities in 1941 he volunteered for service with the paratroops and died (exclaiming 'This is the best darn' football match I ever had') in the Battle of Normandy. Meltzer wanted to be a writer but Dan James recalls that 'nothing he wrote ever quite came off. He was witty, funny – but nothing much ended up on paper.'

Chaplin's staff were astonished when Chaplin engaged Karl Struss as director of photography. After twenty-three years as Chaplin's senior cameraman this was a cruel blow to Rollie Totheroh, who could never afterwards completely forgive his beloved boss. Chaplin had grown dissatisfied with Rollie's camerawork for reasons which were never quite clear. According to Dan James,

> He was having a great war with all the technical people . . . He wasn't satisfied with what Rollie had been giving him; but then he felt that Karl wasn't giving him enough light. He was getting in tree branches and things, to achieve 'mood'. It might have been 'mood', but it wasn't what Chaplin wanted.

The problem for a director making only one film every four or five years was that in the interval conditions in Hollywood had changed. Each time that Chaplin made a film he found himself bedevilled by new technical people whom he neither understood nor needed. He had a running feud with the script girl – a personage hitherto unknown on a Chaplin film.

> He was always fighting against what he called 'chi-chi' – over-attention to detail of make-up, costumes and such. The script girl would stop him in a scene and say, 'But Mr Chaplin, last time you held your arm this way.' He would yell, and say '****! Who *cares*? If they're going to watch my hand we might as well throw the whole thing out of the window.'
>
> Then one day in the cutting room he noticed that Paulette entered a door and came through the other side wearing a completely different dress. He was triumphant. So much for the script girl!

The Great Dictator was to make particular demands on the wardrobe department, and Chaplin engaged Paul (Ted) Tetrick, who had been around Hollywood since the 1920s working at various times in movies, real estate and the clothing business, to deal with it. Tetrick, useful in all sorts of aspects of production, was to work on both Chaplin's subsequent American films. Winifred Ritchie, the widow of Billie Ritchie, who had learned her skill in making trick costumes back in the Karno days and had long been indispensable during Chaplin productions, was again employed on *The Great Dictator*.

The role of Hannah was intended for Paulette, who reported for work at the studio on 29 July. She and Chaplin had spent a good deal of the previous year apart. While he went to Pebble Beach in the early half of 1938, Paulette flew to Florida, and during most of the rest of the year she was at work in Hollywood, while he stayed away from the studio. Already in March, while hardly finished with marriage rumours, the newspapers talked of impending divorce. Paulette's contract with the studio expired on 31 March 1938, and she had sought an earlier release to sign with the Myron Selznick agency. She was hired for *The Great Dictator* at $2500 a week; Chaplin was furious when she brought her agent (probably Selznick himself) to demand bigger billing.

She and Chaplin continued to live together in the Summit Drive house throughout the production of the film. As Chaplin nicely expressed it, 'Although we were somewhat estranged we were friends and still married.' To the Chaplin sons, now mischievous early teenagers, and to casual acquaintances, their relationship seemed much as before. At the studio, the staff were however aware of the change. Dan James remembers, 'You belonged to the Paulette faction or to the Charlie faction. You couldn't be both.' Sometimes, he felt, the strain showed when Chaplin and Paulette were working together.

'There was some anger on both sides. But he worked very hard with her. Sometimes he would make twenty-five or thirty takes. He would stand in her place on the set and try and give her the tone and the gestures. It was a method he had been able to use in silent films: it could not work so well with a talking picture.'

The final stencilled copies of the script were completed on Sunday 3 September 1939 – the day that Britain declared war on Germany. Three days later Chaplin began to rehearse and on 9 September shooting began on the first ghetto sequence. Filming was to continue with hardly a day's break apart from (most weeks) Sundays until the end of March 1940. By that time Chaplin would have shot most of the 477,440 feet of film which were eventually to be exposed. The length of the finished picture was 11,625 feet.

It is interesting, but perhaps not too surprising, to discover that Chaplin kept the shooting of his two roles quite distinct. First, until the end of October, he worked on the scenes of the ghetto, in the character of the barber. With the bulk of those completed, November was spent on more complicated action and location scenes, like the war scenes, particularly those involving Reginald Gardiner and the crashed 'plane. Chaplin had devised some very funny business with the aeroplane. Taking over the controls, Charlie manages to turn it upside down without either himself or his companion (Gardiner) being aware of it. They only notice with some concern that the sun is shining up from below them, that a watch released from a pocket leaps (apparently) into the air and sways there on its taut chain, and that they are passed by flocks of upside-down seagulls. Reginald Gardiner suffered much more than Chaplin from the experience of being strapped upside down, and only managed his lines and air of insouciance with great difficulty.

There were interludes and distractions in the work at the studio that November. Not all were welcome: a plagiarism suit brought by Michael Kustoff on account of *Modern Times* came to trial before Federal Judge McCormick, and kept Reeves busy. Chaplin himself was in court on 18 November when the case was decided in his favour.

More welcome was the arrival of another of Chaplin's English relatives. Betty Chaplin was the elder daughter of Cousin Aubrey. She had kept in touch with Sydney during her childhood. She was not happy in England; her marriage had broken down and she welcomed the chance to leave England, just then in the period of the 'phoney war'. She was lucky to get onto the last passenger ship to leave for America, with no clothes, money or passport, but with a diplomatic visa obtained from Joseph Kennedy, then Ambassador in London.

She arrived on 11 November. That day the Kustoff hearings were in progress; Chaplin had decided to change the entire set and lighting for the roof-top escape scene, and no one from the studio had time to meet Betty off the Superchief. Hal Roach's daughter Maggie stepped in to collect her from the railway station but on arrival at the studio, already nervous, she was advised that Chaplin was in a very difficult mood. She was heartened to find Wyn Ritchie, whom she knew from earlier visits to Hollywood, having a cup of coffee with Ted Tetrick, whom she introduced as 'the breaker of all the hearts of Hollywood'.

Betty was to marry Tetrick eight years later. Chaplin, taking a serious view of his responsibility for his young half-cousin, regularly complained because the marriage was so long delayed. He also continued to urge Betty to take American citizenship. When she countered that he had never done so, he would only reply that he was too old. (Betty became an American citizen on 9 December 1949.) Betty broke her own share of hearts among the studio staff, but her first and final choice was Ted Tetrick.

On 15 November 1939 Douglas Fairbanks and his new wife Sylvia, the former Lady Ashley, visited the location in Laurel Canyon where Chaplin was filming. Chaplin thought he looked older and stouter, though he was still as full of enthusiasm. He had always been Chaplin's favourite audience, and as so many times before, Chaplin showed Fairbanks his sets and expounded his plans. Although he was filming in the Barber's concentration camp costume, Chaplin put on his Hynkel* uniform to show his visitors, and, wearing it, was photographed with them. They all lunched together.

It was the last time he saw the man whom he later said had been his only close friend. At four o'clock in the morning of 12 December, Douglas Fairbanks Junior telephoned Chaplin to tell him that his father had died just over three hours earlier, in his sleep. There was no shooting at the Chaplin studio on the day of his funeral, 15

* In the final script the spelling was changed from Hinkle to Hynkel.

December. 'It was a terrible shock,' wrote Chaplin, 'for he belonged so much to life . . . I have missed his delightful friendship.'

As December came Chaplin began his Hynkel scenes. The supreme actor, Chaplin always became totally subsumed into the role he was playing, as colleagues throughout his career have testified. When, for the first time, he adopted the uniform and role of an autocratic and villainous character, even he was momentarily disconcerted by the effect. Reginald Gardiner remembered that when Chaplin first appeared on the set ready to shoot in his Hynkel uniform, he was noticeably more cool and abrupt than when he had been playing the Jewish barber. Gardiner recalled further that when he was driving with Chaplin – already in uniform – to a new location, Chaplin suddenly became uncharacteristically abusive about the driver of a car that was obstructing them. He quickly recovered himself, and recalled with laughter an earlier discussion about the false sense of superiority a uniform can produce. 'Just because I'm dressed up in this darned thing I go and do a thing like that.'

Although work on *The Great Dictator* proceeded on a much tighter schedule and pre-set plan than any previous Chaplin film, there was no fixed daily routine in the studio. Much, of course, depended upon Chaplin's own somewhat unpredictable time of arrival, although for the first time he appears to have delegated considerable responsibility for preparation and in some cases shooting to his assistants. Two daily reports from December give some idea of the way the day might go at the Chaplin studios during this period.

> December 16
>
> Rehearsals 9 a.m. on stage 1. Hynkel's office with Gilbert, Daniell, 3 girls, 2 guards. Rehearsed all scenes in office – mapped out new business. Lunch 12.45–1.45. Lining up on set till 3 p.m. when C.C. arrived on set. He then asked for a secretary to work in F5 (which was not according to plan in a.m.). Then rehearsed until 4 p.m. Male secretary arrived on set 4.15 ready. C.C. decided to continue to use guard, 1st shot 4 p.m. Finished at 7.10 p.m.

In the final three hours of this day, 2780 feet of film (about thirty minutes' running time) were exposed. Scene F was the first scene in Hynkel's palace.

> December 30
>
> Rushes 8.20 a.m. Shooting 9.30 a.m. C.C. came on set made minor changes. Returned on set made up at 11 a.m. 1st shot 11.55 a.m . Lunch 1.20–2.20. 1st shot 3 p.m. Continued scenes in Banquet Room till 7.20 p.m. when company finished.

That day 3570 feet of film (almost forty minutes' running time) were shot.

Dan James recalls going on location in the San Fernando Valley to film the rally scenes in which Chaplin, spouting wild Teutonic gibberish, miraculously caricatures Hitler's oratorical style. The inspired concoction of sibilants and gutturals seems to have been improvised; there is hardly a hint in the script of the sounds Chaplin would produce.

> We must have gone back to that scene a dozen times. The first time was in San Fernando Valley, with all the extras standing there in front of him. He said, 'Just keep the cameras rolling.' He would keep up that gibberish talk for 700 feet of film.
>
> The temperatures were over 100, but he would go on interminably, it seemed, and then in between he would amuse the extras by doing scenes from *Sherlock Holmes* or demonstrating pratfalls. At the end of the day he would be deadly gray, sweating, exhausted, with a towel wrapped around his neck. He would collapse into his car, and you would think, 'My God, he'll never be back tomorrow.' But he was.
>
> In the end we reshot most of the scene in the studio, and then it wasn't possible to match the light quality, so I think that what we used was mostly the studio stuff. But some of the shots made on that outdoor lot were breathtaking.

Just before Christmas Chaplin shot the scene which remains the most haunting and the most inspired of the film: Hynkel's ballet with the terrestrial globe. The first hint of a symbolic scene of this sort is a random story note dating from 15 February 1939:

> SCENE WITH MAP: cutting it up to suit himself, cutting off bits of countries with a pair of scissors.

The dance with the globe was to go far beyond this elementary notion. While the gibberish speech appears so precise and planned that it is surprising to discover that it was improvised, the dance with the globe seems to soar so freely in its inspiration that it is hard to imagine that it could be written down. Yet it was. In the complete version of the script, the description of Chaplin's *pas seul* occupies four pages, opening,

> HYNKEL GOES TO THE GLOBE – and caresses it – trance-like. Soft strains of Peer Gynt* waft into the room. Hynkel picks up the globe, bumps it into the air with his left wrist. It floats like a balloon and drops back into his hands. He bumps it with his right wrist and catches it. He dominates the world – kicks it viciously away. Sees himself in the mirror – plays God! Beckons, the world floats into his hand. Then he bumps it high in the air with his right wrist. He leaps up (on wire), catches the globe and brings it down . . .

Chaplin continued to develop his ideas for the scene, and by December a new version of the libretto had been substituted in the script. It is now actually headed 'Dance Routine', and is arranged in ten movements.

> I. Hynkel moves hypnotically toward the globe (one hand on hip – one outstretched). He lifts it from its stand. There is a moment of magical concentration. The globe becomes a balloon. Hynkel bounces it from wrist to wrist and off the top of his head. He finds he can do what he likes with it. The world is his oyster. He laughs ecstatically as he plays with it with nonchalance.
>
> II. Now he shows his power. He grips the globe, taps his foot. He changes his grip so that his right hand is above – his left hand underneath.
>
> III. Then he gets a transition – becomes sensuous about the world. It nearly gets away from him.
>
> IV. In revenge he grabs it angrily, kicks it away viciously.
>
> V. It returns to him. Gratified by his manifest power over it, Hynkel plays nonchalantly with the globe again – with silly gestures. Kicks it away with a comedy kick.
>
> VI. He catches the globe – authoritatively taps it from wrist to wrist as he stands before his desk.
>
> VII. Gracefully he leans back over the desk and gets very Greek about the whole thing. He bounces the globe from toe to head to rear. He's carried away with the beauty of it.
>
> VIII. He gets to his feet on the far side of the desk – becomes mystic about the world, tosses it high in the air, leaps after it to the desk top where he catches it.
>
> IX. Again he tosses it up, leaps from the desk to get it (slow motion).

* In the outcome the Prelude to *Lohengrin* proved more appropriate.

x. He catches it roughly (anger business). Laughs demoniacally. The globe pops. He picks up the skin forlornly and bursts into tears.

The particular attention that Chaplin was to give to the balloon dance indicates that he was well aware that it would remain one of his great virtuoso scenes. He spent three days (21, 22 and 23 December) on the main shooting, and then made some retakes on 6 January. The first three days of February 1940 seem to have been entirely taken up with running and rerunning the material, and on 6 February and again on 15 February Chaplin did further retakes.

Carter De Haven, who plays the Ambassador in the film, was later to attempt to get into the plagiarism game by claiming the ballet with the globe as his idea. Any doubt, however, was finally put to rest when Kevin Brownlow and David Gill, preparing their *Unknown Chaplin* film series, unearthed some forgotten home movies of a party at Pickfair somewhere in the early 1920s. Chaplin, in classical Grecian costume and crowned with a laurel wreath, performs a dance with a balloon which is the unmistakable prototype for *The Great Dictator*. No doubt Chaplin was remembering his party trick of nearly twenty years ago when he noted in the script description of the globe ballet, 'Then he slides to the table top to perform a series of Greek postures' (first version) and 'Gracefully he leans back over the desk and gets very Greek about the whole thing.'

In January 1940 Jack Oakie joined the cast to play Benzino Napaloni, the Dictator of Bacteria. When Chaplin first proposed the role to him, Oakie questioned the suitability of casting an Irish–Scottish American in a caricature of Mussolini. What, asked Chaplin, would be funny about an Italian playing Mussolini? Chaplin did perceive a problem however when he discovered that Oakie was at the time dieting to lose weight. According to Charles Chaplin Junior, Chaplin brought his own cook, George, to the studio and had him tempt Oakie with the richest and most fattening dishes he could devise. When he found his strategy was succeeding, and that Oakie was increasingly growing to resemble Mussolini in stature, he cheerfully nicknamed him 'Muscles'.[5]

Charles Junior considered that 'one of the pleasantest things about the new film was the affable relationship between Dad and Jack Oakie. Jack has a tough hide and was able to take Dad's drive in stride. Dad, on his part, has always had great admiration for Jack.' Others on the set observed that working in his scenes with Oakie brought out a certain competitive spirit in Chaplin. It was not jealousy: rationally Chaplin knew that his supremacy was unassailable. Rather it was Chaplin's legacy from the Karno and Keystone training: the essential and driving motive for a comedian must always be to outdo the rest. Chaplin's own script for *The Great Dictator* often gave the better comedy business to Oakie. Chaplin's professional instinct still drove him to top it with his own comedy. He would sense the reaction of the unit, and he played the comic game with the same intensity as he played tennis. As with tennis, he did not like to lose: finishing a scene in which he felt that Oakie had scored the biggest laughs from the bystanders, he could hardly conceal his irritation. Charles Junior, a very reliable witness, despite his youth at the time, recalled one day when Oakie had tried every trick he knew to do the impossible and steal a scene from Chaplin. In the middle of the scene, Chaplin grinned and offered advice: 'If you really want to steal a scene from me, you son-of-a-bitch, just look straight into the camera. That'll do it every time.'[6]

Chaplin undoubtedly found these duels of comedy nostalgic and stimulating. He was less happy with some of his actors from the legitimate theatre. In particular he found it very hard to work against Henry Daniell's measured timing. 'He developed a hatred for Daniell,' recalls Dan James. 'He really thought Daniell was trying to sabotage him. The trouble was that he had a respect for Daniell because he was a real stage actor, and couldn't bring himself to explain what was wrong. Poor Daniell knew that Chaplin was not pleased with him, but he never understood why. On the other hand he was crazy about Reggie Gardiner, though once he had got him, he never really gave Reggie any funny stuff.'

By the middle of February practically all the studio scenes had been shot, and Chaplin moved out onto location to shoot the First World War scenes for the opening of the film and the scene of Hynkel being arrested while out duck shooting, filmed at Malibu Lake. The war scenes involved the series of gags with Chaplin and the enormous Big Bertha gun, and for one day's shooting the Chaplin children were taken to watch. Fourteen-year-old Sydney was so overcome with mirth at his father's antics following the explosion of the gun that he laughed aloud. When he discovered who had wrecked the sound take, Chaplin flew at him in fury, saying 'Do you know your laugh just cost me fifteen thousand dollars?'

'In a twinkling, from being the funniest man alive, Dad had become the most furious.' The two boys feared some awful retribution; but then Chaplin began to laugh, and proudly called out to the crew, 'Even my own son thinks I'm funny.' To Sydney he added, 'Well, it was fifteen thousand dollars' worth of laugh, but if you appreciated it that much, it's all right . . . Just don't let it happen again, son.'[7]

One series of scenes shot during this period was destined never to be seen. Chaplin's first idea for the final scene of the speech, in which (in the words of the early treatment) 'the clown turns into the prophet' was extremely ambitious. He intended the speech to be laid over scenes supposed to take place in Spain, China, a German street and a Jewish ghetto in Germany. As Chaplin's speech came into their consciousness, a Spanish firing squad would throw down their arms; a Japanese bomber pilot would be overcome by wonder, and instead of bombs, toys on parachutes would rain down on the Chinese children below; a parade of goose-stepping German soldiers would break into waltz-time; and a Nazi storm-trooper would risk his life to save a little Jewish girl from an oncoming car. A couple of days were actually spent in shooting material for the sequence, but it was discarded.

By the end of March 1940, the main shooting was all finished, the labourers were already beginning to clear the studio, and Chaplin had a rough-cut of the film ready to show to a few friends such as Constance Collier in early April. The climactic scene, the final speech made by the little barber who has been mistaken for the Great Dictator, remained to be shot. Moreover Chaplin was to polish and tinker with the film more than with any other that he made. During the next six months he would suddenly decide to put up a set again; and he was still doing retakes of the ghetto scenes in late September, after he had already previewed the film. Redubbing of the sound went on practically until the première on 15 October 1940.

From April to June Chaplin laboured over the text of his big speech, between working on the editing of the film. His two young Marxist assistants were of no help to him: 'Bob and I said to him, "Couldn't you just say some simple little thing?" But Charlie wanted to make some great statement to the world. When he finally came to shoot it, we were exiled from the set. He said, "I can't do it with you two there. I can feel your hostility."'[8] The utopian idealism and unashamed emotionalism of the speech evidently offended their Communist orthodoxy. Others were anxious about the speech on more pragmatic grounds. Tim Durant remembered,

> He made a speech about humanity, and there was a great argument about that . . . that it did not belong . . . in the picture. It was unaesthetic. It was wrong to have Charlie go out there and propagandize . . . The film salesmen said, 'You'll lose a million dollars . . . for doing that' and he said, 'Well I don't care if it's five million. I'm gonna do it.' So he did, you know, and of course it did cost him quite a bit.[9]

Chaplin's judgement was not swayed. On 24 June he recorded the speech, which in its final screen form runs six minutes. It has remained one of the most controversial passages in all his works, but today Chaplin's judgement seems to us correct. Simply and succinctly the speech sums up his fears and his hopes for a world in the throes of its most terrible war:

> The way of life can be free and beautiful, but we have lost the way. Greed has poisoned men's souls – has barricaded the world with hate – has goose-stepped us into misery and bloodshed. We have developed speed, but we have shut ourselves in. Machinery that gives abundance has left us in want. Our knowledge has made us cynical; our cleverness, hard and unkind. We think too much and feel too little. More than machinery we need humanity. More than cleverness we need kindness and gentleness. Without these qualities, life will be violent and all will be lost.

Chaplin's critics, from left and right, accused him of cliché and truism. The most striking aspect of the speech, though, is that more than forty years afterwards, not one phrase of it has dated or lost its force, even if the optimism of the final lines ('We are coming out of the darkness into the light! We are coming into a new world . . .!') can hardly be said to have been fulfilled.

Music played a less important role in *The Great Dictator* than in Chaplin's previous sound films; the score was completed in a bare three weeks. On this occasion Chaplin's musical collaborator was Meredith Willson. Many of the music sessions took place at the Chaplin house, and Charles Junior was an interested observer. The musicians, he noted, were really musical secretaries, working to Chaplin's dictation. He would hum a tune or play it on the piano, and the musicians would take it down and play it back for his approval. It might take several tries before the tune gave him complete satisfaction. He had very clear ideas on the scoring, and liked to describe what he wanted by reference to a composer or an instrumental label: 'We should make this Wagnerian,' he would say, or,

'This part should be more Chopin. Let's make this light and airy, a lot of violins. I think we could use an oboe effect in this passage.'[10] Often the musicians were startled by the unorthodox timing Chaplin would demand to suit a special piece of action, but

> Dad's dramatic instinct as it related to music was brilliant . . . The musicians turned gray and were on the verge of nervous breakdown by the time it was over, but whatever they suffered they couldn't say that working with Dad was ever dull. He gave them a free performance at every session, because he didn't just hum or sing, or knock out a tune on the piano. He couldn't stay quiet that long. He would start gesturing with the music, acting out the parts of the various people in the scene he was working on, but caricaturing their movements to evoke a total response in himself. At those times his acting was closer than ever to ballet.[11]

Many more weeks of retakes, cutting and recutting, recording and re-recording, predubbing, dubbing and redubbing followed, until finally on 1 September a complete print of the picture was ready. The first audience that Sunday afternoon consisted of Paulette, Mr and Mrs King Vidor, Mr and Mrs Lewis Milestone, the three assistants, James, Meltzer and Wheeler Dryden, and Steve Pallos, who was invited as Alexander Korda's representative. Three days later, after further changes (mainly restoration of the conspiracy sequence, which he had previously decided to cut) the picture was shown to the United Artists people. Joseph Breen, the film industry censor, also saw the film: subsequently he was to ask for the deletion of the word 'lousy' from the dialogue.

Still anxious, Chaplin decided on a series of sneak previews. The first was at the Riverside Theatre on 5 September, attended by most of the staff. Noting the reaction, Chaplin set to recutting to speed up the picture, and ordered rebuilding of the ghetto street set for some retakes. Wheeler Dryden had by this time taken over the job of writing the daily studio reports. One day he notes, 'The music of the newly edited "Conspiracy" sequence was a difficult task, but Mr Chaplin stuck to it all day.' His no less characteristic comment on a second sneak preview at the UA Theatre, Long Beach on 20 September runs, 'The reaction accorded to the production showed unmistakably that the changes Mr Chaplin has made since the first "Sneak Preview" have improved the picture immeasurably.' All the same Chaplin decided on more retakes, and next day poor Wheeler writes, 'Wheeler Dryden spent whole day and several hours after dinner locating actors needed.'

Not until the end of September was Chaplin sufficiently satisfied to order the final dubbing of the picture. On the evening of 3 October he invited a select group of guests to see the finished work. They were James Roosevelt, Patricia Morison, Gene Tierney, Mrs Rockwell Kent, Anita Loos, the Aldous Huxleys, the John Steinbecks and the Lewis Milestones. Tim Durant, Dan James and Robert Meltzer also attended.

Between this showing and the press previews, which took place eleven days later at the Carthay Circle Theatre, Los Angeles and the Astor Theatre, New York, Chaplin made still further changes to the sound. They were, Wheeler noted, 'just minor changes, but important ones'.

For the first time since work began on the film, Chaplin permitted himself to relax. Wheeler's painstaking notes sometimes recorded social occasions:

> September 25
>
> 4.30. Countess of Jersey (Virginia Cherrill) visited C.C. in cutting room, looked at some scenes and drove him home from studio at 6.08.
>
> October 1
>
> At 6.45 p.m. Tim Durant, a friend of Mr Chaplin's arrived at stu'o. Shortly after Mr C. left the sound stage, dressed in clothes brought from his home by his valet, and at 7.30 p.m. Mr C. was driven from studio to attend social engagement. He drove out of studio in Tim Durant's car.
>
> October 2
>
> Lunch was called at 1.15 p.m., after which, at 3.43 p.m., Mr C. was driven by Jack Kneymeyer, in the latter's automobile, to Mr C.'s residence, where he and Kneymeyer played a game of tennis.
>
> October 3
>
> Heard remainder of dubbed tracks; gave instructions for few changes. *Afternoon*: tennis with Jack Kneymeyer.

Chaplin was understandably nervous about the reception of *The Great Dictator*. The rest of Hollywood had discreetly avoided making overt anti-Nazi films. A Gallup poll at the time of the outbreak of war in Europe showed 96 per cent opposition to America's entry into the war. Since the Depression a fiercely isolationist spirit had developed. Moreover the quantity of threatening letters Chaplin received testified to the strength of pro-Fascist feeling in the United States. He seriously discussed with Harry Bridges of the Longshoremen's Union having some of his men at the opening in case of a pro-Nazi demonstration.

Chaplin gambled that he was likely to get a more sympathetic press in New York than on the West Coast. He therefore decided to have the world première in New York on 15 October, with simultaneous press previews in New York and Los Angeles the day before. Favouring the East in this way was to rebound badly. When he eventually returned to Hollywood after an absence of almost four months in the East, he invited a group of the local press people to a conference at the house. He quickly realized how mortal was the offence he had committed: the press men refused a drink. 'You left here ignoring the press,' they told him, 'and we don't like it.' They were subsequently to punish him for it.

The American critics were on the whole guarded. Generally they admired the audacity of the undertaking and the sustained brilliance of the comedy, though Paul Goodman qualified a genuinely enthusiastic view with asides on 'calamitous music' (Meredith Willson's), 'feeble dialogue' and 'persistent lapses in style'. Most however had an uneasy sense that things had gone beyond the point where Hitler could be made a simple buffoon and his storm-troopers, Keystone Kops. On the other hand Paul Goodman found 'the invective against Hynkel is to my taste all-powerful: disgust expressed by the basic tricks of low vaudeville, gibberish, belching, dirty words and radio static. You will not find the like outside of Juvenal . . . On the other hand the personal Hynkel is not the political Hitler.' Goodman concluded that the film was 'something different, and something better, than the "grandiose failure" of the worried reviewers.' Unlike them, he did not find the last speech in any way out of character, for 'if this isn't meant from the heart, we have been deceived for twenty-five years.'

Another reviewer of special perception was Rudolph Arnheim, who wrote with the awareness of a recent refugee from Hitler's Germany:

> Charles Chaplin is the only artist who holds the secret weapon of mortal laughter. Not the laugh of superficial gibing that self-complacently underrates the enemy and ignores the danger, but rather the profound laughter of the sage who despises physical violence, even the threat of death, because behind it he has discovered the spiritual weakness, stupidity, and falseness of his antagonist. Chaplin could have opened the eyes of a world enchained by the spell of force and material success. But instead of

> unmasking the common enemy, fascism, Chaplin unmasked a single man, 'The Great Dictator'. And that is why I feel that this good film should have been better.[12]

In London *The Great Dictator* opened on 16 December 1940, at the height of the Blitz, when Hitler was a very real and present enemy. The British seemed to delight in Chaplin's ridicule, with none of the reserve felt by the Americans. The British above all loved the prime joke of the physical resemblance of Old Adolf and the funniest man in the world. The critic of the *New Statesman and Nation* called the film 'the best heartener we could have, with war standing still or going for or against us'; and in the *Spectator* Basil Wright found in it 'undeniable greatness, both in its pure comedy and its bold contrast between the small people of the ghetto or the slums and the big people of the Fascist chancelleries, equating both in terms of fantasy and in terms of the adored Chaplin himself.'

The final speech, which the political right felt smacked of Communism and the left suspected of sentimentality, seemed not to embarrass the larger audience. It was widely quoted and reprinted. Chaplin's old friend Rob Wagner devoted a page to it in the 16 November issue of his magazine *Rob Wagner's Script*; Archie Mayo, mainly remembered as the director of *The Petrified Forest*, used it as his Christmas card for 1940, comparing it to Lincoln's Gettysburg Address; and in England the Communist Party put it out as a special pamphlet.

16

MONSIEUR VERDOUX

The whole of Chaplin's life had been marked by dramatic contrasts. The decade which followed the release of *The Great Dictator* was to see both the most bitter period of his public and professional career and the achievement in his personal life of the happiness and success that hitherto persistently eluded him. Chaplin thrilled the audience at the première of *The Great Dictator* by introducing Paulette as 'my wife'. This delayed admission of the marriage made news across the world, yet it was oddly timed, since both partners were by then aware that the marriage had already run its course. For two years they had been drifting apart, apparently without great acrimony. They had even arrived separately in New York – Chaplin from California with Tim Durant, Paulette from Mexico where she had been visiting a new friend, Diego Rivera. Charles Junior suggested, realistically, that Chaplin calculated that a clarification in Paulette's status would disarm the club women of America, whose moral disapprobation could be harmful to the box office success of the new picture. He also believed Chaplin may have hoped that this public announcement might help to patch up the marriage.

It did not. After the première Paulette returned to Hollywood to perform her last duties as hostess at the Summit Drive house, entertaining H. G. Wells, who was on a lecture tour, for two weeks. Chaplin stayed on in New York for four months, until February 1941. In December he heard from Alf Reeves that Paulette had left the house and moved into a beach house lent to her by her agent, Myron Selznick.

Paulette was to get a divorce in Mexico in 1942 on the grounds of incompatibility and separation for more than a year. Chaplin seems to have had grudging admiration for Paulette's shrewdness over the settlement she won from him. It was rumoured to be in the region of one million, but was probably one third of that. Paulette also got the *Panacea*. The divorce proceedings (heard *in absentia* before Judge Javier Rosas Seballas in the Civil Court at Juarez) corroborated that the marriage had taken place in Canton in 1936.

Paulette's career as a Paramount contract star flourished for most of the next decade: her craving for independence was undoubtedly one of the main causes of the split with Chaplin. She had met Burgess Meredith while co-starring with Fred Astaire in *Second Chorus* (1940) and married him in 1944. That marriage ended with another Mexican divorce in June 1949, and in 1958 she married Erich Maria Remarque. Relations between Chaplin and Paulette remained quite cordial after the split, and the Chaplin sons continued to see her from time to time. They felt particularly keenly the loss of Paulette's vivid and cheering presence in the household. 'It's just one of those sad things, son,' Chaplin would tell Charles Junior. 'That's life for you.'

Quite apart from the separation, the year 1941 began badly. The very mixed critical and public reception of his film revealed, to Chaplin's growing distress, the extent of pro-Nazi feeling in the United States. In January he was delighted to accompany a Hollywood delegation to the inauguration of President Roosevelt, whom he had first met as Secretary of the Navy during the First World War, and whom he had since come to regard as the greatest president in United States history. Roosevelt's reception was cool however, and his only comment on *The Great Dictator* was to complain at the difficulties it had caused with pro-Axis countries in Latin America. As part of the celebrations Chaplin was to broadcast the final speech from *The Great Dictator* to a radio audience of sixty million. In the middle of it, perhaps from nerves, his throat went dry and his voice broke; it was two minutes before anyone could find some water in a folded sheet of paper so that he could continue. He carried it off triumphantly, and the audience filled the hiatus with applause; but it was the kind of nightmare of embarrassment that always haunted him.

On his return to Hollywood in February 1941 Chaplin had to concern himself not only with the Kustoff suit against *Modern Times*, but also with two insubstantial but irritating suits relating to *The Great Dictator*.

He remained a favourite target of the Federal tax authorities. This time their claim for a large supplementary payment was thrown out of court, while Chaplin was upheld in his contention that he had overpaid by $24,938. The court victory did not lessen the irritation or prevent unfavourable publicity: in 1947 the vituperative Westbrook Pegler, in his syndicated column 'Fair Enough' (*sic*) would interpret the judgement as showing Chaplin 'caught in the act of cheating the Government of an enormous debt for taxes'. It was hardly surprising that Chaplin willingly returned to New York on 26 March 1941, to appear as a character witness for Joseph M. Schenck who was being sued for income tax evasion. This time Chaplin remained in New York a month. His son Charles believed that he stayed on because he was considering a story about immigrants in New York which he thought of filming there, with Paulette as his leading lady. Charles Junior considered that this idea was the nucleus of *A King in New York*, though nothing seems to have been written at this time either on this story, or on another idea about the love of a drunken has-been star for a little chorus girl who doesn't even know he exists – perhaps the prototype for *Limelight*.

He returned to California on 30 April, but for the next six weeks stayed away from the studio. He was lonely, dispirited, and given to expressing dissatisfaction with his achievements. He enjoyed the companionship of his sons more than at any other time in his life. They were often taken along as chaperons when he dined with actresses who were often nearer their age than their father's. One date at this time was the 22-year-old Carole Landis, who had just arrived at stardom but was to commit suicide in 1948 at the age of twenty-nine. Another was the Viennese-born actress Hedy Lamarr, who had just co-starred with Clark Gable in two films. Although they could never have been regarded as 'dating', Chaplin and Garbo had a high mutual regard: she laughed with abandon at his jokes and impersonations; he regularly proposed films that they should do together – wonderful fantasies with which she played along happily if sceptically.

Chaplin seems at this period to have become unusually gregarious, largely as a result of his passion for tennis. His old Sunday ritual of quiet English teas was now supplanted by weekly tennis parties which grew larger and larger, as friends brought friends, and became a *rendezvous* for the Hollywood élite. The most welcome guests were the great professional players of the time, Budge, Perry, Tilden,

Pauline Betz and Helen Wills. Most of the domestic staff had Sunday free, but the entertainment always included tea and coffee, chicken sandwiches and the indispensable crumpets. Among the guests in this early summer of 1941 was Joan Barry.

At this time she was twenty-two. As Joan Berry she had arrived in Hollywood from Brooklyn in 1940, badly screen-struck but with no prospects. She was working as a waitress when she had her break, and was picked out by J. Paul Getty, the oil millionaire, as pretty enough to form part of the female entourage to accompany him to Mexico for the inauguration of Avila Camacho. In Mexico she caught the attention of a veteran film executive, A. C. Blumenthal, who gave her a letter of introduction to Tim Durant. Durant invited her and another girl to dine with himself and Chaplin. Chaplin thought her cheerful and pleasant, but attached no importance to the encounter. Next Sunday Durant brought her to the weekly tennis party. Chaplin invited them to dinner at Romanoffs; after that Joan Barry pursued him with a persistence which, although her eagerness made him uneasy, eventually won through. She was by no means unattractive, and Chaplin found himself involved in an affair with her.

His uneasiness about the girl was dissipated when he discovered, as he thought, that she had acting talent. Sinclair Lewis and Sir Cedric Hardwicke, who had played the leading role of Canon Skerritt in the New York production, drew his attention to Paul Vincent Carroll's play *Shadow and Substance*, and Chaplin decided it would make a good film subject. One evening Joan Barry read the part of Brigid to him with such effect that he at once made screen tests of her. Having bought the screen rights of the play for $20,000, at the end of June he put Joan Barry under a year's contract. Chaplin remembered that she was paid $250 a week; but though his memory was rarely at fault in matters of money the sum seems rather high. The salary of $75 rising to $100, which Charles Junior remembered, seems more in accordance with Chaplin studio scales.

There is no question about Chaplin's sincerity in believing that he could make Joan Barry into an actress. He had certainly neither the need nor the temperament to waste money wooing girls with contracts, even had there been any cause to woo Barry, who so determinedly threw herself at him. He said, and no doubt meant it, that she had 'all the qualities of a new Maude Adams' and told his sons, 'She has a quality, an ethereal something that's truly marvellous . . . a talent as great as any I've seen in my whole life . . .' Chaplin sent

Barry to Max Reinhardt's drama school, paid for elaborate dental work for her, and showed off her talents in Shakespearean snippets at parties.

Durant and other friends became alarmed at signs of Barry's mental instability before Chaplin himself apparently noticed it. By the spring of 1942 the signs could not be ignored. She began to drive up to the house, very drunk, in the small hours, and on one occasion crashed her Cadillac in the drive. On at least one occasion she began smashing windows when Chaplin refused to open up to her. Abhorring drunkenness, Chaplin was particularly anxious that, as an employee of the studios, her escapades should not become public. He discovered that she had not been attending the Reinhardt classes for weeks.

By mutual agreement the contract was cancelled on 22 May 1942 (it was due to expire on 25 July). As part of the settlement, Chaplin paid off $5000 of Barry's debts, and provided one-way tickets for her and her mother to return to New York, which they did on 5 October. Chaplin hoped and believed that he was at last rid of this unfortunate and troublesome girl.

In June 1941 Chaplin returned to work at the studio for the first time since the completion of *The Great Dictator*. Much of the rest of that year was taken up in preparing a sound re-issue of *The Gold Rush*. Chaplin wrote a new musical accompaniment, which was recorded under the direction of Max Terr; the titles were replaced by a commentary spoken by Chaplin himself. The words of the commentary were largely similar to the original titles: throughout the film Chaplin calls the hero 'The Little Fellow'. Chaplin brought in an editor, Harold McGhean, and trimmed the film slightly, excluding, besides the sub-titles, fifty-seven feet (thirty-eight seconds at normal sound speed of twenty-four frames per second) from the original length. The major change was the lingering fade-out kiss between Chaplin and Georgia Hale, modified to a chaster ending in which they simply walk off hand in hand.

Throughout 1942, and even after the departure of Barry, he continued to work on the script of *Shadow and Substance*. In Chaplin's hands Paul Vincent Carroll's play could have been a fascinating film subject. Written in 1934, the play was produced at the Abbey Theatre, Dublin in January 1937. It is the story of Brigid, a simple Irish girl who sees visions of her namesake, the holy Saint Brigid, and who works in the household of the Reverend Canon Thomas Skerritt. The Canon's two assistant priests represent the poles of rational and superstitious faith. A riot in the local town over the same conflict of belief results in Brigid's death, and leads the Canon to question his own faith and his sinful pride.

Chaplin's adaptation as completed late in 1942 is excellent, though he is much less interested in the issues of Catholicism than in the human and humanist content of the play. Clearly, sympathetic chords were touched in him by lines like 'Every year scores of decent Christians in America sprinkle negroes with petrol and burn them because they love God and his justice.' The film script retains the main dramatic line, while reducing the dialogue by at least one third, and reorganizing a number of the minor characters.

It concludes with a song, which seems to be Chaplin's own addition to the text:

Ecce homo
Ecce homo
His crown
Just a barren wreath of thorns
There in the darkness
He wore
Just a barren wreath of thorns

But in the starlight
I saw
A rose
So red
Blooming on his crown of thorns.

Glory
Glory
A rose
So red a rose
Blooming on his crown of thorns.

On the back of this last page of the script, Chaplin has added some manuscript notes, including reflections on humour. It is not clear if they are notes for additional dialogue or simply *aides-mémoire*:

> Tensions are vital to life. One should never completely relax unless one wants to feel the poetry of slowly dying.
>
> Nonsense is not the proper word for humour. Fun is more appropriate . . .

> Wisdom is the seed of humour.
>
> Humour is the gauge that indicates excess in statement, action, attitude or manner.

On 7 December 1941 the Japanese attacked Pearl Harbour and America entered the war on the Allied side. This caused Chaplin domestic disruption since the Japanese servants were immediately interned. The house was re-staffed with English, whom Chaplin found tiresomely slow after more than twenty years of the swift, efficient, intuitive attentions of the Japanese. Spiritually the war affected Chaplin deeply, and both his sons were soon to be drafted for service. He was particularly chagrined by the widespread anti-Soviet feeling among many Americans who were happy to watch the mounting Russian casualties on the Eastern Front on the principle that in time it would produce the mutual destruction of both Nazis and Communists. Chaplin was eager to contribute his own war effort.

His opportunity came in May 1942. He received a telephone call from the American Committee for Russian War Relief asking if he could stand in for Ambassador Davies, who was ill, at a mass meeting in San Francisco the following day. He agreed, but as the time for his performance approached was overtaken by his old stage-fright at the prospect of facing an audience. He was not reassured by learning that he was expected to hold the platform for an hour. He was helped however by a couple of glasses of champagne and by the irritation he felt at the timidity of the preceding speakers, careful not to appear too enthusiastic about the Soviet ally. When it came to his turn, Chaplin startled his audience of between eight and ten thousand people by addressing them as 'Comrades!' and then going on to explain, 'I assume there are many Russians here tonight, and the way your countrymen are fighting and dying at this very moment, it is an honour and a privilege to call you comrades.' The enthusiasm of the audience spurred him on to an excited Shakespearean paraphrase:

> I am not a Communist. I am a human being, and I think I know the reactions of human beings. The Communists are no different from anyone else; whether they lose an arm or a leg, they suffer as all of us do, and die as all of us die. And the Communist mother is the same as any other mother. When she receives the tragic news that her sons will not return, she weeps as other mothers weep. I do not have to be a Communist to know that. And at this moment Russian mothers are doing a lot of weeping and their sons a lot of dying . . .

The excitement of both speaker and audience escalated, and as a finale Chaplin called upon the enthusiastic multitude to send ten thousand telegrams to the President demanding the opening of a second front in Europe: 'Stalin wants it, Roosevelt has called for it – so let's all call for it – let's open a second front now!' Chaplin's fears that he might have gone too far – even without considering the dubious military implications of a second front at that juncture – were not dispelled by John Garfield's wondering remark at a dinner party after the event: 'You have a lot of courage!'

Dan James and his wife Lilith were present that night, and Lilith recalls that after the speech, 'everyone was scared of him, so they handed him over to us. It was a tremendous speech. It was a very bold political stand to take at that time.'

The experience seems to have given Chaplin a new taste for public speaking. Even he was not clear to what extent he was inspired by idealism or by the rediscovery of the heady and fearsome stimulus of applause. (In *Limelight*, when Terry challenges Calvero's assertion that he hates the theatre he replies: 'I hate the sight of blood, but I still have it in my veins.') Two months after the San Francisco speech he was asked to address a mass meeting in Madison Square by radio-telephone. The rally had been organized by the Council of the Congress of Industrial Organizations and was attended by sixty thousand trades unionists and others. Chaplin spent the whole of the previous day (21 July) preparing his speech, which lasted fourteen minutes and was heard with rapt attention. Again he called for a second front.

> Let us aim for victory in the spring. You in the factories, you in the fields, you in uniforms, you citizens of the world, let us work and fight towards that end. You, official Washington, and you, official London, let us make this our aim – victory in the spring!

'As usual,' commented Charles Junior, 'his enthusiasm ran away with him.' Despite (or perhaps, Chaplin felt, because of) Jack Warner's advice to refuse, he accepted an invitation to speak at a rally in Carnegie Hall organized by the Artists' Front to Win the War, even at that time regarded as a dangerously leftist organization. However, the platform was shared with such politically respectable celebrities as Orson Welles, Pearl Buck and Rockwell Kent. Chaplin arrived in New York on 15 October, the day before the rally, accompanied by Tim Durant and Edward Chaney, his new English valet. In New York he was met by Charles Junior, who recalled his father's habitual pre-performance nerves and nausea. There was also an amiable reunion with Paulette, whose divorce had become effective on 4 June.

Chaplin's platform appearance was the usual sucess. On returning to the Waldorf-Astoria he discovered that Joan Barry had been telephoning repeatedly. She called again, and when later she arrived at the hotel Chaplin took care that Durant stayed with them throughout the visit which he later recalled as lasting no more than half an hour. Barry told them that she had now moved into the Pierre Hotel, owned by J. Paul Getty.

Chaplin stayed on in New York for ten days after the rally, though he sensed that since his Second Front speeches he was no longer welcome at the homes of some of his former hosts. Speaking invitations continued to come, and to be accepted; conscientious as he was, Chaplin began to spend more time on the preparation of each successive speech. He spent much of the previous week dictating an address for a 'Salute to Our Russian Ally' meeting held at Orchestra Hall Chicago on 25 November. From Chicago he went on to New York to speak at an 'Arts for Russia' dinner at the Hotel Pennsylvania on 3 December. This brief but in the long run highly significant phase of Chaplin's activities was rounded off early in 1943. In February he prepared a speech to be recorded at the office of the Soviet consul for subsequent broadcast in Russia. On Sunday 7 March he made a speech which was transmitted to Britain from the Los Angeles studio of CBS. It was presented as a Transatlantic Call to Lambeth, and painted a vivid picture of the London that Chaplin remembered from his boyhood. He concluded: 'I remember the Lambeth streets, the New Cut and the Lambeth Walk, Vauxhall Road. They were hard streets, and one couldn't say they were paved with gold. Nevertheless, the people who lived there are made of pretty good metal.'

Now Joan Barry returned to Hollywood, apparently using $300 Chaplin had given her at the Waldorf-Astoria to pay the fare. After pestering him with telephone calls, on the night of 23 December Barry used a ladder to break into Chaplin's house, where she produced a gun and threatened to kill herself. Chaplin's distress was aggravated when his two sons arrived at the house in the middle of the affair. Unwilling to involve them, he asked them to go to their rooms and only told them the following morning what had occurred. Barry was later to assert that intimacy had taken place on this occasion. Chaplin's version, that he locked the door between his room and the bathroom which lay between the rooms they occupied, seems, in the circumstances, more credible. She left the following morning when Chaplin gave her some money. A week or so later she was back, and this time Chaplin was obliged to call the police. She was given a ninety-day suspended sentence and ordered to leave town. An employee of the Chaplin studios handed her a railroad ticket and $100. In May 1943, six months pregnant, she was back again. Chaplin believed that Hedda Hopper had advised her to get publicity by having herself arrested, which her second court appearance achieved for her. She was sentenced to thirty days for vagrancy, spending most of the time in hospital on account of her condition.

By the purely Chaplinesque twist of fate, at the very moment that this disturbed young woman was tormenting him and storing up still worse trouble for the future, Chaplin met Oona O'Neill. Oona was the daughter of Eugene O'Neill by his second wife Agnes Boulton, but was only a child when her parents divorced. Oona was gifted with beauty, charm and acute intelligence tempered by remarkable shyness. In the spring of 1942, not quite seventeen, she had been nominated Debutante Number One of the year. Having taken her Vassar entrance examinations, she had decided instead upon an acting career, and arrived in Hollywood where her mother and stepfather were already living. She made a screen test for a role in *The Girl From Leningrad* which was to be produced by Eugene Frenke, the husband of Anna Sten. The test still survives to indicate what a striking screen personality she might have been. The beauty is both radiant and fragile, the personality at once diffident and eager. Even in this forty-year-old fragment of film, the presence remains vivid.

Her agent, Minna Wallace, knew that Chaplin was looking for someone to play Brigid in *Shadow and Substance*. She mentioned Oona O'Neill to Chaplin, who was not optimistic about the prospect of the daughter of America's most celebrated tragic dramatist. Minna Wallace however arranged a dinner party at which she and Oona were joined by Durant (whose father had been a friend of O'Neill's) and Chaplin. Chaplin was instantly enchanted by Oona's looks, appeal, gentleness and smile, but he was still nervous that the role of Brigid was beyond an actress of her years and small experience. Had he at this time seen the Eugene Frenke screen test he might well have felt that, different as she was from the voluptuous Joan Barry, she could have brought a quality of magic to the role.

According to Rollie Totheroh, shortly after the meeting Oona herself arrived at the studio and with that mixture of timidity and determination that is so bewildering and appealing in her refused to be put off by all the efforts of Totheroh and Alf Reeves, who were understandably nervous, after the recent experience with Joan Barry, at the arrival of another youngster who looked even less than her seventeen and a half years. Meanwhile Minna Wallace alarmed Chaplin with reports that Fox were interested in her client. Chaplin offered Oona a contract.

Charles Junior and his brother were at once won by Oona when they met her at the house, but quickly realized that they had an insuperable rival: 'Whenever Oona was with our father a rapt expression would come into her eyes. She would sit quietly, hanging on his every word. Most women are charmed by Dad, but in Oona's case it was different. She worshipped him, drinking in every word he spoke, whether it was about his latest script, the weather or some bit of philosophy. She seldom spoke, but every now and then she would come up with one of those penetrating remarks that impressed even our father with her insight.'[1] The extraordinary, perfect love affair that resulted and which brought Chaplin happiness that compensated for everything else that had happened and would happen to him was not long delayed. Chaplin recalled that – despite his nervousness about the discrepancy in their age – they decided to marry after completing the filming of *Shadow and Substance*. The decision must have been rapid. According to the studio records, *Shadow and Substance* was definitively shelved on 29 December 1942, no more than two months after the meeting at Minna Wallace's house.

Already by November 1942 Chaplin was working on a new idea, which was eventually to become *Monsieur Verdoux*, and no doubt it is the much richer possibilities it offered which made him decide to scrap a year's work on the *Shadow and Substance* script. The idea had taken seed when Orson Welles visited the house and suggested he would like to direct a documentary reconstruction of the career of Landru, the celebrated French wife-murderer, with Chaplin playing the principal role. Welles had as yet done no work on a script, and a few days afterwards Chaplin telephoned him to say that his suggestions had given him the idea for a comedy. Although the film would have only the remotest connexion with the real-life Landru,

Chaplin suggested that Welles might accept a payment of $5000, since his proposition had originally stimulated the idea. The offer was not in any way altruistic: Chaplin had by this time had too much experience of plagiarism claims, and wanted to forestall any such possibility in this case. Welles agreed with the proviso that, after seeing the film, he should have the right to a screen credit: 'Idea suggested by Orson Welles'. Chaplin agreed, though in later years he resented Welles's pride in being the author of the germinal idea for *Verdoux*. Chaplin worked almost continuously on the script from November 1942 until the start of production in April 1946. The production was referred to as *Landru* until March 1943, when it became known as 'Production No 7: Bluebeard'. The title then became simply *Verdoux*; *Monsieur Verdoux* seems to have been finally adopted in June 1946.

The early part of 1943 passed pleasantly, without trouble. Oona and her mother spent a lot of time at the house; so did young Charles and Sydney, who were now approaching draft age. In the weeks after Christmas, Chaplin screened *City Lights*, *The Circus*, *The Idle Class* and *Shoulder Arms* at the studio for the O'Neills and other friends. There was a portent of trouble in May when Joan Barry telephoned the house and informed the butler, for no apparent reason, that she was pregnant. On 4 June she gave the same information to the press, this time adding that Chaplin was the father of her unborn child. Thus began a two-year nightmare which was to be described by one Los Angeles attorney, Eugene L. Trope, as 'a landmark in the miscarriage of justice'.

On the day of Joan Barry's announcement to the press her mother, Gertrude Berry, as guardian of the unborn child, filed a paternity suit against Chaplin, asking for $10,000 for pre-natal care, $2500 a month for support of the unborn child, and $5000 court costs. Chaplin's lawyers countered with a brief statement in his name: 'Miss Barry states her unborn child was conceived in December last. The first claim made upon me by Miss Barry was in May and was accompanied by a demand of $150,000. I am not responsible for Miss Barry's condition.' Chaplin claimed that these May demands specified $75,000 for the child and $75,000 for the mother, with nothing for Barry herself, and were made under threat of exposure to the press. Chaplin indignantly refused to settle, even though Tim Durant, who was acting as middleman, was convinced that it was a *bona fide* once and for all settlement. According to Charles Junior,

Chaplin's refusal was not in consideration of money – he was aware that to fight the case would be much more costly, win or lose – but out of a sense of justice: 'He was indignant because he was innocent. It was all part of the strain of stubborn integrity which runs through him and which is such an admirable and exasperating characteristic.'[2]

Californian law on divorce and paternity always gives the benefit of doubt to the woman, and the mere allegation that a man is father is sufficient grounds for forcing him to support both woman and child until settlement of the suit. So the lawyers on both sides agreed and filed with the Superior Court payments to be made pending the outcome of the case. Chaplin agreed to pay $2500 cash and $100 a week for Barry's support, as well as $500 thirty days before the birth, $1000 at the birth and $500 a month for the succeeding four months. For her part, Barry agreed to permit blood tests on the infant to help determine the child's paternity, when it reached the age of four months. As reported by the *New York Times* the Barry lawyers agreed that 'If at least two of the doctors say "no", the suit would be dropped; if they said "maybe" (a positive "yes" is impossible from blood tests) the girl will be free to press her claims.'

The affair provided a field day for the press. Chaplin, to escape reporters or process servers, hid out as soon as the story broke in the home of Eugene Frenke and Anna Sten on Layton Drive, Los Angeles; Oona visited him there and also stayed. It remained a long-standing joke with the Frenkes that the lovers were so preoccupied that they forgot to repay the Frenkes' ration coupons which they used up during the stay. They had already decided to marry on 1 June when Oona, having then passed her eighteenth birthday, would no longer need the parental consent which she rightly anticipated would not have been forthcoming from her father, though her mother was wholehearted in her approval of the match. Now Durant and the lawyers felt it would be advisable for Oona to return East until the Barry storm blew over. It was Oona who overruled this, doggedly insisting that at this time more than at any other her place, as the woman Chaplin loved and was loved by, was at his side.

Harry Crocker was entrusted with arrangements for the marriage, and in return was permitted to photograph the ceremony and give the news as an exclusive to his colleague on the Hearst press, Louella Parsons. Always inclined to take a directly contrary view to her arch rival Hedda Hopper, Miss Parsons had remained as friendly towards

Chaplin as Miss Hopper was vituperative – though the peak of Hopper's vilification was yet to come. On Tuesday 15 June Chaplin and Oona, accompanied by Crocker and Catherine Hunter, Chaplin's secretary, drove to Santa Barbara. Soon after eight the following morning they registered at the court house to receive a license, and then made as rapid a getaway as possible to avoid the press who had already been alerted by the court clerk. They were quietly married by a 78-year-old Justice of the Peace, Clinton Pancoast Moore. When they got outside they discovered that Mr Moore had taken down Chaplin's name as 'Chapman'. It was a mistake few people had made in the thirty years since Keystone had telegraphed the Karno Company in quest of a new star. Mr Moore obligingly corrected it.

Chaplin and Oona stayed on in Santa Barbara almost six weeks, and miraculously the press failed to hunt them out. Chaplin veered from depression to bliss. Unrecognized, they went for country walks in the evenings, and Oona read aloud to relieve Chaplin's darker moods.

They returned to Beverly Hills on 26 July, and Chaplin immediately resumed work on the script, now called *Bluebeard*. There was other work to be done at the studio also. Brigadier-General Osborn, Director of the Special Services Division of the army, had requested that Chaplin might make prints of *Shoulder Arms* available to the Armed Forces Institute Film Services. Chaplin was delighted that his 25-year-old picture was still reckoned to have a value for morale, and Totheroh set about revising and restoring a perfect new negative. In January Chaplin saw the new print, as well as *The Gold Rush*, in the company of Oona and a party of friends, and decided that it would be a good idea to do the same for all his old films, in each case assembling the negatives to obtain a good protection print for special use if required at any time. The negatives, when placed in proper order, were to be deposited with Pathé's Hollywood laboratory. Totheroh spent most of the next year or so preparing these definitive negatives and library prints of the First National films. They were to prove invaluable years later when Chaplin decided to reissue a number of his early films with music.

On the night of 2 October 1943 Joan Barry gave birth to a baby girl, whom she named Carol Ann. Meanwhile the Federal courts were concocting a new case against Chaplin in relation to Barry, and during the next weeks were taking depositions from dozens of witnesses, including Chaplin's entire staff, his sons, and even Oona, who had never met Joan Barry. On 10 February 1944 Chaplin was indicted by a Federal grand jury. The charges were that he had violated the Mann Act, a piece of legislation dating from 1910 and designed to combat commercial prostitution. The Act made it illegal to transport a woman across state lines for immoral purposes, and Chaplin was alleged on 5 October 1942 to have 'feloniously transported and caused to be transported Joan Barry from Los Angeles to the city of New York . . . with the intent and purpose of engaging in illicit sex relations.' A further charge joined Chaplin with six other people, including the police judge who was involved in Barry's first arrest on vagrancy charges, on a rather obscure indictment of conspiring to deprive Miss Barry of her civil rights.

The Mann Act charge was itself pretty far-fetched and depended on proving that Chaplin engaged in sexual relations with Miss Barry on the occasion of his visit to New York for his Second Front speech, and that moreover that had been his intention in paying her fare to New York a couple of weeks earlier. At the trial which began on 25 February, Chaplin's counsel, the celebrated lawyer Jerry Giesler, pinpointed the absurdity of the Government's position. He asked the jury in his summing up if it was likely that Chaplin would transport Barry 3000 miles for the purpose of a single alleged intimacy when she 'would have given her body to him at any time or place'. There was, added Giesler, 'no more evidence of Mann Act violation than there is evidence of murder'. The Government, however, pressed its case doggedly with a procession of witnesses. Barry went on the stand first to assert that intimacy had taken place during the New York visit, and that this meeting had been discussed before her departure from Hollywood for New York. The prosecuting attorney also called the travel agent who had supplied one-way tickets to New York for Barry and her mother; three railroad men who testified that the tickets had been used; the credit manager of the Waldorf-Astoria who confirmed that Chaplin was registered there, as everyone agreed he was, at the time under discussion; the night elevator operator from the hotel; and Chaplin's valet, Edward Chaney. Giesler, for the defence, cross-examined Barry about her visits to Tulsa. J. Paul Getty was called to testify for the defence that he knew Barry and had frequented her company in 1941, and in Tulsa in November 1942.

The last witness, on 30 March, was Chaplin himself, who denied any immoral intent in providing railroad tickets for Joan Barry and her mother, and denied any intimacy with her at any period after

May 1942. Giesler's memoirs recall Chaplin as 'the best witness I've ever seen in a law court. He was effective even when he wasn't being cross-examined but was merely sitting there, lonely and forlorn, at a far end of the counsel table. He is so small that only the toes of his shoes touched the floor.'

The jury of seven women and five men were out almost three hours and took four ballots to arrive at a unanimous vote of 'Not Guilty'. After the trial the judge and the prosecution attorney, Charles Carr, congratulated Chaplin, and he shook hands with each member of the jury and thanked them in turn. He was too moved to speak when one of them, Edythe Lewis, told him, 'It's all right, Charlie. It's still a free country.' At Summit Drive Oona fainted when she heard the news on the radio.

The verdict was an immense relief; but Chaplin had suffered much from the days sitting in court hearing the attorneys sieving through the unsavoury evidence of Barry's love life. During preliminary hearings he had also been furious at the indignity of being fingerprinted while, quite irregularly, the press were permitted to photograph him. This incident was stored up for subsequent use in *A King in New York*.

Between the indictment and the trial, Joan Barry's baby had been submitted to blood tests conducted by three physicians, one representing Barry, one representing Chaplin, and one a neutral observer, Dr Newton Evans. The results were released by the attorneys for both parties on 15 February 1944, and showed conclusively that Chaplin could not be the father of the child. Research had established that parents of blood type O (Chaplin) and A (Joan Barry) cannot produce a child of blood type B, as the baby proved to be. As a result of the tests, Chaplin's lawyer Loyd Wright optimistically filed for a dismissal of the paternity suit. The motion was overruled by Superior Court Judge Stanley Mosk, who enigmatically declared that 'the ends of justice will best be served by a full and fair trial of the issues'. Referring to the previous judge's approval of the blood test, when Mrs Berry's original suit had been filed, Judge Mosk said that it did not appear to him that the court then intended 'more than mere approval of the blood test for the parties and the infant without expressing ultimate determination of the law suit'.

Mrs Berry had of course been party to the agreement to drop the suit if the tests proved negative. This was neatly sidestepped by taking the guardianship of Carol Ann away from her grandmother and assigning it to the court. It was now therefore the Court of Los Angeles that was suing Chaplin on Carol Ann's behalf. The new trial was set for December 1944. Convinced as he was that the results of the blood test must wholly vindicate him, the months of waiting were still an anxious period for Chaplin.

Life with Oona, who was now pregnant with her first child, provided joyful distraction. In May they spent a ten-day holiday in Palm Springs, and passed most of June on the East Coast. On 1 August their first child, Geraldine was born. Shortly afterwards they advertised for a nanny and among the applicants was Edith McKenzie, a Scot who had worked for many years in the United States. When Oona asked her on the phone how old she was Miss McKenzie said evasively, 'Why don't you wait and see me for yourself?' (She was just past forty). Oona saw her and took to this slim, forthright, capable woman at once. Renamed 'Kay-Kay' a few months later by the infant Geraldine, she was to remain for over forty years an indispensable member of the household, and every Chaplin child's closest friend and confidante.

Kay-Kay vividly remembers how Chaplin watched and held his first daughter with as much joyful wonder as a twenty-year-old first-time father. In fact his two sons, now grown up, were both in the army. Less than three weeks after Geraldine was born there was a melancholy reminder of his first unhappy marriage: Mildred Harris died at the age of forty-three in the Cedars of Lebanon Hospital. Chaplin sent a spray of orchids, roses and gladioli to the funeral.

Lion Feuchtwanger, who was among Chaplin's current friends, had commented after the Mann Act trial, 'You are the one artist of the theatre who will go down in American history as having aroused the political antagonism of a whole nation.' On this score Chaplin was reassured when General Eisenhower personally requested the preparation of a dubbed French version of *The Great Dictator* for release in newly-liberated France under the Office of War Information. Chaplin happily gave his consent, and the required prints and tracks were shipped on 21 November.

The Carol Ann Barry paternity trial opened on 13 December 1944 before Judge Henry Willis. Chaplin was so confident that the scientific evidence must win the day that he did not this time hire the skilful Giesler (in the previous trial some friends had advised him that to hire such a heavyweight criminal pleader in itself might imply guilt) but a capable, unsensational attorney, Charles A. (Pat) Millikan. Neither Chaplin nor Millikan had reckoned on being faced by Joseph Scott as attorney for the prosecution. Scott was a craggy-faced old lawyer of the all-stops-out histrionic school. His ardent belief in God, Country and the Republican Party added the strength of personal feeling to his pursuit of the defendant. Scott put Joan Barry on the stand, before a jury of seven women and five men, to describe the events of the night she broke into Chaplin's house brandishing a pistol. She explained that she told Chaplin on that occasion, 'I am almost out of my mind. I have waited and waited. You haven't called me. I don't know what to do.' She insisted that the child was conceived on that occasion, and that she had had relations with no other man since she had met Chaplin. Before she left in the morning of 24 December, she said, Chaplin promised to pay her a regular $25 per week. It was at that point that she had handed over the gun to him. Scott examined Chaplin, who insisted that there had been no intimacy between him and the girl since early in 1942, and that when Barry had told him that she was pregnant and he was responsible, he had replied that it was 'impossible'. Scott's final stroke was to have the jury gaze for three quarters of a minute at Chaplin and Carol Ann, held in her mother's arms and standing at a distance of eight feet from Chaplin, urging them to recognize facial resemblances. The child was fourteen months old.

Millikan's defence was in principle much stronger, relying simply upon two main witnesses. Dr Newton Evans, the independent physician who had conducted the blood tests, demonstrated the laboratory methods used to arrive at the definite conclusion that Chaplin could not be the father of Carol Ann. A Tulsa lawyer, O. C. Lassiter, described a conversation he had had with Barry on 28 January 1943, when he was Assistant County Counsel and was dismissing an unspecified charge against her. She had told him that she had 'gone overboard' for an oil man – presumably Getty – whom she had accompanied from California to Florida in November 1942; that she had come to Tulsa to be with him, and had spent two nights with him at the Mayo Hotel in Tulsa when he had suggested marrying her if he could get rid of his wife. He had now left, however, and she could not find him. In court Barry denied that such a conversation had taken place.

Logic may not have been on Scott's side but he preferred to appeal to emotion. Throughout the trial he persistently abused Chaplin in terms which shocked even experienced reporters, and which had their effect in wounding and exciting Chaplin. Some instances of his invective were 'grey-headed old buzzard', 'little runt of a Svengali' and 'lecherous hound', Chaplin lied, he said, 'like a cheap cockney cad'. 'The reptile looked upon her [Barry] as so much carrion. Finally he took her up to the house and read her a script about Bluebeard' (a reference which must relate to one of the later meetings of Chaplin and Barry). Scott evidently impressed part of the jury and, more important, he threw Chaplin off balance. At one point Chaplin was stung into crying out to the judge, 'Your Honour, I've committed no crime. I'm only human. But this man is trying to make a monster out of me.' Scott succeeded in manoeuvring Chaplin into a state in which the audience saw him as a man angry and cornered. In his final argument he exhorted the jury:

> There has been no one to stop Chaplin in his lecherous conduct all these years – except you. Wives and mothers all over the country are watching to see you stop him dead in his tracks. You'll sleep well the night you give this baby a name – the night you show him the law means him as well as the bums on Skid Row.

If Scott's abuse was to be taken seriously, it was a name the child would hardly thank them for giving her. Chaplin, along with everyone who knew him, was stunned by this unjust vilification. Even taking into account the publicity surrounding his unfortunate divorces, Chaplin had led a life of exceptional discretion by Hollywood standards, and his time with Paulette demonstrated his essential yearning for domesticity. The sticky label of 'libertine' was rarely more unjustly applied.

The jury may have been impressed by Scott's oratory, but they were less convinced by Joan Barry's evidence. After four hours and forty minutes of deliberation the jury could not reach a verdict: the vote was seven to five in favour of acquittal. Judge Clarence L. Kincaid offered to arbitrate. Scott for the prosecution was prepared to accept the offer, but Chaplin (who had missed the final days of the trial because of a foot injury which hospitalized him) was set on complete exoneration, and refused.

The retrial lasted from 4 April to 17 April 1944, and was heard before Judge Kincaid. It was adjourned on 14 April because of the death of President Roosevelt. This time the jury consisted of eleven women and one man. Joseph Scott stepped up his emotional assault upon the jury even more than at the first trial. The jury, in the words of a writer in *Southern California Law Review*, 'let sentimental consideration turn logic out of doors, and failed dismally in its task of weighing the evidence.' They brought in a verdict of 'Guilty' by an eleven to one vote. The stand-out juror was a housewife called Mary James, who said of her vote: 'I am not upholding Mr Chaplin at all . . . Only I don't think he was the father of the child.'

The evidence of the blood tests was totally disregarded. At that time only ten states, which did not include California, allowed blood tests to be introduced in evidence to disprove paternity. The legal notoriety of the Chaplin case may have encouraged wider subsequent recognition of the test. In 1953 California introduced legislation to prevent pursuance of paternity cases where blood tests had conclusively proved that the defendant could not be father of the child.

Judge Kincaid ruled as a result of the verdict that Chaplin should make payments of $75 a week to Carol Ann – who was now legally entitled to adopt the name of Chaplin – with increases to $100 as her needs grew, until she reached the age of twenty-one. Apart from that the Berry/Barry family finally disappeared from Chaplin's life, though the damage they had done and the embarrassment and smears that he had suffered as a result of the trial were permanent. A year or so later Joan Barry married and had two more children before separating from her husband. In 1953 she was found in a dazed state in Torrance, California, whither she had once trekked from Mexico. She was committed to Patton State Hospital for care.

Through his lawyers, Wright and Millikan, Chaplin filed a motion for a new trial, but after four weeks' consideration the motion was denied on 6 June 1945. Though a further trial might have gratified his sense of justice, Chaplin was repelled and exhausted by the affair, and he knew that nothing could now retrieve the damage to the reputation he had so valued throughout his professional life. His consolation was his new family and, as always, work. He took enormous pleasure in screening for Oona his old films, many of which she had never had the opportunity to see. Apart from all her other qualities, Oona was the best audience he had ever had. However often she saw his films she would giggle with as little inhibition as any child at Charlie's antics; Chaplin, who always saw himself on screen with an objective, critical detachment, would join her.

Monsieur Verdoux

Despite the irritations and interruptions of the Barry affair, work had continued on the script of *Monsieur Verdoux*, and preparations for production began in 1945. Practically none of Chaplin's earlier drafts and working notes for *Verdoux* have survived, so it is not possible to trace the kind of evolution which we can discover in the case of his other films. Only three manuscript pages in Chaplin's hand, and headed 'Notes for Verdoux', somehow escaped whatever was the fate of the rest of the papers. The use of the name indicates that the notes belong to a late stage of the writing. The name Verdoux seems not to have been adopted until the latter part of 1945 – the main character was originally called 'Varnay', a name which still crops up, through secretarial slips, in the finished script. It is not clear whether the aphoristic notes are suggestions for dialogue, or whether they represent reflections on the philosophic content of the film. In either event it does not seem far-fetched to see in the tone of irony and disillusion Chaplin's personal reaction to his recent months in the pillory:

> When all the world turns against a man he becomes holy.
>
> Where there are no facts, sentiments prevail.
>
> Virtues are less acquired than vices.
>
> It is more important to understand crime than to condemn it.
>
> Good is in everything – even in evil.
>
> The most profound eloquence is silence, a deep wordless understanding.
>
> Evil has its attendant good.
>
> In the last analysis there is no reason for anything.
>
> Violence is patience's last resort.
>
> Soul is the possible, and the world is the actual. This concept is the deep inner feeling in man.
>
> The soul is the becoming.
> The world is the become.
> Life is the state of becoming.
>
> The soul is the still to be accomplished.
> The world is the accomplished,
> And life is the accomplishing.

The most compleat concept of meaning is beauty.

Living becomes a habit which at times I wish I could break.

A reputation is the concern of cooks and butlers.

The surviving versions of the script are almost exactly in the form of the finished film, except for an opening scene which was never shot, and some emendations to the dialogue required by the censorship of the Breen Office. The only resemblance to the story of Landru is Verdoux's profession, which is that of murdering rich widows and investing their fortunes. The front for his operations is an apparently inoperative furniture business. When he is not otherwise occupied by his demanding business, Verdoux returns to his country cottage, cherished child and invalid wife. He meets a beautiful young woman, down on her luck and working as a prostitute, whom he takes home, intending to use her as a guinea pig for a new poison, but instead persuades her that life is after all worth living. When he meets her again years later, their roles in life have changed: she has become the mistress of an armaments manufacturer, whose business is flourishing on the eve of a new world war; Verdoux's careful investments have been wiped out since the Stock Market crash. At this point Verdoux's past catches up on him and he is arrested and put on trial. At his trial and execution he shows mild surprise rather than remorse, since his mode of life has only carried to logical extremes the philosophies on which contemporary capitalist society is built.

JUDGE: (*to Verdoux*) Have you anything to say before sentence is passed upon you?

VERDOUX: (*rises*) Yes, Monsieur . . . I have . . . However remiss the prosecutor has been in paying me any compliment, he at least admits that I have brains. (*turning to prosecutor*) Thank you, Monsieur . . . I have . . . And for thirty years I used them honestly, but after that nobody wanted them. So I was forced to go into business for myself. But I can assure you it was no life of ease. I worked very hard for what I got, and for the little I received I gave very much . . . As for being a mass murderer, does not the world encourage it? Is it not building weapons of destruction for the sole purpose of mass killing? Has it not blown unsuspecting women and children to pieces, and done it very scientifically? As a mass killer, I am an amateur by comparison . . . To be shocked by the nature of my crime is nothing but a pretence . . . a sham!

> You wallow in murder . . . you legalize it . . . you adorn it with gold braid! You celebrate it and parade it! Killing is the enterprise by which your System prospers . . . upon which your industry thrives. However, I have no desire to lose my temper, because very shortly I shall lose my head . . . Nevertheless, upon leaving this spark of earthly existence, I have this to say . . . I shall see you all very soon.

(This is from the original script: the Breen Office required some cuts to make the speech more acceptable to the mood of post-War America.)

Later, awaiting execution, Verdoux tells a reporter who protests that other people don't conduct their business in Verdoux's way:

> Oh, don't they? That's the history of many a big business. One murder makes a villain . . . millions a hero. Numbers sanctify, my good friend.

In an interview shortly before the release of the picture, Chaplin stated:

> The picture has moral value, I believe. Von Clausewitz said that war is the logical extension of diplomacy; M. Verdoux feels that murder is the logical extension of business. He should express the feeling of the times we live in – out of catastrophe come people like him. He typifies the psychological disease and depression. He is frustrated, bitter, and at the end, pessimistic. But he is never morbid; and the picture is by no means morbid in treatment . . . Under the proper circumstances, murder can be comic.[3]

Under the proper circumstances relations with the Breen Office could be comic too, as well as irritating. Chaplin devotes a dozen pages of his autobiography to his dealings with the Office over *Verdoux*, and the correspondence and a marked copy of the script remain in the Chaplin archive. In initially disapproving the script in its entirety, they said they were passing over 'those elements which seem to be anti-social in their concept and significance . . . the sections of the story in which Verdoux indicts the 'System' and impugns the present-day social structure'. (It is interesting that they failed to acknowledge that the film was supposed to take place in France, between the wars.) The whole nature of Verdoux's *modus vivendi*, they found, had 'about it a distasteful flavour of illicit sex, which in our judgement is not good'. Specific elements to which they raised objection included a scene which suggested that Verdoux had actually slept with one of the 'wives' he had murdered; all dialogue which made it evident that the girl he picked up in the street was a prostitute and later suggestions that she had become prosperous and was the mistress of a munitions manufacturer. They wanted to be sure that

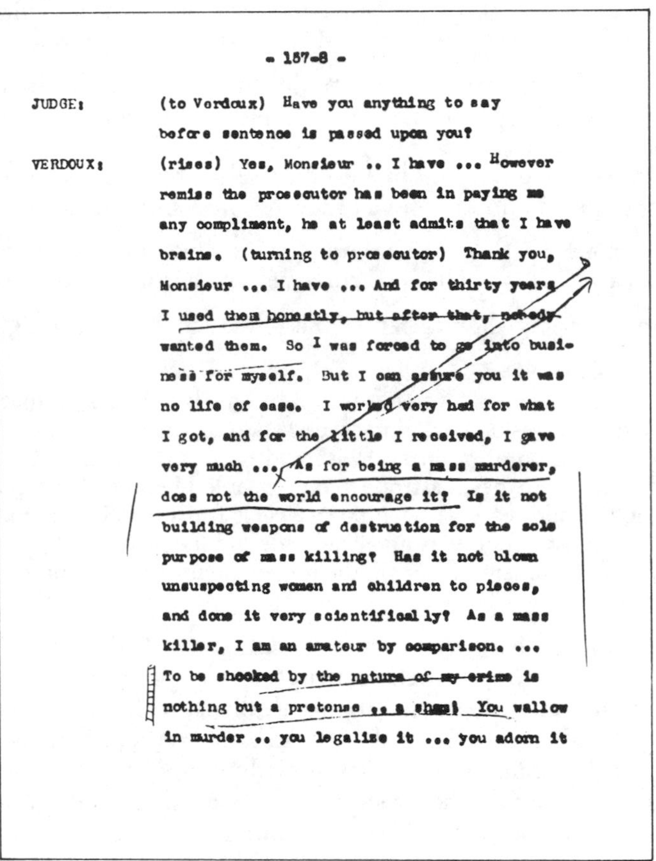

- 157-8 -

JUDGE: (to Verdoux) Have you anything to say before sentence is passed upon you?

VERDOUX: (rises) Yes, Monsieur .. I have ... However remiss the prosecutor has been in paying me any compliment, he at least admits that I have brains. (turning to prosecutor) Thank you, Monsieur ... I have ... And for thirty years I used them honestly, but after that, nobody wanted them. So I was forced to go into business for myself. But I can assure you it was no life of ease. I worked very hard for what I got, and for the little I received, I gave very much ... As for being a mass murderer, does not the world encourage it? Is it not building weapons of destruction for the sole purpose of mass killing? Has it not blown unsuspecting women and children to pieces, and done it very scientifically? As a mass killer, I am an amateur by comparison. ... To be shocked by the nature of my crime is nothing but a pretense .. a sham! You wallow in murder .. you legalize it ... you adorn it

Script for Verdoux's speech from the dock, marked up by the Breen Office.

there was no 'showing of, or suggestion of, toilets in the bathroom', objected to a *double entendre* about 'scraping her bottom'; and required the removal of the word 'voluptuous' and the phrase 'indecent moon' which Chaplin had treasured since he savoured it a quarter of a century before in the company of H. G. Wells.

On 11 March 1946 Chaplin accepted Joseph Breen's invitation to go to his office and discuss the script. Breen himself was amiable and even constructive. Chaplin realized however, from the attitude of one of his assistants, a 'tall, dour young man' who greeted him with the words, 'What have you against the Catholic Church?' that a good deal of their anxiety centred upon Verdoux's exchanges with the priest at the end of the film:

VERDOUX: What can I do for you, my good man?

PRIEST: (*benevolently*) Nothing, my son. I want to help you . . . if I can. I've come to ask you to make your peace with God.

VERDOUX: (*affectionately*) Dear father . . . I am at peace with God . . . my conflict, at this moment, is with Man.

PRIEST: Have you no remorse for your sins?

VERDOUX: Who knows what sin is . . . born, as it was, from heaven . . . from God's fallen angel? Who knows what ultimate destiny it serves? (*with politeness*) After all, what would you be doing without sin?

(*footsteps are heard along the corridor*)

PRIEST: They are coming . . . let me pray for you.

VERDOUX: (*politely*) As you wish. But I don't think these gentlemen want to be kept waiting.

(*enter executioner and prison officials*)

PRIEST: May the Lord have mercy on your soul.

VERDOUX: Why not? After all . . . it belongs to him.

The rejected opening sequence of the film began with a montage of scenes showing American business booming: busy brokers on the stock exchange: a business man in his office, all ready for golf; a millionaire on a luxury yacht. A voice over the action explains, 'In the glorious days of '28, everybody made money except those who worked for it'; and Monsieur Verdoux is seen diligently working away as a clerk in a big Parisian bank. A parallel sequence follows, with the stock exchange in panic, the business man shooting himself, the ruined millionaire falling dead over the side of his yacht, a broker swallowing a cyanide capsule and expiring with a grimace of distaste.

In the bank, Verdoux receives with his pay packet a notice of dismissal and the camera moves in to close-up of a hopeless, tragic face. Over dissolves of Depression scenes, the voice continues, 'In the lean years that followed, many changes occurred in the lives of people . . . millionaires became paupers and commodores became stevedores. But Monsieur Verdoux, ex-bank teller of Paris, became something else, a man of many aliases who, in spite of the depression, did well for himself.' Verdoux is next seen busy and prosperous, an elegant *boulevardier* who now goes to work on his next victim.

As work progressed, Chaplin realized that he needed to place the Stock Market crash and Depression later in the film, to explain Verdoux's ruin. A much simpler Stock Market scene was therefore introduced at a later point, and this beginning was abandoned. In its place Chaplin devised a faster, neater opening. Over a shot of a grave marked 'Henri Verdoux, 1880–1937' his voice is heard saying 'Good evening. I was a bank clerk until the Depression of 1930,' and then goes on laconically to explain the nature of his business.

Few of the old collaborators remained. There was still the ever-faithful Totheroh; and half-brother Wheeler Dryden was now promoted to the post of associate director. The other associate director was Robert Florey, a friend and dedicated admirer for thirty years. Since he had written his first book about Chaplin in 1927, Florey had become a director of some distinction in his own right, and had just enjoyed one of his greatest successes with *The Beast With Five Fingers*. He was proud, even so, to accept a subordinate role on a film directed by his lifelong idol, and for Chaplin he was a valuable asset for the technical advice he was able to offer on the French settings. Henry Bergman, a kind of mascot since 1915, was now too ill to work, and died shortly after shooting had begun. Sydney was living in California again, and Chaplin wanted him to play the role of Detective Morrow who arrests Verdoux but unwisely accepts his hospitality in the shape of a glass of poisoned wine. Sydney's wife Gypsy opposed this, since she did not want to see Sydney worried sick by Charlie's extravagance as, she said, he had been during *The Great Dictator*.

Perhaps at some urging of nostalgia, Chaplin decided that the role of the matronly Madame Grosnay might suit Edna Purviance. Edna, who was now over fifty and many years retired, was as much alarmed as flattered by the prospect. On 18 March 1946 she arrived at the

Chaplin studios for the first time in more than twenty years, during which neither Chaplin nor Totheroh had seen her. The reunion was emotional for all three, though Chaplin affected a breezy nonchalance as if they had been together the day before. Edna had grown stout, and there was not much reminder of her old beauty, but she had still the same charm and humour. She read for the part – not badly, Chaplin conceded – and spent the next month at the studio, testing and rehearsing. Gradually it became evident that it would not work: the sophistication of a Continental *grande dame* was not in her line. When Edna returned home, both she and Chaplin were relieved. Her presence was too melancholy a reminder of the old times when everything lay in the future. They were never to meet again, though in the last pages of his autobiography Chaplin quotes with affection two letters she wrote to him in Switzerland in her last years – knowing full well that she would never receive any answer, for Chaplin was no letter writer. Edna died of cancer in 1958 at the age of sixty-two.

The part of Madame Grosnay eventually went to an English actress, Isobel Elsom, who was singing in the chorus of *The Quaker Girl* at the Adelphi at the time that Chaplin was touring for Karno. She had subsequently made a distinguished stage career, and moved to the United States in the late 1930s. The cast mostly called for character actresses, among whom were the formidable Almira Sessions and the Australian-born Marjorie Bennett, who was to appear again for Chaplin in *Limelight*.

It was most probably at the suggestion of Robert Florey, who had directed her nine years before in *Mountain Music*, that Chaplin cast the comedienne Martha Raye in the role of the terrible Annabella, the most indestructible of Verdoux's victims. The decision was taken after a screening of Raye's most recent film, *Four Jills and a Jeep*, in the studio screening room. During her first days on the set the ebullient Martha Raye was awed by Chaplin, who had been a hero for her since her show business childhood. Recognizing that this was inhibiting her work, she took the plunge, and started to address him familiarly as 'Chuck'. He took it in good part and in turn called her 'Maggie'. (Her real name is Margaret Reed). After that she grew even bolder, and alarmed the unit by calling 'Lunch' if she felt the morning's work had gone on too long. Instead of the anticipated fury, Chaplin accepted this in good part also, perhaps because he justly admired the skilful partnering the actress was giving him.

His casting of the young prostitute was less successful. Marilyn

Nash was good-looking and charming, but all too clearly without experience or great natural talent. Chaplin's own doubts about her were indicated by the number of times he re-screened the elaborate test he had shot of her, and the time he spent patiently rehearsing her. Problems with Miss Nash accounted for several lost days on the schedule. On the second day of shooting the scene in which Verdoux takes the girl to his furniture warehouse, Miss Nash left the studio, ill and unable to work. That afternoon Chaplin tested two girls, Barbara Woodell and Randy Stuart, for the role. He settled on Randy Stuart. Marilyn Nash returned to work on the following day, which was Saturday, but for the next four days of shooting Chaplin took the unusual measure of working with both girls in the part, evidently fearing that Miss Nash might be incapable of continuing. Finally however Miss Stuart was paid off and Marilyn Nash completed the film, pleasantly though somewhat without colour.

The filming of *Monsieur Verdoux* was unlike any previous Chaplin film. Apart from this incident, the work proceeded quickly and efficiently, with none of those pauses for reconsideration and reflection which had been so essential to the Chaplin method. The reason was not any change in Chaplin's temperament, or even because he began with a wholly realized script. It reflected rather the change in Hollywood which followed the end of the war. The years 1945 and 1946 saw much union trouble in the industry, and a prolonged strike had forced up studio wages by 25 per cent. Moreover the unions were now imposing tough minimum requirements on staffing, and, even more than during *The Great Dictator*, Chaplin found himself engaging technicians whom he did not require and whose function he did not even understand. For some years the soaring costs of running a studio had necessitated renting out studio space between films. The cost of the idle days that had been part of the studio routine in years gone by would now have been prohibitive.

There were more painful reminders of passing time. Since Christmas Alf Reeves had been ailing and in the first week of April 1946, when production had just officially got under way, he died. Alf had been associated with Chaplin since 1910, at first as his boss with Karno's companies; later as a shrewd, loyal, incorruptible and skilled employee who had discreetly guided the studio's affairs and watched with patient, paternal concern over Chaplin's private life. At the end of March when it was clear that Reeves, now nearing seventy, could not be expected to return to work, Chaplin had interviewed a prospective replacement, John McFadden, who was appointed general manager on 8 April.

McFadden had been recommended to Chaplin by his lawyer Loyd Wright, and arrived at the studio with new-broom efficiency. From the start he aroused the hostility of the unit, but particularly Rollie Totheroh, who was understandably angry when McFadden began to destroy the old footage he had stored (with frequent grumbles) for almost thirty years.

> He told the cutter to get rid of a lot of stuff, to burn it up. 'I'm making a new Chaplin. The old Chaplin is forgotten, see?' He called in *The Gold Rush* after our second release, that was still out making money with the sound track. 'Don't show that stuff to the public any more. That's the old Chaplin; forget that' . . . But Charlie could be taken in by a lot of guys like that, you see.[4]

Relations at the studio became so bad that Chaplin called the unit together and asked for their cooperation. As Totheroh saw Chaplin entrusting property affairs to the new man, and McFadden using studio facilities in ways of which the jealous Totheroh did not approve, he finally plucked up courage to take Chaplin aside:

> I said, 'You know what's going on here? He's just robbing you right and left and what he intends to do later . . . and you're going to give him permission.' It's a wonder Charlie didn't give him his stocks and his bonds to handle. And Charlie said 'Honest?' 'Yes.' 'Well,' he said, 'just keep an eye on him. I'll get rid of him but we're so far into things now I can't very well change in the middle of the stream. He knows about expenses that have already gone out. Just wait.'[5]

One week after the last shot of *Monsieur Verdoux*, with cutting only just begun, McFadden left the studio.

There was no substance in Totheroh's accusations, but they reflected the general dislike of McFadden. Even so, he introduced something which had never been seen before in the Chaplin studios – a shooting schedule. The work was broken down in advance into sixty shooting days and it was to everyone's credit – including McFadden for the practicability of his schedule – that the film fell only seventeen days behind.

Shooting was completed in the first week of September 1946 and during the remainder of the year Chaplin was cutting and working on his musical score with Rudi Schrager. The music – the most notable theme is the perky little '*boulevardier*' motif for Verdoux –

was ready to record by mid-January; but it was six weeks more before Chaplin was satisfied with the RCA Studios' work on recording and dubbing. He had become as perfectionist over sound as he was about his own performances, and perhaps more so than in his judgement of images: contemporary critics pointed out some rather obvious backdrops and some bad cutting matches in *Verdoux*. By the beginning of March the first finished prints of the film were ready and on 11 March 1947 the film was shown to the Breen Office examiners, who passed it without demur. During March Chaplin arranged private showings of the film for friends and visitors, including Gabriel Pascal, and was greatly heartened by their enthusiasm. On 21 March he and Oona, accompanied by Watson the English butler, took a train for New York, nervous but optimistic about the world première there.

The première was at the Broadway Theatre, New York on 11 April, the same day as the West Coast press preview at the Academy Theatre, Hollywood. A Chaplin première still attracted crowds and excitement. Mary Pickford accompanied the Chaplins. Miss Pickford was grabbed by a radio interviewer, and her companions always wondered how she would have continued her statement if she had not been separated from the microphone just as she had begun, 'Two thousand years ago Christ was born and tonight . . .'

The show was a gruelling experience. The bad publicity of the Barry trials and the growing rumbles of political propaganda against him had clearly done their work, and from the start it was apparent that an element of the première audience were there intent on demonstrating their resentment: from the start of the film there was scattered hissing, which stirred in Chaplin all his old terrors of the live audience. Even many of the well-disposed, however, were puzzled by the dark irony of the film. Eventually Chaplin could no longer bear to stay, and waited in the lobby until the film ended, leaving Oona inside with Mary. The supper party afterwards for 150 guests was an ordeal; this time Oona left early.

There was to be a far worse ordeal the following day. United Artists had arranged a press conference for Chaplin in the Grand Ballroom of the Gotham Hotel at 55th Street just off 5th Avenue. The room was crowded and Chaplin started off the proceedings with an attempt at grim jocularity: 'Proceed with the butchery . . . fire ahead at this old grey head.' The first questions were already barbed: Had he not failed to give Orson Welles proper credit for his contribution to *Monsieur Verdoux*? Had *The Great Dictator* been shown in the

Soviet Union, and was it true that he was part of a motion picture combine to transfer American films to the Soviet Union? (Chaplin said that it was definitely untrue.) Then, 'There have been several stories in the past accusing you more or less of being a fellow traveller, a Communist sympathizer. Could you define your present political beliefs, sir?'[6] Chaplin replied,

> Well, I think that is very difficult to do these days, to define anything politically. There are so many generalities, and life is becoming so technical that if you step off the curb – if you step off the curb with your left foot, they accuse you of being a Communist. But I have no political persuasion whatsoever. I've never belonged to any political party in my life, and I have never voted in my life! . . . Does that answer your question?

It did not: the questioner persisted: was he a Communist sympathizer? Again Chaplin attempted a serious answer to the question:

> A Communist sympathizer? That has to be qualified again. I don't know what you mean by a 'Communist sympathizer'. I'd say this – that during the war, I sympathized very much with Russia because I believe that she was holding the front, and for that I have a memory and I feel that I owe her thanks. I think that she helped contribute a considerable amount of fighting and dying to bring victory to the Allies. In that sense I am sympathetic.

At this point the assault was taken over by one James W. Fay, the representative of the Catholic War Veterans' paper and the Catholic War Veterans of New York County. (Some years later Fay was to become President of the League of Catholic Lawyers in New York, and National Commander of the Catholic War Veterans.) Fay's line of questioning had the insuperable advantage of a wonderful absence of logic, which enabled him to side-step Chaplin's careful answers. The dialogue is a horror comic of the Cold War mind:

FAY: Last week you reported, not as a taxpayer . . . you were a well-paying guest. Don't you realize, Mr Chaplin, that veterans while assuming all the obligations of a citizen at the same time pay their share of taxes as well?

CHAPLIN: I didn't say they didn't.

FAY: I know that, but you are giving that implication, sir.

CHAPLIN: I don't see how. I think you have misinterpreted my remark. I never meant it that way.

FAY: Mr Chaplin, you also said you are not a nationalist of any country, is that correct?

CHAPLIN: True.

FAY: Therefore, you feel that you can pay your way on your taxes without assuming any of the moral responsibilities or obligations of the particular country you are living in?

CHAPLIN: When you say, when you do what you are told – when you are living in a country you assume all the responsibilities – wherever you're residing.

FAY: I don't believe you do, Mr Chaplin.

CHAPLIN: Well, that's a – that's a question where we both differ.

FAY: All right. Now, Mr Chaplin, the *Daily Worker* on October 25 1942 reported [that] you stated, in an address before the Artists' Front to Win the War, a Communist front group: 'I'm not a citizen, I don't need citizenship papers, and I've never had patriotism in that sense for any country, but I'm a patriot to humanity as a whole. I'm a citizen of the world. If the Four Freedoms mean anything after this war, we don't bother about whether we are citizens of one country or another.' Mr Chaplin, the men who advanced in the face of enemy fire, and the poor fellows who were drafted like myself, and their families and buddies, resent that remark. And we want to know, now, if you were properly quoted.

CHAPLIN: I don't know why you resent that. That is a personal opinion. I am – four-fifths of my family are Americans. I have four children, two of them were on those beachheads. They were with Patton's Third Army. I am the one-fifth that isn't a citizen. Nevertheless, I – I – I've done my share, and whatever I said, it is not by any means to be meant to be derogatory to your Catholic – uh – uh – uh – GIs.

FAY: It's not the Catholic GIs, Mr Chaplin, it's the GIs throughout the United States!

CHAPLIN: Well, whatever they are, if they take exception to the fact that I am not a citizen and that I pay my taxes and that seventy per cent of my revenue comes from uh – uh – uh – abroad, then I apologize for paying that hundred per cent on seventy per cent.

FAY: I think that is a very evasive answer, Mr Chaplin, because so do those veterans pay their taxes, too.

CHAPLIN: Yes?

FAY: Whether their revenue comes from elsewhere or not.

CHAPLIN: The problem is – what is it that you are objecting to?

FAY: I'm objecting to your particular stand that you have no patriotic feelings about this country or any other country.

CHAPLIN: I think you're . . .

FAY: You've worked here, you've made your money here, you went around in the last war when you should have been serving Great Britain, you were here selling bonds, so it stated in the paper that I read, and I think that you as a citizen here – or rather a resident here – taking our money should have done more!

CHAPLIN: (*after a pause*) Well, that's another question of opinion and, as I say, I think it is rather dictatorial on your part to say as how I should apply my patriotism. I have patriotism and I had patriotism in this war and I showed it and I did a good deal for the war effort but it was never advertised. Now, whether you say that you object to me for not having patriotism is a qualified thing. I've been that way ever since I have been a young child. I can't help it. I've travelled all over the world, and my patriotism doesn't rest with one class. It rests with the whole world – the pity of the whole world and the common people, and that includes even those that object to me – that sort of patriotism.

The questioners who followed Fay were equally determined to pursue Chaplin's political opinions, rather than to talk about the film. Chaplin's replies were forthright and uncompromising. He was asked about his wartime activities:

> I spoke what was in my heart, what was in my mind and what I felt was right and manly of me to do. I appealed both to Great Britain and the United States – said that we should have a second front. Our boys were over there and so forth, and I wasn't alone in that. It appears it's come out now that General Marshall and President Franklin Roosevelt and other people were of the same opinion. And then I made several speeches along that line for the unification and for the unity of the Allied cause – which at that time was being disrupted. We know the technique of the Nazis. They started by condemning the Communists, and that was their technique in order to bring around the jingoism and the war that followed – and it was very obvious to see that they were trying to disunite

us in this country. We were all fresh at that time, and so the Administration wanted unity – and I made several speeches on behalf of the Administration for that purpose, and I felt that I served that purpose better, doing that sort of thing, than trying to do a floor-show, because that is not quite my business. I'm not very good at that sort of thing. And I thought I would use my effort in another direction. I made several speeches to factory workers and also several records for French distribution and for foreign consumption.

Asked if he was a friend of Hanns Eisler he replied that he was very proud of the fact. Pressed to say if he knew that Eisler was a Communist he said he only knew that 'he is a fine artist and a great musician and a very sympathetic friend'. When eventually some questioners got round to the film, he was asked if he himself shared Verdoux's conviction that contemporary civilization was making mass murderers of us:

Yes . . . Well, all my life I have always loathed and abhorred violence. Now I think these weapons of destruction – I don't think I'm alone in saying this, it's a cliché by now – that the atomic bomb is the most horrible invention of mankind, and I think it is being proven so every moment. I think it is creating so much horror and fear that we are going to grow up a bunch of neurotics.

Would he permit his own children to see *Monsieur Verdoux*?

Why not? . . . Not all of it's beyond them . . . I know there are a lot of pictures that I wouldn't allow my children to see that are supposed to be very forthright, high moral purpose, that I wouldn't send my children because it's absolutely a false notion of life. Something that doesn't exist. A lot of pictures are very dishonest. So-called boy meets girl . . .

Chaplin parried the attacks with skill and total honesty. He seemed taken aback, though clearly touched, suddenly to find he had at least one defender. James Agee of *Time* stood up in the balcony. He was so angry that his words were barely coherent, but his sentiments were clear:

What are people who care a damn about freedom – who really care for it – think of a country and the people in it, who congratulate themselves upon this country as the finest on earth and as a 'free country', when so many of the people in this country pry into what a man's citizenship is, try to tell him his business from hour to hour and from day to day and exert a public moral blackmail against him for not becoming an American citizen – for his political views and for not entertaining troops in the manner – in the way that they think he should. What is to be thought of a . . . country where those people are thought well of . . .

Agee followed up this indignant outburst by devoting three successive monthly columns in the *Nation* to *Monsieur Verdoux*. When, later, he arrived in Hollywood to be the writer of John Huston's *The African Queen*, Agee became a personal friend of the Chaplins, and a visitor at Summit Drive.

The transcript of the *Verdoux* press conference was preserved by George Wallach, who was present as a producer-director for radio and recorded the whole affair on a portable sound recorder. After the conference he asked Chaplin if he would like to hear the recording, and Chaplin invited him to his suite on the seventeenth floor of the hotel. He remembered that Chaplin sat cross-legged on a high-back upholstered chair:

> . . . as he listened to the questions and his answers, he relived each and every moment. He would turn to Oona, his wife, who was sitting on the bed, and say 'How was that?' or 'Did you think that was all right?' And she reacted to him rather than to the recording.
>
> Chaplin's back was quite straight and he held his clasped hands under his chin and rocked slightly back and forth – as if he were shadow-boxing with the words coming out of the speaker. He thanked me after the recording had run its course, and I headed back to the studio, where I put together a thirty-minute program that was broadcast that same evening.
>
> Somehow, thinking back after almost a quarter-century to Chaplin sitting in that chair – listening to the recording – I see in him the personification of the universal underdog. The underdog who, somehow, *does* win in the end.[7]

17

LIMELIGHT

Chaplin returned to California. Back home with Oona and the children he rapidly recovered from the ordeal of *Monsieur Verdoux*. He had still confidence in the American public's affection and moreover 'I had an idea and under its compulsion I did not give a damn what the outcome would be; the film had to be made.' Nor did he give a damn about Representative J. Parnell Thomas and the House Committee on Un-American Activities: or at least he was not going to allow them (as so many others in Hollywood did) to curb his opinions or his associations. 'A democracy is a place where you can express your ideas freely – or it isn't a democracy,' he said. In the opinion of his son, Charles, 'He always felt he belonged here in America, with its promise of freedom in thought and belief and its emphasis on the importance of the individual.'[1] Some of his best friends in Hollywood felt that he should have shut up and not made unnecessary enemies, but Chaplin to his credit always valued his friends and feelings more than he did his enemies. He made no secret of his support for the Liberal, Henry A. Wallace. His dinner guests included Harry Bridges, Paul Robeson and the 'Red Dean' of Canterbury, the Very Reverend Hewlett Johnson, whom he had met on his 1931 tour. In the late 1930s he had met Hanns Eisler, a refugee from Nazi Germany, and had remained friendly with him and his wife. Through the Eislers he met Bertolt Brecht.

As early as December 1946, Ernie Adamson, chief counsel for the Un-American Activities Committee, announced that among people who would be subpoenaed to testify at public hearings in Washington would be James Roosevelt, Will Rogers Jr and Chaplin; but no more was heard of it at that time. In May 1947 Chaplin was again quizzed by the press about his unwillingness to take American citizenship, and again he gave the same answer: 'I am an internationalist, not a nationalist, and that is why I do not take out citizenship.' On 12 June Chaplin became the subject of a heated debate in Congress. Representative John T. Rankin of Mississippi (who was also a member of the House Un-American Activities Committee) told the House:

> I am here today demanding that Attorney General Tom Clark institute proceedings to deport Charlie Chaplin. He has refused to become an American citizen. His very life in Hollywood is detrimental to the moral fabric of America. In that way he can be kept off the American screen, and his loathsome pictures can be kept from before the eyes of the American youth. He should be deported and gotten rid of at once.

Chaplin was much more angered by an NBC broadcast given by Hy Gardner. Chaplin immediately filed a $3 million suit in the federal court, alleging that Gardner had defamed him by calling him a Communist and liar, and moreover that NBC had tapped his private telephones. The case was to drag on inconclusively for several years. In July the newspapers learned from Representative Thomas that HUAC now intended to issue a subpoena requiring Chaplin to testify before his Committee. Chaplin did not wait for the subpoena: on 21 July the press reprinted the text of a dignified but sarcastic message which he had sent by telegram to Thomas:

> From your publicity I note that I am to be quizzed by the House Un-American Activities Committee in Washington in September. I understand I am to be your single 'guest' at the expense of the taxpayers. Forgive me for this premature acceptance of your headlines newspaper invitation [*sic*].
>
> You have been quoted as saying you wish to ask me if I am a Communist. You sojourned for ten days in Hollywood not long ago,* and could have asked me the question at that time, effecting something of an economy, or you could telephone me now – collect. In order that you may be completely up-to-date on my thinking I suggest you view carefully my latest production, *Monsieur Verdoux*. It is against war and the futile slaughter of our youth. I trust you will not find its humane message distasteful.
>
> While you are preparing your engraved subpoena I will give you a hint on where I stand. I am not a Communist. I am a peacemonger.

* Investigating Hanns Eisler.

FRANK F. BARHAM. PUBLISHER

TUESDAY, APRIL 15, 1947

Chaplin Should Be Taken at His Word And Barred From U.S.

Charlie Chaplin, self-proclaimed "citizen of the world" and "man without a country," is fast nearing the end of the trail as far as the United States is concerned.

The complacent self-worship of the man, in a New York press conference, is amazing.

In boasting that he was neither a patriot nor an American citizen, he said, in part:

> **"I am not a nationalist of any country...You might say I am a citizen of the world...I never voted in my life...I did a great deal for the war effort...I made a speech in favor of opening a second front in 1942...I believe that voting for people...leads to Fascism."**

What a moral nonenity this Chaplin is!

In joining the ranks of subversives who have the overthrow of the American way of life as their avowed objective, he insults the American people, the very people who poured millions into his lap.

He has been what he terms "a paying guest" in this country too long.

He has shirked every responsibility of the American citizen.

He brags that he has never cast a vote in his life.

Even permitting him to remain in the United States insults the intelligence of the American people.

He boasts that he is a man without a country.

He should be taken at his word and should be denied the privilege even of being "a paying guest" in the United States.

Leading article from the *Los Angeles Herald-Express,* indicating the violence of McCarthyist attacks on Chaplin.

The fearlessness and fierce humour of this message give credibility to Chaplin's description of how he imagined behaving if he were eventually called before the Committee:

> I'd have turned up in my tramp outfit – baggy pants, bowler hat and cane – and when I was questioned I'd have used all sorts of comic business to make a laughing stock of the inquisitors.
>
> I almost wish I could have testified. If I had, the whole Un-American Activities thing would have been laughed out of existence in front of the millions of viewers who watched the interrogations on TV.[2]

This might have been his greatest performance. Unhappily for history it was not to take place. He was subpoenaed, but three times the date was postponed until eventually he received a 'surprisingly courteous' reply to his telegram, saying that his appearance would not be necessary and that he could consider the matter closed. Perhaps they realized that such a comedian might steal the show.

In November Chaplin was again defying America's Cold War repressions. Deportation proceedings were now proceeding against Hanns Eisler. Chaplin cabled Pablo Picasso asking him to head a committee of French artists to protest to the United States Embassy in Paris about 'the outrageous deportation proceedings against Hanns Eisler here, and simultaneously send me copy of protest for use here'. 'I doubt,' reflected his son Charles,

> if the incongruity of asking a confirmed Communist to intercede for a man accused of Communism in a non-Communist country ever even entered my father's head. He was an artist appealing to another artist to come to the aid of a third artist. But to many people his move smacked of insolence, and the newspapers roundly castigated him for his lack of etiquette rather than for any subversion. How can you call such an open move subversion?[3]

The New York chapter of the Catholic War Veterans did so, however, and sent a telegram to the Attorney General and the Secretary of State demanding 'an investigation of the activities of Charles Chaplin'. The activities in question were the cable to Picasso – 'noted French artist and (self-admitted) Communist' – and an 'alleged attempt to interfere with the activities of a duly elected representative of our citizens'. Almost two years later, when the Senate Judiciary Committee was seeking legislation to expel subversive citizens from the United States, Senator Harry P. Cain revived the

Picasso incident as a reason to deport Chaplin: 'It skirts perilously close to treason,' he declared.

In an atmosphere of growing fear, Chaplin bore up bravely and refused to be intimidated or silenced. Even so it was not surprising that for his new film subject he turned nostalgically backwards to the London of his youth. He even planned to make the film in London, and partly with this in mind decided in the spring of 1948 to go there, taking Oona to show her for the first time the scenes of his boyhood. He had not reckoned with the United States Government, however. When reservations were already made on the *Queen Elizabeth* and at the Savoy, the Immigration Department stalled on Chaplin's application for the re-entry permit which he needed as an alien. Instead they telephoned and asked him to report to the Federal Building. He told them he was busy that day and asked to come the following day, which was Saturday. They replied that they would save him the trouble and call on him. When the deputation arrived, it consisted of a stenographer, FBI man and an immigration officer, who told him that he had the right to demand Chaplin's evidence under oath. The unexpected inquisition lasted for four hours. It began with personal questions about Chaplin's racial origins and sex life. Asked if he had ever committed adultery he countered, 'What is a healthy man who has lived in this country for over thirty-five years supposed to reply?' He found the inquiries into his life, thought and opinions 'most personal, insulting and disgusting'. Asked about his political views he refused as usual to shuffle. He told them frankly, 'that I was decidedly liberal; that I was for Wallace, and that I have no hate for the Communists, and that I believe that they, the Communists, saved our way of life. They were combating 280 divisions of the Germans at a time when we, the Allies, were unprepared.'[4]

Chaplin was told that the re-entry permit would be granted but that he would be required to sign a transcript of the interrogation. Pat Millikan, Chaplin's lawyer, was deeply impressed by the diplomacy with which Chaplin had conducted the affair but advised him not to sign until he was sure he actually intended to sail for England. Chaplin in fact decided against the trip. As soon as wind of his intention to leave the country reached the Treasury, they put in a claim for $1 million's worth of tax and demanded a bond of $1.5 million if he left the country.

To add to his private problems, Chaplin now found himself 'a half-owner in a United Artists that was $1 million in debt'. His co-owner was Mary Pickford. It was a depressed period for Hollywood at large, and most of the other stock-holders had sold back their shares. The repayments had depleted the company's reserves, and *Monsieur Verdoux*, which it had been hoped would bring United Artists back into profit, already promised losses. Chaplin and Pickford found themselves in conflict. Pickford insisted on firing Arthur Kelly, who had resumed his role as Chaplin's representative in the company. In turn Chaplin insisted that Pickford should dispense with her representative also. They then failed to agree on an arrangement under which one of them might buy out the other's interest. Various outside offers in turn faded away, and when an Eastern theatre circuit offered $12 million for United Artists, Pickford and Chaplin again failed to agree upon their respective roles in the arrangement. (The circuit's offer consisted of $7 million in cash and $5 million in stock. Chaplin proposed that he should take $5 million cash down and leave the remainder for Pickford. On reflection Pickford decided that since she would have to wait two years for the balance of her money, even though she made two million dollars more, the advantage was Chaplin's.) When they eventually sold out some years later it was for considerably less.

In post-war Hollywood, studio space was too valuable for Chaplin to leave the studio idle between pictures. During the years that Chaplin was preparing *Limelight*, the studio was regularly rented out to small independent production units such as Cathedral Films, who made dozens of religious shorts there such as *The Conversion of Saul* or *The Return to Jerusalem*. One of these rentals was in its way historic. On 5 and 25 May 1949 Walter Wanger rented the sound stage to make some screen tests with Greta Garbo, who had not appeared in a film for seven years, since *Two-Faced Woman* (1942). It was the star's last appearance before the cameras. Historic, or at least ominous, in another way were the rentals of studio space to Procter and Gamble for the production of some of the earliest television commercials.

The secret of Chaplin's fortitude in weathering the storms of the late 1940s was the unqualified success and happiness of his marriage. On 7 March 1946, when their first child Geraldine was nineteen months old, Oona gave birth to a son, Michael. During the time that Chaplin was writing *Limelight* the Chaplins had two more daughters,

Josephine Hannah, born on 28 March 1949, and Victoria, born 19 May 1951. Geraldine's Hollywood birthday parties were family events. On her fourth birthday Rollie Totheroh came to the house and shot 1000 feet of film of the occasion; unfortunately it seems not to have been preserved. Among other relaxations there were still the summer weekends on a new yacht. From time to time friends would be taken down to the studio to see *Monsieur Verdoux* and some of Chaplin's older films. The new generation of Chaplin children were introduced to the films, too; on 5 December 1950 Oona took Geraldine, Michael and Josephine to the studio to see *The Gold Rush* for the first time. Between the births of Josephine and Victoria, Chaplin and Oona made four trips to New York. Their only brief period of separation was on the last of these, in January 1951, when Chaplin made the journey as usual by train while Oona flew.

Most of the time, though, Chaplin was busy with the script of *Limelight* – at this period still called *Footlights*. In all he was to spend more than three years on it – the longest time for any scenario. The title *Footlights* is first mentioned in the studio records in the second week of September 1948, but he had been dictating story ideas since the start of that year. Arthur Kelly, in New York, was asked to register the titles *Limelight* and *The Limelight* on 6 September 1950, and the 'dramatic composition' was sent for copyright five days later. As late as January 1951 Chaplin was still regularly dictating new script material to his then secretary Lee Cobin. The script as completed was filmed virtually without alteration, though before the film was released one or two scenes were eliminated.

Chaplin's approach to *Limelight* was altogether exceptional. He first set it down in the form of a novel running to something like a hundred thousand words. This incorporated two lengthy 'flashback' digressions in which he related the biographies of his two main characters, the clown Calvero and the young dancer Terry Ambrose, before the beginning of the story. Much later Chaplin was to say that the idea for *Limelight* was suggested by his memory of the famous American comedian Frank Tinney, whom he had seen on stage when he first came to New York, at the height of Tinney's popularity. Some years later he saw him again and recognized with shock that 'the comic Muse had left him'. This gave him the idea for a film which would examine the phenomenon of a man who had lost his spirit and assurance. 'In *Limelight* the case was age; Calvero grew old and introspective and acquired a feeling of dignity, and this divorced him from all intimacy with the audience.' Chaplin, in his sixties, must inevitably have taken a subjective view of this peril. Moreover he was in process of witnessing, painfully, how fickle a mass public can be.

The full 'novel' form of *Limelight* indicates, however, that this was a much more complex series of autobiographical reflexions. At one level the young Calvero is the young Chaplin: 'In his youth he yearned to be a musician but could not afford any kind of instrument upon which to learn. Another longing was to be a romantic actor, but he was too small and his diction too uncultured. Nevertheless, emotionally, he believed himself to be the greatest actor living.' At another level though, Calvero, the stage artist who loses heart and nerve and becomes a victim of drink, is Chaplin's own father. Brought up by his mother, Chaplin had in his innocence always thought of her as the injured party, abandoned by her ne'er-do-well husband. Much later – and particularly after his own life provided domestic stability – he began to reconsider his feelings about his father. Perhaps after all Hannah had been unfaithful and promiscuous: the affair with Leo Dryden certainly suggests it. The description of Calvero's marriage

In his youth he yearned to be a musician but could afford an instrument upon which to learn; Another was to be a romantic actor, but he was too small and his diction too uncultured. Nevertheless, he believed himself to be the greatest actor living. Necessity made him turn to comedy, he loathed, because it demanded of him, an intimacy with his audience which he did not feel and which never came natural to him.

Calvero was not gregarious. He was shy and reserved and difficult to know. At times strange, melancholy and austere.

Chaplin's revisions to the first page of Calvero's story - a section of the 'novel' version of *Limelight*.

to Eva Morton, her infidelity and the consequent despair which drives him to alcoholism, is undoubtedly Chaplin's own attempt to explore his parents' problematic relationship.

Terry is also given a biography. It is clear that these flashback stories were never intended to figure in any eventual scenario, but were Stanislavskian studies to provide background for the characters. Terry's mother resembles the adult Hannah Chaplin. She is seen as a woman worn by suffering but still beautiful, bent over a sewing machine, slaving to make a meagre living for herself and her two children. These two children parallel the close sibling relationships that figure so large in the Chaplin history: Charles Senior and his protective brother Uncle Spencer, Hannah and Kate, Chaplin and Sydney, young Charles and young Sydney. Especially since Aunt Kate remains such a mysterious and fascinating figure in Chaplin's childhood, it is intriguing to speculate how much of her and Hannah there is in Chaplin's picture of the relationship of Terry and her elder sister Louise. It has seemed important, for the intimations they may give of Chaplin's own reflections on his family history, to record the content of the *Limelight* 'novel' at some length in the pages that follow. The 'novel' is in itself notable for the Dickensian relish of Chaplin's descriptions of Victorian life and the theatre of his boyhood. The story begins much like the film, with Terry's attempted suicide in Mrs Alsop's lodging house – 'supine, a little over the edge of the iron bed'. Outside a barrel organ plays 'Why did I leave my little back room in Bloomsbury?' In flashback we see the story of Terry's youth.

> *The daughter of the fourth son of an English lord and a servant girl, Terry lives with her widowed mother and her older sister Louise in a poor room off Shaftesbury Avenue. Louise loses her job in a stationery shop, and the mother is taken off to hospital. Life improves somewhat when Louise starts to bring home a little money. Terry discovers with shock how she earns it, when she wanders with some other children into Piccadilly and sees Louise at work as a street walker.*
>
> *Before Terry is ten, her mother dies and Louise becomes the mistress of a South American with 'a small, luxurious flat in Bayswater'. She sends Terry to boarding school and pays for her dancing lessons. When Terry is seventeen Louise emigrates to South Africa. Terry becomes a dancer at the Alhambra. On the threshold of success, however, she is struck down with rheumatic fever. When she leaves hospital she goes to work at the stationer's and toy shop where Louise was formerly employed, Sardou*

he 1931 world tour. Chaplin at the Iajestic Hotel, Nice, between rank J. Gould and Florence Gould, ie noted socialites of the Cote 'Azur and Chaplin's hosts. ydney is on Mrs Gould's left.

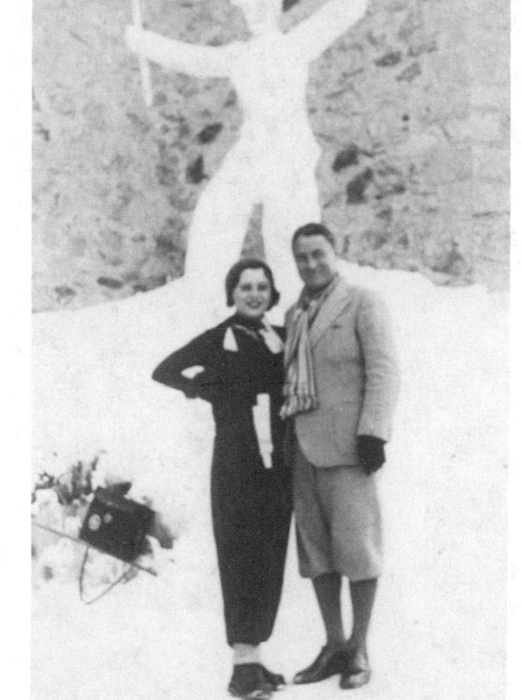

he 1931 world tour. Sydney with Iay Reeves in front of a snowman harlie at St Moritz.

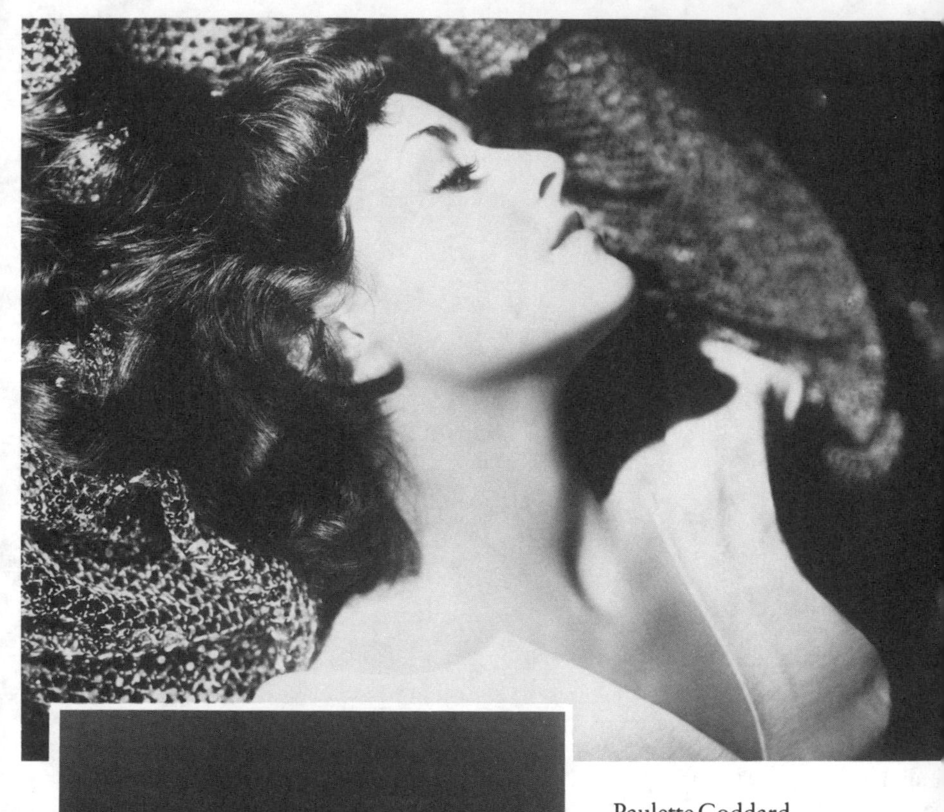

Paulette Goddard, photographed by Hurrell.

Paulette Goddard and Chaplin at the première of *Modern Times*

Right: Paulette Goddard, photographed by Hurrell.

Principal members of the Chaplin unit at about the period of *Modern Times*. Back row: Mark Marlatt, assistant cameraman; Girwood Averill, projectionist; Morgan Hill, assistant cameraman; William Bogdonoff, construction. Front row: Joe Van Meter; Henry Bergman; Roland Tother Della Steele, secretary and script girl; Allan Garcia, casting.

ıaplin as Napoleon at a fancy-dress
rty given by Marion Davies at
n Simeon, 1925. Also in the group
: (left to right) Douglas Fairbanks,
ary Pickford, William Randolph
earst and Princess Bibesco.

ft: set design for the department
ɔre skating sequence in
odern Times.

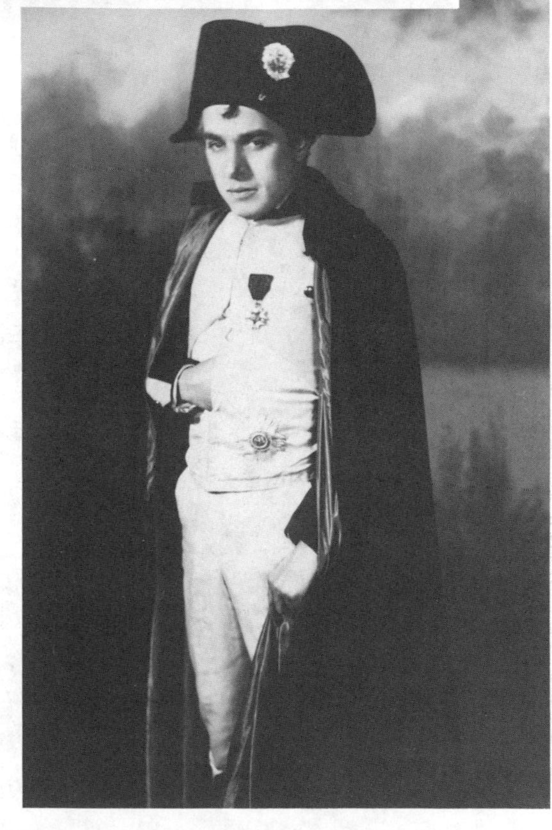

ıaplin as Napoleon. When he posed
r a series of photographs in
aracter in the mid 1930s, Chaplin
pears to have used the old costume
ɔm the Davies fancy-dress party.

The Great Dictator.

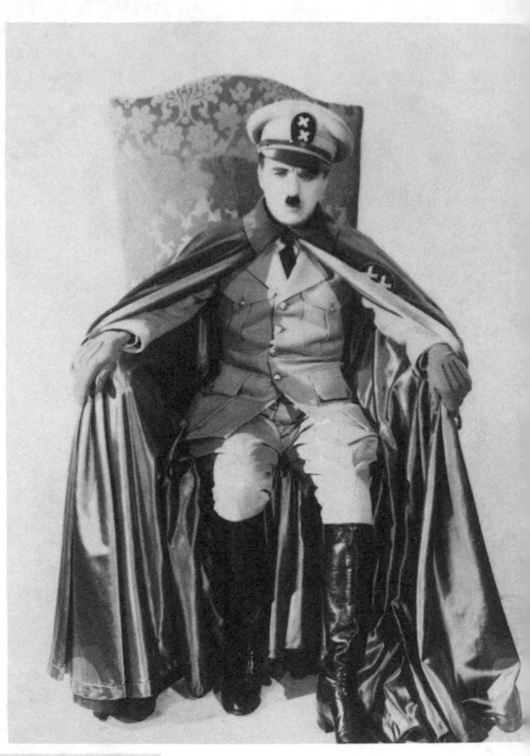

The Great Dictator: Chaplin an
Roland Totheroh on the camera
crane.

The last meeting with Douglas Fairbanks, on the set of *The Great Dictator.*

Above: Chaplin at a music recording session for *The Great Dictator.*

Below: Chaplin at the New York press conference for *The Great Dictator.*

Monsieur Verdoux: Chaplin and Marilyn Nash

Above left: With Oona in Hollywood, 1944.

Below left: Chaplin and Martha Raye in *Monsieur Verdoux*.

Chaplin directing Somerset Maugham's 'Rain' at the Circle Theatre, Hollywood, 1948. From left to right: William Schallert, June Havoc, Earle Herdan, Jerry Kilburn, Chaplin, Jerry Epstein, Sydney Chaplin Jr.

Limelight: Chaplin as Calvero with his half-brother Wheeler Dryden as the Doctor, and Claire Bloom as Terry.

Limelight: the screen debuts of Geraldine, Josephine and Michael Chaplin.

Limelight: after thirty-five years of trying, Chaplin finally managed to find a place for his flea circus routine.

Chaplin and Oona backstage at the Comedie Française, Winter 1952.

Top: Chaplin and Sophia Loren at a press conference conference to announce *The Countess from Hong Kong* at the Savoy Hotel, London, November 1, 1965.

Bottom: *The Countess from Hong Kong*: Chaplin on the set with Sophia Loren and Margaret Rutherford.

Top: Chaplin, Oona and their youngest son Christopher, c. 1967.

Bottom: Chaplin and Oona at the launch of his book *My Life in Pictures*, 1974.

Chaplin, with Oona and Geraldine, arrives at Heathrow in March 1973.

Manoir de Ban, Corsier-sur-Vevey, Switzerland.

The Chaplin Studio, Sunset and La Brea, 1983.

Chaplin: Last official portrait, 1977.

and Company: 'a small establishment, overstocked with newspapers, magazines, stationery requisites, indoor games and other miscellany. The shop was close, oppressive, and had a pungent odour of ink, leather goods and the paint of toys . . . Sardou and Company was Mr Sardou, there being no company.'

It is in Sardou's that she encounters a young composer, Ernest Neville. She loses her job when, out of pity for his evident poverty, she deliberately makes a mistake with his change.

> *Autumn was near, and London was preparing for her coming theatrical season. Dancing troupes, acrobats, trick cyclists, conjurors, jugglers and clowns were renting Soho's clubrooms and vacant warehouses for rehearsals. Theatrical props, costumes and wigmakers were feeling the season's rush. A recumbent giant that would cover the whole stage and that breathed mechanically, was being built in parts for the Drury Lane pantomime, so large that a ballet could enter out of its breast coat pocket.*
>
> *Special devices for Cinderella's transformation scene; pumpkins to be transformed into white horses, contrived by aid of mirrors; paraphernalia for flying ballets, cycloramic tricks, horizontal bars and tight-ropes. Orders for new conjuring tricks, odd musical instruments, padded wigs and slapstick contraptions of all kinds, all to be ready for Christmas.*

Terry, six months after her collapse, desperate for work, takes a job at Northrups' Pickle Factory. Her hands become stained yellow with the pickle and at weekends she wears black gloves to hide them. One Saturday night she walks into a room over a Soho pub where a 'Mr John' is rehearsing some dancers. He is 'a brutish-looking man with a broken nose, a large ugly mouth and a voice low and woolly that sounded like the drawing of a bow over a loose, bass string of a violin.' Terry asks 'Mr John' for a job. He auditions her, but after dancing she collapses. The dancers are frightened when they see her yellow hands, and take her to hospital where she remains eighteen weeks. Meanwhile 'Mr John' and his wife befriend her, and before leaving with his troupe for an American tour he gives her a sovereign. Leaving hospital she moves into a room at Mrs Alsop's for five shillings a week. (Mrs Alsop wisely requires two weeks in advance; after six weeks Terry is four weeks' rent in arrears.)

While scanning the job advertisements, Terry notices that Sir Thomas Beecham will conduct a new symphony by Mr Ernest Neville. She uses one-and-sixpence of her precious remaining four shillings to buy a gallery ticket. Afterwards she sees Neville leaving the Albert Hall with Sir Thomas Beecham. She speaks to him and reminds him that she was the girl in Sardou's but he does not pursue the conversation. It is at this point that she returns to her room and attempts to commit suicide.

From this point the 'novel' coincides with the scenario of the finished film. Calvero returns to find the girl in a gas-filled room, sends for a doctor, and takes her under his wing. As she begins to recover, he tells her his own life story – the Calvero 'novel'.

> *Many years ago Calvero had suffered unrequited love for a young woman who had run away with his rival to South Africa, where she married. In course of time her daughter, having run off with a young doctor, arrives in England. Abandoned by her young man the girl, Eva Morton, appeals for help to Calvero, about whom she has heard from her mother. In a short time they become lovers, following a blissful summer's day on the Thames.*
>
> > *It was a day of flamboyant color; of white flannels and gay parasols; of baskets of strawberries, bright yellow pears and large blue grapes; it was a day of lemon and pink ices, and cool drinks in long-necked bottles; a day of occasional guitars and the rippling of punts and rowboats, gliding through the water.*
> >
> > *And so it was that Calvero and Eva spent the week-end at Hanby. On their way back, they stopped for dinner at a small inn at Staines, and spent the night there. Soon after, Calvero gave up his rooms in Belgravia and moved to a flat off Oxford Street, where he and Eva lived as man and wife, and within three months they were married.*
>
> *Very soon, however, Calvero realizes that Eva is being unfaithful to him:*
>
> > *She . . . understood her own love for him which had a special place in her heart, but which did not wholly occupy it: no man ever could. She realized that her desire was insatiable and verged on being pathological, yet she looked upon it as something separate and apart from herself and her life with Calvero . . .*
> >
> > *Of her unfaithfulness she wanted to tell him. She hated deception because she had a deep regard for him. She wanted to make a clean breast of everything and tell him that she could never be faithful to any man, but she felt that Calvero would not tolerate any compromise. And she was right. His nature demanded the full possession of the thing it loved. His reason might conceive a true justification for her promiscuity, yet to acquiesce to it, he knew that such a love would slowly die from its own poison.**
>
> *Matters come to a head when Eva has an affair with a rich Manchester factory owner called Eric Addington. Calvero discovers the affair while playing principal clown in the Drury Lane pantomime, with Addington and Eva watching him from a box. Having introduced some wry comedy*

* Perhaps seeking to explore the break-up of his parents' marriage, Chaplin undoubtedly also views the problem of the man whose 'nature demanded the full possession of the thing it loved' through the memory of his own experiences with Edna, May Reeves and Paulette.

about the heartbroken cuckold into his stage business, he afterwards accuses the couple. Eva leaves him for ever.

Calvero begins to drink. The more he drinks the less appeal he has to his audience. He is advised by his dresser, who was once a famous clown himself,

> *'The more you think, the less funny you become. The trouble with me,' he continued, '. . . I never thought. It was women that killed my comedy. But you – you think too much.'*
>
> *And the dresser was right. Calvero was instinctively analytical and introspective. He had to know and understand people, to know their fallibilities and weaknesses. It was the means by which he achieved his particular type of comedy. The more he knew about people, the more he knew himself; an estimation that was not very flattering; with the consequence that he became self-conscious and had to be half-drunk before going on stage.*

Calvero's mind fails under the strain. He wanders for six weeks in a state of amnesia, and is then confined for three years in an institution. On his release he is aged and changed. He attempts to make a comeback in the theatre, but succumbs once more to drink. The audience walks out on him. 'His engagements grew less, as well as the salary he was asking, until his vaudeville engagements ceased entirely.' Calvero sinks to work as an extra, though he remains a celebrity in The Queen's Head where he mingles with people he knew in his better days – vaudevillians, agents, critics, jockeys, tipsters. A particular friend is Claudius, the armless wonder. Claudius recognizes Calvero's impecunious state and offers him a loan. Calvero is obliged to take the money from Claudius's wallet himself, and in doing so sees a photograph of a youth. Claudius explains that it is his nephew whom he has educated since the death of his sister, the boy's mother. Calvero has to button up Claudius's coat for him before he goes out into the cold. (Calvero is later able to repay Claudius's loan, since he stakes half of it on a 3–1 winner.) 'It was after one of these dialectic – not to say alcoholic – afternoons that he came home and found Terry Ambrose, unconscious in her back room.'

It is from this point that the 'novel' version of the story follows the essential line of the film script, apart from some inconsiderable differences of detail and plot mechanism. The result of the friendship and mutual encouragement between Calvero and Terry is that she is cured of the psychosomatic fear that she will never be able to dance again, while he is heartened to attempt a comeback. While Terry's career prospers until she becomes principal dancer at the Empire, however, Calvero's once more fades. Terry convinces herself that she is in love with this benefactor, old enough to be her father; but when she once more meets Neville, the young composer (she is to dance in his ballet), Calvero understands her heart better than she does herself, and discreetly disappears from her life.

Calvero is rediscovered, and the manager of the Empire, Mr Postant arranges a benefit performance for him, at which he will be the star. In the 'novel' version, Chaplin has not yet worked out the mechanics of the end. In the film, the performance takes place, and Calvero has one more triumph with the public. When he takes his bow, carried in the drum into which he has fallen as the climax of the act, the audience applauds wildly, unaware that he has suffered a heart attack. He dies as his protégée dances on the stage, in illustration of the archaic, 1920s-style title that prefaces the film: 'The glamor of Limelight, from which age must fade as youth enters.'*

A number of passages exclusive to the 'novel' version of *Limelight* are interesting for their autobiographical and factual references. At one moment Calvero tells Terry that he is going to see a new flat in Glenshaw Mansions – where, of course, the Chaplin brothers had their first bachelor apartment. The illness which is to prove fatal to Calvero is a circumstantial recollection of the elder Chaplin's last days, and the last time his son saw him alive, in the saloon of The Three Stags in Kennington Road:

> The doctors had warned him only a few months ago that further dissipation would be extremely dangerous to his health. It was eleven o'clock in the saloon bar of the White Horse, Brixton, that Calvero, in the midst of his febrile hilarity, collapsed into unconsciousness and was taken to St Thomas's Hospital.

(Charles Chaplin Senior died in St Thomas's.)

Calvero's exhortation to Terry could be the credo of Chaplin's whole working life:

> She must always adhere to the living truth within herself. She must be deeply selfish. That was essential to her art, for her art was her true happiness.

An intriguing scene which was eliminated fom the final film script introduced a historical figure, the great juggler Cinquevalli. Attempting a comeback at the Alhambra, Calvero meets Cinquevalli at the morning rehearsal. The juggler tells him that he intends that evening to perform a new trick with billiard balls that he has been rehearsing for seven years. That night they share a dressing room. Cinquevalli returns from the stage and Calvero asks him how the new trick went.

* In 1905 the stage manager of the Duke of York's Theatre, whose kindness to him in his boyhood Chaplin always remembered, was called William Postance.

Cinquevalli says that it received no applause: he had made it look too easy. Calvero says that he should have fumbled it a couple of times. Cinquevalli replies that he is not yet good enough to do that.

> 'I shall need a little more practice.'
>
> 'I see,' said Calvero ironically. 'And now I suppose it'll take another ten years to learn how to miss it.'
>
> Cinquevalli smiled. 'That's right,' he replied.
>
> 'That's depressing,' said Calvero.
>
> 'Why?' he asked.
>
> 'I can't laugh at that. It's frightening. Perfection must be imperfect before we can appreciate it. The world can only recognize things by the hard way.'
>
> 'That should be encouraging. The world can only recognize virtue by our mistakes.'
>
> 'If that were the truth,' said Calvero, 'I'd be a saint by now.'

To judge from his notes, Chaplin seems to have considered retaining this scene in the film, placing it immediately before Calvero's final appearance on the stage, and setting it in the wings. Finally, though, it was discarded altogether.

Chaplin was fascinated by the problems of creating a ballet, 'The Death of Columbine', for the film. In the past he had always composed his music after the film was finished. In this case the music had to come first. He began to work on the twenty-five minute ballet sequence* with the arranger Ray Rasch in December 1950. Rasch continued to work with him on the ballet several days a week until the following October. A special problem was to compose a forty-five second solo to which André Eglevsky, the dancer Chaplin wanted for the role, could match his choreography for the Blue Bird Pas de Deux. In September the music was recorded with a fifty-piece orchestra under Keith R. Williams. André Eglevsky and his partner Melissa Hayden flew in for two days from New York to hear the music and rehearse some of the dancing. Chaplin was extremely nervous as to their verdict, but they were apparently quite satisfied that his music was suitable for ballet.

Chaplin told his sons that he expected *Limelight* to be his greatest picture and his last. As contented in his family life as he was disillusioned with post-war America, he spoke from time to time of

* Much shorter in the completed film.

retiring. Had he done so, *Limelight*, going right back to his beginnings, would have been a perfect ending to his career. It was, in any event, to round off the Hollywood period. The film was something of a family affair. As the juvenile lead, the young composer Neville, he cast his tall, handsome younger son by Lita Grey, Sydney Chaplin. Sydney remembered that his father asked him to play the part in June 1948, three years before he was to begin the film. Much later he discovered that his role was that of a starving musician, 'and as at this time I weighed over eighteen stone, had access to plenty of food, and what is called a crew haircut, father suggested that I should go on a diet and grow my hair.'[5]

Charles Junior had a small role as a clown in the ballet. Geraldine, Michael and Josephine were to appear in the opening of the film, as three urchins who watch with curiosity Calvero's drunken return to his home. Geraldine even had a line to speak – her first in movies. In the part of the doctor who looks after Terry after her suicide attempt, Chaplin cast Wheeler Dryden, a lean, somewhat wizened figure, wearing spectacles and with an emphatically British accent. Although Wheeler had been around the studio since *The Great Dictator*, this was the first time that his relationship with the Chaplin brothers had been made public by the studio:

> Our mother and my father separated and Charlie and I never met again until I came to America in 1918 [*sic*]. Charles was already famous.
>
> We both agreed that it would be better for me to make good on my own. This is the first time our relationship has been disclosed.
>
> We have both remained British subjects. Not that we are un-American, but although we are fond of America, we do not feel it necessary to give up our British heritage.[6]

Chaplin's major problem was to find a leading lady. She had to have, said Chaplin, 'beauty, talent and a great emotional range'. She also had to be very young and preferably English.

> An advertisement was placed in the papers reading 'Wanted: young girl to play leading lady to a comedian generally recognized as the world's greatest', and for another year Father saw and tested just about every applicant who seemed even vaguely suitable for the part. It was the first time that Father had written a film in which the girl's part was equal to his, and so it was terribly important that he made the right decision.[7]

Sydney somewhat exaggerates the length of the search: the first girls were interviewed in February 1951 and the choice was made by

August. Sydney himself was given the job of screening applicants, with the help of Chaplin's secretary of the time, Lee Cobin. The playwright Arthur Laurents, who was currently friendly with the Chaplins, recommended the twenty-year-old Claire Bloom whom he had seen in London in *Ring Round the Moon* (Christopher Fry's adaptation of Anouilh's *L'Invitation au château*) at the Globe Theatre. Laurents himself telephoned Miss Bloom to ask her to send some photographs of herself to the Chaplin studio. The idea seemed so fanciful and remote to the young actress that she put the whole thing out of her mind until a few weeks later when she received a cable, 'WHERE ARE THE PHOTOGRAPHS? CHARLES CHAPLIN.' When the photographs arrived, Harry Crocker, who had now rejoined Chaplin as business manager, telephoned from California to say Chaplin wanted to test her for the part. Since the theatre management would only release her from *Ring Round the Moon* for one week, it was agreed that she should fly to New York, and Chaplin would meet her there to make the test. Miss Bloom was chaperoned by her mother; Chaplin brought with him his assistant Jerry Epstein. From the moment he met the Blooms at the airport, Chaplin talked with great excitement of his plans:

> He said the love story – so he described it – took place in the London of his childhood. The opening scenes were in the Kennington slums where he was born. The agents' offices where he had endlessly waited for work, the dressing rooms in the dreary provincial theatres, the digs, the landladies – all his melancholy theatrical memories were to be the film's backdrop. He reminisced about the Empire Theatre, the smart music hall of its day, frequented by the smartest courtesans; he talked of his early triumph as a boy actor in a stage adaptation of *Sherlock Holmes* . . . When we went to his rooms for lunch, he continued with his memories of London and seemed desperate to hear that nothing he had known had changed. In the last few years he had been deeply homesick, he said, but he didn't dare to leave America for fear that the U.S. Government wouldn't allow him to re-enter the country. His family, home, studios, money – everything was in America . . .
>
> In the evening Chaplin would take us and Jerry Epstein to dinner at the most elegant restaurants. At the Pavillon and the '21' Club he spoke endlessly of his early poverty; the atmosphere he was creating for *Limelight* brought him back night after night to the melancholy of those years at home with his mother and brother. He spoke either of the early poverty or of his troubles with the U.S. Government, troubles I wasn't quite able to grasp until I had spent a while in Hollywood.[8]

Chaplin rehearsed Miss Bloom every day throughout the week. A little reluctantly he permitted her to see the script, though she was not allowed to take it to her room but returned it to Epstein every night. Like other players of younger generations, she was surprised by Chaplin's singular method of direction: 'Chaplin was the most exacting director, not because he expected you to produce wonders of your own but because he expected you to follow unquestioningly his every instruction. I was surprised at how old-fashioned much of what he prescribed seemed – rather theatrical effects that I didn't associate with the modern cinema.'[9]

At the end of the week the screen tests were made at Fox Studios. Epstein was behind the camera while Chaplin worked in front of the camera with Miss Bloom: 'I was trying out for the role, Jerry hoped he would please Chaplin as assistant director, and Chaplin was watching the script he had worked on for three years finally come before the camera, so everyone was tense.'[10] She was later to discover that Chaplin's methods in directing the tests were the same that he would use in front of the cameras:

> I was close to panic . . . only until I saw that Chaplin intended to give me every inflection and every gesture exactly as he had during rehearsal. This didn't accord with my high creative aspirations, but in the circumstances it was just fine. I couldn't have been happier – nor did I have any choice. Gradually, imitating Chaplin, I gained my confidence, and by the time we came to the actual filming I was enjoying myself rather like some little monkey in the zoo being put through the paces by a clever, playful drillmaster.[11]

Claire Bloom recalled Chaplin's care in choosing the costumes for the tests, talking of the way his mother had worn such a dress or how Hetty Kelly had worn a shawl: 'I quickly realized, even then, that some composite young woman, lost to him in the past, was what he wanted me to bring to life.' She also remembered with amusement the embarrassment of Chaplin and Epstein when they realized that no one had seen her legs, which, since she played a dancer, were going to be important. Somewhat transparently they included a tutu and tights among the costumes she tried, even though no dance sequence was to be included in the tests.

The young actress returned to London with the promise that she would have some news after ten days, and the encouragement that Chaplin had intoduced her to someone in a restaurant as 'a marvellous young actress'. In fact four months passed with no news except for a wire from Harry Crocker saying that she would hear further in a fortnight (which she did not). Despondency – especially after the *Daily Express* printed an article saying that Chaplin did not like the test that had cost him so much to make – gave way to resignation.

Chaplin was much occupied during this period. He arrived back from New York on the 'Santa Fe Chief' on 1 May, and ran the Bloom tests the same evening. Oona was nearing the end of her pregnancy, and on 19 May gave birth to Victoria. Two days later, while mother and baby were still in St John's Hospital, Chaplin moved out of 1085 Summit Drive to temporary accommodation at 711 North Beverly Drive, while the builders moved in to the old home. The growing family and their nurses demanded more room. The pipe organ was usurped. The majestic hall was divided with a new floor to provide more bedrooms. The alterations cost some $50,000 and looked a clear indication of the Chaplins' intention of staying. 'My father,' remembered Charles Junior, 'was so proud of these rooms he liked to take his guests upstairs to show them off.'

He was in fact still not convinced that Claire Bloom was the right choice. Again and again he would run her tests. Often he would invite guests to see some film at the studio, and then slip in the tests as well in order to get their views. Meanwhile he continued to interview other actresses and look at films in which there were likely young candidates. The strongest contender was an actress called Joan Winslow, who was brought from New York to Hollywood to go through the same process of extensive rehearsal and screen testing as Miss Bloom had undergone in New York. She stayed ten days, and was actually shown the Bloom tests. Finally, however, Chaplin made up his mind and Miss Bloom's agent received the fateful call from Harry Crocker. The contract gave her three months' work at $15,000 plus travel expenses and a weekly allowance for herself and her mother.

The Blooms arrived in Hollywood on 29 September 1951, and at dinner at Summit Drive, with Oona and Epstein, Chaplin explained how Miss Bloom would spend the seven weeks till shooting began. Like Chaplin himelf, she had to diet. She was to begin each day by going with Oona to exercise at the gymnasium, then rehearse from eleven until four and round off the day with an hour's ballet class. Generally the rehearsals took place in the garden at Summit Drive. Miss Bloom was again struck by Chaplin's insistence on his boyhood memories. When they went for a costume fitting he told her, 'My mother used to wear a loose knitted cardigan, a blouse with a high neck and a little bow, and a worn velvet jacket.' 'Melancholy,' she noted, 'was a word he was to use frequently when speaking of his plans for *Limelight*.'

The Blooms came to know the Chaplins at a time when their social life was much quieter than in the past. As Charles Chaplin Junior commented:

> It must not be supposed that my father's fight for his convictions was made without sacrifice. When I came back from the East to play my part in *Limelight* I was saddened to see the effect his stand had had on his own life. It was no longer considered a privilege to be a guest at the home of Charlie Chaplin. Many people were actually afraid to be seen there lest they, too, should become suspect.
>
> Tim Durant, the irreconcilable Yankee, solid as a New England rock in his loyalty, was around, and he did his best to bring back some of the old life, noting the irony the while. Once his phone had rung steadily with people calling him, offering him favors, wining him, dining him in the hope that he would extend them an invitation to the Chaplin home. Now it was Tim's turn to phone them and beg them to come up for a game of tennis. But they all backed out. The little tennis house and green lawn where once my father had held a gracious court were practically deserted on Sunday afternoons. I think my father must have been the loneliest man in Hollywood those days.[12]

There were still Saturday night dinner parties for one or two friends. Claire Bloom met there James Agee, the shy film critic who had become a friend since his passionate defence of *Monsieur Verdoux* and had now arrived in Hollywood as a screenwriter; Clifford Odets; and Oona's girlhood friend Carole Marcus, then married to William Saroyan and later to Walter Matthau.

Not many of the old studio staff remained, and once again Karl Struss was to replace Roland Totheroh as cinematographer. As Claire Bloom remembers it,

> the first three days' filming had to be scrapped, because Chaplin was dissatisfied with the camera work of his old associate Rollie Totheroh. He then engaged Karl Struss, a more up-to-date technician, to replace Totheroh, and this cast a gloom over the set. Totheroh had shot most of Chaplin's earlier films and, as he was no longer young, it was clear that this was probably the last job of his career . . . Chaplin, generous and

> loyal as he could be in pensioning his workers, was utterly ruthless when it came to the standards he'd set for his film.[13]

Totheroh was credited as 'photographic consultant'. Jerry Epstein remembers him taking special care over the filming of Chaplin himself. 'He would watch everything and say "Head up . . . head up, now . . . We don't want to see those double chins . . . gotta look pretty."'[14]

The visual recreation of the London of Chaplin's memories was all-important. After another designer had submitted some unsuccessful sketches, Chaplin had his production manager call Eugene Lourié. Lourié had emigrated from Russia in 1919, and had worked as a designer in France since silent days. In the 1930s he began an association with Jean Renoir, which continued after Renoir moved to Hollywood during the war. It is possible that Chaplin had noted Lourié's work in Renoir's *Diary of a Chambermaid*, in which Paulette Goddard had starred. Lourié remembers that the production manager telephoned and asked him if he knew London and had worked there (he had, while designing a ballet for the De Basil company in 1933) and told him that the studio would pay minimum rates. Lourié was not told the identity of the producer until he reported to the studio. 'I was pleased. I had a great admiration for Chaplin – but I was sorry I didn't ask for more money.' Chaplin suggested that before making a definite commitment, Lourié should read the script and work for a fortnight on some sketches. This approach impressed Lourié: 'In Hollywood they mostly hire film architects like stage hands.'[15]

Chaplin was pleased with Lourié's drawings.

> He had talked to me exclusively about London. I had a nostalgic feeling for the place, although I had lived there only three months when I was designing the ballet for De Basil. Later, though, I visited Georges Périnal there, and he took me all over. He took me to the other bank of the river, where Chaplin had been brought up. I remember that at that time of night the streets were very dark. The only lighted windows were the undertakers' shops. It was very curious to me, those lit windows with coffins inside. Anyway, he liked my ideas, and said, 'Well, start.' Then he took me into his drawing room and played me the music he had composed for the film.

The first set which Chaplin needed, so that he could start rehearsals with Claire Bloom, was the apartment at Mrs Alsop's.

He was very anxious to have the view from the window – high brick houses and sad-looking urban back yards. Instead of using the usual painted backgrounds, I built it three-dimensional in miniature. I took a lot of time to dress it, with drying washing and lights in the windows for the night scenes. In the finished picture though I saw practically nothing of it. It looked to me just like a painted background![16]

After the first day's work in this apartment set, Chaplin took Lourié aside and told him, 'I need more distance between the door and the stove. I rehearse it like a ballet. I need a particular distance to get in all the steps. Can we change it?' Lourié, anticipating possible changes, had made the walls of the set three feet longer than was, apparently, necessary. He was able to make the change without difficulty, so that Chaplin could carry on with his rehearsals the following morning.

He was very impressed. I think from that day he had more confidence in me. At the beginning he was very cautious with me. The second thing which gave him confidence I think was when I showed him the three-dimensional model I made for the set for the pantomime. I made it in very forced perspective, with the ceiling sloping down to two feet from the stage. He liked it. After that he would say, 'Mr Lourié, give me a composition for the frame.'

For the exteriors we could not go to London, of course. Travel was restricted then, and we were working on a shoestring budget. For the street I had to build it or find it. I actually found it. It was a New York brownstone street at the Paramount studio – a very old set, which very much resembled London. I showed it to Chaplin. He said 'It's wonderful.' We slightly remodelled it. We changed the entrances to the houses, and built exteriors for two pubs and the physician's office.

He had a very strong visual impression, though he could not always express it in words. He would draw things, though. I have two or three sketches that he made – I think of street lamps for the Victoria Embankment scene. We used back projection for the scene and one lamp and one bench – the bench may still be around his old studio somewhere.

Vincent Korda was extremely helpful. He sent me lots of research about the old Empire Theatre – old photographs. And he sent out the studio stills man at night to photograph the Embankment. I wanted a point opposite Scotland Yard, with Big Ben in the background. I asked him to photograph the scene every hour from dark until dawn, so that I could choose the light.

Basically the film was shot in the studio. We needed a theatre – several theatres in fact, since he wanted to do a montage of the dancer's international tours. The choice was between using the Pasadena Playhouse or one of the two theatre sets at Universal (it had been built for *Phantom of the Opera*, and was still called 'the Phantom stage') and RKO – Pathé. We chose Pathé. It was a complete theatre, so that we could do the backstage stuff there too. And it's much easier working in a studio than in a real theatre, because you can change things as you please.

I was very excited to find some old backdrops from *The Kid* in the studio. And then I found some old scene painters from the 1880s to make the backdrops for the stage scenes.[17]

Jerry Epstein and Wheeler Dryden were credited as assistant producers, although Eugene Lourié does not remember Wheeler as being very active on the film apart from his appearance as an actor. 'He was around all the time though, because he was then living in a house at the studio.' Robert Aldrich worked on the film as associate director.

I think he was brought in because Chaplin felt he wanted someone with a lot of professional experience of studio work. But Aldrich always wanted more artistic shots. Chaplin did not think in 'artistic' images when he was shooting. He believed that action is the main thing. The camera is there to photograph the actors. I worked with Sacha Guitry, and he had exactly the same approach.[18]

Without any significant departure from the script, Chaplin worked with the same discipline as on *Monsieur Verdoux*. He fell two weeks behind the tight shooting schedule he had given himself, and Claire Bloom's engagement lasted (to her delight) longer than the envisioned three months. Even so the film was finished in fifty-five shooting days, including four days for retakes. This was a very far cry from the interminable shooting histories of *The Kid* or *City Lights*. Sydney Chaplin Junior recorded some impressions of his father at work:

We started with some bedroom scenes which lasted three weeks. Then came the street scenes, and it was while these were being shot that I noticed one of the extras was wearing a strange, mustard-coloured suit which looked to me quite terrible. I called Father's attention to this, and he laughed and said it was strange but he'd had a suit just like it at one time. Of course, the one worn by the extra was rented from a firm of costumiers, but, without quite knowing why, the extra looked at the label in the inside pocket. It read: 'Made for Mr Charlie Chaplin, 1918'.

Another time it was Father who objected to a jacket I was wearing. 'Just look at the length of its sleeves compared with those of your shirt,' he complained. 'Get the tailor to lengthen them (the jacket sleeves) straightaway.' I went away, rolled up my shirt sleeves a little, and came back. 'Now that's more like it,' said Father.

> He is, of course a really wonderful director, using the right approach all the time, knowing instinctively how to treat each different artist. There was one old actor who was so nervous of playing with Father that he kept muffing his lines. To put him at his ease, Father muddled his own lines on purpose, and after that the old actor was at ease and the scene was exactly right the next time through.
>
> And, of course, as well as being the film's director Father was also its principal actor. His difficulty was to imagine how he would look in a scene which he wouldn't actually be able to see until it was filmed, and his method was to work out the moves in advance and have his stand-in go through them while he watched through the camera. One moment he'd be behind the camera, the next up 40 ft of scaffolding explaining something to an electrician, the next strolling around on the stage demonstrating some point to another actor . . .
>
> It was hardly surprising that Father ran himself practically ragged. He was always the first to arrive at the studios in the morning and the last to leave at night. His wife Oona would come down about midday with some sandwiches and fruit pie for him. He'd go home at night exhausted and after dinner start right away planning the next day's work.
>
> I only remember one major crisis, that was over a very emotional scene between Father and Claire. He spent the whole day on this scene which on the screen lasts a bare three minutes, and he still wasn't satisfied – chiefly with his own performance. So he spent the next day re-shooting it, and the day after that. Finally there was a terrific take which had all the stage hands weeping and at the end wildly applauding. For the first time in three days Father allowed himself a smile.
>
> The following day the people who were developing the film rang up to say that owing to some technical difficulty that piece of film had been destroyed. Father hit the ceiling when he heard this; but he didn't have the heart to tell Claire. He just said that he still wasn't satisfied and that he wanted to try it again.[19]

Claire Bloom found herself particularly apprehensive about the scene in which she suddenly finds that she can walk again, since she always had difficulty in weeping to order. Chaplin clearly had none of the inhibitions he experienced in directing Jackie Coogan. Before the scene began he criticized her acting and became so angry that she burst into tears. The camera crew had been forewarned and snatched the scene in a single take. 'Chaplin had judged perfectly what would do the job – rather like Calvero understanding what magic would be required to make Theresa walk again.'

In general, however, Chaplin remained patient and understanding with his actors. Eugene Lourié remembered him as being charming to his two sons. Charles Junior, though he evidently worshipped his father, had a different impression:

> And now, at last, it was Syd's and my turn to be targets of that drive for perfection which ever since our childhood we had seen focused upon others. After that experience I was more than ever convinced that my father's towering reputation and his seething intensity make it almost impossible for those working under him to assert their own personality. No one in the world could direct my father as he directs himself, but I feel that lesser actors in his pictures might profit from being directed by someone else.
>
> With Syd and me he was, I believe, even more exacting than with the others. As his sons we could not appear to be favored, and so he went to the opposite extreme and even tended to make examples of us. He was especially tough on Syd as the young romantic lead, and sometimes I heard people commiserating with him. But I never heard Syd himself complain. He kept his equanimity and learned from my father and was rewarded by being praised in the reviews for his fine performance.[20]

Sydney and Claire Bloom became romantically attached during the filming. She remembered that away from the set Sydney would be 'wickedly funny about his strong-minded father's eccentricities, but once Sydney reported to begin his role in the film, he lacked all defensive wit and, confronted with those paternal "eccentricities", became nervous and wooden on the set.'[21]

Just before Christmas 1951 the unit moved to the RKO–Pathé studios for the theatre sequences. The backstage scenes were filmed first, and on the last day of the year, Chaplin began to shoot the performance scenes on stage. For the ballet scenes, Melissa Hayden and Claire Bloom were ingeniously doubled: 'When the camera was close enough to permit me to do so [I was required] to wheel into frame and out as fast as possible – whereupon Melissa would take over again. The effect was so convincing that for years afterwards I was complimented on my dancing.[22]

Today the most touching aspect of *Limelight* is the appearance of Buster Keaton in a double act with Chaplin, in a crazy musical duet.* It was the only time the two greatest comedians of silent pictures

* Keaton arrived in Hollywood in 1917, more than three years after Chaplin. While Keaton was still working with Roscoe Arbuckle at the Balboa Studios, Chaplin visited their set, was photographed fooling with them and recalled that when Buster was a child performer in vaudeville he had bounced him on his knee while appearing on the same bill.

appeared together, and the only time since 1916 that Chaplin had worked with a comic partner. Keaton plays a crumbling and myopic pianist, who is assailed, the moment he takes his seat at the piano, by an avalanche of tumbling sheet music. Chaplin–Calvero, as the violinist, has his own problems: his legs for some inexplicable reason keep shrinking up inside his wide trousers. The unhappy consequences of Buster's attempt to give his friend an 'A' escalate until the piano strings burst in all directions while Calvero's violin is trodden underfoot. Eventually, after Calvero has produced a new violin, the performance begins. Calvero moves from a poignant melody which reduces him to tears to a demonic *vivace* which eventually precipitates him into the pit. He falls into the bass drum, and is carried therein to the stage to take his bow.

Keaton worked on the film for three weeks, from 22 December to 12 January. It was a sweet gesture of Chaplin's to employ him: Keaton had not worked in comedy for years and was all but forgotten. (The previous year, Billy Wilder had introduced him into *Sunset Boulevard* as one of Norma Desmond's Hollywood 'ghosts'.) On the set he was reserved to the point of isolation. He arrived, Jerry Epstein recalls, with the little flat hat he had worn in his own films, and had to be gently told that Chaplin already had a costume and business worked out for him. The whole unit was enchanted to see, however, that once on stage, Chaplin and Keaton became two old comedy pros, each determined to upstage the other. 'Chaplin would grumble,' Eugene Lourié recalls. 'He would say, "No, this is *my* scene."' Claire Bloom, too, felt that 'some of his gags may even have been a little too incandescent for Chaplin because, laugh as he did at the rushes in the screening room, Chaplin didn't see fit to allow them all into the final version of the film.'

Chaplin evidently took particular delight in creating the wonderful pastiches of Edwardian music hall songs and acts. 'Spring Song' led into a charming patter act and dance with Claire Bloom dressed in bonnet and tutu. In 'Oh for the Life of a Sardine' he perfectly parodied the vocal style of George Bastow, one of the last '*lions comiques*' and creator of 'Captain Gingah'. He must, however, have found most satisfaction with 'I'm an Animal Trainer', for here, after more than thirty years of trying, he at last managed to introduce into a film the flea circus business he had first performed on the set of *The Kid*. Chaplin resisted the efforts of his assistants to persuade him to add audience reaction and laughter on the sound track. He was (rightly) convinced that in a full cinema the audience would provide the necessary reaction, and that it would be authentic. He failed to forsee the possibility of the films being shown in thinly-filled cinemas or, worse, on the television screen. Seen in these circumstances, with no laughter or acknowledgement of an audience's presence, the sequences have a somewhat spectral and eerie quality.*

Eugene Lourié was present when the songs were filmed: 'He was very demanding with himself, shooting the vaudeville songs. He'd say, "We'll do it again. I can do it better than that." Sometimes we would shoot fifteen times.'[23] The last shot of the picture was made on 25 January 1952, and Chaplin immediately began cutting and assembling the film. The Blooms – very sad to forsake the family atmosphere of the film and the studio – left California on the 'Santa Fe Chief' on 13 February.

Chaplin spent most of the next three months cutting, and at the beginning of May ordered the rebuilding of several sets for retakes. At this point, yet another Chaplin joined the cast. Some of the new shots required Terry to be seen through the open door of Calvero's apartment, and Oona doubled for Claire Bloom in these scenes. On 15 May Chaplin showed a roughcut to James Agee and Sidney Bernstein, and was gratified by their reactions. By 2 August the final prints were ready for a preview at the Paramount Studios Theatre, which held two hundred people and on this occasion was packed. Sidney Skolsky, the celebrated *Variety* writer, recorded the event two days later:

> The guest list ranged from such celebrities as Humphrey Bogart to Doris Duke to several old ladies and men who had worked with Chaplin since *The Gold Rush* back in 1924 . . . Chaplin and his assistant, Jerry Epstein, ran the picture at two in the afternoon, because Chaplin wanted to check the print personally. Chaplin, who wrote, produced, directed and starred in the picture, had to do everything personally. He even ushered at this preview showing. Then when the lights in the projection room were off and the picture started, this little gray-haired man sat at the dial-controls in the rear of the room and regulated the sound for the picture. It was the most exciting night I have ever spent in a projection room . . .
>
> There was drama and history in the room. There was comedy and drama on the screen, and there was a backdrop of drama running along with the picture *Limelight* itself . . .

* The songs are in fact Calvero's dreams or nightmares of his past fame and failure.

> The projection room lights went up. The entire audience from Ronald Colman to David Selznick to Judge Pecora to Sylvia Gable stood up and applauded and shouted 'Bravo'. It was as if all Hollywood was paying tribute to Charlie Chaplin . . . Then the little gray-haired fellow walked up to the platform. He said: 'Thank you. I was very scared. You are the first people in the world to have seen the picture. It runs two hours and thirty minutes. I don't want to keep you any longer. I do want to say "Thank you –"' and that's as far as Chaplin got. A woman in the audience shouted, 'No! No! Thank you,' and then others in the audience took these words and shouted them to Chaplin . . . Somehow I think this is the key to *Limelight*. It doesn't matter whether some people think it is good and some people think it is great. The degree doesn't matter. This is no ordinary picture made by an ordinary man. This is a great hunk of celluloid history and emotion, and I think everybody who is genuinely interested in the movies will say, 'Thank you'.

Chaplin had decided that the world première of *Limelight* should be in London and that he would take Oona and the children there for the occasion and a prolonged holiday afterwards. It would be Oona's first visit to England. They planned to miss the Hollywood press show and the New York opening; and left California on the first lap of their journey on 6 September. The night before, Tim Durant gave a send-off clambake party for them at his home. The guests included Arthur Rubinstein and Marlon Brando, who was the only one who arrived in dinner jacket. Chaplin thrilled them with an outstanding party piece, a dance with Katharine Dunham in which he perfectly reproduced and reflected her mannerisms, personality and grace. But Charles Junior sensed that his father was preoccupied, and the following day when Tim Durant drove Chaplin and Oona to Union Station, Chaplin told him that he had a premonition that he would not return.

The Chaplins arrived in New York with Harry Crocker, who was to accompany them to Europe to take charge of publicity, on the 'Santa Fe Chief' on 9 September. A week later they were joined by the four children, accompanied by their nurses, Edith McKenzie ('Kay-Kay') and Doris Foster Whitney. The week in New York was somewhat restricted. Chaplin's lawyer had warned him that a suit was in process against United Artists and that an attempt might be made to serve a summons on him, which could prejudice the entire trip. Chaplin, not for the first time, had to stay in hiding, though he seems to have left the Sherry-Netherlands on one or two occasions, at least. Edith Piaf was playing in New York, and says in her memoirs that Chaplin came to see her performance and visited her backstage.

At Crocker's urging he attended a lunch with the editorial staff of *Time* and *Life*, an event he found frigid and unfriendly and which failed to achieve favourable notices from the magazines. He also attended the New York press show of *Limelight.* There was no repetition of the open hostility of the *Verdoux* press conference, but Chaplin found the atmosphere at the show uneasy and unfriendly. He was gratified, however, by many of the subsequent reviews.

Daily Mail

NO. 17,575 THREE HALFPENCE — FOR QUEEN AND COMMONWEALTH — SATURDAY, SEPTEMBER 20, 1952

U.S. MAY BAN CHAPLIN

Attorney-General Orders an Inquiry Into His Readmission

Comment

TURDAY, SEPT. 20, 1952.

TOO MUCH 'LAYTIME?

HE ARCHBISHOP OF CANTERBURY has set the cat nong the pigeons with s remarks about telesion, although on his turn from America yesrday he emphasised at he was not "agin"

said: "There is a danger increasing our amenities dlessly when we, as a poor .tion, should be concen-ating on getting on with

REASONS ARE KEPT SECRET

Surprise Move as Film Star Brings Family to London

From Daily Mail Reporter

NEW YORK, Friday.

CHARLES CHAPLIN, who left New York for London 48 hours ago, has been barred from re-entering the United States until a Government inquiry decides whether he can return.

The U.S. Attorney-General, Mr. James McGranery, announced in Washington tonight that he had ordered the Immigration Service to bar him until the inquiry. No further statement was made.

SENATOR ACCEPTS CASH AID

Eisenhower May Ask His Team Mate to Quit

From WILLIAM HARDCASTLE
ON THE STEVENSON CAMPAIGN TOUR, Friday.

SENATOR Richard Nixon, Mr. Eisenhower's Vice-Presidential running mate, has accepted a £5,700 election fund from "millionaire backers" in California.

This disclosure has given Governor Stevenson's chances of being elected President in November an important boost,

On Wednesday 17 September 1952 the Chaplin family embarked for England on the *Queen Elizabeth*. Still evading the process-server, Chaplin boarded the ship at five in the morning, and did not dare show himself on deck. Consequently the devoted James Agee, who had come to see him off, failed to see him as he waved his hat feverishly out of a porthole. Chaplin and Agee were never to meet again: the critic died a couple of years later of a heart attack. Once at sea, process-servers left behind, Chaplin experienced a sense of freedom. He felt 'like another person. No longer was I a myth of the film world, or a target of acrimony, but a married man with a wife and family on holiday.'

The *Queen Elizabeth* had been at sea two days when the radio brought extraordinary news. The United States Attorney General, James McGranery, had rescinded Chaplin's re-entry permit, and ordered the Immigration and Naturalization Service to hold him for hearings when – or if – he attempted to re-enter the country. These hearings, he said, 'will determine whether he is admissible under the laws of the United States'. The Justice Department added that the action was being taken under the US Code of Laws on Aliens and Citizenship, Section 137, Paragraph (c), which permits the barring of aliens on grounds of 'morals, health or insanity, or for advocating Communism or associating with Communist or pro-Communist organizations'. In response to questions, the Attorney General said that this course of action had been planned for some time but that he had waited until Chaplin had left the country before acting. Chaplin, in other words, had no longer the right to return to the place which for the past forty years he had made his home, and to which he had attracted so much love and lustre.

18

Exile

When the *Queen Elizabeth* docked at Southampton, six-year-old Michael Chaplin had been mislaid (he was eventually found in the ship's gymnasium) which gave the reporters time to interview Chaplin before he boarded the train for London. He was tactful in avoiding a direct reply to the American Government's action, since all he possessed was still in the United States and he was terrified that they would devise some means of confiscating it. He indicated that he would return and face any charges:

> The US Government does not go back on anything it says. It will not go back on my re-entry permit.
>
> These are days of turmoil and strife and bitterness. This is not the day of great artists. This is the day of politics.
>
> People are now only too willing to take issue about everything. But I am very philosophical about it all. I try my best.
>
> I do not want to create any revolution. All I want to do is create a few more films. It might amuse people. I hope so . . .
>
> I've never been political. I have no political convictions. I'm an individualist, and I believe in liberty.[1]

He told them that he had an idea for a new film about a displaced person arriving in the New World. A head wound has given the man a complaint called cryptosthenia, which causes him to speak in an ancient language. Since no one can understand him at the immigration barriers, he is allowed to pass all the language tests. Chaplin mimed the interrogation scene for the reporters. Knowing Chaplin's extreme secrecy about the ideas of his films, he cannot have been very serious about this idea: it was simply an attraction for the press.

More seriously he told them about his anxiety to show London to his wife and children, to explore it again himself. He recalled how 'music first entered my soul' (he never varied the phrase) when he heard the street musicians playing 'The Honeysuckle and the Bee'. 'I was seven and now I'm sixty-three, but I'll never forget it.' He appears to have carried with him his first cuttings book, since the newsmen said that he displayed his first notice from 1903 for *Jim, a Romance of Cockayne*.

Although not quite so numerous as on his previous visits, the crowds were there at Southampton, and at Waterloo, where scores of people broke through the police cordons to touch him. More people were waiting outside the Savoy. Mr and Mrs Marriott, the Festival of Britain Pearly King and Queen, brought him a basket of flowers adorned with boots, bowler and walking stick and inscribed from the people of London. At this time Chaplin was especially touched by such sentimental gestures. On the day of his arrival he gave a press conference:

> In Mr Chaplin, face to face, one looks of course for signs of his tragi-comic screen creation. One sees instead a small friendly man, white-haired, his complexion pinker than usual from the lighting of the little stage from which he addresses the hungry journalists through a microphone. When he descends from his stage he is lost. The swarm slowly circles the room with him as its centre, and when someone, guided by a friendly secretary, succeeds in reaching that centre there is ludicrously little time to conduct the personal conversation which, indeed, one shrinks from forcing on him.[2]

The British public and press were enchanted and intrigued by their first sight of Oona. Shy and retiring though she was, a short statement was wheedled out of her: 'I'm happy to stay in the background and help where I'm needed. Perhaps that is why I am the only one of his four wives he took to London, and I am very proud.'

She was asked what Chaplin was like as a husband: 'Charlie is a half-and-half personality. One half is difficult – the other easy. But I find we manage very happily. He is an attentive husband and a wonderful father.' Chaplin had told reporters when the *Queen Elizabeth* docked at Cherbourg, 'I will go back.' In London he said, 'I expect to go back,' and Oona commented: 'It would come as no shock to me if he decided to stay in England.'

After ten years of coldness in America, Chaplin was gratified by the fan letters that awaited him at the Savoy, many of them imploring him to remain. In the *News Chronicle* Lionel Hale, writing 'as a Tory and a friend of America', declared that

> there is always some good in folly, and the good might be that England, and the London streets which are so greatly changed from the days of fog and gas-light and bare-foot boys, might, after so long a time, have once again as one of its gallant inhabitants one of the greatest artists of the era, Mr Charles Spencer Chaplin.[3]

In the House of Commons there were some heated questions to the Foreign Secretary, Mr Eden, with MPs demanding that he make representations to the US Government to allow Chaplin to re-enter the country without let or hindrance. Nor was all American opinion in favour of the Attorney General. A US Congressman visiting Britain spoke of the affair as 'persecution'. A leader in the *New York Times* said that those who had followed Chaplin through the years could not easily regard him as a dangerous person:

> No political situation, no international menace, can destroy the fact that he is a great artist who has given infinite pleasure to many millions, not in any one country but in all countries. Unless there is far more evidence against him than is at the moment visible, the Department of State will not dignify itself or increase the national security if it sends him into exile.[4]

Attorney General McGranery was meanwhile employing the style of innuendo characteristic of McCarthyist technique. 'If what has been said about him is true,' he hinted darkly, 'he is, in my opinion, an unsavoury character.' He claimed that when the public knew the facts on which he was basing his move to bar the comedian from re-entering the United States, it would realize that his action had been justified. McGranery alleged that Chaplin had been accused in the press of being a member of the Communist Party and also of 'grave moral charges'. He declined to be specific about the charges, since he said that this would assist Chaplin in his defence. He would only add further that 'He has been charged with making leering, sneering statements about the country whose gracious hospitality has enriched him.'

McGranery was forced to admit that he had taken his action without consulting any other government departments. It was believed, in fact, that the State Department and many Washington officials had been dismayed by the adverse reaction from all parts of the world. McGranery, though, had evidently been for some time under pressure from right wing and McCarthyist elements. Senator Richard Nixon, using the notepaper of the Senate Committee on Labor and Public Welfare, had written to Hedda Hopper on 29 May 1952 – four months before Chaplin's departure:

> Dear Hedda:
>
> I agree with you that the way the Chaplin case has been handled has been a disgrace for years. Unfortunately, we aren't able to do much about it when the top decisions are made by the likes of Acheson and McGranery. You can be sure, however, that I will keep my eye on the case and possibly after January we will be able to work with an Administration which will apply the same rules to Chaplin as they do to ordinary citizens.

The Senator signed himself cordially, 'Dick Nixon'.

Chaplin was invigorated by his explorations of London. From his balcony in the Savoy he could see the river and the new Waterloo Bridge, which he did not like at all, 'only that its road led over to my boyhood'.[5] At that time something still remained of the Kennington he had known as a boy, and on this and subsequent visits Oona was to come to know it as well as he did himself. Alone, he preferred to make his trips on foot or by bus and tube; and he was rarely recognized. On his first evening in London he went to The Scotch House, a pub near Leicester Square, where the landlord was an old Karno colleague, Jimmy Russell, one of many interpreters of the awful boy in *Mumming Birds*, but Russell, to his subsequent chagrin, was not there that night. In the afternoons, while the children made their own excursions with their nannies, Chaplin and Oona would have tea at Fortnums.

Compared with their last years in California these weeks in London were a whirl of social activity. On their first night, they dined at Douglas Fairbanks Junior's house; the Oliviers were also guests. The following evening they went to the Old Vic to see Claire Bloom playing Juliet to Alan Badel's Romeo. Some days later Chaplin took Miss Bloom for a walk around Covent Garden market, and she was touched by the way the market traders all saluted him affectionately with 'Hello, Guv'nor'. The Chaplins went to a Toscanini concert and afterwards met the great old man. They saw Emlyn Williams in his Dickens readings, and afterwards dined with him along with Noël Coward, Alec Guinness and Binkie Beaumont. They were entertained as guests of the Variety Club at the Savoy, and at a lunch given by the Critics' Circle. Chaplin was so much more accessible at this time than on any other London visit before or after that it was confidently predicted that he would appear both in the Royal Variety Performance and the Royal Film Performance. He did not. He had told the *Times* reporter that there was no chance of his appearing again on stage. '"You have to be in constant practice," he said. And the fact that one reminded him of the pleasure it would give and how inconceivable it was that a music-hall actor should ever lose his sense of craft could not persuade him to change his mind.'

Chaplin did however agree to an unscripted half-hour interview on the BBC Light Programme. His interviewers were Dilys Powell, Sir Michael Balcon, Paul Holt, John Mills and Robert Mackenzie. He told them how in his early days he 'used to write with a camera' (in this he anticipated the French director Astruc's concept of the *camera-stylo*). By that he meant that he used to go on the set in the morning without an idea. Then he would start, get excited, and in his excitement begin to invent. He told them that this was a contrast to the long, leisurely and thorough preparations he made for his latest films. Of *Limelight* he told them that he had set the film in London partly out of a feeling of nostalgia, partly because he wanted to say something about kindliness and humanity, for which London seemed to him a fitting setting. The film was not autobiographical except in so far that it, like his other work, inevitably expressed something of its creator's personality.

He had much to say about personality. His conception of a film was as a setting for a striking personality, which the story and everything else existed only to display. In the days of the silent films, he believed, the personality of the actor counted for more than in the present day. So much more was left to the spectator's imagination. The film actors then belonged, as it were, to poetry and to fairyland. 'But we cannot go back to silent films, and perhaps I merely romanticize them.'

This was the only recorded occasion on which he said that he had learnt much about the use of music from Fred Karno, who had used music for its incongruity – some stately eighteenth-century air, perhaps, to accompany the adventures of tramps, to underline the satire.

When the word 'genius' came up more than once, Chaplin laughingly said that it no longer embarrassed him. Indeed he had become quite 'shameless' about hearing himself called one. 'We have so many of them in Hollywood.' He liked to think the word meant merely an individual stylist who did things conscientiously and sometimes perhaps remarkably well. For his own part, he said, he had never written down to the public. He had always done the very best he could.

The world première of *Limelight* was given at the Odeon, Leicester Square, on 23 October, in aid of the Royal London Society for Teaching and Training the Blind, and in the presence of Princess Margaret. The Press Show was held in the theatre the same morning. Claire Bloom appeared with Chaplin at the top of the foyer stairs; when she threw her arms around him and kissed him ('He had finally made me natural with him in life as well') they were warmly applauded. Miss Bloom was working in the theatre in the evening and so could not attend the première, but Chaplin appeared on stage, to great enthusiasm. It was the first film première in Britain to be covered by live television.

Leaving their children happily on the farm of their friend Sir Edward Beddington-Behrens, the Chaplin parents and Harry Crocker moved on to Paris for the French première. There they were even more handsomely fêted. They were invited to lunch with the President, and at the British Embassy; Chaplin was made an officer of the Légion d'Honneur and an honorary member of the Société des Auteurs et Compositeurs Dramatiques. The première was attended by members of the cabinet and the diplomatic corps, though the American Ambassador was a notable absentee. At the Comédie Française, they were guests of honour at a special gala performance of Molière's *Don Juan*. Harry Crocker was anxious about the effect on Chaplin's publicity of a dinner with Aragon, Picasso and Sartre. Later Chaplin and Oona visited Picasso's studio, 'the most deplorable, barnlike garret', stacked with priceless masterpieces by Picasso's contemporaries. Chaplin did not speak French and Picasso did not speak English.

> The interpreters were doing their best but the thing was dragging. Then I had the idea of getting Chaplin alone and seeing if maybe all by ourselves we couldn't establish some kind of communication. I took him upstairs to my painting studio and showed him the pictures I had been working on recently. When I finished, I gave him a low bow and a flourish to let him know it was his turn. He understood at once. He went into the bathroom and gave me the most wonderful pantomime of a man washing

> and shaving, with every one of those little involuntary reflexes like blowing the soapsuds out of his nose and digging them out of his ears. When he had finished that routine, he picked up two toothbrushes and performed that marvellous Dance of the Rolls, from the New Year's Eve dinner sequence in *The Gold Rush*. It was just like the old days.

Unfortunately Picasso, violently opposed to all sentimentality, did not like *Limelight*. 'When he starts reaching for the heartstrings, maybe he impresses Chagall, but it doesn't go down with me. It's just bad literature.' He could not reconcile himself either to the physical changes that time had effected in Chaplin:

> The real tragedy lies in the fact that Chaplin can no longer assume the physical appearance of the clown because he's no longer slender, no longer young, and no longer has the face and expression of his 'little man', but that of a man who's grown old. His body isn't really him any more. Time has conquered him and turned him into another person. And now he's a lost soul – just another actor in search of his individuality, and he won't be able to make anybody laugh.

Picasso's young wife felt that the painter's response to *Limelight* may have been affected by the resemblances between the film's story and their personal situation.

In the United States the vilification continued. The American Legion began a campaign of picketing shows of *Limelight*, and several major theatrical chains – Fox, Loews and RKO – were persuaded to withdraw the film within a short period of its first showings. Hedda Hopper published a notorious attack in her nationally syndicated column: 'No one can deny [that Chaplin] is a good actor. That doesn't give him the right to go against our customs, to abhor everything we stand for, to throw our hospitality back in our faces . . . I abhor what he stands for . . . Good riddance to bad rubbish.' The American press was not unanimous. *The Nation* (4 October 1952) said: 'Whatever his political views may be . . . Charlie Chaplin can hardly be regarded as an overt threat to American institutions . . . Chaplin is an artist whose shining talent has for decades cast its luster upon his adopted country and brought joy to the world.' On 30 October, the Hollywood Foreign Press Association awarded a scroll of merit to *Limelight*. It was accepted on behalf of his father by Charles Chaplin Junior.

Chaplin was still in touch with the studio and still working, if at a distance, on his film. In November he sent instructions to cut out of *Limelight* the sequences involving the armless wonder, Claudius. As he became more and more convinced that he would not now attempt to return to the United States, he had to face the problem of removing his fortune to Europe. Providently, nearly all his personal assets were contained in a safe deposit box, and immediately before departing for Europe he had made the necessary arrangements for Oona to have access to it. Since he was personally unable to return to the United States, the only solution was for Oona to travel to Hollywood. The ten days that she was away – practically the first time that they had been separated since their marriage nine years before – was a period of terrible anxiety for Chaplin, terrified as he was that the American authorities would discover some way to prevent her leaving the country again. Oona left London by plane on 17 November: at that time New York was still an overnight journey. From New York she flew to Hollywood, accompanied by Arthur Kelly. They arrived on 20 November and left again on 23 November. In only two complete days, Oona, inexperienced as she still was in business affairs, had as far as possible to wind up the Chaplin assets in the United States.

She discovered that since they had left the FBI had interrogated the servants in an attempt to find some evidence of moral turpitude in the household. It was evident that the Bureau was desperate to uncover something – anything – that could substantiate the Attorney General's innuendoes. Everyone connected with Chaplin, including Tim Durant and his lawyer, was questioned, along with all the principals in the Barry case. The details of Paulette's Mexican divorce were re-examined. Even Lita was questioned about her marriage of more than a quarter of a century earlier. She proudly refused to give them any information that could be used to smear her one-time husband.

The most pitiable victim of the FBI harassment was Wheeler Dryden. Since he had first been employed at the studio, he had become devoted to Chaplin. More than devoted, indeed; Wheeler venerated his illustrious half-brother. Even today in the Chaplin archives there remain little packages, neatly wrapped and tied, and labelled in Wheeler's writing, for example, 'Script, incomplete, *but with a note in Mr Chaplin's own hand.*' On the set he would follow Chaplin at a respectful distance, warding off the importunate, seeing that

Chaplin's meditations were not disturbed, bringing him dates and fruit, always ready with anything he needed. Sometimes he might attempt a helpful suggestion, and bore it patiently if Chaplin's dismissal of it was brusque. He carefully collected every discarded relic of the studio and Chaplin; the accumulating hoard of bric-à-brac may have contributed to his estrangement from his wife. (They had married during the making of *The Great Dictator* and had one son, later a well-known jazz musician, Spencer Wheeler.) Though he retained the grand manner of an old English Shakespearean, Wheeler was a timid man. He felt himself abandoned when first Charles and then Sydney left California; and he was terrified by the FBI interrogations. He began to suspect that the FBI were poisoning his food, and refused to leave his house. Ted and Betty Tetrick would from time to time persuade him to go out for a walk, but wherever they went he carefully noted down the streets, as if he feared that the Tetricks, too, were going to abandon him. Wheeler died on 30 September 1957, aged 65.

Oona arrived back in London on 27 November 1952, and a few days later the family left for Switzerland. Since Chaplin was not to return to the United States, Swiss residence was likely to be the most advantageous from a financial point of view. While looking for a permanent home, they moved into the Beau Rivage in Lausanne – an old-style grand hotel much favoured by exiled monarchs. From Lausanne they travelled to Rome for the Italian première of *Limelight*. Chaplin was invested with the order Al Merito della Republica, though the occasion was somewhat marred by a demonstration by right-wing extremists who pelted Chaplin with vegetables. Later he said that he had been mostly struck by the comedy of the incident and laughed at it. He refused to prosecute the youthful offenders.

The Chaplins quickly found their house. In January they moved into the Manoir de Ban at Corsier sur Vevey, which they first rented from a former American ambassador. Only a month later they bought it for a reported $100,000. The house is an elegant villa with thirty-seven acres of park, orchard and garden. It has fifteen rooms on three floors. On the ground floor is a handsome drawing room with French doors opening onto a colonnaded terrace which was a focal spot of the household during the summer. At either end of the drawing room double doors lead into the dining room and the library, where Chaplin came to spend more and more of his time when he was at home. A fine elliptical stone staircase (which had a special fascination for the children because the wife of a former owner was said to have been killed by falling down it) leads to the first floor, with guest suites and the main bedrooms. Chaplin's bedroom was simply furnished. He designed the furniture himself. It is in pale wood, with something of the 1930s in its rational austerity, something Edwardian in its proportions and Victorian in its evident sturdiness. The style, as he was accustomed to say, is Chaplin. Oona gave much attention to enlarging and decorating her suite, with its fine views over Lake Leman to the mountains beyond. Her paintings include an Eakins of the artist's studio, in which the nude model is probably Oona's grandmother. The third floor, reached by a more modest staircase or the lift installed by the previous owner, was the realm of the children and their nannies. In the wandering catacombs beneath the house, Chaplin, though no drinker himself, established a cellar, and later built an atmospherically conditioned vault to store his films. One room in the cellars is reserved for the great bulk of Chaplin archives; the scripts, studio records, cutting books and glass negatives of still photographs.

Chaplin felt some anxiety about the cost of staffing such a large estate; while the children were growing up the servants generally numbered around a dozen. In later years the Manoir's domestic machine depended largely on Italians: the butler and cook Gino and Mirella Terni, who arrived in 1958, and the chauffeur Renato, a gentle man of distinguished appearance who took over the post from his brother Mario in 1965.

Chaplin's most urgent need was for a secretary. A friend suggested Rachel Ford. Miss Ford had lived in Paris practically all her life, but remained very British in her appearance and her brisk, no-nonsense approach to life. During the war she had risen to the highest rank possible for a woman in the Free French Army. Afterwards she worked for the European Movement, organizing international conferences. She was persuaded to consider a temporary job with Chaplin because she had inherited from her father a passion for his screen creations. When she arrived at the Manoir, the Chaplins were still unpacking, and Miss Ford felt that she was not at her most presentable: she was wearing a man's boot on one foot and a woman's shoe on the other, having suffered a scald. She was accompanied by a dog on a string – he had lost his leash. She explained in her forthright manner that she could not type, had no experience as a secretary and was only free for a few weeks between conferences. She was to stay for more than thirty years. She was to identify herself wholly with the interests of the Chaplins, who found in her an administrator of integrity, astuteness, skill and unwavering determination. Chaplin was to be delighted by her doggedness, for instance in pursuing any infringement of his copyrights. Miss Ford seemed to find the same invigoration in dealing with legal complexities that others might find in bridge or chess. At her first meeting with the Chaplins, she was dazzled by Oona's beauty and youthfulness and, as someone 'who has never even known what shyness meant' she was struck by the shyness of both of them. From the start it was clear that Miss Ford's role was to be more that of manager than secretary; and a secretary with the typing skills that she disclaimed, Mme Eileen Burnier, was engaged.

Having settled in, Chaplin announced, 'I want to have six months of peace and quietness in this house. We will not go in for big parties, and large receptions, but keep to ourselves.' They were to keep to this resolve, though they saw themselves as part of the local community, went shopping, complained if things went wrong, and from time to time appeared at some festive event (which was always good for the receipts). One serious disadvantage of the house had been overlooked, and was to cause some differences between Chaplin and the local authorities. The Chaplins had seen and bought the property in the quiet of winter, and no one apparently troubled to tell them of the proximity of the Stand de Guémont, where since 1874 the ablebodied male citizens of Vevey had done their training in marksmanship. In 1955 Chaplin lodged a formal protest against the noise nuisance. The canton authorities, eager to accommodate such a distinguished resident, made concessions about certain agreed quiet days, but were adamant that the Stand must stay: 'The township of Vevey will do all in the realm of the possible to diminish the noise due to the proximity of a shooting range. But we stress that under the terms of the Federal ordinance on militia shooting, we must furnish freely a range and we intend to do so.' As long as Chaplin lived the dispute went on, with intermittent protests and the occasional arrival of experts to measure the decibels. The noise nuisance was not ameliorated by the growing traffic on a motorway skirting the estate. In moments of irritability Chaplin would threaten to sell up and move to the Riviera.

Noise or no noise, Chaplin now felt confident about pulling up his last roots in America. Early in March, while the family were on holiday on the Riviera, the studio and the house in Beverly Hills were put up for sale. The studio was sold six months later to a firm of New York real estate agents for $700,000 – considerably less than the asking price. In April Chaplin formally handed back his United States re-entry permit, with a public statement:

> I have been the object of lies and vicious propaganda by powerful reactionary groups who, by their influence and by aid of America's yellow press, have created an unhealthy atmosphere in which liberal minded individuals can be singled out and persecuted. Under these conditions I find it virtually impossible to continue my motion picture work, and I have therefore given up my residence in the United States.

The following February, when the Chaplins arrived at Heathrow for a week's holiday in London, Oona had a British passport. The week before she had renounced her own American citizenship. The final link with the United States would be severed in March 1955, when Chaplin sold off his remaining interests in United Artists.

Chaplin made no concessions to the opinions of the 'yellow press' of America, which naturally howled I-told-you-so when he lunched with Chou-en-Lai in July 1954 while the Chinese Premier was attending the Geneva Conference. Curiosity alone would have forced Chaplin to accept the invitation. A couple of years later when Chaplin was in London preparing *A King in New York* he met Bulganin and Khrushchev at Claridges. The meeting was cordial, though Chaplin diplomatically avoided meeting the American Ambassador, Harold Stassen, who was also present. There were more attacks in May 1954 when Chaplin accepted a £5000 Peace Prize from a Communist World Peace organization. Clearly either to accept or to refuse the prize would have been invidious; Chaplin dealt tactfully with the problem by giving most of the money away. In October he arrived in Paris to present £2000 to the Abbé Pierre to build shelters for the homeless of the city. The following week he came to London and in a ceremony at Lambeth Town Hall gave a further £2000 to the Mayor, Major Herbert White, to be used for the old and poor of the borough. A lot of the Lambeth old and poor turned up for the occasion to give him a riotous local boy's welcome.

There was no question of retirement. Less than six months before his death, terribly frail, Chaplin was still reported to be saying, 'To work is to live – and I want to live.' A year or two before that he had said, 'I can't stop . . . ideas just keep popping into my head.' In his mid-sixties he was exploding with the will and need to work. By the end of 1953 he was talking confidently about his new film, though he would not reveal its subject: 'This industry is a monster which grabs at everything. Every grain of an idea I get I have to hang on to jealously.' He was looking for a boy of twelve to play in it, so clearly the project was already *A King in New York*, which he officially announced (as *The Ex-King*) in May 1954. At that time he thought it would be 'more or less a musical'.

Throughout most of 1954 and 1955 he was working on the script, though in the early part of the time he was still reconsidering *Shadow and Substance* also, so that Isobel Deluz, who was brought in as stenographer for the work, was at times not quite clear which of the two scripts she was supposed to be taking down, or whether it was a memorandum of some general purpose gag or line. She recalled how delighted he was one day when a particularly moving scene he had half-dictated, half-performed, so affected her that she began to cry. 'That's the tear-jerker attack that really wows them at the box-office,' he observed cheerfully.

> Chaplin was never fluent in his dictation, and he seldom finished a sentence. He constantly flipped backwards and forwards in the text or jumped to another sequence. It would go this way:–
>
> 'I love you – I love you,' (He lowers his eyes bashfully). 'That's it, got it. Just like that. I – I love you. Just make a note of that somewhere; may need it later on. Now, got those other pages? All right (reading) good. That's all. I won't do any more today. The tennis pro's arrived. Must get in some exercise or my figure will get fat . . .'

Chaplin would correct the transcripts of the dictation sessions in longhand: the creation of a script was a constantly revolving process of dictation, typing, correction and retyping.

By the autumn of 1955 the script was far enough advanced to begin preparing production, and Chaplin invited Jerry Epstein, his assistant producer on *Limelight*, to be his associate producer in *A King in New York*. Epstein arrived in Europe and joined the household at the Manoir de Ban, where he was to become a favourite and confidant of all the Chaplin children. A new production company, Attica, was established. (When a new company was later set up to handle distribution of all the Chaplin films, it was called Roy Export

Company Establishment, in humorous acknowledgement of Chaplin's determinedly Anglo-Saxon pronunciation of the French title of *A King in New York*, *Un Roi à New York*.) Studio facilities were to be rented at Shepperton Studios, and in November 1955 Oona arrived in London to arrange accommodation during the production period. She decided on the Great Fosters Hotel at Egham, which had the advantages of being quiet, rich in historical associations, and within easy reach of the studios.

Chaplin, naturally, was to play the main role of the exiled king who arrives in New York full of optimism for his plans for world peace, but is quickly caught up in the materialist frenzy and political paranoia of contemporary America. He needed a leading lady for the role of the go-getting but attractive young advertising agent who persuades him to submit to the lucrative humiliations of acting in television commercials. Jerry Epstein already knew Kay Kendall, who had recently had considerable screen success with her appearances in *Genevieve*, *Doctor in the House* and *The Constant Husband*. Oona shared his admiration for the comedienne, and Chaplin was infected by their enthusiasm. No doubt his own interest in her was further stimulated by knowing that she was the granddaughter of one of the great idols of the music halls of his youth, Marie Kendall, who had created the song 'Just Like The Ivy'. Epstein incautiously reported to Miss Kendall Chaplin's favourable reaction to his suggestion. Unfortunately he and Oona made the mistake of arranging for Chaplin to see *Genevieve*, which had been a considerable critical and commercial success. Chaplin did not like the film at all, and decided that on no account would he wish to work with Miss Kendall, whereupon Epstein had the uneasy task of deflecting Miss Kendall's hopes. Time has corroborated Chaplin's view of *Genevieve*, though not perhaps of Kay Kendall's elegant talent. He decided upon Dawn Addams, whom he had met when she was filming in Hollywood, shortly before his own departure. She was attractive, and her performance in the film was to prove professional and sporty. The second female role, of the King's estranged Queen, was given to Maxine Audley, an actress with the same aristocratic bearing and fine features as Claire Bloom, and who had recently been playing principal roles at the Shakespeare Memorial Theatre in Stratford.

For the part of the King's long-suffering Ambassador, Chaplin auditioned a number of veteran stage actors and finally chose Oliver Johnston, an actor who had played for most of his career in honourable obscurity, but provided a charming and effective comic foil. Other local character actors in the cast were Jerry Desmonde, who had worked as partner with Sid Field and Norman Wisdom; and Sidney James, who was shortly to establish a new career for himself as a star of the *Carry On* comedies. In the role of the King's lawyer he cast the American–Jewish stage comedian Harry Green – who had, as it happened, begun his career as a real-life lawyer. Green's performance was expert and funny, but Chaplin always had the uneasy sense that Green was upstaging him.

After the King, the most important dramatic role was to be that of the small boy whose parents are victims of the McCarthyist witch-hunt, and whom the King befriends – becoming suspect himself as a result of the association. In late 1953, as we have seen, he was searching for a boy to play this part, and it seems to have been only shortly before embarking on production that he had the idea of casting his own son, Michael: originally he had planned to give Michael the tiny part of the boy in the progressive school who uses his forefinger impartially to form *gateaux* and pick his nose. The boy enjoyed the work: 'I tried hard to do what my father wanted and we got along fine.'[6]

It is important to recognize the courage of Chaplin in undertaking a film, at a time when most men have already retired, in quite new conditions that were far less favourable to creation than the working situation he had known for the past forty years. He was no longer master of his own studio, with familiar craftsmen, who knew his whims, on call. The only official member of the unit who had known the Hollywood studio was Epstein. There were no longer the endless script conferences with the opportunities they provided to test ideas on trusted familiars. Certainly there was no longer the luxury there once had been of time to stop and reflect and try scenes over again some different way. The long pauses between production periods had for long meant that each time Chaplin returned to work there was a marked increase in crewing requirements and production costs. Now the pressures to maintain a tight schedule were aggravated by the added burden of studio rental.

The strains unquestionably show in the finished film. The presence of someone as fearlessly brash as Sutherland or James might have trimmed the script of its wordiness; and someone might have had courage to save Chaplin from mis-pronouncing 'nuclear' as 'nucular'. Circumscribed facilities did not restrain his ambition. His script required the staging of a revolution, while New York had to be recreated from London locations. Georges Périnal was a great photographer who had worked with Clair and Korda and Cavalcanti, but perhaps he lacked Totheroh's resourcefulness and understanding of Chaplin's needs. The London-made New York has a shabby, makeshift look quite absent from the suggestive, mythical cities of *City Lights* and *Modern Times*.

As Chaplin had once taken on the tyranny of European dictators, so now he turned his attack upon the destructive paranoia that had overtaken America. Whether the attack succeeded or failed, the importance of *A King in New York* was that Chaplin was the only film maker with the courage to make it at a time when McCarthyism still prevailed. He was aware before he began the film that he must totally discount the huge American market; in fact *A King in New York* was not screened in the United States until 1976.

The film begins, for old times' sake, with a sub-title: 'One of the minor annoyances of modern life is a revolution.' The exiled King Shahdov of Estrovia seeks refuge in the United States where he hopes to pursue his plans for the peaceful uses of atomic energy. Unfortunately his crooked Prime Minister (Jerry Desmonde) has absconded with the funds that were to have financed these plans. The King and his loyal ambassador Jaume (Oliver Johnston) are initiated into various aspects of contemporary American life – music, movie-going, television and a soirée attended by representatives of the media and intelligentsia. The King visits a progressive school where he meets a precocious child, Rupert Macabee, who reads Marx and assaults the King with a torrent of radical and libertarian oratory. He also encounters an attractive young advertising agent, and ekes out the rapidly diminishing royal funds by appearing in commercials.

The King meets the boy Rupert again, wandering homeless in the wintry streets: he has run away from school to avoid the efforts of the Un-American Activities Committee to question him about his parents' political loyalties and friends. The FBI take the boy away, and the King himself is called before the Committee. His appearance is a fiasco: he manages to get entangled with a fire hose and to soak the Committee with water. He is cleared of any Communist taint but decides to leave America just the same. Before his departure he visits Rupert, but he finds the once spirited child cowed and ashamed. To help his parents he has named names.

Some incidents in the film can be connected with Chaplin's own recent experiences. On arrival at the airport, Shahdov tells reporters how moved he is to be in the United States: all the time he is being fingerprinted by immigration officials. Chaplin had not forgotten his personal humiliation during the Barry affair, when the press was invited to photograph him being fingerprinted. Another incident that can be traced to actual experience is the scene in which the King, fearing a subpoena from the Committee, takes flight at the sight of a sinister pursuer in dark glasses – only to discover, when finally cornered, that the man simply wants his autograph. In his last days in America, fearful of writ-servers, Chaplin slipped out of his hotel each day to lunch at the '21' Club. Al Reuter, the well-known autograph collector and dealer, happened to be working at the club at that time. Al came off duty at 3 p.m. – about the time that Chaplin left the club – and so, on several successive days, he put on his dark glasses and trailed Chaplin, autograph book in hand. Each day Chaplin eluded him until the last, when Al finally caught him and got an autograph from his visibly relieved quarry.

It could be objected – and was widely objected – that fire hoses are as ineffectual against McCarthyism as slapstick against dictators. In a review of the film in the *Evening Standard*, for the most part highly appreciative, the playwright John Osborne wrote:

> In some ways *A King in New York* must be his most bitter film. It is certainly the most openly personal. It is a calculated, passionate rage clenched uncomfortably into the kindness of an astonishing comic personality. Like the king in his film, he has shaken the dust of the United States from his feet, and now he has turned round to kick it carefully and deliberately in their faces. Some of it is well aimed – some is not.
>
> In fact, for such a big, easy target, a great deal of it goes fairly wide. What makes the spectacle of misused energy continually interesting is once again the technique of a unique comic artist.

It is true that some of Chaplin's targets – rock and roll, CinemaScope, sex films – seem marginal to his main theme, and hardly worthy. One part of the film has triumphantly retained its force: the drama of Rupert Macabee, the child robbed of his innate honour. Just as in *The Kid*, Chaplin traces the injustice of a society to its ultimate and most vulnerable victim. The difference is that while The Kid was physically deprived, it is Rupert's conscience and soul that are abused.

Michael Chaplin's performance was admirable: Rupert is a volatile and fiery little pup, as touching in the anger of his protest, 'I'm sick and tired of people asking if I'm this, if I'm that,' as in his final break-down. Chaplin and his wife would afterwards indulge in friendly sparring as to whether Coogan or Michael was the better actor, with his mother always favouring Michael. His parents had wanted Michael to change his name to John Bolton for the role, so as not to trade upon the name of Chaplin, but the child insisted upon his own name. Much later he recalled, 'The only advice my father gave me on acting was: "What you have to try to achieve is to be as natural as possible."'

Shooting lasted from 7 May to 28 July 1956: the twelve-week schedule was the shortest for any Chaplin feature. From August to October Chaplin was in Paris, editing the film. Shortly after his arrival in Paris, on 25 August, he gave a press conference about the forthcoming film, from which American press men were banned. He told the press confidently that it would be his best and funniest film, though he was not giving much away: 'In it I have tried to throw into relief the contrast that exists in a big city, as much in the streets as among the inhabitants.'

One day during the time he was editing in Paris, Chaplin and Oona chanced to eat in the same restaurant as Paulette Goddard and her current husband, the German novelist Erich Maria Remarque. They joined each other, and the meeting was very affable. Remarque and Paulette lived for a time in Switzerland, though the Chaplins and the Remarques never met by design. 'We live on different mountains,' said Paulette.

Work on the film continued throughout the first half of 1957. On 23 May Oona gave birth to their sixth child who was to be named Jane.*

The film was released on 12 September 1957. Before that Chaplin had previewed it for friends. One of them was J. B. Priestley, who wrote:

> It is always a particular pleasure to hear an artist you admire and like describe what he hopes to do, and then afterwards to see for yourself what he has done. Especially if you are not disappointed in the result.
>
> This new film left me with no feelings of disappointment. Chaplin seems to me to have brought off something very difficult, just as he did in *Modern Times* and *The Great Dictator*.

* Chaplin was to have eight children by Oona: Geraldine (1944), Michael (1946), Josephine Hannah (1949), Victoria (1951), Eugene (1953), Jane (1957), Annette (1959) and Christopher (1962).

He has turned film clowning into social satire and criticism, without losing his astonishing ability to make us laugh.

This seems to me – and my standards are high – a wonderful thing to do. Many persons, including a large number who write for a living, will not agree with me. The truth is, this post-war period of ours is rapidly turning into a sour age, in which a great many peevish little men like nothing better than to sneer at anybody of real stature.

And Charles Chaplin has stature. He is, in fact, one of the most remarkable men of our time.

To begin with, he is one of the very few men who have compelled the film industry to serve them, who have been its masters and not its slaves. Sooner or later most film men, no matter how brilliant they may be, are beaten by the front offices, the distributors, the exhibitors, the trade . . .

There is not to my mind a hint of Communist savagery and inhumanity in the satire, for Chaplin, like most genuine artists, is at heart a genial and gentle anarchist and the laughter he provokes only clears and sweetens the air.

Despite Priestley's fears, the British press was largely favourable and at worst respectful. A fine critic who was himself a screenwriter, Paul Dehn, concluded,

Its narrative may be incoherent, its cutting slack, its camera-work primitive and its decor (by glossy Hollywood standards) abominably shoddy, but it says more in its brief, tragi-comic compass than all this year's glossy Hollywood pictures laid end to end; and the more you see it, the more it will have to say – which I take to be a symptom of greatness.

The press was as friendly when the film opened in Paris on 24 September. Chaplin had the American press barred from the première at the Gaumont Palace. This had the effect of excluding one of Chaplin's most loyal and dedicated supporters and devotees, Gene Moskowitz of *Variety*, one of the most generous and best-loved critics in the world. Moskowitz commented sadly, 'For a man demanding liberty and individual freedom of expression for himself, it is a negative action.' Chaplin evidently deigned to communicate with one or two American correspondents. Ed Murrow for one had the opportunity to ask him why he had not shown any positive side of the United States. Chaplin replied frankly:

If you give both sides it becomes bloody dull. I'm not a highbrow – I'm an instinctive artist. Whatever I do is for effect.

The motion picture is not for preachment, and if I've preached here I'm wrong. I'm loading the dice for something more important than politics – the affirmation of the man.

Another American who spoke to Chaplin at this time was Ella Winter who, with her husband Donald Ogden Stewart, had also been forced into exile in these times. The Ogden Stewarts remained friends of the Chaplins until their deaths; shortly before the film was released Ella Winter visited Chaplin in Vevey. Her interview was published in *The Observer* on the same day as Kenneth Tynan's review, which was neither hostile nor admiring. Chaplin had talked incessantly to her about the film.

> Chaplin was agog to know how people had liked his new film at a recent private showing. 'Did they laugh? What did they say? Didn't you like the part where . . .?' I reported in detail and he listened avidly. 'It's good, my best picture, it's entertainment, don't you think?' His agile, speckled hands gestured with every word. 'They say a lot about it that's nonsense, it's not political, not "anti" anything.'
>
> 'But tell me, didn't you like . . .?' He couldn't get enough. He is always possessed by his work and this picture has given him greater anxiety than his others. It's the first one he has made outside the United States.
>
> 'I had to get used to a new crew, different methods of work, but there were advantages – not least that it cost 25 per cent less.' He appreciated many things about the British technicians. 'They're slower, but more thorough . . .
>
> 'Of course I do everything. I create the whole thing. A film isn't just a product of mass production to me. I'm an individualist.'
>
> 'You haven't chosen colour or a wide screen . . .?'
>
> 'No . . . I paint on a small canvas.' He was pacing up and down the porch to keep up with his thought.
>
> 'I'd rather see a man stir his teacup with a spoon than see a volcano erupting. I want my camera to be like the proscenium of a theatre, come close to the actor, not lose his contour, bring the audience to him. Economy of action has gone through all my work. People have an idea that motion pictures must be elaborate, vast, spectacular, in some ways perhaps rightly, but I prefer to intensify personality rather than feature grand canyons on a wide screen. I prefer the shadow of a train passing over a face, rather than a whole railway station . . .'
>
> 'About America –' I started.
>
> He talked about it in snatches. 'What are they so sore about? There was a time when they put out the red carpet, literally, on every platform when I went from Los Angeles to New York. The crowd adored me. Now all that nonsense . . . people who spend time disparaging me . . . Actually I'm a Puritan. I haven't had the time to live the lives some of them attribute to me . . . or the energy. I've made eighty-five pictures.'*

* *A King in New York* was in fact his eightieth film.

We talked a while about the astonishing face of calumny. Then I asked why, when so many early films appear old-fashioned, his wear well.

'My clowning's realistic, that's why it doesn't go out of date. When I dip my fingers in a fingerbowl and wipe them on an old man's beard, I do it as if it were normal behaviour. So they still laugh at me.' And he laughed at himself as he thought of himself doing it.

'They call me old-fashioned,' he said, a bit wistfully. 'I don't know why. I suppose I ignore the "modern techniques", whatever that is. I don't like camera trickery – that's for technicians or track layers. All it leaves for the actor is to make Magnavox eyes or a CinemaScope mouth. It's too simple to shoot through a nostril or the fireplace. It can hurt an actor's talent, too. I don't like actors to be so swamped. Anyway, that's my preference,' he finished aggressively. 'Others may do it differently; that's my personal taste and my style.

'. . . As for politics, I'm an anarchist. I hate governments and rules and fetters . . . Can't stand caged animals . . . People must be free.'

Suddenly he put a thumb in each armhole. 'Greatest little comedian in the world,' he smiled, and he sat down. Then he was on his feet again. 'My picture isn't political. I'm anxious only that people laugh. The film is a satire; a clown must satirize; I've never made a picture that didn't.' After a moment he added, 'This is my most rebellious picture. I refuse to be part of that dying civilization they talk about.'

In the United States the campaign against Chaplin still persisted. In March 1958 the Hicksville Public Library was obliged to cancel a programme of four Chaplin pictures because of objections by local citizens. When Hollywood Boulevard's 'Walk of Fame' – one thousand bronze stars set into the pavement, each in honour of a different film actor or actress – was laid down, Chaplin's name was omitted because of protests from property owners in the area. In 1956 the American Internal Revenue Service announced that they would seek to claim $1.1 million in back taxes due for the last three years of operation in the United States. By 1958 the estimate had been revised to $542,000 with interest bringing the total to $700,000. In December 1958, however, the claim was definitively settled for $330,000, (with interest, $425,000). So Chaplin paid off the United States.

During these years Chaplin seems to have become more accessible to interviewers – though he had always braced himself to the necessity of grinning and bearing newsmen when there was a new film to be publicized. In one of these interviews, with Frederick Sands, he voiced his satisfaction at being back at work, with no prospect of retirement:

> The credit for that goes to Oona. She urged me on, because she found me restive doing nothing.
>
> After taking the decision to go back to work I became a much happier man.
>
> Now I put in a regular six to eight hours of work every day. Usually I finish about five and take a steam bath to keep me fit. In the summer I play lots of tennis . . .
>
> I have no intention of ever retiring again.
>
> I am putting every ounce of energy into writing my memoirs. They will be very long. I have much to tell and at my age I must hurry to complete them.
>
> Every time I think, so much comes back to my mind which I had long forgotten. Seventy years IS a long time.
>
> And then there is my new film, with the little man in the bowler hat back again – in colour.

Asked why he had abandoned the Tramp character in the first place, Chaplin replied:

> It's personal. Old friends are like old shoes, you know. All very fine, but we discard them.
>
> Little fellow just didn't fit in . . . there were periods in the atomic age during which I couldn't see room for him.
>
> I was no longer stimulated by him due to the changing of time. You cannot go on composing in one key . . .
>
> But now I shall bring him back – same as he was, yes, the same as he was . . . Of course, a little older.

He talked a good deal at this time about bringing back the Tramp. To another 1959 interviewer he said, 'I was wrong to kill him. There was room for the Little Man in the atomic age.' His interest in the character had been reawakened by working over *A Dog's Life*, *Shoulder Arms* and *The Pilgrim* which, with the assistance of Jerry Epstein, he edited and re-assembled as *The Chaplin Revue*. As severe as ever in the cutting room, he edited out moments which he thought no longer worked well. As a prologue to the omnibus he cut together some of the *How to Make Movies* material of the old Chaplin Studios. This was the first time the public had seen these scenes of the young Chaplin out of costume. As an introduction to *Shoulder Arms* he included some actuality footage of the First World War; and his own reconstruction of the landscapes of battle were not diminished by this juxtaposition. Throughout the work Oona sat beside him, sewing, and he complained humorously that whenever he wanted to throw out some scene, she pleaded for its retention. Chaplin wrote and recorded a new score for the assembly, and for *The Pilgrim* composed a country pastiche, 'Bound for Texas', which was recorded by the popular singer Matt Munro. *The Chaplin Revue* was released in September 1959.

In April 1959 Chaplin celebrated his seventieth birthday. 'I don't feel a day over sixty-nine,' he said. 'If only I could live long enough to do all the things I want to do!' He received over a thousand letters of congratulation from every part of the world. The guests at his birthday dinner included the dancer Noelle Adam who was soon to become the wife of his son Sydney, and Sydney Bernstein, the British cinema and television magnate, who presented Chaplin with a telescope. Another gift gave him some pleasure: thanks to the determined efforts of Miss Ford, the day before his birthday Roy Export and Lopert Films were granted a writ to seize copies of *Modern Times* that were being illegally distributed in the United States.

Chaplin's birthday was reported in newspapers across the world; and he was asked for his views on the future of mankind. 'I hope,' he said, 'we shall abolish war and settle all differences at the conference table . . . I hope we shall abolish all hydrogen and atom bombs before they abolish us first.' In more intimate interviews he never tired of sharing his wonder at the idyllic personal life he had achieved. Two years earlier, at the time of Jane's birth, he had declared, touchingly, 'With Oona to look after me and the children to inspire me, I cannot grow old, and nothing can hurt me.' In a 1959 interview he enlarged upon the secret of his happiness:

> I love my wife and she loves me. That is why we are so happy.
>
> If you don't demand too much from each other – that, I think, comes nearest to being a formula for happiness in marriage. The rest takes care of itself through tolerance. In the sixteen years of our marriage, we have been separated only once – for five days [*sic*] when Oona went on a business trip to America.
>
> She is my inspiration, and she is a good critic. She has a natural talent, and her criticism is constructive. To get her reactions to anything I do, I let her see my day's output of work. She never discusses anything or proffers an opinion unless I ask her. Sometimes I disagree with her opinion, only to find a week later that she was right.
>
> We have a profound respect for each other's taste and views, and this makes for a most agreeable atmosphere in the home . . . We can be thoroughly relaxed with each other and enjoy our own company without

> having to indulge in conversation . . . Oona feels that she has no talents except as a wife and mother.
>
> She is a very busy woman and leaves me at ten o'clock every morning. I just dally over breakfast, which I enjoy. I like my coffee and orange juice and bacon and eggs. Frightfully English, I know. When I've finished, I try to detain Oona with conversation, but she always runs out on me. At ten on the dot she gets up from the table and tells me: 'No, you get to work . . .'
>
> We like to invite friends on Sundays when most of the staff are off, and Oona and I potter about the kitchen preparing our own meal. Oona is a wonderful cook and there is never a mess of dishes in sight . . .
>
> The children? They have a place in our life and we enjoy them. They are very amusing, and they can be very irritating too. We see to it that their lives are fully occupied.

Oona told the interviewer: 'We encourage the children to become independent. We keep them busy with ballet lessons, music, even writing. It's working wonders developing their personalities.' Chaplin added, 'I never get impatient having children around. Far from disturbing me in my work they are an asset. You know, I thrive on youth and merriness. But get this [here he prodded a finger at the interviewer], our happiness is not governed by the children. We would be just as happy – just Oona and I.'

Oona, notoriously reticent in face of the press, made her own contribution to the interview,

> I am married to a young man.
>
> People think of Charlie as my father, but age counts for nothing in this house. To me he seems younger every day. There is certainly no father fixation about my feeling for Charlie. He has made me mature and I keep him young.
>
> I never consciously think about Charlie's age for 364 days of the year. Only his birthday is the annual shock for me. But I can feel the way some people stare at me with puzzlement and then look back at him, wondering how we have kept it up; whether it's just a façade.
>
> My security and stability with Charlie stem, not from his wealth, but from the very difference in years between us. Only young women who have married mature men will know what I mean.[7]

About this time the writer Ian Fleming was taken to dinner at the Manoir by Noël Coward. He found it 'wonderful to see two people bask unaffectedly in each other's love'. Shy and reticent as they could be in other ways, the Chaplins would kiss and embrace quite unselfconsciously, whoever was present. On the occasion of this visit, Fleming found Chaplin wearing a plum-coloured smoking jacket: it made him feel 'like a millionaire', he explained. At dinner he entertained his guests with a vivid description, illustrated by mime, of an imaginary film he would make, to be called *Around Romance in Eighty Days*. (This was the era of Mike Todd's much-publicized Jules Verne adaptation.) The film, he said, would be a mixture of half a dozen spectaculars – *Ben Hur*, *South Pacific* and *Anna Karenina* among them. It would include a chariot race. The villain, with huge knives on his chariot wheels would overtake the hero ('a chap called Gulliver or Don Quixote or one of those'). The hero would respond by leaning out of his own chariot to slice a side of ham on the knives. He would then eat the meat to renew his strength to win the race. Chaplin was still talking of reviving the Little Fellow: Mrs Fleming suggested that the theme might be 'the Little Man who never had it so good' (it was also the Macmillan period), and Chaplin seemed to like the idea.[8]

Chaplin and Oona would make occasional trips to London or Paris; there were also family holidays. In July and August 1961 Chaplin took his family to the Far East, and in spring 1962 they made their first trip to Ireland, where Chaplin acquired a taste for salmon fishing. Michael Chaplin recalled a charming comedy scene from the trip:

> When you're seventy-two and you believe that you've had all the experiences and are prepared to sit back and think out the rest of your life, it's maybe a little tough to try to start playing the 'my boy and I are just great pals' type of father . . . but on that Irish holiday my father tried. He took me fishing, ready to show me just how it's done . . .
>
> The object of the lesson was to show me how to cast a fly and play the trout. For fifteen minutes I stood by him on the bank of a stream while he talked about the theory of dropping a hooked piece of feather just where some fish would be coming up for his last breath.
>
> 'The touch,' he said. 'You must have the touch . . . here, I'll show you . . .'
>
> He threw the rod back, the line went swishing through the air, then he whipped the rod forward . . .
>
> A big nothing.
>
> Father tugged, obviously thinking that he'd got the line caught on a branch.
>
> I took a quick glance over his shoulder, right to where he'd just about ripped the back out of his raincoat.

'I think it's caught on your raincoat,' I said, very tactfully . . .

Gratefully, but embarrassed, he unhooked himself and wound the line in.

We plodded home at dusk, with my father coyly trying to hold together the torn halves of his raincoat.[9]

The 1962 holiday – the last on which all the children would be together with their parents – also included visits to Venice, London and Paris. It was widely reported that Chaplin would visit the Soviet Union in the near future. The only foundation for this story was that when he had met a delegation of Soviet writers they had courteously suggested that he might visit Russia and he had as courteously replied, 'With pleasure.'

In June of that year, Chaplin was invested by the University of Oxford with the honorary degree of Doctor of Letters. The only disagreeable note to the occasion was the publicity given to the objections of the historian Hugh Trevor-Roper, who declared that the value of honorary degrees would be degraded by this award to a mere film comedian. This had no effect, however, and on 27 June Chaplin arrived at the Senate House, dressed in a dark suit and academic robes of scarlet and grey, to receive his degree. Others honoured at the same time were Dean Rusk, the American Secretary of State, Yehudi Menuhin and Graham Sutherland. The crowds, though, were for Chaplin. Geraldine, who had come from London where she was studying at the Royal Ballet School, had to battle her way to the door and even then had great difficulty in proving her identity. The Vice-Chancellor greeted Chaplin with the words, 'Illustrious man, without doubt star of the first magnitude, you who have been a source of the greatest pleasure to so many people for so many years . . .'

The Public Orator, A. N. Bryan-Brown, introduced Chaplin with a quotation from Juvenal:

Nil habet infelix paupertas durius in se
Quam quod ridiculos homines facit.

[The hardest blow poverty yields is that the poor are laughed at.]

Chaplin, he continued, invited laughter,

per bracas illas fluitantes, calceos divaricatos, petasum orbiculatum constantem simul at instabilem, bacillum flexibile, exiguum denique labri superioris ornamentum.

[with his baggy trousers, his turned out boots, his bowler, cane and toothbrush moustache.]

In all his films, said the Public Orator, 'are to be found the humour and generosity of one who sympathizes with the underdog.' Beauty, said Chaplin, in his speech of acceptance, is in the eye of the beholder: 'There are those who can see either art or beauty in a rose lying in the gutter, or the sudden slant of sunlight across an ash-can, or even in the tumbling of a clown.' When it was over, Chaplin said that he would have 'needed a heart of stone' not to be moved by the reception. Sir Maurice Bowra introduced Chaplin to Dean Rusk. 'There was no bitterness between us, no bitterness at all,' Chaplin said later.

A note of bitterness was, however, introduced by some elements of the American press. The reactionary *Philadelphia Inquirer*[10] had a report headed 'Buffoonery at Oxford', and found the event 'a snide attempt to place Chaplin on the same plane with Dean Rusk in its distribution of honours that most Americans will find unpalatable.' The *New York Times* however took advantage of the occasion to say, 'We do not believe the Republic would be in danger if the present Administration lifted the ban that was imposed in 1952, and if yesterday's unforgotten little tramp were allowed to amble down the gangplank of an American port.'

Nine days later, the University of Durham followed Oxford's lead and awarded Chaplin an honorary degree of D.Litt. The Durham Public Orator, Karl Britton, was something of a film critic, it seemed. Chaplin, he said, had produced some of the great comic art of the age – comedy 'often enriched and sometimes endangered by sentiment,' and with a political message 'that arose out of a deep view of man's small situation in the world.'

Durham invested Chaplin with his degree on 6 July, after which Chaplin had to hurry back to Switzerland in time for the birth of his eighth child. He arrived home on Sunday 7 July, went to bed that night, but had to get up again around 3 a.m. to rush Oona to the Clinique Montchoisi in Lausanne. At 5.30 a.m. on the morning of 8 July she gave birth to a boy who was named Christopher James. The family was now complete.

Chaplin was fifty-five when Geraldine, his first child by Oona, was born; and seventy-three when their last child, Christopher, arrived.

It was a remarkable and challenging undertaking to bring up a young family at an age when most men are relaxing into the sinecure role of grandfather. Ordinary considerations of age and declining energy seemed irrelevant to Chaplin, but problems still remained in rearing this large brood. Chaplin's dreams had been formed in his youth. It would be natural for him to want to provide for his children the paternal discipline and protection that he had been denied in his own youth, yet for children of the 1960s this ideal could appear somewhat archaic and restrictive. Even though to Oona Chaplin remained a young man, the generation gap was undoubtedly exaggerated in their household. Despite his life-long dream of domesticity, Chaplin was still dedicated to work, and that work continued, as it had always done, to take precedence over everything and everyone else. The children learned that above all they must never intrude upon Daddy's work; to make sure that they did not was a heavy part of the nurses' charge. Francis Wyndham, a wise and sympathetic observer who knew the Chaplins, remarked another obstacle to ideal domesticity:

> The only flaw in their domestic harmony – occasional misunderstandings with their children as each in turn ceases to be a child – springs from the very intensity and completeness of their mutual happiness. The delight which Charlie and Oona take in each other's company tends to isolate them in a self-sufficient world of love. This atmosphere is utterly charming for their friends, but its effect on a nearer relationship might be unintentionally exclusive. If Chaplin has failed to achieve a wholly unselfish sympathy with his children, he has triumphantly succeeded in eliminating any dichotomy between 'love' and 'admiration' in his attitude towards the woman in his life.[11]

Chaplin may have had problems in being a father; at the same time it is never easy to be the child of a great man. All the Chaplin children to some degree found themselves isolated from their school contemporaries. They lived in a grand house in a park, with servants and money; and the great men of the world paid homage to their parents. With success and fortune, and through bitter experience, Chaplin had learned to mistrust, in the first instance, any proffered friendship or intimacy; and in their turn the children had to learn this unchildlike lesson. Friends were rigorously vetted and rarely encouraged.

Throughout his life Chaplin had been subject to sudden outbursts of temper which were generally soon forgotten. At other times, though, the difficulty he had in delivering a reprimand was a byword at the studio, where someone else was always deputed to perform such unpleasant tasks on Chaplin's behalf. As the children grew up, he found the same difficulty in telling them off when it was necessary. Gentle and shy even in the face of her own children, Oona was no better equipped for the task, and much of the time the task of delivering reproaches and reprimands was deputed to Kay-Kay or Miss Ford, neither of whom felt any inhibitions in the matter. A certain reticence and evasion became characteristic of the relationship between the Chaplin parents and children.

Chaplin tended to be less severe with the younger children than with the older ones born in the United States. If there was any slight resentment among the children about this discrimination, it was from the younger ones who felt deprived of the discipline they saw doled out to their elders. When Chaplin did get angry with them, the older girls were more adept than Michael at deflecting their father's displeasure. Kay-Kay recalled how effectively Geraldine, then aged five, dealt with a prolonged telling-off from her father. Fixing him with a baleful stare, she yanked her baby sister Josephine to her feet, exhorting her, 'C'mon. Let's get out of here.' Chaplin's wrath could not withstand such an exit line.

Geraldine was to be the first rebel, when she left home to study at the Royal Ballet School. Michael soon followed. He became particularly irked by parental intervention in his friendships, and eventually left home. His adventures provided a field-day for the press and acute embarrassment and annoyance to his parents. He became (briefly) a junkie, enrolled in RADA, acted in pictures, recorded pop songs, married and provided Chaplin and Oona with their first grandchild. At one point in 1965 he claimed National Assistance. Chaplin and the rest of the family happened to be passing through London at the time on their way to the annual Easter holiday in Ireland, and Oona was obliged to give the press an uncharacteristically severe statement in which she said, 'the young man is a problem, and I am sorry he was given National Assistance. He has stubbornly refused an education for three years and therefore he should get a job and go to work. If I do not wish to indulge him as a beatnik, that is my privilege – sincerely, Oona Chaplin.'[12]

Despite his aberrations, Michael Chaplin was clearly a young man of individuality, charm and warmth; and before his father's death, he was to be fully reconciled with the family. During the periods of estrangement from Geraldine and Michael, Oona, when she and Chaplin were in London, would make the excuse of shopping expeditions to slip away and visit them. Chaplin was supposed to know nothing of these trips, but there were no real secrets between them and it is pretty certain that he was tacitly aware that she was keeping a maternal eye on their children. They were both grateful, too, for the fatherly concern of Jerry Epstein, who was by this time permanently resident in London.

Chaplin had begun to write his memoirs after finishing *A King in New York*. In 1960 he told Ian Fleming that he had finished five hundred pages and had only some twenty more to go. Fleming may have misunderstood, because three more years of work remained to be done. Chaplin also complained to Fleming that his secretary was forever trying to improve his English. 'He said he was not surprised, as he had taught himself the language and suspected that his secretary knew it far better than he did but, even so, he liked his own version and hoped that some of what he had actually written would survive the process of editing by his publishers.'[13] Chaplin's daily routine while writing the book was to rise at seven, to take a dip in his swimming pool, whatever the weather, to take his breakfast, and afterwards kiss Oona goodbye as if he was going off to his office. He would then work until midday and lunch. The older children took turns to lunch with their parents. After a siesta, Chaplin would return to work until five, when he had tea and, in fine weather, played a little tennis. Dinner at the Manoir was always at seven. When it was over Chaplin would continue to work in the library until ten. *My Autobiography* went through the same cycles of dictation, typing, correction and retyping as the scripts. Chaplin took great delight in reading aloud to visitors the sections he had most recently written. Lillian Ross was so privileged and remembered how on an autumn afternoon in 1962 'I sat with him on his terrace as he read parts of his book manuscript to me, the tortoiseshell-rimmed glasses a bit down on his nose, his reading dramatic to the point of melodrama, his devotion to his subject unselfconscious and complete.'[14]

Since Chaplin had never co-operated with any biographer (at least since his early misfortunes with Rose Wilder Lane in 1916) the autobiography was a major publishing prize. The lucky winner was The Bodley Head. The managing director Max Reinhardt had been introduced to the Chaplins in 1958, and undoubtedly his urging and encouragement were important to its production. Reinhardt was admirably patient. As early as 1958 he had sounded out *The Sunday Times* about serial rights. Leonard Russell, the Literary Editor, recalled delicately asking if Chaplin would be using a 'ghost':

> Mr Reinhardt looked shocked, offended even. Surely we couldn't think that Chaplin, a man who wrote his own scripts, directed his own films, composed his own music, would seek outside help with his own memoirs: every word would be written by Chaplin – he would swear an affidavit on that. 'Never mind,' said Mr Reinhardt, looking for the waiter, 'I hope to have something to show you before very long.'
>
> But years passed, and nothing happened – we thought that Chaplin must have given up. Then early in 1962 Mr Reinhardt produced an uncorrected draft of the first third of the book. We read it. It was magnificent – a splendid serial in itself.
>
> Chaplin, however, wasn't ready to negotiate the newspaper rights: first he must finish the book. There was nothing to do but wait. And while we were waiting, the word got round that Chaplin was writing his autobiography, with the result that frenzied and fantastic offers for the serial rights came from the United Kingdom, from the United States, from most of the countries of Europe. Chaplin ignored them and Mr Reinhardt, presumably, exercised his customary diplomacy.
>
> Mr Chaplin went on writing and rewriting [in point of fact his actual and uninterrupted time on the book was a mere two years] and our frustration deepened.[15]

It was later revealed that when Ian Fleming visited Vevey it was as an undercover agent for *The Sunday Times* with the assignment of wringing an agreement from Chaplin. The mission was bungled since Fleming became far too interested in the author's view of things, and in urging Chaplin to permit no editorial interventions in his work. In the end, however, *The Sunday Times* managed to secure premier publication of the book.

As a trailer, *The Sunday Times* published in their magazine section a profile of Chaplin, by the distinguished theatre critic Harold Clurman, which had already appeared in *Esquire* (November 1962). Clurman had been a guest at the Manoir, and was permitted to read the manuscript of *My Autobiography*. Before he began reading, he was told by Chaplin, 'I'm really surprised how well America comes off!' 'I had supposed when I read a press report to this effect,' Clurman wrote afterwards,

> that his benign attitude might be a matter of tactics (though Chaplin has never been notably tactful), but face-to-face with him I felt sure his moderation was genuine, a mellowness which is not the sign of any weakening, but rather a growth in breadth and wisdom. For the first time in my long acquaintance with Chaplin, I had the feeling that he was not only an artist of genius, but a man who might be considered – or had become – wise.
>
> When I speak of 'wisdom', I do not mean correct in opinion or even reliable in judgement. I mean that Chaplin's whole personality has become integrated and has attained the finest balance that his talents and nature could achieve – and these are sufficiently rich and human enough to make a man to be cherished.
>
> So when Charlie began to let fly with statements which might be added up to a sort of credo, I had no inclination to contradict him, or to test their objective validity. Everything he said – even when paradoxical or perhaps wildly 'wrong' – seemed right for him and could be so interpreted that some basic truth, some corrective to his exaggerations might be distilled from his sallies.
>
> I could not quarrel with his concern about the armaments race. I smiled in comprehension of his anarchistically aesthetic declaration, 'I can't stand Communists with their *system* and systems . . . I hate systems.' Again and again he exclaimed, 'Life is full of poetry', and though this is not exactly a 'scientific' statement, his person made his meaning entirely clear.
>
> He went on to discuss matters of acting craft. He had learned much, he said, from his first director. 'I believe in theatricalism. (His word, not mine.) Theatricalism is poetry . . . I don't believe in The Method.' (I did not tell him that I had heard Stanislavsky say to an actress: 'If my system' – which is also known as The Method – 'troubles you, forget it.') 'I believe in theatricalism,' Charlie continued, 'even in "tricks" – actors' tricks . . . I don't like Shakespeare on the stage; he interferes with the actor's freedom, with his virtuosity.' And as his spirit almost lifted him from his seat, so that I feared that he might become airborne at any moment. I could see that in his way he was more Shakespearean than many professional Shakespeareans . . .
>
> What struck me . . . was that, though I was not at all tempted to interrupt his outbursts, I might easily have done so without offence. In former years I had the impression that, though he was sharply observant, he hardly listened to anyone. He was always 'on' – telling stories, doing imitations, recitations, pantomimes, delivering himself of fire-cracker pronouncements – providing himself and others with a constant spectacle

> of irrepressible energy and imagination. No one got a chance to speak in his presence. (Hardly anyone desired to.) But now Charlie was also ready to listen.

As Clurman left the Manoir, he asked Chaplin how his book would end: 'What's the conclusion?'

> 'That I am content to look out at the lake and at the mountains and feel that, with my family around me there is nothing more and nothing better,' he answered. He pointed toward the sky and the open space around – in a gesture which pleaded to say more than his words might convey, while his expression was one of naïve bafflement at his inability to define the ineffable.

While the book was in the last stages of production, Chaplin celebrated his seventy-fifth birthday. This time his message to the world combined melancholy and optimism: 'Where is all the fun, the gaiety, the laughter? Everyone is much too serious these days.' He was still gravely troubled by the existence of nuclear weapons, but now 'I am a humanitarian and therefore I believe in humanity and its ability to survive . . . I think, like the British, we will all muddle through somehow.' During the summer he attended a Callas gala performance at the Paris Opera, and was observed by the press greeting Princess Grace of Monaco on the steps of the theatre. He considered writing an opera himself, and thought *Tess of the D'Urbervilles* a likely subject. He also spoke of writing a slapstick comedy for his son Sydney.

My Autobiography was published in September 1964. The first printing was eighty thousand copies, and the book was selected by the Book of the Month Club in America, and by the largest Italian and German book clubs. Chaplin was reputed to have received an advance of half a million dollars for British and American rights, not to mention the nine pounds of caviare given him by the USSR in consideration of the right to reprint a thousand words in *Izvestia*.

The reviews were almost unanimous about the book, which finally ran to more than five hundred printed pages. The first eleven of its thirty-one chapters, ending at the moment that he signed with the Mutual Company, can stand comparison with any autobiography for their colour and vitality. Chaplin's writing is energetic, and his pleasure in words is infectious. Words he particularly likes, like 'ineffable' and 'concupiscence' he may use too often; but even the occasional slight misapplication of some word can endow it with something new and arresting. His phrasing is vivid. The chronicle of the childhood is such a Dickensian mixture of colour and tragedy that some reviewers were sceptical of its truth. Documentary research constantly vindicates Chaplin's record.

From the twelfth chapter onwards, however, some disappointment is almost inevitable. Chaplin is much more concerned to describe his social life and the celebrities he had known than to reveal anything about his films, the way he made them, life in his studio and his collaborators. Chaplin artlessly exposed himself to charges of snobbery: 'If we were not so preoccupied with our family, we could have quite a social life in Switzerland, for we live relatively near the Queen of Spain and the Count and the Countess Chevreau d'Antraigues, who have been most cordial to us, and there are a number of film stars and writers who live near.'[16]

The preface of the present work has already speculated on the reasons for Chaplin's reticence about his work: his declared belief that 'if people know how it's done, all the magic goes'; the possibility that the ultimate secret of his creation was mysterious even to him; the possibility that he felt that the daily routines of his working life would be simply boring to readers. Even then it was hard to understand how he could devote pages to Randolph Hearst or H. G. Wells, yet not make even a passing reference to loyal collaborators who had given so much to the films; people like Totheroh, Bergman, Mack Swain, Eric Campbell or Georgia Hale. Is it far-fetched to look for a deep-rooted psychological explanation of the increasing reluctance to acknowledge collaborators in his work? The perceptive Francis Wyndham wrote that 'the rich and famous and fulfilled man whom the world sees still considers himself a victim maimed for life by that early catastrophic shock'. Perhaps it was a necessary part of the therapy, essential to his confidence, always to tell himself that he had conquered the world and raised himself from poverty and nonentity to universal fame and affection unaided. No other film maker ever so completely dominated every aspect of the work, did every job. If he could have done so Chaplin would have played every role and (as his son Sydney humorously but perceptively observed) sewn every costume. Chaplin had both the compulsion to do everything and the need to know that he had done everything.

Whatever psychological explanations may be adduced, many were hurt by these omissions in *My Autobiography*. Most vocally offended was Robert Florey, who had begun to write about Chaplin more than forty years before, had published an affectionate biography in 1927 and had maintained his loyalty until this time. His review in *Paris-Match* was very largely an appreciation of those dozens of people left out of the autobiography, including Georgia Hale, Wheeler Dryden, Henry Bergman, Albert Austin, Stan Laurel and Mabel Smith, 'who regularly (if not infallibly) predicted the future for him'.

For all its lacunae the autobiography was a very considerable achievement – wonderfully readable, amiably opinionated, disarmingly frank, sometimes pompous and the next moment self-deprecatory in poking fun at the writer's own human vanities and affections. It was widely translated and the warmth of the reception across the world seemed to give new energy to Chaplin. As soon as the book was finished he set about preparing a new film. Jerry Epstein was to be producer and Universal provided distribution backing. The film was *A Countess From Hong Kong*.

19

A COUNTESS FROM HONG KONG and the final years

The subject of *A Countess From Hong Kong* was a refurbishment of *Stowaway*, the script Chaplin had written for Paulette almost thirty years before. Only random pages and notes have survived from the original *Stowaway* script: the rest seems to have been cannibalized in compiling the new screenplay. There were few changes to the story. In the early version the Countess came from Shanghai; now she was from Hong Kong. The hero, Ogden Mears, was changed from a big game hunter to a millionaire and diplomat. *Stowaway* would probably have compared very well with the average situation comedy of the late 1930s. The dialogue was crisp and light and Chaplin felt able to adopt it in large part for *A Countess From Hong Kong*.

The new script opens in traditional Chaplin style with a subtitle: 'As a result of two world wars, Hong Kong was crowded with refugees.' Some of the most glamorous of these are employed as taxi-girls at 'The Palace of Beautiful Women' where, for a few dollars, American sailors may dance with former White Russian baronesses and countesses. (Neither Chaplin nor the critics were greatly bothered about the chronology: after two world wars, exiles from the Revolution of 1917 might well be supposed to be past the dancing age.) One of these aristocratic taxi-girls, the beautiful Natascha Alexandroff, finds herself dancing with Ogden Mears, an American millionaire doing the night spots of Hong Kong.

Ogden returns to his suite on the luxury liner after his heavy night out and the next morning discovers that Natascha has stowed away there. The likely embarrassment of the situation is compounded by the news that he has just been appointed United States Ambassador to Arabia. Ogden is softened by Natascha's recital of her sad life story, of how she fled to Shanghai from Russia and became a gangster's mistress at the tender age of fourteen. Now she seeks only the escape that an American passport could provide. Ogden reluctantly hides her in his suite, which results in a succession of alarms and embarrassments. To obtain the necessary American passport for Natascha, Ogden arranges a marriage of convenience with Hudson, his valet – who is all too clearly not the marrying kind. At Honolulu Ogden's wife comes aboard. Natascha dives over the side of the ship into the harbour. Ogden and his wife come to an amicable divorce agreement. Millionaire and pauper countess are happily reunited in a tango.

While Chaplin was preparing *A Countess From Hong Kong*, the last personal link with his childhood was broken. At 11 p.m. on 16 April 1965 – Chaplin's seventy-sixth birthday – his brother Sydney died in Nice. He was eighty. His death occurred at the Hotel Ruhl, where he and his Niçoise wife Gypsy spent each winter. The following day Chaplin arrived in Nice for the cremation in Marseilles. Sydney's ashes were buried in Montreux.

The two brothers had seen each other frequently during the last years of Sydney's life and no doubt their sessions of reminiscence, as well as delighting Gypsy, Oona and the family, contributed much to *My Autobiography*. Sydney and Gypsy generally visited Switzerland during the summers, and both were adored by the children at Vevey. Gypsy was amusing, charming and elegant, and maintained an intriguing air of mystery: she would never discuss her life before her marriage to Sydney. Sydney, who had never had a family of his own, loved children. The young Chaplins for their part were enchanted by his still prodigious facility for inventing gags and jokes. From Nice he would write long letters to the older children, with page upon page of jokes. (He kept carbon copies to be sure that he did not repeat himself next time.) On visits to the Manoir he found a mischievous way of teasing his younger brother. He would tell the girls some mildly off-colour or racist joke and send them off in fits of giggles to retail it to their father. Sydney would then sit innocently by, hearing his brother raging in the distance, 'Never let me hear jokes like that in this house!' Geraldine and Josephine remember too, though, how in old age their cheerful and ebullient uncle would sit at the window of the Manoir watching the beauty of the sun setting over the mountains, and cry.

During the summer of 1965 Chaplin was co-recipient with Ingmar Bergman of the Erasmus Prize. On 11 November he gave a press conference for two hundred journalists at the Savoy Hotel to announce his plans for *A Countess From Hong Kong*. Sophia Loren was present. The writer was there on that occasion:

> Is it thrilling, asked a friend, to see him in the flesh for the first time? And the answer is that somehow it isn't: more of a puzzle rather, to try to find in this spry, well-fed, lively, neatly turned-out figure in dark glasses (and not nearly as small as I had always imagined) either the old Charlie, or a man well on his way toward eighty. Bright-eyed, clear-voiced, quick-talking, he is, if not exactly youthful, fairly ageless. It is, of course, from use that he is able to remain quite untroubled by being the focus of a heavy stampede of pressmen and photographers such as was produced by his press conference at the Savoy . . .
>
> There is never much to be learned from this kind of affair; anyone who is good at it, like Chaplin, knows exactly what he wants to say, and however irrelevant the questions may be, the answers will all quickly come back to the point. And the point in this instance was that Mr Chaplin was going to make a new film. For the first time in nearly half a century he would not be his own producer: 'And it's wonderful. I don't have to worry. I can extend myself as I please, and it is only my fault if the picture doesn't come off.' No expense would be spared. The film would be in colour and have a fourteen-week shooting schedule. What was the budget? 'I don't think that's anybody's business,' he said, but very amiably.
>
> Mr Chaplin had, he said, two great stars, Marlon Brando and Sophia Loren. He had seen Sophia in a film and known at once that she was perfect for the part. What was the film? He really couldn't remember; it was so long ago. Was it *Marriage, Italian Style?* No, no, it wasn't that. Was it *Yesterday, Today and Tomorrow*? Yes. Yes – that was the film. Anyway, she was perfect for the part . . .
>
> The picture would be called *A Countess From Hong Kong*. He had wanted to call it *The Countess*, but someone already had rights on that title. He had had the screenplay since the time of *The Great Dictator*, but he'd up-dated it. He would not say much about the story, except that it is set in the period just after the Second World War, and a lot of the action takes place aboard ship.
>
> Asked to be more precise, Mr Chaplin said he was sorry but he was

tired; which he clearly was not. He would only add modestly that, 'the situation is riotously funny but justified and believable . . . It is not slapstick, but comedy of character, taken from life.

'I have no role myself, thank God! No, it's not the first time I've directed and not played. Around 1924 [*sic*] I made a film called *A Woman of Paris* . . . Of course, I may walk on, like Hitchcock does . . .'

Chaplin said that his son Sydney would play in it. 'He's a very good comedian and I think he will contribute to the lift and hilarity of the screenplay.' (Chaplin always chooses his words carefully, if sometimes curiously.) Inevitably the columnists asked if his son Michael would play. Chaplin was grave. 'I'm not answering any personal questions . . .' and when the newsman tried to insist, 'Don't try to get smart-alecky with me . . .' He was not so solemn when asked about America. He had no plans to go there unless it happened to be in connexion with the picture, but in any case he had no quarrel with Hollywood. 'I wrote a book, and I think America came out of it pretty well. I happen to like Hollywood. Anyway I don't think that's pertaining much to the picture.'

Mr Chaplin answered a few more questions. How did it feel to be at work again? 'Marvellous. Thank God I'm still active. I can still think up two or three laughs. I'm getting on, but right now I have everything before me. The whole world is my oyster.' ('His what?' the reporter who had quizzed him about his son asked a friend.) What did he think about A. J. P. Taylor's new book, in which Taylor linked him with Shakespeare as a cultural influence? 'I think he has damn' good judgement,' said Mr Chaplin merrily. ('Linked him with who?' asked the same reporter.)[1]

Shooting began on 25 January 1966. Intrepid as ever, Chaplin – who was to celebrate his seventy-seventh birthday in the course of the filming – now undertook his first film in colour and on the anamorphic screen which he had derided in *A King in New York*. This was also the first time that he had cast and directed major international stars – Sophia Loren and Marlon Brando. As in *A Woman of Paris* he allotted himself only a brief walk-on. He was fortunate to have a director of photography, Arthur Ibbetson, and a designer, Don Ashton, who revered him and were responsive and sympathetic to his demands. Moreover in terms of production the film was comparatively simple. Though the action required skilful playing, it was mostly set in interiors, particularly the adjoining rooms of Ogden's ship-board suite. Despite an interruption when Chaplin suffered a bad bout of 'flu, shooting was completed in fourteen working weeks. Charles Chaplin directed what was to prove his last scene on Wednesday 11 May 1966, fifty-two years and three months after his Keystone debut.

Much later Marlon Brando spoke disparagingly of the experience of working on the film: schooled in 'Method' acting he was bewildered by Chaplin's intuitive and pragmatic approach to performance, and not resourceful enough easily to submit himself to Chaplin's requirement that his actors should reproduce his own interpretation of a part. The film critic Penelope Gilliatt visited the set, and described how Brando one day told Chaplin that he did not understand the character's motivation at a particular point in the action. Chaplin cheerfully replied that he did not understand the motivation either, but that it probably did not amount to much. He went on to explain to Brando exactly how to play the action: that way, he said, it would come off. This sort of thing must certainly have been disconcerting for the actor; but Mrs Gilliatt remarked upon Brando's conscientiousness in following Chaplin's minute instructions on every line or gag. Sophia Loren adored Chaplin and proved wonderfully responsive to his direction. Chaplin thought Patrick Cargill's performance as Hudson the valet entirely admirable: 'I've never done anything as *funny*,' he told Francis Wyndham. In supporting roles he had Tippi Hedren, his son Sydney and Oliver Johnston. Chaplin liked his unit, and it was one of his happiest shooting periods.

Among the visitors to the set during the shooting of *A Countess From Hong Kong* was Kevin Brownlow, the historian of the silent cinema, who had accompanied Gloria Swanson to Pinewood. It was the first time that Swanson had been on a Chaplin set since she appeared in *His New Job* in 1915.*

> Finally, Chaplin had to leave to go on the set. Miss Swanson perched on a ladder to get a better view over the obstructing lights. Sophia Loren, devastating in her low-cut white dress, was joined by Marlon Brando in a blue dressing gown, looking furious. A wave of tension followed him as he shuffled from behind the camera onto the set.
>
> Chaplin seemed oblivious. As he directed Loren, and then Brando, I scribbled down the directions verbatim. He tried to work out a way in which Loren could walk over to Brando, holding a glass. He paid no attention to dialogue. I heard him give only one dialogue direction. He may have written the words, but he could not remember them. 'So-and-so-and-so-and-so etcetera,' would be his delivery of an average line.

* On this occasion, Swanson insisted she had not played in the film.

The associate producer, Jerry Epstein, paced behind him, reading the correct lines from a script. The set was a cabin of a luxury liner; at one point, Chaplin stood by the cabin door and looked across at Epstein.

'This walk lays an egg,' he said, and laughed. Then he stalked back to his director's chair beneath the camera and shouted, 'Go over there, make up your mind, take it.'

The action did not proceed smoothly. Brando, sullen, kept saying, 'All right, all right.' He did not seem to be listening as Chaplin instructed him again. Finally, Chaplin got up and walked back onto the set.

'You go, open the door, "Excuse me-so-and-so-and-so."' He paused, and gave a classical, balletic Chaplin gesture. 'All right, you're here . . . come to the door . . . and say, "I'm etcetera, etcetera."'

Brando came in and did a tolerably good, if lifeless scene, ignoring the Chaplinesque gesture; at the end he uttered, 'Oh, no!'

Chaplin interjected a long-drawn-out, 'O-o-oh, n-o-o-o!' Then he hurried in to make adjustments. 'We'll have to do the same choreography.' He went through the moves, ignoring the dialogue, and then turned to the director of photography, Arthur Ibbetson.

'I think that will be the first close-up till we get it natural and sincere,' he said, crossing his chest with his arm to indicate the limit of the close-up.

He stood by and watched a run-through of the scene. Then he said, 'I think that's all right,' and took his hat off, revealing a shock of pure white hair.

Gloria Swanson leaned forward: 'You can see why actors find him difficult,' she whispered. 'This is a simple scene, and he's making much ado about nothing . . .'

Having worked out a bit of business for Brando, Chaplin did it himself, combining Chaplinesque grace with the suggestive vulgarity of the music hall. He picked up an imaginary glass of Alka-Seltzer and drained the contents, leaning his head right back. Then he gave a funny belch, and laughed at his audience – the rows of technicians, who laughed back. Brando gave no visible reaction. Chaplin did it again; he took the non-existent glass, drank deeply, and burped. It didn't quite work. 'We'll put that on sound,' he said, gesturing vaguely off set.

Then, still thinking out the scene, he walked up and down, clenched fist held at forehead in classical style.*

When Brando tried the scene, he used a real glass with no contents, and took a short draft. Chaplin sprang forward.

'No – you're going to take longer to do that, you know.' The old

* In 1982, when searching with his co-director David Gill for material for *Unknown Chaplin*, Brownlow was thrilled to find some shots of Chaplin in the same attitude, taken during the making of *The Count* just fifty years before *A Countess From Hong Kong*.

professional advising the young apprentice. And he demonstrated the whole gesture, going all the way back, swallowing the Alka-Seltzer, and belching at the end of it. Brando followed most of Chaplin's instructions, but he then achieved two startlingly realistic belches which effectively killed the comedy.

Rumours about Brando's temperamental behaviour were circulating widely at this stage of the production. Later, press reports indicated that all was harmonious. But at this point, it was clear that Brando was expected to imitate Chaplin rather than to develop his own performance. For such a great dramatic actor, such direction must have been bewildering.

For the onlooker, however, such direction was miraculous. It was as exciting as watching a Chaplin film no one knew existed; first he played the Brando role, then he skipped over and did the Loren part. One was aggressively masculine, the other provocative and feminine, yet both remained pure Charlie. It is a real loss to the cinema that Chaplin refused to allow a film to be made about the production.

On the way back to London Gloria Swanson reflected:

> Well, wasn't *that* a nostalgic time for me. To walk on that set and be greeted with open arms! He looked as fit as a fiddle. He was bouncing in and out of his chair. Frankly, he didn't look a day older than when I'd last seen him, seven years ago. Did you notice that he isn't as articulate with words as he is in pantomime, when showing people what he wants? What an artist. I suppose he is the most creative man it is possible to meet.[2]

A week before the end of shooting, Chaplin got into costume for his final film role. He plays an elderly steward who is a victim of severe *mal de mer*. It was a favourite joke for him, and he played his exit scene in the same silent mime as in his earliest screen appearances.

Chaplin composed seventeen musical themes, which were orchestrated by Eric James and conducted by Lambert Williamson. The theme song, 'This is my Song', was to become a popular hit. The film was ready for release in the New Year. Chaplin had found it 'such fun to do, I thought the whole world was going to go mad for it.' However he had misgivings at the London press show, when the projector kept breaking down and the image was badly focused.* The notices confirmed his worst fears. The kindest adopted a patronizing 'more in sorrow than in anger' tone. A major problem with the film

* On the foyer steps he encountered a total stranger. 'They're ruining my film,' he wailed, and passed on.

was that, in the year of *Bonnie and Clyde*, *The Dirty Dozen*, *The Graduate*, *Weekend* and *Belle de Jour*, a gentle romantic comedy was an almost incomprehensible anachronism.

Chaplin, publicly at least, took a bravely truculent stance in the face of the rebuffs and declared to the press that the British critics were 'bloody idiots'. He felt this opinion vindicated when the film opened in Europe. *Paris-Match* said that the film was 'a charming comedy [which] did not deserve the severity of the British Press.' *Le Figaro*'s headline was 'In London Thorns – In Paris Roses', and *Paris Jour*'s was 'Paris makes Chaplin even with London'. In Italy *Unità* also had a headline: 'Demolishing Critical Reviews of British and American Press are Unjustified'; and in Sweden the critic of *Dagens Nyhatet* said 'It is difficult to understand the objections raised by the English critics . . . His picture of the world, naïvely warm and generous, unveiling and disarming, uncoils again.' Not all the English-speaking critics were without sympathy. In New York William Wolf wrote in *Cue* Magazine, 'I have returned from a second look at *A Countess From Hong Kong*. Again, I found it charming, funny and a welcome change of pace from our frenetic, super-sophisticated milieu. Chaplin could never be counted on to come up with the expected, and that is a mark of his genius.'

Chaplin spoke at length of his reactions to the reviews in a long interview with Francis Wyndham, which provides fascinating insights into Chaplin's view of the world as he witnessed it in his seventies:

> With my next film, I won't open in London. I'll open in Kalamazoo or somewhere and leave London till later. I don't understand what's happening there now. I think they're swinging drunk. It's a peculiar sort of desperation and somnambulism, a negation of art, of any sort of simplicity. When the swinging thing is over, what will they have left? I don't believe there is such a thing as fashion. Who the hell creates the fashion anyway? Anybody can – something very facile that catches on and everybody imitates. Cynics – so what? Life is cynical if we think only in terms of birth and death. It's too easy. How ironic that my theme song for the *Countess* is a big hit all over the world. They throw away the flesh of the peach . . .
>
> Soon they'll come to their senses and start having a good time. Every once in a while you see a ray of light, someone behind the camera with a sensitive hand. But more often on TV than in the cinema. I saw a TV play called *The Caretaker* which was very mysterious and interesting. And I was amused by *Goldfinger*: one scene I thought so funny, when the whole army falls down gassed during the robbery of Fort Knox! But

Dr Zhivago seemed very banal to me – that ridiculous scene when he writes a poem by candlelight! And *Blow-up* was so slow and boring. I wouldn't go on for hours to work up to an eventual striptease. Or pretend that this man doesn't notice a murder.

So much has been done already. I saw a bit of a Beatle film, and it had that old, old gag, a bubble bath! We did all this stop action business in 1914: it was very dull then and nobody paid much attention. Knock 'em down, drag 'em up, all those impossible Keystone gimmicks – it's all right, but they put it on in such a pretentious way now. There's a quick phase for thinking it smart and swinging. It's just what a little boy would do, the most inarticulate thing really, like dribbling. It says nothing – but the intellectuals find it very profound.

The reviews of my pictures have always been mixed. The only one *everybody* praised was *The Kid* – and then they went too far, talked about Shakespeare. Well, it wasn't *that*! But what shocked me about the English reviews of the *Countess* was the fact that they were unanimous. And they seemed so personal, an attack on *me*. All they were interested in was 'Chaplin has a flop'. In the old days, critics could slaughter quite a good play with just one quip. But there was nothing like that – these were so dull! Why couldn't they poke fun at it? Where's *their* humour, for God's sake? They picked on such puerile things to say – 'Brando is wooden' – but that's just the whole point!

I think it's the best thing I've done. I can be more objective about it than the pictures I've acted in, which can be very irksome and give me terrible inferiority complexes. It's full of invention, which I always like, and though it seems to be very simply constructed, it took a long time to motivate it, to work out the cause and effect. And it has great charm – what more do they want? Things like *The Gold Rush* – one, two, three, pantry cakey – it's so easy. A situation comedy like the *Countess* is much more difficult to keep going . . . The humour of the *Countess* may not be mechanical, but the situations are excruciating. The critics now are terrified of being old-fashioned, but this picture is ten years ahead of its time.

I think it is the first time it's ever happened – a realistic treatment of an incredible situation. That was the thing that excited me. My other films were something else entirely, caricatures of Cruikshank's drawings are caricatures. But this is Cruikshank. The characters react realistically in impossible situations . . . At first Brando was frightened of a funny part, terrified of business, but I told him not to worry as the character was meant to be humourless. And he brought off the realism. Except in the belch scene, which we couldn't get right. He thought the point was the belch – but the point was the man's dignified behaviour. And Sophia does a little quiet clowning. She wanted to be much more facetious but I said, give the audience a treat, let them do some of it for you.

Between you and me and the gatepost, it's a very sad story. This man who leaves his icicle of a wife for a girl who's a whore. I think the end, where they're dancing, is tragic. Perhaps his love for her is just a passing thing, as happens to us all.

At first, when I read the reviews, I wondered. Then I went again the next day, and regained all my confidence. Because the audience were loving it . . .

The visual thing in *Countess* is very obvious. That's its great charm, that it *is* obvious. I was always having trouble with people saying, 'Put the camera there', or 'You must have a close-up now'. I want to make films as I *feel* – there aren't any rules. The fuss they make about continuity! You see a handkerchief in somebody's pocket in one shot, and in the next it's gone. Who cares? If the shot is funny, I keep it in. It's a question of values – if the audiences are looking at the *handkerchief* something's wrong with the scene anyhow! In *Shoulder Arms* there's a bit where I have a gun on my back, then I get my finger caught in a mouse-trap and the gun has disappeared then it's back again in the next shot. Glaring – but *nobody* has ever commented on it.

Now I'm working on another film. The trouble is that as I get older, I get more and more interested in beauty. I want things to be beautiful. I'm wondering whether this isn't a moribund period of art. Aesthetics have gone into things like space and science – those beautiful airships: utility at its height. No artist could compete with that.[3]

Chaplin put a brave face on things, but those closest to him understood that he had suffered a severe blow from the criticism of his film. The year brought other irritations. As a result of the publicity attendant on his claim for National Assistance benefits for himself, his wife and child, Michael Chaplin was approached by the publishers Leslie Frewin in March 1965. On 17 April he and his wife Patrice signed contracts agreeing to write his life story in conjunction with two journalists, Charles Hamblett and Tom Merritt, who were to receive a proportion of the royalties. A book was rather swiftly written, in which the two 'ghosts' attributed to young Chaplin an awful, breezy hip style and vocabulary. Michael at first approved the text, but then changed his mind and appealed to the family lawyers, the formidable Richards, Butler and Co. On 26 August Richards, Butler wrote to Leslie Frewin, claiming to avoid and repudiate the agreement of 17 April on the grounds that the plaintiff was a minor. They further alleged that the text contained material seriously defamatory both of the plaintiff and of other persons. Through Richards, Butler (and, as a minor, suing by Patrice as 'his wife and next friend') Michael sought an interlocutory injunction to prevent publication of the book until the trial. The injunction was granted by Mr Justice Waller on 20 September but the Court of Appeal supported the defendant's appeal on 25 October. Michael was given leave to appeal to the House of Lords and duly lodged his petition. The appeal was withdrawn, however, after the parties got together and agreed on a revised text. Michael agreed to make a substantial contribution from the royalties which would accrue to him when the book was published, to reimburse the publishers for the costs and expenses in which his change of heart had involved him.

Despite the objectionable period style and the title (*I Couldn't Smoke the Grass on My Father's Lawn . . .*) the book, which emerged at the end of the year, is often touching as an intelligent, generous and sensitive youth's reflections on the difficulties of being son to a genius. Despite his resentments at what he perceived as heavy-handed and unsympathetic parental regulation of his life (he instances the employment of private detectives to frighten him off 'unsuitable' friendships), the book still affirms real affection and admiration for both parents:

> My father is not like any other father. Complex, gifted, strangely creative, his irrationalities have never been those of the average commuter. He was, and is, to put it mildly, a bit of a handful as a father. I first became aware of the general impression that he is an exceptional man through the reactions of other people towards him. Visitors whose names at the time didn't mean a thing but who, in retrospect, turned out to be Noël Coward, Graham Greene, Jean Cocteau, Truman Capote, Ian Fleming, and sundry other types, and who greeted him like a god on furlough from Olympus. There was also a fairly constant traffic of suitably awed interviewers, photographers, intellectuals, painters, actors, socialites and name-droppers; and whenever these showed up at the Manoir de Ban, my father's spread in Switzerland, they cast and, in turn, reflected the aura of greatness around the old guy.
>
> There must have been a time when my unformed infant instincts and undeveloped mind simply sensed and felt this man as a kindly, volatile, moody, gay, self-absorbed, inventive, funny, affectionate, stern, sad, brilliant, autocratic, irrational, snobbish, splendid, silly, unjust, loving, perceptive, indifferent, sensitive, cruel, jolly, extension-in-reverse of my own flesh and thought and feelings; a time when I was, quite naturally, just another limb of the father-octopus. There must have been a time, perhaps in the big house in Beverly Hills, California, which was our home before my father settled in Europe, when I may have been able to take

for granted my surroundings and family and my father as head of the household.

But I cannot remember such a time . . .

To be the son of a great man can be a disadvantage; it is like living next to a huge monument; one spends one's life circling around it, either to remain in the shade, or to avoid its shadow. But then people brought up in an orphanage, when trying to find out where they stand in relation to the world, often spend the rest of their lives searching for such a monument.[4]

While he was still editing *A Countess From Hong Kong*, on 11 October 1966, Chaplin was walking with Jerry Epstein outside Pinewood Studios when he tripped on a piece of uneven pavement and broke his ankle. Epstein helped him into the studio first aid centre, and he was taken to Slough hospital where his foot was encased in a 12-inch plaster. 'This is most humiliating,' was Chaplin's comment. 'It is just a nuisance. I'll be back in a day or so.' He was right. He was outstandingly fit for his age, and was soon about again. But it was the first time in his life that he had broken a limb; and it was the end of that phenomenal mobility that had permitted him to play tennis right up to this time. It is possible that around this time also he had the first of a series of almost imperceptible strokes. From this moment Charles Chaplin was obliged to acknowledge the onset of old age.

Not that old age could stem the phenomenal urge to create. He launched immediately into a new idea, *The Freak*, a dramatic comedy about a young girl who awakes one morning to find that she has sprouted wings. The role was designed for his third daughter, Victoria. Geraldine and Josephine had already embarked on acting careers (both appear briefly in *A Countess From Hong Kong*). Chaplin considered however that Victoria had supremely inherited the gift of comedy. The talent was all the more piquant for her extraordinary, luminous beauty, concentrated in the same searching, melancholy eyes as Chaplin's own Tramp. Over the next two years Chaplin worked doggedly on writing and revising the script, and the wings which Victoria was to wear in the film were made and tried.

In 1969 Victoria met and fell in love with Jean-Baptiste Thierrée, a young French actor who had had a considerable success in Alain Resnais's film *Muriel*, but whose heart was set on making a career as a clown and creating his own circus. Without telling her parents,

Victoria left home to join him. Shortly afterwards they were married, and Victoria also dedicated herself to becoming a circus performer. It was for a time a bitter blow to Chaplin, who saw it as a serious set-back to his plans for *The Freak*. Meanwhile Oona and Jerry Epstein, who was to have produced the film, had been forced to recognize that Chaplin's physical strength was not any more likely to be equal to his creative will.

Since *A Countess From Hong Kong*, he had too, suffered a personal bereavement which struck him hard. Charles Chaplin, his elder son by Lita Gray, died at his mother's home in California on 20 March 1968. He was forty-three. Charles Chaplin Junior, as his book about his own relations with his father, *My Father, Charlie Chaplin* (1960) attests, was a charming, warm-hearted young man, whose life had not been fortunate. His career as an actor had not been as rewarding as his brother's; he had acquired a drinking problem during his army service; and he had suffered from two failed marriages. His death resulted from a badly-tended injury received in a fall, which produced a fatal thrombosis.

By the start of the 1970s, Chaplin's energies were engaged on the renewed exploitation of his old films. He had for some time considered leasing out the distribution rights in them. In this way he could secure a very considerable advance and pass on to someone else the task of turning the films to the maximum profit. Both Jerry Epstein and Sydney Chaplin were interested in being involved in such an arrangement. On one occasion Sydney was so sure that he could persuade his father to let him take on distribution that he took to Vevey a potential partner, the producer Sandy Lieberson – who was subsequently to become head of production for, successively, Twentieth Century Fox and Goldcrest Films. Sydney and Lieberson arrived for lunch, which proceeded with great cordiality until Sydney ventured to speak of his proposition, at which Chaplin became enraged. Lieberson still recalls the dreadful embarrassment at being witness to the family row which followed, and their eventual ignominious retreat from the Manoir.

Rachel Ford recommended as a suitable candidate for the distribution deal a former United Artists executive, Moses Rothman, whose effectiveness as a salesman was held in awe throughout Hollywood. Rothman formed a company punningly named Black Inc. to distribute the Chaplin films, and advanced $6,000,000 against the 50 per cent of net proceeds which would go to Chaplin's Roy Export Company

Establishment. Black Inc. were reputed to have recouped the initial advance from sales to Japan alone.

Rothman proved both an astute businessman and a master publicist. Part of the agreement was that Chaplin would assist in publicizing the re-release of the films by discreet and undemanding personal appearances; the acclamation which resulted from these seems to have given Chaplin much interest and satisfaction in his last years. It also provided work to compensate for the set-back to *The Freak*, though it is unlikely that Chaplin ever gave up hope of making the film. In 1970 he composed a new score for *The Circus* and recorded the theme song 'Swing, Little Girl' himself: at eighty he still possessed a pleasant and hardly shaky baritone. In November 1971 Chaplin attested his satisfaction with the Black Inc. deal by throwing in, as a present, *The Kid* and *The Idle Class* (with new musical scores) which had been excluded from the original arrangement.

The world now competed to heap honours upon him. In 1971 the Twenty-fifth Cannes Film Festival made a special award for his total *oeuvre*; at the same time he was invested as Commander of the Légion d'Honneur. Now, at last, America wanted to make amends. The Academy of Motion Picture Arts and Sciences decided to award him an Honorary 'Oscar', and proffered a joint invitation with the Lincoln Center Film Society in New York. The old McGranery prohibitions on his return had long been forgotten. Chaplin was at first hesitant about accepting the invitation: according to Ted Tetrick he was finally swayed by the prospect of inspecting a new camera that was likely to facilitate process work on *The Freak*. The Chaplins decided to have a few days' holiday and rest in Bermuda (where Oona was born and still owned a property she had inherited from her father) before travelling to the United States. They arrived in New York on 2 April 1972, to be greeted at Kennedy Airport by a hundred or so newsmen. Chaplin blew them kisses as he rather slowly descended the steps from the plane and made his way to a waiting limousine, which drove them to the Plaza. That evening Gloria Vanderbilt Cooper, a girlhood friend of Oona's, gave a party for them in her town house. The guests included Lillian Gish, Adolph Green, Geraldine Fitzgerald, Truman Capote and George Plimpton. The following evening the Chaplins attended a cocktail party in their hotel (they arrived late) before going on to the Philharmonic Hall for the gala performance in tribute to him and in aid of Lincoln Center Film Society. The audience consisted of 1500 people who had paid

$10 and $25 admission, and a further 1200 who had paid $100 and $250 for the dressy champagne reception afterwards. They cheered his entrance into the hall; they cheered the films – *The Kid* and *The Idle Class* – and at the end gave him an astonishing and moving ovation. Many of the audience, like Chaplin himself, were in tears. When the applause permitted, he spoke into a microphone: 'This is my renaissance,' he said. 'I'm being born again. It's easy for you, but it's very difficult for me to speak tonight, because I feel very emotional. However, I'm glad to be among so many friends. Thank you.'

The champagne reception proved a greater ordeal. Chaplin had requested that his table not be cordoned off. In consequence, said *Time*, the crowd 'made a surging subway jam of black ties and décolletage, pressing around the table.' Somebody produced a derby and Chaplin mugged a little for the photographers. When Congresswoman Bella Abzug leaned across his table he exclaimed to her in excitement, 'The audience. The audience. *Everybody* was in the audience.' Among those who managed to fight their way to his table were Claire Bloom and Paulette, who talked to him for a couple of minutes. Most of his life Chaplin had been used to crowds and, for all the confusion, *Time* noted that when he left with Oona, protected by policemen, 'his face was alight with pleasure.'

He had initially been nervous about his reception in the United States, but this first experience gave him confidence. The following day he walked in a quiet part of Central Park and lunched at the '21' Club as the guest of a Manhattan councilman, Carter Burden. When he entered the dining room there was a burst of applause, and a waiter proudly told him that he had served him the last time he lunched at the '21', in 1952. 'Well, thank you,' said Chaplin. 'I didn't think I'd ever be back, you know.' Among those who came to his table to pay their respects was George Jessel, a pillar of the right, and Jack Gilford. He did not remember Jessel and did not know Gilford: 'I didn't know many actors in California,' he recalled; 'I was mostly alone there. It was always hard for me to make friends. I was shy and inarticulate. Doug Fairbanks was my only real friend, and I was a showpiece for him at parties.'

After lunch Richard Avedon, who had photographed Chaplin when he passed through the city in 1952, came to the suite in the Plaza for a new sitting. After that the Chaplins went to Gracie Mansion where Mayor Lindsay presented him with the Handel Medallion, New York's highest cultural award. The photographers asked him to smile and Chaplin, now full of the old confidence, cracked back, 'I'm afraid my teeth might fall out,' and cupped his hand beneath his chin.

At the end of the week Chaplin flew to Hollywood with Oona to receive his special Oscar for his 'incalculable effect in making motion pictures the art form of the century'. Candice Bergen accompanied them, on a reporting assignment for *Life*:

> During the flight, he crossed to the other side of the plane to see the Grand Canyon. His face lit up. 'Oh, yes, this is the place where Doug Fairbanks did a handstand on the precipice. He told me about it.'
>
> As they got nearer Los Angeles, he grew more and more nervous, sure he shouldn't have come. He looked fearful and trapped but made a brave attempt to fight it. 'Oh well,' he sighed, 'it wasn't so bad. After all, I met Oona there.'[5]

As he drove through the city he was disappointed to find it changed and unfamiliar. The new owners of his old studio, A. & M. Records, were very proud of the Chaplin connexion, had voluntarily sought to have the buildings declared a national monument and thus protected against alteration, and had established a Chaplin museum in the reception area. They planned to welcome Chaplin back there, and had decorated the place with scores of specially printed flags bearing his portrait. Chaplin could not face it. He arranged to pass the studio on Sunday, when it was closed, and contented himself with looking through the gates.

Some familiar faces from long ago appeared among the worshipping crowds. One was Tim Durant:

> When Charlie arrived, I got a call from a Mrs Walter Matthau. She was a great friend of Oona's and she said, 'I'm giving a lunch for Charlie and would you come next Sunday?' I said, 'Yes, I'll come up right after church. It'll be great to see him' . . . Greer Garson was here in the church, and I asked her to go up with me . . . As I came in, I saw this small table. They were waiting for us: we were a little bit late. I think Lewis Milestone and his wife were there, and one or two others . . . Charlie was across and as I sat down I looked over at him and he seemed to be preoccupied with the people coming up there. He hardly recognized me, you know. We were there about half an hour, and still he didn't respond at all. I tried to catch his eye a few times, and he'd go to move away. He was talking rather aimlessly to people as they came up, not remembering their names, I'm sure. I know how he used to fake that – call them dear friend and so forth. I'd done it myself. I felt, well, Charlie's forgotten about me. I felt rather badly about it, but strangely enough, when the lunch was over he

got up on his feet and he came over to me and looked me right in the eye and said, 'Tim, you and I were buddies once.' Well, tears came to my eyes – I couldn't help it. I sort of grasped him and hugged him and I said, 'Listen, we still are, Charlie.' So I said goodbye to him, and I thought, this is it . . . But then his English secretary called and asked me to come over – they had a cottage at the Beverly Hills Hotel. So I went over there, and as I came in, Charlie opened the front door.

He was talking to a very good-looking young girl, which was typical. She looked about seventeen or eighteen – remember he married all those girls you know, and they all wanted careers and they didn't want Charlie after a while. They weren't as good an audience as I was. Anyway he was talking to her, and the first thing he said to her as he saw me, he said, 'Look at that man there,' he said; 'Now you keep away from him. He's a dangerous man. Don't have anything to do with him, remember that now.'

He was kidding, you know; and I walked in and he introduced me to his granddaughter; and I had a lovely visit with him there.[6]

On another occasion he met Georgia Hale. Georgia had kept her figure and wore blonde shoulder-length hair and long eyelashes. Chaplin affected indignation that she should seem so young while he was suffering the infirmities of age. 'Perhaps, after all, it is your faith,' he told her. 'You should have shared it with me.' It was an ironic joke: in the days of their friendship he had always forbidden her even to speak about religion in his presence.[7]

There was a still more touching reunion. At one of the Hollywood functions which Chaplin attended, Jackie Coogan and his wife were present. They attempted to approach Chaplin's table but Walter Matthau, aiming to protect Chaplin from harassment, fiercely barred their way. 'Either he didn't recognize Jackie,' Coogan's son, Anthony speculates, 'or he *did* recognize him and remembered that there was a time when Jackie could be quite a trouble-maker.' Somehow the Coogans were got past the bodyguard. Jackie was now the bald, stout, 57-year-old man who played Uncle Fester. Chaplin had hardly seen him since he was the Kid, yet he took one look at him and burst into tears. They threw their arms around each other and Chaplin said, 'What a pleasure to see you . . . little boy.' Then, while Jackie and Oona were talking, he gripped Mrs Coogan's arm and pulled her till her face was close to his, and murmured emphatically: 'You must never forget. Your husband is a genius.'[8]

The Oscar show was another great emotional occasion. Chaplin and Oona watched it on a television monitor in a dressing room backstage, delightedly recognizing friends in the audience. Chaplin had had an irrational fear that nobody would turn up. When he accepted his presentation, he was too overcome to stammer out more than a tearful thankyou but he managed a bit of business with a derby, making it spring up from his head as he had in the old silents.

> Afterward, as he talked about the ceremony, his eyes were bright and childlike, wide with wonder, round with glee. 'It almost made me cry – and *this* one,' he cocked his head at a beaming Oona, 'this one kept saying, "*Oh, don't snivel.*"
>
> 'It was *so emotional* and the *audience – their* emotion. I thought some of them might hiss, but they were so *sweet* – all those famous people, all those artists. You know, they haven't done this to me before. It surpasses everything.'
>
> He looked around for his Oscar and couldn't see it. '*Oh, no,*' he wailed, 'all those sweet people and I've *lost* it.' It was retrieved and put back serenely.
>
> More and more he began to look like an English schoolboy, grinning impishly, rolling his eyes up innocently, pointing a freckled hand to himself, announcing playfully, 'The genius . . .'
>
> Suddenly summoning that old agility, he flew from his chair. Eyes twinkling, he said, with mock impatience, 'Let's go and celebrate, for God's sake!'
>
> And happily humming his song 'Smile!' he took Oona's arm and stepped out grandly through the door.[9]

Two years later, away from the euphoria, Chaplin commented in his book *My Life in Pictures*, 'I was touched by the gesture, but there was a certain irony about it somehow.'

In September 1972 he was given a special award of the Golden Lion of the Venice Film Festival. On the final day of the Festival, St Mark's Square was converted into a huge open-air cinema for a showing of *City Lights*. It was arranged that Chaplin would appear on a balcony overlooking the square for the beginning of the screening, and would then be taken to receive his presentation from the wife of the President of Italy. The schedule was tight, and to avoid delay the police had cleared the route on the Grand Canal between the Square and the Palace. Chaplin's appearance in the Square was the signal for overwhelming enthusiasm. At last the projection began, and Chaplin sat down with the rest to enjoy the film. Oona, Rachel Ford and the rest of his entourage began to be rather agitated about the timing, and urged that they should leave. 'I'll wait until I've seen the fight scene,' he said amiably but firmly. And so he did.

Back in Switzerland he set to work on a new book, *My Life in Pictures*. Max Reinhardt of The Bodley Head had had the idea of a book which might supplement *My Autobiography*, with a greater emphasis on Chaplin's work. This sumptuous collection of private and studio photographs, many never reproduced before, seemed a happy solution. Chaplin evidently enjoyed revisiting the past again, though Rachel Ford was often justifiably nervous for the safety of the precious archives as she watched Chaplin and Reinhardt on their knees in a sea of fragile photographs that washed about the floor. Chaplin's brief caption comments provided some new insights, though occasionally now the phenomenal memory seemed to fail him. Clare Sheridan's son is inexplicably mixed up with his own children, for example; while (never too good on names) he adopted the long-standing error of filmographers, who credited Phyllis Allen with an appearance in *The Kid*. Not the least merit of this fine production was Francis Wyndham's introduction, with its sensitive appreciation and moving portrait of Chaplin in old age. In October 1974 Chaplin was in London for the launch of the book. He told journalists that he would never be able to retire 'because ideas just keep popping into my head'.

He was in London again in March 1975, with most of the family, to receive a knighthood from the Queen. The investiture was unquestionably his occasion. During the long wait for the Queen, the string orchestra of the Welsh Guards introduced the theme from *A Countess From Hong Kong* into their selections from light opera, and just before Her Majesty arrived, a solo pianist played 'Smile'. When it was time for his investiture and the name 'Sir Charles Chaplin' was called out, the orchestra went into the theme from *Limelight*.

Chaplin had hoped to be able to walk the ten-yard distance to the Queen, but his legs were too uncertain and a palace steward wheeled him in a chair. Chaplin said that he was 'dumbfounded' by the Queen's smile. 'She thanked me for all that I had done. She said my films had helped her a great deal.' As he waited with the other guests through the rest of the ceremony, his untiring eye for a gag was caught by the sudden collapse of the bandmaster's music stand. As he left the Palace he had the director's presence of mind in asking the television cameramen not to shoot the now laborious process of climbing into his car.

After the investiture there was a family party at the Savoy. Chaplin now found it tiring to do much talking and spent most of the time sitting quietly, simply watching the others. In the course of the party however there was a telephone call fom the Prime Minister, who said he wished to pay his respects. In due course Harold Wilson arrived with Marcia Williams. At once Chaplin was on his feet, straight-backed and sprightly, the old 'prop smile' as brilliant and charming as sixty years before. An actor's resources are mysterious.

The ideas were still popping into his head: the next one was to compose a musical score for the only one of his great silent features that remained without synchronized sound. After half a century he at last felt able to return to *A Woman of Paris*, which had remained a rather sensitive memory for him since its rejection by the audiences of 1923. Seeing it again, his original enthusiasm for the film was revived. Over-sensitive to the possible response of modern audiences, however, he made some cuts where he thought the film would appear too sentimental. He could have been bolder: the great scene between Marie and Jean's mother over Jean's body was certainly stronger in the original form, with Chaplin's sentiment unrestrained.

The sympathetic Eric James collaborated on transcription and orchestration. Chaplin composed several effective new themes; but the effort of creating eighty minutes of music was too demanding and themes were borrowed from his earlier scores to supplement the new material. The critics of the refurbished *Woman of Paris* were to be ecstatic about the rediscovery of the film, but inclined to dismiss the score as inadequate. This is unappreciative. Like all Chaplin's film scores, this one recreates the method and style of Victorian theatre music – an idiom which seems wholly appropriate to this fine melodrama, outside time, but at least as closely linked to the nineteenth century as to the twentieth.

Chaplin attended the recording sessions at Anvil Studios at Denham. The writer sat with him through one of these sessions; it was here that the idea for the present book was first discussed with him. I had taken him some of the photographs of the Karno fun factory which now appear in this book, and he was particularly intrigued by one of Karno himself, the autocrat at his desk in a cluttered Edwardian office. I asked him if preparing the score for *A Woman of Paris* had been a lengthy job to which he answered, 'Not long – inspiration mostly.' Although he was still quite chubby, he seemed by this time terribly fragile. He could no longer walk unaided. It was clear that his mind was still as lively as it had been, but he was constantly frustrated by the breakdown between the thought and the realization or expression of it. He was terribly sensitive. In a break in the recording some of the musicians pretended to quarrel; this pretence of aggression distressed him acutely.

The score was the last completed work of that phenomenal creation, a working life that had spanned three quarters of a century. After this he did not often leave his home. His son Eugene, who had remained in Vevey, described his father's life in the last years in an interview given to *The National Enquirer*. He said that gout prevented him from walking, and that he no longer cared to have visitors to the house. He read and re-read his favourite Dickens novel, *Oliver Twist*. Sometimes he would tinker a little with the script of *The Freak*. (The final words of *My Life in Pictures* were 'I mean to make it some day.') Sometimes in the evening the family would watch his old films on their 16mm projector. When the others laughed, said Eugene, he would sit up straight and grin happily, 'with a whimsical smile'. While the children were growing up he had stood out against allowing television into the Manoir, but now he grew to appreciate it. He enjoyed watching the news programmes, and even though he did not speak French seemed to have no problem at all in understanding them. He liked to see American films; and with French shows would entertain himself with wicked mimicry of the performers. He did not like to talk about old friends. He had no religion, and never went to church, but he had no fear of death: 'When I go, I go,' he would say. He would sit for hours with Oona, holding hands and hardly exchanging a word. 'She is able to share that strange solitude of his,' said his son.

When the weather was fine, Renato the chauffeur or Gino the butler would drive Chaplin and Oona to a quiet spot by the lake, where they would sit together for an hour or two until the car collected them again. They bought an electric runabout so that he could still inspect his park.

On 15 October 1977 Chaplin made his last trip outside the Manoir. With Oona, Victoria, her husband Jean-Baptiste and their children, he attended a performance of the Circus Knie in Vevey. The visits of the circus had been occasions for the Chaplin family since their arrival in Switzerland. Generally they gave a party at the house for the artists.

Now his strength began to ebb very fast. He needed constant nursing. For weeks Oona insisted on attending him herself, until the family and staff began seriously to fear for her own health and she was persuaded to share the duties with a nurse. At Christmas the family, with the exception of Geraldine, who was working in Spain, assembled at the Manoir for the traditional celebration. There was now a tribe of grandchildren. On Christmas Eve Monsieur Inmoos came up from the village dressed as Santa Claus, as he had for the past twenty years, to distribute the presents from the tree. (Monsieur Inmoos said that Chaplin saw him many times, but never in any other garb but this.) The children's presents to him were delivered to Chaplin's bedroom, and the door was left open so that he might hear the younger ones' reactions to Santa Claus.

During that night, in the small hours of Christmas Day 1977, Charles Chaplin died peacefully in his sleep.

In Hollywood the young painter Mark Stock, who idolized Chaplin and had made a fine series of lithograph portraits, heard the news on the radio early in the morning of Christmas Day. Somewhere in the deserted city he found fresh flowers. He drove to the gates of Chaplin's old house and left a rose there. He placed another on the gate of the studio. He found that by climbing up the gate he could draw down the studio flag to half mast: it stayed like that for many days. Finally he went to the Hollywood Cemetery intending to place a rose on Hannah's grave; but a spray of fresh blooms already lay there.

The funeral was held on 27 December 1977 at 11 a.m. at the Anglican Church in Vevey. As Chaplin had wished, it was an unpretentious family affair. The service was conducted by the Rev. Robert Thomson and the Rev. David Miller, in the presence of the British Ambassador, Allen Keir Rothnie. The coffin was covered with a black and silver pall. Immediately after the ceremony Oona left for Crans-sur-Sierre.

Chaplin, with his taste for the macabre, might have found an ideal scenario in the bizarre events that followed barely two months later. On 2 March 1978 the superintendent of the Vevey Cemetery, Etienne

Buenzod, reported for work to find Chaplin's grave opened up and the coffin gone. The world's press competed in fantastic explanations of this crime. Was it the belated revenge of a neo-Nazi group for *The Great Dictator*? An anti-Semitic protest against the burial of a Jew (*sic*) in a Christian cemetery? Or simply fanatical enthusiasts determined to possess the mortal remains of their idol? Within a few days it became clear that it was a case of posthumous kidnapping, as the first telephone call from a mysterious 'M. Cohat' (or 'Rochat') demanded 600,000 Swiss francs for the return of the body.

The culprits eventually proved to be a pathetic pair of Keystone incompetents. Roman Wardas was a 24-year-old unemployed Polish automobile mechanic. Gantcho Ganev, aged 38, was a Bulgarian defector employed as a mechanic in Lausanne. They had been inspired by a news item about the theft of the body of an Italian industrialist, Salvatore Mataressa, and hoped to raise enough money in this way to set themselves up in a garage. Their first mishap was to choose an exceedingly wet night for the exhumation. In the rain it took two hours to dig up the grave and then the ground was much too muddy for them to carry out their original intention of hiding the coffin deeper in the same hole. As it was, they were obliged to struggle through the cemetery with the lead-lined casket, load it on their car and find some other hiding place.

Oona from the start refused to have any dealings with body-snatchers. The family lawyer, Jean-Felix Paschoud, quoted her as saying, 'My husband is in heaven and in my heart.' Perhaps too she remembered the firm line that Chaplin himself had always advocated with kidnappers. The matter had to be treated with delicacy, however, since when the ransom money proved not to be immediately forthcoming, the body-snatchers began to threaten violence against the younger children. After Christopher was threatened with having his legs shot up, he was given an unseen police escort to and from school each day.

From the start Monsieur Paschoud had decided that they were dealing with amateurs: 'If we had parleyed we would eventually have got the coffin back for fifty francs,' he said. The Chaplins and the police had simply to sit it out. In all the kidnappers were to make twenty-seven telephone calls. Geraldine undertook to deal with them, and maintained a fine performance as the weeks went by, keeping the body-snatchers dangling with her vocal representations of grief and concern. A practice 'drop' went farcically wrong. Bit by bit

Wardas and Ganev grew lazy. At first they had moved around and far afield to make their calls but eventually they simply used Lausanne call-boxes. When the police realized this, they waited for a call that was fixed for an appointed time, and then kept watch on every call-box in Lausanne. A number of innocent callers received nasty shocks, but Wardas and Ganev were apprehended.

The coffin was found buried in a cornfield just outside the village of Noville on the eastern end of Lake Geneva, some twenty kilometres from Vevey. It was a place where Wardas was accustomed to go fishing. Oona was touched that they had chosen so peaceful a spot for Chaplin to rest in; and after the coffin was removed, the farmer who owned the land erected a simple wooden cross, ornamented with a cane, in memory.

Wardas and Ganev were put on trial at Vevey in December. The principal witness was Geraldine. Wardas was sentenced to four and a half years' imprisonment and Ganev received a suspended sentence of eighteen months, for 'disturbing the peace of the dead and attempted extortion'.

In the days following Chaplin's death, all the great men of his profession delivered their eulogies. René Clair, doyen of the French cinema, wrote:

> He was a monument of the cinema of all countries and all times. He inspired practically every film maker. I was myself especially sensitive to that extraordinary mixture of comedy and sentiment. It was said that *Modern Times* found its themes in *A Nous la Liberté*. I am happy and proud if I, whom he had so much influenced, was able for once in turn to influence him.
>
> Charles Chaplin, who has given us so many gifts with each of his films, took from us, this Christmas Day, the most beautiful gift the cinema made to us.

Laurence Olivier said, 'He was, perhaps, the greatest actor of all time'; and Jean-Louis Barrault called him

> the supreme example of the perfection of the actor and the creative genius: whether it comes from the theatre or is expressed by the cinema. He is above all an extraordinary mime, and what he teaches, in mime, is that he attains the maximum by immobility, an immobility full and entire. In sum, he has shown us the peak of the art of mime.

The great French film comedian Jacques Tati said,

> Without him I would never have made a film. With Keaton he was the master of us all. His work is always contemporary, yet eternal, and what he brought to the cinema and to his time is irreplaceable.

For Federico Fellini he was

> a sort of Adam, from whom we are all descended . . . There were two aspects of his personality; the vagabond, but also the solitary aristocrat, the prophet, the priest and the poet.

The simplest tribute – yet perhaps also the most touching, because it intimated atonement by the very section of America which, so long ago, had abused and rejected Charles Chaplin – was spoken by Bob Hope:

> 'We were fortunate to have lived in his time.'

Chaplin's presence had dominated Oona's entire adult life. After his death she tried bravely to create a new social existence for herself, but her natural shyness and Charlie's commanding memory made it hard. She bought an apartment in New York and renewed old friendships there; but after a year or two sold it again (thrilled by her profit on the price). She was amused and flattered when the tabloid press tried to make romances out of friendships with Ryan O'Neal and David Bowie, her neighbour in Switzerland. For a while in the mid eighties there seemed to be a serious affair with the script writer Walter Bernstein; but the friendship ended.

As the children left home, life at the Manoir became more lonely. She amused herself redecorating the house and buying pictures; but the fun of spending was always shadowed by the thought of Charlie's respect for money. As she became lonelier she retreated more and more into herself, staying in her rooms, watching videos for hours. Latterly her only outings were trips to the hairdresser in Vevey.

In August 1991 an operation revealed that she had incurable cancer. She returned from hospital to the Manoir, where her daughters came home to care for her in the last days. She died near midnight on 27 September 1991 and was buried alongside Charlie in the big grave in the churchyard at Corsier.

NOTES

CHAPTER 1: A London boyhood

1 Suffolk Parish Registers, *passim*.
2 1851 Census return.
3 Will of Shadrach Chaplin at Principal Probate Office, Somerset House.
4 Marriage certificate in General Registry Office.
5 Death Certificate in General Registry Office.
6 Birth Certificate in General Registry Office.
7 Birth Certificate in General Registry Office.
8 Now in possession of Lady Chaplin.
9 Marriage Certificate in General Registry Office.
10 Marriage Certificate in General Registry Office.
11 Marriage Certificate in General Registry Office.
12 Death Certificate in General Registry Office.
13 Birth Certificate in General Registry Office.
14 Birth Certificate in General Registry Office.
15 1871 Census: Parish of St Mary Newington, Schedule 321.
16 Birth Certificate in General Registry Office.
17 Death Certificate in General Registry Office.
18 Marriage Certificate in General Registry Office.
19 *The Era*, 18 June 1887.
20 Programme in collection of Professor E. J. Dawes.
21 *The Era*, August 1890.
22 Letter in Sydney Chaplin Archive, Vevey.
23 *The Era*.
24 Letter from Wheeler Dryden to Edna Purviance. See p. 217.
25 Lambeth Board of Guardians, Lunacy Examinations Book, 1893, p.196, GLC Archives.
26 St Saviour Union (Southwark). Order for Reception of a Pauper Lunatic, GLC Archives.
27 *American Magazine*, November 1918.

28 Renfrew Road (Lambeth) Workhouse Register, GLC Archives.
29 School Register, GLC Archives.
30 Southwark Workhouse Register, GLC Archives.
31 Chaplin. *My Autobiography*, 1964, though correspondence of St Saviour Board of Guardians and Norwood Schools (GLC Archives) establishes the name as 'Hindom' not 'Hindrum' as Chaplin remembered it.
32 *Pearson's Weekly*, 21 September 1921.
33 Letter now in Vevey Archives.
34 Walter Monnington and Frederick J. Lampard. *Our London Poor Law Schools*, London, 1898.
35 *Ibid.*
36 *Strand Magazine*, volume 17, no. 12, pp.88–95.
37 St Saviour (Southwark) Board of Guardians Minutes, GLC Archives.
38 Letter from Dr Shepherd to CC, 1916, in Vevey Archives.
39 Will of Spencer Chaplin, dated 18 May 1897, at Principal Probate Office, Somerset House.
40 St Saviour (Southwark) Board of Guardians Minutes, GLC Archives.
41 Correspondence of St Saviour (Southwark) Board of Guardians, GLC Archives.
42 Renfrew Road (Lambeth) Workhouse Register, GLC Archives.
43 Lambeth Board of Guardians, Lunacy Examinations Book, 12 September 1898, GLC Archives.
44 *Motion Picture Classic.*
45 Renfrew Road (Lambeth) Workhouse Register, GLC Archives.
46 Kennington Road Schools Register, GLC Archives.
47 *Glasgow Weekly Herald*, 9 October 1921.
48 *The Magnet*, 14 July 1900.
49 Armitage Street School Register. The school registers have now disappeared, but the entry was illustrated in a Manchester newspaper in 1921.
50 Alfred Jackson interviewed in *The Star*, 3 September 1921.
51 Charles Douglas Stuart and A. J. Park. *The Variety Stage*, London, 1895.
52 Alfred Jackson, *loc. cit.*
53 *Winnipeg Tribune*, 29 November 1912
54 Renfrew Road (Lambeth) Workhouse Register, GLC Archives.
55 Sydney Hill – Continuous Certificate of Discharge.
56 Sydney Hill – Seaman's Allotment Note.
57 Sydney Hill – Continuous Certificate of Discharge.
58 *Manchester Daily Chronicle*, 14 September 1921.
59 Post Office directories, *passim.*
60 Newspaper cutting, source unidentified.
61 May Reeves. *Charlie Chaplin intime. Souvenirs receuillis par Claire Goll*, 1935.
62 Lambeth Board of Guardians, Lunacy Reception Order, 9 May 1903, GLC Archives.
63 Charles Chaplin Jr. *My Father, Charlie Chaplin*, 1960.

CHAPTER 2: The young professional

1 Charles Chaplin. *My Autobiography.*
2 Letter to Sydney Chaplin, August 1913. See p.97.

3 Bert Herbert interviewed in *the Star*, 3 September 1921.
4 Licensing records, GLC Archives.
5 Edith Scales quoted in *Empire News*, 8 March 1931.
6 Edith Scales, *loc. cit.*
7 *Ashton-under-Lyne Reporter*, 21 November 1903.
8 *Ibid.*
9 Edith Scales, *loc. cit.*
10 *Ibid.*
11 *Ibid.*
12 Sydney Hill – Continuous Certificate of Discharge.
13 Lambeth Board of Guardians, Lunacy Reception Order, 18 March 1905.
14 *The Era.*
15 *The Era Annual*, 1906.
16 Will Murray, interviewed in *Glasgow Weekly Herald*, 10 September 1921.
17 *Ibid.*
18 Dan Lipton quoted in *Daily Graphic*, 1 September 1921.
19 Will Murray, *loc. cit.*
20 Fred Goodwins, article in *Pearson's Weekly*.
21 Interview with Richard Meryman, 1968.
22 In conversation with writer, c.1954.

CHAPTER 3: With the Guv'nor

1 Syndicated newspaper interview.
2 *The Theatre*, London, April 1880.
3 Stan Laurel, quoted in John McCabe's *Charlie Chaplin*, 1978.
4 Fred Goodwins, *op. cit.*
5 Letter in Vevey Archive.
6 Stan Laurel, *loc. cit.*
7 Birth certificate in General Registry.
8 Charles Chaplin. *My Trip Abroad*, 1922.
9 Charles Chaplin. *A Comedian Sees the World*, 1932.
10 Manuscript scenario in Vevey Archive.
11 Newspaper cutting, source unidentified. Most of these early reviews from Karno days are preserved in Chaplin's first cuttings book, but have been pasted in without reference to date or source.
12 Stan Laurel, *loc. cit.*
13 Newspaper cutting, source unidentified.
14 Stan Laurel, *loc. cit.*
15 Alf Reeves interview, *Photoplay*, August 1934. Preserved in Reeves' own cuttings book.
16 Alf Reeves, *loc. cit.*
17 Newspaper cutting, source unidentified.
18 Newspaper cutting, source unidentified.
19 Newspaper cutting, source unidentified.
20 Newspaper cutting, source unidentified.
21 Newspaper cutting, source unidentified.
22 Stan Laurel, *loc. cit.*

23 Newspaper cutting, source unidentified.
24 Letter in Vevey Archive.
25 Newspaper cutting, source unidentified.
26 'Whimsical' Walker. *From Sawdust to Windsor Castle*, 1922.
27 Newspaper interview, source unidentified.
28 Letter from CC to Sydney Chaplin in Vevey Archive.
29 Stan Laurel, *loc. cit.*
30 Newspaper cutting, 1921, source unidentified.

CHAPTER 4: In Pictures

1 Mack Sennett. *King of Comedy* (as told to Cameron Shipp), 1954.
2 Letter in Kevin Brownlow collection.
3 This version is quoted, without source, in John McCabe's *Charlie Chaplin*.
4 Original contract and draft in Vevey Archive.
5 Walter Kerr. *The Silent Clowns*, 1975.
6 *Ibid.*
7 Charles Chaplin. *My Autobiography*.
8 Hans Koenekamp in interview with author, December 1983.
9 *Ibid.*
10 Walter Kerr, *op. cit.*

CHAPTER 5: Essanay

1 Roland Totheroh interviewed by Timothy J. Lyons in *Film Culture*, Spring 1972.
2 *Ibid.*
3 *Ibid.*
4 Fred Goodwins, article in *Pearsons Weekly*.
5 *Ibid.*
6 Lambeth Board of Guardians, Settlement Examination Book, GLC Archives.

CHAPTER 6: Mutual

1 Syndicated newspaper article.
2 *Ibid.*
3 *Ibid.*
4 *Ibid.*
5 Syndicated newspaper interview with Kitty Kelly.
6 Roland Totheroh, *loc. cit.*
7 *Ibid.*
8 *Ibid.*
9 *Ibid.*
10 Terry Ramsaye. 'Chaplin – and how he does it' in *Photoplay*, September 1917.
11 Newspaper interview, source unidentified.
12 Roland Totheroh, *loc. cit.*
13 Edward Sutherland in interview with Robert Franklin.
14 *New York Tribune*.

15 This and subsequent correspondence relating to *Charlie Chaplin's Own Story* is preserved in the Vevey Archive.
16 Langford Reed. *The Chronicles of Charlie Chaplin*, 1917.
17 *Ibid.*
18 *Ibid.*
19 Kevin Brownlow. *The Parade's Gone By*, 1968.
20 Constance Collier. *Harlequinade. The Story of My Life*, 1929.
21 Gerith von Ulm. *Charles Chaplin, King of Tragedy*, 1940.
22 Walter Kerr. *The Silent Clowns.*
23 Mutual press release, 1 February 1917.
24 *Reel Life*, February 1917.
25 Mutual press release, February 1917.
26 Syndicated newspaper interview by Karl Kitchen.
27 Newspaper cutting, source unidentified.
28 Carlyle T. Robinson. *La verité sur Charles Chaplin. Sa vie, ses amours, ses déboires*, 1935 (translated from French original).
29 *Ibid.*
30 *Ibid.*
31 *Ibid.*
32 *Ibid.*
33 *Ibid.*
34 *Cincinnati Star*, 8 February 1917.
35 *NYC Mail*, 23 December 1918.
36 Newspaper cutting, source unidentified.
37 Correspondence in possession of Mrs Wyn Ray Evans, Ritchie's daughter.
38 Newspaper cutting, source unidentified.

CHAPTER 7: Penalties and rewards of independence

1 Interview in *Exhibitors' Trade Review*, 28 April 1917.
2 Letter from Sydney Chaplin to CC, in Vevey Archive.
3 Interview in *Cleveland Leader*, date not known.
4 Lita Grey Chaplin. *My Life with Chaplin*, 1966.
5 Roland Totheroh interviewed by Timothy J. Lyons in *Film Culture*, Spring 1972.
6 Frank Harris in *Contemporary Portraits*, 1924.
7 Detectives' report in Vevey Archive.
8 Edward Sutherland in interview with Robert Franklin.
9 Wyn Ray Evans in interview with author, December 1983.

CHAPTER 8: Escape to independence

1 Charles Chaplin. *My Trip Abroad*, 1922. All subsequent quotations from Chaplin in this chapter are from the same source.
2 Newspaper cutting in Vevey scrapbooks, source unidentified.
3 Newspaper cutting in Vevey scrapbooks, source unidentified.
4 Thomas Burke. 'A Comedian' in *City of Encounters*, 1932.
5 Clare Sheridan. *My American Diary*, 1922.
6 *Ibid.*
7 *Ibid.*

CHAPTER 9: *A Woman of Paris*

1 Edward Sutherland, *loc. cit.*
2 Adolphe Menjou: *It Took Nine Tailors*, 1952.
3 Edward Sutherland, *loc. cit.*
4 *Ibid.*
5 Adolphe Menjou, *op. cit.*
6 Edward Sutherland, *loc. cit.*
7 Cutting preserved in Edna Purviance collection, now owned by Inman Hunter, Esq.
8 Adolphe Menjou, *op. cit.*
9 *Ibid.*
10 Edward Sutherland, *loc. cit.*
11 Adolphe Menjou, *op. cit.*
12 Work notes, Vevey Archive.
13 Adolphe Menjou, *op. cit.*
14 Edward Sutherland, *loc. cit.*
15 Roland Totheroh, *loc. cit.*
16 Adolphe Menjou, *op. cit.*
17 *Ibid.*
18 *Ibid.*
19 *Detroit Free Press*, 16 October 1923.
20 *Boston Globe*, 23 March 1923.
21 *Ibid.*
22 *Ibid.*
23 *Ibid.*
24 *Ibid.*
25 *Los Angeles Times*, 29 January 1923.
26 *Ibid.*
27 *Boston Globe*, 23 March 1923.
28 Charles Chaplin, Jr. *My Father, Charlie Chaplin.*
29 *Ibid.*

CHAPTER 10: *The Gold Rush*

1 Charles Chaplin. *My Autobiography*, 1964.
2 Syndicated press article, June 1924.
3 *Ibid.*
4 Souvenir programme, *The Gold Rush*, 1925.
5 *Ibid.*
6 *Los Angeles Daily News*, 28 November 1924.
7 Georgia Hale in interview with author, December 1983.
8 *Ibid.*
9 *Ibid.*
10 *Ibid.*
11 *Ibid.*
12 *The Star*, 25 September 1925.
13 *The Star*, 28 September 1925.
14 Information from Dr Hans Feld, then critic of *Filmkurier*, Berlin.

Notes to Text

CHAPTER 11: *The Circus*

1 Interview with Henry Bergman, in cutting from unidentified source.
2 James Agee. 'Comedy's Greatest Era' in *Life*, 5 September 1949.
3 Harry Crocker in unpublished interview, c. 1955.
4 Press brochure issued by Studio.
5 Robert Florey. *Charlie Chaplin. Ses debuts, ses films, ses aventures*, 1927.
6 *Ibid.*

CHAPTER 12: *City Lights*

1 Harry Crocker, *loc. cit.*
2 Jean Cocteau, *My Journey Round the World*,
3 Interview with Richard Meryman, 1968.
4 Virginia Cherrill, in telephone conversation with author, December 1983.
5 Interview with Richard Meryman, 1968.
6 Carlyle T. Robinson. *La verité sur Charles Chaplin. Sa vie, ses amours, ses déboires.*
7 Georgia Hale in interview with author, December 1983.
8 *Ibid.*
9 Robert Parrish, *Growing Up in Hollywood.*
10 Interview with Richard Meryman, 1968.
11 James Agee, *loc. cit.*
12 Charles Chaplin. *My Trip Abroad.*
13 Interview with Richard Meryman, 1968.
14 Ivor Montagu. *With Eisenstein in Hollywood*, 1967.
15 *Ibid.*
16 *Ibid.*
17 Luis Buñuel. *My Last Breath*, 1983.
18 *Ibid.*
19 Georgia Hale, *loc. cit.*
20 Luis Buñuel, *op. cit.*

CHAPTER 13: Away from it all

1 Charles Chaplin. *A Comedian Sees the World.*
2 The *Daily Express.*
3 Thomas Burke, *loc. cit.*
4 *Ibid.*

CHAPTER 14: *Modern Times*

1 Georgia Hale in interview with author, December 1983.
2 Charles Chaplin. *My Autobiography.*
3 *Screenland*, October 1932.
4 *Chicago American*, 29 September 1932.
5 Charles Chaplin Jr. *My Father, Charlie Chaplin*, 1960.
6 *Budgepost Post*, 16 September 1932.

7 *Boston Globe*, 4 September 1932.
8 Lita Grey Chaplin. *My Life with Chaplin.*
9 Letter to Sydney Chaplin in Vevey Archive.
10 Charles Chaplin, Jr. *My Father, Charlie Chaplin.*
11 *Ibid.*
12 Thomas Burke, *op. cit.*
13 *Ibid.*
14 Charles Chaplin, Jr, *op. cit.*
15 Jean Cocteau: *My Voyage Round the World.*
16 *Ibid.*
17 *Ibid.*
18 *Ibid.*
19 *Ibid.*

CHAPTER 15: *The Great Dictator*

1 Charles Chaplin. *My Autobiography.*
2 The story was published, in English translation, in Peter Cotes and Thelma Niklaus' *The Little Fellow.*
3 Tim Durant in interview with Kevin Brownlow and David Gill, 1980.
4 All quotations from Dan James in this chapter are from an interview with the author, December 1983.
5 Charles Chaplin, Jr, *op. cit.*
6 Dan James, *loc. cit.*
7 Charles Chaplin, Jr, *op. cit.*
8 Dan James, *loc. cit.*
9 Tim Durant, *loc. cit.*
10 Charles Chaplin, Jr, *op. cit.*
11 *Ibid.*
12 *Films*, 1946.

CHAPTER 16: *Monsieur Verdoux*

1 Charles Chaplin, Jr, *op. cit.*
2 *Ibid.*
3 Quoted in Theodore Huff. *Charlie Chaplin* 1951.
4 Roland Totheroh interviewed by Timothy J. Lyons in *Film Culture*, Spring 1972.
5 *Ibid.*
6 All quotations from the press conference are from the transcript by George Wallach, published in *Film Comment*, Winter 1969.
7 *Film Comment*, Winter, 1969.

CHAPTER 17: *Limelight*

1 Charles Chaplin Jr, *op. cit.*
2 Interview with Margaret Hinxman.
3 Charles Chaplin Jr, *op. cit.*
4 Letter to Sydney Chaplin in Vevey Archive.

5 Article in *Everybody's*.
6 Press interview, source unidentified. Wheeler had in fact advertised the relationship in advertisements in *The Stage Yearbook* in the 1920s.
7 Sydney Chaplin Jr, *op. cit.*
8 Claire Bloom. *Limelight and After*, 1982.
9 *Ibid.*
10 *Ibid.*
11 *Ibid.*
12 Charles Chaplin Jr, *op. cit.*
13 Claire Bloom, *op. cit.*
14 Private communication to author.
15 Eugene Lourié in interview with author, December 1983.
16 *Ibid.*
17 *Ibid.*
18 *Ibid.*
19 Sydney Chaplin Jr, *op. cit.*
20 *Ibid.*
21 Claire Bloom, *op. cit.*
22 *Ibid.*
23 Eugene Lourié, *loc. cit.*

CHAPTER 18: *Exile*

1 *News Chronicle*, 24 September 1952.
2 *The Times*, 24 September 1952.
3 *News Chronicle*, 22 September 1952.
4 *New York Times*, 21 September 1952.
5 Charles Chaplin. *My Autobiography*.
6 Michael Chaplin in *I Couldn't Smoke the Grass on My Father's Lawn*, 1966.
7 *Daily Herald*, 16 April 1959.
8 *Sunday Times*, 21 August 1964.
9 Michael Chaplin, *op. cit.*
10 24 June 1962.
11 Introduction to *My Life in Pictures*, 1974.
12 Michael Chaplin, *op. cit.*
13 *Sunday Times*, 21 August 1964.
14 Lillian Ross in *Moments With Chaplin*, 1980.
15 *Sunday Times*, 1964.
16 Charles Chaplin. *My Autobiography*.

CHAPTER 19: *A Countess From Hong Kong*

1 David Robinson: 'Chaplin Meets the Press' in *Sight and Sound*, Winter 1965–66.
2 Kevin Brownlow: *The Parade's Gone By*. (1968).
3 *Sunday Times*.
4 Michael Chaplin, *op. cit.*
5 *Life*, 21 April 1972.
6 Interview with Kevin Brownlow and David Gill, 1980.

7 Georgia Hale, *loc. cit.*
8 Interview with Anthony Coogan, December 1983.
9 *Life*, 21 April 1972.

APPENDIX I
Chaplin chronology

1786		Shadrach Chaplin I (CC's great-great-grandfather) born.
1807–8		Sophia Chaplin (CC's great-grandmother) born.
1814		Shadrach Chaplin II (CC's great-grandfather) born.
1834–5		Spencer Chaplin (CC's grandfather) born.
1839	16 April	Charles Frederick Hill (CC's maternal grandfather) born.
		Mary Ann Terry (CC's maternal grandmother) born.
1854	15 May	Mary Ann Terry (CC's maternal grandmother) marries Henry Lamphee Hodges.
	30 October	Spencer Chaplin marries Ellen Elizabeth Smith (both minors) at St Margaret's Church, Ipswich.
1855	June	Spencer William Tunstill Chaplin (CC's uncle) born.
1858	18 December	Mary Ann Hodges, née Terry (CC's maternal grandmother) widowed by death of Henry Lamphee Hodges, aged thirty-four.
1861	16 August	Charles Frederick Hill (widower) marries Mary Ann Hodges (widow) (CC's maternal grandfather and grandmother) at St Mary's Church, Lambeth.

1863	18 March	Charles Chaplin (CC's father) born at 22 Orcus Street, Marylebone.
1865	6 August	Hannah Harriett Pedlingham Hill (CC's mother) born at 11 Camden Street, Walworth.
1870	18 January	Kate Hill (CC's aunt) born at 39 Bronti Place, Walworth.
1871		Census returns show Charles Hill lodging at 77 Beckway Street, Walworth, with wife, Mary Ann, stepson Henry and daughters Hannah and Kate.
1873	2 October	Death of Ellen Chaplin (CC's grandmother) at 15 Rillington Place, aged thirty-five.
1885	16 March	Sidney John Hill (Sydney Chaplin; CC's brother) born.
	29 April	Sidney Hill's birth registered.
	22 June	Charles Chaplin Senior marries Hannah Hill at St John's Church, Larcom Street.
1886	2 January	Hannah Chaplin ('Lily Harley') appears in Belfast.
	27 May	Hannah Chaplin ('Lily Harley') appears in benefit at South London Palace.
1887	20 June	Hannah Chaplin ('Lily Harley') appears at Folly Theatre Manchester.
	20 June	First recorded professional appearance of Charles Chaplin Senior, at Poly Variety Theatre.
1889	16 April	BIRTH OF CHARLES CHAPLIN.
	Autumn/Winter	Charles Chaplin Senior appearing at several London music halls.
1890		Publication of Charles Chaplin Senior's song successes, 'Eh, boys?' and 'Everyday Life'.
	3 March	Sydney Chaplin enrolled at King and Queen Street School, Southwark (remains until May).
	5 May	Sydney Chaplin enrolled at Addington Street School, Lambeth.
	16 August	Charles Chaplin Senior appearing at Union Square Theatre, New York (remains until 6 September).

	11 November	Sydney Chaplin enrolled at Flint Street School, Southwark.
1891		Publication of Charles Chaplin Senior's song success, 'As the Church Bells Chime'.
	November	Leo Dryden sings 'The Miner's Dream of Home' and is paid £20 for publication rights by Francis, Day and Hunter – 'the most they have ever paid for a song'.
1892	31 August	Birth of Wheeler Dryden (CC's half-brother).
1893		Publication of Charles Chaplin Senior's song success, 'Oui, Tray Bong'.
	19 February	Mary Ann Hill (CC's grandmother) admitted to infirmary. Charles Hill is living at 97 East Street.
	23 February	Mary Ann Hill committed to asylum. Charles Hill is living at 87 St George's Road.
	1 March	Mary Ann Hill removed to Banstead Asylum.
	8 October	Birth of Henrietta Florence Kelly at 12 Guinea St, Bristol.
1895	29 June	Hannah Chaplin admitted (as 'Lilian Chaplin') to Lambeth Infirmary (remains until 30 July).
	1 July	Sydney Chaplin admitted to Lambeth Workhouse (remains until 4 July).
	4 July	Sydney Chaplin transferred to Norwood Schools (remains until 17 September).
	17 September	Sydney transferred to Lambeth Workhouse and discharged to care of father.
	10 October(?)	CC enrolled at Addington Street School, Lambeth.
1896		Publication of Charles Chaplin Senior's song success, 'She Must Be Witty'.
	8 February	Hannah Chaplin (as 'Lily Chaplin') performs at Hatcham Liberal Club.
	30 May	CC and Sydney admitted to Newington Workhouse.
	9 June	St Saviour Parish Board of Guardians requires

		Charles Chaplin Senior to pay 15s. weekly towards support of CC and Sydney.
	18 June	CC and Sydney transferred to Hanwell Schools.
	June/July	Hannah Chaplin admitted to Champion Hill Infirmary.
	1 July	Board of Guardians reports to Local Government Board that Charles Chaplin Senior agrees to contribute to sons' support.
	18 November	Sydney Chaplin transferred to Training Ship *Exmouth*.
1897		Throughout entire year CC remains at Hanwell Schools; Sydney Chaplin at Training Ship *Exmouth*.
	29 May	Death of Spencer Chaplin (CC's grandfather).
	10 August	Hannah Chaplin visits CC at Hanwell.
	16 September	Board of Guardians applies for warrant for Charles Chaplin Senior for non-payment of sons' support, and offers £1 for information leading to his arrest.
	11 November	Reported to Board of Guardians that Spencer Chaplin (CC's uncle) has paid £44.8s. due from Charles Chaplin Senior.
	16 November	Board of Guardians, through Spencer Chaplin, requests Charles Chaplin Senior to take responsibility for sons within fourteen days.
	20 December	Hannah Chaplin and her father Charles Hill seek baptism at Christchurch Nonconformist Church, Westminster Bridge Road. Resulting decision to be baptized on 10 January 1898.
	23 December	Warrant issued against Charles Chaplin Senior for neglecting to maintain his children.
1898	18 January	CC discharged from Hanwell Schools.
	18 January	Charles Chaplin Senior arrested for non-payment of support for sons.

	20 January	Sydney Chaplin discharged from Training Ship *Exmouth*.
	22 July	CC, Sydney and Hannah admitted to Lambeth Workhouse.
	30 July	CC and Sydney transferred to Norwood Schools.
	12 August	CC and Sydney transferred to Lambeth Workhouse; CC, Sydney and Hannah discharged from Lambeth Workhouse (Hannah's day's outing).
	13 August	CC, Sydney and Hannah readmitted to Lambeth Workhouse.
	15 August	CC and Sydney transferred to Norwood Schools.
	6 September	Hannah admitted to Lambeth Infirmary.
	15 September	Hannah transferred to Cane Hill Asylum.
	21 September	Board of Guardians seeks to make Charles Chaplin Senior take charge of his sons.
	27 September	CC and Sydney transferred to Lambeth Workhouse, and discharged to care of father.
	12 October	Board of Guardians informed that Charles Chaplin Senior has failed to enroll his sons in school.
	12 November	Hannah discharged from Cane Hill Asylum.
	26 December	CC with Eight Lancashire Lads at Theatre Royal, Manchester.
		Charles Chaplin Senior at Tivoli, Manchester (remains until 7 January 1899).
1899	9 January	CC enrolled at Armitage Street School, Ardwick, Manchester.
	5 May	Death of Spencer Chaplin (CC's uncle). Charles Chaplin Senior becomes nominal licensee of Queen's Head.
	20 July	Charles Hill (Chaplin's grandfather) admitted to Lambeth Infirmary, from 39 Methley Street.

	2 August	Charles Hill transferred from Lambeth Infirmary to Lambeth Workhouse.
1900	23 April	CC enrolled in St Mary the Less School, Newington (remained until 3 May).
	September	Charles Chaplin Senior's last recorded stage appearance, at Granville Theatre of Varieties, Walham Green.
	12 November	CC enrolled in St Francis Xavier School, Liverpool.
1901	6 April	Sydney Chaplin embarks to Cape as assistant steward and bandsman on *Norman* (returns 31 May).
	29 April	Charles Chaplin Senior admitted to St Thomas's Hospital.
	9 May	Charles Chaplin Senior dies in St Thomas's Hospital, aged thirty-seven.
	1 September	Sydney Chaplin embarks for New York as steward on *Haverford* (discharged in New York, 2 October).
	5 October	Sydney Chaplin engaged as steward on *St Louis*, New York to Southampton (discharged in Southampton, 23 October).
1902	September	Sydney Chaplin embarks for Cape as steward and bugler on *Kinfairns Castle* (returns 25 October).
	8 November	Sydney Chaplin's second voyage as steward and bugler on *Kinfairns Castle* (returns 27 December).
1903	17 January	Sydney Chaplin's third voyage as steward and bugler on *Kinfairns Castle* (returns 7 March).
	24 March	Sydney Chaplin's fourth voyage as steward and bugler on *Kinfairns Castle* (returns 9 May).
	5 May	Hannah Chaplin admitted to Lambeth Infirmary.
	9 May	Hannah Chaplin committed as lunatic (next of kin: son, CC).
	11 May	Hannah Chaplin transferred to Cane Hill Asylum (remains until 2 January 1904).

	6 July	CC plays Sam in *Jim, A Romance of Cockayne* at Royal County Theatre, Kingston.
	12 July	CC plays Sam in *Jim, A Romance of Cockayne* at Grand Theatre, Fulham.
	27 July	CC plays Billy in *Sherlock Holmes* for first time, Pavilion Theatre, East London (H. A. Saintsbury as Holmes).
	10 August	Tour of *Sherlock Holmes*, with CC as Billy, begins at Theatre Royal, Newcastle.
	(?) December	Sydney Chaplin joins cast of *Sherlock Holmes* tour.
1904	2 January	Hannah Chaplin discharged from Cane Hill Asylum; joins sons on tour.
	11 June	First *Sherlock Holmes* tour ends.
	20 August	Production of *From Rags to Riches*, starring CC, announced.
	29 August	Charles Hill (CC's grandfather) admitted to Renfrew Road Workhouse from 24 Chester Street.
	21 October	Charles Hill discharged from Renfrew Road Workhouse.
	31 October	CC joins second *Sherlock Holmes* tour, with Kenneth Rivington as Holmes.
	10 November	Sydney Chaplin embarks on last voyage, as assistant steward and bugler on *Dover Castle* to Natal.
1905	6 March	Hannah Chaplin readmitted to Lambeth Infirmary.
	16 March	Hannah Chaplin committed as lunatic (next of kin: Kate Hill).
	18 March	Hannah Chaplin transferred to Cane Hill Asylum (remains until 9 September 1912).
	22 April	Second *Sherlock Holmes* tour ends.
	12 August	CC joins third *Sherlock Holmes* tour, with H. Lawrence Layton as Holmes (Harry Yorke Company).

	13 September	*Clarice*, with William Gillette, opens at Duke of York's Theatre, London.
	30 September	CC leaves third *Sherlock Holmes* tour.
	3 October	*The Painful Predicament of Sherlock Holmes* added as afterpiece to *Clarice* at Duke of York's: CC plays Billy.
	17 October	*Sherlock Holmes* replaces *Clarice* at Duke of York's: CC plays Billy.
	19 October	Funeral of Henry Irving, CC attends.
	20 November	Royal Gala Performance of *Sherlock Holmes*.
1906	1 January	CC joins fourth *Sherlock Holmes* tour (Harry Yorke Company).
	3 March	Fourth *Sherlock Holmes* tour ends.
	March	CC joins company of Wal Pink's *Repairs*.
	19 March	*Repairs* tour opens at Hippodrome, Southampton.
	12 May	CC leaves tour of *Repairs* at Grand Palace, Clapham.
	May	CC joins *Casey's Court Circus* Company.
	9 July	Sydney Chaplin signs first contract with Fred Karno: one year at £3 per week (£6 if required to work in USA).
	Oct/Nov	Sydney Chaplin with Karno Company in USA.
1907	24 June	Sydney Chaplin signs second contract with Fred Karno: two years at £4 per week, one-year option.
	20 July	Tour of *Casey's Court Circus* ends.
	Autumn	CC attempts single act at Foresters' Music Hall.
1908	February	CC given trial by Fred Karno.
	21 February	CC's first contract with Fred Karno: £3.10s. per week first year; £4 per week second year; third year option at same rate.
		During the year CC and Sydney take flat at 15 Glenshaw Mansions, Brixton Road.
	Autumn	Meets Hetty Kelly.

Year	Date	Event
	Autumn	CC appears in Karno's *Mumming Birds* in Paris.
1909		During the year CC plays in *The Football Match*, *Mumming Birds*.
	3 March	Charles Hill (CC's grandfather) admitted to Renfrew Road Workhouse from 15 Glenshaw Mansions.
	4 September	Charles Hill discharged from Renfrew Road Workhouse.
	31 December	CC plays in *The Football Match* at Oxford Music Hall.
1910		During the year CC plays additionally in *Skating* and *Jimmy the Fearless*.
	19 September	CC signs second contract with Fred Karno, to run from 6 March 1911: three years at £6, £8 and £10 per week and a three-year option.
		Embarks with Karno American Company on SS *Cairnrona*.
	3 October	Karno US tour begins at Colonial Theatre, New York, with *The Wow-Wows*.
	26 December	New York Karno Company presents *A Harlequinade in Black and White* (possibly devised by CC) at American Music Hall.
1911		Karno US tour continues throughout year.
	January	Alf Reeves (Karno tour manager) marries Amy Minister.
1912	June	CC returns to England at end of Karno US tour.
	July/August	CC touring in France and Channel Islands with Karno Company.
	9 September	Hannah Chaplin transferred from Cane Hill Asylum to Peckham House, Peckham Road.
	2 October	CC embarks on *Oceanic* with Karno Company for second US tour.
1913	25 September	CC signs contract with Kessel and Bauman to join Keystone Film Company on 16 December, at $150 per week for one year.

	8 October	CC acquires 200 shares in Vancouver Island Oil Company Ltd (nos. 10826–11025).
	29 November(?)	CC's last performance with Karno Company, at Empress, Kansas City.
	16 December	CC's contract with Keystone Film Company commences.
1914	January	Commences work at Keystone Studios.
	2 February	*Making a Living* released.
	7 February	*Kid Auto Races* released.
	9 February	*Mabel's Strange Predicament* released.
	28 February	*Between Showers* released.
	2 March	*A Film Johnnie* released.
	9 March	*Tango Tangles* released.
	16 March	*His Favorite Pastime* released.
	26 March	*Cruel, Cruel Love* released.
	4 April	*The Star Boarder* released.
	18 April	*Mabel at the Wheel* released.
	20 April	*Twenty Minutes of Love* released.
	27 April	*Caught in a Cabaret* released.
	4 May	*Caught in the Rain* released.
	7 May	*A Busy Day* released.
	1 June	*The Fatal Mallet* released.
	4 June	*Her Friend the Bandit* released.
	11 June	*The Knockout* released.
	13 June	*Mabel's Busy Day* released.
	20 June	*Mabel's Married Life* released.
	9 July	*Laughing Gas* released.
	1 August	*The Property Man* released.
	10 August	*The Face on the Bar Room Floor* released.
	18 August	*Recreation* released.

	27 August	*The Masquerader* released.
	31 August	*His New Profession* released.
	7 September	*The Rounders* released.
	24 September	*The New Janitor* released.
	10 October	*Those Love Pangs* released.
	26 October	*Dough and Dynamite* released.
	29 October	*Gentlemen of Nerve* released.
	7 November	*His Musical Career* released.
	9 November	*His Trysting Place* released.
	14 November	*Tillie's Punctured Romance* released.
		Sydney Chaplin arrives at Keystone.
		CC signs contract with Essanay for $1250 per week to make fourteen films in 1915.
	5 December	*Getting Acquainted* released.
	7 December	*His Prehistoric Past* released.
		At end of month arrives in Chicago.
1915	January	CC working in Essanay Chicago Studio.
	1 February	*His New Job* released.
		CC moves to Essanay Studio, Niles, California.
	15 February	*A Night Out* released.
	11 March	*The Champion* released.
	18 March	*In The Park* released.
	1 April	*A Jitney Elopement* released.
	11 April	*The Tramp* released.
	May	Mark Hampton Co. for Charles Chaplin Advertising Service Company sues Art Novelty Co. for producing Chaplin statuettes.
	28 May	Board of Guardians seeks to return Hannah Chaplin to Cane Hill Asylum, since sons' payments to Peckham House Hospital are in arrears.

	21 June	*Work* released.
	12 July	*A Woman* released.
	9 August	*The Bank* released.
	27 August	Hetty Kelly marries Lieutenant Alan Edgar Horne at registry office in Parish of St George, Hanover Square.
		Keystone sues Chaplin Film Co. along with A. G. Levi and Lemun Film Co. for copyright infringement and accounting of profits relating to *Dough and Dynamite*.
		Himalaya Films, the distributors in France, name Chaplin 'Charlot'.
	4 October	*Shanghaied* released.
	20 November	*A Night in the Show* released.
	18 December	*Charlie Chaplin's Burlesque on Carmen* released.
1916		CC forms Charles Chaplin Music Corporation, with Sydney Chaplin and Herbert Clark (offices at 233 South Broadway, Los Angeles).
	22 January	Kate Mowbray (Kate Hill, CC's aunt) dies at 99 Gower Street, London.
	20 February	CC appears in benefit at Hippodrome, New York; donates half his fee to Actors' Fund.
	25 February	Subscription lists opened on Lone Star Film Corporation ($400,000 7% preferred stock; $25,000 common stock).
	26 February	CC signs with Mutual Film Corporation for $10,000 per week, with bonus of $150,000.
	27 February	In Boston, Rev. Frederick E. Heath preaches sermon on 'Charles Chaplin's Half Million'.
	22 March	CC attacked by London *Daily Mail* for clause in contract forbidding return for war service in British forces.
	27 March	Lone Star Studio opened.
	22 April	Essanay releases expanded version of *Charlie Chaplin's Burlesque on Carmen*.

	12 May	Chaplin seeks injunction to prevent release of *Charlie Chaplin's Burlesque on Carmen.*
	15 May	*The Floorwalker* released.
	25 May	CC appeals against adverse ruling on *Carmen* case.
	27 May	*Police* released.
	12 June	*The Fireman* released.
	24 June	CC's appeal against *Carmen* ruling fails in Supreme Court.
	10 July	*The Vagabond* released.
	7 August	*One A.M.* released.
	4 September	*The Count* released.
	1 October	CC institutes proceedings to prevent publication of *Charlie Chaplin's Own Story.*
	2 October	*The Pawnshop* released.
	8 November	CC cables requesting to negotiate for rights in Hall Caine's *The Prodigal Son.*
	12 November	Nationwide Chaplin psychic impulse reported in USA.
	13 November	*Behind the Screen* released.
	December	Paderewski visits studio.
	4 December	*The Rink* released.
	9 December	Al Woods cables CC the offer of half of profits plus weekly salary stipulated by CC, to appear in a musical comedy during 1917–18. Woods includes film rights to CC, in consideration of split of profits. Chaplin refuses.
		Publication of *Charlie Chaplin's Own Story* prevented.
1917	22 January	*Easy Street* released.
	8 February	In Cincinnati, hold-up man disguises himself as CC.
	31 March	CC plays in Tragics v. Comics ball game in Washington Park, Los Angeles.

	16 April	*The Cure* released.
	15 May	*Variety* report (incorrectly) Chaplin pictures to be distributed by Artcraft.
	June	John Jasper succeeds Henry P. Caulfield as general manager of Lone Star Studio. Carlyle Robinson appointed press representative.
	17 June	*The Immigrant* released.
		CC signs 'million-dollar contract' with First National Exhibitors' Circuit (salary: $1,075,000 per year).
	4 August	CC issues press statement: 'I am ready and willing to answer the call of my country.'
		British High Command forbids wearing of CC toothbrush moustache in army, as likely cause for ridicule.
	22 October	*The Adventurer* released.
	Autumn	CC begins work on building new studio on La Brea Avenue, Los Angeles.
1918	January	CC moves into new studio.
	15 January	Begins shooting *A Dog's Life* (working title: *I Should Worry*).
	23 January	Harry Lauder visits studio; Lauder and CC shoot 745 feet of comedy together.
	25 January	Lauder visits studio with Douglas Fairbanks.
	7 February	Artificial lights first used in studio (for night scene).
	11 February	*A Dog's Life* abandoned; CC begins new film, *Wiggle and Son*.
	12 February	*Wiggle and Son* abandoned; CC resumes *A Dog's Life*.
	26 March	Begins cutting *A Dog's Life*, 'working night and day'; completes it on 31 March.
	1 April	CC leaves Hollywood for Washington on Liberty Bond Tour.

	8 April	In New York for Liberty Loan appeal (rest of month on Liberty Bond tour).
	14 April	*A Dog's Life* released.
	15 April	John Jasper resigns as studio manager.
	9 May	CC announced to appear at benefit for Child Welfare Association of England and Ireland, but is not present.
	27 May	Begins to shoot *Shoulder Arms* (working title: *Camouflage*).
	8 June	Solar eclipse prevents shooting.
	13 June	Mrs Lee (mother of child actor Frankie Lee) paid $2 for use of her sweater in kitchen scene.
	18 July	CC receives and replies to letter from Henrietta Horne (née Hetty Kelly).
	11 August	Essanay release *Triple Trouble.*
	15 August	CC begins work on *The Bond.*
	22 August	Completes *The Bond.*
	31 August	CC begins cutting *Shoulder Arms* (though shooting continues).
	20 October	*Shoulder Arms* released.
	23 October	CC marries Mildred Harris, and moves into 2000 De Mille Drive.
	4 November	Begins work on *Sunnyside.*
		Death of Henrietta Horne (née Hetty Kelly). CC will not learn of death until 1921.
	7 November	Premature national holiday for Armistice.
	11 November	Holiday for real Armistice.
	15 November	Bishop of Birmingham visits studio.
	16 December	*The Bond* released.
1919	1–18 January	CC and Edna Purviance absent from studio.
	15 January	Statement of intent to form United Artists.
	19–28 January	Studio closed down.

29 January	*Sunnyside* abandoned.
	CC begins work on *A Day's Pleasure* (working title: *Putting It Over*).
5 February	Resumes work on *Sunnyside*.
	Contracts of incorporation for United Artists signed.
15 April	CC completes shooting *Sunnyside*.
17 April	Certificates of incorporation for United Artists filed.
21 May	CC begins rehearsals for *A Day's Pleasure* (working title: *Charlie's Picnic*), but does no shooting until 30 June.
26 May	Elsie Codd, CC's English press representative, arrives in Hollywood.
15 June	*Sunnyside* released.
7 July	CC's first son, Norman Spencer Chaplin, born.
8–9 July	Desultory shooting on *A Day's Pleasure*.
10 July	4 pm: Norman Spencer Chaplin dies.
11 July	Burial of Norman Spencer Chaplin, Inglewood Cemetery.
21 July	CC begins auditioning young children for *The Waif*.
30 July	Begins shooting *The Waif* (first version of *The Kid*).
8 August	Publicity film of CC in aeroplane shot at San Diego.
18 August	Commences 'new version' of *The Waif*.
17 September	Jackie Coogan 'lost and licked'.
	Towards end of month CC apparently abandons work on *The Kid*.
1–4 October	Shoots flea and flophouse material now identified as *The Professor*.
7 October	Resumes work on *A Day's Pleasure* (working title now *The Ford Story*).

	19 October	Completes *A Day's Pleasure.*
	14 November	Resumes work on *The Kid* (now known by definitive title).
	15 December	*A Day's Pleasure* released.
	22–27 December	CC gives Jackie Coogan holiday to visit grandmother in San Francisco, as Christmas present.
1920	14 January	CC begins cutting *The Kid* (though shooting continues).
	18 March	News stories on Chaplin marital troubles.
	4 April	Mildred Harris Chaplin begins divorce proceedings, charging mental cruelty.
	7 April	CC and Louis B. Mayer fight in Alexandria Hotel dining room.
	19 April	CC tests possible replacement for Edna Purviance in *The Kid.*
	9 June	Lillita McMurray (Lita Grey) shoots her first scenes in *The Kid.*
	3 August	Mildred Harris Chaplin's suit for divorce.
		During most of the rest of the year, and while cutting *The Kid*, Chaplin is in New York.
	13 November	Mildred Harris Chaplin granted divorce.
1921	22 January	CC begins preparing *The Idle Class* (working title: *Home Again*).
	6 February	*The Kid* released.
	15 February	CC begins shooting *The Idle Class.*
	29 March	Hannah Chaplin is admitted into America.
	25 July	CC completes shooting *The Idle Class.*
		At end of month CC goes to Catalina with Edward Knoblock and Carlyle Robinson to work on scenario.
	6 August	CC begins work on *Pay Day* (working title: *Come Seven*).

	22 August	Begins shooting *Pay Day*: completes eight scenes (348 feet).
	27 August	Leaves Los Angeles for New York and European trip.
	3 September	Sails from New York on *Olympic*.
	9 September	Arrives in London.
	19 September	Arrives in Paris.
	24 September	Arrives in Berlin.
	25 September	*The Idle Class* released.
	30 September	Weekend with H. G. Wells and family.
	6 October	Returns to Paris. Decorated by French Government.
	7 October	Flies back to London.
	7–9 October	Weekend with H. G. Wells and family.
	10 October	Sails from London in *Olympic*.
	17 October	Arrives in New York.
	30 October	Plagiarism suit brought by L. Loeb *re Shoulder Arms*.
	31 October	CC arrives back in Los Angeles.
	6 November	CC looks for locations for *Pay Day*.
	8 November	Trip with Clare and Dickie Sheridan.
	26 November	Begins shooting *Pay Day*.
1922	27 January	CC begins cutting *Pay Day*.
	7 February	Completes shooting and cutting of *Pay Day*.
	1 April	Begins preparing *The Pilgrim*.
	2 April	*Pay Day* released.
	10 April	CC begins shooting *The Pilgrim*.
	1–6 May	New generator installed at studio.
	15 July	CC completes *The Pilgrim*.
	Summer	Meets Peggy Hopkins Joyce.

	October	CC and Pola Negri meet at Actors' Fund Pageant.
	3 October	Mildred Harris Chaplin files for bankruptcy.
	27 November	CC begins shooting *A Woman of Paris.*
1923	25 January	Jesse Lasky announces that Pola Negri's contract with Paramount would not preclude marriage to Chaplin.
	28 January	Chaplin–Negri press conference to announce engagement.
	26 February	*The Pilgrim* released.
	1 March	Pola Negri breaks engagement.
	2 March	Pola Negri and CC announce reconciliation and re-engagement.
	25 June	CC completes shooting of *A Woman of Paris.*
	28 June	Chaplin–Negri engagement definitively broken off.
	29 September	CC completes editing of *A Woman of Paris.*
	1 October	Première of *A Woman of Paris*, Criterion Theatre, Hollywood.
		New York première of *A Woman of Paris*, Lyric Theatre.
	15 October	CC addresses American Child Health Association in Detroit.
	12 December	*Suspicion*, a play by George Appell and Wheeler Dryden (Chaplin's half-brother) produced at Egan Theatre, Los Angeles.
	29 December	'The Lucky Strike', scenario of *The Gold Rush*, registered for copyright.
1924	January	CC preparing *The Gold Rush.*
	8 February	Begins shooting *The Gold Rush.*
	2 March	Lita Grey signed as leading lady for *The Gold Rush.*
	April	Unit shoots on location at Truckee.
	1 May	Unit returns from Truckee.

	22 September	Studio shooting halted. Does not resume until 2 January 1925.
	19 November	Death of Thomas Ince.
	26 November	CC marries Lita Grey in Guaymas, Mexico.
	22 December	Tests made of Georgia Hale: announcement that she would replace Lita Grey in leading role.
1925	2 January	Shooting of *The Gold Rush* resumed.
	February	First rumours of marital disharmony.
	20 February	CC wins suit against Charles Amador for infringement of a comic character.
	20 April	Begins cutting *The Gold Rush*.
	5 May	Birth of son, Charles Spencer Chaplin.
	26 June	Première of *The Gold Rush* at Grauman's Egyptian Theatre, Los Angeles.
	28 June	'Official' birth date of Charles Spencer Chaplin Junior.
	3 July	CC finishes cutting *The Gold Rush*.
	12 July	Decision in Amador case overturned.
	29 July	CC leaves Los Angeles for New York.
	16 August	New York première of *The Gold Rush* at Strand Theatre.
	1 October	Hannah Chaplin's residence permit temporarily renewed.
	15 October	CC returns to Los Angeles.
	2 November	Begins preparation of *The Circus*.
	31 December	Georgia Hale's contract terminates.
1926	2 January	Commencement of Merna Kennedy's contract.
	11 January	CC begins shooting *The Circus*.
	16 January	Josef von Sternberg begins work on *Sea Gulls*, or *A Woman of the Sea*, produced by CC.
	9 March	Von Sternberg begins shooting *A Woman of the Sea*.

	30 March	Birth of Sydney Earle Chaplin.
	1 June	Von Sternberg completes shooting *A Woman of the Sea.*
	16 June	Raquel Meller visits set of *The Circus.*
	7 September	Chaplin is bearer at Rudolph Valentino's funeral.
	28 September	Fire at studio.
	30 November	Lita Grey leaves Chaplin home, with children.
	5 December	Studio operations temporarily suspended.
1927	8 January	CC sues Jim Tully over biographical article in *Pictorial Review.*
	10 January	Lita Grey files divorce complaint.
	18 January	Chaplin safe and vault opened by receivers.
	March	CC invited by Soviet film organization to visit USSR to escape 'hypocrisy'.
	20 April	CC agrees to pay one million dollars settlement on claim for back taxes.
	2 June	CC answers Lita Grey's complaint.
	9 June	Guards taken off duty, as receiver leaves studio.
	22 August	Hearing of divorce suit. Lita Grey granted divorce (final decree 25 August 1928).
	23 August	CC and Alf Reeves return to studio.
	6 September	Work on *The Circus* resumed after eight months' suspension.
	28 October	Preview of *The Circus* at Alexandra Theatre, Glendale.
	17 November	Further preview at Bard & West Adams Theatre, following reshoots and further editing.
	19 November	*The Circus* completed.
	December	CC works on musical score for *The Circus* with Arthur Kay.
	24 December	CC considering material for next film.
1928	6 January	World première of *The Circus* at Strand Theatre, New York.

27 January — Première of *The Circus* at Grauman's Chinese Theatre, Los Angeles.

7 March — Trial of CC's suit against First National for unpaid royalties on *The Kid*. Decision in CC's favour, 17 March.

5 May — CC begins preparation of *City Lights*.

28 August — Death of Hannah Chaplin at Glendale Hospital, California.

1 November — Virginia Cherrill put under contract.

27 December — CC begins shooting *City Lights*.

1929 25 February — CC becomes ill with ptomaine poisoning; contracts 'flu, and does not resume shooting until 1 April.

10 June — Work begins to move studio buildings fifteen feet, for widening of La Brea. Last until end July.

28 June — CC replaces Henry Clive with Harry Myers.

7 September — CC fires Harry Crocker.

24 September — Winston Churchill and party visit studio.

11 November — Georgia Hale brought in to replace Virginia Cherill. Remains on payroll until 30 November.

12 November — Virginia Cherrill removed from payroll (returns 21 November).

16 November — Gordon Pollock replaces Eddie Gheller as cameraman.

1930 24 February — Death of Mabel Normand.

5 October — Shooting of *City Lights* completed.

8 November — CC begins work on musical score.

1931 19 January — Preview of *City Lights* at Tower Theatre.

30 January — CC attends world première of *City Lights* at Los Angeles Theatre.

31 January — CC leaves Los Angeles on start of world trip.

6 February — CC attends New York opening of *City Lights*, George Cohan Theatre.

	13 February	Sails for Europe on *Mauretania* with Ralph Barton and Kono.
	19 February	Arrives at Southampton, travels by train to London.
	20 February	Visits Hanwell Schools.
	27 February	Attends London première of *City Lights*, Dominion Theatre.
	March	Visits Berlin, Vienna, Venice.
	27 March	Travels from Venice to Paris to receive the Légion d'Honneur.
	April	Visits Riviera.
	23 April	Alf Reeves reports sackings of studio staff.
	28 April	CC in Algiers with Sydney Chaplin and May Reeves, then returns to Riviera.
	May	Carlyle Robinson sent from Paris to New York.
	30 May	CC in Juan-les-Pins with May Reeves.
	20 June	Boris Evelinoff put in charge of Chaplin Paris office.
	15 July	Carlyle Robinson put in charge of Chaplin New York office.
	August	CC in Spain and Paris.
	September	CC in London.
	22 September	Meeting with Gandhi.
		Weekend at Chartwell.
	10 November	Weekend with Astors at Cliveden.
	December	Makes trip to North of England.
	26 December	CC in St Moritz with the Fairbankses, Sydney Chaplin and May Reeves, where he stays until March 1932.
1932	January	Carlyle Robinson dismissed.
	12 March	CC and Sydney Chaplin leave for Far East. Farewell to May Reeves.

	3 April	Edna Purviance, ill and without money, appeals for help to CC.
	23 April	CC and Sydney in Singapore; CC becomes ill with fever.
	7 May	CC and Sydney leave Singapore for Japan.
	14 May	Arrive Tokyo.
	2 June	CC, Sydney and Kono leave Yokohama in *Hikawa Maru*.
	10 June	CC and Kono arrive in Hollywood. Sydney Chaplin returns to Europe.

[NOTE: The exact dates of Chaplin's itinerary during this 1931–2 trip are extremely elusive: at this distance in time, one must be grateful for sightings *en route* which the foregoing dates largely represent.]

	27 June	CC releases article on Economic Solution to press.
	July	Until February 1933, Chaplin is occupied in writing series of articles, 'A Comedian Sees the World', for *Woman's Home Companion*.
	July	First meeting with Paulette Goddard.
	25 August	Loyd Wright (lawyer) files CC's petition objecting to sons working in motion pictures.
	27 August	CC in court for petition.
	2 September	Decision in CC's favour.
	15 October	CC served with subpoena to appear in court, 26 October.
	26 October	CC in court on Lita Grey Chaplin's appeal. Decision in his favour.
1933	March	Buys yacht, *Panacea*. Spends much of this summer on it.
	25 March	First record of work on *Modern Times*.
	21 June	Original and only negative of *A Woman of the Sea* or *Sea Gulls* destroyed in presence of witnesses.
		Work on *Modern Times* and preparations for production continue to end of year.

	23 October	CC speaks for National Recovery Act on Columbia Broadcasting System.
	7/9 December	CC at Hearst Ranch, San Simeon.
	29/31 December	CC at Yosemite.
1934		Preparations for *Modern Times* continue.
	16 May	Kono resigns, is given position with United Artists in Tokyo.
	4 September	Paulette Goddard signs contract with studio.
	11 October	CC begins shooting *Modern Times*.
	16 December	Douglas Fairbanks and Lady Mountbatten visit set.
	28 December	Sound tests of CC and Paulette Goddard.
1935	17 July	Title *Modern Times* officially announced.
	30 August	Shooting on *Modern Times* completed.
	27 November	H. G. Wells arrives in Hollywood as guest of CC; stays until 24 December.
	4 December	CC has row with Al Newman over music for film.
	22 December	Sound for *Modern Times* completed.
	28 December	Preview of *Modern Times* in San Francisco, followed by cuts and redubbing.
1936	5 January	Preview of *Modern Times* at Alexander Theatre, Glendale.
	5 February	*Modern Times* opens at Rivoli, New York.
	12 February	*Modern Times* Hollywood première at Grauman's Chinese Theatre.
	17 February	CC embarks on *Coolidge* with Paulette and Mrs Goddard and Frank Yonamori (valet) for San Francisco *en route* for Honolulu.
	26 February	They arrive in Honolulu but decide to go on to Hong Kong.
	7 March–22 May	Travelling to Yokohama, Kobe, Shanghai, Hong Kong, Manila, Saigon, French Indo-China, Japan.

	22 April	CC erroneously reported dead in Indo-China.
	22 May	Leave Japan for California on *Coolidge*; arrive 3 June.
	11 June	Death of Nathan Burkan, for long CC's lawyer.
		During rest of year CC works on *Stowaway*, *Regency* and Napoleon project. This work continues into 1937.
1937	23 April	Sonores Tobis Films bring suit for plagiarism of *A Nous la Liberté*. (Suit dismissed 19 November 1939.)
	26 May	*Regency* laid aside.
	1 October	Paulette Goddard takes screen test for role of Scarlett O'Hara in *Gone With the Wind*.
1938		Chaplin spends much of year at Pebble Beach, working intermittently on projects.
	October	Begins work on *The Great Dictator*.
1939	9 January	Work begins on sound-proofing studio stages (finished 10 February).
	21 January	Sydney Chaplin arrives in Hollywood from Europe.
	25 March	Wheeler Dryden arrives in Hollywood to work at studio.
	23 June	Title *The Great Dictator* registered.
	9 September	CC begins shooting *The Great Dictator*.
		House Un-American Activities Committee begins investigations.
	15 November	Douglas Fairbanks visits studio with wife: last meeting with CC.
	12 December	Death of Douglas Fairbanks (funeral, 15 December).
1940	28 March	CC completes main shooting of *The Great Dictator*.
	29 March	Begins cutting *The Great Dictator*.
	23 June	Resumes shooting, including final speech.

	3 July	Resumes cutting.
	22 July	Begins work on recording and music.
	5 September	Preview at Riverside Theatre, Riverside, followed by cutting, reshooting and redubbing.
	20 September	Preview at Long Beach, followed by further retakes and redubbing.
	11 October	CC goes to New York; remains until 10 February 1941.
	15 October	World première of *The Great Dictator* at Capitol and Astor Theatres, New York. CC present.
	14 November	Hollywood première of *The Great Dictator*, Carthay Circle Theatre.
1941	26 March–30 April	CC in New York.
	15 April	Konrad Bercovici brings plagiarism suit over *The Great Dictator*.
	9 June	CC begins work on reissue of *The Gold Rush*, with sound track.
	26(?) June	Puts Joan Berry (Barry) under contract.
		CC working on *Shadow and Substance*.
1942		CC continues work on *Shadow and Substance*.
	18 May	Speech for Russian War Relief in San Francisco.
	19 May	New version of *The Gold Rush* opens at Paramount, Hollywood and Paramount, Los Angeles.
	22 May	Joan Barry's contract cancelled by mutual consent.
	4 June	Paulette Goddard granted divorce (marriage revealed to have taken place in Far East, 1936).
	22 July	CC speaks by radio-telephone to Madison Square Second Front rally.
	12 October	Leaves for New York with Tim Durant and Edward Chaney (valet).
	16 October	Speaks at 'Artists' Front to Win the War' rally, Carnegie Hall.

	30 October	Returns to Los Angeles.
		Meets Oona O'Neill.
	November	Begins work on script for *Landru (Monsieur Verdoux)*.
	25 November	Speaks at 'Salute Our Russian Ally' meeting, Orchestra Hall Chicago.
	3 December	Speaks at 'Arts for Russia' dinner, Hotel Pennsylvania, New York.
	10 December	Returns home from New York and Chicago.
	23 December	Joan Barry breaks into Chaplin house, carrying gun.
	29 December	*Shadow and Substance* shelved.
1943		CC works on *Landru (Monsieur Verdoux)* script throughout year.
	7 March	Broadcasts 'Lambeth Walk' talk to Britain from CBS studio.
		Records speech at Soviet consul's office to be sent to USSR.
	4 June	Joan Barry accuses CC of being father of unborn child.
	16 June	CC marries Oona O'Neill at Carpenteria, Santa Barbara.
	26 June	CC and Oona Chaplin return from Carpenteria.
	14 September	CC's deposition in Barry case.
	2 October	Joan Barry gives birth to girl, Carol Ann.
1944	10 February	CC indicted by Federal Grand Jury on Mann Act charges and for conspiring with Los Angeles police and others to deprive Barry of civil rights in having her held on vagrancy charges.
	14 February	CC in court.
	15 February	Blood tests prove CC not father of Barry's child.
	21 February	CC arraigned.
	25 February	CC in court to plead against Mann Act charges.

	26 February	CC in court – pleads not guilty in Mann Act case.
	9 March	CC in court – pleads not guilty in conspiracy case.
	21 March	Mann Act case opens.
	4 April	CC found not guilty on Mann Act charges.
	4–15 May	CC and Oona in Palm Springs.
	15 May	Violation of civil rights charges dropped.
	29 May–30 June	CC and Oona absent on New York trip.
	20 July	Death of Mildred Harris.
	1 August	Birth of daughter to CC and Oona, Geraldine Leigh Chaplin.
	26 September	CC dictates article to 'youth of Soviet Russia'.
	13 December	Opening of Barry paternity trial.
	30 December	CC injures foot: in Cedars of Lebanon Hospital until 2 January.
1945	2 January	Paternity suit jury fail to agree (7–5 in favour of CC). Retrial ordered.
	26 January	Work begins on *Landru (Monsieur Verdoux)*. Marilyn Nash tested.
	20 February	CC issues statement to press.
	4 April	Opening of new paternity trial.
	17 April	Paternity trial verdict for Barry (11 votes to 1).
	22–27 April	CC and Oona in Palm Springs.
	10 May	CC files motion for new trial.
	6 June	Motion for new trial denied.
	16 June	CC in court *re* Barry support.
1946	11 February	Script of *Monsieur Verdoux* sent for copyright.
	7 March	Birth of Michael John Chaplin.
	11 March	CC has interview with Joseph Breen.
	18 March	Edna Purviance arrives at studio with view to playing in film.

	7 April	Death of Alf Reeves.
	8 April	John McFadden appointed General Manager of studio.
	10 April	Funeral of Alf Reeves.
	21 May	Begins shooting *Monsieur Verdoux*.
	5 September	Shooting completed.
1947	11 April	World première of *Monsieur Verdoux*, Broadway Theatre, New York.
	12 April	Hostile press conference in New York.
	12 June	Congressman John Rankin demands Chaplin's deportation.
	20 July	CC publicly accepts invitation from House Un-American Activities Committee to testify.
	23 September	Accepts subpoena for HUAC investigations.
	November	Sends telegram to Pablo Picasso in support of Hanns Eisler.
	17 December	Catholic War Veterans urge Justice and State Departments to investigate and arrange for CC's deportation.
1948		By start of year, CC working on story of *Footlights (Limelight)*.
	13 September	Begins dictating *Footlights*: work on script continues throughout following year.
1949	28 March	Josephine Hannah Chaplin born at St John's Hospital, Santa Monica.
	5 May	Walter Wanger rents studio for tests of Greta Garbo.
	3–18 August	CC and Oona on trip to New York.
1950	17 January–13 February	CC and Oona on trip to New York.
	8 April	*City Lights* reissued. Opened Globe Theatre, New York.
	6 September	Title *Limelight* registered.

	11 September	Script of *Limelight* sent for copyright.
	17 September–8 October	CC and Oona on trip to New York.
	December	CC begins working on music for *Limelight*.
1951	11–22 January	CC and Oona on trip to New York.
	February	CC begins interviewing actresses for *Limelight*.
	22–28 April	CC in New York to test Claire Bloom.
	19 May	Birth of daughter, Victoria, at St John's Hospital, Santa Monica.
	21 May	Start of enlargement of house at 1085 Summit Drive. Alterations completed 29 June.
	18 September	Claire Bloom sails on *Mauretania* from London.
	19 November	CC begins main shooting of *Limelight*.
1952	25 January	Main shooting completed.
	15 May	Roughcut of *Limelight* shown to James Agee and Sidney Bernstein.
	2 August	Preview at Paramount Studio.
	6 September	Chaplins leave Hollywood.
	17 September	Chaplin family sails from New York on *Queen Elizabeth*.
	19 September	Re-entry permit rescinded.
	23 September	Chaplins arrive in London.
	23 October	Première of *Limelight*, Odeon, Leicester Square, London.
	17–27 November	Oona Chaplin on trip to Los Angeles to wind up business affairs.
1953	January	Many theatres in USA cancel showings of *Limelight*.
	5 January	Chaplins move into Manoir de Ban, Corsier sur Vevey, Switzerland.
	March	Holiday on French Riviera.

	6 March	*Limelight* named Best Film by Foreign Language Press Critics in USA.
	10 April	CC surrenders US re-entry permit.
	23 August	Birth of son, Eugene Anthony.
	September 18	Studio sold to Webb and Knapp.
1954	10 February	Oona Chaplin renounces US citizenship.
	2 May	CC announces he will make film called *The Ex-King (A King in New York).*
	27 May	Awarded World Peace Council Prize.
	18 July	Meets Chou En Lai in Geneva.
	10 October	Makes personal appearance in ring of Knie Circus in Vevey.
		Distributes Peace Prize money to poor of Paris and Lambeth.
1955		Preparing *A King in New York.*
	1 March	CC sells remainder of stock in United Artists.
1956	24 April	CC meets Bulganin and Khrushchev at Claridges.
	25 May	Is made honorary member of ACTT.
	May–July	Shooting *A King in New York.*
	15 June	US Internal Revenue Service claims for back taxes.
	10 August	Reissue of *The Gold Rush* in Britain.
	25 August	Press conference in Paris.
	August–October	Editing, recording, dubbing *A King in New York* in Paris.
1957		CC continues work on *A King in New York* during early part of year.
	23 May	Birth of daughter, Jane Cecil.
	12 September	London première of *A King in New York.*
	24 September	CC bars US newsmen from Paris première.
	30 September	Death of Wheeler Dryden, in Hollywood.
1958	13 January	Death of Edna Purviance.

	21 February	CC's name excluded from Los Angeles 'Walk of Fame'.
	November	CC works on *The Chaplin Revue*.
	30 December	Settles US tax claims.
1959	16 April	Seventieth birthday. Chaplin says he will bring back The Little Fellow.
	24 September	*The Chaplin Revue* released.
	3 December	Birth of daughter, Annette Emily.
1960	July	Holiday in Ireland.
	20 December	Death of Mack Sennett.
1961	July	Holiday in Far East.
1962	April	Holiday in Switzerland, Ireland, London, Paris, Venice.
	27 June	Receives honorary doctorate from Oxford.
	6 July	Receives honorary doctorate from Durham University.
	8 July	Birth of son, Christopher James.
1963	June	Roy Export Company wins case against Atlas Films for unauthorized distribution of *The Gold Rush*.
	September	CC seeks suppression of brochure for rejuvenation treatment, quoting CC as successful patient.
1964		CC talks of writing opera, and slapstick comedy for Sydney Chaplin Junior.
	June	Attends Callas Gala at Paris Opera.
	September	Publication of *My Autobiography*.
1965	16 April	Death of Sydney Chaplin Senior.
	2 June	CC receives Erasmus Prize with Ingmar Bergman.
	1 November	London Press Conference to announce *A Countess From Hong Kong*.
1966	25 January	CC begins shooting *A Countess From Hong Kong*.

	11 May	Completes shooting *A Countess From Hong Kong*.
	11 October	CC breaks ankle.
1967	2 January	*A Countess From Hong Kong* opens.
	18 June	Death of Roland Totheroh.
1968		CC works on *The Freak*.
	20 March	Death of Charles Chaplin Junior.
1970		CC composes new score for *The Circus*.
		Black Inc. takes distribution of Chaplin films.
1971	31 October	CC is awarded Grande Medaille de Vermeil by City of Paris.
1972	March	CC's name added to Los Angeles 'Walk of Fame'.
	2 April	CC arrives in New York.
	3 April	Appears at show at Philharmonic Hall, Lincoln Center.
	6 April	Is awarded Handel Medallion, New York.
	16 April	Is awarded Special Academy Award, in Hollywood.
	3 September	Is awarded Golden Lion at Venice Film Festival.
1974	October	Publication of *My Life in Pictures*.
1975	4 March	CC is knighted by HM Queen Elizabeth II.
1976	30 June	CC is reported as saying: 'To work is to live – and I love to live'.
1977	15 October	CC makes last trip from home – to see Knie Circus in Vevey.
	25 December	CC dies in his sleep at Manoir de Ban, Corsier sur Vevey.
	27 December	Funeral at Vevey.
1978	1 March	Theft of body.
	17 March	Recovery of body.
	11–14 December	Trial of Ganev and Wardas for theft of body.

1980	14 January	Leicester Square hoax: *papier maché* statue of CC erected.
	27 September	Parc Charles Chaplin inaugurated in Vevey.
	19 December	Plaque placed on 287 Kennington Road. Unveiled by Sir Ralph Richardson.
1981	14 April	Statue by John Doubleday placed in Leicester Square. Unveiled by Sir Ralph Richardson.
1982	22 August	Bronze replica of Doubleday statue erected in Parc Charles Chaplin in Vevey.
1988		Oona Chaplin gives permission for Richard Attenborough to base a film on Chaplin's *My Autobiography*.
1991	27 September	Oona Chaplin dies at the Manoir de Ban, Corsier sur Vevey, Switzerland.
1991	16 November	Jerry Epstein dies in London.
1992	14 July	Henriette (Gypsy) Chaplin, widow of Sydney Chaplin, dies at the Hotel Beau Rivage, Lausanne, Switzerland, at 93 years.
1992	December	Release of film biography, *Chaplin*, produced and directed by Richard Attenborough and based on Chaplin's *My Autobiography* and *Chaplin: His Life and Art* by David Robinson.

ACADEMY AWARDS

Chaplin twice received special Oscars from the American Motion Picture Academy. At the first Academy Awards in 1928 he received a special award 'for Versatility and Genius for Writing, Acting, Directing and Producing *The Circus*'. His second 'Oscar' came in 1972 (see above and pp 621–5).

APPENDIX II

Tours of 'The Eight Lancashire Lads', 1898–1900

Chaplin is believed to have been with the troupe throughout the period detailed below. It is possible that the troupe did not perform at all during the weeks for which there is no record.

	week commencing:	
1898	26 December	Theatre Royal, Manchester (*Babes in the Wood*).
1899	2 January	Theatre Royal, Manchester (*Babes in the Wood*).
	9 January	Theatre Royal, Manchester (*Babes in the Wood*).
	16 January	Theatre Royal, Manchester (*Babes in the Wood*).
	23 January	Theatre Royal, Manchester (*Babes in the Wood*).
	30 January	Theatre Royal, Manchester (*Babes in the Wood*).
	6 February	Theatre Royal, Manchester (*Babes in the Wood*).
	13 February	Theatre Royal, Manchester (*Babes in the Wood*).
	27 February	Grand Theatre, Manchester.
	6 March	Grand Theatre, Manchester.
	3 April	Oxford Music Hall, Oxford Street, London.
	10 April	Oxford Music Hall, Oxford Street, London.
	17 April	Oxford Music Hall, Oxford Street, London.
	24 April	Oxford Music Hall, Oxford Street, London.
	1 May	Oxford Music Hall, Oxford Street, London.

	8 May	Oxford Music Hall, Oxford Street, London.
	15 May	Oxford Music Hall, Oxford Street, London.
	29 May	Empire, Cardiff.
	5 June	Empire, Swansea.
	17 July	Empire, Nottingham.
	2 October	Paragon, Mile End Road, London.
	9 October	Paragon, Mile End Road, London.
	16 October	Paragon, Mile End Road, London.
	23 October	Paragon, Mile End Road, London.
	6 November	Oxford Music Hall, Oxford Street, London.
	13 November	Oxford Music Hall, Oxford Street, London.
	20 November	Oxford Music Hall, Oxford Street, London.
	27 November	Oxford Music Hall, Oxford Street, London.
	5 December	Oxford Music Hall, Oxford Street, London.
	12 December	Oxford Music Hall, Oxford Street, London.
	19 December	Oxford Music Hall, Oxford Street, London.
	26 December	New Alexandra Theatre, Stoke Newington, London (pantomime: *Sinbad the Sailor*).
1900	1 January	New Alexandra Theatre, Stoke Newington, London.
	8 January	New Alexandra Theatre, Stoke Newington, London.
	15 January	New Alexandra Theatre, Stoke Newington, London.
	22 January	New Alexandra Theatre, Stoke Newington, London.
	29 January	New Alexandra Theatre, Stoke Newington, London.
	5 February	New Alexandra Theatre, Stoke Newington, London.
	26 February	Empire Theatre, Newcastle-upon-Tyne.

5 March	Empire Palace, South Shields.
12 March	Empire Palace, Glasgow.
19 March	Royal, Holborn (Holborn Empire), London.
26 March	Empire Palace, Edinburgh.
2 April	Empire Palace, Birmingham.
9 April	Empire Palace, Birmingham.
16 April	Tivoli Music Hall, Strand, London.
23 April	Tivoli Music Hall, Strand, London.
30 April	Tivoli Music Hall, Strand, London.
7 May	Tivoli Music Hall, Strand, London.
14 May	Tivoli Music Hall, Strand, London.
21 May	Tivoli Music Hall, Strand, London.
28 May	Tivoli Music Hall, Strand, London.
4 June	Canterbury Music Hall, London.
6 August	Camberwell Palace of Varieties, London.
20 August	Oxford Music Hall, Oxford Street, London.
27 August	Oxford Music Hall, Oxford Street, London.
3 September	Oxford Music Hall, Oxford Street, London.
10 September	Oxford Music Hall, Oxford Street, London.
17 September	Palace Theatre, Hull.
24 September	Empire Palace, Sheffield.
1 October	Empire Palace, Leeds.
8 October	Empire Theatre, Bradford.
15 October	Palace Theatre, Manchester.
22 October	Palace Theatre, Manchester.
29 October	Empire Theatre, Liverpool.
5 November	Empire Theatre, Liverpool.
12 November	Empire Theatre, Dublin.
19 November	Empire Theatre, Dublin.

Tours of 'The Eight Lancashire Lads', 1898–1900

26 November	Empire Theatre, Belfast.
3 December	Empire Theatre, New Cross.
24 December	According to Chaplin the Lancashire Lads appeared in the pantomime *Cinderella* at the London Hippodrome, which ran from 24 December to 13 April 1901.

APPENDIX III

Tours of 'Sherlock Holmes', 1903-1906

Chaplin is thought to have played the role of Billy throughout these tours, in the absence of any record of performances missed through illness or other causes.

1903	week commencing:	
		Charles Frohman's Northern Company **H. A. SAINTSBURY as Holmes**
	27 July	Pavilion Theatre, Whitechapel Road, London.
	10 August	Theatre Royal, Newcastle.
	17 August	Lyceum Theatre, Sheffield.
	26 October	Theatre Royal, Bolton.
	2 November	Royal Court Theatre, Wigan.
	9 November	Theatre Royal, Ashton under Lyne.
	16 November	New Theatre Royal, Stockport.
	23 November	Gaiety Theatre, Burnley.
	30 November	New Theatre Royal, Rochdale.
	7 December	Victoria Theatre, Broughton.
	14 December	Theatre Royal, Bury.
	21 December	Theatre Royal, Dewsbury.
	28 December	Royalty Theatre and Opera House, Barrow.

1904	4 January	Royal Opera House, Wakefield.
	11 January	Queen's Theatre, Leeds.
	18 January	Grand Theatre, West Hartlepool.
	25 January	Grand Theatre, West Hartlepool.
	1 February	Grand Opera House, York.
	4 February	Grand Opera House, Harrogate.
	8 February	Theatre Royal, Jarrow.
	15 February	Theatre Royal, Middlesbrough.
	22 February	Avenue Theatre, Sunderland.
	29 February	Theatre Royal, North Shields.
	7 March	Prince of Wales Theatre, Grimsby.
	14 March	His Majesty's Theatre, Aberdeen.
	21 March	His Majesty's Theatre, Dundee.
	28 March	Paisley Theatre, Paisley.
	4 April	His Majesty's Theatre, Carlisle.
	11 April	Royal Princess's Theatre, Glasgow.
	18 April	Grand Theatre, Glasgow.
	25 April	Grand Theatre, West Hartlepool.
	2 May	Grand Theatre, Hyson Green, Nottingham.
	9 May	Theatre Royal, Aldershot.
	16 May	Theatre Royal, Bradford.
	23 May	His Majesty's Opera House, Blackpool.
	30 May	Royal West London Theatre, Church Street, Edgware Road.
	6 June	Royal West London Theatre, Church Street, Edgware Road.
		Charles Frohman's Midland Company KENNETH RIVINGTON as Holmes
	31 October	New Theatre Royal, King's Lynn (two-day engagement only).

	7 November	Theatre Royal, Shrewsbury.
	14 November	Royal Court Theatre, Warrington.
	21 November	*No engagement traced*
	28 November	Prince of Wales Theatre, Mexborough.
	5 December	Lyceum Theatre, Sheffield.
	12 December	Theatre Royal, Barnsley.
	19 December	*No engagement traced*
1905	2 January	Theatre Royal, Darlington.
	9 January	Theatre Royal, Dumfries (three-day engagement only).
	16 January	*No engagement traced*
	23 January	Theatre Royal, Perth.
	30 January	New Century Theatre, Motherwell.
	6 February	Theatre Royal, Greenock.
	13 February	*No engagement traced*
	20 February	Royal Worcester Theatre, Bootle.
	27 February	Princes' Theatre, Accrington.
	6 March	Theatre Royal, Hyde.
	13 March	*No engagement traced*
	20 March	Theatre Royal and Opera House, Merthyr Tydfil.
	27 March	*No engagement traced*
	3 April	Theatre Royal, Tonypandy.
	10 April	*No engagement traced*
	17 April	Poole's Opera House, Perth.

Harry Yorke's Company
H. LAWRENCE LAYTON as Holmes

12 August	Theatre Royal, Blackburn.
19 August	Theatre Royal, Hull.
26 August	Theatre Royal, Dewsbury.

	4 September	Theatre Royal, Huddersfield.
	11 September	Queen's Theatre, Manchester.
	18 September	Rotunda Theatre, Liverpool.
	25 September	Court Theatre, Warrington.
		From 3–14 October Chaplin played the role of Billy in William C. Gillette's *The Painful Predicament of Sherlock Holmes* at the Duke of York's Theatre, St Martin's Lane, London.
		From 17 October to 2 December Chaplin played the role of Billy in William C. Gillette's revival of *Sherlock Holmes* at the Duke of York's Theatre, London. Royal Gala performance, 20 November.
1906		**Harry Yorke's Company**
	1 January	Grand Theatre, Doncaster.
	8 January	*No engagement traced*
	15 January	New Theatre, Cambridge.
	22 January	Pavilion Theatre, Whitechapel Road, London.
	29 January	Dalston Theatre, London.
	5 February	Carlton Theatre, Greenwich.
	12 February	Crown Theatre, Peckham.
	19 February	Lyceum Theatre, Crewe.
	26 February	Theatre Royal, Rochdale.

Frohman at times had three *Sherlock Holmes* companies touring at the same time. Other boys who played the part of Billy the page included Walter Hicks, Cedric Walters and Ernest Hollern. The last named took over from Chaplin when he left the 1905 tour to play the role at the Duke of York's. Chaplin left the company on 30 September: nevertheless he received a favourable notice in *The Era* for his performance at the Theatre Royal, Preston in the week of 2 October. Presumably his sudden departure had not permitted time to alter the programmes. It is a useful lesson that contemporary documentation must always be regarded with caution.

APPENDIX IV

Tours of 'Casey's Court Circus', 1906-1907

Chaplin is believed to have remained with the company throughout the tour.

1906	week commencing:	
	3 March	Advertisement in *The Era* announces *'Casey's Court Circus'* is 'copyrighted and to be produced shortly'.
	17 March	Advertisement in *The Era* announces *'Casey's Court Circus'* is 'in active rehearsal'.
	14 May	Empire Theatre, Bradford.
	21 May	Olympia Theatre, Liverpool.
	28 May	Coliseum Theatre, Glasgow.
	4 June	Empire Theatre, Newcastle.
	11 June	Empire Theatre, Leeds.
	18 June	*No engagement traced*
	25 June	Empire Theatre, Sheffield.
	2 July	Empire Theatre, Ardwick.
	9 July	Empire Theatre, Nottingham.
	16 July	Palace Theatre, Leicester.
	23 July	Bordsley Palace Theatre, Birmingham.
	30 July	Palace Theatre, Halifax.

Tours of 'Casey's Court Circus', 1906–1907

	6 August	Richmond Theatre, London.
	13 August	*No engagement traced*
	20 August	Holloway Empire, London.
	27 August	New Cross Empire, London.
	3 September	*No engagement traced*
	10 September	Shepherds Bush Empire, London.
	17 September	Stratford East Empire, London.
	24 September	Surrey Theatre of Varieties, London.
	1 October	Empire, Cardiff.
	8 October	*No engagement traced*
	15 October	*No engagement traced*
	22 October	*No engagement traced*
	29 October	Palace Theatre, Southampton.
	5 November	*No engagement traced*
	12 November	*No engagement traced*
	19 November	*No engagement traced*
	26 November	*No engagement traced*
	3 December	Palace Theatre, Blackburn.
	10 December	Palace Theatre, Bath.
	17 December	Sadlers Wells, London.
	24 December	Empire, South Shields.
	31 December	*No engagement traced*
1907	7 January	*No engagement traced*
	14 January	*No engagement traced*
	21 January	Empire Theatre, Belfast.
	28 January	Empire Theatre, Dublin.
	4 February	Olympia Theatre, Liverpool.
	11 February	*No engagement traced*
	18 February	*No engagement traced*

25 February	*No engagement traced*
4 March	Palace Theatre, West Hartlepool.
11 March	*No engagement traced*
18 March	Zoo and Hippodrome, Glasgow.
25 March	*No engagement traced*
1 April	Empire Theatre, Newcastle-upon-Tyne.
8 April	Hippodrome, Manchester.
15 April	*No engagement traced*
22 April	Empire Palace, Leeds.
29 April	Empire Palace, Birmingham.
6 May	Empire Theatre, Nottingham.
13 May	Hackney Empire, London.
20 May	Holloway Empire, London.
27 May	New Cross Empire, London.
3 June	Stratford Empire, London.
10 June	Shepherds Bush Empire, London.
17 June	Palace Theatre, Leicester.
24 June	Foresters' Music Hall, Bethnal Green, London.
1 July	Surrey Theatre of Varieties, London.
8 July	*No engagement traced*
15 July	Sadlers Wells, London.

APPENDIX V

Three Keystone scenarios

The three shot-by-shot scripts which follow have been recreated from the best available copies of the films, and are believed to represent the complete and original form Chaplin intended. They have been selected to illustrate the rapid progress and variety of Chaplin's approach to film craft in the formative year he spent at Keystone.

CAUGHT IN THE RAIN

Caught in the Rain was probably his first effort as a director: he was only allowed to make it with his own guarantee of $1500 against loss. It is evidently made with great care: Chaplin has conscientiously studied the post-Griffith shot-by-shot method of film construction, and in fact the single reel contains rather more shots than the average Keystone production. The *mise-en-scène* of each shot and scene is already admirable, within the studio formula of only a dozen fixed camera set-ups: the bench, the refreshment stand, the drinking fountain, the road crossing, the saloon doorway, the hotel exterior, the hotel lobby, the balcony and the ground beneath it, and the usual Keystone composite setting of a room on either side of a hallway.

TITLE: A BIG THIRST AND A LITTLE WIFE

1 A bench in the park. Mack Swain and Alice Davenport sit side by side. Mack gets up and exits to –
2 Refreshment stand. Mack takes a drink.
3 The Bench (as shot 1). Alice plucks a rose.

TITLE: A WRECKER OF HOMES

4 A drinking fountain. Charlie, trying to take a drink, soaks himself.
5 The Bench. Alice laughs flirtatiously; then remembers herself.
6 The Drinking Fountain. Charlie exits to –
7 The Bench. Charlie sits down – on Alice's rose.

TITLE: 'SOMETHING ATTACKED ME IN THE REAR'

8 The Bench. Charlie flirts with Alice, but she is unresponsive.

TITLE: 'WE SEEM TO BE GETTING ALONG WELL TOGETHER'

9 The Bench. Alice remains unresponsive.
10 Refreshment Stand. Mack notices what is going on.

TITLE: 'MY WIFE – WITH A LADY-KILLER!'

11 Refreshment Stand. Mack is clearly angry.
12 The Bench. Alice tells Charlie off.
13 Refreshment Stand. Mack fiercely exits towards –
14 The Bench. Charlie rests his feet on Alice's knee. Mack enters scene and yells at both of them. As he abuses Alice, he keeps hitting Charlie with his elbow.

TITLE: 'TAKE A BACK SEAT – YOU RUSTY ROMEO'

15 The Bench. Mack shoves Charlie into the bushes and goes off with Alice.
16 The Bench. Charlie gets up, brushes himself off and exits.
17 A road. Mack and Alice.
18 Saloon – exterior. Charlie at door of saloon.

TITLE: LOVE IS A THIRSTY BUSINESS

19 Saloon – exterior. Charlie licks his lips, then drags himself into the saloon by his own ear.
20 Hotel – exterior. Mack angrily shoves Alice into the door.
21 Hotel lobby – interior.
22 Saloon – exterior. Charlie emerges, evidently drunk. He leans on a convenient cop (who remains impassive in shock) then strikes a match on him.

TITLE: 'A STRIKING FELLOW LIKE YOU SHOULD BE A MATCH FOR ANYONE'

23 Saloon – exterior. Charlie flicks his match at the cop, but beats a hasty retreat when the cop threatens him with his truncheon.
24 Hotel lobby. Mack and Alice.
25 A road. Charlie crosses, narrowly escaping the cars which rush past him.
26 Hotel corridor with rooms to left and right. Mack and Alice enter room at right.
27 First Hotel Room. Mack and Alice enter.
28 Hotel – exterior. Charlie follows an attractive girl who enters the door. She slams the door in his face, but he enters after her.
29 Hotel lobby. Charlie enters and trips over an old man's gouty leg.
30 First hotel room. Mack and Alice. Mack is drinking.
31 Hotel lobby. Charlie whispers to receptionist, while pointing to a group of girls.

TITLE: 'WHO DOES THE HAT WITH THE FEATHERS BELONG TO?'

32 Hotel lobby. Charlie casually throws the hotel register at the gouty gentleman.
33 First hotel room. Mack and Alice quarrelling.

TITLE: 'AFTER TWENTY YEARS OF MARRIED LIFE I FIND YOU FLIRTING WITH A SCAVENGER'

34 First hotel room. Mack and Alice quarrelling.
35 Hotel lobby. Charlie attempts to ascend the stairs, but slides down on his face. He tries again, and this time bowls over the gouty man who is also making the ascent. At the next try the gouty man falls on top of Charlie who hits the receptionist in revenge. He tries again, his body leaning backwards at a 45-degree angle.
36 First hotel room. Mack and Alice still quarrelling.
37 Hotel lobby. Charlie is now wearing the girl's feather hat, d'Artagnan style. The girl grabs back her hat and goes upstairs, which is incentive enough for Charlie finally to make the ascent successfully.
38 Hotel corridor (as shot 26). Charlie passes the gouty gentleman, and aims a passing kick at him.
39 First hotel room. Mack and Alice.
40 Hotel corridor. Charlie inspects lock of first hotel room.
41 First hotel room. Mack and Alice, reconciled at last.
42 Hotel corridor. Charlie attempts to unlock first hotel room with a cigarette instead of a key.

TITLE: 'AH, LOCKED!'

43 First hotel room. Charlie enters. Mack and Alice, sitting on the bed, are at first unaware of his presence as he sprinkles the contents of Mack's bottle on his head as if it were brilliantine, combs his hat, takes a drink, and wipes his mouth on Alice's hat. Mack finally remonstrates.

TITLE: 'OUT YOU GO – YOU HE-VAMP'

44 First hotel room. Mack throws Charlie out.
45 Hotel corridor. As Charlie emerges from the room the gouty man, passing by, sees him and hurriedly flees.
46 First hotel room. Mack and Alice are quarrelling again.
47 Hotel corridor. Charlie enters Second Hotel Room, on left.
48 Second hotel room. Charlie does a long undressing routine. He wipes his shoes on his dickey and his brow on his collar. He then becomes entangled in his trousers. He is already wearing his pyjamas under his outer clothes.
49 First hotel room. Alice is in bed; Mack exits.
50 Second hotel room. Charlie gets into bed, having first removed hair brush from between the sheets.
51 Hotel – exterior. Mack comes out of door.
52 Second hotel room. As an afterthought, Charlie puts his boots under the pillow for safety.

TITLE: MIDNIGHT – THE SLEEP WALKING

53 First hotel room. Somnambulant Alice gets out of bed and opens the door.
54 Hotel – exterior. A sudden shower of rain soaks Mack.
55 Hotel corridor. Alice walks from door of first hotel room to door of second hotel room.
56 Second hotel room. Alice enters door and sits on bed. Charlie wakens, alarmed.

TITLE: 'WHOEVER SENT YOU MUST HAVE OWED ME A GRUDGE'

57 Second hotel room. Alice picks up Charlie's trousers and begins to go through the pockets. Charlie snatches them away and hides them under his pillow.
58 First hotel room. Mack re-enters, finds Alice gone, and begins to call out.
59 Second hotel room. Charlie is very alarmed.
60 Hotel corridor. Charlie comes out of his room at the same time as Mack. Charlie affects nonchalance in face of Mack's anger.

TITLE: 'I'M ITCHING TO THROTTLE SOMEONE'

61 Corridor. Charlie and Mack. Mack exits.
62 Second hotel room. Charlie re-enters to find Alice is now in his bed. He collapses on the bed. This awakens Alice, who is shocked by her situation.
63 Hotel corridor. Charlie peeks out of the door of his room, and sees it is empty.
64 Second hotel room. Charlie pushes Alice out into corridor.
65 Hotel corridor. Charlie pushing Alice out of door.
66 Hotel lobby. Mack questions receptionist, then returns upstairs.
67 First hotel room. Charlie enters with Alice.

TITLE: 'KEEP CALM – I'LL BE QUITE ALL RIGHT'

68 First hotel room. Charlie snatches a drink. Alice becomes hysterical.
69 Hotel corridor. Mack returns.
70 First hotel room. Charlie and Alice in consternation. Alice pushes Charlie out of the window.
71 Balcony outside window. Charlie in pouring rain.
72 First hotel room. Alice makes up to Mack.
73 Balcony outside window. Charlie suffering in the rain.
74 Exterior, below the balcony. A policeman yells at Charlie, ordering him down.
75 Balcony. Charlie signals helplessness.
76 Exterior, below the balcony. Policeman fires gun at Charlie.
77 Balcony. Charlie terrified.
78 Exterior, below the balcony. The policeman fires again.
79 First hotel room. Charlie suddenly re-enters through the window.
80 Hotel – exterior. The Keystone Kops arrive.
81 Hotel corridor. Charlie flees from first hotel room, managing to kick the gouty man who happens to be passing.
82 Hotel lobby. The Keystone Kops rush in.
83 Hotel corridor. Charlie rushes back into his room.
84 Second hotel room. Charlie firmly shuts the door behind him.
85 First hotel room. Mack exits.
86 Hotel corridor. Coming out of his room, Mack rushes into arms of the Keystone Kops. They fall like ninepins (or like Keystone Kops).
87 Second hotel room. Charlie listens at door.
88 Corridor. The Kops pick themselves up.
89 Second hotel room. Charlie leaps at the door.
90 Hotel corridor. Charlie's door, bursting open, knocks over the Kops once more. They flee in terror. Charlie kicks Mack into –
91 Second hotel room. Mack is kicked through the door.

92 Hotel corridor. Alice, emerging from her room, faints in Charlie's arms.
93 Second hotel room. Mack in state of collapse.
94 Hotel corridor. Charlie and Alice in state of collapse.

THE NEW JANITOR

Caught in the Rain was released on 4 May 1914. *The New Janitor*, released on 24 September, came less than five months, and fourteen films, later. Chaplin is already much more assured. Again he follows the Keystone ground rules, with a mere eight camera set-ups and ninety shots. Using only seven brief titles, he fashions a brilliant and clear narrative, with suspense and a new element of sentiment. Now Chaplin is creating a real comic drama rather than an animated strip cartoon. The editing builds its own dynamic, in the Griffith manner, rather than simply joining a step-by-step progression of shots. Thus in shots 43 to 56 and 66 to 79, Chaplin skilfully uses cutting between parallel actions to create suspense. At the same time, as in shot 79, he is now prepared to abandon the fast Keystone cutting and allow a piece of dramatic or comic action to run on unbroken as long as it seems to require. Gags and character touches, like Charlie's troubles in cleaning the window or his melodramatic response to dismissal, are at once integrated into the story and given time to develop.

1 Stairway and elevator, ground floor. Charlie, the janitor, carrying a broom and feather duster, attempts to enter the elevator in the wake of a well-dressed gentleman, but the elevator boy slams the gate in his face. Charlie toils up the stairs.

TITLE: THE TOP FLOOR

2 Stairway and elevator, top floor. Elevator boy emerges, but darts back into elevator as Charlie, mopping his brow, toils to the top of the stairs.
3 Hallway between two offices. Charlie walks away from camera, twirling his pan and duster behind him.
4 Manager's office (room to left of hall). Manager reads letter.

TITLE: 'WILL CALL TODAY TO COLLECT THAT GAMBLING DEBT. HAVE THE MONEY READY FOR ME, OR I'LL EXPOSE YOU. LUKE CONNOR'

5 Manager's office. Manager reads letter, gets up from chair anxiously.
6 Hallway. Charlie hangs hat on hall-stand. It falls off again, and he gives it a back-kick. *[This looks like an accident: retakes were not encouraged at Keystone.]* Enters Manager's office.
7 Manager's office. Charlie enters, knocks on door *after* entering. He removes wastepaper basket, gets it upside down, spilling contents. In retrieving contents, and stuffing them back into basket, he includes a file which Manager has just dropped. Manager is angry. Charlie drops lady-like curtsey on leaving.
8 Hallway. Charlie juggles wastepaper basket but drops it. Picks up broom, pan and duster and enters Boss's office. He gets the brush stuck across the doorway, so carefully steps over it.

9 Boss's office. Charlie walks up and down, dusts telephone.
10 Hallway. Secretary hangs up hat, looks lovingly at Manager's hat hanging there, enters Boss's office.
11 Boss's office. Secretary enters. Charlie continues to dust while casting abstracted, admiring glances at her. Yawning, he inadvertently feather-dusts her bottom as she is bending over her desk.

TITLE: LUKE CONNOR

12 Manager's office. Villainous man enters: altercation with Manager.
13 Boss's office. Still admiring the secretary, Charlie wipes his shoes with his handkerchief. Secretary leaves office by back door.
14 Manager's office. Manager and Connor still arguing. Manager shushes Connor.
15 Hallway. Secretary overhearing conversation.
16 Manager's office. Manager and Connor still arguing.

TITLE: 'I'LL GET IT BY FIVE O'CLOCK'

17 Manager's office. Manager and Connor in conversation.
18 Hallway. Secretary listening.
19 Manager's office. Connor exits.
20 Boss's office. Charlie sits on window ledge cleaning windows, almost falls out, signifies heart palpitations.
21 Exterior window, overlooking street far below. Charlie leans out of window backwards.
Exterior building at street level. Boss with two ladies.
22 Boss's office. Charlie in window, wringing out cloth.
23 Exterior building at street level. Water falls on Boss and ladies. The ladies are outraged; the Boss shakes his fist in direction of window.
24 Boss's office. Charlie, in window, knocks out his bucket.
25 Exterior window, overlooking street. Charlie's bucket falling.
26 Exterior building at street level. Bucket falls on Boss.
27 Boss's office. Charlie in window talking to (unseen) Boss below. Struggling with the sash, it falls and almost knocks him out of window.
28 Exterior building at street level. Irate Boss enters door.
29 Boss's office. Charlie at window, still shouting down to street, and again almost precipitated out by falling sash.
30 Stairway and elevator, ground floor. Distressed Boss enters lift under amused gaze of lift boy.
31 Staircase and elevator, top floor. Boss storms out of elevator.
32 Hallway. Boss, holding head, charges into office door.
33 Boss's office. Charlie still leaning out of window. Boss rushes in and kicks him. Charlie mildly excuses himself.

TITLE: BOUNCED

34 Boss's office. Boss dismisses Charlie, who runs through a repertory of shrugs, bows, half-turns with startled turns back. He backs towards door, falling over when he gets there.
35 Hallway. Charlie exits backwards through the door, which is slammed on him, knocking him on his back.

TITLE: GOING DOWN

36 Stairway and elevator, top floor. Charlie as usual shut out of lift.
37 Boss's office. Manager enters and gives paper to Boss, still grumbling about his troubles with Charlie.
38 Stairway and elevator, ground floor. Charlie descends stairs, falling on his bottom on last step. Retrieving broom and dustpan, he uses dustpan to protect bottom against further injury.
39 The Janitor's Room. Charlie enters, the dustpan now held to his head.
40 Boss's office. As Manager exits, Boss puts papers in safe.
41 Manager's office. Manager enters, thoughtful.
42 Boss's office. Secretary now at typewriter. Boss picks up hat and stick, instructs Secretary, and leaves.
43 Manager's office. Manager sits at desk, still thoughtful.
44 Boss's office. Secretary tidies up and exits.
45 Hallway. Secretary comes out of office.
46 Manager's office. Manager furtively approaches door.
47 Hallway. Secretary puts on hat and exits.
48 Manager's office. Manager furtively opens door and exits to –
49 Hallway. Manager enters from office.
50 Staircase and elevator. Secretary rings for lift.
51 Hallway. Manager crosses to Boss's office.
52 Boss's office. Manager enters, pulls down blinds, goes to safe.
53 Stairway and elevator. Secretary remembers something, and turns back from elevator.
54 Boss's office. Manager opens safe.
55 Hallway. Secretary approaches office door and opens it.
56 Boss's office. Secretary enters and sees Manager open safe. They look at each other. Manager leaves; the Secretary is very suspicious.
57 Manager's office. Manager enters, takes bag, listens at door.
58 Boss's office. Secretary listening at door. She exits into –
59 Hallway. Secretary crosses, points accusingly at door of Manager's office, then kneels and looks through keyhole.
60 Manager's office. Manager listening at keyhole.
61 Hallway. Shocked, the Secretary recoils from door.
62 Manager's office. Manager goes to open door.
63 Hallway. Secretary retreats into Boss's office.
64 Manager's office. Manager swiftly exits.
65 Hallway. Manager puts on hat, starts to leave, but then goes to door of Boss's office.
66 Boss's office. The alarmed secretary enters, goes to the desk and hides behind it. The Manager enters, makes for the safe, opens it, begins to hurl out the contents, until he finds a wad of notes. At this moment he notices the Secretary. He points at her; she points back. Manager begins to struggle with Secretary, threatening to throw her out of window. She attempts to open the desk to reach for the telephone, but the Manager knocks her to the floor.
67 The Janitor's Room. Charlie, preparing to leave, shrugs.
68 Manager's Room. Manager and Secretary struggling.

TITLE: THE PORTER'S BUTTON

69 Boss's office. As Manager pushes Secretary back across the rolltop desk, her hand reaches for a button at the side.

70 The Janitor's office. Charlie on the point of leaving.

71 Bell ringing.

72 The Janitor's office. Charlie irritatedly mouths 'Shut up.'

73 Boss's office. Manager holds girl over desk, then throws her unconscious to the ground.

74 The Janitor's office. Charlie leaves, with a backward glance.

75 Staircase and elevator, ground floor. Charlie enters . . . indicates indecision . . . indecision . . . but finally sets off up the stairs.

76 Boss's office. Manager returns to rifling safe.

77 Staircase and elevator, top floor. Charlie reaches top landing, collapsing in exhaustion. After taking a breather, he pulls himself to his feet, and exits to left of screen.

78 Hallway. Charlie enters, right of screen. He pauses to light a cigarette, throws down the match and gives it a back-kick. Then, swinging his cane, he enters the Boss's office.

79 Boss's office. Charlie enters, sees man rifling safe, and swipes him on the bottom with his cane, demanding what he has been doing to the girl. Manager produces a gun, but Charlie flicks it out of his hand with his cane. The man hits out, misses, and Charlie fells him with a kick. Charlie turns his back and bends down, but as the Manager prepares to attack him from the rear, points the gun at him between his legs. Charlie neatly rights himself by stepping over his gun arm, and backs the man at gun-point against the safe. They circle each other, and Charlie tells the Manager to pick up the girl, which he does, placing her on a chair. They circle again until the Manager is again backed against the safe. He tries to take advantage of a moment's inattention, but fails to catch Charlie out. Charlie picks up the telephone, but talks into the wrong end of it. They continue to circle each other: when Charlie reaches the window, he fires his gun out of it.

80 Exterior of building at street level. A policeman, flirting with a girl, looks up, attracted by the shots.

81 Boss's office. Charlie accidentally shoots his own foot.

82 Exterior building at street level. Policeman hastily exits.

83 Boss's office. Charlie shoots gun in time to fend off the Manager's counter-attack.

84 Staircase and elevator, ground floor. Policeman rushes upstairs.

85 Hallway. Boss in leisure clothes approaches office.

86 Boss's office. Boss enters, and, misjudging the situation, assaults Charlie, despite the efforts of the Secretary, who has now regained consciousness, to explain all.

87 Hallway. Boss's attack precipitates Charlie into the arms of the Policeman. When Policeman grabs him, Charlie kicks him into –

88 Manager's office. Policeman tumbles into door.

89 Hallway. Policeman re-enters, and grabs Charlie.

90 Manager's office. Manager, Secretary and Boss. Policeman enters, holding

Charlie, but Boss points accusing finger at Manager. As Policeman leads Manager away, Charlie briefly menaces him with the telephone, which he has momentarily mistaken for the pistol. Boss hands Charlie a reward, which he quickly counts before shaking Boss's hand in gratitude.

HIS MUSICAL CAREER

His Musical Career was released on 7 November, towards the end of Chaplin's time with Keystone. At first sight it seems a regression in terms of narrative: in fact, he is boldly experimenting with quite a different style, much closer to that of his maturity. Having recognized that cutting is a convenience, not an obligation, he dispenses with the rapid editing which Keystone inherited from Griffith, and conceives the film in a series of much more extended shots which provide a stage for uninterrupted comedy routines.

TITLE: MR RICH BUYS A PIANO

1 Piano Shop. Charley Chase sells a piano to Mr Rich.
2 Back Room of Shop. Mack and Charlie are piano movers. Mack incredulously gazes at Charlie's antics which include oiling his elbows with an oil can.
3 Piano Shop. Charley Chase treats a Shabby Old Man very differently from Mr Rich.

TITLE: 'IF YOU CAN'T KEEP UP YOUR PAYMENTS, I'LL TAKE BACK YOUR PIANO'

4 Piano Shop. Shabby Old Man sadly leaves.
5 Back Room of Shop. Charlie reposes on piano as Charley Chase enters.

TITLE: 'TAKE THIS PIANO TO 666 PROSPECT STREET AND BRING ONE BACK FROM 999 PROSPECT STREET'

6 Charley Chase regards his unenthusiastic workers.

TITLE: 'NO TIME TO LOSE'

7 Piano Shop. In their struggles with the piano, Charlie manages to leave all the heavy work to Mack.
8 Shop – exterior. Charlie manages to drop entire weight of piano onto Mack – gazes in sympathetic surprise at Mack's struggling form beneath piano.
9 Sidewalk. Mack and Charlie load piano onto cart drawn by minute donkey.
10 Home of Shabby Old Man. Shabby Old Man tells Beautiful Daughter sad tale of piano.
11 CU. Mack and Charlie on donkey cart, with street behind. *[camera apparently mounted on front of cart]*. Charlie uses a clay pipe like straw to drink from Mack's huge jar of beer, while Mack's attention is engaged by traffic.
12 House – exterior. Weight of piano weighs down cart, lifting little donkey into the air.

TITLE: TAKING MR RICH'S PIANO TO 999 PROSPECT INSTEAD OF 666

13 House – exterior. Cart draws up. Mack and Charlie unload piano.
14 Long stairway to house. Mack and Charlie struggle with piano.

15 House – interior. Daughter reports arrival of piano. Shabby Old Man delighted.
16 Long stairway to house. Piano slides down stairs.
17 CU. Suffering Mack on stairs.
18 Long stairway to house. Mack and Charlie struggle up with piano.
19 House – interior. Charlie toils in with piano on his back. Shabby Old Man and Daughter are indecisive about where to put it, as Charlie staggers around room.
20 Long stairway to house. Mack and Charlie, relieved of their burden, descend. Charlie falls down last steps.
21 Sidewalk. Mack and Charlie get back on cart. Charlie is almost left behind.

TITLE: COMING TO GET THE OLD MAN'S SUPPOSED PIANO AT MR RICH'S

22 Sidewalk outside Mr Rich's house. Mack and Charlie drive up on cart and dismount. Charlie politely raises hat to donkey.
23 Entrance to Mr Rich's house. Mack and Charlie.

TITLE: THEY WALKED RIGHT IN

24 Mr Rich's House – interior. Mack and Charlie curiously inspect all the ornaments and decorations of the house. They begin to remove the piano. Mrs Rich appears and protests. She calls the Footman, but Mack and Charlie knock him down and exit with piano.
25 Mr Rich's House – exterior. Mack and Charlie carry out piano.
26 Sidewalk. Mr Rich arrives. General Keystone mêlée.

APPENDIX VI
Filmography

The record of the early Chaplin films has been a matter of accretion over the years since 1944, when Theodore Huff compiled his pioneer 'Index to the Films of Charles Chaplin'. Five years before that, in *The Rise of the American Film*, Lewis Jacobs considered that it was already an impossible task to compile an accurate listing of the Chaplin Keystone films. Huff nevertheless achieved a complete record of the Chaplin films, apart from the mysterious *The Professor* which is recorded here for the first time in any filmography. Huff also made a brave beginning in listing the credits and casts of the films; and his remains the basis of all subsequent filmographies. His errors – like crediting Roland Totheroh as Chaplin's cameraman at Essanay – have also been perpetuated.

The early 1970s saw efforts to augment the credits: Denis Gifford's 1974 biography, *Chaplin*, contained the most comprehensive filmography to that date, due to conscientious work in identifying players from the screen. This however introduced some new errors: any passing virago was optimistically identified as Phyllis Allen, while the misapprehension that Edna Purviance appeared as an extra in *Monsieur Verdoux* and *Limelight* was unquestioningly followed by subsequent filmographers. Some of the errors (though not the last) persisted as late as the filmography included in the present writer's *Chaplin: The Mirror of Opinion* (1983).

Inevitably the present filmography relies to an extent upon the work of Huff and his successors, and in the case of the early films cannot claim to be comprehensive or definitive. The source for credits that are included here for the first time is generally the studio records preserved in the Chaplin private archive at Vevey.

The system of numbering established in Uno Asplund's 1971 filmography, *Chaplin's Films*, and adopted by Timothy J. Lyons' *Charles Chaplin: A Guide to References and Resources* and the present writer's *Chaplin: The Mirror of*

Opinion, is again followed here to avoid the confusion which might result from the existence of two systems. As far as may be ascertained, the footages given for films are those of the original release prints.

I THE KEYSTONE FILMS 1914

General Credits:

Production: The Keystone Film Company

Producer: Mack Sennett

Photography: According to Hans Koenekamp, who was at Keystone from 1913 and photographed *Mabel's Strange Predicament*, any Keystone cameraman might work any day on any production. Asked (in 1983) who shot *Tillie's Punctured Romance*, he replied 'Who *didn't*?' Previous filmographies have generally credited Frank D. Williams or E. J. Vallejo *(Making a Living)* with the photography of Chaplin's films, but other members of the Keystone camera team must have also worked on the Chaplin pictures.

1 Making A Living

Director: Henry Lehrman
Scenario: ?Reed Heustis

Cast:	Charles Chaplin	(Slicker)
	Virginia Kirtley	(Girl)
	Alice Davenport	(Mother)
	Henry Lehrman	(Reporter)
	Minta Durfee	(Woman)
	Chester Conklin	(Policeman/Bum)

Released: 2 February 1914
Length: 1030 feet.

2 Kid Auto Races at Venice

Director: Henry Lehrman
Scenario: Henry Lehrman

Cast:	Charles Chaplin	(Tramp)
	Henry Lehrman	(Film Director)
	Frank D. Williams	(Cameraman)
	Billy Jacobs	(Boy)
	Charlotte Fitzpatrick	(Girl)
	Thelma Salter	(Girl)
	Gordon Griffith	(Boy)

Released: 7 February 1914
Length: 572 ft (released on a 'split reel' with an interest film, *Olives and their Oil.*)

3 Mabel's Strange Predicament

Director:	Henry Lehrman and Mack Sennett	
Scenario:	Henry Lehrman	
Cast:	Charles Chaplin	(Tramp)
	Mabel Normand	(Mabel)
	Chester Conklin	(Husband)
	Alice Davenport	(Wife)
	Harry McCoy	(Lover)
	Hank Mann	
	Al St John	
Released:	9 February 1914	
Length:	1016 ft.	

4 Between Showers

Director:	Henry Lehrman	
Scenario:	?Reed Heustis	
Cast:	Charles Chaplin	(Masher)
	Ford Sterling	(Rival Masher)
	Chester Conklin	(Policeman)
	Emma Clifton	(Girl)
	Sadie Lampe	(Policeman's Lady Friend)
Released:	28 February 1914	
Length:	1020 ft	

5 A Film Johnnie

Director:	George Nichols	
Scenario:	Craig Hutchinson	
Cast:	Charles Chaplin	(The Film Johnnie)
	Roscoe Arbuckle	(Fatty)
	Virginia Kirtley	(The Keystone Girl)
	Minta Durfee	(Actress)
	Mabel Normand	(Mabel)
	Ford Sterling	(Ford)
	Mack Sennett	(Himself)
Released:	2 March 1914	
Length:	1020 ft	

6 Tango Tangles

Director/Scenario: Mack Sennett

Cast:	Charles Chaplin	(Tipsy Dancer)
	Ford Sterling	(Band Leader)
	Roscoe Arbuckle	(Musician)
	Chester Conklin	(Policeman)
	Minta Durfee	(Check Girl)

Released: 9 March 1914
Length: 734 ft

7 His Favorite Pastime

Director: George Nichols
Scenario: Craig Hutchinson

Cast:	Charles Chaplin	(Drinker)
	Roscoe Arbuckle	(Drinker)
	Peggy Pearce	(Wife)

Released: 16 March 1914
Length: 1009 ft

8 Cruel, Cruel Love

Director: George Nichols
Scenario: Craig Hutchinson

Cast:	Charles Chaplin	(Lord Helpus)
	Chester Conklin	(Butler)
	Minta Durfee	(Girl)
	Alice Davenport	(Maid)

Released: 26 March 1914
Length: 1025 ft

9 The Star Boarder

Director: George Nichols
Scenario: Craig Hutchinson

Cast:	Charles Chaplin	(The Star Boarder)
	Minta Durfee	(Landlady)
	Edgar Kennedy	(Landlady's Husband)
	Gordon Griffith	(Their Son)
	Alice Davenport	(Landlady's Friend)

Released: 4 April 1914
Length: 1020 ft

10 Mabel At The Wheel

Directors: Mabel Normand, Mack Sennett
Scenario: ?Mabel Normand, Mack Sennett

Cast:	Charles Chaplin	(Villain)
	Mabel Normand	(Mabel)
	Harry McCoy	(A Car Racer, Mabel's Boyfriend)
	Chester Conklin	(Mabel's Father)
	Mack Sennett	(A Rube)
	Al St John	(Villain's Henchman)
	Fred Mace	(Dubious Character)

	Joe Bordeaux	(Dubious Character)
	Mack Swain	(Spectator)
Released:	18 April 1914	
Length:	1900 ft	

11 Twenty Minutes of Love

Director/Scenario: Charles Chaplin

Cast:	Charles Chaplin	(Pickpocket)
	Minta Durfee	(Woman)
	Edgar Kennedy	(Lover)
	Gordon Griffith	(Boy)
	Chester Conklin	(Pickpocket)
	Joseph Swickard	(Victim)
	Hank Mann	(Sleeper)
Released:	20 April 1914	
Length:	1009 ft	

12 Caught in a Cabaret

Director:	Mabel Normand	
Scenario:	?Mabel Normand and Charles Chaplin	
Cast:	Charles Chaplin	(Waiter)
	Mabel Normand	(Mabel)
	Harry McCoy	(Lover)
	Chester Conklin	(Waiter)
	Edgar Kennedy	(Café Proprietor)
	Minta Durfee	(Dancer)
	Phyllis Allen	(Dancer)
	Joseph Swickard	(Father)
	Alice Davenport	(Mother)
	Gordon Griffith	(Boy)
	Alice Howell	
	Hank Mann	
	Wallace MacDonald	
Released:	27 April 1914	
Length:	1968 ft	

13 Caught in the Rain

Director/Scenario: Charles Chaplin

Cast:	Charles Chaplin	(Tipsy Hotel Guest)
	Mack Swain	(Husband)
	Alice Davenport	(Wife)
	Alice Howell	(A Woman)
Released:	4 May 1914	
Length:	1015 ft	

14 A Busy Day

Director/Scenario: ?Charles Chaplin

Cast:	Charles Chaplin	(Wife)
	Mack Swain	(Husband)
	Phyllis Allen	(The Other Woman)
Released:	7 May 1914	
Length:	441 ft	

15 The Fatal Mallet

Director/Scenario: Mack Sennett

Cast:	Charles Chaplin	(Suitor)
	Mabel Normand	(Mabel)
	Mack Sennett	(Rival Suitor)
	Mack Swain	(Man)
Released:	1 June 1914	
Length:	1120 ft	

16 Her Friend the Bandit

Director:	?	
Scenario:	?	
Cast:	Charles Chaplin	(Bandit)
	Mabel Normand	(Mabel)
	Charles Murray	(Count De Beans)
Released:	4 June 1914	
Length:	1000 ft approx.	

17 The Knockout

Director:	Charles Avery	
Cast:	Roscoe Arbuckle	(Fatty)
	Minta Durfee	(Woman)
	Edgar Kennedy	(Cyclone Flynn)
	Charles Chaplin	(Referee)
	Al St John	(Boxer)
	Hank Mann	(Boxer)
	Mack Swain	(Spectator)
	Mack Sennett	(Spectator)
	Alice Howell	(Spectator)
	Charles Parrott*	(Policeman)
	Eddie Cline	(Policeman)
	Joe Bordeaux	(Policeman)
	*Charley Chase	
Released:	11 June 1914	
Length:	1960 ft	

18 Mabel's Busy Day

Director/Scenario: ?Mabel Normand

Cast:	Charles Chaplin	(Tipsy Nuisance)
	Mabel Normand	(Mabel)
	Chester Conklin	(Police Sergeant)
	Slim Summerville	(Policeman)
	Billie Bennett	(Woman)
	Harry McCoy	
	Wallace MacDonald	
	Edgar Kennedy	
	Al St John	
	Charles Parrott*	
	Mack Sennett	
	Henry Lehrman(?)	
	*Charley Chase	
Released:	13 June 1914	
Length:	998 ft	

19 Mabel's Married Life

Director:	Charles Chaplin	
Scenario:	Charles Chaplin and Mabel Normand	
Cast:	Charles Chaplin	(Mabel's Husband)
	Mabel Normand	(Mabel)
	Mack Swain	(Sporty Ladykiller)
	Alice Howell	(Mack's Wife)
	Hank Mann	(Friend)
	Charles Murray	(Man in Bar)
	Harry McCoy	(Man in Bar)
	Wallace MacDonald	(Delivery Boy)
	Al St John	(Delivery Boy)
Released:	20 June 1914	
Length:	1015 ft	

20 Laughing Gas

Director/Scenario: Charles Chaplin

Cast:	Charles Chaplin	(Dentist's Assistant)
	Fritz Schade	(The Dentist)
	Alice Howell	(Dentist's Wife)
	Joseph Sutherland	(Assistant)
	George Slim Summerville	(Patient)
	Joseph Swickard	(Patient)
	Mack Swain	(Patient)
Released:	9 July 1914	
Length:	1020 ft	

21 The Property Man

Director/Scenario: Charles Chaplin

Cast:	Charles Chaplin	(The Property Man)
	Fritz Schade	(Garlico)
	Phyllis Allen	(Hamlene Fat)
	Àlice Davenport	(Actress)
	Charles Bennett	(Actor)
	Mack Sennett	(Man in Audience and Spectator)
	Norma Nichols	(Vaudeville Artist)
	Joe Bordeaux	(Old Actor)
	Harry McCoy	
	Lee Morris	
Released:	1 August 1914	
Length:	1858 ft	

22 The Face on the Bar Room Floor

Director:	Charles Chaplin	
Scenario:	Charles Chaplin, after the poem by Hugh Antoine d'Arcy.	
Cast:	Charles Chaplin	(Artist)
	Cecile Arnold	(Madeline)
	Fritz Schade	(The Lover Who Stole Her)
	Vivian Edwards	(A Woman)
	Chester Conklin	(Drinker)
	Harry McCoy	(Drinker)
	Hank Mann	(Drinker)
	Wallace MacDonald	(Drinker)
Released:	10 August 1914	
Length:	1020 ft	

23 Recreation

Director/Scenario: Charles Chaplin

Cast:	Charles Chaplin	(Tramp)
	Charles Murray(?)	(Seaman on Park Bench)
	Norma Nichols	(Girl)
Released:	18 August 1914	
Length:	462 ft (released as a 'split reel' with a scenic film, *The Yosemite*.)	

24 The Masquerader

Director/Scenario: Charles Chaplin

Cast:	Charles Chaplin	(Film Actor)
	Roscoe Arbuckle	(Film Actor)
	Chester Conklin	(Film Actor)
	Charles Murray	(Film Director)
	Fritz Schade	(Villain)

	Minta Durfee	(Leading Lady)
	Cecile Arnold	(Actress)
	Vivian Edwards	(Actress)
	Harry McCoy	(Actor)
	Charles Parrott*	(Actor)
	*Charley Chase	
Released:	27 August 1914	
Length:	1030 ft	

25 His New Profession

Director/Scenario: Charles Chaplin

Cast:	Charles Chaplin	(Charlie)
	Minta Durfee	(Woman)
	Fritz Schade	(Uncle)
	Charles Parrott*	(Nephew)
	Cecile Arnold	(Girl)
	Harry McCoy	(Cop)
	*Charley Chase	
Released:	31 August 1914	
Length:	1015 ft	

26 The Rounders

Director/Scenario: Charles Chaplin

Cast:	Charles Chaplin	(Reveller)
	Roscoe Arbuckle	(His Friend and Neighbour)
	Phyllis Allen	(Charlie's Wife)
	Minta Durfee	(Fatty's Wife)
	Al St John	(Bellhop)
	Fritz Schade	(Diner)
	Wallace MacDonald	(Diner)
	Charles Parrott*	(Diner)
	*Charley Chase	
Released:	7 September 1914	
Length:	1010 ft	

27 The New Janitor

Director/Scenario: Charles Chaplin

Cast:	Charles Chaplin	(Janitor)
	Fritz Schade	(Boss)
	Jack Dillon	(Villainous Manager)
	Minta Durfee	(Secretary)
	Al St John	(Elevator Boy)
Released:	24 September 1914	
Length:	1020 ft	

28 Those Love Pangs

Director/Scenario: Charles Chaplin

Cast:	Charles Chaplin	(Masher)
	Chester Conklin	(Rival)
	Cecile Arnold	(Girl)
	Vivian Edwards	(Girl)
	Edgar Kennedy	(Girls' Friend)
	Norma Nichols	(Landlady)
	Harry McCoy	(Cop)
Released:	10 October 1914	
Length:	1010 ft	

29 Dough and Dynamite

Director/Scenario: Charles Chaplin (Sennett is generally credited with collaboration on the scenario.)

Cast:	Charles Chaplin	(Waiter)
	Chester Conklin	(Waiter)
	Fritz Schade	(Bakery Proprietor)
	Norma Nichols	(His Wife)
	Cecile Arnold	(Waitress)
	Vivian Edwards	(Waitress)
	Phyllis Allen	(Customer)
	Jack Dillon	(Customer)
	Edgar Kennedy	(Striking Baker)
	George Slim Summerville	(Striking Baker)
	Charles Parrott*	(Striking Baker)
	Wallace MacDonald	(Striking Baker)
	*Charley Chase	
Released:	26 October	
Length:	2000 ft	

30 Gentlemen of Nerve

Director/Scenario: Charles Chaplin

Cast:	Charles Chaplin	(Impecunious Track Enthusiast)
	Mack Swain	(Ambrose, His Friend)
	Mabel Normand	(Mabel)
	Chester Conklin	(Walrus)
	Phyllis Allen	(His Wife)
	Edgar Kennedy	(Policeman)
	Charles Parrott*	(Spectator)
	Alice Davenport	(Waitress)
	*Charley Chase	
Released:	29 October 1914	
Length:	1030 ft	

31 His Musical Career

Director/Scenario: Charles Chaplin

Cast:	Charles Chaplin	(Piano Mover)
	Mack Swain	(Ambrose, his Partner)
	Charles Parrott*	(Piano Store Manager)
	Fritz Schade	(Mr Rich)
	Joe Bordeaux	(Mr Poor)
	Alice Howell	(Mrs Rich)
	Norma Nichols	(Miss Poor)
	*Charley Chase	
Released:	7 November 1914	
Length:	1025 ft	

32 His Trysting Place

Director/Scenario: Charles Chaplin

Cast:	Charles Chaplin	(Husband)
	Mabel Normand	(Mabel, His Wife)
	Mack Swain	(Ambrose)
	Phyllis Allen	(Ambrose's Wife)
Released:	9 November 1914	
Length:	2000 ft	

33 Tillie's Punctured Romance

Director:	Mack Sennett	
Scenario:	Mack Sennett, from the play, *Tillie's Nightmare*.	
Cast:	Marie Dressler	(Tillie Banks, a Country Lass)
	Charles Chaplin	(Charlie, a City Slicker)
	Mabel Normand	(Mabel, his Girl Friend)
	Mack Swain	(John Banks, Tillie's Father)
	Charles Bennett	(Douglas Banks, Tillie's Uncle)
	Charles Murray	(Detective)
	Charles Parrott*	(Detective)
	Edgar Kennedy	(Restaurant Proprietor)
	Harry McCoy	(Pianist)
	Minta Durfee	(Maid)
	Phyllis Allen	(Wardress)
	Alice Davenport	(Guest)
	George Slim Summerville	(Policeman)
	Al St John	(Policeman)
	Wallace MacDonald	(Policeman)
	Joe Bordeaux	(Policeman)
	G. G. Ligon	(Policeman)
	Gordon Griffith	(Newsboy)

	Billie Bennett	(Girl)
	Rev D. Simpson	(Himself)
	*Charley Chase	
Released:	14 November 1914	
Length:	6000 ft.	

34 Getting Acquainted

Director/Scenario: Charles Chaplin

Cast:	Charles Chaplin	(Spouse)
	Phyllis Allen	(His Wife)
	Mack Swain	(Ambrose)
	Mabel Normand	(Ambrose's Wife)
	Harry McCoy	(Policeman)
	Edgar Kennedy	(A Passing Turk)
	Cecile Arnold	(Girl)
Released:	5 December 1914	
Length:	1025 ft	

35 His Prehistoric Past

Director/Scenario: Charles Chaplin

Cast:	Charles Chaplin	(Weakchin)
	Mack Swain	(King Lowbrow)
	Gene Marsh	(Lowbrow's Favourite Wife)
	Fritz Schade	(Cleo)
	Cecile Arnold	(Cave Woman)
	Al St John	(Cave Man)
Released:	7 December 1914	
Length:	2000 ft	

II THE ESSANAY FILMS 1915–1916

General Credits:

Production:	The Essanay Film Manufacturing Company
Producer:	Jesse T. Robbins
Director:	Charles Chaplin
Scenario:	Charles Chaplin
Photography:	Harry Ensign from *A Night Out* onwards: photographer of *His New Job* unknown.
Assistant Director:	Ernest Van Pelt (believed to have worked on all Essanay films after *His New Job*).
Scenic Artist:	E. T. Mazy (believed to have worked on all Essanay films from *Work* onwards).

36 His New Job

Cast:	Charles Chaplin	(Film Extra)
	Ben Turpin	(Film Extra)
	Charlotte Mineau	(Film Star)
	Charles Insley	(Film Director)
	Leo White	(Actor)
	Frank J. Coleman	(Assistant Director)
	Bud Jamison	(Unpunctual Star)
	Gloria Swanson	(Stenographer)
	Agnes Ayres	(Secretary)
	Billy Armstrong	(Extra)

Filmed at the Essanay Chicago Studios

Released: 1 February 1915
Length: 1896 ft

37 A Night Out

Cast:	Charles Chaplin	(Reveller)
	Ben Turpin	(Fellow Reveller)
	Bud Jamison	(Head Waiter)
	Edna Purviance	(His Wife)
	Leo White	('French' Dandy)
	Fred Goodwins	

Filmed at the Essanay Niles Studio

Released: 15 February 1915
Length: 1856 ft

38 The Champion

Cast:	Charles Chaplin	(Aspiring Pugilist)
	Lloyd Bacon	(Trainer)
	Edna Purviance	(His Daughter)
	Leo White	(Would-be Briber)
	Bud Jamison	(Champion)
	Billy Armstrong	(Sparring Partner)
	Carl Stockdale	(Sparring Partner)
	Paddy McGuire	(Sparring Partner)
	Ben Turpin	(Salesman)
	G. M. ('Broncho Billy') Anderson	(Enthusiastic Spectator)

Filmed at the Essanay Niles Studio

Released: 11 March 1915
Length: 1938 ft

39 In the Park

Cast:	Charles Chaplin	(Charlie)
	Edna Purviance	(Nursemaid)
	Leo White	(Elegant Masher)
	Margie Reiger	(His Fancy)
	Lloyd Bacon	(Hot Dog Seller)
	Bud Jamison	(Edna's Beau)
	Billy Armstrong	(Thief)
	Ernest Van Pelt	(Policeman)

Filmed on location

Released: 18 March 1915
Length: 984 ft

40 A Jitney Elopement

Cast:	Charles Chaplin	(Suitor, the Fake Count)
	Edna Purviance	(The Girl)
	Fred Goodwins	(Her Father)
	Leo White	(The Count)
	Lloyd Bacon	(Butler)
	Paddy McGuire	(Ancient Servant)
	Carl Stockdale	(Policeman)
	Ernest Van Pelt	(Policeman)
	Bud Jamison	(Policeman)

Filmed at the Essanay Niles Studio

Released: 1 April 1915
Length: 1958 ft

41 The Tramp

Cast:	Charles Chaplin	(The Tramp)
	Edna Purviance	(The Farmer's Daughter)
	Fred Goodwins	(The Farmer)
	Lloyd Bacon	(Edna's Fiancé)
	Paddy McGuire	(Farmhand)
	Billy Armstrong	(Poet)
	Leo White	(Hobo)
	Ernest Van Pelt	(Hobo)

Filmed at the Essanay Niles Studio and locations

Released: 11 April 1915
Length: 1896 ft

42 By the Sea

Cast:	Charles Chaplin	(Stroller)
	Billy Armstrong	(Holiday-maker)
	Margie Reiger	(His Wife)
	Bud Jamison	(Jealous Husband)
	Edna Purviance	(His Wife)
	Paddy McGuire	(Refreshment Stand Proprietor)
	Carl Stockdale	(Policeman)

Filmed on location at Crystal Pier

Released: 29 April 1915
Length: 971 ft

43 Work

Cast:	Charles Chaplin	(Decorator's Apprentice)
	Charles Insley	(His Boss)
	Edna Purviance	(Housemaid)
	Billy Armstrong	(Householder)
	Marta Golden	(His Wife)
	Leo White	(Gentleman Caller)
	Paddy McGuire	(Hod Carrier)

Filmed at the Bradbury Mansion studio

Released: 21 June 1915
Length: 2017 ft

44 A Woman

Cast:	Charles Chaplin	(Charlie; and 'The Woman')
	Edna Purviance	(Daughter)
	Marta Golden	(Mother)
	Charles Insley	(Father)
	Margie Reiger	(Father's Lady Friend)
	Billy Armstrong	(Father's Friend)
	Leo White	(Gentleman in Park)

Filmed at the former Majestic Studio

Released: 12 July 1915
Length: 1788 ft

45 The Bank

Cast:	Charles Chaplin	(Janitor)
	Edna Purviance	(Secretary)
	Carl Stockdale	(Cashier)
	Billy Armstrong	(Janitor)
	Charles Insley	(Manager)
	Lawrence A. Bowes	(Important Customer)
	John Rand	(Salesman)

	Leo White	(Client)
	Fred Goodwins	(Doorkeeper *and* Bank Robber)
	Bud Jamison	(Chief Bank Robber)
	Frank J. Coleman	(Bank Robber)
	John Rand	(Bank Robber)
	Lloyd Bacon	(Bank Robber)
	Paddy McGuire	(Bank Robber)
	Wesley Ruggles	
	Carrie Clark Ward	

Filmed at the former Majestic Studio

Released: 9 August 1915
Length: 1985 ft

46 Shanghaied

Cast:	Charles Chaplin	(Charlie)
	Edna Purviance	(Owner's Daughter)
	Wesley Ruggles	(Owner)
	John Rand	(Captain)
	Bud Jamison	(Mate)
	Billy Armstrong	(Cook)
	Lawrence A. Bowes	(Seaman)
	Paddy McGuire	(Seaman)
	Leo White	(Seaman)
	Fred Goodwins	(Seaman)

Filmed at the former Majestic Studio

Released: 4 October 1915
Length: 1771 ft

47 A Night in the Show

Cast:	Charles Chaplin	(Mr Pest *and* Mr Rowdy)
	Edna Purviance	(Lady in the Stalls)
	Charlotte Mineau	(Lady in the Stalls)
	Dee Lampton	(The Mischievous Fat Boy)
	Leo White	(Man in Stalls *and* Conjuror)
	Wesley Ruggles	(Man in Gallery)
	John Rand	(Orchestra Conductor)
	James T. Kelley	(Musician *and* Singer)
	Paddy McGuire	(Musician)
	May White	(Fat Lady in Foyer *and* Snake Charmer)
	Bud Jamison	(Edna's Husband in Stalls *and* Singer)
	Phyllis Allen	(Lady in Audience)
	Fred Goodwins	(Gentleman in Audience)
	Charles Insley	(Gentleman in Audience)
	Carrie Clark Ward	(Woman in Audience)

Filmed at the former Majestic Studio

Released:	20 November 1915
Length:	1735 ft

48 Charlie Chaplin's Burlesque on Carmen

Cast:	Charles Chaplin	(Darn Hosiery)
	Edna Purviance	(Carmen)
	Ben Turpin	(Don Remendado)
	Leo White	(Officer of the Guard)
	John Rand	(Escamillo)
	Jack Henderson	(Lilias Pasta)
	May White	(Frasquita)
	Bud Jamison	(Soldier)
	Wesley Ruggles	(A Vagabond)
	Frank J. Coleman	
	Lawrence A. Bowes	

Filmed at the former Majestic Studio

The film was expanded from two reels to four, without Chaplin's authority, after he had left the studio. The new version was assembled by Leo White, who also shot new material for it. Chaplin unsuccessfully took legal action against Essanay.

Released:	22 April 1916
Length:	3986 ft

49 Police

Cast:	Charles Chaplin	(Ex-Convict)
	Edna Purviance	(Daughter of the House)
	Wesley Ruggles	(Jailbird and Thief)
	James T. Kelley	(Drunk)
	Leo White	(Fruit Seller *and* Doss House Proprietor *and* Policeman)
	John Rand	(Policeman)
	Fred Goodwins	(Fake Preacher)
	Billy Armstrong	(Dubious Character)
	Bud Jamison	(Dubious Character)

Filmed at the former Majestic Studio

Released:	27 May 1916
Length:	2050 ft

III THE MUTUAL FILMS 1916–1917

General Credits:

Production:	Lone Star Mutual
Producer:	Charles Chaplin
Director:	Charles Chaplin

Scenario:	Charles Chaplin (Story collaboration credit on *The Floorwalker, The Fireman* and *The Vagabond* to Vincent Bryan.)
Photography:	*The Floorwalker, The Fireman* and *The Vagabond*: Frank D. Williams. Assistant: Roland Totheroh. From *One A.M.*: Roland Totheroh
Scenic Artist:	E. T. Mazy (said to have worked on *The Floorwalker, The Fireman* and *One A.M.*)

Filmed at the Lone Star Studios, Hollywood.

51 The Floorwalker

Cast:	Charles Chaplin	(Impecunious Customer)
	Eric Campbell	(Store Manager)
	Edna Purviance	(His Secretary)
	Lloyd Bacon	(Assistant Manager)
	Albert Austin	(Shop Assistant)
	Leo White	(Elegant Customer)
	Charlotte Mineau	(Beautiful Store Detective)
	James T. Kelley	(Lift Boy)
Released:	15 May 1916	
Length:	1734 ft	

52 The Fireman

Cast:	Charles Chaplin	(Fireman)
	Edna Purviance	(The Girl)
	Lloyd Bacon	(Her Father)
	Eric Campbell	(Fire Chief)
	Leo White	(Owner of Burning House)
	Albert Austin	(Fireman)
	John Rand	(Fireman)
	James T. Kelley	(Fireman)
	Frank J. Coleman	(Fireman)
Released:	12 June 1916	
Length:	1921 ft	

53 The Vagabond

Cast:	Charles Chaplin	(Street Musician)
	Edna Purviance	(Girl Stolen by Gypsies)
	Eric Campbell	(Gypsy Chieftain)
	Leo White	(Old Jew *and* Old Gypsy Woman)
	Lloyd Bacon	(The Artist)
	Charlotte Mineau	(Girl's Mother)
	Albert Austin	(Trombonist)
	John Rand	(Trumpeter, Band Leader)

	James T. Kelley	(Musician *and* Gypsy)
	Frank J. Coleman	(Musician *and* Gypsy)
Released:	10 July 1916	
Length:	1956 ft	

54 One A.M.

Cast:	Charles Chaplin	(Drunk)
	Albert Austin	(Taxi Driver)
Released:	7 August 1916	
Length:	2000 ft	

55 The Count

Cast:	Charles Chaplin	(Tailor's Apprentice)
	Edna Purviance	(Miss Moneybags, the Heiress)
	Eric Campbell	(The Tailor)
	Leo White	(The Count)
	May White	(Large Lady)
	Charlotte Mineau	(Mrs Moneybags)
	Albert Austin	(Guest)
	Stanley Sanford	(Guest)
	John Rand	(Guest)
	James T. Kelley	(Butler)
	Leota Bryan	(Young Girl)
	Loyal Underwood	(Small Guest)
	Eva Thatcher	(Cook)
	Frank J. Coleman	(Policeman *and* Guest in Pierrot costume)
Released:	4 September 1916	
Length:	2000 ft	

56 The Pawnshop

Cast:	Charles Chaplin	(Pawnbroker's Assistant)
	Henry Bergman	(The Pawnbroker)
	Edna Purviance	(His Daughter)
	John Rand	(The Other Assistant)
	Albert Austin	(Customer with Alarm Clock)
	Wesley Ruggles	(Dramatic Customer with Ring)
	Eric Campbell	(Burglar)
	James T. Kelley	(Old Bum *and* Lady with Goldfish)
	Frank J. Coleman	(Policeman)
Released:	2 October 1916	
Length:	1940 ft	

57 Behind the Screen

Cast:	Charles Chaplin	(Property Man's Assistant)
	Eric Campbell	(Property Man)
	Edna Purviance	(Aspiring Actress)
	Henry Bergman	(Director of Historical Film)
	Lloyd Bacon	(Director of Comedy Film)
	Albert Austin	(Scene Shifter)
	John Rand	(Scene Shifter)
	Leo White	(Scene Shifter)
	Frank J. Coleman	(Producer)
	Charlotte Mineau	(Actress)
	Leota Bryan	(Actress)
	Wesley Ruggles	(Actor)
	Tom Wood	(Actor)
	James T. Kelley	(Cameraman)
Released:	13 November 1916	
Length:	1796 ft	

58 The Rink

Cast:	Charles Chaplin	(Waiter and Skating Enthusiast)
	Edna Purviance	(Society Girl)
	James T. Kelley	(Her Father)
	Eric Campbell	(Mr Stout)
	Henry Bergman	(Mrs Stout *and* Angry Diner)
	Lloyd Bacon	(Guest)
	Albert Austin	(Chef *and* Skater)
	Frank J. Coleman	(Restaurant Manager)
	John Rand	(Waiter)
	Charlotte Mineau	(Edna's Friend)
	Leota Bryan	(Edna's Friend)
Released:	4 December 1916	
Length:	1881 ft	

59 Easy Street

Cast:	Charles Chaplin	(Vagabond recruited to Police Force)
	Edna Purviance	(Missionary)
	Eric Campbell	(Scourge of Easy Street)
	Albert Austin	(Clergyman *and* Policeman)
	Henry Bergman	(Anarchist)
	Loyal Underwood	(Small but Fecund Father *and* Policeman)
	Janet Miller Sully	(His Wife *and* Mission Visitor)
	Charlotte Mineau	(Ungrateful Woman)
	Tom Wood	(Chief of Police)
	Lloyd Bacon	(Drug Addict)

	Frank J. Coleman	(Policeman)
	John Rand	(Mission Visitor *and* Policeman)
Released:	22 January 1917	
Length:	1757 ft	

60 The Cure

Cast:	Charles Chaplin	(Alcoholic Gentleman at Spa)
	Edna Purviance	(Fellow Guest at Spa)
	Eric Campbell	(Gentleman with Gout)
	Henry Bergman	(Masseur)
	Albert Austin	(Male Nurse)
	John Rand	(Male Nurse *and* Masseur)
	James T. Kelley	(Ancient Bell Boy)
	Frank J. Coleman	(Proprietor)
	Leota Bryan	(Nurse)
	Tom Wood	(Patient)
	Janet Miller Sully	(Spa Visitor)
	Loyal Underwood	(Spa Visitor)
Released:	16 April 1917	
Length:	1834 ft	

61 The Immigrant

Cast:	Charles Chaplin	(Immigrant)
	Edna Purviance	(Immigrant)
	Kitty Bradbury	(Her Mother)
	Albert Austin	(Slavic Immigrant *and* Diner)
	Henry Bergman	(Slavic Woman Immigrant *and* Artist)
	Loyal Underwood	(Small Immigrant)
	Eric Campbell	(Head Waiter)
	Stanley Sanford	(Gambler on Ship)
	James T. Kelley	(Shabby Man in Restaurant)
	John Rand	(Tipsy Diner who cannot pay)
	Frank J. Coleman	(Ship's Officer *and* Restaurant Owner)
	Tom Harrington	(Marriage Registrar)
Released:	17 June 1917	
Length:	1809 ft	

62 The Adventurer

Cast:	Charles Chaplin	(Escaped Convict)
	Edna Purviance	(A Girl)
	Henry Bergman	(Her Father *and* a Docker)
	Marta Golden	(Her Mother)
	Eric Campbell	(Her Suitor)
	Albert Austin	(Butler)
	Toraichi Kono	(Chauffeur)

	John Rand	(Guest)
	Frank J. Coleman	(Fat Warder)
	Loyal Underwood	(Small Guest)
	May White	(Stout Lady)
	Janet Miller Sully	
	Monta Bell	
Released:	22 October 1917	
Length:	1845 ft	

IV THE FIRST NATIONAL FILMS 1918–1923

General Credits:

Production:	Chaplin–First National
Producer:	Charles Chaplin
Director:	Charles Chaplin
Scenario:	Charles Chaplin
Photographer:	Roland Totheroh
Second Camera:	Jack Wilson
Assistant:	Charles ('Chuck') Riesner
Production Designer:	Charles D. Hall

Filmed at the Chaplin Studio on Sunset and La Brea

62a How to Make Movies

A comedy-documentary showing the premises and personnel of the new Chaplin studios. The film seems never to have been assembled, although a title list was prepared. This was used by Kevin Brownlow and David Gill to reconstruct Chaplin's intended film, and it was seen for the first time in its entirety at the 1981 London Film Festival. Some parts of the film had previously been used by Chaplin in *The Chaplin Revue* however.

63 A Dog's Life

Cast:	Charles Chaplin	(Tramp)
	Edna Purviance	(Bar Singer)
	Mut	(Scraps)
	Sydney Chaplin	(Lunch Wagon Owner)
	Henry Bergman	(Man in Employment Agency *and* Lady in Dance Hall)
	Charles Riesner	(Clerk in Employment Agency *and* Drummer)
	Albert Austin	(Crook)
	Tom Wilson	(Policeman)
	M. J. McCarty	(Unemployed Man)

Mel Brown	(Unemployed Man)
Charles Force	(Unemployed Man)
Bert Appling	(Unemployed Man)
Thomas Riley	(Unemployed Man)
Slim Cole	(Unemployed Man)
Ted Edwards	(Unemployed Man)
Louis Fitzroy	(Unemployed Man)
Dave Anderson	(Unemployed Man)
Granville Redmond	(Proprietor of Dance Hall)
Minnie Chaplin	(Dramatic Lady in Dance Hall)
Alf Reeves	(Man at Bar)
N. Tahbel	(Hot Tamaly Man)
Rob Wagner	(Man in Dance Hall)
I. S. McVey	(Musician)
J. F. Parker	(Musician)
Al Blake	
Loyal Underwood	
James T. Kelley	
Fred Starr	
Janet Miller Sully	
Grace Wilson (Mrs Tom Wilson)	
Jerry Ferragoma	

Jack Duffy, Richard Dunbar, Edward Miller, Billy Dul, Bruce Randall, Brand O'Ree, Bill White, John Lord, Jim O'Niall, H. C. Simmons, J. L. Fraube, Jim Habif, Florence Parellee, Miss Cullington, Margaret Dracup, Ella Eckhardt, Sarah Rosenberg, Lottie Smithson, Lillian Morgan, Jean Johnson, Fay Holderness, Dorothy Cleveland, J. Miller, Minnie Eckhardt, Mrs Rigoletti.
(People in Dance Hall)

Production started:	15 January 1918
Production finished:	9 April 1918
Released:	14 April 1918
Length	2674 ft

64 The Bond

Cast:	Charles Chaplin	
	Edna Purviance	
	Sydney Chaplin	(The Kaiser)
	Henry Bergman	(John Bull)
	Dorothy Rosher	(Cupid)

[Dorothy Rosher worked 17 and 19 August, at a rate of $10 per day.]

Production started:	15 August 1918	
Production finished:	22 August 1918	
Released:	16 December 1918	
Length:	685 ft	

64a (Chaplin–Lauder Charity Film)

Cast:	Charles Chaplin	(Himself)
	Harry Lauder	(Himself)

Filmed: 22 January 1918
Apparently never completed or released
Length: 745 ft (unedited)

65 Shoulder Arms

Cast:	Charles Chaplin	(Recruit)
	Edna Purviance	(French Girl)
	Sydney Chaplin	(Sergeant *and* the Kaiser)
	Jack Wilson	(German Crown Prince)
	Henry Bergman	(Fat German Sergeant *and* Field Marshal von Hindenburg)
	Albert Austin	(American Soldier *and* German Soldier *and* Kaiser's Chauffeur)
	Tom Wilson	(Training Camp Sergeant)
	John Rand	(American Soldier)
	Park Jones	(American Soldier)
	Loyal Underwood	(Small German Officer)
	W. G. Wagner, J. T. Powell, W. Herron, W. Cross, G. E. Marygold	(Motorcyclists)
	C. L. Dice, G. A. Godfrey, L. A. Blaisdell, W. E. Allen, J. H. Warne	(Motorcyclists – alternative group*)
	Roscoe Ward, Ed Hunt, M. J. Donovan, E. B. Johnson, Fred Graham, Louis Orr, Al Blake, Ray Hanford, Cliff Brouwer, Claude McAtee, F. S. Colby, Jack Shalford, Joe Van Meter, Guy Eakins, Jack Willis, Charles Cole, T. Madden	(American and German Soldiers)
	Harry Goldman, Jack Willis, Mark Faber, E. H. Devere, Fred Everman, A. North, Charles Knuske, O. E. Haskins, Tom Hawley, W. E. Graham, James Griffin, W. A. Hackett, E. Brucker, J. H. Shewry, Sam Lewis, R. B. McKenzie, K. Herlinger, A. J. Hartwell	(Additional players in street set, with Kaiser's car)

In Cut Sequences

	Marion Feducha	(Small Boy)
	Alf Reeves	(Draft Board Sergeant)
	Albert Austin	(Draft Board Doctor)
	Peggy Prevost	(Draft Board Clerk)
	Nina Trask	(Draft Board Clerk)

*Since the motorcyclists wore goggles, different groups could be used for different days' shooting. The motorcyclists were paid $5 a day, except for Wagner and Powell, who provided their own bikes and so received $7.50 a day.

Production started:	27 May 1918
Production finished:	16 September 1918
Released:	20 October 1918
Length:	3142 ft

66 Sunnyside

Cast:	Charles Chaplin	(Farm Handyman)
	Edna Purviance	(Village Belle)
	Tom Wilson	(Boss)
	Tom Terriss	(Young Man from the City)
	Henry Bergman	(Villager *and* Edna's Father)
	Loyal Underwood	(Fat Boy's Father)
	Tom Wood	(Fat Boy)
	Helen Kohn	(Nymph)
	Olive Burton	(Nymph)
	Willie Mae Carson	(Nymph)
	Olive Alcorn	(Nymph)
	Park Jones	
	Granville Redmond	
	Al Blake	
	Shorty Hendricks	
	Lulu Jenks	
	George Cole	
	David Kohn	
	Tom Harrington	

Zasu Pitts worked in a number of scenes from 4 to 25 November; but her role appears to have been cut from the finished film.

In Cut Sequence

Albert Austin (Man being Shaved)

Locations: Phelps Ranch, Lasky Ranch, Country Road in Beverly Hills, Bridge in San Fernando Road, exterior of Edna's home.

Production started:	4 November 1918
Production finished:	15 April 1919
Released:	15 June 1919
Length:	2769 ft

67 A Day's Pleasure

Cast:	Charles Chaplin	(Father)
	Edna Purviance	(Mother)
	Marion Feducha	(Small Boy)
	Bob Kelly	(Small Boy)
	Jackie Coogan	(Smallest Boy)
	Tom Wilson	(Large Husband)
	Babe London	(His Seasick Wife)
	Henry Bergman	(Captain *and* Man in Car)
	Loyal Underwood	(Angry Little Man in Street)
	Albert Austin	
	Jessie Van Trump	

At the start of shooting, the role of Charlie's wife was taken by the 495-lb. Tom Wood

Location:	San Pedro pleasure boat, *Ace*.
Production started:	21 May 1919
Production interrupted:	30 July–7 October 1919
Production finished:	19 October 1919
Released:	15 December 1919
Length:	1714 ft

68 The Kid

Cast:	Charles Chaplin	(Tramp)
	Edna Purviance	(Mother)
	Jackie Coogan	(The Kid)
	Baby Hathaway	(The Kid as a Baby)
	Carl Miller	(Artist)
	Granville Redmond	(His Friend)
	May White	(Policeman's Wife)
	Tom Wilson	(Policeman)
	Henry Bergman	(Night Shelter Keeper)
	Charles Riesner	(Bully)
	Raymond Lee	(His Kid Brother)
	Lillita McMurray (Lita Grey)	(Flirtatious Angel)

Edith Wilson	(Lady With Pram)
Baby Wilson	(Baby in Pram)
Nellie Bly Baker	(Slum Nurse)
Albert Austin	(Man in Shelter)
Jack Coogan Sr	(Pickpocket *and* Guest *and* Devil)
Edgar Sherrod	(Priest)
Beulah Bains	(Bride)
Robert Dunbar	(Bridegroom)
Kitty Bradbury	(Bride's Mother)
Rupert Franklin	(Bride's Father)
Flora Howard	(Bridesmaid)
Elsie Sindora	(Bridesmaid)
Walter Lynch	(Tough Cop)
Dan Dillon	(Bum)
Jules Hanft	(Physician)
Silas Wilcox	(Cop)
Kathleen Kay	(Maid)
Minnie Stearns	(Fierce Woman)
Frank Campeau	(Welfare Officer)
F. Blinn	(His Assistant)
John McKinnon	(Chief of Police)

Elsie Young, V. Madison, Evans Quirk, Bliss Chevalier, Grace Keller, Irene Jennings, Florette Faulkner, Martha Hall, Estelle Cook, J. B. Russell, Lillian Crane, Sarah Kernan, Philip D'Oench, Charles I. Pierce

(Extras in Wedding Scene)

Elsie Codd (Chaplin's English publicity representative), Mother Vinot (studio sewing lady), Louise Hathaway, Amada Yanez and Baby

(Extras in Alley Scene)

Clyde McAtee, Frank Hale, Ed Hunt, Rupert Franklin, Frances Cochran, George Sheldon

(Extras in Reception Scene)

Sadie Gordon, Laura Pollard, L. Parker, Ethel O'Neil, L. Jenks, Esther Ralston, Henry Roser

(Extras in Heaven Scene)

Production started:	21 July 1919
Production finished:	30 July 1920
Released:	6 February 1921
Length:	5250 ft

68a Nice and Friendly

Cast:		
	Charles Chaplin	(Villain)
	Lord Louis Mountbatten	(Hero)
	Lady Edwina Mountbatten	(Heroine)
	Jackie Coogan	
	Colonel Robert M. Thompson	
	Frederick Neilson	
	Eulalie Neilson	

Improvised sketch, never released.

69 The Idle Class

Cast:		
	Charles Chaplin	(Tramp *and* Husband)
	Edna Purviance	(Neglected Wife)
	Mack Swain	(Her Father)
	Henry Bergman	(Sleeping Hobo)
	Allan Garcia	(His Neighbour on a Park Bench *and* Guest)
	John Rand	(Golfer *and* Guest)
	Rex Storey	(Pickpocket *and* Guest)
	Lillian McMurray	(Maid)
	Lillita McMurray	(Maid)
	Loyal Underwood	(Guest)
	Mrs Parker	
	Lolita Parker	
	Howard Olsen	
	Edward Knoblock	
	Granville Redmond	
	Carlyle Robinson	
	Joe Van Meter	

Bruce Belamator, William Thompson, William Hackett, Jack Mortimer, B. W. McComber, Charles Aber, Jim Collins, Jack Sydney, Duffy Kirk, Jack Lott, George Bastian, Howard Johnston, Joe Campbell, Richard Brewster, Mrs Ross Lang, Miss Helene Calverley, Margaret Rishell, Miss M. Parsons, Gertrude Pedlar, Ruth Darling, Joe Flores, Miss Grace, Carl Brown, Anita Walton, Miss Egbert, Lura Anson, Catherine Vidor, Gladys Webb, Mary Land, California Truman, Marie Crist, Lottie Cruz, Helen McMullin, Hugh Saxon, Harold Kent, Harold McNulty, Helen McKee, Gladys Baxter, Dolly Rich, Robert Badger, Jack Woods, C. S. Steele, Fred Wilson, E. C. Holkin, Miss Wicks, Mary Ann Bennett, Harriett Bennett, Vera Wilder, Ethel Childers, Anita Simons, Melissa Ledgerwood, Nel Foltz, Ruth Foster, Evelyn Burns, Jean Temle, Bertha Feducha,

Pearl Palmer, Arnold Triller, Jack Underhill, John Sweeny, Clyde McCoy, George Milo, William Moore, George Mistler, J. A. Beaver, Charles Meakins, W. R. Denning, L. Chandler, L. Swisher, R. Pennell, Jules Hanft, Bob Palmer, Walter Bacon, Art Hanson, Harry Tenbrook, Bill Carey, Joe Anderson, Paul Mertz (Extras)

Production started: 29 January 1921
Production finished: 25 June 1921
Released: 25 September 1921
Length: 1916 ft

70 Pay Day

Cast:

Charles Chaplin	(Labourer)
Phyllis Allen	(His Wife)
Mack Swain	(Foreman)
Edna Purviance	(Foreman's Daughter)
Sydney Chaplin	(Charlie's Mate *and* Lunch Wagon Proprietor)
Albert Austin	(Workman)
John Rand	(Workman)
Loyal Underwood	(Workman)
Henry Bergman	(Drinking Companion)
Allan Garcia	(Drinking Companion)

Pete Griffin, Joe Griffin, Harry Tenbrook, Ethel Childers, Edith Blythe, Virginia Bodle, Helen Kapp, La Belle Raymond, Sylvia Menier (Extras)

Production started: 6 August 1921
Production interrupted by European tour, September–October 1921
Production finished: 23 February 1922
Released: 2 April 1922
Length: 1950 ft

71 The Pilgrim

Cast:

Charles Chaplin	(Escaped Convict)
Edna Purviance	(Girl)
Kitty Bradbury	(Her Mother, Charlie's Landlady)
Mack Swain	(Deacon)
Loyal Underwood	(Elder)
Charles Riesner	(Thief)
Dinky Dean (Riesner)	(Horrid Child)

	Sydney Chaplin	(His Father)
	May Wells	(His Mother)
	Henry Bergman	(Sheriff on Train)
	Tom Murray	(Local Sheriff)
	Monta Bell	(Policeman)
	Raymond Lee	(Boy in Congregation)
	Frank Antunez	(Bandit)
	Joe Van Meter	(Bandit)
	Phyllis Allen	(Member of Congregation)
	Florence Latimer	(Member of Congregation)
	Edith Bostwick	(Member of Congregation)
	Laddie Earle	(Member of Congregation)
	Louis Troester	(Member of Congregation)
	Beth Nagel	(Member of Congregation)
	Mrs C. Johnson	(Member of Congregation)
	Marion Davies	(Member of Congregation)
	Miss Evans	
	Frank Liscomb	
	S. D. Wilcox	
	Robert Traughbur	
	Carlyle Robinson	
	Jack McCredie	
	Charles Hafler	
	Bill Carey	
	Paul Mason	
	McNeill	

Sarah Barrows, Donnabelle Ouster, Gallie Frey, Della Glowner, Theresa Gray, Cecile Harcourt, Anna Hicks, Martha Harris, Mary Hamlett, Ethel Kennedy, Emily Lamont, Agnes Lynch, Mildred Pitts, Katherine Parrish, Edna Rowe, Mabel Shoulters, Georgia Sherrart, Rose Wheeler, George Bradford, George Carruthers, J. Espan, F. F. Guenste, Lee Glowner, Harry Hicks, Carl Jensen, Tom Ray, James J. Smith, S. H. Williams, Paul Wilkins, H. Wolfinger

(Extras in Church Scene)

Production started:	1 April 1922
Production finished:	15 July 1922
Première:	26 February 1923, Strand Theatre, New York.
Length:	3647 ft.

71a The Professor

Cast:	Charles Chaplin	(Professor Bosco)
Production started:	30 September 1919	

Production finished:	?(Film possibly assembled from out-takes from other pictures.)

Never released, but declared by Chaplin to be ready for release in November 1922.

Length:	An edited sequence of some 450 feet survives, along with a few out-takes apparently from another sequence. Chaplin's correspondence with Sydney in 1923, however, refers to *The Professor* as a two-reeler – i.e. approximately 2000 feet.

V THE UNITED ARTISTS' FILMS 1923–1952

72 A Woman of Paris

Production:	Regent–United Artists	
Producer:	Charles Chaplin	
Director:	Charles Chaplin	
Scenario:	Charles Chaplin	
Photography:	Roland Totheroh	
Second Camera:	Jack Wilson	
Assistant:	Edward Sutherland	
Literary Editor:	Monta Bell	
Art Director:	Arthur Stibolt	
Research:	Jean de Limur, Henri d'Abbadie d'Arrast	
Cast:	Edna Purviance	(Marie St Clair)
	Adolphe Menjou	(Pierre Revel)
	Carl Miller	(Jean Millet)
	Lydia Knott	(Jean's Mother)
	Charles French	(Jean's Father)
	Clarence Geldert	(Marie's Father)
	Betty Morrissey	(Fifi)
	Malvina Polo	(Paulette)
	Henry Bergman	(Head Waiter)
	Harry Northrup	(Man About Town)
	Nellie Bly Baker	(Masseuse)
	Miss Delante (?Stella De Lanti)	(Revel's Fiancée)
	Charles Chaplin	(Porter)
Production started:	27 November 1922	
Production finished:	29 September 1923	
Première:	1 October 1923, Criterion Theatre, Hollywood	
Length:	7557 ft	

73 The Gold Rush

Production:	Chaplin–United Artists
Producer:	Charles Chaplin
Director:	Charles Chaplin
Scenario:	Charles Chaplin
Photography:	Roland Totheroh
Cameramen:	Jack Wilson, Mark Marlatt
Art Director:	Charles D. Hall
Assistant Directors:	Charles Riesner, Henri d'Abbadie d'Arrast, Eddie Sutherland
Production Manager:	Alfred Reeves

Cast:	Charles Chaplin	(Lone Prospector)
	Georgia Hale	(Georgia)
	Mack Swain	(Big Jim McKay)
	Tom Murray	(Black Larson)
	Betty Morrissey	(Georgia's Friend)
	Kay Desleys	(Georgia's Friend)
	Joan Lowell	(Georgia's Friend)
	Malcolm Waite	(Jack Cameron)
	Henry Bergman	(Hank Curtis)
	John Rand	(Prospector)
	Heinie Conklin	(Prospector)
	Albert Austin	(Prospector)
	Allan Garcia	(Prospector)
	Tom Wood	(Prospector)
	Stanley Sanford	(Barman)
	Barbara Pierce	(Manicurist)
	A. J. O'Connor	(Officer)
	Art Walker	(Officer)
	Daddy Taylor	(Ancient Dancing Prospector)
	Margaret Martin	(Squaw)
	Princess Neela	(Squaw)
	Frank Aderias	(Eskimo Child)
	Leona Aderias	(Eskimo Child)
	E. Espinosa	(Eskimo)
	Ray Morris	(Eskimo)
	Fred Karno Jr	

Jack Adams, Sam Allen, Claude Anderson, Harry Arras, F. J. Beauregard, William Bell, Francis Bernhardt, E. Blumenthal, William Bradford, George Brock, William Butler, Pete Brogan, R. Campbell, Leland Carr, H. C. Chisholm, Harry Coleman, Harry De Mors, Jimmy Dime, W. S. Dobson, John Eagown, Aaron Edward, Elias Elizaroff, Leon Fary, Richard Foley, Charles Force, J. C. Fowler, Ray Grey, William Hackett, James

Hammer, Ben Hart, R. Hausner, Tom Hawley, Jack Herrick, Jack Hoefer, George Holt, Tom Hutchinson, Carl Jenson, Harry Jones, Bob Kelly, John King, Bob Leonard, Francis Lowell, Clyde McAtee, John McGrath, Chris Martin, John Millerta, Chris Martin, Mr Myers, George Neely, H. C. Oliver, William Parmalee, Jack Phillips, Art Price, Frank Rice, E. M. Robb, C. F. Roarke, J. Ryan, J. J. Smith, Joe Smith, C. B. Steele, Armand Triller, John Tully, Jack Vedders, John Wallace, Sharkey Weimar, Ed Wilson, C. Whitecloud, H. Wolfinger, Dave Wright, Ah Yot, George Young, Ed Zimmer, Lillian Adrian, Rebecca Conroy, Donnabella Custer, Kay De Lay, Inez Gomez, Mildred Hall, Gypsy Hart, Helen Hayward, Josie Howard, Jean Huntley, Gladys Johnson, Helen Kassler, Geraldine Leslie, Joan Lowell, Ruth Milo, Marie Muggley, Florence Murth, Lillian Rosino, Edna Rowe, Jane Sherman, Nina Trask, Mary Williams, Marie Willis, Lillian Reschm, Nellie Noxon, Dolores Mendes, Cecile Cameron, Joan Lowell, Betty Pierce, Marta Belfort, Dorothy Crane, Bessie Eade, James Darby, Frank E. Stockdale, Freddie Lansit, George Lesley, P. Nagle, M. Farrell, S. Murphy.

(People in Dance Hall)

Shooting began with Lita Grey as leading lady. Georgia Hale took over the role in December 1924

Production started:	December 1923
Production completed:	21 May 1925
Première:	26 June 1925, Grauman's Egyptian Theatre, Hollywood
Length:	8555 ft

Reissue Version

Director:	Charles Chaplin
Narrator:	Charles Chaplin
Music:	Charles Chaplin
Musical Director:	Max Terr
Editor:	Harold McGhean
Released:	16 April 1942
Length:	8498 ft

74 The Circus

Production:	Chaplin–United Artists
Producer:	Charles Chaplin
Director:	Charles Chaplin
Scenario:	Charles Chaplin
Photography:	Roland Totheroh

Cameramen:	Jack Wilson, Mark Marlatt	
Assistant Director:	Harry Crocker	
Art Director:	Charles D. Hall	
Editor:	Charles Chaplin	
Cast:	Charles Chaplin	(Tramp)
	Merna Kennedy	(Equestrienne)
	Allan Garcia	(Circus Proprietor)
	Harry Crocker	(Rex, the High Wire Walker)
	Henry Bergman	(Old Clown)
	Stanley Sanford	(Chief Property Man)
	George Davis	(Magician)
	Betty Morrissey	(Vanishing Lady)
	John Rand	(Assistant Property Man *and* Clown)
	Armand Triller	(Clown)
	Steve Murphy	(Pickpocket)
	Bill Knight	(Cop)
	Jack Pierce	(Man operating Ropes)
	H. L. Kyle	
	Eugene Barry	
	L. J. O'Connor	
	Hugh Saxon	
	Jack Bernard	
	Max Tyron	
	A. Bachman	
	William Blystone	
	Numi	(Lion)
	Bobby	(Monkey)
	Josephine	(Monkey)
	Jimmy	(Monkey)
	In Cut Sequences	
	Doc Stone	(Twin Prize Fighters)
Production started:	2 November 1925	
Production interrupted:	5 December 1926–3 September 1927	
Production finished:	19 November 1927	
Première:	6 January 1928, Strand Theatre, New York	
Length:	6500 ft	

Reissue Version

Director:	Charles Chaplin
Music:	Charles Chaplin
Musical Director:	Eric James

Song 'Swing, Little Girl' composed and sung by Charles Chaplin.
Released: 1970
Length: 6431 ft

75 **City Lights**

Production:	Chaplin–United Artists
Producer:	Charles Chaplin
Director:	Charles Chaplin
Scenario:	Charles Chaplin
Photography:	Roland Totheroh
Cameramen:	Mark Marlatt, Gordon Pollock
Assistant Directors:	Harry Crocker, Henry Bergman, Albert Austin
Art Director:	Charles D. Hall
Music:	Charles Chaplin
Arranger:	Arthur Johnson
Music Director:	Alfred Newman
Editor:	Charles Chaplin

Musical Themes used in addition to original compositions: 'Star-Spangled Banner', 'Hail, Hail, The Gang's All Here', 'Dixie', 'I Hear You Calling Me', 'Home, Sweet Home', 'La Violetera' (Jose Padilla), 'Swanee River', 'How Dry Am I', 'St Louis Blues' (W. S. Handy)

Cast:	Charles Chaplin	(The Tramp)
	Virginia Cherrill	(The Blind Girl)
	Florence Lee	(Her Grandmother)
	Harry Myers	(Millionaire)
	Hank Mann	(Boxer)
	Eddie Baker	(Referee)
	Tom Dempsey	(Boxer)
	Eddie McAuliffe	(Boxer who leaves in a hurry)
	Willie Keeler	(Boxer)
	Victor Alexander	(Knocked-out Boxer)
	Tony Stabeman	(Victorious Boxer, later knocked-out)
	Emmett Wagner	(Second)
	Joe Herrick, A. B. Lane, Cy Slocum, Ad Herman, Jack Alexander	(Extras in Boxing Scene)
	T. S. Alexander	(Doctor)
	Allan Garcia	(Butler)
	Henry Bergman	(Mayor *and* Janitor)
	Albert Austin	(Street Sweeper *and* Burglar)
	Joe Van Meter	(Burglar)
	John Rand	(Tramp)
	Spike Robinson	(Man Who Throws Away Cigar)

	Tiny Ward	(Man on Lift in front of Art Shop)
	Mrs Hyams	(Flower Shop Assistant)
	James Donnelly	(Foreman)
	Harry Ayers	(Cop)
	Stanhope Wheatcroft	(Man in Café)
	Jean Harlow	(Extra in Restaurant Scene)
	Mrs Pope (Harlow's Mother)	(Extra in Restaurant Scene)
	Florence Wicks	(Woman Who Sits on Cigar)
	Mark Strong	(Man in Restaurant)
	Mrs Garcia	(Woman at left of table in Restaurant)
	Peter Diego	(Man in mix-up with Coat and Hat)
	Betty Blair	(Woman at centre of table in Restaurant)
	Robert Parrish	(Newsboy)
	Margaret Oliver, Charlie Hammond, Milton Gowman	(Extras in Street Scene)
	In Cut Sequence	
	Harry Crocker	(Window Dresser)
	Charles Lederer	(Express Boy)
	Edith Wilson	(Younger Lady Looking in Window)
	Blanche Payson	(Older Lady Looking in Window)
Production started:	31 December 1927	
Production finished:	22 January 1931	
Première:	30 January 1931, Los Angeles Theatre	
London Première:	27 February 1931, Dominion Theatre	
Length:	8093 ft	

76 Modern Times

Production:	Chaplin–United Artists
Producer:	Charles Chaplin
Director:	Charles Chaplin
Scenario:	Charles Chaplin
Photography:	Roland Totheroh, Ira Morgan
Assistant Directors:	Carter De Haven, Henry Bergman
Art Directors:	Charles D. Hall, Russell Spencer
Music:	Charles Chaplin
Arrangers:	Edward Powell, David Raksin
Musical Director:	Alfred Newman

Musical themes used in addition to original compositions: 'Halleluiah, I'm a Bum', 'Prisoners' Song' (C. Massey), 'How Dry Am I', 'In the Evening By the Moonlight' (Bland), 'Je cherche après Titine' (Duncan and Daniderff)

Cast:	Charles Chaplin	(A Worker)
	Paulette Goddard	(Gamine)
	Henry Bergman	(Café Owner)
	Stanley J. Sanford	(Big Bill *and* Worker)
	Chester Conklin	(Mechanic)
	Hank Mann	(Burglar)
	Louis Natheaux	(Burglar)
	Stanley Blystone	(Sheriff Couler)
	Allan Garcia	(Company Boss)
	Sam Stein	(Foreman)
	Juana Sutton	(Woman with Buttoned Bosom)
	Jack Low	(Worker)
	Walter James	(Worker)
	Dick Alexander	(Convict)
	Dr Cecil Reynolds	(Prison Chaplain)
	Myra McKinney	(Chaplain's Wife)
	Lloyd Ingraham	(Prison Governor)
	Heinie Conklin	(Workman)
	John Rand	(Convict)
	Murdoch McQuarrie	
	Wilfred Lucas	
	Edward le Saint	
	Fred Maltesta	
	Ted Oliver	
	Edward Kimball	
Production started:	September 1933	
Production finished:	12 January 1936	
Première:	5 February 1936, Rivoli Theatre, New York	
London Première:	11 February 1936, Tivoli Theatre	
Length:	8126 ft	

77 **The Great Dictator**

Production:	Chaplin–United Artists
Producer:	Charles Chaplin
Director:	Charles Chaplin
Scenario:	Charles Chaplin
Photography:	Karl Struss, Roland Totheroh
Assistant Directors:	Dan James, Robert Meltzer, Wheeler Dryden

Art Director:	J. Russell Spencer	
Editor:	Willard Nico	
Music:	Charles Chaplin, with paraphrases of Wagner, Brahms	
Musical Director:	Meredith Willson	
Sound:	Percy Townsend, Glenn Rominger	
Coordinator:	Henry Bergman	
Cast:	Charles Chaplin	(Adenoid Hynkel *and* The Barber)
	Paulette Goddard	(Hannah)
	Jack Oakie	(Benzino Napaloni)
	Henry Daniell	(Garbitsch)
	Reginald Gardiner	(Schultz)
	Billy Gilbert	(Herring)
	Maurice Moskovich	(Mr Jaeckel)
	Emma Dunn	(Mrs Jaeckel)
	Bernard Gorcey	(Mr Mann)
	Paul Weigel	(Mr Agar)
	Grace Hayle	(Madame Napaloni)
	Carter De Haven	(Ambassador)
	Chester Conklin	(Customer in Barber's Shop)
	Hank Mann	(Storm Trooper)
	Eddie Gribbon	(Storm Trooper)
	Richard Alexander	(Storm Trooper)
	Leo White	(Hynkel's Barber)
	Lucien Prival	(Officer)
	Pat Flaherty	
	Harry Semels	
	Esther Michaelson	
	Florence Wright	
	Robert O. David	
	Eddie Dunn	
	Peter Lynn Hayes	
	Nita Pike	
	Jack Perrin	
	Max Davidson	
	Nellie V. Nichols	
Production started:	1 January 1939	
First shot:	9 September 1939	
Final shot:	2 October 1940	
Première:	15 October 1940, Capitol and Astor Theatres, New York	
London Première:	16 December 1940, Prince of Wales, Gaumont, Haymarket, Marble Arch, Pavilion Theatres	
Length:	11,628 ft	

78 Monsieur Verdoux

Production:	Chaplin–United Artists	
Producer:	Charles Chaplin	
Director:	Charles Chaplin	
Scenario:	Charles Chaplin	
Photography:	Curt Courant, Roland Totheroh	
Cameraman:	Wallace Chewning	
Associate Directors:	Robert Florey, Wheeler Dryden	
Assistant Director:	Rex Bailey	
Art Director:	John Beckman	
Editor:	Willard Nico	
Music:	Charles Chaplin	
Musical Director:	Rudolph Schrager	
Sound:	James T. Corrigan	
Costumes:	Drew Tetrick	
Make-up:	William Knight	
Hair Stylist:	Hedvig M. Jornd	
Narrator:	Charles Chaplin	
Cast:	Charles Chaplin	(Monsieur Henri Verdoux)
	Martha Raye	(Annabella Bonheur)
	Isobel Elsom	(Marie Grosnay)
	Marilyn Nash	(The Girl)
	Robert Lewis	(Monsieur Bottello)
	Mady Correl	(Madame Verdoux)
	Allison Roddan	(Peter Verdoux)
	Audrey Betz	(Madame Bottello)
	Ada-May	(Annette)
	Marjorie Bennett	(Maid)
	Helen High	(Yvonne)
	Margaret Hoffman	(Lydia Floray)
	Irving Bacon	(Pierre Couvais)
	Edwin Mills	(Jean Couvais)
	Virginia Brissac	(Carlotta Couvais)
	Almira Sessions	(Lena Couvais)
	Eula Morgan	(Phoebe Couvais)
	Bernard J. Nedell	(Prefect)
	Charles Evans	(Detective Morrow)
	Arthur Hohl	(Estate Agent)
	John Harmon	(Joe Darwin)
	Vera Marshe	(Mrs Darwin)
	William Frawley	(Jean La Salle)
	Fritz Lieber	(Priest)
	Fred Karno Jr	(Mr Karno)
	Barry Norton	(Guest)

Pierre Watkin	(Attorney)
Cyril Delevanti	(Postman)
Charles Wagenheim	(Friend)
Addison Richards	(M. Millet)
James Craven	(Friend)
Franklin Farnum	(Victim)
Herb Vigran	(Reporter)
Boyd Irwin	(Warder)
Paul Newland	(Guest)
Joseph Crehan	(Broker)
Wheaton Chambers	(Druggist)
Frank Reicher	(Doctor)
Wheeler Dryden	(Salesman)
Thérèse Lyon	(Jeannette)
Lester Mathews	(Prosecuting Attorney)
Richard Abbot	(Defence Attorney)
Garnett Monks	(Foreman of Jury)
Joseph Granby	(Court Clerk)
Julius Cramer	(Executioner)
Art Miller	(Guard)
Albert Petit	(Spectator)
Barbara Slater	(Flower Girl)
Ella Ethridge	(Woman in Street)
Christine Ell	(Maid)
Lois Conklin	(Flower Girl)
Alicia Adams	(Flower Girl)
Elisabeth Dudgeon	(Old Hag)
John Harmon	(Joe, friend of Annabella)
Vera Marshe	(Vicki, friend of Annabella)
Daniel de Jonghe	(Waiter)
George Dees	(Waiter)
Carlo Schipa	(Waiter)
Albert D'Arno	(Waiter)
Bert le Baron	(Doorman at Café Royal)
Jean Bittner	(Diner in Café Royal)
Munnel Petroff	(Diner in Café Royal)
Tom Wilson	
Phillips Smalley	

Production started:	April 1946
Opening shot:	3 June 1946
Final shot:	5 September 1946
Production finished:	4 March 1947
Première:	11 April 1947, Broadway Theatre, New York
Length:	11,132 ft

79 Limelight

Production:	Celebrated–United Artists	
Producer:	Charles Chaplin	
Director:	Charles Chaplin	
Scenario:	Charles Chaplin	
Photography:	Karl Struss	
Photographic Consultant:	Roland Totheroh	
Assistant Producers:	Wheeler Dryden, Jerome Epstein	
Associate Director:	Robert Aldrich	
Art Director:	Eugene Lourié	
Editor:	Joseph Engel	
Choreography:	Charles Chaplin, André Eglevsky, Melissa Hayden	
Music:	Charles Chaplin	
Musical Director:	Ray Rasch	
Songs:	Charles Chaplin, Ray Rasch	
Cast:	Charles Chaplin	(Calvero)
	Claire Bloom	(Terry)
	Buster Keaton	(Partner)
	Sydney Chaplin	(Neville)
	Norman Lloyd	(Bodalink)
	Marjorie Bennett	(Mrs Alsop)
	Wheeler Dryden	(Doctor *and* Clown)
	Nigel Bruce	(Mr Postant)
	Barry Bernard	(John Redfern)
	Leonard Mudie	(Doctor)
	Snub Pollard	(Musician)
	Loyal Underwood	(Musician)
	Julian Ludwig	(Musician)
	André Eglevsky	(Harlequin)
	Melissa Hayden	(Columbine)
	Charles Chaplin Jr	(Pantomime Policeman)
	Geraldine Chaplin	(Child)
	Michael Chaplin	(Child)
	Josephine Chaplin	(Child)
	Jack Deery	(Emissary – Dress Circle)
	Major Sam Harris	(Old Fogey in Dress Circle)
	Dorothy Ford	(Patrician Lady in Dress Circle)
	Elizabeth Root, Millicent Patrick, Judy Landon, Sherry Moreland, Valerie Vernon, Eric Wilson, Cyril Delevanti,	

	Leonard Mudi,	
	Frank Hagrey	(Extras in Dress Circle)
	Oona O'Neill Chaplin	(Double for Terry, in brief long-shot)
	Stapleton Kent	
	Mollie Blessing	
Production started:	12 November 1951	
Opening shot:	19 November 1951	
Final shot:	25 January 1952	
Première:	23 October 1952, Odeon Theatre, Leicester Square, London	
US Première:	23 October 1952, Astor and Trans Lux Theatres, New York	
Length:	12,636 ft	

VI THE BRITISH PRODUCTIONS 1957–1967

80 A King in New York

Production:	Attica-Archway
Producer:	Charles Chaplin
Director:	Charles Chaplin
Scenario:	Charles Chaplin
Photography:	Georges Périnal
Camera Operator:	Jeff Seaholme
Assistant Director:	René Dupont
Associate Producer:	Jerome Epstein
Art Director:	Allan Harris
Editor:	John Seabourne
Assistant:	Tony Bohy
Music:	Charles Chaplin
Arranged by:	Boris Sarbek
Conducted by:	Leighton Lucas
Sound Supervisor:	John Cox
Sound Recording:	Bert Ross, Bob Jones
Sound Editor:	Spencer Reeve
Sound System:	Westrex
Special Effects:	Wally Veevers
Continuity:	Barbara Cole
Make-up:	Stuart Freeborn
Hair Stylist:	Helen Penfold
Wardrobe Supervisor:	J. Wilson-Apperson

Production Controller:	Mickey Delamar	
Production Manager:	Eddie Pike	
Furs:	Deanfield	
Studio:	Shepperton	
Cast:	Charles Chaplin	(King Shahdov)
	Maxine Audley	(Queen Irene)
	Jerry Desmonde	(Prime Minister Voudel)
	Oliver Johnston	(Ambassador Jaume)
	Dawn Addams	(Ann Kay – TV Specialist)
	Sidney James	(Johnson – TV Advertiser)
	Joan Ingrams	(Mona Cromwell – Hostess)
	Michael Chaplin	(Rupert Macabee)
	John McLaren	(Mr Macabee)
	Phil Brown	(Headmaster)
	Harry Green	(Lawyer Green)
	Robert Arden	(Liftboy)
	Alan Gifford	(School Superintendent)
	Robert Cawdron	(US Marshal)
	George Woodbridge	(Member of Atomic Commission)
	Clifford Buckton	(Member of Atomic Commission)
	Vincent Lawson	(Member of Atomic Commission)
	Shani Wallis	(Singer)
	Joy Nichols	(Singer)
	Nicholas Tannar	(Butler)
	George Truzzi	(Comedian)
	Laurie Lupino Lane	(Comedian)
	Macdonald Parke	
Released:	12 September 1957	
Length:	9891 ft	

81 A Countess From Hong Kong

Production:	Universal
Producer:	Jerome Epstein
Director:	Charles Chaplin
Scenario:	Charles Chaplin
Photography:	Arthur Ibbetson
Assistant Director:	Jack Causey
Production Designer:	Don Ashton
Art Director:	Robert Cartwright
Set Decorator:	Vernon Dixon
Editor:	Gordon Hales
Music:	Charles Chaplin

Chaplin: His Life and Art

Musical Director:	Lambert Williamson	
Musical Associate:	Eric James	
Sound:	Michael Hopkins	
Sound Recording:	Bill Daniels, Ken Barker	
Production Supervisor:	Denis Johnson	
Titles:	Gordon Shadrick	
Colour:	Technicolor. CinemaScope.	
Cast:	Marlon Brando	(Ogden Mears)
	Sophia Loren	(Countess Natascha Alexandroff)
	Sydney Chaplin	(Harvey Crothers)
	Tippi Hedren	(Martha Mears)
	Patrick Cargill	(Hudson)
	Margaret Rutherford	(Miss Gaulswallow)
	Michael Medwin	(John Felix)
	Oliver Johnston	(Clark)
	John Paul	(Captain)
	Angela Scoular	(Society Girl)
	Peter Bartlett	(Steward)
	Bill Nagy	(Crawford)
	Dilys Laye	(Saleswoman)
	Angela Pringle	(Baroness)
	Jenny Bridge	(Countess)
	Maureen Russell	(Countess)
	Jackie Dee	(Girl in Dance Hall)
	Ray Marlowe	(American in Dance Hall)
	Arthur Gross	(Immigration Officer)
	Balbina	(Maid)
	Geraldine Chaplin	(Girl in Ballroom)
	Janine Hill	(Girl in Ballroom)
	Christine Rogers	(Girl in Ballroom)
	Pat Hagan	(Girl in Ballroom)
	Gerry Howes	(Man in Ballroom)
	Anthony Chin	(Hawaiian)
	Burnell Tucker	(Receptionist)
	Leonard Trolley	(Purser)
	Lee Lowe	(Electrician)
	Francis Dux	(Head Waiter)
	Cecil Cheng	(Taxi Driver)
	Ronald Rubin	(Sailor)
	Michael Spice	(Sailor)
	Ray Marlowe	(Sailor)
	Josephine Chaplin	(Young Girl)

	Victoria Chaplin	(Young Girl)
	Harold Korn	(Officer)
	Holly Grey	(Steward)
	Kevin Manser	(Photographer)
	Marianne Stone	(Reporter)
	Lew Luton	(Reporter)
	Bill Edwards	(Reporter)
	Drew Russell	(Reporter)
	John Sterland	(Reporter)
	Paul Carson	(Reporter)
	Paul Tamarin	(Reporter)
	Carol Cleveland	(Nurse)
	Charles Chaplin	(An Old Steward)
Released:	2 January 1967	
Length:	11,033 ft	

VII FILM PRODUCED BY CHAPLIN

A Woman of The Sea (*Working title*: Sea Gulls)

Production:	Charles Chaplin Film Corporation	
Producer:	Josef von Sternberg	
Director:	Josef von Sternberg	
Scenario:	Josef von Sternberg	
Photography:	Eddie Gheller, Paul Ivano	
Cameraman:	Mark Marlatt	
Art Director:	Charles D. Hall	
Assistants:	George Ruric, Charles Hammond, Riza Royce	
Cast:	Edna Purviance	(Joan)
	Eve Southern	(Magdalen)
	Charles French	(Their Father)
	Raymond Bloomer	(Peter, the Fisherman)
	Gayne Whitman	(The Novelist from the City)

The film was never released; on 24 June 1933 the negative was formally burnt.

VIII COMPILATION FILM

80a The Chaplin Revue

Production:	Roy Film Establishment–United Artists
Producer:	Charles Chaplin
Director:	Charles Chaplin
Scenario:	Charles Chaplin
Music:	Charles Chaplin
Musical Director:	Eric James

Song, 'Bound
For Texas': Charles Chaplin
Sung by: Matt Munro
Narrator: Charles Chaplin

Compiled from *A Dog's Life, Shoulder Arms, The Pilgrim* and *How to Make Movies*

Released: 25 September 1959
Length: 11,150 ft

IX UNAUTHORIZED FILMS: ESSANAY PERIOD

49a The Essanay–Chaplin Revue

5-reel anthology of *The Tramp, His New Job* and *A Night Out.*

Released: 23 September 1916

50 Triple Trouble

Producer: Jesse J. Robbins for Essanay
Directors: Charles Chaplin and Leo White
Scenario: Leo White

Cast:	Charles Chaplin	(Janitor)
	Edna Purviance	(Maid)
	Leo White	(Count)
	Billy Armstrong	(Cook *and* Thief)
	James T. Kelley	(Singing Derelict)
	Bud Jamison	(Tramp)
	Wesley Ruggles	(Crook)
	Albert Austin	(Man)

An amalgam, assembled by White, of scenes from *Police* and an uncompleted Essanay Chaplin short, *Life*, with new material directed by White.

Released: 11 August 1918
Length: 2000 ft approximately

50a Chase Me Charlie

7-reel montage of Essanay films, edited by Langford Reed.

Released: May 1918
Length: 6500 ft approximately

X OTHER FILM APPEARANCES

His Regeneration (1915)

An Essanay Broncho Billy film, in which Chaplin plays himself.

Filmography

The Nut (1921)

Production: Douglas Fairbanks–United Artists
Director: Theodore Reed
Starring: Douglas Fairbanks

Chaplin appears as himself

Souls For Sale (1923)

Production: Rupert Hughes–Metro Goldwyn Mayer
Director: Rupert Hughes

Chaplin appears as himself, along with many other Hollywood stars.

Show People (1928)

Production: Cosmopolitan–MGM
Director: King Vidor
Starring: Marion Davies

Chaplin appears as himself.

The Gentleman Tramp (1975)

Production: Filmverhuurkantoor 'De Dam' D.V.-Audjeff
Director: Richard Patterson

Compilation documentary, with newly filmed scenes of Chaplin at home in Corsier sur Vevey.

APPENDIX VII

Shooting schedules and ratios

		SCHEDULES		RATIOS		
DATE	TITLE	SHOOTING DAYS	IDLE* DAYS	TOTAL FOOTAGE SHOT	LENGTH OF FINISHED FILM	SHOOTING RATIO
1918	A Dog's Life	59	17	35,887 ft	2674 ft	13.4
1918	Shoulder Arms			43,937	3142	14
1919	Sunnyside	76	103	59,559	2769	21.5
1919	A Day's Pleasure			38,921	1714	22.7
1920	The Kid	154	117	278,573	5250	53
1921	The Idle Class	53	78	27,078	1916	14.1
1922	Pay Day	31	164	33,914	1950	17.4
1922	The Pilgrim	51	153	46,166	3647	12.7
1923	A Woman of Paris			130,115	7557	17.1
1925	The Gold Rush	170	235	231,505	8555	27
1927	The Circus	170	467	211,104	6500	32.5
1931	City Lights	179	504	314,256	8093	38.8
1936	Modern Times	147	263	213,961	8126	26.3
1940	The Great Dictator	168	391	477,440	11,628	41
1946	Monsieur Verdoux	80		313,726	11,132	28.2
1952	Limelight	55		239,481	12,636	19

*This is a comparative term. Although the number of 'idle days' recorded in the studio records of each film included some periods of total inactivity, the figure also included time spent on preparation of sets and costumes, rehearsing, cutting and (later) music and recording.

APPENDIX VIII

Chaplin, Epstein and the Circle Theatre

Towards the end of his three-decade residence in the United States, the chance to resume an active contact with the live theatre seems to have revived something of the old passion implanted in Chaplin when he was a boy performer. His contacts with the Circle Theatre also began the association with Jerome (Jerry) Epstein as collaborator, friend and confidant which was to last for thirty years, until Chaplin's death.

Epstein was a friend of Chaplin's younger son Sydney, with whom he was associated in establishing the theatre in 1946. The Circle began in a modest way, giving its performances in the homes of any friends with large enough drawing rooms, but its very first production, *The Adding Machine*, directed by Epstein with Sydney Chaplin in the leading role, attracted favourable notice. Sydney had already introduced Epstein to his father and Oona when they all met at a show of *Les Enfants du Paradis*; and the Chaplins came to see Sydney's performance. 'Charlie was a wonderful audience,' Epstein recalled, 'and he just got to like the theatre. He would come all the time. When he'd nothing else to do, he would drive down in his little Ford, and sit with me in the box office. And then of course all his friends began to come to the theatre and they brought friends. Fanny Brice came; and Constance Collier took us up in a big way, and brought Katharine Hepburn and George Cukor, and Gladys Cooper and Robert Morley and any English people who happened to be in Hollywood. When we did *Ethan Frome* we borrowed props from the studio. Charlie was so impressed by our production of *Time of Your Life* that he contacted Saroyan and asked him to give us a play, which he did: it was *Sam Ego's House*.

'Then one day he was watching a rehearsal of *The Skin Game*, and asked "Do you mind if I suggest something . . .?" and of course in no time he had taken over the whole show. He was marvellous. His instinct was amazing – his feeling for the play, stage pictures, timing, exits, entrances, everything.

Of course he acted out every part himself, and some of the actors as a result became little Charlie Chaplins. It was an unforgettable experience for them, though at this stage of the production it was very confusing for them too, altering everything they had already done.

'After that ne did five other productions. Of course he had not the patience to do them from the beginning, but he would come in at the end and give his touches. The next one was *Hindle Wakes*. Then he wanted to do *Rain*, which he said had never been done correctly. He considered that Jeanne Eagels' performance had been overrated and that the Reverend Davidson was always done wrong. Sadie was June Havoc – that was the first time we had a real star, but she had come to the theatre and wanted to do the part.

'I had called Albert Camus in North Africa to ask if we could produce *Caligula*, and Charlie did it. It was a disaster: no one understood the play, least of all the actors. Although Charlie's participation was never made public, or printed in the programme, he took it very personally when the play had bad notices, and I had to dissuade him from firing off letters to the press. Sydney was delighted when Frank Eng wrote in his review that he, Sydney, was the only one who understood the play – because he understood no more of it than anyone else!

'Charlie devised some wonderful gags for *School for Scandal* and even added a line. Marie Wilson played Lady Teazle, and the eighteenth-century dresses dramatically showed off her magnificent breasts. I had devised a card game, in which Wheeler Dryden stood behind Marie. Charlie suggested that when Wheeler peered over her shoulder, and Marie held the cards to her, Wheeler should simply say, "Madam, I was not looking at your cards." It really brought the house down.

'Constance Collier would sit in on the rehearsals and there would be some very funny sparring between them. Constance would criticize, and he would become very mad. "But Charlie – you haven't read the play," she would say; and he would snap back, "I don't need to. *I know what it's about.*"

'In all, the Circle presented more than a hundred plays. Eventually we had three theatres, the Circle, the Coronet and the Cast. The Cast was attached to the Circle, and shared the same backstage and dressing rooms: one night an actor actually walked onto the wrong stage. Our regular people included Kathleen Freeman and Strother Martin; Alan Pakula directed a very good *Antigone*, and Shelley Winters directed *Thunder Rock*. In 1950 some of our actors broke away to form their own theatre (Charlie was indignant), and that company included Jack Nicholson and Richard Dreyfus.'

The final production of the Circle was *What Every Woman Wants*, which Constance Collier recommended. In her book *Moments With Chaplin*, Lillian Ross gives a vivid picture both of the atmosphere of the theatre, and of Chaplin tirelessly putting his actors – who included his two sons and Ruth Conte – through an energetic five-hour rehearsal. (He thought nothing of working through until 6 a.m. – with Oona calling from time to time to inquire when he was coming home.) Lillian Ross recalls verbatim some of his direction: 'You must not act. You . . . *must* give the audience the impression that you've just read the script. It's phoney now. We don't talk that way. Just state it. Don't make it weary. You're too young for that. Let's get away from acting. We don't want acting. We want reality. Give the audience the feeling that they're looking through the keyhole. This will be maudlin and sticky as hell if you act . . .' Later he told them, 'Keep it simple. Too many gestures are creeping in. I don't like that. If the audience notices a gesture you're gone. Gestures are not to be seen. And I'm a gesture man. It's hard for me to keep them down . . . Thank God, I can see myself on the screen the next day . . . I'm essentially an entrance and exit man . . . Good exits and entrances. That's all theatre is. And punctuation. That's all it is.'

Epstein felt that a lot of inspiration for *Limelight* came from this contact with the Circle Theatre. 'He had always said, "When I make my film you're going to work with me." I never took it seriously of course; but then when he came to make *Limelight* he took me as his assistant. And after that I just kept on working with him.

'The writer Dudley Nichols – he did *Stagecoach* – was one of our first fans; and as a result of their meetings in the theatre he and his wife became quite friendly with Charlie and Oona. I remember him telling me one day, "You're young. And you'll remember these as the happiest days of your life." '

APPENDIX IX
The FBI v. Chaplin

The extensive files on Chaplin maintained by the Federal Bureau of Investigation over a period of more than fifty years – they total more than nineteen hundred pages – only became available to the author when the present book was practically completed. The information they provide adds little to the material in the body of the book, apart from corroboration and a mass of circumstantial detail in such matters as the Barry trials. In general they reveal much more about the methods of the FBI than about the life of Chaplin. It seems appropriate however to make some comment here upon their contents.

What is alarming in the files is not any investigative skill or deviousness in the methods of the Bureau, but rather the degree of sloppiness and stupidity that many of the reports reveal. An inordinate amount of time seems to have been devoted to processing hearsay, rumours, poison-pen letters and cranky unsolicited correspondence, along with the public revelations of Hedda Hopper, Ed Sullivan and other syndicated gossip columnists. The Bureau's biographical data on Chaplin, which served, periodically rehashed, for more than thirty years, was derived from Gerith von Ulm's 1940 book *Charlie Chaplin, King of Tragedy*, a record only intermittently trustworthy. Throughout the files the Bureau perpetuated such inaccuracies as that Chaplin had married Mildred Harris in London (von Ulm had this right, at least) and that he was Jewish. In this connection, they happily gleaned a piece of colourful misinformation from *Who's Who in American Jewry*, wherein it was claimed that Chaplin was the son of a family called Thonstein, who had emigrated from Eastern Europe and settled in London in 1850. After this they generally headed reports on Chaplin 'alias Charlie Chaplin; alias Israel Thonstein', which gave a nicely sinister touch to things.

The first record of the Bureau's interest in Chaplin dates from 15 August 1922, when an agent called A. A. Hopkins passed on the information that Chaplin had given a reception for a prominent labour leader, William Z.

Foster, who was visiting Los Angeles. The event had been attended by many of the 'Parlor Bolsheviki' and such Hollywood radicals as William De Mille and Rob Wagner. Will Hays had arrived in Hollywood a few months before this to set up the office of Motion Picture Producers and Distributors of America, Inc., a self-regulatory industry body; and Chaplin was alleged to have told Foster in the course of the evening that he had no use for Hays: 'We are against any kind of censorship, and particularly against presbyterian censorship.'

He also pointed out to his guests a pennant bearing the words 'Welcome Will Hays', pinned over the men's lavatory at the studio. J. Edgar Hoover and his associates were so impressed by Agent Hopkins' report on this and other evidence of the infiltration of Communist ideas into the film industry, that they instituted further investigation. Meanwhile Hopkins' information was passed on to Will Hays himself, who recalled broodingly that Chaplin had not participated in the welcoming activities when he arrived in Hollywood, which led him to think that 'the party mentioned is really a little odd in his mental processes to say the least, in the direction which you mention. I did not know he had gone so far, however, as the report indicates.' Hays added a pledge to discuss 'ways and means of making certain that there is no seditious propaganda allowed to get into anything'.

Subsequent reports dealt with the alleged visit to Chaplin of a Communist organizer of the Garment Workers' Union, bearing the sinister name of Plotkin, to appeal for funds for striking railroad workers; and a rumour that Chaplin was the anonymous Hollywood donor of $1000 to the Communist Party of America, at Christmas 1922. Periodically over the next thirty years the Bureau would re-examine their growing file of reports (invariably unsubstantiated) of donations by Chaplin to Communist causes.

These early reports coincided with America's most rabid Red Scare until the 1940s, and in the interim the FBI seem to have lost interest in Chaplin. They were back in action, however, from the moment he spoke at the meeting arranged by Russian War Relief, Inc. on 3 December 1942. The following day an unidentified agent, who had posed as a sympathizer, sent back a detailed transcript of Chaplin's speech which included such enthusiastic phrases as 'I am not a Communist, but I am pretty pro-Communist.'

After this, evidence of 'Red sympathies' was laboriously piled up against him. The Second Front speeches were duly noted. In August 1943 he was Master of Ceremonies at a reception for the distinguished Soviet director Mikhail Kalatozov. In May 1946 he attended a film show and party on a Soviet ship in Long Beach harbour, and jokingly called American customs men 'Gestapo'. On leaving, he was photographed 'with John Garfield, alias Jules Garfinkle and Lewis Milestone, Russian born film director'. The endless rumours of contributions to the Party culminated in Hedda Hopper's inventive sneers about 'Charlie Chaplin, who contributed $25,000 to the

Communist cause and $100 to the Red Cross'. The Bureau 'monitored' his bank account and found a lot of money but no sign of contributions to Communist causes.

Everything was grist to the Bureau's slow-grinding mill. In August 1947 we find Hoover himself requesting by urgent teletype a copy of an article in praise of Chaplin that had appeared in *Pravda.* It hardly seemed to matter to the Director that the item – an appreciative notice of the first Chaplin films to appear in the Soviet Union – had appeared in 1923. A week later, a memorandum proposes that the *Pravda* piece might make an excellent item for the gossip columnist Louella Parsons. In the end it was sent to Hedda Hopper. It is interesting to discover that the FBI was not only using the gossip of these viperish ladies as evidence, but was also feeding information to them. There is at least an acknowledgement that the procedure might be irregular in the instruction (ignored) on the Louella Parsons memorandum: 'To be destroyed after action is taken and not sent to files.'

Nothing, however negative, was disregarded. It was enough for some leftish organization to express its admiration for Chaplin, or to say that it might invite him to attend a function, for an addition to the files. A soldier charged with a security offence snapped 'Sure I'm a Communist . . . so is Charlie Chaplin.' It was reported by the Army to the FBI, and stayed on Chaplin's record to the end; for no detail, however meaningless or insubstantial, was ever erased, once it was on the files. In April 1943 Chaplin was seen at a showing of the Soviet classic, *Baltic Deputy.* He attended a Shostakovich concert. It was recorded as a sign of undesirable radical views that he was signatory to a letter from eight hundred labour, religious and social leaders who urged Roosevelt to prevent racial outbreaks and lauded his stand against discrimination.

At the time of Chaplin's departure from the United States in 1952, all this was summarized in a 125-page report with the classification 'Information pertaining to Questions of Communist Party Membership of Charles Chaplin', 'Individual Associates of Chaplin who are Reported to be Communist Party Members' (they included Hanns and Gerhardt Eisler, Lion Feuchtwanger and Theodore Dreiser), and 'Affiliation of Charles Chaplin with Groups Declared to be Communist Subversive Groups or Reputedly Controlled or Influenced by the Communist Party'.

The investigation into Chaplin's supposed subversive activities was temporarily eclipsed however by the Joan Barry case. Barry made her first public charges that Chaplin was the father of her unborn child on 4 June 1943. The FBI initiated investigations on 17 August, when Hoover put Special Agent Hood on the case to collect evidence to support the Mann Act charges and the case for violation of civil liberties brought against Chaplin and six other defendants. Three days later Hoover issued a teletype requesting that the investigation be expedited, and during the next four months the Bureau were tireless. They interviewed scores of witnesses, and the secret evidence they collected fills more than four hundred pages. One of their most helpful informants was Hedda Hopper. They seemed to have bugged telephones and hotel rooms (with devices they called 'microphone technicals'). They put stops on border posts to prevent Chaplin's leaving the country if he had been so inclined.

The Bureau's investigations reveal much more about Joan Barry than emerged in the trials, showing her as perhaps the most pitiable figure in the affair, trapped between the lines of the war which Hoover and the FBI were waging against Chaplin. The files reveal that her true name was Mary Louise Gribble. She had adopted the name of her step-father, Mr Berry, and was variously known as Joan Berry, Joan Barry, Mary Louise Barry, Joan Barratt, Mary L. Barratt, Joanne Berry, Jo Anne Berry, Bettie Booker, Joan Spencer, Mrs Mark Warner, Catherine McLaren and Mary L. Spencer.

This indecision over her names perhaps reflects her real mental confusion, which became increasingly acute towards the end of her association with Chaplin. Chaplin appears to have been considerate and generous during most of their time together; Barry complained that it was his friends, notably Tim Durant (who had first introduced them), who mistreated her in trying to break up the liaison. Perhaps the most singular revelation of the FBI files is the admission that 'never did either BERRY or her attorney request this investigation or express a desire for the Government to take action against CHAPLIN'. It is also revealed that the prosecution did not always have an easy time in presenting Mrs Berry in the required role of a concerned and loving mother: Gertrude Berry was reported to have a drink problem and to quarrel frequently with her daughter; and on one occasion she disappeared from their home.

When the trials ended in failure for the prosecution (the Mann Act jury decided in Chaplin's favour and the civil rights violation charges were dropped on instructions from the Attorney General), the Bureau exchanged letters of commiseration and compliments with the attorneys, and contemplated bringing charges of perjury against some of the witnesses. (After the civil case on Carol Ann Barry's paternity they contemplated, in the same spirit, investigating whether blood tests could be faked by chemical additions to the blood stream. Wiser counsels prevailed.)

With the peak of the McCarthy witch hunts, investigation of Chaplin's suspected subversive sympathies was once more stepped up. Chaplin's friendship with Hanns Eisler, whose brother was a declared Communist, attracted grave suspicion; after his telegram to Picasso seeking support for Eisler the Bureau constituted an investigation 'to determine whether or not Chaplin was or is engaged in Soviet espionage'. Shortly after this, in February 1948, Chaplin applied for a re-entry permit since he planned to visit Britain and then return to California via the Far East. On 17 April officials of the Immigration and Naturalization Service went to his house and conducted an interview which lasted for four hours and was recorded verbatim by a stenographer (cf. p. 548). Chaplin handled the interview with tremendous skill and frankness; a couple of years later the FBI's Los Angeles office said that further interviews with Chaplin were 'not recommended . . . the interview for the most part was inconclusive because CHAPLIN would either deny allegations, explain them in his own manner or state that he did not remember'.

Nevertheless in November 1948 Chaplin was placed on the Security Index. The newspaper morgues were combed anew. Incriminating new evidence was discovered, such as that in 1929 Chaplin had been a member of something called 'The Russian Eagle Supper Club'. News items about his failure to appear in the 1931 Royal Variety Show, and his thoughts on patriotism delivered on that occasion, were brought up against him. There was even an attempt to introduce Hetty Kelly into the case. A disgruntled former employee sent the Bureau off on a wild goose chase involving a fictitious courier who had brought a secret message to Chaplin from an agent in Moscow. A tip-off that there would be a clandestine meeting at Summit Drive launched a surveillance operation on the house, but of course no one arrived.

Despite these setbacks, in November 1949 the FBI had a request from the Assistant Attorney General, Alexander Campbell, for the Chaplin files, since a 'Security-R investigation was pending'. The files were disappointing: on 29 December there came the admission: 'It has been determined that there are no witnesses available who could offer testimony that Chaplin has been a member of the Communist Party in the past, is now a member, or has contributed funds to the Communist Party.' There was some consolation in 1950 when Louis F. Budenz, a former managing editor of the *Daily Worker* and a marathon namer of names, included Chaplin in his list of four hundred 'concealed Communists' and alleged substantial contributions to Party funds. He turned out to be a singularly unreliable witness.

The final phase of the war on Chaplin came in 1952. On 25 August a Mr Noto of the Immigration and Naturalization Service telephoned the FBI to say that Chaplin was intending to sail for England in September, and to ask for information. On 16 September Hoover told the Los Angeles office that Chaplin had been issued with a re-entry permit, and that they should advise head office of any information on his tour abroad. A note at the foot of the message comments, 'INS has advised that even though he was given a re-entry permit, this permit gives no guarantee he will be allowed to return to the United States.' Already, on 9 September, McGranery had met with J. Edgar Hoover and told him that he 'was considering taking steps to prevent the re-entry into this country of Charlie Chaplin . . . because of moral turpitude'. The files on the Barry case were turned up again: 'See that all is included in memo to A.G.,' scribbled Hoover.

On 19 September Attorney General McGranery announced that Chaplin's re-entry permit would not be honoured. The FBI files show however that the Immigration and Naturalization service remained very nervous about their position:

> Mr Farrell stated bluntly that at the present INS does not have sufficient information to exclude Chaplin from the United States if he attempts to re-enter. Mr Mackey interposed that INS could, of course, make it difficult for Chaplin to re-enter, but in the end, there is no doubt Chaplin would be admitted. Mr Mackey pointed out that if INS attempted to delay Chaplin's re-entry into the United States, it would involve a question of detention which might well rock INS and the Department of Justice to its foundations.
>
> Mr Farrell advised further that while INS does not have sufficient information on which to exclude Chaplin if he attempts to re-enter before December 24 1952, INS hopes that under the new Immigration and Nationality Act (Public Law 414, 82nd Congress), effective on and after that date, it will be able to make a case against Chaplin sufficient to exclude him. Mr Farrell expressed the view that if Chaplin's lawyer was astute, he would have Chaplin return to the United States before the effective date of the new law.

Chaplin however did not return. He chose to make his home in Europe. After this the FBI mainly contented itself with monitoring the press reports on his movements and activities. When he handed back his re-entry permit the Bureau were alerted to the possibility that it might be 'an effort on his part to give the impression he is not returning to the United States while actually he may attempt to return unnoticed by United States officials', and cautioned their agents to vigilance. In 1954 the Army Censorship intercepted and passed on to the FBI a letter from Mrs Eisler in Vienna to Oona in Switzerland, in which she expressed a hope that *Limelight* could be shown not only in Austria but also in the Soviet Union and China. In 1955 Charles Chaplin Junior acted in a German film with the export title of *Yankee Business*, which persuaded the Bureau that subversive views might be inherited.

In 1957 the Bureau analyzed the European press reaction to *A King in New York* and concluded that 'the State Department could be put on the spot. Either a move by State to prevent importation of the film or a hands-off policy could subject it to criticism. Any criticism of State would inure to Communist benefit as a discrediting of the United States Government.'

When Chaplin was given his Oxford degree in 1962 the *New York Times* published its editorial speculating that 'We do not believe the Republic would be in danger . . . if yesterday's unforgotten little tramp were allowed to amble down the gangplank of an American port.' This apparently stirred Judge McGranery to ask for the old files once again. The Judge grumbled to the FBI liaison officer that *The Times* had alleged that as Attorney General he had blocked Chaplin's return to the United States. He said that this was simply not true: 'he had insisted that Chaplin be subject to the same hearing procedures as anyone else, and should not be given preferential treatment because of his wealth and notoriety.'

Nine years later Ambassador Davis sent a telegram from Bern to the Attorney General and the Under-Secretary of State, noting that Brandeis University was to honour Chaplin with an award the following year. He 'recommended swift waiving of Chaplin's ineligibility to avoid unfavorable publicity for U.S.'.

Even after this, and Chaplin's return to the United States, the FBI file was not quite closed. The final documents relate to the theft of Chaplin's body in 1978. Somehow it seems appropriate that the FBI's contribution to the investigation was a series of interviews with psychics.

APPENDIX X
A Chaplin Who's Who

AGEE, James. (1909–1955) Screenwriter, novelist, poet, critic. Chaplin's most vigorous and distinguished US defender in the McCarthy years, notably in his *Verdoux* criticisms and *Life* essay, 'The Golden Age of Comedy'. Own screenplays: *The Quiet One* (1950), *The African Queen* (1951), *The Night of the Hunter* (1955).

ALDRICH, Robert. (1918–1983) Director. Associate director of *Limelight*. Was also assistant to Renoir, Milestone, Wellman, Rosson, Polansky, Losey. Own first film: *Big Leaguer* (1953); later work included *Kiss Me Deadly* (1955), *Whatever Happened to Baby Jane?* (1962).

ALLEN, Phyllis. Actress, *Caught in a Cabaret, A Busy Day, The Property Man, The Rounders, Dough and Dynamite, Gentlemen of Nerve, His Trysting Place, Tillie's Punctured Romance, Getting Acquainted, Pay Day.* Began career in vaudeville and musical comedy; screen debut 1910 with Selig Company. Keystone 1913–1916; later Fox, Vitagraph.

ANDERSON, G. M. ('Broncho Billy') (1883–1971) The first great Western star, Anderson made some 400 one-reelers between 1907 and 1914. Co-founder of Essanay Company (1907), which engaged Chaplin in 1914–15. Explained principle of own films: 'We don't change the stories – only the horses.' Reappeared on screen 1967 in *The Bounty Killer*. Special Academy Award, 1957. Appears as actor in *The Champion*.

ARBUCKLE, Roscoe. (1887–1933) Actor, *A Film Johnnie, Tango Tangles, His Favorite Pastime, The Knockout, The Masquerader, The Rounders.* Began career in vaudeville and musical comedy, touring with Leon Errol. Film debut, Selig Company 1909. Keystone 1913. Two-reeler partners included Mabel Normand and Buster Keaton. At peak of career earned $1000 a day, but was ruined by scandal in 1921 when an actress, Virginia Rappe, died in the course of a party given by Arbuckle at the St Francis Hotel, San Francisco.

Attempted come-back as director in late 1920s under pseudonym, Will B. Goodrich.

ARMSTRONG, Billy (1891–?). Actor, *The Champion, In the Park, The Tramp, By the Sea, Work, A Woman, The Bank, Shanghaied, Police, Triple Trouble.* Began career in music hall, with Karno companies and Harry Tate Company. Film debut, Essanay 1915; later Horsley, Cub Comedies, L-Ko and Keystone, including *Skirts* (1921).

d'ARRAST, Henri d'Abbadie. (Argentina, 1897–France, 1968) Research assistant, *A Woman of Paris,* and for a time a regular companion of Chaplin in Hollywood. Had brief and stormy career as director of sparkling social comedies at Paramount: *Service for Ladies, A Gentleman of Paris* (both 1927), *Laughter* (1912), *Topaze* (1933). Retired to Europe.

AUDLEY, Maxine. (1923–1992) Actress, *A King in New York.* Stage from 1940; films from 1947 (*Anna Karenina*).

AUSTIN, Albert. (Birmingham, England, 1885–Hollywood, 1953) Actor, *The Floorwalker, The Fireman, The Vagabond, One A.M., The Count, The Pawnshop, Behind the Screen, The Rink, Easy Street, The Cure, The Immigrant, The Adventurer, A Dog's Life, Shoulder Arms, Sunnyside, A Day's Pleasure, The Kid, Pay Day, The Gold Rush, City Lights.* Also assistant director. Early career in musical comedy and music hall; arrived in America with Karno companies; stock in Denver for two years before film debut with Chaplin at Mutual. Other films as actor included *Suds.* Directed *Trouble* (1922), *A Prince of a King* (1923), both with Jackie Coogan.

AYRES, Agnes. (Agnes Hinkle) (Carbondale, Illinois 1896–Hollywood, 1940) Actress, *His New Job.* Debut at Essanay. Later known as 'The O.Henry Girl'. Starring roles in *The Sheik* (1921), *The Ten Commandments* (1924), *Son of the Sheik* (1926).

BACON, Lloyd. (1889–1955) Director. Actor in *The Champion, In the Park, A Jitney Elopement, The Tramp, The Bank, The Floorwalker, The Fireman, The Vagabond, Behind the Screen, The Rink, Easy Street.* Debut as director with Mack Sennett, 1921. Later films included *The Singing Fool* (1928), *Forty-Second Street* (1933), *A Slight Case of Murder* (1937), *The French Line* (1954).

BAKER, Nellie Bly. (b. 1894) Actress, *The Kid, A Woman of Paris.* Originally employed at the Chaplin Studio as a secretary (she is seen bringing Chaplin his morning mail in *How To Make Movies*); her appearancces in Chaplin films led to a career as a character player throughout the 1920s, including von Sternberg's *The Salvation Hunters.*

BARTON, Ralph. (1891–1931) Artist and illustrator. Reported First World War in pictures for British magazine *Puck,* though subsequently developed pathological dislike of British. Illustrated *Gentlemen Prefer Blondes* and *Contes Drolatiques*; many caricatures in *New Yorker, Vanity Fair, Liberty, Harpers*. Accompanied Chaplin – whom he considered 'the greatest man alive' – on the first stage of his 1931 world trip, but returned to New York where he killed himself. In his suicide note he deplored 'beautiful lost Carlotta' (Monterey); but Eugene O'Neill, then married to Carlotta, told reporters, 'I never saw Barton in my life. Mrs O'Neill hasn't seen him in five years. He made no attempt to see her at any time.' Barton was married four times.

BAUMAN, Charles O. Co-founder with Adam Kessel of Keystone. Was bookmaker, exhibitor, producer from 1909 when founded New York Motion Picture Company (with Kessel).

BELL, Monta. (1891–1958) Director. Assisted Chaplin in writing *My Trip Abroad* and was literary editor on *A Woman of Paris*. Early career: reporter on *Washington Post*; actor in stock. Director debut, *The Snob* (1924); later films include *The King on Main Street* (1925), *The Torrent* (1926), *China's Little Devils* (1945).

BENNETT, Marjorie. (1894–1982) Actress, *Monsieur Verdoux*, *Limelight*. Sister of Enid Bennett and long active in Hollywood as character player.

BERGMAN, Henry. (1868–1946, Hollywood) Actor, *The Pawnshop, Behind the Screen, The Rink, Easy Street, The Cure, The Immigrant, The Adventurer, A Dog's Life, The Bond, Shoulder Arms, Sunnyside, A Day's Pleasure, The Kid, The Idle Class, Pay Day, The Pilgrim, The Gold Rush, The Circus, City Lights, Modern Times*. Coordinator, *The Great Dictator*. Originally on operatic and musical stage; films from 1914 (Henry Lehrman's L-Ko Company). From 1916 worked exclusively at Chaplin studios as actor and assistant. Also owned Hollywood restaurant, 'Henry's'.

BLOOM, Claire. (b. 1931) Actress, *Limelight*. Trained at Guildhall Schools of Speech and Drama, Central School of Speech Training. Stage from 1946: *Ring Round the Moon* (1950); several seasons at Old Vic. Films from 1948 (*The Blind Goddess*), including *Look Back in Anger* (1959), many in USA, and in Europe with director Krzysztof Zanussi. Autobiography, *Limelight and After*, 1982.

BODIE, 'Dr' Walford. (1870–1939). Music hall performer, at first as ventriloquist, later performing 'miraculous' electrical cures for all ills. Chaplin impersonated him during the *Casey's Court Circus* tour.

BRANDO, Marlon (b. 1924) Actor, *A Countess From Hong Kong*. Studied painting; worked as lift boy; Stella Adler's 'Dramatic Workshop' 1943; summer stock 1944; Broadway 1944 (*I Remember Mama*); films from 1950.

BRUCE, Nigel. (1895–1953) Actor, *Limelight*. Stage (in England) from 1920; films from 1930. Born in US to English parents, Bruce specialized in quintessentially British characters. His most famous screen role was Doctor Watson in numerous *Sherlock Holmes* pictures – a fact which undoubtedly recommended him to Chaplin.

BRYAN, Vincent (1877–?) Writer, assisted Chaplin at Essanay and Mutual. Early career in theatre, writing plays, vaudeville sketches, songs. Began screen career at Keystone; later with Goldwyn.

BURKAN, Nathan. Noted film industry lawyer who represented Chaplin's legal interests from his arrival in Hollywood.

BURKE, Thomas. (1886–1945, London) Novelist and essayist. Their common south London background and mutual admiration brought Burke and Chaplin together; and the friendship resulted in Burke's remarkable study of Chaplin, 'A Comedian', in *City of Encounters*. The most notable film adaptation of a Burke story was D. W. Griffith's *Broken Blossoms*, from *The Chink and the Child*.

CAMPBELL, Eric (1880–1917) Actor, *The Floorwalker, The Fireman, The Vagabond, The Count, The Pawnshop, Behind the Screen, The Rink, Easy Street, The Cure, The Immigrant, The Adventurer*. Early career, D'Oyly Carte company, Karno Company. Had appeared in films in London and New York before Hollywood.

CARGILL, Patrick (b. 1918) Actor, *A Countess From Hong Kong*. Sandhurst and Indian Army. Stage, in repertory, from 1939. West End debut in revue, *High Spirits* (1953). Films from 1952.

CARROLL, Paul Vincent. (1900–1968) Dramatist. Author of *Shadow and Substance* (1934), of which Chaplin proposed a screen adaptation.

CHAPLIN, Albert. Younger brother of Charles Chaplin Senior. Emigrated before 1900 to South Africa where he achieved considerable prosperity and raised a large family. Paid funeral expenses for Charles Chaplin Senior.

CHAPLIN, Annette Emily. (b. 1959) Chaplin's youngest daughter. In 1984 made debut as screen actress in *A Sense of Wonder*.

CHAPLIN, Aubrey. (1889–1932) Chaplin's cousin, son of Charles Chaplin Senior's older brother, Spencer. After death of father became youngest licensee in London. Father of Betty and Pauline Chaplin.

CHAPLIN, Betty (May). Daughter of Aubrey Chaplin. Emigrated to USA in 1939, where she married Drew Tetrick, costumier on later Chaplin films.

CHAPLIN, Charles, Senior. (1863–1901) Father of Charles Chaplin. See Chapter I, *passim*.

CHAPLIN, Charles Spencer, Junior. (1925–1968) Chaplin's elder son by his second marriage. Brought up by mother, Lita Grey, though increasingly in contact with father during boyhood and adolescence. Army; indifferent stage and screen career. Appeared in *Limelight*. Wrote *My Father, Charlie Chaplin* (1960) in collaboration with N. and M. Rau.

CHAPLIN, Christopher James. (b. 1962) Chaplin's youngest son. Able musician; in 1984 made debut as screen actor in *Where is Parsifal?*

CHAPLIN, Eugene Anthony. (b. 1953) Chaplin's second son and fifth child by his marriage to Oona O'Neill. Has worked as recording engineer in Montreux, later as proprietor of curio shop in Vevey.

CHAPLIN, Geraldine Leigh. (b. 1944) First child of Chaplin's marriage to Oona O'Neill. First film appearance in *Limelight*. Appeared in ballroom scene in *A Countess From Hong Kong*. Royal Ballet School and stage experience as dancer. In 1965 made adult film debut in *Par un beau matin d'été*, dir. Jacques Deray. Subsequently many films, notably *Doctor Zhivago* and works by Carlos Saura and Robert Altman.

CHAPLIN, Hannah Harriett Pedlingham (née Hill). (1865–1928) Chaplin's mother. See Chapters 1, 2, 3 *passim*.

CHAPLIN, Jane Cecil. (b. 1957) Chaplin's sixth child and fourth daughter by marriage to Oona O'Neill. Experimental film maker.

CHAPLIN, Josephine Hannah. (b. 1949) Chaplin's second daughter. As child appeared in *Limelight*. As adult, work on stage and in films and television.

CHAPLIN, Lita Grey. (Lillita McMurray) (b.1908) Chaplin's second wife (marriage dissolved) and mother of Charles Spencer and Sydney Earle Chaplin. See Chapters 10, 11 *passim*.

CHAPLIN, Michael John. (b. 1946) First son of Chaplin and Oona O'Neill. Appeared in *Limelight* and *A King in New York*. Subsequently RADA, work as pop musician and actor. Now works own smallholding in France.

CHAPLIN, Mildred Harris. (1901–1944) Child actress from 1910; reputed to have appeared in the Babylonian sequence of *Intolerance*. Her career prospered after the publicity derived from marriage to Chaplin in October 1918, and she was put under contract by Louis B. Mayer, with whom she had worked in *The Warrens of Virginia* (1918). After the Chaplin divorce her popularity declined rapidly, though she appeared in more than fifty films, the last, Alan Crosland's *Lady Tubby*, in 1933. De Mille used her as an extra, along with other of his former stars, in *Reap The Wild Wind* (1941). Later vaudeville, night clubs. Died of pneumonia, following surgery.

CHAPLIN, Norman Spencer. (Born and died July 1919). Chaplin's first child, by Mildred Harris, born severely handicapped and survived only three days.

CHAPLIN, Oona O'Neill. (1926–1991) Chaplin's fourth wife. Daughter of Eugene O'Neill. See Chapters 16 *et seq.*

CHAPLIN, Paulette Goddard. (Pauline Levy) (b. 1911) Actress, *Modern Times, The Great Dictator*. Chaplin's third wife (1936). On stage from 1927 (chorus of *Rio Rita*); films from 1931. After marriage to Chaplin dissolved, continued to work in films until 1966 *(Time of Indifference)*. Married Erich Maria Remarque. See Chapters 14, and 15, *passim.*

CHAPLIN, Pauline (Pauline Mason). (b. 1928) Youngest child of Aubrey Chaplin (q.v.), by second wife, Louise Ella Orton. As licensee of the Princess of Wales, 11 Circus Road, NW8, she represented the fourth generation of Chaplins to manage public houses in London.

CHAPLIN, Spencer. (1834–1897) Chaplin's grandfather; apprenticed as butcher, but became publican. See Chapter 1.

CHAPLIN, Spencer William Tunstill. (1855–1900) Brother of Charles Chaplin Senior and uncle of Charles Chaplin. Publican, notably of The Queen's Head. See Chapter 1.

CHAPLIN, Sydney. (1885–1965) Chaplin's half-brother. See text, *passim.* Films with Chaplin: *A Dog's Life, The Bond, Shoulder Arms, Pay Day, The Pilgrim.* Other films: *Gussle the Golfer* (1914), *Gussle's Day of Rest* (1914), *Gussle Rivals Jonah* (1915), *Gussle's Backward Way* (1915), *Gussle's Wayward Path* (1915), *Gussle Tied to Trouble* (1915), *Submarine Pilot* (1915), *That Springtime Feeling* (1915), *Giddy, Gay and Ticklish* (1915), *Hushing the Scandal* (1915), *No Mother to Guide Him* (1919), *King, Queen, Joker* (1921), *Her Temporary Husband* (1923), *The Rendezvous* (1923), *The Perfect Flapper* (1924), *Galloping Fish* (1924), *The Man on the Box* (1925), *Oh! What a Nurse* (1926), *The Fortune Hunter* (1927), *The Missing Link* (1927), *A Little Bit of Fluff* (1928).

CHAPLIN, Sydney Earle. (b. 1926) Second son of Chaplin by Lita Grey. Actor, *Limelight, A Countess From Hong Kong*. Stage, films; now virtually retired.

CHAPLIN, Victoria. (b. 1951) Chaplin's third daughter. Intended for leading role in *The Freak*, Chaplin's last and unrealized film project. With her husband, Jean-Baptiste Thierrée, formed and runs 'Le Cirque Imaginaire'. Appeared in *A Countess From Hong Kong*, as dancer in ballroom.

CHASE, Charley. (Charles Parrott) (1895–1940) Actor, *The Knockout, Mabel's Busy Day, The Masquerader, His New Profession, The Rounders,*

Dough and Dynamite, Gentlemen of Nerve, His Musical Career, Tillie's Punctured Romance. Early career in vaudeville and burlesque, as Irish monologuist. Film debut, Keystone, 1914. Acted, wrote and directed hundreds of two-reelers for Keystone, Roach (Laurel and Hardy series) and Columbia.

CHERRILL, Virginia. (Virginia Cherrill Martini) (b. 1908) Actress, *City Lights*. Previous career: Chicago society girl. Later films include *Charlie Chan's Latest Case* (1933), *White Heat* (1934), *Troubled Waters* (1935). Husbands include Irving Adler, William Rhinelander Stewart, Cary Grant, Earl of Jersey.

CLINE, Edward. (1892–1961) Actor, *The Knockout*. Stage, then actor and gagman with Sennett. Later notable director of comedy, including *Sherlock Junior* (Buster Keaton) and several films with W. C. Fields.

CODD, Elsie. Chaplin's British press representative from 1918 through early 1920s. Appears as extra in *The Kid*. Seems to have operated from 264 Eastern Road, Kemp Town, Brighton. 'I should like the British press,' she wrote, 'to feel that they can rely upon me as Chaplin's sole press representative for this country for the only true and reliable information about him and his work – that which reaches me direct from the studio.'

CONKLIN, Chester. (Jules Cowles) (1888–1971) Actor, *Making a Living, Mabel's Strange Predicament, Between Showers, Tango Tangles, Cruel, Cruel Love, Mabel at the Wheel, Twenty Minutes of Love, Caught in a Cabaret, Mabel's Busy Day, The Face on the Bar Room Floor, The Masquerader, Those Love Pangs, Dough and Dynamite, Gentlemen of Nerve, Modern Times, The Great Dictator*. Early career, circus clown, vaudeville, stock and road companies. Film debut, Majestic Company, c. 1913; Keystone from 1913; innumerable shorts. Remained in films until 1967 *(Big Hand for a Little Lady)*.

CONKLIN, Heinie (or Charles). (1880–1959) Actor, *Modern Times*. Film debut, Keystone; one of original Keystone Kops. Later many silent features.

COOGAN, Jackie. (1914–1984) Child actor, *The Kid*. Discovered by Chaplin when appearing in father's vaudeville act. (See Chapter 7, *passim*.)

COOKE, Alfred Alistair. (b. 1908) Journalist, broadcaster, film critic. Worked with Chaplin on Napoleon script. See pp. 475–6.

COURANT, Curt (or Kurt). (b. c. 1895) Cameraman, *Monsieur Verdoux*. Born and worked in Germany from 1920 (with Fritz Lang, etc), Great Britain from 1933, France from 1937 (with Jean Renoir, Max Ophuls).

CROCKER, Harry. (1895–1958) Actor, assistant, *The Circus, City Lights*. Later Chaplin's publicist. Son of prominent San Francisco banking family, took up screen career. A familiar of the San Simeon circle, was also columnist for Hearst newspapers.

DANIELL, Henry. (1894–1963) Actor, *The Great Dictator*. Stage; then films from 1929, including Cukor's *Camille*, with Garbo. Last film appearance, *My Fair Lady* (1964).

DAVENPORT, Alice. Actress, *Making a Living, Mabel's Strange Predicament, Cruel, Cruel Love, The Star Boarder, Caught in a Cabaret, Caught in the Rain, The Property Man, Gentlemen of Nerve, Tillie's Punctured Romance*. Stage from infancy; films from 1911 (Nestor), with daughter Dorothy D. One of original Keystone Company, 1912. Later with Fox, Sunshine Comedies.

DAVIES, Marion. (1897–1961) Actress, comedienne and long-time mistress of William Randolph Hearst. For years a friend of Chaplin, who made guest appearance in her film *Show People*, directed by another of his friends, King Vidor.

DE HAVEN, Carter. (1886–?) Assistant director, *Modern Times*; actor, *The Great Dictator*. Long vaudeville career in partnership with wife, Flora. Films from 1915 until early 1920s. Father of actress Gloria De Haven.

DELLUC, Louis. (1890–1924) Pioneer French film critic and author of first serious book-length appreciation of Chaplin, *Charlot* (1921).

DESMONDE, Jerry. (James Robert Sadler) (1908–1967) Actor, *A King in New York*. Variety experience, especially as straight man to comedians like Sid Field and Norman Wisdom. Films from 1946 *(London Town)*.

DORO, Marie. (1882–1956) Actress, played leading role of Alice Faulkner in Gillette's 1905 production of *Sherlock Holmes* at Duke of York's Theatre, London. The adolescent Chaplin worshipped her from afar; much later, as a Hollywood star, met her again. In 1916, when she was working with the Jesse L. Lasky Feature Play Company, Chaplin was guest at a house-warming given by Miss Doro and her husband Elliott Dexter, and presented her with a miniature cine camera he had had specially made.

DRESSLER, Marie. (Leila Koerber) (1869–1934) Actress, *Tillie's Punctured Romance*. Stage career in vaudeville and musicals, notably *Tillie's Nightmare*. When stage career faltered, returned to the screen with singular success (*Let Us be Gay, Anna Christie*, 1929), and at the time of her death was one of Hollywood's top box-office stars.

DRYDEN, Leo. (George Dryden Wheeler) (1863–1939) Music hall star and father of Chaplin's half-brother Wheeler Dryden. Specializing in enthusiastically patriotic and imperialist ballads, he enjoyed huge success in the early 1890s with 'The Miner's Dream of Home'.

DRYDEN, Wheeler. (1892–1957) Chaplin's half-brother, the son of Leo Dryden and Hannah Chaplin. Taken from his mother by Dryden as a baby, Wheeler seems to have been brought up in India. He reappeared in the lives of the Chaplin brothers around 1918, and received a money allowance from the studio, though he made his own career as actor and (occasionally) playwright. Assistant to Sydney Chaplin in his British film ventures in late 1920s. Joined Chaplin Studios as assistant director on *The Great Dictator* and remained until Chaplin's departure from USA in 1952. Last days troubled by paranoid fears of persecution by FBI.

DURFEE, Minta. (1897, Los Angeles–1975, Los Angeles) Actress, *Making a Living, A Film Johnnie, Tango Tangles, Cruel, Cruel Love, The Star Boarder, Twenty Minutes of Love, Caught in a Cabaret, The Knockout, The Masquerader, His New Profession, The Rounders, The New Janitor, Tillie's Punctured Romance*. Musical comedy, vaudeville, stock. Keystone from 1913–16. Married Roscoe Arbuckle. After retirement ran dress shop in Hollywood.

EPSTEIN, Jerry. (1924–1991) Chaplin's close associate from *Limelight* onwards. First met Chaplin when running Hollywood theatre, The Circle, in association with Sydney Earle Chaplin; Chaplin directed productions there. Assistant on *Limelight*; associate producer on *A King in New York* and producer on *A Countess From Hong Kong*. Directed *The Adding Machine*.

FAIRBANKS, Douglas. (Elton Thomas Ullman) (1883–1939) Swashbuckling, all-American star of the 1910s and 1920s. Married Mary Pickford; co-founder with Pickford, Chaplin and D. W. Griffith of United Artists. Late in life Chaplin said Fairbanks was the only close friend he had ever had.

FISKE, Minnie Maddern. (1865–1932) One of the most respected American stage actresses of the early twentieth century, Mrs Fiske made her debut at the age of three. Her 1916 essay, 'The Art of Charlie Chaplin' in *Harpers* did much to stimulate the evaluation of Chaplin as a serious artist.

FLOREY, Robert. (1900–1979) French cinephile with passionate admiration both for Hollywood and Chaplin. In 1927 wrote monograph on Chaplin in series *Les Grands Artistes de l'Ecran*. Later, working in Hollywood as assistant to such directors as von Sternberg, Vidor and King, he came to know Chaplin personally. Associate director on *Monsieur Verdoux*. As director, Florey made two horror classics, *The Beast With Five Fingers* and *Murders in the Rue Morgue*.

GARDINER, Reginald. (1903–1980). Actor, *The Great Dictator*. Trained as an architect, but decided to study at RADA instead. Stage debut, London; film debut in *Born to Dance* (1936). Subsequently made career as character actor in American films, playing silly-ass British roles. In 1950s and 1960s returned to the stage, and played Doolittle in Broadway production of *My Fair Lady*.

GILLETTE, William C. (1855–1937) Actor and dramatist, noted for restraint and comedy style. Most famous role was *Sherlock Holmes* which he revived in London in 1905 (Duke of York's Theatre) with Chaplin in the role of Billy.

GODDARD, Paulette, see CHAPLIN, Paulette.

GOODWINS, Fred (1891–?) Actor, *A Night Out, A Jitney Elopement, The Tramp, The Bank, Shanghaied, A Night in The Show, Police*. Journalist, then on stage with George Alexander, Charles Frohman. Screen with Edison, Imp, Horsley companies. Also acted as unofficial press representative for Chaplin at Essanay.

GOULD, Florence. (1895–1983) American philanthropist, art patron, Riviera hostess and collector. Wife of Frank J. Gould. Entertained Chaplin in Nice, where the Goulds were then proprietors of The Majestic Hotel, during his 1931 world tour.

GOULD, Frank J. (d. 1956) American millionaire, son of railway king, George J. Gould, creator of 'Gould System' of railways in American southwest. Amateur archaeologist, and Riviera hotelier and host. Wives included Edith, sister of Hetty and Arthur Kelly (q.v.), and Florence Gould (q.v.).

GREY, Lita, see CHAPLIN, Lita Grey.

GRIFFITH, Gordon. (b. 1907) Child actor at Keystone, *Kid Auto Races, The Star Boarder, Twenty Minutes of Love, Caught in a Cabaret, Tillie's Punctured Romance*. Stage at one year with mother, Katherine G. Remained in pictures until 1926: appearances included *Tarzan of the Apes, Huckleberry Finn, Little Annie Rooney*. Later assistant director at Monogram Pictures, and production manager, *The Jolson Story*.

HALE, Georgia. (1903/6–1985) Actress, *The Gold Rush*. Arrived in Hollywood after winning beauty contest. Worked as extra until von Sternberg made her star of his first film *The Salvation Hunters* (1924). Remained in pictures until 1928 (Paul Fejös's *The Last Moment*). Afterwards worked as dance teacher. Close but intermittent friendship with Chaplin continued until 1943.

HALL, Charles D. (1899–1959) Art director with Chaplin Studios on First National Films, *The Gold Rush, The Circus, City Lights, Modern Times*. Previously worked with Karno companies. Later films included James Whale pictures, among them *The Bride of Frankenstein* and *Showboat*. Continued in films until 1951 (Robert Florey's *The Vicious Years*).

HARRINGTON, Tom. Chaplin's valet and amanuensis during his early bachelor days in Hollywood.

HARRIS, Mildred, see CHAPLIN, Mildred Harris.

HEDREN, Tippi. (Nathalie Hedren) (b. 1935) Actress, *A Countess From Hong Kong*. Best known for roles in Hitchcock's *The Birds* and *Marnie*. In 1981 made *Roar*, based on her husband and family's experiments in coexistence with wild animals.

HILL, Charles Frederick. (b. c. 1839) Chaplin's maternal grandfather, a boot-maker. See Chapter 1, *passim*.

HILL, Kate. (1870–1916) Chaplin's maternal aunt. See Chapters 1 and 5, *passim*.

HILL, Mary Ann. (c. 1839–1892) Chaplin's maternal grandmother. See Chapter 1, *passim*.

HORNE, Sir Alan Edgar. (1889–1984) 2nd Bt, created 1939; succeeded father, Sir Edgar Horne, 1941. Husband of Henrietta Florence (Hetty) Kelly (q.v.), whom he married in 1915, when he was Captain in Surrey Yeomanry.

INCE, Thomas H. (1882–1924) Outstanding early Hollywood producer, who systematized film-making methods and is credited with the general adoption of the film script. Died mysteriously following a trip on W.R. Hearst's yacht: Chaplin has frequently figured as one of several characters in the rumours surrounding the event.

JACKSON, John William. Founder and proprietor of The Eight Lancashire Lads. Previously a school teacher. See Chapter 2, *passim*.

JAMES, Dan. (b. 1911) Assistant on *The Great Dictator*. Educated Yale; worked for family firm of china importers, then became interested in left wing politics. Wrote *Winter Soldiers* (1942), *Bloomer Girl* (1944). While blacklisted worked on scripts of *The Giant Behemoth* and *Gorgo* as 'Daniel Hyatt'. In 1983 published prize-winning novel, *Famous All Over Town* – inspired by experiences as volunteer social worker among *chicanos* of East Los Angeles—under pseudonym 'Danny Santiago'.

JAMES, Sidney. (1913–1976) Actor, *A King in New York*. Arriving in Britain from South Africa in 1946, he soon established himself as a popular comedy player, specializing in cockney and American characters. His major success came with the *Carry On* film series.

JAMISON (or JAMIESON), Bud (William). (1894–1944) Actor, *His New Job, A Night Out, The Champion, In the Park, A Jitney Elopement, By the Sea, The Bank, Shanghaied, A Night in the Show, Charlie Chaplin's Burlesque on Carmen, Police*. Before joining Chaplin at Essanay, was café entertainer. Continued in films until 1940 *(Captain Caution)*.

JOHNSTON, Oliver. (1889–1966) Actor, *A King in New York, A Countess From Hong Kong*. Son of producer and actor Herbert Jenner, was educated at

RADA. On stage from 1910 till retirement in 1947. Returned to stage in 1951, and played in television, including early series, *The Grove Family.*

KARNO, Fred. (1886–1941) Music hall performer, producer and manager. See Chapter 3, *passim.*

KARNO, Fred, Junior. Son of Fred Karno. Accompanied Chaplin on Karno tours of United States; later worked on *The Gold Rush* and *Monsieur Verdoux.*

KEATON, Joseph Francis (Buster). (1896–1966) One of the great comic stars of the silent screen. Entered films in 1917, after many years since early childhood in vaudeville. Early shorts with Roscoe Arbuckle, then star in his own right. After a series of brilliant feature comedies in the 1920s his career declined with the new economies of sound films. His appearance in *Limelight* teamed the two comic geniuses of the twentieth century.

KELLEY, James T. Actor, *A Night in the Show, Police, The Floorwalker, The Fireman, The Vagabond, The Count, The Pawnshop, Behind the Screen, The Rink, The Cure, The Immigrant, A Dog's Life.* Irish-born stage veteran of stock and vaudeville, who always played elderly and decrepit roles in Chaplin films. Also worked at Universal, Rolin and Roach studios.

KELLY, Arthur. (1890–1955) Brother of Hetty Kelly and Chaplin's representative in United Artists. Began career at twenty-one when he joined Frank J. Gould Enterprises in USA (Gould had married another Kelly sister, Edith). Major in British tank corps in First World War, after which joined United Artists as treasurer. 1924, head of UA foreign sales, and subsequently in charge of domestic sales. 1944, Vice President and US representative for Eagle Lion Pictures. Rejoined UA as Executive Vice President, 1947. Resigned 1950 to establish own television company.

KELLY, Henrietta Florence (Hetty). (1893–1918) Chaplin's first love; subsequently married Alan Edgar Horne (q.v.). See Chapters 3 and 8, *passim.*

KENNEDY, Edgar. (1890–1948) Actor, *The Star Boarder, Twenty Minutes of Love, Caught in a Cabaret, The Knockout, Mabel's Busy Day, Those Love Pangs, Dough and Dynamite, Gentlemen of Nerve, Tillie's Punctured Romance, Getting Acquainted.* Vaudeville and musical comedy, films (at Keystone) from 1914. Credited as inventor of 'the slow burn', he became a comedy star in his own right, notably in sound shorts. Later films included *Duck Soup, A Star is Born.*

KENNEDY, Merna. (1908–1944) Actress, *The Circus.* Musical comedy, as dancer, from childhood. Later films include *King of Jazz* and *Broadway.* Last picture, *I Like It that Way* (1934).

KESSEL, Adam, Junior. Co-founder, with Charles O. Bauman (q.v.), of New York Motion Picture Company and its affiliate, Keystone Film Company.

KNOBLOCK, Edward. (Edward Knoblauch) (1874–1945) Actor and later dramatist and screenwriter. A naturalized British subject, he became friendly with Chaplin through Fairbanks, and was in London at the time of Chaplin's 1921 visit. Appeared as extra in *The Idle Class.*

KONO, Toraichi. (1888–?) Chaplin's valet and general assistant from 1916–1934. Emigrated to US c. 1906. Appears in *The Adventurer*, *The Circus.* After leaving Chaplin's service worked briefly in United Artists' Tokyo office.

LAUDER, Sir Harry. (1870–1950) Great Scottish star of the British music halls. Visited Chaplin Studios in 1918 and shot film with Chaplin, intended to raise money for Lauder's war charity fund.

LAUREL, Stan. (1895–1965) Created role of *Jimmy the Fearless*, later taken over by Chaplin, with Karno Company. Accompanied Chaplin on 1910 and 1912 Karno tours of USA. From 1917 in films as star in own right; from 1926 as partner to Oliver Hardy. During vaudeville days did Chaplin impersonation in 'The Keystone Trio'.

LEHRMAN, Henry, nicknamed 'Pathé' by D. W. Griffith. (1886–1946) Director, *Making a Living, Kid Auto Races at Venice, Mabel's Strange Predicament, Between Showers.* Originally tram conductor, then director at Biograph, Imp, Kinemacolor, Keystone, Sterling, L-Ko (Lehrman–Knockout). Continued to direct until 1929 *(New Year's Eve)*; then writer. Was fiancé of Virginia Rappe, whose death in the course of a party precipitated the Fatty Arbuckle trial (1921) in which Lehrman was main prosecution witness.

LIMUR, Jean de. Research assistant, *A Woman of Paris.* Of aristocratic birth, came to USA after war service as aviator and was actor in Fairbanks's *The Three Musketeers.* Later assistant to De Mille and Rex Ingram, then directed early sound films, *The Letter* and *Jealousy.* Returned to Europe and continued to direct in France and Italy until 1944 *(La Grande Meute).*

LOREN, Sophia. (Sofia Scicolone) (b. 1934) Actress, *A Countess From Hong Kong.* In films from 1950, became a major international star in the 1960s. Married to producer Carlo Ponti.

LOURIÉ, Eugene. (1895–1991) Art director on *Limelight.* Emigrating to Paris after the Russian Revolution, Lourié trained as a painter, but became involved with emigré film-makers. As a designer he worked with outstanding success with Jean Renoir in the 1930s, and joined him in Hollywood during the 1940s. Later directed monster films, *The Beast From 20,000 Fathoms* (1953) and *The Colossus of New York* (1958).

McGUIRE, Paddy. Actor, *The Champion, A Jitney Elopement, The Tramp, By the Sea, Work, The Bank, Shanghaied, A Night in the Show.* Musical comedy; films from 1915 (Essanay). Later with Vogue and Triangle Keystone companies. Specialized in 'rubes' and Irish characters.

McMURRAY, Lillian. Mother of Lita Grey. Survived to the late 1980s.

MANN, Hank. (David W. Liebman) (1888–1971) Actor, *Mabel's Strange Predicament, Twenty Minutes of Love, Caught in a Cabaret, The Knockout, Mabel's Married Life, The Face on the Bar Room Floor, City Lights, Modern Times, The Great Dictator*. Stage, then films (Keystone) from 1914. In films until 1957 *(Man of a Thousand Faces)*.

MARCELINE. (1873–1927) French clown. Chaplin saw and admired him when he was appearing in the pantomime *Cinderella* at the newly opened London Hippodrome, where Marceline remained a popular star for several seasons. Chaplin records that he later saw him in the USA when Marceline's talent and confidence had deserted him.

MENJOU, Adolphe (1890–1963) Actor, *A Woman of Paris*. Cornell University, First World War service, then vaudeville and stage. Screen from 1912 at Vitagraph; but only achieved principal roles from 1921 *(The Three Musketeers)*. Continued in films until 1959 *(Pollyanna)*. Notable later performance in Kubrick's *Paths of Glory*. Reckoned one of Hollywood's best-dressed men. One of the most voluble 'friendly' witnesses in Hollywood Un-American Activities investigations.

MINEAU, Charlotte (b. 1891) Actress, *His New Job, A Night in the Show, The Floorwalker, The Vagabond, The Count, Behind the Screen, The Rink, Easy Street*. Previously with Selig, George Ade Fables, Swedie series; later films include *Sparrows*, with Mary Pickford.

MORRISSEY, Betty. (d. 1950) Actress, *A Woman of Paris, The Gold Rush, The Circus*. Discovered by Erich Von Stroheim, who used her in *Merry-Go-Round* (1922). Screen career continued throughout 1920s, until *The Circus*.

MURRAY, Charles K. (1872–1941) Actor, *Her Friend the Bandit, Mabel's Married Life, The Masquerader, Tillie's Punctured Romance*. Twenty years in vaudeville in Murray and Mack act, then films with Biograph, Keystone. Prolific later career, including *Cohens and Kellys* series.

MURRAY, Tom. (b. 1893–) Actor, *The Pilgrim, The Gold Rush* (Black Larson). Vaudeville, in black-face double act, Gillihan and Murray. Films from 1914, with Eagle Film Company. First Hollywood film, *My Boy*, with Jackie Coogan.

MURRAY, Will. (1877–1955) Managed *Casey's Circus Company* during Chaplin's tour. First stage appearance 1890; first London appearance, 1892. Gymnastic speciality act, Lord, Murray and Lord; then teamed with Arthur Woodville as The Freans. Joined Casey's Court in 1906, and continued to tour the act until 1950. Casey's Court *alumni* included besides Chaplin, Stan Laurel, Stanley Lupino, Jack Edge, Hal Jones, Leslie Strange, George Doonan, the Terry Twins, Jerry Verno, Tom Gamble, Jimmy Russell.

MYERS, Harry. (1882–1938) Actor, *City Lights*. Stage; films from 1908 at Biograph; then Lubin and Vim Comedies series with wife, Rosemary Thelby. Starring roles in 1920s (including *A Connecticut Yankee at King Arthur's Court, Exit Smiling*); continued in films until 1936 *(San Francisco, Hollywood Boulevard)*.

NEWMAN, Alfred. (1901–1970) Composer and musical director. Worked on *City Lights* but walked off *Modern Times* after disagreement with Chaplin. Began his career as a child prodigy at the piano, composed more than 250 film scores, and won nine Oscars (rarely for his best work).

NORMAND, Mabel. (1892–1930) Actress, *Mabel's Strange Predicament, Mabel at the Wheel, Caught in a Cabaret, The Fatal Mallet, Her Friend the Bandit, Mabel's Busy Day, Mabel's Married Life, Gentlemen of Nerve, His Trysting Place, Tillie's Punctured Romance, Getting Acquainted*. Photographic model. Entered films at Vitagraph, then Biograph and Keystone (1912). Features included *Mickey* and *Molly-O*. Later career troubled by scandals; died of tuberculosis.

NORTHRUP, Harry. Actor, *A Woman of Paris*. Character actor much in demand during 1920s (*Four Horsemen of the Apocalypse* etc).

OAKIE, Jack. (Lewis Delaney Offield) (1893–1978) Actor, *The Great Dictator*. After early work as chorus boy in musical comedy and as song-and-dance man in vaudeville, Oakie arrived in Hollywood in 1927 and established himself as a comedian. Debut in *Finders Keepers*. Later films include *It Happened Tomorrow, Lover Come Back* (1962).

O'NEILL, Oona, see CHAPLIN, Oona O'Neill.

PARRISH, Robert. (b. 1916) Actor, *City Lights* (newsboy). Subsequently became film editor and (from 1951) director. Autobiography: *Growing Up in Hollywood*, 1976.

PARSONS, Louella. (1880–1972) Columnist on Hearst newspapers known for her malice but generally (unlike Hedda Hopper) cordial to Chaplin. Was a member of party on Hearst boat trip which proved fatal for Thomas Ince.

PEARCE, Peggy. (b. 1896) Actress, *His Favorite Pastime*; also Chaplin's first Hollywood girlfriend. Films from 1913 (Biograph, Keystone).

PERINAL, Georges. (1897–1965) Director of photography, *A King in New York*. Outstanding cinephotographer whose career began in 1913; notable collaborations with René Clair, Alexander Korda, Michael Powell and Emeric Pressburger.

PICKFORD, Mary. (1893–1979) Dominant star of 1910s and 1920s; wife of Douglas Fairbanks; friend of Chaplin and co-founder of United Artists. Stage debut 1898; film debut 1909 under D. W. Griffith at Biograph. An outstanding businesswoman, she was in constant competition with Chaplin to be the highest earner in Hollywood in the period of the First World War. Retired from acting in 1933.

POLLARD, Snub. (1886–1962) Actor, *Limelight.* Arrived in US from Australia with Juvenile Opera Company; joined Broncho Billy at Essanay in 1913. Subsequently many slapstick shorts. In sound period became character player: career continued until 1961 *(Pocketful of Miracles).*

POLO, Malvina (or Malvine). Actress, *A Woman of Paris.* Daughter of serial star Eddie Polo (1875–1961) who claimed Italian descent from Marco Polo. Also played half-wit girl in Von Stroheim's *Foolish Wives.*

POSTANCE, William. Stage Manager at Duke of York's Theatre, London, in 1905 when Chaplin played there. Chaplin remembered his kindness, and paid tribute to him in the character 'Mr Postant' in *Limelight.*

PURVIANCE, Edna Olga. (1896–1958) Actress, *A Night Out, The Champion, In the Park, A Jitney Elopement, The Tramp, By the Sea, Work, A Woman, The Bank, Shanghaied, A Night in the Show, Charlie Chaplin's Burlesque on Carmen, Police, The Floorwalker, The Fireman, The Vagabond, The Count, The Pawnshop, Behind the Screen, The Rink, Easy Street, The Cure, The Immigrant, The Adventurer, A Dog's Life, The Bond, Shoulder Arms, Sunnyside, A Day's Pleasure, The Kid, The Idle Class, Pay Day, The Pilgrim, A Woman of Paris.* Afterwards (1926) starred in von Sternberg's *Sea Gulls* (produced by Chaplin; never released) and Henri Diamant-Berger's *Education du Prince* (in France); then retired. The correct pronunciation of 'Purviance' is with the accent on the 'i', pronounced as the letter of the alphabet. Chaplin used to joke that the name was in fact unpronounceable, and that she should change it to Edna Pollolobus.

RAKSIN, David. (b. 1912) Arranger of music for *Modern Times.* Composer, conductor, author, lecturer and teacher. Son of conductor of orchestras for silent films; studied piano in Philadelphia, then composition with Isadore Freed and Arnold Schoenberg. Was working as Broadway arranger when Chaplin asked him to go to Hollywood to assist on score for *Modern Times.* Subsequently remained active in Hollywood, where he composed music for more than a hundred films, including *Laura.* President, Composers and Lyricists Guild of America.

RAYE, Martha. (b. 1916) Actress, *Monsieur Verdoux.* Gifted, wide-mouthed American comedienne. Daughter of vaudeville artists (Reed and Hooper); had experience in musical comedy, radio, vaudeville and band work before making her first film in 1936 *(Rhythm on the Range).* Many films until 1970; then television work.

REEVES, Alfred. (1876–1946) General Manager, Chaplin Film Corporation, 1918–1946. Son of a lion tamer who lost an arm to the animals; worked in circus, then management for Fred Karno. Managed Karno's US tours from 1905. Chose Chaplin for 1910 tour. Brother of Billie Reeves, Karno player who later did Chaplin imitation.

REEVES, Amy. Wife of Alf Reeves. Karno artist (as Amy Minister) who played the Saucy Soubrette in *Mumming Birds*, and accompanied Chaplin on 1910 and 1912 Karno US tours. Settled in Hollywood from 1918 and befriended Hannah Chaplin during her last days there.

REEVES, Billie. (1866–1945) Brother of Alfred Reeves; Karno player, who preceded Chaplin in *Mumming Birds*. Began his career as a performer at seven, and was acrobat, clown, bareback rider, animal trainer and tamer like his father. Also knockabout skater and member of Fletcher's Skaters. Remained in America after Karno tour, in vaudeville and later in films (Lubin). In one year made fifty-three films, at $1000 each. In 1918 did vaudeville tour with drunk sketch, 'The Right Key But The Wrong Flat'.

REEVES, May. Young woman, apparently of Czech origin, who was Chaplin's companion during much of his 1931 holiday and wrote her memoirs of the period, *Charlie Chaplin intime*, edited by Claire Goll (1935).

REYNOLDS, Dr Cecil. Hollywood neighbour of Chaplin, who played prison chaplain in *Modern Times*. Died by suicide.

RIESNER, Charles Francis. (1887–1962) Actor, *A Dog's Life, The Kid, The Pilgrim*; assistant director, First National Films and *The Gold Rush*. Left Chaplin to direct Sydney Chaplin pictures *(The Man on the Box, The Better 'Ole)*. Later films include Buster Keaton's *Steamboat Bill Jr*. Last film made in Italy, *L'Ultima Cena* (1950). Before joining Chaplin in January 1918 Riesner had ten years experience on the stage; featured on Keith and Orpheum vaudeville circuits, and as star of musical comedy, *Stop, Look, Listen*. His son DEAN RIESNER was a child actor in *The Pilgrim* who later became successful screenwriter.

RITCHIE, Billy. (1877–1921) Vaudeville and musical comedy; then Karno Company. Created role of Drunk in *Mumming Birds*. Following Karno tour, remained in US starring in vaudeville, on Broadway, and Orpheum Circuit. On screen in L-Ko comedies, was persuaded by Henry Lehrman to undertake Chaplin impersonation. Died from injuries received from ostrich during making of a film. His wife WINIFRED RITCHIE, also a former Karno player, was expert in making trick costumes, and worked frequently at Chaplin studios. Daughter WYN married Ray Evins, Hollywood song-writer ('Buttons and Bows' 'Che Sara, Sara' etc). Winifred and Wyn were among Hannah Chaplin's selected Hollywood friends.

ROBINSON, Carlyle T. Chaplin's press representative from 1917 to 1932. Accompanied him on 1921 and 1931 European trips. Appears in *The Idle Class, The Pilgrim*. Was educated in New York, and worked in a bank before turning to journalism. Was obituary reporter for Brooklyn Standard Union before moving to California to work as press agent for motion picture companies.

RUGGLES, Wesley. (1889–1972) Actor, *The Bank, Shanghaied, A Night in the Show, Charlie Chaplin's Burlesque on Carmen, Police, The Pawnshop, Behind the Screen*. Stage, then films at Keystone (1914) as Keystone Kop, and in Sydney Chaplin 'Gussle' shorts. Director from 1917 *(For France)*. Later films include *I'm No Angel*, with Mae West. Last picture, *London Town* (1940), in England.

RUTHERFORD, Margaret Taylor. (1892–1972) Actress in *A Countess From Hong Kong*. Well-loved English character actress. Originally teacher of music and speech; stage from 1925; films from 1936 *(Dusty Ermine)*.

ST JOHN, Al. (1893–1963) Actor, *Mabel's Strange Predicament, Mabel at the Wheel, The Knockout, Mabel's Busy Day, Mabel's Married Life, The Rounders, The New Janitor, Tillie's Punctured Romance, His Prehistoric Past*. Nephew of Roscoe Arbuckle. Musical comedy, then Keystone from 1914. Later, bearded, made career as Western character actor, Al 'Fuzzy' St John, in a career extending to the 1950s.

SAINTSBURY, H. A. (1869–1939) Actor and dramatist. Educated St John's College, Hurstpierpoint, then engaged as clerk at Bank of England. Stage debut 1887. Played wide repertory of Shakespearean roles but his favourite part remained Sherlock Holmes, which he acted more than 1400 times. Chaplin made his first appearances on the legitimate stage under Saintsbury, in Saintsbury's own *Jim, A Romance of Cockayne* and in a touring production of *Sherlock Holmes*.

SENNETT, Mack. (1880–1960) Producer. See Chapter 4, *passim*.

STERLING, Ford. (1880–1939) Actor, *Between Showers, A Film Johnnie, Tango Tangles*. Began career in circus as Keno the Boy Clown; later stock, vaudeville, musical comedy. Films from 1911 at Biograph; then in original Keystone Company (1912). Formed own company in 1914, but later returned to Sennett. Career continued until 1935 *(Black Sheep)*.

STERNBERG, Josef von. (1894–1969) Impressed by Sternberg's first film, *The Salvation Hunters*, Chaplin financed and produced Sternberg's *Sea Gulls* (or *A Woman From the Sea*), starring Edna Purviance. The film was never shown however, and the negative was destroyed in 1933. Later most famous for his films with Marlene Dietrich.

STOCKDALE, Carl. (b. 1874) Actor, *The Champion, A Jitney Elopement,*

By the Sea, The Bank. University of North Dakota; amateur, then professional stage. Films from 1912, at Essanay. Early roles included Belshazzar's Father in Griffith's *Intolerance*. Career continued in sound films until 1941 *(Dangerous Lady)*.

STRUSS, Karl. (1891–1981) Photographer, *The Great Dictator*, *Limelight*. Work as Hollywood cameraman began with Cecil B. De Mille in 1920 and included *Ben Hur* (1926).

SULLY, Janet Miller. Actress, *Easy Street, The Cure, The Adventurer, A Dog's Life*. In 1918 *Motion Picture Magazine* reported that she had just played '68 comedies with George Ovey without a break'.

SUMMERVILLE, George ('Slim'). (1892–1946) Actor, *Mabel's Busy Day, Laughing Gas, Dough and Dynamite, Tillie's Punctured Romance*. Vaudeville and musical comedy; films (at Keystone) from 1913; was also gagman for Sennett. Remained in films as character player until death: most famous later performances in *All Quiet on the Western Front* and *Tobacco Road*.

SUTHERLAND, Edward A. (1895–1974) Assistant director, *A Woman of Paris, The Gold Rush*. Nephew by marriage of Thomas Meighan. Educated Paris and US. Stage and musical comedy. Screen from 1914 in Helen Holmes serial. Director from 1925 *(Coming Through)*. Later films included *The Old Army Game* and *Poppy*, both with W. C. Fields. Continued to direct until 1956 (*Bermuda Affair*, in England). Wives included Louise Brooks.

SWAIN, Mack. (1876–1935) Heavyweight actor, *Caught in the Rain, A Busy Day, The Fatal Mallet, The Knockout, Mabel's Married Life, Laughing Gas, Gentlemen of Nerve, His Musical Career, His Trysting Place, Tillie's Punctured Romance, Getting Acquainted, His Prehistoric Past, The Idle Class, Pay Day, The Pilgrim, The Gold Rush*. The son of Mormon pioneers (his middle name was Moroni, from the trumpeter angel on the Mormon temple), he established his own infant minstrel troupe at the age of seven. At fifteen toured with Martin Josey Minstrel Show. 1900, Kempton and Graves Stock Company, Chicago. Films from 1913, at Keystone. Career interrupted by blacklisting, but revived after *The Gold Rush*. Last appearance in 1932, *The Midnight Patrol*.

SWANSON, Gloria. (1897 or 1898–1983) Actress, *His New Job*. One of the greatest Hollywood stars of the 1920s, Swanson for long denied that she appeared in this film. Later she acknowledged it, but claimed that she deliberately tried not to give a comedy performance so as to avoid getting typed as a slapstick artist.

SWICKARD, Joseph. (d. 1938) Actor, *Twenty Minutes of Love, Caught in a Cabaret, Laughing Gas*. In films from 1912; established career as character actor in the 1920s, notably in *The Four Horsemen of the Apocalypse*.

Continued in films until death: last appearance in Frank Capra's *You Can't Take It With You* (1938).

TERRELL, Maverick. (b. 1875) University of Indiana Law School, writer of plays and magazine fiction. Said by Theodore Huff (*Charlie Chaplin*, 1951) to have assisted Chaplin in writing Essanay and Mutual comedies.

TETRICK, Paul Drew (Ted). Hollywood producer and costumier, worked on costumes for *The Great Dictator, Monsieur Verdoux* and planned costumes for *The Freak*. Married to Betty Chaplin (q.v.).

TOTHEROH, Roland H. (1890–1964) Photographer on Chaplin films from 1916 to 1952. Early career as cartoonist; amateur ball player. Photographer at Essanay, shooting Broncho Billy Westerns, from 1913. Retired after Chaplin's departure from Hollywood.

TURPIN, Ben. (1874–1940) Actor, *His New Job, A Night Out, The Champion*. With his puny physique and crossed eyes, one of the most singular figures in silent slapstick comedy. Eleven years in vaudeville with Sam T. Jack's Burlesque Company, then films at Essanay (1915). In later years played support to comedy stars: last appearance with Laurel and Hardy in *Saps at Sea* (1940).

WALLIS, Shani. (b. 1933) Singer in *A King in New York*. Child performer; debut on television, 1948; RADA; stage musicals. Films from 1956 *(The Extra Day)*. Chaplin selected her after seeing her in pantomime at Golders Green Hippodrome.

WELLES, Orson. (1915–1985) Director and actor. Suggested original idea for *Monsieur Verdoux*, and is so credited in the film.

WHITE, Leo. (1887–1948) Actor, *His New Job, A Night Out, The Champion, In the Park, A Jitney Elopement, The Tramp, Work, A Woman, The Bank, Shanghaied, A Night in the Show, Charlie Chaplin's Burlesque on Carmen, Police, The Floorwalker, The Fireman, The Vagabond, The Count, Behind The Screen, The Great Dictator*. With Karno; later in operetta. In films from 1915 (at Essanay); then George Ade Comedies, Billy West comedies, Hal Roach. For Essanay compiled four-reel version of *Charlie Chaplin's Burlesque on Carmen* and *Triple Trouble*. Career continued until 1942 *(Yankee Doodle Dandy)*.

WILLIAMS, Frank D. (b. 1893) Chaplin's cameraman on *The Floorwalker, The Fireman, The Vagabond*. Previously with Essanay and Keystone, where he may also have filmed Chaplin. Highly innovative, Williams is credited with the invention of the travelling matte, and was responsible for trick work on *King Kong* and *The Invisible Man*.

WILLSON, Meredith. (1902–1984) Music arranger, *The Great Dictator*. Accomplished pianist and flautist, studied at New York Institute of Musical

Art (now Juilliard School). Flute and piccolo with J. P. Sousa Band, then first flautist with New York Philharmonic, under Toscanini. Musical director for ABS and NBC. Major Broadway successes with two musicals, *The Music Man* (1957) and *The Unsinkable Molly Brown* (1960).

WILSON, Jack. (John) Second cameraman at Chaplin Studios from First National Pictures to *City Lights*. Wife EDITH WILSON was bit actress in *The Kid*, *City Lights* (cut sequence).

WOOD, Tom. Young, 495-lb. actor in *Sunnyside*. Was originally cast as Charlie's wife in *A Day's Pleasure* but the role was eventually taken by Edna Purviance.

BIBLIOGRAPHY

This bibliography aims only to list some of the major works among the several hundred books that have been devoted to Chaplin's life and career, along with a few early rarities and curiosities. For a comprehensive bibliography the reader is directed to Lennart Eriksson's admirable compilation (see below) and its various updatings.

ADELER, Edwin and WEST, Con. *Remember Fred Karno*, John Long, London, 1939.

AMENGUAL, Barthélemy (and others). *Charles Chaplin*. Premier Plan, 28 Société d'Etudes de Recherches et Documentation Cinématographiques, Lyon, 1952.

ASPLUND, Uno. *Chaplin's Films*. Translated from Swedish, *Chaplin i Sverige*, by Paul Britten Austin. David & Charles, Newton Abbot, 1973.

ATASHEVA, Pera M. (ed.) *Charles Spencer Chaplin*.Volume II in a series on film history, edited by Sergei M. Eisenstein and Sergei I. Yutkevitch. Essays by M. BLEIMAN, Grigori KOZINTSEV, S. I. YUTKEVITCH and S. M. EISENSTEIN. Goskinoizdat, 1945.

BAZIN, André.*Charlie Chaplin*. Preface by François Truffaut. Collection 7e Art. Editions du Cerf, Paris, 1973.

BESSY, Maurice, and FLOREY, Robert. *Monsieur Chaplin, ou le rire dans la nuit*, Jacques Damase, Paris, 1952.

BESSY, Maurice, and LIVIO, Robin. *Charles Chaplin*, Denoel, Paris, 1972.

BOWMAN, William Dodgson. *Charlie Chaplin. His Life and Art*, Routledge, London, 1931. Reprint: Haskell, New York, 1974.

BROWN, Albert T. *The Charlie Chaplin Fun Book*, 1915.

BROWNLOW, Kevin. *The Parade's Gone By*, Alfred A. Knopf, New York, 1968/Secker & Warburg, London, 1968.

CHAPLIN, Charles. *A Comedian Sees the World*, Crowell, New York, 1933.

CHAPLIN, Charles. *My Autobiography*, The Bodley Head, London, 1964/Simon & Schuster, New York, 1964/Penguin Books, Harmondsworth, 1966/Fireside Books, New York, 1978. Translations in Arabic, Armenian, Bulgarian, Chinese, Czech, Danish, Dutch, Finnish, French, Georgian, German (publication in Austria, West Germany and East Germany), Greek, Hungarian, Icelandic, Italian, Japanese, Latvian, Norwegian, Polish, Portuguese, Rumanian, Russian, Serbo-Croat, Spanish, Swedish.

CHAPLIN, Charles. *My Early Years*, The Bodley Head, London, 1979. The first eleven chapters of *My Autobiography*.

CHAPLIN, Charles. *My Life in Pictures*. Introduction by Francis Wyndham. The Bodley Head, London 1974/Grosset & Dunlap, New York, 1976.

CHAPLIN, Charles. *My Trip Abroad*, Harper & Brothers, New York, 1922. Translations in Bulgarian, Chinese, Czech, French, German, Polish, Portuguese, Russian, Spanish, Swedish, Yiddish.

CHAPLIN, Charles. *My Wonderful Visit*, Hurst & Blackett, London, 1922. English edition of *My Trip Abroad*.

CHAPLIN, Charles, Jr. (with N. and M. RAU) *My Father, Charlie Chaplin*, Random House, New York, 1960/Longmans, London, 1960.

CHAPLIN, Lita Grey (with Morton COOPER). *My Life With Chaplin, An Intimate Memoir*, Grove Press, 1966.

CHAPLIN, Michael. *I Couldn't Smoke the Grass on My Father's Lawn*, Leslie Frewin, London, 1966/G. P. Putnam's Sons, New York, 1966.

The Charlie Chaplin Book, Street & Smith, New York, 1915.

The Charlie Chaplin Book, Sabriel Sons & Co., New York, 1916.

CODD, Elsie. 'Charlie Chaplin's Methods' in *Cinema: Practical Course in Cinema Acting in Ten Complete Lessons*, Volume II, Lesson 2. Standard Art Book Company, London, 1920.

COOKE, Alistair. 'Charles Chaplin' in *Six Men*. Alfred A. Knopf, New York, 1977/The Bodley Head, London, 1978/Berkley Publishing Corporation, New York, 1978/Penguin Books, Harmondsworth, 1978.

COTES, Peter and NIKLAUS, Thelma. *The Little Fellow. The Life and Work of Charles Spencer Chaplin*. Foreword by W. SOMERSET MAUGHAM. Paul Elek, London, 1951/Philosophical Library Inc., New York, 1951. Reprint: Citadel Press, New York, 1965.

DELL, Draycott M. *The Charlie Chaplin Scream Book*, Fleetway, London, 1915.

DELLUC, Louis. *Charlot*, Maurice de Brunoff, Paris, 1921. English translation by Hamish MILES: *Charlie Chaplin*, John Lane/The Bodley Head, London, 1922.

ERIKSSON, Lennart. *Books on/by Chaplin*, Lennart Eriksson, Vasteras, Sweden, 1980. The best and most comprehensive bibliography.

FLOREY, Robert. *Charlie Chaplin. Ses débuts, ses films, ses aventures.* Preface by Lucien Wahl. Collection 'Les Grands Artistes de l'Ecran'. Jean-Pascal, Paris, 1927.

FOWLER, Gene. *Father Goose. The Story of Mack Sennett*, Covici Friede, New York, 1934.

GALLAGHER, J. P. *Fred Karno, Master of Mirth and Tears*, Robert Hale, London, 1971.

GIFFORD, Denis. *The Movie Makers*, Macmillan, London, 1974/Doubleday, New York, 1974.

GOLD, Michael. *Charlie Chaplin's Parade*, Harcourt, Brace & Co., New York, 1930.

HAINING, *The Legend of Charlie Chaplin*, W. H. Allen, London, 1983. Anthology of writings by or about Chaplin.

HEMBUS, Joe. *Charlie Chaplin und seine Filme. Eine Dokumentation*, Wilhelm Heyne, Munich, 1972/1973.

HOYT, Edwin P. *Sir Charlie*, Robert Hale, London, 1977.

HUFF, Theodore. *An Index to the Films of Charles Chaplin.* 'Sight and Sound' Index No. 3, British Film Institute, London, 1944. Revised as *The Early Work of Charles Chaplin*, British Film Institute, 1961.

HUFF, Theodore. *Charlie Chaplin*, Henry Schuman, New York, 1951/ Cassell, London, 1952. Reprints: Pyramid Books, New York, 1964/Arno Press, New York, 1972.

JACOBS, David. *Chaplin, The Movies and Charlie*, Harper & Row, New York, 1975.

JACOBS, Lewis. *The Rise of the American Film*, Harcourt, Brace & Co., New York, 1939.

KERR, Walter. *The Silent Clowns*, Alfred A. Knopf, New York, 1975.

LAHUE, Kalton C. *World of Laughter*, Norman, Oklahoma, 1966.

LAHUE, Kalton C. *Kops and Custards*, Norman, Oklahoma, 1967.

LEPROHON, Pierre. *Charlot, ou la Naissance d'un Mythe*, Editions Corymbe, Paris, 1935.

LEPROHON, Pierre. *Charles Chaplin*, Jacques Melot, Paris, 1946.

LUFT, Friedrich. *Vom grossen schönen Schweigen. Arbeit und Leben des Charles Spencer Chaplin*, Rembrandt Verlag, Berlin, 1957, 1963.

LYONS, Timothy J. (and others). 'Chaplin and Sound' in *Journal of the University Film Association*, Vol XXXI, No. 1, Winter 1979. University Film Association, Houston, 1979.

LYONS, Timothy J. *Charles Chaplin: a Guide to References and Resources*, G. K. Hall, Boston, 1979.

McCABE, John. *Charlie Chaplin*, Doubleday, New York, 1978/Robson Books Limited, London, 1978.

McCAFFREY, Donald W. *Focus on Chaplin*, Prentice-Hall, New Jersey, 1971. An Anthology of writings by and about Chaplin.

McCAFFREY, Donald W. *4 Great Comedians: Chaplin, Lloyd, Keaton, Langdon*, Tantivy Press, London/A. S. Barnes & Co., New York, 1968.

McDONALD, Gerald D., CONWAY, Michael and RICCI, Mark. *The Films of Charlie Chaplin*, Citadel Press, New York, 1965.

McDONALD, Gerald D. *The Picture History of Charlie Chaplin*, Nostalgia Press, New York, 1965.

MANNING, Harold. 'Charlie Chaplin's Early Life: Fact and Fiction' in *Historical Journal of Film, Radio and Television*, Vol. III – Number 1, March 1983. Carfax, Oxford, 1983. Valuable contribution to the record of Chaplin's early years.

MANVELL, Roger. *Chaplin*. Introduction by J. H. Plumb. Little, Brown, Boston, 1974/Hutchinson, London, 1975.

MARTIN, Marcel. *Charles Chaplin*. Collection 'Cinema d'Aujourd'hui' no. 43. Editions Seghers, Paris, 1966. New edition, 1972.

MINNEY, R. J. *Chaplin: The Immortal Tramp. The Life and Work of Charles Chaplin*, George Newnes, London, 1954.

MITRY, Jean. *Charlot et la 'fabulation' chaplinesque*, Editions Universitaires, Paris, 1957.

MITRY, Jean. *Tout Chaplin*, Editions Seghers, Paris, 1972.

MONTGOMERY, John. *Comedy Films 1894–1954*. Preface by Norman Wisdom. George Allen & Unwin, London, 1954, 1968.

MOSS, Robert. 'Charlie Chaplin' in *Pyramid History of the Movies*, Pyramid Publications, New York, 1975.

OLEKSY, Walter. *Laugh, Clown, Cry – The Story of Charlie Chaplin*, Raintree Editions, Milwaukee, 1976.

PAYNE, Robert. *The Great Charlie*. Foreword by G. W. Stonier. André Deutsch, London, 1952/Hermitage House, New York, 1952.

QUIGLEY, Isabel. *Charlie Chaplin, Early Comedies*, Studio Vista/Dutton Paperback, London, 1968.

RAMSAYE, Terry. *A Million and One Nights. A History of the Motion Picture*, Simon & Schuster, New York, 1926/Frank Cass, London, 1964.

REED, Langford. *The Chronicles of Charlie Chaplin*, Cassell, London, 1917.

REEVES, May. *Charlie Chaplin intime. Souvenirs receuillis par Claire Goll*, NRF, Gallimard, Paris, 1935.

ROBINSON, Carlyle T. *La vérité sur Charles Chaplin. Sa vie, ses amours, ses déboires.* Translated by René Lelu. Editions de Mon Ciné, Paris, 1935.

ROBINSON, David. *Chaplin: The Mirror of Opinion*, Secker Warburg, London, 1983.

ROBINSON, David. *The Great Funnies. A History of Film Comedy*, Studio Vista/Dutton Paperback, London, 1969.

SADOUL, Georges. *Vie de Charlot. Charles Spencer Chaplin, ses films et son temps*, Les Editeurs Francaïs Réunis, Paris, 1952, 1953, 1957. Definitive edition: Spes, Lausanne/L'Herminier, Paris, 1978.

SANDS, Frederick. *Charlie and Oona – The Story of a Marriage.* Translated from German, *Herr und Frau Chaplin. Die Geschichte einer Ehe* by Marianne Pasetti. Kindler Verlag, Munich, 1977.

SAVIO, Francesco. (ed.) *Il Tutto Chaplin*, Mostra Internazionale d'Arte Cinematografica di Venezia, Venice, 1972.

SEN, Mrinal. *Charlie Chaplin*, Grantha Prakash, Calcutta, 1974, 1980.

SENNETT, Mack (as told to Cameron SHIPP). *King of Comedy*, Doubleday, New York, 1954.

SOBEL, Raoul and FRANCIS, David. *Chaplin, Genesis of a Clown*, Quartet Books, London, 1977/Horizon Press, New York, 1978.

SULLIVAN, Ed. *Chaplin vs. Chaplin.* Foreword by Walter E. Hurst and Frank Bacon. Marvin Miller Enterprises, Los Angeles, 1965.

TRAUBERG, Leonid. *Mir Naisnanku (The World Inside Out)*, Isskustvo, Moscow, 1984.

TURCONI, Davide. *Mack Sennett, il 're de comiche'*, Mostra Internazionale d'Arte Cinematografica di Venezia, Edizioni dell'Ateneo, Rome, 1961.

TYLER, Parker. *Chaplin, Last of the Clowns*, Vanguard Press, New York, 1947. Reprint: Horizon Press, New York, 1972.

von ULM, Gerith. *Charlie Chaplin, King of Tragedy. An unauthorized Biography*, Caxton Printers, Idaho, 1940. Interesting since largely based on information supplied by Toraichi Kono.

INDEX

Index